THE
WRITERS
DIRECTORY
THIRTIETH EDITION

THE WRITERS DIRECTORY

THIRTIETH EDITION
VOLUME 3: H-L

Editor
Lisa Kumar

ST. JAMES PRESS
A part of Gale, Cengage Learning

GALE
CENGAGE Learning

Detroit • New York • San Francisco • New Haven, Conn • Waterville, Maine • London

GALE
CENGAGE Learning·

Writers Directory, 30th Edition

Project Editor: Lisa Kumar

Editorial Support Services: Natasha Mikheyeva

Manufacturing: Rita Wimberley

For product information and technology assistance, contact us at
Gale Customer Support, 1-800-877-4253.
For permission to use material from this text or product,
submit all requests online at **www.cengage.com/permissions.**
Further permissions questions can be emailed to
permissionrequest@cengage.com

Gale
27500 Drake Rd.
Farmington Hills, MI, 48331-3535

ISBN-13: 978-1-4144-8712-0 (set)   ISBN-10: 1-4144-8712-6 (set)
ISBN-13: 978-1-4144-8713-7 (vol. 1)   ISBN-10: 1-4144-8713-4 (vol. 1)
ISBN-13: 978-1-4144-8714-4 (vol. 2)   ISBN-10: 1-4144-8714-2 (vol. 2)
ISBN-13: 978-1-4144-9901-7 (vol. 3)   ISBN-10: 1-4144-9901-9 (vol. 3)
ISBN-13: 978-1-4144-9902-4 (vol. 4)   ISBN-10: 1-4144-9902-7 (vol. 4)
ISBN-13: 978-1-4144-9903-1 (vol. 5)   ISBN-10: 1-4144-9903-5 (vol. 5)
ISBN-13: 978-1-4144-9904-8 (vol. 6)   ISBN-10: 1-4144-9904-3 (vol. 6)

ISSN 0084-2699

Printed in the United States of America
1 2 3 4 5   16 15 14 13 12

FD156

Contents

Preface

The *Writers Directory* is the newly revised and expanded thirtieth edition of this acclaimed reference work. It lists 26,615 writers—writing under 29,776 names—from all countries of the world who have had at least one work published in English.

The Directory is published in 6 individual volumes, with content divided as follows:

Volume 1: Lists entries from A-C
Volume 2: Lists entries from D-G
Volume 3: Lists entries from H-L
Volume 4: Lists entries from M-Q
Volume 5: Lists entries from R-U
Volume 6: Lists entries from V-Z, Obituaries, Index to Writing Categories, and Country of Citizenship Index

The *Directory* lists approximately 26,526 living writers of fiction and non-fiction who have published at least one full-length work in English. Listees run the gamut from the best-known, best selling authors of fiction and the most prominent non-fiction writers to those writers just embarking on their literary careers. The thirtieth edition includes nearly 1,000 writers whose listings have not appeared in a previous edition of *The Writers Directory*.

The **Obituaries** Section contains the entries for approximately 89 writers whose listings have appeared in previous editions of *The Writers Directory* and whose passing was made known to us in preparing this edition.

Compilation Methods

Selection of writers to appear in *The Writers Directory* is based primarily on reference value. Biographical and career information is researched for each writer, then a copy of the entry is sent to the writer for his or her approval and updates. By this process, the editors can assure comprehensive, current information. At the same time, entries in the previous edition were rigorously reviewed with an eye toward their current research value. As a result, some writers' entries have been retired to make way for those of new writers.

How to Read a Citation

Entries in *The Writers Directory* contain some or all of the following elements (please note that this is a sample entry for demonstration purposes only):

▌1▐ WILLIAMS, Mae. ▌2▐ (Allison May Williams) ▌3▐ Also writes as William Allison. ▌4▐ American (born Malta), ▌5▐ b. 1945. ▌6▐ **Genres:** Novels, Biography. ▌7▐ **Career:** Freelance writer. ▌8▐ **Publications:** Paris, L'amour, 1972; (ed.) Running through the Weeds, 1982; (as William Allison) Louis, My Love (biography), 1987; The Waves at My Back, 1997. ▌9▐ **Address:** 27500 Drake Rd., Farmington Hills, MI 48331U.S.A. ▌10▐ **Online address:** maewil@aol.com ▌11▐ Died 1997.

▌1▐ Name of writer with fuller name information in parentheses

▌2▐ Full name of writer if different from writing name or pseudonyms but not used for writing

▌3▐ Pseudonym information

▌4▐ Nationality—if birthplace is different from nationality, it will follow the nationality in parentheses

▌5▐ Birth year

▌6▐ Genres—corresponds to **Index to Writing Categories**

▌7▐ Brief career information

▌8▐ Publications: title, year of publication, pseudonym if used, special awards

▌9▐ Address

▌10▐ Online address and/or web site

▌11▐ Death notation and year (in **Obituaries** Section only)

Cross references appear in the following form:

To main entry in main section: **ALLISON, William.** See **WILLIAMS, Mae.**

From main section to main entry in **Obituaries** section: **WILLIAMS, Mae.** See Obituaries.

From pseudonym in main section to main entry in **Obituaries** section: **ALLISON, William.** See **WILLIAMS, Mae** in the Obituaries.

Writers (and cross references) are listed alphabetically by surname which are sorted letter-by-letter. In cases where surnames are identical, writers are listed first by surname, then by given and middle names, and finally by suffixes such as Jr., Sr., II, or III. Surnames beginning with a prefix (such as Du, Mac, or Van), however spaced, are listed alphabetically under the first letter of the prefix and treated as if there were no space. Other compound surnames, hyphenated names, and names with apostrophes are alphabetized as if there were no space or punctuation. Surnames beginning with Saint or St. appear after names beginning with Sains and before names beginning with Sainu.

Entries in the **Obituaries** Section follow the same style as those in the main entries with the addition of the notation *Died* and the death year (if known) at the end of the entry.

Features

The Writers Directory contains many features to enhance its usefulness:

Boldface Rubrics allow quick and easy scanning for specifics on genre, career, publication, and mailing and online addresses.

The Obituaries Section lists the entries for those writers whose listing appeared in previous editions of The Writers Directory and whose passing was made known to us in preparing this edition. Cross references have been provided in the main body of the Directory to those deceased writers.

Indexing

The Writers Directory includes two indexes. In the **Index to Writing Categories**, one can locate writers by the type of works they write. New categories are added to The Writers Directory as needed to reflect new topics of interest and to define a writer's body of work more accurately. The **Country of Citizenship Index** lists writers by their country of citizenship as provided by the writer. Users are advised that one writer with multiple citizenship may appear under one country grouping (e.g., Canada-England) while another with the same citizenships may appear under a different grouping (e.g., England-Canada) depending on how the writer submitted the information.

The **Index to Writing Categories and Country of Citizenship Index** can be found in Volume 6 of the Directory following the **Obituaries** Section.

Also Available in Electronic Formats

Licensing. *The Writers Directory* is available for licensing. The complete database is provided in a fielded format and is deliverable on such media as disk or CD-ROM. For more information, contact Gale's Business Development Group at 1-800-877-GALE, or visit us on our web site at gale. cengage. com.

Online. *The Writers Directory* is accessible as part of Gale's Biography in Context database, as well as through the Gale Biographies database (File GALBIO) through Lexis-Nexis. For more information on Biography in Context, visit us on our web site at gale.cengage.com. For more information on Gale Biographies, contact LexisNexis, P.O. Box 933, Dayton, OH 45401-0933; phone (937) 865-6800; toll- free: 800-227-4908.

Suggestions Welcome

Comments and suggestions from users of *The Writers Directory* on any aspect of the product as well as suggestions for writers to be included in a future edition are cordially invited. Please write:

The Editor

The Writers Directory

St. James Press

Gale, a part of Cengage Learning

27500 Drake Rd.

Farmington Hills, Michigan 48331-3535.

Entry in *The Writers Directory* is at the discretion of the editor.

Abbreviations Used In The Writers Directory

A

AB	Alberta
ABC	American Broadcasting Company
ACT	Australian Capital Territory
AK	Alaska
AL	Alabama
Apt.	Apartment
AR	Arkansas
Assn.	Association
Assoc.	Associate
Asst.	Assistant
Ave.	Avenue
AZ	Arizona

B

b.	born
BBC	British Broadcasting Corporation
BC	British Columbia
Beds.	Bedfordshire
Berks.	Berkshire
Bldg.	Building
Blvd.	Boulevard
Brig.	Brigadier
Bros.	Brothers
Bucks.	Buckinghamshire

C

CA	California
Cambs.	Cambridgeshire
Can.	Canada
Capt.	Captain
CBC	Canadian Broadcasting Company
CBS	Columbia Broadcasting System (US)
CIA	Central Intelligence Agency (US)
CO; co.	Colorado; Company; County
Co-ed.	Co-editor
Co-trans.	Co-translator
Col.	Colonel
Contrib.	Contributor; Contributing
Corp.	Corporation
CPA	Certified Public Accountant
Cres.	Crescent
CT; Ct.	Connecticut; Court

D

DC	District of Columbia
DE	Delaware
Dept.	Department
Derbys.	Derbyshire
Dir.	Director
Div.	Division
Dr.	Doctor; Drive

E

E.	East
Ed.	Editor; Edition
Exec.	Executive

F

FBI	Federal Bureau of Investigation (US)
FL	Florida
Ft.	Fort

G

GA	Georgia
Gen.	General
Glam.	Glamorgan
Glos.	Glouchestershire
Gov.	Governor
Govt.	Government

H

Hants.	Hampshire
HE	His Eminence; His/Her Excellency
Herts.	Hertfordshire
HI	Hawaii
HM	His/Her Majesty
HMS	His/Her Majesty's Ship; His/Her Majesty's Service
Hon.	Honorable; Honorary

I

IA	Iowa
ID	Idaho
IL	Illinois
IN	Indiana
Inc.	Incorporated
Inst.	Institute
Intl.	International

J

Jr.	Junior

K

KS	Kansas
KY	Kentucky

L

LA	Louisiana
Lab.	Laboratory
Lancs.	Lancashire
Leics.	Leicestershire
LI	Long Island
Lincs.	Lincolnshire
Lt.	Lieutenant
Ltd.	Limited

M

MA	Massachusetts
Mag.	Magazine
Maj.	Major
MB	Manitoba
MD	Maryland
ME	Maine
Mgr.	Manager
MI	Michigan
Middx.	Middlesex
MN	Minnesota
MO	Missouri
MP	Member of Parliament
MT; Mt.	Montana; Mount, Mountain

N

N.	North
NASA	National Aeronautics and Space Administration
NATO	North Atlantic Treaty Organization
NB	New Brunswick
NBC	National Broadcasting System (US)
NC	North Carolina
NE	North East
NF	Newfoundland
NH	New Hampshire
NJ	New Jersey
NL	Newfoundland and Labrador
NM	New Mexico
No.	Number

Northants.	Northamptonshire
Notts.	Nottinghamshire
nr.	Near
NS	Nova Scotia
NSW	New South Wales
NT	Northern Territory (Australia); Northwest Territories (Canada)
NU	Nunavut
NV	Nevada
NW	North West
NWT	Northwest Territories
NY	New York
NYC	New York City

O

OH	Ohio
OK	Oklahoma
ON	Ontario
OR	Oregon
Orch.	Orchestra
Org.	Organization
Oxon.	Oxfordshire

P

PA	Pennsylvania
PE, PEI	Prince Edward Island
PEN	Poets, Playwrights, Essayists, Editors, Novelists
Pl.	Place
PO	Post Office
Pres.	President
Prof.	Professor
Prog.	Program
Publrs.	Publishers
Publs.	Publications

Q

QC	Quebec
QLD	Queensland

R

Rd.	Road
Rep.	Representative
Rev. ed.	Revised edition
RI	Rhode Island
RR	Rural Route
Rte.	Route

S

S.	South
SA	South Australia
Salop.	Shropshire
SC	South Carolina
Sch.	School
SD	South Dakota
SE	South East
Sec	Secretary
SK	Saskatchewan
Soc.	Society
Sq.	Square
Sr.	Senior
St.	Saint; Street
Staffs.	Staffordshire
Ste.	Suite
Supt.	Superintendent
SW	South West

T

Tas.	Tasmania
Terr.	Terrace
TN	Tennessee
Trans.	Translator; Translation
Treas.	Treasurer
TX	Texas

U

UK	United Kingdom
UN	United Nations
Unesco	United Nations Educational, Scientific and Cultural Organization

Unicef	United Nations Children's Emergency Fund
Univ.	University
US;	USA United States, United States of America
USS	United States Ship; United States Service
USSR	Union of Soviet Socialist Republics
UT	Utah

V

VA	Virginia
VIC	Victoria
Vol(s).	Volume(s)
VT	Vermont

W

W.	West
WA	Washington; Western Australia
Warks.	Warwicks; Warwickshire
WHO	World Health Organization
WI	Wisconsin
Wilts.	Wiltshire
Worcs.	Worcestershire
WV	West Virginia
WY	Wyoming

Y

YM-YWHA	Young Men's-Young Women's Hebrew Association
YMCA	Young Men's Christian Association
Yorks.	Yorkshire
YWCA	Young Women's Christian Association
YT	Yukon Territory

H

HAAR, Charles M(onroe). American/Belgian (born Belgium), b. 1920. **Genres:** Regional/Urban Planning. **Career:** Harvard University, assistant professor, 1952-54, associate professor, 1954-55, professor of law, 1955-72, Louis D. Brandeis professor of law, 1972-91, Louis D. Brandeis professor emeritus of law, 1991-; U.S. Department of Housing and Urban Development, Metropolitan Development, assistant secretary, 1966-69; Massachusetts Institute of Technology, faculty, Joint Center for Urban Studies, chairman, 1969-; Zelda Zinn Foundation, director; Charles River Associates, director; Doxiadis Associates, vice president; Regional and Urban Planning Inc., president. Writer. **Publications:** Land Planning Law in a Free Society, 1959; Land-Use Planning, 1959, (with M.A. Wolf) 4th ed. as Land Use Planning: A Casebook on the Use, Misuse and Reuse of Urban Land, 1989; Federal Credit and Private Housing, 1960; Report to the President from the Panel on Automobile Junkyards, 1965; The End of Innocence, 1972; (with D.S. Iatridis) Housing the Poor in Suburbia, 1974; Between the Idea and the Reality, 1975; Financing the Solar Home, 1977; (co-author) Transfer of Development Rights: A Primer, 1981; (with D.W. Fessler) The Wrong Side of the Tracks, 1986; (with D.W. Fessler) Fairness and Justice: Law in the Service of Equality, 1987; (with J.S. Kayden) Landmark Justice: The Influence of William J. Brennan Jr. on America's Communities, 1988; Suburbs Under Siege, Race, Space and Audacious Judges, 1996; Mastering Boston Harbor: Courts, Dolphins and Imperiled Waters, 2005; (with M.A. Wolf) Land use Planning and the Environment, 2010. EDITOR: Law and Land, 1964, 2nd ed. as Property and Law, 1985; The Golden Age of American Law, 1966; Final Report, 1974; (co-ed.) Casenote Legal Briefs. Property: Adaptable to Courses Utilizing Haar and Liebman's Casebook on Property and law, 1978; Housing in the Eighties: Financial and Institutional Perspective, 1984; Cities, Law and Social Policy: Learning from the British, 1984; Judges, Politics and Flounders: Perspectives on the Cleaning up of Boston Harbor, 1986; (with J.S. Kayden) Zoning and the American Dream: Promises still to Keep, 1989; Zoning at Sixty: Mediating Public and Private Rights, 1990. **Address:** Harvard University Law School, 305 Langdell, 563 Massachusetts Ave., Cambridge, MA 02138, U.S.A. **Online address:** haar@law.harvard.edu

HAAR, James. American (born United States), b. 1929. **Genres:** Music, Poetry, Essays, History, Reference. **Career:** Harvard University, instructor, 1960-63, assistant professor, 1963-67; University of Pennsylvania, associate professor of music, 1967-69; New York University, professor of music, 1969-78; University of North Carolina, professor of music, now distinguished professor emeritus. Writer. **Publications:** The Tugendsterne of Harsduörffer and Staden: An Exercise in Musical Humanism, 1965; Essays on Italian Poetry and Music in the Renaissance, 1350-1600, 1986; (with I.A. Fenlon) The Italian Madrigal in the Early Sixteenth Century: Sources and Interpretation, 1988; The Science and Art of Renaissance Music, 1998; Collected Secular Works, 2001. EDITOR: Chanson and Madrigal 1480-1530: Studies in Comparison and Contrast. A Conference at Isham Memorial Library, September 13-14, 1961, 1964; The Duos of Gero, 1975; (with L.F. Bernstein) Primo libro de' madrigali italiani et canzoni Francese: A due Voci, 1980; (with L. Lockwood) Masses Based on Solmisation Themes, 2002; European Music, 1520-1640, 2006. Contributor to journals. **Address:** Department of Music, University of North Carolina, CB Ste. 3320, Hill Hall, 145 E Cameron Ave., Chapel Hill, NC 27599-3320, U.S.A.

HAAS, Dan. American (born United States), b. 1957. **Genres:** Education, Young Adult Fiction. **Career:** Millbrook Middle School, special education teacher, 1987-. Writer. **Publications:** You Can Call Me Worm, 1997. **Address:** Millbrook Middle School, PO Box AA, Millbrook, NY 12545, U.S.A. **Online address:** parkhaas@taconic.net

HAAS, Jeffrey. American (born United States), b. 1942?. **Genres:** Criminology/True Crime. **Career:** Legal Assistance Foundation, on staff, 1967-69; People's Law Office, co-founder and criminal defense and civil rights lawyer, 1969-2004; Action Coalition of Taos, co-founder, 2002-; Foundation for Self Sufficiency in Central America, chair. Writer. **Publications:** The Assassination of Fred Hampton: How the FBI and the Chicago Police Murdered a Black Panther, 2010. **Address:** Santa Fe, NM , U.S.A. **Online address:** jeff@hamptonbook.com

HAAS, Lawrence J. American (born United States), b. 1956. **Genres:** Politics/Government, Economics, Business/Trade/Industry. **Career:** Daily Register, municipal reporter, 1980-82; Pittsburgh Post-Gazette, state house correspondent, 1982-83; United Press Intl., state capital bureau chief, 1983-85; Bond Buyer, budget and tax reporter, 1985-87; National Journal, budget and tax reporter, 1987-92; National Academy of Public Administration, special assistant, 1992-; Manning Selvage & Lee, senior vice president and director of public affairs, 2001-05; Georgetown University's Government Affairs Institute, visiting senior fellow; public affairs consultant; White House, communications strategist, Office of Management and Budget, communications director; Yale University, special assistant and director of public affairs; American Foreign Policy Council, senior fellow. **Publications:** Running on Empty: Bush, Congress and the Politics of a Bankrupt Government, 1990; The Washington Almanac: A Guide to Federal Policy, 1992, rev. ed., 1993. Contributor to periodicals. **Address:** American Foreign Policy Council, 509 C St. NE, Washington, DC 20002, U.S.A. **Online address:** larry@larryhaasonline.com

HAASE, Donald. American (born United States), b. 1950. **Genres:** Literary Criticism And History. **Career:** University of Cincinnati, Charles P. Taft fellow, 1972-73; The Carolina Quarterly, managing editor, 1974-75; German Academic Exchange Service, fellow, 1976-77; Miami University, visiting assistant professor of German, 1979-81; Wayne State University, Department of German and Slavic Studies, assistant professor, 1981-86, associate professor, 1986-2004, professor of German, 2004-, career development chair, 1988-89, head, 1989-, chair, 1989-2007, Germany Programs, director of junior year, 1993-95, Department of Classical and Modern Languages, Literatures, and Cultures, interim associate chair, 2007, College of Liberal Arts and Sciences, associate dean, 2008-. **Publications:** EDITOR: The Reception of Grimms' Fairy Tales, 1993; (intro.) English Fairy Tales, 2002; Fairy Tales and Feminism: New Approaches, 2004; Fairy-Tale Studies series, 2004; Greenwood Encyclopedia of Folktales and Fairy Tales, 2008. Work appears in anthologies. Contributor of articles to journals. **Address:** Department of German & Slavic Studies, Wayne State University, 2155 Old Main, 4841 Cass Ave., Detroit, MI 48201, U.S.A. **Online address:** d.haase@wayne.edu

HABEGGER, Alfred (Carl). American (born United States), b. 1941. **Genres:** Novellas/Short Stories, Literary Criticism And History, Biography.

Career: University of Kansas, assistant professor, 1966-71, associate professor, 1971-82, professor of English, 1982-96, professor emeritus, 1996-; University of Bucharest, Fulbright lecturer, 1972-73; National Endowment for the Humanities, fellow, 1978-79, 1986-87, 1991-92, 1997-98; Hall Center for the Humanities, research fellow, 1988, 1990; independent biographer, 1996-. Writer. **Publications:** (Ed.) The Bostonians, 1976; Gender, Fantasy, and Realism in American Literature, 1982; Henry James and the Woman Business, 1989; The Father: A Life of Henry James, Sr., 1994; My Wars Are Laid Away in Books: The Life of Emily Dickinson, 2001. Contributor of articles to journals. **Address:** Department of English, University of Kansas, 1445 Jayhawk Blvd., Rm. 3001, Lawrence, KS 66045, U.S.A.

HABEL, Janette. *See* **GRIMALDI, Janette Pienkny.**

HABER, Julian Stuart. American (born United States) **Genres:** Novels, Mystery/Crime/Suspense. **Career:** Cook Children's Medical Center, pediatrician; Christian University, Department of Communications Disorders and Science, adjunct professor; American Academy of Pediatrics, Committee on Disabilities, staff. Writer. **Publications:** ADHD: The Great Misdiagnosis, 2000, rev. ed., 2003; Blood Avenger, 2005; They Were Soldiers in Peace and War: Stories of the Men and Women, Jewish War Veterans Martin Hochster Post 755 Fort Worth, Texas, 2006; A Nail In The Body of Christ, 2010. **Address:** 1300 W Lancaster Ave., Fort Worth, TX 76102, U.S.A.

HABER, Karen. American (born United States), b. 1955. **Genres:** Science Fiction/Fantasy, Young Adult Fiction, Art/Art History, Writing/Journalism. **Career:** Writer and journalist. **Publications:** (With R. Silverberg) The Mutant Season, 1990; Thieves' Carnival (novella), 1990; The Mutant Prime, 1991; Mutant Star, 1992; Mutant Legacy, 1993; Woman without a Shadow, 1995; The War Minstrels, 1996; Star Trek Voyager: Bless the Beasts, 1996; Sister Blood, 1997; (co-author) Science of the X-Men, 1999; (with T. Lockwood) Transitions: The Art of Todd Lockwood, 2003; Crossing Infinity (YA science fiction), 2005; Masters of Science Fiction and Fantasy Art, 2011. EDITOR: (with R. Silverberg) Universe (anthology), vol. I, 1990, vol. II, 1992, vol. III, 1994; Meditations on Middle-Earth, 2001; (with R. Silverberg) Fantasy: The Best of 2001, 2002; (with R. Silverberg) Science Fiction: The Best of 2002, 2003; (with R. Silverberg) Fantasy: The Best of 2002, 2003; Exploring the Matrix, 2003; (with J. Strahan) Science Fiction: The Best of 003, 2004; Year's Best Fantasy, 2004; Kong Unbound: The Cultural Impact, Pop Mythos and Scientific Plausibility of a Cinematic Legend, 2005. Contributor of articles to journals. Works appear in anthologies. **Address:** PO Box 13160, Sta. E, Oakland, CA 94661, U.S.A. **Online address:** karenhaber@yahoo.com

HABERMAN, David L. American (born United States), b. 1952. **Genres:** Natural History, Environmental Sciences/Ecology, Essays. **Career:** Indiana University, professor of religion. Writer. **Publications:** Acting as a Way of Salvation: A Study of Raganuga Bhakti Sadhana, 1988; Journey through the Twelve Forests: An Encounter with Krishna, 1994; (with L. Stevenson) Ten Theories of Human Nature, 1998, 5th ed., 2009; (ed. with L.L. Patton) Notes from a Mandala: Essays in Honor of Wendy Doniger, 2003; (trans. and intro.) The Bhaktirasamrtasindhu of Rupa Gosvamin, 2003; River of Love in an Age of Pollution: The Yamuna River of Northern India, 2006. Contributor of articles to journals. **Address:** Department of Religious Studies, College of Arts and Sciences, 230 Sycamore Hall, Bloomington, IN 47405-7005, U.S.A. **Online address:** dhaberma@indiana.edu

HABERMAN, Jacob. American/Swiss (born Switzerland), b. 1932. **Genres:** Novels, Biography, Adult Non-fiction. **Career:** Congregation Ramath Orah, rabbi, 1954-60; Haberman Group, staff, 1960-. Writer and lawyer. **Publications:** Maimonides and Aquinas: A Contemporary Appraisal, 1979; (trans. and intro.) The Microcosm of Joseph Ibn Saddiq, 2003. **Address:** Haberman Group, 315 Central Pk. W, New York, NY 10025, U.S.A.

HABERMAN, Richard. American (born United States), b. 1945. **Genres:** Mathematics/Statistics. **Career:** University of California, Department of Applied Mechanics and Engineering Sciences, lecturer, 1971-72, Institute of Geophysics and Planetary Physics, post-doctoral researcher, 1971-72; Rutgers University, assistant professor of mathematics, 1972-77; Ohio State University, assistant professor of mathematics, 1977-78; Southern Methodist University, Department of Mathematics, associate professor, 1978-85, professor, 1985-. Writer. **Publications:** Mathematical Models: Mechanical Vibrations, Population Dynamics, and Traffic Flow: An Introduction to Applied Mathematics, 1977; Elementary Applied Partial Differential Equations: With

Fourier Series and Boundary Value Problems, 1983, 3rd ed., 1998; Applied Partial Differential Equations, 1983, 4th ed. as Applied Partial Differential Equations: With Fourier Series and Boundary Value Problems, 2004; (with S.L. Campbell) Introduction to Differential Equations with Boundary Value Problems, 1996; (with S.L. Campbell) Introduction to Differential Equations with Dynamical Systems, 2008. **Address:** Department of Mathematics, Southern Methodist University, 209D Clements Hall, Dallas, TX 75275-0156, U.S.A. **Online address:** rhaberma@smu.edu

HABERS, Walther A(drianus). Dutch (born Netherlands), b. 1926. **Genres:** Novels, Literary Criticism And History. **Career:** Dutch Ground Nut Association, chair; police officer. Writer. **Publications:** Involved (novel), 1994. Contributor to periodicals. **Address:** Reviusrondeel 197, Capelle IJssel, 2902 EE, Netherlands. **Online address:** waltherh@hetnet.nl

HABGOOD *See* **Habgood, John Stapylton.**

HABGOOD, John Stapylton. (Habgood). British (born England), b. 1927. **Genres:** Ethics, Sciences, Theology/Religion, Natural History, Medicine/Health. **Career:** Cambridge University, university demonstrator in pharmacology, 1950-53, King's College, fellow, 1952-55; Westcott House, vice-principal, 1956-62; Saint John's Episcopal Church, rector, 1962-67; University of Birmingham, Queen's College, principal, 1967-73; Durham County, bishop, 1973-; retired, 1995. Writer. **Publications:** Religion and Science, 1964, as Truths in Tension: New Perspectives on Religion and Science, 1965; A Biologist Looks at Life, 1965; The Proliferation of Nuclear Technology, 1977; A Working Faith: Essays and Addresses on Science, Medicine and Ethics, 1980; Church and Nation in a Secular Age, 1983; Confessions of a Conservative Liberal, 1988; Making Sense, 1993; Faith and Uncertainty, 1997; Being a Person, 1998; Varieties of Unbelief, 2000; The Concept of Nature, 2002. CO-AUTHOR: Soundings, 1962; The Bible Tells Me So: Broadcast Talks on the Authority of the Bible, 1967; Christianity and Change, 1971; Queen's Sermons, 1973; Explorations in Ethics and International Relations, 1981; In Search of Christianity, 1986; Changing Britain, 1987; Liberating Life, 1990; The Divine Risk, 1990; Can Scientists Believe?, 1990; Tradition and Unity, 1991; The Weight of Glory, 1991; Using the Bible Today, 1991; Challenges in Medical Care, 1992; Treasure in the Field, 1993; Christian Values in Europe, 1993; Humanity Environment and God, 1993; Veritatis Splendor: A Response, 1994; The Sense of the Sacramental, 1995; The Christian Family, 1996; Seeing Ourselves, 1998; Community, Unity, Communion, 1998. Contributor to books. **Address:** 18 The Mount, Malton, NY YO17 7ND, England.

HABILA, Helon. Nigerian/British (born England), b. 1967?. **Genres:** Novels, Young Adult Fiction. **Career:** Federal Polytechnic, literature lecturer, 1997-99; University of East Anglia, writer-in-residence, 2002-, writing fellow; Bard College, Chinua Achebe fellow, 2005-06; Virginia Quarterly Review, contributing editor; Vanguard Newspaper, arts editor; George Mason University, faculty in creative writing. Writer. **Publications:** Waiting for an Angel, 2002; New Writing 14, 2006; Measuring Time: A Novel, 2007; (with K. George) Dreams, Miracles and Jazz: New Adventures in African Fiction, 2008; Oil on Water, 2010; (ed. and intro.) Granta Book of the African Short Story, 2011. **Address:** DGA Ltd., 55 Monmouth St., London, GL WC2H 9DG, England. **Online address:** h.habila@uea.ac.uk

HABINEK, Thomas N. American (born United States), b. 1953?. **Genres:** Literary Criticism And History, Classics, Translations. **Career:** National Institute for the Foodservice Industry, assistant editor, 1976; UCLA, assistant professor of classics, 1981-84; University of California, assistant professor of classics, associate professor of classics and rhetoric, professor of classics and rhetoric, 1984-92, faculty assistant, 1998; University of Southern California, Department of Classics, professor of classics, 1992-, chair, 1993-96, 2002-. **Publications:** The Colometry of Latin Prose, 1985; (ed. with A. Schiesaro) The Roman Cultural Revolution, 1997; The Politics of Latin Literature: Writing, Identity and Empire in Ancient Rome, 1998; Ancient Rhetoric and Oratory, 2004; The World of Roman Song: From Ritualized Speech to Social Order, 2005; Evolution, Cognition and the Humanities: Classical and Contemporary Approaches to Human Nature and Culture, forthcoming; (trans.) Cicero On Living and Dying Well, 2012. **Address:** Department of Classics, University of Southern California, THH 256, Los Angeles, CA 90089-0352, U.S.A. **Online address:** habinek@usc.edu

HABITO, Ruben L.F. (Ruben Leodegario Flores Habito). American (born United States), b. 1947?. **Genres:** Theology/Religion, History. **Career:** Sophia University, professor, 1976-89; Southern Methodist University, Perkins School of Theology, professor, 1989-; Maria Kannon Zen Center, founder and teacher, 1990-. Writer. **Publications:** IN ENGLISH: Total Liberation: Zen Spirituality and the Social Dimension, 1986; Healing Breath: Zen Spirituality for a Wounded Earth, 1993, rev. ed. as Healing Breath: Zen for Christians and Buddhists in a Wounded World, 2006; Originary Enlightenment: Tendai Hongaku Doctrine and Japanese Buddhism, 1996; (ed. with D.A. Pittman and T.C. Muck) Ministry and Theology in Global Perspective: Contemporary Challenges for the Church, 1996; Living Zen, Loving God, 2004; Experiencing Buddhism: Ways of Wisdom and Compassion, 2005; (ed. with K. Inaba) The Practice of Altruism: Caring and Religion in a Global Perspective, 2006; (foreword) The Flowing Bridge: Guidance on Beginning Zen Koans, 2007; (foreword) The Essential Shinran: A Buddhist Path of True Entrusting, 2007. IN JAPANESE: (with Y. Keizō) Kaihō no shingaku ga toikakeru mono: Ajia no genjitsu to Nihon no kadai, 1985; (with Y. Keizō) Kaihō no shingaku to Nihon: Shūkyō to seiji no kōsaten kara, 1985; Yameru Nihon o mitsumete: Ningen kaihō to shūkyō no saisei, 1988; Kore kara no Firipin to Nihon: Minsai kōryū no susume, 1988; (with C. Keiko) Akino seiken to Firipin shakai: Watashi no tsutaetai Firipin, 1989; (with T. Junshō) Seisho to Shinran no yomikata: Kaihō no shingaku to undō no Kyōgaku, 1989; Shinran to Kiristokyō no deai kara: Nihon-teki kaihō no reisei, 1989. Contributor of books. **Address:** Perkins School of Theology, Southern Methodist University, PO Box 750133, Dallas, TX 75275-0133, U.S.A. **Online address:** rhabito@smu.edu

HACHIGIAN, Nina L. American (born United States), b. 1967. **Genres:** Technology, Engineering. **Career:** Center for American Progress, senior vice president; U.S. National Security Council, special assistant to Jim Steinberg, the Deputy National Security Advisor & National Security Advisor Samuel R. Berger, 1998-99; RAND Corp., senior political scientist; Center for Asia-Pacific Policy, director; Federal Trade Commission, U.S. Chair Robert Pitofsky, attorney-advisor; O'Melveny & Myers, attorney; Ninth Circuit Court, clerk; Stanford University Center for International Security and Cooperation, visiting scholar. Writer. **Publications:** (ed. with C. Bernard) Khaled M. Abou El Fadl, Democracy and Islam in the New Constitution of Afghanistan, 2003; (with L. Wu) The Information Revolution in Asia, 2003; (with M. Sutphen) The Next American Century: How the U.S. Can Thrive as Other Powers Rise, 2008. Contributor to periodicals. **Address:** Los Angeles, CA, U.S.A. **Online address:** nhachigian@americanprogress.org

HACKBARTH, Steven (L.). American/German (born Germany), b. 1945. **Genres:** Education, Communications/Media, Philosophy. **Career:** NYC Board of Education, computer specialist teacher, 1994-; University of Southern California, Office of Student Services, director; USC Department of Policy, Planning and Administration, adjunct faculty, 1977-91; UNICEF, consultant, 1992-93; Tech Trends, consulting editor; Educational Technology Magazine, contributing editor. **Publications:** The Educational Technology Handbook: A Comprehensive Guide: Process and Products for Learning, 1996. **Address:** The Lillie Devereux Blake School, 45 E 81st St., New York, NY 10028, U.S.A. **Online address:** hackbarths@aol.com

HACKE, Daniela Alexandra. Swiss (born Switzerland), b. 1966. **Genres:** Human Relations/Parenting, Sex. **Career:** University of Zurich, staff. Writer. **Publications:** Women, Sex, and Marriage in Early Modern Venice, 2004. Contributor to books. **Address:** Historisches Seminar, University of Zurich, Karl Schmid-Str. 4, Zurich, CH-8006, Switzerland. **Online address:** dahacke@hist.uzh.ch

HACKELSBERGER, Christoph. German (born Germany), b. 1931. **Genres:** History, Architecture, Education. **Career:** Freelance architect, 1960-; Akademie der Bildenden Künste, honorary professor, 1992. Writer. **Publications:** IN GERMAN: Das k.k. oesterreichische Festungsviereck in Lombardo-Venetien, 1980; Ein Architekt sieht Müenchen, 1981; Müenchen und seine Isar-Brüecken, 1981; (contrib.) Zeit im Aufriss, Architektur in Bayern nach, 1945, 1983; Plädeoyer füer eine Befreiung des Wohnens aus den Zwäengensinnloser Perfektion, 1985; Die aufgeschobene Moderne: ein Versuch zur Einordnung der Architektur der Fünfziger Jahre, 1985; Lebensraum Stadt, 1985; Die k.k. Franzensfeste: ein Monumentalwerk der Befestigungskunst des 19. Jahrhunderts, 1986; Zweitausendzwölf, 1986; Beton: Stein der Weisen?, 1988; Hundert Jahre deutsche Wohnmisere, und kein Ende?, 1990; Architektur eines labilen Jahrhunderts, 1991; U-Bahn-Architektur in Munchen: Subway Architecture in Munich, 1997; Türme sind Träume: der Killesbergturm vom Jörg Schlaich, 2001; Flughafen München, 2004; Detlef

Schreiber, Architekt und Städteplaner/Detlef Schreiber, Architect and Town Planner, 2006. **Address:** Hofmark 9, 84181 Neufraunhofen, Neufraunhofen, 84181, Germany.

HACKER, Barton C(lyde). American (born United States), b. 1935. **Genres:** History, Bibliography. **Career:** University of Chicago, lecturer in history of science, 1965-66; University of Houston, research associate in history, 1966-69; National Aeronautics and Space Administration, Manned Spacecraft Center, historian, 1966-69; Iowa State University, assistant professor of history and mechanical engineering, 1970-75; Massachusetts Institute of Technology, Oral History Program and Archives for the History of 20th-Century Science and Technology, research associate, 1975-77; Reynolds Electrical and Engineering Co., Dosimetry Research Project, historian, 1978-86; Oregon State University, visiting professor, adjunct professor of history of technology, 1986-91; University of California, Lawrence Livermore National Laboratory, laboratory historian, 1992-98; Smithsonian Institution, National Museum of American History, Division of Armed Forces History, curator of military history, 1998-. Writer. **Publications:** The Military and the Machine: An Analysis of the Controversy Over Mechanization in the British Army, 1919-1939, 1968; (with J.M. Grimwood and P.J. Vorzimmer) Project Gemini Technology and Operations: A Chronology, 1969; An Annotated Index to Volumes 1 through 10 of Technology and Culture, 1959-1969, 1976; (with J.M. Grimwood) On the Shoulders of Titans: A History of Project Gemini, 1978; The Dragon's Tail: Radiation Safety in the Manhattan Project, 1942-1946, 1987; An Annotated Index to Volumes 1 through 25 of Technology and Culture, 1959-1984, 1991; Elements of Controversy: The Atomic Energy Commission and Radiation Safety in Nuclear Weapons Testing, 1947-1974, 1994; World Military History Bibliography: Premodern and Nonwestern Military Institutions and Warfare, 2003; World Military History Annotated Bibliography: Premodern and Nonwestern Military Institutions, 2005; American Military Technology: The Life Story of a Technology, 2006; (ed. with M. Vining and M. Gordon) Science in Uniform, Uniforms in Science: Historical Studies of American Military and Scientific Interactions, 2007. Contributor of articles to journals. **Address:** Division of Military History & Diplomacy, National Museum of American History, 14th St. & Constitution Ave. NW, MRC 623, PO Box 37012, Washington, DC 20013-7012, U.S.A. **Online address:** hacker1@coral.llnl.gov

HACKER, Jacob S. American (born United States), b. 1971. **Genres:** Social Sciences, Medicine/Health, Sports/Fitness, Politics/Government. **Career:** U.S. Department of Education, Jacob Javits fellow, 1994; Harvard University, research associate, 1995-96, Society of Fellows, junior fellow, 1999-2002; Yale University, Robert M. Leylan fellow in social sciences, 1996, teaching fellow, 1996-97, Peter Strauss Family assistant professor of political science, 2005-, Stanley B. Resor professor of political science; Brookings Institution, Robert Hartley research fellow, 1997-98; Institution for Social and Policy Studies, resident fellow. Writer. **Publications:** NONFICTION: The Road to Nowhere: The Genesis of President Clinton's Plan for Health Security, 1997; The Divided Welfare State: The Battle over Public and Private Social Benefits in the United States, 2002; (with P. Pierson) Off Center: The Republican Revolution and the Erosion of American Democracy, 2005; The Great Risk Shift, 2006; (ed. with J. Soss and S. Mettler) Remaking America: Democracy and Public Policy in an Age of Inequality, 2007; (ed.) Health at Risk: America's Ailing Health System-and How to Heal it, 2008; (co-ed.) The Interplay of Politics and Policy in America's Struggle against Poverty and Inequality, forthcoming; (with P. Pierson) Winner-Take-All Politics: How Washington Made the Rich Richer-and Turned its Back on the Middle Class, 2010; (ed. with A. O'Leary) Shared Responsibility, Shared Risk: Government, Markets and Social Policy in the Twenty-First Century, 2011. Contributor to periodicals. **Address:** Department of Political Science, Yale University, 77 Prospect St., Rm. A105, PO Box 208301, New Haven, CT 06511, U.S.A. **Online address:** jacob.hacker@yale.edu

HACKER, Kenneth L. American (born United States), b. 1951. **Genres:** Communications/Media, Psychology, Politics/Government, Technology. **Career:** Telecommunications system consultant, 1981-83; Michigan Technological University, assistant professor of speech and communication, 1986-90; New Mexico State University, Department of Communication Studies, visiting assistant professor, 1990-91, associate professor of communication studies, 1992-, professor of communication studies; San Juan College, lecturer, 1992; Dona Ana Community College, lecturer, 1997. Writer. **Publications:** (Contrib.) Mathematical Modelling for Information Technology, 1988; Verbal and Nonverbal Communication for Technical Professionals, 1988; (contrib.)

Communication and Culture, 1989; (ed.) Candidate Images in Presidential Elections, 1995; (contrib.) Theory and Research in Political Communication, 1996; (contrib.) The Clinton Presidency: Images, Issues, and Communication Strategies, 1996; (ed. with J. van Dijk) Digital Democracy: Issues of Theory and Practice, 2000; Presidential Candidate Images, 2004; (with J. van Dijk) Democracy in a Network Society, 2010. Contributor to books and periodicals. **Address:** Department of Communication Studies, New Mexico State University, Rm. 304, Speech Bldg., PO Box 30001, Las Cruces, NM 88003-8001, U.S.A. **Online address:** comstudy@nmsu.edu

HACKER, Marilyn. American (born United States), b. 1942. **Genres:** Poetry, Translations. **Career:** George Washington University, Jenny McKean Moore chair in writing, 1974; Columbia University, American Studies Institute, adjunct professor in creative writing, 1979-81; State University of New York, writer-in-residence, 1988; Columbia University, writer-in-residence, 1988; University of Cincinnati, George Elliston poet-in-residence, 1988; American University, distinguished writer-in-residence, 1989; State University of New York, visiting professor of creative writing, 1990; University of Utah, visiting professor of creative writing, 1995; Barnard College, visiting professor of creative writing, 1995; Brandeis University, Fannie Hurst visiting professor of poetry, 1996; Washington University, Fannie Hurst writer-in-residence, 1997; Hofstra University, professor of creative writing, 1997-99; City College of New York, director of creative writing M.A. Program, 1999-, Division of Humanities and the Arts, professor of English, 2003-; City University of New York, professor of French; Academy of American Poets, chancellor. Writer. **Publications:** The Terrible Children, 1967; (with T.M. Disch and C. Platt) Highway Sandwiches, 1970; Presentation Piece, 1974; Separations, 1976; Taking Notice, 1980; Assumptions, 1985; Love, Death, and the Changing of the Seasons, 1986; (contrib.) Five Poems of Marilyn Hacker: Soprano and Chamber Ensemble, 1989; Going Back to the River: Poems, 1990; The Hang-Gliders Daughter: New and Selected Poems, 1990; (contrib.) Hub of Ambiguity: For Soprano and Eight Players, 1984, 1992; Selected Poems, 1965-1990, 1994; Winter Numbers: Poems, 1994; Squares and Courtyards, 2000; First Cities: Collected Early Poems, 1960-1979, 2003; Desesperanto: Poems, 1999-2002, 2003; Names: Poems, 2010; Unauthorized Voices: Essays on Poets and Poetry, 1987-2009, 2010. TRANSLATOR: Claire Malroux, Edge, 1996; C. Malroux, A Long-Gone Sun: A Poem, 2000; V. Khoury-Ghata, Here There Was Once a Country, 2001; V. Khoury-Ghata, She Says, 2003; C. Malroux, Birds and Bison: Poems, 2004; V. Khoury-Ghata, A House at the Edge of Tears, 2005; Essays on Departure: New and Selected Poems, 2006; (and ed.) G. Goffette, Charlestown Blues: Selected Poems, 2007; V. Khoury-Ghata, Nettles: Poems, 2008; M. Étienne, King of a Hundred Horsemen, 2008; E. Moses, He and I, 2009; H. Kaddour, Treason: Poems, 2010. **Address:** Department of English, City College of New York, NA 6/235, 160 Convent Ave., New York, NY 10110, U.S.A. **Online address:** marilyn.hacker@gmail.com

HACKETT, Helen. British (born England), b. 1961. **Genres:** Literary Criticism And History, Romance/Historical. **Career:** University of Oxford, Merton College, junior research fellow, 1988-90; University College London, faculty, 1990-, reader in English, Centre for Early Modern Exchanges, co-director, 2009-. Writer. **Publications:** Virgin Mother, Maiden Queen: Elizabeth I and the Cult of the Virgin Mary, 1995; Women and Romance Fiction in the English Renaissance, 2000; Shakespeare and Elizabeth: The Meeting of Two Myths, 2009. Contributor to books and periodicals. **Address:** Department of English Language and Literature, University College London, Gower St., London, GL WC1E 6BT, England. **Online address:** h.hackett@ucl.ac.uk

HACKETT, Jeremy. British (born England), b. 1954?. **Genres:** Adult Non-fiction, Art/Art History, Social Sciences, History. **Career:** Hackett Ltd., co-founder and chairman. Writer. **Publications:** Mr. Classic, 2006. Contributor to periodicals. **Address:** Hackett Ltd., The Clove Bldg., 4 Maguire St., London, GL SE1 2NQ, England.

HACKETT, Joyce. American (born United States), b. 1961?. **Genres:** Novels, Adult Non-fiction, Romance/Historical. **Career:** George Washington University, Jenny McKean Moore writer-in-Washington, 2004-05; American Academy-Berlin, Holtzbrinck fellow, 2006; Netherlands Institute for Advanced Studies in the Humanities and Social Sciences, writer-in-residence, 2010-11. **Publications:** Disturbance of the Inner Ear, 2002; Manhattanville, forthcoming; Reconstruction, forthcoming. Contributor to periodicals

and magazines. **Address:** c/o Author Mail, Carroll & Graf Publishers, 245 W 17th St., 11th Fl., New York, NY 10011-5300, U.S.A. **Online address:** nanookindc@yahoo.com

HACKETT, Robert A(nthony). Canadian/British (born England), b. 1952. **Genres:** Communications/Media, Language/Linguistics, History, Social Sciences, Reference, Young Adult Non-fiction, Politics/Government. **Career:** Simon Fraser University, assistant professor, 1984-92, associate professor of communications, 1992-, professor, News Watch Canada, co-director, 1993-2003; Canadian Centre for Policy Alternatives, research associate. Writer. **Publications:** Pie in the Sky: A History of the Ontario Waffle, 1980; News and Dissent, 1991; Engulfed, 1993; (with Y. Zhao) Sustaining Democracy?: Journalism and the Politics of Objectivity, 1998; (co-author) The Missing News: Filters and Blind Spots in Canada's Press, 2000; (ed. with Y. Zhao) Democratizing Global Media: One World, Many Struggles, 2005; (with W.K. Carroll) Remaking Media: The Struggle to Democratize Public Communication, 2006. **Address:** School of Communication, Simon Fraser University, K9653, 8888 University Dr., Burnaby, BC V5A 1S6, Canada. **Online address:** hackett@sfu.ca

HACKL, Erich. Swiss/Austrian (born Austria), b. 1954. **Genres:** Novels, Young Adult Non-fiction, Essays, Young Adult Fiction, Translations. **Career:** Universidad Complutense, lecturer, 1977-79; University of Vienna, lecturer, 1981-90. Writer. **Publications:** Auroras Anlass, 1987; Sidonie, 1988; Abschied von Sidonie: Erzählung, 1989; Köenig Wamba, 1991; Sara und Simón: eine endlose Geschichte, 1995; In Fester Umarmung: Geschichtenund Berichte, Diogenes (essays), 1996; Entwurf einer Liebe auf den ersten Blick, 1999; Materialien zu Abschied von Sidonie, 2000; Der Träumer Krivanek, 2000; Lexikon der österreichischen Spaienkämpfer 1936-1939, 2003; Hagenwil-les-deux-Eglises: Ein Gespräch mit Niklaus Meienberg (essay), 2003; Bruiloft van Auschwitz, 2003; Anprobieren eines Vaters, 2004; Narratives of Loving Resistance: Two Stories, 2006; Als ob ein Engel, 2007; The Wedding in Auschwitz, 2009. EDITOR: (co-ed.) Lesebuch Dritte Welt: Band 2, 1984; Hier istniemand gestorben, 1985; Das Herz des Himmels, 1986; (with C.T. Solinis) Geschichten aus der Geschichte des Spanischen Buergerkriegs, 1986; Wien, Wien allein, 1987; Zugvoegel set jeher, 1987; (with M.L. Garcia) Spanien: Im Schatten der Sonne, 1989; (trans.) Idea Vilariño: An Liebe, 1994; (and trans.) A.M. Rodas: Gedichte der erotischen Linken, 1995; Alfredo Bauer: Hexenprozess in Tucuman und andere Chroniken aus der neuen Welt, 1996; Henriette Haill, Strassenballade, 1996; Album Gurs, Ein Fundstück aus dem Widerstand, 2000; Die Hochzeit von Auschwitz, 2002; Anprobiesen eines Vaters: Geschichtenund Erwägungen, 2004; (with P. Schultze-Kraft) Das Meschuggene Jahr: Roman, 2005; Das Y im Namen dieser Stadt, Ein Steyr Lesebuch, 2005. **Address:** c/o Diogenes Verlag, Sprecherstr 8, Zurich, CH-8032, Switzerland.

HACKLER, George. American (born United States), b. 1948. **Genres:** Administration/Management, Business/Trade/Industry, Economics, History. **Career:** Alpine Avalanche, owner, editor, and publisher, 1972-76; Texas State Senate, press secretary, 1976-78; El Paso Chamber of Commerce, business development officer, 1978; Southwest Publications Inc., owner, editor and publisher, 1981-95; Corporate Press, founder. Writer. **Publications:** An Act of Faith: 25 Golden Rules for Small Business Success, 2002; Butterfield Trail in New Mexico, 2005. **Address:** PO Box 2445, Corrales, NM 87048, U.S.A. **Online address:** ghack73586@aol.com

HACKNEY, Rod. See **HACKNEY, Rod(erick Peter).**

HACKNEY, Rod(erick Peter). (Rod Hackney). British (born England), b. 1942. **Genres:** Architecture, Songs/Lyrics And Libretti, History. **Career:** Government of Libya, housing architect, 1967-68; assistant to Arne Jacobsen, 1968-71; Rod Hackney Architect, principal, 1972-; Castward Ltd., founder, 1983; University of Paris VI, visiting professor, 1984; Times/RIBA Community Enterprise Scheme, chair, 1985-89, president, 1987-89; Young Architect World Forum, president, 1985; Building Communities, International Community Architecture Conference, president, 1986; Inner City Trust, chair of trustees, 1986; University of Nottingham, special professor, 1987; Union Internationale des Architectes, president, 1988-91; North Wales Centre, National Trust, president. Writer. **Publications:** Highfield Hall, 1982; The Good, the Bad, and the Ugly: Cities in Crisis, 1990; Good Golly, Miss Molly (musical), 1991. Contributor to periodicals. **Address:** Rod Hackney & Associates, St. Peter, Windmill St., Macclesfield, CH SK11 7HS, England.

HADAS, Rachel. American (born United States), b. 1948. **Genres:** Humanities, Poetry, Literary Criticism And History, Writing/Journalism, Essays, Translations. **Career:** Rutgers University, Department of English, instructor, 1980-81, assistant professor, 1982-87, associate professor, 1987-92, professor, 1992-2006, Board of Governors professor, 2006-; Columbia University, Department of English, faculty, 1992, 1993; Princeton University, Hellenic Studies Program, faculty, 1995, Creative Writing Program, faculty, 1996. Poet, essayist and translator. **Publications:** POETRY: Starting from Troy, 1975; Slow Transparency, 1983; A Son from Sleep, 1987; Pass It On, 1989; Living in Time, 1990; Mirrors of Astonishment, 1992; Other Worlds Than This: Translations, 1994; The Empty Bed, 1995; The Double Legacy: Reflections on a Pair of Deaths, 1995; Halfway down the Hall: New and Selected Poems, 1998; Merrill, Cavafy, Poems and Dreams, 2000; Indelible, 2001; Laws: Poems, 2004; The River of Forgetfulness: Poems, 2006; The Ache of Appetite, 2010. OTHER: Trelles, by Stephanos Xenos, 1978; (ed. and intro. with C. Mandel and M. Silverman) Saturday's Women: Eileen W. Barnes Award Anthology, 1982; Form, Cycle, Infinity: Landscape Imagery in the Poetry of Robert Frost, 1985; (with C. Barber) Unending Dialogue: Voices from an AIDS Poetry Workshop, 1991; Three Poets in Conversation: Dick Davis, Rachel Hadas, Timothy Steele, 2006; Classics: Essays, 2007; Greek Poets: Homer to the Present, 2010; Strange Relation: A Memoir of Marriage, Dementia and Poetry, 2011. **Address:** Department of English, Rutgers University, 520 Hill Hall, 360 Dr. Martin Luther King Jr. Blvd., Newark, NJ 07102-1801, U.S.A. **Online address:** rhadas@rutgers.edu

HADDAD, Gladys. American (born United States), b. 1930. **Genres:** Area Studies, Art/Art History, Film, History, Humanities, Literary Criticism And History, Local History/Rural Topics, Women's Studies And Issues, Autobiography/Memoirs, Biography, Documentaries/Reportage. **Career:** South Euclid-Lyndhurst, school teacher, 1952-63; Lake Erie College, professor of American studies and administrator, academic dean and executive assistant, 1963-89, professor of American studies emerita, 1989-; Case Western Reserve University, founder, director of western reserve studies symposium, 1985-, adjunct professor of American studies, professor of American studies and director of western reserve studies symposia, 1990-, archivist, researcher; Western Reserve Historical Society, administrator, 1989-. Writer and producer for films. **Publications:** Laukhuff's Book Store of Cleveland: An Epilogue, 1997; Flora Stone Mather: Daughter of Cleveland's Euclid Avenue and Ohio's Western Reserve, 2007. EDITOR: (with H.F. Lupold) Ohio's Western Reserve: A Regional Reader, 1988; (with D.R. Anderson) Anthology of Western Reserve Literature, 1992. **Address:** Interdisciplinary Centers and Programs, Case Western Reserve University, 101 Clark Hall, 11130 Bellflower Rd., Cleveland, OH 44106-7120, U.S.A. **Online address:** gmh3@po.cwru.edu

HADDEN, Sally E. American (born United States) **Genres:** History, Law. **Career:** University of Toledo, assistant professor of history and adjunct lecturer in law, 1993-95; Florida State University, faculty, assistant professor of history and assistant professor of law, 1995-2002, associate professor of history and associate professor of law, 2002-10; Harvard University, Summer School Program, instructor, 2001-07, 2009-; Western Michigan University, Department of History, associate professor of history, 2010-. Writer. **Publications:** Slave Patrols: Law and Violence in Virginia and the Carolinas, 2001; (ed. with A. Brophy) The Blackwell Companion to American Legal History, 2012; (ed. with P. Minter) Signposts, 2012. **Address:** Department of History, Western Michigan University, 4408 Friedmann Hall, Kalamazoo, MI 49008-5334, U.S.A. **Online address:** sally.hadden@wmich.edu

HADDOCK, Lisa (Robyn). American (born United States), b. 1960. **Genres:** Novels, Young Adult Fiction. **Career:** University of Tulsa, news editor and managing editor of Collegian, 1981-82, editor-in-chief, 1982-83; Neighbor Newspapers, intern, 1982; St. Louis Globe-Democrat, clerk, 1984; teacher, 1985; Tulsa World, copy editor, 1986-89; The Record, religion and values editor, copy editor and layout editor, 1989-; New Jersey Faith Forum, editor. **Publications:** Edited Out, 1994; Final Cut, 1995; The Virgin Mary Prayer Kit, 2011. **Address:** Fair Winds Press, 400 1st Ave. N, Ste. 300, Minneapolis, MN 55401, U.S.A.

HADLEY, Dawn M. British (born England), b. 1967. **Genres:** History. **Career:** University of Sheffield, faculty. Writer. **Publications:** (Ed. with J.D. Richards) Cultures in Contact: Scandinavian Settlement in England in the Ninth and Tenth Centuries, 2000; (as D.M. Hadley) The Northern Danelaw: Its Social Structure, C. 800-1100, 2000; (as D.M. Hadley) Death in Medieval England, 2001; The Vikings in England: Settlement, Society and Culture,

2007. **Address:** University of Sheffield, Western Bank, Sheffield, SY S10 2TN, England. **Online address:** d.m.hadley@sheffield.ac.uk

HADLEY, Joan. See HESS, Joan.

HAEGER, John Denis. American (born United States), b. 1942. **Genres:** History, Biography. **Career:** Central Michigan University, Department of history, assistant professor, 1968-72, associate professor, 1972-78, professor, 1978-, research professor, 1979, head, 1982-85, College of Arts and Sciences, dean, College of Graduate Studies/Office of Research, associate dean, 1988-89, interim dean, dean, Institute for Social and Behavioral Research, board director, 1988-89, School of Graduate Studies, assistant vice president for research and dean, 1990-; Northern Arizona University, president, 2001-; Towson University, provost and vice president for academic affairs. United Way of Northern Arizona, chair; Translational Genomics Research Institute, director. Writer. **Publications:** (Ed. with M.P. Weber) The Bosses, 1974, rev. ed., 1979; The Investment Frontier: New York Businessmen and the Economic Development of the Old Northwest, 1981; John Jacob Astor: Business and Finance in the Early Republic 1991. Works appear in anthologies. Contributor of articles to journals. **Address:** Northern Arizona University, S San Francisco St., PO Box 4092, Flagstaff, AZ 86011-4120, U.S.A. **Online address:** john.haeger@nau.edu

HAENEL, Wolfram. German (born Germany), b. 1956. **Genres:** Children's Fiction, Plays/Screenplays, Novels, Education. **Career:** Landestheater Hannover, photographer and graphic artist, 1983-85; Georg Buechner Gymnasium, high school teacher, 1985-86; Atelier fuer Werbegestaltung, public relations assistant, copywriter, photographer and graphic artist, 1986-88; Theaterwerkstatt Hannover, drama producer and playwright, 1988-91. **Publications:** FOR CHILDREN IN ENGLISH TRANSLATION: Der kleine Mann und der Baer, 1993; Waldemar und die weite Welt, 1994; Mia, die Strandkatze, 1994; Lila und der regenbogenbunte Dinosaurier, 1994; Romeo liebt Julia, 1995; Anders hat sich verlaufen, 1996; Angst um Abby, 1996; Eine falle fur familie bar, 1997; Das gold am ende des regenbogens, 1997; Willi, der strandhun, 1999; Schiffshund in not, 1999; Oskar, der kleine elefant, 2000; Little Elephant Runs Away, 2001; Weekend with Grandmother, 2002; Als die Schneemannes Weihnachten feiesten, 2004. FOR CHILDREN IN GERMAN: Willi Wolle, 1987; Mimmi an der Nordsee, 1990; Die Teddybaeren-Bande, 1994; Ein Huhn haut ab, 1995; Anna Nass, 1996; Ein Pferd fuer Runder Mond: Indianer-Geschichten, 1996; Der kleine Mann und Familie Bar, 1997; Lasses letzter Urlaub: Ferien-Geschichten, 1997; Der kleine Haewelmann, 1997; Anna Nass, die neue kommt, 1997; Mein schwein, die drei rauber, dochen und ich, 1997; Giftiges gold oder grossvaters esel, 1997; Lola und Glatze, 1998; Lasse und das geheimnis der leuchtturmwarter, 1998; (with U. Gerold) Jetzt will ich aber schlafen: zwei Gutenachtgeschichten, 1998; Die rauber vom Geistermoor, 1998; Anna Nass kusst Alexander, 1998; Das Weihnachtswunschtraumbett, 1999; Die sache mit den weihnachtsmannern, 1999; Geheimpirat Herr Holtermann, 1999; Die wilden ponys von Dublin, 2000; Wie der Zauberlehrling die pommes frites erfand, 2000; Der tag, an dem lehrer roth verschwand, 2001; Oskar, der klein elefant, haut ab, 2001. OTHER: (with U. Gerold) Irland (guide book), 1991; (with U. Gerold) Irland (picture book), 1995; Irgendwo woandess (novel), 2002. **Address:** c/o Ulrike Gerold, Atelier fuer Werbegestaltung, Luisenstrasse 15, Hildesheim, D-31141, Germany.

HAENN, Nora. American (born United States), b. 1967. **Genres:** Economics, Social Sciences, Environmental Sciences/Ecology. **Career:** Western Carolina University, visiting assistant professor, 1997-98; American Ethnologist, assistant editor for reviews, 1998-99; Arizona State University, assistant professor, 1999-2005, associate professor, 2005-07; North Carolina State University, associate professor of anthropology and international studies, 2007-. Writer. **Publications:** Fields of Power, Forests of Discontent: Culture, Conservation, and the State in Mexico, 2005; (ed. with R.R. Wilk) The Environment in Anthropology: A Reader in Ecology, Culture and Sustainable Living, 2005; (with E. Johnson and M.G. Buckwalter) The Teaching Road Map: A Pocket Guide For High School And College Teachers, 2009. **Address:** Department of Sociology & Anthropology, North Carolina State University, Rm. 229, 1911 Bldg., Ste. 334, PO Box 8107, Raleigh, NC 27695-7107, U.S.A. **Online address:** nora_haenn@ncsu.edu

HAERI, Shahla. American/Iranian (born Iran) **Genres:** Cultural/Ethnic Topics. **Career:** Harvard University, Center for Middle Eastern Studies, faculty associate, 1986-; Brown University, Pembroke Center for Teaching and

Research on Women, postdoctoral fellow, 1986-87; New York University, Department of Anthropology, assistant professor, 1990-91; Boston University, Department of Anthropology, assistant professor, 1993-2004, director of women's studies program, 1997-98, 2001-, associate professor, 2005-; Comparative Studies of South Asia, Africa, and the Middle East, associate editor, 2002-; Women's Studies, research fellow and visiting associate professor, 2006-07; Graduate Consortium of Women's Studies, board director, 2006-; Cultural anthropologist and writer. **Publications:** Law of Desire: Temporary Marriage in Shi'i Iran, 1989; No Shame for the Sun: Lives of Professional Pakistani Women, 2002. Contributor to periodicals. **Address:** Department of Anthropology, College of Arts & Sciences, Boston University, 704 Commonwealth Ave., Ste. 101, Boston, MA 02215, U.S.A. **Online address:** shaeri@bu.edu

HAFERTEPE, Kenneth. American (born United States), b. 1955. **Genres:** Architecture, Photography. **Career:** University of Texas, assistant instructor, 1981-86, lecturer in American studies, 1986; French Legation Museum, tour guide and historian, 1986-87; Neill-Cochran Museum House, resident manager, 1987-90; Historic Deerfield Inc., director of academic programs, 1990-; Smith College, adjunct assistant professor, 1990-; Baylor University, Department of Museum Studies, faculty, 2000-, interim chair, assistant professor; University of Massachusetts, Department of Museum Studies, assistant professor; Chumney and Associates, architectural historian and photographer; Williams Co., architectural historian and photographer. **Publications:** America's Castle: The Evolution of the Smithsonian Building and Its Institution, 1840-1878, 1984; A History of the French Legation in Texas: Alphonse Dubois de Saligny and His House, 1989; A History of Ashton Villa: A Family and Its House in Victorian Galveston, Texas, 1991; Abner Cook: Master Builder on the Texas Frontier, 1991; (ed. with J.F. O'Gorman) American Architects and Their Books to 1848, 2001; (ed. with J.F. O'Gorman) American Architects and Their Books, 1840-1915, 2007. Contributor of articles to periodicals. Works appear in anthologies. **Address:** Department of Museum Studies, Baylor University, Mayborn 1809, PO Box 97154, Waco, TX 76798-7154, U.S.A. **Online address:** kenneth_hafertepe@baylor.edu

HAFFENDEN, John. British (born England), b. 1945. **Genres:** Art/Art History, Biography, Autobiography/Memoirs, Reference, Writing/Journalism, Young Adult Fiction, Essays. **Career:** Oxford College of Further Education, faculty; University of Exeter, faculty; University of Sheffield, faculty, 1975-, professor of English, 1994-, research professor in English literature. Writer. **Publications:** John Berryman: A Critical Commentary, 1980; The Life of John Berryman, 1982; William Empson, vol. I: Among the Mandarins, 2005, vol. II: Against the Christians, 2006. EDITOR: (and intro.) Henry's Fate & Other Poems, 1967-1972, 1978; Novelists in Interview, 1985; (and intro.) The Royal Beasts and Other Works, 1986; (and intro.) Argufying: Essays on Literature and Culture, 1987; Essays on Renaissance Literature, vol. I: Donne and the New Philosophy, 1994, vol. II: The Drama, 1995; W.H. Auden: The Critical Heritage, 1993; The Strengths of Shakespeare's Shrew: Essays, Memoirs and Reviews, 1996; (and intro.) Berryman's Shakespeare, 1999; The Complete Poems of William Empson, 2001; Selected Letters of William Empson, 2006. **Address:** University of Sheffield, Rm. 1.15, Sir William Empson House, Jessop W 1 Upper Hanover St., Shearwood Rd., Sheffield, SY S10 2TD, England. **Online address:** j.haffenden@sheffield.ac.uk

HAFNER, Katie. American (born United States), b. 1957. **Genres:** Documentaries/Reportage, Music, Biography, Information Science/Computers, Technology. **Career:** Computerworld, reporter, 1983; San Diego Union, reporter, 1984-85; Business Week, staff writer, 1986-89; freelance and book writer, 1990-94; Newsweek, contributing editor and technology correspondent, 1994-98; New York Times, computer technology reporter, 1998-. **Publications:** (With J. Markoff) Cyberpunk: Outlaws and Hackers on the Computer Frontier, 1991; The House at the Bridge: A Story of Modern Germany, 1995; (with M. Lyon) Where Wizards Stay up Late: The Origins of the Internet, 1996; The Well: A Story of Love, Death and Real Life in the Seminal Online Community, 2001; Das Haus an Der Brücke: Die Villa Schöningen in Potsdam und ihre Bewohner, 2004; Romance on Three Legs: Glenn Gould's Obsessive Quest for the Perfect Piano, 2008. Contributor to periodicals. **Address:** c/o Author Mail, Avalon Publishing Group, 245 W 17th St., 11th Fl., New York, NY 10011, U.S.A. **Online address:** katieh@zilker.net

HAFNER-BURTON, Emilie M. American (born United States), b. 1973. **Genres:** Business/Trade/Industry, Economics. **Career:** Nuffield College, University of Oxford, postdoctoral research fellow, 2003-06; Stanford Law School, associate fellow, 2003-06, Center for International Security and Cooperation, visiting fellow, 2008-09; Princeton University, Woodrow Wilson School for International and Public Affairs, assistant professor of politics and public policy, 2006-09; University of California, associate professor and director, Laboratory on International Law and Regulation, staff, 2009-. Writer. **Publications:** Forced to Be Good: Why Trade Agreements Boost Human Rights, 2009. Contributor to journals and periodicals. **Address:** CA, U.S.A. **Online address:** ehafner@ucsd.edu

HAFVENSTEIN, Joel. Afghani/American (born United States), b. 1976?. **Genres:** Autobiography/Memoirs. **Career:** Chemonics, staff. Writer and consultant. **Publications:** Opium Season: A Year on the Afghan Frontier (memoir), 2007. Contributor to periodicals. **Address:** Lyons Press, 246 Goose Ln., PO Box 480, Guilford, CT 06437, U.S.A.

HAGA, Enoch John. American (born United States), b. 1931. **Genres:** Education, Genealogy/Heraldry, Information Science/Computers, Mathematics/Statistics, Essays, Medicine/Health, Technology. **Career:** California Medical Facility, business teacher, 1956-60; Stanislaus State College (now California State College), assistant professor of business, 1960-61; Amador Valley High School, chairman, teacher in business education, 1964-92; Sacramento State College (now California State University at Sacramento), visiting assistant professor, 1967-69; Chabot College, instructor in business, 1970-; Automedica, founder, co-editor, 1970-76; Ohlone College, instructor in philosophy (logic), part-time, 1972-; California Institute of Asian Studies, vice president, 1972-75; Pacific Institute of East-West Studies, president, 1975-76; Business Education Certification Council and Data Education Certification Council, director, 1975-; Enoch Haga Publisher, owner. **Publications:** Understanding Automation: A Data Processing Curriculum Guide and Reference Text, 1965; Simplified Computer (Arithmetic, Logic, Input, Flowcharting) series, vol. I, 1971, vol. II, 1972; The 2000-Year History of the Haga-Helgoy and Krick-Keller Families, Ancestors and Descendants, 1994; Before the Apple Drops: 15 Essays on Dinosaur Education, 1994; Exploring Prime Numbers on Your PC, 1994; TARO solution: A Complete Guide to Interpreting the Tarot, 1994; How to Prepare Your Genealogy for Publication on Your Home Computer, 2001; Exploring Prime Numbers on Your PC and the Internet: With Directions To Prime Number Sites on the Internet, 2001, rev. ed. 2007. EDITOR: (with M.F. Ronayne) Total Systems, 1962; Automated Educational Systems, 1967; Computer Techniques in Biomedicine and Medicine: Simulation and Modeling, Health Care and Image Processing, 1973. **Address:** Enoch Haga Publisher, PO Box 489, Folsom, CA 95763-0489, U.S.A. **Online address:** enochhaga@msn.com

HAGAN, Stephen. Australian (born Australia), b. 1959?. **Genres:** Novels. **Career:** University of Southern Queensland, associate lecturer. Writer. **Publications:** The N Word: One Man's Stand, 2005. **Address:** Darling Heights, QL, Australia. **Online address:** hagans@usq.edu.au

HAGEDORN, Jessica Tarahata. American/Filipino (born Philippines), b. 1949?. **Genres:** Poetry, Novellas/Short Stories, Novels, Plays/Screenplays, Social Sciences, Literary Criticism And History, Young Adult Fiction. **Career:** Writer. **Publications:** Four Young Women, 1973; Dangerous Music, 1975; Pet Food and Tropical Apparitions, 1981; Dogeaters (novel), 1990; Two Stories, 1992; Danger and Beauty, 1993, rev. ed., 2002; (ed. and intro.) Charlie Chan is Dead, 1993, rev. ed., 2004; The Gangster of Love (novel), 1996; (with M. Roth) Burning Heart: A Portrait of the Phillipines, 1999; Dogeaters: A Play About the Philippines, 2003; Dream Jungle (novel), 2003; (contrib.) Fred Wilson: So Much Trouble in the World-Believe It or Not!, 2006; Toxicology, 2011. Work appears in anthologies. Contributor to periodicals. **Address:** Harold Schmidt Literary Agency, 415 W 23rd St., Ste. 6F, New York, NY 10011, U.S.A.

HAGEDORN, John M. American (born United States), b. 1947. **Genres:** Urban Studies, Social Work, Criminology/True Crime. **Career:** Impact Press Service, journalist, 1978-80; Sherman Park Community Association, interim director, community organizer and coordinator of anti-crime programs, 1982-83; Community Relations-Social Development Commission, Youth Diversion Project, director, 1983-85; University of Wisconsin, Urban Research Center, project director, 1985-88, principal investigator and project director, 1991-96; Milwaukee County Department of Health and Human Service, youth program coordinator, 1988-91; Marquette University, instructor, 1988; Milwaukee Area Technical College, instructor, 1988; Aurora University, instructor, 1992-96; University of Illinois, Department of Criminal Justice, assistant professor,

1996-99, associate professor 1999-, senior reseaerch fellow, Kenneth B. Clark Center for the Study of Violence in Communities, director. Writer. **Publications:** (With P. Macon) People and Folks: Gangs, Crime, and the Underclass in a Rustbelt City, 1988, 2nd ed., 1998; Forsaking Our Children: Bureaucracy and Reform in the Child Welfare System, 1995; (ed. with M. Chesney-Lind) Female Gangs in America: Essays on Girls, Gangs and Gender, 1999; (with J. Moore) Female Gangs: A Focus on Research, 2001; (ed.) Gangs in the Global City: Alternatives to Traditional Criminology, 2007; World of Gangs: Armed Young Men and Gangsta Culture, 2008. Contributor of articles to journals and books. **Address:** Department of Criminology, Law & Justice, University of Illinois, 4050C Behavioral Sciences Bldg., 1007 W Harrison St., Chicago, IL 60607-7140, U.S.A. **Online address:** huk@uic.edu

HAGELIN, Aiban. Argentine/Chilean (born Chile), b. 1934. **Genres:** Psychology, Sciences. **Career:** Buenos Aires, training analyst and medical doctor, 1962-. Philosopher of science and writer. **Publications:** Narcissism: Myth and Theory in Freud's Works, 1985; (co-ed.) On Freud's Observations on Transference-Love, 1993; Autism; Incest; Cannibalism. **Address:** Ayacucho 203070, Buenos Aires, 1112, Argentina.

HAGEN, George. American/British (born England), b. 1958. **Genres:** Novels. **Career:** Screenwriter, cartoonist and freelance journalist. **Publications:** NOVELS: The Laments, 2004; Tom Bedlam, 2007. Contributor to periodicals. **Address:** New York, NY , U.S.A. **Online address:** george@georgehagen.com

HAGEN, Steve. American (born United States), b. 1945. **Genres:** Theology/Religion, Sciences. **Career:** Zen priest, 1979; Dharma Field Meditation and Learning Center, head teacher. Writer. **Publications:** How the World Can Be the Way It Is: An Inquiry for the New Millennium into Science, Philosophy and Perception, 1995; Buddhism Plain and Simple, 1997; (ed.) You Have to Say Something: Manifesting Zen Insight, 1998; (intro.) The Iron Flute: 100 Zen Koans, 2000; Buddhism Is Not What You Think: Finding Freedom beyond Beliefs, 2003; Meditation Now or Never, 2007. **Address:** Dharma Field Zen Center, 3118 W 49th St., Minneapolis, MN 55410, U.S.A.

HAGER, Alan. American (born United States), b. 1940. **Genres:** Literary Criticism And History, Mystery/Crime/Suspense, Novellas/Short Stories, Intellectual History, Writing/Journalism, Classics, Music, Education, Mythology/Folklore, Sports/Fitness, Theatre. **Career:** University of California, associate of subject A (remedial) and associate of English, 1968-76, professor of English; Dominican College of San Rafael, visiting assistant professor of English, 1972, University of Oklahoma, instructor in English, 1977-79; Loyola University of Chicago, assistant professor of English, 1979-88; Robert Morris College, acting assistant professor of English, 1989; University of Illinois, visiting lecturer of English, 1989-93; State University of New York, assistant professor, 1993-96, associate professor, 1996-99, professor of English, 2000-05, emeritus professor 2005-. Writer. **Publications:** Shakespeare's Political Animal: Schema and Schemata in the Canon, 1990; Dazzling Images: The Masks of Sir Philip Sidney, 1991; The Toll Booth: A Dicky Getz Novel, 2004; Bedtime Confidential, a Novel, 2006. EDITOR: (contrib.) Major Tudor Authors: A Bio-Bibliographical Critical Sourcebook, 1997; Understanding Romeo and Juliet: A Student Casebook to Issues, Sources and Historic Documents, 1999; The Age of Milton: An Encyclopedia of Major 17th-Century British and American Authors, 2004; Encyclopedia of British Writers: 16th and 17th Centuries, 2005; Encyclopedia of British Writers, 18th Century, 2005. Contributor of articles to periodicals. **Address:** Department of English, State University of New York, PO Box 2000, Cortland, NY 13045, U.S.A. **Online address:** hagera@cortland.edu

HAGER, Betty. American (born United States), b. 1923. **Genres:** Novellas/Short Stories, Mythology/Folklore, Novels, Travel/Exploration. **Career:** Writer. **Publications:** TALES FROM THE BAYOU SERIES: Old Jake and the Pirate's Treasure, 1980; Miss Tilly and the Haunted Mansion, 1994; Marcie and the Shrimp Boat Adventure, 1994; Marcie and the Monster of the Bayou, 1994. OTHER: The Gift of the Dove (adult novel), 1991. **Address:** c/o Sandy Mackey, Quillco Agency, 3104 W Cumberland Ct., Westlake Village, CA 91362-3524, U.S.A.

HAGERMAN, Edward. Canadian (born Canada), b. 1939. **Genres:** History, International Relations/Current Affairs, Military/Defense/Arms Control, Technology, Local History/Rural Topics, Social Sciences, Chemistry. **Career:** Ohio State University, instructor in history, 1965-70; York University,

assistant professor, 1970-76, associate professor, 1976-2002, professor of history, 2002-04, professor emeritus, 2004-. Writer. **Publications:** The American Civil War and the Origins of Modern Warfare: Ideas, Organization and Field Command, 1988; (with S. Endicott) The United States and Biological Warfare: Secrets from the Early Cold War and Korea, 1998. **Address:** Department of History, Atkinson College, York University, 730 Atk, 4700 Keele St., Toronto, ON M3J 1P3, Canada. **Online address:** hagerman@yorku.ca

HAGERTY, Barbara Bradley. American (born United States), b. 1959?. **Genres:** Theology/Religion, Humanities. **Career:** Christian Science Monitor, news reporter, Tokyo, correspondent; Japan, correspondent; Asia, correspondent, senior correspondent, 1982-93; National Public Radio, staff, 1995-, U.S. Justice Department, correspondent, 1998-2003, religion correspondent, 2003-. **Publications:** Fingerprints of God: The Search for the Science of Spirituality, 2009. Contributor to periodicals. **Address:** c/o Raphael Sagalyn, The Sagalyn Agency, 4922 Fairmont Ave., Ste. 200, Bethesda, MD 20814, U.S.A.

HAGERTY, Devin T. American (born United States), b. 1962?. **Genres:** Politics/Government, Social Sciences, History. **Career:** University of Sydney, lecturer; University of Maryland, Department of Political Science, associate professor, professor. Writer. **Publications:** Preventing Nuclear Proliferation in South Asia, 1995; The Consequences of Nuclear Proliferation: Lessons from South Asia, 1998; (ed.) South Asia in World Politics, 2005; (with S. Ganguly) Fearful Symmetry: India-Pakistan Crises in the Shadow of Nuclear Weapons, 2005. **Address:** Department of Political Science, University of Maryland, Baltimore County, 1000 Hilltop Cir., Baltimore, MD 21250, U.S.A. **Online address:** dhagerty@umbc.edu

HAGGER, Nicholas. British (born England), b. 1939. **Genres:** Novellas/Short Stories, Plays/Screenplays, Poetry, History, Philosophy, Autobiography/Memoirs, Travel/Exploration. **Career:** Gregory, Rowcliffe & Co. (solicitors), articled clerk, 1957-58; University of Baghdad, lecturer in English, 1961-62; Tokyo University of Education, professor, 1963-67; Kcio University, professor, 1963-67; University of Libya, lecturer, 1968-70; Oaklands School, principal, 1982-; Oak-Tree Books Ltd., editorial director, 1984-86; Coopersale Hall School, principal, 1989-; Normanhurst School, principal, 1996-; Otley Hall (historic house), proprietor, 1997-2004. Poet, philosopher and historian. **Publications:** HISTORY: The Fire and the Stones: A Grand Unified Theory of World History and Religion, 1991; The Syndicate: The Story of the Coming World Government, 2004; The Secret History of the West: The Influence of Secret Organisations on Western History from the Renaissance to the 20th Century, 2005; The Light of Civilization: How the Vision of God has Inspired All the Great Civilizations, 2006; The Secret Founding of America: The Real Story of Freemasons, Puritans and The Battle for the New World, 2007; The Rise and Fall of Civilizations: Why Civilizations Rise and Fall and What Happens When They End, 2008; The Secret American Dream: The Real Story of Liberty's Empire and the Rise of a World State, 2011. POETRY: Selected Poems: A Metaphysical's Way of Fire, 1991; Collected Poems: A White Radiance 1958-1993, 1994; Overlord, The Triumph of Light: An Epic Poem Based on the Events of 1944-1945, 4 vols., 1994-96; Overlord: The Triumph of Light: 1944-1945, 2006; Classical Odes: Poems on England, Europe and a Global Theme, and of Everyday Life in the One, 2006; Collected Poems 1958-2005, 2006; Armageddon: The Triumph of Universal Order, An Epic Poem on The War on Terror and of Holy-War Crusaders, 2010. CRITICISM: A New Philosophy of Literature: The Fundamental Theme and Unity of World Literature, 2012. PHILOSOPHY: The Universe and the Light: A New View of the Universe and Reality, 1993; The One and the Many: Universalism and the Vision of Unity, 1999; The New Philosophy of Universalism: The Infinite and the Law of Order, 2009; The World Government: A Blueprint for a Universal World State, 2010. AUTOBIOGRAPHICAL: A Mystic Way: A Spiritual Autobiography, 1994; Awakening to the Light: Diaries, vol. I, 1958-1967, 1994. VERSE PLAYS: The Warlords: From D-Day to Berlin, 1995; The Tragedy of Prince Tudor: A Nightmare, 1999; Collected Verse Plays, 2007. STORIES: A Spade Fresh with Mud: Collected Stories, vol. I, 1995; A Smell of Leaves and Summer: Collected Stories, vol. II, 1995; Wheeling Bats and a Harvest Moon: Collected Stories, vol. III, 1999; The Warm Glow of the Monastery Courtyard: Collected Stories, vol. IV, 1999; Collected Stories: A Thousand and One Mini-Stories or Verbal Paintings, 2007. EYEWITNESS HISTORY/TRAVELOGUES: The Last Tourist in Iran, 2008; The Libyan Revolution, 2009; A View of Epping Forest, 2012. Contributor to magazines. **Address:** PO Box 289, Loughton, EX IG10 4WD, England. **Online address:** info@nicholashagger.co.uk

HAGUE, D. C. *See* **HAGUE, Douglas (Chalmers).**

HAGUE, Douglas (Chalmers). (D. C. Hague). British (born England), b. 1926. **Genres:** Education, Economics, Business/Trade/Industry, Young Adult Non-fiction. **Career:** University of London, assistant lecturer, 1947-50, lecturer, 1950-57, reader in political economy, 1957; University of Sheffield, Newton Chambers professor of economics, 1957-63, Department of Business Studies, head, 1962-63; Duke University, visiting professor, 1960-61; University of Manchester, Manchester Business School, professor of applied economics, 1963-65, professor of managerial economics 1965-81, deputy director 1978-81; Carnegie Corp's Anglo-American Project on Accountability, British chairman, 1968-72; Oxford University, Centre for Management Studies, professorial fellow, Oxford Strategy Unit, chairman, 1981-, Economic and Social Research Council, chairman, 1983-87; University of Manchester, 1981-; Oxford Strategy Network, chairman, 1984; Templeton College, associate fellow, 1983, professorial fellow, 1981-83, Strategic Leadership Programme, chairman. Writer. **Publications:** Costs in Alternative Locations: The Clothing Industry, 1952; (with A. Stonier) A Textbook of Economic Theory, 1953, 5th ed., 1980; (with W. Stonier) The Essentials of Economics, 1955; The Economics of Man-Man Fibres, 1957; (ed.) Inflation, 1962; International Trade Theory in a Developing World, 1963; (ed.) Price Formation in Various Economies, 1967; Managerial Economics, 1969; (ed. with B.L. Smith) The Dilemma of Accountability in Modern Government, 1971; Pricing in Business, 1971; (with W.E.F. Oakeshott and A.A. Strain) Devaluation and Pricing Decisions: A Case Study Approach, 1974; (ed. with M.E. Beesley) Britain in the Common Market: A New Business Opportunity, 1974; (with W.J.M. Mackenzie and A. Barker) Public Policy and Private Interests: The Institutions of Compromise, 1975; (with G. Wilkinson) The IRC: An Experiment in Industrial Intervention, 1983; (ed. with B. Csikós-Nagy and G. Hall) The Economics of Relative Prices, 1984; (ed.) Stability and Progress in the World Economy, 1985; (ed. with K. Jungenfelt) Structural Adjustment in Developed Open Economies, 1985; (ed. with L.H. Dupriez) Economic Progress, 2nd ed., 1987; (ed.) The Management of Science, 1990; Beyond Universities, 1991; Transforming the Dinosaurs, 1993. **Address:** Templeton College, University of Oxford, Oxford, OX OX1 5NY, England. **Online address:** douglas@oxfordstrategy.freeserve.co.uk

HAGUE, William. British (born England), b. 1961. **Genres:** Politics/Government, Biography. **Career:** Young Conservatives, chair, 1977-79; Oxford Union, president, 1981; Oxford University, president, 1981; Conservative Association, president, 1981; McKinsey & Co., management consultant, 1985-88; House of Commons, Chancellor of the Exchequer, parliamentary private secretary, 1990-93, Department of Social Security, undersecretary of state for England, 1993-94, minister of state for social security and disabled people, 1994-95, secretary of state for Wales, 1995-97, leader of Conservative Party and leader of the opposition, 1997-2001, shadow foreign minister, 2005-; International Democratic Union, chair, 1999-; JCB, political and economic advisor, 2001-; AES Engineering, non-executive director, 2001-; Terra Firma Capital Partners, political advisor, 2002-. Writer. **Publications:** A Fresh Future for the Conservative Party, 1997; Speaking with Conviction: A Collection of Speeches, 1998; William Pitt the Younger, 2005; William Wilberforce: The Life of the Great Anti-Slave Trade Campaigner, 2007. **Address:** Conservative Party, 30 Millbank, London, GL SW1P 4DP, England. **Online address:** whague@conservative-party.org.uk

HAGY, Alyson. American (born United States), b. 1960. **Genres:** Novellas/Short Stories, Novels, Young Adult Fiction. **Career:** University of Virginia, lecturer in literature and creative writing, 1985-86; University of Michigan, lecturer in composition and creative writing, 1986-95; University of Wyoming, Department of English, assistant professor, 1995-, associate professor, professor. Writer. **Publications:** STORIES: Madonna on Her Back, 1986; Hardware River, 1991; Graveyard of the Atlantic, 2000; Ghosts of Wyoming, 2010. NOVELS: Keeneland, 2000; Snow, Ashes, 2007; Boleto, 2012. Contributor to periodicals. **Address:** Department of English, University of Wyoming, Hoyt 408, 1000 E University Ave., Laramie, WY 82071, U.S.A. **Online address:** ahagy@uwyo.edu

HAGY, James William. American (born United States), b. 1936. **Genres:** Local History/Rural Topics, Archaeology/Antiquities, History, Humanities. **Career:** College of Charleston, associate professor, 1969-77, professor, 1977-97, retired, 1997; American Academy in Rome, School of Classical Studies, Dr. Russell Scott director, 1976; University of South Carolina, Institute for Southern Studies, fellow, 1987, 1989. Writer. **Publications:** Castle's

Woods: Frontier Virginia Settlement, 1769-1799, 1966; Castle's Woods and Early Russell County, 1769-1799, 1979; People and Professions of Charleston, South Carolina, 1782-1802, 1992; This Happy Land: The Jews of Colonial and Antebellum Charleston, 1993; To Take Charleston: The Civil War on Folly Island, 1993; City Directories for Charleston, South Carolina: For the Years 1803, 1806, 1807, 1809, and 1813, 1995; (comp.) Charleston, South Carolina City Directories: For the Years 1816, 1819, 1822, 1825, and 1829, 1996; Edge of America: Folly Beach, A Pictorial History, 1997; Directories For the City of Charleston, South Carolina: For the Years 1830-31, 1835-36, 1837-38, and 1840-41, 1997; Directories for the City of Charleston, South Carolina: For the Years 1849, 1852, and 1855, 1998; On the Eve of the Civil War: The Charleston, S.C., Directories for the Years 1859 and 1860: With Additional Information From the City Census of 1861, 2000; The Folly Beach Book: A Pictorial History, 1696-2009, 2009. Works appear in anthologies. Contributor of articles to journals. **Address:** 645 Buckinon Dr., Oviedo, FL 32765-8113, U.S.A.

HAHM, Sung Deuk. (Sŏ'ng-dŭk Ham). Korean (born Korea (South)), b. 1963. **Genres:** Politics/Government. **Career:** West Virginia University, assistant professor of public administration, 1992-94; Yonsei University, professor of political science, 1992-2005; Harvard University, John F. Kennedy School of Government, researcher, 1992-94; Ronald Reagan Center for Public Affairs, research associate, 1993-94; Georgetown University, assistant professor of public policy and business administration, 1994-97, McDonough School, faculty associate, Georgetown Center for Asian Public Policy, director, 1995-97; Basil Blackwell (publisher), managing editor of governance, 1995-97, Department of Government, visiting professor of international relations, 2003; Korea University, assistant professor of public administration and director of advanced program in policy studies, 1996-, professor of political economy; Duke University, Asia/Pacific Studies Institute, Department of Political Science, visiting professor of international relations, 2002; United Nations Educational, Scientific and Cultural Organization, Division of Social Science Research and Policy, director, 2003-05; Princeton University, Department of East Asian Studies, visiting professor of international relations; University of Southern California, Korean Studies Institute, director, School of International Relations, Department of Political Science, professor of international relations, 2005-07; Rand Corp., senior political scientist, 2007-. **Publications:** After Development: Transformation of the Korean Presidency and Bureaucracy, 1997; (co-author) Tijit'ŏl kwallyo k'iugi, 2000; Hanguk ŭi taetongnyŏng kwa kwŏllyoŏk, 2000; Kim Yŏng-sam chŏngbu ŭi sŏnggong kwa silpae, 2001; Yŏngbuin non, 2001; Taetongnyŏng pisŏsilchang non, 2002; (co-author) Changgwannon, 2003. Contributor to journals. **Address:** Department of Public Administration, College of Political Science & Economics, Korea University, 5-1, Anam-dong, Sungbuk-ku, Seoul, 136-701, Korea (South). **Online address:** hahm33@hotmail.com

HAHN, Frank H(orace). British/German (born Germany), b. 1925. **Genres:** Economics. **Career:** University of Birmingham, lecturer, 1948-58, reader, 1958-60; Cambridge University, Faculty of Economics and Politics, lecturer, 1960-66, professor of economics, 1972-92, professor emeritus, 1992-, Churchill College, founding fellow fellow, 1960-66; Review of Economic Studies, managing editor, 1963-66; London School of Economics, professor of economics, 1967-72; Econometric Society, president, 1968-69; Royal Econometric Society, president, 1986-89; Universita di Siena, professore ordinario, 1989-, professor emeritus, 2000-; Harvard University, visiting professor; University of California, visiting professor; Massachusetts Institute of Technology, visiting professor. **Publications:** On the Stability of Growth Equilibrium, 1966; (with K.J. Arrow) General Competitive Analysis, 1971; The Share of Wages in the National Income, 1972; On the Notion of Equilibrium in Economics an Inaugural Lecture, 1973; (co-author) Attualità di Keynes, 1983; Money and Inflation, 1983; Equilibrium and Macroeconomics, 1984; Money, Growth, and Stability, 1985; Three Lectures on Monetary Theory, 1986; (with R. Solow) A Critical Essay on Modern Macroeconomic Theory, 1995; (with F. Petri) General Equilibrium, 2002. EDITOR: (with F.P.R. Brechling) The Theory of Interest Rates, 1965; Readings in the Theory of Growth, 1971; (with M. Hollis) Philosophy and Economic Theory, 1979; The Economics of Missing Markets, Information, and Games, 1989; (with B.M. Friedman) Handbook of Monetary Economics, 1990; The Market: Practice and Policy, 1992; (ed. with F. Farina and S. Vannucci) Ethics, Rationality, and Economic Behaviour, 1996; (ed. with F. Coricelli and M. di Matteo) New Theories in Growth and Development, 1997. **Address:** Cambridge University, The Old Schools, Trinity Ln., Cambridge, CB CB2 1TN, England. **Online address:** frank.hahn@econ.cam.ac.uk

HAHN, Gordon M. American/German (born Germany), b. 1955. **Genres:** Politics/Government. **Career:** American University, visiting assistant professor, 1995; Hoover Institution, archival research coordinator, 1997-2000; Center for Terrorism and Intelligence Studies, senior researcher; San Jose State University, Department of Political Science, lecturer, 2002-03; Stanford University, visiting lecturer in political science; Monterey Institute of International Studies, senior researcher, Graduate School of International Policy Studies, visiting assistant professor. Writer. **Publications:** Russia's Revolution from Above, 1985-2000: Reform, Transition, and Revolution in the Fall of the Soviet Communist Regime, 2002; Russia's Islamic Threat, 2007. Contributor to journals and periodicals. **Address:** CETI Research, 25 Metro Dr., Ste. 500, San Jose, CA 95110, U.S.A.

HAHN, Mary Downing. American (born United States), b. 1937. **Genres:** Children's Fiction, Young Adult Fiction, Mystery/Crime/Suspense, Ghost Writer, Horror, Novels, Science Fiction/Fantasy, Bibliography, Bibliography. **Career:** Art teacher, 1960-61; Hutzler's Department Store, clerk, 1963; Navy Federal Credit Union, clerk, 1963-65; University of Maryland, English Instructor, 1970-75; Cover to Cover, freelance artist, 1973-75; WETA-TV, freelance artist, 1973-75; Prince George's County Memorial Library System, children's librarian associate, 1975-91; full-time writer, 1991-. **Publications:** The Sara Summer, 1979; The Time of the Witch, 1982; Daphne's Book, 1983; The Jellyfish Season, 1985; Wait Till Helen Comes: A Ghost Story, 1986; Tallahassee Higgins, 1987; Following the Mystery Man, 1988; December Stillness, 1988; The Doll in the Garden, 1989; The Dead Man in Indian Creek, 1990; The Spanish Kidnapping Disaster, 1991; Stepping on the Cracks, 1991; The Wind Blows Backward, 1993; Time for Andrew, 1994; Look for Me by Moonlight, 1995; The Gentleman Outlaw and Me-Eli: A Story of the Old West, 1996; Following My Own Footsteps, 1996; As Ever, Gordy, 1998; Anna All Year Round, 1999; Promises to the Dead, 2000; Anna on the Farm, 2001; Hear the Wind Blow, 2003; Old Willis Place: A Ghost Story, 2004; Janey and the Famous Author, 2005; Witch Catcher, 2006; The Gentleman Outlaw and Me, 2007; Deep and Dark and Dangerous, 2007; All the Lovely Bad Ones: A Ghost Story, 2008; Closed for the Season: A Mystery Story, 2009; Ghost of Crutchfield Hall, 2010; Haunting Tales, 2011; Mister Death's Blue-Eyed Girls, 2012. Works appear in anthologies. Contributor to periodicals. **Address:** 9746 Basket Ring Rd., Columbia, MD 21045-3416, U.S.A. **Online address:** mdh12937@aol.com

HAHN, Michael T. American (born United States), b. 1953. **Genres:** Novels, Biography, Autobiography/Memoirs, Young Adult Fiction. **Career:** Musician and writer. **Publications:** Ethan Allen: A Life of Adventure, 1994; Ann Story: Vermont's Heroine of Independence, 1996; Alexander Twilight: Vermont's African-American Pioneer, 1998; Dad's Deer Tactics: Tom Hahn's Hunting Secrets Revealed by His Son, 2003; Butte, 2008; Champ's Mate, forthcoming. Contributor to books and periodicals. **Address:** 869 Kittredge Rd., Orleans, VT 05860, U.S.A.

HAHN, Steven C. American (born United States), b. 1968. **Genres:** Social Sciences, History, Politics/Government, Social Sciences. **Career:** St. Olaf College, assistant professor of American history, associate professor of history. Writer. **Publications:** The Invention of the Creek Nation, 1670-1763, 2004; (intro.) Verner Crane, The Southern Frontier, 1670-1732, 2004. Contributor to journals. **Address:** Department of History, St. Olaf College, Holland Hall 535, 1520 St. Olaf Ave., Northfield, MN 55057, U.S.A. **Online address:** hahn@stolaf.edu

HAHN, Susan. American (born United States), b. 1941. **Genres:** Poetry. **Career:** TriQuarterly magazine, editor. **Publications:** (Ed. with R. Gibbons) Fiction of the Eighties: A Decade of Stories from TriQuarterly, 1990; Harriet Rubin's Mother's Wooden Hand, 1991; Incontinence, 1993; (ed. with R. Gibbons) TriQuarterly New Writers, 1996; Confession, 1997; Holiday, 2001; Mother in Summer, 2002; Self/Pity, 2005; The Scarlet Ibis: Poems, 2007; The Note She Left: Poems, 2008. **Address:** TriQuarterly, 629 Noyes St., Evanston, IL 60208-4302, U.S.A.

HAIDT, Jonathan. American (born United States), b. 1963. **Genres:** Adult Non-fiction. **Career:** University of Chicago, post-doctoral fellow, 1992-94; John D. and Catherine T. MacArthur Foundation, Program on Mental Health and Human Development, post-doctoral associate, 1994-95; Revista Psicologia: Reflexao & Critica, associate editor, 1994-98; University of Virginia, Department of Psychology, assistant professor, 1995-2001, associate professor, 2001-09, professor, 2009-; Indian Psychological Abstracts, associate editor, 1997-2000; Princeton University Center for Human Values, Laurance S. Rockefeller visiting professor for distinguished teaching, 2006-07; University of California, Sage Center, visiting distinguished fellow, 2008. **Publications:** (Ed. with C.L.M. Keyes) Flourishing: Positive Psychology and the Life Well-Lived, 2003; The Happiness Hypothesis: Finding Modern Truth in Ancient Wisdom, 2006; The Righteous Mind: Why Good People are Divided by Politics and Religion, 2012. **Address:** Department of Psychology, University of Virginia, 102 Gilmer Hall, PO Box 400400, Charlottesville, VA 22904-4400, U.S.A. **Online address:** haidt@virginia.edu

HAIG, Kathryn. Scottish (born Scotland), b. 1947. **Genres:** Romance/Historical, Literary Criticism And History. **Career:** Civil Service, computer programmer, 1975-78; Computer Ltd., computer programmer, 1978-80; ICL Ltd., computer programmer, 1980-82. Writer. **Publications:** Shadows on the Sun, 1992; Secret Sins, 1993; Apple Blossom Time, 1998; A Time to Dance, 2000. **Address:** c/o Carol Smith, 25 Hornton Ct., Kensington High St., London, GL WS 7RT, England. **Online address:** kathrynhaig@btinternet.com

HAIGHT, Roger. American (born United States), b. 1936. **Genres:** Theology/Religion, Language/Linguistics. **Career:** Ateneo de Davao High School, teacher, 1961-64; Ateneo de Manila University, Loyola School of Theology, assistant professor, 1973-75; Jesuit School of Theology, assistant professor, 1975-79, associate professor, 1979-81, Department of Systematic Theology, chair, 1976-79, Master of Theology and Ministry Program, director, 1978-79; Papal Seminary-Pune, visiting professor, 1977; Regis College, Toronto School of Theology, associate professor, 1981-90; Hekima College, visiting professor, 1987, 1991; Weston School of Theology, Department of Theology, professor, 1990-, chair, 1992-; Woodstock Theological Center, visiting fellow, 2003-04; Union Theological Seminary, adjunct professor of theology, 2004-, visiting professor; Catholic Theological Society of America, president. Writer. **Publications:** The Experience and Language of Grace, 1979; An Alternative Vision: An Interpretation of Liberation Theology, 1985; Dynamics of Theology, 1990; Jesus, Symbol of God, 1999; Christian Community in History, vol. I: Historical Ecclesiology, 2004, vol. II: Comparative Ecclesiology, 2005; The Future of Christology, 2005. **Address:** Union Theological Seminary, BT 409, 3041 Broadway, New York, NY 10027-5701, U.S.A. **Online address:** rdhaight@aol.com

HAIKEN, Elizabeth. American (born United States) **Genres:** Medicine/Health, Fash Ion/Costume, Adult Non-fiction. **Career:** University of British Columbia, Department of History, assistant professor, 2000; University of Tennessee, assistant professor of history. Writer. **Publications:** Venus Envy: A History of Cosmetic Surgery, 1997. Contributor to periodicals. **Address:** c/o Author Mail, Johns Hopkins University Press, 2715 N Charles St., Baltimore, MD 21218-4363, U.S.A.

HAILES, Julia. British (born England), b. 1961. **Genres:** Environmental Sciences/Ecology, Food And Wine. **Career:** Sustainability Ltd., director and secretary, 1987-95; Out of this World, non-executive director, 1994-2000; Jupiter Global Green Investment Trust, non-executive director, 2001-06; Haller Foundation, co-founder and trustee, 2003-; Ecos Trust, patron. Writer. **Publications:** Green Pages: The Business of Saving the World, 1987; The New Green Consumer Guide, 2007. WITH J. ELKINGTON: The Green Consumer Guide, 1988; (and T. Burke) Green Pages, 1988; The Green Consumer's Supermarket Shopping Guide, 1989; Green Consumer, 1990, rev. ed., 1993; (and D. Hill) The Young Green Consumer Guide, 1990; (and P. Knight) The Green Business Guide, 1991; Holidays That Don't Cost the Earth, 1992; The LCA Sourcebook, 1993; Who Needs It?, 1995; Manual 2000, 1998; The New Foods Guide, 1999. **Address:** Hodder & Stoughton, 338 Euston Rd., London, GL NW1 3BH, England. **Online address:** julia@juliahailes.com

HAILEY, Elizabeth Forsythe. American (born United States), b. 1938. **Genres:** Novels. **Career:** Yale University Press, editorial assistant, 1961-62; Tandem Productions, creative consultant for syndicated television series Mary Hartman, 1976; Columbia Broadcasting System Inc. (CBS), co-producer of television series another day, 1977; Hollins University, Wyndham Robertson writer-in-residence, 1998. **Publications:** A Woman of Independent Means, 1978; Life Sentences, 1982; Joanna's Husband and David's Wife, 1986; Home Free, 1991. Contributor to books. **Address:** c/o Molly Friedrich, Aaron M. Priest Literary Agency, 708 3rd Ave., New York, NY 10017, U.S.A.

HAILEY, (Elizabeth) Kendall. American (born United States), b. 1966. **Genres:** Novels, Plays/Screenplays, Biography. **Career:** Writer. **Publica-**

tions: (Co-author) The Bar Off Melrose, 1987; The Day I Became an Autodidact: And the Advice, Adventures, and Acrimonies That Befell Me Thereafter, 1988. Contributor to periodicals. **Address:** c/o Molly Friedrich, Aaron M. Priest Literary Agency Inc., 122 E 42nd St., New York, NY 10168, U.S.A.

HAIN, Peter. (Peter Gerald Hain). British/Kenyan (born Kenya), b. 1950. **Genres:** Mystery/Crime/Suspense, Civil Liberties/Human Rights, Politics/Government. **Career:** Union of Communication Workers, research officer, 1976-91; Parliament for Neath, labour member, 1991-; Welsh office minister, 1991-99, parliamentary under-secretary of state, 1997-99; foreign minister, 1999-2002, energy minister, 2001, Department of Trade and Industry, minister of state, 2001, Europe minister, 2001-02; privy councilor, 2001-; secretary of State for Wales, 2002-08, 2009-10; European Union Convention, government representative, 2002-03; leader of house of commons, 2003-05; State of Northern Ireland, secretary, 2005-07; secretary of work and pensions, 2007-08; secretary of state for labour; shadow secretary of State for Wales, 2010-. Writer. **Publications:** Don't Play with Apartheid: The Background to the Stop the Seventy Tour Campaign, 1971; Radical Liberalism and Youth Politics, 1973; Radical Regeneration, 1975; Mistaken Identity: The Wrong Face of the Law, 1976; (ed.) Community Politics, 1976; (with S. Hebditch) Radicals and Socialism, 1978; (co-ed.) Policing the Police, vol. I, 1979, vol. II, 1980; Neighbourhood Participation, 1980; (ed.) The Crisis and the Future of the Left: The Debate of the Decade, 1980; The Democratic Alternative: A Socialist Response to Britain's Crisis, 1983; Political Trials in Britain, 1984; Political Strikes: The State and Trade Unionism in Britain, 1986; Proportional Misrepresentation: The Case Against PR in Britain, 1986; A Putney Plot?, 1987; The Peking Connection, 1995; Ayes to the Left: A Future for Socialism, 1995; Sing the Beloved Country: The Struggle for the New South Africa, 1996; The End of Foreign Policy, 2001; New Designs For Europe, 2002; The Future Party, 2004; Mandela, 2010; Outside In, 2012. Contributor to periodicals. **Address:** House of Commons, Westminster, London, GL SW1A 0AA, England. **Online address:** hainp@parliament.uk

HAIN, Peter Gerald. *See* **HAIN, Peter.**

HAINES, David W. American (born United States), b. 1947. **Genres:** Anthropology/Ethnology, History. **Career:** Republic of Vietnam, education adviser and civil affairs specialist, 1969-70; U.S. Office of Refugee Resettlement, research and policy analyst, 1980-84; Virginia Department of Information Technology, management consultant, 1988-89; Virginia Worker's Compensation Commission, senior manager, 1990-97; George Mason University, associate professor, full professor of anthropology, 1997-, director of undergraduate program in anthropology, sociology and anthropology. Writer. **Publications:** Refugee Resettlement in the United States: An Annotated Bibliography on the Adjustment of Cuban, Soviet and Southeast Asian Refugees, 1981; Cultural Anthropology: Adaptations, Structures, Meanings, 2005; The Limits of Kinship: South Vietnamese Households, 1954-1975, 2006; Safe Haven? A History of Refugees in America, 2010. EDITOR: (and contrib.) Refugees in the United States: A Reference Handbook, 1985; Refugees as Immigrants: Cambodians, Laotians, and Vietnamese in America, 1989; (and contrib.) Refugees in America in the 1990s: A Reference Handbook, 1996; (with K.E. Rosenblum and contrib.) Illegal Immigration in America: A Reference Handbook, 1999; (with C.A. Mortland) Manifest Destinies: Americanizing Immigrants and Internationalizing Americans, 2001. Contributor to books and periodicals. **Address:** Department of Sociology and Anthropology, George Mason University, Rm. B 322, Robinson Hall, Ste. 3G5, 4400 University Dr., Fairfax, VA 22030, U.S.A. **Online address:** dhaines1@gmu.edu

HAINES, Kathryn Miller. American (born United States), b. 1971. **Genres:** Novels, Young Adult Fiction. **Career:** University of Pittsburgh, Center for American Music, associate director and librarian; Mystery's Most Wanted, artistic director. Writer. **Publications:** ROSIE WINTER MYSTERY SERIES: The War against Miss Winter, 2007; The Winter of Her Discontent, 2008; Winter in June, 2009; When Winter Returns, 2010. NOVEL: The Girl is Murder, 2011, The Girl is Trouble, 2012. **Address:** Center for American Music, University of Pittsburgh, 106A Stephen Foster Memorial, 4301 Forbes Ave., Pittsburgh, PA 15260, U.S.A. **Online address:** kathrynmillerhaines@mac.com

HAINSWORTH, D(avid) R(oger). Australian/British (born England), b. 1931. **Genres:** History. **Career:** Mitchell Library, research fellow, 1960-62; James Cook University, lecturer in history, 1963-65; University of Adelaide, lecturer, 1965-70, senior lecturer, 1970-78, associate professor of history, 1979-, visiting research fellow, now retired. Writer. **Publications:** Simeon

Lord, 1968; Builders and Adventurers: The Traders and the Emergence of the Colony of New South Wales, 1788-1821, 1969; Sydney Traders: Simeon Lord and His Contemporaries, 1788-1821, 1971; Stewards, Lords and People: The Estate Steward and His World in Later Stuart England, 1992; Swordsmen in Power: War and Politics under the English Republic, 1649-1660, 1997; (with C. Churches) The Anglo-Dutch Naval Wars 1652-1674, 1998. EDITOR: Commercial Papers of Sir Christopher Lowther of Whitehaven, 1611-1644, 1977; The Correspondence of Sir John Lowther of Whitehaven, 1693-1698: A Provincial Community in Wartime, 1983; (with C. Walker) The Correspondence of Lord Fitzwilliam of Milton and Francis Guybon His Steward, 1697-1709, 1990. Works appear in anthologies. Contributor to journals. **Address:** 6 Tyne St., Gilberton, SA 5081, Australia. **Online address:** drogerh@mail.mdt.net.au

HAINSWORTH, Peter (R. J.). British (born England) **Genres:** Essays, Poetry, Literary Criticism And History, inspirational/Motivational Literature. **Career:** Oxford University, Lady Margaret Hall, professor of Italian, University lecturer in Italian, fellow, 1979-2003, emeritus fellow, 2003-, now professor emeritus. **Publications:** (Ed. and intro. with T.G. Griffith) Selected Poems of Petrarch, 1971; (ed. with M. Caesar) Writers and Society in Contemporary Italy: A Collection of Essays, 1984; Petrarch the Poet: An Introduction to the Rerum Vulgarium Fragmenta, 1988; (co-ed.) The Languages of Literature in Renaissance Italy, 1988; (ed. with D. Robey) The Oxford Companion to Italian Literature, 2002; (ed. with M. McLaughlin) Biographies And Autobiographies In Modern Italy: A Festschrift For John Woodhouse, 2007; (ed. with M. McLaughlin and L. Panizza) Petrarch in Britain: Interpreters, Imitators, and Translators over 700 Years, 2007; (ed., trans. and intro.) Essential Petrarch, 2010; Italian Literature: A Very Short Introduction, 2012. Contributor to periodicals. **Address:** Lady Margaret Hall, Oxford University, Oxford, GL OX2 6QA, England. **Online address:** peter.hainsworth@lmh.ox.ac.uk

HAIRSTON, William. American (born United States), b. 1928. **Genres:** Novels, Plays/Screenplays, Novellas/Short Stories, Young Adult Fiction, Poetry. **Career:** Greenwich Mews Theatre, production coordinator and co-producer, 1963; NYSF Mobile Theatre Unit, co-director of community relations, 1965; Arena Stage, assistant, 1965-66; District of Columbia, executive office of the mayor, executive manager, 1970-90; DC Pipeline, publisher and editor, 1973-79. **Publications:** The World of Carlos (novel), 1968; Sex and Conflict: Four Novellas (short stories), 1993; Ira Aldridge (The London Conflict), 1998; Space Out: A Space Adventure, 1998; Showdown at Sundown, 1998; History of the National Capital Area Council/Boy Scouts of America, 1998; Passion and Politics (novel), 2001; Poetry and Prose of Passion and Compassion (poetry), 2002; Swan Song, 2003. Contributor of articles to books and magazines. Works appear in anthologies. **Address:** 5501 Seminary Rd., Ste. 511-S, Falls Church, VA 22041-3904, U.S.A.

HAIZLIP, Shirlee Taylor. American (born United States), b. 1937. **Genres:** Adult Non-fiction, Biography. **Career:** WBNB-TV, general manager, 1975-81; WNET-TV, director of corporate communications, 1981-86; National Center for Film and Video Preservation, executive director, 1989-93; Allergy Center, editorial director; Tufts University, instructor; The Ebell of Los Angeles, president. **Publications:** The Sweeter the Juice, 1994; (with H.C. Haizlip) In the Garden of Our Dreams: Memoirs of a Marriage, 1998; Finding Grace: Two Sisters and the Search for Meaning Beyond the Color Line, 2004. Contributor to periodicals and newspapers. Works appear in anthologies. **Address:** 1754 N Serrano Ave., Penthouse B, Los Angeles, CA 90027, U.S.A. **Online address:** haizlip@earthlink.net

HAJDU, David. American (born United States), b. 1955. **Genres:** Film, Biography, Essays, Young Adult Non-fiction. **Career:** New School, instructor, 1980; Video Review magazine, founding editor, 1980-84; University of Chicago, faculty, nonfiction writer-in-residence; Syracuse University, professor of public communications, professor of journalism; Columbia University, affiliated faculty, professor of journalism; Entertainment Weekly, senior editor, general editor, 1990-99. **Publications:** (Ed.) Video Review's Best on Home Video, 1985; How to Shoot Your Kids on Home Video: Moviemaking for the Whole Family, 1988; (with R. Hemming) Discovering Great Singers of Classic Pop: A New Listener's Guide to the Sounds and Lives of the Top Performers and Their Recordings, Movies and Videos, 1991; Lush Life: A Biography of Billy Strayhorn, 1996; Positively 4th Street, 2001; Ten-Cent Plague: The Great Comic-Book Scare and How it Changed America, 2008; Heroes and Villains: Essays on Music, Movies, Comics and Culture, 2009. Contributor of articles to periodicals. **Address:** Farrar, Straus & Giroux, 18 W 18th St., New York, NY 10011, U.S.A. **Online address:** davidhajdu@aol.com

HAJDUSIEWICZ, Babs Bell. American (born United States), b. 1944. **Genres:** Poetry, Animals/Pets, Children's Non-fiction, Children's Fiction, Language/Linguistics, Picture/Board Books, Mythology/Folklore, Music, Social Sciences, Biography, Humor/Satire. **Career:** Teacher, 1965-72; Putnam-West Hendricks Cooperative, director of special education, 1972-73; Northville Public Schools, director, 1973-75; Eastern Michigan University, instructor and teacher trainer, 1978-80; Pee Wee Poetry, founder and director, 1979-89; Ohio Community Education, instructor, 1981-82; Cleveland State University, instructor and teacher trainer, 1981-83; Parenting Education, instructor, 1981-82; Westshore Montessori Association, administrative consultant, 1983-84; education consultant, 1983-84; freelance writer, 1986-; Booking the Future: Reader to Reader, founder and director, 1993; Reading Realm, consultant. **Publications:** Help from Dainty Dinosaur, 1988; How Can I Dainty Dinosaur?, 1988; It Will Be Fun Dainty Dinosaur, 1988; Why Dainty Dinosaur?, 1988; Up and down Dainty Dinosaur, 1988; You Are Here Dainty Dinosaur, 1988; When Will I Dainty Dinosaur?, 1988; You Have a Friend Dainty Dinosaur, 1988; Two Homes for Dainty Dinosaur, 1988; Where Is It Dainty Dinosaur?, 1988; What Is It Dainty Dinosaur?, 1988; Who Did This Dainty Dinosaur?, 1988; Poetry Works!, 1991; I Would If I Could, 1991; Fluffy Snowflakes, 1991; Rico's Shadow, 1991; Poetry Works! The Second Stanza, 1992; Busy People, 1993; Poetry Works! The First Verse, 1993; Jacks and More Jacks, 1994; Mary Carter Smith: African-American Storyteller, 1995; My Faces, 1996; What Hangs from the Tree?, 1996; How Do I Feel?, 1996; Words Words Words, 1997; Words and More Words, 1997; Dont Go out in Your Underwear: Poems, 1997; More! Phonics through Poetry: Teaching Phonemic Awareness Using Poetry, 1999; Peaceful Me, 2002; The Bridge Is Up!, 2004; Sputter, Sputter, Sput, 2008. **Address:** Reading Realm, PO Box 19013, Atlanta, GA 31126, U.S.A. **Online address:** babs@ilikeme.com

HAJI, Nafisa. American (born United States), b. 1969?. **Genres:** Novels. **Career:** Writer and educator. **Publications:** The Writing on My Forehead (novel), 2009. **Address:** CA , U.S.A. **Online address:** contact@nafisahaji.com

HAJRATWALA, Minal. American (born United States), b. 1972?. **Genres:** Autobiography/Memoirs. **Career:** The Community Crier, reporter, 1989; Santa Clara University, Santa Clara Magazine, copy editor, 1992-93; San Jose Mercury News, perspective editor, reader representative and reporter, 1992-2000; Columbia University, National Arts Journalism Program, fellow, 2000-01; Avatars High-Performance Consulting, founder and principal. **Publications:** Leaving India: My Family's Journey from Five Villages to Five Continents (memoir), 2009. Works appear in anthologies. **Address:** Houghton Mifflin Harcourt, 222 Berkeley St., Boston, MA 02116, U.S.A. **Online address:** contact@minalhajratwala.com

HAKAK, Lev. American (born United States), b. 1944?. **Genres:** Poetry, History, Translations, Essays, Young Adult Fiction. **Career:** Hebrew University of Jerusalem, teacher, 1963-70; University of California-Berkeley, lecturer in Near Eastern Studies, 1974-76; University of Judaism-San Francisco, acting assistant professor, 1974-76; University of Judaism-Los Angeles, College of Judaic Studies (joint program), visiting assistant professor, 1975-76, 1977-78, teaching associate of Hebrew language and literature; University of California-Los Angeles, Department of Near Eastern Languages and Cultures, teaching associate of Hebrew language and literature, 1971-74, professor of Hebrew language and literature, 1976-; Tel-Aviv University, advisor and teacher in Hebrew language and literature; University of Southern California, teaching associate of Hebrew language and literature; Hebrew Union College, teaching associate of Hebrew language and literature. **Publications:** (with T. Hakak) 'Oked be-'od aviv (poetry), 1961; Modes of Organization in Modern Hebrew Free Verse, 1974; Ha-Asufim (fiction), 1977, trans. as Stranger among Brothers, 1984; 'Im arba'ah meshorerim: Avraham Ben Yitshak, Amir Gilboa, Natan Zakh, Shlomoh Zamir, 1979; Im eshkah'ekh: sipurim, 1981; Perakim be-sifrut Yehude ha-Mizrah bi-Medinat Yisra'el, 1985; Le-horish shir 'Ivri be-Los Ang'eles, 1988; Bayit 'al giv'ah (fiction), 1993; Equivocal Dreams: Studies in Modern Hebrew Literature, 1993; Modern Hebrew Literature Made into Films, 2001; Nitsane ha-yetsirah ha- 'Ivrit ha-hadashah be-Vavel (title means: 'The Budding of Modern Hebrew Creativity in Babylon'), 2003; Igrot ha-Rav Shelomoh Bekhor Hutsin (title means: 'The Collected Essays of Rabbi Shelomo Bekhor Hutsin'), 2005; Hasid mul hot'im: Sefer Tokhehot usar Shel Ezra Ha-Bavli; Be-tseruf, Hadarah u- mavo (ethics), 2008; The Emergence of Modern Hebrew Creativity in Babylon from 1735-1950, 2009. Contributor of books, poems and articles to periodicals. **Address:** Department of Near Eastern Languages and Cultures, University of California, MC 151105, 378 Humanities Bldg., 415 Portola Plz., Los Angeles, CA 90095-1511, U.S.A. **Online address:** hakak@humnet.ucla.edu

HAKALA, Dee. American (born United States), b. 1958. **Genres:** Adult Non-fiction, Self Help. **Career:** Laubach Literacy Volunteer Service, tutor, 1989-93; Lake Charles Memorial Hospital, developer, instructor and program director of exercise programs, 1991-93; American Council on Exercise, fitness instructor, 1991-, personal trainer, 1993-; MWR Sports, program director, fitness instructor and personal trainer, 1993-94; P.L.A.Y., creator, facilitator, 1994-97; Advanced Health and Fitness Club, program director, fitness instructor and personal trainer, 1998-99; American College of Sports Medicine, health and fitness trainer, 1996-; Young Women's Christian Association, program director, 2001-; C.H.O.I.C.E.S. VVV with De Inc., president and chief executive officer; New Face of Fitness, founder; Rush Copley Healthplex, personal trainer and fitness instructor. Writer. **Publications:** (With M. D'Orso) Thin Is Just a Four Letter Word: Living Fit for All Shapes and Sizes, 1997; Hungry Heart, forthcoming. **Address:** c/o David Black, David Black Literary Agency, 156 5th Ave., Ste. 608, New York, NY 10010-7789, U.S.A. **Online address:** deevvv@aol.com

HALAM, Ann. See **JONES, Gwyneth A(nn).**

HALBERSTADT, Hans. American (born United States), b. 1944. **Genres:** Military/Defense/Arms Control. **Career:** Writer. **Publications:** (With R. Hill and J. Hill) Stained Glass: Music for the Eye, 1976; USCG-Always Ready, 1986; Airborne: Assault from the Sky, 1988; Green Berets: Unconventional Warriors, 1988; NTC: A Primer of Modern Land Combat, 1989; Army Aviation, 1990; Desert Storm Ground War, 1991; The Wild Weasels: History of US Air Force Sam Killers, 1965 to Today, 1992; Mikoyan MiG-29: Design and Development of Russia's Super Fighter, 1992; (with A. Velovich and P. Palovic) Sukhoi Su-27: Design and Development of Russia's Super Interceptor, 1992; US Marine Corps, 1993; The American Fire Engine, 1993; (with T. Murphy) Illustrated Cessna Buyer's Guide, 1993; US Navy SEALS, 1993; Desert Rats: The British 4 and 7 Armoured Brigades, WW II to Today, 1993; (with T. Murphy) Illustrated Piper Buyer's Guide, 1993; Combines & Harvesters, 1994; Giant Dump Trucks, 1994; War Stories of the Green Berets: The Viet Nam Experience, 1994, new ed. as War Stories of the Green Berets, 2004; SWAT Team: Police Special Weapons and Tactics, 1994; Threshers at Work, 1995; (with G. Stubblefield) Inside the US Navy SEALs, 1995; (with A. Halberstadt) The American Train Depot & Roundhouse, 1995; US Navy SEALs in Action, 1995, 2nd ed. as U.S. Navy SEALs, 2006; Modern Diesel Locomotives, 1996; Steam Tractors, 1996; Demolition Equipment, 1996; The American Family Farm, 1996; Orchard Tractors, 1996; US Aircrew Combat Flight & Survival Gear, 1996; Military Vehicles: From World War I to the Present, 1998; (co-author) U.S. Special Forces: Airborne Rangers, Delta & U.S. Navy SEALs, 1999; (with E. Halberstadt) Abrams Company, 1999; Seaplanes, 1999; Working Steam: Vintage Locomotives Today, 1999; Woodies, 2000; Classic Trains, 2001; Fire Engines, 2002; The World's Great Artillery: From the Middle Ages to the Present Day, 2002; (with F. Antenori) Roughneck Nine-One: The Extraordinary Story of a Special Forces A-Team at War, 2006; Battle Rattle: The Stuff a Soldier Carries, 2006; (with G. Mast) To Be a Paratrooper, 2007; Trigger Men: Shadow Team, Spider-man, the Magnificent Bastards, and the American Combat Sniper, 2008. **Address:** St. Martin's Press, 175 5th Ave., New York, NY 10010, U.S.A. **Online address:** hans.halberstadt@gmail.com

HALBERTAL, Tova Hartman. Israeli/Canadian (born Canada), b. 1958?. **Genres:** Theology/Religion. **Career:** Jerusalem Women's Counseling Center, clinician; Hebrew University, School of Education, lecturer; Bar Ilan University, professor of gender studies and education. Shira Hadasha, Orthodox congregation, co-founder, 2002. Writer. **Publications:** Appropriately Subversive: Modern Mothers in Traditional Religions, 2002; Feminism Encounters Traditional Judaism: Resistance and Accommodation, 2007. Contributor of articles to periodicals. **Address:** Department of Gender Studies, Bar-Ilan University, Ramat Gan, 52900, Israel.

HALDAR, Achintya. American/Indian (born India), b. 1945?. **Genres:** Engineering, Technology. **Career:** Kuljian Corp., student engineer, 1967; Paharpur-Marley Cooling Tower Engineers, design engineer, 1968-70; Engineers India Ltd., junior engineer, 1970-72; Marco Steel Supply Co., designer, 1972; University of Illinois, teaching and research assistant, 1972-76; Bechtel

Power Corp., staff engineer, 1976-78; Illinois Institute of Technology, assistant professor of civil engineering, 1978-79; Georgia Institute of Technology, School of Civil Engineering, assistant professor, 1979-85, associate professor, 1985-88; University of Arizona, professor of civil engineering and engineering mechanics, 1988-; Hong Kong University of Science Technology, visiting professor, 1995-2002; Institute of Theoretical and Applied Mechanics, visiting professor, 2002; Indian Institute of Science, visiting professor, 2009. Writer. **Publications:** Probability Concepts in Engineering Planning and Design, vol. I: Basic Principles: Solution Manual, 1975; (ed. with B.M. Ayyub and A. Guran) Uncertainty Modeling in Vibration, Control and Fuzzy Analysis of Structural Systems, 1997; (ed. with B.M. Ayyub and A. Guran) Uncertainty Modeling in Finite Element, Fatigue and Stability of Systems, 1997; (with S. Mahadevan) Probability, Reliability and Statistical Methods in Engineering Design, with Solutions Manual, 2000; (with S. Mahadevan) Reliability Assessment Using Stochastic Finite Element Analysis, 2000; (ed.) Recent Developments in Reliability-Based Civil Engineering, 2006; (ed.) Health Assessment of Engineered Structures: Bridges, Buildings and Other Infrastructures, 2012. Contributor to books and journals. **Address:** Department of Civil Engineering and Engineering, Mechanics, University of Arizona, Rm. 206, Civil Engineering Bldg., PO Box 210072, Tucson, AZ 85721, U.S.A. **Online address:** haldar@u.arizona.edu

HALDEMAN, Joe (William). (Robert Graham). American (born United States), b. 1943. **Genres:** Novels, Novellas/Short Stories, Horror, Science Fiction/Fantasy, Plays/Screenplays, Poetry. **Career:** Writer, 1970-; Science Fiction and Fantasy Writers of America, treasurer, 1970-73, president, 1992-94; University of Iowa, teaching assistant, 1975; Astronomy Magazine, editor, 1976; Massachusetts Institute of Technology, visiting professor, 1983-84, adjunct professor, 1983-; University of North Florida, faculty. **Publications:** War Year, 1972; The Forever War, 1975; (as Robert Graham) Attar 1: Attar's Revenge, 1975; (as Robert Graham) Attar 2: War of Nerves, 1975; Mindbridge, 1976; Planet of Judgment, 1977; All My Sins Remembered, 1977; Infinite Dreams (short stories), 1978; World without End, 1979; Worlds: A Novel of the Near Future, 1981; (with J.C. Haldeman) There is No Darkness, 1983; Worlds Apart, 1983; The Forever War (stage play), 1984; Dealing in Futures (short stories), 1985; Tool of the Trade, 1987; Buying Time, 1989; The Hemingway Hoax, 1990; More Than the Sum of His Parts, 1991; Worlds Enough and Time: The Conclusion of the Worlds Trilogy, 1992; Vietnam and Other Alien Worlds (essays, poetry, stories), 1993; 1968: A Novel, 1995; None So Blind (short stories), 1996; Forever Peace, 1997; Saul's Death and Other Poems (poetry), 1997; Forever Free, 1999; The Coming, 2000; Guardian, 2002; Worlds, 2002; (with H. Harrison and R. Matheson) Dogs of War, 2002; Camouflage, 2004; Old Twentieth, 2005; War Stories, 2005; A Separate War and Other Stories, 2006; The Accidental Time Machine, 2007; Marsbound, 2008; Starbound, 2010; Earthbound, 2011. EDITOR: Cosmic Laughter, 1974; Study War No More, 1977; Nebula Award Stories 17, 1983; (with M.H. Greenberg and C.G. Waugh) Body Armor: 2000, 1986; (with M.H. Greenberg and C.G. Waugh) Supertanks, 1987; (intro.) The Best of John Brunner, 1988; (M.H. Greenberg and C.G. Waugh) Spacefighters, 1988; (with M.H. Greenberg) Future Weapons of War, 2007. Contributor to periodicals. **Address:** 5412 NW 14th Ave., Gainesville, FL 32605, U.S.A. **Online address:** haldeman@mit.edu

HALDON, J. F. See **HALDON, John F.**

HALDON, John. See **HALDON, John F.**

HALDON, John F. Also writes as J. F. Haldon, John Haldon. American/British (born England) **Genres:** History, Military/Defense/Arms Control. **Career:** Universities of Athens, staff; University of Birmingham, Centre for Byzantine, Ottoman and Modern Greek Studies, director, 1995-, School of Historical Studies, head, 2000-04; Princeton University, professor of history and Hellenic studies, 2005-, graduate studies, director, 2009-; Dumbarton Oaks Center for Byzantine Studies, senior fellow, 2007-10; University of Birmingham, reader in history. Writer. **Publications:** Recruitment and Conscription in the Byzantine Army 550-950: A Study on the Origins of the Stratiotika, 1979; Byzantine Praetorians: An Administrative, Institutional and Social Survey of the Opsikion and Tagmata, 580-900, 1984; (trans. and intro.) Constantine VII Porphyrogenitus, Three Treatises on Imperial Military Expeditions, 1990; Byzantium in the Seventh Century: The Transformation of a Culture, 1990; The State and the Tributary Mode of Production, 1993; State, Army and Society in Byzantium: Approaches to Military, Social and Administrative History, 6th-12th Centuries, 1995; Warfare, State and Society in the Byzan-

tine World, 565-1204, 1999; Byzantium: A History, 2000; (with L. Brubaker) Byzantium in the Iconoclast Era (c. 680-850): The Sources: An Annotated Survey, 2001; The Byzantine Wars: Battles and Campaigns of the Byzantine Era, 2001; Byzantium at War: AD 600-1453, 2002; Palgrave Atlas of Byzantine History, 2005; (ed.) General Issues in the Study of Medieval Logistics: Sources, Problems and Methodologies, 2006; (ed.) Byzantine Warfare, 2007; (with J. Haldon and S. Turnbull) Fall of Constantinople: The Ottoman Conquest of Byzantium, 2007; (co-ed.) Oxford Handbook of Byzantine Studies, 2008; (ed.) Social History of Byzantium, 2009; Money, Power and Politics in Early Islamic Syria: A Review of Current Debates, 2009; Problems and Perspectives in Byzantine Social and Economic History, 2010; Byzantium in the Iconoclast Period: A History, forthcoming. Contributor to books. **Address:** Department of History, Princeton University, 220 Dickinson Hall, Princeton, NJ 08544-1017, U.S.A. **Online address:** jhaldon@princeton.edu

HALE, Antoinette. See **STOCKENBERG, Antoinette.**

HALE, Douglas. (Douglas D. Hale). American (born United States), b. 1929. **Genres:** Genealogy/Heraldry, History, Military/Defense/Arms Control, Local History/Rural Topics, Biography. **Career:** University of North Carolina, assistant professor of history, 1961-63; Oklahoma State University, Department of History, professor of history, 1963-82, professor emeritus, 1982-. Writer. **Publications:** The Germans from Russia in Oklahoma, 1980; The Third Texas Cavalry in the Civil War, 1993; (co-author) Nonparametric Comparative Statecs and Stability; Wanderers between Two Worlds: German Rebels in the American West, 1830-1860, 2004. **Address:** Department of History, Oklahoma State University, 501 Life Sciences W, Stillwater, OK 74078-3054, U.S.A.

HALE, Douglas D. See **HALE, Douglas.**

HALE, Henry E. American (born United States), b. 1966. **Genres:** Politics/Government, History. **Career:** Tufts University, Fletcher School of Law and Diplomacy, adjunct professor, 1997-98; Harvard University, Strengthening Democratic Institutions (SDI) Project, research associate, 1998-2000; European University, Department of Political Science and Sociology, visiting professor, 1999; Indiana University, assistant professor of political science, 2000-05; George Washington University, Elliott School of International Affairs, Department of Political Science, assistant professor, 2005-08, associate professor, 2008-, Institute for European, Russian and Eurasian Studies, director, 2009-, European and Eurasian Studies MA Program, director, 2009-; Demokratizatsiya (The Journal of Post-Soviet Democratization), executive editor, 2007-. Writer. **Publications:** Why Not Parties in Russia? Democracy, Federalism and the State, 2006; The Foundations of Ethnic Politics: Separatism of States and Nations in Eurasia and the World, 2008; (ed. with R. Sakwa and S. White) Developments in Russian Politics 7, 2010. Contributor to books and periodicals. **Address:** Department of Political Science, Elliott School of International Affairs, George Washington University, 1957 E St. NW, Ste. 412, Washington, DC 20052, U.S.A. **Online address:** hhale@gwu.edu

HALE, Janice E(llen). American (born United States), b. 1948. **Genres:** Education. **Career:** Third Avenue Child Development Center, teacher, 1968; Georgia State University, research assistant, 1973-73; lecturer, 1974; Clark College, assistant professor to associate professor of early childhood education, 1974-80; University of California, lecturer of communications program, 1979; Laboratory of Comparative Human Cognition University, research fellow, 1979; Yale University, research associate, 1979-81, lecturer in Afro-American studies, 1980-81, research affiliate, 1981-83, visiting professor; University of Connecticut, lecturer in psychology, 1980; Jackson State University, associate professor of early childhood education, 1981-84; Cleveland State University, College of Education, associate professor, 1984-90; Vision for Children Early Childhood Education Program, president, 1986-93; Wayne State University, College of Education, research enhancement professor, professor, 1991-, Institute for the Study of the African American Child, founding director, 2006-. Writer. **Publications:** Black Children: Their Roots, Culture and Learning Styles, 1982, rev. ed., 1986; Unbank the Fire: Visions for the Education of African-American Children, 1994; Learning while Black: Creating Educational Excellence for African-American Children, 2001. **Address:** College of Education, Wayne State University, Rm. 213, 5462 Gullen Mall, Detroit, MI 48201, U.S.A. **Online address:** janiceehale@cs.com

HALE, John. (John Barry Hale). British (born England), b. 1926. **Genres:** Novels, Plays/Screenplays, Young Adult Fiction, Romance/Historical. **Career:** Lincoln Repertory Theatre, founder and artistic director, 1955-58; Arts

Theatre, artistic director, 1958-59; Bristol Old Vic Theatre, artistic director, 1959-61; freelance director, 1961-; freelance writer, 1965-; Greenwich Theatre, associate artistic director, 1968-71; resident playwright, 1975-76. **Publications:** NOVELS: The Grudge Fight, 1964; A Fool at the Feast, 1966; Kissed the Girls and Made Them Cry, 1966; The Paradise Man: A Black and White Farce, 1969; The Fort, 1973; The Love School, 1975; Lovers and Heretics, 1976; The Whistle Blower, 1984. **Address:** c/o Stephen Durbridge, Lemon, Unna & Durbridge Ltd., 24 Pottery Ln., London, GL W11 4LZ, England.

HALE, John Barry. *See* **HALE, John.**

HALE, John R. American (born United States), b. 1951. **Genres:** History. **Career:** University of Louisville, director of liberal studies; Greater Louisville Rowing Foundation, founder. Writer. **Publications:** Lords of the Sea: The Epic Story of the Athenian Navy and the Birth of Democracy, 2009. **Online address:** jrhale@louisville.edu

HALE, Nathan G. American (born United States), b. 1922. **Genres:** Psychology, History, Medicine/Health. **Career:** University of California-Berkeley, lecturer in history, 1965-69; University of California-Riverside, professor of history, 1970-79, professor emeritus, 1979-; Stanford University, visiting professor, 1982-83. Writer. **Publications:** (With K.R. Beutner) Emotional Illness: How Families Can Help, 1957; Freud and the Americans, vol. I: The Beginnings of Psychoanalysis in the United States, 1876-1917, 1971, vol. II: The Rise and Crisis of Psychoanalysis in America, 1917-1985, 1995; The Freud Bashers, forthcoming. EDITOR AND INTRODUCTION: James Jackson Putnam and Psychoanalysis: Letters Between Putnam, Sigmund Freud, William James, Ernest Jones, Sandor Ferenczi, and Morton Prince, 1971; Psychotherapy and Multiple Personality: Selected Papers of Morton Prince, 1975. Contributor to books. **Address:** Department of History, University of California, 900 University Ave., 1212 HMNSS Bldg., Riverside, CA 92521, U.S.A.

HALE, Robert D(avid). American (born United States), b. 1928. **Genres:** Novels, Literary Criticism And History, Photography, Autobiography/Memoirs, Essays, Young Adult Fiction. **Career:** Westwinds Bookshop, manager, 1953-57, owner, 1983-90; Curtiss Johnson Publications, managing editor, 1957-61; Connecticut College Bookshop, general manager, 1961-69; Hathaway House Bookshop, president, 1969-77; American Booksellers Association, associate executive director, 1977-83. Writer. **Publications:** (Comp. and ed. with K.H. Pillsbury and J. Post) Duxbury Book, 1637-1987, 1987; (ed. with A. Marshall and J.N. Showalter) Manual on Bookselling: How to Open and Run Your Own Bookstore, 3rd ed., 1980, (ed. with A. Marshall and G. Curwen) 4th ed., 1987; (contrib.) Massachusetts (photography and essays), 1992. NOVELS: The Elm at the Edge of the Earth, 1990; The Cloud Dweller, 2003. Contributor to books. **Address:** 374 High St., Pembroke, MA 02359, U.S.A.

HALE, Shannon. American (born United States), b. 1974. **Genres:** Novels, Children's Fiction, Science Fiction/Fantasy, Graphic Novels. **Career:** Allen Communication, instructional designer; Avaltus, instructional designer. Writer. **Publications:** BAYERN SERIES: The Goose Girl, 2003; Enna Burning, 2004; River Secrets, 2006; Forest Born, 2009. NOVELS: Princess Academy, 2005; Austenland, 2007; Book of a Thousand Days, 2007; (with D. Hale) Rapunzel's Revenge, 2008; Actor and the Housewife, 2009; (with D. Hale) Calamity Jack, 2010; Midnight in Austenland, 2012; Palace of Stone, 2012; Daisy Danger, 2012. **Address:** Bloomsbury Children's Books, 175 5th Ave., 8th Fl., New York, NY 10010-7703, U.S.A. **Online address:** squeetus@hotmail.com

HALES, Dianne R. American (born United States), b. 1950. **Genres:** Novels, Medicine/Health, Sports/Fitness. **Career:** Author and journalist. **Publications:** (Co-author) An Invitation to Health: Your Personal Responsibility, 1980, 14th ed. as An Invitation to Health: Choosing to Change, 2011; The Complete Book of Sleep: How Your Nights Affect Your Days, 1981; (with H.A. deVries) Fitness after Fifty, 1982; (with R.K. Creasy) New Hope for Problem Pregnancies: Helping Babies Before They're Born, 1982; (with R.E. Hales) The U.S. Army Total Fitness Program, 1985; Case Histories, 1987; How to Sleep like a Baby, Wake up Refreshed, and Get More out of Life, 1987; The Family, 1988; Pregnancy and Birth, 1989; Depression, 1989; (with T.R.B. Johnson) Intensive Caring: New Hope for High-risk Pregnancy, 1990; Your Health, 1991; (with R.E. Hales) Caring for the Mind: The Comprehensive Guide to Mental Health, 1995; Just Like a Woman: How Gender Science Is Redefining What Makes Us Female, 1999; (with R.E. Hales) The Mind/

Mood Pill Book, 2000; An Invitation to Fitness and Wellness, 2001; (with D.W. Helmering) Think Thin, Be Thin, 2005; Invitation to Wellness: Making Healthy Choices, 2006; (with K.W. Christian) Invitation to Personal Change, 2009; La Bella Lingua: My Love Affair with Italian, the World's Most Enchanting Language, 2009. Contributor of articles to magazines. **Address:** c/o Author Mail, Bantam Dell Books, 1745 Broadway, 10th Fl., New York, NY 10019-4368, U.S.A. **Online address:** dianne@becomingitalian.com

HALES, Steven D(ouglas). American (born United States), b. 1966. **Genres:** Philosophy. **Career:** Georgia State University, visiting assistant professor of philosophy, 1992-94; Bloomsburg University, Department of Philosophy, professor of philosophy, 1994-. Writer. **Publications:** (Ed.) Metaphysics: Contemporary Readings, 1999; (with R. Welshon) Nietzsche's Perspectivism, 2000; (ed.) Analytic Philosophy: Classic Readings, 2002; Relativism and the Foundations of Philosophy, 2006; (ed.) Beer & Philosophy: The Unexamined Beer isn't Worth Drinking, 2007; (with S.C. Lowe) Delight in Thinking: An Introduction to Philosophy Reader, 2007; (ed.) What Philosophy Can Tell You About Your Dog, 2008; (ed.) What Philosophy Can Tell You About Your Cat, 2008; (ed.) A Companion to Relativism, 2011. Contributor to periodicals. **Address:** Department of Philosophy, Bloomsburg University, 400 E 2nd St., Bloomsburg, PA 17815-1301, U.S.A. **Online address:** hales@bloomu.edu

HALEVI, Zev ben Shimon. *See* **KENTON, Warren.**

HALEY, Gail E(inhart). American (born United States), b. 1939. **Genres:** Children's Fiction, Novellas/Short Stories, Illustrations, inspirational/Motivational Literature, Young Adult Non-fiction. **Career:** Manuscript Press, vice-president, 1965-; Appalachian State University, writer-in-residence; Gail Haley Collection of the Culture of Childhood, curator. Writer, artist and illustrator. **Publications:** SELF-ILLUSTRATED: My Kingdom for a Dragon, 1962; The Wonderful Magical World of Marguerite: With the Entire Cast of Characters Including Rocks, Roses, Daisies, Violets, Snails, Butterflies, Breezes, and Above All-the Sun, 1964; Round Stories About Things That Live on Land, 1966; Round Stories About Things That Live in Water, 1966; Round Stories About Things That Grow, 1966; Round Stories About Our World, 1966; (reteller) A Story, A Story: An African Tale, 1970; Noah's Ark, 1971; Jack Jouett's Ride, 1973; The Abominable Swamp Man, 1975; The Post Office Cat, 1976; Go Away, Stay Away!, 1977; Costumes for Plays and Playing, 1978; Gail Haley's Costume Book, vol. I: Dress Up and Have Fun, 1979, vol. II: Dress Up and Play, 1980; The Green Man, 1979; A Story, a Day, 1979; Birdsong: Story and Pictures, 1984; Jack and the Bean Tree, 1986; Marguerite, 1988; Jack and the Fire Dragon, 1988; Sea Tale, 1990; (reteller) Puss in Boots, 1991; Mountain Jack Tales, 1992; Dream Peddler, 1993; Two Bad Boys: A Very Old Cherokee Tale, 1996; My Father's Beast, 2006. NON-FICTION: Play People: Puppetry in Education, 1988; (with D.M. Considine) Visual Messages: Integrating Imagery into Instruction, 1992, 2nd ed., 1999; (with L.E. Lacy and D.M. Considine) Imagine That: Developing Critical Thinking And Critical Viewing Through Children's Literature, 1994. Illustrator of books by others. Contributor of articles to periodicals. **Address:** Teacher Ideas Press, PO Box 1911, Santa Barbara, CA 93116-1911, U.S.A. **Online address:** info@gailehaley.com

HALFMANN, Janet. American (born United States), b. 1944. **Genres:** Picture/Board Books, Children's Fiction, Children's Non-fiction, Animals/Pets, Education, Environmental Sciences/Ecology, History, Natural History, Biography, E-books, Marine Sciences/Oceanography. **Career:** Country Kids, managing editor; Golden Books, manager, editor and writer. Freelance author, 1997-. **Publications:** BUGS SERIES: Dragonflies, 1999; Grasshoppers, 1999; Ants, 1999; (with A. Richardson) Bugbook, 1999; Fireflies, 1999. DESIGNING THE FUTURE SERIES: Mosques, 2000; Greek Temples, 2000; Theaters, 2000. LIFEVIEWS SERIES: Life in the Sea, 2000; Life in a Garden, 2000; Life in a Tree, 2001; Life in a Pond, 2001; Life in a Tide Pool, 2001; Life under a Stone, 2001. LET'S INVESTIGATE SERIES: Peanuts, 2002; Spiders, 2002. NATURE'S PREDATORS SERIES: Scorpions, 2003; Lizards, 2004; Mongoose, 2005. SMITHSONIAN BACKYARD SERIES: Red Bat at Sleepy Hollow Lane, 2004; Canada Goose at Cattail Lane, 2005; Alligator at Saw Grass Road, 2006; Little Black Ant on Park Street, 2009; Garter Snake at Willow Creek Lane, 2011. SMITHSONIAN OCEANIC SERIES: Pelican's Catch, 2004; Dolphin's Rescue: The Story of a Pacific White-Sided Dolphin, 2005; Polar Bear Horizon, 2006; Hermit Crab's Home: Safe in a Shell, 2007; Narwhal: Unicorn of the Sea, 2008. OTHER CHILDREN'S NONFICTION: Skyscrapers, 2003; Plant Tricksters, 2003; The Tallest Building, 2004; Seven Miles to Freedom: The Robert Smalls Story, 2008; Star of the Sea: A Day in the Life of a Starfish, 2011; Eggs 1, 2, 3: Who Will the Babies Be? 2012. CHILDREN'S FICTION: Little Skink's Tail, 2007; Fur and Feathers, 2010; Good Night, Little Sea Otter, 2010; Home in the Cave, 2012. Contributor to magazines. **Address:** South Milwaukee, WI , U.S.A. **Online address:** janet@janethalfmann.com

HALFORD, Graeme S(ydney). Australian (born Australia), b. 1937. **Genres:** Psychology, Education. **Career:** University of Newcastle, lecturer, 1965-70, senior lecturer in psychology, 1971-72; Queen's University, associate professor of psychology, 1972-75; University of Queensland, senior lecturer, 1975-79, reader, 1980-89, professor of psychology, 1989-, personal chair; Australian Journal of Psychology, associate editor, 1986-91; Queensland Academy of the Arts and Sciences, vice president, 2001. **Publications:** (Ed. with J.A. Keats and K.F. Collis) Cognitive Development: Research Based on a Neo-Piagetian Approach, 1978; The Development of Thought, 1982; Children's Understanding: The Development of Mental Models, 1993; (ed. with T.J. Simon) Developing Cognitive Competence: New Approaches to Process Modelling, 1995; Mathematics Education: Models and Processes, 1995. **Address:** School of Psychology, University of Queensland, Rm. MC-417, Brisbane, QL 4072, Australia. **Online address:** gsh@psy.uq.edu.au

HALKIN, Ariela. Israeli (born Israel), b. 1942. **Genres:** Literary Criticism And History, Young Adult Fiction. **Career:** Tel Aviv University, teacher of history. Writer. **Publications:** The Enemy Reviewed: German Popular Literature through British Eyes between the Two World Wars, 1995. **Address:** 11 Hashikma St., Savyon, 56518, Israel. **Online address:** halkin@netvision.net.il

HALL, Ann C. American (born United States), b. 1959. **Genres:** Literary Criticism And History, Young Adult Fiction. **Career:** Marquette University, assistant professor of English, 1989-91; Contemporary American Theatre Co., education director, 1991-94; Ohio Dominican University, Division of Literature and Languages, assistant professor, 1994-98, department chair, 1997, associate professor of English, full professor, 1998-. Writer. **Publications:** A Kind of Alaska: Women in the Plays of O'Neill, Pinter and Shepard, 1993; (ed.) Delights, Desires and Dilemmas: Essays on Women and the Media, 1998; (ed. with M.J. Bishop) Pop-Porn: Pornography in American Culture, 2007; (ed.) Making the Stage: Essays on the Changing Concept of Theatre, Drama and Performance, 2008; (ed. with M.J. Bishop) Mommy Angst: Motherhood in American Popular Culture, 2009; Phantom Variations: The Adaptations of Gaston Leroux's Phantom of the Opera, 1925 to the Present, 2009. Contributor to journals. **Address:** Division of Literature and Languages, Ohio Dominican University, 1216 Sunbury Rd., Columbus, OH 43219, U.S.A. **Online address:** halla@ohiodominican.edu

HALL, Bert S(tewart). American (born United States), b. 1945. **Genres:** History, Technology, Art/Art History. **Career:** State University of New York at Buffalo, assistant professor of history, 1972-77; University of Toronto, Institute for the History and Philosophy of Science and Technology, associate professor of history, 1977-, professor. Writer. **Publications:** Technological Illustrations, 1976; (ed. with D.C. West) On Pre-Modern Technology and Science: A Volume of Studies in Honor of Lynn White, Jr., 1976; Technological Illustrations of the So-Called Anonymous of the Hussite Wars: Codex Latinus Monacensis, 1979; Tools in Medieval Life, 1981; (ed. with S. Campbell and D. Klausner) Health, Disease and Healing in Medieval Culture, 1991; Weapons and Warfare in Renaissance Europe: Gunpowder, Technology and Tactics, 1997; (intro.) History of Greek Fire and Gunpowder, 1998. **Address:** Victoria College, University of Toronto, IHPST, Rm. 316, Toronto, ON M5S 1K7, Canada. **Online address:** bert.hall@utoronto.ca

HALL, Blaine H(ill). American (born United States), b. 1932. **Genres:** Librarianship, Literary Criticism And History, Bibliography, Language/Linguistics, Reference, Autobiography/Memoirs. **Career:** Teacher, 1960-61; Brigham Young University, instructor in English, 1963-72, Harold B. Lee Library, senior English and American literature librarian, 1972-96, professor emeritus of library science, 1996-. Writer. **Publications:** (With C.I. Bradshaw and M.E. Wiggins) Using the Library: The Card Catalog, 1971; Collection Assessment Manual for College and University Libraries, 1985; (with G.L. Cronin) Saul Bellow: An Annotated Bibliography, 2nd ed., 1987; (with G.L. Cronin) Jerzy Kosinski: An Annotated Bibliography, 1991; (with G.L. Cronin and C. Lamb) Jewish American Fiction Writers: An Annotated Bibliography, 1991; (ed. with G. Bach) Conversations with Grace Paley, 1997. **Address:** Brigham Young University, 5220 HBLL, Provo, UT 84602, U.S.A. **Online**

address: bhall11@att.net

HALL, Brian. American (born United States), b. 1959. **Genres:** Novels, Politics/Government, Travel/Exploration, Children's Fiction. **Career:** Harvard University, LeBaron Russell Briggs travel fellow, 1981; freelance writer, 1984-. **Publications:** Stealing from a Deep Place: Travels in Southeastern Europe, 1988; The Dreamers: A Novel, 1989; The Impossible Country: A Journey through the Last Days of Yugoslavia, 1994; The Saskiad (novel), 1997; Madeleine's World: A Child's Journey from Birth to Age Three, 1997; I Should Be Extremely Happy in Your Company: A Novel of Lewis and Clark, 2003; Fall of Frost: A Novel, 2008. Contributor to periodicals. **Address:** c/o David Chalfant, IMG Literary, 825 7th Ave., New York, NY 10019, U.S.A.

HALL, Carl W. American (born United States), b. 1924. **Genres:** Agriculture/Forestry, Engineering, Food And Wine, Technology, Business/Trade/Industry, Economics, Biography, Bibliography, Bibliography. **Career:** University of Delaware, instructor, assistant professor, 1948-51; Michigan State University, assistant professor, professor of agricultural engineering and chairman of department, 1951-70; ACA Engineering Consultants, president, 1960-70; Washington State University, professor of mechanical engineering and dean of College of Engineering, 1970-82, University Research Foundation, president, 1973-82; ESCOE Inc., engineer, 1979; National Science Foundation, deputy assistant director, directorate for engineering, 1982-90; Engineering Information Services, engineer, 1990-. Writer. **Publications:** Drying Farm Crops, 1957; (ed. with C.B. Richey and P. Jacobson) Agricultural Engineers' Handbook, 1961; Agricultural Engineering Index, 1907-1960, vol. I, 1961, vol. II: (with G.E. Hall) Agricultural Engineering Index, 1961-1970, 1972, vol. III: (with J.A. Basselman) Agricultural Engineering Index, 1971-1980, 1982, vol. IV: (with J. Basselman) Agricultural Engineering Index, 1981-1985, 1986; vol. V: Agricultural Engineering Index, 1986-1990, 1991; (with D.C. Davis) Processing Equipment for Agricultural Products, 1963, 2nd ed. (with D.C. Davis), 1979; (with T.I. Hedrick) Drying Milk and Milk Products, 1966, 2nd ed., 1971; (with F. Salas) Equipo para Procesamiento de Productos Agricolas, 1968; (with G.M. Trout) Milk Pasteurization, 1968; (with A.W. Farrall and A.L. Rippen) Encyclopedia of Food Engineering, 1971, 2nd ed., 1986; (ed. with M.L. Esmay) Agricultural Mechanization in Developing Countries, 1973; Perspectives on Technological Progress: A Treatise on the Past, Present and Future of Engineering Contributions and Effects, 1973; (with D.B. Brooker and F.W. Bakker-Arkema) Drying Cereal Grains, 1974; (with R.W. Crain, Jr. and G.W. Hinman) Perspectives on Energy, 1974; (with W.J. Harper) Dairy Technology and Engineering, 1976; Errors in Experimentation, 1977; Dictionary of Drying, 1979; Drying and Storage of Agricultural Crops, 1980; Biomass as an Alternative Fuel, 1981; (with G.W. Hinman) Dictionary of Energy, 1983; (ed. with D. Pimentel) Food and Energy Resources, 1984; Bibliography of Biomass Energy: Including Items Published Separately as Books, Booklets, Bulletins, Dissertations, Pamphlets and Reports, 1985; (ed. with D. Pimentel) Food and Natural Resources, 1989; (ed. with O. Kitani) Biomass Handbook, 1989; (ed. with W. Vergara and N.E. Hay) Natural Gas: Its Role and Potential in Economic Development, 1990; (with D. Brooker and F.W. Bakker-Arkema) Drying and Storage of Grains and Oilseeds, 1992; (ed. with W.C. Olsen) Literature of Agricultural Engineering, 1992; The Age of Synthesis: A Treatise and Sourcebook, 1995; Laws and Models: Science, Engineering and Technology, 2000; A Biographical Dictionary of People in Engineering: From Earliest Records until 2000, 2008. **Address:** 2454 N Rockingham St., Arlington, VA 22207-1033, U.S.A.

HALL, David C. Spanish/American (born United States), b. 1943. **Genres:** Mystery/Crime/Suspense, Novels. **Career:** Summit School of English, teacher, 1975-79; English Three, teacher, 1980-, now retired. Writer. **Publications:** CRIME NOVELS: (trans.) Cuatro dias (title means: 'Four Days'), 1984; (trans.) No quiero hablar de Bolivia (title means: 'The Real Thing'), 1988; Return Trip Ticket, 1992. **Address:** Avenida Virgen de Montserrat 18, Sant Cugat del Valles, Barcelona, 08190, Spain. **Online address:** dchall01@gmail.com

HALL, David Ian. British (born England), b. 1956. **Genres:** Air/Space Topics. **Career:** Royal Military College of Canada, lecturer in history; King's College London, senior lecturer in defense studies, 1998-; Joint Services Command and Staff College, Defence Studies: The Journal, founding editor; Royal Navy, director; Royal Air Force, academic air power specialist. **Publications:** Strategy for Victory: The Development of British Tactical Air Power, 1919-1943, 2008. **Address:** Department of Defence Studies, Joint Services Command and Staff College, King's College London, Faringdon Rd., Shrivenham, Swindon, WT SN6 8TS, England. **Online address:** dhall.jscsc@defenceacademy.mod.uk

HALL, David Locke. American (born United States), b. 1955. **Genres:** Politics/Government, Military/Defense/Arms Control, Law. **Career:** Department of Justice, assistant U.S. attorney. Writer. **Publications:** The Reagan Wars: A Constitutional Perspective on War Powers and the Presidency, 1991. **Address:** Westview Press Inc., 5500 Central Ave., Boulder, CO 80301-2877, U.S.A.

HALL, Donald (Andrew). American (born United States), b. 1928. **Genres:** Children's Fiction, Poetry, Art/Art History, Literary Criticism And History, Young Adult Fiction, Biography, Autobiography/Memoirs. **Career:** Paris Review, poetry editor, 1953-62; British Broadcasting Corp., broadcaster, 1959-80; Harvard University, Society of Fellows, junior fellow, 1954-57; University of Michigan, assistant professor, associate professor, 1957-66, professor of English, 1966-76; full-time freelance writer, 1975-; Bennington College graduate writing seminars, poet-in-residence, 1993-; Library of Congress, Poet Laureate, 2006-07; Oxford Poetry, editor. **Publications:** Donald Hall: Poems, 1952; Exile: The Newdigate Prize Poem, 1952; To the Loud Wind and Other Poems, 1955; Exiles and Marriages, 1955; The Dark Houses, 1958; Andrew the Lion Farmer, 1959; String Too Short to Be Saved: Childhood Reminiscences, 1961; A Roof of Tiger Lilies: Poems, 1964; Henry Moore: The Life and Work of Great Sculptor, 1966; (intro.) A Choice of Whitman's Verse, 1968; The Alligator Bride, 1968; Marianne Moore: The Cage and the Animal, 1970; As the Eye Moves: A Sculpture by Henry Moore, 1970; The Yellow Room Love Poems, 1971; The Gentleman's Alphabet Book, 1972; Writing Well, 1973, 9th ed., 1998; Playing Around, 1974; A Blue Wing Tilts at the Edge of the Sea, 1975; Dock Ellis in the Country of Baseball, 1976; Remembering Poets, 1978; Goatfoot Milktongue Twinbird: Interviews, Essays, and Notes on Poetry 1970-76, 1978; Kicking the Leaves, 1978; Ox Cart Man, 1979; To Keep Moving, 1980; (comp.) To Read Literature, 1981, 3rd ed., 1992; The Weather for Poetry, 1982; The Man Who Lived Alone, 1984; Fathers Playing Catch with Sons, 1985; The Happy Man, 1986; The Ideal Bakery, 1987; The Bone Ring, 1987; Seasons at Eagle Pond, 1987; Poetry and Ambition, 1988; The One Day, 1988; Anecdotes of Modern Art, 1990; Old and New Poems, 1990; Here at Eagle Pond, 1990; Their Ancient Glittering Eyes, 1991; The Museum of Clear Ideas, 1993; Life Work, 1993; Lucy's Christmas, 1994; The Farm Summer 1942, 1994; I am the Dog, I am the Cat, 1994; Death to the Death of Poetry, 1994; Principal Products of Portugal, 1995; Lucy's Summer, 1995; When Willard Met Babe Ruth, 1996; Without, 1998; The Old Life, 1996; Old Home Day, 1996; Three Donald Hall Songs, 1997; The Milkman's Boy, 1997; The Purpose of a Chair, 2000; The Painted Bed, 2002; Willow Temple, 2003; Breakfast Served Any Time All Day (essays), 2003; The Best Day the Worst Day: Life with Jane Kenyon, 2005; White Apples and the Taste of Stone: Selected Poems 1946-2006, 2006; Eagle Pond, 2007; (co-author) Seven American Poets in Conversation, 2008; Unpacking the Boxes: A Memoir of a Life in Poetry, 2008. EDITOR: The Harvard Advocate Anthology, 1950; (with R. Pack and L. Simpson) New Poets of England and America, 1957; Whittier, 1961; (with R. Pack) New Poets of England and America: Second Selection, 1962; Contemporary American Poetry, 1962; (with S. Spender) The Concise Encyclopedia of English and American Poets and Poetry, 1963; (with W. Taylor) Poetry in English, 1963; The Faber Book of Modern Verse, rev. ed., 1965; The Modern Stylists, 1968; Man and Boy: An Anthology, 1968; American Poetry: An Introductory Anthology, 1969; The Pleasures of Poetry, 1971; (with D.L. Emblen) A Writer's Reader, 1976, 9th ed., 2002; The Oxford Book of American Literary Anecdotes, 1981; Claims for Poetry, 1982; To Read Poetry, 1982; The Contemporary Essay, 1984, 3rd ed., 1995; The Oxford Book of Children's Verse in America, 1985; To Read Fiction, 1987; (and intro.) The Essential Robinson, 1994; The Oxford Illustrated Book of American Children's Poems, 1999; The Back Chamber, 2011. **Address:** Gerald McCauley Agency Inc., PO Box 844, Katonah, NY 10536, U.S.A.

HALL, Douglas. American (born United States) **Genres:** Cultural/Ethnic Topics, Novels, History. **Career:** University of Maryland, professor in European Division. Writer. **Publications:** The Trinity: An Analysis of St. Thomas Aquinas's Expositio of the De Trinitate of Boethius, 1992. **Address:** c/o Author Mail, Brill Academic Publishers, PO Box 9000, PA Leiden, 2300, Netherlands.

HALL, Edith. British (born England), b. 1959. **Genres:** Intellectual History, Language/Linguistics. **Career:** Oxford University, Lincoln College, lecturer,

1985-86, Magdalen College, lecturer, 1989-90, university lecturer in classics and Somerville College, fellow, 1995-2001, Archive of Performances of Greek and Roman Drama (APGRD), co-founder and co-director, consultant director; Cambridge University, research fellow, 1987-89; University of Reading, lecturer, 1990-95; University of Durham, Leverhulme professor of Greek cultural history and Leverhulme chair of Greek cultural history, 2001-06; University of London, Royal Holloway, research professor of classics and drama, 2006-, research chair, Centre for the Reception of Greece and Rome, director, through 2011; University of Wisconsin-Madison, Swarthmore College, visiting professor; Miami University, visiting professor; Royal Shakespeare Co., consultant; ENO, consultant; National Theatre, consultant; Northern Broadsides, consultant; Abbey Theatre, consultant; Live Theatre, consultant. Writer. **Publications:** Inventing the Barbarian: Greek Self-Definition through Tragedy, 1989; (ed. and intro.) Antigone; Oedipus the King; Electra, 1994; (ed.) Aeschylus, 1996; (ed. with F. Macintosh and O. Taplin) Medea in Performance 1500-2000, 2000; (ed. with P. Easterling) Greek and Roman Actors: Aspects of an Ancient Profession, 2002; (ed. with F. Macintosh and A. Wrigley) Dionysus since 69: Greek Tragedy at the Dawn of the Third Millennium, 2004; (with F. Macintosh) Greek Tragedy and the British Theatre, 1660-1914, 2005; (co-ed.) Agamemnon in Performance 458 BC to AD 2004, 2005; The Theatrical Cast of Athens: Interactions between Ancient Greek Drama and Society, 2006; (ed. with A. Wrigley) Aristophanes in Performance 421 BC-AD 2007: Peace, Birds, Frogs, 2007; (ed. with E. Bridges and P.J. Rhodes) Cultural Responses to the Persian Wars: Antiquity to the Third Millennium, 2007; Return of Ulysses, 2008; (ed. with R. Wyles) New Directions in Ancient Pantomime, 2008; (ed. with S. Goldhill) Sophocles and the Greek Tragic Tradition, 2009; (contrib.) Through the Gate, 2009; Greek Tragedy: Suffering Under the Sun, 2010; (ed. with S. Harrop) Theorising Performance: Greek Drama, Cultural History and Critical Practice, 2010; (ed. with R. Alston and J. McConnell) Ancient Slavery and Abolition: From Hobbes to Hollywood, 2011. **Address:** Department of Drama & Theatre Studies, Royal Holloway, University of London, Rm. 31 Founders W, Egham Hill, Egham, SR TW20 0EX, England. **Online address:** edith.hall@rhul.ac.uk

HALL, Gimone. Also writes as Shannon Willow, Shannon Willow. American (born United States), b. 1940. **Genres:** Novels, Romance/Historical. **Career:** Romantic Times Critique Service, critic; Writer's Digest School, teacher; Million Wishes Romance Writing School, founder and director; Corpus-Christi Caller-Times, news reporter, 1962. **Publications:** The Blue Taper, 1970; Witch's Suckling, 1970, 3rd ed., 1973; Devil's Walk, 1971; The Juliet Room, 1973; The Silver Strand, 1974; Hide My Savage Heart, 1977; Rapture's Mistress, 1978; Fury's Sun, Passion's Moon, 1979; Ecstasy's Empire, 1980; The Jasmine Veil, 1982; Rules of the Heart, 1984; The Kiss Flower, 1985; (as Shannon Willow) Texas Jewel, 1993. Contributor to magazines. **Address:** Million Wishes Romance Writing School, Million Wishes Farm, 55 Brennan Rd., Ottsville, PA 18942, U.S.A. **Online address:** romance@epix.net

HALL, H(ugh) Gaston. British/American (born United States), b. 1931. **Genres:** Poetry, Literary Criticism And History, Essays, Translations. **Career:** Yale University, instructor in French, 1958-60; University of Glasgow, lecturer in French, 1960-64; University of California, assistant professor, 1963; Monash University, senior lecturer in French, 1965; University of Warwick, senior lecturer, 1966-74, reader in French, 1974-89, School of Spanish, chairman, 1984-87, emeritus reader, 1989-; City University of New York, visiting professor, 1970-72. Writer. **Publications:** Molière: Tartuffe, 1960; Quadruped Octaves, 1983; Comedy in Context: Essays on Moliere, 1984; Alphabet Aviary (poems), 1986; Moliere's Le Bourgeois Gentilhomme: Context and Stagecraft, 1990; Richelieu's Desmarets and the Century of Louis XIV, 1990; Sonnets, 2002; Reptile Rhymes (poems), 2002; Domestic Tales and Other Poems, 2002; Sketches (poems), 2003; Quatrains (poems), 2004. TRANSLATOR: F. Simone, The French Renaissance, 1970; J. de La Fontaine, Forty Fables, 2002. EDITOR: Les Visionnaires, 1963, rev. ed., 1995; (and intro.) Les Femmes Savantes, 1974; L'Amant auteur et valet: Comédie, 1978; Melanges a la memoire de F. Simone, 4 vols., 1980-84; Critical Bibliography of French Literature, vol. III A, 1983; W.E. Sly Jr., Poems, 2002. **Address:** University of Warwick, Coventry, WW CV4 7AL, England.

HALL, Ivan P(arker). American (born United States), b. 1932?. **Genres:** Area Studies, Business/Trade/Industry. **Career:** Military intelligence staff, 1954-56; United States Information Service, staff, 1958-61; Philadelphia Bulletin, correspondent, 1970-77; Washington Star, correspondent, 1970-77; Modern Japanese History, visiting lecturer, 1971; Japan-U.S. Friendship Commission, Japan representative and associate executive director, 1977-84;

Tsukuba University, professor of international cultural relations and intellectual history, 1985-93; Keio University, professor of international cultural relations and intellectual history, 1985-93; Gakushuin University, professor of international cultural relations and intellectual history, 1985-93; Japan Policy Research Institute, board adviser, 1993-; Harvard-Yenching Institute, consultant; Harvard's Japan Fund Drive, consultant. Writer. **Publications:** Mori Arinori, 1973; Cartels of the Mind: Japan's Intellectual Closed Shop, 1997; Bamboozled! How America Loses the Intellectual Game with Japan and Its Implications for Our Future in Asia, 2002. Contributor to periodicals. **Address:** Japan Policy Research Institute, Center for the Pacific Rim, University of San Francisco, LM280, 2130 Fulton St., San Francisco, CA 94117-1080, U.S.A. **Online address:** ivanphall@hotmail.com

HALL, Joan Wylie. American (born United States), b. 1947. **Genres:** Literary Criticism And History, Women's Studies And Issues, Reference. **Career:** Franklin News-Herald, general reporter, 1966-69; University of Notre Dame, teaching assistant, 1971-72, adjunct instructor, 1973-74; Saint Mary-of-the-Woods College, instructor, 1974-78; Harvard University, preceptor for junior English tutorials, 1983-84; University of Mississippi, instructor, 1979-83, 1984-2008, lecturer, 2008-. Writer. **Publications:** Shirley Jackson: A Study of the Short Fiction, 1993; (ed.) Conversations with Audre Lorde, 2004. Contributor to journals. **Address:** Department of English, University of Mississippi, 135 Bondurant Hall, PO Box 1848, University, MS 38677-1848, U.S.A. **Online address:** egjwh@olemiss.edu

HALL, J(ohn) C(live). *See* Obituaries.

HALL, Jonathan M. British (born England) **Genres:** History. **Career:** Marlboro College, Oxford University, teaching fellow, 1988-89; Cambridge University, undergraduate supervisor, 1989-96, Downing College, resident fellow, 1993-96, affiliated lecturer, 1995-96; University of Chicago, assistant professor, 1996-; Athens Summer School, British School, lecturer, 1992-93. Writer. **Publications:** Ethnic Identity in Greek Antiquity, 1997; Hellenicity: Between Ethnicity and Culture, 2002; A History of the Archaic Greek World ca. 1200-479 BCE, 2006. **Address:** Department of History, University of Chicago, 1126 E 59th St., PO Box 60, Chicago, IL 60637, U.S.A. **Online address:** jhall@uchicago.edu

HALL, Karen L. American (born United States), b. 1956. **Genres:** Novels. **Career:** Silkwood, Twentieth Century-Fox, production coordinator, 1983; American Broadcasting Co.(ABC), assistant, producer, 1987-88, creative consultant, 1994-95. Television series producer and writer. **Publications:** Dark Debts, 1996. Contributor to periodicals. **Address:** 11812 San Vicente Blvd., Ste. 200, Los Angeles, CA 90049-6622, U.S.A. **Online address:** khall356@earthlink.net

HALL, Kathleen (Mary). British (born England), b. 1924. **Genres:** Literary Criticism And History, Translations, Poetry. **Career:** British Ministry of Supply, assistant principal, 1945-46; Queen's University, assistant lecturer, 1953-55; University of Southampton, lecturer, 1955-69, senior lecturer in French, 1969-85. Writer. **Publications:** Pontus de Tyard and His Discours Philosophiques, 1963; (ed. with K. Cameron and F. Higman) Abraham Sacrifiant, 1967; (ed. with C.N. Smith) Dramatic Works, 1972; (ed.) Cléopâtre Captive, 1979; (with M.B. Wells) Du Bellay: Poems, 1985; Rabelais: Pantagruel and Gargantua, 1991; (trans. and into Esperanto) R. Kipling, La Zodiakidoj Kaj Aliaj Rakontoj, 1997. **Address:** 37 Granville Ct., Oxford, OX OX3 OHS, England.

HALL, Kirsten Marie. American (born United States), b. 1974. **Genres:** Children's Fiction, Animals/Pets, Novellas/Short Stories. **Career:** Random House, editorial assistant. **Publications:** Bunny, Bunny, 1989; Who Says?, 1989; A Visit to France, 1991; Puppies: A Pop-Up Book, 1993; Kittens, 1993; Hot Summer Fun Friendship Bracelets, 1994; The Tooth Fairy, 1994; Ballerina Girl, 1994; My Brother, the Brat, 1995; A Bad, Bad Day, 1995; I See a Bug, 1995; I'm a Princess, 1995; Boo!, 1995; Duck, Duck, Goose, 1995; My Trucks, 1995; Our Tea Party, 1996; At the Carnival, 1996; Madame Boskey's Fortune-Telling Kit, 1996; Noah's Ark, 1997; Princess Florella, 1997; Really Gross Stuff, 1998; Bad Jokes and Worse Riddles, 1998; Dinosaur Facts, 1998; Weird Animal Facts, 1998; My Best Friend, 1998; Who Loves Me Best?, 1999; The Princess Who Never Smiled, 1999; We Are All Different, 1999; A Practical Guide to Handwriting, 1999; Princess Daisy Finds a Friend, 1999; Last Night I Danced With a Stranger: A Guide to Dream Analysis, 2000; My Best Friend, 2001; Magical World of Fairies, 2001; Magical World of Ballet,

2001; Going Batty, 2001; Busy Chipmunk, 2001; Making Tracks, 2002; I'm So Sared!, 2002; Green Thumbs, 2002; Big Sled Race, 2002; Help!: All About Telling Time, 2003; First Day of School: All About Shapes and Sizes, 2003; Double Trouble: All About Colors, 2003; Deep Sea Adventures: A Chapter Book, 2003; Buried Treasure: All About Using a Map, 2003; Birthday Beastie: All About Counting, 2003; Vote for Me: All About Civics, 2003; Top Secret, 2003; Oops!: All About Opposites, 2003; I'm not Scared, 2003; Mystery at the Museum, 2003; Little Lies: All About Math, 2003; On the Farm, 2004; My New School, 2004; Let's Trade: All About Trading, 2004; Kids in Sports: A Chapter Book, 2004; Hide-And-Seek: All About Location, 2004; Grandma's House, 2004; Good Times: All About the Seasons, 2004; Big Race: All About Safety, 2004; Bear for You, 2004; Zoom, Zoom, Zoom, 2004; What a Mess!: All About Numbers, 2004; Tug-of-War: All About Balance, 2004; Slider's Pet: All About Nature, 2004; Perfect Day: All About the Five Senses, 2004; Tracking Animals: A Chapter Book, 2005; Revamp your Room, 2005; My New Town, 2005; Animal Touch: El tacto en los animals, 2006; Discover the Real You, 2006; Animal Hearing: El oído en los, 2006; Animal Sight: La vista de los animals, 2006; Animal Smell: El olfato en los animals, 2006; Animal Taste: El gusto en los animals, 2006; African Elephant: The World's Biggest Land Mammal, 2007; Great Bustard: The World's Heaviest Flying Bird, 2007; Leatherback Turtle: The World's Heaviest Reptile, 2007; Glow-in-the-dark Zombie Science, 2009; Up Close and Gross, 2009; (with C. Schulz) Hospitality, 2010. **Address:** 86 Woodbury St., Providence, RI 02906-3510, U.S.A. **Online address:** kirhall@aol.com

HALL, Lee. American (born United States), b. 1934. **Genres:** Art/Art History, Biography, History. **Career:** State University of New York College-Potsdam, assistant professor of art, 1958-60; Keuka College, Art Department, associate professor of art and department chair, 1960-62; Winthrop University, associate professor of art, 1962-65; Drew University, assistant professor, 1965-67, associate professor, 1967-70, professor of art, 1970-74, Art Department, chair, 1965-74; National Endowment for Humanities, consultant, 1969-75, panelist 1972-80; State University of New York College-Purchase, dean of visual arts, 1974-75; Rhode Island School of Design, president, 1975-83; Academy for Educational Development, senior vice president and director of arts and communications, 1984-92. Artist and writer. **Publications:** Wallace Herndon Smith: Paintings, 1987; Abe Ajay, 1990; Betty Parsons: Artist, Dealer, Collector, 1991; Common Threads: A Parade of American Clothing, 1992; Elaine and Bill, Portrait of a Marriage: The Lives of Willem and Elaine de Kooning, 1993; Olmsted's America: An Unpractical Man and His Vision of Civilization, 1995; Athena: Biography, 1997; Living in the Future: International House, New York: 75 Years, 2000. Contributor to journals. **Address:** 14 Silverwood Terr., South Hadley, MA 01075-1237, U.S.A. **Online address:** lhall82115@aol.com

HALL, Lesley A(nn). British (born England), b. 1949?. **Genres:** Adult Nonfiction, Science Fiction/Fantasy, Sex. **Career:** India Office Records, archives assistant, 1973-75, research assistant, 1975-79; Wellcome Institute for the History of Medicine, Contemporary Medical Archives Centre, assistant archivist, 1979-89, senior assistant archivist, 1989-. Writer. **Publications:** A Brief Guide to Sources for the Study of Afghanistan in the India Office Records, 1981; Hidden Anxieties: Male Sexuality, 1900-1950, 1991; (with J. Dixon and J. Sheppard) A Guide to the Contemporary Medical Archives Centre, 1995; (with R. Porter) The Facts of Life: The Creation of Sexual Knowledge in Britain, 1680-1950, 1995; Sex, Gender, and Social Change in Britain since 1880, 2000; (ed. with R. Davidson) Sex, Sin, and Suffering: Venereal Disease and European Society since 1870, 2001; (ed.) Outspoken Women: An Anthology of Women's Writing on Sex, 1870-1969, 2005. Works appear in anthologies. Contributor of articles to periodicals. **Address:** Contemporary Medical Archives Centre, Wellcome Institute for the History of Medicine, 183 Euston Rd., London, GL NW1 2BE, England. **Online address:** lesleyah@primex.co.uk

HALL, Lincoln. Australian (born Australia), b. 1955?. **Genres:** Young Adult Fiction. **Career:** World Expeditions, freelance guide, 1978; Gondwana Publishing & Photography, owner, 1990-; Adventure West, freelance facilitator, 1991-2002; Gondwana Publishing, editor, 1993-2007; Out There Magazine, founder and managing editor, 1993-96; DIDJ, online publication for Microsoft Corp., contributing editor, 1996-97; Expanse Magazine, editor-at-large, advisor, contributing editor, 1997-98; Saxton Speakers Bureau, creative director, 2006-10; Beyond Survival, creative director, 2006-. **Publications:** White Limbo: The First Australian Climb of Mt. Everest, 1985; The Loneliest Mountain: The Dramatic Story of the First Expedition to Climb Mt. Minto,

Antarctica, 1989; Douglas Mawson: The Life of an Explorer, 2000; Dead Lucky: Life after Death on Mount Everest, 2007; Alive in the Death Zone: Mount Everest Survival, 2008. Contributor to periodicals. **Address:** Random House Books, 100 Pacific Hwy., Level 3, North Sydney, NW 2060, Australia. **Online address:** lincolnhall.net@gmail.com

HALL, Linley Erin. American (born United States), b. 1979?. **Genres:** Children's Non-fiction. **Career:** Arizona State University, Ira A. Fulton School of Engineering, science writer and editor, 2002-03; freelance writer, 2003-; Humanistic Mathematics Network Journal, part-time production manager; University of California, Santa Cruz Public Information Office, science writing internship; Stanford University Medical Center Office of Communication and Public Affairs, science writing internship. Freelance writer and editor. **Publications:** (ed.) The Laws of Motion: An Anthology of Current Thought, 2006; Who's Afraid of Marie Curie? The Challenges Facing Women in Science and Technology, 2007; Careers in Biotechnology, 2007; (ed.) Critical Perspectives on Energy and Power, 2007; Starvation in Africa, 2007. **Address:** San Francisco, CA , U.S.A. **Online address:** lhall@nasw.org

HALL, Lynn. American (born United States), b. 1937. **Genres:** Novellas/ Short Stories, Children's Fiction, Novels, Mystery/Crime/Suspense, Young Adult Non-fiction. **Career:** Children's writer, 1968-. **Publications:** The Shy Ones, 1965; The Secret of Stonehouse, 1968; Ride a Wild Dream, 1969; Too Near the Sun, 1969; Gently Touch the Milkweed, 1970; A Horse Called Dragon, 1971; Sticks and Stones, 1972; The Famous Battle of Bravery Creek, 1972; Dog Stories, 1972; The Siege of Silent Henry, 1972; Flash: Dog of Old Egypt, 1973; Barry: The Bravest Saint Bernard, 1973; Riff, Remember, 1973; To Catch a Tartar, 1973; Troublemaker, 1974; Bob, Watchdog of the River, 1974; Stray, 1974; Kids and Dog Shows, 1975; New Day for Dragon, 1975; Captain, Canada's Flying Pony, 1975; Flowers of Anger, 1976; Owney, The Traveling Dog, 1977; Dragon Defiant, 1977; Shadows, 1977; Careers for Dog Lovers, 1978; The Mystery of Pony Hollow, 1978; The Mystery of the Lost and Found Hound, 1979; The Whispered Horse, 1979; The Mystery of the Schoolhouse Dog, 1979; Dog of the Bondi Castle, 1979; The Leaving, 1980; Dragon's Delight, 1980; The Mystery of Stubborn Old Man, 1980; The Mystery of Plum Park Pony, 1980; The Haunting of the Green Bird, 1980; The Mystery of the Stubborn Old Man, 1980; The Disappearing Grandad, 1980; The Ghost of the Great River Inn, 1980; The Mysterious Moortown Bridge, 1981; The Mystery of the Caramel Cat, 1981; The Horse Trader, 1981; Danza!, 1981; Half the Battle, 1982; Tin Can Tucker, 1982; Denison's Daughter, 1983; Megan's Mare, 1983; The Mystery of Pony Hollow Panda, 1983; The Boy in the Off-White Hat, 1984; Uphill All the Way, 1984; The Something-Special Horse, 1985; The Giver, 1985; Tazo and Me, 1985; Just One Friend, 1985; If Winter Comes, 1986; The Solitary, 1986; Danger Dog, 1986; Mrs. Portree's Pony, 1986; Letting Go, 1987; Flyaway, 1987; Ride a Dark Horse, 1987; In Trouble Again, Zelda Hammersmith?, 1987; A Killing Freeze, 1988; Zelda Strikes Again!, 1988; The Secret Life of Dagmar Schultz, 1988; Murder at the Spaniel Show, 1988; Where Have All the Tigers Gone?, 1989; Dagmar Schultz and the Powers of Darkness, 1989; Dagmar Schultz and the Angel Edna, 1989; Here Comes Zelda Claus: And Other Holiday Disasters, 1989; Murder in a Pig's Eye, 1990; Fair Maiden, 1990; Halsey's Pride, 1990; The Tormentors, 1990; Flying Changes, 1991; Dagmar Schultz and the Green-eyed Monster, 1991; The Soul of the Silver Dog, 1992; Windsong, 1992; The More I See of Men, 1992; Decisions, 1992; The Mystery of the Phantom Pony, 1993; Dog Showing for Beginners, 1994; Love's Return, 1996. Contributor to periodicals. **Address:** Random House Inc., 1745 Broadway, New York, NY 10019, U.S.A.

HALL, Marie Beth. American (born United States), b. 1933. **Genres:** Military/Defense/Arms Control, Women's Studies And Issues, History. **Career:** Pan American World Airways, flight purser, 1954-62; U.S. Department of Energy, Federal Energy Regulatory Commission, writer and editor, 1978-2002; Northern Virginia Swim League, division coordinator. **Publications:** (With J. Ebbert) Crossed Currents: Navy Women from WWI to Tailhook, 1993; Crossed Currents: Navy Women in a Century of Change, 1993, 3rd. Ed., 1999; The First, the Few, the Forgotten: Navy and Marine Corps Women in World War I, 2002. **Address:** 5808 Hampton Forest Way, Fairfax, VA 22030-7253, U.S.A.

HALL, Martha Lacy. American (born United States), b. 1923. **Genres:** Novellas/Short Stories, Young Adult Fiction, Young Adult Non-fiction, Literary Criticism And History. **Career:** Louisiana State University Press, editor, 1968-78, managing editor, 1979-84, fiction editor, 1984-. **Publications:** FIC-TION: Call It Living, 1981; Music Lesson: Stories, 1984; The Apple-Green Triumph and Other Stories, 1990. NONFICTION: An Historical Sketch of Magnolia, Mississippi: Centennial Celebration, Magnolia, Mississippi, 1856-1956, 1956. Contributor to periodicals. **Address:** c/o Nat Sobol, Sobel Weber Associates Inc., 146 E 19th St., New York, NY 10003, U.S.A. **Online address:** marthatheauthor@earthlink.net

HALL, Matthew. American (born United States), b. 1958. **Genres:** Mystery/ Crime/Suspense. **Career:** Editor of medical textbooks and writer. **Publications:** Nightmare Logic, 1989; The Art of Breaking Glass: A Thriller, 1997; Victims and Policy Making: A Comparative Perspective, 2010. **Address:** c/o Laurie Liss, Harvey Klinger Inc., 301 W 53rd St., New York, NY 10019, U.S.A. **Online address:** petithall@dcdu.com

HALL, Meredith. American (born United States), b. 1949?. **Genres:** Biography, Autobiography/Memoirs. **Career:** University of New Hampshire, writing teacher. Writer. **Publications:** Without a Map: A Memoir, 2007. Contributor to Anthologies. **Address:** University of New Hampshire, 310 Hamilton Smith Hall, Durham, NH 03824, U.S.A.

HALL, M. R. British (born England), b. 1967. **Genres:** Mystery/Crime/ Suspense. **Career:** Barrister, screenwriter and producer. **Publications:** The Coroner, 2009; The Disappeared, 2009; The Redeemed, 2011. **Address:** c/o Zoe Waldie, Rogers Coleridge & White, 20 Powis Mews, London, GL W11 1JN, England. **Online address:** matthew@m-r-hall.com

HALL, Parnell. American (born United States), b. 1944. **Genres:** Mystery/ Crime/Suspense, Novels, Young Adult Fiction. **Career:** Marlboro Theater Co., actor, 1968, 1970-74; Windsor Mountain School, teacher, 1974-75; Berkshire Community College, teacher, 1975; Stockbridge School, teacher, 1975-76; screenwriter, 1977-84; Claims Investigation Bureau, private detective, 1985-87; novelist, 1987-. **Publications:** STANLEY HASTINGS NOVELS: Detective: A Novel, 1987; Murder: A Novel, 1987; Favor: A Novel, 1988; Strangler, 1989; Client: A Novel, 1990; Juror, 1990; Shot, 1991; Actor, 1993; Blackmail, 1994; Movie, 1995; Trial, 1996; Scam, 1997; Suspense, 1998; Cozy: A Stanley Hastings Mystery, 2001; Manslaughter, 2003; Hitman, 2007; Caper, 2010. STEVE WINSLOW NOVELS AS J.P. HAILEY: The Baxter Trust, 1988; The Anonymous Client, 1989; The Underground Man, 1990; The Naked Typist, 1990; The Wrong Gun, 1992. PUZZLE LADY SERIES: A Clue for the Puzzle Lady, 1999; Last Puzzle & Testament, 2000; Puzzled to Death, 2001, 2nd ed., 2002; Puzzle in a Pear Tree, 2002; With This Puzzle, I Thee Kill, 2003; And a Puzzle to Die on: A Puzzle Lady Mystery, 2004; Stalking the Puzzle Lady, 2005; You Have The Right to Remain Puzzled, 2006; The Sudoku Puzzle Murders, 2008; Dead Man's Puzzle, 2009; The Puzzle Lady vs. The Sudoku Lady, 2010; Kenken Killings: A Puzzle Lady Mystery, 2011. OTHERS: $10,000 in Small, Unmarked Puzzles, 2012. **Address:** c/o Donald Maass, Donald Maass Literary Agency, 160 W 95th St., Ste. 1B, New York, NY 10025, U.S.A. **Online address:** parnellh@pipeline.com

HALL, Peter (Geoffrey). British (born England), b. 1932. **Genres:** Geography, Regional/Urban Planning. **Career:** London School of Economics, reader in geography, 1965-67; University of Reading, professor of geography, 1968-89; University of California, professor, 1980-92, professor emeritus of city and regional planning, 1992-; University College London, Bartlett professor of planning, 1992-; University of Melbourne, Department of Mathematics and Statistics, professor and ARC Federation fellow; Australian National University, Centre for Mathematics and its Application, professor. Writer. **Publications:** The Industries of London, 1962; London 2000, 1963, 2nd. ed., 1969; The World Cities, 1966, 3rd ed., 1984; Acton Essays, 1968; (coauthor) Regional Planning in Britain, 1969; Theory and Practice of Regional Planning, 1970; (with M. Batty and D. Starkie) The Impact of Fares-Free Public Transport Upon Urban Land Use and Activity Patterns, 1974; Urban and Regional Planning, 1974, 5th ed., 2010; Europe 2000, 1977; Great Planning Disasters, 1980; Growth Centres in the European Urban System, 1980; London 2001, 1986; Cities of Tomorrow, 1988; Technopoles of the World, 1994; Cities in Civilization, 1998; London Voices London Lives, 2007. CO-AUTHOR: An Advanced Geography of North-West Europe, 1967; Containment of Urban England, 1973; Planning and Urban Growth: An Anglo-American Comparison, 1973; Can Rail Save the City, 1985; High-Tech America, 1986; Western Sunrise, 1987; Sociable Cities, 1999; Urban Future 21, 2000; Working Capital, 2002; The Polycentric Metropolis, 2006; London Voices London Lives, 2007. EDITOR: Labour's New Frontiers, 1964; Land Values, 1965; Von Thunen's Isolated State, 1966; (with D. Banister) Transport and Public

Policy Planning, 1980; The Inner City in Context, 1981; Silicon Landscapes, 1985; Cities of the 21st Century, 1991. **Address:** Bartlett School of Planning, University College London, 22 Gordon St., London, GL WC1H 0QB, England. **Online address:** p.hall@ucl.ac.uk

HALL, Robert. *See* **WUBBELS, Lance.**

HALL, Rodney. Australian/British (born England), b. 1935. **Genres:** Novels, Poetry, Literary Criticism And History, Race Relations, Biography, Young Adult Non-fiction, Young Adult Fiction. **Career:** Freelance scriptwriter and actor, 1957-67; Overland Magazine, advisory editor, 1962-78; film critic, 1966-67; American Broadcasting Commission, film critic, 1966-67; The Australian Newspaper, poetry editor, 1967-78; Australian National University, fellow, 1968; Australian Department of Foreign Affairs, lecturer, 1970, 1972; New England University School of Music, tutor, 1977-80; Australian Council for the Arts, youth officer, 1971-73, chair, 1990-93; Canberra School of Music, lecturer in recorder, 1979-83. **Publications:** Penniless Till Dommsday, 1962; Forty Beads on a Hangman's Rope: Fragments of Memory, 1963; (with S. Andrews) Social Services and the Aborigines, 1963; The Autobiography of a Gorgon, 1968; Focus on Andrew Sibley, 1968; J.S. Manifold: An Introduction to the Man and His Work (biography), 1978; (with D. Moore) Australia: Image of a Nation, 1983; Journey Through Australia, 1988; (contrib.) An Australian Place, 1991; (contrib.) Sydney Harbour, 1993; Dream More Luminous than Love, 1994; Writer and the World of the Imagination, 1995; The Yandilli Trilogy, 1995. POETRY: Eyewitness: Poems, 1967; The Law of Karma: A Progression of Poems, 1968; Heaven, In a Way, 1970; The Soapbox Omnibus, 1973; Selected Poems, 1975; Black Bagatelles, 1978; The Most Beautiful World (verse), 1981; A Return to the Brink, 1999; (with M. Williams) The Unforgiving Poem, 2000; Owner of My Face, 2000. NOVELS: The Ship on the Coin, 1971; A Place among People, 1976; Just Relations, 1982; Kisses of the Enemy, 1987; Captivity Captive, 1988; The Second Bridegroom, 1991; The Grisly Wife, 1993; The Island in the Mind, 1996; The Day We Had Hitler Home, 2000; The Last Love Story, 2004; Love Without Hope, 2007; Popeye Never Told You, 2010. EDITOR: (with T.W. Shapcott) New Impulses in Australian Poetry, 1968; Australian Poetry 1970, 1970; Poems from Prison, 1973; Voyage into Solitude, 1978; Second Month of Spring, 1980; The Collins Book of Australian Poetry, 1981; Collected Poems, 1987. **Address:** c/o Fran Bryson, Bryson Agency Australia Private Ltd., Flinders Ln., PO Box 226, Melbourne, VI 8009, Australia.

HALL, Roger (Leighton). New Zealander (born New Zealand), b. 1939. **Genres:** Children's Fiction, Plays/Screenplays, Anthropology/Ethnology. **Career:** Berhampore School, teacher, 1966, 1968-69; University of Otago, Burns fellow, 1977-78, Department of English, teaching fellow, 1979-94; Fortune Theatre Board, chairman, 1983-85; Monitor, founder. Writer. **Publications:** PLAYS: Glide Time: A Play in Four Acts Set in the Public Service, 1977; Middle-Age Spread, 1978; State of the Play, 1979; Prisoners of Mother England, 1980; Fifty-Fifty, 1981; Hot Water, 1982; Footrot Flats (musical), 1983; Multiple Choice, 1983; Love off the Shelf (musical), 1986; The Share Club, 1987; Conjugal Rites, 1990; By Degrees, 1993; Take a Chance on Me, 2001; A Way of Life, 2001. CHILDREN'S BOOKS: Captain Scrimshaw in Space, 1979; How the Crab Got a Hard Back, 1979; Sam, Max and Harold Meet Dracula, 1990; Penguin Trouble, 1991; My Aunt Went Shopping, 1991; Mum's Photo, 1993; Julie Rescues Big Mack, 1994; Putting on a Concert: And The Television News, 1994; The Tiger and the Mad Millionaire, 1994. OTHER: Otago, The University, 1994; Bums on Seats: The Backstage Story, 1998. Contributor to periodicals. **Address:** 298 York Pl., Dunedin, 9016, New Zealand. **Online address:** roger.h@xtra.co.nz

HALL, Russ. American (born United States), b. 1949?. **Genres:** Mystery/Crime/Suspense, Novels. **Career:** Writer. **Publications:** World Gone Wrong, 1996; The Blue-eyed Indian, 1997; Wildcat Did Growl, 2000; Island, 2001; Bent Red Moon: A Western Story, 2005. ESBETH WALTERS MYSTERY NOVEL SERIES: No Murder before Its Time, 2003; Black Like Blood: An Esbeth Walters Mystery, 2005; Goodbye, She Lied: An Esbeth Walters Mystery, 2007. **Address:** Marble Falls, TX , U.S.A. **Online address:** russhall3@yahoo.com

HALL, Sarah. British (born England), b. 1974?. **Genres:** Art/Art History, Novels. **Career:** St. Andrews University, Undergraduate Creative Writing Program, creative writing teacher; Aberystwyth University, honorary fellow. Writer. **Publications:** Haweswater (novel), 2003; The Electric Michelangelo (novel), 2005; The Carhullan Army, 2007 in US as Daughters of the North:

A Novel, 2008; How to Paint a Dead Man, 2009. Contributor of periodicals. **Address:** c/o Author Mail, Faber and Faber Ltd., 3 Queen Sq., London, GL WC1N 3AU, England.

HALL, Simon. British (born England), b. 1976?. **Genres:** Civil Liberties/Human Rights, History, Military/Defense/Arms Control. **Career:** Cambridge University, lecturer; University of Leeds, School of History, senior lecturer in American history, 2003-, director of admissions, 2004-06, director of learning and teaching, 2007-08. Writer. **Publications:** Peace and Freedom: The Civil Rights and Antiwar Movements of the 1960s, 2005; American Patriotism, American Protest: Social Movements Since the Sixties, 2010. Contributor to journals. **Address:** School of History, University of Leeds, Woodhouse Ln., Leeds, WY LS2 9JT, England. **Online address:** s.d.hall@leeds.ac.uk

HALL, Stacey A. American (born United States), b. 1957. **Genres:** Business/Trade/Industry, Economics. **Career:** Perfect Customers Inc., vice president of sales and marketing. Writer and consultant. **Publications:** (With J. Brogniez) Attracting Perfect Customers: The Power of Strategic Synchronicity, 2001. **Address:** Perfect Customers Inc., 4711 Contenta Ridge, Santa Fe, NM 87507-6603, U.S.A. **Online address:** info@perfectcustomer.com

HALL, Steffie. *See* **EVANOVICH, Janet.**

HALL, Steven. British (born England), b. 1975?. **Genres:** Novels. **Career:** Producer and writer. **Publications:** The Raw Shark Texts (novel), 2007. **Address:** c/o Simon Trewin, PFD, Drury House, 34-43 Russell St., London, GL WC2B 5HA, England. **Online address:** info@steven-hall.org

HALL, Susan Bard. American (born United States), b. 1954. **Genres:** Animals/Pets, Travel/Exploration, Food And Wine, Reference. **Career:** Commodity News Services, reporter, copy editor, assistant bureau chief, 1977-79; Chicago Board of Trade, staff writer in public relations department, 1979-80; Mid America Commodity Exchange, local trader and broker, 1980-82; National Futures Association, manager of public affairs department, 1982-83; Letters Etcetera, owner and freelance writer, 1983-. **Publications:** Midway Airlines: The First Ten Years, 1979-1989, 1989; Purr-fect Places to Stay: Beds & Breakfasts, Country Inns, and Hotels with Resident Cats, 1999. Contributor to books and periodicals. **Address:** Letters Etcetera, 360 E Randolph St., Chicago, IL 60601-5069, U.S.A. **Online address:** susanandnormanhall@prodigy.net

HALL, Thor. American/Norwegian (born Norway), b. 1927. **Genres:** Theology/Religion, Translations, Cultural/Ethnic Topics. **Career:** Clergyman of United Methodist Church, assistant pastor and minister in Norway, 1946-47, 1951-53; Methodist Church in Norway, national director of Christian education, 1953-57; Duke University, assistant professor of preaching and theology, 1962-68, associate professor, 1968-72; University of Tennessee, LeRoy A. Martin distinguished professor of religious studies, 1972-94, Martin professor emeritus, 1994-. Writer. **Publications:** (Ed.) The Unfinished Pyramid, Ten Sermons by Charles P. Bowles, 1967; A Theology of Christian Devotion, 1969; A Framework for Faith, 1970; The Future Shape of Preaching, 1971; Whatever Happened to the Gospel?, 1973; Advent-Christmas, 1975; Directory of Systematic Theologians in North America, 1977; Anders Nygren, 1978; Systematic Theology Today, 1978; The Evolution of Christology, 1982; Pentecost 1, 1991. Contributor to periodicals. **Address:** University of Tennessee, 615 McCallie Ave., Chattanooga, TN 37403, U.S.A. **Online address:** thorhall@ix.netcom.com

HALL, Timothy L. American (born United States), b. 1955. **Genres:** Law, Education, Theology/Religion. **Career:** U.S. Court of Appeals for the Fifth Circuit, judicial clerk, 1983-84; Hughes & Luce, litigation associate, 1984-89; University of Mississippi, assistant professor, 1989-93, associate professor, 1993-99, Mitchell, McNutt, Threadgill, Smith and Sams lecturer in law, 1997-99, professor of law, 1999-, associate provost, 2002-, Jessie Puckett Jr. lecturer, executive director of a campaign, 2005, associate vice chancellor of academic affairs, through 2007; University of Texas, visiting professor, 1994; Austin Peay State University, president, 2007-. Writer. **Publications:** The Labor of Love: Creating an Enduring Romance in Your Marriage, 1996; (with M.L. Harrington) The University of Mississippi: In Principle and Practice, 3rd ed., 1997, 4th ed., 1998; Separating Church and State: Roger Williams and Religious Liberty, 1998; Entering the University, 2nd ed., 2001; Supreme Court Justices: A Biographical Dictionary, 2001; American Religious Leaders, 2003; Religion in America, 2007. EDITOR: Magill's Legal Guide, 3 vols., 2000; U.S. Laws, Acts, and Treaties, 2003; U.S. Legal System, 2004. EDITOR AND CONTRIBUTOR: Ready Reference: American Justice, 1996; Ready Reference: Censorship, 3 vols., 1997; Civil Rights Encyclopedia, 3 vols., 1997; Ready Reference: Women's Issues, 3 vols., 1997; Ready Reference: Family Life, 3 vols., 1998. Contributor to journals. **Address:** Austin Peay State University, 601 College St., Clarksville, TN 37044, U.S.A. **Online address:** hallt@apsu.edu

HALLAHAN, William H(enry). American (born United States), b. 1925. **Genres:** Mystery/Crime/Suspense, History, Young Adult Fiction, Novels, Young Adult Non-fiction, Military/Defense/Arms Control. **Career:** Hallahan Inc., president, 1970-91; N.W. Ayer, copywriter, copy chief and creative director; writer, 1972-. **Publications:** FICTION: The Dead of Winter, 1972; The Ross Forgery, 1973; The Search for Joseph Tully: A novel, 1974; Catch Me, Kill Me: A Novel, 1977; Keeper of the Children, 1978; The Trade, 1981; The Monk: A Novel, 1983; Foxcatcher, 1986; Tripletrap, 1989. NONFICTION: Misfire: The History of How America's Small Arms have Failed Our Military, 1994; The Day the Revolution Began: 19 April 1775, 1999; Day the Revolution ended, 19 October 1781, 2004. OTHERS: The Day the American Revolution Began, 2001; Modern Masters of Horror, 1981; The New Tenant, 1981. **Address:** c/o Author Mail, John Wiley & Sons Inc., 111 River St., Hoboken, NJ 07030-5774, U.S.A.

HALLAM, Elizabeth. See REASONER, Livia Jane Washburn.

HALLAM, Elizabeth. See WASHBURN, Livia J.

HALLAM, Elizabeth M. British (born England), b. 1950. **Genres:** History, Military/Defense/Arms Control. **Career:** University of Reading, tutor, 1975-76; The National Archives, Public Record Office, assistant keeper, 1976-93, director of national advisory and public services, 1993-2005, National Council, chair; House of Lords, director of information services and librarian, 2005-; University College London, visiting professor. Writer. **Publications:** Capetian France, 987-1328, 1980; (intro.) English Royal Marriages: The French Marriages of Edward I and Edward II, 1299 and 1307, 1981; (with J. Everard) 2nd ed., 2001; The Itinerary of Edward II and His Household, 1307-1328, 1984; The Domesday Project Book, 1986; Domesday Book through Nine Centuries, 1986; The Wars of the Roses: From Richard II to the Fall of Richard III at Bosworth Field, 1988; Gods and Goddesses, 1995; Domesday Souvenir Guide, 2000. EDITOR: The Plantagenet Chronicles, 1986; Chronicles of the Age of Chivalry, 1987; The Four Gothic Kings: The Turbulent History of Medieval England and the Plantagenet Kings 1216-1377, 1987; Chronicles of the Wars of the Roses, 1988; Chronicles of the Crusades, 1989; The Plantagenet Encyclopedia, 1990; Saints, Who They Are and How They Help You, 1994; (with A. Prescott) The British Inheritance, 1999; Domesday Book: New Perspectives, 2001. Contributor to books and periodicals. **Address:** House of Lords, Saint Margaret St., Westminster, London, GL SW1A 0PW, England. **Online address:** elizabeth.hallam-smith@nationalarchives.gov.uk

HALLAM, Livia. See WASHBURN, Livia J.

HALLAS, James H(enry). American (born United States), b. 1952. **Genres:** Military/Defense/Arms Control, History. **Career:** Glastonbury Citizen, editor and publisher, 1979-. **Publications:** The Devil's Anvil: The Assault on Peleliu, 1994; Squandered Victory, 1995; Killing Ground on Okinawa, 1996; (ed.) Doughboy War: The American Expeditionary Force in World War I, 2000. **Address:** Glastonbury Citizen, 87 Nutmeg Ln., PO Box 373, Glastonbury, CT 06033, U.S.A. **Online address:** devanuil@aol.com

HALLCOX, Jarrett. American (born United States) **Genres:** Law, Criminology/True Crime. **Career:** National Forensic Science Institute, forensic training specialist, director; National Forensic Academy, program director and program manager. Consultant and writer. **Publications:** (With A. Welch) Bodies We've Buried: Inside the National Forensic Academy, the World's Top CSI Training School, 2006; (with A. Welch) Behind the Yellow Tape: On the Road with Some of America's Hardest Working Crime Scene Investigators, 2009. Contributor to periodicals. **Address:** c/o Laurie Abkemeier, DeFiore & Co., 47 E 19th St., 3rd Fl., New York, NY 10003, U.S.A. **Online address:** jhallcox@utk.edu

HALLÉ, Francis. French (born France), b. 1938. **Genres:** Earth Sciences, Botany. **Career:** Orstom, botanist, 1960-68; University of Montpellier, professor, 1972-99, professor emeritus, 1999-; Biotrop, team leader, 1978-80; writer and botanist, 1999-. **Publications:** Etude biologique et morphologique de la tribu des Gardéniées (Rubiacées), 1967; (with R.A.A. Oldeman and P.B. Tomlinson) Tropical Trees and Forests, 1978; Un monde sans hiver, 1993; Eloge de la plante: pour une nouvelle biologie, 1999; (with D. Cleyet-Marrel and G. Ebersolt) Le radeau des cimes, 2000; Architecture des plantes, 2004; (ed.) Aux origines des plantes, 2008; La Condition Tropicale: Une Histoire Naturelle, économique et sociale des Basses Latitudes, 2010; Arbres: petite conférence, 2011. **Address:** University of Montpellier, 39 rue de l'Université, Montpellier, 34000, France. **Online address:** francishalle@wanadoo.fr

HALLENDY, Norman. Canadian (born Canada), b. 1932. **Genres:** Anthropology/Ethnology, Social Sciences. **Career:** Smithsonian Institution, research associate; Arctic Institute of North America, research associate; Canadian Museum of Civilization, research fellow; Nunavut Research Institute, research fellow; World Archaeological Congress, associate; Tukilik Foundation, director. Writer. **Publications:** SELF-ILLUSTRATED: Inuksuit: Silent Messengers of the Arctic, 2001. OTHER: Tukiliit: The Stone People Who Live in the Wind, 2009. **Address:** D&M Publishers Inc., 2323 Quebec St., Ste. 201, Vancouver, BC V5T 4S7, Canada. **Online address:** tukilik@rogers.com

HALLER, Hermann (W). American/Swedish (born Sweden), b. 1945. **Genres:** Language/Linguistics, History, Social Sciences. **Career:** City University of New York, Queens College, assistant professor, 1974-79, associate professor, 1980-83, professor of Romance languages, 1984-96, professor of Italian, 1996-, Department of European Languages and Literatures, chair 1999-2004, Graduate Center, Ph.D Program in Comparative Literature, head, doctoral specialization in Italian, 2003-; Brown University, visiting professor, 1980; Johns Hopkins University, visiting professor, 1993; Middlebury College, visiting professor, 1996; University of Trento, visiting professor, 1996; University of Foreigners, visiting professor, 1996. **Publications:** Der deiktische Gebrauch des Demonstrativums im Altitalienisch, 1973; Il panfilo veneziano. Edizione critica con introduzione e glossario (bilingual Italian/Latin), 1982; (ed. and trans.) The Hidden Italy: A Bilingual Edition of Italian Dialect Poetry, 1986; Una lingua perduta e ritrovata: l'italiano degli Italo-Americani, 1993; The Other Italy: The Literary Canon in Dialect, 1999; La festa delle lingue, 2002; Tra Napoli e New York: le macchiette italo-americane di Eduardo Migliaccio: testi con introduzione e glossario, 2006. Contributor of articles to periodicals. **Address:** Department of European Languages and Literatures, Queens College, City University of New York, Rm. 207, King Hall, 65-30 Kissena Blvd., Flushing, NY 11367-1597, U.S.A. **Online address:** hhaller@gc.cuny.edu

HALLETT, Charles A(rthur). American (born United States), b. 1935?. **Genres:** Plays/Screenplays, Literary Criticism And History, Theatre. **Career:** City University of New York, Brooklyn College, lecturer in English, 1966-67; Fordham University, assistant professor, 1967-71, associate professor, 1971-81, professor of English, 1981-2010, professor emeritus, 2010-; University of Warwick, visiting fellow, 1978; Loyola University, visiting professor, 1994. Writer. **Publications:** Middleton's Cynics: A Study of Middleton's Insight into the Moral Psychology of the Mediocre Mind, 1975; Aaron Burr (three-act play), 1976; (with E.S. Hallett) The Revenger's Madness: A Study of Revenge Tragedy Motifs, 1980; (with E.S. Hallett) Analyzing Shakespeare's Action: Scene vs. Sequence, 1991; Boris Godunov: A Melodrama, 2010; (with E.S. Hallett) The Artistic Links Between William Shakespeare and Sir Thomas More: Radically Different Richards, 2011. Work appear in anthologies. Contributor to professional journals. **Address:** 534 River Rd., Lyme, NH 03768, U.S.A. **Online address:** hallett@fordham.edu

HALLETT, Michael A. American (born United States), b. 1965. **Genres:** Law, History. **Career:** Middle Tennessee State University, assistant professor; University of North Florida, Department of Criminology and Criminal Justice, associate professor, professor of criminal justice and chair, Center for Criminal Justice Policy Research, director. Writer. **Publications:** (With D.J. Palumbo) U.S. Criminal Justice Interest Groups: Institutional Profiles, 1993; (ed.) Activism and Marginalization in the AIDS Crisis, 1997; Private Prisons in America: A Critical Race Perspective, 2006. **Address:** Department of Criminology & Criminal Justice, University of North Florida, Rm. 2130, Bldg. 51, 1 University of North Florida Dr., Jacksonville, FL 32224-7699, U.S.A. **Online address:** mhallett@unf.edu

HALLIBURTON, David (Garland). American (born United States), b. 1933. **Genres:** Literary Criticism And History, History. **Career:** University of California, assistant professor of English, 1966-72, associate professor of

English and comparative literature, 1972-80; Stanford University, professor of English, 1980-2000, professor emeritus, 2000-. Writer. **Publications:** Edgar Allan Poe: A Phenomenological View, 1973; Poetic Thinking: An Approach to Heidegger, 1981; The Color of the Sky: A Study of Stephen Crane, 1989; The Fateful Discourse of Worldly Things, 1997. Contributor to periodicals. **Address:** Department of English, Stanford University, Bldg. 460, Margaret Jacks Hall, Stanford, CA 94305-2153, U.S.A. **Online address:** hallibur@stanford.edu

HALLIDAY, Ayun. American (born United States), b. 1965. **Genres:** Humor/Satire. **Career:** Neo-Futurists, actor; East Village Inky, writer, illustrator and publisher; BUST Magazine, columnist. **Publications:** The Big Rumpus: A Mother's Tale from the Trenches, 2002 in UK as Mama Lama Ding Dong: A Mother's Tale from the Trenches, 2006; No Touch Monkey! And Other Travel Lessons Learned Too Late, 2003; Job Hopper: The Checkered Career of a Down-market Dilettante, 2005; Dirty Sugar Cookies: Culinary Observations, Questionable Taste, 2006; Always Lots of Heinies at the Zoo, 2009; Peanut, 2011. Works appear in anthologies. **Address:** Brooklyn, NY , U.S.A. **Online address:** ayun@ayunhalliday.com

HALLIDAY, Gemma. American (born United States) **Genres:** Mystery/Crime/Suspense, Young Adult Fiction. **Career:** Writer. **Publications:** HIGH HEELS MYSTERY SERIES: Spying in High Heels, 2006; Killer in High Heels, 2007; Undercover in High Heels, 2007; Alibi in High Heels, 2008; Mayhem in High Heels, 2009; Fearless in High Heels, 2011. HOLLYWOOD HEADLINES SERIES: Hollywood Scandals, 2009; Hollywood Confessions, 2010; Hollywood Confessions, 2011. DEADLY COOL SERIES: Deadly Cool, 2011; Social Suicide, 2012. OTHER WORKS: Play Nice, 2012. ANTHOLOGIES: Dreams & Desires, vol. I, 2007, vol. II, 2008, vol. III, 2009; These Boots Were Made For Strutting, 2008. **Address:** Los Gatos, CA , U.S.A. **Online address:** gemmahalliday@gmail.com

HALLIDAY, Mark. American (born United States), b. 1949?. **Genres:** Poetry, Literary Criticism And History. **Career:** Ohio University, Department of English, professor, 1996-; Indiana University, faculty; Western Michigan University, faculty. Writer. **Publications:** POETRY: Little Star, 1987; Tasker Street, 1992; Selfwolf, 1999; Jab, 2002; Keep This Forever, 2008. CRITICISM: (ed. with A. Grossman) Against Our Vanishing: Winter Conversations with Allen Grossman on the Theory and Practice of Poetry, 1981; Stevens and the Interpersonal, 1991; (with A. Grossman) The Sighted Singer: Two Works on Poetry for Readers and Writers, 1992. Contributor to periodicals. **Address:** Department of English, Ohio University, 357 Ellis Hall, Athens, OH 45701, U.S.A. **Online address:** hallidam@ohio.edu

HALLIDAY, Nigel Vaux. British (born England), b. 1956. **Genres:** Art/Art History, Theology/Religion. **Career:** Houghton College, faculty; Wheaton College, faculty; Biola University, faculty; Point Loma Nazarene College, faculty. Writer and art historian. **Publications:** More Than a Bookshop: Zwemmer's and Art in the 20th Century, 1991. **Address:** Rake Industries, Canhouse Ln., Ste. F1, Rake, Petersfield, HM GU31 5DU, England. **Online address:** enquiries@nigelhalliday.org

HALLIDAY, Stephen. British (born England) **Genres:** Engineering, History, Food And Wine. **Career:** British Rail, management trainee and depot manager, 1964-68; CPC Ltd., distribution manager, resource planning manager, product manager and sales manager, 1968-80; Hammick's Bookshop's, marketing director, 1980-81; Buckinghamshire Business School, lecturer in marketing, 1981-, principal lecturer. Writer. **Publications:** Which Business?: How to Select the Right Opportunity for Starting Up, 1987, 2nd ed., 1990; The Great Stink of London: Sir Joseph Bazalgette and the Cleansing of the Victorian Capital, 1999; Underground to Everywhere: London''s Underground Railway in the Life of the Capital, 2001; Making the Metropolis: Creators of Victoria's London, 2003; Water: A Turbulent History, 2004; Great Filth: The War Against Disease in Victorian England, 2007; Newgate: London's Prototype of Hell, 2007; Our Troubles with Food: Fears, Fads and Fallacies, 2009. Contributor to periodicals. **Address:** Buckinghamshire Business School, Buckinghamshire Chilterns University College, Gorelands Ln., Chalfont St. Giles, BK HP8 4AD, England. **Online address:** stephen.halliday@bcuc.ac.uk

HALLIDAY, William R(oss). American (born United States), b. 1926. **Genres:** Earth Sciences, Natural History, Recreation, Travel/Exploration. **Career:** Western Speleological Survey, director, 1955-81, director of research, 1981-96; Department of Labor and Industries, medical director, 1971-76; Intl.

Glaciospeleological Survey, assistant director, 1972-76; Washington State Division of Vocational Rehabilitation, medical director, 1976-82; N.W. Occupational Health Center, staff physician, 1983-84; N.W. Vocational Rehabilitation Group, medical director, 1984; Comprehensive Medical Rehabilitation Center, medical director, 1984-87; Hawaii Speleological Survey, chairman, 1989-98; Intl. Union of Speleology Commission on Volcanic Caves, chairman, 1990-98. Writer. **Publications:** Adventure is Underground, 1959; Caves of California: A Special Report of the Western Speleological Survey in Cooperation with the National Speleological Society, 1962; Caves of Washington, 1963; Depths of the Earth: Caves and Cavers of the United States, 1966, rev. ed., 1976; (with F.K. Walsh) Discovery and Exploration of the Oregon Caves: Oregon Caves National Monument, 1971; American Caves and Caving: Techniques, Pleasures, and Safeguards of Modern Cave Exploration, 1974, rev. ed., 1982; Ape Cave, 1983; (with R. Nymeyer) Carlsbad Cavern: The Early Years, 1991; Floyd Collins of Sand Cave: A Photographic Memorial, 1998; (foreword) Hawaiian Volcanoes, 2005. **Address:** c/o L.B. Halliday, 6530 Cornwall Ct., Nashville, TN 37205, U.S.A.

HALLIGAN, Marion (Mildred Crothall). Australian (born Australia), b. 1940. **Genres:** Novels, Novellas/Short Stories, Children's Fiction, Plays/Screenplays, Essays, Young Adult Non-fiction, Literary Criticism And History. **Career:** Teacher, 1963-65, 1974-86. Australian National Word Festival, chair, 1987-92; Charles Sturt University, writer-in-residence, 1990; Literature Board of Australia Council, chair, 1992-95; Monash University, writer-in-residence; Latrobe University, writer-in-residence. **Publications:** NOVELS: Self Possession, 1987; Spider Cup, 1990; Lovers' Knots: A Hundred-Year Novel, 1992; Wishbone, 1994; The Golden Dress, 1998; The Fog Garden, 2001; The Point, 2003; The Apricot Colonel, 2006; Murder on the Apricot Coast, 2008; Valley of Grace, 2009. SHORT-STORY COLLECTIONS: The Living Hothouse, 1988; The Hanged Man in the Garden, 1989; The Worry Box, 1993; Collected Stories, 1997; (ed. with R. Fitzgibbon) Gift of Story: Three Decades of UQP Short Stories, 1998. ESSAYS: Eat My Words, 1990; Cockles of the Heart, 1996; The Taste of Memory, 2004. JUVENILE: The Midwife's Daughters, 1997. OTHER: Out of the Picture, 1996; (with L. Frost) Those Women Who Go to Hotels, 1997; (ed.) Storykeepers, 2001. Works appear in anthologies. Contributor to periodicals. **Address:** Margaret Connolly and Associates, PO Box 945, Wahroonga, NW 2076, Australia. **Online address:** wishbone@grapevine.com.au

HALLINAN, Timothy. American (born United States), b. 1942?. **Genres:** Novels, Young Adult Fiction. **Career:** Stone/Hallinan (a public relations firm), founder and partner; Hallinan Consulting, founder. Songwriter and musician. **Publications:** SIMEON GRIST SUSPENSE SERIES: The Four Last Things, 1989; Everything but the Squeal, 1990; Skin Deep, 1991; Incinerator, 1992; The Man with No Time, 1993; The Bone Polisher, 1995. POKE RAFFERTY SUSPENSE SERIES: A Nail through the Heart, 2007; The Fourth Watcher: A Novel of Bangkok, 2008; Breathing Water, 2009; The Queen of Patpong, 2010. **Address:** HarperCollins Publishers Inc., 10 E 53rd St., New York, NY 10022-5244, U.S.A.

HALLISSY, Margaret. American (born United States), b. 1945. **Genres:** Literary Criticism And History, Cultural/Ethnic Topics, History, Women's Studies And Issues. **Career:** Adelphi University, adjunct lecturer, 1974; Long Island University, C.W. Post Campus, adjunct lecturer, 1974-75, adjunct assistant professor, 1975-77, assistant professor, 1977-82, associate professor, 1982-87, professor of English, 1987-, Office of Life Experience Credit, coordinator, 1979-81, Office of Interdisciplinary Studies, director, 1981-84, Writing Center, director, 1986-88, Honors Program, faculty, American Studies Program, faculty. Writer. **Publications:** Venomous Woman: Fear of the Female in Literature, 1987; Clean Maids, True Wives, Steadfast Widows: Chaucer's Women and Medieval Codes of Conduct, 1993; A Companion to Chaucer's Canterbury Tales, 1995; Reading Irish-American Fiction: The Hyphenated Self, 2006. Contributor to journals. **Address:** Department of English, Long Island University, C.W. Post Campus, 720 Northern Blvd., Brookville, NY 11548, U.S.A. **Online address:** margaret.hallissy@liu.edu

HALLO, William W. American/German (born Germany), b. 1928. **Genres:** Archaeology/Antiquities, History, Literary Criticism And History, Theology/Religion. **Career:** University of Chicago, Oriental Institute, research assistant, 1954-56; Hebrew Union College, Jewish Institute of Religion, instructor, 1956-58, assistant professor of Bible and Semitic languages, 1958-62; Yale University, associate professor of Assyriology, 1962-65, professor of Assyriology, 1965-75, William M. Laffan professor of Assyriology and Babylonian literature, 1975-2002, William M. Laffan professor emeritus of Assyriology and Babylonian literature, 2002-, Babylonian Collection, curator, 1963-2001, Yale Near Eastern Researches, editor, 1968-2002; Columbia University, visiting professor, 1970-71, 1980; Hebrew University, Institute for Advanced Studies, fellow, 1978-79; Jewish Theological Seminary, visiting professor, 1982-83. **Publications:** Early Mesopotamian Royal Titles, 1957; (with J.J.A. van Dijk) The Exaltation of Inanna, 1968; (trans.) F. Rosenzweig, The Star of Redemption, 1971; (with W.K. Simpson) The Ancient Near East, 1971, 2nd ed., 1998; Sumerian Archival Texts, 1973; (intro.) Early Near Eastern Seals in the Yale Babylonian Collection, 1979; (contrib.) The Torah, 1981; (with S.G. Beld and P. Michalowski) The Tablets of Ebla, 1984; The Book of the People, 1991; Origins: The Ancient Near Eastern Background of Some Modern Western Institutions, 1996; World's Oldest Literature: Studies in Sumerian Belles-Lettres, 2010. EDITOR: Essays in Memory of E.A. Speiser, 1968; (with C.D. Evans and J.B. White) Scripture in Context, 1980; (with C.D. Evans and J.B. White) Essays on the Comparative Method, 1980; (with J.C. Moyer and L.G. Perdue) Scripture in Context II, 1983; (co-ed.) Heritage: Civilization and the Jews, 2 vols., 1984; (with B.W. Jones and G.L. Mattingly) The Bible in the Light of Cuneiform Literature: Scripture in Context III, 1990; (with K.L. Younger, Jr. and B.F. Batto) The Biblical Canon in Comparative Perspective: Scripture in Context IV, 1991; (with K.L. Younger, Jr.) The Context of Scripture, 3 vols., 1997-2003; Ki Baruch Hu: Ancient Near Eastern, Biblical, and Judaic Studies in Honor of Baruch A. Levine, 1999. Contributor of articles to journals. **Address:** Department of Linguitics, Yale University, SSS 1001, 370 Temple St., PO Box 208366, New Haven, CT 06520-8366, U.S.A. **Online address:** william.hallo@yale.edu

HALLOCK, John W(esley) M(atthew). American (born United States), b. 1959. **Genres:** Biography, Gay And Lesbian Issues, Literary Criticism And History, Autobiography/Memoirs, History. **Career:** Temple University, lecturer. Writer and counselor. **Publications:** The American Byron: Homosexuality and the Fall of Fitz-Greene Halleck (biography), 2000. Contributor to books. **Address:** 1232 Waverly Walk, Philadelphia, PA 19147-1135, U.S.A.

HALLOWELL, Edward McKey. American (born United States), b. 1949. **Genres:** Self Help, Children's Fiction, Adult Non-fiction, Psychology. **Career:** Harvard Medical School, faculty, 1983-2004; Hallowell Center for Cognitive and Emotional Health, founder and child and adult psychiatrist. Writer. **Publications:** (With W.J. Grace, Jr.) What Are You Worth?, 1989; (with M. Thompson) Finding the Heart of the Child, 1993; (with J.J. Ratey) Answers to Distraction, 1994 as Attention Deficit Disorder, 1996; (with J.J. Ratey) Driven to Distraction: Attention Deficit Disorder in Children and Adults, 1994 as Driven to Distraction: Recognizing and Coping with Attention Deficit Disorder from Childhood Through Adulthood, 1995; When You Worry About the Children You Love, 1996; Worry: Controlling It and Using It Wisely, 1997 as Worry: Hope and Help for a Common Condition, 1998; ADHD (Attention-Deficit Hyperactivity Disorder): Achieving Success in School and in Life, 1999; Connect, 1999 as Connect: Twelve Vital Ties that Open Your Heart, Lengthen Your Life and Deepen Your Soul, 2001; (with J. Reichenberg-Ullman and R. Ullman) Ritalin-Free Kids: Safe and Effective Homeopathic Medicine for ADHD and Other Behavioral and Learning Problems, 2nd ed., 2000; Human Moments: How to Find Meaning and Love in Your Everyday Life, 2001; The Childhood Roots of Adult Happiness: Five Steps to Help Kids Create and Sustain Lifelong Joy, 2002; A Walk in the Rain with a Brain, 2002; Dare to Forgive: The Power of Letting Go and Moving On, 2004; (with J.J. Ratey) Delivered from Distraction: Getting the Most of Life With Attention Deficit Disorder, 2005; Crazy Busy: Overstretched, Overbooked and About to Snap: Strategies for Coping in a World Gone ADD, 2006; (with C.A. Corman) Positively ADD: Real Success Stories to Inspire Your Dreams, 2006; Superparenting for ADD: An Innovative Approach to Raising Your Distracted Child, 2008; (with S. Hallowell and M. Orlov) Married to Distraction: Restoring Intimacy and Strengthening Your Marriage in an Age of Interruption, 2010; Shine: Using Brain Science to Get the Best from Your People, 2011. **Address:** Hallowell Center for Cognitive and Emotional, Health, 144 North Rd., Sudbury, MA 01776, U.S.A. **Online address:** hallowellevents@drhallowell.com

HALLOWELL, Janis. American (born United States) **Genres:** Novels. **Career:** Lighthouse Writers Workshop, instructor, 2004. Author and graphic designer. **Publications:** The Annunciation of Francesca Dunn, 2004; She Was: A Novel, 2008. Contributor to periodicals. **Address:** Anderson Grinberg Literary Management Inc., 266 W 23rd St., Ste. 3, New York, NY 10011-2323, U.S.A. **Online address:** info@janishallowell.com

HALLOWELL, Tommy. *See* **HILL, Thomas.**

HALLWAS, John E. American (born United States), b. 1945. **Genres:** Plays/Screenplays, Area Studies, History, Literary Criticism And History, Autobiography/Memoirs, Humanities. **Career:** Western Illinois University, assistant professor, associate professor, 1970-81, director of regional collections, 1979-, professor of American literature, 1981-2004, distinguished professor, 1992-93, distinguished professor emeritus, 2004-; Carl Sandburg College, visiting lecturer, 1976; Monmouth College, visiting lecturer, 1979; Spoon River College, part-time faculty, 1987-; Black Hawk College, visiting lecturer, 1990; University of Illinois, visiting lecturer, 1995. Writer. **Publications:** The Western Illinois Poets (monograph), 1975; The Poems of H.: The Lost Poet of Lincoln's Springfield, 1982; Western Illinois Heritage, 1983; Thomas Gregg: Early Illinois Journalist and Author (monograph), 1983; McDonough County Heritage, 1984; (intro.) Life in Prairie Land, 1988; (intro.) The Illinois, 1989; Macomb: A Pictorial History, 1990; (intro.) Chicago Poems: Carl Sandburg, 1992; The Bootlegger: A Story of Small-Town America, 1998; First Century: A Pictorial History of Western Illinois University, 1999; (intro.) The Drums of the 47th, 1999; Keokuk and the Great Dam, 2001; McDonough County Historic Sites, 2002. EDITOR: (with D.J. Reader) The Vision of This Land: Studies of Vachel Lindsay, Edgar Lee Masters, and Carl Sandburg, 1976; Western Illinois University Libraries: A Handbook, 1980; (with J. Cain-Tyson and V. Hicken) Tales from Two Rivers, vol. I, 1981, vol. II, 1982, vol. III, 1984, (with D.R. Pichaske) vol. IV, 1987, (with A.J. Lindsey) vol. V, 1990, (with Lindsey) vol. VI, 1996; (co-author) Teaching the Middle Ages, vol. II, 1985; Illinois Literature: The Nineteenth Century, 1986; Studies in Illinois Poetry, 1989; (co-author) Prairie State Books Series, 1987-2002; Spoon River Anthology: An Annotated Edition, 1992; The Legacy of the Mines: Memoirs of Coal Mining in Fulton County, Illinois, 1993; (with R.D. Launius) Cultures in Conflict: A Documentary History of the Mormon War in Illinois, 1995; (with R.D. Launius) Kingdom on the Mississippi Revisited: Nauvoo in Mormon History, 1996; The Bootlegger: A Story of Small-Town America, 1998; Keokuk and the Great Dam, 2001; McDonough County Historic Sites, 2002; Dime Novel Desperadoes: The Notorious Maxwell Brothers, 2008; (with J. Hancks and K. Nichols) Tales from Two Rivers, vol. VII, 2009; Remembering McDonough County, 2009. Contributor to periodicals. **Address:** Department of English, Western Illinois University, 1 University Cir., Macomb, IL 61455-1390, U.S.A. **Online address:** je-hallwas@wiu.edu

HALLWOOD, Jan. British (born England) **Genres:** Autobiography/Memoirs, Biography, Business/Trade/Industry. **Career:** Writer. **Publications:** (With S. Morris) Living with Eagles: Marcus Morris, 1998. Contributor to periodicals. **Address:** The Lutterworth Press, PO Box 60, Cambridge, CI CB1 2NT, England.

HALPERIN, James L(ewis). American (born United States), b. 1952. **Genres:** Novels, Antiques/Furnishings, Young Adult Fiction, Novellas/Short Stories. **Career:** Heritage Galleries and Auctioneers, co-chairperson, 1982-. Writer. **Publications:** How to Grade U.S. Coins, 1990; The Truth Machine (novel), 1996; The First Immortal (novel), 1997; Beginner's Luck: the Assassination of Adolf Hitler, 1999; Y2K: Three Scenarios, 1999; (co-author) The Rare Coin Estate Handbook, 2000. **Address:** Heritage Auctions, 3500 Maple Ave., 17th Fl., Dallas, TX 75219-3941, U.S.A. **Online address:** jim@heritagecoin.com

HALPERIN, Joan Ungersma. American (born United States), b. 1932. **Genres:** Art/Art History, Humanities, Politics/Government. **Career:** University of Chicago, instructor in French, 1964-65; Wesleyan University, instructor in French, 1965-66; University of Maine, associate professor, 1967-69, associate professor of French, 1969-70; Saint Mary's College of California, professor of French, 1974-, chair of department of modern languages, 1985-90, 1993-94, now professor emeritus. Writer. **Publications:** (Ed.) Oeuvres plus que completes, vol. I: Chroniques d'art, vol. II: Les Lettres, les moeurs, 1970; Oeuvres plus que complètes. Textes réunis et présentés par, 1970; Studies in the Fine Arts, vol. VI: Félix Fénéon and the Language of Art Criticism, 1980; Félix Fénéon: Aesthete and Anarchist in Fin-de-Siècle Paris, 1988; Correspondence, 1989. Contributor to periodicals. **Address:** Department of Modern Languages, School of Liberal Arts, Saint Mary's College of California, PO Box 4730, Moraga, CA 94575, U.S.A. **Online address:** halperin@stmarys-ca.edu

HALPERIN, Jonathan L. American (born United States), b. 1949. **Genres:**

Medicine/Health. **Career:** Boston City Hospital, research assistant in hematology, 1971; St. Elizabeth's Hospital, Brighton, research assistant in hematology, 1972; Boston University, University Hospital, intern in medicine, 1975-76, resident in internal medicine, 1976-77, clinical and research fellow in peripheral vascular diseases, 1977-78, Evans Medical Foundation, clinical and research fellow, 1977-78; fellow in cardiology, 1978-80; Lynn Hospital, staff physician, 1978-80; Mount Sinai Medical Center, cardiology liaison to division of cardiothoracic surgery, 1980-85, assistant professor, 1980-85, associate professor, 1986-93, professor of medicine, 1993-96, Robert and Harriet Heilbrunn professor of medicine, 1996-, director of clinical services of division of cardiology, 1983-; City University of New York, Mount Sinai School of Medicine, assistant professor, 1980-85, associate professor of medicine, 1986-93, professor of medicine, 1993-96, Robert and Harriet Heilbrunn professor of medicine, 1996-; Zena and Michael A. Wiener Cardiovascular Institute, associate director of clinical services, 1983-; Mount Sinai Hospital, associate attending physician for cardiology, 1983-, professor of cardiology. Writer. **Publications:** (With R. Levine) Bypass: A Cardiologist Reveals What Every Patient Needs to Know, 1985; (co-ed. and contrib.) Managing Your Health: Strategies for Lifelong Good Health, 1991. Contributor to books and periodicals. **Address:** Mount Sinai Medical Center, 1190 5th Ave., 1st Fl., New York, NY 10029, U.S.A. **Online address:** jonathan.halperin@mssm.edu

HALPERN, Cynthia Leone. American (born United States), b. 1952. **Genres:** History, Politics/Government, Theatre. **Career:** Cabrini College, Department of Romance Languages and Literatures, adjunct professor, 1984-, associate professor, 1994-, professor and chair; Holy Family College, assistant professor of Spanish. Writer. **Publications:** The Political Theater of Early Seventeenth-Century Spain, with Special Reference to Juan Ruiz de Alarcón, 1993. **Address:** Department of Romance Languages and Literatures, Cabrini College, Rm. 366, Founder's Hall, 610 King of Prussia Rd., Radnor, PA 19087-3698, U.S.A. **Online address:** cynthia.halpern@cabrini.edu

HALPERN, Daniel. (Angela McCabe). American (born United States), b. 1945. **Genres:** Novellas/Short Stories, Poetry, Food And Wine. **Career:** Antaeus Magazine, editor, 1969-94; Ecco Press, co-founder and editor-in-chief, 1971-91, editorial director, 1991-, president and publisher; Bobbs-Merrill Co., freelance editor, 1971-81; New School for Social Research, instructor, 1971-76; Columbia University, instructor, 1975-95, Graduate Writing Program, chair, 1980-84; Princeton University, instructor, 1975-76, 1987-88; National Poetry Series, founder and director, 1978-. **Publications:** Traveling on Credit, 1972; (as Angela McCabe) The Keeper of Height, 1974; (trans. with P. Paley) M. Attik, Songs of Mririda, Courtesan of the High Atlas, 1974; The Lady Knife-Thrower, 1975; (with G. Mayer and F. Elon) Treble Poets 2, 1975; Street Fire, 1975; Life among Others, 1978; Seasonal Rights, 1982; (with J. Strand) The Good Food: Soups, Stews and Pastas, 1985; Tango, 1987; (with J. Wilmot) Halpern's Guide to the Essential Restaurants of Italy, 1990; Foreign Neon, 1991; Something Shining, 1999. EDITOR: The American Poetry Anthology, 1975; The Art of the Tale, 1986 in UK as The Penguin of International Short Stories 1945-85, 1989; The Antaeus Anthology, 1986; (co-ed.) On Nature, 1987; On Reading, 1987; Literature as Pleasure, 1987; (with J.C. Oates) Reading the Fights, 1988; Writers on Artists, 1988; Our Private Lives: Journals, Notebooks and Diaries, 1989 in UK as Journals, Notebooks and Diaries; Not for Bread Alone: Writers on Food, Wine, and the Art of Eating, 1993; Autobiographical Eye, 1993; (with N.T. di Giovanni and F. MacShane) Borges on Writing, 1994; (with J.W. Carter) On Music, 1994; Holy Fire: Nine Visionary Poets and the Quest for Enlightenment, 1994; Who's Writing This?, 1995; (with D. Frank) Nature Reader, 1996; Art of the Story: An International Anthology of Contemporary Short Stories, 1999. Contributor to periodicals. **Address:** HarperCollins Publishers, Ecco Press Ltd., 10 E 53rd St., New York, NY 10022-5244, U.S.A. **Online address:** dan.halpern@harpercollins.com

HALPERN, Jake. Indian/American (born United States), b. 1975?. **Genres:** Writing/Journalism, Travel/Exploration, Social Sciences, Young Adult Fiction. **Career:** Yale University, Morse College, fellow. Freelance journalist and radio producer. **Publications:** Braving Home: Dispatches from the Underwater Town, the Lava-Side Inn, and Other Extreme Locales, 2003; Fame Junkies: The Hidden Truths Behind America's Favorite Addiction, 2007; (with P. Kujawinski) Dormia, 2009; (with P. Kujawinski) World's End, 2011; The Shadow Tree, forthcoming. **Address:** c/o Author Mail, Houghton Mifflin Harcourt, 222 Berkeley St., Boston, MA 02116, U.S.A. **Online address:** jakehalpern@yahoo.com

HALPERN, Julie. American (born United States), b. 1975. **Genres:** Novels, Picture/Board Books, Children's Fiction. **Career:** Writer and librarian. **Publications:** Toby and the Snowflakes (picture book), 2004; Get Well Soon (young-adult novel), 2007; Into the Wild Nerd Yonder (young-adult novel), 2009; Don't Stop Now, 2011. **Address:** PO Box 8583, Gurnee, IL 60031-7018, U.S.A. **Online address:** julie@juliehalpern.com

HALPERN, Paul. American (born United States), b. 1961. **Genres:** Physics, Sciences, Mathematics/Statistics, Education. **Career:** Brookhaven National Lab, research assistant, 1983; Astronomy Centre, research assistant, 1985; Rudjer Boskovic Institute, research assistant, 1989; Hamilton College, visiting assistant professor of physics, 1987-88; University of the Sciences in Philadelphia, assistant professor of physics, 1988-92, associate professor of mathematics and physics, 1992-99, professor of mathematics and physics, 1999-, fellow in the humanities, 2001-; University of the Arts, adjunct associate professor of liberal arts, 1997; Haverford College, visiting professor of physics, 2004-05. Writer. **Publications:** Time Journeys: A Search for Cosmic Destiny and Meaning, 1990; Cosmic Wormholes: The Search for Interstellar Shortcuts, 1993; A Naval History of World War I, 1994; The Cyclical Serpent: Prospects for an Ever-Repeating Universe, 1995; The Structure of the Universe, 1997; The Quest for Alien Planets: Exploring Worlds Outside the Solar System, 1997; Countdown to Apocalypse: Asteroids, Tidal Waves, and the End of the World, 1998; The Pursuit of Destiny: A History of Prediction, 2000; Faraway Worlds: Planets Beyond our Solar System, 2004; Great Beyond: Higher Dimensions, Parallel Universes and the Extraordinary Search for a Theory of Everything, 2004; (with P. Wesson) Brave New Universe: Illuminating the Darkest Secrets of the Cosmos, 2006; What's Science Ever Done for Us?: What the Simpsons can Teach Us about Physics, Robots, Life and the Universe, 2007; Collider: The Search for the World's Smallest Particles, 2009; Cosmological Conundrums: Illuminating the Darkest Secrets of the Universe, forthcoming. Contributor to journals. **Address:** Department of Mathematics, Physics and Statistics, University of the Sciences in Philadelphia, 600 S 43rd St., Philadelphia, PA 19104-4495, U.S.A. **Online address:** p.halper@usp.edu

HALPERN, Sue. American (born United States), b. 1955. **Genres:** Sciences, Novels. **Career:** Columbia University, research associate, 1985-87; Bryn Mawr College, assistant professor, 1987-88; Middlebury College, Guggenheim fellow; Face of Democracy, director. Writer. **Publications:** Migrations to Solitude, 1992; Four Wings and a Prayer, 2001; Book of Hard Things, 2003; Introducing-Sasha Abramowitz, 2005; I Can't Remember What I Forgot: The Good News From the Front Lines of Memory Research, 2008. Contributor to popular magazines and newspapers. **Address:** Middlebury College, Middlebury, VT 05753, U.S.A.

HALPIN, Brendan. American (born United States), b. 1968?. **Genres:** Novels, Children's Fiction, Sports/Fitness. **Career:** Writer. **Publications:** It Takes a Worried Man: A Memoir, 2002; Losing My Faculties: A Teacher's Story, 2003; Donorboy, 2004; Long Way Back, 2006; Dear Catastrophe Waitress, 2007; How Ya Like Me Now, 2007; Forever Changes, 2008; I can See Clearly Now: A Novel, 2009; (with E. Franklin) Half Life of Planets, 2010; (with E. Franklin) Shutout, 2010; Jenna & Jonah's Fauxmance, 2011; (with T. Cook) Notes From The Blender, 2011. **Address:** Douglas Stewart, Sterling Lord Literistic Inc., 65 Bleecker St., 12th Fl., New York, NY 10012, U.S.A. **Online address:** brendan@brendanhalpin.com

HALPIN, Marlene. American (born United States), b. 1927. **Genres:** How-to Books, Theology/Religion, Education, inspirational/Motivational Literature, Cultural/Ethnic Topics. **Career:** Molloy College, Rockville Centre, academic dean and professor of philosophy, 1963-74; Aquinas Institute of Theology, coordinator of continuing education and professor of philosophy, 1974-81; Notre Dame University, Clergy Institute of Retreat Instructors, consultant, 1981-82; Diocese of Kalamazoo, Ministry Formation Program, director, 1982-; St. Augustine's School, Grades K-8, director of prayer room, 1982-. Writer, photographer and educator. **Publications:** (With P. Conway) Grammar-Logic-Rhetoric, 1964; (with M.L. Brill and W.H. Genne) Write Your Own Wedding, 1973, rev. ed., 1985; Planned Continuing Education: A Study of Needs Assessment Processes, 1979; Imagine That!: The Use of Phantasy in Spiritual Direction, 1982; Creator of Calendars (photography and poetry) for Holy Cross Health Systems, 1983, 1984; Puddles of Knowing: Engaging Children in Our Prayer Heritage, 1984; The Continuing Formation of Priests: Growing in Wisdom, Age and Grace, 1984; Inside Out (photography and poetry), 1985; Forgiving: Present Perfect, 1987; Leading Prayer:

Plain and Simple, 1990; At Home with God: A Child's Book of Prayer, vol. I, 1993, vol. II-IV, 1995; Imagine That, Too!: Imagination and Self-Discovery, 1994; Following Jesus: A Way of the Cross for Children, 1995; Right Side Up: A Book of Reflections for People Living with Serious Illness, 1995; At Home with God: A Book of Prayer for Young People, 1995; Grandparents: Passing on Our Religious Heritage, 1997; Caregivers: Reflections on Coping with Caregiving, 1998; The Ball of Red String: A Guided Meditation for Children, 1998; 189 Ways to Contact God, 1999. Contributor to books. **Address:** 215 N Westnedge Ave., Kalamazoo, MI 49007, U.S.A. **Online address:** mhalpin@dioceseofkalamazoo.org

HALSALL, Guy. British (born England), b. 1964. **Genres:** History. **Career:** University of London, Birkbeck College, lecturer; University of York, Vanbrugh College, professor of history, 2003-. Writer. **Publications:** Early Medieval Cemeteries: An Introduction to Burial Archaeology in the Post-Roman West, 1995; Settlement and Social Organization: The Merovingian Region of Metz, 1995; (ed.) Violence and Society in the Early Medieval West, 1998; (ed.) Humour, History, and Politics in Late Antiquity and the Early Middle Ages, 2002; Warfare and Society in the Barbarian West, 450-900, 2003; (ed. with W. Davies and A. Reynolds) People and Space in the Middle Ages, 300-1300, 2006; Barbarian Migrations and the Roman West, 376-568, 2007; Cemeteries and Society in Merovingian Gaul: Selected Studies in History and Archaeology, 1992-2009, 2010. **Address:** Department of History, Vanbrugh College, University of York, Rm. V/215, York, NY YO10 5DD, England. **Online address:** grwh2@york.ac.uk

HALSEY, A(lbert) H(enry). British (born England), b. 1923. **Genres:** Sociology, Autobiography/Memoirs, Education, History. **Career:** University of Birmingham, lecturer, senior lecturer, 1954-62; Center for Advanced Study of the Behavioral Sciences, fellow, 1956-57; University of Chicago, visiting professor, 1959-60; University of Oxford, Department of Social and Administration Studies, director, 1962-, Nuffield College, professorial fellow, 1962-, Department of Sociology, professor, now professor emeritus. Writer. **Publications:** (With J.E. Floud and F.M. Martin) Social Class and Educational Opportunity, 1956; (with J.E. Floud and C.A. Anderson) Education, Economy and Society, 1961; Ability and Educational Opportunity, 1962; (with G.N. Ostergaard) Power in Co-operatives, 1965; The Civil Service, 1969; (with M. Trow) The British Academics, 1971; Academic Freedom and the Idea of a University, 1976; (with A.F. Heathand J.M. Ridge) Origins and Destinations, 1980; Change in British Society, 1981, 4th ed., 1995; (with N. Dennis) English Ethical Socialism, 1988; British Social Trends Since 1900, 1988, rev. ed., 1999; The Decline of Donnish Dominion, 1992, rev. ed., 1995; No Discouragement: An Autobiography, 1996; Twentieth Century British Social Trends, 2000; A History of Sociology in Britain: Science, Literature and Society, 2004; Changing Childhood, 2009. EDITOR: Trends in British Society Since 1900, 1972; Educational Priority, 1972; E.P.A. Problems and Policies, 1972; Traditions of Social Policy, 1976; Heredity and Environment, 1977; (with J. Karabel) Power and Ideology in Education, 1977; (with D. Butler) Policy and Politics, 1978; British Social Trends Since 1900: A Guide to the Changing Social Structure of Britain, 1988; (with R. Jowell and B. Taylor) Quality of Life in London, 1995; (co-ed.) Education: Culture, Economy, and Society, 1997; (with J. Webb) Twentieth-Century British Social Trends, 2000; (with W.G. Runciman) British Sociology Seen from Without and Within, 2005. **Address:** Department of Sociology, University of Oxford, Manor Rd., Oxford, OX OX1 3UQ, England. **Online address:** chelly.halsey@nuffield.ox.ac.uk

HALSTEAD, Ted. American (born United States), b. 1968?. **Genres:** Politics/Government, History. **Career:** Redefining Progress, founder, 1993, executive director; New America Foundation, founder, 1999-, president and chief executive officer, 1999-2007; Harvard University, John F. Kennedy School of Government, Montgomery fellow; World Policy Institute, senior fellow. Political analyst and writer. **Publications:** (With M. Lind) The Radical Center: The Future of American Politics, 2001; (ed.) Real State of the Union: From the Best Minds in America, Bold Solutions to the Problems Politicians Dare not Address, 2004. Contributor to periodicals. **Address:** New America Foundation, 1899 L St. NW, Ste. 400, Washington, DC 20036, U.S.A. **Online address:** president@newamerica.net

HALTER, Marek. French/Polish (born Poland), b. 1936. **Genres:** Autobiography/Memoirs, Novels, Literary Criticism And History. **Career:** European Foundation for Science, Art, and Culture, president. Writer and artist. **Publications:** Le fou et les rois (autobiography), 1976; La vie incertaine de Marco Mahler, 1979; Le Mémoire d'Abraham, 1983; Un Homme, un cri, 1991; La

Mémoire inquiète: il y a cinquante ans, le ghetto de Varsovie, 1993; (with E. Laurent) Fous de la paix, 1994; Le Messie, 1996; Les Mystères de Jérusalem: Roman (novel), 1999; Le Judaïsme raconté à mes filleuls, 1999; Le Vent des Khazars: Roman (novel), 2001; Tsippora: Roman, 2003; Marie: Roman, 2006; Je me suis rveillé en colère, 2007; Reine de Saba: roman, 2008; Kabbaliste de Prague, 2010; Jewish Odyssey, 2010; Histoires du peuple juif, 2010; Inconnue de Birobidjan, 2012. CANAAN TRILOGY SERIES: Sarah: Roman, 2003; Lilah: Roman, 2004; Zipporah, Wife of Moses: A Novel, 2005. Illustrator of books by others. **Address:** 13 rue des Minimes, Paris, 75003, France.

HALTON, Francesca. See **ROCHBERG, Francesca.**

HALTZMAN, Scott. American (born United States), b. 1960?. **Genres:** Natural History, Human Relations/Parenting. **Career:** NRI Community Services, medical director; Brown University, professor; DrScott.com, founder and editor; 365Reasons.com, founder and editor; Best Life, editorial consultant. **Publications:** (Foreword) 28 Days, 2005; (with T.F. DiGeronimo) The Secrets of Happily Married Men: Eight Ways to Win Your Wife's Heart Forever, 2006; (with T.F. DiGeronimo) Secrets of Happily Married Women: How to Get More Out of Your Relationship by Doing Less, 2008; (with T.F. DiGeronimo) Secrets of Happy Families: Eight Keys to Building a Lifetime of Connection and Contentment, 2009. Contributor to periodicals. **Address:** 365Reasons.com, 147 County Rd., Barrington, RI 02806, U.S.A. **Online address:** dr.scott@365reasons.com

HALVERSON, Cathryn. Japanese/American (born United States), b. 1968?. **Genres:** Autobiography/Memoirs, Women's Studies And Issues, History. **Career:** Kobe City College of Foreign Studies (now Kobe City University of Foreign Studies), associate professor of English. Writer. **Publications:** Maverick Autobiographies: Women Writers and the American West, 1900-1936, 2004. Contributor to periodicals. **Address:** Kobe City University of Foreign Studies, Kobe City, 651-2102, Japan. **Online address:** p200296@inst.kobe-cufs.ac.jp

HALVORSON, Marilyn. Canadian (born Canada), b. 1948. **Genres:** Children's Fiction, Young Adult Fiction, Local History/Rural Topics, Animals/Pets. **Career:** Didsbury School, teacher, 1968-71; Sundre School, teacher, 1974-90, now retired. Rancher and writer. **Publications:** Cowboys Don't Cry, 1984; Let It Go, 1985; Nobody Said It Would Be Easy, 1987; Hold on, Geronimo, 1988; Dare, 1988; Bull Rider, 1989; Stranger on the Run, 1992; To Everything a Season: A Year in Alberta Ranch Country, 1991; But Cows Can't Fly, 1993; Blue Moon, 1994; Cowboys Don't Quit, 1994; Brothers and Strangers, 1996; Stranger on the Line, 1997; Blood Brothers, 2004. **Address:** RR 2, Ste. 14, PO Box 9, Sundre, AB T0M 1X0, Canada. **Online address:** halatsundre@telus.net

HAM, Sŏ'ng-dŭk. See **HAHM, Sung Deuk.**

HAMALAINEN, Pekka J. American (born United States), b. 1967?. **Genres:** History, Social Commentary. **Career:** Southern Methodist University, Clements Center for Southwest Studies, fellow, 2001-02; University of Helsinki, Helsinki Collegium for Advanced Studies, fellow, 2003-05; Stanford University, Center for Advanced Study in the Behavioral Sciences, fellow, 2009-10; University of California, Department of History, associate professor, professor. Writer. **Publications:** When Disease Makes History: Epidemics and Great Historical Turning Points, 2006; The Comanche Empire, 2008. Contributor to periodicals. **Address:** Department of History, University of California, 4218 HSSB, Santa Barbara, CA 93106-9410, U.S.A. **Online address:** hamalainen@history.ucsb.edu

HÄMÄLÄINEN, Pertti (Olavi). Finnish (born Finland), b. 1952. **Genres:** Travel/Exploration, Information Science/Computers. **Career:** Kwayyis International Oy, owner, 1988-, chief executive director, 1993-. Writer and consultant. **Publications:** Yemen: A Travel Survival Kit, 1988, 4th ed., 1999; Mikroverkot, 1992; (co-author) Middle East on a Shoestring, 1994, 3rd ed., 2000; (co-author) Africa on a Shoestring, 7th ed., 1995; (co-author) Experimental Travel, 2005. **Address:** Kwayyis International Oy, Tehtaankatu 16 B, Helsinki, 00140, Finland. **Online address:** pertti.hamalainen@kwayyis.fi

HAMAMOTO, Darrell Y. American (born United States), b. 1953. **Genres:** Novels, Social Sciences, Language/Linguistics, Humanities. **Career:** University of California, associate professor, 1995-, professor of Asian American studies, School of Arts and Sciences, program coordinator; Yellow Entertainment Network, president. Writer. **Publications:** Nervous Laughter: Television Situation Comedy and Liberal Democratic Ideology, 1989; Monitored Peril: Asian Americans and the Politics of TV Representation, 1994; (ed. with R.D. Torres) New American Destinies: A Reader in Contemporary Asian and Latino Immigration, 1997; (ed. with S. Liu) Countervisions: Asian American Film Criticism, 2000. **Address:** Asian American Studies Program, University of California, 3119 Hart Hall, Davis, CA 95616, U.S.A. **Online address:** dyhamamoto@ucdavis.edu

HAMAND, Maggie. British (born England), b. 1953?. **Genres:** Novels, Writing/Journalism. **Career:** Bedford Square Press, editor; Complete Creative Writing Course, co-founder, 1998-; Morley College, creative writing instructor; Holloway Prison, writer-in-residence, 2000-01; Maia Press, founder and director, 2003-; London University of the Arts, Royal Literary Fund fellow, 2004-07. Journalist. **Publications:** The Resurrection of the Body (novel), 1994; The Rocket Man (novel), 1995; Uncut Diamonds: A Selection of New Writing, 2003; Creative Writing for Dummies, 2009. Work appear in anthologies. **Address:** Greagory & Co., 3 Barb Mews, Hammersmith, London, GL W6 7PA, England. **Online address:** maggie.h@blueyonder.co.uk

HAMBLIN, Robert W(ayne). American (born United States), b. 1938. **Genres:** Poetry, Documentaries/Reportage, Biography, Novellas/Short Stories, Literary Criticism And History, Bibliography. **Career:** Sparrows Point High School, English teacher and baseball coach, 1960-62; University of Mississippi, Department of English, teaching assistant, 1964-65; Southeast Missouri State University, instructor, 1965-66, assistant professor, 1967-70, associate professor, 1971-77, professor of English, 1978-; Cape Girardeau Civic Center, president of board, 1978-81; Brodsky Collection, curator, 1983-89; National Endowment for the Humanities Summer Seminars for School Teachers, director, 1985-87, Center for Faulkner Studies, director, 1989-. Writer. **Publications:** (With L.D. Brodsky) William Faulkner, A Perspective From the Brodsky Collection, October 2, 1979-December 13, 1979, 1979; (with L.D. Brodsky) Selections From the William Faulkner Collection of Louis Daniel Brodsky: A Descriptive Catalogue, 1979; (contrib.) A Cosmos of My Own: Faulkner and Yoknapatawpha, 1980, 1981; (with L.D. Brodsky) Faulkner: A Comprehensive Guide to the Brodsky Collection, vol. I: The Bio-bibliography, 1982, vol. II: The Letters, 1984, vol. III: The De Gaulle Story, 1984, vol. IV: Battle Cry, 1985, vol. V: Manuscripts and Documents, 1988; Brodsky, the Evolution of a Faulkner Collector/Scholar at Work, 1983; (with L.D. Brodsky) Faulkner and Hollywood: A Retrospective from the Brodsky Collection, 1984; Perpendicular Rain (poems), 1986; (ed. with L.D. Brodsky) Country Lawyer and Other Stories for the Screen, 1987; (ed. with L.D. Brodsky) Stallion Road: A Screenplay, 1989; (contrib.) Faulkner and the Craft of Fiction, 1989; From the Ground Up: Poems of One Southerner's Passage to Adulthood, 1992; Win or Win: A Season with Ron Shumate, 1993; (ed. with C.A. Peek) A William Faulkner Encyclopedia, 1999; (ed. with S. Hahn) Teaching Faulkner: Approaches and Methods, 2001; (ed. with A.J. Abadie) Faulkner in the Twenty-first Century: Faulkner and Yoknapatawpha, 2000, 2003; Mind the Gap: Poems by an American in London, 2003; (ed. with C.A. Peek) Companion to Faulkner Studies, 2004; Keeping Score: Sports Poems for Every Season, 2007; (with A.N. Fargnoli and M. Golay) Critical Companion to William Faulkner: A Literary Reference to His Life and Work, 2008; About a Little Girl: A William Carlos Williams Poem and Its Legacy, 2008; (ed. with M. Speight) Faulkner and Twain, 2009; Crossroads: Poems of a Mississippi Childhood, 2010. Contributor to books and journals. **Address:** Department of English, Southeast Missouri State University, Grauel 318 M, One University Pl., PO Box 2650, Cape Girardeau, MO 63701, U.S.A. **Online address:** rhamblin@semo.edu

HAMBLY, Barbara. American (born United States), b. 1951. **Genres:** Science Fiction/Fantasy, Novels. **Career:** Science Fiction Writers of America, president, 1994-96; teacher. Writer. **Publications:** DARWATH SERIES: The Time of the Dark, 1982; The Walls of Air, 1983; The Armies of Daylight, 1983; Mothers of Winter, 1996; Icefalcon's Quest, 1998. OTHER NOVELS: The Quirinal Hill Affair, 1983, as Search the Seven Hills, 1987; Dragonsbane, 1985; Those Who Hunt the Night, 1988 in UK as Immortal Blood; Beauty and the Beast (novelization of television script), 1989; Song of Orpheus (novelization of television script), 1990; Stranger at the Wedding, 1994 in UK as Sorcerer's Ward; Bride of the Rat God, 1994; Travelling with the Dead, 1995; Star Wars: Children of the Jedi, 1995; Traveling with the Dead, 1995; Mother of Winter, 1996 A Free Man of Color, 1997; Star Wars: Planet of

Twilight, 1997; Fever Season, 1998; Graveyard Dust, 1999; Dragonshadow, 1999; Sold Down the River, 2000; Knight of the Demon Queen, 2000; Die Upon a Kiss, 2001; (with M.S. Zicree) Magic Time, 2001; Dragonstar, 2002; Wet Grave, 2002; Sisters of the Raven, 2002; Days of the Dead, 2003; Dead Water, 2004; (with M. Shayne and C. Harris) Night's Edge, 2004; Circle of the Moon, 2005; The Emancipator's Wife, 2005; Renfield: Slave of Dracula, 2006; Patriot Hearts: A Novel of the Founding Mothers, 2007; Homeland: A Novel, 2009; Blood Maidens, 2010; Dead and Buried, 2010; Ran Away, 2011; A Thousand Waters, 2011; The Shirt on His Back, 2011. SUN WOLF SERIES: The Ladies of Mandrigyn, 1984; The Witches of Wenshar, 1987; The Unschooled Wizard, 1987; The Dark Hand of Magic, 1990. STAR TREK BOOKS: Ishmael: A Star Trek Novel, 1985; Ghost Walker, 1991; Crossroad, 1994. THE WINDROSE CHRONICLES: The Silent Tower, 1986; The Silicon Mage, 1988; Darkmage, 1988; Dog Wizard, 1992. SUN-CROSS SERIES: The Rainbow Abyss, 1991; Magicians of the Night, 1992; Sun-Cross, 1992. EDITOR: Women of the Night, 1994; Sisters of the Night, 1995; (with G.A. Effinger) Budayeen Nights, 2003. Works appear in anthologies. **Address:** c/o Author Mail, Del Rey Books, 201 E 50th St., New York, NY 10022, U.S.A. **Online address:** info@barbarahambly.com

HAMBLYN, Richard. British (born England), b. 1965?. **Genres:** Geography. **Career:** Nottingham University, postdoctoral research fellow. Writer and geologist. **Publications:** The Invention of Clouds: How an Amateur Meteorologist Forged the Language of the Skies, 2001; (ed.) Earthly Powers, 1660-1834, vol. III, 2003; (ed. and intro.) The Storm, 2005; (with M.J. Callanan) Data Soliloquies, 2009; Terra: Tales of the Earth, 2009. **Address:** c/o Author Mail, Farrar, Straus & Giroux, 19 Union Sq. W, New York, NY 10003-3304, U.S.A. **Online address:** richard.hamblyn@nottingham.ac.uk

HAMBOURG, Maria Morris. American (born United States), b. 1949. **Genres:** Art/Art History, Photography. **Career:** Museum of Modern Art, Department of Photography, curatorial intern, 1975-76, exhibitions assistant, 1976, research assistant, 1978-79, consultant, 1980-83; Princeton University, visiting professor, 1984; Metropolitan Museum of Art, Department of Prints and Photography, associate curator 1985-91, Department of Photographs, associate curator, 1992, curator in charge, 1992-; New York University, Institute of Fine Arts, adjunct associate professor, 1989. Writer. **Publications:** (With J. Chambord) Charles Marville: Photographs of Paris at the Time of the 2nd Empire, 1981; (with J. Szarkowski) The Work of Atget, vol. I: Old France, 1981, vol. II: The Art of Old Paris, 1982, vol. III: The Ancien Regime, 1983, vol. IV: Modern Times, 1985; (contrib.) Observations, 1984; Photographers and Authors: A Collection of Portraits of 20th-Century Writers, 1984; (with C. Phillips) The New Vision: Photography between the Wars: Ford Motor Company Collection at the Metropolitan Museum of Art, New York, 1989; (with S.S. Phillips) Helen Levitt, 1991; (co-author) The Waking Dream: Photography's First Century: Selections from the Gilman Paper Company Collection, 1993; (with C. Phillips) Nueva visión: fotografía de entraguerras: Ford Motor Company collection en el Metropolitan Museum of Art, Nueva York, 1994; (with F. Heilbrun and P. Néagu) Nadar, 1995; (with P. Schimmel) Sigmar Polke Photoworks, 1995; Sugimoto, 1995; Georgia O'Keeffe: A Portrait by Alfred Stieglitz, 1997; Paul Strand circa 1916, 1998; (intro.) Carleton Watkins: The Art of Perception, 1999; (co-author) Walker Evans, 2000; Earthly Bodies: Irving Penn's nudes, 1949-1950, 2002; (contrib.) Richard Avedon Portraits, 2002; Thomas Struth 1977-2002, 2002; (with D.A. Mellor) Guest, 2002. **Address:** The Metropolitan Museum of Art, 1000 5th Ave., 82nd St., New York, NY 10028-0198, U.S.A.

HAMBREY, Michael (John). (M. J. Hambrey). Welsh/British (born England), b. 1948. **Genres:** Earth Sciences, Geography, Natural History, Sciences. **Career:** Swiss Federal Institute of Technology, postdoctoral research assistant, 1974-77; Cambridge University, research assistant and senior research associate, 1977-91, St. Edmund's College, fellow, 1978-91; chartered geologist, 1991; Liverpool John Moores University, professor of quaternary geology, 1991-; Aberystwyth University, Centre for Glaciology, staff, 1997-, director, 1998-, professor of glaciology, 1999-; Victoria University of Wellington, visiting fellow; University of British Columbia, visiting professor, 2006. Writer. **Publications:** (Ed. with W.B. Harland) Earth's Pre-Pleistocene Glacial Record, 1981; (co-author) Late Precambrian Geology of the Scottish Highlands and Islands, 1991; (with J.C. Alean) Glaciers, 1992, 2nd ed. 2004; Glacial Environments, 1994; (ed. with A.J. Maltman and B. Hubbard) Deformation of Glacial Materials, 2000; (with J. Dowdeswell) Islands of the Arctic, 2002; (ed. with P. Christoffersen, N.F. Glasser and B. Hubbard) Glacial Sedimentary Processes and Products, 2007. Contributor of articles to journals.

Address: Center for Glaciology, Institute of Geography & Earth Sciences, University of Wales, Aberystwyth, SY23 2AX, Wales.

HAMBREY, M. J. *See* **HAMBREY, Michael (John).**

HAMBURGER, Aaron. American (born United States), b. 1973?. **Genres:** Novellas/Short Stories, Novels, Literary Criticism And History. **Career:** Columbia University, lecturer of creative writing. Writer. **Publications:** The View from Stalin's Head, 2004; Faith for Beginners 2005; Contemporary Berlin, forthcoming. Contributor to periodicals. **Address:** c/o Author Mail, Random House Inc., 1745 Broadway, New York, NY 10019, U.S.A. **Online address:** aaronhamburger@gmail.com

HAMDANI, Sumaiya A. American/Egyptian (born Egypt), b. 1962. **Genres:** Literary Criticism And History. **Career:** The Institute of Ismaili Studies, Department of Academic Research and Publications, visiting research fellow, 1998-99; George Mason University, Department of History and Art History, associate professor, Islamic Studies Program, founding director, 2003-08; Hawwa: Journal of Women in Middle East and Islamic Studies, book review editor. **Publications:** Between Revolution and State: The Path to Fatimid Statehood: Qadi Al-Nu'man and the Construction of Fatimid Legitimacy, 2006. **Address:** Department of History and Art History, George Mason University, B 347 Robinson Hall, MSN 3G1, 4400 University Dr., Fairfax, VA 22030-4444, U.S.A. **Online address:** shamdani@gmu.edu

HAMEL, Gary. American (born United States), b. 1954. **Genres:** Administration/Management. **Career:** Strategos, founder and chair, 1995-; Woodside Institute, director; Management Innovation Lab, co-founder; University of Michigan, visiting professor of international business; London Business School, visiting professor of strategic and international management; Harvard Business School, distinguished research fellow. Writer and consultant. **Publications:** (With C.K. Prahalad) Competing for the Future, 1994; Competence-based Competition, 1994; (with Y.L. Doz) Alliance Advantage: The Art of Creating Value through Partnering, 1998; (ed.) Strategic Flexibility: Managing in a Turbulent Environment, 1998; Leading the Revolution, 2000 as Leading the Revolution: How to Thrive in Turbulent Times by Making Innovation a Way of Life, 2002; (with B. Breen) The Future of Management, 2007. Contributor to periodicals and journals. **Address:** MLab, PO Box 620955, Woodside, CA 94062, U.S.A. **Online address:** ghamel@london.edu

HAMER, Forrest. American (born United States), b. 1956. **Genres:** Poetry. **Career:** Psychologist and psychoanalyst. Writer. **Publications:** POETRY: Call and Response, 1995; Middle Ear, 2000; Rift, 2007. **Address:** 5305 College Ave., Oakland, CA 94618, U.S.A. **Online address:** forrest.hamer@sbcglobal.net

HAMID, Ahmad A. Egyptian/American (born United States), b. 1948. **Genres:** Architecture, Engineering. **Career:** University of Oklahoma, assistant professor, 1979-81; Drexel University, professor of civil engineering, 1982-; consultant in structural engineering. Writer. **Publications:** (Co-author) Masonry Structures: Behavior and Design, 1994, (with R.G. Drysdale) 3rd ed., 2008. **Address:** Department of Civil & Architectural Engineering, Drexel University, Rm. 280-F, Alumni Engineering Labs, 3141 Chestnut St., Philadelphia, PA 19104, U.S.A. **Online address:** hamidaa@drexel.edu

HAMID, Mohsin. American/Pakistani (born Pakistan), b. 1971?. **Genres:** Novels, Literary Criticism And History. **Career:** McKinsey and Co., management consultant, 1997-. Freelance journalist and writer. **Publications:** Moth Smoke, 2000; The Reluctant Fundamentalist, 2007. Contributor of articles to periodicals. **Address:** c/o Jay Mandel, William Morris Agency, 1325 Ave. of the Americas, New York, NY 10019, U.S.A. **Online address:** jman@wmeentertainment.com

HAMILL, Janet. American (born United States), b. 1945. **Genres:** Poetry, Novellas/Short Stories, Music, Songs/Lyrics And Libretti. **Career:** College of Poetry, Northeast Poetry Center, instructor. Poet and short fiction writer. **Publications:** POETRY: Troublante, 1975; The Temple, 1980; Nostalgia of the Infinite, 1992; Lost Ceilings, 1999; Body of Water, 2008. Works appear in anthologies. Contributor to periodicals. **Address:** PO Box 21, Circleville, NY 10919, U.S.A. **Online address:** lostceilings@aol.com

HAMILL, Pete. American (born United States), b. 1935. **Genres:** Novels, Plays/Screenplays, Essays, Documentaries/Reportage. **Career:** Brooklyn Navy Yard, sheetmetal worker, 1951-52; New York Post, reporter, 1960-63, political columnist, 1965-67, 1969-74, columnist, 1988-93, editor-in-chief; Saturday Evening Post, contributing editor, 1964-65; Newsday, columnist; Village Voice, columnist, 1974-; New York Daily News, columnist, 1975-79, editor-in-chief; Mexico City News, editor, 1986-87; Esquire, columnist, 1989-91; New York University, distinguished writer-in-residence, 2005. **Publications:** NOVELS: A Killing for Christ, 1968; The Gift, 1973; Flesh and Blood, 1977; Dirty Laundry, 1978; The Deadly Piece, 1979; The Guns of Heaven, 1983; Loving Women: A Novel of the Fifties, 1990; Snow in August, 1997; Diego Rivera, 1999; Forever: A Novel, 2003; North River: A Novel, 2007; Tabloid City: A Novel, 2011. SHORT STORY COLLECTIONS: The Invisible City: A New York Sketchbook, 1980; Tokyo Sketches, 1993. NEWSPAPER COLUMN COLLECTIONS: Irrational Ravings, 1971; Piecework: Writings on Men and Women, Fools and Heroes, Lost Cities, Vanished Friends, Small Pleasures, Large Calamities, and How the Weather Was, 1996. OTHER: (intro.) Kill the Dutchman!: The Story of Dutch Schultz, 1971; Fighters, 1978; (intro.) Harvey Wang's New York, 1990; (afterword) Tales from the Arabian Nights, 1991; A Drinking Life: A Memoir, 1994; (intro.) The Brooklyn Reader: 30 Writers Celebrate America's Favorite Borough, 1994; (intro.) A Diary of the Century: Tales from America's Greatest Diarist, 1995; Tools as Art: The Hechinger Collection, 1995; Times Square Gym, 1996; News is a Verb: Journalism at the End of the Twentieth Century, 1998; Why Sinatra Matters, 1998; At Sea in the City: New York from the Water, 2002; Downtown: My Manhattan, 2004; New York: City of Islands, 2007; They Are Us, 2010. Contributor to books, periodicals and newspapers. **Address:** International Creative Management, 825 8th Ave., New York, NY 10019, U.S.A. **Online address:** petehamill1@gmail.com

HAMILL, Sam (Patrick). American (born United States), b. 1943. **Genres:** Poetry, Literary Criticism And History, Translations, Essays, Photography. **Career:** Copper Canyon Press, co-founder, editor, 1972-2004; Reed College, writer-in-residence, 1974-; University of Alaska, writer-in-residence, 1974-; South Utah State University, writer-in-residence, 1974-; South Oregon College, writer-in-residence, 1974-; Austin College, writer-in-residence, 1974-; Trinity College, writer-in-residence, 1974-; public schools, artist-in-residence, 1974-90; Department of Correction in Washington, writer-in-residence, 1976-88; Port Townsend Leader, columnist, 1990-93; Poets Against war, founder and director, 2003-; Spectrum, editor; Los Angeles Valley College, newspaper and literary magazine editor; Independent Journal, reporter; Western Electric, telephone installer. **Publications:** POETRY: Heroes of the Teton Mythos, 1973; Petroglyphs, 1975; Uintah Blue (chapbook), 1975; The Calling Across Forever, 1976; The Book of Elegaic Geography, 1978; Triada (also known as Sam Hamill's Triada), 1978; Animae, 1980; Requiem, A Poem, 1983; Fatal Pleasure, 1984; The Nootka Rose, 1987; Passport, 1988; A Dragon in the Clouds, 1989; Mandala, 1991; Destination Zero: Poems 1970-1995, 1995; Gratitude, 1999; Dumb Luck: Poems, 2002; American Voices: Poems for the White House, 2003; Almost Paradise: New and Selected Poems and Translations, 2005; Avocations, 2007; Measured by stone, 2007. ESSAYS: At Home in the World, 1980; Bashō's Ghost (prose & poetry), 1989; A Poet's Work: The Other Side of Poetry, 1998. EDITOR: Faces in the Crowd: An Anthology of Washington High School Student Poetry and Fiction, 1981; Selected Poems of Thomas McGrath 1938-1988, 1988; Collected Poems of Kay Boyle, 1991; T. McGrath, Death Song, 1991; Endless River: Li Po and Tu Fu, A Friendship in Poetry, 1993; The Erotic Spirit: An Anthology of Poems of Sensuality, Love and Longing, 1996; The Gift of Tongues: Twenty-Five Years of Poetry from Copper Canyon Press, 1996; Sacramental Acts: The Love Poems of Kenneth Rexroth, 1997; (co-ed.) Poets Against the War, 2003; (with B. Morrow) The Complete Poems of Kenneth Rexroth, 2003; (trans. with J.P. Seaton) The Poetry of Zen, 2004; (intro.) Toward the Distant Islands New & Selected Poems, 2006. TRANSLATOR: The Lotus Lovers, 1985; Night Traveling, 1985; (with J. Kalpinski) The Same Sea in Us All, 1985; Catullus Redivivus, 1986; Li T'ai-po, Banished Immortal, 1987; (with J. Kaplinski) The Wandering Border, 1987; Lu Chi, The Art of Writing, 1987, Wen fu: The Art of Writing, 1987, rev. ed., 2000; Tu Fu, Facing the Snow, 1988; Basho, Narrow Road to the Interior, 1991; Only Companion: Japanese Poems of Love and Longing, 1991, rev. ed., 1997; The Infinite Moment: Poems from Ancient Greek, 1992; Midnight Flute: Chinese Poems of Love and Longing, 1994; Love Poems from the Japanese, 1994, rev. ed., 1991; The Sound of Water: Haikuby Basho, Buson and Issa, 1997; (with K.M. Gibson) River of Stars: Selected Poems of Yosano Akiko, 1997; Spring of My Life: A Selected Haiku, 1997; The Essential Chuang Tzu, 1998; The Essential Bashō, 1999; Crossing the Yellow River: Three Hundred Poems from the Chinese, 2000; Taote Ching, 2005; L. Tzu, Tao te ching, 2005. Contributor to magazines.

Works appear in anthologies. **Address:** Poets Against War, PO Box 1614, Port Townsend, WA 98368, U.S.A.

HAMILTON, Alastair. Dutch/British (born England), b. 1941. **Genres:** Intellectual History, History, Theology/Religion. **Career:** University of Urbino, professor of English, 1977-88; University of Leiden, C. Louise Thijssen-Schoute professor of the history of ideas, 1986-; University of Amsterdam, professor of radical reformation history, 1987-2001, professor emeritus, 2001-; London University, School of Advanced Study, Warburg Institute, Arcadian visiting research professor. Writer. **Publications:** The Appeal of Fascism: A Study of Intellectuals and Fascism, 1919-1945, 1971; Illusion fasciste: les intellectuels et le fascisme, 1919-1945, 1973; (trans. and intro.) Secret Journal and Other Writings, 1973; Proceso de Rodrigo de Bivar (1539), 1979; The Family of Love, 1981; William Bedwell, the Arabist, 1563-1632, 1985; (ed. and intro.) Cronica. Ordo sacerdotis. Acta HN, 1988; (ed. with J. van den Berg) Anglo-Dutch Renaissance: Seven Essays, 1988; Heresy and Mysticism in Sixteenth-Century Spain: The Alumbrados, 1992; Europe and the Arab World: Five Centuries of Books by European Scholars and Travellers from the Libraries of the Arcadian Group, 1994; (ed. with S. Voolstra and P. Visser) From Martyr to Muppy (Mennonite Urban Professionals): A Historical Introduction to Cultural Assimilation Processes of a Religious Minority in the Netherlands, the Mennonites, 1994; The Apocryphal Apocalypse: The Reception of the Second Book of Esdras (4 Ezra) from the Renaissance to the Enlightenment, 1999; (ed. with A.H. de Groot and M.H. van den Boogert) Friends and Rivals in the East: Studies in Anglo-Dutch Relations in the Levant from the Seventeenth to the Early Nineteenth Century, 2000; Arab Culture and Ottoman Magnificence in Antwerp's Golden Age, 2001; The Family of Love I: Hendrik Niclaes, 2003; (with F. Richard) Andre Du Ryer and Oriental Studies in Seventeenth-Century France, 2003; (ed. with B. Westerweel and M.H. van den Boogert) The Republic of Letters and the Levant, 2005; Copts and the West, 1439-1822: The European Discovery of the Egyptian Church, 2006; An Arabian Utopia: The Western Discovery of Oman, 2010. Contributor to periodicals. **Address:** Opleiding Engels, University of Leiden, PO Box 9515, Leiden, 2300 RA, Netherlands. **Online address:** alastair.hamilton@sas.ac.uk

HAMILTON, Allan J. American (born United States), b. 1950. **Genres:** Medicine/Health. **Career:** Massachusetts General Hospital, assistant in neurosurgery, 1989-90; University of Arizona, assistant professor of neurosurgery, 1990-96, assistant clinical professor in radiation/oncology, 1992-96, Division of Neurosurgery, chief, 1995-2004, associate clinical professor in radiation/oncology, 1996-2000, clinical professor in radiation/oncology, Department of Surgery, associate professor of surgery, 1996-2000, head, 1999-2004, professor of surgery, 2000, professor of psychology, 2001, College of Medicine, Arizona Simulation Technology and Education Center, executive director, 2005-. Writer. **Publications:** The Scalpel and the Soul: Encounters with Surgery, the Supernatural, and the Healing Power of Hope, 2008. Contributor of articles to books and journals. **Address:** Department of Surgery, Arizona Health Sciences Ctr., University of Arizona, Rm. 4307, 1501 N Campbell Ave., PO Box 245207, Tucson, AZ 85724-5207, U.S.A. **Online address:** info@ranchobosque.com

HAMILTON, Bernard. British (born England), b. 1932?. **Genres:** History, Theology/Religion. **Career:** University of Nottingham, professor, now professor emeritus of crusading history. Writer. **Publications:** Albigensian Crusade, 1974; Monastic Reform, Catharism, and the Crusades, 1979; The Latin Church in the Crusader States, 1980; The Medieval Inquisition, 1981; Religion in the Medieval West, 1986, 2nd ed., 2003; (trans. with J. Hamilton) Christian Dualist Heresies in the Byzantine World, 1998; The Crusades, 1998; (contrib.) The Crusades and Their Sources: Essays Presented to Bernard Hamilton, 1998; Crusaders, Cathars, and the Holy Places, 1999; The Leper King and His Heirs, 2000; The Christian World of the Middle Ages, 2003; (intro.) Contra Patarenos, 2004. EDITOR: (with B. Arbel and D. Jacoby) Latins and Greeks in the Eastern Mediterranean after 1204, 1989; (with C.F. Beckingham) Prester John, the Mongols and the Ten Lost Tribes, 1996. **Address:** Department of History, University of Nottingham, University Pk., Nottingham, NT NG7 2RD, England.

HAMILTON, Carl. (Earl Hamilton). Swedish (born Sweden), b. 1956?. **Genres:** Popular Culture, Biography, Translations, Business/Trade/Industry, Education. **Career:** Aftonbladet (newspaper), columnist and political commentator. **Publications:** Absolut: Historien om Flasken, 1994, trans. as Absolut: Biography of a Bottle, 2000; Krönika II: Från Silicon Valley Till ådalen, 1998. **Address:** c/o Author Mail, Texere, 55 E 52nd St., New York, NY 10055, U.S.A. **Online address:** carl.hamilton@aftonbladet.se

HAMILTON, Carol (Jean Barber). American (born United States), b. 1935. **Genres:** Young Adult Fiction, Poetry, Novels. **Career:** Elementary schoolteacher, 1957-82; Academic Center for Enrichment, teacher of elementary gifted education, 1982-93; Rose State College, adjunct professor of English, 1988-96; University of Central Oklahoma, adjunct faculty, 1996-2002. Writer. **Publications:** Daring the Wind, 1985; Once the Dust, 1992; Legends of Poland, 1992; Contrapuntal, forthcoming. JUVENILE NOVELS: The Dawn Seekers, 1987; The Mystery of Black Mesa, 1995; I'm Not from Neptune, 2003. NOVELS: POETRY: Deserts, Dry Places, and Other Aridities, 1978; Legerdemain, 2000; Gold: Greatest Hits, 2002; Breaking Bread, Breaking Silence, 2002; Vanishing Point, 2004; Shots On, 2008. Contributor of articles to periodicals. **Address:** 9608 Sonata Ct., Midwest City, OK 73130, U.S.A. **Online address:** hamiltoncj@earthlink.net

HAMILTON, Earl. *See* **HAMILTON, Carl.**

HAMILTON, Hugo. (Hugo O). Irish (born Ireland), b. 1953. **Genres:** Novels, Autobiography/Memoirs, Young Adult Fiction. **Career:** University of Bucharest, Irish literature, lecturer, 1994-96; University of York, writer-in-residence, 1998. **Publications:** NOVELS: Surrogate City, 1990; The Last Shot, 1992; The Love Test, 1995; Dublin Where the Palm Trees Grow, 1996; Headbanger, 1996; Sad Bastard, 1998; Disguise, 2008. MEMOIR: The Speckled People (autobiography), 2003; Harbor Boys: A Memoir, 2006; Sailor in the Wardrobe, 2006; Hand in the Fire, 2010. **Address:** Rogers Coleridge and White Literary Agency, 20 Powis Mews, London, GL W11 1JN, England. **Online address:** info@hugohamilton.net

HAMILTON, James. British (born England), b. 1948?. **Genres:** Biography, Art/Art History, Adult Non-fiction. **Career:** University of Manchester, curator, 1966-72; Portsmouth Museums, curator, 1972-74; Wakefield Art Gallery, curator, 1974-78; Mappin Art Gallery, curator, 1978-84; Yorkshire Contemporary Arts Group, curator, 1984-89; Tate Gallery, Turner Fellow, 1996-98; St. Anthony's College, fellow, 1998-99; University of Birmingham, curator, Barber Institute of Fine Arts, honorary reader. Writer. **Publications:** Arthur Rackham: A Biography, 1990; William Heath Robinson, 1992; The Sculpture of Austin Wright, 1994; Wood Engraving and the Woodcut in Britain c. 1890-1990, 1994; William Heath Robinson, 1995; Turner: A Life, 1998; Turner and the Scientists, 1998; Fields of Influence: Conjunctions of Artists and Scientists 1815-1860, 2001; Faraday: The Life, 2002; A Life of Discovery: Michael Faraday Giant of the Scientific Revolution, 2002; Hughie O'Donoghue: Painting Memory Myth, 2003; Turner: The Late Seascapes, 2003; Turner: The Late Seascapes, 2003; London Lights: Minds that Moved the City that Shook the World 1805-51, 2007; Turner e l'Italia, 2008; Turner & Italy, 2009. **Address:** 2A N Parade, Banbury Rd., Oxford, CH OX2 6LX, England. **Online address:** j.h.hamilton@binternet.com

HAMILTON, J(ames) Scott. Canadian (born Canada), b. 1956. **Genres:** Anthropology/Ethnology, Archaeology/Antiquities, History. **Career:** Lakehead University, associate professor of archaeology, 1988, professor and department chair, 1995-. Writer. **Publications:** (With D.V. Burley and K.R. Fladmark) Prophecy of the Swan: The Upper Peace River Fur Trade of 1794-1823, 1996. Contributor to journals. **Address:** Department of Anthropology, Lakehead University, 955 Oliver Rd., Thunder Bay, ON P7B 5E1, Canada. **Online address:** shamilto@lakeheadu.ca

HAMILTON, Jane. American (born United States), b. 1957. **Genres:** Novels, Literary Criticism And History, Young Adult Fiction. **Career:** Apple farmer, 1979-; freelance author, 1982-. **Publications:** NOVELS: The Book of Ruth, 1988 in UK as The Frogs Are Still Singing, 1989; A Map of the World, 1994; The Short History of a Prince: A Novel, 1998; Disobedience, 2000; When Madeline was Young, 2006; Laura Rider's Masterpiece, 2009. Contributor of articles to periodicals. **Address:** c/o Bantam Doubleday, Dell Publishing Group Inc., 1540 Broadway, New York, NY 10036, U.S.A.

HAMILTON, Jessica. *See* **GREENHALL, Ken.**

HAMILTON, John Maxwell. American (born United States), b. 1947. **Genres:** Communications/Media, Economics, International Relations/Current Affairs, Biography, Writing/Journalism, Essays. **Career:** Milwaukee Journal, reporter, 1967-69; U.S. Marine Corps, officer, 1969-73; freelance journalist, 1973-78, 1986-88; Agency for International Development, special assistant, 1979-81; U.S. House of Representatives Foreign Affairs Committee, associate, 1981-82; World Bank, senior counselor, 1983-86, 1988-92; Public Radio International, Marketplace, commentator, 1991-2002; Louisiana State University, Manship School of Mass Communication, director, 1992-94, dean, 1994-2010, Hopkins P. Braezeale professor, 1998-, executive vice-chancellor and provost, 2010-. Writer. **Publications:** Main Street American and the Third World, 1986; Edgar Snow: A Biography, 1988; Entangling Alliances: How the Third World Shapes Our Lives, 1990; (with G.A. Krimsky) Hold the Press: The Inside Story on Newspapers, 1996; Casanova was a Book Lover: And Other Naked Truths and Provocative Curiosities about the Writing, Selling, and Reading of Books, 2000; Journalism's Roving Eye: A History of American News Gathering Abroad, 2009. **Address:** Academic Affairs, Exec Vice Chancellor & Provost, Louisiana State University, 146 Thomas Boyd Hall, Tower Dr., Baton Rouge, LA 70803, U.S.A. **Online address:** jhamilt@lsu.edu

HAMILTON, Marci A. American (born United States), b. 1957. **Genres:** Politics/Government. **Career:** U.S. Court of Appeals (3rd circuit), law clerk, 1989; U.S. Supreme Court, law clerk, 1989-90; Yeshiva University, Benjamin N. Cardozo School of Law, assistant professor, 1990-93, associate professor, 1993-95, professor of law, 1995-2000; Princeton Theological Seminary, visiting scholar, 1997-98, 2004; Princeton Theological Seminary, fellow, 1997-98; Emory University School of Law, visiting professor of law, 1999; New York University School of Law, visiting professor, 2000-01; Princeton University, visiting professor & Kathleen & Martin Crane Fellow, program in law & public affairs, 2007- 08. Writer. **Publications:** God vs. the Gavel: Religion and the Rule of Law, 2005; Justice Denied: What America Must Do to Protect Its Children, 2008. **Address:** Benjamin N. Cardozo School of Law, Yeshiva University, 55 5th Ave., Ste. 104, New York, NY 10003, U.S.A. **Online address:** hamilton02@aol.com

HAMILTON, Marybeth. British (born England), b. 1958. **Genres:** Young Adult Fiction, Young Adult Non-fiction. **Career:** University of London, Birkbeck College, reader in American History, 1993-, teacher in American History, professor. Historian and writer. **Publications:** When I'm Bad, I'm Better: Mae West, Sex and American Entertainment, 1995; (contrib.) Movie Censorship and American Culture, 1996; (contrib.) Listen Again: A Momentary History of Pop Music, 2007; In Search of the Blues, 2008. Contributor of books to periodicals and journals. **Address:** School of History, Classics and Archaeology, Birkbeck College, University of London, Rm. 162, Malet St., London, GL WC1E 7HX, England. **Online address:** marybeth.hamilton@bbk.ac.uk

HAMILTON, Neil (W.). American (born United States), b. 1945. **Genres:** Urban Studies, Transportation, Education. **Career:** Gray, Plant, Mooty, Mooty and Bennett, associate attorney, 1970-71; Krieg, Devault, Alexander and Capehart, associate attorney, 1971-72; U.S. Army Finance School, instructor in accounting, 1971-72; Airlangga University, visiting professor of law, International Legal Center, fellow, 1972-74; Case Western Reserve University, assistant professor of law, 1977-80; William Mitchell College of Law, trustees professor of regulatory policy, 1980-2001; Midwest Corporate Counsel Center, president and executive director, 1985-90; University of St. Thomas, professor of law, 2001-, Mentor Program, director, 2001-02, interim associate dean for academic affairs, 2002, associate dean for academic affairs, 2003-05, Thomas Holloran Center for Ethical Leadership in the Professions, founding director, 2006-. Writer. **Publications:** (With P.R. Hamilton) Governance of Public Enterprise: A Case Study of Urban Mass Transit, 1981; (with R. Wasserstrom) Solid Waste Disposal in the United States: Rate Regulation is not the Answer, 1989; Zealotry and Academic Freedom: A Legal and Historical Perspective, 1995; Academic Ethics: Problems and Materials on Professional Conduct and Shared Governance, 2002. Contributor of articles to journals. **Address:** School of Law, University of St. Thomas, MSL 400, 1000 LaSalle Ave., Minneapolis, MN 55403-2015, U.S.A. **Online address:** nwhamilton@stthomas.edu

HAMILTON, Peter F. British (born England), b. 1960. **Genres:** Science Fiction/Fantasy, Young Adult Fiction, Novellas/Short Stories, Novels, Literary Criticism And History. **Career:** Writer. **Publications:** GREG MANDEL TRILOGY: Mindstar Rising, 1993; A Quantum Murder, 1994; The Nano Flower, 1995. NIGHT'S DAWN TRILOGY: The Reality Dysfunction, 1996; A Second Chance at Eden, 1996; The Neutronium Alchemist, 1997; The Naked God, 1999; The Confederation Handbook, 2000. THE REALITY DYSFUNCTION: Emergence, 1996; Expansion, 1997. THE NEUTRONIUM

ALCHEMIST: Consolidation, 1997; Conflict, 1998; THE NAKED GOD: Flight, 2000; Faith, 2000. JUVENILE FICTION: Lightstorm, 1998. NOVELS: Watching Trees Grow, 2000; (ed.) Futures: Four Novellas, 2001; Fallen Dragon, 2002; Misspent Youth, 2002. VOID TRILOG: The Dreaming Void, 2007; The Temporal Void, 2008; The Evolutionary Void, 2010. COMMONWEALTH SAGA: Pandora's Star, 2004; Judas Unchained, 2005. Works appear in anthologies. Contributor to magazines. **Address:** Macmillan Publishers Ltd., 25 Eccleston Pl., London, GL SW1W 9NF, England.

HAMILTON, Priscilla. *See* **GELLIS, Roberta (Leah Jacobs).**

HAMILTON, Richard. American (born United States), b. 1943. **Genres:** Art/Art History, How-to Books, Poetry. **Career:** Bryn Mawr College, assistant professor, associate professor, 1971-88, Paul Shorey professor of Greek, 1988-, Bryn Mawr Commentaries Inc., founder, editor. Writer. **Publications:** Epinikion: General Form in the Odes of Pindar, 1974; The Architecture of Hesiodic Poetry, 1989; Choes and Anthesteria: Athenian Iconography and Ritual, 1992; Treasure Map: A Guide to the Delian Inventories, 2000; (ed. with J.S. Rusten) Thucydidean Narrative and Discourse, 2011. **Address:** Department of Greek, Latin & Classical Stuides, Bryn Mawr College, Thomas Hall 246, 101 N Merion Ave., Bryn Mawr, PA 19010-2899, U.S.A. **Online address:** rhamilto@brynmawr.edu

HAMILTON, Saskia. American (born United States), b. 1967. **Genres:** Poetry. **Career:** Folger Shakespeare Library, poetry coordinator, 1992-97; Lannan Foundation, director of literary programs, 1997-99; Kenyon College, visiting instructor, 2000-01; Stonehill College, assistant professor of English, 2001-02; Barnard College, associate professor of English, 2002-, director of womens poets. Writer. **Publications:** As for Dream (poetry), 2001; (ed.) The Letters of Robert Lowell, 2005; Divide These, 2005; (ed. with T. Travisano) Words in Air: The Complete Correspondence Between Elizabeth Bishop and Robert Lowell, 2008; (ed.) Poems, 2010. Contributor to periodicals. **Address:** Barnard College, Columbia University, 3009 Broadway, New York, NY 10027, U.S.A. **Online address:** shamilton@barnard.edu

HAMILTON, Sharon Jean. Canadian/Scottish (born Scotland), b. 1944. **Genres:** Education, Adult Non-fiction, Women's Studies And Issues, Autobiography/Memoirs. **Career:** Teacher, 1964-72; high school English teacher and department head, 1972-83; University of Manitoba, assistant professor of English, 1986-87; Indiana University-Purdue University (IUPUI), assistant professor, 1987-92, associate professor of English, 1992-96, acting associate dean of external affairs, 1994-95, director of campus writing, 1995-, professor, 1996-99, associate vice chancellor for academic affairs, associate dean of the faculties, chancellor's professor, 1999-, Urban Universities Portfolio Project, director, Faculty Colloquium for Excellence in Teaching, director, chancellor's professor emerita of English. Writer. **Publications:** (With E. Hansen) Sourcebook for Collaborative Learning in the Arts and Sciences, 1992; (ed. with K. Bosworth) Collaborative Learning in Higher Education: Underlying Processes and Effective Techniques, 1994; My Name's Not Susie: A Life Transformed by Literacy, 1995. Contributor of articals to books and journals. **Address:** School of Liberal Arts, Indiana University-Purdue University, Cavanaugh Hall 441, 425 University Blvd., Indianapolis, IN 46202, U.S.A. **Online address:** shamilto@iupui.edu

HAMILTON, Tim. American (born United States), b. 1966. **Genres:** Graphic Novels. **Career:** Writer, illustrator and cartoonist. **Publications:** (Adaptor) Robert Louis Stevenson's Treasure Island: The Graphic Novel, 2005; (with R. Nieves) Welcome Back, Mr. Moto, 2008; (adaptor) Ray Bradbury's Fahrenheit 451: The Authorized Adaptation, 2009. **Address:** New York, NY, U.S.A. **Online address:** hamiltontim@hotmail.com

HAMILTON-PATERSON, James. Italian/British (born England), b. 1941. **Genres:** Marine Sciences/Oceanography, Poetry, Novels, Novellas/Short Stories. **Career:** Teacher, 1965-66; St. Stephen's Hospital, staff, 1966-68; Times Literary Supplement, freelance journalist, 1968-74; New Statesman, reporter, freelance journalist, 1969-74; NOVA Magazine, feature editor, 1975. Novelist. **Publications:** Flight Underground (juvenile), 1969; The House in the Waves (juvenile), 1970; A Very Personal War: The Story of Cornelius Hawkridge, 1971 in US as The Greedy War, 1972; Option Three (poems), 1974; (with C. Andrews) Mummies: Death and Life in Ancient Egypt, 1978; Hostage! (juvenile), 1978; Dutch Alps (poems), 1984; The View from Mount Dog, 1986; Playing with Water: Passion and Solitude on a Philippine Island, 1987; Gerontius, 1989; Radio Play, 1990; That Time in Malomba in UK as

The Bell Boy, 1990; Science Fiction Stories, 1991; The Great Deep: The Sea and its Thresholds in UK as Seven-Tenths, 1992; Ghosts of Manila, 1994; Griefwork: A Novel, 1993; The Music: Stories, 1995; (contrib.) Sea Change: The Seascape in Contemporary Photography, 1998; Three Miles Down: A Hunt for Sunken Treasure, 1998; America's Boy: The Rise and Fall of Marcos and Other Misadventures of U.S. Colonialism in the Philippines, 1999; Book on Smell, 1999; Loving Monsters, 2001; Cooking with Fernet Branca, 2004; Amazing Disgrace, 2006; Rancid Pansies, 2008; Seven Tenths: The Sea and its Thresholds, 2009; Empire of the Clouds: When Britain's Aircraft Ruled the World, 2010. Contributor to periodicals. **Address:** John Johnson Ltd., Clerkenwell House, 45-47 Clerkenwell Green, London, GL EC1R 0HT, England.

HAMLIN, Dallas. *See* **SCHULZE, Dallas.**

HAMLYN, D(avid) W(alter). British (born England), b. 1924. **Genres:** Philosophy, Psychology, Humanities. **Career:** Oxford University, Corpus Christi College, research fellow, 1950-53, Jesus College, lecturer in philosophy, 1953-54; University of London, Birkbeck College, lecturer, 1954-63, reader, 1963-64, professor of philosophy and head of department, 1964-88, Mind, editor, 1972-84, head of department of classics, 1981-86, vice-master of the college, 1983-88, emeritus professor, 1988-, fellow. Writer. **Publications:** The Psychology of Perception: A Philosophical Examination of Gestalt Theory and Derivative Theories of Perception, 1957, rev. ed., 1969; Sensation and Perception: A History of the Philosophy of Perception, 1961; (trans. and intro.) Aristotle's De Anima, Books II-III, 1968, rev. ed. as De Anima: Books II and III with Passages from Book I, 1993; The Theory of Knowledge, 1970; Experience and the Growth of Understanding, 1978, vol. XI, 2009; Schopenhauer, 1980; Perception, Learning, and the Self: Essays in the Philosophy of Psychology, 1983; Metaphysics, 1984; A History of Western Philosophy, 1987; The Penguin History of Western Philosophy, 1990; In and Out of the Black Box: On the Philosophy of Cognition, 1990; Being a Philosopher: The History of a Practice, 1992; Understanding Perception: The Concept and Its Conditions, 1996. Contributor to periodicals. **Address:** Birkbeck College, University of London, Malet St., Bloomsbury, London, GL WC1E 7HX, England.

HAMM, Diane Johnston. American (born United States), b. 1949. **Genres:** Children's Non-fiction, Young Adult Non-fiction, Young Adult Fiction. **Career:** Freelance writer, 1971-; Teacher and community extension worker, 1973-75; Community School, workshop counselor, 1981-83; Health Clinic, counselor, 1990-. **Publications:** FOR CHILDREN: Grandma Drives a Motor Bed, 1987; How Many Feet in the Bed, 1991; Laney's Lost Momma, 1991; Rock-A-Bye Farm, 1992. FOR YOUNG ADULTS: Bunkhouse Journal, 1990; Second Family, 1992; Daughter of Suqua, 1997. Contributor to periodicals. **Address:** 345 Luther St. S, Salem, OR 97302-5218, U.S.A.

HAMM, Richard F. American (born United States), b. 1956. **Genres:** Law, History. **Career:** University of Virginia, instructor, 1983-86; Princeton University, lecturer in history, 1987-88; University of New Hampshire, lecturer in history, 1988-90; University at Albany, assistant professor, 1990-96, associate professor, 1996-2004, professor, 2004-, chair, 2007-. Writer. **Publications:** Shaping the Eighteenth Amendment: Temperance Reform Legal Culture and the Polity 1880-1920, 1995; Murder Honor and Law: 4 Virginia Homicides between Reconstruction and the Great Depression, 2003. **Address:** Department of History, State University of New York, 145C Social Sciences, 1400 Washington Ave., Albany, NY 12222, U.S.A. **Online address:** hamm@albany.edu

HAMM, Theodore Alton. American (born United States), b. 1966. **Genres:** Politics/Government. **Career:** Brooklyn Rail, founding editor, 2000-; New York University, associate professor of urban studies. **Publications:** Rebel and a Cause: Caryl Chessman and the Politics of the Death Penalty in Postwar California, 1948-1974, 2001; The New Blue Media: How Michael Moore, MoveOn.org, Jon Stewart, and Company Are Transforming Progressive Politics, 2008. Contributor to periodicals. **Address:** Arthur L. Carter Journalism Institute, New York University, 20 Cooper Sq., 6th Fl., New York, NY 10003, U.S.A. **Online address:** h27@nyu.edu

HAMMEL, Bob. American (born United States), b. 1937?. **Genres:** Novels, Sports/Fitness, Autobiography/Memoirs, Biography. **Career:** Huntington Herald-Press, sports writer, 1954-66; Fort Wayne News-Sentinel, sports writer, 1954-66; Peru Tribune, sports writer, 1954-66; Kokomo Morning Times, sports writer, 1954-66; Indianapolis News, sports writer, 1954-66; Herald-Telephone (then Bloomington Herald-Times), sports editor and columnist, 1966-96; U.S. Basketball Writers Association, president; Football Writers Association of America, president; National Sportscasters and Sportswriters Association, president. **Publications:** Beyond the Brink with Indiana, 1987; (with J. Russo) Super Scout: Thirty-five Years of Major League Scouting, 1992; A Banner Year at Indiana, 1993; Hoosiers-Classified: Indianas Love Affair with One-Class Basketball, 1997; (with K. Klingelhoffer) Glory of Old IU, Indiana University, 1999; (with B. Knight) Knight: My Story, 2002; Bill Cook Story: Ready, Fire, Aim!, 2008. **Address:** Indiana University Press, 601 N Morton St., Bloomington, IN 47404, U.S.A.

HAMMELL, Ian. *See* **EMERY, Clayton.**

HAMMERSCHMIDT-HUMMEL, Hildegard. German (born Germany), b. 1944. **Genres:** Literary Criticism And History. **Career:** University of Mainz, professor of English literature and culture, 1977-; University of Marburg, faculty, 1977-; German Consulate General, consul for cultural affairs, 1979-82; Shakespeare Picture Archive, head, 1982-2005. Writer. **Publications:** Das historische Drama in England (1956-1971): Erscheinungsformen un Entwicklungstendenzen, 1972; Die Importgüter Der Handelsstadt London Als Sprach-und Bildbereich des elisabethanischen Dramas, 1979; (ed. with M. Eksteins) Nineteenth-Century Germany: A Symposium, 1983; Die Shakespeare-Illustrationen des Frankfurter Malers Victor Müller im Städelschen Kunstinstitut: Unbekannte Zeichnungen und Entwürfe zu Shakespeares Dramen, 1990; Die Traumtheorien des 20. Jahrhunderts und die Träume der Figuren Shakespeares: Mit einem Abriss philosophischer und Literarischer Traumauffassungen von der Antike bis zur Gegenwart, 1992; Annette oder Die Landschaft unseres inneren Lebens, 1992; Das Geheimnis um Shakespeares Dark Lady: Dokumentation einer Enthüllung, 1999; Die verborgene Existenz des William Shakespeare: Dichter und Rebell im katholischen Untergrun, 2001; Die ShakespeareIllustration (1594-2000): Bildkünstlerische Darstellungen zu den Dramen William Shakespeares: Katalog, Geschichte, Funktion und Deutung. Mit Kunstlerlexikon, Klassifizierter Bibliographie und Registern, 2003; William Shakespeare: Seine Zeit, Sein Leben, Sein Werk, 2003; Die authentischen Gesichtszüge William Shakespeares: Die Totenmaske des Dichters und Bildnisse aus drei Lebensabschnitten, 2006; Und das Flower-Porträt von William Shakespeare ist doch echt. Neueste Untersuchungen beweisen erneut seine Authentizität, 2010. **Address:** Georg Olms Verlag AG, Hagentorwall 7, Hildesheim, 31134, Germany. **Online address:** h.hammerschmidt-hummel@t-online.de

HAMMERSLOUGH, Jane. American (born United States) **Genres:** Young Adult Non-fiction, Children's Fiction, Animals/Pets. **Career:** New York Post, columnist. Journalist. **Publications:** JUVENILE BOARD BOOKS: Aladdin's Lamp, 1992; Firehouse Dogs, 1992; The Little Mermaid, 1992; Pinocchio, 1992. OTHERS: Everything You Need to Know About Teen Motherhood, 1990, rev. ed., 2001; The Home Alone Survival Guide (juvenile), 1993; Everything You Need to Know About Skin Care, 1994; Dematerializing: Taming the Power of Possessions, 2002; Into the Rain Forest, 2003; Langur Monkey's Day, 2003; Monkeying Around, 2003; Snakes! Face-to Face: Based on the Animal Planet Program: The Jeff Corwin Experience, 2003; Wild in the U.S.A., 2003; Owl Puke, 2004; Dino Poop, 2006; The Search for Vile Things, vol. I, 2008. Contributor to periodicals. **Address:** c/o Author Mail, Perseus Publishing, 11 Cambridge Ctr., Cambridge, MA 02142, U.S.A.

HAMMES, John A. (John Anthony Hammes). American (born United States), b. 1924. **Genres:** Psychology, Theology/Religion. **Career:** University of Georgia, Department of Psychology, assistant professor, 1956-62, associate professor of psychology, 1962-68, professor of psychology, 1968-90, head, 1969-, professor emeritus of psychology, 1990-, Civil Defense Research, director, 1962-68. **Publications:** To Help You Say the Rosary Better, 1962; To Help You Follow the Way of the Cross, 1964; Humanistic Psychology: A Christian Interpretation, 1971; Human Destiny: Exploring Today's Value Systems, 1978; The Way of the Cross in Scripture and Meditation: Stations for Each Friday During Lent, 1979; In Praise of God, 1983, vol. II, 1987; Ascend to Your Father: An Introduction to Marian Meditation, 1987; One-Month Scriptural Rosary, 1999. **Address:** Department of Psychology, University of Georgia, Psychology Bldg., Athens, GA 30602-3013, U.S.A. **Online address:** jhammes@uga.edu

HAMMES, John Anthony. *See* **HAMMES, John A.**

HAMMOND, Andrew. Saudi/Egyptian/Scottish (born Scotland), b. 1970. **Genres:** Novels. **Career:** Middle East Times, editor; Reuters (multimedia news agency), senior correspondent; Cairo Times (weekly magazine), co-founder. **Publications:** Pop Culture Arab World! Media, Arts and Lifestyle, 2005; What the Arabs Think of America, 2007. **Address:** Reuters Saudia Ltd., Al Thalateen Commercial Center Bldg., 2nd Fl., Corner Olaya Thalateen & Dabab St., PO Box 62422, Riyadh, 11585, Saudi Arabia. **Online address:** andrew-hammond@reuters.com

HAMMOND, Gerald (Arthur Douglas). Also writes as Dalby Holden, Arthur Douglas. British (born England), b. 1926. **Genres:** Novels, Mystery/Crime/Suspense. **Career:** Navy, Army and Air Force Institutes, assistant architect, 1952-53; Aberdeen County Council, assistant architect, 1953-60; University of Dundee, assistant resident architect, 1960-69; Livingston Development Corp., deputy chief architect and planning officer, 1969-82; Chartered Institute of Arbitrators, fellow and chair. Writer. **Publications:** NOVELS AS ARTHUR DOUGLAS: The Goods, 1985; Last Rights, 1986; A Worm Turns, 1988. CRIME NOVELS AS GERALD HAMMOND: Fred in Situ, 1965; The Loose Screw, 1966; Mud in His Eye, 1967; Dead Game, 1979; The Reward Game, 1980; The Revenge Game, 1981; Fair Game, 1982; The Game, 1982; Cousin Once Removed, 1984; Sauce for the Pigeon, 1984; Pursuit of Arms, 1985; Silver City Scandal, 1986; The Executor, 1986; The Worried Widow, 1987; Adverse Report, 1987; Stray Shot, 1989; Dog in the Dark, 1989; A Brace of Skeet, 1990; Whose Dog Are You?, 1991; Let Us Prey, 1991; Home to Roost, 1991; A Very Wrong Number, 1991; In Camera, 1992; Cash & Carry, 1992; Doghouse, 1992; Snatch Crop, 1993; Give a Dog a Name, 1993; Thin Air, 1994; The Curse of the Cockers, 1994; Sting in the Tail, 1995; Hook or Crook, 1995; Mad Dogs and Scotsmen, 1995; Carriage of Justice, 1996; Sink or Swim, 1996; Bloodlines, 1998; Follow that Gun, 1998; Fine Tune, 1998; Twice Bitten, 1999; A Running Jump, 1998; Flamescape, 1998; A Shocking Affair, 1999; Dogsbody, 1999; Dead Weight, 2000; Into the Blue, 2000; Illegal Tender, 2001; Grail for Sale, 2002; The Dirty Dollar, 2002; Into the Blue, 2000; The Snatch, 2003; Down the Garden Path, 2003; The Hitch, 2004; Outpost, 2004; Dead Letters, 2005; Cold in the Heads, 2006; Cold Relations, 2006. OTHER: (as Dalby Holden) Doldrum (crime novel), 1987; The Language of Horse Racing, 2000; Hisor Her Grace, 2004; Saving Grace, 2004; Heirs and Graces, 2005; His or Her Grace, 2005; On the Warpath, 2006; Keeper Turned Poacher, 2006; A Dead Question, 2007; Waking Partners, 2007; Loving Memory, 2007; Hit and Run, 2008; Crash, 2008; Well and Good, 2009; Silent Intruder, 2010; The Fingers of One Foot, 2010; A Dog's Life, 2010; Snitch, 2010; With My Little Eye, 2011. Contributor to periodicals. **Address:** CEILIDH, St. Eunan's Rd. E, Aboyne, Aberdeenshire, AB34 5HH, Scotland. **Online address:** gerald983@aol.com

HAMMOND, Herb(ert L.). Canadian/American (born United States), b. 1945. **Genres:** Environmental Sciences/Ecology, Chemistry, Engineering, Sciences, Earth Sciences. **Career:** Hammond Builders Supply, part-time retail salesperson and builder of custom cabinets, 1960-67; U.S. Forest Service, cruiser checker in white pine blister rust control, 1964; Weyerhaeuser Co., field research assistant, 1966; University of Washington, graduate research assistant in forest resources, 1972-73; Crown Zellerbach Corp., Courtenay Division, forester, 1973-74; Selkirk College, instructor in forest ecology and silviculture, 1974-82, Department of Forest Resources, chair, 1979-81, forestry extension coordinator, 1981-82; Silva Ecosystem Consultants Ltd., president, 1976-, Silva Forest Foundation, founder; Slocan Valley Watershed Alliance, co-chair, 1982-; British Columbia Watershed Protection Alliance, chair, 1984-88. Writer and consultant. **Publications:** Reforestation Syllabus, 1982, rev. ed., 1984; British Columbia Watershed Protection Alliance Handbook, 1988; Seeing the Forest among the Trees: The Case for Wholistic Forest Use, 1991; (with S. Hammond) Community Guide to the Forest: Ecology, Planning and Use, 1992; Maintaining Whole Systems on Earth's Crown: Ecosystem-based Conservation Planning for the Boreal Forest, 2007. Contributor to books. **Address:** Silva Forest Foundation, PO Box 9, Slocan Park, BC V0G 2E0, Canada. **Online address:** hhammond@netidea.com

HAMMOND, John Craig. American (born United States), b. 1974. **Genres:** Politics/Government. **Career:** University of Kentucky, adjunct instructor, 2004-05, Purdue University Calumet, assistant professor, 2005-08; Pennsylvania State University, faculty, 2008-. Writer. **Publications:** Slavery, Freedom, and Expansion in the Early American West, 2007; (ed. with M. Mason) Contesting Slavery: The Politics of Bondage and Freedom in the New American Nation, 2011. Contributor to periodicals and journals. **Address:** U.S.A. **Online address:** jch24@psu.edu

HAMMOND, Warren. American (born United States) **Genres:** Novels, Science Fiction/Fantasy. **Career:** Writer. **Publications:** Kop, 2007; Ex-Kop, 2008. **Address:** Tor Books, 175 5th Ave., New York, NY 10010, U.S.A. **Online address:** warren.hammond@hotmail.com

HAMMOND, Wayne G(ordon). American (born United States), b. 1953. **Genres:** Bibliography, Literary Criticism And History, Biography. **Career:** Williams College, Chapin Library of Rare Books, assistant librarian, 1976-. Writer. **Publications:** The Graphic Art of C.B. Falls, 1982; (with D.A. Anderson) J.R.R. Tolkien: A Descriptive Bibliography, 1993; (with C. Scull) J.R.R. Tolkien: Artist and Illustrator, 1995; (ed. with C. Scull) Roverandom, 1998; (ed. with C. Scull) Farmer Giles of Ham, 1999; Arthur Ransome: A Bibliography, 2000; (ed. with C. Scull) The Lord of the Rings by J.R.R. Tolkien, 2004; (with C. Scull) The Lord of the Rings: A Reader's Companion, 2005; (ed. with C. Scull) The Lord of the Rings, 1954-2004: Scholarship in Honor of Richard E. Blackwelder, 2006; (with C. Scull) The J.R.R. Tolkien Companion and Guide, 2006; (with R.L. Volz) Gunnar A. Kaldewey: Artist Books for a Global World, 2006. Contributor to periodicals. **Address:** Chapin Library of Rare Books, Williams College, Southworth Schoolhouse, 96 School St., Apt. 3, PO Box 426, Williamstown, MA 01267, U.S.A. **Online address:** wayne.g.hammond@williams.edu

HAMMOUDI, Abdellah. American/Moroccan (born Morocco), b. 1945?. **Genres:** Translations, Social Sciences, Theology/Religion, Cultural/Ethnic Topics. **Career:** Mohammed V University, Agronomic Institute, professor, 1972-89; Princeton University, Faisal visiting professor, 1990-, Department of Anthropology, professor, 1991-, Institute for the Transregional Study of the Contemporary Middle East, North Africa, and Central Asia, founding director, 1995-2004. Writer. **Publications:** La victime et ses masques: essai sur le sacrifice et la mascarade au Maghreb, 1988; (ed. with S. Schaar) Algeria's Impasse, 1995; Master and Disciple: The Cultural Foundations of Moroccan Authoritarianism, 1997; Wa'y al-mujtama' bi-dhātih, 1998; Shaykh wa-al-murīd, 2000; (ed. with R. Leveau) Monarchies arabes: transitions et dérives dynastiques, 2002; Une saison à la Mecque: récit de pèlerinage, 2005; (ed. with D. Bauchard and R. Leveau) Démocratie, est-elle soluble dans l'Islam, 2007; (ed. with J. Borneman) Being There: The Fieldwork Encounter and the Making of Truth, 2009; (with M. Zaranīn) Riḥān al-thaqāfī wa-hamm al-qaṭī'ah, 2011. Contributor to newspapers. **Address:** Department of Anthropology, Princeton University, 124 Aaron Burr Hall, Princeton, NJ 08544-1011, U.S.A. **Online address:** hammoudi@princeton.edu

HAMPSON, (Margaret) Daphne. British (born England), b. 1944. **Genres:** Ethics, Intellectual History, Theology/Religion, Women's Studies And Issues. **Career:** University of North Carolina, instructor in British history, 1970-71; University of Stirling, lecturer, 1974-76; University of St. Andrews, lecturer in systematic theology, 1977-94, senior lecturer, 1994-99, reader, 1999-2001, professor of post-Christian thought, 2001-02, professor emeritus, 2002-; Oxford University, Faculty of Theology, affiliate, 2002; Cambridge University, Clare Hall, visiting fellow, 2005. Writer. **Publications:** Theology and Feminism, 1990; After Christianity, 1996, rev. ed., 2002; (ed.) Swallowing a Fishbone? Feminist Theologians Debate Christianity, 1996; Christian Contradictions: The Structures of Lutheran and Catholic Thought, 2001; Kierkegaard: Exposition and Critique, forthcoming. **Address:** 17 Earl St., Oxford, OX OX2 0JA, England. **Online address:** daphne.hampson@theology.ox.ac.uk

HAMPSON, Norman. *See* Obituaries.

HAMPSON, Robert (Gavin). British (born England), b. 1948. **Genres:** Poetry, Literary Criticism And History. **Career:** University of London, Royal Holloway and New Bedford College, lecturer, 1978-94, senior lecturer, 1994-96, acting head of department, 1994, reader in English literature, 1996-2000, professor of modern literature, 2000-, head of the department, 1996-97, 2002-. Writer. **Publications:** POETRY: Degrees of Addiction, 1975; How Nell Scored, 1976; A Necessary Displacement, 1978; A Feast of Friends, 1982; A City at War, 1985; A Human Measure, 1989; Unicorns, 1989; Seaport, 1995; A New Hampshire Sampler, 1996; Assembled Fugitives: Selected Poems 1973-1998, 2001; C for Security, 2002. LITERARY CRITICISM: Joseph Conrad: Betrayal and Identity, 1992; Cross-cultural Encounters in Joseph Conrad's Malay Fiction, 2000. EDITOR: (with C. Watts) Lord Jim, 1986; Something of Myself, 1987; Victory, 1989; (with P. Barry) New British Poetries: The Scope of the Possible, 1993; (and intro.) Heart of Darkness, 1995; R. Kipling, Soldiers Three (In Black and White), 1998; Nostromo, 2000; (with T. Davenport) Ford Madox Ford: A Reappraisal, 2002; (with W. Montgomery)

Frank O'Hara Now, 2010; Conrad's Secrets, forthcoming. **Address:** Department of English, University of London, Royal Holloway, Egham Hill, Egham, SR TW20 0EX, England. **Online address:** r.hampson@rhul.ac.uk

HAMPTON, Wilborn. American (born United States), b. 1940?. **Genres:** Communications/Media, Environmental Sciences/Ecology, History, Young Adult Non-fiction, Autobiography/Memoirs, International Relations/Current Affairs. **Career:** United Press Intl. (UPI), cub reporter, 1963, foreign correspondent; New York Times, editor and theater critic. **Publications:** Kennedy Assassinated!: The World Mourns: A Reporter's Story, 1997; Meltdown: A Race against Nuclear Disaster at Three Mile Island: A Reporter's Story, 2001; September 11, 2001: Attack on New York City, 2003; Elvis Presley, A Twentieth Century Life, 2007; War in the Middle East: A Reporter's Story, 2007; Babe Ruth: A Twentieth-Century Life, 2009; Horton Foote: America's Storyteller, 2009. **Address:** Candlewick Press, 2067 Massachusetts Ave., 5th Fl., Cambridge, MA 02140, U.S.A.

HAMPTON-JONES, Hollis. American (born United States) **Genres:** Dance/Ballet, Novels, Psychology. **Career:** Writer. **Publications:** Vicious Spring (novel), 2003. Contributor to periodicals. **Address:** c/o Author Mail, Riverhead Books Publicity, 375 Hudson St., New York, NY 10014-3658, U.S.A.

HAMRIN, Robert. (Robert D. Hamrin). American (born United States), b. 1946. **Genres:** Economics, Business/Trade/Industry, Administration/Management, Essays, Human Relations/Parenting. **Career:** Joint Economic Committee of Congress, staff economist, 1974-83; Environmental Protection Agency, senior policy economist and director of benefits staff, 1979-82; economic advisor to Senator Gary Hart, 1982-83; National Association of Manufacturers, advisor; economic consultant and author, 1983-96; Great Dads, founder, 1996, president. Educator. **Publications:** (Comp. with R.H. Haveman) The Political Economy of Federal Policy, 1973; (co-author) Broadening the Ownership of New Capital: ESOPs and Other Alternatives, 1976; Managing Growth in the 1980's: Toward a New Economics, 1980; Environmental Quality and Economic Growth, 1981; A Renewable Resource Economy, 1983; America's New Economy: The Basic Guide, 1988; Straight from a Dad's Heart: 12 Keys to Joy-Filled Fathering, 1993; (with J. Jasinowski) Making It in America: Proven Paths to Success from Fifty Top Companies, 1995; Great Dads: Building Loving Lasting Relationships with Your Kids, 2002. Contributor to books and journals. **Address:** Great Dads, PO Box 7537, Fairfax Station, VA 22039, U.S.A.

HAMRIN, Robert D. *See* **HAMRIN, Robert.**

HAN, Béatrice. (Beatrice Han-Pile). British/French (born France), b. 1963. **Genres:** Adult Non-fiction, History. **Career:** University of Paris IV, assistant, 1987-91; University of Reims, assistant, 1992-95; University of Amiens, assistant, 1996-97; University of Essex, reader, 1997-, professor of philosophy, director of graduate studies. Writer. **Publications:** L'ontologie manquée de Michel Foucault: Entre l'historique et le transcendental, 1998; Foucault's Critical Project: Between the Transcendental and the Historical, 2002; Transcendence without Religion, 2005. **Address:** Department of Philosophy, University of Essex, Rm. 5B.143, Wivenhoe Pk., Colchester, CO4 3SQ, England. **Online address:** beatrice@essex.ac.uk

HAN, Suzanne Crowder. American (born United States), b. 1953. **Genres:** Children's Fiction, Novels, Translations, Mythology/Folklore, Travel/Exploration, Young Adult Non-fiction, Animals/Pets, Literary Criticism And History, Literary Criticism And History. **Career:** Korean Overseas Informational Service, editorial consultant, 1981-88; Franciscan Preschool and Kindergarten, preschool and kindergarten teacher, 1991-92. Freelance writer. **Publications:** CHILDREN'S FICTION: Let's Color Korea: Traditional Lifestyles, 1989; Let's Learn about Korea: Customs, 1992; (contrib.) Customs of Korea, 1992; Let's Visit Seoul, 1993; Let's Visit Korea, 1993, rev. ed. 2006; The Rabbit's Judgment, 1994; The Rabbit's Escape, 1995; The Dried Persimmon, 1997; The Rabbit's Tail: A Story from Korea, 1999. FOR ADULTS: Korea, 1986; Seoul, 1986; Kyongju, 1988; Chejudo, 1988; Notes on Things Korean, 1997. TRANSLATOR: Han Mahlsook, Arumdaun yongga, 1981 (title means: 'Hymn of the Spirit'), 1983; Son So-hui, Nampung, 1975 (title means: 'The Wind from the South'), 1988. **Address:** UN Village, D Apt. 302, Hannam-dong, Yongsan-gu, Seoul, 140-210, Korea (South). **Online address:** hancrowd@nuri.net

HANBURY-TENISON, Robin. British (born England), b. 1936. **Genres:** Children's Fiction, Civil Liberties/Human Rights, Travel/Exploration. **Career:** Survival Intl., president and co-founder, 1969-, chairman, 1969-81; Royal Geographical Society, vice president, 1982-86; Camel Valley and Bodmin Moor Protection Society, president, 1984-; Cornwall Wildlife Trust, president, 1988-95; British Field Sports Society, chief executive, 1995-98; Geographical Magazine, columnist, 1995-98. Writer. **Publications:** The Rough and the Smooth (exploration), 1969; A Question of Survival for the Indians of Brazil, 1973; A Pattern of Peoples: A Journey among the Tribes of the Outer Indonesian Islands, 1975; Mulu: The Rain Forest, 1980; The Aborigines of the Amazon Rain Forest: The Yanomami, 1982; Worlds Apart: An Explorer's Life, 1984; White Horses over France: From the Camargue to Cornwall, 1985; A Ride along the Great Wall, 1987; Fragile Eden: A Ride through New Zealand, 1989; Spanish Pilgrimage: A Canter to St. James, 1990; (ed.) The Oxford Book of Exploration, 1993, 2nd ed., 2005; (ed.) The Seventy Great Journeys in History, 2006; Land of Eagles: Riding through Europe's Forgotten Country, 2009; The Great Explorers, 2010. CHILDREN'S BOOKS: Jake's Escape, 1996; Jake's Treasure, 1998; Jake's Safari, 1998. **Address:** Survival International, 6 Charterhouse Bldg., London, GL EC1M 7ET, England. **Online address:** robin@cabilla.co.uk

HANC, John. American (born United States), b. 1955. **Genres:** Sports/Fitness, History, Biography. **Career:** Writer. **Publications:** (With R. Reiman) Combating Your Child's Cholesterol: A Pediatrician Shows You How, 1993; The Essential Runner: A Concise Guide to the Basics for All Runners, 1994; The Essential Marathoner: A Concise Guide to the Race of Your Life, 1996; (with F.G. Joyner) Running for Dummies, 1999; (with J. Berman and F. Fleegler) The FORCE Program: The Proven Way to Fight Cancer through Physical Activity and Exercise, 2001; Jones Beach: An Illustrated History, 2007; The Coolest Race on Earth: Mud, Madmen, Glaciers, and Grannies at the Antarctica Marathon, 2009; (with P. Southerland) Not Dead Yet: My Race Against Disease-from Diagnosis to Dominance, 2011; (with P. Hammerness and M. Moore) Organize Your Mind, Organize Your Life: Train Your Brain to Get More Done in Less Time, 2012. Contributor to periodicals. **Address:** Runner's World, 135 N 6th St., Emmaus, PA 18098, U.S.A.

HANCOCK, Brian. American/South African (born South Africa), b. 1957?. **Genres:** Novels, Sports/Fitness. **Career:** Writer. **Publications:** Spindrift: True Tales from Scattered Parts of the Planet, 2000, rev. ed. as The Risk in Being Alive: One Man's Adventures across the Planet, 2003; Maximum Sail Power: The Definitive Guide to Sails, Sail Technology, and Performance, 2003; Grabbing the World, 2010; Grabbing the Dream, 2011. **Address:** c/o Author Mail, Nomad Press, 2456 Christian St., White River Junction, VT 05001, U.S.A. **Online address:** brian@brianhancock.org

HANCOCK, Ian (Robert). Australian (born Australia), b. 1940. **Genres:** History, Biography, Politics/Government, Military/Defense/Arms Control. **Career:** University of Melbourne, tutor, 1962; Monash University, lecturer in history, 1965-69; Australian National University, senior lecturer, 1970, reader in history, 1986-, Department of History, head, 1986-91; Research School of Social Sciences, History Program, honorary visiting fellow, 2000, honorary visiting fellow, 2001-07, National Centre of Biography, biography fellow, 2010-; Liberal Party of Australia, pre-eminent historian. Writer. **Publications:** White Liberals, Moderates, and Radicals in Rhodesia, 1953-1980, 1984; (with P. Godwin) Rhodesians Never Die: The Impact of War and Political Change on White Rhodesia, c. 1970-1980, 1993; A Handbook of Vlax Romani, 1995; National and Permanent?: The Federal Organisation of the Liberal Party of Australia 1944-1965, 2000; John Gorton: He Did it his Way, 2002; The Liberals: A History of the NSW Division of the Liberal Party of Australia 1945-2000, 2007. **Address:** National Centre of Biography, Research School of Social Sciences, Australian National University, Coombs Bldg., Ste. 9, Canberra, AC 0200, Australia. **Online address:** ihancock@webone.com.au

HAND, Dana. *See* **HOWARTH, William (Louis).**

HAND, Geoffrey Joseph Philip. Irish/British (born England), b. 1931. **Genres:** History, Law, Theology/Religion. **Career:** University of Edinburgh, assistant lecturer in history, 1960-61; University of Southampton, lecturer in history, 1961-65; University College, lecturer, 1965-71, professor of legal history, 1971-; European University Institute, professor-designate of law, 1975-; University of Birmingham, Birmingham Law School, Barber professor of jurisprudence, 1980-92, professor emeritus, 1992-; Irish Jurist Publishing Co., director. Writer. **Publications:** English Law in Ireland, 1290-1324, 1967; Church in the English Lordship, 1216-1307, 1968; The Church in Ireland;

1216-1307, 1968; Report of the Irish Boundary Commission 1924, 1970; (with L. Cross) English Legal System, 5th ed., 1971, (ed. with D.J. Bentley) 6th ed., 1977; (ed. with J. Georgel and C. Sasse) European Electoral Systems Handbook, 1979; (ed. with J. Georgel and C. Sasse) Wahlrecht der Neun: Wahlsysteme in d. Europ. Gemeinschaft, 1979; (co-author) The European Parliament: Towards a Uniform Procedure for Direct Elections, 1981; (with J. McBride) Droit Sans Frontières, 1991. Contributor to journals and newspapers. **Address:** Birmingham Law School, University of Birmingham, Edgbaston, Birmingham, WM B15 2TT, England.

HANDELAND, Lori. American (born United States), b. 1961?. **Genres:** Novels. **Career:** Writer. **Publications:** NOVELS: Second Chance, 1994; D.J.'s Angel, 1995; Shadow Lover, 1995; Charlie and the Angel, 1995; Full Moon Dreams, 1996; Enchanted Crossings, 1997; Dreams of an Angel, 1998; By Any Other Name, 1998; Dreams of an Eagle, 1998; When You Wish, 2000; Mother of the Year, 2000; Loving a Legend, 2000; An Outlaw for Christmas, 2001; Then He Kissed Her, 2003; Dates from Hell, 2006; Moon Fever, 2007; Mothers of the Year, 2008; Shakespeare Undead, 2010. ROCK CREEK SIX SERIES: Reese, 2001; Rico, 2001; Nate, 2002. LUCHETTI BROTHERS SERIES: The Daddy Quest, 2003; The Brother Quest, 2004; The Husband Quest, 2004; A Soldier's Quest, 2005; The Mommy Quest, 2006. NIGHT CREATURE SERIES: Blue Moon, 2004; Hunter's Moon, 2005; Dark Moon, 2005; Crescent Moon, 2006; Midnight Moon, 2006; Rising Moon, 2007; Hidden Moon, 2007; Thunder Moon, 2008; Marked by the Moon, 2010. PHOENIX CHRONICLES SERIES: Any Given Doomsday, 2008; Doomsday Can Wait, 2009; Apocalypse Happens, 2009; Chaos Bites, 2010. Contributor to books. **Address:** Milwaukee, WI , U.S.A. **Online address:** lhandel120@aol.com

HANDELMAN, Stephen. American (born United States), b. 1947. **Genres:** Area Studies, International Relations/Current Affairs, Politics/Government, Social Sciences. **Career:** New York Free Press, assistant editor, 1967-69; New York Times, news assistant, 1967-68; Penticton Herald/Prince George Citizen, reporter, 1969-71; Miami News, reporter, 1973-74; Toronto Star, reporter, 1974-76, political writer, 1977-80, bureau chief in Middle East and Europe, 1981-87, bureau chief in Moscow, 1987-92; Columbia University, Harriman Institute of Post-Soviet Studies, associate fellow, 1994-; Time Magazine, columnist, 1998; Americas Quarterly, consulting managing editor; The City University of New York, John Jay College, Center on Media, Crime and Justice, director, 2007-; The New School, adjunct professor; Pace University, adjunct professor; Rutgers University, adjunct professor; Moscow Correspondents Association, co-founder. **Publications:** Uncommon Kingdom: The British in the 1980s, 1988; Crime and Corruption in Russia/Briefing Of the Commission On Security and Cooperation in Europe, 1994; Comrade Criminal: Russia's New Mafiya in UK as Comrade Criminal: The Theft of the Second Russian Revolution, 1995; (with K. Alibek) Biohazard: The Chilling True Story of the Largest Covert Biological Weapons Program in the World, Told from the Inside By the Man Who Ran it, 1999. Contributor to periodicals. **Address:** Center on Media, Crime and Justice, John Jay College, The City University of New York, 555 W 57th St., Ste. 604B, New York, NY 10019, U.S.A. **Online address:** shandelman@jjay.cuny.edu

HANDLER, Daniel. *See* **SNICKET, Lemony.**

HANDLER, David. (Russell Andrews). American (born United States), b. 1952. **Genres:** Novels, Plays/Screenplays, Ghost Writer. **Career:** Writer, producer and syndicated columnist. **Publications:** NOVELS: Kiddo, 1987; Boss, 1988. STEWART HOAG MYSTERY NOVELS: The Man Who Died Laughing, 1988; The Man Who Lived by Night, 1989; The Man Who Would Be F. Scott Fitzgerald, 1991; The Woman Who Fell from Grace, 1991, 2nd ed., 1992; The Boy Who Never Grew Up: A Stewart Hoag Novel, 1992; The Man Who Cancelled Himself: A Stewart Hoag Novel, 1995; The Girl Who Ran Off with Daddy: A Stewart Hoag Novel, 1996; The Man Who Loved Women to Death: A Stewart Hoag Mystery, 1997. AS RUSSELL ANDREWS: (with P. Gethers) Gideon, 1999; Icarus, 2001; Anonymus, 2002; Aphrodite, 2004; Midas, 2005; Hades, 2007. BERGER AND MITRY MYSTERY NOVELS: The Cold Blue Blood: A Berger & Mitry Mystery, 2001; The Hot Pink Farmhouse, 2002; The Bright Silver Star, 2003; The Burnt Orange Sunrise, 2004; Sweet Golden Parachute, 2006; Sour Cherry Surprise, 2008; Click to Play, 2009; OTHERS: Shimmering Blond Sister: A Berger and Mitry Mystery, 2010; Blood Red Indian Summer, 2011. **Address:** 7 Library Ln., Old Lyme, CT 06371, U.S.A. **Online address:** david@davidhandlerbooks.com

HANDLER, Marisa. American/South African (born South Africa), b. 1976?. **Genres:** Biography, Autobiography/Memoirs, Social Sciences. **Career:** Activist, teacher and writer. **Publications:** Loyal to the Sky: Notes from an Activist, 2007. Contributor to publications. **Address:** Berrett-Koehler Publishers, 235 Montgomery St., Ste. 650, San Francisco, CA 94104, U.S.A. **Online address:** marisahandler@gmail.com

HANDLER, Richard. American (born United States), b. 1950. **Genres:** Politics/Government, History, Social Sciences, Criminology/True Crime, Anthropology/Ethnology. **Career:** Lake Forest College, assistant professor, 1980-86; University of Virginia, Department of Anthropology, professor and associate dean, 1986-, Global Development Studies Program, director. Writer. **Publications:** Nationalism and the Politics of Culture in Quebec, 1988; (with D. Segal) Jane Austen and the Fiction of Culture: An Essay on the Narration of Social Realities, 1990, rev. ed., 1999; (ed. and intro.) Schneider on Schneider: The Conversion of the Jews and Other Anthropological Stories, 1995; (with E. Gable) The New History in an Old Museum: Creating the Past at Colonial Williamsburg, 1997; (ed.) Excluded Ancestors, Inventible Traditions, 2000; (ed.) Significant Others: Interpersonal and Professional Commitments in Anthropology, 2004; Critics against Culture: Anthropological Observers of Mass Society, 2005; (ed.) Central Sites, Peripheral Visions: Cultural and Institutional Crossings in the History of Anthropology, 2006. **Address:** College and Graduate School of Arts & Sciences, University of Virginia, 203 Monroe Hall, PO Box 400772, Charlottesville, VA 22904, U.S.A. **Online address:** rh3y@virginia.edu

HANDLEY, Eric Walter. British (born England), b. 1926. **Genres:** Classics, History, Art/Art History, Mythology/Folklore. **Career:** University College, lecturer, 1946-61, reader, 1961-67, professor of Greek, 1967-84; Institute of Classical Studies, director, 1967-84; British Academy, foreign secretary, 1979-88; Cambridge University, Regius professor of Greek, 1984-94; Trinity College, fellow, 1984-; Royal Academy of Arts, professor of ancient literature, 1990-. Writer. **Publications:** (With J. Rea) The Telephus of Euripides, 1957; (ed.) The Dyskolos of Menander, 1965; (with A. Hurst) Relire Menandre, 1990; (with J.M. Bremer) Aristophane, 1993; (co-author) The Oxyrhynchus Papyri, vol. LIX, 1992, vol. LXIV, 1997; (with R. Green) Images of the Greek Theatre, 1995. **Address:** Trinity College, Cambridge, CB CB2 1TQ, England.

HANDLEY, Paul M. American (born United States), b. 1955. **Genres:** Biography. **Career:** Journalist. **Publications:** The King Never Smiles: A Biography of Thailand's Bhumibol Adulyadej, 2006. **Address:** Yale University Press, 302 Temple St., PO Box 209040, New Haven, CT 06511-8909, U.S.A. **Online address:** phandley1@yahoo.com

HANDS, D. Wade. American (born United States), b. 1951. **Genres:** Economics, Business/Trade/Industry, Science Fiction/Fantasy, Essays, Social Sciences. **Career:** Indiana University, associate instructor in economics, 1976-80; University of Puget Sound, assistant professor, 1980-86, associate professor, 1986-92, professor of economics, 1992-97, distinguished professor of economics, 1997-. Writer. **Publications:** Introductory Mathematical Economics, 1991, 2nd ed., 2004; Testing, Rationality, and Progress: Essays on the Popperian Tradition in Economic Methodology, 1992; (ed. with J.B. Davis and U. Maki) The Handbook of Economic Methodology, 1998; Reflection without Rules: Economic Methodology and Contemporary Science Theory, 2001; (ed. with P. Mirowski) Agreement on Demand: Consumer Theory in the Twentieth Century, 2006. CONTRIBUTOR: Non-Natural Social Science: Reflecting on the Enterprise of More Heat than Light, 1993; New Perspectives in Economic Methodology, 1994; Economics and Methodology: Crossing Boundaries, 1998; Critical Realism in Economics: Development and Debate, 1999. Works appear in anthologies. Contributor of articles to journals. **Address:** Department of Economics, University of Puget Sound, 1500 N Warner St., PO Box 1057, Tacoma, WA 98416-1057, U.S.A. **Online address:** hands@ups.edu

HANDY, Lowell K. American (born United States), b. 1949. **Genres:** Librarianship, Theology/Religion, Bibliography, Reference. **Career:** Loyola University of Chicago, senior lecturer, 1987-2002; American Theological Library Association, senior indexer-analyst, 1988-. Writer. **Publications:** A Realignment in Heaven: An Investigation into the Ideology of the Josianic Reform, 1987; Among the Host of Heaven: The Syro-Palestinian Pantheon as Bureaucracy, 1994; The Educated Person's Thumbnail Introduction to the Bible,

1997; Entertaining Faith: Reading Short Stories in the Bible, 2000; Jonah's World: Social Science and the Reading of Prophetic Story, 2007. EDITOR: (with L. Bouchard and L. Richesin) Interpreting Disciples: Practical Theology in the Disciples of Christ, 1987; Index to Book Reviews in Religion: An Author, Title and Classification Index to Reviews of Books Published in and of Interest to the Field of Religion, 1969-1974, 1993; (with R.D. Hudgens) Index to Book Reviews in Religion: An Author, Title and Classification Index to Reviews of Books Published in and of Interest to the Field of Religion, 1993; The Age of Solomon: Scholarship at the Turn of the Millennium, 1997; Psalm 29 through Time and Tradition, 2009. CONTRIBUTOR: International Christian Literature Documentation Project: A Subject, Author and Corporate Name Index to Nonwestern Christian Literature, 1993; (ed. with S.W. Holloway) The Pitcher Is Broken: Memorial Essays for Goesta W. Ahlstroem, 1995; (ed. with S.I. Johnston) Religions of the Ancient World, 2004; (ed. with S.W. Holloway) Orientalism, Assyriology and the Bible, 2006. Contributor of articles to books and journals. **Address:** American Theological Library Association, 300 S Wacker Dr., Ste. 2100, Chicago, IL 60606-6701, U.S.A. **Online address:** lhandy@atla.com

HANDY, Rollo. American (born United States), b. 1927. **Genres:** Philosophy, Economics. **Career:** University of South Dakota, Department of Philosophy, assistant professor, professor and head, 1954-60; Union College, associate professor of philosophy, 1960-61; State University of New York, Department of Philosophy, associate professor and acting chair, professor and chair, 1961-67, now professor emeritus, Faculty of Educational Studies, provost, 1967-76; American Institute for Economic Research, president, 1976-91, president emeritus, 1991-. Writer. **Publications:** (With P. Kurtz) A Current Appraisal of the Behavioral Sciences, 1964, (with E.C. Harwood) rev. ed., 1973; Methodology of the Behavioral Sciences, Problems and Controversies, 1964; (with E.C. Harwood) Useful Procedures of Inquiry, 1964; (comp. and ed. with E.H. Madden and M. Farber) Philosophical Perspectives on Punishment, 1968; (co-ed.) The Behavioral Sciences, 1968; (comp. and ed. with E.H. Madden and M. Farber) The Idea of God, 1968; Value Theory and the Behavioral Sciences, 1969; The Measurement of Values, 1970. Contributor of articles to journals. **Address:** Department of Philosophy, State University of New York, 135 Park Hall, Buffalo, NY 14260-4150, U.S.A. **Online address:** rhandy@aol.com

HANES, Frank Borden. American (born United States), b. 1920. **Genres:** Novels, Poetry, Literary Criticism And History. **Career:** Twin City Sentinel, reporter; Winston-Salem Journal & Sentinel, columnist, 1946-49; Winston-Salem Operetta Association, president, 1949; Winston-Salem Arts Council, staff, 1957; Chatham Manufacturing Co., director, 1960-87; Merchant's Development Co., director, 1961-; University of North Carolina, Friends of Library, president, 1961-2001; Hanes Dye & Finishing Co., director, 1971-86; Old Salem Inc., chairman; Summit School, chairman. Writer. **Publications:** Abel Anders, 1951; The Bat Brothers, 1953; Journey's Journal, 1956; The Fleet Rabble, 1961; Jackknife John, 1964; The Seeds of Ares, 1977; The Garden of Nonentities, 1983. Contributor to periodicals. **Address:** 1057 W Kent Rd., Winston-Salem, NC 27104-1131, U.S.A.

HANHIMÄKI, Jussi M. (Jussi Markus Hanhimäki). Finnish (born Finland), b. 1965. **Genres:** History. **Career:** Massachusetts Institute of Technology, instructor, 1989-90, lecturer, 1990-91; Boston University, adjunct professor, 1990-91; United States Institute of Peace, researcher, 1991-92; Bishop's University, assistant professor, 1992-93; Harvard University, research fellow, 1993-94, Charles Warren fellow, 1993-94; Social Sciences and Humanities Research Council of Canada, post-doctoral fellow, 1993-95; Ohio University, research fellow, 1994-95; London School of Economics, lecturer in international history, 1995-2000; London School of Economics and Political Science, faculty, MA/MSc Program in the Theory and History of International Relations, director, 1997-2000; Graduate Institute of International and Development Studies, professor of international history and politics, 2000-, Finland distinguished professor, 2006-, head, 2008-11, Program for the Study of Global Migration, director, 2008-11; United Nations High Commissioner for Refugees, project director, 2008-10; Norwegian Nobel Institute, visiting fellow, 1997, senior fellow, 2001; University of Helsinki, docent, 2002-. Writer. **Publications:** NONFICTION: Rinnakkaiseloa patoamassa: Yhdysvallat ja Paasikivien linja 1948-1956, 1996; Scandinavia and the United States: An Insecure Friendship, 1997; Containing Coexistence: America, Russia, and the Finnish Solution, 1997; (ed. with O.A. Westad) The Cold War: A History in Documents and Eyewitness Accounts, 2003; The Flawed Architect: Henry Kissinger and American Foreign Policy, 2004; United Nations: A Very Short

Introduction, 2008; (ed. with B. Germond and G. Soutou) Routledge Handbook of Transatlantic Security, 2010. FORTHCOMING: Global Visions and Parochial Politics: The Persistent Dilemma of American Foreign Policy from 1776 to the Present; The Cold War: A Transnational History; Refugee Politics and the Cold War; Transatlantic Relations Since 1945: An Introduction; The Rise and Fall of Détente, 1961-1979. **Address:** Graduate Institute of International, Development Studies, VC 319, 16 chemin de la Voie-Creuse, 132 Rue de Lausanne, Case postale 36, Geneva, 1211, Switzerland. **Online address:** hanhimak@hei.unige.ch

HANHIMÄKI, Jussi Markus. *See* **HANHIMÄKI, Jussi M.**

HANKIN, C(herry) A(nne). New Zealander (born New Zealand), b. 1937. **Genres:** History, Novellas/Short Stories, Literary Criticism And History, Biography, Young Adult Fiction. **Career:** Teacher, 1960-65; University of Canterbury, lecturer, reader in English, 1971-95, senior lecturer in English. Writer. **Publications:** EDITOR: Critical Essays on the New Zealand Novel, 1977; (intro.) It was So late, and other stories, 1978; Life in a Young Colony: Selections From Early New Zealand Writing, 1981; The Letters of John Middleton Murry to Katherine Mansfield, 1983; Letters Between Katherine Mansfield and John Middleton Murry, 1991. OTHER: Katherine Mansfield and Her Confessional Stories, 1983. Contributor of articles to journals and periodicals. **Address:** 5 Stratford St., Christchurch, 8041, New Zealand.

HANKIN, Elizabeth R. *See* **HANKIN, Elizabeth Rosemary.**

HANKIN, Elizabeth Rosemary. Also writes as Elizabeth R. Hankin, Elizabeth Gill. British (born England), b. 1950. **Genres:** Novels, Adult Non-fiction, Geography. **Career:** Journalist, 1970-75. **Publications:** NOVELS AS ELIZABETH GILL: The Singing Winds, 1995; Far from My Father's House, 1995; Under a Cloud-Soft Sky, 1996; The Road to Berry Edge, 1997; Snow Angels, 1999; Black Prince, 2000; The Homecoming, 2003; When Day Is Done, 2004; Where Curlews Cry, 2004; The Preacher's Son, 2005; The Foxglove Tree, 2006; Home to the High Fells, 2006; The Secret, 2007; Swan Island, 2007; Silver Street, 2008; Sweet Wells, 2008; Paradise Lane, 2009; Dream Breakers, 2009; Snow Hall, 2010; Dragon's Field, 2011. NOVELS AS ELIZABETH R. HANKIN: The Phantom Hills, 1981; Farewell to the Enemy, 1981; Fire Flowers, 1984; Lady Diamond, 1985; October's Night, 1986. **Address:** Judith Murdoch Literary Agency, 19 Chalcot Sq., London, GL NW1 8YA, England.

HANLEY, William. American (born United States), b. 1931. **Genres:** Novels, Plays/Screenplays, Novellas/Short Stories. **Career:** Clerk and writer. **Publications:** Whisper Into My Good Ear, 1963; Mrs. Dally Has a Lover and Other Plays, 1963; Slow Dance on the Killing Ground, 1964; Today Is Independence Day, 1967; Flesh and Blood, 1968; No Answer, 1968; Blue Dreams: Or, The End of Romance and the Continued Pursuit of Happiness (novel), 1971; Mixed Feelings (novel), 1972; Leaving Mount Venus (novel), 1977; Something about Amelia, 1984. **Address:** Georges Borchardt Inc., 136 E 57th St., New York, NY 10020, U.S.A.

HANLON, Gregory. Canadian (born Canada), b. 1953. **Genres:** History, Local History/Rural Topics, Social Sciences, Demography, Criminology/True Crime, Anthropology/Ethnology, Military/Defense/Arms Control. **Career:** York University, history teacher, 1983-88; University of California, visiting assistant professor of history, 1988-89; Dalhousie University, associate professor, 1989-97, professor of history, 1997-, university research professor; Universite de Laval, adjunct professor, 1993; Universite de Paris-Sorbonne, visiting adjunct professor, 1996. Writer. **Publications:** L'Univers des gens de bien: Culture et comportements des elites urbainesen Aquitaine au 17e siecle, 1989; Community and Confession in Seventeenth-Century France: Catholic and Protestant Coexistence in Aquitaine, 1993; The Twilight of a Military Tradition: Italian Aristocrats and European Conflicts, 1560-1800, 1998; Early Modern Italy (1550-1800): Three Seasons in European History, 2000; Storia dell'Italia moderna(1550-1800), 2002; Human Nature in Rural Tuscany: An Early Modern History, 2007; Vita rurale in Terra di Siena: Natura umana e storia, 2008; Early Modern Italy: A Comprehensive Bibliography of Titles in English and French, 2010. Contributor to periodicals. **Address:** Department of History, Dalhousie University, 3176 McCain Arts & Social Science Bldg., Halifax, NS B3H 3J5, Canada. **Online address:** ghanlon@dal.ca

HANLON, Patrick. American (born United States) **Genres:** Business/Trade/Industry, Economics, Marketing. **Career:** Thinktopia, founder and chief executive officer. Writer. **Publications:** Primal Branding: Create Zealots for Your Brand, Your Company, and Your Future, 2006. **Address:** Thinktopia Inc., 2751 Hennepin Ave. S, Ste. 4, Minneapolis, MN 55408-1002, U.S.A. **Online address:** pathanlon@thinktopia.com

HANNAFORD, Peter (Dor). American (born United States), b. 1932. **Genres:** Biography, Communications/Media, History, Politics/Government. **Career:** Helen A. Kennedy Advertising, account executive, 1956; Kennedy-Hannaford Inc., vice-president, 1957-62, president, 1962-67; Merritt College, instructor in advertising, 1964-67; Kennedy, Hannaford & Dolman Inc., partner and president, 1965-67; Pettler and Hannaford Inc., president, 1967-69, chairman, 1975-95; Children's Hospital Medical Center of Northern California, 1967-70; Mutual Advertising Agency Network, national president, 1968-69; Wilton, Coombs & Colnett Inc., vice-president, 1969-72; California Governor's Consumer Fraud Task Force, vice-chairman, 1972-; Hannaford & Associates, president, 1973; Tahoe Regional Planning Agency, staff, 1973-74; Office of the Governor of California, director of public affairs, 1975; White House Preservation Fund, staff, 1981-89; The Franklin Firm, Carman Group Inc., manager, managing director, 1996-; speechwriter and advisor to president Ronald Reagan. Writer. **Publications:** The Reagans: A Political Portrait, 1983; Talking Back to the Media, 1986; (with C.D. Hobbs) Remembering Reagan, 1994; (ed.) Recollections of Reagan: A Portrait of Ronald Reagan, 1997; (ed.) My Heart Goes Home: A Hudson Valley Memoir, 1997; (ed. and comp.) The Quotable Ronald Reagan, 1998; (ed. and comp.) The Essential George Washington: Two Hundred Years of Observations on the Man, the Myth, the Patriot, 1999; (comp. and ed.) The Quotable Calvin Coolidge: Sensible Words for a New Century, 2001; Ronald Reagan and His Ranch: The Western White House, 1981-89, 2002; Reagan's Roots, 2012. Contributor to magazines. **Address:** Bill Adler Books Inc., 10 E 39th St. Lbby, New York, NY 10016, U.S.A. **Online address:** pdh3292@aol.com

HANNAH, James. American (born United States), b. 1951. **Genres:** Novellas/Short Stories, History, Literary Criticism And History. **Career:** Texas A&M University, lecturer, 1981-87, assistant professor, 1989-93, associate professor, 1993-, professor, associate department head; Murray State University, assistant professor, 1987-89. Writer. **Publications:** Desperate Measures (stories), 1988; Sign Languages: Stories, 1993; Tobias Wolff: A Study of the Short Fiction, 1996; (ed.) The Great War Reader (anthology), 2000. Work appears in anthologies. Contributor to periodicals. **Address:** Department of English, Texas A & M University, 227D Blocker Bldg., PO Box 4227, College Station, TX 77843, U.S.A. **Online address:** james.hannah@qatar.tamu.edu

HANNAH, Sophie. British (born England), b. 1971. **Genres:** Poetry, Children's Fiction, Criminology/True Crime, Mystery/Crime/Suspense, Novels, Young Adult Fiction. **Career:** Portico Library, writer-in-residence, 1994-97; University of Cambridge, Trinity College, fellow commoner in creative arts, 1997-99; Manchester Metropolitan University, creative writing lecturer, 1998-2005; University of Oxford, Wolfson College, fellow, 1999, 2001; BBC2's Newsnight Review, critic; Lucy Cavendish College, fellow commoner. Writer. **Publications:** POETRY: Early Bird Blues, 1993; Second Helping of Your Heart, 1994; The Hero and the Girl Next Door, 1995; Hotels Like Houses, 1996; Leaving and Leaving You, 1999; Love Me Slender: Poems about Love, 2000; (trans.) T. Jannson, The Book about Moomin, Mymble and Little My (for children), 2001; (trans.) T. Jannson, Who Will Comfort Toffle? (for children), 2001; The Box Room (for children), 2001; First of the Last Chances, 2003; (co-author) Leeds Stories 2, 2005; Selected Poems, 2006; Pessimism for Beginners, 2007; FICTION: Carrot the Goldfish (children's fiction), 1992; Gripless, 1999; Cordial and Corrosive: An Unfairy Tale, 2000; The Superpower of Love, 2002; We All Say What We Want (short stories), 2007; The Fantastic Book of Everybody's Secrets (short stories), 2008; CRIME FICTION: Little Face, 2006; Hurting Distance, 2007; The Point of Rescue, 2007; Wrong Mother, 2009; Dead Lie Down, 2010; A Room Swept White, 2010; Lasting Damage, 2011; Kind of Cruel, 2012. The Carrier, forthcoming. Works appear in anthologies. Contributor to periodicals. **Address:** Rogers, Coleridge & White Ltd., 20 Powis Mews, London, GL W11 1JN, England. **Online address:** sophie@sophiehannah.com

HANNAM, June. British (born England), b. 1947. **Genres:** Biography, Bibliography. **Career:** Teacher, 1970-71; North East London Polytechnic, associate lecturer in history, 1971-73; University of the West of England, lecturer, senior lecturer, 1973-86, department head, 1985-97, principal lecturer in humanities, social science and history, 1987-, associate dean, professor; Royal Historical Society, fellow. Writer. **Publications:** Isabella Ford, 1855-1924,

1989; (comp. with A. Hughes and P. Stafford) British Women's History: A Bibliographical Guide, 1996; (with M. Auchterlonie and K. Holden) International Encyclopedia of Women's Suffrage, 1999; (with K. Hunt) Socialist Women: Britain, 1880s to 1920s, 2002; Feminism, 2007. Contributor of articles to periodicals. **Address:** School of History, University of the West of England, Rm. 1CK19, Frenchay Campus, Coldharbour Ln., Bristol, BS16 1QY, England. **Online address:** june.hannam@uwe.ac.uk

HANNAN, Chris(topher John). Scottish (born Scotland), b. 1958. **Genres:** Plays/Screenplays. **Career:** Dramatist and writer. **Publications:** Purity, 1984; Klimkov: Life of a Tsarist Agent, 1984; The Orphan's Comedy, 1986; Gamblers, 1987; The Baby, 1990; The Evil Doers, 1990; Elizabeth Gordon Quinn, 1990, rev. ed., 2006; The Pretenders, 1991; Shining Souls, 1996; Dr. Finlay, 1996; Missy, 2008; The Three Musketeers and the Princess of Spain, 2010; The God of Soho, 2011. **Address:** Alan Brodie Representation Ltd., The Courtyard, 55 Charterhouse St., Paddock Ste., London, GL EC1M 6HA, England. **Online address:** contact@chrishannan.co.uk

HANNAN, Peter. American (born United States), b. 1954?. **Genres:** Young Adult Fiction, Novels, Children's Fiction. **Career:** Nickelodeon Television, CatDog Series, creator and executive producer. Writer and artist. **Publications:** The Adventures of a Huge Mouth, 1990; The Battle of Sillyville: Live Silly or Die!, 1991; Escape from Camp Wannabarf, 1991; School after Dark, 1991; Sillyville or Bust, 1991; (contrib.) Speak! Children's Illustrators Brag about Their Dogs, 1993; (contrib.) Purr! Children's Illustrators Brag about Their Cats, 2004; Wally, King of Flurbs (four-book series), 2009; SUPER GOOFBALLS SERIES: SELF- ILLUSTRATED: That Stinking Feeling, 2007; Goofballs in Paradise, 2007; Super Underwear-and Beyond!, 2007; Attack of the 50-foot Alien Creep-oids!, 2007; Doomed in Dreamland, 2007; Battle of the Brain-Sucking Robots, 2008; Greatest Snowman in the World!, 2010; Freddy! Locked in Space, 2011; Freddy, Deep-Space Food Fighter, 2011; Freddy! King of Flurb, 2011; My Big Mouth: 10 Songs I Wrote That Almost Got Me Killed, 2011; Not a Pretty Picture, 2012. Contributor to periodicals. **Address:** Peter Hannan Productions, 9301 Wilshire Blvd., Ste. 507, Beverly Hills, CA 90210, U.S.A. **Online address:** peter@peterhannan.com

HANNANT, Larry. Canadian (born Canada), b. 1950?. **Genres:** History, Politics/Government, Social Sciences. **Career:** University of Victoria, Department of History, professor, 1992-97, adjunct associate professor, Great Unsolved Mysteries in Canadian History Project, director; Camosun College, professor of history, 1997-. Writer. **Publications:** The Infernal Machine: Investigating the Loyalty of Canada's Citizens, 1995; (ed. and intro.) Politics of Passion: Norman Bethune's Writing and Art, 1998. **Address:** Department of History, Camosun College, Y 232, 3100 Foul Bay Rd., Victoria, BC V8P 5J2, Canada. **Online address:** hannant@camosun.bc.ca

HANNAY, Alastair. Norwegian/British (born England), b. 1932. **Genres:** Philosophy, Translations, Young Adult Non-fiction, Social Sciences. **Career:** Norwegian Research Council, research fellow, 1968-71; University of Oslo, Department of philosophy senior lecturer, 1972-74, professor, 1990-96, professor emeritus, 1996-; University of Trondheim, associate professor, 1975-75, professor of philosophy, 1975-86; University of California-Berkeley, visiting professor, 1982; University of California-San Diego, visiting professor, 1985, 1988 and 1991; Stockholm University, visiting professor. Writer. **Publications:** Mental Images: A Defence, 1971; (ed. with A. Naess) Invitation to Chinese Philosophy, 1972; Kierkegaard, 1982, rev. ed., 1992; Human Consciousness, 1990; (ed. with A. Feenberg) Technology and the Politics of Knowledge, 1995; (ed. with G.D. Marino) Cambridge Companion to Kierkegaard, 1998; Kierkegaard: A Biography, 2001; Kierkegaard and Philosophy, 2003; On the Public, 2005. TRANSLATOR and INTRODUCTION: A. Naess, Four Modern Philosophies, 1968; S. Kierkegaard, Fear and Trembling: A Dialectical Lyric, 1984; The Sickness unto Death, 1988; Kierkegaard, Either/Or, 1992; Kierkegaard, Papers and Journals, 1996; Kierkegaard, A Literary Review, 2001; Fear and Trembling, 2006; (ed.) Concluding Unscientific Postscript to the Philosophical Crumbs, 2009. Contributor to books. **Address:** Department of Philosophy, University of Oslo, Rm. 534 NT, PO Box 1024, Oslo, 0316, Norway. **Online address:** r.a.hannay@filosofi.vio.nu

HANNESSON, Rögnvaldur. Norwegian/Icelander (born Iceland), b. 1943. **Genres:** Business/Trade/Industry, Economics, Administration/Management. **Career:** University of Tromsø, lecturer, 1975; University of Bergen, senior lecturer, 1976-83; Norwegian School of Economics & Business Administration, professor, 1983-; International Institute of Fisheries Economics and

Trade, chair, 1987-90; Food and Agriculture Organization (FAO), consultant; Organization for Economic Cooperation and Development, consultant; World Bank, consultant. Writer. **Publications:** Economics of Fisheries: Some Problems of Efficiency, 1974; Fisheries Economics: An Introduction, 1975; Bioeconomic Analysis of Fisheries, 1993; Fisheries Mismanagement: The Case of the North Atlantic Cod, 1996; Petroleum Economics: Issues and Strategies of Oil and Natural Gas Production, 1998; Investing for Sustainability: The Management of Mineral Wealth, 2001; (ed. with W.E. Schrank and R. Arnason) The Cost of Fisheries Management, 2003; The Privatization of the Oceans, 2004; (ed. with M. Barange and S.F. Herrick, Jr.) Climate Change and the Economics of the World's Fisheries: Examples of Small Pelagic Stocks, 2006. Contributor of articles to journals. **Address:** Norwegian School of Econ & Business Admin, Helleveien 30, Bergen, N-5045, Norway. **Online address:** rognvaldur.hannesson@nhh.no

HANNIBAL, Edward L. American (born United States), b. 1936. **Genres:** Novels, Advertising/Public Relations, Novellas/Short Stories, Education. **Career:** Kenyon & Eckhardt (advertising agency), copywriter, 1962-64; Norman, Craig & Kummel (advertising agency), copywriter, 1964-65; Benton & Bowles (advertising agency), associate creative director, 1965-68; Wayne Jervis & Associates (advertising agency), creative director, 1968-69; Grey Advertising Inc., associate creative director, 1975-, president, retired, 2003. **Publications:** Chocolate Days, Popsicle Weeks, 1970; Dancing Man, 1973; Liberty Square Station (novel), 1977 as Better Days, 1979; (with R. Boris) Blood Feud, 1979; A Trace of Red, 1982. **Address:** 461 Old Stone Hwy., East Hampton, NY 11937-3154, U.S.A. **Online address:** edhannibalsr@yahoo.com

HANNIGAN, Katherine. American (born United States), b. 1962?. **Genres:** Novels, Young Adult Fiction. **Career:** Iowa State University, instructor in drawing, assistant professor of art and design, 2001-04; Head Start, education coordinator and assistant professor of art and design; Rochester Institute of Technology, instructor; Buffalo State College, instructor; Niagara County Community College, instructor. Writer. **Publications:** Ida B: . . . and Her Plans to Maximize Fun, Avoid Disaster, and (Possibly) Save the World, 2004; Emmaline and the Bunny, 2009; Delly Pattison, 2011. **Address:** c/o Author Mail, HarperCollins Children's Books, 10 E 53rd St., New York, NY 10022, U.S.A. **Online address:** hannigan@iastate.edu

HANNUM, Hurst. American (born United States), b. 1945. **Genres:** Food And Wine, Law, International Relations/Current Affairs, Civil Liberties/Human Rights. **Career:** Northern Ireland Civil Rights Association, legal adviser, 1972-75; Institute of International Law and Economic Development, attorney, 1977-79; Procedural Aspects of International Law Institute, executive director, 1979-89; University College, Faculty of Law, lecturer, 1982; University of Virginia, lecturer, 1986-87; American University, adjunct professor of law, 1987-89; Tufts University, Fletcher School of Law and Diplomacy, associate professor of international law, 1990-96, professor, 1996-, academic dean, 1995-96, Center for Human Rights and Conflict Resolution, co-director, 2000-; Harvard Law School, visiting professor, 1991; University of Hong Kong, Sir Y.K. Pao professor of public law, 2006-08. Writer. **Publications:** (With R.S. Blumberg) The Fine Wines of California, 1971, rev. ed. 1984; (with R.S. Blumberg) Brandies and Liqueurs of the World, 1976; (with R.B. Lillich) Materials on International Human Rights and U.S. Constitutional Law, 1985; The Right to Leave and Return in International Law and Practice, 1987; Autonomy, Sovereignty, and Self-Determination, 1990, rev. ed., 1996; (ed. with R.B. Lillich) International Human Rights: Problems of Law, Policy, and Practice, 3rd ed., 1995, (ed. with J. Anaya and D. Shelton) 5th ed., 2011. EDITOR: Guide to International Human Rights Practice, 1984, 4th ed., 2004; (with E.L. Lutz and K.J. Burke) New Directions in Human Rights, 1989; Documents on Autonomy and Minority Rights, 1993; (with D.D. Fischer) U.S. Ratification of the International Covenants on Human Rights, 1993; (with E.F. Babbitt) Negotiating Self-Determination, 2006. Contributor to periodicals. **Address:** Fletcher School of Law and Diplomacy, Tufts University, 250C Mugar Hall, 160 Packard Ave., Medford, MA 02155, U.S.A. **Online address:** hurst.hannum@tufts.edu

HAN-PILE, Beatrice. See **HAN, Béatrice.**

HANSCOMBE, Gillian E(ve). British/Australian (born Australia), b. 1945. **Genres:** Novels, Poetry, Gay And Lesbian Issues, Literary Criticism And History, Women's Studies And Issues, Social Sciences, Psychology, Mystery/Crime/Suspense, Mystery/Crime/Suspense. **Career:** Hitchin College of F.E.

Herts, assistant lecturer, 1969-70; Queens College, assistant lecturer, 1970-74; Jews' College, assistant lecturer, 1970-74; Gay News, journalist, 1981-83; freelance writer, 1984-. **Publications:** Hecate's Charms, 1976; (with J. Forster) Rocking the Cradle: Lesbian Mothers: A Challenge in Family Living, 1981; Between Friends, 1982; The Art of Life: Dorothy Richardson and the Development of Feminist Consciousness, 1982; (with A. Lumsden) Title Fight: The Battle for Gay News, 1983; William Golding: Lord of the Flies, 1986, rev. ed., 2004; (with S. Namjoshi) Flesh and Paper (poetry), 1987; (ed. with M. Humphries) Heterosexuality, 1987; (with V.L. Smyers) Writing for Their Lives: The Modernist Women, 1900-1940, 1987; Stan Barstow: Joby, 1988; Sybil: The Glide of Her Tongue (poetry), 1992; Figments of a Murder, 1995; (contrib.) Conversations of Love, 1996; The Interloper, 1996. **Address:** Grindon Cottage, Combpyne Ln., Rousdon Nr, Lyme Regis, DS DT7 3XW, England. **Online address:** gillhans@freeuk.com

HÄNSEL, Marion. Belgian/French (born France), b. 1949. **Genres:** Novels, Autobiography/Memoirs. **Career:** Man's Films (movie production co.), founder; Walloon Film Promotion, president, 1988-90, 1996-97, 2002-03. Writer, director and producer. **Publications:** Equilibres, 1977; Dust, 1985; Between the Devil and the Deep Blue Sea, 1995; Clouds: Letters to My Son, 2001; La femme de Gilles, 2004. Contributor to periodicals. **Address:** Man's Films, 65 Ave. Mostinck, Brussels, 1150, Belgium.

HANSELL, Michael H. See **HANSELL, Mike.**

HANSELL, Michael Henry. See **HANSELL, Mike.**

HANSELL, Mike. Also writes as Michael H. Hansell, Michael Henry Hansell. Scottish (born Scotland), b. 1940. **Genres:** Animals/Pets, Natural History. **Career:** University of Khartoum, lecturer in zoology, 1966-68; University of Glasgow, assistant lecturer, 1968-71, lecturer, 1971-85, senior lecturer, 1985-2000, professor of animal architecture, emeritus professor of animal architecture, 2005-, honorary senior research fellow. Zoologist and writer. **Publications:** (as Michael H. Hansell) Animal Architecture and Building Behaviour, 1984; Bird Nests and Construction Behaviour, 2000; Animal Architecture, 2005; Built by Animals: The Natural History of Animal Architecture, 2007. Contributor to books and periodicals. **Address:** Dept of Biomed/Life Sci, Ecology, Evolutionary Bio, University of Glasgow, Graham Kerr Bldg., Glasgow, G12 8QQ, Scotland. **Online address:** m.hansell@bio.gla.ac.uk

HANSEN, Ann Larkin. American (born United States), b. 1958. **Genres:** Animals/Pets. **Career:** Writer. **Publications:** Beef Cattle: Keeping a Small-Scale Herd for Pleasure and Profit, 2006; Organic Farming Manual, 2010; A Landowner's Guide to Managing Your Woods, 2011. THE FARM SERIES: All Kinds of Farms, 1996; Crops on the Farm, 1996; Farm Kids, 1996; Farm Machinery, 1996; Farmers, 1996; Seasons on the Farm, 1996. FARM ANIMALS SERIES: Cattle, 1998; Chickens, 1998; Goats, 1998; Pigs, 1998; Sheep, 1998; Uncommon Farm Animals, 1998. POPULAR PET CARE SERIES: Birds, 1997; Cats, 1997; Dogs, 1997; Fish, 1997; Hamsters and Gerbils, 1997; Turtles, 1997. Contributor to magazines and journals. **Address:** 19351 165th St., Bloomer, WI 54724, U.S.A. **Online address:** shansenwin@bright.net

HANSEN, Ann Natalie. American (born United States), b. 1927?. **Genres:** History, Literary Criticism And History, Theology/Religion. **Career:** Martha Kinney Cooper Ohioana Library Association, research assistant and editor, 1951-54; Columbus Dispatch, editorial staff, 1954-58; At the Sign of the Cock, publisher, 1974-2004. **Publications:** (Ed.) Ohio, 1954; Westward the Winds: Being Some of the Main Currents of Life in Ohio, 1788-1873, 1974; So You're Going Abroad: How to Do It, 1984; The English Origins of the Mary and John Passengers, 1985; The Dorchester Group: Puritanism and Revolution, 1987; Oxford Goldsmiths before 1800, 1996. **Address:** 2341 Brixton Rd., Columbus, OH 43221-3119, U.S.A.

HANSEN, Brooks. American (born United States), b. 1965. **Genres:** Novels, Young Adult Fiction. **Career:** Writer. **Publications:** (With N. Davis) Boone, 1990; The Pilgrimage of Gustav Uyterhoeven, 1993; The Chess Garden, or, The Twilight Letters of Gustav Uyterhoeven, 1995; Caesar's Antlers (young adult), 1997; Perlman's Ordeal, 1999; Monsters of St. Helena, 2003; Brotherhood of Joseph: A Father's Memoir of Infertility and Adoption in the 21st Century, 2008; John the Baptizer: A Novel, 2009. **Address:** c/o Amanda Urban, International Creative Management, 40 W 57th St., New York, NY 10019, U.S.A. **Online address:** bbrux@mindspring.com

HANSEN, Chadwick. (Chadwick Clarke Hansen). American (born United States), b. 1926. **Genres:** History, Literary Criticism And History, Music, Biography, Autobiography/Memoirs. **Career:** Pennsylvania State University, instructor, professor, 1955-71, assistant professor, 1960-65, associate professor of English, 1965-70, professor of English and American studies, 1970-71; University of Minnesota, professor, 1971-74; University of Illinois, professor of English, 1974-75, 1976-91, professor emeritus, 1991-; University of Iowa, professor of English, 1975-76. Writer. **Publications:** (With D. Austin and R.W. Condee) Modern Fiction: Form and Idea in the Contemporary Novel and Short Story, 1959; (co-author) The American Renaissance: The History and Literature of an Era, 1961; Witchcraft at Salem, 1969; (ed. with A. Hodes) Selections from the Gutter: Portraits from the Jazz Record, 1977; (with A. Hodes) Hot Man: The Life of Art Hodes, 1992. Contributor to journals. **Address:** 1325 N State Pkwy., Chicago, IL 60610-2170, U.S.A.

HANSEN, Chadwick Clarke. *See* **HANSEN, Chadwick.**

HANSEN, Debra Gold. American (born United States), b. 1953. **Genres:** Women's Studies And Issues, History. **Career:** Oral History Review, associate editor, 1980-87; Claremont Colleges, Honnold Library, history bibliographer and reference librarian, 1984-89; Journal of Orange County Studies, resources editor, 1988-92; Pomona College, assistant coordinator of bibliographic instruction, 1988-89; Anaheim Public Library, archivist, 1989-90; San Jose State University, assistant professor of library and information science, 1989-; California State University, instructor, 1990; California State Archives, California State Legislature Oral History Project, editor, 1991-93. **Publications:** Strained Sisterhood: Gender and Class in the Boston Female Anti-Slavery Society, 1993. Contributor to journals. **Address:** California State University, 800 N State College Blvd., PO Box 34080, Fullerton, CA 92831-3599, U.S.A.

HANSEN, Drew D. American (born United States), b. 1964?. **Genres:** Adult Non-fiction, History. **Career:** Susman Godfrey L.L.P., associate attorney, partner. Writer. **Publications:** The Dream: Martin Luther King, Jr., and the Speech that Inspired a Nation, 2003. Contributor of articles to journals and periodicals. **Address:** Susman Godfrey L.L.P. Attorneys at Law, 1201 3rd Ave., Ste. 3800, Seattle, WA 98101-3000, U.S.A. **Online address:** dhansen@susmangodfrey.com

HANSEN, Eric K. American (born United States), b. 1947?. **Genres:** Westerns/Adventure, Travel/Exploration, Natural History. **Career:** Writer. **Publications:** Stranger in the Forest: On Foot across Borneo, 1988; Motoring with Mohammed: Journeys to Yemen and the Red Sea, 1991; The Traveler: An American Odyssey in the Himalayas, 1993; Orchid Fever: A Horticultural Tale of Love, Lust, and Lunacy, 2000, The Bird Man and the Lap Dancer: Close Encounters with Strangers, 2004. **Address:** Pantheon Books, 1745 Broadway, New York, NY 10019, U.S.A. **Online address:** ekhansen@ix.netcom.com

HANSEN, G. Eric. American (born United States), b. 1938. **Genres:** Cultural/Ethnic Topics, Social Sciences, Economics, Sociology. **Career:** Wellesley College, faculty member, 1963-64; Massachusetts Institute of Technology, faculty member, 1964-69; Haverford College, faculty member, 1969-73; San Francisco State University, faculty member, 1973-77; Saint Mary's College of California, professor of international political economy, 1977-, director of graduate business programs, 1979-89, School of Economics and Business Administration, associate dean. Writer. **Publications:** The Culture of Strangers: Globalization, Localization, and the Phenomenon of Exchange, 2002. Contributor to books and periodicals. **Address:** Graduate Business Program, School of Economics & Business Administration, St. Mary's College of California, Moraga, CA 94575, U.S.A.

HANSEN, Gregory. American (born United States), b. 1962. **Genres:** Biography. **Career:** Florida Folklife Program, folk arts coordinator, 1980-90, education coordinator, 2000-02; Arkansas State University, associate professor of folklore and English. Writer and folklorist. **Publications:** A Florida Fiddler: The Life and Times of Richard Seaman, 2007. **Address:** Department of English, Arkansas State University, PO Box 1150, State University, AR 72467-1150, U.S.A. **Online address:** ghansen@astate.edu

HANSEN, James R. American (born United States) **Genres:** Biography, Sciences, History. **Career:** NASA Langley Research, historian, 1981-85; University of Maine, professor, 1984-85; Auburn University, professor of history, 1986-, department chair, 1992-96, University Honors College, director, 2006-; Virginia Air and Space Museum and Hampton Roads History Center, vice president; Space Restoration Society, board director; University of Central Florida, faculty; National Air and Space Museum, staff; U.S. Air Force Academy, staff; U.S. Air Force Air War College, staff; American Society of Mechanical Engineers, staff. Writer. **Publications:** NASA HISTORY SERIES: Engineer in Charge: A History of the Langley Aeronautical Laboratory, 1917-1958, 1987; Spaceflight Revolution: NASA Langley Research Center from Sputnik to Apollo, 1995; (with D.B. Taylor, J. Kinney and J.L. Lee) The Wind and Beyond: A Documentary Journey into the History of Aerodynamics in America, 6 vols., 2003. OTHERS: (with F.E. Weick) From the Ground Up: The Autobiography of an Aeronautical Engineer, 1988; The Bird Is on the Wing: Aerodynamics and the Progress of the American Airplane (Centennial of Flight Series), 2004; First Man: The Life of Neil A. Armstrong (biography), 2005; (with A.J. McDonald) Truth, Lies and O-Rings: Inside the Space Shuttle Challenger Disaster, 2009. Contributor to periodicals. **Address:** Department of History, Auburn University, 308-B Thach Hall, Auburn, AL 36849, U.S.A. **Online address:** hansejr@auburn.edu

HANSEN, Jennifer. American/German (born Germany), b. 1972. **Genres:** Novels, Essays, Biography. **Career:** Writer. **Publications:** (Ed.) Anne Frank, 2003; For Love of Bread, forthcoming. **Address:** Greenhaven Press Inc., 10911 Technology Pl., San Diego, CA 92127, U.S.A. **Online address:** chefjhansen@yahoo.com

HANSEN, Jim Michael. American (born United States), b. 1949?. **Genres:** Law, Mystery/Crime/Suspense. **Career:** Writer and lawyer. **Publications:** BRYSON COVENTRY THRILLERS: Night Laws, 2006; Shadow Laws, 2006. Deadly Laws, 2007; Fatal Laws, 2007; Immortal Laws, 2008; Bangkok Laws, 2008; Voodoo Laws, 2009; Ancient Laws, 2009. **Address:** 218 S McIntyre Way, Golden, CO 80401, U.S.A. **Online address:** jimmichaelhansen@yahoo.com

HANSEN, Karen V. American (born United States), b. 1955. **Genres:** Sociology, Women's Studies And Issues. **Career:** Foote, Cone and Belding/Honig, project director, 1980-81; URSA Institute, research associate, 1981-84; University of California, acting instructor in sociology, 1989, Berkeley Center for Working Families, associate senior researcher; Brandeis University, assistant professor, 1989-95, associate professor of sociology, 1995-, professor of sociology and women's and gender studies, Marver and Sheva Bernstein faculty fellow, 1993-94, chair of sociology; Radcliffe College, Bunting Institute, fellow, 1991-92, Harvard University, Andrew W. Mellon faculty fellow in women's studies, 1991-92. Writer. **Publications:** A Very Social Time: Crafting Community in Antebellum New England, 1994; Not-So-Nuclear Families: Class, Gender and Networks of Care, 2005. EDITOR and CONTRIBUTOR: (with I.J. Philipson) Women, Class and the Feminist Imagination: A Socialist-Feminist Reader, 1990; (with A.I. Garey) Families in the U.S.: Kinship and Domestic Politics, 1998; (with A.I. Garey) At the Heart of Work and Family: Engaging the Ideas of Arlie Hochschild, 2011. Contributor to books and journals. **Address:** Department of Sociology, Brandeis University, 209 Pearlman, 415 South St., PO Box 071, Waltham, MA 02454-9110, U.S.A. **Online address:** khansen@brandeis.edu

HANSEN, Keith A. American (born United States) **Genres:** Sciences. **Career:** Stanford University, Ford Dorsey Program in International Policy Studies, consulting professor of international relations; U.S. national security and strategic nuclear arms, negotiator. Writer. **Publications:** The Comprehensive Nuclear Test Ban Treaty: An Insider's Perspective, 2006; (with T. Graham) Spy Satellites: And Other Intelligence Technologies That Changed History, 2007; (with T. Graham, Jr.) Preventing Catastrophe: The Use and Misuse of Intelligence in Efforts to Halt the Proliferation of Weapons of Mass Destruction, 2009. Contributor to periodicals. **Address:** Ford Dorsey Program in International Policy, Studies, Stanford University, Encina Hall W, 2nd Fl., Stanford, CA 94305-6045, U.S.A.

HANSEN, Maren Tonder. American (born United States), b. 1952?. **Genres:** Adult Non-fiction, Agriculture/Forestry. **Career:** Pacifica Graduate Institute, faculty, adjunct faculty; Joseph Campbell Library, founding member. Writer. **Publications:** Increasing Organic Agriculture at the Local Level: A Manual for Consumers, Grocers, Farmers and Policy Makers, 1992; Mother-Mysteries, 1997; Teachers of Myth, 2005. **Address:** Pacifica Graduate Institute, 249 Lambert Rd., Carpinteria, CA 93013-3019, U.S.A.

HANSEN, Mark Victor. American (born United States), b. 1948. **Genres:** inspirational/Motivational Literature, Autobiography/Memoirs, Novellas/ Short Stories. **Career:** M.V. Hansen & Associates Inc., chief executive officer; Soul Enterprises Inc., co-founder; One Minute Millionaire L.L.C., president. Author. **Publications:** Future Diary, 1983; (with J. Canfield) Chicken Soup for the Soul: 101 Stories to Open the Heart and Rekindle the Spirit, 1993; (with Canfield) A 2nd Helping of Chicken Soup for the Soul: 101 More Stories to Open the Heart and Rekindle the Spirit, 1995; (with J.D. Batten) The Master Motivator: Secrets of Inspiring Leadership, 1995; (with Canfield and D.V. Wentworth) Chicken Soup for the Soul Cookbook: 101 Stories with Recipes from the Heart, 1995; (with Canfield) The Aladdin Factor, 1995; (with Canfield) A 3rd Helping of Chicken Soup for the Soul: 101 More Stories to Open the Heart and Rekindle the Spirit, 1996; (with B. Nichols and P. Hansen) Out of the Blue: Delight Comes into Our Lives, 1996; (with Canfield and P. Hansen) Condensed Chicken Soup for the Soul, 1996; Dare To Win, 1996; (with Canfield and B. Spilchuk) A Cup of Chicken Soup for the Soul: Stories to Open the Heart and Rekindle the Spirit, 1996; (with Canfield and K. Kirberger) Chicken Soup for the Teenage Soul: 101 Stories of Life, Love and Learning, 1997; (with Canfield) A Fifth Portion of Chicken Soup for the Soul: 101 More Stories to Open the Heart and Rekindle the Spirit, 1998; (with Canfield and R. Camacho) Chicken Soup for the Country Soul: Stories Served Up Country Style and Straight from the Heart, 1998; (with Canfield and Kirberger) Chicken Soup for the Teenage Soul II: 101 More Stories of Life, Love and Learning, 1998; (with Canfield and Kirberger) Chicken Soup for the Teenage Soul, 1998; (with Canfield) The Best Night Out with Dad (children's book), 1998; The Power of Focus, 2000; (with R.G. Allen) The One Minute Millionaire, 2002; Miracle of Tithing: A Little Book of Answers to Questions About Tithing, 2002; (co-author) Chicken Soup for the Soul Celebrates Teachers, 2003; (co-author) Chicken Soup for the Soul Celebrates Mothers, 2003; (co-author) Chicken Soup for the Soul Celebrates Cats and the People Who Love Them, 2004; (with J. Canfield and J. McPherson) Chicken Soup for the Soul: Cartoons for Teachers, 2004; (co-ed.) Chicken Soup to Inspire a Woman's Soul: Stories Celebrating the Wisdom, Fun and Freedom of Midlife, 2004; (with J. Canfield and S.J. Wohlmuth) Chicken Soup for the Soul Celebrates Dogs and the People Who Love Them, 2004; (with J. Canfield and M. Adams) Chicken Soup for the Soul Nascar Xtreme Race Journal for Kids, 2005; (with J. Canfield and M.H. White) Chicken Soup for the Soul: Daily Inspirations for Women, 2005; (co-ed.) Weight Loss, 2005; (co-ed.) Heart Disease, 2005; (comp. with J. Canfield) Chicken Soup for the Soul: Cartoons for Golfers, 2005; (co-author) Chicken Soup for the Soul: The Book of Christmas Virtues: Inspirational Stories to Warm the Heart, 2005; (comp. with J. Canfield and D. Reber) Chicken Soup for the Teenage Soul's the Real Deal: Friends: Best, Worst, Old, New, Lost, False, True, and More, 2005; (co-ed.) Chicken Soup for the Soul Healthy Living: Menopause, 2005; (co-author) Chicken Soup for the Latino Soul, 2005; (with J. Canfield and L. Brystan) Chicken Soup for the Soul Celebrates Grandmothers, 2005; (co-ed.) Asthma, 2005; (comp. with J. Canfield) Chicken Soup for the Grandma's Soul: Stories to Honor and Celebrate the Ageless Love of Grandmothers, 2005; (with R.G. Allen) Cracking the Millionaire Code: Your Key to Enlightened Wealth, 2005; (ed. with J. Canfield and S.L. Hendrix) Chicken Soup for the Soul Healthy Living: Back Pain, 2005; (with J. Canfield and L. Godwin) Stress, 2005; (with A. Linkletter) How to Make the Rest of Your Life the Best of Your Life, 2006; (co-author) Chicken Soup for the Soul: Recipes for Busy Moms, 2006; (with J. Canfield and T. Peluso) Chicken Soup for the Shopper's Soul: Celebrating Bargains, Boutiques & the Perfect Pair of Shoes, 2006; (comp. with J. Canfield and D. Reber) Chicken Soup for the Teenage Soul's the Real Deal: Challenges: Stories About Sisses, Losses, Messes, Stresses & More, 2006; (with J. Canfield and T. Peluso) Chicken Soup for the Dieter's Soul: Inspiration and Humor to Get You Over the Hump, 2006; (comp. with J. Canfield and L. Thieman) Chicken Soup for the Christian Soul II: Stories of Faith, Hope, and Healing, 2006; (with J. Canfield and P. Lorenz) Chicken Soup for the Dieter's Soul: Daily Inspirations, 2006; (with J. Canfield and M.O. Kelly) Chicken Soup for the Breast Cancer Survivor's Soul: Stories to Inspire, Support and Heal, 2006; (comp. with J. Canfield) To Mom, with Love: Special Wishes from Me to You, 2006; (ed. with J. Canfield and B. Hoggwerf) Diabetes, 2006; (co-ed.) Arthritis, 2006; (comp. with J. Canfield and L. Nichols) Chicken Soup for the African American Woman's Soul: Laughter, love and Memories to Honor the Legacy of Sisterhood, 2006; (with J. Canfield and A. Unkovich) Chicken Soup for the Soul in the Classroom, 2007; (comp. with J. Canfield and P. Lorenz) Chicken Soup for the Chocolate Lover's Soul: Indulging in Our Sweetest Moments, 2007; (comp. with J. Canfield and P. Aubery) Chicken Soup for the New Mom's Soul: Touching Stories About the Miracles of Motherhood, 2007; (comp. with J. Canfield) Chicken Soup for the Soul Christmas: Stories to Warm your Heart and Share with Your Family During the Holidays, 2007; (comp. with J. canfield and P. Aubery) Chicken Soup for the Working Mom's Soul: Humor and Inspiration for Moms Who Juggle It All, 2007; (comp. with J. canfield and T. Peluso) Chicken Soup for the Coffee Lover's Soul: Celebrating the Perfect Blend, 2007; (with J. Canfield and L. Thieman) Chicken Soup for the Nurse's Soul, Second Dose: More Stories to Honor and Inspire Nurses, 2007; (comp. with J. Canfield and D.H. Poneman) Chicken Soup for the American Idol Soul, 2007; (co-ed.) Chicken Soup for the Soul in Menopause: Living and Laughing Through Hot Flashes and Hormones, 2007; (with J. Canfield and J.R. Hawthorne) Life Lessons for Loving the Way You Live: 7 Essential Ingredients for Finding Balance and Serenity, 2007; (with J. Canfield and T. Peluso) Chicken Soup for the Wine Lover's Soul: A Toast to the Perfect Occasion, 2007; (with J. Canfield and P. Lorenz) Chicken Soup for the Tea Lover's Soul: Stories Steeped in Comfort, 2007; (with J. Canfield and A. Frontera) Chicken Soup for the Soul: Kids in the Kitchen: Tasty Recipes and Fun Activities for Budding Chefs, 2007; (with J. Canfield and A. Newmark) Chicken Soup for the Soul: Inspiration and Support for Preteens From Kids Just Like Them: Our 101 Best Stories, 2008; (with J. Canfield and L. Thieman) Chicken Soup for the Adopted Soul: Stories Celebrating Forever Families, 2008; (with J. Canfield and A. Newmark) Chicken Soup for the Soul: Teens Talk Relationships: Stories About Family, Friends and Love, 2008; (comp. with J. Canfield) Chicken Soup for the Soul: Loving Our Cats: Heartwarming and Humorous Stories About Our Feline Family Members, 2008; Chicken Soup for the Soul Love Stories, 2008; (comp. with J. Canfield) Chicken Soup for the Soul: Happily Ever After: Fun and Heartwarming Stories About Finding and Enjoying your Mate, 2008; (comp. with J. Canfield) Chicken Soup for the Soul: Divorce and Recovery: 101 Stories About Surviving and Thriving After Divorce, 2008; (comp. with J. Canfield) Chicken Soup for the Soul: Christmas Cheer: Stories About the Love, Inspiration, and Joy of Christmas, 2008; (comp. with J. Canfield) Chicken Soup for the Soul: Christian Teen Talk: Christian Teens Share their Stories of Support, Inspiration and Growing Up, 2008; (comp. with J. Canfield) Chicken Soup for the Soul: Christian Kids: Stories to Inspire, Amuse, and Warm the Hearts of Christian Kids and their Parents, 2008; (comp. with J. Canfield) Chicken Soup for the Soul: A Tribute to Moms, 2008; (with J. Canfield and A. Newmark) Chicken Soup for the Soul: Teens Talk High School, 2008; (with J. Canfield and A. Newmark) Chicken Soup for the Soul: Teens Talk Getting In.To College, 2008; (with J. Canfield and A. Newmark) Chicken Soup for the Soul: Tales of Golf and Sport: the Joy, Frustration and Humor of Golf and Sport, 2008; (with J. Canfield and L. Thieman) Chicken Soup for the Soul: Living Catholic Faith: 101 Stories To Offer Hope, Deepen Faith and Spread Love, 2008; (comp. with J. Canfield) Chicken Soup for the Soul: Woman To Woman: Women Sharing Their Stories of Hope, Humor and Inspiration, 2008; (comp. with J. Canfield) Chicken Soup for the Soul: the Wisdom of Dads: Stories About Fathers and Being a Father, 2008; (comp. with J. Canfield) Chicken Soup for the Soul: Teens Talk Tough Times: Stories About the Hardest Parts of Being a Teenager, 2008; (comp. with J. Canfield) Chicken Soup for the Soul: Stories of Faith: Inspirational Stories of Hope, Devotion, Faith and Miracles, 2008; (comp. with J. Canfield) Chicken Soup for the Soul: Our 101 Best Stories: Dads & Saughters: Stories About the Special Relationship Between Fathers and Daughters, 2008; (comp. with J. Canfield) Chicken Soup for the Soul: Older & Wiser: Stories of Inspiration, Humor, and Wisdom About Life at a Certain Age, 2008; (comp. with J. Canfield) Chicken Soup for the Soul: Moms know Best: Stories of Appreciation for Mothers and Their Wisdom, 2008; (comp. with J. Canfield) Chicken Soup for the Soul: Moms & Sons: Stories by Mothers and Sons, In Appreciation of Each Other, 2008; (comp. with J. Canfield) Chicken Soup for the Soul Loving Our Dogs: Heartwarming and Humorous Stories About Our Companions and Best Friends, 2008; (comp. with J. Canfield) Chicken Soup for the Soul: Our 101 Best Stories: On Being a Parent: Inspirational, Humorous, and Heartwarming Stories About Parenthood, 2008; (comp.) Chicken Soup for the Soul: Preteens Talk: Inspiration and Support for Preteens from Kids Just Like Them, 2008; (comp.) Chicken Soup for the Soul Presents Teens Talkin' Faith, 2008; (with R.G. Allen) Cash in a Flash: Fast Money in Slow Times, 2009; (comp. with J. Canfield) Chicken Soup for the Soul: What I Learned from the Dog, 2009; (comp.) Chicken Soup for the Soul: What I Learned from the Cat: 101 Stories About Life, Love and Lessons, 2009; (with J. Canfield and S.M. Heim) Chicken Soup for the Soul: Twins and More: 101 Stories Celebrating Double Trouble and Multiple Blessings, 2009; (with J. Canfield and M. Adler) Chicken Soup for the Soul and Golf Digest Present the Golf Book: 101 Great Stories from the Course and the Clubhouse, 2009; (comp.) Chicken Soup for the Soul: The Story Behind the Song: The Exclusive Personal Stories Behind 101 of your Favorite Songs, 2009; (comp.) Chicken Soup for the Soul: Tough

Times, Tough People: 101 Stories About Overcoming the Economic Crisis and Other Challenges, 2009; (comp. with J. Canfield and J. Geffen) Chicken Soup for the Soul: The Story Behind the Song: The Exclusive Personal Stories Behind 101 of Your Favorite Songs, 2009; (comp. with J. Canfield) Chicken Soup for the Soul: Thanks Mom: 101 Stories of Gratitude, Love and Good Times, 2009; (with J. Canfield and W. Walker) Chicken Soup for the Soul: Power Moms: 101 Stories Celebrating the Power of Choice for Stay-At-Home and Work-From-Home Moms, 2009; (comp. with J. Canfield and D. Waltrip) Chicken Soup for the Soul: NASCAR: 101 Stories of Family, Fortitude and Fast Cars, 2009; (comp. with J. Canfield and K. Healy) Chicken Soup for the Soul Extraordinary Teens: Personal Stories and Advice from Today's Most Inspiring Youth, 2009; (comp. with J. Canfield and A. Newmark) Chicken Soup for the Soul: Teacher Tales: 101 Inspirational Stories from Great Teachers and Appreciative Students, 2010; (with J. Canfield and A. Newmark) Chicken Soup for the Soul: Think Positive: 101 Inspirational Stories About Counting your Blessings and Having a Positive Attitude, 2010; (comp. with J. Canfield and L. Thieman) Chicken soup for the Soul: A Book of Miracles: 101 True Stories of Healing, Faith, Divine Intervention, and Answered Prayers, 2010; (comp. with J. Canfield and S.M. Heim) Chicken Soup for the Soul: New Moms: 101 Inspirational Stories of Joy, Love, and Wonder, 2011; (comp. with J. Canfield and R. Rudder) Chicken Soup for the Soul Country Music: The Inspirational Stories Behind 101 of your Favorite Country Songs, 2011. **Address:** Mark Victor Hansen & Associates Inc., PO Box 7665, Newport Beach, CA 92658-7665, U.S.A.

HANSEN, Matthew Scott. American (born United States), b. 1953?. **Genres:** Business/Trade/Industry, Adult Non-fiction, Mystery/Crime/Suspense, Novels, Young Adult Non-fiction, Autobiography/Memoirs. **Career:** Carsey-Werner Productions, writer; Fox Television, writer. **Publications:** (With B. Zmuda) Andy Kaufman Revealed!: Best Friend Tells All, 1999; (with B. Eubanks) It's in the Book, Bob!, 2004; The Shadow Killer, 2007. WITH L. BREWER: House of Cards: Confessions of an Enron Executive, 2002; Confessions of an Enron Executive: A Whistleblower's Story, 2004. **Address:** c/o Nicholas Ellison, The Nicholas Ellison Agency, 55 5th Ave., New York, NY 10003-4301, U.S.A. **Online address:** matt@matthewscotthansen.com

HANSEN, Poul Einer. Danish (born Denmark), b. 1939. **Genres:** Environmental Sciences/Ecology, Mathematics/Statistics, Translations. **Career:** Royal Veterinary and Agricultural University, associate professor of mathematics, 1963-2005, Danish Informatics Network in the Agricultural Sciences, secretary. Writer. **Publications:** Beregningsmetoder, 1972; (ed. with S.E. Joergensen) Introduction to Environmental Management, 1991; (trans.) The Count of Monte Cristo, 1991. **Address:** Department of Mathematics & Physics, Royal Veterinary and Agricultural University, Rm. T637, Thorvaldsensvej 40, Copenhagen V, DK-1871, Denmark. **Online address:** peh@kvl.dk

HANSEN, Suzanne. American (born United States) **Genres:** Social Commentary, Social Sciences, Biography, Autobiography/Memoirs. **Career:** Writer. **Publications:** You'll Never Nanny in This Town Again! The Adventures and Misadventures of a Hollywood Nanny (memoir), 2003 as You'll Never Nanny in This Town Again: The True Adventures of a Hollywood Nanny, 2005. **Address:** c/o Sharlene Martin, Literary Management/Film Rights, Martin Literary Management, 17328 Ventura Blvd., Ste. 138, Encino, CA 91316, U.S.A.

HANSEN-HILL, N. D. New Zealander/American (born United States) **Genres:** Novels, E-books, Mystery/Crime/Suspense, Young Adult Fiction, Literary Criticism And History. **Career:** Novelist and artist. **Publications:** NOVELS: Grave Images, 2000; Graven Image, 2000; Lightning Play, 2000; Light Plays, 2000; Lightning Play, 2000; Vision, 2001; Grave Imagery, 2002; Static, 2002; Gilded Folly, 2007. TREES SERIES: Trees, 1996; Crystals, 2000; Mud, 2000; Shades, 2001; Fire, 2002; Light, 2002. ELF CHRONICLES SERIES: Elf, 2002; Trolls, 2002. OTHERS: Glass Works, 2008; Erratic, 2008; Gray Beginnings, 2008; The Hollowing, 2008. **Address:** c/o Author Mail, Fictionwise, 407 Main St., Chatham, NJ 07928, U.S.A. **Online address:** sfnovels@gmail.com

HANSFORD, Thomas G. American (born United States), b. 1971. **Genres:** Politics/Government, Law. **Career:** University of South Carolina, assistant professor, 2001-06; University of California, faculty senator, 2004-06, assistant professor of political science, 2006-08, associate professor of political science, 2008-, undergraduate director of political science, 2007-09, 2010-11.

Writer. **Publications:** (With J.F. Spriggs II) The Politics of Precedent on the U.S. Supreme Court, 2006. Contributor to professional journals. **Address:** Merced School of Social Sciences, Humanities & Arts, University of California, 5200 N Lake Rd., PO Box 2039, Merced, CA 95343-5001, U.S.A. **Online address:** thansford@ucmerced.edu

HANSKI, Ilkka. Finnish (born Finland), b. 1953. **Genres:** Biology, Sciences, Natural History. **Career:** Academy of Finland, junior research scientist, 1981-87, senior research scientist, 1988, 1991-92, research professor, 1996-2006; University of Helsinki, acting professor of zoology, 1988-91, professor of zoology, 1993-, Department of Ecology and Evolutionary biology, professor, Metapopulation Research Group, Department of Biological and Environmental Sciences, professor. Writer. **Publications:** Distributional Ecology and Abundance of Dung and Carrion-Feeding Beetles (Scarabaeidae) in Tropical Rain Forests in Sarawak, 1983; (ed. with Y. Cambefort) Dung Beetle Ecology, 1991; (ed. with M.E. Gilpin) Metapopulation Biology: Ecology, Genetics, and Evolution, 1997; Metapopulation Ecology, 1999; (ed. with O.E. Gaggiotti) Ecology, Genetics, and Evolution of Metapopulations, 2004; (ed. with P.R. Ehrlich) On the Wings of Checkerspots: A Model System for Population Biology, 2004; The Shrinking World: Ecological Consequences of Habitat Loss, 2005. **Address:** Department of Biological, Environmental Sciences, University of Helsinki, Viikinkaari 1, PO Box 65, Helsinki, 00014, Finland. **Online address:** ilkka.hanski@helsinki.fi

HANSON, Anne E. See YLVISAKER, Anne.

HANSON, David D. American (born United States), b. 1968. **Genres:** Business/Trade/Industry, Economics, Social Sciences, Humor/Satire. **Career:** New York Public Library, information associate, 1992-95; Dreyfus Corp., senior research specialist, 1995-97; Kansas City Public Library, fiction specialist, 1998; writer, 1998-. **Publications:** Dumb as I Wanna Be: 101 Reasons to Hate Dennis Rodman (humor), 1998; The Spring Habit, 2004; Limits to Free Trade: Non-tariff Barriers in the European Union, Japan and United States, 2010. Works appear in anthologies. **Address:** 7230 Gleason Rd., Shawnee, KS 66227, U.S.A. **Online address:** dhanson193@aol.com

HANSON, Neil. British (born England), b. 1948. **Genres:** Novels, History, Autobiography/Memoirs, Biography. **Career:** Author and broadcaster, 1977-. **Publications:** (Ed.) Presences of Nature: Words and Images of the Lake District, 1982; (Ed. with S. Jones) Directory of Exhibition Spaces, 1983; Blood, Mud, and Glory: The Inside Story of Wigan's Year, 1991; The Custom of the Sea, 2000; (with K. Jessop) Goldfinder, 2001; The Dreadful Judgment, 2001; The Great Fire of London, 2002; The Confident Hope of a Miracle, 2003; Unknown Soldiers 2005; First Blitz: The Secret German Plan to Raze London to the Ground in 1918, 2008; Priestley's Wars: The War Writings of J.B. Priestley, 2008; Monk Eastman: The Gangster Who Became A War Hero, 2010. Contributor to periodicals. **Address:** c/o Mark Lucas, Lucas Alexander Whitley, 14 Vernon St., London, GL W14 0RJ, England. **Online address:** neilhanson@blueyonder.co.uk

HANSON, Paul R. American (born United States), b. 1952. **Genres:** History. **Career:** Arizona State University, visiting assistant professor of history, 1981-83; Linfield College, visiting assistant professor, 1984; Butler University, Department of History, acting instructor, 1981-83, assistant professor, 1984-88, associate professor of history, 1988-96, department chair, 1991-, professor, 1996-, Change and Tradition Program, coordinator, 1986-89, dean of liberal arts and sciences, 2002-05. Writer. **Publications:** Revolutionary France (textbook), 1987; Provincial Politics in the French Revolution: Caen and Limoges, 1789-1794, 1989; The Jacobin Republic Under Fire: The Federalist Revolt in the French Revolution, 2003; Historical Dictionary of the French Revolution, 2004; Contesting the French Revolution, 2009; French Revolutionaries Divided: The Federalist Revolt of 1793, forthcoming. Contributor to books. **Address:** Department of History, Butler University, 237 Jordan Hall, 4600 Sunset Ave., Indianapolis, IN 46208, U.S.A. **Online address:** phanson@butler.edu

HANSON, Peter G. Canadian (born Canada), b. 1947. **Genres:** Psychology, Medicine/Health. **Career:** University of Toronto, Women's College Hospital, intern, 1971-72; Toronto Argonauts football club, team doctor, 1972-74; physician, 1972-87; Kings Ranch Health Spa and Fitness Resort, director, 1990; acupuncturist, 1992-; Porter Memorial Hospital, medical acupuncturist; National Stress Test, writer. **Publications:** The Joy of Stress, 1985; Stress for

Success, 1991; Counterattack!, 1994. **Address:** Hanson Peak Performance Clinic, 3300 E 1st Ave., Ste. 600, Denver, CO 80206, U.S.A. **Online address:** peter@peterhansonmd.com

HANSON, Philip. British (born England), b. 1936. **Genres:** Economics, Advertising/Public Relations, Technology, Politics/Government, Social Sciences. **Career:** British Treasury, economic assistant, 1960-61; University of Exeter, lecturer in economics, 1961-67; University of Michigan, visiting professor, 1967-68, 1977; University of Birmingham, lecturer, 1968-73, senior lecturer, 1973-80, reader, 1980-87, professor of Soviet economics, professor of the political economy of Russia and Eastern Europe, 1987-2002, professor emeritus of the political economy of Russia and Eastern Europe, 2002-, Center for Russian and East European Studies, director, 2001-02; Foreign and Commonwealth Office, senior research officer, 1971-72; Soviet Economy, contributing editor, 1985-; Harvard University, Russian Research Center, Mellon senior fellow, 1986-87; United Nations Economic Commission for Europe, senior economic affairs officer, 1991-92; Kyoto University, Institute of Economic Research, visiting professor, 2000; Soedertoerns University, visiting professor, 2004; The Royal Institute of International Affairs, Russia and Eurasia Programme, associate fellow. Consultant and writer. **Publications:** The Wage-Packet: How the Economy Works, 1967; The Consumer in the Soviet Economy, 1968; Development of Advertising in the Soviet Union, 1970; Advertising and Socialism, 1974; External Influences on the Soviet Economy Since the Mid-1950's: The Import of Western Technology, 1975; USSR: The Foreign Trade Implications of the 1976-80 Plan, 1976; Produkitonsstruktur, Nachfragestruktur und Aussenhandel der USSR, 1979; Trade and Technology in Soviet-Western Relations, 1981; Economic Relations Between Communist and Capitalist Nations in Europe, 1985; Soviet Foreign Trade Policies in the 1980s, 1986; (with K. Pavitt) The Comparative Economics of Research Development and Innovation in East and West: A Survey, 1987; Western Economic Statecraft in East-West Relations: Embargoes, Sanctions, Linkage, Economic Warfare, 1988; Some Schools of Thought in the Soviet Debate on Economic Reform, 1989; The Baltic States: The Economic and Political Consequences of the Secession of Estonia, Latvia and Lithuania from the USSR, 1990; From Stagnation to Catastroika: Commentaries on the Soviet Economy, 1983-1991, 1992; The Rise and Fall of the Soviet Economy: An Economic History of the USSR from 1945, 2003. EDITOR: (with K. Dawisha) Soviet-East European Dilemmas: Coercion, Competition and Consent, 1981; (with M. Kirkwood) Alexander Zinoviev as Writer and Thinker: An Assessment, 1988; (with J. Gibson) Transformation from Below: Local Power and the Political Economy of Post-Communist Transitions, 1996; (with M.J. Bradshaw) Regional Economic Change in Russia, 2000. Contributor to journals. **Address:** The Royal Institute of International Affairs, Chatham House, 10 St. James's Sq., London, GL SW1Y 4LE, England. **Online address:** p.hanson@bham.ac.uk

HANSON, Sue. *See* **HANSON, Susan F.**

HANSON, Susan F. (Sue Hanson). American (born United States), b. 1955. **Genres:** How-to Books, History. **Career:** Delco Electronics, programmer, 1978-80; Compunet, programmer, 1981-83; McDonnell Douglas, training specialist, 1984-87; Fullerton College, instructor, 1986; Cerritos College, instructor, 1987; Parkland College, instructor, 1991, 1997, 1999; U.S. Army Corps of Engineers, Construction Engineering Research Laboratory, geographic information specialist, 1991-94; Happy Viking Crafts, co-owner, 1998-. Writer. **Publications:** (As Sue Hanson) All about Mancala: Its History and How to Play, 2003; All about Classic Board Games, forthcoming. **Address:** Happy Viking Crafts, PO Box 35, Mahomet, IL 61853, U.S.A. **Online address:** happyviking@prairienet.org

HAN SUYIN. Swiss/Chinese (born China), b. 1917. **Genres:** Novels, International Relations/Current Affairs, Travel/Exploration, Autobiography/Memoirs, Romance/Historical. **Career:** Beijing Hospital, typist, 1931; medical practitioner, 1948-63; Nanyang University, lecturer in contemporary Asian literature, language and psychology; writer, 1963-; American Christian mission hospital, staff. Consultant. **Publications:** Destination Chungking, 1942, rev. ed., 1953; A Many-Splendoured Thing, 1952; From One China to the Other, 1956; And the Rain My Drink, 1956; The Mountain Is Young, 1958; Cast But One Shadow, 1962; Two Loves, 1962; Winter Love, 1963, new ed. 1994; Four Faces, 1964; The Crippled Tree, Biography, History, Autobiography, 1965; A Mortal Flower, China: Autobiography, History, 1966; China in the Year 2001, 1967; Birdless Summer, China, Autobiography, History, 1968; Asia Today; Two Outlooks, 1969; Kai Tsao Chung-kuo Ta Ti Ti Tou Cheng, 1970; Êrh Ling Ling i Nien Ti Chung-Kuo, 1970; The Morning Deluge: Mao

Tse Tung and the Chinese Revolution, 1893-1954, 1972; Zao Chen De Hong Liu/The morning Deluge, 1974; Wind in the Tower: Moa Tsetung and the Chinese Revolution, 1949-75, 1975; Lhasa, étoile-fleur, 1976; Lhasa, the Open City: A Journey to Tibet, 1977; Hsi-tsang Chi Hsing/Tibets Bigleap, 1976; La Peinture Chinoise, 1977; Huai Nian Mao Zedong, 1977; La Chine au Mille Visages, 1978; Les 100 Fleurs, 1978; La Peinture Chinoise, 1978; 1900-1938: La Chine Aux Mille Visages, 1979; China 1890-1938, 1979; Chine: Terre, Eau et Hommes, 1980; My House Has Two Doors, 1981; Phoenix Harvest, 1981; Till Morning Comes: A Novel, 1982; Diao Xie Di Hua Duo: Han Suyin Zi Zhuan, 1982; Shang Can Di Shu: Wo Di Fu Mu He Tong Nian: Han Suyin Zi Zhuan, 1983; The Enchantress, 1985; A Share of Loving, 1987; Han Suyin's China, 1988; Fleur de Soleil, 1988; Tigers and Butterflies, 1990; Les Yeux de Demain, 1992; Wind In My Sleeve, 1992; (co-author) Le Sel de la semaine, 1994; Eldest Son: Zhou Enlai and the Making of Modern China, 1989-76, 1994; (with S. Dali and M.A. Yi) Ming Tian di Yan Jing, 2000; Can Feng Yin Lu, 2005. Contributor to books and periodicals. **Address:** 37 Montoie, Lausanne, 1007, Switzerland.

HANTOVER, Jeffrey Philip. American (born United States) **Genres:** Novels. **Career:** Vanderbilt University, faculty; National Social Service Agency, director; Gap Inc., staff. Writer. **Publications:** Boston, 2008; The Jewel Trader of Pegu (novel), 2008. Contributor to books. **Address:** Marly Rusoff & Associates Inc., PO Box 524, Bronxville, NY 10708, U.S.A. **Online address:** jhantover@gmail.com

HANZO, L(ajos). Hungarian (born Hungary), b. 1952. **Genres:** Technology. **Career:** Telecommunications Research Institute, staff member, 1976-87; University of Southampton, School of Electronics and Computer Science, faculty, 1986-, professor of communications, chair in telecommunications, Communications Research Group, head; Tsinghua University, chaired professor; IEEE Press, editor-in-chief. Writer. **Publications:** (With W. Webb) Modern Quadrature Amplitude Modulation, 1994; (with R. Steele) Mobile Radio Communications: Second and Third Generation Cellular and WATM Systems, 2nd ed., 1999; (with W. Webb and T. Keller) Single-and Multi-Carrier Quadrature Amplitude Modulation: Principles and Applications for Personal Communications, WLANs and Broadcasting, 2000; (with P. Cherriman and J. Streit) Wireless Video Communications: Second to Third Generation Systems and Beyond, 2001; (with F. Clare, A. Somerville and J.P. Woodward) Voice Compression and Communications: Principles and Applications for Fixed and Wireless Channels, 2001; (with T.H. Liew and B.L. Yeap) Turbo Coding, Turbo Equalisation and Space-Time Boding for Transmission over Fading Channels, 2002; (with C.H. Wong and M.S. Yee) Adaptive Wireless Transceivers: Turbo-Coded, Turbo-Equalised and Space-Time Coded CDMA, TDMA and OFDM Systems, 2002; (with J.S. Blogh) Third-Generation Systems and Intelligent Wireless Networking: Smart Antennas and Adaptive Modulation, 2002. (with M. Mandunster, B.J. Choi and T. Keller) OFDM and MC-CDMA for Broadband Multi-user Communications, WLANs and Broadcasting, 2003; (co-author) Single and Multi-Carrier DS-CDMA: Multi-User Detection, Space-Time Spreading, Synchronisation, Networking and Standards, 2003; (co-author) Quadrature Amplitude Modulation: From Basics to Adaptive Trellis-Coded, Turbo-Equalised and Space-Time Coded OFDM, CDMA and MC-CDMA Systems, 2004; (co-author) Video Compression and Communications: From Basics to H.261, H.263, H.264, MPEG2, MPEG4 for DVB and HSDPA-style Adaptive Turbo-Transceivers, 2007; (with F.C. Somerville and J. Woodard) Voice and Audio Compression for Wireless Communications, 2007; (co-author) Near-Capacity Multi Functional MIMO Systems: Sphere-Packing, Iterative Detection and Cooperation, 2009; (co-author) Near-capacity Variable Length Coding: Regular and Exit-chart Aided Irregular Designs, 2010; (A.M. Jiang and L. Wang) MIMO-OFDM for LTE, WIFI and WIMAX: Coherent Versus Non-coherent and Cooperative Turbo-transceivers, 2010; Turbo Coding, Turbo Equalisation and Space-Time Coding: Exit-Chart Aided Near-Capacity Designs for Wireless Channels, 2011. **Address:** School of Electronics & Computer Science, University of Southampton, Highfield, Southampton, SO17 1BJ, England. **Online address:** lh@ecs.soton.ac.uk

HAPKE, Laura. American (born United States), b. 1946. **Genres:** Literary Criticism And History, Women's Studies And Issues, History, Social Sciences. **Career:** Pace University, professor of English, 1990-. Writer. **Publications:** Conventions of Denial: Prostitution in Late Nineteenth-Century American Anti-vice Narrative, 1982; Girls Who Went Wrong: Prostitutes in American Fiction, 1885-1917, 1989; Tales of the Working Girl: Wage-earning Women in American Literature, 1890-1925, 1992; Daughters of the Great Depression: Women, Work and Fiction in the American 1930s, 1995; Labor's Text: The

Worker in American Fiction, 2001; Sweatshop: The History of an American Idea, 2004; Labor's Canvas: American Working-Class History and the WPA Art of the 1930s, 2008; (ed. with L.A. Kirby) A Class of Its Own: Re-Envisioning American Labor Fiction, 2008. Contributor to journals and periodicals. **Address:** Department of English, Pace University, Rm. 1522, 1 Pace Plz., New York, NY 10038-1598, U.S.A. **Online address:** lhapke@tiac.net

HAQQANI, Husain. American/Pakistani (born Pakistan), b. 1956. **Genres:** Theology/Religion, Young Adult Non-fiction, Military/Defense/Arms Control. **Career:** Arabia-The Islamic World Review, East Asian correspondent, 1980-84; Far Eastern Economic Review, Pakistan and Afghanistan correspondent, 1984-88; Voice of America, contributor, 1986-88; Chief Minister of Punjab, special assistant, 1988-90; Pakistan Prime Minister Ghulam Mustafa Jatoi, special assistant, 1990; Pakistan Prime Minister Nawaz Sharif, special assistant and principal spokesman, 1990-92; Pakistan ambassador to Sri Lanka, 1992-93; Pakistan Prime Minister Benazir Bhutto, spokesman, 1993-95; House Building Finance Corp., chair, 1995-96; Communications Research Strategies (consulting firm), founder, 1996-2002; Johns Hopkins University, School of Advanced International Studies, adjunct professor; Boston University, Center for International Relations, director, associate professor of international relations, professor of international relations; Hudson Institute's Project on the Future of the Muslim World, co-chair; Current Trends in Islamist Thought journal, editor; Pakistan ambassador to the United States; John Hopkins University, School of Advanced International Studies, professorial lecturer. Journalist, diplomat and educator. **Publications:** Ikkīsvīn Sadī Men Ulte Pãon, 1997; Pakistan: Between Mosque and Military, 2005. Contributor to books and periodicals. **Address:** Department of International Relations, Boston University, Rm. 110, 152 Bay State Rd., Boston, MA 02215, U.S.A. **Online address:** haqqani@bu.edu

HARADA, Masako. (Satoko Kizaki). Japanese/Chinese (born China), b. 1939. **Genres:** Novels, Novellas/Short Stories, Young Adult Fiction. **Career:** Writer. **Publications:** FICTION AS SATOKO KIZAKI: Rasoku, (title means: 'Barefoot'), 1982; Umi-to Rosoku (short stories), 1985; Aogiri (short stories), 1985; Shizumeru tera (novel), 1987, Nami-Half-way (short stories), 1988; Sanzoku-no-Haka, 1989; Kagami-no-Tani, 1990; Toki-no-Shizuku, 1991; Atonaki-Niwa-ni, 1991; Shiawase No Chiisana Tobira, 1994. Contributor to periodicals. **Address:** 473-1-411 Iwase, Matsudo-Shi, Chiba-Ken, 271, Japan.

HARAKAS, Exetastes. See HARAKAS, Stanley Samuel.

HARAKAS, Stanley Samuel. (Exetastes Harakas). American (born United States), b. 1932. **Genres:** Theology/Religion. **Career:** Greek Orthodox Archdiocese of America, ordained priest, 1956; Holy Cross Greek Orthodox Theological School, instructor, 1966-67; St. Vladimirs Theological Seminary, visiting professor, 1970-71; Hellenic College, dean, 1971-75; Holy Cross Orthodox School of Theology, assistant professor, associate professor, 1967-72, dean, 1970-80, professor, 1972-, Archbishop Iakovos professor of Orthodox theology, 1986-95, Archbishop Iakovos professor of Orthodox theology emeritus, 1995-; Boston University, visiting professor, 1975-76; Boston College, visiting professor, 1976-80; The Hellenic Chronicle, columnist, 1980-2000; John XIII Institute, visiting professor, 1982-83; Emmanuel College, visiting professor, 1986-87; University of Thessalonike, visiting professor, 1988; University of South Florida, Department of Religion, associate professor, 1997-98, 1998-99; National Herald, columnist, 1997-2004; Tampa's University of South Florida, Interdisciplinary Center for Hellenic Studies, honorary professor, 2000; Savior Greek Orthodox Church Atlanta, Georgia, priest, 2001; Savior Greek Orthodox Church-New parish, 2002. Writer. **Publications:** Guidelines for Marriage in the Orthodox Church, 1970; Living the Liturgy: A Practical Guide for Participating in the Divine Liturgy of the Eastern Orthodox Church, 1974; (trans.) George Stavropoulos, Partakers of Divine Nature, 1976; (as Exetastes Harakas) Contemporary Issues: Orthodox Christian Perspectives, 1976, rev. ed., 1982; Something Is Stirring in World Orthodoxy: An Introduction to the Forthcoming Great and Holy Council of the Orthodox Church (booklet), 1978; The Melody of Prayer: How to Personally Experience the Divine Liturgy (booklet), 1979; For the Health of Body and Soul (booklet), 1980; Contemporary Moral Issues Facing the Orthodox Christian, 1982; Let Mercy Abound: Social Concern in the Greek Orthodox Church, 1983; Toward Transfigured Life, 1983; The Orthodox Church: 455 Questions and Answers, 1987; Proclaiming God's Word Today: Preaching Concerns in the Greek Orthodox Archdiocese of North and South America, 1989; Health and Medicine in the Eastern Orthodox Tradition, 1990; Living

the Faith: The Praxis of Eastern Orthodox Ethics, 1992; Of Life and Salvation: Reflections on Living the Christian Life, 1996; Wholeness of Faith and Life: Orthodox Christian Ethics, 1999; Orthodox Christian Beliefs: Real Answers to Real Questions from Real People, 2002; Orthodox Christian Beliefs About the Bible: Real Answers to Real Questions From Real People, 2003. Contributor of articles. **Address:** Greek Orthodox Archdiocese of America, 8 E 79th St., New York, NY 10075, U.S.A. **Online address:** rharakas@aol.com

HARBERGER, Arnold C. American (born United States), b. 1924. **Genres:** Economics, History. **Career:** Cowles Commission for Research in Economics, research assistant, 1949-; Johns Hopkins University, assistant professor of political economy, 1949-53; International Monetary Fund, economist, 1950-, 1989-, 2002-03; University of Chicago, associate professor of economics, 1953-59, professor of economics, 1959-76, Gustavus F. and Ann M. Swift distinguished service professor in economics, 1977-91, Economics Department, chairman, 1964-71, 1975-80, Center for Latin American economic studies, director, 1965-91, Gustavus F. and Ann M. Swift distinguished service professor emeritus, 1991-; U.S. Department of Agriculture, consultant, 1955; MIT Center for International Studies (New Delhi), economist and visiting professor, 1961-62; U.S. Treasury Department, consultant, 1962-; Organization of American States, consultant, 1962-76; International Bank for Reconstruction and Development, consultant and lecturer, 1963-; U.S. Department of State, consultant, 1963-77, 1984-; International Bank for Reconstruction and Development, consultant, 1963-; The Ford Foundation, consultant, 1965-76; U.S. Department of Commerce, consultant, 1965; Inter-American Development Bank, consultant and lecturer, 1968-; U.S. Council of Economic Advisers, consultant, 1969-74; Asian Development Bank, consultant and lecturer, 1971-; Harvard University, visiting professor, 1971-72; International Labor Organization, consultant, 1971-72; Princeton University, visiting professor, 1973-74; Indonesian Ministry of Finance, consultant, 1974, 1981; Bolivian Ministry of Finance, consultant, 1976; Canadian Department of Regional Economic Expansion, consultant, 1975-78; U.S. Department of Labor, consultant, 1976; U.S. Postal Service, consultant, 1976-78; Caribbean Development Bank, consultant and lecturer, 1978; Canadian Department of Employment and Immigration, consultant, 1980-; Ministry of Finance-China, Central Institute of Finance and Banking, lecturer, 1983-; University of California, visiting professor, 1983-84, professor of economics, 1984-; University of Paris, visiting professor, 1986; Institute for the Economy in Transition (Moscow), visiting professor, 2003. Writer and consultant. **Publications:** (Contrib.) Demand for Durable Goods, 1960; Inflation Problem in Latin America, 1966; Project Evaluation, 1972; Taxation and Welfare, 1974; Capitalismo y Genocidio Economico: Carta Abierta a la Escuela de Economia de Chicago a Proposito De su Intervencion en Chile, 1976; Cuatro Momentos de laeconomia Chilena. Version de las Conferencias Ofrecidas, 1976; Institucionalidad Economica e Integracion Financiera con el Exterior: Cinco Trabajos y Comentarios Efectuados Bajo el Patrocinio del Institutode Estudios Bancarios Guillermo Subercaseaux y un Estudio sobre el Neo Proteccionismo y la Banca Privada, 1979; Estudios, 1979; Política Ecónomica y Crecimiento Económico, 1985; Modern Developments in Public Finance: Essays in Honor of Arnold Harberger, 1987; Growth, Industrialization and Economic Structure: Latin America and East Asia Compared; Reflections on Social Project Evaluation, 1988; The Economist and the Real World, 1989; Anatomy of Crises, 1997; Indonesian Crisis Revisited, 1998; Notes on the Indonesian Crisis, 1998; (co-author) Puti Ekonomicheskogo Rosta: Mezhdunarodnyi Opyt, 2001; On the Process of Growth and Economic Policy in Developing Countries, 2005. EDITOR: (with M.J. Bailey) Taxation of Income from Capital, 1969; World Economic Growth, 1984; (with G.P. Jenkins) Cost-Benefit Analysis, 2002. Contributor to books and journals. **Address:** University of California, 8273 Bunche Hall, PO Box 951477, Los Angeles, CA 90095-1477, U.S.A. **Online address:** harberger@econ.ucla.edu

HARBISON, Beth. (Elizabeth McShulskis Harbison). American (born United States), b. 1966. **Genres:** Novels. **Career:** Writer, novelist and chef. **Publications:** Shoe Addicts Anonymous, 2007; Secrets of a Shoe Addict, 2008; Hope in A Jar, 2009; Thin, Rich, Pretty, 2010; Always Something There to Remind Me, 2011; When in Doubt, Add Butter, 2011. AS ELIZABETH M. HARBISON: The Bread Machine Baker, 1995; (with M. McGowan) A Taste for Love: Romantic Meals for Two, 1996; Loaves of Fun: A History of Bread with Activities and Recipes from around the World, 1997; Four Seasons with the Bread Machine Baker, 2001; AS ELIZABETH HARBISON: A Groom for Maggie, 1997; Wife without a Past, 1997; Two Brothers and a Bride, 1998; True Love Ranch, 1998; Afterglow, 1999; Emma and the Earl, 1999; Plain Jane Marries the Boss, 1999; Annie and the Prince, 1999; His Secret Heir,

2001; A Pregnant Proposal, 2001; Mission Creek Mother-to- Be, 2002; Drive Me Wild, 2002; Midnight Cravings, 2003; Princess Takes a Holiday, 2003; The Secret Princess, 2004, Taming of the Two, 2005; Diary of a Domestic Goddess, 2005; How to Get Your Man, 2005; If the Slipper Fits, 2006; A Dash of Romance, 2006; Falling for the Boss, 2006. **Address:** Jane Rotrosen Agency, 318 E 51st St., New York, NY 10022, U.S.A. **Online address:** mail@bethharbison.com

HARBISON, Elizabeth McShulskis. *See* **HARBISON, Beth.**

HARBURG, Ernie. American (born United States), b. 1926. **Genres:** Songs/Lyrics And Libretti, Film, Theatre. **Career:** Council for Rural Welfare, Rural Welfare Department, research assistant, 1953; Wisconsin State Department of Public Welfare, research assistant, 1954-57; University of Michigan, Institute for Social Research, study director, 1957-64, associate professor of nursing, 1964-70, research scientist in psychology, 1965-82, research scientist in epidemiology, 1973-82, senior research scientist emeritus in psychology and epidemiology, 1973-, Program for Urban Health Research, director, 1964-; Del Rio Bar Inc., president, 1970-2004; Harburg Foundation, president, 1981-, co-owner; New York University, adjunct professor of psychology, 1982-; The Yip Harburg Foundation, president, 1982-; The Musical Theater Foundation, director, 1983-. Writer. **Publications:** (With S.J. Cardinal) Survey of the Dental Care and Needs of Patients in the Wisconsin State and County Mental Hospitals, 1955-1957, 1958; (as Ernie Harburg with H. Meyerson) Who Put the Rainbow in The Wizard of Oz? Yip Harburg, Lyricist, 1993; (with B. Rosenberg) The Broadway Musical: Collaboration in Commerce and Art, 1993; (co-author) Liberty, Equality, Consensus and All that Jazz at the Del Rio Bar, 2009. Contributor to journals. **Address:** The Harburg Foundation, Rm. 813, 225 Lafayette St., New York, NY 10012, U.S.A.

HARCLERODE, Peter. British (born England), b. 1947?. **Genres:** Military/Defense/Arms Control, History, Art/Art History. **Career:** Writer. **Publications:** The Elite and Their Support, 1987; Go to It!: The Illustrated History of the 6th Airborne Division, 1990; Para!: Fifty Years of the Parachute Regiment, 1992; Arnhem: A Tragedy of Errors, 1994; (with B. Pittaway) The Lost Masters: The Looting of Europe's Treasurehouses, 1999; (with B. Pittaway) Lost Masters: World War II and The Looting of Europe's Treasurehouses, 2000; Equinox: Warfare, 2000; Secret Soldiers: Special Forces in the War Against Terrorism, 2000; Fighting Dirty: The Inside Story of Covert Operations from Ho Chi Minh to Osama bin Laden, 2001; (with D. Reynolds) Commando: The Illustrated History of Britain's Green Berets from Dieppe to Afghanistan, 2003; Wings of War: Airborne Warfare 1918-1945, 2005; Fighting Brigadier: The Life of Brigadier James Hill DSO** MC, 2010. **Address:** Peters Fraser & Dunlop, 34-43 Russell St., Drury House, London, GL WC2B 5HA, England. **Online address:** sirmoori@globalnet.co.uk

HARCOURT, Geoffrey Colin. Australian (born Australia), b. 1931. **Genres:** Economics. **Career:** University of Adelaide, lecturer to professor, 1958-67, senior lecturer, 1962-65, reader in economics, 1965-97, professor of economics, 1967-85, Caretaker chairman, 1979-, chair, 1982, professor emeritus of economics, 1988-; University of Cambridge, university lecturer in economics and politics, 1964-66, 1982-90, Trinity Hall, fellow, 1964-66, reader in the history of economic theory, 1990-98, emeritus reader in the history of economic theory, 1998-; Australian Economic Papers, joint editor, 1967-85; Cambridge Journal of Economics, associate editor, 1976-82, joint editor, 1983-; Journal of Post Keynesian Economics, academic board, 1978-; Manchester School of Economic and Social Studies, correspondent editor, 1982-96; Jesus College, lecturer in economics, fellow, 1982-98, president, 1988-92, emeritus fellow, 1998-; University of Toronto, visiting professor, 1997, 1980; University of New South Wales, honorary professor, 1997, 1999, visiting professorial fellow, 2008-; University of Melbourne, Sugden fellow, 2002. **Publications:** (With P.H. Karmel and R.H. Wallace) Economic Activity, 1967; Some Cambridge Controversies in the Theory of Capital, 1972; Theoretical Controversy and Social Significance: An Evaluation of the Cambridge Controversies, 1982; The Social Science Imperialists, 1982; Controversies in Political Economy, 1986; On Political Economists and Modern Political Economy, 1992; Post-Keynesian Essays in Biography, 1993; Capitalism, Socialism and Post-Keynesianism (essays), 1995; (contrib.) Capital Controversy, 1997; (contrib.) Markets, Unemployment, and Economic Policy, 1997; (contrib.) Keynes, Post-Keynesianism and Political Economy, 1999; 50 Years a Keynesian and Other Essays, 2001; Selected Essays on Economic Policy, 2001; Structure of Post-Keynesian Economics: The Core Contributions of the Pioneers, 2006; On Skidelsky's Keynes and Other Essays, 2011; The Making

of a Post-Keynesian Economist, 2012. EDITOR: (with R.H. Parker) Readings in the Concept and Measurement of Income, 1969, 2nd ed., 1986; (with N.F. Laing) Capital and Growth: Selected Readings, 1971; Keynes and His Contemporaries, 1985; (with J.S. Cohen) International Monetary Problems and Supply-Side Economics: Essays in Honour of Lorie Tarshis, 1986; (with M. Baranzini) The Dynamics of the Wealth of Nations: Growth, Distribution and Structural Change: Essays in Honour of Luigi Pasinetti, 1993; (with A. Roncaglia and R. Rowley) Income and Employment in Theory and Practice, 1995; (with P.A. Riach) A Second Edition of the General Theory, 1997; L' Economie Rebelle de Joan Robinson, 2001; (with H. Lim and U.K. Park) Editing Economics: Essays in Honour of Mark Perlman, 2002; (with P. Kerr) Joan Robinson: Critical Assessments of Leading Economists, 5 vols., 2002; (with C. Bliss and A.J. Cohen) Capital Theory, 2005; Joan Robinson, 2009. **Address:** Jesus College, University of Cambridge, Jesus Ln., Cambridge, CB5 8BL, England. **Online address:** fellows-secretary@jesus.cam.ac.uk

HARD, Charlotte (Ann). British (born England), b. 1969. **Genres:** Children's Fiction, Sports/Fitness. **Career:** Children's book illustrator, 1990-. Writer. **Publications:** SELF-ILLUSTRATED: One Green Island, 1995 in UK as One Green Island: An Animal Counting Gamebook, 1996. Contributor to periodicals. Illustrator of books by others. **Address:** 54 Chapel Ln., Headingley, Leeds, LS6 3BW, England.

HARDCASTLE, Bob. American (born United States), b. 1940. **Genres:** Novels, Money/Finance, Business/Trade/Industry. **Career:** Baltimore Orioles Baseball Team, professional baseball player; Southern Illinois University, teacher and coach; financial planner, 1964-; Delta Investment Services Inc., president and chief executive officer. Writer. **Publications:** (Ed.) Gilbert and Sullivan's London, 1988; Hardcastle's Money Talk, 1994; (with R.A. Esperti and R.L. Peterson) Wealth Enhancement & Preservation: Practical Answers from America's Experts, 1996; (contrib.) 21st Century Wealth: Essential Financial Planning Principles, 2000; (with A. Vlamis) Money Minutes: How to Grow and Manage Your Money One Easy Idea at a Time, 2008. Contributor to magazines. **Address:** Delta Investment Services Inc., 16100 Chesterfield Pkw. W, Ste. 150, Chesterfield, MO 63017, U.S.A. **Online address:** delta@moneytalk.org

HARDCASTLE, Michael. (David Clark). British (born England), b. 1933. **Genres:** Children's Fiction, Children's Non-fiction, Horror. **Career:** Newspaper reporter, 1956-59; Bristol Evening Post, literary editor, 1959-65; Liverpool Daily Post, chief feature writer, 1965-67; freelance writer, 1967-. **Publications:** Soccer Is Also a Game, 1966; Shoot on Sight, 1967; Redcap, 1967; Aim for the Flag, 1967; The Chasing Game, 1968; Goal, 1969; Dive to Danger, 1969; Shilling a Mile, 1969; Stop that Car!, 1970; Reds and Blues, 1970; Strike, 1970; Smashing, 1970; Don't Tell Me What To Do, 1970; The Hidden Enemy, 1970; Come and Get Me, 1971; Live in the Sky, 1971; Shelter, 1971; A Load of Trouble, 1971; Blood Money, 1971; It Wasn't Me, 1971; In the Net, 1971; Playing Ball, 1972; Goals in the Air, 1972; Island Magic, 1973; United!, 1973; Away from Home, 1974; Free Kick, 1974; The Demon Bowler, 1974; The Big One, 1974; The Chase, 1974; On the Run, 1974; Heading for Goal, 1974; Last Across, 1974; The Match, 1974; Dead of Night, 1974; Road Race, 1974; A Hard Man, 1974; Catch, 1974; Day in the Country, 1974; The Long Drop, 1974; Flare Up, 1975; Get Lost, 1975; Life Underground, 1975; Money for Sale, 1975; Where the Action Is, 1976; The First Goal, 1976; Breakaway, 1976; Go and Find Him, 1977; River of Danger, 1977; The Great Bed Race, 1977; Night Raid, 1977; On the Ball, 1977; Shooting Star, 1977; The Saturday Horse, 1977; Strong Arm, 1977; Fire on the Sea, 1977; Holiday House, 1977; Crash Car, 1977; Goal in Europe, 1978; Soccer Special, 1978; Top of the League, 1979; Top Soccer, 1979; The Switch Horse, 1980; Top Fishing, 1980; Go for Goal, 1980; Racing Bike, 1980; Snake Run, 1980; Hot Wheels, 1980; Half a Team, 1980; Behind the Goal, 1980; Kick Off, 1980; Top Speed, 1980; Gigantic Hit, 1982; Roar to Victory, 1982; Attack!, 1982; Fast from the Gate, 1983; Caught Out, 1983; The Team That Wouldn't Give In, 1984; Hooked!, 1984; Tiger of the Track, 1985; Double Holiday, 1985; Winning Rider, 1985; One Kick, 1986; James and the TV Star, 1986; No Defence, 1986; The Shooters, 1986; Snookered!, 1987; Quake, 1987; Mascot, 1987; The Rival Games, 1988; The Magic Party, 1988; The Green Machine, 1989; Kickback, 1989; Splashdown, 1989; Jump In, 1989; Lucky Break, 1990; Joanna's Goal, 1990; Mark England's Cap, 1990; Walking the Goldfish, 1990; Penalty, 1990; Second Chance, 1991; Soccer Star, 1991; James and the House of Fun, 1991; The Away Team, 1992; Own Goal; 1992; Dog Bites Goalie and Other Soccer Stories, 1993; Shooting Boots, 1993; Soccer Star, 1993; One Good Horse; 1994; You Won't Catch Me, 1994; Soccer Captain, 1994;

Puzzle, 1995; Winning Goal, 1995; Please Come Home, 1995; Puzzle, 1995; The Fastest Bowler in the World, 1996; Matthew's Goals, 1997; Hit it!, 2006; Archie's Amazing Game, 2006; My Brother's a Keeper, 2007; Sam's Goal, 2007. AS DAVID CLARK: Goalie, 1972; Splash, 1972; Run, 1973; Top Spin, 1973; Grab, 1974; Winner, 1974; Volley, 1975; Roll Up, 1975. Contributor to periodicals. **Address:** 17 Molescroft Pk., Beverley, NY HU17 7EB, England.

HARDEN, Blaine. (Blaine Charles Harden). American (born United States), b. 1952. **Genres:** Environmental Sciences/Ecology, Geography, History. **Career:** Trenton Times, reporter, 1976-78; Washington Post, reporter, 1978-83, foreign correspondent and bureau chief, 1984-89, foreign correspondent, 1986-93, bureau chief of Eastern Europe, 1989-93, investigative reporter, 1995-96, political reporter, 1996-97, bureau chief, 1997-98, Tokyo bureau chief; Washingtonian, senior writer, 1983-84; New York Times, metro desk, reporter, 1999-2000, writer, 1999-, national correspondent, 2001-. **Publications:** Africa: Dispatches from a Fragile Continent, 1990; A River Lost: The Life and Death of the Columbia, 1996. **Address:** c/o Raphael Sagalyn, Sagalyn Literary Agency, 7201 Wisconsin Ave., Ste. 675, Bethesda, MD 20814, U.S.A.

HARDEN, Blaine Charles. *See* HARDEN, Blaine.

HARDER, Leland. American (born United States), b. 1926. **Genres:** Theology/Religion, Social Sciences. **Career:** Mennonite Church, pastor, 1952-57; Mennonite Biblical Seminary, professor, 1958-83; Great Plains Seminary Education Program, director, 1983-86; Church Member Profile Research Project, associate director, 1988-92; A Family History, publisher. Writer. **Publications:** Steinbach and its Churches., 1970; (with J.H. Kouffman) Anabaptists Four Centuries Later: A Profile of Five Mennonite and Brethren in Christ denominations, 1975; The Pastor-People Partnership: The Call and Recall of Pastors from a Believer's Church Perspective, 1983; (ed.) Perspectives on the Nurturing of Faith, 1983; (ed.) The Sources of Swiss Anabaptism, 1985; (ed. with L. Driedger) Anabaptist-Mennonite Identities in Ferment, 1990; Doors to Lock and Doors to Open: The Discerning People of God, 1993; (with S.W. Harder) The Blumstein Legacy: A Six Generation Family Saga, 1998. **Address:** PO Box 363, North Newton, KS 67117, U.S.A. **Online address:** ldharder@southwind.net

HARDER, Robert O. American (born United States), b. 1945. **Genres:** History. **Career:** Target Stores Inc., manager; Montgomery Ward & Co., vice president; full-time writer, 2004-. **Publications:** Flying from the Black Hole: The B-52 Bombardiers of Vietnam, 2009. **Address:** Chicago, IL, U.S.A. **Online address:** rnd.harder@att.net

HARDESTY, Larry (Lynn). American (born United States), b. 1947. **Genres:** Education, Librarianship, Bibliography, Language/Linguistics, Art/Art History. **Career:** Roman Catholic high school, teacher, 1969-70; Kearney State College, assistant reference librarian and instructor in educational media, 1973-74, user services coordinator, 1974-75, Library Learning Program, director, 1975; DePauw University, instructor, 1975-79, head of library reference department, 1975-83, project librarian, 1976-77, project director, 1977-82, assistant professor, 1979-83; Eckerd College, associate professor, 1983-91, director of library services, 1983-95, professor of library services, 1991-95; Austin College, professor and college librarian, 1995-2004; University of Nebraska, dean of the library, 2004-06; Winona State University, interim university librarian, 2006-. Writer. **Publications:** The Use of Slide-Tape Presentations in Academic Libraries, 1978; Faculty and the Library: The Undergraduate Experience, 1991. EDITOR: (with J. Hastreiter and D. Henderson) Bibliographic Instruction in Practice: A Tribute to the Legacy of Evan Ira Farber, 1993; Books Bytes and Bridges: Libraries and Computer Centers in Academic Institutions, 2000; The Role of the Library in the First College Year, 2007. COMPILER: (with J. Hastreiter and D. Henderson) Mission Statements for College Libraries, 1985, 2nd ed., 1999; (with J.M. Tucker and J. Schmitt) User Instruction in Academic Libraries: A Century of Selected Readings, 1986; (with J. Hastreiter and D. Henderson) Periodicals in College Libraries, 1987. Contributor of articles to journals and books. **Address:** Krueger Library, Winona State University, PO Box 5838, Winona, MN 55987-5838, U.S.A. **Online address:** lhardesty@winona.edu

HARDESTY, Sarah. *See* ROBERTS, Nora.

HARDIE, Sean. Irish/British (born England), b. 1947. **Genres:** Novels, Plays/Screenplays. **Career:** British Broadcasting Corp-TV, senior film pro-

ducer for current affairs, 1969-79, senior producer for entertainment, 1979-81, head of entertainment, 1981-85; full-time writer, 1985-. Radio and television broadcaster and producer. **Publications:** NOVELS: (with J. Lloyd) Prince Harry's First Quiz Book, 1985; The Last Supper, 1990; Right Connections, 1991; Table for Five, 1991; Till the Fat Lady Sings, 1993. Contributor to periodicals. **Address:** Toby Eady Associates Ltd., 9 Orme Ct., 3rd Fl., London, GL W2 4RL, England. **Online address:** seanhardie@gmail.com

HARDIN, John A. American (born United States), b. 1948. **Genres:** History. **Career:** University of Louisville, Department of History, lecturer, 1972-79, faculty, 1984; Kentucky State University, instructor, 1972-74, 1976-78, assistant professor of history, 1976-84, Department of History and Political Science, assistant professor and area coordinator, 1978-80, Division of Behavioral and Social Sciences, assistant professor, 1980-84; University of Kentucky, Department of History, visiting assistant professor, 1980-81; Eastern Washington University, Black Education Program, assistant professor, 1984-90, associate professor, 1990-91; Western Kentucky University, associate professor of history, 1991-2009, professor of history, 2009-, Potter College of Arts, Humanities and Social Sciences, assistant dean, 1997-2002, assistant to provost, 2002-05. Writer. **Publications:** Onward and Upward: A Centennial History of Kentucky State University, 1886-1986, 1987; Fifty Years of Segregation: Black Higher Education in Kentucky, 1904-1954, 1997; (co-ed.) Community Memories: A Glimpse of African American Life in Frankfort, Kentucky, 2003; A Commemoration of WKU's Integration/1956-2006, 2006. Contributor of articles to books and periodicals. **Address:** Department of History, Western Kentucky University, 223A Cherry Hall, 1906 College Heights Blvd., Ste. 21086, Bowling Green, KY 42101-1086, U.S.A. **Online address:** john.hardin@wku.edu

HARDIN, Russell. American (born United States), b. 1940?. **Genres:** Adult Non-fiction, History. **Career:** Columbia University, Research Institute on Communist Affairs, junior fellow, 1971-72; University of Pennsylvania, assistant professor of political science and public policy analysis, 1972-76; Stanford University, Hoover Institution, national fellow, 1975-76, visiting professor, 1999-2000, professor of political science, 2001-03; University of Maryland, associate professor of government and politics, 1976-81; University of Chicago, visiting associate professor, 1979-81, associate professor, 1981-83, professor of political science, philosophy, and public policy, 1983-92, Mellon Foundation professor, 1987-92, professor of political science and philosophy, 1992-93; Australian National University, Research School of the Social Sciences, visiting fellow, 1987, 1990; Northwestern University School of Law, Jack N. Pritzker distinguished visiting professor, 1990; New York University, professor of politics, 1993-, chair, 1993-98, Helen Gould Shepard professor in the social sciences; Center for Advanced Study in Behavioral Sciences, fellow, 1996-97. Writer. **Publications:** (Ed. with B. Barry) Rational Man and Irrational Society? An Introduction and Sourcebook, 1982; Collective Action, 1982; (co-ed.) Nuclear Deterrence: Ethics and Strategy, 1985; Morality within the Limits of Reason, 1988; One for All: The Logic of Group Conflict, 1995; (ed. with I. Shapiro) Political Order, 1996; Liberalism, Constitutionalism, and Democracy, 1999; Trust and Trustworthiness, 2002; Indeterminacy and Society, 2003; (ed.) Distrust, 2004; (with K.S. Cook and M. Levi) Cooperation without Trust?, 2005; David Hume: Moral and Political Theorist, 2007; Dmitri Esterhaats: A Novel, 2007; (with I. Creppell and S. Macedo) Toleration on Trial, 2008; How do You know?: The Economics of Ordinary Knowledge, 2009; (ed. with K.S. Cook and M. Levi) Whom can We Trust?: How Groups, Networks, and Institutions Make Trust Possible, 2009. Contributor to journals and periodicals. **Address:** Department of Politics, New York University, 726 Broadway, New York, NY 10003-9580, U.S.A. **Online address:** russell.hardin@nyu.edu

HARDING, James. British (born England), b. 1969. **Genres:** Business/Trade/Industry, Economics, Politics/Government, History. **Career:** European Commission, Japan Unit, speechwriter, 1993-94; Financial Times, reporter, 1994-, correspondent, 1996-99, Shanghai bureau chief, 1996-2003, media editor, 1999-2002, Washington bureau chief, 2002-06; The Times, business editor, 2006-07, editor, 2007-. **Publications:** Alpha Dogs: The Americans Who Turned Political Spin into a Global Business, 2008. **Address:** The Times, 1 Virginia St., London, GL E98 1RL, England. **Online address:** james.harding@thetimes.co.uk

HARDING, Les. Canadian (born Canada), b. 1950. **Genres:** Children's Non-fiction, History, Local History/Rural Topics, Young Adult Non-fiction, Theology/Religion, Adult Non-fiction, Trivia/Facts, Transportation, Transportation. **Career:** Statistics Canada, reference librarian, 1977-78; Transport Canada, librarian, 1980-82; Waterloo Regional Library, indexer, 1983-84; University of Waterloo, reference librarian, 1985-90, Government of Newfoundland, reference librarian, 1991-92; writer, 1993-. **Publications:** The Voyages of Lesser Men: Thumbnail Sketches in Canadian Exploration, 1991, rev. ed., 1999; Historic St. John's: City of Legends, 1992; A Book in Hand is Worth Two in the Library, 1994; Journeys of Remarkable Women: Their Travels on the Canadian Frontier, 1994; (with G. Brannon) Carto-Quotes: An Inspirational Companion for the Map-Maker and the Map-User, 1996; Dead Countries of the 19th and 20th Centuries: Aden to Zululand, 1998; Exploring the Avalon, 1998; McCurdy and the Silver Dart, 1998; Elephant Story: Jumbo and P.T. Barnum Under the Big Top, 1999; Damn the Mosquitoes! More Travellers on the Canadian Frontier, 2001; Holy Bingo, the Lingo of Eden, Jumpin' Jehosophat, and the Land of Nod: A Dictionary of the Names, Expressions, and Folklore of Christianity, 2006; The Newfoundland Railway 1898-1969: A History, 2008; They Knew Marilyn Monroe: Famous Persons in the Life of the Hollywood Icon, 2012. Contributor to journals. **Address:** 18 Guzzwell Dr., St. John's, NL A1A 3X1, Canada. **Online address:** leslie_l_harding@yahoo.com

HARDING, Paul. *See* **DOHERTY, P(aul) C.**

HARDING, Paul. American (born United States), b. 1967. **Genres:** Novels. **Career:** University of Iowa, instructor; Harvard University, instructor. Writer. **Publications:** Tinkers, 2009. **Address:** Bellevue Literary Press, 550 1st Ave., New York, NY 10016, U.S.A. **Online address:** pharding@fas.harvard.edu

HARDING, Robyn. Canadian (born Canada), b. 1969?. **Genres:** Novels, Young Adult Fiction. **Career:** Advertising executive and writer. **Publications:** The Journal of Mortifying Moments, 2004; The Secret Desires of a Soccer Mom, 2006; Secrets and Wives, 2006; Unravelled, 2007; My Parents are Sex Maniacs, 2009; Mom, Will This Chicken Give Me Man Boobs?, 2009; Chronicles of a Midnight Crisis, 2010; Girl's Night Out, forthcoming. Contributor to periodicals. **Address:** c/o Author Mail, Ballantine Books, 1745 Broadway, New York, NY 10019, U.S.A. **Online address:** info@robynharding.com

HARDING, Stephan. British/Venezuelan (born Venezuela), b. 1953?. **Genres:** Sciences. **Career:** National University, visiting professor in wildlife management; Schumacher College, co-founder, 1990-, Master's of Science Degree in Holistic Science, coordinator, resident ecologist and tutor, 1991-; University of Oslo, Arne Naess chair in social justice and the environment, 2007; Gaia Coach Institute, faculty; Smithsonian Institute, ecologist; University of Oxford, Animal Ecology Research Group, ecologist. Writer. **Publications:** Animate Earth: Science, Intuition and Gaia, 2006. **Address:** Schumacher College, The Old Postern, Dartington, Totnes, DN TQ9 6EA, England. **Online address:** stephan@schumachercollege.org.uk

HARDT, Michael. Swiss/American (born United States), b. 1960. **Genres:** History, Politics/Government, Philosophy, Military/Defense/Arms Control. **Career:** University of Southern California, instructor in Italian; Duke University, associate professor and director of graduate studies, 1994-, professor of literature and Italian, chair of literature; The European Graduate School, professor of political literature. Writer. **Publications:** A Stranger and Afraid, 1943; Papsttum und Okumene: Ansätze eines Neuverständnisses für einen Papstprimat in der protestantischen Theologie des 20. Jahrhunderts, 1981; Savage Anomaly, 1991; Gilles Deleuze: An Apprenticeship in Philosophy, 1993; Labor of Dionysus: A Critique of the State-Form, 1994; Radical Thought in Italy: A Potential Politics, 1996; (with A. Negri) Empire, 2000; (ed. with K. Weeks) The Jameson Reader, 2000; (contrib.) Guide: Cinque Lezioni Su Lmpero e Dintorni, 2003; (with A. Negri) Multitude: War and Democracy in the Age of Empire, 2004; (contrib.) Reflections on Empire, 2008; (foreword) Labor of Job: the Biblical Text as a Parable of Human Labor, 2009; (with A. Negri) Commonwealth, 2009. Contributor to journals and periodicals. **Address:** European Graduate School, Media & Communications Division, Alter Kehr 20, Leuk-Stadt, CH-3953, Switzerland. **Online address:** hardt@duke.edu

HARDWICK, Phil. American (born United States), b. 1966. **Genres:** Mystery/Crime/Suspense, Novels, How-to Books, Biography. **Career:** Mississippi Valley Gas Co., vice president of community and economic development; Mississippi State University, John C. Stennis Institute of Government, coordinator of capacity development, 2003-; The Hardwick Company L.L.C., presi-

dent. Writer. **Publications:** MISSISSIPPI MYSTERIES SERIES: Two Hours of Real Estate: One Minute at a Time, 1993; Found in Flora, 1997; Captured in Canton, 1997; Justice in Jackson, 1997; Newcomer in New Albany, 1997; Vengeance in Vicksburg, 1998; Collision in Columbia, 1998; Conspiracy in Corinth, 1999; Captured in Canton, 1999; Cover-up in Columbus, 2001; Sixth Inning in Southaven, 2002; Letters from Lexington, 2007. **Address:** The Hardwick Company L.L.C., PO Box 23631, Jackson, MS 39225, U.S.A. **Online address:** phil@philhardwick.com

HARDY, Antoinette. *See* **STOCKENBERG, Antoinette.**

HARDY, Barbara (Gladys). (Barbara (Nathan) Hardy). British (born England), b. 1924. **Genres:** Literary Criticism And History, Autobiography/Memoirs, Novels, Poetry, Essays, History. **Career:** University of London, Royal Holloway College, professor, 1965-70, honorary fellow, Birkbeck College, Department of English and Humanities, professor of English, 1970-89, professor emeritus, 1989-, honorary fellow; University College of Swansea, honorary professor of English; University of Wales, honorary fellow. Writer. **Publications:** The Novels of George Eliot: A Study in Form, 1959; Twelfth Night, 1964; Wuthering Heights, 1964; The Appropriate Form: An Essay on the Novel, 1964; Jane Eyre, 1965; Charles Dickens: The Later Novels, 1968; The Moral Art of Dickens: Essays, 1970; The Exposure of Luxury: Radical Themes in Thackeray, 1972; Tellers and Listeners: The Narrative Imagination, 1975; A Reading of Jane Austen, 1975; The Advantage of Lyric: Essays on Feeling in Poetry, 1977; Dramatic Quicklyisms: Malapropic Wordplay Technique in Shakespeare's Henriad, 1979; Particularities: Readings in George Eliot, 1982; Charles Dickens: The Writer and His Work, 1983; Forms of Feeling in Victorian Fiction, 1985; Collected Essays, vol. I, 1987; Shakespeare's Self-Conscious Art, 1989; Tennyson and the Novelists, 1993; Swansea Girl: A Memoir, 1994; London Lovers: A Novel, 1996; Henry James: The Later Writing, 1996; Shakespeare's Storytellers: Dramatic Narration, 1996; Thomas Hardy: Imaging Imagination, 2000; Dylan Thomas: An Original Language, 2000; Severn Bridge: Collected and New Poems, 2001; George Eliot: A Critic's Biography, 2006; Dickens and Creativity, 2008. EDITOR: Middlemarch: Critical Approaches to the Novel, 1967; (and intro.) Daniel Deronda, 1967; Critical Essays on George Eliot, 1970; The Trumpet Major, 1974; Laodicean, 1975; Not So Quiet, 1988. Contributor to periodicals. **Address:** Department of English & Humanities, Birkbeck College, University of London, 43-46 Gordon Sq., Malet St., Bloomsbury, London, GL WC1E 7HX, England.

HARDY, Barbara (Nathan). *See* **HARDY, Barbara (Gladys).**

HARDY, B. Carmon. (Blaine Carmon Hardy). American (born United States), b. 1934. **Genres:** History, Race Relations, Theology/Religion. **Career:** Brigham Young University, assistant professor of history, 1961-66; California State University, professor of history, 1966, now professor emeritus; University of Illinois, faculty. Writer. **Publications:** (Comp. and ed. with N.S. Hatch) Stalwarts South of the Border, 1985; Solemn Covenant: The Mormon Polygamous Passage, 1992; The World and the West: A Book of Readings, vol. I, 1994, vol. II, 1995; (ed.) Doing the Works of Abraham: Mormon Polygamy: Its Origin, Practice and Demise, 2007. **Address:** Department of History, California State University, 800 N State College Blvd., Fullerton, CA 92834, U.S.A. **Online address:** chardy@fullerton.edu

HARDY, Blaine Carmon. *See* **HARDY, B. Carmon.**

HARDY, Edward. American (born United States), b. 1957. **Genres:** Novels, Human Relations/Parenting, Children's Fiction. **Career:** Burlington Times Union, reporter and editor; Lawrence Eagle-Tribune, reporter and editor; Cornell University, faculty of creative writing; Boston College, faculty of creative writing; Brown University, Department of English, visiting lecturer. **Publications:** Geyser Life (novel), 1996; Keeper and Kid, 2008. Contributor to publications and books. **Address:** Department of English, Brown University, 70 Brown St., PO Box 1852, Providence, RI 02912, U.S.A. **Online address:** ehhardy@gmail.com

HARDY, Gayle J. American (born United States), b. 1942. **Genres:** Civil Liberties/Human Rights, Adult Non-fiction, Politics/Government, Women's Studies And Issues, Bibliography, Reference, Biography, Autobiography/Memoirs, Autobiography/Memoirs. **Career:** State University of New York, Lockwood Library, Circulation Department, head, 1974-85, senior assistant librarian, 1985-91, associate librarian-subject specialist for information and library studies, communication and communicative disorders, 1992-99. Writer. **Publications:** American Women Civil Rights Activists: Biobibliographies of 68 Leaders, 1825-1992, 1993; (with J.S. Robinson) Subject Guide to U.S. Government Reference Sources, 2nd ed., 1996. Contributor to books and periodicals. **Address:** 10805 Boyd Dr., Clarence, NY 14031-2203, U.S.A.

HARDY, John Philips. Australian (born Australia), b. 1933. **Genres:** Literary Criticism And History, Novellas/Short Stories, Humanities, Essays, Poetry, Human Relations/Parenting. **Career:** Magdalen College, junior research fellow, 1962-65; University of Toronto, University College, visiting assistant professor, 1965-66; University of New England, professor of English and head of department, 1966-72; Australian National University, professor of English, 1973-87, head of department, 1973-75; Bond University, foundation professor of humanities, 1988-93. Writer. **Publications:** Dictionary Johnson, 1967; Reinterpretations: Essays on Poems by Milton, Pope and Johnson, 1971; Samuel Johnson: A Critical Study, 1979; Jane Austen's Heroines: Intimacy in Human Relationships, 1984. EDITOR: (co-ed.) Johnson, Boswell and Their Circle: Essays Presented to Lawrence Fitzroy Powell, 1965; The Political Writings of Dr. Johnson: A Selection, 1968; (and intro.) The History of Rasselas, Prince of Abissinia, 1968; Johnson's Lives of the Poets: A Selection, 1971; (with A. McCredie) The Classical Temper in Western Europe: Papers from the Annual Symposium of the Australian Academy of the Humanities, 1983; Stories of Australian Migration, 1988; (with A. Frost) Studies from Terra Australis to Australia, 1989; (with A. Frost and I. Moutinho) European Voyaging towards Australia, 1990. **Address:** 26 Rawson St., Deakin, Canberra, AC 2600, Australia.

HARDY, Lyndon (Maurice). American (born United States), b. 1941. **Genres:** Science Fiction/Fantasy, Novels. **Career:** TRW Systems, center manager, 1966-96, engineer, 1996-; Alodar Systems Inc., owner, president, 1992-. Writer and physicist. **Publications:** NOVELS: Master of the Five Magics, 1980; Secret of the Sixth Magic, 1984; Riddle of the Seven Realms, 1988; Magic in Triplicate, 2003. **Address:** Alodar Systems Inc., 19616 Redbeam Ave., Torrance, CA 90503-1134, U.S.A. **Online address:** lynhardy@aol.com

HARDY, Michael C. American (born United States), b. 1972. **Genres:** History, Military/Defense/Arms Control, Humanities. **Career:** Watauga County Public Library, circulation president, 1998; Caldwell Community College, library assistant, 1999. Writer. **Publications:** The Thirty-Seventh North Carolina Troops: Tar Heels in the Army of Northern Virginia, 2003; The ca. 1840 McElroy House: A Glimpse of Yancey County, North Carolina's History, 2004; Avery County: Images of America, 2005; A Short History of Old Watauga County, 2005; The Battle of Hanover Court House, 2006; Images of America: Caldwell County, 2006; Remembering North Carolina's Confederates, 2006; Remembering Avery County: Old Tale from North Carolina's Youngest County, 2007; (with R.M. Hardy) A Heinous Sin The 1864 Brooksville Bayport Raid, 2009; Mitchell County: Images of America, 2009; Fifty-Eighth North Carolina Troops: Tar Heels in the Army of Tennessee, 2010; North Carolina in the Civil War, 2011. Contributor to periodicals. **Address:** PO Box 393, Crossnore, NC 28616-0393, U.S.A.

HARDY, Richard Earl. American (born United States), b. 1938. **Genres:** Psychology, Sociology. **Career:** U.S. Department of Health, Education, and Welfare, rehabilitation adviser, 1963-66; South Carolina Department of Rehabilitation, chief psychologist, 1966-68; Medical College of Virginia/Virginia Commonwealth University, associate professor of rehabilitation counseling, chair of department and director of graduate studies, 1967-, professor emeritus and chair emeritus, 1996-; Charles C. Thomas Publishing, editor, 1972-. **Publications:** Introduction to Correctional Rehabilitation, 1972; Drug Dependence and Rehabilitation Approaches, 1972; Applied Psychology in Law Enforcement and Corrections, 1973; Rehabilitation of the Drug Abuser with Delinquent Behavior; Climbing Ghetto Walls, 1973; Alcohol Dependence and Rehabilitation Approaches, 1974; (with Gandy and Martin) Rehab Counseling and Services, 1987; Hemingway: A Psychological Portrait, 1988; Gestalt Psychotherapy, 1991; Hispaniola Episode, 1992; (with Gandy and Martin) Rehabilitation Counseling: Mental and Physical Disabilities, 1999; Woodpeckers Don't Get Headaches, 2001. WITH J.G. CULL: (ed.) Social and Rehabilitation Services for the Blind, 1972; Counseling Strategies with Special Populations, 1973; (ed.) Rehabilitation of the Urban Disadvantaged, 1973; Neglected Older American, 1973; (ed.) Law Enforcement and Correctional Rehabilitation, 1973; The Big Welfare Mess: Public Assistance and Rehabilitation Approaches, 1973; Fundamentals of Criminal Behavior and Correctional Systems, 1973; Adjustment to Work, 1973; Understanding Disability for Social and Rehabilitation Services, 1973; Applied Volunteerism in Community Development, 1973; Vocational Rehabilitation: Profession and Process, 1973; Types of Drug Abusers and their Abuses, 1974; (ed.) Counseling High School Students, 1974; Administrative Techniques of Rehabilitation Facility Operations, 1974; Rehabilitation Techniques in Severe Disability, 1974; Problems of Disadvantaged and Deprived Youth, 1974; (ed.) Counseling and Rehabilitating the Diabetic, 1974; Volunteerism: An Emerging Profession, 1974; Organization and Administration of Drug Abuse Treatment Programs, 1974; Deciding on Divorce, 1974; (ed.) Mental Retardation and Physical Disability, 1974; (ed.) Group Counseling and Therapy Techniques in Special Settings, 1974; (ed.) Educational and Psychosocial Aspects of Deafness, 1974; (ed.) Creative Divorce through Social and Psychological Approaches, 1974; Counseling and Rehabilitating the Cancer Patient, 1974; (ed.) Career Guidance for Young Women, 1974; (ed.) Severe Disabilities: Social and Rehabilitation Approaches, 1974; (ed.) Psychological and Vocational Rehabilitation of the Youthful Delinquent, 1974; Problems of Adolescents, 1974; Modification of Behavior of the Mentally Retarded, 1974; (ed.) Behavior Modification of the Mentally Ill, 1974; Therapeutic Needs of the Family: Problems, Descriptions, and Therapeutic Approaches, 1974; (ed.) Techniques and Approaches in Marital and Family Counseling, 1974; Services of the Rehabilitation Facility, 1974; Organization and Administration of Service Programs for the Older American, 1975; Fundamentals of Juvenile Criminal Behavior and Drug Abuse, 1975; Drug Language and Lore, 1975; (ed.) Rehabilitation Facility Approaches in Severe Disabilities, 1975; (ed.) Career Guidance for Black Adolescents, 1975; (ed.) Problems of Runaway Youth, 1976; Hemingway, a Psychological Portrait, 1977; (ed.) Physical Medicine and Rehabilitation Approaches in Spinal Cord Injury, 1977; Considerations in Rehabilitation Facility Development, 1977; (ed. with C.W. Hoehne) Ophthalmological Considerations in the Rehabilitation of the Blind, 1977; The Brass Chalice, A Book of Drug Prevention for Children, Youth and Parents, 1994. OTHERS: (and ed. With J.G. Cull, L. Gandy and E.D. Martin, Jr.) Counseling in the Rehabilitation Process, 2nd ed., 1999. Contributor to journals. **Address:** Department of Rehabilitation Counseling, Virginia Commonwealth University, PO Box 980330, Richmond, VA 23298-0330, U.S.A. **Online address:** richardehardy@cs.com

HARDY, Robert Earl. American (born United States), b. 1957. **Genres:** Biography, Autobiography/Memoirs, Music. **Career:** Writer and musician. **Publications:** A Deeper Blue: The Life and Music of Townes Van Zandt (biography), 2008. **Address:** University of North Texas Press, Rm. 174, Stovall Hall, 1400 Highland St., 1155 Union Cir. Ste. 311336, Denton, TX 76201, U.S.A. **Online address:** deeperblue@verizon.net

HARE, David. British (born England), b. 1947. **Genres:** Plays/Screenplays, Songs/Lyrics And Libretti, Economics, Literary Criticism And History, Anthropology/Ethnology. **Career:** Portable Theatre Co., co-founder and director, 1968-71; Royal Court Theatre, literary manager, 1969-70, resident dramatist, 1970-71; Nottingham Playhouse, resident dramatist, 1973; Joint Stock Theatre Group, co-founder and director, 1975-80; Greenpoint Films, co-founder, 1982; National Theatre, associate director, 1984-. Writer, author and filmmaker. **Publications:** Writing Left-handed, 1991; Asking Around: Background to the David Hare Trilogy, 1993; Via Dolorosa, 1998; Acting Up: A Diary, 1999; (adaptor) Platonov, 2001; The Breath of Life, 2002; Collected Screenplays, 2002; The Hours, 2003; Obedience, Struggle & Revolt, 2005; The Permanent Way, or, La Voie Anglaise, 2007; The Verticle Hour, 2007; (and intro.) Plays Three, 2008; Berlin/Wall, 2009. PUBLISHED PLAYS: Slag, 1971; The Great Exhibition, 1972; (with H. Brenton) Brassneck, 1974; Knuckle, 1974; Fanshen, 1976; Teeth n Smiles, 1976; Plenty, 1978; Deeds, 1978; Licking Hitler, 1978; A Map of the World, 1982, rev. ed., 1983; (with H. Brenton) Pravda: A Fleet Street Comedy, 1985; The Asian Plays: Fanshen, Saigon, A Map of the World, 1986; The Bay at Nice and Wrecked Eggs, 1986; The History Plays: Plenty, Knuckle, Licking Hitler, 1986; Heading Home, Wetherby and Dreams of Leaving, 1991; Skylight, 1995; Mother Courage and Her Children, 1996; David Hare: Plays 1: Slag, Teeth n Smiles, Knuckle, Licking Hitler, Plenty, 1996; David Hare: Plays 2: Fanshen, A Map of the World, Saigon, The Bay at Nice, The Secret Rapture, 1997; The Secret Rapture and Other Plays, 1997; The Blue Room: Freely Adapted from Arthur Schnitzler's La Ronde, 1998; Amy's View, 1998; The Judas Kiss, 1999; My Zinc Bed, 2000; Stuff Happens, 2004; The Vertical Hour, 2006; Gethsemane, 2008; Power of Yes: A Dramatist Seeks to Understand the Financial Crisis, 2009; South Downs, 2011. **Address:** Casarotto Ramsay & Associates Ltd., National House, 60-66 Wardour St., London, GL W1V 4ND, England.

HARE-DUKE, Michael (Geoffrey). Scottish/Indian (born India), b. 1925. **Genres:** Novellas/Short Stories, Poetry, Psychology, Theology/Religion, Social Sciences. **Career:** Ordained Deacon, 1952; priest, 1953; St. Johns Wood Church, curate, 1952-56; St. Mark's Bury, vicar, 1956-62; Clinical Theology Centre, pastoral director, 1962-64; St. Paul's Daybrook, vicar, 1964-68; East Midlands Headquarters, officiating chaplain to the forces, 1968-69; Scottish Episcopal Church, bishop, 1969-94, retired; Age Concern Scotland, chairman, 1994-2000. Writer. **Publications:** (Co-author) The Caring Church, 1963; (co-author) First Aid in Counselling, 1968; Understanding the Adolescent, 1969; The Break of Glory, 1970; Sigmund Freud, 1972; Good News, 1978; Stories, Signs and Sacraments in the Emerging Church, 1982; Pastoral Care, 1984; Praying for Peace: Reflections on the Gulf Crisis, 1991; Hearing the Stranger, Poems, Reflections and Hymns, 1994; Exits and Entrances, 1997; One Foot in Heaven: Growing Older and Living to the Full, 2001. Contributor to periodicals. **Address:** 2 Balhousie Ave., Perth, CN PH1 5HN, Scotland. **Online address:** bishmick@blueyonder.co.uk

HARER, John B. American (born United States), b. 1948. **Genres:** Civil Liberties/Human Rights, Librarianship. **Career:** Jewelcor Jewellers and Distributors, warehouse manager, 1972-74; Williamsport Area School District, librarian, 1975-79; American International School, librarian, 1979-80; Radford University, McConnell Library, head of circulation, 1980-83; Towson State University, Cook Library, head of circulation, 1983-88, adjunct professor, 1986-87; Literacy Volunteers of America, tutor, 1993-; Texas A&M University, Sterling C. Evans Library, head of access services, 1988-96, head education reference edms, 1996-2000; Catawba College, Corriher-Linn-Black Library, director of the library, 2001-04; East Carolina University, College of Education, Department of Library Science, assistant professor, 2004-. Writer. **Publications:** Intellectual Freedom: A Reference Handbook, 1992; (with S.R. Harris) Censorship of Expression in the 1980s: A Statistical Survey, 1994; (with J.E. Harrell) People for and against Restricted or Unrestricted Expression, 2002; (with S. Munden) The Alexander Technique Resource Book: A Reference Guide, 2009. **Address:** Department of Library Science, East Carolina University, 1105 Joyner Library, Greenville, NC 27858, U.S.A. **Online address:** harerj@ecu.edu

HAREVEN, Gail. Israeli (born Israel), b. 1959?. **Genres:** Novels, Novellas/Short Stories, Young Adult Non-fiction. **Career:** University of Illinois, visiting professor, 2006. Writer and columnist. **Publications:** Agadah Hadashah, 1986; Tikvah, im nit'akesh: 'im 'olim ve-'im 'atsmenu, 1992; Aruhat tsohorayim 'im Ima, 1993; Ha-Sipur ha-amiti, 1994; Muzah (novel), 1995; Ha-Boker haragti ish, 1997; Eretz Zolelei Ha-Begadim, 1997; Ha-Derekh le-Gan 'Eden, 1999; She-ahavah nafshi, 2000; Haye mal'akh, 2003; Ha-Ish ha-nakhon, 2005; (with A. Olmert) Sefat kir, 2007; Ha-Shekarim ha-aharonim shel ha-guf, 2008. **Address:** Melville House, 145 Plymouth St., Brooklyn, NY 11201, U.S.A.

HARFORD, Tim. British (born England), b. 1973. **Genres:** Economics, How-to Books. **Career:** Financial Times, columnist, senior columnist, 2003-; Shell Oil Co., scenario expert; International Finance Corp., economist; Nuffield College, visiting fellow; Cass Business School, senior visiting fellow. **Publications:** (With M. Klein) The Market for Aid, 2005; The Undercover Economist: Exposing Why the Rich Are Rich, the Poor Are Poor-and Why You Can Never Buy a Decent Used Car!, 2006; The Logic of Life: The Rational Economics of an Irrational World, 2008; Dear Undercover Economist: Priceless Advice On Money, Work, Sex, Kids and Life's Other Challenges, 2009; Adapt: Why Success Always Starts With Failure, 2011. Contributor to periodicals. **Address:** Felicity Bryan Literary Agency, 2a N Parade Ave., Oxford, OX OX2 6LX, England. **Online address:** undercovereconomist@gmail.com

HARGARTEN, Stephen W. American (born United States), b. 1949. **Genres:** Documentaries/Reportage, Medicine/Health. **Career:** Medical College of Wisconsin, Department of Emergency Medicine, chairman and professor of emergency medicine, 1985-, Firearm Injury Center, director, Injury Research Center, director and associate dean of global health. Writer. **Publications:** (With T.A. Karlson) Reducing Firearm Injury and Death: A Public Health Sourcebook on Guns, 1997. **Address:** Department of Emergency Medicine, Froedtert Hospital, Medical College of Wisconsin, 9200 W Wisconsin Ave., Milwaukee, WI 53226-3522, U.S.A. **Online address:** hargart@mcw.edu

HARGREAVES, John D(esmond). Scottish/British (born England), b. 1924. **Genres:** History, Biography, Autobiography/Memoirs, Bibliography, Essays. **Career:** British Civil Service, staff, 1948; University of Manchester, assistant lecturer, lecturer in history, 1948-52; Fourah Bay College, senior lecturer in history, 1952-54; University of Aberdeen, lecturer, 1954-62, visiting professor, 1970-71, professor of history and chair of department, 1962-85, part-time faculty, 1982, Burnett-Fletcher professor of history, professor emeritus, 1985-; Union College, visiting professor, 1960-61; University of Ibadan, visiting professor, 1970-71. Writer. **Publications:** Problems of Constitutional Development in West Africa: An Outline for Group Discussion, 1953; A Life of Sir Samuel Lewis, 1958; Prelude to the Partition of West Africa, 1963; West Africa: The Former French States, 1967; (ed. and intro.) The Expansion of Europe: A Selection of Articles from History Today, 1968; (co-ed.) Nations and Empire, 1969; (ed.) France and West Africa: An Anthology of Historical Documents, 1969; West Africa Partitioned, 2 vols., 1974-85; The End of Colonial Rule in West Africa: Essays in Contemporary History, 1976; Aberdeenshire to Africa: Northeast Scots and British Overseas Expansion, 1981; (contrib.) An African Miscellany for John Hargreaves, 1983; Decolonization in Africa, 1988, 2nd ed., 1996; (ed. with A. Forbes) Aberdeen University, 1945-1981: Regional Roles and National Needs, 1989; Sierra Leone, De Stevens À Momoh, 1989; Academa and Empire, 1994; (contrib.) Imperialism, Decolonization and Africa: Studies Presented to John Hargreaves: With an Academic Memoir and Bibliography, 1999. Contributor of articles to periodicals. **Address:** School of Divinity, History and Philosophy, King's College, University of Aberdeen, Crombie Annexe, Meston Walk, Aberdeen, AB24 3FX, Scotland.

HARGROVE, Erwin C. American (born United States), b. 1930. **Genres:** Politics/Government, Social Sciences. **Career:** Brown University, faculty, 1960-76, Department of Political Science, professor, chair, 1971-73; Vanderbilt University, professor of political science, 1976, Alexander Heard professor, 1985-86, Vanderbilt Institute for Policy Studies, director, 1976-85, chair, 1992-94, now professor emeritus; The Urban Institute, senior fellow. Writer. **Publications:** Presidential Leadership: Personality and Political Style, 1966; Professional Roles in Society and Government: The English Case, 1972; The Power of the Modern Presidency, 1974; The Missing Link: The Study of the Implementation of Social Policy, 1975; (with E.C. Hargrove) Presidency: A Question of Power, 1975; (ed. with P.K. Conkin) TVA 50 Years of Grass-Roots Bureaucracy, 1983; (with M. Nelson) Presidents, Politics and Policy, 1984; (ed. with S.A. Morley) The President and the Council of Economic Advisors, 1984; (ed. with J.W. Doig) Leadership and Innovation, 1987; Jimmy Carter as President, 1988; (ed. with J.C. Glidewell) Impossible Jobs in Public Management, 1990; (ed. with J.W. Doig) Leadership and Innovation: Entrepreneurs in Government, 1990; Prisoners of Myth: The Leadership of the Tennessee Valley Authority, 1933-1990, 1994; The President as Leader: Appealing to the Better Angels of Our Nature, 1998; (ed.) Future of the Democratic Left in Industrial Democracies, 2003; (ed. with J.E. Owens) Leadership in Context, 2003; Effective Presidency: Lessons on Leadership from John F. Kennedy to George W. Bush, 2008. **Address:** 662 Timber Ln., Nashville, TN 37215, U.S.A. **Online address:** erwin.c.hargrove@vanderbilt.edu

HARING, Bruce. American (born United States) **Genres:** Adult Non-fiction, Music, Biography, Autobiography/Memoirs. **Career:** Billboard, editor; Daily Variety, editor; USA Today, reporter, 1995-; Star-Ledger, music critic; JM Northern Media L.L.C., founder and chief executive officer, 1999-; DIY Convention, managing director and chairman. **Publications:** Off the Charts: Ruthless Days and Reckless Nights Inside the Music Industry, 1996; Beyond the Charts: MP3 and the Digital Music Revolution, 2000; (with D. McDaniels) King of Rock: Respect, Responsibility, and My Life with Run-DMC, 2001; How Not to Destroy Your Career in Music: Avoiding the Common Mistakes Most Musicians Make, 2005. **Address:** JM Northern Media L.L.C., 7095 Hollywood Blvd., Ste. 864, Hollywood, CA 90028, U.S.A. **Online address:** bruce@jmnorthernmedia.com

HARING, Lee. American (born United States), b. 1930. **Genres:** Area Studies, Literary Criticism And History, Mythology/Folklore, Third World, Social Sciences. **Career:** Guilford College, assistant professor of English, 1953-56; City University of New York, Brooklyn College, lecturer, 1957-61, instructor, 1961-67, assistant professor, 1967-73, associate professor, 1973-81, professor, 1981-99, professor of English emeritus, 1999-. Writer. **Publications:** The Gypsy Laddie, 1962; Folk Songs for Guitar, 1964; The Folklore Component in Malagasay, 1979; Malagasy Tale Index, 1982; Verbal Arts in Madagascar, 1992; Collecting Folklore in Mauritius, 1992; Ibonia, Epic of Madagascar, 1994; Ann Koleksyonn Folklor Moris, 2001; Indian Ocean Folktales: Madagascar, Comoros, Mauritius, Reunion, Seychelles, 2002; (trans. and ed. with

D. Auleear) Indian Folktales from Mauritius, 2006; Stars and Keys: Folktales and Creolization in the Indian Ocean, 2007. **Address:** Department of English, Brooklyn College, City University of New York, 2900 Bedford Ave., Brooklyn, NY 11210, U.S.A. **Online address:** lharing@hvc.rr.com

HARKER, Michael P. American (born United States), b. 1950. **Genres:** Photography. **Career:** Frank Woods Photography, photographer, 1975-76; Rend Lake College, teacher of adult photography, 1976; Wilson and Lund Inc., custom photographic laboratory technician, 1976-78; Tom Simmons Photography, assistant photographer and manager of photography laboratory, 1980; Vicomm Inc., photographer and manager of photography laboratory, 1981-83; Scott Community College, teacher of adult photography, 1982; freelance commercial photographer, 1983-85; Quad City Times, staff news photographer, 1984; Tucker/Thompson Photographics Inc., director, photographer and manager of studio and laboratory 1985-86; Rockwell Avionics and Communications, staff photographer, 1986-94; Silver Nitrate Photography, owner, photographer and writer, 1994-97; University of Iowa, ophthalmic photographer, 1997-; Lee Williams Enterprises, photographic technician; Deere and Co., photographic technician, public-relations photographer. **Publications:** Harker's One-Room Schoolhouses: Visions of an Iowa Icon, 2008; Family Farmers of the Heartland, forthcoming; Iowa's Rural School Houses, forthcoming; Iowa's Classic County Courthouses, forthcoming. **Address:** Department of Ophthalmology and Visual Sciences, University of Iowa, 200 Hawkins Dr., Iowa City, IA 52242, U.S.A. **Online address:** harker@harkerphotography.com

HARKINS, Anthony. American (born United States) **Genres:** History. **Career:** Emerson Preparatory School, teacher, 1988-90; University of Wisconsin, writing instructor, 1998-99, assistant professor of history, 1999; Iowa State University, instructor, 2000-01; Princeton University, Princeton Writing Program, instructor, 2001-03; Western Kentucky University, assistant professor of history, 2003-. Writer. **Publications:** Hillbilly: A Cultural History of an American Icon, 2004. (co-ed.) Media Section, 2006: Billy DeBeck's Impact on American Culture, 2005. Contributor to periodicals. **Address:** Western Kentucky University, 218 Cherry Hall, 1906 College Heights Blvd., Ste. 21806, Bowling Green, KY 42101, U.S.A. **Online address:** anthony.harkins@wku.edu

HARKNESS, Deborah E. American (born United States), b. 1965. **Genres:** Natural History, Sciences, Philosophy. **Career:** Colgate University, assistant professor, 1994-97; University of California, assistant professor, 1997-99, associate professor, 1999-2004; University of Southern California, associate professor, 2004-07, professor of history, 2007-; The History Channel, consultant and presenter, 2006-07. Writer, historian, consultant and presenter. **Publications:** John Dee's Conversations with Angels: Cabala, Alchemy, and the End of Nature, 1999; The Jewel House: Elizabethan London and the Scientific Revolution, 2007. Contributor to books and periodicals. **Address:** Department of History, University of Southern California, 153 Social Sciences Bldg., Los Angeles, CA 90089-0034, U.S.A. **Online address:** deharkne@email.usc.edu

HARKNETT, Terry. See **GILMAN, George G.**

HARLAN, Judith. American (born United States), b. 1949. **Genres:** Adult Non-fiction, Local History/Rural Topics, Social Commentary, Biography, Social Sciences, Reference. **Career:** Harbor Times, editor, 1980-81; Murphy Organization, news copywriter, 1982-83; Freebies, editor, 1984-85; Oxnard College, instructor, 1991-; Harlan Editorial Inc., owner. **Publications:** American Indians Today: Issues and Conflicts, 1987; Hispanic Voters: A Voice in American Politics, 1988; Sounding the Alarm: A Biography of Rachel Carson, 1989; Bilingualism in the United States: Conflict and Controversy, 1991; Puerto Rico: Deciding Its Future, 1996; Girl Talk: Staying Strong, Feeling Good, Sticking Together, 1997; Feminism: A Reference Handbook, 1998; Mamphela Ramphele: Ending Apartheid in South Africa, 2000. Contributor to periodicals. **Address:** c/o Author Mail, Feminist Press, 365 5th Ave., Ste. 5406, New York, NY 10016, U.S.A. **Online address:** judith_harlan@yahoo.com

HARLAN, Rex. See **BUSLIK, Gary.**

HARLAND, Christina. See **PEMBERTON, Margaret.**

HARLAND, Richard. Australian (born Australia), b. 1947. **Genres:** Science Fiction/Fantasy, Novels. **Career:** Writer, 1997-; University of New South Wales, tutor; University of Wollongong, senior lecturer in English,

visiting fellow, part-time lecturer, through 2011. **Publications:** Testimony, 1981; Superstructuralis, 1987; Beyond Superstructuralism: The Syntagmatic Side of Language, 1993; The Vicar of Morbing Vyle, 1993; The Dark Edge, 1997; Taken by Force, 1998; Literary Theory from Plato to Barthes, 1999; Hidden from View, 1999; Ferren and the Angel, 2000; Ferren and the White Doctor, 2002; Ferren and the Invasion of Heaven, 2003; Walter Wants to Be a Werewolf, 2003; The Black Crusade, 2004; Sassycat, 2005; Worldshaker, 2009; Liberator, 2011. WOLF KINGDOM SERIES: Escape, 2008; Under Siege, 2008; Race to the Ruins, 2008; The Heavy Crown, 2008. Works appear in anthologies. Contributor to journals. **Address:** Selwa Anthony Agency, PO Box 714, Broadway, NW 2007, Australia. **Online address:** richard@richardharland.net

HARLEE, J. V. See **LEESE, Jennifer L. B.**

HARLEMAN, Ann. American (born United States), b. 1945. **Genres:** Novellas/Short Stories, Language/Linguistics, Literary Criticism And History, Poetry, Translations, Novels. **Career:** Rutgers University, assistant professor of English, 1973-74; University of Washington, assistant professor, 1974-79, associate professor of English, 1979-84; Dartmouth College, visiting professor, 1981-82; Massachusetts Institute of Technology, visiting associate professor of English, 1984-86; Brown University, research associate in American civilization, 1986-; Wheaton College, Cole distinguished professor, 1992-93; Northeastern University, visiting professor; Wesleyan University, visiting professor; Rhode Island School of Design, adjunct professor, Department of English, senior lecturer. Writer. **Publications:** Happiness, 1994; Bitter Lake: A Novel, 1996; Thoreau's Laundry: Stories, 2007; The Year She Disappeared: A Novel, 2008. OTHERS: Graphic Representation of Models in Linguistic Theory, 1976; (contrib.) The Critical Temper IV, 1979; (with B.A. Rosenberg) Ian Fleming: A Critical Biography, 1989; (contrib.) The Writer's Handbook, 1989, rev. ed., 1993; (trans.) R. Zernova, Mute Phone Calls, 1991; (contrib.) Russia Accordingto Women, 1991. Contributor to periodicals. **Address:** Rhode Island School of Design, 2 College St., Providence, RI 02903-2784, U.S.A. **Online address:** ann_harleman@brown.edu

HARLEY, Bill. American (born United States), b. 1954. **Genres:** Children's Fiction, Songs/Lyrics And Libretti, Novels, Picture/Board Books. **Career:** Providence Learning Connection, founder; Stone Soup Coffeehouse, co-founder; Spellbinders, co-founder; Round River Records, co-founder, 1984-; Pokanoket Watershed Alliance, vice-president; National Public Radio, commentator, 1991-; Round River Productions, founder. Writer and performing artist. **Publications:** FOR CHILDREN: Carna and the Boots of Seven Strides, 1994; Ready-to-Tell Tales, 1994; Nothing Happened, 1995; Sarah's Story, 1996; Sitting Down to Eat, 1996; Bear's All-night Party, 2001; Participation and Democracy at Work: Essays in Honor of Harvie Ramsay, 2005; (comp.) Dear Santa: The Letters of James B. Dobbins, 2005; The Amazing Flight of Darius Frobisher, 2006; Dirty Joe, the Pirate: A True Story, 2008; The Night of the Spadefoot Toads, 2008; Lost and Found, 2012. Contributor to periodicals. **Address:** Round River Productions, 301 Jacob St., Seekonk, MA 02771, U.S.A.

HARLEY, Willard F. American (born United States), b. 1941. **Genres:** Human Relations/Parenting, Psychology, Self Help, Romance/Historical. **Career:** Westmont College, head of psychology department, 1968-71; Bethel College and Seminary, professor of psychology, 1972-77; Harley Clinics, president, 1976-93; Marriage Builders, president, 1993-. Writer. **Publications:** Get Growing, Christian!, 1975; His Needs, Her Needs, 1986, rev. ed., 2011; Marriage Insurance, 1988; Love Busters, 1992, rev. ed. as Love Busters: Protecting Your Marriage from Habits That Destroy Romantic Love 2008; Five Steps to Romantic Love, 1994, rev. ed., 2009; Give and Take, 1996; Your Love and Marriage, 1997; Four Gifts of Love, 1998; (with J.H. Chalmers) Surviving an Affair, 1998; Fall in Love, Stay in Love, 2000; Buyers, Renters and Freeloaders, 2000; I Cherish You, 2002; His Needs, Her Needs for Parents: Keeping Romance Alive, 2003; Defending Traditional Marriage: It Starts With You, 2005; I Promise You: Preparing for a Marriage that Will Last a Lifetime, 2006; Effective Marriage Counseling: The His Needs, Her Needs Guide to Helping Couples, 2010; Draw Close, 2011. **Address:** Marriage Builders Inc., 12568 Ethan Ave. N, White Bear Lake, MN 55110, U.S.A. **Online address:** bharley@marriagebuilders.com

HARLINE, Craig E. American (born United States) **Genres:** Biography, Autobiography/Memoirs, History, Theology/Religion. **Career:** Brigham Young

University, professor of history, 1992-; Catholic University, visiting professor and research fellow, 1996, 2001; University of Antwerp, visiting professor, 2006. Writer. **Publications:** Pamphlets, Printing and Political Culture in the Early Dutch Republic, 1987; (ed.) The Rhyme and Reason of Politics in Early Modern Europe, 1992; (with E. Put) A Bishop's Tale: Mathias Hovius among His Flock in Seventeenth-Century Flanders, 2000; The Burdens of Sister Margaret: Inside a Seventeenth-Century Convent, rev. ed., 2000; Miracles at the Jesus Oak: Histories of the Supernatural in Reformation Europe, 2003; Sunday: A History of the First Day from Babylonia to the Super Bowl, 2007; Conversions, 2011. **Address:** Department of History, Brigham Young University, 2115 JFSB, 150 E Bulldog Blvd., Provo, UT 84602-6707, U.S.A. **Online address:** craig_harline@byu.edu

HARLING, Robert. American (born United States), b. 1951?. **Genres:** Plays/Screenplays, Young Adult Fiction. **Career:** Actor, 1979-87; playwright, 1987-; screenwriter, 1989-. **Publications:** Steel Magnolias, 1988. **Address:** Creative Artists Agency, 9830 Wilshire Blvd., Beverly Hills, CA 90212-1825, U.S.A.

HARLOW, Michael. New Zealander/American (born United States), b. 1937?. **Genres:** Poetry, Music, Psychology, Children's Fiction, Humanities, Crafts. **Career:** Writer. **Publications:** The Book of Quiet, 1974; Edges, 1974; (ed.) Christchurch Teachers College Centennial 1977, 1977; The Identikit, 1978; Texts, Identities, 1978; Nothing But Switzerland and Lemonade, 1980; Today Is the Piano's Birthday, 1981; Vlaminck's Tie, 1985; Take a Risk, Trust Your Language, Make a Poem, 1985; Giotto's Elephant, 1991; Cassandra's Daughter (poems), 2005; Tram Conductor's Blue Cap, 2009. **Address:** Alchemy House, 122 Earnscleugh Rd., Alexandra, 9320, New Zealand. **Online address:** m.harlow@xtra.co.nz

HARLOW, Rosie. British/Scottish (born Scotland), b. 1961. **Genres:** Children's Non-fiction. **Career:** South Oxfordshire Countryside Education Trust, teacher, 1985-87; Hill End Residential Environment Centre, Oxford County Council, teacher, 1987-88; Sutton Courtenay Field Study Centre, Oxford County Council, head of centre, 1989-93. Writer. **Publications:** (With G. Morgan) 175 Amazing Nature Experiments, 1992. FUN WITH SCIENCE SERIES WITH S. MORGAN: Trees and Leaves, 1991; Energy and Growth, 1991; Observing Minibeasts, 1991; Cycles and Seasons, 1991; Nature: Experiments, Tricks, Things to Make, 1992; Nature in Danger, 1995; Pollution and Waste, 1995; Garbage and Recycling, 1995. YOUNG DISCOVERER'S ENVIRONMENT SERIES: Energy and Power, 1995; Nature in Danger, 1995; Pollution and Waste, 1995; Rubbish and Recycling, 1995. Contributor to periodicals. **Address:** 12 Sunningwell Rd., Oxford, OX OX1 45X, England.

HARMAN, Oren Solomon. Israeli (born Israel), b. 1973. **Genres:** Biology. **Career:** Harvard University, Bertram J. and Barbara B. Cohn fellow, 2000-01, instructor, 2001-02; Hebrew University of Jerusalem, Sidney M. Edelstein postdoctoral fellow, 2002-03, adjunct lecturer, 2003-05, Lady Davis Fellowship Trust Postdoctoral Fellow, 2003-04, Golda Meir Postdoctoral Fellow, 2004-05, adjunct senior lecturer, 2005-08; Bar Ilan University, adjunct lecturer, 2003-05, senior lecturer, 2006-, Graduate Program in Science, Technology, and Society, chair, 2009-. Writer. **Publications:** The Man Who Invented the Chromosome: The Life of Cyril Darlington, 2004; (ed. and intro. with M.R. Dietrich) Rebels, Mavericks, and Heretics in Biology, 2008; The Price of Altruism: George Price and the Search for the Origins of Kindness, 2010. Contributor to periodicals. **Address:** Department of History and Philosophy of Science, Bar-Ilan University, Ramat Gan, 52900, Israel. **Online address:** harmano@mail.biu.ac.il

HARMAN, Patricia. American (born United States), b. 1943. **Genres:** Autobiography/Memoirs. **Career:** Growing Tree Natural Foods Cooperative, co-founder. Writer. **Publications:** The Blue Cotton Gown: A Midwife's Memoir, 2008. **Address:** Morgantown, WV , U.S.A. **Online address:** pharmancnm@comcast.net

HARMEL, Kristin. American (born United States), b. 1979. **Genres:** Novels, Young Adult Fiction, Mystery/Crime/Suspense, Romance/Historical. **Career:** People, reporter, 2001-; The Daily Buzz, television book reviewer; Saint Petersburg Times, sports reporter. Journalist. **Publications:** How to Sleep with a Movie Star, 2006; The Blonde Theory, 2007; Art of French Kissing, 2007; When You Wish, 2008; Italian for Beginners, 2009; After, 2010. Contributor to magazines. **Address:** c/o Author Mail, Warner Books, 1271 Ave. of the Americas, New York, NY 10020, U.S.A. **Online address:** kristin@kristinharmel.com

HARMETZ, Aljean. American (born United States) **Genres:** Film, History. **Career:** New York Times, culture and entertainment correspondent, 1978-90, hollywood film correspondent, 1981-, Sunday Arts and Leisure Section, correspondent, 1990-; Esquire Magazine, contributing editor, 1990-. **Publications:** Making of the Wizard of Oz, 1977; Rolling Breaks and Other Movie Business, 1983; Round Up the Usual Suspects: The Making of Casablanca: Bogart, Bergman, and World War II, 1992; On the Road to Tara: The Making of Gone with the Wind, 1996; Off the Face of the Earth, 1997; (ed. with S.B. Casmier and C. Lawrence) A Deadly Dozen: Tales of Murder from Members of Sisters in Crime/Los Angeles, 2000; The Making of Casablanca: Bogart, Bergman, and World War II, 2002. **Address:** c/o Candida Donadio, Donadio & Olson Inc., 121 W 27th St., Ste. 704, New York, NY 10001-6262, U.S.A.

HARMON, Alexandra Sasha. American (born United States), b. 1945. **Genres:** History, Economics. **Career:** University of Washington, associate professor of American Indian studies, 1995-. Writer and lawyer. **Publications:** Indians in the Making: Ethnic Relations and Indian Identities around Puget Sound, 1998; (ed.) The Power of Promises: Rethinking Indian Treaties in the Pacific Northwest, 2008; Rich Indians: Native People and the Problem of Wealth in American History, 2010. Contributor to periodicals and journals. **Address:** American Indian Studies Center, University of Washington, C514 Padelford, Seattle, WA 98195, U.S.A. **Online address:** aharmon@u.washington.edu

HARMON, Dan. *See* **HARMON, Daniel E(lton).**

HARMON, Daniel E(lton). (Dan Harmon). American (born United States), b. 1949. **Genres:** Children's Non-fiction, Adult Non-fiction, Biography, History. **Career:** Sandlapper: The Magazine of South Carolina, assistant editor, 1971-73, associate editor and art director, 1989-; Dispatch-News, reporter and editor, 1973-83; Bruner Publishing Co., writer and editor, 1973-83; RPW Publishing Corp., editor, 1983-97; Hornpipe Vintage Publications, author and editor, 1997-; freelance editor, 1997-. **Publications:** (Ed. as Dan Harmon) Martin Luther: The Great Reformer, 1995; Civil War Generals, 1997; The Tortured Mind: The Many Faces of Manic Depression, 1998; (ed. as Dan Harmon) Life after Death, 1998; (as Dan Harmon) Fighting Units of the American War of Independence, 1999; Life out of Focus: Alzheimer's Disease and Related Disorders, 1999; (as Dan Harmon) Anorexia Nervosa: Starving for Attention, 1999; More Clean Jokes for Kids, 1999; Juan Ponce de Leon and the Search for the Fountain of Youth, 2000; Nigeria: 1880 to the Present: The Struggle, the Tragedy, the Promise, 2000; Schizophrenia; Losing Touch with Reality, 2000; West Africa, 1880 to the Present: A Cultural Patchwork, 2001; The FBI, 2001; Jacques Cartier and the Exploration of Canada, 2001; Egypt: 1880 to the Present: Desert of Envy, Water of Life, 2001; La Salle and the Exploration of the Mississippi, 2001; The U.S. Armed Forced, 2001; (as Dan Harmon) The Titanic, 2001; The Attorney General's Office, 2001; Sudan: 1880 to the Present: Crossroads of a Continent in Conflict, 2001; The Chalk Town Train, and Other Tales, 2001; Bible Challenge: Small Facts from the Big Book, 2002; Jolliet and Marquette: Explorers of the Mississippi River, 2002; Lord Cornwallis: British General, 2002; The Food and Drug Administration, 2002; The Environmental Protection Agency, 2002; Robert Peary and the Quest for the North Pole, 2002; Davy Crockett, 2002; Southeast Africa: 1880 to the Present: Reclaiming a Region of Natural Wealth, 2002; The Ultimate Joke Book: 100s of Great Clean Jokes, 2002; Defense Lawyers, 2002; Billy the Kid, 2002; Central and East Africa: 1880 to the Present: From Colonialism to Civil War, 2002; John Burgoyne: British General, 2002; Andrew Jackson, 2003; Early French Explorers of North America, 2003; Explorers of the South Pacific: A Thousand Years of Exploration, from the Polynesians to Captain Cook and Beyond, 2003; Hudson River, 2003; (with C.L. Reece) Men and women of the Bible: More Than One Hundred Intriguing Stories, 2003; Woodrow Wilson, 2003; (as Dan Harmon) Book of Clean Jokes, 2004; Taught to Lead: The Education of the Presidents of the United States, 2004; Libya, 2004, rev. ed., 2010; Turkey, 2004, rev. ed., 2010; (with C. Reece and J. Reece-DeMarco) 128 of the Greatest Stories from the Bible: Amazing and True Tales of the Men, Women and Children Who Shaped History, 2005; Ayatollah Ruhollah Khomeini, 2005; Kyrgyzstan, 2005; Obesity, 2007; Algeria, 2008; Careers in Explosives and Arson Investigation, 2008; Pervez Musharraf: President of Pakistan, 2008; Fish, Meat and Poultry: Dangers in the Food Supply, 2008; Al Gore and Global Warming, 2009; Chemical and Biological Weapons: Agents of War and Terror, 2009; Hallucinogens: The Dangers of Distorted Reality, 2009; New Medicines: Issues of Approval, Access and Product Safety, 2009; Careers in the Corrections System, 2010; Minnesota: Past and Present, 2010; Jobs In Environmental Cleanup And Emergency Hazmat Response, 2010; Frequently Asked Questions About Overscheduling And Stress, 2010; First Car Smarts, 2010; First Job Smarts, 2010; South Carolina: Past and Present, 2010; Washington: Past and Present, 2010; Careers in Internet Security, 2011; A Career as an Electrician, 2011; Leukemia: Current and Emerging Trends in Detection and Treatment, 2012; How to Start Your Own Band, 2012; Managing Your Band, 2012; (with H.M. Lily) Frequently Asked Questions About Alcohol Abuse and Binge Drinking, 2012. **Address:** Hornpipe Vintage Publications, PO Box 18428, Spartanburg, SC 29318, U.S.A. **Online address:** d@danieleltonharmon.com

HARMON, Kate. See GIBSON, Marley.

HARMON, Louise. American (born United States), b. 1949. **Genres:** Law, Politics/Government, Sports/Fitness. **Career:** Touro College, Jacob D. Fuchsberg Law Center, professor of law, associate dean for for academic affairs and faculty development; State University of New York, Center for Indian Studies, senior research fellow, 2003. Writer. **Publications:** (With D.W. Post) Cultivating Intelligence: Power, Law, and the Politics of Teaching, 1996; Fragments on the Deathwatch, 1998. **Address:** Jacob D. Fuchsberg Law Center, Touro College, Rm. 405, 225 Eastview Dr., Central Islip, NY 11722-4539, U.S.A. **Online address:** lharmon@tourolaw.edu

HARMON, Maurice. Irish (born Ireland), b. 1930. **Genres:** Songs/Lyrics And Libretti, Literary Criticism And History, Bibliography, Biography. **Career:** Harvard University, teaching fellow and research assistant, 1955-58; Lewis and Clark College, Department of English, instructor, 1958-63; University of Notre Dame, Department of English, assistant professor, 1961-64; University College, lecturer in English, 1965-74, associate professor, 1976-90, professor of Anglo-Irish literature and drama 1984-90, professor emeritus of Anglo-Irish literature and drama, 1990-; Irish University Review, founder and editor, 1970-87; Ohio State University, distinguished visiting professor, 1973-74; International Association for the Study of Anglo-Irish Literature, chairman, 1979-82; Royal Irish Academy, vice president, 1986-89; Marshall University, John Drinko professor of liberal arts, 1992; Kobe College-Japan, visiting professor, 1997-98. **Publications:** Seán O'Faoláin: A Critical Introduction, 1966; Modern Irish Literature, 1800-1967; A Reader's Guide, 1968; The Poetry of Thomas Kinsella: With Darkness for a Nest, 1974; Select Bibliography for the Study of Anglo-Irish Literature and Its Background: An Irish Studies Handbook, 1977; (with R. McHugh) A Short History of Anglo-Irish Literature from Its Origins to the Present, 1982; Austin Clarke, 1896-1974: A Critical Introduction, 1989; The Book of Precedence, 1994; A Stillness at Kiawah, 1996; No Author Better Served: The Correspondence of Samuel Beckett and Alan Schneider, 1998; The Last Regatta, 2000; The Colloquy of the Old Men, 2001; Tales of Death and Other Poems, 2001; The Dolman Poem: A Celebration, 2001; Doll with Two Backs and Other Poems, 2004; Selected Essays, 2006; Thomas Kinsella: Designing for the Exact Needs, 2008; Mischievous Boy, and Other Poems, 2008; (trans. and intro.) The Dialogue of the Ancients of Ireland: a New Translation of Acallam na Senórach, 2009; When Love is Not Enough: New & Selected Poems, 2010. EDITOR: Fenians and Fenianism (essays), 1968; The Celtic Master (essays), 1969; King Lear, 1970; Romeo and Juliet, 1970; King Richard II, 1971; J.M. Synge Centenary Papers 1971, 1972; Coriolanus, 1972; (with P. Rafroidi) The Irish Novel in Our Time, 1976; Richard Murphy: Poet of Two Traditions: Interdisciplinary Studies, 1978; Irish Poetry after Yeats: Seven Poets, 1979; Image and Illusion: Anglo-Irish Literature and Its Contexts: A Festschrift for Roger McHugh, 1979; The Irish Writer and the City, 1984; No Author Better Served: The Correspondence of Samuel Beckett & Alan Schneider, 1998. Contributor to periodicals. **Address:** School of English & Drama, University College Dublin, Belfield, DU 4, Ireland. **Online address:** morris.harmon@ucd.ie

HARMON, Sandra. American (born United States) **Genres:** Novels, Autobiography/Memoirs, How-to Books, Criminology/True Crime. **Career:** Journalist, writer and producer. **Publications:** Girl Like Me, 1975; (with P.B. Presley) Elvis and Me, 1985; (with P. Allen) Getting to I Do, 1994; (with Allen) Staying Married and Loving It!: How to Get What You Want from Your Man Without Asking, 1997; Dream Weaver Magic Maker, 2000; Mafia Son: The Scarpa Mob Family, the FBI and a Story of Betrayal, 2009. **Address:**

HarperCollins Publishers Inc., 10 E 53rd St., New York, NY 10022, U.S.A. **Online address:** shtvshow@aol.com

HARNACK, Curtis. American (born United States), b. 1927. **Genres:** Novels, Novellas/Short Stories, Poetry, History, Autobiography/Memoirs, Travel/Exploration, Young Adult Fiction, Biography. **Career:** United Nations Secretariat, collator of documents, 1951-52; Grinnell College, instructor in English, 1952-53, 1954-56, admissions counselor, 1953-54; University of Iowa, instructor in writers workshop, 1957-58, visiting lecturer in writers workshop, 1959-60; University of Tabriz, Fulbright professor of American literature, 1958-59; Sarah Lawrence College, literature faculty, 1960-71; Corporation of Yaddo, president, 1971-87, now retired; School of American Ballet, president, 1992-97. Writer. **Publications:** (Ed. with P. Engle) Prize Stories: The O. Henry Memorial Collection, 1958; The Work of an Ancient Hand, 1960; Love and Be Silent, 1962; Persian Lions, Persian Lambs: An American's Odyssey in Iran, 1965; We Have All Gone Away, 1973; Under My Wings Everything Prospers, 1977; Limits of the Land, 1979; Gentlemen on the Prairie, 1985; The Attic: A Memoir, 1993. Contributor to magazines. **Address:** c/o Timothy Seldes, Russell & Volkening Inc., 50 W 29th St., Ste. 7E, New York, NY 10001-4227, U.S.A. **Online address:** curharnack@aol.com

HARNER, Michael J(ames). American (born United States), b. 1929. **Genres:** Anthropology/Ethnology, Novels. **Career:** Arizona State University, assistant professor of anthropology, 1958-61; University of California, senior museum anthropologist, associate research anthropologist, 1961-67; Lowie Museum of Anthropology, assistant director, 1961-66, visiting associate professor, 1971, 1972, visiting professor, 1975; Columbia University, visiting associate professor, associate professor of anthropology, 1966-70; Yale University, visiting associate professor of anthropology, 1970; New School for Social Research, associate professor, 1970-77, professor of anthropology, 1973-77, chairman of department, 1973-87; Foundation for Shamanic Studies, founder and president, 1985-; Center for Shamanic Studies, founder and director. Writer. **Publications:** (With A.L. Kroeber) Mohave Pottery, 1955; The Jívaro: People of the Sacred Waterfalls, 1972; (ed.) Hallucinogens and Shamanism, 1973; Shuar: Pueblo de las cascadas sagradas, 1978; (with A. Meyer) Cannibal (novel), 1979; The Way of the Shaman: A Guide to Power and Healing, 1980. **Address:** Foundation for Shamanic Studies, PO Box 1939, Mill Valley, CA 94942, U.S.A.

HARNER, Stephen M. (Churchill East). Chinese/American (born United States), b. 1949. **Genres:** Economics, Politics/Government, Cultural/Ethnic Topics, Business/Trade/Industry. **Career:** U.S. Department of State, foreign service officer, 1975-80; Citibank N.A., vice-president of offices in Japan and Taiwan, 1981-91, Corporate Banking-Osaka, credit officer, 1981-82, Corporate Banking-Nagoya, credit officer, 1983-86, MNC Subsidiaries Unit, credit officer, 1987-88, Transaction Banking Group, credit officer, 1988-89, Private Banking Group, credit officer, 1990-91; Merrill Lynch International Bank, chief, 1991-93; Deutsche Bank AG, chief representative, 1995-98; American Express Financial Advisors Japan Inc., president, 1999; S.M. Harner and Co., president, 2000-, owner. Writer. **Publications:** Living and working in the People's Republic of China: A Cultural Guide, 1980; Living and Working in Shanghai, 1996; (with S. Yabuki) China's New Political Economy, rev. ed., 1999; Japan's Financial Revolution and How American Firms are Profiting, 2000. **Address:** S. M. Harner & Co., Rm. 1205, Harcourt House, 12th Fl., 39 Gloucester Rd., Wanchai, 852, Hong Kong. **Online address:** smharnerco@yahoo.com

HARNESS, Kelley. (Kelley Ann Harness). American (born United States), b. 1960. **Genres:** Music, Art/Art History. **Career:** University of Minnesota, School of Music, associate professor of musicology. Musicologist and writer. **Publications:** Echoes of Women's Voices: Music, Art, and Female Patronage in Early Modern Florence, 2006. Contributor of to journals. **Address:** School of Music, University of Minnesota, 100 Ferguson Hall, 2106 4th St. S, Minneapolis, MN 55455-0441, U.S.A. **Online address:** harne005@umn.edu

HARNESS, Kelley Ann. See HARNESS, Kelley.

HARNEY, Elizabeth. Canadian (born Canada) **Genres:** Young Adult Nonfiction. **Career:** Smithsonian Institution, National Museum of African Art, International Art Museums Division, curator, 1999-2003, 2000-04; University of Toronto, assistant professor, associate professor. Writer. **Publications:** Ethiopian Passages: Contemporary Art from the Diaspora, 2003; In Senghor's Shadow: Art, Politics and the Avant-garde in Senegal, 1960-1995, 2004. Address: Department of Art, University of Toronto, Rm. 6036 , Sidney Smith Hall, 100 St George St., Toronto, ON M5S 3G3, Canada. **Online address:** e.harney@utoronto.ca

HARNOIS, Albert J. American (born United States), b. 1945. **Genres:** Business/Trade/Industry, Money/Finance, Biography, Information Science/Computers. **Career:** Textron Financial Corp., vice president, internal audit. Writer. **Publications:** EDP Auditing: A Functional Approach, 1991; Accounting and Auditing in a New Environment: A Guide to Personal Survival Skills and Professional Growth, 1994; Growing Up With Guilt, 1996; Trail of Evidence, 2010. **Address:** 122 Morris St., Cumberland, RI 02864, U.S.A. **Online address:** aharnois@tfc.textron.com

HARNUM, Robert. American (born United States) **Genres:** Novels, Translations, Young Adult Fiction. **Career:** University of Connecticut, faculty; La Grande école de Commerce de Rouen, faculty. High school teacher and writer. **Publications:** Le Festin Des Lions, 1998; La dernière Sentinelle (novel), 1999, trans. as Exile in the Kingdom, 2001; Poursuite, 2001; Une Rhapsodie Américaine, 2002. **Address:** University Press of New England, 23 S Main St., PO Box 979, Hanover, NH 03755-2048, U.S.A.

HAROIAN-GUERIN, Gil. (Gil Harootunian). American (born United States), b. 1957. **Genres:** Literary Criticism And History, Gay And Lesbian Issues, Young Adult Fiction. **Career:** Syracuse University, instructor in writing program, 1995-. Writer. **Publications:** The Fatal Hero: Diana, Diety of the Moon, as an Archetype of the Modern Hero in English Literature, 1996, 2nd ed., 1998; (ed.) The Personal Narrative: Writing Ourselves as Teachers and Scholars, 1999; (ed. with L. Gray-Rosendale as Gil Harootunian) Fractured Feminisms: Rhetoric, Context and Giland Contestation, 2003. **Address:** Writing Program, Syracuse University, HBC 234, Syracuse, NY 13244, U.S.A. **Online address:** gharoian@mailbox.syr.edu

HAROLD, Christine. American (born United States), b. 1969. **Genres:** Language/Linguistics, Art/Art History. **Career:** University of Washington, assistant professor, 2007-; University of Georgia, assistant professor of speech communication. Writer and educator. **Publications:** Our Space: Resisting the Corporate Control of Culture, 2007. Contributor to periodicals. **Address:** Department of Communication, University of Washington, PO Box 353740, Seattle, WA 98195-3740, U.S.A. **Online address:** charold@u.washington.edu

HAROLD, Clive. See **HUTSON, Shaun P.**

HAROOTUNIAN, Gil. See **HAROIAN-GUERIN, Gil.**

HARPAZ, Beth J. American (born United States), b. 1961?. **Genres:** Social Commentary, Women's Studies And Issues. **Career:** Associated Press, travel editor, 1988-; Staten Island Advance, staff; Bergen Record, staff; Exceptional Parent Magazine, staff. **Publications:** The Girls in the Van: Covering HillaAssociated Pressry, 2001; Finding Annie Farrell: A Family Memoir, 2004; 13 is the New 18: And Other Things my Children Taught Me While I was Having a Nervous Breakdown being Their Mother, 2009. **Address:** c/o Author Mail, St. Martins Press, 175 5th Ave., New York, NY 10010, U.S.A. **Online address:** bethharpaz@hotmail.com

HARPENDING, Henry. American (born United States), b. 1944. **Genres:** History. **Career:** University of Utah, distinguished professor and Thomas chair. Writer. **Publications:** (With G. Cochran) The 10, 000 Year Explosion: How Civilization Accelerated Human Evolution, 2009. Contributor to journals. **Address:** Department of Anthropology, University of Utah, Rm. 102, 270 South 1440 East, Salt Lake City, UT 84112-0060, U.S.A. **Online address:** henry.harpending@anthro.utah.edu

HARPER, Andrew. See **CLEGG, Douglas.**

HARPER, Hill. American (born United States), b. 1966. **Genres:** Social Sciences. **Career:** Actor, business person, public speaker and writer. **Publications:** Letters to a Young Brother: MANifest Your Destiny, 2006; Letters to a Young Sister: DeFINE Your Destiny, 2008; The Conversation, 2009; Wealth Cure, 2011. **Address:** Principato-Young Entertainment, 9465 Wilshire Blvd., Ste. 430, Beverly Hills, CA 90212, U.S.A. **Online address:** hillharperintern@gmail.com

HARPER, Jean. American (born United States), b. 1958?. **Genres:** Auto-

biography/Memoirs. **Career:** Indiana University East, assistant professor of English, associate professor, 1999-; Ball State University, Department of English, assistant professor, 2000-03; Earlham College, Department of Art, visiting instructor, 2000, 2002, Earlham School of Religion, visiting professor, 2011. Novelist. **Publications:** Rose City: A Memoir of Work, 2005; Horses and Divorces, forthcoming. Contributor to journals. **Address:** Department of English, University of Indiana East, 267 Whitewater Hall, 2325 Chester Blvd., Richmond, IN 47374, U.S.A. **Online address:** jeharper@indiana.edu

HARPER, Jo. American (born United States), b. 1932. **Genres:** Children's Fiction, Young Adult Fiction, Children's Non-fiction, Young Adult Non-fiction. **Career:** Junior high school, librarian, 1951-52; High school teacher of English, Spanish and humanities, 1964-68; Texas A&I University, instructor in English, 1968-70; Rockingham Community College, instructor in English and Spanish, 1971-77; Armstrong State College, assistant professor of English and Spanish and foreign student adviser, 1977-80; Texas Southern University, director of intensive English for foreign students, 1980-84; University of Houston, lecturer in English, 1984-96; Spring Branch Education Center, teacher of English to at-risk high school students, 1996-99; Houston Community College, instructor in English, 1999-, adjunct instructor in English. Writer. **Publications:** PICTURE BOOKS: The Harper's Voices-Caves and Cowboys: Family Song Book, 1988; Pals, Potions, and Pixies: Family Songbook, 1988; Jalapeno Hal, 1993; Outrageous, Bodacious Boliver Boggs!, 1996; Deaf Smith: Scout, Spy, and Texas Hero, 1996; Bigfoot Wallace: Texas Ranger and Mier Survivor, 1997; The Legend of Mexicatl, 1998; (with J. Harper) Prairie Dog Pioneers, 1998; Como los Perros de la Pradera, 1998; Bigfoot Wallace, 1999; Ollie Jolly, Rodeo Clown, 2002; Mayor Jalapeno Hal, 2003; (with J. Harper) Finding Daddy: A Story of the Great Depression, 2005. OTHERS: Delfino's Journey (young adult novel), 2001; Wilma Rudolph: Olympic Runner (middle grade biography), 2004; (with J. Harper) Teresa's Journey, 2006; I Could Eat You Up!, 2007; Birth of the Fifth Sun: And Other Mesoamerican Tales, 2008; (with J. Harper) Mier Men, 2011. **Address:** 1605 Huge Oaks, Houston, TX 77055, U.S.A. **Online address:** jo.harper@hccs.edu

HARPER, Judith E. American (born United States), b. 1953?. **Genres:** Adult Non-fiction, Biography. **Career:** Adirondack Explorer, freelance writer; Northwoods Magazine, freelance writer; The Boston Globe, freelance writer; Worcester Telegram and Gazette, freelance writer; Adirondack Safaris (tourism Co.), owner and hiking guide. Historian and educator. **Publications:** Susan B. Anthony: A Biographical Companion, 1998; Women during the Civil War: An Encyclopedia, 2004. NONFICTION FOR YOUNG READERS: Maya Angelou, 1999; Inuit, 1999; African Americans and the Revolutionary War, 2000; Andrew Johnson: Our Seventeenth President, 2002; John F. Kennedy: Our Thirty-fifth President, 2002; Unique Places, 2005. Contributor to periodicals. **Address:** Adirondack Safaris, PO Box 122, Johnsburg, NY 12843, U.S.A. **Online address:** juditheharper@gmail.com

HARPER, Julia. See **HOYT, Elizabeth.**

HARPER, Kenneth. See **MILES, Keith.**

HARPER, Lila Marz. American (born United States), b. 1955. **Genres:** Literary Criticism And History. **Career:** Central Washington University, instructor in English, 1989-, Honors College, General Education Writing Program, Department of Computer Science, senior lecturer, 1989-2010. Writer. **Publications:** Solitary Travelers: Nineteenth-Century Women's Travel Narratives and the Scientific Vocation, 2001; (ed.) Flatland, 2010. Contributor to books and periodicals. **Address:** Department of English, Central Washington University, 403-G Language & Literature Bldg., 400 E University Way, Ellensburg, WA 98926-7556, U.S.A. **Online address:** harperl@cwu.edu

HARPER, Michael S(teven). American (born United States), b. 1938. **Genres:** Poetry. **Career:** Pasadena City College, teacher, 1962; Contra Costa College, instructor in English, 1964-68; Lewis and Clark College, poet-in-residence, 1968-69; Reed College, visiting professor, 1968-69; California State College (now University), associate professor of English, 1970; Brown University, associate professor, 1970-73, professor, 1973-, I.J. Kapstein professor of English, 1983-, university professor, 1990-, director of writing program, poet laureate emeritus; Hayward State College, faculty, 1971; Harvard University, visiting professor, 1974-77; Yale University, visiting professor, 1976; Carleton College, Benedict distinguished professor of English, 1979; University of Cincinnati, visiting professor and Elliston poet, 1979; Colgate University, national humanities distinguished professor, 1985; University of

Alabama, visiting professor, 1987; University of Delaware, distinguished minority professor, 1988; MacAlester College, distinguished minority professor, 1989; New York University, Berg professor, distinguished visiting professor of literature, 1992; University of Houston, poet-in-residence, 1993; University of Virginia, REA Professor, 1998; Kenyon College, faculty, 1999; Bowdoin College, visiting professor, 2001. **Publications:** POETRY: Dear John, Dear Coltrane, 1970; History Is Your Own Heartbeat, 1971; Photographs, Negatives: History as Apple Tree, 1972; Song: I Want a Witness 1972; Debridement, 1973; Nightmare Begins Responsibility, 1974; Images of Kin: New and Selected Poems, 1977; Rhode Island: Eight Poems, 1981; Healing Song for the Inner Ear, 1985; Honorable Amendments: Poems, 1995; (ed.) Collected Poems of Sterling A. Brown, 1996; Songlines in Michaeltree: New and Collected Poems, 2000; Selected Poems, 2002; Debridement/Song: I Want a Witness, 2002; Use Trouble, 2009. OTHERS: (comp.) Leaving Eden: Poems, 1974; (comp.) Robert Hayden, 1978; (ed. with R.B. Stepto) Chant of Saints: A Gathering of Afro-American Literature, Art and Scholarship, 1979; (comp.) The Collected Poems of Sterling A. Brown, 1980; (ed. with J. Wright) Carleton Miscellany, 1980; (contrib.) Black American Literature and Humanism, 1981; (ed. with A. Walton) Every Shut Eye Ain't Asleep: An Anthology of Poetry by African Americans since 1945, 1994; (ed. with A. Walton) The Vintage Book of African-American Poetry, 2000. Works appear in anthologies. Contributor to periodicals. **Address:** Department of Literary Arts, Brown University, Providence, RI 02912-1923, U.S.A. **Online address:** michael_harper@brown.edu

HARPER, Piers. British (born England), b. 1966. **Genres:** Children's Fiction, Illustrations. **Career:** Author and illustrator of children's books, 1991-; Walker Books Ltd., editor and advisor. **Publications:** SELF-ILLUSTRATED: Snakes and Ladders (and Hundreds of Mice!): A Weird and Wonderful Tower Maze, 1997; If You Love a Bear, 1998; Checkmate at Chess City, 2000; B as in Bible, 2000; Snow Bear, 2002. OTHERS: (re-teller) How the World Was Saved and Other Native American Tales, 1994; Turtle Quest, 1997. Illustrator of books by others. **Address:** 40 Marne Ave., Ravenstown, Flookburgh, Grange-Over-Sands, CM LA11 7LH, England.

HARPER, Rachel M. American (born United States), b. 1972?. **Genres:** Novels, Young Adult Fiction. **Career:** Spalding University, MFA in Writing Program, faculty. Writer. **Publications:** Brass Ankle Blues, 2006; This Side of Providence, forthcoming. Contributor to journals. **Address:** c/o Maria Massie, Lippincott Massie McQuilkin, 27 W 20th St., Ste. 305, New York, NY 10011, U.S.A. **Online address:** mail@rachelmharper.com

HARPER, Susan (Rice). American (born United States), b. 1943. **Genres:** Local History/Rural Topics, Young Adult Fiction, Novellas/Short Stories. **Career:** San Francisco State University, lecturer in creative writing, 1980-93; Commerce Public Library, director, 1986-93. Writer. **Publications:** The Oakland Paramount, Lancaster-Miller, 1981; The Year of the Buck: And Other Stories, 1992. **Address:** Bureau of Jewish Education, 639 14th Ave., San Francisco, CA 94118, U.S.A.

HARPER, Tara K. American (born United States), b. 1961. **Genres:** Science Fiction/Fantasy, Novels. **Career:** The World Newspaper, science journalist, special reporter, 1983; Tektronix Inc., senior technical writer and editor, 1984-90; National Institute of Standards and Technology, technical writer and editor, 1988-; American National Standards Institute, technical writer and editor, 1988-; American Society for Quality Control, technical writer and editor, 1988-; Cascade Microtech Inc., technical documentation specialist, 1990-; Campfire, wilderness skills trainer, 1991-; Fowler Middle School, creative writing adviser, 1992-; Hillsboro School District, mentor, 1992-93; Tigard High School, creative writing teacher for alternative education programs, 1992-; Youth Contact, director, 1992-; Saint Andrew's Lutheran Church, creative adviser with youth programs, 1993; Youth Treatment Center, director. **Publications:** Wolfwalker, 1990; Shadow Leader, 1991; Lightwing, 1992; Storm Runner, 1993; Cat Scratch Fever, 1994; Cataract, 1995; Grayheart, 1996; Wolf's Bane, 1997; Silver Moons, Black Steel, 2001; Wolf in Night, 2005; Ghost Wolf, 2007. **Address:** c/o James Allen, PO Box 278, Milford, PA 18337, U.S.A.

HARPER-SCOTT, J. P. E. British (born England), b. 1977. **Genres:** Music. **Career:** University of London, Royal Holloway, Department of Music, lecturer, tutor for postgraduate admissions, 2005-. **Publications:** Elgar's Musical Language, 2003; Edward Elgar, Modernist, 2006; (ed. with J. Rushton) Elgar Studies, 2007; Elgar: An Extraordinary Life, 2007; (ed. with J. Samson) An Introduction to Music Studies, 2009. **Address:** Department of Music, Royal Holloway, University of London, Egham Hill, Egham, ES TW20 0EX, England. **Online address:** j.p.e.harper-scott@rhul.ac.uk

HARPHAM, Wendy S(chlessel). American (born United States), b. 1954. **Genres:** Medicine/Health, Sciences. **Career:** Presbyterian Hospital of Dallas, Department of Internal Medicine, attending physician, 1983-. Writer, public speaker and consultant. **Publications:** Diagnosis, Cancer: Your Guide through the First Few Months, 1992, rev. ed. as Diagnosis, Cancer: Your Guide to the First Months of Healthy Survivorship, 2003; After Cancer: A Guide to Your New Life, 1994; When a Parent Has Cancer: A Guide to Caring for Your Children, 1997; (with L. Numeroff) The Hope Tree: Kids Talk about Breast Cancer, 1999; Happiness in a Storm: Facing Illness and Embracing Life as a Healthy Survivor, 2005; Only 10 Seconds to Care: Help and Hope for Busy Clinicians, 2009. Contributor to books, journals and periodicals. **Address:** PO Box 835574, Richardson, TX 75083-5574, U.S.A. **Online address:** harpham@tx.rr.com

HARPUR, Tom. Canadian (born Canada), b. 1929. **Genres:** Ethics, Theology/Religion, Essays, Self Help. **Career:** Ordained Anglican, priest, 1956; Saint John's York Mills, curate, 1956-57; Saint Margaret's-in-the-Pines, rector, 1957-64; Trinity College, lecturer, 1960-62; Wycliffe College, lecturer in ancient philosophy, 1960-62, professor of New Testament and Greek, 1964-71; Toronto School of Theology, affiliate, 1964-71, part-time lecturer on the Theology, 1984-87; Toronto Star, religion editor, 1971-83; Toronto School of Theology, lecturer in theology, 1983-86; writer, 1986-. **Publications:** (With C. Templeton) Jesus, 1975; The Road to Bethlehem: 2000 Years Later, 1977; Harpur's Heaven and Hell (essays), 1983; For Christ's Sake, 1987; Communicating the Good News Today, 1987; Always on Sunday, 1988; Life after Death, 1991; God Help Us, 1992; The Uncommon Touch: An Investigation of Spiritual Healing, 1994; Harpur versus Hancock, 1994; The Divine Lover: A Celebration of Romantic Love for Lovers of All Ages, 1994; Would You Believe?, 1996, rev. ed. as Would You Believe? Finding God without Losing Your Mind, 2001; The Thinking Person's Guide to God: Overcoming the Obstacles to Belief, 1996; Prayer: The Hidden Fire: A Practical and Personal Approach, 1996; Finding the Still Point: A Spiritual Response to Stress, 2002; The Pagan Christ: Recovering the Lost Light, 2004; The Spirituality Of Wine, 2004; Living Waters, 2006; Water Into Wine, 2007; Born Again: My Journey from Fundamentalism to Freedom a Spiritual Memory, 2011; There is Life After Death, 2011. Contributor to periodicals. **Address:** PO Box 3216, Meaford, ON N4L 1A5, Canada. **Online address:** thestar@bmts.com

HARRE, Rom. British/American/New Zealander (born New Zealand), b. 1927. **Genres:** Psychology, Sciences, Education, Social Sciences. **Career:** Kings College, instructor in physics, 1948-53; University of Leicester, lecturer, 1957-60; Oxford University, Linacre College, lecturer in philosophy of science, 1960-97, fellow, 1965-97, emeritus fellow, 1997-; State University of New York, adjunct professor, 1973-98; Georgetown University, Department of Psychology, distinguished research professor, 1989-, adjunct professor; American University, distinguished adjunct professor; Oxford University, lecturer in philosophy of science; London School of Economics, Centre for Natural and Social Science (CPNSS), director. Writer. **Publications:** An Introduction to the Logic of the Sciences, 1960; Theories and Things, 1961; Matter and Method, 1964; The Anticipation of Nature, 1965; The Method of Science, 1970; The Principles of Scientific Thinking, 1970; The Philosophies of Science, 1972; (with P.F. Second) The Explanation of Social Behaviour, 1973; (with E.H. Madden) Causal Powers, 1975; (with J. Hawthorn) A Selective Bibliography of Philosophy of Science, 1977; (with P. Marsh and E. Rosses) The Rules of Disorder, 1978; (with J. Morgan and C. O'Neill) Nicknames: Their Origins and Social Consequences, 1979; Social Being: A Theory for Social Psychology, 1979; Great Scientific Experiments: Twenty Experiments That Changed Our View of the World, 1981; Introduction To the Logic of the Sciences, 1983; Personal Being: A Theory for Individual Psychology, 1984; (with D. Clarke and N. de Carlo) Motives and Mechanisms: An Introduction to the Psychology of Action, 1985; Philosophies of Science, 1985; Varieties of Realism: A Rationale for the Natural Science, 1986; (with P. Muhlhausler) Pronouns and People: The Linguistic Construction of Social and Personal Identity, 1990; Physical Being: A Theory for a Corporeal Psychology, 1991; Laws of Nature, 1993; (with G. Gillett) The Discursive Mind, 1994; (with J.L. Aronson and C. Way) Realism Rescued: How Scientific Progress is Possible, 1995; (with M. Krausz) Varieties of Relativism, 1996; Singular Self: An

Introduction to the Psychology of Personhood, 1998; Greenspeak: A Study of Environmental Discourse, 1999; One Thousand Years of Philosophy: From Rāmānujato Wittgenstein, 2000; Cognitive Science: A Philosophical Introduction, 2002; Great Scientific Experiments: Twenty Experiments That Changed Our View of the World, 2002; (with M.A. Tissaw) Wittgenstein and Psychology: A Practical Guide, 2005; Key Thinkers in Psychology, 2006; Pavlov's Dogs and Schrödinger's Cat: Scenes from the Living Laboratory, 2009; (with S. Tan and P. Pfordhresher) Psychology of Music: From Sound to Significance, 2010. EDITOR: Early Seventeenth Century Scientists, 1965; The Principles of Linguistic Philosophy, 1965; The Sciences: Its Aims and Methods, 1967; How I See Philosophy, 1968; Some Nineteenth Century British Scientists, 1969; Scientific Thought 1900-1960, 1969; Problems of Scientific Revolution, 1975; Life Sentences, 1976; Personality, 1976; (with E.J. Jensen) The Philosophy of Evolution, 1982; (with M.V. Cranach) The Analysis of Action: Recent Theoretical and Empirical Advances, 1982; (with V. Reynolds) The Meaning of Primate Signals, 1984; (with R. Lamb) The Dictionary of Personality and Social Psychology, 1986; The Physical Sciences Since Antiquity, 1986; The Social Construction of Emotions, 1986; (with H.R. Brown) Philosophical Foundations of Quantum Field Theory, 1988; Anglo-Ukrainain Studies in the Analysis of Scientific Discourse: Reason and Rhetoric, 1993; (with R. Harris) Linguistics and Philosophy: The Controversial Interface, 1993; (with J.A. Smith and L.V. Langenhove) Rethinking Methods in Psychology, 1995; (with J.A. Smith and L.V. Langenhove) Rethinking Psychology, 1995; (with P. Stearns) Discursive Psychology in Practice, 1995; (with G. Parrott) The Emotions: Social, Cultural and Biological Dimensions, 1996; (with L.V. Langenhove) Positioning Theory: Moral Contexts of Intentional Action, 1999; (with F.M. Moghaddam) Self And Others: Positioning Individuals and Groups in Personal, Political and Cultural Contexts, 2003; Modeling: Gateway to the Unknown: A Work, 2004; (with F.M. Moghaddam and N. Lee) Global Conflict Resolution Through Positioning Analysis, 2008; People and Societies: Rom Harré and Designing the Social Sciences, 2010; (with F. Moghaddam) Words of Conflict, Words of War, 2010; (with F. Moghaddem) Psychology for the Third Millennium: Integrating Mainstream and Normative Human Science, 2012. CO-EDITOR: Encyclopedic Dictionary of Psychology, 1983; The Dictionary of Developmental and Educational Psychology, 1986; The Dictionary of Ethology and Animal Learning, 1986; The Dictionary of Physiological and Clinical Psychology, 1986. Contributor to journals and periodicals. **Address:** Department of Psychology, Georgetown University, 301 D White Gravenor, PO Box 571001, Washington, DC 20057-1001, U.S.A. **Online address:** harre@georgetown.edu

HARRELL, Beatrice Orcutt. American (born United States), b. 1943. **Genres:** Mythology/Folklore, Cultural/Ethnic Topics, Novels, History. **Career:** Indian Health Care, social service counselor, 1975-77; Green Bay Packaging, personnel assistant, 1987-91; Sapulpa Indian Education, tutor, 1995-. Writer. **Publications:** (Reteller) How Thunder and Lightning Came to Be: A Choctaw Legend, 1995; Choctaw Mother (story), 1995; Longwalker's Journey: A Novel of the Choctaw Trail of Tears, 1999. Contributor to periodicals. **Address:** 13962 Hickory Pl., Glenpool, OK 74033, U.S.A.

HARRI, Kitty. See SEWELL, Kitty.

HARRIES, Karsten. German (born Germany), b. 1937. **Genres:** Architecture, Art/Art History, Philosophy, Ethics. **Career:** Yale University, instructor in philosophy, 1961-63, assistant professor, 1965-66, associate professor, 1966-70, professor of philosophy, 1970-, Brooks and Suzanne Ragen professor of philosophy, 2006-, director of graduate studies; University of Texas, assistant professor of philosophy, 1963-65. Writer. **Publications:** The Meaning of Modern Art: A Philosophical Interpretation, 1967; The Bavarian Rococo Church: Between Faith and Aestheticism, 1983; The Broken Frame, 1989; (ed. with C. Jamme) Martin Heidegger: Kunst, Politik, Technik, 1992, trans. as Martin Heidegger: Politics, Art, and Technology, 1994; The Ethical Function of Architecture, 1996; Infinity and Perspective, 2001; (with T. Myers and L. Woods) Lebbeus Woods: Experimental Architecture, 2004; Art Matters: A Critical Commentary on Heidegger's The Origin of the Work of Art, 2009; Between Nihilism and Faith: A Commentary on Either/Or, 2010. Contributor of articals to journals. **Address:** Department of Philosophy, Yale University, Connecticut Hall 107, 157 Church St., PO Box C108, New Haven, CT 06520-8306, U.S.A. **Online address:** karsten.harries@yale.edu

HARRIES, Patrick. Swiss/South African (born South Africa), b. 1950. **Genres:** Social Sciences. **Career:** University of Cape Town, instructor, 1975-80, lecturer, 1980-87, senior lecturer, 1987-93, associate professor,

1993-2000; University of Basel Africa, Centre for African Studies and Centre of Excellence, manager; University of Lausanne, visiting professor, 1991-92; Ecole des Hautes Etudes en Sciences Sociales, visiting professor, 1992; Maison des Sciences de l'Homme, visiting professor; Humboldt University, visiting professor, 1996; Institut d'Etudes Politiques de Paris, visiting professor, 2000; University of Wisconsin, visiting professor, 2001; University of Basel, professor of history, 2001-; University of Cape Town, visiting professor, 2001-03; University of Stellenbosch, Institute for Advanced Studies, fellow, 2002. Writer. **Publications:** Work, Culture, and Identity: Migrant Laborers in Mozambique and South Africa, c. 1860-1910, 1994; Butterflies and Barbarians: Swiss Missionaries and Systems of Knowledge in South-East Africa, 2007. Contributor to books and periodicals. **Address:** Switzerland. **Online address:** patrick.harries@unibas.ch

HARRIFORD, Daphne. See HARRIS, Marion (Rose).

HARRIGAN, Patrick J. Canadian/American (born United States), b. 1941. **Genres:** History, Education, Reference. **Career:** University of Waterloo, professor of history, through 1969, now distinguished professor emeritus; Princeton University, Shelby Cullom Davis fellow. Writer. **Publications:** (With V. Negila) Lycéens et Collégiens sous le Second Empire: étude Statistiquesur les Fonctions Sociales de L'enseignement Secondaire Public, D'après L'enquête de Victor Duruy (1864-1865): Introduction Suivie de 148 Tableaux, 1979; (ed. with D. Baker) The Making of Frenchmen: Current Directions in the History of Education in France, 1679-1979, 1980; Mobility, Elites and Education in French Society of the Second Empire, 1980; (with R. Grew) School, State and Society: The Growth of Elementary Schooling in Nineteenth-Century France, 1991; The Detroit Tigers: Club and Community 1945-1995, 1997. **Address:** Department of History, University of Waterloo, 153 Hagey Hall, Waterloo, ON N2L 3G1, Canada. **Online address:** harrigan@uwaterloo.ca

HARRIGER, Katy J(ean). American (born United States), b. 1957. **Genres:** Politics/Government, Social Sciences. **Career:** University of Connecticut, Department of Political Science, teaching assistant, 1979-84, instructor in political science, 1983-84; Wake Forest University, Department of Political Science, instructor, 1985-86, assistant professor, 1986-91, associate professor, 1991-2002, Zachary T. Smith professor, 2002-, Teaching and Learning Center, director, 1997-99, chair, 2007-. Writer. **Publications:** Independent Justice: The Federal Special Prosecutor in American Politics, 1992; The Special Prosecutor in American Politics, 2000; (with L. Fisher) American Constitutional Law, 2009, 9th ed., 2011. EDITOR: Separation of Powers: Commentary & Documents, 2003; (with J.J. McMillan) Speaking of Politics: Preparing College Students for Democratic Citizenship through Deliberative Dialogue, 2007. Works appear in anthologies. Contributor of articles to periodicals and journals. **Address:** Department of Political Science, Wake Forest University, Tribble C-309, PO Box 7568, Winston-Salem, NC 27109, U.S.A. **Online address:** harriger@wfu.edu

HARRILL, Ronald. American (born United States), b. 1950. **Genres:** Biography, Autobiography/Memoirs, Children's Fiction. **Career:** First Union National Bank, systems analyst, assistant vice president, 1978-. Author, lecturer and storyteller. **Publications:** Makeda, Queen of Sheba, 1995. **Address:** 2311 Holly Ln., Shelby, NC 28150, U.S.A.

HARRIMAN, Steven. See SPRUILL, Steven.

HARRINGTON, Anne. American (born United States), b. 1960. **Genres:** History. **Career:** Harvard University, professor of the history of science and department chair, Mind, Brain and Behavior Initiative, co-director, Harvard Summer School, Study Abroad Program in London lecturer; MacArthur Foundation Research Network on Mind-Body Interactions, consultant; Biosocieties, co-editor. **Publications:** Medicine, Mind and the Double Brain: A Study in Nineteenth-Century Thought, 1987; (ed.) So Human a Brain: Knowledge and Values in the Neurosciences, 1992; Reenchanted Science: Holism in German Culture from Wilhelm II to Hitler, 1996; (ed.) The Placebo Effect: An Interdisciplinary Exploration, 1997; (ed. with R.J. Davidson) Visions of Compassion: Western Scientists and Tibetan Buddhists Examine Human Nature, 2002; (ed. with A. Zajonc) The Dalai Lama at MIT, 2006; The Cure Within: A History of Mind-Body Medicine, 2008. **Address:** Department of History of Science, Harvard University, Science Ctr., 1 Oxford St., 3rd Fl., Cambridge, MA 02138, U.S.A. **Online address:** aharring@fas.harvard.edu

HARRINGTON, David. See BLAKE, Mark R.

HARRINGTON, John P. American (born United States), b. 1952. **Genres:** Literary Criticism And History, Art/Art History. **Career:** St. Peter's college, assistant professor of English and director of composition, 1985-86; The Cooper Union, assistant professor, 1986-91, associate professor, 1991-96, professor of humanities, 1996, dean of faculty of humanities and social sciences, 1992-2002, The Cooper Union Academic Council of Deans, chair, Cooper Union Library, director, The Humanities Gallery, founder and director; Irish Studies Review, editor, 1997-; Rensselaer Poltecnic Institute, School of Humanities, Arts and Social Sciences, chief executive officer, dean and professor of humanities, 2002-09; Fordham University, Faculty of Arts and Sciences, dean and professor of English, 2009-. **Publications:** The English Traveller in Ireland: Accounts of Ireland and the Irish Through Five Centuries, 1990; The Irish Beckett, 1991; (ed.) Modern Irish Drama, 1991, 2nd ed. as Modern and Contemporary Irish Drama, 2009; Irish Play on the New York Stage, 1874-1966, 1997; (ed. with E.J. Mitchell) Politics and Performance in Contemporary Northern Ireland, 1999; The Life of the Neighborhood Playhouse on Grand Street, 2007; Modem and Contemporary Irish Drama, 2008; (co-ed.) The Future of Irish Studies, 2006; (ed.) Irish Theater in America, 2009. **Address:** Faculty of Arts and Sciences, Fordham University, 416 Dealy Hall, Bronx, NY 10458, U.S.A. **Online address:** jharrington15@fordham.edu

HARRINGTON, Karen. American (born United States), b. 1967. **Genres:** Novels. **Career:** Writer. **Publications:** Janeology: A Novel, 2008. **Address:** Plano, TX , U.S.A. **Online address:** kharrin2003@yahoo.com

HARRINGTON, Kathleen. American (born United States) **Genres:** Romance/Historical, Medicine/Health, Novels, Young Adult Fiction. **Career:** Writer. **Publications:** HISTORICAL-ROMANCE NOVELS: Cherish the Dream, 1990; Warrior Dreams, 1992; Sunshine and Shadow, 1993; Montana Angel, 1994; Promise Me, 1995; Dream Catcher, 1996; Fly with the Eagle, 1997; Enchanted by You, 1998; The MacLean Groom, 1999; BOOKS ON AUTISM: Autism in Adolescents & Adults, 1998; Giving Parents Reasons for Hope, Encouragement for Parents, Guidance for Help, 2000. **Address:** Avon Books, 10 E 53rd St., New York, NY 10022, U.S.A.

HARRINGTON, Philip S(tuart). American (born United States), b. 1956. **Genres:** Astronomy, Recreation, Meteorology/Atmospheric Sciences, Sciences, Adult Non-fiction. **Career:** Hayden Planetarium, planetarium professional, 1979-81; Vanderbilt Planetarium, instructor, 1982-97; Unisys Corp., mechanical engineer, 1983-92; Brookhaven National Laboratory, supervisor of course development, 1992-; Suffolk County Community College, adjunct instructor, 1998-, adjunct professor; Dowling College, adjunct professor; Astronomy Magazine, contributing editor; Westport (CT) Astronomical Society, founding member. **Publications:** Touring the Universe Through Binoculars: A Complete Astronomer's Guidebook, 1990; (with W. Harrington) Short Bike Rides in and Around NYC, 1992; (with E. Pascuzzi) Astronomy for All Ages: Discovering the Universe Through Activities for Children and Adults, 1994, 2nd ed., 2000; Star Ware: The Amateur Astronomer's Ultimate Guide to Choosing, Buying and Using Telescopes and Accessories, 1994, 4th ed., 2007; Eclipse!: The What, Where, When, Why and How Guide to Watching Solar and Lunar Eclipses, 1997; The Deep Sky: An Introduction, 1997; The Space Shuttle: A Photographic History, 2003; Star Watch: The Amateur Astronomer's Guide to Finding, Observing and Learning About Over 125 Celestial Objects, 2003; (with R.H. Sanderson) The Illustrated Timeline of the Universe: A Crash Course in Words & Pictures, 2006; Cosmic Challenge, 2010. Contributor to magazines. **Address:** PO Box 732, Upton, NY 11973-0732, U.S.A. **Online address:** phil@philharrington.net

HARRIOTT, Peter. American (born United States), b. 1927. **Genres:** Engineering. **Career:** E.I. duPont de Nemours, engineer, 1949; General Electric Co., research engineer, 1952-53; Cornell University, assistant professor, 1953-54, associate professor, 1954-65, professor of chemical engineering, 1965-, Fred Hoffman Rhodes professor of chemical engineering, 1975-, now professor emeritus. Writer and consultant. **Publications:** Process Control, 1964; (with W.L. McCabe and J.C. Smith) Unit Operations of Chemical Engineering, 4th ed., 1985, 7th ed., 2005; Chemical Reactor Design, 2003. **Address:** School of Chemical & Biomolecular Engineering, Cornell University, 120 Olin Hall, Ithaca, NY 14853-5201, U.S.A. **Online address:** ph@cheme.cornell.edu

HARRIS, Alan. American (born United States), b. 1944. **Genres:** Astronomy. **Career:** University of California-Los Angeles, graduate research assistant, 1966-67, 1973-75, visiting associate professor of earth and science; Space

Division Rockwell Intl., staff, 1968-70; Santa Monica College, physics instructor, 1970-71; Immaculate Heart High School, physical teacher, 1970-73; Jet Propulsion Lab, technical staff, 1974-91, senior member of technical staff, 1991-97, senior research scientist, 1998-2002; NATO Advanced Study Institute on Origin of the Solar System, faculty, 1976; University of California-Santa Barbara, visiting associate professor, 1978; Earth and Planetary Physics Group, supervisor, 1983-92; U.S. Delegation, deputy chairman, 1985-93; Table Mountain Observatory, science manager, 1985-88; International Astronomical Union, organizing commissioner, 1985-88, vice president, 1988-91, president, 1991; CRAF Proposal Review Panel, subgroup chairman, 1986; Dynamical Astronomy of AAS, vice chairman, 1990-91, chairman, 1991-92; University of Paris, visiting professor, 1992-93, 1999; Division of Planetary Sciences, secretary, 1995-2001; Space Science Institute, senior research scientist, 2002-. Writer. **Publications:** (With P. Weissman) The Great Voyager Adventure, 1990. Contributor to books on astronomical subjects. **Address:** Space Science Institute, 4750 Walnut St., Ste. 205, Boulder, CO 80301, U.S.A. **Online address:** harrisaw@colorado.edu

HARRIS, Anne L. American (born United States), b. 1964?. **Genres:** Science Fiction/Fantasy, Novels, Sex, Young Adult Fiction. **Career:** U.S. Department of Defense, operations research analyst. Small-town reporter and public relations writer. **Publications:** NOVELS: The Nature of Smoke, 1996; Accidental Creatures, 1998; Inventing Memory, 2004; Facing the Wind, 2006. **Address:** c/o Author Mail, Tor Books, 175 5th Ave., 14th Fl., New York, NY 10010, U.S.A. **Online address:** annesible@gmail.com

HARRIS, Archibald. *See* **FLEISSNER, Robert F.**

HARRIS, Bob. *See* **HARRIS, Robert J.**

HARRIS, Brayton. American (born United States), b. 1932. **Genres:** Military/Defense/Arms Control, Writing/Journalism, Autobiography/Memoirs. **Career:** U.S. Selective Service System, assistant director, 1980-81; Boerger/Harris Ltd., partner; Pratt & Whitney, public relations representative, 1984-90; B.F. Goodrich Aerospace, director of communications, 1990-98; Crown and Anchor Development Inc., executive vice president, 2001-. Customer Relations Threeway Inc., vice president; Martin County Council for the Arts, vice president. Writer. **Publications:** (With M. McGuire and R. Dunlap) Three San Francisco Playwights: Three One Act Plays, 1962; Age of the Battleship, 1890-1922, 1965; Johann Gutenberg and the Invention of Printing, 1972; (with J. Kirschenbaum) U.S. Navy Diving Manual, 1972; (with J. Kirschenbaum) Safe Boat: A Comprehensive Guide to the Purchase, Equipping, Maintenance and Operation of a Safe Boat, 1990; The Navy Times Book of Submarines: A Political, Social and Military History, 1997; Blue & Gray in Black & White: Newspapers in the Civil War, 1999; (ed.) The Civil War: Ironweed American Newspapers and Periodicals Project, 2002; Admiral Nimitz, 2012. **Address:** 6521 Mission Rd., Mission Hills, KS 66208, U.S.A. **Online address:** brayton@harris.net

HARRIS, Carla A. American (born United States), b. 1962. **Genres:** inspirational/Motivational Literature, Business/Trade/Industry, Self Help. **Career:** Morgan Stanley, Department of Mergers and Acquisitions, investment banker, 1985-91, managing director for global capital markets, 1999-, Equity Private Placement Group, director, 2003-. Writer. **Publications:** Expect to Win: Proven Strategies for Success from a Wall Street Vet, 2009. **Address:** Morgan Stanley, 1585 Broadway, New York, NY 10036, U.S.A.

HARRIS, Charles Wesley. American (born United States), b. 1928?. **Genres:** Politics/Government, Urban Studies, History, Social Sciences. **Career:** Texas College, assistant professor, 1950-53; Tuskegee Institute, assistant professor, 1954-56; University of Wisconsin, James Found fellow, 1956-58; Grambling State University, associate professor, 1959-61; Coppin State College, associate professor, 1961-66, Division of Social Sciences, chairperson, 1967-68, director of graduate studies, 1969-70; U.S. Civil Service Commission, associate director of executive Institutes, 1966-67; Xerox Corp., research associate, 1968; Howard University, professor of political science, 1970-, department head, 1974-77, College of Liberal Arts, associate dean, 1988-92; Library of Congress, Congressional Research Service, senior specialist and chief of government division, 1971-74; Woodrow Wilson International Center for Scholars, fellow, 1992-94. Writer. **Publications:** A Research Brief on Councils of Governments and the Central City, 1970; Regional Councils of Government and the Central City, 1970; Resolving the Legislative Veto Issue: A Review of Proposals and Opinions, 1979; (with A. Thornton) Perspectives of Political

Power in the District of Columbia: The Views and Opinions of 110 Members of the Local Political Elite, 1981; Congress and the Governance of the Nation's Capital: The Conflict of Federal and Local Interests, 1995; Foreign Capital City Governance: Representation, Governmental Structure, Finances and Intergovernmental Relations in Six Capital Cities, 1997. Contributor to books and professional journals. **Address:** 13908 Turnmore Rd., Silver Spring, MD 20906, U.S.A.

HARRIS, Christine. Australian (born Australia), b. 1955. **Genres:** Novellas/Short Stories, Romance/Historical, Science Fiction/Fantasy, Children's Fiction, Young Adult Fiction, Plays/Screenplays, Picture/Board Books, Humor/Satire, Humor/Satire, Children's Non-fiction. **Career:** Jenny Piper Promotions, staff, 1986-87; writer, 1988-; Myer Bookstore, sales assistant, 1990-74. **Publications:** SHORT STORY COLLECTIONS: Outer Face, 1992; Buried Secrets, 1993; Widdershins, 1995, as Party Animals, 1997; (with C. Carmichael and M. Clark) Deadly Friends, 1997; Fortune Cookies, 1998; Warped, 2000. NOVELS FOR YOUNG ADULTS: Strike!, 1994; Baptism of Fire, 1996; Foreign Devil, 1999; Outback: The Diary of Jimmy Porter 1927-28, 2005. CHILDREN'S FICTION: Torture Chamber, 1997; Slime Time, 1997; Hairy Legs, 2001; Halfway Round the World, 2001; Brain Drain, 2001; Windbag, 2001; Psycho Gran, 2001; Jamil's Shadow, 2002; Cool Bananas, 2007; Audrey of the Outback, 2008; Audrey Goes to Town, 2008; Audrey's Big Secret, 2009. SCIENCE-FICTION NOVELS: Pitt Man, 1996; Suspicion, 1998; Masks, 1998; Jigsaw, 1998; Shadows, 1998; Omega, 2000; Head Space, 2004; Spygirl, vol. I: Secrets, 2004, vol. II: Fugitive, 2004, vol. III: Nightmare 2005, vol. IV: Danger, 2005, vol. V: Twisted, 2007; Freaks, 2007; Mask of the Jackal, 2008. FOR CHILDREN: Sleeping In (picture book), 1997; I Don't Want to Go to School (picture book), 1999; Snowy's Rescue, 2008. EDITOR-NON-FICTION: No Bed of Roses, 1993; Old Yanconian School Daze, 1995; What a Line!, 1995; In Looking-Glass Land, 1996. OTHER: Trees in My Ears: Children from around the World Talk to Christine Harris, 1992; Countdown (novel), 1995; A Real Corpse, 1997; Odd Balls: Jokes and Funny Stories, 1998; The Little Book of Elephants (humor and nonfiction), 1999; Break a Leg (plays), 2001. **Address:** PO Box 478, Mount Barker, SA 5251, Australia. **Online address:** christine@christineharris.com

HARRIS, Claire. Canadian (born Canada), b. 1937. **Genres:** Novellas/Short Stories, Poetry, Essays, Young Adult Fiction. **Career:** Poetry Goes Public, editor, 1976-79; Dandelion (magazine), poetry editor, 1981-89; Blue Buffalo, co-founder, 1982, managing editor, 1982-84; Catholic high school, teacher, through 1994. **Publications:** Translation into Fiction, 1984; Fables from the Women's Quarters, 1984; Travelling to Find a Remedy, 1986; The Conception of Winter, 1989; Drawing down a Daughter, 1992; (ed. with E. Alford) Kitchen Talk: An Anthology of Writings by Canadian Women, 1992; (with D. Brand and M.N. Philip) Grammar of Dissent: Poetry and Prose, 1995; Dipped in Shadow, 1996; She (novella), 2000; Under Black Light: New and Selected Poems, forthcoming. Contributor to magazines. Works appear in anthologies. **Address:** 300 Meredith Rd. NE, Ste. 701, Calgary, AB T2E 7A8, Canada.

HARRIS, C. Nelson. American (born United States), b. 1964. **Genres:** Novels, Adult Non-fiction, History. **Career:** Ridgewood Baptist Church, pastor, 1989-98; City of Roanoke, vice mayor, 1996-2003, mayor, 2004-08; Virginia Heights Baptist Church, pastor, 1999-; Virginia Western Community College, adjunct faculty of religion and philosophy. Writer. **Publications:** The Seventeenth Virginia Cavalry, 1994; Roanoke in Vintage Postcards, 2002; Images of Rail: Norfolk & Western Railway, 2003; Norfolk and Western Railway Stations and Depots, 2009. **Address:** Virginia Heights Baptist Church, 2014 Memorial Ave. SW, Roanoke, VA 24015, U.S.A.

HARRIS, Deborah Turner. Scottish/American (born United States), b. 1951. **Genres:** Science Fiction/Fantasy, Novels, History, Literary Criticism And History. **Career:** Teacher of English literature and composition, 1974-83; part-time writer, 1983-87; writer, 1987-. **Publications:** MAGES OF GARILLON SERIES: The Burning Stone, 1987; The Gauntlet of Malice, 1988; Spiral of Fire, 1989. ADEPT SERIES WITH K. KURTZ: The Adept, 1991; The Lodge of the Lynx, 1992; The Templar Treasure, 1993; Dagger Magic: A Novel of the Adept, 1995; Death of an Adept: A Novel of the Adept, 1996. CALEDON SERIES: Caledon of the Mists, 1994; Queen of Ashes, 1995; City of Exile, 1997. WITH ROBERT J. HARRIS: The City Of Brass, 1995; The Company Of Three, 1998; Last Kingdom, 1999; Cusade Of Fire, 2002. KNIGHTS TEMPLAR SERIES WITH K. KURTZ: The Temple and the Stone, 1998; The Temple and the Crown, 2001. OTHER: (contrib.) Tales of the Knights Templar, 1995. **Address:** Virginia Kidd Agency, 538

E Harford St., PO Box 278, Milford, PA 18337, U.S.A. **Online address:** debby@harris-authors.com

HARRIS, Denise Michelle. American (born United States), b. 1970. **Genres:** Novels. **Career:** Christian Preschool, teacher; ANG Newspapers, advertising sales staff; San Jose Mercury News, advertising sales staff; The Weather Channel, advertising sales staff. Novelist. **Publications:** Sweet Bye-Bye, 2004. **Address:** c/o Author Mail, Warner Books, 1271 Ave. of the Americas, New York, NY 10020-1300, U.S.A. **Online address:** dniceh@yahoo.com

HARRIS, Dudley Arthur. South African (born South Africa), b. 1925. **Genres:** Chemistry, Horticulture, Sciences. **Career:** South African Council for Scientific and Industrial Research, 1948-51; J. Muller Labs, director, analytical and consulting chemist, 1953-81. Writer. **Publications:** Hydroponics: The Gardening Without Soil: Easy-to-Follow Instructions for the Flatweiler, Hobbyist and Commercial Grower, 1966, 4th ed., 1974; Hydroponics, 1975, 7th ed., 1987; The Illustrated Guide to Hydroponics, 1994. **Address:** A22 Larmenier Village, 1 Derry St., Vredehoek, Capetown, 8001, South Africa.

HARRIS, Elizabeth. American (born United States), b. 1944. **Genres:** Novels, Novellas/Short Stories, Young Adult Fiction, Literary Criticism And History. **Career:** University of Texas, Department of English, assistant professor, 1976-83, associate professor, 1983-. Writer. **Publications:** The Ant Generator (stories), 1991. Contributor to journals. **Address:** Department of English, University of Texas, 1 University Sta. B5000, PAR 29, Austin, TX 78712-1164, U.S.A.

HARRIS, Elizabeth. See CLARE, Alys.

HARRIS, Fredrick C. American (born United States), b. 1962. **Genres:** Theology/Religion, Politics/Government, Humanities. **Career:** University of Rochester, Center for the Study of African-American Politics, director, Frederick Douglass Institute for African and African-American Studies, director; Columbia University, professor of political science, Institute for Research in African-American Studies, director. Writer. **Publications:** Something Within: Religion in African-American Political Activism, 1999; (ed. with R.D. Smith) Black Churches and Local Politics: Clergy Influence, Organizational Partnerships, and Civic Empowerment, 2005; (with V. Sinclair-Chapman and B.D. McKenzie) Countervailing Forces in African-American Civic Activism, 1973-1994, 2006; The Price of the Ticket: Barack Obama and the Rise and Fall of Black Politics, 2012. Contributor to journals. **Address:** Department of Political Science, University of Rochester, 732 Intl Affairs Bldg. 7th Fl., 420 W 118th St., PO Box 3320, Rochester, NY 14627-0146, U.S.A. **Online address:** fh2170@columbia.edu

HARRIS, Fred R(oy). American (born United States), b. 1930. **Genres:** Novels, Politics/Government, Autobiography/Memoirs. **Career:** Harris, Newcomrbe, Redman and Doolin, founder and managing partner, 1956-64; Democratic Party, National chair, 1969-70; Peoples Policy Center (public interest and research organization), president, 1973-75; American University, adjunct professor of government, 1973-76; University of New Mexico, visiting professor, 1976, professor of political science, 1977-, now professor emeritus, Institute for Public Policy, director, 1985-87, University Partnership Program, director, 1989-91; University of Oklahoma, visiting professor of political science, 1981-; Democratic Party of New Mexico, state chair, 1998-99; Common Cause New Mexico, state chair, 1999-. Writer. **Publications:** NON-FICTION: Alarms and Hopes: A Personal Journey, a Personal View, 1968; (ed.) Social Science and National Policy, 1970, 2nd ed., 1973; Now Is the Time: A New Populist Call to Action, 1971; (with J.V. Lindsay) State of the Cities: Report, 1972; The New Populism, 1973; Potomac Fever, 1977; America's Democracy: The Ideal and Reality, 1980, 3rd ed., 1986; 1980 Elections: The Voters Turn Toward Reagan and the Republicans, 1980; (with P.L. Hain) America's Legislative Processes: Congress and the States, 1983; 1984 Elections, 1985; (with D. Cooper) Estudios sobre Estados Unidos y su Relaion Bilateral con Meico, 1986; (ed.) Readings on the Body Politic, 1987; (with R. Roberts and M.S. Elliston) Understanding American Government, 1988; (ed. with R.W. Wilkins) Quiet Riots: Race and Poverty in the United States, 1988; (with G. Wasserman) America's Government, 1990; (ed.) Los Obstaculos para el Desarrollo, 1991; Deadlock or Decision: The U.S. Senate and the Rise of National Politics, 1993; In Defense of Congress, 1995; (ed. with L.A. Curtis) Locked in the Poorhouse: Cities, Race and Poverty in the United States, 1998; (ed.) Baby Bust: Who Will do the Work? Who will Pay the Taxes?, 2006; Does People Do It?: A Memoir, 2008. NOVELS: Coyote Revenge, 1999; Easy Pickin's, 2000; Following the Harvest, 2004. Contributor to periodicals. **Address:** Department Political Science, University of New Mexico, 2059 Social Sciences Bldg., 1915 Roma NE, PO Box 05-3070, Albuquerque, NM 87131-0001, U.S.A. **Online address:** fharris@unm.edu

HARRIS, George A. American (born United States), b. 1950. **Genres:** Psychology, Sciences. **Career:** Veterans Administration Hospital, intern; Goodwill Industries, staff psychologist, 1975-76; Jackson County Department of Corrections, intern, counselor, 1976-77, training coordinator, 1977-78; Washburn University of Topeka, assistant professor of criminal justice, 1978-; National Institute of Corrections, consultant; Western Interstate Commission for Higher Education, consultant. Writer. **Publications:** Broken Ears, Wounded Hearts, 1983; (with D. Watkins) Counseling the Involuntary and Resistant Client, 1987; (ed.) Tough Customers: Counseling Unwilling Clients, 1991; Overcoming Resistance: Success in Counseling Men, 1995. Contributor to journals. **Address:** American Correctional Association, 4380 Forbes Blvd., Lanham, MD 20706-4322, U.S.A.

HARRIS, Helen(a) (Barbara Mary). British (born England), b. 1927. **Genres:** Agriculture/Forestry, Archaeology/Antiquities, Area Studies, Local History/Rural Topics, Reference. **Career:** Ministry of Agriculture, dairy adviser, 1948-56; The Devon Historian, honorary editor, 1985-2005. **Publications:** The Industrial Archaeology of Dartmoor, 1968, rev. ed., 1992; The Industrial Archaeology of the Peak District, 1971, rev. ed., 1992; (with M. Ellis) The Bude Canal, 1972; The Grand Western Canal, 1973, rev. ed., 1996; How to Survive Vision Loss, 1994; The Haytor Granite Tramway and Stover Canal, 1994, rev. ed., 2002; The Church on the Hill (Buckfastleigh), 1996; Devon's Century of Change, 1998; A Handbook of Devon Parishes: A Complete Guide for Local and Family Historians, 2004. **Address:** Hirondelles, 22 Churchill Rd., Whitchurch, Tavistock, DN PL19 9BU, England.

HARRIS, James F. (James Franklin Harris). American (born United States), b. 1941. **Genres:** Philosophy, Ethics, Theology/Religion. **Career:** Transylvania University, assistant professor of philosophy, 1966-67; University of Georgia, assistant professor of history, 1967-73; College of William and Mary, associate professor of philosophy, 1975-80, professor of philosophy, 1980-, Francis S. Haserot endowed chair in philosophy, 1982-2009, chairman, 1990-97, 2000-05, Francis S. Haserot professor or philosophy, through 2009, Francis S. Haserot professor emeritus, 2009-, adjunct professor of philosophy, 2009-; The International Journal for Philosophy of Religion, associate editor. **Publications:** Ethics and Academics, 1968; (ed. and intro. with R.H. Severens) Analyticity, 1970; Against Relativism: A Philosophical Defense of Method, 1992; (with M.H. Waymack) Single-malt Whiskies of Scotland, 1992; (ed. as James Franklin Harris) Logic, God, and Metaphysics, 1992; Philosophy at 33 1/3 RPM: Themes of Classic Rock Music, 1993; (with M.H. Waymack) The Book of Classic American Whiskeys, 1995; Anglo-American, Analytic Philosophy of Religion, 2002; The Ascent of Man: A Philosophy of Human Nature, 2011. **Address:** Department of Philosophy, College of William and Mary, Rm. 121, James Blair Hall, 250 James Blair Dr., PO Box 8795, Williamsburg, VA 23185, U.S.A. **Online address:** jfharr@wm.edu

HARRIS, James Franklin. See HARRIS, James F.

HARRIS, Jana. American (born United States), b. 1947. **Genres:** Novels, Poetry. **Career:** University of California, Lawrence Hall of Science, Project SEED Inc., educational mathematics consultant, 1970-76; Intersection Inc., Women-in-poetry Program, co-coordinator, 1972-73; San Francisco State University, instructor, 1972-78; Modesto Junior College, instructor in creative writing, 1975-78; Alameda County Neighborhood Arts Program, poet-in-residence, 1977-78; City University of New York, instructor in creative writing, 1980-; Manhattan Theatre Club, Writers in Performance Series, acting director, 1980-86; University of Washington, instructor, 1986-; University of Wyoming, St. Catherine's College, writer-in-residence; Switched-on Gutenberg, founder and editor. **Publications:** This House That Rocks with Every Truck on the Road (poetry), 1976; Letters from the Promised Land: Alaska Poems, 1976; Pin Money (poetry), 1977; The Book of Common People: Poems in a Dime Store Sack, 1978; The Clackamas (poetry), 1980; Alaska (novel), 1980; Who's That Pushy Bitch? (poetry), 1981; Manhattan as a Second Language and Other Poems, 1982; The Sourlands (poetry), 1989; Oh How Can I Keep on Singing? (poems), 1993; The Dust of Everyday Life (epic poem), 1997; The Pearl of Ruby City (novel), 1998; We Never Speak

of It: Idaho-Wyoming Poems, 1889-90, 2003; Horses Never Lie about Love, 2011. Contributor of articles to books and periodicals. **Address:** Robin Straus Agency Inc., 229 E 79th St., Ste. 5A, New York, NY 10065, U.S.A. **Online address:** jnh@u.washington.edu

HARRIS, Jonathan. British (born England), b. 1961?. **Genres:** History. **Career:** University of London, Royal Holloway College, lecturer. Writer and historian. **Publications:** Greek Emigrés in the West, 1400-1520, 1995; Byzantium and the Crusades, 2003; (ed.) Palgrave Advances in Byzantine History, 2005; Constantinople: Capital of Byzantium, 2007. **Address:** Department of History, Royal Holloway College, University of London, Egham, SR TW20 0EX, England. **Online address:** jonathan.harris@rhul.ac.uk

HARRIS, Jose. British (born England) **Genres:** Politics/Government, Biography, Sociology. **Career:** Oxford University, St. Catherine's College, tutorial fellow in history, 1978-97, reader in modern history, 1990-97, professor, 1997-, professor emeritus of modern history; British Academy, fellow. Writer. **Publications:** Unemployment and Politics, 1886-1914, 1972; William Beveridge: A Biography, 1977, 2nd ed., 1997; Private Lives, Public Spirit: A Social History of Britain, 1870-1914, 1993; Beveridge, Titmuss, and Trends in Social Policy at the Start of the Twenty-First Century, 2000; (trans. with M. Hollis and ed.) Community and Civil Society, 2001; (ed.) Civil Society in British History: Ideas, Identities, Institutions, 2003; Gemeinschaft und Gesellschaft, forthcoming. **Address:** St. Catherine's College, Oxford University, Manor Rd., Oxford, OX OX1 3UJ, England. **Online address:** jose.harris@stcatz.ox.ac.uk

HARRIS, Kristina. See SELESHANKO, Kristina.

HARRIS, Leonard. American (born United States), b. 1933?. **Genres:** Novels, Plays/Screenplays, Communications/Media, Mystery/Crime/Suspense. **Career:** New York World Telegram and Sun, reporter, 1960-66; WCBS-TV News, critic, 1966-74; Fordham University, adjunct associate professor, 1969-74; Hunter College, staff, 1974-75; Soho News, Broadway theatre critic, 1977-78; The Hollywood, reporter, 1982; CBS Morning Program, writer, 1986-91; Miss America Pageant, writer, 1990-92; CBS Tournament of Roses and CBS Coming Up Roses, writer, 1993-2001; CBS All-American Thanksgiving Parade, writer, 1996-2000. **Publications:** The Masada Plan, 1976; Don't Be No Hero, 1978; The Hamptons, 1981. **Address:** 330 E 71st St., New York, NY 10021, U.S.A.

HARRIS, Leslie M. American (born United States), b. 1965. **Genres:** History, Social Sciences. **Career:** University of Maryland, postdoctoral fellow, 1994-95; Emory University, assistant professor, 1995-2001, associate professor of history, 2001-, associate professor of African American studies, 2003-, associate chair of African American studies, 2003-04, chair of African American studies, 2004-06; Columbia University, Ford Foundation, postdoctoral fellow, 1998-99. Writer. **Publications:** In the Shadow of Slavery: African Americans in New York City, 1626-1863, 2003; (ed. with I. Berlin) Slavery in New York, 2005. Contributor to books and periodicals. **Address:** Department of History, Emory University, Bowden Hall, Atlanta, GA 30322, U.S.A. **Online address:** lharr04@emory.edu

HARRIS, Margaret. British (born England), b. 1951?. **Genres:** Psychology, Social Sciences. **Career:** University of London, reader in developmental psychology; University of Oxford Brookes, School of Social Sciences and Law, professor, chair, 2006-; Institute for Research in Child Development, director. Writer and psychologist. **Publications:** (With M. Coltheart) Language Processing in Children and Adults: An Introduction, 1986; Language Experience and Early Language Development: From Input to Uptake, 1992; (ed. with G. Hatano) Learning to Read and Write, 1999; (with G. Butterworth) Developmental Psychology: A Students Handbook, 1999; Exploring Developmental Psychology: Understanding Theory and Methods, 2008. Contributor to periodicals. **Address:** Department of Psychology, Oxford Brookes University, Headington Campus, Gipsy Ln., Oxford, OX OX3 0BP, England. **Online address:** m.harris@rhul.ac.uk

HARRIS, Marion (Rose). Also writes as Rose Young, Henry Charles, Rose Glendower, Daphne Harriford, Keith Rogers. British/Welsh (born Wales), b. 1925. **Genres:** Novels, Adult Non-fiction, Food And Wine. **Career:** Builder's Merchant, private secretary to managing director, 1942-46; freelance journalist, 1946-; Regional Feature Service, editor, 1964-71; W. Foulsham & Company Ltd., editorial controller, 1974-83; Irish Leather and Footwear Journal, correspondent; Futura, correspondent. Consultant. **Publications:** Fresh Fruit Dishes, 1963; Making a House a Home, 1964; The Awful Slimmer Book, 1967; Flower Arranging, 1968; Teach Your Mum Flower Arranging, 1968; (as Daphne Harriford) Around the Home, 1974; (as Keith Rogers) Plumbing Repairs and Maintenance, 1974; (as Henry Charles) Twenty-Five Easy to Grow Vegetables: In Any Size Plot, 1975; (as Rose Young) When the Clouds Clear, 1975; (as Rose Young) Love Can Conquer, 1976; Captain of Her Heart, 1976; (as Rose Young) Secret of Abbey Place, 1977; Just a Handsome Stranger, 1983; The Queen's Windsor, 1985; Soldiers' Wives, 1986; Officers' Ladies, 1987; The Heart of the Dragon, Book 1: Nesta, 1988, Book 2: Amelda, 1989; (as Rose Glendower) Sighing for the Moon, 1991; To Love & Love Again, 1994. AS ROSIE HARRIS: The Turn of the Tide, 2002; Through Troubled Waters, 2002; Patsy of Paradise Place, 2003; One Step Forward, 2003; Looking for Love, 2003; Pins and Needles, 2004; Winnie of the Waterfront, 2004; The Cobbler's Kids, 2005; Sunshine and Showers, 2005; At Sixes and Sevens, 2005; Megan of Merseyside, 2006; The Power of Dreams, 2006; Sunshine and Shadows, 2006; A Mother's Love, 2006; Sing for Your Supper, 2007; Waiting for Love, 2007; Love Against All Odds, 2007; A Dream of Love, 2008; A Love Like Ours, 2008; Love Changes Everything, 2009; The Quality of Love, 2009; Whispers of Love, 2010; Ambitious Love, 2010; The Price of Love, 2011; A Brighter Dawn, 2011. **Address:** Walpole Cottage, Long Dr., Slough, BK SL1 8AJ, England. **Online address:** marionharris@btinternet.com

HARRIS, Mary Emma. American (born United States), b. 1943. **Genres:** Art/Art History. **Career:** Detroit Institute of Arts, curator in education department, 1969-70, lecturer; North Carolina Museum of Art, Black Mountain College Research Project, research director, 1970-73; Smithsonian Institution, lecturer; Black Mountain College Project Inc., chair and project director; Pratt Institute, lecturer; Black Mountain College, curator, 1987; Sheridan Square Triangle Viewing Garden, board director, director of gardening. Writer. **Publications:** (With R.M. Robinson) The Proud Heritage of Cleveland Heights, Ohio, 1966; The Arts at Black Mountain College, 1987; Remembering Black Mountain College (exhibit catalogue), 1996; Starting at Zero: Black Mountain College, 1933-57, 2005; (contrib.) Sewell Sillman: Pushing Limits, 2010. Contributor of articals to periodicals. **Address:** Black Mountain College Project Inc., PO Box 607, Village Sta., New York, NY 10014-0607, U.S.A. **Online address:** harris@bmcproject.org

HARRIS, Neil. American (born United States), b. 1938?. **Genres:** Art/Art History, History, Social Sciences. **Career:** Harvard University, instructor, assistant professor of history, 1965-69; University of Chicago, Department of History, associate professor, 1969-72, professor of history, 1972-90, chair, 1985-88, Preston and Sterling Morton professor of history and of art history, 1990-2007, Preston and Sterling Morton professor emeritus of history and of art history, 2007-; Johns Hopkins University, Boucher lecturer, 1971; Yale University, Cardozo Lecturer, visiting professor, 1974; National Humanities Institute, director, 1975-77; Pfizer College, Kemper lecturer, 1980; Whitney Museum of American Art, Tandy lecturer, 1982; Ecole des Hautes Etudes en Sciences Sociales, director d'etudes, 1985. Writer. **Publications:** The Artist in American Society: The Formative Years, 1790-1860, 1966; (ed. with D.J. Rothman and S. Thernstrom) History of the United States, 1969; (ed. with D.J. Rothman and S. Thernstrom) American History: Source Readings, 1600 to the Present, 1969; (ed. and intro.) The Land of Contrasts: 1880-1901, 1970; History and the Role of the City in American Life, 1972; Humbug: The Art of P.T. Barnum, 1973; Winterthur and America's Museum Age, 1981; The WPA Guide to Illinois, 1983; (contrib.) Art, Design and the Modern Corporation: The Collection of Container Corporation of America, a Gift to the National Museum of American Art (art history/catalog), 1985; (contrib.) William Rimmer, a Yankee Michelangelo, 1985; Masterworks of Louis Comfort Tiffany, 1989; Cultural Excursions: Marketing Appetites and Cultural Tastes in Modern America, 1990; Grand Illusions: Chicago's World's Fair of 1893, 1993; Planes, Trains and Automobiles: The Transportation Revolution in Children's Picture Books, 1995; (contrib.) The First Hundred Years: The Denver Art Museum, 1996; Building Lives: Construction Rites and Passages, 1999; Chicago Apartments: A Century of Lakefront Luxury, 2004; (contrib.) Seurat and the Making of La Grande Jatte, 2004; The Chicagoan: A Lost Magazine of the Jazz Age, 2008. Contributor to books. **Address:** Department of History, University of Chicago, 1126 E 59th St., Chicago, IL 60637-1580, U.S.A. **Online address:** nh16@uchicago.edu

HARRIS, Paul. Scottish/British (born England), b. 1948. **Genres:** History, Biography, Documentaries/Reportage, International Relations/Current Affairs, Trivia/Facts, Art/Art History, Photography. **Career:** IPRC, chief analyst.

Writer and photographer. **Publications:** When Pirates Ruled the Waves, 2nd ed., 1968, 4th ed., 1970; The Garvie Trial: The Crime That Shocked Scotland, 1969; To Be a Pirate King, 1971; Oil, 1975; A Concise Dictionary of Scottish Painters, 1976; Broadcasting from the High Seas: 1858 to 1976, 1977; (comp.) Scotland: An Anthology, 1985; Glasgow and the Clyde at War, 1986; Aberdeen and the North East at War, 1987; (with T. Miah) Tommy Miah Presents the Best of Bangladesh, 1987; Cooking with Beer, 1987; Edinburgh since 1900, 1987; Tyneside at War, 1987; Aberdeen since 1900, 1988; By Appointment: The Story in Pictures of Royal Deeside and Balmoral, 1988; Edinburgh: The Fabulous Fifties, 1988; A Little Scottish Cookbook, 1988; Disaster! One Hundred Years of Wreck, Rescue, and Tragedy in Scotland, 1989; Glasgow since 1900, 1989; Life in a Scottish Country House: The Story of A.J. Balfour and Whittingehame House, 1989; (with J. Halsby) The Dictionary of Scottish Painters, 1600-1960, 1990, (with J. Halsby) 4th ed., 2010; Somebody Else's War: Frontline Reports from the Balkan Wars, 1992; (with Miah) Tommy Miah Presents the Secrets of the Indian Masterchefs: Mouthwatering Dishes from Bangladesh, India and Pakistan, 1993; Somebody Else's War, 1993; Cry Bosnia, 1995; Glasgow: The People's Story, 1996; (with Miah) A True Taste of Asia, 1996; (with I. Elphick) TN Foulis: The History and Bibliography of an Edinburgh Publishing House, 1998; Audi, 1999; Scotland's Century 1900-2000: One Hundred Years of Photographs, 1999; Producing Your Own Showcase, 2001; Fractured Paradise: Images of Sri Lanka, 2001; Delightfully Imperfect: A Year in Sri Lanka at the Galle Face Hotel, 2007; War In Paradise: The Tragedy of Sri Lanka, forthcoming; Looking For Trouble, forthcoming; The World Directory of Special Forces, forthcoming. EDITOR: Investing in Scottish Pictures, 1977; The DC Thomson Bumper Fun Book, 1977; The Rhythm of the Glass: Drinking, a Celebration, 1977; The Grizedale Experience: Sculpture, Arts, and Theatre in a Lakeland Forest, 1991; Story of Scotland's Flag, 1992; Ifor On Ifor, 1996. Contributor of articles to periodicals. **Address:** Whittingehame House, Haddington, LT EH41 4QA, Scotland. **Online address:** journoharris@compuserve.com

HARRIS, Paul. American (born United States), b. 1972. **Genres:** Novels. **Career:** Guardian, correspondent; The Observer, U.S. correspondent, 2003-. Journalist. **Publications:** The Secret Keeper (novel), 2009. **Address:** Penguin Group Inc., 375 Hudson St., New York, NY 10014, U.S.A. **Online address:** paul.harris@observer.co.uk

HARRIS, Phil. See **HARRIS, Philip Robert.**

HARRIS, Philip Robert. (Phil Harris). American (born United States), b. 1926. **Genres:** Novels, Administration/Management, Education. **Career:** St. Francis College, vice president, 1956-64; Pennsylvania State University, visiting professor, 1965-66; Leadership Resources Inc., senior associate, 1966-69; Temple University, visiting professor, 1967-69; Copley International Corp., vice president, 1970-71; Harris International Ltd., president, 1972-; California Space Institute, research associate, 1984-90; Netrologic Inc., senior scientist, 1989-93; Lunar Power System Coalition, executive director/editor, 1990-93; United Societies in Space, executive vice president, Space Governance Journal, founding executive editor, 1993-98. **Publications:** Organizational Dynamics, 1973; Effective Management of Change, 1976; New Worlds, New Ways, New Management, 1983; Management in Transition, 1985; High Performance Leadership, 1989, 2nd ed., 1994; Living and Working in Space, 1992, 2nd ed., 1996; (with G.F. Simons and C. Vázquez) Transcultural Leadership, 1993; (with R.T. Moran and W.G. Stripp) Developing Global Organizations, 1993; New Work Culture Series, 3 vols., 1994-98; Twenty Reproducible Assessment Instruments, 1995; (with F. Elashmawi) Multicultural Management 2000: Essential Cultural Insights for Global Business Success, 1998; New Work Culture: HRD Transformational Management Strategies, 1998; Launch Out (novel), 2003; Managing the Knowledge Culture, 2005; Future Possibilities, 2006; Space Enterprise: Living and Working Offworld, 2009; Toward Human Emergence, 2009; Lunar Pioneers, 2010; Developing High Performance Leaders, 2011. EDITOR: Regents Study Guide to State Scholarships, 1949; Official Guide to Catholic Educational Institutions, 1959; Impact (textbook), 1965; (with G. Malin) Innovations in Global Consultation, 1980; Global Strategies for Human Resource Development, 1984; Innovations in Global Consultation, 1984. CO-AUTHOR: Insight Series, 4 vols., 1957-64; It's Your Education, 1959; It's Your Future, 1965; It's Your Personality, 1965; (with D. Harris) Improving Management Communication Skills, 1978; Managing Cultural Differences, 1979, 8th ed., 2011; (with R.T. Moran) Managing Cultural Synergy, 1982; Multicultural Management, 1992, 2nd ed., 2000; Multicultural Law Enforcement, 1995, 5th ed., 2011. **Address:** 2702 Costebelle Dr., La Jolla, CA 92037-3524, U.S.A. **Online address:** philharris@aol.com

HARRIS, Randy Allen. Canadian (born Canada), b. 1956. **Genres:** Language/Linguistics. **Career:** Queen's University, teaching assistant, 1979-80; Dalhousie University, teaching assistant, 1981-82; University of Alberta, teaching assistant, 1982-83, department of linguistics, lecturer, 1983-85, 1990-91; Grant MacEwan Community College, Department of English, lecturer, 1984-85; Rensselaer Polytechnic Institute Writing Center, teaching assistant, 1986-88; Bell-Northern Research, usability expert, 1988-90; University of Waterloo, associate professor of English, 1992-2000, professor, 2000-, associate chair and director of graduate studies, 2011-. Writer. **Publications:** Functor Comprehension in Broca's Aphasia, 1985; Acoustic Dimensions of Functor Comprehension in Broca's Aphasia, 1988; The Linguistics Wars, 1993. EDITOR: Technical Communication in Canada, 1994; (ed.) Landmark Essays in the Rhetoric of Science, 1997; Rhetoric of Science in Canada, 2000; (ed. and intro.) Rhetoric and Incommensurability, 2005; Voice Interaction Design: Crafting the New Conversational Speech Systems, 2005. **Address:** Department of English, University of Waterloo, Waterloo, ON N2L 3G1, Canada. **Online address:** raha@watarts.uwaterloo.ca

HARRIS, Robert (Dennis). British (born England), b. 1957. **Genres:** Military/Defense/Arms Control, Biography, Novels, Young Adult Non-fiction. **Career:** British Broadcasting Corp. (BBC-TV), researcher and film director, 1978-81; Newsnight, reporter, 1981-87; Panorama, reporter, 1985-87; Observer, political editor, 1987-89; Thames TV, political reporter for This Week, 1988-89; Sunday Times, political columnist, 1989-92. **Publications:** (With J. Paxman) A Higher Form of Killing: The Secret Story of Gas and Germ Warfare, 1982 in US as A Higher Form of Killing: The Secret Story of Chemical and Biological Warfare, 1982; Gotcha!: The Media, the Government and the Falklands Crisis, 1983; The Making of Neil Kinnock, 1984; Selling Hitler, 1986; Good and Faithful Servant: The Unauthorized Biography of Bernard Ingham, 1990; Fatherland (novel), 1992; The Media Trilogy, 1994; Enigma, 1995; Archangel, 1998; Pompeii, 2003; Imperium: A Novel of Ancient Rome, 2006; The Ghost, 2007; Conspiracy, 2008; Lustrum, 2009; Conspirata: A Novel of Ancient Rome, 2010; The Fear Index, 2011. **Address:** The Old Vicarage, Kintbury, Kintbury, BR R915 OTR, England.

HARRIS, Robert J. (Bob Harris). Scottish (born Scotland), b. 1955?. **Genres:** Young Adult Non-fiction, Intellectual History, Novels, Children's Fiction, Romance/Historical. **Career:** Writer. **Publications:** SCOTTISH QUARTET HISTORICAL NOVELS FOR YOUNG ADULTS: (with J. Yolen) Queen's Own Fool, 2000; (with J. Yolen) Girl in a Cage, 2002; (with J. Yolen) Prince across the Water, 2004; (with J. Yolen) The Rogues, 2007; YOUNG HEROES NOVEL SERIES: (with J. Yolen) Odysseus in the Serpent Maze, 2001; (with J. Yolen) Hippolyta and the Curse of the Amazons, 2002; (with J. Yolen) Atalanta and the Arcadian Beast, 2003; (with J. Yolen) Jason and the Gorgon's Blood, 2004; YOUNG LEGENDS NOVEL SERIES: Leonardo and the Death Machine, 2005; Will Shakespeare and the Pirate's Fire, 2006; OTHER: (as Bob Harris with A. McFadzean) The Knox Factor, 2008. Contributor to periodicals. **Address:** HarperCollins Children's Books, 10 E 53rd St., New York, NY 10022, U.S.A. **Online address:** bob@harris-authors.com

HARRIS, Robie H. American (born United States), b. 1940. **Genres:** Children's Fiction, Children's Non-fiction, Picture/Board Books, Adult Non-fiction. **Career:** Freelance writer, 1975-; Bank Street College of Education's School for Children, writer and teacher and director of after-school program; Smallwood Drive School, teacher; Children's Museum, consultant. **Publications:** NONFICTION: (with E. Levy) Before You Were Three: How You Began to Walk, Talk, Explore and Have Feelings, 1977; It's Perfectly Normal: Changing Bodies, Growing Up, Sex and Sexual Health, 1994, 3rd ed., 2009; It's So Amazing: A Book about Eggs, Sperm, Birth, Babies and Families, 1999. FICTION: Don't Forget to Come Back, 1978; Rosie's Double Dare, 1980; I Hate Kisses, 1981; Rosie's Razzle Dazzle Deal, 1982; Hot Henry, 1987; Messy Jessie, 1987; Rosie's Rock 'n' Roll Riot, 1990; Rosie's Secret Spell, 1991; Happy Birth Day!, 1996; Hi, New Baby!, 2000; Goodbye, Mousie, 2001; I Am not Going to School Today!, 2003; I'm So Mad, 2005; I'm not Sleepy, 2005; I Love Messes!, 2005; I'm All Dressed!, 2005; All About Us Books, forthcoming. GROWING UP STORIES SERIES: Hello Benny! What It's Like to Be a Baby, 2002; Go! Go! Maria: What It's Like to Be 1, 2003 Maria: What It's Like to be 2, 2003; Sweet Jasmine, Nice Jackson, What It's Like to Be 2-And to Be Twins!, 2004. OTHER: It, 2002; David Dinosaur-rrr!: What It's Like To Be 3, 2005; It's Not the Stork!: A Book about Girls, Boys, Babies, Bodies, Families and Friends, 2006; Maybe a Bear Ate It!, 2008; Mail Harry to the Moon!, 2008; The Day Leo Said I Hate You, 2008; What's in There?: A Book about before You were Born, 2010; Who has

What?, 2011; When Lions Roar!, forthcoming; Who's in my Family, forthcoming. **Address:** 2 Brighton St., Ste. 2, Belmont, MA 02478-4008, U.S.A. **Online address:** authorappearance@candlewick.com

HARRIS, Robin. American/British (born England), b. 1952. **Genres:** Politics/Government, History. **Career:** British Government, special adviser at the treasury, 1981-83, Home Office, special adviser, 1983-85, Conservative Research Department, director, 1985-89; Heritage Foundation, senior visiting fellow. Journalist and speech writer. **Publications:** Valois Guyenne: A Study of Politics, Government, and Society in Late Medieval France, 1994; A Tale of Two Chileans: Pinochet and Allende, 1999; Dubrovnik: A History, 2003; Talleyrand: Betrayer and Saviour of France, 2007. Contributor to periodicals. **Address:** The Heritage Foundation, 214 Massachusetts Ave. NE, Washington, DC 20002-4999, U.S.A.

HARRIS, Rosemary. American (born United States) **Genres:** Mystery/Crime/Suspense, Literary Criticism And History. **Career:** Waldenbooks, staff; Crown Publishers, staff; American Express Travel Related Services, staff; WNET, staff; ABC, staff; Kultur, staff; Winstar, staff. Writer. **Publications:** The Political Organization of the Mbembe, Nigeria, 1965; Pushing Up Daisies: A Dirty Business Mystery, 2008; The Big Dirt Nap: A Dirty Business Mystery, 2009; The Big Dirt Nap: A Dirty Business Mystery, 2009; Dead Head, 2010; Slugfest, 2011. **Address:** c/o Sarah Melnyk, St. Martin's, 175 5th Ave., New York, NY 10010, U.S.A. **Online address:** rosemary@rosemaryharris.com

HARRIS, Rosemary (Jeanne). British (born England), b. 1923. **Genres:** Mystery/Crime/Suspense, Romance/Historical, Children's Fiction, Young Adult Fiction, Mythology/Folklore, Novellas/Short Stories, Novels, Literary Criticism And History, Literary Criticism And History. **Career:** The Times, children's book reviewer, 1970-73. Writer. **Publications:** The Summer House, 1956; Voyage to Cythera, 1958; Venus with Sparrows, 1961; All My Enemies, 1967; The Nice Girl's Story, 1968 in US as Nor Evil Dreams, 1973; A Wicked Pack of Cards, 1969; (ed. with X. Howard-Johnston) Christian Appeals from Russia, 1969; Sea Magic and Other Stories of Enchantment, 1974, rev. ed. as (ed.) The Lotus and the Grail: Legends from East and West, 1974; The Double Snare, 1974; Three Candles for the Dark, 1976; (ed.) Love and the Merry-go-round, 1988; Ticket to Freedom, 1992; Haunting of Joey Mbasa, 1996. JUVENILES: The Moon in the Cloud (first book in trilogy), 1968; The Shadow on the Sun (second book in trilogy), 1970; The Seal-Singing, 1971; The Child in the Bamboo Grove, 1971; The Bright and Morning Star (third book in trilogy), 1972; The King's White Elephant, 1973; Sea Magic and Other Stories of Enchantment, 1974; The Flying Ship, 1975; The Little Dog of Fo, 1976; I Want to Be a Fish, 1977; (contrib.) Young Winter's Tales, 1978; A Quest for Orion, 1978; Beauty and the Beast, 1979; Green Finger House, 1980; Tower of the Stars, 1980; The Enchanted Horse, 1981; Janni's Stork, 1982; Zed, 1982; (adaptor) Johanna Spyri, 1983; Summers of the Wild Rose, 1987; Colm of the Islands, 1989; Ticket to Freedom, 1991; The Wildcat Strike, 1995. **Address:** A. P. Watt Ltd., 20 John St., London, GL WC1N 2DR, England.

HARRIS, Roy. British (born England), b. 1931. **Genres:** Language/Linguistics, History, Art/Art History. **Career:** Ecole Normale Superieure, lecturer, 1956-57; University of Leicester, assistant lecturer, 1957-58, lecturer, 1958-60; Oxford University, medieval and modern languages faculty, 1961-76, Keble College, fellow and tutor, 1967-76, professor of the romance languages, 1976-77, Worcester College, professor of general linguistics and fellow, 1978-88, professor emeritus of general linguistics, 1988-; Language and Communication, editor, 1980-; Ecole Pratique des Hautes Etudes, directeur d'etudes associe, 1991-92. **Publications:** Synonymy and Linguistic Analysis, 1973; On the Possibility of Linguistic Change, 1977; Communication and Language, 1978; The Language-Makers, 1980; The Language Myth, 1981; (trans.) Course in General Linguistics, by de Saussure, 1983; (ed.) Approaches to Language, 1983; (ed. with C.N. Bailey) Developmental Mechanisms of Language, 1985; The Origin of Writing, 1986; Language Machine, 1987; Reading Saussure: A Critical Commentary on the Cours de linguistique générale, 1987; (ed.) Linguistic Thought in England, 1914-1945, 1988; Language, Saussure and Wittgenstein: How to Play Games with Words, 1988; (ed.) Linguistic Thought in England, 1914-1945, 1988; Foundations of Linguistic Theory: Selected Writings of Roy Harris, 1990; Sémiologie de l'écriture, 1993; (ed. with R. Harré) Linguistics and Philosophy: The Controversial Interface, 1993; British Linguistics in the Nineteenth Century, 1994; Signs of Writing, 1995; The Language Connection, 1996; Signs, Language and Communication: Integrational and Segregational Approaches, 1996; (with T.J. Taylor) Western Tradition from Socrates to Saussure, 1997; (ed. with G. Wolf) Integrational Linguistics: A First Reader, 1998; Introduction to Integrational Linguistics, 1998; (ed.) Foundations of Indo-European Comparative Philology 1800-1850, 1999; Rethinking Writing, 2000; Saussure and His Interpreters, 2001; The Necessity of Artspeak: The Language of the Arts in the Western Tradition, 2003; History, Science, and the Limits of Language: An Integrationist Approach, 2003; The Linguistics of History, 2004; Semantics of Science, 2005; Integrationist Notes and Papers 2003-2005, 2006; (with C. Hutton) Definition in Theory and Practice: Language, Lexicography and the Law, 2007; Mindboggling: Preliminaries to a Science of the Mind, 2008; Integrationist Notes and Papers 2006-2008, 2009; Rationality and the Literate Mind, 2009; After Epistemology, 2009; The Great Debate About Art, 2010. **Address:** 2 Paddox Close, Oxford, OX OX2 7LR, England.

HARRIS, Ruth Elwin. British (born England), b. 1935. **Genres:** Novels. **Career:** Educator and writer. **Publications:** QUANTOCKS QUARTET NOVEL SERIES: The Silent Shore, 1986; The Beckoning Hills, 1987; The Dividing Sea, 1989; Beyond the Orchid House, 1994. OTHER: (ed.) Billie: The Nevill Letters, 1914-1916, 1991; Frances' Story, 2002; Gwen's Story, 2002; Julia's Story, 2002; Sarah's Story, 2002; Giving Thanks, 2003. Contributor to periodicals. **Address:** c/o Author Mail, Walker Books Ltd., 87 Vauxhall Walk, London, GL SE11 5HJ, England.

HARRIS, Stacy. American (born United States), b. 1952. **Genres:** Music, Biography, Autobiography/Memoirs. **Career:** Stacy's Music Row Report, publisher and executive director. Writer and educator. **Publications:** Comedians of Country Music, 1978; (with R.K. Krishef and S. Harris) The Carter Family: Country Music's First Family, 1978; The Best of Country: The Essential CD Guide, 1993. Works appear in anthologies. Contributor to periodicals. **Address:** Windsor Twr., 4215 Harding Rd., Nashville, TN 37205, U.S.A. **Online address:** harrisstacy@juno.com

HARRIS, Steve. British (born England), b. 1954. **Genres:** Horror, Novels. **Career:** Writer. **Publications:** Adventureland, 1990 in US as The Eyes of the Beast, 1993; Wulf, 1991; Hoodoo Man, 1992; Angels, 1993; Black Rock, 1996; The Devil on May Street, 1997; Challenging the Wolf (chapbook), 1997; Straker's Island, 1998; Miami Five Fifteen, forthcoming; The Switch, forthcoming. **Address:** Trafalgar Square Books, 388 Howe Hill Rd., PO Box 257, North Pomfret, VT 05053-0257, U.S.A.

HARRIS, Terrell. See DOUGAN, Terrell Harris.

HARRIS, (Theodore) Wilson. (Kona Waruk). British/Guyanese (born Guyana), b. 1921. **Genres:** Novels, Poetry, Literary Criticism And History, Essays, Young Adult Fiction, Young Adult Non-fiction. **Career:** British Guiana Government, assistant government surveyor, 1942-44, government surveyor, 1944-54, senior surveyor, 1955-58; writer, 1958-; State University of New York, visiting lecturer, 1970; Yale University, visiting lecturer, 1970; University of West Indies, writer-in-residence, 1970; University of Toronto, writer-in-residence, 1970; University of Texas, visiting professor, 1972, 1981-83; University of Aarhus, visiting professor, 1973; Newcastle University, writer-in-residence, 1979; University of California, Regents lecturer, 1983; University of Queensland, writer-in-residence, 1986. **Publications:** FICTION: Palace of the Peacock, 1960; The Far Journey of Oudin, 1961; The Whole Armour, 1962; The Secret Ladder, 1963; Heartland, 1964; The Eye of the Scarecrow, 1965; The Waiting Room, 1967; Tumatumari, 1968; Ascent to Omai, 1970; The Sleepers of Roraima, 1970; The Age of the Rainmakers, 1971; Black Marsden: A Tabula Rasa Comedy, 1972; Companions of the Day and Night, 1975; Da Silva da Silva's Cultivated Wilderness and Genesis of the Clowns, 1977; The Tree of the Sun, 1978; The Angel at the Gate, 1983; The Carnival, 1985; The Guyana Quartet, 1985; Carnival, 1985; The Infinite Rehearsal, 1987; The Four Banks of the River of Space, 1990; Resurrection at Sorrow Hill, 1993; Jonestown, 1996; The Dark Jester, 2001; The Mask of the Beggar, 2003. POETRY: (as Kona Waruk) Fetish, 1951; The Well and the Land, 1952; Eternity to Season, 1954, 2nd ed., 1978. OTHERS: Tradition and the West Indian Novel, 1965; Tradition, The Writer and Society: Critical Essays, 1967; (with S.R. Cudjoe) History, Fable and Myth in the Caribbean and Guianas, 1970, rev. ed., 1995; Fossil and Psyche, 1974; Explorations: A Selection of Talks and Articles, 1966-81, 1981; The Womb of Space: The Cross-Cultural Imagination, 1983; The Radical Imagination (essays), 1992; Merlin and Parsifal: Adversarial Twins, 1997; (contrib.) Biografi del possibile, 2005; The Ghost of Memory, 2006. Contributor to periodicals. Works

appear in anthologies. **Address:** Faber & Faber Ltd., Bloomsbury House, 74-77 Great Russell St., London, GL WC1B 3DA, England.

HARRIS, Thomas (E.). American (born United States), b. 1944. **Genres:** Administration/Management, Business/Trade/Industry, Communications/Media, Industrial Relations. **Career:** George Washington University, instructor, 1967-70; Rutgers University, lecturer, 1970-78, director of debate, instructor, consultant; University of Evansville, professor, 1980-89, consultant/trainer; University of Alabama, assistant professor, associate professor, 1989-96, professor of communication studies and graduate program director, 1996-2009, professor emeritus, 2009-; Kelsey Group Inc., senior consultant, 2008-, training coordinator. Writer. **Publications:** Alcoholism: The Six Billion Dollar Problem, 1984; Analysis of the Clash over Issues between Booker T. Washington and W.E.B. DuBois, 1993, rev. ed., 2005; Applied Organizational Communication: Perspectives, Principles and Pragmatics, 1993; Conflict and Diversity, 1997; (with J.C. Sherblom) Small Group and Team Communication, 1999, 5th ed., 2010; Applied Organizational Communication: Principles and Pragmatics for Future Success, 2002. Contributor to periodicals. **Address:** Kelsey Group Inc., PO Box 1053, Northport, AL 35476, U.S.A. **Online address:** tharris@ua.edu

HARRIS, Thomas Walter. (T. H. Darling). American (born United States), b. 1930. **Genres:** Plays/Screenplays, Novels. **Career:** Appeal Printing Co., affiliate, 1948-49; Bureau of Internal Revenue, affiliate, 1956-57; Los Angeles Public Library, librarian in literature and fiction department, 1961-; University of California, teacher of playwriting, 1966-; Inner City Cultural Center, teacher of mass communications, 1968; Audrey Skirball-Kenis Theater Collection, collector and editor, 1996-; Studio West, director; Los Angeles Citizens Co., executive producer and director. **Publications:** PLAYS: (as Tom Harris) Daddy Hugs and Kisses, 1960; OTHER: Always with Love, 1970; No Time to Play, 1977. **Address:** 630 W 5th St., Los Angeles, CA 90071, U.S.A.

HARRIS, Walter A. American (born United States), b. 1929. **Genres:** Economics, Politics/Government, Social Sciences. **Career:** Midwood High School, teacher of social studies; Port Richmond High School, assistant principal; Sheepshead Bay High School, principal; Kolburne School Inc., director of education; Stageworks on the Hudson, director of development. Writer. **Publications:** Workbook: The Modern Economy in Action, 1968; Introductory Economics, 1970; Economics for Everybody, 1973, 3rd ed., 2003; Teacher's Manual for Economics for Everybody, 1973, 3rd ed., 2003; (with G. Antell) Current Issues in American Democracy, 1975, 2nd ed., 1992; Western Civilization, 1982; Economics, Institutions and Analysis, 4th ed., 2004; Teacher's Manual for Economics, Institutions and Analysis, 4th ed., 2004. **Address:** Hativat Givati 11/1, Netanya, 42463, Israel. **Online address:** barbarawalt@yahoo.com

HARRIS, William V. American/British (born England), b. 1938. **Genres:** History, Economics, Literary Criticism And History. **Career:** Columbia University, Department of History, instructor, 1965-, professor, 1976-, chairman, 1988-94, William R. Shepherd professor of history, 1995-, Center for the Ancient Mediterranean, director. Writer. **Publications:** Rome in Etruria and Umbria, 1971; War and Imperialism in Republican Rome, 327-70 B.C., 1979; (ed. with R.S. Bagnall) Studies in Roman Law in Memory of A. Arthur Schiller, 1986; Ancient Literacy, 1989; (ed.) Inscribed Economy, 1993; (ed.) The Transformations of Vrbs Roma in Late Antiquity, 1999; Restraining Rage: The Ideology of Anger Control in Classical Antiquity, 2001; (ed. with G. Ruffini) Ancient Alexandria between Egypt and Greece, 2004; (ed. with E.L. Cascio) Noctes Campanae: Studi di Storia Antica ed Archeologia dell'Italia Preromana e Romana in Memoria di Martin W. Frederiksen, 2005; (ed.) The Spread of Christianity in the First Four Centuries: Essays in Explanation, 2005; (ed.) Rethinking the Mediterranean, 2005; (ed. with B. Holmes) Aelius Aristides between Greece, Rome, and the Gods, 2008; (ed.) The Monetary Systems of the Greeks and Romans, 2008; Dreams and Experience in Classical Antiquity, 2009; Rome's Imperial Economy: Twelve Essays, 2011. **Address:** Department of History, Columbia University, 624 Fayerweather Hall, 1180 Amsterdam Ave., PO Box 2515, New York, NY 10027, U.S.A. **Online address:** wvh1@columbia.edu

HARRIS-LACEWELL, Melissa Victoria. (Melissa Victoria Harris-Perry). American (born United States), b. 1973. **Genres:** Theology/Religion, Politics/Government, International Relations/Current Affairs. **Career:** University of Chicago, Center for the Study of Race, Politics, and Culture, Department of Political Science, assistant professor, 1999-2005; Princeton University, associate professor of politics and African American studies, 2006-10; Tulane University, professor of political science, Anna Julia Cooper Project, Gender, Race, and Politics in the South, director; Nation Magazine, columnist. **Publications:** Barbershops, Bibles, and BET: Everyday Talk and Black Political Thought, 2004; (as Melissa V. Harris-Perry) Sister Citizen: Shame, Stereotypes, and Black Women in America, 2011. Contributor to books, periodicals and journals. **Address:** c/o Annette Luba-Lucas, Anderson Literary Management L.L.C., 12 W 19th St., New York, NY 10011, U.S.A. **Online address:** info@melissaharrislacewell.com

HARRISON, Ann Tukey. American (born United States), b. 1938. **Genres:** History, Women's Studies And Issues, Medicine/Health, Language/Linguistics. **Career:** University of Wisconsin, instructor, 1961-63, assistant professor, 1962-65; Michigan State University, professor, 1965, now professor emeritus; Mount Holyoke College, Ruth Dean lecturer, 1976. Writer. **Publications:** (Ed. with G.J. Joyaux) Lectures de France et d'outre-mer, 1967; Charles d'Orléans and the Allegorical Mode, 1974; (ed.) The Danse Macabre of Women: Ms. fr. 995 of the Bibliothèque nationale, 1994. **Address:** Department of French, Classics and Italian, Michigan State University, East Lansing, MI 48824, U.S.A. **Online address:** harris10@msu.edu

HARRISON, Antony H. American (born United States), b. 1948. **Genres:** Poetry, Art/Art History, Literary Criticism And History. **Career:** North Carolina State University, Department of English, assistant professor, 1974-80, associate professor, 1980-87, professor of English, 1987-, director of graduate programs, 2005-06, head of department, 2006-, distinguished professor of English, 2009-. Writer. **Publications:** The Craft of Pure Expression: Passion, Pantheism, and Courtly Love in the Works of A. C. Swinburne, 1974; Christina Rossetti in Context, 1988; Swinburne's Medievalism: A Study in Victorian Love Poetry, 1988; Victorian Poets and Romantic Poems: Intertextuality and Ideology, 1990; (ed. with B. Taylor) Gender and Discourse in Victorian Literature and Art, 1992; (ed.) The Letters of Christina Rossetti, vol. I, 1997, vol. IV, 2004; Victorian Poets and the Politics of Culture: Discourse and Ideology, 1998; (ed. with M. Arseneau and L.J. Kooistra) The Culture of Christina Rossetti: Female Poetics and Victorian Contexts, 1999; (ed.) The Letters of Christina Rossetti, vol. I, 1998, vol. II, 1999; (ed. with R. Cronin and A. Chapman) Companion to Victorian Poetry, 2002; (co-ed.) The Blackwell Companion to Victorian Poetry, 2002; The Cultural Production of Matthew Arnold, 2006; (ed.) Christina Rossetti: Selected Writings, 2007; (co-ed.) The Correspondence of Dante Gabriel Rossetti, 2008; The Cultural Production of Matthew Arnold, 2010. Victorian Taste: A Reconsideration, forthcoming. **Address:** Department of English, North Carolina State University, Tompkins 249, PO Box 8105, Raleigh, NC 27695-8105, U.S.A. **Online address:** tony_harrison@ncsu.edu

HARRISON, Brady. American (born United States), b. 1963?. **Genres:** Literary Criticism And History. **Career:** University of Montana, professor of English. Writer. **Publications:** Agent of Empire: William Walker and the Imperial Self in American Literature, 2004; (ed.) Soldiers of Fortune, 2006; (ed.) All Our Stories Are Here: Critical Perspectives on Montana Literature, 2009. Contributor to periodicals. **Address:** Department of English, University of Montana, LA 114, 32 Campus Dr., Missoula, MT 59812-0003, U.S.A. **Online address:** brady.harrison@mso.umt.edu

HARRISON, Brian (Howard). British (born England), b. 1937. **Genres:** History, Humanities. **Career:** Nuffield College, junior research fellow, 1964-67; Corpus Christi College, fellow and tutor in modern history and politics, 1967-2000, reader in modern British history, 1990-2000, professor of modern British history, 1996-, now emeritus fellow; Oxford Dictionary of National Biography, editor, 2000-04. **Publications:** (Ed. with G. Barlow) History at the Universities: A Comparative and Analytical Guide to History Syllabuses at Universities in the United Kingdom, 1966; (with B. Trinder) Drink and Sobriety in an Early Victorian Country Town: Banbury 1830-1860, 1969; Drink and the Victorians: The Temperance Question in England, 1815-1872, 1971, 2nd ed., 1994; Dictionary of British Temperance Biography, 1973; Separate Spheres: The Opposition to Women's Suffrage in Britain, 1978; (ed. with P. Hollis) Robert Lowery, Radical and Chartist, 1979; Peaceable Kingdom: Stability and Change in Modern Britain, 1982; (with C. Ford) Hundred Years Ago: Britain in the 1880s in Words and Photographs, 1983; Prudent Revolutionaries: Portraits of British Feminists between the Wars, 1987; (ed. and contrib.) The History of the University of Oxford, vol. VIII: Twentieth Century Oxford, 1994; (ed.) Corpuscles: A History of Corpus Christi College, Oxford in the Twentieth Century, 1994; The Transformation of Brit-

ish Politics 1860-1995, 1996; (ed. and contrib. with P. Burke and P. Slack) Civil Histories: Essays Presented to Sir Keith Thomas, 2000; Great Britons: The Great Debate, 2002; (ed.) The Oxford Dictionary of National Biography: In Association with the British Academy: From the Earliest Times to the Year 2000, 2004; Seeking a Role: The United Kingdom, 1951-1970, 2009; Finding a Role?: The United Kingdom, 1970-1990, 2010. **Address:** Corpus Christi College, Merton St., Oxford, OX OX1 4JF, England. **Online address:** harrisob@oup.co.uk

HARRISON, C. C. (Christy Hubbard). American (born United States) **Genres:** History, Mystery/Crime/Suspense, Romance/Historical, Novels. **Career:** Writer. **Publications:** The Charmstone, 2007; Running from Strangers, 2008; Picture of Lies, 2011. AS CHRISTY HUBBARD: Sage Cane's House of Grace and Favor, 2009. **Address:** Five Star Publishing, 295 Kennedy Memorial Dr., Waterville, ME 04901, U.S.A. **Online address:** arizonaauthor@cox.net

HARRISON, Chip. See **BLOCK, Lawrence.**

HARRISON, Colin. (Colin Young Harrison). American (born United States), b. 1960. **Genres:** Novels, Children's Fiction, Mystery/Crime/Suspense. **Career:** Harper's Magazine, associate editor, 1988-92, senior editor, 1992-94, deputy editor, 1994-2000; Columbia University, adjunct assistant professor, 1993-2000; Scribner, vice president and senior editor, 2000-, executive editor. **Publications:** Break and Enter, 1990; Bodies Electric: A Novel, 1993; Manhattan Nocturne: A Novel, 1996; Afterburn, 2000; The Havana Room, 2004; Finder, 2008; Risk, 2009. **Address:** c/o Kris Dahl, International Creative Management, 40 W 57th St., New York, NY 10019-4001, U.S.A. **Online address:** colin.harrison@simonandschuster.com

HARRISON, Colin Young. See **HARRISON, Colin.**

HARRISON, David Lakin. British (born England), b. 1926. **Genres:** Natural History, Travel/Exploration, Sciences, Animals/Pets. **Career:** St. Thomas's Hospital, house physician, 1951-52; general medical practitioner, 1956-; Harrison Zoological Museum, curator of mammals, 1970-, director, chairman of trustees. Writer. **Publications:** (With P.J.J. Bates) The Mammals of Arabia, 1964, vol. II, 1968; Note on the Occurrence of the Large Free-Tailed Bat, Otomops Martiensseni Matschie, 1897 (Chiroptera: Molossidae) in Rhodesia, 1965; (with R.L. Peterson) Second and Third Known Specimens of the African Molossid Bat, Tadarida Lobata, 1970; Note on the Occurrence of the Giant African Free-Tailed Bat, Tadarida Africana (Dobson, 1876) in Tanzania, With Some Observations on the Characters of the Species, 1971; Mammals of the Arabian Gulf, 1981; (with P.J.J. Bates) Bats of the Indian Subcontinent, 1997. SELF-ILLUSTRATED: Footsteps in the Sand, 1959. **Address:** Harrison Institute, Bowerwood House, 15 St Botolph's Rd., Sevenoaks, KT TN13 3AQ, England.

HARRISON, Elizabeth Fancourt. See Obituaries.

HARRISON, Gary. (Gary Lee Harrison). American (born United States), b. 1949. **Genres:** Literary Criticism And History. **Career:** State University of New York College, tutor at writing center, 1979-80; Western States Technical Assistance Resource, staff writer and editor, 1980, managing editor, 1980-81; Product Development Assistance Systems, staff writer and editor, 1980; University of Santa Clara, adjunct lecturer in English, 1982-83; University of New Mexico, assistant professor, 1987-93, associate professor, 1993-2001, professor, 2001-, director of graduate studies in English, 1995-99, associate dean of graduate studies, presidential teaching fellow, 2008-. Writer. **Publications:** AS GARY LEE HARRISON: Wordsworth's Vagrant Muse: Poetry, Poverty and Power, 1994. EDITOR: (with D. Assael) Handicapped Children's Early Education Program: 1980-81 Overview and Directory, 1981; (with D. Mirkes) From Process to Product, 1981; (co-ed.) Western Literature in a World Context, 2 vol., 1995; (co-ed.) Bedford Anthology of World Literature, 6 vol., 2004. Contributor to journals and books. **Address:** Department of English, University of New Mexico, 107 Humanities Bldg., 1 University of New Mexico, Albuquerque, NM 87131-0001, U.S.A. **Online address:** garyh@unm.edu

HARRISON, Gary Lee. See **HARRISON, Gary.**

HARRISON, Harry. Irish/American (born United States), b. 1925. **Genres:** Novellas/Short Stories, Science Fiction/Fantasy, Children's Fiction, Young

Adult Fiction, Novels, Humor/Satire. **Career:** Freelance commercial artist, 1946-55. Writer. **Publications:** Planet of the Damned, 1962; War with the Robots (short stories), 1962; Bill, the Gallactic Hero, 1965; Two Tales and 8 Tomorrows (short stories), 1965; Plague from Space, 1965; Make Room! Make Room!, 1966; The Technicolor Time Machine, 1967; (ed.) World of Wonder (juvenile), 1968; (ed.) Farewell, Fantastic Venus! A History Of The Planet Venus In Fact and Fiction, 1968; The Man from P.I.G., 1968; (ed.) Apeman, Spaceman: Anthropological Science Fiction, 1968; Captive Universe, 1969; Four For the Future: An Anthology on the Themes of Sacrifice and Redemption, 1969; Worlds of Wonder: Sixteen Tales of Science Fiction, 1969; (ed.) Year 2000: An Anthology, 1970; Daleth Effect: A Science Fiction Novel, 1970; Nova 1: An Anthology of Original Science Fiction Stories, 1970; In Our Hands, the Stars, 1970; Prime Number (short stories), 1970; One Step from Earth (short stories), 1970; The Jupiter Legacy, 1970; Spaceship Medic (children), 1970; Science Fiction Omnibus on Pollution, 1971; The Light Fantastic: Science Fiction Classics From the Mainstream, 1971; Astounding Analog Reader, 1972; (ed.) Ahead of Time, 1972; Nova 2, 1972; (L.E. Stover) Stonehenge. 1972; Tunnel through the Deeps in UK as A Transatlantic Tunnel, Hurrah!, 1972; Montezuma's Revenge, 1972; Nova 3, 1973; (ed. with C. Pugner) A Science Fiction Reader, 1973; Star Smashers of the Galaxy Rangers, 1973; (ed.) Nova 4, 1974; The Men from P.I.G. and R.O.B.O.T. (for children), 1974; The California Iceberg (for children), 1974; Queen Victoria's Revenge, 1974; Decade, the 1940's, 1975; (co-ed.) Hell's Cartographers: Some Personal Histories of Science Fiction Writers, 1975; California Iceberg, 1975; (co-ed.) Science Fiction Novellas, 1975; (ed. with B. Aldiss) Best SF: 1967 to 1975, 1975; (co-ed.) Decade the 1950s, 1976; (with G. Dickson) The Lifeship, 1976; The Best of Harry Harrison, 1976; Skyfall, 1977; Great Balls of Fire, 1977; Mechanism, 1978; (with M. Edwards) Spacecraft in Fact and Fiction, 1979; Planet Story, 1979; The QE2 Is Missing, 1980; Homeworld, 1980; Wheelworld, 1981; Starworld, 1981; Planet of No Return, 1981; Invasion, Earth, 1982; Rebel in Time, 1983; West of Eden, 1984; Winter in Eden, 1986; Return to Eden, 1988; The Planet of the Robot Slaves, 1989; (with M. Minsky) The Turning Option, 1992; The Hammer and the Cross, 1993; One King's Way, 1994; Galactic Dreams, 1994; (with J. Holm) King and Emperor, 1996; Stars and Stripes Forever, 1995; Stars and Stripes in Peril, 2000; 50 in 50: A Collection of Short Stories, One for Each of Fifty Years, 2001; Stars & Stripes Triumphant, 2003; Toy Shop and Two Others, 2009; Essential Harry Harrison, 2010; The K-Factor, 2010; Arm of the Law, 2010; The Repairman, 2010; Toy Shop, 2010; The Misplaced Battleship, 2010. DEATH-WORLD SERIES: Deathworld, 1960; Deathworld Two, 1964; Deathworld Three, 1968. THE STAINLESS STEEL RAT SERIES: The Stainless Steel Rat, 1961; The Stainless Steel Rat's Revenge, 1970; The Stainless Steel Rat Saves the World, 1972; The Stainless Steel Rat Wants You!, 1978; The Stainless Steel Rat for President, 1982; The Adventures of the Stainless Steel Rat, 1983; You Can Be the Stainless Steel Rat, 1985; A Stainless Steel Rat is Born, 1985; The Stainless Steel Rat Gets Drafted, 1987; Stainless Steel Visions, 1992; The Stainless Steel Rat Sings the Blues, 1994; Stainless Steel Rat Goes to Hell, 1996; Stainless Steel Rat Joins the Circus, 1999; The Stainless Steel Rat Returns, 2010. Contributor to periodicals and journals. **Address:** Sobel Weber Associates Inc., 146 E 19th St., New York, NY 10003-2404, U.S.A. **Online address:** hhwebsite@gmail.com

HARRISON, Jim. American (born United States), b. 1937. **Genres:** Novels, Poetry, Novellas/Short Stories, Adult Non-fiction, Literary Criticism And History, Young Adult Fiction. **Career:** State University of New York, assistant professor of English, 1965-66; Warner Brothers Co., screenwriter. **Publications:** Plain Song, 1965; Walking, 1967; Locations, 1968; Outlyers and Ghazals, 1971; Wolf (novel), 1971; A Good Day to Die (novel), 1973; Letters to Yesenin, 1973; Farmer (novel), 1976; Legends of the Fall (novella), 1979; Warlock (novel), 1981; Selected & New Poems, 1961-1981, 1982; (with Diana Guest) Natural World, 1983; Sundog (novel), 1984; The Theory and Practice of Rivers (poetry), 1986; Confusion Reigns: A Quick and Easy Guide to the Most Easily Mixed-Up Words, 1987; Dalva (novel), 1988; The Woman Lit by Fireflies (novella), 1990; Just Before Dark (non-fiction), 1991; Julip (novellas), 1994; After Ikkyū and Other Poems, 1996; The Road Home, 1998; The Shape of the Journey: New and Collected Poems, 1998; The Beast God Forgot to Invent, 2000; The Boy Who Ran to the Woods, 2000; Raw and the Cooked: Adventures of a Roving Gourmand, 2001; Off to the Side: A Memoir, 2002; (with T. Kooser) Braided Creek: A Conversation in Poetry, 2003; True North: A Novel, 2004; Summer He Didn't Die, 2005; Saving Daylight, 2006; Returning to Earth, 2007; English Major, 2008; In Search of Small Gods, 2009; (with G. Snyder) The Etiquette of Freedom: Gary Snyder, Jim Harrison and The Practice of the Wild, 2010; The Farmer's Daughter, 2010;

The Great Leader, 2011; Songs of Unreason, 2011. Works appear in anthologies. Contributor of poems to periodicals. **Address:** PO Box 135, Lake Leelanau, MI 49653, U.S.A.

HARRISON, John F(letcher) C(lews). British (born England), b. 1921. **Genres:** History, Social Commentary, Bibliography, Essays, Education, Social Sciences. **Career:** University of Leeds, lecturer in history, 1947-58, deputy director of adult education, 1958-61; University of Wisconsin, professor of history, 1961-70, Institute for Research in the Humanities, visiting research professor, 1977-78; Australian National University, visiting research fellow, 1968-69, 1977; University of Sussex, professor of social history, 1970-82, professor emeritus, 1982-. Writer. **Publications:** History of the Working Men's College 1854-1954, 1954; (co-author) Chartist Studies, 1959; Learning and Living, 1790-1960: A Study in the History of the English Adult Education Movement, 1961; (ed.) Society and Politics in England, 1780-1960: A Selection of Readings and Comments, 1965; (ed. and intro.) Utopianism and Education: Robert Owen and the Owenites, 1968; Quest for the New Moral World: Robert Owen and the Owenites in Britain and America: A Quest for the New Moral World, Scribner in UK as Robert Owen and the Owenites in Britain and America, 1969; The Early Victorians, 1832-1851, 1971 in UK as Early Victorian Britain, 1832-51, 1979; Birth and Growth of Industrial England, 1714-1867, 1973; (ed. and contrib.) Eminently Victorian, 1974; Bibliography of the Chartist Movement, 1837-1976, 1978; The Second Coming: Popular Millenarianism, 1780-1850, 1979; English Common People: A Social History from the Norman Conquest to the Present, 1984; Common People of Great Britain: A History from the Norman Conquest to the Present, 1985; Late Victorian Britain, 1875-1901, 1991; Scholarship Boy: A Personal History of the Mid-Twentieth Century, 1995; (contrib.) Living and Learning: Essays in Honour of J.F.C. Harrison, 1996; History of the Working Men's College, 1854-1954, 2007. **Address:** Mill Cottage, 2 Sandford Mill Close, Cheltenham, GC GL53 7QZ, England.

HARRISON, J. Richard. American (born United States), b. 1947. **Genres:** Business/Trade/Industry, Administration/Management, Cultural/Ethnic Topics, Social Sciences, Sociology. **Career:** Siren Records, vice president, 1976-78; University of California, Graduate Student Association, executive director, 1976-78, lecturer in business administration, 1981; California State University, lecturer in management sciences, 1979-81; Pepperdine University, instructor in business and management, 1982; University of Arizona, assistant professor of management, 1983-85; TPF Corp., director, 1984-85; University of Texas, School of Management, assistant professor, 1985-91, associate professor of management, 1991-, associate dean for academic affairs, 1991-95, Ph.D. Program coordinator, 1986-91, Russian Institute, director, 1992-96; Memorial Hospital of Southern Oklahoma, consultant, 1987-92; BancOne, 1993, Rockwell Intl., consultant, 1994; Baylor University Medical Center, consultant, 1996; U.S. Department of Defense, consultant, 2002; Hot Earth Films, president, 2007-. Writer. **Publications:** (With G.R. Carroll) Culture and Demography in Organizations, 2006. Contributor to books and periodicals. **Address:** School of Management, University of Texas, SM43, 80 W Campbell Rd., PO Box 830688, Richardson, TX 75080-3021, U.S.A. **Online address:** harrison@utdallas.edu

HARRISON, Kathryn. American (born United States), b. 1961. **Genres:** Novels, Autobiography/Memoirs, Essays, Adult Non-fiction, Human Relations/Parenting, Theology/Religion, Travel/Exploration, Women's Studies And Issues, Biography, Mystery/Crime/Suspense, Classics, Medicine/Health, Literary Criticism And History. **Career:** Hunter College, professor; Master of Fine Arts Program in Creative Writing, reviewer. Writer. **Publications:** Thicker than Water, A Novel, 1991; Exposure, A Novel, 1993; Poison, A Novel, 1995; The Kiss A Memoir, 1997; The Binding Chair, or A Visit from the Foot Emancipation Society: A Novel, 2000; (intro.) The Scarlet Letter, 2000; (intro.) Lady Chatterly's Lover, 2001; The Seal Wife, A Novel, 2002; The Road to Santiago, A Travel Memoir, 2003; Seeking Rapture: Scenes from a Woman's Life, 2003; Saint Therese of Lisieux, A Biography, 2003; The Mother Knot, A Memoir 2004; (intro.) Becoming a Man, 2004; Envy: A Novel, 2005; While they Slept: An Inquiry into the Murder of a Family, 2008; Enchantments, 2012. **Address:** c/o Amanda Urban, International Creative Management Inc., 825 8th Ave., New York, NY 10019, U.S.A. **Online address:** kathryn@kathrynharrison.com

HARRISON, Kathy A. American (born United States), b. 1952. **Genres:** Autobiography/Memoirs, Biography, Politics/Government. **Career:** Writer. **Publications:** Another Place at the Table: A Story of Shattered Childhoods

Redeemed by Love (memoir), 2003; One Small Boat: The Story of a Little Girl, Lost then Found, 2006; Just in Case: How to be Self-Sufficient When the Unexpected Happens, 2008. Contributor to periodicals. **Address:** c/o Maureen Walters, Curtis Brown Ltd., 10 Astor Pl., New York, NY 10003, U.S.A.

HARRISON, Kim. See **COOK, Dawn.**

HARRISON, Kim. (Dawn Cook). American (born United States), b. 1966?. **Genres:** Young Adult Fiction, Horror, Novels, Mystery/Crime/Suspense. **Career:** Writer, 2002-. **Publications:** (With A. Harrison) Seek, Share, Serve, 2002; Dead Witch Walking, 2004; Every Which Way but Dead, 2005; The Good, the Bad, and the Undead, 2005; A Fistful of Charms, 2006; (co-author) Dates from Hell, 2006; For a Few Demons More, 2007; (with L. Sands, M.M. Liu and V. Pettersson) Holidays are Hell, 2007; (co-author) Prom Nights from Hell, 2007; (ed. with M.H. Greenberg) Hotter than Hell, 2008; The Outlaw Demon Wails, 2008; Once Dead, Twice Shy: A Novel, 2009; (with J. Frost, M. Marr and V. Pettersson) Unbound, 2009; White Witch, Black Curse, 2009; Early to Death, Early to Rise, 2010; Black Magic Sanction, 2010; Something Deadly this Way Comes, 2011; Pale Demon, 2011; The Hollows Insider, 2011; Blood Work, 2011; A Perfect Blood, 2012; Blood Crime, 2012. AS DAWN COOK: First Truth, 2002; Hidden Truth, 2002; Forgotten Truth, 2003; Lost Truth, 2004; The Decoy Princess, 2005; Princess at Sea, 2006. **Address:** PO Box 36653, Rock Hill, SC 29732, U.S.A. **Online address:** kimharrison@comporium.net

HARRISON, Kyle. American (born United States), b. 1970?. **Genres:** Biography, Information Science/Computers, Autobiography/Memoirs, Business/Trade/Industry. **Career:** Andersen Consulting, management consultant; Platinum Concepts, co-founder, 1999. Writer. **Publications:** (With J. Lusk) The MouseDriver Chronicles: The True-Life Adventures of Two First-Time Entrepreneurs, 2002. Contributor to periodicals. **Address:** Perseus Books, 11 Cambridge Ctr., Cambridge, MA 02142, U.S.A.

HARRISON, Lisi. American/Canadian (born Canada), b. 1975. **Genres:** Novels. **Career:** Music Television Productions, director of production development, senior director, 2003. Writer. **Publications:** A CLIQUE NOVEL: Sealed with a Diss, 2004; The Clique, 2004; Best Friends for Never, 2004; Invasion of the Boy Snatchers, 2005; Revenge of the Wannabes, 2005; Dial L for Loser, 2006; The Pretty Committee Strikes Back, 2006; It's Not Easy Being Mean, 2007; Bratfest at Tiffany's, 2008; Kristen, 2008; Dylan, 2008; Claire, 2008; Massie, 2008; Alicia, 2008; P.S. I Loathe You, 2009; Alphas, 2009; Boys r Us, 2009; Cliquetionary: The Wit and Wisdom of the Clique, 2009; Charmed and Dangerous: The Rise of the Pretty Committee: The Clique Prequel, 2009; Monster High, 2010, Movers & Fakers: An Alphas Novel, 2010; My Little Phony, 2010; Belle of the Brawl, 2010; Movers and Fakers, 2010; These Boots are made for Stalking, 2010; A Tale of Two Pretties, 2011; Top of the Feud Chain, 2011. **Address:** c/o Author Mail, Little Brown Co., 1271 Ave. of the Americas, New York, NY 10020, U.S.A.

HARRISON, Lowell H. American (born United States), b. 1922. **Genres:** History, Biography, Education, Military/Defense/Arms Control. **Career:** New York University, instructor, 1947-50, Foreign Students Center, assistant director, 1950-51; West Texas State University, Social Sciences Division, associate professor, 1952-57, department head, 1957-67, chairman, 1962-67; Western Kentucky University, professor of history and graduate adviser, 1967-88, faculty regent, 1971-74. Writer. **Publications:** John Breckinridge: Western Statesman, 1952; John Breckinridge, Jeffersonian Republican, 1969; The Civil War in Kentucky, 1975; George Rogers Clark and the War in the West, 1976; (ed. with N.L. Dawson) A Kentucky Sampler, 1977; The Anti-Slavery Movement in Kentucky, 1978; (with J.D. Bennett) Writing History Papers: An Introduction, 1979; (ed.) Kentucky's Governors, 1792-1985, 1985, rev. ed., 2004; Western Kentucky University, 1987; Kentucky's Road to Statehood, 1992; (ed.) The Kentucky Encyclopedia, 1992; (with J.C. Klotter) A New History of Kentucky, 1997; Lincoln of Kentucky, 2000. **Address:** 1800 Westen St., Apt. 2306, Bowling Green, KY 42104-5851, U.S.A.

HARRISON, Michael. British (born England), b. 1939. **Genres:** Children's Fiction, Poetry, Humor/Satire, Mythology/Folklore, Mystery/Crime/Suspense, Literary Criticism And History. **Career:** Teacher, 1961-94. Writer. **Publications:** FOR CHILDREN: FICTION: Bags of Trouble (comedy), 1988; Trouble Abroad (comedy), 1990; Trouble in Store (comedy), 1991; It's My Life (thriller), 1997; Facing the Dark (thriller), 1997; Junk Mail (poems), 1998; At the Deep End (thriller), 2001; Carried Away (thriller), 2003. OTH-

ERS: Scolding Tongues: The Persecution of Witches (history for children), 1987; (comp. with C. Stuart-Clark) The Oxford Treasury of Children's Stories, 1994; (comp. with C. Stuart-Clark) The Oxford Treasury of World Stories, 1998. EDITOR: POETRY ANTHOLOGIES: Catch the Light, 1982; Upright Downfall, 1983; The Candy-Floss Tree, 1984; The Crystal Zoo, 1985; Bright Lights Blaze Out, 1986; Splinters: A Book of Very Short Poems, 1988. POETRY ANTHOLOGIES WITH C. STUART-CLARK: The New Dragon Book of Verse, 1977 as The Dragon Book of Verse, 1997; Poems 1, 1979; Poems 2, 1980; Narrative Poems, 1981; Noah's Ark, 1983; (comp.) The Oxford Book of Christmas Poems, 1983; Writing Poems, 1985; The Oxford Treasury of Children's Poems, 1988; The Young Dragon Book of Verse, 1989; Peace and War: A Collection of Poems, 1989; The Oxford Book of Story Poems, 1990; A Year Full of Poems, 1991; The Oxford Book of Animal Poems, 1992; Writing Poems Plus, 1992; Bright Star Shining: Poems for Christmas, 1993; (comp.) The Oxford Treasury of Classic Poems, 1996; The New Oxford Treasury of Children's Poems, 1997; The Oxford Treasury of Time Poems, 1998; One Hundred Years of Poetry for Childrens, 1999; The Oxford Treasury of Christmas Poems, 1999. **Address:** 65 Bainton Rd., Oxford, CW OX2 7A9, England.

HARRISON, Neil E. American/British (born England), b. 1949. **Genres:** Environmental Sciences/Ecology, International Relations/Current Affairs, Politics/Government, Business/Trade/Industry, Social Sciences. **Career:** Price Waterhouse, manager, 1976-81; Colorado Aggregate, president, 1981-83; Unibind USA, president, 1983-85; Business Health Systems America, vice president, 1984-87; Fernandez & Associates, technical director, 1988-93; University of Wyoming, assistant professor, 1993-2000, adjunct professor, 1994-2001; Sustainable Development Institute, founder, executive director and senior fellow, 2000-. Writer. **Publications:** Constructing Sustainable Development, 2000; (ed. with G.C. Bryner) Science and Politics in the International Environment, 2004; (ed.) Complexity in World Politics: Concepts and Methods of a New Paradigm, 2006; (ed.) Selected Topics in National and Regional Institutions and Infrastructures, 2008. Contributor to books. **Address:** Sustainable Development Institute, PO Box 423, Laramie, WY 82073-0423, U.S.A. **Online address:** harrison@sd-institute.org

HARRISON, Roy M(ichael). British (born England), b. 1948. **Genres:** Chemistry, Environmental Sciences/Ecology, Meteorology/Atmospheric Sciences. **Career:** Imperial Chemical Industries Ltd., laboratory technician, 1966; University of London, postdoctoral research assistant in public health engineering, 1972-74; University of Lancaster, Department of Environmental Sciences, lecturer, 1974-84; University of Essex, Department of Chemistry and Biological Chemistry, reader, 1984-91, Institute of Aerosol Science, director 1985-91; University of Birmingham, Queen Elizabeth II Birmingham centenary professor of environmental health, 1991-93, director, 1993-2000, Institute of Public and Environmental Health, director, 1991-, Division of Environmental Health and Risk Management, head, 1999-, professor, School of Geography, Earth and Environmental Sciences, deputy head, 2003-, Natural Environment Research Council on Environment, Pollution abd Human Health, leader, 2007-. Writer and consultant. **Publications:** (With D.P.H. Laxen) Lead Pollution Causes and Control, 1981; (with W.R. Johnston, S. Rapsomanikis and S.J. de Mora) Introductory Chemistry for the Environmental Sciences, 1991, (with S.J. de Mora), 2nd ed., 1996; (with L. Butterwick and Q. Merritt) Handbook for Urban Air Improvement, 1992. EDITOR: Pollution, 1983, 4th ed., 2001; (with R. Perry) Handbook of Air Pollution Analysis, 2nd ed., 1986; (co-ed.) Acid Rain, 1987; (with S. Rapsomanikis) Environmental Analysis Using Chromatography Interfaced with Atomic Spectroscopy, 1989; (with R.S. Hamilton) Highway Pollution, 1991; Understanding Our Environment, 1992, 3rd ed., 1999; (with M. Radojevic) Atmospheric Acidity, 1992; (with F.E. Warner) Radioecology after Chernobyl, 1993; (with R.E. Hester) Mining and its Environmental Impact, 1994; (with R.E. Hester) Waste Incineration and the Environment, 1994; (with R.E. Hester) Waste Treatment and Disposal, 1995; (with R.E. Hester) Agricultural Chemicals and the Environment, 1996; (with R.E. Hester) Contaminated Land and its Reclamation, 1997; (with R. van Grieken) Atmospheric Particles, 1998; (with R.E. Hester) Issues in Environmental Science and Technology, 20 vols., 1994-2004; (with R.E. Hester) Chemistry in the Marine Environment, 2000; (with R.E. Hester) Food Safety and Food Quality, 2001; (with R.E. Hester) Assessment and Reclamation of Contaminated Land, 2001; Global Environmental Change, 2002; (with R.E. Hester) Sustainability and Environmental Impact of Renewable Energy Sources, 2003; (with R.E. Hester) Transport and the Environment, 2004; (with R.E. Hester) Sustainability in Agriculture, 2005; (with R.E. Hester) Alternatives to Animal Testing, 2006; (with R.E. Hester)

Chemicals in the Environment, 2006; Introduction to Pollution Science, 2006; (with R.E. Hester) Biodiversity Under Threat, 2007; (with R.E. Hester) Nanotechnology, 2007; Principles of Environmental Chemistry, 2007; (with R.E. Hester) Environmental Forensics, 2008; (with R.E. Hester) Air Quality in Urban Environments, 2009; (with R.E. Hester) Electronic Waste Management, 2009. **Address:** Division of Environmental Health, University of Birmingham, Edgbaston, Birmingham, WM B15 2TT, England. **Online address:** r.m.harrison@bham.ac.uk

HARRISON, Russell (T.). American (born United States), b. 1944. **Genres:** Literary Criticism And History. **Career:** St. Peter's College, adjunct professor of English, 1984-87; Hudson County Community College, adjunct professor of English, 1984-87; Palacky University, senior Fulbright lecturer in American literature, 1987-89; Hofstra University, New College, adjunct and associate, 1989-90, assistant professor of writing studies and composition, 1990-, adjunct assistant professor, 1998-; writer, 1994-; Minsk State Linguistic University, senior Fulbright lecturer in American literature, 1996-98. **Publications:** Against the American Dream: Essays on Charles Bukowski, 1994; Patricia Highsmith, 1997. Contributor to periodicals. **Address:** Hofstra University, 311 Mason Hall, 1000 Fulton Ave., Hempstead, NY 11550, U.S.A. **Online address:** russell.t.harrison@hofstra.edu

HARRISON, Sarah. British (born England), b. 1946. **Genres:** Novels, Children's Fiction, Writing/Journalism, inspirational/Motivational Literature. **Career:** International Publishing Corp., magazine journalist, 1967-70. Writer, journalist, broadcaster and public speaker. **Publications:** FICTION: The Flowers of the Field, 1980; A Flower That's Free, 1984; Hot Breath, 1985; An Imperfect Lady, 1988; Cold Feet, 1989; The Forests of the Night, 1991; Foreign Parts, 1992; Be an Angel, 1993; Both Your Houses, 1995; Life after Lunch, 1996; Flowers Won't Fax, 1997; That Was Then, 1998; Heaven's on Hold, 1999; The Grass Memorial, 2002; The Dreaming Stones, 2003; A Dangerous Thing, 2003; The Divided Heart, 2003; Swan Music, 2005; The Nightingale's Nest, 2006; The Next Room, 2006; The Red Dress, 2006; A Spell of Swallows, 2007; Rose Petal Soup, 2008; Matters Arising, 2009; Secrets of Our Hearts, 2010; Returning the Favour, 2010. CHILDREN'S BOOKS: In Granny's Garden, 1980; Laura from Lark Rise series, 4 vols., 1986. NONFICTION: How to Write a Blockbuster, 1995. Contributor of articles to magazines, books and periodicals. **Address:** A.P. Watt, Sheila Crowley, 20 John St., London, GL WC1N 2DR, England. **Online address:** novel.sarah@virgin.net

HARRISON, Sue. American (born United States), b. 1950. **Genres:** Novels, Young Adult Fiction, Romance/Historical, Mythology/Folklore. **Career:** Lake Superior State University, public relations writer, 1985-88, adjunct instructor in writing, 1988-90. **Publications:** Mother Earth Father Sky, 1990; My Sister the Moon, 1992; Brother Wind, 1994; SISU (young adult novel), 1997; Song of the River, 1997; Cry of the Wind, 1998; Call Down the Stars, 2001. **Address:** c/o Jennie Dunham, Dunham Literary Inc., 156 5th Ave., Ste. 823, New York, NY 10010-7002, U.S.A. **Online address:** sue@sueharrison.com

HARRISON, Suzan. American (born United States), b. 1956. **Genres:** Literary Criticism And History, Politics/Government, Young Adult Fiction. **Career:** Eckerd College, assistant professor, 1989-95, Writing Excellence Program, associate professor, 1995-, director, 1992-93, Writing Center, director, 1995-96, Letters Collegium, chairperson, 1998-2000, associate dean of faculty and professor of rhetoric, 2000-. Writer. **Publications:** (Contrib.) Gender and Academe: Feminist Pedagogy and Politics, 1994; Eudora Welty and Virginia Woolf: Gender, Genre and Influence, 1997; (ed. with H. Pollock) Eudora Welty and Politics: Did the Writer Crusade?, 2001; (contrib.) Political Welty, forthcoming. Contributor to books and journals. **Address:** Writing Excellence Program, Eckerd College, 4200 54th Ave. S, PO Box 12560, St. Petersburg, FL 33711, U.S.A. **Online address:** harrisms@eckerd.edu

HARRISON, Tony. (T. W. Harrison). British (born England), b. 1937. **Genres:** Plays/Screenplays, Poetry, Translations, Literary Criticism And History, Theatre. **Career:** Ahmadu Bello University, lecturer, 1962-66; Charles University, lecturer, 1966-67; University of Newcastle, northern arts fellow in poetry, 1967-68, 1976-77; Durham University, northern arts fellow in poetry, 1967-68, 1976-77; University of Wales, Gregynog Arts fellow, 1973-74; National Theatre, resident dramatist, 1977-78. Writer and translator. **Publications:** POETRY: (as T.W. Harrison) Earthworks, 1964; Newcastle is Peru, 1969; The Loiners, 1970; (ed. and intro.) Poems of Palladas of Alexandria, 1973; From The School of Eloquence and Other Poems, 1978; Continuous:

Fifty Sonnets from The School of Eloquence, 1981; A Kumquat for John Keats, 1981; U.S. Martial, 1981; Selected Poems, 1984; V., 1985; The Fire Gap: A Poem with Two Tails, 1985; V. and Other Poems, 1990; A Cold Coming: Gulf War Poems, 1991; The Gaze of the Gorgon, 1992; The Common Chorus, 1992; Poetry or Bust, 1993; A Maybe Day in Kazakhstan, 1994; (with S. Armitage and S. O'Brien) Penguin Modern Poets 5, 1995; The Shadow of Hiroshima and Other Film/Poems, 1995; Permanently Bard: Selected Poetry, 1995; Prometheus, 1998; Laureate's Block and Other Occasional Poems, 2000; Collected Film Poetry, 2007; Collected Poems, 2007. OTHERS: (as T.W. Harrison trans. with J. Simmons) Aikin Mata: The Lysistrata of Aristophanes, 1966; Voortrekker, 1972; (trans.) Molière, The Misanthrope, 1973; Phaedra Britannica, 1975; (trans., ed. and intro.) Palladas: Poems, 1975; The Passion, 1977; Bow Down, 1977; A Source Book of Dinghies, 1978; (trans.) The Bartered Bride, 1978; (with P. Sharpe) Looking Up, 1979; (trans.) Aeschylus, The Oresteia, 1981; Medea: A Sex-War Opera, 1985; The Mysteries, 1985; Dramatic Verse, 1973-1985, 1985; Theater Works, 1973-1985, 1986; The Mother of Muses, 1989; Losing Touch, 1990; The Trackers of Oxyrhynchus: The Delphi Text 1988, 1990; Square Rounds, 1992; Black Daisies for the Bride, 1993; (with V. Hugo) Le roi s'amuse/The Prince's Play, 1996; Plays, 1996; Plays 3, 1996; Prometheus, 1998; Plays 1: The Mysteries, 1999; Tony Harrison: Plays Two, 2002; (trans.) Plays 4: The Orestia/The Common Chorus, 2002; Plays 5, 2004; (trans.) Hecuba/Euripides, 2005; Under the Clock, 2005; Fram, 2008. Contributor to magazines, periodicals and newspapers. **Address:** c/o Gordon Dickerson, 2 Crescent Grove, London, GL SW4 7AH, England.

HARRISON, Trevor (W.). Canadian (born Canada), b. 1952?. **Genres:** Politics/Government, Public/Social Administration, Sociology. **Career:** Alberta Department of Social Services, child protection worker, 1980-83; Fort McMurray Integrated Services, director, 1986-87; City Counselling Services, supervisor, 1987-88; University of Alberta, sessional lecturer, 1990-97, visiting professor, 1997-2002, Parkland Institute, research director, 1996-97, 2000-04, research coordinator, 2004-08; University of Lethbridge, associate professor, 2002-04, professor of sociology, associate chair, 2003-04, chair, 2004-10, Fulbright visiting research chair, interim director, 2007-10, board director, 2008-, Prentice Institute for Global Population and Economy, associate director. Writer. **Publications:** Of Passionate Intensity: Right-Wing Populism and the Reform Party of Canada, 1995; Requiem for a Lightweight: Stockwell Day and Image Politics, 2002; (with J. Friesen) Canadian Society in the Twenty-first Century: An Historical Sociological Approach, 2004; Twenty-First Century Japan: A New Sun Rising, 2008. EDITOR: (with G. Laxer) The Trojan Horse: Alberta and the Future of Canada, 1995; (with J.L. Kachur) Contested Classrooms: Education, Globalization, and Democracy in Alberta, 1999; The Return of the Trojan Horse: Alberta and the New World (Dis)Order, 2005. **Address:** Department of Sociology, University of Lethbridge, University Hall, Rm. A876, 4401 University Dr., Lethbridge, AB T1K 3M4, Canada. **Online address:** trevor.harrison@uleth.ca

HARRISON, T. W. See **HARRISON, Tony.**

HARRIS-PERRY, Melissa Victoria. See **HARRIS-LACEWELL, Melissa Victoria.**

HARRIST, Robert E. American (born United States), b. 1951. **Genres:** Art/Art History. **Career:** Columbia University, Department of Art History and Archaeology, associate professor, 1997-2001, Jane and Leopold Swergold professor of Chinese art history and chair, 2001-; Cambridge University, Slade professor of fine art, 2006-07; Oberlin College, faculty. Writer. **Publications:** Power and Virtue: The Horses in Chinese Art, 1997; Painting and Private Life in Eleventh-Century China: Mountain Villa by Li Gonglin, 1998; (with W.C. Fong) The Embodied Image: Chinese Calligraphy from the John B. Elliott Collection, 1999; (intro.) Paintings by Xu Jin: Tradition and Innovation in Chinese Fine Brushwork=Xu Jin Hua Ji, 2005; The Landscape of Words: Stone Inscriptions from Early and Medieval China, 2008. Contributor to books. **Address:** Columbia University, 2960 Broadway, New York, NY 10027-6902, U.S.A. **Online address:** reh23@columbia.edu

HARROD, Tanya. American (born United States), b. 1951. **Genres:** Crafts. **Career:** Open University, tutor, 1978-79; The Independent on Sunday, correspondent, 1989-94; Cardiff Institute of Higher Education, History and Theory of Art and Design, external examiner, 1990-93; London Arts Board, Visual Arts and Crafts, advisor, 1994-95; University of East Anglia, visiting fellow, 1995-97; Royal College of Art, Department of Design History, lecture, 1998, visiting professor, 2000-; British Library, National Sound Archive, Crafts Lives for the National Life Story Collection, advisor, 1999-. Writer. **Publications:** Alison Britton: Ceramics in Studio, 1990; Factfile on the History of the Crafts Council, 1994; Obscure Objects of Desire?: Reviewing the Crafts in the Twentieth Century, 1996; Contemporary Applied Arts: Fifty Years of Craft, 1998; The Crafts in Britain in the Twentieth Century, 1999; (with R.L. Goldberg) Carol McNicoll, 2003; (ed.) Ann Stokes: Artists' Potte, 2009. **Address:** Royal College of Art, Kensington Gore, London, GL SW7 2EU, England. **Online address:** tanya@harrod4.demon.co.uk

HARROD-EAGLES, Cynthia. Also writes as Emma Woodhouse, Emma Bennett, Elizabeth Bennett. British (born England), b. 1948. **Genres:** Novels, Mystery/Crime/Suspense, Romance/Historical, Science Fiction/Fantasy, Novellas/Short Stories. **Career:** Coca Cola Co., sales manager; BBC, pensions officer; writer, 1979-. **Publications:** The Waiting Game, 1972; Shadows on the Mountain, 1973; Hollow Night, 1980; Deadfall, 1982; The Orange Tree Plot, 1989; The Horsemasters, 2001; The Longest Dance, 2001; Julia, 2002; The Colonel's Daughter, 2006; Measure of Days, 2007; Harte's Desire, 2007; The Foreign Field, 2008; Fallen Kings, 2009; The Dancing Years, 2010; The Winding Road, 2011. AS EMMA WOODHOUSE: A Rainbow Summer, 1976; A Well-Painted Passion, 1976; Romany Magic, 1977; Love's Perilous Passage, 1978; On Wings of Love, 1978; Never Love a Stranger, 1978. AS ELIZABETH BENNETT: Title Role, 1980; The Unfinished, 1983; Even Chance, 1984; Last Run, 1984; I, Victoria, 1996. MORLAND DYNASTY SERIES: The Founding, 1980; The Dark Rose, 1981; The Princeling, 1981 in US as The Distant Wood, 1982; The Oak Apple, 1982 in US as The Crystal Crown, 1982; The Black Pearl, 1982; The Long Shadow, 1983; The Chevalier, 1984; The Maiden, 1985; The Flood-Tide, 1986; The Tangled Thread, 1987; The Emperor, 1988; The Victory, 1989; The Regency, 1990; The Campaigners, 1991; The Reckoning, 1992; The Devil's Horse, 1993; The Poison Tree, 1994; The Abyss, 1995; The Hidden Shore, 1996; The Winter Journey, 1997; The Outcast, 1998; The Mirage, 1999; The Cause, 2000; The Homecoming, 2001; The Question, 2002; The Dream Kingdom, 2003; The Restless Sea, 2004; The White Road, 2005; The Burning Roses, 2006; The Golden Wind, 2007. THE KIROV TRILOGY: Anna, 1991; Emily, 1992; Fleur, 1993. STORIES: Real Life, 1999. BILL SLIDER SERIES (crime novels): Orchestrated Death, 1992; Death Watch, 1993; Necrochip, 1993; Death to Go, 1994; Dead End, 1994; Grave Music, 1995; Blood Lines, 1996; Killing Time, 1998; Shallow Grave, 1999; Blood Sinister, 1999; Gone Tomorrow, 2001; Dear Departed, 2004; Game Over, 2008; Fell Purpose, 2009; Body Line, 2011; Kill My Darling, 2011. **Address:** c/o Author Mail, Time Warner Books, Brettenham House, Lancaster Pl., London, GL WC2E 7EN, England. **Online address:** messages@cynthiaharrodeagles.com

HARROW, Judy. American (born United States), b. 1945. **Genres:** Theology/Religion. **Career:** Wiccan high priestess and coven leader; Cherry Hill Seminary (Pagan seminary), chair of pastoral counseling department; Covenant of the Goddess, Northeast Local Council, officer, 1983, national first officer, 1984, Grand Council, co-chair, 1985, national public information officer, 1993-95; New Jersey ASERVIC, president. Writer. **Publications:** Wicca Covens, 1999; Spiritual Mentoring: A Pagan Guide, 2002; (co-author) Devoted to You: Honoring Deity in Wiccan Practice, 2003. Contributor to periodicals. **Address:** c/o Jennie Dunham, Dunham Literary Inc., 156 5th Ave., Ste. 625, New York, NY 10010-7002, U.S.A. **Online address:** judyharo@comcast.net

HARROW, Kenneth W. American (born United States), b. 1943. **Genres:** Literary Criticism And History, Education, Reference. **Career:** Michigan State University, Department of Humanities, instructor, 1966 70, assistant professor, 1970-75, associate professor, 1976-81, professor, 1981-89, Humanities and English Department, faculty, 1987, Department of English, professor, 1989-, Graduate Program in Comparative Literature, director, 2000-02; University of Darak, faculty, 1989-90; University of Yaounde, Fulbright senior lecturer, 1977 79; Université Cheikh Anta Diop, Fulbright senior lecturer, 2005-06. Writer. **Publications:** Less Than One and Double: A Feminist Reading of African Women's Writing, 2002; Postcolonial African Cinema: From Political Engagement to Postmodernism, 2007. EDITOR: (with J. Ngaté and C. Zimra) Crisscrossing Boundaries in African Literatures, 1986, 1991; Faces of Islam in African literature, 1991; Thresholds of Change in African Literature: The Emergence of a Tradition, 1994; Marabout and the Muse: New Approaches to Islam in African Literature, 1996; African Cinema: Postcolonial and Feminist Readings, 1999; (with M. Eke and E. Yewah) Af-

rican Images: Recent Studies and Text in Cinema, 2000; (with K. Mpoche) Language, Literature and Education in Multicultural Societies: Collaborative Research on Africa, 2008. **Address:** Department of English, Michigan State University, 17E Morrill Hall, East Lansing, MI 48824-1036, U.S.A. **Online address:** harrow@msu.edu

HARROWER, Elizabeth. Australian (born Australia), b. 1928. **Genres:** Novels, Young Adult Fiction. **Career:** Australian Broadcasting Commission, staff, 1959-60; Sydney Morning Herald, reviewer, 1960; Macmillan and Company Ltd., publisher, 1961-67. Writer. **Publications:** Down in the City, 1957; The Catherine Wheel, 1960; The Watch Tower, 1966; The Long Prospect, 1966. Work appears in anthologies. **Address:** 5 Stanley Ave., Mosman, NW 2088, Australia.

HARSANYI, David. American (born United States) **Genres:** Novels. **Career:** Denver Post, columnist & editorial board member. **Publications:** Nanny State: How Food Fascists, Teetotaling Do-gooders, Priggish Moralists, and Other Boneheaded Bureaucrats Are Turning America into a Nation of Children, 2007. Contributor to periodicals. **Address:** Sloan Harris, International Creative Management, 825 8th Ave., New York, NY 10019, U.S.A. **Online address:** david@davidharsanyi.com

HARSCH, Rich. American (born United States), b. 1959?. **Genres:** Novels, Mystery/Crime/Suspense, Literary Criticism And History. **Career:** Writer. **Publications:** Driftless Zone, 1997; Billy Verite, 1998; The Sleep of the Aborigines, 2002. Contributor to periodicals. **Address:** c/o Warren Frazier, John Hawkins and Associates Inc., 71 W 23rd St., Ste. 1600, New York, NY 10010, U.S.A.

HARSENT, David. (Jack Curtis). British (born England), b. 1942. **Genres:** Novels, Poetry. **Career:** Poet and novelist; Times Literary Supplement, fiction critic, 1965-73; Spectator, poetry critic, 1970-73; Arrow Publishing, editorial director, 1977-79; Andre Deutsch, editor-in-chief and director, 1979-91; Hallam University, distinguished writing fellow, 2005-, visiting professor; Royal Holloway University, honorary research fellow, Royal Society of Literature, fellow; Sheffield Hallam University, distinguished writing fellow, 2005, visiting professor. **Publications:** Tonight's Lover, 1968; A Violent Country, 1969; Ashridge, 1970; After Dark, 1973; Truce, 1973; Dreams of the Dead, 1977; (ed.) New Poetry 7, 1981; Mister Punch, 1984; From an Inland Sea (novel), 1985; Playback, 1987; (ed. with M. Susko) Savramena Britanska Poezija, 1988; Selected Poems, 1989; Gawain (libretto), 1991; Storybook Hero, 1992; News from the Front, 1993; The Sorrow of Sarajevo (versions of poems by G. Simic), 1996; Sprinting from the Graveyard (versions of poems by G. Simic), 1997; The Potted Priest, 1997; A Bird's Idea of Flight, 1998; (ed.) Another Round at the Pillars: Essays, Poems and Reflections on Ian Hamilton, 1999; Marriage (poetry), 2002; Legion, 2005; Selected Poems, 1969-2005, 2007; The Minotaur: Libretto, 2008; Night, 2011. AS JACK CURTIS: Crow's Parliament, 1987; Glory, 1988; Point of Impact, 1991; Sons of the Morning, 1992; Conjure Me, 1994; Mirrors Kill, 1995; The Confessor, 1998. Contributor to periodicals. **Address:** c/o Charles Walker, 12-26 Lexington St., London, GL W1F 0LE, England.

HART, Alison. (Alice Leonhardt). American (born United States), b. 1950. **Genres:** Children's Fiction, Young Adult Fiction. **Career:** Special education teacher, 1976-94; Blue Ridge Community College, adjunct instructor, 1995-. Writer. **Publications:** Shadow Horse, 1999, rev. ed., 2010; Chase: A Police Story, 2002; Rescue: A Police Story, 2002; Fires of Jubilee, 2003; Return of the Gypsy Witch, 2003; Anna's Blizzard, 2005; A Spy on the Home Front: A Molly Mystery, 2005; Gabriel's Horses, 2007; Gabriel's Triumph, 2007; Gabriel's Journey, 2008; Bell's Star, 2009; Emma's River, 2010; Taking the Reins, 2010; Whirlwind, 2010; Dive Right In! 2011; Risky Chance 2011. RIDING ACADEMY SERIES: A Horse for Mary Beth, 1994; Andie out of Control, 1994; Jina Rides to Win, 1994; Mary Beth's Haunted Ride, 1994; Andie Shows Off, 1994; Jina's Pain-in-the-Neck Pony, 1995; The Craziest Horse Show Ever, 1995; Andie's Risky Business, 1995; Trouble at Foxhall, 1995; Foxhunt!, 1995; Lauren Rides to the Rescue, 1995; Haunted Horseback Holiday, 1996. LINDA CRAIG SERIES: Kathy in Charge, 1990; The Riding Club, 1990; A Horse for Jackie, 1990; The Glimmering Ghost, 1990; The Silver Stallion, 1990. AS ALICE LEONHARDT: Melanie's Last Ride, 1998; A Home for Melanie, 1998; Ocean Life: Tide Pool Creatures, 2000; Living Legend, 2000; The Bad Luck Filly, 2000; Perfect Image, 2000; Star's Chance, 2001; The Case of the Jingle Bell Jinx, 2001; The Case of the High Seas Secret, 2001; Racing Image, 2001; Team Player, 2001; Perfect Challenge, 2002;

The Case of the Mall Mystery, 2002; Faith in a Long Shot, 2003. **Address:** Peachtree Publishers, 1700 Chattahoochee Ave., Atlanta, GA 30318, U.S.A. **Online address:** alison@alisonhartbooks.com

HART, Andre. *See* **FREEMANTLE, Brian (Harry).**

HART, Bret. Canadian (born Canada), b. 1957. **Genres:** Sports/Fitness, Biography, Autobiography/Memoirs, Art/Art History. **Career:** Writer and actor. **Publications:** Bret Hitman Hart: The Best There Is, the Best There Was, the Best There Ever Will Be, 2000; Hitman: My Real Life in the Cartoon World of Wrestling, 2008. Contributor to periodicals. **Address:** World Wrestling Federation, PO Box 3857, Stamford, CT 06905-0857, U.S.A. **Online address:** office@brethart.com

HART, Brian. American (born United States), b. 1976?. **Genres:** Novels. **Career:** Writer. **Publications:** Then Came the Evening (novel), 2010. **Address:** PO Box 283, McCall, ID 83638, U.S.A.

HART, Carolyn G(impel). American (born United States), b. 1936. **Genres:** Novels, Mystery/Crime/Suspense, Children's Fiction, History, Horror, Young Adult Fiction, Ghost Writer. **Career:** Norman Transcript, reporter, 1958-59; Sooner Newsmakers (University of Oklahoma alumni news), editor, 1959-60; freelance writer, 1961-82, 1986-; University of Oklahoma, School of Journalism and Mass Communications, assistant professor, 1982-85; Sisters in Crime, co-founder and president. **Publications:** CRIME NOVELS: Flee from the Past, 1975; A Settling of Accounts, 1976; The Rich Die Young, 1983; Death by Surprise, 1983; Castle Rock, 1983; Skulduggery, 1984. DEATH ON DEMAND MYSTERIES: Death on Demand, 1987; Design for Murder, 1988; Something Wicked, 1988; Honeymoon with Murder, 1989; A Little Class on Murder, 1989; Deadly Valentine, 1990; The Christie Caper, 1991; Southern Ghost, 1992; Mint Julep Murder, 1995; Yankee Doodle Dead, 1998; White Elephant Dead, 1999; Sugarplum Dead, 2000; April Fool Dead, 2002; Secrets and Other Stories of Suspense, 2002; Engaged to Die, 2003; Letter from Home, 2003; (co-author) The Sunken Sailor, 2004; Murder Walks the Plank, 2004; Death of the Party, 2005; Dead Days of Summer, 2006; Death Walked In, 2008; Dare to Die, 2009; Laughed 'Til He Died, 2010; Ghost in Trouble, 2010; Dead by Midnight, 2011; Death Comes Silently, 2012. HENRIE O MYSTERIES: Dead Man's Island, 1993; Scandal in Fair Haven, 1994; Death in Lovers' Lane, 1997; Death in Paradise, 1998; Death on the River Walk, 1999; Resort to Murder, 2001; Set Sail for Murder: A Henrie O Mystery, 2007. BAILEY RUTH MYSTERIES: Ghost At Work, 2008; Merry, Merry Ghost, 2009. FOR CHILDREN: The Secret of the Cellars (for children), 1964; Dangerous Summer (for children), 1968; No Easy Answers, 1970; Rendezvous in Veracruz, 1970; Danger, High Explosives!, 1972. OTHERS: (with C.F. Long) The Sooner Story, 1890-1980 (history), 1980; Escape from Paris (novel), 1982; The Devereaux Legacy (novel), 1984; Brave Hearts (novel), 1987; Crime on Her Mind (short stories), 1999; (co-author) Motherhood Is Murder, 2003; What the Cat Saw, 2012. EDITOR: Crimes of the Heart (anthology), 1995; Love and Death (anthology), 2001. Contributor to books. **Address:** 1705 Drakestone Ave., Oklahoma City, OK 73120, U.S.A. **Online address:** chart@carolynhart.com

HART, Catherine. American (born United States), b. 1948. **Genres:** Romance/Historical, Sports/Fitness. **Career:** Dental assistant, 1965-66; dispensing optician, 1966-67. Writer, 1983-. **Publications:** ROMANCE FICTION: Fire and Ice, 1984; Silken Savage, 1985; Ashes and Ecstasy, 1985; Satin and Steel, 1986; Summer Storm, 1987; Forever Gold, 1988; Night Flame, 1989; Fallen Angel, 1989; Sweet Fury, 1990; Christmas Romance: Love Stories, 1990; Tempest, 1991; Temptation, 1992; Splendor, 1993; Irresistible, 1994; Dazzled, 1994; Mischief, 1995; Charmed, 1996; Horizons, 1997; Impulsive, 1998. Work appears in anthologies. **Address:** Maria Carvainis Agency, 235 W End Ave., New York, NY 10023, U.S.A.

HART, Charles (A.). American (born United States), b. 1940. **Genres:** Medicine/Health, Self Help, Human Relations/Parenting. **Career:** University of Washington Hospitals, training administrator, 1972-78; Troubleshooters for the Handicapped, writer and trainer, 1983-85; Association for Retarded Citizens, communication specialist, 1987-90; Allied Arts of Seattle, director. **Publications:** Without Reason: A Family Copes with Two Generations of Autism, 1989; A Parent's Guide to Autism, 1993. **Address:** c/o Susan Ginsburg, Writers House Inc., 21 W 26th St., New York, NY 10010, U.S.A.

HART, Christine. Canadian (born Canada), b. 1978?. **Genres:** Novels. Ca-

reer: Bridges.com, features writer, 2002-04; YES Canada, article writer, 2003-04; Cahoots Magazine, columnist, 2005-09. **Publications:** Watching July (children's book), 2008; Best Laid Plans, 2009. Contributor to magazines. **Address:** Victoria, BC , Canada. **Online address:** contact@christine-hart.com

HART, Christopher. American (born United States), b. 1957. **Genres:** Art/Art History, Children's Non-fiction, How-to Books, Cartoons. **Career:** Writer for film and television studios, 1981-97. Illustrator. **Publications:** How to Draw Cartoons for Comic Strips, 1988; Making Funny Faces: Cartooning for Kids, 1992; Everything You Ever Wanted to Know about Cartooning but Were Afraid to Draw, 1994; How to Draw Cartoon Animals, 1995; How to Draw Comic Book Heroes and Villains, 1995; Christopher Hart's Portable Cartoon Studio, 1996; Christopher Hart's Portable Animation Studio, 1996; Christopher Hart's Portable Action Hero Comic Book Studio, 1997; How to Draw Animation, 1997; Drawing on the Funny Side of the Brain: How to Come Up with Jokes for Cartoons and Comic Strips, 1998; How to Draw Comic Book Bad Guys and Gals, 1998; How to Draw Cartoon Dogs, Puppies and Wolves, 1998; How to Draw Comic Book Bad Guys, 1999; How to Draw Cartoon Cats, Kittens, Lions and Tigers, 1999; How to Draw Fantasy Characters, 1999; How to Draw Halloween, Christmas and Seasonal Characters, 1999; How to Draw Knights, Kings, Queens and Dragons, 1999; Cartooning for the Beginner, 2000; How to Draw Cartoon Baby Animals, 2000; How to Draw Sports Cars, Monster Trucks and Fighter Jets, 2000; Human Anatomy Made Amazingly Easy, 2000; How to Draw Fast Cars, Monster Trucks and Fighter Jets, 2000; How to Draw Great-Looking Comic Book Women, 2000; How to Draw Aliens, Mutants and Mysterious Creatures, 2001; Kids Draw Baby Animals, 2001; Kids Draw Cats, Kittens, Lions and Tigers, 2001; Kids Draw Dogs, Puppies and Wolves, 2001; Kids Draw Funny and Spooky Holiday Characters, 2001; Manga Mania: How to Draw Japanese Comics, 2001; Drawing Cutting Edge Comics, 2001; Kids Draw Dinosaurs, 2001; Kids Draw Angels, Elves, Fairies and More, 2001; Kids Draw Anime, 2002; Anime Mania: How to Draw Characters for Japanese Animation, 2002; Merwin: Master of Disguise, 2002; Mecha Mania: How to Draw the Battling Robots, Cool Spaceships and Military Vehicles of Japanese Comics, 2002; Draw Manga!, 2003; Manga Mania Fantasy Worlds: How to Draw the Amazing Worlds of Japanese Comics, 2003; Manga Mania Villains: How to Draw the Dastardly Characters of Japanese Comics, 2003; Police Puppies, 2003; Kids Draw Animals, 2003; Drawing Faeries: A Believer's Guide to Sketching Faeries When They're Not Looking, 2004; Kids Draw Manga, 2004; Manga Mania Shoujo: How to Draw the Charming and Romantic Characters of Japanese Comics, 2004; Xtreme Art: Draw Manga Villains!, 2004; Cartoon Cool: How to Draw New Retro-Style Characters, 2005; Doing your Masters Dissertation: Realizing Your Potential as a Social Scientist, 2005; Draw Manga Monsters!, 2005; Drawing Cutting Edge Fusion: American Comics with a Manga Influence, 2005; Kids Draw Manga Shoujo, 2005; Manga Mania Bishoujo: How to Draw the Alluring Women of Japanese Comics, 2005; Draw Mini Manga!, 2006; Drawing Crime Noir for Comics & Graphic Novels, 2006; Drawing Faeries: Keys to the Kingdom, 2006; Kids Draw Manga Fantasy, 2006; Manga Mania Chibi and Furry Characters: How to Draw the Adorable Mini-People and Cool Cat-Girls of Japanese Comics, 2006; Manga Mania Magical Girls and Friends: How to Draw the Super-Popular Action-Fantasy Characters of Manga, 2006; (ed.) Cognitive Linguistics in Critical Discourse Analysis: Application and Theory, 2007; Drawing Animals Made Amazingly Easy, 2007; Drawing Dragons and Those Who Hunt Them, 2007; Kids Draw Manga Monsters, 2007; Manga Mania Shoujo Sketchbook, 2007; Kid's Draw Manga Monsters, 2007; Simplified Anatomy for the Comic Book Artist: How to Draw the New Streamlined Look of Action-Adventure Comics!, 2007; Manga Mania Occult and Horror: How to Draw the Elegant and Seductive Characters of the Dark, 2007; Manga Mania Fantasy Sketchbook, 2007; Shonen: Drawing Action-Style Japanese Comics, 2008; Astonishing Fantasy Worlds: The Ultimate Guide to Drawing Adventure Fantasy Art, 2008; Cartoonist's Big Book of Drawing Animals, 2008; Draw a Circle, Draw Anything!: Learn to Draw Starting with Simple Shapes, 2008; Draw a Square, Draw Anything!: Learn to Draw Starting with Simple Shapes, 2008; Reformed, 2008; Cartooning: the Ultimate Character Design Book, 2008; Draw a Triangle, Draw Anything!: Learn to Draw Starting with Simple Shapes, 2008; Drawing Wizards, Witches and Warlocks, 2008; Manga Mania Romance: Drawing Shojo Girls and Bishie Boys, 2008; Manga for the Beginner: Everything You Need to Know to Get Started Right Away!, 2008; Drawing the New Adventure Cartoons: Cool Spies, Evil Guys and Action Heroes, 2008; Kids Draw Big Book of Everything Manga, 2009; Xtreme Art: Ultimate Book of Trace-and-Draw Manga, 2009; Superheroes and Beyond: How to Draw the Leading and Supporting Characters of Today's Comics, 2009; Manga Mania Girl Power!: Drawing

Fabulous Females for Japanese Comics, 2009; Humongous Book of Cartooning, 2009; Figure it Out!: The Beginner's Guide to Drawing People, 2009; Drawing Vampires: Gothic Creatures of the Night, 2009; Manga for the Beginner Shoujo: Everything You Need to Start Drawing the Most Popular Style of Japanese Comics, 2010; Manga for the Beginner Chibis: Everything You Need to Start Drawing the Super-cute Characters of Japanese Comics, 2010; Drawing Fantastic Furries: The Ultimate Guide to Drawing Anthropomorphic Characters, 2010; Cartoon Cute Animals: How to Draw the Most Irresistible Creatures on the Planet, 2010; Basic Anatomy for the Manga Artist: Everything you Need to Start Drawing Authentic Manga Characters, 2011; Basic Drawing Made Amazingly Easy, 2011; Young Artists Draw Manga, 2011. Contributor of articles to magazines. **Address:** 5 Brightfield Ln., Westport, CT 06880, U.S.A. **Online address:** chart72873@aol.com

HART, Ellen. American (born United States), b. 1949. **Genres:** Mystery/Crime/Suspense, Novels. **Career:** Ambassador College, teaching assistant, 1972-75; University of Minnesota, kitchen manager, Compleat Scholar Program, teacher; Hamline University, Compleat Scholar Program, teacher; The Loft Literary Center, mystery writing teacher, 1995-. Writer. **Publications:** MYSTERIES: Hallowed Murder, 1989; Vital Lies, 1990; Stage Fright, 1992; A Killing Cure, 1993; A Small Sacrifice, 1994; This Little Piggy Went to Murder, 1994; For Every Evil, 1995; Faint Praise, 1995; Robber's Wine, 1996; The Oldest Sin, 1996; Murder in the Air, 1997; (co-author) Murder, They Wrote, 1997; Wicked Games, 1998; Hunting the Witch, 1999; Slice and Dice, 2000; Dial M for Meat Loaf, 2001; The Merchant of Venus, 2001; Immaculate Midnight, 2002; Death on a Silver Platter, 2003; An Intimate Ghost, 2004; No Reservations Required, 2005; The Iron Girl, 2005; Night Vision, 2006; The Mortal Groove, 2007; Sweet Poison, 2008; Mirror and the Mask, 2009; Cruel Ever After, 2010; The Lost Women of Lost Lake, 2011. **Address:** Seal Press, 300 Queen Anne Ave. N, PO Box 375, Seattle, WA 98109-4512, U.S.A. **Online address:** ellenhart@earthlink.net

HART, Jan Siegel. American (born United States), b. 1940. **Genres:** Children's Fiction, Literary Criticism And History. **Career:** Novits Department Store, staff. Writer, publisher and speaker. **Publications:** Hanna, the Immigrant, 1991; The Many Adventures of Minnie, 1992; More Adventures of Minnie, 1994. **Address:** 1041 Clarence Rd., Temple, TX 76501-6652, U.S.A. **Online address:** jshauthor@sbcglobal.net

HART, JoeAnn. American (born United States), b. 1955?. **Genres:** Food And Wine, Novels, Humor/Satire, Novellas/Short Stories, Writing/Journalism, Animals/Pets, Homes/Gardens, Literary Criticism And History, Literary Criticism And History. **Career:** Rural New England Magazine, columnist on farming and gardening, 1997-2001. **Publications:** Addled, 2007. Contributor to journals and periodicals. **Address:** Little, Brown and Co., 1271 Ave. of the Americas, New York, NY 10020-1300, U.S.A. **Online address:** joeann@joeannhart.com

HART, John Fraser. American (born United States), b. 1924. **Genres:** Geography, Photography, History, Travel/Exploration. **Career:** University of Georgia, assistant professor, 1949-53, associate professor of geography, 1953-55; Indiana University, assistant professor, 1955-58, associate professor, 1958-63, professor of geography, 1963-67, acting head of department, 1956-58; University of Minnesota, professor of geography, 1967-; Annals of the Association of American Geographers, executive director, 1965-66, editor, 1970-75, president, 1979-80. Writer. **Publications:** The British Moorlands: A Problem in Land Utilization, 1955; America's Farms and Ranches, 1957; Ireland, 1957; Illinois and Indiana, 1959; Kentucky and Tennessee, 1960; Geographic Manpower, 1966; The Southeastern United States, 1967; U.S. and Canada, 1967; (ed. with K.B. Raitz) Preliminary List of Topographic Maps Illustrating Aspects of the Cultural Geography of the United States, 1970; (ed.) Regions of the United States, 1972; (comp.) Selected Geographical Serials Published in the United States, 1972; Manpower in Geography, 1972; The Look of the Land, 1975; (with K.B. Raitz) Cultural Geography on Topographic Maps, 1975; (with H.B. Johnson and C. Mather) Upper Coulee Country, 1975; The South, 1976; (contrib.) Midwest and Great Plains, 1979; (contrib.) West, 1979; (ed.) Our Changing Cities, 1991; The Land That Feeds Us, 1991; The American Farm: How Farming Shaped the Landscape of America, 1998; The Rural Landscape, 1998; (with M.J. Rhodes and J.T. Morgan) The Unknown World of the Mobile Home, 2002; Changing Scale of American Agriculture, 2003; My Kind of County: Door County, Wisconsin, 2008; (ed. and intro.) Love of the Land: Selected Writings of John Fraser Hart, 2008; (S.S. Ziegler) Landscapes of Minnesota: A Geography, 2008.

Address: Department of Geography, University of Minnesota, Rm. 558 Social Sciences, 414 Social Sciences Bldg., 267 19th Ave. S, Minneapolis, MN 55455, U.S.A. **Online address:** frase002@umn.edu

HART, John Mason. American (born United States), b. 1935. **Genres:** Area Studies, History. **Career:** University of North Dakota, assistant professor of history, 1969-73; University of Houston, associate professor, 1973-78, Department of History, professor of Mexican history, 1978-, chairman, 1989-90, interim and associate chair, John and Rebecca Moores professor of history; Southwestern Council on Latin American Studies, president, 1983; Rocky Mountain Council on Latin American Studies, director, 1983-2000; University of California, Center for U.S.-Mexican Studies, visiting fellow, 1987; Escuela Nacional de Antropologia e Historia, distinguished visiting professor; Instituto Nacional de Antropologia e Historia, distinguished visiting professor. Writer. **Publications:** Los anarquistas Mexicanos, 1974; El anarquismo y la clase obrera mexicana, 1980; Revolutionary Mexico, 1987; Anarchism and the Mexican Working Class, 1860-1931, 1987; El Mexico revolucionario: gestacion Y proceso de la revolucion mexicana, 1990; (ed.) Border Crossings: Mexican and Mexican-American Workers, 1998; Empire and Revolution: The Americans in Mexico since the Civil War, 2002; The Silver of the Sierra Madre: John Robinson, Boss Shepherd, and the People of the Canyons, 2008. Contributor to journals. **Address:** Department of History, University of Houston, 538 Agnes Arnold Hall, 4800 Calhoun Rd., Houston, TX 77204-3785, U.S.A. **Online address:** jhart@uh.edu

HART, Jonathan (Locke). Canadian (born Canada), b. 1956. **Genres:** Novellas/Short Stories, Plays/Screenplays, Poetry, Theatre, Essays. **Career:** University of Alberta, lecturer in English, 1984-85, assistant professor, 1987-92, associate professor of English and adjunct professor of comparative literature, 1992-95, professor, 1995-, Comparative Literature, program director, 2004-10; Trent University, assistant professor of English, 1985-86; Harvard University, tutor, 1986-87, Kirkland House, associate, 1992-93; Cambridge University, Clare Hall, visiting fellow, 1993-94, Churchill College, overseas fellow, 2007-08; Princeton University, visiting professor of history and Canadian studies, 2000-02. Writer. **Publications:** Theater and World: The Problematics of Shakespeare's History, 1992; Northrop Frye: The Theoretical Imagination, 1994; Imagining Culture, 1996; (with R.W. Bauman) Explorations in Difference: Law, Culture, and Politics, 1996; (ed.) Reading the Renaissance: Culture, Poetics, and Drama, 1996; Breath and Dust, 2000; Representing the New World, 2001; Dream China, 2002; Columbus, Shakespeare and the Interpretation of the New World, 2003; Comparing Empires: European Colonialism from Portuguese Expansion to the Spanish-American War, 2003; Dream Salvage, 2003; Contesting Empires: Opposition, Promotion, and Slavery, 2005; Interpreting Cultures: Literature, Religion, and the Human Sciences, 2006; Empires and Colonies, 2008; Shakespeare: Poetry, History, and Culture, 2009; City of the End of Things: Essays on Civilization and Empire, 2009; Dreamwork, 2010; Shakespeare and His Contemporaries, 2010; Musing, 2011; Literature, Theory History, 2011. Contributor to periodicals. **Address:** Department of English, University of Alberta, 3-35 Humanities Ctr., Edmonton, AB T6G 2E5, Canada. **Online address:** jonathan.hart@ualberta.ca

HART, Kevin. American/Australian/British (born England), b. 1954. **Genres:** Literary Criticism And History, Poetry. **Career:** Geelong College, Department of Philosophy and Religious Studies, co-ordinator, 1979-83; University of Melbourne, lecturer in philosophy, 1985-86, lecturer in English, 1986-87; Deakin University, senior lecturer in literary studies, 1987-90; Monash University, associate professor of English, 1991-, professor; Notre Dame University, chair in English literature; University of Virginia, Department of Religious Studies, Edwin B. Kyle professor of Christian studies, chair. Writer. **Publications:** Nebuchadnezzar, 1976; The Departure, 1978; The Lines of the Hand: Poems 1976-79, 1981; Your Shadow: Poems 1980-83, 1984; (ed.) Shifting Frames: English/Literature/Writing, 1988; The Trespass of the Sign: Deconstruction, Theology and Philosophy, 1989, 2nd ed., 2000; The Buried Harbour: Selected Poems of Giuseppe Ungaretti, 1990; Peniel, 1991; A.D. Hope, 1992; The Oxford Book of Australian Religious Verse, 1994; New and Selected Poems, 1995; Dark Angel, 1996; Losing the Power to Say I, 1996; Wicked Heat (poetry), 1999; Nineteen Songs, 1999; Samuel Johnson and the Culture of Property (criticism), 1999; How to Read a Page of Boswell, 2000; Madonna, 2000; Flame Tree: Selected Poems, 2002; The Dark Gaze: Maurice Blanchot and the Sacred, 2004; (ed. with G.H. Hartman) The Power of Contestation: Perspectives on Maurice Blanchot, 2004; (ed. with Y. Sherwood) Derrida and Religion: Other Testaments, 2004; Nowhere Without

No: In Memory of Maurice Blanchot, 2004; (ed.) Nowhere Without No: In Memory of Maurice Blanchot, 2004; Postmodernism: A Beginner's Guide, 2004; Night Music (poetry), 2004; (ed.) Counter-experiences: Reading Jean-Luc Marion, 2007; Young Rain, 2008; Slow movement, oder, Das Halbe und das Ganze=Slow Movement, or, Half and Whole, 2009; (ed.) Clandestine Encounters: Philosophy in the Narratives of Maurice Blanchot, 2010; (ed. with M.A. Signer) Exorbitant: Emmanuel Levinas Between Jews and Christians, 2010; Morning Knowledge, 2011. **Address:** Department of Religious Studies, University of Virginia, Halsey Hall, PO Box 400126, Charlottesville, VA 22904-4126, U.S.A. **Online address:** kevin.hart@arts.monash.edu.au

HART, Lenore. American (born United States) **Genres:** Novels, Novellas/Short Stories, Young Adult Fiction, Adult Non-fiction, Children's Fiction. **Career:** New College of Florida, writer-in-residence, 2005; Sweetbriar College, Virginia Center for the Creative Arts, fellow; Flagler College, visiting writer; Eastern Shore Community College, faculty; Florida State University, faculty; George Mason University, faculty; Florida Community College, faculty; Poynter Institute, faculty; Christopher Newport University, faculty; Eckerd College, faculty; Cape May Institute, faculty; The U.S. Naval Academy, faculty; Old Dominion University, faculty, visiting writer; Tidewater College, faculty; Wilkes University, Graduate Writing Program, teacher; Florida Arts Council, writer-in-residence; National Endowment for the Arts, writer-in-residence; Elizabethtown College, visiting writer. **Publications:** Waterwoman, 2002; (with L. Carrier) T. Rex at Swan Lake, 2004; Ordinary Springs, 2005; The Treasure of Savage Island, 2005; Becky: The Life and Loves of Becky Thatcher, 2008; The Raven's Bride, 2011; Nevermore; Black River; Svart Frikt. **Address:** c/o Author Mail, Dutton Children's Books, 375 Hudson St., New York, NY 10014-3658, U.S.A.

HART, (Margaret Eleanor) Anne. Canadian (born Canada) **Genres:** Novellas/Short Stories, Poetry, Biography, Novels, Documentaries/Reportage. **Career:** Newfoundland Public Library Services, part-time cataloger, 1969-72; Memorial University of Newfoundland, librarian, 1973-74, Center for Newfoundland Studies, assistant head, 1974-77, head, 1977-98, honorary research librarian, 1999-. Writer. **Publications:** (Co-ed. and comp.) Newfoundland and Confederation, 1977; The Life and Times of Miss Jane Marple, 1985; The Life and Times of Hercule Poirot, 1990; Cyberscribes 1: The New Journalists, 1997; (co-ed. and comp.) My Inside Self: Writings and Pictures by Children of Newfoundland and Labrador, 1980; (contrib.) The Woman Who Mapped Labrador: The Life and Expedition Diary of Mina Hubbard, 2005. **Address:** Center for Newfoundland Studies, Queen Elizabeth II Library, Memorial University of Newfoundland, St. Johns, NL A1B 3Y1, Canada. **Online address:** ahart@morgan.ucs.mun.ca

HART, Maxwell. *See* **SKIPP, John.**

HART, Melissa. American (born United States), b. 1970. **Genres:** Autobiography/Memoirs. **Career:** University of Oregon, School of Journalism, faculty; University of California, Extension Program, faculty. Writer. **Publications:** The Assault of Laughter (memoir), 2005; Gringa: A Contradictory Girlhood, 2009. Contributor to newspapers and periodicals. **Address:** University of Oregon, 1275 Allen Hall, Eugene, OR 94703, U.S.A. **Online address:** melissah@uoregon.edu

HART, Mitchell B. American (born United States), b. 1959. **Genres:** Social Sciences. **Career:** Florida International University, assistant professor, 1995-2001, associate professor, 2001-03, Program in Jewish Studies, director, 1997-2000; Oxford Centre for Jewish and Hebrew Studies, Skirball fellow, 2001; University of Michigan, Program in Judaic Studies, Padnos visiting professor, 2002-03; University of Florida, associate professor, 2003-09, professor and Alexander Grass chair in Jewish history, 2009-. Writer. **Publications:** Social Science and the Politics of Modern Jewish Identity, 2000; The Healthy Jew: The Symbiosis of Judaism and Modern Medicine, 2007; (ed.) Jewish Blood: Reality and Metaphor in History, Religion, and Culture, 2009; (ed.) Jews on Race: A Reader, 2010. Contributor to books and journals. **Address:** Department of History, University of Florida, 025 Keene-Flint Hall, Gainesville, FL 32611, U.S.A. **Online address:** hartm@ufl.edu

HART, Peter. British (born England), b. 1955. **Genres:** Military/Defense/Arms Control, History. **Career:** Imperial War Museum Sound Archive, oral historian, 1981-2008. Writer. **Publications:** (With N. Steel) Defeat at Gallipoli, 1995; To the Last Round: The South Notts Hussars, 1939-1942, 1996; (with N. Steel) Tumult in the Clouds: The British Experience of the War in the Air, 1914-1918, 1997; At the Sharp End: From Le Paradis to Kohima: 2nd Battalion, the Royal Norfolk Regiment, 1998; The Heat of the Battle: The 16th Battalion Durham Light Infantry, 1943-1945, 1999; (with N. Steel) Passchendaele: The Sacrificial Ground, 2000; Somme Success: The Royal Flying Corps and the Battle of the Somme, 1916, 2001; (with N. Steel) Jutland, 1916: Death in the Grey Wastes, 2003; Bloody April: Slaughter in the Skies over Arras, 1917, 2005; The Somme, 2005 in US as The Somme: The Darkest Hour on the Western Front, 2009; Aces Falling: War above the Trenches, 2007; 1918: A Very British Victory, 2008. **Address:** England. **Online address:** pmhart@btinternet.com

HARTCUP, Guy. British (born England), b. 1919. **Genres:** Military/Defense/Arms Control, Sciences, History, Reference. **Career:** British Air Ministry, Air Historical Branch, historian, 1948-59; International Atomic Energy Agency, English editor, 1961-62; British Cabinet Office, Historical Section, assistant historian, 1962-64; H.M. Treasury, Historical Section, historian, 1964-76; Royal Commission on Civil Liability and Compensation, general editor, 1976-. **Publications:** Origins and Development of Operational Research in the Royal Air Force, 1963; The Challenge of War: Britain's Scientific and Engineering Contributions to World War Two, 1970; The Achievement of the Airship: A History of The Development of Rigid, Semi-Rigid, and Non-Rigid Airships, 1974; Code Name Mulberry: The Planning, Building, and Operation of The Normandy Harbours, 1977; Camouflage: A History of Concealment and Deception at War, 1980; (with T.E. Allibone) Cockcroft and the Atom, 1984; The War of Invention: Scientific Development, 1914-18, 1988; The Silent Revolution: The Development of Conventional Weapons, 1945-85, 1993; The Effect of Science on the Second World War, 2000. **Address:** 3 Chestnut Ave., E Sheen, London, GL SW14 8NT, England.

HART-DAVIS, Duff. British (born England), b. 1936. **Genres:** Novels, History, Biography. **Career:** Sunday Telegraph, feature writer, 1969-75, literary editor, 1975-76, assistant editor, 1977-78; The Independent, country columnist, 1986-. **Publications:** Behind the Scenes on a Newspaper, 1964; The Megacull, 1968; The Gold of St. Matthew in US as The Gold Trackers, 1968; Spider in the Morning, 1972; Ascension: The Story of a South Atlantic Island, 1972; Peter Fleming (biography), 1974; Monarchs of the Glen: A History of Deer-stalking in the Scottish Highlands, 1978; The Heights of Rimring, 1980; (with C. Strong) Fighter Pilot, 1981; Level Five, 1982; Fire Falcon, 1983; The Man-Eater of Jassapur, 1985; Hitler's Games, 1986; Armada, 1988; Country Matters, 1988; The House the Berrys Built, 1990; Horses of War, 1991; Wildings: The Secret Garden of Eileen Soper, 1991; Further Country Matters, 1992; When the Country Went to Town, 1997; Raoul Millais, 1998; Fauna Britannica: The Practical Guide to Wild & Domestic Creatures of Britain, 2002; Audubon's Elephant, 2003; Audubon's Elephant: America's Greatest Naturalist and the Making of the Birds of America, 2004; Honorary Tiger: The Life of Billy Arjan Singh, 2005; Philip de Laszlo: His Life and Art, 2010; The War that Never was, 2011. EDITOR: End of an Era: Letters and Journals of Sir Alan Lascelles 1887-1920, 1986; The Prince of Wales, 1988; The Mammoth Book of Spy Thrillers, 1989; In Royal Service: Letters and Journals of Sir Alan Lascelles, vol. II, 1920-36, 1989; Pavilions of Splendour: An Architectural History of Lord's, 2004; King's Counsellor: Abdication and War: The Diaries of Sir Alan Lascelles, 2006. **Address:** Owlpen Farm, Uley, Dursley, GC GL11 5BZ, England.

HARTE, Amanda. American (born United States) **Genres:** Romance/Historical, Novels. **Career:** Writer. **Publications:** NOVELS: Silver Thorns, 1996; Midnight Sun, 1999; North Star, 2000; Strings Attached, 2000; Moonlight Masquerade, 2001; Imperfect Together, 2001; Rainbows at Midnight, 2002; Carousel of Dreams, 2002; Dancing in the Rain, 2003; Whistling in the Dark, 2004; Laughing at the Thunder, 2004; Bluebonnet Spring, 2005; Painted Ponies, 2006; Dream Weaver, 2007; The Brass Ring, 2007. HIDDEN FALLS SERIES: Stargazer, 2008; The Golden Thread, 2008. AS AMANDA CABOT: TEXAS DREAMS TRILOGY: Paper Roses, 2009; Scattered Petals, 2010; Tomorrow's Garden, 2011. Works appear in anthologies. **Address:** PO Box 21596, Cheyenne, WY 82003-7030, U.S.A. **Online address:** amanda.harte@sff.net

HARTE, Lara. Irish (born Ireland), b. 1975. **Genres:** Novels, Romance/Historical, Young Adult Fiction. **Career:** Writer and librarian. **Publications:** NOVELS: First Time, 1996; Losing it, 1999; Wild Geese, 2003; Honour Bound, 2007. Contributor to periodicals. **Address:** c/o Author Mail, Weidenfeld & Nicolson Ltd., Orion House, 5 Upper Saint Martin's Ln., London, GL WC2H 9EA, England. **Online address:** laraharte@eircom.net

HARTEIS, Richard. American (born United States), b. 1946. **Genres:** Poetry, Adult Non-fiction, Literary Criticism And History. **Career:** American University, poet-in-residence, 1995-96. Health-care consultant and writer. **Publications:** POETRY: Fourteen Women, 1979; Morocco Journal: Love, Work, Play, 1981; Internal Geography, 1987; Keeping Heart, 1996; Revenant, 2010. EDITOR: (trans. with others) Poets of Bulgaria, 1986; (with W. Meredith) Window on the Black Sea: Bulgarian Poetry in Translation, 1992. OTHER: Marathon: A Story of Endurance and Friendship (nonfiction), 1989; Sapphire Dawn (fiction), 1999; Provence, 2000. Contributor to periodicals. **Address:** 3915 S Flagler Dr., Apt. 118, West Palm Beach, FL 33405, U.S.A. **Online address:** rfhar@concoll.edu

HARTER, Karen. American (born United States), b. 1952?. **Genres:** Young Adult Fiction, Psychology, Novels, Literary Criticism And History. **Career:** The Valley Church, pastor. Writer. **Publications:** Where Mercy Flows, 2006; Autumn Blue, 2007. Contributor to periodicals. **Address:** c/o Deidre Knight, The Knight Agency Inc., 570 East Ave., Madison, GA 30650, U.S.A.

HARTER, Penny. (Penny Bihler). American (born United States), b. 1940. **Genres:** Poetry, Adult Non-fiction, Young Adult Non-fiction, Children's Non-fiction. **Career:** Consultant, 1972-; New Jersey State Council on Arts, Poets-in-Schools Program, consultant, 1973-79; Woodbridge Township Board of Education, Arts Magnet High School, teacher of writing, 1978-83; From Here Press, editor, 1979-; Madison High School and Junior School, teacher, 1983-91; Union County College, adjunct instructor, 1987-89; Santa Fe Preparatory School, teacher, 1991-2002; Oak Knoll School of the Holy Child, teacher, 2002-05. **Publications:** POETRY: (as Penny Bihler) House by the Sea, 1975; (with W.J. Higginson) Used Poems, 1978; The Orange Balloon (haiku), 1980; Lovepoems, 1981; White Flowers in the Snow (poems and stories), 1981; From the Willow: Homage to Takechi no Kurohito (haiku), 1983; Hiking the Crevasse: Poems on the Way to Divorce, 1983; In the Broken Curve (haiku), 1984; The Price of Admission, 1986; The Monkey's Face (haiku), 1987; At the Zendo (poems and journal), 1993; Stages and Views, 1994; Shadow Play, Night Haiku (children's haiku), 1994; Grandmother's Milk, 1995; Turtle Blessing, 1996; Lizard Light: Poems from the Earth, 1998; Buried in the Sky, 2001; Along River Road, 2005; Night Marsh, 2008; Beastie Book: An Alphabestiary, 2009; Recycling Starlight, 2010. NONFICTION: (with W.J. Higginson) The Haiku Handbook: How to Write, Share, and Teach Haiku, 1985; (with Higginson) Met on the Road: A Transcontinental Haiku Journal, 1993. EDITOR: (co-ed.) Advance Taken to Boardwalk: 28 New Jersey Poets, 1977; (with W.J. Higginson) Union County Literature Today, 1980; Between Two Rivers: Ten North Jersey Poets, 1981; (co-ed.) An Anthology of Haiku by People of the United States and Canada, 1988; A Haiku Path: The Haiku Society of America 1968-1988, 1994. **Address:** PO Box 1402, Summit, NJ 07902-1402, U.S.A. **Online address:** penhart@att.net

HARTIG, John H. American (born United States), b. 1952. **Genres:** Environmental Sciences/Ecology. **Career:** University of Michigan, Great Lakes Research Division, research assistant, 1976-78; Michigan Department of Natural Resources, water quality specialist, 1978-82; International Joint Commission, environmental scientist, 1985-98; Wayne State University, adjunct professor, 1992-2002; Greater Detroit American Heritage River Initiative, river navigator, 1999-2004; Detroit River International Wildlife Refuge, refuge manager, 2004-. Writer. **Publications:** (Ed. with M.A. Zarull) Under RAPs: Toward Grassroots Ecological Democracy in the Great Lakes Basin, 1992; (ed. with J.R.M. Kelso) Methods of Modifying Habitat to Benefit the Great Lakes Ecosystem, 1995; (ed.) Honoring Our Detroit River: Caring for Our Home, 2003; Burning Rivers: Revival of Four Urban-Industrial Rivers That Caught on Fire, 2010. Contributor to periodicals. **Address:** Detroit River International Wildlife Refuge, 9311 Groh Rd., Large Lakes Research Sta., Grosse Ile, MI 48138, U.S.A. **Online address:** john_hartig@fws.gov

HARTIGAN, John. American (born United States), b. 1964. **Genres:** Race Relations, Social Sciences. **Career:** Knox College, assistant professor, 1996-99; University of North Texas, assistant professor, 1999-2001; University of Texas, Department of Anthropology, assistant professor, 2001-02, associate professor of anthropology, 2002-09, professor, 2010-, Americo Paredes Center for Cultural Studies, director, 2007-. Writer. **Publications:** Racial Situations: Class Predicaments of Whiteness in Detroit, 1999; Odd Tribes: Toward a Cultural Analysis of White People, 2005; Race In The 21st Century: Ethno-

graphic Approaches, 2009; What Can You Say?: Americas National Conversation On Race, 2010; Race and Science: Biology, Genes and Culture, forthcoming. Contributor of articles to books and journals. **Address:** Department of Anthropology, Americo Paredes Center for Cultural Studies, University of Texas, 4 158 Student Activity Center Bldg., PO Box C3200, Austin, TX 78712-0303, U.S.A. **Online address:** hartigan@mail.utexas.edu

HARTJE, Tod D(ale). American (born United States), b. 1968. **Genres:** Sports/Fitness, Biography. **Career:** Wilson's Suede and Leather, accounting intern, 1989; Soviet Elite League (Sokol Kiev), professional hockey player, 1989-90; Winnipeg Jets Hockey Club (Moncton Hawks), professional hockey player, 1990-92; Service Ltd., assistant, 1991; Little Caesar Enterprises Inc., marketing and media intern, 1991; Hartje Pro Edge Hockey Training, owner and director, 1991-. Writer. **Publications:** (With L. Martin) From Behind the Red Line: An American Hockey Player in Russia, 1992. **Address:** c/o Moncton Hawks, PO Box 2940, Sta. A, Moncton, NB E1C 8T8, Canada.

HARTLAND, Michael. Also writes as Michael Leonard James, Ruth Carrington. British (born England), b. 1941. **Genres:** Mystery/Crime/Suspense, Novels. **Career:** British Government Service, Minister for the Arts, private secretary to Jennie Lee, 1966-68; Planning Unit of Margaret Thatcher, State for Education, secretary, 1970-73; United Nations International Atomic Energy Agency, director, 1978-82; writer, 1982-; University of Exeter, honorary fellow, 1985; The Times, book reviewer, travel and feature writer; Sunday Times, book reviewer, travel and feature writer; Daily Telegraph, resident thriller critic, 1993-, book reviewer; Sunday Express, book reviewer; Guardian, travel and feature writer. **Publications:** Down among the Dead Men, 1983; Seven Steps to Treason, 1984; The Third Betrayal, 1986; Frontier of Fear: A Novel, 1988; The Year of the Scorpion, 1991; Traicion En Oriente, 1991; (as Ruth Carrington) Dead Fish, 1998; Great Guns of Barbados, 2009. Contributor of articles to magazines. **Address:** Hartland Press Ltd., Cotte Barton, Branscombe, Seaton, DN EX12 3BH, England.

HARTLE, Anthony E. (Anthony Elwood Hartle). American (born United States), b. 1942. **Genres:** Ethics, Military/Defense/Arms Control, History, Young Adult Non-fiction. **Career:** United States Military Academy, instructor and assistant professor, 1971-74, associate professor, 1982-88, professor of philosophy, 1988-2004, Department of English, chair, deputy head, 1994-2004; Cambridge University, visiting fellow, 1991-92. Writer. **Publications:** (Ed. with J. Kekes) Dimensions of Ethical Thought, 1987; Moral Issues in Military Decision Making, 1989, 2nd ed., 2004. Contributor to periodicals. **Address:** University Press of Kansas, 2502 Westbrooke St., Lawrence, KS 66045-4444, U.S.A.

HARTLE, Anthony Elwood. See **HARTLE, Anthony E.**

HARTLEY, Aidan. Kenyan (born Kenya), b. 1965?. **Genres:** Autobiography/Memoirs, Genealogy/Heraldry. **Career:** Reuters News Agency, foreign correspondent; Financial Times, foreign correspondent; London Times, foreign correspondent; African Environment News Services, co-founder. Writer. **Publications:** The Zanzibar Chest: A Story of Life, Love, and Death in Foreign Lands, 2003; Wild Life: Adventures on an African Farm, 2008. **Address:** c/o Rosie Gailer, HarperCollinsPublishers, 77-85 Fulham Palace Rd., London, GL W6 8JB, England. **Online address:** info@thezanzibarchest.com

HARTLEY, Hal. American (born United States), b. 1959. **Genres:** Plays/Screenplays, Adult Non-fiction, Humor/Satire. **Career:** Possible Films, owner. Writer and director. **Publications:** Simple Men: Trust, 1992; Amateur, 1994; Flirt, 1996; Henry Fool, 1998; Hal Hartley: Collected Screenplays, vol. I: The Unbelievable Truth, Trust, Simple Men, 2002; True Fiction Pictures and Possible Films, 2008. **Address:** Possible Films, 302A W 12th St., Ste. 334, PO Box 334, New York, NY 10014-1947, U.S.A. **Online address:** info@possiblefilms.com

HARTLEY, Steven W. American (born United States), b. 1956?. **Genres:** Marketing, Advertising/Public Relations, Business/Trade/Industry, Economics. **Career:** University of Denver, Department of Marketing, teaching assistant, 1978-80, instructor, 1980-83, research associate, 1981-82, assistant professor, 1983-88, associate professor, 1988-92, chairman, 1989-94, 2002-07, professor of marketing, 1992-, EVM Program, Walter Koch Endowed Chair and director, 2003-07; Control Data Corp., staff, 1979; Rosemount Inc., staff, 1977-78, 1980; Minnesota Valley Engineering, staff, 1976. Writer. **Publications:** (With C.H. Patti and S.L. Kennedy) Business-to-Business Advertising, 1991; (with R.A. Kerin and W. Rudelius) Marketing: The Core, 10th ed., 2010. **Address:** Department of Marketing, University of Denver, 2101 S University Blvd., Denver, CO 80208, U.S.A.

HARTMAN, Donald K. American (born United States), b. 1959. **Genres:** Bibliography, Reference. **Career:** State University of New York, Lockwood Library, staff, associate librarian, reference coordinator, economics subject specialist; Epoch Books Inc., co-owner. Writer. **Publications:** (With J. Drost) Themes and Settings in Fiction: A Bibliography of Bibliographies, 1988; (with G. Sapp) Historical Figures in Fiction, 1994; Historical Figures in Nineteenth Century Fiction, 1999. EDITOR: Fairground Fiction: Detective Stories of the World's Columbian Exposition: Containing Reprints of Emma Murdoch Van Deventer's Against Odds, a Detective Story, and John Harvey Whitson's Chicago Charlie, the Columbian Detective, 1992. Contributor to periodicals. **Address:** Lockwood Library, State University of New York, Reference/Collection Development, 521 Lockwood Library, N Campus, Buffalo, NY 14260, U.S.A. **Online address:** unldon@buffalo.edu

HARTMAN, Geoffrey H. American/German (born Germany), b. 1929. **Genres:** Poetry, Literary Criticism And History, Essays, Humanities. **Career:** Yale University, Sterling fellow, 1952-53, Morse faculty fellow, 1958-59, Department of English, instructor and assistant professor, 1955-62, professor of English and comparative literature, 1967-74, Karl Young professor, 1974-94, Mellon Term professor, 1992-97, Sterling professor of English and comparative literature, 1994-97, emeritus professor, 1997-, Council on the Humanities, chair, 1973-75, Department of Comparative Literature, chair, 1984-86, Center for Cultural Sociology, senior fellow; University of Chicago, Department of English, visiting lecturer, 1960-61; University of Iowa, associate professor and professor of English and comparative literature, 1962-65; Cornell University, professor, 1965-67, School of Criticism and Theory, honorary senior fellow; Guggenheim Foundation, fellow, 1969-70, 1986-87; Northwestern University, School of Criticism and Theory, director, 1981-85, 1985-87; Hebrew University, Institute for Advanced Studies, fellow, 1985-86, 1988-89, Lady Davis fellow, 1988-89; University of Warwick, Center for Research in Philosophy and Literature, honorary associate fellow; New School University, distinguished visiting professor of humanities, 2000-03. Writer. **Publications:** The Unmediated Vision: An Interpretation of Wordsworth, Hopkins, Rilke, and Valery, 1954, new ed., 1966; Andre Malraux, 1960; Wordsworth's Poetry 1787-1814, 1964; Beyond Formalism: Literary Essays 1958-1970, 1970; The Fate of Reading and Other Essays, 1975; Akiba's Children (poetry), 1978; Criticism in the Wilderness: The Study of Literature Today, 1980, 2nd ed., 2007; Saving the Text: Literature, Derrida, Philosophy, 1981; Easy Pieces, 1985; State of the Art of Criticism, 1987; The Unremarkable Wordsworth, 1987; Minor Prophecies: The Literary Essay in the Culture Wars, 1991; Preserving Living Memory: The Challenge and Power of Videotestimony, 1995; The Longest Shadow: In the Aftermath of the Holocaust, 1996; The Fateful Question of Culture, 1997; Critic's Journey: Literary Reflections, 1958-1998, 1999; Scars of the Spirit: The Struggle against Inauthenticity, 2002; A Scholar's Tale: Intellectual Journey of a Displaced Child of Europe, 2007; The Third Pillar, 2011. EDITOR: Hopkins: A Collection of Critical Essays, 1966; (and intro.) Selected Poetry and Prose of William Wordsworth, 1970; (and foreword) New Perspectives on Coleridge and Wordsworth, 1972; (with D. Thorburn) Romanticism: Vistas, Instances, Continuities, 1973; (and intro.) Psychoanalysis and the Question of the Text, 1978; (and intro.) Selected Poetry and Prose of Wordsworth, 1980; (with P. Parker) Shakespeare and the Question of Theory, 1985; (with S. Budick) Midrash and Literature, 1986; Bitburg in Moral and Political Perspective, 1986; Holocaust Remembrance: The Shapes of Memory, 1994; (with K. Hart) Power of Contestation: Perspectives on Maurice Blanchot, 2004; (with D.T. O'Hara) The Geoffrey Hartman Reader, 2004. Contributor to periodicals. **Address:** Koerner Center, Yale University, 149 Elm 216, Comparative Literature, PO Box 208302, New Haven, CT 06520, U.S.A. **Online address:** geoffrey.hartman@yale.edu

HARTMAN, Honor. See JAMES, (Darryl) Dean.

HARTMAN, Saidiya V. American (born United States) **Genres:** Literary Criticism And History, Autobiography/Memoirs, Young Adult Non-fiction, Humanities. **Career:** University of California, president's fellow; Columbia University, Department of English and Comparative Literature, professor, 2006-, Institute for Research on Women and Gender, director. Writer. **Publications:** (With B.J. Wright) Lorna Simpson: For the Sake of the Viewer, 1992; Scenes of Subjection: Terror, Slavery, and Self-Making in Nineteenth-Century America, 1997; Lose Your Mother: A Journey along the

Atlantic Slave Route, 2007. **Address:** Columbia University, 602 Philosophy Hall, 2960 Broadway, New York, NY 10027-6902, U.S.A. **Online address:** svh2102@columbia.edu

HARTMAN, Victoria. American (born United States), b. 1942. **Genres:** Humor/Satire. **Career:** Henry Holt, senior designer; Lothrop, Lee and Shepard, art director, 1967-74; freelance book designer, 1974-. Writer. **Publications:** The Silly Joke Book, 1987; Westward Ho Ho Ho!: Jokes from the Wild West, 1992; The Silliest Joke Book Ever, 1993; Too Cool Jokes for School, 1996. Contributor to periodicals. **Address:** 164 Halsey St., Southampton, NY 11968-4012, U.S.A. **Online address:** harken2@optonline.net

HARTMANN, Dennis L. American (born United States), b. 1949. **Genres:** Earth Sciences, Environmental Sciences/Ecology, Meteorology/Atmospheric Sciences, Sciences. **Career:** Princeton University, Geophysical Fluid Dynamics Program, research assistant, 1971-75; McGill University, Montreal, research associate in meteorology, 1975-76; National Center for Atmospheric Research, visiting scientist, 1976-77; University of Washington, assistant professor, 1977-83, associate professor, 1983-88, professor of atmospheric sciences, 1988-, chair, 2002-07, Quaternary Research Center, adjunct faculty, 1978-, College of the Environment, interim dean, 2008-10; Oxford University, Department of Atmospheric Physics, visiting scientist, 1985; École Normale Superieure, visiting scientist, 1986; European Centre for Medium Range Weather Forecasts, visiting scientist, 1993-94; University of Reading, Department of Meteorology, visiting professor, 1993-94; AAAS Section on Atmospheric and Hydrospheric Sciences, chair, 1998. Writer. **Publications:** Global Physical Climatology, 1994. Contributor of articles to journals and magazines. **Address:** Department of Atmospheric Sciences, University of Washington, 408 Atmospheric Sciences-Geophysics (ATG) Bldg., PO Box 351640, Seattle, WA 98195-1640, U.S.A. **Online address:** dennis@atmos.washington.edu

HARTMANN, Ernest L. American/Austrian (born Austria), b. 1934. **Genres:** Medicine/Health, Psychiatry, Psychology, Education, Reference. **Career:** Newton-Wellesley Hospital, Sleep Disorders Center, director; Massachusetts Mental Health Center, residency in psychiatry, 1960-62; National Institute of Mental Health, clinical associate, 1962-64, career investigator, 1964-69; Boston State Hospital, Sleep and Dream Laboratory, director, 1964-85; Tufts University, School of Medicine, assistant professor, 1964-69, professor of psychiatry, 1969-; Peter Bent Brigham Hospital, Sleep clinic, director. Writer. **Publications:** The Biology of Dreaming, 1967; (co-author) Adolescents in a Mental Hospital, 1968; (ed. and contrib.) Sleep and Dreaming, 1970; The Functions of Sleep, 1973; The Sleeping Pill, 1978; The Nightmare: The Psychology and Biology of Terrifying Dreams, 1985; The Sleep Book: Understanding and Preventing Sleep Problems in People Over 50, 1987; Boundaries in the Mind: A New Psychology of Personality, Basic Books, 1991; Dreams and Nightmares: The New Theory on the Origin and Meaning of Dreams, 1998, rev. ed., 2002; The Nature and Functions of Dreaming, 2011. Contributor of articles to journals. **Address:** School of Medicine, Tufts University, 27 Clark St., Newton, MA 02459, U.S.A. **Online address:** ehdream@aol.com

HARTMANN, Thom. American (born United States), b. 1951. **Genres:** How-to Books, Adult Non-fiction. **Career:** Radio reporter, news anchor, talk-show host and disc jockey, 1968-78; New England Salem Children's Village, co-founder, 1978; The Hunter School, co-founder, 1997; Michigan Healing Arts Center, co-founder; Sirius Satellite Radio Channel 146, talk-show host, 2002-; Goddard College, visiting faculty. Writer. **Publications:** Attention Deficit Disorder: A Different Perception, 1993, 2nd ed., 1997; Focus Your Energy: Hunting for Success in Business with Attention Deficit Disorder, 1994; ADD Success Stories: A Guide to Fulfillment for Families with Attention Deficit Disorder: Maps, Guidebooks, and Travelogues for Hunters in This Farmer's World, 1995; Beyond ADD: Hunting for Reasons in the Past and the Present, 1996; Healing ADD: Simple Exercises That Will Change Your Daily Life, 1998; The Last Hours of Ancient Sunlight: Waking Up to Personal and Global Transformation, 1999, rev. ed., 2004; The Greatest Spiritual Secret of the Century, 2000; Unequal Protection: The Rise of Corporate Dominance and the Theft of Human Rights, 2002; ADHD Secrets of Success: Coaching Yourself to Fulfillment in the Business World, 2002; The Edison Gene: ADHD and the Gift of the Hunter Child, 2003; The Prophet's Way: A Guide to Living in the Now, 2004; We the People: A Call to Take Back

America, 2004; What Would Jefferson Do? A Return to Democracy, 2004; (with L. Waldron) Ultimate Sacrifice: John and Robert Kennedy, the Plan for a Coup in Cuba, and the Murder of JFK, 2005, rev. ed., 2006; Screwed: The Undeclared War against the Middle Class and What We Can Do about It, 2006; Walking Your Blues Away: How to Heal the Mind and Create Emotional Well-Being, 2006; Cracking the Code: How to Win Hearts, Change Minds and Restore America's Original Vision, 2007; Threshold: the Crisis of Western Culture, 2009; (with L. Waldron) Legacy of Secrecy: the Long Shadow of the JFK Assassination, 2008; Rebooting the American Dream: 11 Ways to Rebuild Our Country, 2010. Contributor to periodicals. **Address:** KPOJ Radio, 4949 SW Macadam Ave., Portland, OR 97239, U.S.A. **Online address:** thom@thomhartmann.com

HARTNETT, Sonya. (Cameron S. Redfern). Australian (born Australia), b. 1968. **Genres:** Young Adult Fiction, Novels, Animals/Pets, Science Fiction/Fantasy. **Career:** Writer. **Publications:** FOR YOUNG ADULTS: Trouble All the Way, 1984; Sparkle and Night Flower, 1986; The Glass House, 1990; Wilful Blue, 1994; Sleeping Dogs, 1995; The Devil Latch, 1996; Black Foxes, 1996; Princes, 1998; All My Dangerous Friends, 1998; (co-author) There Must Be Lions: Stories about Mental Illness, 1998; Stripes of the Sidestep Wolf, 1999; Thursday's Child, 2000; Of a Boy, 2000; Forest, 2001; What the Birds See, 2003; The Silver Donkey: A Novel for Children, 2004; Surrender, 2005; (as Cameron S. Redfern) Landscape with Animals, 2006; The Ghost's Child, 2007; Sadie and Ratz: Aussie Nibble, 2008; Butterfly, 2009; The Midnight Zoo, 2010. **Address:** 15A Cain Ave., Northcote, VI 3070, Australia.

HARTOONIAN, Gevork. American (born United States), b. 1947. **Genres:** Architecture. **Career:** Mirick, Pearson, Batcheler (architects), architect, 1984-87; Spring Garden College, adjunct faculty, 1988-90; Kling-Linquist Partnership Inc., architect, 1988-96; Drury College, assistant professor, 1990-; Hammons School of Architecture, lecturer, 1991-92; University of Texas, visiting assistant professor, 1993-95; Rice University, interim lecturer, 1995; Parsons School of Design, visiting associate professor, 1996; Pratt Institute, visiting associate professor, adjunct associate professor, 1997-; Columbia University, visiting professor, adjunct associate professor, 1997-; University of Canberra, associate professor of architecture, 1998-; University of Sydney, masters program in architecture, lecturer and coordinator. Writer. **Publications:** Ontology of Construction: On Nihilism of Technology in Theories of Modern Architecture, 1994; Modernity and Its Other: A Post-Script to Contemporary Architecture, 1997; Crisis of the Object: The Architecture of Theatricality, 2006; (co-author P. Drew and P. Goad) Australian Architecture: Living the Modern, 2007; (ed.) Walter Benjamin and Architecture, 2010; Toward a Critical Practice in Architecture, 2010; Mental Life of the Architectural Historian, 2011; Architecture and Spectacle, 2011. Contributor of articles to periodicals. **Address:** School of Design & Architecture, Canberra University, Rm. B29, 7A Bldg., North Rd., Canberra, AC 2601, Australia. **Online address:** gevork.hartoonian@canberra.edu.au

HARTSHORNE, Thomas L. American (born United States), b. 1935. **Genres:** Cultural/Ethnic Topics, History, Social Sciences. **Career:** Kent State University, instructor in history, 1962-65, assistant professor of history, 1962-66; Cleveland State University, assistant professor, 1966-69, associate professor of history, 1969-2001, associate professor of history, emeritus, 2001-. Writer. **Publications:** The Distorted Image: Changing Conceptions of the American Character since Turner, 1968; (co-ed.) The Social Fabric, 1987, 11th ed., 2009. **Address:** Department of History, College of Liberal Arts & Social Sciences, Cleveland State University, 2121 Euclid Ave., Cleveland, OH 44115-2214, U.S.A. **Online address:** t.hartshorne@csuohio.edu

HARTWIG, Manfred. German (born Germany), b. 1950. **Genres:** Animals/Pets, Children's Non-fiction. **Career:** Fossil Power Plants, deputy director for marketing and sales; Siemens Power Generation, vice president of supply management; Berggorilla Patenschaft, co-founder. Writer. **Publications:** (With P.H. Bürgel) Bei den Berggorillas, 1989 in US as Gorillas, 1992. **Address:** Mecklenburger Str. 10, Adelsdorf, 91325, Germany. **Online address:** manfred.hartwig@t-online.de

HARTWIG, Michael J. American (born United States), b. 1953. **Genres:** Human Relations/Parenting. **Career:** White Rock Young Men's Christian Association, aquatics and coach of swim team, director, 1972-75; International High School, teacher, 1975-77; North American College, College Bookstore, director, 1979-80; Roman Catholic parish, 1979-87, assistant pastor, 1980-83; Immaculate Conception Parish, middle school and high school teacher,

coordinator of Hispanic ministries and instructor in continuing education, 1980-83; John Paul I Catechetical Institute, lecturer, 1983-87; Holy Trinity Seminary, vice rector, 1983-85, academic dean, 1986-87; University of Dallas, adjunct instructor, 1983-85; Brookhaven College, Philosophy, adjunct instructor, 1988; Eastern Connecticut State University, director of advising program and secretary in education department, 1989-91; University of New Haven, adjunct instructor, 1990-91; Albertus Magnus College, associate professor of religion and philosophy, 1991-99, Peace, Justice and Global Issues Studies, coordinator, 1991-94; Saint Francis School of Nursing, adjunct faculty, 1991-97; Yale University, Mellon visiting faculty, 1995-96; Cambridge College, adjunct faculty, 1998; Emmanuel College, adjunct professor, 1998-; Fisher College, adjunct faculty, 1998-2000; Hartwig-Baker and Associates, operator of ethics consulting business, 1998-2000; Charter Oak College, adjunct faulty, 1998-; University of Massachusetts, College of Public and Community Service, adjunct faculty, 1999-; WTS/Raptim Transport Service, Academic Travel Division and Academic Travel Consultant, director, 1999-; Vinfen Corp., Academic Affairs, acting director, 1999-2000; Mental Health Center, consultant. Writer. **Publications:** The Poetics of Intimacy and the Problem of Sexual Abstinence, 2000; What Happens after Consent? A Process Model of Informed Consent, forthcoming. Contributor to periodicals. **Address:** Charter Oak College, 55 Paul J. Manafort Dr., New Britain, CT 06053-2150, U.S.A. **Online address:** portamjh@aol.com

HARUF, Kent. American (born United States), b. 1943. **Genres:** Novels, Children's Fiction. **Career:** Teacher, 1976-86; Nebraska Wesleyan University, assistant professor, 1986-91; Southern Illinois University, associate professor, 1991-2000, now professor emeritus. Writer. **Publications:** The Tie That Binds: A Novel, 1984; Where You Once Belonged: A Novel, 1990; Plainsong, 1999; Eventide: A Novel, 2004; (with P. Brown) West of Last Chance, 2008. Contributor to periodicals. **Address:** Department of English, Southern Illinois University, 2380 Faner Hall, 1000 Faner Dr., PO Box 4503, Carbondale, IL 62901, U.S.A.

HARVARD, Jane. See **ADIELE, Faith.**

HARVEY, (Brian) Peter. British (born England), b. 1951. **Genres:** Theology/Religion, History, Philosophy. **Career:** University of Sunderland (formerly Sunderland Polytechnic), faculty, 1976-, lecturer, senior lecturer in religious studies and philosophy, reader in Buddhist studies, 1992, professor of Buddhist studies, 1996-; Samatha Trust, meditation teacher, 1977-; U.K. Association for Buddhist Studies, co-founder, 1996-, president, 2002-06; Buddhist Studies Review, editor, 2006-. **Publications:** An Introduction to Buddhism: Teachings, History, and Practices, 1990; The Selfless Mind: Personality, Consciousness and Nirvana in Early Buddhism, 1990; An Introduction to Buddhist Ethics: Foundations, Values, and Issues, 2000; (ed.) Buddhism, 2001. Contributor to periodicals. **Address:** University of Sunderland, Priestman Bldg., City Campus, Green Terr., Sunderland, TW SR1 3PZ, England. **Online address:** peter.harvey@sunderland.ac.uk

HARVEY, Caroline. See **TROLLOPE, Joanna.**

HARVEY, Clay. (Leo Atkins). American (born United States) **Genres:** Novels, Recreation, Literary Criticism And History, Young Adult Fiction. **Career:** Novelist. **Publications:** NOVELS: A Flash of Red, 1996; A Whisper of Black, 1997; Dwelling in the Gray, 2000. NONFICTION: Popular Sporting Rifle Cartridges, 1984; The Hunter's Rifle, 1988, rev. ed. as The Rifles, The Cartridges, and the Game, 1991. AS LEO ATKINS: Deadbeat, 1999; Dead Run, 2000; Play Dead, 2000. Contributor to periodicals. **Address:** Putnam Berkley Group Inc., 375 Hudson St., New York, NY 10014, U.S.A.

HARVEY, David. American/British (born England), b. 1935. **Genres:** Adult Non-fiction, Geography, History. **Career:** University of Bristol, lecturer in geography, 1961-69; Johns Hopkins University, associate professor of geography, 1969-73, professor of geography, 1973-89, 1993-2001; University of Oxford, Halford Mackinder professor of geography, 1987-93; City University of New York, Graduate Center, professor, distinguished professor of anthropology, 2001-; London School of Economics, Miliband fellow. Writer. **Publications:** Explanation in Geography, 1969; Society, the City, and the Space-Economy of Urbanism, 1972; A Question of Method for a Matter of Survival, 1973; Social Justice and the City, 1973, rev. ed., 2009; The Limits to Capital, 1982, new ed., 2006; The Urbanization of Capital: Studies in the History and Theory of Capitalist Urbanization, 1985; Consciousness and the Urban Experience: Studies in the History and Theory of Capitalist Urbanization, 1985; The Condition of Postmodernity: An Enquiry into the Origins of Cultural Change, 1989; The Urban Experience, 1989; (ed. with T. Hayter) The Factory and the City: The Story of the Cowley Automobile Workers in Oxford, 1993; Justice, Nature, and the Geography of Difference, 1996; (with J. Beverley and P. Cohen) Subculture and Homogenization, 1998; Spaces of Hope, 2000; Spaces of Capital: Towards a Critical Geography, 2001; The New Imperialism, 2003; Paris, Capital of Modernity, 2003; A Brief History of Neoliberalism, 2005; Spaces of Global Capitalism, 2006; (intro.) Communist Manifesto, 2008; Cosmopolitanism and the Geographies of Freedom, 2009; Companion to Marx's Capital, 2010; Enigma of Capital, 2010. **Address:** Ph.D. Program in Anthropology, The Graduate Center, City University of New York, Rm. 5111, 365 5th Ave., New York, NY 10016-4309, U.S.A. **Online address:** dharvey@gc.cuny.edu

HARVEY, David Allen. American (born United States), b. 1971?. **Genres:** Politics/Government. **Career:** New College of Florida, assistant professor, 2000-, professor of History, Division of Social Sciences, chair. Writer. **Publications:** Constructing Class and Nationality in Alsace, 1830-1945, 2001; Beyond Enlightenment: Occultism and Politics in Modern France, 2005. **Address:** Division of Social Sciences, New College of Florida, 5800 Bay Shore Rd., Sarasota, FL 34243-2109, U.S.A. **Online address:** dharvey@ncf.edu

HARVEY, Hazel (Mary). British (born England), b. 1936. **Genres:** Translations, Local History/Rural Topics, Autobiography/Memoirs, Biography. **Career:** Harrap (publisher), lexicographer, 1957-58; University of Exeter, lecturer, 1961-64; University of London, National Extension College, tutor, 1975-. Writer. **Publications:** (Trans. with D. Harvey) Karl Reinhardt, Sophocles, 1979; (trans. with D. Harvey and F. Robertson) Richard Heinze, Virgil's Epic Technique, 1993; Exeter Past, 1996; A Better Provision: The Royal Devon & Exeter Hospital, 1948-1998, 1998; (ed.) Memories of Exeter, 1999; (ed.) Two Thousand Years in Exeter, 2004. **Address:** 53 Thornton Hill, Exeter, DN EX4 4NR, England.

HARVEY, Jack. See **RANKIN, Ian (James).**

HARVEY, John. Also writes as John J. McLaglen, Terry Lennox, James Mann, William S. Brady, Thom Ryder. British (born England), b. 1938. **Genres:** Novels, Mystery/Crime/Suspense, Westerns/Adventure, Children's Fiction, Young Adult Fiction, Poetry, inspirational/Motivational Literature. **Career:** English and drama teacher, 1963-74; writer, 1975-; University of Nottingham, part-time film and literature teacher, 1979-86; Nottingham News and Trader, film reviewer, 1981-86. **Publications:** (As Thom Ryder) Avenging Angel, 1975; (as Thom Ryder) Angel Alone, 1975; Amphetamines and Pearls, 1976; The Geranium Kiss, Sphere, 1976; (as Jon Barton) Kill Hitler, 1976; (as Jon Barton) Forest of Death, 1977; (as Jon Barton) Lightning Strikes, 1977; Junkyard Angel, 1977; Neon Madman, 1977; Frame, Methuen, 1979; Blind, Methuen, 1981; (as James Mann) Endgame, 1982; (as Terry Lennox) Dancer Draws a Wild Card, 1985; (as James Mann) Vandal, 1988; Now's the Time, 1999; In A True Light: A Novel of Crime, 2002; Flesh and Blood, 2004; Ash & Bone, 2005; Darkness & Light, 2006; Gone to Ground, 2007; Trouble in Mind, 2007; Cold in Hand, 2008; Far Cry, 2009; A Darker Shade of Blue, 2010; Good Bait, 2012. NOVELIZATIONS: (as Michael Syson) The Eagle's Wing, 1978. POETRY: Provence (poetry), 1978; The Old Postcard Trick (poetry), 1985; Neil Sedaka Lied (poetry), 1987; The Downeast Poems, 1989; (with S. Dymoke) Sometime Other Than Now, 1989; Ghosts of a Chance, 1992; Territory, 1992; Bluer Than This, 1998. JUVENILE: What about It, Sharon?, 1979; Reel Love, 1982; Sundae Date, 1983; What Game Are You Playing?, 1983; Footwork, 1984; Last Summer, First Love, 1986; Wild Love, 1986; Daylight Robbery!, 1987; Hot Property!, 1987; Kidnap!, 1987; Downeast to Danger, 1988; Runner!, 1988; Terror Trap!, 1988; Nick's Blues, 2005. CHARLIE RESNICK MYSTERY SERIES: Lonely Hearts, 1989; Rough Treatment, 1990; Cutting Edge, 1991; Off Minor, 1992; Wasted Years, 1993; Cold Light, 1994; Living Proof, 1995; Easy Meat, 1996; Still Water, 1997; Last Rites, 1998. EDITOR: Blue Lightning (crime anthology), 2003; Men from Boys (crime anthology), 2005. AS WILLIAM S. BRADY: HAWK AND PEACEMAKER SERIES: Blood Money, 1979; Blood Kin, 1980; Killing Time, 1980; Dead Man's Hand, 1981; Desperadoes, 1981; Whiplash, 1981; Death and Jack Shade, 1982; Sierra Gold, 1982; Border War, 1983; Killer!, 1983; War Party, 1983; The Lost, 1984. AS L.J. COBURN: CALEB THORN SERIES: The Raiders, 1977; Bloody Shiloh, 1978. AS J.B. DANCER: LAWMEN SERIES: Evil Breed, 1977; Judgment Day, 1978; The Hanged Man, 1979. AS JON HART: MERCENARIES SERIES: Black Blood, 1977; Guerrilla Attack!, 1977; High Slaughter, 1977; Triangle of

Death, 1977; Death Raid, 1978. AS JOHN B. HARVEY: HART THE REGULATOR SERIES: Blood Trail, 1980; Cherokee Outlet, 1980; The Silver Lie, 1980; Tago, 1980; Blood on the Border, 1981; Ride the Wide Country, 1981; Arkansas Breakout, 1982; John Wesley Hardin, 1982; California Bloodlines, 1983; The Skinning Place, 1983. AS WILLIAM M. JAMES: APACHE SERIES: Blood Rising, 1979; Blood Brother, 1980; Death Dragon, 1981; Death Ride, 1983; The Hanging, 1983. AS JOHN J. McLAGLEN: HERNE THE HUNTER SERIES: River of Blood, 1976; Death in Gold, 1977; Shadow of the Vulture, 1977; Cross-Draw, 1978; Vigilante!, 1979; Billy the Kid, 1980; Sun Dance, 1980; Till Death, 1980; Dying Ways, 1982; Hearts of Gold, 1982; Wild Blood, 1983. AS J.D. SANDON: GRINGOS SERIES: Border Affair, 1979; Cannons in the Rain, 1979; Mazatlan, 1980; Wheels of Thunder, 1981; Durango, 1982. **Address:** c/o Sarah Lutyens, Lutyens & Rubinstein, 231 Westbourne Park Rd., London, GL W11 1EB, England. **Online address:** john@mellotone.co.uk

HARVEY, John F(rederick). American (born United States), b. 1921. **Genres:** Librarianship, Information Science/Computers. **Career:** John Crerar Library, assistant cataloger, 1944-45, assistant librarian, 1945-47; University of Chicago Library, administrative assistant, 1949-50; Parsons College, librarian and professor of library science, 1950-53; Kansas State Teachers College of Pittsburg (now Pittsburg State University), professor, head librarian, chairman of department of library science, 1953-58; Drexel Institute of Technology (now Drexel University), director of libraries, 1958-63, Graduate School of Library Science, dean and professor, 1958-67; University of Tehran, professor of library sciences, 1967-71, chairman of department, 1967-68; Iranian Documentation Centre and Tehran Book Processing Centre, founder, technical director, 1968-71; University of New Mexico, dean of Library Services, 1972-74; Hofstra University, dean of library services, 1974-76. Writer and consultant, 1976-78. **Publications:** The Librarian's Career: A Study of Mobility, 1957; (comp. with P. Temple) A Directory of Library Periodicals Published in the Continental United States, 1957; (with L. Shores and R. Jordan) The Library College, 1964; (ed.) Data Processing in College and Public Libraries, 1966; (comp. with D. Rodda) Directory of Church Libraries, 1970; (ed.) Proceedings, 1970; Iranian Senior College Library Standards, 1971; Toward a Definition of International and Comparative Library Science, 1972; (ed.) Comparative and International Library Science, 1977; Church and Synagogue Libraries, 1980; (with E.M. Dickinson) Affirmative Action in Libraries, 1982; (ed. with P. Spyers-Duran) Austerity Management in Academic Libraries, 1984; (ed. with F.L. Carroll) Internationalizing Library and Information Science Education, 1987; Scholarly Religious Libraries in North America: A Statistical Examination, 1998; Popular Religious Libraries in North America: A Statistical Examination, 1998. **Address:** 82 Wall St., Ste. 1105, New York, NY 10005-3682, U.S.A. **Online address:** john.f.harvey@usa.net

HARVEY, Karen D. American (born United States), b. 1935. **Genres:** Education, Cultural/Ethnic Topics, Anthropology/Ethnology, History, Social Sciences. **Career:** Teacher, 1956-74; University of Denver, professor, 1978-84, director of teacher education, 1978-84, assistant dean, associate dean of academic affairs, 1991-; Cherry Creek Schools, director of staff development, 1984-91. Writer and consultant. **Publications:** (With L.D. Harjo and J.K. Jackson) Teaching about Native Americans, 1990; Indians of the Great Plains, 1993; (with L.D. Harjo) Indian Country: A History of Native People in America, 1994; (with L.D. Harjo) Indian Country Teachers' Guide, 1994; (with L.D. Harjo and L. Welborn) How to Teach about American Indians: A Guide for the School Library Media Specialist, 1995; (ed., contrib. and intro.) American Indian Voices, 1995; (with L.D. Harjo and J.K. Jackson) Teaching about Native Americans, 1998; (with L.D. Harjo) Indian Country: A History of Native People in America, 1998. **Address:** 2211 S Josephine, Denver, CO 80208, U.S.A.

HARVEY, Kenneth J. Canadian (born Canada), b. 1962. **Genres:** Young Adult Fiction, Novels, Poetry, Novellas/Short Stories, Mystery/Crime/Suspense, Young Adult Non-fiction. **Career:** University of New Brunswick, writer-in-residence; Memorial University, writer-in-residence. Poet. **Publications:** No Lies: And Other Stories, 1985; Directions for an Opened Body (stories), 1990; Brud: A Parable, 1992; The Hole That Must Be Filled (stories), 1994; Stalkers, 1994; Kill the Poets: Anti verse, 1995; The Great Misogynist, 1996; Heart to Heart, 1996; Nine-tenths Unseen: A Psychological Mystery, 1996; We Must Let Him Know, 1997; Lift Up Your Eyes (poems), 1997; The Woman in the Closet (mystery novel), 1998; As Time Winds Down, 1998; Everyone Hates a Beauty Queen: Provocative Opinions and Irrelevant Humor, 1998; The Flesh So Close: Stories, 1998; Skin Hound (There Are No Words):

A Transcomposite Novel, 2000; Sense the Need, 2000; (with E.M. Nash) Little White Squaw: A White Woman's Story of Abuse, Addiction and Reconciliation, 2002; Artists United, 2003; The Town That Forgot How to Breathe, 2003; Heaven Only, 2004; Shack: The Cutland Junction Stories, 2004; The Path of Life, 2005; Inside, 2006; Blackstrap Hawco, 2008; Reinventing the Rose, 2011. Contributor to periodicals. **Address:** Publicity Department, Saint Martin's Press, 175 5th Ave., New York, NY 10010, U.S.A. **Online address:** kennethjharvey@hotmail.com

HARVEY, P(aul) D(ean) A(dshead). British (born England), b. 1930. **Genres:** Geography, History, Social Sciences. **Career:** Warwick County Record Office, assistant archivist, 1954-56; British Museum, Department of Manuscripts, assistant keeper, 1957-66; Royal Historical Society, fellow, 1961; Society of Antiquaries, fellow, 1962; University of Southampton, lecturer, 1966-70, senior lecturer in medieval economic and social history, 1970-78; Surtees Society, vice president, 1978; University of Durham, professor, 1978-85, professor emeritus of medieval history, 1985-. Writer. **Publications:** (With H. Thorpe) Printed Maps of Warwickshire 1576-1900, 1959; A Medieval Oxfordshire Village: Cuxham 1240-1400, 1965; The History of Topographical Maps: Symbols, Pictures and Surveys, 1980; Manorial Records, 1984; Medieval Maps, 1991; Maps in Tudor England, 1993; (with A. McGuinness) Guide to British Medieval Seals, 1996; Mappa Mundi: The Hereford World Map, 1996; Editing Historical Records, 2001; Maps in the Age of Bede, 2006; Manors and Maps in Rural England, from the Tenth Century to the Seventeenth, 2010. EDITOR: (with W. Albert) Portsmouth and Sheet Turnpike Commissioners' Minute Book 1711-1754, 1973; Manorial Records of Cuxham, Oxfordshire, circa 1200-1359, 1976; The Peasant Land Market in Medieval England, 1984; (with R.A. Skelton) Local Maps and Plans from Medieval England, 1986; Hereford World Map: Medieval World Maps and Their Context, 2006. Contributor to periodicals. **Address:** Deparment of History, Durham University, 43 N Bailey, Durham, DU DH1 3EX, England.

HARVEY, Paul William. American (born United States), b. 1961. **Genres:** Cultural/Ethnic Topics. **Career:** University of California, lecturer, 1992; University of Colorado, Colorado College, visiting professor, 1991, 1993, 1996, assistant professor, 1996-2000, associate professor, 2000-04, professor of history, 2004-. Writer. **Publications:** Redeeming the South: Religious Cultures and Racial Identities among Southern Baptists, 1865-1925, 1997; (ed. with P. Goff) Themes in Religion and American Culture, 2004; (ed. with P. Goff) The Columbia Documentary History of Religion in America since 1945, 2005; Freedom's Coming: Religious Culture and the Shaping of the South from the Civil War through the Civil Rights Era, 2005. Contributor to journals. **Address:** Department of History, University of Colorado, Colorado Springs, CO 80933-7150, U.S.A. **Online address:** pharvey@mail.uccs.edu

HARVEY, Robert C. American (born United States), b. 1937. **Genres:** Art/Art History, Biography, Cartoons, Humor/Satire, Theology/Religion. **Career:** Wyandotte High School, English teacher, 1964-69; National Council of Teachers of English, Educational Resources Information Center Clearinghouse, assistant director, 1969-70, convention director, 1971-97, retired, 1977. Freelance commercial artist, writer and cartoonist. **Publications:** Restless Heart: Breaking the Cycle of Social Identity, 1973; The Art of the Funnies: An Aesthetic History, 1994; The Art of the Comic Book: An Aesthetic History, 1996; The Genius of Winsor McCay, 1998; Children of the Yellow Kid: The Evolution of the American Comic Strip, 1998; A Gallery of Rogues: Cartoonists' Self-Caricatures, 1998; (with G. Arriola) Accidental Ambassador Gordo: The Comic Strip Art of Gus Arriola, 2000; To the Isles Afar Off, 2009. EDITOR AND COMPILER: Cartoons of the Roaring Twenties, vol. I: 1920-22, 1991, vol. II, 1923-25, 1992; Milton Caniff Conversations, 2002. Contributor of articles to magazines and periodicals. **Address:** 2701 Maplewood Dr., Champaign, IL 61821, U.S.A. **Online address:** rc_harvey@q.com

HARVEY, Steven. American (born United States), b. 1949. **Genres:** Poetry, Adult Non-fiction, Music, Autobiography/Memoirs. **Career:** English teacher, 1974-76; Young Harris College, professor of English, 1976-, G. Milton Goolsby and Ophelia Roberts Goolsby chair of English; John C. Campbell Folk School, writing instructor, 1995-. Writer. **Publications:** Powerlines (poems), 1976; A Geometry of Lilies: Life and Death in an American Family (nonfiction), 1993; (ed.) In a Dark Wood: Personal Essays by Men on Middle Age, 1996; Lost in Translation (nonfiction), 1997; Bound for Shady Grove, 2000. Works appear in anthologies. Contributor of articles to periodicals. **Address:** Department of English, Young Harris College, 1 College St., PO Box 68, Young Harris, GA 30582, U.S.A. **Online address:** sharvey@yhc.edu

HARVEY, Susan Ashbrook. American (born United States), b. 1953?. **Genres:** Adult Non-fiction, History, Translations. **Career:** University of Birmingham, Department of Theology, instructor in Syriac, 1978-82, assistant in New Testament Greek, 1981-82, Centre for Byzantine Studies, instructor in Syriac, 1978-82, Department of Extramural Studies, lecturer in theology, 1980-82; University of North Carolina, Department of Religious Studies, lecturer in New Testament studies and Christian origins, 1982-83; University of Rochester, Department of Religious and Classical Studies, assistant professor of religious studies, 1983-87; Brown University, Department of Religious Studies, assistant professor of religious studies, 1987-91, associate professor of religious studies, 1991-2002, director of graduate studies, 1992-93, 1995-2000, 2001-04, professor of religious studies, 2002-08, director of undergraduate studies, 2005-07, Willard Prescott and Annie McClelland Smith professor of religious studies, 2008-, Program in Ancient Studies, director, 1997-2000. Writer. **Publications:** (Trans. and intro. with S.P. Brock) Holy Women of the Syrian Orient, 1987; Asceticism and Society in Crisis: John of Ephesus and the Lives of the Eastern Saints, 1990; Scenting Salvation: Ancient Christianity and the Olfactory Imagination, 2006; (ed. with D.G. Hunter) Oxford Handbook of Early Christian Studies, 2008; (trans. and intro. with O. Münz-Manor) Jacob of Sarug's Homily on Jephthah's Daughter, 2009; Song And Memory: Biblical Women In Syriac Tradition, 2010. **Address:** Department of Religious Studies, Brown University, 59 George St., PO Box 1927, Providence, RI 02912, U.S.A. **Online address:** susan_harvey@brown.edu

HARVEY, Thomas. Singaporean/American (born United States), b. 1956. **Genres:** Politics/Government, Theology/Religion. **Career:** Fuxin Mining Institute, English instructor; Guangzhou Foreign Language Institute, instructor in American cultural studies; Trinity Avenue Presbyterian Church, director of Christian education; Trinity Theological College, lecturer of systematic theology and ethics, 1997-; The Oxford Centre for Mission Studies, dean, 2008-. Writer and educator. **Publications:** Acquainted with Grief: Wang Mingdao's Stand for the Persecuted Church in China, 2002; Tension, Tradition and Transformation: Global Christianity's Impact on Theology and Ethics, forthcoming. Contributor to periodicals. **Address:** Department of Theology and Ethics, Trinity Theological College, 490 Upper Bukit, Timah, 678093, Singapore. **Online address:** tharvey@ttc.edu.sg

HARVIE, Christopher (Thomas). Scottish (born Scotland), b. 1944. **Genres:** History. **Career:** Held Labour Party posts, 1962-80; Edinburgh University, tutorial assistant in history, 1968-69; Open University, lecturer in history, 1969-80, acting head, 1975, 1978-80, senior lecturer in history, 1978-80; Merton College, visiting research fellow, 1973; Edinburgh University, visiting research fellow, 1978-79; University of Tuebingen, professor of British studies, 1980-, deputy director of seminar, 1981-82, director, 1982-83, 1986-87, 1989, 1992-2003, 2001-02; Strathclyde University, visiting professor of history, 1988-89; Scottish Centre for Social and Economic Research, vice-president, 1990-99; University College, honorary research fellow, 1994; University of Wales, honorary professor of politics, 1996; Strathclyde University, honorary professor of history, 1999-; Scottish Association for Public Transport, president, 2002-. Writer. **Publications:** War and Society in the Nineteenth Century, 1973; The Lights of Liberalism: University Liberals and the Challenge of Democracy, 1860-1886, 1976; Scotland and Nationalism: Scottish Society and Politics, 1707-1977, 1977, 4th ed., 2004; No Gods and Precious Few Heroes: Scotland, 1914-1980, 1981, 3rd ed. as No Gods and Precious Few Heroes: Twentieth-Century Scotland, 1997; Against Metropolis, 1982; (with A. Marwick) Britain Today: The Economy, 1985, rev. ed., 1993; Britain Today: Politics and Society, 1985, rev. ed., 1992; The Centre of Things: Political Fiction in Britain from Disraeli to the Present, 1991; Cultural Weapons, Scotland and Survival in a New Europe, 1992; (contrib.) The Oxford History of Britain, vol. IV: The Eighteenth Century and the Age of Industry, 1992; Fool's Gold: The Story of North Sea Oil, 1994; The Rise of Regional Europe, 1994; Europe and the Welsh Nation, 1995; Travelling Scot: Scotus Viator: Essays on the History, Politics and Future of the Scots, 1999; (with P. Jones) The Road to Home Rule: Images of Scotland's Cause, 1999; Nineteenth-Century Britain: A Very Short Introduction, 2000; Deep-Fried Hillman Imp: Scotland's Transport, 2001; Scotland: A Short History, 2002; Mending Scotland: Essays in Regional Economics, 2004; Floating Commonwealth: Politics, Culture and Technology on Britain's Atlantic Coast, 1860-1930, 2008; Broonland: The Last Days of Gordon Brown, 2010; Scotland the Brief: A Short History of a Nation, 2010. EDITOR: (with G. Martin and A. Scharf) Industrialisation and Culture, 1830-1914, 1970; (with A. Marwick, C. Knightly and K. Wrightson) The Illustrated Dictionary of British History, 1981; (with I. Donnachie and I.S. Wood) Forward: Labour Politics in Scotland, 1888-1988, 1989; (and intro.) The Thirty Nine Steps, 1999. **Address:** University of Tuebingen, 50 Wilhelmstrasse, Tuebingen, 72074, Germany. **Online address:** christopher.harvie@uni-tuebingen.de

HARVOR, Beth. *See* **HARVOR, Elisabeth.**

HARVOR, Elisabeth. (Beth Harvor). Canadian (born Canada), b. 1936. **Genres:** Novels, Novellas/Short Stories, Poetry, inspirational/Motivational Literature, Young Adult Fiction. **Career:** Algonquin College, conductor of workshops on women and writing, 1973-76; Concordia University, sessional lecturer, 1986-87, 1995-97, writer-in-residence, 1996-97; York University, sessional lecturer in writing program, 1987-93; Ottawa Public Library and Carleton University, writer-in-residence, 1993-94; University of New Brunswick, writer-in-residence, 1994-95, instructor, 1995; Humber School for Writers, instructor, 1996-98, 2000-03; Saskatoon Public Library, writer-in-residence, 1998-99. Writer. **Publications:** STORIES: Women and Children, 1973, rev. ed. as Our Lady of All the Distances, 1991; If Only We Could Drive Like This Forever, 1988, rev. ed., 2004; Let Me Be the One, 1996. POEMS: Fortress of Chairs, 1992; The Long Cold Green Evenings of Spring, 1997; (ed.) A Room at the Heart of Things: The Work That Came to Me, 1997; Open Door in the Landscape, 2010. NOVELS: Excessive Joy Injures the Heart, 2000; (contrib.) Rising to a Tension: New Short Fiction by Thirteen Writers [under] 25, 2003; All Times Have Been Modern, 2004. Works appear in anthologies. Contributor to periodicals and newspapers. **Address:** c/o Writers' Union of Canada, 90 Richmond St. E, Ste. 200, Toronto, ON M5E 1C7, Canada. **Online address:** eharvor@sympatico.ca

HARWIT, Eric. American (born United States), b. 1962?. **Genres:** Business/Trade/Industry, Communications/Media. **Career:** University of Hawaii, professor of Asian studies. Writer. **Publications:** China's Automobile Industry: Policies, Problems, and Prospects, 1995; China's Telecommunications Revolution, 2008. Contributor to journals. **Address:** U.S.A. **Online address:** harwit@hawaii.edu

HARWOOD, (Henry) David. British (born England), b. 1938. **Genres:** Children's Fiction, Children's Non-fiction, Demography, Gerontology/Senior Issues, Medicine/Health, Sports/Fitness. **Career:** Medical Research Council, administrative officer, 1960-66; freelance writer, typographical designer and photographer, 1966-70; Wiltshire County Council, youth and community service officer, 1970-74; Filton Technical College, lecturer and marketing officer, 1974-96; Age Concern South Gloucestershire, chief officer, 1996. **Publications:** Scouts in Action, 1963; Scouts on Safari, 1965; The Scout Handbook, 1967; Scouts Indeed!, 1967; Alert to Danger!, 1969; How to Read Maps, 1970; Exploring Your Neighborhood, 1970; Scouts, 1971; Cub Scouts, 1971; The Extension Activities Handbook, 1972; (ed.) Cub Scout Annual, 1977; Learn about Camping, 1977; Car Games, 1978; Butterflies, 1990; Alumni Relations, 1995; Survey of People Aged 50+ in South Gloucestershire, 1997; Goat Health and Welfare: A Veterinary Guide, 2006. EDITOR: (with V. Peters) The Bronze Arrow, 1973; (with V. Peters) The Silver Arrow, 1973; (with V. Peters) The Gold Arrow, 1973; The International Cub Scout Book, 1980; Older & Bolder: Extending Learning Opportunities for Older People, 1999. **Address:** The Scout Association, Gilwell Park, Chingford, GL E4 7QW, England.

HARWOOD, John. Australian (born Australia), b. 1946. **Genres:** Novels, Ghost Writer, Young Adult Fiction, Biography, Autobiography/Memoirs, Humanities. **Career:** Flinders University, professor of English. Writer. **Publications:** Olivia Shakespear and W. B. Yeats: After Long Silence, 1989; Eliot to Derrida: The Poverty of Interpretation, 1995; The Ghost Writer, 2004; Séance, 2008. **Address:** c/o Author Mail, Harcourt, 6277 Sea Harbor Dr., Orlando, FL 32887-0001, U.S.A.

HARWOOD, John. American (born United States), b. 1956. **Genres:** Politics/Government. **Career:** St. Petersburg Times, state capital correspondent, political editor, Washington correspondent, 1978-91; Wall Street Journal, political editor, congressional correspondent, 1991-97, political editor and chief political correspondent, 1997-; New York Times, political correspondent; CNBC, chief Washington correspondent, 2006-. Journalist. **Publications:** (with G. Seib) Pennsylvania Avenue: Profiles in Backroom Power, 2008. **Address:** Wall Street Journal, 1025 Connecticut Ave. NW, Washington, DC 20036-5405, U.S.A. **Online address:** johnharwood@news.wsj.com

HARWOOD, Melanie. *See* **MURPHEY, Cecil B(laine).**

HARWOOD, Ronald. British/South African (born South Africa), b. 1934. **Genres:** Novels, Plays/Screenplays, Biography, Novellas/Short Stories, Young Adult Non-fiction, Plays/Screenplays. **Career:** Balliol College, visitor in theatre, 1986; English P.E.N., president, 1989-93; International P.E.N., president, 1993-97. Writer. **Publications:** All the Same Shadows, 1961 in US as George Washington September Sir!, 1961; The Guilt Merchants, 1963; The Girl in Melanie Klein, 1969; Sir Donald Wolfit: His Life and Work in the Unfashionable Theatre, 1971; Articles of Faith, 1973; The Genoa Ferry, 1976; César and Augusta, 1978; One. Interior Day Adventures in the Film Trade, 1978; A Family, 1978; The Dresser, 1980; After the Lions, 1982; The Ordeal of Gilbert Pinfold, 1983; All the World's a Stage, 1984; Tramway Road, 1984; The Deliberate Death of a Polish Priest, 1985; Interpreters, 1985; J.J. Farr, 1987; Mandela, 1987; Ivanov, 1989; Reflected Glory, 1992; Home, 1993; The Faber Book of Theatre, 1993; The Handyman, 1996; Taking Sides, 1997; Quartet & Equally Divided, 1999; Mahler's Conversion, 2001; Ronald Harwood's Adaptations: From Other Works Into Films, 2007; Heavenly Ivy: An Entertainment, 2010. EDITOR: (co-ed.) New Stories 3, 1978; A Night at the Theatre, 1982; The Ages of Gielgud, 1984; Dear Alec: Guinness at 75, 1989; Faber Book of the Theatre, 1993. **Address:** Judy Daish Associates Ltd., 2 St. Charles Pl., London, GL W10 6EG, England.

HASAN, Anjum. Indian (born India), b. 1972?. **Genres:** Novels, Poetry, Literary Criticism And History. **Career:** India Foundation for the Arts, Arts Connect, communications editor. **Publications:** Street on the Hill, 2006; Lunatic in My Head, 2007; Neti, Neti=Not This, Not This, 2009. Contributor to periodicals. **Address:** Zubaan Books, 128 B, 1st Fl.,, Shahpur Jat, New Delhi, DH 110049, India. **Online address:** a.hasan@kent.ac.uk

HASAN, Ruqaiya. Australian/Indian (born India) **Genres:** Novels, Language/Linguistics, Art/Art History, Psychology. **Career:** Macquarie University, professor, emeritus professor of linguistics, 1994-. Writer. **Publications:** The Language of Eight-Year-Old Children, 1964; The Language of Nine-Year-Old Children, 1965; The Language of Ten-Year-Old Children, 1966; Child Language Survey: Grammatical Analysis Code, 1967; The Written Language of Nine and Ten Year Old Children, 1967; Grammatical Cohesion in Spoken and Written English, 1968; (with S. Lushington) The Subject-Matter of English, 1968; The Language of Eleven-Year-Old Children: Transcript Number 4A, 1968; (with M.A.K. Halliday) Cohesion in English, 1976; Linguistics, Language and Verbal Art, 1985; Language, Context and Text: Aspects of Language in a Social-Semiotic Perspective, 1985; Ways of Saying, Ways of Meaning: Selected Papers of Ruqaiya Hasan, 1996; The Collected Works of Ruqaiya Hasan, 2005; Language, Society and Consciousness, 2005; Semantic Variation: Meaning in Society and in Sociolinguistics, 2009; Language and Education: Learning and Teaching in Society, 2010; Context in the System and Process of Language, vol. IV, 2012; Describing Language: Form and Function, vol. V, 2012; Unity in Discourse: Texture and Structure, vol. VI, 2012; Verbal Art: A Social Semiotic Perspective, 2013. EDITOR: Discourse on Discourse: Workshop Reports from the Macquarie Workshop on Discourse Analysis, February 21-25, 1983, 1985; (with J.R. Martin) Language Development: Learning Language, Learning Culture, 1989; (with P.H. Fries) On Subject and Theme: A Discourse Functional Perspective, 1995; (with G. Williams) Literacy in Society, 1996; (with C. Cloran and D.G. Butt) Functional Descriptions: Theory in Practice, 1996; (with O.N. Koul and S.I. Hasanain) Linguistics, Theoretical And Applied: A Festschrift for Ruqaiya Hasan, 2004; (with C. Matthiessen and J. Webster) Continuing Discourse on Language: A Functional Perspective, 2005. **Address:** Department of Linguistics, Macquarie University, C5A Bldg., Rm. 508, 5th Fl., Balaclava Rd., North Ryde, NW 2109, Australia. **Online address:** rhasan@laurel.ocs.mq.edu.au

HASBURGH, Patrick. American (born United States) **Genres:** Novels, Humor/Satire. **Career:** Television writer, editor and producer. **Publications:** Aspen Pulp, 2004. Contributor to periodicals. **Address:** c/o Author Mail, Thomas Dunne Books, 175 5th Ave., New York, NY 10010-7703, U.S.A.

HASELEY, Dennis. American (born United States), b. 1950. **Genres:** Children's Fiction, Young Adult Fiction, Photography, Novels. **Career:** Jewish Board of Family and Children's Services, therapist, 1982-86; writer, 1982-; private practice in psychotherapy, 1984-. Educator. **Publications:** FOR CHILDREN: The Scared One, 1983; The Old Banjo, 1983; The Pirate Who Tried to Capture the Moon, 1983; The Soap Bandit, 1984; The Kite Flier, 1986; The Cave of Snores, 1987; My Father Doesn't Know about the Woods and Me, 1988; Ghost Catcher, 1991; The Thieves' Market, 1991; Horses with Wings, 1993; Crosby, 1996; A Story for Bear, 2002; Photographer Mole, 2004; Invisible Moose, 2005; Sky Writer, 2008. YOUNG-ADULT NOVELS: The Counterfeiter, 1987; Shadows, 1991; Dr. Gravity, 1992; Getting Him, 1994; Amazing Thinking Machine, 2002; Trick of the Eye, 2004; Twenty Heartbeats, 2008. Contributor to periodicals. **Address:** Wendy Schmalz Agency, PO Box 831, Hudson, NY 12534-0831, U.S.A.

HASENFELD, Yeheskel. American (born United States), b. 1937. **Genres:** Social Sciences, Institutions/Organizations, History. **Career:** University of Michigan, School of Social Work, assistant professor, 1970-79, professor, 1979-86, associate dean, 1981-86; University of California, School of Public Policy and Social Research, professor, 1987-. Writer. **Publications:** Manpower Placement: Service Delivery for the Hard-to-Employ, 1973; (comp. with R.A. English) Human Service Organizations: A Book of Readings, 1974; Human Service Organizations, 1983; (with H. Shmid and D. Bar-Gal) Minhal ha-matnas: tehu pe'ulah veu-tifkud, 1987; Ha-Nihul shel sherute enosh: Mah tsafui ba-'atid?, 1997; Mi-revahah la- 'avodah, hafratah ve-ezrahut hevratit: Bi-re'i ha-metsiy'ut, 2006. EDITOR: (with R.C. Sarri) Brought to Justice? Juveniles, the Courts, and the Law, 1976; (with R.C. Sarri) The Management of Human Services, 1978; Administrative Leadership in the Social Services: The Next Challenge, 1989; Human Services as Complex Organizations, 1992; (with B. Gidron and S.N. Katz) Mobilizing for Peace: Conflict Resolution in Northern Ireland, Israel/ Palestine, and South Africa, 2002. WITH J.F. HANDLER: The Moral Construction of Poverty: Welfare Reform in America, 1991; We the Poor People: Work, Poverty, and Welfare, 1997; Blame Welfare, Ignore Poverty and Inequality, 2007. **Address:** Department of Social Welfare, School of Public Policy and Social Research, University of California, 3250 Public Policy Bldg., PO Box 951656, Los Angeles, CA 90095-1656, U.S.A. **Online address:** zekeh@ucla.edu

HASHMI, (Aurangzeb) Alamgir. Pakistani (born Pakistan), b. 1951. **Genres:** Literary Criticism And History, Poetry, Novellas/Short Stories, Essays, Translations, Reference, Classics, Theatre, Theatre, Social Sciences. **Career:** Pakistan Broadcasting Corp., broadcaster, lecturer, editor and translator, 1968-74, 1988-; Government College, instructor, 1971-72, tutor in English, 1972-73; Forman Christian College, lecturer in English, 1973-74; University of Louisville, lecturer in English, 1975-78; University of Bahawalpur, assistant professor of English, 1979-80; University of Zurich, lecturer in English, 1980-85, visiting lecturer in English, 1982-; University of Bern, lecturer, 1982; University of Basel, lecturer, 1982; International Islamic University, associate professor of English, 1985-86; University of Fribourg, visiting professor of English and comparative literature, 1985-; Federal Government Postgraduate College for Men, visiting professor of English literature, 1986; University of Azad Jammu and Kashmir, professor of English and head of department, 1986-87; Quaid-i-Azam University, visiting professor of American and African literatures, 1986; Townsend Poetry Prize, founder, 1986; Pakistan Ministry of Foreign Affairs, Foreign Service Training Institute, course director, 1988-; Pakistan Institute of Development Economics, Publications Division, literary editor and chief, 1988-2011; University of Iceland, visiting professor of English and comparative literature, 1999-2000; The Literature Podium, founding president, 2011-. **Publications:** The Oath and Amen: Love Poems, 1976; (ed.) Pakistani Literature, 1978, 2 vols., 2nd ed. as Pakistani Literature: The Contemporary English Writers, 1987; America Is a Punjabi Word, 1979; An Old Chair, 1979; My Second in Kentucky: Poems, 1981; Commonwealth Literature: An Essay Towards the Re-Definition of a Popular/Counter Culture, 1983; This Time in Lahore: New Poems, 1983; Ezra Pound, 1983; Neither This Time/Nor That Place, 1984; (ed. and contrib.) The Worlds of Muslim Imagination, 1986; Pakistani Literature: The Contemporary English Writers, 1987; Inland and Other Poems, 1988; The Commonwealth, Comparative Literature and the World, 1988; The Poems of Alamgir Hashmi, 1992; Sun and Moon and Other Poems, 1992; (ed.) Encyclopedia of Post-Colonial Literatures in English, 1994; A Choice of Hashmi's Verse, 1997; Pakistani Short Stories in English, 1997; (co-ed.) Post-Independence Voices in South Asian Writings, 2001; The Ramazan Libation: Selected Poems, 2003; (ed.) Your Essence, Martyr, 2011. Contributor to books and periodicals. **Address:** 1542 Service Rd. W, G-11/2, Islamabad, 44000, Pakistan. **Online address:** alamgirhashmi@hotmail.com

HASKELL, Guy H. American (born United States), b. 1956. **Genres:** Area Studies, Medicine/Health, Social Sciences, Autobiography/Memoirs, Novels. **Career:** Indiana University, associate instructor in near eastern languages and culture, 1978-80, 1982-85, Kinesiology Department, adjunct faculty; Bnai Brith Hillel Foundation, interim director, 1981-82; Oberlin College, lecturer, 1985-88, Judaic and Near Eastern studies, assistant professor, 1988-94, director, 1991-94; Emory University, Judaic and Near Eastern languages and literatures, visiting assistant professor, 1994-98; Quinsigamond Community College, Department of Emergency Medical Services, associate professor, director, 1998-2000; Bloomington Hospital, Indiana Emergency Medical Services Academy, academic director, 2000-03; Monroe County Indiana, deputy prosecutor, 2007-; Journal of Emergency Medical Services, columnist; State University of New York, faculty; Wooster College, faculty; Ohio State University, faculty. **Publications:** From Sofia to Jaffa: The Jews of Bulgaria and Israel, 1994; Emergency Medical Technician-Basic Pearls of Wisdom, 1999; EMT-Intermediate P.O.W., 1999, 2nd ed., 2009; Paramedic P.O.W., 2000; Pediatric Advanced Life Support, 2005, 3rd ed., 2007; (ed.) PALS Review, 2006. Contributor to books and journals. **Address:** Office of the Monroe County Prosecutor, 301 N College Ave., Bloomington, IN 47404, U.S.A. **Online address:** ghaskell@indiana.edu

HASKELL, Molly. American (born United States), b. 1939. **Genres:** Film, Women's Studies And Issues, Autobiography/Memoirs, Plays/Screenplays, Adult Non-fiction, Art/Art History, History, Literary Criticism And History, Young Adult Non-fiction. **Career:** Barnard College, associate professor of film, 1989-; Columbia University, adjunct professor of film; Sarah Lawrence College, Graduate Writing Program, staff. Writer and film critic. **Publications:** From Reverence to Rape: The Treatment of Women in the Movies, 1973, 2nd ed., 1987; Love and Other Infectious Diseases: A Memoir, 1990; Holding My Own In No Man's Land: Women and Men, Film and Feminists, 1997; (intro.) Leading Men: The 50 Most Unforgettable Actors of the Studio Era, 2006; (intro.) Leading Ladies: The 50 Most Unforgettable Actresses of the Studio Era, 2006; Frankly, My Dear: Gone with the Wind Revisited, 2009. Contributor to periodicals. **Address:** 19 E 88th St., New York, NY 10128, U.S.A. **Online address:** haskmoll@gmail.com

HASKETT, Robert. (Robert Stephen Haskett). American (born United States), b. 1952. **Genres:** History. **Career:** University of Oregon, assistant professor, 1987-93, associate professor, 1993-2003, professor of Latin American history, 2003-, director of the history department undergraduate program. Writer. **Publications:** Indigenous Rulers: An Ethnohistory of Town Government in Colonial Cuernavaca, 1991; (ed. with S. Schroeder and S. Wood) Indian Women of Early Mexico, 1997; Visions of Paradise: Primordial Titles and Mesoamerican History in Cuernavaca, 2005. Contributor to books and journals. **Address:** Department of History, University of Oregon, 355 McKenzie Hall, Eugene, OR 97403-1288, U.S.A. **Online address:** rhaskett@uoregon.edu

HASKETT, Robert Stephen. See **HASKETT**, Robert.

HASKINS, Michael. American (born United States) **Genres:** Novels. **Career:** Key West Citizen, business editor/writer. **Publications:** Chasin' the Wind (novel), 2008. Contributor to periodicals. **Address:** Key West, FL , U.S.A. **Online address:** info@michaelhaskins.net

HASKINS, Scott (M.). (Andre Hawkins). American (born United States), b. 1953. **Genres:** Antiques/Furnishings, Social Sciences, History. **Career:** Lombardy regional conservation center, conservator, 1975-78; Brigham Young University, director of conservation, 1978-84; Art Conservation Laboratories, chief paintings conservator, 1984-86; Fine Art Conservation Laboratories, chief conservator, 1984-, director, 1986-. Writer and consultant. **Publications:** The Emergency Care Book for Your Possessions, 1994; How to Save Your Stuff from a Disaster: Complete Instructions On How to Protect and Save Your Family History, Heirlooms and Collectibles, 1996. **Address:** Fine Art Conservation Laboratories, PO Box 23557, Santa Barbara, CA 93121, U.S.A. **Online address:** artdoc@earthlink.net

HASLAM, Gerald William. American (born United States), b. 1937. **Genres:** Novels, Novellas/Short Stories, Literary Criticism And History, Autobiography/Memoirs, Essays, Humor/Satire, Children's Fiction, Young Adult Fiction, Young Adult Fiction. **Career:** San Francisco State College, instructor in English, 1966-67; Sonoma State University, professor of English, 1967-97, professor emeritus, 1997-; Union Graduate School, adjunct professor, 1984-; The National Faculty, adjunct professor, 1984-; KQED-FM, commentator, 1997-2004; University of San Francisco, Fromm Institute, adjunct professor, 2001-; Osher Lifelong Learning Institute, adjunct professor, 2003-; Los Angeles Times Magazine West, contributing writer, 2006-. Educator and writer. **Publications:** EDITOR: (and intro.) Western Writing, 1974; Afro-American Oral Literature, 1974; (with J.D. Houston) California Heartland: Writing from the Great Central Valley, 1978; (with J.G. Taylor) A Literary History of the American West, 1987; Many California's: Literature from the Golden State, 1992, 2nd ed., 1999; (with A.R. Haslam) Where Coyotes Howl and Wind Blows Free: Growing up in the West (juvenile), 1995; Jack London's Golden State: Selected California Writings, 1999. FICTION: Okies: Selected Stories, 1973; Masks: A Novel, 1976; The Wages of Sin: Stories, 1980; Hawk Flights: Visions of the West, 1983; Snapshots: Glimpses of the Other California, 1985; The Man Who Cultivated Fire and Other Stories, 1987; That Constant Coyote: California Stories, 1990; Condor Dreams and Other Fictions, 1994; The Great Tejon Club Jubilee, 1996; (J.E. Haslam) Manuel and the Madman, 2000; Straight White Male, 2000. NONFICTION: The Language of the Oil Fields: Examination of an Industrial Argot, 1972; Voices of a Place: The Great Central Valley, 1986 as Voices of a Place: Social and Literary Essays from the Other California, 1987; Baiting the Hook, 1990; Coming of Age in California: Personal Essays, 1990, 2nd ed., 2000; The Other California: The Great Central Valley in Life and Letters, 1990, rev. ed., 1994; (with S. Glasser) Out of the Slush Pile, 1993; (with A.H. Russell and R. Chon) Workin' Man Blues: Country Music in California, 1999; (with J. Haslam) In Thought and Action: The Enigmatic Life of S. I. Hayakawa, 2011. OTHER: Forgotten Pages of American Literature, 1970; William Eastlake, 1970; Jack Schaefer, 1976; Prettyfields: A Work in Progress, 1987; Lawrence Clark Powell, 1992; The Great Central Valley: California's Heartland, 1993; The Horned Toad, 1995; Grace Period: A Novel, 2006. **Address:** PO Box 969, Penngrove, CA 94951-0969, U.S.A. **Online address:** ghaslam@sonic.net

HASLAM, Jonathan George. British (born England), b. 1951. **Genres:** Social Sciences, History. **Career:** University of Birmingham, lecturer, 1975-84; Johns Hopkins University, associate professor, 1984-86; University of Cambridge, King's College, senior research fellow, 1988-92, Department of Politics and International Studies, professor of history of international relations, 1992-, Corpus Christi College, fellow, 1994-; Stanford University, visiting associate professor, 1986-87, Quondam Visiting Professor of History, 1994, 2005; University of California, visiting associate professor, 1987-88; Yale University, visiting professor of history, 1996; Harvard University, visiting professor of government, 2001. Writer. **Publications:** Soviet Foreign Policy, 1930-33: The Impact of the Depression, 1983; The Soviet Union and the Struggle for Collective Security in Europe, 1933-39, 1984; (ed. with G.W. Lapidus) Reforming Socialist Systems: The Chinese and Soviet Experiences: A Conference Report, 1987; The Soviet Union and the Politics of Nuclear Weapons in Europe, 1969-87, 1990; The Soviet Union and the Threat from the East, 1933-41: Moscow, Tokyo, and the Prelude to the Pacific War, 1992; (ed. with T. Hasegawa and A. Kuchins) Russia and Japan: An Unresolved Dilemma between Distant Neighbors, 1993; The Vices of Integrity: A Biography of E.H. Carr, 1999; No Virtue Like Necessity: Realist Thought in International Relations since Machiavelli, 2002; The Nixon Administration and the Death of Allende's Chile: A Case of Assisted Suicide, 2005; Russia's Cold War: From the October Revolution to the Fall of the Wall, 2011. IN RUSSIAN-CO-EDITOR: Rossiia I SShA: Diplomaticheskie Otnosheniia 1900-1917, 1999; Sovetsko-Amerikanskie Otnosheniia: Gody Nepriznaniia, 1918-1926, 2002; Sovetsko-Amerikanskie Otnosheniia: Gody Nepriznaniia, 1927-1933, 2002. **Address:** Department of Politics and International Studies, University of Cambridge, Alison Richard Bldg., 1st Fl., 7 West Rd., Cambridge, CB CB3 9DT, England. **Online address:** jgh1001@cam.ac.uk

HASLAM, Nicholas. British (born England), b. 1939. **Genres:** Autobiography/Memoirs. **Career:** Vogue, assistant art director; Show, art director; NH Design, founder and interior designer; Tatler Magazine, contributing editor; British Vogue, contributing editor; Ritz Newspaper, gossip columnist. **Publications:** Sheer Opulence, 2002; Redeeming Features (memoir), 2009. Contributor to periodicals. **Address:** NH Design, 243-247 Pavilion Rd., London, GL SW1X 0BP, England. **Online address:** info@nh-design.co.uk

HASLER, Julie. (Julie S. Hasler). Canadian (born Canada), b. 1963. **Genres:** Philosophy, Politics/Government, Social Sciences, Crafts, Homes/Gardens. **Career:** Review (newspaper), pasteup artist, 1978-80; Welwyn Hatfield Line, bus driver, 1986-87. Writer. **Publications:** (As Julie S. Hasler) Cats and Kittens Charted Designs, 1986; Kate Greenaway Alphabet Charted Designs, 1986; Peter Rabbit Iron-On Transfer Patterns, 1987; (as Julie S. Hasler) Wild Flowers in Cross Stitch: Charted Designs, 1988; (as Julie S. Hasler) Dogs and Puppies in Cross Stitch: Charted Designs, 1988; Kate Greenaway Cross Stitch Designs, 1989; Kate Greenaway Iron-On Transfer Patterns, 1990; The Little Tale of Benjamin Bunny, 1990; The Little Tale of Tom Kitten, 1991; The Crafty Cat Workbasket, 1991; Needlepoint Designs: Cushions, Pictures, Cov-

ers, 1991; Egyptian Charted Designs, 1992; Cats & Kittens in Cross Stitch, 1992; (as Julie S. Hasler) Decorative Charted Designs for Children's Clothing and Accessories, 1993; Decorative Charted Designs: 114 Motifs, 1993; Wild Animals in Cross Stitch, 1993; (with V. Janitch) 500 Cross Stitch Charted Designs, 1993; Cuddly Cats and Kittens in Cross Stitch, 1993; Silhouettes in Cross Stitch, 1993; Cats: A Cross Stitch Alphabet, 1993; Teddy Bears in Cross Stitch, 1994; Christmas in Cross Stitch, 1994; Julie Hasler's Cross Stitch Designs, 1994; Nursery Cross Stitch, 1995; Clowns in Cross Stitch, 1996; Cross Stitch Gifts for Special Occasions, 1996; (with Janitch) Five Hundred Flower and Animal Charted Designs, 1996; Julie Hasler's Cross Stitch Projects, 1996; Julie Hasler's Fantasy Cross Stitch, Zodiac Signs, Mythical Beasts, and Mystical Characters, 1997; (with Janitch) 500 Alphabets in Cross Stitch, 1998; Needlepoint Cats, 1998; Native American Cross Stitch, 1999. Contributor to needlecraft books and periodicals. **Address:** David & Charles Publishing, F&W Media International Ltd., Brunel House, Forde Close, Newton Abbot, DN TQ12 4PU, England.

HASLER, Julie S. See **HASLER, Julie.**

HASLETT, Adam. American (born United States), b. 1970. **Genres:** Novellas/Short Stories, Novels. **Career:** The University of Iowa, visiting professor; Columbia University, visiting professor, adjunct assistant professor. Attorney and writer. **Publications:** You Are Not a Stranger Here (stories), 2002; Adam Haslett on George Washington Rules of Civility, 2004; Union Atlantic: A Novel, 2009. Contributor to periodicals. **Address:** c/o Author Mail, Nan A Talese, Doubleday, 1540 Broadway, New York, NY 10036, U.S.A.

HASLUCK, Nicholas. Australian (born Australia), b. 1942. **Genres:** Novels, Novellas/Short Stories, Poetry, Children's Fiction, Essays. **Career:** Keall Brinsden (law firm), partner, 1970-84; Australia Council, deputy chairman, 1978-82; Freshwater Bay Press, proprietor, 1982-2000; Literature Board, chairman, 1998-2001; Commonwealth Writers Prize, chairman, 2006-; Supreme Court of Western Australia, judge. Writer. **Publications:** POETRY: Anchor and Other Poems, 1976; (with W. Grono) On the Edge, 1981; (with C.J. Koch) Chinese Journey, 1985; A Dream Divided, 2005. STORIES: The Hat on the Letter O and Other Stories, 1978, rev. ed., 1990. NOVELS: Quarantine, 1978, 2nd ed., 1979; The Blue Guitar, 1980; The Hand That Feeds You: A Satiric Nightmare, 1982; The Bellarmine Jug, 1984; Truant State, 1987; The Country Without Music, 1991; The Blosseville File, 1992; A Grain of Truth, 1994; Our Man K, 1999. ESSAYS: Collage: Recollections and Images of the University of Western Australia, 1987; Offcuts from a Legal Literary Life, 1993; The Chance of Politics, 1997; (ed. and author of intro.) The Legal Labyrinth: The Kisch Case and Other Reflections on Law and Literature, 2003; Somewhere in the Atlas, 2007. **Address:** 14 Reserve St., Claremont, WA 6010, Australia. **Online address:** hasluck@iinet.net.au

HASPIEL, Dean. American (born United States), b. 1967. **Genres:** Cartoons, Graphic Novels. **Career:** Upstart Studios, assistant illustrator; ACT-I-VATE.com, founder. Writer, artist, cartoonist and director. **Publications:** Daydream Lullabies: A Billy Dogma Experience, 1999; Opposable Thumbs, 2001; Boy In My Pocket, 2003; Aim To Dazzle, 2004; The Quitter, 2005; (contrib.) Scary Summer, 2007; (with J. Lynch) Mo and Jo: Fighting Together Forever, 2008. Illustrator of books by others. **Address:** 335 Court St., Ste. 131, Brooklyn, NY 11231, U.S.A. **Online address:** dean.haspiel@verizon.net

HASSAN, Aftab Syed. American/Pakistani (born Pakistan), b. 1952. **Genres:** Education, Information Science/Computers, Medicine/Health, Sciences. **Career:** Chesapeake Bay Tidewater Administration, fish physiology, research associate, 1979-88; Emerson Preparatory Institute, head of mathematics department, 1979-89, head of science department, 1979-89; Georgetown University, Department of Community and Academic Family Medicine, program coordinator for health careers programs, 1983-87; Betz Publishing Company Inc., Medical College Admission Test and Dental Admission Test Books, technical editor and coordinating author, 1984-90, Division of Scientific and Educational Research, director, 1991-94; Charles R. Drew University of Medicine and Science, consulting professor, 1985-86, Center for Educational Achievement, director, 1994-; University of California, instructor, 1986; Metropolitan Accounting Associates, vice president, 1987-88; Metropolitan Accounting and Research, owner, 1988-91; Washington Information Group, accounting manager and strategic research planner, 1988-90; Williams & Wilkins Educational Services, vice-president for academic development and strategic planning, 1994-; Planning at Metro Academic Research Institute, Academic Development and Strategic, consultant and vice president. Writer.

Publications: (With A. Braestrup) Skills Development in Reading, Writing and Quantitative on the MCAT, 4th ed., 1984; (with Braestrup) The MCAT Primer, 1985; (co-author) A Complete Preparation for the MCAT, 6th ed., 1991; (co-author) Preparing for the DAT, 1992; Establishing Nonparametric Discrimination Variables with Frequency Analysis for Two Pseudo-Identical Manuscripts, 1992; Design of Biological Sciences Software: Using Immersion Approach with Enhanced Problem Solving, 1992; (co-author) Dental Admission Test: The Betz Guide, 1993; A Personal MCAT Prep Planner, 1993; Preparing for the Optometry Admission Test: The Betz Guide, 2nd ed., 1993; Allied Health Professions Admission Test: The Betz Guide, 1994; Pharmacy College Admission Test: The Betz Guide, 1994; Veterinary Entrance Tests VETs: The Betz Guide, 1996. **Address:** American Society Landscape Architects, 636 Eye St. NW, Washington, DC 20001-3736, U.S.A.

HASSAN, Ihab (Habib). American/Egyptian (born Egypt), b. 1925. **Genres:** Literary Criticism And History, Autobiography/Memoirs. **Career:** Rensselaer Polytechnic Institute, instructor in English, 1952-54; Wesleyan University, instructor, 1954-55, assistant professor, 1955-58, associate professor, 1958-62, professor of English, 1962-63, Benjamin L. Waite professor of English, 1964-70, chairman of department, 1963-64, 1968-69, College of Letters, director, 1964-66, director of center for humanities, 1969-70; Indiana University, School of Letters, fellow, 1964; American Seminars at Salzburg, tutor, 1965, 1975; Fulbright lecturer, 1966-67, 1974-75; University of Wisconsin Milwaukee, Vilas research professor, 1970-99; Woodrow Wilson International Center for Scholars, visiting fellow, 1972; Kyoto Seminars in American Studies, Fulbright lecturer, 1974; Camargo Foundation, senior fellow, 1974-75; University of London, Institute of United States Studies, honorary research fellow, 1988; University of California, Humanities Research Institute, fellow, 1990; Seijo University, visiting professor, 1991. Writer. **Publications:** Radical Innocence: Studies in the Contemporary American Novel, 1961; Crisedu Heros Dans Le Roman Americain Contemporain, 1963; The Literature of Silence: Henry Miller and Samuel Beckett, 1968; The Dismemberment of Orpheus: Toward a Postmodern Literature, 1971, 2nd ed., 1982; Contemporary American Literature, 1945-1972: An Introduction, 1973; Paracriticisms: Seven Speculations of the Times, 1975; The Right Promethean Fire: Imagination, Science and Cultural Change, 1980; Out of Egypt: Scenes and Fragments of an Autobiography, 1986; The Postmodern Turn: Essays in Postmodern Theory and Culture, 1987; Ideology, Pragmatism and the Self: Toward an Independent Criticism, 1988; Selves at Risk: Patterns of Quest in Contemporary American Letters, 1990; Rumors of Change: Essays of Five Decades, 1995; Between the Eagle and the Sun: Traces of Japan, 1996; Return to Postmodernism: Theory, Travel Writing, Autobiography: Festschrift in Honour of Ihab Hassan, 2005; In Quest of Nothing: Selected Essays, 1998-2008. EDITOR: Liberations: New Essays on the Humanities in Revolution, 1971; (with S. Hassan) Innovation/Renovation: New Perspectives on the Humanities, 1983. **Address:** University of Wisconsin--Milwaukee, PO Box 413, Milwaukee, WI 53201, U.S.A.

HASSELSTROM, Linda (Michele). American (born United States), b. 1943. **Genres:** Poetry, Adult Non-fiction, Environmental Sciences/Ecology, Autobiography/Memoirs, Local History/Rural Topics, Regional/Urban Planning, Women's Studies And Issues, Autobiography/Memoirs, Essays. **Career:** Cattle rancher, 1953-; Sioux City Journal, reporter, staff, 1965-66; Christian College (now Columbia College), teacher of journalism, director of student publications, 1966-69; University of Missouri-Columbia, instructor in English, 1969-71; Lame Johnny Press, owner and publisher, 1971-85; Sunday Clothes, editor, 1971-82; National College, instructor in English, 1987-88; Black Hills State College, instructor in English, 1987-88; Oglala Lakota College, teacher, 1989; South Dakota School of Mines, professor of English, 1989-90; Windbreak House Writing Retreats, 1996-; University of Minnesota/Split Rock, online mentor, 2003-10; University of Iowa/Ames, visiting faculty, 2008-. **Publications:** NONFICTION AND POETRY: Book Book: A Publishing Handbook for Beginners and Others, 1979; Caught by One Wing: Poems, 1984; Windbreak: A Woman Rancheron the Northern Plains, 1987; Going over East: Reflections of a Woman Rancher, 1987, 2nd ed., 2001; Roadkill, 1987; Land Circle: Writings Collected from the Land (poems and essays), 1991; Dakota Bones: The Collected Poems of Linda Hasselstrom, 1992; A Roadside History of South Dakota, 1994; Bison: Monarch of the Plains, 1998; Feels Like Far: A Rancher's Life on the Great Plains, 1999; Bitter Creek Junction, 1999; Between Grass and Sky: Where I Live and Work, 2002; When a Poet Dies, 2004; No Place Like Home, 2009. EDITOR: Next-Year Country: One Woman's View, 1978; (intro.) Journal of a Mountain Man: James Lyman, 1984; (with N. Curtis and G. Collier) Leaning into the

Wind: Women Write from the Heart of the West, 1997; (with G. Collier and N. Curtis) Woven on the Wind, 2001; Between Grass and Sky, 2002; (with N. Curtis sand G. Collier) Crazy Woman Creek, 2004. Contributor to books and periodicals. **Address:** Windbreak House Retreats, PO Box 169, Hermosa, SD 57744, U.S.A. **Online address:** info@windbreakhouse.com

HASSEN, Philip Charles. Canadian/American (born United States), b. 1943. **Genres:** Medicine/Health, Sociology. **Career:** Washtenaw County Community Mental Health Center, mental health specialist, 1971-73; Metro-Calgary and Rural General Hospital District, staff; Rockyview General Hospital, assistant administrator, 1974-76; Holy Cross Hospital, assistant administrator, 1976-78; University of Calgary, Faculty of Medicine, assistant professor, 1978-87; Foothills Provincial General Hospital, assistant executive director of services, 1978-81, executive vice president, 1981-87; Canadian School of Management, MBA Program, student preceptor, 1981-; University of Alberta, Masters of Health Administration, student preceptor, 1981-, associate adjunct professor of public health sciences, 2005-; Ottawa University, Masters of Health Administration, student preceptor, 1981-; Toronto University, Masters of Health Administration, student preceptor, 1981-, Department of Health Administration, lecturer, 1988-; Dalhousie University, Masters of Health Administration, student preceptor, 1981-; The Toronto Hospital, chief operating officer and senior vice president, 1987-88; St. Joseph's Health Centre, president, 1988-97; Providence Health Care, chief executive officer, 1997-2000; Vancouver/Richmond Health Board, chief executive officer, 2000-; Vancouver Coastal Health Authority, president and chief executive officer; Canadian Patient Safety Institute, chief executive officer, through 2010; International Society for Quality and Safety, president; Canadian Network for International Surgery, president. **Publications:** (With S. Lindenburger) Rx for Hospitals: New Hope for Medicare in the Nineties, 1993. Contributor to journals. **Address:** Intl Society for Quality in Health Care Ltd., 8-11 Lombard St. E, Dublin, DU 2, Ireland. **Online address:** phassen@cpsi-icsp.ca

HASSLER, Christine. American (born United States), b. 1976. **Genres:** inspirational/Motivational Literature, Self Help. **Career:** American Express, Zync. Writer. **Publications:** 20 Something, 20 Everything: A Quarter-Life Woman's Guide to Balance and Direction, 2005; (comp. and ed.) 20 Something Manifesto: Quarter-Lifers Speak Out about Who They Are, What They Want, and How to Get It, 2008. **Address:** New World Library, 14 Pamaron Way, Los Angeles, CA 94949, U.S.A. **Online address:** christine@campuspeak.com

HASSLER, Donald M(ackey). American (born United States), b. 1937. **Genres:** Science Fiction/Fantasy, Poetry, Literary Criticism And History. **Career:** Crowell-Collier Encyclopedia, writer, 1960; University of Montreal, instructor of English, 1961-65; Kent State University, instructor, associate professor of English, 1965-77, director of experimental programmes, 1973-83, professor of English, 1977-, coordinator of writing certificate program, 1986-; Extrapolation, co-editor, 1986-89, editor, 1990-2002, executive editor, 2002-; Hellas, advisory editor, 1990-; NEOMFA Program, faculty, 2006-. **Publications:** The Comedian as Letter D: Erasmus Darwin's Comic Materialism, 1973; (co-author) On Weighing a Pound of Flesh (verse), 1973; Erasmus Darwin, 1974; Comic Tones in Science Fiction, 1982; Hal Clement, 1982; Patterns of the Fantastic, 1983; Patterns of the Fantastic II, 1984; (co-ed.) Death and the Serpent! Immortality in Science Fiction and Fantasy, 1985; Isaac Asimov, 1991; (co-ed.) The Letters of Arthur Machen to Montgomery Evans, 1994; (co-ed.) Political Science Fiction, 1997; New Boundaries in Political Science Fiction, 2008; Postnational Fantasy, 2011. **Address:** 1226 Woodhill Dr., Kent, OH 44240, U.S.A. **Online address:** extrap@kent.edu

HASTEDT, Glenn Peter. American (born United States), b. 1950. **Genres:** Politics/Government, Economics. **Career:** State University of New York College, assistant professor of political science, 1978-81; James Madison University, assistant professor, 1981-86, associate professor, 1986-91, professor of political science, 1991-, department head, 1999-, director, Justice Studies Department, chair. Writer. **Publications:** American Foreign Policy: Past Present Future, 1988, 8th ed. as American Foreign Policy, 2011; (with K. Knickrehm) Dimensions of World Politics, 1990; (ed. and contrib.) Controlling Intelligence, 1991; (ed. with K. Knickrehm) Toward the Twenty-first Century: A Reader in World Politics, 1994; American Foreign Policy, 1994; (ed.) One World Many Voices: Global Perspectives on Political Issues, 1995; (ed. with D. Charters and S. Farson) Analysis and Estimates, 1996; (ed. with A. Eksterowicz) The Post-Cold-War Presidency, 1996; (with K. Knickrehm) International Politics in a Changing World, 2003; Understanding the War in Iraq: Insights from History, International Politics, and American Foreign

Policy, 2004; Espionage: A Reference Handbook, 2003; Encyclopedia of American Foreign Policy, 2004; (ed. with A.J. Eksterowicz) The President and Foreign Policy: Chief Architect or General Contractor?, 2005; (with A.J. Eksterowicz) Presidencies of George Herbert Walker Bush and George Walker Bush: Like Father Like Son?, 2008; (with A.J. Eksterowicz) The Presidency of the United States: New Issues and Developments, 2009; (with S. Guerrior) American Espionage: A Historical Encyclopedia, 2010; (ed. with A.J. Eksterowicz) Presidents and War, 2010; Spies, Wiretaps and Secret Operations: An Encyclopedia of American Espionage, 2010; (ed. with A.J. Eksterowicz) Wilsonianism and Other Visions of Foreign Policy, 2011; (ed.) Spies, Wiretaps and Secret Operations: An Encyclopedia of American Espionage, 2011. Contributor to books. **Address:** Department of Political Science, James Madison University, 91 E Grace St., PO Box 7705, Harrisonburg, VA 22807, U.S.A. **Online address:** hastedgp@jmu.edu

HASTINGS, Brooke. *See* **GORDON, Deborah Hannes.**

HASTINGS, Graham. *See* **JEFFRIES, Roderic.**

HASTINGS, Max M(acdonald). British (born England), b. 1945. **Genres:** History, Military/Defense/Arms Control, Biography, Documentaries/Reportage. **Career:** British Broadcasting Corp. (BBC), researcher for television historical documentaries, 1963-64, Twenty-Four Hours, current daily affairs commentator, 1970-73, foreign correspondent; Evening Standard, staff, 1965-67, foreign correspondent, 1968-70, editor, 1996-2002; freelance foreign correspondent for television and newspapers, 1973-86; Daily Telegraph, editor, 1986-96, director, 1989-, editor-in-chief, 1990-95; London Evening Standard, editor; The Daily Mail, contributor; Daily Express, columnist. Historian. **Publications:** Fire This Time: America in 1968, 1968; Ulster, 1969: Barricades in Belfast: The Fight for Civil Rights in Northern Ireland, 1970; Montrose: The Kings Champion, 1977; Yoni: The Hero of Entebbe, 1979; Bomber Command: The British Bombing of Germany in World War II, 1979; Game Book: Sporting Around the World, 1979; (with L. Deighton) The Battle of Britain, 1980; Das Reich: Resistance and the March of the 2nd SS Panzer Division Through France, June, 1944, 1981; The Shotgun, 1981; Das Reich: March of the Second SS Panzer Division Through France, 1982; (with S. Jenkins) Battle for the Falklands, 1983; Overlord: D-Day and the Battle for Normandy, 1984; Victory in Europe: D-Day to V-E Day, 1985; (ed.) Oxford Book of Military Anecdotes, 1985, rev. ed., 2002; The Korean War, 1987; (intro.) The Daily Telegraph of the Second World War: Month by Month from 1939 to 1945, 1989; (ed.) Robert Churchill's Game Shooting: The Definitive Book on the Churchill Method of Instinctive Wingshooting for Game and Sporting Clays, 1990; Outside Days, 1995; Scattered Shots, 1999; Editors, 2000; Going to the Wars, 2000; (ed.) Editor: An Inside Story of Newspapers, 2002; Armageddon: The Battle for Germany, 1944-45, 2004; Warriors: Portraits from the Battlefield, 2005; Nemesis: The Battle for Japan, 1944-45, 2007; Retribution: The Battle for Japan, 1944-45, 2008; Finest Years: Churchill as Warlord 1940-45, 2009; Winston's War: Churchill, 1940-1945, 2010; Did You Really Shoot the Television?: A Family Fable, 2010; Inferno, 2011; All Hell Let Loose, 2011. Contributor to books. **Address:** Daily Mail, Northcliffe House, 2 Derry St., London, GL W8 5TT, England.

HASTINGS, Michael. British (born England), b. 1938. **Genres:** Novels, Plays/Screenplays, Poetry, Biography, Young Adult Fiction. **Career:** Writer. **Publications:** NOVELS: The Game, 1958; The Frauds, 1961; Tussy Is Me, 1971; The Nightcomers, 1972; And In the Forest the Indians, 1975. OTHER: Don't Destroy Me, 1956; Love Me, Lambeth (poems), 1961; The Silence of Lee Harvey Oswald, 1966; Three Plays, 1966; Rupert Brooke: The Handsomest Young Man in England, 1967; The Silence of Saint-Just, 1970; Bart's Mornings and Other Tales of Modern Brazil, 1975; Sir Richard Burton, 1978; Three Plays, 1980; Two Plays, 1981; Stars of the Roller State Disco, 1984; A Spy in Winter, 1984; Tom and Viv (play), 1985; (with J. Miller) The Emperor, 1987; Three Political Plays, 1988; (trans.) Roberto Cossa, La Nona, 1989; A Dream of People, 1990; (trans.) Ariel Dorfman, Death and the Maiden, 1991; Unfinished Business and Other Plays, 1994; The Dance of the Mexican Rattle Snake, 2003; Calico, 2004. Contributor to periodicals. **Address:** c/o Andrew Hewson, John Johnson Agency, 45/47 Clerkenwell Green, London, GL EC1R 0HT, England.

HASTORF, Christine Ann. American (born United States), b. 1950. **Genres:** Archaeology/Antiquities, Anthropology/Ethnology, Theology/Religion. **Career:** U.S. Geological Survey, Division of Western Regional Geology, archaeologist, 1977-79, 1980-82; University of Minnesota, assistant

professor, 1983-90, associate professor of anthropology, 1990-93, director of archaeobotany laboratory, 1983-93; University of California, associate professor of anthropology, 1994-, professor of anthropology. Writer. **Publications:** (Ed. with V.S. Popper and contrib.) Current Paleoethnobotany: Analytical Methods and Cultural Interpretation of Archaeological Plant Remains, 1988; (ed. with M.W. Conkey and contrib.) The Uses of Style in Archaeology, 1990, 2nd ed., 1993; Agriculture and the Onset of Political Inequality Before the Inka, 1993; (ed. with S. Johannessen and contrib.) Corn and Culture in the Prehistoric New World, 1994; (with T.N. D'Altroy) Empire and Domestic Economy, 2001. (with D.Y. Arnold) Heads of State: Icons, Power and Politics in the Ancient and Modern Andes, 2008. Contributor to journals. Works appear in anthologies. **Address:** Department of Anthropology, University of California, Rm. 215, 2251 College, Berkeley, CA 94720, U.S.A. **Online address:** hastorf@berkeley.edu

HASTY, Jennifer. American (born United States) **Genres:** Politics/Government, Writing/Journalism, Cultural/Ethnic Topics, Education. **Career:** Newspaper reporter, 1996-97; University of Ghana, research affiliate, 1996-97; Center for Africa and Media, research associate, 1998; Duke University, instructor, 1999; Pacific Lutheran University, assistant professor of anthropology, 1999-2006; Center for Democracy and Development, research fellow, 2004-05; Serious Fraud Office, assistant, 2004-05; University of Pennsylvania, Center for African Studies, research associate, lecturer; University of Leiden, lecturer; University of Amsterdam, lecturer; University of Birmingham, lecturer; Harvard University, lecturer; Rutgers University, lecturer; University of Florida, lecturer; Cornell University, lecturer; Drexel University, adjunct professor, 2006-. Writer. **Publications:** The Press and Political Culture in Ghana, 2005. Contributor to journals and periodicals. **Address:** Department of Culture & Communication, Drexel University, 3234 Powelton Ave., Philadelphia, PA 19104, U.S.A. **Online address:** mary.jennifer.hasty@drexel.edu

HASTY, Will. American (born United States) **Genres:** Literary Criticism And History, Art/Art History, Biography, History. **Career:** Illinois Wesleyan University, Department of Foreign Languages, assistant professor, 1987-88; Yale University, Department of Germanic Languages and Literatures, assistant professor, 1988-93, director of undergraduate studies, 1992-93; University of Florida, Department of Germanic and Slavic Studies, coordinator of undergraduate studies, 1993-99, 2000-04, professor, 1999-2008, chair, 2004-05, 2007-08, Center for Medieval and Early Modern Studies, co-director, 2004-, Department of Languages, Literatures, and Cultures, professor, 2008-, Center for Medieval and Early Modern Studies, co-director, 2008-, Graduate Studies for German, coordinator; University of Birmingham, visiting professor, 1999-2000. Writer. **Publications:** Adventures as Social Performance: A Study of the German Court Epic, 1990; Adventures in Interpretation: The Works of Hartmann von Aue and Their Critical Reception, 1996; Art of Arms: Studies of Aggression and Dominance in Medieval German Court Poetry, 2002. EDITOR: (with J. Hardin) Dictionary of Literary Biography: German Writers and Works of the High Middle Ages, 1170-1280, 1994; (with J. Hardin) Dictionary of Literary Biography: German Writers and Works of the Early Middle Ages, 800-1170, 1995; (with C. Merkes-Frei) Werkheft Literatur: Sinasi Dikmenund Zehra Çirak, 1996; A Companion to Wolfram's Parzival, 1999; A Companion to Gottfried von Strassburg's Tristan, 2003; The Camden House History of German Literature: The Literature of the High Middle Ages, 2006. Contributor of articles to books. **Address:** Department of Languages, Literatures and Cultures, University of Florida, 263 Dauer Hall, 301 Pugh Hall, PO Box 115565, Gainesville, FL 32611-5565, U.S.A. **Online address:** hasty@ufl.edu

HASWELL, Janis Tedesco. American (born United States), b. 1950. **Genres:** Literary Criticism And History, Women's Studies And Issues. **Career:** University of the Incarnate Word, assistant professor of English, 1993-94; Washington State University, visiting assistant professor of English, 1994-96; Texas A&M University, visiting assistant professor, 1996-98, assistant professor, 1998-2000, associate professor of English, 2000-05, professor, 2005-. Writer. **Publications:** (With J. Popham) Introduction to the Raj Quartet, 1985; Pressed against Divinity: W.B. Yeats and the Feminine Mask, 1997; Paul Scott's Philosophy of Place(s): The Fiction of Relationality, 2002; (with R. Haswell) Authoring: An Essay for the English Profession on Potentiality and Singularity, 2010; Behind Paul Scott's Raj Quartet, a Life in Letters, vol. I, vol. II, 2011. **Address:** Department of English, Texas A & M University, 6300 Ocean Dr., Corpus Christi, TX 78412-5813, U.S.A. **Online address:** janis.haswell@tamucc.edu

HASWELL, Richard H(enry). American (born United States), b. 1940. **Genres:** Education, Essays, Novellas/Short Stories. **Career:** University of Washington, Woodrow Wilson fellow, 1961-62; University of Missouri, teaching assistant, 1962-67, Gregory Fellow, 1964; Washington State University, assistant professor, 1967-73, associate professor, 1973-80, professor, 1980-96; Texas A&M University, Haas professor of English, 1996-2005, professor emeritus, 2005-. **Publications:** Gaining Ground in College Writing: Tales of Development and Interpretation, 1991; (with M.-Z. Lu) Comp Tales: An Introduction to College Composition through Its Stories, 2000; (contrib.) Comp Tales: An Introduction to College Composition Through Its Stories, 2008; (with J. Haswell) Authoring: An Essay for the English Pofession on Potentiality and Singularity, 2010; EDITOR: (with J. Ehrstine) A Baker's Dozen: 13 Modern Essays of Excellence, 1974, 3rd ed., 1992; (with J. Ehrstine and R. Wilkinson) The HBJ Reader, 1987; Beyond Outcomes: Assessment and Instruction within a University Writing Program, 2001; (with P.F. Ericsson) Machine Scoring of Student Essays: Truth and Consequences, 2006. Contributor of articles to journals. **Address:** Department of English, Texas A & M University-Corpus Christi, 6300 Ocean Dr., Corpus Christi, TX 78412, U.S.A. **Online address:** rhaswell@falcon.tamucc.edu

HATAB, Lawrence J. American (born United States), b. 1946. **Genres:** Philosophy. **Career:** Fordham University, Denzel Washington's philosophy, teacher; Old Dominion University, Louis I. Jaffe professor of philosophy, university professor, 1976-, faculty senate, 1980-88, department head, 1994-2000, chair. Writer. **Publications:** Nietzsche and Eternal Recurrence: The Redemption of Time and Becoming, 1978; Myth and Philosophy: A Contest of Truths, 1990; A Nietzschean Defense of Democracy: An Experiment in Postmodern Politics, 1995; Ethics and Finitude: Heideggerian Contributions to Moral Philosophy, 2000; Nietzsche's Life Sentence: Coming to Terms with Eternal Recurrence, 2005; Nietzsche's On the Genealogy of Morality: An Introduction, 2008. Contributor of articles to journals and books. **Address:** Department of Philosophy, Old Dominion University, 5115 Hampton Blvd., Norfolk, VA 23529-0083, U.S.A. **Online address:** lhatab@odu.edu

HATCH, Lynda S. American (born United States), b. 1950. **Genres:** Travel/Exploration, Local History/Rural Topics, Education, Social Sciences, Children's Fiction. **Career:** Clover Park School District, teacher, 1971-72; Hillsboro Elementary District, teacher, 1972-78; Bend-La Pine Public Schools, teacher and elementary curriculum specialist, 1978-90; Northern Arizona University, associate professor and coordinator of elementary education, chair of instructional leadership, 1990-99; Washington State University, Boeing distinguished professor of science education, 1999-. Writer. **Publications:** PATHWAYS OF AMERICA SERIES: The Oregon Trail, 1994; Lewis and Clark, 1994; The California Gold Rush Trail, 1994; The Santa Fe Trail, 1995. OTHER: Tools for Teachers: Teaching Curriculum for Home and the Classroom (18 guides), 1994-; Fifty States, 1996; U.S. Presidents, 1996; U.S. Map Skills, 1996; National Parks and Other Park Service Sites, 1999; Our National Parks, 1999; The California Mission Trail, 2000; Circling the World: Festivals and Celebrations, 2000; Endangered Species, 2001. Contributor to periodicals. **Address:** Department of Teaching & Learning, Washington State University, Cleveland 333, PO Box 642132, Pullman, WA 99164-2132, U.S.A. **Online address:** lhatch@wsu.edu

HATCH, Michael F. (Mike Hatch). American (born United States), b. 1947. **Genres:** Novels, Administration/Management, Young Adult Fiction. **Career:** University of Wisconsin, lecturer of Business Administration, 1978, adjunct faculty member, 1993-, adjunct instructor, 1993. Writer, consultant and educator. **Publications:** (As M. Hatch) Horseshoes and Nuclear Weapons, 1997; Production and Inventory Control Handbook-Manufacturing Resource Planning, 1997; Take It to the Limit, 1998. **Address:** University of Wisconsin, 337 Dempsey Hall, 800 Algoma Blvd., Oshkosh, WI 54901, U.S.A. **Online address:** hatch@uwosh.edu

HATCH, Mike. See **HATCH, Michael F.**

HATCHER, Robin Lee. American (born United States), b. 1951. **Genres:** Novels, Romance/Historical, Novellas/Short Stories. **Career:** Novelist and public speaker. **Publications:** NOVELS: Stormy Surrender, 1984; Heart's Landing, 1984; Thorn of Love, 1985; Heart Storm, 1986; Passion's Gamble, 1986; Pirate's Lady, 1987; Gemfire, 1988; The Wager, 1989; Dream Tide, 1990; Promised Sunrise, 1990; Rugged Splendor, 1991; Promise Me Spring, 1991; The Hawk and the Heather, 1992; Devlin's Promise, 1992; A Frontier Christmas (novella collection), 1992; Midnight Rose, 1992; The Magic, 1993;

Where the Heart Is, 1993; Forever, Rose, 1994; Remember When, 1994; A Purrfect Romance (novella collection), 1995; Liberty Blue, 1995; Chances Are, 1996; Kiss Me, Katie!, 1996; In His Arms, 1998; Hometown Girl, 1999; Taking Care of the Twins, 1999; Daddy Claus, 1999; Catching Katie, 2003; Speak to Me of Love, 2003; Legacy Lane, 2004; Beyond the Shadows: A Love Story, 2004; Veterans way, 2005; Victory Club, 2005; Loving Libby, 2005; Diamond Place, 2006; A Carol for Christmas, 2006; Another Chance to Love You, 2006; Sweet Dreams Drive, 2007; Return to Me, 2007; Trouble in Paradise, 2007; Hearts Evergreen, 2007; Home to Harts Crossing, 2008; Wagered Heart: A Novel, 2008; Home to Hart's Crossing, 2008; When Love Blooms, 2008; The Perfect Life: A Novel, 2008; Bundle of Joy, 2008; A Vote of Confidence, 2009; Fit to be Tied, 2009; Matter of Character: The Sisters of Bethlehem Springs, 2010. CHRISTIAN FICTION: Dear Lady, 1997; Patterns of Love, 1998; The Forgiving Hour, 1999; Whispers from Yesterday, 1999; The Shepherd's Voice, 2000; (with A.E. Hunt and D. Bedford) The Story Jar, 2001; Ribbon of Years, 2001; Firstborn, 2002; Promised to Me, 2003. OTHERS: Belonging, 2011; Heart of Gold, 2012. Contributor to periodicals. **Address:** RobinSong Inc., PO Box 1455, Meridian, ID 83680, U.S.A. **Online address:** rlhreadermail@gmail.com

HATFIELD, Juliana. American (born United States), b. 1967. **Genres:** Autobiography/Memoirs. **Career:** Ye Olde Records, founder, 2005-. Writer and musician. **Publications:** When I Grow Up: A Memoir, 2008. **Address:** Ye Olde Records, PO Box 398110, Cambridge, MA 02139, U.S.A. **Online address:** admin@julianahatfield.com

HATFIELD, Kate. See **WRIGHT, Daphne.**

HATFIELD, Phyllis. American (born United States), b. 1944. **Genres:** Biography, Autobiography/Memoirs, History. **Career:** Northwest Independent Editors Guild, co-founder; University of Washington, faculty. Freelance book editor. **Publications:** (Ed.) The Educated Piano: The Structural Relationships and Specifications Essential for Fine Piano Tone, 1989; Pencil Me In: A Memoir of Stanley Olson, 1994. **Address:** Northwest Independent Editors Guild, 7210 5th Ave. NW, Seattle, WA 98117, U.S.A. **Online address:** info@edsguild.org

HATHAWAY, Barbara. American (born United States), b. 1944?. **Genres:** Novels, Literary Criticism And History. **Career:** Writer. **Publications:** Missy Violet and Me, 2004; Letters to Missy Violet, 2012. Contributor periodicals. **Address:** c/o Author Mail, Houghton Mifflin, 222 Berkeley St., Boston, MA 02116-3764, U.S.A.

HATHAWAY, Margaret. American (born United States), b. 1969?. **Genres:** Travel/Exploration, Animals/Pets, Environmental Sciences/Ecology, Natural History. **Career:** Magnolia Bakery, manager. Journalist. **Publications:** The Year of the Goat: 40, 000 Miles and the Quest for the Perfect Cheese, 2007; Living with Goats: Everything You Need to Know to Raise Your Own Backyard Herd, 2010. **Address:** Lyons Press, 246 Goose Ln., PO Box 480, Guilford, CT 06437-2186, U.S.A. **Online address:** margaret@yearofthegoat.net

HATHORN, Libby. Australian (born Australia), b. 1943. **Genres:** Novels, Novellas/Short Stories, Children's Fiction, Plays/Screenplays, Songs/Lyrics And Libretti, Education. **Career:** Teacher, 1965-81; consultant and senior education officer, 1981-86; Sydney University, occasional lecturer in English and children's literature, 1982-; full-time writer, 1987-; University of Technology, writer-in-residence, 1990; Woollahra Library, writer-in-residence, 1992; Edith Cowan University, writer-in-residence, 1992. **Publications:** FOR CHILDREN FICTION: Stephen's Tree, 1979; Lachlan's Walk, 1980; The Tram to Bondi Beach, 1981; Paolo's Secret, 1985; All about Anna, 1986; Looking Out for Sampson, 1987; Freya's Fantastic Surprise, 1988; The Extraordinary Magics of Emma McDade, 1989; Stuntumble Monday, 1989; The Garden of the World, 1989; Thunderwith, 1989; Jezza Sez, 1990; So Who Needs Lotto?, 1990; Love Me Tender, 1992; The Lenski Kids and Dracula, 1992; Valley under the Rock, 1993; Way Home, 1993; There and Back, 1993; Feral Kid, 1994; Grandma's Shoes, 1994; What a Star, 1994; Looking for Felix, 1994; Surprise Box, 1994; The Wonder Thing, 1995; The Climb, 1996; Chrysalis, 1997; Rift, 1998; Sky Sash So Blue, 1998; Magical Ride, 1999; A Face in the Water, 2000; The Gift, 2000; Wattle Pattern Plate, 2001; The River, 2001; The Wishing Cupboard, 2002; Over the Moon, 2003; The Great Big Animal Ask, 2004; Caravan Kids, 2006. POETRY: Talks with My Skateboard, 1991. OTHER: (ed.) The Blue Dress (stories), 1991; Help for Young Writers, 1991; Good to Read (textbook), 1991; Who? (stories), 1992; Zahara's Rose, 2009. FOR YOUNG ADULTS FICTION: Ghostop, 1999; (with G. Crew) Dear Venny, Dear Saffron, 1999; The Painter, 2001. POETRY: Volcano Boy, 2001; Letters To a Princess, 2007; Georgiana: Women of Flowers, 2008. Contributor to periodicals. **Address:** PO Box 433, Woollahra, NW 2025, Australia. **Online address:** hatorders@gmail.com

HATKOFF, Amy. American (born United States) **Genres:** Film, Social Work, Writing/Journalism, Animals/Pets, Human Relations/Parenting. **Career:** Children's Aid Society, Homeless Families Service Program, director and special events coordinator, 1987-89; Women's Group (support group), founder, 1988, director, 1988-; The Hadar Foundation, executive director, 1993-96; Jewish Board of Family and Children's Services, Institute for Infants, Children & Families, director; ParentWise, founder. Advocate, parenting educator, filmmaker and writer. **Publications:** (With K.K. Klopp) How to Save the Children, 1992; You Are My World: How a Parent's Love Shapes a Baby's Mind, 2007; Inner World of Farm Animals: Their Amazing Social, Emotional, and Intellectual Capacities, 2009. Contributor to periodicals. **Address:** 136 E 76th St., Apt. 6E, New York, NY 10021, U.S.A. **Online address:** amyhatkoff@yahoo.com

HATOUM, Milton. Brazilian (born Brazil), b. 1952. **Genres:** Poetry, Novels, Young Adult Fiction. **Career:** University of Amazonas, professor of French literature, 1984-99; University of California, visiting professor of Latin-American literature, 1996, writer resident; Yale University, writer resident; Stanford University, writer resident. **Publications:** Um rio entre ruinas (poetry), 1978; (contrib.) Amazonas, palavras e imagens de um rio entre ruínas, 1979; Relato de um Certo Oriente (novel), 1989; Cidades, 1993; Tree of the Seventh Heaven, 1994; Dois irmãos, 2000; Brothers, 2002; Tale of a Certain Orient, 2004; Cinzas do norte, 2005; Orfãos do Eldorado, 2008; Ashes of the Amazon, 2008; A Cidade Ilhada: Contos, 2009; Norte, 2009; (contrib.) Amazônia de Euclides, 2010. Contributor of articles to periodicals. **Address:** Rua Recife, 1128 Casa 14-B, Manaus, AZ 69057-002, Brazil.

HATTENDORF, John B(rewster). American (born United States), b. 1941. **Genres:** History, Local History/Rural Topics, Marine Sciences/Oceanography, Military/Defense/Arms Control, Transportation, Travel/Exploration. **Career:** Office of the Chief of Naval Operations, assistant head of ships' histories section and research section, 1967-69; U.S. Naval War College, instructor and research associate, 1972-73, assistant professor, associate professor of strategy, 1977-81, professor of naval history, 1983-84, Ernest J. King professor of maritime History, 1984-, director of department of advanced research, 1988-2003, Naval War College Museum, chairman, Maritime History Department, 2003-, director, 2003-; National University of Singapore, visiting professor, 1981-83; Salve Regina College, faculty, 1988-92; University of Freiburg i B., visiting professor, 1991; Frank Munson Institute of American Maritime History, faculty, 1990-, director, 1995-2001; St. Antony's College, senior associate, 1986; Pembroke College, visiting fellow, 2002-02. Writer. **Publications:** A Dusty Path, 1964; (with J.D. Hayes) The Writings of Stephen B. Luce, 1975; On His Majesty's Service, 1983; (with B.M. Simpson III and J.R. Wadleigh) Sailors and Scholars, 1984; Two Beginnings, 1984; (with L.C. Hattendorf) A Bibliography of the Works of Alfred Thayer Mahan, 1986; England in the War of the Spanish Succession, 1987; The Evolution of the U.S. Navy's Maritime Strategy, 1977-1987, 1989; (with D.H. King and W. Estes) A Sea of Words, 1995; (with D.H. King) Harbors and High Seas, 1996; (with D.H. King) Every Man Will Do His Duty, 1997; (co-author) America and the Sea, 1998; John Robinson's Account of Sweden 1688, 1998; Naval History and Maritime Strategy: Collected Essays, 2000; Semper Eadem: A History of Trinity Church in Newport, 1698-1998, 2001; The Boundless Deep: The European Conquest of the Seas, 1450-1830, 2003; The Evolution of the U.S. Navy's Maritime Strategy, 1977-1987, 2004; Newport, the French Navy, and American Independence, 2005; Faces of the Naval War College, 2009; Talking About Naval History, 2011. EDITOR: (with R.S. Jordan) Maritime Strategy and the Balance of Power, 1989; (with M.H. Murfett) The Limitations of Military Power, 1990; Mahan on Naval Strategy, 1991; The Influence of History on Mahan, 1991; (co-ed.) British Naval Documents, 1204-1960, 1993; (with J. Goldrick) Mahan Is Not Enough, 1993; Ubi Sumus?, 1994; St. Barthelemy and the Swedish West Indies Company, 1995; Josiah Burchett's Transactions at Sea, 1995; Doing Naval History (essays), 1995; Maritime History, vol. I, The Age of Discovery, 1996; vol. II: The 18th Century and the Classic Age of Sail, 1997; Naval Policy and Strategy in the Mediterranean, 1999; (with R.W. Unger) War at Sea in the Middle Ages and the Renaissance, 2002; U.S. Naval Strategy in the 1990s: Selected Documents, 2006; The Oxford Encyclopedia of Maritime History, 2007; U.S. Naval Strategy on the 1970s: Selected

Documents, 2007; U.S. Naval Strategy on the 1980s: Selected Documents, 2009. XIth-XIVth, XVIth-XIXth International Seapower Symposium, Report of the Proceedings, 1992- 1998, 2004-2010. **Address:** Maritime History Department (Code 37), U.S. Naval War College, 686 Cushing Rd., Newport, RI 02841-1207, U.S.A. **Online address:** john.hattendorf@usnwc.edu

HATTERSLEY, Roy (Sydney George). British (born England), b. 1932. **Genres:** Autobiography/Memoirs, Biography, Novels, Politics/Government, Young Adult Fiction, Social Sciences. **Career:** Journalist, 1956-64; Minister of Pensions and National Insurance, parliamentary private secretary, 1964-67; Campaign for a European Political Community, director, 1966-67; Ministry of Labor, joint parliamentary secretary, 1967-68, Department of Employment and Productivity, joint parliamentary secretary, 1968-69; Defense for Administration, minister, 1969-70; Harvard University, Institute of Politics, visiting fellow, 1971, 1972; Foreign and Commonwealth Office, minister of state, 1974-76; Prices and Consumer Protection, secretary of state, 1976-79; Home Affairs, opposition spokesman, 1980-83, 1987-92; Lustie, columnist, 1980-81, 1988-; Punch, columnist, 1982-88; Treasury Affairs, opposition spokesman, 1983-87; Labour Party, deputy leader, 1983-92; International Business Machines Corp., consultant; Guardian, columnist. **Publications:** The Overload Performance of Powder Couplings: The Prevention of the Fire Hazard, 1957; Nelson: A Biography, 1974; Goodbye to Yorkshire, 1976; Politics Apart, 1982; A Yorkshire Boyhood, 1983; Press Gang, 1983; Endpiece Revisited, 1984; Choose Freedom: The Future for Democratic Socialism, 1987; Economic Priorities for a Labour Government, 1987; The Maker's Mark, 1990; In That Quiet Earth, 1991; Skylark's Song, 1994; Between Ourselves, 1994; Who Goes Home?: Scenes from a Political Life, 1995; (intro.) Churchill's Favourite Socialist: A Life of A.V. Alexander, 1995; In Praise of Ideology, 1997; Fifty Years On: A Prejudiced History of Britain since the War, 1998; Buster's Diaries As Told to Roy Hattersley, 1998; Blood & Fire: William and Catherine Booth and Their Salvation Army, 1999; Buster's Diaries: A True Story of a Dog and His Man, 2000; Life of John Wesley: A Brand from the Burning, 2003; Edwardians, 2005; Campbell-Bannerman, 2006; Borrowed Time: The Story of Britain Between the Wars, 2007; In Search of England, 2009; David Lloyd George: The Great Outsider, 2010. Contributor to journals. **Address:** Guardian, Kings Pl., 90 York Way, London, GL N1 9GU, England.

HATTON, Caroline. American/French (born France), b. 1957?. **Genres:** Children's Fiction, Young Adult Fiction, Adult Non-fiction, Young Adult Non-fiction, Translations, Chemistry, Medicine/Health, Sports/Fitness, Sports/Fitness, Botany. **Career:** Writer, translator and scientist. **Publications:** Vero and Philippe, 2001; Surprise Moon, 2004; The Night Olympic Team: Fighting to Keep Drugs out of the Games, 2008. Contributor to children's magazines and scientific periodicals. **Address:** CA , U.S.A. **Online address:** ch@carolinehatton.com

HAUG, James. American (born United States), b. 1954?. **Genres:** Poetry, Young Adult Fiction, Literary Criticism And History. **Career:** Poet. **Publications:** POETRY: The Stolen Car, 1989; Fox Luck, 1998; Walking Liberty, 1999; A Plan Of How To Catch Amanda, 2007; Legend of the Recent Past, 2009. Contributor to books. **Address:** 15 Washington Ave., Northampton, MA 01060, U.S.A. **Online address:** alix1@mediaone.net

HAUGEN, Hayley Mitchell. American/British (born England), b. 1968?. **Genres:** Children's Non-fiction, Young Adult Fiction, Adult Non-fiction. **Career:** Sheila-Na-Gig, co-founder, editor, publisher, 1990-2000; Seattle Review, editorial assistant, 1993-95; Quarter after Eight, co-editor-in-chief, 2002-04; Hotel Amerika (literary magazine), assistant editor, 2005-; Ohio University, visiting instructor in English. **Publications:** Teen Suicide, 1997; Teenage Alcoholism, 1997; Endangered Habitats and Species: The Wolf, 1998; (ed.) Readings on Wuthering Heights, 1998; (ed.) Readings on A Doll's House, 1998; The Death Penalty: Contemporary Issues Companion, 1998; (ed.) Readings on Black Boy, 2000; (ed.) Readings on Native Son, 2000; (ed.) Readings on the Short Stories of Edgar Allan Poe, 2001; A Complete History of the Death Penalty, 2001; Eagles, 2002; (ed.) Readings on The Metamorphosis, 2002; Life in a Coral Reef, 2003; (ed.) Teen Smoking, 2004; (ed.) Violent Children, 2004; Daniel Handler: The Real Lemony Snicket, 2005; Epilepsy, 2005; Life in a Forest, 2005; Monsters: Gargoyles, 2006; Life in a Grassland, 2006; (ed.) Racism, 2008; (ed. with S. Musser) Internet Safety, 2008; (co-ed.) Disaster Relief, 2010; (ed. with O. Ferguson) Is Childhood Becoming Too Sexualized?, 2010; (ed. with O. Ferguson) Age of Consent, 2010; (ed.) Lupus, 2010; (ed.) The American Dream in John Steinbeck's of Mice and Men, 2010; People with Disabilities, 2011; (ed.) Race in Ralph Ellison's Invisible Man, 2011. Contributor to periodicals. **Address:** Department of English, Ohio University, 360 Ellis Hall, 1 Park Place Dr., Athens, OH 45701, U.S.A. **Online address:** grimmgirl@aol.com

HAUGHT, James A(lbert). (Jim Haught). American (born United States), b. 1932. **Genres:** Theology/Religion, Children's Non-fiction, Sex, Sciences, Horror, Essays. **Career:** Daily Mail, apprentice printer, 1951-53; Gazette, reporter, 1953-, investigator, 1970-82, associate editor, 1983-92, editor, 1993-; Free Inquiry magazine, senior editor (part-time), 1996-. **Publications:** Holy Horrors: An Illustrated History of Religious Murder and Madness, 1990, rev. ed., 2002; Science in a Nanosecond: Illustrated Answers to 100 Basic Science Questions (for children), 1990; The Art of Lovemaking: An Illustrated Tribute, 1992; Holy Hatred: Religious Conflicts of the '90s, 1995; 2000 Years of Disbelief: Famous People with the Courage to Doubt, 1996; Honest Doubt: Essays on Atheism in a Believing Society, 2007; Amazon Moon (novel), 2007; Fading Faith: The Rise of the Secular Age, 2010. Contributor of articles to magazines. **Address:** The Charleston Gazette, 1001 Virginia St. E, Charleston, WV 25301, U.S.A. **Online address:** haught@wvinter.net

HAUGHT, Jim. *See* **HAUGHT, James A(lbert).**

HAUGHTON, Rosemary Luling. American/British (born England), b. 1927. **Genres:** Novels, Children's Non-fiction, Mythology/Folklore, Theology/Religion, Philosophy. **Career:** Wellspring House Inc., co-founder, associate director, director, now director emeritus. Educator, broadcaster on theology and writer. **Publications:** Jesus with Me, 1950; Thérèse Martin: The Story of St. Therese of Lisieux, 1957; The Family Book, 1959; The Children: Heirs to the Kingdom, 1961; Six Saints for Parents, 1963; The Family God Chose, 1964; The Young St. Mark, 1965; A Home for God's Family, 1965; The Carpenter's Son, 1965; The Boy from the Lake, 1965; Beginning Life in Christ: The Gospel in Christian Education, 1966; On Trying to be Human, 1966; The Young Moses, 1966; The Young Thomas More, 1966; (with A.M. Cocagnac) Bible for Young Christians: The Old Testament, 1966; The Transformation of Man, 1967; (with C. Heenan) Dialogue: The State of the Church Today, 1968; Why Be a Christian?, 1968; Elizabeth's Greeting, 1968; Matthew's Good News of Jesus, 1968; Problems of Christian Marriage, 1968; The Gospel Where It Hits Us, 1975; John's Good News of Jesus, 1968; Act of Love, 1968; Holiness of Sex, 1965; Why the Epistles were written, 1969; Love, 1970; Paul and the World's Most Famous Letters, 1970; Theology of Marriage, 1971; The Theology of Experience in UK as The Knife-Edge of Experience, 1972; Mystery of Sexuality, 1972; In Search of Tomorrow, 1972; Tales From Eternity: The World of Faerie and the Spiritual Search, 1973; The Liberated Heart, 1974; The Drama of Salvation, 1975; Feminine Spirituality. Reflections on the Mysteries of the Rosary, 1976; The Catholic Thing, 1980; The Passionate God, 1981; The Re-Creation of Eve, 1985; Song in a Strange Land: The Wellspring Story and the Homelessness of Women, 1990; (co-author) To Do Justice and Right Upon the Earth: Papers from the Virgil Michel Symposium on Liturgy and Social Justice, 1993; The Tower that Fell, 1997; Images for Change: The Transformation of Society, 1997; Gifts in the Ruins: Rediscovering What Matters Most, 2004. **Address:** Templegate Publishing Co., 302 E Adam St., PO Box 5152, Springfield, IL 62705, U.S.A.

HAUPTMAN, Don. American (born United States), b. 1947. **Genres:** Language/Linguistics, Marketing, Humor/Satire, Art/Art History, Reference. **Career:** Don Hauptman Inc., owner. Creative consultant and writer. **Publications:** Cruel and Unusual Puns: A Celebration of Spoonerisms, 1991; Acronymania: A Celebratory Roundup of Nomenclature Yielding Mischief: Abbreviations, Neologisms, Initialisms, Acronyms!, 1993. Contributor to journals. **Address:** Don Hauptman Inc., 61 W 62nd St., Ste. 22G, New York, NY 10023-7022, U.S.A. **Online address:** donhauptman@nyc.rr.com

HAUPTMAN, Judith. American (born United States), b. 1943?. **Genres:** Theology/Religion, History. **Career:** Jewish Theological Seminary, faculty, 1973-, E. Billi Ivry Professor of Talmud and Rabbinic Culture; 92nd Street Y, instructor; City College of New York, visiting professor of Talmud; Hebrew Union College, visiting instructor and as assistant professor of Talmud; Seminario Rabinico Latinamericano, visiting associate professor of Talmud; Ohel Ayalah Project, founder. Rabbi, theologian and writer. **Publications:** Development of the Talmudic Sugya: Relationship between Tannaitic and Amoraic Sources, 1988; Rereading the Rabbis: A Woman's Voice, 1998; (contrb.) Atarah le-Hayim: mehkarim ba-sifrut ha-Talmudit veha-rabanit li-khevod Professor Hayim Zalman Dimitrovski, 2000; Rereading the Mishnah: A New Approach to Ancient Jewish Texts, 2005. Contributor to periodicals. **Address:** Jewish Theological Seminary, 3080 Broadway, New York, NY 10027-4650, U.S.A. **Online address:** juhauptman@jtsa.edu

HAUPTMAN, Laurence Marc. American (born United States), b. 1945. **Genres:** Cultural/Ethnic Topics, History, Biography, Autobiography/Memoirs, Humanities, Politics/Government. **Career:** State University of New York, professor of history, 1971-99, distinguished professor of history, 1999-, now distinguished professor emeritus of history; New York University, faculty, 1974, 1981; Nelson A. Rockefeller Institute of Government, senior fellow, 1986; University of New Mexico, faculty, 1987; St. Bonaventure University, faculty, 1992; University of Oklahoma, Wilma Mankiller lecturer, 2005; Seneca Nation of Indians, consultant; Indian Rights Association, consultant; U.S. Small Business Administration, consultant. Writer. **Publications:** EDITOR: Library of World Peace Studies, 1978; (with J. Campisi) Neighbors and Intruders: An Ethnohistorical Exploration of the Indians of Hudson's River, 1978; (with J. Campisi) The Oneida Indian Experience: Two Perspectives, 1988; (with J.D. Wherry) The Pequots in Southern New England: The Fall and Rise of an American Indian Nation, 1990; A Seneca Indian in the Union Army: The Civil Wars Letters of Sergeant Isaac Newton Parker, 1861-1865, 1995; (with L.G. McLester III) The Oneida Indian Journey: From New York to Wisconsin, 1784-1860, 1999; (with L.G. McLester III) Nation within a Nation: Voices of the Oneidas in Wisconsin, 2010; Tonawanda Senecas' Heroic Battle Against Removal: Conservative Activist Indians, 2011. OTHERS: The Iroquois and the New Deal, 1981; The Iroquois Struggle for Survival: World War II to Red Power, 1986; Formulating American Indian Policy in New York State, 1970-1986, 1988; The Iroquois and the Civil War Year: From Battlefield to Reservation, 1993; Tribes & Tribulations: Misconceptions about American Indians and Their Histories, 1995; Between Two Fires: American Indians in the Civil War, 1995; Conspiracy of Interests: Iroquois Disposession and the Rise of the New York State, 1999; (with L.G. McLester) Chief Daniel Bread and the Oneida Nation Indians of Wisconsin, 2002; (with L.G. McLester) Oneida Indians in the Age of Allotment, 1860-1920, 2006; Seven Generations of Iroquois Leadership: The Six Nations Since 1800, 2008. Contributor to journals. **Address:** Department of History, State University of New York, JFT 916, 75 S Manheim Blvd., Ste. 6, New Paltz, NY 12561, U.S.A. **Online address:** hauptmal@newpaltz.edu

HAUPTMAN, Robert. American (born United States), b. 1941. **Genres:** Ethics, Librarianship, Literary Criticism And History, Travel/Exploration, Reference. **Career:** University of Oklahoma, humanities librarian and assistant professor of bibliography, 1980-84; St. Cloud State University, reference librarian and professor of library science, 1984-2005, now professor emeritus; Library Trends, special editor, 1991, reference librarian, 1992; Journal of Information Ethics, founding editor, 1992-. **Publications:** Twenty Poems Adjuring Death, 1973; The Pathological Vision: Jean Genet, Louis-Ferdinand Celine, and Tennessee Williams, 1984; Ethical Challenges in Librarianship, 1988; (with C. Anderson) Technology and Information Services: Challenges for the 1990s, 1993; Ethics and Librarianship, 2002; (with F. Hartemann) The Mountain Encyclopedia: An A-Z Compendium of More Than 2, 300 Terms, Concepts, Ideas, and People, 2005; Documentation: A History and Critique of Attribution, Commentary, Glosses, Marginalia, Notes, Bibliographies, Works-Cited Lists, and Citation Indexing and Analysis, 2008; Authorial Ethics, 2011. EDITOR: (with M.K. Ewing) Reference Librarian and Implications of Mediation, 1992; (with R. Stichler) Ethics, Information and Technology: Readings, 1998; (with S. Motin) The Holocaust: Memories, Research, Reference, 1998. Works appear in anthologies. Contributor of articles to periodicals. **Address:** 150 Allen Rd., South Burlington, VT 05403, U.S.A. **Online address:** hauptman@stcloudstate.edu

HAUPTMAN, William (Thornton). American (born United States), b. 1942. **Genres:** Plays/Screenplays, Novels, Novellas/Short Stories, Travel/Exploration. **Career:** Adelphi College, instructor, 1973-75; Yale University, School of Drama, instructor, 1976; University of Texas, Michener Center for Writers, faculty. Writer. **Publications:** Comanche Cafe, 1977; Heat, 1977; Domino Courts, and Comanche Cafe, 1977; Gillette: A Play, 1985; Big River: The Adventures of Huckleberry Finn: A Musical Play, 1986; Good Rockin' Tonight: A Collection of Short Stories, 1988; Comanche Cafe and Domino Courts, 1989; The Storm Season (novel), 1992; Journey to the West, forthcoming. Contributor to periodicals. **Address:** c/o Rick Leed, Agency for the Performing Arts, 45 W 45th St., 4th Fl., New York, NY 10036, U.S.A. **Online address:** whauptman2@aol.com

HAUSER, Marc D. (Marc David Hauser). American (born United States), b.

1959. **Genres:** Psychology. **Career:** Harvard University, assistant professor, 1992-95, associate professor, 1995-98, professor of psychology, organismic, evolutionary biology & biological anthropology, 1998-; adjunct professor in the graduate school of education, 2001-, co-director of the mind, brain & behavior program, 2003-; Harvard University, director; Makerere University, department of zoology, honorary lecturer. Writer. **Publications:** The Evolution of Communication, 1996; (ed. with M. Konishi) The Design of Animal Communication, 1999; Wild Minds: What Animals Really Think, 2000; (ed. with S. Dehaene, J.R. Duhamel and G. Rizzolatti) From Monkey Brain to Human Brain, 2005; (ed. with F. Cushman and M. Kamen) People, Property or Pets?, 2006; Moral Minds: How Nature Designed Our Universal Sense of Right and Wrong, 2006. **Address:** Department of Psychology, Harvard University, 33 Kirkland St., Cambridge, MA 02138, U.S.A. **Online address:** mdh@wjh.harvard.edu

HAUSER, Marc David. See **HAUSER, Marc D.**

HAUSER, Susan Carol. American (born United States), b. 1942. **Genres:** Poetry, Autobiography/Memoirs, Essays, Reference, Natural History, Adult Non-fiction, Institutions/Organizations. **Career:** Bowling Green State University, Department of English, faculty, 1973; Anoka-Ramsey Community College, Department of English, instructor, 1974-75; University of Minnesota, Department of Extension Offerings, instructor, 1975; Bemidji State University, writer and editor, 1980-98, Department of English, instructor, 1984-86, 1990-91, assistant professor, 1986-88, professor, 1998-2010. **Publications:** Meant to Be Read Out Loud, 1988; Girl to Woman: A Gathering of Images, 1992; Redpoll on a Broken Branch, 1992; What the Animals Know, 1992; Which Way to Look, 1992; Full Moon: Reflections on Turning Fifty, 1996; Nature's Revenge: The Secrets of Poison Ivy, Poison Oak, Poison Sumac and Their Remedies, 1996; Sugartime: The Hidden Pleasures of Making Maple Syrup with a Primer for the Novice Sugarer, 1997; Wild Rice Cooking: Harvesting, History, Natural History, Lore & Recipes, 2000; You Can Write a Memoir, 2001; Outwitting Poison Ivy: How to Prevent and Treat the Effects of Poison Ivy, Poison Oak and Poison Sumac, 2001; Outside After Dark: New & Selected Poems, 2001; Outwitting Ticks, 2001; Field Guide to Poison Ivy, Poison Oak and Poison Sumac, 2008; Field Guide to Ticks, 2008; My Kind of River Journey: Seeking Passage on the Mississippi, 2011. Contributor to books and periodicals. **Address:** 21963 Erica Ln. NW, Puposky, MN 56667, U.S.A. **Online address:** schauser@paulbunyan.net

HÄUSLER, Thomas. Swiss (born Switzerland), b. 1968. **Genres:** Sciences, Medicine/Health. **Career:** McKinsey and Co., business consultant, 1997-98; Facts magazine, reporter, 1998-, chief science editor, 1999-2007; Swiss Public Radio, science reporter, 2007-. Freelance writer. **Publications:** Viruses vs. Superbugs: A Solution to the Antibiotics Crisis?, 2006; (contrib.) Phanomen Mensch, 2008; (contrib.) Planet Erde, 2008. Contributor to scientific journals and periodicals. **Address:** Palgrave Macmillan Ltd., Houndmills, Basingstoke, Hampshire, RG21 6XS, England. **Online address:** thaeusler@vtxmail.ch

HAUSMANN, Winifred Wilkinson. (Winifred Wilkinson). American (born United States), b. 1922. **Genres:** Self Help, Theology/Religion. **Career:** Unity Church, minister, 1957-58; United Center of Cleveland, minister, 1958-66, co-minister, 1966-85, minister, 1985-88, minister emeritus, 1988-; Ordained Unity minister, 1959. Writer. **Publications:** (As Winifred Wilkinson) Focus on Living, 1967; (as Winifred Wilkinson) Miracle Power for Today, 1969; Your God-Given Potential: Unfolding the Twelve Spiritual Powers, 1978, rev. ed., 1999; How to Live Life Victoriously, 1982; Dealing with Stress through Spiritual Methods, 1985; A Guide to Love-Powered Living: Keys to Millennium-Living Today, 1986. **Address:** 327 Katey Rose Ln., Cleveland, OH 44143-2429, U.S.A.

HAUTH, Katherine B. American (born United States), b. 1940. **Genres:** Environmental Sciences/Ecology, Animals/Pets, Children's Fiction. **Career:** South Milwaukee High School, teacher, 1962-65; University of Washington, personnel analyst, 1966-76; King County, personnel analyst, 1966-76; writer, 1976-. **Publications:** Night Life of the Yucca: The Story of a Flower and a Moth, 1996; What's for Dinner?: Quirky, Squirmy Poems from the Animal World, 2010. **Address:** Roberts Rinehart Publishers, 5360 Manhattan Cir., Ste. 101, Boulder, CO 80303, U.S.A.

HAVARD, Bill. See **HAVARD, Cyril (William Holmes).**

HAVARD, C. W. H. See **HAVARD, Cyril (William Holmes).**

HAVARD, Cyril (William Holmes). Also writes as Bill Havard, C. W. H. Havard. British (born England), b. 1925?. **Genres:** Medicine/Health, Reference. **Career:** St. Bartholomews Hospital, casualty physician, 1964-66. Writer. **Publications:** AS C.W.H. HAVARD: Lectures in Medicine, 1967, 2nd ed., 1969; (ed.) Fundamentals of Current Medical Treatment, rev. ed., 1968; (ed. and contrib.) Frontiers of Medicine, 1973; (with M.R. Wills and P.J. Royalance) The Laboratory Investigation of Endocrine Disorders, 1979, (as Bill Havard with M.R. Wills) 2nd ed., 1983; (ed.) Current Medical Treatment, 3rd ed., 1970, 5th ed., 1983. OTHER: (as Cyril Havard) Medical Eponyms: Diseases, Syndromes and Signs, 1998. **Address:** 8 Upper Wimpole St., London, GL W1M 7TD, England.

HAVAZELET, Ehud. American/Israeli (born Israel), b. 1955. **Genres:** Novellas/Short Stories, Novels, Young Adult Fiction. **Career:** Stanford University, Jones lecturer, 1985-89, Wallace Stegner fellow; Oregon State University, associate professor, 1989-99; Warren Wilson MFA Program for Writers, faculty, 1995; University of Oregon, Creative Writing Program, associate professor of creative writing, 1999-, professor. Writer. **Publications:** What is it then Between Us?, 1988; Like Never Before, 1998; Bearing the Body, 2007. Contributor to periodicals and journals. **Address:** Creative Writing Program, University of Oregon, 211 Alder Bldg., 5243 University of Oregon, Eugene, OR 97403-5243, U.S.A. **Online address:** havazele@uoregon.edu

HAVEL, Geoff. Australian (born Australia), b. 1955. **Genres:** Children's Fiction. **Career:** Education Department of Western Australia, primary teacher, 1980-. Writer. **Publications:** Ca-a-r Ca-a-a-a-r (picture book), 1996; Punzie, ICQ! (picture book), 1999; The Real Facts of Life, 2001; Grave of the Roti Men, 2003; Babies Bite: More Real Facts of Life, 2004; The Master, 2009; Water, 2010. Contributor to periodicals. **Address:** Fremantle Arts Center Press, PO Box 158, North Fremantle, WA 6159, Australia. **Online address:** ghavel@smartchat.net.au

HAVEL, Harvey. American/Pakistani (born Pakistan), b. 1971. **Genres:** Novels, Novellas/Short Stories, Writing/Journalism, Literary Criticism And History. **Career:** CBS-TV, CBS Evening News, production assistant, 1991-92, 1996, CBS-Radio, CBS News Radio, assistant, 1996-98; Bergen Community College, teacher; State University of New York, lecturer; College of Saint Rose, lecturer, 2007-. Writer. **Publications:** NOVELS: Noble McCloud, 1999; The Imam, 2000; Freedom of Association, 2006; From Poets to Protagonists, 2008. **Address:** 123 Ryckman Ave., Ste. 1R, Albany, NY 12208, U.S.A. **Online address:** harveyhavel@hotmail.com

HAVEMAN, Robert Henry. American (born United States), b. 1936. **Genres:** Economics. **Career:** Vanderbilt University, Department of Economics, instructor, 1960-62; Grinnell College, Department of Economics, instructor, assistant professor, associate professor, professor, 1962-70; Brookings research professor, 1965-66; Economy in Government, senior economist, 1968-69; Resources for the Future Inc., research associate, 1969-70; University of Wisconsin, Department of Economics, professor of economics, 1970-; John Bascom professor of economics and public affairs, 1984-, professor emeritus of economics and public affairs, chair, 1993-96, Institute for Research on Poverty, director, 1971-76, faculty affiliate; Netherlands Institute for Advanced Study in the Social Sciences and Humanities, fellow, 1975-76, 1996-97; Erasmus University, Tinbergen professor, 1984-85; La Follette Institute of Public Affairs, director, 1988-91; Australia National University, Institute for Research on Poverty, adjunct professor; International Institute of Public Finance, vice president, 1988-93, president, 1997-2000; Midwest Economics Association, president, 1992-93; International Institute of Public Finance, executive vice president, 1993-97. Writer. **Publications:** Water Resource Investment and the Public Interest, 1965; (with K. Knopf) The Market System, 1966, 4th ed., 1981; (with J.V. Krutilla) Unemployment, Idle Capacity and the Evaluation of Public Expenditures, 1968; The Economics of the Public Sector, 1970, 2nd ed., 1976; The Economic Performance of Public Investments, 1972; (with C.J. Cicchetti) Optimality in Producing and Distributing Public Outputs, 1972; (with A.M. Freeman and A.V. Kneese) The Economics of Environmental Policy, 1973; (with I. Garfinkel) Economic Inequality and the Utilization of Earnings Capacity, 1975; Poverty, Income Distribution and Social Policy: The Last Decade and the Next, 1976; (with F. Golladay) The Economic Impacts of Tax-Transfer Policy: Regional and Distributional Effects, 1977; A Decade of Federal Anti-Poverty Programs: Achievements, Failures and Lessons, 1977; (with I. Garfinkel) Earnings Capacity, Poverty and Inequality, 1977; (with S. Danziger) Economic Concept of Solidarity: Its Application to Poverty and Income Distribution Policy in the United States, 1978; (with B. Berelson) On Allocating Resources for Fertility Reduction in Developing Countries, 1979; (with G. Christainsen) Jobs and the Environment, 1979; (with R. Burkhauser) Disability Policy in the United States, 1982; (with R.V. Burkhauser) Disability and Work: The Economics of American Policy, 1982; (with S. Oliner and M. David) Investment in Equipment, Structures and Research Capital under the Reagan Tax Acts, 1983; (with V. Halberstadt and R.V. Burkhauser) Public Policy toward Disabled Workers: Cross-National Analyses of Economic Impacts, 1984; (with G. Burtless) Policy Lessons from Three Labor Market Experiments, 1984; (with R.V. Burkhauser) United States Policy Toward the Disabled and Employment Handicapped, 1984; (with R. Burkhauser and V. Halberstadt) Public Policy Toward Disabled Workers, 1985; (with G. Burtless) Taxes, Transfers and Labor Supply: The Evolving Views of U.S. Economists, 1985; (with B. Wolfe and J. Warlick) Behavioral Responses to Social Security Retrenchment: Estimates from a Trichotomous Choice Model, 1985; Poverty Policy and Poverty Research, 1987; Starting Even: An Equal Opportunity Program to Combat the Nation's New Poverty, 1988; (with B. Wolfe) Succeeding Generations: On the Effects of Investments in Children, 1994; Earnings Inequality: The Influence of Changing Opportunities and Choices, 1996; (with A. Bershadker and J.A. Schwabish) Human Capital in the United States from 1975 to 2000: Patterns of Growth and Utilization, 2003. EDITOR: (with J. Margolis) Public Expenditures and Policy Analysis, 1970, 3rd ed., 1983; (co-ed.) Benefit-Cost Annual-1971; (with R. Hamrin) The Political Economy of Federal Policy, 1973; (co-ed.) Benefit-Cost and Policy Analysis-1972, 1973 and 1974, 3 vols., 1973-75; Decade of Federal Antipoverty Programs: Achievements, Failures and Lessons, 1977; (with B. Zellner) Policy Studies Review Annual, 1979; (with K. Hollenbeck) Microeconomic Simulation Models for Public Policy Analysis, 1980, 2 vols., 1982; (with J. Palmer) Jobs for Disadvantaged Workers, 1982; Public Finance and Public Employment, 1982; (with B. Wolfe) Succeeding Generations: On the Effects of Investments in Children, 1994; (with D.S. Nightingale) Work Alternative: Welfare Reform and the Realities of the Job Market, 1995; (with S.H. Danziger) Understanding Poverty, 2001. **Address:** Department of Economics, University of Wisconsin, 204 Observatory Hill Office Bldg., 1225 Observatory Dr., Madison, WI 53706, U.S.A. **Online address:** haveman@lafollette.wisc.edu

HAVENS, Candace. American (born United States), b. 1963. **Genres:** Romance/Historical. **Career:** Tribune Media, columnist; FYI Television, syndicated entertainment columnist and managing editor; KSCS, weekly radio show host. Journalist and broadcaster. **Publications:** Joss Whedon: The Genius behind Buffy (nonfiction), 2003; Charmed & Dangerous, 2005; Charmed & Ready, 2006; Charmed and Deadly, 2007; The Demon King and I, 2008; Like a Charm, 2008; Dragons Prefer Blondes, 2009; Take Me If You Dare, 2010. Works appear in anthologies. **Address:** TX , U.S.A. **Online address:** candacehavensbooks@gmail.com

HAVERTY, Anne. Irish (born Ireland), b. 1959?. **Genres:** Novels, Poetry, Biography, Young Adult Fiction, Anthropology/Ethnology, Novellas/Short Stories. **Career:** Novelist and poet. **Publications:** Constance Markievicz: Irish Revolutionary (biography), 1993; One Day as a Tiger (novel), 1997; The Beauty of the Moon (poems), 1999; Ladies' Night at Finbar's Hotel, 2000; The Far Side of a Kiss (novel), 2001; The Free and Easy, 2006. Contributor to periodicals. **Address:** c/o Chatto & Windus, Random House UK, 20 Vauxhall Bridge Rd., London, GL SW1V 2SA, England. **Online address:** annehaverty@ireland.com

HAVET, Jose (L.). Canadian/Belgian (born Belgium), b. 1937. **Genres:** Sociology, Area Studies, International Relations/Current Affairs, Local History/Rural Topics, Cartoons, Third World, Women's Studies And Issues. **Career:** Teacher, 1961-63; International Institute of Differing Civilizations, research assistant, 1969; Universidad San Francisco-Xavier, visiting professor of sociology, 1970-71; Accion Cultural Loyola, researcher, 1971-72; University of Pittsburgh, teaching fellow, 1972-76; Universidad Interamericana de Puerto Rico, assistant professor of sociology, 1976-80, co-ordinator of sociology and anthropology program, 1978-79; University of Ottawa, Institute for International Development and Cooperation, assistant professor, 1980-84, associate professor, 1984-89, professor of sociology, 1989-2003, professor emeritus, deputy director of research, 1988-89. Writer. **Publications:** The Diffusion of Power: Rural Elites in a Bolivian Province, 1985. EDITOR: (and intro.) Le village et le bidonville: Retention et migration des populations rurales d'Afrique, 1986; (and intro.) L'etude du Developpement International au Canada: Evolution, Recherche et Enseignement, 1987; (and intro.) Staying On: Retention and Migration in Peasant Societies, 1988; (ed. with L. Dignard) Women in Micro and Small Scale Enterprise Development, 1995; (ed. and intro.) Identities, State, Markets: Looking at Social Change in Latin America, 1999. Contributor of articles to journals. **Address:** University of Ottawa, Tabaret Hall, 75 Laurier Ave. E, Ottawa, ON K1N 6N5, Canada. **Online address:** jhavet@uottawa.ca

HAVIARAS, Stratis. (Strates Chaviaras). American/Greek (born Greece), b. 1935. **Genres:** Novels, Poetry, Art/Art History, Translations, History. **Career:** Harvard University, University Library, acquisitions specialist, Gifts and Exchange Division, head, 1968-74, Woodberry Poetry Room, curator of the poetry collection, 1974-2000, Harvard Review, founding editor, 1992-2007; National Book Centre of Greece, director. **Publications:** POETRY IN GREEK: Lady with a Compass, 1963; Berlin, 1965; Night of the Stiltwalker, 1967; Apparent Death, 1972. IN ENGLISH: (trans.) 35 Post-War Greek Poets, 1972; (with P. Hannigan and J. Batki) Kiss: A Collaboration (art), 1976; Crossing the River Twice (verse), 1976; When the Tree Sings (novel), 1979; The Heroic Age (novel), 1984; Millennial Afterlives: A Retrospective (short fiction), 2000; (trans.) C.P. Cavafy, The Canon: The Original One Hundred and Fifty-Four Poems, 2007. AS STRATeS CHAVIARAS: Hotan tragoudousan ta dentra: mythistorema, 1980; Herōika chronia: mythistorema, 1999. **Address:** 19 Clinton St., Cambridge, MA 02139, U.S.A. **Online address:** haviaras@hudce7.harvard.edu

HAVIL, Julian. British (born England), b. 1952. **Genres:** Mathematics/Statistics, History, Sciences. **Career:** Winchester College, master of mathematics, now retired. Author. **Publications:** Gamma: Exploring Euler's Constant, 2003; Nonplussed!: Mathematical Proof of Implausible Ideas, 2007; Impossible?: Surprising Solutions to Counterintuitive Conundrums, 2008. **Address:** Princeton University Press, 41 William St., Princeton, NJ 08540-5237, U.S.A. **Online address:** jrh@wincoll.ac.uk

HAWES, Judy. American (born United States), b. 1913. **Genres:** Children's Fiction, Children's Non-fiction, Animals/Pets. **Career:** Teacher, 1958-76; Coleman School, teacher. Writer. **Publications:** Fireflies in the Night, 1963, rev. ed., 1991; Bees and Beelines, 1964; Watch Honeybees with Me, 1964; Shrimps, 1966; Ladybug, Ladybug, Fly away Home, 1967; Why Frogs Are Wet, 1968; What I Like about Toads, 1969; The Goats Who Killed the Leopard (A Story of Ethiopia), 1970; My Daddy Longlegs, 1972; Spring Peepers, 1975. **Address:** 79 Abbington Terr., Glen Rock, NJ 07452, U.S.A. **Online address:** hawesglenrocknew@juno.com

HAWES, Louise. American (born United States), b. 1943. **Genres:** Novels, Children's Fiction, Young Adult Fiction, Picture/Board Books. **Career:** State of New Jersey, Department of Community Affairs, Division on Aging, public information director, 1967-69; Supermarkets General Corp., Pathmark News, assistant editor, 1970-72; Barbizon School, instructor in advertising and writing, 1978-79; Stanley H. Kaplan Educational Centers, advertising manager, 1980-; freelance writer, 1985-; Spalding University, instructor in M.F.A. writing program; Vermont College, M.F.A. Writing for Children program, co-founder. **Publications:** Nelson Malone Meets the Man from Mush-Nut, 1986; Nelson Malone Saves Flight 942, 1988; Tales from the Cafeteria No. 2: Things That Go Bump in Your Soup, 1995; Tales from the Cafeteria No. 1: Spaghetti and Spooks, 1995; Rosey in the Present Tense, 1999; Willem de Kooning: The Life of an Artist, 2002; Waiting for Christopher, 2002; The Vanishing Point: A Story of Lavinia Fontana, 2004; Mutis Necklace: The Oldest Story in the World, 2006; Anteaters Don't Dream and Other Stories, 2007; Black Pearls: A Faerie Strand, 2008; (co-author) Fallen Angel 2010. **Address:** Houghton Mifflin Childrens Books, 222 Berkeley St., 8th Fl., Boston, MD 02116-3764, U.S.A. **Online address:** mail@louisehawes.com

HAWK, Alex. See GARFIELD, Brian (F. W.).

HAWKE, Ethan. American (born United States), b. 1970. **Genres:** Novels, Film, Plays/Screenplays. **Career:** Malaparte Theater Co., co-founder and artistic director, 1993-2000. Novelist and actor. **Publications:** NOVELS: The Hottest State, 1997; Ash Wednesday, 2002; Manhattan Story, 2003. OTHER: (foreword) New York's Unique & Unexpected Places, 2009. **Address:** Creative Artists Agency, 2000 Ave. of the Stars, Los Angeles, CA 90067, U.S.A.

HAWKE, Gary Richard. New Zealander (born New Zealand), b. 1942. **Genres:** Economics, History. **Career:** Victoria University of Wellington, lecturer, 1968-70, reader, 1971-73, professor of economic history, 1974-2007, emeritus professor, 2007-, Institute of Policy Studies, director, 1987-98, School of Government, head, 2003-07; Stanford University, visiting fellow, 1972-73; New Zealand Economic Papers, editor, 1973-77; University of Oxford, All Souls College, visiting fellow, 1977-78. **Publications:** Railways and Economic Growth in England and Wales, 1840-1870, 1970; The Development of the British Economy, 1870-1914, 1970; Between Governments and Banks: A History of the Reserve Bank of New Zealand, 1973; The Evolution of the New Zealand Economy, 1977; Economics for Historians, 1980; Government in the New Zealand Economy, 1982; The Making of New Zealand, 1982; Adaptable Kiwis or Drought: Responses to Refrigeration in Australia and New Zealand, 1985; Diversity and Injustice, 1996; The Thoroughbred among Banks in New Zealand, 1872-1947, The Early Years, 1997. EDITOR: (with K. Guerin) A History of the Bank of New Zealand, 1862-1982, 1990; (with R.W. Baker) Anzus Economics: Economic Trends and Relations Among Australia, New Zealand and the United States, 1992; Changing Politics? The Electoral Referendum, 1993; Improving Policy Advice, 1993; Employment and the Future of Work: Harkness Employment Conference 9-19 May, 1995 Parkroyal Hotel, Wellington, 1996; Guardians for the Environment: Proceedings of a Symposium to Mark the First Decade and to Provide Directions for the New Zealand Parliamentary Commissioner for the Environment with Support from the Officers of the Parliament Committee and Russell McVeagh, 1997; Free Trade in the New Millennium, 1999. Contributor to journals. **Address:** New Zealand Institute of Economic Research, PO Box 3479, Wellington, 6140, New Zealand. **Online address:** gary.hawke@vuw.ac.nz

HAWKE, Richard. Also writes as Tim Cockey. American (born United States), b. 1955?. **Genres:** Novels, Mystery/Crime/Suspense. **Career:** Writer. **Publications:** AS RICHARD HAWKE: Speak of the Devil: A Novel, 2006; Cold Day in Hell: A Novel, 2007; House of Secrets: A Novel, 2010. HITCHCOCK SEWELL SERIES AS TIM COCKEY: The Hearse You Came In On, 2000; Hearse of a Different Color, 2001; Hearse Case Scenario, 2002; Murder in the Hearse Degree, 2003; Backstabber, 2004. **Address:** Random House Inc., 1745 Broadway, New York, NY 10019, U.S.A. **Online address:** tcockey@mindspring.com

HAWKE, Rosanne Joy. Australian (born Australia), b. 1953. **Genres:** Novels, Young Adult Fiction, Science Fiction/Fantasy, Children's Fiction. **Career:** Teacher, 1975-, 1986-91, 1993-96; acting principal, 1988, 1990; writer, 1994-. **Publications:** Re-Entry, 1995; Jihad: A Girls Quest to Settle the Past and Say Goodbye, 1996; The Keeper, 2000; A Kiss in Every Wave, 2001; Sailmaker, 2002; Borderland, 2002; Zenna Dare, 2002; Wolfchild, 2003; Yardil, 2004; Soraya the Storyteller, 2004; Across the Creek, 2004; The Collector, 2004; The Last Virgin in Year Ten, 2006; Mustara, 2006; Marrying Ameera, 2010. **Address:** Jacinta di Mase Management, 342 St. Geroges Rd., North Gitzroy, VI 3068, Australia. **Online address:** hawknest@rosannehawke.com

HAWKE, Simon. Also writes as J. D. Masters, S. L. Hunter, Nicholas Valentin Yermakov. American (born United States), b. 1951. **Genres:** Novels, Science Fiction/Fantasy, Mystery/Crime/Suspense, Literary Criticism And History, Young Adult Fiction. **Career:** Pima Community College, instructor, 1995-98; Elon College, instructor, 1998-; Guilford Technical Community College, instructor, 1998-; North Carolina A&T University, instructor, 1999-. Writer. **Publications:** AS NICHOLAS YERMAKOV: Journey from Flesh, 1981; Last Communion, 1981; Fall into Darkness, 1982; (with G.A. Larson) Battlestar Galactica, Number 6: The Living Legend, 1982; Clique, 1982; (with G.A. Larson) Battlestar Galactica, Number 7: War of the Gods, 1982; Epiphany, 1982; Jehad, 1984; The Ivanhoe Gambit, 1984; The Timekeeper Conspiracy, 1984; The Pimpernel Plot, 1984; The Nautilus Sanction, 1985; The Lilliput Legion, 1989; The Cleopatra Crisis, 1990; The Six-Gun Solution, 1991. AS J.D. MASTERS: Steele, 1989; Cold Steele, 1989; Killer Steele, 1990; Jagged Steele, 1990; Renegade Steele, 1990; Target Steele, 1990. AS S.L. HUNTER: Fugitive Steele, 1991; Molten Steele, 1991. OTHERS: The Zenda Vendetta, 1985; The Khyber Connection, 1986; The Argonaut Affair, 1987; The Wizard of Fourth Street, 1987; The Dracula Caper, 1988; Shapechanger Scenario, 1988; The Wizard of Whitechapel, 1988; The Wizard of Sunset Strip, 1989; The Wizard of Rue Morgue, 1990; The Hellfire Rebellion, 1990; Batman, 1991; The Samurai Wizard, 1991; The Wizard of Santa Fe, 1991; Sons of Glory, 1992; The Reluctant Sorcerer, 1992; The Nine Lives of Catseye Gomez, 1992; Call to Battle Sons of Glory, 1993; The Inadequate Adept (sequel to The Reluctant Sorcerer), 1993; The Wizard of Love-

craft's Café, 1993; Romulan Prize, 1993; The Wizard of Camelot, 1993; Dark Sun: The Outcast, 1993; Dark Sun: The Nomad, 1994; Patrian Transgression, 1994; Dark Sun: The Seeker, 1994; The Whims of Creation, 1995; Dark Sun: The Broken Blade, 1995; The Iron Throne, 1995; The Ambivalent Magician, 1996; War, 1996; The Last Wizard, 1997; A Mystery of Errors, 2000; The Slaying of the Shrew, 2001; Much Ado about Murder, 2002; The Merchant of Vengeance, 2003. Contributor to periodicals. **Address:** Tom Doherty Associates L.L.C., Tor Books, 175 5th Ave., New York, NY 10010, U.S.A. **Online address:** simonhawke@aol.com

HAWKES, G(ary) W(arren). American (born United States), b. 1953. **Genres:** Novellas/Short Stories, Novels. **Career:** Lycoming College, Professor of English, creative writing program, co-director, The Tributary, faculty advisor, professor of English, 1989-. Writer. **Publications:** Spies in the Blue Smoke: Stories, 1992; Playing Out of the Deep Woods: Stories, 1995; Surveyor, 1998; Semaphore, 1998; Gambler's Rose, 2000. **Address:** Department of English, Lycoming College, 700 College Pl., Williamsport, PA 17701-5157, U.S.A. **Online address:** hawkes@lycoming.edu

HAWKES, Judith. American (born United States), b. 1949. **Genres:** Novels, Horror. **Career:** Saint Ann's School, computer programmer, 1974-91, martial arts instructor, 1990-. Writer. **Publications:** Julian's House (novel), 1989; My Soul to Keep (novel), 1996; The Heart of a Witch, 1999. **Address:** John Farquharson Ltd., 250 W 57th St., New York, NY 10019, U.S.A.

HAWKES, Kevin. American (born United States), b. 1959. **Genres:** Children's Fiction, Illustrations, Humor/Satire. **Career:** Xam Inc., animation assistant, 1985; Gibby Studios, photo retoucher, 1985-86; freelance illustrator, 1987-; writer, 1990-. **Publications:** FOR CHILDREN AND SELF-ILLUSTRATED: Then the Troll Heard the Squeak, 1991; His Royal Buckliness, 1992; Library Lion, 2006; Wicked Big Toddlah, 2007; Wicked Big Toddlah Goes To New York, 2007 OTHER: (with A, Isaacs) Meanwhile Back at the Ranch, 2013. Contributor to periodicals. Illustrator of books by others. **Address:** 5 Robie St., Gorham, ME 04038, U.S.A. **Online address:** info@kevinhawkes.com

HAWKINS, Andre. See HASKINS, Scott (M.).

HAWKINS, Anne Hunsaker. American (born United States), b. 1944. **Genres:** Humanities, Medicine/Health, Literary Criticism And History, Autobiography/Memoirs, Young Adult Fiction. **Career:** Pennsylvania State University, College of Medicine, associate professor of humanities, 1990-, professor, university professor emeritus, The Doctors Kienle Center for Humanistic Medicine, director; Dermanities, contributor. Writer. **Publications:** Archetypes of Conversion: The Autobiographies of Augustine, Bunyan and Merton, 1985; Reconstructing Illness: Studies in Pathography, 1993, 2nd ed., 1999; (ed. with J.O. Ballard and T. Blaisdell) Time to Go: Three Plays on Death and Dying, with Commentary on End-of-Life Issues, 1995; Small, Good Thing: Stories of Children with HIV and Those Who Care for Them, 2000; (ed. with M.C. McEntyre) Teaching Literature and Medicine, 2000. **Address:** Department of Humanities, Pennsylvania State University, Rm. H134, 500 University Dr., PO Box 850, Hershey, PA 17033, U.S.A. **Online address:** ahh1@psu.edu

HAWKINS, Bradford A(lan). American (born United States), b. 1952. **Genres:** Biology, Environmental Sciences/Ecology, Sciences. **Career:** Texas A&M University, postdoctoral fellow in entomology, 1984; University of Puerto Rico, assistant professor of biology, 1985-86; University of York, postdoctoral fellow in biology, 1986-88; University of Texas, lecturer in zoology, 1988-89; Imperial College, Centre for Population Biology, staff research scientist, 1990-94; University of California, School of Biological Sciences, assistant professor, 1994-96, associate professor of ecology and evolutionary biology, 1996-, professor of ecology and evolutionary biology. Writer. **Publications:** (Ed. with W. Sheehan) Parasitoid Community Ecology, 1994; Pattern and Process in Host-Parasitoid Interactions, 1994; (ed. with H.V. Cornell) Theoretical Approaches to Biological Control, 1999; (ed. with T. Tscharntke) Multitrophic Level Interactions, 2002. Contributor to journals. **Address:** Department of Ecology & Evolutionary Biology, University of California, 455 Steinhaus Hall, Irvine, CA 92697-2525, U.S.A. **Online address:** bhawkins@uci.edu

HAWKINS, Hunt. American (born United States), b. 1943. **Genres:** Poetry, Psychology, Children's Fiction. **Career:** Kurasini International Education

Centre, teacher, 1966-67; Texas Southern University, instructor and Woodrow Wilson teaching intern, 1968-70; Stanford University, teaching assistant, 1972-73; University of Minnesota, visiting assistant professor of English, 1977-78; Florida State University, assistant professor, 1978-83, associate professor, 1983-94, professor of English, 1994-2004, chair, 1999-2006, James M. McCrimmon professor, 2004-06, English Honors Program, director, 1980-85, 1991-97, director of English studies and assistant chair, 1985-88, director of undergraduate studies, 1991-97, Creative Writing Program, acting director, 1996-97; Joseph Conrad Society, vice president, 1996-98, president, 1998-2000, Joseph Conrad Today, editor, 1997-2000; South Atlantic Association of Departments of English, president, 2003-04; University of South Florida, professor of English, 2006-; South Atlantic Modern Language Association, vice president, 2007-08, president, 2009; South Atlantic Graduate Education Consortium, president. **Publications:** The Domestic Life (poetry), 1994; (ed. with B.W. Shaffer) Approaches to Teaching Conrad's Heart of Darkness and The Secret Sharer, 2002. Works appear in anthologies. Contributor to periodicals. **Address:** Department of English, University of South Florida, CPR-360A, 4202 E Fowler Ave., Tampa, FL 33620-5550, U.S.A. **Online address:** hhawkins@cas.usf.edu

HAWKINS, Regina Trice. American (born United States), b. 1938. **Genres:** Biography, Autobiography/Memoirs. **Career:** Buckhead Brokers, referral agent; Georgia Women of Achievement, board director. Writer. **Publications:** Hazel Jane Raines, Pioneer Lady of Flight, 1996. **Address:** 2724 Barnesville Hwy., Thomaston, GA 30286, U.S.A. **Online address:** reghawk@mediaone.net

HAWKS, Kate. See GODWIN, Parke.

HAWKS, Tony. British (born England), b. 1960. **Genres:** Sports/Fitness. **Career:** Writer. **Publications:** Round Ireland with a Fridge, 2000; Playing the Moldovans at Tennis, 2001; One Hit Wonderland, 2007; A Piano in the Pyrenees: The Ups and Downs of an Englishman in the French Mountains, 2007. **Address:** St. Martin's Press, 175 5th Ave., New York, NY 10010, U.S.A. **Online address:** tony@tony-hawks.com

HAWKSLEY, Lucinda. British (born England) **Genres:** History, Young Adult Fiction, Biography, Autobiography/Memoirs. **Career:** Educator and writer. **Publications:** The Virgin Encyclopedia of Rock, 1998; (with D. Hardley) The Magic & Mystery of Scotland, 1998; Essential Pre-Raphaelites, 1999; Endangered Animals, 2000; A Tale of Two Cities, 2002; (ed. with I. Whitelaw) Yoga, 2003; Lizzie Siddal: The Tragedy of a Pre-Raphaelite Supermodel, 2004; Katey: The Life and Loves of Dickens's Artist Daughter, 2006. Contributor to books and periodicals. **Address:** c/o Christopher Sinclair Stevenson, Sinclair-Stevenson Ltd., 3 South Terr., London, GL SW7 2TB, England. **Online address:** info@lucindahawksley.com

HAWLEY, Ellen. American (born United States), b. 1947. **Genres:** Novels. **Career:** A View from the Loft, editor, 1982-99. Freelance editor. **Publications:** Trip Sheets (fiction), 1998; Open Line (fiction), 2008. **Address:** U.S.A. **Online address:** ellenhawley@yahoo.com

HAWLEY, John C(harles). American (born United States), b. 1947. **Genres:** Literary Criticism And History, Theology/Religion. **Career:** High school English teacher, 1972-74; Georgetown University Hospital, assistant chaplain, 1977; Roman Catholic congregations, assistant pastor, 1977; Mercy Hospital, assistant chaplain, 1978; University of Pennsylvania, teaching fellow, 1978-81, assistant chaplain at Newman Center, 1979-82; St. John's, Belize, assistant pastor, 1978, 1982-84, 1986, 1989; South Asian Review, associate editor; America magazine, literary editor and weekly columnist, 1983-84; Santa Clara University, assistant professor, 1986-92, associate professor of English, 1992-2005, professor of English, 2005-, Student Communications Board, chairperson, 1988-91, 1997-, department chair, 2005-09. Writer. **Publications:** (Ed.) Reform and Counterreform: The Dialectics of the Word in Western Christianity since Luther, 1994; (contrib.) Saving Beauty: Further Studies in Hopkins, 1994; (contrib.) Left Margins: Cultural Studies and Composition Pedagogy, 1995; Writing the Nation: Self and Country in the Post-Colonial Imagination, 1996; (ed.) Through a Glass Darkly: Essays in the Religious Imagination, 1996; (ed.) Cross-Addressing: Resistance Literature and Cultural Borders, 1996; (contrib.) Aspects of Islam in African Literature, 1996; (contrib.) Ideas of Home: Literature of Asian Migration, 1997; (ed.) The Postcolonial Crescent: Islam's Impact on Contemporary Literature, 1998; (ed.) Christian Encounters with the Other in UK as Historicizing Christian

Encounters with the Other, 1998; (ed.) Divine Aporia: Postmodern Conversations About the Other, 2000; (ed.) Postcolonial and Queer Theories: Intersections and Essays, 2001; (ed.) Postcolonial, Queer: Theoretical Intersections, 2001; (ed.) Encyclopedia of Postcolonial Studies, 2001; (contrib.) Flashes of the Fantastic: Selected Essays from the War of the Worlds Centennial, 2004; Amitav Ghosh: An Introduction, 2005; (ed. with R. Krishnaswamy) The Postcolonial and the Global, 2008; (ed.) India in Africa, Africa in India: Indian Ocean Cosmopolitanisms, 2008; (ed.) LGBTQ America Today: An Encyclopedia, 2009. Contributor to books and periodicals. **Address:** Department of English, Santa Clara University, Rm. 301, 500 El Camino Real, Santa Clara, CA 95053, U.S.A. **Online address:** jhawley@scu.edu

HAWLEY, Noah. American (born United States), b. 1967?. **Genres:** Novels, Plays/Screenplays. **Career:** Legal Aid Society, staff; Fox Searchlight, director of short films. Novelist, film maker and photographer. **Publications:** A Conspiracy of Tall Men, 1998; Other People's Weddings, 2004; The Punch, 2008; Good Father, 2012. Contributor to periodicals. **Address:** c/o Author Mail, St. Martins Press, 175 5th Ave., New York, NY 10010, U.S.A. **Online address:** noah@26keys.com

HAWLEY, Richard A. American (born United States), b. 1945. **Genres:** Novels, Poetry, Education, Social Commentary, Autobiography/Memoirs, Essays. **Career:** Cleveland's University School, teacher, 1968-86, dean of students, 1973-79, History Department, chairman, Upper School, director, 1988-2005, headmaster, 1995-2005; International Boys Schools Coalition, founding president. Writer and consultant. **Publications:** Aspects of Vision, 1976; With Love to My Survivors, 1982; (ed.) Coming through School, 1982; Purposes of Pleasure, 1983; The Headmaster's Papers, 1983, (foreword and afterword) rev. ed., 1992; A School Answers Back: Responding to Student Drug Use, 1984; Building Drug-Free Schools: An Educator's Guide to Policy, Curriculum & Community Consensus, 1986; St. Julian, 1987; Seeing Things: A Chronicle of Surprises, 1987; The Big Issues in the Adolescent Journey, 1988; The Big Issues in the Passage to Adulthood, 1988; Think about Drugs and Society: Responding to an Epidemic, 1988; In Praise of the Teaching Life, 1988; Hail, University!, 1990; Boys Will Be Men: Maculinity in Troubled Times, 1993; The Romance of Boys Schools, 1994; Papers from the Headmaster: Reflections on a World Fit for Children, 1996; The Headmaster's Wife: A Novel, 2000; Hard Lessons and Other Talks to the School, 2002; The Headmaster's Poems, 2002; Paul and Juliana, 2003; Icarus in Our Midst: A Reflection on Boys at Risk, 2004; Beyond the Icarus Factor, 2008; Twenty-One Visits to a Darkly Sun-Tanned Angel, 2009; (with M. Reichert) Teaching Boys, 2009; Reaching Boys/Teaching Boys, 2010; The Guru, 2011. FORTHCOMING: The Boyhood of Jonathan Force; The Figure of Icarus; Souls in Boxes; The Source of Longing. Contributor to periodicals. **Address:** 1266 Rte. 125, PO Box 28, Ripton, VT 05766, U.S.A. **Online address:** richardhawley32@gmail.com

HAWORTH-ATTARD, Barbara. Canadian (born Canada), b. 1953. **Genres:** Novels. **Career:** Writer and educator. **Publications:** NOVELS: The Three Wishbells, 1995; Dark of the Moon, 1995; Home Child, 1996; Truth Singer, 1996; Buried Treasure, 1998; WyndMagic, 1999; Love-Lies-Bleeding, 1999; Flying Geese, 2001; Irish Chain, 2002; Theories of Relativity, 2003; A Trail of Broken Dreams: The Gold Rush Diary of Harriet Palmer: Overland to the Cariboo, 1862, 2004; Forget-Me-Not, 2005; A Is for Angst, 2007; Haunted, 2009; My Life from Air-bras to Zits, 2009. Works appear in anthologies. **Address:** c/o Scott Treimel, 434 Lafayette St., New York, NY 10003, U.S.A. **Online address:** battard@rogers.com

HAWTHORNE, Fran. American (born United States), b. 1952?. **Genres:** Business/Trade/Industry, Politics/Government, Medicine/Health. **Career:** Fortune, writer and editor; Business Week, writer and editor; Crain's New York Business, writer and editor; Institutional Investor, writer, editor and senior contributing editor; Bergen Record, writer and editor. **Publications:** Teach Yourself Visually Investing Online, 2000; The Merck Druggernaut: The Inside Story of a Pharmaceutical Giant, 2003; Inside the FDA: The Business and Politics behind the Drugs We Take and the Food We Eat, 2005; Pension Dumping: The Reasons, the Wreckage, the Stakes for Wall Street, 2008; The Overloaded Liberal: Shopping, Investing, Parenting, and Other Daily Dilemmas in An Age of Political Activism, 2009; Ethical Chic: The Inside Story of the Companies We Think We Love, 2012. Contributor to periodicals. **Address:** Beacon Press, 25 Beacon St., Boston, MA 02108, U.S.A. **Online address:** fran@hawthornewriter.com

HAWTHORNE, Rachel. *See* **HEATH, Lorraine.**

HAWVERMALE, Lance. *See* **O'ROURKE, Erin.**

HAXTON, Brooks. American (born United States), b. 1950. **Genres:** Poetry. **Career:** Syracuse University, Department of English, adjunct professor, 1981-82, associate professor, 1993-, professor; George Washington University, adjunct professor, 1982-84; American University, adjunct professor, 1983-84; George Mason University, adjunct professor, 1984-85, teacher of creative writing; University of Maryland, adjunct professor, 1984-85, teacher of creative writing; Sarah Lawrence College, visiting poet, 1985, teacher of creative writing; Warren Wilson College, resident poet, 1990-, teacher of creative writing. Writer. **Publications:** POETRY: The Lay of Eleanor and Irene, 1985; Dominion, 1986; Dead Reckoning, 1989; Traveling Companion, 1989; The Sun at Night, 1995; Nakedness, Death and the Number Zero, 2001; Selected Poems, 2002; Uproar: Antiphones to the Psalms, 2004; They Lift their Wings to Cry, 2008. TRANSLATIONS: Dances for Flute and Thunder: Praises, Prayers and Insults: Poems from the Ancient Greek, 1999; Fragments: the Collected Wisdom of Heraclitus, 2001. OTHER: Tennessee Williams, 1994. Contributor of articles to periodicals. **Address:** Department of English, Syracuse University, 432 Hall of Languages, Syracuse, NY 13244, U.S.A. **Online address:** bhaxton@syr.edu

HAY, Elizabeth (Jean). (Elizabeth Smith). British/Indian (born India), b. 1936. **Genres:** Biography. **Career:** BBC Radio News, producer, 1961-70, producer of current affairs, 1970-78, BBC World Service, head of current affairs, 1984-87, English Services, controller, 1987-94. Writer. **Publications:** AS ELIZABETH SMITH: Healing Herbs, 1978; Sambo Sahib: The Story of Little Black Sambo and Helen Bannerman, 1981; Sayonara Sambo, 1994. **Address:** 12 Highbury Terr., London, GL N5 1UP, England. **Online address:** elizabeth.smith226@gmail.com

HAY, Samuel A. American (born United States), b. 1937. **Genres:** Literary Criticism And History, Theatre, Young Adult Fiction, Social Sciences, Biography, Autobiography/Memoirs. **Career:** Drama teacher, 1960-; University of Maryland, assistant professor of English, 1971-72, assistant professor of African American studies, 1972-73; Purdue University, Africana Studies and Research Center, director, 1974-78; Washington University, Black Studies Program, director and professor of theater, 1978-79; Morgan State University, Department of Communication and Theater Arts, professor and chair, 1979-84; University of California, faculty; Morgan State University, faculty; Washington University, faculty; Purdue University, faculty; University of Maryland, faculty; Lafayette College, visiting professor of government and law; North Carolina Agricultural and Technical State University, Department of Performing Visual Arts and Theater, chair. Writer. **Publications:** African American Theatre: An Historical and Critical Analysis, 1994; Ed Bullins: A Literary Biography, 1997. Contributor to journals. **Address:** Wayne State University Press, Leonard N. Simons Bldg., 4809 Woodward Ave., Detroit, MI 48201-1309, U.S.A.

HAY, Sheridan. American/Australian (born Australia) **Genres:** Novels, Young Adult Fiction. **Career:** Strand Bookstore, staff; Parsons School of Design, instructor. Writer. **Publications:** The Secret of Lost Things, 2006. **Address:** c/o Elaine Koster, Elaine Koster Literary Agency, 55 Central Pk. W, Ste. 6, New York, NY 10023, U.S.A.

HAY, William Anthony. American (born United States), b. 1968. **Genres:** History, Politics/Government, Humanities. **Career:** University of Virginia, Miller Center of Public Affairs, Presidential Oral History Project, research associate, 1999-2000; Foreign Policy Research Institute, Orbis: A Journal of World Affairs, book review editor, 2001-09, associate editor, 2007-09, research fellow, 2000-02, senior fellow, 2002-; Mississippi State University, assistant professor of history, 2003, associate professor of history; Southern Conference on British Studies, secretary and treasurer; Royal Historical Society, fellow, 2009. Writer. **Publications:** The Whig Revival, 1808-1830, 2005; (ed. with H. Sicherman) Is There Still a West?: The Future of the Atlantic Alliance, 2007. Contributor to periodicals. **Address:** Department of History, Mississippi State University, 214 Allen Hall, PO Box H, Mississippi State, PA 39762, U.S.A. **Online address:** wilhay6248@aol.com

HAYASHI, Nancy. American (born United States), b. 1939. **Genres:** Young Adult Fiction, Illustrations. **Career:** Higbee's Department Store, layout artist, 1964-66; Bowes Advertising, art director, 1966-75; Baxter, Gurian and Mazzei Advertising, art director, 1975-77. Writer. **Publications:** SELF-ILLUSTRATED FOR MIDDLE-GRADE READERS: Cosmic Cousin (mystery), 1988; (with P.K. Feder) Did You Lose the Car Again?, 1990; The Fantastic Stay-Home-from-School Day, 1992; Superbird to the Rescue, 1995. Illustrator of books by others. **Address:** 3507 Landa St., Los Angeles, CA 90039-3525, U.S.A.

HAYASHI, Robert T. American (born United States), b. 1963?. **Genres:** Natural History, Social Sciences. **Career:** University of Wisconsin, assistant professor of English; Amherst College, Department of English, assistant professor, Department of American Studies, assistant professor, Department of European Studies, faculty, Department of Environmental Studies, faculty. Writer. **Publications:** Haunted by Waters: A Journey through Race and Place in the American West, 2007. Contributor to journals. **Address:** Department of English, Amherst College, 13 Johnson Chapel, PO Box AC 2234, Amherst, MA 01002-5000, U.S.A. **Online address:** rhayashi@amherst.edu

HAYCOCK, Kate. British (born England), b. 1962. **Genres:** Sports/Fitness, Theatre, Food And Wine, Film, History, Children's Fiction. **Career:** Aston Technology, management trainee, 1986-87; Acton College, lecturer in computing and business, 1987-89; Gamester Kenyon, public relations account executive, 1989-90. Writer. **Publications:** Fitness, 1990; Plays, 1990; Pasta, 1991; Skiing, 1991; Gymnastics, 1991; Science Fiction Films, 1992; Shelter, 1993; Dealing with Eating Disorders, 1994; Dealing with Family Break-Up, 1995. **Address:** 64 Beaks Hill Rd., Kings Norton, Birmingham, WM B38 8BY, England. **Online address:** kate@rpmguiding.com

HAYDEN, Brian (Douglas). Canadian/American (born United States), b. 1946. **Genres:** Anthropology/Ethnology, Archaeology/Antiquities, Social Sciences. **Career:** American Stock Exchange, research worker, 1964; Virginia Commonwealth University, instructor in sociology and anthropology, 1973-74; Simon Fraser University, instructor, 1974-76, assistant professor, 1976-78, associate professor, 1978-84, professor of archaeology, 1984-, now professor emeritus of archaeology; Dinosaur National Monument, field assistant, 1965-66; Coxoh ethno-archaeological Project in Mexico and Guatemala, principal investigator and field director, 1977-85; Villatoro Mastodon Site, principal investigator, 1978. Writer. **Publications:** Paleolithic Reflections: Lithic Technology of the Western Desert Aborigines, 1979; Palaeolithic Reflections: Lithic Technology and Ethnographic Excavation among Australian Aborigines, 1979; (with A. Cannon) The Structure of Material Systems: Ethnoarchaeology in the Maya Highlands, 1984; (with T.A. Lee, Jr.) San Pablo Cave and El Cayo on the Usumacinta River, Chiapas, Mexico, 1988; Archaeology: The Science of Once and Future Things, 1993; The Pithouses of Keatley Creek: Complex Hunter-Gatherers of the Northwest Plateau, 1997; Shamans, Sorcerers, and Saints: The Prehistory of Religion, 2003; L'Homme et l'inégalité, 2008. EDITOR AND CONTRIBUTOR: Settlement Patterns of the Draper and White Sites: 1973 Excavations, 1979; Lithic Use-Wear Analysis, 1979; Lithic Studies among the Contemporary Highland Maya, 1987; A Complex Culture of the British Columbia Plateau: Traditional Stl'atl'imx Resource Use, 1992; The Ancient Past of Keatley Creek, vol. I: Taphonomy, 2000, vol. II: Socioeconomy, 2000, vol. III: Excavations, 2004; (with M. Dietler) Feasts: Archaeological and Ethnographic Perspectives on Food, Politics and Power, 2001. Works appear in anthologies. Contributor to books and journals. **Address:** Department of Archaeology, Simon Fraser University, 8888 University Dr., Burnaby, BC V5A 1S6, Canada. **Online address:** bhayden@sfu.ca

HAYDEN, C. J. American (born United States), b. 1956. **Genres:** Business/Trade/Industry, Marketing, Self Help, inspirational/Motivational Literature, How-to Books, Adult Non-fiction, E-books, Advertising/Public Relations, Reference. **Career:** Telelearning Inc., product manager, 1986-87; Morrison & Foerster, systems consultant and administrator, 1987-90; Winston HR Solutions, management consultant, 1990-92; Wings for Business L.L.C., entrepreneurship coach and author, 1992-; Mills College, adjunct faculty, 1994-95; Coaches Training Institute, faculty, 1996-2002, John F. Kennedy University, instructor, 2000-01. **Publications:** Get Clients Now!: A 28-Day Marketing Program for Professionals, Consultants and Coaches, 1999, 2nd ed., 2007; Get Hired Now!: A 28-Day Program for Landing the Job You Want, 2005; The One-Person Marketing Plan Workbook, 2007. Contributor to periodicals. **Address:** Wings for Business L.L.C., PO Box 225008, San Francisco, CA 94122, U.S.A. **Online address:** info@tsgetclientsnow.com

HAYDEN, Eric William. British (born England), b. 1919. **Genres:** Children's Fiction, Theology/Religion, Novellas/Short Stories, Poetry. **Career:** Whitley Bay Baptist Church, pastor, 1948-52; Shrewsbury Baptist Church, pastor, 1952-56; Spurgeon's Tabernacle, pastor, 1956-62; Leominster Baptist Church, pastor, 1962-73; Donnington Wood Baptist Church, pastor, 1973-76; Longhope and Ruardean Hill Baptist Churches, pastor, 1976-. Writer. **Publications:** Church Publicity, 1952; Faith's Glorious Achievement, 1958; Spurgeon on Revival, 1962; History of Spurgeons Tabernacle, 1962, rev. ed., 1992; Preaching Through the Bible, 1964, vol. II, 1966; Everyday Yoga for Christians, 1966; Bible Object Lessons, vol. III, 1968; When God Takes Over, 1969; Miracle of Time, 1970; Searchlight on Spurgeon, 1973; Jimmy in Space, 1973; Jimmy Plays Cricket, 1974; Traveller's Guide to Spurgeon Country, 1974; Sermon Outlines series, 6 vols., 1974-80; Joshua Thomas, 1976; (contrib.) The American Baptist Heritage in Wales, 1976; Just the Girl You Want and Other Stories, 1977; Meditation: The Key to Expanded Consciousness, 1978; Praying for Revival, 1978; The Adventures of Bobby Wildgoose, 1980; Learning to Cope with Agoraphobia, 1983; Letting the Lion Loose, 1984; God's Answer for Fear, 1985; God's Answer for Pressure, 1987; People Like Us, 1989; Highlights in the Life of C.H. Spurgeon, 1990; The Spurgeon Family, 1993; The Light of the World, 1993; He Won Them for Christ, 1993; (with P. Hayden) Lectures on C.H. Spurgeon, 1994; Poems and Letters of C.H. Spurgeon, 1994; The Unforgettable Spurgeon, 1996; My Spurgeon Souvenirs, 1996. **Address:** 7 Nanfan & Dobyn Pl., Newent, GC GL18 1TF, England.

HAYDON, Elizabeth. American (born United States), b. 1965?. **Genres:** Science Fiction/Fantasy, Children's Fiction, Westerns/Adventure. **Career:** Writer and educational book editor. **Publications:** Rhapsody: Child of Blood, 1999; Prophecy: Child of the Earth, 2000; Destiny: Child of the Sky, 2001; Requiem for the Sun, 2002; Elegy for a Lost Star, 2004; (comp.) The Floating Island: The Lost Journals of Ven Polypheme, 2006; The Assassin King, 2006; (comp.) The Thief Queen's Daughter, 2007; Dragon's Lair, 2008; The Tree of Water, forthcoming. **Address:** Tor Books, 175 5th Ave., New York, NY 10010, U.S.A. **Online address:** elizabethhaydon@hotmail.com

HAYDUK, Ron. American (born United States), b. 1958. **Genres:** Adult Non-fiction, Social Commentary, Politics/Government. **Career:** City University of New York, adjunct instructor in political science, 1989-98, Borough of Manhattan Community College, Department of Political Science, assistant professor, 2000-05, deputy chair, 2004-06, associate professor, 2005-, professor of social sciences and human services; John Jay College, adjunct instructor, 1989; Hunter College, adjunct instructor, 1991-92; Baruch College, adjunct instructor, 1997-98; City College Internship Program in Government and Politics, faculty coordinator; New York University, adjunct instructor, 1995; Touro College, assistant professor of political sciences, 1997-2000; Columbia University, adjunct instructor in political science, 1999; Immigrant Voting Project, co-founder and co-director, 2004-; New York City Voter Assistance Commission, coordinator; Brecht Forum, board director. Consultant and writer. **Publications:** (Contrib.) Defense of the Alien, 2001; (ed. with K. Mattson) Democracy's Moment: Reforming the American Political System for the 21st Century, 2002; From Act Up to the WTO: Urban Activism and Community Building in Era of Globalization, 2002; (contrib.) U.S. Progressive Political Movements in the 21st Century, 2003; (contrib.) Surviving Sprawl: Culture, Ecology and Politics, 2003; Gatekeepers to the Franchise: Shaping Election Administration in New York, 2005; Democracy for All: Restoring Immigrant Voting Rights in the United States, 2006. Contributor to periodicals. **Address:** Department of Social Science, Borough of Manhattan Community College, Rm. N615, 199 Chambers St., New York, NY 10007, U.S.A. **Online address:** ron@ronhayduk.com

HAYES, Belinda. See LANAGAN, Margo.

HAYES, Bill. American (born United States), b. 1961?. **Genres:** Novels, Autobiography/Memoirs. **Career:** Writer. **Publications:** Sleep Demons: An Insomniac's Memoir, 2001; Five Quarts: A Personal and Natural History of Blood, 2005; The Anatomist: A True Story of "Gray's Anatomy,", 2008. **Address:** Wendy Weil, 232 Madison Ave., Ste. 1300, New York, NY 10016, U.S.A.

HAYES, Charles Langley. See HOLMES, B(ryan) J(ohn).

HAYES, Christopher L. American (born United States), b. 1958. **Genres:** Gerontology/Senior Issues, Business/Trade/Industry, Psychology. **Career:** Project T.L.C., director of social service and personnel, 1978-79; Project

PACE Inc., executive director, 1979-83; Coastline Community College, faculty, 1980-82; Santa Ana College, faculty, 1981-83; Catholic University of America, Center for the Study of Pre-Retirement and Aging, director of education, training and acting director, 1984-85, director of the center, 1985-86; Long Island University, assistant professor, 1986-89, National Center for Women and Retirement Research, director, 1988-, Master's Program in Gerontology, director, 1988-, associate professor of psychology, 1989, professor of Gerontology; In These Times, Schumann Center, writing fellow, 2005-06; The Nation Institute, Puffin foundation writing fellow, 2006-07; The Nation, editor; Harvard University, Edmond J Safra Foundation Center for Ethics, fellow. **Publications:** (Co-author) The Euro-American Elderly in the United States: A Manual for Service Providers and Ethnic Leaders, 1986; (ed. with R.A. Kalish and D. Guttmann) The European-American Elderly: A Guide for Practice, 1986; (with J. Deren) Employment and Retirement Issues for Mid-Life Women, 1988; (with J. Deren) Looking Ahead to Your Financial Future, 1988; (ed. with J. Deren) Pre-Retirement Planning for Women: Programs Design and Research, 1990; (with D. Anderson and M. Blau) Our Turn: The Good News about Women and Divorce, 1993; (ed.) Women in Mid-Life: Planning for Tomorrow, 1993; (with D.Y. Anderson) Gender, Identity, and Self-Esteem: A New Look At Adult Development, 1996; (with K. Kelly) Money Makeovers: How Women can Control Their Financial Destiny, 1998. Works appear in anthologies. Contributor to periodicals. **Address:** National Center for Women and Retirement Research, Long Island University, Southampton Campus, Southampton, NY 11968, U.S.A. **Online address:** christopher.hayes@liu.edu

HAYES, Daniel. American (born United States), b. 1952. **Genres:** Novels, Young Adult Fiction. **Career:** Waterford Central Catholic School, English teacher, 1975-84; Troy High School, English teacher, 1984-; Hudson Valley Community College, creative writer. **Publications:** The Trouble with Lemons, 1991; Eye of the Beholder, 1992; No Effect, 1994; Flyers, 1996; My Kind of Crazy, forthcoming. Contributor to periodicals. **Address:** Jennifer DeChiara Literary Agency, 31 E 32nd St., Ste. 300, New York, NY 10016, U.S.A. **Online address:** hayesdm@aol.com

HAYES, Dawn Marie. American (born United States), b. 1968. **Genres:** History. **Career:** New York University, teaching assistant, 1991-94, administrative assistant, 1993, 1996, web master & web designer, 1996-97; College of Staten Island, adjunct lecturer, 1996-98; Iona College, assistant professor, 1998-2002, Department of History and Political Science, web master & web designer, 1999-2002; Borough of Manhattan Community College, City University of New York, assistant professor, 2002-03; Montclair State University, assistant professor, 2003-06, newsletter editor, 2005-, associate professor, 2006-, director of Sicily summer study abroad program, 2006-; International Catholic History Discussion List (H-Catholic) Web site, list editor, 2004-. Educator, writer and administrator. **Publications:** Body and Sacred Place in Medieval Europe, 1100-1389, 2003. **Address:** Department of History, Montclair State University, 426 Dickson Hall, Montclair, NJ 07043, U.S.A. **Online address:** dawn.hayes@montclair.edu

HAYES, Derek. Canadian (born Canada), b. 1947?. **Genres:** History, Geography. **Career:** City Planning Department, planner. Historian and writer. **Publications:** Historical Atlas of British Columbia and the Pacific Northwest: Maps of Exploration: British Columbia Washington Oregon Alaska Yukon, 1999; First Crossing: Alexander Mackenzie His Expedition across North America and the Opening of the Continent, 2001; Historical Atlas of the North Pacific Ocean: Maps of Discovery and Scientific Exploration 1500-2000, 2001; Historical Atlas of Canada: Canada's History Illustrated with Original Maps, 2002; Historical Atlas of the Arctic, 2003; Canada: An Illustrated History, 2004; America Discovered: A Historical Atlas of North American Exploration, 2005; Historical Atlas of Vancouver and Lower Fraser Valley, 2005; Historical Atlas of the United States: With Original Maps, 2007; Historical Atlas of California: With Original Maps, 2007; Historical Atlas of Toronto, 2008; Historical Atlas of the American West, 2009; Historical Atlas of the North American Railroad, 2010; Historical Atlas of Washington and Oregon, 2011. **Address:** c/o Author Mail, D & M Publishing Group/Douglas & McIntyre, 2323 Quebec St., Ste. 201, Vancouver, BC V5T 4S7, Canada. **Online address:** derek@derekhayes.ca

HAYES, Joe. American (born United States), b. 1945. **Genres:** Children's Fiction, Novels. **Career:** Sunnyside High School, teacher; Writer. **Publications:** The Day It Snowed Tortillas, 1982, 3rd ed., 1985; Coyote & Native American Folk Tales, 1983; The Checker Playing Hound Dog: Tall Tales

From a Southwestern Storyteller, 1986; No Way, Jose!/De Ninguna Manera, Jose!: A Story in Two Languages, 1986; La Llorona/The Weeping Woman: An Hispanic Legend, 1987, 3rd ed., 2004; Monday, Tuesday, Wednesday, Oh!/Lunes, Martes, Miercoles, O!, 1987; Terrible Tragadabas: A Story in Two Languages: El terrible Tragadabas, 1987; A Heart Full of Turquoise: Pueblo Indian Tales, 1988; Mariposa, Mariposa: A Story in Two Languages, 1988; The Wise Little Burro: Holiday Tales from Near and Far, 1990; That's Not Fair! Earth Friendly Tales, 1991; Everyone Knows Gato Pinto: More Tales from Spanish New Mexico, 1992; Soft Child: How Rattlesnake Got Its Fangs: A Native American Folktale, 1993; Antonio's Lucky Day, 1993; The Butterflies Trick Coyote, 1993; Watch Out for Clever Women/Cuidado con las Mujeres Astutas, 1994; Where There's a Will, There's a Way/Donde hay Ganashay Manas, 1995; Grandfather Horned Toad, 1996; A Spoon for Every Bite: Una Cuchara Para Cada Bocado, 1996, rev. ed., 2005; Here Comes the Storyteller, 1996; (with S. Franco) Modelo Antiguo: A Novel of Mexico City, 1997; (ed. and trans.) J. Manuel Espinosa, Cuentos de Cuanto hay: Tales from Spanish New Mexico, 1998; Tell Me A Cuento: Cuéntame Un Story, 1998; Little Gold Star: A Cinderella Cuento: Estrellita de Oro, 2000; El Cucuy!: A Bogeyman Cuento, 2001; Juan Verdades: The Man Who Could Not Tell a Lie, 2001; Pájaro Verde: The Green Bird, 2002; Day it Snowed Tortillas: Eldía que nevó tortillas: A Classic From the American Southwest, 2003; Ghost Fever: Mal de Fantasma, 2004; La llorona /The Weeping Woman: An Hispanic Legend Told in Spanish and English, 3rd ed., 2004; Spoon for Every Bite/Una Cuchara Para Cada Bocado, 2005; (trans. with S. Franco) Celebrate Martin Luther King, Jr. Day with Mrs. Park's Class, 2006; The Gum-Chewing Rattler, 2006; (trans. with S. Franco) Celebrate Cinco de Mayo with the Mexican Hat Dance, 2006; Dance, Nana, dance/Baila, Nana, Baila: Cuban Folktales in English and Spanish, 2007; (trans. with S. Franco) Celebrate Kwanzaa with Boots and Her Kittens, 2007; (trans. with S. Franco) Celebra un powwow con Sandy Starbright, 2007; The Love-Sick Skunk, 2010; Coyote Under the Table=El Coyote Debajo De La Mesa: Folktales Told in Spanish and English, 2011. Works appear in anthologies. **Address:** Cinco Puntos Press, 701 Texas, El Paso, TX 79901, U.S.A.

HAYES, Rosemary. British (born England) **Genres:** Children's Fiction, Novels, Natural History, Young Adult Fiction. **Career:** Anglia Young Books, owner. Writer and consultant. **Publications:** FOR CHILDREN: Race against Time, 1988; The Fox in the Wood, 1989; Flight of the Mallard, 1989; Scent of Danger, 1989; The Gremlin Buster, 1990; Dreamchild, 1990; Seal Cry, 1991; Mission from the Marsh: King Alfred and the Vikings, 1991; The Smell That Got Away, 1992; Herbie's Place, 1994; The Grabbing Bird, 1996; The Amazing Mr. Mulch, 1996; Mr. Mulch's Magic Mixtures, 1996; Jumble Power, 1996; The Big Shrink, 1996; The Slippery Planet, 1996; The Treasure Cave, 1996; The Peace Ring, 1996; The Magic Sword, 1996; The Silver Fox, 1997; Holly and the Dream Fixer, 1998; The Big Shrink, 2000; Play a Part, 2000; (ed. with R. Brown) Write Here, Write Now, 2001; Follow That Lion!, 2001; Blood Ties, 2001; Troubled Waters, 2003; The Gangbusters, 2004; To the Edge of the Ocean, 2004; Bright Horizon, 2004; Mixing It, 2007; Secrets and Spies, 2007; Payback, 2009; Ghost Ride, 2010; The Blue-Eyed Aborigine, 2010; (with C. Herbert) Rising Above Bullying: From Despair to Recovery, 2011. **Address:** c/o Author Mail, Hodder Headline, 338 Euston Rd., London, GL NW1 3BH, England. **Online address:** r.hayes@btinternet.com

HAYES, Stephen F. American (born United States) **Genres:** Young Adult Non-fiction, Social Sciences. **Career:** National Journal Hotline, senior writer; Georgetown University, Institute on Political Journalism, director; The Weekly Standard, senior writer; Cable News Network, commentator. **Publications:** The Connection: How Al Qaeda's Collaboration with Saddam Hussein Has Endangered America, 2004; Cheney: The Untold Story of America's Most Powerful and Controversial Vice President, 2007. Contributor to periodicals. **Address:** The Weekly Standard, 1150 17th St. NW, Ste. 505, Washington, DC 20036, U.S.A.

HAYFLICK, Leonard. American (born United States), b. 1928. **Genres:** Biology, Medicine/Health. **Career:** Sharp and Dohme, research assistant in bacteriology, 1951-52; University of Texas Medical Branch, Department of Microbiology, McLaughlin research fellow in infection and immunity, 1956-58; Wistar Institute of Anatomy and Biology, associate, 1958-68; University of Pennsylvania, assistant professor of research medicine, 1966-68; Stanford University, school of medicine, professor of medical microbiology, 1968-76, senator-at-large for basic medical sciences, 1970-73; Children's Hospital Medical Center, senior research cell biologist, 1976-81; University of Florida, professor of zoology and professor of microbiology and immunology,

1981-86, Center for Gerontology Studies of the College of Liberal Arts and Sciences, director, 1981-87; Genentech Inc., consultant, 1982-; University of California, School of Medicine, professor of anatomy, cell biology and aging, 1988-. Writer. **Publications:** How and Why We Age, 1994; Has Anyone Ever Died of Old Age?, 2003. EDITOR: (co-ed.) Biology of the Mycoplasma, 1967; The Mycoplasmatales and the L-Phase of Bacteria, 1969; (co-ed.) Handbook of the Biology of Aging, 1977. Contributor to journals. **Address:** School of Medicine, University of California-San Francisco, 36991 Greencroft Close, PO Box 89, The Sea Ranch, CA 95497, U.S.A. **Online address:** len@gene.com

HAYFORD, Charles W. American (born United States), b. 1941. **Genres:** Cultural/Ethnic Topics, History, Bibliography. **Career:** Harvard College, teaching fellow, 1967-71; Oberlin College, instructor, assistant professor, 1971-76; International Asian Studies Program, associate director, 1978-81; Chinese University of Hong Kong, Honorary lecturer, 1978-81; University of Chicago, Center for East Asian Studies, coordinator of outreach, 1981-87; Northwestern University, Department of History, department associate, 1981-, visiting professor, 1988, 1991, 2008-09; Journal of Asian Studies, book review editor, 1990-94; University of Illinois, visiting associate professor, 1992; Stanford University, visiting professor, 1995-96; University of Iowa, visiting professor, 1997, 1999; University of Illinois at Chicago, visiting professor, visiting associate professor, 1992-95, 1997-98; Harvard University, Harvard Summer School, faculty, 2002-08; Journal of American-East Asian Relations, editor, 2006-. Writer. **Publications:** To the People: James Yen and Village China, 1990; (comp.) China, 1997; Bibliography of American-East Asian Relations, 2002; Blog Frog In A Well, 2007. Contributor to journals. **Address:** Department of History, Lake Forest College, 555 N Sheridan Rd., Lake Forest, IL 60045, U.S.A. **Online address:** chayford@aol.com

HAYGOOD, Wil. American (born United States), b. 1954. **Genres:** Biography, Documentaries/Reportage, Art/Art History, Music. **Career:** Call and Post, reporter, 1977-78; Community Information and Referral, hotline operator, 1978-79; R.H. Macy's, retail manager, 1980-82; Charleston Gazette, copy editor, 1982-84; Pittsburgh Post-Gazette, reporter, 1984-85; Boston Globe, staff writer, 1985-2001, foreign correspondent; Washington Post, Style Section, staff writer, 1991-. **Publications:** Two on the River, 1986; King of the Cats: The Life and Times of Adam Clayton Powell, Jr. (biography), 1993; The Haygoods of Columbus, 1997; In Black and White: The Life of Sammy Davis, Jr., 2003; Sweet Thunder: The Life and Times of Sugar Ray Robinson, 2009. Contributor to periodicals. **Address:** Style Section, Washington Post, 1150 15th St. NW, Washington, DC 20071, U.S.A.

HAYMAN, Carol Bessent. American (born United States), b. 1927. **Genres:** Poetry, Communications/Media, Gerontology/Senior Issues, inspirational/ Motivational Literature, Local History/Rural Topics, Self Help, Autobiography/Memoirs, Young Adult Fiction, Young Adult Fiction. **Career:** Louisburg College, trustee, 1964-71, poet-in-residence, 1982; Carteret Community College, adjunct teacher, instructor in creative writing, 1985-; Beaufort, poet laureate, 1989-; County Commissioners of Carteret County, poet laureate, 1993-; Carteret Writers, president; News-Times, columnist, 1999-; North Carolina Inc., Poetry Council, president, 1996-98. **Publications:** Keepsake, 1962; These Lovely Days, 1971; A Collection of Writings, 1972; What Is Christmas?, 1974; (ed.) The Bessent Story, 1978; Images and Echoes of Beaufort-by-the-Sea, 1993. Contributor of articles to periodicals. **Address:** Mount Olive College Press, 634 Henderson St., Mount Olive, NC 28365, U.S.A.

HAYMAN, David. American (born United States), b. 1927. **Genres:** Literary Criticism And History. **Career:** Assistant de langue anglaise, 1951-53; University of Texas, instructor, 1955-57, assistant professor, 1957-59, associate professor of English, 1959-65; University of Iowa, professor of English, 1965-73; University of Paris VIII, Anglo-American literature, professor, 1972-73; University de Paris, professor of English, 1972-73; University of Wisconsin, professor of comparative literature, 1973-89, chair, 1973-77, Evjue-Bascom professor of comparative literature, 1989-96, professor emeritus, 1997-; Goethe University, professor of English and American literature, 1984-85; Coimbra University, professor of English, 1994. Writer. **Publications:** Joyce et Mallarmae, 1956; (ed.) A First-Draft Version of Finnegan's Wake, 1963; Louis Ferdinand Céline, 1965; Ulysses: The Mechanics of Meaning, 1970; (with E. Rabkin) Form in Fiction: An Introduction to the Analysis of Narrative Prose, 1974; (ed. with C. Hart) James Joyce's Ulysses: Critical Essays, 1974; Finnegans Wake: A Facsimile of Buffalo Notebooks VI.B.13-16, 1978; (co-ed.) The James Joyce Archive, 1978; (ed. with E. Anderson) In the Wake of the Wake, 1978; Guia del Ulyses, 1979; Visiona New York: Entretiens Avec David Hayman, 1981; (ed.) Philippe Sollers, Writing and the Experience of Limits, 1983; Re-Forming the Narrative: Toward a Mechanics of Modernist Fiction, 1987; The Wake in Transit, 1990; (with S. Slate) Probes: Genetic Studies in Joyce, 1995. **Address:** Department of Comparative Literature, University of Wisconsin-Madison, 934 Van Hise Hall, 1220 Linden Dr., Madison, WI 53706-1525, U.S.A. **Online address:** dhayman@facstaff.wisc.edu

HAYMAN, Richard. British (born England), b. 1959. **Genres:** Archaeology/Antiquities, History. **Career:** National Trust, archaeologist, 1983-85; Merthyr Tydfil Heritage Trust, archaeologist, 1985-88; Ironbridge Gorge Museum, archaeologist, 1994-. Writer and photographer. **Publications:** Riddles in Stone: Myths, Archaeology, 1997; (with W. Horton and S. White) Archaeology and Conservation in Ironbridge, 1999; (with W. Horton) Ironbridge: History and Guide, 1999; Wrought Iron, 2000; Trees: Woodlands and Western Civilization, 2003; Riddles in Stone: Myths, Archaeology and the Ancient Britons, 2006; Concise Guide to the Parish Church, 2007; Church Misericords and Bench Ends, 2009; The Green Man, 2010. **Address:** Ironbridge Gorge Museum Trust, Coach Rd., Coalbrookdale, Shropshire, GL TF8 7DQ, England.

HAYMAN, Ronald. British (born England), b. 1932. **Genres:** Plays/Screenplays, Literary Criticism And History, Theatre, Autobiography/Memoirs, Biography. **Career:** Northampton Repertory Co., assistant producer, 1962-63; University of London, Department of English Literature, lecturer. Writer. **Publications:** (Co-author) Situation de la littérature anglaise d'aprés-guerre, 1955; Harold Pinter, 1968, 4th ed., 1980; Samuel Beckett, 1968, 3rd ed., 1980; John Osborne, 1968; John Arden, 1968; Robert Bolt, 1969; John Whiting, 1969; Techniques of Acting, 1969; Arthur Miller, 1970; Tolstoy, 1970; Arnold Wesker, 1970, 3rd ed., 1979; John Gielgud, 1971; Edward Albee, 1971; Arguing with Walt Whitman: An Essay on His Influence on 20th Century American Verse, 1971; Eugène Ionesco, 1972; One Hundred Years of Drama: A Selected List, 1972; Playback, 1973; The Set-Up, 1974; Playback 2, 1974; The First Thrust, 1975; The Novel Today 1967-1975, 1976; Leavis, 1976; Tom Stoppard, 1977, 4th ed., 1982; How to Read a Play, 1977, rev. ed., 1999; Artaud and After, 1977; De Sade: A Critical Biography, 1978; Theatre and Anti-Theatre: New Movements Since Beckett, 1979; British Theatre Since 1955: A Reassessment, 1979; Nietzsche: A Critical Life, 1980; K: A Biography of Kafka, 1981; Brecht: A Biography, 1983; Fassbinder, Film Maker, 1984; Brecht: The Plays, 1984; Günter Grass, 1985; Secrets: Boyhood in a Jewish Hotel, 1985; Writing Against: A Biography of Sartre, 1986; Sartre: A Life, 1987; Proust: A Biography, 1990; The Death and Life of Sylvia Plath, 1991; Tennessee Williams: Everyone Else is an Audience, 1993; Playing the Wife, 1995; Thomas Mann, 1995; Playing the Wife: A Play, 1996; Hitler and Geli, 1997; A Life of Jung, 1999; Marquis De Sade, 2003. EDITOR: Collected Plays of John Whiting, vol. II, 1969; J. Whiting, The Art of the Dramatist and Other Pieces, 1970; The German Theatre, 1975; My Cambridge, 1977; Plays One, 1998; At Ease in a Bright Red Tie: Writing on Theatre, 1999; Plays Two, 2001. Contributor to periodicals. **Address:** Gillon Aitken Associates, 18-21 Cavaye Pl., London, GL SW10 9PT, England.

HAYMAN, Walter Kurt. British/German (born Germany), b. 1926. **Genres:** Mathematics/Statistics, Sciences. **Career:** University of Exeter, lecturer, 1947-53, reader, 1953-56; University of London, professor of pure mathematics, 1956-85, professor emeritus, 1985-, senior research fellow, 1995-; University of York, professor of mathematics, 1985-93, professor emeritus, 1993-; Imperial college, senior research investigator, now professor emeritus. Writer. **Publications:** Multivalent Functions, 1958, 2nd ed., 1994; Meromorphic Functions, 1964; Transfinite Diameter and Its Applications, 1966; Research Problems in Function Theory, 1967; Functions Multivalents, 1968; (with P.B. Kennedy) Subharmonic Functions, vol. I, 1976, vol. II, 1989; (ed. with J. Clunie) Proceedings, 1974; Lectures on Approximation and Value Distribution, 1982; Conformal Mapping Problem Arising in Elasticity, 1983. **Address:** Department of Mathematics, Imperial College, South Kensington Campus, Rm. 6M43, 180 Queen's Gate, London, GL SW7 2AZ, England. **Online address:** w.hayman@imperial.ac.uk

HAYNES, C. Rayfield. American (born United States), b. 1943. **Genres:** Sociology, Biography, Young Adult Fiction, Autobiography/Memoirs, Adult Non-fiction. **Career:** U.S. Government, school teacher and principal, 1966-71; University of Miami, assistant professor, 1975-76; University of Wisconsin-Madison, assistant professor, 1976-79; clinical psychologist, 1979-. Writer. **Publications:** Growing Up Colored in Mississippi, 1992; The Ghost, 1995. **Address:** 222 W Brown Rd., Mesa, AZ 85201-3422, U.S.A.

HAYNES, David. American (born United States), b. 1955. **Genres:** Novels, Young Adult Fiction, Writing/Journalism, Business/Trade/Industry. **Career:** C.V. Mosby Publishing Co., associate editor, 1978-81; teacher, 1981-93; writer, 1993-; Mankato State University, visiting writer, 1994; Writer's Center, teacher, 1994-95; National Board for Professional Teaching Standards, teacher-in-residence, 1994-; Hamline University, teacher, 1995; Warren Wilson College, M.F.A. Program for Writers, faculty, 1996-97. **Publications:** ADULT NOVELS: Right by my Side, 1993; Somebody Else's Mama, 1995; Heathens, 1996; Live at Five, 1996; All American Dream Dolls, 1997; Full Matilda, 2004. JUVENILE FICTION: Right by My Side (young adult novel), 1993; Business as Usual (west 7th Wildcats 1), 1997, rev. ed., 2001; The Gumma Wars (West 7thWildcats 2), 1997; (ed. with J. Landsman) Welcome to Your Life: Writings for the Heart of Young America, 1998; The Everyday Magic of Walterlee Higgins, 1998. Contributor to periodicals. **Address:** Milkweed Editions, 1011 Washington Ave. S, Ste. 300, Minneapolis, MN 55415-1246, U.S.A.

HAYNES, Duncan H(arold). (Dirk Wyle). American (born United States), b. 1945. **Genres:** Mystery/Crime/Suspense, Novels, Sciences, Travel/Exploration. **Career:** University of Miami, assistant professor, 1973-77, associate professor, 1977-82, professor of pharmacology, 1982-2001; Pharma-Logic Inc., founder and principal, 1983-. Writer. **Publications:** MYSTERY NOVELS AS DIRK WYLE: Pharmacology Is Murder, 1998; Biotechnology Is Murder, 2000; Medical School Is Murder, 2001; Amazon Gold: A Ben Candidi Mystery, 2003; Bahamas West End is Murder: A Ben Candidi Mystery, 2005. Contributor to books and journals. **Address:** 4051 Barbarossa Ave., Miami, FL 33133, U.S.A. **Online address:** dirk@dirk-wyle.com

HAYNES, Gary (Anthony). American (born United States), b. 1948. **Genres:** Anthropology/Ethnology, Adult Non-fiction. **Career:** Catholic University of America, Department of Anthropology, teaching assistant, 1974-76, visiting assistant professor, 1981, Archeology Laboratory, director, 1977-78; Smithsonian Institution, research associate, 1981-85; George Washington University, Department of Anthropology, associate professorial lecturer, 1982; University of Nevada, Department of Anthropology, assistant professor, 1985-88, associate professor, 1988-95, professor, 1995-; Nevada Archaeologist, editor, 1987-92; International Union for Quaternary Research, Commission on Humans and Biosphere, president, 2003-11. **Publications:** Mammoths, Mastodonts, and Elephants: Biology, Behavior, and the Fossil Record, 1991; Early Settlement of North America: The Clovis Era, 2002; Clovis Era in a Mammoth-Haunted Continent, 2002; (ed.) American Megafaunal Extinctions At The End Of The Pleistocene, 2009; The Forest with a Desert Heart: Human Fortunes in an African Wilderness, forthcoming. Contributor to journals. **Address:** Department of Anthropology, University of Nevada, 512 Ansari Business Bldg., 1664 N Virginia St., Reno, NV 89557-0096, U.S.A. **Online address:** gahaynes@unr.edu

HAYNES, Jane. British (born England), b. 1944. **Genres:** Psychology, Writing/Journalism. **Career:** Intheconsultingroom.com (professional site for psychoanalysts), partner; University of London, Birkbeck College, qualified student counselor; Eastern European Institute for Psychoanalytic Studies, clinical consultant. Writer and relational psychotherapist. **Publications:** Who Is It That Can Tell Me Who I Am? The Journal of a Psychotherapist, 2007. EDITOR: (with A. Shearer) When a Princess Dies: Reflections from Jungian Analysts, 1998; (with H. Zinkin and R. Gordon) Dialogue in the Analytic Setting: Selected Papers of Louis Zinkin on Jung and on Group Analysis, 1998; (with J. Miller) Inconceivable Conceptions: Psychological Aspects of Infertility and Reproductive Technology, 2003. Contributor to books and periodicals. **Address:** London, GL , England. **Online address:** author@intheconsultingroom.com

HAYNES, Jim. (James Almand). French/American (born United States), b. 1933. **Genres:** Philosophy, Theatre, Travel/Exploration, Autobiography/Memoirs, Essays, Reference. **Career:** Paperback Bookshop and Gallery, founder and proprietor, 1959-64; Traverse Theatre, founder and co-artistic director, 1962-67; Arts Laboratory, co-founder and co-artistic director, 1967-69; University of Paris VIII, associate professor of media studies, 1969-99; Videoheads, co-founder and co-director, 1968-; Handshake Editions, founder and director, 1979-. Writer. **Publications:** Workers of the World, Unite and Stop Working! A Reply to Marxism, 1978; Everything Is!, 1980; Thanks for Coming! An Autobiography, 1984; Very Rough and Very Self-indulgent Year by Year Chronology, 2005; On all Fronts: Australia's World War II, 2010. EDITOR: Traverse Plays, 1965; (with J. Pasle-Green) Hello, I Love You! Voices from within the Sexual Revolution, 1974; More Romance, Less Romanticism, 1982; Homage to Henry (tribute to Henry Miller), 1982; Czech-Slovakia, Hungary, Bulgaria, 1993; Lithuania, Latvia, Estonia, 1993; Round the World in 33 Days, 2002. TRAVEL GUIDE SERIES: (Ed.) People to People...: Poland; Romania; Baltic Republics; Russia. Contributor to periodicals. **Address:** Atelier A-2, 83 rue de la Tombe Issoire, Paris, 75014, France. **Online address:** jim_haynes@wanadoo.fr

HAYNES, John Earl. American (born United States), b. 1944. **Genres:** History, Politics/Government, Social Sciences. **Career:** University of California, Bush leadership lellow, 1974; Historians of American Communism (newsletter), editor, 1982-2003, president, 1992-95; Library of Congress, Manuscript Division, 20th-century political historian, 1987-; Central European University, lecturer, 2001. **Publications:** Dubious Alliance: The Making of Minnesota's DFL Party, 1984; Communism and Anti-Communism in the United States: An Annotated Guide to Historical Writings, 1987; (with H. Klehr) The American Communist Movement, 1992; (with H. Klehr and F.I. Firsov) The Secret World of American Communism, 1995; Red Scare or Red Menace? American Communism and Anticommunism in the Cold War Era, 1996; (with H. Klehr and K. Anderson) The Soviet World of American Communism, 1998; (ed.) Calvin Coolidge and the Coolidge Era, 1998; (with H. Klehr) Venona: Decoding Soviet Espionage in America, 1999; (with H. Klehr) In Denial: Historians, Communism and Espionage, 2002; (with H. Klehr) Early Cold War Spies: The Espionage Trials that Shaped American Politics, 2006; (with H. Klehr and A. Vassiliev) Spies: The Rise and Fall of the KGB in America, 2009. Contributor to books and periodicals. **Address:** Manuscript Division, Library of Congress, Rm. LM 101, James Madison Memorial Bldg., 101 Independence Ave. SE, Washington, DC 20540-4680, U.S.A. **Online address:** jhay@loc.gov

HAYNES, Jonathan. American (born United States), b. 1952. **Genres:** Film, Literary Criticism And History. **Career:** American University, visiting assistant professor of English and director of freshman writing program, 1980-82; Tufts University, visiting assistant professor of English, 1982-83; Albion College, assistant professor of English, 1983-85; Bennington College, professor of English, 1985-94; Long Island University, Southampton College, Humanities Division, associate professor, 1998-2005, Brooklyn Campus, professor of English, 2005-. Writer. **Publications:** The Humanist as Traveler: George Sandys's Relation of a Journey Begun An. Dom. 1610, 1986; The Social Relations of Jonson's Theatre, 1992; (with O. Okome) Cinema and Social Change in West Africa, 1995. EDITOR: Nigerian Video Films, 1997, (and intro.) rev. ed., 2000. Works appear in anthologies. Contributor to periodicals. **Address:** Department of English, Long Island University, 1 University Plz., Brooklyn, NY 11201, U.S.A. **Online address:** jonathan.haynes@liu.edu

HAYNES, Melinda. American (born United States), b. 1955?. **Genres:** Novels, Literary Criticism And History. **Career:** Archdiocese of Mobile, Catholic Week, typesetter, 1987-95. Writer. **Publications:** NOVELS: Mother of Pearl, 1999; Chalktown, 2001; Willem's Field, 2003. Contributor to periodicals. **Address:** c/o Author Mail, Hyperion Books, 77 W 66th St., 11th Fl., New York, NY 10023-6201, U.S.A.

HAYNES, Stephen R. American (born United States), b. 1958. **Genres:** Theology/Religion, Education. **Career:** Rice University, Department of Religious Studies, teaching assistant, 1985-86; Emory University, Department of Religion, teaching associate, 1987-88; University of Durham, St. Chad's College, Centre for the Study of Literature and Theology, research fellow, 1988-89; Rhodes College, Department of Religious Studies, assistant professor of religious studies, 1989-95, associate professor of religious studies, 1995-, chair, 1996-, Albert B. Curry chair of religious studies, 1997-, professor; Columbia Theological Seminary, visiting professor of continuing education, 1992; Idlewild Presbyterian Church, parish associate. Writer. **Publications:** Prospects for Post-Holocaust Theology, 1991; (ed. with S.L. McKenzie) To Each Its Own Meaning: An Introduction to Biblical Criticisms and Their Application, 1993, rev. ed., 1999; Reluctant Witnesses: Jews and the Christian Imagination, 1995; Holocaust Education and the Church-Related College: Restoring Ruptured Traditions, 1997; (ed. with J.K. Roth) The Death of God Movement and the Holocaust: Radical Theology Encounters the Shoah, 1999; (ed.) Professing in the Postmodern Academy: Faculty and the Future of Church-Related Colleges, 2002; Noah's Curse: The Biblical Justification of American Slavery, 2002; The Bonhoeffer Phenomenon: Portraits of a Protestant Saint, 2004; The Bonhoeffer Legacy: Post-Holocaust Perspectives, 2006; (with L.B. Hale) Bonhoeffer for Armchair Theologians, 2009; The Last Segre-gated Hour: The Memphis Kneel-Ins and the Campaign for Southern Church Desegregation, 2013. Contributor to books and journals. **Address:** Department of Religious Studies, Rhodes College, 403 Clough Hall, 2000 N Pkwy., Memphis, TN 38112-1690, U.S.A. **Online address:** haynes@rhodes.edu

HAYNES, Sybille (Edith). British/German (born Germany), b. 1926. **Genres:** Romance/Historical, Archaeology/Antiquities, Travel/Exploration, History. **Career:** British Museum, Greek and Roman Department, voluntary assistant, 1951-76. Writer. **Publications:** Etruscan Bronze Utensils, 1965; Etruscan Sculpture, 1971; Land of the Chimaera, 1974; Zwischen Maander and Taurus, 1977; Die Tochter der Augurs, 1981; Etruscan Bronzes, 1985; The Augur's Daughter, 1987; Etruscan Civilization: A Cultural History, 2000; Kulturgeschichte der Etrusker, 2005. **Address:** 24 Hereford Sq., London, SW7 4TS, England.

HAYNIE, Barbara. American (born United States), b. 1947. **Genres:** Air/Space Topics, Literary Criticism And History. **Career:** Writer, landscape designer and artist. **Publications:** The Terrain of Paradise, 2002; Falling Through the Cracks, 2005. Contributor to periodicals. **Address:** c/o Author Mail, Five Star Publishing, 295 Kennedy Memorial Dr., Waterville, ME 04901-4535, U.S.A. **Online address:** tbhaynie@msn.com

HAYS, Kelley Ann. See **HAYS-GILPIN, Kelley.**

HAYS, Peter L. American/German (born Germany), b. 1938. **Genres:** Literary Criticism And History, Art/Art History, Biography, Autobiography/Memoirs. **Career:** Ohio State University, instructor in English, 1965-66; University of California, assistant professor, 1966-72, associate professor, 1972-77, department chair, 1974-77, senior Fulbright lecturer, 1977-78, professor of English and comparative literature, 1977-2004, professor emeritus, 2004-; Johannes Gutenberg University, instructor. Writer. **Publications:** The Limping Hero: Grotesques in Literature, 1971, 2nd ed., 2000; Ernest Hemingway, 1990; A Concordance to Hemingway's In Our Time, 1990; (ed. and contrib.) Teaching Hemingway's The Sun Also Rises, 2003; (with K. Nicholson) Arthur Miller's Death of a Salesman, 2008; The Critical Reception of Hemingway's The Sun Also Rises, 2011. Contributor to journals. **Address:** Department of English, University of California, 1 Shields Ave., Davis, CA 95616, U.S.A. **Online address:** plhays@ucdavis.edu

HAYS, Thomas Anthony. See **HAYS, Tony.**

HAYS, Tommy. American (born United States) **Genres:** Fash Ion/Costume. **Career:** University of North Carolina, Master of Liberal Arts Program, lecturer, Great Smokies Writing Program, executive director; South Carolina Governor's School for the Arts and Humanities, teacher; Murray State University, Master of Fine Arts, teacher. Writer. **Publications:** Sam's Crossing (novel), 1992; In the Family Way (novel), 1999; Pleasure was Mine, 2005. **Address:** c/o Neeti Madan, Sterling Lord Literistic Inc., 65 Bleecker St., New York, NY 10012, U.S.A. **Online address:** hays@main.nc.us

HAYS, Tony. (Thomas Anthony Hays). American (born United States), b. 1957. **Genres:** Novels, Mystery/Crime/Suspense, Archaeology/Antiquities, History, Politics/Government, Young Adult Fiction. **Career:** Young Men's Christian Association, English instructor, 1992; Motlow State Community College, English instructor, 1992-94; freelance writer and investigative reporter, 1994-; South East European University, visiting author, 2007-; Overseas Security Advisory Council, founding chairperson. **Publications:** FICTION: Murder on the Twelfth Night, 1993; Murder in the Latin Quarter, 1993; The Trouble with Patriots, 2002. OTHER: (comp. as Thomas A. Hays) Hardin County, Tennessee, Records, 1820-1860, 1985; Volunteers: Tennesseans in the War with Mexico, 1986; Hardin County Hodgepodge, 1987; On the Banks of the River: A History of Hardin County, 1996; Shiloh Stories: Fact, Fiction and Folklore from the Battle of Shiloh, 2000; Killing Way, 2009; The Divine Sacrifice, 2010; The Beloved Dead, 2011; Stolen bride, 2012. Contributor of articles and short fiction to periodicals. **Address:** The Literary Group International, 14 Penn Plz., Ste. 925, New York, NY 10122, U.S.A. **Online address:** tony@tonyhays.com

HAYS-GILPIN, Kelley. (Kelley Ann Hays). American (born United States), b. 1960. **Genres:** Archaeology/Antiquities, Social Sciences, Art/Art History. **Career:** University of Michigan, Museum of Anthropology, Great Lakes Archaeological Services, field and laboratory assistant, 1980-82; Black Mesa Archaeological Project, field and laboratory assistant, 1981, assistant crew chief, 1982; Walter P. Reuther Library of Labor and Urban Affairs, archival assistant in collections processing and reference services, 1983; Bureau of Land Management, archaeological technician, 1983; University of Arizona, Department of Anthropology, teaching assistant, 1984, Department of Women's Studies, research assistant, 1984; Arizona State Museum, Homol'ovi Research Program, research assistant, 84-88, field lab director, 1986-87, research associate, 1988-89; University of Arizona, Department of Anthropology, lecturer, 1990-91; SWCA Inc., project archaeologist, 1990-91, ceramic specialist, 1991-92; Museum of Northern Arizona, research associate, 1991-, Edward Bridge Danson Chair of Anthropology; Northern Arizona University, Ceramic Analysis, instructor, 1992, Animas-La Plata Archaeological Project, principal investigator for ceramic analysis, 1992-93, adjunct professor, 1992-97, Navajo Nation Archaeology Department, archaeologist III and ceramic specialist, 1992-97, Department of Anthropology, assistant professor, 1997-2003, associate professor, 2003-. Writer. **Publications:** (With A.C. Deegan and E.A. Morris) Prehistoric Sandals from Northeastern Arizona: The Earl H. Morris and Ann Axtell Morris Research, 1998; (ed. with D.S. Whitley) Reader in Gender Archaeology, 1998; (with E.V. Hartesveldt) Prehistoric Ceramics of the Puerco Valley, Arizona, 1998; Ambiguous Images: Gender and Rock Art, 2004; (ed. with D.S. Whitley) Belief in the Past: Theoretical Approaches to the Archaeology of Religion, 2008. AS KELLEY ANN HAYS: (ed. with E.C. Adams) Homol'ovi II: Archaeology of an Ancestral Hopi Village, Arizona, 1991. Works appear in anthologies. **Address:** Department of Anthropology, Northern Arizona University, Rm. 101D, Bldg. 98D, South San Francisco St., PO Box 15200, Flagstaff, AZ 86011-5200, U.S.A. **Online address:** kelley.hays-gilpin@nau.edu

HAYSLIP, Le Ly. American/Vietnamese (born Vietnam), b. 1949. **Genres:** Autobiography/Memoirs. **Career:** East Meets West Foundation, founder, 1987-; Global Village Foundation, president and founder, 1999-. Writer. **Publications:** (With J. Wurts) When Heaven and Earth Changed Places: A Vietnamese Woman's Journey from War to Peace, 1989; (with J. Hayslip) Child of War, Woman of Peace, 1993; (contrib.) The Making of Oliver Stone's Heaven and Earth, 1993. **Address:** Global Village Foundation, PO Box 130656, Carlsbad, CA 92013, U.S.A. **Online address:** lely@globalvillagefoundation.org

HAYT, Elizabeth. American (born United States), b. 1961?. **Genres:** History. **Career:** Museum of Modern Art, Department of Education, teacher, 1990-96; Manhattan College, assistant professor, 1993; New York Times, fashion columnist. **Publications:** Duane Hanson, 2000; I'm No Saint: A Nasty Little Memoir of Love and Leaving, 2005. Contributor to periodicals. **Address:** Levine/Greenberg Literary Agency, 307 7th Ave., Ste. 2407, New York, NY 10001, U.S.A. **Online address:** elizabeth@elizabethhayt.com

HAYTER, Teresa. British (born England), b. 1940?. **Genres:** Social Commentary, Civil Liberties/Human Rights, Economics, Environmental Sciences/Ecology, Geography, Industrial Relations, International Relations/Current Affairs, Organized Labor, Politics/Government, Race Relations, Social Sciences, Urban Studies. **Career:** Writer, researcher and political activist. **Publications:** (With A. Moyes) World III, 1964; French Aid, 1966; Aid as Imperialism, 1971; Hayter of the Bourgeoisie, 1971; The Creation of World Poverty, 1981, 2nd ed., 1990; (with C. Watson) Aid: Rhetoric and Reality, 1985; Exploited Earth: Britain's Aid and the Environment, 1989; (ed. with D. Harvey) The Factory and the City: The Story of the Cowley Automobile Workers in Oxford, 1993; Urban Politics: Accommodation or Resistance?, 1997; Open Borders: The Case against Immigration Controls, 2000, 2nd ed., 2004. **Address:** Pluto Press, 345 Archway Rd., London, GL N6 5AA, England. **Online address:** teresahayter@riseup.net

HAYTHORNTHWAITE, Philip John. British (born England), b. 1951. **Genres:** History, Military/Defense/Arms Control, Social Sciences. **Career:** H. Gerrard Ltd., director, 1970-. Writer. **Publications:** Uniforms of the Napoleonic Wars, 1973; Uniforms of Waterloo, 1974; Uniforms of the American Civil War, 1975; World Uniforms and Battles 1815-50, 1976; Uniforms of the Retreat from Moscow 1812, 1976; Uniforms of the Peninsular War 1807-14, 1978; Weapons and Equipment of the Napoleonic Wars, 1979, rev. ed. 1996; Uniforms of the French Revolutionary Wars 1789-1802, 1981; The English Civil War, 1982; Uniforms of 1812: Napoleon's Retreat from Moscow, 1982; Napoleon's Line Infantry, 1983; Napoleon's Light Infantry, 1983; Napoleon's Guard Infantry, 2 vols., 1984-85; Civil War Soldiers, 1985; The Alamo and War of Texan Independence, 1986; Austrian Army of the Napoleonic Wars, 2 vols., 1986; The Poster Book of the Civil War, 1987; Uniforms Illustrated: The Boer War, 1987; British Infantry of the Napoleonic Wars, 1987; Uni-

forms Illustrated: The Victorian Colonial Wars, 1988; Napoleon's Military Machine, 1988; Napoleon's Specialist Troops, 1988; Wellington's Military Machine, 1989; Wellington's Specialist Troops, 1989; World War I: 1914, 1989; World War I: 1915, 1989; World War I: 1916, 1990; Austrian Specialist Troops of the Napoleonic Wars, 1990; Napoleonic Source Book, 1990; World War I: 1917, 1990; World War I: 1918, 1990; Frederick the Great's Cavalry, 1991; Frederick the Great's Infantry, 1991; Invincible Generals, 1991; Frederick the Great's Specialist Troops, 1992; World War I Source Book, 1992; Napoleon's Campaigns in Italy, 1993; Nelson's Navy, 1993; A Photohistory of World War I, 1993; The British Cavalryman 1792-1815, 1994; Armies of Wellington, 1994; Austrian Cavalry 1740-80, 1994; Austrian Infantry 1740-80, 1994; Austrian Specialist Troops 1740-80, 1995; Colonial Wars Source book, 1995; Die Hard!: Dramatic Actions from the Napoleonic Wars, 1996; Uniforms of Waterloo: 16-18 June 1815, 1996; Napoleon: The Final Verdict, 1996; Uniforms of the French Revolutionary Wars, 1789-1802, 1997; Imperial Guardsman, 1997; Who Was Who in the Napoleonic Wars, 1998; Waterloo Men: The Experience of Battle, 16-18 June 1815, 1999; Corunna 1809, 2001; Napoleon's Commanders 1792-1809, 2001; Weapons & Warfare: Napoleonic Infantry, 2001; Napoleonic Cavalry, 2001; British Rifleman 1797-1815, 2002; (ed. with R.M. Johnston) In the Words of Napoleon: The Emperor Day By Day, 2002; Napoleon's Commanders 1809-1815, 2002; Wellington's Army: The Uniforms of the British Soldier, 1812-1815, 2002; Peninsular War Almanac, 2004; Gallipoli 1915, 2004; Corunna 1809: Sir John Moore's Fighting Retreat, 2005; Russian Army of the Napoleonic Wars 2: Cavalry, 2005; Wellington: The Iron Duke, 2007; Waterloo Armies: Men, Organization and Tactics, 2007; British Napoleonic Infantry Tactics: 1792-1815, 2008. **Address:** Park Hill, Parrock Rd., Barrowford, Nelson, LC BB9 6QF, England.

HAYWARD, Jennifer (Poole). American (born United States), b. 1961. **Genres:** Literary Criticism And History. **Career:** Teacher, 1983-86; College of Wooster, Department of English, assistant professor, associate professor, 1992-, professor; Great Lakes College Association, New Writers Awards, judge, 1994-96. Writer. **Publications:** Consuming Pleasures: Active Audiences and Serial Fictions from Dickens to Soaps, 1997; (ed.) Journal of a Residence in Chile During the Year 1822; and, A Voyage from Chile to Brazil in 1823, 2003; (ed. with M.S. Caballero) Maria Graham's Journal of a Residence in Chile, 2003; (ed.) Maria Graham's Journal of a Voyage to Brazil, 2010. Contributor to periodicals. **Address:** Department of English, College of Wooster, Kauke Hall, 400 E University St., Wooster, OH 44691, U.S.A. **Online address:** jhayward@wooster.edu

HAYWARD, Philip. Australian/British (born England), b. 1956. **Genres:** Art/Art History, Music. **Career:** West Surrey College of Art, lecturer in media studies, 1988-90; University of London, new technologies projects officer, 1989-90; Macquarie University, senior lecturer in mass communications, 1991-, professor, Research Program, coordinator; Southern Cross University, Division of Research, Higher Degree Research Unit, director; Shima: The International Journal of Research into island Cultures, co-editor. **Publications:** Pop Music Business, 1989; (with R. Coyle) Apparition: Holographic Art in Australia, 1995; Music at the Borders: Not Drowning, Waving and Their Engagement with Papua New Guinean Culture (1986-96), 1998; Tide Lines: Music, Tourism & Cultural Transition in the Whitsunday Islands, 2001; Hearing the Call: Music and Social History on Lord Howe Island, 2002; Bounty Chords: Music, Dance and Cultural Heritage on Norfolk and Pitcairn Islands, 2006; (with R. Coyle) 3-D Images: Australian Holography, forthcoming. EDITOR: Picture This: Media Representations of Modern Art, 1988; Culture, Technology, and Creativity, 1990; From Pop to Punk to Postmodernism, 1992; (with T. Wollen) Future Visions: New Technologies of the Screen, 1993; Sound Alliances: Indigenous Peoples, Cultural Politics, and Popular Music in the Pacific, 1998; Widening the Horizon: Exoticism in Post-war Popular Music, 1999; Outback and Urban, 2003; Off the Planet: Music, Sound and Science Fiction Cinema, 2004; (with G. Walden) Roots and Crossovers, 2004; Terror Tracks: Music, Sound and Horror Cinema, 2009. **Address:** Division of Research, Southern Cross University, PO Box 157, Lismore, NW 2480, Australia. **Online address:** philip.hayward@scu.edu.au

HAYWOOD, Chelsea. British/Canadian (born Canada), b. 1983?. **Genres:** Autobiography/Memoirs. **Career:** Writer and memoirist. **Publications:** 90-Day Geisha: My Time as a Tokyo Hostess (memoir), 2008. Contributor to newspapers. **Address:** London, GL , England. **Online address:** chelseahaywood@hotmail.com

HAYWOOD, Gar Anthony. (Ray Shannon). American (born United States),

b. 1954. **Genres:** Mystery/Crime/Suspense, Bibliography, Theology/Religion, Children's Fiction, Young Adult Fiction, Novels. **Career:** Bell Atlantic, field engineer, 1976-88; freelance novelist, 1988-. **Publications:** Fear of the Dark, 1988; Not Long for This World: An Aaron Gunner Mystery, 1990; Schwarz, Weiss, Tot, 1990; You Can Die Trying, 1993; Going Nowhere Fast, 1994; Bad News Travels Fast, 1995; It's Not a Pretty Sight: An Aaron Gunner Mystery, 1996; When Last Seen Alive: An Aaron Gunner Mystery, 1997; All the Lucky Ones are Dead: An Aaron Gunner Mystery, 1999; Cemetery Road, 2010; Assume Nothing, 2011. AS RAY SHANNON: Man Eater, 2003; Firecracker, 2004. **Address:** Severn House Publishers, 110 E 59th St., 22th Fl., New York, NY 10022, U.S.A. **Online address:** talktogar@garanthonyhaywood.com

HAYWOOD, Kathleen M. American (born United States), b. 1950. **Genres:** Medicine/Health, Sports/Fitness. **Career:** University of Missouri, professor and associate dean, 1976-, American Academy, Kinesiology and Physical Education, fellow, interim dean. Writer. **Publications:** Life Span Motor Development, 1986, 5th ed., 2009; (with T. Loughery) Motor Development, 1987; (with C.F. Lewis) Teaching Archery: Steps to Success, 1989; (with C.F. Lewis) Archery: Steps to Success, 1989, 3rd ed., 2006; (with N. Getchell) Learning Activities for Life Span Motor Development, 2001; (with M.A. Roberton and N. Getchell) Advanced Analysis of Motor Development, 2012. **Address:** University of Missouri, 201 Education Admin Bldg., 1 University Blvd., St. Louis, MO 63121-4400, U.S.A. **Online address:** kathleen_haywood@umsl.edu

HAYWOOD, Stephen Patrick. *See* **HAYWOOD, Steve.**

HAYWOOD, Steve. (Stephen Patrick Haywood). British (born England), b. 1949. **Genres:** Novels, Mystery/Crime/Suspense, Travel/Exploration, Transportation. **Career:** Westminster Press Group, journalist; Time Out, journalist; City Limits, co-founder; Thames Television, producer; British Broadcasting Corp., producer and editor; Just TV, owner and producer. Writer. **Publications:** Murderous Justice (novel), 1991; Fruit Flies Like a Banana (travel), 2004; One Man and a Narrowboat: Slowing Down Time on England's Waterways, 2009; Narrowboat Dreams, 2010. Contributor to magazines and newspapers. **Address:** 18 Quentin Rd., Blackheath, London, GL SE13 5DF, England. **Online address:** sphaywood@aol.com

HAZARD, Ann. American (born United States), b. 1952. **Genres:** Novels, Food And Wine, Self Help, Travel/Exploration. **Career:** R.E. Hazard Jr. Inc. (general building contractors), new project administrator, 1974-76, marketing and administration manager, 1982-85, corporate communications manager, 1988-92; Robert G. Fisher Construction Company Inc., project administrator, 1976-79; WESTEC Services Inc., personnel administrator, 1979-80; TRW Colorado Electronics, technical writer, 1980-82; Child Protective Services for the County of San Diego, case analyst with Voices for Children, 1987-88; Childcare Connection Inc. (nanny placement agency), owner, 1986-88; San Diego Child Protective Services, case analyst, 1987-88; Mission Valley Young Men's Christian Association, board director, 1988-93; freelance writer, 1992-. **Publications:** Cooking with Baja Magic (cookbook): Mouth-Watering Meals from the Enchanted Kitchens and Campfires of Baja, 1997; Cartwheels in the Sand (novel), 1999; Agave Sunsets (travel stories), 2002; Rise Up and Walk (self-help), 2001; Cooking With Baja Magic Dos, 2005. **Address:** Renegade Enterprises, PO Box 1505, Solana Beach, CA 92075, U.S.A. **Online address:** mobeyel@aol.com

HAZELWOOD, Robert R. Also writes as Roy Hazelwood. American (born United States), b. 1938. **Genres:** Law, Criminology/True Crime. **Career:** Federal Bureau of Investigation, agent, 1971-78, Behavioral Science Unit, supervisory agent, 1978-93, retired, 1993; Academy Group Inc., forensics consultant. Writer and speaker. **Publications:** (With P.E. Dietz and A.W. Burgess) Autoerotic Fatalities, 1983; (ed. with A.W. Burgess) Practical Aspects of Rape Investigation: A Multidisciplinary Approach, 1987, 4th ed., 2009; (as Roy Hazelwood with S.G. Michaud) The Evil That Men Do: FBI Profiler Roy Hazelwood's Journey into the Minds of Sexual Predators, 1998; (as Roy Hazelwood with S.G. Michaud) Dark Dreams: Sexual Violence, Homicide, and the Criminal Mind, 2001. Contributor to journals. **Address:** c/o Author Mail, St. Martin's Press, 175 5th Ave., New York, NY 10010, U.S.A.

HAZELWOOD, Roy. *See* **HAZELWOOD, Robert R.**

HAZLEHURST, Cameron. Australian/British (born England), b. 1941. **Genres:** History, Politics/Government, Biography. **Career:** Monash Univer-
sity, teaching fellow in history, 1964-65; Oxford University, Nuffield College, junior research fellow, 1968-70, Queen's College, junior research fellow, 1970-72, University College, lecturer in politics, 1969-72; Jonathan Cape Ltd., historical adviser, 1968-72; Australian National University, Institute of Advanced Studies, fellow, 1972-88, senior fellow, 1988-92, Humanities Research Centre, adjunct professor, 2006-; Australian Department of Urban and Regional Development, assistant secretary, 1974-75; Queensland University of Technology, School of Humanities, foundation professor and head, 1992-97; Flaxton Mill House, managing director, 1997-; University of South Australia, Hawke Institute, adjunct professor of government, 2002-05. Australian National University Research School of Humanities and the Arts, adjunct professor, 2006-.Writer. **Publications:** Politicians at War, July 1914 to May 1915: A Prologue to the Triumph of Lloyd George, 1971; (with C. Woodland) A Guide to the Papers of British Cabinet Ministers 1900-1951, 1974; Menzies Observed, 1979; Gordon Chalk: A Political Life, 1987; (with C. Forster) Australian Statisticians and the Development of Official Statistics, 1988; (with G. Terrill and S. Mendra) Government Communication, 1993; (with C. Woodland) A Liberal Chronicle: The Political Journal and Papers of J.A. Pease, 1st Lord Gainford 1908-1910, 1994; (with S. Whitehead and C. Woodland) A Guide to the Papers of British Cabinet Ministers, 1900-1964, 1996. EDITOR: W.S. Churchill, The People's Rights, 1970; The Lloyd George Liberal Magazine, 1974; The History of the Ministry of Munitions, 1974; (with J.R. Nethercote) Reforming Australian Government: The Coombs Report and Beyond, 1977; Australian Conservatism, 1979; The Mastermind Book, 1979; The Mastermind General Knowledge Book, 1982; (with K.M. Hazlehurst) Gangs and Youth Subcultures: International Subcultures, 1998. **Address:** Flaxton Mill House Pty Ltd., PO Box 60, Mapleton, QL 4560, Australia. **Online address:** cameron.hazlehurst@gmail.com

HAZLETT-STEVENS, Holly. American (born United States), b. 1969. **Genres:** Psychology, Self Help. **Career:** University of Nevada, assistant professor of psychology, 2002-, associate professor of psychology. Writer. **Publications:** (With D.A. Bernstein and T.D. Borkovec) New Directions in Progressive Relaxation Training: A Guidebook for Helping Professionals, 2000; Women Who Worry Too Much: How to Stop Worry & Anxiety from Ruining Relationships, Work, & Fun, 2005; Psychological Approaches to Generalized Anxiety Disorder: A Clinician's Guide to Assessment and Treatment, 2008. Contributor to periodicals. **Address:** Department of Psychology, University of Nevada, Rm. 323, Mack Social Science, 1664 N Virginia St., Reno, NV 89557, U.S.A. **Online address:** hhazlett@unr.edu

HAZO, Samuel (John). American (born United States), b. 1928. **Genres:** Autobiography/Memoirs, Novels, Poetry, Literary Criticism And History. **Career:** Shady Side Academy, teacher of Latin, 1953-55; Duquesne University, instructor, 1955-58, assistant professor, 1958-60, associate professor, 1960-61, professor of English, 1964-, now professor emeritus, College of Arts and Sciences, dean, 1961-66; International Poetry Forum, director, 1966-; University of Detroit, distinguished visiting professor, 1968. Writer. **Publications:** Discovery and Other Poems, 1959; The Quiet Wars (verse), 1962; Hart Crane: An Introduction and Interpretation, 1963 as Smithereened Apart: A Critique of Hart Crane, 1978; The Christian Intellectual: Studies in the Relation of Catholicism to the Human Sciences, 1963; A Selection of Contemporary Religious Poetry, 1963; Listen with the Eye (verse), 1964; My Sons in God: Selected and New Poems, 1965; Blood Rights (verse), 1968; (with G. Nama) Twelve Poems, 1970; Seascript: A Mediterranean Logbook (fiction), 1971; (with A.A. Said) The Blood of Adonis (verse), 1971; Once for the Last Bandit: New and Previous Poems, 1972; Quartered (verse), 1974; Inscripts (fiction), 1975; The Very Fall of the Sun (novel), 1978; To Paris (verse), 1981; The Wanton Summer Air (novel), 1982; Thank a Bored Angel (verse), 1983; The Feast of Icarus (essays), 1984; The Color of Reluctance (verse), 1986; The Pittsburgh that Starts within You (memoir), 1986; Nightwords (verse), 1987; Silence Spoken Here (verse), 1988; Stills (fiction), 1989; The Rest is Prose (essays), 1990; The Past Won't Stay Behind You (poetry), 1993; The Pages of Day and Night (verse), 1995; The Holy Surprise of Right Now (verse), 1996; Latching the Fist (verse), 1996; As They Sail (poetry), 1999; Spying for God (essays), 1999; (trans.) The Pages of Day and Night, 2000; Just Once: New and Previous Poems, 2002; Pittsburgh that Stays Within You, 2005; Flight to Elsewhere, 2005; Power of Less: Essays on Poetry and Public Speech, 2005; (trans. with P.B. Kelley) Lebanon: Poems of Love and War, 2006; Song of the Horse: A Selection of Poems, 1958-2008, 2008; This Part of the World: A Novel, 2008; Like a Man Gone Mad: Poems in a New Century, 2010; The Stroke of a Pen, 2011. **Address:** 785 Somerville Dr., Pittsburgh, PA 15243, U.S.A. **Online address:** samhazo1@earthlink.net

HAZUKA, Tom. American (born United States), b. 1956?. **Genres:** Novels, Poetry, Young Adult Fiction, Novellas/Short Stories. **Career:** Quarterly West, co-editor, 1987-89; Central Connecticut State University, professor, 1992-. **Publications:** (Ed. with J. Thomas and D. Thomas) Flash Fiction: Very Short Stories, 1992; (ed. with J.P. Maney) A Celestial Omnibus: Short Fiction on Faith, 1997; The Road to the Island: A Novel, 1998; In the City of the Disappeared: A Novel, 2000; (with C.J. Jones) Method to March Madness: An Insider's Look at the Final Four, 2006; (ed. with M. Budman) You have Time for this: Contemporary American Short Stories, 2007; Last Chance for First, 2008; Exile in Gringolandia, forthcoming. Contributor of articles to periodicals. **Address:** Department of English, Central Connecticut State University, 309 Willard Hall, 1615 Stanley St., New Britain, CT 06050, U.S.A. **Online address:** hazukaj@ccsu.edu

HAZZARD, Shirley. American/Australian (born Australia), b. 1931. **Genres:** Novels, International Relations/Current Affairs, Young Adult Non-fiction, Novellas/Short Stories. **Career:** British Intelligence, staff, 1947-48; Combined Services Intelligence, Hong Kong, staff, 1947-48; British High Commissioner's Office, staff, 1949-50; United Nations Headquarters, General Service Category, staff, 1951-61. Writer. **Publications:** Cliffs of Fall and Other Stories, 1963; The Evening of the Holiday, 1966; People in Glass Houses: Portraits from Organization Life, 1967; The Bay of Noon: A Novel, 1970; Defeat of an Ideal: A Study of the Self-destruction of the United Nations, 1973; The Transit of Venus, 1980; Coming of Age in Australia, 1985; Countenance of Truth: The United Nations and the Waldheim Case, 1990; (contrib. with N. Richardson) City of Secrets: Photographs of Naples, 1997; Greene on Capri: A Memoir, 2000; The Great Fire, 2003; (with F. Steegmuller) Ancient Shore: Dispatches from Naples, 2008. Works appear in anthologies. Contributor to periodicals. **Address:** Sheil Land Associates Ltd., 52 Doughty St., London, GL WC1N 2LS, England.

HEACOX, Kim. American (born United States), b. 1951. **Genres:** Travel/Exploration, Photography, Autobiography/Memoirs, Biography, Novels. **Career:** U.S. National Park Service, park ranger, 1977-85. Writer and photographer. **Publications:** California State Parks, 1987; Bush Pilots of Alaska, 1989; Alaska's National Parks, 1990; Iditarod Spirit, 1991; In Denali, 1992; Visions of a Wild America: Pioneers of Preservation, 1996; Alaska's Inside Passage, 1997; Antarctica: The Last Continent, 1998; Alaska Light, 1998; Shackleton: The Antarctic Challenge, 1999; The Denali Road Guide: A Traveler's Guide to the Wildlife and Wilderness of Denali National Park, 1999; Caribou Crossing, 2001; American Idea: The Making of the National Parks, 2001; Making the National Parks: An American Idea, 2004; Only Kayak: A Journey Into the Heart of Alaska, 2005; Jimmy Bluefeather, 2008; Kingdom of Strictest Meridian: Antarctica in an Age of Global Warming, 2008; Fixing a Hole in the Ocean, forthcoming; Old Ben and the Cedar Canoe, forthcoming. Contributor to periodicals. **Address:** PO Box 359, Gustavus, AK 99826, U.S.A.

HEAD, David M. American (born United States), b. 1951. **Genres:** Biography, History, Autobiography/Memoirs. **Career:** Middle Georgia College, assistant professor of history, 1982-90; University System of Georgia, assistant professor in charge of studies abroad program, 1984; South Georgia College, associate professor of history, 1990-93; John Tyler Community College, professor of history, 1993-. Writer. **Publications:** The Ebbs and Flows of Fortune: The Life of Thomas Howard, Third Duke of Norfolk, 1995. Contributor to periodicals and journals. **Address:** John Tyler Community College, 13101 Jefferson Davis Hwy., Chester, VA 23831-5316, U.S.A. **Online address:** dhead@jtcc.edu

HEAD, Dominic. British (born England), b. 1962. **Genres:** Literary Criticism And History, Novellas/Short Stories, Young Adult Fiction, Novels. **Career:** University of Warwick, Department of English and Comparative Literary Studies, tutor, 1988-89; University of Keele, Department of English, lecturer, 1989; Open University, tutor, 1990; University of Central England, School of English, lecturer, 1990-97, senior lecturer, 1997-98, reader, 1998-; University of Wolverhampton, lecturer, 1998; University of Nottingham, School of English Studies, professor of modern English literature and head of school, faculty of arts. Writer. **Publications:** The Modernist Short Story: A Study in Theory and Practice, 1992; Nadine Gordimer, 1994; J.M. Coetzee, 1997; The Cambridge Introduction to Modern British Fiction, 1950-2000, 2002; (ed.) The Cambridge Guide to Literature in English, 2006; The State of the Novel: Britain and Beyond, 2008; The Cambridge Introduction to J.M. Coetzee, 2009. Contributor of articles to periodicals. **Address:** School of English Stud-

ies, University of Nottingham, Rm. A50 Trent, University Pk., Trent, NG7 2RD, England. **Online address:** dominic.head@nottingham.ac.uk

HEAD, John. American (born United States), b. 1951?. **Genres:** Adult Non-fiction, Novels. **Career:** Detroit Free Press, reporter; USA Today, reporter; Atlanta Journal-Constitution, mental health reporter, features writer and columnist; Penn Foundation, chair. **Publications:** We Were the Land's: The Biography of a Homeplace, 1999; Standing in the Shadows: Understanding and Overcoming Depression in Black Men, 2004. Contributor to periodicals. **Address:** c/o Author Mail, Broadway Books, 1745 Broadway, 18th Fl., New York, NY 10019-4368, U.S.A. **Online address:** jhnfhead@aol.com

HEADLEY, Bernard D. American (born United States) **Genres:** Horror, Novels. **Career:** Northeastern Illinois University, professor, professor emeritus of criminology and criminal justice, chair of sociology and criminal justice; University of the West Indies, visiting professor of criminology, 1993-94, professor of criminology. Writer. **Publications:** The Jamaican Crime Scene: A Perspective, 1994; The Atlanta Youth Murders and the Politics of Race, 1998. **Address:** c/o J. D. Tremblay, Southern Illinois University Press, 1915 University Press Dr., PO Box 6806, Carbondale, IL 62901, U.S.A. **Online address:** b-headley@neiu.edu

HEADLEY, Jason. American (born United States), b. 1973?. **Genres:** Novels, Young Adult Fiction. **Career:** Cohn Wells, copywriter, 1997-99; Tenth Dimension, associate creative director, 1999-2000; writer, 2000-. **Publications:** Small Town Odds: A Novel, 2004; Pure Spirits, 2008. Contributor to periodicals. **Address:** Chronicle Books, 680 2nd St., San Francisco, CA 94107-2015, U.S.A. **Online address:** jason@jasonheadley.com

HEADLEY, John M. American (born United States), b. 1929. **Genres:** History, Theology/Religion, Social Sciences, Essays. **Career:** University of Massachusetts, instructor in history, 1959-61; Yale University, St. Thomas More Project, research associate, 1961-62; University of British Columbia, instructor in history, 1962-64; University of North Carolina, assistant professor, 1964-66, associate professor, 1966-70, professor of European history, 1970-, distinguished university professor, now professor emeritus; Southeastern Institute for Medieval and Renaissance Studies, chairman, 1967. Writer. **Publications:** Luther's View of Church History, 1963; Responsio ad Lutherum, 1969; (contrib.) The Meaning of the Renaissance and the Reformation, 1973; The Emperor and His Chancellor: A Study of the Imperial Chancellery under Gattinara, 1983; (ed. with J.B. Tomaro) San Carlo Borromeo: Catholic Reform and Ecclesiastical Politics in the Second Half of the Sixteenth Century, 1988; Tommaso Campanella and the Transformation of the World, 1997; Church, Empire and World: The Quest for Universal Order, 1520-1640, 1997; (ed. with H.J. Hillerbrand and A.J. Paplas) Confessionalization in Europe, 1555-1700: Essays in Honor and Memory of Bodo Nischan, 2004; Europeanization of the World: On the Origins of Human Rights and Democracy, 2008; The Problem with Multiculturalism, 2012. Contributor to journals. **Address:** Department of History, University of North Carolina, CB 3195, Hamilton Hall, Chapel Hill, NC 27599-3915, U.S.A. **Online address:** headley@email.unc.edu

HEADLEY, Maria Dahvana. American (born United States), b. 1977. **Genres:** Biography. **Career:** Writer. **Publications:** The Year of Yes, 2006; Queen of Kings, 2011. **Address:** The Gernet Co., 136 E 57th St., New York, NY 10022, U.S.A. **Online address:** theyearofyes@hotmail.com

HEADLEY, Victor. British/Jamaican (born Jamaica), b. 1960. **Genres:** Novels, Young Adult Fiction. **Career:** Writer. **Publications:** Yardie, 1992; Excess, 1993; Yush!, 1994; Fetish, 1995; Here Comes the Bride, 1996; The Best Man, 1999; Off Duty, 2001; Seven Seals, Seven Days, 2002. **Address:** X Press, 55 Broadway Marker, London, GL E8 4PH, England. **Online address:** cicely.dayes@btinternet.com

HEADRICK, Daniel R. American (born United States), b. 1941. **Genres:** History, Technology. **Career:** Tuskegee Institute, instructor, 1968-71, assistant professor, 1971-73, associate professor of history, 1973-75; Roosevelt University, associate professor, 1975-82, professor of social sciences and history, 1982-2007, professor emeritus of social science and history, 2007-; Hawaii Pacific University, visiting professor, 2000. Writer. **Publications:** Ejercito y politica en Espana, 1866-1898, 1981; The Tools of Empire: Technology and European Imperialism in the Nineteenth Century, 1981; The Tentacles of Progress: Technology Transfer in the Age of Imperialism, 1851-1945, 1988;

The Invisible Weapon: Telecommunications and International Politics, 1851-1945, 1991; Colonialism, Health and Illness in French Equatorial Africa, 1885-1935, 1994; The Earth and Its Peoples, 1997; When Information Came of Age: Technologies of Knowledge in the Age of Reason and Revolution, 1700-1850, 2000; Technology: A World History, 2009; Power Over Peoples: Technology, Environments and Western Imperialism, 1400 to the Present, 2010. Works appear in anthologies. Contributor of articles to journals. **Address:** 96 Colony Rd., New Haven, CT 06511-1620, U.S.A. **Online address:** dan.headrick@att.net

HEADY, Harold F(ranklin). *See* Obituaries.

HEAL, Gillian. (Gillian Ferguson). British (born England), b. 1934. **Genres:** Children's Fiction, Illustrations. **Career:** Halfpenny Houses (toy designers and manufacturers), co-founder, 1972, toy designer, 1972-2000. Writer and graphic designer. **Publications:** SELF-ILLUSTRATED FOR CHILDREN: The Halfpennys Find a Home, 1994; Jack and the Beanstalk, 1995; Tom Thumb, 1995; Rapunzel, 1996; Grandpa Bear's Fantastic Scarf, 1997; Thumbelina and Rumpelstiltskin, 1997; Hansel and Gretel, 1998; Opa Bar und Sein Langer, Bunter Schal, 1998; Cinderella, 1999; Aunt Lily's Great Adventure, 2000; Red Riding Hood, forthcoming. **Address:** Overskern, Churchill Way, Appledore, Bideford, DN EX39 1PA, England. **Online address:** gillian@gillianhealpaintings.co.uk

HEALD, Suzette. British/Scottish (born Scotland), b. 1943. **Genres:** Anthropology/Ethnology, Sociology, Social Sciences, Politics/Government. **Career:** University of Lancaster, lecturer, senior lecturer, 1971-99; University of Botswana, associate professor, 1997-99; Brunel University, professor of social anthropology, 2000-; London School of Economics, Crisis States Research Centre, senior research fellow. Writer. **Publications:** Controlling Anger: The Sociology of Gisu Violence, 1989; (ed. with A. Deluz) Anthropology and Psychoanalysis: An Encounter through Culture, 1994; (comp. and ed.) Praise Poems of the Kuria: In Kuria with English Translations, 1997; Manhood and Morality: Sex, Violence and Ritual in Gisu Society, 1999. **Address:** School of Social Sciences, Brunel University, SS144, Kingston Ln., Uxbridge, GL UB8 3PH, England. **Online address:** suzette.heald@brunel.ac.uk

HEALD, Tim(othy Villiers). British (born England), b. 1944. **Genres:** Novels, Novellas/Short Stories, Mystery/Crime/Suspense, Biography. **Career:** Sunday Times, columnist, reporter, 1965-67; Town Magazine, feature editor, 1967; Daily Express, feature writer, 1967-72; freelance journalist, 1972-; Weekend Magazine, associate editor, 1977-78; The Observer, Pendennis column, author, 1990; University of Tasmania, writer-in-residence, 1997-99; FRSL, 2000; University of South Australia, writer-in-residence, 2001; St. John's College, University of Sydney, NSW, 2007. **Publications:** MYSTERY NOVELS: Unbecoming Habits, 1973; Blue Blood Will Out, 1974; Deadline, 1975; Let Sleeping Dogs Die, 1976; Just Desserts, 1977; Murder at Moose Jaw, 1981; Masterstroke, 1982; Red Herrings, 1985; Brought to Book, 1988; Business Unusual, 1989; Death and the Visiting Fellow, 2004; A Death on the Ocean Wave 2007. NOVELS: It's a Dog's Life, 1971; Caroline R., 1980; Class Distinctions, 1984; Stop Press, 1998. BIOGRAPHY: John Steed: An Authorized Biography, 1977; (with M. Mohs) H.R.H.: The Man Who Will Be King, 1979; The Duke: A Portrait of Prince Philip, 1991; Barbara Cartland: A Life of Love, 1994; Denis: The Authorised Biography of the Incomparable Compton, 1994; Brian Johnston, The Authorised Biography, 1995. OTHER: The Making of Space 1999, 1976; Small Masterpiece, 1982; Networks, 1983; Old Boy Networks: Who We Know and How We Use Them, 1984; The Character of Cricket, 1986; By Appointment: 150 Years of the Royal Warrant, 1989; Philip: A Portrait of the Duke of Edinburgh, 1991; Honourable Estates, 1992; Beating Retreat: Hong Kong under the Last Governor, 1997; A Peerage for Trade, 2001; Village Cricket, 2004; Princess Margaret, A Life Unravelled, 2007; Death in the Opening Chapter, 2011; Poison at the Pueblo, 2011. EDITOR: The Newest London Spy, 1988; My Lord's, 1990; A Classic English Crime, 1991; A Classic Christmas Crime, 1995. **Address:** Roselands, Blind Ln., Bower Hinton, Martock, SM TA12 6LG, England. **Online address:** tim@timheald.com

HEALEY, Denis (Winston). British (born England), b. 1917. **Genres:** Economics, International Relations/Current Affairs, Politics/Government. **Career:** International Department of Labour Party, secretary, 1945-52; S.E. Leeds, member of parliament, 1952-55; Leeds East, labour member of Parliament, 1955-82; Foreign affairs of Parliament, deputy spokesman, 1958-62; secretary of state for defence, 1964-70; Exchequer, chancellor, 1974-79; La-

bour Party, deputy leader, 1980-83. Writer. **Publications:** Western Europe: The Challenge of Unity, 1950; (with J. Freeman) Rearmament-How Far?, 1951; The Curtain Falls, 1951; New Fabian Essays, 1952; Neutralism, 1955; Fabian International Essays, 1956; A Neutral Belt in Europe, 1958; NATO and American Security, 1959; The Race against the H Bomb, 1960; Labor Britain and the World, 1963; Managing the Economy, 1980; Healey's Eye, 1980; Labor and World Society, 1985; Beyond Nuclear Deterrence, 1986; The Time of My Life, 1989; When Shrimps Learn to Whistle: Signposts to the Nineties, 1990; My Secret Planet, 1992; Denis Healey's Yorkshire Dales, 1995; Healey's World: Travels with My Camera, 2002. Contributor to periodicals. **Address:** House of Lords, Information Service, London, GL SW1A 0PW, England.

HEALEY, Judith Koll. American (born United States), b. 1939. **Genres:** History, Poetry, Novels. **Career:** JKH Executive Consulting, owner; Weyerhaeuser Family Foundation, manager; Laura Jane Musser Fund, manager; Counsel on Foundations, consultant. Writer. **Publications:** The Canterbury Papers, 2004; The Rebel Princess, 2009. **Address:** c/o Author Mail, HarperCollins Publishers Inc., 10 E 53rd St., 7th Fl., New York, NY 10022-5244, U.S.A. **Online address:** info@thecanterburypapers.com

HEALY, Erin M. American (born United States), b. 1970. **Genres:** Novels, Horror. **Career:** Christian Parenting Today, assistant editor, editor, 1990; WordWright Editorial Services, owner and consultant, 2002-; WaterBrook Press, book editor. **Publications:** (With J. Trent) My Mother's Hands: Celebrating Her Special Touch, 2000; Managing Your Time: You and God, You and Others, You and Your Kids (Bible study), 2003; (with T. Dekker) Kiss (thriller novel), 2008; (with T. Dekker) Burn (thriller novel), 2010; Never Let You Go (thriller novel), 2010; Promises she keeps, 2010; Bakers Wife, 2011; (with T. Dekker) Llamas, 2011. **Address:** c/o Dan Raines, Creative Trust Inc., 5141 Virginia Way, Ste. 320, Brentwood, TN 37027, U.S.A. **Online address:** erin@erinhealy.com

HEALY, Gene. American (born United States), b. 1970. **Genres:** Politics/Government. **Career:** Cato Institute, vice president; Liberty, contributing editor. Political scientist. **Publications:** (Ed.) Go Directly to Jail: The Criminalization of Almost Everything, 2004; (with T. Lynch) Power Surge: The Constitutional Record of George W. Bush, 2006; The Cult of the Presidency: America's Dangerous Devotion to Executive Power, 2008. Contributor to periodicals. **Address:** Cato Institute, 1000 Massachusetts Ave. NW, Washington, DC 20001-5403, U.S.A. **Online address:** ghealy@cato.org

HEALY, Jeremiah. (Terry Devane). American (born United States), b. 1948. **Genres:** Mystery/Crime/Suspense, Young Adult Fiction, Novels. **Career:** New England School of Law, assistant professor, 1978-80, associate professor, 1980-83, professor of law, 1983-96. Writer. **Publications:** Blunt Darts, 1984; The Staked Goat in UK as The Tethered Goat, 1986; So Like Sleep, 1987; Swan Dive, 1988; Yesterday's News: A Novel of Suspense, 1989; Right to Die: A John Cuddy Mystery, 1991; Shallow Graves: A John Cuddy Mystery, 1992; Foursome: A John Cuddy Novel, 1993; Act of God, 1994; Rescue, 1995; Invasion of Privacy, 1996; The Only Good Lawyer, 1998; The Stalking of Sheilah Quinn, 1998; The Concise Cuddy: A Collection of John Francis Cuddy Stories, 1998; Holiday Fairy: A Christmas Story, 1998; Spiral, 1999; Turnabout, 2000; Cuddy Plus One, 2002; Off-Season and Other Stories, 2003. AS TERRY DEVANE: Uncommon Justice, 2001; Juror No.11, 2002; A Stain upon the Robe, 2003. **Address:** 186 Commonwealth Ave., Ste. 31, Boston, MA 02116, U.S.A. **Online address:** jeremiah_healy@yahoo.com

HEALY, Maureen. American (born United States) **Genres:** History, Military/Defense/Arms Control. **Career:** Oregon State University, associate professor of history. Writer. **Publications:** Vienna and the Fall of the Habsburg Empire: Total War and Everyday Life in World War I, 2004. **Address:** Oregon State University, Department of History, 302B Milam Hall, Corvallis, OR 97331, U.S.A. **Online address:** mhealy@oregonstate.edu

HEALY, Sophia (Warner). American (born United States), b. 1938. **Genres:** Novels, Literary Criticism And History. **Career:** Bennington College, teacher of drawing and print making, 1968-82; Trout Paper, director, 1980-; 8 1/2 by 11, co-founder and co-editor, 1983-. **Publications:** Lone Stars, 1989; The Robber Girl My Imaginary Youth, 2006. Contributor to periodicals. **Address:** c/o Melanie Jackson, Melanie Jackson Agency, 250 W 57 St., Ste. 1119, New York, NY 10107, U.S.A.

HEANEY, Seamus. Irish (born Ireland), b. 1939. **Genres:** Poetry, Literary Criticism And History, Translations, Young Adult Non-fiction, Novellas/Short Stories. **Career:** Teacher, 1962-63; St. Joseph's College of Education, lecturer, 1963-66; Queen's University, lecturer in English, 1966-72; University of California, visiting lecturer, 1970-71; freelance writer, 1972-75; Carysfort College, lecturer, 1976-82, Department of English, head, through 1982; Harvard University, visiting lecturer, 1979, visiting professor, 1982-85, Boylston professor of rhetoric and oratory, 1984-97, Ralph Waldo Emerson poet-in-residence, 1998-2006; Oxford University, professor of poetry, 1989-94; St. Columb's College, faculty. Translator. **Publications:** Death of a Naturalist, 1966; Eleven Poems, 1967; (with D. Hammond and M. Longley) Room to Rhyme, 1968; A Lough Neagh Sequence, 1969; (with J. Montague) The Northern Muse, 1969; Door into the Dark, 1969; Night Drive: Poems, 1970; Boy Driving His Father to Confession, 1970; Land, 1971; Servant Boy, 1971; (ed. with A. Brownjohn and J. Stallworthy) New Poems 1970-71, 1971; Soundings: An Annual Anthology of New Irish Poetry, 1972; Wintering Out, 1972; (ed.) Soundings, 1974; North, 1975; The Fire I' the Flint: Reflections on the Poetry of Gerard Manley Hopkins, 1975; Bog Poems, 1975; Stations, 1975; (with D. Mahon) In their Element, 1977; After Summer, 1978; Robert Lowell: A Memorial Address and an Elegy, 1978; Hedge School, 1979; Field Work, 1979; Gravities, 1979; Selected Poems, 1980; Preoccupations: Selected Prose, 1968-78, 1980; Sweeney Praises the Trees, 1981; Sweeney Astray: A Version from the Irish, 1982; (ed. with T. Hughes) The Rattle Bag: An Anthology of Poetry, 1982; An Open Letter, 1983; Station Island, 1984; Hailstones, 1984; Sweeney Astray, 1984; The Haw Lantern, 1987; The Government of the Tongue, 1988; (ed. and intro.) The Essential Wordsworth, 1988; The Place of Writing, 1989; (with M. Longley) Upstairs Outlook: An Evening of Poetry, 1989; New Selected Poems 1966-1987, 1990; The Tree Clock, 1990; Seeing Things, 1991; The Cure at Troy, 1991; The Cure at Troy: A Version of Sophocles' Philoctetes, 1991; Sweeney's Flight, 1992; The Midnight Verdict, 1993; (ed.) The May Anthology of Oxford and Cambridge Poetry, 1993; Keeping Going, 1993; The Redress of Poetry, 1995; (trans. with S. Barańczak) J. Kochanowski, Laments, 1995, rev. ed., 2009; (with J. Brodsky and D. Walcott) Homage to Frost, 1996; The Spirit Level (poetry), 1996; Crediting Poetry: The Nobel Lecture, 1996; (with T. Hughes) The School Bag, 1997; Opened Ground: Poems, 1966-1996, 1998; (contrib.) Diary of One Who Vanished: A Song Cycle, 2000; Yeats, 2000; Sounding Lines: The Art of Translating Poetry, 2000; Beowulf: A New Verse Translation, 2000; Electric Light, 2001; Something to Protect, 2001; (intro.) A Way of Life, Like Any Other, 2002; The Debateable Land: Ireland's Border Counties, 2002; Finders Keepers: Selected Prose, 1971-2001, 2002; (trans.) Beowulf: A Verse Translation, 2002; Talking with Poets, 2002; (with L. O' Flynn) The Poet and the Piper, 2003; (intro.) There You Are: Writing on Irish and American Literature and History, 2003; The Burial at Thebes: A Version of Sophocles' Antigone, 2004; Anything Can Happen: A Poem and Essay, 2004; (contrib.) Perspectives on Equality: The Second Seamus Heaney Lectures, 2005; District and Circle, 2006; Riverbank Field, 2007; (contrib.) Touched by Robert Burns, 2008; Articulations, 2008; (trans.) Beowulf: An Illustrated Edition, 2008; Spelling It Out: In Honour of Brian Friel on His 80th Birthday, 2009; (trans.) R. Henryson, The Testament of Cresseid and Seven Fables, 2009; (co-author) From the Republic of Conscience: Stories Inspired by the Universal Declaration of Human Rights, 2009; Human Chain, 2010; (contrib.) Brian Bourke: Five Decades 1960s-2000s, 2010; (contrib.) Mirror up to Nature, 2010. Contributor to books. **Address:** The Gallery Press, Loughcrew, Oldcastle, ME 1, Ireland.

HEARD, Alex. American (born United States), b. 1957. **Genres:** History, Social Sciences. **Career:** Nashville Tennessean, reporting intern, 1979; Washington Monthly, editorial intern, 1980-81; Education Week, staff writer, 1982- 83; Vanity Fair, freelance writer, 1984-86; New Republic, freelance writer, 1984-86; Harper's, freelance writer, 1984-86; Washington Post, weekly humor columnist, 1986-88; freelance writer, 1988-92; Outside magazine, senior editor and writer, 1992-96, editorial director; New York Times, editor and writer, 1996-98; Wired Magazine, executive editor, 1999-. **Publications:** Apocalypse Pretty Soon: Travels in End-Time America, 1999; The Eyes of Willie McGee: A Tragedy of Race, Sex, and Secrets in the Jim Crow South, 2010. Contributor to periodicals. **Address:** Santa Fe, NM , U.S.A. **Online address:** alexheard@yahoo.com

HEARD, Anthony Hazlitt. South African (born South Africa), b. 1937. **Genres:** History. **Career:** Cape Times, junior reporter, 1955-64, assistant editor, 1967-71, leader-page editor, 1967-, editor, 1971-87; Financial Mail, cape editor, 1964-65; South African Morning Newspapers Bureau, senior correspondent, 1966; Freelance writer, 1987-94; Harvard University, visit-

ing Nieman fellow, 1987-88; University of Arkansas, associate professor, visiting fulbright fellow, 1989, 1992; University of the Western Cape, media consultant, 1990-94; Minister Kader Asmal in South Africa Government, Minister of Water Affairs and Forestry, special adviser, 1994-99; Minister in Presidency, special adviser, 2000-. **Publications:** The Cape of Storms; A Personal History of the Crisis in South Africa, 1990, rev. ed., 1991. **Address:** Mill St., PO Box 12189, Cape Town, 8010, South Africa. **Online address:** heardt@mweb.co.za

HEARDEN, Patrick J. American (born United States), b. 1942. **Genres:** History. **Career:** Case Western Reserve University, visiting assistant professor, 1971-72; University of South Dakota, visiting assistant professor, 1972-75; University of Missouri-Columbia, visiting assistant professor, 1975-76, 1977-79; University of Wisconsin-Madison, visiting assistant professor, 1976-77, 1981-82; University of Arizona, visiting assistant professor, 1979-80; Purdue University, professor, 1983-. Writer. **Publications:** Independence & Empire: The New South's Cotton Mill Campaign, 1865-1901, 1982; Roosevelt Confronts Hitler: America's Entry into World War II, 1987; (ed.) Vietnam: Four American Perspectives, 1990; Architects of Globalism: Building a New World Order during World War II, 2002; The Tragedy of Vietnam, 4th ed., 2012. **Address:** Department of History, Purdue University, University Hall, 672 Oval Dr., West Lafayette, IN 47907, U.S.A. **Online address:** phearden@purdue.edu

HEARN, Chester G. American (born United States), b. 1932. **Genres:** History, Humanities, inspirational/Motivational Literature, Marine Sciences/Oceanography, Meteorology/Atmospheric Sciences, Military/Defense/Arms Control, Theology/Religion, Biography, Biography. **Career:** Combustion Engineering, vice-president for manufacturing, 1973-90; Philip A. Crosby Associates Inc., consultant, 1990-93; CJ Quality Associates, vice president, 1997-98; Young Men's Christian Association of Milton, president of board of directors. Writer. **Publications:** Gray Raiders of the Sea: How Eight Confederate Warships Destroyed the Union's High Seas Commerce, 1992; Mobile Bay and the Mobile Campaign: The Last Great Battles of the Civil War, 1993; George Washington's Schooners: The First American Navy, 1995; The Capture of New Orleans, 1862, 1995; Admiral David Dixon Porter: The Civil War Years, 1996; Six Years of Hell: Harpers Ferry During the Civil War, 1996; Companions in Conspiracy, 1996; When the Devil Came Down to Dixie: Ben Butler in New Orleans, 1997; Admiral David Glasgow Farragut: The Civil War Years, 1998; (with S.A. Hearn) Safe in the Arms of Jesus: The Story of Fanny Crosby, 1998; Ellet's Brigade: The Strangest Outfit of All, 2000; The Impeachment of Andrew Johnson, 2000; Naval Battles of the Civil War, 2000; The American Soldier in World War II, 2000; An Illustrated History of the U.S. Navy; An Illustrated History of the U.S. Marines; Tracks in the Sea: Matthew Fontaine Maury and the Mapping of the Oceans, 2002; Illustrated Directory of the U.S. Marine Corps, 2003; Sorties into Hell: The Hidden War on Chichi Jima, 2003; Circuits in the Sea: The Men, the Ships and the Atlantic Cable, 2004; The Maccabees, 2004; Herod the Great, 2004; Carriers in Combat: The Air War at Sea, 2005; Spies and Espionage: A Directory, 2006; Army: An Illustrated History: The U.S. Army from 1775 to the 21st Century, 2006; Marines: An Illustrated History: The U.S. Marine Corps from 1775 to the 21st Century, 2007; Navy: An Illustrated History: The U.S. Navy from 1775 to the 21st Century, 2007; Air Force: An An llustrated History: The U.S. Air Force from 1907 to the 21st Century, 2008; Lincoln, The Cabinet and the Generals, 2010. Contributor to magazines and periodicals. **Address:** 5266 Wolf Run Village Ln., Erie, PA 16505, U.S.A.

HEARN, Julie. British (born England), b. 1958?. **Genres:** Children's Fiction, History, Novels, Young Adult Fiction. **Career:** Journalist, editor and educator. **Publications:** Follow Me Down, 2003 in US as Sign of the Raven, 2005; The Merrybegot, 2005; The Minister's Daughter, 2005; Hazel, 2007; Ivy: A Novel, 2008; Rowan the Strange, 2009. Contributor to periodicals. **Address:** c/o Author Mail, The Felicity Bryan Literary Agency, 2a N Parade Ave., Oxford, OX OX2 6LX, England.

HEARN, Lian. *See* **RUBINSTEIN, Gillian (Margaret Hanson).**

HEARN, Otis. *See* **TRENERRY, Walter N.**

HEARON, Shelby. American (born United States), b. 1931. **Genres:** Novels, Autobiography/Memoirs, Biography, Animals/Pets, Art/Art History, Young Adult Fiction, Animals/Pets. **Career:** Freelance writer, 1966-; University of Texas, visiting lecturer, 1978-80; Bennington College, Summer Program Fiction Workshop, teacher, 1980; Ohio Wesleyan University, writer-in-residence, 1989; University of Massachusetts, visiting distinguished professor, 1994-96; Middlebury College, visiting distinguished professor, 1996-98. **Publications:** NOVELS: Armadillo in the Grass, 1968; The Second Dune, 1973; Hannah's House, 1975; Now and Another Time, 1976; A Prince of a Fellow, 1978; (with B. Jordan) Barbara Jordan: A Self-Portrait (biography), 1979; Painted Dresses, 1981; Afternoon of a Faun, 1983; Group Therapy, 1984; A Small Town, 1985; Five Hundred Scorpions, 1987; Owning Jolene, 1989; Hug Dancing, 1991; Life Estates, 1994; Footprints, 1996; Ella in Bloom, 2001; Year of The Dog, 2007. Works appear in anthologies. Contributor of articles to periodicals and books. **Address:** University of Texas Press, PO Box 7819, Austin, TX 78713-7819, U.S.A. **Online address:** shelby.shelby@verizon.net

HEARST, Dorothy. American (born United States), b. 1966. **Genres:** Novels. **Career:** Jossey-Bass, acquisitions editor. **Publications:** Promise of the Wolves, 2008. **Address:** c/o Mollie Glick, Jean V. Naggar Literary Agency, 216 E 75th St., Ste. 1E, New York, NY 10021, U.S.A. **Online address:** dorothy@dorothyhearst.com

HEARTH, Amy. See HEARTH, Amy Hill.

HEARTH, Amy Hill. (Amy Hearth). American (born United States), b. 1958. **Genres:** Children's Fiction. **Career:** New York Times, reporter on assignment, 1988-92, drama critic. **Publications:** (with S.L. Delany) On My Own at 107: Reflections on Life without Bessie, 1997; (with N. Salsitz and A.P. Salsitz) In a World Gone Mad: A Heroic Story of Love, Faith and Survival, 2001; The Delany Sisters Reach High (children's book), 2003; (with N. Pelosi) Know Your Power: A Message to America's Daughters, 2008; Strong Medicine Speaks: A Native American Elder Has Her Say: An Oral History, 2008. WITH SARAH LOUISE DELANY AND A. ELIZABETH DELANY: Having Our Say: The Delany Sisters First 100 Years, 1993; The Delany Sisters Book of Everyday Wisdom, 1994. Contributor to periodicals. **Address:** c/o Mel Berger, William Morris Agency, 1325 Ave. of the Americas, New York, NY 10019, U.S.A. **Online address:** contact@amyhillhearth.com

HEATER, Derek Benjamin. British (born England), b. 1931. **Genres:** Education, History, International Relations/Current Affairs, Politics/Government. **Career:** RAF, education officer, 1954-57; assistant master, 1957-62; Brighton College of Education, lecturer in history, 1962-76, Department of History, head, 1966-76; Politics Association, founder and chairman, 1969-73; Teaching Politics, editor, 1973-79; Brighton Polytechnic, Faculty of Social and Cultural Studies, dean, 1976-79, Humanities Department, head, 1976-83. **Publications:** Political Ideas in the Modern World, 1962, 4th ed., 1972; Order and Rebellion: A History of Europe in the Eighteenth Century, 1964; The Cold War, 1964; (with G. Owen) World Affairs, 1972; Contemporary Political Ideas, 1974; History Teaching & Political Education, 1974; Britain and the Outside World, 1976; (with B. Crick) Essays on Political Education, 1977; Peace and War, 1978; Essays on Contemporary Studies, 1979; World Studies: Education for International Understanding in Britain, 1980; Our World This Century, 1982; Peace through Education: The Contribution of the Council for Education in World Citizenship, 1984; Our World Today, 1985; Reform and Revolution, 1987; Case Studies in Twentieth-Century World History, 1988; Refugees, 1989; Citizenship: The Civic Ideal in World History, Politics, and Education, 1990, 3rd ed., 2004; The Idea of European Unity, 1992; (with G.R. Berridge) Introduction to International Politics, 1993; The Remarkable History of Rottingdean, 1993; (with D. Oliver) The Foundations of Citizenship, 1994; National Self-Determination: Woodrow Wilson and His Legacy, 1994; United Nations: How it Works and What it Does, 2nd ed., 1994; World Citizenship and Government: Cosmopolitan Ideas in the History of Western Political Thought, 1996; The Theory of Nationhood: A Platonic Symposium, 1997; Keeping Faith: A History of Sutton Grammar School, 1998; What is Citizenship?, 1999; World Citizenship: Cosmopolitan Thinking and Its Opponents, 2002; A History of Education for Citizenship, 2004; A Short History of Citizenship, 2004; Brief History of Citizenship, 2004. EDITOR: The Teaching of Politics, 1969; (with J. Gillespie) Political Education in Flux, 1981. **Address:** 3 The Rotyngs, Rottingdean, Brighton, BN2 7DX, England.

HEATH, Chip. American (born United States), b. 1963. **Genres:** Business/Trade/Industry, Economics. **Career:** University of Chicago Graduate School of Business, assistant professor, associate professor, 1991-97; Duke University, Fuqua School, associate professor, 1997-2000; Stanford University Graduate School of Business, Thrive Foundation for Youth Professor of Organizational Behavior, 2000-. Writer. **Publications:** (with J.G. March) A Primer on Decision Making: How Decisions Happen, 1994; (ed. with G.A. Fine and V.C. Vincent) Rumor Mills: The Social Impact of Rumor and Legend, 2004; (with D. Heath) Made to Stick: Why Some Ideas Survive and Others Die, 2007. Contributor to periodicals and journals. **Address:** Stanford Graduate School of Business, Stanford University, 518 Memorial Way, Stanford, CA 94305-5015, U.S.A. **Online address:** chip.heath@stanford.edu

HEATH, Dwight B. (Dwight Braley Heath). American (born United States), b. 1930. **Genres:** Anthropology/Ethnology, History, Sociology, Psychology, Social Sciences. **Career:** Yale University, reader in anthropology, 1958-59; Brown University, research professor, instructor, 1959-60, assistant professor, 1960-62, associate professor, 1963-70, professor of anthropology, 1970-; U.S. Peace Corps, consulting anthropologist, 1961-63; Special Operations Research Office, consulting anthropologist, 1962-63; Research Institute for the Study of Man, research associate, 1964-65; World Health Organization, consultant in mental health, 1973-80. Writer. **Publications:** A Journal of the Pilgrims at Plymouth: Mourt's Relation, 1963, rev. ed., 1986; (with C.J. Erasmus and H.C. Buechler) Land Reform and Social Revolution in Bolivia, 1969; Historical Dictionary of Bolivia, 1972; (with A.M. Cooper) Alcohol Use and World Cultures: A Comprehensive Bibliography of Anthropological Sources, 1981; (intro. and comp.) Alcohol and Data Research, 1996; Drinking Occasions, 2000. EDITOR: (and intro. with R.N. Adams) Contemporary Cultures and Societies of Latin America: A Reader in the Social Anthropology of Middle and South America, 1965, 3rd ed., 2002; (contrib.) Classification of Highland Communities in Latin America, 1967; (with M.W. Everett and J.O. Waddell) Cross-Cultural Approaches in the Study of Alcohol, 1976; (with J.O. Waddell and M.D. Topper) Cultural Factors in Alcohol Research and Treatment of Drinking Problems, 1981; International Handbook on Alcohol and Culture, 1995. **Address:** Department of Anthropology, Brown University, PO Box 1921, Providence, RI 02912, U.S.A.

HEATH, Dwight Braley. See HEATH, Dwight B.

HEATH, Jennifer. American/Australian (born Australia) **Genres:** Novels, Art/Art History, Literary Criticism And History. **Career:** Writer. **Publications:** Super Colon, 1992; Black Velvet: The Art We Love to Hate, 1994; On the Edge of Dream: Celtic Tales for Grown Women, 1995; A House White with Sorrow (novel), 1996; (with N. Berry) Cerridwen and the Cauldron of Knowledge (juvenile fiction), 1997; On the Edge of Dream: The Women in Celtic Myth and Legend, 1998; Echoing Green: The Garden in Myth and Memory, 2000; Scimitar and the Veil: Extraordinary Women of Islam, 2004; (ed.) Veil: Women Writers on its History, Lore, and Politics, 2008; Primal Picnics: Writers Invent Creative Myths for their Favorite Foods, 2010; (ed. with A. Zahedi) Land of the Unconquerable: The Lives of Contemporary Afghan Women, 2011; The Jewel and the Ember: Love Stories of the Islamic World, forthcoming. **Address:** 4125 Nassau Pl., Boulder, CO 80301-6029, U.S.A. **Online address:** heathcollom@comcast.net

HEATH, Lorraine. Also writes as Jade Parker, Rachel Hawthorne. American/British (born England), b. 1954. **Genres:** Romance/Historical, Young Adult Fiction. **Career:** Novelist, 1993-. **Publications:** HISTORICAL ROMANCE NOVELS: Sweet Lullaby, 1994; Parting Gifts, 1994; The Ladies Man, 1995; Always to Remember, 1996; Texas Destiny, 1997; Texas Glory, 1998; Texas Splendor, 1999; To Tame a Texan Anthology, 1999; A Rogue in Texas, 1999; (as Rachel Hawthorne) Rome, 2000; Never Love a Cowboy, 2000; (as Rachel Hawthorne) London, 2000; (as Rachel Hawthorne) Paris, 2000; Never Marry a Cowboy, 2001; The Outlaw and the Lady, 2001; (as Rachel Hawthorne) Nick & the Nerd, 2001; (as Rachel Hawthorne) Older Guy, 2001; Samantha and the Cowboy, 2002; To Marry an Heiress, 2002; Amelia and the Outlaw, 2003; Love with a Scandalous Lord, 2003; Hard Lovin' Man, 2003; (as Rachel Hawthorne) Caribbean cruising, 2004; Smooth Talkin' Stranger, 2004; An Invitation to Seduction, 2004; As an Earl Desires, 2005; (as Rachel Hawthorne) Island Girls, 2005; A Matter of Temptation, 2005; Promise Me Forever, 2006; (with G. Gentry and T. Bodwell) My Heroes Have Always Been Cowboys, 2006; Duke of Her Own, 2006; (as Rachel Hawthorne) Love on the Lifts, 2006; (as Rachel Hawthorne) Thrill Ride, 2006; (as Rachel Hawthorne) Trust Me, 2007; (as Rachel Hawthorne) Boyfriend League, 2007; Just Wicked Enough, 2007; (as Jade Parker) To Catch a Pirate, 2007; (as Rachel Hawthorne) Snowed In, 2007; In Bed With the Devil, 2008; (as Rachel Hawthorne) Labor of Love, 2008; (as Jade Parker) Caitlin, 2008; (as Jade Parker) Robyn, 2008; (as Jade Parker) Whitney, 2008; (as Rachel Hawthorne) Suite Dreams, 2008; Between the Devil and Desire, 2009; Surrender to the Devil, 2009; Midnight Pleasures with a Scoundrel, 2009; Dark Guardian, 2009; (as Rachel Hawthorne) Shadow of the Moon, 2009; (as Rachel Hawthorne) Moonlight, 2009; (as Rachel Hawthorne) Full Moon, 2009; (as Rachel Hawthorne) Dark of the Moon, 2009; Waking Up With the Duke, 2011; She Tempts the Duke, 2012. Contributor to books. Works appear in anthologies. **Address:** PO Box 250034, Plano, TX 75025-0034, U.S.A. **Online address:** lorraine-heath@sbcglobal.net

HEATH, Malcolm (Frederick). British (born England), b. 1957. **Genres:** Classics, Politics/Government, History, Poetry. **Career:** Oxford University, Hertford College, junior research fellow, 1984-87; University of St. Andrews, lecturer in Greek, 1987-88; University of Leeds, Department of Classic lecturer in classics, 1988-91, reader, 1991-2000, professor of Greek language and literature, 2000-, Leeds International Classical Studies Online Journal, editor, 2002-. Writer. **Publications:** The Poetics of Greek Tragedy, 1987; Political Comedy in Aristophanes, 1987; Unity in Greek Poetics, 1989; Hermogenes on Issues: Strategies of Argument in Later Greek Rhetoric, 1995; Aristotle: Poetics, 1996; (ed. with F. Cairns) Roman Poetry and Prose, Greek Poetry, Etymology, Historiography, 1996; Interpreting Classical Texts, 2002; Menander: A Rhetor in Context, 2004. Contributor to journals. **Address:** Department of Classics, University of Leeds, Leeds, LS2 9JT, England. **Online address:** m.f.heath@leeds.ac.uk

HEATH, Sandra. *See* **WILSON, Sandra.**

HEATH, Sebastian E. American (born United States), b. 1955. **Genres:** Animals/Pets, Social Sciences. **Career:** Oleoducto Nor Peruano, industrial radiographer, 1975-76; University of Maryland, instructor in biology, 1984-85; Marquis Downs, veterinarian, 1987-88; Montclair Veterinary Hospital, associate, 1988-89; University of Florida, clinical instructor of rural animal medicine service, 1989-90, assistant professor of large animal clinical sciences, 1990-91; Purdue University, School of Veterinary Medicine, section chief for large animal medicine, 1991-94, assistant professor of veterinary clinical services, 1998-, Center for the Human-Animal Bond, disaster management consultant; Federal Emergency Management Agency, project coordinator for animals in disaster, 1996-98; Tripler Army Medical Center, adjunct faculty, 1996-97; Pan American Health Organization, consultant; U.S. Agency for International Development, Livestock Development Programs, technical advisor and administrative assistant. Writer. **Publications:** (With A. O'Shea) Rescuing Rover: A First Aid & Disaster Guide for Dog Owners, 1999; Animal Management in Disasters, 1999. **Address:** 1650 Harvard St. NW, Washington, DC 20009-3737, U.S.A. **Online address:** heathseb@paho.org

HEATH, Veronica. British (born England), b. 1927. **Genres:** Animals/Pets, Food And Wine, Natural History, Sports/Fitness. **Career:** The Guardian Newspaper, freelance journalist. **Publications:** Susan's Riding School, 1956; Ponies in the Heather, 1959; Come Riding with Me, 1964; Come Show Jumping with Me, 1966; Ponies and Pony Management, 1966; Come Pony Trekking with Me, 1966; Ponies, 1969; Beginner's Guide to Riding, 1971; The Family Dog, 1972; So You Want to Be a Show Jumper, 1974; So You Want to Own a Pony, 1974; Let's Own a Pony, 1974; Riding for Beginners, 1978; Perfect Cooking with Game, 1983; A Dog at Heel, 1987, rev. ed., 1999; Geordie Cook Book, 1995; A Gundog Handler's Guide to Picking Up, 1999; Taste of Northumberland, 2001. **Address:** The Guardian Newspaper, Kings Pl., 90 York Way, London, GL N1 9GU, England.

HEATH, William. American (born United States), b. 1942. **Genres:** Poetry, Literary Criticism And History, Novels. **Career:** University of Seville, Fulbright lecturer, 1979-81; Mount St. Mary's University, Department of English, professor, 1981-2007, professor emeritus, 2007-; Kenyon College, faculty; Transylvania University, faculty; Vassar College, faculty; Monocacy Valley Review, editor, 1985-93; Hood College, Libman professor. Novelist. **Publications:** POETRY: The Walking Man, 1994. NOVELS: The Children Bob Moses Led, 1995; Blacksnake's Path: The True Adventures of William Wells, 2008. Contributor to magazines. **Address:** Department of English, Mount St. Mary's University, 212 Knott Academic Ctr., 16300 Old Emmitsburg Rd., Emmitsburg, MD 21727-7700, U.S.A. **Online address:** heath@msmary.edu

HEATHER, Peter. British/Irish (born Ireland), b. 1960. **Genres:** History, Translations, Politics/Government, Philosophy. **Career:** Oxford University, Worcester College, Murray resident fellow in history, tutor in medieval history and lecturer in modern history; Yale University, instructor; University College London, instructor; King's College London, Department of History,

chair of medieval history and professor of medieval history, 2008-. Writer. **Publications:** (With J. Matthews) The Goths in the Fourth Century, 1991; (as P.J. Heather) Goths and Romans, 332-489, 1991; (afterword) The Huns, 1996; The Goths, 1996; (ed.) The Visigoths from the Migration Period to the Seventh Century: An Ethnographic Perspective, 1999; (trans. and intro. with D. Moncur) Themistius, Politics, Philosophy, and Empire in the Fourth Century: Select Orations of Themistius, 2001; The Fall of the Roman Empire: A New History of Rome and the Barbarians, 2006; Empires and Barbarians: The Fall of Rome and the Birth of Europe, 2010; Der Untergang des Römischen Weltreichs, 2010. **Address:** Department of History, King's College, Rm. K6.45, Strand, London, GL WC2R 2LS, England. **Online address:** peter.heather@kcl.ac.uk

HEBER, R. *See* **COX, Richard (Hubert Francis).**

HECHT, Jeff(rey Charles). American (born United States), b. 1947. **Genres:** Natural History, Sciences, Technology, Young Adult Non-fiction, Physics, Science Fiction/Fantasy. **Career:** Laser Focus World, managing editor, 1974-81, contributing editor, 1992-; freelance writer, 1981-; Lasers and Applications, contributing editor, 1982-91; New Scientist, correspondent, 1984-. **Publications:** (With D.W. Allen) Controversies in education, 1974; (with D. Teresi) Laser: Supertool of the 1980s, 1982; Beam Weapons: The Next Arms Race, 1984; Laser Pioneer Interviews: With an Introduction to Laser History, 1985, rev. ed., 1992; The Laser Guidebook, 1986, 2nd ed., 1992; Understanding Fiber Optics, 1987, 5th ed., 2006; Optics: Light for a New Age (juvenile), 1987; Understanding Lasers, 1988, 3rd ed. as Understanding Lasers: An Entry-Level Guide, 2008; Shifting Shores: Rising Seas, Retreating Coastlines (juvenile), 1990; Vanishing Life: The Mystery of Mass Extinctions (juvenile), 1993; Laser, Light of a Million Uses, 1998; City of Light: The Story of Fiber Optics, 1999, rev. ed., 2004; (with B. Hitz and J.J. Ewing) Introduction to Laser Technology, 2001, 4th ed., 2012; Beam: The Race to Make the Laser, 2005. Contributor of fiction to periodicals. **Address:** 525 Auburn St., Auburndale, MA 02466-1739, U.S.A. **Online address:** jeff@jeffhecht.com

HECHT, Jennifer Michael. American (born United States), b. 1965. **Genres:** Anthropology/Ethnology, Biography, Psychology, History. **Career:** Mannes College, instructor in history, 1993-94; Nassau Community College, associate professor of history, 1994-2006; New York Institute for the Humanities, fellow, 2004. Writer. **Publications:** The Next Ancient World (poetry), 2001; The End of the Soul: Scientific Modernity, Atheism and Anthropology in France, 2003; Doubt: A History: The Great Doubters and Their Legacy of Innovation, from Socrates and Jesus to Thomas Jefferson and Emily Dickinson, 2003; Funny, 2005; The Happiness Myth: Why What We Think is Right is Wrong: A History of What Really Makes Us Happy, 2007. Works appear in anthologies. Contributor of periodicals. **Address:** c/o Author Mail, HarperCollins Publishers, 10 E 53rd St., New York, NY 10022, U.S.A. **Online address:** hechtjm@aol.com

HECHT, Michael L. American (born United States), b. 1949. **Genres:** Communications/Media, Cultural/Ethnic Topics, Speech/Rhetoric. **Career:** University of Illinois-Urbana-Champaign, instructor in communication, 1975-76; University of Montana, assistant professor of communication, 1976-78; California State University, assistant professor of communication, 1978-79; Xerox Corp., Systemix Division, data analyst and project manager, 1979-81; University of Southern California, assistant professor of communication, 1979-83; Arizona State University, assistant professor, 1983-85, associate professor, 1985-89, professor of communication, 1989-97; Penn State University, professor, 1997-2005, Department of Sociology, affiliated professor, 1998-, Department of Communication Arts and Sciences, head, 1999-2003, liberal arts research professor, 2005-07, distinguished professor, 2007-. Writer. **Publications:** (With M.J. Collier and S. Ribeau) African American Communication, 1993, 2nd ed. (with R.L. Jackson and S. Ribeau), 2003; (co-author) Adolescent Relationships and Drug Abuse, 2000; (with R.R. Baldwin, S.L. Faulkner and S.L. Lindsley) Conceptualizing Culture, forthcoming. EDITOR: (with J.A. DeVito and L.K. Guerrero) The Nonverbal Communication Reader, 1989, 3rd ed. (with L. Guerrero and J.A. DeVito), 2008; Communicating Prejudice, 1998. **Address:** Department of Communication Arts & Sciences, Pennsylvania State University, 229 Sparks Bldg., University Park, PA 16802, U.S.A. **Online address:** mhecht@psu.edu

HECKERT, Connie K(aye Delp). American (born United States), b. 1948. **Genres:** Children's Fiction, Human Relations/Parenting, Local History/Rural

Topics, Adult Non-fiction, Young Adult Fiction. **Career:** Iowa State University Veterinary Clinics, medical records librarian, 1968-73; freelance writer, 1972-; Peoria Engineering, proofreader, 1975; Illowa Health Systems Agency, assistant health planner, 1977-78; Black Hawk College, instructor, 1985; St. Ambrose University, adjunct assistant professor of English, 1985-93; Society of Children's Book Writers and Illustrators-Iowa, regional adviser, 2000-; Augustana College, Department of English, faculty, 2002; National League of American Pen Women Inc., president. Newspaper correspondent and speaker. **Publications:** FOR CHILDREN: Miss Rochelle and the Lost Bell, 1985; Dribbles, 1993. FOR ADULTS: Lyons: 150 Years North of the Big Tree, 1985; The Swedish Connections, 1986; The First 100 Years: A Pictorial History of Lindsay Park Yacht Club, 1987; (with K.M. Becker) To Keera with Love: Abortion, Adoption or Keeping the Baby, 1987; (with V. Berry) Roots and Recipes: Six Generations of Heartland Cookery, 1995; The Mel Foster Story: 75 Years of Shaping the Quad-Cities, 1997; Alcoa Davenport Works: The First Fifty, 1998; The Kahl Legacy: The History, the Man, the Vision, 2000; The Writing Group Book, 2003; (ed.) The First Fifty Years: Per Mar Security Services. Contributor to periodicals. **Address:** Society of Children's Book, Writers and Illustrators, PO Box 1436, Bettendorf, IA 52722-0024, U.S.A. **Online address:** hecklit@aol.com

HECKLER, Cheryl. American (born United States), b. 1959. **Genres:** Biography, Autobiography/Memoirs. **Career:** Ecumenical News Intl., staff; New York Times, writer; Miami University, associate professor of English and journalism. Journalist and historian. **Publications:** (With D. Ariail) The Carpenter's Apprentice: The Spiritual Biography of Jimmy Carter, 1996; Heart and Soul of a Nation: How the Spirituality of Our First Ladies Changed America, 1997; An Accidental Journalist: The Adventures of Edmund Stevens, 1934-1945, 2007. Contributor to newspapers and periodicals. **Address:** Department of English, Miami University, 336 Bachelor Hall, Oxford, OH 45056, U.S.A. **Online address:** heckler_cheryl@yahoo.com

HECKMAN, Robert A. American (born United States), b. 1965. **Genres:** Archaeology/Antiquities, Art/Art History, Social Sciences, Sociology. **Career:** Statistical Research Inc., archaeologist and project director, 1992-. Writer. **Publications:** (With B.K. Montgomery and S.M. Whittlesey) Prehistoric Painted Pottery of Southeastern Arizona, 2000. **Address:** Statistical Research Inc., 4425 Juan Tabo Blvd. NE, Ste. 112, PO Box 14700, Albuquerque, NM 87111-2681, U.S.A. **Online address:** rheckman@sricrm.com

HECKSCHER, Charles. American (born United States), b. 1949. **Genres:** Organized Labor, Business/Trade/Industry, Economics. **Career:** Harvard University, John F. Kennedy School of Government, Harman fellow, 1979-81; consultant, 1979-; Communications Workers of America, research economist, 1981-84; Harvard University, Harvard Business School, assistant professor, 1986-91, associate professor of human resource management, 1991-92, Harvard Law School, co-director of project on employment relations, 1988-96; Rutgers University, Department of Labor Studies and Employment relations, chair, 1992-98, professor, 1992-, acting extension director, 2006, School of Management and Labor Relations, director of center for workplace transformation, 1998-; Institut des Études Politiques, visiting professor, 1996; University of Pennsylvania, Wharton School, visiting professor, 2008-09. Writer. **Publications:** The New Unionism: Employee Involvement in the Changing Corporation, 1988; (ed. with A. Donnellon and contrib.) The Post-Bureaucratic Organization: New Perspectives on Organizational Change, 1994; White-Collar Blues: Management Loyalties in an Age of Corporate Restructuring, 1995; (co-author) Agents of Change: Crossing the Post-Industrial Divide, 2003; (ed. with P.S. Adler) The Firm as a Collaborative Community: Reconstructing Trust in the Knowledge Economy, 2006; Collaborative Enterprise: Managing Speed and Complexity in Knowledge-based Businesses, 2007. Contributor to books and journals. **Address:** Center for Workplace Transformation, Rutgers School of Management and Labor Relations, Rutgers University, 50 Labor Center Way, New Brunswick, NJ 08901-8553, U.S.A. **Online address:** cch@heckscher.us

HECKSCHER, Morrison H. American (born United States), b. 1941?. **Genres:** Art/Art History. **Career:** Metropolitan Museum of Art, Print Department, Chester Dale fellow, 1966, curator in American wing, 1968-78, curator of American decorative arts, 1978-98, Department of American Decorative Arts, Anthony W. and Lulu C. Wang curator, 1998-2001, Lawrence A. Fleischman chair of the American wing, 2001-. Writer. **Publications:** The Orga-

nization and Practice of Philadelphia Cabinetmaking Establishments, 1790-1820, 1964; American Furniture in the Metropolitan Museum of Art: Late Colonial Period-the Queen Anne and Chippendale Styles, vol. II, 1985; (with L.G. Bowman) American Rococo, 1750-1775: Elegance in Ornament, 1992; (with L. Zabar) John Townsend: Newport Cabinetmaker, 2005; Creating Central Park, 2008. Contributor to books and periodicals. **Address:** Metropolitan Museum of Art, 1000 5th Ave., New York, NY 10028-0198, U.S.A.

HEDDERWICK, Mairi. British/Scottish (born Scotland), b. 1939. **Genres:** Children's Fiction, Travel/Exploration, Illustrations, Reference, Sports/Fitness, History. **Career:** Art teacher, 1962-64; Malin Workshop, artist, designer and owner, 1969-80; freelance writer, illustrator and public speaker, 1980-; Highlands and Islands, community cooperatives advisor, 1986-89. **Publications:** FOR CHILDREN: Katie Morag Delivers the Mail, 1984; Katie Morag and the Two Grandmothers, 1985; Katie Morag and the Tiresome Ted, 1986; Katie Morag and the Big Boy Cousins, 1987; Peedie Peebles' Summer or Winter Book in US as P.D. Peebles' Summer or Winter Book, 1989; Katie Morag and the New Pier, 1993; Dreamy Robbie!, 1993; Robbie's First Day at School, 1993; Robbie's Trousers, 1993; Peedie Peebles Colour Book, 1994; The Tale of Carpenter MacPheigh, 1994; Robbie's Birthday, 1994; Robbie and Grandpa, 1994; Katie Morag and the Wedding, 1995; Katie Morag's Island Stories, 1995; The Big Katie Morag Storybook, 1996; Katie Morag and the Grand Concert, 1997; Oh No, Peedie Peebles!, 1997; The Second Katie Morag Storybook, 1998; Katie Morag's Rainy Day Book, 1999; Katie Morag and the Riddles, 2001; Katie Morag's Island Stories, 2003; A Walk with Grannie, 2003; Katie Morag, of Course, 2003; Katie Morag and the Birthdays, 2005; Katie Morag and the Dancing Class, 2007. ADULT NON-FICTION: Mairi Hedderwick's Views of Scotland, 1981; An Eye on the Hebrides: Illustrated Travel, 1989, new ed., 2011; Highland Journey: A Sketching Tour of Scotland Retracing the Footsteps of Victorian Artist John T. Reid, 1992, new ed., 2009; Sea Change: The Summer Voyage from East to West Scotland of the Anassa, 1999, new ed., 2011. OTHERS: Last Laird of Coll, 2011. Illustrator of books by others. Contributor to periodicals. **Address:** Curtis Brown Group Ltd., Haymarket House, 28-29 Haymarket, London, GL SW1Y 4SP, England.

HEDEEN, Stanley. American (born United States), b. 1943?. **Genres:** History. **Career:** Xavier University, College of Arts and Sciences, former dean, professor emeritus, acting chair of communication arts. Writer. **Publications:** Natural History of the Cincinnati Region, 2006; Big Bone Lick: The Cradle of American Paleontology, 2008. Contributor to periodicals. **Address:** Xavier University, 3800 Victory Pkwy., Cincinnati, OH 45207, U.S.A. **Online address:** hedeen@xavier.edu

HEDGES, Joseph. *See* **GILMAN, George G.**

HEDIN, Robert (Alexander). American (born United States), b. 1949. **Genres:** Poetry, Translations. **Career:** Sheldon Jackson College, instructor in English, 1973-76; University of Alaska-Anchorage, visiting assistant professor of creative writing, 1976-77; Ecole Nationale d'Administration, teacher of English, 1978; University of Alaska-Fairbanks, visiting assistant professor of English, 1979-80; Midnight Sun Writers Symposium, director, 1980; Wake Forest University, poet-in-residence, 1980-92, 1995-96; North Carolina Writers' Network, board director, 1989-91; Loft Literacy Center, instructor, 1993-94, 1996-97; Associated Colleges of the Twin Cities, visiting writer-in-residence, 1995-96; University of Minnesota, lecturer, 1995-96, Edelstein-Keller Minnesota writer of distinction, 2001-02; Loft Literary Center, instructor, 1996-97; Anderson Center for Interdisciplinary Studies, executive director, 1997-; Great River Review, editor, 1997-; Saint Olaf College, visiting poet in residence, 1999-2000, visiting poet-in-residence, 2000-01. **Publications:** POETRY: Snow Country, 1975; At the Home-Altar, 1979; County O, 1984; Tornadoes, 1990; The Old Liberators: New and Selected Poems and Translations, 1998. EDITOR OF ANTHOLOGIES: (with D. Stark) In the Dreamlight, 1984; (with G. Holthaus) Alaska: Reflections on Land and Spirit, 1989; (with G. Holthaus) The Great Land: Reflections on Alaska, 1994; The Great Machines: Poems and Songs of the American Railroad, 1996; The Zeppelin Reader, 1998; Perfect in Their Art, 2003; Old Glory: American War Poems from the Revolutionary War to the War on Terrorism, 2004; Where One Voice Ends Another Begins: 150 years of Minnesota Poetry, 2007. TRANSLATOR: In Lands Where Light Has Another Color: Poems of Rolf Jacobsen, 1990; Night Music: Poems of Rolf Jacobsen, 1994; B. Sortland, The Dream Factory,

2001; O.H. Hauge, The Bullfinch Rising from the Cherry Tree, 2001; (with R. Bly and R. Greenwald) The Roads Have Come to an End Now: Selected and Last Poems of Rolf Jacobsen, 2001; (with R. Bly) O.H. Hauge, Passing the Arctic Circle, 2003; (with R. Bly) The Dream We Carry: Selected and Last Poems of Olav H. Hauge, 2008. Works appears in anthologies. Contributor of articles to periodicals. **Address:** PO Box 59, Frontenac, MN 55026, U.S.A. **Online address:** info@roberthedin.com

HEDIN, Thomas F. American (born United States), b. 1944. **Genres:** Art/Art History, Social Sciences. **Career:** University of Minnesota, professor of art history, 1973-2007. Writer and historian. **Publications:** The Sculpture of Gaspard and Balthazard Marsy: Art and Patronage in the Early Reign of Louis XIV, With a Catalogue Raisonne, 1983; (with R.W. Berger) Diplomatic Tours in the Gardens of Versailles Under Louis XIV, 2008. **Address:** University of Minnesota, Rm. 317H, D198, 10 University Dr., Duluth, MN 55812, U.S.A. **Online address:** thedin@d.umn.edu

HEEFNER, Wilson A. American (born United States), b. 1931. **Genres:** Military/Defense/Arms Control, Biography, History. **Career:** University of Maryland, School of Medicine, assistant professor, 1966-68; Dameron Hospital, pathologist, 1968-88. Writer. **Publications:** Twentieth Century Warrior: The Life and Service of Major General Edwin D. Patrick, 1995; Patton's Bulldog: The Life and Service of General Walton H. Walker, 2001; Dogface Soldier: The Life of General Lucian K. Truscott, Jr., 2010. **Address:** 7205 Park Woods Dr., Stockton, CA 95207-1409, U.S.A. **Online address:** w.heefner@comcast.net

HEER, David M(acAlpine). American (born United States), b. 1930. **Genres:** Demography. **Career:** U.S. Bureau of the Census, Population Division, Social Statistics Branch, statistician, 1957-61; University of California, lecturer in sociology and assistant research sociologist, 1961-64; Harvard University, assistant professor, 1964-68, associate professor of demography, 1968-72; University of Southern California, Population Research Laboratory, director, 1972-2000, professor of sociology, 1995-. Writer. **Publications:** After Nuclear Attack: A Demographic Inquiry, 1965; Society and Population, 1968, (with J. Grigsby) 3rd ed., 1992; (with P. Herman) A Human Mosaic: An Atlas of Ethnicity in Los Angeles County, 1980-1986, 1990; Undocumented Mexicans in the United States, 1990; Immigration in America's Future: Social Science Findings and the Policy Debate, 1996; Kingsley Davis: A Biography and Selections from His Writings, 2005. EDITOR: Social Statistics and the City, 1968; Readings on Population, 1968. **Address:** Population Research Laboratory, University of Southern California, AHF B52, 3616 Trousdale Pkwy, Los Angeles, CA 90089-0377, U.S.A. **Online address:** dheer@ucsd.edu

HEERBOTH, Sharon. *See* LEON, Sharon.

HEERMA VAN VOSS, Lex. Dutch (born Netherlands), b. 1955. **Genres:** History, Social Sciences. **Career:** University of Utrecht, assistant professor of social and economic history, 1991-94, professor, 2000-, Faculty of Social Sciences, endowed chair; International Institute of Social History, associate director of research, 1994-. Writer. **Publications:** (Ed. with H. Diederiks) Industrial Conflict: Papers Presented to the Fourth British-Dutch Conference on Labour History, 1988; (with F.H. Hoon) Working Class and Popular Culture, 1988; The North Sea and Culture in Early Modern History, 1996; Dock Workers 1790-1970: International Explorations in Comparative Labour History, 2000; Petitions in Social History, 2001; (ed. with M. van der Linden) Class and Other Identities: Gender Religion and Ethnicity in the Writing of European Labor History, 2002; (with P. Pasture and J. De Maeyer) Between Cross and Class: Comparative Histories of Christian Labour in Europe, 1840-2000, 2005; (ed. with E.H. Kuperus and E.N. Meerkerk) The Ashgate Companion to the History of Textile Workers, 1650-2000, 2009. **Address:** International Institute of Social History, Cruquiusweg 31, Amsterdam, 1019, Netherlands. **Online address:** lhv@iisg.nl

HEERTJE, Arnold. Dutch (born Netherlands), b. 1934. **Genres:** Economics, Marketing, Money/Finance, Politics/Government, Technology. **Career:** Baarnsch Lyceum, faculty, 1963-64; University of Amsterdam, faculty of economics, 1963-, professor of economics, 1964-99, professor of history of economic thought, 1997-2005, professor emeritus, 2006-. Writer and advisor. **Publications:** Het Elasticteitsbegrip in de Theoretische Economie, 1957; De Kern van de Economie, 1962; Geldontwaarding, 1968; Inleiding tot de Commerciele Economie, 1968; Elemtaire Commerciele Economie, 1969; Export

en Welvaart, 1970; Grundbegriffe der Volswirtschaftslehre, 1970-71; Economie en Recht Voor het Agrarisch Onderwijs, 1971; Economie en Technische Ontwekkeling, 1973; Terugblikken en Vooruitzien, 1976; De Verwording ven de Econonmie: Voor de Arbeider, Ondernemer en Kruidenier Verklaard: Waarin Opgenomen de Dood van een Courer, 1976; Economics and Technical Change, 1977; Echte Econonmie: Misverstanden over en Misstanden in de Economie, 1977; Basic Economics, 1980; De Nederlandse Economen, 1980; (with H. Cohen) Het Officieuze Circuit: Een Witboek over Zwart en Grijs Geld, 1980; (with F.J. Hogendoorn) Geld, Rollen of Stilstaan?: Een Praktisch Boek over Geld voor Praktische Mensen, 1981; Hoe Slecht Gaat het Werkelijk met Onze Economie?: Economische Dagboekaantekeningen uit de Sombere Jaren 1974-1980, 1981; The Black Economy, 1982; (with F.W. Rushing and F. Skidmore) Economics, 1983; (with P. Barthelemy) L'économie Souterraine, 1984; The U.S.A. in the World Economy, 1984; (with R.J.G.M. Widdershoven and J. Vischjager) Het Cijfer van de Rechter, 1991; (with P. Barthelemy and P. Pieretti) Principes d'economie Politique, 1992; (with H.D. Wenzel) Grundlagen der Volkswirtschaftslehre, 1997; Markt-Meesters: Portretten van Vooraanstaande Liberale Economen, 2004; Schumpeter on the Economics of Innovation And the Development of Capitalism, 2006. EDITOR: (with J.S. Cramer and P. Venekamp) Relevance and Precision: From Quantitative Analysis to Economic Policy: Essays in Honor of Pieter de Wolff, 1976; Schumpeter's Vision: Capitalism, Socialism and Democracy after Forty Years, 1981; Investir dans l'avenir de l'Europe, 1983; Investing in Europe's Future, 1983; Innovation, Technical and Financial, 1988; (with J.E. Stinglitz) The Economic Role of the State, 1989; (with M. Perlman) Evolving Technology and Market Structure: Studies in Schumpeterian Economics, 1990; (with J. Van Daal) Economic Thought in the Netherlands: 1650-1950, 1992; World Savings: An International Survey, 1993; The Makers of Modern Economics, vol. I, 1993, vol. II, 1995, vol. III, 1997, vol. IV, 1999; (with J. Polak) European Transport Economics, 1993; (with D. Walker and H.D. Doel) Welfare Economics and the Theory of Economic Policy, 1995; (with J. Polak) Analytical Transport Economics: An International Perspective, 2000. Contributor to periodicals. **Address:** Department of Economics, University of Amsterdam, Spui 21, Amsterdam, 1012 WX, Netherlands. **Online address:** joab@hccrtje.nl

HEFER, Hayim (Baruch). Israeli/Polish (born Poland), b. 1925. **Genres:** Adult Non-fiction, Poetry. **Career:** Yediot Ahronot, columnist; El-Hamam Satirical Theater, co-founder, 1960; Cultural Affairs for the West Coast, staff. Writer and translator. **Publications:** Milim la-manginot, 1961; Tarnegolim 'al Gesher ha-Yarkon: Pizmonim, 1968; Yig'al, 1970; (with D. Ben-Amotz) Tel-Aviv Ha-ketanah: Hizayon, 1980; Af Milah ra ah, 1998. Contributor to periodicals. **Address:** 53 Arlozoroff St., Tel Aviv, 4, Israel.

HEFFER, Simon (James). British (born England), b. 1960. **Genres:** History, Biography, Writing/Journalism. **Career:** Medical journalist, 1983-85; freelance journalist, 1985-86; Daily Telegraph, leader writer, 1986-91, deputy correspondent, 1987-88, political sketch writer, 1988-91, political columnist, 1990-91, deputy editor and political columnist, 1994-95; Spectator, deputy editor, 1991-94; Evening Standard, columnist, 1991-93; Daily Mail, columnist, 1993-94, 1995-. Writer. **Publications:** (Ed. with C. Moore) A Tory Seer: The Selected Journalism of T.E. Utley, 1989; Moral Desperado: A Life of Thomas Carlyle, 1995; Power and Place: The Political Consequences of King Edward VII, 1998; Like the Roman: The Life of Enoch Powell, 1998; The End of the Peer Show?, 1998; Nor Shall My Sword: The Reinvention of England, 1999; Vaughan Williams, 2001; (ed.) The Great British Speeches, 2007. **Address:** c/o Daily Mail, Northcliffe House, 2 Derry St., London, GL W8 5TT, England. **Online address:** simon.heffer@telegraph.co.uk

HEFFERNAN, Nancy Coffey. American (born United States), b. 1936?. **Genres:** History, Area Studies, Novellas/Short Stories, Social Sciences, Biography. **Career:** Writer. **Publications:** WITH ANN PAGE STECKER: New Hampshire: Crosscurrents in Its Development, 1986, 3rd ed., 2004; Sisters of Fortune: Being the True Story of How Three Motherless Sisters Saved Their Home in New England and Raised Their Younger Brother While Their Father Went Fortune Hunting in the California Gold Rush, 1993. OTHER: (with L. Judson) What's In a Name?: The Heroes and Heroines Baby Name Book, 1990. Contributor to periodicals. **Address:** University Press of New England, 23 S Main St., Hanover, NH 03755, U.S.A.

HEFFRON, Doris. British/Canadian (born Canada), b. 1944. **Genres:** Novels, Young Adult Fiction, Essays. **Career:** Oxford University, Department for Continuing Studies, lecturer and tutor in literature, 1969-80; Open University, lecturer, 1972-78; National University of Malaysia, lecturer in creative writing, 1978; writer, 1978-; Writers' Union of Canada, staff; PEN Canada, board of director; Native Men's Residence, board of director; Wainfleet Public Library, writer-in-residence, 1989-90. Writer. **Publications:** NOVELS: A Shark in the House, 1996; City Wolves, 2008. ESSAYS: More than Words Can Say, 1990. YOUNG ADULT NOVELS: A Nice Fire and Some Moonpennies, 1971; Crusty Crossed, 1976; Rain and I, 1982. **Address:** GL , England. **Online address:** dheffron@sympatico.ca

HEGAMIN, Tonya C. American (born United States), b. 1975?. **Genres:** Children's Fiction. **Career:** Writer. **Publications:** M+ O 4evr, 2008; (with M. Nelson) Pemba's Song: A Ghost Story, 2008; Most Loved in All the World, 2009. **Address:** Houghton Mifflin's Children's Books, 222 Berkeley St., Boston, MA 02116, U.S.A. **Online address:** tonyacheriehegamin@gmail.com

HEGARTY, Frances. (Frances Fyfield). British (born England), b. 1948. **Genres:** Mystery/Crime/Suspense, Novels, Horror. **Career:** Crown Prosecution Service, solicitor, 1975-. Lawyer and writer. **Publications:** MYSTERY NOVELS AS FRANCES FYFIELD: A Question of Guilt, 1988; Not That Kind of Place, 1990; Shadows on the Mirror, 1991; Deep Sleep, 1991; Shadow Play, 1993; Perfectly Pure and Good, 1994; A Clear Conscience, 1994; Without Consent, 1997; Blind Date, 1998; Staring at the Light, 2000; Undercurrents, 2001; The Nature of the Beast, 2001; Seeking Sanctuary, 2003; Looking Down, 2004; Safer Than Houses, 2005; The Art of Drowning, 2006; Blood from Stone, 2008; Cold to the Touch, 2009; Gold Digger, 2012. MYSTERY NOVELS AS FRANCES HEGARTY: Trial by Fire, 1990; The Playroom, 1991; Deep Sleep, 1992; Half Light, 1992; Let's Dance, 1995. Contributor to periodicals. **Address:** Little, Brown Book Group, 100 Victoria Embankment, London, GL EC4Y 0DY, England. **Online address:** frances@francesfyfield.co.uk

HEGEDUS, Bethany. American (born United States), b. 1974?. **Genres:** Novels. **Career:** Writers' League of Texas, office manager; Burke County High School, English and theater teacher; Hunger Mountain Journal, Children and Young Adult Section, co-editor. **Publications:** Between Us Baxters (novel), 2009; Truth with a Capital T (novel), 2010. **Address:** Serendipity Literary Agency L.L.C., 305 Gates Ave., Brooklyn, NY 11216, U.S.A. **Online address:** bethany@writersleague.org

HEGEMAN, Mary Theodore. (Mary Theodore). American (born United States), b. 1907?. **Genres:** Education, History, Biography, Human Relations/Parenting, Social Sciences. **Career:** St. Coletta School, principal, 1947-64, superintendent, 1964-70, director of public relations, 1970-87. Writer. **Publications:** (As Mary Theodore) The Challenge of the Retarded Child, 1959, 3rd ed. 1969; Developmental Disability: A Family Challenge, 1984; A Short Life of Saint Coletta, 1987; History of St. Coletta School, 1989. **Address:** St. Coletta School, N4637 County Rd Y, Jefferson, WI 53549, U.S.A.

HEGENBERGER, John. American (born United States), b. 1947. **Genres:** How-to Books, Art/Art History, Photography, Literary Criticism And History. **Career:** This Week, arts and entertainment editor. **Publications:** Collector's Guide to Comic Books, 1990; Collector's Guide to Treasures of the Silver Screen, 1991. **Address:** William Morris Agency, 1350 Ave. of the Americas, New York, NY 10019, U.S.A.

HEIDAR, Knut (Martin). Norwegian (born Norway), b. 1949. **Genres:** Politics/Government, Social Commentary. **Career:** Institute for Social Research, research assistant, senior research assistant, 1972-74; University of Oslo, Department of Political Science, faculty, 1975-92, associate professor, 1980-92, professor of political science, 1992-, Faculty of Social Sciences, dean, 2007-12, Institutt for Statsvitenskap, faculty; University of Warwick, visiting researcher, 1986-87; University of Denver, visiting researcher, 1998. Writer. **Publications:** Norske Politiske Fakta 1884-1982, 1983; Partidemokrati på prøve: Norske Partieliter I Demokratisk Perspektiv, 1988; (with L. Svåsand) Partiene I en Brytningstid, 1994; (with E. Berntzen) Vesteuropeisk Politikk, 3rd ed., 1998; Statsvitenskapelige Utsyn: Politiske Tema Og Tenkemåter i enOppbruddstid, 2001; Norway: Elites on Trial, 2001; (with J. Saglie) Hva Skjer Med Partiene?, 2002. EDITOR: (with L. Svåsand) Partier Uten Grenser?, 1997; (with P. Esaiasson) Beyond Westminster and Congress: The Nordic Experience, 2000; (with R. Koole) Parliamentary Party Groups in European Democracies: Political Parties Behind Closed Doors, 2000; Statsvitenskapelige Utsyn: Politiske Tema Og Tenkemåter I En Oppbruddstid, 2001; Nordic Politics: Comparative Perspectives, 2004. **Address:** Institutt for Statsviten-

skap, University of Oslo, Blokk B, Moltke Moes vei 31, Eilert Sundts hus, PO Box 1097, Oslo, 0851, Norway. **Online address:** knut.heidar@stv.uio.no

HEIDBREDER, Robert K. Canadian/American (born United States), b. 1947. **Genres:** Poetry, Children's Fiction, Children's Non-fiction. **Career:** Vancouver School Board, primary school teacher, 1975-2005; Queen's University, honorary lecturer, 2003; University of British Columbia, professor, professor emeritus of English and Canadian literature. Writer. **Publications:** Don't Eat Spiders (poems), 1985; (comp. and contrib.) I Hate Dinosaurs, 1992; Eenie Meenie Manitoba: Playful Poems from Coast to Coast, 1996; Python Play and Other Recipes for Fun (poems), 2000; I Wished for a Unicorn, 2000; See Saw Saskatchewan: More Playful Poems from Coast to Coast, 2002; Drumheller Dinosaur Dance, 2004; (with R. Mate) Crocodiles Say..., 2005; A Sea-Wishing Day, 2007; Lickety-Split, 2007; Shake-Awakes, forthcoming; A Black and Bittern Night, forthcoming; Sock-Hop Sunday, forthcoming. **Address:** Department of English, University of British Columbia, 397-1873 East Mall, Vancouver, BC V6T 1Z1, Canada.

HEIDE, Florence Parry. *See* Obituaries.

HEIDE, Kathleen M. American (born United States), b. 1954. **Genres:** Criminology/True Crime. **Career:** University of South Florida, assistant professor, 1981-87, associate professor, 1987-94, professor of criminology, 1994-, associate dean, 2001-03, interim dean, 2003-05, Center for Mental Health Education, Assessment and Therapy, licensed psychotherapist; State of Florida, mental health counselor. Writer. **Publications:** Why Kids Kill Parents: Child Abuse and Adolescent Homicide, 1992; Young Killers: The Challenge of Juvenile Homicide, 1999; (with L. Merz-Perez) Animal Cruelty: Pathway to Violence Against People, 2003. Works appear in anthologies. Contributor of articles to periodicals. **Address:** Department of Criminology, College of Arts and Sciences, University of South Florida, 4202 E Fowler Ave., SOC 311, Tampa, FL 33620-8100, U.S.A. **Online address:** kheide@cas.usf.edu

HEIDEL, R. Andrew. American (born United States), b. 1969. **Genres:** Poetry, Young Adult Fiction, Novellas/Short Stories. **Career:** Avon Books, publicist, senior publicist, 1996-. Writer. **Publications:** Beyond the Wall of Sleep: A Collection of Prose and Poetry, 1988-1997, 1997, 2nd ed., 1998; Desperate Moon, 2006; Lilith, forthcoming. **Address:** Avon Books, 1350 Ave. of the Americas, New York, NY 10019, U.S.A.

HEIDENRY, John. (John M. Heidenry). American (born United States), b. 1939. **Genres:** Communications/Media, Sex, Sports/Fitness, Mystery/Crime/Suspense. **Career:** Social Justice Review, assistant editor, 1957-61; St. Louis Review, St. Louis reporter, 1961-63, editor, 1977-82; Herder and Herder, managing editor, 1963-72; St. Louis Literary Supplement, co-founder, 1977; Penthouse Forum, executive editor, editor, 1982-89; freelance writer, 1989-2000; St. Louis Magazine, editor; Maxim Magazine, interim editor; Continuum Publishing Group, consultant editor; The Week, executive editor, 2000-07, contributing editor, 2007-. **Publications:** Test Your Sex I.Q., 1988; Theirs Was the Kingdom: Lila and DeWitt Wallace and the Story of the Reader's Digest, 1993; What Wild Ecstasy: The Rise and Fall of the Sexual Revolution, 1997; The Boys Who Were Left Behind: The 1944 World Series between the Hapless St. Louis Browns and the Legendary St. Louis Cardinals, 2006; The Gashouse Gang: How Dizzy Dean, Leo Durocher, Branch Rickey, Pepper Martin, and Their Colorful, Come-from-Behind Ball Club Won the World Series-and America's Heart-During the Great Depression, 2007; Zero at the Bone: The Playboy, the Prostitute, and the Murder of Bobby Greenlease, 2009. EDITOR: More Letters from Penthouse, 1989; Erotica from Penthouse, 1990. **Address:** c/o Andrew Blauner, 135 Charles St., New York, NY 10014, U.S.A. **Online address:** jmheidenry@aol.com

HEIDENRY, John M. *See* **HEIDENRY, John.**

HEIDLER, David S(tephen). American (born United States), b. 1955. **Genres:** History, Biography. **Career:** Salisbury State University, assistant professor of history, 1984-93; Colorado State University, visiting professor of history, 1994-99. Writer. **Publications:** WITH J.T. HEIDLER: Old Hickory's War: Andrew Jackson and the Quest for Empire, 1996; The War of 1812, 2002; Manifest Destiny, 2003; Daily Life in the Early American Republic, 1790-1820: Creating a New Nation, 2004; Mexican War, 2006; Indian Removal: A Norton Casebook, 2007; Henry Clay: The Essential American, 2010. EDITED WITH J.T. HEIDLER: Encyclopedia of the War of 1812, 1997; Encyclopedia of the Mexican-American War, 1999; Encyclopedia of the American Civil War, 2000; Daily Lives of Civilians in Wartime Modern America: From the Indian Wars to the Vietnam War, 2007; Daily Lives of Civilians in Wartime Early America, 2007. OTHER: Pulling the Temple Down: The Fire-Eaters and the Destruction of the Union, 1994. **Address:** 187 Dolomite Dr., Colorado Springs, CO 80919, U.S.A. **Online address:** david@djheidler.com

HEIDLER, Jeanne T(wiggs). American (born United States), b. 1956. **Genres:** History, Biography, Military/Defense/Arms Control, Politics/Government. **Career:** Salisbury State University, assistant professor of history, 1985-93; United States Air Force Academy, assistant professor, 1993-96, associate professor of history, 1996-99, professor of history, 1999-. Writer. **Publications:** WITH D.S. HEIDLER: Old Hickory's War: Andrew Jackson and the Quest for Empire, 1996; (ed.) Encyclopedia of the War of 1812, 1997, rev. ed., 2004; (ed.) Encyclopedia of the Mexican-American War, 1999; (ed.) Encyclopedia of the American Civil War: A Political, Social, and Military History, 2000; The War of 1812, 2002; Manifest Destiny, 2003; Daily Life in the Early American Republic, 1790-1820, 2004; Mexican War, 2006; Indian Removal: A Norton Casebook, 2006; (ed.) Daily Lives of Civilians in Wartime Modern America: From the Indian Wars to the Vietnam War, 2007; (ed.) Daily Lives of Civilians in Wartime Early America: From the Colonial Era to the Civil War, 2007; Henry Clay: The Essential American, 2010. **Address:** Department of History, United States Air Force Academy, 2354 Fairchild Dr., Ste. 6F-101, USAF Academy, CO 80840, U.S.A. **Online address:** jeanne.heidler@usafa.edu

HEILBRUNN, Jacob. American (born United States) **Genres:** History, Politics/Government, International Relations/Current Affairs. **Career:** National Interest, senior editor and contributor; New Republic, senior editor. **Publications:** They Knew They Were Right: The Rise of the Neocons, 2008. Contributor to journals. **Address:** Washington, DC , U.S.A. **Online address:** jheilbrunn@nationalinterest.org

HEIM, Michael Henry. American (born United States), b. 1943. **Genres:** Politics/Government, Translations, Adult Non-fiction. **Career:** Harvard University, teaching fellow, 1966-69, visiting associate professor, 1985-86; University of Wisconsin, assistant professor, 1970-72; University of California, assistant professor, 1972-79, visiting assistant professor, 1977-78, associate professor, 1979-86, professor, 1986-; University of California, visiting assistant professor, 1977-78. Writer. **Publications:** NONFICTION: Contemporary Czech, 1976; The Russian Journey of Karel Havlicek Borovsky, 1979. TRANSLATOR: The Letters of Anton Chekhov, 1973 as Anton Chekhov's Life and Thought: Selected Letters and Commentary, 1996; B. Hrabal, The Death of Mr. Baltisberger, 1975; M. Kundera, The Book of Laughter and Forgetting, 1980; M. Kundera, The Joke, 1982; V. Aksyonov, The Island of Crimea, 1983; M. Ageyev, Novel With Cocaine, 1984; M. Kundera, The Unbearable Lightness of Being, 1984; M. Kundera, Jacques and His Master: An Homage to Diderot in Three Acts, 1985; H. Troyat, Chekhov, 1986; (with A.W. Bouis) V. Aksyonov, In Search of Melancholy Baby, 1987; D. Kis, The Encyclopedia of the Dead, 1989; S. Sokolov, Astrophobia, 1990; B. Hrabal, Too Loud a Solitude, 1990; P. Esterhazy, Helping Verbs of the Heart, 1991; F. Roziner, A Certain Finkelmeyer, 1991; D. Ugresic, Fording the Stream of Consciousness, 1991; (with C. Hawkesworth) D. Ugresic, In the Jaws of Life, 1992; E. Uspensky, Uncle Fedya, His Dog, and His Cat (children's book), 1993; J. Neruda, Prague Tales, 1993; M. Tsernianski, Migrations, vol. I, 1994; (and afterword) G. Konrad, The Melancholy of Rebirth: Essays from Post-Communist Central Europe, 1989-1994 (nonfiction) by 1995; B. Hrabal, Dancing Lessons for the Advanced in Age, 1995; (in collaboration with S. Karlinsky) Anton Chekhov's Life and Thought: Selected Letters and Commentary, 1997; D. Kis, The Encyclopedia of the Dead, 1997; J. Hirsal, A Bohemian Youth, 1997; D. Kis, Early Sorrows: For Children and Sensitive Readers, 1998; A. Tisma, The Book of Blam, 1998; M. Ageyev, Novel with Cocaine, 1998; P. Matvejević, Mediterranean: A Cultural Landscape, 1999; G. Grass, My Century, 1999; (and intro.) A. Chekhov, The Essential Plays, 2003; T. Mann, Death in Venice, 2004; K. Chukovsky, Diary, 1901-1969, 2005; D. Ugresic, Lend Me your Character, 2005; D. Ugresic, Ministry of Pain, 2006; G. Grass, Peeling the Onion, 2007; B. Schlink, Homecoming, 2008; H. Claus, Wonder, 2009; B. Hrabal, Death of Mr. Baltisberger, 2010; Dancing Lessons for the Advanced in Age, 2011. EDITOR: (with O. Matich) The Third Wave: Russian Literature in Emigration, 1984; (with Z. Meyerstein and D. Worth) Readings in Czech, 1985; Magic Prague, 1993; Talks With

T.G. Masaryk (nonfiction), 1995; G. Conrád, Guest in My Own Country: A Hungarian Life, 2007; T. Mora, Day in Day Out, 2007. OTHERS: Un Babel fericit, 1999; (contrib.) Between Texts, Languages and Cultures, 2008; Contributor of articles to journals. **Address:** Department of Slavic Languages & Literatures, University of California, 316 Humanities Bldg., 405 Hilgard Ave., PO Box 951502, Los Angeles, CA 90095, U.S.A. **Online address:** heim@humnet.ucla.edu

HEIM, Scott. American (born United States), b. 1966. **Genres:** Novels, Poetry. **Career:** Novelist and poet. **Publications:** Saved from Drowning: Poems, 1993. NOVELS: Mysterious Skin, 1995; In Awe, 1997; We Disappear, 2008. Contributor to periodicals. **Address:** c/o Dorian Karchmar, William Morris Agency, 1325 Ave. of the Americas, New York, NY 10019, U.S.A. **Online address:** scottheim@aol.com

HEIM, S. Mark. American (born United States), b. 1950. **Genres:** Theology/Religion, History, Social Sciences. **Career:** Andover Newton Theological School, faculty, 1982-, Samuel Abbot professor of Christian theology. Theologian and writer. **Publications:** Is Christ the Only Way? Christian Faith in a Pluralistic World, 1985; Salvations: Truth and Difference in Religion, 1995; The Depth of the Riches: A Trinitarian Theology of Religious Ends, 2001; Saved from Sacrifice: A Theology of the Cross, 2006. EDITOR: (with T. Stylianopoulos) Spirit of Truth: Ecumenical Perspectives on the Holy Spirit: Papers of the Holy Spirit Consultation, October 24-25, 1985, Brookline, Massachusetts, 1986; Faith to Creed: Ecumenical Perspectives on the Affirmation of the Apostolic Faith in the Fourth Century: Papers of the Faith to Creed Consultation, Commission on Faith and Order, NCCCUSA, October 25-27, 1989-Waltham, Massachusetts, 1991; Grounds for Understanding: Ecumenical Resources for Responses to Religious Pluralism, 1998. Contributor to books, periodicals and journals. **Address:** Andover Newton Theological School, 210 Herrick Rd., Newton Center, MA 02459-2248, U.S.A. **Online address:** mheim@ants.edu

HEIMANN, Judith M(oscow). American (born United States), b. 1936. **Genres:** Biography, Military/Defense/Arms Control, History. **Career:** American University, Foreign Area Studies Program, researcher, 1968-72; U.S. Embassy, vice consul, 1972-75, assistant attache, 1975-78, second secretary, 1978-80, Indochinese Refugee Program, coordinator, 1991-92; U.S. Mission to the European Economic Community, first secretary, 1980-84; U.S. Department of State, EEC Political Affairs, officer-in-charge, 1984-86; U.S. Consulate, consul general, 1987-91. Writer. **Publications:** (Co-author) Area Handbook for Indonesia March, 1970; The Most Offending Soul Alive: Tom Harrisson and His Remarkable Life, 1998; The Airmen and the Headhunters: A True Story of Lost Soldiers, Heroic Tribesmen and the Unlikeliest Rescue of World War II, 2007. Contributor to periodicals. **Address:** Houghton Mifflin Harcourt Co., 222 Berkeley St., 9th Fl., Boston, MA 02116-3748, U.S.A.

HEIMS, Steve J(oshua). American/German (born Germany), b. 1926. **Genres:** Environmental Sciences/Ecology, History, Intellectual History, Physics, Sciences, Biography. **Career:** National Advisory Commission for Aeronautics, research scientist, 1955-58; Brandeis University, research fellow and assistant professor of physics, 1960-65; Wayne State University, associate professor of physics, 1966-69; Boston University, visiting professor of history and philosophy of science, 1970-71; University of New Hampshire, visiting faculty, 1975-84; Brandeis University, visiting faculty, 1975-84; University of Massachusetts, visiting faculty, 1975-84; Boston College, visiting faculty, 1975-84; Lesley College, visiting faculty, 1975-84; Worcester Polytechnic Institute, visiting faculty, 1975-84. Writer. **Publications:** (Intro.) The Human Use of Human Beings: Cybernetics and Society, 1949; John von Neumann and Norbert Wiener: From Mathematics to the Technologies of Life and Death, 1980; (ed. and contrib.) Passages from Berlin: Recollections of Former Students and Staff of the Goldschmidt Schule, 1987; The Cybernetics Group, 1991; Constructing a Social Science for Postwar America: The Cybernetics Group 1946-1953, 1993. Contributor of articles to periodicals. **Address:** 14 Babson St., Gloucester, MA 01930-3604, U.S.A.

HEIN, Christoph. German (born Germany), b. 1944. **Genres:** Novels, Plays/Screenplays, Translations, Autobiography/Memoirs, Biography, Essays, Young Adult Fiction, Young Adult Non-fiction, Young Adult Non-fiction. **Career:** Volkesbuhne (People's Stage), dramaturge and director's assistant, 1971-74, house author, 1974-79; Universities of Kentucky, visiting dramatist; New York University, visiting dramatist; Vanderbilt University, visiting dramatist; Amherst College, visiting dramatist; freelance writer, 1979-.

Publications: NOVELS: Einladung zum Lever bourgeois, 1980; Nachfahrt und fruherMorgen, 1982; Cromwell, under andere Stucke, 1981; Der fremde Freund, 1982; Drachenblut (Dragon blood), 1983; Nachtfahrt und fruher Morgen, 1982; Das Wildpferdunterm Kachelofen: Ein schones dickes Buch von Jakob Borg und seinen Freunden, 1984; Die wahre Geschichte des Ah Q, 1984; Horns Ende (Horn's End), 1985; Schlotel oder Was solls: Stucke und Essays, 1986; Offentlich arbeiten: Essais und Gesprache, 1987; Die Ritter der Tafelrunde: Komodie, 1989; Der Tangospieler, 1989; Als Kind habeich stalin gesehen: Essais und Reden, 1990; Die funfte Grundrechenart: Aufsatze und Reden, 1990; Bridge Freezes before Roadway, 1990; Das Napoleon-Spiel, 1993; Willenbrock: A Novel, 2003. OTHERS: Das Wildpferd unterm Kachelofen (children's book), 1984; (with U. Schreiber and Autorengruppe) Kunst als Opposition, 1990; Als Kind habe ich Stalin gesehen, 1990; Der Bund proletarisch revolutionarer Schriftsteller Deutschland: Biography eines Kulturpolitischen Experiments in der Weimarer Republik (nonfiction), 1991; Exekution eines Kalbes und andere Erzahlungern, 1994; Randow: eine Komödie, 1994; Von allem Anfang an, 1997; Bruch; In Acht und Bann; Zaungäste; Himmel auf Erden: Stücke, 1999; Willenbrock: Roman, 2000; Ort, das Jahrhundert: Essais, 2003; Landnahme: Roman, 2004; In seiner frühen Kindheit ein Garten: Roman, 2005; Goldene Vlies, 2005; Stücke, 2005; Frau Paula Trousseau: Roman, 2007. (contrib.) Nachdenken uber Deutschland: Herausgegeben von Dietmar Keller (speeches by Gunther Grass and others), 1990-1991. Contributor to periodicals. **Address:** c/o Suhrkamp-Verlag, PF 10 19 45, Frankfurt am Main, 60019, Germany.

HEINBUCH, Jean (M.). (Hine Book). American (born United States), b. 1953. **Genres:** Art/Art History, Homes/Gardens. **Career:** Native American Art Forms, instructor and consultant. Writer. **Publications:** SELF-ILLUS-TRATED: A Quillwork Companion, 1990; A Beadwork Companion, Eagle's View, 1992. **Address:** PO Box 116, Weippe, ID 83553, U.S.A.

HEINE, Art. *See* **HEINE, Arthur J.**

HEINE, Arthur J. (Art Heine). American (born United States), b. 1940. **Genres:** Administration/Management, Business/Trade/Industry, Self Help, Young Adult Non-fiction, Reference, Education. **Career:** Vocational Technical School, instructor, 1963-67; instructor, 1968-84; instructor and curriculum writer, 1984-; King's Point Civic League, officer, 1987-91, president, 1991-92. **Publications:** Surviving after High School: Overcoming Life's Hurdles, 1991; (as Art Heine with J. Heine) Book Selling 101: A Marketing Primer for Authors and Publishers, 1995. **Address:** J-MART Enterprises, 787 Biltmore Dr., PO Box 8884, Virginia Beach, VA 23454-3437, U.S.A.

HEINE, Steven. American (born United States), b. 1950. **Genres:** Poetry, Philosophy, Mythology/Folklore. **Career:** Villanova University, lecturer in religious studies, 1982-87; LaSalle University, assistant professor, 1987-91; Pennsylvania State University, associate professor of religious studies, 1991-96; Florida International University, professor of religion and director of the Institute for Asian Studies, 1997-. Writer. **Publications:** Existential and Ontological Dimensions of Time in Heidegger and Dogen, 1985; A Blade of Grass: Japanese Poetry and Aesthetics in Dogen Zen, 1989; A Dream within a Dream: Studies in Japanese Thought, 1991; Dogen and the Koan Tradition: A Tale of Two Shōbōgenzō Texts, 1994; The Zen Poetry of Dogen: Verses from the Mountain of Eternal Peace, 1997; Shifting Shape, Shaping Text: Philosophy and Folklore in the Fox Koan, 1999; (with D.S. Wright) The Koan: Texts and Contexts in Zen Buddhism, 2000; Opening a Mountain: Koans of the Zen Masters, 2002; White Collar Zen: Using Zen Principles to Overcome Obstacles and Achieve Your Career Goals, 2005; Did Dogen Go to China? What He Wrote and When He Wrote It, 2006; Zen Skin, Zen Marrow: Will the Real Zen Buddhism Please Stand Up?, 2008. EDITOR: A Study of Dogen: His Philosophy and Religion, 1992; (with C.W. Fu) Japan in Traditional and Postmodern Perspectives, 1995; Buddhism and Interfaith Dialogue: Part One of a Two-Volume Sequel to Zen and Western Thought, 1995; Zen and Comparative Studies: Part Two of a Two-Volume Sequel to Zen and Western Thought, 1997; (with D.S. Wright) The Koan: Texts and Contexts in Zen Buddhism, 2000; Zen and the Modern World: A Third Sequel to Zen and Western Thought, 2003; (with C.S. Prebish) Buddhism in the Modern World: Adaptations of an Ancient Tradition, 2003; (with D.S. Wright) The Zen Canon: Understanding the Classic Texts, 2004; (with D.S. Wright) Zen Classics: Formative Texts in the History of Zen Buddhism, 2006; (with D.S. Wright) Zen Ritual: Studies of Zen Buddhist Theory in Practice, 2008. Contributor to journals. **Address:** Institute for Asian Studies, Florida International University, DM 300, Miami, FL 33199, U.S.A. **Online address:** heines@fiu.edu

HEINEMAN, Kenneth J. American (born United States), b. 1962. **Genres:** History, Education, Politics/Government, Social Sciences. **Career:** U.S. Department of the Interior, National Park Service, historian, 1987; Historical Society of Western Pennsylvania, historian, 1988-89; University of Toledo, visiting assistant professor of history, 1989-90; Pennsylvania State University, New Kensington Campus, visiting instructor in history, 1989; Iowa State University, visiting assistant professor of history, 1990-91; Ohio University, Lancaster Campus, assistant professor of history, 1991-95, associate professor of history, 1995-2000, professor of history, 2000-; Angelo State University, Department of History, professor and department chair, 2009-. Writer. **Publications:** Campus Wars: The Peace Movement at American State Universities in the Vietnam Era, 1993; God Is a Conservative: Religion, Politics, and Morality in Contemporary America, 1998; A Catholic New Deal: Religion and Reform in Depression Pittsburgh, 1999; Put Your Bodies Upon the Wheels: Student Revolt in the 1960s, 2001. Contributor of articles to periodicals. **Address:** Department of History, Ohio University, Brasee Hall, Bentley Annex, 4th Fl., 1 Park Pl., Athens, OH 45701-2979, U.S.A. **Online address:** heineman@ohio.edu

HEINRICH, Will. American (born United States), b. 1978?. **Genres:** Communications/Media, Novels, Young Adult Fiction. **Career:** Harper's Magazine, intern, 2001; The New York Observer, art critic. Writer. **Publications:** The King's Evil, 2003. **Address:** c/o Author Mail, Simon & Schuster Inc., 1230 Ave. of the Americas, New York, NY 10020, U.S.A. **Online address:** stranger@willheinrich.com

HEINZ, Brian J(ames). American (born United States), b. 1946. **Genres:** Children's Non-fiction, Children's Fiction. **Career:** Middle Country School District, elementary teacher, 1974-78; William Floyd School District, elementary science teacher, 1978-; New York State Department of Education, regional elementary science mentor, 1985-95; State University of New York, Center for Science, Math and Technology Education, adjunct instructor, 1987-92. Writer. **Publications:** SELF-ILLUSTRATED: Beachcraft Bonanza, 1986. OTHERS: Beachcrafts, Too!, 1988; The Alley Cat, 1993; Introduction to Space, 1994; The Wolves, 1996; Kayuktuk: An Arctic Quest, 1996; The Monster's Test, 1996; Nanuk: Lord of the Ice, 1998; Butternut Hollow Pond, 2000; The Barnyard Cat, 2000; Cheyenne Medicine Hat, 2006; Red Fox at McCloskey's Farm, 2006; Nathan of Yesteryear and Michael of Today, 2007; A Coming of Winter in the Adirondacks, 2010. Contributor to magazines. **Address:** Ballyhoo Books, PO Box 534, Shoreham, NY 11786, U.S.A. **Online address:** bheinz@optonline.net

HEIR, Theron. *See* **RICHTEL, Matt.**

HEISEL, Sharon E(laine). American (born United States), b. 1941. **Genres:** Young Adult Fiction, Mystery/Crime/Suspense. **Career:** Sacred Heart Junior High School, science teacher, 1978-87; Providence Hospital, health educator, 1988-93; McLoughlin Middle School, science teacher, 1998-. Writer. **Publications:** A Little Magic, 1991; Wrapped in a Riddle, 1993; Eyes of a Stranger, 1996; Precious Gold, Precious Jade, 2000. Contributor to periodicals. **Address:** Jean V. Naggar Literary Agency, 216 E 75th St., New York, NY 10021-2921, U.S.A.

HEISING, Willetta L. American (born United States), b. 1947. **Genres:** Mystery/Crime/Suspense, Novels, History, Adult Non-fiction. **Career:** Wayne State University, instructor in geography, 1970-71; Model Cities Program, city planner, 1971-73; Chatham Supermarkets, site location analyst, 1973-74; Marketing Research and Private Banking, National Bank of Detroit, facilities planning, 1974-92; The Writing Co., owner, 1992-94; Purple Moon Press, publisher, 1994-. Writer. **Publications:** Detecting Women: A Reader's Guide and Checklist for Mystery Series Written by Women, 1994, 3rd ed., 1998; Detecting Women 2 Pocket Guide: A Checklist for Mystery Series Written by Women, 1995, 3rd. ed, 1998; Detecting Women 2: A Reader's Guide and Checklist for Mystery Series, 1996; Detecting Men Pocket Guide: A Checklist for Mystery Series Written by Men, 1997; Detecting Men: A Reader's Guide and Checklist for Mystery Series Written by Men, 1998; Willetta's Guide to Private Eye Series, 2002; Wiletta's Guide to Police Detective Series, 2002. Contributor to periodicals. **Address:** Purple Moon Press, 3319 Greenfield Rd., Ste. 317, Dearborn, MI 48120-1212, U.S.A. **Online address:** willetta@purplemoonpress.com

HEITMILLER, David A. American (born United States), b. 1945. **Genres:** Documentaries/Reportage, Self Help, Business/Trade/Industry, Money/

Finance. **Career:** Sunbeam Appliance Co., branch manager, 1969-76; U.S. West Communications, product manager, 1977-94. Writer. **Publications:** (With J. Blix) Getting a Life: Real Lives Transformed by Your Money or Your Life, 1997 as Getting a Life: Strategies for Simple Living Based on the Revolutionary Program for Financial Freedom, 1999. **Address:** c/o Beth Vesel, Sanford J. Greenburger Associates Inc., 55 5th Ave., New York, WA 10003, U.S.A. **Online address:** david@gettingalife.org

HEITZMANN, Kristen. American (born United States) **Genres:** Novels, Young Adult Fiction, Architecture. **Career:** People of Praise, music minister. Writer. **Publications:** Honor's Quest, 1998; Honor's Price, 1998; Honor's Pledge, 1998; Honor's Disguise, 1999; The Rose Legacy, 2000; Honor's Reward, 2000; Sweet Boundless, 2001; The Tender Vine, 2002; Twilight, 2002; A Rush of Wings, 2003; The Still of Night, 2003; Secrets, 2004; Halos, 2004; Unforgotten, 2005; Freefall, 2006; Echoes, 2007; Edge of Recall, 2008; Rules of Contact, 2009; Indivisible: A Novel, 2010; Indelible, 2011. Contributor to periodicals. **Address:** Bethany House Publishers, 11400 Hampshire Ave. S, Minneapolis, MN 55438, U.S.A.

HEJINIAN, Lyn. American (born United States), b. 1941. **Genres:** Poetry, Translations, Novels, Biography, Autobiography/Memoirs. **Career:** Tuumba Press, editor, 1976-84; Poetics Journal, editor; University of California, Department of English, professor. **Publications:** POETRY: A Thought Is the Bride of What Thinking, 1976; A Mask of Motion, 1977; Writing Is an Aid to Memory, 1978; Gesualdo, 1978; Redo, 1984; The Guard, 1984; (with K. Robinson) Individuals, 1988; The Hunt, 1991; The Cell, 1992; The Cold of Poetry, 1994; (trans.) Xenia: Poems by Arkadii Dragomoshchenko, 1994; A Border Comedy, 1999; The Fatalist: Poetry, 2003; Saga/circus, 2008. NOVELS: My Life, 1980; Oxota: A Short Russian Novel, 1991. OTHERS: My life, 1987; (trans.) Arkadii Dragomoshchenko, 1990; Leningrad: American Writers in the Soviet Union, 1991; (trans. with E. Balashova) Arkadi Dragomoschenko, 1993; Two Stein Talks, 1995; Wicker, 1996; The Little Book of A Thousand Eyes, 1996; Guide, Grammar, Watch, and The Thirty Nights, 1996; A Book from A Border Comedy, 1997; The Traveler and the Hill; and, The Hill, 1998; Sight, 1998; Chartings, 2000; Sunflower, 2000; The Language of Inquiry, 2000; Happily, 2000; A Border Comedy, 2001; The Beginner, 2001; Slowly, 2002; (ed.) The Best American Poetry, 2004; (with E. Clark) The Lake, 2004. Contributor to periodicals. **Address:** Omnidawn Publishing, PO Box 5224, Richmond, CA 94805-5224, U.S.A. **Online address:** lynhejinian@earthlink.net

HEKKANEN, Ernest. Canadian/American (born United States), b. 1947. **Genres:** Novels, Novellas/Short Stories, Plays/Screenplays, Travel/Exploration. **Career:** New Orphic Review (literary journal), editor-in-chief. **Publications:** (Contrib. with) Second Impressions, 1981; Chasing after Carnivals, 1985; Medieval Hour in the Author's Mind, 1987, rev. ed., 2003; The Violent Lavender Beast, 1988; From a Town Now Dreaming, 1995; Journeys That Bring Us Here, 1996; The Wedding Cycle, 1996; (with M. Schraner) Black Snow: An Imaginative Memoir, 1996; Turning Life into Fiction: An Aesthetic Manifesto, 1996; The Soul You Call Your Own, 1997; Beyond the Call: A One-Act Play, 1997; The House of Samsara, 1997; You Know Me Better than That, 1998; The Last Thing My Father Gave Me, 1998; Bridge over the Tampere Rapids and Other Finnish Stories, 1998; Those Who Eat at My Table, 1998; (with E. Roy) Good Ol' Boy: Willis V. McCall, 1999; Dementia Island, 1999; My Dog is More than Just a Dog to Me, 1999; Straying from Luminosity, 1999; The Well, 2000; Sometimes I Have These Incendiary Dreams, 2000; Harbinger of Fall, 2000; The Lambing: A Passion Play in One Act, 2000; Man's Sadness, 2000; The Island of Winged Wonders, 2000; Exhuming Carl Jung: A Burlesque, 2001; The Shipwrecked Heart: Tales of the Fantastic and the Macabre, 2001; The Radio Interview, 2001; The Misadventures of Bumbleberry Finn, 2001; The Clown Act, 2001; The Flat Earth Excavation Company: A Surreal Fiction Anthology, 2002; The Expulsion; or Goodbye Chubby Chickens Goodbye, 2002; Up & Coming, 2003; The Big Dave (and Little Wife) Convention, 2004; Melancholy and Mystery of a Street, 2004; The Life of Bartholomew G., 2005; Kafka: The Master of Yesno: A Critical Study of the Writer and His Work, 2006; Shadows on a Cave Wall, 2007; Of a Fire Beyond the Hills, 2008; Surreal & Postmodern, 2010. **Address:** New Orphic Publishers, 706 Mill St., Nelson, BC V1L 4S5, Canada.

HELD, Peter. *See* **VANCE, Jack.**

HELD, Virginia. American (born United States), b. 1929. **Genres:** Economics, Philosophy, Politics/Government, Ethics, Women's Studies And Issues. **Career:** The Reporter (magazine), staff, 1954-65; Columbia University, Barnard College, lecturer in philosophy, 1964-66; City University of New York, Hunter College, lecturer, 1965-69, assistant professor, 1969-72, associate professor, 1973-77, professor of philosophy, 1977-96, distinguished professor, 1996-2001, professor emeritus, 2001-, Graduate School, associate professor, 1973-77, professor of philosophy, 1977-96, distinguished professor, 1996-2001, Ph.D. Program, deputy executive officer, 1980-84, distinguished professor, 1996-; Yale University, visiting lecturer, 1972. Writer. **Publications:** Bewildered Age: A Report on Morals and Values in Today's Society, 1962; The Public Interest and Individual Interests, 1970; (comp.) Property, Profits, and Economic Justice, 1980; (co-author) Women's Realities, Women's Choices, 1983, 2nd ed., 1995; Rights and Goods: Justifying Social Action, 1984; Feminist Morality: Transforming Culture, Society, and Politics, 1993; (contrib.) Norms and Values: Essays on the Work of Virginia Held, 1998; Ethics of Care: Personal, Political, and Global, 2006; How Terrorism is Wrong: Morality and Political Violence, 2008. EDITOR: (with K. Nielsen and C. Parsons) Philosophy and Political Action: Essays Edited for the New York Group of the Society for Philosophy and Public Affairs, 1972; (with S. Morgenbesser and T. Nagel) Philosophy, Morality, and International Affairs: Essays Edited for the Society for Philosophy and Public Affairs, 1974; Justice and Care: Essential Readings in Feminist Ethics, 1995. **Address:** Department of Philosophy, Hunter College, City University of New York, Rm. 1413, West Bldg., 695 Park Ave., New York, NY 10065, U.S.A. **Online address:** vheld@hunter.cuny.edu

HELFGOTT, Gillian. Australian (born Australia), b. 1931. **Genres:** Autobiography/Memoirs. **Career:** Astrologer, lecturer in astrology and writer. **Publications:** (With A. Tanskaya) Love You to Bits and Pieces: Life with David Helfgott, 1996. Contributor to periodicals and books. **Address:** Penguin Books Australia, 487 Maroondah Hwy., PO Box 257, Ringwood, VI 3134, Australia. **Online address:** helfgott@bigpond.com

HELGELAND, Brian. American (born United States), b. 1961. **Genres:** Plays/Screenplays, Film, Young Adult Fiction. **Career:** Writer, producer and director. **Publications:** A Nightmare on Elm Street 4: (with S. Pierce) The Dream Master, 1988; (with C. Hanson) L.A. Confidential: The Screenplay, 1997; (and intro.) A Knight's Tale: The Shooting Script, 2001. **Address:** Directors Guild of America, 7920 W Sunset Blvd., Los Angeles, CA 90046-3300, U.S.A.

HELLEINER, Gerald K(arl). Canadian/Austrian (born Austria), b. 1936. **Genres:** Economics, International Relations/Current Affairs, Third World, Business/Trade/Industry. **Career:** Yale University, instructor, assistant professor, 1961-65; University of Toronto, associate professor, 1965-71, professor, 1971-99, professor emeritus, 1999-, Munk School of Global Affairs (formerly Munk Centre for International Studies), distinguished research fellow, 1998-; University College, Dar es Salaam, director of the Economic Research Bureau, 1966-68; Economic Society of Tanzania, vice-president, 1967-68; North-South Institute, deputy chair, 1976-90, chair, 1990-92; International Development Research Centre, board of directors, 1985-91; International Food Policy Research Institute, director and chairman, 1988-94; Group of 24, research coordinator, 1991-99; African Capacity Building Foundation, executive board, 1997-2003; Order of Canada, officer, 2002; International Lawyers and Economists against Poverty, chairman and chair emeritus, 2003-09. Writer. **Publications:** Peasant Agriculture, Government, and Economic Growth in Nigeria, 1966; Handel Och Bistand I Tanzania, 1968; International Trade and Economic Development, 1972; Beyond Growth Rates and Plan Volumes: Planning for Africa in the 1970s, 1975; World Market Imperfections and the Developing Countries, 1978; International Economic Disorder: Essays in North-South Relations, 1980; Economic Theory and North-South Negotiations on a New International Economic Order, 1980; Intra-firm Trade and the Developing Countries, 1981; (with C.F. Diaz-Alejandro) Handmaiden in Distress: World Trade in the 1980s, 1982; The New Global Economy and the Developing Countries: Essays in International Economics and Development, 1990; Trade, Trade Policy, and Industrialization Reconsidered, 1995; Global Development Fifty Years after Bretton Woods: Essays in Honour of Gerald K. Helleiner, 1997. EDITOR: Agricultural Planning in East Africa, 1968; A World Divided: The Less Developed Countries in the International Economy, 1976; For Good or Evil: Economic Theory and North-South Negotiations, 1982; The IMF and Africa in the 1980s, 1983; Africa and the International Monetary Fund, 1986; The Other Side of International Development Policy: Non-Aid Economic Relations with Developing Countries in Canada, Denmark, the Netherlands, Norway and Sweden, 1990; Trade Policy, Industrialization and Development: New Perspectives, 1992; Trade Policy and Industrialization in Turbulent Times, 1994; (with G.A. Cornia) From Adjustment to Development in Africa: Conflict, Controversy, Convergence, Consensus?, 1994; Manufacturing for Export in the Developing World: Problems and Possibilities, 1995; (co-ed.) Poverty, Prosperity and the World Economy: Essays in Memory of Sidney Dell, 1995; The International Monetary and Financial System: Developing Country Perspectives, 1996; Capital Account Regimes and the Developing Countries, 1998; Non-Traditional Export Promotion in Africa: Experience and Issues, 2002. **Address:** Department of Economics, University of Toronto, Max Gluskin House, 150 St. George St., Toronto, ON M5S 3G7, Canada. **Online address:** ghellein@sympatico.ca

HELLENGA, Robert. American (born United States), b. 1941. **Genres:** Adult Non-fiction, Mystery/Crime/Suspense. **Career:** Knox College, assistant professor, 1968-76, distinguished writer-in-residence, 1976-, associate professor, 1976-, George Appleton Lawrence distinguished service professor, now George Appleton Lawrence distinguished service professor emeritus of English; Newberry Library Seminar in Humanities, faculty fellow, co-director, 1973-74; Associated Colleges of the Midwest, Florence Program, director, 1981-82. **Publications:** The Sixteen Pleasures, 1994; The Fall of a Sparrow, 1998; Blues Lessons, 2002; Philosophy Made Simple, 2006; The Italian Lover, 2007; Snakewoman of Little Egypt, 2010. Contributor to periodicals. **Address:** Department of English, Knox College, 2 E South St., Galesburg, IL 61401, U.S.A. **Online address:** henry@dclagency.com

HELLER, Agnes. American/Australian/Hungarian (born Hungary), b. 1929. **Genres:** Sociology, Philosophy, History. **Career:** University of Budapest, assistant professor of philosophy, 1955-58; La Trobe University, senior lecturer and reader of sociology, 1978-83; New School for Social Research, Department of Philosophy, professor of philosophy, 1984-88, chair, 1986-89, Hannah Arendt visiting professor of philosophy and political science, Hannah Arendt professor of philosophy, 1988-. Writer. **Publications:** Portrévázlatok az etika történetéböl, 1976; Theory of Need in Marx, 1976; Instinkt, Aggression, Charakter: Einl. zu e. marxist. Sozialanthropologie, 1977; OAUMLsztönök; Az érzelmek elmélete, 1978; Philosophie des linken Radikalismus: e. Bekenntnis zur Philosophie, 1978; (with F. Fehér) Diktatur über die Bedürfnisse: sozialistische Kritik osteuropäischer Gesellschaftformationen, 1979; Theory of Feelings, 1979, 2nd ed., 2009; Renaissance Man, 1981; Theory of History, 1982; (with F. Fehér and G. Márkus) Dictatorship Over Needs, 1982; (ed.) Lukács Reappraised, 1983; Lukács Revalued, 1983; (with F. Feher) Hungary 1956 Revisited: The Message of a Revolution-A Quarter of a Century After 1983; Radical Philosophy, 1984; Power of Shame: A Rational Perspective, 1985; (ed. with F. Feher) Reconstructing Aesthetics: Writings of the Budapest School, 1986; (with F. Feher) Doomsday or Deterrence?: On the Antinuclear Issue, 1986; (with F. Feher) Eastern left, Western Left: Totalitarianism, Freedom and Democracy, 1987; Beyond Justice, 1987; General Ethics, 1988; (with F. Feher) Postmodern Political Condition, 1988; (with F. Feher) Jalta után: Kelet-Európa hosszú forradalma Jalta ellen, 1990; Can Modernity Survive?, 1990; Philosophy of Morals, 1990; (with F. Ferenc and M. György) Diktatúra a szükségletek felett, 1990; (with F. Feher) From Yalta to Glasnost: The Dismantling of Stalin's Empire, 1991; (with F. Feher) Grandeur and Twilight of Radical Universalism, 1991; (with F. Feher) Kelet-Európa dicsöséges forradalmai, 1992; Szilveszteri szimpózium, 1992; Philosophy of History in Fragments, 1993; általános etika, 1994; Nietzsche és a Parsifal: prolegomena egy személyiségetikához, 1994; Leibniz egzisztenciális metafizikája, 1995; Ethics of Personality 1996; Morálfilozófia, 1996; Költészet és gondolkodás, 1998; Theory of Modernity, 1999; (co-author) Janeiro, Brazil Crise dos paradigmas em ciências sociais e os desafios para o século XXI, 1999; Zsidó Jézus feltámadása, 2000; Time is Out of Joint: Shakespeare as Philosopher of History, 2001; (with F. Feher) Marx és a modernitás, 2002; (contrib.) Cronofagia: la contrazione del tempo e dello spazio nell era della globalizzazione, 2003; Pikareszk Auschwitz árnyékában: négy tanulmány, 2003; Immortal Comedy: The Comic Phenomenon in Art, Literature and Life, 2005; Megtestesülés: filozófiai esszék, 2005; Iimhol vagyok: a Genezis könyvének filozófiai értelmezései, 2006; Trauma, 2006; Sámson: Erósz és Thanatosz a Biírák könyvében, 2007; (with G. Márkus) Trauma, History, Philosophy: With Feature Essays, 2007; New York Nosztalgia, 2008; Kertész Imre: négy töredék, 2009; A Short History of My Philosophy, 2010; Aesthetics and Modernity: Essays, 2011. **Address:** Department of Philosophy, New School for Social Research, 6 E 16th St., New York, NY 10003, U.S.A. **Online address:** hellera@newschool.edu

HELLER, Henry. Canadian/American (born United States), b. 1938.

Genres: History, Intellectual History. **Career:** University of Manitoba, lecturer, 1963-66, assistant professor, 1966-69, associate professor, 1969-79, professor of history, 1979-. Writer. **Publications:** (ed.) Guillaume Brionnet and Marguerite d'AngoulEme, Correspondance, 15211524, 1971; The Conquest of Poverty: The Calvinist Revolt in Sixteenth Century France, 1986; Iron and Blood: Civil Wars in Sixteenth-Century France, 1991; Labour, Science, and Technology in France, 1500-1620, 1996; Anti-Italianism in Sixteenth-Century France, 2003; The Bourgeois Revolution in France, 1789-1815, 2006; The Cold War and the New Imperialism: A Global History, 1945-2005, 2006. **Address:** Department of History, University of Manitoba, 403 Fletcher Argue Bldg., Winnipeg, MB R3T 5V5, Canada. **Online address:** heller@cc.umanitoba.ca

HELLER, Jane. American (born United States), b. 1950?. **Genres:** Novels, Young Adult Non-fiction. **Career:** Coward, McCann and Geoghegan, publicity assistant; New American Library, publicity manager; Dell/Delacorte, publicity director; Jove, vice president and director of advertising, promotion and publicity. Writer. **Publications:** (With B.A. Castorri) Mental Aerobics: Exercises for a Stronger, Healthier Mind, 1992; Cha Cha Cha, 1994; The Club, 1995; Infernal Affairs, 1996; Princess Charming, 1997; Crystal Clear, 1998; Sis Boom Bah, 1999; Name Dropping, 2000; Female Intelligence, 2001; The Secret Ingredient, 2002; Lucky Stars, 2003; Best Enemies, 2004; An Ex to Grind, 2005; Some Nerve, 2006; Confessions of a She-fan: The Course of True Love with the New York Yankees, 2009; You'd Better Not Die Or I'll Kill You: A Caregiver's Survival Guide To Keeping You in Good Health and Good Spirits, 2012. **Address:** c/o Ellen Levine, Trident Media Group L.L.C., 41 Madison Ave., 36th Fl., New York, NY 10010-2257, U.S.A. **Online address:** jane@janeheller.com

HELLER, Marvin J. American (born United States), b. 1940. **Genres:** Theology/Religion, Bibliography. **Career:** Writer. **Publications:** Printing the Talmud: A History of the Earliest Printed Editions of the Talmud, 1992; Printing the Talmud: A History of the Individual Treatises Printed from 1700 to 1750, 1999; The Sixteenth Century Hebrew Book: An Abridged Thesaurus, 2003; Studies in the Making of the Early Hebrew Book, 2008; The Seventeenth Century Hebrew Book: An Abridged Thesaurus, 2011. Contributor to periodicals. **Address:** 1028 E 28th St., Brooklyn, NY 11210, U.S.A. **Online address:** mjh1mjh@yahoo.com

HELLER, Michael. American (born United States), b. 1937. **Genres:** Poetry, Adult Non-fiction, Autobiography/Memoirs, Essays, Essays, Novellas/Short Stories, Literary Criticism And History. **Career:** Norelco, chief technical writer, 1963-65; English teacher, 1965-66; freelance writer, 1966-67, 1999-; New York University, American Language Institute, staff, 1967; Washington Square College, teacher in English, 1967-, acting director, 1986-87, academic coordinator, 1987-92, retired, 1999; Naropa Institute, visiting professor; University of Notre Dame, visiting professor; City University of New York, visiting professor. **Publications:** POETRY: Two Poems, 1970; Accidental Center, 1972; Figures of Speaking, 1977; Knowledge, 1979; Marginalia in a Desperate Hand, 1985; In the Builded Place: Poems, 1989; Wordflow: New and Selected Poems, 1997; Exigent Futures: New and Selected Poems, 2003; Uncertain Poetries: Selected Essays, 2005; Eschaton, 2009; Two Novellas: Marble Snows and The Study, 2009; Speaking The Estranged: Essays on the Work of George Open, 2009. OTHERS: Conviction's Net of Branches: Essays on the Objectivist Poets and Poetry, 1985; (ed. and intro.) Carl Rakosi: Man and Poet, 1993; Six Poems, 1993; Living Root: A Memoir, 2000; Earth and Cave, 2006; Beckmann Variations and Other Poems, 2010; This Constellation Is A Name: Collected Poems 1965-2010, 2012. **Address:** 346 E 18th St., Apt. 3C, New York, NY 10003, U.S.A. **Online address:** mh7@nyu.edu

HELLER, Steven. American (born United States), b. 1950. **Genres:** Art/Art History, Design, Fash Ion/Costume. **Career:** Evergreen Review, art director, 1967-73; New York Times, art director, 1974-86, senior art director, 1986-; Pushpin Editions, co-director, 1983-; School of Visual Arts, instructor, 1985-99, Department of Master of Fine Arts Design, co-chair, 1997-, chairperson, 1998-2000, MFA Designer as Author Program, co-founder and co-chair, 1997-; Book Review, art director, 1986-. Writer. **Publications:** The Book of Waters, 1979; The Empire State Building Book, 1979; Sin City Fables, 1980; War Heads, 1982; Art against War, 1984; (with R.E. Shikes) The Art of Satire, 1984; The Fifties Revisited, 1985; The Little Theatre, 1985; (with L. Talarico) Design Career, 1987; (with S. Chwast) Graphic Style, 1987; (with K. Pomeroy) Designing with Illustration, 1988; (with Cohen and S. Chwast) Trylon and Perisphere: The 1939 New York World's Fair, 1988; (with A. Fink)

Low-Budget, High-Quality Design, 1988; Communications, 1988; (with G. Anderson) Graphic Wit, 1989; (with K. Jacobs) Angry Graphics: Protest Posters of the Reagan/Bush Era, 1990; (with V.G. Levi and S. Chwast) You Must Have Been a Beautiful Baby, 1990; (with S. Guarnaccia) School Days, 1991; (with J. Lasky) Borrowed Design, 1991; (with G. Anderson) The Savage Mirror, 1992; (with L. Fili) Italian Art Deco, 1993; (with L. Fili) Dutch Moderne, 1994; (with S. Guarnaccia) Designing for Children, 1994; (with A. Fink) That's Entertainment, 1995; Carta Italiana, 1995; (with G. Anderson) American Typeplay, 1996; (with Fili) Streamline, 1996; (ed.) Japanese Modern, 1996; (with S. Chwast) Jackets Required, 1920-1950, 1996; (with T. Fernandes) The Business of Illustration, 1997; (with L. Fili) Deco Espana, 1997; 101 Best Posters of Europe and America, 1997; (with E. Pettit) Newsletters Now!, 1997; (with A. Fink) Faces on the Edge, 1997; (with L. Fili) French Modern, 1997; (with L. Fili) Deco Type, 1997; (with L. Fili) Cover Story, 1998; (with T. Fernandes) Magazines Inside & Out, 1998; Food Wrap, 1998; Belle Letters, 1998; Design Dialogues, 1998; German Modern, 1998; The Education of a Graphic Designer, 1998, 2nd ed., 2005; Papier Francias, 1999; The Italian Art Deco Address Book, 1999; (with D. Drenan) The Digital Designer, 1999; (with M. Barson) Teenage Confidential, 1999; Design Literacy, 1999, 2nd ed. as Design Literacy: Understanding Graphic Design, 2004; (ed. with M. Finamore) Design Culture, 1999; British Art Deco, 1999; Typology, 1999; On Becoming a Graphic Designer, 1999, (with T. Fernandes) 3rd ed. as Becoming a Graphic Designer: A Guide to Careers in Design, 2006, 4th ed., 2010; Paul Rand, 1999; Less Is More, 1999; The Swastika, 2000; Wedding Bell Blues, 2000; Sex Appeal, 2000; Letterforms, 2000; Design Connoisseur, 2000; Graphic Design Time Line, 2000; The Education of an Illustrator, 2000; Genius Rules, 2001; Texts on Type, 2001; Graphic Style, 2001; Graphic Design History, 2001; Red Scared, 2001; The Education of an E-Designer, 2001; Counter Culture, 2001; The Graphic Design Reader, 2002; The Education of a Design Entrepreneur, 2002; Design Humor, 2002; Cuba Style, 2002; From Merz to Emigre and Beyond, 2003; Citizen Designer, 2003; Teaching Design, 2003; (with V.G. Levi) Times Square Style: Graphics from the Great White Way, 2004; (with M. Arisman) Inside the Business of Illustration, 2004; (with M. Ilić) Handwritten: Expressive Lettering in the Digital Age, 2004; (with L. Fili) Euro Deco: Graphic Design Between the Wars, 2004; (with G. Anderson) Designer's Guide to Astounding Photoshop Effects, 2004; (with L. Fili) Stylepedia: A Guide to Graphic Design Mannerisms, Quirks and Conceits, 2006; Nigel Holmes: On Information Design, 2006; (with G. Anderson) New Vintage Type: Classic Fonts for the Digital Age, 2007; (with M. Ilić) Anatomy of Design: Uncovering the Influences and Inspirations in Modern Graphic Design, 2007; (with M. Arisman) Marketing Illustration: New Venues, New Styles, New Methods, 2008; (with S. Chwast) Illustration: A Visual History, 2008; (with M. Ilić) Icons of Graphic Design, 2008; (with L. Talarico) Design Entrepreneur: Turning Graphic Design into Goods that Sell, 2008; (with D. Womack) Becoming a Digital Designer: A Guide to Careers in Web, Video, Broadcast, Game, + Animation Design, 2008; (with L. Talarico) Design School Confidential: Extraordinary Class Projects from International Design Schools, 2009; (contrib.) Design for Obama, 2009; Pop: How Graphic Design Shapes Popular Culture, 2010; (with E.L. Cohen) Born Modern: The Life and Work of Alvin Lustig, 2010; (with G. Anderson) New Ornamental Type: Decorative Lettering in the Digital Age, 2010; (with L. Talarico) Graphic: Inside the Sketchbooks of the World's Great Graphic Designers, 2010; (with K. Bonansinga) Up Against the Wall: Posters of Social Protest, 2010; (with L. Fili) Scripts: Elegant Lettering from Design's Golden Age, 2011; (with L. Fili) Typography Sketchbooks, 2011; (with M. Ilić) Stop, think, go, do, 2012; (with G. Anderson) New Modernist Type, 2012; Comics Sketchbooks, 2012; (foreword) Elegantissima, 2012. EDITOR: Man Bites Man, 1980; Jules Feiffer's America, 1982; Seymour Chwast: The Left-Handed Designer, 1985; Innovators of American Illustration, 1986; (with S. Chwast) The Sourcebook of VisualIdeas, 1989; Looking Closer, 1996; (with W. Drenttel and M. Bierut) Looking Closer II, 1999; (with W. Drenttel and M. Bierut) Looking Closer 3, 1999; (with W. Drenttel and M. Bierut) Looking Closer 4, 2002; (with M. Venezky) The Push Pin Graphic: A Quarter Century of Innovative Design and Illustration, 2004; Education of a Typographer, 2004; (with M. Dooley) The Education of a Comics Artist: Visual Narrative in Cartoons, Graphic Novels and Beyond, 2005; (with M. Arisman) Teaching Illustration: Course Offerings and Class Projects from the Leading Undergraduate and Graduate Programs, 2006; (with V. Vienne) Education of an Art Director, 2006; (with W. Drenttel and M. Bierut) Looking Closer 5, 2006; (with C.H. Traub and A.B. Bell) The Education of a Photographer, 2006; (with M. Dooley) Teaching Motion Design: Course Offerings and Class Projects from the Leading Undergraduate and Graduate Programs, 2008; Design Disasters: Great Designers, Fabulous Failures, and Lessons Learned, 2008; I Heart Design: Significant Graphic De-

sign Selected by Designers, Illustrators, and Critics, 2010. COMPILER: Artists' Christmas Cards, 1978; (and ed. with S. Chwast) The Art of New York, 1983; (and ed. with B. Cohen and S. Chwast) New York Observed: Artists and Writers Look at the City, 1650 to the Present, 1987; (with A. Fink) Covers & Jackets!, 1993. INTRODUCTION: Illustration Now! 4, 2011; Mono Taxali, 2011; Identify. Basic Principles of Identity Design in the Iconic Trademarks of Chermayeff & Geismar, 2011; Menu Design in America, 2011; Illustration Now! Portraits, 2011; R.O. Blechman: Poche Illustrateur, 2011; Soy Cuba: Cuban Cinema Posters From After the Revolution, 2011; The Electric Information Age Book, 2012. Contributor to periodicals. **Address:** School of Visual Arts, 209 E 23rd St., New York, NY 10010-3994, U.S.A. **Online address:** sheller@sva.edu

HELLER, Zoë. American/British (born England), b. 1965. **Genres:** Novels, Young Adult Fiction. **Career:** London Sunday Times, staff writer; Vanity Fair, staff writer; Harper's, staff writer; Independent, staff writer; New Yorker, staff writer; Daily Telegraph, columnist. **Publications:** Everything You Know, 1999; What Was She Thinking? Notes on a Scandal in UK as Notes on a Scandal, 2003; The Believers, 2008. **Address:** Rogers, Coleridge & White Ltd., 20 Powis Mews, London, GL W11 1JN, England.

HELLMAN, Hal. American (born United States), b. 1927. **Genres:** History, Physics, Sciences, Technology, Biography, Mathematics/Statistics. **Career:** Singer/General Precision Inc., technical information manager, 1956-66; New York University, adjunct associate professor of science and technical writing, 1982-90; Sensor Technology, editor, 1984-92. **Publications:** Navigation-Land, Sea and Sky, 1966; The Art and Science of Color, 1967; Controlled Guidance Systems, 1967; Light and Electricity in the Atmosphere, 1968; The Right Size, 1968; Transportation in the World of the Future, 1968, rev. ed., 1974; High Energy Physics, 1968; Lasers, 1968; Spectroscopy, 1968; Communications in the World of the Future, 1969; Defense Mechanisms: From Virus to Man, 1969; The City in the World of the Future, 1970; Helicopters and Other VTOLs, 1970; Atomic Particle Detection, 1970; Energy and Inertia, 1970; Biology in the World of the Future, 1971; (with M. Klass) The Kinds of Mankind: An Introduction to Race and Racism, 1971; The Lever and the Pulley, 1971; Feeding the World of the Future, 1972; Population, 1972; Energy in the World of the Future, 1973; (ed.) Epidemiological Aspects of Carcinogenesis, 1973; (ed.) Psychosocial and Cultural Determinants of Population Policy: Proceedings of Workshop, 1975; Technophobia: Getting Out of the Technology Trap, 1976; (with L. Kowalski) Understanding Physics, 1978; Deadly Bugs and Killer Insects, 1978; Computer Basics, 1983; Industrial Sensors-A Report on Leading Edge Technology, 1985; Intelligent Sensors-The Merging of Electronics and Sensing, 1988; The Story of Gold, 1996; Beyond Your Senses: The New World of Sensors, 1997; Great Feuds in Science; Ten of the Liveliest Disputes Ever, 1998; Great Feuds in Medicine, 2001; Great Feuds in Technology, 2004; Great Feuds in Mathematics, 2006. Contributor to periodicals. **Address:** c/o Faith Hamlin, Sanford J. Greenburger Associates, 55 5th Ave., New York, NY 10003, U.S.A. **Online address:** hal.hellman@earthlink.net

HELLMAN, Stephen. (Stephen M. Hellman). Canadian/American (born United States), b. 1943. **Genres:** Politics/Government, Translations, History, Social Commentary. **Career:** York University, Department of Political Science, assistant professor, 1971-76, associate professor, 1976-89, professor, 1990-. Writer. **Publications:** (Trans.) Maria Antonietta Macciocchi, Letters from Inside the Italian Communist Party, 1974; (co-author) European Politics in Transition, 1987, 3rd ed., 1997; Italian Communism in Transition: The Rise and Fall of the Historic Compromise in Turin, 1975-1980, 1988; (ed. with G. Pasquino) Italian Politics: A Review, Frances Pinter, vol. VII, 1992, vol. VIII, 1993. **Address:** Depaertment of Political Science, York University, S662 Ross Bldg., 4700 Keele St., Toronto, ON M3J 1P3, Canada. **Online address:** shellman@yorku.ca

HELLMAN, Stephen M. *See* **HELLMAN, Stephen.**

HELLMANN, Libby Fischer. American (born United States), b. 1949?. **Genres:** Novels. **Career:** Writer. **Publications:** An Eye for Murder, 2002; A Picture of Guilt, 2003; An Image of Death, 2004; A Shot to Die For, 2005; (ed.) Chicago Blues, 2007; Easy Innocence, 2008; Doubleback, 2009; Set the Night on Fire, 2010; Nice Girl Does Noir, 2010; ToxiCity, 2011; The Last Page (A novella), 2011. **Address:** IL 07933, U.S.A. **Online address:** libbyfh@comcast.net

HELLSTRÖM, Börge. Swedish (born Sweden), b. 1957?. **Genres:** Young Adult Fiction. **Career:** KRIS (Criminals Return into Society), co-founder. Novelist. **Publications:** (With A. Roslund) The Beast, 2005; (with A. Roslund) Box 21 in UK as The Vault, 2009. **Address:** Sweden. **Online address:** info@roslund-hellstrom.se

HELLSTROM, Ward. American (born United States), b. 1930. **Genres:** Literary Criticism And History. **Career:** University of Florida, assistant professor, 1961-67, associate professor, 1967-71, professor of English, 1971-; Victorian Newsletter, editor, 1978-; Western Kentucky University, professor of English, dean of arts, humanities and social sciences, 1981-92. **Publications:** On the Poems of Tennyson, 1972; Children and Childhood in the Nineteenth Century in England and American, 1985. **Address:** Department of English, University of Florida, Gainesville, FL 32601, U.S.A. **Online address:** wardhellstrom@wku.edu

HELLYER, Jill. Australian (born Australia), b. 1925. **Genres:** Novels, Poetry, Young Adult Fiction. **Career:** Australian Society of Authors, foundation executive secretary, 1963-71; freelance writer and editor, 1971-. **Publications:** The Exile (verse) 1969; Not Enough Savages (novel), 1975; (ed.) Fifty Years in Psychiatry, 1980; Song of the Humpback Whales (verse), 1981; The Listening Place, 2007; As Always, forthcoming. Contributor to periodicals. **Address:** 25 Berowra Rd., Mount Colah, NW 2079, Australia.

HELLYER, Paul T. Canadian (born Canada), b. 1923. **Genres:** Economics, Politics/Government, Business/Trade/Industry. **Career:** Fleet Aircraft Manufacturing Company Ltd., Engineering Department, junior draftsperson, group leader, 1942-44; Mari-Jane Fashions, proprietor, 1945-56; House of Commons, Davenport riding representative, 1949-57, Trinity riding representative, 1958-74; member of parliament, 1949-57, 1958-74; Curran-Hall Ltd., president, 1951-62; Trepil Realty Ltd., president, 1951-62; Minister of National Defence of Canada, parliamentary assistant, 1956-57, associate minister, 1957, minister, 1963-67, minister of transport, 1967-69, acting prime minister, 1968-69, deputy prime minister; Hendon Estates Ltd., president, 1959-62; York University, distinguished visitor, 1969-70; Toronto Sun, columnist, 1974-84. Writer. **Publications:** Agenda: A Plan for Action, 1971; Exit Inflation, 1981; Jobs for All: Capitalism on Trial, 1984; Canada at the Crossroads, 1990; Damn the Torpedoes: My Fight to Unify Canada's Armed Forces, 1990; Funny Money: A Common Sense Alternative to Mainline Economics, 1994; Surviving the Global Financial Crisis: The Economics of Hope for Generation X, 1996; Arundel Lodge: A Little Bit of Old Muskoka, 1996; The Evil Empire: Globalization's Darker Side, 1997; Stop: Think, 1999; Goodbye Canada, 2001; One Big Party: To Keep Canada Independent, 2003; Former Liberal Deputy Prime Minister of Canada Paul Hellyer Speaks Out on Canadian Sovereignty, and Free Trade in the Context of Corporate Globalization, 2005; Light at the End of the Tunnel: A Survival Plan for the Human Species, 2010; A Miracle in Waiting: Economics That Make Sense, 2010. **Address:** 506, 65 Harbour Sq., Toronto, ON M5J 2L4, Canada. **Online address:** cap-pac@istar.ca

HELMER, Diana Star. American (born United States), b. 1962. **Genres:** Children's Fiction, Plays/Screenplays, Children's Non-fiction, Sports/Fitness, Human Relations/Parenting, Young Adult Fiction, History. **Career:** Writer. **Publications:** Belles of the Ballpark, 1993; Panda Bears, 1997; Women Suffragists, 1998; The Believers, 2000; Give Me Liberty, 2000; We're behind You, George Washington, 2000; Half Free, 2000; The Secret Soldier, 2000; Once upon a War, 2001; Diary of a War Child, 2001; (with T.S. Owens) The Statue of Liberty, 2003. BEARS SERIES: Black Bears, 1997; Brown Bears, 1997; The Koala: The Bear That's Not a Bear, 1997; Pandas, 1997; Polar Bears, 1997; Famous Bears, 1997. LET'S TALK ABOUT SERIES: Adoption, 1999; Feeling Sad, 1999; Having a New Brother or Sister, 1999; Moving to a New Place, 1999; When Your Mom or Dad Is Unhappy, 1999; When Someone You Love Is in a Nursing Home, 1999. WITH T.S. OWENS: Inside Collectible Card Games, 1996; The History of Baseball, 2000; The History of Basketball, 2000; The History of Figure Skating, 2000; The History of Football, 2000; The History of Hockey, 2000; The History of Soccer, 2000; NASCAR, 2000; The War between Bosses and Workers, 2003; Cat Who Came for Tacos, 2003. WITH T.S. OWENS: GAME PLAN SERIES: Football, 1998; Baseball, 1999; Basketball, 1999; Hockey, 1999; Soccer, 2000; Stock Car Racing, 2001. WITH T.S. OWENS: TEAMWORK IN ACTION SERIES: The Charlotte Sting in Action, 1999; The Cleveland Rockers in Action, 1999; The Houston Comets in Action, 1999; The Los Angeles Sparks in

Action, 1999; The New York Liberty in Action, 1999; The Phoenix Mercury in Action, 1999; The Sacramento Monarchs in Action, 1999; The Utah Starzz in Action, 1999. **Address:** c/o Barbara S. Kouts, Barbara S Kouts Literary Agency, PO Box 558, Bellport, NY 11713-0558, U.S.A.

HELMER, Marilyn. Canadian (born Canada) **Genres:** Children's Fiction, Picture/Board Books, Novels. **Career:** Author. **Publications:** The Boy, the Dollar and the Wonderful Hat, 1992; Boathouse Treasure (Novel), 1998; Fog Cat, 1998; Mr. McGratt and the Ornery Cat, 1999; Once-Upon-A-Time Retold Fairy Tales Series: Three Tales of Three, 2000; Three Prince Charming Tales, 2000; Three Tales of Enchantment, 2001; Three Teeny Tiny Tales, 2001; (reteller) Three Barnyard Tales, 2002; Three Tales of Trickery, 2002; Three Tuneful Tales, 2003; Dinosaurs on the Beach (novel), 2003; Three Royal Tales, 2003; Kids-Can-Read Riddle Books: Critter Riddles, 2003; Yummy Riddles, 2003; Spooky Riddles, 2003; Yucky Riddles, 2003; Three Cat and Mouse Tales, 2004; Three Tales of Adventure, 2004; Funtime Riddles, 2004; Recess Riddles, 2004; One Splendid Tree, 2005; The North Wind and the Sun, 2005; Hare and Turtle Two Pourquoi Tales, 2007; The North Wind and the Sun An Aesop's Fable, 2007; Hickory's Problem, 2007; Hare and Turtle Two Pourquoi Tales, 2007; Sharing Snowy, 2008; Fossil Hunters, 2009; Adventures at Camp Lots-o-Fun, 2010; Walli Goggin's Halloween, 2011. Contributor to periodicals. Works appear in anthologies. **Address:** 137 White Bark Way, RR, Ste. 1, Belwood, ON N0B 1J0, Canada. **Online address:** marilyn@marilynhelmer.com

HELMER, Roberta. See SKYE, Christina.

HELMINSKI, Kabir. (Kabir Edmund Helminski). American (born United States), b. 1947. **Genres:** Theology/Religion, Translations. **Career:** Threshold Society (non-profit education foundation), co-founding director; Threshold Books (publisher), director, 1980-99; Book Foundation, co-director. Writer. **Publications:** (Trans. as Edmund Helminski) The Ruins of the Heart: Selected Lyric Poetry of Jelaluddin Rum, 1981; (trans. with R. Algan) The Drop That Became the Sea: Lyric Poems of Yunus Emre, 1989; Rumi-Daylight: A Daybook of Spiritual Guidance, 1990; (as Kabir Edmund Helminski) Living Presence: A Sufi Way to Mindfulness and the Essential Self, 1992; (trans. as Kabir Edmund Helminski) Love Is a Stranger: Selected Lyric Poetry of Jelaluddin Rumi, 1993; (trans. with C.A. Helminski) Jewels of Remembrance: A Daybook of Spiritual Guidance: Containing 365 Selections from the Wisdom of... Rumi, 1996; (ed.) The Knowing Heart: A Sufi Path of Transformation, 1999; (ed.) The Pocket Rumi Reader, 2001; (with H.A. Hassaballa) The Beliefnet Guide to Islam, 2006; (with G.B. Muhammad) The Book of Language: Exploring the Spiritual Vocabulary of Islam, 2006; (trans. with A. Rezwani) Love's Ripening: Rumi on the Heart's Journey, 2008; (ed.) The Pocket Rumi, 2008; (trans. with C. Helminski and R. Algan) Rumi's Sun: The Teachings of Shams of Tabriz, 2008; (trans. with C. Helminski) Rumi Daybook, 2012. **Address:** 303 Potrero St., Santa Cruz, CA 95060-2741, U.S.A.

HELMINSKI, Kabir Edmund. See HELMINSKI, Kabir.

HELMKE, Gretchen. American (born United States), b. 1967. **Genres:** Writing/Journalism, Politics/Government, Law. **Career:** University of Rochester, assistant professor of political science, 2000-01, 2002-08, associate professor, 2008-, Comparative Politics Workshop, organizer, 2006-; University of Notre Dame, The Helen Kellogg Institute for International Studies, visiting fellow, 2000, assistant professor of political science, 2001-02; Woodrow Wilson International Center for Scholars, fellow. Writer. **Publications:** (Ed. with J. Gershman, K. Baker and J. Cavanagh) Trading Freedom: How Free Trade Affects Our Lives, Work, and Environment, 1992; Courts under Constraints: Judges, Generals and Presidents in Argentina, 2005; (contrib.) The Politics of Institutional Weakness: Argentine Democracy, 2005; (ed. with S. Levitsky) Informal Institutions and Democracy: Lessons from Latin America, 2006; (ed. with J. Rios-Figueroa.) Courts in Latin America, 2011; Institutions on the Edge: The Origins and Consequences of Institutional Instability in Latin America, forthcoming. Contributor to periodicals. **Address:** Department of Political Science, University of Rochester, Harkness Hall 334, Rochester, NY 14627, U.S.A. **Online address:** hlmk@mail.rochester.edu

HELMREICH, Anne. (Anne L. Helmreich). American (born United States) **Genres:** Adult Non-fiction, Art/Art History, Homes/Gardens. **Career:** University of Pittsburgh, teaching assistant, 1987-88, Art Gallery, assistant director, 1988-89; Art Institute of Chicago, Department of Prints and Drawings, intern, 1990-91; Northwestern University, teaching assistant, 1990-91; National Gallery of Art, Center for Advanced Study in the Visual Arts, graduate lecturing fellow, 1992-93, research assistant, 1993-96; Texas Christian University, Department of Art and Art History, associate professor of art history, 1996-2003; Yale Center for British Art, visiting fellow, 2002; Case Western Reserve University, Department of Art History and Art, associate professor of art history, 2004-, Baker-Nord Center for the Humanities, associate director, 2006-07, director, 2007-. Writer. **Publications:** (Contrib.) The Victorians: British Painting, 1837-1901, 1996; (contrib.) Victorian Urban Settings, 1996; (contrib.) Nature and Ideology: Natural Gardens in the 20th Century, 1997; (contrib.) Gendering the Landscape, 2000; (contrib.) John Everett Millais: Beyond the Pre-Raphaelite Brotherhood, 2001; The English Garden and National Identity: The Competing Styles of Garden Design, 1870-1914, 2002; (contrib.) Art, Nation, and Gender: Ethnic Landscapes, Myths, and Mother-Figures, 2003; (contrib.) Art, Culture and National Identity in Fin-de-Siecle Europe, 2003; (contrib. as Anne L. Helmreich) Keywords in American Landscape Design, 2010. Contributor to periodicals. **Address:** Department of Art History and Art, Case Western Reserve University, 11201 Euclid Ave., Cleveland, OH 44106-7110, U.S.A. **Online address:** anne.helmreich@case.edu

HELMREICH, Anne L. *See* **HELMREICH, Anne.**

HELMS, Mary W. American (born United States), b. 1938. **Genres:** Anthropology/Ethnology, History, Crafts, Art/Art History, Social Sciences, Politics/Government. **Career:** Wayne State University, instructor in anthropology, 1965-67; Syracuse University, assistant professor of anthropology, 1967-68; Northwestern University, lecturer in anthropology, 1969-79; University of North Carolina-Greensboro, professor of anthropology, 1979-, department head, 1979-85, now professor emeritus. Writer. **Publications:** Asang: Adaptations to Culture Contact in a Miskito Community, 1971; Middle America: A Culture History of Heartland and Frontiers, 1975; Ancient Panama: Chiefs in Search of Power, 1979; Cuna Molas and Cocle Art Forms: Reflections on Panamanian Design Styles and Symbols (monograph), 1981; Ulysses' Sail: An Ethnographic Odyssey of Power, Knowledge, and Geographical Distance, 1988; Craft and the Kingly Ideal: Art, Trade, and Power, 1993; Creations of the Rainbow Serpent: Polychrome Ceramic Designs from Ancient Panama, 1995; Access to Origins: Affines, Ancestors, and Aristocrats, 1998; The Curassow's Crest: Myths and Symbols in the Ceramics of Ancient Panama, 2000. EDITOR: (with F.O. Loveland) Frontier Adaptations in Lower Central America, 1976; (with J.R. Bort) Panama in Transition: Local Reactions to Development Policies (monograph), 1983. Contributor to books and journals. **Address:** Department of Anthropology, University of North Carolina, 426 Graham Bldg., PO Box 26170, Greensboro, NC 27412-5001, U.S.A.

HELMS, Robert B(rake). American (born United States), b. 1940. **Genres:** Medicine/Health, Economics, Politics/Government. **Career:** Loyola College, assistant professor of economics, associate professor of economics, professor, 1971-73; American Enterprise Institute for Public Policy Research, Center for Health Policy Research, director, 1974-81, resident director of health policy studies, 1990-; U.S. Department of Health and Human Services, deputy assistant secretary for planning and evaluation, 1981-84, assistant secretary for planning and evaluation, 1984-89; American Pharmaceutical Institute, executive director, 1989-90. Writer. **Publications:** Natural Gas Regulation: An Evaluation of FPC Price Controls, 1974. EDITOR: Drug Development and Marketing, 1975; The International Supply of Medicines, 1980; Drugs and Health: Economic Issues and Policy Objectives, 1981; American Health Care, 1988; American Health Policy: Critical Issues for Reform, 1993; Health Care Policy and Politics: Lessons from Four Countries, 1993; Health Policy Reform: Competition and Controls, 1993; Competitive Strategies in the Pharmaceutical Industry, 1995; Medicare in the Twenty-first Century: Seeking Fair and Efficient Reform, 1999; The Political Economy of Health Care Reforms, 2001; Uncle Sam, M.D., 2009. Contributor to books and journals. **Address:** American Enterprise Institute for, Public Policy Research, 1150 17th St. NW, Washington, DC 20036, U.S.A. **Online address:** rhelms@aei.org

HELNWEIN, Mercedes. Austrian/American (born United States), b. 1979. **Genres:** Novels. **Career:** Writer. **Publications:** The Potential Hazards of Hester Day (novel), 2008. **Address:** Los Angeles, CA , U.S.A. **Online address:** mercedeshelnwein@yahoo.com

HELPRIN, Mark. American (born United States), b. 1947. **Genres:** Novels, Novellas/Short Stories, Autobiography/Memoirs, Military/Defense/Arms Control, Literary Criticism And History, Young Adult Fiction. **Career:** Harvard University, instructor; Claremont Institute for the Study of Statesman-

ship and Political Philosophy, senior fellow; Hudson Institute, senior fellow. Journalist and commentator. **Publications:** A Dove of the East: And Other Stories, 1975; Refiner's Fire: The Life and Adventures of Marshall Pearl, a Foundling, 1977; Ellis Island and Other Stories, 1981; Winter's Tale, 1983; (ed. with S. Ravenel) Best American Short Stories 1988; Swan Lake, 1989; A Soldier of the Great War, 1991; Memoir from Antproof Case, 1995; A City in Winter, 1996; The Veil of Snows, 1997; The Pacific and Other Stories, 2004; Freddy and Fredericka, 2005; Digital Barbarism: A Writer's Manifesto, 2009. Contributor to periodicals and journals. **Address:** Claremont Institute, 937 W Foothill Blvd., Ste. E, Claremont, CA 91711-3362, U.S.A.

HELVARG, David. American (born United States), b. 1951. **Genres:** History, Sciences, Natural History, Environmental Sciences/Ecology, Biography, Autobiography/Memoirs. **Career:** Reporter, 1973; San Diego Newsline, editor, 1974-79; print reporter, 1974-79; print, radio and television reporter, 1979-83; television news and documentary producer, 1983-93; writer and television producer, 1993-; Blue Frontier Campaign, founder and president. **Publications:** The War Against the Greens: The Wise-Use Movement, the New Right and Anti-Environmental Violence, 1994, rev. ed., 2004; Blue Frontier: Saving America's Living Seas, 2001, 2nd ed., 2006; (ed.) The Ocean and Coastal Conservation Guide 2005-2006, 2005; 50 Ways to Save the Ocean, 2006; Rescue Warriors: The U.S. Coast Guard, America's Forgotten Heroes, 2009; Saved by the Sea: A Love Story With Fish, 2010. Contributor to magazines and newspapers. **Address:** Blue Frontier Campaign, PO Box 19367, Washington, DC 20036, U.S.A.

HELWIG, Maggie. Canadian/British (born England), b. 1961. **Genres:** Novels, Novellas/Short Stories, Poetry, Essays. **Career:** University of Toronto, The Varsity, editor, 1986-87; What Magazine, contributing editor, 1987-90; The Nerve, associate editor, 1987-89; Lowlife Publishing, founder, managing editor, 1987-, production manager; CRASH, editor, 1991-; Canadian Action for Indonesia and East Timor, researcher, 1998-2001; PEN Canada, director, 2004-05; Anglican Church of Canada, Parish outreach facilitator, 2007-10; Church of St. Timothy, assistant curate, 2011-. **Publications:** POETRY: Walking through Fire, 1981; Tongues of Men and Angels: Poems, 1985; Eden, 1987; Because the Gunman, 1988; Talking Prophet Blues, 1989; Graffiti for J.J. Harper, 1991; Eating Glass, 1994; One Building in the Earth: New and Selected Poems, 2002. ESSAYS: Apocalypse Jazz, 1993; Real Bodies, 2002. SHORT STORIES: Gravity Lets You Down, 1997. NOVELS: Where She Was Standing, 2001; Between Mountains, 2004. OTHER: (ed. with M. Jarman) Coming Attractions 02, 2002; (ed.) Speaking in Tongues: PEN Canada Writers in Exile, 2005; Girls Fall Down, 2008. **Address:** c/o Lesley Thorne, Gillon Aitken Associates, 18-21 Cavaye Pl., London, GL SW10 9PT, England. **Online address:** maggie@maggiehelwig.com

HELY, Sara. Scottish/British (born England), b. 1930?. **Genres:** Novels, Novellas/Short Stories, Romance/Historical, Literary Criticism And History, Young Adult Fiction. **Career:** Writer. **Publications:** The Legend of the Green Man, 1972; The Sign of the Serpent, 1984; War Story, 2003. Contributor to periodicals. **Address:** c/o Author Mail, St. Martin's Press, 175 5th Ave., New York, NY 10010, U.S.A.

HEMINGS, T. J. *See* **REITER, Victoria (Kelrich).**

HEMINGWAY, Edith M. (Edith Morris Hemingway). American (born United States), b. 1950?. **Genres:** Novels. **Career:** Hood College, academic advisor; Carroll Community College, coordinator of admissions and academic advisor; teacher, 2004-. **Publications:** NOVELS: (with J.C. Shields as Edith Morris Hemingway) Broken Drum, 1996; (with J.C. Shields as Edith Morris Hemingway) Rebel Hart, 2000; Road to Tater Hill, 2009. Works appear in anthologies. **Address:** MD , U.S.A. **Online address:** edie@ediehemingway.com

HEMINGWAY, Edith Morris. *See* **HEMINGWAY, Edith M.**

HEMINGWAY, Hilary. American (born United States), b. 1961?. **Genres:** Novels, Sciences, Science Fiction/Fantasy. **Career:** Writer. **Publications:** (With J.P. Lindsay) Dreamland: A Novel of the UFO Cover-Up, 1995; (with J.P. Lindsay) Dreamchild, 1998; (with J.P. Lindsay) Hunting with Hemingway: Based on the Stories of Leicester Hemingway, 2000; (with C. Brennen) Hemingway in Cuba, 2003. Contributor to periodicals. **Address:** c/o Author Mail, Rugged Land L.L.C., 401 W St., 2nd Fl., New York, NY 10014, U.S.A.

HEMINGWAY, Lorian. American (born United States), b. 1951. **Genres:** Novels, Novellas/Short Stories, Young Adult Fiction. **Career:** Writer, 1965-; Lorian Hemingway Short Story Competition, founder, director, coordinator and judge, 1980-. **Publications:** Walking into the River (novel), 1992; Walk on Water (memoir), 1998; World Turned Over: A Killer Tornado and the Lives it Changed Forever, 2002; Key West: The Pirate Heart, 2010; Forsaking All Others, forthcoming. Work represented in anthologies. **Address:** Lorian Hemingway Short Story Competition, PO Box 993, Key West, FL 33041, U.S.A.

HEMINWAY, John. American (born United States), b. 1944. **Genres:** Sciences, Travel/Exploration, Biography, Geography, History, Natural History, Politics/Government, Recreation, Sciences, Third World, Zoology, Westerns/Adventure, Travel/Exploration, Documentaries/Reportage, Plays/Screenplays, Archaeology/Antiquities, Earth Sciences, Environmental Sciences/Ecology. **Career:** Writer, director and producer. **Publications:** The Imminent Rains: A Visit among the Last Pioneers of Africa, 1968; No Man's Land: The Last of White Africa, 1983; No Man's Land: A Personal Journey into Africa, 1989; African Journeys: A Personal Guidebook, 1990; Travels: Banana Boat, 1991; Travels: Journey to a Lost Japan, 1991; Travels: For the Colors-a Journey Through Italy, 1991; Travels: Last Train Across Canada, 1991; Travels: In Search of Paradise, 1991; Travels: The Sacred Way, 1991; Travels: L.A. is it with John Gregory Dunne, 1991; Travels: The Africa Passion; Disney Magic: The Launching of a Dream, 1998; Yonder: A Place in Montana, 2000; Evolution: The Mind's Big Bang, 2001; Flight: The True Story of A Heroine Of Africa, 2012. **Address:** 141 Village Crossing Way, Bozeman, MT 59715, U.S.A. **Online address:** bar20@aol.com

HEMMING, John Henry. British/Canadian (born Canada), b. 1935. **Genres:** History, Anthropology/Ethnology, Geography, Environmental Sciences/Ecology, Sciences. **Career:** Maclean-Hunter Publishing Co., assistant editor, 1957-59; Brintex Exhibitions Ltd., managing editor, 1963-70; Royal Geographical Society, director and secretary, 1975-96; Hemming Group Ltd., joint chairman. **Publications:** The Conquest of the Incas, 1970, rev. ed., 1983; (co-author) Tribes of the Amazon Basin, Brazil, 1973; Conquistador Dog Texts, 1976; Red Gold: The Conquest of the Brazilian Indians, 1978; The Search for El Dorado, 1978, rev. ed., 2001; Machu Picchu, 1981; (contrib.) Monuments of the Incas, 1982, rev. ed., 2010; (intro.) The New Incas, 1983; (ed.) Change in the Incas, vol. II., 1984; (ed.) Change in the Amazon Basin, 2 vols., 1985; Amazon Frontier: The Defeat of the Brazilian Indians, 1987; (with J. Ratter and A. dos Santos) Maracá, Roraima/Brasil, 1988; Roraima: Brazil's Northernmost Frontier, 1990; (with J. Ratter) Maracá Rainforest Island, 1993; (ed.) Rainforest Edge: Plant and Soil Ecology of Maracá Island, Brazil, 1994; (ed.) The Forest Frontier, 1995; (foreword) Atlas of Exploration, 1997, 2nd ed., 2008; The Golden Age of Discovery, 1998; Die if You Must: Brazilian Indians in the Twentieth Century, 2003; Tree of Rivers: The Story of the Amazon, 2008. Contributor to periodicals. **Address:** Hemming Group Ltd., 32 Vauxhall Bridge Rd., London, GL SW1V 2SS, England. **Online address:** j.hemming@hgluk.com

HEMMING, Laurence Paul. British (born England), b. 1962. **Genres:** Theology/Religion, History, Essays. **Career:** University of London, Heythrop College, research fellow, 1998-99, lecturer in theology, 1999-2000, assistant dean of research students, 2000-01, dean of research students, 2001-04, dean of research, 2004-07; Catholic University of Leuven, research fellow, 2002-03; St. Mary's University College, research fellow, 2007-08; Lancaster University, Institute for Advanced Studies, senior research fellow, 2008-. Philosopher, theologian and writer. **Publications:** Radical Orthodoxy? A Catholic Enquiry, 2000; Heidegger's Atheism: The Refusal of a Theological Voice, 2002; Benedict XVI: Fellow Worker for the Truth: An Introduction to His Life and Thought, 2005; Postmodernity's Transcending: Devaluing God, 2005; Worship as a Revelation: The Past, Present and Future of Catholic Liturgy, 2008. EDITOR: Radical Orthodoxy? A Catholic Enquiry, 2000; (with S.F. Parsons) Restoring Faith in Reason: With a New Translation of the Encyclical Letter, Faith and Reason of Pope John Paul II: Together with a Commentary and Discussion, 2003; (with L. Boeve) Divinising Experience: Essays in the History of Religious Experience from Origen to Ricœur, 2004; (with S.F. Parsons) Corpus Mysticum: The Eucharist and the Church in the Middle Ages: Historical Survey, 2007; (with S.F. Parsons) Redeeming Truth: Considering Faith and Reason, University of Notre Dame Press (Notre Dame, IN), 2007. Contributor to books and periodicals. **Address:** London, GL , England. **Online address:** laurence.hemming@btinternet.com

HEMPHILL, Kenneth S. American (born United States), b. 1948. **Genres:** Theology/Religion, Reference. **Career:** Calvary Baptist Church, youth pastor, 1968-70; Wolf Creek Baptist Church, pastor, 1970-72; Meadow Hill Baptist Church, youth and education worker, 1973; Temple Southern Baptist Church, interim pastor, 1975, director; Wingate College, instructor in religion, 1976-77; First Baptist Church, pastor, 1977-92; First Baptist Church of Norfolk, pastor, 1981-; Norfolk Baptist Association, chair, 1983; Southern Baptist Center for Church Growth, director, 1992-94; Southwestern Baptist Theological Seminary, president, 1994, distinguished professor of evangelism and church growth, 2005-; Southern Baptist Convention, director. Writer. **Publications:** Spiritual Gifts: Empowering the New Testament Church, 1988; (with R.W. Jones) Growing an Evangelistic Sunday School, 1989; The Official Rule Book for the New Church Game, 1990; The Bonsai Theory of Church Growth, 1991; Mirror, Mirror on the Wall: Discovering Your True Self through Spiritual Gifts, 1992; LifeAnswers: Making Sense of Your World, 1993; The Antioch Effect: 8 Characteristics of Highly Effective Churches, 1994; Revitalizing the Sunday Morning Dinosaur: A Sunday School Growth Strategy for the 21st Century, 1996; Ten Best Practices: To Make Your Sunday School Work, 2001; Names of God, 2001; Prayer of Jesus: The Promise and Power of Living in the Lord's Prayer, 2001; EKG (Empowering Kingdom Growth): The Heartbeat of God, 2004; We Can: Devotions Empowered by Biblical Statements of Faith, 2005; Parenting with Kingdom Purpose, 2005; He Is: Devotions Empowered by Biblical Statements of Faith, 2006; We Are: Devotions Empowered by Biblical Statements of Faith, 2006; But God: Devotions Empowered by Biblical Statements of Faith, 2006; Making Change: A Transformational Guide to Christian Money Management, 2006; God Will: Devotions Empowered by Biblical Statements of Faith, 2008; Eternal Impact: The Passion of Kingdom-Centered Communities, 2008; God Is, 2008; You are Gifted: Your Spiritual Gifts and the Kingdom of God, 2009. **Address:** Casa Bautista de Publicaciones, 7000 Alabama St., PO Box 4255, El Paso, TX 79914, U.S.A. **Online address:** khemphill@sbts.edu

HEMPTON, Gordon. American (born United States), b. 1953. **Genres:** Environmental Sciences/Ecology, Natural History. **Career:** Writer and sound recording engineer. **Publications:** (With J. Grossmann) One Square Inch of Silence: One Man's Search for Natural Silence in a Noisy World, 2009. **Address:** Sound Tracker, PO Box 550, Port Angeles, WA 98362, U.S.A. **Online address:** gordon@soundtracker.com

HEMSTOCK, Gillian. Canadian (born Canada), b. 1956. **Genres:** Young Adult Non-fiction, Novels, Science Fiction/Fantasy. **Career:** Writer. **Publications:** YOUNG-ADULT NOVELS AS MITZI DALE: Round the Bend, 1988; The Sky's the Limit, 1990; On My Own, 1991; Bryna Means Courage, 1993; What's Tuesday?, 1997; The Great and Awful Summer, 2007. OTHERS: (with F. McEnaney) The Careerfree Life, 1986; (with F. McEnaney) Luminosity, 1998; (with F. McEnaney) Sea Change, 2003. **Address:** Nimbus Publishing, PO Box 9166, Halifax, NS B3K 5M8, Canada. **Online address:** bankscorners@hotmail.com

HEN, Yitzhak. Israeli (born Israel), b. 1963. **Genres:** History. **Career:** University of Haifa, Department of History, lecturer, 1994-2002; Ben-Gurion University of the Negev, Department of General History, faculty, 2002-, Anna and Sam Lopin professor of history, Anna and Sam Lopin chair of history, 2008-. Writer. Historian. **Publications:** Culture and Religion in Merovingian Gaul, A.D. 481-751, 1995; (ed.) The Sacramentary of Echternach, 1997; Sof ha-elef ha-rishon: Dat, hevrah ve-tarbut ba-me ah ha-a sirit, 2000; (ed. with M. Innes) The Uses of the Past in the Early Middle Ages, 2000; The End of the First Millenium, Religion, Society and Culture in the Tenth Century, 2000; (ed.) De Sion exibit lex et verbum Domini de Hierusalem: Studies on Medieval Law, Liturgy, and Literature in Honor of Amnon Linder, 2001; The Royal Patronage of Liturgy in Frankish Gaul to the Death of Charles the Bald (877), 2001; (ed. with Miri Eliav-Feldon) Nashim, Zkenim va Taf: Kovets Ma'amarim Lichvoda shel Shulamith Shahar, 2001; (ed. with R. Meens) The Bobbio Missal: Liturgy and Religious Culture in Merovingian Gaul, 2004; Roman Barbarians: The Royal Court and Culture in the Early Medieval West, 2007; (ed. with M. Becher) Wilhelm Levison (1876-1947): Ein juedisches Forscherleben zwischen wissenschaftlicher Anerkennung und politischem Exil,, 2010; (ed. with Iris Shagrir) Liroth veLaga'at: Aliya Laregel uMekomot Kdoshim Bba Yahaduth, ba Natzruth ubaIslam. Mechkarim Lichvod Ora Limor, 2011. FORTHCOMING: Western Arianism: Politics and Religious Culture in the Early Medieval West; (ed. with M. Deisenberger and M. Pollheimer) Sermo doctorum: Compilers, Preachers and their Audiences in the Early Medieval West; (ed. with O. Limor and T.F.X. Noble) Barbarians and

Jews: Jews and Judaism in the Early Medieval West; (ed.) The Brill Companion to Early Medieval Western Liturgy. **Address:** Department of General History, Ben-Gurion University of the Negev, Diller Bldg., Rm. 313, PO Box 653, Beer Sheva, 84105, Israel. **Online address:** yhen@bgu.ac.il

HENARE, Amiria J.M. (Amiria Salmond). British (born England), b. 1973. **Genres:** Anthropology/Ethnology. **Career:** University of Cambridge, Museum of Archaeology and Anthropology, assistant curator for anthropology. Writer. **Publications:** Museums, Anthropology, and Imperial Exchange, 2005; (ed. with M. Holbraad and S. Wastell) Thinking Through Things: Theorising Artefacts in Ethnographic Perspective, 2006. **Address:** Museum of Archaeology & Anthropology, University of Cambridge, Downing St., Cambridge, CB2 3DZ, England. **Online address:** ajms2@cam.ac.uk

HENBEST, Nigel. British (born England), b. 1951. **Genres:** Astronomy, Children's Non-fiction, Air/Space Topics, Reference, Sciences. **Career:** University of Leicester, research assistant, 1976-77; New Scientist, astronomy consultant, 1980-92; BBC World Service, broadcaster; British Radio, broadcaster; British and American Television, producer and scriptwriter; British Astronomical Association Journal, editor, 1985-87; Pioneer Productions, co-founder and director; Hencoup Enterprises (consultants), founder and director; Science and Engineering Research Council, media consultant; Royal Greenwich Observatory, consultant. **Publications:** Exploding Universe, 1979; Spotter's Guide to the Night Sky, 1979; (with L. Mots) The Night Sky, 1979; Mysteries of the Universe, 1981; (with M. Marten) The New Astronomy, 1983, 2nd ed., 1996; (ed.) Observing the Universe, 1984; The Universe: A Computer-Generated Voyage through Time and Space, 1992; The Planets: A Guided Tour of Our Solar System through the Eyes of America's Space Probes, 1994. WITH H. COUPER: Space Frontiers, 1978; The Restless Universe, 1982; Astronomy, 1983; Physics, 1983; All About Space, 1983; The Sun, 1986; New Worlds: In Search of Planets, 1986; The Moon, 1986; Galaxies and Quasars, 1986; Space Probes and Satellites, 1987; Telescopes and Observatories, 1987; The Space Atlas, 1992; The Guide to the Galaxy, 1994; How the Universe Works, 1994; Black Holes, 1996; Big Bang, 1996; Is Anybody Out There?, 1998; To the Ends of the Universe, 1998; DK Space Encyclopedia, 1999, rev. ed. as DK Encyclopedia of Space, 2009; Universe, 2000; Extreme Universe, 2001; Mars: The Inside Story of the Red Planet, 2001; Philip's Stargazing, 2004; The History of Astronomy, 2007. **Address:** Collins Cottage, Lower Rd., Loosley Row, BK HP27 0PF, England. **Online address:** nigel@hencoup.com

HENDERSON, Bonnie. American (born United States), b. 1954. **Genres:** History. **Career:** Sunset magazine, associate editor, through 1990; Journalist and public affairs writer, 1990-; Seaside Signal, reporter and editor; Grants Pass Daily Courier, reporter. **Publications:** Archeology Notes: Southwestern Pennsylvania and Adjacent Areas, 1978; Best Hikes with Children in Western & Central Oregon, 1992, 2nd ed., 1999; Exploring the Wild Oregon Coast, 1994; 120 Hikes on the Oregon Coast, 2nd ed., 1999; Best Hikes with Kids: Oregon, 2007; Day Hiking: Oregon Coast, 2007; Strand: An Odyssey of Pacific Ocean Debris, 2008. Contributor to books. **Address:** OR , U.S.A. **Online address:** bonnie@bonniehendersonwrites.com

HENDERSON, F(rancis) M(artin). Australian (born Australia), b. 1921?. **Genres:** Engineering, Technology, Mathematics/Statistics, Sciences. **Career:** Department of Scientific and Industrial Research, engineer, senior engineer; University of Canterbury, senior lecturer, 1952-63, professor, 1964-68; University of Newcastle, Department Civil Engineering, professor, 1968-82, professor emeritus, 1982-. Writer. **Publications:** Elliptic Functions with Complex Arguments, 1960; Open Channel Flow, 1966. **Address:** 3 Ashby St., Dudley, NW 2290, Australia.

HENDERSON, Harold. American (born United States), b. 1948. **Genres:** Adult Non-fiction, Education, Reference. **Career:** Illinois Times, staff writer, 1980-85; Chicago Reader, staff writer, 1985-2008. **Publications:** Seizing the Day: How to Take the Day Off and Change Your Life, 1983; Catalyst for Controversy: Paul Carus of Open Court, 1993; Let's Kill Dick and Jane: How the Open Court Publishing Company Fought the Culture of American Education, 2006. **Address:** St. Augustine's Press Inc., 17917 Killington Way, PO Box 2285, South Bend, IN 46614-9973, U.S.A.

HENDERSON, J. A. (Jan-Andrew Martin Henderson). British/Scottish (born Scotland), b. 1962. **Genres:** Children's Fiction. **Career:** Black Hart Entertainment (a ghost tour company), founder and proprietor, 1998-. Writer.

Publications: The Town below the Ground: Edinburgh's Legendary Underground City, 1999; The Emperor's New Kilt: The Two Secret Histories of Scotland, 2000; The Ghost That Haunted Itself: The Story of the McKenzie Poltergeist, 2001; Edinburgh: City of the Dead, 2004; The Wee Book of Edinburgh, 2004; Who Wants to Be an Edinburgher, 2004. CHILDREN'S FICTION: Secret City, 2004; Hunting Charlie Wilson, 2005; Bunker 10, 2007; Crash, 2008; Colony, 2009. **Address:** Edinburgh, Scotland. **Online address:** janandrewhenderson@hotmail.com

HENDERSON, Jan-Andrew Martin. See HENDERSON, J. A.

HENDERSON, Jeff. American (born United States), b. 1964. **Genres:** Food And Wine, Biography. **Career:** Cafe Bellagio, sous chef, executive chef, 2004-, through 2006; Marriott Hotel, chef; Ritz-Carlton Hotel, chef; Hotel Bel-Air, chef; Gadsby's restaurant, dishwasher; Caesars Palace Hotel, chef de cuisine; Urban Educational Consulting, president and chief executive officer; Posh Urban Cuisine, owner. Writer. **Publications:** (Trans., intro. and contrib.) Aristophanes' Clouds, 1992; Cooked: From the Streets to the Stove, from Cocaine to Foie Gras, 2007; Chef Jeff Cooks: In the Kitchen with America's Inspirational New Culinary Star, 2008. **Address:** The Henderson Group Inc., 3275 N Fort Apache Rd., Ste. 150, Las Vegas, NV 89129, U.S.A. **Online address:** info@chefjeffhenderson.com

HENDERSON, Kristin. American (born United States) **Genres:** History, Autobiography/Memoirs, Travel/Exploration, Military/Defense/Arms Control. **Career:** Journalist. **Publications:** Driving by Moonlight: A Journey through Love, War, and Infertility (memoir), 2003; While They're at War: The True Story of American Families on the Homefront, 2006; Sisterhood of War, forthcoming. Contributor of articles to magazines and journals. **Address:** c/o Author Mail, Houghton Mifflin Co., 222 Berkeley St., 8th Fl., Boston, MA 02116-3764, U.S.A. **Online address:** kh@kristinhenderson.com

HENDERSON, Lauren. British (born England), b. 1966?. **Genres:** Novels, Novellas/Short Stories, Young Adult Non-fiction. **Career:** Journalist. **Publications:** FICTION: My Lurid Past, 2003; Don't Even Think about It, 2004; Exes Anonymous, 2005. SAM JONES MYSTERY SERIES: Dead White Female, 1996; Too Many Blondes, 1996; The Black Rubber Dress, 1997; The Strawberry Tattoo, 1999; Chained!, 2000; Freeze My Margarita, 2000; Pretty Boy, 2002. SCARLETT WAKEFIELD MYSTERY SERIES FOR YOUNG ADULTS: Kiss Me, Kill Me, 2008; Kisses and Lies, 2009; Kiss in the Dark, 2010. OTHERS: (ed. with S. Duffy) Tart Noir (anthology), 2002; (ed. with C. Manby and S. Mlynowski) Girls' Night In, 2004; Jane Austen's Guide to Dating, 2005; Jane Austen's Guide to Romance: The Regency Rules, 2006. Contributor to periodicals. **Address:** David Higham Associates, 5-8 Lower John St., Golden Sq., London, GL W1F 9HA, England.

HENDERSON, Meg. Scottish (born Scotland), b. 1948?. **Genres:** Novels, Young Adult Fiction. **Career:** Journalist and author. **Publications:** Finding Peggy, 1994; The Holy City, 1997; Bloody Mary, 1999; Chasing Angels, 2000; The Last Wanderer, 2002; Second Sight, 2004; John McNamee: An Autobiography, 2004; Daisy's Wars, 2005; A Scent of Bluebells, 2006; Ruby, 2010. **Address:** c/o Author Mail, HarperCollins Canada Ltd., 55 Ave. Rd., Ste. 2900, Toronto, ON M5R 3L2, Canada.

HENDERSON, Richard (Jud). American (born United States), b. 1924. **Genres:** Recreation, Travel/Exploration, Transportation, Sports/Fitness, Illustrations. **Career:** Henderson-Atherton Studio, founder and partner, 1951; freelance writer and illustrator. **Publications:** (Ed. and comp.) Dangerous Voyages of Captain Andrews, 1966; (with B.S. Dunbar) Sail and Power: A Manual of Seamanship for the United States Naval Academy, 1967, 4th ed., 1991; The Racing-Cruiser, 1970, 2nd ed., 1983; Sea Sense, 1972, 3rd ed., 1991; The Cruiser's Compendium, 1973; Better Sailing: Error Analysis in Sailing and Seamanship, 1977; East to the Azores: A Guide to Offshore Passage-Making, 1978; (with R. Scharff) Encyclopedia of Sailing, 1978; Choice Yacht Designs, 1979; Philip L. Rhodes and His Yacht Designs, 1981; (with R.W. Carrick) John G. Alden and His Yacht Designs, 1983; The Racing Cruiser, 1983; (with W.J. Kotsch) Heavy Weather Guide, 2nd ed., 1984; 53 Boats You Can Build, 1985; Understanding Rigs and Rigging, 1985; Sailing at Night, 1987; Sailing in Windy Weather, 1987; First Sail, 1993; Essential Seamanship, 1994; Chesapeake Sails: A History of Yachting on the Bay, 1999. SELF-ILLUSTRATED: First Sail for Skipper, 1960; Hand, Reef and Steer, 1965, rev. ed., 1978; Singlehanded Sailing: The Experiences and Techniques of the Lone Voyagers, 1967, 2nd ed., 1988. **Address:** Cornell Maritime Press

Inc., 101 Water Way, PO Box 456, Centreville, MD 21617, U.S.A. **Online address:** judsalhen@toad.net

HENDERSON, Timothy J. American (born United States), b. 1957. **Genres:** Novels. **Career:** Yale University, faculty; Auburn University, faculty, 1996-, professor of history, distinguished research professor. Writer. **Publications:** The Worm in the Wheat: Rosalie Evans and Agrarian Struggle in the Puebla-Tlaxcala Valley of Mexico, 1906-1927, 1998; (ed. with G.M. Joseph) The Mexico Reader: History, Culture, Politics, 2002; A Glorious Defeat: Mexico and its War with the United States, 2007; The Mexican Wars for Independence, 2009; Beyond Borders: A Concise History of Mexican Migration to the United States, 2011. **Address:** Department of History, Auburn University Montgomery, 345 Liberal Arts, 7051 Senators Dr., PO Box 244023, Montgomery, AL 36117, U.S.A. **Online address:** thender1@aum.edu

HENDERSON, William Darryl. American/Canadian (born Canada), b. 1938. **Genres:** Military/Defense/Arms Control, Sociology, Psychology. **Career:** U.S. Military Academy, assistant professor of social science, 1970-74, instructor for leadership and military psychology; Joint Security Area for Panmunjom, deputy commander, Office of the Deputy Secretary of Defense, staff assistant, executive assistant to the assistant secretary of defense legislative affairs, battalion commander, U.S. Army Research Institute for the Behavioral and Social Sciences, commander, Army Reserve command, senior adviser, International Military Staff, senior arms control planner; Canadian Department of Justice, consultant; Canadian Defense Department, consultant. Writer. **Publications:** (Ed.) Handbook of World Conflicts, 1970; Infantryong Fought: A Study of Motivation and Control in a Modern Army in Combat, 1979; Why the Vietcong Fought, 1979; Cohesion: The Human Element in Combat, 1985; The Hollow Army: How the U.S. Army Is Oversold and Undermanned, 1990. Contributor to books. **Address:** 19880 Lark Way, Saratoga, CA 95070, U.S.A.

HENDRA, Jessica. American (born United States), b. 1965. **Genres:** Autobiography/Memoirs, Literary Criticism And History, Humor/Satire. **Career:** Actress and writer. **Publications:** (With B. Morrison) How to Cook Your Daughter (memoir), 2005; (with J. Stainhauer) Beverly Hills Adjacent, 2009. **Address:** Sterling Lord Literistic Inc., 65 Bleecker St., New York, NY 10012-2420, U.S.A. **Online address:** jessicahendra@jessicahendra.com

HENDRICKS, Christopher E. (Christopher Edwin Hendricks). American (born United States), b. 1963?. **Genres:** History. **Career:** Armstrong Atlantic State University, assistant professor, 1993-99, associate professor, 1999-2006, professor of history, 2006-; College of William and Mary, visiting professor and instructor; University of Alabama, visiting professor and instructor; Hampton University, visiting professor and instructor; Wake Forest University, visiting professor and instructor. Writer. **Publications:** The Backcountry Towns of Colonial Virginia, 2006. Contributor of essays and articles to periodicals and journals. **Address:** Department of History, Armstrong Atlantic State University, Savannah, GA 31419-1997, U.S.A. **Online address:** chris.hendricks@armstrong.edu

HENDRICKS, Christopher Edwin. *See* **HENDRICKS, Christopher E.**

HENDRICKS, Judith Ryan. American (born United States), b. 1947?. **Genres:** Novels. **Career:** Journalist, copywriter, computer instructor and writer. **Publications:** Bread Alone, 2001; Isabels Daughter, 2003; The Bakers Apprentice, 2005; The Laws of Harmony: A Novel, 2009. **Address:** William Morrow & Co., 10 E 53rd St., 7th Fl., New York, NY 10022, U.S.A. **Online address:** jr@judihendricks.com

HENDRICKS, Obery M(ack). American (born United States), b. 1953. **Genres:** Novels, Theology/Religion. **Career:** Investment advisor, 1977-86; Payne Theological Seminary, president; New York Theological Seminary, professor of biblical interpretation; Drew University, professor; Wall Street, investment executive; Princeton Theological Seminary, visiting professor; African Methodist Episcopal Church, ordained elder. Writer. **Publications:** Living Water (novel), 2003; The Politics of Jesus: Rediscovering the True Revolutionary Nature of the Teachings of Jesus and How They Have Been Corrupted, 2006; The Universe Bends Toward Justice: Radical Reflections on the Bible, the Church and the Body Politic, 2011. **Address:** New York Theological Seminary, 475 Riverside Dr., Ste. 500, New York, NY 10115, U.S.A. **Online address:** obhendr@nyts.edu

HENDRICKS, Patricia. American (born United States) **Genres:** Young Adult Fiction, Theology/Religion. **Career:** Christos Center for Spiritual Formation, executive director and spiritual direction preparation program coordinator. Writer. **Publications:** Hungry Souls, Holy Companions: Mentoring a New Generation of Christians, 2006. **Address:** Christos Center for Spiritual Formation, 1212 Holly Dr., Lino Lakes, MN 55038, U.S.A. **Online address:** patchristoscenter@msn.com

HENDRICKS, Vicki (Due). American (born United States), b. 1951. **Genres:** Novels, Novellas/Short Stories, Mystery/Crime/Suspense. **Career:** Broward Community College, professor, 1981-. Writer. **Publications:** NOVELS: Miami Purity, 1995; Iguana Love, 1998; Voluntary Madness, 2000; Sky Blues, 2001; Cruel Poetry, 2007. SHORT STORY COLLECTION: Florida Gothic Stories, 2010. Works appear in anthologies. **Address:** Broward Community College, 7200 Pines Blvd., Pembroke Pines, FL 33024, U.S.A. **Online address:** vickih@vickihendricks.com

HENDRICKSON, R. J. *See* **JENSEN, Ruby Jean.**

HENDRICKSON, Ryan C. American (born United States), b. 1969. **Genres:** Military/Defense/Arms Control, History, Politics/Government. **Career:** University of Nebraska, Department of Political Science, teaching assistant, 1992-97; Lambuth University, Department of Political Science, assistant professor, 1997-99; Eastern Illinois University, Department of Political Science, assistant professor, 1999-2003, department graduate coordinator, 2003-, associate professor, 2003-08, professor, 2008-. Writer, political scientist and military historian. **Publications:** The Clinton Wars: The Constitution, Congress and War Powers, 2002; Diplomacy and War at NATO: The Secretary General and Military Action after the Cold War, 2006. Contributor to books and periodicals. **Address:** Department of Political Science, Eastern Illinois University, Coleman Hall 2325, 600 Lincoln Ave., Charleston, IL 61920-3099, U.S.A. **Online address:** cfrch@eiu.edu

HENDRIX, Scott H. American (born United States), b. 1942. **Genres:** History, Theology/Religion, Sociology. **Career:** Princeton Theological Seminary, James Hastings Nichols professor, 1998-, now professor emeritus; Tenth International Congress for Luther Research, plenary lecturer, 2002. Writer. **Publications:** Ecclesia in Via: Ecclesiological Developments in the Medieval Psalms Exegesis and the Dictata Super Psalterium (1513-1515) of Martin Luther, 1974; Luther and the Papacy: Stages in a Reformation Conflict, 1981; Tradition and Authority in the Reformation, 1996; (with G. Gassmann) Fortress Introduction to the Lutheran Confessions, 1999; (trans., ed. and intro.) U. Rhegius, Preaching the Reformation: The Homiletical Handbook of Urbanus Rhegius, 2003; Recultivating the Vineyard: The Reformation Agendas of Christianization, 2004; (ed. with S.C. Karant-Nunn) Masculinity in the Reformation Era, 2008. **Address:** Princeton Theological Seminary, 64 Mercer St., PO Box 821, Princeton, NJ 08542-0803, U.S.A.

HENDRY, Diana. Scottish/British (born England), b. 1941. **Genres:** Novellas/Short Stories, Children's Fiction, Young Adult Fiction, Poetry. **Career:** Sunday Times, assistant literature editor, 1958-60; Western Mail, reporter and feature writer, 1960-65; freelance journalist, 1965-80; Clifton College, instructor in English, 1987-90; Bristol Polytechnic, adjunct lecturer, 1987-; University of Bristol, Department of Continuing Education, instructor, 1987-92; University of the West of England, tutor; Open University, tutor, 1991-92; McConomy & Company Ltd., non-executive director; Dumfries & Galloway Royal Infirmary, writer-in-residence; Edinburgh University, Royal Literary Fund, fellow, 2008-10. **Publications:** Midnight Pirate, 1984; Fiona Finds Her Tongue, 1985; Hetty's First Fling, 1985; The Not Anywhere House, 1989; The Rainbow Watchers, 1989; The Carey Street Cat, 1989; Christmas on Exeter Street, 1989; Sam Sticks and Delilah, 1990; A Camel Called April, 1990; A Moment for Joe, 1990; Double Vision (young adult novel), 1990; The Thing-in-a-Box, 1992; Wonderful Robert and Sweetie-Pie Nell, 1992; Kid Kibble, 1993; Back Soon!, 1993; Why Father Christmas Was Late for Hartlepool, 1994; The Awesome Bird, 1995; Happy Old Birthday Owl, 1995; Flower Street Friends, 1995; Dog Donovan, 1995; The Thing-on-Two-Legs, 1995; Dog Dottington, 1995; Fiona Says..., 1998. JUNIOR FICTION: Harvey Angell, 1991; Strange Goings-On, 1995; Harvey Angell and the Ghost Child, 1997; Minders, 1998; Harvey Angell Beats Time, 2000; The Crazy Collector, 2001; You Can't Kiss It Better, 2003; Swan Boy, 2004; Catch a Gran, 2006. CHILDREN BOOKS: The Very Noisy Night, 1998; The Very

Busy Day, 2001; No Homework Tomorrow, 2003; The Very Snowy Christmas, 2005; Oodles of Noodles, 2008. POETRY FOR ADULTS: Making Blue, 1995; Borderers, 2001; Twelve Lilts: Psalms and Responses, 2003; (with T. Pow) Sparks!, 2005; Late Love and Other Whodunnits, 2008. **Address:** 23 Dunrobin Pl., Edinburgh, EH3 5HZ, Scotland. **Online address:** diana.hendry@btinternet.com

HENDRY, Joy (McLaggan). British/Scottish (born Scotland), b. 1953. **Genres:** Poetry, Communications/Media, Intellectual History, Literary Criticism And History, Philosophy, Theatre, Women's Studies And Issues, Writing/Journalism, Writing/Journalism. **Career:** Chapman: Scotland's Quality Literary Magazine, co-editor, 1972-76, editor, 1976-; Register House, civil servant, 1974-75; Knox Academy, teacher of English, 1977-84; writer, 1984-; Oxford Brookes University, professor of social anthropology, 1980-, Europe Japan Research Centre, director; The Scotsman, radio critic, 1987-97; Scottish Poetry Library, deputy convener. **Publications:** Marriage in Changing Japan, 1981; Becoming Japanese, 1986; Understanding Japanese Society, 1987, 3rd ed. 2003; Wrapping Culture: Politeness, Presentation, and Power in Japan and Other Societies, 1993; An Anthropologist in Japan: Glimpses of Life in the Field, 1999; Other People's Worlds: An Introduction to Cultural and Social Anthropology, 1999, 2nd ed. as Sharing Our Worlds: An Introduction to Cultural and Social Anthropology, 2008; The Orient Strikes Back: A Global View of Cultural Display, 2000; Reclaiming Culture: Indigenous People and Self-Representation, 2005; Introduction to Social Anthropology, 2008. EDITOR: Poems and Pictures of Wendy Wood, 1985; (with I. Evans) The Land for the People, 1985; (with R.J. Ross) Sorley MacLean: Critical Essays, 1986; (with R. Ross) Norman MacCaig: Critical Essays, 1990; Edwin Morgan, 1991; (with A. Campbell) Norman MacCaig: A Celebration: Tributes from Writers in Honour of Norman MacCaig's Birthday, 1996; The Drawings of Sydney Goodsir Smith, Poet, 1998; Interpreting Japanese Society: Anthropological Approaches, 1998; (with C.W. Watson) An Anthropology of Indirect Communication, 2001; (with M. Raveri) Japan at Play: The Ludic and Logic of Power, 2002; (with H.W. Wong) Dismantling the East-West Dichotomy, 2006. Contributor to periodicals. **Address:** Department of Anthropology & Geography, School of Social Sciences & Law, Oxford Brookes University, Gipsy Ln., Oxford, OX OX3 0BP, England. **Online address:** jhendry@brookes.ac.uk

HENEGHAN, Judith. (Judith Anderson). British (born England), b. 1965. **Genres:** Novels. **Career:** University of Winchester, faculty member teaching creative writing. Writer, book editor and columnist. **Publications:** Stonecipher (children's novel), 2005 in US as The Magician's Apprentice, 2008. **Address:** HM , England **Online address:** judith.anderson@winchester.ac.uk

HENEHAN, Mary Pat. American (born United States), b. 1942. **Genres:** Medicine/Health. **Career:** Saint Paul's Hospital, obstetrical-gynecological nurse, 1965-69; Saint Paul's School of Nursing, adjunct faculty, 1965-69; Saint Louis University, adjunct faculty, 1974-76, adjunct assistant professor, 1996-; Seton Medical Center, director of nursing, 1976-79; University of Texas, adjunct faculty, 1976-79; Saint Vincent's College, affiliate of pastoral ministry and parish missions programs, 1979-81; Daughters of Charity, formation counselor, 1981-85; De Paul Health Center, vice president for mission services, 1984-87; Care and Counseling Inc., counselor and psychotherapist, 1987-90; Missouri Baptist Health Center, psychiatric home health nurse, 1988-96; Appleton and Associates, counselor, 1988-92; Counseling and Educational Associates Inc., president and therapist, 1991-; Aquinas Institute of Theology, adjunct faculty, 1997-99; Washington University, adjunct faculty, 2003-; American Association for Marriage and Family Therapy, supervisor. Writer. **Publications:** Integrating Spirit and Psyche: Using Women's Narratives in Psychotherapy, 2003. Contributor to journals. **Address:** 16 Bon Hills Dr., Saint Louis, MO 63132, U.S.A. **Online address:** marypat@moamft.org

HENG, Liu. Chinese (born China), b. 1954?. **Genres:** Novels, Plays/Screenplays, Young Adult Fiction. **Career:** Beijing Literature, editor, 1979-. **Publications:** Dogshit Food, 1985; Fuxi Fuxi, 1987; Hei di xue, 1988; Dong xi nan bei feng, 1989; Qiuju da guan si, 1993; Fu xi fu xi, 1993; Meishi Touzhe Le, 2000; Liu Heng, 2000; Quan sheng, 2000; Lang wo, 2001; Gou ri de liang shi, 2003. **Address:** c/o Author Mail, Grove/Atlantic Inc., 841 Broadway, 4th Fl., New York, NY 10003, U.S.A.

HENGGELER, Scott Walter. American (born United States), b. 1950. **Genres:** Psychology, Human Relations/Parenting. **Career:** University of Virginia, Children and Youth Center, pediatric clinical psychology intern,

1974-76, visiting assistant professor, 1977; Memphis State University, assistant professor, 1976-81, associate professor, 1981-86, professor of psychology, 1986-88, Psychological Services Center, clinical director of psychology, 1976-84, Delinquency Project, director, 1978-83; Family and Health Institute of Memphis, director, 1981-88; Human Affairs Intl., director of Memphis Office, 1983-88; U.S. International University, professor of human behavior, 1988-92; University of Nebraska, Law and Psychology Program, affiliate, 1989-94; San Diego State University, adjunct professor, 1990-92; University of South Carolina, School of Medicine, clinical professor, 1992-2000; Medical University of South Carolina, professor of psychiatry and behavioral sciences, 1992-, Family Services Research Center, director, 1992-; Violent Offenders, Tall Trees Residential Program, consultant; South Carolina Department of Mental Health, consultant; Memphis Federal Corrections Institute, consultant. Writer. **Publications:** (Ed. with Alberto B. Santos) Innovative Approaches for Difficult-to-Treat Populations, 1977; (ed.) Delinquency and Adolescent Psychopathology: A Family-Ecological Systems Approach, 1982; Developmental Clinical Psychology and Psychiatry, 1989; Delinquency in Adolescence, 1989; (with C.M. Borduin) Family Therapy and Beyond: A Multisystemic Approach to Treating the Behavior Problems of Children and Adolescents, 1990; (with G.B. Melton and J.R. Rodrigue) Pediatric and Adolescent AIDS: Research Findings From the Social Sciences, 1992; (ed. with A.B. Santos and contrib.) Innovative Services for Difficult to Treat Populations, 1994; (co-author) Multisystemic Treatment of Antisocial Behavior in Children and Adolescents, 1998, 2nd ed., 2009; (co-author) Multisystemic Therapy, 1998, 2nd ed., 2009; (ed.) Serious Emotional Disturbance in Children and Adolescents: Multisystemic Therapy, 2002; (co-author) Contingency Management for Adolescent Substance Abuse, 2012. Works appear in anthologies. Contributor to journals. **Address:** Department of Psychiatry and Behavioral Sciences, Medical University of South Carolina, McClennan Banks Bldg., 4th Fl., 326 Calhoun St., Ste. MC406, Charleston, SC 29401, U.S.A. **Online address:** henggesw@musc.edu

HENIG, Jeffrey R. American (born United States), b. 1951. **Genres:** Politics/Government, Education. **Career:** George Washington University, Department of Political Science, assistant professor, 1977-84, associate professor, 1984-91, professor of political science, 1991-2002, chair, 1997-2000, 2001-02, Undergraduate Urban Affairs Program, director, 1977-89, School of Public and International Affairs, associate dean, 1985-87, Center for Washington Area Studies, director, 1990-2002; Columbia University, professor of political science and education, 2002-, Graduate Program in Politics and Education, director, 2002-. Writer. **Publications:** Gentrification in Adams Morgan: Political and Commercial Consequences of Neighborhood Change, 1982; Neighborhood Mobilization: Redevelopment and Response, 1982; Citizens against Crime: An Assessment of the Neighborhood Watch Program in Washington, D.C., 1984; Public Policy and Federalism: Issues in State and Local Politics, 1985; Rethinking School Choice: Limits of the Market Metaphor, 1994; (with R.C. Hula, M. Orr and D.S. Pedescleaux) The Color of School Reform: Race, Politics, and the Challenge of Urban Education, 1999; (with H. Feigenbaum and C. Hamnett) Shrinking the State: The Political Underpinnings of Privatization, 1999; (with C.N. Stone, B.D. Jones and C. Pierannunzi) Building Civic Capacity: The Politics of Reforming Urban Schools, 2001; (ed. with W.C. Rich) Mayors in the Middle: Politics, Race, and Mayoral Control of Urban Schools, 2003; Spin Cycle: How Research Is Used in Policy Debates: The Case of Charter Schools, 2008; (ed. with K.E. Bulkley and H.M. Levin) Between Public and Private: Politics, Governance, and the New Portfolio Models for Urban School Reform, 2010. Contributor to books, periodicals and journals. **Address:** Columbia University, 525 W 120th St., New York, NY 10027, U.S.A. **Online address:** henig@exchange.tc.columbia.edu

HENKE, Shirl. American (born United States) **Genres:** Romance/Historical, Novels, Young Adult Fiction. **Career:** Writer and educator. **Publications:** ROMANCE NOVELS. Golden Lady, 1986; Love Unwilling, 1987; Capture the Sun, 1988; Summer Has No Name, 1991; Bouquet, 1994; A Fire in the Blood, 1994; Love a Rebel, Love a Rogue, 1994; Broken Vows, 1995; McCrory's Lady, 1995; Bride of Fortune, 1996; The Endless Sky, 1998; Sundancer, 1999; Wicked Angel, 2001; Wanton Angel, 2002; Yankee Earl, 2003; Rebel Baron, 2004; Texas Viscount, 2004; Finders Keepers, 2005; Sneak and Rescue, 2006; River Nymph, 2008; (with J. Henke) Pale Moon Stalker, 2008; (with J. Henke) Chosen Woman, 2009. GONE TO TEXAS TRILOGY: Cactus Flower, 1988; Moon Flower, 1989; Night Flower, 1990. DISCOVERY DUET: Paradise and More, 1991; Return to Paradise, 1992. HOUSE OF DREAMS SERIES: Love Lessons at Midnight, 2010. NIGHT WIND SERIES: Night Wind's Women, 1991; White Apache's Woman, 1993; Deep as the Rivers, 1997. ROCKY MOUNTAIN SERIES: Terms of Love, 1992; Terms of Surrender, 1993. Works appear in anthologies. Contributor to periodicals. **Address:** St. Martin's Press, 175 5th Ave., New York, NY 10010-7703, U.S.A. **Online address:** shirl@shirlhenke.com

HENKIN, Joshua. American (born United States), b. 1964. **Genres:** Novels, Young Adult Non-fiction. **Career:** Tikkun Magazine, assistant editor, 1987-89; freelance writer, 1993-; University of Michigan, instructor in creative writing, 1997-; Unterberg Poetry Center, instructor in fiction writing, 1999-; Sarah Lawrence College, faculty of writing, 2000-; City University of New York, Brooklyn College, Department of English, professor, Master of Fine Arts Program, coordiantor. **Publications:** Swimming across the Hudson (novel), 1997; Matrimony, 2007. Contributor of articles to periodicals. **Address:** Department of English, Brooklyn College, City University of New York, Rm. 2308, Boylan Hall, 2900 Bedford Ave., Brooklyn, NY 11210, U.S.A. **Online address:** jhenkin@brooklyn.cuny.edu

HENLEY, Arthur. Also writes as Webb Jones. American (born United States), b. 1921. **Genres:** Plays/Screenplays, Medicine/Health, Psychology, Sociology, Travel/Exploration, Humor/Satire, Young Adult Fiction. **Career:** Fairchild Instruments Co., technical writer, 1944; Arthur Henley Productions, writer and producer, 1945-61; freelance writer, 1961-; Brides, columnist, 1969-70; New York University, lecturer in creative writing, 1970-71. Consultant. **Publications:** Demon in My View, 1966; Make Up Your Mind, 1967; (with R.L. Wolk) Yes Power, 1969; (with R.L. Wolk) The Right to Lie, 1970; Schizophrenia: Current Approaches to a Baffling Problem, 1971; (with M. Weisinger) The Complete Alibi Handbook, 1972; (with A.J. Montanari) The Montanari Book, 1972; (with A.J. Montanari) What Other Child Care Books Won't Tell You, 1973; (with A.J. Montanari) The Difficult Child, 1973; Human Resources and Population Policies, 1974; (with D.L. Brooks) Don't Be Afraid of Cataracts, 1978, rev. ed. 1983; Phobias: The Crippling Fears, 1987, rev. ed., 1988; Schizophrenia: Advances in Diagnosis and Treatment, 1987; Lily and Joel: A Novel of Life, Love and Audio Tapes, 1992. Works appear in anthologies. Contributor to periodicals. **Address:** 73-37 Austin St., Forest Hills, NY 11375-6219, U.S.A. **Online address:** ah55@webtv.net

HENLEY, Marian. American (born United States), b. 1954. **Genres:** Autobiography/Memoirs, Graphic Novels, Humor/Satire. **Career:** Writer and freelance and syndicated cartoonist. **Publications:** Maxine!, 1987; Laughing Gas: The Best of Maxine, 2002. SELF-ILLUSTRATED: The Shiniest Jewel: A Family Love Story: A Memoir, 2008. **Address:** Springboard Press, 237 Park Ave., New York, NY 10017, U.S.A. **Online address:** mkeyhenley@gmail.com

HENLEY, Patricia. American (born United States), b. 1947. **Genres:** Novels, Novellas/Short Stories, Poetry. **Career:** Purdue University, professor of English, 1987-. Writer. **Publications:** POEM: Learning to Die: Poems, 1979. STORIES: Friday Night at Silver Star: Stories, 1986; The Secret of Cartwheels: Short Stories, 1992; Back Roads, 1996; Worship of the Common Heart: New and Selected Stories, 2000; Other Heartbreaks: Stories, 2011. NOVELS: Hummingbird House, 1999; In the River Sweet, 2002. Works appear in anthologies. **Address:** Department of English, Purdue University, 428 Heavilon Hall, 500 Oval Dr., West Lafayette, IN 47907, U.S.A. **Online address:** phenley@purdue.edu

HENNEBERGER, Melinda. American (born United States) **Genres:** Adult Non-fiction, Politics/Government. **Career:** New York Times, reporter, Washington correspondent, Rome bureau chief; Newsweek, reporter; Politics Daily, editor-in-chief; Commonweal, columnist. Journalist. **Publications:** If They Only Listened to Us: What Women Voters Want Politicians to Hear, 2007. Contributor to journals. **Address:** Simon & Schuster Inc., 1230 Ave. of the Americas, New York, NY 10020-1513, U.S.A. **Online address:** melinda.henneberger@slate.com

HENNESSEY, Thomas W. British/American (born United States) **Genres:** History, Military/Defense/Arms Control, Social Sciences, Humanities. **Career:** Queen's University, staff; Canterbury Christ Church University, professor of history, 1998-, reader; University of Ulster, Centre for the Study of Conflict, research fellow. Writer. **Publications:** A History of Northern Ireland, 1920-1996, 1997; Dividing Ireland: World War I and Partition, 1998; The Northern Ireland Peace Process: Ending the Troubles?, 2000; Northern

Ireland: The Origins of the Troubles, 2005; The Evolution of the Troubles, 1970-72, 2007; (with C. Thomas) Spooks: The Unofficial History of MI5, 2009. **Address:** Department of History and American Studies, Canterbury Christ Church University, North Holmes Rd., Canterbury, KT CT1 1QU, England.

HENNESSY, John J(oseph). American (born United States), b. 1958. **Genres:** History, Military/Defense/Arms Control. **Career:** Manassas National Battlefield, staff historian, 1981-85; New York State Office of Historic Preservation, historian, 1986-91; National Park Service, exhibit planner, 1991-95; Save Historic Antietam Foundation, director, 1992-; Fredericksburg and Spotsylvania National Military Park, assistant superintendent, 1995-, chief historian. Writer. **Publications:** An End to Tennessee: The First Battle of Manassas, 1989; First Battle of Manassas: An End to Innocence, 1989; Return to Bull Run: The Campaign and Battle of Second Manassas, 1993; (ed.) Fighting with the Eighteenth Massachusetts: The Civil War Memoir of Thomas H. Mann, 2000. **Address:** Fredericksburg & Spotsylvania National Military, Park, 120 Chatham Ln., Fredericksburg, VA 22405-2508, U.S.A.

HENNESSY, Peter. British (born England), b. 1947. **Genres:** History, Politics/Government. **Career:** Times Higher Education Supplement, reporter, 1971-74; The Times, reporter, 1974-76, Whitehall correspondent, 1976-82, leader writer, 1982-84; Institute of Contemporary British History, co-founder, 1986; BBC Radio 4's Analysis, presenter, 1987-92; The Independent, Whitehall, Watch, columnist, 1987-91; University of London, Director Magazine, columnist, 1989; University of Strathclyde, visiting professor of government, 1989-; Queen Mary and Westfield College, professor of contemporary history, 1992-, Attlee professor of contemporary British history; The Financial Times, lobby correspondent, economist. **Publications:** (With C. Bennett) A Consumer's Guide to Open Government, 1980; (with K. Jeffery) States of Emergency: British Governments and Strikebreaking since 1919, 1983; (with A. Arends) Mr. Attlee's Engine Room, 1983; (with M. Cockerell and D. Walker) Sources Close to the Prime Minister: Inside the Hidden World of the News Manipulators, 1984; (with S. Morrison and R. Townsend) Routine Punctuated by Orgies: The Central Policy Review Staff, 1970-83, 1985; (with Sir D. Hague) How Adolph Hitler Reformed Whitehall, 1985; What the Papers Never Said, 1985; Cabinet, 1986; The Great and the Good: An Inquiry Into the British Establishment, 1986; (ed. with A. Seldon) Ruling Performance: British Governments from Attlee to Thatcher, 1987; Whitehall, 1989, rev. ed., 2001; Never Again: Britain 1945-51, 1992; The Hidden Wiring: Unearthing the British Constitution, 1995; Muddling Through: Power, Politics and the Quality of Government in Postwar Britain, 1996; The Prime Minister: The Office and Its Holders, 1998; Secret State: Whitehall and the Cold War, 2002, 2nd ed. as Secret State: Preparing for the Worst, 1945-2010, 2010; Having It So Good: Britain in the Fifties, 2006; Cabinets and the Bomb, 2007; (ed.) New Protective State: Government, Intelligence and Terrorism, 2007. **Address:** Department of History, Queen Mary & Westfield College, University of London, Arts 2.23, Mile End Rd., London, GL E1 4NS, England. **Online address:** p.j.hennessy@qmul.ac.uk

HENNESY, Carolyn. American (born United States), b. 1962?. **Genres:** Novels. **Career:** Writer. **Publications:** PANDORA SERIES YOUNG ADULT NOVELS: Pandora Gets Jealous, 2008; Pandora Gets Vain, 2008. **Address:** Los Angeles, CA 90004, U.S.A. **Online address:** carolyn@carolynhennesy.com

HENNEY, Carolee Wells. American (born United States), b. 1928. **Genres:** Novels, Children's Fiction, Poetry. **Career:** Hampton School System, elementary teacher, 1968-88; Virginia Living Museum, interpreter, 1993-2001. Writer. **Publications:** Calbert and His Adventures, 1990; Tac and Tuk, 1992; The B&O Engineer (poem), forthcoming. Contributor to periodicals. **Address:** 407 Wormley Creek Dr., Yorktown, VA 23692-4215, U.S.A. **Online address:** chenney@marketplacepublicity.com

HENNING, Ann. (Ann Henning Jocelyn). Irish/British/Swedish (born Sweden), b. 1948. **Genres:** Children's Fiction, Plays/Screenplays, Poetry, Adult Non-fiction, Translations, Astronomy. **Career:** Radio 1, writer; Gothenburg University, Department of Art History, lecturer. Playwright and translator. **Publications:** (Trans.) Love's Gravity, 1977; Modern Astrology, 1983; The Connemara Whirlwind, 1990; The Connemara Stallion, 1991; The Connemara Champion, 1994; The Cosmos and You (nonfiction), 1995; Honeylove the Bear Cub, 1995; (as Ann Henning Jocelyn) Keylines (poetry), 2000; Keylines for Living, 2007. Contributor to periodicals. **Address:** 4 The Boltons, London, GL SW10 9TB, England.

HENRICKSSON, John. American (born United States), b. 1926. **Genres:** Environmental Sciences/Ecology, Natural History, Autobiography/Memoirs. **Career:** State of Minnesota, Department of Tourism, publicity director, 1952-62. Writer. **Publications:** Rachel Carson: The Environmental Movement, 1991; (ed.) North Writers, vol. I: A Strong Woods Collection, 1991, vol. II: Our Place in the Woods, 1997; A Wild Neighborhood, 1997; Gunflint Cabin: A Northwoods Memoir, 2008. **Address:** c/o Linda Strommer, StrommerGroup, 2510 Wilshire Ct., Mendota Heights, MN 55120, U.S.A. **Online address:** henricksson@aol.com

HENRIKSEN, Margot A. American (born United States) **Genres:** History. **Career:** University of Hawaii-Manoa, Department of History, associate professor. Writer. **Publications:** Dr. Strangelove's America: Society and Culture in the Atomic Age, 1997. **Address:** Department of History, University of Hawaii Manoa, Sakamaki Hall B402, 2530 Dole St., Honolulu, HI 96822-2283, U.S.A. **Online address:** henrikm@hawaii.edu

HENRIOT, Christian. French (born France) **Genres:** Air/Space Topics, History. **Career:** Jean Moulin-Lyon 3 University, Department of Chinese, Vietnamese and Korean Studies, associate professor, 1985-92, chair, 1985-90, professor, 1992-98, Research Center on Modern East Asia, director and founder, 1987-92; Lumière-Lyon 2 University, Ecole Normale Supérieure-LSH, Institute of East Asian Studies, CNRS, director and founder, 1993-2002, Department of History, professor, 1998-; Institut Universitaire de France, junior research fellow, 1994-99, senior fellow, 2007-; European Journal of East Asian Studies, co-founder, 2000-04, editor, 2000-; French National Center for Scientific Research, Division of Social Sciences and Humanities, deputy director, 2002-05; Stanford University, Stanford Humanities Center, senior research fellow, 2006-07. **Publications:** (Ed.) La Femme en Asie Orientale: Politique, Société, Littérature, Université Jean Moulin-Lyon III, 1988; (ed.) Shanghai dans les années 1980: études urbaines, 1989; Shanghai, 1927-1937: élites locales et Modernisation dans la Chine Nationaliste, 1991; (ed. with A. Delissen) Les métropoles chinoises au XXe siècle, 1995; (with S. Lu) La Réforme des Entreprises en Chine: Les Industries Shanghaiennes entre etat et Marché, 1996; (ed.) Chinese Urban History Workshop: A Reader, 1996; Belles de Shanghai: Prostitution et Sexualité en Chine aux XIXe-XXe siècle, 1997; (with A. Roux) Shanghai années 30: plaisirs et violences, 1998; (coauthor) Atlas de Shanghai: Espaces et Représentations de 1849 à nos jours, 1999; (ed. with R. Bickers) New Frontiers: Imperialism's New Communities in East Asia, 1842-1953, 2000; (ed. with G. Dubois-Taine) Cities of the Pacific Rim: Diversity and Sustainability, 2001; Prostitution in Shanghai: A Social History, 2001; (ed. with W. Yeh) In the Shadow of the Rising Sun: Shanghai Under Japanese Occupation, 2003; Shanghai: An Interpretive History, 1840-1949, forthcoming. Contributor to periodicals. **Address:** Institute of East Asian Studies, Lumière-Lyon 2 University, 15, Parvis René Descartes, Lyon, 69342, France. **Online address:** christian.henriot@univ-lyon2.fr

HENRY, Chad. American (born United States), b. 1946. **Genres:** Plays/Screenplays. **Career:** Denver Center Theater Co., affiliate, literary associate; actor; director; composer; author. **Publications:** Dog Breath Victorious (novel), 1999. Contributor to periodicals. **Address:** Denver Center Theater Co., 1101 13th St., Denver, CO 80204, U.S.A. **Online address:** gregcat@msn.com

HENRY, Charles P. American (born United States), b. 1947?. **Genres:** Young Adult Non-fiction. **Career:** Denison University, faculty; Howard University, faculty; University of California, faculty member, professor of African American studies, 1981-; University of Bologna, Distinguished Fulbright Chair in American History and Politics, 2003; University of Tours, Fulbright-Tocqueville Distinguished Chair, 2006; National Council on the Humanities, member, 1994-2000; Amnesty International USA, director & chair, 1986-88. Writer. **Publications:** NONFICTION: Culture and African American Politics, 1990; (ed.) Ralph J. Bunche: Selected Speeches and Writings, 1995; Ralph Bunche: Model Negro or American Other?, 1999; (ed.) Foreign Policy and the Black (Inter)national Interest, 2000; Long Overdue: The Politics of Racial Reparations, 2007. Contributor of articles to journals. **Address:** Department of African American Studies, University of California, 660 Barrows Hall, Ste. 2572, Berkeley, CA 94720, U.S.A. **Online address:** cphenry@berkeley.edu

HENRY, DeWitt (Pawling). American (born United States), b. 1941. **Genres:** Novels, Autobiography/Memoirs, Education, Literary Criticism And History, Novellas/Short Stories. **Career:** Simmons College, instructor of English, 1971-72; Ploughshares Inc., founding editor and director, 1971-95, interim director, editor-in-chief and director, 2007-08; Emerson College,

prose writer-in-residence, 1973-74, adjunct professor, 1982-83, assistant professor 1983-89, acting chair, 1987-88, Publishing and Literature Division, chair of writing, 1989-93, associate professor, 1989-2006, professor of creative writing and literature, 2006-; Book Affairs Inc., director, 1975-82. **Publications:** The Marriage of Anna Maye Potts: A Novel, 2001; Safe Suicide: Narratives, Essays and Meditations, 2008; Sweet Dreams: A Family History, 2011. EDITOR: (and intro.) The Ploughshares Reader: New Fiction for the Eighties, 1985; Other Sides of Silence: New Fiction from Ploughshares, 1992; (with J.A. McPherson) Fathering Daughters: Reflections by Men, 1998; Breaking into Print: Early Stories and Insights into Getting Published a Ploughshares Anthology, 2000; Sorrow's Company: Writers on Loss and Grief, 2001. **Address:** Writing Literature & Publishing Division, Emerson College, 120 Boylston St., Boston, MA 02116-4624, U.S.A. **Online address:** dewitt_henry@emerson.edu

HENRY, Gordon D. American (born United States), b. 1955. **Genres:** Novels, Cultural/Ethnic Topics, Humanities, Poetry. **Career:** Ferris State University, assistant professor, 1988-92; Michigan State University, assistant professor of English, 1993-, associate professor, professor. Writer, lecturer and storyteller. **Publications:** Outside White Earth, 1986; The Light People: A Novel, 1994; (with G.L. Cornell) Ojibwa, 2004; The Failure of Certain Charms and Other Disparate Signs of Life, 2008; Stories Through Theories/Theories Through Stories: North American Indian Writing, Storytelling and Critique, 2009; Aphorisms for Long Knives; The Golden Arrow. **Address:** Department of English, Michigan State University, 225B Morrill Hall, East Lansing, MI 48824, U.S.A. **Online address:** henryg@msu.edu

HENRY, Julie. (Julie Mears Henry). American (born United States), b. 1965. **Genres:** Medicine/Health. **Career:** Ad Lib Books L.L.C., owner; American Academy of Family Physicians, manager of practice management and professional support, 1998-. Writer. **Publications:** (With J. Valancy) On Your Own: Starting a Medical Practice from the Ground Up, 2001; (as Julie Mears Henry) A Matter of Time (romance novel), 2004; (with H. Larson and J. Rubin) Home Emergency Pocket Guide, 2007; (with P. Derr) RN Pocket Guide, 2008; Getting Cancer: Diagnosis, Symptoms & Treatment, 2008; Getting Answers About Cancer: Understanding the Symptoms, Diagnosis and Treatment, 2009. **Address:** American Academy of Family Physicians, 11400 Tomahawk Creek Pkwy., Leawood, KS 66211-2680, U.S.A. **Online address:** jhenryrn2@att.net

HENRY, Julie Mears. See **HENRY, Julie.**

HENRY, Maeve. British/Irish (born Ireland), b. 1960. **Genres:** Novels, Young Adult Fiction. **Career:** Oxford Intensive School of English, English and foreign language teacher, 1987-. Writer. **Publications:** The Witch King, 1987; A Gift for a Gift: A Ghost Story, 1990; Listen to the Dark, 1993; A Summer Dance, 1994; (contrib.) The River Shannon, 1996; Midwinter, 1997; Just a Boy, 2001. Contributor to periodicals. **Address:** c/o Felicity Bryan, 2A N Parade, Banbury Rd., Oxford, OX OX2 6PE, England.

HENRY, Patrick. American (born United States), b. 1940. **Genres:** Literary Criticism And History. **Career:** Rice University, instructor in French, 1968-69; Whitman College, Department of Foreign Languages and Literatures, instructor in French, 1969-70, assistant professor, 1976-79, chair, 1979-82, associate professor, 1979-88, professor of French, 1988-, Cushing Eells professor of philosophy and literature, now Cushing Eells professor emeritus of philosophy and literature, Great Works Freshman Core Curriculum Program, chair, 1986-88; University of Strasbourg, Fulbright lecturer in American literature, 1971-72; Willamette University, assistant professor of French, 1973-76; Johns Hopkins University Press, Philosophy and Literature, co-editor, 1982-2002, editor emeritus, 2002-. **Publications:** Voltaire and Camus: The Limits of Reason and the Awareness of Absurdity, 1975; Montaigne in Dialogue: Censorship and Defensive Writing, Architecture and Friendship, the Self and the Other, 1987; We Only Know Men: The Rescue of Jews in France During the Holocaust, 2007. EDITOR: (and contrib.) An Inimitable Example: The Case for the Princesse de Clèves, 1992; Approaches to Teaching Montaigne's Essays, 1993; Jewish Resistance to the Nazis, 2012. Contributor of articles to journals. **Address:** Department of Foreign Languages & Literatures, Whitman College, 345 Boyer Ave., Walla Walla, WA 99362, U.S.A. **Online address:** henrypg@whitman.edu

HENRY, Patti Callahan. American (born United States) **Genres:** Novels. **Career:** Clinical nurse specialist and writer. **Publications:** NOVELS: Losing the Moon, 2004; Where the River Runs, 2005; When Light Breaks, 2006; Between the Tides, 2007; The Art of Keeping Secrets, 2008; Driftwood Summer, 2009. **Address:** c/o Kimberly Whalen, Trident Media Group, 41 Madison Ave., 36th Fl., New York, NY 10010, U.S.A.

HENRY, Paul. Welsh/British (born England), b. 1959?. **Genres:** Poetry. **Career:** University of Glamorgan, lecturer in creative writing. Writer and singer. **Publications:** POETRY: Time Pieces, 1991; Captive Audience, 1996; The Milk Thief, 1998; The Slipped Leash, 2002; The Breath of Sleeping Boys and Other Poems, 2004; Ingrid's Husband, 2007; The Brittle Sea, 2010; Mari d'Ingrid; The Black Guitar, forthcoming. Contributor to periodicals. **Address:** c/o Author Mail, Seren Books, 57 Nolton St., Bridgend, CF31 3AE, Wales. **Online address:** enquiries@paulhenrywales.co.uk

HENRY, Stuart (Dennis). American/British (born England), b. 1949. **Genres:** Criminology/True Crime, Public/Social Administration, Sociology, Business/Trade/Industry, Politics/Government. **Career:** University of London, Institute of Psychiatry, Addiction Research Unit, research sociologist, 1975-78; University of Middlesex, Centre for Occupational and Community Research, research fellow, 1978-79; Nottingham Polytechnic, senior lecturer in social studies, 1979-83; Old Dominion University, assistant professor of sociology and criminal justice, 1984-87; Eastern Michigan University, associate professor, 1987-92, professor of sociology and criminal justice, 1992-98, Criminal Justice Program, coordinator; Critical Criminologist, co-editor, 1997-2000; Valparaiso University, Department of sociology, professor and chair, 1998-99; Wayne State University, College of Lifelong Learning, director and associate dean, 1999-2002, College of Urban, Labor and Metropolitan Affairs, Department of Interdisciplinary Studies, professor and chair, 2002-06; San Diego State University, School of Public Affairs, professor of criminal justice, 2006-10, director, 2006-10; University of Kent, visiting professor of criminology, 2008-; University of Texas, Arlington, Interdisciplinary Studies Program, professor and director, 2010-. Writer. **Publications:** (With D. Robinson) Self-Help and Health: Mutual Aid for Modern Problems, 1977; The Hidden Economy: The Context and Control of Borderline Crime, 1978; Private Justice: Toward Integrated Theorizing in the Sociology of Law, 1983; (with R. Cantor and S. Rayner) Making Markets: An Interdisciplinary Perspective on Economic Exchange, 1992; (with E.H. Pfuhl) The Deviance Process, 3rd ed., 1993; (with W.J. Einstadter) Criminological Theory: An Analysis of its Underlying Assumptions, 1995, 2nd ed., 2006; (with D. Milovanovic) Constitutive Criminology: Beyond Postmodernism, 1996; (with M. Lanier) Essential Criminology, 1998, 3rd ed., 2009; (with R. Cantor and S. Rayner) Markets, Distribution, and Exchange after Societal Cataclysm, 2001. EDITOR: Informal Institutions: Alternative Networks in the Corporate State in UK as Can I Have It in Cash?, 1981; The Informal Economy, vol. CDXCIII: The Annals of the American Academy of Political and Social Science, 1987; (with R. Eaton) Degrees of Deviance: Student Accounts of Their Deviant Behavior, 1990, 2nd ed., 1999; (with L.A. Ferman and L.E. Berndt) Work beyond Employment in Advanced Capitalist Countries: Classic and Contemporary Perspectives on the Informal Economy, vol. I: Concepts, Evidence, and Measurement, vol. II: Revisions and Criticism, 1993; Social Control: Aspects of Non-State Justice, 1994; Employee Dismissal: Justice at Work, 1994; Inside Jobs, 1994, rev. ed. as Careers in Criminal Justice: The Inside Story, 2001; (with W. Einstadter) The Criminology Theory Reader, 1998; (with D. Milovarovic) Constitutive Criminology at Work: Applications to Crime and Justice, 1999; (with W.G. Hinkle) School Violence, 2000; (with M. Lanier) What Is Crime? Controversy Over the Nature of Crime and What To Do About It, 2001; (with M. Lanier) The Essential Criminology Reader, 2006; (with T. Augsburg) Politics of Interdisciplinary Studies: Essays on Transformations in American Undergraduate Programs, 2009; (with S.A. Lukas) Recent Developments in Criminological Theory: Toward Disciplinary Diversity and Theoretical Integration, 2009; Social Deviance, 2009; (with M. Lanier) Essential Criminology, 2010. Contributor to periodicals. Works appear in anthologies. **Address:** Interdisciplinary Studies, School of Urban and Public Affairs, University of Texas, Rm. 501A, University Hall, PO Box 19588, Arlington, TX 76019-0588, U.S.A. **Online address:** stuart.henry@uta.edu

HENRY, Sue. American (born United States), b. 1940. **Genres:** Mystery/Crime/Suspense, Novels, Young Adult Fiction. **Career:** University of Alaska, instructor in writing, now retired; education administrator and grant writer. Writer. **Publications:** ALASKA MYSTERY SERIES: Murder on the Iditarod Trail, 1991; Termination Dust, 1995; Sleeping Lady: An Alex Jensen Mystery, 1996; Death Takes Passage: An Alex Jansen Alaska Mystery, 1997; Deadfall: An Alaska Mystery, 1998; Murder on the Yukon Quest: An Alaska Mystery,

1999; Beneath the Ashes: An Alaska Mystery, 2000; Dead North: An Alaska Mystery, 2001; Cold Company: An Alaska Mystery, 2002; Death Trap: An Alaska Mystery, 2003; Murder at Five Finger Light: A Jessie Arnold Mystery, 2005; Degrees of Separation: A Jessie Arnold Mystery, 2008; Cold As Ice, 2010. MAXIE AND STRETCH MYSTERY SERIES: The Serpents Trail: A Maxie and Stretch Mystery, 2004; The Tooth of Time: A Maxie and Stretch Mystery, 2006; The Refuge: A Maxie and Stretch Mystery, 2007; End of the Road: A Maxie and Stretch Mystery, 2009. **Address:** c/o Author Mail, Avon Books, 10 E 53rd St., New York, NY 10022, U.S.A.

HENSLEY, Dennis. American (born United States), b. 1964. **Genres:** Novels, Film, Gay And Lesbian Issues. **Career:** Detour Magazine, columnist. Journalist. **Publications:** Misadventures in the (213), 1998; Screening Party, 2002. Contributor to periodicals. **Address:** HarperCollins Publishers, 10 E 53rd St., New York, NY 10022-5244, U.S.A. **Online address:** dhensley@aol.com

HENSLEY, William L. Iggiagruk. American (born United States), b. 1941?. **Genres:** Autobiography/Memoirs. **Career:** Northwest Alaska Native Association (NANA) Regional Corp., founder; Alaska Federation of Natives, director, executive director, president, cochair; Alaska State Legislature, representative, senator; Alyeska Pipeline Service Co., manager of federal government relations. Writer. **Publications:** Fifty Miles from Tomorrow: A Memoir of Alaska and the Real People, 2009. **Address:** PO Box 110274, Anchorage, AR 99511-0274, U.S.A. **Online address:** aglak@williehensley.com

HENTOFF, Nat(han Irving). American (born United States), b. 1925. **Genres:** Novels, Young Adult Fiction, Civil Liberties/Human Rights, Music, Social Commentary, Autobiography/Memoirs, History, Photography, Photography. **Career:** WMEX (radio station), writer, producer and announcer, 1944-53; Sorbonne, Fulbright fellow, 1950; Down Beat Magazine, columnist, 1952, associate editor, 1953-57; Village Voice, columnist, 1957-; New Yorker, staff writer, 1960-86; Washington Post, columnist, 1984-2000; Washington Times, columnist, 2000-; New York University, adjunct associate professor; United Media Newspaper Syndicate, columnist; Legal Times, columnist; editor, publisher, columnist; The Jazz Review, co-founder, co-editor, through 1961; Free Inquiry, columnist; Wall Street Journal, columnist; Jazz Times, columnist; WorldNetDaily.com, contributing columnist, 2008-; Cato Institute, senior fellow, 2009. **Publications:** The Jazz Life, 1961; The Peace Agitator, 1963; The New Equality, 1964; Jazz Country, 1965; Call the Keeper: A Novel, 1966; Our Children Are Dying, 1966; A Doctor Among the Addicts, 1968; I'm Really Dragged but Nothing Gets Me Down, 1968; Onwards!: A Novel, 1968; Journey into Jazz, 1968; A Political Life: The Education of John V. Lindsay, 1969; (intro.) Black Anti-Semitism and Jewish Racism, 1969; In the Country of Ourselves, 1971; (co-author) State Secrets: Police Surveillance in America, 1974; The Jazz Life, 1975; This School is Driving Me Crazy: A Novel, 1976; Jazz Is, 1976; Does Anybody Give a Damn?: On Education, 1977; The First Freedom: The Tumultuous History of Free Speech in America, 1980; (foreword) Giants of Black Music, 1980; Does This School Have Capital Punishment?, 1981; Blues for Charlie Darwin, 1982; The Day They Came to Arrest the Book: A Novel, 1982; (intro.) Live at the Village Vanguard, 1982; The Man from Internal Affairs, 1983; (with T. Keefe and H. Levine) The 1984 Calendar: An American History, 1983; (intro.) Jazzmen, 1985; Boston Boy: A Memoir, 1986; American Heroes: In and Out of School, 1987; Indivisible Fight for Life, 1987; John Cardinal O'Connor: At the Storm Center of a Changing American Catholic Church, 1988; (intro.) Jazz Giants, 1988; Free Speech for Me-But Not for Thee: How the American Left and Right Relentlessly Censor Each Other, 1992; Listen to the Stories: Nat Hentoff on Jazz and Country Music, 1995; Speaking Freely: A Memoir, 1997; Living the Bill of Rights: How to Be an Authentic American, 1998; (co-author) Is There a Duty to Die?: And Other Essays in Bio-Ethics, 2000; (intro.) Remembering Bix: A Memoir of the Jazz Age, 2000; The Nat Hentoff Reader, 2001; The War on the Bill of Rights and the Gathering Resistance, 2003; (contrib.) Phil Stern: A Life's Work, 2003; American Music Is!, 2004; (with W. Smith and M. McFadden) Insisting on Life, 2005; At the Jazz Band Ball: Sixty Years on the Jazz Scene, 2010. EDITOR: (with N. Shapiro) Hear Me Talkin' to Ya, 1955; (with N. Shapiro) The Jazz Makers, 1957; (with A.J. McCarthy) Jazz: New Perspectives on the History of Jazz by Twelve of the World's Foremost Jazz Critics and Scholars, 1959; The Essays of A.J. Muste, 1967. **Address:** Cato Institute, 1000 Massachusetts Ave. NW, Washington, DC 20001-5403, U.S.A.

HEPER, Metin. Turkish (born Turkey), b. 1940. **Genres:** History, Politics/Government, Translations. **Career:** Middle East Technical University, assistant professor, 1970-74; Bogazici University, assistant professor, 1974-76, associate professor, 1976-81, professor of public administration, 1981-88, associate chair, 1982-85, department head, 1985-88, Faculty of Economics and Administrative Sciences, associate dean, 1983-85; Harvard University, research associate, 1977-78, visiting professor, research fellow; University of Connecticut, visiting professor, 1981-82; University of Manchester, Simon Senior research fellow, 1986-87; Bilkent University, professor of political science and public administration and chairperson of department, 1988-98, 2002-, Center for Turkish Politics and History, director, 1998-, Faculty of Economics, Administrative and Social Sciences, associate dean, 1988-89, dean, 1996-98, 2005-10, provost, 2010-; Princeton University, visiting professor and research fellow, 1995-96; Brandeis University, Madeleine Haas Russell visiting professor of non-Western and comparative politics, 2003-04. Writer. **Publications:** Decision-Making in the Middle East Technical University, 1973; (with C.L. Kim and S. Pai) Role of Bureaucracy and Regime Types: A Comparative Study of Turkish and Korean Higher Civil Servants, 1977; Gecekondu Policy in Turkey: An Evaluation, with a Case Study of Rumelihisarüstü Squatter Area in Istanbul, 1978; (with A.U. Berkman) Development Administration in Turkey, 1980; The State Tradition in Turkey, 1985; Historical Dictionary of Turkey, 1994, (with N.B. Criss) rev. ed., 2009; Ismet Inönü: The Making of a Turkish Statesman, 1998; State and Kurds in Turkey: The Question of Assimilation, 2008. EDITOR AND CONTRIBUTOR: Turkey: Past Achievement and Future Prospects, 1983; (with I. Raphaeli) Islam and Politics in the Modern Middle East, 1984; Dilemmas of Decentralization, 1986; Democracy and Local Government, 1987; The State and Public Bureaucracies, 1987; (with A. Evin) The State, Military and Democracy, 1988; Local Government in Turkey, 1989; (with J. Landau) Political Parties and Democracy in Turkey, 1991; Strong State and Economic Interest Groups, 1991; (with A. Oncu and H. Kramer) Turkey and the West, 1993; (with Evin) Politics in the Third Turkish Republic, 1994; (with B. Rockman and A. Kazancigil) Institutions and Democratic Statecraft, 1997; (with S. Sayari) Political Leaders and Democracy in Turkey, 2002; (with B. Rubin) Political Parties in Turkey, 2002. UNTRANSLATED WORKS: Kisa âmme idaresi bibliyografyasi, 1958-1966, 1966; Modernleşme ve bürokrasi, 1973; Burokratik Yonetim Gelenegi (Bureaucratic Ruling Tradition), 1974; Tü rk kamu bürokrasisinde gelenekçilik ve modernleşme: siyaset sosyoloji[si] açisindan bir inceleme, 1977; Turkiye'de Kent Gocmeni ve Burokratik Orgutler (Urban Migrant and Bureaucratic Organizations in Turkey), 1983. Contributor to books and journals. **Address:** Department of Political Science, Bilkent University, Rm. EA-G16, Engineering Faculty Bldg., Ankara, 06800, Turkey. **Online address:** heper@bilkent.edu.tr

HEPPENHEIMER, T. A. *See* **HEPPENHEIMER, Thomas A.**

HEPPENHEIMER, Thomas A. (T. A. Heppenheimer). American (born United States), b. 1947. **Genres:** Air/Space Topics, Physics, Technology, History, Engineering, Humanities. **Career:** Forum for the Advancement of Students in Science and Technology, technical vice president, 1971-73; Science Applications Inc., scientist, 1972-73; Rockwell International Corp., technical staff in systems engineering, 1973-74; California Institute of Technology, research fellow in planetary science, 1974-75; Max Planck Institute for Nuclear Physics, Alexander von Humboldt research fellow, 1976-78; K.R.G. Inc., vice president, 1978-82; freelance writer, 1978-; University of California, instructor, 1988-90; American Institute of Aeronautics and Astronautics, associate fellow. Writer. **Publications:** Colonies in Space, 1977; Toward Distant Suns, 1979; The Real Future, 1983; The Man-Made Sun: The Quest for Fusion Power, 1984; Superconductivity: Research, Applications and Potential Markets, 1987; The Coming Quake: Science and Trembling on the California Earthquake Frontier, 1988; (ed. and contrib.) Anti Submarine Warfare: The Threat, The Strategy, The Solution, 1989, 2nd ed., 1992; Hypersonic Technologies and the National Aerospace Plane, 1990; Air Traffic Control, 1995; Turbulent Skies: The History of Commercial Aviation, 1995; Countdown: A History of Space Flight, 1997; The Space Shuttle Decision: NASA's Search for a Reusable Space Vehicle, 1999; A Brief History of Flight: From Balloons to Mach 3 and Beyond, 2001; History of the Space Shuttle, vol. I: Development of the Space Shuttle, 1965-72, vol. II: Development of the Space Shuttle, 1972-81, 2002; First Flight: The Wright Brothers and the Invention of the Airplane, 2003; Flight: A History of Aviation in Photographs, 2004; Facing the Heat Barrier: A History of Hypersonics, 2006. Contributor to books and journals. **Address:** Center for Space Science, 11040 Blue Allium Ave., Fountain Valley, CA 92708, U.S.A. **Online address:** taheppenheimer@yahoo.com

HEPPNER, Cheryl M. American (born United States), b. 1951. **Genres:** Autobiography/Memoirs, E-books, Biography. **Career:** Handley Library, staff, 1977-85; Cheryl A. Heppner Public Relations, public relations consultant, 1979-91; Virginia Department for the Deaf and Hard of Hearing, outreach specialist, 1986-91; Northern Virginia Resource Center for Deaf and Hard of Hearing Persons, executive director, 1991-; Telecommunications for the Deaf Inc., vice-president, 1993; Shenandoah Valley Independent Living Center, co-founder. Writer. **Publications:** Seeds of Disquiet: One Deaf Woman's Experience, 1992. **Address:** Northern Virginia Resource Center, for Deaf and Hard of Hearing Persons, 3951 Pender Dr., Ste. 130, Fairfax, VA 22030-6035, U.S.A. **Online address:** cheppner@nvrc.org

HEPPNER, P(uncky) Paul. American (born United States), b. 1951. **Genres:** Psychology, Medicine/Health. **Career:** University of Minnesota, counselor, 1976; Tomah Veterans Administration Hospital, psychology trainee, 1977; University of Nebraska, counselor, 1977-78; Colorado State University, intern, 1979; University of Missouri, assistant professor, 1979-84, associate professor, 1984-88, professor of psychology, 1988-, senior staff psychologist in counseling services, 1979-88, associate chair of department, 1990-98, Frederick A. Middlebush professor of social sciences, 1990-95, Counseling Center, adjunct psychologist, 1991-; University of London, Goldsmith's College, visiting fellow in psychology, 1987; Counseling Psychologist, editor, 1997-2002. **Publications:** (Ed.) Pioneers in Counseling and Human Development: Personal and Professional Perspectives, 1990; (with D. Kivlighan and B.E. Wampold) Research Design in Counseling, 1992, 3rd ed., 2008; (with N.A. Fouad and N. Hansen) First and Second Generations in the Counseling Profession: Personal and Professional Perspectives, 2002; (with M.J. Heppner) Writing and Publishing Your Thesis, Dissertation, and Research: A Guide for Students in the Helping Professions, 2004. Works appear in anthologies. Contributor to journals. **Address:** Department of Educational Psychology, University of Missouri, 16 Hill Hall, Columbia, MO 65211, U.S.A. **Online address:** heppnerp@missouri.edu

HEPWORTH, Noel P. British (born England), b. 1934?. **Genres:** Money/Finance, Politics/Government, Economics. **Career:** London Borough of Croydon, director of finance, 1972-80; Chartered Institute of Public Finance and Accountancy, director, 1980-96, now retired; Institute of Public Finance, chairman, 1996-. Writer. **Publications:** Finance of Local Government, 1970, 7th ed., 1984; (with J. Odling-Smee and A. Grey) Housing Rents, Costs, and Subsidies, 1978; The Reform of Local Government, 1985; What Future for Local Government, 1988. **Address:** NLA Tower, 12/16 Addiscombe Rd., Croydon, SR CR0 0XT, England.

HERALD, Kathleen. *See* **PEYTON, K. M.**

HERBACH, Geoff. American (born United States), b. 1969?. **Genres:** Novels, Young Adult Fiction, Sports/Fitness. **Career:** Minnesota State University, faculty of creative writing; Lit 6, performer and radio playwright; Electric Arc Radio Show, performer. **Publications:** The Miracle Letters of T. Rimberg (novel), 2008; Stupid Fast, 2011; Nothing Special, 2012. **Address:** Sourcebooks Fire, 18 W 18th St., New York, NY 10011, U.S.A. **Online address:** geoff.herbach@gmail.com

HERBERT, Brian. American (born United States), b. 1947. **Genres:** Mystery/Crime/Suspense, Science Fiction/Fantasy, Humor/Satire, Novels, Biography. **Career:** Crowell Collier McMillan, sales manager, 1966; Fireman's Fund America, underwriter, 1968-73; Insurance Co. of North America, underwriter, 1973-77; Stanley Scott & Co., broker, 1977-84. **Publications:** HUMOR: Classic Comebacks, 1981; Incredible Insurance Claims, 1982. SCIENCE FICTION/FANTASY NOVELS: Sidney's Comet, 1983; The Garbage Chronicles, 1985; Sudanna, Sudanna, 1985; (with F. Herbert) Man of Two Worlds, 1986; Prisoners of Arionn, 1987; The Race for God, 1990; (with M. Landis) Memorymakers, 1991; (with M. Landis) Blood on the Sun, 1996; Timeweb, 2006. SCIENCE FICTION/FANTASY NOVELS WITH K.J. ANDERSON: Dune: House Atreides, 1999; Dune: House Harkonnen, 2000; Dune: House Corrino, 2001; Dune: The Butlerian Jihad, 2002; Dune: The Machine Crusade, 2003; Dune: The Battle of Corrin, 2004; The Road to Dune, 2005; Hunters of Dune, 2006; Web and The Stars, 2007; Sandworms of Dune, 2007; Paul of Dune, 2008; The Winds of Dune, 2009; The Throne of Dune; Leto of Dune, 2011; Tales of Dune, 2011; The Sisterhood of Dune, 2012. NON FICTION: (with F. Herbert) The Notebooks of Frank Herbert's Dune, 1988; Dreamer of Dune: The Biography of Frank Herbert, 2003; The Forgotten Heroes: The Heroic Story of the United States, 2004; Merchant Marine, 2004; Webdancers, 2008. EDITOR: The Songs of Muad'Dib (collection of F. Herbert's poetry), 1992; Never as It Seems, 1992; A Bird of Passage, 1995. OTHERS: (intro.) Dune Messiah, 2008; (with K.J. Anderson) Hellhole, 2011. Contributor of articles to periodicals. **Address:** c/o Robert Gottlieb, Trident Media Group, 41 Madison Ave., 36th Fl., New York, NY 10010, U.S.A.

HERBERT, Gilbert. Israeli/South African (born South Africa), b. 1924. **Genres:** Architecture, Social Sciences, Art/Art History. **Career:** Architectural consultant, 1947-68; University of the Witwatersrand, lecturer in architecture, 1947-61; South African Architectural Record, associate editor, 1949-60; University of Adelaide, reader in architecture and town planning, 1961-68, acting dean, 1964; Technion: Israel Institute of Technology, associate professor, 1968-72, professor, 1972-92, Faculty of Architecture and Town Planning, dean, 1973-74, Architectural Heritage Research Centre, founder and chair, Mary Hill Swope professor of architecture, 1974-92, professor emeritus, 1992-; Bezalel Academy of Art and Design, adjunct professor, 1970-72, 1976-78. **Publications:** The Synthetic Vision of Walter Gropius, 1959; Martienssen and the International Style: The Modern Movement in South African Architecture, 1975; Pioneers of Prefabrication: The British Contribution in the Nineteenth Century, 1978; The Dream of the Factory-Made House: Walter Gropius and Konrad Wachsmann, 1984; (with S. Sosnovsky) Bauhaus on the Carmel and the Crossroads of the Empire: Architecture and Planning in Haifa during the British Mandate, 1993; (with I. Heinze-Greenberg) The Beginnings of Modern Architecture in Israel: The First Power Stations, 1921-1932, 1996; The Search for Synthesis: Selected Writings on Architecture and Planning, 1997; Reshit ha-adrikhalut ha-modernit be-Erets Yiśrael: taḥanot ha-koaḥ ha-rishonot, 1921-1932, 1997; (with M. Donchin) Speculations on a Black Hole: Adler & Sullivan and the Planning of the Chicago Auditorium Building, 1998; (with I. Heinze-Greenberg and S. Sosnovsky) In Search of Excellence: The Architecture and Building Projects of the Electric Industry in the Land of Israel 1921-1942, 2003; Symbols of a New Land: Architects and the Design of the Passenger Ships of Zim, 2006. **Address:** Faculty of Architecture & Town Planning, Technion Israel Institute of Technology, Haifa, 32000, Israel. **Online address:** herbert2@bezeqint.net

HERBERT, Ivor. British/South African (born South Africa), b. 1925. **Genres:** Novels, Plays/Screenplays, Sports/Fitness, Biography, Travel/Exploration, Autobiography/Memoirs. **Career:** Charterhouse Finance Corp., executive, 1949-54; London Evening News, staff writer, 1954-66; Sunday Express, contract contributor, 1973-81; Mail on Sunday, chief travel writer and racing editor, 1981-2002; Equus Productions, partner. **Publications:** Eastern Windows, 1953; Arkle: The Story of a Champion, 1966; Point-to-Point: A Story of Steeplechasing, 1967; The Queen Mother's Horses, 1967; (with P. Smyly) The Winter Kings, 1968; The Way to the Top, 1969; Over Our Dead Bodies! (novel), 1972; The Diamond Diggers: South Africa 1866 to the 1970's, 1972; (with J. Cusack) Scarlet Fever: A Lifetime with Horses, 1972; Winter's Tale: A Study of a Stable, 1974; Red Rum: Ivor Herbert's Full and Extraordinary Story of a Horse of Courage, 1974; Come Riding, 1975; The Filly (novel), 1977; Six at the Top, 1977; Spot the Winner: Inside Racing with Whitbread, 1978; Longacre, 1978; (ed.) Horse Racing: The Complete Guide to the World of the Turf, 1980; (with J. O'Brien) Vincent O'Brien's Great Horses, 1984; Revolting Behaviour, 1987; Thoroughbreds, 1987; Herbert's Travels, 1987; (with M. Rimell) Reflections on Racing, 1989; Spot the Winner, 1990; (with R. Anne) Riding through My Life, 1991. Contributor of articles to periodicals. **Address:** The Old Rectory, Bradenham, High Wycombe, BK HP14 4HD, England.

HERBERT, James. British (born England), b. 1943. **Genres:** Novels, Horror, Science Fiction/Fantasy, Biography, Graphic Novels, Mystery/Crime/Suspense, Adult Non-fiction, Young Adult Fiction, Young Adult Fiction. **Career:** John Collings Advertising, staff, 1963-66; Ayer, Barker, Hegemann, art director in advertising, 1966-69, group head, 1969-71, associate director, 1971-77; writer, 1971-. **Publications:** The Rats, 1974; The Fog, 1975; The Survivor, 1976; Fluke, 1977; The Spear, 1978; Lair, 1979; The Dark, 1980; The Jonah, 1981; Shrine, 1983; Domain, 1984; Moon, 1985; The Magic Cottage, 1986; Sepulchre, 1987; Haunted, 1988; Creed, 1990; Portent, 1992; Dark Places (non-fiction), 1993; The City (graphic novel), 1993; The Ghosts of Sleath, 1994; '48, 1996; Others, 1999; Once..., 2001; Nobody True, 2003; The Secret of Crickley Hall, 2006; Ash, 2010. BIOGRAPHIES: By Horror Haunted, 1992; Devil in the Dark, 2003. **Address:** c/o Bruce Hunter, David Higham Associates, 5-8 Lower John St., Golden Sq., London, GL W1F 9HA, England. **Online address:** info@james-herbert.co.uk

HERBERT, Sandra (Swanson). American (born United States), b. 1942.

Genres: Sciences, Biography, History. **Career:** Smithsonian Institution, visiting curator, 1967-68; University of Maryland-College Park, lecturer in history, 1969-72; University of Maryland-Baltimore County, assistant professor, 1973-78, associate professor, 1978-86, professor of history, 1986-, now professor emeritus, Department of History, chair, 1995, Program on Human Context of Science and Technology, director, 2000. Writer. **Publications:** EDITOR: (and intro.) The Red Notebook of Charles Darwin, 1980; (co-ed.) Charles Darwin's Notebooks, 1836-1844, 1987. OTHERS: Charles Darwin, Geologist, 2005; Charles Darwin and the Question of Evolution: A Brief History with Documents, 2011. Contributor to journals and periodicals. **Address:** Department of History, University of Maryland, 726 Administration Bldg., 1000 Hilltop Cir., Baltimore, MD 21250, U.S.A. **Online address:** herbert@umbc.edu

HERBSMAN, Cheryl Renee. American (born United States), b. 1968. **Genres:** Novels. **Career:** Writer. **Publications:** Breathing, 2009. **Address:** CA , U.S.A. **Online address:** cheryl@cherylreneeherbsman.com

HERBST, Jurgen. American/German (born Germany), b. 1928. **Genres:** Education, History, Autobiography/Memoirs. **Career:** Wesleyan University, instructor, 1958-59, assistant professor, 1959-65, associate professor of history, 1965-66; Yale University, visiting lecturer, 1962-64; University of Wisconsin, Department of Educational Policy Studies, professor of educational policy studies and of history, 1966-94, professor emeritus, 1994-. Writer. **Publications:** The German Historical School in American Scholarship, 1965; The History of American Education, 1973; From Crisis to Crisis: American College Government, 1636-1819, 1982; And Sadly Teach: Teacher Education and Professionalization in American Culture, 1989; The Once and Future School: Three Hundred and Fifty Years of American Secondary Education, 1996; Requiem for a German Past: A Boyhood among the Nazis, 1999; School Choice and School Governance: A Historical Study of the United States and Germany, 2006; Women Pioneers of Public Education: How Culture Came to the Wild West, 2008. EDITOR: Our Country, 1963; (co-ed.) History of Elementary School Teaching and Curriculum, vol. I, 1990; (co-ed.) Aspects of Antiquity in the History of Education, vol. III, 1992; (with H. Geitz and J. Heideking) German Influences on Education in the United States to 1917, 1995; (with J. Heideking and M. Depaepe) Mutual Influences on Education: Germany and the United States in the Twentieth Century, 1997. Contributor to magazines. **Address:** Department of Educational Policy Studies, University of Wisconsin, 1000 Bascom Mall, Madison, WI 53706, U.S.A. **Online address:** jherbst22@compuserve.com

HERBST, Phil(ip H.). American (born United States), b. 1944. **Genres:** Language/Linguistics, Reference, Social Sciences, Politics/Government. **Career:** State University of New York College, instructor in anthropology, 1971-74; Follett Corp., American Publishers Co., educational sales representative, 1974-75; Chicago Daily News/Sun Times, educational consultant, 1975-79; freelance editor, 1979-81; American Society of Clinical Pathologists Press, product development editor, 1981-85; Scott, Foresman/Little, Brown, project editor, 1985-90; New Trier Extension, instructor in anthropology, 1990; Harold Washington College, lecturer in English, 1995-96; Evanston Township High School, instructor in English, 1996-97. **Publications:** The Multicultural Dictionary: A Usage Guide to Ethnic and Racial Words, 1993; The Color of Words: An Encyclopaedic Dictionary of Ethnic Bias in the United States, 1997; Wimmin, Wimps and Wallflowers: An Encyclopaedic Dictionary of Gender and Sexual Orientation Bias in the United States, 2001; Power of Words, Teaching Tolerance, 2001; Talking Terrorism: A Dictionary of the Loaded Language of Political Violence, 2003. Contributor of articles to periodicals. **Address:** 2415 Central St., Ste. D, Evanston, IL 60201-1413, U.S.A. **Online address:** tkherbst@earthlink.net

HERDING, Klaus. German (born Germany), b. 1939. **Genres:** Art/Art History, Social Commentary, Adult Non-fiction, Translations. **Career:** National Gallery, assistant, 1968-70; Technical University of Berlin, research assistant, 1971-74; Free University of Berlin, assistant professor of art history, 1974; University of Hamburg, professor of art history, 1975-93, head of faculty of cultural sciences, 1987-88; L'Ecole des Hautes Etudes, director of studies, 1988-90; Getty Center of the History of Art and the Humanities, research fellow, 1992-93; University of Frankfurt, professor of art history, 1993-2005, head of faculty of cultural sciences, 1994-95, professor emeritus, 1996-. Writer. **Publications:** Pierre Puget: Das Bildnerische Werk, 1970; Propylaen Kunstgeschichte, 1970; (with H.E. Mittig) Kunst und Alltag im NS-System: Albert Speers Berliner Strassenlaternen, 1975; Egalitaet und Autoritaet in

Courbets Landschaftsmalerei, 1975; Realismus als Widerspruch: d. Wirklichkeit in Courbets Malerei, 1978; (with G. Otto) Karikaturen: Nervoese Auffangsorgane des Inneren und aeusseren Lebens, 1980; Malerei und Theorie: Das Courbet-Colloquium, 1979; Staedtische Galerie im Staedelschen Kunstinstitut Frankfurt am Main, 1980; La Revolution Francaise et l'Europe, 1989; (with R. Reichardt) Die Bildpublizistik der Französcischen Revolution, 1989; Im Zeichen der Aufklärung: Studien zur Moderne, 1989; Courbet: To Venture Independence, 1991; Pablo Picasso: Les Demoiselles d'Avignon: die Herausforderung der Avantgarde, 1992; Changements et continuité dans la création artistique des révolutions politiques: Actes, 1992; Aufklärung anstelle von Andacht: Kulturwissenschaftliche Dimensionen Bildender Kunst, 1997; Freuds Leonardo: Eine Auseinandersetzung mit psychoanalytischen Theorien der Gegenwart, 1998; Psychische Energien Bildender Kunst: Festschrift Klaus Herding, 2002; Kunstwerke der Goethe-Universitaet, 2002; Pathos, Affekt, Gefuehl: Die Emotionen in den Kuensten, 2004; (with G. Gehrig) Orte des Unheimlichen: die Faszination verborgenen Grauens in Literatur und bildender Kunst, 2006; (with A. Krause-Wahl) Wie sich Gefühle Ausdruck verschaffen, 2007; 1968: Kunst, Kunstgeschichte, Politik, 2008; (with H. Schmidt) Irene Bisang, 2008; Handbuch psychoanalytischer Begriffe für die Kunstwissenschaft, 2009. EDITOR/CO-EDITOR: (with W. Hofmann) Courbet und Deutschland, 1978; Realismus als Widerspruch, 1978; Das Courbet-Colloquium im Staedel, 1980; Courbet, Gustave, 1819-1877: Les Voyages Secrets de Monsieur Courbet: Unbekannte Reiseskizzen aus Baden, Spa und Biarritz: Staatliche Kunsthalle Baden-Baden, 1984; (trans. and intro.) Proudhon's Art Theory, 1988; (with M. Hollein) Courbet - A Dream of Modern Art, 2010. **Address:** Kunstgeschichtliches Institut, Hausener Weg 120, 3. OG, Frankfurt, D-60489, Germany. **Online address:** herding@kunst.uni-frankfurt.de

HERENDEEN, Ann Wyman. American (born United States), b. 1955?. **Genres:** Novels. **Career:** Writer, media planner and librarian. **Publications:** Phyllida and the Brotherhood of Philander: A Novel, 2008; Pride/Prejudice: A Novel of Mr. Darcy, Elizabeth Bennet, and Their Other Loves, 2010. **Address:** U.S.A. **Online address:** ann@annherendeen.com

HERF, Jeffrey. American (born United States), b. 1947. **Genres:** History, Politics/Government, Military/Defense/Arms Control, Biography. **Career:** Ohio University, associate professor of history; University of Maryland, Department of History, professor. Writer. **Publications:** Reactionary Modernism: Technology, Culture, and Politics in Weimar and the Third Reich, 1984; War By Other Means: Soviet Power, West German Resistance, and the Battle of the Euromissiles, 1991; East German Communists and the Jewish Question: The Case of Paul Merker, 1994; Divided Memory: The Nazi Past in the Two Germanys, 1997; Jewish Enemy: Nazi Propaganda During World War II and the Holocaust, 2006; (ed.) Anti-Semitism and Anti-Zionism in Historical Perspective: Convergence and Divergence, 2007; Nazi Propaganda for the Arab World, 2009. **Address:** Department of History, University of Maryland, 2136 Francis Scott Key Hall, College Park, MD 20742-7315, U.S.A. **Online address:** jherf@umd.edu

HERL, Joseph. American (born United States) **Genres:** Politics/Government, Music. **Career:** Concordia University, Department of Music, associate professor of music, 2000-. Writer and musician. **Publications:** Six Hymn Inventions: For Organ, 1997; (ed. with P. Grime) Hymnal Supplement 98 Handbook, 1998; (contrib.) The Hymn Tune Index: A Census of English-Language Hymn Tunes in Printed Sources from 1535 to 1820, 1998; Worship Wars in Early Lutheranism: Choir, Congregation, and Three Centuries of Conflict, 2004. **Address:** Department of Music, Concordia University, 106 Music Ctr., 800 N Columbia Ave., Seward, NE 68434, U.S.A. **Online address:** joseph.herl@cune.edu

HERMAN, Barbara. American (born United States), b. 1945. **Genres:** Philosophy, Ethics, Adult Non-fiction, Humanities, Essays. **Career:** Massachusetts Institute of Technology, assistant professor of philosophy, 1973-80; University of Southern California, visiting assistant professor, 1980-81, assistant professor to professor of philosophy and law, 1981-94; Princeton University, visiting associate professor, 1987; Ethics, associate editor, 1991-94; University of California, Griffin Professor of Philosophy, 1994-2006, professor of law, 2006-. **Publications:** Morality As Rationality: A Study of Kant's Ethics, 1990; The Practice of Moral Judgment, 1993; Screening for Acceptable Risk, 1994; (ed. with A. Reath and C.M. Korsgaard) Reclaiming the History of Ethics: Essays for John Rawls, 1997; (ed.) Lectures On the History of Moral Philosophy, 2000; Moral Literacy, 2007. Contributor to books and journals.

Address: Department of Philosophy, University of California, 405 Hilgard Ave., 385 Charles E. Young Dr., 1242 Law Bldg., Los Angeles, CA 90095, U.S.A. **Online address:** herman@humnet.ucla.edu

HERMAN, Bernard L. American (born United States), b. 1951?. **Genres:** Art/Art History, Local History/Rural Topics, Food And Wine. **Career:** University of Delaware, Department of Art History, professor, chair, Edward F. and Elizabeth Goodman Rosenberg professor; University of Memphis, School of Urban Affairs and Public Policy, faculty; University of North Carolina, adjunct faculty, George B. Tindall distinguished professor of American studies and folklore. Writer. **Publications:** Americo-Liberian Folk Architecture, 1988; The Stolen House: Material Culture, History, and Metaphor in the Early Republic, 1992; (with L.A.D. Cunzo) Historical Archaeology and the Study of American Culture, 1996; (with G.M. Lanier) Everyday Architecture of the Mid-Atlantic: Looking at Buildings and Landscapes, 1997; Town House: Architecture and Material Life in the Early American City, 1785-1830, 2005; Architectural Definitions in Gee's Bend: The Architecture of the Quilt, 2006; (ed.) Thornton Dial: Thoughts on Paper, 2011. **Address:** Department of American Studies, University of North Carolina, 227 Greenlaw Hall, PO Box 3520, Chapel Hill, NC 27599-3520, U.S.A. **Online address:** blherman@email.unc.edu

HERMAN, Didi. British/Canadian (born Canada), b. 1961. **Genres:** Gay And Lesbian Issues, Law, Social Commentary, Ethics, Sex. **Career:** Middlesex University, School of Law, lecturer, 1990-91; Keele University, Department of Law, lecturer, 1992-95, senior lecturer, 1995-97, reader, 1997-98, professor of law and social change, 1998-2004; University of Kent, Law School, professor of law and social change, 2004-. Writer. **Publications:** Rights of Passage: Struggles for Lesbian and Gay Legal Equality, 1994; The Antigay Agenda: Orthodox Vision and the Christian Right, 1997; Sexuality in the Legal Arena, 2000; (with D. Buss) Globalizing Family Values: The Christian Right in International Politics, 2003; (co-ed.) Intersectionality and Beyond: Law, Power, and the Politics of Location, 2008. EDITOR WITH C. STYCHIN: Legal Inversions: Lesbians, Gay Men, and The Politics of Law, 1995; Reflections, New Directions: Gender, Sexuality, and Law, 1999; Law and Sexuality: The Global Arena, 2001; Unfortunate Coincidence: Jews, Jewishness and English Law, 2011. **Address:** Law School, Eliot College, University of Kent, Canterbury, KT CT2 7NS, England. **Online address:** d.herman@kent.ac.uk

HERMAN, Eleanor. American (born United States), b. 1960. **Genres:** History, Sex, Biography, Romance/Historical. **Career:** Nations and Partners for Peace (publication of North Atlantic Treaty Organization), associate publisher. Writer. **Publications:** Sex with Kings: Five Hundred Years of Adultery Power Rivalry and Revenge, 2004; Sex With the Queen: 900 Years of Vile Kings, Virile Lovers and Passionate Politics, 2006; Mistress of the Vatican: The True Story of Olimpia Maidalchini, the Secret Female Pope, 2008; King Peggy: An American Secretary, Her Royal Destiny, and the Inspiring Story of How She Changed an African Village, 2011. Contributor to periodicals. **Address:** c/o Dorian Karchmar, William Morris Agency, 1325 Ave. of Americas, New York, NY 10019, U.S.A. **Online address:** eherman@mistressofthevatican.com

HERMAN, Ellen. American (born United States), b. 1957. **Genres:** History, Psychology, Medicine/Health, Social Sciences, Women's Studies And Issues, Intellectual History. **Career:** Harvard University, social studies faculty; University of Oregon, Department of History, professor. Writer. **Publications:** The Romance of American Psychology: Political Culture in the Age of Experts, 1940-1970, 1995; Psychiatry, Psychology, and Homosexuality, 1995; Kinship by Design: A History of Adoption in the Modern United States, 2008. **Address:** Department of History, University of Oregon, 335 McKenzie Hall, Eugene, OR 97403-1288, U.S.A. **Online address:** eherman@uoregon.edu

HERMAN, John E. American (born United States), b. 1957. **Genres:** History. **Career:** Virginia Commonwealth University, assistant professor, associate professor of Chinese history, 2002-, VCU-Fudan Partnership, director, 2005-, VCU-China Relations, director, 2005-; Institute for Advanced Study, School of Historical Studies, faculty, 2010-11; University of Virginia, East Asia Center, associate. Writer. **Publications:** Amid the Clouds and Mist: China's Colonization of Guizhou, 1200-1700, 2007. Contributor to books and periodicals. **Address:** Department of History, Virginia Commonwealth University, 912 W Franklin St., Richmond, VA 23284-2001, U.S.A. **Online address:** jeherman@vcu.edu

HERMAN, Michael. British (born England), b. 1929. **Genres:** Military/

Defense/Arms Control, Education. **Career:** Government Communications Headquarters, intelligence practitioner for Great Britain, 1952-87; Nuffield College, Gwilym Gibbon research fellow, 1987-88, associate, 1988-94; Birmingham University, lecturer, 1992; King's College, lecturer, 1992-95, honorary research fellow; University of Oxford, St. Antony's College, senior associate, 2000-03, Aberystwyth University, departmental fellow, 2001-; Oxford Intelligence Group, director; Keele University, honorary research fellow. Writer. **Publications:** Intelligence Power in Peace and War, 1996; Intelligence Services in the Information Age: Theory and Practice, 2001. Contributor to books. **Address:** Cambridge University Press, 40 W 20th St., New York, NY 10011-4211, U.S.A. **Online address:** mhe24@aol.com

HERMAN, Michelle. American (born United States), b. 1955. **Genres:** Novels, Novellas/Short Stories, Adult Non-fiction. **Career:** Associated Press, reporter, 1976; freelance editor, 1976-84; Ohio State University, Department of English, associate professor of English, 1988-, professor of English, M.F.A. Program in Creative Writing, director, The Journal, co-editor. **Publications:** Missing, 1990; A New and Glorious Life, 1998; Middle of Everything: Memoirs of Motherhood, 2005; Dog, 2005. Works appear in anthologies. Contributor to periodicals. **Address:** Department of English, Ohio State University, 165 Denney Hall, 164 W 17th Ave., Columbus, OH 43210-1326, U.S.A. **Online address:** herman.2@osu.edu

HERMAN, Richard. American (born United States), b. 1939. **Genres:** Mystery/Crime/Suspense, Military/Defense/Arms Control, Literary Criticism And History, Young Adult Fiction. **Career:** U.S. Air Force Academy, assistant professor of geography, 1972-75, chief of operative plans in the Netherlands, 1980-83. Writer. **Publications:** MILITARY AND POLITICAL THRILLERS: The Warbirds, 1989; Force of Eagles, 1990; Firebreak, 1991; Call to Duty, 1993; Dark Wing, 1994; Iron Gate, 1996; The Power Curve, 1997; Against All Enemies, 1998; Edge of Honor, 1999; The Trojan Sea, 2001; The Last Phoenix, 2002; A Far Justice, 2010. **Address:** John Hawkins & Associates Inc., 71 W 23rd St., Ste. 1600, New York, NY 10010, U.S.A.

HERMAN, Stephen L. American (born United States), b. 1946. **Genres:** Education, Physics, Sciences. **Career:** Lee College, teacher of electrical technology; Baytown, teacher of electrical technology; Randolph Technical College, teacher of electrical technology. Writer. **Publications:** (With W.N. Alerich) Industrial Motor Control, 1985, 6th ed., 2010; Electronics for Industrial Electricians, 1985, 3rd ed., 1995; (with B.L. Sparkman) Electricity and Controls for Heating, Ventilating and Air Conditioning, 4th ed., trans. as Electricity and Controls for HVAC/R, 1986, 6th ed., 2009; (with J.R. Duff) Alternating Current Fundamentals, (with J.R. Duff) 3rd ed., 1987, 8th ed., 2011; Practical Problems in Mathematics for Electronic Technicians, (with C.G. Garrard) 4th ed., 1987, 6th ed., 2004; (with R.L. Smith) Electrical Wiring: Industrial, 6th ed., 1987, 13th ed., 2008; Practical Problems in Mathematics for Electricians, (with C.G. Garrard) 4th ed., 1987, 8th ed., 2011; (with W.N. Alerich) Industrial Motor Control, 1990, 6th ed., 2010; Delmar's Standard Textbook of Electricity, 1993, 5th ed., 2010; Experiments in Electricity: For Use with the Lab-Volt EMS Training System, 1993, 3rd ed., 2004; (with R.L. Smith) Electrical Wiring Industrial, 9th ed., 1996, 14th ed., 2010; Electrical Studies for Trades, 1997, 4th ed., 2009; (with D.E. Singleton) Delmar's Standard Guide to Transformers, 1997, 3rd ed., 2004; Electrician's Technical Reference: Theory and Calculations, 1998; (with W.N. Alerich) Electric Motor Control, 6th ed., 1998, 9th ed., 2010; Electrician's Technical Reference: Transformers, 1999; Electrician's Technical Reference: Industrial Electronics, 1999; Electrical Transformers and Rotating Machines, 1999, 3rd ed., 2011; Electricity and Controls for HVAC, 2000, 6th ed., 2010; The Complete Lab Manual for Industrial Electricity, 2001, 3rd ed., 2009; Electronics for Electricians, 4th ed., 2002, 6th ed., 2012; Residential Construction Academy: Electrical Principles, 2003, 2nd ed., 2011; The Complete Laboratory Manual for Electricity, 2nd ed., 2003, 3rd ed., 2009; Understanding Motor Controls, 2006, 2nd ed., 2012; Direct Current Fundamentals, 7th ed., 2007, 8th ed., 2011; Instructor's Resource Guide to Accompany Residential Construction Academy: Electrical Principles, 2nd ed., 2011. **Address:** Delmar Cengage Learning, Executive Woods, 5 Maxwell Dr., Clifton Park, NY 12065-2919, U.S.A.

HERMANN, Iselin C. Danish (born Denmark), b. 1959. **Genres:** Novels, Young Adult Fiction. **Career:** V. Folketeateret and Gladsaxe Theatre, instructor assistant, 1979-81; Christian Ejlers publishers, publishing secretary, 1982-84; Forest Books, publishing secretary, 1984-91, editor, co-editor; Brondum/Aschehoug, publishing manager, 1991-97; Danish Institute, Governing Board, staff. **Publications:** (With G. Forester) Prioritaire: A Correspondence

Published by Jean-Luc Foreur, 1998; Vilmer I Vildrede, 2001; Dampe, 2002; Fadul and the Big Blunder as Fadul og hele fadaelsen, 2005. **Address:** c/o Author Mail, Grove/Atlantic Inc., 841 Broadway, 4th Fl., New York, NY 10003, U.S.A.

HERMANN, L. William. See **LICHT, H. William (Bill).**

HERMANN, Nellie. American (born United States), b. 1978. **Genres:** Novels. **Career:** Columbia University Medical School, Program in Narrative Medicine, writing teacher. Writer. **Publications:** The Cure for Grief: A Novel, 2008. **Address:** U.S.A. **Online address:** info@nelliehermann.com

HERMANS, Hubert J. M. Dutch (born Netherlands), b. 1937. **Genres:** Psychology. **Career:** Asthma Center, assistant psychologist and diagnostician, 1963-65; Catholic University of Nijmegen, Psychology Laboratory, staff, 1965-72, associate professor, 1972-80, full-professor, 1980-2002, professor emeritus, 2002-; International Journal for Dialogical Science, chief-editor, 2005-. **Publications:** (With H. Kempen) The Dialogical Self: Meaning as Movement, 1993; (with E. Hermans-Jansen) Self-Narratives: The Construction of Meaning in Psychotherapy, 1995; (ed. with G. Dimaggio) The Dialogical Self in Psychotherapy, 2004; (ed. with Piotr K. Oleś) The Dialogical Self: Theory and Research, 2005; (with A. Hermans-Konopka) Dialogical Self Theory: Positioning and Counter-Positioning in a Globalizing Society, 2010; (ed. with T. Gieser) Handbook of Dialogical Self Theory, 2011. Contributor to periodicals. **Address:** Department of Clinical Psychology and Personality, Catholic University of Nijmegen, PO Box 9104, Nijmegen, 6500 HE, Netherlands. **Online address:** hhermans@psych.kun.nl

HERMES, Jules. American (born United States), b. 1962. **Genres:** Documentaries/Reportage, Biography. **Career:** International Commentary Service, senior writer, 1989-90; F.L.I.P. Writers and Photographers, writer and photographer, 1990-93; Carolrhoda Books Inc., writer and photographer, 1991-95; Global Volunteers, media coordinator, 1995-; American Refugee Committee Intl., public relations director, 1997-. Writer. **Publications:** Children of India, 1993; Children of Micronesia, 1994; Children of Morocco, 1995; The Dalai Lama: A Biography, 1995; Children of Bolivia, 1996; Children of Guatemala, 1997. **Address:** Hermes House Press L.L.C., 1197 Village Cove NE, Atlanta, GA 30319-5308, U.S.A. **Online address:** pr@archq.org

HERMES, Patricia. American (born United States), b. 1936. **Genres:** Young Adult Fiction, Novels. **Career:** Rollingcrest Junior High School, teacher of English and social studies, 1957-58; Delcastle Technical High School, teacher of homebound children, 1972-73; writer, 1977-; Norfolk Public School System, writer-in-residence, 1981-; teacher, 1981-82; Scared Heart University, teacher of English and writing, 1986-87. **Publications:** What If They Knew?, 1980; Nobody's Fault?, 1981; You Shouldn't Have to Say Good-bye, 1982; Who Will Take Care of Me?, 1983; Friends Are Like That, 1984; A Solitary Secret, 1985; Kevin Corbett Eats Flies, 1986; A Place for Jeremy, 1987; A Time to Listen: Preventing Youth Suicide, 1987; Heads, I Win, 1988; Be Still My Heart, 1989; I Hate Being Gifted, 1990; Mama, Let's Dance: A Novel, 1991; My Girl, 1991; Take Care of My Girl: A Novel, 1992; Someone to Count On, 1993; My Girl II, 1994; I'll Pulverize You, William, 1994; Nothing but Trouble, Trouble, Trouble, 1994; Everything Stinks, 1995; Thirteen Things Not to Tell a Parent, 1995; On Winter's Wind, 1995; Christmas Magic, 1996; Turkey Trouble, 1996; Fly Away Home, 1996; Something Scary, 1996; When Snow Lay Soft on the Mountain, 1996; Boys Are Even Worse than I Thought, 1996; My Secret Valentine, 1997; Zeus and Roxanne, 1997; Calling Me Home, 1998; Cheat the Moon, 1998; Our Strange New Land: Elizabeth's Diary, 2000; In God's Novel, 2000; Westward to Home: Joshua's Journal, 2001; The Starving Time, 2001; A Perfect Place: Joshua's Oregon Trail Diary, Book Two, 2001; Sweet By and By, 2002; Season of Promise, 2002; The Wild Year, 2003; Summer Secrets, 2004; The Brothers' War, 2005; Emma Dilemma and the New Nanny, 2006; Salem Witch-Elizabeth's Story, 2006; (with S. Rosner) The Self-sabotage Cycle: Why We Repeat Behaviors that Create Hardships and Ruin Relationships, 2006; Emma Dilemma and the Two Nannies, 2007; Emma Dilemma and the Soccer Nanny, 2008; You Shouldn't Have to Say Goobye, 2008; Koda, 2009; Emma Dilemma and the Camping Nanny, 2009; Emma Dilemma, The Nanny, and the Secret Ferret, 2010; Emma Dilemma, The Nanny, and the Best Horse Ever, 2011; Black Cloud, 2012. Contributor to books and periodicals. **Address:** 1414 Melville Ave., Fairfield, CT 06825-2021, U.S.A. **Online address:** patriciahermes@snet.net

HERNANDEZ, Jaime. (Los Bros Hernandez). American (born United

States), b. 1959?. **Genres:** Cartoons. **Career:** Graphic artist, writer and comics creator. **Publications:** (As Los Bros Hernandez with G. Hernandez and M. Hernandez) Love and Rockets, 1982; Return of Mr. X, 1986; The Lost Women: And Other Stories, 1988; Whoa Nellie! (collection), 2000; Locas: The Maggie and Hopey Stories, 2004; Maggie and Hopey Color Fun, 2004. Contributor to periodicals. **Address:** c/o Author Mail, Fantagraphics Books, 7563 Lake City Way NE, Seattle, WA 98115-4218, U.S.A.

HERNANDEZ, Jo Farb. American (born United States), b. 1952. **Genres:** Art/Art History, Cultural/Ethnic Topics, Mythology/Folklore, Popular Culture, Photography, Adult Non-fiction, Documentaries/Reportage, Anthropology/Ethnology, Architecture, Area Studies, Crafts. **Career:** University of California, Museum of Cultural History, curatorial assistant, 1974-75, lecturer, 1999-2000; Dallas Museum of Fine Arts, curator and educational assistant, 1976-77; East Texas State University, Department of Commerce, adjunct professor, 1977; Triton Museum of Art, assistant, 1977-78, director, 1978-85; John F. Kennedy University, adjunct professor of museum studies, 1979; Monterey Peninsula Museum of Art, director, 1985-93, consulting curator, 1994-; Curatorial and Museum Management Services, principal, 1993-; San Jose State University, School of Art and Design, professor and director of Natalie and James Thompson Art Gallery, 2000-. Writer. **Publications:** (With S.R. Hernandez) The Day of the Dead: Tradition and Change in Contemporary Mexico, 1979; Crime and Punishment: Reflections of Violence in Contemporary Art, 1984; Three from the Northern Island: Contemporary Sculpture from Hokkaido, 1984; Anders Aldrin, 1990; (with C. Shere) The Expressive Sculpture of Alvin Light, 1990; Lorser Feitelson: Exploration of the Figure, 1919-1929, 1990; Two Sides of the Same Reality: The World and I, 1990; (with M. Levy) Alan Shepp: The Language of Stone, 1991; The Quiet Eye: Poetry of Shoji Hamada and Bernard Leach, 1991; (with C. Berney and A. White) Armin Hansen: The Jane and Justin Dart Collection, 1993; (with N. Boas) Wonderful Colors: The Paintings of August Francois Gay, 1993; Jeanette Maxfield Lewis: A Centennial Celebration, 1994; Jeremy Anderson: The Critical Link/A Quiet Revolution, 1995; (with J. Beardsley and R. Cardinal) A.G. Rizzoli: Architect of Magnificent Visions, 1997; Misch Kohn: Beyond the Tradition, 1998; (with P. Karlstrom) Fire and Flux/An Undaunted Vision: The Art of Charles Strong, 1998; Mel Ramos: The Galatea Series, 2000; Holly Lane: Small Miracles, 2001; (with F. Gualdoni and E. Mascelloni) Mel Ramos, 2001; (co-author) Irvin Tepper: When Cups Speak/Life with the Cup, 2002; (with P. Sanders) Sam Richardson, 2002; (contrib.) Color in Space, 2002; (with P. Linhares and M. Tromble) Marc D'Estout: Domestic Objects, 2003; (co-author) Peter Shire: Go Beyond the Ordinary, 2004; Forms of Tradition in Contemporary Spain, 2005; Gerald Walburg, 2007. Contributor to books and periodicals. **Address:** Natalie and James Thompson Art Gallery, School of Art & Design, San Jose State University, 116 Art Bldg., 1 Washington Sq., San Jose, CA 95192-0089, U.S.A. **Online address:** jo.hernandez@sjsu.edu

HERNÁNDEZ, Lisa. American (born United States) **Genres:** Travel/Exploration, Antiques/Furnishings, Literary Criticism And History. **Career:** Los Angeles City College, instructor in English, adjunct faculty. Editor. **Publications:** (Ed. with T. Benitez) Palabras Chicanas: An Undergraduate Anthology, 1988; Migrations and Other Stories, 2007. Contributor to periodicals. **Address:** Department of English, Los Angeles City College, SCI 218W1/W2, 855 N Vermont Ave., Los Angeles, CA 90029, U.S.A. **Online address:** hernanla@lacitycollege.edu

HERNANDEZ, Los Bros. *See* **HERNANDEZ, Jaime.**

HERNANDEZ-EHRISMAN, Laura. American (born United States), b. 1972. **Genres:** History. **Career:** San Antonio Community College, 1994-96; University of Texas at Austin, tutor, 1997, teaching assistant, 1998-2000, assistant instructor, 2001-03; Saint Phillip's College, adjunct faculty, 2001; Saint Edwards University, instructor, 2004, adjunct professor, 2008; Southern Methodist University, instructor, 2005. **Publications:** Inventing the Fiesta City: Heritage and Carnival in San Antonio, 2008. **Online address:** laurae@stedwards.edu

HERNDON, Ernest. American (born United States), b. 1955. **Genres:** Novels, Children's Fiction, Travel/Exploration, Essays, Young Adult Fiction. **Career:** Enterprise-Journal, reporter, 1979-, outdoors editor, religion editor, staff writer. **Publications:** FOR CHILDREN: The Secret of Lizard Island, 1994; Night of the Jungle Cat, 1994; Smugglers on Grizzly Mountain, 1994; Sisters of the Wolf, 1996; Trouble at Bamboo Bay, 1996; Deathbird of Paradise,

1997; Little People of the Lost Coast, 1997. OTHERS: In the Hearts of Wild Men, 1986; (with T. Seabourne) Self-Defense: A Body-Mind Approach (textbook), 1987; Morning Morning True: A Novel of Intrigue in New Guinea, 1988; Island Quarry: A Novel of Suspense, 1990; Backwater Blues: A Novel of Faith and Fury, 1991; Double-Crossed in Gator Country, 1994; Canoeing Mississippi, 2001; Canoeing Louisiana, 2003; Nature Trails and Gospel Tales: Stories of Grace from the Wilds of Mississippi, 2004; Paddling the Pascagoula, 2005. Works appear in anthologies. Contributor to periodicals. **Address:** Enterprise-Journal, 112 Oliver Emmerich Dr., PO Box 2009, McComb, MS 39648-6330, U.S.A. **Online address:** eherndon@enterprise-journal.com

HERNDON, Nancy. Also writes as Nancy Fairbanks, Elizabeth Chadwick. American (born United States), b. 1934. **Genres:** Novels, Mystery/Crime/Suspense. **Career:** Foley's Department Store, advertising writer and proof reader, 1957; Darcy Advertising Co., advertising proof reader, 1958; Howland's Department Store, advertising copywriter, 1959; New York University, lecturer in English, 1959-61; University of Mississippi, lecturer in English, 1962-63; Florida Atlantic University, lecturer in English, 1965-66; University of Texas, lecturer in English, 1976-81; Rice University, faculty; New York University, faculty. Writer. **Publications:** MYSTERY NOVELS AS NANCY HERNDON: Widows' Watch, 1995; Acid Bath, 1995; Lethal Statues, 1996; Hunting Game, 1996; Time Bombs, 1997; C.O.P. Out, 1998; Casanova Crimes, 1999. AS ELIZABETH CHADWICK: Wanton Angel, 1989; Widows' Fire, 1990; Virgin Fire, 1991; The Wild Hunt, 1991; Bride Fire, 1992; Reluctant Lovers, 1993; Children of Destiny, 1993; Shields of Pride, 1994; Elusive Lovers, 1994; Daughters of the Grail, 1995; First Knight: A Novel, 1995; The Conquest, 1997; The Love Knot, 1998; The Champion, 1998; The Marsh King's Daughter, 2000; Lords of the White Castle, 2002; The Winter Mantle, 2002; The Falcons of Montabard, 2004; The Greatest Knight: The Unsung Story of the Queen's Champion, 2009; For the King's Favor, 2010; The Scarlet Lion, 2010; To Defy a King, 2011; Lady of the English, 2011. AS NANCY FAIRBANKS: Crime Brûlée, 2001; Truffled Feathers, 2001; Death à l'Orange, 2002; Chocolate Quake: A Culinary Mystery with Recipes, 2002; Holy Guacamole!, 2004; Perils of Paella, 2004; Shadows and strongholds, 2005; Mozzarella Most Murderous, 2005; Bon Bon Voyage, 2006; Three-Course Murder, 2006; French Fried, 2006; Turkey Flambé, 2007; Blood Pudding, 2009. **Address:** 6504 Pino Real Dr., El Paso, TX 79912, U.S.A. **Online address:** nancyfairbanks@nancyfairbanks.com

HERNDON, Terry (Eugene). American (born United States), b. 1939. **Genres:** Education, Adult Non-fiction. **Career:** Teacher at public schools, 1962-67; National Education Association, urban representative, 1967-68, specialist in negotiations, 1968, executive director, 1973-83; Michigan Education Association, executive director, 1969-73; Integrated Teaching Corp., chair, 1984; WEA Insurance Group, president, 1985-; WEA Insurance Corp., chief executive officer, through 1998, executive director, 1998-99, consultant, 1998-; National Foundation for the Improvement of Education, president; Center for Education on Nuclear War, president. Writer. **Publications:** We, the Teachers: Terry Herndon on Education and Democracy, 1983. Contributor to journals. **Address:** Herndon, Mays & Skornicka, 5712 Odana Rd., Madison, WI 53719-1221, U.S.A.

HERO, Rodney E. American (born United States), b. 1953. **Genres:** Politics/Government, Race Relations, History, Young Adult Non-fiction. **Career:** University of Colorado-Colorado Springs, assistant professor, 1980-86, associate professor, 1986-88; University of Colorado-Boulder, associate professor, 1989-93, professor, 1993-2000; University of Notre Dame, professor of political science, 2000-. Writer. **Publications:** NONFICTION: Latinos and the U.S. Political System: Two-Tiered Pluralism, 1992; Faces of Inequality: Social Diversity in American Politics, 1998; The Politics of Democratic Inclusion, 2005; Racial Diversity and Social Capital: Equality and Community in America, 2007. Contributor of articles to periodicals. **Address:** University Notre Dame, 217 O'Shaughnessy Hall, Notre Dame, IN 46556-5639, U.S.A. **Online address:** rhero@nd.edu

HERON, Ann. American (born United States), b. 1954. **Genres:** Young Adult Non-fiction, Gay And Lesbian Issues, Psychology, Politics/Government. **Career:** Affiliated with Alyson Publications, 1980-84; Nolo Press, staff, 1985-, vice president of information technology, 1999-2003, chief operations officer, 2003-. Writer. **Publications:** (Ed.) One Teenager in Ten: Writings By Gay and Lesbian Youth, 1983; (with M. Maran) How Would You Feel If Your Dad Was

Gay?, 1991; (ed.) Two Teenagers in Twenty: Writings by Lesbian and Gay Youth, 1994. **Address:** Nolo Press, 950 Parker St., Berkeley, CA 94710-2524, U.S.A. **Online address:** ann-heron@ndo.com

HERR, Michael. American (born United States), b. 1940. **Genres:** Novels, Plays/Screenplays, Autobiography/Memoirs, Biography, Young Adult Non-fiction, Children's Non-fiction, Art/Art History. **Career:** Esquire Magazine, correspondent, 1967-69. **Publications:** Dispatches (memoir), 1977; (with G. Peellaert) The Big Room (biographies), 1986; (with S. Kubrick and G. Hasford and foreword) Full Metal Jacket: The Screenplay, 1987; Walter Winchell: A Novel, 1990; Kubrick, 2000. Contributor of articles to journals. **Address:** c/o Author Mail, Grove/Atlantic Inc., 841 Broadway, 4th Fl., New York, NY 10003-4704, U.S.A.

HERRICK, James A. American (born United States), b. 1954?. **Genres:** Adult Non-fiction, Speech/Rhetoric, Theology/Religion, Intellectual History, Popular Culture, Science Fiction/Fantasy, Mythology/Folklore, Technology, Technology. **Career:** University of California, Department of Rhetoric, teaching assistant, 1976-79; University of Wisconsin, Department of Communication Arts, teaching assistant, 1979-84; Hope College, Department of Communication, assistant professor, 1984-90, associate professor, 1990-93, department chair, 1993-2003, professor, 1997-, Guy Vander Jagt professor of communication, 2001-, interim chair, 2007-08; Lithuania Christian College, professor, 2004. Writer. **Publications:** Critical Thinking: The Analysis of Arguments, 1990; Argumentation: Understanding and Shaping Arguments, 1995, 4th ed., 2011; The History and Theory of Rhetoric: An Introduction, 1997, 5th ed., 2011; The Radical Rhetoric of the English Deists: The Discourse of Skepticism, 1680-1750, 1997; The Making of the New Spirituality: The Eclipse of the Western Religious Tradition, 2003; Scientific Mythologies: How Science And Science Fiction Forge New Religious Beliefs, 2008. Contributor to journals and periodicals. **Address:** Department of Communication, Hope College, Rm. 125 Martha Miller Ctr., 257 Columbia Ave., Holland, MI 49423-3615, U.S.A. **Online address:** herrick@hope.edu

HERRICK, Steven. Australian (born Australia), b. 1958. **Genres:** Poetry, Novels, Picture/Board Books, Adult Non-fiction, Children's Non-fiction. **Career:** Writer. **Publications:** CHILDREN POETRY: My Life, My Love, My Lasagne, 1997; Poetry to the Rescue, 1998; The Spangled Drongo (verse-novel), 1999; Love Poems and Leg-Spinners, 2001; Tom Jones Saves the World, 2002; Do-wrong Ron, 2003; Naked Bunyip Dancing, 2005; Untangling Spaghetti, 2009. CHILDREN NOVELS: Rhyming Boy, 2008. PICTURE BOOKS: The Place Where the Planes Take Off, 1995. FOR YOUNG ADULTS: POETRY: Caboolture, 1990; Water Bombs: A Book of Poems for Teenagers, 1992. NOVELS IN VERSE: Love, Ghosts, & Nose Hair, 1996; A Place Like This, 1998; The Simple Gift, 2000; By the River, 2004; Lonesome Howl, 2006 in US as The Wolf, 2007; Cold Skin, 2007. NOVELS: Slice, 2010; Black Painted Fingernails, 2011. FOR ADULTS POETRY: The Esoteric Herrick: Poems & Things, 1982; The Sound of Chopping, 1994. **Address:** PO Box 640, Katoomba, NW 2780, Australia. **Online address:** stevenherrick@gmail.com

HERRIN, Lamar. American (born United States), b. 1940. **Genres:** History, Novels, Autobiography/Memoirs, Young Adult Fiction. **Career:** State University College of New York at Buffalo, instructor, 1964-66; University of Cincinnati, instructor of English, 1966-69, teaching assistant of English, 1975-76; Dublin School of English, professor of English, 1971-73; Northern Kentucky State College, instructor of English, 1973-74; Cornell University, assistant professor of English, 1977-83, associate professor of English, 1983-89, professor of English, 1989-2006, professor emeritus, 2006-, Cornell University's Study Abroad Program in Spain, director. Writer. **Publications:** The Rio Loja Ringmaster, 1977; American Baroque, 1981; The Unwritten Chronicles of Robert E. Lee, 1989; The Lies Boys Tell, 1991; House of the Deaf, 2005; Romancing Spain: A Memoir, 2006. Contributor to periodicals. **Address:** Department of English, Cornell University, 234 Goldwin Smith Hall, Ithaca, NY 14853-3201, U.S.A. **Online address:** wlh4@cornell.edu

HERRING, Adam. American (born United States), b. 1967?. **Genres:** Art/Art History, History. **Career:** Southern Methodist University, Meadows School of the Arts, associate professor of art history, director of graduate studies. Writer. **Publications:** Art and Writing in the Maya Cities, AD 600-800:

A Poetics of Line, 2005. **Address:** Meadows School of the Arts, Southern Methodist University, PO Box 750356, Dallas, TX 75275-0356, U.S.A. **Online address:** aherring@smu.edu

HERRING, Eric. British (born England), b. 1961. **Genres:** Politics/Government, International Relations/Current Affairs. **Career:** University College of Wales, tutor, 1986-87; University of Bristol, lecturer, 1989-2001, conveyor, 2002-. Writer. **Publications:** Strategic Concepts and Nuclear Threats: Testing Schelling and Morgan, 1988; Building Democracy? The International Dimension of Democratisation in Eastern Europe, 1994; Keyguide to Information Sources in Strategic Studies, 1994; Danger and Opportunity: Explaining International Crisis Outcomes, 1995; (with B. Buzan) The Arms Dynamic in World Politics, 1998; Preventing the Use of Weapons of Mass Destruction, 2000; Iraq in Fragments: The Occupation and Its Legacy, 2006. **Address:** School of Sociology, Politics and International, Studies, University of Bristol, 2.4 10 Priory Rd., Clifton, Bristol, BS8 1TY, England. **Online address:** eric.herring@bristol.ac.uk

HERRING, Mark. See **HERRING, Mark Youngblood.**

HERRING, Mark Youngblood. Also writes as Mark Herring. American (born United States), b. 1952. **Genres:** Bibliography, Librarianship, How-to Books, Engineering. **Career:** Educational tutor, 1975-78; King College, director, 1979-88; Oklahoma Baptist University, dean of library services, 1992-99; Winthrop University, dean of library services, 1999-. Writer. **Publications:** Controversial Issues in Librarianship: An Annotated Bibliography, 1960-1984, 1987; Ethics and the Professor: An Annotated Bibliography, 1970-1985, 1988; (as Mark Y. Herring) Organizing Friends Groups: A How-to-Do-It Manual for Librarians, 1993; (as Mark Y. Herring) The Pro-Life/Choice Debate: Historical Guides to Controversial Issues in America, 2003; (as Mark Herring) Raising Funds with Friends Groups: A How-to-Do-It Manual for Librarians, 2004; (as Mark Y. Herring) Genetic Engineering, 2006; (as Mark Y. Herring) Fool's Gold, 2007. Contributor of articles to books and periodicals. **Address:** Dacus Library, Winthrop University, 200 Tillman Hall, 701 Oakland Ave., Rock Hill, SC 29733, U.S.A. **Online address:** herringm@winthrop.edu

HERRING, Peg. American (born United States), b. 1950. **Genres:** Romance/Historical, Plays/Screenplays. **Career:** Onaway High School, instructor in communications, drama, English, and history, 1975-2002; Onaway United Methodist Church, choir director. Writer. **Publications:** PLAYS: Rumpelstiltskin, 2006; Hansel and Gretel: A Comedy, 2006. OTHERS: Macbeth's Niece (historical romance novel), 2008; Her Highness' First Murder: A Simon and Elizabeth Mystery (historical mystery), 2010. Works appear in anthologies. Contributor to periodicals. **Address:** c/o Mary Sue Seymour, Seymour Agency, 475 Miner Street Rd., Canton, NY 13617, U.S.A.

HERRING, Phillip F. American (born United States), b. 1936. **Genres:** Literary Criticism And History, Social Sciences. **Career:** University of Texas, instructor in English, 1964-65, Humanities Research Center, special assistant, 1996-, adjunct professor; University of Virginia, assistant professor of English, 1965-70; University of Wisconsin, associate professor of English, 1970-74, professor of English, 1974-96. Writer. **Publications:** Joyce's Uncertainty Principle, 1987; Djuna: The Life and Work of Djuna Barnes, 1995. EDITOR: Joyce's Ulysses Notesheets in the British Museum, 1972; Joyce's Notes and Early Drafts for Ulysses: Selections from the Buffalo Collection, 1977; (with O. Stutman) Collected Poems: With Notes Toward the Memoirs, 2005. Contributor to books and journals. **Address:** c/o Jeremy Solomon, First Books, 2040 N Milwaukee Ave., Chicago, IL 60647, U.S.A. **Online address:** pherring@mail.utexas.edu

HERRINGTON, Anne J. American (born United States), b. 1948. **Genres:** Education, Writing/Journalism. **Career:** Johnson State College, director of developmental skills, 1973-82, acting dean of students, 1976-77; State University of New York, research assistant in the writing in non-academic settings project, 1980-81; Pennsylvania State University, assistant professor, 1983-86; University of Massachusetts, professor, 1986-, director of undergraduate writing program, 1990-96, acting chair, 1997, chair in English department, 2000-06, Western Massachusetts Writing Project, director, 2007-; National Writing Project, director; Bard College, visiting faculty member; Northeastern University, faculty member, 1989. Writer. **Publications:** (Ed. with C. Moran) Writing, Teaching, and Learning in the Disciplines, 1992; (with M. Curtis) Persons in Process: Four Stories of Writing and Personal

Development in College, 2000; (ed. with C. Moran and A. Herrington) Genre across the Curriculum, 2005; (ed. with K. Hodgson and C. Moran) Teaching the New Writing: Technology, Change, and Assessment in the 21st-century Classroom, 2009. **Address:** Department of English, University of Massachusetts, 265 Bartlett Hall, Amherst, MA 01003, U.S.A. **Online address:** anneh@english.umass.edu

HERRINGTON, Terri. *See* **BLACKSTOCK, Terri.**

HERRMANN, Luke John. British/German (born Germany), b. 1932. **Genres:** Art/Art History, Translations, Architecture. **Career:** Illustrated London News, assistant editor, 1955-58; Oxford University, Ashmolean Museum, Department of Western Art, assistant keeper, 1958-67; University of Leicester, Paul Mellon Foundation lecturer, 1967-70, senior lecturer and head of department, 1970-73, professor of art history, 1973-87, now professor emeritus. Writer. **Publications:** (Trans.) L. Muenz and P. Bruegel, Bruegel's Drawings, 1961; J.M.W. Turner, 1775-1851, 1963; Il Paesaggio Nella Pittura Inglese dell'Ottocento, 1967; Ruskin and Turner: A Study of Ruskin as a Collector of Turner, Based on His Gifts to the University of Oxford: Incorporating a Catalogue Raisonné of the Turner Drawings in the Ashmolean Museum, 1968; British Landscape Painting of the Eighteenth Century, 1973; Turner: Paintings, Water Colours, Drawings and Prints, 1975, 2nd ed., 1986; Royal Academy Diploma Works, 1921-1981: A Selection of Paintings, Drawings, Prints and Sculpture from the Diploma Collections of the Royal Academy of Arts: Catalogue, 1982; Paul and Thomas Sandby, 1986; Turner Prints: The Engraved Work of J.M.W. Turner, 1990; Katalog der Albertina, Band VII, Die Englische Schule, 1992; Englische Schule: Zeichnungen und Aquarelle Britischer Künstler, 1992; (with T. Cubberley) Catalogue of the Drawings by James Hakewill in the British School at Rome Library, 1992; Twilight of the Grand Tour: A Catalogue of the Drawings by James Hakewill in the British School at Rome Library, 1992; Nineteenth Century British Painting, 2000; (ed. with E. Joll and M. Bublin) The Oxford Companion to J.M.W. Turner, 2001; J.M.W. Turner, 2007. **Address:** Department of the History of Art and Film, University of Leicester, University Rd., Leicester, LE LE1 7RH, England.

HERRMANNS, Ralph. Swedish/German (born Germany), b. 1933. **Genres:** Novels, Children's Fiction, Plays/Screenplays, Art/Art History, Biography, Autobiography/Memoirs, Young Adult Fiction, Education, Education. **Career:** Bonnier Group, foreign correspondent; Ediciones Albon Medillin, editor-in-chief and publisher, 1962-64; Ahlen and Akerlunds Foerlag, editor-in-chief, 1964-66; Time-Life Inc., traveling correspondent, 1966-67; Dagens Industries, art commentator, 1991-2001. **Publications:** Lee Lan Flies the Dragon Kite, 1961; Barnen vid Nordpolen, 1963; Our Car Julia, 1963; Car Named Julia, 1964; Children of the North Pole, 1964; Bilen Julia, 1964; River Boy, 1965; Flickan som hade brattom, 1967; Den fortrollade ladan, 1968; The Abominable Snowman, 1969; In Search of the Abominable Snowman, 1970; Pojken Som vile måla världens Vackraste Tavla, 1970; The World's Most Beautiful Painting, 1970; Natten och drommen, 1972; Joan Miro, 1972; Posters by Miro, 1974; Carl Gustaf von Rosen: A Biography, 1975; Royal Palace of Stockholm's, 1978; A World of Islands, 1980; En fest för ögat, 1980; Och solen gick ned över profeterna, 1981; Gösta Werner, A Biography, 1981; Den enes brod, 1982; Jenny Nystrom's Art, 1982; Why New York?, 1982; Israel talar, 1982; år i Jenny Nyströms Sverige, 1983; Tank pa de dagar, 1984; Slott och herremanshus, 1985; Lognens triumf, 1985; Blott doden, blott doden, 1986; Hunden i Konsten, 1987; Hasten hos manniskan, 1990; Tapies, 1993; 1900-talets maleri, 1994; Haberlands, 1996; Detjudiska Prag, 1997; Portratten pa Gripsholm, 1998; Miro, 2001; Karl-Axel Pehrson, 2001; Botero, 2001; Calatrava, 2001. **Address:** Brannkyrkagatan 77, Stockholm, 118 23, Sweden. **Online address:** rh@moviemakers.se

HERROLD, Tracey. *See* **DILS, Tracey E.**

HERRON, Carolivia. American (born United States), b. 1947. **Genres:** Novels, Literary Criticism And History, Children's Fiction. **Career:** Harvard University, assistant professor of Afro-American studies and comparative literature, 1986-90; Mount Holyoke College, Epicenter for the Study of Epic Literature, director, 1988-, associate professor of English, 1990-92; National Endowment for the Humanities, Curriculum Development Program, board director, 1988-90; Carleton College, visiting professor, 1989; California State University, professor of English; Epicenter Literary Software (multimedia company), founder. Writer. **Publications:** Thereafter Johnnie (novel), 1991; (ed.) Selected Works of Angelina Weld Grimké, 1991; Nappy Hair

(children's fiction), 1997; Always an Olivia: A Remarkable Family History, 2007. Contributor of articles to journals. **Address:** Epicenter Literary Software, 6514 7th St. NW, Washington, DC 20012, U.S.A. **Online address:** carolivia@carolivia.org

HERRON, William G. (William George Herron). American (born United States), b. 1933. **Genres:** Novels, Psychology, Young Adult Fiction. **Career:** Manhattanville College of the Sacred Heart, instructor in psychology, 1957-58; St. Vincent's Hospital, intern in clinical psychology, 1958-59; St. Bonaventure University, Department of Psychology, associate professor and chairman, 1959-65; Cattaraugus County Mental Health Clinic, supervisory clinical psychologist, 1961-65; St. John's University, administrator, professor, 1965-2000, co-director of clinical training, 1965-, School Psychology Program, director, Clinical Psychology Ph.D. Program, founding coordinator; West Bergen Mental Health Center, chief psychologist, 1966-70; Fairleigh Dickinson University, Contemporary Center for Advanced Psychoanalytic Studies, dean of training, 2000-04; Adelphi University, professor, now retired; Derner Institute, faculty. Writer. **Publications:** (With R.E. Kantor) Reactive and Process Schizophrenia, 1966; (co-author) Contemporary School Psychology, 1970, 2nd ed., 1984; F. Quantmeyer Hose No. 7 (novel), 1972; The Doctor Talks to You About Understanding Psychotherapy: A Discussion, 1979; (with M. Herron and J. Handron) School Psychology: A Challenge for Change, 1980; (with S. Rouslin) Issues in Psychotherapy, 1982; (with S.R. Welt) Narcissism and the Psychotheropist, 1990; (with S.R. Welt) Money Matters: The Fee in Psychotherapy and Psychoanalysis, 1992; (ed. with R. Javier and A. Bergman) Domestic Violence: Assessment and Treatment, 1996; (ed. with R. Javier) Personality Development and Psychotherapy in Our Diverse Society, 1998; Narcissism and the Relational World, 1999; (with W.G. Herron) Patterns of Desire: Sexual Diversity in Psychoanalysis, 2006. **Address:** 5 Pascack Rd., Woodcliff Lake, NJ 07677-8317, U.S.A.

HERRON, William George. *See* **HERRON, William G.**

HERSCHLER, Mildred Barger. American (born United States) **Genres:** Children's Fiction, Young Adult Fiction, Novels, Biography. **Career:** Moundsville Journal, reporter and staff writer; Research Institute of America, editor, 1973-75; Sales Executives Clubs of New York, editor and advertising manager, 1976-81; freelance writer, 1982-. **Publications:** Frederick Douglass (juvenile biography), 1969; The Walk into Morning (historical novel), 1993; The Darkest Corner (young adult novel), 2000. **Address:** Front Street Inc., 862 Haywood Rd., Asheville, NC 28806, U.S.A. **Online address:** mbhersch@aol.com

HERSHBERGER, Mary. American (born United States) **Genres:** Politics/Government, Biography, Ethics, Philosophy. **Career:** University of Georgia, faculty; Virginia Tech University, faculty; Eastern Mennonite University, faculty; Ohio State University, faculty; Makerere University, faculty; Capital University, associate professor of history, professor of history. Writer. **Publications:** Traveling to Vietnam: American Peace Activists and the War, 1998; Jane Fonda's War: A Political Biography of an Antiwar Icon, 2005; (ed.) Jane Fonda's Words of Politics and Passion, 2006. Contributor to journals. **Address:** c/o Author Mail, New Press, 38 Greene St., 4th Fl., New York, NY 10013, U.S.A. **Online address:** mhershbe@capital.edu

HERSHENHORN, Esther. American (born United States), b. 1945. **Genres:** Children's Fiction, Humor/Satire. **Career:** Society of Children's Book Writers and Illustrators, advisor; University of Chicago, Graham School, faculty of writing. Writer. **Publications:** There Goes Lowell's Party, 1998; Illinois: Fun Facts and Games, 2000; The Confe$$ion$ and $ecret$ of Howard J. Fingerhut, 2002; Chicken Soup by Heart, 2002; Fancy That, 2003; S is for Story: A Writer's Alphabet, 2009; Little Illinois, 2011. **Address:** c/o Author Mail, Holiday House, 425 Madison Ave., Ste. 12, New York, NY 10017, U.S.A. **Online address:** esthersh@aol.com

HERSHEY, Kathleen M. American (born United States), b. 1934. **Genres:** Mystery/Crime/Suspense, Young Adult Fiction. **Career:** Writer and librarian. **Publications:** Cotton Mill Town, 1993; Secret on Cemetery Hill, forthcoming. Works appear in anthologies. Contributor to magazines. **Address:** c/o Kendra Marcus, BookStop Literary Agency L.L.C., 67 Meadow View Rd., Orinda, CA 94563, U.S.A.

HERSHEY, Mary. American (born United States) **Genres:** Children's Fiction. **Career:** Va Greater Los Angeles Healthcare System, lead administrator,

1993-; Mary Hershey Coaching, author and coach, 1998-; Empower Coaching Systems, consultant. Writer and social worker. **Publications:** My Big Sister Is So Bossy: She Says You Can't Read This Book, 2005; The One Where the Kid Nearly Jumps to His Death and Lands in California, 2007; 10 Lucky Things that Have Happened to Me Since I Nearly Got Hit by Lightning, 2008; Love and Pollywogs from Camp Calamity, 2010. **Address:** Author Mail, Razorbill/Penguin Putnam, 375 Hudson St., New York, NY 10014, U.S.A. **Online address:** books@maryhershey.com

HERSHEY, Olive. American (born United States), b. 1941?. **Genres:** Novels, Poetry, Plays/Screenplays, Young Adult Fiction. **Career:** St. Stephens Episcopal School, teacher of English, 1973-78; Wall Street Transcript, editor, 1980; University of Houston, lecturer in English, 1983-88; Rice University, visiting assistant professor of fiction writing and English, 1988-. **Publications:** Floating Face Up (poems), 1984; Truck Dance: A Novel, 1989. **Address:** c/o Liz Darhansoff, Darhansoff & Verrill Literary Agency, 1220 Park Ave., New York, NY 10128, U.S.A.

HERSHMAN, Marcie. American (born United States), b. 1951?. **Genres:** Novels, Autobiography/Memoirs, Essays. **Career:** Cambridge Women's School, instructor in creative writing, 1974-76; Boston Center for Adult Education, instructor in fiction, 1974-76; Boston Globe, book reviewer and arts correspondent, 1975-82; Fisher Junior College, Department of Continuing Education, instructor, 1975-78; Young Women's Christian Association, writer and community liaison in non-traditional jobs program, 1977; Lesley College (now Lesley University), instructor in American literature, 1978-80; MFA Writing Program, writing faculty, 2008-10; Massachusetts College of Pharmacy and Allied Health Sciences, visiting assistant professor of English, 1980; Tufts University, lecturer in English, creative writing faculty, 1981-; Emerson College, instructor in MFA writing program, 1982-99; Radcliffe College, Bunting Institute, fellow in fiction, 1992-93; Warren Wilson College, MFA Writing Program, staff, 1998; Fine Arts Work Center, faculty, 1999-; Brandeis University, Fannie Hurst writer-in-residence, 1999-2001; Bennington College, M.F.A. Writing Program, visiting associate faculty, 2002; University of Minnesota, Split Rock Arts Program, on-line mentor, 2003-. **Publications:** Tales of the Master Race (novel), 1991; Safe in America (novel), 1995; Speak to Me: Grief, Love and What Endures (memoir), 2001. Works appear in anthologies. **Address:** Department of English, Tufts University, 210 E Hall, Medford, MA 02155, U.S.A. **Online address:** marcie.hershman@tufts.edu

HERSHOCK, Martin J. American (born United States), b. 1962. **Genres:** History, Cultural/Ethnic Topics. **Career:** University of Michigan Dearborn, adjunct lecturer, 1992-97; Hobart and William Smith Colleges, assistant professor, 1997-99; University of Michigan Dearborn, assistant professor of social sciences, 1999-. Writer. **Publications:** The Paradox of Progress: Economic Change, Individual Enterprise and Political Culture in Michigan, 1837-1878, 2003; (ed. with P. Finkelman) The History of Michigan Law, 2006. **Address:** Department of Social Sciences, University of Michigan, Dearborn, MI 48128, U.S.A. **Online address:** mhershoc@umd.umich.edu

HERSHON, Joanna (Brett). American (born United States), b. 1972?. **Genres:** Novels. **Career:** Columbia University, Undergraduate Creative Writing, faculty. Writer. **Publications:** Swimming, 2001; The Outside of August, 2003; The German Bride (novel), 2008. Contributor to periodicals. **Address:** c/o Author Mail, Ballantine Books/Random House, 1745 Broadway, New York, NY 10019, U.S.A. **Online address:** joahersh@gmail.com

HERSPRING, Dale R. American (born United States), b. 1940. **Genres:** Politics/Government, Military/Defense/Arms Control. **Career:** U.S. Department of State, Bureau of Politico-Military Affairs, arms control specialist, U.S. Embassy-Warsaw, consular officer, U.S. Embassy-Moscow, political-military affairs officer, Office of East European Affairs, deputy director, Office of Security Analysis, director, Policy Planning Council, senior staff, foreign service officer, 1971-91; Georgetown University, adjunct professor, 1982-93; University of Maryland, adjunct professor, 1988-89; Columbia University, Harriman Institute for the Advanced Study of the Soviet Union, adjunct professor, 1990-91; National War College, professor, 1991-93; George Washington University, adjunct professor, 1992-93; Kansas State University, professor of political science, 1993-, Department of Political Science, head, 1993-2000, university distinguished professor; University of Kansas, visiting professor, 1998-, Center for Russian and East European Studies, fellow. Writer. **Publications:** East German Civil-Military Relations: The Impact of Technology, 1949-1972, 1973; (ed. with I. Volgyes) Civil-Military Relations in Communist Systems, 1978; (with R.F. Laird) The Soviet Union and Strategic Arms, 1984; The Soviet High Command, 1964-1969, 1990; Russian Civil-Military Relations, 1996; Requiem for an Army: The Demise of the East German Military, 1998; Soldiers, Commissars and Chaplains: Civil-Military Relations since Cromwell, 2001; (ed.) Putin's Russia, 2003, (ed. with S.K. Wegren) 4th ed. as After Putin's Russia: Past Imperfect, Future Uncertain, 2010; The Pentagon and the Presidency, 2005; Kremlin & the High Command: Presidential Impact on the Russian Military from Gorbachev to Putin, 2006; (with H.J. Wiarda and E.M. Skelley) Development on the Periphery, 2006; Rumsfeld's Wars: The Arrogance of Power, 2008. Contributor of articles to books and periodicals. **Address:** Department of Political Science, Kansas State University, 244 Waters Hall, Manhattan, KS 66506, U.S.A. **Online address:** falka@ksu.edu

HERTZ, Deborah. American (born United States), b. 1949. **Genres:** History, Theology/Religion. **Career:** Pittsburgh State University, assistant professor of history, 1978-79; State University of New York, assistant professor, 1980-88, associate professor of history, 1988-96, Center for Research in Womens Studies, director, 1989-90; Harvard University, Andrew W. Mellon faculty fellow in the humanities, 1984-85; Hebrew University, Fulbright professor, 1987-88; Harvard Divinity School, Women's Studies in Religion Program, research associate and visiting lecturer, 1991-92; University of Haifa, visiting senior lecturer, 1994-95; Sarah Lawrence College, professor of history, 1996-2003; University of California, professor of history, Herman Wouk chair in modern Jewish studies 2004-. Writer. **Publications:** Jewish High Society in Old Regime Berlin, 1988; (ed.) Briefe an eine freundin: Rahel Varnhagen an Rebecca Friedländer, Kiepenheuer, 1988; Jewish High Society in Old Regime Berlin, 2005; How Jews Became Germans: The History of Conversion and Assimilation in Berlin, 2007; Journeys to Emancipation: Jewish Women in Radical Politics, 1869-1914, forthcoming; Why Jewish Women Became Radicals in Russia and Beyond, 1869-1915, forthcoming; (ed. with S. Bentley and F. Hertz) A Torn Family Reunited in Reading Greatgrandpa David's South Saint Paul Diary, forthcoming; Jewish Historical Society of the Upper Midwest, forthcoming. **Address:** Department of History, University of California, 9500 Gilman Dr., La Jolla, CA 92093-0104, U.S.A. **Online address:** dhertz@ucsd.edu

HERTZKE, Allen D. American (born United States), b. 1950. **Genres:** Politics/Government. **Career:** Congressional Campaign, assistant campaign director, 1972; U.S. Senate Campaign, rural director, 1974; National Demonstration Water Project, program development specialist and lobbyist, 1976-78; Environmental Protection Agency, assistant director for public participation, 1978-80; Community Development and Energy Conservation, extension agent, 1980-82; Carl Albert Congressional Research Center, assistant director, 1986-98; University of Oklahoma, professor of political science, presidential professor, Carl Albert Congressional Research Center, assistant director, 1989-98, director of religious studies, 2002-, founding director of the religious studies program, 2002-08. Consultant and writer. **Publications:** Representing God in Washington: The Role of Religious Lobbies in the American Polity, 1988; (ed. with R. Peters) The Atomistic Congress: An Interpretation of Congressional Change, 1992; Echoes of Discontent: Jesse Jackson, Pat Robertson and the Resurgence of Populism, 1993: (with R.B. Fowler) Religion and Politics in America: Faith, Culture and Strategic Choices, 1995, 2nd ed., 1999; Freeing God's Children: The Unlikely Alliance for Global Human Rights, 2004; (with E.L. Cleary) Representing God at the Statehouse: Religion and Politics in the American States, 2006; Tocqueville's Ghost: the Challenge of Religious Politics in America, forthcoming. Contributor to periodicals. **Address:** Department of Political Science, University of Oklahoma, 205 Dale Hall Twr., 455 W Lindsey St., Norman, OK 73019, U.S.A. **Online address:** ahertzke@ou.edu

HERYANTO, Ariel. Australian/Indonesian (born Indonesia), b. 1954?. **Genres:** Politics/Government, Social Sciences, Local History/Rural Topics. **Career:** University of Melbourne, Asia Institute, convenor of Indonesian program, assistant international dean of the faculty of arts. Writer. **Publications:** Perdebatan Sastra Kontekstual, 1985; (co-author) Pers: Hukum Dan Kekuasaan, 1994; Language of Development and Development of Language: The Case of Indonesia, 1995; (co-author) Bahasa Dan Kekuasaan: Politik Wacana Di Panggung Orde Baru, 1996; Perlawanan Dalam Kepatuhan: Esai-esai Budaya, 2000; (ed. with S.K. Mandal) Challenging Authoritarianism in Southeast Asia: Comparing Indonesia and Malaysia, 2003; State Terrorism and Political Identity in Indonesia: Fatally Belonging, 2006; (ed.) Popular Culture in Indonesia: Fluid Identities in Post-Authoritarian Politics, 2008.

Contributor to periodicals. **Address:** Asia Institute, University of Melbourne, Sidney Myer Asia Centre Bldg., Level 2, Corner of Swanston St., Carlton, VI 3010, Australia. **Online address:** arielh@unimelb.edu.au

HERZ, Rachel. American/Canadian (born Canada), b. 1963. **Genres:** Psychology, Adult Non-fiction, Social Sciences. **Career:** Brown University, Department of Psychology, visiting professor, 2000-05, 2008, Chronobiology Summer Behavioral Sciences Research Apprenticeship Program, faculty, E.P. Bradley Sleep and Chronobiology Research Lab, faculty, 2004-, Medical School, Department of Psychiatry and Human Behavior, visiting professor, 2004-11, adjunct professor, 2011-, Department of Cognitive, Linguistic and Psychological Sciences, visiting professor, 2004-11; Institute of Food Technologists, distinguished lecturer, 2004-. Writer and consultant. **Publications:** The Scent of Desire, 2007; (co-author) Sensation & Perception (textbook), 2006, 2nd ed., 2008; 3rd ed., 2012; That's Disgusting, 2012. CONTRIBUTOR: Memory for Odors, 1995; Advances in Chemical Signals in Vertebrates, 1999; Compendium of Olfactory Research, 2001; Olfaction, Taste and Cognition, 2002; Applied Developmental Science Encyclopedia, 2004; Trends in Experimental Psychology Research, 2005; The Smell Culture Reader, 2006; Encyclopedia of Perception, 2010; Sensory Marketing, 2010; The Neurobiology of Sensation and Reward, 2011. Contributor to many periodicals. **Address:** Department of Cognitive, Linguistic & Psych Sci, Brown University, 190 Thayer St., Providence, RI 02912, U.S.A. **Online address:** rachel_herz@brown.edu

HERZBERG, Nancy K. American (born United States), b. 1951. **Genres:** Biography, Anthropology/Ethnology, Economics, Travel/Exploration, Autobiography/Memoirs. **Career:** East Tennessee Research Corp., grant writer and paralegal, 1973-74; Inter-Cooperative Council, University of Michigan, membership coordinator, 1974-76; Consumers Cooperative Association of Eau Claire, director of membership education, 1977-78; consultant, 1979-84; National Cooperative Bank, Upper Midwest Regional Office, technical assistance officer, 1980-83; International Alliance for Sustainable Agriculture, co-founder, 1983; Passamaquoddy Tribe, coordinator of Passamaquoddy women's project and grant writer, 1985-87; University of New England, Rural Health Project, grant writer-social and global awareness, curriculum reform and coordinator, 1987-92; American Indian Science and Engineering Society, grant writer and project development coordinator, 1992-94; Winds of Change Magazine, American Indian Education and Opportunity, editorial associate, 1993-95; The Wheetley Co., associate editor, 1994-95. **Publications:** A Journey of a Thousand Miles Begins with a Single Step: The Story of the Passamaquoddy Women's Project, 1986; (co- author) Perspectives on Economic Development in Indian Country, 1990; (ed.) From Roots to Roses: The Autobiography of Tilda Kemplen, 1992. Contributor to periodicals. **Address:** c/o S. Boldrey, 4048 Rose Ave., Western Springs, IL 60558-1075, U.S.A.

HERZFELD, Michael (F.). American/British (born England), b. 1947. **Genres:** Anthropology/Ethnology, History. **Career:** Vassar College, assistant professor of anthropology, 1978-80; Indiana University, Research Center for Language and Semiotic Studies, associate, 1980-85, Department of Anthropology, assistant professor, 1980-83, associate professor, 1983-87, chair, 1987-90, professor of anthropology and semiotics, 1988-91, Undergraduate Certificate Program in Semiotic Studies, chair, 1981-85, Folklore Institute, fellow, Russian and East European Institute, faculty, West European National Resource Center, faculty; Semiotic Society of America, associate executive director, 1982-84; International Summer Institute for Semiotic and Structural Studies, director and faculty, 1983, 1985; Modern Greek Studies Association, vice president, 1988-90, 1991; Society for the Anthropology of Europe, president, 1990-92; Harvard University, Department of Anthropology, professor of anthropology, 1991-, Peabody Museum of Archaeology and Ethnology, curator, 1991-, Center for European Studies, social anthropologist, Greek Study Group, co-chair; Université Paris X, senior research scientist, 1992; Università di Padua, visiting faculty, 1992; University of Manchester, Honorary Lord Simon Visiting Professor, 1994; American Ethnologist, editor, 1994-98; Ecole des Hautes Etudes en Sciences Sociales, director, 1995; Università di Roma, professor, 1999-2000; University of Melbourne, Department of Anthropology, visiting faculty, 2005-10; University of Malta, visiting professor, 2006. **Publications:** Ours Once More: Folklore, Ideology, and the Making of Modern Greece, 1982; The Poetics of Manhood: Contest and Identity in a Cretan Mountain Village, 1985; Anthropology through the Looking-Glass: Critical Ethnography in the Margins of Europe, 1987; A Place in History: Social and Monumental Time in a Cretan Town, 1991; The Social Production of Indifference: Exploring the Symbolic Roots of Western Bureaucracy, 1992; Cultural

Intimacy: Social Poetics in the Nation-State, 1997, 2nd ed., 2005; Portrait of a Greek Imagination: An Ethnographic Biography of Andreas Nenedakis, 1997; Anthropology: Theoretical Practice in Culture and Society, 2001; Body Impolitic: Artisans and Artifice in the Global Hierarchy of Value, 2004; Evicted from Eternity: The Restructuring of Modern Rome, 2009. EDITOR: (with P. Bouissac and R. Posner) Iconicity: Essays on the Nature of Culture: Festschrift for Thomas A. Sebeok on his 65th Birthday, 1986; (with L. Melazzo) Semiotic Theory and Practice: Proceedings of the Third International Congress of the IASS, Palermo, 1984, 1988; Mouton de Gruyter 1988; Property, Production and Family in Neckarhausen, 1700-1870, 1994. Contributor to journals. **Address:** Department of Anthropology, Harvard University, Rm. 380, William James Hall, 33 Kirkland St., Cambridge, MA 02138, U.S.A. **Online address:** herzfeld@fas.harvard.edu

HERZIG, Alison Cragin. American (born United States), b. 1935. **Genres:** Children's Fiction, Young Adult Fiction, History. **Career:** Editors Ink, writer and founding partner; National Magazine, art dealer, fiction editor and writer. **Publications:** Shadows on the Pond, 1985; The Boonsville Bombers, 1991; The Big Deal, 1992; Bronco Busters, 1998. WITH J.L. MALI: A Word to the Wise, 1978; Oh Boy! Babies!, 1980; A Season of Secrets, 1982; Thaddeus, 1984; The Ten-Speed Babysitter, 1987; Sam and the Moon Queen, 1990; Mystery on October Road, 1991; The Wimp of the World, 1994; Weekly Reader Children's Book Club Presents Silly Steggy, 1993. **Address:** 15 W 81st St., New York, NY 10024, U.S.A.

HERZOG, Brad. American (born United States), b. 1968. **Genres:** Children's Fiction, Children's Non-fiction, Sports/Fitness, Travel/Exploration. **Career:** Ithaca Journal, sports reporter, 1990-92; freelance writer and screenwriter, 1992-. **Publications:** The Sports 100, 1995; States of Mind, 1999; Small World, 2004; Turn Left at the Trojan Horse, 2010. NOVELS FOR CHILDREN: Freddy in the Fridge, 2000; The Hero in the Mirror, 2000; The Monster's New Friend, 2000; The Runaway Ball, 2000. NONFICTION: The Everything You Want to Know about Sports Encyclopedia, 1994; Heads Up!, 1994; Seventh-Inning Stretch: Time-out for Baseball Trivia, 1994; MVP Sports Puzzles, 1995; Hoopmania!: The Jam-Packed Book of Basketball Trivia, 1995; The Sports One Hundred: The One Hundred Most Important People in American Sports History, 1995; Soccer, 1996; Hot Summer Stars, 1997; The Fifty Greatest Athletes of Today, 1998; 2000: A Celebration of Sports, 1999; Olympics 2000: Stars and Stats, 2000; 20 Greatest Athletes of the 20th Century, 2000; Laugh Locker, 2000; Shake, Rattle and Roll, 2002; Having a Ball, 2002; Dare to Be Different: Athletes Who Changed Sports, 2003; K is for Kick: A Soccer Alphabet, 2003; H is for Home Run: A Baseball Alphabet, 2004; T is for Touchdown: A Fooball Alphabet, 2004; P is for Putt: A Golf Alphabet, 2005; R is for Race: A Stock Car Alphabet, 2006; E is for Extreme: An Extreme Sports Alphabet, 2007; A is for Amazing Moments: A Sports Alphabet, 2008; S is for Save the Planet: A How-to-be-Green Alphabet, 2009; Full Count: A Baseball Number Book, 2009; I Spy with My Little Eye Baseball, 2011; G is for Gold Medal: An Olympics Alphabet, 2011; Little Baseball, 2011; Little Football, 2011; Little Basketball, 2011; Little Soccer, 2011. Contributor of articles to magazines. **Address:** c/o Laura Rennert, Andrea Brown Agency, 208 Lexington Dr., Menlo Park, CA 94025, U.S.A. **Online address:** brad@bradherzog.com

HERZOG, Dagmar. American (born United States), b. 1961. **Genres:** History, Politics/Government, Social Sciences. **Career:** Brown University, teaching assistant, 1985-87, 1988-90, instructor, 1990-91; Michigan State University, assistant professor, 1991-97, associate professor, 1997-2005; Harvard University, Andrew W. Mellon faculty fellow, 1993-94; City University of New York, Graduate Center, professor, 2005. Writer. **Publications:** Lessons and Legacies, 1991; Intimacy and Exclusion: Religious Politics in Pre-revolutionary Baden, 1996; (ed. and intro.) Sexuality and German Fascism, 2004; Sex after Fascism: Memory and Morality in Twentieth-Century Germany, 2005; (ed. with G. Bischof and A. Pelinka) Sexuality in Austria, 2007; Sex in Crisis: The New Sexual Revolution and the Future of American Politics, 2008; (ed. with D. Fuda, S. Hoffmann and T. van Rahden and contrib.) Demokratie im Schatten der Gewalt: Geschichten des Privaten im deutschen Nachkrieg, 2008; (ed. and intro.) Brutality and Desire: War and Sexuality in Europe's Twentieth Century, 2008. CONTRIBUTOR: German Ideologies since 1945: Studies in the Political Thought and Culture of the Bonn Republic, 2003; Fascism and Neofascism: Critical Writings on the Radical Right in Europe, 2004; Between Marx and Coca Cola: Youth Cultures in Changing European Societies, 1960-1980, 2005; Gray Zones: Ambiguity and Compromise in the Holocaust and Its Aftermath, 2005; Wo 1968 liegt: Reform und Revolte in der

Geschichte der Bundesrepublik, 2006; Die Gegenwart Gottes in der modernen Gesellschaft: Transzendenz und religiose Vergemeinschaftung in Deutschland, 2006; German History from the Margins, 2006; Conflict, Catastrophe and Continuity: Essays on Modern German History, 2007; Socialist Modern, 2008; Frauengesundheit, Migration und Kultur in einer globalisierten Welt, 2008; (ed. with S. Spector and H Puff) After the History of Sexuality: German Genealogies With and Beyond Foucault, 2012. Contributor to journals and periodicals. **Address:** Department of History, Graduate Ctr., City University of New York, Rm. 5111, 365 5th Ave., New York, NY 10016, U.S.A. **Online address:** dherzog@gc.cuny.edu

HERZOG, Melanie Anne. American (born United States), b. 1956?. **Genres:** Art/Art History. **Career:** Edgewood College, professor of art history, chair and director of women's and gender studies. Writer. **Publications:** (With B. Gordon and F. Potter) American Indian Art: The Collecting Experience: Elvehjem Museum of Art, University of Wisconsin-Madison, May 7-July 3, 1988; Elizabeth Catlett: An American Artist in Mexico, 2000; Elizabeth Catlett: In the Image of the People, 2005; Milton Rogovin: The Making of a Social Documentary Photographer, 2006. Contributor to books. **Address:** Edgewood College, 1000 Edgewood College Dr., Madison, WI 53711, U.S.A. **Online address:** mherzog@edgewood.edu

HERZOG, Tobey C. American (born United States), b. 1946. **Genres:** Literary Criticism And History, History, Military/Defense/Arms Control. **Career:** Wabash College, professor of English, 1976-, faculty marshal, 1985-, English Department, chair, 1992-95, Humanities Division, chair, 1998-2002; Anne and Andy Ford Chair in the Liberal Arts, 2010-; R.R. Donnelley, writing consultant, 1980-. Writer. **Publications:** Vietnam War Stories: Innocence Lost, 1992; Tim O'Brien, 1997; Writing Vietnam, Writing Life: Caputo, Heinemann, O'Brien, Butler, 2008. Contributor to books and periodicals. **Address:** Department of English, Wabash College, 209 Center Hall, PO Box 352, Crawfordsville, IN 47933, U.S.A. **Online address:** herzogt@wabash.edu

HESCHEL, Susannah. American (born United States), b. 1956. **Genres:** Theology/Religion. **Career:** Case Western Reserve University, faculty; Princeton University, visiting professor; University of Cape Town, visiting professor; University of Frankfurt, visiting professor; Dartmouth College, Eli Black professor of Jewish studies. Writer and historian. **Publications:** Transforming Jesus from Jew to Aryan: Protestant Theologians in Nazi Germany, 1995; Abraham Geiger and the Jewish Jesus, 1998; The Aryan Jesus: Christian Theologians and the Bible in Nazi Germany, 2008. EDITOR: (and intro.) On Being a Jewish Feminist: A Reader, 1983; Moral Grandeur and Spiritual Audacity: Essays, 1996; (with D. Biale and M. Galchinsky) Insider/Outsider: American Jews and Multiculturalism, 1998; (with R.P. Ericksen) Betrayal: German Churches and the Holocaust, 1999; (with F.E. Udoh, M. Chancey and G. Tatum) Redefining First-Century Jewish and Christian Identities: Essays in Honor of Ed Parish Sanders, 2008. Contributor of articles to periodicals. **Address:** U.S.A. **Online address:** susannah.heschel@dartmouth.edu

HESLAM, Peter S. British/Dutch (born Netherlands), b. 1963. **Genres:** Business/Trade/Industry, Economics, Ethics, Theology/Religion, Third World. **Career:** University of Hull, tutor, 1988-89; Commonwealth House, deputy warden, 1990-92; Church of England, ordained minister and curate, 1996-99; Cambridge Theological Federation, tutor, 1997-99, director of studies, 1999-2000; Ridley Hall, tutor, 2000-; London Institute for Contemporary Christianity, director of capitalism project, 2000-04, associate lecturer in social and economic ethics, 2004-; University of Cambridge, Transforming Business, director, chief coordinator, researcher, prolific writer; Royal Society of Arts, fellow; Trinity Western University, Centre for Entrepreneurial Leaders, adviser. **Publications:** Creating a Christian Worldview: Abraham Kuyper's Lectures on Calvinism, 1998; Globalization: Unravelling the New Capitalism, 2002; (ed.) Globalization and the Good, 2004. Contributor to journals. **Address:** London Institute for Contemporary Christianity, St. Peter's, Vere St., London, GL W1G 0DQ, England. **Online address:** peter.heslam@licc.org.uk

HESLEP, Robert Durham. American (born United States), b. 1930. **Genres:** Education, Philosophy, Women's Studies And Issues, Law. **Career:** Harvard School, instructor in English and history, 1958-63; Pestalozzi-Froebel Teachers College, lecturer in educational philosophy, 1959-61; Edinboro State College, associate professor of education and philosophy, 1963-65; University of Georgia, College of Education, professor of philosophy of education, 1965-67, associate professor of educational leadership, 1967-72, professor of educational leadership, 1972-2001, emeritus professor of educational leader-

ship, 2001-. Writer. **Publications:** Thomas Jefferson and Education, 1969; (ed.) Philosophy of Education, 1971; (ed. with W.T. Blackstone) Social Justice and Preferential Treatment: Women and Racial Minorities in Education and Business, 1977; The Mental in Education: A Philosophical Study, 1981; Professional Ethics and the Georgia Public School Administrator, 1988; Education in Democracy: Education's Moral Role in the Democratic State, 1989; La Educacion en Democracia: La Funcion Moral de la en Educacion en el Estrado Democratico, 1993; Moral Education for Americans, 1995; Philosophical Thinking in Educational Practice, 1997; A Philosophical Guide for Decision Making by Educators: Developing a Set of Foundational Principles, 2002; Ten Basic Questions About Education: How the Concept of Education Shapes the Practice of Education, 2006. Contributor of articles to periodicals. **Address:** College of Education, University of Georgia, G-3 Aderhold Hall, Athens, GA 30602, U.S.A.

HESLEWOOD, Juliet. British (born England), b. 1951. **Genres:** Art/Art History, Mythology/Folklore, Children's Fiction. **Career:** Writer, playwright and art historian. **Publications:** JUVENILE: Tales of Sea and Shore (legends and folktales), 1983; Earth, Air, Fire and Water (legends and folktales), 1985; Introducing Picasso: Painter, Sculptor, 1993; Tales of Two Rivers, the Dordogne and the Lot, 1994; The Magic Sandals of Hualachi (Inca myth), 1995; The History of Western Painting: A Young Person's Guide, 1996; The History of Western Sculpture: A Young Person's Guide, 1996. TRANSLATOR: The Valleys of the Lot and Cele, 1993; The Segala, 1994; The Causse, 1995. **Address:** Frances Lincoln Publishers, 4 Torriano Mews, Torriano Ave., London, GL NW5 2RZ, England. **Online address:** juliet.heslewood@worldonline.fr

HESS, Alan. American/South African (born South Africa), b. 1952?. **Genres:** Architecture, Photography, History. **Career:** San Jose Mercury News, architecture critic, 1986-. Writer and photographer. **Publications:** Some British Industries: Their Expansion and Achievements, 1936-1956, 1957; Googie: Fifties Coffee Shop Architecture, 1986; Viva Las Vegas: After-Hours Architecture, 1993; (with A. Weintraub) Hyperwest: American Residential Architecture on the Edge, 1996; (contrib.) The Architecture of John Lautner, 1999, rev. ed., 2001; (contrib.) Rancho Deluxe: Rustic Dreams and Real Western Living, 2000; (with A. Danish) Palm Springs Weekend: The Architecture and Design of a Mid-Century Oasis, 2001; The Ranch House, 2004; Googie Redux: Ultramodern Roadside Architecture, 2004; (contrib.) Frank Lloyd Wright: The Houses, 2005; (contrib.)Oscar Niemeyer Houses, 2006; (contrib.) Frank Lloyd Wright: Prairie Houses, 2006; (contrib.) Organic Architecture: The Other Modernism, 2006; Forgotten Modern: California Houses 1940-1970, 2007; (contrib.) Frank Lloyd Wright: Mid-century Modern, 2007; (with M. Stern) Julius Shulman: Palm Springs, 2008; Sony Alpha Dslr-a200 Digital Field Guide, 2008; (contrib.) Frank Lloyd Wright: The Buildings, 2008; Sony Alpha Dslr-a700 Digital Field Guide, 2008; Constructing the Academy of Sciences, 2008; Exposure Digital Field Guide, 2009; Oscar Niemeyer Buildings, 2009; Casa Modernista: A History of the Brazil Modern House, 2010; IPad Fully Loaded, 2010; Composition Digital Field Guide, 2010; IPad 2 Fully Load, 2011; All Access, 2012. **Address:** San Jose Mercury News, 750 Ridder Park Dr., San Jose, CA 95190, U.S.A. **Online address:** alan@alanhessphotography.com

HESS, Bill. American (born United States) **Genres:** Documentaries/Reportage, Travel/Exploration, Literary Criticism And History, Social Sciences, History. **Career:** Tundra Times, reporter, photographer and editor, 1981-85; Fort Apache Scout Newspaper, editor, reporter and photographer; Uiñiq Magazine, founder; Alaska's Village Voices, editor and producer; Eyak Echo, staff. **Publications:** Taking Control: The North Slope Borough, the Story of Self Determination in the Arctic, 1993; Gift of the Whale: The Iñupiat Bowhead Hunt, a Sacred Tradition, 1999. **Address:** c/o Author Mail, Sasquatch Books, 119 S Main, Ste. 400, Seattle, WA 98104, U.S.A.

HESS, David J. American (born United States), b. 1956. **Genres:** Sciences, Social Sciences, Technology. **Career:** Colgate University, Interdisciplinary Writing Program, visiting assistant professor, 1987-89; Rensselaer Polytechnic Institute, Department of Science and Technology Studies, assistant professor, 1989, associate professor, 1994, professor, 1998, chair, 2000-04, Program in Ecological Economics, Values and Policy, director, 2006-11; Vanderbilt University, professor of sociology, 2011-. Writer. **Publications:** Spirits and Scientists, 1991; Science in the New Age, 1993; Samba in the Night: Spiritism in Brazil, 1994; Science and Technology in a Multicultural World, 1995; (with R. Da Matta) The Brazilian Puzzle, 1995; Can Bacteria Cause Cancer?, 1997; Science Studies: An Advanced Introduction, 1997; (ed. with

M.J. Wooddell) Women Confront Cancer, 1998; (ed.) Evaluating Alternative Cancer Therapies, 1999; (ed. and intro.) Studying Those Who Study Us: An Anthropologist in the World of Artificial Intelligence, 2001; Selecting Technology, Science and Medicine, 2001; Alternative Pathways in Science and Industry: Activism, Innovation and the Environment in an Era of Globalization, 2007; Localist Movements in a Global Economy: Sustainability, Justice and Urban Development in the United States, 2009. **Address:** Department of Science and Technology Studies, Rensselaer Polytechnic Institute, Sage Bldg., 5th Fl., 110 8th St., Troy, NY 12180-3590, U.S.A. **Online address:** hessd@rpi.edu

HESS, Edward. *See* **BUNGERT, D. Edward.**

HESS, Elizabeth. American (born United States) **Genres:** Adult Non-fiction, Animals/Pets. **Career:** Writer. **Publications:** (With B. Ehrenreich, G. Jacobs) Re-making Love: The Feminization of Sex, 1986; Lost and Found: Dogs, Cats and Everyday Heroes at a Country Animal Shelter, 1998; Nim Chimpsky: The Chimp Who would be Human, 2008. Contributor to periodicals. **Address:** c/o Harcourt Brace & Co., 15 E 26th St., New York, NY 10010, U.S.A.

HESS, Gary R. American (born United States), b. 1937. **Genres:** International Relations/Current Affairs, Biography, History. **Career:** Bowling Green State University, Department of History, professor of history, 1964-, chairman, 1973-81, 1985-92, distinguished research professor, now distinguished research professor emeritus, College of Arts and Sciences, acting dean, 1981-82; Society for Historians of American Foreign Relations, president, 1991; University of Hawaii, John A. Burns distinguished visiting professor, 1993. Writer. **Publications:** Sam Higginbotham of Allahabad: Pioneer of Point IV to India, 1967; America Encounters India, 1941-1947, 1971; (ed.) America and Russia: Cold War Confrontation to Coexistence, 1973; The United States at War, 1941-1945, 1986, 3rd ed., 2010; The United States' Emergence as a Southeast Asian Power, 1940-1950, 1987; Vietnam and the United States: Origins and Legacy of War, 1990, rev. ed., 1998; Presidential Decisions for War: Korea, Vietnam, and the Persian Gulf, 2001, 2nd ed. as Presidential Decisions for War: Korea, Vietnam, the Persian Gulf, and Iraq, 2009; Vietnam: Explaining America's Lost War, 2009; Bowling Green State University, 1910-2010, 2010. **Address:** Department of History, Bowling Green State University, 128 Williams Hall, Bowling Green, OH 43403-0001, U.S.A. **Online address:** ghess@bgnet.bgsu.edu

HESS, Joan. (Joan Hadley). American (born United States), b. 1949. **Genres:** Mystery/Crime/Suspense, Romance/Historical, Novels, Criminology/True Crime, Young Adult Fiction. **Career:** Art teacher in Fayetteville, 1980-84; freelance writer, 1984-. **Publications:** NOVELS: Future Tense, 1987; To Kill a Husband; A Mystery Jigsaw Puzzle Thriller, 1995. CLAIRE MALLOY: Strangled Prose, 1986; Murder at the Murder at the Mimosa Inn, 1986; Dear Miss Demeanor, 1987; Really Cute Corpse, 1988; Diet to Die for, 1989; Roll Over and Play Dead, 1991; Death by the Light of the Moon, 1992; Poisoned Pins: A Claire Malloy Mystery, 1993; Tickled to Death: A Claire Malloy Mystery, 1994; Busy Bodies: A Clare Malloy Mystery, 1995; Closely Akin to Murder: A Claire Malloy Mystery, 1996; Holly, Jolly Murder, 1997; Conventional Corpse: A Claire Malloy Mystery, 2000; Out on a Limb: A Claire Malloy Mystery, 2002; The Goodbye Body, 2005; Damsels in Distress, 2007; Mummy Dearest, 2008. ARLY HANKS: Malice in Maggody: An Ozarks Murder Mystery, 1987; Mischief in Maggody: An Ozarks Murder Mystery, 1988; Much Ado in Maggody, 1989; Madness in Maggody, 1991; Mortal Remains in Maggody, 1991; Maggody in Manhattan: An Arly Hanks Mystery, 1992; O Little Town of Maggody, 1993; Martians in Maggody: An Arly Hanks Mystery, 1994, 2nd ed., 1995; Miracles in Maggody: An Arly Hanks Mystery, 1995; Maggody Militia: An Arly Hanks Mystery, 1997; Misery Loves Maggody: An Arly Hanks Mystery, 1998; Murder@maggody.com, 2000; Joan Hess Presents Malice Domestic 9, 2000; Maggody and the Moonbeams: An Arly Hanks Mystery, 2001; Muletrain to Maggody: An Arly Hanks Mystery, 2004; Malpractice in Maggody: An Arly Hanks Mystery, 2006; The Merry Wives of Maggoddy, 2009. OTHERS: (as Joan Hadley) The Nightblooming Cereus, 1986; (as Joan Hadley) Deadly Ackee, 1988; Red Rover, Red Rover, 1988; (as Joan Hadley) Death of a Romance Writer and Other Stories, 2002; Deadly Ackee and Other Stories of Crime and Catastrophe, 2003; Big Foot Stole My Wife!: And Other Stories, 2003; Deader Homes and Gardens, 2012. Contributor of articles and to magazines. **Address:** c/o Dominick Abel, 146 W 82nd St., Apt. 1B, New York, NY 10024, U.S.A.

HESS, Mary E. American (born United States), b. 1963. **Genres:** Theol-

ogy/Religion, Education, Technology. **Career:** National Assault Prevention Center, director of adolescent programming, 1986-87; Governor's Committee, communications director to the First Lady, 1987-89; Rails-to-Trails Conservancy, Ohio Chapter, director, 1989-90; Cambridge Forum, media coordinator, 1990-91; Public Conversations Project, research assistant, 1991-92; Boston College, Institute of Religious Education and Pastoral Ministry, consultant to master's program, 1994-97, postdoctoral research fellow, director of religious education and director of challenge of media culture project, 1997-2000, lecturer in religious education, 1997-2000; Luther Seminary, associate professor of educational leadership, 2000-. Writer. **Publications:** Media Literacy and Religious Education: Engaging Popular Culture to Enhance Religious Experience, 1998; (ed. with P. Horsfield and A.M. Medrano) Belief in Media: Cultural Perspectives on Media and Christianity, 2004; Engaging Technology in Theological Education: All That We Can't Leave Behind, 2005; (with P. Horsfield, A. Medrano and J.C. Henrííquez) Medios y Creencias: Perspectivas Culturales del Cristianismo en el Entorno Mediático, 2007; (ed. with S.D. Brookfield) Teaching Reflectively in Theological Contexts: Promises and Contradictions, 2008. Contributor of articles to journals and periodicals. **Address:** Luther Seminary, 2481 Como Ave., St. Paul, MN 55108, U.S.A. **Online address:** mhess@luthersem.edu

HESS, Richard S. American (born United States), b. 1954. **Genres:** History, Theology/Religion, Reference. **Career:** Denver Seminary, faculty, 1997-, Earl S. Kalland professor of Old Testament and Semitic languages; International Christian College, lecturer in the old testament and Hebrew; Roehampton University, reader in Old Testament. Writer. **Publications:** Studies in the Personal Names of Genesis 1-11, 1993; Amarna Personal Names, 1993; Joshua: An Introduction and Commentary, 1996; Song of Songs, 2005; Israelite Religions: An Archaeological and Biblical Survey, 2007; (with F.I. Anderson) Names in the Study of Biblical History: David, YHWH Names, and the Role of Personal Names, 2007. EDITOR: (with G.J. Wenham and P.E. Satterthwaite) He Swore an Oath: Biblical Themes from Genesis 12-50, 1994; (with D.T. Tsumura) I Studied Inscriptions from before the Flood: Ancient Near Eastern, Literary, and Linguistic Approaches to Genesis 1-11, 1994; (with P.E. Satterthwaite and G.J. Wenham) The Lord's Anointed: Interpretation of Old Testament Messianic Texts, 1995; (with G.J. Wenham) Make the Old Testament Live: From Curriculum to Classroom, 1998; (with S.E. Porter) Translating the Bible: Problems and Prospects, 1999; (with G.J. Wenham) Zion, City of Our God, 1999; (with M.D. Carroll) Family in the Bible: Exploring Customs, Culture, and Context, 2003; (with M.D. Carroll) Israel's Messiah in the Bible and the Dead Sea Scrolls, 2003; (with G.A. Klingbeil and P.J. Ray, Jr.) Critical Issues in Early Israelite History, 2008; (with E.A. Martens) War in the Bible and Terrorism in the Twenty-first Century, 2008. Contributor of articles to books and journals. **Address:** Denver Seminary, 6399 S Santa Fe Dr., Littleton, CO 80120-2912, U.S.A. **Online address:** rick.hess@denverseminary.edu

HESSE, Karen. American (born United States), b. 1952. **Genres:** Children's Fiction, Young Adult Fiction, Picture/Board Books, Novels, Children's Nonfiction, Biography. **Career:** Writer, 1969-; University of Maryland, leave benefit coordinator, 1975-76; Mental Health Care and Hospice, affiliate, 1988-; Newfane Elementary School, board chair, 1989; teacher; librarian. **Publications:** Wish on a Unicorn, 1991; Letters form Rifka, 1992; Lavender (chapter book), 1993; Phoenix Rising, 1994; A Time of Angels, 1995, rev. ed., 2000; The Music of Dolphins, 1996; Out of the Dust, 1997; Just Juice (chapter book), 1998; A Light in the Storm: The Civil War Diary of Amelia Martin, 1999, 2nd ed., 2003; Stowaway, 2000; Witness, 2001; Aleutian Sparrow, 2003; The Stone Lamp: Eight Stories of Hanukkah through History, 2003; Young Hans Christian Andersen, 2005; Spuds, 2008; Brooklyn Bridge, 2008; What You Wish For: A Book for Darfur, 2011. PICTURE BOOKS: Poppy's Chair, 1993; Lester's Dog, 1993; Sable, 1994; Come on, Rain, 1999; The Cats in Krasinski Square, 2004. Contributor to periodicals. **Address:** c/o of Author Mail, Scholastic Books, 555 Broadway, New York, NY 10012-3919, U.S.A.

HESSE, Mary Brenda. British (born England), b. 1924. **Genres:** Archaeology/Antiquities, Philosophy, Sciences, History. **Career:** University of Leeds, lecturer in mathematics, 1951-55; University of London, University College, lecturer in history and philosophy of science, 1955-59; Cambridge University, lecturer, 1960-68, university reader, 1968-75, professor of philosophy of science, 1975, Stanton lecturer, 1977-80, now professor emeritus; Yale University, visiting professor, 1962-63; University of Minnesota, visiting professor, 1966; University of Chicago, visiting professor, 1968; University of Notre Dame, visiting professor, 1972; University of Edinburgh, Gifford lecturer,

1983. Writer. **Publications:** Science and the Human Imagination: Aspects of the History and Logic of Physical Science, 1954; Forces and Fields: The Concept of Action at a Distance in the History of Physics, 1961; Models and Analogies in Science, 1963, rev. ed., 1966; In Defence of Objectivity (lecture), 1973; The Structure of Scientific Inference, 1974; (ed. with L.J. Cohen) Applications of Inductive Logic: Proceedings of a Conference at the Queen's College, Oxford 21-24, August 1978, 1980; Revolutions and Reconstructions in the Philosophy of Science, 1980; (with M.A. Arbib) The Construction of Reality, 1986. Contributor to journals. **Address:** Department of History and Philosophy of Science, University of Cambridge, Free School Ln., Cambridge, CB CB2 3RH, England.

HESSINGER, Rodney. American (born United States) **Genres:** Young Adult Fiction. **Career:** Hiram College, associate professor of history. Writer. **Publications:** Seduced, Abandoned and Reborn: Visions of Youth in Middle-Class America, 1780-1850, 2005. **Address:** Hiram College, PO Box 67, Hiram, OH 44234, U.S.A. **Online address:** hessingerrj@hiram.edu

HESTER, Katherine L. American (born United States), b. 1964. **Genres:** Novellas/Short Stories, Young Adult Fiction. **Career:** Fiction writer. **Publications:** Eggs for Young America (short stories), 1997. Contributor of articles to periodicals. **Address:** Penguin Group, 375 Hudson St., New York, NY 10014, U.S.A.

HESTER, M(arvin) Thomas. American (born United States), b. 1941. **Genres:** Literary Criticism And History, Translations, Biography, Art/Art History. **Career:** University of Florida, lecturer, 1966-69; North Carolina State University, Department of English, assistant professor, 1972-76, associate professor, 1977-82, professor, 1983-, University Honors Council, director, 1985-87, alumni distinguished professor, 1989-; John Donne Journal, founder and co-editor. **Publications:** (Ed. with J. Durant) A Fair Day in the Affections, 1980; Kinde Pitty and Brave Scorn: John Donne's Satyres, 1982; (with R.V. Young) Justus Lipsius: Epistolica institutio, 1990; (ed. with R.V. Young) John Donne: Selected Prose, 1990; (ed.) Seventeenth-Century British Non-Dramatic Poets, vol. I, 1992, vol. II, 1993, vol. III, 1993; (ed.) John Donne's Desire of More: The Subject of Anne More Donne in his Poetry, 1996; (ed. and trans. with R.V. Young) Principles of Letter-Writing: A Bilingual Text of Justi Lipsi Epistolica Institutio, 1996; (ed. and intro. with R.P. Sorlien and D. Flynn) John Donne's Marriage Letters in The Folger Shakespeare Library, 2005; (ed. with J. Kahan) Talking Renaissance Texts, 2009; The Oxford Handbook of John Donne, 2011. **Address:** Department of English, North Carolina State University, 269 Tompkins Hall, PO Box 8105, Raleigh, NC 27695, U.S.A. **Online address:** hesterats@unity.ncsu.edu

HETHERINGTON, Stephen Cade. Australian (born Australia), b. 1959. **Genres:** Philosophy. **Career:** West Virginia University, assistant professor of philosophy, 1987-90; University of New South, School of History and Philosophy, lecturer, 1990-94, senior lecturer, 1994-2000, associate professor, 2001-, professor; Springer, editor. **Publications:** Epistemology's Paradox: Is a Theory of Knowledge Possible?, 1992; Knowledge Puzzles: An Introduction to Epistemology, 1996; Good Knowledge, Bad Knowledge: On Two Dogmas of Epistemology, 2001; Reality? Knowledge? Philosophy!: An Introduction to Metaphysics and Epistemology, 2003; (ed.) Epistemology Future, 2006; Self-Knowledge: Beginning Philosophy Right Here and Now, 2007; Yes, But How Do You Know?: Introducing Philosophy through Sceptical Ideas, 2009; How to Know: A Practicalist Conception of Knowledge, 2011; (comp.) Epistemology: The Key Thinkers, 2012. Contributor of articles to journals. **Address:** School of History and Philosophy, University of New South Wales, Rm. 337, Morven Brown Bldg., Sydney, NW 2052, Australia. **Online address:** s.hetherington@unsw.edu.au

HETTCHE, Thomas. German (born Germany), b. 1964. **Genres:** Novels, Young Adult Fiction. **Career:** Writer. **Publications:** Ludwig Muss Sterben, 1989; Inkubation, 1992; Nox, 1995; Das Sehen Gehört zu den Glänzenden und Farbigen Dingen, 1997; Animationen, 1999; Der Fall Arbogast: Kriminalroman, 2001; The Arbogast Case, 2003; Woraus wir Gemacht Sind: Roman, 2006. **Address:** Kiepenheuer & Witsch, Bahnhofsvorplatz 1, Köln, 50667, Germany. **Online address:** gfaehndrich@kiwi-koeln.de

HEUER, Jennifer Ngaire. American (born United States), b. 1969. **Genres:** History, Civil Liberties/Human Rights. **Career:** Middlebury College, assistant professor of history; University of Massachusetts, assistant professor of history. Writer. **Publications:** The Family and the Nation: Gender and Citizenship in Revolutionary France, 1789-1830, 2005. **Address:** University of Massachusetts, 300 Massachusetts Ave., Amherst, MA 01003, U.S.A. **Online address:** heuer@history.umass.edu

HEUER, Karsten. Canadian (born Canada), b. 1968?. **Genres:** Children's Fiction, Young Adult Fiction, Travel/Exploration. **Career:** Parks Canada, park ranger, Banff National Park, park ranger, Ivvavik National Park, park ranger. Writer and biologist. **Publications:** Walking the Big Wild: From Yellowstone to the Yukon on the Grizzly Bears' Trail, 2002; Being Caribou: Five Months on Foot with an Arctic Herd, 2005; Being Caribou: Five Months on Foot With a Caribou Herd, 2007. Contributor to magazines. **Address:** 637 3rd St., Canmore, AB T1W 2H9, Canada. **Online address:** feedback@necessaryjourneys.ca

HEUSER, Beatrice. British/Thai (born Thailand), b. 1961. **Genres:** History, International Relations/Current Affairs, Military/Defense/Arms Control, Social Sciences. **Career:** University of Reims, lecturer, 1991; University of London, King's College, Department of War Studies, professor of international and strategic studies, 1991-2003, chair of international and strategic studies, 2000-03; Military History Research Institute of the Bundeswehr, director of research, 2003-07; University of Potsdam, staff; Graduate School of Journalism in Lille, staff; University of the Bundeswehr, staff; The University of Reading, chair in international relations in the school of politics, professor. Writer. **Publications:** Western Containment Policies in the Cold War: The Yugoslav Case, 1948-1953, 1989; (ed.) Nuclear Weapons and the Future of European Security, 1991; (ed. with R. O'Neill) Securing Peace in Europe, 1945-62: Thoughts for the Post-Cold War Era, 1992; Transatlantic Relations: Sharing Ideals and Costs, 1996; NATO, Britain, France and the FRG: Nuclear Strategies and Fares for Europe 1949-2000, 1997; Nuclear Mentalities?: Strategies and Belief in Britain, France, and the FRG, 1998; (ed. with C. Buffet) Haunted by History: Myths in International Relations, 1998; (with F. Géré and A. Baer) Réflexions sur le 'Nucléaireinterdit', 1998; The Bomb: Nuclear Weapons in Their Historical, Strategic and Ethical Context, 1999; (ed. with A.V. Hartmann) Thinking War, Peace and World Orders from Antiquity until the 20th century, 2001; Reading Clausewitz, 2002 trans. as Clausewitz Lesen!: Eine Einführung, 2005; (ed. and intro.) Carl von Clausewitz: On War, 2007; The Evolution of Strategy from Vegetius to the Present, 2008; Den Krieg Denken: Die Entwicklung der Strategie seit, 2009 in UK as The Evolution of Strategy: Thinking War from Antiquity to the Present, 2010; (ed. and intro.) The Strategy Makers, 1650-1850: Thoughts on War and Society, 2010. **Address:** Depart mentof Politics and International Relations, University of Reading, PO Box 218, Reading, BR RG6 6AA, England. **Online address:** d.b.g.heuser@reading.ac.uk

HEVIA, James L. American (born United States), b. 1947. **Genres:** History, Adult Non-fiction, Language/Linguistics. **Career:** Pennsylvania State University, Department of History, teaching assistant, 1972-74; University of Chicago, resident head, 1981-85, Social Science Undergraduate Core Program, lecturer, 1993, The College, senior lecturer, 2004-08, International Studies Program, director, 2004-, International History and the New Collegiate Division, professor; Purdue University, visiting assistant professor of history, 1988; Indiana State University, assistant professor of history, 1988-92; Shandong University, visiting professor of history, 1991; University of North Carolina, Department of History, visiting professor of history, 1991-92, assistant professor of history, 1998-2004, chair of curriculum in international and area studies, 1999-2004; North Carolina Agricultural and Technical State University, assistant professor of history, 1992-98. Writer. **Publications:** Cherishing Men from Afar: Qing Guest Ritual and the Macartney Embassy of 1793, 1995; Huai rou yuan ren: Magaerni shi Hua de Zhong Ying li yi chong tu, 2002; English Lessons: The Pedagogy of Imperialism in Nineteenth-Century China, 2003; Secret Archive: British India Army Intelligence and the Construction of Geo-strategic Asia, forthcoming; Making China Perfectly Equal, forthcoming. Contributor of articles to books and journals. **Address:** Department of History, University of Chicago, 124 Pick Hall, 5828 S University Ave., Chicago, IL 60637-1553, U.S.A. **Online address:** jhevia@uchicago.edu

HEWETT, Joan. American (born United States), b. 1930. **Genres:** Children's Non-fiction, Young Adult Fiction, Law, Transportation, Animals/Pets, Children's Fiction. **Career:** Writer. **Publications:** NONFICTION: The Mouse and the Elephant, 1977; Watching Them Grow: Inside a Zoo Nursery, 1979; Fly Away Free, 1981; When You Fight the Tiger, 1984; Motorcycle on Patrol: The Story of a Highway Officer, 1986; On Camera: The Story of a

Child Actor, 1987; Getting Elected: The Diary of a Campaign, 1989; Laura Loves Horses, 1990; Hector Lives in the United States Now: The Story of a Mexican-American Child, 1990; Public Defender: Lawyer for the People, 1991; Tiger, Tiger, Growing Up, 1993; Tunnels, Tracks and Trains: Building a Subway, 1995; Flamingo Chick Grows Up, 2001; Kangaroo Joey Grows Up, 2002; Harbor Seal Pup Grows Up, 2002; Tiger Cub Grows Up, 2002; Koala Joey Grows Up, 2004; Monkey Baby Grows Up, 2004; Giraffe Calf Grows Up, 2004; Penguin Chick Grows Up, 2004. OTHER: Rosalie, 1987. **Address:** c/o Author Mail, Carolrhoda, 241 1st Ave. N, Minneapolis, MN 55401, U.S.A.

HEWITT, Geof. (Geof George F. Hewitt). American (born United States), b. 1943. **Genres:** Poetry, Education, Literary Criticism And History. **Career:** Epoch Magazine, assistant editor, 1964-66; The Trojan Horse Magazine, editor-in-chief, 1965-66; The Kumquat Press, founding editor, 1966-; Johns Hopkins University, instructor in English, 1966-67; University of Iowa, instructor in English, 1967-69; University of Hawaii, instructor in English, 1969-70; Cornell Alumni News, contributor editor, 1970-75; Union Institute and University, faculty. **Publications:** Poem and Other Poems, 1966; Waking Up Still Pickled, 1967; Quickly Aging Here: Some Poets of the 1970s, 1969; Stone Soup, 1974; I Think They'll Lay My Egg Tomorrow, 1976; Working for Yourself: How to be Successfully Self-employed, 1977; Just Worlds, 1989; A Portolio Primer: Teaching, Collecting, and Assessing Student Writing, 1995; Today You are My Favorite Poet: Writing Poems with Teenagers, 1998; Hewitt's Guide to Slam Poetry and Poetry Slam: For Teachers and Performers, 2005. EDITOR: Selected Poems of Alfred Starr Hamilton, 1969; Living in Whales: Stories and Poems from Vermont Public Schools, 1972. **Address:** Kumquat Press, PO Box 51, Calais, VT 05648, U.S.A. **Online address:** geof.hewitt@myunion.edu

HEWITT, Geof George F. *See* **HEWITT, Geof.**

HEWITT, Richard. American (born United States), b. 1950. **Genres:** Plays/Screenplays, Travel/Exploration, Psychology. **Career:** Freelance writer, 1975-. **Publications:** (With C. McGinn) Wisboroughs: Make a New Start with a Fresh View on Life, 1995; A Cottage in Portugal, 1996; Regresso á casa em Portugal, 1999; Children's Delights: Four In One, 2002; Portugal Redux: Another Cottage in Portugal, forthcoming. Contributor to periodicals. **Address:** Don Congdon Associates, 156 5th Ave., New York, NY 10010, U.S.A.

HEWITT, W(arren) E(dward). Canadian (born Canada), b. 1954. **Genres:** Sociology, International Relations/Current Affairs, Politics/Government, Social Sciences, Urban Studies, Theology/Religion, Young Adult Non-fiction, History, History. **Career:** McMaster University, assistant professor of sociology, 1985-86; University of Lethbridge, assistant professor of sociology, 1986-89; Cooper-Thompson Associates Ltd., vice-president and researcher, 1989-; University of Western Ontario, assistant professor, 1989-93, associate professor, 1993-2001, associate dean of faculty of social sciences, 1998-2001, professor of sociology, 2001-, associate vice-president (research), 2001-04, vice president research and international relations, 2004-; Canadian Journal of Latin American and Caribbean Studies, managing editor. **Publications:** Base Christian Communities and Social Change in Brazil, 1991. EDITOR: The Sociology of Religion: A Canadian Focus, 1993; Introduction to Sociology: A Canadian Focus, 1994, rev. ed., 2000; (with J. Burdick) The Church at the Grassroots in Latin America: Perplexities on Thirty Years of Activism, 2000. Contributor to journals. Works appear in anthologies. **Address:** Department of Sociology, University of Western Ontario, Rm. 5306, StvH 2107, Social Science Ctr., London, ON N6A 5C2, Canada. **Online address:** hewitt@uwo.ca

HEWSON, John. Canadian/British (born England), b. 1930. **Genres:** Language/Linguistics, Art/Art History, Local History/Rural Topics. **Career:** Memorial University of Newfoundland, assistant professor of French, 1960-64, associate professor of French, 1964-68, professor of linguistics, 1968-, university research professor, 1985-90, Henrietta Harvey professor, 1997-, professor emeritus. Writer. **Publications:** Oral French Pattern Practice, 1963; La Pratique du francais, 1965; Article and Noun in English, 1972; Beothuk Vocabularies, 1978; (with B. Francis) The Micmac Grammar of Father Pacifique, 1990; A Computer Generated Dictionary of Proto-Algonquian, 1993; The Cognitive System of the French Verb, 1997; (with V. Bubenik) Tense and Aspect in Indo-European Languages: Theory, Typology, Diachrony, 1997; Workbook for Historical Romance Linguistics, 1998; The French Language in Canada, 2000; (with V. Bubenik) From Case to Adposition: The Develop-

ment of Configurational Syntax in Indo-European Languages, 2006; Grammatical Change in Indo-European Languages, 2009. **Address:** Department of Linguistics, Memorial University of Newfoundland, SN-3050D, St. John's, NL A1B 3X9, Canada. **Online address:** jhewson@mun.ca

IIEY, Jeanne A. K. Italian (born Italy), b. 1963. **Genres:** International Relations/Current Affairs, Economics, Social Sciences, Politics/Government. **Career:** Ohio State University, Department of Political Science, instructor, 1989-91; FLACSO, Quito and Ecuador, visiting researcher and instructor, 1991; Miami University, Department of Political Science and International Studies Program, assistant professor, associate professor, 1992-2004, Miami University Dolibois European Center, core professor in social science, 1998-99, director of international studies program, 2002-, professor, 2004-, interim dean; La Facultad Latinoa Americana de Ciencias Sociales, Quito and Ecuador, graduate program in international relations, visiting assistant professor, 1994; Centre Universitaire de Luxembourg, visiting associate professor, 1999-2000; University of New England, College of Arts and Sciences, dean, Writer. **Publications:** Theories of Dependent Foreign Policy and the Case of Ecuador in the 1980s, 1995; (with L. Neack and P.J. Haney) Foreign Policy Analysis: Continuity and Change in Its Second Generation, 1995; (ed.) Small States in World Politics: Explaining Foreign Policy Behavior, 2003; (ed. with F.O. Mora) Latin American and Caribbean Foreign Policy, 2003. **Address:** College of Arts and Sciences, University of New England, Rm. 405, Decary Hall, Biddeford, ME 04005, U.S.A. **Online address:** heyja@muohio.edu

HEYEN, William. American (born United States), b. 1940. **Genres:** Novellas/Short Stories, Poetry, Essays, Literary Criticism And History. **Career:** Springville High School, English teacher, 1961-62; State University of New York-Cortland, instructor in English, 1963-65; State University of New York-Brockport, assistant professor, 1967-70, associate professor, 1970-73, professor of English and poet-in-residence, 1973-2000, professor emeritus, 2000-; University of Hannover, senior Fulbright lecturer, 1971-72; National Endowment for the Arts, fellow, 1973-74, 1984-85; New York Foundation for the Arts, fellow, 1984; University of Hawaii, visiting professor, 1985; Chautauqua Institution, leader of poetry workshops, 1993. Writer. **Publications:** (Comp. with W. Taggart) What Happens in Fort Lauderdale, 1968; The Mower, 1970; Depth of Field: Poems, 1970; (comp.) Profile of Theodore Roethke, 1971; The Fireman Next Door, 1971; The Trail Beside the River Platte, 1973; The Pigeons, 1973; Noise in the Trees: Poems and a Memoir, 1974; Mermaid, 1975; The Pearl, 1976; Cardinals, 1976; Of Palestine: A Meditation, 1976; Pickerel, 1976; Dusk, 1976; Eighteen Poems and a Story, 1976; The Trench, 1976; The Carrie White Auction at Brockport, 1976; XVII Machines, 1976; Ars Poetica, 1976; Mare, 1976; Darkness, 1977; Fires, 1977; The Elms Home, 1977; The Swastika Poems, 1977; Son Dream/Daughter Dream, 1978; From This Book of Praise: Poems and a Conversation with William Heyen, 1978; The Ash, 1978; Witness, 1978; Lord Dragonfly, 1978; Brockports Poems, 1978; The Descent, 1979; The Children, 1979; Long Island Light: Poems and a Memoir, 1979; Evening Dawning, 1979; The Snow Hen, 1979; Abortion, 1979; Mantle, 1979; The City Parables, 1980; The Shy Bird, 1980; Our Light, 1980; My Holocaust Songs, 1980; 1829-1979: The Bells, 1980; December 31, 1979: The Candle, 1980; The Ewes Song, 1980; Bean, 1981; Blackberry Light: Sections 19-32 of The Chestnut Rain, A Poem in Progress, 1981; Lord Dragonfly: Five Sequences, 1981; The Trains, 1981; The Berries, 1982; Jesus: Three Poems, 1983; Along This Water, 1983; Ram Time, 1983; Ensoulment, 1983; The Numinous, 1983; Erika: Poems of the Holocaust, 1984; Wenzel/The Ghost, 1984; Winter Letter to Dave Smith, 1984; Eight Poems for Saint Walt, 1985; The Cabin, 1985; The Spruce in Winter, 1985; At West Hills, Long Islands, 1985; The Trophy, 1986; Vic Holyfield and the Class of 1957: A Romance, 1986; The Chestnut Rain, 1986; Brockport Sunflowers, 1986; The Amber, 1986; The Bells, 1987; Mother and Son, 1987; What Do You Have to Lose?, 1987; Four from Brockport, 1988; Brockport, New York: Beginning with, 1988; Americans, 1988; (with L.D. Brodsky) Falling from Heaven: Holocaust Poems of a Jew and a Gentile, 1991; Pterodactyl Rose: Poems of Ecology, 1991; The Shore, 1991; Ribbons: The Gulf War: A Poem, 1992; The Tower, 1993; The Host: Selected Poems, 1965-90, 1994; With Me Far Away: A Memoir, 1994; Crazy Horse in Stillness: Poems, 1996; Pig Notes and Dumb Music: Prose on Poetry, 1998; Diana, Charles and the Queen: Poems, 1998; Annuli, 2001; Shoah Train: Poems, 2003; The Rope: Poems, 2003; The Hummingbird Corporation: Stories, 2003; Home: Autobiographies, 2004; The Confessions of Doc Williams and Other Poems, 2006; Poetics of Hiroshima & Other Poems, 2008; The Angel Voices: A Poem, 2010. EDITOR: American Poets in 1976, 1976; I Would Also Like to Mention Aluminum: A Conversation with William Stafford, 1976; The Generation of 2000: Contemporary

American Poets, 1984; (with E. Spires) The Pushcart Prize Fifteen: 1990-91, Best of the Small Presses, 1990; September 11, 2001: American Writers Respond, 2002. Contributor of articles to periodicals. **Address:** 142 Frazier St., Brockport, NY 14420, U.S.A. **Online address:** wheyen@rochester.rr.com

HEYER, Carol. American (born United States), b. 1950. **Genres:** Science Fiction/Fantasy, Children's Fiction, Plays/Screenplays, Art/Art History, Illustrations. **Career:** Lynn-Davis Productions, staff artist and writer, 1982-86; Lynn-Wenger Productions, staff writer and artist, 1986-88; Hollywood Film School, artist, 1986-88; Touchmark, writer and illustrator, 1988-. **Publications:** SELF-ILLUSTRATED: Beauty and the Beast, 1989; The Easter Story, 1990; Excalibur, 1991; The Christmas Story, 1991; Robin Hood, 1993; The Sleeping Beauty in the Wood, 1996; The First Easter, 2002; The First Christmas, 2003; Zippity Zinger, 2004; Humphrey's First Christmas, 2007; Crow and the Pitcher: A Tale About Problem Solving, 2007; Little Shepherd's Christmas, 2011; Humphrey's First Palm Sunday, 2012. **Address:** Touchmark, 925 Avenida de los Arboles, Thousand Oaks, CA 91360, U.S.A. **Online address:** carolheyer@carolheyer.com

HEYES, (Nancy) Eileen. American (born United States), b. 1956. **Genres:** History, Biography, Novels, Young Adult Fiction, Children's Fiction, Education. **Career:** Editor and staff writer for newspapers, 1979-2004; freelance writer, 1990-; News & Observer, children's book review columnist, 1995-2001. **Publications:** Children of the Swastika: The Hitler Youth, 1993; Adolf Hitler, 1994; Tobacco U.S.A.: The Industry behind the Smoke Curtain, 1999; O'Dwyer & Grady Starring In: Acting Innocent, 2002; O'Dwyer & Grady Starring In: Tough Act to Follow, 2003. Contributor to newspapers and periodicals. **Address:** Sterling Lord Literistic, 65 Bleecker St., 2 Old New Milford Rd., PO Box 335, New York, NY 10012, U.S.A. **Online address:** eileenh@eileenheyes.com

HEYHOE, Kate. American (born United States), b. 1955. **Genres:** Food And Wine, Travel/Exploration. **Career:** Gourmet Guide (online periodical), co-founder, 1994; Global Gourmet (online periodical), editor, 1996-. **Publications:** SELF-ILLUSTRATED: (with T. Way) Macho Nachos: 50 Toppings, Salsas and Spreads for Irresistible Snacks and Light Meals, 2003; (with T. Way) A Chicken in Every Pot: Global Recipes for the World's Most Popular Bird, 2004. OTHERS: Cooking with Kids for Dummies, 1999; (with S. Hock) Harvesting the Dream: The Rags-to-Riches Tale of the Sutter Home Winery, 2004; Great Bar Food at Home, 2007; (with C.B. Stubblefield) The Stubb's Bar-B-Q Cookbook, 2007; Cooking Green: Reducing Your Carbon Footprint in the Kitchen: The New Green Basics Way, 2009. Contributor to magazines. **Address:** Forkmedia L.L.C., PO Box 2261, Wimberley, TX 78676-2261, U.S.A. **Online address:** egg@globalgourmet.com

HEYMAN, Abigail. American (born United States), b. 1942. **Genres:** Human Relations/Parenting, Women's Studies And Issues, Autobiography/Memoirs, Documentaries/Reportage, Travel/Exploration. **Career:** Magnum Photos Inc., photographer, 1974-; Archive Pictures, partner, 1981-87; International Center for Photography, director of documentary and photojournalism full-time studies program, 1986-88; New School for Social Research, faculty; Center for Concerned Photography, faculty; Country Photography Workshop, faculty; Aperion Photography Workshops, faculty; freelance photo-journalist. Writer. **Publications:** Growing Up Female: A Personal Photo-Journal, 1974; Butcher, Baker, Cabinet-Maker: Photographs of Women at Work, 1978; Dreams and Schemes: Love and Marriage in Modern Times, 1987; (co-ed.) Flesh and Blood: Photographers' Images of Their Own Families, 1992. Contributor to magazines. **Address:** Magnum Photos Inc., 15 W 46th St., New York, NY 10036, U.S.A.

HEYMAN, Jacques. British (born England), b. 1925?. **Genres:** Architecture, Engineering, Essays. **Career:** Cambridge University, demonstrator, 1951, lecturer, 1954, senior lecturer, 1962-64, reader, 1968, professor of engineering, 1971-92, head of department, 1983-92, professor emeritus, 1992-. Writer. **Publications:** (With L. Baker and M.R. Horne) The Steel Skeleton, vol. II, 1956; Plastic Design of Portal Frames, 1957; Beams and Framed Structures, 1964, 2nd ed., 1974; (ed. with F.A. Leckie) Engineering Plasticity: Papers for a Conference held in Cambridge, March 1968, 1968; (with J. Baker) Plastic Design of Frames, 2 vols., 1969-71; Coulomb's Memoir on Statics: An Essay in the History of Civil Engineering, 1972; Equilibrium of Shell Structures, 1977; Elements of Stress Analysis, 1982; The Masonry Arch, 1982; The Stone Skeleton: Structural Engineering of Masonry Architecture, 1995; Estructuras de Fabrica, 1995; Teoría, Historia y Restauración de Estructuras de Fábrica;

Colección de Ensayos, 1995; Elements of the Theory of Structures, 1996; Arches, Vaults and Buttresses: Masonry Structures and Their Engineering, 1996; Structural Analysis: A Historical Approach, 1998; The Science of Structural Engineering, 1999; Análisisde Estructuras: Un Estudio Histórico, 2004; Essays in the History of the Theory of Structures: In Honour of Jacques Heyman, 2005; Elements of Stress Analysis, 2008; Plastic Design of Frames, 2008; Basic Structural Theory, 2008. **Address:** Department of Engineering, University of Cambridge, The Old Schools, Trinity Ln., Cambridge, CB CB2 1TN, England. **Online address:** jh10002@eng.cam.ac.uk

HEYMAN, Josiah McC(onnell). American (born United States), b. 1958. **Genres:** Anthropology/Ethnology, Law, Social Sciences. **Career:** Michigan Technological University, assistant professor of anthropology and science, technology and society, 1989-94, associate professor, 1994-2000, professor, 2000-02; University of Texas at El Paso, professor of anthropology and chair of department of sociology and anthropology, 2002-. Writer. **Publications:** Life and Labor on the Border: Working People of Northeastern Sonora, Mexico, 1886-1986, 1991; Finding a Moral Heart for U.S. Immigration Policy: An Anthropological Perspective, 1998; (ed.) States and Illegal Practices, 1999. **Address:** Department of Sociology and Anthropology, The University of Texas, Rm. 110, 500 W University Ave., Old Main, El Paso, TX 79968, U.S.A. **Online address:** jmheyman@utep.edu

HEYWARD, Vivian H. American (born United States), b. 1947. **Genres:** Sports/Fitness, Medicine/Health. **Career:** High school physical education teacher, 1968-70; University of Illinois, graduate teaching assistant, 1971-72, Physical Fitness Research Laboratory, research assistant, 1972-74; University of New Mexico, assistant professor, 1974-79, associate professor, 1979-84, professor of exercise science, 1984-97, Regents professor of exercise science, 1997-2000, Regents professor emeritus of exercise science, 2000-; certified health and fitness instructor, 1985-. Writer. **Publications:** Designs for Fitness: A Guide to Physical Fitness Appraisal and Exercise Prescription, 1984; Advanced Fitness Assessment and Exercise Prescription, 1991, 6th ed., 2010; (with L.M. Stolarczyk) Applied Body Composition Assessment, 1996, 2nd ed., 2004. **Address:** University of New Mexico, 1102 Johnson Ctr., 1 University of New Mexico, Albuquerque, NM 87131, U.S.A. **Online address:** vheyward@unm.edu

HEYWOOD, Andrew. British (born England), b. 1952. **Genres:** Philosophy, Politics/Government, Social Sciences. **Career:** Farnborough College, Department of Political Studies, head, 1981-86; Orpington College, course director for political studies, history and law, 1986-, director of studies, 1996-2003; Croydon College, vice principal; University of London, chief examiner. Freelance author and consultant. **Publications:** Political Ideologies: An Introduction, 1992, 4th ed., 2007, trans. as Zheng Zhi De Yi Shi Xing Tai, 2009; Political Ideas and Concepts: An Introduction, 1994, 3rd ed. as Political Theory: An Introduction, 2004; Politics, 1997, 3rd ed., 2007; Key Concepts in Politics, 2000; Essentials of U.K. Politics, 2007, 2nd ed. as Global Politics, 2011. Contributor to books and periodicals. **Address:** 15 Chuters Grove, Epsom, SR KT17 4AS, England. **Online address:** heywoodas@tiscali.co.uk

HEYWOOD, Colin. British (born England), b. 1947. **Genres:** History. **Career:** University of Loughborough, lecturer in economic history, 1973-88; University of Nottingham, senior lecturer in economic and social history, 1988-2004, modern French history, reader, 2004-, professor, faculty of arts. Writer. **Publications:** Cotton industry in France, 1750-1850: An Interpretative Essay, 1977; Childhood in Nineteenth-Century France: Work, Health, and Education among the Classes Populaires, 1988; The Development of the French Economy, 1750-1914, 1992; A History of Childhood: Children and Childhood in the West from Medieval to Modern Times, 2001; Growing Up in France: From the Ancien Regime to the Third Republic, 2007; (ed.) A Cultural History of Childhood and the Family, vol. V: The Age of Empire, 2010. **Address:** School of History, University of Nottingham, Rm. B10 Lenton Grove, University Pk., Nottingham, NT NG7 2RD, England. **Online address:** colin.heywood@nottingham.ac.uk

HEZLEP, William (Earl). American (born United States), b. 1936. **Genres:** Mystery/Crime/Suspense, Children's Fiction, Young Adult Fiction, Plays/Screenplays, Art/Art History. **Career:** Actor 1962-65; Wayne State University, instructor, 1965-68; Southwest State University, assistant professor, 1968-72, associate professor and department chairman, 1973-76, professor of theatre arts, 1976-2005, professor emeritus, 2005-; Southwest Summer Theatre, director, 1968-77; L.S.U. The Pittsburgh Playhouse, actor. Writer. **Publica-**

tions: TRAVELERS PLAY SERIES (FOR CHILDREN): Nessie, 1981; Pharaoh's Dagger, 1982; Cayman Duppy, 1984; Travelers, 1987; Ghost Town, 1992; Pharoah's [sic] Dagger, 1992; Red Cloud's Revenge, 1994; Treasure of the Mayans, 1994; Tower of London, 1995; Merlin's Cave, 1996; How Come Christmas?, 1996; Shipwrecked, 1999; Kokopelli's Cave, 2002; Trouble in the Mountains, 2002; Bog Bodies, 2004; Bigfoot!, 2004; Plays of the Past, 2004; Plays of the Present, 2004; Curse of the Tomb Raiders, 2005; Time Travelers, 2006; Past and Present, 2010. OTHERS: Pipestone Cafe, 1977; Winterkill, 1978; It's a Living, 1979; Time Pockets, 1979; Computer Bait, 1983; Obit for a Polar Bear, 1985; Runestone 2005. **Address:** Theatre Program, Southwest Minnesota State University, 1501 State St., Marshall, MN 56258, U.S.A. **Online address:** hezlep@southwest.msus.edu

HIAASEN, Carl. American (born United States), b. 1953. **Genres:** Mystery/Crime/Suspense, Humor/Satire, Young Adult Fiction, Essays. **Career:** Cocoa Today, reporter, 1974-76; Miami Herald, reporter, 1976-, columnist, 1985-; Barry College, professor, 1978-79. **Publications:** (With W.D. Montalbano) Powder Burn, 1981; (with W.D. Montalbano) Trap Line, 1982; (with W.D. Montalbano) A Death in China, 1984; Tourist Season, 1986; Double Whammy, 1987; Skin Tight, 1989; Native Tongue, 1991; Strip Tease, 1993; Stormy Weather, 1995; (co-author) Naked Came the Manatee, 1997; Lucky You, 1997; Team Rodent: How Disney Devours the World (essay), 1998; (contrib.) Kick Ass, 1999; Sick Puppy, 2000; Paradise Screwed, 2001; Basket Case, 2002; Skinny Dip, 2004; Nature Girl, 2006; (ed. and intro.) Best American Mystery Stories 2007, 2007; The Downhill Lie, 2008; Scat, 2009; Star Island, 2010; Chomp, 2012. FOR YOUNG ADULTS: Hoot, 2002; Flush, 2005. **Address:** c/o Author Mail, Random House Children's Books, 1745 Broadway, New York, NY 10019, U.S.A. **Online address:** chiaasen@miamiherald.com

HIAM, Alexander. (Alexander Watson Hiam). American (born United States), b. 1957. **Genres:** Administration/Management, Business/Trade/Industry, Marketing. **Career:** Silicon Valley of California, staff, 1980-88; Alexander Hiam and Associates (consulting and training firm), director, 1988-; INSIGHTS for Training & Development, founder. Writer. **Publications:** The Vest-Pocket CEO: Decision-Making Tools for Executives, 1990; The Vest-Pocket Marketer, 1991; (with S. Angle) Adventure Careers: Your Guide to Exciting Jobs, Uncommon Occupations and Extraordinary Experiences, 1992; (with C. Schewe) The Portable MBA in Marketing, 1992, 2nd ed., 1998; (co-author) Closing the Quality Gap: Lessons from America's Leading Companies, 1992; Does Quality Work?: A Review of Relevant Studies, 1993; Quality Function Deployment: Adding Value to Products and Processes, 1994; (with S. Angle) Adventure Careers, 1995; (co-author) Exploring the World of Business, 1996; (with R.J. Lewicki) Think before You Speak, 1996; (with K.W. Olander) The Entrepreneur's Complete Sourcebook, 1996; (ed. as Alexander Watson Hiam) The Portable Conference on Change Management, 1997; Marketing for Dummies, 1997, 3rd ed., 2009; The Manager's Pocket Guide to Creativity, 1998; (with R.J. Lewicki) The Fast-Forward MBA in Negotiation and Deal-Making, 1999; Streetwise Motivating and Rewarding Employees: New and Better Ways to Inspire Your People, 1999; Streetwise Twenty-Four Hour MBA: Power Workshops for Business Success, Including Leadership, Marketing, Finance, Motivating Employees and Business Communications, 2000; Marketing Kit for Dummies, 2000, 3rd ed., 2009; Making Horses Drink: How to Lead and Succeed in Business, 2002; (co-author) Managing by Defining Moments: Innovative Strategies for Motivating Five Very Different Generational Cohorts-Postwar, Leading-Edge Baby Boomer, 2002; Motivational Management: Inspiring Your People for Maximum Performance, 2003; Strategic Type Leadership Indicator Video, 2004; Dealing With Conflict: Participant Coursebook, 2004; Mastering Business Negotiation: A Working Guide to Making Deals and Resolving Conflict, 2006; (with L.G. Rastelli) Marketing, 2007. Contributor to periodicals. **Address:** John Wiley & Sons Inc., 10475 Crosspoint Blvd., Indianapolis, IN 46256, U.S.A. **Online address:** alexawh@gmail.com

HIAM, Alexander Watson. *See* **HIAM, Alexander.**

HIATT, Howard H(aym). American (born United States), b. 1925. **Genres:** Medicine/Health. **Career:** Cornell University, Medical College, New York Hospital, research fellow, 1951-53; National Institute for Arthritis and Metabolic Disorders, investigator, 1953-55; Harvard University, instructor, 1955-57, assistant professor, 1957-63, professor of medicine, 1963-, Herrman L. Blumgart professor of medicine, 1963-72, School of Public Health, dean, 1972-84, Harvard AIDS Institute, Center for Policy and Education, head, 1988-90; Beth Israel Hospital, associate in medicine, 1955-63, physician-in-chief, 1963-72; Imperial Cancer Research Fund Laboratory, visiting scientist, 1969-70; Brigham and Women's Hospital, senior physician, 1985-, Division of Global Health Equity, co-founder and associate chief; American Academy of Arts and Sciences, secretary, 1991-97. Writer. **Publications:** (Ed. with D.S. Feingold) Beth Israel Hospital Seminars in Medicine, 1969; (ed. with J.D. Watson and J.A. Winsten) Origins of Human Cancer, vol. I: Incidence of Cancer in Humans, vol. II: Mechanisms of Carcinogenesis, vol. III: Human Risk Assessment, 1977; America's Health in the Balance: Choice or Chance?, 1987; Medical Lifeboat: Will There Be Room for You in the Health Care System?, 1989; (co-author) A Measure of Malpractice: Medical Injury, Malpractice Litigation, and Patient Compensation, 1993. **Address:** Department of Medicine, Brigham and Women's Hospital, 75 Francis St., Boston, MA 02115-6110, U.S.A. **Online address:** hhiatt@partners.org

HIBBING, John R. American (born United States), b. 1953. **Genres:** Politics/Government, Social Sciences. **Career:** Oakland University, Department of Political Science, visiting instructor, 1980-81; University of Nebraska, Department of Political Science, assistant professor, 1981-85, associate professor, 1985-90, professor of political science, 1990-2001, chair of department, 1991-93, Foundation Regents university professor, 2001-; University of Essex, NATO fellow and visiting fellow, 1984-85; Legislative Studies Quarterly, editorial board, 1984-88, 1990-92, 2001-04, co-editor, 1992-93; American Political Science Review, editorial board, 1985-89; Institute of Regional Studies, visiting professor, 1990; American Journal of Political Science, editorial board, 1991-94; American Politics Quarterly, associate editor, 1987-90, co-editor, 1991-92, editorial board, 1992-; Congress and The Presidency, editorial board, 1995-; Journal of Politics, editorial board, 1998-2001; Rutgers University, Eagleton Institute, visiting research professor, 2002-03; Midwest Political Science Association, vice president, 2004-05. **Publications:** Choosing to Leave: Voluntary Retirement from the U.S. House of Representatives 1982; Congressional Careers: Contours of Life in the U.S. House of Representatives, 1991; (with E. Theiss-Morse) Congress as Public Enemy: Public Attitudes toward American Political Institutions, 1995; (with E. Theiss-Morse) Stealth Democracy: Americans' Beliefs about How Government Should Work, 2002. EDITOR: (with J.G. Peters) The Changing World of the U.S. Senate, 1990; (with E. Theiss-Morse) What Is It about Government that Americans Dislike, 2001. Works appear in anthologies. Contributor to political science journals. **Address:** Department of Political Science, University of Nebraska, 511 Oldfather Hall, Lincoln, NE 68588-0328, U.S.A. **Online address:** jhibbing@unl.edu

HIBBS, John. (John Blyth). British (born England), b. 1925. **Genres:** Poetry, Economics, Marketing, Transportation, Economics, Politics/Government. **Career:** Premier Travel Ltd., personal assistant, 1950-52; Corona Coaches Ltd., managing director, 1956-60; British Railways, traffic survey officer and market research officer, 1961-67; City of London Polytechnic, senior lecturer, 1967-69, principal lecturer in transport, 1969-73; University of Central England (now Birmingham City University), principal lecturer, 1973-83, director of transport studies, 1983-90, professor of transport management, 1987-90, professor emeritus transport management, 1990-; Proceedings of the Chartered Institute of Transport, editor, 1991-. Writer. **Publications:** Transport for Passengers: A Study in Enterprise without Licence, 1963, 2nd ed., 1971; (as John Blyth) New Found Land, 1963; (as John Blyth) Being a Patient, 1965; The History of British Bus Services: With Eleven Maps Drawn by Eric Axten, 1968, 2nd ed., 1989; Transport Studies: An Introduction, 1970, 3rd ed., 1999; (ed.) The Omnibus: Readings in the History of Road Passenger Transport, 1971; How to Run the Buses, 1972; People and Transport, 1972; The Bus and Coach Industry: Its Economics and Organization, 1975; (with R. Seaton) The Teaching of Transport Studies, Organisation of Teachers of Transport Studies, 1976; Transport Without Politics?: A Study of the Scope for Competitive Markets in Road, Rail and Air, 1982; Bus and Coach Management, 1985; Regulation: An International Study of Bus and Coach Licensing, 1985; The Country Bus, 1986; The Bus and Coach Operator's Handbook, 1987; The Country Chapel, 1988; Marketing Management in the Bus and Coach Industry, 1989; Looking Upwards, 1991; (with G. Roth) Tomorrow's Way: Managing Roads in a Free Society, 1992; On the Move: A Market for Mobility on the Roads, 1993; Glossary of Economic and Related Terms for the Use of Students on Transport Courses, 1993; Transport Policy: The Myth of Integrated Planning, 2000; Transport Economics & Policy: A Practical Analysis of Performance, Efficiency and Marketing Objectives, 2003; A Country Busman, 2003. Contributor to journals. **Address:** Birmingham City University,

City North Campus, Birmingham, WM B42 2SU, England. **Online address:** john.hibbs@uce.ac.uk

HIBBS, Thomas S. American (born United States), b. 1960?. **Genres:** Theology/Religion, Cultural/Ethnic Topics, Essays. **Career:** Thomas Aquinas College, faculty; Boston College, professor of philosophy; Baylor University, professor of ethics and culture, distinguished professor of ethics and culture, Honors College, dean. Writer. **Publications:** NONFICTION: Dialectic and Narrative in Aquinas: An Interpretation of the Summa Contra Gentiles, 1995; The Enchiridion on Faith, Hope and Love, 1996; (ed. with J. O'Callaghan) Recovering Nature: Essays in Natural Philosophy, Ethics and Metaphysics in Honor of Ralph McInerny, 1999; Shows about Nothing: Nihilism in Popular Culture from The Exorcist to Seinfeld, 1999, 2nd ed., 2011; On Human Nature, 1999; Virtue's Splendor: Wisdom, Prudence and the Human Good, 2001; Aquinas, Ethics and Philosophy of Religion: Metaphysics and Practice, 2007; Arts of Darkness: American Noir and the Quest for Redemption, 2008; (with M. Fujimura) Rouault-fujimura: Soliloques, 2009. Contributor of articles to periodicals. **Address:** Baylor University, 1 Bear Pl., Waco, TX 76798-7014, U.S.A.

HICHWA, John S. American (born United States), b. 1938. **Genres:** Sports/Fitness, Education, inspirational/Motivational Literature, Medicine/Health. **Career:** Teacher, 1960-65; Old Lyme Country Club, teaching tennis professional, 1960-65; John Read Middle School, physical education teacher, 1965-95, Project Adventure Program, founder, teacher, 1982-95; Country Club of Fairfield, teaching tennis professional, 1966-80; Sportime Intl., consultant. Writer. **Publications:** Right Fielders are People Too: An Inclusive Approach to Teaching Middle School Physical Education, 1998. **Address:** 10 Beauiles Ln., Redding, CT 06896, U.S.A. **Online address:** toy1993@mindspring.com

HICK, John (Harwood). British (born England), b. 1922. **Genres:** Theology/Religion, Philosophy, Humanities. **Career:** Cornell University, assistant professor of philosophy, 1956-59; Princeton Theological Seminary, Stuart professor of Christian philosophy, 1959-64; Cambridge University, lecturer in divinity, 1964-67; University of Birmingham, H.G. Wood professor of theology, 1967-82, H.G. Wood professor emeritus, 1982-; Claremont Graduate University, Danforth professor of philosophy of religion, 1980-92, professor emeritus, 1992-. Writer. **Publications:** Faith and Knowledge: A Modern Introduction to the Problem of Religious Knowledge, 1957, 2nd ed., 1966; Philosophy of Religion, 1963, 4th ed., 1990; Evil and the God of Love, 1966, 2nd ed., 1977; Theology's Central Problem, 1968; Christianity at the Centre, 1968, 2nd ed. as The Center of Christianity, 1978; Arguments for the Existence of God, 1971; Biology and the Soul, 1972; God and the Universe of Faiths, 1973, rev. ed., 1977; Death and Eternal Life, 1976, 3rd ed., 1994; God Has Many Names, 1980, 2nd ed., 1982; Problems of Religious Pluralism, 1985; An Interpretation of Religion: Human Responses To The Transcendent, 1989, 2nd ed., 2005; (with N. Smart and D. Burrell) Hermeneutics, Religion Pluralism and Truth: Lectures, 1989; John Hick: An Autobiography, 1990; Disputed Questions in Theology and the Philosophy of Religion, 1993; The Metaphor of God Incarnate: Christology in a Pluralistic Age, 1993, 2nd ed., 2006; The Second Christianity, 1994; (with M. Goulder) Why Believe in God?, 1994; A Christian Theology of Religions: The Rainbow of Faiths in UK as The Rainbow of Faiths, 1995; (co-author) Four Views on Salvation in a Pluralistic World, 1996; The Fifth Dimension: An Exploration of the Spiritual Realm, 1999; The New Frontier of Religion and Science: Religious Experience, Neuroscience and The Transcendent, 2007; Who or What is God?: And Other Investigations, 2009; Between Faith and Doubt: Dialogues on Religion and Reason, 2010. EDITOR: The Existence of God, 1964; Faith and the Philosophers, 1964; Classical and Contemporary Readings in the Philosophy of Religion, 1964, 3rd ed., 1990; (intro.) The Existence of God, 1964; (with A.C. McGill) The Many-Faced Argument: Recent Studies on the Ontological Argument for the Existence of God, 1967; Truth and Dialogue in World Religions: Conflicting Truth-Claims, 1974; The Myth of God Incarnate, 1978; (with B. Hebblethwaite) Christianity and Other Religions, 1981, 2nd ed., 2000; (with H. Askari) The Experience of Religious Diversity, 1985; (with P.F. Knitter) The Myth of Christian Uniqueness: Toward A Pluralistic Theology of Religions, 1987; (with E. Meltzer) Three Faiths-One God: A Jewish, Christian, Muslim Encounter, 1989; (with L. Hempel) Gandhi's Significance for Today, 1989; A John Hick Reader, 1990; Dialogues in the Philosophy of Religion, 2001. **Address:** Depatment of Philosophy, Theology & Religion, University of Birmingham, Edgbaston, Birmingham, WM B15 2TT, England. **Online address:** j.h.hick@bham.ac.uk

HICKEN, Mandy. (Marilyn E. Hicken). British (born England), b. 1937. **Genres:** Adult Non-fiction, Bibliography, Young Adult Fiction. **Career:** Chesterfield Borough Library, chief cataloger, 1962-74; Derbyshire Library Service, special services librarian, 1974-80, group librarian, 1980-97; director. Writer. **Publications:** (With R. Prytherch) Now Read On: A Guide to Contemporary Popular Fiction, 1990, 2nd ed., 1994; A History of Brimington, 1990; (comp. as Marilyn E. Hicken) Cumulated Fiction Index, 1980-1989, 1990; Filmed Books and Plays, 1991. **Address:** Manor House Farm, 76 Manor Rd., Brimington, Chesterfield, DB S43 1NN, England. **Online address:** mhicken@talk21.com

HICKEN, Marilyn E. *See* **HICKEN, Mandy.**

HICKEY, Caroline. American (born United States), b. 1976?. **Genres:** Children's Fiction, Adult Non-fiction. **Career:** Writer. **Publications:** Cassie Was Here, 2007; Isabelle's Boyfriend, 2008. **Address:** Writers House, 21 W 26th St., New York, NY 10010, U.S.A. **Online address:** caroline@carolinehickey.com

HICKEY, Donald R. American (born United States), b. 1944. **Genres:** History, Biography, Military/Defense/Arms Control, Reference. **Career:** University of Illinois, visiting lecturer, 1972-73; University of Colorado, visiting assistant professor, 1973-75; University of California, lecturer, 1976-77; Wayne State College, assistant professor, professor of history, 1978-; U.S. Army Command and General Staff College, John F. Morrison professor of military history, 1991-92; U.S. Naval War College, visiting professor of strategy, 1995-96. Writer and historian. **Publications:** The War of 1812: A Forgotten Conflict, 1989; (with S.A. Wunder and J.R. Wunder) Nebraska Moments: Glimpses of Nebraska's Past, 1992, new ed., 2007; The War of 1812: A Short History, 1995; Don't Give Up the Ship!: Myths of the War of 1812, 2006; (ed. with C.D. Clark) Citizen Hamilton: The Wit and Wisdom of an American Founder, 2006; (with R.E. Eshelman and S.S. Sheads) War of 1812 in the Chesapeake: A Reference Guide to Historic Sites in Maryland, Virginia, and the District of Columbia, 2010; (with C.D. Clark) The Rockets' Red Glare: An Illustrated History of the War of 1812, 2011. Contributor to books, periodicals and journals. **Address:** Department of History, Wayne State College, 247 Connell Hall, 1111 Main St., Wayne, NE 68787-1181, U.S.A. **Online address:** dohicke1@wsc.edu

HICKEY, Georgina. American (born United States), b. 1968. **Genres:** History, Women's Studies And Issues, Sociology. **Career:** Georgia Southern University, assistant professor of history, 1996-2001; University of Michigan, Department oh History, assistant professor, 2001-04, associate professor and chair, 2004-, Women in Learning and Leadership Program, director. Writer and historian. **Publications:** Hope and Danger in the New South City: Working-Class Women and Urban Development in Atlanta, 1890- 1940, 2003. Contributor to books and journals. **Address:** Department of Social Sciences, University of Michigan, 4901 Evergreen Rd., Dearborn, MI 48128-1491, U.S.A. **Online address:** ghickey@umd.umich.edu

HICKMAN, Bert G(eorge). American (born United States), b. 1924. **Genres:** Economics, Adult Non-fiction, Autobiography/Memoirs, Business/Trade/Industry. **Career:** Stanford University, instructor in economics, 1949-51, professor of economics, 1966, now professor emeritus of economics; National Bureau of Economic Research, research associate, 1951-52; Northwestern University, assistant professor of economics, 1952-54; Council of Economic Advisors, senior staff, 1954-56; Brookings Institution, research associate, 1956-57, senior staff, 1958-66; University of California, visiting professor, 1960-61. Writer. **Publications:** The Korean War and the United States Economic Activity, 1950-52, 1955; Growth and Stability of Post War Economy, 1960; On a New Method of Capacity Estimation, 1964; Investment Demand and U.S. Economic Growth, 1965; Investment Demand in the Sixties, 1966; (with R.M. Coen) Annual Growth Model of the U.S. Economy, 1976. EDITOR: Quantitative Planning of Economic Policy: A Conference of the Social Science Research Council Committee on Economic Stability, 1965; (ed.) Econometric Models of Cyclical Behavior, 1972; (ed.) Global International Economic Models: Selected Papers from an IIASA Conference, 1983; (ed. with F.G. Adams) Global Econometrics: Essays in Honor of Lawrence R. Klein, 1983; International Monetary Stabilization and the Foreign Debt Problem, 1984; Macroeconomic Impacts of Energy Shocks, 1987; (with H.G. Huntington and J.L. Sweeney) Macroeconomic Impacts of Energy Shocks: Contributions from Participating Modelers, 1987; (ed.) International Productivity and Competitiveness, 1992; (with L. Klein) LINK Proceedings, 1991-

1992, Studies in Applied International Economics, vol. I, 1998. **Address:** Department of Economics, Stanford University, 337 Landau, Ralph Landau Economics Bldg., 579 Serra Mall, Stanford, CA 94305-6072, U.S.A. **Online address:** bhickman@stanford.edu

HICKOK, Ralph. American (born United States), b. 1938. **Genres:** Sports/Fitness. **Career:** Green Bay Press-Gazette, general assignment reporter, 1954-57; Gloucester Daily Times, general assignment reporter, 1960-61; Celina Daily Standard, sports editor, 1961-63; New Bedford Standard-Times, feature writer and editor of sunday magazine, 1963-73; Southeastern Advertising Agency Inc., chief copywriter, 1973-92; SEA Tourism/Travel Research, director of data processing, 1992-; hickoksports.com, owner. **Publications:** Who Was Who in American Sports, 1971; The New Encyclopedia of Sports, 1977; The Encyclopedia of North American Sports History, 1992, 2nd ed., 2002; The Pro Football Fan's Companion, 1995; Who's Who of Sports Champions, 1995. Contributor to magazines. **Address:** Hickok Sports, 60 Orchard St., New Bedford, MA 02740, U.S.A.

HICKS, Barbara. Also writes as Charlotte Nichols, JoAnn Barbour, Barbara Jean Hicks. American (born United States), b. 1953. **Genres:** Novels, Literary Criticism And History. **Career:** WASL University, special program manager. Writer, educator and consultant. **Publications:** (As Charlotte Nichols with P. Knoll) For the Love of Mike, 1984; (as Charlotte Nichols with P. Knoll) Eye of the Beholder, 1985; (as JoAnn Barbour) One on One, 1991. AS BARBARA JEAN HICKS: pictures by Alexis Deacon. Tea for Two, 1996; Coming Home, 1996; (with L. McCourtney and K.M. Ball) Mistletoe, 1996; Snow Swan, 1997; (with K. Ball and D. Noble) Hearts Delight, 1998; All That Glitters: A Romantic Comedy, 1998; China Doll, 1998; An Unlikely Prince, 1998; Twice in a Blue Moon, 1999; Cupid's Chase, 1999; Loves Me Loves Me Not, 2000; Restoration and Romance: For the Love of an Old House, 2001; The Queen of the World and the Handyman, 2001; Jitterbug Jam: A Monster Tale, 2005; I Like Colors, 2006; I Like Black and White, 2006; The Secret Life of Walter Kitty, 2007; Monsters Don't Eat Broccoli, 2009; Be Wize, Give Love, 2009. Contributor to periodicals. **Address:** Farrar, Straus and Giroux, 19 Union Sq. W, New York, NY 10001, U.S.A. **Online address:** bjhicks@ix.netcom.com

HICKS, Barbara Jean. See HICKS, Barbara.

HICKS, Brian. American (born United States), b. 1966?. **Genres:** Novels, Mystery/Crime/Suspense, History. **Career:** Post and Courier, senior writer, 1997-, metro columnist. **Publications:** (With T. Bartelme) Into the Wind, Around Alone: The Story of the World's Longest Race, 1999; (with S. Kropf) Raising the Hunley: The Remarkable History and Recovery of the Lost Confederate Submarine, 2002; Ghost Ship: The Mysterious True Story of the Mary Celeste and Her Missing Crew, 2004; When the Dancing Stopped: The Real Story of the Morro Castle Disaster and its Deadly Wake, 2006; Toward the Setting Sun: John Ross, The Cherokees, and the Trail of Tears, 2011. **Address:** The Post and Courier, 134 Columbus St., Charleston, SC 29403-4800, U.S.A. **Online address:** bhicks@postandcourier.com

HICKS, Douglas A. American (born United States), b. 1967. **Genres:** Theology/Religion, Money/Finance, Economics. **Career:** Clarendon Hill Church, parish associate, 1995-98; University of Virginia, assistant professor, 1998-2004, associate professor, 2004-10, professor of leadership studies and religion, 2010-, Bonner Center for Civic Engagement, founding director, 2004-07, executive director, 2007-09; Bon Air Presbyterian Church, parish associate, 1998-2009; Harvard Divinity School, visiting assistant professor, 2003; Union Theological Seminary, visiting associate professor, 2006-07; Presbyterian School of Christian Education, visiting associate professor, 2006-07; Universidad de Granada, visiting researcher, 2007; Second Presbyterian Church, parish associate, 2010-; Harvard University, Pluralism Project, research affiliate. Writer and ordained Presbyterian minister. **Publications:** Inequality and Christian Ethics, 2000; Religion and the Workplace: Pluralism, Spirituality, Leadership, 2003; (ed. with J.T. Wren and T.L. Price) International Library of Leadership, 3 vols., 2004; (ed. with M. Valeri) Global Neighbors: Christian Faith and Moral Obligation in Today's Economy, 2008; With God on All Sides: Leadership in a Devout and Diverse America, 2009; Money Enough: Everyday Practices for Living Faithfully in the Global Economy, 2010. Contributor of articles to books, journals and periodicals. **Address:** Jepson School of Leadership Studies, University of Richmond, 28 Westhampton Way, Richmond, VA 23173, U.S.A. **Online address:** dhicks@richmond.edu

HICKS, L. Edward. American (born United States), b. 1949. **Genres:** Bi-ography, Politics/Government, Social Sciences. **Career:** High school teacher and coach, 1968-76; Fullerton Junior College, adjunct instructor, 1970-76; BD Hicks Enterprises Inc., vice-president, president, 1976-90; University of Memphis, instructor, 1987-91; Christian Brothers University, instructor in European history, 1990-91; Faulkner University, professor of history, 1991-, Humanities and Fine Arts Division, head, 1991-93, Department of Behavioral and Social Science, head, 1991-2002, chairman. Writer. **Publications:** Sometimes in the Wrong, But Never in Doubt: George S. Benson and the Education of the New Religious Right, 1995. Contributor to journals. **Address:** Department of Social & Behavioral Science, Faulkner University, Rm. 305-B, Greer Hall, 5345 Atlanta Hwy., Montgomery, AL 36109-3323, U.S.A.

HICKS, Robert. American (born United States), b. 1951?. **Genres:** Novellas/Short Stories. **Career:** Franklin's Charge: A Vision and Campaign for the Preservation of Historic Open Space, founder and president; Ogden Museum of Southern Art, director; Historic Carnton Plantation, director, president, 1997. Writer. **Publications:** Nashville: The Pilgrims of Guitar Town, 2000; The Widow of the South, 2005; (ed. with J. Stelter and J. Bohlinger) A Guitar and a Pen: Stories by Country Music's Greatest Songwriters, 2008; A Separate Country, 2009. **Address:** c/o Author Mail, Warner Books, 1271 Ave. of the Americas, New York, NY 10020, U.S.A. **Online address:** contactrobert@aol.com

HICOK, Bob. American (born United States), b. 1960?. **Genres:** Poetry. **Career:** Western Michigan University, visiting instructor in English, 2002-; Virginia Tech, associate professor of creative writing. Poet. **Publications:** POETRY: Bearing Witness, 1991; The Legend of Light, 1995; Plus Shipping, 1998; Animal Soul, 2001; Insomnia Diary, 2004; This Clumsy Living, 2007; Words for Empty and Words for Full, 2010. Contributor of poems to periodicals. Works appear in anthologies. **Address:** Department of English, Virginia Tech, 323 Shanks Hall 0112, Blacksburg, VA 24061, U.S.A. **Online address:** bob.hicok@wmich.edu

HIÇYILMAZ, Gaye. British (born England), b. 1947. **Genres:** Children's Fiction, Young Adult Fiction, Travel/Exploration, Romance/Historical, Novels. **Career:** Writer and educator. **Publications:** Against the Storm (children's novel), 1992; The Frozen Waterfall, 1994; Watching the Watcher, 1996; And the Stars Were Gold, 1997; Coming Home, 1998; Smiling for Strangers, 2000; Girl in Red, 2000; In Flame, 2002. **Address:** c/o Rosemary Bromley, Juvenalia, Avington, Winchester, HM SO21 1DB, England.

HIDER, James. Israeli/British (born England), b. 1968?. **Genres:** Young Adult Non-fiction. **Career:** Times, Middle East correspondent. Writer. **Publications:** The Spiders of Allah: Travels of an Unbeliever on the Frontline of Holy War (nonfiction), 2009. Contributor to periodicals. **Address:** Jerusalem, Israel. **Online address:** jameshider@spidersofallah.com

HIEATT, Constance B(artlett). American/Canadian (born Canada), b. 1928. **Genres:** Children's Fiction, Food And Wine, Literary Criticism And History, Translations. **Career:** City University of New York, City College, faculty, 1959-60, Queensborough Community College, assistant professor, 1960-64, associate professor of English, 1964-65; Yale University, faculty; Saint John's University, associate professor, 1965-67, professor of English, 1967-69; University of Western Ontario, professor of English, 1969-93, professor emeritus, 1993-. Writer. **Publications:** CO-EDITOR: (and trans. and adapter) The Canterbury Tales of Geoffrey Chaucer, 1961; (and trans.) The Canterbury Tales of Geoffrey Chaucer, 1964; (with A.K. Hieatt) Selected Poetry, 1970; Curye on Inglysch, 1985; La Novele Cirurgerie, 1990; Beginning Old English, 1994; (and trans.) Tale of the Alerion, 1994; (with M.J. Toswell) Prosody and Poetics in the Early Middle Ages, 1995; (and trans.) Libellus de arte coquinaria: An Early Northern Cookery Book, 2000. OTHERS: The Realism of Dream Visions: The Poetic Exploitation of the Dream Experience in Chaucer and His Contemporaries, 1967; (trans.) Beowulf and Other Old English Poems, 1967, 2nd ed., 1982; Essentials of Old English: Readings with Keyed Grammar, 1968; (ed.) The Miller's Tale of Geoffrey Chaucer, 1970; (trans.) Karlamagnús Saga: The Saga of Charlemagne and His Heroes, I, vol. IV, 1975, vol. X, 1980; (S. Butler) Pleyn Delit: Medieval Cookery for Modern Cooks, 1976, 2nd ed., 1996; (with S. Butler) Pain, vin et veneison: un livre de cuisine médiévale, 1977; An Ordinance of Pottage, 1988; (with B. Shaw and D. Macrae-Gibson) Beginning Old English: An Elementary Grammar for Use with Computerized Exercises, 1994; (with T. Nutter) Concordance of English Recipes: Thirteenth through Fifteenth Centuries, 2006; (ed.) Gathering of Medieval English Recipes, 2008. ADAPTER: Sir Gawain and the Green

Knight, 1967; The Knight of the Lion, 1968; The Knight of the Cart, 1969; The Joy of the Court, 1971; The Sword and the Grail, 1972; The Castle of Ladies, 1973; The Minstrel Knight, 1974. **Address:** 335 Essex Meadows, Essex, CT 06426, U.S.A. **Online address:** constance.hieatt@yale.edu

HIESTAND, Emily (L.). American (born United States), b. 1947. **Genres:** Poetry, Social Commentary, Travel/Exploration. **Career:** Curriculum designer, 1971-73; Hiestand Design Associates, principal and senior designer, 1973-88; Artemis Ensemble, founder and creative director, 1988-; Orion Magazine, literary and poetry editor, 1991-2001, princiapal editor; University of Alabama, visiting poet, 1992; Elements Communications, creative director, 2000-; Boston University, visiting poet; Communicators (media consultants for the peace and social justice community), co-director; Atlantic Monthly, editor; MIT School of Humanities, Arts, and Social Sciences, communications director. **Publications:** Green the Witch-Hazel Wood (poems), 1989; The Very Rich Hours (travel literature), 1992; Angela the Upside-Down Girl: And Other Domestic Travels (essays), 1999; (ed. with A, Zellman) The Good City: Writers Explore 21st Century Boston, 2004. Works appear in anthology. **Address:** c/o Jill Kneerim, Kneerim & Williams, Fish & Richardson PC, 225 Franklin St., Boston, MA 02110, U.S.A. **Online address:** hiestand@mit.edu

HIETALA, Thomas R. American (born United States), b. 1952. **Genres:** Social Sciences, History, Biography, Autobiography/Memoirs. **Career:** Yale University, lecturer in history, 1979-80; Dartmouth College, visiting assistant professor of history, 1980-85; Grinnell College, assistant professor, 1985-89, associate professor, 1989-99, professor of history, 1999-. Writer. **Publications:** Manifest Design: Anxiety and Aggrandizement, 1985, rev. ed. as Manifest Design: American Exceptionalism and Empire, 2003; The Fight of the Century: Jack Johnson, Joe Louis, and the Struggle for Racial Equality, 2002. **Address:** 215 Mears Cottage, 1213 6th Ave., Grinnell, IA 50112-1690, U.S.A.

HIGDON, Hal. American (born United States), b. 1931. **Genres:** Children's Fiction, Children's Non-fiction, Sports/Fitness. **Career:** The Kiwanis Magazine, assistant editor, 1957-59; freelance magazine writer, 1959-; Runner's World, contributing editor; Roadrunner Tours, partner. **Publications:** The Union vs. Dr. Mudd, 1964; Heroes of the Olympics, 1965; Pro Football, USA, 1967; The Horse That Played Center Field, 1968; Stars of the Tennis Courts, 1969; The Business Healers, 1970; The Electronic Olympics, 1971; Thirty Days in May, 1971; On the Run from Dogs and People, 1971; Champions of the Tennis Court, 1971; Finding the Groove, 1973; Find the Key Man, 1974; The Last Series, 1974; Six Seconds to Glory, 1975; The Crime of the Century, 1975; Showdown at Daytona, 1976; Summer of Triumph, 1977; Fitness after Forty, 1977; (with R. Offen and J. Starr) Together, 1977; Complete Diet Guide: For Runners and Other Athletes, 1978; Hitting, Pitching & Fielding, 1978; Beginner's Running Guide, 1978; (with J. Milkereit) Runner's Cookbook, 1979; Johnny Rutherford, Indy Champ, 1980; The Marathoners, 1980; The Team That Played in the Space Bowl, 1981; The Masters Running Guide, 1990; Run Fast: How to Train for a 5-K or 10-K Race, 1992; Marathon: The Ultimate Training and Racing Guide, 1993, 3rd ed., 2005; Falconara: A Family Odyssey, 1993; Boston: A Century of Running, 1995; Hal Higdon's How to Train, 1997; Hal Higdon's Smart Running, 1998; Leopold and Loeb: The Crime of the Century, 1999; (with D. Summers) Run, Dogs, Run,!, 2000; Run Fast: How to Beat Your Best Time Every Time, 2000; Marathoning A to Z, 2002; Masters Running: A Guide to Running and Staying Fit after 40, 2005; Marathon: A Novel, 2009. **Address:** Roadrunner Press, 2815 Lake Shore Dr., Long Beach, IN 46360-1619, U.S.A.

HIGGINBOTHAM, Elizabeth. American (born United States), b. 1948. **Genres:** Women's Studies And Issues, Race Relations. **Career:** University of Massachusetts, Afro-American Studies Concentration Program, adjunct lecturer, 1972-74, Department of Sociology, adjunct lecturer, 1975-76; University of Pittsburgh, instructor, 1977-79, assistant professor, 1979-81; Columbia University, assistant professor, 1981-83, Division of Urban Planning, urban sociologist; University of Memphis, research professor, 1983-92, assistant professor, 1985-88, associate professor 1988-95, professor of sociology and social work, 1995-98, Center for Research on Women, associate director, 1992-94, acting director, 1994-96; University of Michigan, Center for Afroamerican and African Studies and Women's Studies, visiting professor in black gender studies, 1996-97; University of Delaware, Department of Sociology and Criminal Justice, professor, 1998-; Eastern Sociological Society, Robin M. Williams Jr. distinguished lecturer, 2003-04. Writer. **Publications:** Too Much to Ask: Black Women in the Era of Integration, 2001. EDITOR:

(co-ed.) Women of Color and Southern Women: A Bibliography of Social Science Research, 1975-1988, 1988; (with M. Romero) Women and Work: Exploring Race, Ethnicity, and Class, 1997; (with M.L. Anderson) Race and Ethnicity in Society: The Changing Landscape, 2006, 2nd ed., 2008. Contributor of articles to periodicals. **Address:** Department of Sociology & Criminal Justice, University of Delaware, 322 Smith Hall, Newark, DE 19716, U.S.A. **Online address:** ehiggin@udel.edu

HIGGINBOTHAM, Jay. American (born United States), b. 1937. **Genres:** Novels, Plays/Screenplays, Autobiography/Memoirs, Social Commentary, Travel/Exploration, Autobiography/Memoirs, Writing/Journalism. **Career:** Mississippi House of Representatives, assistant clerk; State House of Representatives, assistant clerk, 1955-61; Mobile County, Alabama Public Schools, teacher, 1962-73; Mobile Public Library, Local History Department, head, 1973-83; Special Collection Department, acting head, 1979-80, research consultant, 1980-; Mobile Municipal Archives, founder and director, 1983, now retired. Writer. **Publications:** The Mobile Indians, 1966; The World Around, 1966; Pascagoula: Singing River City, 1967; Family Biographies: Brief Portraits of Some Ancestors and Members of the Higginbotham Family of Pascagoula, 1967; Pascagoula Indians, 1967; Fort Maurepas: The Birth of Louisiana, 1968; Mobile: City by the Bay, 1968; The Journal of Sauvole, 1969; Brother Holyfield: A Novel, 1972; (trans. and ed. with F. Escoffier) A Voyage to Dauphin Island in 1720: The Journal of Bertet de la Clue, 1974; Old Mobile: Fort Louis de la Louisiane, 1702-1711, 1977; Fast Train Russia, 1983; Autumn in Petrishchevo, 1987; The Vital Alliance, 1988; Discovering Russia: People and Places, 1989; Kazula, 1993; Man, Nature and the Infinite: Random Thoughts and Impressions from the Journals, Interviews, Letters, Speeches and Notebooks of Jay Higginbotham, 1961-1997, 1998; Mauvila, 2000; Alma, 2002; Narrow is the Way, 2004; One Man In The Universe, 2005; Selected Writings of Jay Higginbotham, 2008. Contributor to newspapers, magazines and journals. **Address:** 60 N Monterey St., Mobile, AL 36604-1348, U.S.A.

HIGGINS, Aidan. Irish (born Ireland), b. 1927. **Genres:** Novels, Novellas/Short Stories, Autobiography/Memoirs. **Career:** Domas Advertising, copywriter; John Wright's Marionettes in Europe, puppet-operator, 1958-60. Writer. **Publications:** Felo de Se, 1960 in US as Killachter Meadow, 1960, rev. ed. as Asylum and Other Stories, 1978; Langrishe, Go Down, 1966; Images of Africa, 1971; Balcony of Europe, 1972; (ed. and intro.) A Century of Short Stories, 1977; Scenes from a Receding Past, 1977; (ed.) Colossal Gongorr and the Turkes of Mars, 1979; Bornholm Night Ferry, 1983; Helsingor Station and Other Departures, 1987; Ronda Gorge and Other Precipices, 1987; Lions of the Grunewald, 1993; Donkey's Years: Memories of a Life as Story Told, 1995; (intro.) Samuel Beckett: Photographs, 1996; Flotsam and Jetsam, 1997; Dog Days, 1998; The Whole Hog: A Sequel to Donkey's Years and Dog Days, 2000; As I was Riding Down Duval Boulevard with Pete La Salle, 2002; A Bestiary, 2004; Windy Arbours, 2005; Bornholm Night-ferry, 2006; Darkling Plain, 2010. **Address:** c/o Secker & Warburg, Michelin House, 81 Fulham Rd., London, GL SW3 6RB, England.

HIGGINS, Gina O'Connell. American (born United States), b. 1950. **Genres:** Psychology, Social Sciences. **Career:** Lesley College, lecturer and clinical placement supervisor in special education, 1974-76, assistant professor of special education, 1976-81; Middlesex Community College, lecturer, 1974-75; Tufts University, lecturer, 1974-75; North Shore Children's Hospital, psychology intern, 1981-82, Medical Educational Evaluation Clinic, diagnostician, 1982-87, Mental Health Center, psychotherapist and intake diagnostician, 1982-86; Clinical Developmental Institute, associate fellow, 1985-86, fellow, 1990-; Harvard University, Clinical Developmental Institute, associate, faculty, 1986, 1990, clinical instructor, 1993-94, clinical associate, 1994-2000; Massachusetts General Hospital, staff psychologist, 1993-2000. Writer. **Publications:** Resilient Adults: Overcoming a Cruel Past, 1994. Contributor to books. **Address:** 1 Salem Green, Ste. 555, Salem, MA 01970, U.S.A.

HIGGINS, Ian (Kevin). Australian (born Australia), b. 1959. **Genres:** Literary Criticism And History. **Career:** La Trobe University, senior tutor in English literature, 1985-91; Australian National University, lecturer in English, 1991-97, senior lecturer, 1997-2005, reader, 2005-. Writer. **Publications:** Swift's Politics: A Study in Disaffection, 1994; Jonathan Swift, 2004; (ed. with C. Rawson) Jonathan Swift: Gulliver's Travels, 2005; (ed. with C. Rawson) Jonathan Swift: The Essential Writings: Authoritative Texts, Contexts, Criticism, 2010. Contributor to journals and books. **Address:** English Program, Australian National University, Canberra, AC 0200, Australia. **Online address:** ian.higgins@anu.edu.au

HIGGINS, Joanna. American (born United States), b. 1945. **Genres:** Novellas/Short Stories, Children's Fiction, Novels, Literary Criticism And History, Mystery/Crime/Suspense. **Career:** Grand Rapids Junior College, instructor in English, 1968-69; University of Maryland, instructor in English, 1970-71; Keystone Junior College, instructor in English, 1974-77; University of Hawaii-Hilo, assistant professor of English, 1977-78; University of Hawaii, West Oahu College, assistant professor of English, 1978-79; State University of New York, adjunct creative writing faculty, 1982; writer, 1982-. **Publications:** The Magic Crystal, 1987; Quest for the Golden Flower, 1988; In the Treasure House of the Ten Masters, 1990; The Importance of High Places: Stories and A Novella, 1993; (with A.M. Odams) Commercial Dispute Resolution, 1996; A Soldier's Book, 1999; Dead Center, 2011. Contributor to periodicals. **Address:** Bowbridge Rd., RR 1, PO Box 1544, Little Meadows, PA 18830, U.S.A.

HIGGINS, Kathleen M(arie). American (born United States), b. 1954. **Genres:** Philosophy. **Career:** The University of Texas, faculty, 1982-, professor, 1995-; University of California, visiting assistant professor, 1986-87; University of Auckland, visiting professor; Australian National University, Department of Philosophy, visiting fellow; Canberra School of Music, visiting fellow. Writer. **Publications:** Nietzsche's Zarathustra, 1987, rev. ed. 2010; The Music of Our Lives, 1991; (with R.C. Solomon) A Short History of Philosophy, 1996; (with R.C. Solomon) A Passion for Wisdom: A Very Brief History of Philosophy, 1997; Comic Relief, 2000; (with R.C. Solomon) What Nietzsche Really Said, 2000. EDITOR: (with R.C. Solomon) Reading Nietzsche, 1988; (with R.C. Solomon) The Philosophy of (Erotic) Love, 1992; (with L. Bowie and M. Michaels) Thirteen Questions: An Introduction to Ethics, 1992, 2nd ed. as Thirteen Questions in Ethics and Social Philosophy, 1998; (with R.C. Solomon) From Africa to Zen: An Invitation to World Philosophy, 1993, 2nd ed., 2003; (with R.C. Solomon) Routledge History of Philosophy, vol. VI: The Age of German Idealism, 1993; (with R.C. Solomon) World Philosophy: A Text with Readings, 1995; (with B. Magnus) The Cambridge Companion to Nietzsche, 1996; Aesthetics in Perspective, 1996; (with R.C. Solomon) The Big Questions, 8th ed., 2010. **Address:** The University of Texas at Austin, Philosophy, 1 University Sta., C3500, Austin, TX 78712, U.S.A. **Online address:** kmhiggins@austin.utexas.edu

HIGGINS, Michael W. (Michael William Higgins). Canadian (born Canada), b. 1948. **Genres:** Biography, Theology/Religion, History, Geography. **Career:** St. Michael's College School, instructor in English, and religious studies and theology, 1973-82; St. Paul's University, Ontario College, instructor in religious studies and theology, 1973-82; Erindale College, instructor in religious studies and theology, 1973-82; St. Jerome's University, associate dean and vice president and academic dean, 1982-2006, president and vice chancellor, 1999-2006, Center for Catholic Experience, director, Institute for Studies in Theological Renewal, director, Department of Religious Studies, chair; University of Waterloo, Department of Religious Studies, chair; University of Toronto, president and vice chancellor, 1999-2006; St. Thomas University, president and vice chancellor, 2006-; Canadian Broadcasting Corp., scriptwriter and radio documentarian. Writer, columnist, commentator, researcher, consultant, broadcaster and administrator. **Publications:** (ed. with D. Grayston) Thomas Merton: Pilgrim in Process, 1983; Heretic Blood: The Spiritual Geography of Thomas Merton, 1998; The Muted Voice: Religion and the Media, 2000; Stalking the Holy: The Pursuit of Saint-Making, 2006. WITH D.R. LETSON: My Father's Business: A Biography of His Eminence G. Emmett Cardinal Carter, 1990; The Jesuit Mystique, 1995; Power and Peril: The Catholic Church at the Crossroads, 2002. Contributor to periodicals and journals. **Address:** St. Thomas University, 51 Dineen Dr., Fredericton, NB E3B 5G3, Canada.

HIGGINS, Michael William. *See* **HIGGINS, Michael W.**

HIGGINS, Peter M. Australian (born Australia), b. 1956. **Genres:** Sciences, History. **Career:** Henrietta Barnett Girls School, instructor in mathematics, 1978-79; California State University, Department of Mathematics, assistant professor, 1983-90; University of Essex, Department of Mathematical Sciences, professor, 2000-, department head, 2005-10. Writer. **Publications:** (Ed. with S.M. Goberstein) Semigroups and Their Applications: Proceedings of the International Conference Algebraic Theory of Semigroups and Its Applications, 1987; Techniques of Semigroup Theory, 1992; Mathematics for

the Curious, 1998; Mathematics for the Imagination, 2002; Nets, Puzzles, and Postmen: An Exploration of Mathematical Connections, 2007; Number Story: From Counting to Cryptography, 2008. Contributor to journals. **Address:** Department of Mathematical Sciences, University of Essex, Rm. 6.317, Wivenhoe Pk., Colchester, EX CO4 3SQ, England. **Online address:** peteh@essex.ac.uk

HIGGINS, Rosalyn. (Rosalyn Cohen Higgins). British (born England), b. 1937. **Genres:** International Relations/Current Affairs, Military/Defense/Arms Control, Politics/Government, Law. **Career:** Yale University, Law School, graduate fellow, 1959-61; University of London, London School of Economics, junior fellow in international studies, 1961-63, visiting fellow, 1974-78, professor of international law, 1981-95, chair of international law, 1985-, honorary fellow; Royal Institute of International Affairs, research specialist in international law and United Nations affairs and international lawyer, 1963-74; Brookings Institution, visiting fellow, 1960; University of Kent, professor and chair of international law, 1978-81; International Court of Justice, president, 2006-09; Girton College, honorary fellow. Writer. **Publications:** The Development of International Law through the Political Organs of the United Nations, 1963; Conflict of Interests: International Law in a Divided World, 1965; The Administration of United Kingdom Foreign Policy through the United Nations, 1966; United Nations Peacekeeping: Documents and Commentary, vol. I: The Middle East, 1969, vol. II: Asia, 1971, vol. III: Africa, 1980, vol. IV: Europe, 1981; (with M. Harbottle) United Nations Peacekeeping: Past Lessons and Future Prospects, 1972; Problems and Process: International Law and How We Use It, 1994; (intro.) United Nations Forces: A Legal Study, 2008; Role of the International Court of Justice in the Contemporary World, 2008; Themes and Theories: Selected Essays, Speeches, and Writings in International Law, 2009. EDITOR: (with J.E.S. Fawcett) International organization: Law in Movement: Essays in Honour of John McMahon, 1974; (with M. Flory) Libertaé de Circulation des Personnes en Droit International, 1988; (with M. Flory) Terrorism and International Law, 1997. **Address:** 18 Hallgate, Blackheath Pk., London, GL SE3 9SG, England.

HIGGINS, Rosalyn Cohen. *See* **HIGGINS, Rosalyn.**

HIGGINS, Simon (Richard). Australian/British (born England), b. 1958. **Genres:** Young Adult Fiction, Novels. **Career:** Police officer, 1986-94; novelist, 1996-. **Publications:** FOR YOUNG ADULTS: Doctor Id, 1998; Thunderfish, 1999; Jade Draper in the Dream Web Files, 1999; Cybercage, 2000; Beyond the Shaking Time, 2000; Under No Flag, 2001; The Stalking Zone, 2002; In the Jaws of the Sea, 2003; The Dream Web Files, 2003; Tomodachi: The Edge of the World, 2007. MOONSHADOW SERIES: Moonshadow: Eye of the Beast, 2008 in US as Rise of the Ninja, 2010; The Nightmare Ninja, 2011; Moonshadow: The Wrath of Silver Wolf, forthcoming. Contributor to books and magazines. **Address:** Jenny Darling and Associates, PO Box 235, Richmond, VI 3121, Australia.

HIGGINSEN, Vy. American (born United States) **Genres:** Plays/Screenplays, Young Adult Fiction, Novels, Young Adult Non-fiction. **Career:** Ebony magazine, advertising and sales manager, 1970-71; WBLS-FM, on-air personality, 1971-75; Unique, publisher, 1974-78; Mama Foundation for the Arts, chief executive officer and executive director. Writer. **Publications:** Let the Music Play Gospel, 1988; (with T. Bolden) Mama, I Want to Sing (young adult novel), 1992; (comp.) This Is My Song: A Collection of Gospel Music for the Family, 1995; This Is My Story, forthcoming. **Address:** Mama Foundation for the Arts, 149 W 126th St., New York, NY 10027, U.S.A. **Online address:** mamaofc@aol.com

HIGGS, Liz Curtis. American (born United States), b. 1956?. **Genres:** Novels, Young Adult Non-fiction, Picture/Board Books, Adult Non-fiction, Young Adult Fiction, Reference. **Career:** Radio broadcaster, 1978-88; public speaker, 1978-; Today's Christian Woman Magazine, columnist. **Publications:** Does Dinner in a Bucket Count? Ninety Laughs for the '90s Woman, 1993; One Size Fits All: And Other Fables, 1993; Especially for a Woman, 1994; Only Angels Can Wing It, 1995; The Pumpkin Patch Parable, 1995; Reflecting His Image: Discovering Your Worth in Christ from A to Z, 1996; Forty Reasons Why Life Is More Fun after the Big 4-0, 1997; Mirror, Mirror on the Wall, Have I Got News for You!: An A to Z Faith Lift for Your Sagging Self-Esteem, 1997; The Sunflower Parable, 1997; The Parable of the Lily, 1997; The Pine Tree Parable, 1997; Go Away, Dark Night, 1998; Help! I'm Laughing and I Can't Get Up, 1998; While Shepherds Washed Their Flocks and Other Funny Things Kids Say and Do, 1998; Bad Girls of the Bible: And

What We Can Learn from Them, 1999; Mixed Signals, 1999; One Fun Day!, 1999; Bookends, 2000; The Best of Liz Curtis Higgs, 2000; Really Bad Girls of the Bible: More Lessons from Less-than-Perfect Women, 2000; (with C. Zane and K. Ball) Three Weddings and a Giggle, 2001; Devotions for a Sensational Life, 2001; Mad Mary: A Bad Girl from Magdala, Transformed at His Appearing, 2001; Rise and Shine, 2001; Thorn in My Heart, 2001; Fair Is the Rose, 2004; Unveiling Mary Magdalene: Workbook, 2004; Loved By God, 2004; Whence Came a Prince, 2005; Embrace Grace: Welcome to the Forgiven Life, 2005; Grace in Thine Eyes, 2006; Slightly Bad Girls of the Bible: Flawed Women Loved by a Flawless God, 2007; My Heart's in the Lowlands: Ten Days in Bonny Scotland, 2007; Here Burns My Candle, 2010; Mine Is the Night, 2011. **Address:** PO Box 43577, Louisville, KY 40253-0577, U.S.A. **Online address:** liz@lizcurtishiggs.com

HIGH, Linda Oatman. American (born United States), b. 1958. **Genres:** Novels, Children's Fiction, Young Adult Fiction, Poetry, Songs/Lyrics And Libretti, Picture/Board Books, Adult Non-fiction, Novellas/Short Stories, Novellas/Short Stories. **Career:** Writer. **Publications:** YOUNG ADULT NOVELS: Maizie, 1995; Hound Heaven, 1995; The Summer of the Great Divide, 1996. NOVELS: A Stone's Throw from Paradise, 1997. FOR CHILDREN: A Christmas Star, 1997; Beekeepers, 1998; Barn Savers, 1999; Under New York, 2001; Winter Shoes for Shadow Horse, 2001; Last Chimney of Christmas Eve, 2001; A Humble Life: Plain Poems, 2001; Strum a Song of Angels: Poems about Music, 2002; The President's Puppy, 2002; The Girl on the High-Diving Horse: An Adventure in Atlantic City, 2003; Sister Slam and the Poetic Motormouth Road Trip, 2004; City of Snow: The Great Blizzard of 1888, 2004. OTHERS: Don't Cramp My Style: Stories About that Time of the Month, 2004; Cool Bopper's Choppers, 2007; The Cemetery Keepers of Gettysburg, 2007; Tenth Avenue Cowboy, 2008; Planet Pregnancy, 2008; Boomers Cruise, Too: Groovy Cruises for Cool Baby Boomers, forthcoming; Pigs In Wigs, forthcoming; Gargantua The Great, forthcoming. **Address:** 1209 Reading Rd., Narvon, PA 17555, U.S.A. **Online address:** lohigh@frontiernet.net

HIGHAM, Robin. American/British (born England), b. 1925. **Genres:** Administration/Management, Air/Space Topics, Archaeology/Antiquities, History, Military/Defense/Arms Control, Bibliography, Language/Linguistics, Art/Art History, Art/Art History. **Career:** Webb School of California, instructor, 1950-52; University of Massachusetts, instructor, 1954-57; University of North Carolina-Chapel Hill, assistant professor, 1957-63; British Overseas Airways Corp., historian, 1960-66, 1976-78; Kansas State University, associate professor, 1963-66, professor of history, 1966-98, graduate faculty lecturer, 1971, emeritus, 1998-; Military Affairs, editor, 1968-88; Aerospace Historian, editor, 1970-88; Journal of the West, ed., 1977-; Sunflower University Press, founder and president, 1977-; Greenwood Press, advisory editor, 1993-. **Publications:** Britain's Imperial Air Routes, 1918 to 1939: The Story of Britain's Overseas Airlines, 1960; An Introduction to Maritime, Naval, and Aeronautical History, 1960; The British Rigid Airship, 1908-1931, 1961; Armed Forces In Peacetime; Britain, 1918-1940, A Case Study, By Robin Higham, 1962; The Military Intellectuals in Britain, 1918-1939, 1966; (with D.H. Zook) A Short History of Warfare, 1966; Air Power: A Concise History, 1972, 3rd ed., 1988; The Compleat Academic, 1975, rev. ed., 1993; Diary of a Disaster: British Aid to Greece, 1940-1941, 1986; Bases of Air Strategy: Building Airfields for the RAF, 1914-1945, 1998; Research on World War I: A Handbook, 2003; 100 Years of Air Power and Aviation, 2003; Who Do We Think We Are?: Canada's Reasonable and (Less-Reasonable) Accomodation Debates, 2009; Two Roads to War: The French and British Air Arms from Versailles to Dunkirk, 2012. EDITOR: Bayonets in the Street, 1969, 2nd ed., 1989; Civil Wars in the Twentieth Century, 1972; A Guide to the Sources of British Military History, 1972; Intervention or Abstention, 1975; Guide to the Sources of United States Military History, 1975; (with D.J. Mrozek) Guide to the Sources of United States Military History, Supplement I, 1981; (with D.J. Mrozek) Guide to the Sources of United States Military History, Supplement II, 1985; (with D.J. Mrozek) Guide to the Sources of United States Military History, Supplement III, 1993; The Rise of the Wheat State: A History Of Kansas Agriculture, 1861-1986, 1987; (with C.D. Bright) Historical Dictionary of the U.S. Air Force, 1992; (with T. Veremis) The Metaxas Dictatorship: Aspects of Greece, 1936-1940, 1993; Kansas Morning: A Turn-of-The-Century Midwestern Boyhood, 1996; (with D.J. Mrozek) Guide to the Sources of United States Military History, Supplement IV, 1997; World War II in Europe, Africa, and the Americas, With General Sources: A Handbook of Literature and Research, 1997; (with A.T. Siddall) Flying Combat Aircraft I, 1978; (with C. Williams) Flying Combat Aircraft II, 1978; Flying Combat Aircraft III, 1981; Flying Combat Aircraft IV, 1998; (with J.W. Kipp) Soviet Aviation and

Air Power, 1978; (with J.W. Kipp) The Garland Military History Bibliographies, 1978-92; (with D.J. Mrozek and J.L.A. Newell) The Martin Marauder and the Franklin Allens: A Wartime Love Story, 1980; (with J.T. Greenwood and V. Hardesty) Russian Aviation and Air Power in the Twentieth Century, 1998; A Handbook on Air Ministry Organization, 1998; Dictionary of Contemporary Chinese Military History, 1999; Writing Official Military History, 1999; A Guide to the Sources of United States Military History Supplement IV, 1998; Official Military History I and II, 2000; Official Military Historical Offices and Sources, 2000; (with F.W. Kagan) The Military History Of Tsarist Russia, 2002; (with F.W. Kagan) The Military History of the Soviet Union 1917-1991, 2002; (with D.A. Graff) A Military of History of China, 2002; (with D.E. Showalter) Researching World War I: A Handbook, 2003; (with S.J. Harris) The Defense of Air Forces, 2004; Flying American Combat Aircraft of WWII: 1939-45, 2004; Flying American Combat Aircraft: The Cold War, 2005; (with S.J. Harris) Why Air Forces Fail: The Anatomy of Defeat, 2006; (with D.A. Graff) A Military History of China, 2012. FORTHCOMING: The Overlooked Civilization; Options of Difficulties; Peacekeeping; BOAC-The Inside Story; The Grecian Sea; (with M. Parillo) A Handbook to Railway Research Worldwide; Roads to 1940-The French and British Air Forces; The Invisible Infrastructure of the U.S. Civil War; The Defeat and Fall of Air Forces. **Address:** Department of History, Kansas State University, 208 Eisenhower Hall, Manhattan, KS 66506-1002, U.S.A. **Online address:** rhigham@ksu.edu

HIGHFIELD, (John) Roger (Loxdale). (J. R. L. Highfield). British (born England), b. 1922. **Genres:** History, Geography, Social Sciences, Adult Non-fiction, Education. **Career:** Oxford University, Merton College, fellow, 1949-89, lecturer in history, 1951-89, emeritus fellow, 1989-. Writer. **Publications:** (With C. Brooke) Oxford and Cambridge, 1988; (with G.H. Martin) History of Merton College, Oxford, 1997. EDITOR: The Early Rolls of Merton College, 1964; (with B. Smalley and J. Hale) Europe in the Late Middle Ages, 1965; Spain in the Fifteenth Century, 1369-1516, 1972; (with R. Jeffs) The Crown and Local Communities in England and France in the Fifteenth Century, 1983. **Address:** Merton College, Oxford University, Merton St., Oxford, OX OX1 4TD, England.

HIGHLAND, Monica. See SEE, Carolyn.

HIGHTMAN, Jason. (J. P. Hightman). American (born United States), b. 1971?. **Genres:** Novels, Animals/Pets, Children's Non-fiction. **Career:** Writer, director and producer. **Publications:** SIMON ST. GEORGE SERIES: The Saint of Dragons, 2004; Samurai, 2006. NOVELS: (as J.P. Hightman) Spirit, 2008. **Address:** c/o Author Mail, HarperCollins Publishers, 10 E 53rd St., 11th Fl., New York, NY 10022-5244, U.S.A. **Online address:** jason@jasonhightman.com

HIGHTMAN, J. P. See HIGHTMAN, Jason.

HIGHTOWER, Lynn S. American (born United States), b. 1956?. **Genres:** Novels, Mystery/Crime/Suspense, inspirational/Motivational Literature, Women's Studies And Issues, Children's Fiction. **Career:** Full-time fiction writer; University of California-Los Angeles, lecturer in novel writing. **Publications:** DAVID SILVER SERIES: Alien Blues, 1991; Alien Eyes, 1993; Alien Heat, 1994; Alien Rites, 1995. LENA PADGETT SERIES: Satan's Lambs: A Novel, 1993; Fortunes of the Dead: A Novel, 2003; When Secrets Die, 2005. SONORA BLAIR MYSTERY SERIES: Flashpoint, 1995; Eyeshot, 1996; No Good Deed, 1998; The Debt Collector, 2000. NOVELS: High Water, 2002. Works appear in anthologies. **Address:** Delacorte Press, 1540 Broadway, New York, NY 10036, U.S.A. **Online address:** lynn@lynnhightower.com

HIGHTOWER, Scott. American (born United States), b. 1952. **Genres:** Poetry. **Career:** Fordham University, poet-in-residence; The Journal, contributing editor; Drew University, adjunct faculty; New York University, Gallatin School of Individualized Study, adjunct faculty. **Publications:** Tin Can Tourist, 2001; Natural Trouble, 2003; Part of the Bargain, 2005; Self-Evident, 2012; Hontanares, 2012. Contributor to periodicals. **Address:** Gallatin School of Individualized Study, New York University, 1 Washington Pl., 8th Fl., New York, NY 10003, U.S.A. **Online address:** shightower@nyc.rr.com

HIGHWAY, Tomson. Canadian (born Canada), b. 1951. **Genres:** Plays/Screenplays, Novels, Children's Fiction, Young Adult Fiction. **Career:** Native Earth Performing Arts Inc. artistic director, 1986-92; University of Toronto, writer-in-residence, adjunct professor; Concordia University, writer-in-residence; Simon Fraser University, writer-in-residence; Brandon University, Stanley Knowles distinguished visiting professor. **Publications:** Aria (monologues), 1987; The Rez Sisters (two-act play) 1988; Dry Lips Oughta Move to Kapuskasing, 1989; (with R. Highway and B. Merasty) The Sage, the Dancer, and the Fool (play), 1989; Kiss of the Fur Queen (novel), 1998; Caribou Song, 2001; Dragonfly Kites: Pimihakanisa, 2002; Fox on the Ice, 2003; Comparing Mythologies, 2003; Rose, 2003; Ernestine Shuswap Gets Her Trout: A String Quartet for Four Female Actors, 2005; Pimooteewin, 2008; Iskooniguni iskweewuk, 2010. **Address:** Playwrights Canada, 54 Wolseley St., 2nd Fl., Toronto, ON M5T 1A5, Canada. **Online address:** hghwyt@aol.com

HILBERRY, Conrad Arthur. American (born United States), b. 1928. **Genres:** Poetry, Music, Adult Non-fiction. **Career:** DePauw University, instructor, 1954-56, assistant professor, 1956-60, associate professor of English literature, 1960-61; Associated Colleges of the Midwest, program associate, 1961-62; North Central Association of Colleges and Secondary Schools, consultant, examiner, 1959-; Kalamazoo College, associate professor, 1962-67, professor of English literature, 1967-, now professor emeritus of English; Florence J. Lucasse fellow, 1979; Antioch College, associate director of study of liberal arts colleges, 1965-67. Writer. **Publications:** POETRY: Encounter on Burrows Hill and Other Poems, 1969; Rust, 1974; Man in the Attic, 1980; House Marks, 1980; Moon Seen as a Slice of Pineapple, 1984; Jacob's Dancing Tune, 1986; Sorting the Smoke: New and Selected Poems, 1990; Player Piano: Poems, 1999; Taking Notes on Nature's Wild Inventions, 1999; The Fingernail of Luck, 2005; After-music: Poems, 2008. OTHER: Luke Karamazov (case study), 1987; The Lagoon, 1989. EDITOR: The Poems of John Collop, 1962; (with M. Keeton) Struggle and Promise: A Future for Colleges, 1969; (with H. Scott and J. Tipton) The Third Coast: Contemporary Michigan Poets, 1976; (with M. Delp and H. Scott) Contemporary Michigan Poetry: Poems from the Third Coast, 1988; (with M. Delp and J. Kearns) New Poems from the Third Coast: Contemporary Michigan Poetry, 2000. **Address:** Department of English, Kalamazoo College, 1200 Academy St., Kalamazoo, MI 49006, U.S.A. **Online address:** hilberry@core.com

HILBERT, Richard A. American (born United States), b. 1947. **Genres:** Anthropology/Ethnology, Sociology. **Career:** Gustavus Adolphus College, teacher of sociology, 1978-81, 1983-, Department of Sociology and Anthropology, professor and head, 1991-. Writer. **Publications:** The Classical Roots of Ethnomethodology: Durkheim, Weber, and Garfinkel, 1992; Duck King, 1998. Works appear in anthologies. Contributor of articles to journals. **Address:** Department of Sociology and Anthropology, Gustavus Adolphus College, 129 Social Science Ctr., 800 W College Ave., St. Peter, MN 56082, U.S.A. **Online address:** rhilbert@gac.edu

HILBORN, Robert C. American (born United States), b. 1943. **Genres:** Physics. **Career:** State University of New York at Stony Brook, research associate and lecturer, 1971-73; Oberlin College, assistant professor to professor, 1973-86; Amherst College, professor of physics, 1986-94, Amanda and Lisa Gross emeritus professor of physics, 1994-, associate dean of the faculty, 2000-03; University of Nebraska-Lincoln, research professor of physics and science director for the Center for Science, Mathematics and Computer Education; National Task Force on Undergraduate Physics, founding chair, 1999-; University of Texas, professor and head of science and mathematics education, 2008-, workshop chair. Writer. **Publications:** Chaos and Nonlinear Dynamics: An Introduction for Scientists and Engineers, 1994, 2nd ed., 2000; (ed. with G.M. Tino) Spin-Statistics Connection and Commutation Relations: Experimental Tests and Theoretical Implications: Anacapri, Capri Island, Italy, 31 May-3 June 2000, 2000. **Address:** Department of Science/Mathematics Education, University of Texas at Dallas, 800 W Campbell Rd., PO Box 830688, Mail Sta. FN33, Richardson, TX 75080-0688, U.S.A. **Online address:** rhilborn@utdallas.edu

HILBURN, Robert. American (born United States), b. 1939. **Genres:** History. **Career:** Los Angeles Times, chief rock critic, 1970-2005; Valley Times Today, staff; Los Angeles Unified School District, public information officer. Writer. **Publications:** Springsteen, 1985; Corn Flakes with John Lennon: And Other Tales from a Rock N Roll Life, 2009. **Address:** 4335 Van Nuys Blvd., Ste. 385, Sherman Oaks, CA 91403, U.S.A. **Online address:** robert.hilburn@gmail.com

HILDEBRAND, Ann Meinzen. American/Canadian (born Canada), b. 1933. **Genres:** Children's Non-fiction, Literary Criticism And History, Biography, History, Illustrations. **Career:** Kent State University, part-time

instructor, 1965-76, visiting assistant professor, 1976-86, visiting associate professor, 1986-93, visiting professor of children's and adolescent literature, 1993-, visiting professor of English, 1993-98, professor emeritus of English, 1998-. Writer. **Publications:** Jean and Laurent de Brunhoff: The Legacy of Babar, 1991; (with W.H. Hildebrand) Anne Chamberlain: A Writer's Story (monograph), 2001. Works appear in anthologies. Contributor to journals. **Address:** 11 Glenside Dr., Munroe Falls, OH 44262, U.S.A. **Online address:** ahildeb0@kent.edu

HILDEBRAND, John. American (born United States), b. 1949. **Genres:** Literary Criticism And History, Natural History, Social Sciences. **Career:** University of Alaska, instructor in English, 1974-76; University of Wisconsin, assistant professor of English, 1977-, professor of English, now professor emeritus of English. Writer. **Publications:** Reading the River: A Voyage Down the Yukon, 1988; Mapping the Farm: The Chronicle of a Family, 1995; A Northern Front: New and Selected Essays, 2005. Works appear in anthologies. Contributor to periodicals and magazines. **Address:** Department of English, University of Wisconsin, 403 Hibbard Humanities Hall, Eau Claire, WI 54702-4004, U.S.A. **Online address:** hildebjs@uwec.edu

HILDEBRAND, Klaus. German (born Germany), b. 1941. **Genres:** History, Translations, Social Sciences. **Career:** University of Mannheim, research assistant, 1967-72; University of Bielefeld, professor of modern history, 1972-74; University of Frankfurt, professor, 1974-77; University of Muenster, professor, 1977-82; University of Bonn, professor, 1982-, chair of modern history, acting chair, 2008-, now professor emeritus. Writer. **Publications:** IN GERMAN: Bundesrepublik Deuchchlarest, 1963-67; Bethmann Hollweg, der Kanzler ohne Eigenschaften? Urteile der Geschichtsschreibung. Eine Kritische Bibliographie, 1970; Das Deutsche Reich und die Sowjetunion im Internationalen System: 1918-1932: Legitimität Oder Revolution?, 1977; (ed.) Wem gehört die Deutsche Geschichte?: Deutschlands Weg vom alten Europa in die Europäische Moderne: Symposium, 1987; (with J. Schmaedeke and K. Zernack) 1939, an der Schwelle zum Weltkrieg: Die Entfesselung des Zweiten Weltkrieges und das Internationale System, 1990; Das Vergangene Reich: Deutsche Aussenpolitik von Bismarck bis Hitler, 1871-1945, 1995; Das Deutsche Reich im Urteil der Grossen Maechte und Europäischen Nachbarn (1871-1945), 1995; No Intervention: Die Pax Britannica und Preussen 1865/66-1869/70: Eine Untersuchung zur Englischen Weltpolitik im 19. Jahrhundert, 1997; (with H. Moller) Die Bundesrepublik Deutschland und Frankreich: Dokumente 1949-1963, 1997. IN ENGLISH TRANSLATION: Vom Reich zum Weltreich. Hitler, NSDAP u. Koloniale Frage 1919-1945, 1969; Deutsche Aussenpolitik, 1933-45, 1970, 4th ed., 1980; Kalküloder Dogma?, 1971, 4th ed., 1980; Das Dritte Reich, 1979, 6th ed., 2003; Staatskunst oder Systemzwang, 1989; (intro.) The Manichaean Trap: American Perceptions of the German Empire, 1871-1945, 1995. EDITOR: (with J. Becker) Internationale Beziehungen (1929-1933), 1980; (with K.F. Werner) Deutschland und Frankreich, 1936-1939: 15. Deutsch-Französisches Historikerkolloquim des Deutschen Historischen Instituts Paris (Bonn, 26.-29. September 1979), 1981; (with R. Pommerin) Deutsche Frage undeuropäisches Gleichgewicht: Festschrift für Andreas Hillgruber zum 60. Geburtstag, 1985; Integration und Souveränität: Die Aussenpolitik der Bundesrepublik Deutschland, 1949-1982: Intégrationet souveraineté: La Politique étrangère de la République Fédérale d'Allemagne de 1949 à 1982, 1991; (with A. Wenger and U. Wirsching) Geschichtswissenschaft und Zeiterkenntnis: von der Aufklärung bis zur Gegenwart; Festschrift zum 65. Geburtstag von Horst Möller, 2008. OTHERS: Internationale Beziehungen in der Weltwirtschaftskrise 1929-1933: Referateund Diskussionsbeiträge eines Augsburger Symposions, 29. März bis1. April 1979, 1980; Kalkül zwischen Macht und Ideologie: der Hitler-Stalin-Pakt: Parallelen bis heute?, 1980; The Third Reich, 1984; Deutschland, 1949-1989: Sonderdruck der Texte zum Kalender 1989 des Gesamtdeutschen Instituts, 1989; Deutsche Aussenpolitik 1871-1918, 1989; Zwischen Politik undReligion: Studien zur Entstehung, Existenz und Wirkung des Totalitarismus, 2003; (with E. Kolb) Otto von Bismarck im Spiegel Europas, 2006; (ed. with D. Hein and A. Schulz) Historie und Leben: der Historiker als Wissenschaftler und Zeitgenosse, 2006; Gesamtausgabe des Briefwechsels von Leopold von Ranke, 2007. **Address:** Institute of History, University of Bonn, Rm. 104, Konviktstrabe 11, Bonn, 53113, Germany. **Online address:** klaus.hildebrand@uni-bonn.de

HILDEBRAND, Verna. (Verna Lee Hildebrand). American (born United States), b. 1924. **Genres:** Education, Human Relations/Parenting, Young Adult Non-fiction, Social Sciences. **Career:** Kansas State University, instructor, 1953-54, 1959, instructor in student counseling center, 1958; Oklahoma

State University, instructor, 1955-56; Texas Tech University, assistant professor of home and family life, 1962-67; Michigan State University, Department of Family and Child Ecology, professor, 1967-96, professor emeritus, 1996-. Writer. **Publications:** Introduction to Early Childhood Education, 1971, 6th ed., 1997; A Laboratory Workbook for Introduction to Early Childhood Education, 1971, 8th ed., 2009; Guiding Young Children, 1975, (with P. Hearron) 8th ed., 2009; Parenting and Teaching Young Children, 1981, 3rd ed., 1990; (with J.R. Hildebrand) China's Families: Experiment in Societal Change, 1981; Management of Child Development Centers, 1984, 7th ed., 2011; Fundamentos de Educacion Infantil: Jardin de ninos y preprimariam, 1987; Parenting: Rewards and Responsibilities, 1993, 7th ed., 2003; (co-ed.) Knowing and Serving Diverse Families, 1996, 3rd ed., 2008. **Address:** Department of Human Development and Family Studies, College of Social Science, Michigan State University, 7 Human Ecology Bldg., East Lansing, MI 48824, U.S.A.

HILDEBRAND, Verna Lee. *See* **HILDEBRAND, Verna.**

HILDEBRANDT, Erik A(lan). American (born United States), b. 1966. **Genres:** Military/Defense/Arms Control, Adult Non-fiction. **Career:** Cleared Hot Media Inc., owner. Writer. **Publications:** Blue Water Ops: On the Front Line of Naval Aviation, 1997; Fly Navy: Celebrating the First Century of Naval Aviation, 2000; Front Row Center: Inside the Great American Airshow, 2000; Heritage Flight: America's Air Force Celebrates 100 Years of Aviation, 2003; Front Row Center 2: Inside the World's Greatest Air Shows, 2004; Anytime Baby! Hail & Farewell to the U.S. NAVY F-14 Tomcat, 2006; Front Row Center 3: Inside the Great American Airshow, 2007; Front Row Center 4: Inside the Great American Air Show, 2009. **Address:** Cleared Hot Media Inc., 10390 118th St. N, Stillwater, MN 55082, U.S.A. **Online address:** erik@vulturesrow.com

HILDEN, Joanne (M.). American (born United States), b. 1957. **Genres:** Medicine/Health, Psychology. **Career:** Cleveland Clinic, Children's Hospital, Pediatric Palliative Medicine, director, Department of Pediatric Hematology and Oncology, chair. Writer. **Publications:** (With D.R. Tobin and K. Lindsey) Shelter from the Storm: Caring for a Child with a Life-threatening Condition, 2003. **Address:** Department of Pediatric Hematology/Oncology, The Children's Hospital, The Cleveland Clinic, Desk S20, 9500 Euclid Ave., PO Box 931517, Cleveland, OH 44195, U.S.A. **Online address:** hildenj@ccf.org

HILDERBRAND, Elin. American (born United States) **Genres:** Young Adult Fiction, Novels, Romance/Historical. **Career:** Nantucket Preservation Trust, director. Writer. **Publications:** The Beach Club, 2000; Nantucket Nights, 2002; Summer People, 2003; The Blue Bistro, 2005; Love Season, 2006; Barefoot: A Novel, 2007; A Summer Affair: A Novel, 2008; The Castaways: A Novel, 2009; The Island, 2010; Silver Girl, 2011. Contributor to journals. **Address:** Nantucket Preservation Trust, 55 Main St., PO Box 158, Nantucket, MA 02554, U.S.A.

HILDRETH, Denise. American (born United States), b. 1969?. **Genres:** Novels, Young Adult Fiction. **Career:** Teacher, 1997-. Songwriter. **Publications:** NOVELS: Savannah from Savannah, 2004; Savannah Comes Undone, 2005; Savannah by the Sea, 2006; Flies on the Butter, 2007; The Will of Wisteria, 2007; Hurricanes in Paradise, 2010. **Address:** PO Box 680488, Franklin, TN 37068-0488, U.S.A. **Online address:** revolution@denisehildreth.com

HILDT, Elisabeth. German (born Germany), b. 1966. **Genres:** Medicine/Health, Sciences, Engineering. **Career:** European Network for Biomedical Ethics, scientific coordinator, 1996-98; Technik-Theologie-Naturwissenschaften, Wissenschaftliche Mitarbeiterin, researcher in biomedical ethics, 1998-2000; Ludwig-Maximilians-Universitat Munich, Institute of Medical Psychology, postdoctoral fellow, 2000-02; Tubingen University, Interdepartmental Centre for Ethics in the Sciences and Humanities, assistant professor, 2002-. Writer. **Publications:** Hirngewebetransplantation und Personale Identitat, 1996; (ed. with D. Meth) In Vitro Fertilisation in the 1990s: Towards a Medical, Social and Ethical Evaluation, 1998; (ed. with S. Graumann) Genetics in Human Reproduction, 1999; (with B. Hepp) Organtransplantationen: Heteronome Effekte in der Medizin, 2000; Autonomie in der biomedizinischen Ethik: Genetische Diagnostik und selbstbestimmte Lebensgestaltung, 2006; (with Herausgeber and L. Kovács) Was bedeutet genetische Information?, 2009. Contributor to books and journals. **Address:** Inst of Microbiology and Interdisciplinary Fields, Eberhard-Karls-University Tubingen, Auf der Morgenstelle 28, Tubingen, 72076, Germany. **Online address:** e.hildt@lrz.uni-muenchen.de

HILL, Ann M. American (born United States), b. 1945. **Genres:** Education, Human Relations/Parenting, Design, Librarianship. **Career:** Teacher, 1975-93; high school media specialist, 1993-96; Washington Township High School, educational media specialist, 1996-; Mount Laurel Library, reference librarian, 2002-. Writer. **Publications:** (With J.D. Fisher) Tooting Your Own Horn: Web-Based Public Relations for the Twenty-first Century Librarian, 2002. **Address:** Washington Township High School, 519 Hurffville-Crosskeys Rd., Sewell, NJ 08080, U.S.A. **Online address:** ahill@wtps.org

HILL, Anthony (Robert). Australian (born Australia), b. 1942. **Genres:** Novellas/Short Stories, Children's Fiction, Young Adult Fiction, Antiques/Furnishings, History, Adult Non-fiction. **Career:** Melbourne Herald, journalist, 1960-75; Australian Financial Review, journalist, 1976-77; self-employed, 1977-82; freelance journalist, 1982-89; Office of the Governor-General of Australia, speechwriter, 1989-99; Writer, 1999-. **Publications:** JUVENILE FICTION: Birdsong, 1988; The Burnt Stick, 1994; Spindrift, 1996; The Grandfather Clock, 1996. OTHER: The Bunburyists (nonfiction), 1985; Antique Furniture in Australia, 1988; Growing Up and Other Stories, 1999; Soldier Boy, 2001; Forbidden, 2002; Young Digger, 2002; The Shadow Dog, 2003; Animal Heroes, 2005, Harriet 2006, Captain Cook's Apprentice 2008. **Address:** Penguin Books Australia Ltd., 250 Camberwell Rd., Camberwell, VI 3124, Australia. **Online address:** anthony@anthonyhillbooks.com

HILL, A. W. American (born United States), b. 1951?. **Genres:** Novels. **Career:** Columbia College, Department of Film and Video, production manager and instructor in music for filmmakers, 1980, instructor in music composition, 1999-, M.F.A. Program in Music Composition for the Screen, director, 2006-; Disney, music supervisor at film studies, 1989-96, vice president of music production; MGM, music supervisor at film studies; Fox, music supervisor at film studies; Warner Brothers, music supervisor at film studies; Sony, music supervisor at film studies. Writer. **Publications:** Enoch's Portal (novel), 2002; The Last Days of Madame Rey, 2007; Nowhere-Land: A Stephan Raszer Investigation, 2009. **Address:** Publishers Group West, 1700 4th St., Berkeley, CA 94710, U.S.A. **Online address:** awhillpubs@sbcglobal.net

HILL, Barry. Australian (born Australia), b. 1943. **Genres:** Poetry, History, Criminology/True Crime, Social Sciences. **Career:** Full-time freelance writer, 1975-; RMIT, School of Architecture, lecturer in philosophy, 1977-78; University of Melbourne, tutor in creative writing, 1995-99, lecturer, 1999-2002, English Literary Studies, The Australian Centre, fellow, senior fellow, honorary fellow; The Australian, poetry editor. **Publications:** The Schools, 1977; A Rim of Blue, 1978; Near the Refinery, 1980; Headlocks & Other Stories, 1983; The Best Picture, 1988; Raft: Poems, 1983-1990, 1990; Sitting In, 1991; Ghosting William Buckley, 1993; The Rock: Travelling to Uluru, 1994; The Inland Sea, 2001; Broken Song: T.G.H. Strehlow and Aboriginal Possession, 2002; The Enduring Rip: A History of Queenscliff, 2004; The War Sonnets, 2006; Necessity: Poems 1996-2006, 2007; (with J. Wolseley) Lines for Birds, 2011. **Address:** The Australian Centre, University of Melbourne, 137 Barry St., Carlton, VI 3053, Australia. **Online address:** bhill@unimelb.edu.au

HILL, Brian W. British (born England), b. 1932. **Genres:** Biography, History, Autobiography/Memoirs. **Career:** University of East Anglia, reader in history, 1963-, now retired. Writer. **Publications:** (Ed.) Edmund Burke on Government, Politics, and Society, 1975; The Growth of Parliamentary Parties, 1689-1742, 1976; British Parliamentary Parties, 1742-1832: From the Fall of Walpole to the First Reform Act, 1985; Robert Harley, Speaker, Secretary of State, and Premier Minister, 1988; Sir Robert Walpole: Sole and Prime Minister, 1989; The Early Parties and Politics in Britain, 1688-1832, 1996; British Political Parties: 1689 to the Present, forthcoming. **Address:** St. Martin's Press, 175 5th Ave., New York, NY 10010, U.S.A.

HILL, Carol. (Carol Dechellis Hill). American (born United States), b. 1942. **Genres:** Novels, Plays/Screenplays, Social Commentary, Poetry, Literary Criticism And History. **Career:** Crown Publishers, publicist, 1965-67; Bernard Geis Associates Inc., publicist, 1967-69; Pantheon Books, publicist, 1969-71, editor, 1971-73; Random House, publicity manager, 1973-74; William Morrow & Company Inc., senior editor, 1974-76; Harcourt Brace Jovanovich, senior editor, editor-in-chief, vice-president, publisher, 1976-79; writer, 1980-. **Publications:** WITH K. HARRISON: The Mouse Driver Chronicles, 2002; The Mouse Driver Chronicles: The True-Life Adventures of Two First-Time Entrepreneurs, 2003. OTHERS: Jeremiah 8: 20, 1970; Subsistence USA, 1973; Let's Fall in Love, 1974; Montessori on a Limited

Budget: A Manual for the Amateur Craftsman, 1975; An Unmarried Woman, 1978; Montessori for a Home Based Curriculum: A Study, with Particular Attention to the Day Care Education Project, Ithaca, N.Y., 1978; The Eleven Million Mile High Dancer, 1985 in UK as Amanda and The Eleven Million Mile High Dancer, 1988; Henry James' Midnight Song, 1993. Contributor to magazines and periodicals. **Address:** c/o Lynn Nesbit, Janklow and Nesbit Associates Inc., 598 Madison Ave., New York, NY 10022-1610, U.S.A.

HILL, Carol Dechellis. *See* **HILL**, Carol.

HILL, Charles E. (Charles Evan Hill). American (born United States), b. 1956. **Genres:** Theology/Religion, History. **Career:** Northwestern College, faculty member; Reformed Theological Seminary, professor of new testament. Writer and commercial artist. **Publications:** Regnum Caelorum: Patterns of Future Hope in Early Christianity, 1992, 2nd ed. as Regnum Caelorum: Patterns of Millennial Thought in Early Christianity, 2001; (ed. with F.A. James, III) The Glory of the Atonement: Biblical, Historical & Practical Perspectives: Essays in Honor of Roger Nicole, 2004; The Johannine Corpus in the Early Church, 2004; From the Lost Teaching of Polycarp: Identifying Irenaeus' Apostolic Presbyter and the Author of Ad Diognetum, 2006. Contributor to books and journals. **Address:** Reformed Theological Seminary, 1231 Reformation Dr., Oviedo, FL 32765-7197, U.S.A. **Online address:** chill@rts.edu

HILL, Charles Evan. *See* **HILL**, Charles E.

HILL, David. New Zealander (born New Zealand), b. 1942. **Genres:** Children's Fiction, Young Adult Fiction, Plays/Screenplays, Novels. **Career:** School teacher, 1965-82; Writer, 1982-. **Publications:** FOR CHILDREN: The Games of Nanny Miro, 1990; See Ya Simon, 1992; Kick Back, 1995; The Winning Touch, 1995; Take It Easy, 1995; Help Yourself, 1995; Old Bones, 1995; Hats Off!, 1995; Seconds Best, 1996; Cold Comfort, 1996; Fat, Four-eyed and Useless, 1997; Treasure Deep, 1997; Good Move, 1997; Ganging Up, 1997; Give It Hoops, 1998; Boots 'n All, 1998; Comes Naturally, 1998; Time Out, 1999; Just Looking, Thanks, 1999; Impact, 2000; The High Wind Blows, 2000; Afterwards, 2000; The Sleeper Wakes, 2000; The Name of the Game, 2001; Where All Things End, 2002; Right Where It Hurts, 2002; No Safe Harbour, 2003; Journey to Tangiwai, 2003; No Big Deal, 2003; Coming Back, 2004; Running Hot, 2005; Bodies and Soul, 2005; Aim High, 2006; Duet, 2007; The Forgotten Children, 2007; Black Day, 2007. FOR ADULTS: The Seventies Connection, 1980; Moaville Magic, 1985; Ours But to Do, 1986; Taranaki, 1987; The Boy, 1988; More from Moaville, 1988; A Time to Laugh, 1990; The Year in Moaville, 1991; Hill Sides, 2006; River Runs, 2008. TEXTBOOKS: On Poetry: Twelve Studies of Work by New Zealand Poets, 1984; Response to the Short Story, 1985; (with S. Davey) Just Write, 1989; Gossip Writing, 1993; (with C. Ryan) You Know Something: Research using the Encyclopedia, 1994; (with C. Ryan) Right Number: Research using the Telephone Book, 1994; (with C. Ryan) Having a Word: Research using the Thesaurus, 1994; Life on Other Planets, 1997. **Address:** 21 Timandra St., New Plymouth, 4312, New Zealand. **Online address:** david.hill@clear.net.nz

HILL, Elizabeth Starr. American (born United States), b. 1925. **Genres:** Children's Fiction. **Career:** Princeton Adult School, teacher. Writer, actor and painter. **Publications:** The Wonderful Visit to Miss Liberty, 1961; The Window Tulip, 1964; Evan's Corner, 1967, rev. ed., 1990; Master Mike and the Miracle Maid, 1967; Pardon My Fangs, 1969; Bells: A Book to Begin On, 1970; Ever-After Island, 1977; Fangs Aren't Everything, 1985; When Christmas Comes, 1989; The Street Dancers, 1991; Broadway Chances, 1992; The Banjo Player, 1993; Curtain Going Up!, 1995; Bird Boy, 1999; Chang and the Bamboo Flute, 2002; Wildfire!, 2004. **Address:** Wendy Schmalz Agency, PO Box 831, Hudson, NY 12534, U.S.A.

HILL, Geoff. British/Irish (born Ireland), b. 1956. **Genres:** Transportation, History. **Career:** Fodor's, editor; News Letter, features editor. **Publications:** The Ulster Joke Book, 1987; Smith, 1993; Battle for Zimbabwe: The Final Countdown, 2003; What Happens After Mugabe?, 2005; Way to Go: Two of the Worlds Great Motorcycle Journeys, 2005; The Road to Gobblers Knob: From Chile to Alaska on a Motorbike, 2007; Anyway, Where Was I?: Geoff Hills Alternative A-Z of the World, 2008; (with C. O'Carroll) Oz: Around Australia on a Triumph, 2010. Contributor of articles to newspapers. **Address:** Carn Industrial Estate, 2 Esky Dr., Craigavon, BT63 5YY, Northern Ireland.

HILL, Geoffrey. British/American (born United States), b. 1932. **Genres:** Poetry, Literary Criticism And History, History. **Career:** University of Leeds, senior lecturer in English, 1954-80, professor of English, 1976-80; University of Bristol, Churchill Fellow, 1980; University of Oxford, Keble College, honorary fellow; University of Cambridge, Emmanuel College, teaching fellow, 1981-88, honorary fellow; Cambridge University, university lecturer, 1981-88; Trinity College, Clark lecturer, 1986; University of Warwick, Center for Research in Philosophy and Literature, associate fellow; Boston University, Editorial Institute, co-director, 1988-2004, university professor, university professor emeritus, 2006-, College of Arts and Sciences, professor of literature and religion, 1988-2006, professor emeritus of literature and religion, 2006-; University of Oxford, professor of poetry, 2010. Writer. **Publications:** Poems, 1952; For the Unfallen: Poems 1952-1958, 1959; Preghiere, 1964; (with E. Brock and S. Smith) Penguin Modern Poets 8, 1966; King Log, 1968; Mercian Hymns, 1971; Somewhere Is Such a Kingdom: Poems 1952-1971, 1975; Tenebrae, 1978; (contrib.) Brand, 1978; The Mystery of the Charity of Charles Péguy, 1984; The Lords of Limit: Essays on Literature and Ideas, 1984; Collected Poems, 1985; The Enemy's Country: Words, Contexture and Other Circumstances of Language, 1991; Illuminating Shadows: The Mythic Power of Film, 1992; New & Collected Poems, 1952-1992, 1994; Canaan, 1996; The Triumph of Love, 1998; Speech! Speech!, 2000; The Orchards of Syon, 2002; Style and Faith: Essays, 2003; (co-author) Three Bromsgrove Poets, 2003; Scenes from Comus, 2005; Way to Go: Two of the World's Great Motorcycle Journeys, 2005; Without Title, 2007; A Treatise of Civil Power, 2007; Collected Critical Writings, 2008; Selected Poems, 2009; Clavics, 2011. Contributor to periodicals. **Address:** Department of Religion, College of Arts and Sciences, Boston University, 145 Bay State Rd., Boston, MA 02215-1719, U.S.A.

HILL, Gerald N. American (born United States), b. 1929. **Genres:** History, Politics/Government, Law. **Career:** California Governor's Housing Commission, executive director, 1961-63; California Democratic Council, president, 1966-69; Democratic National Convention, delegate, 1968, 1992; Golden Gate University, instructor in law, 1970-71, arbitrator and pro tem judge. Writer. **Publications:** (Ed. and contrib.) Housing in California, 1963; (with K.T. Hill) Nolo's Plain-English Law Dictionary, 2009. WITH K.T. HILL: The Aquino Assassination: The True Story and Analysis of the Assassination of Philippine Senator Benigno S. Aquino, Jr., 1983; Real Life Dictionary of American Politics: What They're Saying and What It Really Means, 1994; Real Life Dictionary of the Law: Taking the Mystery out of Legal Language, 1995; Sonoma Valley: The Secret Wine Country: A Witty and Accurate Guide to Maximizing Your Enjoyment!, 1996; Napa Valley: Land of Golden Vines, 1999; Monterey and Carmel: Eden by the Sea, 1999; Northwest Wine Country: Wines New Frontier, 1999; Santa Barbara & the Central Coast: California's Riviera, 2000; Facts on File Dictionary of American Politics, 2001; People's Law Dictionary: Taking the Mystery Out of Legal Language, 2002; Encyclopedia of Federal Agencies and Commissions, 2004; Victoria & Vancouver Island: A Personal Tour of an Almost Perfect Eden, 2004. **Address:** c/o Michael Hamilburg, Mitchell J. Hamilburg Agency, 292 S La Cienega Blvd., Ste. 312, Beverly Hills, CA 90211, U.S.A.

HILL, Harvey. American (born United States), b. 1965. **Genres:** Politics/Government, Humanities, History. **Career:** Emory University, Candler School of Theology, teaching assistant and teaching associate, 1991-94, assistant instructor, 1995-96; Berry College, assistant professor of religion, 1996-2002, associate professor of religion, 2002-, chair of department, 2002-; Spring Hill College, adjunct lecturer, 1999; Smith College, research associate and lecturer, 2007-09. Educator and writer. **Publications:** (Ed. With L. Barmann) Personal Faith and Institutional Commitment: Roman Catholic Modernist and Anti-Modernist Autobiography, 2002; The Politics of Modernism: Alfred Loisy and the Scientific Study of Religion, 2002; (with L. Sardella and C.J.T. Talar) By Those Who Knew Them: French Modernists Left, Right, and Center, 2008. Contributor to journals. **Address:** Department of Religion and Philosophy, Berry College, 2277 Martha Berry Hwy. NW, PO Box 550, Mount Berry, GA 30149, U.S.A. **Online address:** hhill@berry.edu

HILL, Ingrid. American (born United States) **Genres:** Novellas/Short Stories, Novels, Literary Criticism And History, Young Adult Fiction. **Career:** Writer. **Publications:** Dixie Church Interstate Blues, 1989; Ursula, Under: A Novel, 2004; The Ballad of Rappy Valcour, forthcoming. Contributor to periodicals. **Address:** c/o Author Mail, Workman Publishing, 708 Broadway, New York, NY 10003-9555, U.S.A.

HILL, Janet Muirhead. American (born United States), b. 1942. **Genres:** Children's Fiction, Young Adult Fiction, Westerns/Adventure, Novels. **Career:** MJH Enterprises Business, co-owner, 1984-89; home care provider, 1990-92; Alone Together, publisher, writer and editor, 1997-2007; Raven Publishing, founder, publisher, editor-in-chief, 1997-, president, 2003-. **Publications:** Miranda and Starlight (juvenile fiction), 2002, rev. ed., 2003; Starlights Courage, 2002, rev. ed., 2007; Starlight, Star Bright, 2003; Starlights Shooting Star, 2003; Starlight Shines for Miranda, 2004; Starlight Comes Home, 2004; Dannys Dragon, 2006; Kyleahs Tree, 2008, rev. ed., 2011; Kendalls Storm, 2011. Contributor of short stories to magazines. **Address:** Raven Publishing, 125 Cherry Creek Rd., PO Box 2866, Norris, MT 59745, U.S.A. **Online address:** author@janetmuirheadhill.com

HILL, Johnson. *See* **KUNHARDT, Edith.**

HILL, Jonathan D. American (born United States), b. 1954. **Genres:** Anthropology/Ethnology, Social Sciences. **Career:** Indiana University, instructor in anthropology, 1982-83; University of Georgia, visiting assistant professor of anthropology, 1983-86; Southern Illinois University, assistant professor, 1986-89, associate professor of anthropology, 1990-95, professor, 1996-, Department of Anthropology, chair, 1999-; University of California, visiting associate professor, 1993-94. Writer. **Publications:** Keepers of the Sacred Chants: The Poetics of Ritual Power in an Amazonian Society, 1993; Made-from-Bone: Trickster Myths, Music and History from the Amazon, 2009. EDITOR: Rethinking History and Myth: Indigenous South American Perspectives on the Past, 1988; Anthropological Discourses and the Expression of Personhood in South American Inter-Ethnic Relations, 1993; History, Power and Identity: Ethnogenesis in the Americas, 1492-1992, 1996; Comparative Arawakan Histories: Rethinking Language Family and Culture Area in Amazonia, 2002. Contributor to books and journals. **Address:** Department of Anthropology, Southern Illinois University, 3231 Faner Hall, 1000 Faner Dr., PO Box 4502, Carbondale, IL 62901-4502, U.S.A. **Online address:** jhill@siu.edu

HILL, Justin. British/Bahamian (born Bahamas), b. 1971?. **Genres:** Novels, Social Sciences, Young Adult Fiction. **Career:** City University of Hong Kong, visiting specialist; Lingnan University, honorary fellow; Asian Literary Review, contributing editor; Hong Kong University, faculty; Shaoyang University, faculty. **Publications:** A Bend in the Yellow River, 1997; The Drink and Dream Teahouse, 2001; Ciao Asmara: A Classic Account of Contemporary Africa, 2002; Passing Under Heaven, 2004; Shieldwall, 2011. Contributor to magazines and periodicals. **Address:** The Viney Agency, 23 Erlanger Rd., Telegraph Hill, London, SE14 5TF, United Kingdom. **Online address:** hi@justinhillauthor.com

HILL, Kathleen Thompson. American (born United States), b. 1941. **Genres:** History, Law, Politics/Government, Travel/Exploration, Food And Wine. **Career:** Democratic National Convention, delegate, 1992; University of British Columbia, lecturer on political science, 2000-; Sonoma State University, lecturer on political science, 2000-; Cultural and Fine Arts Commission of Sonoma, chairperson; Peace Corps, intern; Sonoma Magazine, Food and Wine editor; Boston Globe, food and travel correspondent; A Million Cooks, foodcaster. **Publications:** Festivals U.S.A.: Western States, 1982; (with G.N. Hill) The Aquino Assassination: The True Story and Analysis of the Assassination of Philippine Senator Benigno S. Aquino, Jr., 1983; Festivals U.S.A., 1983; (ed.) Sonoma Poets: A Collection, 1986, 2nd ed., 1995; Santa Barbara and Central Coast, 1991, rev. ed., 2001; (with G.N. Hill) Real Life Dictionary of American Politics: What They're Saying and What It Really Means, 1994, rev. ed. as Facts on File Dictionary of American Politics, 2001; (with G.N. Hill) Real Life Dictionary of the Law: Taking the Mystery out of Legal Language, 1995, rev. ed. as People's Law Dictionary, 2002; Victoria and Vancouver Island, 1997, 4th ed., 2004; (with G.N. Hill) Hill Guides to Sonoma Valley, 1998, 5th ed., 2005; Northwest Wine Country, 1998, rev. ed., 2000; Napa Valley, 1999, rev. ed., 2003; Monterey and Carmel, 1999, rev. ed., 2001; (with G.N. Hill) Encyclopedia of Federal Agencies and Commissions, 2004; (ed. with G.N. Hill and Nolo) Nolo's Plain-English Law Dictionary, 2009; Career Opportunities in the Food and Beverage Industry, 2010. Contributor to magazines and newspapers. **Address:** 631 4th St. E, PO Box 654, Sonoma, CA 95476, U.S.A. **Online address:** hilltopub@aol.com

HILL, Laban Carrick. American (born United States), b. 1960?. **Genres:** Young Adult Fiction, Novels, Mystery/Crime/Suspense, Horror. **Career:** New Yorker, senior copywriter and marketing analyst, 1982-86; Sterling Publishing, senior copywriter, 1990-91; Bantam Publishing, senior copywriter, 1991-93; Pine Manor College, teacher; Columbia University, teacher; City University of New York, Bernard M. Baruch College, instructor in composition and English as a second language, 1993-94; Eating Well Books, marketing and promotion director, 1994-96; St. Michael's College, lecturer in English and writing, 1994-2000; Greater Burlington Girls Soccer League, vice president, 1997-2003; Flechter Free Library, commissioner, 2003-; U.S. Embassy in Egypt, lecturer, 2006; Vermont College, adjunct faculty, 2006; University of Vermont, adjunct faculty, 2006; University of Cape Coast, visiting professor of creative writing, 2008; Ghana Poetry Project, co-founder, 2009. Writer. **Publications:** Monster Dots, 1993; Clinton Street Crime Wave, 1994; Watch Out for Room 13, 1996; Bugged Out!, 1996; The Evil Pen Pal, 1997; Stampede!: Choose Your Own Adventure, 1997; The Toy Shop of Terror, 1997; Welcome to Horror Hospital, 1997; Jonathan Franzen's The Corrections (Spark Notes), 2003; Harlem Stomp!: A Cultural History of the Harlem Renaissance, 2003; The Spy's Survival Handbook, 2004; Casa Azul: An Encounter with Frida Kahlo (young-adult novel), 2005; America Dreaming: How Youth Changed America in the Sixties, 2007; A Brush with Napoleon: An Encounter with Jacques-Louis David, 2007; Dave the Potter, 2011; DJ Kool Herc, 2012. X-TREME MYSTERIES NOVEL SERIES: Deep Powder, Deep Trouble, 1998; Spiked Snow, 1998; Out of Line, 1998; Lost Wake, 1998; Half Pipe Rip-off, 1998; Rocked Out: A Summer X Games Special, 1998; Crossed Tracks, 1998; Total White Out, 1998. Works appear in anthologies. Contributor to periodicals. **Address:** c/o Author Mail, Watson-Guptill Publications Inc., 770 Broadway, New York, NY 10003-9522, U.S.A. **Online address:** labanhill@yahoo.com

HILL, Lynda Marion. American (born United States), b. 1951?. **Genres:** Social Commentary, Literary Criticism And History. **Career:** Temple University, College of Liberal Arts, assistant professor of English. Writer. **Publications:** Social Rituals and the Verbal Art of Zora Neale Hurston, 1996. **Address:** Departmentt of English, College of Liberal Arts, Temple University, 1038 Anderson Hall, 1114 Polett Walk, Philadelphia, PA 19122-6090, U.S.A. **Online address:** lynda.hill@temple.edu

HILL, Lynn. American (born United States), b. 1961?. **Genres:** Autobiography/Memoirs. **Career:** Lynn Hill Climbing Camps, owner. Writer. **Publications:** (With G. Child) Climbing Free: My Life in the Vertical World (autobiography), 2002. **Address:** PO Box 383, Eldorado Springs, CO 80025-0383, U.S.A. **Online address:** lynn@lynnhillblogs.com

HILL, Marion Moore. American (born United States), b. 1937. **Genres:** Mystery/Crime/Suspense, Adult Non-fiction, Young Adult Fiction. **Career:** Writer and educator. **Publications:** SCRAPPY LIBRARIAN MURDER MYSTERIES: Bookmarked for Murder, 2002; Death Books a Return, 2008. DEADLY PAST MURDER MYSTERIES: Deadly Will, 2006; Deadly Design: A Deadly Past Mystery, 2009. OTHER: Nanette, forthcoming. Contributor to periodicals. **Address:** c/o Ms. Arlene Johnson, Arlene Johnson & Associates, 406 S Boulder Ave., Ste. 454, Tulsa, OK 74103-3825, U.S.A. **Online address:** marion@marionmoorehill.com

HILL, Pamela. (Sharon Fiske). British/Kenyan (born Kenya), b. 1920. **Genres:** Mystery/Crime/Suspense, Romance/Historical, Novels, Young Adult Fiction. **Career:** Teacher, 1958-74, 1965-70. Novelist. **Publications:** NOVELS: The King's Vixen, 1954 in UK as Flaming Janet: A Lady of Galloway, 1954; (contrib.) The Crown and the Shadow: The Story of Francoise D'Aubigne, Marquise de Maintenon, 1955 in UK as Shadow of Palaces: The Story of Francoise d'Aubigne, Marquise De Maintenon, 1955; Marjorie of Scotland, 1956; Here Lies Margot, 1957; Maddalena, 1963; Forget Not Ariadne, 1965; Julia, 1967; The Devil of Aske, 1972; The Malvie Inheritance, 1973; The Incumbent, 1974 in US as The Heatherton Heritage, 1976; Whitton's Folly, 1975; Norah Stroyan in US as Norah, 1976; The Green Salamander, 1977; Csar's Woman, 1977 as Tsar's Woman, 1985; Stranger's Forest, 1978; Homage to a Rose, 1979; Daughter of Midnight, 1979; Daneclere, 1980; Fire Opal, 1980; A Place of Ravens, 1980; (as Sharon Fiske) Summer Cypress, 1981; Knock at a Star, 1981; This Rough Beginning, 1981; Dutchess Cain, 1982; The House of Cray, 1982; The Fairest One of All, 1982; The Copper-Haired Marshal, 1983; Bride of Ae, 1983; Children of Lucifer, 1984; Still Blooms the Rose, 1984; The Governess, 1984; Sable for the Count, 1985; My Lady Glamis, 1985; Venables, 1986; Digby, 1987; Fenfallow, 1987; The Sutburys, 1988; Jeannie Urquahart, 1988; The Sisters, 1988; The Renegade's Moon, 1988, The Woman in the Cloak, 1988; Trevithick, 1989; Artemia, 1989; The Loves of Ginevra, 1990; Vollands, 1990; Dark Star Passing, 1990;

The Brocken, 1990; The Sword and the Flame, 1991; A The Silver Runaways, 1992; Angel and Sons, 1992; Mercer, 1992; O Madcap Duchess, 1993; Aunt Lucy, 1993; The Parson's Children, 1994; The Man from the North, 1994; Journey beyond Innocence, 1994; The Charmed Descent, 1995; The Inadvisable Marriages, 1995; Curtmantle, 1996; Murder in Store, 1996; Alice the Palace: A Particularly Important Bull Terrier, 1996; Saint's Names for Confirmation, 1996; The Supplanter, 1998; The Small Black Knife, 1998; Aunt Lucy, 1999; The Lion's Daughter, 1999; Countess Isabel, 1999; Bailie's Wake, 2000; The Gods Return, 2000; Venus Rising, 2003; A Tale of Strawberries: Shakespeare's Journeys in Scotland, 2005; Prinny Remembers, 2006; Lady Kate, 2007; Jacobites, 2008; Milady's Aesthetician Series: Microdermabrasion, 2009, 2nd ed. as Milady's Aesthetician Series: Peels and Chemical Exfoliation, 2009. OTHERS: The Enamel Eye, 2008; Milady's Medispa Dictionary, 2010; Botox, Dysport, Dermal Fillers and Sclerotherapy, 2011. **Address:** Hale Robert Ltd., Clerkenwell House, 45-47 Clerkenwell Green, London, GL EC1R 0HT, England.

HILL, Reginald (Charles). Also writes as Charles Underhill, Patrick Ruell, Dick Morland. British (born England), b. 1936. **Genres:** Novels, Novellas/Short Stories, Mystery/Crime/Suspense, Plays/Screenplays, Young Adult Fiction. **Career:** Teacher, 1962-67; Doncaster College of Education, lecturer in English literature, 1967-82; writer, 1980-. **Publications:** CRIME NOVELS: Fell of Dark, 1971; A Fairly Dangerous Thing, 1972; A Very Good Hater, 1974; Another Death in Venice, 1976; The Spy's Wife, 1980; Who Guards the Prince?, 1982; Traitor's Blood, 1983; Guardians of the Prince, 1983; No Man's Land, 1985; The Collaborators, 1987; The Stranger House, 2005; The Woodcutter, 2010. DALZIEL AND PASCOE SERIES: A Clubbable Woman, 1970; An Advancement of Learning, 1971; Ruling Passion, 1973; An April Shroud, 1975; A Pinch of Snuff, 1978; A Killing Kindness, 1980; Deadheads, 1983; Exit Lines, 1984; Child's Play, 1986; Underworld, 1988; Bones and Silence, 1990; One Small Step, 1990; Recalled to Life, 1992; Pictures of Perfection, 1994; The Wood Beyond, 1995; Asking for the Moon (short stories), 1996; On Beulah Height, 1998; Arms and the Women, 1999; Dialogues of the Dead, 2001; Death's Jest Book, 2002; Good Morning, Midnight, 2004; For Love Nor Money, 2005; Secrets of the Dead, 2005; Death Comes for the Fat Man as The Death of Dalziel, 2007; The Last National Serviceman, 2007; A Cure for All Diseases as The Price of Butcher's Meat, 2008; Midnight Fugue, 2009. JOE SIXSMITH SERIES: Blood Sympathy, 1993; Born Guilty, 1995; Killing the Lawyers, 1997; Singing the Sadness, 1999; The Roar of the Butterflies, 2008. AS DICK MORLAND: Heart Clock, 1973; Albion! Albion!, 1974 as Singleton's Law, 1997. AS PATRICK RUELL: The Castle of the Demon, 1971; Red Christmas, 1972; Death Takes the Low Road, 1974; Urn Burial, 1976, The Long Kill, 1986; Death of a Dormouse, 1987; Dream of Darkness, 1989; The Only Game, 1991. AS CHARLES UNDERHILL: Captain Fantom, 1978; The Forging of Fantom, 1979. COLLECTIONS: Pascoe's Ghost: And Other Brief Chronicles of Crime, 1979; There Are No Ghosts in the Soviet Union, 1987; Brother's Keeper, 1992. OTHERS: Who Guards a Prince, 2010. **Address:** AP Watt Ltd., 20 John St., London, GL WC1N 2DR, England.

HILL, Robert S. Australian (born Australia), b. 1954. **Genres:** Botany. **Career:** James Cook University, tutor in botany, 1979-80; University of Tasmania, lecturer in botany, 1980-87, senior lecturer in plant science, 1988-90, reader in plant science, 1991, associate professor in plant science, 1991-92, professor in plant science, 1993-99; Geological Society of Australia, Southern Connection, founding member and bulletin editor, 1991-2004; Palynological and Palaeobotanical Association of Australasia, president 1994-97; Australian Systematic Botany Society, newsletter editor 1998-2001; University of Adelaide, research fellow, 1999-2003, School of Earth and Environmental Sciences, head, 2003-, executive dean, 2006-, faculty of sciences, 2006-, Academic Board, chair, 2007-09, council, 2007-; South Australian Museum, head of science, 2001-; Australian Institute of Biology, president 2001-03. Writer. **Publications:** History of the Australian Vegetation: Cretaceous to Recent, 1994; Ecology of the Southern Conifers, 1995; (ed. with T.T. Veblen, J. Read) The Ecology and Biogeography of Nothofagus Forests, 1996; The Vegetation of Tasmania, 1999. **Address:** Department of Environmental Biology, University of Adelaide, Rm. G, Darling Bldg., Adelaide, SA 5005, Australia. **Online address:** bob.hill@adelaide.edu.au

HILL, Roccie. American (born United States), b. 1952. **Genres:** Novels. **Career:** Writer, filmmaker and journalist. **Publications:** Three Minutes on Love (novel), 2008. **Address:** CA, U.S.A. **Online address:** roccie@rocciehill.com

HILL, Ronald C. American (born United States), b. 1937. **Genres:** Transportation, Travel/Exploration, Art/Art History. **Career:** Anstine, Hill, Richards & Simpson, attorney, 1969-, of counsel. Writer. **Publications:** (With J.T. Brouws) Railroading West, 1975, rev. ed., 1979; Rio Grande in the Rockies, 1977, 2nd ed., 1979; (with D. Stanley) Rails in the Northwest, 1978; (with R.H. Kindig) Union Pacific 8444, 1978; (ed. with R.H. Kindig) Locomotive 346: The First One Hundred Years, 1981; Rio Grande West, 1982; (with W.E. Botkin and R.H. Kindig) Union Pacific 3985, 1985; (with W.E. Botkin and V. Hand) Union Pacific: Mainline West, 1986; Mountain Mainlines of the West, 1988; Colorful Colorado Railroads in the 1960s, 1992; (with A. Chione) The Railroad Artistry of Howard Fogg, 1999. Contributor of articles to books and periodicals. **Address:** Anstine, Hill, Richards & Simpson, 899 Logan St., Ste. 406, Denver, CO 80203-2988, U.S.A. **Online address:** rhill@ahrs-law.com

HILL, Russell. American (born United States), b. 1935. **Genres:** Novels, Natural History, Mystery/Crime/Suspense, Young Adult Fiction, Poetry. **Career:** Tamalpais High School District, instructor in English; California teacher, editor. **Publications:** Reflections of the Future, 1975; Letters from the Mines (poetry), 1978; Cold Creek Cash Store, as Edge of the Earth, 1986; Lucy Boomer, 1992; The Search for Sheepheaven Trout, 2003; Heeler, 2005; Robbie's Wife, 2007; The Lord God Bird, 2009; Dog Sox, 2011; Lubbock, 2011; Deadly Negatives, 2012; The Ghost Trout, forthcoming; Ivory Blouse, forthcoming. **Address:** Frederick Hill Associates, 1842 Union St., San Francisco, CA 94123, U.S.A. **Online address:** russellhillwriter@gmail.com

HILL, Sarah H. American (born United States) **Genres:** History. **Career:** Oglethorpe University, lecturer, 1995; DeKalb College, honors lecturer, 1995, 1997; Emory University, adjunct assistant professor, 1996-; Georgia Chapter National Trail of Texas Association, research chair, 1997-; North Carolina Heritage Trails project, consultant, 1999-; Qualla Arts and Crafts, consultant; McKissick Museum, consultant; Cumberland Gap Interpretive Center Project, consultant. Writer. **Publications:** Weaving New Worlds: Southeastern Cherokee Women and Their Basketry, 1997; (with S.E. Vrooman) Native Lands: Indians & Georgia, 1999. Contributor to books and periodicals. **Address:** 3210 W Andrews Dr. NW, Atlanta, GA 30305, U.S.A. **Online address:** sarahhill@mindspring.com

HILL, Selima (Wood). British (born England), b. 1945. **Genres:** Poetry, Novels, Romance/Historical. **Career:** Morley College of Further Education, staff, 1967-75; Tetric Bookshop, assistant manager, 1980-85; University of East Anglia, writing fellow, 1991; Royal Festival Hall Dance Festival, writer-in-residence, 1992; South Bank Center, reader-in-residence, 1998; University of Exeter, fellow, 2003-04; Poetry School in London, tutor. **Publications:** Saying Hello at the Station, 1984; My Darling Camel, 1988; The Accumulation of Small Acts of Kindness, 1989; A Little Book of Meat, 1993; Trembling Hearts in the Bodies of Dogs, 1994; My Sister's Horse, 1996; Violet, 1997; Bunny, 2001; Portrait of My Lover as a Horse, 2002; Mr. Silver-Shoes, 2003; Lou-Lou, 2004; Red Roses, 2006; Gloria: Selected Poems, 2008; The Hat, 2008; Fruitcake, 2009; Advice On Wearing Animal Prints, 2009. Contributor to magazines and newspapers. Works appear in anthologies. **Address:** Bloodaxe Books Ltd., Highgreen, Tarset, PO Box 15N, New Castle upon Tyme, NM NE48 1RP, England.

HILL, Susan (Elizabeth). British (born England), b. 1942. **Genres:** Novels, Novellas/Short Stories, Children's Fiction, Plays/Screenplays, Picture/Board Books, Autobiography/Memoirs, Translations, Essays, Essays. **Career:** Novelist, playwright, critic, 1960-; Coventry Evening Telegraph, literary critic, 1963-68; Daily Telegraph, monthly columnist, 1977-; King's College, fellow, 1978; Bookshelf, Radio 4, staff, 1986-87; Long Barn Books, founder, 1996-. **Publications:** The Enclosure, 1961; Do Me a Favour, 1963; Gentleman and Ladies, 1969; A Change for the Better, 1969; I'm the King of the Castle, 1970; Strange Meeting, 1971; The Albatross in US as The Albatross and Other Stories, 1971; The Bird of Night, 1972; The Custodian, 1972; A Bit of Singing and Dancing (short stories), 1973; In the Springtime of the Year: A Novel, 1974; The Cold Country and Other Plays for Radio, 1975; The Magic Apple Tree: A Country Year, 1982; The Woman in Black, 1983; Through the Kitchen Window, 1984; One Night at a Time (for children), 1984; Go Away, Bad Dreams!, 1984; Through the Garden Gate, 1986; Mother's Magic (for children), 1986; Shakespeare Country, 1987; The Lighting of the Lamps, 1987; Lanterns across the Snow (novella), 1988; The Spirit of the Cotswolds, 1988; Can It Be True? (for children), 1988; Family (autobiography), 1989; Suzie's Shoes (for children), 1989; (with T. Hill) The Collaborative Classroom: A Guide to Co-operative Learning, 1990; Stories from Codling Village, 1990;

I've Forgotten Edward, 1990; I Won't Go There Again, 1990; Pirate Poll, 1991; (trans. with J. Tittler) A. Ortiz, Juyungo: The First Black Ecuadorian Novel, 1991; The Mist in the Mirror, 1992; The Glass Angels, 1992; Mrs. De Winter, 1993; Beware, Beware, 1993; King of Kings, 1993; The Christmas Collection, 1994; (with R. Stuart) Reflections from a Garden, 1995; Listening to the Orchestra (stories), 1996; Simba's A-Z, 1998; Service of Clouds, 1999; Stuart Sets Sail, 2001; Stuart Hides Out, 2001; Stuart at the Library, 2001; Stuart at the Fun House, 2001; Backyard Bedtime, 2001; The Boy Who Taught the Beekeeper to Read, 2003; Ruby Bakes a Cake, 2004; Pure in Heart: A Simon Serrailler Crime Novel, 2005; Ruby Paints a Picture, 2005; Risk of Darkness: A Simon Serrailler Crime Novel, 2006; Ruby's Perfect Day, 2006; Various Haunts of Men: A Simon Serrailler Crime Novel, 2007; Man in the Picture: A Ghost Story, 2007; Vows of Silence: A Simon Serrailler Crime Novel, 2008; The Battle for Gullywith, 2008; Beacon, 2008; Spider-Man Versus Electro, 2009; Spider-Man Versus Kraven, 2009; Howard's End is on the Landing, 2009; The Shadows in the Street, 2010; (contrib.) Strike Three, Marley!, 2010; Spider-Man versus the Scorpion, 2010; Spider-Man versus the Green Goblin, 2010; Small Hand, 2010; (contrib.) Snow Dog, Marley, 2010; A Kind Man, 2011; The Betrayal of Trust, 2011. EDITOR: (and intro.) The Distracted Preacher and Other Stories, 1979; People: Essays & Poems, 1983; Ghost Stories, 1984; (with J. Hancock) Literature-Based Reading Programs at Work, 1988; The Random House Book of Ghost Stories, 1991; (and intro.) Spirit of Britain: An Illustrated Guide to Literary Britain, 1994; (and intro.) Contemporary Women's Short Stories, 1995; (with S. Topley) Counting My Chickens: And Other Home Thoughts, 2002. Contributor to magazines. **Address:** c/o Vivien Green, Sheil Land Associates Ltd., 52 Doughty St., London, GL WC1N 2LS, England. **Online address:** mail@susan-hill.com

HILL, Thomas. (Tommy Hallowell). American (born United States), b. 1960. **Genres:** Young Adult Fiction, Humor/Satire, Business/Trade/Industry, Law, Humor/Satire. **Career:** Freelance writer, 1984-89; Nick at Nite/TV Land, copywriter and creative director, 1989-. **Publications:** (With A. Zybell) The Tax Reform Act of 1986: Tax Shelters, 1986; (with S. Slavkin) Salute Your Shorts: Life at Summer Camp, 1986; (with A. Hill) Otherwise Engaged, 1988; What to Expect When Your Wife Is Expanding, 1993, rev. ed. as What to Expect When Your Wife is Expanding: A Reassuring Month-by-Month Guide for the Father-to-be, Whether He Wants Advice or Not, 2007; (with D. Friedman) Pat the Stimpy, 1993; Nick at Nites' Classic TV Companion, 1996; What the Heck Were You Expecting?: A Complete Guide for the Perplexed Father, 2000. AS TOMMY HALLOWELL: Varsity Coach: Fourth and Goal (young adult), 1986; Varsity Coach: Out of Bounds (young adult), 1987; The Alden All Stars: Duel on the Diamond, 1990; The Alden All Stars: Jester in the Backcourt, 1990; The Alden All Stars: Shot from Midfield, 1990; The Alden All Stars: Last Chance Quarterback, 1990. **Address:** Nick at Nite/TV Land, 1515 Broadway, 45th Fl., New York, NY 10036, U.S.A.

HILL, Thomas E(nglish). American (born United States), b. 1937. **Genres:** Philosophy. **Career:** Macalester College, instructor, 1962-63; Johns Hopkins University, assistant professor of philosophy, 1965-66; Pomona College, assistant professor, 1966-68; University of California, faculty, 1968-84, full professor, 1982-84, acting chair, 1983-84; Stanford University, visiting associate professor, 1980; University of North Carolina, professor, 1984-, William Rand Kenan, Jr. professor, 1994-95, Kenan professor, 1996-; University of Minnesota, visiting professor, 1994. Writer. **Publications:** Autonomy and Self-Respect, 1991; Dignity and Practical Reason in Kant's Moral Theory, 1992; Respect, Pluralism, and Justice: Kantian Perspectives, 2000; Human Welfare and Moral Worth: Kantian Perspectives, 2002; (ed. with A. Zweig) Groundwork for the Metaphysics of Morals, 2002; The Importance of Moral Rules and Principles, 2007; (ed.) Blackwell Guide to Kant's Ethics, 2008. Contributor to philosophy journals. **Address:** Department of Philosophy, University of North Carolina, 214-B Caldwell Hall, Chapel Hill, NC 27599-3125, U.S.A. **Online address:** thill@email.unc.edu

HILL, Tobias. British (born England), b. 1970. **Genres:** Poetry, Novels, Novellas/Short Stories. **Career:** Apex School, teacher, 1993-94; Sunday Telegraph's, rock critic, 1998-2001. Editor and writer. **Publications:** Year of the Dog (poetry), 1995; Midnight in the City of Clocks (poetry), 1996; Skin (short stories), 1997; Zoo (poetry), 1998; Underground, (novel) 1999; The Love of Stones (novel), 2001; The Cryptographer, 2003; Nocturne in Chrome and Sunset Yellow, 2006; The Lion Who Ate Everything, 2008; The Hidden, 2009. **Address:** c/o Victoria Hobbs, Toby Eady Associates, 9 Orme Ct., London, GL W2 4RL, England.

HILL, Tracey. British (born England), b. 1964. **Genres:** Literary Criticism And History, Young Adult Fiction. **Career:** University of Essex, faculty; WEA, staff; Bath Spa University, School of Humanities and Cultural Industries, Department of English and Cultural Studies, faculty, 1993, head; University of the West of England, Early Modernist Network, founder. Writer. **Publications:** (Ed.) Decadence and Danger: Writing, History, and the Fin de Siecle, 1997; Anthony Munday and Civic Culture: Theatre, History and Power in Early Modern London, 1580-1633, 2004; Pageantry and Power: A Cultural History of the Early Modern Lord Mayor's Show, 1585-1639, 2010. **Address:** Department of English, Bath Spa University, NP. NE.208, Newton Pk., Newton St., Bath, SM BA2 9BN, England.

HILL, William. American (born United States), b. 1959. **Genres:** Science Fiction/Fantasy, Horror, Novels. **Career:** Nortel Telecommunications, employee relations staff, 1983-86; Vistawall/Butler Manufacturing, human resources manager, 1987-89; writer, 1989-; Diamond Peak, ski patroller, 1995-2010. **Publications:** Dawn of the Vampire, 1991; Vampire's Kiss, 1994; The Magic Bicycle, 1997; California Ghosting, 1998; The Vampire Hunters, 1998; Chasing Time-The Magic Bicycle Two, 1999; The Wizard Sword, 2000; Vegas Vampires, 2004; Dragon Pawns: Jules and the Runt Dragon, 2005; The Vampire Hunters Stalked, 2006; Impatient Fire: Jules and the Runt Dragon, 2009. **Address:** Otter Creek Press, 3154 Nautilus Rd., Middleburg, FL 32068, U.S.A. **Online address:** otterpress@aol.com

HILLARD, Darla. American (born United States), b. 1946. **Genres:** Environmental Sciences/Ecology, Natural History, Travel/Exploration, Sciences. **Career:** Snow Leopard Conservancy, program coordinator. Writer. **Publications:** Vanishing Tracks: Four Years among the Snow Leopards of Nepal, 1989. **Address:** Snow Leopard Conservancy, 18030 Comstock Ave, Sonoma, CA 95476, U.S.A.

HILLES, Rick. American (born United States) **Genres:** Poetry. **Career:** University of Michigan, faculty; University of Wisconsin, faculty; Vanderbilt University, assistant professor of creative writing; James Merrill House, James Merrill writer-in-residence, 2007. Writer. **Publications:** A Visionary's Company & Other Poems, 2000; Preparing for Flight (poetry), 2005; Brother Salvage: Poems, 2006; Boundary Waters, 2012. Contributor to journals. **Address:** Department of English, Vanderbilt University, 427 Benson Hall, 2301 Vanderbilt Pl., Nashville, TN 37235-0002, U.S.A. **Online address:** rick.hilles@vanderbilt.edu

HILLES, Robert. Canadian (born Canada), b. 1951. **Genres:** Poetry, Novellas/Short Stories, Adult Non-fiction, Novels, Autobiography/Memoirs. **Career:** Dandelion, managing editor; League of Canadian Poets, executive; DeVry Institute of Technology, faculty. Writer. **Publications:** POETRY: Look the Lovely Animal Speaks, 1980; The Surprise Element, 1982; An Angel in the Works, 1983; Outlasting the Landscape, 1989; Finding the Lights On, 1991; A Breath at a Time, 1992; Cantos From a Small Room, 1993; Nothing Vanishes, 1996; Breathing Distance, 1997; Wrapped within Again, 2003; Partake, 2010. OTHER: Raising of Voices (prose), 1993; Near Morning (short fiction collection), 1995; Kissing the Smoke (nonfiction), 1996; Somewhere Between Obstacles and Pleasure, 1999; Higher Ground, 2001; Gradual Ruin: A Novel, 2004; Calling the Wild, 2005; Slow Ascent, 2006; Solo, forthcoming; The Smallest Detail, forthcoming. Contributor to periodicals. Works appear in anthologies. **Address:** Black Moss Press, 2450 Byng Rd., Windsor, ON N8W 3E8, Canada. **Online address:** rhilles@shaw.wave.ca

HILLGARTH, J(ocelyn) N(igel). British (born England), b. 1929. **Genres:** History, Literary Criticism And History. **Career:** Warburg Institute, senior research fellow, 1959-62; University of Texas, visiting lecturer, 1964-65; Harvard University, assistant professor of history, 1965-70; Boston College, associate professor, 1970-73, professor of history, 1973-77; University of Toronto, Pontifical Institute of Medieval Studies and Centre for Medieval Studies, professor of history, 1977-95, professor emeritus, 1995-; Hebrew University of Jerusalem, Lady Davis visiting professor, 1980. Writer. **Publications:** (With J.G. Pastor) Manuscritos lulianos de la Biblioteca Pública de Palma, por Jesús García Pastor, J.N. Hillgrath, 1965; (ed.) The Conversion of Western Europe 350-750, 1969; Ramon Lull and Lullism in Fourteenth Century France, 1971; Problem of a Catalan Mediterranean Empire 1229-1327, 1975; (co-author) Cultura I Historia a Mallorca, Menorcal Eivissa, 1976; The Spanish Kingdoms, 1250-1516, vol. I, 1976, vol. II, 1978; (intro.) Chronicle, Pere III of Catalonia, 2 vols., 1980; Vida de Ramon Llull: Les Fonts Escrites I la Iconografia Coetanies, 1982; (with G. Silano) Register Notule Communium 14 of the Diocese of Barcelona (1345-1348): A Calendar with Selected Documents, 1983; Private Life: Autobiographical Writings, 1984; Visigothic Spain, Byzantium and the Irish, 1985; (ed.) Christianity and Paganism 350-750: The Conversion of Western Europe, 1986; Readers and Books in Majorca, 1229-1550, 1991; Who Read Thomas Aquinas?, 1992; The Liber Communis Curiae of the Diocese of Majorca, 1364-1374, 1992; (ed. with J. Fontaine) Le septième siècle, changements et continuités, 1992; Ramon Llull I el Naixement del Illúlisme, 1998; The Mirror of Spain, 1500-1700: The Formation of a Myth, 2000; Nous Horitzons Culturals a Mallorca al Final de l'Edat Mitjana, 2000; (contrib.) Religion, Text and Society in Medieval Spain and Northern Europe: Essays in Honor of J.N. Hillgarth, 2002; Spain and the Mediterranean in the Later Middle Ages: Studies in Political and Intellectual History, 2003; (ed. with J. Jeffs) Maurice Baring: Letters, 2007; Visigoths in History and Legend, 2009. **Address:** Pontifical Institute of Mediaeval Studies, University of Toronto, 59 Queen's Park Cres. E, Toronto, ON M5S 2C4, Canada.

HILLIER, Jim. British (born England), b. 1941. **Genres:** Film, Documentaries/Reportage, Humor/Satire, Reference. **Career:** South East London College of Further Education, lecturer in English, liberal studies and film, 1964-68; Schools Council of the Nuffield Foundation Humanities Project, film research officer, 1968-69; British Film Institute, teacher, adviser, 1969-73, Educational Advisory Service, deputy head, 1974-78, acting head of education department, 1976-78; University of Reading (formerly Bulmershe College of Higher Education), senior lecturer in film studies, 1979-. Writer. **Publications:** (With A. Lovell) Studies in Documentary, 1972; (with A. Lipstadt) Roger Corman's New World, 1981; The New Hollywood, 1992; (with S. Blandford and B.K. Grant) The Film Studies Dictionary, 2001. EDITOR: (contrib.) New Cinema in Finland, 1972; (contrib.) Cinema in Finland: An Introduction, 1975; Cahiers du Cinéma, vol. I: The 1950's: Neo Realism, Hollywood, New Wave, 1985, Cahiers du Cinéma, vol. II, 1960-68: New Wave, New Cinema, Re-evaluating Hollywood, 1986; (with P. Wollen) Howard Hawks: American Artist, 1996; (ed.) The Hillier Gardener's Guide to Trees and Shrubs, 1997; American Independent Cinema, 2001; (with B.K. Grant) 100 Documentary Films, 2009. CONTRIBUTOR: The Films of Jean-Luc Godard, 1968; Film in English Teaching, 1972; Focus on Bonnie and Clyde, 1973; Media Culture, 1978; Oblike in Metode Filmske in Televizijske Vzgoje (title means: Handbook for Methodology of Film and Television Study), 1978; Images of Alcoholism, 1979. Contributor to periodicals. **Address:** Department of Film, Theatre & Television, The University of Reading, Bulmershe Ct., Woodlands Ave., Reading, BR RG6 1HY, England. **Online address:** j.m.hillier@reading.ac.uk

HILLIS, Bryan V. Canadian (born Canada), b. 1956. **Genres:** Theology/Religion. **Career:** Saskatchewan Government Insurance, corporate business analyst, 1981-82; Memorial University, lecturer, 1988; York University, lecturer, 1988-89; University of Regina, Luther College, assistant professor, 1989-94, associate professor, 1994-2001, dean, 1995-2005, professor, 2001-; South Saskatchewan Youth Orchestra, board director, 2003-, president; Saskatchewan Games Council, board director, 2006-. Writer. **Publications:** Can Two Walk Together Unless They Be Agreed?: American Religious Schisms in the 1970s, 1991. Contributor to periodicals. **Address:** Luther College, University of Regina, LC 101, 1500 Royal St., Regina, SK S4S 0A2, Canada. **Online address:** bryan.hillis@uregina.ca

HILLMAN, Barry (Leslie). British (born England), b. 1942. **Genres:** Plays/Screenplays, Poetry, Photography. **Career:** Northamptonshire County Council, local government officer, 1974-. Writer. **Publications:** Endymion Rampant (poetry), 1964; Happy Returns, 1970; Partly Furnished, 1971; Roly-Poly, 1973; Two Can Play at That Game, 1975; The Dispossessed, 1975; Face the Music, 1975; (with R. Newton) Bibs and Bobs, 1975; Six for the Charleston, 1976; (with R. Newton) Odds and Sods, 1977; The Queen and the Axe, 1978; The Guests, 1978; (with R. Newton) A Few Minor Dischords, 1978; These Little Songs (poetry), 1979; Castle on the Rocks, 1979; Never the Blushing Bride, 1981; The Establishment at Arles, 1982; Beyond Necessity, 1981; Three's a Crowd, 1982; The Amazing Dancing Bear (play), 1985; Iron Magnolias, 1994; Housewarming, 1999; Till the Devil Be Up, 2000; At the End of the Day, 2000; An Enemy of the People (adaptation), 2000; A Night at the Moulin Rouge, 2001; A Simple Ceremony, 2002. **Address:** Northamptonshire County Council, Northampton House, Wellington St., Northampton, NN 1 3RR, England.

HILLMAN, David (A.). American (born United States) **Genres:** Art/Art History. **Career:** University of Cambridge, King's College, senior lecturer, professor of English. Writer. **Publications:** (Ed.) Authority and Representation in Early Modern Discourse, 1996; (ed. with C. Mazzio) The Body in Parts: Fantasies of Corporeality in Early Modern Europe, 1997; (ed. with A. Phillips) Book of Interruptions, 2007; Shakespeare's Entrails: Belief, Scepticism, and the Interior of the Body, 2007. **Address:** Department of English, King's College, University of Cambridge, Rm. H3 Right, King's Parade, Cambridge, CB2 1ST, England. **Online address:** dah54@cam.ac.uk

HILLMAN, Elizabeth. British (born England), b. 1942. **Genres:** Poetry, Children's Fiction. **Career:** San Diego State University Library, clerk, 1970-74; National Steel and Shipbuilding Co., engineering aide, 1975-80. Writer. **Publications:** Tudo Bem! (Haiku chapbook), 1989; Apitos Da Brisa (Haiku chapbook), 1989; Min-Yo and the Moon Dragon, 1992. **Address:** 41 Love Ln., Oldswinford, Stourbridge, WM DY8 2DH, England.

HILLMAN, Elizabeth Lutes. American (born United States), b. 1967?. **Genres:** Military/Defense/Arms Control. **Career:** U.S. Air Force, officer; U.S. Air Force Academy, instructor in history; Yale University, instructor in history; Rutgers School of Law, professor of law, director of faculty development, Marshall-Brennan Fellowship Program, co-director; University of California Hastings College of the Law, professor of law, 2008-. Writer. **Publications:** Defending America: Military Culture and the Cold War Court-martial, 2005; (with E.R. Fidell and D.H. Sullivan) Military Justice: Cases and Materials, 2007. Contributor to books. **Address:** Rutgers School of Law, 217 N 5th St., Camden, NJ 08102, U.S.A. **Online address:** hillmane@uchastings.edu

HILLMAN, Richard S. American (born United States), b. 1943?. **Genres:** Novels, Politics/Government, History, Young Adult Fiction. **Career:** Tufts University, Getulio Vargas Foundation School of Administration, Fletcher School of Law and Diplomacy, Latin American teaching fellow, 1969-70; St. John Fisher College, assistant professor, 1971-75, associate professor, 1975-81, professor of political science, 1981-, Department of Political Science, chairman, 1976-80, 1981-86, 1988-91, 1993-95, 1996-98, 2001, Vere C. Bird professor of political science and international studies, Vere C. Bird senior professor of political science and international studies, 1988-, Institute for the Study of Democracy and Human Rights, director, 1997-, now distinguished professor emeritus; Central University of Venezuela, visiting professor, 1999, 2000; US Department of State, Bureau of Intelligence and Research, consultant. Writer. **Publications:** (With T.J. D'Agostino) Distant Neighbors in the Caribbean: The Dominican Republic and Jamaica in Comparative Perspective, 1992; Democracy for the Privileged: Crisis and Transition in Venezuela, 1994; (with E.C.D. Silva) De una a otra gobernabilidad: el desbordamiento de la democracia venezolana, 1997; (ed. with T.J. D'Agostino) Understanding Contemporary Latin America, 1997, 4th ed., 2011; (ed. with J.A. Peeler and E.C.D. Silva) Democracy and Human Rights in Latin America, 2002; (ed. with T.J. D'Agostino) Understanding the Contemporary Caribbean, 2003, 2nd ed., 2009. **Address:** Institute for the Study of Democracy/Human Rights, St. John Fisher College, 124 Basil Hall, 3690 East Ave., Rochester, NY 14618, U.S.A. **Online address:** hillman@sjfc.ecu

HILL-MILLER, Katherine C(ecelia). American (born United States) **Genres:** Writing/Journalism, Language/Linguistics, Biography, Young Adult Non-fiction. **Career:** City University of New York, Kingsborough Community College, adjunct lecturer in English, 1972-73; College of William and Mary, assistant professor of English, 1978-80; Long Island University, C.W. Post Center, assistant professor, 1980-84, associate professor, 1984-89, professor of English, 1989-2003, director of the poetry center, 1982-85, director of the composition program, 1993-2000, College of Liberal Arts and Sciences, dean, 2003-. Writer. **Publications:** (With S. Weidenborner) Writing Effective Paragraphs, 1974; The Bantam Book of Spelling, 1986; My Hideous Progeny: Mary Shelley, William Godwin and the Father-Daughter Relationship, 1995; From the Lighthouse to Monk's House: A Guide to Virginia Woolf's Literary Landscapes, 2001. Works appear in anthologies. Contributor to periodicals. **Address:** College of Liberal Arts and Sciences, Long Island University, C.W. Post Campus, Administration Bldg., 720 Northern Blvd., Brookville, NY 11548-1300, U.S.A. **Online address:** katherine.hill-miller@liu.edu

HILLS, Philip James. British (born England), b. 1933?. **Genres:** Education, Information Science/Computers, Sciences, Technology, Communications/Media, Chemistry, Physics, Reference, Reference. **Career:** Netherthorpe Grammar School, Department of Chemistry, senior science master and head, 1959-64; University of Sheffield, Institute of Education, lecturer in education and science, 1964-69; University of Surrey, Institute for Educational Technology, lecturer in educational technology, 1972-; University of Cambridge, Center for Research into Human Communication and Learning, head, 1986-; International Journal of Information Management, editor. **Publications:** Small Scale Chemistry for Ordinary Level, 1961; Small Scale Organic Preparations, 1964; Chemical Equilibria, 1969; (with H. Peden and P. Hills) Sources of Funding for Research and Publication, 1983; (with M. McLaren) Teaching Communication Skills, 1987; Educational Futures, 1987; Publish or Perish, 1989, 2nd ed., 1999; Management Information Systems: The Human/ Computer Interface, 1990; (with H. Lewis) Time Management for Academics, 1999; Aspects of Human Communication, vol. I: As Others See Us, 2004. EDITOR: (with L.J. Hayness, C.R. Palmer and D.S. Trickey) Alternatives to the Lecture, 1974; (with J. Gilbert) Aspects of Educational Technology, vol. II, 1977; Information Package on Teaching and Learning Methods for Librarians, 1979; The Future of the Printed Word: The Impact and the Implications of the New Communications Technology, 1980; Trends in Information Transfer, 1982; (with M. McLaren) Communication Skills, 1986; (with M. McLaren) Communication Skills: A International Review, 1987; (with N. Dower and M. Bartlet) Nonsense on Stilts?: A Quaker View of Human Rights, 2008. AS P.J. HILLS: Small Scale Physical Chemistry, 1966; (with J.A. Leisten) Studies in Atomic Structure, 1969; Study to Succeed, 1973; The Self-Teaching Process in Higher Education, 1976; (with L. Lincoln and L.P. Turner) Evaluation of Tape-Slide Guides for Library Instruction, 1977; (ed.) Tape Slide Presentations and Teaching Packages for Library User Education, 1977; (ed.) Study Courses and Counselling: Problems and Possibilities, 1979; Teaching and Learning as a Communications Process, 1979; (with H. Barlow) Effective Study Skills, 1980; (ed.) Dictionary of Education, 1982; Teaching, Learning and Communication, 1986; Educating for a Computer Age, 1987. **Address:** Centre for Research into Human Communication and, Learning, University of Cambridge, Old School House, Little Fransham, Dereham, NF NR19 2JP, England.

HILLYER, Barbara. American (born United States), b. 1934. **Genres:** Human Relations/Parenting, Women's Studies And Issues, Sociology, Psychology, Social Sciences. **Career:** University of Oklahoma, assistant professor, 1976-82, director of women's studies, 1976-88, associate professor of women's studies and human relations, 1982-, professor and chair of human relations; United Ministry Center, board director, 1993-96. Writer. **Publications:** Feminism and Disability, 1993. **Address:** Department of Human Relations, University of Oklahoma, Rm. 728, 601 Elm Ave., Norman, OK 73019, U.S.A. **Online address:** bghillyer@ou.edu

HILMES, Michele. American (born United States), b. 1953. **Genres:** Communications/Media, Social Commentary, Adult Non-fiction. **Career:** New York University, Alternate Media Center and Interactive Telecommunications Program, research assistant, administrative assistant, 1979-82; Spring Hill College, assistant professor, 1987-92, chair for communication arts department, 1989-90; University of Wisconsin-Madison, professor for media and cultural studies, director for Wisconsin Center for Film and Theater Research, 2003-, associate chair for communication arts, 2004-06, director of graduate studies, 2009-; University of Central England, visiting international fellow. **Publications:** Hollywood and Broadcasting: From Radio to Cable, 1990; Radio Voices: American Broadcasting, 1922-1952, 1997; Only Connect: A Cultural History of U.S. Broadcasting, 2001, 2nd ed., 2006; (ed. with J. Loviglio) Radio Reader: Essays on the Cultural History of American Radio, 2001; Connections: A Broadcast History Reader, 2003; (ed.) Television History Book, 2003; (ed.) NBC: America's Network, 2007. Only Connect: A Cultural History of Broadcasting in the United States, 2007; Network Nations: A Transnational History of British and American Broadcasting, 2011. FORTHCOMING: Network Nations: How the Broadcasting Battle between the U.S. and Great Britain Shaped Twentieth Century Culture; Photography in Sound: Aural Aesthetics in the Visual Age. **Address:** Department of Communication Arts, University of Wisconsin-Madison, 6040 Vilas Hall, 821 University Ave., Madison, WI 53706-1412, U.S.A. **Online address:** mhilmes@wisc.edu

HILSMAN, Gordon J. American (born United States), b. 1941?. **Genres:** Theology/Religion, Adult Non-fiction, Sex. **Career:** Diocese of Dubuque, Ordained Roman Catholic priest, 1967; clinical pastoral educator, 1974; Franciscan Health System, St. Joseph Medical Center, Clinical Pastoral Education Program, manager, 1991-, supervisor. Writer. **Publications:** Intimate Spirituality: The Catholic Way of Love and Sex, 2007. **Address:** St. Joseph Medical Center, Franciscan Health System, 1717 S J St., PO Box 2197, Tacoma, WA 98405-4933, U.S.A. **Online address:** gordonhilsman@fhshealth.org

HILSMAN, Roger. American (born United States), b. 1919. **Genres:** International Relations/Current Affairs, Politics/Government. **Career:** Princeton University, research assistant, Center of International Studies, research associate, 1954-56; Woodrow Wilson School of Public and International Affairs, lecturer, 1955-56; Library of Congress, Foreign Affairs Division, chief, 1956-58, Legislative Reference Service, deputy director for research, 1958-61; George Washington University, lecturer in international relations, 1957; Johns Hopkins University, School of Advanced International Studies, lecturer in international relations, 1957-61; Columbia University, lecturer in international relations, 1958; U.S. Department of State, Bureau of Intelligence and Research, director, 1961-63, Far Eastern Affairs, assistant secretary of state, 1963-64; Columbia University, Department of Government, School of International Affairs, professor, 1964, now emeritus professor. Writer. **Publications:** Strategic Intelligence and National Decisions, 1956; (co-author) Military Policy and National Security, 1956; (co-author) NATO and American Security, 1958; (co-author) Alliance Policy in the Cold War, 1958; (co-author) The Guerrilla and How to Fight Him, 1960; Sino-Soviet Economic Offensive through June 30, 1962, 1962; (with R.C. Good) Foreign Policy in the Sixties, 1965; To Move a Nation, 1967; The Politics of Policy Making in Defense and Foreign Affairs, 1971; The Crouching Future, 1975; To Govern America, 1979; Strategic Intelligence and National Decisions, 1981; The Politics of Governing America, 1985; Politics of Policy Making in Defense and Foreign Affairs: Conceptual Models and Bureaucratic Politics, 1987; American Guerrilla: My War Behind Japanese Lines, 1990; George Bush vs. Saddam Hussein: Military Success! Political Failure?, 1992; The Cuban Missile Crisis: The Struggle over Policy, 1996; From Nuclear Military Strategy to a World without War; A History and a Proposal, 1999. **Address:** Government & Community Affairs, Columbia University, 2960 Broadway, New York, NY 10027, U.S.A. **Online address:** rh21@columbia.edu

HILTERMANN, Joost R. American/Dutch (born Netherlands), b. 1956. **Genres:** History, Politics/Government. **Career:** Al-Haq, analyst, 1985-88, research director, 1988-90; Human Rights Watch, Iraq Documents Project, director, 1992-94, Arms Division, executive director, 1994-2002; International Crisis Group, deputy program director for the Middle East and North Africa, 2002-, project director for the Middle East, 2002-07. Writer and human rights activist. **Publications:** Israel's Deportation Policy in the Occupied West Bank and Gaza: A Report Commissioned by Al-Haq (report), 1986, 2nd ed., 1988; Al-Haq's Response to the Chapter on Israel and the Occupied Territories, in the State Department's Country Reports on Human Rights Practices for 1984, 1986; Behind the Intifada: Labor and Women's Movements in the Occupied Territories, 1991; (ed. and contrib.) Bureaucracy of Repression: The Iraqi Government in Its Own Words (report), 1994; (co-author) Playing with Fire: Weapons Proliferation, Political Violence, and Human Rights in Kenya (report), 2002; A Poisonous Affair: America, Iraq, and the Gassing of Halabja, 2007. Contributor to books and periodicals. **Address:** International Crisis Group, 1629 K St. NW, Ste. 450, Washington, DC 20006, U.S.A. **Online address:** jhiltermann@crisisgroup.org

HILTON, (Andrew John) Boyd. British (born England), b. 1944. **Genres:** History, Economics, Social Sciences, Business/Trade/Industry. **Career:** Oxford University, Christ Church, research lecturer, 1969-74; Cambridge University, Trinity College, fellow and lecturer in history, 1974-, senior tutor, 1983-88, professor, reader in modern British history, 1996-. Writer. **Publications:** Corn, Cash, Commerce: The Economic Policies of the Tory Government, 1815-1830, 1977; The Age of Atonement: The Influence of Evangelicalism on Social and Economic Thought, 1795-1865, 1988; Mad, Bad and Dangerous People?: England, 1783-1846, 2006; (with M. Lucas and D. Walliams) Inside Little Britain, 2007. **Address:** Trinity College, University of Cambridge, Cambridge, CM CB2 1TQ, England. **Online address:** ajbh1@cam.ac.uk

HILTON, Boyd. See **HILTON, Boyd John Boyd.**

HILTON, Boyd John Boyd. (Boyd Hilton). British (born England), b. 1944. **Genres:** Economics. **Career:** Oxford University, research lecturer, 1969-74; Cambridge University, Trinity College, fellow and lecturer, 1974-, senior tutor, 1983-88, reader in modern British history, 1996-. Writer. **Publications:** Corn, Cash, Commerce: The Economic Policies of the Tory Governments, 1815-1830, 1977; The Age of Atonement: The Influence of Evangelicalism on Social and Economic Thought, 1795- 1865, 1988; A Mad, Bad and Dangerous People? England, 1783-1846, 2006; (with M. Lucas and D. Walliams) Inside Little Britain, 2007. Contributor to books and periodicals. **Address:** Trinity

College, Cambridge University, Cambridge, CB CB2 1TQ, England. **Online address:** ajbh1@cam.ac.uk

HILTON, George Woodman. American (born United States), b. 1925. **Genres:** Sports/Fitness, Theatre, Transportation, History, Business/Trade/Industry. **Career:** University of Maryland, instructor, 1949-51, 1954-55; Stanford University, assistant professor, 1955-60; University of California-Berkeley, lecturer in business administration, 1961-62; International Bank for Reconstruction and Development, consultant, 1961, 1964; University of California-Los Angeles, lecturer, 1962-63, associate professor, 1963-66, professor of economics, 1966-92, professor emeritus, 1993-. Writer. **Publications:** Cable Railways of Chicago, 1954; (with J.F. Due) The Electric Interurban Railways in America, 1960; The Truck System, 1960; The Great Lakes Car Ferries, 1962; The Ma and Pa, a History of the Maryland & Pennsylvania Railroad, 1963, rev. ed., 1999; Toledo, Port Clinton and Lakeside Railway, 1964; Staten Island Ferry, 1964; The Night Boat, 1968; The Transportation Act of 1958, 1969; The Cable Car in America, 1971, rev. ed., 1997; Federal Transit Subsidies, 1974; Northeast Railroad Problem, 1975; (with R. Plummer and J. Jobé) Illustrated History of Paddle Steamers, 1976; Monon Route, 1978; Amtrak: The National Railroad Passenger Corporation, 1980; American Narrow Gauge Railroads, 1990; (ed.) The Annotated Baseball Stories of Ring W. Lardner, 1914-1919, 1995; Eastland: Legacy of the Titanic, 1995; The Front Page, 2002; Lake Michigan Passenger Steamers, 2002. **Address:** Department of Economics, University of California, Bunche Hall 8283, PO Box 147703, Los Angeles, CA 90095, U.S.A.

HILTON, Joni. American (born United States), b. 1956?. **Genres:** inspirational/Motivational Literature, Novels, Food And Wine. **Career:** Hour Family (syndicated television specials), co-host; Holy Cow, founder and chief executive officer. Journalist and broadcaster. **Publications:** Braces, Gym Suits, and Early-Morning Seminary: A Youthquake Survival Manual, 1985; Five-Minute Miracles: 373 Quick Daily Projects for You and Your Kids to Share, 1992; Guilt-free Motherhood: How to Raise Great Kids and Have Fun Doing It, 1996; Honey on Hot Bread and Other Heartfelt Wishes, 1997; Family Fun Book: More than 400 Amazing, Amusing, and All-around Awesome Activities for the Entire Family!, 1998; The Once-a-Week Cooking Plan: The Incredible Cooking Program That Will Save You Twenty Hours a Week (and Have Your Family Begging for More!), 1999; Housekeeping Secrets My Mother Never Taught Me, 2001; Cooking Secrets My Mother Never Taught Me, 2001; Power of Prayer, 2004. NOVELS: Dating: No Guts, No Glory (for teens), 1989; As the Ward Turns, 1991; Around the Ward in Eighty Days, 1993; Scrambled Home Evenings, 1994; That's What Friends Are For (for teens), 1997; Stop the Ward: I Want to Get Off!, 1999; Ten-Cow Wives' Club, 2005. Contributor to periodicals. **Address:** c/o Joyce Holland, D4EO Literary Agency, 7 Indian Valley Rd., Weston, CT 06883-1018, U.S.A. **Online address:** joni@jonihilton.com

HILTON, Margery. British (born England) **Genres:** Romance/Historical, Novels, Young Adult Fiction, Literary Criticism And History. **Career:** Writer. **Publications:** The Dutch Uncle, 1966; Young Ellis, 1966; Darling Rhadamanthus, 1966; The Grotto of Jade, 1967; Girl Crusoe, 1969; Interlude in Arcady, 1969; The Flower of Eternity, 1970; Bitter Masquerade, 1970; The House of the Amulet, 1970; Frail Sanctuary, 1970; The Inshine Girl, 1970; Miss Columbine and Harley Quinn, 1970; Time of Curtain Fall, 1970; A Man Without Mercy, 1971; The Whispering Grove, 1971; Trust in Tomorrow, 1971; Dear Conquistador, 1972; The Spell of the Enchanter, 1972; Miranda's Marriage, 1973; The Beach of Sweet Returns, 1975; The House of Strange Music, 1976; The Dark Side of Marriage, 1978; Snow Bride, 1979; The Velvet Touch, 1979; Way of a Man, 1981. **Address:** Harlequin, Mills & Boon Ltd., Eton House, 18-24 Paradise Rd., Richmond, SR TW9 1SR, England.

HILTON, Matt. British (born England), b. 1966?. **Genres:** Mystery/Crime/Suspense, Horror. **Career:** Writer. **Publications:** Dead Men's Dust, 2009; Judgement and Wrath, 2009; Slash and Burn, 2010. **Address:** CM , England. **Online address:** matthiltonbooks@live.co.uk

HILTON, Suzanne. American (born United States), b. 1922. **Genres:** Children's Non-fiction, Genealogy/Heraldry, History, Sciences, Young Adult Non-fiction. **Career:** Westminster Press, Department of Advertising, researcher and copywriter. Writer. **Publications:** How Do They Get Rid of It?, 1970; How Do They Cope With It?, 1970; It's Smart to Use a Dummy, 1971;

It's A Model World, 1972; Beat It, Burn It, and Drown It, 1974; The Way It Was-1876, 1975; Who Do You Think You Are?: Digging for Your Family Roots, 1976; Yesterday's People: The Upper Dublin Story, 1976; Here Today and Gone Tomorrow: The Story of America's World's Fairs, 1978; Getting There: Frontier Travel Without Power, 1980; We the People: The Way We Were 1783-1793, 1981; Faster Than a Horse: Moving West with Engine Power, 1983; (ed. and contrib.) Montgomery County, The Second Hundred Years 1880-1980, 1983; The World of Young Tom Jefferson, 1986; World of Young Herbert Hoover, 1987; World of Young George Washington, 1987; World of Young Andrew Jackson, 1988; A Capital Capital City, 1790-1814, 1992; Miners, Merchants, and Maids (Settlers of the West Series), 1995. **Address:** 3320-108th St. NW, Gig Harbor, WA 98332, U.S.A.

HILTY, James W. American (born United States), b. 1939. **Genres:** History, Regional/Urban Planning, Education. **Career:** History teacher at public schools, 1965; Ohio State University, assistant track coach, 1965-66; Temple University, instructor to professor of history, 1970-, associate dean and acting dean of graduate school, 1979-81, assistant vice president for academic affairs, 1982, director of university planning, 1982-84, department head, 1988-94, Ambler Campus, dean, 2005-09, professor of community and regional planning, 2007-; University of Pennsylvania, adjunct professor, 1976; Villanova University, visiting professor, 1996. Writer. **Publications:** John F. Kennedy: An Idealist without Illusions (monograph), 1976; Robert Kennedy, Brother Protector, 1997; Temple University: 125 Years of Service to Philadelphia, the Nation and the World, 2009. Contributor to periodicals. **Address:** Department of History, Temple University, 1st Fl., Administration Bldg., Philadelphia, PA 19122, U.S.A. **Online address:** james.hilty@temple.edu

HIM, Chanrithy. American/Cambodian (born Cambodia), b. 1965. **Genres:** Autobiography/Memoirs. **Career:** Khmer Adolescent Project, research associate; Oregon Health Sciences University, medical interpreter. Writer. **Publications:** When Broken Glass Floats: Growing up under the Khmer Rouge, 2000. Contributor to journals. **Address:** c/o Author Mail, W. W. Norton & Company Inc., 500 5th Ave., New York, NY 10110, U.S.A. **Online address:** chanrithy@chanrithyhim.com

HIME, James (L.). American (born United States), b. 1954. **Genres:** Novels, Mystery/Crime/Suspense. **Career:** Baker & Botts (law firm), associate, 1976-, partner, 1985-90, 1992-95; Gerald Hines, fund manager, 1995-. Writer and attorney. **Publications:** JEREMIAH SPUR MYSTERY SERIES: The Night of the Dance, 2003; Scared Money, 2004; Where Armadillos Go to Die, 2009; Three Thousand Bridges, forthcoming. **Address:** c/o Author Mail, St. Martin's Press, 175 5th Ave., New York, NY 10010-7703, U.S.A. **Online address:** jim_hime@hines.com

HIMELFARB, Richard. American (born United States), b. 1963. **Genres:** Politics/Government, Adult Non-fiction. **Career:** Hofstra University, assistant professor of political science, 1993-, associate professor of political science. Writer. **Publications:** Catastrophic Politics: The Rise and Fall of the Medicare Catastrophic Coverage Act of 1988, 1995; (ed. with R. Perotti) Principle Over Politics?: The Domestic Policy of the George H. W. Bush Presidency, 2004. **Address:** Department of Political Science, Hofstra University, 203D Barnard Hall, 1000 Fulton Ave., Hempstead, NY 11550, U.S.A. **Online address:** richard.i.himelfarb@hofstra.edu

HIMELSTEIN, Morgan Y. American (born United States), b. 1926. **Genres:** Literary Criticism And History, Music, Theatre, Translations. **Career:** University of Rochester, instructor in English, 1948-50; Adelphi University, instructor, 1957-60, assistant professor of English, 1957-64, associate professor, 1964-, professor of English, through 1993, director of graduate studies in English, 1965-74, emeritus professor of English, 1993-. Writer. **Publications:** Drama Was a Weapon: The Left-Wing Theatre in New York, 1929-1941, 1963. OPERA TRANSLATIONS: Offenbach: La Grande Duchesse de Gerolstein, 1977; Offenbach: La Perichole, 1982; Offenbach: Orphee aux Enfers, 1985; J. Strauss: Die Fledermaus, 1990. **Address:** Department of English, Adelphi University, Rm. 216, Harvey Hall, 1 S Ave., PO Box 701, Garden City, PA 11530-0701, U.S.A.

HIMELSTEIN, Shmuel. Israeli (born Israel), b. 1940. **Genres:** Theology/Religion, Humor/Satire, Translations, History. **Career:** Jewish Day School, teacher, 1964-68, assistant principal, 1968-70; Jewish Day School, principal, 1970-73; Jewish Day School, principal, 1973-75; Winnipeg Hebrew School, principal; Joseph Wolinsky Collegiate, principal; Ramat Shapira World Youth

Academy Beit Wein, general director. Translator and editor. **Publications:** (Trans.) Y. Rappel, Kisufim le-Erets-ha-Ḳodesh (title means: 'Yearning for the Holy Land: Hasidic Tales of Israel'), 1986; The Jewish Primer: Questions and Answers on Jewish Faith and Culture, 1990; A Touch of Wisdom, A Touch of Wit, 1991; (trans.) Íture Torah (title means: 'Torah Gems'), 1992; (ed.) Grand mufti: Haj Amin al-Hussaini, Founder of the Palestinian National Movement, 1993; Words of Wisdom, Words of Wit: A Veritable Storehouse of Jewish Experience-Its Honey and Space, 1993; (trans.) J. Erlich, Shabes (title means: 'Sabbath'), 1999; (ed. with F. Skolnik and S. Himelstein) New Encyclopedia of Judaism, 2002; Touch of Wisdom, a Touch of Wit: A Sparkling Treasury of Jewish Anecdotes, Ideas and Advice, 2002; (trans.) Y. Leibowitz, Hearot le-farashiyot ha-shavua (title means: 'Accepting the Yoke of Heaven: Commentary on the Weekly Torah Portion'), 2002; (co-ed.) Student's Ecyclopedia of Judaism, 2004; Passover Haggadah: Around The Seder Table, 2008. **Address:** 22 Shear Yashuv St., Jerusalem, 97280, Israel.

HIMKA, John-Paul. Canadian/American (born United States), b. 1949. **Genres:** History, Politics/Government, Race Relations, Theology/Religion, Essays. **Career:** University of Alberta, visiting assistant professor, 1977-81, 1984-85, postdoctoral fellow, 1982-84, assistant professor of history, professor of history, 1985-. Historian and writer. **Publications:** Socialism in Galicia: The Emergence of Polish Social Democracy and Ukrainian Radicalism, 1860-1890, 1983; (with F.A. Swyripa) Sources for Researching Ukrainian Family History, 1984; The Greek Catholic Church and Ukrainian Society in Austrian Galicia, 1986; Galician Villagers and the Ukrainian National Movement in the Nineteenth Century, 1988; Galicia and Bukovina: A Research Handbook about Western Ukraine: Late 19th and 20th Centuries, 1990; (with J.T. Flynn and J. Niessen) Religious Compromise, Political Salvation: The Greek Catholic Church and Nation-Building in Eastern Europe, 1993; Religion and Nationality in Western Ukraine: The Greek Catholic Church and Ruthenian National Movement in Galicia, 1867-1900, 1999. EDITOR: (with I.L. Rudnytsky) Rethinking Ukrainian History, 1981; (and trans. and intro.) R. Rosdolsky, Engels and the Nonhistoric Peoples: The National Question in the Revolution of 1848, 1986; (with H. Torke) German-Ukrainian Relations in Historical Perspective, 1994; (with Z. Gitelman, L. Hajda and R. Solchanyk) Cultures and Nations of Central and Eastern Europe: Essays in Honor of Roman Szporluk, 2000; (with A. Zayarnyuk) Letters from Heaven: Popular Religion in Russia and Ukraine, 2006. Contributor to journals. **Address:** University of Alberta, 2-72 Tory Bldg., Edmonton, AB T6G 2H4, Canada. **Online address:** john-paul.himka@ualberta.ca

HIMMEL, Richard L. American (born United States), b. 1950. **Genres:** History, Biography, Adult Non-fiction, Education. **Career:** University of North Texas, librarian, university archivist, 1985-2006, assistant director for special collections, 1989-, Department of History, adjunct faculty. Writer. **Publications:** (With R.S. La Forte) Down the Corridor of Years: A Centennial History of the University of North Texas in Photographs, 1890-1990, 1989; (ed. with R.S. La Forte and R.E. Marcello) With Only the Will to Live: Accounts of Americans in Japanese Prison Camps, 1941-1945, 1994. Contributor to history journals. **Address:** University Library, University of North Texas, 1155 Union Cir., PO Box 5188, NT Sta., Denton, TX 76203-5188, U.S.A. **Online address:** rhimmel@library.unt.edu

HIMMELFARB, Gertrude. American (born United States), b. 1922. **Genres:** History, Intellectual History, Social Commentary. **Career:** City University of New York, Brooklyn College, professor of history, 1965-78, Graduate School, distinguished professor, 1978-88, distinguished professor emeritus of history, 1988-; British Institute of the United States, board director, 1985-; Woodrow Wilson Center, trustee, 1985-96; Institute for Contemporary Studies, board director, 1986-; National Endowment for the Humanities, Jefferson lecturer, 1991. Writer. **Publications:** Lord Acton: A Study in Conscience and Politics, 1952; Darwin and the Darwinian Revolution, 1959; Victorian Minds, 1968; On Liberty and Liberalism: The Case of John Stuart Mill, 1974; The Idea of Poverty, 1984; Marriage and Morals among the Victorians, 1986; The New History and the Old, 1987, rev. ed., 2004; Poverty and Compassion: The Moral Imagination of the Late Victorians, 1991; On Looking into the Abyss: Untimely Thoughts on Culture and Society, 1994; The De-Moralization of Society: From Victorian Virtues to Modern Values, 1995; (intro.) Memoir on Pauperism, 1997; One Nation, Two Cultures, 1999; The Roads to Modernity: The British, French and American Enlightenments, 2004; The Past and The Present: Episodes in Intellectual and Cultural History, 2005; The Jewish Odyssey of George Eliot, 2009; The People of the Book: Philosemitism in England, from Cromwell to Churchill, 2011. EDI-

TOR: Acton, Essays on Freedom and Power, 1948; (and intro.) Malthus, On Population, 1960; Essays on Politics and Culture, 1962; On Liberty, 1974; Memoir on Pauperism, 1997; The Spirit of the Age: Victorian Essays, 2007; Jews and Gentiles, 2007; The Neoconservative Persuasion: Selected Essays, 1942-2009, 2011. Contributor to books. **Address:** Graduate School, City University of New York, Rm. 5111, 365 5th Ave., New York, NY 10016, U.S.A.

HIMRICH, Brenda L. American (born United States), b. 1954. **Genres:** Children's Non-fiction, Sciences, Technology. **Career:** Writer. **Publications:** (With S. Thornley) Electrifying Medicine: How Electricity Sparked a Medical Revolution, 1995. **Address:** 1082 Lovell, Roseville, MN 55113, U.S.A. **Online address:** brenda@brendahimrich.net

HINCHMAN, Lewis P(atrick). American (born United States), b. 1946. **Genres:** Humanities, Essays. **Career:** State University of New York College-Potsdam, adjunct assistant professor of philosophy, 1979-82; St. Lawrence University, adjunct assistant professor, 1980-82; Clarkson University, adjunct assistant professor, 1981-82, assistant professor, 1982-87, associate professor of government, 1987-94, professor of political science, 1994-, now professor emeritus; Carl Von Ossietzlay University, visiting professor of politics, 2000. Writer. **Publications:** Hegel's Critique of the Enlightenment, 1984; (ed. with S.K. Hinchman) Hannah Arendt: Critical Essays, 1994; (ed. with S.K. Hinchman) Memory, Identity, Community: The Idea of Narrative in the Human Sciences, 1997; Hiking Tropical Australia: Queensland and Northern New South Wales, 1999; (with L. Hinchman.) Media Democracy: How the Media Colonize Politics, 2002. Contributor to journals and books. **Address:** Department of Humanities & Social Sciences, Clarkson University, 274 Bertrand H. Snell Hall, 8 Clarkson Ave., Potsdam, NY 13699-5750, U.S.A. **Online address:** hinchman@clarkson.edu

HINCHMAN, Sandra K(uracina). American (born United States), b. 1950. **Genres:** Literary Criticism And History, Travel/Exploration. **Career:** St. Lawrence University, professor of government, 1975-, Munsil professor of government. Writer. **Publications:** Hiking the Southwest's Canyon Country, 1990, 3rd ed., 2004. EDITOR (with L.P. Hinchman) Hannah Arendt: Critical Essays, 1994; (with L.P. Hinchman) Memory, Identity, Community: The Idea of Narrative in the Human Sciences, 1997. **Address:** Department of Government, St. Lawrence University, 23 Romoda Dr., Canton, NY 13617, U.S.A. **Online address:** shinchman@stlawu.edu

HINDE, Thomas. British (born England), b. 1926. **Genres:** Novels, History, Travel/Exploration, Autobiography/Memoirs, Young Adult Fiction, Adult Non-fiction, Young Adult Fiction. **Career:** Shell International Petroleum Co., public relations officer, 1953-58; Shell Company of East Africa, Nairobi, 1958-60; freelance writer, 1960-64; University of York, Granada Arts Fellow, 1964-65; University of Illinois, visiting professor of English, 1965-67; Boston University, visiting professor, 1969-70. **Publications:** Mr. Nicholas, 1952; Happy as Larry, 1957; For the Good of the Company, 1961; A Place Like Home, 1962; The Cage, 1962; (comp.) Spain: A Personal Anthology, 1963; Ninety Double Martinis, 1963; The Day the Call Came, 1964; Games of Chance: The Interviewer and the Investigator, 1965; (contrib.) Writers on Themselves, 1965; The Village, 1966; High, 1968; Bird, 1970; Generally a Virgin: A Novel, 1972; Agent, 1974; Our Father, 1975; (with S. Hinde) On Next to Nothing: A Guide to Survival Today, 1976; (with S.N. Chitty) The Great Donkey Walk, 1977; The Cottage Book: A Manual for Maintenance, Repair and Construction, 1979; Sir Henry and Sons: A Memoir, 1981; Daymare, 1981; Stately Gardens of Britain, 1983; Field Guide to the English Country Parson, 1984; Forests of Britain, 1985; (with C. Chitty) Just Chicken, 1985; (ed.) The Domesday Book: England's Heritage, Then and Now, 1985; Capability Brown: The Story of a Master Gardener, 1986; Courtiers: Nine Hundred Years of English Court Life, 1986; Tales from the Pumproom: Nine Hundred Years of Bath, the Place, Its People and Its Gossip, 1988; Imps of Promise: A History of the King's School, Canterbury, 1990; (ed. and intro.) Looking-Glass Letters, 1991; Paths of Progress: A History of Marlborough College, 1992; Highgate School: A History, 1993; King's College School, A History, 1995; Carpenter's Children, A History of the City of London School, 1995; University of Greenwich, 1996; The Martlet and the Griffen: A History of Abingdon School, 1997. **Address:** Curtis Brown Ltd., 28-29 Haymarket, Haymarket House, London, GL SW1Y 4SP, England. **Online address:** thomas.chitty@ukgateway.net

HINDESS, Barry. Australian/British (born England), b. 1939. **Genres:** Politics/Government, Social Sciences. **Career:** University of Liverpool, lecturer, professor of sociology, 1968-87; Australian National University, professor of political science, 1987-, professor emeritus of political science. Writer. **Publications:** The Decline of Working Class Politics, 1971; The Use of Official Statistics in Sociology: A Critique of Positivism and Ethnomethodology, 1973; (with P. Hirst) Pre-Capitalist Modes of Production, 1975; Philosophy and Methodology in the Social Sciences, 1977; (with P. Hirst) Mode of Production and Social Formation, 1977; (with Hirst, T. Cutler and A. Hussain) Marx's Capital and Capitalism Today, vol. I, 1977, vol. II, 1978; Parliamentary Democracy and Socialist Politics, 1983; Freedom, Equality, and the Market: Arguments on Social Policy, 1987; Politics and Class Analysis, 1987; Choice, Rationality, and Social Theory, 1988; Political Choice and Social Structure, 1989; Discourses of Power: From Hobbes to Foucault, 1996. EDITOR: Sociological Theories of the Economy, 1977; Reactions to the Right, 1990; (with M. Dean) Governing Australia, 1998; (with M. Jolly) Thinking Peace, Making Peace, 2001; Corruption and Democracy in Australia, 2004; (with M. Sawyer) Us and Them: Elites and Anti-elitism in Australia, 2004; (with L. Sousa and P. Larmour) Governments, NGOs and Anti-Corruption: The New Integrity Warriors, 2009. **Address:** Research School of Social Sciences, Australian National University, PO Box 1956, Canberra, AC 2601, Australia. **Online address:** b.hindess@anu.edu.au

HINDLE, Steve. British (born England), b. 1965. **Genres:** History. **Career:** University of Warwick, Warwick Research fellow, 1995-2001, Department of History, senior lecturer, 2001-04, professor, 2004-, head, 2010-11, Centre for the Study of the Renaissance, director, 2004-07; The Huntington Library, W.M. Keck Foundation, director of research, 2011-, coordinator for fellowship program, 2011-. Writer and historian. **Publications:** (Ed. with P. Griffiths and A. Fox) The Experience of Authority in Early Modern England, 1996; The State and Social Change in Early Modern England, 1550-1640, 2000; The Birthpangs of Welfare: Poor Relief and Parish Governance in Seventeenth-Century Warwickshire, 2000; (ed. with H. Falvey) This Little Commonwealth: Layston Parish Memorandum Book, 1607-1650 & 1704-1747, 2003; On the Parish?: The Micro-politics of Poor Relief in Rural England, 1550-1750, 2004. **Address:** Department of History, University of Warwick, Humanities Bldg., University Rd., Coventry, CV4 7AL, England. **Online address:** steve.hindle@warwick.ac.uk

HINDS, Gareth. American (born United States), b. 1971?. **Genres:** Graphic Novels. **Career:** Writer, 1994-; game developer, 1994-2006; Massachusetts College of Art, instructor, 2001. **Publications:** GRAPHIC NOVELS: SELF-ILLUSTRATED: Bearskin, 1997; Beowulf, 2007; King Lear, 2007; The Merchant of Venice, 2008; The Odyssey, 2010. Works appear in anthologies. **Address:** Candlewick Press Inc., 99 Dover St., Somerville, MA 02144, U.S.A. **Online address:** gareth@garethhinds.com

HINDS, Maurene J. American (born United States) **Genres:** Children's Fiction, Education, How-to Books, Illustrations. **Career:** American Military University, faculty. Writer. **Publications:** Focus on Body Image: How You Feel about How You Look, 2002; You Have the Right to Know Your Rights: What Teens Should Know, 2005; Furman v. Georgia and the Death Penalty Debate: Debating Supreme Court Decisions, 2005; Grant Writing Made Easy, 2005; The Ferguson Guide to Resumes and Job Hunting Skills: A Step-by-Step Guide to Preparing for Your Job Search, 2005; John Steinbeck: Banned, Challenged and Censored, 2008; Fighting the AIDS and HIV Epidemic: A Global Battle, 2008; Witchcraft on Trial: From the Salem Witch Hunts to the Crucible, 2009; Halle Berry, 2009; Reader's Guide to Richard Wright's Black Boy, 2010; Legal Issues: The Salem Witch Trials, forthcoming. **Address:** c/o Author Mail, Enslow Publishers Inc., 40 Industrial Rd., PO Box 398, Berkeley Heights, NJ 07922-0398, U.S.A. **Online address:** maureneh@msn.com

HINDS, P(atricia) Mignon. American (born United States) **Genres:** Children's Fiction, Children's Non-fiction, Adult Non-fiction, Animals/Pets, Inspirational/Motivational Literature. **Career:** Mignon Communications L.L.C., president and founder; Essence Books, director. Writer. **Publications:** Kittens Need Someone to Love, 1981; Puppies Need Someone to Love, 1981; Baby Pig, 1988; Baby Calf, 1989; A Day in the Life of Morgan Freeman, 1994; (ed.) Essence: 25 Years Celebrating Black Women, 1995; What I Want to Be, 1995; My Best Friend, 1996; The King's Daughters, 1997; (ed.) Essence Total Makeover: Body, Beauty, Spirit, 1999; (ed.) 21st Century Sister: The Essence 5 Keys to Success, 2000; (ed. with S.L. Taylor) Black Men in their Own Words, 2002; The Good Sense Handbook: 52 Weeks of Inspired Thoughts, 2009. **Address:** Mignon Communications L.L.C., 333 E 55th St., Ste. 6B, New York, NY 10022, U.S.A. **Online address:** pmignon@msn.com

HINE, Darlene Clark. American (born United States), b. 1947. **Genres:** Cultural/Ethnic Topics, History, Women's Studies And Issues. **Career:** South Carolina State College, assistant professor of history and coordinator of black studies, 1972-74; Purdue University, assistant professor, 1974-79, associate professor, 1979-85, professor of history, 1985-87, Africana Studies and Research Center, interim director, 1978-79, vice-provost, 1981-86; Arizona State University, distinguished visiting professor, 1985; Michigan State University, John A. Hannah distinguished professor of history, 1987-2004, John A. Hannah adjunct professor of history, 2004-; Consortium of Social Science Associations, director, 1987-91; University of Delaware, distinguished visiting professor of women's studies, 1989-90; Northwestern University, professor of African American studies and professor of history, 2004-, Department of African American Studies, chair, 2008-11. Consultant and writer. **Publications:** Black Victory, 1979, rev. ed., 2003; When the Truth is Told, 1981; Black Women in White, 1989; (with N. McKay and R.L. Harris Jr.) Black Studies in the United States: Three Essays, 1990; Hine Sight, 1994; Culture, Consciousness and Community: The Making of an African American Women's History, 1994; Speak Truth to Power: Black Professional Class in United States History, 1996; (with K. Thompson) A Shining Thread of Hope, 1998; (with S. Harrold and W. Hine) The African-American Odyssey (textbook), 2 vols., 2000, 5th ed., 2011; (with W.C. Haine and S. Harrold) African Americans: A Concise History, 2004, 3 rd ed., 2009; (with W.C. Haine and S. Harrold) The African-American Odyssey: Combined Volume, 2nd ed., 2006; African-American History, 2006, 2nd ed., 2010. EDITOR: Black Women in the Nursing Profession: An Anthology of Historical Sources, 1985; Black Women in the Middle West Project, 1985; (contrib.) The State of Afro-American History, 1986; Black Women in the United States, 1619-1989, 16 vols., 1990; Black Women's History: Theory and Practice, 1990; Black Women in American History. From Colonial Times through the Nineteenth Century, 1990; Black Women in American History: The Twentieth Century, 1990; (with C. Carson, D. Garrow and V. Harding) Eyes on the Prize, A History of the Civil Rights Era, 1991; (with E.B. Brown and R. Terborg-Penn) Black Women in America, 2 vols., 1993; (with C. Carson) Milestones in African American History, 16 vols., 1994; (with L. Reed and W. King) We Specialize in the Wholly Impossible: A Reader in Black Women's History, 1995; (with D.B. Gaspar) More Than Chattel: Black Women and Slavery in the Americas, 1996; Facts on File Encyclopedia of Black Women in America, 1997; (with E. Jenkins) A Question of Manhood, vol. I, 1999, vol. II, 2001; (with J. McLeod) Crossing Boundaries, 1999; (with E.B. Higginbotham and L. Litwack) The Harvard Guide to African-American History, 2001; (with D.V. Gaspar) Beyond Bondage: Free Women of Color in the Americas, 2004, (with T.D. Keaten and S. Small) Black Europe and the African Diaspora, 2009. Contributor of articles to journals. **Address:** Department of African American Studies, Northwestern University, Crowe 5-134, 1860 S Campus Dr., Evanston, IL 60208, U.S.A. **Online address:** d-hine@northwestern.edu

HINE, Robert V. American (born United States), b. 1921. **Genres:** History, Novels, Autobiography/Memoirs. **Career:** Huntington Library, research fellow, 1951-53; University of California-Riverside, instructor, 1954-55, assistant professor, 1955-61, associate professor, 1961-66, professor of history, 1966-90, professor emeritus of history, 1990-; University of California-Irvine, School of Humanities, professor of history, now professor emeritus. Writer. **Publications:** California's Utopian Colonies, 1953; (ed.) William Andrew Spaulding: An Autobiographical Account, 1961; (ed. and epilogue) The Irvine Ranch, 1962; Edward Kern and American Expansion, 1962; (foreword) Sun Chief: The Autobiography of a Hopi Indian, 1963; (ed. with E.R. Bingham) The Frontier Experience: Readings in the Transmississippi West, 1963; Bartlett's West: Drawing the Mexican Boundary, 1968; (ed. with S. Lottinville) Soldier in the West: Letters of Theodore Talbot during His Services in California, Mexico and Oregon, 1845-53, 1972; (ed. with E.R. Bingham) The American Frontier: Readings and Documents, 1972; The American West: An Interpretive History, 1973; Community on the American Frontier: Separate but Not Alone, 1980; In the Shadow of Frémont: Edward Kern and the Art of Exploration, 1845-1860, 2nd ed., 1982; Josiah Royce: From Grass Valley to Harvard, 1992; Second Sight, 1993; Reflections of a Lifetime Reader: Second Sight, Reflections of a Once-Blind Professor, 1994; Broken Glass: A Family's Journey through Mental Illness, 2006; (with J.M. Faragher) Frontiers: A Short History of the American West, 2007; I Have Seen the Fire: A Novel Inspired by the Life of Sarah Royce, 2008; Dynamite and Dreams: A Novel Based on the Life of Job Harriman, 2008. **Address:** School of Humanities, University of California, HTC 200, 19191 Harvard Ave., Ste. 233, PO Box 3275, Irvine, CA 92612, U.S.A. **Online address:** rvhine@uci.edu

HINE BOOK. *See* **HEINBUCH, Jean (M.).**

HINES, James R. American (born United States), b. 1937. **Genres:** Sports/Fitness, History, Biography. **Career:** Christopher Newport University, professor of music, 1975-2010, professor emeritus, 2010-. Writer. **Publications:** Figure Skating: A History, 2006; The English Style: Figure Skating's Oldest Tradition, 2008; Historical Dictionary of Figure Skating, 2011. **Address:** 5356 Pine Shadow Ln., North Port, FL 34287, U.S.A. **Online address:** jhines@cnu.edu

HINES, Jeanne. Also writes as Valerie Sherwood, Rosamond Royal. American (born United States), b. 1922. **Genres:** Romance/Historical, Novels, Literary Criticism And History, Children's Fiction, Mystery/Crime/Suspense. **Career:** Washington Star, columnist (book critic); Georgetowner, columnist (book critic); National Art Academy, faculty; novelist, 1973-. Art director and freelance commercial artist. **Publications:** The Slashed Portrait, 1973; Tidehawks, 1974; Talons of the Hawk, 1975; Brides of Terror, 1976; Scarecrow House, 1976; The Keys to Queenscourt, 1976; The Legend of Witchwynd, 1976; The Third Wife, 1977. AS VALERIE SHERWOOD: This Loving Torment, 1977; These Golden Pleasures, 1977; This Towering Passion, 1978; Her Shining Splendor, 1980; Bold Breathless Love, 1981; Rash Reckless Love, 1982; Wild Willful Love, 1982; Rich Radiant Love, 1983; Lovely Lying Lips, 1983; Born to Love, 1984; Lovesong, 1985; Windsong, 1986; Nightsong, 1986; To Love a Rogue, 1987; Lisbon, 1989; Her Crowning Glory, 1988; The Mistress, 1991. AS ROSAMOND ROYAL: Rapture, 1979. Works appear in anthologies. Contributor to magazines. **Address:** Severn House Publishers Ltd., 110 E 59th St., 22th Fl., New York, NY 10017-6220, U.S.A.

HINES, Joanna. British (born England), b. 1949. **Genres:** Novels, Mystery/Crime/Suspense, Psychology, Theology/Religion. **Career:** St. Mary's University College, The Royal Literary Fund, fellow, 2004-07. Writer. **Publications:** NOVELS: Dora's Room, 1993; The Cornish Girl, 1994; The Fifth Secret, 1995; The Puritan's Wife, 1996; Autumn of Strangers, 1997; The Lost Daughter, 1999; Improvising Carla, 2001; Surface Tension, 2002; Angels of the Flood, 2004; The Murder Bird, 2006. **Address:** c/o Jennifer Kavanagh, 44 Langham St., London, GL W1W 7AU, England. **Online address:** joanna@joannahines.co.uk

HINES, (Melvin) Barry. British (born England), b. 1939. **Genres:** Novels, Plays/Screenplays, Young Adult Fiction. **Career:** L.C.C., teacher, 1960-62; Barnsley Education Authority, teacher, 1963-68; West Riding County Council Education Authority, teacher, 196872; University of Sheffield, fellow in creative writing, 1972-74; Matlock College of Education, East Midlands Arts fellow in creative writing, 1975-77; University of Wollongong, fellow in creative writing, 1979; Sheffield City Polytechnic, Arts Council, fellow, 1982-84. Writer. **Publications:** The Blinder, 1966; Continental Size Six, 1966; A Kestrel for a Knave, 1968; First Signs, 1972; Speech Day, 1973; Gamekeeper, 1975; Kes: A Play of the Novel, 1976; The Price of Coal: The Scripts of the Two Television Plays Meet the People and Back to Reality, 1979; Looks and Smiles, 1981; Unfinished Business, 1983; The Heart of It, 1994; Elvis over England, 1999. **Address:** Lemon Unna & Durbridge Ltd., 24 Pottery Ln., London, GL W11 4LZ, England.

HINES, Robert S. (Robert Stephan Hines). American (born United States), b. 1926. **Genres:** Music, Songs/Lyrics And Libretti. **Career:** General Motors Corp., choral director, 1952-57; Our Saviour Lutheran Church, director of music, 1952-57; Southern Illinois University, assistant professor of music, 1957-61; University of Michigan, visiting professor, 1960; Northwestern University, visiting lecturer, 1960; Wichita State University, Department of Choral-Voice, associate professor, professor of music, chairman, 1961-71; University of Texas, visiting lecturer, 1968; University of Miami, visiting professor, 1971-72; University of Hawaii, Department of Music, professor, 1972-80, chairman of department, 1980-84, emeritus professor, 1994-, College of Arts and Humanities, dean, 1984-94. Writer. **Publications:** (As Robert Stephan Hines) The Composer's Point of View: Essays on Twentieth-century Choral Music by Those Who Wrote It, 1963; (co-ed.) Selected Lists of Choral Music, 1968; (ed. as Robert Stephan Hines) The Orchestral Composer's Point of View: Essays on Twentieth-century Music by Those Who Wrote It, 1970; Singer's Manual of Latin Diction and Phonetics, 1975; (with A.R. Trubitt) Ear Training and Sight-Singing: An Integrated Approach, vol. I, 1979, vol. II, 1980; (ed.) Magnificat in C Major: From Vesperae de Domenica, 1988; (ed.) Blow Ye the Trumpet: For Five-Part Chorus of Mixed Voices A Cappella=Canite Tuba, 1990; (ed.) Kyrie: From Litaniae de Venerabili Altaris Sacramento: For Four-Part Chorus of Mixed Voices and Solos with Keyboard Accompaniment, 1992; (as Robert Stephan Hines) Choral Composition: A Handbook for Composers, Arrangers, Conductors, and Singers, 2001; (as Robert Stephan Hines) Singers' Liturgical Latin: Rules for Pronunciation Plus Standard Texts with IPA Transcriptions and English Translations, 2003. Contributor to periodicals. **Address:** Department of Music, University of Hawaii, 2411 Dole St., Honolulu, HI 96822, U.S.A. **Online address:** hines@hawaii.edu

HINES, Robert Stephan. *See* **HINES, Robert S.**

HINES, Thomas S(pight). American (born United States), b. 1936. **Genres:** Architecture, Biography, History. **Career:** University of California, School of the Arts and Architecture, Department of History, professor, 1968-, now professor emeritus; University of Exeter, Fulbright fellow, 1984-85; American Academy of Arts and Sciences, faculty, 1994. Writer. **Publications:** Burnham of Chicago: Architect and Planner, 1974, 2nd ed., 2009; (with A. Drexler) The Architecture of Richard Neutra: From International Style to California Modern, 1980; Richard Neutra and the Search for Modern Architecture: A Biography and History, 1982; (with R.J. Clark) Los Angeles Transfer: Architecture in Southern California, 1880-1980, 1983; William Faulkner and the Tangible Past: The Architecture of Yoknapatawpha, 1996; Irving Gill and the Architecture of Reform, 2000; Architecture of the Sun: Los Angeles Modernism, 1900-1970, 2010. **Address:** Department of History, University of California, 1317 Perloff Hall, 405 Hilgard Ave., Los Angeles, CA 90095-1473, U.S.A. **Online address:** hines@history.ucla.edu

HINEY, Tom. South African (born South Africa), b. 1970?. **Genres:** Biography, Autobiography/Memoirs, History. **Career:** Observer, writer; Spectator, writer. Biographer. **Publications:** Raymond Chandler: A Biography, 1997; (ed. with F. MacShane) The Raymond Chandler Papers: Selected Letters and Non-Fiction, 1909-1959, 2000; On the Missionary Trail: A Journey Through Polynesia, Asia, and Africa with the London Missionary Society, 2000; On the Missionary Trail: The Classic Georgian Adventure of Two Englishmen, Sent on a Journey Around the World, 1821-29, 2000. Contributor to periodicals. **Address:** c/o Author Mail, Grove/Atlantic Inc., 841 Broadway, 4th Fl., New York, NY 10003, U.S.A.

HING, Bill Ong. American (born United States), b. 1949?. **Genres:** Young Adult Non-fiction, Politics/Government, Social Sciences. **Career:** Immigration Law Unit, San Francisco Neighborhood Legal Assistance Foundation, staff attorney and director, 1974-79; University of San Francisco, School of Law, adjunct faculty, 1976-79, professor of law, 2010-; New College School of Law, adjunct faculty, 1977-83; Golden Gate University Law School, associate professor, 1979-85; Immigrant Legal Resource Center (ILRC), founder, volunteer director, volunteer legal counsel, 1982-; Stanford Law School, acting professor and associate professor, 1985-97; East Palo Alto Community Law Project, acting executive director, 1987; University of California-Berkeley, Boalt Hall School of Law, chancellor's distinguished professorship, 1993, visiting professor, 1996-97; Baker & Mackenzie, counsel, 1996-2007; University of California-Davis, visiting professor, 1997-2000, professor of law, 2000-10, professor emeritus, 2010-. Writer. **Publications:** Handling Immigration Cases, 1985, 2nd ed., 1995; Making and Remaking Asian America through Immigration Policy, 1850-1990, 1993; (ed. with R. Lee) Reframing the Immigration Debate, 1996; To Be an American: Cultural Pluralism and the Rhetoric of Assimilation, 1997; Immigration and the Law: A Dictionary, 1999; A Quick Reference to IRCA, 2000; Defining America through Immigration Policy, 2004; Deporting Our Souls: Values, Morality, and Immigration Policy, 2006; Ethical Borders: NAFTA, Globalization, and Mexican Migration, 2010. Contributor of articles to journals. **Address:** School of Law, University of California, 2083 King Hall, 400 Mrak Hall Dr., Davis, CA 95616-5201, U.S.A. **Online address:** bhing@usfca.edu

HINGLE, Metsy. American (born United States) **Genres:** Novels. **Career:** Writer. **Publications:** NOVELS: Seduced, 1994; Surrender, 1996; Backfire, 1996; Lovechild, 1997; The Kidnapped Bride, 1997; Switched at the Altar, 1998; The Bodyguard and the Bridesmaid, 1998; Dad in Demand, 1999; Secret Agent Dad, 1999; The Baby Bonus, 2000; The Wager, 2001; Wife with Amnesia, 2001; Navy SEAL Dad, 2002; And the Winner Gets ... Married!, 2002; Behind the Mask, 2002; The Marriage Profile, 2002; Flash Point, 2003; Passionately Ever After, 2003; Deadline, 2004; Black Silk, 2006; The Rags-to-Riches Wife, 2006; What the Millionaire Wants..., 2008. Works appear in anthologies. **Address:** PO Box 3224, Covington, LA 70433, U.S.A. **Online address:** metsy@metsyhingle.com

HINN, Benny. American/Israeli (born Israel), b. 1952. **Genres:** Theology/Religion, Autobiography/Memoirs. **Career:** Evangelist, 1975-83; Orlando Christian Center, founder and pastor, 1983-99. Writer and television host. **Publications:** Good Morning, Holy Spirit, 1990; The Anointing, 1992; The Blood: Its Power from Genesis to Jesus to You, 1993, new ed., 2001; Lord, I Need a Miracle, 1993; Welcome, Holy Spirit: How You Can Experience The Dynamic Work Of The Holy Spirit In Your Life, 1995; This Is Your Day for a Miracle, 1996; Biblical Road to Blessing, 1997; Promises of Healing from Every Book in the Bible, 1998; He Touched Me (autobiography), 1999; Kathryn Kuhlman: Her Spiritual Legacy and Its Impact on My Life, 1999; The Blood Study Guide, 2001; Blood in the Sand, 2009; Sangre en la arena, 2009. **Address:** Benny Hinn Ministries, PO Box 162000, Irving, TX 75016-2000, U.S.A.

HINNEFELD, Joyce. American (born United States), b. 1961?. **Genres:** Medicine/Health, Novellas/Short Stories, Novels. **Career:** Moravian College, assistant professor of English, associate professor of English, 1997-, Writing Center, director; College of New Rochelle, teacher; Siena College, teacher; State University of New York, teacher; Dutchess Community College, teacher. Writer. **Publications:** Everything You Need to Know When Someone You Love Has Alzheimer's Disease, 1994; Tell Me Everything, and Other Stories, 1998; In Hovering Flight, 2008; Stranger Here Below, 2010. Contributor to periodicals. Works appear in anthologies. **Address:** Department of English, Moravian College, Rm. 200, Zinzendorf Hall, 1200 Main St., Bethlehem, PA 18018-6650, U.S.A. **Online address:** hinncfcldj@moravian.edu

HINOJOSA, Gilberto Miguel. American (born United States), b. 1942. **Genres:** History. **Career:** KWEX-TX, Voces del Seminario, program director, 1967-68; Bexar County Archives, assistant archivist, 1968-69; Lowell Junior High School, history teacher, 1969-70; Laredo Junior College, instructor, 1970-71; University of Texas at Austin, teaching assistant, 1971-74, assistant instructor, 1975-76, adjunct faculty, Mexican American Cultural Center, 1980-; Pan American University, assistant instructor, 1974; University of Texas at San Antonio, instructor, 1976-79, assistant professor, 1979-84, associate professor of history, 1984-93, assistant vice-president for academic affairs, 1988-90, Division of Behavioral and Cultural Sciences, discipline coordinator for history, 1992-93; Juarez-Lincoln University, adjunct faculty, 1976-78; Institute of Texan Cultures, lecturer, 1979-; Universidad Autonoma de Nuevo Leon, visiting Fulbright professor, 1981-82, Crane Publishing, associate editor, 1981-; Yturria Papers Collection, archivist, 1986-; University of the Incarnate Word, Incarnate Word College, discipline coordinator, 1992-93, associate professor, 1993-95, professor of history, 1995-, College of Arts and Sciences, dean, 1995-99, dean of humanities and fine arts, 1993-95. Writer. **Publications:** A Borderlands Town in Transition: Laredo, 1755-1870, 1983; (with M.A. Bruni) Viva la Virgen de Guadalupe! A History of Our Lady of Guadalupe Parish, 1988; (ed. with G.E. Poyo) Tejano Origins in Eighteenth-Century San Antonio, 1991; (ed. with J.P. Dolan) Mexican Americans and the Catholic Church, 1900-1965, 1994. Contributor of articles to books and periodicals. **Address:** College of Humanities, Arts and Social Sciences, University of the Incarnate Word, 4301 Broadway, San Antonio, TX 78209, U.S.A. **Online address:** hinojosa@universe.uiwtx.edu

HINOJOSA, Maria (de Lourdes). American/Mexican (born Mexico), b. 1961. **Genres:** Documentaries/Reportage, Criminology/True Crime, Autobiography/Memoirs. **Career:** WKCR FM, host, 1980-92; National Public Radio, production assistant, 1985-86, freelance reporter and producer, 1988-89, New York Bureau, staff reporter, 1990-96, anchor and managing editor, 1993-; WNYC Radio, staff reporter, 1989-90; CNN, correspondent, 1997-2005; Latino USA, managing editor, 2002-; PBS News Magazine, senior correspondent, 2005-10; The Futuro Media Group, president, 2010-. **Publications:** Crews: Gang Members Talk to Maria Hinojosa, 1995; Raising Raul: Adventures Raising Myself and My Son, 1999. **Address:** Latino USA, 1 University Sta. A0704, 2609 University Ave., Ste. 3.108, Austin, TX 78712, U.S.A. **Online address:** mhinojosa@kut.org

HINRICHS, Ernest H(enry). American (born United States), b. 1922. **Genres:** Military/Defense/Arms Control, History, Communications/Media. **Career:** Writer. **Publications:** Listening In: Intercepting German Trench Communications in World War I, 1996. Contributor to articles and dental journals. **Address:** 270 Ridgecrest Cir., Ste. 311, Lewisburg, PA 17837, U.S.A.

HINSON, E. Glenn. American (born United States), b. 1931?. **Genres:** Theology/Religion, inspirational/Motivational Literature, History, Autobiography/Memoirs, Classics, Education. **Career:** First Baptist Church, pastor, 1957-59; Baptist Theological Seminary, professor of spirituality, John Loftis professor of church history; Southern Baptist Theological Seminary, instructor in New Testament, 1959-60, instructor in church history, 1960-62, professor of church history, 1962-92, senior professor, now retired; Wake Forest University, professor of religion, 1982-84. Writer. **Publications:** The Church: Design for Survival, 1967; (co-author) Glossolalia, 1967; Seekers After Mature Faith, 1968; I and II Timothy and Titus, 1971; A Serious Call to a Contemplative Life Style, 1974, rev. ed., 1993; Soul Liberty, 1975; Jesus Christ, 1977; The Integrity of the Church, 1978; The Reaffirmation of Prayer, 1979; A History of Baptists in Arkansas, 1980; The Early Church Fathers, 1980; The Evangelization of the Roman Empire, 1981; The Priesthood of Believers, 1982; Are Southern Baptists Evangelicals?, 1983; Understandings of the Church, 1986; Religious Liberty, 1991; A Serious Call to a Contemplative Lifestyle, 1993; Vozes do Christiano Primitivo, 1993; The Church Triumphant: A History of Christianity up to 1300, 1995; The Early Church, 1996; Love at the Heart of Things: A Biography of Douglas V. Steele, 1998; Spiritual Preparation for Christian Leadership, 1999; Who Interprets the Bible for Baptists?, 2003; Companions in Christ: A Small-Group Experience in Spiritual Formation, 2006. EDITOR: The Early Church Fathers, 1975; Doubleday Devotional Classics, 3 vols., 1978; Spirituality in Ecumenical Perceptive, 1993. **Address:** Retired, 651 Upland Rd, Louisville, KY 40206, U.S.A. **Online address:** glennhinson@iglou.com

HINTON, Lynne. Also writes as Jackie Lynn. American (born United States) **Genres:** Novels, Mystery/Crime/Suspense, Young Adult Fiction. **Career:** Ordained Baptist minister, 1990; Hospice of Rockingham County, chaplain, 1990-; Mount Hope United Church of Christ, pastor, 1992; First Congregational United Church of Christ, pastor, 1998; Charlotte Observer, columnist. **Publications:** (As J. Lynne Hinton) Meditations for Walking, 1999; Friendship Cake, 2000; The Things I Know Best, 2001; Garden of Faith, 2002; Forever Friends, 2003; The Last Odd Day, 2004; The Arms of God, 2005; Order of Things, 2009; Christmas Cake, 2009; Wedding Cake, 2010; Pie Town, 2011. (as Jackie Lynn) SHADY GROVE MYSTERY SERIES: Down by the Riverside, 2006; Jacob's Ladder, 2007; Swing Low, Sweet Chariot, 2008. **Address:** c/o Author Mail, Publicity Department, St. Martin's Press, 175 5th Ave., New York, NY 10010, U.S.A.

HINTON, Michael. British (born England), b. 1927. **Genres:** Self Help, Ethics, Philosophy, Education, Theology/Religion, History, Cultural/Ethnic Topics. **Career:** Dover Grammar School for Boys, headmaster, 1960-68; Sevenoaks School, headmaster, 1968-70; Broadoak School in Weston-Super-Mare, headmaster, 1971-84; Parish of Shepherdswell, minister, 1985-95. Writer. **Publications:** A History of the Town of Reading, 1954; Ethics, 1974; Authority, 1974; Comprehensive Schools: A Christian's View, 1979; The Anglican Parochial Clergy: A Celebration, 1994; The 100-Minute Bible, 2005. **Address:** 212 The Gateway, Dover, KT CT16 1LL, England. **Online address:** michael@hintonm.demon.co.uk

HINTON, S(usan) E(loise). American (born United States), b. 1950. **Genres:** Children's Fiction, Young Adult Fiction, Novels, Picture/Board Books, Literary Criticism And History, Classics, Horror. **Career:** Writer. **Publications:** YOUNG ADULT NOVELS: The Outsiders, 1967; That Was Then, This Is Now, 1971; Rumble Fish, 1975; Tex, 1979; Taming the Star Runner, 1988; Hawkes Harbor, 2004; Some of Tim's Stories, 2007. OTHER: Big David, Little David, 1995; The Puppy Sister, 1995. Contributor to periodicals. **Address:** Delacorte Press, 1745 Broadway, 9th Fl., New York, NY 10019-4368, U.S.A. **Online address:** sehinton@sehinton.com

HINZE, Bradford E. American (born United States), b. 1954?. **Genres:** Adult Non-fiction, Theology/Religion, History. **Career:** Marquette University, theology faculty; Fordham University, professor of theology. Writer. **Publications:** Narrating History, Developing Doctrine: Friedrich Schleiermacher and Johann Sebastian Drey, 1993; (ed. with D.L. Dabney) Advents of the Spirit: An Introduction to the Current Study of Pneumatology, 2001; (ed.) The Spirit in the Church and the World, 2004; (ed. with I.A. Omar) Heirs of Abraham: The Future of Muslim, Jewish and Christian Relations, 2005; Practices of Dialogue in the Roman Catholic Church: Aims and Obstacles, Lessons and Laments, 2006. Contributor to periodicals. **Address:** Department of Theology, Fordham University, Rm. 158, Duane Library, Rose Hill Campus, Bronx, NY 10458, U.S.A. **Online address:** bhinze@fordham.edu

HIONIDOU, Violetta. British (born England) **Genres:** Economics, Social Sciences. **Career:** University of Liverpool, Department of Geography, research fellow, 1993-95; University of Southampton, Department of Social Statistics, lecturer, 1995-98, Department of Sociology and Social Policy, senior postdoctoral research fellow, 1999-2002; University of Crete, Department of Sociology, lecturer in social statistics, 2004; Newcastle University, School of Historical Studies, lecturer in modern history. Writer. **Publications:** Famine and Death in Occupied Greece, 1941-1944, 2006. Contributor of articles to books and journals. **Address:** School of Historical Studies, Faculty of Humanities, Arts & Social Sciences, Newcastle University, Armstrong Bldg., Newcastle upon Tyne, NE1 7RU, England. **Online address:** violetta.hionidou@ncl.ac.uk

HIPPERSON, Carol Edgemon. American (born United States), b. 1950?. **Genres:** Military/Defense/Arms Control, History, Education. **Career:** Writer, librarian, educator and military historian. **Publications:** The Belly Gunner, 2001; Radioman: An Eyewitness Account of Pearl Harbor and World War II in the Pacific, 2008; Probably From the Point of View of a Marine, forthcoming. Contributor to periodicals. **Address:** Stringer Literary Agency, PO Box 770365, Naples, FL 34107, U.S.A. **Online address:** carol@carolhipperson.com

HIRABAYASHI, Lane Ryo. American (born United States), b. 1952. **Genres:** Cultural/Ethnic Topics, Anthropology/Ethnology, History, Antiques/Furnishings. **Career:** University of California, visiting professor, 1996-97, Department Asian American Studies, lecturer, 1981-82, professor, 2006-, chair and Aratani endowed chair, 2007-10, George and Sakaye Aratani professor in Japanese American redress, internment and community, 2006-; California State University, lecturer in Asian American studies, 1982; San Francisco State University, lecturer, 1983, associate professor, 1984-88, professor of Asian American studies, 1988-91; Japanese Community Youth Council, board director, 1984-91; University of Colorado, associate professor of Asian American studies and anthropology, 1991-, professor of Asian American studies and anthropology, 1991-, Asian American Studies, coordinator, 1992-; Asian American Theater Co., musician; Japanese American National Museum, consultant. Writer. **Publications:** Asian American Community Studies: Selected References, 1982; (with G. Tanaka) The Early Gardena Valley and the Issei (monograph), 1986; The Delectable Berry: Japanese American Contributions to the Development of the Strawberry Industry on the West Coast (monograph), 1989; Cultural Capital: Mountain Zapotec Regional Associations in Mexico City, 1993; The Politics of Fieldwork: Research in an American Concentration Camp, 1999; (with J. Xing) Reversing the Lens: Ethnicity, Race, Gender and Sexuality through Film, 2003; Japanese American Resettlement through the Lens: Hikaru Iwasaki and the WRA's Photographic Section, 1943-1945, 2009. EDITOR: (and intro.) Inside an American Concentration Camp: Japanese American Resistance in Poston, 1995; (with T. Altamirano and contrib.) Migrants, Regional Identities and Latin American Cities, 1996; Teaching Asian America: Diversity and the Problem of Community, 1998; (with A. Kikumura-Yano and J.A. Hirabayashi) New Worlds, New Lives: Globalization and People of Japanese Descent in the Americas and from Latin America in Japan, 2002; (with A. Kikumura-Yano and J.A. Hirabayashi) On Common Ground: The Japanese American National Museum and the Culture of Collaborations, 2005. Contributor to books and academic journals. **Address:** Department of Asian American Studies, University of California, 3331 Rolfe Hall, PO Box 957225, Los Angeles, CA 90095-7225, U.S.A. **Online address:** lane.hirabayashi@colorado.edu

HIRATA, Hosea. American/Canadian (born Canada), b. 1952. **Genres:** Poetry, History. **Career:** Princeton University, assistant professor; Tufts University, professor, director of Japanese Program and chair of Department of German, Russian, and Asian Languages and Literatures. Poet, educator and filmmaker. **Publications:** The Poetry and Poetics of Nishiwaki Junzaburo: Modernism in Translation, 1993; Discourses of Seduction: History, Evil, Desire, and Modern Japanese Literature, 2005. Contributor to books, periodicals and journals. **Address:** Dept of German, Russian, & Asian Lang and Lit, Tufts University, Olin Ctr., 180 Packard Ave., Medford, MA 02155-5831, U.S.A. **Online address:** hosea.hirata@tufts.edu

HIRO, Dilip. British/Pakistani (born Pakistan) **Genres:** Novels, Plays/Screenplays, Poetry, History, International Relations/Current Affairs, Race Relations. **Career:** Writer. **Publications:** The Indian Family in Britain, 1967; Triangular View: A Novel, 1969; Black British, White British, 1971, rev. ed. as Black British, White British: A History of Race Relations in Britain, 1991; To Anchor a Cloud: A Play in Three Acts, 1972; The Untouchables of India, 1975, rev. ed., 1982; Inside India Today, 1976; Two One-Act Plays: Apply, Apply, No Reply and a Clean Break, 1978; Interior, Exchange, Exterior, 1980; Inside the Middle East, 1982; Iran Under the Ayatollahs, 1985; Iran: The Revolution Within, 1988; Islamic Fundamentalism, 1988; Holy Wars: The Rise of Islamic Fundamentalism, 1989; The Longest War: The Iran-Iraq Military Conflict, 1989; Desert Shield to Desert Storm: The Second Gulf War, 1992; Lebanon: Fire and Embers: A History of the Lebanese Civil War, 1993; Between Marx and Muhammad: The Changing Face of Central Asia, 1993; Dictionary of the Middle East, 1996; Middle East, 1996; Sharing the Promised Land: A Tale of the Israelis and Palestinians, 1999; Neighbors, Not Friends: Iraq and Iran After the Gulf Wars, 2001; War Without End: The Rise of Islamist Terrorism and the Global Response, 2002; India: A Concise History, 2002; Iraq: In the Eye of the Storm, 2002; India: The Rough Guide Chronicle, 2002; Essential Middle East: A Comprehensive Guide, 2003; Secrets and Lies: Operation Iraqi Freedom and After, 2004; Iranian Labyrinth: Journeys Through Theocratic Iran and its Furies, 2005; Iran Today, 2006; The Timeline History of India, 2006; Babur Nama, 2006; Blood of The Earth: The Battle for the World's Vanishing Oil Resources, 2007; Inside Central Asia: A Political and Cultural History Of Uzbekistan, Turkmenistan, Kazakhstan, Kyrgyzstan, Tajikistan, Turkey and Iran, 2009; After Empire: The Birth of a Multipolar World, 2010; Apocalyptic Realm: Jihad in South Asia, 2011. **Address:** c/o Bruce Hunter, David Higham Associates, 5-8 Lower John St., Golden Sq., London, GL W1F 9HA, England.

HIROTA, Dennis. Japanese (born Japan), b. 1946?. **Genres:** Theology/Religion. **Career:** Ryukoku University, professor of Shin Buddhism; Harvard Divinity School, visiting professor of Buddhism. Writer. **Publications:** (With Y. Ueda) Shinran: An Introduction to His Thought, with Selections from the Shin Buddhism Translation Series, 1989; (trans. and intro.) No Abode: The Record of Ippen, 1997; (trans. and intro.) The Collected Works of Shinran, 1997; Asura's Harp: Engagement with Language as Buddhist Path, 2006. EDITOR: Wind in the Pines: Classic Writings of the Way of Tea as a Buddhist Path, 1995; Toward a Contemporary Understanding of Pure Land Buddhism: Creating a Shin Buddhist Theology in a Religiously Plural World, 2000. (and trans.) Wandering Spirits and Temporary Corpses: Studies in the History of Japanese Religious Tradition, 2004. Contributor to periodicals. **Online address:** dhirota@let.ryukoku.ac.jp

HIRSCH, Edward. American (born United States), b. 1950. **Genres:** Poetry, How-to Books. **Career:** Wayne State University, assistant professor, 1979-82, associate professor of English, 1982-85; University of Houston, associate professor, 1985-88, professor of English, 1985-2002; John Simon Guggenheim Memorial Foundation, president, 2003-; Washington Post, columnist, 2002-05; DoubleTake Magazine, poetry editor. **Publications:** For the Sleepwalkers: Poems, 1981; Wild Gratitude: Poems, 1986; The Night Parade: Poems, 1989; (intro.) (ed. and intro.) Transforming Vision: Writers on Art, 1994; Earthly Measures: Poems, 1994; (intro.) Reading the Water, 1997; On Love: Poems, 1998; How to Read a Poem: And Fall in Love with Poetry, 1999; Responsive Reading, 1999; The Demon and the Angel: Searching for the Source of Artistic Inspiration, 2002; Lay Back the Darkness: Poems, 2003; (ed. with C. Baxter and M. Collier) A William Maxwell Portrait: Memories and Appreciations, 2004; (ed.) Selected Poems, 2005; Poet's Choice, 2006; (comp. and intro.) To a Nightingale, 2007; Special Orders: Poems, 2008; The Making of a Sonnet, 2008; (ed. with E. Boland) The Living Fire: New and Selected Poems 1975-2010, 2010; Sobbing Superpower, 2011. Contributor to periodicals. **Address:** John Simon Guggenheim Memorial Foundation, 90 Park Ave., New York, NY 10016, U.S.A. **Online address:** eh@gf.org

HIRSCH, E(ric) D(onald). American (born United States), b. 1928. **Genres:** Education, Literary Criticism And History, Psychology. **Career:** Yale University, instructor, 1956-60, assistant professor, 1960-63, associate professor of English, 1963-66; University of Virginia, Department of English, professor, 1966-72, William R. Kenan professor, 1973-84, university professor of education and humanities, Linden Kent Memorial professor, 1989-2001, Linden Kent Memorial professor emeritus, 2001-, chair, 1968-71, 1981-82, director of composition, 1971; Oxford University, Bateson Lecturer, 1983; Core Knowledge Foundation, founder, 1986-; Cultural Literacy Foundation, founder, 1986-; Albert Shanker Institute, director, 1997; Hoover Institution, distinguished visiting fellow, 1999-2006; Marian University, national faculty. Writer. **Publications:** Wordsworth and Schelling: A Typological Study of Romanticism, 1960; Innocence and Experience: An Introduction to Blake, 1964, 2nd ed., 1975; Validity in Interpretation, 1967; Prinzipien der Interpretationen, 1972; The Aims of Interpretation, 1976; The Philosophy of Composition, 1977; Cultural Literacy: What Every American Needs to Know, 1987; (intro.) Collected Poems of Elma Stuckey, 1987; (with J. Kett and J. Trefil) Dictionary of Cultural Literacy, 1988, 3rd ed. as The New Dictionary of Cultural Literacy, 2002; (ed.) A First Dictionary of Cultural Literacy: What Our Children Need to Know, 1989, 3rd ed. as The New First Dictionary of Cultural Literacy: What Your Child Needs to Know, 2004; The Schools We Need and Why We Don't Have Them, 1996; (ed. with J. Holdren) Books to Build On: A Grade by Grade Resource Guide for Parents and Teachers, 1996; The Knowledge Deficit: Closing the Shocking Education Gap for American Children, 2006; The Making of Americans: Democracy and Our Schools, 2009. EDITOR: CORE KNOWLEDGE SERIES: What Your First Grader Needs to Know: Fundamentals of a Good First-Grade Education, 1991, rev. ed., 1998; What Your Second Grader Needs to Know: Fundamentals of a Good Second-Grade Education, 1991, rev. ed., 1998; What Your Third Grader Needs to Know: Fundamentals of a Good Third-Grade Education, 1992, rev. ed., 2001; What Your Fourth Grader Needs to Know: Fundamentals of a Good Fourth-Grade Education, 1992, rev. ed., 2004; What Your Fifth Grader Needs to Know: Fundamentals of a Good Fifth-Grade Education, 1993, rev. ed., 2005; What Your Sixth Grader Needs to Know: Fundamentals of a Good Sixth-Grader Education, 1993, rev. ed., 2006; (with J. Holdren) What Your Kindergartner Needs to Know: Preparing Your Child for a Lifetime of Learning, 1996; (ed. with M. Davis) Czars and Czarinas: A History of Old Russia for Young Readers, 2001; (with S.A. Wright) Core Knowledge: Grade K, Kindergarten, 2004; (with S.A. Wright) Core Knowledge, Grade 1, 2004; (with L. Bevilacqua) What Your Preschooler Needs to Know: Read-alouds to Get Ready for Kindergarten, 2008. Contributor to periodicals. **Address:** Core Knowledge Foundation, 801 E High St., Charlottesville, VA 22902-5125, U.S.A. **Online address:** edh9k@virginia.edu

HIRSCH, James (S.). American (born United States), b. 1962. **Genres:** Documentaries/Reportage, History, Adult Non-fiction, Social Sciences. **Career:** New York Times, news staff/reporter, 1986-89; Wall Street Journal, reporter, 1989-98; Close Concerns, principal. **Publications:** Hurricane: The Miraculous Journey of Rubin Carter, 2000; Riot and Remembrance: The Tulsa Race War and Its Legacy, 2002; Two Souls Indivisible: The Friendship that Saved Two POWs in Vietnam, 2004; Cheating Destiny: Living With Diabetes, America's Biggest Epidemic, 2006; Willie Mays: The Life, the Legend, 2010. **Address:** 17 Hollow Ridge Rd., Needham, MA 02494, U.S.A. **Online address:** jimhirsch@rcn.com

HIRSCH, Pam. British (born England), b. 1947. **Genres:** Literary Criticism And History, Biography, Education. **Career:** Literature and history teacher, 1972-78; Cambridgeshire College of Arts and Technology and Newnham Language Center, teacher, 1981-83; nursery school principal, 1983-88; Homerton College, senior lecturer in English and research mentor, 1992-2001; University of Cambridge, lecturer in English literature, history of education, Newnham College, lecturer in faculty of education, graduate tutor, 2001-. Writer. **Publications:** Barbara Leigh Smith Bodichon, 1827-1891: Feminist, Artist and Rebel, 1998; (ed. with M. Hilton) Practical Visionaries: Women, Education and Social Progress, 1790-1930, 2000; (with M. McBeth) Teacher Training at Cambridge: The Initiatives of Oscar Browning and Elizabeth Hughes, 2004; The Constant Liberal: The Life and Work of Phyllis Bottome, 2010; Reframing Literacy, forthcoming. Contributor of articles to books and periodicals. **Address:** Faculty of Education, University of Cambridge, 184 Hills Rd., Homerton Site, Cambridge, CB CB2 2PQ, England. **Online address:** ph211@cam.ac.uk

HIRSCH, Seev. Israeli/German (born Germany), b. 1931. **Genres:** Business/Trade/Industry, Economics, Adult Non-fiction, International Relations/Current Affairs, Industrial Relations. **Career:** Tel-Aviv University, faculty, 1965, Department of Accounting, head, 1966-68, Leon Recanati Graduate School of Business Administration, dean, 1970-73, associate professor, 1971-78, senior lecturer, 1976-71, professor, 1978-81, Jaffee professor, 1981-95, professor emeritus, 1995-, College of Management, MBA program, director, 1995-; Economic Development Institute, visiting fellow, 1976. Writer. **Publications:** Location of Industry and International Competitiveness, 1967; Identification and Exploitation of the Export Potential of Industrial Firms in Israel, 1969; The Export Performance of Six Manufacturing Industries: A Comparative Study of Denmark, Holland and Israel, 1971; (co-author) Profiles of Six Export Oriented Industries A&B, 1973; Rich Man's, Poor Man's and Every Man's Goods: Aspects of Industrialization, 1977; Towards Peace in the Middle East: How Can Business Contribute?, 1977; Economic Inte-

gration of Israel in the EEC: The Relationship between the Domestic and International Sectors in Economic Development, 1978; (with R. Arad and A. Tovias) The Economics of Peacemaking: Focus on the Egyptian-Israeli Situation, 1983; (with R. Arad and A. Tovias) Kalkalah shel aóiyatshalom, 1984; (with I. Ayal and S. Kalish) Israel as a Bridge to the United States and the European Economic Community, 1987; (with I. Ayal and S. Kalish) Free Trade Areas and International Production Sharing: An Economic Model for Identifying Potential Bridge Goods, 1988; (with S. Kalish and S. Katznelson) Effects of Knowledge and Service Intensities on Domestic and Export Performance, 1988; (with H. Ben-Shahar and G. Fishelson) Economic Cooperation and Middle East Peace, 1989; (ed. with T. Almor) Outsiders Response to European Integration, 1996; (with N. Hashai) The Arab-Israeli Trade Potential: The Role of Distance-Sensitive Products, 1999. **Address:** Leon Recanati Graduate School of Business Admin, Tel Aviv University, Rm. 425, PO Box 39010, Tel Aviv, 69978, Israel. **Online address:** hirsch@post.tau.ac.il

HIRSCHFELD, Lawrence A. American (born United States), b. 1947. **Genres:** Anthropology/Ethnology, Psychology. **Career:** University of Wisconsin, assistant scientist in anthropology, 1983-89, research associate in psychology, 1984-85; Centre Nationale de la Recherche Scientifique, Laboratoire de Psycho-Biologie de l'Enfant, researcher, 1987-88, Centre de Recherche en Epistemologie Appliquee, Groupe de Recherche sur la Cognition, head of research, 1988-89; University of Michigan, assistant professor, 1989-96, associate professor of anthropology and psychology, 1996-, professor of anthropology and psychology, Institute for Social Research, Research Center for Group Dynamics, faculty associate, 1992-, Graduate Program in Culture and Cognition, co-director, 1993-. Writer. **Publications:** (Ed. with S.A. Gelman) Mapping the Mind: Domain Specificity in Cognition and Culture, 1994; Race in the Making: Cognition, Culture, and the Child's Construction of Human Kinds, 1996; (ed. with R. Viale and D. Andler) Biological and Cultural Bases of Human Inference, 2006. Contributor to books and journals. **Address:** Department of Psychology and Anthropology, New School for Social Research, Rm. 323, 65 5th Ave., New York, NY 10011, U.S.A. **Online address:** hirschfl@newschool.edu

HIRSCHFELDER, Arlene B. American (born United States), b. 1943. **Genres:** Children's Non-fiction, Cultural/Ethnic Topics, Young Adult Non-fiction, Bibliography, Adult Non-fiction. **Career:** Association on American Indian Affairs, scholarship director and education consultant, 1969-91; New School for Social Research, faculty, 1984-96; Smithsonian Institution/National Museum of the American Indian, faculty, 1994-95. Writer. **Publications:** (Comp.) American Indian Authors: A Representative Bibliography, 1970; (comp.) American Indian and Eskimo Authors: A Comprehensive Bibliography, 1973; This Land Is Ours: A Native American Anthology and Teachers Guide, 1978; Annotated Bibliography of the Literature on American Indians Published in State Historical Society Publications: New England and Middle Atlantic States, 1982; American Indian Stereotypes in the World of Children: A Reader and Bibliography, 1982, (with P.F. Molin and Y. Wakim) 2nd ed., 1999; (with M.G. Byler and M. Dorris) Guide to Research on North American Indians, 1983; American Indian Desk Calendar, 1985; Happily May I Walk: American Indians and Alaska Natives Today, 1986; (with P.F. Molin) Encyclopedia of Native American Religions: An Introduction, 1992; (ed. with B.R. Singer) Rising Voices: Writings of Young Native Americans, 1992; (with M.K. de Montano) Native American Almanac: A Portrait of Native America Today, 1993; American Indian Lives: Artists and Craftspeople, 1994; Artists and Craftspeople, 1994; (with D. Hirschfelder) The Tobacco Chronicles: Tobacco in the United States, 1880-1995: Tobacco Practices, Policies and Research among American Indians and Alaska Natives, 1995; (ed.) Native Heritage: Personal Accounts by American Indians, 1790 to the Present, 1995; Kick Butts: A Kids Action Guide to a Tobacco-Free America, 1998; Encyclopedia of Smoking and Tobacco, 1999; Native Americans: A History in Photographs, 2000; Photo Odyssey: Solomon Carvalhos Remarkable Western Adventure, 1853-54, 2000; (with Y. Beamer) Native Americans Today: Resources and Activities for Educators, Grades 4-8, 2000; (with Y.W. Dennis) Children of Native America Today, 2003; Squanto, 1585?-1622, 2004; (with M. Ajmera, Y.W. Dennis and C. Pon) Children of the U.S.A, 2008; (with Y.W. Dennis) A Kids Guide to Native American History: More Than 50 Activities, 2010; Tobacco, 2010; (with P.F. Molin) The Extraordinary Book of Native American Lists, 2012. Contributor to books and periodicals. **Address:** 170 Copley Ave., Teaneck, NJ 07666-4100, U.S.A. **Online address:** arlene0417@aol.com

HIRSCHHORN, Clive. British/South African (born South Africa), b. 1940. **Genres:** Film, Biography, Art/Art History. **Career:** Empire Films, publicist,

1960-62; ABC-TV, story editor, 1962-63; Daily Mail, pop columnist, 1964-65; Sunday Express London, film critic, 1966-69, drama critic, 1966-96; Applause Magazine, editor. **Publications:** Gene Kelly, 1975; The Films of James Mason, 1975; The Warner Bros. Story, 1979; The Hollywood Musical, 1981; The Universal Story, 1983, rev. ed., 2000; The Columbia Story, 1990; Mae West: An Interview & Biography, 2009. **Address:** c/o Eleanor Knowles Dugan, Grand Cyrus Press, 1024 Sacramento St., San Francisco, CA 94108-2003, U.S.A. **Online address:** cliveh@cwcom.net

HIRSCHMAN, Jack. American (born United States), b. 1933. **Genres:** Poetry, Translations, Theology/Religion. **Career:** Dartmouth College, instructor, 1959-61; University of California, assistant professor, 1961-66; Left Curve, editor. **Publications:** Fragments, 1953; A Correspondence of Americans, 1960; Two, 1964; Interchange, 1964; Kline Sky, 1965; (ed.) Artaud Anthology, 1965; Yod, 1966; London Seen Directly, 1967; Wasn't It Like This in the Woodcut, 1967; William Blake, 1967; (with A. Benveniste) A Word in Your Season, 1967; Ltd. Interchangeable in Eternity: Poems of Jackruthdavidcelia Hirschman, 1967; Jerusalem: A Three Part Poem, 1968; Aleph, Benoni and Zaddik, 1968; Jerusalem, 1968; Shekinah, 1969; Broadside Golem, 1969; Black Alephs: Poems 1960-1968, 1969; NHR, 1970; Scintilla, 1971; Soledeth, 1971; DT, 1971; The Burning of Los Angeles, 1971; HNYC, 1971; Les Vidanges, 1972; The R of the Ari's Raziel, 1972; Adamnan, 1972; Aur Sea, 1974; KS/An Essay on Kabbala Surrealism, 1973; Cantillations, 1973; Djackson, 1974; Time of the People Changed to Prayer, 1974; Cockroach Street, 1975; The Cool Boyetz Cycle, 1975; Stump 2 Athens, 1975; Kashtaninyah Segodnyah, 1975; Lyripol, 1976; The Arcanes of Le Comte de St. Germain, 1977; The Jonestown Arcane, 1979; The Proletarian Arcane, 1980; Class Questions, 1981; The Cagliostro Arcane, 1981; The Donmeh Arcane, 1982; The David Arcane, 1982; Salt Point, 1983; Kallatumba, 1984; The Necessary Is, 1984; Sun, Stay, 1987; The Bottom Line, 1988; The Satin Arcane, 1991; The Triana Arcane, 1991; Endless Threshold, 1992; The Back of a Spoon, 1992; Heartbeat Arcane, 1993; The Xibalba Arcane, 1994; The Arcane on a Stick, 1995; The Graffiti Arcane, 1995; Culture and Struggle, 1995; The Green Chakra Arcane, 1996; L'Arcano di Pasolini, 1996; L'Arcano di Shupsl, 1996; The Grit Arcane, 1997; Arcani, 1999; Sunsong, 2000; The Archaic Now Arcane, 2000; (ed.) 500, 000 Azaleas, 2001; (ed. with P. Laraque) The Open Gate, 2001; The Lotus Bikini Arcane, 2002; Front Lines: Selected Poems, 2002; Fists on Fire, 2003; I Was Born Murdered, 2004; Dodici Arcani, 2004; (ed.) Art on the Line: Essays by Artists About the Point Where Their Art and Activism Intersect, 2002; The Arcanes, 2006; Only Dreaming Sky: Poems, 2007; All That's Left, 2008. TRANSLATOR: (with V. Erlich) V. Mayakovsky, Electric Iron, 1970; A. Artaud, Love Is a Tree, 1972; R. Depestre, A Rainbow for the Christian West, 1972; L. Pasamanik, The Exiled Angel, 1973; S. Mallarme, Igitur, 1973; A. Djafer, Wail for the Arab Beggars of the Casbah, 1973; J. Cocteau, The Crucifixion, 1976; J. Maier, The Book of Noah, 1976; A. Voznesensky, Kaligrunes, 1976; A. Kohav, Four Angels in Profile, Four Beasts in Full Face, 1976; A. Abulafia, The Path of the Names, 1976; A. Kohav, Orange Voice, 1976; N. Belyaeva, Hunger, 1977; A. Kohav, Emigroarium: A Roaratory!, 1977; E. Levi, Dove Rose, 1979; R. Depestre, Vegetations of Splendor, 1980; S. Calí, Yossiph Shyryn, 1980; Jabixshak, 1982; P. Neruda, Elegy, 1983; K. Gogou, Three Clicks Left, 1983; A. Gjakova, Communist, 1984; R. Dalton, Clandestine Poems, 1985; P. Laraque, Slingshot, 1989; D. Lefteria, In Memory of the Children, 1994; A. Past, The Sea on its Side: Poetry, 1994; R. Scotellaro, Seven Poems, 1994; (with A. Beske) P. Celan, Light-Force, 1996; F. Brugnaro, Fist of Sun, 1998; S. Mallarme, A Fling of Two Die Never Will Abolish Chance, 1998; K. Gogou, The Month of the Frozen Grapes, 1998; M. Heidegger, Imaginings, 1999; F. Brugnaro, Partial Portrait of Maria, 2000; S. Mallarme, To Marry the Notion, 2000; F. Carlini, A Mountain Under a Bridge: Eleven Poems, 2001; M. Heidegger, Slow Lightning: The Poems of Martin Heidegger, 2001; P.P. Pasolini, The Book of Crosses, 2001; J. Baudrillard, Stucco Angel, 2001; A. Zuccolo, Chorale for Geese and a Solo Voice, 2001; A. Kruchenych, Suicide Circus: Selected Poems, 2001; J. Stalin, Joey: The Poems of Joseph Stalin, 2001; M. Licheri, Sabotages, 2002; A. Lombardo, Even the Fish Are Drunk, 2002; A. Masala, Taliban, 2002; G. Daniel, Suggar Point, 2002; S. Notarnicola, Liberty, Understand?!, 2002; A. Masala, In the Executioner's House, 2003; P. Molinier, The Magic Glee Clubs, 2003; P. Celan, 40 Poems, 2004; E. Ugolini, Incandescences, 2004; U. Pierri, Steel Away, 2004; L. Lucchesinno, Erotic Verses, 2004. **Address:** Left Curve, 15 W 37th St., New York, NY 10018-6223, U.S.A.

HIRSH, Michael. American (born United States), b. 1957?. **Genres:** Writing/Journalism, Politics/Government, Social Commentary. **Career:** Institutional Investor, Asia bureau chief, 1992-94; Newsweek, senior writer, 1994-97;

Newsweek Intl., senior editor, 1994-97, bureau correspondent, 1997, diplomatic correspondent covering foreign policy, senior editor and chief diplomatic correspondent, 1999-2000, managing editor of issues, 2001, Newsweek USA, foreign editor of international news coverage, 2001-02, Washington Bureau, senior editor of business and economics, 2002-, national economics correspondent; U.S. State Department, staff, 1998-99 U.S. Department of Treasury, staff, 1998-99; National Journal, chief correspondent. **Publications:** At War with Ourselves: Why America Is Squandering Its Chance to Build a Better World, 2003; Capital Offense: How Washington's Wise Men Turned America's Future Over to Wall Street, 2010. Contributor to periodicals. **Address:** Newsweek, 251 W 57th St., New York, NY 10019-1894, U.S.A. **Online address:** mhirsh@nationaljournal.com

HIRSHFELD, Alan. American (born United States), b. 1951. **Genres:** Astronomy, Sciences, History, Philosophy. **Career:** University of Massachusetts, professor of physics, 1978-; Harvard College Observatory, associate. Writer. **Publications:** (Ed. with R.W. Sinnott) Sky Catalogue 2000.0, 1982, 2nd ed., 1991, vol. I: Stars to Magnitude 8.0, vol. II: Double Stars, Variable Stars and Nonstellar Objects, 1985; Parallax: The Race to Measure the Cosmos, 2001; Electric Life of Michael Faraday, 2006; Eureka Man: The Life and Legacy of Archimedes, 2009. **Address:** Department of Physics, University of Massachusetts, Rm. 208B, Group II Bldg., 285 Old Westport Rd., North Dartmouth, MA 02747-2300, U.S.A. **Online address:** ahirshfeld@umassd.edu

HIRSHFIELD, Jane. American (born United States), b. 1953. **Genres:** Poetry, Literary Criticism And History, Translations. **Career:** Freelance editor, 1983-; University of San Francisco, lecturer in creative writing, 1991-98; Northern Michigan University, adjunct professor, 1994; University of Minnesota, adjunct professor, 1995; University of California, visiting associate professor, 1995; Bennington College, MFA Writing Seminars, core faculty, 1999-2004; University of Cincinnati, Elliston visiting poetry professor, 2000. **Publications:** POETRY: Alaya, 1982; Of Gravity & Angels, 1988; The October Palace, 1994; The Lives of the Heart, 1997; Given Sugar, Given Salt, 2001; (with R. Bly) Mirabai: Ecstatic Poems, 2004; After: Poems, 2006; Come, Thief, 2011. OTHER: (trans. with M. Aratani) The Ink Dark Moon: Poems by Ono no Komachi and Izumi Shikibu, 1988, rev. ed., 1990; (ed.) Women in Praise of the Sacred: 43 Centuries of Spiritual Poetry by Women, 1994; Nine Gates: Entering the Mind of Poetry: Essays, 1997; (ed.) Bloodaxe Poetry Introductions 3, 2007. Contributor of poems and translations to anthologies, periodicals. **Address:** c/o Michael Katz, 367 Molino Ave., Mill Valley, CA 94941, U.S.A.

HIRSHMAN, Linda R. American (born United States), b. 1944. **Genres:** Women's Studies And Issues, Sex. **Career:** Arizona Foundation for Women, board director, 1995; Brandeis University, Allen Berenson distinguished visiting professor of philosophy and women's studies, 1998-, now retired; University of Iowa, Mason Ladd distinguished visitor at law school, 1999. Lawyer and Writer. **Publications:** (With J.E. Larson) Hard Bargains: The Politics of Sex, 1998; The Woman's Guide to Law School, 1999; Get to Work: A Manifesto for Women of the World, 2006. Contributor to periodicals. **Address:** c/o Philippa Brophy, Sterling Lord Literistic, 65 Bleecker St., New York, NY 10012, U.S.A. **Online address:** lrhirshman@cs.com

HIRSH-PASEK, Kathy. American (born United States), b. 1953. **Genres:** Language/Linguistics, How-to Books. **Career:** Sperry Univac Inc., consultant research psychologist on software ease of use, 1980-84; Rutgers University, Medical College, Department of Psychiatry, assistant professor, 1981-85; Swarthmore College, Department of Psychology, assistant professor, 1982-84; Infant Speech Perception Laboratory, director, 1982-84; Haverford College, Department of Psychology, assistant professor, 1984-87, Infant Language and Perception Laboratory, director, 1984-87; Temple University, Department of Psychology, assistant professor, 1987-90, Infant Language and Perception Laboratory, director, 1987-, associate professor, 1990-97, professor of psychology, 1997-, Stanley and Debra Lefkowitz professor of psychology, The Debra and Stanley Lefkowitz faculty fellow; International Society for Infant Studies, treasurer, 2004-10. Writer. **Publications:** (Ed. with L. Rescorla and M. Hyson) Academic Instruction in Early Childhood: Challenge or Pressure?, 1991; (with R.M. Golinkoff) The Origins of Grammar: Evidence from Early Language Comprehension, 1996; (with R.M. Golinkoff) How Babies Talk: The Magic and Mystery of Language in the First Three Years of Life, 1999; (with R.M. Golinkoff and D. Eyer) Einstein Never Used Flash Cards: How Our Children Really Learn and Why They Need to Play More And Memorize Less, 2003; (ed. with D.G. Singer and R.M. Golinkoff) Play-Learning: How

Play Motivates and Enhances Children's Cognitive and Social-Emotional Growth, 2006; (ed. with R.M. Golinkoff) Action Meets Word: How Children Learn Verb, 2006; (with L. Berk, D.G. Singer and R.M. Golinkoff) A Mandate for Playful Learning in Preschool: Presenting the Evidence, 2009. Contributor to books and periodicals. **Address:** Department of Psychology, Temple University, Rm. 1701, Weiss Hall, N 13th St., Philadelphia, PA 19122-6085, U.S.A. **Online address:** khirshpa@temple.edu

HISCHAK, Thomas S. American (born United States), b. 1951. **Genres:** Plays/Screenplays, Theatre, Literary Criticism And History, Film, Art/Art History. **Career:** Point Park College, instructor, 1978-82; Delaware Theater Co., Wilmington, worked in audience development, 1982-83; State University of New York College, Cortland, professor of theater, 1983-. Writer and educator. **Publications:** PLAYS: Murder by Membership Only, 1980; The Gift of the Magi, 1984; A New Style for Murder, 1991; Murder on Reserve: A Mystery Play in Two Acts, 1994; Murder in Bloom: A Mystery Comedy in Two Acts, 1995; Murder by the Book, 1995; Little Women, 1995; Tiny Tim's Christmas, 1997; Rutherford Wolf, 1997; The Phony Physician, 1997; Willabella Witch's Last Spell, 1999; Cinderella Inc., 2000; (adapted) Molière's Tartuffe: A Comedy in Five Scenes, 2001; Curst Be He that Moves My Bones, 2002; Popularity, 2004; Ladies, Sigh No More, 2004; David Copperfield, 2005; Six Characters in Search of a Life, 2008; Christie, 2009. BOOKS: The Last Leaf, 1991; Word Crazy: Broadway Lyricists from Cohan to Sondheim, 1991; Stage It with Music: An Encyclopedic Guide to the American Musical Theatre, 1993; The American Musical Theatre Song Encyclopedia, 1995; American Theatre: A Chronicle of Comedy and Drama, 1930-1969, 1996; The Theatregoer's Almanac: A Collection of Lists, People, History and Commentary on the American Theatre, 1997; The American Musical Film Song Encyclopedia, 1999; Film It with Music: An Encyclopedic Guide to the American Movie Musical, 2000; American Theatre: A Chronicle of Comedy and Drama, 1969-2000, 2000; The Tin Pan Alley Song Encyclopedia, 2002; Boy Loses Girl: Broadway's Librettists, 2002; Enter the Players: New York Actors in the Twentieth Century, 2003; Through the Screen Door: What Happened to the Broadway Musical When It Went to Hollywood, 2004; (with G. Bordman) Oxford Companion to American Theatre, 3rd ed., 2004; American Plays and Musicals on Screen: 650 Stage Productions and Their Film and Television Adaptations, 2005; Theatre as Human Action: An Introduction to Theatre Arts, 2006; Enter the Playmakers: Directors and Choreographers on the New York Stage, 2006; Swine of Avon, 2006; The Rodgers and Hammerstein Encyclopedia, 2007; Oxford Companion to the American Musical: Theatre, Film and Television, 2008; Broadway Plays and Musicals: Descriptions and Essential Facts of More Than 14, 000 Shows Through 2007, 2008; (with M.A. Robinson) The Disney Song Encyclopedia, 2009; Off-Broadway Musicals since 1919: From Greenwich Village Follies to the Toxic Avenger, 2011. Contributor to books. **Address:** Department of Performing Arts, State University of New York Cortland, Rm. 216, Dowd Fine Arts Ctr., PO Box 2000, Cortland, NY 13045, U.S.A. **Online address:** hischakt@cortland.edu

HISE, Greg. American (born United States), b. 1953. **Genres:** Urban Studies, History, Geography, Social Sciences. **Career:** University of California, instructor, 1988-90; University of Southern California, School of Urban Planning and Development, School of Policy, Planning, and Development, assistant professor, 1992-98, associate professor of urban history, 1998-2008; California Institute of Technology, Division of Humanities and Social Sciences, visiting associate professor, 1997-98; Rutgers University, Center for Historical Analysis, senior fellow, 2001-02, Natural History Museum of Los Angeles County, research associate, 2005-; University of Nevada, Department of History, professor, 2008-. Writer. **Publications:** (Ed. with M.J. Dear and H.E. Schockman) Rethinking Los Angeles, 1996; Magnetic Los Angeles: Planning the Twentieth-Century Metropolis, 1997; (with W. Deverell) Eden by Design: The 1930 Olmsted-Bartholomew Plan for the Los Angeles Region, 2000; (ed. with W. Deverell) Land of Sunshine: An Environmental History of Metropolitan Los Angeles, 2005; (ed. with W. Deverell) Companion to Los Angeles, 2010. **Address:** Department of History, University of Nevada, Rm. B-313, Wright Hall, 4505 Maryland Pkwy., PO Box 45020, Las Vegas, NV 89154-9900, U.S.A. **Online address:** hise@unlv.edu

HISE, Phaedra. American (born United States), b. 1964. **Genres:** Novels. **Career:** Fortune Small Business Magazine, contributor; Inc. (magazine), staff writer, 1990-95; Virginia Living Magazine, contributing editor; freelance journalist, 1995; James River Writers Festival, co-chair, 2003, 2004; COLLOQUY Magazine, senior editor. **Publications:** Growing Your Business Online: Small-Business Strategies for Working the World Wide Web, 1996;

301 Ways to Use Technology, 1998; (with R. Ryan) Entrepreneur America: Lessons from inside Rob Ryans High-Tech Start-up Boot Camp, 2001; Pilot Error: Anatomy of a Plane Crash, 2002; (with M. Paxton) Secret Lives of Hoarders: True Stories of Tackling Extreme Clutter, 2011. **Address:** Dystel & Goderich Literary Management, 1 Union Sq. W, Ste. 904, New York, NY 10003, U.S.A. **Online address:** phaedra@aerobat.com

HISLOP, Victoria. British (born England), b. 1959?. **Genres:** Novels, Young Adult Fiction, History. **Career:** Freelance writer. **Publications:** The Island, 2005; The Return, 2009; The Thread, 2011. Contributor to periodicals. Works appear in anthologies. **Address:** c/o David Miller, Rogers, Coleridge & White, 20 Powis Mews, London, GL W11 1JN, England. **Online address:** info@victoriahislop.com

HITCHCOCK, Lydia. See **JORDAN, Penny.**

HITCHCOCK, Tim. British/American (born United States), b. 1957. **Genres:** History, Economics, Social Work, Literary Criticism And History. **Career:** University of North London, lecturer, principal lecturer, senior lecturer in early-modern British history, 1989-98; University of Hertfordshire, reader in eighteenth-century history, 1998-2002, Faculty of Humanities, Languages and Education, associate dean, 2001-06, professor of eighteenth-century history, 2002-, Social Sciences, Arts and Humanities Research Institute, head, 2004-08, Old Bailey Online Project, co-director. Writer and historian. **Publications:** Richard Hutton's Complaints Book: The Notebook of the Steward of the Quaker Workhouse at Clerkenwell, 1711- 1737, 1987; (ed. with L. Davidson, T. Keirn and R.B. Shoemaker) Stilling the Grumbling Hive: The Regulation of Social and Economic Problems in England, 1689-1750, 1992; (with R. Shoemaker) Economic Growth and Social Change in the Eighteenth-Century English Town, 1996; (ed. with P. King and P. Sharpe) Chronicling Poverty: The Voices and Strategies of the English Poor, 1640-1840, 1997; English Sexualities, 1700-1800, 1997; (ed. with M. Cohen) English Masculinities, 1660-1800, 1999; (ed. with J. Black) Chelsea Settlement and Bastardy Examinations, 1733-1766, 1999; (ed. with H. Shore) The Streets of London from the Great Fire to the Great Stink, 2003; Down and Out in Eighteenth-Century London, 2004; (with R. Shoemaker) Tales from the Hanging Court, 2006. Contributor to books, periodicals and journals. **Address:** University of Hertfordshire, College Ln., Hatfield, HF AL10 9AB, England. **Online address:** t.hitchcock@herts.ac.uk

HITCHENS, Peter Jonathan. British (born England), b. 1951. **Genres:** History, Politics/Government, Social Commentary, Theology/Religion. **Career:** Swindon Evening Advertiser, reporter, 1973-76; Coventry Evening Telegraph, journalist, 1976; Daily Express, labour, political and education reporter, deputy political editor, 1977-90, Moscow correspondent, 1990-92, Washington correspondent, 1993-95, assistant editor, 1995-2000, columnist, 1997-2000; Mail on Sunday, journalist, correspondent and columnist, 2001-. **Publications:** The Abolition of Britain: From Winston Churchill to Princess Diana, 2000; Monday Morning Blues, 2000; A Brief History of Crime: The Decline of Order, Justice and Liberty in England, 2003; The Broken Compass: How Left and Right Lost Their Meaning, 2009; The Rage Against God, 2010. **Address:** The Mail on Sunday, 2 Derry St., London, GL W8 5TS, England. **Online address:** peter.hitchens@mailonsunday.co.uk

HITCHINGS, Henry. British (born England), b. 1974. **Genres:** Novellas/Short Stories, Reference. **Career:** London Evening Standard, theatre critic, 2009-. Journalist. **Publications:** Dr. Johnson's Dictionary: The Extraordinary Story of the Book That Defined the World in US as Defining the World: The Extraordinary Story of Dr. Johnson's Dictionary, 2005; The Secret Life of Words: How English Became English, 2008; How to Really Talk About Books You Haven't Read, 2008; The Language Wars: A History of Proper English, 2011. Contributor to periodicals. **Address:** c/o Author Mail, John Murray Publishers, 338 Euston Rd., London, GL NW1 3BH, England.

HITCHINS, Keith. American (born United States), b. 1931. **Genres:** History, Language/Linguistics. **Career:** Wake Forest University, instructor in history, 1958-60, 1962-64, assistant professor, 1964-65; Rice University, assistant professor, 1965-67; University of Illinois, associate professor, 1967-69, professor of history, 1969-. Writer. **Publications:** The Rumanian National Movement in Transylvania, 1780-1849, 1969; Rumanian Studies, 1970, vol. II, 1971-72, vol. III, 1973-75, vol. IV, 1976-79, vol. V, 1980-86; Studien zur modernen Geschichte Transsilvaniens, 1971; Cultură i nationalitate în

Transilvania, 1972; The Nationality Problem in Austria-Hungary, 1974; (ed.) Studies in East European Social History, 1977; Orthodoxy and Nationality: Andreiu Saguna and the Rumanians of Transylvania, 1846-1873, 1977; Hungarica 1961-1974, 1981; Studies on Romanian National Consciousness, 1983; The Idea of Nation: The Romanians of Transylvania, 1691-1849, 1985; Constiinta nationala si actiune politica la Romanii din Transilvania, vol. I: (1700-1868), 1987, vol. II: (1868-1918), 1992; (ed.) Great Historians from Antiquity to 1800, 1989; (ed.) Great Historians of the Modern Age, 1991; (with I.N. Beju) Biserica Ortodaxă Română in secolul XVIII: conscripții, statistici, 1991; Rumania, 1866-1947, 1994; The Romanians, 1774-1866, 1996; Mit ș i realitate în istoriografia românească, 1997; A Nation Discovered: Romanian Intellectuals in Transylvania and the Idea of Nation, 1700-1848, 1999, 1999; A Nation Affirmed: The Romanian National Movement in Transylvania, 1860-1914, 1999; (with M. Milin) Relații româno-americane, 1859-1901: documente diplomatice ș i consulare, 2001; The Identity of Romania, 2009; (ed. with L. Stanciu and D. Dumitran) Despre Biserica romanilor din Transilvania. Documente externe (1744-1754), 2009; Ion I. C. Bratianu at the Paris Peace Conference, 1919, 2011. Contributor to periodicals. **Address:** Department of History, University of Illinois, 446-G Gregory Hall, 810 S Wright St., Urbana, IL 61801-3644, U.S.A. **Online address:** khitchin@illinois.edu

HITT, David. American (born United States), b. 1975. **Genres:** Air/Space Topics. **Career:** The Huntsville Times, graphic artist, 1991-92; The Enterprise-Tocsin, news editor and reporter, 1996-98, 1999-2002; Boone Newspapers Inc., editor and general manager, 1998-99; National Aeronautics and Space Administration (NASA), Marshall Space Flight Center, senior technical writer and editor, 2002-11; Face2Face Improv Inc., actor, 2006-. Journalist. **Publications:** (With O. Garriott and J. Kerwin) Homesteading Space: The Skylab Story, 2008. **Address:** University of Nebraska Press, 1111 Lincoln Mall, Lincoln, NE 68588-0630, U.S.A. **Online address:** dhitt@alltheseworlds.net

HITTINGER, Russell (F.). American (born United States), b. 1949. **Genres:** Philosophy, Theology/Religion. **Career:** Fordham University, assistant professor of philosophy, 1987-91; Pace University, adjunct professor, 1988-89; Princeton University, visiting assistant professor, 1988, 1989-91; New York University, visiting professor, 1990, lecturer, 1993; Catholic University of America, associate professor of philosophy, 1991-96, Columbus School of Law, adjunct faculty; American Enterprise Institute for Public Policy Research, adjunct research fellow, 1991-96; Yale University, lecturer, 1991; Pontifical University, visiting professor, 1991, 1994; Franklin J. Matchette Foundation, lecturer, 1992; American Public Philosophy Institute, director, 1992; Wabash College, Goodrich lecturer, 1992; Harvard University, lecturer, 1992; Mount Saint Mary's College, lecturer, 1993; Cornell University, lecturer, 1993; University of Notre Dame, lecturer, 1994; University of Tulsa, School of Law, research professor of law, 1996-, Department of Philosophy and Religion, Warren professor of Catholic studies, 1996-, William K. Warren chair of Catholic studies, 2002-05, research professor of law, faculty advisor; University of Notre Dame, Notre Dame Center for Ethics and Culture, senior research fellow, 2000-01; Università Regina Apostolorum, visiting professor, 2001, 2004; Warren Medical Research Center, director of ethics, 2004-; Emory University, Center for the Study of Law and Religion, senior fellow Christian jurisprudence, 2005-09; Catholic University of Ruzomberok, faculty of philosophy, visiting professor, 2005; Providence College, Robert J. Randall distinguished visiting professor in Christian culture, 2007-08. Writer. **Publications:** (Ed.) Linking the Human Life Issues, 1986; A Critique of the New Natural Law Theory, 1987; (ed. and intro.) Treatise on Law, 1994; The First Grace: Rediscovering the Natural Law in a Post-Christian World, 2003, 2nd ed., 2007; Thomas Aquinas and the Rule of Law, 2007. Contributor to journals. **Address:** Department of Philosophy and Religion, University of Tulsa, 205 Chapman Hall, 600 S College Ave., Tulsa, OK 74104-3189, U.S.A. **Online address:** francis-hittinger@utulsa.edu

HITZ, Frederick P(orter). American (born United States), b. 1939. **Genres:** Novels, History, Literary Criticism And History, Politics/Government. **Career:** University of Ife, Law Department, assistant lecturer, 1964-65; U.S. Department of State, foreign service officer, 1967-73, congressional relations officer, 1974-75; U.S. Department of Defense, deputy assistant secretary of legislative affairs, 1975-77; U.S. Department of Energy, director of congressional affairs, 1977-78; Central Intelligence Agency, legislative counsel, 1978-81, deputy director, 1980, inspector general, 1990-98; Schwabe, Williamson & Wyatt (law firm), partner, 1982-90; Princeton University, Woodrow Wilson School of Public and International Affairs, lecturer, 1998-2006;

University of Virginia, Department of Politics, visiting lecturer, 1998-, Frank Batten School of Leadership and Public Policy, visiting lecturer, 1998-, School of Law, lecturer, 2002-, Center for National Security Law, senior fellow, adjunct professor. Writer. **Publications:** The Great Game: The Myth and Reality of Espionage, 2004; Why Spy?: Espionage in an Age of Uncertainty, 2008. **Address:** School of Law, University of Virginia, Rm. 232 Cabell Hall, 580 Massie Rd., Charlottesville, VA 22903-1738, U.S.A. **Online address:** fph7w@virginia.edu

HIX, Simon. British (born England), b. 1968. **Genres:** Politics/Government. **Career:** Brunel University, lecturer in European politics, 1996-97; London School of Economics and Political Science, lecturer, 1997-2000, senior lecturer, 2000-01, reader in European Union politics and policy, 2001-04, professor of European and comparative politics, 2004-, Political Science and Political Economy research Group, director; Norwegian School of Management, external professor, 1999-2000; Wimbledon Park Primary School, governor; University of California, visiting professor, 2000-01; Stanford University, visiting professor, 2001; College of Europe, external professor, 2002-03; Institut d' Études Politiques, visiting professor, 2003; Hertie School of Governance, external professor, 2004-09; Korean Institute for International Economic Policy, visiting professor, 2005; Barcelona Institute of International Studies, visiting professor, 2008; Institute for Advanced Studies, visiting professor, 2009. Writer. **Publications:** (With C. Lord) Political Parties in the European Union, 1997; (with J. Niessen) Reconsidering European Migration Policies: The 1996 IGC and the Reform of the Maastricht Treaty, 1997; (with P. Dunleavy and H. Margetts) Counting on Europe: Proportional Representation and the June 1999 Elections to the EP, 1998; The Political System of the European Union, 1999; (ed. with K.H. Goetz) Europeanised Politics? European Integration and National Political Systems, 2001; (with U. Lesse) Shaping a Vision: A History of the Party of European Socialists 1957-2002, 2002; Linking National Politics to Europe, 2002; (with M. Marsh) Predicting the Future: The Next European Parliament, 2004; (with H. Jun) An East Asian Single Market? Lessons from the European Union, 2005; (with A.G. Noury and G. Roland) Democratic Politics in the European Parliament, 2007; What's Wrong with the European Union and How to Fix It, 2008. Contributor to books and journals. **Address:** Department of Government, London School of Economics and Political Science, Rm. CON.H307, London, GL WC2A 2AE, England. **Online address:** s.hix@lse.ac.uk

HJORTSBERG, William. American (born United States), b. 1941. **Genres:** Novels, Novellas/Short Stories, Plays/Screenplays. **Career:** Montana State University, Department of Media and Theatre Arts, adjunct professor. Writer. **Publications:** Alp, 1969; Gray Matters, 1971; Symbiography (novella), 1973; Toro! Toro! Toro!, 1974; Falling Angel, 1978; Tales and Fables (short stories), 1985; Nevermore, 1994; Odd Corners: The Slip-Stream World of William Hjortsberg, 2004. **Address:** c/o Ben Camardi, The Harold Matson Co., 276 5th Ave., Ste. 713, New York, NY 10001, U.S.A. **Online address:** contact@williamhjortsberg.com

HO, Minfong. American/Myanmar (born Myanmar), b. 1951. **Genres:** Young Adult Fiction, Children's Fiction, Novellas/Short Stories, Literary Criticism And History, Poetry. **Career:** Straits Times Newspaper, journalist, 1974-75; Chiengmai University, lecturer in English, 1975-76; Cornell University, teaching assistant in English literature, 1978-80; Catholic Relief Services, Thai-Cambodian Border, nutritionist and relief worker, 1980; Singapore University, writer-in-residence, 1983. **Publications:** FOR YOUNG ADULTS: FICTION: Sing to the Dawn, 1975; Rice without Rain, 1990; The Clay Marble, 1991. FOR CHILDREN: (with S. Ros) Two Brothers, 1995; (trans. and comp.) Maples in the Mist: Children's Poems from the Tang Dynasty, 1996; Hush!: A Thai Lullaby (poetry), 1996; (with S. Ros) Brother Rabbit: A Cambodian Tale, 1997; Stone Goddess, 2003; Peek!: A Thai Hide-and-Seek, 2004; Journeys: An Anthology of Short Stories, 2008. FOR ADULTS: Tanjong Rhuand Other Stories, 1986; Motherless Malik, forthcoming; Jataka Tales: A Selection of Buddha's Birth Stories, forthcoming; Surviving the Peace, forthcoming; Duty Free, forthcoming; Mosaic: An Anthology of Short Stories from Southeast Asia, forthcoming. OTHERS: (with S. Clark) Sing to the Dawn: The Musical, 1996. **Address:** c/o Tracey Adams, McIntosh and Otis Inc., 310 Madison Ave., New York, NY 10017, U.S.A. **Online address:** minfong@aol.com

HOAG, Tami. American (born United States), b. 1959. **Genres:** Mystery/Crime/Suspense, Novels. **Career:** Writer, 1987-. **Publications:** QUAID HORSES SERIES: Rumor Has It, 1988; Man of Her Dreams, 1989; Tempestuous, 1990. HENNESSY SERIES: The Trouble with J.J., 1988; Magic, 1990. RAINBOW CHASERS SERIES: Heart of Gold, 1990; Keeping Company, 1990; Reilly's Return, 1990. DOUCETTE SERIES: The Restless Heart, 1991; Lucky's Lady, 1992; Cry Wolf, 1993. DEER LAKE SERIES: Night Sins, 1995; Guilty As Sin, 1996. KOVAC/LISKA SERIES: Ashes to Ashes, 1999; Dust to Dust, 2000; Prior Bad Acts, 2006. ELENA ESTES SERIES: Dark Horse, 2002; The Alibi Man, 2007. NOVELS: McKnight in Shining Armor, 1988; Straight from the Heart, 1989; Mismatch, 1989; Sarah's Sin, 1991; Heart of Dixie, 1991; Last White Knight, 1992; Still Waters, 1992; Taken By Storm, 1992; Dark Paradise, 1994; A Thin Dark Line, 1997; Kill the Messenger, 2004; Person of Interest, 2008. DEEPER THAN THE DEAD SERIES: Deeper than the Dead, 2010; Secrets to the Grave, 2010; Down the Darkest Road, 2011. **Address:** c/o Andrea Cirillo, Jane Rotrosen Agency, 318 E 51st St., New York, NY 10022, U.S.A. **Online address:** tami@tamihoag.com

HOAGLAND, Edward. American (born United States), b. 1932. **Genres:** Novels, Novellas/Short Stories, Travel/Exploration, Autobiography/Memoirs, Essays, Photography, Biography. **Career:** Novelist and essayist, 1954-; New School for Social Research, instructor, 1963-64; Rutgers University, instructor, 1966; Sarah Lawrence College, faculty, 1967, 1971; City University of New York, instructor, 1967-68; University of Iowa, instructor, 1978, 1982; Columbia University, instructor, 1980-81; Bennington College, instructor, 1987-2002; Brown University, instructor, 1988; University of California, instructor, 1990, 1992; Beloit College, instructor, 1995. **Publications:** NOVELS: Cat Man, 1956; The Circle Home, 1960; The Peacock's Tail, 1965; Seven Rivers West, 1986. TRAVEL: Notes from the Century Before: A Journal from British Columbia, 1969; African Calliope: A Journey to the Sudan, 1979. ESSAYS: The Courage of Turtles: Fifteen Essays about Compassion, Pain, and Love Essays, 1970; The Moose on the Wall: Field Notes from the Vermont Wilderness, 1974; Red Wolves and Black Bears, 1976; The Tugman's Passage, 1982; Hearts Desire: The Best of Edward Hoagland: Essays from Twenty Years, 1988; Balancing Acts: Essays, 1992; Tigers & Ice: Reflections on Nature and Life, 1999; Compass Points: How I Lived, 2001; Hoagland on Nature: Essays, 2003; Early in the Season, 2008. OTHERS: Walking the Dead Diamond River, 1973; (ed. and intro.) The Edward Hoagland Reader, 1979, (ed.) The Penguin Nature Library, 29 vols., 1985-2002; (ed. with R. Atwan) The Best American Essays 1999, 1999; (contrib.) Step Right this Way: The Photographs of Edward J. Kelty, 2002. STORIES: City Tales, 1986; The Final Fate of the Alligators, 1992; Sex and the River Styx, 2011. Contributor to periodicals. **Address:** PO Box 51, Barton, VT 05822-0051, U.S.A.

HOAR, Jere (Richmond). American (born United States), b. 1929. **Genres:** Novels, Novellas/Short Stories, Communications/Media, Writing/Journalism, Mystery/Crime/Suspense. **Career:** Troy Messenger, reporter, 1947-49; Oxford Eagle, news editor, 1953-54; Journal of Southern Commerce, news editor, 1953-54; Iowa Publication Magazine, editor, 1954-56; University of Mississippi, assistant professor, 1956-59, associate professor, 1959-67, professor of journalism, 1967-86, professor emeritus, 1986-; Freeland and Gafford Law Office, preceptorship in law, 1966-67, 1969-71. **Publications:** OTHER: Drama was a Weapon: The Left-Wing Theatre in New York, 1929-1941, 1963. SHORT STORIES: Body Parts, 1997. NOVELS: The Hit, 2002. Contributor of articles to magazines and periodicals. Works appear in anthologies. **Address:** c/o Author Mail, University Press of Mississippi, 3825 Ridgewood Rd., Jackson, MS 39211-6492, U.S.A. **Online address:** jrhoar@watervalley.net

HOARE, Philip. British (born England), b. 1958. **Genres:** Art/Art History, History, Literary Criticism And History, Biography. **Career:** Roughtrade Records, buyer and designer; Operation Twilight, owner and manager; Max Rock Grove, co-manager; Virgin Records Ltd., retail buyer; University of Plymouth, The Marine Institute, artist-in-residence. Writer. **Publications:** Serious Pleasures: The Life of Stephen Tennant, 1990; Noël Coward: A Biography, 1995; (ed.) The Sayings of Noël Coward, 1997; Wilde's Last Stand: Decadence, Conspiracy and the First World War, 1998; Oscar Wilde's Last Stand: Decadence, Conspiracy and the Most Outrageous Trial of the Century, 1998; (contrib.) Icons of Pop, 1999; Spike Island: The Memory of a Military Hospital, 2001; England's Lost Eden: Adventures in a Victorian Utopia, 2005; (with C. Heath) Pet Shop Boys, Catalogue, 2006; (contrib.) David Austen, 2007; Leviathan, or, The Whale, 2009; Whale, 2010; (with J. Millar) Tania Kovats, 2010. Contributor to periodicals. **Address:** c/o Gillon Aitken, Aitken Alexander Associates, 18-21 Cavaye Pl., London, GL SW10 9PT, England.

HOBAN, Russell. *See* Obituaries.

HOBBET, Anastasia. American (born United States), b. 1954. **Genres:** Novels. **Career:** Writer and freelance journalist. **Publications:** Pleasure of Believing (novel), 1997; Small Kingdoms (novel), 2010. **Address:** CA , U.S.A. **Online address:** anastasiahobbet@gmail.com

HOBBS, Anne Stevenson. British (born England), b. 1942. **Genres:** Art/Art History, Adult Non-fiction, Natural History, Language/Linguistics. **Career:** British Museum, curator, 1964-66; Victoria and Albert Museum's National Art Library, curator, 1966-90, curator of special collections, 1966-90; Frederick Warne curator of children's literature, 1990-; violinist; pianist. Writer. **Publications:** (Ed. with J.I. Whalley) Beatrix Potter, the V and A Collection: The Leslie Linder Bequest of Beatrix Potter Material, 1985; (ed.) Fables: Five Hundred Years of Illustration and Text, 1986; (co-ed.) Beatrix Potter, 1866-1943: The Artist and Her World, 1987; Beatrix Potter's Art, 1990; (trans.) Naissance de Pierre Lapin, 1992; (with E. Jay and M. Noble) A Victorian Naturalist: Beatrix Potter's Drawings from the Armitt Collection, 1992; The Linder Collection of the Works and Drawings of Beatrix Potter, 1996; (intro.) Les Champignons, 1996; (contrib.) The Beatrix Potter Collection of Lloyd Cotsen: Published on the Occasion of His 75th Birthday, 2004. Contributor to newsletters. **Address:** Archive of Art & Design, Victoria & Albert Museum, 23 Blythe Rd., London, GL WI4 0QF, England.

HOBBS, Dick. British (born England), b. 1951. **Genres:** Business/Trade/Industry, Economics, Criminology/True Crime. **Career:** Durham University, instructor, 1990-2005; London School of Economics, professor of sociology, head of sociology department, 2005-; University of Oxford, Center for Criminal Research, resident fellow; Polytechnic of Central London, instructor. Writer. **Publications:** Keeping Our Home Warm, 1985; Doing the Business: Entrepreneurship, the Working Class, and Detectives in the East End of London, 1988; Bad Business: Professional Crime in Modern Britain, 1995; Policing Matters: Policing Changes, 1996; Bouncers: Violence and Governance in the Night-Time Economy, 2003. EDITOR: (with T. May) Interpreting the Field: Accounts of Ethnography, 1993; Professional Criminals, 1995; (with R. Wright) The Sage Handbook of Fieldwork, 2006; (with R. Hornsby) Gun Crime, 2008; (ed. with D. Downes and T. Newburn) Eternal Recurrence of Crime and Control: Essays in Honour of Paul Rock, 2010; (ed.) Ethnography in Context, 2011. Contributor to books, periodicals and journals. **Address:** London School of Economics and Political Science, Houghton St., London, GL WC2A 2AE, England. **Online address:** r.hobbs@lse.ac.uk

HOBBS, Valerie. American (born United States), b. 1941. **Genres:** Children's Fiction, Young Adult Fiction, Young Adult Fiction, Novels. **Career:** English teacher, 1971-74; University of California, lecturer in writing, 1981-2001, emeritus lecturer in writing program, 2001-. Writer. **Publications:** How Far Would You Have Gotten If I Hadn't Called You Back?, 1995; Get It While It's Hot-Or Not, 1996; Tender, 2001; Sonny's War, 2002; Stefan's Story, 2003; Letting Go of Bobby James Or How I Found Myself of Steam, 2004; Defiance, 2005; Call it a Gift, 2005; Sheep, 2006; Anything but Ordinary, 2007; Lucy in the Sky, 2010; Minnie McClary Speaks Her Mind, 2012. CHILDREN'S FICTION: Carolina Crow Girl, 1999; Charlie's Run, 2000; The Last Best Days Of Summer, 2010; Maggie and Oliver or A Bone of One's Own, 2011. Works appear in anthologies. Contributor to periodicals and magazines. **Address:** Barbara Markowitz, 117 N Mansfield Ave., Los Angeles, CA 90036, U.S.A. **Online address:** valhobbs@cox.net

HOBBY, Elaine (Ann). British (born England), b. 1956. **Genres:** Literary Criticism And History, Medicine/Health, Women's Studies And Issues, Autobiography/Memoirs. **Career:** Workers' Education Association, part-time tutor in women's studies, 1980-81; Princeton University, Harkness fellow, 1981-83; Huntington Library, Harkness fellow, 1981-83; Waltham Forest Women's Centre, director, 1983-85; Cambridgeshire College of Arts and Technology, lecturer in English and general studies, 1985-87; Cambridge Women's Resources Centre, part-time tutor in English and women's studies, 1987-88; Loughborough University, professor of seventeenth-century studies, 1988-, head, 2006-. Writer. **Publications:** Virtue of Necessity: English Women's Writing, 1649-1688, 1988. EDITOR: (co-ed.) Her Own Life: Autobiographical Writings by Seventeenth-Century Women, 1989; (with C. White) What Lesbians Do in Books, 1991; The Midwives Book, 1999; The Birth of Mankind, 2008. Contributor of articles to periodicals. **Address:** Department of English & Drama, Loughborough University, Rm. NN 0.10, Martin Hall Bldg., East Pk., Loughborough, LE LE11 3TU, England. **Online address:** e.a.hobby@lboro.ac.uk

HOBERMAN, Mary Ann. American (born United States), b. 1930. **Genres:** Children's Fiction, Poetry. **Career:** Writer, 1955-; The Pocket People (children's theater group), founder, 1968-75; Fairfield University, adjunct professor, 1980-83; C.G. Jung Center, program coordinator, 1981. **Publications:** CHILDREN'S BOOKS: All My Shoes Come in Two's, 1957; How Do I Go?, 1958; Hello and Good-by, 1959; What Jim Knew, 1963; Not Enough Beds for the Babies, 1965; A Little Book of Little Beasts, 1973; The Looking Book, 1973, rev. ed., 2002; The Raucous Auk, 1973; Nuts to You and Nuts to Me, 1974; I Like Old Clothes, 1976; Bugs, 1976; A House is a House for Me, 1978; Yellow Butter, Purple Jelly, Red Jam, Black Bread: Poems, 1981; The Cozy Book, 1982, rev. ed., 1995; Mr. and Mrs. Muddle, 1988; A Fine Fat Pig, and Other Animal Poems, 1991; Fathers, Mothers, Sisters, Brothers: A Collection of Family Poems, 1991; The Cozy Book, 1995; One of Each, 1997; The Seven Silly Eaters, 1997; The Llama Who Had No Pajama, 1998; Miss Mary Mack: A Hand-Clapping Rhyme, 1998; And to Think That We Thought We Would Never Be Friends, 1999; The Marvelous Mouse Man, 1999; The Eensy Weensy Spider, 2000; The Two Sillies, 2000; Michael Finnegan, 2001; There Once Was a Man Named Michael Finnegan, 2001; It's Simple, Said Simon, 2001; You Read to Me, I'll Read to You: Very Short Stories to Read Together, 2001; (with N.B. Westcott) Sing-along Songs, 2001; Bill Grogan's Goat, 2002; The Marvelous Mouse Man, 2002; Right outside My Window, 2002; (contrib.) Mary Had a Little Lamb, 2003; You Read to Me, I'll Read to You: Very Short Fairy Tales to Read Together, 2004; Whose Garden Is It?, 2004; Yankee Doodle, 2004; (with N.B. Westcott) Sing-along Stories 3: More Favorite Songs to Sing Together, 2005; You Read to Me, I'll Read to You: Very Short Mother Goose Tales to Read Together, 2005; I'm Going to Grandma's, 2007; Mrs. O'Leary's Cow, 2007; You Read to Me, I'll Read to You: Very Short Scary Tales to Read Together, 2007; Strawberry Hill, 2009; All Kinds of Families, 2009. EDITOR: My Song Is Beautiful: Poems and Pictures in Many Voices, 1994; I Know an Old Lady Who Swallowed a Fly, 2004; (with L. Winston) The Tree That Time Built: A Celebration of Nature, Science, and Imagination, 2009. Contributor to periodicals. **Address:** Gina Maccoby Literary Agency, PO Box 60, Chappaqua, NY 10514-0060, U.S.A. **Online address:** mahoberm@optonline.net

HOBHOUSE, Hermione. British (born England), b. 1934. **Genres:** Architecture, Biography, History. **Career:** Associated-Rediffusion Television, researcher and scriptwriter, 1956-58; Granada Television, researcher and scriptwriter, 1958-63; Architectural Association School, faculty, 1973-78; Survey of London, general editor, 1983-94, retired, 1994. Architectural historian and reviewer. **Publications:** The Ward of Cheap in the City of London: A Short History, 1958; (with C.G. Trust) A Regency Survival in Clapham, 1967; Thomas Cubitt: Master Builder, 1971, 2nd ed., 1995; Lost London: A Century of Demolition and Decay, 1971 in US as Lost London, 1972; History of Regent Street, 1975, rev. ed., 2008; (with R. Gloucester) Oxford & Cambridge, 1980; Prince Albert: His Life and Work, 1983; (ed.) Survey of London, vol. XLII: Southern Kensington, 1986; (ed. with A. Saunders) Good and Proper Materials: The Fabric of London Since the Great Fire: Papers Given at a Conference Organised by the Survey of London at the Society of Antiquaries on 21 October 1988, 1989; Survey of London Monograph 17, 1991; (ed.) Survey of London, vol. XLIII-XLIV: Poplar, Blackwater & The Isle of Dogs, 1994; London Survey'd: The Work of the Survey of London, 1894-1994, 1994; (with Galletti) Gärten in Italien, 1999; The Crystal Palace and the Great Exhibition: Art, Science, and Productive Industry: A History of the Royal Commission for the Exhibition of 1851, 2001. **Address:** Westcombe Stables, Westcombe, Evercreech, Shepton Mallet, SM BA4 6ES, England.

HOBSBAWM, Eric (John Ernest). (Francis Newton). British/Egyptian (born Egypt), b. 1917. **Genres:** History, Music, Adult Non-fiction, Essays, Politics/Government. **Career:** University of London, Birkbeck College, lecturer in history, 1947-59, reader in history, 1959-70, professor of economic and social history, 1971-82, professor emeritus, 1982-, president; Cambridge University, King's College, fellow in history, 1949-55, honorary fellow, 1973-; Stanford University, visiting professor, 1960; Massachusetts Institute of Technology, visiting professor, 1967; British Academy, professor, 1970; Universidad Nacional Autonoma de Mexico, visiting professor, 1971; Cornell University, Andrew D. White professor-at-large, 1976-82; New School for Social Research, visiting professor, 1984-97, university professor of politics and society, 1984-98, university professor emeritus and senior lecturer, 1989-. Writer. **Publications:** (Ed.) Labour's Turning Point, 1880-1900: Extracts from Contemporary Sources, 1948, 2nd ed., 1974; (as Francis Newton) The Jazz Scene, 1959, rev. ed., 1993; Social Bandits and Primitive Rebels in UK as Primitive Rebels: Studies in Archaic Forms of Social Movement in the 19th and 20th Centuries, 1960, 3rd ed., 1971; The Age of Revolution, 1789-1848, 1962; Labouring Men: Studies in the History of Labour, 1964, 2nd ed., 1965; (ed. and intro.) Pre-capitalist Economic Formations, 1964; Takufat ha-mahapekhah, 1965; Sociologie du Jazz, 1966; Industry and Empire: The Making of Modern English Society in UK as Industry and Empire: An Economic History of Britain since 1750, 1968, rev. ed., 1999; (with G.F.E. Rudé) Captain Swing: A Social History of the Great English Uprising, 1968; Industrie und Empire. Britische Wirtschaftsgeschichte seit 1750, 1969; Bandits, 1969; Convención, un Caso de neofeudalismo, 1970; En Torno a los Origenes dela Revolucion Industrial, 1971; (contrib.) Historical Studies Today, 1972; Revolutionaries: Contemporary Essays, 1973; Crisis & the Outlook, 1975; The Age of Capital, 1848-1875, 1975, rev. ed., 1996; Giorgio Napolitano: Intervista sul PCI, 1976; La Politique du Parti Communiste Italien: Entretien Avec Eric J. Hobsbawm, 1976; The Italian Road to Socialism: An Interview, 1977; Pensamiento Revolucionario de Gramsci, 1978; Revolución Industrial y Revuelta Agraria: El Capitán Swing, 1978; (ed.) Peasants in History: Essays in Honour of Daniel Thorner, 1980; (co-author) The Forward March of Labour Halted?, 1981; (intro.) Communist Cartoons: Cartoons from The Communist, 1921-1922, 1982; Culture, Ideology and Politics: Essays for Eric Hobsbawm, 1982; (ed.) History of Marxism, 1982; (ed.) Marxism in Marx's Day, 1982; (ed. with T. Ranger) The Invention of Tradition, 1983; Workers: Worlds of Labour in UK as Worlds of Labour: Further Studies in the History of Labour, 1984; (contrib.) The Power of the Past: Essays for Eric Hobsbawm, 1984; The Age of Empire, 1875-1914, 1987; Politics for a Rational Left: Political Writing, 1977-1988 (essays), 1989; Echoes of the Marseillaise: Two Centuries Look Back on the French Revolution, 1990; Nations and Nationalism Since 1780: Programme, Myth, Reality, 1990, 2nd ed., 1992; The Age of Extremes: The Short Twentieth Century, 1914-1991, 1994; The Age of Extremes: A History of the World, 1914-1991, 1994; Age of Extremes: The Short Twentieth Century, 1914-1991, 1994; (intro.) The Condition of the Working Class in England: From Personal Observation and Authentic Sources, 1994; On History, 1997; Uncommon People: Resistance, Rebellion and Jazz, 1998; (intro.) The Communist Manifesto: A Modern Edition, 1998; (with M. Weitzmann) 1968, Magnum dans le Monde, 1998; Behind the Times: The Decline and Fall of the Twentieth-Century Avant-Gardes, 1999; The New Century, 1999; Historien Engagé, 2000; On the Edge of the New Century, 2000; Interesting Times: A Twentieth-Century Life, 2002; (contrib.) Shi xue jia, 2002; Optimisme de la Volonté: d'un Siècle à l'autre, 2003; Nationen und Nationalismus: Mythos und Realität seit 1780, 2005; Globalisation, Democracy and Terrorism, 2007; On Empire: America, War, and Global Supremacy, 2008; (intro.) Antonio Gramsci, 2010; How to Change the World, 2011. Contributor to periodicals. **Address:** Department of History, Classics and Archaeology, Birkbeck College, University of London, Rm. G02, 30 Russell Sq., London, GL WC1B 5DQ, England.

HOBSON, Anthony Robert Alwyn. Also writes as A. R. A. Hobson. Welsh/British (born England), b. 1921. **Genres:** History, Librarianship, Reference. **Career:** Sotheby and Co., director, 1949-71, associate, 1971-77; University of Cambridge, Sandars reader in bibliography, 1973-74; Pierpont Morgan Library, Franklin Jasper Walls lecturer, 1979; University of Pennsylvania, Rosenbach fellow, 1990; University of Oxford, Lyell reader in bibliography, 1990-91; British Academy, fellow, 1992-. Writer. **Publications:** French and Italian Collectors and Their Bindings, 1953; Great Libraries, 1970; Apollo and Pegasus: An Enquiry into the Formation and Dispersal of a Renaissance Library, 1975; Cyril Connolly as a Book Collector, 1983; Humanists and Bookbinders: The Origins and Diffusion of the Humanistic Bookbinding 1459-1559, with a Census of Historiated Plaquette and Medallion Bindings of the Renaissance, 1989; (with P. Culet) Italian and French 16th Century Bookbindings, 1991; Bookbinding & Other Bibliophily, 1994; Legature bolognesi del Rinascimento, 1998; Renaissance Book Collecting: Jean Grolier and Diego Hurtado, Their Books and Bindings, 1999; (ed.) Ronald Firbank, Letters to His Mother 1920-1924, 2001; (ed.) Actes et Communications, 2002; (ed.) Association Internationale de Bibliophilie, XIXe Congrès, Prague, 1995: Actes et Communications, 2003; (ed. with C. de Hamel) Bartolomeo Sanvito: The Life & Work of a Renaissance Scribe, 2009. **Address:** The Glebe House, Whitsbury, Fordingbridge, HM SP6 3QB, England.

HOBSON, A. R. A. See HOBSON, Anthony Robert Alwyn.

HOBSON, Fred Colby. American (born United States), b. 1943. **Genres:** Literary Criticism And History, Social Commentary, Adult Non-fiction, Essays. **Career:** Journal and Sentinel, editorial writer, 1969-70; University of Alabama, assistant professor, 1972-75, associate professor, 1975-80, professor of English, 1980-86; University of Hull, visiting professor, 1982; Louisiana State University, professor of English, 1986-89, Fleming lecturer, 1998, The Southern Review, co-editor, 1986-89; University of Mississippi, Ford Foundation, Center for Southern Studies, lecturer, 1988; University of North Carolina at Chapel Hill, professor of English, 1989-, Southern Literary Journal, co-editor, 1989-, Institute for the Arts and Humanities, fellow, 1991, Lineberger professor in the humanities, 1997-; Mercer University, Lamar Memorial lecturer, 1989. **Publications:** Serpent in Eden: H.L. Mencken and the South, 1974; Southern Mythmaking: The Savage and the Ideal, 1978; Tell about the South: The Southern Rage to Explain, 1983; The Southern Writer in the Postmodern World, 1991; Mencken: A Life, 1994; But Now I See: The White Southern Racial Conversion Narrative, 1999; The Silencing of Emily Mullen and Other Essays, 2005; Off the Rim: Basketball and Other Religions in a Carolina Childhood, 2006; A Southern Enigma, 2008; The Savage South, forthcoming. EDITOR: (with R.F. Bogardus) Literature at the Barricades: The American Writer in the 1930's, 1982; (and intro.) South-Watching: Selected Essays of Gerald W. Johnson, 1983; (with V. Fitzpatrick and B. Jacobs) Thirty-Five Years of Newspaper Work, H.L. Mencken's, 1994; The Literature of the American South: A Norton Anthology, 1997; South to the Future: An American Region in the Twenty-First Century, 2002; William Faulkner's Absalom, Absalom!: A Casebook, 2003. **Address:** Department of English, University of North Carolina, Greenlaw Hall, CB, Ste. 3520, Chapel Hill, NC 27599-3520, U.S.A. **Online address:** fhobson@email.unc.edu

HOBSON, J(ohn) Allan. American (born United States), b. 1933. **Genres:** Psychiatry, Bibliography, Psychology, Autobiography/Memoirs. **Career:** Bellevue Hospital, intern-in-medicine, 1959-60; Massachusetts Mental Health Center, resident in psychiatry, 1960-61, 1964-66, senior psychiatrist, 1965-67, director of laboratory of neurophysiology, 1967, principal psychiatrist, 1967-, director of group psychotherapy training program, 1972-80; National Institute of Mental Health, clinical associate, 1961-63; University of Lyon, National Institute of Mental Health, special fellow, 1963-64; Harvard Medical School, research associate in physiology department, 1964-67, instructor in psychiatry, 1966-67, associate in psychiatry, 1967-69, assistant professor, 1969-74, associate professor, 1974-78, professor of psychiatry, 1978-, now professor emeritus of psychiatry, Beth Israel Deaconess Medical Center, Department of Psychiatry, professor; Brown University, lecturer in psychiatry, 1972-74, director of behavioral science teaching program, 1980-86; University of Bordeaux, visiting scientist and lecturer, 1973; University of Edinburgh, Sandoz Lecturer, 1975; Italian National Health Research Institute, lecturer, 1978; Universita degli Studi, Istituto di Psicologia, visiting professor, 1983; University of Messina, visiting professor, 1992. Writer. **Publications:** (With R.W. McCarley) Neuronal Activity in Sleep: An Annotated Bibliography, 1971, 2nd ed., 1977; (ed. with M.A.B. Brazier) The Reticular Formation Revisited, 1980; States of Brain Mind, 1988; The Dreaming Brain, 1988; (ed. and intro.) States of Brain and Mind, 1988; (ed. and intro.) Abnormal States of Brain and Mind, 1989; Sleep, 1989; Sleep and Dreams, 1992; The Chemistry of Conscious States: How the Brain Changes Its Mind, 1994; Dreaming as Delirium: How the Brain Goes out of Its Mind, 1999; (contrib.) States of Mind: New Discoveries about How Our Brains Make Us Who We Are, 1999; Consciousness, 1999; The Dream Drug Store: Chemically Altered States of Consciousness, 2001; Dream Drugstore: Chemically Altered States of Consciousness, 2001; (with J.A. Leonard) Out of Its Mind: Psychiatry in Crisis: A Call for Reform, 2002; Dreaming: An Introduction to the Science of Sleep, 2002; 13 Dreams Freud Never Had: The New Mind Science, 2005; Dreaming: A Very Short Introduction, 2005; Dream Life: An Experimental Memoir, 2011. Contributor to books. **Address:** Division of Sleep Medicine, Harvard Medical School, 401 Park Dr., 2nd Fl. E, Boston, MA 02215, U.S.A. **Online address:** allan_hobson@hms.harvard.edu

HOBSON, John M. British (born England), b. 1962. **Genres:** Business/Trade/Industry, Economics. **Career:** La Trobe University, instructor, 1991-97; University of Sydney, instructor, 1997-2004; University of Sheffield, reader, 2004, professor of politics and international relations. Writer. **Publications:** (With L. Weiss) States and Economic Development: A Comparative Historical Analysis, 1995; The Wealth of States: A Comparative Sociology of International Economic and Political Change, 1997; The State and International Relations, 2000; (ed. with S. Hobden) Historical Sociology of International Relations, 2002; The Eastern Origins of Western Civilisation, 2004, 8th ed., 2009; (ed. with L. Seabrooke) Everyday Politics of the World Economy, 2007; Selected Writings of John A. Hobson 1932-1938: The Struggle for the International Mind, 2011; The Eurocentric Conception of World Politics, 2012. CONTRIBUTOR: Anatomy of Power: Essays on the Work

of Michael Mann, 2006; Europe and Asia: Towards a New Cosmopolitanism, 2006; Writing Civilizations, 2008. Contributor to books and journals. **Address:** Department of Politics, University of Sheffield, 1.32 Elmsfield, Northumberland Rd., Sheffield, SY S10 2TU, England. **Online address:** j.m.hobson@sheffield.ac.uk

HOCHMAN, Elaine S(chwartz). American (born United States) **Genres:** Architecture, Photography. **Career:** Metropolitan Museum of Art, staff member, 1957-58; New School for Social Research, faculty, 1969-; New York City Real Estate Developers, architectural consultant, 1970-; Art Ventures International Inc., president, 1985-. Writer. **Publications:** Architects of Fortune: Mies van der Rohe and the Third Reich, 1989; Architects of Fortune: Mies van der Rohe and the Third Reich, 1990; Bauhaus: Crucible of Modernism, 1997; La Bauhaus Crisol De La Modernidad, 2002. Contributor of essays to journals. **Address:** Fromm Intl., 1919 Stanley St., Northbrook, IL 60062, U.S.A.

HOCHMAN, Gloria. American (born United States), b. 1943. **Genres:** Adult Non-fiction. **Career:** National Adoption Center, director of communications and marketing, 1977-. Writer. **Publications:** Heart Bypass: What Every Patient Must Know, 1982; (with E.W. Beal) Adult Children of Divorce: Breaking the Cycle and Finding Fulfillment in Love, Marriage, and Family, 1991; (with P. Duke) A Brilliant Madness: Living with Manic-Depressive Illness, 1992. Contributor to periodicals. **Address:** National Adoption Center, 1500 Walnut St., Ste. 701, Philadelphia, PA 19102, U.S.A. **Online address:** ghochman@adopt.org

HOCHMAN, Jiri. Czech (born Czech Republic), b. 1926. **Genres:** Novels, History, Politics/Government, Autobiography/Memoirs. **Career:** Ohio State University, associate professor of journalism, 1974-78, professor emeritus, 1984-. Writer and editor. **Publications:** European Crossroads, 1957; Spain Twenty Years Later, 1959; Cuban Diary, 1961; Algerian Report, 1964; Deer Creek (novel), 1970, 3rd ed., 1992; Chronicle of Regentship in Bohemia, 1972, 2nd ed., 1991; Letters from Prison, 1973; Boehmisches Happening, 1977; The Other Way Round, 1980; The Soviet Union and the Failure of Collective Security, 1934-38, 1985; (with A. Dubcek) Hope Dies Last: Dubcek by Dubcek (autobiography), 1993; Historical Dictionary of the Czech State, 1998, 2nd ed., 2010. **Address:** School of Communication, Ohio State University, 103 Putter Dr., Palm Coast, FL 32164, U.S.A. **Online address:** jirhoch@pcfl.net

HOCK, Randolph. American (born United States), b. 1944. **Genres:** Information Science/Computers, Travel/Exploration, Reference. **Career:** Massachusetts Institute of Technology, chemistry librarian, 1971-73; DIALOG Information Services, representative, 1972-82, regional director, 1982-92; University of Pennsylvania, data services librarian, 1973-74; Knight-Ridder Information Services, regional director, 1992-96; Online Strategies, founder and principal, 1996-. Writer. **Publications:** The Extreme Searchers Guide to Web Search Engines: A Handbook for the Serious Searcher, 1999, 2nd ed., 2001; The Extreme Searchers Internet Handbook: A Guide for the Serious Searcher, 2004, 3rd ed., 2010; Yahoo! to the Max: An Extreme Searcher Guide, 2005; Traveler's Web: An Extreme Searcher Guide to Travel Resources on the Internet, 2007. **Address:** Online Strategies, 9919 Corsica St., Vienna, VA 22181, U.S.A. **Online address:** ran@onstrat.com

HOCKENBERRY, John. American (born United States), b. 1956. **Genres:** Documentaries/Reportage, Sciences, Mystery/Crime/Suspense. **Career:** Massachusetts Institute of Technology, Media Lab, distinguished fellow; National Public Radio, stringer, 1980-81; National Broadcasting Co., correspondent, 1996. **Publications:** Moving Violations: War Zones, Wheelchairs and Declarations of Independence, 1995; A River Out of Eden: A Novel, 2001. Contributor to periodicals. **Address:** Watkins Loomis Agency, PO Box 20925, New York, NY 10025, U.S.A. **Online address:** john.hockenberry@nbc.com

HOCKENSMITH, Sean M. American (born United States), b. 1972. **Genres:** Self Help, Philosophy, inspirational/Motivational Literature, Sports/Fitness. **Career:** Dynamic Life Publishing, owner. Writer. **Publications:** Smashing the Wall of Fear: Dynamic Strategies to Overcome the Obstacles in Your Life, 1997; Getting into the Zone, forthcoming. **Address:** Dynamic Life Publishing, 3310 Graham Ave., Windber, PA 15963-2537, U.S.A. **Online address:** sean@seanhockensmith.com

HOCKENSMITH, Steve. American (born United States), b. 1968. **Genres:** Novels, Young Adult Fiction. **Career:** Journalist, magazine editor. **Publications:** Holmes on the Range, 2006; On the Wrong Track, 2007; Black Dove, 2008; Crack in the Lens, 2009; Pride and Prejudice and Zombies: Dawn of the Dreadfuls, 2010; Pride and Prejudice and Zombies: Dreadfully Ever After, 2011; World's Greatest Sleuth!: A Holmes on the Range Mystery, 2011. Contributor to periodicals. **Address:** Elyse Cheney, Elyse Cheney Literary Associates, 156 5th Ave., Ste. 1134, New York, NY 10010, U.S.A. **Online address:** mrcineshock@yahoo.com

HOCKING, Mary (Eunice). British (born England), b. 1921. **Genres:** Novels, History, Young Adult Fiction, Horror. **Career:** Local government officer, 1946-70. Writer. **Publications:** NOVELS: The Winter City, 1961; Visitors to the Crescent, 1962; The Sparrow, 1964; The Young Spaniard, 1965; Ask No Question, 1967; A Time of War, 1968; Checkmate, 1969; The Hopeful Traveller, 1970; The Climbing Frame, 1971; Family Circle, 1972; Daniel Come to Judgement, 1974; The Bright Day, 1975; The Mind Has Mountains, 1976; Look Stranger!, 1979; He Who Plays the King, 1980; March House, 1981; Good Daughters (first novel in trilogy), 1984; Indifferent Heroes (second novel in trilogy), 1985; Welcome Strangers (third novel in trilogy), 1986; An Irrelevant Woman, 1987; A Particular Place, 1989; Letters from Constance, 1991; The Very Dead of Winter, 1993; The Meeting Place, 1996. **Address:** 3 Church Row, Lewes, ES BN7 2PU, England.

HOCKNEY, David. American/British (born England), b. 1937. **Genres:** Design, Photography, Art/Art History, Illustrations. **Career:** Maidstone College of Art, instructor, 1962; University of Iowa, lecturer, 1964; University of Colorado, lecturer, 1965; University of California-Los Angeles, lecturer, 1966-67, honorary chair of drawing, 1980; University of California-Berkeley, lecturer, 1966-67. Writer. **Publications:** Six Fairy Tales From the Brothers Grimm With Original Etchings, 1970; Paintings, Prints, and Drawings, 1960-1970; David Hockney, 1976; The Blue Guitar, 1977; Travels with Pen, Pencil and Ink, 1978; Paper Pools, 1980; David Hockney: Looking at Pictures in a Book, 1981; (with S. Spender) China Diary, 1982; Cameraworks, 1984; Martha's Vineyard: My Third Sketchbook from the Summer of 1982, 1985; Hockney on Photography: Conversations with Paul Joyce, 1988; Picasso, 1990; That's the Way I See It, 1993; Grimms' Fairy Tales, 1993; David Hockney's Dog Days, 1998; (foreword) Brandt: The Photography of Bill Brandt, 1999; Secret Knowledge: Rediscovering the Lost Techniques of the Old Masters, 2001, new ed., 2006; Egyptian Journeys, 2002; (comp.) Hockney's Pictures, 2004; Hockney on Art, 2008. AUTHOR OF INTRODUCTION: Draw: How to Master the Art, 1994; Making It New: Collected Essays and Writings of Henry Geldzahler, 1994; Icons and Legends: The Photography of Michael Childers, 2003. COLLECTIONS: 72 Drawings Chosen by the Artist, 1971; 18 Portraits, 1977; David Hockney Prints, 1954-77, 1979; Pictures, 1979; David Hockney, 23 Lithographs, 1980; David Hockney Photographs, 1982; Hockney's Photographs, 1982; Kasmin's Hockneys: 45 Drawings, 1983; David Hockney in America, 1983; Hockney Posters, 1983; David Hockney: Graphics, 1992; Off the Wall, 1994 in US as David Hockney: Poster Art, 1995. Illustrator of books by others. **Address:** 7508 Santa Monica Blvd., West Hollywood, CA 90046-6407, U.S.A. **Online address:** info@davidhockney.com

HODDINOTT, R(alph) F(ield). British (born England), b. 1913. **Genres:** Archaeology/Antiquities, Architecture, Art/Art History, History, Anthropology/Ethnology, Cultural/Ethnic Topics, Social Sciences. **Career:** British Council, lecturer in and teacher of English, 1939-41; United Nations Relief and Rehabilitation Administration, chief public relations officer, 1945-47, International Refugee Organization, public information officer, 1947-52; Central Office of Information, staff, 1967-. Writer. **Publications:** Early Byzantine Churches in Macedonia and Southern Serbia: A Study of Origins and the Initial Development of East Christian Art, 1963; Bulgaria Antiquity: An Archaeological Introduction, 1975; The Thracians, 1981; (with A. Fol and B. Nikolov) The New Thracian Treasure from Rogozen, Bulgaria, 1986; (contrib.) The Rogozen Treasure, 1987; (co-author) APMOE (Thessalonica), 1992. **Address:** 11 Sydney House, Woodstock Rd., Chiswick, London, GL W4 1DP, England.

HODEL, Steve. American (born United States), b. 1941?. **Genres:** Mystery/Crime/Suspense, Adult Non-fiction. **Career:** Los Angeles Police Department, police officer to Detective II, 1963-83, senior field homicide detective, 1983-, Detective III, through 1986; Hodel Investigations, founder, 1986-. Writer. **Publications:** Black Dahlia Avenger: A Genius for Murder, 2003, rev. ed., 2006; (with R. Pezzullo) Most Evil: Avenger, Zodiac and the Fur-

ther Serial Murders of Dr. George Hill Hodel, 2009. **Address:** 12400 Ventura Blvd., PO Box 378, Studio City, CA 91604, U.S.A. **Online address:** skh@stevehodel.com

HODES, Martha. American (born United States) **Genres:** History, Humanities, Race Relations, Biography, Writing/Journalism. **Career:** New York University, professor of history. Writer. **Publications:** White Women, Black Men: Illicit Sex in the Nineteenth-Century South, 1997; (ed.) Sex, Love, Race: Crossing Boundaries in North American History, 1999; The Sea Captain's Wife: A True Story of Love, Race and War in the Nineteenth Century, 2006; Mourning Lincoln: Personal Grief and the Meaning of the American Civil War, forthcoming. **Address:** Department of History, New York University, 53 Washington Sq. S, New York, NY 10012, U.S.A. **Online address:** martha.hodes@nyu.edu

HODGE, Paul William. American (born United States), b. 1934. **Genres:** Astronomy, Physics, Sciences. **Career:** Harvard University, teaching fellow, 1956-58, Agassiz fellow, 1957-58, 1959-60, Margaret Weyerhauser Jewitt fellow, 1958-59, Parker fellow, 1959-60, lecturer in astronomy, 1960-61; California Institute of Technology, research fellow, 1960-61; University of California, instructor, 1961-62, assistant professor of astronomy, 1962-65; University of Washington, Department of Astronomy, co-founder, associate professor, 1965-69, professor of astronomy, 1969, now professor emeritus, associate dean of the graduate school, 1971-73, associate dean of arts and sciences, 1978-79, chairman of department, 1987-90; Astronomical Society of the Pacific, director, 1968-74, vice-president, 1973-74; Astronomical Journal, editor, 1984-2004. **Publications:** (With F.W. Wright and D. Hoffleit) An Annotated Bibliography on Interplanetary Dust, 1961; (with J.C. Brandt) Solar System Astrophysics, 1964; Henbury Meteorite Craters, 1965; Galaxies and Cosmology, 1965; (with F.W. Wright) The Large Magellanic Cloud, 1967; An Atlas and Catalog of HII Regions in Galaxies, 1966; Physics and Astronomy of Galaxies and Cosmology, 1966; Concepts of the Universe, 1967; The Revolution in Astronomy, 1970; Estimates of Magnitudes of the Brightest Stars in the Clusters of the Large Magellanic Cloud, 1970; Color-Magnitude Diagrams for Five Stellar Associations in the Large Magellanic Cloud, 1970; Color-Magnitude Diagrams of Five Faint Clusters of the Large Magellanic Cloud, 1971; Slides for Astronomy, 1971; Galaxies, 3rd ed., 1972; Astronomy Study Guide, 1973; Concepts of Contemporary Astronomy, 1974, 2nd ed., 1979; (with F.W. Wright) The Small Magellanic Cloud, 1977; An Atlas of the Andromeda Galaxy, 1981; Interplanetary Dust, 1981; (with R.C. Kennicutt) HII Regions in Galaxies, 1982; (ed.) Galaxies and the Universe, 1984; (contrib.) Space and Mankind, 1984; (comp.) Universe of Galaxies, 1984; (contrib.) Structure and Evolution of the Magellanic Clouds, 1984; (contrib.) Milky Way Galaxy, 1985; Galaxies, 1996; (contrib.) Luminous Stars and Associations in Galaxies, 1986; The Andromeda Galaxy, 1992; Meteoritic Craters and Impact Structures of the World, 1993; Meteorite Craters and Impact Structures of the Earth, 1994; Higher than Everest: An Adventurer's Guide to the Solar System, 2001; (with B.P. Skelton and J. Ashizawa) Atlas of Local Group Galaxies, 2002; (with W.H. Waller) Galaxies and the Cosmic Frontier, 2003. **Address:** Department of Astronomy, University of Washington, Rm. B355, Physics-Astronomy Bldg., 3910 15th Ave. NE, PO Box 351580, Seattle, WA 98195-1580, U.S.A. **Online address:** hodge@astro.washington.edu

HODGE, Susie. British (born England), b. 1960?. **Genres:** Children's Non-fiction, Biography, History, Animals/Pets, Adult Non-fiction. **Career:** Saatchi & Saatchi, copy writer; JWT, copy writer. Royal Society of Arts, fellow; University of London, governor. Artist, art historian, illustrator and educator. **Publications:** Ancient Egyptian Art, 1998, rev. ed., 2006; Ancient Greek Art, 1998, rev. ed., 2006; Ancient Roman Art, 1998, rev. ed., 2006; Prehistoric Art, 1998, rev. ed., 2006; Best Grades at GCSE Art and Design, 2000; Drawing Is Fun!, 2000; Claude Monet, 2002; How to Draw Portraits: A Step-by-Step Guide for Beginners with Ten Projects, 2003; Pablo Picasso, 2004; How to Paint like the Impressionists: A Practical Guide to Re-Creating Your Own Impressionist Paintings, 2004; How to Draw Animals: A Step-by-Step Guide for Beginners with Ten Projects, 2004; (co-author) Period Living and Traditional Homes Escapes, 2004; Art and Design at Key Stage Three, 2004; The Forbidden City, 2005; Medieval Europe, 2005; How to Draw People: A Step-by-Step Guide for Beginners with Ten Projects, 2005; Picture Frames, 2005; The Secret History of the Knights Templar, 2006; Victorian Art, 2006; The Life of Leonardo Da Vinci, 2006; Tudor Art, 2006; Mountains, 2007; Oceans, 2007; Puppets, 2007; Masks, 2007; Ocean Survival, 2008; Mountain Survival, 2008; How to Draw Dinosaurs, 2008; Toxic!: Killer Cures and Other Poisonings, 2008; Israel, 2008; Celebrity Snapper: Taking the Ultimate Celebrity

Photo, 2008; The Complete Guide to Painting Pictures from Photos, 2008; Latin and Ballroom Dance, 2008; How to Draw Dogs, 2009; How to Survive Modern Art, 2009; Latin and Ballroom, 2009; Art And Design Teacher's Handbook, 2010; Resources for Teaching History: 11-14, 2010; Resources for Teaching History: 14-16, 2010; Monet, 2010; The Great Artists, 2010; Dinosaurs, 2011; Animals, 2011. **Address:** c/o Author Mail, Gareth Stevens Publishing Inc., 330 W Olive St., Ste. 100, Milwaukee, WI 53212, U.S.A. **Online address:** susiehodge@hotmail.com

HODGES, Andrew. British (born England), b. 1949?. **Genres:** Gay And Lesbian Issues, Biography, Mathematics/Statistics. **Career:** Oxford University, Wadham College, tutorial fellow. Writer, mathematician, physicist and biographer. **Publications:** (with D. Hutter) With Downcast Gays: Aspects of Homosexual Self-Oppression, 1977, 2nd ed., 1979; Alan Turing: The Enigma (biography), 1983, new ed., 2000; Turing, 1999; One to Nine: The Inner Life of Numbers, 2008. Contributor to books and periodicals. **Address:** Wadham College, Oxford University, Oxford, OX OX1 3PN, England. **Online address:** andrew@synth.co.uk

HODGINS, Jack. Canadian (born Canada), b. 1938. **Genres:** Novels, Novellas/Short Stories, Children's Fiction, Travel/Exploration, Writing/Journalism, Young Adult Fiction, Young Adult Non-fiction, Travel/Exploration, Travel/Exploration. **Career:** Nanaimo District Senior Secondary School, teacher, 1961-81; Simon Fraser University, writer-in-residence, 1977; University of Ottawa, writer-in-residence, 1979, visiting professor, 1981-83; full-time writer, 1979-; University of Victoria, visiting professor, 1983-85, Department of Writing, professor of creative writing, 1985-2002. **Publications:** STORIES: Spit Delaney's Island: Selected Stories, 1976, 2nd ed., 2011; The Barclay Family Theatre, 1981; Beginnings, 1983; Damage Done by The Storm: Stories, 2004. EDITOR: (with W.H. New) Voice and Vision, 1972; The Frontier Experience, 1975; The West Coast Experience, 1976; Letters to Omar, 2010; Forest Horses: A Novel. NOVELS: The Invention of the World, 1977; The Resurrection of Joseph Bourne: Or a Word or Two on Those Port Annie Miracles, 1979; The Honorary Patron, 1987; Left Behind in Squabble Bay (for children), 1988; Innocent Cities, 1990; The Macken Charm, 1995; Broken Ground, 1998; Distance, 2003; The Master of Happy Endings, 2010. OTHERS: (with B. Nesbitt) Teaching Short Fiction, 1977; (with B. Nesbitt) Teacher's Resource Book to Transition II: Short Fiction, 1978; Over Forty in Broken Hill: Unusual Encounters Outback and Beyond (travel), 1992; A Passion for Narrative: A Guide for Writing Fiction (non-fiction), 1993, rev. ed., 2001. Contributor to books and periodicals. Works appear in anthologies. **Address:** 2640 MacDonald Dr. E, Victoria, BC V8N 1X9, Canada. **Online address:** info@jackhodgins.ca

HODGKISS, Alan Geoffrey. British (born England), b. 1921. **Genres:** Geography, History, Biography, Autobiography/Memoirs, Illustrations. **Career:** Warrington Rural District Council, surveying assistant, 1939-46; University of Liverpool, experimental officer, 1946-83; Society of University Cartographers Bulletin, editor, 1964-73; Canadian Cartographer, contributing editor, 1965-75. **Publications:** SELF-ILLUSTRATED: Maps for Books and Theses, 1970. OTHERS: (ed. with J.A. Patmore) Merseyside in Maps, 1970; Discovering Antique Maps, 1971, new ed., 1977; (contrib.) Jamaica in Maps, 1974; Understanding Maps: A Systematic History of Their Use and Development, 1981; (ed. with W.T.S. Gould) Resources of Merseyside, 1982; (with J.J. Bagley) Lancashire: A History of the County Palatine in Early Maps, 1985; (with A.F. Tatham) Keyguide to Information Sources: Cartography, 1986; Memories of a Nobody, 2006. **Address:** 25 Burnham Rd., Allerton, Liverpool, MS L18 6JU, England.

HODGSON, Barbara L. Canadian (born Canada), b. 1955?. **Genres:** Novels, Young Adult Non-fiction, Picture/Board Books. **Career:** Douglas & McIntyre (publisher), assistant, book designer, Trade Publishing Division, art director, 1982-89; Simon Fraser University, sessional instructor, 1990, lecturer in book design; Emily Carr School of Art and Design, instructor, 1990-93; Barbara Hodgson Design, principal, 1991-; Byzantium Books (book packaging company), founding partner, 1993-. Writer. **Publications:** Medcards: The Total Medication Reference Guide, 1984; Kubla Khan: A Pop-up Version of Coleridge's Classic, 1994; The Tattooed Map, 1995; Paris out of Hand, 1996; The Rat: A Perverse Miscellany, 1997; The Sensualist: A Novel, 1998; Opium: A Portrait of the Heavenly Demon, 1999; In the Arms of Morpheus: The Tragic History of Laudanum, Morphine, and Patent Medicines, 2001; Hippolyte's Island, 2001; No Place for a Lady: Tales of Adventurous Women Travelers, 2002; Heroines, 2002; Good and Evil in the Garden, 2003; The

Lives of Shadows, 2004; Dreaming of East: Western Women and the Allure of the Orient, 2005; Italy Out of Hand: A Capricious Tour, 2005; Italy Out of Hand: A Capricious History, 2005; Trading in Memories, 2007; (with C. Cohen) The WunderCabinet: Curious Worlds of Barbara Hodgson and Claudia Cohen, 2011. Contributor to periodicals. **Address:** Barbara Hodgson Design, 402 W Pender St., Ste. 404, Vancouver, BC V6B 1T6, Canada.

HODGSON, Geoffrey M. British (born England), b. 1946. **Genres:** Economics, Business/Trade/Industry, Social Sciences, Intellectual History. **Career:** STL Research, computer programmer, 1964-65; Levenshulme High School, teacher of mathematics, 1968-72; Manchester Metropolitan University, lecturer, senior lecturer in economics, 1974-81; Bennington College, visiting professor of economics, 1980-81; University of Northumbria, principal lecturer in economics, 1981-87, reader in economics, 1987-90, professor of economics, 1990-92; University of Manchester, Hallsworth research fellow in political economy, 1984-85; University of Cambridge, university lecturer in economics, 1992-98, reader in institutional and evolutionary economics, 1998; University of Hertfordshire, research professor in business studies, 1999-; Trinity College, global visiting professor, 2001-; University of Aix-en-Provence III, visiting professor, 2002; University of Lyon II, visiting professor, 2002; University of Rheims, visiting professor, 2004-06, 2008; Huazhong Agricultural University, visiting professor, 2004; University of Strasbourg, visiting professor, 2005; Nanjing University of Finance and Economics, visiting professor, 2006; University of Athens, visiting professor, 2007. Writer. **Publications:** Socialism and Parliamentary Democracy, 1977; Labour at the Crossroads, 1981; Hodgson Family, 1982; Capitalism, Value, and Exploitation, 1982; The Democratic Economy, 1984; Economics and Institutions: A Manifesto for a Modern Institutional Economics, 1988; After Marx and Sraffa: Essays in Political Economy, 1991; Hodgson Surname: Its Norse Origins and Cumbrian Location, 1993; Economics and Evolution: Bringing Life Back Into Economics, 1993; Economics and Utopia: Why the Learning Economy is Not the End of History, 1999; Evolution and Institutions: Critical Essays on the Reconstruction of Economics, 1999; How Economics Forgot History: The Problem of Historical Specificity in Social Science, 2002; Evolution of Institutional Economics: Agency, Structure, and Darwinism in American institutionalism, 2004; Economics in the Shadows of Darwin and Marx: Essays on Institutional and Evolutionary Themes, 2006; Hodgson Saga, 2006; (with T. Knudsen) Darwin's Conjecture, 2010; The Political Economy of Utopia, forthcoming. EDITOR: (with E. Screpanti) Rethinking Economics: Markets, Technology and Economic Evolution, 1991; The Economics of Institutions, 1993; (with W. Samuels and M. Tool) The Elgar Companion to Institutional and Evolutionary Economics, 1994; Economics and Biology, 1995; The Foundations of Evolutionary Economics: 1890-1973, 1998; Modern Reader in Institutional and Evolutionary Economics: Key Concepts, 2002; Recent Developments in Institutional Economics, 2003; The Evolution of Institutional Economics, 2004; Economics in the Shadows of Darwin and Marx, 2006; The Evolution of Economic Institutions: A Critical Reader, 2007; (with M. Itoh and N. Yokokawa) Capitalism in Evolution: Global Contentions-East and West, 2007. Contributor to journals. **Address:** The Business School, University of Hertfordshire, De Havilland Campus, Hatfield, HF AL10 9AB, England. **Online address:** g.m.hodgson@herts.ac.uk

HODGSON, Harriet. American (born United States), b. 1935. **Genres:** How-to Books, Human Relations/Parenting, Medicine/Health, Poetry. **Career:** Rochester Post-Bulletin, freelance special features writer; KSMQ, Parenting Today, producer and host; Open to Hope Foundation, contributing writer. Freelance journalist. **Publications:** Just for You, 1978; I Made It Myself!, 1979; E Is for Energy, M Is for Me; 1980; Artworks, 1986; Gameworks, 1986; A Parent's Survival Guide: How to Cope When Your Kid is Using Drugs, 1986; Toyworks, 1986; Contraptions, 1987; My First Fourth of July Book (poetry), 1987; Parents Recover Too, 1988; Rochester: City of the Prairie, 1989; When You Love a Child, 1992; Powerplays Leader's Guide, 1993; Powerplays: How Teens Can Pull the Plug on Sexual Harassment, 1993; Heart Surgery and You: A Guide for Teens, 1994; Heart Surgery and You: An Activity Book for Gradeschoolers, 1994; Heart Surgery and You: An Activity Book for Preschoolers, 1994; Alzheimer's: Finding the Words, 1995; The Alzheimer's Caregiver, 1998; Smart Aging, 1999; Food Label Detective, 2002, rev. ed., 2006; Grieving Too Soon, 2002; Why Do I Feel This Way?, 2002; Good Samaritan Dental Clinic, 2004; Catching the Exercise Thief, 2004; Cracking the Health Words Code, 2005; Smiling Through Your Tears: Anticipating Grief, 2005; Writing to Recover Affirmations Calendar, 2008; Writing to Recover Journal, 2008; Writing to Recover: The Journey from Loss and Grief to a New Life, 2008; 101 Affirmations to Ease Your Grief

Journey: Words of Comfort, Words of Hope, 2010; The Spiritual Woman: Quotes to Refresh and Sustain Your Soul, 2010; Happy Again! Your New and Meaningful Life After Loss, forthcoming. Contributor to books and periodicals. Works appear in anthologies. **Address:** 1107 Foxcroft Ln. SW, Rochester, MN 55902-3411, U.S.A. **Online address:** harriethodgson@charter.net

HODGSON, Peter C. American (born United States), b. 1934. **Genres:** Theology/Religion. **Career:** United Presbyterian Church, ordained clergyman; Trinity University, assistant professor of religion, 1963-65; Vanderbilt University, assistant professor, 1965-69, associate professor, 1969-73, professor of theology, 1973-97, Graduate Department of Religion, chairman, 1975-80, 1990-97, Graduate Department of Religion Long-Range, Charles G. Finney professor of theology, 1997-2003, Divinity faculty, chair, emeritus, 2003-. Writer. **Publications:** The Formation of Historical Theology: A Study of Ferdinand Christian Baur, 1966; Jesus Word and Presence: An Essay in Christology, 1971; Children of Freedom: Black Liberation in Christian Perspective, 1974; New Birth of Freedom: A Theology of Bondage and Liberation, 1976; Revisioning the Church: Ecclesial Freedom in the New Paradigm, 1988; God in History: Shapes of Freedom, 1989; Winds of the Spirit: A Constructive Christian Theology, 1994; God's Wisdom: Toward a Theology of Education, 1999; Mystery beneath the Real: Theology in the Fiction of George Eliot, 2000; Theology in the Fiction of George Eliot: The Mystery beneath the Real, 2001; Christian Faith: A Brief Introduction, 2001; Hegel and Christian Theology: A Reading of the Lectures on the Philosophy of Religion, 2005; Liberal Theology: A Radical Vision, 2007. EDITOR: (trans.) Ferdinand Christian Baur on the Writing of Church History, 1968; (intro.) The Life of Jesus Critically Examined, 1972; (trans.) Christian Religion: Lectures on the Philosophy of Religion, vol. III, The Revelatory, Consummate, Absolute Religion, 1979; (with R.H. King) Christian Theology: An Introduction to Its Traditions and Tasks, 1985; (trans.) Lectures on the Philosophy of Religion, vol. I, 1984, vol. II, 1987, vol. III, 1985; (with R.H. King) Readings in Christian Theology, 1985; (and trans.) G.W.F. Hegel: Theologian of the Spirit, 1997; (trans.) Lectures on the Proofs of the Existence of God, 2007; (ed. And trans. With R.F. Brown) Lectures on the Philosophy of World History, vol. I: Manuscripts of the Introduction and the Lectures of 1822-1823, 2011. Contributor to periodicals. **Address:** Vanderbilt University, The Divinity School, 411 21st Ave. S, Nashville, TN 37240-1121, U.S.A.

HØECK, Klaus. Danish (born Denmark), b. 1938. **Genres:** Poetry. **Career:** University of Copenhagen, faculty; City of Copenhagen, mail carrier. Poet. **Publications:** POETRY: Yggdrasil: Indvendig rejse udvendig, 1966; Mitrenf-snee: Indvendig rejse udvendig, 1967; Fluch dem Kapitalismus, 1970; Rejse, vol. I: Yggdrasil, vol. II: Lejre, vol. III: Alpha, vol. IV: Omega, vol. V: Hymne, 1973; Transformations, 1974; Pentagram, 1976; Projekt Perseus: Data og science fiction digte, 1977; Ulrike Marie Meinhof: Et digt; Firdobbelt sonetkreds: 1. bind af en trilogi, 1977; Topia eller Che Guevara: digte et epos, 1978; Skygger at efterårsdigt, 1978; Dylan Forever, 1979; Winterreisse: Dobbelte sonetkredse, 1979; (with A. Schnack) Bowie, Bowie, 1980; (with A. Schnack and F.P. Jac) Nul, 1980; (with A. Schnack) Eno one, 1980; (with A. Schnack) Renaldo and Clara, 1980; Canzone: Digte fra Norrebro, 1981; Sorte sonetter et digt, 1981; (with A. Schnack) Eno zebra, 1982; Metamorphoses, 1983; (with A. Schnack) Eno high, 1983; (with A. Schnack) Blåvand Revisited: Et topografisk digt i 4 moduler, 1984; Marienbad: digte, 1984; International Klein Bleu, 1984; (with A. Schnack) Jaevngøgn, 1985; Hjem, 1985; Blackberry Winter, 1987; Udvalgte digte, 1988; Lukas O'Kech: En digtroman, 1988; Heptameron, 1989; Salme, 1991; Eventyr, 1992 as The Woods, 1998; Hommage, 1995; 1001 digt: Med 18 ordsnit, 1995; Honeymoon, 1997; In Nomine, 2001; Hsieh, 2004; (trans. with J. Irons) 100 Danish Poems, 2011. Contributor to periodicals. **Address:** Hedebovej 84, Veflinge, 5474, Denmark.

HOEDEMAKER, Bert. Also writes as Libertus A. Hoedemaker, L. A. Hoedemaker. Dutch (born Netherlands), b. 1935. **Genres:** Theology/Religion. **Career:** Educator, 1967-; state university, professor, 1981-; University of Groningen, professor, now emeritus professor of Ecumenics and Mission; Writer. **Publications:** Faith in Total Life, 1966; The Theology of H. Richard Niebuhr, 1970; Masihkah benih tersimpan?, 1990; (with A. Houtepen, T. Witvliet) Oecumene als leerproces: inleiding in de oecumenica, 1993; Discussies rond Kerkelijke presentie in een oude stadswijk, 1993; (ed. and contrib.) Missiology: An Ecumenical Introduction, 1995; Secularization and Mission, 1998; Met Anderen Tot Christen: Zending in een Postmissionair Tijdperk, 2000; World Christianity Reconsidered: Questioning the Questions of Ecumenism and Missiology, 2001. **Address:** University of Groningen, Oude

Boteringestraat 44, PO Box 72, Groningen, 9712 GL, Netherlands. **Online address:** l.a.hoedemaker@theol.rug.nl

HOEDEMAKER, L. A. See **HOEDEMAKER, Bert.**

HOEDEMAKER, Libertus A. See **HOEDEMAKER, Bert.**

HØEG, Peter. Danish (born Denmark), b. 1957. **Genres:** Novels, Mystery/Crime/Suspense. **Career:** Writer, 1983-. **Publications:** Forestilling om det Tyvende århundrede: Roman, 1988; Fortllinger om Natten, 1990; Frøken Smillas Fornemmelse for Sne: Roman, 1992; Måske Egnede: Roman, 1993; Smilla's Sense of Snow, 1995; Kvinden og Aben: Roman, 1996; Miss Smilla's Feeling For Snow, 1997; The Woman and the Ape, 1997; (intro.) Point of View, 1998; (with B. Haveland) Tales of the Night, 1999; Stille Pige: Roman, 2006; Quiet Girl, 2007; Elefantpassernes børn: Roman, 2010. **Address:** c/o Author Mail, Random House, 1745 Broadway, Ste. B1, New York, NY 10019-4305, U.S.A. **Online address:** peter@peterhoeg.com

HOEHNE, Marcia. American (born United States), b. 1951. **Genres:** Children's Fiction, Young Adult Fiction, Young Adult Non-fiction. **Career:** Kaukauna Public Schools, paraprofessional, 1970-73; Kaukauna Public Library, affiliated, 1975-79; La Leche League Intl., leader, 1980-86, district adviser, 1983-86; writer, 1988-; freelance editor, 2000-; Institute of Children's Literature, instructor, 2000-. **Publications:** The Journey of Emilie, 1999; Anne Bradstreet: America's Puritan Poet, 2007. THE ADVENTURES OF JENNA V. SERIES: A Place of My Own, 1993; A Pocket in My Heart, 1994; The Fairy Tale Friend, 1994; Sunflower Girl, 1995. CAROLINE GRADE MYSTERIES SERIES: The Music Box Test, 1994; The Paper Route Treasure, 1994. **Address:** Institute of Children's Literature, 93 Long Ridge Rd., West Redding, CT 06896, U.S.A. **Online address:** donmar@athenet.net

HOEK, D. J. American (born United States), b. 1970. **Genres:** Biography, Bibliography, Music, History. **Career:** Wichita State University, music and media catalog librarian, 1999-2001; Kent State University, head of music library, 2001-04, adjunct instructor in library and information science, 2002-04; Northwestern University, head of music library, 2004-, Alice Berline Kaplan Institute Library, fellow, 2010-11. Writer. **Publications:** Steve Reich: A Bio-Bibliography, 2002; Analyses of Nineteenth- and Twentieth-Century Music, 1940-2000, 2007. Contributor to periodicals. **Address:** Music Library, Northwestern University, 1970 Campus Dr., Evanston, IL 60208-2300, U.S.A. **Online address:** djhoek@northwestern.edu

HOEPPNER, Edward Haworth. American (born United States), b. 1951. **Genres:** Poetry, Literary Criticism And History, History. **Career:** Writer. **Publications:** Echoes and Moving Fields (critical study), 1994; Rain through High Windows (poetry), 2000; Ancestral Radio (poetry), 2008. **Address:** Department of English, Oakland University, 536 O'Dowd Hall, Rochester, MI 48309-4479, U.S.A. **Online address:** hoeppner@oakland.edu

HOERDER, Dirk. American/German (born Germany), b. 1943. **Genres:** History, Essays, Bibliography. **Career:** Free University of Berlin, John F. Kennedy Institute for North American Studies, assistant, 1969-75, part-time teacher, 1975-77; Harvard University, Center for West European Studies, John F. Kennedy memorial fellow, 1973-74, Charles Warren Center, Charles Warren fellow, 1974-75; University of Bremen, part-time teacher, 1975-77, professor of the social history of North America, 1977-2008, Labor Migration Project, director, 1978-93, now retired; York University, visiting professor, 1991-92, Robarts Centre for Canadian Studies, research associate, 2000-01; German Historical Institute, annual lecturer, 1992; Duke University, Center for International Studies, visiting professor, 1995; University of Toronto, Robert F. Harney Program in Ethnic, Immigration and Pluralism Studies, Diefenbaker visiting professor, 1996-97; Université de Paris 8-Vincennes-Saint Denis, visiting professor, 2002, 2005-06; Arizona State University, distinguished visiting professor of history, 2006-, College of Liberal Arts and Sciences, Department of History, professor, now professor emeritus. Writer. **Publications:** People and Mobs, Crowd Action in Massachusetts during the American Revolution, 1765-1780, 1971; Crowd Action in Revolutionary Massachusetts, 1765-1780, 1977; das sind eben alles Bilder der Strasse, 1979; (with C. Harzig) Why did You Come?: The Proletarian Mass Migration, 1986; People on the Move: Migration, Acculturation and Ethnic Interaction in Europe and North America, 1993; Creating Societies: Immigrant Lives in Canada, 1999; Cultures in Contact: World Migrations in the Second Millennium, 2002; (with C. Harzig, D. Gabaccia) What is Migration History?,

2009; To Know Our Many Selves: From the Study of Canada to Canadian Studies, 2010. EDITOR: (and comp.) Violence in the United States, Riots, Strikes, Protest and Suppression, 1973; (and comp.) Studies on the Interaction of Society and Culture in American Past and Present: A Bibliography of Dissertations, 1938-1973, 1975; (and comp.) American Labor History: Research, Teaching and Bibliographic Aids, 1976; (and comp.) Protest, Direct Action, Repression: Dissent in American Society from Colonial Times to the Present, 1977; Plutokraten und Sozialisten: Berichte deutscher Diplomaten und Agenten über die amerikanische Arbeiterbewegung 1878-1917, 1981; American Labor and Immigration History, 1877-1920s, 1982; Essays on the Scandinavian-North American Radical Press, 1880s-1930s, 1984; (with C. Harzig) The Press of Labor Migrants in Europe and North America, 1880s-1930s, 1985; (and intro.) Struggle a Hard Battle (essays), 1986; (with D. Knauf) Einwandererland USA, Gastarbeiterland BRD, 1987; (co-author) The Settling of North America, 1995; J.N. Jodlbauer, Dreizehn Jahre in Amerika, 1910-1923, 1996; (with Y. Hébert and I. Schmitt) Negotiating Transcultural Lives: Belongings and Social Capital among Youth in Comparative Perspective, 2005 in Canada, 2006; (with D.R. Gabaccia) Connecting Seas and Connected Ocean Rims: Indian, Atlantic and Pacific Oceans and China Seas Migrations from the 1830s to the 1930s, 2011; (with N. Faires) Migrants and Migration in Modern North America: Cross-border Lives, Labor Markets and Politics, 2011. EDITOR AND CONTRIBUTOR: Labor Migration in the Atlantic Economies, 1985; (with C. Harzig) The Immigrant Labor Press in North America, 1840s-1970s: An Annotated Bibliography, vol. I: Migrants from Northern Europe, vol. II: Migrants from Eastern and Southeastern Europe, vol. III: Migrants from Southern and Western Europe, 1987; (with D. Knauf) Fame, Fortune, and Sweet Liberty, 1992; (with H. Rössler) Distant Magnets, 1993; (with I. Blank and H. Rossler) Roots of the Transplanted, vol. I: Late 19th-Century East Central and Southeastern Europe, vol. II: Plebeian Culture, Class and Politics in the Life of Labor Migrants, 1994; (with J. Nagler) People in Transit, 1995; The Settling of North America: The Atlas of the Great Migrations into North America from the Ice Age to the Present, 1995; (with L.P. Moch) European Migrants, 1996; (with R.O. Schultze) Socio-Cultural Developments in the Metropolis, 2000; (with C. Harzig and A. Shubert) Historical Practice Of Diversity: Transcultural Interactions from the Early Modern Mediterranean to the Postcolonial World, 2003. Contributor to books and journals. **Address:** Department of History, Arizona State University, Coor Hall, PO Box 874302, Tempe, AZ 85287-4302, U.S.A. **Online address:** hoerder@uni-bremen.de

HOERR, John. American/German/British (born England), b. 1930. **Genres:** History, Organized Labor, Novels, Politics/Government, History. **Career:** United Press Intl., wire service reporter in Newark and Trenton, 1956-57, wire service reporter in Chicago, 1958-60; Daily Tribune, reporter, 1957-58; Business Week, correspondent from Detroit, 1960-63, correspondent from Pittsburgh, 1965-69, labor editor, 1975-79, associate editor, 1979-85, senior writer, 1985-91; freelance writer in Detroit, 1963-64; WQED-TV (PBS), labor reporter, commentator and producer, 1969-74; freelance writer in New Jersey and Massachusetts, 1991-. **Publications:** And the Wolf Finally Came: The Decline of the American Steel Industry, 1988; We Can't Eat Prestige: The Women Who Organized Harvard, 1997; Harry, Tom, and Father Rice: Accusation and Betrayal in America's Cold War, 2005; Monongahela Dusk, 2009. **Address:** 4303 Pheasant Ln., Middleboro, MA 02346, U.S.A. **Online address:** wolfcame@verizon.net

HOESTLANDT, Jo(celyne). French (born France), b. 1948. **Genres:** Children's Fiction, History, Young Adult Fiction, Literary Criticism And History, Translations, Picture/Board Books. **Career:** Teacher, 1969-72. Writer. **Publications:** Le Petit Pousse, 1980; Le Moulin a Paroles: Abecedaire, 1980; La Rentree de Mamans, 1990, trans. as Back to School with Mom: A Story, 1992; La Grande Peur Sous les étoiles, 1993; Emile Billede Clown, 1995; Star of Fear, Star of Hope, 1995; Les Passants de Noël, 1996; Les Amoureux de Léonie, 1996; La Géante solitude, 1997; Pique et pique écoleet drame, 1997; Le Virus de la rentrée, 1997; Petite poupée s'enva-t-en guerre, 1997; Peur bleue chez les souris grises, 1998; Le Pouvoird'Aimé, 1998; Mon meilleur ami, 1998; Une journée pleine desecrets, 1998; Et les petites filles dansent, 1999; La Boîte àBisous, 1999; Charlotte, la poupée et le chat, 1999; Coup dethéâtre à l'école, 1999; La Balançoire, 1999; Mémé, t'as du courrier, 1999; Simon et la commode pas commode, 1999; Lucien et les fleurs du balcon, 1999; Marie et les riquiquis duplancher, 1999; Juliette et les animaux du zoo, 1999; Mes petitesétoiles, 2000; Mon petit papa de rien du tout, 2000; Le Châteaufort et le château faible, 2000; Oh, les belles letters, 2000; La Nuitde la rentrée, 2000; La Maison de mon grand-père, 2000; Drôled'endroit pour des vacances, 2000; Un bonheur de Noël, 2000; Réponds-moi quand je t'écris, 2001; Miranda, reine du cirque, 2001; Le Petit monstrem, 2001; A pas de louve, 2001; Portraits en piedsdes princes et princesses, 2001; Joyeux Noël les monsters, 2001; Le Prince sans rire, 2002; Ma vie ce n'est pas de la tarte, 2002; Lesfrayeurs de la baby-sitter, 2002; Quel stress pour la maîtresse, 2002; Poings de côté, 2002; Un petit kangourou trop doudou !, 2003; Lamaîtresse est amoureuse, 2003; Cousin contre cousine, 2003; Journée poubelle pour Gaëlle, 2003; Drôlement mordu, 2003; Maman ne sait pas dire non, 2003; Tempête aGRV la maison, 2003; L'arche de Zoé, 2003; Un mouchoir de ciel bleu, 2003; Mimosa et les Bonshommes de craie, 2004; La demoiselle d'horreur, 2004; Parfaite et Rouspète, 2004; Oh, la barbe !, 2004; Tu peux toujours courir!, 2005; Trois Soleils, 2005; Gris-Gris et Perlimpinpin, 2005; Le songe de Constantin, 2005; Les belles espérances, 2005; Mon p'tit vieux, 2006; Le petit homme qui monte, qui monte, 2006; L'été où j'aigrandi, 2006; Faut pas pousser Mémé, 2006; Le cahier d'amour, 2006; L'auteur de mes jours, 2006; Un anniversaire camion, 2007; Gran, You've Got Mail!, 2008. **Address:** Delacorte Press, 1745 Broadway, 10th Fl., New York, NY 10019, U.S.A. **Online address:** js.hoestlandt@caramail.com

HOEZEE, Scott E. American (born United States), b. 1964. **Genres:** Theology/Religion. **Career:** Christian Reformed Church, pastor, 1990-93; Newaygo County Habitat for Humanity, founding member and president, 1991-93; Calvin Christian Reformed Church, minister of preaching and administration, 1993-2005; Christian Reformed Ministers Institute, corresponding secretary, 1993-96; Theological Inquiry, pastor-in-residence, 2000; Calvin Theological Seminary, Center for Excellence in Preaching, director, 2005-. Writer. **Publications:** The Riddle of Grace: Applying Grace to the Christian Life, 1996; Flourishing in the Land: A Hundred Year History of Christian Reformed Home Missions in North America, 1996; Speaking as One: A Look at the Ecumenical Creeds, 1997; Remember Creation: God's World of Wonder and Delight, 1998; Speaking of Comfort: A Look at the Heidelberg Catechism, 1998; Proclaim the Wonder: Engaging Science on Sunday, 2003; Grace Through Every Generation: The Ongoing Story of the Christian Reformed Church in North America, 2006; Expecting: Devotions for Advent, 2010. Contributor of articles to periodicals. **Address:** Calvin Theological Seminary, 3233 Burton SE, Grand Rapids, MI 49546, U.S.A. **Online address:** hoezee@calvinseminary.edu

HOFF, Al. American (born United States), b. 1964. **Genres:** Humor/Satire, Economics. **Career:** Writer. **Publications:** Thrift Score (nonfiction), 1997; If You Like Pina Coladas: The Humor and Weirdness of Personal Ads, 1999; Funny Personal Ads, forthcoming. **Address:** PO Box 90282, Pittsburgh, PA 15224, U.S.A. **Online address:** al@girlreporter.com

HOFF, B. J. American (born United States), b. 1940?. **Genres:** Novels, Romance/Historical, inspirational/Motivational Literature, Young Adult Non-fiction, Theology/Religion. **Career:** Church music director, music teacher and writer. **Publications:** THE MOUNTAIN SONG LEGACY: A Distant Music, 2006; The Wind Harp, 2006; The Song Weaver, 2007. RIVERHAVEN YEARS SERIES: Rachel's Secret, 2008; Where Grace Abides, 2009; River of Mercy, 2010. THE AMERICAN ANTHEM SERIES: Prelude, 2002; Cadence, 2003; Jubilee, 2004. EMERALD BALLAD SERIES: Song of the Silent Harp, 1991; Heart of the Lonely Exile, 1991; Land of a Thousand Dreams, 1992; Sons of an Ancient Glory, 1993; Dawn of the Golden Promise, 1993. THE SONG OF ERIN SERIES: Cloth of Heaven (historical novel), 1997; Ashes and Lace (historical novel), 1999; Song of Erin, 2008. DAYBREAK MYSTERIES SERIES: Storm at Daybreak, 1986; The Domino Image, 1987 as The Captive Voice, 1987; The Tangled Web, 1988; Vow of Silence, 1988; Dark River Legacy, 1990. NOVELS: Mists of Danger (novel), 1986, rev. ed. as Masquerade, 1996; The Penny Whistle (novel), 1996; American Anthem, 2009. DALTON SAGA SERIES: To Love and to Honor, 1986; A Whisper in the Wind, 1987. ST. CLARE TRILOGY SERIES: Winds of Graystone Manor, 1985. NON-FICTION: Thorns and Thrones, 1991; God's Abundant Love: One Minute Devotions, 2003. COLLECTION: Songs of a Christmas Night (poetry), 2000. **Address:** c/o Janet Kobobel Grant, Books & Such Literary Agency, 2 Mission Cir., Ste. 122, PO Box 170, Santa Rosa, CA 95409-5370, U.S.A.

HOFF, Joan. (Joan Hoff Wilson). American (born United States), b. 1939. **Genres:** Biography, History, Women's Studies And Issues, Law, Politics/Government, Business/Trade/Industry, Humanities. **Career:** California State University at Sacramento, assistant professor of U.S. diplomatic history, 1967-70; Arizona State University, associate professor, 1970-76, professor of U.S.

foreign relations, 1976-81; Indiana University at Bloomington, professor of history and foreign relations, 1981-95; Center for the Study of the Presidency, president and chief executive officer, 1995-97; Ohio University at Athens, professor of history, Contemporary History Institute, director, 1997-2000; James Pinckney Harrison visiting professor of history and research fellow, 2000-01; Montana State University, Department of History and Philosophy, research professor of history, distinguished research professor, 2001-; Hoff & Associates consultant L.L.C., staff, 2003-. Writer. **Publications:** American Business and Foreign Policy, 1920-1933, 1971; (ed.) The Twenties: The Critical Issues, 1972; Ideology and Economics: U.S. Relations with the Soviet Union, 1918-1933, 1974; (as Joan Hoff Wilson) Herbert Hoover: Forgotten Progressive, 1975; (as Joan Hoff Wilson with A. Sachs) Sexism and the Law: A Study of Male Beliefs and Legal Bias in Britain and the United States, 1978; (ed. with E.W. Hawley and R. Zieger) Herbert Hoover as Secretary of Commerce, 1921-1928: Studies in New Era Thought and Practice, 1981; (ed. as Joan Hoff-Wilson with M. Lightman) Without Precedent: The Life and Career of Eleanor Roosevelt, 1984; (ed. as Joan Hoff Wilson) Rights of Passage: The Past and Future of the ERA, 1986; Wellington's Marriage: A Soldier's Wife, 1987; (ed. with S. Gubar) For Adult Users Only: The Dilemma of Violent Pornography, 1989; Law, Gender and Injustice: A Legal History of U.S. Women, 1991, rev. ed. 1994; Watergate Revisited, 1993; Nixon Reconsidered, 1994; (ed. with M. Coulter) Voices of Irish Women: Past and Present, 1995; (ed. with R.H. Ferrell) Dictionary of American History, 1996; (ed. with D. Ink) The Nixon Presidency, 1996; (with M. Yeates) The Cooper's Wife is Missing: The Trails of Bridget Cleary, 2000; A Faustian Foreign Policy from Woodrow Wilson to George W. Bush: Dreams of Perfectibility, 2008. Contributor to periodicals. **Address:** Department of History and Philosophy, Montana State University, 2-155 Wilson Hall, PO Box 172320, Bozeman, MT 59717-3440, U.S.A. **Online address:** joanhoff1@aol.com

HOFF, Mary (King). American (born United States), b. 1956. **Genres:** Adult Non-fiction, Children's Fiction, Novels, Animals/Pets, Natural History, Sciences. **Career:** Writer. **Publications:** WITH M.M. RODGERS: Our Endangered Planet: Rivers and Lakes, 1991; Our Endangered Planet: Oceans, 1991; Our Endangered Planet: Groundwater, 1991; Our Endangered Planet. Life on Land, 1992; Our Endangered Planet: Atmosphere, 1995. OTHERS: Living Together, 2002; Pollination, 2003; Mimicry and Camouflage, 2003; Migration, 2003; Metamorphosis, 2003; Life at Night, 2003; Handling Heat, 2003; Coping with Cold, 2003; Communication, 2003; Tigers, 2004; Monkeys, 2006; Polar Bears, 2006; Koalas, 2006; Swans, 2006; Penguins, 2007; Crocodiles, 2007; Snakes, 2007. Contributor to periodicals. **Address:** c/o Author Mail, Creative Education Inc., 123 S Broad St., Mankato, MN 56001-3612, U.S.A.

HOFFER, Peter T(homas). American (born United States), b. 1942. **Genres:** Psychology, History, Translations, Biography. **Career:** Lincoln University, instructor, 1971-75, assistant professor of German, 1975-82; University of the Sciences, assistant professor, 1982-87, associate professor of German, 1988-94, professor of German, 1994-; Library of Congress, Sigmund Freud Archives, official translator. Writer. **Publications:** Klaus Mann, 1978. TRANSLATOR: (with A. Hoffer) Sigmund Freud, A Phylogenetic Fantasy: Overview of the Transference Neuroses, 1987; The Correspondence of Sigmund Freud and Sandor Ferenczi, vol. I: 1908-1914, 1993, vol. II: 1914-1920, 1996, vol. III: 1920-1933, 2000. Contributor of articles to journals. **Address:** University of the Sciences, E Bldg., Rm. 204, 600 S 43rd St., PO BOX 102, Philadelphia, PA 19104-4495, U.S.A. **Online address:** p.hoffer@usp.edu

HOFFMAN, Alice. American (born United States), b. 1952. **Genres:** Novels, Plays/Screenplays, Picture/Board Books, Science Fiction/Fantasy, Children's Fiction, Literary Criticism And History. **Career:** Brandeis University, Women's Studies Research Center, visiting research associate; freelance writer, 1975-; Stanford University, fellow, 1975. **Publications:** NOVELS: Property of, 1977; The Drowning Season, 1979; Angel Landing, 1980; White Horses, 1982; Fortune's Daughter, 1985; Illumination Night, 1987; At Risk, 1988; Seventh Heaven, 1990; Turtle Moon, 1992; Second Nature, 1994; Practical Magic, 1995; Here on Earth, 1997; Local Girls, 1999; The River King, 2000; Tevá Sheni, 2000; Blue Diary, 2001; The Probable Future, 2003; Blackbird House, 2004; The Ice Queen, 2005; Skylight Confessions, 2007. YOUNG ADULT NOVELS: Aquamarine, 2001; Indigo, 2002; Green Angel, 2003; Water Tales, 2003; The Foretelling, 2005; Incantation, 2006; The Third Angel, 2008; Story Sisters, 2009; Green Witch, 2010; Red Garden, 2011; The Dovekeepers, 2011; Green Heart, 2012. CHILDREN'S BOOKS: Fireflies: A Winter's Tale, 1997; Horsefly, 2000; Moondog, 2004. Contributor to periodi-

cals. **Address:** Elaine Markson Agency, 44 Greenwich Ave., New York, NY 10011-8347, U.S.A.

HOFFMAN, Allan M. American (born United States), b. 1948. **Genres:** Administration/Management, Education. **Career:** Columbia University, Institute for the Study of Higher Education Teachers College, Kellogg fellow, 1973-74; State University of New York, College of Health Related Professions, director of continuing education, assistant professor, faculty of health sciences, 1976-79; University of Southern California, Medical Education, assistant clinical professor, 1982-87, Medical Education and Family Medicine, associate clinical professor, 1987-93, clinical professor of family medicine, 1993-98, St. Francis Medical Center, director of medical education and clinical professor; University of La Verne, adjunct professor, 1987-99; Compton College, associate dean, 1990-93; California State University, associate professor, associate dean, dean, 1993-98; Des Moines University, Osteopathic Medical Center, professor and dean, 1998-2004, Center For The Prevention Of Community Violence, director, 1999; Hartnell College, vice president, 2004-. Writer. **Publications:** History of an Idea, 1981. EDITOR AND CONTRIBUTOR: (with D. Julius) Managing Community and Junior Colleges: Perspectives for the Next Century, 1994; (with Julius) Total Quality Management: Implications for Higher Education, 1995; Schools: Violence and Society, 1996; (with R. Fenske and J. Schuh) Violence on Campus: Defining the Problems, Strategies for Action, 1998; (with R. Summers) Managing Colleges and Universities: Issues for Leadership, 2000; (with R.W. Summers) Teen Violence: A Global View, 2001; (with R.W. Summers) Domestic Violence: A Global View, 2002; (with R.W. Summers) Elder Abuse: A Public Health Perspective, 2006; (with S.D. Spangehl) Innovations in Higher Education: Igniting the Spark for Success, 2011 Contributor to journals. **Address:** Hartnell College, 411 Central Ave., Salinas, CA 93901, U.S.A. **Online address:** drallan52@sbcglobal.net

HOFFMAN, Amy Beth. American (born United States), b. 1952?. **Genres:** Autobiography/Memoirs, Gay And Lesbian Issues, Medicine/Health. **Career:** South End Press, editor; Unitarian Universalist World, editor; University of Massachusetts, writing and literature instructor; Emerson College, writing and literature instructor; Pine Manor College, M.F.A. in Creative Nonfiction, faculty; Massachusetts Foundation for the Humanities and the Women's Lunch Place, development director; Gay Community News, features editor, managing editor, 1978-82; Bad Attitude, co-publisher, 1980; Women's Review of Books, editor-in-chief, 2003-04, 2006-. **Publications:** Hospital Time (memoir), 1997; An Army of Ex-lovers: My Life at the Gay Community News (memoir), 2007. Contributor to periodicals. **Address:** Women's Review of Books, Wellesley Centers for Women, Wellesley College, 106 Central St., Wellesley, MA 02481, U.S.A. **Online address:** amybhoffman@earthlink.net

HOFFMAN, Andrew Jay. *See* **HOFFMAN, Andy.**

HOFFMAN, Andy. (Andrew Jay Hoffman). American (born United States), b. 1956. **Genres:** Novels, Literary Criticism And History, Biography. **Career:** Running Press, editor, 1976-77; Headlands Press, editor, 1977-79; University of Oregon, instructor in writing, 1979-81; U.S. Magazine, copy chief, 1981-82; Brown University, Graduate School, special assistant to the dean, 1986-90; Central Connecticut State University, assistant professor of English, 1990-91; freelance writer and editor, 1991-; Goosewing, founder and chief executive officer, 1999-2003; Bristol Community College, Teaching American History Projects, director, 2003-; WGBH, American History and Civics Initiative, director; Madison Couch Productions, chief executive officer. **Publications:** Twain's Heroes, Twain's Worlds: Mark Twain's Adventures of Huckleberry Finn, A Connecticut Yankee in King Arthur's Court, and Pudd'nhead Wilson, 1988; Beehive, 1992; Inventing Mark Twain: The Lives of Samuel Langhorne Clemens, 1997. **Address:** c/o. Elaine Markson, Elaine Markson Literary Agency Inc., 44 Greenwich Ave., New York, NY 10011, U.S.A. **Online address:** jamall@juno.com

HOFFMAN, Bruce. American (born United States), b. 1954?. **Genres:** International Relations/Current Affairs, Military/Defense/Arms Control, Politics/Government, History. **Career:** Rand Corp., International Policy Department, staff of senior research, 1981-94, Army Research Division, director of strategy and doctrine program, 1993-94, director, 1998-, Counterterrorism and Counterinsurgency, corporate chair, vice-president, 2001-04, Center for Middle East Public Policy, acting director, 2004; Saint Andrews University, Department of International Relations, chair, 1994-98, Center for the Study of Terrorism and Political Violence, director, 1994-98, reader in international relations; U.S. Military Academy, Combating Terrorism Center, senior fellow; University of Utah, Institute of Public and International Affairs, International Security Programs, distinguished fellow and senior fellow; Institute for Counter-Terrorism, Interdisciplinary Center, visiting professor; Australian Strategic Policy Institute, visiting fellow, 2007; Nanyang Technological University, S. Rajaratnam School of International Studies, visiting professor, S. Rajaratnam professor of strategic studies, 2009; All Souls College, visiting professor, 2009; Georgetown University, Edmund A. Walsh School of Foreign Service, professor, Center for Peace and Security Studies, director, Security Studies Program, director. Writer. **Publications:** The PLO and Israel in Central America: The Geopolitical Dimension, 1988; The Potential Terrorist Threat to Commercial Nuclear Facilities, 1988; British Air Power in Peripheral Conflict, 1919-1976, 1989; Insider Crime: The Threat to Nuclear Facilities and Programs, 1990; (with K. Gardela) The Rand Chronology of International Terrorism for 1986, 1990; Recent Trends and Future Prospects of Iranian Sponsored International Terrorism, 1990; (with J.M. Taw) Defense Policy and Low-Intensity Conflict: The Development of Britain's Small Wars Doctrine during the 1950s, 1991; (with J.M. Taw and D. Arnold) Lessons for Contemporary Counterinsurgencies: The Rhodesian Experience, 1991; (with K. Gardela) The Rand Chronology of International Terrorism for 1987, 1991; (with S. Sayari) Urbanization and Insurgency: The Turkish Case, 1976-1980, 1991; (with K. Gardela) The Rand Chronology of International Terrorism for 1988, 1992; (with J.M. Taw) A Strategic Framework for Countering Terrorism and Insurgency, 1992; (with J. Duncan and C. Meyer) Force-On-Force Attacks: Their Implications for the U.S. Defense of Nuclear Facilities, 1993; (with T. Downes-Le Guin) The Impact of Terrorism on Public Opinion, 1988 to 1989, 1993; Holy Terror: The Implications of Terrorism Motivated by a Religious Imperative, 1993; Responding to Terrorism Across the Technological Spectrum, 1994; (with J.M. Taw) The Urbanization of Insurgency: The Potential Challenge to U.S. ARMY Operations, 1994; (with K.J. Riley) Domestic Terrorism: A National Assessment of State and Local Preparedness, 1995; Inside Terrorism, 1998, rev. ed., 2006; Terrorism and Weapons of Mass Destruction: An Analysis of Trends and Grounds, 1999; Transnational Threats: Blending Law Enforcement and Military Strategies, 2000; (co-author) Security in the Nation's Capital and the Closure of Pennsylvania Avenue: An Assessment 2002; Terrorismus Der Krieg Unerklärte: Neue Gefahren Politischer Gewalt, 2002; (with K. Cragin) Arms Trafficking and Colombia, 2003; Al Qaeda, Trends in Terrorism and Future Potentialities: An Assessment, 2003; (with S. Chubin and W. Rosenau) The United States, Europe and the Wider Middle East, 2004; Insurgency and Counterinsurgency in Iraq, 2004; (with A. Kasupski) The Victims of Terrorism: An Assessment of Their Influence and Growing Role in Policy, Legislation and the Private Sector, 2007; (co-author) Radicalization of Diasporas and Terrorism: A Joint Conference by the RAND Corporation and the Center for Security Studies, ETH Zurich, 2007; Anonymous Soldiers, 2014. Contributor to periodicals. **Address:** Edmund A. Walsh School of Foreign Service, Georgetown University, Mortara Bldg., 3600 N St. NW, Washington, DC 20007, U.S.A. **Online address:** brh6@georgetown.edu

HOFFMAN, Carl. American (born United States), b. 1960. **Genres:** Documentaries/Reportage, History, Travel/Exploration, Crafts, Military/Defense/Arms Control. **Career:** Freelance writer, 1984-; National Geographic Traveler, contributing editor; Wired, contributing editor; Popular Mechanics, contributing editor. **Publications:** Hunting Warbirds: The Obsessive Quest for Lost Aircraft of World War II, 2001; The Lunatic Express: Discovering the World ...via Its Most Dangerous Buses, Boats, Trains and Planes, 2010; Somewhere in Eden, forthcoming. Contributor to periodicals and magazines. **Address:** 5239 Sherier Pl. NW, Washington, DC 20016-3323, U.S.A. **Online address:** carlhoffmn@earthlink.net

HOFFMAN, Daniel. American (born United States), b. 1923. **Genres:** Poetry, Literary Criticism And History, Mythology/Folklore. **Career:** Columbia University, lecturer in English, 1947-48, 1952-56; Rutgers University, lecturer in English, 1948-50; Temple University, instructor in English, 1950-52; Faculte des Lettres, visiting professor of American studies, 1956-57; Swarthmore College, assistant professor, 1957-60, associate professor, 1960-65, professor of English literature, 1965-66; Indiana University, fellow of school of letters, 1959; Tufts University, Phi Beta Kappa poet, 1963; University of Cincinnati, Elliston lecturer in poetry, 1964; University of Pennsylvania, professor of English, 1966-83, poet-in-residence, 1978-93, Felix E. Schelling professor of English, 1983-93, emeritus, 1993-; Academy of American Poets, chancellor, 1974-98; Kings's College, faculty, 1991-92. Writer. **Publications:** Paul Bunyan, Last of the Frontier Demigods, 1952; An Armada of Thirty Whales,

1954; The Poetry of Stephen Crane, 1957; A Little Geste, 1960; Form and Fable in American Fiction, 1961; The City of Satisfactions, 1963; Instructions to a Medium to be Transmitted to the Shade of W.B. Yeats: The Latter Having Responded in a Seance Held On 13 June 1965, Its Hundredth Birthday, 1965; Barbarous Knowledge, 1967; Striking the Stones, 1968; Broken Laws, 1970; Poe Poe Poe Poe Poe Poe Poe, 1972; The Center of Attention, 1974; Able was I Ere I Saw Elba: Selected Poems, 1977; Moonlight Dries No Mittens: Carl Sandburg Reconsidered, 1978; Brotherly Love, 1981; Hang-Gliding from Helicon: New and Selected Poems 1948-1988, 1988; Faulkner's Country Matters: Folklore and Fable in Yoknapatawpha, 1989; Words to Create a World, 1993; Middens of the Tribe, 1995; Zone of the Interior: A Memoir 1942-1947, 2000; Darkening Water: Poems, 2002; (trans.) A Play of Mirrors: Poems by Ruth Domino, 2002; Beyond Silence: Selected Shorter Poems 1948-2003, 2003; Makes You Stop and Think: Sonnets, 2005; Whole Nine Yards: Longer Poems, New And Selected, 2009. EDITOR: The Red Badge of Courage and Other Stories, 1957; American Poetry and Poetics, 1962; (with S. Hynes) English Literary Criticism: Romantic and Victorian, 1963; New poets, 1970; In Memory of Loring Williams, 1974; The Harvard Guide to Contemporary American Writing, 1979; Ezra Pound and William Carlos Williams, 1983. **Address:** Department of English, University of Pennsylvania, Rm. 127, Fisher-Bennett Hall, 3340 Walnut St., Philadelphia, PA 19104-6273, U.S.A.

HOFFMAN, Donna R. American (born United States), b. 1969. **Genres:** Social Sciences, Politics/Government, International Relations/Current Affairs. **Career:** Phillips University, adjunct instructor in political science, 1997-98; University of Oklahoma, graduate teaching associate, 1997-2000; University of Northern Iowa, Department of Political Science, head of department, assistant professor, 2001-07, associate professor, 2007-. Writer. **Publications:** (With A.D. Howard) Addressing the State of the Union: The Evolution and Impact of the President's Big Speech, 2006. Contributor to periodicals and journals. **Address:** Department of Political Science, University of Northern Iowa, 333 Sabin Hall, Cedar Falls, IA 50614-0404, U.S.A. **Online address:** donna.hoffman@uni.edu

HOFFMAN, Elizabeth Cobbs. Also writes as Elizabeth Anne Cobbs. American (born United States), b. 1956. **Genres:** International Relations/Current Affairs, Essays, History. **Career:** Center for Women's Studies and Services, staff, 1972-83, president, 1983-94; University of California, lecturer, 1988-89; San Diego State University, associate professor, 1989-98, Dwight E. Stanford professor of American foreign relations, 1998-, Dwight E. Stanford chair in U.S. foreign relations; Stanford University, Hoover Institution, national fellow, 2012. Writer. **Publications:** (As Elizabeth Anne Cobbs) The Rich Neighbor Policy: Rockefeller and Kaiser in Brazil, 1992; All You Need is Love: The Peace Corps and the Spirit of the 1960s, 1998; (ed. with J. Gjerde) Major Problems in American History: Documents and Essays, 2002, 3rd ed., 2010; In the Lion's Den, 2009; Broken Promises: A Novel of the Civil War, 2011. **Address:** Department of History, San Diego State University, 4123 AH, 5500 Campanile Dr., San Diego, CA 92182-8147, U.S.A. **Online address:** ehoffman@mail.sdsu.edu

HOFFMAN, Eva. American/Polish (born Poland), b. 1945. **Genres:** Autobiography/Memoirs, Travel/Exploration, History. **Career:** University of New Hampshire, assistant professor of literature, 1975-76; Tufts University, assistant professor of art history and coordinator of survey course, 1990-2001, assistant professor of literature, 1976-77, associate professor, 2001-, ARTIFACT, director, 1994-2007, Undergraduate Studies, director, 2001-, Art History Survey Course, coordinator, 2001-, Middle Eastern Studies Program, director, 2007-; New York Times, editor, 1980-82, Arts and Leisure, deputy editor, 1982-85; Wellesley College, visiting assistant professor, 1983; Rhode Island School of Design, assistant professor of art history, 1985-88; New York Times Book Review, editor, 1987-89; Massachusetts Institute of Technology, visiting professor. **Publications:** Lost in Translation: A Life in a New Language, 1989; Exit into History: A Journey through the New Eastern Europe, 1993; Shtetl: The Life and Death of a Small Town and the World of Polish Jews, 1997; The Secret: A Fable for Our Time, 2001; The Secret: A Novel, 2002; After Such Knowledge: Memory, History, and the Legacy of the Holocaust, 2004; Illuminations, 2008; Appassionata, 2009; Time, 2009. Cotributor to periodicals. **Address:** c/o Georges Borchardt, 136 E 57th St., New York, NY 10022, U.S.A. **Online address:** evah@mit.edu

HOFFMAN, Jay. (Jay R. Hoffman). American (born United States), b. 1961. **Genres:** Sports/Fitness, How-to Books. **Career:** Philadelphia Eagles,

National Football League player; New York Jets, National Football League player; Tampa Bay Bandits, U.S. Football League player; University of Connecticut, football team coach, 1988-92, basketball team coach, 1990-91; Israel's National Youth Basketball Team, coach, 1997; Detroit Lions', Strength and Conditioning Program, coordinator; Journal of Strength and Conditioning Research, associate editor; College of New Jersey, Department of Health and Exercise Science, associate professor, professor and chair of department, 2000-; National Strength and Conditioning Association, vice president, president, 2009-. Writer. **Publications:** (Contrib.) Exercise and Sport Science, 2000; Physiological Aspects of Sport Training and Performance, 2002; (contrib.) Handbook on Basketball: Olympic Handbook of Sport Medicine, 2003; (contrib.) The Endocrinology of Physical Exercise and Sport, 2005; Norms for Fitness, Performance and Health, 2006; (with N.A. Ratamess) A Practical Guide to Developing Resistance-Training Programs, 2006, 2nd ed., 2008. Contributor to periodicals. **Address:** Department of Health and Exercise Science, College of New Jersey, Packer Hall 216, 2000 Pennington Rd., PO Box 7718, Ewing, NJ 08628, U.S.A. **Online address:** hoffmanj@tcnj.edu

HOFFMAN, Jay R. *See* **HOFFMAN**, Jay.

HOFFMAN, Kerry Cohen. *See* **COHEN**, Kerry.

HOFFMAN, Mary (Margaret). (Mary Lassiter). British (born England), b. 1945. **Genres:** Children's Fiction, Education, Writing/Journalism. **Career:** Writer, 1970-; Milton Keynes Open University, lecturer in education, 1975-80; BBC-TV, reading consultant, 1977-79. **Publications:** FOR ADULTS: Reading, Writing, and Relevance, 1976; (as Mary Lassiter) Our Names, Ourselves, 1983. FOR CHILDREN: White Magic, 1975; (with C. Callery) Buttercup Buskers' Rainy Day, 1982; Tiger, 1983; Monkey, 1983; Elephant, 1983; Panda, 1983; Lion, 1985; Zebra, 1985; Hippo, 1985; Gorilla, 1985; (with W. Hall) The Return of the Antelope, 1985; Whales and Sharks, 1986; (with T. Weston) Dangerous Animals, 1986; Beware, Princess!, 1986; The Second-hand Ghost, 1986; King of the Castle, 1986; A Fine Picnic, 1986, 1994; Animal Hide and Seek, 1986; The Perfect Pet, 1986; Clothes for Sale, 1986; Wild Cat, 1986; Giraffe, 1986; Snake, 1986; Bear, 1986; Wild Dog, 1987; Seal, 1987; Antelope, 1987; Bird of Prey, 1987; Nancy No-Size, 1987; Specially Sarah, 1987; My Grandma Has Black Hair, 1988; Dracula's Daughter, 1988; All about Lucy, 1989; Min's First Jump, 1989; Mermaid and Chips, 1989; Dog Powder, 1989; Catwalk, 1989; Just Jack, 1990; Leon's Lucky Lunchbreak, 1991; The Babies' Hotel, 1991; Amazing Grace, 1991; Maxin the Jungle, 1991; The Ghost Menagerie, 1992; Henry's Baby, 1993; Cyril MC, 1993; Bump in the Night, 1993; Amazing Mammals, 1993; Boundless, Grace, 1995; Earth, Fire, Water, Air, 1995; Trace in Space, 1996; A Vanishing Tail, 1996; Quantum Squeak, 1996; Special Powers, 1997; A First Bible Storybook, 1997; An Angel Just Like Me, 1997; Comet, 1997; Sun, Moon and Stars, 1998; A Twist in the Tail, 1998; Virtual Friend, 1998; Clever Katya, 1998; A First Book of Myths, 1999; Three Wise Women, 1999; Starring Grace, 2000; Women of Camelot, 2000; Brother and Sister Tales, 2000; Parables, 2000; A Treasury of Nursery Stories, 2000; Miracles, 2001; The Colour of Home, 2002; Stravaganza Series, City of Masks, 2002; Animals of the Bible, 2002; Encore, Grace!, 2003, Seven Wonders of the World, 2003; City of Stars, 2003, City of Flowers, 2005; Bravo, Grace!, 2005, Princess Grace, 2007; The Falconer's Knot, 2007; Kings and Queens of the Bible, 2008; City of Secrets, 2008; Troubadour 2009; City of Ships 2010; The Great Big Book of Families 2010; David 2011. EDITOR: Ip, Dip, Sky Blue, 1990; Stacks of Stories, 1997; Lines in the Sand, 2003. **Address:** Rogers, Coleridge & White, 20 Powis Mews, London, GL W11 1JN, England. **Online address:** maryhoffman@maryhoffman.co.uk

HOFFMAN, Mat. American (born United States), b. 1972. **Genres:** Young Adult Fiction, Sports/Fitness, Autobiography/Memoirs, Biography. **Career:** Hoffman Bikes, founder; Hoffman Sports Association, founder; Hoffman Promotions, founder; Hoffman Enterprises Inc., founder; Entertainment and Sports Programming Network, producer, director and host. Writer. **Publications:** (With M. Lewman) The Ride of My Life (autobiography), 2002. **Address:** c/o Brian Dubin, Artist Brand Alliance L.L.C., 11 E 86th St., New York, NY 10028, U.S.A.

HOFFMAN, Michael J. American (born United States), b. 1939. **Genres:** Novels, Literary Criticism And History, History, Essays. **Career:** Washington College, instructor of English, 1962-64; University of Pennsylvania, assistant professor of English, 1964-67; University of California, assistant professor, 1967-71, graduate chairman, 1971-72, 1995-98, associate profes-

sor, 1971-75, professor of English, 1975-2001, chairman, 1984-89, professor emeritus, 2001-, Academic Affairs, assistant vice chancellor, 1974-83, Humanities Institute, director, 1986-91, coordinator of writing programs, 1991-94, master undergraduate adviser, 1994-95. Writer. **Publications:** The Development of Abstractionism in the Writings of Gertrude Stein, 1965; The Buddy System (novel), 1971; The Subversive Vision: American Romanticism in Literature, 1972; Gertrude Stein, 1976; (comp.) Critical Essays on Gertrude Stein, 1986. EDITOR: (with P.D. Murphy) Essentials of the Theory of Fiction, 1988, 3rd ed., 2005; (with P.D. Murphy) Critical Essays on American Modernism, 1992. **Address:** Department of English, University of California, Voorhies Hall, 1 Shields Ave., Davis, CA 95616, U.S.A. **Online address:** mjhoffman@ucdavis.edu

HOFFMAN, Paul E. American (born United States), b. 1943. **Genres:** History, Translations. **Career:** Louisiana State University, professor of history and Paul W. and Nancy W. Murrill distinguished Professor. Writer. **Publications:** The Spanish Crown and the Defense of the Caribbean, 1535-1585: Precedent, Patrimonialism and Royal Parsimony, 1980; Spain and the Roanoke Voyages (booklet), 1987; A New Andalucia and a Way to the Orient: The American Southeast during the Sixteenth Century, 1990, rev. ed., 2004; (trans.) C.M. Hudson, The Juan Pardo Expeditions: Explorations of the Carolinas and Tennessee, 1566-1568, 1990; Luisiana (Spanish language history of Spanish Louisiana), 1992; (with C.E. Pearson) The Last Voyage of El Nuevo Constante: The Wreck and Recovery of an Eighteenth-Century Spanish Ship off the Louisiana Coast, 1995; A History of Louisiana before 1813, 1996; (comp. with C.E. Pearson) El Nuevo Constante: Investigation of an Eighteenth Century Spanish Shipwreck off the Louisiana Coast, 1998; Florida's Frontiers, 2002; (ed.) The Louisiana Purchase and Its Peoples: Perspectives from the New Orleans Conference, 2004. **Address:** Department of History, Louisiana State University, 221C Himes Hall, Baton Rouge, LA 70803, U.S.A. **Online address:** hyhoff@lsu.edu

HOFFMAN, Ronald. American (born United States), b. 1941. **Genres:** History, Theology/Religion, Politics/Government, Economics, Cultural/Ethnic Topics, Biography, Autobiography/Memoirs, Romance/Historical, Romance/Historical. **Career:** University of Maryland, assistant professor, 1969-73, associate professor of history, 1973-92, professor of history, 1992-95; College of William and Mary, Omohundro Institute for Early American History and Culture, director, 1992-, professor of history, 1993-, William E. Pullen professor of American history, 2004-09. Writer. **Publications:** A Spirit of Dissension: Economics, Politics and the Revolution in Maryland, 1973; (co-author) The Pursuit of Liberty, 1983; (with S.D.Mason) Princes of Ireland, Planters of Maryland: A Carroll Saga, 1500-1782, 2000; Carroll Family of Maryland, 2008. EDITOR: (with I. Berlin) Slavery and Freedom in the Age of American Revolution, 1983; The Economy of Early America: The Revolutionary Period, 1763-1790, 1988; (with M. Sobel and F.J. Teute) Through a Glass Darkly: Reflections on Personal Identity in Early America, 1997; (with S.D. Mason) Princes of Ireland, Planters of Maryland: A Carroll Saga, 1500-1782, 2000; (with S.D. Mason and E.S. Darcy) Dear Papa, Dear Charley, 2001. EDITOR WITH P.J. ALBERT: Diplomacy and Revolution: The Franco- American Alliance of 1778, 1981; Sovereign States in an Age of Uncertainty, 1981; (with P.J. Albert) Arms and Independence: The Military Character of the American Revolution, 1984; (with T.W. Tate) An Uncivil War: The Southern Backcountry During the American Revolution, 1985; (with P.J. Albert) Peace and the Peacemakers: The Treaty of 1783, 1986; Women in the Age of the American Revolution, 1989; We Shall Overcome: Martin Luther King, Jr. and the Black Freedom Struggle, 1990; (with H. Belz) To Form a More Perfect Union: The Critical Ideas of the Constitution, 1992; (with C. Carson) Of Consuming Interests: The Style of Life in the Eighteenth Century, 1994; Religion in a Revolutionary Age, 1994; The Transforming Hand of Revolution: Reconsidering the American Revolution as a Social Movement, 1996; Launching the Extended Republic: The Federalist Era, 1996; The Bill of Rights: Government Proscribed, 1997; (with F.E. Hoxie) Native Americans and the Early Republic, 1999. **Address:** Department of History, College of William and Mary, OIEAHC, PO Box 8795, Williamsburg, VA 23187-8795, U.S.A. **Online address:** ieahc1@wm.edu

HOFFMAN, Valerie J. American (born United States), b. 1954. **Genres:** Theology/Religion, Intellectual History, Third World. **Career:** University of Illinois, Spertus College of Judaica, instructor in Arabic, 1978; University of Illinois, assistant professor, 1986-94, associate professor, 1994-2011, professor 2011-; Ecole des Hautes Etudes en Sciences Sociales, lecturer, 1993. Writer. **Publications:** Sufism, Mystics and Saints in Modern Egypt, 1995;

The Essentials of Ibadi Islam, 2011. Contributor of articles to journals. **Address:** Department of Religion, University of Illinois, 707 S Mathews Ave., Urbana, IL 61801, U.S.A. **Online address:** vhoffman@illinois.edu

HOFFMAN, Wayne. American (born United States), b. 1970?. **Genres:** Novels. **Career:** Washington Blade, contributor; Billboard, senior editor; New York Blade (weekly newspaper), co-editor, arts editor and managing editor, 1997; Forward, managing editor, 2003-. **Publications:** Laura's War, 2004; Hard, 2006; (ed.) What we Brought Back: Jewish Life after Birthright, 2010. Contributor to periodicals. Works appear in anthologies. **Address:** New York, NY , U.S.A. **Online address:** waynewriter@aol.com

HOFFMAN, William M(oses). American (born United States), b. 1939. **Genres:** Plays/Screenplays, Songs/Lyrics And Libretti, Gay And Lesbian Issues. **Career:** Barnes & Noble, editorial assistant, 1960-61; Hill & Wang, assistant editor, 1961-67, associate editor and drama editor, 1967-68; Wolf Co., founder and director, 1968; Scripts magazine, literary adviser, 1971-72; Lincoln Center Student Program, artist-in-residence, 1971-72; Eugene O'Neill Foundation, lecturer, 1971; Changing Scene, artist-in-residence, 1972; University of Massachusetts, visiting lecturer, 1973; Cable Arts Foundation, drama adviser, 1973; New York State Council on the Arts, CAPS Program, playwriting consultant, 1975-77; American Conservatory Theatre, playwright-in-residence, 1978; La Mama, playwright-in-residence, 1978-79; Massachusetts Arts and Humanities Foundation, playwriting consultant, 1978; Hofstra University, Star professor, 1980-; One Life to Live, staff writer, 1991-92; City University of New York, Lehman College, associate professor of journalism, communications and theatre, professor. **Publications:** PLAYS: Thank You, Miss Victoria, 1965; A Quick Nut Bread to Make Your Mouth Water, 1970; As Is, 1985, rev. ed., 1990. LIBRETTI: The Cloisters: A Song Cycle, 1968; Wedding Song, 1984; Ghosts of Versailles, 1991; Ghosts of Versailles: The Aria of the Worm, 1993; Ghosts of Versailles: They Wish They Could Kill Me, 1993; Ghosts of Versailles: As Summer Brings a Wistful Breeze, 1993; Ghosts of Versailles: Come Now, My Darling: Quartet, SSAB, 1993; Jack and Jill, 1994; (contrib.) A Petition to the the Governor: For Soprano, Tenor, Baritone and Piano, 2005. EDITOR: New American Plays, 4 vols., 1968-71; Gay Plays: The First Collection, 1979. OTHERS: Fine Frenzy (poems), 1972. **Address:** Lehman College, City University of New York, Rm. 214, Music Bldg., 250 Bedford Park Blvd. W, Bronx, NY 10468, U.S.A. **Online address:** william.hoffman@lehman.cuny.edu

HOFFMANN, Donald. American (born United States), b. 1933. **Genres:** Architecture, Travel/Exploration. **Career:** City News Bureau of Chicago, staff; Illinois State Register, staff, 1954-56; Kansas City Star, general assignment reporter, 1956-65, art and architecture critic, 1965-90; Journal of the Society of Architectural Historians, assistant editor, 1970-71. **Publications:** (Ed. and intro.) The Meanings of Architecture: Buildings and Writings, 1967; The Architecture of John Wellborn Root, 1973; Frank Lloyd Wright's Fallingwater: The House and Its History, 1978, rev. ed., 1993; Frank Lloyd Wright's Robie House, 1984; Frank Lloyd Wright: Architecture and Nature, 1986; Frank Lloyd Wright's Hollyhock House, 1992; Understanding Frank Lloyd Wright's Architecture, 1995; Frank Lloyd Wright's Dana House, 1996; Frank Lloyd Wright, Louis Sullivan, and the Skyscraper, 1998; Frank Lloyd Wright's House on Kentuck Knob, 2000; Mark Twain in Paradise: His Voyages to Bermuda, 2006. Contributor to journals. **Address:** 6441 Holmes St., Kansas City, MO 64131-1110, U.S.A.

HOFFMANN, Peter (Conrad Werner). Canadian/German (born Germany), b. 1930. **Genres:** History, Translations. **Career:** University of Maryland, lecturer in history, 1961-65; Schiller College, lecturer, 1964-65; University of Northern Iowa, assistant professor, 1965-68, associate professor of history, 1968-70; McGill University, professor of history, 1970-, William Kingsford professor of history, 1988-. Writer. **Publications:** Die diplomatischen Beziehungen zwischen Württemberg und Bayern im Krimkrieg und bis zum Beginn der Italienischen Krise 1853-1858, 1963; (trans.) John J. McCloy II: Die Verschwörung gegen Hitler: Ein Geschenk an die deutsche Zukunft, 1963; Widerstand, Staatsstreich, Attentat: Der Kampf der Opposition gegen Hitler, 1969, 4th ed., 1985; Die Sicherheit des Diktators: Hitlers Leibwachen, Schutzmassnahmen, Residenzen, Hauptquartiere, 1975; The History of the German Resistance 1933-1945, 1977, 3rd ed., 1996; Hitler's Personal Security, 1979; Widerstand gegen Hitler, 1979, 4th ed., 1994; German Resistance to Hitler, 1988; (contrib.) Germans against Nazism: Nonconformity, Opposition and Resistance in the Third Reich: Essays in Honour of Peter Hoffmann, 1990; Claus Schenk Graf von Stauffenberg und seine Brüder, 1992; Stauffen-berg: A Family History, 1905-1944, 1995, 2nd ed., 2003; Stauffenberg und der 20. Juli 1944, 1998; Stauffenbergs Freund, 2007; Carl Goerdeler and the Jewish Question, 1933-1942, 2011. **Address:** Department of History, McGill University, Rm. 615, Leacock Bldg., 855 Sherbrooke St. W, Montreal, QC H3A 2T7, Canada.

HOFFMANN, Roald. American/Polish (born Poland), b. 1937. **Genres:** Plays/Screenplays, Poetry, Sciences. **Career:** Harvard University, Society of Fellows, junior fellow, 1962-65; Cornell University, faculty, 1965-, Frank H. T. Rhodes professor of humane letters, now Frank H. T. Rhodes professor emeritus of humane letters. Writer. **Publications:** (With R.B. Woodward) Conservation of Orbital Symmetry, 1970; The Metamict State (poems), 1987; Solids and Surfaces: A Chemist's View of Bonding in Extended Structures, 1988; Gaps and Verges (poems), 1990; (with V. Torrence) Chemistry Imagined: Reflections on Science, 1993; The Same and Not the Same, 1995; (with S.L. Schmidt) Old Wine, New Flasks: Reflections on Science and Jewish Tradition, 1997; Memory Effects (poems), 1999; (with C. Djerassi) Oxygen (play), 2001; Soliton (poems) 2002; Catalista (poems, Spanish), 2002. Works appear in anthologies. Contributor of articles to journals and magazines. **Address:** Department of Chemistry and Chemical Biology, Cornell University, Rm. 222, Baker Laboratory, Ithaca, NY 14853-1301, U.S.A. **Online address:** rh34@cornell.edu

HOFFMANN, Stanley. American/Austrian (born Austria), b. 1928. **Genres:** International Relations/Current Affairs, Politics/Government, Essays, Area Studies. **Career:** French Political Science Association, assistant, 1952-53; Harvard University, instructor, 1955-57, assistant professor, 1957-59, associate professor, 1959-63, professor of government, 1963-80, Center for European Studies, chairman, 1969-95, Paul and Catherine Buttenwieser University professor, 1997-, Douglas Dillon professor of the civilization of France, 1980-96; Institut d'études Politiques de Paris, faculty. Writer. **Publications:** Organisations internationales et pouvoirs politiques des Etats, 1954; (co-author) Le Mouvement Poujade, 1956; (ed.) Contemporary Theory in International Relations, 1960; (co-author) In Search of France, 1963; The State of War: Essays on the Theory and Practice of International Politics, 1965; (ed. and intro.) Conditions of World Order, 1968; (ed. with K. Deutsch) The Relevance of International Law: Essays in Honour of Leo Gross, 1968; Gulliver's Troubles: Or, the Setting of American Foreign Policy, 1968; Decline or Renewal?: France Since the 1930's, 1974; La Politique des Sciences Sociales en France, 1975; Sur la France, 1976; Primacy or World Order, 1978; Duties beyond Borders, 1981; (with W.G. Andrews) The Fifth Republic at Twenty, 1981; (ed. with W.G. Andrews) The Impact of the Fifth Republic on France, 1981; (ed. with P. Kitromilides) Culture and Society in Contemporary Europe: A Casebook, 1981; (with C. Vance) Building the Peace: U.S. Foreign Policy for the Next Decade, 1982; Dead Ends, 1983; La nouvelle guerre froide, 1983; Living with Nuclear Weapons, 1983; (ed. with C. Maier) The Marshall Plan: A Retrospective, 1984; Janus and Minerva, 1986; (ed. with A. Gould and C.S. Maier) The Rise of the Nazi Regime: Historical Reassessments, 1986; (ed. with G. Ross and S. Malzacher) The Mitterrand Experiment: Continuity and Change in Modern France, 1987; (ed. with D.P. Fidler) Rousseau on International Relations, 1991; (ed. with R.O. Keohane) The New European Community, 1992; (with R.O. Keohane and J.S. Nye) After the Cold War, 1993; The Tanner Lecture on Human Values, 15 vols., 1994; The European Sisyphus: Essays on Europe, 1964-1994, 1995; The Ethics and Politics of Humanitarian Intervention, 1996; World Disorders: Troubled Peace in the Post-Cold War Era, 1998; (ed. with D.F. Thompson) Redeeming American Political Thought, 1998; (ed.) Political Thought and Political Thinkers, 1998; Amériquevraiment impériale: entretiens sur le vif avec Frédéric Bozo, 2003; America Goes Backward, 2004; Out Of Iraq, 2004; (with F. Bozo) Gulliver Unbound: America's Imperial Temptation and The War in Iraq, 2004; Chaos and Violence: What Globalization, Failed States and Terrorism Mean for U.S. Foreign Policy, 2006; (ed. with C. McDonald) Rousseau and Freedom, 2010. Contributor to books. **Address:** Center for European Studies, Harvard University, 27 Kirkland St., Cambridge, MA 02138, U.S.A. **Online address:** shhoffm@fas.harvard.edu

HOFFSCHWELLE, Mary S. American (born United States), b. 1955. **Genres:** Education, History. **Career:** Middle Tennessee State University, Department of History, professor. Writer. **Publications:** Rebuilding the Rural Southern Community: Reformers, Schools, and Homes in Tennessee, 1900-1930, 1998; The Rosenwald Schools of the American South, 2006; "We Will Independent Be": African American Place Making and the Struggle to Claim Space in the U.S, forthcoming; Designing Modern Childhoods, forthcoming.

Address: Middle Tennessee State University, Rm. 273, Peck Hall,, 1301 E Main St., PO Box 23, Murfreesboro, TN 37132-0001, U.S.A. **Online address:** mhoffsch@mtsu.edu

HOFLER, Robert. American (born United States) **Genres:** Homes/Gardens, Psychology, Sex, Sports/Fitness, Humor/Satire. **Career:** Journalist; Variety, theater reporter, 1999-2005, senior editor, 2005-. Buzz, Life, editor; U.S. magazines, editor. **Publications:** (With C. Hiller) Complete Sexenders Program: For Those Who should Quit but Can't Break the Habit, 1983; (with G. Haubner) Foolproof Bride, 1984; (with C. Zarco) Wild Style, 1985; (with Werner and F. Busen) Tae Kwon Do for Beginners: A Karate Program of Fitness and Self-defense, 1987; The Man Who Invented Rock Hudson: The Pretty Boys and Dirty Deals of Henry Willson, 2005; Variety's the Movie that Changed My Life: 120 Celebrities Pick the Films that Made a Difference, 2009; Party Animals: A Hollywood Tale of Sex, Drugs and Rock n Roll Starring the Fabulous Allan Carr, 2010. **Address:** Variety, 5900 Wilshire Blvd., Ste. 3100, Los Angeles, CA 90036, U.S.A. **Online address:** bob.hofler@variety.com

HOFMANN, Michael. American/German (born Germany), b. 1957. **Genres:** Poetry, Literary Criticism And History, Translations, Novels, Plays/Screenplays. **Career:** University of Michigan, visiting associate professor, 1994; University of Florida, Department of English, lecturer, 1994-200, professor, 2009-; Rutgers University, visiting writer, 2003; New School University, visiting professor; Barnard College, visiting professor; Columbia University, visiting professor. Writer, poet and translator. **Publications:** POETRY: Nights in the Iron Hotel, 1983; Acrimony, 1986; K.S. in Lakeland: New and Selected Poems, 1990; Corona, Corona, 1993; Approximately Nowhere, 1999. TRANSLATOR: (and intro.) Castle Gripsholm, 1985; Bloesch, 1988 in US as Cow, 1990; (with C. Middleton) Balzac's Horse and Other Stories, 1989; The Legend of the Holy Drinker, 1989; (with S. Whiteside) Emotion Pictures: Reflections on the Cinema, 1990; Emotion Pictures: Reflections on the Cinema, 1990; The Logic of Images, 1991; The Story of Mr. Sommer, 1992; Right and Left, 1992; (and intro.) Death in Rome, 1993; The Lord Chandos Letter, 1995; The Film Explainer, 1995; The Land of the Green Plums, 1996; (and intro.) The Man Who Disappeared, 1997; The Act of Seeing, 1997; The Pollen Room, 1998; The String of Peaks, 1998; Rebellion, 1999; Agnes, 2000; My Time with Antonioni, 2000; The Collected Stories, 2001; The Wandering Jews, 2000; On Film, 2001; Luck, 2002; The Hothouse, 2002; (and intro.) The Radetzky Mark, 2002; Junge, The Snowflake Constant, 2002; Amerika: The Man Who Disappeared, 2002; Luck, 2002; (and intro.) Collected Stories of Joseph Roth, 2002; (and intro.) What I saw, 2003; (and intro.) A Sad Affair, 2003; (and intro.) Storm of Steel, 2003; I Saw: Reports from Berlin, 1920-1933, 2003; I Saw: Reports from Berlin, 1920-1933, 2003; (and intro.) Report from a Parisian Paradise: Essays from France, 1925-1939, 2004; Unformed Landscape, 2004; Jungk, Tigor, 2004; (and intro.) The Stalin Front: A Novel of World War II, 2004; Jungk, The Perfect American, 2004; (intro.) Storm of Steel, 2004; (and intro.) Lichtenberg and the Little Flower Girl, 2004; Party in the Blitz: The English Years, 2005; An Innocent Soldier, 2005; Ashes for Breakfast: Selected Poems, 2005; Frost, 2006; In Strange Gardens and Other Stories, 2006; (and ed.) Voyage that Never Ends: Fictions, Poems, Fragments, Letters, 2007; (and intro.) Metamorphosis and Other Stories, 2007; On a Day Like This: A Novel, 2007; Seventh Well, 2008; (afterword) Child of All Nations, 2008; Selected Poems, 2009; (ed.) Alone in Berlin, 2009; Gunter Eich: Selected Poems, 2010; Inheritance, 2010; Leviathan, 2011; Seven Years, 2011; (ed.) Joseph Roth, 2012; We're Flying, 2012. PLAYS: The Double-Bass, 1987; The Good Person of Sichuan, 1989. CRITICISM: Behind the Lines, 2001; (intro.) John Berryman, 2004. (ed.) Robert Lowell, 2006. OTHER: (ed. with J. Lasdun) After Ovid: New Metamorphoses, 1994; (ed.) Twentieth-Century German Poetry: An Anthology, 2006. Contributor to periodicals. Works appear in anthologies. **Address:** Department of English, University of Florida, 4211D Turlington Hall, 4008 Turlington Hall, PO Box 117300, Gainesville, FL 32611-7310, U.S.A. **Online address:** mhofmann@ufl.edu

HOFSCHRÖER, Peter. British (born England) **Genres:** Novels, Military/Defense/Arms Control. **Career:** Military book dealer; Harper Collins, publishing and international sales; Interactive Magic, managing director, 1996-99; CDV, president; JoWooD, intl. sales director, 1999-2001; MPS Software Distribution, sales director; Psygnosis, sales manager; MicroProse Software, German sales manager; IncaGold P.L.C., sales manager, chief operations officer. Writer. **Publications:** Prussian Line Infantry, 1792-1815, 1984; Prussian Cavalry of the Napoleonic Wars, 1985; Prussian Cavalary of the Napoleonic Wars 2: 1807-15, 1986; Prussian Reserve Foreign and Militia Troops, 1806-

15, 1987; Hanoverian Army of the Napoleonic Wars, 1989; 1815, the Waterloo Campaign: Wellington and His German Allies and the Battles of Ligny and Quatre Bras, 1998; 1815, the Waterloo Campaign: The German Victory: From Waterloo to the Fall of Napoleon, 1999; Wellington's Smallest Victory: The Duke, the Model Maker, and the Secret of Waterloo, 2004; Leipzig, 1813: The Battle of the Nations, 2005; Lutzen & Bautzen, 1813: The Turning Point, 2005; Waterloo, 1815: Quatre Bras and Ligny, 2005; Waterloo 1815: Wavre, Plancenoit and the Race to Paris, 2006; (trans. and ed.) On Wellington: A Critique of Waterloo, 2010. **Address:** IncaGold, 28 Victoria St., Douglas, IM IM1 2LE, England.

HOFSTADTER, Douglas (Richard). American (born United States), b. 1945. **Genres:** Information Science/Computers, Language/Linguistics, Philosophy, Translations, Technology, Adult Non-fiction. **Career:** Indiana University, College of Arts and Sciences, from assistant professor to associate professor of computer science, 1977-84, Center for Research on Concepts and Cognition, director, 1988-, college professor of cognitive science and computer science, adjunct professor of history and philosophy of science, philosophy, comparative literature and psychology, 1988-2007, distinguished professor of cognitive science and comparative literature, 2007-; University of Michigan, Walgreen Professor of Cognitive Science, 1984-88. Writer. **Publications:** Göedel, Escher, Bach, an Eternal Golden Braid, 1979; (with D.C. Dennett) The Mind's I: Fantasies And Reflections On Self And Soul, 1981; Metamagical Themas: Questing For The Essence Of Mind And Pattern, 1985; Ambigrammi: Un Microcosmo Ideale Per Lo Studio Della Creatività, 1987; Fluid Concepts and Creative Analogies: Computer Models of The Fundamental Mechanisms of Thought, 1995; Le Ton beau de Marot: In Praise of the Music of Language, 1997; (trans.) A.S. Pushkin, Eugene Onegin: A Novel in Verse, 1999; (ed. and foreword) Gödel's Proof, 2001; (contrib.) Virtual Music: Computer Synthesis of Musical Style, 2001; I am a Strange Loop, 2007; (trans. and intro.) W. Veltroni, The Discovery of Dawn, 2008; (trans.) F. Sagan, Chamade, 2009; (trans.) F. Sagan, That Mad Ache: A Novel, 2009. Contributor to periodicals. **Address:** Center for Research on Concepts and Cognition, Indiana University, 510 N Fess Ave., 819 Eigenmann, 1900 E 10th St., Bloomington, IN 47408-3822, U.S.A. **Online address:** dughof@indiana.edu

HOFSTRA, Warren R. American (born United States), b. 1947. **Genres:** History, Adult Non-fiction, Military/Defense/Arms Control. **Career:** Shenandoah University, Department of History, professor, 1978-. Writer. **Publications:** A Separate Place: The Formation of Clarke County, 1986; (ed.) George Washington and the Virginia Backcountry, 1998; (ed. with K.E. Koons) After the Backcountry: Rural Life in the Great Valley of Virginia, 1800-1900, 2000; (ed. with K.R. Hardwick) Virginia Reconsidered: New Histories of the Old Dominion, 2003; The Planting of New Virginia: Settlement and Landscape in the Shenandoah Valley, 2004; (ed.) Cultures in Conflict: The Seven Years' War in North America, 2007; (ed. with K. Raitz) Great Valley Road of Virginia: Shenandoah Landscapes from Prehistory to the Present, 2010; (ed.) Ulster to America: The Scots-Irish Migration Experience, 1680-1830, 2011. Contributor to periodicals. **Address:** Department of History, Shenandoah University, Gregory 154, 1460 University Dr., Winchester, VA 22601-5100, U.S.A. **Online address:** whofstra@su.edu

HOGAN, David Gerard. American (born United States), b. 1959. **Genres:** Adult Non-fiction, Food And Wine, Biography, History. **Career:** Rogers State College, instructor, 1988-89; Heidelberg College, associate professor of history, 1989-, professor of history. Writer. **Publications:** Selling 'em by the Sack: White Castle and the Creation of American Food, 1997. **Address:** Department of History, Heidelberg College, 7 Pfleiderer, 310 E Market St., Tiffin, OH 44883-2462, U.S.A. **Online address:** dhogan@heidelberg.edu

HOGAN, J. Michael. American (born United States), b. 1953. **Genres:** Communications/Media, Politics/Government, Speech/Rhetoric. **Career:** Cold Mountain Press, associate editor, 1972-76; University of Wisconsin-Madison, Department of Communication Arts, teaching assistant, 1975-80, assistant director of debate and forensics, 1977-79, College of Agriculture and Life Sciences, instructor of public speaking, 1980; Cochise College, writer-in-residence, 1977-78; University of Virginia, assistant professor of rhetoric and communication studies, 1981-86; Southwest Legal Services, vice president, 1984-87; Indiana University-Bloomington, adjunct professor of American studies, 1986-97, Department of Speech Communication, associate professor, 1986-95, professor of speech communication, 1995-97; Pennsylvania State University, Department of Communication Arts and Sciences, professor, 1997-2009, graduate officer, 1999-2003, Center for Civic Engagement and

Center for Democratic Deliberation, professor of rhetoric, director, 2006-, co-director, 2006-11, liberal arts research professor, 2010-. **Publications:** The Panama Canal in American Politics: Domestic Advocacy and the Evolution of Policy, 1986; The Nuclear Freeze Campaign: Rhetoric and Foreign Policy in the Telepolitical Age, 1994; Woodrow Wilson's Western Tour: Rhetoric, Public Opinion and the League of Nations, 2006; (co-author) Public Speaking and Civic Engagement, 2008, 2nd. ed., 2011; (with S.J. Parry-Giles) The Handbook of Rhetoric and Public Address, 2010. EDITOR: Rhetoric and Community: Studies in Unity and Fragmentation, 1998; Rhetoric and Reform in the Progressive Era, 2003. Contributor of articles to journals. **Address:** Department of Communication Arts and Sciences, Pennsylvania State University, 234 Sparks Bldg., University Park, PA 16802-5201, U.S.A. **Online address:** jmh32@psu.edu

HOGAN, Linda. American (born United States), b. 1947. **Genres:** Novels, Novellas/Short Stories, Plays/Screenplays, Poetry, Animals/Pets, Environmental Sciences/Ecology. **Career:** University of Colorado, instructor in creative writing, fiction and native American literature, 1977-79, professor of English and creative writing, 1989-98, professor emeritus; Newberry Library, D'Arcy McNickle Memorial fellow, 1980; Colorado College, TRIBES program, assistant professor, 1982-84; University of Oklahoma, professor; University of Minnesota, associate professor of American studies and American Indian studies, 1984-89; Orion Magazine, advisor; Chickasaw Nation, writer-in-residence; Black Earth Institute, fellow. **Publications:** POETRY: Calling Myself Home, 1979; Daughters, I Love You, 1981; Eclipse, 1984; Seeing through the Sun, 1985; Savings, 1988; The Book of Medicines, 1993. PLAYS: A Piece of Moon, 1981; Mean Spirit, 1986; Aunt Moon, 1986; Indios: A Poem to be Spoken, 2011. NOVELS: Mean Spirit, 1990; Red Claw, 1994; Solar Storms, 1995, Power, 1997. OTHER: That Horse (stories), 1985; Dwellings (essays), 1995; Woman Who Watches over the World: A Native Memoir, 2001; (with B. Peterson) Sightings: The Mysterious Journey of the Gray Whale, 2002; Rounding the Human Corners, 2008: People of the Whale, 2008. EDITOR: (with C. Buechal and J. McDaniel) The Stories We Hold Secret, 1985; (with B. Peterson and D. Metzger) Intimate Nature: The Bond between Women and Animals, 1997; (with B. Peterson) The Sweet Breathing of Plants, 2001; (with B. Peterson) Face to Face, 2004; The Inner Journey: Views from Native Traditions, 2009. Work appears in anthologies. Contributor to periodicals. **Address:** Department of English, University of Colorado, PO Box 226, Boulder, CO 80309, U.S.A.

HOGAN, Mary. American (born United States), b. 1957. **Genres:** Romance/Historical, Young Adult Fiction. **Career:** Teen Magazine, editor. Novelist. **Publications:** YOUNG ADULT FICTION: The Serious Kiss, 2005; Perfect Girl, 2007; Pretty Face, 2008. SUSANNA SERIES; YOUNG ADULT FICTION: Susanna Sees Stars, 2006; Susanna Hits Hollywood, 2008; Susanna Covers the Catwalk, 2008; Susanna Falls in Love...in London in US as Susanna Loves London, 2009. **Address:** New York, NY , U.S.A. **Online address:** maryhogan@msn.com

HOGAN, Michael William. American (born United States), b. 1950. **Genres:** Young Adult Fiction, Mystery/Crime/Suspense. **Career:** Writer, artist and attorney. **Publications:** Man Out of Time, 2003; Burial of the Dead, 2008. Contributor of short fiction to journals. **Address:** Cleveland, OH , U.S.A. **Online address:** h-hogan@sbcglobal.net

HOGAN, Patrick Colm. American (born United States), b. 1957. **Genres:** Literary Criticism And History, Cultural/Ethnic Topics, Essays. **Career:** University of Kentucky, assistant professor of English, 1983-87; University of Connecticut, assistant professor, 1987-90, associate professor of English, 1990-96, acting department head, 1994-95, professor of English, 1996-, Comparative Literature and Cultural Studies, faculty, 1990-, India Studies, faculty, 2003-, Cognitive Science, faculty, 2003-. Writer. **Publications:** The Politics of Interpretation: Ideology, Professionalism and the Study of Literature, 1990; Joyce Milton, the Theory of Influence, 1995; On Interpretation: Meaning and Inference in Law, Psychoanalysis and Literature, 1996; Colonialism and Cultural Identity: Crises of Tradition in the Anglophone Literatures of India, Africa and the Caribbean, 2000; Philosophical Approaches to the Study of Literature, 2000; The Culture of Conformism: Understanding Social Consent, 2001; Cognitive Science, Literature and the Arts: A Guide for Humanists, 2003; The Mind and Its Stories: Narrative Universals and Human Emotion, 2003; Empire and Poetic Voice: Cognitive and Cultural Studies of Literary Tradition and Colonialism, 2004; Understanding Indian Movies: Indian Culture, the Human Brain and Cinematic Imagination, 2008;

Understanding Nationalism: On Narrative, Cognitive Science and Identity, 2009; Affective Narratology: The Emotional Structure of Stories, 2011; What Literature Teaches Us About Emotion, 2011. EDITOR: (with L. Pandit) Criticism and Lacan: Essays and Dialogue on Language, Structure and the Unconscious, 1990; (with L. Pandit) Literary India: Comparative Studies in Aesthetics, Colonialism and Culture, 1995; (with L. Pandit) Rabindranath Tagore: Universality and Tradition, 2003; Cambridge Encyclopedia of the Language Sciences, 2010. **Address:** Department of English, University of Connecticut, 215 Glenbrook Rd., U-4025, Storrs, CT 06269-4025, U.S.A. **Online address:** patrick.hogan@uconn.edu

HOGAN, Ron. American (born United States) **Genres:** Law, Art/Art History. **Career:** Duttons Brentwood Bookstore, staff; Amazon.com, review editor; Beatrice Web site, creator and editor, 1995-, online marketing consultant, 2010-; writer, 2000-; Galley Cat, senior editor, 2005-09. **Publications:** (With B.M. Gesser and T.N. Turner) Vault Guide to the Top Boston Law Firms, 2003; (co-author) Vault Guide to the Top Government and Nonprofit Legal Employers, 2003; The Stewardess Is Flying the Plane! American Films of the 1970s, 2005; Getting Right With Tao: A Contemporary Spin on the Tao Te Ching, 2010. **Address:** c/o Author Mail, Bullfinch Press, 1271 Ave. of the Americas, New York, NY 10020, U.S.A. **Online address:** ronhogan@beatrice.com

HOGE, Hilary. American (born United States), b. 1954. **Genres:** Women's Studies And Issues, Human Relations/Parenting, Social Sciences. **Career:** Harvard University Medical School, resident in psychiatry, 1988; Boston Philharmonic Orchestra, violinist. Writer. **Publications:** Women's Stories of Divorce at Childbirth: When the Baby Rocks the Cradle, 2002. **Address:** 1680-A Beacon St., Brookline, MA 02445-2180, U.S.A. **Online address:** hhoge@massmed.org

HOGELAND, William. American (born United States) **Genres:** History, Biography. **Career:** Freelance writer. **Publications:** The Whiskey Rebellion: George Washington, Alexander Hamilton, and the Frontier Rebels Who Challenged America's Newfound Sovereignty, 2006; Inventing American History, 2009; Declaration: The Nine Tumultuous Weeks When America Became Independent, May 1-July 4, 1776, 2010. Contributor to periodicals. **Address:** c/o Author Mail, Scribner Publishing, 1230 Ave. of the Americas, New York, NY 10020, U.S.A. **Online address:** whogeland@earthlink.net

HOGENDORN, Jan Stafford. American (born United States), b. 1937. **Genres:** Economics. **Career:** Boston University, instructor of economics, 1963-64; Colby College, assistant professor, 1966-69, associate professor, 1969-76, professor, 1976-77, Grossman professor of economics, 1977-2003, Grossman professor emeritus, 2003-. Writer. **Publications:** Managing the Modern Economy, 1972, 2nd ed., 1975; Markets in the Modern Economy, 1974; Modern Economics: An Introduction, 1975; Nigerian Groundnut Exports: Origins and Early Development, 1978; (with H. Gemery) The Uncommon Market, 1979; (with W. Brown) The New International Economics, 1979; The Grossman Lectures at Colby College 1977-1983, 1984; (with M. Johnson) The Shell Money of the Slave Trade, 1986; Economic Development, 1987, rev. ed., 1996; (with P. Lovejoy) Slow Death for Slavery, 1993; Modern Economics, 1995; International Economics in the Age of Globalization, 2000. **Address:** Department of Economics, Colby College, 4000 Mayflower Hill, Waterville, ME 04901-8852, U.S.A. **Online address:** jshogend@colby.edu

HOGG, David S. American (born United States), b. 1971. **Genres:** Theology/Religion. **Career:** Southeastern Baptist Theological Seminary, faculty, 2002-. Writer. **Publications:** Anselm of Canterbury: The Beauty of Theology, 2004. **Address:** Southeastern Baptist Theological Seminar, PO Box 1889, Wake Forest, NC 27588, U.S.A. **Online address:** dhogg@sebts.edu

HOGG, James (Dalby). British (born England), b. 1937. **Genres:** Biography, Humor/Satire, Autobiography/Memoirs, History. **Career:** British Broadcasting Corp. (BBC-TV), reporter, 1965-. Writer. **Publications:** (Ed.) Lord Emsworth's Annotated Whiffle: The Care of the Pig, 1992; The Queen Mother Remembered, 2002. **Address:** Noon's Folly Cottage, Melbourn, Royston, CB SG8 7NG, England. **Online address:** jmshogg@aol.com

HOGG, Patrick Scott. Scottish (born Scotland), b. 1961?. **Genres:** Literary Criticism And History, Poetry. **Career:** Writer. **Publications:** Robert Burns: The Lost Poems, 1997; (ed. with A. Noble) The Canongate Burns: The Complete Poems and Songs of Robert Burns, 2001. Robert Burns: The Patriot

Bard, 2008. **Address:** Canongate Books, 14 High St., Edinburgh, LT EH1 1TE, Scotland. **Online address:** ps.hogg@blueyonder.co.uk

HOGGARD, James. American (born United States), b. 1941. **Genres:** Novels, Novellas/Short Stories, Plays/Screenplays, Poetry, Essays, Translations. **Career:** University of Kansas, teaching assistant, 1963-65; Midwestern State University, instructor, 1966-68, assistant professor, 1968-72, associate professor, 1972-77, professor, 1977-, McMurtry distinguished professor of English, 1997-2001, Perkins-Prothro distinguished professor of English, 2001-, Midwestern State University Press, director. Writer. **Publications:** NON-FICTION: Elevator Man (non-fiction), 1983. POETRY: Eyesigns, 1977; The Shaper Poems, 1983; Two Gulls, One Hawk, 1983; Breaking an Indelicate Statue, 1986; Medea in Taos, 2000; Rain in a Sunlit Sky, 2000; Wearing The River, 2005; Triangles of Light: The Edward Hopper Poems, 2009. NOVELS: Trotter Ross, 1981, rev. ed., 1999; Mayor's Daughter, 2011. STORIES: Riding the Wind and Other Tales, 1997; Patterns of Illusion: Stories and a Novella, 2002. TRANSLATOR: The Art of Dying, 1988; Love Breaks, 1991; Chronicle of My Worst Years, 1994; Alone against the Sea: Poems from Cuba, 1998; Stolen Verses and Other Poems, 2000; Splintered Silences, 2000; Ashes In Love: Translations of Poems by Oscar Hahn, 2009. **Address:** Department of English, Midwestern State University, 211 Bea Wood Hall, 3410 Taft Blvd., Wichita Falls, TX 76308, U.S.A. **Online address:** james.hoggard@mwsu.edu

HOGGART, Richard. British (born England), b. 1918. **Genres:** Communications/Media, Cultural/Ethnic Topics, Education, Literary Criticism And History, Essays, Social Sciences, Reference. **Career:** University of Hull, extra-mural staff tutor in English literature, 1946-56, senior staff tutor, 1957-59; University of Rochester, visiting professor of English, 1956-57; University of Leicester, senior lecturer in English, 1959-62; Royal Shakespeare Theatre, governor, 1962-88; University of Birmingham, professor of English, 1962-73, Centre for Contemporary Cultural Studies, founder, 1964-, director, 1964-73; UNESCO, assistant director-general, 1971-75; University of Sussex, Institute of Development Studies, visiting fellow, 1975; University of London, Goldsmith's College, warden, 1976-84, retired, 1984. Writer. **Publications:** (Ed. with J. Hewett) Four in Hand: An Excursion, 1945; Auden: An Introductory Essay, 1951, rev. ed., 1966; The Uses of Literacy: Changing Patterns in English Mass Culture, 1957, rev. ed., 1998; W.H. Auden, 1957, rev. ed., 1966; Prefabricated Thinking, 1958; (ed.) W.H. Auden: A Selection, 1961; Teaching Literature, 1963; Schools of English and Contemporary Society, 1963; The Critical Movement, 1964; Higher Education and Cultural Change, 1965; (intro.) The Road to Wigan Pier, 1965; (with M.C. Bradbrook) W.H. Auden and T.S. Eliot, 1965; A Question of Time: Some Problems in Autobiographical Writing, 1965; (ed.) The Way of All Flesh, 1966; (ed.) Your Sunday Paper, 1967; Contemporary Cultural Studies: An Approach to the Study of Literature and Society, 1969; Speaking to Each Other, 2 vols., 1970; La Culture Du Pauvre; Études sur le style De Vie Des Classes Populaires en Angleterre, 1971; On Culture and Communication, 1972 in UK as Only Connect: On Culture and Communication, 1972; Only Connect (Reith Lectures), 1972; An Idea and Its Servants: UNESCO from Within, 1978; An English Temper: Essays on Education, Culture and Communications, 1982; (ed. with J. Morgan) The Future of Broadcasting: Essays on Authority, Style and Choice, 1982; (ed.) Professionalism and Flexibility In Learning, 1982; (with D. Johnson) An Idea of Europe, 1987; A Local Habitation, 1988; (ed.) Liberty and Legislation, 1989; A Sort of Clowning: Life and Times 1940-59, 1990; An Imagined Life: Life and Times 1959-91, 1992; (ed.) Oxford Illustrated Encyclopedia of Peoples and Cultures, 1992; Townscape with Figures, 1994; A Measured Life: The Times and Places of an Orphaned Intellectual, 1994; The Way We Live Now, 1995, rev. ed. as The Tyranny of Relativism: Culture and Politics in Contemporary English Society, 1998; First and Last Things, 1999; Between Two Worlds: Politics, Anti-Politics and the Unpolitical, 2002; Everyday Language and Everyday Life, 2003; Mass Media in a Mass Society: Myths and Reality, 2004; Promises to Keep: Thoughts in Old Age, 2005. Contributor to books and periodicals. **Address:** 19 Mount Pleasant, Norwich, NF NR2 2DH, England. **Online address:** richardhoggart@onetel.net.uk

HOGUE, James K. American (born United States), b. 1954. **Genres:** Military/Defense/Arms Control, History, Humanities. **Career:** Woodrow Wilson School of International and Public Affairs, postdoctoral fellow, 1998-99; University of North Carolina, associate professor of history, 1999-. Writer and historian. **Publications:** Uncivil War: Five New Orleans Street Battles and the Rise and Fall of Radical Reconstruction, 2006; (with J.M McPherson) Ordeal by Fire: The Civil War and Reconstruction, 2009. Contributor to periodicals and journals. **Address:** Department of History, University of North Carolina, 232 Garinger, 9201 University City Blvd., Charlotte, NC 28223-0001, U.S.A. **Online address:** jhogue@uncc.edu

HOHENEGGER, Beatrice. American/Italian (born Italy) **Genres:** History. **Career:** Tricom (film production Co.) creative development coordinator; Getty Publications, translator and editor; Houghton Mifflin Harcourt Publishing Co., translator and editor; McGraw-Hill, translator and editor; Wiley & Sons, translator and editor. Photographer, curator and historian. **Publications:** Liquid Jade: The Story of Tea from East to West, 2006; (ed.) Steeped in History: The Art of Tea, 2009. **Address:** Fowler Museum, University of California, 308 Charles E. Young Dr. N, PO Box 951549, Los Angeles, CA 90095, U.S.A. **Online address:** beatrice@beatricehohenegger.com

HOILE, David. British (born England), b. 1960?. **Genres:** Politics/Government, Law. **Career:** House of Commons, private secretary and research assistant, 1986-90; National Center for Public Policy Research, visiting research fellow, 1988-; Westminster Associates, political consultant, 1988-; Mozambique Institute, executive director, 1991-95; European-Sudanese Public Affairs Council (ESPAC), public affairs consultant and director. Writer. **Publications:** Understanding Sanctions, 1988; Mozambique: A Nation in Crisis, 1989; Mozambique, Resistance and Freedom: A Case for Reassessment, 1994; (ed.) Mozambique 1962-93: A Political Chronology, 1994; Farce Majeure: The Clinton Administration's Sudan Policy 1993-2000, 2000; (ed.) Search for Peace in the Sudan: A Chronology of the Sudanese Peace Process 1989-2001, 2002; Images of Sudan: Case Studies in Propaganda and Misrepresentation, 2003; Darfur in Perspective, 2005; Darfur: The Road to Peace, 2008. **Address:** European-Sudanese Public Affairs Council (ESPAC), 1 Northumberland Ave., London, GL WC2N 5BW, England. **Online address:** director@espac.org

HOKANSON, (Anthony) Drake. American (born United States), b. 1951. **Genres:** Travel/Exploration, Air/Space Topics, Transportation, Area Studies, Essays, Photography, Writing/Journalism, Agriculture/Forestry, Politics/Government. **Career:** Johnson County Regional Planning Commission, photographer and producer, 1973; University of Iowa, Office of Public Information, photojournalist, manager of photography unit, 1974-82, instructor, 1982-84, lecturer in journalism and mass communication, 1984-88; Lakeland College, Summer Writing Festival, instructor, 1987-, assistant professor of writing, 1991-97, Tokyo branch, 1995; City University, lecturer, 1989; Winona State University, assistant professor of mass communication, 1997-; University of Nebraska, Center for Great Plains Studies, associate fellow, 1997-. Writer and photographer. **Publications:** Lincoln Highway: Main Street Across America, 1988, rev. ed., 1999; Transportation and the Iowa Landscape, 1989; Landforms of Iowa (photographs), 1991; (foreword) A Complete Official Road Guide of the Lincoln Highway, 1924, 1993; Reflecting a Prairie Town: A Year in Peterson, 1994; Land of the Fragile Giants: Landscapes, Environments and Peoples of the Loess Hills (photographs), 1994; A Sense of Place, A Sense of Time (photographs), 1994; Plain Pictures: Images of the American Prairie, 1996; Wisconsin Then and Now: A Rephotographic Essay (photographs), 1998; Wisconsin Revisited: A Rephotographic Essay (photographs), 1998; (with C. Kratz) Watching for the Ferris Wheel, 2000; A Look at the Land in Iowa: A Portrait of the Land, 2000; (co-ed.) Ica from the Air: An Aviator's Story, 2004; America from the Air: An Aviator's Story, 2004; (with C. Kratz) Purebred & Home-Grown: America's County Fairs, 2008. Contributor of articles to books and periodicals. **Address:** Department of Mass Communication, Winona State University, B-10 Phelps Hall, PO Box 5838, Winona, MN 55987, U.S.A. **Online address:** dhokanson@winona.edu

HOLAHAN, Susan. American (born United States), b. 1940?. **Genres:** Poetry, Literary Criticism And History. **Career:** University of Rochester, teacher; Yale University, teacher; Newsday, editor; Yale University Press, editor. **Publications:** Sister Betty Reads the Whole You (poetry), 1998. Contributor to journals, periodicals, magazines and newspapers. **Address:** PO Box 155, East Middlebury, VT 05740-0155, U.S.A.

HOLBROOK, David (Kenneth). See Obituaries.

HOLBROOK, Sara. American (born United States) **Genres:** Novels, Children's Non-fiction, Picture/Board Books, Poetry, Young Adult Non-fiction, Education, Reference. **Career:** Writer and educator. **Publications:** FOR CHILDREN POETRY: The Dog Ate My Home Work, 1990, 2nd ed., 1996; Kid Poems for the Not-So-Bad, 1992 as I Never Said I Wasn't Difficult, 1997;

Nothing's the End of the World: Poems, 1995; Am I Naturally This Crazy?, 1996; Which Way to the Dragon!: Poems for the Coming-on-Strong, 1996; Walking on the Boundaries of Change: Poems of Transition, 1998. OTHERS: Feelings Make Me Real, 1990; Some Families, 1990; What's So Big about Cleveland, Ohio? (picture book), 1997; Wham! It's a Poetry Jam: Discovering Performance Poetry, 2002; Isn't She Ladylike, 2002; By Definition: Poems of Feelings, 2003; Practical Poetry: A Nonstandard Approach to Meeting Content-Area Standards, 2005; (with M. Salinger) Outspoken!: How to Improve Writing and Speaking Skills Through Poetry Performance, 2006; (with A. Wolf) More than Friends: Poems from Him and Her, 2008; High Definition: Unforgettable Vocabulary-Building Strategies Across Genres and Subjects, 2010; Zombies: Evacuate the School, 2010; Weird? (Me Too!): Let's be Friends, 2010. FOR ADULTS: Chicks up Front (poetry), 1998. Contributor to periodicals. **Address:** 7326 Presley Ave., Mentor, OH 44060, U.S.A. **Online address:** sara@saraholbrook.com

HOLBROOK, Teri. American (born United States) **Genres:** Mystery/Crime/Suspense, Young Adult Fiction, Reference. **Career:** Georgia State University, faculty. Mystery novelist. **Publications:** A Far and Deadly Cry, 1995; The Grass Widow, 1996; Sad Water, 1999; Der Junge am Fenster, 1999; Letzte Glut, 2000; The Mother Tongue, 2001; Schrei im Wind, 2001; Des Teufels Wort, 2002. Works appear in anthologies. **Address:** Bantam Books, 1540 Broadway Ste., 9E, New York, NY 10036, U.S.A. **Online address:** btholbrook@compuserve.com

HOLCOMB, Brent H. American (born United States), b. 1950. **Genres:** History, Genealogy/Heraldry. **Career:** South Carolina Magazine of Ancestral Research, editor. **Publications:** South Carolina Magazine of Ancestral Research, 1973; 1800 Lexington County Census, 1974; Anson County, N.C., Deed Abstracts, 1974; Two 1787 Tax Lists: Ninety Six District, South Carolina, 1974; Anson County, North Carolina Wills and Estates, 1749-1795, 1975; North Carolina Land Grants in South Carolina, 1975; Mecklenburg County, North Carolina Deed Abstracts. vol. I, 1763-1768, 1976; Probate Records of South Carolina, 1977; Marriage and Death Notices from Pendleton (S.C.) Messenger, 1807-1851, 1977; Bedenbaugh-Betenbaugh Family of South Carolina, 1978; Marriage and Death Notices from Camden, South Carolina Newspapers, 1816-1865, 1978; Memorialized Records of Lexington District, South Carolina, 1814-1825, 1978; Ninety Six District, South Carolina, Journal of the Court of Ordinary, Inventory Book, Will Book, 1781-1786, 1978; Saint David's Parish, South Carolina, Minutes of the Vestry, 1768-1832, Parish Register, 1819-1924, 1979; Bladen County, North Carolina, Abstracts of Early Deeds, 1738-1804, 1979; Brief Guide to South Carolina Genealogical Research and Records, 1979; Marriage and Death Notices from the Lutheran Observer, 1831-1861, And the Southern Lutheran, 1861-1865, 1979; Marriage and Death Notices from the Southern Christian Advocate, 1979; Marriage, Death, and Estate Notices from Georgetown, S.C. Newspapers, 1791-1861, 1979; (with E.O. Parker) Mecklenburg County, North Carolina Deed Abstracts, 1763-1779, 1979; (ed. with E.O. Parker) Chester County, South Carolina Minutes of the County Court, 1785-1799, 1979; (ed.) Union County, South Carolina, Minutes of the County Court, 1785-1799, 1979; Anson County, North Carolina, Deed Abstracts, 1749-1766, Abstracts of Wills & Estates, 1749-1795, 1980; Index to the 1850 Mortality Schedule of South Carolina, 1980; Index to the 1850 Mortality Schedule of South Carolina, 1980; Marriage and Death Notices from the Charleston Observer, 1827-1845, 1980; Mecklenburg County, North Carolina Abstracts of Early Wills, 1763-1790 (1749-1790), 1980; North Carolina Land Grants in South Carolina, 1980; (ed.) Spartanburgh [sic] County, South Carolina, Minutes of the County Court, 1785-1799, 1980; Guide and Index to the Records of Washington Equity District (Greenville, Laurens, and Newberry), 1808-1821, 1981; Lancaster County, South Carolina Deed Abstracts, 1787-1811, 1981; Marlborough County, South Carolina Minutes of the County Court, 1785-1799, and Minutes of the Court of Ordinary, 1791-1821, 1981; Marriage and Death Notices from Columbia, South Carolina, Newspapers, 1792-1839, 1982; Orangeburgh District, South Carolina Returns in Partition from the Court of Equity, 1824-1837, 1982; Rucker Family of South Carolina, 1752-1983, 1983; Lineage & Descendants of John Wesley Harrelson, Marion County, South Carolina, 1756-1984, 1984; Ancestors and Descendants of Charles Humphries (d. 1837) of Union District, South Carolina, 1677-1984: Including Records from Virginia, North Carolina, South Carolina, Mississippi, and Other States, 1985; Guide to South Carolina Genealogical Research and Records, 1986; Kershaw County, South Carolina, Minutes of the County Court, 1791-1799, 1986; North Carolina Land Grants in South Carolina, 1986; Record of Deaths in Columbia, South Carolina, and Elsewhere as Recorded by John Glass, 1859-1877, 1986;

Greer and Related Families: Sanders, Sims, Glenn, Christmas, Smith, Ferris, and Carver, of the Carolinas and Virginia, 1987; Union County, South Carolina, Will Abstracts, 1787-1849, 1987; (ed.) Bute County, North Carolina Minutes of the Court of Pleas and Quarter Sessions, 1767-1779, 1988; Ancestors and Descendants of Mercer Silas Bailey (1841-1926), 1767-1988, 1988; Marriage and Death Notices from Columbia, South Carolina, Newspapers, 1838-1860, Including Legal Notices from Burnt Counties, 1988; Jackson of North Pacolet: Descendants of Samuel Jackson, Sr. (Died 1796, Spartanburg County, South Carolina), 1991; Death and Obituary Notices from the Southern Christian Advocate, 1867-1878, 1993; Marriage Notices from the Southern Christian Advocate, 1867-1878, 1994; (ed.) Tryon County, North Carolina Minutes of the Court of Pleas and Quarter Sessions, 1769-1779, 1994; Bedenbaugh-Betenbaugh Family: Descendants of Johann Michael Bidenbach: From Germany to South Carolina, 1752, 1995; Parish Registers of Prince George Winyah Church, Georgetown, South Carolina, 1815-1936, 1996; Petitions for Land from the South Carolina Council Journals, 1996; Guide to South Carolina Genealogical Research and Records, 1998; Union County, South Carolina Deed Abstracts, 1998; Newberry County, South Carolina Deed Abstracts, 1999; York County, South Carolina Will Abstracts: 1787-1862 (1770-1862), 2002; (ed.) Charleston District, South Carolina, Journal of the Court of Ordinary, 1812-1830, 2002; Death and Marriage Notices from the Watchman and Observer, 1845-1855, 2004; Laurens County, South Carolina Minutes of the County Court, 1786-1789, 2004; Chester County, South Carolina, Deed Abstracts, 2005; Kershaw County, South Carolina, Minutes of the County Court, 1791-1799, 2005; Chester County, South Carolina, Will Abstracts, 1787-1838 [1776-1838], 2006; South Carolina's Royal Grants, 2006; York County, South Carolina Deed Abstracts, 2008; (comp.) Marriage and Death Notices from the Southern Presbyterian, 2009. **Address:** South Carolina Magazine of Ancestral Research, PO Box 21766, Columbia, SC 29221, U.S.A. **Online address:** scmar@juno.com

HOLDEFER, Charles. French/American (born United States), b. 1959. **Genres:** Novels. **Career:** Universite de Poitiers, instructor in language, 1989-; University of Oregon, visiting associate professor, 2007; University of Iowa, instructor. Writer. **Publications:** Apology for Big Rod, or, The Defiler, 1997; Nice, 2001; (ed. with A. McKeown) Philip Larkin and the Poetics of Resistance, 2006; The Contractor, 2007; Back in the Game, 2012; Prospects of Joy, forthcoming. Contributor to books and periodicals. **Address:** Permanent Press, 4170 Noyac Rd., Sag Harbor, NY 11963-2809, U.S.A. **Online address:** mail@charlesholdefer.com

HOLDEN, Anthony (Ivan). British (born England), b. 1947. **Genres:** Biography, Translations, Sports/Fitness, Autobiography/Memoirs, Humor/Satire. **Career:** Evening Echo, reporter, 1970-73; London Sunday Times, general reporter, 1973-77; Observer, chief U.S. correspondent, 1979-81; Punch Magazine, transatlantic cables columnist, 1979-81; Times, features editor and assistant editor, 1981-82; BBC Radio 4, presenter of in the air, 1982-84; freelance writer, 1982-85, 1986-; Today, executive editor, 1985-86. **Publications:** (Ed. and trans.) Agamemnon, 1969; (trans. and intro.) Greek Pastoral Poetry; Theocritus, Bion, Moschus, The Pattern Poems, 1974; The St. Albans Poisoner: The Life and Crimes of Graham Young, 1974; Prince Charles: A Biography in UK as Charles, Prince of Wales, 1979; Their Royal Highnesses: The Prince and Princess of Wales, 1981; (intro.) Great Royal Front Pages, 1983; Anthony Holden's Royal Quiz: The Penguin Master quiz, 1983; Of Presidents, Prime Ministers, and Princes: A Decade in Fleet Street, 1984; The Queen Mother, 1985, rev. ed., 1993; (trans. with A. Holden) L. da Ponte, Mozart's Don Giovanni, 1987; King Charles III: A Biography, 1988; Olivier, 1988; Laurence Olivier, 1990; (ed.) The Last Paragraph: The Journalism of David Blundy, 1990; Big Deal: A Year as a Professional Poker Player, 1990 in UK as Big Deal: One Year as a Professional Poker Player, 2002; A Princely Marriage: Charles and Diana, the First Ten Years, 1991; The Tarnished Crown: Princess Diana and the House of Windsor, 1993; Behind the Oscar: The Secret History of the Academy Awards, 1993; Tchaikovsky: A Biography, 1995; Diana: A Life & a Legacy, 1997; Charles at Fifty, 1998; Charles: A Biography, 1998; (ed. with F. Kermode) The Mind Has Mountains, 1999; (ed. with U. Owen) There Are Kermodians: A Liber Amicorum for F. Kermode, 1999; William Shakespeare: His Life and Work, 1999 in US as William Shakespeare: The Man Behind the Genius: A Biography, 2000, rev. ed. as William Shakespeare: An Illustrated Biography, 2002; The Drama of Love, Life & Death in Shakespeare, 2002; Wit in the Dungeon: The Remarkable Life of Leigh Hunt: Poet, Revolutionary, and The Last of the Romantics, 2005; The Man Who Wrote Mozart: The Extraordinary Life of Lorenzo Da Ponte, 2006; Bigger Deal: A Year on the New Poker Circuit, 2007; Olivier, 2007; Holden on Hold' Em,

2008. Contributor of articles to periodicals and magazines. **Address:** Rogers, Coleridge & White Ltd., 20 Powis Mews, London, GL W11 1JN, England.

HOLDEN, Craig. American (born United States) **Genres:** Novels. **Career:** New Mexico State University, visiting writer; University of Michigan, faculty; University of Toledo, faculty. Writer. **Publications:** NOVELS: The River Sorrow, 1994; The Last Sanctuary, 1996; Four Corners of Night, 1999; The Jazz Bird, 2002; The Narcissist's Daughter, 2005; Matala, 2008. **Address:** NM , U.S.A. **Online address:** craig@craigholden.com

HOLDEN, Dalby. *See* **HAMMOND, Gerald (Arthur Douglas).**

HOLDEN, Greg. American (born United States), b. 1957?. **Genres:** Novels, Technology, Information Science/Computers. **Career:** Chicago Tribune, copy clerk, editorial assistant, 1978-79; Journal-news Publications, writer, 1979-83; University of Chicago, Office of University Publications, writer to assistant director, 1983-95; Desktop Publishing Consultant, staff, 1987-89; full-time freelance writer and website designer, 1996-; Stylus Media (Web site design Co.), owner, project manager/writer/editor, 2009-. **Publications:** Publishing on the Web, 1995; (with T. Webster) Mastering Netscape 2.0 for Macintosh, 1995; Official Online Marketing with Netscape Book: Build Your Business with the Power of Netscape, 1996; Mastering Netscape 4.0 for Macintosh, 1996; Creating Web Pages for Kids and Parents, 1997; Small Business Internet for Dummies, 1998; Windows 98 Registry, 1998; Cliffs Notes on Buying and Selling on eBay, 1999; Apache Server Commentary, 1999; Starting an Online Business for Dummies, 1999, 6th ed., 2010; Internet Auctions for Dummies, 1999; Apache Server for Windows, 1999; Tips and Tactics for Using the Internet to Run Your Business, 2000; Literary Chicago: A Book Lovers Tour of the Windy City, 2001; Dreamweaver 4 Visual Insight, 2001; E-commerce Essentials with Microsoft FrontPage Version 2002, 2001; Microsoft FrontPage: Version 2002 Plain and Simple, 2002; How to Do Everything with Your eBay Business, 2003, 2nd ed., 2005; (with J. Ballew) The Complete Idiot's Guide to Adobe Photoshop Elements 2.0, 2003; (with W.R. Stanek) Faster Smarter Microsoft Office FrontPage 2003, 2004; Karma Kids: Answering Everyday Parenting Questions with Buddhist Wisdom, 2004; EBay Poweruser's Bible, 2004, 2nd ed., 2007; Norton Internet Security for Dummies, 2004; How to Do Everything with eBay, 2004; Degunking eBay, 2005; The Collector's Guide to eBay: The Ultimate Resource for Buying Selling and Valuing Collectibles, 2005; Absolute Beginner's Guide to Online Dating, 2005; (with J. Finlayson) Fundraising on eBay: How to Raise Big Money on the World's Greatest Online Marketplace, 2005; Selling Beyond eBay: Foolproof Ways to Reach More Customers and Make Big Money on Rival Online Marketplaces, 2006; Secrets of eBay Millionaires: Inside Success StoriesAnd Proven Money-Making Tips from eBay's Greatest Sellers, 2006; How to do Everything With Microsoft Office Live, 2007; 1000 Best eBay Powerseller Secrets, 2007; (with A. Borelli) Affiliate Millions: Make a Fortune Using Search Marketing on Google and Beyond, 2007; Go Google: 20 Ways to Reach More Customers and Build Revenue with Google Business Tool, 2008; Introducing Microsoft Expression Studio: Using Design, Web Blend and Media to Create Professional Digital Content, 2008; Booklover's Guide to the Midwest: A Literary Tour, 2008; Brilliant Home Networking for the Over 50s, 2009; Brilliant Microsoft Excel 2007: Tips & Tricks, 2009; (contrib.) Guide to Firewalls and Network Security with Intrusion Detection and VPNs, 2nd ed., 2009; Computer Basics for the Over 50s in Simple Steps, 2009; (co-author) E-business, 2009; Brilliant Home & Wireless Networks, 2009; Laptop Basics for the Over 50s in Simple Steps, 2010; Microsoft Excel 2010 in Simple Steps, 2010; Using the Internet for the Over 50s, 2010; Microsoft Office 2010 in Simple Steps, 2010; Business Reports for Busy People: Timesaving, Ready-to-Use Reports for Any Occasion, 2011; Expression Web Designer Bible, forthcoming. **Address:** Stylus Media, 1826 W Cornelia, Chicago, IL 60657, U.S.A. **Online address:** gholden@interaccess.com

HOLDEN, Peter. British (born England), b. 1948. **Genres:** Adult Non-fiction, Animals/Pets, Children's Non-fiction, Natural History, Zoology, Reference. **Career:** Freelance genealogist, 1968-69; Royal Society for the Protection of Birds (RSPB), assistant education officer, 1969-74, Young Ornithologists Club, national organizer, 1974-92, RSPB Youth and Volunteer Department, head, 1992-. Writer. **Publications:** (With J.T.R. Sharrock) The RSPB Book of British Birds, 1978; (ed. with P. Gonsalves) Alternative Tourism: A Resource Book, 1985; (ed. with J. Horlemann and G.F. Pfäfflin) Tourism, Prostitution, Development: Documentation, 1985; (ed. with P. Gonsalves) Alternative Tourism: A Resource Book, 1985; Alternative Tourism: Report of the Workshop on Alternative Tourism with a Focus on Asia, Chiang Mai, Thailand,

April 26-May 8, 1984, 1988; (contrib.) Tourism, an Ecumenical Concern: The Story of the Ecumenical Coalition on Third World Tourism, 1988; Collins Wild Guide to Birds, 1996; (with B. Oddie) Bird in the Nest, 1997; (with J.T.R. Sharrock) RSPB Guide to British Birds, 2002; FOR CHILDREN: Spotter's Guide to Birds, 1978; Spotter's Guide to Birds of Prey, 1981; First Book Birds, 1984; Migrants and Migration, 1994. **Address:** Royal Society for the Protection of Birds, The Lodge, Sandy, BD SG19 2DL, England.

HOLDEN, Philip (Joseph). Singaporean/British (born England), b. 1962. **Genres:** Literary Criticism And History. **Career:** University of Florida, teaching assistant, 1984-86; Hunan Normal University, foreign expert, 1986-87; Nanyang Technological University, National Institute of Education, lecturer, 1994-97, assistant professor of literature and cultural studies, 1998-2000; Open University, part-time tutor and part-time counselor, 1996-97, 1998-99; University of Warwick, Centre for British and Comparative Cultural Studies, visiting fellow, 1997-98; National University of Singapore, Department of English Language and Literature, assistant professor, 2000-02, associate professor, 2003-. Writer. **Publications:** Orienting Masculinity, Orienting Nation: W. Somerset Maugham's Exotic Fiction, 1996; Modern Subjects/Colonial Texts: Hugh Clifford & the Discipline of English Literature in the Straits Settlements & Malaya, 1895-1907, 2000; (ed. with R.J. Ruppel) Imperial Desire: Dissident Sexualities and Colonial Literature, 2003; (ed. with M. Ng) Reading Chinese Transnationalisms: Society, Literature, Film, 2006; Autobiography and Decolonization: Modernity, Masculinity, and the Nation-State, 2008. Contributor of articles to books and periodicals. **Address:** Department of English Language & Literature, Faculty of Arts and Social Sciences, National University of Singapore, AS5 05-26, Block AS5, 7 Arts Link, Singapore, 117570, Singapore. **Online address:** ellhpj@nus.edu.sg

HOLDER, Nancy L. Also writes as Wendi Davis, Nancy L. Jones, Laurel Chandler. American (born United States), b. 1953. **Genres:** Horror, Romance/Historical, Novels, Ghost Writer, Mystery/Crime/Suspense. **Career:** Writer. **Publications:** ROMANCE NOVELS AS WENDI DAVIS: Teach Me to Love, 1982; Sealed with a Kiss, 1984. ROMANCE NOVELS AS NANCY L. JONES: Jessie's Song, 1983. ROMANCE NOVELS AS LAUREL CHANDLER: Treasure of Love, 1983; Heart's Victory, 1983; Shades of Moonlight, 1984; Boundless Love, 1984. ROMANCE NOVELS: The Greatest Show on Earth, 1984; Winner Take All, 1984; Finders Keepers, 1985; His Fair Lady, 1985; Out of This World, 1985; Emerald Fire, 1986; Once in Love With Amy, 1986. HORROR NOVELS: Rough Cut, 1990; The Ghosts of Tivoli, 1992; Cannibal Dwight's Special Purpose, 1992; (with M. Tem) Making Love, 1993; Dead in the Water, 1994; (with M. Tem) Witch-Light, 1996; Measure of a Man (Highlander), 1997. BUFFY THE VAMPIRE SLAYER SERIES: (with C. Golden) Halloween Rain, 1997; The Angel Chronicles, 1998, vol. III, 1999; Blooded, 1998; (with C. Golden) Child of the Hunt, 1998; Immortal, 1999; (with C. Golden) Out of the Madhouse, 1999; The Gatekeeper Trilogy, 1999; (with C. Golden) Ghost Roads, 1999; (with C. Golden) Sons of Entropy, 1999; Sunnydale High Yearbook, 1999; The Book of Fours, 2001; The Journals of Rupert Giles, 2002; Tales of the Slayer, vol. III, 2003. OTHERS: Wings and Other Poems, 1972; The Six Families, 1998; Spying Eyes, 1998; The Watcher's Guide, vol. I, 1998, vol. II, 2003; Scarabian Nights, 1999; Up, Up and Away, 1999; Feline Felon, 1999; City of, 1999; Legacies and Lies, 1999; Eight Spells a Week, 1999; Invasions, 2000; Ivanhound, 2000; Millennium Madness, 2000; The Evil that Men Do, 2000; Not Forgotten, 2000; (with J. Mariotte) Burning, 2001; (with J. Mariotte) Door to Alternity, 2001; (with J. Mariotte) Long Way Home, 2001; Pearl Harbor, 1941, 2001; (with J. Mariotte and M. Hart) Angel: The Casefiles, 2002; (with C. Golden) The Longest night, 2002; (with J. Mariotte) Endangered Species, 2002; (with D.Viguie) Witch, 2002; Chosen, 2003; (with D. Viguie) Spellbound, 2003; Silence, 2003; (with D. Viguie) Legacy, 2003; Hauntings, 2003; Blood and Fog, 2003; (with D. Viguie) Curse, 2003; Heat, 2004; Spirited, 2005; Keep Me In mind, 2005; Queen of the Slayers, 2005; (co-ed.) Outsiders, 2005; Carnival of Souls, 2006; Pretty Little Devils, 2006; Daughter of the Flames, 2006; Daughter of the Blood, 2006; Rose Bride: A Retelling of The White Bride and the Black Bride, 2007; Disclosure, 2008; Legacy and Spellbound, 2008; Witch and Curse, 2008; Son of the Shadows, 2008; Son of the Sea, 2008; Zorro in the Valley of the Shadow, 2008; Possessions, 2009; (with D. Viguie) Resurrection, 2009; Sex as a Weapon: The Domino Lady, 2009; Cry Me a River, 2009; Crusade, 2010; The Evil Within, 2010; Tough Love, 2010; Chicks in Capes, 2010; The Screaming Season, 2011; Damned, 2011; Ramping Up for a Decade with Joss Whedon, 2011; (with D. Viguie) Unleashed, 2011. **Address:** c/o Howard Morhaim, Howard Morhaim Literary Agency Inc., 30 Pierrepont St., Brooklyn, NY 11201, U.S.A. **Online address:** nancy@nancyholder.com

HOLDGATE, Martin W. British (born England), b. 1931. **Genres:** Biology, Environmental Sciences/Ecology, History, Autobiography/Memoirs, Earth Sciences. **Career:** Gough Island Scientific Survey, senior scientist, 1955-56; Victoria University of Manchester, lecturer in zoology, 1956-57; Durham University, university lecturer, 1957-60; Scott Polar Research Institute, assistant director of research, 1960-63; British Antarctic Survey, chief biologist, 1963-66; Nature Conservancy, deputy director of research, 1966-70; Central Unit of Environmental Pollution, Department of the Environment, director, 1970-74; Institute of Terrestrial Ecology, Natural Environment Research Council, director, 1974-76, Departments of Environment and Transport, director general, 1976-; Departments of the Environment and Transport, chief scientist, 1976-88; International Union for Conservation of Nature and Natural Resources, director-general, 1988-94, now retired. **Publications:** History of Appleby, County Town of Westmorland, 1956, rev. ed., 1970; Mountains in the Sea: The Story of the Gough Island Expedition, 1958; (with N.M. Wale) Man and Nature in the Tristan de Cunha Islands, 1976; (co-author) Forces of Nature, 1977; (contrib.) Breakdown and Restoration of Ecosystems, 1978; A Perspective of Environmental Pollution, 1979; (co-author) Climate Change: Meeting the Challenge, 1989; Environment of Tomorrow's World, 1990; From Care to Action: Making a Sustainable World, 1996; The Green Web: A Union for World Conservation, 1999; Penguins and Mandarins, 2003. EDITOR: (ed. with R. Carrick and J. Prevost) Antarctic Biology, 1964; Antarctic Ecology, 1970; The Restoration of Damaged Ecosystems, 1976; (with G.F. White) Environmental Issues, 1977; The World Environment 1972-82: A Report, 1982. **Address:** Institute of Terrestrial Ecology, 68 Hills Rd., Cambridge, CB2 1LA, United Kingdom. **Online address:** martin@fellbeck.fsnet.co.uk

HOLDHEIM, W(illiam) Wolfgang. American/German (born Germany), b. 1926. **Genres:** Literary Criticism And History, Philosophy, Translations. **Career:** Ohio State University, instructor, 1955-57; Brandeis University, instructor, 1957-58, assistant professor, 1958-61, associate professor of European languages and literature, 1961-64; Washington University, professor of French and comparative literature, 1964-69; Free University of Berlin, Fulbright visiting professor, 1968-69; Cornell University, professor of comparative literature, 1969-75, Frederic J. Whiton professor of liberal studies, 1975-90, professor emeritus, 1990; University of California, visiting professor, 1980. Writer. **Publications:** Benjamin Constant, 1961; (trans.) Ressentiment, 1961; Theory and Practice of the Novel, 1968; Der Justizirrtum als literarische Problematik, 1969; Die Suche nach dem Epos, 1978; Hermeneutic Mode: Essays on Time in Literature and Literary Theory, 1984. Contributor of articles to journals. **Address:** Cornell University, Goldwin Smith Hall, Rm. 247, Ithaca, NY 14853, U.S.A. **Online address:** csspeast@sgi.net

HOLEMAN, Linda. (Linda Gay Freeman). Canadian (born Canada), b. 1949. **Genres:** Novellas/Short Stories, Children's Fiction, Young Adult Fiction, Novels. **Career:** Frontier School Division, classroom and resource teacher, 1974-76; Ryerson School, Fort Garry School Division, classroom and resource teacher, 1977-84; writer, 1994-; University of Winnipeg, Continuing Education Division, creative writing instructor, 1996-; Winnipeg Public Library, writer-in-residence, 1999-2000. **Publications:** FOR YOUNG ADULTS: STORIES: Saying Good-bye, 1995; Toxic Love, 2003. NOVELS: Promise Song, 1997; Mercy's Birds, 1998; Raspberry House Blues, 2000; Search of the Moon King's Daughter, 2002; The Linnet Bird, 2004; The Moonlit Cage, 2005; In a Far Country, 2008; The Saffron Gate, 2010. FOR CHILDREN: Frankie on the Run, 1995. FOR ADULTS: Flying to Yellow (short stories), 1996; Devil's Darning Needle (short stories), 1999. Contributor to books and periodicals. **Address:** c/o Sarah Heller, Helen Heller Agency Inc., 216 Heath St. W. Ste. 4, Toronto, ON M5P 1N7, Canada. **Online address:** readers.forum@lindaholeman.com

HOLIFIELD, E. Brooks. American (born United States), b. 1942. **Genres:** Theology/Religion, History, Medicine/Health. **Career:** Quinnipiac College, part-time instructor, 1967-69; Yale Divinity School, teaching assistant, 1968-69, teaching associate, 1969-70; Emory University, Candler School of Theology, assistant professor, 1970-75, associate professor, 1975-80, professor, 1980-84, Charles Howard Candler Professor of American Church History, 1984-, department chair, 1977-79, director of graduate division, 1979-83, Center for the Interdisciplinary Study of Religion, fellow, 2004-; University of Mississippi, Center for the Study of Southern Culture, national consultant, 1979-85. Writer. **Publications:** The Covenant Sealed: The Development of Puritan Sacramental Theology in Old and New England, 1570-1720, 1974; The Gentlemen Theologians: American Theology in Southern Culture, 1795-1860, 1978; A History of Pastoral Care in America: From Salvation to Self-Realization, 1983; Health and Medicine in the Methodist Tradition: Journey toward Wholeness, 1986; Era of Persuasion: American Thought and Culture, 1521-1680, 1989; Theology in America: Christian Thought from the Age of the Puritans to the Civil War, 2003; God's Ambassadors: A History of the Christian Clergy in America, 2007. Contributor of articles to books and journals. **Address:** Candler School of Theology, Emory University, 1531 Dickey Dr., Atlanta, GA 30322-1003, U.S.A. **Online address:** eholifi@emory.edu

HOLLAND, Antonio F. American (born United States), b. 1943. **Genres:** History, Education, Military/Defense/Arms Control. **Career:** Lincoln University, instructor, professor of history, 1970-. Writer. **Publications:** (With L.J. Greene and G.R. Kremer) Missouri's Black Heritage, 1980, rev. ed., 1993; The Soldiers' Dream Continued: A Pictorial History of Lincoln University of Missouri, 1991; Nathan B. Young and the Struggle over Black Higher Education, 2006. **Address:** Lincoln University, 415 Martin Luther King Hall, 812 E Dunklin St., Jefferson City, MO 65101, U.S.A. **Online address:** hollanda@lincolnu.edu

HOLLAND, David. American (born United States), b. 1959. **Genres:** Novels, Mystery/Crime/Suspense, Young Adult Fiction. **Career:** WHAS Radio, creative director; freelance journalist; college teacher; Kentucky Center for the Performing Arts, public relations director. **Publications:** NOVELS: Murcheston: The Wolf's Tale, 2000; Devil in Bellminster: An Unlikely Mystery, 2002; Devil's Acre: An Unlikely Mystery, 2003; Devil's Game: An Unlikely Mystery, 2005. **Address:** 84WHAS Radio, 4000 Radio Dr., Ste. 1, Louisville, KY 40218, U.S.A. **Online address:** holland.d@insightbb.com

HOLLAND, James R. American (born United States), b. 1944. **Genres:** Music, Travel/Exploration, Biography, Natural History, Art/Art History, Autobiography/Memoirs. **Career:** National Geographic Magazine, photographer trainee, 1966-67, contract photographer, 1967-68; Christian Science Center, film producer, 1969-75; The Christian Science Center, film editor, producer; National Geographic Television, still photographer. Writer. **Publications:** The Amazon, Text and Photos, 1971; Mr. Pops, 1972; Tanglewood, 1973; W.O'K's Weird Wacky Wonderful World: The Art of William O'Keefe, 2006; Klan Rally, 2007; Diamonds are Waiting for You: Crater of Diamonds, Where Dreams Can and Do Come True, 2007; Klan Rally, 2008; Fisheyes, 2008; Adventure Photographer, 2009; Santa's Elves Revolt and Politics: Puns and Parody. Contributor of articles to journals. **Address:** A Bit of Boston Books, PO Box 990262, Boston, MA 02199-0262, U.S.A.

HOLLAND, Jo. See **HOLLAND, JoJean.**

HOLLAND, JoJean. Also writes as Veronica DeTerre, JoJean, Jo Holland. American (born United States), b. 1936. **Genres:** Young Adult Non-fiction, Food And Wine, Mystery/Crime/Suspense. **Career:** Dallas County Community College District, biology instructor, 1989-2001, retired, 2001. Writer. **Publications:** (As Jo Holland) One Little Branch, 1988; (as JoJean) Twilight in the Vineyard, 1988, rev. ed., 2007; (as Veronica DeTerre) AVAM: Avenging America, 2003. **Address:** 804 Brockden Dr., Mesquite, TX 75149-3274, U.S.A. **Online address:** jdaout@sbcglobal.net

HOLLAND, Julie. American (born United States), b. 1965. **Genres:** Psychiatry. **Career:** Mount Sinai Medical Center, resident, 1992-96, chief resident of schizophrenia research ward, 1994-95; Bellevue Hospital, Comprehensive Psychiatric Emergency Program, attending psychiatrist, 1996-2005; New York University, Langone Medical Center, clinical assistant professor of psychiatry, 1996-. Writer. **Publications:** (Ed.) Ecstasy: The Complete Guide: A Comprehensive Look at the Risks and Benefits of MDMA, 2001; Weekends at Bellevue: Nine Years on the Night Shift at the Psych ER, 2009. Contributor to periodicals and journals. **Address:** Langone Medical Center, New York University, 550 1st Ave., New York, NY 10016, U.S.A. **Online address:** jholland@inch.com

HOLLAND, Max (Mendel). American (born United States), b. 1950. **Genres:** Business/Trade/Industry, History, Politics/Government, Biography, Young Adult Non-fiction. **Career:** Lincoln Star, copy editor, 1975-76; Voice of America, news writer, 1976; Center for International Policy, fellow, 1977-80; U.S. Representative Toby Moffett, aide, 1980; Nation, Washington Bureau, columnist, 1982-86, contributing editor, 1986-; Wilson Quarterly, contributing editor, 1991-; University of Virginia, Miller Center of Public Affairs, research fellow, 1998-2003. **Publications:** When the Machine Stopped:

A Cautionary Tale from Industrial America (nonfiction), 1989; The CEO Goes to Washington: Negotiating the Halls of Power, 1994; A Need to Know: Inside the Warren Commission, 2002; From Industry to Alchemy: Burgmaster, a Machine Tool Company, 2002; (comp.) The Kennedy Assassination Tapes: The White House Conversations of Lyndon B. Johnson Regarding the Assassination, the Warren Commission, and the Aftermath, 2004; (ed.) Lyndon B. Johnson, the Kennedy Assassination, and the Transfer of Power, November 1963-January 1964, 2005; Why Mark Felt became Deep Throat, 2012. Contributor to periodicals. **Address:** W. W. Norton & Company Inc., 500 5th Ave., New York, NY 10110, U.S.A.

HOLLAND, Norman N. (Norman Norwood Holland). American (born United States), b. 1927. **Genres:** Literary Criticism And History, Psychology. **Career:** Massachusetts Institute of Technology, instructor, 1955-56, assistant professor, 1956-63, associate professor of English, 1963-66; State University of New York, professor, 1966-79, English Department, chairman, 1966-68, Center for the Psychological Study of the Arts, director, 1970-, McNulty professor, 1979-83; University of Florida, Marston-Milbauer professor, 1983-, now emeritus. Writer. **Publications:** The First Modern Comedies, 1959; The Shakespearean Imagination, 1964; Psychoanalysis and Shakespeare, 1966; The Dynamics of Literary Response, 1968; Poems in Persons, 1973, rev. ed., 2000; Five Readers Reading, 1975; Laughing, 1982; The I, 1985; The Brain of Robert Frost, 1988; (ed.) The Second Part of King Henry IV: With New Dramatic Criticism and an Updated Bibliography, 1988, rev. ed., 2002; (ed. with S. Homan and B.J. Paris) Shakespeare's Personality, 1989; Holland's Guide to Psychoanalytic Psychology and Literature-and-Psychology, 1990; The Critical I, 1992; Death in a Delphi Seminar: A Postmodern Mystery, 1995; Meeting Movies, 2006; Literature and the Brain, 2009. **Address:** 5000 SW 25th Blvd., Apt. 3117, Gainesville, FL 32608-8931, U.S.A. **Online address:** nholland@post.harvard.edu

HOLLAND, Norman Norwood. See **HOLLAND, Norman N.**

HOLLAND, Noy. American (born United States), b. 1960. **Genres:** Novels, Novellas/Short Stories. **Career:** Hotchkiss School, instructor, 1983-; Esquire, editorial assistant, 1984-85; Charles Scribner's Sons, assistant to the senior editor, 1986-87; New York Association for New Americans, instructor, 1990; University of Florida, instructor, 1992-94; Phillips Academy, writer-in-residence, 1994-96; University of Massachusetts, Department of English, assistant professor, 1997-, associate professor, professor, MFA Program, director, 1997-. **Publications:** The Spectacle of the Body: Stories, 1994; What Begins with Bird, 2005. Contributor to periodicals. **Address:** Department of English, University of Massachusetts, 465 Bartlett Hall, PO Box 30515, Amherst, MA 01003-0515, U.S.A. **Online address:** fholland@english.umass.edu

HOLLAND, Robert Gray. American (born United States), b. 1941. **Genres:** Education, Politics/Government. **Career:** Richmond Times-Dispatch, education writer and news bureau chief, 1963-69, editorial writer and associate editor, 1970-92, columnist and editor of "Op-Ed" page, 1992-99; Washington and Lee University, director of public relations, 1969-70; Lexington Institute, senior fellow, 1999-. **Publications:** The Story of the Prince Edward Free Schools, 1963; The Student Journalist and the Literary Magazine, 1970; Not with My Child You Don't: A Citizens Guide to Eradicating OBE and Restoring Education, 1995; Charlie Dollarhide: A Novel of Sports and Mystery, 2002; To Build a Better Teacher: The Emergence of a Competitive Education Industry, 2003. Contributor to periodicals. **Address:** Lexington Institute, 1600 Wilson Blvd., Ste. 900, Arlington, VA 22209, U.S.A. **Online address:** rholl1176@aol.com

HOLLANDER, David. American (born United States) **Genres:** Novels, Young Adult Fiction, Mystery/Crime/Suspense. **Career:** State University of New York, Purchase College, writing instructor; Sarah Lawrence College, writing instructor, 2001-; Teachers and Writers Collaborative, instructor in the public school writing program. Writer. **Publications:** L.I.E.: A Novel, 2000. Contributor to books. **Address:** Sarah Lawrence College, Rm. 1, 1 Mead Way, Bronxville, NY 10708-5940, U.S.A. **Online address:** dholland98@hotmail.com

HOLLANDER, Jack M. American (born United States) **Genres:** Sciences, Social Sciences, Economics. **Career:** University of California, professor emeritus of energy and resources. Writer. **Publications:** (With C.M. Lederer

and I. Perlman) Table of Isotopes, 6th ed., 1967; (ed. with G.T. Goodman and L.A. Kristoferson) The European Transition from Oil: Societal Impacts and Constraints on Energy Policy, 1981; (ed.) The Energy-Environment Connection, 1992; The Real Environmental Crisis: Why Poverty, Not Affluence, Is the Environment's Number One Enemy, 2003. **Address:** Atmospheric Sciences, Lawrence Berkeley National Laboratory, 1 Cyclotron Rd., PO Box 73, Berkeley, CA 94720, U.S.A. **Online address:** jmhollander@lbl.gov

HOLLANDER, John. American (born United States), b. 1929. **Genres:** Children's Fiction, Poetry, Literary Criticism And History. **Career:** Harvard University, Society of Fellows, junior fellow, 1954-57; Connecticut College, lecturer, 1957-59; Partisan Review, poetry editor, 1959-65; Yale University, instructor, 1959-61, assistant professor, 1961-63, associate professor, 1963-66, professor of English, 1977-, A. Bartlett Giamatti professor of English, 1986-95, Sterling professor of English, 1995-, Sterling professor emeritus of English, 2007-; Princeton University, Christian Gauss seminarian, 1962; Indiana University, Linguistic Institute and School of Letters, visiting professor, 1964, Institute for Advanced Study, fellow, 1986; City University of New York, Hunter College, professor of English, 1966-77; University of Cincinnati, Elliston poetry professor, 1969; Churchill College, overseas fellow, 1967-68; Harper's Magazine, contributor editor, 1969-71. **Publications:** POETRY: A Crackling of Thorns, 1958; Movie-Going and Other Poems, 1962; A Beach Vision, 1962; A Book of Various Owls (children's), 1963; Visions from the Ramble, 1965; The Quest of the Gole (children's), 1966; Philomel, 1968; Types of Shape, 1969; Images of Voice: Music and Sound in Romantic Poetry, 1970; The Night Mirror, 1971; Town and Country Matters: Erotica and Satirica, 1972; Selected Poems, 1972; The Head of the Bed, 1974; Tales Told of the Fathers, 1975; Reflections on Espionage, 1976; Spectral Emanations: New and Selected Poems, 1978; In Place, 1978; Blue Wine and Other Poems, 1979; Looking Ahead. 1982; Powers of Thirteen, 1984; A Hollander Garland. Newton, 1985; In Time and Place, 1986; Harp Lake, 1988; Some Fugitives Take Cover, 1988; Tesserae, 1993; Selected Poetry, 1993; The Gazer's Spirit: Poems Speaking to Silent Works of Art, 1995; Figurehead and Other Poems, 1999; Picture Window: Poems, 2003; Draft of Light, 2008. CRITICISM: Vision and Resonance: Two Senses of Poetic Form, 1975, rev. ed., 1985; William Bailey, 1990; The Work of Poetry, 1997; The Poetry of Everyday Life, 1998. OTHERS: The Untuning of the Sky: Ideas of Music in English Poetry 1500-1700, 1961; The Immense Parade on Supererogation Day (for children), 1972; Rhyme's Reason: A Guide to English Verse, 1981, 3rd ed., 2001; The Figure of Echo: A Mode of Allusion in Milton and After, 1981; (with S. Steinberg) Dal Vero, 1983; Melodious Guile: Fictive Pattern in Poetic Language, 1988; American Poetry: The Nineteenth Century, 2 vols., 1993; (contrib.) Never Again would Birds' Song be the Same, 2002; (contrib.) Of Challenge and of Love, 2009. EDITOR: Selected Poems, 1961; (with H. Bloom) The Wind and the Rain: An Anthology of Poems for Young People, 1961; (with A. Hecht) Jiggery-Pokery: A Compendium of Double Dactyls, 1967; Poems of Our Moment, 1968; Modern Poetry: Essays in Criticism, 1968; American Short Stories since 1945, 1968; (co-ed.) The Oxford Anthology of English Literature, 2 vols., 1973; (with R. Brower and H. Vendler) I.A. Richards: Essays in His Honor, 1973; (with I. Howe and D. Bromwich) Literature as Experience, 1979; The Poetics of Influence, 1988; The Essential Rossetti, 1990; Spoon River Anthology, 1992; Animal Poems, 1994; Garden Poems, 1996; Marriage Poems, 1997; Nineteenth Century American Poetry, 1996; Committed to Memory: 100 Best Poems to Memorize, 1996; Frost, 1997; Marriage Poems, 1997; (with E.L. Haralson) Encyclopedia of American Poetry, 1998; The Best American Poetry, 1998; War Poems, 1999; (with J.D. McClatchy) Christmas Poems, 1999; Sonnets, 2001; (with J. Weber) Words for Images: A Gallery of Poems, 2001; Crossing Boundaries, 2002; American Wits, 2003; American Poetry, 2004; Poetry for Young People: Animal Poems, 2004; Poems Bewitched and Haunted, 2005; O. Henry, 2005; (and intro.) Tricks of the Light: New and Selected Poems, 2007. **Address:** Department of English, Yale University, SSS 1002, 63 High St., PO Box 208302, New Haven, CT 06520-8302, U.S.A. **Online address:** john.hollander@yale.edu

HOLLANDER, Nicole. American (born United States), b. 1939. **Genres:** Cartoons, Graphic Novels, Children's Fiction, Humor/Satire. **Career:** Cartoonist, 1979-; Sylvia Products, head. Writer. **Publications:** COLLECTED CARTOONS: I'm in Training to Be Tall and Blonde, 1979; Ma, Can I Be a Feminist and Still Like Men?: Lyrics from Life, 1980; That Woman Must Be on Drugs: A Collection of Sylvia, 1981; Mercy, It's the Revolution and I'm in My Bathrobe: More Sylvia, 1982; My Weight Is Always Perfect for My Height-Which Varies: More Sylvia, 1982; Sylvia on Sundays, 1983; (ed. with S. Morrow and R. Wolin) Drawn Together: Relationships Lampooned, Harpooned and Cartooned, 1983; Hi, This is Sylvia: I Can't Come to the Phone Right Now, So When You Hear the Beep, Please Hang Up, 1983; Okay, Thinner Thighs for Everyone, 1984; Never Tell Your Mother This Dream, 1985; The Whole Enchilada: A Spicy Collection of Sylvia's Best, 1986; Never Take Your Cat to a Salad Bar: New Sylvia Cartoons, 1987; You Can't Take It with You, So Eat It Now; Everyday Strategies from Sylvia, 1989; Tales from the Planet Sylvia, 1990; (co-author) Sylvia's Real Good Advice, 1991; Everything Here is Mine: An Unhelpful Guide to Cat Behavior, 1992; Female Problems: An Unhelpful Guide, 1995; My Cat's Not Fat, He's Just Big-Boned, 1998; Cats With Attitude, 2002; (with R. Barreca) The ABC Of Vice: An Insatiable Women's Guide, 2003; Psycho Kitties, 2006; Tales Of Graceful Aging from the Planet Denial, 2007; Nobody Owns A Cat: An Unhelpful Guide to Cat Behavior, 2007; Sylvia Chronicles: 30 Years of Graphic Misbehavior from Reagan to Obama, 2010. Contributor to periodicals. **Address:** Adams Media Corp., 57 Littlefield St., Ste. 2, Avon, MA 02322-1914, U.S.A.

HOLLANDER, Samuel. Israeli/Canadian/British (born England), b. 1937. **Genres:** Economics, Autobiography/Memoirs. **Career:** Princeton University, assistant-in-instruction, 1962-63; University of Toronto, assistant professor, 1963-66, associate professor, 1966-70, professor, 1970-84, university professor, 1984-98, university professor emeritus, 1998; McMaster University, lecturer, 1966-68; University of Florence, professor, 1973-74; London School of Economics, professor, 1974-75; Hebrew University, Lady Davis professor, 1979-80; Ben-Gurion University of the Negev, professor, 2000-06, research associate, 2006-. Writer. **Publications:** The Sources of Increased Efficiency: A Study of DuPont Rayon Plants, 1965; The Economics of Adam Smith, 1973; The Economics of David Ricardo, 1979; The Economics of John Stuart Mill, 2 vols., 1985; Classical Economics, 1987; Ricardo, The New View: Collected Essays I, 1995; The Economics of Thomas Robert Malthus, 1997; Collected Essay II, 1997; The Literature of Political Economy, 1997; John Stuart Mill on Economic Theory and Method, 2000; Jean-Baptiste Say and the Classical Canon in Economics: The British Connection in French Classicism, 2005; The Economics of Karl Marx: An Analysis and Application, 2008; Essays on Friedrich Engels and Marxian Political Economy, 2011. **Address:** Department of Economics, Ben-Gurion University of the Negev, PO Box 653, Beer-Sheva, 84105, Israel. **Online address:** sholland@bgu.ac.il

HOLLANDSWORTH, James G. American (born United States), b. 1944. **Genres:** History, Psychology. **Career:** Duke University Medical Center, Highland Hospital, psychiatric social worker, 1972-73; Community Mental Health Center of Palm Beach County, clinical and community psychology intern, 1975-76; University of Southern Mississippi, assistant professor, 1976-79, associate professor, 1979-84, professor of psychology, 1984-, director of training, 1987-89, assistant vice-president for academic affairs, 1989-94, assistant commissioner for academic affairs, 1994-96, associate vice-president for academic affairs, 1997, associate provost, 1998-, dean of graduate school, now retired. Writer. **Publications:** Physiology and Behavior Therapy: Conceptual Guidelines for the Clinician, 1986; The Physiology of Psychological Disorders: Schizophrenia, Depression, Anxiety and Substance Abuse, 1990; The Louisiana Native Guards: The Black Military Experience during the Civil War, 1995; Pretense of Glory: The Life of General Nathaniel P. Banks, 1998; Absolute Massacre: The New Orleans Race Riot of July 30, 1866, 2001; Portrait of a Scientific Racist: Alfred Holt Stone of Mississippi, 2008. **Address:** c/o Author's Mail, Louisiana State University Press, PO Box 25053, Baton Rouge, LA 70894, U.S.A. **Online address:** jgh@netdoor.com

HOLLAR, David W(ason). American (born United States), b. 1960. **Genres:** Bibliography, Natural History, Sciences, Reference. **Career:** Roanoke-Chowan Community College, instructor in science, 1986-89; Rockingham Community College, instructor in biology, 1989-2001; Wright State University, School of Medicine, postdoctoral research scientist, 2001-; University of Tennessee, Graduate School of Medicine, Department of Medical Genetics, assistant professor, 2003-; National Institutes of Health, postdoctoral fellow; Maternal and Child Health Journal, editor. **Publications:** The Origin and Evolution of Life on Earth: An Annotated Bibliography, 1992. Works appear in anthologies. **Address:** Department of Medical Genetics, Rockingham Community College, UT Graduate School of Medicine, PO Box 38, Wentworth, NC 27375, U.S.A. **Online address:** david.hollar@wright.edu

HÖLLDOBLER, Bert(hold Karl). American/German (born Germany), b. 1936. **Genres:** Biology, Zoology, Animals/Pets. **Career:** University of Frankfurt, Zoological Institute, scientific assistant, 1966-69, professor of zoology, 1971-72; Harvard University, Department of Biology, research associate in zoology, 1969-71, professor of biology, 1973-90, Alexander Agassiz professor of zoology, 1982-90, Museum of Comparative Zoology, research associate, 1990-; University of Arizona, adjunct professor, 1989-; University of Würzburg, professor of zoology, 1989-2004, chair of behavioral physiology and sociobiology, chair of department of biology, 1993-95; University of Mainz, Johannes Gutenberg Stiftungs professor, 2001; Cornell University, Andrew D. White professor-at-large, 2002-08; Arizona State University, foundation professor of life sciences, 2004-. Writer. **Publications:** (Ed. with M. Lindauer) Experimental Behavioral Ecology and Sociobiology: In Memoriam Karl von Frisch, 1886-1982, 1985; (with V.T. Eisner and M. Lindauer) Chemische ökologie, Territorialität, Gegenseitige Verständigung, 1986; (with E.O. Wilson) The Ants, 1990; (co-author) Tier und Mensch: Unterschiede und ähnlichkeiten: Vorträge, 1993; (with E.O. Wilson) Journey to the Ants: A Story of Scientific Exploration, 1994; (co-author) Herbivory In Leaf-Cutting Ants, 2003; (with E.O. Wilson) Superorganism: The Beauty, Elegance, and Strangeness of Insect Societies, 2009; (with E.O. Wilson) Leafcutter Ants: Civilization by Instinct, 2011. Contributor to journals. **Address:** Center for Social Dynamics and Complexity, School of Life Sciences, Arizona State University, 427 E Tyler Mall, PO Box 874701, Tempe, AZ 85287-4701, U.S.A. **Online address:** bert.hoelldobler@asu.edu

HOLLENBERG, Donna Krolik. American/Canadian (born Canada), b. 1942. **Genres:** Literary Criticism And History, Poetry, History. **Career:** Simmons College, instructor, 1985-90; University of Connecticut, assistant professor, 1991-97, associate professor, 1997-2004, professor, 2004-. Writer. **Publications:** H.D.: The Poetics of Childbirth and Creativity, 1991; Between History and Poetry: The Letters of H.D. and Norman Holmes Pearson, 1997; (ed.) H.D. and Poets After, 2000; A Poet's Revolution: The Life of Denise Levertov, forthcoming. **Address:** Department of English, University of Connecticut, CLAS Rm. 214, 215 Glenbrook Rd., Ste. 4025, Storrs, CT 06269-4025, U.S.A. **Online address:** donna.hollenberg@uconn.edu

HOLLERAN, Andrew. (Eric Garber). American (born United States), b. 1944?. **Genres:** Novels, Novellas/Short Stories, Dance/Ballet. **Career:** American University, instructor in creative writing, 2000, distinguished adjunct-in-residence. Writer. **Publications:** Dancer from the Dance (novel), 1978; Nights in Aruba (novel), 1983; The Normal Heart, 1985; Ground Zero (essays), 1988; (afterword) Men on Men 4, 1992; The Beauty of Men, 1996; In September the Light Changes: Stories, 1999; Grief, 2006; Chronicle of a Plague, Revisited: AIDS and its Aftermath, 2008. Contributor to periodicals. Works appear in anthologies. **Address:** Department of Litrature, American University, Battelle T01-12, 4400 Massachusetts Ave. NW, Washington, DC 20016, U.S.A. **Online address:** egarber@msn.com

HOLLEY, Margaret. American (born United States), b. 1944. **Genres:** Poetry, Literary Criticism And History. **Career:** Franklin College, professor of literature, 1972-80; Bryn Mawr College, instructor in English, Creative Writing Program, director, assistant to the president, 1981-2000; American Committee for the Weizmann Institute of Science, faculty. Writer. **Publications:** The Dark Horses (chapbook), 1980; The Poetry of Marianne Moore: A Study in Voice and Value, 1987; (ed.) Higher Spheres: More Poems, 1988; The Mayflower (chapbook), 1989; The Smoke Tree, 1991; Morning Star, 1992; Beyond Me: Voices of the Natural World, 1993; Kyrie for One Voice (chapbook), 1993; Kore in Bloom, 1998; Walking through the Horizon, 2006. Contributor to books and periodicals. **Address:** American Committee for the Weizmann Institute, of Science, 7975 N Hayden Rd., Ste. B124, Scottsdale, AZ 85258, U.S.A. **Online address:** margaret.holley@att.net

HOLLI, Betsy B. American (born United States), b. 1933. **Genres:** Communications/Media, Medicine/Health, Education. **Career:** Rush Presbyterian-St. Luke's Medical Center, health center nutritionist, 1965-69; University of Illinois, Medical Center, professor, 1969-70; Dominican University, professor of nutrition sciences, 1970-2004, professor emeritus of nutrition sciences, 2004-. Writer. **Publications:** (With R.J. Calabrese) Communication and Education Skills: The Dietitian's Guide, 1986, (co-author) 5th ed. as Communication and Education Skills for Dietetics Professionals, 2009. Contributor to professional journals. **Address:** Department of Nutrition Sciences, Dominican University, 7900 W Division St., River Forest, IL 60305, U.S.A. **Online address:** holli@dom.edu

HOLLI, Melvin George. American (born United States), b. 1933. **Genres:** Cultural/Ethnic Topics, History, Biography, Essays. **Career:** University of Michigan, curator of historical collections, 1963-64; University of Illinois,

Department of History, associate professor, 1965-76, professor of history, 1976-, department chairman, 1991-94, now professsor emeritus. Writer. **Publications:** Reform in Detroit: Hazen S. Pingree and Urban Politics, 1969; (intro.) My Story, 1971; (ed.) Detroit: Fur Trading Post to Industrial Metropolis, 1701-1976, 1976; (ed. with P. Jones) The Ethnic Frontiers: Essays in the History of Group Survival in Chicago and the Midwest, 1977; (ed. with P. Jones) Ethnic Chicago, 1981, rev. ed., 1984; (ed.) Biographical Dictionary of American Mayors 1820-1980, 1981; (ed. with P.M. Green) The Making of the Mayor, Chicago 1983, 1984; (with P.M. Green) The Mayors: The Chicago Political Tradition, 1987, 3rd ed., 2005; (with P.M. Green) Bashing Chicago Traditions: Harold Washington's Last Campaign, 1989; (with P.M. Green) Restoration 1989: Chicago Elects a New Daley, 1991; (ed. with P. d'A. Jones) Ethnic Chicago: A Multi-Cultural Portrait, 1994; The American Mayor: The Best and Worst Big City Leaders, 1999; (with P.M. Green) A View from Chicago's City Hall: Mid-Century to Millennium, 1999; (with R. Beuttler and R. Remini) The University of Illinois at Chicago: A Pictorial History, 2000; The Wizard of Washington: Emil Hurja, Franklin Roosevelt and the Birth of Public Opinion Polling, 2002; World War II Chicago, 2003; (with P.M. Green) View From Chicago's City Hall: Mid-century to Millennium, 2008. **Address:** Department of History, University of Illinois, 1001 University Hall, 601 S Morgan St., PO Box 198, Chicago, IL 60607-7109, U.S.A. **Online address:** mholli@uic.edu

HOLLIDAY, Alesia. Also writes as Jax Abbott, Alyssa Day. American (born United States) **Genres:** Novellas/Short Stories, Adult Non-fiction, Novels. **Career:** Writer. **Publications:** E-mail to the Front: One Wife's Correspondence with Her Husband Overseas, 2003; (with N. Neale and S. Rowe) Shop 'til Yule Drop, 2004; (as Jax Abbott) Super What?, 2004; American Idle, 2004; (with B. Brandt, D. Kauffman and E. McCarthy) The Naked Truth, 2005; Nice Girls Finish First, 2005; (as Jax Abbott) Super 16, 2005; Murder by Mass Tort, 2006; Blondes Have More Felons, 2006; Seven Ways to Lose Your Lover, 2006; Blonde Justice, 2007. AS ALYSSA DAY: WARRIORS OF POSEIDON SERIES: Atlantis Rising, 2007; Atlantis Awakening, 2007; Wild Hearts in Atlantis, 2007; Atlantis Unleashed, 2008; Shifter's Lady, 2008; Atlantis Unmasked, 2009; Atlantis Redeemed, 2010; Atlantis Betrayed, 2010; Vampire in Atlantis, 2011; Heart of Atlantis, 2012. Contributor to books. **Address:** Berkley Sensation Books, 375 Hudson St., New York, NY 10014, U.S.A. **Online address:** mail@alyssaday.com

HOLLIFIELD, James F. American (born United States), b. 1954. **Genres:** Politics/Government. **Career:** Duke University, instructor in political science, 1982-84; Brandeis University, assistant professor of political science, 1985-92; Harvard University, Minda de Gunzburg Center for European Studies, research associate, 1986-92, Harvard's Center for International Affairs, associate, 1991-92, French Study Group, co-chair; Auburn University, alumni associate professor of political science, 1992-; Centre National de la Recherche Scientifique, Centre d'Etudes et de Recherches Internationales, associate director of research, director of research, 1992-93; U.S. Department of State, consultant; U.S. Department of Labor, consultant; Organization for Economic Cooperation and Development, consultant; Southern Methodist University, Dedman College of Humanities and Sciences, professor of political science, International and Area Studies Program, director, 1996-2006, John Goodwin Tower Center for Political Studies, director, 2001-. Writer. **Publications:** (Ed. with G. Ross) Searching for the New France, 1991; Immigrants, Markets, and States, 1992; (ed. with W.A. Cornelius and P.L. Martin) Controlling Immigration, 1994; State and Public Policy, 1995; (ed. with C. Jillson) Pathways to Democracy: The Political Economy of Democratic Transitions, 2000; (ed. with C.B. Brettell) Migration theory: Talking across Disciplines, 2000, 2nd ed., 2008; (contrib.) Herausforderung Migration, 2006. **Address:** Department Political Science, Southern Methodist University, 222 Carr Collins, 2nd Fl., PO Box 750117, Dallas, TX 75205, U.S.A. **Online address:** jhollifi@smu.edu

HOLLINDALE, Peter. British (born England), b. 1936. **Genres:** Literary Criticism And History, Children's Fiction. **Career:** Cathedral Choir School, assistant English master, 1959-62; Clifton College, assistant master in English, 1962-65; University of York, lecturer, 1965-75, reader in English and educational studies, 1965-99, senior lecturer in English and education, 1975-. Writer. **Publications:** A Critical Commentary on Shakespeare's King Henry IV, vol. II, 1971; Choosing Books for Children, 1974; Ideology and the Children's Book, 1988; William Shakespeare: A Midsummer Night's Dream, 1992; Signs of Childness in Children's Books, 1997; (with A. Fine) An Interview with A. Fine, 1999. EDITOR: As You Like It, 1974; Shakespeare:

King Henry IV, vol. I, 1975; Lord Jim, 1982; Volpone, 1985; (and intro.) Black Beauty, 1992; (and intro.) Admirable Crichton, 1995; Negative Equity: Information from Household Interview Surveys, 1996; Housing Equity Withdrawal, 1996; (and intro.) Peter Pan in Kensington Gardens, and Peter and Wendy, 2008. Contributor to journals. **Address:** Department of English and Related Literature, University of York, 14 E Jackson Blvd., Ste. 1802, York, NY YO1 5DD, England.

HOLLINGS, Robert L. American (born United States), b. 1953. **Genres:** Bibliography, Politics/Government, Social Sciences, Business/Trade/Industry, Money/Finance. **Career:** Screen Tech Inc., shipping and receiving supervisor, 1978-82; State of Utah, Division of Healthcare Financing, Bureau of Provider and Client Services, Department of Health, health program representative, 1984; public policy analyst, 1996-98; Arizona Department of Economic Security, Office of Audit and Management Services, program compliance auditor, 1998-; Glendale Community College, adjunct instructor in sociology, 1998-. Writer. **Publications:** The General Accounting Office: An Annotated Bibliography, 1991, rev. ed., 1995; Nonprofit Public Policy Research Organization: A Sourcebook on Think Tanks in Government, 1993; Reinventing Government: An Analysis and Annotated Bibliography, 1996; (comp. with C. Pike-Nase) Professional and Occupational Licensure in the United States: An Annotated Bibliography and Professional Resource, 1997. **Address:** Office of Audit and Management Services, Arizona Department of Economic Security, 1140 E Washington, Ste. 104, Phoenix, AZ 85034, U.S.A. **Online address:** hollingsr@juno.com

HOLLINGSHEAD, Greg. Canadian (born Canada), b. 1947. **Genres:** Novels, Novellas/Short Stories, Essays. **Career:** University of Alberta, professor of English, 1975-, now professor emeritus; Banff Centre, director of writing programs, 1999-. Writer. **Publications:** STORIES: Famous Players, 1982; White Buick, 1992; The Roaring Girl, 1995. NOVELS: Spin Dry, 1992; The Healer, 1998; Bedlam, 2004. Works appear in anthologies. **Address:** Department of English, University of Alberta, 3-5 Humanities Ctr., Edmonton, AB T6G 2E5, Canada. **Online address:** g.h@ualberta.ca

HOLLINGSWORTH, A. B. (Alan B. Hollingsworth). American (born United States), b. 1949. **Genres:** Young Adult Fiction, Medicine/Health, Sports/Fitness. **Career:** University of California, fellow in surgical pathology, 1977; University of Oklahoma, Health Sciences Center, resident in general surgery, Institute for Breast Health, founding medical director, 1989-99, G. Rainey Williams professor of surgical breast oncology, 1998-99, G. Rainey Williams chair of surgical breast oncology; Mercy Women's Center, medical director of breast program, 1999-; Mercy Health Center, Mercy Cancer Resource Center, medical director, 1999-; Breast MRI of Oklahoma L.L.C., medical director, 2003-; NeoMatrix L.L.C., scientific advisor, 2005-; Daniel Freeman Marina Hospital, chief of surgery. Writer. **Publications:** (As Alan B. Hollingsworth) The Truth about Breast Cancer Risk Assessment, 2000; Flatbellies: It's Not about Golf, It's About Life, 2001; University Boulevard, 2003. Contributor to journals. **Address:** NeoMatrix L.L.C., 19800 MacArthur Blvd., Ste. 690, Irvine, CA 92612, U.S.A.

HOLLINGSWORTH, Alan B. See **HOLLINGSWORTH, A. B.**

HOLLINGSWORTH, Margaret. Canadian/British (born England), b. 1940?. **Genres:** Novels, Plays/Screenplays, Novellas/Short Stories, Literary Criticism And History, Young Adult Fiction. **Career:** Journalist, librarian and teacher, 1960-68; Fort William Public Library, librarian, 1968-72; Concordia University, writer-in-residence; University of Western Ontario, writer-in-residence; Stratford Shakespeare Festival, writer-in-residence; University of Victoria, assistant professor, 1980-82, associate professor, 1992-2002, now professor emeritus; David Thompson University Centre, assistant professor, 1981-83. **Publications:** PLAYS: Dance for My Father, 1976; Alli Alli Oh, 1979; Mother Country, 1980; Operators; Bushed: Two plays, 1981; Ever Loving, 1981; Islands, 1983; Willful Acts (collection), 1985, rev. ed., 1998; Endangered Species (collection), 1988; In Confidence, 1994; Numbrains, 1995; Commonwealth Games, 1998; Numbrains, forthcoming. SHORT STORIES: Smiling Under Water, 1989. NOVEL: Be Quiet, 2003. **Address:** c/o Playwrights Canada, 8 York St. 6th Fl., Toronto, ON M5J 1R2, Canada. **Online address:** mail@margarethollingsworth.com

HOLLINGSWORTH, Mary. (Scribbler). American (born United States), b. 1947. **Genres:** Children's Fiction, Plays/Screenplays, Poetry, Songs/Lyrics And Libretti, Adult Non-fiction, Children's Non-fiction, inspirational/Motivational Literature, Picture/Board Books, Picture/Board Books. **Career:** Sweet Publishing, managing editor, 1984-95; Richland Hills Church of Christ, Music Outreach Ministry, co-leader, 1985-2001; Richland Hills Singers, president, 1985-94; Shady Oaks Studio, owner, author, editor and consultant, 1988-; A Capella Junction, owner, 1991-; Creative Enterprises Studio, managing director. **Publications:** JUVENILES: International Children's Story Bible, 1991; (reteller) My Little Bible, 1991; The Captain, the Countess, and Cobby the Swabby: A Book about Honour, 1992; Parrots, Pirates, and Walking the Plank: A Book about Obeying, 1992; A Girl's Diary of Prayers, 1992; A Boy's Book of Prayers, 1992; (as Mary Shrode) Just Imagine! with Barney, 1992; Journey to Jesus: A Four-in-One Story, 1993; The Kids-Life Bible Storybook, 1994, rev. ed. as The Kids-Life Bible, 1998; The Children's Topical Bible, 1994; Bumper and Noah, 1994; Songs and Rhymes for Wiggle Worms, 1995; Who Is Jesus?, 1995; What Does Jesus Say?, 1995; The Story of Jesus, 1995; Bumper the Dinosaur, 1996; Bumper the Dinosaur Bible Stories: Two Stories in One Book, 1996; Into My Heart: A Treasury of Songs and Rhymes, 1996; The Preschooler's Picture-Reading Bible, 1998; The Amazing Expedition Bible: Linking God's Word to the World, 1998; Hugs for Kids: Stories, Sayings and Scriptures to Encourage and Inspire, 2000; Tall Body, Short Body, 2000; The Upside-Down, Inside-Out, Backwards, Oopsie Daisy Book, 2000; Little Taps on the Shoulder from God, 2002; My Bible Journey, 2002; Mary Hollingsworth's Love Notes from God, 2003. CHILDREN OF THE KING SERIES: The King's Alphabet: A Bible Book about Letters, 1988; The King's Numbers: A Bible Book about Counting, 1988; The King's Workers: A Bible Book about Serving, 1990; The King's Manners: A Bible Book about Courtesy, 1990; The King's Animals: A Bible Book about God's Creatures, 1991; The King's Children: A Bible Book about God's People, 1991. GOD'S HAPPY FOREST SERIES: Polka Dots, Stripes, Humps, 'n' Hatracks: How God Created Happy Forest, 1990; Twizzler, the Unlikely Hero: Bigger is not Always Better, 1990; Christmas in Happy Forest: Love is the Greatest Gift, 1990. MY VERY FIRST BOOK SERIES: My Very First Book of Bible Heroes, 1993; My Very First Book of Bible Lessons, 1993; My Very First Book of Bible Words, 1993; My Very First Book of Prayers, 1993; My Very First Book of God, 1994; My Very First Book of God's Animals-and Other Creatures, 1994; My Very First Book of Bible Questions, 1994; My Very First Book of Bible Fun Facts, 1994. AS SCRIBBLER: Charlie and the Shabby Tabby: Learning How to Be a Real Friend, 1989; Charlie and the Missing Music: Learning about God's Concern for the Lost, 1989; Charlie and the Jinglemouse: Learning about God's Forgiveness, 1989; Charlie and the Gold Mine: Learning What's Really Valuable in Life, 1989. OTHERS: Help! I Need a Bulletin Board, 1975; For Mom with Love, 1987; A Few Hallelujahs for Your Ho-Hums: A Lighthearted Look at Life, 1988; Just between Friends, 1988; It's a One-derful Life! A Single's Celebration, 1989; Rainbows, 1989; Apple Blossoms: A Tribute to Teachers, 1990; (with C.A. Greeson and M. Washburn) The Grief Adjustment Guide: A Pathway through Pain, 1990; (with C.A. Greeson and M. Washburn) The Divorce Recovery Guide, 1991; (comp.) Together Forever: Reflections on the Joys of Marriage, 1993; (comp.) On Raising Children: Lessons on Love and Limits, 1993; (with F. Kendall and A. Kendall) Speaking of Love, 1995; Getting to Know Jesus: First Steps to Knowing God, 1995; The Everyday Study Bible: New Century Version, 1996; The Last Journey (musical), 1997; (with M.N. Young) Living Lights, Shining Stars: Ten Secrets to Becoming the Light of the World, 1997; Suddenly One Morning (musical adaptation), 1998; Hugs for Women: Stories, Sayings, and Scriptures to Encourage and Inspire, 1998; Arise!, 1999; Fireside Stories: Heartwarming Tales of Life, Love, and Laughter, 2000; (comp.) Fireside Stories of Faith, Family, and Friendship, 2000; (with P. Stiger) The Joy of Tea, 2002; Love Notes from Heaven, 2002; (foreword) Mary Hollingsworth's Love Notes from God for Busy Moms, 2003; (with P. Boultinghouse) Big Hugs for Women: Stories, Sayings, and Scriptures to Encourage and Inspire, 2009. EDITOR: You've Gotta Be Kidding!: Inspirational Stories, Quotes, and Quips, 2005; Just Call Them Laugh Lines!: Inspirational Stories, Quotes, and Quips on Feeling Young at Heart, 2005; View from the Pew!, 2005; Contagious Joy!: Joyful Devotions to Lift Your Spirits, 2006; Funny Bone Fitness: Inspirational Stories, Quotes, and Quips about Dieting and Fitness, 2006; Happily Ever Laughter: Inspirational Stories, Quotes and Quips about Love and Marriage, 2006; Main Street Mirth: Inspirational Stories, Quotes and Quips from around Town, 2006; Medical Mayhem: Inspirational Stories, Quotes, and Quips on Health and Getting Well, 2006; Parents Wanted: Inspirational Stories, Quotes, and Quips on Parenting, 2006; Animal Antics, 2006; Cash in on Laughter: Inspirational Stories, Quotes, and Quips about Money and Life, 2007; On the Highway to Humor, 2007; Holiday Hilarity: Inspirational Stories, Quotes, and Quips about the Special Times of the Year, 2007; Jest Patriotic, 2007; Miracles and Animals, 2007; Miracles and

Mysterious Visitors, 2007; Miracles of Christmas, 2007; Miracles of Love, 2007; Miracles Every Day, 2007; Miracles of Renewal, 2007; And God Said Let There be Laughter!: Humorous and Inspiring Stories, Quotes, and Quips, 2008; Miracles in Tough Times, 2008; Miracles of Nature: When Miracles Happen: True Stories of God's Divine Touch, 2008; Christmas Miracles: True Stories of Joy and Wonder, 2008. Contributor of articles to periodicals. **Address:** Creative Enterprises Studio, 1507 Shirley Way, Bedford, TX 76022-6737, U.S.A. **Online address:** info@maryhollingsworth.com

HOLLINS, Etta R(uth). American (born United States), b. 1942. **Genres:** Education. **Career:** Elementary school teacher, 1964-65; California State Department of Youth Authority, classroom teacher, 1966-69; social studies teacher and department head at middle schools, 1969-72; primary resource teacher at public schools, 1972-73; administrator of public schools, 1975-79; Education Service Center, full-time consultant in social studies and multicultural education, 1979-82; coordinator of teacher training program for public schools, 1982-84; University of Utah, assistant professor of educational studies, 1984-86; Weber State College, assistant professor of teacher education, 1986-87; Delaware State University, associate professor of education and head of department, 1987-88; California State University, professor of teacher education, 1988-95; Pacific Lutheran Seminary, lecturer, 1990; Jackson State University, Joseph H. Jackson distinguished lecturer, 1994; Washington State University, professor of teaching and learning and department head, 1995-98; Wright State University, College of Education and Human Services, professor of education and associate dean, 1998-2000; University of Southern California, Rossier School of Education, professor and chairman of teacher education. Writer. **Publications:** A Conceptual Framework for Selecting Instructional Approaches and Materials for Inner City Black Youngsters, 1989; Culture in School Learning: Revealing the Deep Meaning, 1996, 2nd ed., 2008. EDITOR: (with J.E. King and W.C. Hayman and contrib.) Teaching Diverse Populations: Formulating a Knowledge Base, 1994; Transforming Curriculum for a Culturally Diverse Society, 1996; (with J.E. King and W.C. Hayman and contrib.) Preparing Teachers for Cultural Diversity, 1997; (with E.I. Oliver and contrib.) Pathways to Success in School: Culturally Responsive Teaching, 1999; (with R.H. Sheets) Racial and Ethnic Identity in School Practice: Aspects of Human Development, 1999; Learning to Teach in Urban Schools: The Transition from Preparation to Practice, 2011. Contributor of articles to books and journals. **Address:** Rossier School of Education, University of Southern California, WPH 1002 B, 3470 Trousdale Pkwy., Los Angeles, CA 90089-4038, U.S.A. **Online address:** ehollins@usc.edu

HOLLIS, Edward Christopher Rexworthy. Scottish/British (born England), b. 1970. **Genres:** Architecture. **Career:** Richard Murphy Architects, architect, 1995-99; Napier University, lecturer and programme leader, 1999-2004; Edinburgh College of Art, head of interior design department and instructor, 2004-; Nicholas Groves Raines Architects, staff. Writer. **Publications:** (Ed.) Thinking Inside the Box: A Reader in Interior Design for the 21st Century, 2007; The Secret Lives of Buildings: From the Ruins of the Parthenon to the Vegas Strip in Thirteen Stories, 2009. **Address:** Edinburgh College of Art, Lauriston Pl., Edinburgh, EH3 9DF, Scotland. **Online address:** e.hollis@eca.ac.uk

HOLLIS, Stephanie. British (born England), b. 1946. **Genres:** Literary Criticism And History, Bibliography. **Career:** University of Auckland, lecturer, 1972-76, Old and Middle English and Old Icelandic, senior lecturer, 1977-94, associate professor of English, 1995-, Centre for Medievaland Early Modern Studies, director, now professor emeritus. Writer. **Publications:** Anglo-Saxon Women and the Church, 1992; (with M. Wright) Annotated Bibliographies of Old and Middle English IV: Old English Prose of Secular Learning, 1992; (co-ed.) Writing the Wilton Women: Goscelin's Legend of Edith and Liber Confortatorius, 2004; (ed. with A. Barratt) Migrations: Medieval Manuscripts in New Zealand, 2007. Contributor to journals. **Address:** Department of English, University of Auckland, Rm. 527, 1-11 Short St., Level 5, Auckland, 1, New Zealand. **Online address:** s.hollis@auckland.ac.nz

HOLLIS, Tim. American (born United States), b. 1963. **Genres:** Popular Culture, History, Business/Trade/Industry. **Career:** Campbell's Publishing, editor-in-chief, 1986-. **Publications:** Cousin Cliff: 40 Magical Years in Television, 1991; Dixie before Disney: 100 Years of Roadside Fun, 1999; Hi There, Boys and Girls: America's Local Children's TV Programs, 2001; Florida's Miracle Strip: From Redneck Riviera to Emerald Coast, 2004; Birmingham's Theater and Retail District, 2005; Glass Bottom Boats & Mermaid Tails: Florida's Tourist Springs, 2006; (with G. Ehrbar) Mouse Tracks: The Story of Walt

Disney Records, 2006; Birmingham Broadcasting (Al), 2006; Six Flags over Georgia, 2006; The Land of the Smokies: Great Mountain Memories, 2007; Vintage Birmingham Signs, 2008; Ain't that a Knee-Slapper: Rural Comedy in the Twentieth Century, 2008; Selling the Sunshine State: A Celebration of Florida Tourism Advertising, 2008; Stone Mountain Park, 2009; See Rock City: The History of Rock City Gardens, 2009; Christmas Wishes: A Catalog of Vintage Holiday Treats and Treasures, 2010; Pizitz: Your Store, 2010; (with M. Soward) Lost Attractions of Sevier County, 2011; Wish You Were Here, 2011. **Address:** Campbell's Publishing, PO Box 310727, Birmingham, AL 35231, U.S.A. **Online address:** campholl@aol.com

HOLLO, Anselm (Paul Alexis). American/Finnish (born Finland), b. 1934. **Genres:** Poetry, Autobiography/Memoirs, Essays, Translations. **Career:** Journalist and book and film reviewer, 1950-58; Finnish Lumber Export Co., commercial correspondent; United Nations Atomic Energy Agency, interpreter; British Broadcasting Corp., program assistant and coordinator, 1958-67; State University of New York, Department of English, visiting professor, 1967-69; University of Iowa, Creative Writing Program, lecturer, 1968-73, Center for New Performing Arts, lecturer in English, 1970-71, Translation Workshop, head, 1971-72; Bowling Green State University, visiting professor, 1972-73; Hobart and William Smith Colleges, visiting professor, 1973-75; Michigan State University, distinguished visiting poet, 1974; University of Maryland, associate professor of literature and creative writing, 1975-77; Southwest Minnesota State College, visiting lecturer in creative writing, 1977-78; Sweet Briar College, Margaret Bannister distinguished writer-in-residence, 1978-81; Naropa Institute, faculty, 1981-84, Graduate Writing and Poetics Department, associate professor, 1989-, professor; Kerouac School of Poetics, poet-in-residence, 1981, associate lecturer in poetry and poetics, 1986-89; New College of California, visiting lecturer in poetics, 1981-83; Maryland Institute College of Art, lecturer, 1983-84; Black Mountain College Symposium, faculty, 1983-84; University of Colorado, Creative Writing Department, visiting professor of poetry, 1985. **Publications:** Sateiden Valilla, 1956; St. Texts and Finnpoems, 1961; Loverman, 1961; Some poems, 1962; Red cats., 1962; We Just Wanted to Tell You, 1963; And What Else Is New, 1963; History, 1964; Trobar: Loytaa (poetry), 1964; Negro verse, 1964; And It is a Song: Poems, 1965; Faces & Forms, 1965; Here We Go, 1965; The Claim, 1966; The Going-On Poem, 1966; Poems/Runoja, 1967; Isadora and Other Poems, 1967; Leaf Times, 1967; The Man in the Tree-Top Hat, 1968; The Coherences, 1968; Tumbleweed: Poems, 1968; (with J. Esam and T. Raworth) Haiku, 1968; Waiting for a Beautiful Bather: Ten Poems, 1969; Double Talk, 1969; Maya: Works, 1959-69, 1970; Gee Apollinaire: Birth of a Poem, A Documentary Poem, 1970; America del Norte and Other Peace Herb Poems, 1970; Message, 1970; (with J. Marshall and S. Hamod) Surviving in America, 1972; Sensation 27, 1972; Alembic, 1972; Some Worlds, 1974; Lingering Tangos, 1976; Sojourner Microcosms: New and Selected Poems 1959-1977, 1977; Heavy Jars, 1977; Curious Data, 1978; Lunch in Fur, 1978; With Ruth in Mind, 1979; Finite Continued, 1980; No Complaints, 1983; Pick Up the House, 1986; Outlying Districts, 1987; Near Miss Haiku (poetry), 1990; Space Baltic: The Science Fiction Poems, 1962-1987, 1991; High Beam: 12 Poems, 1993; (with J. Dalrymple-Hollo) West Is Left on the Map, 1993; Survival Dancing, 1995; Corvus: New Poems, 1995; Caws and Causeries: Around Poetry and Poets, 1999; Rue Wilson Monday, 2000; Notes on the Possibilities and Attractions of Existence: Selected Poems 1965-2000, 2001; So the Ants Made It to the Cat Food, 2002; The Guy in the Little Room, 2002; Guests of Space, 2007. EDITOR: Jazz Poems, 1963; Negro Verse, 1964; (with G. Harding) Modern Swedish Poetry in Translation, 1979; (with G. Malanga) A Purchase in the White Botanica: The Collected Poetry of Piero Helicze, 2001. TRANSLATOR: (intro.) Selected Poems of Paavo Haavikko, 1974; L. Malle, Au Revoir les Enfants, 1988; I, Eternal Child: Paintings and Poems, 1988; Egon Schiele: The Poems, 1988; Kullervon Tarina=Kullervo's Story, 1989; P.S. Jungk, Frans Werfel: The Story of a Life, 1990; Paavo Haavikko: Selected Poems, 1949-1989, 1991; J. Kross, The Czar's Madman, 1991; R. Liksom, One Night Stands, 1993; Sarajevo: A War Journal, 1993; J. Kross, Professor Martens' Departure, 1994; And Still Drink More!: A Kayankaya Mystery, 1994; The Poems of Hipponax of Ephesus, 1996; Starfall: A Triptych, 1997; One Death to Die: A Kayankaya Mystery, 1997; Day in Ostrobothnia, 2001; A. Tuuri, A Day in Ostrobothnia, 2001; Trilogy, 2003; J. Arjouni, More Beer: A Kayankaya Mystery, 2011. EDITOR and TRANSLATOR: A. Ginsberg, Kaddisch, 1962; Red Cats: Selection from Three Russian Poets, 1962; G. Corso, In der Fluchtigen Hand der Zeit, 1963; A. Ginsberg, Huuto ja Muita Runoja, 1963; A. Ginsberg, Kuolema van Goghin Korvalle, 1963; (with M. Lahtela) Idan ja Lannen Runot, 1963; Selected Poems by Andrei Voznesensky, 1964; Nain Ihminen Vastaa, 1964; R.G. Dienst, Five

Feet Two, 1965; Word from the North: New Poetry from Finland, 1965; P. Saarikoski, Helsinki: Selected Poems, 1967; P. Haavikko, Selected Poems, 1968; A. Blok, The Twelve and Other Poems, 1971; (with G. Harding) Recent Swedish Poetry in Translation, 1979; Pentti Saarikoski: Poems 1958-80, 1984. **Address:** Writing & Poetics, Naropa Institute, 2130 Arapaho Ave., Boulder, CO 80302, U.S.A.

HOLLOS, Marida. (Marida C. Hollos). American/Hungarian (born Hungary), b. 1940. **Genres:** Geography, Local History/Rural Topics, Environmental Sciences/Ecology, Anthropology/Ethnology. **Career:** University of Chicago, Eastern Norway Isolation Project, research associate, 1969; Ethnographic Museum, research associate, 1971-72; University of Oslo, Institutt for Etnografi, lecturer, 1972-74; Brown University, Department of Anthropology, assistant professor, 1974-84, associate professor, 1984-2001, professor, 2001-; National Museum of Canada, Canadian Centre for Folk Culture Studies, research fellow, 1975-76; Hungarian Academy of Sciences, research scientist, 1976-77, 1980; Harvard University, Peabody Museum of Anthropology, research fellow, 1981-83; University of Port Harcourt, research scientist, 1982-83; University of Benin, Department of Sociology and Anthropology, visiting Fulbright professor, 1984-86; Eotvos Lorand University, visiting Fulbright professor, 1990-91. Writer and anthropologist. **Publications:** Growing Up in Flathill: Social Environment and Cognitive Development, 1974; (ed. with B.C. Maday) New Hungarian Peasants: An East Central European Experience with Collectivization, 1983; (with P.E. Leis) Becoming Nigerian in Ijo Society, 1989; Scandal in a Small Town: Understanding Modern Hungary Through the Stories of Three Families, 2001. **Address:** Department of Anthropology, Brown University, PO Box 1921, Providence, RI 02912, U.S.A. **Online address:** marida_hollos@brown.edu

HOLLOS, Marida C. See **HOLLOS, Marida.**

HOLLOWAY, Harry (Albert). American (born United States), b. 1925. **Genres:** Politics/Government, Social Sciences, History. **Career:** University of Texas, instructor, 1957-61, assistant professor of political science, 1961-62; University of Oklahoma, associate professor, 1962-66, professor of political science, 1961-91, professor emeritus of political science, 1991-; American Association of University Professors, Oklahoma Chapter, president, 1995. Writer. **Publications:** (With J.R. Soukup and C. McCleskey) Party and Factional Division in Texas, 1964; The Politics of the Southern Negro: From Exclusion to Big City Organization, 1969; (with J. George) Public Opinion: Coalitions, Elites, and Masses, 1979, 2nd ed., 1986; (with F.S. Meyers) Bad Times for Good Ol' Boys: The Oklahoma County Commissioner Scandal, 1993. **Address:** Department of Political Science, The University of Oklahoma, Rm. 205, 455 W Lindsey St., Norman, OK 73019-2001, U.S.A. **Online address:** hholloway1@cox.net

HOLLOWAY, Karla F. C. American (born United States), b. 1949. **Genres:** Literary Criticism And History, Biography, Autobiography/Memoirs, Women's Studies And Issues. **Career:** Old Dominion University, instructor in English, 1972-74; Western Michigan University, assistant professor, 1978-82, associate professor of English, 1982-86; North Carolina State University, professor of English, 1988-93; Duke University, professor of English and African-American literature, 1993-, William R. Kenan Jr. Professor of English and dean of humanities and social sciences, James B. Duke professor of English and professor of law, women's studies and African & African American studies, faculty; John Hope Franklin Center, founding co-director; Franklin Humanities Institute, founding co-director. **Publications:** The Character of the Word: The Texts of Zora Neale Hurston, 1987; (with S.A. Demetrakopoulos) New Dimensions of Spirituality: A Biracial and Bicultural Reading of the Novels of Toni Morrison, 1987; Moorings and Metaphors: Figures of Culture and Gender in Black Women's Literature, 1992; Codes of Conduct: Race, Ethics, and the Color of Our Character, 1994; Passed On: African American Mourning Stories: A Memorial Collection, 2002; BookMarks: Reading in Black and White: A Memoir, 2006; Private Bodies/Public Texts: Locating (a) Narrative Bioethics, 2011. Contributor of periodicals. **Address:** Department of English, Duke University, 304 F Allen Bldg., Durham, NC 27708-0015, U.S.A. **Online address:** khollow@fas.harvard.edu

HOLLOWAY, Richard (Frederick). Scottish (born Scotland), b. 1933. **Genres:** Theology/Religion, Ethics, Social Commentary, inspirational/Motivational Literature, Adult Non-fiction, Politics/Government, History, Philosophy, Philosophy. **Career:** St Ninian's, curate, 1959-63; St. Margaret and St. Mungo's Church, priest in charge, 1963-68; Edinburgh Theological

College, lecturer, 1968-72; Old St. Paul's Church, rector, 1968-80; Church of the Advent, rector, 1980-84; St. Mary Magdalen Church, vicar, 1984-86; Harvard University, William Belden Noble lecturer, 1985; Scottish Episcopal Church, bishop of Edinburgh, 1986-2001, primus, 1992-2001; Gresham College, professor of divinity, 1997-2001. Writer. **Publications:** Let God Arise, 1972; New Vision of Glory, 1974; A New Heaven, 1979; Beyond Belief: The Christian Encounter with God, 1981; Signs of Glory, 1983; Paradoxes of Christian Faith and Life, 1984 in US as Suffering, Sex and Other Paradoxes, 1985; The Killing: Meditations on the Death of Christ, 1985; The Way of the Cross in US as A Death in Jerusalem, 1986; Seven to Flee, Seven to Follow, 1986; The Sidelong Glance: Politics, Conflict and the Church, 1986; Crossfire: Faith and Doubt in an Age of Certainty, 1988; When I Get to Heaven, 1988; Another Country, Another King, 1988; Anger, Sex, Doubt and Death, 1992; The Stranger in the Wings, 1994; (with B. Avery) Churches and How to Survive Them, 1994; Behold Your King, 1995; Limping Towards the Sunrise, 1995; Dancing on the Edge, 1997; Godless Morality: Keeping Religion Out of Ethics, 1999; Doubts and Loves: What Is Left of Christianity, 2001; On Forgiveness: How Can We Forgive the Unforgivable?, 2002; Sword and the Cross: Four Turbulent Episodes in the History of Christian Scotland, 2003; How to Read the Bible, 2007; Looking in the Distance: The Human Search for Meaning, 2007; Between the Monster and the Saint, 2008. EDITOR: The Anglican Tradition, 1984; Who Needs Feminism?: Male Responses to Sexism in the Church, 1991. **Address:** 6 Blantyre Terr., Edinburgh, EH10 5AE, Scotland. **Online address:** doc.holloway@virgin.net

HOLLOWAY, Sara. British (born England) **Genres:** Human Relations/Parenting. **Career:** Granta Books, senior editor, editorial director, publishing director. **Publications:** (Ed.) Family Wanted: True Stories of Adoption, 2005. Contributor to periodicals. **Address:** Granta Books, 12 Addison Ave., London, GL W11 4QR, England. **Online address:** sholloway@granta.com

HOLLOWAY, Sue (A.). American (born United States), b. 1944. **Genres:** Poetry, Natural History, Essays, Ethics, Sciences. **Career:** Southern Connecticut State University, adjunct professor, Foundations of Education/Women's Studies Departments, 1991-2000; Teachers' Creative Workshop, founder and facilitator, 1993-95; InterCity Cultural Development Project, mentor, 1999-2000; TWR Associates, qualitative researcher; Southern Connecticut Library Council, lecturer and workshop facilitator. Writer. **Publications:** (Co-ed.) A Community of Young Poets (poetry), 1995; Chronicles of Healing Self with Nature (poetry), 1995, rev. ed., 2000; Artemis' Arrow (poetry; audiotape), 1999; Swan in the Grail (nonfiction), 1999. Works appear in anthologies. Contributor of essays to journals. **Address:** 168 Thimble Islands Rd., Branford, CT 06405-5747, U.S.A.

HOLM, Tom. American (born United States), b. 1946. **Genres:** History, Military/Defense/Arms Control, Novels. **Career:** University of Arizona, assistant professor, 1980-86, associate professor, 1986-95, professor of political science, 1995-; Readjustment Counseling Services, advisor. Political scientist and writer. **Publications:** Strong Hearts, Wounded Souls: Native American Veterans of the Vietnam War, 1996; The Great Confusion in Indian Affairs: Native Americans and Whites in the Progressive Era, 2005; Code Talkers and Warriors: Native Americans and World War II, 2007; The Osage Rose (novel), 2008. Contributor to books and periodicals. **Address:** Department of American Indian Studies, University of Arizona, 1103 E 2nd St., PO Box 210076, Tucson, AZ 85721-0076, U.S.A. **Online address:** holm@email.arizona.edu

HOLMAN, Sheri. American (born United States), b. 1966. **Genres:** Novels, Young Adult Fiction. **Career:** Aaron M. Priest Literary Agency, aide, 1996-; Penguin Group, Department of Marketing, assistant; The Moth, founding member. Writer. **Publications:** FICTION: A Stolen Tongue, 1997; The Dress Lodger, 2000; Sondok: Princess of the Moon and Stars, 2002; The Mammoth Cheese: A Novel, 2003; The Witches on the Road Tonight, 2011. OTHER: (contrib.) The Secret Currency of Love, 2009. **Address:** c/o Deb Seager, Grove/Atlantic Inc., 841 Broadway, 4th Fl., New York, NY 10003-4704, U.S.A. **Online address:** sheri@sheriholman.com

HOLMAN, Susan R. American (born United States), b. 1956?. **Genres:** Medicine/Health, Social Sciences, Novels. **Career:** Brigham and Women's Hospital, Department of Medicine, Office of Faculty Services, medical writer and editor, 1988-2004; American Journal of Archaeology, associate editor, 1999; Nutrition Today, managing editor, 2000-03; Harvard University, School of Public Health, François-Xavier Bagnoud Center for Health and Human Rights, writer, Health and Human Rights: An International Journal, editor,

2007-. Nutritionist and researcher. **Publications:** Essentials of Nutrition for the Health Professions, 1987; Domitian, the Younger: A Novel, 1994; Watchmen of the House (novel), 1997; The Hungry Are Dying: Beggars and Bishops in Roman Cappadocia, 2001; (ed.) Wealth and Poverty in Early Church and Society, 2008; God Knows There's Need: Christian Responses to Poverty, 2009. Contributor of articles to books and journals. **Address:** Poverty Studies, PO Box 380252, Cambridge, MA 02238-0252, U.S.A. **Online address:** povertystudies@aol.com

HOLMES, Amanda. Canadian (born Canada), b. 1972. **Genres:** Adult Non-fiction. **Career:** McGill University, Department Of Hispanic Studies, assistant professor, 2001-07, director of graduate studies, 2004-07, associate professor, 2007-, chair of the department, 2008-11, director of graduate studies, 2011-. Writer. **Publications:** City Fictions: Language, Body, and Spanish American Urban Space, 2007; (ed. with R. Young) Cultures of the City: Mediating Identities in Urban Latin/o America, 2010. Contributor to journals. **Address:** Department of Hispanic Studies, McGill University, Rm. 425, 688 Sherbrooke St. W, Montreal, QC H3A 3R1, Canada. **Online address:** amanda.holmes@mcgill.ca

HOLMES, Arthur F(rank). American/British (born England), b. 1924. **Genres:** Philosophy, Theology/Religion. **Career:** Wheaton College, assistant professor, 1953-57, associate professor, 1957-66, professor of philosophy, 1966-, emeritus professor of philosophy, 1994-, chairman. Writer. **Publications:** Christianity and Philosophy, 1960; Christian Philosophy in the Twentieth Century, 1969; Faith Seeks Understanding, 1971; The Idea of a Christian College, 1975, rev. ed., 1987; All Truth is God's Truth, 1977; Contours of a World View, 1983; Ethics: Approaching Moral Decisions, 1984, 2nd ed., 2007; Shaping Character: Moral Education in the Christian College, 1991; Fact, Value and God, 1997; Building the Christian Academy, 2001. EDITOR: War and Christian Ethics, 1975, 2nd ed., 2005; The Making of a Christian Mind, 1985; New Dictionary of Christian Ethics and Pastoral Theology, 1995. **Address:** Department of Philosophy, Wheaton College, 501 College Ave., Wheaton, IL 60187, U.S.A.

HOLMES, B(ryan) J(ohn). Also writes as Ethan Wall, Charles Langley Hayes. British (born England), b. 1939?. **Genres:** Novellas/Short Stories, Westerns/Adventure, Reference, Novels, Young Adult Fiction. **Career:** North Staffordshire Polytechnic, faculty; University of Derby, lecturer. Writer. **Publications:** NOVELS: The Avenging Four, 1978; Hazard, 1979; Blood, Sweat and Gold, 1980; Gunfall, 1980; A Noose for Yanqui, 1981; Shard, 1982; Bad Times at Backwheel, 1982; On the Spin of a Dollar, 1983; Guns of the Reaper, 1983; Another Day, Another Dollar, 1984; Dark Rider, 1987; I Rode with Wyatt, 1989; A Legend Called Shatterhand, 1990; Dollars for the Reaper, 1990; Shatterhand and the People, 1992; The Last Days of Billy Patch, 1992; Blood on the Reaper, 1992; The Coffin for the Reaper, 1994; Viva Reaper!, 1996; The Shard Brand, 1996; Smoking Star, 1997; Comes the Reaper, 1998; Crowfeeders, 1999; Jake's Women, 2002; (with J. Sadler) Yuma Breakout, 2008. REFERENCE: Pocket Crossword Dictionary, 2001; Bradford's Guide to Solving Crosswords: Cracking the Code, 2002; Solving Cryptic Crosswords, 2003. AS CHARLES LANGLEY HAYES: NOVELS: Montana Hit, 1993; Dakota Hit, 1995; Utah Hit, 1995; Wyoming Hit, 2005. AS ETHAN WALL: NOVELS: Loco, 1991; All Trails Lead to Dodge, 1993; High Plains Death, 1997; North of the Bravo, 2001; Rio Grande Shoot-out, 2004; Three Graves to Fargo, 2004. **Address:** Robert Hale Ltd., 45-47 Clerkenwell Green, London, GL EC1R 0HT, England.

HOLMES, Diana. British (born England), b. 1949. **Genres:** Literary Criticism And History, Language/Linguistics, Cultural/Ethnic Topics. **Career:** University of Wolverhampton, lecturer in French, 1975-80, senior lecturer, 1984-90, principal lecturer in French, 1990; North London Polytechnic, part-time lecturer in French, 1981-84; University of Birmingham, visiting lecturer, 1986-87; Keele University, lecturer, 1992-94, senior lecturer, 1994-95, professor of French and head of French studies, 1995-99; University of Leeds, professor of French, 1999-. Writer. **Publications:** (Contrib.) France: Image and Identity, 1986; Colette, 1991; (contrib.) Violence and Conflict in French Culture, 1995; Women in Context: French Women Writers, 1848-1994, 1996; French Women's Writings, 1848-1994, 1996; (contrib.) French Erotic Fiction: Women's Desiring Writing, 1880-1990, 1996; (with R. Ingram) Francois Truffaut, 1998; Why Europe?: Problems of Culture and Identity, vol. II, 1999; (ed. with A. Smith) 100 Years of European Cinema: Entertaining Ideologies, 2000; Rachilde: Decadence, Gender and the Woman Writer, 2001; (ed. with C. Tarr) A Belle Epoque?: Women in French Society and Culture 1890-1914,

2005; (ed. with C. Tarr) A Belleepoque?: Women and Feminism In French Society and Culture, 1890-1914, 2006; (ed. with J. Gaffney) Celebrity and Stardom in France, 2006; Romance and Readership in Twentieth Century France, 2006. Contributor to periodicals. **Address:** Department of French, University of Leeds, Woodhouse Ln., Leeds, WY LS2 9JT, England. **Online address:** d.holmes@leeds.ac.uk

HOLMES, Hannah. American (born United States), b. 1963?. **Genres:** Environmental Sciences/Ecology. **Career:** Casco Bay Weekly, news editor, 1988; Garbage Magazine, writer and associate editor, 1989-2001; Discovery Channel Online, writer. **Publications:** The Secret Life of Dust: From the Cosmos to the Kitchen Counter the Big Consequences of Little Things, 2001; Suburban Safari: A Year on the Lawn, 2005; The Well-dressed Ape: A Natural History of Myself, 2008; Quirk: Brain Science Makes Sense of Your Peculiar Personality, 2011. Contributor to magazines.. **Address:** Tessler Literary Agency, 27 W 20th St., Ste. 1003, New York, NY 10011, U.S.A. **Online address:** info@hannahholmes.net

HOLMES, John. See **SOUSTER, Raymond.**

HOLMES, Jon Richard. British (born England), b. 1973. **Genres:** Music, Art/Art History, Photography. **Career:** The Sunday Times, travel writer, 1999-. **Publications:** Rock Star Babylon: Outrageous Rumors, Legends, and Raucous True Tales of Rock and Roll Icons, 2007; Status Quo and the Kangaroo: And Other Rock Apocryphals, 2007. **Address:** c/o Vivienne Clore, The Richard Stone Partnership, 85 New Cavendish St., De Walden Ct., Ste. 3, London, GL W1W 6XD, England. **Online address:** jon@jonholmes.net

HOLMES, Katie. Australian (born Australia) **Genres:** Literary Criticism And History, Homes/Gardens. **Career:** La Trobe University, associate professor, History Program, cordinator, 1994-; freelance writer, 1996-; University of Melbourne, teacher; Australia's National University, teacher; University College, Keith Cameron chair in Australian history, 2010. **Publications:** Spaces in Her Day: Australian Women's Diaries of the 1920s and 1930s, 1995; (ed. with P. Grimshaw and M. Lake) Women's Rights and Human Rights: International Historical Perspectives, 2001; (ed. with S.K. Martin and K. Mirmohamadi) Green Pens: A Collection of Garden Writing, 2004; (with S.K. Martin and K. Mirmohamadi) Reading the Garden: The Settlement of Australia, 2008; Between the Leaves: Stories of Australian Women, Writing and Gardens, 2011. **Address:** History Program, La Trobe University, Rm. E135, David Myers Bldg., St. Leonards, Melbourne, VI 3086, Australia. **Online address:** k.holmes@latrobe.edu.au

HOLMES, Leslie (Templeman). Australian/British (born England), b. 1948. **Genres:** Politics/Government, Administration/Management, Economics. **Career:** University of Wales, lecturer in political science, 1976-78; University of Kent at Canterbury, lecturer, senior lecturer in political science, 1978-83; University of Melbourne, lecturer, senior lecturer, 1983-88, professor of political science, 1988-, department head, 1988-93, deputy department head, 1998-99, Faculty of Arts, Research and Graduate Studies, associate dean, 1990-91, 2005-06, MA in Comparative Politics Program, director, 1990-96, Contemporary Europe Research Centre, director, 1997-2000, Private International Relations program, principal academic overseer, 1999-2001, MA in International Studies, director, 2000-, deputy director, 2001-, Masters in International Politics, director, 2000-03, Division of Political Science, deputy head, 2008; Harvard University, Russian Research Center, visiting fellow, 1993; Central European University, visiting professor, 2001. Writer. **Publications:** The Policy Process in Communist States: Industrial Administration and Politics, 1981; (ed.) The Withering Away of the State?: Party and State under Communism, 1981; Politics in the Communist World, 1986; The End of Communist Power: Anti-Corruption Campaigns and Legitimation Crisis, 1993; Post-Communism: An Introduction, 1997; (ed. with W. Roszkowski) Changing Rules: Polish Political and Economic Transformation in Comparative Perspectives, 1997; (ed. with P. Murray) Europe: Rethinking the Boundaries, 1998; (ed. with P. Murray) Citizenship and Identity in Europe, 1999; (with J.S. Dryzek) Post Communist Democratization Political Discourses across Thirteen Countries, 2002; Rotten States?: Corruption, Post-Communism and Neoliberalism, 2006; (ed.) Terrorism, Organised Crime and Corruption: Networks and Linkages, 2007; Communism: A Very Short Introduction, 2009; (ed.) Trafficking and Human Rights, 2010. Contributor to journals. Works appear in anthologies. **Address:** Department of Political Science, University of Melbourne, Level 2, 234 Queensberry St., Carlton, VI 3052, Australia. **Online address:** leslieth@unimelb.edu.au

HOLMES, Mary Tavener. American (born United States), b. 1954. **Genres:** Art/Art History, Biography, Literary Criticism And History. **Career:** College of the City University of New York, assistant professor, 1985-92, Cooper Hewitt Masters Program, instructor, 1992-93; Houston Museum of Fine Art, special curator, 1986; Frick Museum, curator, 1992. Writer. **Publications:** (With G.T.M. Shackelford) The Magic Mirror: The Portrait in France, 1700-1900, 1986; Nicolas Lancret, 1690-1743, 1992; (with P. Stein) Eighteenth-Century French Drawings in New York Collections (catalogue), 1999; Nicolas Lancret: Dance Before a Fountain, 2006; My Travels with Clara, 2007; A Giraffe Goes to Paris, 2010; (with J.C. Harris) The Elephant from Baghdad, 2012. **Address:** 7 W 81st St., New York, NY 10024, U.S.A.

HOLMES, Mary Z(astrow). American (born United States), b. 1943. **Genres:** Romance/Historical, Novels, Children's Fiction. **Career:** Raintree Publishers, general manager and publisher, 1981-85; Agridata Resources, executive vice president, 1982-87; freelance writer and consultant, 1987-; Stone Bank Books, founding partner; SRA Ltd., editorial manager; Lyons & Carnahan, senior editor; SVE, mathematics editor. **Publications:** (Ed.) Super Dictionary, 1978; Cross of Gold: 1615, 1992; Two Chimneys: 1628, 1992; Thunder Foot: 1730, 1992; Year of the Sevens: 1777, 1992; See You in Heaven: 1836, 1992; For Bread: 1893, 1992; Dear Dad: 1942, 1992; Dust of Life: 1980, 1992. **Address:** 6910 Reynolds Dr., Oconomowoc, WI 53066, U.S.A.

HOLMES, Megan. American (born United States), b. 1959. **Genres:** Art/Art History, inspirational/Motivational Literature. **Career:** Harvard University, Department of Art History and Architecture, teaching fellow, 1984-88; Johns Hopkins University, Department of the History of Art, visiting assistant professor, 1994-96; Florida State University, Study Abroad Program, visiting assistant professor of art history, 1994; University of Michigan, Department of History of Art, associate professor of Italian renaissance art history, 2001-, director of graduate studies, 2005-06, associate chair, 2008-09, 2010-, Medieval and Early Modern Studies Program, faculty. Writer. **Publications:** (Contrib.) Picturing Women in Renaissance and Baroque Italy, 1997; Fra Filippo Lippi the Carmelite Painter, 1999; (contrib.) Coming About? A Festschrift for John Shearman, 2002; (contrib.) The Art Market in Italy, 2003; (contrib.) Italian Renaissance Cities: Artistic Exchange and Cultural Translation, 2004; (contrib.) The Miraculous Image in Late Medieval and Renaissance Culture, 2004. **Address:** Department of History of Art, University of Michigan, 150B Tappan Hall, 855 S University Ave., Ann Arbor, MI 48109-1357, U.S.A. **Online address:** holmesml@umich.edu

HOLMES, Raymond. See **SOUSTER, Raymond.**

HOLMES, Richard. British (born England), b. 1945. **Genres:** Poetry, Literary Criticism And History, Biography, Translations. **Career:** University of East Anglia, professor of biographical studies, 2001-07. Writer. **Publications:** One for Sorrow, Two for Joy (poem), 1970; Thomas Chatterton: The Case Reopened, 1970; Shelley: The Pursuit, 1974, new ed., 2003; (trans. and intro.) T. Gautier, My Fantoms, 1976; Coleridge, 1982; (contrib.) The Chimeras/Nerval (essays), 1984; Footsteps: Adventures of a Romantic Biographer, 1985; (with R. Hampson) Kipling: Something of Myself, 1987; Coleridge: Early Visions, 1989; Dr. Johnson & Mr. Savage, 1994; Coleridge: Darker Reflections, 1804-1834, 1999; Sidetracks: Explorations of a Romantic Biographer, 2000; The Age of Wonder: How the Romantic Generation Discovered the Beauty and Terror of Science, 2008; Thomas Lawrence Portraits, 2010. EDITOR: Shelley on Love: An Anthology, 1980; (and intro.) A Short Residence in Sweden, Norway, and Denmark, 1987; Coleridge: Selected Poems, 1996; (and intro.) Johnson on Savage: An Account of the Life of Mr. Richard Savage, Son of the Earl Rivers, 2002; Defoe on Sheppard and Wild, 2002; Gilchrist on Blake, 2002; Godwin on Wollstonecraft, 2002; Scott on Zelide, 2002; Southey on Nelson, 2002; A Dream Biography. Contributor to periodicals. **Address:** David Godwin Associates Ltd., 55 Monmouth St., London, GL WC2H 9DG, England.

HOLMES, Rupert. British (born England), b. 1947. **Genres:** Novels, Mystery/Crime/Suspense, Music. **Career:** Musician, playwright and novelist. **Publications:** The Mystery of Edwin Drood, 1986; Accomplice: A Comedy Thriller, 1991; Where the Truth Lies, 2003; Swing: A Mystery, 2005; The McMasters Guide To Homicide: Murder Your Employer, 2010; (with P. Manley) Essential Boat Maintenance: A Comprehensive Guide to Boat Improvement, Refitting, and Repair, 2011; False Information. **Address:** The Holmes Line, 717 White Plains Rd., Ste. 114, PO Box 303, Scarsdale, NY 10583, U.S.A. **Online address:** email@rupertholmes.com

HOLMES, Sara Lewis. American (born United States) **Genres:** Young Adult Fiction, Children's Fiction. **Career:** Writer. **Publications:** Letters from Rapunzel, 2007; Operation Yes, 2009. Contributor to periodicals. **Address:** Arthur A. Levine Books, 557 Broadway, New York, NY 10012, U.S.A. **Online address:** email@saralewisholmes.com

HOLROYD, Michael. British (born England), b. 1935. **Genres:** Literary Criticism And History, Biography, Young Adult Non-fiction, Art/Art History, Essays, Autobiography/Memoirs, Human Relations/Parenting. **Career:** Writer, 1964-; National Book League, chairman, 1976-78; Pennsylvania State University, visiting fellow, 1979. **Publications:** Hugh Kingsmill: A Critical Biography, 1964; Lytton Strachey, 2 vols., 1967-68, rev. ed., 1973; A Dog's Life, 1969; Unreceived Opinions, 1973; Augustus John: A Biography, 2 vols., 1974-75, rev. ed., 1976; (with M. Easton) The Art of Augustus John, 1975; Bernard Shaw, vol. I: The Search for Love, 1856-1898, 1988, vol. II: The Pursuit of Power, 1898-1918, 1989, vol. III: The Lure of Fantasy, 1918-1950, 1991, vol. IV: The Last Laugh, 1950-1991, 1991; Pygmalion and Major Barbara, 1992; The Shaw Companion, 1993; Lytton Strachey: The New Biography, 1994; (contrib.) Themes and Variations, 1996; Augustus John: The New Biography, 1996; Basil Street Blues, 2000; (intro.) The Whispering Gallery: Leaves from a Diplomat's Diary by Hesketh Pearson, 2000; (intro.) A Month in the Country, 2000; Works on Paper: The Craft of Biography and Autobiography, 2002; (intro.) Swedish Reflections: From Beowulf to Bergman, 2003; Mosaic: A Family Memoir Revisited in UK as Mosaic: Portraits in Fragments, 2004; A Strange Eventful History: The Dramatic Lives of Ellen Terry, Henry Irving, and Their Remarkable Families, 2008; A Book of Secrets: Illegitimate Daughters, Absent Fathers, 2011. EDITOR: (and intro.) The Best of Hugh Kingsmill, 1970; The Genius of Shaw, 1979; (and intro. with P. Levy) The Shorter Strachey, 1980; (and intro. with R. Skidelsky) God's Fifth Column, 1981; Essays by Divers Hands, XLII, 1982; Peterley Harvest: The Private Diary of David Peterley, 1985. Contributor to periodicals. **Address:** A. P. Watt Ltd., 20 John St., London, GL WC1N 2DR, England.

HOLSTAD, Scott Cameron. American (born United States), b. 1966. **Genres:** Poetry, Young Adult Fiction, Adult Non-fiction. **Career:** Big Head Press, editor, 1990-; APIPA, document control technician, 1991; California State University, lecturer, 1993-94; TSI Pubs, editorial coordinator, 1994-96; DeVry Institute of Technology, associate professor of English, 1995; Zellweger Uster, technical writer, 1999-2000; City of Knoxville, technical writer, 2000-. **Publications:** Street Poems, 1991; Industrial Madness, 1991; Dancing with the Lights Out, 1992; (with P. Weinman) Grungy Ass Swaying, 1993; Junction City, 1993; Binge, 1994; Distant Visions, Again and Again, 1994; Places, 1995; Never-Ending Cigarettes, 1999; Shrapnel, 1999; (with M.B. Simon) Shadows before the Maiming, 1999; Hang Gliding on X, 1999; The Napalmed Soul, 1999; Artifacts, 2002; Cells, 2005. Contributor to periodicals. **Address:** 733 Villa Crest Dr., Knoxville, TN 37923-6313, U.S.A. **Online address:** scott@scottcholstad.com

HOLSTI, Kalevi J. Canadian/Swiss (born Switzerland), b. 1935. **Genres:** International Relations/Current Affairs, Essays, Politics/Government, History. **Career:** University of British Columbia, instructor, 1961-63, assistant professor, 1963-67, associate professor, 1967-71, professor of political science, 1971, University Killam professor emeritus, 2000-, Centre for International Relations, research associate; Institute of International Relations, director, 1970-71; International Studies Association, president, 1986-87. Writer. **Publications:** Suomen Ulkopolitiikka Suuntaansa Etsimassa, 1963; International Politics: A Framework for Analysis, 1967, 7th ed., 1995; (co-author) Why Nations Realign: Foreign Policy Restructuring in the Postwar World, 1982; The Dividing Discipline: Hegemony and Diversity in International Theory, 1985; Peace and War: Armed Conflicts and International Order, 1648-1989, 1991; Change in the International System: Essays on the Theory and Practice of International Politics, 1991; The State, War and the State of War, 1996; Political Sources of Humanitarian Emergencies, 1997; Taming the Sovereigns: Institutional Change in International Politics, 2004. Contributor of articles to journals. **Address:** Department of Political Science, University of British Columbia, Rm. 207, C472-1866 Main Mall, Vancouver, BC V6T 1Z1, Canada. **Online address:** holsti@interchange.ubc.ca

HOLSTI, Ole Rudolf. American/Swiss (born Switzerland), b. 1933. **Genres:** International Relations/Current Affairs, Politics/Government, Sports/Fitness. **Career:** Stanford University, Department of Political Science, instructor, 1962-65, acting assistant professor, 1963-65, assistant professor, 1965-67, Studies in International Conflict and Integration, research coordinator and associate director, 1962-67; University of British Columbia, Department of Political Science, associate professor, 1967-71, professor, 1971-74; Journal of Conflict Resolution, associate editor, 1967-72; International Studies Association, president, 1969-70, 1975-77, 1979-80; Western Political Quarterly, editor, 1970-79; Duke University, Department of Political Science, George V. Allen professor, 1974-, chairman, 1978-83, director of undergraduate studies, 1992-98, George V. Allen professor emeritus, 1998-; University of California, professor of political science, 1978-79; International Studies Quarterly, associate editor, 1980-; University Press of America, editor, 1980-; International Society of Political Psychology, vice president, 1993-95. **Publications:** Content Analysis: A Handbook with Application for the Study of International Crisis, 1963; (with D.J. Findlay and R.R. Fagen) Enemies in Politics, 1967; Content Analysis for the Social Sciences and Humanities, 1969; (co-author) The Analysis of Communication Content: Developments in Scientific Theories and Computer Techniques, 1969; Crisis Escalation War, 1972; (with T. Hopmann and J.D. Sullivan) Unity and Disintegration in International Alliances: Comparative Studies, 1973; (with J.N. Rosenau) Vietnam, Consensus, and the Belief Systems of American Leaders, 1977; (ed. with A.L. George and R.M. Siverson) Change in the International System, 1980; The Three-Headed Eagle: Who Are the Cold War Internationalists, Post-Cold War Internationalists, and Isolationists?, 1981; (J.R. Rosenau) Consensus and Change in Foreign Policy: Opinions among American Leaders, 1982; American Leadership in World Affairs: Vietnam and the Breakdown of Consensus, 1984; (with P. Hopmann and J.D. Sullivan) Unity and Disintegration in International Alliances, 1985; Public Opinion and American Foreign Policy, 1996, rev. ed., 2004; Encyclopedia of U.S. Foreign Relation, 1997; (co-author) On the Cutting Edge of Globalization, 2005; Making American Foreign Policy, 2006; To See Ourselves as Others See Us: How Publics abroad View the United States after 9/11, 2008; American Public Opinion on the Iraq War, 2011. **Address:** Department of Political Science, Duke University, 301B Perkins Library, Durham, NC 27708-0204, U.S.A. **Online address:** holsti@duke.edu

HOLST-WARHAFT, Gail. Australian (born Australia), b. 1941?. **Genres:** Literary Criticism And History, Music, Poetry, Translations. **Career:** Cornell University, Institute for European Studies, acting director, 2000-03, Department of Classics and Comparative Literature, adjunct associate professor, 2003-, adjunct professor, co-director, 2003-04, director, 2004-05; Onassis Foundation, visiting professor, 2007-08. Poet, translator and musician. **Publications:** Road to Rembetika: Music of a Greek Sub-Culture: Songs of Love, Sorrow and Hashish, 1975, 3rd ed., 1983; Theodorakis: Myth and Politics in Modern Greek Music, 1980; Dangerous Voices: Women's Laments and Greek Literature, 1992; (trans.) I. Kambenellis, Mauthausen, 1995; (ed. with D.R. McCann) The Classical Moment: Views from Seven Literatures, 1999; The Cue for Passion: Grief and Its Political Uses, 2000; (trans.) Collected Poems of Nikos Kavadias, 2006; Penelope's Confession, 2007; (ed. with T. Steenhuis) Losing Paradise: The Water Crisis in the Mediterranean, 2010. Contributor to books and periodicals. **Address:** Institute for European Studies, Cornell University, 120 Uris Hall, Ithaca, NY 14853-7601, U.S.A. **Online address:** glh3@cornell.edu

HOLT, A. J. See HYDE, Christopher.

HOLT, David. American (born United States), b. 1946. **Genres:** Music, Young Adult Fiction, Social Sciences, Horror. **Career:** Warren Wilson College, Appalachian Music Program, founder and director, 1975. Musician, editor, historian and writer. **Publications:** Ready-to-Tell Tales: Surefire Stories from America's Favorite Storytellers, 1994; (ed. with B. Mooney) The Storytellers Guide: Storytellers Share Advice for the Classroom Boardroom Showroom Podium Pulpit and Center Stage, 1996; (with B. Mooney) Spiders in the Hairdo: Modern Urban Legends, 1999; (with B. Mooney) More Ready-to-Tell Tales from around the World, 2000; (with B. Mooney) Exploding Toilets: Modern Urban Legends, 2004. Contributor to periodicals. **Address:** c/o Betty Nichols, High Windy Productions, PO Box 28, Fairview, NC 28730, U.S.A.

HOLT, Ian. American (born United States), b. 1964. **Genres:** Horror. **Career:** Actor, screenwriter and radio host. **Publications:** (With D. Stoker) Dracula: The Un-Dead, 2009. **Address:** New York, NY, U.S.A. **Online address:** ian@draculatheun-dead.com

HOLT, James Clarke. British (born England), b. 1922. **Genres:** History, Humanities. **Career:** University of Nottingham, assistant lecturer, 1949-51, lecturer, 1951-61, senior lecturer and professor of medieval history, 1961-62; University of Reading, professor of history and dean, 1966-78, faculty of letters and social sciences, 1972-76; University of Cambridge, Emmanuel College, professorial fellow, 1978-81, professor of medieval history, 1978-88, honorary fellow, 1985-2005, now professor emeritus, Fitzwilliam College, master, 1981-88, honorable fellow, 2005-; Queen's College, honorable fellow, 1998-; Royal Historical Society, president, 1980-84; University of Oxford, Merton College, honorary fellow. Writer. **Publications:** The Northerners: A Study in the Reign of King John, 1961; King John, 1963; (ed.) Praestita Roll 14-18 John, Roll of Summonses 1214, Scutage Roll 16 John, 1964; Magna Carta, 1965, 2nd ed., 1992; The Making of Magna Carta, 1965; (ed.) Magna Carta and the Idea of Liberty, 1972; The University of Reading: The First Fifty Years, 1977; Robin Hood, 1982, rev. ed., 1989; (ed. with J. Gillingham) War and Government in the Middle Ages: Essays in Honour of J.O. Prestwich, 1984; Magna Carta and Medieval Government, 1985; (ed. with R. Mortimer) Acta of Henry II and Richard I, 1986; (ed.) Domesday Studies: Papers Read at the Novocentenary Conference of the Royal Historical Society and the Institute of British Geographers, Winchester, 1986, 1987; (ed.) Foundations for the Future: The University of Cambridge, 1995; Colonial England, 1066-1215, 1997. **Address:** Fitzwilliam College, University of Cambridge, Storey's Way, 1 Brookside Cambridge, Cambridge, CB CB2 1JE, England.

HOLT, Marilyn Irvin. American (born United States), b. 1949. **Genres:** History, Local History/Rural Topics, Biography, Autobiography/Memoirs. **Career:** Madison College, instructor in English, 1967-85; School teacher, 1970-79; Illinois State Historical Library, editor, 1983-86; Kansas State Historical Society, director of publications, 1986-90; University of Kansas, adjunct faculty, 1988-96. Historian. **Publications:** The Orphan Trains: Placing Out in America, 1992; Model Ts, Pep Chapels, and a Wolf at the Door: Kansas Teenagers, 1900-1941, 1995; Linoleum, Better Babies and the Modern Farm Woman, 1890-1930, 1995; Indian Orphanages, 2001; Children of the Western Plains: The Nineteenth-Century Experience, 2003; Mamie Doud Eisenhower: The General's First Lady, 2007. Contributor to journals. **Address:** 902 N Buckeye Ave., Abilene, KS 67410, U.S.A. **Online address:** mih@att.net

HOLT, Michael (Paul). British (born England), b. 1929. **Genres:** Children's Fiction, Recreation, Mathematics/Statistics, Sciences, Education, Young Adult Fiction. **Career:** Gas Council, research physicist in industrial laboratory, 1956-59, head of electronics laboratory, 1959-62; World Book Encyclopedia, senior science and mathematics editor, 1962-64; Ginn and Co., senior science and mathematics editor, 1965-67; Richmond Institute, lecturer in adult education, 1967-69; University of London, Goldsmiths College, lecturer in mathematics, 1967-68, senior lecturer in mathematics, 1968-70; free-lance educational writer, 1970-; Society of Authors, Educational Writers Group, chairman, 1971-73; Keele University, lecturer in mathematics; Association of Science Education, lecturer in mathematics; Oxford Mathematical Association, lecturer in mathematics. Writer. **Publications:** (With D.T.E. Marjoram) Mathematics Through Experience, 1966; What Is the New Maths?, 1968; Science Happenings, 6 books, 1969; Mathematics in Art, 1971; (with R. Ridout) Joe's Trip to the Moon, 1971; (with R. Ridout) The Train Thief, 1971; Exercises, 4 books, 1972; (with Z.P. Dienes) Zoo, 1972; (with R. Ridout) The Big Book of Puzzles, 3 vols., 1972-79; (with Z.P. Dienes) Let's Play Math, 1973; (with D.T.E. Marjoram) Mathematics in a Changing World, 1973; Inner Ring Maths, 1973; Maths, 6 books, 1973-74; (with R. Ridout) All Round English, 1974; (with R. Ridout) Life Cycle Books, 4 books, 1974; Monkey Puzzle Books, 6 books, 1974; Ready for Science, 6 books, 1974; Maps, Tracks, and the Bridges of Königsberg: A Book about Networks, 1975; Fun with Numbers, 1976; Math Puzzles and Games, 1977; More Math Puzzles and Games, 1978; Figure It Out Books, 4 vols., 1978-81; (with A. Rothery) Mathsworks, books, 1979; The Puma Puzzle Book, 1980; Basic Skills in Maths, 1981; Answer Me This, 1981; Holt Counting Board, 1981; The Bumper Quiz Book, 1981; (with A. Rothery) Maths Alive, 1982; The Amazing Invisible Ink Puzzle Books, 1982; (with A. Ward) Wide Range Science Story Books 1-2, 1982; The Amazing Invisible Ink Puzzle Books, 1983; Basic Arithmetic Puzzles: Adding and Subtracting, Multiplying and Dividing, 1983; The Dr. Who Quiz Book of Dinosaurs Magic, Science, 3 vols., 1983; (with A. Ward) Wide Range Science Story Books 3-4, 1984; The Dr. Who Book of Space, 1984; Now I Can Count to 3 Count to 5, 1984; Basic Arithmetic Puzzles: Fractions, Decimals, 1984; Now I Can Count to 10, 1985; Dr. Who Book of Puzzles, 1985; The Pan Pocket Puzzler, 1985; Crisis in Space, 1986; Getting on with Maths, 6 vols., 1986; The Great Spy Race, 1987; The Riddle of the Sphinx, 1987; Match and Sort, 6 vols., 1989; Getting Ahead in Maths, 1990; Inventions, 1990; The Sarbanes-Oxley Act: Overview and Implementation Procedures Manual, 2005. Contributor of articles to journals. **Address:** Highley, Whitbourne, Worcester, WM WR6 5RZ, England.

HOLT, Stephen. Australian (born Australia), b. 1949. **Genres:** Biography, History, Social Sciences. **Career:** Writer. **Publications:** Manning Clark and Australian History 1915-1963, 1982; A Veritable Dynamo: Lloyd Ross and Australian Labor, 1901-1987, 1996; A Short History of Manning Clark, 1999; (with R. Fitzgerald) Alan the Red Fox Reid: Pressman Par Excellence, 2010. **Address:** UNSW Press, University of New South Wales, Sydney, NW 2052, Australia. **Online address:** stephenholt34@hotmail.com

HOLT, (Wilma) Geraldene. British (born England) **Genres:** Food And Wine, Homes/Gardens, Horticulture, Food And Wine. **Career:** Jane Grigson Trust, chairman, honorary secretary; teacher, 1964-78; Guild of Food Writers, vice president, 1999. Writer. **Publications:** Geraldene Holt's Cake Stall, 1980; Geraldene Holt's Travelling Food, 1982; (comp.) Devon Air Cookbook, 1982; Budget Gourmet, 1984; French Country Kitchen, 1987; Tuckbox Treats, 1987; Recipes from a French Herb Garden, 1989; The Gourmet Garden: The Fruits Of The Garden Transported To The Table, 1990; French Country Kitchen, 1990; Geraldene Holt's Book of Herbs, 1991; (ed.) A Cup of Tea: An Afternoon Anthology Of Fine China And Tea Traditions, 1991; Geraldene Holt's Complete Book of Herbs, 1991; Geraldene Holt's Country House Cooking, 1996; Diary Of A French Herb Garden, 2002. **Address:** David Godwin Associates, 55 Monmouth St., London, GL WC2H 9DG, England. **Online address:** wgh@geraldeneholt.com

HOLTE, James Craig. American (born United States), b. 1949. **Genres:** Theology/Religion, Cultural/Ethnic Topics, Literary Criticism And History. **Career:** University of Cincinnati, instructor in English, 1976; University of New Orleans, instructor in English, 1976-81; East Carolina University, associate professor of English, 1981-, professor of English, director of graduate studies in English; WWNO-Radio, film critic; The Journal of the Fantastic in the Arts, special editor. **Publications:** The Ethnic I: A Sourcebook for Ethnic-American Autobiography, 1988; The Conversion Experience in America: A Sourcebook on Religious Conversion Autobiography, 1992; Dracula in the Dark: The Dracula Film Adaptations, 1997; (and ed.) The Fantastic Vampire: Studies in the Children of the Night Selected Essays from the Eighteenth International Conference on the Fantastic in the Arts, 2002. Contributor of articles to periodicals. **Address:** Department of English, East Carolina University, Rm. Bate 2211, 2211 Bate Bldg., Greenville, NC 27858-4353, U.S.A. **Online address:** holtej@mail.ecu.edu

HOLTER, Knut. Norwegian (born Norway), b. 1958. **Genres:** Theology/Religion, Reference, Cultural/Ethnic Topics, History. **Career:** School of Mission and Theology, associate professor, 1993-2002, professor of Old Testament studies, 2003-; University of Stellenbosch, professor, 2006-. Writer. **Publications:** Second Isaiah's Idol-Fabrication Passages, 1995; Yahweh in Africa: Essays on Africa and the Old Testament, 2000; (ed. with M. Getui and V. Zinkuratire) Interpreting the Old Testament in Africa, 2001; Old Testament Research for Africa: A Critical Analysis and Annotated Bibliography of African Old Testament Dissertations, 1967-2000, 2002; Deuteronomy 4 and the Second Commandment, 2003; (ed.) Let My People Stay!: Researching the Old Testament in Africa, 2006; Contextualized Old Testament Scholarship in Africa, 2008. **Address:** School of Mission and Theology, Misjonsveien 34, Misjonsmarka 12, Stavanger, N 4024, Norway. **Online address:** knut.holter@mhs.no

HOLTHE, Tess Uriza. American (born United States), b. 1966. **Genres:** Novels, Literary Criticism And History. **Career:** Writer. **Publications:** When the Elephants Dance (novel), 2002; The Five-Forty-Five to Cannes, 2007. Contributor to periodicals. **Address:** c/o Mary Ann Naples, Creative Culture Inc., 47 E 19th St., 3rd Fl., New York, NY 10003, U.S.A.

HOLTON, Woody. American (born United States), b. 1959. **Genres:** History. **Career:** Clean Up Congress, founder, 1990; Bloomsburg University, faculty; University of Richmond, associate professor of history and American studies. Writer. **Publications:** Forced Founders: Indians, Debtors, Slaves, and the Making of the American Revolution in Virginia, 1999; From the Labours of Others': The War Bonds Controversy and the Origins of the Constitution in New England, 2004; Unruly Americans and the Origins of the Constitution, 2007; Abigail Adams, 2009; Enslaved Americans and the Revolutionary War: A Brief History With Documents, 2009; Black Americans in the Revolutionary Era: A Brief History with Documents, 2009. **Address:** Department of History, University of Richmond, 317 Ryland Hall, 28 Westhampton Way, Richmond, VA 23173, U.S.A. **Online address:** aholton@richmond.edu

HOLTORF, Cornelius. (Cornelius J. Holtorf). Swedish/German (born Germany), b. 1968. **Genres:** Archaeology/Antiquities, History, Cultural/Ethnic Topics, Essays. **Career:** University of Cambridge, Department of Archaeology, teacher, 1999-2002; Lund University, Department of Archaeology and Ancient History, assistant professor, 2005-08, docent, 2007; University of Kalmar, Department of Humanities, associate professor, 2008-11; Linnaeus University, professor of archaeology, 2011-; European Journal of Archaeology, editor. **Publications:** (With C. Holtorf) Zwischenprüfung: 23 Studentische Essays Zur Frage: Wo Stehen Wir Heute?, 1992; (ed. with A. Gazin-Schwartz) Archaeology and Folklore, 1999; From Stonehenge to Las Vegas: Archaeology as Popular Culture, 2005; Archaeology Is a Brand! The Meaning of Archaeology in Contemporary Popular Culture, 2007; (ed. with A. Piccini) Contemporary Archaeologies: Excavating Now, 2009. **Address:** Institutionen för kulturvetenskaper, Linnéuniversitetet, Kalmar, SE-391 82, Sweden. **Online address:** cornelius.holtorf@lnu.se

HOLTORF, Cornelius J. *See* **HOLTORF, Cornelius.**

HOLTZ, Nairne. Canadian (born Canada), b. 1967?. **Genres:** Young Adult Fiction, Novels. **Career:** Writer. **Publications:** (Ed. with C. Lake) No Margins: Writing Canadian Fiction in Lesbian, 2006; The Skin Beneath (novel), 2007; This One's Going to Last Forever (novella and short stories), 2010. Contributor to periodicals. **Address:** Montreal, QC , Canada. **Online address:** nholtz@gmail.com

HOLTZMAN, Wayne Harold. American (born United States), b. 1923. **Genres:** Education, Psychology, Psychiatry, Sciences. **Career:** University of Texas, assistant professor, 1949-53, associate professor, 1953-59, professor of psychology and education, 1959-70, Hogg Foundation for Mental Health, associate director, 1955-64, president, 1970-, Hogg professor of psychology and education, 1970-, now Hogg professor emeritus in psychology and education, College of Education, dean, 1964-70; Social Science Research Council, faculty research fellow, 1953-54; Texas Psychological Association, president, 1956-57; Southwestern Psychological Association, president, 1958-59; Interamerican Society of Psychology, vice-president, 1962-64, president, 1966-67; National Science Foundation, chairman, 1972-73; International Union of Psychological Science, secretary-general, 1972, president, 1984-88; Learning Research and Development Center, chairman, 1976-86; Menninger Clinic, vice chairman, 1988-; International Council of Psychology, fellow; Society for Projective Techniques, fellow. Writer. **Publications:** (With W.F. Brown) Survey of Study Habits and Attitudes, 1953; (with J.S. Thorpe, J.D. Swartz and E.W. Herron) Inkblot Perception and Personality, 1961; (co-ed.) Personality Factors on the College Campus, 1962; (with B.M. Moore) Tomorrow's Parents, 1965; (with J.F. Santos, S. Bouquet and P. Barth) The Peace Corps in Brazil, 1966; (with O.G. Brim, Jr. and R.S. Crutchfield) Intelligence: Perspectives 1965, 1966; (ed.) Computer-Assisted Instruction, Testing and Guidance, 1970; (ed.) Interpreting Personality Theories, 1970; (with W.F. Brown) A Guide to College Survival, 1972, rev. ed., 1987; (ed.) Personalized Psychology, 1975; (with R. Diaz-Guerrero and J.D. Swartz) Personality Development in Two Cultures, 1975; (co-author) Introduction to Psychology, 1978; (co-ed.) Introductory Psychology in Depth, 1978; (co-ed.) Impact of Educational Television on Young Children, 1981; (with K.A. Heller and S. Messick) Placing Children in Special Education, 1982; American Families and Social Policies for Services to Children, 1983; Texas Universities and Mexico, 1984; Beyond the Rorschach, 1988; (ed. with T.H. Bornemann) Mental Health of Immigrants and Refugees, 1990; School of the Future, 1992; (ed.) Shared Opportunities for Schools and Communities: Eighth Robert Lee Sutherland Seminar, 1993; (ed. with S.K. Hoppe) Search for a Common Language in Psychiatric Assessment, 1994; (ed.) Psychiatric Assessment of Mexican-origin Populations: Proceedings of the Ninth Robert Lee Sutherland Seminar in Mental Health, 1995; Holtzman Inkblot Technique Research Guide, 1999; History of the International Union of Psychology and Science, 2000. **Address:** Department of Psychology, College of Liberal Arts, University of Texas, LAC 4.408A, 1 University Sta. A8000, Austin, TX 78712-0187, U.S.A. **Online address:** wayne.holtzman@mail.utexas.edu

HOLUB, Joan. American (born United States), b. 1956?. **Genres:** Children's Fiction, Mythology/Folklore, Children's Non-fiction, Picture/Board Books, Animals/Pets, Illustrations, Graphic Novels, Young Adult Fiction, Mathematics/Statistics, Humor/Satire, Cartoons, Biography. **Career:** Communications Plus, art director, 1980-89; Scholastic Inc., associate art director of children's trade books, 1989-91; author and illustrator, 1991-. **Publications:** Pajama Party, 1998; Space Dogs on Planet K-9, 1998; I Have a Weird Brother Who Digested a Fly, 1999; The Spooky Sleepover, 1999; Backwards Day, 2000; Light the Candles: A Hanukkah Lift-the-Flap Book, 2000; Abby Cadabra, Super Speller, 2000; Lost and Found in Jump Start Town, 2000; My Soccer Mom from Mars, 2001; Scat Cats!, 2001; Silly Bears, 2001; Why Do Cats Meow?, 2001; Why Do Dogs Bark?, 2001; The Garden That We Grew, 2001; The Pizza That We Made, 2001; The Gingerbread Kid Goes to School, 2002; Company's Coming: A Passover Lift-the-Flap Book, 2002; Hooray for St. Patrick's Day!, 2002; Jack and the Jellybeanstalk, 2002; Turkeys Never Gobble, 2002; Kwanzaa Kids, 2002; Why Do Horses Neigh?, 2003; Why Do Rabbits Hop?: And Other Questions About Rabbits, Guinea Pigs, Hamsters, and Gerbils, 2003; Yankee Doodle Riddles: American History Fun, 2003; Apples and Honey: A Rosh Hashanah Lift-the-Flap Book, 2003; Dragon Dance: A Chinese New Year Lift-the-Flap Book, 2003; Fourth of July, Sparkly Sky, 2003; Riddle-iculous Math, 2003; Why Do Birds Sing?, 2004; Geogra-Fleas!: Riddles all Over the Map, 2004; Why Do Snakes Hiss?: And Other Questions about Snakes, Lizards, and Turtles, 2004; The Halloween Queen, 2004; Who was Johnny Appleseed?, 2005; Happy Easter Eggs, 2005; (with J. Hannah) The Man Who Named the Clouds, 2006; Glorious Grandmas, 2006; Marvelous Moms, 2006; Who Was Marco Polo?, 2007; Knuckleheads, 2008; Five Spring Fairies: A Counting Book with Flaps and Pop-ups, 2008; Bed, Bats, & Beyond, 2008; Shampoodle, 2009; Groundhog Weather School, 2009; Apple Countdown, 2009; Who was Jim Henson?, 2010; Twinkle, Star of the Week, 2010; (with G. Hallowell) Wagons Ho!, 2011; What Does Cow Say?, 2011; A Kiss For You!, 2011; Who Was Babe Ruth?, 2012; Zero the Hero, 2012; Ballet Stars, 2012. DOLL HOSPITAL SERIES: Tatiana Comes to America: An Ellis Island Story, 2002; Goldie's Fortune: A Story of the Great Depression, 2002; Glory's Freedom: A Story of the Underground Railroad, 2003; Saving Marissa, 2003; Danielle's Dollhouse Wish, 2003; Charlotte's Choice, 2004. ANT HILL SERIES: More Snacks! A Thanksgiving Play, 2006; Big Heart! A Valentine's Day story, 2007; Good Luck! A St. Patrick's Day Story, 2007; Scaredy Pants! A Halloween Story, 2007; Spring is Here! A Story about Seeds, 2008; Snow Day!, 2008; Picnic! A Day in the Park, 2009. YOUNG PRINCESSES AROUND THE WORLD SERIES: Elizabeth and the Royal Pony: Based on a True Story of Elizabeth I of England, 2007; Cleopatra and the King's Enemies: Based On a True Story of Cleopatra in Egypt, 2007; Isabel Saves the Prince: Based on a True Story of Isabel I of Spain, 2007; Lydia and the Island Kingdom: A Story Based on the Real Life of Princess Liliuokalani of Hawaii, 2007. GODDESS GIRLS SERIES WITH S. WILLIAMS: Athena the Brain, 2010; Persephone the Phony, 2010; Aphrodite the Beautiful, 2010; Artemis the Brave, 2010; Athena the Wise, 2011; Aphrodite the Diva, 2011; Artemis the Loyal, 2011; Medusa the Mean, 2012; The Girl Games (super special), 2012. SELF-ILLUSTRATED FOR CHILDREN: Pen Pals, 1997; Boo Who? A Spooky Lift-the-Flap Book, 1997; Ivy Green, Cootie Queen, 1998; Red, Yellow, Green: What Do Signs Mean?, 1998; Happy Monster Day!, 1999; Eek-A-Boo! A Spooky Lift-the-Flap Book, 2000; Abby Candabra, Super Speller, 2000; How to Find Lost Treasure in All Fifty States... and Canada, Too!, 2000; Cinderdog and the Wicked Stepcat, 2001; Vincent van Gogh: Sunflowers and Swirly Stars, 2001; The Haunted States of America: Haunted Houses and Spooky Places in All Fifty States 2001; The Valley of the Golden Mummies, 2002; (with D. Regan) Animals, 2002; (with D. Regan) Cars and Trucks, 2002; (with D. Regan) Dinosaurs, 2003; (with D. Regan) Magical Creatures, 2003; Somebunny Loves Me, 2003; What Can Our New Baby Do?, 2004; Ivy Queen, Cootie Queen, 2004. Illustrator of books by others. Contributor to periodicals. **Address:** NC , U.S.A. **Online address:** joanholub@aol.com

HOLYFIELD, Evander. American (born United States), b. 1962. **Genres:** Autobiography/Memoirs. **Career:** Amateur boxer, 1972-84; professional boxer, 1984-; Evander Holyfield Buick & Subaru, partner; Real Deal Records, founder; Black Family Channel, partner. Writer. **Publications:** (with B. Holyfield) Holyfield: The Humble Warrior (memoir), 1996; (with L. Gruenfeld) Becoming Holyfield: A Fighter's Journey (memoir), 2008. **Address:** Holyfield Foundation, 794 Evander Holyfield Hwy., Fairburn, GA 30213, U.S.A.

HOLZ, Cynthia. Canadian/American (born United States), b. 1950?. **Genres:** Novels. **Career:** Business Week, correspondent, 1976-78; Ryerson Polytechnic University, teacher of creative writing, 1990-2008; Toronto Public Library, writer-in-residence, 1999. **Publications:** Home Again (short stories), 1989; Onlyville (novel), 1994; The Other Side, 1997; Semi-Detached, 1999; A Good Man, 2003; Benevolence, 2011. Contributor to periodicals. **Address:** Toronto, ON , Canada. **Online address:** cholz@cynthiaholz.com

HOM, Sharon K. (Sharon Kang Hom). American/Hong Kong (born Hong Kong), b. 1951. **Genres:** Social Sciences, Autobiography/Memoirs, Essays, Poetry. **Career:** Bar Association, Human Rights Watch, advisor, 1995-, Committee on Asian Affairs, advisor, 1998-; Tsinghua University, School of Law, Clinical Legal Education Workshop, faculty and program director, 2000; China Center for American Law Study, faculty and program director; City University of New York, School of Law, professor, now professor emeritus; Human Rights in China, executive director. Writer. **Publications:** (Contrib.) Fa lü jiao xue xin Fang fa gai lue: Meiguo fa lu jiao xue fang fa zai Zhongguo di Chang shi: Zhong Ying wen dui Zhao, 1990; (with A.H. Kastely and D.W. Post) Contracting Law, 1996, 4th ed., 2006; (ed.) Chinese Women Traversing Diaspora: Memoirs, Essays and Poetry, 1999; (ed. with S. Mosher) Challenging China: Struggle and Hope in an Era of Change, 2007. **Address:** Human Rights in China Head Office, 350 5th Ave., Ste. 3311, New York, NY 10118, U.S.A. **Online address:** hom@mail.law.cuny.edu

HOM, Sharon Kang. *See* **HOM, Sharon K.**

HOMAN, Madeleine. American (born United States) **Genres:** Business/Trade/Industry. **Career:** Straightline Coaching, owner and president, 1994-2001; The Ariel Group, course author and leader, 1995-2000; International Coach Federation, founder and founding board member, 1996-2006, vice president for professional development; Bregman Partners, director, 1998-2000; Ken Blanchard Companies, Coaching.com, co-founder, 2000-, vice president of coaching services, leadership coach, 2010-; CD2, general manager, 2009-; Coach University, senior trainer; CD2Learning, general manager, 2011-. Writer. **Publications:** (With S. Blanchard) Leverage Your Best, Ditch the Rest: The Coaching Secrets Top Executives Depend On, 2004; (with L.J. Miller) Coaching in Organizations: Best Coaching Practices from the Ken Blanchard Companies, 2008. Contributor to periodicals. **Address:** Coaching Services, Ken Blanchard Companies, 125 State Pl., Escondido, CA 92029-1323, U.S.A. **Online address:** mhb@mhblanchard.com

HOMAN, Sidney. American (born United States), b. 1938. **Genres:** Literary Criticism And History, Theatre, Language/Linguistics. **Career:** University of Illinois, assistant professor of English, 1965-69; Boston University, associate professor of English, 1969-72; University of Florida, professor of English and theater, 1977-; Jilin University, People's Republic of China, visiting professor, 1986-; Acrosstown Repertory Theatre, artistic director. Writer. **Publications:** (Ed.) Midsummer Night's Dream, 1970; (ed.) Shakespeare's More Than Words Can Witness: Essays on Visual and Nonverbal Enactment in the Plays, 1980; When the Theater Turns to Itself: The Aesthetic Metaphor in Shakespeare, 1981; Beckett's Theaters: Interpretations for Performance, 1984; Shakespeare's Theater of Presence: Language, Spectacle, and the Audience, 1986; (ed.) Shakespeare and the Triple Play: From Study to Stage to Classroom, 1988; The Audience As Actor and Character: The Modern Theater of Beckett, Brecht, Genet, Ionesco, Pinter, Stoppard, and Williams, 1989; (ed. with N.N. Holland and B.J. Paris) Shakespeare's Personality, 1989; Filming Beckett's Television Plays: A Director's Experience, 1992; (with S. Dugan, S. Langsner and T. Pender) Pinter's Odd Man Out: Staging and Filming Old Times, 1993; Staging Modern Playwrights: From Director's Concept to Performance, 2003; Directing Shakespeare: A Scholar Onstage, 2004; Fish in the Moonlight: Growing Up in the Bone Marrow Unit, 2008; The Führer and the Dove, forthcoming; One Wednesday in New York City, forthcoming. **Address:** Department of English, University of Florida, 4109 Turlington Hall, PO Box 117300, Gainesville, FL 32611-7310, U.S.A. **Online address:** shakes@ufl.edu

HOMBERGER, Eric. (Eric Ross Homberger). British/American (born United States), b. 1942. **Genres:** History, Literary Criticism And History, Photography, Urban Studies. **Career:** University of Exeter, temporary lecturer in American literature, 1969-70; University of East Anglia, lecturer, 1970-88, reader in English and American literature, 1988-, professor of American studies, now professor emeritus of American studies; University of New Hampshire, visiting professor of American literature, 1991-92. Writer. **Publications:** A Chronological Checklist of the Periodical Publications of Sylvia Plath, 1970; (comp.) Ezra Pound: The Critical Heritage, 1972; The Art of the Real: Poetry in England and America since 1939, 1977; American Writers and Radical Politics 1900-1939: Equivocal Commitments, 1986; John le Carre, 1986; John Reed, 1990; The Historical Atlas of New York City, 1994; Scenes from the Life of a City: Corruption and Conscience in Old New York, 1994; The Penguin Historical Atlas of North America, 1995; Mrs Astor's New York: Money and Social Power in a Gilded Age, 2002; New York City: A Cultural and Literary Companion, 2003; The Historical Atlas of New York City: A Visual Celebration of 400 Years of New York City's History, 2005. EDITOR: (with W. Janeway and S. Schama) The Cambridge Mind: Ninety Years of the Cambridge Review 1879-1969, 1970; (with H. Klein and J. Flower) The Second World War in Fiction, 1984; (with J. Charmley) The Troubled Face of Biography, 1988; (with J. Biggart) John Reed and the Russian Revolution: Uncollected Articles, Letters and Speeches on Russia, 1917-1920, 1992. **Address:** School of American Studies, University of East Anglia, Norwich Research Pk., Norwich, NR4 7TJ, England. **Online address:** e.homberger@uea.ac.uk

HOMBERGER, Eric Ross. *See* **HOMBERGER, Eric.**

HOMEL, David. Canadian/American (born United States), b. 1952. **Genres:** Novels, Plays/Screenplays, Essays, Translations. **Career:** Concordia University, part-time professor of arts and science, 1983-. Writer and filmmaker. **Publications:** TRANSLATOR: L. Caron, The Draft Dodger, 1980; S. Martel, The King's Daughter, 1980; M. Corriveau, A Perfect Day for Kites, 1981; G. Bureau, Mona: A Mother's Story, 1981; R. Lalonde, Sweet Madness, 1982; Archambault Prison Theatre Collective, No Big Deal!, 1982; R. Marteau, Mount Royal, 1983; C. Brouillet, Dear Neighbor, 1984; J. Renaud, Broke City, 1984; M. Raboy, Media and Messages, 1984; R. Marteau, Pig-Skinning Day, 1984; R. Ducharme, Ha! Ha!, 1986; C. Couture and J. Rousseau, The Life of a Document: A Global Approach to Archives and Records Management, 1987; F. Simard, Talking It Out: The October Crisis from Inside, 1987; R. Marteau, River without End, 1987; D. Laferrière, How to Make Love to a Negro, 1988; R. Marteau, Voyage to Vendee, 1988; R. Simard and M. Vastel, The Nephew: Making of a Mafia Hitman, 1988; M. Begin, Canada's Right to Health, 1988; M. Corriveau, Seasons of the Sea, 1989; D. Sernine, Those Who Watch over the Earth, 1990; D. Cote, The Invisible Empire, 1990; (with W. Grady) M. Henrie, The Mandarin Syndrome, 1990; D. Laferrière, Eroshima, 1991; P. Bourgault, Now or Never!, 1991; C. Marchand, Vanishing Villages, 1992; D. Laferrière, An Aroma of Coffee, 1993; L. Caron and F. Poche, Montreal: A Scent of the Islands, 1994; D. Laferrière, Dining with the Dictator, 1994; D. Laferrière, Why Must a Black Writer Write about Sex?, 1994; D. Pennac, Better than Life, 1994; D. Laferrière, Down among the Dead Men, 1997; D. Laferrière, A Drifting Year, 1997; Y. Beauchemin, Second Fiddle, 1998; P. Poloni, Olivo Oliva, 1999; (with F. Reed) S. Kokis, Funhouse, 1999; (with F. Reed) M. Desjardins, Fairy Ring, 2000; (with F. Reed) M. Proulx, The Heart is an Involuntary Muscle, 2003; P. Poloni, Olivo Oliva, 2005; (with F. Reed) M. Desjardins, All That Glitters, 2005; (with F. Reed) S. Lamothe, The Baldwins, 2006; (with F. Reed) M. Desjardins, A Covenant of Salt, 2007; (with F. Reed) M. Proulx, Wildlives, 2009; E. Ehrenberg, The Weariness of the Self: Diagnosing the History of Depression, 2010; H. Laroche, The Last Genet, 2010; D. Laferrière, I Am a Japanese Writer, 2010; F. Cusset, The Inverted Gaze, 2011; D. Laferrière, The Return, 2011. NOVELS: Electrical Storms, 1988; Rat Palms, 1992; Sonya & Jack, 1995; Get on Top, 1999; The Speaking Cure, 2003; Travels with My Family, 2006; On the Road Again! More Travels with My Family, 2008; Midway, 2010; Summer in the City, 2012. NONFICTION: Mapping Literature: The Art and Politics of Translation, 1988. OTHER: The World is a Document, 2002. **Address:** French Department, Concordia University, 1455 De Maisonneuve Blvd. W, Montreal, QC H3G 1N2, Canada. **Online address:** dhomel@alcor.concordia.ca

HOMER, William Innes. American (born United States), b. 1929. **Genres:** Art/Art History, Photography, Biography. **Career:** Sewell C. Biggs Museum of American Art, curator, 1955-56, 1958, trustee; Princeton University, Department of Art and Archaeology, instructor, 1955-59, The Art Museum, assistant director, 1956-57, lecturer, 1959-61, assistant professor of art history, 1961-64; University Portraits and the Boudinot Collection, curator, 1956-57; Cornell University, Department of the History of Art, associate professor, 1964-66; University of Delaware, Department of Art History, professor, 1966-84, professor emeritus, 2000-, chairman, 1966-81, 1986-93, H. Rodney Sharp professor of art history, 1984-99, acting chairman, 1986-87. Writer and consultant. **Publications:** Georges Seurat, 1957; Catalogue of the Ceramic Sculpture of Carl Walters, 1883-1955, 1958; Seurat and the Science of Painting, 1964; (with V. Organ) Robert Henri and His Circle, 1969; (ed.) Avant-Garde Painting & Sculpture in America 1910-25, 1975; Alfred Stieglitz and the American Avant-Garde, 1977; The Photographs of Gertrude Kasebier, 1979; Eakins at Avondale and Thomas Eakins, 1980; Brandywine River Museum of the Brandywine Conservancy, Chadds Ford, Pennsylvania, 1980; (ed. and intro.) Heart's Gate: Letters Between Marsden Hartley & Horace Traubel, 1906-1915, 1982; Seven/Eight, A Comparative Exhibition of the Canadian Group of Seven and the American Painters, the Eight: The Heckscher Museum, Huntington, New York, June 20-August 1, 1982, 1982; Alfred Stieglitz and the Photo-Secession, 1983; Pictorial Photography in Philadelphia: The Pennsylvania Academy's Salons, 1898-1901: March 9-April 18, 1984, 1984; (with L. Goodrich) Albert Pinkham Ryder: Painter of Dreams, 1989; Brandywine Valley to the Bay: Art From Private Collections, October 3 through November 3, 1991, University Gallery, University of Delaware, 1991; Thomas Eakins: His Life and Art, 1992, 2nd ed., 2002; The Language of Contemporary Criticism Clarified, 1999; (contrib.) Stieglitz and the Photo-Secession, 1902, 2002; (ed.) Paris Letters of Thomas Eakins, 2009. Contributor to periodicals and journals. **Address:** Department of Art History, University of Delaware, 318 Old College, Newark, DE 19716-2516, U.S.A. **Online address:** whomer@udel.edu

HOMES, A. M. American (born United States), b. 1961. **Genres:** Novels, Novellas/Short Stories, Adult Non-fiction, Young Adult Non-fiction. **Career:** Writer. **Publications:** NOVELS: Jack, 1989; In a Country of Mothers, 1993; The End of Alice, 1996; Music for Torching, 1999; This Book Will Save Your Life, 2006. STORIES: The Safety of Objects, 1990; (with R. Rudolph) Cecily Brown, 2000; Things You Should Know, 2002; Speed: Art, 2003-2009, 2009. NONFICTION: Los Angeles: People, Places, and the Castle on the Hill, 2002; Wave Music, 2005. OTHERS: Appendix A: An Elaboration on the Novel The End of Alice, 1996; (contrib.) On the Street: 1980-1990, 2006; The Mistress's Daughter (memoir), 2007; (contrib.) Petah Coyne: Everything That Rises Must Converge, 2010. Contributor to books and periodicals. **Address:** The Wylie Agency, 250 W 57th St., Ste. 2114, New York, NY 10107, U.S.A. **Online address:** info@amhomesbooks.com

HOMSHER, Deborah. American (born United States), b. 1952. **Genres:** Criminology/True Crime, Young Adult Fiction, Law. **Career:** Ithaca College, English Department, instructor, 1988-94; Cornell University, Southeast Asia Program, managing editor of publications, 1995-. **Publications:** From Blood to Verdict: Three Women on Trial, 1993; Women and Guns: Politics and the Culture of Firearms, 2001; The Rising Shore-Roanoke, 2007. Contributor to periodicals. **Address:** Southeast Asia Program, Cornell University, 213 Kahin Ctr., 640 Stewart Ave., Ithaca, NY 14850-3857, U.S.A. **Online address:** dlh10@cornell.edu

HONAN, Park. British/American (born United States), b. 1928. **Genres:** Literary Criticism And History, Biography. **Career:** Connecticut College, instructor, 1959-61, assistant professor of English, 1961-62; Brown University, assistant professor, 1962-65, associate professor of English, 1965-68; University of Birmingham, lecturer, 1968-72, senior lecturer, 1968-76, reader in English, 1976-83; Marlowe Society, vice president; University of Leeds, professor of English and American literature, 1984-93, chair, 1984-, now professor emeritus. Writer. **Publications:** Browning's Characters: A Study in Poetic Technique, 1961; (with W. Irvine) The Book, The Ring, and The Poet: A Biography of Robert Browning, 1974; Matthew Arnold: A Life, 1981; Jane Austen: Her Life, 1988; Authors' Lives: On Literary Biography and the Arts of Language, 1990; Shakespeare: A Life, 1998; Christopher Marlowe: Poet & Spy, 2005. Contributor to books and periodicals. **Address:** School of English, University of Leeds, Woodhouse Ln., Leeds, WY LS2 9JT, England. **Online address:** park.honan@tiscali.co.uk

HOND, Paul. American (born United States) **Genres:** Novels, Young Adult Fiction, Literary Criticism And History. **Career:** Writer. **Publications:** The Baker: A Novel, 1997; (co-author) Men Seeking Women: Love and Sex Online, 2001; Mothers and Sons: A Novel, 2005. Contributor to periodicals. **Address:** Barbara J. Zitwer Agency, 525 W End Ave., Ste. 11H, New York, NY 10024, U.S.A.

HONDERICH, Ted. British/Canadian (born Canada), b. 1933. **Genres:** Philosophy, Politics/Government, Social Sciences, Biography, Essays. **Career:** University of Sussex, lecturer in philosophy, 1962-64; University College of London, Department of Philosophy, lecturer, 1964-72, tutor, 1965-74, reader, 1972-83, professor, 1983-88, head, 1987-92, Grote professor of the philosophy of mind and logic, 1988-98, Grote professor of the philosophy of mind and logic emeritus, 1998-; Yale University, visiting professor, 1970; City University of New York, Graduate Centre, visiting professor, 1971; The Royal Institute of Philosophy, vice chairman, 1995-2005, chairman, 2005-; University of Bath, visiting professor, 2003-. Writer. **Publications:** Punishment:

The Supposed Justifications, 1969, rev. ed. as Punishment: The Supposed Justifications Revisited, 2006; Three Essays on Political Violence, 1976, rev. ed. as Violence for Equality: Inquiries in Political Philosophy, 1980, rev. ed. as Terrorism for Humanity: Inquiries in Political Philosophy, 2003; Political Violence, 1976; A Theory of Determinism: The Mind, Neuroscience and Life-Hopes, 1988; Conservatism: Burke, Nozick, Bush, Blair?, 1990, rev. ed., 2005; Mind and Brain, 1990; How Free Are You?: The Determinism Problem, 1993, 2nd. ed., 2002; Philosopher: A Kind of Life, 2001; After the Terror, 2002, rev. ed., 2003; On Political Means and Social Ends, 2003; On Consciousness, 2004; On Freedom and Determinism, 2004; Humanity, Terrorism, Terrorist War: Palestine, 9-11, Iraq, 7-7, 2006; Right and Wrong and Palestine, 9/11, Iraq, 7/7, 2006; Radical Externalism: Honderich's Theory of Consciousness Discussed, 2006. EDITOR: International Library of Philosophy and Scientific Method Series, 1970; Essays on Freedom of Action, 1973; Social Ends and Political Means, 1976; The Arguments of Philosophers Series, 1979; (with M. Burnyeat) Philosophy as It Is, 1979; (and intro.) Philosophy through Its Past, 1984; Morality and Objectivity: A Tribute to J.L. Mackie, 1984; Oxford Companion to Philosophy, 1995, 2nd. ed., 2005; The Philosophers: Introducing Great Western Thinkers, 1999. **Address:** Department of Philosophy, University College London, Gower St., London, GL WC1E 6BT, England. **Online address:** t.honderich@ucl.ac.uk

HONE, Joseph. American/British/Irish (born Ireland), b. 1937. **Genres:** Mystery/Crime/Suspense, Travel/Exploration, Romance/Historical, Novels, Young Adult Fiction. **Career:** Egyptian Ministry of Education, teacher of English, 1957-58; Rupert Hart-Davis Publishers, editorial assistant, 1958-59; Envoy Productions, co-founder and co-producer, 1960-62; BBC, radio producer, 1963-67; U.N. Secretariat, information officer, 1967-68; freelance writer and broadcaster 1968-; College of William and Mary, writer-in-residence, 1983-84; Sweet Briar College, writer-in-residence, 1983-84; Hamish Hamilton Publishers, part-time editor; Wroxton College, teacher. **Publications:** The Private Sector, 1971; The Sixth Directorate, 1975; The Dancing Waiters: Collected Travels, 1975; The Paris Trap, 1977; (ed.) Irish Ghost Stories, 1977; The Oxford Gambit, 1980 in UK as The Flowers of the Forest, 1981; Gone Tomorrow: Some More Collected Travels, 1981; The Valley of the Fox, 1982; Africa of the Heart: A Personal Journey, 1986 in UK as Children of the Country: Coast-to-Coast across Africa, 1986; Duck Soup in the Black Sea: Further Collected Travels, 1988; Summer Hill (novel), 1990; Return to Summer Hill (novel), 1992; Firesong (novel), 1997; Wicked Little Joe, 2009. **Address:** Wroxton College, Fairleigh Dickinson University, 285 Madison Ave., Madison, NJ 07940, U.S.A.

HONERKAMP, Nicholas. American (born United States), b. 1950. **Genres:** Archaeology/Antiquities, Business/Trade/Industry, History, Industrial Relations. **Career:** University of Florida, Department of Anthropology, assistant adjunct instructor, 1978-79; Jeffrey L. Brown Institute of Archaeology, director, 1980-; University of Tennessee, Department of Sociology, Anthropology and Geography, assistant professor, 1981-86, associate professor, 1986-89, UC Foundation associate professor, 1989-93, professor, 1993-, Department of Sociology, Anthropology and Geography, acting head, 2003-07, Department's Institute of Archaeology, director. Writer. **Publications:** Colonial Life on the Georgia Coast, 1977; Union Railyards Site: Industrial Archaeology in Chattanooga, Tennessee, 1984; (with R.B. Council and M.E. Will) Industry and Technology in Antebellum Tennessee: The Archaeology of Bluff Furnace, 1992; Perspectives from Historical Archaeology: The Archaeology of Plantation Life, 2009; Mulberry Grove: Life and Times on a Tidewater Georgia Plantation, forthcoming. Contributor to professional journals. **Address:** Department of Sociology, Anthropology and, Geography, University of Tennessee, 104 Brock Hall, 615 McCallie Ave., Chattanooga, TN 37403-2598, U.S.A. **Online address:** nick-honerkamp@utc.edu

HONEYCUTT, Natalie. American (born United States), b. 1945. **Genres:** Young Adult Fiction, Novels, Human Relations/Parenting, Children's Fiction. **Career:** Writer. **Publications:** Invisible Lissa, 1985; The All New Jonah Twist, 1986; Josie's Beau, 1987; The Best-Laid Plans of Jonah Twist, 1988; Ask Me Something Easy, 1991; Juliet Fisher and the Foolproof Plan, 1992; Whistle Home, 1993; Lydia Jane and the Baby-Sitter Exchange, 1993; Twilight in Grace Falls, 1997; Granville Jones: Commando, 1998. **Address:** PO Box 1078, McCloud, CA 96057-1078, U.S.A.

HONEYGOSKY, Stephen R(aymond). American (born United States), b. 1948. **Genres:** Theology/Religion, Literary Criticism And History. **Career:** St. Vincent Archabbey, member of monastic community, 1969-; St. Vincent

College, director of campus ministry, 1980-86, assistant professor, 1986-90; St. Vincent Seminary, dean of students, 1988-89; University of Pittsburgh, lecturer, 1991-; St. Bruno Church, associate pastor, 1992-96; St. Benedict Church, pastor, 1996-; Seton Hill University, chaplain, associate professor of English, director of campus ministry, 2005-; Pennsylvania State University, adjunct faculty, Campus Ministry, director, Benedictine Community, rector. Writer. **Publications:** Milton's House of God: The Invisible and Visible Church, 1993; (ed. and contrib.) Religion & Spirituality: Bridging the Gap, 2006. **Address:** Department of English, Seton Hill University, 1 Seton Hill Dr., PO Box 991, Greensburg, PA 15601, U.S.A.

HONEYMAN, Brenda. *See* CLARKE, Brenda.

HONG, Lily Toy. American (born United States), b. 1958. **Genres:** Mythology/Folklore, Illustrations, Biography, Children's Fiction. **Career:** Hallmark Cards Inc., artist-designer and production artist, 1983-86; freelance writer and illustrator, 1988-. **Publications:** SELF-ILLUSTRATED: How the Ox Star Fell from Heaven, 1991; The Moon in the Well, 1992; Two of Everything: A Chinese Folktale, 1992; (with K. Hatch) Marco Polo and Kublai Khan: A Great Friendship, 1993; Jungle Spots, 1997. OTHER: The Empress and the Silkworm, 1995. Illustrator of books by others. Contributor to periodicals. **Address:** Albert Whitman & Co., 6340 Oakton St., Morton Grove, IL 60053-2723, U.S.A.

HONIGSBAUM, Mark. British (born England), b. 1960?. **Genres:** Documentaries/Reportage, Sciences. **Career:** Observer, chief reporter; University College London, Wellcome Trust Centre for the History of Medicine, researcher; University of Zurich, Institute for Medical History, research associate. Writer and journalist. **Publications:** The Fever Trail: In Search of the Cure for Malaria, 2002; Valverde's Gold: In Search of the Last Great Inca Treasure, 2004; Living with Enza: The Forgotten Story of Britain and the Great Flu Pandemic of 1918, 2009. Contributor to periodicals. **Address:** c/o Author Mail, Farrar, Straus & Giroux Inc., 18 W 18th St., New York, NY 10011, U.S.A. **Online address:** mark.honigsbaum@guardian.co.uk

HONNEF, Klaus. German (born Germany), b. 1939. **Genres:** Photography, Novels, Romance/Historical. **Career:** Aachener Nachrichten, editor, 1965-70; Center for contemporary art, artistic director, 1968-70; Westfaelischer Kunstverein, director, 1970-74; Rheinisches Landesmuseum Bonn, chief exhibition officer, 1974-94, curator of photography, 1994-99; Kassel Art Academy, honorary professor, 1986-. **Publications:** Concept Art, 1971; Verkehrskultur, 1972; 150 Maler, Jochem und Rudi, 1976; 200 Jahreamerikanische Malerei, 1776-1976: eine Ausstellung des Rheinischen Landes museums Bonn und der Botschaft der Vereinigten Staaten von Amerika, 1976; Karl Blossfeldt: Fotografien 1900-1932, 1976; 400 Jahre Zoo: im Spiegel der Sammlung Werner Kourist, Bonn, 1976; Gerhard Richter, 1977; Jahre Fotografie, 1977; Kunst der Gegenwart, 1990; Andy Warhol, 1992; Pantheon der Photography, 1992; (contrib.) Vorher müsst ihr uns erschiessen, 2001; (contrib. with G. Freund and H.V. Amelunxen) In Memoriam Gisèlle Freund, 2001; (with H. Newton) Helmut Newton: Portraits, 2005; (contrib. with J. Strauss and Herausgeber) Armin Mueller-Stahl: Portraits: Malerei und Zeichnung=Painting and Drawing, 2006; Kuba: Bilder einer Revolution, 2008; Images of Women, 2008; (with P. Lodermeyer) Hiller, 2009; (M.G. Bau) Hannes Kilian 1909-1999, 2009. EDITOR: (with P. Pachnicke) John Heartfield, 1993; Die Verlassenen Schuhe, 1993; Heribert C. Ottersbach: Wider die Vollendung, 1993; Hermann Claasen: Werkverzeichni, 1993; (with G. Nothhelfer) Lange Augenblicke: Diefotografischen Bilder von 1970-1992, 1993; Elisabeth Marx, 1994; (with H.A. Peters) Karl Marx: Gemalde, 1994; (with W. Muller) Nie Wieder Krieg!: Bilder aus dem zerstorten Koln, 1994; (and contrib.) John Heartfield: Dokumentation: Reaktionen auf eine Ugewohnliche Ausstellung, 1994; (with V. Loers) Axel Hutte, Landschaft, 1995; Die andere Seite der Schonheit: Die Sammlung Michael Horbach, 1995; (with U. Breymayer) Ende und Anfang: Photographen in Deutschland um 1945, 1995; Der Fixierte Blink: Deutschlandund das Rheinland im Fokus der Fotografie: Auswahlkatalog der Fotografishen Sammlungen im Rheinischen Landesmuseum Bonn und der Sammlung Gesellschaft Photo- Archi, 1996; (and contrib.) Asylbilder, 1996; (and contrib.) Frosty Fire: Recent Photographs, 1996; Kunst im Hotel, 1996; Zeitgleich, 1996; Deutsche Fotografie: Macht eines Mediums1870-1970, 1997; German Photography 1870-1970: Power of a Medium, 1997; (with F. Weyers) Und sie Haben Deutschland verlassen mussen: Fotografen und ihreBilder 1928-1997, 1997; (and contrib. with M. Mettner) Der Mann: Eine Hommage, 1998; (with Kuratoren and G.H. Harling) Bilder, die noch Fehlten: Zeitgenossische Fotografie: Eine Ausstellung des Deutschen Hygiene-Museums und

der Deutschen Behindertenhilfe-Aktion Mensche e.V. unter Schirmherrschaft des Bundesprasidenten Johannes Rau, 2000; (with T. Quinn and B. Schecker) Sensation des Alltäglichen, 2001; Melanie Manchot: Love Is a Stranger: Photographs, 1998- 2001, 2001; Euro Press Photo Awards, 2002; (with G.H. Harling) Von Körpern und anderen Dingen, 2003; (and contrib.) Anke Erlenhoff: 1993-2003, 2003; Pop Art, 2004; (co-ed.) Andreas Horlitz: Arbeiten=works, 2005. **Address:** Rheinisches Landesmuseum Bonn, Colmantstrasse 14, Bonn, D-53115, Germany.

HONNOLD, RoseMary. American (born United States), b. 1954. **Genres:** Human Relations/Parenting. **Career:** Coshocton Public Library, librarian assistant, 1984-88, bookmobile assistant manager, 1988-98, Young Adult Services, co-ordinator, 1983-, bookmobile assistant manager, 1988-98; RoseMary Honnold, consultant, 2002-; Neal-Schuman Publishers, author, 2002-09, library series editor, 2008-09; YALSA, editor, 2008-09; Young adult library reference site, creator and maintainer; See YA Around Web site, creator and maintainer; Voice of Youth Advocates Magazine, editor-in-chief, 2009-. **Publications:** 101+ Teen Programs That Work, 2003; (with S.A. Mesaros) Serving Seniors: A How-To-Do-It Manual for Librarians, 2004; (ed.) More Teen Programs That Work, 2005; The Teen Reader's Advisor, 2006; Get Connected: Tech Programs for Teens, 2007. **Address:** Young Adult Services, Coshocton Public Library, 655 Main St., Coshocton, OH 43812-1697, U.S.A. **Online address:** honnolro@oplin.org

HONORÉ, Carl. British/Canadian/Scottish (born Scotland), b. 1967?. **Genres:** Novels, Human Relations/Parenting, Adult Non-fiction. **Career:** Freelance journalist, 1991-96; Houston Chronicle, London correspondent, 1996-98; National Post, London correspondent, 1998-2001; writer and speaker, 2001-. **Publications:** In Praise of Slowness: Challenging the Cult of Speed, 2004; (foreword) Discovery of Slowness: A Novel, 2005; Under Pressure: How The Epidemic of Hyper-parenting is Endangering Childhood in US as Under Pressure: Rescuing Our Children From The Culture Of Hyper-parenting, 2008. **Address:** c/o Patrick Walsh, Conville and Walsh, 2 Ganton St., Soho, London, GL W1F 7QL, England. **Online address:** carl@carlhonore.com

HONORÉ, Tony. British (born England), b. 1921. **Genres:** Law, History. **Career:** University of Nottingham, assistant lecturer, 1948-49; Oxford University, fellow, Law of Queen's College, praelector, 1949-64, Roman-Dutch Law, Rhodes reader, 1957-71, Civil Law of All Souls College, religious professor, 1971-88, Regius Professor of Civil Law, now professor emeritus; McGill University, visiting professor, 1961; University of Cape Town, visiting professor, 1964; University of Witwatersrand, visiting professor, 1964. Writer. **Publications:** (With R.W. Lee) The South African Law of Obligations, 1950, 2nd ed., 1978; (with Lee) The South African Law of Property, Family Relations and Succession, 1954, 2nd ed., 1983; (with H.L.A. Hart) Causation in the Law, 1959, 2nd ed., 1985; Gaius, 1962; The South African Law of Trusts, 1966, (co-author) 5th ed., 2002; Justinian's Digest: Work in Progress: An Inaugural Lecture Delivered Before the University of Oxford on 12 May 1971, 1971; Tribonian, 1978; Sex Law, 1978; Sex Law in England, 1978; (with J. Menner) Concordance to the Digest Jurists, 1980; Emperors and Lawyers, 1981, 2nd ed., 1994; The Quest for Security: Employees, Tenants, Wives, 1982; Ulpian: Pioneer of Human Rights, 1982, 2nd ed., 2002; Family, Things and Succession, 1983; The Legal Mind: Essays for Tony Honore, 1986; Making Law Bind: Essays Legal and Philosophical, 1987; Honorés South African Law of Trusts, 1992, 5th ed., 2006; About Law: An Introduction, 1995; Law in the Crisis of Empire, 379-455 AD: The Theodosian Dynasty and its Quaestors with a Palingenesia of Laws of the Dynasty, 1998; Responsibility and Fault, 1999; Responsibility and Fault, 1999; Relating to Responsibility: Essays for Tony Honoré on his Eightieth Birthday, 2001; Justinian's Digest: Character and Compilation, 2010. **Address:** All Souls College, University of Oxford, 13 Beaumont St., Oxford, OX OX1 2LP, England. **Online address:** tony.honore@all-souls.ox.ac.uk

HONRI, Peter. British (born England), b. 1929. **Genres:** Film, Industrial Relations, Music, Organized Labor, Theatre, Art/Art History. **Career:** Music Hall Investigations, joint managing director. Writer. **Publications:** Peter Honri Presents-Working the Halls: The Honris in One Hundred Years of British Music Hall, 1973; Working the Halls, 1973; John Wilton's Music Hall: The Handsomest Room in Town, 1985; Music Hall Warriors, 1997. Contributor to magazines. **Address:** Pollinger Ltd., 9 Staple Inn, Holborn, London, GL WC1V 7QH, England.

HOOD, Ann. American (born United States), b. 1956. **Genres:** Novels, Novellas/Short Stories. **Career:** Trans World Airlines (TWA), flight attendant, 1979-86; New York University, fiction writing instructor, Department of English, Faculty of Arts and Science, adjunct instructor. **Publications:** NOVELS: Somewhere Off The Coast of Maine, 1987; Waiting to Vanish, 1988; Three-Legged Horse, 1989; Something Blue, 1991; Places to Stay the Night, 1993; Properties of Water, 1995; Ruby: A Novel, 1998; Knitting Circle, 2007; Comfort: A Journey through Grief, 2008; How I Saved My Father's Life (and Ruined Everything Else), 2008; Red Thread: A Novel, 2010. OTHER: Creating Character Emotions, 1998; Do Not Go Gentle, 2000; Ornithologist's Guide to Life, 2004; Little Lion, 2011; Angel of the Battlefield, 2011; Jewel of the Earth, 2012. Contributor to periodicals. **Address:** c/o Gail Hochman, Brandt & Brandt Literary Agents Inc., 1501 Broadway, New York, NY 10036, U.S.A. **Online address:** ah17@nyu.edu

HOOD, Daniel. American (born United States), b. 1967. **Genres:** Science Fiction/Fantasy, Novels, Novellas/Short Stories, Travel/Exploration. **Career:** IMP (publisher), art director, 1989-94; Wall Street Journal Europe, desktop manager, 1994-96; Faulkner and Gray (publisher), managing editor, 1996-2000; Daily News Express, business editor, 2000-01; AMG, managing editor, 2002-. **Publications:** The End of Trading Season, 1993; The Wealth of Kingdoms, 1993; Cap Renvoort's Luck, 1994; A Minor Odyssey, 1994; The Siege of Bahorel's Bed, 1994; Fanuilh, 1994; Things Fall Apart, 1995; Biouniversity, 1995; Wizard's Heir, 1996; Beggar's Banquet, 1997; A Familiar Dragon, 1997; Scales of Justice, 1998; Scipio, 1998; King's Cure, 2000; (with B. Dunn) New York: The Unknown City, 2004. **Address:** Donald Maass Literary Agency, 121 W 27th St., Ste. 801, New York, NY 10001, U.S.A. **Online address:** dan.hood@sff.net

HOOD, Ken. *See* DUNCAN, Dave.

HOOD, Lynley (Jane). New Zealander (born New Zealand), b. 1942. **Genres:** Law, Social Sciences, Biography, Criminology/True Crime. **Career:** University of Otago, Medical School, research physiologist, 1965-68, Robert Burns Fellow, 1991; freelance writer, 1973-; PEN, vice-president and local secretary. **Publications:** Sylvia! The Biography of Sylvia Ashton-Warner, 1988; Who Is Sylvia? The Diary of a Biography, 1990; Minnie Dean-Her Life and Crimes, 1994; A City Possessed and the Christchurch Civic Creche Case, 2001. Contributor to magazines. **Address:** Richards Literary Agency, PO Box 31240, Milford, 0741, New Zealand. **Online address:** enquiries@lynleyhood.org

HOOD, Mary. American (born United States), b. 1946. **Genres:** Novels. **Career:** University of Georgia, visiting author, 1993; University of Mississippi, John and Renee Grisham chair of visiting Southern writer, 1996; Berry College, writer-in-residence, 1997-98; Centre College, visiting writer, 1999; Reinhardt College, writer-in-residence, 2001, Oxford College of Emory University, writer-in-residence, 2009. **Publications:** How Far She Went, 1984; And Venus Is Blue, 1986; Familiar Heat, 1995. Contributor to periodicals. **Address:** c/o Liz Darhansoff, Darhansoff and Verrill Literary Agents, 236 W 26th St., Ste. 802, New York, NY 10001, U.S.A. **Online address:** maryhood@aol.com

HOOD, Stuart (Clink). Scottish (born Scotland), b. 1915. **Genres:** Communications/Media, Novels, Translations, Romance/Historical. **Career:** Royal College of Art, professor of film; BBC Television Service, controller, 1961-63; BBC Television, controller, 1963-; Rediffusion London, controller; ACCT, vice president. Writer and executive. **Publications:** FICTION: The Circle of the Minotaur and The Fisherman's Daughter, 1950; Since the Fall, 1955; In and Out the Windows, 1974; A Storm from Paradise, 1985; The Upper Hand, 1987; The Brutal Heart, 1989; A Den of Foxes, 1991; Book of Judith, 1995. NONFICTION: Pebbles from My Skull (memoirs), 1963 as Carlino, 1985; A Survey of Television, 1967; The Mass Media, 1972; Radio and Television, 1975; On Television, 1980, (with T. Tabary-Petersenn) 4th ed., 1997; (with G. O'Leary) Questions of Broadcasting, 1990; Fascism for Beginners (juvenile), 1993, in North America as Introducing Fascism, 1994; (with H. Bresheeth and L. Jansz) Introducing the Holocaust (juvenile), 1994. TRANSLATOR: On the Marble Cliffs, 1970; Moscow, 1976; Raids and Reconstructions: Essays on Politics, Crime and Culture, 1976; One Hundred Poems without a Country, 1978; 100 Poems Without a Country, 1978; Love Poems, 1991; (intro.) Theorem, 1992; The Letters of Pier Paolo Pasolini, 1992; Appearances, 1992; Sodomies in Eleven-Point, 1993; The Way Back, 1994; Tartar Steppe, 1995; Uses and Abuses: Journeys, Sleepwalkings and Fool's Errands, 1997. EDITOR:

(intro.) Elizabeth: Almost by Chance a Woman (play), 1987; The Tricks of the Trade (play), 1991; Behind the Screens: The Structure of British Broadcasting in the 1990s, 1994. Contributor to periodicals. **Address:** Carcanet Press Ltd., 4th Fl., Conavon Ct., 12-16 Blackfriars St., Manchester, M3 5BQ, England.

HOODBHOY, Pervez. (Pervez Amirali Hoodbhoy). Pakistani (born Pakistan), b. 1950. **Genres:** Sciences, Plays/Screenplays. **Career:** Quaid-e-Azam University, physicist, 1973-, professor and chairman; Mashal, chairman. Writer. **Publications:** Islam and Science: Religious Orthodoxy and the Battle for Rationality, 1991; M.A. Beg Memorial Volume, 1991; Muslims & Science: Religious Orthodoxy and the Struggle for Rationality, 1991; (ed.) Education and the State: Fifty Years of Pakistan, 1998. **Address:** Department of Physics, Quaid-e-Azam University, Islamabad, 45320, Pakistan. **Online address:** hoodbhoy@lns.mit.edu

HOODBHOY, Pervez Amirali. *See* HOODBHOY, Pervez.

HOOFT, Hendrik (G. A.). Canadian/Dutch (born Netherlands), b. 1939. **Genres:** History, Politics/Government. **Career:** Attorney, 1966-71; Pierson Heldring and Pierson Bank, executive vice president, 1971-75; Oryx Investments, president and chief executive officer, 1975-80; Woodmont Head Management Ltd., president and chief executive officer, 1980-. Writer. **Publications:** De burgher en de burgemeester, 1994, trans. as Patriot and Patrician: To Holland and Ceylon in the Steps of Henrik Hooft and Pieter Ondaatje, Champions of Dutch Democracy, 1999. Contributor of articles to newspapers and periodicals. **Address:** 9 High Point Rd., Don Mills, ON M3B 2A3, Canada.

HOOK, Brendan. Australian (born Australia), b. 1963. **Genres:** Children's Fiction, Literary Criticism And History. **Career:** Moonee Valley Instrumental Music Program, music teacher, 1991-. Writer. **Publications:** Harry the Honkerzoid, 1997; Planet of the Honkerzoids, 1998. Contributor to periodicals. **Address:** 5 McLean Ave., Bentleigh, VI 3204, Australia. **Online address:** brendan@geoffhook.com

HOOK, Geoffrey R(aynor). (Jeff Hook). Australian (born Australia), b. 1928. **Genres:** Cartoons, Illustrations, Children's Fiction. **Career:** Davies Brothers Ltd., press artist, 1951-64; The Sun News-Pictorial, founder, 1964; Herald and Weekly Times, editorial cartoonist, 1964-93, Sunday Herald-Sun, editorial cartoonist, 1993-. Writer. **Publications:** AUTHOR AND ILLUSTRATOR AS JEFF HOOK: (with D. Rankine) Kangapossum and Crocoroo, 1969; Jamie the Jumbo Jet, 1971; Hook Book: Cartoons by Jeff of the Sun, 1978; The Hook Book No. 2, 1979, The Penguin Hook, 1984; The Laugh's on Us: Cricket's Finest Tell Their Funniest, 1989; Ashes: Battles and Bellylaughs, 1990; More Laughs on Us, 1991; Just for Kicks, 1992; Boom, Bust and Polka Dots, 1992; Look Who's Laughing Now, 1995. **Address:** 2 Montana St., Glen Iris, VI 3146, Australia. **Online address:** geoff@geoffhook.com

HOOK, Jeff. *See* HOOK, Geoffrey R(aynor).

HOOK, Jonathan B(yron). American (born United States), b. 1953. **Genres:** History, Anthropology/Ethnology. **Career:** High school teacher of mathematics and English and football coach, choral music teacher, 1978-79, 1990-91; American high school teacher of television production and coach of football and wrestling, 1980-81; University of Texas, instructor, 1982-85; Houston Community College, instructor, 1988-90; Lee College, instructor, 1990-91; Intertribal Council of Houston, board director, 1992; Project Nicaragua, founding board director, 1993-97; Houston Community College, instructor, 1993-94; University of Houston, instructor, 1995; American Indian Resource Center, inaugural president, 1997-2003, founding board director, 1998; University of Northern Iowa, instructor, 2000-03; U.S. Environmental Protection Agency, Office of Environmental Justice and Tribal Affairs, inaugural director, 2003-08; University of North Texas, International Indigenous and American Indian Initiatives, inaugural director, 2009, Department of Philosophy and Religion, research professor, 2009-. Writer and consultant. **Publications:** The Alabama-Coushatta Indians, 1997. Contributor to periodicals. **Address:** Department of Philosophy & Religion Studies, University of North Texas, 310M EESAT, 1704 W Mulberry, Denton, TX 76201, U.S.A. **Online address:** jonathan.hook@unt.edu

HOOKER, Jeremy. Welsh/British (born England), b. 1941. **Genres:** Poetry, Literary Criticism And History, Autobiography/Memoirs, Essays, Novellas/Short Stories. **Career:** University College of Wales, lecturer in twentieth-century English literature, 1965-84; Winchester School of Art, fellow, 1981-

83; Kibbutz Gezer, writer-in-residence, 1985; Bath Spa University College, course director, creative writing, 1988-96, professor, through 1994; LeMoyne College, visiting professor, 1994-95; University of Glamorgan, Department of English, professor, 1995-2005, professor emeritus, 2005-, Humanities and Social Sciences, faculty; University of Groningen, faculty. Writer. **Publications:** (Contrib.) Poetry Introduction I, 1969; (ed.) Poems '71, 1971; The Elements, 1972; John Cowper Powys, 1973; Soliloquies of a Chalk Giant, 1974; David Jones: An Exploratory of the Writing, 1975; Solent Shore, 1978; Landscape of the Daylight Moon, 1978; John Cowper Powys and David Jones: A Comparative Study, 1979; Englishman's Road, 1980; (ed. with G. Lewis) Alun Lewis: Selected Poems, 1981; Poetry of Place: Essays and Reviews 1970-1981, 1982; A View from the Source: Selected Poems 1967-69, 1982; Itchen Water, 1982; (ed. and intro.) Selected Stories, 1986; The Presence of the Past: Essays on Modern British and American Poetry, 1987; Master of the Leaping Figures, 1987; In Praise of Windmills, 1990; (with L. Grandjean) Their Silence a Language, 1992; Writers in a Landscape, 1996; Inwards Where All the Battle Is: A Selection of Alun Lewis's Writings from India, 1997; Our Lady of Europe, 1997; (with L. Grandjean) Groundwork, 1998; (intro.) At Home on the Earth: A New Selection of the Later Writings of Richard Jefferies, 2001; Welsh Journal, 2001; Imagining Wales: A View of Modern Welsh Writing in English, 2001; Adamah, 2001; (ed. and intro.) Ship of Swallows: A Selection of Short Stories, 2005; Cut of the Light: Poems, 1965-2005, 2006; Moment of Earth: Poems & Essays in Honour of Jeremy Hooker, 2007. Contributor to books and periodicals. **Address:** Department of English, University of Glamorgan, 102 Forest Hall, Pontypridd, PW CF37 1DL, Wales. **Online address:** jhooker1@glam.ac.uk

HOOKER, J. N. *See* **HOOKER, John.**

HOOKER, John. Also writes as J. N. Hooker. American (born United States), b. 1949. **Genres:** Ethics, Mathematics/Statistics, Cultural/Ethnic Topics. **Career:** Oak Ridge National Laboratory, research staff, 1979-84; Centre for AI and Robotics, visiting research scientist, 1989, 1992; Aarhus University, visiting professor, 1991-92; Africa University, visiting professor, 1997; Monash University, visiting professor, 1997; Shanghai Economic Management College, visiting professor, 1998; Bilkent University, visiting professor, 1999; Hong Kong Polytechnic University, visiting professor, 2001; Carnegie Mellon University, 1984-, T. Jerome Holleran professor of business ethics and social responsibility, professor of operations research, Center for International Corporate Responsibility, founding director; London School of Economics, visiting professor, 2008, part-time visiting professor 2009-11. Writer. **Publications:** (As J.N. Hooker with V. Chandru) Optimization Methods for Logical Inference, 1999; (as J.N. Hooker) Logic-Based Methods for Optimization: Combining Optimization and Constraint Satisfaction, 2000; Working across Cultures, 2003; (ed. with P. Madsen) International Corporate Responsibility: Exploring the Issues, 2004; (ed. with A. Colk and P. Madsen) Perspectives on International Corporate Responsibility, 2005; (as J.N. Hooker) Integrated Methods for Optimization, 2007; (ed. with J. Hulpke and P. Madsen) Controversies in International Corporate Responsibility, 2007; (ed. with M. Dobashi and P. Madsen) A Survey of International Corporate Responsibility, 2009; Business Ethics as Rational Choice, 2011. **Address:** Tepper School of Business, Carnegie Mellon University, 5000 Forbes Ave., Pittsburgh, PA 15213, U.S.A. **Online address:** john@hooker.tepper.cmu.edu

HOOKER, Morna Dorothy. British (born England), b. 1931. **Genres:** Theology/Religion, Biography. **Career:** King's College, lecturer, 1961-70, fellow; Oxford University, lecturer, 1970-76; Linacre College, fellow, 1970-76; Keble College, lecturer, 1972-76; Cambridge University, Lady Margaret's Professor of Divinity, 1976-98, professor emerita, 1998-; Robinson College, fellow, Theological Society, president; Journal of Theological Studies, co-editor, 1985-; Studiorum Novi Testamenti Societas, president; Linacre College, honorary fellow. **Publications:** Jesus and the Servant, 1959; Fire on the Earth, 1965; The Apostle Paul: Three Lectures Given on B.B.C. Television by C.F. Evans, Morna Hooker, J.C. O'Neill, 1966; To know Christ and to Make Him Known: 4 Bible Studies, 1967; The Son of Man in Mark: A Study of the Background of the Term "Son of Man" and Its Use in St. Mark's Gospel, 1967; What about the New Testament, 1975; Interchange and Atonement, 1978; Pauline Pieces, 1979; Studying the New Testament, 1979; A Preface to Paul, 1980; The Message of Mark, 1983; Trial and Tribulation in Mark XIII, 1983; Continuity and Discontinuity: Early Christianity in Its Jewish Setting, 1986; From Adam to Christ: Essays on Paul, 1990; A Commentary on the Gospel of St. Mark, 1991; The Gospel According to St. Mark, 1993;

Not Ashamed of the Gospel: New Testament Interpretations of the Death of Christ, 1995; The Signs of a Prophet: The Prophetic Actions of Jesus, 1997; Beginnings: Keys that Open the Gospels, 1997; Paul: A Short Introduction, 2003; Endings: Invitations To Discipleship, 2003; Paul: A Short Introduction, 2003. EDITOR/CO-EDITOR: What about the New Testament?: Essays in Honour of Christopher Evans, 1975; Paul and Paulinism: Essays in Honour of C.K. Barrett, 1982; Early Christian Thought in Its Jewish context, 1996; Not in Word Alone, 2003. **Address:** Robinson College, Grange Rd., Cambridge, CB CB3 9AN, England.

HOOKS, Bell. American (born United States), b. 1952. **Genres:** Philosophy, Race Relations, Women's Studies And Issues, Essays, Adult Non-fiction, Education, Politics/Government, Cultural/Ethnic Topics, Cultural/Ethnic Topics, Social Sciences, Geography. **Career:** University of Southern California, English instructor and senior lecturer in ethnic studies, 1976-79; San Francisco State University, faculty; University of California, faculty; Yale University, assistant professor of Afro-American studies and English, 1985-; Oberlin College, associate professor of women's studies and American literature, 1988-94; City University of New York, City College, distinguished professor of English, 1994-; Berea College, Appalachian Center, distinguished professor in residence in Appalachian studies, 2004-. Social critic and writer. **Publications:** Ain't I a Woman: Black Women and Feminism, 1981; Feminist Theory: From Margin to Center, 1984, 2nd ed., 2000; Talking Back: Thinking Feminist, Thinking Black, Between-the-Lines, 1989; Yearning: Race, Gender, and Cultural Politics, Between-the-Lines, 1990; (with C. West) Breaking Bread: Insurgent Black Intellectual Life, 1991; A Woman's Mourning Song, Writers and Readers, 1992; Black Looks: Race and Representation, 1992; Sisters of the Yam: Black Women and Self-recovery, 1993, 2nd ed., 2005; Outlaw Culture: Resisting Representations, 1994; Emma Amos: Changing the Subject: Painting and Prints, 1994; Teaching to Transgress: Education As the Practice of Freedom, 1994; Art on My Mind: Visual Politics, 1995; Killing Rage: Ending Racism, 1995; (foreword) Gumbo YA YA: Anthology of Contemporary African-American Women Artists, 1995; Bone Black: Memories of Girlhood, 1996; Reel to Real: Race, Sex, and Class at the Movies, 1996; Wounds of Passion: A Writing Life, 1997; Remembered Rapture: The Writer at Work, 1999; Happy to Be Nappy (for children), 1999; All about Love: New Visions, 2000; Feminism Is for Everybody: Passionate Politics, 2000; Where We Stand: Class Matters, 2000; Salvation: Black People and Love, 2001; Homemade Love, 2002; Be Boy Buzz, 2002; Communion: Female Search for Love, 2002; Rock My Soul: Black People and Self-Esteem, 2003; Teaching Community: A Pedagogy of Hope, 2003; We Real Cool: Black Men and Masculinity, 2004; Skin Again, 2004; Will to Change: Men, Masculinity and Love, 2004; (with A. Mesa-Bains) Homegrown: Engaged Cultural Criticism, 2006; When Angels Speak of Love: Poems, 2007; Grump Groan Growl, 2008; Belonging: A Culture of Place, 2009; Teaching Critical Thinking: Practical Wisdom, 2009. Contributor to periodicals. **Address:** Appalachian Center, Berea College, Rm. 128A, Bruce Bldg., 205 N Main St., CPO 2166, Berea, KY 40404, U.S.A.

HOOKS, Gregory M. American (born United States), b. 1953. **Genres:** Sociology, Politics/Government, Regional/Urban Planning, Military/Defense/Arms Control. **Career:** University of Wisconsin, Department of Rural Sociology, research assistant, 1980-84; Indiana University, Department of Sociology, assistant professor, 1985-90; Washington State University, Department of Sociology, assistant professor, 1990-93, associate professor, 1993-2001, director of graduate studies, 1993-96, professor, 2001-, chair, 2001-09, Boeing distinguished professor of environmental sociology, 2008-11; Open Society Institute, Soros senior justice fellow, 2005-07; McMaster University, visiting research chair in health, science and the environment, 2009-. Writer. **Publications:** Forging the Military-Industrial Complex: World War II's Battle of the Potomac, 1991; (with R. Hodson and S. Rieble) Customized Training in the Workplace, 1991; (ed. with L.M. Lobao and A.R. Tickamyer) Sociology of Spatial Inequality, 2007. Contributor to journals. **Address:** Department of Sociology, Washington State University, Wilson Hall 204D, PO Box 644020, Pullman, WA 99164-4020, U.S.A. **Online address:** ghooks@wsu.edu

HOOLEY, D(aniel) M. American (born United States), b. 1950. **Genres:** Classics, Young Adult Fiction. **Career:** Carleton College, lecturer in classics, 1985-88; Princeton University, Perkins lecturer in classics and humanities, 1988-89; Allegheny College, assistant professor of classics, 1989-92; University of Missouri, Department of Classics, assistant professor, 1992-96, associate professor, 1996-2007, professor, 2007-, chair, 2002-05. **Publications:** The Classics in Paraphrase: Ezra Pound and Modern Translators of Latin Poetry,

1988; The Knotted Thong: Structures of Mimesis in Persius, 1997; Blackwell's Introductions to the Classical World, 2005; Roman Satire, 2007. Contributor of articles to periodicals. **Address:** Department of Classical Studies, University of Missouri-Columbia, 420 General Classroom Bldg., Columbia, MO 65201, U.S.A. **Online address:** hooleyd@missouri.edu

HOOPER, Chloe. Australian (born Australia), b. 1973?. **Genres:** Children's Non-fiction, Mystery/Crime/Suspense. **Career:** Melbourne Grammar, writer-in-residence; Shelford Girls School, writer-in-residence; Lauriston Girls School, writer-in-residence. **Publications:** A Child's Book of True Crime, 2002; The Tall Man: Death and Life on Palm Island, 2008; Tall Man: The Death of Doomadgee, 2009; The Engagement, 2012. Works appear in anthologies. Contributor to journals. **Address:** c/o Author Mail, Scribner Publicity, 1230 Ave. of the Americas, New York, NY 10020-1513, U.S.A.

HOOPER, Dan. American (born United States), b. 1976. **Genres:** Sciences, Astronomy. **Career:** U.S. Department of Energy, Fermi National Accelerator Laboratory, David Schramm fellow, associate scientist in theoretical astrophysics, 1994-; Oxford University, postdoctoral researcher; University of Chicago, Department of Astronomy and Astrophysics, assistant professor. Writer. **Publications:** Dark Cosmos: In Search of Our Universe's Missing Mass and Energy, 2006; Nature's Blueprint: Supersymmetry and the Search for a Unified Theory of Matter and Force, 2008. **Address:** Fermi National Accelerator Laboratory, U.S. Department of Energy, Wilson Hall 6 W, PO Box 500, Batavia, IL 60510, U.S.A. **Online address:** dhooper@uchicago.edu

HOOPER, Kay. (Kay Robbins). American (born United States), b. 1957. **Genres:** Novels, Novellas/Short Stories, Mystery/Crime/Suspense, Romance/Historical, Horror, Science Fiction/Fantasy. **Career:** Novelist, 1980-. **Publications:** Lady Thief, 1981; Breathless Surrender, 1982; Mask of Passion, 1982; Breathless Surrender, 1982; On the Wings of Magic, 1983; C.J.'s Fate, 1984; If There Be Dragons, 1984; Pepper's Way, 1984; Something Different, 1984; Illegal Possession, 1985; Rafe, The Maverick, 1986; Rebel Waltz, 1986; Time After Time, 1986; Larger than Life, 1986; The Shamrock Trinity: Rafe, the Maverick, 1986; Adelaide, The Enchantress, 1987; In Serena's Web, 1987; Matilda, the Adventuress, 1987; Rafferty's Wife, 1987; Rafferty's Wife, 1987; Zach's Law, 1987; Raven on the Wing, 1987; Velvet Lightning, 1988; Captain's Paradise, 1988; Outlaw Derek, 1988; Summer of the Unicorn, 1988; Shades of Gray, 1988; The Fall of Lucas Kendrick, 1988; Unmasking Kelsey, 1988; Golden Flames, 1988; It Takes a Thief, 1989; Aces High, 1989; Golden Threads, 1989; The Glass Shoe, 1989; What Dreams May Come, 1990; Star Crossed Lovers, 1990; Through the Looking Glass, 1990; The Lady and the Lion, 1990; Crime of Passion, 1991; The Matchmaker, 1991; The Haviland Touch, 1991; House of Cards, 1991; The Delaney Christmas Carol: Christmas Future, 1992; The Touch of Max, 1993; Hunting the Wolfe, 1993; The Trouble with Jared, 1993; The Wizard of Seattle, 1993; All for Quinn, 1993; The Haunting of Josie, 1994; Amanda, 1995; After Caroline, 1996; Finding Laura, 1997; Haunting Rachel, 1998; Stealing Shadows, 2000; Hiding in the Shadows, 2000; Out of the Shadows, 2000; Touching Evil, 2001; Whisper of Evil, 2002; Enchanted, 2003; Sense of Evil, 2003; Once a Thief, 2003; Always a Thief, 2003; I'd Kill for That, 2004; Elusive, 2004; Hunting Fear, 2004; Enemy Mine, 2005; Chill of Fear, 2005; Sleeping With Fear, 2006; Blood Dreams, 2007; Blood Sins, 2008; Blood Ties, 2010. NOVELLAS: Holiday Spirit, 1991; Masquerade, 1994; Almost an Angel, 1995; Arts Magica, 1999. AS KAY ROBBINS: Return Engagement, 1982; Elusive Dawn, 1983; Kissed by Magic, 1983; Taken by Storm, 1983; Moonlight Rhapsody, 1984; Eye of the Beholder, 1985; Belonging to Taylor, 1986; On Her Doorstep, 1986. Contributor to periodicals. **Address:** PO Box 370, Bostic, NC 28018, U.S.A. **Online address:** kay@kayhooper.com

HOOPER, Maureen Brett. American (born United States), b. 1927. **Genres:** Children's Fiction, Young Adult Fiction, Novels, Music, Social Sciences, Human Relations/Parenting. **Career:** Los Angeles Unified School District, music teacher, 1949-62; University of California, senior lecturer of music education, 1962-91, lecturer emeritus, 1991-; American Suzuki Institute West, director. Writer and consultant. **Publications:** The Violin Man (middle grade novel), 1991; The Christmas Drum (picture book), 1994; Highlights Fun to Play Recorder Book, 2000; Silent Night: A Christmas Carol Is Born, 2001. **Address:** Department of Music, Herb Alpert School of Music, University of California Los Angeles, 2539 Schoenberg Music Bldg., PO Box 951616, Los Angeles, CA 90095-1616, U.S.A.

HOOPER, Meredith Jean. Australian (born Australia), b. 1939. **Genres:**
Science Fiction/Fantasy, Children's Fiction, Air/Space Topics, Art/Art History, Children's Non-fiction, Picture/Board Books, History, Mythology/Folklore, Natural History, Sciences, Technology, Travel/Exploration. **Career:** University of Adelaide, tutor in history, 1961; Voluntary Service Overseas, administrator, 1964-65; freelance writer, 1968-; Commonwealth Journal of International Affairs, editorial board, staff, 1988-; Royal Institution and History of Science and Technology, visiting research fellow, 1988-; Australian National Antarctic Research Expedition, visiting writer, 1994; NJF Artists and Writers Program, grantee, 1998-99, 2002. **Publications:** NONFICTION: Land of the Free, 1968; The Gold Rush in Australia, 1969; Everyday Inventions, 1972; The Story of Australia, 1974; More Everyday Inventions, 1976; Doctor Hunger and Captain Thirst, 1982; Kangaroo Route, 1985; God 'Elp All of Us, 1986; Cleared for Take-Off, 1986; (with M. Clark and S. Ferrier) History of Australia, 1988; How High Is the Sky?, 1990; Earth and Space, 1990; A for Antarctica, 1991; I for Invention, 1992; Balls, Bangs and Flashes, 1994; Germs, Jabs and Laughing Gas, 1994; The Feast, 1994; The Planets, 1994; Looking after the Egg, 1994; Count Down to Take Off, 1995; The Pebble in My Pocket, 1996; January, 1996; Entering the Ark, 1996; Hunting in the Marshes, 1996; Dinosaur, 1996; Osprey, 1996; Seal, 1996; The Bridge, 1996; The Forest, 1996; The Harbour, 1996; Coral Reef, 1997; Desert, 1997; Rainforest, 1997; The Tomb of Nebamma, 1997; A Book of Hours, 1997; Noah's Ark, 1997; Journey to Antarctica, 1997; The Colour of Light, 1997; Honey Biscuits, 1997; Cow, a Bee, a Cookie and Me, 1997; The Drop in My Drink, 1998; A Song for Planet Earth, 1998; The Pear Tree, 1998; Tigers, 1999; River Story, 2000; Ice Trap!, 2000; Gandali the Whale, 2000; Antarctic Adventure, 2000; Animals in the Ark, 2000; Who Built the Pyramid?, 2001; Race to the Pole, 2002; Gold: A Treasure Hunt through Time, 2002; Sticky.Jam, 2003; Woolly Jumper, 2003; The Island That Moved: How Shifting Forces Shape Our Earth, 2004; Egyptian Tomb, 2008. FICTION: Seven Eggs, 1985; The Journal of Watkin Stench, 1988; Evie's Magic Lamp, 1990; The Great Stone Circle, 1992; The Lost Purse, 1994; Monkeys, 1994; Tom's Rabbit, 1998; The Pole-Seekers, 2000; Dog's Night, 2000; (with M.P. Robertson) The Endurance: Shackleton' Sperilous Expedition in Antarctica, 2000; Thank You for My Yukky Present, 2001; Ponko and the South Pole, 2002; Emily and Alfie, 2006; Celebrity Cat: With Paintings from Art Galleries around the World, 2007. OTHER: Antarctic Journal: The Hidden Worlds of Antarctica's Animals, 2000; Longest Winter: Scott's Other Heroes, 2011. **Address:** David Higham Associates Ltd., 5-8 Lower John St., Golden Sq., London, GL W1R 4HA, England.

HOOPES, John W. American (born United States), b. 1958. **Genres:** Anthropology/Ethnology, Archaeology/Antiquities, History. **Career:** National Museum of Costa Rica, excavation supervisor, 1978-79, laboratory supervisor, 1983; Yale University, Laboratory of Archaeology, research assistant and photographer, 1980-81; Soil Systems Inc., archaeologist, 1981; New Mexico Archaeological Services Inc., archaeological consultant, 1981-82; Harvard University, Tozzer Library, Anthropological Literature, editor, 1987-88, Peabody Museum of Archaeology and Ethnology, research associate, 1988-89; State University of New York, Department of Anthropology, visiting assistant professor, 1988-89; University of Kansas, Department of Anthropology, assistant professor, 1989-94, associate professor, 1994-, Museum of Anthropology, assistant curator, 1989-94, courtesy curator, 1994-, Center of Latin American Studies, acting director, 1997, associate chair, 2001-08, Natural History Museum and Biodiversity Institute, 2008-, Global Indigenous Nations Studies, director, 2008-11. **Publications:** (Ed. with W.K. Barnett) The Emergence of Pottery: Technology and Innovation in Ancient Societies, 1995; Mayfield's Quick View Guide to the Internet for Anthropology, 1997; (ed. with J. Quilter) Gold and Power in Ancient Costa Rica, Panama, and Colombia: A Symposium at Dumbarton Oaks, 9 and 10 October 1999, 2003; Ancient Central American, 2004; The Archaeology Of Central America, 2009. **Address:** Department of Anthropology, University of Kansas, Rm. 622, 1415 Jayhawk Blvd., Lawrence, KS 66045-7594, U.S.A. **Online address:** hoopes@ku.edu

HOOSE, Phillip M. American (born United States), b. 1947?. **Genres:** Adult Non-fiction, Children's Non-fiction, Young Adult Non-fiction, Novels. **Career:** Nature Conservancy, staff, 1977-; songwriter and performing musician, 1984-; Children's Music Network, co-founding member, 1986-. Writer. **Publications:** Building an Ark: Tools for the Preservation of Natural Diversity through Land Protection, 1981; Hoosiers: The Fabulous Basketball Life of Indiana, 1986, rev. ed., 1995; Necessities: Racial Barriers in American Sports, 1989. FOR CHILDREN: It's Our World, Too!: Stories of Young People Who Are Making a Difference, 1993; (with H. Hoose) Hey, Little Ant, 1998; We Were There, Too!: Young People in U.S. History, 2001; The Race to

Save the Lord God Bird, 2004; Perfect, Once Removed: When Baseball Was All the World to Me, 2006; Claudette Colvin: Twice Toward Justice, 2009; Moonbird: A Year on the Wind with the Great Survivor B95, 2012. **Address:** Children's Music Network, 10 Court St., PO Box 22, Arlington, MA 02476, U.S.A. **Online address:** hoose@gwi.net

HOOVER, Dwight Wesley. American (born United States), b. 1926. **Genres:** History, Bibliography, Biography, Sciences, Social Commentary. **Career:** Bethune-Cookman College, professor of history, chair of department, head of division of social science, 1953-55, 1958; Kansas State University, assistant professor of general studies, 1958-59, professor of history, 1967-91; Ball State University, assistant professor, 1959-63, associate professor, 1963-67, professor, 1967-77, professor emeritus, 1977-; University of Virginia, professor of historical sociology, 1977-79; Jozsef Attila University, Fulbright lecturer in American studies, 1991-92; Doshisha University, visiting professor, 1992; Kansai Gaidai, visiting professor, 1996-97. Writer. **Publications:** Henry James, Sr. and the Religion of Community, 1969; (contrib.) New Movements in the Study and Teaching of History, 1970; A Teacher's Guide to American Urban History, 1971; The Red and the Black, 1976; Cities, 1976; A Pictorial History of Indiana, 1980; (co-ed.) Family History, 1980; Science and History, 1981; Magic Middletown, 1986; (with D.C. Tambo and J.D. Hewitt) Middletown: An Annotated Bibliography, 1988; Middletown: The Making of a Documentary Film Series, 1992; A Good Day's Work: An Iowa Farm in the Great Depression, 2007. EDITOR/CO-EDITOR: Understanding Negro History, 1968; American Society in the 20th Century, 1972; Readings in Twentieth Century American Social History, 1972; Conspectus of History: Focus on Biography, 1975; Conspectus of History: Focus on Issues in World Diplomacy, 1975. Contributor to journals. **Address:** Department of History, Ball State University, Burkhardt Rm. 200, Muncie, IN 47306, U.S.A. **Online address:** jmhdwh@aol.com

HOOVER, H(elen) M(ary). American (born United States), b. 1935. **Genres:** Science Fiction/Fantasy, Novels, Social Sciences, Children's Fiction, Politics/Government. **Career:** Writer. **Publications:** SCIENCE FICTION FOR CHILDREN: Children of Morrow, 1973; The Lion's Cub (historical fiction), 1974; Treasures of Morrow, 1976; The Delikon, 1977; The Rains of Eridan, 1977; The Lost Star, 1979; Return to Earth: A Novel of the Future, 1980; This Time of Darkness, 1980; Another Heaven, Another Earth, 1981; The Bell Tree, 1982; The Shepherd Moon: A Novel of the Future, 1984; (contrib.) Literature for Today's Young Adults, 1985; Anatomy of Wonder: A Critical Guide to Science Fiction, 1987; Journey Through the Empty, 1987; Orvis, 1987; The Dawn Palace: The Story of Medea, 1988; Away Is a Strange Place to Be, 1990; Only Child, 1992; The Winds of Mars, 1995; (with C.M. Brenner and W.J. Williams) The Whole Truth and Other Myths: Retelling Ancient Tales, 1996. **Address:** Russell & Volkening Inc., 50 W 29th St., Ste. 7E, New York, NY 10001, U.S.A.

HOOVER, Paul. American (born United States), b. 1946. **Genres:** Poetry, Translations, Literary Criticism And History. **Career:** University of Illinois Press, assistant editor, 1973-74; Columbia College, poet-in-residence and professor of English, 1974-2003, School of the Art Institute of Chicago, Poetry Center, founding member, 1974, president, 1975-78; Bard College, fellow, 1988-; San Francisco State University, visiting professor, 2003-05, professor, 2006-. **Publications:** POETRY: Harpin Turns, 1973; The Monocle Thugs, 1977; Letter to Einstein Beginning Dear Albert, 1979; Somebody Talks a Lot, 1983; Nervous Songs, 1986; Idea, 1987; Saigon, Illinois, 1988; The Novel: A Poem, 1990; Viridian, 1997; Totem and Shadow: New & Selected Poems, 1999; Rehearsal in Black, 2001; Winter (Mirror), 2002; Poems in Spanish, 2005; Edge and Fold, 2006; Sonnet 56, 2009; Desolation: Souvenir, 2012. OTHERS: (ed.) Postmodern American Poetry: A Norton Anthology, 1994, 2nd ed., 2012; Fables of Representation (essays), 2004; (co-ed. and trans.) Selected Poems of Friedrich Hoelderlin, 2008; (co-ed. and trans.) Black Dog, Black Night: Contemporary Vietnamese Poetry, 2008; (co-ed. and trans.) Beyond the Court Gate: Selected Poems of Nguyen Trai, 2010. **Address:** Department of Creative Writing, San Francisco State University, 1600 Holloway, San Francisco, CA 94132, U.S.A. **Online address:** viridian@hotmail.com

HOPCKE, Robert H(enry). American (born United States), b. 1958. **Genres:** Psychology, Sex, Adult Non-fiction, Theology/Religion, Gay And Lesbian Issues, Politics/Government. **Career:** Unitas Personal Counseling, intern, senior intern, supervisor, 1981-86, staff clinical supervisor, 1986-89; Operation Concern, co-ordinator of AIDS prevention program, 1989-95, vice-president and chair, 2001-05; Center of Symbolic Studies, co-founder, 1990-;

Pacific Center for Human Growth in Berkeley, supervisor faculty, 1999-2007, president and chairperson, 2007-; Institute for Transpersonal Psychology in Palo Alto, adjunct faculty, 2003-. Writer and psychotherapist. **Publications:** A Guided Tour of the Collected Works of C.G. Jung, 1989, 2nd ed., 1999; Jung, Jungians, and Homosexuality, 1989; Men's Dreams, Men's Healing, 1990; (trans. with P.A. Schwartz) M. Brusatin, The History of Colors, 1991; (ed. with K.L. Carrington and S. Wirth) Same-Sex Love: A Path to Wholeness, 1993; The Persona: Where Sacred Meets Profane, 1995; There Are No Accidents: Synchronicity and the Stories of Our Lives, 1997; (with L. Rafaty) A Couple of Friends: The Remarkable Friendship between Straight Women and Gay Men, 1999; (trans. with P. Schwartz) V. Lingiardi, Men in Love: Male Homosexualities from Ganymede to Batman, 2002; Living the Mysteries, 2003; Catholics and the Death Penalty: Six Things Catholics Can Do To End Capital Punishment, 2004. (with P.A. Schwartz) Little Flowers of Francis of Assisi: A New Translation, 2006. Contributor to books. **Address:** 2920 Domingo Ave., Ste. 203, Berkeley, CA 94705-2400, U.S.A. **Online address:** rob@symbolics.org

HOPE, Christopher (David Tully). South African/Irish (born Ireland), b. 1944. **Genres:** Novels, Novellas/Short Stories, Children's Fiction, Poetry, Travel/Exploration. **Career:** South British Insurance, underwriter, 1966; Nasionale Pers Publishers, editor, 1966-67; Lintas, copywriter, 1967-75; Durban Sunday Tribune, reviewer, 1968-69; Halesowen Secondary Modern School, English teacher, 1972; Bolt, editor, 1972-73; Gordonstoun School, writer-in-residence, 1978; Royal Society of Literature, fellow, 1990; Franschhoek Literary Festival, founder, 2007. **Publications:** NOVELS: A Separate Development, 1980; Kruger's Alp, 1984; The Hottentot Room, 1986; Life Class, 1986; My Chocolate Redeemer, 1989; Serenity House, 1992; Darkest England, 1996; Me, the Moon and Elvis Presley, 1997; Heaven Forbid, 2002; Brothers Under the Skin, 2003; My Mother's Lovers 2006; Garden of Bad Dreams, 2008; Shooting Angels, 2011. STORIES: Learning to Fly and Other Tales, 1981; Black Swan (novella), 1987; The Love Songs of Nathan J. Swirsky, 1993. FOR CHILDREN: (with Y. Menuhin) The King, The Cat, and the Fiddle, 1983; The Dragon Wore Pink, 1985. TRAVEL: Moscow! Moscow!, 1990; Signs of the Heart: Love and Death in Languedoc, 1999. POETRY: (with M. Kirkwood) Whitewashes, 1971; Cape Drives, 1974; In the Country of the Black Pig and Other Poems, 1981; Englishmen, 1985. OTHER: White Boy Running (memoir), 1988. **Address:** c/o Rogers, Coleridge & White, 20 Powis Mews, London, GL W11 1JN, England. **Online address:** christopher1hope@gmail.com

HOPE, Janet. Australian (born Australia), b. 1972. **Genres:** Sciences. **Career:** Australian Commonwealth Government, Chief General Counsel, barrister, 1997-99. Writer, lawyer and scientific researcher. **Publications:** Biobazaar: The Open Source Revolution and Biotechnology, 2008. **Address:** Centre for Governance of Knowledge and Development, Regulatory Institutions Network, Australian National University, Canberra, AC 0200, Australia. **Online address:** janet.hope@anu.edu.au

HOPE, Margaret. See KNIGHT, Alanna (Cleet).

HOPE, Marjorie (Cecelia). American (born United States), b. 1923. **Genres:** Civil Liberties/Human Rights, Environmental Sciences/Ecology, International Relations/Current Affairs, Politics/Government, Sociology, Humanities. **Career:** East Stroudsburg State College, professor of sociology, 1973-75; Wilmington College, associate professor, professor of sociology, 1975-. Writer. **Publications:** Youth against the World, 1970, rev. ed. as The New Revolutionaries, 1971. WITH J. YOUNG: The Struggle for Humanity: Agents of Nonviolent Change in a Violent World, 1977; The South African Churches in a Revolutionary Situation, 1981; The Faces of Homelessness, 1986; Voices of Hope in the Struggle to Save the Planet, 2000. Contributor of articles to periodicals. **Address:** Department of Sociology and Criminology, Wilmington College, Rm. 208, Social and Behavioral Sciences Bldg., 601 S College Rd., Wilmington, NC 28403, U.S.A.

HOPE, Ronald. British (born England), b. 1921. **Genres:** Geography, History, Travel/Exploration. **Career:** Brasenose College, fellow, 1945-47; Oxford University, fellow and lecturer in economics, 1946-47; College of the Sea, Seafarers Education Service, director, 1947-76; justice of the peace, 1963-70; London Nautical School, chairman; The Marine Society, director, 1976-; Order of the British Empire, officer. Writer. **Publications:** Spare Time at Sea, 1954, rev. ed., 1974; Economic Geography, 1956, 5th ed., 1969; Dick Small in the Half-Deck (novel), 1958; Ships, 1958; The British Shipping Industry,

1959; The Shoregoer's Guide to World Ports, 1963; Introduction to the Merchant Navy, 1965, 4th ed., 1973; In Cabined Ships at Sea: Fifty Years of the Seafarers Education Service, 1969; The Merchant Navy, 1980; A New History of British Shipping, 1990; Poor Jack, 2001. EDITOR: The Harrap Book of Sea Verse, 1960; Seamen and the Sea, 1965; Retirement from the Sea, 1967; Voices from the Sea, 1977; John Masefield: The Sea Poems, 1978; Twenty Singing Seamen, 1979; (and intro.) The Seaman's World, 1982; Sea Pie, 1984. Contributor to periodicals. **Address:** The Marine Society, 202 Lambeth Rd., London, GL SE1 7JW, England.

HOPGOOD, Mei-Ling. Argentine/Chinese (born China), b. 1974?. **Genres:** Autobiography/Memoirs. **Career:** Detroit Free Press, reporter; St. Louis Post-Dispatch, reporter; Cox Newspapers, Washington bureau, reporter. **Publications:** Lucky Girl (memoir), 2009; How Eskimos Keep Their Babies Warm, 2012. Contributor to periodicals. **Address:** Algonquin Books, PO Box 2225, Chapel Hill, NC 27515-2225, U.S.A. **Online address:** info@mei-linghopgood.com

HOPKINS, Antony. British (born England), b. 1921. **Genres:** Music, Autobiography/Memoirs, Children's Fiction, Literary Criticism And History. **Career:** Intimate Opera Co., director, 1952-64; BBC, composer and presenter; Royal College of Music, professor, 1955-70; City University, Gresham professor; Robinson College, fellow. Writer. **Publications:** Talking about Symphonies: An Analytical Study of a Number of Well-Known Symphonies from Haydn to the Present Day, 1961; Talking about Concertos: An Analytical Study of a Number of Well-Known Concertos from Mozart to the Present Day, 1964; Music All around Me: A Personal Choice from the Literature of Music, 1967; Lucy and Peterkin, 1968; (with A. Previn) Music Face to Face, 1971; Talking about Sonatas: A Book of Analytical Studies, Based on a Personal View, 1971; Doctor Musicus, 1971; Sonatine, 1971; Talking about Music: Symphonies, Concertos and Sonatas, 1977; Downbeat Music Guide, 1977; Understanding Music, 1979; The Nine Symphonies of Beethoven, 1981; Early One Morning: A Cantata for Mezzo-Soprano, Male Speaker, Female Chorus and Orchestra, 1981; Songs for Swinging Golfers, 1981; Sounds of Music: A Study of Orchestral Texture, 1982; Beating Time (autobiography), 1982; Musicamusings, 1983; Pathway to Music, 1983; Nightlong: Variations on a Welsh Tune, 1984; The Concertgoer's Companion, vol. I, 1984, vol. II, 1985; Sounds of the Orchestra, 1995; The Seven Concertos of Beethoven, 1996. Contributor to periodicals. **Address:** Woodyard, Ashridge, Berkhamsted, HF HP4 1PS, England.

HOPKINS, Bruce R. American (born United States), b. 1941. **Genres:** Law, Money/Finance, Business/Trade/Industry, Economics. **Career:** George Washington National Law, professional lecturer in law, 1972-91; Powers, Pyles, Sutter & Verville, lawyer, 1992-; University of Kansas School of Law, adjunct professor, 2008-; Welte Suelthaus Polsinelli Shalton, PC, senior partner, attorney and owner. Writer. **Publications:** The Law of Tax-Exempt Organizations, 1977, 10th ed., 2011; Charity Under Siege: Government Regulation of Fund-Raising, 1980; A Tax Guide for College & University Presidents, 1980; Charitable Giving and Tax-Exempt Organizations: The Impact of the 1981 Tax Act, 1982; (with B.S. Anderson) The Counselor and the Law, 4th ed., 1996; Starting and Managing Starting a Nonprofit Organization: A Legal Guide, 1989, 5th ed., 2009; The Law of Fund-Raising, 1991, 4th ed., 2009; (with A.R. Summers) Using Charitable Dollars to Affect Public Policy, 1991; Charity, Advocacy, and the Law: How Nonprofit Organizations Can Use Charitable Dollars to Affect Public Lawfully Policy, 1992; The Tax Law of Charitable Giving, 1993, 4th ed., 2010; Nonprofit Law Dictionary, 1994; (with T.K. Hyatt) The Law of Tax-Exempt Healthcare Organizations, 1995, 3rd ed., 2008; The Legal Answer Book for Nonprofit Organizations, 1996; (with D.B. Tesdahl) Intermediate Sanctions: Curbing Nonprofit Abuse, 1997; (with J. Blazek) Private Foundations: Tax Law and Compliance, 1997, 3rd ed., 2008; The Second Legal Answer Book for Nonprofit Organizations, 1999; The First Legal Answer Book for Fund-Raisers 2000; The Second Legal Answer Book for Fund-Raisers, 2000; The Legal Answer Book for Private Foundations, 2002; The Law of Intermediate Penalties: A Guide for Nonprofits, 2003; The Nonprofits' Guide to Internet Communications Law, 2003; Legal Responsibilities of Nonprofit Boards, 2003, 2nd ed., 2009; The Law of Tax-Exempt Organizations Planning Guide: Strategies and Commentaries, 2004; 650 Essential Nonprofit Law Questions Answered, 2005; The Tax Law of Unrelated Business for Nonprofit Organizations, 2005; Nonprofit Law Made Easy, 2005; The Tax of Unrelated Business Law for Nonprofit Organizations, 2006; The Tax Law of Associations, 2006; (with D.O. Middlebrook) Nonprofit Law for Religious Organizations: Essential Questions & Answers,

2007; Charitable Giving Easy Law Made, 2007; IRS Audits of Tax-Exempt Organizations: Policies, Practices and Procedures, 2008; Private Foundation Law Made Easy, 2008; (co-author) New Form 990: Law, Policy and Preparation, 2009; Fundraising Law Made Easy, 2009; (with V.C. Gross) Nonprofit Governance: Law, Practices and Trends, 2009; (with V.C. Gross and T.J. Schenkelberg) Nonprofit Law for Colleges and Universities: Essential Questions and Answers for Officers, Directors and Advisors, 2011. **Address:** Polsinelli Shalton Flanigan Suelthaus, 700 W 47th St., Ste. 1000, Kansas City, MO 64112, U.S.A. **Online address:** bhopkins@polsinelli.com

HOPKINS, Cathy. British (born England), b. 1953. **Genres:** Young Adult Fiction, Novels. **Career:** Writer, 1987-. **Publications:** MATES, DATES SERIES: Mates, Dates and Inflatable Bras, 2001; Mates, Dates and Cosmic Kisses, 2001; Mates, Dates and Portobello Princesses, 2001; Mates, Dates and Sleepover Secrets, 2002; Mates, Dates and Designer Divas, 2003; Mates, Dates and Mad Mistakes, 2003; Mates, Dates and Pulling Power, 2003, rev. ed. as Mates, Dates and Sequin Smiles, 2004; Mates, Dates and Tempting Trouble, 2004; Mates, Dates and Sole Survivors, 2004; Mates, Dates and Great Escapes, 2004; Mates, Dates and Chocolate Cheats, 2005; Mates Dates and Diamond Destiny, 2005; Mates, Dates Guide to Life, 2005, rev. ed. as Mates, Dates Guide to Life, Love and Looking Luscious, 2005; Mates Dates and Sizzling Summers, 2006; Mates Dates Simply Fabulous: Books 1-4, 2006; Mathy Mates The Secret Story, 2009. TRUTH OR DARE SERIES: White Lies and Barefaced Truths, 2002; Pop Princess, 2002; Teen Queens and Has beens, 2003; Starstruck, 2003; Double Dare, 2005; Midsummer Meltdown, 2006; All Mates Together, 2007; Love Lottery, 2007. CINNAMON GIRL SERIES: This Way to Paradise, 2007; Starting Over, 2007; Looking for a Hero, 2008; Expecting to Fly, 2009. OTHERS: Girl Chasing: How to Improve Your Game, 1989; Sixty-Nine Things to Do When You are Not Busy Doing It, 1991; The Joy of Aromatherapy, 1991; Revenge of the Essex Girls, 1992; Keeping It Up!: How to Make Your Love Affair Last Forever, 1993; Blooming Pregnant!: The Real Facts about Having a Baby, 1993; Divorce for Beginners: How to Get Unhitched Without the Hitches, 1995; The Worlds Best Light-Bulb Jokes, 1995; Thorsons Principles of Aromatherapy, 1996; 101 Shortcuts to Relaxation, 1997; The Wisdom of the Master Cat, 1998; Dead Dudes on Holiday, 2006; Holy Moley Im a Dead Dude, 2006; From Geek to Goddess, 2007; Recipe for Rebellion, 2007; Discount Diva, 2007; Brat Princess, 2007; Star Child, 2008; Bridesmaids' Club, 2009; Double Trouble, 2009; Dancing Queen, 2009; Friend Me, 2009; Besties, 2009; Million Dollar Mates, 2010; Paparazzi Princess, 2011; Catwalk Queen, 2011; Golden Girl, 2012; Time After Time, 2012. **Address:** Piccadilly Press Ltd., 5 Castle Rd., London, GL NW1 8PR, England. **Online address:** cathy@cathyhopkins.com

HOPKINS, Dwight N(athaniel). American (born United States), b. 1953. **Genres:** Theology/Religion, History, Social Sciences. **Career:** University of Chicago, Divinity School, professor of theology, 1996-, director of MA studies, Center for the Study of Race, Politics and Culture, faculty affiliate, Center for East Asian Studies, faculty affiliate, Center for Latin American Studies, faculty affiliate; American Baptist minister. Writer. **Publications:** Black Theology U.S.A. and South Africa: Politics, Culture, and Liberation, 1989; Shoes That Fit Our Feet: Sources for a Constructive Black Theology, 1993; Down, Up, and Over: Slave Religion and Black Theology, 1999; Introducing Black Theology of Liberation, 1999; Heart and Head: Black Theology Past, Present, and Future, 2002; Being Human: Race, Culture, and Religion, 2005; Walk Together Children: Black and Womanist Theologies, Church and Theological Education, 2009. EDITOR: We Are One Voice: Black Theology in South Africa and the USA, 1989; (with G.C.L. Cummings) Cut Loose Your Stammering Tongue: Black Theology in the Slave Narratives, 1991, 2nd ed., 2003; Changing Conversations: Religious Reflection and Cultural Analysis, 1996; Liberation Theologies: Post-Modernity and the Americas, 1997; (ed.) Black Faith and Public Talk: Critical Essay on James H. Cone's Black Theology and Black Power, 1999; Religions/Globalizations: Theories and Cases, 2001; Global Voices for Gender Justice, 2003; (with A.B. Pin) Loving the Body: Black Religious Studies and the Erotic, 2004; (with M. Lewis) Another World is Possible: Spiritualities and Religions of Global Darker Peoples, 2008; (with L.E. Thomas) Walk Together Children: Black and Womanist Theologies, Church, and Theological Education, 2010. **Address:** The Divinity School, University of Chicago, 1025 E 58th St., Swift Hall 306 B, Chicago, IL 60637, U.S.A. **Online address:** dhopkins@uchicago.edu

HOPKINS, George Emil. American (born United States), b. 1937. **Genres:** Air/Space Topics, History, Industrial Relations, Organized Labor, Politics/Government, Transportation, Autobiography/Memoirs. **Career:** Western Illinois University, Department of History, assistant professor, associate professor, professor, 1968-2005, professor emeritus, 2005-. Writer. **Publications:** The Airline Pilots: A Study in Elite Unionization, 1971; Flying the Line: The First Half Century of the Air Line Pilots Association, 1982, vol. II, 2000; (ed.) Pan Am Pioneer: A Manager's Memoir from Seaplane Clippers to Jumbo Jets, 1995. Contributor to periodicals. **Address:** Department of History, Western Illinois University, 1 University Cir., Macomb, IL 61455-1390, U.S.A. **Online address:** ge-hopkins@wiu.edu

HOPKINS, Jackie (Mims). American (born United States), b. 1952. **Genres:** Young Adult Fiction, Young Adult Non-fiction, Picture/Board Books. **Career:** Eastdale Academy, elementary school teacher, 1976-78; Lamkin Elementary, elementary school teacher, 1978-81; Building Rainbows, kindergarten teacher, 1985-88; Matzke Elementary, elementary school teacher, 1988-91, librarian/media specialist, 1994-; Horne Elementary, Houston, librarian/media specialist, 1991-93. Writer. **Publications:** Tumbleweed Tom on the Texas Trail, 1994; The Horned Toad Prince, 2000; The Three Armadillies Tuff, 2002; The Shelf Elf, 2004; The Shelf Elf Helps Out, 2006; The Gold Miner's Daughter: A Melodramatic Fairytale, 2006; Goldie Socks and the Three Libearians, 2007; Joe Bright and the Seven Genre Dudes, 2010; Our Texas, 2010. **Address:** 13223 Golden Valley, Cypress, TX 77429, U.S.A. **Online address:** jackie@jackiemimshopkins.com

HOPKINS, Jasper. American (born United States), b. 1936. **Genres:** Philosophy, Theology/Religion, Translations, History. **Career:** Harvard University, teaching fellow in humanities, 1959-63; Case-Western Reserve University, assistant professor of philosophy, 1963-68; University of Arkansas, visiting associate professor, 1969; University of Massachusetts, associate professor, 1969-70; University of Minnesota, associate professor of philosophy, 1970-74, professor of philosophy, 1974-; University of Graz, visiting professor, 1981-82; University of Munich, visiting professor, 1986-87; Pontificia Università Gregoriana, visiting researcher, 1992-93. Writer. **Publications:** A Companion to the Study of St. Anselm, 1972; Hermeneutical and Textual Problems in the Complete Treatises of St. Anselm, 1976; A Concise Introduction to the Philosophy of Nicholas of Cusa, 1978, 3rd ed., 1986; Nicholas of Cusa on God as Not-Other: A Translation and an Appraisal of De Li Non Aliud, 1979, 3rd ed., 1987; Nicholas of Cusa on Learned Ignorance: A Translation and an Appraisal of De Docta Ignorantia, 1981, 2nd ed., 1985; Nicholas of Cusa's Debate with John Wenck: A Translation and an Appraisal of De Ignota Litteratura and Apologia Doctae Ignorantiae, 1981, 3rd ed., 1988; Nicholas of Cusa's Metaphysic of Contraction, 1983; Nicholas of Cusa's Dialectical Mysticism: Text, Translation and Interpretive Study of De Visione Dei, 1985, 3rd ed., 2001; A New, Interpretive Translation of St. Anselm's Monologion and Proslogion, 1986; Nicholas of Cusa's De Pace Fidei and Cribratio Alkorani: Translation and Analysis, 1990, 2nd ed., 1994; A Miscellany on Nicholas of Cusa, 1994; Philosophical Criticism: Essays and Reviews, 1994; Nicholas of Cusa on Wisdom and Knowledge, 1996; Glaube und Vernunft im Denken des Nikolaus von Kues, 1996, 2nd ed., 2008; Nicholas of Cusa: Metaphysical Speculations, vol. I, 1998, vol. II, 2000; Hugh of Balma on Mystical Theology: A Translation and an Overview of His De Theologia Mystica, 2002; (and trans.) Nicholas of Cusa's Last Sermons: 1457-1463, 2011. EDITOR AND TRANSLATOR: Truth, Freedom and Evil: Three Philosophical Dialogues, 1967; (and intro. with H. Richardson) Trinity, Incarnation and Redemption: Theological Treatises by Anselm of Canterbury, 1970; (with H. Richardson) Anselm of Canterbury, 3 vols., 1974-76. TRANSLATOR: (with H. Richardson) Complete Philosophical and Theological Treatises of Anselm of Canterbury, 2000; Complete Philosophical and Theological Treatises of Nicholas of Cusa, 2 vols., 2001; (and intro.) Nicholas of Cusa's Early Sermons, 1430-1441, 2003; (and intro.) Nicholas of Cusa's Didactic Sermons: A Selection, 2008. **Address:** Department of Philosophy, University of Minnesota, 831 Heller Hall, 271-19th Ave. S, Minneapolis, MN 55455, U.S.A. **Online address:** hopkins@umn.edu

HOPKINS, John. American (born United States), b. 1938. **Genres:** Novels, Novellas/Short Stories, Young Adult Non-fiction, Biography. **Career:** Writer. **Publications:** NOVELS: The Attempt, 1967; Tangier Buzzless Flies, 1972; The Flight of the Pelican, 1984; In the Chinese Mountains, 1990; All I Wanted Was Company, 1999. OTHERS: Rendez-Vous Ultimes (stories), 1991; The Tangier Diaries, 1962-1979, 1998; The South American Diaries, trans. as Carnets d'Amérique du Sud, 1972-1973, 2005; The South American Diaries, 1972-1973, 2008. **Address:** Secker and Warburg, 20 Vauxhall Bridge Rd., London, GL SW1V 2SA, England. **Online address:** theoldparsonage@hotmail.com

HOPKINS, Lee Bennett. American (born United States), b. 1938. **Genres:** Novels, Children's Fiction, Poetry, Children's Non-fiction, Literary Criticism And History, Animals/Pets. **Career:** Public school teacher, 1960-66; Bank Street College of Education, senior consultant, 1966-68; Scholastic Magazines Inc., curriculum and editorial specialist, 1968-74; full-time writer, 1976-; Zebra Wings, host and consultant. **Publications:** (With A.F. Shapiro) Creative Activities for Gifted Children, 1968; Books Are by People: Interviews with 104 Authors and Illustrators of Books For Young Children, 1969; Let Them Be Themselves: Language Arts Enrichment for Disadvantaged Children in Elementary Schools, 1969, 2nd ed. as Let Them Be Themselves: Language Arts for Children in Elementary Schools, 1974; (with M. Arenstein) Partners in Learning: A Child-Centered Approach to Teaching the Social Studies, 1971; Pass the Poetry, Please!: Bringing Poetry into the Minds and Hearts of Children, 1972, 3rd ed., 1998; More Books by More People, 1974; (with M. Arenstein) Do You Know What Day Tomorrow Is?: A Teacher's Almanac, 1975; The Best of Book Bonanza, 1980; (with A.F. Ada and V.J. Harris) A Chorus of Cultures: Developing Literacy through Multicultural Poetry, 1993; The Writing Bug: An Autobiography, 1994; Been to Yesterdays: Poems of a Life, 1995; Pauses: Autobiographical Reflections on 101 Creators of Children's Books, 1995; Blast Off! Poems About Space, 1995; Mother Goose and Her Children, 1999; Alphathoughts: Alphabet Poems, 2003; (and ed.) Days to Celebrate: A Full Year of Poetry, People, Holidays, History, Fascinating Facts and More, 2005; City I Love, 2009; (ed.) Dizzy Dinosaurs, 2011; Full Moon and Star, 2011; Mary's Song, 2012. YOUNG ADULT NOVELS: Mama, 1977; Wonder Wheels, 1980; Mama and Her Boys, 1981. FOR CHILDREN: Important Dates in Afro-American History, 1969; This Street's for Me (poetry), 1970; (with M. Arenstein) Faces and Places: Poems for You, 1970; Happy Birthday to Me!, 1972; When I Am All Alone: A Book of Poems, 1972; Charlie's World: A Book of Poems, 1972; Kim's Place and Other Poems, 1974; I Loved Rose Ann, 1976; A Haunting We Will Go: Ghostly Stories and Poems, 1976; Witching Time: Mischievous Stories and Poems, 1976; Kits, Cats, Lions, and Tigers: Stories, Poems, and Verse, 1979; Pups, Dogs, Foxes, and Wolves: Stories, Poems, and Verse, 1979; Go to Bed: A Book of Bedtime Poems, 1979; How Do You Make an Elephant Float and Other Delicious Food Riddles, 1983; Animals from Mother Goose, 1989; People from Mother Goose, 1989; Baseball Poems, 1993; April Bubbles Chocolate: An ABC of Poetry, 1994; Good Rhymes, Good Times!, 1995; Small Talk: A Book of Short Poems, 1995; All God's Children: A Book of Prayers, 1998; Mother Goose and Her Children, 1999; (ed.) Hoofbeats, Claws & Rippled Fins: Creature Poems, 2002; (ed.) Oh, No! Where are My Pants? And Other Disasters: Poems, 2005; (ed.) Hamsters, Shells, and Spelling Bees: School Poems, 2008. COMPILER: I Think I Saw a Snail: Young Poems for City Seasons, 1969; Don't You Turn Back: Poems by Langston Hughes, 1969; City Talk, 1970; The City Spreads Its Wings, 1970; Me!: A Book of Poems, 1970; Zoo!: A Book of Poems, 1971; Girls Can Too!: A Book of Poems, 1972; (with M. Arenstein) Time to Shout: Poems for You, 1973; (with S. Rasch) I Really Want to Feel Good about Myself: Poems by Former Addicts, 1974; On Our Way: Poems of Pride and Love, 1974; Hey-How for Halloween, 1974; Take Hold!: An Anthology of Pulitzer Prize-Winning Poems, 1974; Poetry on Wheels, 1974; Sing Hey for Christmas Day, 1975; Good Morning to You, Valentine, 1976; Merrily Comes Our Harvest In, 1976; (ed.) Thread One to a Star, 1976; (with M. Arenstein) Potato Chips and a Slice of Moon: Poems You'll Like, 1976; Beat the Drum! Independence Day Has Come, 1977; Monsters, Ghoulies, and Creepy Creatures: Fantastic Stories and Poems, 1977; To Look at Any Thing, 1978; Easter Buds Are Springing: Poems for Easter, 1979; Merely Players: An Anthology of Life Poems, 1979; My Mane Catches the Wind: Poems about Horses, 1979; By Myself: Poems, 1980; Elves, Fairies and Gnomes, 1980; Moments: Poems about the Seasons, 1980; Morning, Noon, and Nighttime, Too!, 1980; I Am the Cat, 1981; And God Bless Me: Prayers, Lullabies and Dream-Poems, 1982; Circus! Circus!, 1982; Rainbows Are Made: Poems by Carl Sandburg, 1982; A Dog's Life, 1983; The Sky Is Full of Song, 1983; A Song in Stone: City Poems, 1983; Crickets and Bullfrogs and Whispers of Thunder: Poems and Pictures, 1984; Love and Kisses (poems), 1984; Surprises: An I Can Read Book of Poems, 1984; Creatures, 1985; Munching: Poems about Eating, 1985; Best Friends, 1986; The Sea Is Calling Me, 1986; Click, Rumble, Roar: Poems about Machines, 1987; Dinosaurs, 1987; More Surprises: An I Can Read Book, 1987; Voyages: Poems by Walt Whitman, 1988; Side by Side: Poems to Read Together, 1988; Still as a Star: Nighttime Poems, 1988; Good Books, Good Times!, 1990; On the Farm, 1991; Happy Birthday: Poems, 1991; Questions: An I Can Read Book, 1992; Through Our Eyes: Poems and Pictures about Growing Up, 1992; To the Zoo: Animal Poems, 1992; Ring out, Wild Bells: Poems of Holidays and Seasons, 1992; Pterodactyls and Pizza: A Trumpet Club Book of Poetry, 1992; Flit,

Flutter, Fly!: Poems About Bugs and Other Crawly Creatures, 1992; School Supplies: A Book of Poems, 1996; Opening Days: Sports Poems, 1996; Song and Dance: Poems, 1997; Marvelous Math: A Book of Poems, 1997; Climb into My Lap: First Poems to Read Together, 1998; Sports! Sports! Sports!: A Poetry Collection, 1999; Spectacular Science: A Book of Poems, 1999; Dinoroars, 1999; Lives: Poems About Famous Americans, 1999; My America: A Poetry Atlas of the United States, 2000; Yummy!: Eating through a Day: Poems, 2000; Home to Me: Poems Across America, 2002; Pet for Me: Poems, 2003; Christmas Presents: Holiday Poetry, 2004; Hanukkah Lights: Holiday Poetry, 2004; Wonderful Words: Poems About Reading, Writing, Speaking, and Listening, 2004; Valentine Hearts: Holiday Poetry, 2005; Halloween Howls: Holiday Poetry, 2005; Got Geography!: Poems, 2006; Behind the Museum Door: Poems to Celebrate The Wonders of Museums, 2007; America at War: A Book of Poems, 2008; Sky Magic: Poems, 2009; Incredible Inventions: Poems, 2009; Amazing Faces, 2010; Give Me Wings: Poems, 2010; I am the Book: Poems, 2010; Sharing the Seasons: A Book of Poems, 2010; Hear My Prayer, 2011; Nasty Bugs, 2012. **Address:** HarperCollins Children's Books, 10 E 53rd St., New York, NY 10022-5244, U.S.A.

HOPKINS, Lisa. British (born England), b. 1962?. **Genres:** Language/Linguistics, Literary Criticism And History. **Career:** Sheffield Hallam University, Humanities Research Centre, professor of English, group leader. Writer. **Publications:** Queen Elizabeth I and Her Court, 1990; Women Who Would Be Kings: Female Rulers of the Sixteenth Century, 1991; John Ford's Political Theatre, 1994; The Shakespearean Marriage: Merry Wives and Heavy Husbands, 1998; Christopher Marlowe: A Literary Life, 2000; Writing Renaissance Queens: Texts by and about Elizabeth I and Mary, Queen of Scots, 2002; The Female Hero in English Renaissance Tragedy, 2002; Giants of the Past: Popular Fictions and the Idea of Evolution, 2004; Screening the Gothic, 2005; A Christopher Marlowe Chronology, 2005; Beginning Shakespeare, 2005; Shakespeare on the Edge: Border-Crossing in the Tragedies and the Henriad, 2005; (with M. Steggle) Renaissance Literature and Culture, 2006; Bram Stoker: A Literary Life, 2007; (ed. with A. Hiscock) Teaching Shakespeare and Early Modern Dramatists, 2007; (ed. with R. Buccola) Marian Moments in Early Modern British Drama, 2007; (ed. with A. Connolly) Goddesses and Queens, 2007; The Cultural Uses of the Caesars on the English Renaissance Stage, 2008; Shakespeare's The Tempest, 2008; Christopher Marlowe, Renaissance Dramatist, 2008; Relocating Shakespeare and Austen on Screen, 2009; (ed.) 'Tis Pity She's a Whore: A Critical Guide, 2010; Drama and the Succession to the Crown, 1561-1633, 2011. **Address:** Humanities Research Center, Sheffield Hallam University, 38-40 Howard St., City Campus, Sheffield, SY S1 1WB, England. **Online address:** l.m.hopkins@shu.ac.uk

HOPKINS, Mary R(ice). American (born United States), b. 1956. **Genres:** Children's Fiction, Local History/Rural Topics, Theology/Religion. **Career:** Sparrow Records, recording artist; Maranatha! Music, recording artist; Big Steps Records, founder. Writer. **Publications:** Hip, Hip, Hip Hippopotamus: A Celebration of God's Creation, 1996; Animal Alphabet: On the Land, in the Sky or Sea, Meet God's Creatures from A to Z, 1997; Noah, 1998; Come Back Home, 2004; Lost and Found, 2004; Safe in the Fold, 2004; Simple Stories Jesus Told: 13 Lessons & Songs for Young Children, 2004; Children's Ministry That Works, 2004. **Address:** Big Steps 4 U, PO Box 362, Montrose, CA 91021, U.S.A. **Online address:** bigsteps@aol.com

HOPKINSON, Amanda. (Caistor). British (born England), b. 1948. **Genres:** Photography, Women's Studies And Issues, Translations. **Career:** University of East Anglia, senior fellow, British Center for Literary Translation, director; Manchester University, visiting professor; City University London, visiting professor. Writer and translator. **Publications:** Julia Margaret Cameron, 1986; (ed.) Lovers and Comrades: Women's Resistance Poetry from Central America, 1989; Desires and Disguises: 5 Latin American Photographers, 1992; The Forbidden Rainbow, 1992; Mexico (children's nonfiction), 1992; (ed.) Contemporary Photographers, 1995; Chicano/Latino Writings, 1996; (ed.) Between Ourselves, 1998; Diary of an Unofficial War Artist, 2000; Martin Chambi, 2001; (ed. and contrib.) Encyclopaedia of Latin American Culture, 2000; Manuel Alvarez Bravo, 2002. TRANSLATOR: C. Alegria, They Won't Take Me Alive, 1987; (and ed.) Lovers and Comrades: Women's Resistance Poetry from Central America, 1988; C. Alegria, Family Album, 1989; C. Boullosa, The Miracle Worker, 1994; D. Eltir, Sacred Cow, 1995; J. Saramago, Journey to Portugal, 1999; R. Piglia, Money to Burn, 2003; D. Manotti, Dead Horsemeat, 2006; P. Coelho: The Devil and Miss Prym, 2007; R. Fogwill, Malvinas Requiem, 2007; D. Manotti, Lorraine Connection, 2008; D. Manotti, Affairs of State, 2009; J. Saramago, The Notebook,

2010; M. Barcelo, Terramare, 2010; M. Ray, Portraits, 2011; Isabel Allende, 2011. **Address:** British Centre for Literary Translation, School of Literature, University of East Anglia, Norwich, NF NR4 7TJ, England. **Online address:** a.hopkinson@uea.ac.uk

HOPKINSON, Christina. British (born England), b. 1969. **Genres:** Novels. **Career:** Thisislondon.com, editor, 1998-2000; The Times, editor, writer, journalist; The Guardian, editor, writer, journalist; The Daily Telegraph, editor, writer, journalist; Grazia Magazine, editor, writer, journalist. **Publications:** The Usborne History of the Twentieth Century, 1993; Izobel Brannigan.com, 2004, Cyber Cinderella, 2005; The Pile of Stuff at the Bottom of the Stairs, 2011. **Address:** Hachette Book Group USA, 237 Park Ave., New York, NY 10017, U.S.A. **Online address:** xtina_hopkinson@yahoo.co.uk

HOPLER, Jay. American (born United States), b. 1970. **Genres:** Poetry, Literary Criticism And History. **Career:** University of South Florida, associate professor of English. Poet. **Publications:** (Ed.) The Killing Spirit: An Anthology of Murder-for-Hire, 1996; Green Squall, 2006. Contributor to periodicals. **Address:** Department of English, University of South Florida, CPR-107, 4202 E Fowler Ave., Tampa, FL 33620-5550, U.S.A. **Online address:** jhopler@usf.edu

HOPPER, Kim. American (born United States) **Genres:** Social Sciences, Sciences. **Career:** National Coalition for the Homeless, president, 1991-93; Columbia University, School of Public Health and Law, adjunct professor, professor of clinical sociomedical sciences; Nathan S. Kline Institute for Psychiatric Research, research scientist, Center to Study Recovery in Social Contexts Method, co-director. Writer. **Publications:** (With E. Baxter) Private Lives/Public Spaces: Homeless Adults on the Streets of New York City, Community Service Society, 1981; (co-author) One Year Later: The Homeless Poor in NYC, 1982; Community Service Society, 1982; (with J. Hamberg) The Making of America's Homeless: From Skid Row to New Poor, Community Service Society, 1984; (with E. Baxter and D. Salerno) Hardship in the Heartland: Homelessness in Eight U.S. Cities, Community Service Society, 1984; (with M. Susser and W. Watson) Sociology in Medicine, 1985; Reckoning with Homelessness, 2003. **Address:** Nathan S. Kline Institute for Psychiatric Research, 140 Old Orangeburg Rd., Orangeburg, NY 10962, U.S.A. **Online address:** hopper@nki.rfmh.org

HOPPING EGAN, Lorraine. American (born United States), b. 1960. **Genres:** Children's Fiction, Young Adult Fiction, Children's Non-fiction, Information Science/Computers, Young Adult Non-fiction, History, How-to Books, Language/Linguistics, Mathematics/Statistics, Meteorology/Atmospheric Sciences, Natural History, Sciences, Adult Non-fiction, Education, Earth Sciences, Criminology/True Crime, Biography, Children's Fiction. **Career:** Scholastic magazines, reporter/editor, 1982-87; DynaMath, editor, 1987; Super Science, editor, 1988-91; Aristoplay Ltd., product development director, 1991-96; Hopping Fun Creations, president, 1996-. **Publications:** NONFICTION: My First Book of Animals A to Z, 1994; Sports Math Mania, 1996; Wild Weather: Tornadoes!, Hurricanes!, Blizzards!, Lightning!, Floods!, 1997-2002; Inventors and Inventions, 1997; Yes You Can Teach Shakespeare, 1999; 25 Super-Cool Board Games to Build Math Skills, 1999; Wild Earth: Avalanche!, Volcano!, Earthquake!, 1999-2003; Today's Weather Is . . . A Book of Experiments, 2000; Sally Ride: Space Pioneer and Jacques Cousteau: Saving Our Seas, Ideas on Trial Series, 2000; Great American History Games, 2000; Interactive Geography: Polar Regions, 2000; Noun Hounds and Other Great Grammar Games, 2001; Best-Ever Vocabulary and Word Study Games, 2001; Hall of Fame Sports Stars, 2001; Race to the Pole, 2001; 15 Primary Source Activities in American History, 2003; Across the Atlantic, 2003; Hatshepsut, 2003; Flight Test Lab: Hovercrafts!, 2004; Bone Detective and Space Rocks, Women's Adventures in Science, 2005; Investigating a Crime Scene and The Body as Evidence, 2007; Elephants Without Borders, 2007; The World of Inventors: Leonardo da Vinci, 2008; Explore Within an Egyptian Mummy, 2008; Chief Joseph: The Voice for Peace, Sterling Biographies, 2010. FICTION: Escape from Antcatraz, 1986; The Balloonatics, 1987; Safari!, 1987; Quest for the Pole, 1988; Kinetic City Super Crew: The 17-Year Drum Corps, Flower Power, The Case of the Unidentified Flashing Object, The Case of the Biggest Little Theme Park in Texas, 1994-96; Choose Your Move Series: Adventures of a Crater Creature, The Lost Pirates of Waylay Bay, The Stormy Voyage of Captain Reckless, 2010-11. BOARD GAMES: Island Alive!, 1990; Feeding Frenzy, 1992; The Play's the Thing, 1992; Top Dog, 1993; In the Land of Egypt, 1994; Who's at Home in the Animal Habitats?, 1994; A Time for Native Americans, 1994; NOVA True Science, 1994; True Math, 1995; Mars 2020, 1996; Panwapa Island, 2006; Speed Racer, 2008. Contributor of articles to periodicals. **Address:** 5606 N Dixboro Rd., Ann Arbor, MI 48105, U.S.A. **Online address:** mail@hoppingfun.com

HORACK, Skip. American (born United States), b. 1976. **Genres:** Novels. **Career:** Stanford University, faculty and Wallace Stegner fellow. Writer and attorney. **Publications:** The Southern Cross: Stories, 2009; The Eden Hunter: A Novel, 2010. Contributor to periodicals. **Address:** Stanford University, 450 Serra Mall, Stanford, CA 94305, U.S.A.

HORADAM, A. F. See **HORADAM, Alwyn Francis.**

HORADAM, Alwyn Francis. (A. F. Horadam). Australian (born Australia), b. 1923?. **Genres:** Mathematics/Statistics. **Career:** University of New England, lecturer, 1947-58, senior lecturer, 1958-63, associate professor of mathematics, 1963-87, Faculty of Science, dean, 1966-68, university ombudsman, 1984, Department of Mathematics, Statistics and Computing Science, head, 1985-87, Robb College, fellow, governor, Duval College, governor, Wright College, governor, University Esquire Bedell, governor, now retired. Writer. **Publications:** Outline Course of Pure Mathematics, 1968; Guide to Undergraduate Projective Geometry, 1970; (with M.E. Dunkley and I.W. Stewart) New Horizons in Mathematics, Book I, 1970, Book II, 1972; (with M.E. Dunkley and I.W. Stewart) Teacher's Manual to New Horizons in Mathematics, Book I, 1970, Book II, 1972. EDITOR: (with W.D. Wallis) Combinatorial Mathematics VI: Proceedings, Armidale, 1979; (with A.N. Philippou and G.E. Bergum) Fibonacci Numbers and Their Applications: Proceedings, 1986; (with G.E. Bergum and A.N. Philippou) Applications of Fibonacci Numbers: Proceedings, vol. II, 1988, vol. III, 1990, vol. IV, 1991, vol. V, 1993, vol. VI, 1996, vol. VII, 1998. **Address:** Springer Publishing Co., 11 W 42nd St., 15th Fl., New York, NY 10036, U.S.A.

HORAK, Jan-Christopher. American/German (born Germany), b. 1951. **Genres:** Film. **Career:** University of Münster, Institut für Publizistik, lecturer, 1980-84; HEIMAT, film researcher, 1981; Edgar Reitz Filmproduktion, film researcher, 1984; International Museum of Photography and Film, associate curator, 1984-87, curator, 1987-90; George Eastman House, senior curator, 1984-94; University of Rochester, professor of English, 1985-94; Munich Filmmuseum, director, 1994-98, senior curator; Hochschule Fernsehen/Film, lecturer in film, 1995-98; Universal Studios, Archives & Collections, founding director, 1998-2000; University of California, visiting professor, 1999-, Moving Image Archives Studies Program, acting director, 2006-, Film & Television Archive, director, 2007-; Hollywood Entertainment Museum, curator, 2000-06; Making Images Move, founder, 2000; Edgar Reitz Films, International Design Center, consultant; U.S. Information Agency, consultant; University of Salzburg, adjunct professor; Wayne State University, adjunct professor; Munich Film Academy, adjunct professor; University of Rochester, adjunct professor. Writer. **Publications:** IN ENGLISH: (trans.) U. Eskildsen, Helmar Lerski: Metamorphosis through Light, 1983; The Dream Merchants: Making and Selling Films in Hollywood's Golden Age, 1989; Lovers of Cinema: The First American Film Avant-Garde, 1919-1945, 1995; Making Images Move: Photographers and Avant-Garde Cinema, 1997. EDITOR: (with H.J. Wulff and K.D. Moeller) Bibliography of Film Bibliographies/Bibliographie der Filmbibliographien, 1987. IN GERMAN: (ed. with U. Eskildsen) Film und Foto der zwanziger Jahre, 1979; (with U. Eskildsen) Helmar Lerski: Lichtbildner, Fotographien und Filme, 1910-1947, 1982; Fluchtpunkt Hollywood: Eine Dokumentation zur Filmemigration nach 1933, 1984, rev. ed., 1986; Anti Nazi Filme der deutschsprachigen Emigration von Hollywood, 1984; (ed. with P.C. Usai and L. Codelli) Prima di Caligari: Cinema Tedesco, 1990; Berge, Licht und Traum Dr. Arnold Fanck und der deutsche Bergfilm, 1998. Contributor of articles and reviews to periodicals. **Address:** School of Theater, Film and Television, UCLA, 102 E Melnitz Hall, PO Box 951622, Los Angeles, CA 90095-1622, U.S.A. **Online address:** jchorak@ucla.edu

HORAN, Elizabeth (Rosa). American (born United States), b. 1956. **Genres:** Literary Criticism And History. **Career:** Cabrillo Community College, instructor in English, 1984; Tufts University, lecturer, 1987-88, visiting assistant professor of English, 1989; Wheelock College, lecturer, 1987-88; Arizona State University, assistant professor of English, associate professor of English and women's studies, 1989-, professor of English, chair of department, 2002-04, Comparative Literature Program, director and associate chair, 1989-2000; University of California, faculty; Catholic University, faculty; University of Costa Rica, faculty; Grand Valley State University, faculty. Writer, translator and public speaker. **Publications:** (Trans. and intro.)

Happiness: Stories by Marjorie Agosin, 1993; Gabriela Mistral: An Artist and Her People, 1994; (trans. and ed.) The House of Memory: Stories by Jewish Women Writers of Latin America, 1999; (trans., intro. and ed.) The Subversive Voice of Carmen Lyra: Selected Works, 2000; (ed. and trans. with D. Meyer) This America of Ours: The Letters of Gabriela Mistral and Victoria Ocampo, 2003; The Secret Lives of Gabriela Mistral: Poet, Teacher, Diplomat, Spy, forthcoming. Works appear in anthologies. Contributor of articles to periodicals. **Address:** Department of English, Arizona State University, PO Box 0302, Tempe, AZ 85287-0302, U.S.A. **Online address:** ehoran@asu.edu

HORAN, Ellen. American (born United States), b. 1956. **Genres:** Novels. **Career:** Vanity Fair, staff writer and freelance contributor; Vogue, staff writer and freelance contributor; House & Garden, staff writer and freelance contributor; Forbes, staff writer and freelance contributor; ARTnews, staff writer and freelance contributor. **Publications:** 31 Bond Street: A Novel, 2010. **Address:** Marly Rusoff and Associates Inc., PO Box 524, Bronxville, NY 10708, U.S.A.

HORAN, Nancy. American (born United States) **Genres:** Novels, Literary Criticism And History, Young Adult Fiction. **Career:** Journalist and writer. **Publications:** Loving Frank: A Novel, 2007. Contributor to periodicals. **Address:** Random House, 1745 Broadway, 3rd Fl., New York, NY 10019, U.S.A. **Online address:** nancy@nancyhoran.com

HORD, Frederick (Lee). (Mzee Lasana Okpara). American (born United States), b. 1941. **Genres:** Poetry, Literary Criticism And History, Essays. **Career:** Wabash College, professor of black studies, 1972-76; Community Service Administration, research director, 1977-80; Frostburg State University, assistant director of minority affairs, 1980-84; Howard University, professor of Afro-American studies, 1984-87; West Virginia University, Center for Black Culture, director, 1987-88; Knox College, director of black studies, 1988-, professor of black studies, chair of black studies; Association for Black Culture Centers, founder and executive director. Writer. **Publications:** POEMS: After H(ours), 1974; Into Africa, the Color Black, 1987; Life Sentences, 1994; Africa to Me, 1999; The Rhythm of Home: Selected Poems, forthcoming. OTHER: Reconstructing Memory: Black Literary Criticism (essays), 1991; (ed. and intro.) I am Because We Are: Readings in Black Philosophy, 1995; Straight Wobblings of My Father, 2000; (ed.) Black Culture Centers: Politics of Survival and Identity, 2005. Contributor to journals. **Address:** Knox College, 2 E South St., Galesburg, IL 61401-4999, U.S.A. **Online address:** fhord@knox.edu

HORGAN, John. American (born United States), b. 1953. **Genres:** Sciences, Social Sciences, Theology/Religion. **Career:** Institute of Electrical and Electronics Engineers, IEEE Spectrum, associate editor, 1983-86; Scientific American, senior writer, 1986-97; freelance writer, 1997-; Stevens Institute of Technology, Center for Science Writings, 2005-, director; The New York Times, writer; Time, writer; Newsweek, writer; The Washington Post, writer; The Los Angeles Times, writer; The New Republic, writer; Slate, writer; Discover, writer; The London Times, writer; The Times Literary Supplement, writer; New Scientist, writer. **Publications:** The End of Science: Facing the Limits of Knowledge in the Twilight of the Scientific Age, 1996; The Undiscovered Mind: How the Human Brain Defies Replication, Medication, and Explanation, 1999; (with F. Geer) Where Was God on September 11? A Scientist Asks a Ground Zero Pastor, 2001; Rational Mysticism: Dispatches from the Border Between Science and Spirituality, 2003. **Address:** Center for Science Writings, Stevens Institute of Technology, Castle Point on Hudson, Hoboken, NJ 07030-5991, U.S.A. **Online address:** email@johnhorgan.org

HORLAK, E. E. See **TEPPER, Sheri S.**

HORLICK, Allan S. American (born United States), b. 1941. **Genres:** History, Intellectual History, Education, Humanities. **Career:** New York University, assistant professor, associate professor of educational history, 1969-76; Trinity School, Department of History, history teacher and head, 1988-; The History of Education Quarterly, associate editor. **Publications:** Country Boys and Merchant Princes; The Social Control of Young Men in New York, 1975; Patricians, Professors, and Public Schools: The Origins of Modern Educational Thought in America, 1994. **Address:** Trinity School, 139 W 91St. St., New York, NY 10024-1326, U.S.A.

HORLOCK, John Harold. British (born England), b. 1928. **Genres:** Engineering, Sciences, Economics. **Career:** University of Liverpool, Harrison professor of mechanical engineering, 1958-66; University of Cambridge, professor of engineering, 1967-74; University of Salford, vice-chancellor, 1974-80; Open University, vice-chancellor, 1981-90. Writer. **Publications:** Axial-Flow Compressors, 1958; Axial-Flow Turbines: Fluid Mechanics and Thermodynamics, 1966; Effect of Change in Axial Velocity on The Potential Flow in Cascades, 1968; Actuator Disk Theory: Discontinuities in Thermo Fluid Dynamics, 1978; Cogeneration: Combined Heat and Power: Thermodynamics and Economics, 1987; Combined Power Plants: Including Combined Cycle Gas Turbine (Ccgt) Plants, 1992; Advanced Gas Turbine Cycles, 2003; Energy: Resources, Utilisation and Policies, 2009. EDITOR: Thermodynamics and Gas Dynamics of Internal-Combustion Engines, 2 vols., 1982-86; Energy for the Future, 1995. **Address:** 2 The Ave., Ampthill, Bedford, MK45 2NR, England. **Online address:** john.horlock1@btinternet.com

HORMATS, Robert D. American (born United States), b. 1943. **Genres:** Business/Trade/Industry, Economics, Military/Defense/Arms Control, History, Politics/Government. **Career:** U.S. National Security Council, senior staff for international economic affairs, senior economic advisor, 1969-77; U.S. Department of State, senior deputy assistant secretary for economic and business affairs, 1977-79, ambassador and deputy U.S. trade representative, 1979-81, assistant secretary of state for economic and business affairs, 1981-82, State for Economic, Business and Agricultural Affairs, under secretary, 2009-; Goldman Sachs, managing director and vice chairman, 1982-; Princeton University, visiting lecturer; Engelhard Hanovia Inc., board director; Irvington Institute for Immunological Research, board director; Freedom House, board director. Writer. **Publications:** Reforming the International Monetary System: From Roosevelt to Reagan, 1987; American Albatross: The Foreign Debt Dilemma, 1988; (ed. with W.E. Brock) The Global Economy: America's Role in the Decade Ahead, 1990; (with J.F. Brown and W.H. Luers) Western Approaches to Eastern Europe, 1992; The Price of Liberty: Paying for America's Wars, 2007. Contributor to journals and periodicals. **Address:** Goldman Sachs, 85 Broad St., New York, NY 10004, U.S.A.

HORN, Gerd-Rainer. British (born England), b. 1955. **Genres:** History, Politics/Government, Biography. **Career:** Montana State University, adjunct assistant professor, 1993-94; Western Oregon University, assistant professor, 1994-97, associate professor, 1997-2000; Catholic University of Leuven, Department of Political Science, research fellow, 1998-99; University of Huddersfield, senior lecturer, 2000-01; University of Warwick, Department of History, lecturer, 2001-05, senior lecturer, 2005-10, professor of twentieth century history, 2010-. Writer. **Publications:** NONFICTION: European Socialists Respond to Fascism: Ideology, Activism and Contingency in the 1930s, 1996; (ed. with E. Gerard) Left Catholicism, 1943-1955: Catholics and Society in Western Europe at the Point of Liberation, 2001; (ed. with P. Kenney) Transnational Moments of Change: Europe 1945, 1968, 1989, 2004; (ed. with B. Gehrke) 1968 und die Arbeiter: Studien zum proletarischen Mai in Europa, 2007; The Spirit of '68: Rebellion in Western Europe and North America, 1956-1976, 2007; Western European Liberation Theology: The First Wave (1924-1959), 2008; (ed.) Letters from Barcelona: An American Woman in Revolution and Civil War, 2009. **Address:** Department of History, University of Warwick, Rm. H332, Humanities Bldg., Coventry, CV4 7AL, England. **Online address:** g-r.horn@warwick.ac.uk

HORN, James. American (born United States) **Genres:** Adult Non-fiction, History, Social Sciences. **Career:** University of Brighton, School of Historical and Critical Studies, head; Omohundro Institute of Early American History and Culture, visiting editor of publications; Thomas Jefferson Foundation, International Center for Jefferson Studies, Saunders director; Colonial Williamsburg Foundation, deputy research division administrator, director of research, John D. Rockefeller Jr. Library, director of research, O'Neill Director, vice president of research, Deputy Research Division, administrator; College of William and Mary, lecturer; Omohundro Institute, research fellow; American Council of Learned Societies, research fellow; Harvard University, Charles Warren Center, research fellow; Royal Historical Society, research fellow. **Publications:** (Ed. with I. Altman) To Make America: European Emigration in the Early Modern Period, 1991; Adapting to a New World: English Society in the Seventeenth-Century Chesapeake, 1994; (ed. with J.E. Lewis and P.S. Onuf) The Revolution of 1800: Democracy, Race and the New Republic, 2002; A Land As God Made It: Jamestown and the Birth of America, 2005; (ed. and intro.) Writings, 2007; A Kingdom Strange: The Brief and Tragic History of the Lost Colony of Roanoke, 2010. **Address:** The College

of William & Mary, 102 Richmond Rd., PO Box 8795, Williamsburg, VA 23187-8795, U.S.A. **Online address:** jhorn@cwf.org

HORN, Jeff. American (born United States) **Genres:** History, Economics. **Career:** Massachusetts Institute of Technology, Dibner Institute for the History of Science and Technology, senior fellow, 2002-03; Manhattan College, Department of history, associate professor, professor and chair, Manhattan College Holocaust Resource Center, associate director, 2000-07, director, 2007-. Writer and historian. **Publications:** Qui parle pour la nation?: les élections et les élus de la Champagne méridionale, 1765-1830, 2004; The Path Not Taken: French Industrialization in the Age of Revolution, 1750-1830, 2006; The Industrial Revolution: Milestones in Business History, 2007; (ed. with L.N. Rosenband and M.R. Smith) Reconceptualizing the Industrial Revolution, 2010. Contributor to periodicals and journals. **Address:** Department of History, Manhattan College, 413 Miguel Hall, 4513 Manhattan College Pkwy., Riverdale, NY 10471, U.S.A. **Online address:** jeff.horn@manhattan.edu

HORN, Michiel. Canadian/Dutch (born Netherlands), b. 1939. **Genres:** History, Trivia/Facts, Translations, Politics/Government, Social Sciences. **Career:** Bank of Montreal, bank officer, 1956-58; York University, Glendon College, lecturer in history, 1968-69, assistant professor, 1969-73, associate professor, 1973-82, associate principal of the college, 1978-81, professor, 1982-, department chair, 1982-93, director of Canadian studies, 1986-89. Writer. **Publications:** The Dirty Thirties: Canadians in the Great Depression, 1972; (with R. Sabourin) Studies in Canadian Social History, 1974; The League for Social Reconstruction: Intellectual Origins of the Democratic Left in Canada, 1930-1942, 1980; A Liberation Album: Canadians in the Netherlands, 1944-45, 1980; (with E. McInnis) Canada, a Political and Social History, 1982; The Great Depression of the 1930s in Canada (booklet), 1984; Years of Despair, 1929-1939, 1986; Becoming Canadian: Memoirs of an Invisible Immigrant, 1997; Academic Freedom in Canada: A History, 1998. EDITOR: (and intro.) A New Endeavour: Selected Political Essays, Letters, and Addresses, 1986; Academic Freedom: The Harry Crowe Memorial Lectures, 1987; The Depression in Canada: Responses to Economic Crisis, 1988. TRANSLATOR: M. Hart, The Sundial, 2004; At the Edge of the Abyss: A Concentration Camp Diary, 1943-1944, 2012. Contributor to periodicals and journals. **Address:** Glendon College, York University, 2275 Bayview Ave., Toronto, ON M4N 3M6, Canada. **Online address:** mhorn@glendon.yorku.ca

HORN, Mike. South African/Swiss (born Switzerland), b. 1966. **Genres:** Adult Non-fiction, Autobiography/Memoirs, Travel/Exploration. **Career:** No Limits Outdoor Activity Sports Center, founder and owner, 1995. Writer and educator. **Publications:** Latitude Zero, 2001; (with J.P. Chatrier) Conquering the Impossible: My 12, 000-Mile Journey Around the Arctic Circle, 2007. **Address:** Mike Horn Expedition Centre, Pl. Centrale, Chateau d'Oex, 1660, Switzerland. **Online address:** mike.horn@bluewin.ch

HORN, Miriam. American (born United States) **Genres:** Women's Studies And Issues, Natural History, Education. **Career:** U.S. News & World Report, senior writer. **Publications:** Rebels in White Gloves: Coming of Age with Hillary's Class, Wellesley '69, 1999; (with F. Krupp) Earth, the Sequel: The Race to Reinvent Energy and Stop Global Warming, 2008. Contributor to periodicals. **Address:** U.S. News & World Report, 1050 Thomas Jefferson St. NW, Washington, DC 20007-3837, U.S.A.

HORN, Stacy. American (born United States), b. 1956. **Genres:** Sociology, History, Sciences, Autobiography/Memoirs. **Career:** Echo Communications Group, founder and director, 1989-. Writer. **Publications:** Cyberville: Clicks, Culture and the Creation of an Online Town, 1998; Waiting for My Cats to Die: A Morbid Memoir, 2001; The Restless Sleep: Inside New York City's Cold Case Squad, 2005; Unbelievable: Investigations into Ghosts, Poltergeists, Telepathy, and Other Unseen Phenomena from the Duke Parapsychology Laboratory, 2009; The Secret Life of Angels, forthcoming. **Address:** Echo Communications Group, 97 Perry St., Ste. 13, New York, NY 10014-7107, U.S.A. **Online address:** horn@echonyc.com

HORN, Tammy. American (born United States), b. 1968. **Genres:** History, Food And Wine, Women's Studies And Issues, Writing/Journalism. **Career:** University of West Alabama, faculty; Eastern Kentucky University, faculty, 2000-02, Environmental Research Institute, senior researcher; Berea College, faculty, 2002-, National Endowment for the Humanities, chair of Appalachian studies, 2006-07; writer, 2008-. **Publications:** Bees in America: How the

Honey Bee Shaped a Nation, 2005; Piping Up: A Notebook about Women and Bees, 2011; Beeconomy: What Women and Bees can Teach us About Local Trade and the Global Market, 2011. **Address:** Environmental Research Institute, Eastern Kentucky University, B-18 Moore Bldg,, 521 Lancaster Ave., Richmond, KY 40475, U.S.A. **Online address:** tammy.horn@eku.edu

HORNBY, Nick. British (born England), b. 1957. **Genres:** Novels, Literary Criticism And History, Autobiography/Memoirs, Essays, Young Adult Nonfiction, Young Adult Fiction. **Career:** New Yorker, pop music critic; English teacher; freelance journalist. Novelist. **Publications:** NOVELS: High Fidelity, 1995; About a Boy, 1998; How to Be Good, 2001; Juliet, Naked, 2009. OTHERS: Contemporary American Fiction (essays), 1992; Fever Pitch (memoir), 1992; (ed.) My Favourite Year: A Collection of New Football Writing, 1993; (ed. with N. Coleman) The Picado Book of Sportswriting, 1996; (ed.) Speaking with the Angel, 2001; Songbook, 2002; 31 Songs, 2003; A Long Way Down, 2005; Otherwise Pandemonium, 2005; Slam, 2007; An Education: The Screenplay, 2009. Contributor to periodicals. **Address:** Penguin Books Ltd., 80 Strand, London, GL WC2R 0RL, England.

HORNBY, Simonetta Agnello. British/Italian (born Italy), b. 1945?. **Genres:** Novels. **Career:** University of Leicester, Department of Law, faculty; Special Educational Needs and Disability Tribunal, part-time chairman, 1999, president. Writer and lawyer. **Publications:** La Mennulara, 2002; The Almond Picker, 2002; The Marchesa, 2007; Boccamurata, 2007; Vento scomposto, 2009; Camera oscura, 2010; La Monaca, 2010. **Address:** c/o Author Mail, Giangiacomo Feltrinelli Editore, via Andegari 6, Milan, 20121, Italy.

HORNE, Alistair (Allan). British (born England), b. 1925. **Genres:** History, Politics/Government, Social Commentary, Biography. **Career:** Cambridge Daily News, journalist, 1950-51; Daily Telegraph, staff correspondent in Germany, 1952-55; freelance writer, 1955-; Mombasa Investment Trust Ltd., director. **Publications:** Back into Power: A Report on the New Germany, 1955; Return to Power: A Report on the New Germany, 1956; The Land Is Bright: A Portrait of America, 1958; Canada and the Canadians, 1961; The Price of Glory: Verdun 1916, 1963; The Fall of Paris: The Siege and the Commune, 1870-71, 1966; Le Siège de Paris, le siège et la Commune, 1870-1871, 1967; To Lose a Battle: France 1940, 1969, rev. ed., 1990; Death of a Generation: From Neuve Chapelle to Verdun and the Somme, 1970; The Terrible Year: The Paris Commune, 1871, 1971; Small Earthquake in Chile: A Visit to Allende's South America, 1972; Small Earthquake in Chile: Allende's South America, 1973; A Savage War of Peace: Algeria, 1954-1962, 1977, rev. ed., 1987; Napoleon, Master of Europe, 1805-1807, 1979; The French Army and Politics, 1870-1970, 1984; Macmillan: The Official Biography, 2 vols., 1988-89; Harold Macmillan, 1989; Small Earthquake in Chile: New, Revised and Expanded Edition of the Classic Account of Allende's Chile, 1990; A Bundle from Britain, 1994; (with D. Montgomery) Monty: The Lonely Leader, 1944-1945, 1994; How Far from Austerlitz?: Napoleon, 1805-1815, 1997; (ed.) Telling Lives: From W.B. Yeats to Bruce Chatwin, 2001; Seven Ages of Paris, 2002; Age of Napoleon, 2004; La Belle France: A Short History, 2005; Kissinger: 1973, The Crucial Year, 2009. Contributor to books and periodicals. **Address:** Simon & Schuster, 1230 Ave. of the Americas, New York, NY 10020, U.S.A.

HORNE, Gerald. (Gerald Charles Horne). American (born United States), b. 1949. **Genres:** Cultural/Ethnic Topics, Literary Criticism And History. **Career:** University of North Carolina, Black Cultural Center, director, Department of Communication Studies, professor; University of Houston, Department of History, John and Rebecca Moores professor, John J. and Rebecca Moores chair. Lawyer and journalist. **Publications:** Black and Red: W.E.B. Du Bois and the Afro-American Response to the Cold War, 1944-1963, 1986; Thinking and Rethinking U.S. History, 1988; Communist Front?: The Civil Rights Congress, 1946-1956, 1988; Studies inBlack: Progressive Views and Reviews of the African American Experience, 1992; Reversing Discrimination: The Case for Affirmative Action, 1992; Studies in Black, 1992; Black Liberation/Red Scare: Ben Davis and the Communist Party, 1993; Race for the Planet: The U.S. and the New World Order, 1994; Fire This Time: The Watts Uprising and the 1960s, 1995; (with M. Young) Testaments of Courage: Selections from Men's Slave Narratives, 1995; Powell v. Alabama: The Scottsboro Boys and American Justice, 1997; Race Woman: The Lives of Shirley Graham Du Bois, 2000; Class Struggle in Hollywood, 1930-1950: Moguls, Mobsters, Stars, Reds, & Trade Unionists, 2001; From the Barrel ofa

Gun: The United States and the War against Zimbabwe, 1965-1980, 2001; (ed. with M. Young) W.E.B. Du Bois: An Encyclopedia, 2001; From the Barrel of a Gun, 2001; Race War: White Supremacy and the Japanese Attack on the British Empire, 2004; Black andBrown: African Americans and the Mexican Revolution, 1910-1920, 2005; Red Seas: Ferdinand Smith and Radical Black Sailors in the United States and Jamaica, 2005; Final Victim of the Blacklist: John Howard Lawson, Dean of the Hollywood Ten, 2006; Color of Fascism: Lawrence Dennis, Racial Passing, and the Rise of Right-Wing Extremism in the United States, 2006; Cold War in a Hot Zone: The United States Confronts Labor and Independence Struggles in the British West Indies, 2007; Deepest South: The United States, Brazil, and the African Slave Trade, 2007; White Pacific: U.S. Imperialism and Black Slavery in the South Seas after the Civil War, 2007; End of Empires: African Americans and India, 2008; Blows against the Empire: U.S. Imperialism in Crisis, 2008; Mau Mau in Harlem?, 2009; W.E.B. Du Bois, 2010. **Address:** Department of History, University of Houston, 546 Agnes Arnold Hall, 4800 Calhoun Rd., Houston, TX 77204-3003, U.S.A. **Online address:** ghorne@mail.uh.edu

HORNE, Gerald Charles. See **HORNE, Gerald.**

HORNE, R(alph) A(lbert). Also writes as Bulot Blaise. American (born United States), b. 1929. **Genres:** Chemistry, Environmental Sciences/Ecology, Marine Sciences/Oceanography, Antiques/Furnishings, Civil Liberties/Human Rights, Sciences, Race Relations, Autobiography/Memoirs, Autobiography/Memoirs. **Career:** University of Vermont, teaching assistant, 1950-52; Columbia University, teaching assistant, 1953; Brookhaven National Laboratory, research assistant, 1953-55, postdoctoral fellow, 1955; Massachusetts Institute of Technology, postdoctoral fellow, 1955-57; Radio Corporation of America, senior scientist, 1957-58; Joseph Kaye and Co., senior scientist, 1958-60; Arthur D. Little Inc., scientific staff, 1960-69; Woods Hole Oceanographic Institute, associate scientist, 1970-71; JBF Scientific Corp., principal scientist, 1971-72; GCA/Technology Division, senior scientist, 1978-80; Free Speech Foundation Inc., founder and president, 1980-; Energy and Environmental Engineering Inc., senior scientist, 1980-85; U.S. Environmental Protection Agency, consultant; U.S. Army Corps of Engineers, consultant. Writer. **Publications:** (Co-author) Investigation of the Transport Properties of Ion Exchange Membranes, 1968; Marine Chemistry: The Structure of Water and the Chemistry of the Hydrosphere, 1969; (ed.) Water and Aqueous Solutions: Structure, Thermodynamics and Transport Processes, 1972; The Chemistry of Our Environment, 1978. AS BULOT BLAISE: Dark Waters, 1993; Starr Lyte, 1996. Contributor of articles to journals. **Address:** Free Speech Foundation Inc., 9 Wellington St., Boston, MA 02118, U.S.A.

HORNE, Richard. British (born England), b. 1973. **Genres:** Mystery/Crime/Suspense, Illustrations. **Career:** Author, illustrator and designer. **Publications:** 101 THINGS SERIES-SELF-ILLUSTRATED: 101 Things to Do before You Die, 2005; (with H. Szirtes) 101 Things to Do before You're Old and Boring, 2006; (with T. Turner) 101 Things You Need to Know And Some You Don't!, 2006; (with T. Turner) 101 Things You Wish You'd Invented And Some You Wish No One Had, 2008. ILLUSTRATOR: Fantastic Beasts and Where to Find Them, 2001; Quidditch through the Ages, 2001; How to Survive a Robot Uprising: Tips on Defending Yourself against the Coming Rebellion, 2005; How to Build a Robot Army: Tips on Defending Planet Earth against Alien Invaders, Ninjas and Zombies, 2007; Where's My Jetpack? A Guide to the Amazing Science Fiction Future That Never Arrived, 2007. **Online address:** yourthings@101thingstodo.co.uk

HORNER, David. Australian (born Australia), b. 1948. **Genres:** Military/Defense/Arms Control, History, Politics/Government, Essays. **Career:** Australian National University, Research School of Pacific and Asian Studies, Strategic and Defence Studies Centre, professor of Australian defence history and official historian, 1990-; Australian Army's Land Warfare Studies Centre, head, 1998-2002; Joint Services College, staff; Official History of Australian Peacekeeping, Humanitarian and Post-Cold War Operations, general editor and official historian, 2004-; Australian Security Intelligence Organisation, official historian. Military analyst. **Publications:** Crisis of Command: Australian Generalship and the Japanese Threat 1941-1943, 1978; (ed. with R. O'Neil) New Directions in Strategic Thinking, 1981; (ed. with R. O'Neil) Australian Defence Policy for the 1980s, 1982; High Command: Australia and Allied Strategy 1939-1945, 1982; (ed.) Commanders: Australian Military Leadership in the Twentieth Century, 1984; Australian Higher Command in the Vietnam War, 1986; SAS, Phantoms of the Jungle: A History of the Australian Special Air Service, 1986 as SAS: Phantoms of the War: A History of the Australian Special Air Service, 1989, rev. ed., 2002; (ed.) Duty First: The Royal Australian Regiment in War and Peace, 1990; (ed.) Reshaping the Australian Army: Challenges for the 1990s, 1991; (ed. with D. Ball) Strategic Studies in a Changing World: Global Regional and Australian Perspectives, 1992; General Vaseys War, 1992; The Gulf Commitment: The Australian Defence Forces First War, 1992; (with J. Penglase) When the War Came to Australia: Memories of the Second World War, 1992; High Command: Australia's Struggle for an Independent War Strategy, 1939-1945, 1992; The Army and the Future: Land Forces in Australia and South-East Asia, 1993; (ed.) The Battles That Shaped Australia: The Australians Anniversary Essays, 1994; The Gunners: A History of Australian Artillery, 1995; Armies and Nation-Building: Past Experience Future Prospects, 1995; Inside the War Cabinet: Directing Australia's War Effort 1939-1945, 1996; (with D. Ball) Breaking the Codes: Australia's KGB Network, 1998; Blamey: The Commander-in-Chief, 1998; Defence Supremo: Sir Frederick Shedden and the Making of Australian Defence Policy, 2000; The Australian Centenary History of Defence, 2001; Making the Australian Defence Force, 2001; The Second World War, 2002; Strategic Command: General Sir John Wilton and Australia's Asian Wars, 2005; In Action with the SAS, 2009; (ed. with P. Londey and J. Bou) Australian Peacekeeping: Sixty Years in the Field, 2009; World War II. The Pacific, 2010; Australia and the New World Order, 2011. **Address:** School of International, Political & Strategic, Studies, College of Asia and the Pacific, Australian National University, Canberra, AC 0200, Australia. **Online address:** david.horner@anu.edu.au

HORNER, Jack. *See* **HORNER, John R(obert).**

HORNER, John R(obert). (Jack Horner). American (born United States), b. 1946. **Genres:** Adult Non-fiction, Children's Non-fiction, History, Animals/Pets, Sciences. **Career:** Princeton University, Museum of Natural History, research assistant, 1975-82; Montana State University, adjunct professor of paleontology, Regents professor of paleontology, Museum of the Rockies, curator of paleontology, 1982-. Writer. **Publications:** (With J. Gorman) Maia: A Dinosaur Grows Up (children's book), 1985; (with J. Gorman) Digging Dinosaurs, 1988, rev. ed., 1990; Cranial Morphology of Prosaurolophus (Ornithischia: Hadrosauridae): With Descriptions of Two New Hadrosaurid Species and an Evolution of Hadrosaurid Phylogenetic Relationships, 1992; (with D. Lessem) Digging Up Tyrannosaurus Rex (children's book), 1992; (with D. Lessem) The Complete T. Rex: How Stunning New Discoveries Are Changing Our Understanding of the World's Most Famous Dinosaur, 1993; (ed. with K. Carpenter and K.F. Hirsch) Dinosaur Eggs and Babies, 1994; (with E. Dobb) Dinosaur Lives: Unearthing an Evolutionary Saga, 1997; (as Jack Horner) Dinosaurs Under the Big Sky, 2001; (as Jack Horner) Digging Up Dinosaurs, 2007; (with J. Gorman as Jack Horner) How to Build a Dinosaur: Extinction Doesn't Have to Be Forever, 2009. Contributor to periodicals. **Address:** Museum of the Rockies, Montana State University, 600 W Kagy Blvd., Bozeman, MT 59717-3480, U.S.A. **Online address:** jhorner@montana.edu

HORNIK, Heidi J. American (born United States), b. 1962. **Genres:** Young Adult Non-fiction. **Career:** Cornell University, The Herbert F. Johnson Museum of Art, registrarial intern, 1983-84; Pennsylvania State University, Department of Art History, instructor, 1985-87, teaching assistant, 1985-88; Baylor University, Department of Art, assistant professor, 1990-98, associate professor, 1998-2004, professor of art history, 2004-, The Martin Museum of Art, director, 1990-2004. Writer. **Publications:** NONFICTION: (ed. with M.C. Parsons) Interpreting Christian Art: Reflections on Christian Art, 2003; (with M.C. Parsons) Illuminating Luke, vol. I: The Infancy Narrative of Christ in Italian Renaissance Painting, 2003, vol. II: The Public Ministry of Christ in Italian Renaissance Painting, 2005, vol. III: The Passion and Resurrection Narratives in Italian Renaissance and Baroque Painting, 2007; Michele Tosini and the Ghirlandaio Workshop in Cinquecento Florence, 2009; (with M.C. Parsons) The Acts of the Apostles Through the Centuries, 2012. **Address:** Department of Art, Baylor University, FAC151, Hooper-Schaefer Fine Arts Ctr., 1 Bear Pl., Ste. 97263, 60 Baylor Ave., Waco, TX 76798-7263, U.S.A. **Online address:** heidi_hornik@baylor.edu

HORNIMAN, Joanne. Australian (born Australia), b. 1951. **Genres:** Novels, Children's Fiction, Young Adult Fiction, Women's Studies And Issues, Biography. **Career:** New South Wales Department of Education's School Magazine, assistant editor, 1973-77; New South Wales Department of Technical and Further Education, teacher. Writer. **Publications:** The End of the World Girl, 1988; The Ghost Lasagna, 1992; Sand Monkeys, 1992; The Serpentine Belt, 1994; Furry-Back and the Lizard-Thing, 1995; Jasmine, 1995; (with

J. Kent) Bad Behaviour, 1996; Billygoat Goes Wild, 1996; Loving Athena, 1997; Sunflower!, 1999; Mahalia, 2001; A Charm of Powerful Trouble, 2002; Secret Scribbled Notebooks, 2004; Little Wing, 2006; My Candlelight Novel, 2008. Contributor to periodicals. **Address:** 602 Cawongla Rd., Via Lismore, NW 2480, Australia. **Online address:** horniman@ccinternet.com.au

HORNING, Alice S. American (born United States), b. 1950. **Genres:** Language/Linguistics, Writing/Journalism. **Career:** Michigan State University, graduate assistant in English, 1971-74; Wayne State University, instructor in English, 1974-77, assistant professor of English, 1977-82; Oakland University, assistant professor, 1982-86, associate professor of rhetoric and linguistics, 1986-94, professor of rhetoric and linguistics, 1994-2009, Rhetoric Program, director, 1998-2008, professor of writing and rhetoric/linguistics, 2009-. Writer. **Publications:** Readings in Contemporary Culture, 1978; Teaching Writing as a Second Language, 1987; The Psycholinguistics of Readable Writing: A Multidisciplinary Exploration, 1993; Revision Revisited, 2002. EDITOR: (with R.A. Sudol) Understanding Literacy: Personality Preference in Rhetorical and Psycholinguistic Contexts, 1997; (with R.A. Sudol) The Literacy Connection, 1999; (with A. Becker) Revision: History, Theory, and Practice, 2006; (with D.F. Dew) Untenured Faculty as Writing Program Administrators: Institutional Practices and Politics, 2007; (with R.A. Sudol) The Literacy Standard, forthcoming; Reading, Writing and Digitizing: Understanding Literacy in the Electronic Age, forthcoming. Works appear in anthologies. Contributor of articles to journals. **Address:** Department of Writing and Rhetoric, Oakland University, 378 O'Dowd Hall, Rochester, MI 48309, U.S.A. **Online address:** horning@oakland.edu

HORNSBY, Alton. American (born United States), b. 1940. **Genres:** History, Race Relations, Politics/Government, History. **Career:** Tuskegee Institute, instructor, 1962-65; Morehouse College, Department of History, assistant professor, 1968-71, associate professor, 1971-74, chairman, 1971-, professor of history, 1974-; Fuller E. Calloway professor of history, 1988, now professor emeritus; Journal of Negro History, editor, 1976-2001; Association of Social and Behavioral Scientists, president; Southern Conference on African American Studies, president. **Publications:** (Ed. and intro.) In The Cage: Eyewitness Accounts of the Freed Negro in Southern Society, 1877-1929, 1971; The Black Almanac, 1972, 4th ed., 1977; The Negro in Revolutionary Georgia, 1977; Chronology of African-American History: Significant Events and People from 1619 to the Present, 1991, 2nd ed., 1997; Milestones in 20th Century African-American History, 1993; Southerners, Too?: Essays on the Black South, 1733-1990, 2004; (ed.) Dictionary of Twentieth Century Black Leaders, 2005, (ed.) Companion to African American History, 2005; (with A.B. Henderson) Atlanta Urban League, 1920-2000, 2005; Biographical History of African Americans, 2005; (with A.M. Hornsby) From the Grassroots: Profiles of Contemporary African American Leaders, 2006; Zell, We Hardly Knew Ye: Senator Zell Miller and The Politics of Region, Gender, Class and Race, 2000-2005, 2007; Black Power in Dixie: A Political History of African Americans in Atlanta, 2009; African Americans in the Post-Emancipation South, 2010; (ed.) Black America, 2011. **Address:** Department of History, Morehouse College, 830 Westview Dr. SW, PO Box 20, Atlanta, GA 30314, U.S.A. **Online address:** hornsbya@aol.com

HORNSBY, Stephen J. American/British (born England), b. 1956?. **Genres:** History, Adult Non-fiction. **Career:** University of Maine, Canadian-American Center, director and professor of geography and Canadian studies. Writer. **Publications:** NONFICTION: (ed. with V.A. Konrad and J.J. Herlan) The Northeastern Borderlands: Four Centuries of Interaction, 1989; Nineteenth-Century Cape Breton: A Historical Geography, 1992; (ed. with J.G. Reid) New England and the Maritime Provinces: Connections and Comparisons, 2005; British Atlantic, American Frontier: Spaces of Power in Early Modern British America, 2005; Surveyors of Empire: Samuel Holland, J.F.W. DesBarres and the Making of the Atlantic Neptune, 2011. **Address:** Canadian-American Center, University of Maine, 154 College Ave., Orono, ME 04473, U.S.A. **Online address:** hornsby@maine.edu

HORNSBY, Wendy. American (born United States), b. 1947. **Genres:** Novels, Mystery/Crime/Suspense. **Career:** Long Beach City College, professor of history, 1975-. Writer. **Publications:** MAGGIE MACGOWEN MYSTERY SERIES: Telling Lies, 1992; Midnight Baby, 1993; Bad Intent, 1994; 77th Street Requiem, 1995; Swimming with Jonah, 1996; A Hard Light, 1997; In the Guise of Mercy, 2009; The Paramour's Daughter, 2010. KATE TEAGUE SERIES: No Harm, 1987; Half a Mind, 1990. COLLECTIONS: (with N. Barrett, Jr. and R. Laymon) Ten Tales, 1994; Nine Sons: Collected Mysteries,

2002. **Address:** c/o Deborah Schneider, Gelfman Schneider Literary Agents Inc., 250 W 57th St., Ste. 2515, New York, NY 10107-0001, U.S.A. **Online address:** wendy@wendyhornsby.com

HORNSCHEMEIER, Paul. American (born United States), b. 1977. **Genres:** Novels, Graphic Novels. **Career:** Margo Mitchell Media Group, founder; University of Chicago, faculty of creative writing. Graphic novelist. **Publications:** Stand on a Mountain, Look Back: Sequential Book Seven, 2001; Mother, Come Home, 2003; The Collected Sequential, 2004; Return of the Elephant, 2004; Let Us Be Perfectly Clear, 2006; The Three Paradoxes, 2006; Forlorn Funnies, vol. I, 2010; Life with Mr. Dangerous, 2011; A New Decade for Eli Guggenheim, forthcoming; Planet, forthcoming. **Address:** PO Box 1365, Evanston, IL 60204, U.S.A. **Online address:** paul@margomitchell.com

HORNSTEIN, Gail A. American (born United States), b. 1951?. **Genres:** Psychology, Biography, Adult Non-fiction, Psychiatry. **Career:** Mount Holyoke College, professor of psychology, 1978-. Writer. **Publications:** To Redeem One Person Is to Redeem the World: The Life of Frieda Fromm-Reichmann, 2000; Agnes's Jacket: A Psychologist's Search for the Meanings Of Madness, 2009. Contributor to books and journals. **Address:** Department of Psychology, Mount Holyoke College, 50 College St., South Hadley, MA 01075-1462, U.S.A. **Online address:** gh@gailhornstein.com

HOROVITZ, Michael. German (born Germany), b. 1935. **Genres:** Poetry, Art/Art History, Literary Criticism And History, Music, Translations, Young Adult Fiction. **Career:** Live New Departures Road Show, director, 1959-; New Departures Magazine, founder, editor and publisher, 1959-; University of Maryland Overseas Program, lecturer in English grammar and literature, 1961-64; World's Best Jam Arts Circuses, director, 1966-; Royal College of Art, tutor, 1966-69; International Poetry Olympics Festivals, director, 1980-. Critic. **Publications:** New Departures, 1959; (trans.) Europa, 1961; Alan Davie, 1963; Declaration, 1965; Strangers: Fauve Poems, 1965; Poetry for the People: A Verse Essay in Bop Prose, 1966; Bank Holiday: A New Testament for the Love Generation, 1967; The Wolverhampton Wanderer: An Epic of Football, Fate and Fun, 1970; Love Poems, 1971; Nineteen Poems of Love, Lust and Spirit, 1971; A Contemplation, 1978; Growing Up: Selected Poems and Pictures 1951-1979, 1979; (trans.) The Egghead Republic, 1979; Midsummer Morning Jog Log: A Poem, 1986; Michael Horovitz Goes Visual, 1987; Bop Paintings, Collages, Drawings and Picture Poems, 1989; Wordsounds and Sightlines: New & Selected Poems, 1994; A New Waste Land: Timeship Earth at Nillennium, 2005. EDITOR: Children of Albion: Poetry of the Underground in Britain, 1969; Poetry Olympics Anthology, 3 vols., 1980-83; A Celebration of and for Francis Horovitz (1938-1983), 1984; Grandchildren of Albion: Illustrated Anthology of Voices and Visions of Younger Poets in Britai, 1992; The POW! Anthology, 1996; The POP! Anthology, 2000; The POM! Anthology, 2001; Jeff Nuttall's Wake, 2004. Contributor to periodicals. **Address:** New Departures / Poetry Olympics, PO Box 9819, London, GL W11 2G6, England.

HOROWITZ, Daniel. American (born United States), b. 1938. **Genres:** Urban Studies, History. **Career:** Wellesley College, instructor in history, 1966-67; Harvard University, instructor, 1967-69, lecturer in history, 1969-70, Radcliffe College, Schlesinger Library, honorary visiting fellow; Skidmore College, assistant professor of history, 1970-72; Scripps College, assistant professor, 1972-78, associate professor, 1978-86, Nathaniel Wright Stephenson professor of history and biography, 1986-88; Carleton College, visiting professor, 1980; University of Michigan, visiting associate professor, 1983-84; Smith College, professor of American studies and history, 1989-, Mary Huggins Gamble professor of American studies, Sylvia Dlugasch Bauman professor of American studies, Daniel Horowitz professor, American Studies Program, director; Occidental College, Ray A. Billington visiting professor, 2010-11. Writer. **Publications:** The Morality of Spending: Attitudes toward the Consumer Society in America, 1875-1940, 1985; Vance Packard and American Social Criticism, 1994; (ed. and intro.) American Social Classes in the 1950s: Selections from Vance Packard's The Status Seekers, 1995; Betty Friedan and the Making of The Feminine Mystique: The American Left, the Cold War and Modern Feminism 1998; Anxieties of Affluence: Critiques of American Consumer Culture, 1939-1979, 2004; Jimmy Carter and the Energy Crisis of the 1970s: A Brief History with Documents, 2005. Contributor of articles to journals. **Address:** American Studies Program, Smith College, 221 Wright Hall, 7 College Ln., Northampton, MA 01063, U.S.A. **Online address:** dhorowit@smith.edu

HOROWITZ, Dave. American (born United States), b. 1973?. **Genres:** Children's Fiction, Adult Non-fiction, Illustrations. **Career:** Writer. **Publications:** (With S.P. Lewis) Selected Climbs in the Northeast: Rock, Alpine, and Ice Routes from the Gunks to Acadia, 2003. SELF ILLUSTRATED: A Monkey among Us, 2004; The Ugly Pumpkin, 2005; Soon, Baboon, Soon, 2005; Beware of Tigers, 2006; Five Little Gefiltes, 2007; Humpty Dumpty Climbs Again, 2008; Twenty-six Princesses, 2008; Duck, Duck, Moose, 2009; Buy My Hats!, 2010; Pretty, Pretty Bunny, 2011. **Address:** c/o Author Mail, G.P. Putnam's Sons Publishing Group, 375 Hudson St., New York, NY 10014, U.S.A. **Online address:** dave@horowitzdave.com

HOROWITZ, Irving Louis. American (born United States), b. 1929. **Genres:** Education, Politics/Government, Social Sciences, Sociology, Philosophy, Sciences. **Career:** College of the City of New York, graduate assistant, 1952; University of Buenos Aires, associate professor of social theory, 1956-58, visiting professor, 1959, 1961, 1963; Central University of Venezuela, visiting professor, 1957; Ford Foundation, International Education Division, consultant, 1959-60; Bard College, assistant professor of sociology, 1960; Hobart and William Smith Colleges, assistant professor of sociology and chair of department of sociology and anthropology, 1960-63; State University of New York, visiting professor, 1960; Syracuse University, visiting professor, 1961; Fulbright-Hays lecturer, 1961, 1969, 1977; University of Rochester, visiting professor, 1962; London School of Economics and Political Science, visiting lecturer, 1962; Transaction Publishers, founding president, 1962-; Washington University, associate professor, 1963-65, professor of sociology, 1965-69; Latin American Research Center, advisory staff, 1964-67, 1967-70; Oxford University Press, consulting editor, 1964-69; University of California, visiting professor, 1966; University of Wisconsin, visiting professor, 1967; Stanford University, visiting professor, 1968-69; Aldine-Atherton Publishers, consulting editor, 1969-72; Rutgers University, graduate professor of sociology, 1969, Hannah Arendt distinguished university professor emeritus of sociology and political science, 1992-; Livingston College, chair of the department of sociology, 1969-73, chair of sociology section for all campuses, 1975-85, Hannah Arendt professor of sociology and political science, 1979-, Bacardi chair Cuban studies, 1992-; University of Calgary, visiting professor, 1970; American University, visiting professor, 1972; Queen's University, visiting professor, 1973; Princeton University, visiting professor, 1976; Boston College, visiting professor, 1976; University of Mexico, visiting professor, 1978; Tokyo University, visiting professor, 1980; Hosei University, visiting professor, 1980; Transaction Publishers, Grant's-in-Publication program, founder, 1983-97, chair of the board, 1997-, editorial director; University of Miami, visiting professor, 1992; The Horowitz Foundation, founder, 1998-; International Society of Political Psychology, founder. **Publications:** Idea of War and Peace in Contemporary Philosophy, 1957, 2nd ed. as War and Peace in Contemporary Social and Philosophy Theory, 1973; Philosophy, Science and the Sociology of Knowledge, 1961; Radicalism and the Revolt against Reason, 1961; The War Game, 1963; Revolution in Brazil, 1964; Three Worlds of Development, 1966, 1972; Professing Sociology, 1968; Sociological Self-Images, 1969; The Struggle Is the Message, 1970; (with W.H. Friedland) The Knowledge Factory, 1970; Foundations of Political Sociology, 1972; Israeli Ecstasies/Jewish Agonies, 1974; (with J.E. Katz) Social Science and Public Policy in the United States, 1975; Genocide, 1976, 5th ed. as Taking Lives, 2001; Ideology and Utopia in the United States 1956-1976, 1977; (with S.M. Lipset) Dialogues on American Politics, 1978; El Comunismo Cubano 1959-1979, 1979; Beyond Empire and Revolution, 1982; C. Wright Mills: An American Utopian, 1983; Winners and Losers, 1984; Communicating Ideas, 1986; Persuasions and Prejudices, 1989; Daydreams and Nightmares, 1990; The Decomposition of Sociology, 1993; Behemoth, 1999; (intro.) Veblen's Century, 2002; Eli Ginzberg: The Economist as a Public Intellectual, 2002; Tributes: Personal Reflections on a Century of Social Research, 2004; Long Night of Dark Intent: A Half Century of Cuban Communism, 2008; Publishing as a Vocation: Studies of an Old Occupation in a New Technological Era, 2010; Hannah Arendt: Radical Conservative, 2012. TRANSLATOR: Gumplowicz, Outlines of Sociology, 1963. EDITOR: Power, Politics and People, 1963; Historia y Elementos de la Sociologia del Conocimiento, 2 vols., 1964; The New Sociology, 1964; Sociology and Pragmatism, 1964; The Rise and Fall of Project Camelot, 1967; (with J. de Castro and J. Gerassi) Latin American Radicalism, 1969; Cuban Communism, 1970, 11th ed., 2003; Masses in Latin America, 1970; The Use and Abuse of Social Science, 1971; (with M.S. Strong) Sociological Realities, 1971; The Troubled Conscience, 1971; (with C. Nanry) Sociological Realities II, 1975; Equity, Income and Policy, 1977; Science, Sin and Scholarship, 1978; Constructing

Policy, 1979; (with J.C. Leggett and M. Oppenheimer) The American Working Class, 1979; Policy Studies Review Annual, vol. V, 1981; Vested Interests, 2002; (with J. Suchliki) Cuban Communism, 2003; Civil Society and Class Politics: Essays on the Political Sociology of Seymour Martin Lipset, 2004; Anarchists, 2005; Idea of War and Peace: The Experience of Western Civilization, 2007. **Address:** Department of Sociology, State University of New Jersey, 54 Joyce Kilmer Ave., Piscataway, NJ 08854-8045, U.S.A. **Online address:** ihorowitz@transactionpub.com

HOROWITZ, Mitch. American (born United States), b. 1965. **Genres:** History. **Career:** Tarcher/Penguin, editor-in-chief. Publisher. **Publications:** Occult America: The Secret History of How Mysticism Shaped Our Nation, 2009. Contributor to periodicals. **Address:** Tarcher/Penguin, 375 Hudson St., New York, NY 10014, U.S.A. **Online address:** mitch.horowitz@us.penguingroup.com

HOROWITZ, Renee B(arbara). American (born United States), b. 1932. **Genres:** Mystery/Crime/Suspense, Novels, Young Adult Fiction. **Career:** U.S. Department of Commerce, Institute for Telecommunication Sciences, writer and editor, 1974-80; University of Colorado, visiting lecturer and instructor, 1974-80; Metropolitan State College, instructor, 1977-79; Sperry Flight Systems, editor in publications engineering, 1980-81; Allied Signal Companies, Documentation and Data Management Group, senior documentation engineer, 1981-86; Arizona State University, associate professor, 1986-91, course coordinator, 1989-, professor of information and management technology, 1991, now professor emerita. **Publications:** MYSTERY NOVELS: Rx for Murder, 1997; Deadly Rx, 1997; Rx Alibi, 2001. Contributor to books and professional journals. **Address:** College of Technology and Applied Sciences, Arizona State University, 699 S Mill Ave., Tempe, AZ 85281, U.S.A. **Online address:** renee@rxmysteries.com

HOROWITZ, Shale A. American (born United States), b. 1965. **Genres:** History, Politics/Government, Military/Defense/Arms Control. **Career:** KNBC-TV, segment producer, 1984; San Francisco Magazine, editorial staff, 1985; University of California, Center for Communication Policy, research fellow, 1994-96; Central European University, visiting assistant professor, 1996-97; University of Wisconsin, assistant professor, 1997-2003, associate professor of political science, 2003-08, professor, 2008-. Writer. **Publications:** (Ed. with U. Heo) The Political Economy of International Financial Crisis: Interest Groups, Ideologies, and Institutions, 2001; (ed. with U. Heo) Conflict in Asia: Korea, China-Taiwan, and India-Pakistan, 2003; (ed. with A. Schnabel) Human Rights and Societies in Transition: Causes, Consequences, Responses, 2004; From Ethnic Conflict to Stillborn Reform: The Former Soviet Union and Yugoslavia, 2005; (ed. with U. Heo and A.C. Tan) Identity and Change in East Asian Conflicts: The Cases of China, Taiwan, and the Koreas, 2007. CONTRIBUTOR: Resurrecting the Phoenix, 1998; Democracy in the New Europe: The Politics of Post-Communism, 1999; Ethnic Conflict and International Politics: Explaining Diffusion and Escalation, 2004; PEcs Political Studies, 2005; Defense and Security: A Guide to National Armed Forces and Security Policies of the World, 2005; Civil Wars of the World, 2005; Neo-Liberalism, 2005. Contributor to periodicals. **Address:** Department of Political Science, University of Wisconsin, Rm. 622, Bolton Hall, 2200 E Kenwood Blvd., PO Box 413, Milwaukee, WI 53201-0413, U.S.A. **Online address:** shale@uwm.edu

HORRIE, Chris(topher). British (born England), b. 1956. **Genres:** Communications/Media, Documentaries/Reportage, Business/Trade/Industry. **Career:** Sanity Magazine, editor, 1980-84; New Statesman, staff reporter, 1985-86; freelance contributor, 1985-99; National Student Magazine, relaunch editor, 1986; Sunday Correspondent Magazine, feature writer and commissioning editor, 1990; London College of Communication, director of studies in journalism and course leader, 1992-99; Business Diary, columnist, 1998-2000; The Observer, freelance feature writer, 2000-03; University of Westminster, visiting lecturer in investigative journalism, 1999-2000, Postgraduate Diploma/MA in Journalism, course director, 2000-07, senior lecturer in journalism, 2000-07, principal lecturer, 2003-07, BA (hons) in Medical Journalism, director, 2003-07; BA Journalism, programme director, 2008; MA Journalism, programme director, 2008; BBC News Online, part-time senior feature writer, 2000-03; University of Winchester, programme director, 2008. Television researcher and producer. **Publications:** (With P. Chippindale) Disaster! The Rise and Fall of News on Sunday, 1987; (with P. Chippindale) Stick It up Your Punter: The Rise and Fall of The Sun, 1990, 3rd

ed., 2005; What Is Islam?, 1990, 3rd ed., 2008; Sick As a Parrot, 1992; (with S. Clarke) Fuzzy Monsters: Fear and Loathing at the BBC, 1994; Live TV, 1999; (with S. Clarke) Citizen Greg: The Extraordinary Story of Greg Dyke and How He Captured the BBC, 2000; Premiership: Unauthorised Business History of the Premier League, 2002; Play It Again, 2007; Chapters on Investigative Journalism and the Law, 2008; (with D. Matthews) True Blue, 2009. Contributor to periodicals. **Address:** Lucas Alexander Whitley Ltd., 14 Vernon St., London, GL W14 0RJ, England. **Online address:** chris@horrie.com

HORROCKS, Dylan. New Zealander (born New Zealand), b. 1966. **Genres:** Novels, Cartoons, Graphic Novels. **Career:** Auckland University, Department of Education, part-time faculty, 1994-96, Department of history, visiting professor, 2004-; full-time comic book artist and writer, 1995-. **Publications:** Hicksville (graphic novel), 1998; Better Luck Next Century (collection of political cartoons), 2001; The Names of Magic, 2002; (intro.) No More Mrs Nice Nun: The Collected Knuckles the Malevolent Nun, 2003; Hicksville: A Comic Book, 2010. **Address:** Victoria University Press, 49 Rawhiti Tce, Kelburn, PO Box 600, Wellington, 006140, New Zealand. **Online address:** dylan@hicksville.co.nz

HORSEY, David. American (born United States), b. 1951. **Genres:** Politics/Government, Novels, Cartoons, Humor/Satire, Social Commentary, Graphic Novels. **Career:** Washington State capitol, political reporter; Daily Journal-American, political reporter, columnist, editorial cartoonist, 1976-79; Seattle Post-Intelligencer, editorial cartoonist, columnist, 1979-; Tribune Media Services, staff, 1986-89; King Features, staff, 1988-2000; Horsey-Words and Pictures, owner, 1993-; Academy of Realist Art, instructor, 1998; Los Angeles Times Syndicate, staff, 2000-. **Publications:** Politics and Other Perversions, 1974; Horsey's Rude Awakenings, 1981; Horsey's Greatest Hits of the '80s, 1989; (ed. with M. Forman) Cartooning AIDS around the World, 1992; The Fall of Man, 1994; One-Man Show, 1999; From Hanging Chad to Baghdad, 2003; Beyond the Border, forthcoming. Contributor to periodicals. **Address:** Seattle Post-Intelligencer, 101 Elliott Ave. W, Ste. 540, PO Box 19099, Seattle, WA 98119, U.S.A. **Online address:** davidhorsey@seattle-pi.com

HORSFIELD, Debbie. British (born England), b. 1955. **Genres:** Plays/Screenplays, Novels, Mystery/Crime/Suspense, Literary Criticism And History. **Career:** Gulbenkian Studio Theatre, assistant administrator, 1978-80; Royal Shakespeare Co., assistant, 1980-83; Liverpool Playhouse, writer-in-residence, 1983-84. **Publications:** The Red Devils Trilogy, 1986. **Address:** The Agency Ltd., 24 Pottery Ln., Holland Pk., London, GL W11 4LZ, England.

HORSLEY, Lee. British/American (born United States), b. 1944?. **Genres:** Theology/Religion, Literary Criticism And History, Politics/Government. **Career:** Lancaster University, reader in literature and culture and senior lecturer in English literature, 1974-; Crimeculture, co-founder, 2002; Pulp Originals, co-editor. **Publications:** (With R. Currie and A. Gilbert) Churches and Churchgoers: Patterns of Church Growth in the British Isles since 1700, 1977; Political Fiction and the Historical Imagination, 1990; Fictions of Power in English Literature, 1900-1950, 1995; The Noir Thriller, 2001, rev. ed., 2009; Twentieth-Century Crime Fiction, 2005; (ed. with C.J. Rzepka) Companion to Crime Fiction, 2010. **Address:** Department of English & Creative Writing, County College, Lancaster University, Lancaster, LC LA1 4YT, England. **Online address:** l.horsley@lancaster.ac.uk

HORSLEY, Richard A. American (born United States) **Genres:** History, Theology/Religion, Essays, Archaeology/Antiquities. **Career:** University of Massachusetts-Boston, research professor, 1996-98, distinguished professor of liberal arts and religious studies, now professor of religion emeritus. Writer. **Publications:** (With J.S. Hanson) Bandits, Prophets, and Messiahs: Popular Movements in the Time of Jesus, 1987; Jesus and the Spiral of Violence: Popular Jewish Resistance in Roman Palestine, 1987; The Liberation of Christmas: The Infancy Narratives in Social Context, 1989; Sociology and the Jesus Movement, 1989, 2nd ed., 1994; (ed. with N.K. Gottwald) Bible and Liberation: Political and Social Hermeneutics, 1993; Galilee: History, Politics, People, 1995; Archaeology, History and Society in Galilee: The Social Context of Jesus and the Rabbis, 1996; (with N.A. Silberman) The Message and the Kingdom: How Jesus and Paul Ignited a Revolution and Transformed the Ancient World, 1997; (ed.) Paul and Empire: Religion and Power in Roman Imperial Society, 1997; 1 Corinthians, 1998; (with J.A. Draper) Whoever Hears You Hears Me: Prophets, Performance, and Tradition in Q, 1999; (ed.) Paul and Politics: Ekklesia, Israel, Imperium, Interpretation: Essays in Honor of Krister Stendahl, 2000; (ed. with J. Tracy) Christmas Unwrapped: Consumerism, Celluloid, Christ, and Culture, 2001; Hearing the Whole Story: The Politics of Plot in Mark's Gospel, 2001; Jesus and Empire: The Kingdom of God and the New World Disorder, 2003; Religion and Empire: People, Power, and the Life of the Spirit, 2003; (ed.) Hidden Transcripts and the Arts of Resistance: Applying the Work of James C. Scott to Jesus and Paul, 2004; (ed.) Paul and the Roman Imperial Order, 2004; (ed.) Christian Origins, 2005; (ed. with J.A. Draper and J.M. Foley) Performing the Gospel: Orality, Memory, and Mark, 2006; (ed.) Oral Performance, Popular Tradition, and Hidden Transcript in Q, 2006; Scribes, Visionaries, and the Politics of Second Temple Judea, 2007; (ed.) In the Shadow of Empire: Reclaiming the Bible as a History of Faithful Resistance, 2008; Jesus in Context: Performance, Power and People, 2008; Covenant Economics: A Biblical Vision of Justice for All, 2009; Revolt of the Scribes: Resistance and Apocalyptic Origins, 2010; Jesus and the Powers: Conflict, Covenant and the Hope of the Poor, 2011. **Address:** Study of Religion, University of Massachusetts, 100 Morrissey Blvd., Boston, MA 02125-3393, U.S.A. **Online address:** richard.horsley@umb.edu

HORSMAN, Reginald. American/British (born England), b. 1931. **Genres:** History. **Career:** University of Wisconsin, instructor, 1958-59, assistant professor, 1959-62, associate professor, 1962-64, professor, 1964-73, distinguished professor of history, 1973-99, distinguished professor emeritus, 1999-. Writer. **Publications:** The Causes of the War of 1812, 1962; Frontier Detroit, 1760-1812, 1964; Matthew Elliott: British Indian Agent, 1964; Expansion and American Indian Policy, 1783-1812, 1967; The War of 1812, 1969; Napoleon's Europe, 1970; The Frontier in the Formative Years, 1783-1815, 1970; Origins of Indian Removal, 1815-1824, 1970; Race and Manifest Destiny: The Origins of American Racial Anglo-Saxonism, 1981; The Diplomacy of the New Republic, 1776-1815, 1985; Josiah Nott of Mobile: Southerner, Physician, and Racial Theorist, 1987; Frontier Doctor: William Beaumont, America's First Great Medical Scientist, 1996; The New Republic: The United States of America, 1789-1815, 2000; Feast or Famine: Food and Drink in American Westward Expansion, 2008. Contributor of articles to journals. **Address:** Department of History, University of Wisconsin, 342 Holton Hall, 2442 E Hartford Ave., PO Box 413, Milwaukee, WI 53211, U.S.A. **Online address:** horsman@uwm.edu

HORSPOOL, David. British (born England), b. 1971?. **Genres:** History, Young Adult Non-fiction, Young Adult Fiction, Military/Defense/Arms Control. **Career:** Times Literary Supplement, history editor; historian. **Publications:** King Alfred: Burnt Cakes and Other Legends, 2006; English Rebel: One Thousand Years of Troublemaking, from the Normans to the Nineties, 2009. **Address:** Times Literary Supplement, Times House, 1 Pennington St., London, GL E98 1BS, England.

HORTON, David (Edward). American (born United States), b. 1931. **Genres:** Young Adult Fiction, Novels, Literary Criticism And History. **Career:** Cardiff Baptist Church, pastor, 1960-64; First Baptist Church, pastor, 1964-72; American Baptists of Michigan, area director, 1972-. Minister and writer. **Publications:** A Legion of Honor: A Novel, 1995; Boys Life Adventure Bible Storybook, 1999; (ed.) The Portable Seminary, 2006. Contributor to periodicals. **Address:** c/o Cygnet Publishing Group, 4821 54th St., Red Deer, AB T4N 2G5, Canada.

HORTON, David M. American (born United States), b. 1949. **Genres:** Criminology/True Crime, Bibliography, Law. **Career:** St. Edward's University, Criminology, Criminal Justice and Forensic Science, professor, chair, Criminal Justice Program, director. Writer. **Publications:** (Comp. with S.S. LaPerla) Criminal Justice Periodicals, 1979; (comp. with M. Kravitz) Female Offender, 1979; (comp. with C. Klein) Bibliographies in Criminal Justice, 1980; (with K. Turner) Lone Star Justice: A Comprehensive Overview of the Texas Criminal Justice System, 1999; Pioneering Perspectives in Criminology: The Literature of 19th Century Criminological Positivism, 2000; (with G.R. Nielsen) Walking George: The Life of George John Beto and the Rise of the Modern Texas Prison System, 2005; (ed. and intro.) Pioneers in Penology: The Reformers, the Institutions, and the Societies, 1557-1900, 2006; (ed. and intro. with C.L. Parish and M.Y. Richter) Pioneering Research in Forensic Science, 2009. **Address:** School of Behavioral and Social Sciences, St. Edward's University, DOYX 248, 3001 S Congress Ave., Austin, TX 78704, U.S.A. **Online address:** davidh@stedwards.edu

HORTON, Frank E. American (born United States), b. 1939. **Genres:** Transportation, Urban Studies, Geography. **Career:** Lake Forest College, instructor in geography, 1964-65; University of Iowa, department of geography assistant professor, 1966-68, department of geography associate professor, 1968-70, Institute of Urban and Regional Research, director, 1968-72, professor of geography, 1970-75, dean for advanced studies, 1972-75; Carnegie-Mellon University, Urban Transportation Program, lecturer, 1970-; Southern Illinois University, professor of geography and vice-president for academic affairs and research, 1975-80, senior consultant, 2000-01, interim president, 2000; University of Wisconsin-Milwaukee, chancellor and professor of geography and urban affairs, 1980-85; University of Oklahoma, president and professor of geography, 1985-88, president emeritus, 1989-; University of Toledo, president, 1989-98, professor of geography and higher education, 1989-2000, emeritus professor and president emeritus, 1999-; Horton & Associates, principal, 1999-. Writer. **Publications:** Non-Residential Trip Generation Analysis, 1965; A Study of Forces Affecting School Organization in Forest Park, Illinois Public Schools, 1965; Further Comments on Non-Residential Trip Generation Analysis, 1966; An Introduction to Urban Geography, 1967; The Geography of Manufacturing and Commerce, 1968; (with W.E. Wagner) Markovian Analysis of Urban Travel Behavior: Pattern Response by Socio-Economic-Occupational Groups, 1968; Remote Sensors as Data Sources for Urban Research and Planning: Final Report, 1971; Quantitative Geography: Achievements and Prospects, 1971; The Application of Remote Sensing Techniques to Intraand Inter-Urban Analysis: Final Report, 1972; Geographical Perspectives on Contemporary Urban Problems, 1973; (with B.L. Berry) Urban Environmental Management: Planning for Pollution Control: An Original Text with Integrated Readings, 1974. EDITOR: Geographic Studies of Urban Transportation and Network Analysis, 1968; Geographic Research in Urban Transportation and Network Analysis, 1968; (with B.J.L. Berry) Geographical Perspectives on Urban Systems with Integrated Readings, 1970; Geographical Perspectives and Urban Problems, 1973. Contributor of articles to journals. **Address:** 288 River Ranch Cir., Bayfield, CO 81122, U.S.A.

HORTON, J(ames) Wright. American (born United States), b. 1950. **Genres:** Earth Sciences. **Career:** University of Southern Maine, assistant professor of geology, 1977-78; U.S. Geological Survey, National Research Council, postdoctoral associate, 1978-80, research geologist, 1980-. Writer. **Publications:** (Co-ed.) Geological Investigations of the Kings Mountain Belt and Adjacent Areas in the Carolinas, 1981; (ed. with N. Rast) Mélanges and Olistostromes of the U.S. Appalachians, 1989; (ed. with V.A. Zulla) The Geology of the Carolinas: Carolina Geological Society Fiftieth Anniversary Volume, 1991; (ed. with E.T. Cleaves) Forum on Geologic Mapping Applications In The Washington-Baltimore Urban Area: Proceedings, Reston, Virginia, April 23, 1997, 1997; (ed. with D.S. Powars and G.S. Gohn) Studies of the Chesapeake Bay Impact Structure: The USGS-NASA Langley Core Hole, Hampton, Virginia, and Related Core Holes and Geophysical Surveys, 2005. Contributor to journals. **Address:** U.S. Geological Survey, 12201 Sunrise Valley Dr., PO Box 926A, Reston, VA 20192-0002, U.S.A. **Online address:** whorton@usgs.gov

HORTON, Madelyn (Stacey). American (born United States), b. 1962. **Genres:** Air/Space Topics, Children's Non-fiction, Documentaries/Reportage, Biography, Autobiography/Memoirs, History. **Career:** University of Louisville, writing instructor, 1984-87. Children's book writer. **Publications:** The Lockerbie Airline Crash, 1991; The Importance of Mother Jones, 1996. **Address:** 3331 Vivienda Cir., Carlsbad, CA 92009, U.S.A.

HORTON, Michael Scott. American (born United States), b. 1964. **Genres:** Adult Non-fiction, Theology/Religion. **Career:** St. Luke's Episcopal Church, curator, 1988, rector, 1988-; Ordained Reformed Episcopal minister, 1998; Christians United for Reformation Inc., founder, president, through 1994; Westminster Seminary California, associate professor of apologetics and historical theology, J. Gresham Machen professor of systematic theology and apologetics; Modern Reformation Magazine, publisher, editor-in-chief; United Reformed Churches of North America, ordained minister; White Horse Inn, president. Writer. **Publications:** Mission Accomplished, 1986; Agony of Deceit, 1990; Made in America: The Shaping of Modern American Evangelicalism, 1991; Putting Amazing Back Into Grace: An Introduction to Reformed Theology, 1991, 2nd ed. as Putting Amazing Back Into Grace: Embracing the Heart of the Gospel, 2002, rev. ed., 2011; The Power Trip, 1992; Christ the Lord, 1992; The Law of Perfect Freedom, 1993; Beyond Culture Wars, 1994; Where in the World Is the Church?: A Christian View of Culture and Your Role in It, 1995; In the Face of God, 1996; We Believe: Recovering the Essentials of the Apostles Creed, 1998; Evangelicals, Catholics and Unity, 1999; A

Better Way: Rediscovering the Drama of God-Centered Worship, 2002; (contrib.) Four Views on Eternal Security, 2002; Covenant and Eschatology: The Divine Drama, 2002; Lord and Servant: A Covenant Christology, 2005; Too Good to Be True: Finding Hope in a World of Hype, 2006; God of Promise: Introducing Covenant Theology, 2006; Covenant and Salvation: Union With Christ, 2007; Christless Christianity: The Alternative Gospel of the American Church, 2008; People and Place: A Covenant Ecclesiology, 2008; Gospel-driven Life: Being Good News People in a Bad News World, 2009; Christian Faith: A Systematic Theology for Pilgrims on the Way, 2011; For Calvinism, 2011; The Gospel Commission: Recovering God's Strategy for Making Disciples, 2011. EDITOR: Agony of Deceit, 1990; Power Religion: The Selling Out of the Evangelical Church?, 1992; Christ the Lord: The Reformation and Lordship Salvation, 1993; A Confessing Theology for Post-Modern Times, 2000; (with R. Lints and M.R. Talbot) Personal Identity in Theological Perspective, 2006. **Address:** Westminster Seminary California, 1725 Bear Valley Pkwy., Escondido, CA 92027, U.S.A. **Online address:** horton@wscal.edu

HORVATH, Betty. American (born United States), b. 1927. **Genres:** Children's Fiction, Human Relations/Parenting, Young Adult Fiction, Children's Non-fiction. **Career:** KWOS Radio Station, continuity writer, 1946-48; KCRC, continuity writer, 1948-49; WIL Radio Station, continuity writer, 1949-50; Palan Advertising Co., continuity writer, 1950-52; Camp Nebagam-on for Boys, secretary, 1952-54. **Publications:** Hooray for Jasper, 1966; Jasper Makes Music, 1967; Will The Real Tommy Wilson Please Stand Up, 1969; The Cheerful Quiet, 1969; Be Nice to Josephine, 1970; Not Enough Indians, 1971; Small Paul and The Bully of Morgan Court, 1971; Jasper and The Hero Business, 1977; Sir Galahad, Mr. Longfellow and Me, 1998. **Address:** 2340 Waite Ave., Kalamazoo, MI 49008, U.S.A. **Online address:** gmabbh@chartermi.net

HORVÁTH, John. American (born United States), b. 1948. **Genres:** Poetry, Literary Criticism And History. **Career:** Tougaloo College, professor of literature and criticism, Department of English, chair, 1992-97; PoetryRepairShop, editor, 1997-; Amateur Poetry Journal, editor, 1999-2000. **Publications:** Cain' Country: A Volume of Oral Poetry, 1977; Illiana Region Poems: Harboring the Enemy, 2000; Conus: The First Tour (chapbook), 2001; Twelve Greatest Poems of John Horváth, 2002. Contributor to periodicals. **Address:** Bookstand Publishing, 305 Vineyard Town Ctr., Ste. 302, Morgan Hill, CA 95037, U.S.A. **Online address:** john@horvath.ws

HORWITZ, Gordon J. American (born United States), b. 1953. **Genres:** History. **Career:** Illinois Wesleyan University, associate professor of history. Writer and historian. **Publications:** In the Shadow of Death: Living Outside the Gates of Mauthausen, 1990; Ghettostadt: Łódz and the Making of a Nazi City, 2008. **Address:** Department of History, Illinois Wesleyan University, CLA 247, 1312 Park St., PO Box 2900, Bloomington, IL 61701, U.S.A. **Online address:** ghorwitz@iwu.edu

HORWITZ, Tony. American (born United States), b. 1958. **Genres:** Travel/Exploration, Young Adult Non-fiction, History, Biography. **Career:** News-Sentinel, reporter, 1983-84; Sydney Morning Herald, reporter, 1985-87; Wall Street Journal, reporter, 1989; The New Yorker, staff writer; Harvard University, Radcliffe Institute for Advanced Study, fellow. **Publications:** One for the Road: Hitchhiking Through the Australian Outback, 1988; Baghdad Without a Map and Other Misadventures in Arabia, 1991; Confederates in the Attic: Dispatches from the Unfinished Civil War, 1998; Blue Latitudes: Boldly Going Where Captain Cook Has Gone Before, 2002; Into the Blue: Boldly Going Where Captain Cook has Gone Before, 2002; (ed.) Devil May Care: Fifty Intrepid Americans and Their Quest for the Unknown, 2003; A Voyage Long and Strange: Rediscovering the New World, 2008; Midnight Rising: John Brown and the Raid that Sparked the Civil War, 2011. **Address:** Wall Street Journal, 1211 Ave. of the Americas, New York, NY 10036, U.S.A. **Online address:** tony@tonyhorwitz.com

HORWOOD, William. British (born England), b. 1944. **Genres:** Novels, Autobiography/Memoirs, Young Adult Non-fiction. **Career:** London Preparatory School, teacher, 1966-68; Campaign, London, news reporter and feature writer, 1968-69; Financial Times, Guardian, Marketing and Reader's Digest, management, marketing and business freelance journalist, 1970-71; Daily Mail, feature editor, 1972-77; Steppenmole Enterprises Ltd., managing director. Writer. **Publications:** NOVELS: (with J. Horwood) Superhealth: A Challenge for All the Family, 1979; The Stonor Eagles, 1982; Lands of Never,

1982; Callanish, 1984; Skallagrigg, 1987; The Boy with No Shoes (memoir), 2004; (with H. Rappaport) Dark Hearts of Chicago, 2007; (with H. Rappaport) The Coburg Conspiracy, 2008; Spring, 2009; Summer, 2011. BOOK OF SILENCE SERIES: Duncton Wood, 1980; Duncton Quest, 1988; Duncton Found, 1989; The Book of Silence, 1990; Duncton Tales, 1991; Duncton Rising, 1992; Duncton Stone, 1993. WIND IN THE WILLOWS SERIES: The Willows in Winter, 1994; Toad Triumphant, 1996; The Willows and Beyond, 1998; The Willows at Christmas, 2001. WILLOWS IN WINTER SERIES: Mole Gets Lost, 1997; Flying into Danger, 1997; Toad in Trouble, 1997. WOLVES OF TIME SERIES: Journeys to the Heartland, 1995; Seekers at the Wulfrock, 1997. OTHERS: Awakening, 2011. **Address:** c/o Author Mail, Headline Book Publishing, 338 Euston Rd., London, GL NW1 3BH, England. **Online address:** william@williamhorwood.co.uk

HOSKYNS, Tam. British (born England), b. 1961. **Genres:** Mystery/Crime/Suspense, Psychology, Young Adult Fiction. **Career:** Actress and writer. **Publications:** CRIME NOVELS: The Talking Cure, 1997; Peculiar Things, 1998. **Address:** c/o Gill Coleridge, Rogers Coleridge & White, 20 Powis Mews, London, GL W11 1JN, England.

HOSOZAWA-NAGANO, Elaine. American (born United States), b. 1954?. **Genres:** Children's Fiction, Literary Criticism And History. **Career:** Writer. **Publications:** Chopsticks from America, 1995. **Address:** c/o Polychrome Publishing Corp., 4509 N Francisco Ave., Chicago, IL 60625-3808, U.S.A.

HOSSACK, Joei Carlton. American/Canadian (born Canada), b. 1944. **Genres:** Travel/Exploration. **Career:** Kraft Foods, office worker and sales representative, 1974-80; Joei's Place (wool and craft store), owner, 1980-89. Writer. **Publications:** Restless from the Start (travel essays), 1997; Everyone's Dream Everyone's Nightmare, 1998; Kiss This Florida, I'm Outta Here, 2000; A Million Miles from Home, 2001; Alaska Bound and Gagged, 2002; Free Spirit: Born to Wander, 2004; Chasing the Lost Dream, 2006; How I Lost 3 Pounds in 30 years of Dieting Without Going Hungry, 2009, Down on the Farm, 2010; Morocco Without a Pit to Hiss In 2010. Contributor to magazines. **Address:** c/o Skeena Press, 13860 70th Ave., Ste. 404, Surrey, BC V3W 0S1, Canada. **Online address:** joeicarlton@hotmail.com

HOSSEINI, Khaled. American/Afghani (born Afghanistan), b. 1965. **Genres:** Young Adult Fiction, Novels. **Career:** The Permanente Medical Group, practicing internist, 1996-2004; physician in internal medicine, 1999-; writer, 2003-; The Khaled Hosseini Foundation, founder, 2007-; United Nations High Commissioner for Refugees, goodwill envoy. Writer. **Publications:** The Kite Runner, 2003; A Thousand Splendid Suns, 2007. **Address:** Elaine Koster Literary Agency L.L.C., 55 Central Pk. W, New York, NY 10023-6003, U.S.A. **Online address:** khaled@khaledhosseini.com

HOSTETTER, Joyce Moyer. American (born United States), b. 1952. **Genres:** Theology/Religion, History, Science Fiction/Fantasy. **Career:** Writer and preschool program director. **Publications:** (with J. Egli) Life to Share: Leader's Guide: Discovering a Biblical Vision for Evangelism, 1991; Best Friends Forever, 1995; Blue, 2006; Healing Water: A Hawaiian Story, 2008; Comfort, 2009. **Address:** NC , U.S.A. **Online address:** moyergirl@twave.net

HOSTROP, Richard W. American (born United States), b. 1925. **Genres:** Education, Librarianship, Travel/Exploration. **Career:** Elementary school teacher, 1950-53, principal, 1953-54; U.S. Department of Defense, high school principal and superintendent, 1954-65; College of the Desert, registrar and teacher of history and psychology, 1965-67; Prairie State College, president, 1967-70; Linnet Books, president, 1970-72; ETC Publications, president, 1972-. Writer. **Publications:** Teaching and the Community College Library, 1968; Orientation to the Two-Year College, 1970; Handbook for Achieving Academic Success, 1970; Learning Inside the Library Media Center, 1972; Managing Education for Results, 1973, 2nd ed., 1975; Education Inside the Library-Media Center, 1973; Watergate: The Waterloo of a President, 1975; United States History Simulations, 1787-1868, 1988; United States History Simulations, 1925-1964, 1990; Scopes Trial: Dropping the Atomic Bomb on Japan: United States Versus Alger Hiss: Mississippi-Summer 1964, 1990; Prairie State-The Civil Rights of Administrators, 1995; Profiles in Courage: Simulations: Based on President John F. Kennedy's Pulitzer Prize Book, 1995; (with L.S. Hostrop) Australia and New Zealand by Campervan and/or Car-with Stopovers in the Cook Islands, Fiji, Hawaii and Tahiti, 1998; (with L.S. Hostrop) Eclectic Guide to Europe for the Serendipitous Traveler, 2002. EDITOR/CO-EDITOR: (with J.A. Mecklenburger and J.A. Wilson) Learning C.O.D.-Can the Schools Buy Success?, 1972; (with J.A. Mecklenburger) Education Vouchers: From Theory to Alum Rock, 1972; Foundations of Futurology in Education, 1973; (with J.A. Mecklenburger and J.A. Wilson) Accountability for Educational Results, 1973; Education... Beyond Tomorrow, 1975; Outstanding Public and Private Elementary Schools in the United States, 1989; The Effective School Administrator, 1990. **Address:** ETC Publications, 1456 Rodeo Rd., Palm Springs, CA 92262, U.S.A.

HOTCHNER, A(aron) E(dward). American (born United States), b. 1920. **Genres:** Novels, Plays/Screenplays, Biography, Adult Non-fiction. **Career:** Cosmopolitan Magazine, articles editor, 1948-50; Newman's Own Inc., executive vice president and treasurer; Hole in the Wall Gang Fund, founding director; freelance writer, 1950-. **Publications:** NOVELS: The Dangerous America, 1958; Treasure, 1970; The Man Who Lived at the Ritz, 1981; Louisiana Purchase, 1996. NONFICTION: Papa Hemingway: A Personal Memoir, 1966 as Papa Hemingway: The Ecstasy and Sorrow, 1983; King of the Hill (memoir), 1972; Looking for Miracles, 1975; Doris Day: Her Own Story, 1976; Sophia, Living and Loving: Her Own Story, 1979; Choice People: The Greats, Near-Greats and Ingrates I Have Known, 1984; (comp. with N. Newman and U. Hotchner) Newman's Own Cookbook, 1985; Hemingway and His World, 1989; Blown Away: The Rolling Stones and the Death of the Sixties, 1990; (with P. Newman) The Hole in the Wall Gang Cookbook: Kid-friendly Recipes for Families to Make Together, 1998; After the Storm, 2001; The Day I Fired Alan Ladd and Other World War II Adventures, 2002; (with P. Newman) Shameless Exploitation in Pursuit of the Common Good, 2003; Everyone Comes to Elaine's: Forty Years of Neighborhood Regulars, Movie Stars, All-Stars, Literary Lions, Financial Scions, Top Cops, Politicians and Power Brokers at the Legendary Hot Spot, 2004; Boyhood Memoirs of A.E. Hotchner, 2007; (ed.) Good Life According to Hemingway, 2008; Paul and Me: Fifty-three Years of Adventures and Misadventures with My Pal Paul Newman, 2010. PLAYS: The White House, 1964. OTHERS: (ed.) Dear Paul Newman, 2002; (intro.) Dear Papa, Dear Hotch, 2005. **Address:** c/o Owen Laster, William Morris Agency, 1325 Ave. of the Americas, New York, NY 10019, U.S.A.

HOUCK, Davis W. American (born United States), b. 1966. **Genres:** Economics. **Career:** Florida Atlantic University, Schmidt College of Arts and Letter, assistant professor of communications, 1996-99; Florida State University, College of Communication, assistant professor, 2000-04, associate professor, 2004-. Writer. **Publications:** (With A. Kiewe) A Shining City on a Hill: Ronald Reagan's Economic Rhetoric, 1951-1989, 1991. (ed. with A. Kiewe) Actor, Ideologue, Politician: The Public Speeches of Ronald Reagan, 1993; Rhetoric as Currency: Hoover, Roosevelt, and the Great Depression, 2001; FDR and Fear Itself: The First Inaugural Address, 2002. (with A. Kiewe) FDR's Body Politics: The Rhetoric of Disability, 2003. (ed. with D.E. Dixon) Rhetoric, Religion, and the Civil Rights Movement, 1954-1965, 2006; (with M.A. Grindy) Emmett Till and the Mississippi Press, 2008; (ed. with D.E. Dixon) Women and the Civil Rights Movement, 1954-1965, 2009; The Speeches of Fannie Lou Hamer: To Tell It like It Is, 2011. Contributor to journals and periodicals. **Address:** School of Communication, Florida State University, Bldg. C, 3121 University Ctr., Tallahassee, FL 32306-2664, U.S.A. **Online address:** dhouck@fsu.edu

HOUCK, Judith A. American (born United States), b. 1963. **Genres:** Trivia/Facts, Sciences, Medicine/Health, Women's Studies And Issues. **Career:** University of Georgia, Department of History, visiting assistant professor, 1999-2000; University of Wisconsin, assistant professor, 2002-08, associate professor, 2008-. Writer and physician. **Publications:** (Contrib.) Controversies in Science & Technology: From Maize to Menopause, 2005; Hot and Bothered: Women, Medicine, and Menopause in Modern America, 2006. Contributor to journals and periodicals. **Address:** Department of Medical History and Bioethics, University of Wisconsin-Madison, 1419 Medical Science Ctr., 1300 University Ave., Madison, WI 53706-1532, U.S.A. **Online address:** jahouck@wisc.edu

HOUGH, Michael. Canadian/French (born France), b. 1928. **Genres:** Regional/Urban Planning, Adult Non-fiction. **Career:** Basil Spence and Partners, assistant architect, 1955-56; landscape architect, 1958-62; University of Toronto, Planning Office, architect, 1962-70, associate professor of landscape architecture, 1963-; Hough, Stansbury and Associates Ltd., principal and director of design, 1964-79; York University, professor of environment studies, 1970-, now FES professor emeritus; Hough, Stansbury and Michalski Ltd.,

partner, 1979-83; Hough, Stansbury Woodland Ltd., founder and partner, 1984-91; ENVision The Hough Group Ltd., founder, partner, 1992-. Writer. **Publications:** City Form and Natural Process: Towards a New Urban Vernacular, 1984, (with S. Barrett) People and City Landscapes, 1987; Out of Place: Restoring Identity to the Regional Landscape, 1990; Cities and Natural Process: A Basis for Sustainability, 1995, 2nd ed., 2004; Anxiety about Crime: Findings from the 1994 British Crime Survey, 1995; (with B.Benson and J. Evenson) Greening the Toronto Port Lands, 1997; (with H. Warburton and P.J. Turnbull) Occasional and Controlled Heroin Use: Not a Problem?, 2005. **Address:** ENVision The Hough Group, 916 The East Mall, Ste. B, Toronto, ON M9B 6K1, Canada. **Online address:** mh@yorku.ca

HOUGH, Peter A. British (born England), b. 1954. **Genres:** Paranormal, Novellas/Short Stories, Science Fiction/Fantasy, Mystery/Crime/Suspense. **Career:** Manchester Unidentified Flying Objects Research Association (MUFORA), chair; Northern Anomalies Research Organisation, investigator. Writer. **Publications:** Witchcraft: A Strange Conflict, 1991; Supernatural Britain, 1995; One in a Million, 1996; (with M. Kalman) The Truth About Alien Abductions, 1997. WITH J. RANDLES: Death by Supernatural Causes?, 1988; Scary Stories, 1991; Looking for the Aliens: A Psychological, Imaginative, and Scientific Investigation, 1991; Spontaneous Human Combustion, 1992; Mysteries of the Mersey Valley, 1993; The Afterlife: An Investigation into the Mysteries of Life after Death, 1993; The Complete Book of UFOs: An Investigation into Alien Contacts & Encounters, 1994; World's Best True UFO Stories, 1994; Strange But True?, 1994; The Encyclopedia of the Unexplained, 1995; Life after Death and The World Beyond: Investigating Heaven and the Spiritual Dimension, 1998; Psychic Detectives: The Mysterious Use of Paranormal Phenomena in Solving True Crimes, 2001. **Address:** 6 Silsden Ave., Lowton, Warrington, CH WA3 1EN, England. **Online address:** peter.hough@tesco.net

HOUGHTON, David Patrick. American (born United States) **Genres:** Politics/Government, International Relations/Current Affairs. **Career:** University of Pittsburgh, teaching assistant, 1990-92, teaching fellow, 1992-96; University of Essex, lecturer in international relations, 1996-2003, M.A. Program in American Government and Politics, joint director, 1997-2001, B.A. Program in Politics and International Relations, director, 1999-2001, M.A. in International Relations Program, director, 2000-03; University of Central Florida, assistant professor, 2003-08, associate professor of political science, 2008-, professor of political science, honors-in-the-major coordinator, 2006-. Political scientist and writer. **Publications:** U.S. Foreign Policy and the Iran Hostage Crisis, 2001; (with D. McKay and A. Wroe) Controversies in American Politics and Society, 2002; (contrib.) Encyclopaedia of Global Perspectives on the United States: Issues and Ideas Shaping International Relations, vol. III, 2007; Political Psychology: Situations, Individuals and Cases, 2009; The Decision Point: Six Case Studies in U.S. Foreign Policy Decision-Making, 2012. Contributor to periodicals. **Address:** Department of Political Science, University of Central Florida, Colbourn Hall 407D, 4000 Central Florida Blvd., Orlando, FL 32816-1356, U.S.A. **Online address:** david.houghton@ucf.edu

HOUGHTON, Eric. (Hugo Rice). British (born England), b. 1930. **Genres:** Children's Fiction, Sports/Fitness. **Career:** Teacher, 1952-85; Hastings International Chess Congress, honorary secretary, 1975-76; writer, 1985-. **Publications:** The White Wall, 1961; They Marched with Spartacus, 1963; Summer Silver, 1963; Mystery of the Old Field, 1964; The Boy beyond the Mist, 1966; The Mouse and the Magician, 1970; A Giant Can Do Anything, 1975; (as Hugo Rice) The Remarkable Feat of King Caboodle, 1978; Steps Out of Time, 1979; Time-Piece, 1981; Gates of Glass, 1987; Walter's Magic Wand, 1990; The Backwards Watch, 1992; The Magic Cheese, 1991; Vincent the Invisible, 1993; Rosie and the Robbers, 1996; The Crooked Apple Tree, 2000. Contributor to periodicals. **Address:** 42 Collier Rd., Hastings, WS TN34 3JR, England.

HOUGHTON, Gordon. British (born England), b. 1965?. **Genres:** Novels, Human Relations/Parenting, Children's Fiction, Young Adult Fiction. **Career:** Zzap!64 Magazine, editor. **Publications:** The Dinner Party, 1998; The Apprentice, 1999 in US as Damned If You Do, 2000. **Address:** St. Martin's Press, 175 5th Ave., New York, NY 10010, U.S.A. **Online address:** gordon@the-burrow.freeserve.co.uk

HOUGHTON, John T(heodore). British/Welsh (born Wales), b. 1931. **Genres:** Meteorology/Atmospheric Sciences, Theology/Religion. **Career:** Royal Aircraft Establishment, research fellow, 1954-57; Oxford University, lecturer in physics, 1958-63, reader, 1963-73, professor of atmospheric physics, 1976-83, Jesus College, fellow, 1960-83, honorary fellow, 1983; Science and Technology Facilities Council, Rutherford Appleton Laboratory, deputy director, 1981-83, honorary scientist, 1992; Meteorological Office, director-general, 1983-91, chief executive, 1990-91, Hadley Centre for Climate Prediction and Research, honorary scientist, World Meteorological Organization, vice president, 1987-91; Scientific Assessment Working Group, Intergovernmental Panel on Climate Change, chair, 1988-2002; UK Royal Commission on Environmental Pollution, chairman, 1992-98; University of Gloucestershire, John Ray Initiative, president, chairman and director, Intergovernmental Panel on Climate Change, chairman, 1988-2002; International Society for Science and Religion, founding member; Victoria Institute, president. Writer and physicist. **Publications:** (With S.D. Smith) Infra-red Physics, 1966; The Physics of Atmospheres, 1977, 3rd ed., 2002; (with F.W. Taylor and C.D. Rodgers) Remote Sounding of Atmospheres, 1984; Does God Play Dice?: A Look at the Story of the Universe, 1988; Global Warming: The Complete Briefing, 1994, 4th ed., 2009; The Search for God: Can Science Help, 1995. EDITOR: (with A.H. Cook and H. Charnock) The Study of the Ocean and the Land Surface from Satellites, 1983; The Global Climate, 1984; (with G.J. Jenkins and J.J. Ephraums) Climate Change: The IPCC Scientific Assessment, 1990; (with B.A. Callander and S.K. Varney) Climate Change 1992: The Supplementary Report to the IPCC Scientific Assessment, 1992; (co-ed.) Climate Change, 1994: Radiative Forcing of Climate Change and an Evaluation of the IPCC IS92 Emission Scenarios, 1995; (co-ed.) Climate Change 1995: The Science of Climate Change, 1996; (co-ed.) Climate Change 2001: The Scientific Basis, 2001. **Address:** John Ray Initiative, University of Gloucestershire, PH201, Francis Close Hall, Cheltenham, GC GL50 4AZ, England. **Online address:** john.houghton@jri.org.uk

HOUGHTON, Katharine. (Katharine Houghton Grant). American (born United States), b. 1945. **Genres:** Plays/Screenplays, Songs/Lyrics And Libretti, Autobiography/Memoirs, Biography, Novels. **Career:** Screen and television, actress on stage, 1965-. Writer. **Publications:** The Prodigal Daughter, 1973; (with J.B. Grant) Two Beastly Tales, 1975; MHG: A Biography, 1989; My Grandmother's House Near the River and the Three Katharines as Katharine Time 3, 1999; The Secret Life of Louisa May Alcott, 2002. **Address:** c/o Grada Fischer, Fischer Ross Group Inc., 249 E 48th St., New York, NY 10017, U.S.A.

HOUK, Randy. (Joey Elliott). American (born United States), b. 1944. **Genres:** Children's Fiction, Animals/Pets. **Career:** Soundworks, president; National Public Radio, director of publishing; Soundprints, founder, president and chief executive officer; Benefactory Inc., president, founder and chief executive officer. Writer and illustrator. **Publications:** CHILDREN'S BOOKS: Ruffle, Coo, and Hoo Doo, 1993; Bentley and Blueberry, 1993; Jasmine, 1993; Hope, 1995; Wolves in Yellowstone, 1995; Chessie, the Travelin' Man, 1997; Rico's Hawk: A Green Chimneys Tale, 1998. CHILDREN'S BOOKS AS JOEY ELLIOTT: Beezle's Bravery, 1989; Scout's New Home, 1989. **Address:** The Benefactory Inc., PO Box 213, Pembroke, MA 02359, U.S.A. **Online address:** randyhouk@aol.com

HOULBROOKE, Ralph (A.). British (born England), b. 1944. **Genres:** History, Theology/Religion. **Career:** University of Reading, lecturer, 1971-88, reader, 1988-, professor, Early Modern Research Centre, director, undergraduate dissertation tutor. Writer. **Publications:** Church Courts and the People during the English Reformation, 1520-1570, 1979; The English Family, 1450-1700, 1984; (ed.) English Family Life, 1576-1716, 1988; (ed. with G. Parfitt) Courtship Narrative of Leonard Wheatcroft, Derbyshire Yeoman, 1986; (ed.) Death, Ritual and Bereavement, 1989; Death, Religion, and the Family in England, 1480-1750, 1998; Magic and Witchcraft in the Diocese of Winchester, 1491-1570, 2004; (ed.) James VI and I: Ideas, Authority and Government, 2006. **Address:** Department of History, University of Reading, Rm. 132, Whiteknights Campus, PO Box 217, Reading, BR RG6 6AH, England. **Online address:** r.a.houlbrooke@reading.ac.uk

HOUSE, James S. American (born United States), b. 1944. **Genres:** Gerontology/Senior Issues, Medicine/Health, Sociology. **Career:** University of Michigan, Detroit Area Study, assistant, 1967-68, associate professor of sociology, 1978-82, professor of sociology, 1982-2005, Department of Sociology, associate chair, 1981-84, chairperson, 1986-90, Department of Epidemiology, research scientist, 1982-2005, Institute for Social Research, Survey Research Center, Department of Epidemiology, associate research scientist, 1978-82, senior research scientist, research professor, 1982-2005, director, 1991-2001,

Population Studies Center, research professor, 2000-, Angus Campbell Collegiate professor of sociology and survey research and research professor, 2005-08, Angus Campbell distinguished university professor of survey research, public policy and sociology and Department of Epidemiology, research professor, 2008-; Duke University, instructor, associate professor of sociology, 1970-78, director of undergraduate studies, 1973-76; University of North Carolina, School of Public Health, Department of Epidemiology, adjunct assistant professor, adjunct associate professor, 1975-78; Institute of Gerontology, associate professor. Writer. **Publications:** Occupational Stress and The Mental and Physical Health of Factory Workers, 1980; Work Stress and Social Support, 1981. EDITOR: (with K.W. Schaie and D. Blazer) Aging, Health Behaviors and Health Outcomes, 1992; (with K.S. Cook and G.A. Fine) Sociological Perspectives on Social Psychology, 1995; (with H. Schuman, F.T. Juster and R.L. Kahn) Telescope on Society: Survey Research and Social Science at the University of Michigan and Beyond, 2004; (with G.A. Kaplan, H. Pollack and R.F. Schoeni) Making Americans Healthier: Social and Economic Policy as Health Policy, 2008. **Address:** Institute for Social Research, University of Michigan, Weill Hall, 735 S Thompson St., Ste. 5219, PO Box 1248, Ann Arbor, MI 48106-1248, U.S.A. **Online address:** jimhouse@isr.umich.edu

HOUSE, John. British (born England), b. 1945. **Genres:** Art/Art History. **Career:** University of East Anglia, faculty, 1969-76; University of East Anglia, lecturer, 1976-80; University College of London, Courtauld Institute of Art, faculty, 1980-87, reader, 1987-95, professor, Walter H. Annenberg professor, 1995-2010, professor emeritus, deputy director, 1996-99; University of Oxford, Slade Professor, 1987; Organizer and curator of exhibitions, art historian and writer. **Publications:** Monet, 1977, rev. ed., 1981; (ed. with M.A. Stevens) Post-Impressionism: Cross-Currents in European Painting, 1979; Impressionist Masterpieces: National Gallery of Art, 1985; Monet: Nature into Art, 1986; Impressionism for England: Samuel Courtauld as Patron and Collector, 1994; (with A. Dumas, J.M. Roos and J.F. McMillan) Impressions of France: Monet, Renoir, Pissarro and Their Rivals, 1995; (with A. Dumas, J.M. Roos and J.F. McMillan) Landscapes of France: Impressionism and Its Rivals, 1995; (contrib. with F. Cohen) Boudin to Dufy: Impressionist and Other Masters from the Musee Des Beaux Arts, 1996; Pierre-Auguste Renoir: La Promenade, 1997; (contrib. with K. Silver) Impressions of the Riviera: Monet, Renoir, Matisse and Their Contemporaries, 1998; (contrib.) The Faces of Impressionism: Portraits from American Collections, 1999; (contrib. with E.C. Childs, R. Thomson and L. DuBard) Vincent Van Gogh and the Painters of the Petit Boulevard, 2001; Impressionism: Paint and Politics, 2004; Turner Whistler Monet, 2004; (contrib.) Manet Face to Face, 2004; (contrib.) Physiognomy in Profile: Lavater's Impact on European Culture, 2005; (with D. Hopkins) Impressionists by the Sea, 2007; (contrib. with N. Ireson and A. Ribeiro) Renoir at the Theatre: Looking at La loge, 2008; (contrib. with E. Reissner and B. Wright) The Courtauld Cézannes; The Genius of Renoir: Paintings from the Clark, 2010; (with M. Lucy) Renoir in the Barnes Foundation, 2012. **Address:** Courtauld Institute of Art, Somerset House, Strand, London, GL WC2R 0RN, England. **Online address:** john.house@courtauld.ac.uk

HOUSE, Silas D. American (born United States), b. 1971. **Genres:** Novels, Novellas/Short Stories, Plays/Screenplays. **Career:** No Depression magazine, music journalist and contributing editor; United States Post Office, substitute rural carrier, 1996-2001; Eastern Kentucky University, writer-in-residence, 2004-05; Lincoln Memorial University, writer-in-residence, 2005-10, Mountain Heritage Literary Festival, director; Spalding University, Creative Writing Program, fiction faculty, 2005-. **Publications:** Clay's Quilt: A Novel, 2001; A Parchment of Leaves: A Novel, 2002; The Coal Tattoo: A Novel, 2004; The Hurting Part (play), 2005; (with J. Howard) Something's Rising: Appalachians Fighting Mountaintop Removal, 2009; Eli the Good, 2009; (ed. with S.S. Burns and M.L. Evans) Coal Country: Rising Up Against Mountaintop Removal Mining, 2009; (ed.) Chinaberry, 2011; Evona Darling, forthcoming; (with N. Vaswani) Same Sun Here, 2012. Contributor to periodicals. Works appear in anthologies. **Address:** c/o Joy Harris, The Joy Harris Literary Agency, 156 5th Ave., Ste. 617, New York, NY 10010-7002, U.S.A. **Online address:** houses@berea.edu

HOUSE, Tom. American (born United States), b. 1962?. **Genres:** Novels, Literary Criticism And History, Young Adult Fiction. **Career:** State University of New York, professor of English. Writer. **Publications:** The Beginning of Calamities: A Novel, 2003. Works appear in anthologies. Contributor to periodicals. **Address:** PO Box 856, Wainscott, NY 11975-0856, U.S.A. **Online address:** tomhouse@housestories.net

HOUSEWRIGHT, David. American (born United States), b. 1955?. **Genres:** Mystery/Crime/Suspense, Novels. **Career:** Minneapolis Star Tribune, reporter; Albert Lea Evening Tribune, reporter; Grand Forks Herald, reporter; University of Minnesota, faculty; The Loft Literary Center, faculty; SASE: The Write Place, faculty. **Publications:** Penance, 1995; Practice to Deceive, 1997; Dearly Departed: A Holland Taylor Mystery, 1999; A Hard Ticket Home, 2004; Tin City, 2005; Pretty Girl Gone, 2006; Dead Boyfriends, 2007; Madman on a Drum, 2008; Jelly's Gold, 2009; Taking of Libbie, SD, 2010; Highway 61, 2011. Contributor to periodicals. **Address:** c/o Alison J. Picard, PO Box 2000, Cotuit, MA 02635, U.S.A. **Online address:** davidhousewright@comcast.net

HOUSHMAND, Zara. American/Iranian (born Iran), b. 1953. **Genres:** Autobiography/Memoirs, Poetry, Novels. **Career:** Worlds Inc., executive producer; Mind and Life Institute, editor. Theater artist. **Publications:** (Ed.) A Passage from Solitude: Training the Mind in a Life Embracing the World: A Modern Commentary on Tibetan Buddhist Mind Training, 1992; (with T. Wangmo) The Lhasa Moon Tibetan Cookbook, 1998; (ed. with R.B. Livingston and B.A. Wallace) Consciousness at the Crossroads: Conversations with the Dalai Lama on Brainscience and Buddhism, 1999; (ed.) Boundless Heart: The Four Immeasurables, 1999; (ed. with A. Zajonc) The New Physics and Cosmology: Dialogues with the Dalai Lama, 2004; (with M.S. Farmanfarmaian) A Mirror Garden, 2007; (with P.L. Luisi) Mind and Life: Discussions with the Dalai Lama on the Nature of Reality, 2009. Works appear in anthologies. **Address:** c/o Tina Bennett, Janklow & Nesbit Associates, 445 Park Ave., New York, NY 10022-8628, U.S.A. **Online address:** zh@mindspring.com

HOUSTON, Alan Craig. American (born United States), b. 1957. **Genres:** Politics/Government. **Career:** University of California, professor of political science; Columbia University, fellow; Princeton University, Center for Human Values, fellow. Writer. **Publications:** Algernon Sidney and the Republican Heritage in England and America, 1991; (ed. with S. Pincus and contrib.) A Nation Transformed: England after the Restoration, 2001; (ed.) Franklin: The Autobiography and Other Writings on Politics, Economics, and Virtue, 2004; Benjamin Franklin and the Politics of Improvement, 2008. **Address:** University of California, 362 Social Sciences Bldg., 9500 Gilman Dr., La Jolla, CA 92093-0521, U.S.A. **Online address:** ahouston@ucsd.edu

HOUSTON, Cecil J(ames). Canadian/Irish (born Ireland), b. 1943. **Genres:** Area Studies, Cultural/Ethnic Topics, Geography, History. **Career:** University of Toronto-Toronto, lecturer, 1972-75, assistant professor, 1975-77, associate professor, 1977-91, professor of geography, 1991-; Torontos Erindale College, associate dean of social sciences and vice principal, 1993-2000; University of Toronto-Mississauga, The Communication, Culture and Information Program, director, 2001; University of Windsor, Faculty of Arts and Social Sciences, professor and dean, 2002-; Canadian Association for Irish Studies, president. Writer. **Publications:** (With W.J. Smyth) Sash Canada Wore: A Historical Geography of the Orange Order in Canada, 1980; (with W.J. Smyth) Irish Emigration and Canadian Settlement: Patterns, Links and Letters, 1990; (with J. Leydon) Ireland: The Haunted Ark, 1996. **Address:** Department of Arts & Social Sciences, University of Windsor, Rm. 101 Chrysler Hall Twr., Windsor, ON N9B 3P4, Canada. **Online address:** chouston@uwindsor.ca

HOUSTON, Gail Turley. American (born United States), b. 1950. **Genres:** Novels, Young Adult Fiction, Children's Fiction, Economics, Education. **Career:** Carl Hayden High School, teacher, 1974-75; Brigham Young University, teaching assistant, 1979-81, assistant professor, 1990-96; University of California, teaching assistant, 1984-88; University of New Mexico, Department of English, assistant professor, 1996, professor and chair, interim chair of undergraduate studies, 1999-2001, director of women's studies, 2003-, interim coordinator for British and Irish literature. Writer. **Publications:** Consuming Fictions: Gender, Class, and Hunger in Dickens's Novels, 1994; Royalties: The Queen and Victorian Writers, 1999; From Dickens to Dracula: Gothic, Economics, and Victorian Fiction, 2005. Contributor to books and journals. **Address:** Department of English Language and Literature, University of New Mexico, Humanities 227, 1 University of New Mexico, PO Box 032170, Albuquerque, NM 87131-0001, U.S.A. **Online address:** english@unm.edu

HOUSTON, Gloria. American (born United States), b. 1940?. **Genres:** Children's Fiction, Young Adult Fiction, Education, Songs/Lyrics And Libretti, Reference, Social Commentary, Travel/Exploration. **Career:** Junior high and high school teacher, 1963-64, 1967-73, 1974-79, 1981-82, 1983; University of South Florida, instructor, 1982-88, visiting professor, 1984, lecturer of childhood education, 1988-, author-in-residence, 1989-94, assistant professor, 1992-, Center for the Study of Child Writing, director, 1992-, founder; Western Carolina University, author-in-residence, 1994-2002. Writer. **Publications:** My Brother Joey Died, 1982; The Year of the Perfect Christmas Tree: An Appalachian Story, 1988; Littlejim, 1990; My Great-Aunt Arizona, 1992; But No Candy, 1992; Mountain Valor, 1994; Littlejim's Gift: An Appalachian Christmas Story, 1994; Old Heckum Beckum Linkumfelt, 1995; Young Will, An American, 1996; Littlejim's Dreams, 1997; Bright Freedom's Song: A Story of the Underground Railroad, 1998; Miss Dorothy and Her Bookmobile, 2001; How Writing Works: Imposing Organizational Structure Within the Writing Process, 2004; Miss Dorothy's Bookmobile, 2006. Contributor of articles to books. **Address:** Department of Communication, University of South Florida, 4202 E Fowler Ave., Tampa, FL 33620, U.S.A. **Online address:** ghinc@ioa.com

HOUSTON, R. B. *See* **RAE, Hugh C(rawford).**

HOUSTON, Velina Hasu. American (born United States), b. 1957. **Genres:** Plays/Screenplays, Poetry, Children's Fiction, Novels, Cultural/Ethnic Topics, Essays. **Career:** Playwright, screenwriter, essayist and poet, 1979-; University of Southern California, School of Theater, visiting professor, 1990-91, associate professor and director of playwriting program, 1991-, now professor, Gender Studies Program, associate, Dramatic Writing, director, associate dean of faculty, resident playwright; University of California, School of Theater, Film and Television, visiting professor, 1993; Doshisha University, visiting professor, 1999-2000. **Publications:** Green Tea Girl in Orange Pekoe Country, 1993; (ed. and contrib.) The Politics of Life, 1993; (ed.) But Still, Like Air, I Rise: New Asian American Plays, 1997; No Passing Zone, 1997; Tea, 2007; Writer's Block Busters: 101 Exercises to Clear the Deadwood and Make Room for Flights of Fancy, 2008. Contributor to periodicals. Works appear in anthologies. **Address:** School of Theatre, University of Southern California, 1029 Childs Way, Los Angeles, CA 90089-0791, U.S.A. **Online address:** greentea@usc.edu

HOUSTON, Victoria. American (born United States), b. 1945. **Genres:** Mystery/Crime/Suspense, Young Adult Non-fiction. **Career:** Writer. **Publications:** NONFICTION: (with H.L. Swan) Alone after School: A Self-Care Guide for Latchkey Children and Their Parents, 1985; Loving a Younger Man: How Women Are Finding and Enjoying a Better Relationship, 1987; Making It Work: Finding the Time and Energy for Your Career, Marriage, Children, and Self, 1990; Restore Yourself: A Woman's Guide to Reviving Her Sexual Desire and Passion for Life, 2001; (with T. Shelby) Michelle and Me: The Incredible True Stories of a K-9 Search-and-Rescue Team, 2002. LOON LAKE MYSTERY SERIES: Dead Angler, 2000; Dead Creek, 2000; Dead Water, 2002; Dead Frenzy, 2003; Dead Hot Mama, 2004; Dead Jitterbug, 2005; Dead Boogie, 2006; Dead Madonna, 2007; Dead Hot Shot, 2008. **Address:** Rhinelander, WI , U.S.A. **Online address:** vhouston@charter.net

HOUSTON, W. Robert. American (born United States), b. 1928. **Genres:** Education, Mathematics/Statistics. **Career:** University of Texas, supervisor of student teachers, 1959-60, research associate, 1960-61; Michigan State University, assistant professor, 1961-63, associate professor, 1963-66, Michigan professor of education, 1967-70, Models Elementary Teacher Education Program, project director, 1968-70; University of Houston, professor of education, 1970-, associate dean, 1973-92; Texas Center for University School Partnerships, executive director, 1990-95, John and Rebecca Moores professor, 1996-; Institute for Urban Education, executive director, 1996-; National Association of Teacher Educators, president. Writer. **Publications:** Strategies and Resources for Developing Competency-Based Teacher Education Program, 1972; Resources for Performance-Based Education, 1973; Competency Assessment, Research, and Evaluation, 1975; Modern Elementary Education Teaching and Learning, 1976; Exploring World Regions, 1977; Assessing School/College/Community Needs, 1978; Emerging Professional Roles in Teacher Education, 1978; Focus on the Future Implications for Education, 1978; Designing Short-Term Instructional Programs, 1979; Staff Development and Educational Change, 1980. CO-AUTHOR: Sir Isaac Newton, 1960; Extending Mathematics Understanding, 1961; Professional Growth through Student Teaching, 1965; Teaching in the Modern Elementary School, 1967; Exploring Regions of Latin America and Canada, 1968; Extending Understandings of Mathematics, 1969; Understanding the Number System, 1969;

The Elementary School Curriculum, 1970; Elementary Education in the Seventies, 1970; Acquiring Competencies to Teach Mathematics in Elementary Schools, 1973; Competency-Based Instructional Design, 1973; Adult Learners, 1981; Touch the Future: Teach!, 1988; Encouraging Reflective Practice in Education, 1990. EDITOR: (co-ed.) Competency-Based Teacher Education, 1972; Exploring Competency-Based Education, 1974; Mirrors of Excellence, 1986; Handbook of Research on Teacher Education, 1990. **Address:** College of Education, University of Houston, 466 FH, 4800 Calhoun Rd., Houston, TX 77004, U.S.A. **Online address:** rhouston@uh.edu

HOUT, Michael. American (born United States), b. 1950. **Genres:** Adult Non-fiction, Sociology, Sciences, History. **Career:** University of Arizona, assistant professor, 1976-82, associate professor, 1982-85; University College, visiting profesor, 1983-84; University of California, associate professor of sociology, 1985-88, professor of sociology, 1988-2006, professor of sociology and demography, 2006-, chair of graduate group in sociology and demography, 1996-97, Department of Demography, chair, Berkeley Population Center, director, Natalie Cohen sociology chair. Writer. **Publications:** Mobility Tables, 1983; Following in Father's Footsteps: Social Mobility in Ireland, 1989; (co-author) Inequality by Design: Cracking the Bell Curve Myth, 1996; (with C.S. Fischer) Century of Difference: How America Changed in the Last One Hundred Years, 2006; (with A. Greeley) The Truth about Conservative Christians: What They Think and What They Believe, 2006; Rationing Opportunity, forthcoming. Contributor to journals. **Address:** Department of Sociology, University of California-Berkeley, 410 Barrows Hall, Berkeley, CA 94720-1980, U.S.A. **Online address:** mikehout@berkeley.edu

HOVANNISIAN, Richard G. American (born United States), b. 1932. **Genres:** History, Theology/Religion. **Career:** Teacher, 1958-62; University of California at Los Angeles, Armenian Studies Program, lecturer, 1962-69, associate professor, 1969-72, Armenian and Near Eastern History, professor, 1972-95, Armenian Educational Foundation, professor of modern Armenian history, professor emeritus, 1995-, G.E. Von Grunebaum Center for Near Eastern Studies, associate director, 1978-95, Guggenheim Fellow, Armenian Educational Foundation, endowed chair in modern Armenian history, 1987; Mount St. Mary's College, Near Eastern and Russian studies, associate professor, 1966-69; Society for Armenian Studies, founder; University of Michigan, Armenian Research Center, director. Writer. **Publications:** Armenia on the Road to Independence, 1967, 4th ed., 1984; The Republic of Armenia, vol. I, 1971, 4th ed., 1996, vol. II, 1982, vol. III-IV, 1996; (contrib.) The Lions of Marash, 1973; The Armenian Holocaust: A Bibliography Relating to the Deportations, Massacres and Dispersion of the Armenian People, 1915-1923, 1978; Ethics in Islam, 1985; Hayastani Hanrapetutyun, 2005; (contrib.) Never Again, Again, Again...: Genocide: Armenia, The Holocaust, Cambodia, Rwanda, Bosnia and Herzegovina, Darfur, 2007. EDITOR: The Armenian Image in History and Literature, 1981; (with S. Vryonis, Jr.) Islam's Understanding of Itself, 1983; The Armenian Genocide in Perspective, 1986; The Armenian Genocide: History, Politics, Ethics, 1992; (with A. Banani and G. Sabagh) Poetry and Mysticism in Islam: The Heritage of Rumi, 1994; (with G. Sabagh) The Thousand and One Nights in Arabic Literature and Society, 1997; The Armenian People from Ancient to Modern Times, 2 vols., 1997; (with G. Sabagh) The Persian Presence in Islamic World, 1998; (with G. Sabagh) The Persian Presence in the Islamic World, 1998; Remembrance and Denial: The Case of the Armenian Genocide, 1998; (with G. Sabagh) Religion and Culture in Medieval Islam, 1999; (with D.N. Myers) Enlightenment and Diaspora: The Armenian and Jewish Cases, 1999; Armenian Van/Vaspurakan, 2000; Armenia at the Dawn of the Century, 2000; Armenian Baghesh/Bitlis and Taron/Mush, 2001; Armenian Kharperpt/Tsopk, 2002; Armenian Karin/Erzerum, 2003; Looking Backward, Moving Forward: Confronting the Armenian Genocide, 2003; Armenian People from Ancient to Modern Times, 2004; Armenian Sebastia/Sivas and Lesser Armenia, 2004; Armenian Tigranakert/Diarbekir and Edessa/Urfa, 2006; The Armenian Genocide: Cultural and Ethical Legacies, 2007; (with S. Payaslian) Armenian Cilicia, 2008; Armenian Pontus: The Trebizond-Black Sea Communities, 2009; (with S. Payaslian) Armenian Constantinople, 2010; Armenian Kars and Ani, 2011. Contributor to journals. **Address:** Department of History, University of California, 6238 Bunche Hall, PO Box 951473, Los Angeles, CA 90095-1473, U.S.A. **Online address:** hovannis@history.ucla.edu

HOVENKAMP, Herb. See HOVENKAMP, Herbert.

HOVENKAMP, Herbert. (Herb Hovenkamp). American (born United States), b. 1948?. **Genres:** Law. **Career:** University of Texas, assistant in-

structor in English and American studies, 1972-76, lecturer in history and American Studies, 1976-79; University of California, Hastings College of Law, associate professor of law, 1980-85; University of Iowa, Ben V. and Dorothy Willie Distinguished Professor of Law and professor of history, 1986-; University of Iowa, College of Law, visiting professor, 1984, Presidential Lecturer; Michigan Law School, visiting professor, 1986; Writer, reviewer and educator. **Publications:** Science and Religion in America, 1800-1860, 1978; Economics and Federal Antitrust Law, 1985; Antitrust, 1986, 4th ed., 2005; (with S.F. Kurtz) Cases and Materials on American Property Law, 1987, 5th ed., 2007; (with E.T. Sullivan) Antitrust Law, Policy, and Procedure: Cases, Materials, Problems, 2nd ed., 1989, 5th ed., 2003; Enterprise and American Law, 1836-1937, 1991; (with R.E. Boyer and S.F. Kurtz) The Law of Property: An Introductory Survey, 4th ed., 1991, 5th ed., 2001; Federal Antitrust Policy: The Law of Competition and Its Practice, 1994, 3rd ed., 2005; (with M.D. Janis and M.A. Lemley) IP and Antitrust: An Analysis of Antitrust Principles Applied to Intellectual Property Law, 2002; (with P. Areeda) Fundamentals of Antitrust Law, 2003; The Antitrust Enterprise: Principle and Execution, 2005; Principles of Property Law, 6th ed., 2005. Contributor to books, periodicals and journals. **Address:** College of Law, University of Iowa, 290 Boyd Law Bldg., Iowa City, IA 52242-1113, U.S.A. **Online address:** herbert-hovenkamp@uiowa.edu

HOVEY, Kate. American (born United States) **Genres:** Poetry, Children's Fiction. **Career:** Metalsmith, teacher and writer. **Publications:** Arachne Speaks, 2001; Voices of the Trojan War, 2004; Ancient Voices, 2004. Contributor to periodicals. **Address:** c/o Author Mail, Margaret K. McElderry Books, Simon Schuster, 1230 Ave. of the Americas, New York, NY 10020, U.S.A. **Online address:** katehovey@juno.com

HOWARD, A. E. Dick. See HOWARD, A(rthur) E(llsworth) Dick.

HOWARD, Alison D. American (born United States), b. 1970. **Genres:** Politics/Government. **Career:** Dominican University of California, adjunct instructor in political science, 2004-. Academic and writer. **Publications:** (with D.R. Hoffman) Addressing the State of the Union: The Evolution and Impact of the President's Big Speech, 2006. Contributor to journals. **Address:** Dominican University of California, 50 Acacia Ave., San Rafael, CA 94901, U.S.A. **Online address:** alison.howard@dominican.edu

HOWARD, A(rthur) E(llsworth) Dick. (A. E. Dick Howard). American (born United States), b. 1933. **Genres:** History, Law, Politics/Government, Novels, Essays. **Career:** Covington & Burlington, associate, 1961-62; U.S. Supreme Court Justice Hugo Black, law clerk, 1962-64; University of Virginia, associate professor, 1964-67, professor of law, 1967-, associate dean, 1967-69, director of graduate program, 1972-, White Burkett Miller professor of law and public affairs, 1976-; General Assembly of Virginia, counsel, 1969-70; Magna Carta Commission of Virginia, vice chair, 1964-65; Virginia Commission on Constitutional Revision, executive director, 1968-69; Woodrow Wilson International Center for Scholars, fellow, 1974-77; Army Judge Advocate General's School, lecturer. Writer. **Publications:** AS A. E. DICK HOWARD: Magna Carta: Text and Commentary, 1964, rev. ed., 1998; (ed.) Magna Carta Commission Essays, 1965; (ed.) The Virginia Lawyer, 1966; The Road from Runnymede: Magna Carta and Constitutionalism in America, 1968; (co-author) Virginia's Urban Corridor, 1970; Commentaries on the Constitution of Virginia, 1974; (with S.A. Newman) Fair Trial and Free Expression: A Background Report Prepared for and Presented to the Subcommittee on Constitutional Rights of the Committee on the Judiciary, United States Senate, 1976; State Aid to Private Higher Eduction, 1977; (with J.W. Baker and T.S. Derr) Church, State and Politics: Final Report of the 1981 Chief Justice Earl Warren Conference on Advocacy in the United States, 1981; Democracy's Dawn: A Directory of American Initiatives on Constitutionalism, Democracy and the Rule of Law in Central and Eastern Europe, 1991; (ed.) The United States Constitution: Roots, Rights and Responsibilities, 1992; (ed. with M.I. Urofsky) Virginia and the Constitution, 1992; (ed.) Constitution Making in Eastern Europe, 1993; Toward the Open Society in Central and Eastern Europe, 1994. CO-AUTHOR: The Courts, Separation of Powers: Final Report of the 1983 Chief Justice Earl Warren Conference on Advocacy in the United States, 1983; The Rehnquist Court: The First Year, 1987; The Bill of Rights, the Courts and the Law: Case Abridgements and Commentary, 1991. Contributor to journals and periodicals. **Address:** School of Law, University of Virginia, WB362A, 580 Massie Rd., Charlottesville, VA 22903, U.S.A. **Online address:** adh3m@virginia.edu

HOWARD, Audrey. British/Australian (born Australia), b. 1929. **Genres:** Romance/Historical, Novels. **Career:** Writer. **Publications:** ROMANCE NOVELS: The Skylark's Song, 1984; The Morning Tide, 1985; Ambitions, 1986; The Juniper Bush, 1987; Between Friends, 1988; The Mallow Years, 1989; Shining Threads, 1990; A Day Will Come, 1992; All the Dear Faces, 1992; There is No Parting, 1993; Echo of Another Time, 1994; The Woman from Browhead, 1994; The Silence of Strangers, 1995; A World of Difference, 1995; Promises Lost, 1996; The Shadowed Hills, 1996; Strand of Dreams, 1997; Tomorrows Memories, 1997; When Morning Comes, 1998; Not a Bird Will Sing, 1998; Beyond the Shining Water, 1999; Angel Meadow, 1999; Rivers of the Heart, 2000; Seasons Will Pass, 2000; Annie's Girl, 2001; A Place Called Hope, 2001; Whispers on the Water, 2002; A Flower in Season, 2002; Painted Highway, 2003; Reflections from the Past, 2003; Distant Images, 2004; As the Night Ends, 2005; Rose Alley, 2006; A Time Like No Other, 2007; The Long Way Home, 2008; The Flight of Swallows, 2009. **Address:** c/o Jodie Marsh, United Agents, 12-26 Lexington St., London, GL W1F 0LE, England.

HOWARD, Clark. American (born United States), b. 1955. **Genres:** Business/Trade/Industry, Economics, Reference, Law. **Career:** WSB-AM, show host, 1991-; WSB-TV Channel 2 Action News, reporter. Writer. **Publications:** Clark Howard's Consumer Survival Kit, 1993, rev. ed., 1995; (with M. Meltzer) Clark Howard's Consumer Survival Kit III, 1998; Get Clark Smart: The Ultimate Guide for the Savvy Consumer, 2000; Get Clark Smart: The Ultimate Guide to Getting Rich from America's Money-Saving Expert, 2001; (with M. Meltzer) Clark's Big Book of Bargains, 2003; (with M. Meltzer) Clark Smart Parents, Clark Smart Kids, 2005; (with M. Meltzer) Clark Smart Real Estate, 2007; Clarkonomics, 2011. **Address:** News/Talk Radio 750 WSB-AM, 1601 W Peachtree St., Atlanta, GA 30309, U.S.A.

HOWARD, Clark. American (born United States), b. 1932?. **Genres:** Novels, Novellas/Short Stories, Mystery/Crime/Suspense, Criminology/True Crime, Sports/Fitness, Young Adult Non-fiction. **Career:** Writer. **Publications:** NOVELS: The Arm, 1967. MYSTERY NOVELS: A Movement Toward Eden, 1969; The Doomsday Squad, 1970; Siberia 10, 1973; The Killings, 1973; Last Contract, 1973; Summit Kill, 1975; Mark the Sparrow, 1975; The Hunters, 1976; The Last Great Death Stunt, 1977; Traces of Mercury, 1979; Hard City, 1990; City Blood, 1994. OTHER: Six against the Rock, 1977; The Wardens, 1979; Zebra: The True Account of the 179 Days of Terror in San Francisco, 1979 in UK as The Zebra Killings, 1980; American Saturday, 1981; Brothers in Blood, 1983; Dirt Rich, 1986; Quick Silver, 1988; Love's Blood: The Shocking True Story of a Teenager Who Would Do Anything for the Older Man She Loved-Even Kill Her Whole Family, 1993; (with M. Meltzer) Clark Howard's Guide to Saving $$ on the Internet, 2001. SHORT STORIES: Crowded Lives and and Other Stories of Desperation and Danger, 1999; Challenge the Widow-Maker, 2000; Derringer Award (novelette), 2003. Contributor to journals. **Address:** PO Box 1527, Palm Springs, CA 92263, U.S.A. **Online address:** rchoward440@cs.com

HOWARD, David A. American (born United States), b. 1942. **Genres:** History, Social Sciences. **Career:** Houghton College, professor of history, 1969-, chair of history and political science. **Publications:** The Royal Indian Hospital of Mexico City, 1980; Conquistador in Chains: Cabeza de Vaca and the Indians of the Americas, 1997. **Address:** Department of History and Political Science, Houghton College, 1 Willard Ave., Houghton, NY 14744-8732, U.S.A. **Online address:** david.howard@houghton.edu

HOWARD, David M. (David M(orris) Howard). American (born United States), b. 1928. **Genres:** Theology/Religion, Young Adult Fiction. **Career:** Latin America Mission, assistant general director, 1953-68, field director, 1958-67, president, 1965-80, 1984-87, 1993-99, retired, 1999; Inter-Varsity Christian Fellowship, campus staff, 1949-51, missions director, 1968-76, assistant to the president, 1976-77; Evangelism Explosion, staff, 1981-82; World Evangelical Fellowship, international director, 1982-92; David C. Cook Foundation, senior vice president, 1992-95. Writer. **Publications:** Hammered as Gold, 1969, as The Costly Harvest, 1975; Student Power in World Evangelism, 1970, as Student Power in World Missions, 1979; How Come, God?, 1972; By the Power of the Holy Spirit, 1973; Words of Fire, Rivers of Tears: The Man Jeremiah, 1975; The Great Commission for Today, 1976; The Dream That Would Not Die, 1986; What Makes a Missionary, 1987; From Wheaton to the Nations, 2001; Not in Vain, 2003; Mysteries of the Bible, 2004. EDITOR: Jesus Christ: Lord of the Universe, Hope of the World, 1974; Declare His Glory Among the Nations, 1977; Interpreting the Psalms: An Exegetical Handbook, 2007. **Address:** 14571 Daffodil Dr., Apt. 2007, Fort Myers, FL 33919-7480, U.S.A.

HOWARD, David M(orris). *See* HOWARD, David M.

HOWARD, Elizabeth Jane. British (born England), b. 1923. **Genres:** Novels, Plays/Screenplays, Novellas/Short Stories, Young Adult Non-fiction, Autobiography/Memoirs. **Career:** British Broadcasting Corp., broadcaster, 1939-46; Inland Waterways Association, secretary, 1947-50; Chatto & Windus Ltd., editor, 1953-56; Weidenfeld & Nicolson Ltd., publisher and editor, 1957; Queen Magazine, book critic, 1957-60. **Publications:** CAZALET CHRONICLES SERIES: The Light Years, 1988; Marking Time, 1991; Confusion, 1993; Casting Off, 1995. NOVELS: The Beautiful Visit, 1950; The Long View, 1956; The Sea Change, 1959; After Julius, 1965; Something in Disguise, 1969; Odd Girl Out, 1972; Getting It Right, 1982; Falling, 1999; Love All, 2008. COLLECTIONS: (with R. Aickman) We Are for the Dark: Six Ghost Stories, 1951; Mr. Wrong, 1975. NON-FICTION: Slipstream: An Memoir, 2002. OTHERS: (with A. Helps) Bettina: A Portrait, 1957; (ed.) The Lover's Companion: The Pleasures, Joys and Anguish of Love, David & Charles, 1978; (with F. Maschler) Howard and Maschler on Food, 1987; (ed.) Green Shades: An Anthology of Plants, Gardens and Gardeners, Aurum, 1991; (with F. Maschler) Cooking for Occasion, 1994; (ed.) Marriage: An Anthology, 1997. Contributor to periodicals. **Address:** Jonathan Clowes Ltd., 10 Iron Bridge House, Bridge Approach, London, GL NW1 8BD, England.

HOWARD, Ellen. American (born United States), b. 1943. **Genres:** Children's Fiction, Novels. **Career:** The Collins Foundation, secretary, 1980-88; Vermont College, MFA Program, Writing for Children and Young Adults, faculty. Writer. **Publications:** Circle of Giving, 1984; When Daylight Comes, 1985; Gillyflower, 1986; Edith Herself, 1987, new ed. 1994; Her Own Song, 1988; Sister, 1990; The Chickenhouse House, 1991; The Cellar, 1992; Gilly's Secret, 1993; The Big Seed, 1993; The Tower Room, 1993; Murphy and Kate, 1995; Different Kind of Courage, 1996; The Log Cabin Quilt, 1996; The Gate in the Wall, 1999; The Log Cabin Christmas, 2000; The Log Cabin Church, 2002; Log Cabin Wedding, 2006; Crimson Cap, 2009. Contributor to periodicals. **Address:** Vermont College of Fine Arts, 36 College St., Montpelier, VT 05602, U.S.A. **Online address:** cfhjreh@comcast.net

HOWARD, Ginnah. American (born United States), b. 1939?. **Genres:** Novels. **Career:** Teacher, retired, 1995. Writer. **Publications:** Night Navigation (novel), 2009. **Address:** Oneonta, NY , U.S.A. **Online address:** nightnavigation@ginnahhoward.com

HOWARD, Heather H. American (born United States), b. 1963?. **Genres:** Novels, Literary Criticism And History, Humor/Satire. **Career:** Writer. **Publications:** Chore Whore: Adventures of a Celebrity Personal Assistant, 2005. Contributor to periodicals. **Address:** c/o Author Mail, HarperCollins Publishers, 10 E 53rd St., Fl. 7, New York, NY 10022, U.S.A.

HOWARD, Jason. American (born United States), b. 1981?. **Genres:** History, Science Fiction/Fantasy. **Career:** Equal Justice Magazine, senior editor and staff writer; MotesBooks, acquisitions editor. Musician. **Publications:** (Ed.) We All Live Downstream: Writings about Mountaintop Removal, 2009; (with S. House) Something's Rising: Appalachians Fighting Mountaintop Removal, 2009. Contributor to periodicals. **Address:** The University Press of Kentucky, 663 S Limestone St., Lexington, KY 40508-4008, U.S.A. **Online address:** jason@jason-howard.com

HOWARD, Joan E. American (born United States), b. 1951. **Genres:** Literary Criticism And History, Biography, Reference, Translations. **Career:** University of New Hampshire, instructor, 1981-87, assistant professor of French, 1987-89; Word Works Editing and Translating, director, 1991- ; Petite Plaisance, director, 2000-. Writer. **Publications:** From Violence to Vision: Sacrifice in the Works of Marguerite Yourcenar, 1992; (trans.) J. Savigneau, Marguerite Yourcenar: Inventing a Life, 1993; (ed.) Actes: Marguerite Yourcenar et la mort, 1993; (trans.) J. Savigneau, Carson McCullers: A Life, 2001. Encyclopedia of New England Culture, forthcoming. **Address:** 110 Willard Ave., Portsmouth, NH 03801-5046, U.S.A. **Online address:** vze265vd@verizon.net

HOWARD, J. Woodford. American (born United States), b. 1931. **Genres:** Law, Politics/Government, Biography. **Career:** Lafayette College, instructor, 1958-59, assistant professor of government and law, 1959-61; Harvard

University, fellow in law and political science, 1961-62; Duke University, assistant professor, 1962-66, associate professor of political science, 1966-67; Johns Hopkins University, associate professor, 1967-69, professor of political science, 1969-75, chair of department, 1973-75, Thomas P. Stran professor, 1975-, now professor emeritus. Writer. **Publications:** (Contrib.) Essays on the American Constitution, 1964; Mr. Justice Murphy: A Political Biography, 1968; (contrib.) Changing Perspectives in Contemporary Political Analysis, 1971; (contrib.) Constitutional Law and Judicial Policy Making, 1972; (contrib.) Courts, Judges, and Politics, 2nd ed., 1974; Courts of Appeals in the Federal Judicial System: A Study of the Second, Fifth, and District of Columbia Circuits, 1981. Contributor to books and periodicals. **Address:** Department of Political Science, Johns Hopkins University, 338 Mergenthaler Hall, 3400 N Charles St., Baltimore, MD 21218-2686, U.S.A. **Online address:** jwhoward@jhu.edu

HOWARD, Kathleen L. American/Canadian (born Canada), b. 1942. **Genres:** History, Photography. **Career:** Motorola, purchasing agent, 1965-87; Newberry Library, researcher, 1986-87; Heard Museum, research associate, 1988-; Historical Perspectives Inc., senior historian. Writer. **Publications:** (With D.F. Pardue) Inventing the Southwest: The Fred Harvey Company and Native American Art, 1996. Contributor to periodicals. **Address:** 10642 E San Salvador Dr., Scottsdale, AZ 85258, U.S.A. **Online address:** kathy.howard@att.net

HOWARD, Madeline. See **EDGERTON, Teresa (Ann).**

HOWARD, Maureen. American (born United States), b. 1930. **Genres:** Novels, Autobiography/Memoirs, Young Adult Fiction, Children's Fiction, Young Adult Non-fiction, Literary Criticism And History, History, Biography, Art/Art History. **Career:** New School for Social Research, lecturer in English and creative writing, 1967-68, 1970-71, 1974-; University of California, lecturer in English and drama, 1968-69; Yale University, Department of English, faculty, 1991-; Columbia University, associate professor, 1993, adjunct professor, professor of writing; Amherst College, instructor; Brooklyn College, instructor. Writer. **Publications:** NOVELS: Not a Word about Nightingales, 1960; Bridgeport Bus, 1965; Before My Time, 1975; Facts of Life (autobiography), 1978; Grace Abounding, 1982; Expensive Habits, 1986; Natural History, 1992; A Lover's Almanac, 1998; Big as Life: Three Tales for Spring, 2001; The Silver Screen, 2004; Rags of Time, 2009. OTHERS: (ed.) Seven American Women Writers of the Twentieth Century, 1977; (ed.) Contemporary American Essays, 1984 as The Penguin Book of Contemporary Essays, 1984; (foreword) Mrs. Dalloway, 1990; (co-ed.) Cabbage and Bones: An Anthology of Irish-American Women's Fiction, 1997; (intro.) Three Novels: 'O Pioneers!, The Song of the Lark and My Antonia, 1998. Contributor to periodicals. **Address:** Watkins Loomis Agency, 133 E 35th St., Ste. 1, PO Box 20925, New York, NY 10016-3886, U.S.A.

HOWARD, M(ichael) C. British/Canadian (born Canada), b. 1945. **Genres:** Economics, Military/Defense/Arms Control, Politics/Government, Social Sciences. **Career:** University of Lancaster, lecturer in economics, 1970-72; University of Leicester, lecturer in economics, 1972-79; University of British Columbia, visiting professor, 1976-77; University of Waterloo, assistant professor, 1979-83, associate professor, 1983-89, professor of economics, 1989-, now distinguished professor emeritus; University of California, professor of economics, 1991-93. Writer. **Publications:** (With J.E. King) The Political Economy of Marx, 1975, 2nd ed., 1985; Modern Theories of Income Distribution, 1979; Profits in Economic Theory, 1983; (with J.E. King) A History of Marxian Economics, vol. I: 1883-1929, 1989, vol. II: 1929-1990, 1992; Contemporary Cultural Anthropology, 1993; The Rationality of Violence, Terrorism and War, 2006; (with J.E. King) The Rise of Neoliberalism in Advanced Capitalist Economies: A Materialist Analysis, 2008. EDITOR: (with J.E. King) The Economics of Marx: Selected Readings of Exposition and Criticism, 1976; (with I.G. Bradley) Classical and Marxian Political Economy: Essays in Honour of Ronald Meek, 1982. Works appear in anthologies. Contributor of articles to journals. **Address:** Department of Economics, University of Waterloo, Hagey Hall of Humanities, Waterloo, ON N2L 3G1, Canada. **Online address:** mchoward@uwaterloo.ca

HOWARD, Michael (Eliot). British (born England), b. 1922. **Genres:** History, Military/Defense/Arms Control. **Career:** University of London, King's College, assistant lecturer, 1947-50, lecturer in history, 1950-53, lecturer in war studies, 1953-61, reader, 1961-63, professor of war studies, 1963-68, faculty of arts dean, 1964-68, now professor emeritus; Stanford University,

visiting professor of European history, 1967; University of Oxford, All Souls College, fellow, 1968-80, Ford's lecturer in English history, 1971, Chichele professor of the history of war, 1977-80, Chichele chair of war, Regius professor of modern history, 1980-89, Regius chair of modern history, professor emeritus of modern history, 1993-; University of Warwick, Radcliffe Lecturer, 1975; Cambridge University, Trevelyan lecturer, 1977; Yale University, Robert A. Lovett professor of naval and military history, 1989-93, Robert A. Lovatt chair of military and naval history; National University of Singapore, Lee Kuan Yew distinguished visiting professor, 1996; International Institute for Strategic Studies, president and co-founder; Council on Christian Approaches to Defence and Disarmament, vice president. Writer. **Publications:** (With J. Sparrow) The Coldstream Guards 1920-1946, 1951; Proud Heritage: A Portrait of Greatness, 1951; Grand Strategy, 1956, vol. IV: 1942-43, 1972; Soldiers and Governments: Nine Studies in Civil-military Relations, 1957; Disengagement in Europe, 1958; The Franco-Prussian War, 1961; (with R. Hunter) Israel and the Arab World, 1967; Lord Haldane and the Territorial Army, 1967; Strategy and Policy in Twentieth-century Warfare, 1967; The Mediterranean Strategy in the Second World War, 1968; Studies in War and Peace, 1970; Central Organisation of Defence, 1970; The Continental Commitment, 1972; British Way in Warfare, 1975; War in European History, 1976; War and the Liberal Conscience, 1978; (co-author) and British Intelligence in the Second World War: Strategic Deception, 1979; Causes of Wars, 1983; Lessons of History, 1991; (with J.F. Guilmartin, Jr.) Two Historians in Technology and War, 1994; Clausewitz on War, 1998; The Invention of Peace, 2000; Clausewitz: A Very Short Introduction, 2002; The First World War, 2003; (trans. with P. Paret) C. Clausewitz, On War, 2006; Liberation or Catastrophe?: Reflections on the History of the Twentieth Century, 2007; First World War: A Very Short Introduction, 2007; War and the Liberal Conscience, 2008; (intro.) A Part of History: Aspects of the British Experience of the First World War, 2008. EDITOR: Wellingtonian Studies, 1959; The Theory and Practice of War, 1965; (with R. Ahmann, A.M. Birke) and Quest for Stability: Problems of West European Security, 1918-1957, 1993; (with G.J. Andreopoulos and M.R. Shulman) The Laws of War: Constraints on Warfare in the Western World, 1994; (with W.R. Louis) The Oxford History of the Twentieth Century, 1998. **Address:** King's College, University of London, Surrey St., Strand, London, GL WC2R 2LS, England.

HOWARD, Patricia. British (born England), b. 1937. **Genres:** Music, Translations, History. **Career:** Holton Park Grammar School, director of music, 1959-60; Open University, tutor in humanities and lecturer in music. Writer. **Publications:** Gluck and the Birth of Modern Opera, 1963; The Operas of Benjamin Britten: An Introduction, 1969; Haydn in London, 1980; Mozart's Marriage of Figaro, 1980; (comp.) C.W. von Gluck, Orfeo, 1981; Haydn's String Quartets, 1984; Beethoven's Eroica Symphony, 1984; (ed.) Benjamin Britten, The turn of the Screw, 1985; Christoph Willibald Gluck: A Guide to Research, 1987, 2nd ed., 2003; Music in Vienna 1790-1800, 1988; Beethoven's Fidelio, 1988; Music and the Enlightenment, 1992; Gluck: An Eighteenth-Century Portrait in Letters and Documents, 1995; (trans.) A Critical Translation from the Italian of Vincenzo Manfredini's Difesa della musica moderna: In Defense of Modern Music (1788), 2002. Contributor to magazines. **Address:** Stepping Stones, Gomshall, SR GU5 9NL, England.

HOWARD, Philip K. (Philip King Howard). American (born United States), b. 1948. **Genres:** Law. **Career:** Sullivan & Cromwell (law firm), associate, 1974-83; Howard, Darby, & Levin, co-founding partner, 1983-99; SEC Task Force of Simplification, special adviser, 1996, 1997; Covington & Burling L.L.P., lawyer, partner, vice-chairman and senior corporate adviser, 1999; Common Good, founder and chair. Writer. **Publications:** The Death of Common Sense: How Law is Suffocating America, 1994; (intro.) A. Gore, Common Sense Government, 1995; The Collapse of the Common Good: How America's Lawsuit Culture Undermines Our Freedom, 2001; Lost art of Drawing the Line: How Fairness went too Far, 2001; History of American Law: Since 1968 in The Oxford Companion to American Law, 2002; The Collapse of the Common Good, 2002; Life Without Lawyers: Liberating Americans from Too Much Law, 2009. Contributor to periodicals. **Address:** Covington & Burling L.L.P., The New York Times Bldg., 620 8th Ave., New York, NY 10018-1405, U.S.A. **Online address:** phoward@cov.com

HOWARD, Philip King. See **HOWARD, Philip K.**

HOWARD, Philip N. American (born United States), b. 1970. **Genres:** Social Commentary. **Career:** Northwestern University, Department Of Sociology, lecturer, 1999-2001; Illinois Institute of Technology, lecturer, 2000; Pew

Trusts' Internet and American Life Project, research fellow, 2000-01; University of Washington, Jackson School of International Studies, Department Of Communication, assistant professor, 2002-, associate professor, Project on Information Technology and Political Islam, director. Political scientist, sociologist and writer. **Publications:** (Ed. with S. Jones) Society Online: The Internet in Context, 2004; New Media Campaigns and the Managed Citizen, 2006; (ed. with A. Chadwick) Routledge Handbook of Internet Politics, 2009; The Digital Origins of Dictatorship and Democracy: Information Technology and Political Islam, 2010. Contributor to journals. **Address:** Department of Communication, Jackson School of International Studies, University of Washington, 141 Communications Bldg., PO Box 353740, Seattle, WA 98195-3740, U.S.A. **Online address:** pnhoward@u.washington.edu

HOWARD, Philip (Nicholas Charles). British (born England), b. 1933. **Genres:** Language/Linguistics, Military/Defense/Arms Control, Travel/Exploration. **Career:** Glasgow Herald, parliamentary correspondent, 1959-64; The Times, reporter and feature writer, 1964-78, senior leader writer and literary editor, 1978-92, columnist, 1992-2010. **Publications:** The Black Watch, 1968; The Royal Palaces, 1970; London's River, 1975; The British Monarchy in the Twentieth Century, 1977; New Words for Old, 1977; Weasel Words, 1978; U and Non-U Revisited, 1978; Words Fail Me, 1981; A Word in Your Ear, 1983; The State of the Language: English Observed, 1984; We Thundered Out: 200 Years of The Times, 1785-1985, 1985; Winged Words, 1988; Word-Watching, 1988; A Word in Time, 1990; (ed.) The Times Bedside Book, 1991; The British Library: A Treasure House of Knowledge, 2008. **Address:** 47 Ladbroke Grove, Apt. 1, London, GL W11 3AR, England.

HOWARD, Rhoda E. *See* **HOWARD-HASSMANN, Rhoda E.**

HOWARD, Roger. British (born England), b. 1938. **Genres:** Novels, Plays/Screenplays, Poetry, Literary Criticism And History, Politics/Government, Theatre, Translations. **Career:** University of Essex, teacher, lecturer in literature, 1979-, fellow, through 2003, retired 2003; Nankai University, faculty, 1965-67; Collets Bookshop, manager, 1967-68; Bookshop 85, manager, 1968-72; University of Peking, lecturer, 1972-74; Mercury Theatre, Colchester, playwright-in-residence, 1976; Theatre Underground, founding director, 1979-, senior lecturer, 1993; University of York, fellow in creative writing, 1976-78; University of East Anglia, Henfield writing fellow, 1979; Universities of Tientsin, faculty; University of Sussex, series editor, 1980-; Theatre Action Press, founder, 1980-; Janus Pannonius University, visiting playwright, 1991. **Publications:** A Phantastic Satire (novel), 1960; From the Life of a Patient (novel), 1961; Four Stories, 1964; To the People (poetry), 1966; Praise Songs (poetry), 1966; The Technique of the Struggle Meeting, 1968; (co-author) New Short Plays, 1968; The Use of Wall Newspapers, 1968; New Plays 1, 1968; Fin's Doubts, 1968; The Hooligan's Handbook, 1971; Method for Revolutionary Writing, 1972; (ed.) Culture and Agitation: Theatre Documents, 1972; Episodes from the Fighting in the East, 1971; Slaughter Night and Other Plays, 1971; Contemporary Chinese Theatre, 1977; Mao Tse-tung and the Chinese People, 1978; Le théâtre chinois contemporain, 1978; The Society of Poets, 1979; A Break in Berlin, 1980; The Siege, 1981; Partisans, 1983; Ancient Rivers, 1984; The Speechifier, 1984; Contradictory Theatres, 1985; (trans.) Sappa, 1985; Senile Poems, 1988; The Tragedy of Mao and Other Plays, 1989; Britannia and Other Plays, 1990; Selected Poems 1966-1996, 1997; Three War Plays, 2004. **Address:** Oberon Books Ltd., 521 Caledonian Rd., London, GL N7 9RH, England. **Online address:** rhoward@essex.ac.uk

HOWARD, Thomas Albert. American (born United States), b. 1967?. **Genres:** Theology/Religion. **Career:** Gordon College, associate professor of history, founding member, Jerusalem & Athens Forum; Valparaiso University, faculty; University of Freiburg im Breisgau, faculty; Humboldt University, faculty; University of Basel, faculty; University of Notre Dame, faculty. Writer. **Publications:** Religion and the Rise of Historicism: W.M.L. de Wette, Jacob Burckhardt and the Theological Origins of Nineteenth-Century Historical Consciousness, 2000; Protestant Theology and the Making of the Modern German University, 2006; (ed. with M.A. Noll and J. Turner) The Future of Christian Learning: An Evangelical and Catholic Dialogue, 2008. Contributor to journals. **Address:** Gordon College, 255 Grapevine Rd., Wenham, MA 01984, U.S.A. **Online address:** tal.howard@gordon.edu

HOWARD, Todd. American (born United States), b. 1964. **Genres:** Novels, Literary Criticism And History, History. **Career:** Freelance writer, 1994-; California State University, English instructor, 1995-2000, Motion Picture Industry, story analyst. **Publications:** Ether (novel), 1999; (ed.) William J.

Clinton (nonfiction), 2001; Understanding The Outsiders (nonfiction), 2001; (ed.) Mark Twain (nonfiction), 2002; Heroin (nonfiction), 2003. Contributor to journals. **Address:** c/o Author Mail, Lucent Books, PO Box 289011, San Diego, CA 92198-9011, U.S.A.

HOWARD, Tracie. American (born United States) **Genres:** Novels, Young Adult Fiction, Mystery/Crime/Suspense. **Career:** Xerox, staff; Johnson and Johnson, staff; American Express, staff; Savoy Magazine, travel and lifestyle editor; Ethos, curator and co-founder. **Publications:** (With D. Carter) Revenge is Best Served Cold, 2001; (with D. Carter) Talk of the Town, 2002; Why Sleeping Dogs Lie, 2003; Never Kiss and Tell, 2004; (with D. Carter) Success is the Best Revenge, 2004; Gold Diggers, 2007; Friends & Fauxs, 2009. **Address:** Broadway Books, 1745 Broadway, 10th Fl., New York, NY 10019, U.S.A.

HOWARD, Walter T. American (born United States), b. 1951. **Genres:** History, Literary Criticism And History. **Career:** University of South Florida, adjunct instructor in history, 1981-90; St. Leo College, Department of History, adjunct instructor, 1987-90; Hillsborough Community College, adjunct instructor, 1988-90; Bloomsburg University, assistant professor, 1990-95, associate professor of history, 1995-2005, professor, 2005-; Park College Prison Program, instructor, 1991-95. Writer. **Publications:** Lynchings: Extralegal Violence in Florida during the 1930s, 1995; (ed.) B.D. Amis: African American Radical: A Short Anthology of His Writings and Speeches, 2007; (ed.) Anthracite Reds: A Documentary History of Communists in Northeastern Pennsylvania During the 1920s, 2004 as (ed.) Anthracite Reds vol. II: A Documentary History of Communists in Northeastern Pennsylvania During the Great Depression, 2004; Forgotten Radicals: Communists in the Pennsylvania Anthracite, 1919-1950, 2005; (ed.) Black Communists Speak on Scottsboro: A Documentary History, 2008. Contributor to magazines. **Address:** Department of History, Bloomsburg University, 114 Old Science Hall, 400 E 2nd St., Bloomsburg, PA 17815, U.S.A. **Online address:** whoward@bloomu.edu

HOWARD-HASSMANN, Rhoda E. (Rhoda E. Howard). Canadian/British/Scottish (born Scotland), b. 1948. **Genres:** Civil Liberties/Human Rights, Politics/Government, Women's Studies And Issues, Gay And Lesbian Issues, Area Studies, International Relations/Current Affairs. **Career:** McMaster University, professor of sociology, 1976-2003, professor emeritus, 2003-; Canadian Journal of African Studies, editor, 1987-92; University of Connecticut, Marsha Lilien Gladstein distinguished visiting professor of human rights, 2001; Mary Washington College, James T. Farmer visiting professor of human rights, 2003; Wilfrid Laurier University, Canada research chair in international human rights, 2003-, Department of Global Studies, professor, Balsillie School of International Affairs, professor; University of Goteborg, Torgny Segerstedt visiting professor of human rights, 2005. Writer. **Publications:** AS RHODA E. HOWARD: Colonialism and Underdevelopment in Ghana, 1978; Human Rights in Commonwealth Africa, 1986; (ed. with J. Donnelly) International Handbook of Human Rights, 1987; Human Rights and the Search for Community, 1995; (with J. Donnelly) Human Rights Self-monitoring, 1996. AS RHODA E. HOWARD-HASSMANN: Compassionate Canadians: Civic Leaders Discuss Human Rights, 2003; (ed. with C.E. Welch, Jr.) Economic Rights in Canada and the United States, 2006; (ed. with M. Gibney, J. Coicaud and N. Steiner) The Age of Apology: Facing up to the Past, 2007; (with A.P. Lombardo) Reparations to Africa, 2008; Can Globalization Promote Human Rights?, 2010. **Address:** Global Studies Program, Wilfrid Laurier University, 4-158 Dr. Alvin Woods Bldg., 75 University Ave. W, Waterloo, ON N2L 3C5, Canada. **Online address:** hassmann@wlu.ca

HOWARTH, Lesley. British (born England), b. 1952. **Genres:** Children's Fiction, Children's Non-fiction, Young Adult Fiction, Novels. **Career:** Writer. **Publications:** NOVELS: The Flower King, 1993; Weather Eye, 1995; The Pits, 1996; Mister Spaceman, 1999; Paulina, 1999; I Managed a Monster, 2000; Ultraviolet, 2001; Carwash, 2002; Drive, 2004; Colossus, 2004; Calling the Shots, 2006. TAKEAWAY TALES: Aliens for Dinner, 1999; Yambusters!, 1999. QUIRX: Welcome to Inner Space, 1997; The Edge of the World, 1998. SERIES: MapHead, 1994; MapHead 2, 1997; MapHead: The Return, 1997. **Address:** The Agency, 24 Pottery Ln., Holland Pk., London, GL W11 4LZ, England.

HOWARTH, Peter. British (born England), b. 1952. **Genres:** Medicine/Health, Sciences. **Career:** University of Southampton, reader; Southampton General Hospital, honorary consultant, Allergy and Severe Asthma Clinic, co-founder. Writer and physician. **Publications:** (With A. Reid) Allergy-Free

Living: How to Create a Healthy, Allergy-Free Home and Lifestyle, 2000; (ed.) Airway Remodeling, 2001. **Address:** Southampton General Hospital, Level F South Block, Tremona Rd., PO Box 825, Southampton, HM SO16 6YD, England. **Online address:** p.h.howarth@southampton.ac.uk

HOWARTH, William (Louis). (Dana Hand). American (born United States), b. 1940. **Genres:** Novels, Film, Literary Criticism And History, Natural History, Young Adult Fiction, Travel/Exploration. **Career:** Princeton University, instructor, 1966-68; assistant professor, 1968-73, associate professor, 1973-81, professor of English, 1981-2008, professor emeritus, 2008-; Writings of Henry D. Thoreau, editor-in-chief, 1972-80; Thoreau Society, president, 1974-75; Princeton Environmental Institute, associate faculty; Center for American Places, board director, chair. Consultant. **Publications:** EDITOR: A Thoreau Gazetteer, 1970; 20th Century Interpretations of Poe's Tales, 1971; The John McPhee Reader, 1976; Walden and Other Writings, 1981; Journal 1, 1837-44 of Henry D. Thoreau, 1984; C. King, Mountaineering in the Sierra Nevada, 1989; (ed. with C.F. Hovde and E.H. Witherell) A Week on the Concord and Merrimack Rivers, 2004. FICTION: (as Dana Hand) Deep Creek: A Novel, 2010. OTHERS: (comp. with C.A. Miller) Nature in American Life: A Preliminary Bibliographical Guide, 1971 and 1972, 1972; The Literary Manuscripts of Henry David Thoreau, 1974; The Book of Concord: Thoreau's Life as a Writer, 1982; (with H.D. Thoreau) Thoreau in the Mountains, 1982; The Book of Concord: Thoreau's Life as a Writer, 1982; (contrib.) The Illustrated a Week on the Concord and Merrimack Rivers, 1983; Traveling the Trans-Canada: From Newfoundland to British Columbia, 1987; Walking with Thoreau: A Literary Guide to the Mountains of New England, 2001. Contributor to periodicals. **Address:** Department of English, Princeton University, 22 McCosh Hall, Princeton, NJ 08544, U.S.A. **Online address:** howarth@princeton.edu

HOWATCH, Susan. British (born England), b. 1940. **Genres:** Novels, Mystery/Crime/Suspense, Theology/Religion, Essays. **Career:** Masons of London, law clerk, 1961-62; R.C.A. Victor Record Corp., secretary, 1964-65; novelist, 1965-; University of London, King's College, fellow, 1999; University of Wales, fellow; Sarum College, fellow. **Publications:** NOVELS: The Dark Shore, 1965; Waiting Sands, 1966; Call in the Night, 1967; The Shrouded Walls, 1968; The Devil on Lammas Night, 1970; Penmarric, 1971; April's Grave, 1973; Cashelmara, 1974; The Rich Are Different, 1977; Susan Howatch Treasury, 1978; Sins of the Fathers, 1980; Five Complete Novels, 1982; The Wheel of Fortune, 1984. NOVELS: ST. BENET'S SERIES: The Wonder Worker in UK as A Question of Integrity, 1997; The High Flyer, 2000; The Heartbreaker, 2003. NOVELS: STAR BRIDGE SERIES: Glittering Images, 1987; Glamorous Powers, 1988; Ultimate Prizes, 1989; Scandalous Risks, 1990; Mystical Paths, 1992; Absolute Truths, 1994. OTHERS: (with J. Peel) In Conversation, 2001; Scandalous Truths: Essays By and About Susan Howatch, 2005. **Address:** Gillon Aitken Associates Ltd., 29 Fernshaw Rd., London, GL SW10 0TG, England.

HOWE, Christine J. British (born England), b. 1948. **Genres:** Education, Language/Linguistics, Psychology. **Career:** Sussex University, lecturer, 1974-76; Strathclyde University, lecturer, 1976-90, senior lecturer, 1990-95, reader, 1995-98, head of department, 1997-, professor of psychology, 1998-; University of Cambridge, professor of education, director of research, Lucy Cavendish College, fellow. Writer. **Publications:** Acquiring Language in a Conversational Context, 1981; Language Learning: A Special Case for Developmental Psychology, 1993; Group and Interactive Learning, 1994; Gender and Classroom Interaction, 1997; Conceptual Structures in Childhood and Adolescence: The Case of Everyday Physics, 1998; Peer Groups and Childrens Development, 2010; (ed. with K. Littleton) Educational Dialogues: Understanding and Promoting Productive Interaction, 2010. **Address:** Faculty of Education, Cambridge University, 184 Hills Rd., Cambridge, CB CB2 8PQ, England. **Online address:** cjh82@cam.ac.uk

HOWE, Fanny. American (born United States), b. 1940. **Genres:** Novels, Children's Fiction, Poetry, Literary Criticism And History. **Career:** Tufts University, lecturer in creative writing, 1968-71; Emerson College, lecturer in creative writing, 1974; Columbia University Extension and School of the Arts, lecturer in creative writing, 1975-78; Yale University, lecturer in poetry, 1976; Harvard Extension, lecturer in fiction, 1977; Massachusetts Institute of Technology, visiting writer and lecturer in fiction and poetry, 1978-87; University of California, professor of writing and literature, 1987-2001, chair of the literature department, now professor emeritus of writing and American literature; Bard College, David and Ruth Schwab III professor of language

and literature and co-director of M.F.A. program (writing), 1991; University of California Study Center, associate director, 1993-95; Mills College, distinguished visiting writer-in-residence, 1996-97; Small Press Traffic, writer-in-residence, 1998; New School for Social Research, writing teacher, 2004; Kenyon College, visiting Richard L. Thomas professor of creative writing, 2005. Writer. **Publications:** Forty Whacks, 1969; Eggs: poems, 1970; First Marriage, 1974; The Amerindian Coastline Poem, 1975; Bronte Wilde: A Novel, 1976; Holy Smoke, 1979; Poems From a Single Pallet, 1980; The White Slave, 1980; The Blue Hills, 1981; Alsace-Lorraine, 1982; Yeah, But, 1982; In the Middle of Nowhere, 1984; Radio City, 1984; For Erato: The Meaning of Life, 1984; Taking Care, 1985; The Race of the Radical, 1985; Robeson Street, 1985; Introduction to the World, 1986; The Lives of a Spirit, 1987; The Vineyard, 1988; Deep North, 1988; Famous Questions: A Novel, 1989; The Quietist, 1992; Saving History, 1993; The End, 1993; O'Clock, 1995; One Crossed Out, 1997; Nord Profond, 1997; Nod, 1998; Q, 1998; Forged, 1999; Indivisible, 2000; Selected Poems, 2000; Economics, 2002; Gone: Poems, 2003; Tis of Thee, 2003; Wedding Dress: Meditations on Word and Life, 2003; On the Ground, 2004; The Lives of a Spirit; Glasstown: Where Something Got Broken, 2005; Radical Love: 5 Novels, 2006; A Wall of Two: Poems of Resistance and Suffering From Kraków to Buchenwald and Beyond, 2007; The Lyrics, 2007; Winter Sun: Notes on a Vocation, 2009; Emergence, 2010; Come and See, 2011. **Address:** Department of Literature, University of California, 139/140 Literature Bldg., 9500 Gilman Dr., La Jolla, CA 92093-0410, U.S.A. **Online address:** fqhowe@aol.com

HOWE, James. American (born United States), b. 1946. **Genres:** Children's Fiction, Children's Non-fiction, Picture/Board Books, Novels, Animals/Pets, Social Commentary. **Career:** Freelance actor and director, 1971-75; Lucy Kroll Agency, literary agent, 1976-81. Writer. **Publications:** (With D. Howe) Bunnicula: A Rabbit Tale of Mystery, 1979; (with D. Howe) Teddy Bear's Scrapbook, 1980; Pinky and Rex and the Just-Right Pet, 1980; The Hospital Book, 1981; Annie Joins the Circus, 1982; Howliday Inn, 1982; The Case of the Missing Mother, 1983; The Celery Stalks at Midnight, 1983; A Night without Stars, 1983; The Day the Teacher Went Bananas, 1984; The Muppet Guide to Magnificent Manners, 1984; How the Ewoks Saved the Trees: An Old Ewok Legend, 1984; Morgan's Zoo, 1984; Mister Tinker in Oz, 1985; What Eric Knew, 1985; Babes in Toyland, 1986; Eat Your Poison, Dear: A Sebastian Barth Mystery, 1986; (contrib.) When You Go to Kindergarten, 1986, rev. ed., 1994; A Love Note for Baby Piggy, 1986; Stage Fright: A Sebastian Barth Mystery, 1986; There's a Monster Under My Bed, 1986; I Wish I Were a Butterfly, 1987; Carol Burnett: The Sound of Laughter, 1987; Nighty-Nightmare, 1987; Fright before Christmas, 1988; Dew Drop Dead, 1990; Pinky and Rex, 1990; Pinky and Rex Get Married, 1990; Hot Fudge, 1990; Creepy-Crawly Birthday, 1991; Pinky and Rex and the Spelling Bee, 1991; Dances with Wolves: A Story for Children, 1991; Pinky and Rex and the Mean Old Witch, 1991; Pinky and Rex Go to Camp, 1992; Return to Howliday Inn, 1992; Pinky and Rex and the New Baby, 1993; Rabbit-Cadabra!, 1993; Bunnicula Fun Book, 1993; Playing with Words, 1994; There's a Dragon in My Sleeping Bag, 1994; Bunnicula Escapes!: A Pop-Up Adventure, 1994; New Nick Kramer, or My Life as a Babysitter, 1995; Pinky and Rex and the Bully, 1996; Pinky and Rex and the Double-Dad Weekend, 1996; Pinky and Rex and the New Neighbors, 1997; The Watcher, 1997; Horace and Morris but Mostly Dolores, 1997; Pinky and Rex and the School Play, 1998; Pinky and Rex and the Perfect Pumpkin, 1998; Bunnicula's Wickedly Wacky Word Games: A Book for Word Lovers & Their Pencils!, 1998; Bunnicula's Pleasantly Perplexing Puzzlers, 1998; Scared Silly: A Halloween Treat, 1999; Bunnicula Strikes Again, 1999; Bunnicula's Frightfully Fabulous Factoids: A Book to Entertain Your Brain!, 1999; Bunnicula's Long-Lasting Laugh Alouds: A Book of Jokes & Riddles to Tickle Your Bunny-Bone!, 1999; Horace and Morris Join the Chorus, 2001; (ed.) Color of Absence: 12 Stories About Loss and Hope, 2001; Misfits, 2001; Howie Monroe and the Doghouse of Doom, 2002; Invasion of the Mind Swappers from Asteroid 6, 2002; It Came from Beneath the Bed!: Tales from the House of Bunnicula, 2002; (ed.) 13: Thirteen Stories that Capture the Agony and Ecstasy of Being Thirteen, 2003; The Amazing Odorous Adventures of Stinky Dog, 2003; Bud Barkin, Private Eye, 2003; The Bunnicula Collection: Three Hare-Raising Tales in One Volume, 2003; Screaming Mummies of The Pharaoh's Tomb II, 2003; The Vampire Bunny, 2004; Kaddish For Grandpa in Jesus' Name, Amen, 2004; Totally Joe, 2005; Scared Silly, 2005; Bunnicula Meets Edgar Allan Crow, 2006; Houndsley and Catina and the Birthday Surprise, 2006; Houndsley and Catina, 2006; Rabbit Cadabra, 2006; Bunnicula-in-a-box, 2006; Creepy-Crawly Birthday, 2007; Houndsley and Catina and the Quiet Time, 2008; Houndsley and Catina

Plink and Plunk, 2009; Horace and Morris Say Cheese: Which Makes Dolores Sneeze!, 2009; Brontorina, 2010; Addie on the Inside, 2011; Otter and Odder, 2012. Contributor to journals. **Address:** c/o Amy Berkower, Writers House Inc., 21 W 26th St., New York, NY 10010-1003, U.S.A.

HOWE, Jeff P. American (born United States), b. 1970. **Genres:** Economics. **Career:** Inside.com, senior editor; Village Voice, writer; Wired magazine, contributing editor. **Publications:** Crowdsourcing: Why the Power of the Crowd Is Driving the Future of Business, 2008. Contributor to periodicals. **Address:** Brooklyn, NY , U.S.A. **Online address:** jeff_howe@wired.com

HOWE, LeAnne. American (born United States), b. 1951. **Genres:** Young Adult Fiction, Poetry. **Career:** Journalist, 1977-89; University of Iowa, team teacher of American Indian and native studies, 1992, 1994, 1995, international media producer, 1994-95; Iowa Arts Council, artist-in-residence, 1993; Smithsonian Institution, Native American intern, 1993; Amideast and UNICEF, lecturer, 1993-94; MacDowell Colony, writer-in-residence, 1995; Atlantic Center for the Arts, writer-in-residence, 1995; Ragdale Foundation, resident, 1996; Newberry Library, Indian Voices in the Academy, fellow, 1996; Carleton College, visiting teacher of Native American literature, 1996-97; Grinnell College, visiting faculty, 1997, lecturer in American studies, 1997-; Wagon Burner Theater Troop, founder and director; University of Illinois, Urbana-Champaign, professor of English and American Indian studies, director of creative writing. **Publications:** Coyote Stories, 1984; A Stand up Reader, 1987; Shell Shaker, 2001; Evidence of Red, 2005; Miko Kings: An Indian Baseball Story, 2007. Contributor of articles to periodicals. Works appear in anthologies. **Address:** Department of English, University of Illinois, 261 English Bldg., 608 S Wright St., Urbana, IL 61801, U.S.A. **Online address:** ileannehowe@gmail.com

HOWE, Leo. British (born England), b. 1949?. **Genres:** History, Theology/Religion, Travel/Exploration. **Career:** University of Cambridge, faculty member. Writer. **Publications:** Being Unemployed in Northern Ireland: An Ethnographic Study, 1990; (ed. with A. Wain) Predicting the Future, 1993; Status Mobility in Contemporary Bali: Continuities and Change, 1995; Hinduism & Hierarchy in Bali, 2001; The Changing World of Bali: Religion, Society and Tourism, 2005. Contributor to books and periodicals. **Address:** Department of Social Anthropology, University of Cambridge, Free School Ln., Cambridge, CB CB2 3RF, England. **Online address:** leh1000@cam.ac.uk

HOWE, Marie. American (born United States), b. 1950?. **Genres:** Poetry, Young Adult Fiction. **Career:** Sarah Lawrence College, faculty; New York University, faculty; Columbia University, School of the Arts, adjunct assistant professor of writing, adjunct faculty. Writer. **Publications:** POETRY: The Good Thief, 1988; Certain Light: 1992: For Baritone and Piano, 1992; What the Living Do: Poems, 1998. OTHERS: (ed. with M. Klein) In the Company of My Solitude: American Writing from the AIDS Pandemic, 1994; The Kingdom of Ordinary Time, 2008. Contributor of poems to periodicals. **Address:** School of the Arts, Columbia University, 305 Dodge Hall, 2960 Broadway, PO Box 1808, New York, NY 10027, U.S.A.

HOWE, Melodie Johnson. American (born United States) **Genres:** Mystery/Crime/Suspense, Young Adult Fiction, Novels. **Career:** Writer. **Publications:** MYSTERY NOVELS: The Mother Shadow, 1989; Beauty Dies, 1994. **Address:** Viking Penguin USA, 375 Hudson St., New York, NY 10014, U.S.A. **Online address:** melodie@melodiejohnsonhowe.com

HOWE, Muriel. Also writes as Kaye Stewart, Mary Munro, Newlyn Nash. British/Irish (born Ireland) **Genres:** Romance/Historical, Young Adult Fiction, Novellas/Short Stories. **Career:** Writer and artist (painter). **Publications:** If there Be One, 1944; The Joyful Tomorrow, 1945; Master of Skelgale, 1946; Until the Day, 1946; Stairs of Sand, 1947; First Affections, 1949; Heatherling, 1950; Private Road to Beyond, 1951; Barbican, 1952; A House of Character, 1953; Winter Staff, 1953; Still They Come, 1955; The Affair At Falconers, 1957; Pendragon, 1958. **Address:** Skelwith Bridge, Ambleside, CM LA22 9NW, England.

HOWE, Neil. American (born United States), b. 1951. **Genres:** Economics, Politics/Government, History, Social Sciences. **Career:** American Spectator, managing editor, 1972-74; freelance writer, consultant on economics and public policy, 1980-; LifeCourse Associates, founding partner, president; Blackstone Group, public policy advisor; Center for Strategic and International Studies, senior associate; Concord Coalition, senior advisor. **Publications:** (With P.G. Peterson) On Borrowed Time: How the Growth in Entitlement Spending Threatens America's Future, 1988; Global Aging: The Challenge of the Next Millennium, 1999; The 2003 Aging Vulnerability Index, 2003; The Graying of the Middle Kingdom, 2004; Long-Term Immigration Projection Methods, 2006; (with R. Jackson, R. Strauss and K. Nakashima) The Graying of the Great Powers: Demography and Geopolitics in the 21st Century, 2008; Millennials and K-12 Schools, 2008; Millennials in the Workplace, 2010; WITH W. STRAUSS: Generations: The History of America's Future, 1584-2069, 1991; 13th Gen: Abort, Retry, Ignore, Fail?, 1993; The Fourth Turning: An American Prophecy, 1997; Millennials Rising: The Next Great Generation, 2000; Millennials Go To College: Strategies for a New Generation on Campus: Recruiting and Admissions, Campus Life and the Classroom; 2003, 2nd ed., 2007; Millennials and the Pop Culture: Strategies for a New Generation of Consumers, 2006; Millennials Go to College Surveys and Analysis: From Boomer to Gen-X Parents, 2006; College Student and Parent Surveys, 2007. Contributor to books and periodicals. **Address:** LifeCourse Associates, 9080 Eaton Park Rd., Great Falls, VA 22066, U.S.A. **Online address:** howe@lifecourse.com

HOWE, (Richard Edward) Geoffrey. (Howe of Aberavon). British/Welsh (born Wales), b. 1926. **Genres:** Politics/Government, History, Social Sciences. **Career:** Parliament for Bebington on Merseyside, member, 1964-66, Reigate, 1970-74, and East Surrey, 1974-92; Queen's Counsel, 1965, bencher, 1969, privy councillor, 1972; solicitor-general, 1970-72; minister for trade and consumer affairs, 1972-74; member of Conservative shadow cabinet, 1974-79; chief front bench spokesman on treasury and economic affairs, 1975-79; chancellor of exchequer, 1979-83; secretary of state for foreign and commonwealth affairs, 1983-89; deputy prime minister, 1989-90; Leader of House of Commons And Lord President of Council, 1989-90; Harvard University, John F. Kennedy School of Government, visiting fellow, 1991-92. Writer. **Publications:** (With C. Jones) Houses to Let, 1956; (with T. Hooson) Work for Wales, 1959; (co-author) Principles in Practice, 1961; Conservative Opportunity, 1965; (with H. Street and G. Bindman) Anti-discrimination Legislation: The Street Report, 1967; (with B. Cooper) Opportunity for Women, 1969; Action for the Consumer, 1973; Too Much Law?: The Effects of Legislation on Economic Growth, 1977; (with M. Thatcher and K. Joseph) The Right Angle: Three Studies in Conservatism, 1978; Europe Tomorrow, 1985; East-West Relations, 1987; Down to Earth Diplomacy, 1988; Conflict of Loyalty (memoir), 1994; Nationalism and the Nation-state, 1995. Contributor of articles to periodicals. **Address:** House of Lords, London, GL SW1A 0PW, England.

HOWE, Stephen. American (born United States), b. 1958?. **Genres:** Politics/Government, History. **Career:** Ruskin College, Politics and History, tutor; University of Bristol, School of Humanities, Department of History, professor in history and cultures of colonialism. Writer. **Publications:** (Ed.) Lines of Dissent: Writing from the New Statesman, 1913-1988, 1988; Anticolonialism in British Politics: The Left and the End of the Empire, 1918-1964, 1993; Afrocentrism: Mythical Pasts and Imagined Homes, 1998; Ireland and Empire: Colonial Legacies in Irish History and Culture, 2000; Empire: A Very Short Introduction, 2002; (ed.) New Imperial Histories Reader, 2010; Intellectual Consequences of Decolonisation, forthcoming. **Address:** Department of History, School of Humanities, University of Bristol, 11 Woodland Rd., Bristol, BS8 1TB, England. **Online address:** stephen.howe@bristol.ac.uk

HOWE, Susan. American (born United States), b. 1937. **Genres:** Poetry, Literary Criticism And History, History. **Career:** WBAI-FM, producer of poetry, 1975-80; Breakwater Books, bookseller, 1985-87; State University of New York, Butler fellow in English, 1988-89, instructor in English, professor of English, 1989-2006; University of Denver, Leo Block chair, 1992-93, visiting poet and Leo Block professor, 1993-94; University of Arizona, visiting poet, 1994; Stanford Humanities Center, distinguished fellow, 1998; Stanford University, Department of English, visiting professor, 1998. Writer. **Publications:** POETRY: The End of Art, 1974; Hinge Picture, 1974; Chanting at the Crystal Sea, 1975; The Western Borders, 1976; Secret History of the Dividing Line, 1978; Cabbage Gardens, 1979; Deep in a Forest of Herods, 1979; The Liberties, 1980; Pythagorean Silence, 1982; Defenestration of Prague, 1983; My Emily Dickinson, 1985; Articulation of Sound Forms in Time, 1987; A Bibliography of the King's Book, or Eikon Basilike, 1989; The Europe of Trusts: Selected Poems, 1990; Singularities, 1990; Incloser, 1992; The Nonconformist's Memorial, 1993; Frame Structures: Early Poems 1974-1979, 1996; Pierce-Arrow, 1999; Bed Hangings, 2001; Europe of Trusts, 2002; The

Midnight, 2003; Souls of the Labadie Tract, 2007. OTHERS: My Emily Dickinson, 1985; The Birth-Mark: Unsettling the Wilderness in American Literary History (criticism), 1990; Kidnapped, 2002; That This, 2010. **Address:** 115 New Quarry Rd., Guilford, CT 06437, U.S.A.

HOWELL, Anthony. British (born England), b. 1945. **Genres:** Novels, Poetry. **Career:** Grenoble University, lecturer in creative writing, 1969-70; Theatre of Mistakes, director, 1972-84; Wallpaper Magazine, editor, 1974-76; Cardiff School of Art, lecturer, 1990-; Softly Loudly Books, editor. **Publications:** Sergei de Diaghileff (1929) (poetry), 1968; Inside the Castle: Poems, 1969; Imruil: A Naturalized Version of His First Ode-Book (pre-Islamic Arabic) 1970; (ed.) Erotic Lyrics, 1970; Femina Deserta, 1971; Anchovy, 1973; Oslo: A Tantric Ode, 1975; The Mekon, 1976; (comp. with F. Templeton) Elements of Performance Art, 1977; Notions of a Mirror: Poems Previously Uncollected, 1964-1982, 1983; Why I May Never See the Walls of China (poems), 1986; In the Company of Others (novel), 1986; Howell's Law (poems), 1990; Near Calvary (selected poems of Nick Lafitte), 1992; First Time in Japan (poems), 1995; Sonnets, 1999; The Analysis of Performance Art: A Guide to Its Theory and Practice, 1999, rev. ed., 2000; Selected Poems, 2000; Dancers in Daylight: Poems 1995-2002, 2003; Oblivion, 2006; Silvae, 2006; Ogre's Wife, 2009; Plague Lands, 2011. **Address:** 80 Sparkford House, Battersea Church Rd., London, GL SW11 3NQ, England. **Online address:** howell.anthony1@googlemail.com

HOWELL, Christopher. American (born United States), b. 1945. **Genres:** Poetry. **Career:** Lynx House Press, founder and director, 1972-, principal editor; Pittsburg State University, visiting writer, 1986-87; Whitman College, distinguished visiting professor, 1987-88; Colorado State University, faculty; Oregon State University, faculty; Willamette University, faculty; Eastern Washington University, Inland Northwest Center for Writers, Creative Writing Program, faculty, Department of English, professor of English and creative writing, 1996-, Eastern Washington University Press, director and senior editor; Emporia State University, director of creative writing, 1996-99; Willow Springs, editor. **Publications:** Why Shouldn't I, 1977; The Crime of Luck, 1977; Though Silence: The Ling Wei Texts: Poems, 1981; Sea Change: Poems, 1985; Simons's Quest, 1990; Sweet Afton, 1991; Memory and Heaven, 1996; Lady of the Fallen Air: Poems from the Chinese, 1998; Just Waking: Poems Uncollected and Otherwise, 1981-1996, 2003; Light's Ladder, 2004; Dreamless and Possible: Poems New and Selected, 2010; Gaze: Poems, 2012. **Address:** Inland Northwest Center for Writers, Eastern Washington University, 501 N Riverpoint Blvd., Ste. 425, Spokane, WA 99202-1647, U.S.A. **Online address:** cnhowell@ewu.edu

HOWELL, David. *See* **WYNNE, John (Stewart).**

HOWELL, David L. American (born United States), b. 1959?. **Genres:** Technology, Sciences. **Career:** University of Texas, Department of History, assistant professor, 1989-92; Princeton University, Departments of East Asian Studies and History, assistant professor, 1993-99, associate professor, 1999-2004, professor of history, 2004-10, Nissan professor in Japanese studies, 2009-10, Department of East Asian Studies, director of graduate studies, 1996-97, 1998-2002, Program in East Asian Studies, acting director, 2001-02, chair, 2005-10; Harvard University, Department of East Asian Languages and Civilizations, professor of Japanese history, 2010-. Writer. **Publications:** (Co-author) Elements of the Structure of Agricultural Education in the United States of America, 1983; Capitalism from Within: Economy, Society and the State in a Japanese Fishery, 1995; Geographies of Identity in Nineteenth-Century Japan, 2005; (ed. with J.C. Baxter and contrib.) History and Folklore Studies in Japan, 2006. CONTRIBUTOR: New Directions in the Study of Meiji Japan, 1997; Basho ukeoisei to Ainu: Kinsei Ezochishi no kochiku o mezashite, 1998; Ainu: Spirit of a Northern People, 1999; Japanese Civilization in the Modern World, vol. XVI: Nation-State and Empire, 2000; Historical Perspectives on Contemporary East Asia, 2000; The Teleology of the Modern Nation-State: Japan and China, 2005; Shuen bunka to mibunsei, 2005; Rokaru hisutorii kara gurobaru hisutorii e: Tabunka no rekishigaku to chiikishi, 2005; Nas honaru hisutorii o manabisuteru, 2006; Looking Modern: East Asian Visual Culture from the Treaty Ports to World War II, 2008; Oxford Encyclopedia of the Modern World, 2008. Contributor to periodicals. **Address:** Department of East Asian Languages and, Civilizations, Harvard University, 2 Divinity Ave., Ste. 233, Cambridge, MA 02138, U.S.A. **Online address:** dhowell@fas.harvard.edu

HOWELL, Dorothy J(ulia). American (born United States), b. 1940.

Genres: Environmental Sciences/Ecology, History, Law, Natural History, Politics/Government. **Career:** Metropolitan Sanitary District of Greater Chicago, microbiologist, 1969-75; Office of the Illinois Attorney General, Environmental Control Division, assistant attorney general, 1975-76; Borg-Warner Corp., attorney, 1976-85; Chemical Waste Management, environmental counsel, 1985-87; Boston University, Center for Technology and Policy, Bell & Howell research fellow, 1987-88; Vermont Law School, visiting professor, 1988-92, assistant professor of environmental law, 1992-96, Environmental Law Center, academic counselor and director of internships, 1993-96; Franklin Pierce Law Center, adjunct professor, 1989-90. Writer. **Publications:** Federal Environmental Release Reporting: Memorandum of Case Law, 1982; (ed. and contrib.) The Complete Library for the Environmental Practitioner, 1984; Intellectual Properties and the Protection of Fictional Characters: Copyright, Trademark, or Unfair Competition? 1990; Scientific Literacy and Environmental Policy: The Missing Prerequisite For Sound Decision Making, 1992; Ecology for Environmental Professionals, 1994; Environmental Stewardship: Images From Popular Culture, 1997. Works appear in anthologies. Contributor to journals. **Address:** 506 Leetes Island Rd., Ste. 3, Branford, CT 06405-3373, U.S.A.

HOWELL, John Christian. American (born United States), b. 1924. **Genres:** Human Relations/Parenting, Sex, Theology/Religion. **Career:** First Baptist Church, pastor, 1950-56; Southwestern Baptist Theological Seminary, fellow, 1954-56; Volunteers of America Maternity Home, chaplain-counselor, 1954-56; West Bradenton Baptist Church, pastor, 1956-60; Midwestern Baptist Theological Seminary, professor of Christian ethics, 1960-99, academic dean, 1976-82, interim vice-president of academic affairs and academic dean, 1994-95, academic dean emeritus, 2003-; Midwest Christian Counseling Center, associate counselor. Writer. **Publications:** Teaching about Sex: A Christian Approach, 1966; Growing in Oneness, 1972; Teaching Your Children about Sex, 1973; Equality and Submission in Marriage, 1979; Senior Adult Family Life, 1979; Christian Marriage: Growing in Oneness, 1983; Church and Family: Growing Together, 1984; Transitions in Mature Marriage, 1989. CONTRIBUTOR: The Gambling Menace, 1966; The Cutting Edge, 1969; Extremism Left and Right, 1972; An Approach to Christian Ethics, 1979. **Address:** Midwestern Baptist Theological Seminary, 5001 N Oak Trafficway, Kansas City, MO 64118, U.S.A.

HOWES, Craig. American/Canadian (born Canada), b. 1955. **Genres:** Documentaries/Reportage. **Career:** University of Hawaii at Manoa, assistant professor, 1980-87, associate professor, 1987-94, professor of English, 1994-, Center for Biographical Research, director, 1997-; Hawaii Literary Arts Council, president, 1983; Biography: An Interdisciplinary Quarterly, editor, 1994-; Study Abroad Program in London, overseas director, 1995. **Publications:** Voices of the Vietnam POWs: Witnesses to Their Fight, 1993; (ed. with M. Fuchs) Teaching Life Writing Texts, 2008; (ed. with J.K.K. Osorio) The Value of Hawaii: Knowing the Past, Shaping the Future, 2010. Works appear in anthologies. Contributor of articles to periodicals. **Address:** Center for Biographical Research, University of Hawaii, 1733 Donaghho Rd., Henke 325, Honolulu, HI 96822, U.S.A. **Online address:** craighow@hawaii.edu

HOWES, Laura L(ouise). American/German (born Germany), b. 1956. **Genres:** Literary Criticism And History. **Career:** Columbia University, teaching associate, 1980-85; Columbia College, assisstant to dean, 1985-87; Barnard College, instructor, 1989-90; University of Tennessee, Department of English, assistant professor, 1990-96, associate professor of English, 1996-, The MARCO Project: Medieval and Renaissance Curriculum and Outreach Project, director and grant co-author, 2001-03, Interdisciplinary Medieval Studies Program, chair, 2001-04, director of undergraduate studies in English, 2004-07, Marco Institute for Medieval And Renaissance Studies, interim director, 2009-10. Writer. **Publications:** Chaucer's Gardens and the Language of Convention, 1997; (ed.) Place, Space, and Landscape in Medieval Narrative, 2007; (ed. with M. Borroff) Sir Gawain and the Green Knight: An Authoritative Translation, Contexts, Criticism, 2010; Trekking the Medieval Landscape: The Representation of Place in Middle English, forthcoming. Contributor of articles to books and journals. **Address:** Department of English, University of Tennessee, 404 McClung Twr., Knoxville, TN 37996-0430, U.S.A. **Online address:** lhowes@utk.edu

HOWEY, John. American (born United States), b. 1933. **Genres:** Architecture, Regional/Urban Planning, History. **Career:** Architect, 1958-73; John Howey and Associates, architect, 1973-. Baypark Inc., president.

Writer. **Publications:** The Sarasota School of Architecture, 1941-1966, 1995; (with S.K. Bailey and D.D. Greer) Florida Architecture: A Celebration, 1912-2000, 2000. Contributor to periodicals. **Address:** John Howey & Associates, 121 W Whiting St., Tampa, FL 33602, U.S.A. **Online address:** jhoweyarch@tampabay.rr.com

HOWEY, Noelle. American (born United States) **Genres:** Adult Non-fiction, Biography. **Career:** National Public Radio, reporter and producer; Cleveland Free Times, book reviewer; Time Out Kids, editorial director; Real Simple Magazine, deputy director. **Publications:** (Ed. with E. Samuels) Out of the Ordinary: Essays on Growing up with Gay, Lesbian and Transgender Parents, 2000; Dress Codes: Of Three Girlhoods My Mother's, My Father's and Mine, 2002. Contributor to periodicals. **Address:** c/o Author Mail, Picador USA, 175 5th Ave., New York, NY 10010, U.S.A.

HOWKER, Janni. British/Cypriot (born Cyprus), b. 1957. **Genres:** Young Adult Fiction, Novels, Novellas/Short Stories, Picture/Board Books, Literary Criticism And History. **Career:** Lancaster University, Department of Sociology, research assistant; Open University, examiner. Writer. **Publications:** Badger on the Barge and Other Stories, 1984; The Nature of the Beast (novel), 1985; Isaac Campion (novel), 1986; Martin Farrell, 1994; The Topiary Garden, 1995; Walk with a Wolf, 1998. **Address:** Walker Books, 87 Vauxhall Walk, London, GL SE11 5HJ, England.

HOWLAND, Ethan. American (born United States), b. 1963. **Genres:** Young Adult Fiction, Animals/Pets, Environmental Sciences/Ecology. **Career:** U.S. Embassy Press Office, reporter, 1989; Central New Jersey Home News, Washington correspondent, 1991; National Wildlife Federation, assistant editor, 1992; Inside EPA's Environmental Policy Alert, associate editor, 1992-94, managing editor, 1994-95; Brazelton Institute, publications editor, 1996-97; Maine Hospital Association, communications manager, 1997-2000; freelance reporter, 2000-. **Publications:** (Co-ed.) EnviroAction, 1992; The Lobster War, 2001. **Address:** 28 Mayland St., Portland, ME 04103-3407, U.S.A. **Online address:** ehowland@maine.rr.com

HOWSAM, Leslie. Canadian (born Canada), b. 1946?. **Genres:** Theology/Religion, Bibliography, Biography, History, Cultural/Ethnic Topics. **Career:** University of Windsor, university professor of history, 1993-; University of Oxford, J.P.R. Lyell Reader in Bibliography, 2005-06; University of Toronto, faculty. Writer. **Publications:** Cheap Bibles: Nineteenth- Century Publishing and the British and Foreign Bible Society, 1991; Scientists since 1660: A Bibliography of Biographies, 1997; Kegan Paul, a Victorian Imprint: Publishers, Books, and Cultural History, 1998; Old Books and New Histories: An Orientation to Studies in Book and Print Culture, 2006; Past into Print: The Publishing of History in Britain 1850-1950, 2009. Contributor of articles to journals. **Address:** University of Windsor, Rm. 2164 CHN, 401 Sunset, Windsor, ON N9B 3P4, Canada. **Online address:** lhowsam@uwindsor.ca

HOY, Claire. Canadian (born Canada), b. 1940. **Genres:** Biography, Politics/Government, Medicine/Health, Social Sciences, Law. **Career:** Toronto Telegram, political columnist, 1966-70; Toronto Star, political columnist, 1970-74; Toronto Sun, political columnist and bureau chief, 1975-87; Global Television Network, political columnist, 1980; Southam News, freelance columnist, 1988-. Writer. **Publications:** Bill Davis: A Biography, 1985; Friends in High Places: Politics and Patronage in the Mulroney Government, 1987; Margin of Error: Pollsters and the Manipulation of Canadian Politics, 1989; (with V. Ostrovsky) By Way of Deception: The Making and Unmaking of a Mossad Officer in UK as By Way of Deception: A Devastating Insider's Portrait of the Mossad, 1990; Clyde Wells: A Political Biography, 1992; The Truth about Breast Cancer, 1995; Nice Work: The Continuing Scandal of Canada's Senate, 1999; Stockwell Day: His Life and Politics, 2000; Canadians in the Civil War, 2004; (with A. Worrall) Punishment in the Community: Managing Offenders, Making Choices, 2005. Contributor to periodicals. **Address:** The Hill Times, 69 Sparks St., Ottawa, ON K1P 5A5, Canada. **Online address:** sallyclaire@sympatico.ca

HOY, David Couzens. American (born United States), b. 1944?. **Genres:** Philosophy, Humanities. **Career:** Yale University, instructor, 1969-70; Princeton University, assistant professor, 1970-76; University of California, assistant professor-in-residence, 1976-77; Columbia University, Barnard College, associate professor, 1977-81; senior lecturer in philosophy; University of California, Santa Cruz, distinguished professor of humanities, professor of philosophy and director of graduate studies, 1981-, now distinguished profes-

sor emeritus. Writer. **Publications:** The Critical Circle: Literature, History and Philosophical Hermeneutics, 1978; (ed.) Foucault: A Critical Reader, 1986; (with T. McCarthy) Critical Theory, 1994; Critical Resistance: From Poststructuralism to Post-Critique, 2004; The Time of Our Lives: A Critical History of Temporality, 2009. **Address:** Department of Philosophy, University of California, A103 Cowell College Annex, 1156 High St., Santa Cruz, CA 95064, U.S.A. **Online address:** hoy@ucsc.edu

HOY, Linda. British (born England), b. 1946. **Genres:** Children's Fiction, Plays/Screenplays, Young Adult Fiction, Literary Criticism And History, Horror. **Career:** Gosforth Comprehensive School, English teacher, 1974-83; Sheffield City Polytechnic (now Sheffield Hallam University), lecturer, 1986-90; York St John University, fellow, 2004-07; University of Sheffield, fellow, 2007-10. Writer. **Publications:** The Alternative Assembly Book, 1985; (ed.) Poems for Peace, 1986. FOR YOUNG PEOPLE: Your Friend Rebecca, 1981; The Damned, 1983; Emmeline Pankhurst, 1985; Kiss File JC 110, 1988; Nightmare Park, 1989; Ring of Death, 1990; Haddock 'N' Chips, 1993; United on Vacation, 1994; The Pit, 1995; Nightmare Express, 1996; Dear Poltergeist, 1996; The Oracle, 1997. Contributor to periodicals. **Address:** David Higham Associates Ltd., 5-8 Lower John St., Golden Sq., London, GL W1R 4HA, England. **Online address:** hoypeloy@blueyonder.co.uk

HOYEM, Andrew. American (born United States), b. 1935. **Genres:** Poetry, Translations, Young Adult Fiction. **Career:** Auerhahn Press, partner, 1961-65; Grabhorn-Hoyem Printers, staff, 1966-73; The Arion Press, founder and director, 1974-, owner, 1974-79, president, 1979-, publisher; M and H Type, president, 1989-. Writer. **Publications:** The Wake, 1963; The Music Room, 1965; (trans.) G. de Nerval, Les Chimères. Chimeras, 1966; (trans. with J.F. Crawford) The Pearl, 1967; Articles: Poems, 1960-1967, 1969; Picture/Poems, 1975; The First Poet Travels to the Moon, 1975; Wilder Bentley the Elder at the Archetype Press, 1982; What If: Poems, 1969-1987, 1987. **Address:** Arion Press, 1802 Hays St., The Presidio, San Francisco, CA 94129-1197, U.S.A.

HOYLE, Carolyn. British (born England) **Genres:** Criminology/True Crime, Humanities. **Career:** Oxford University, Centre for Criminology, university lecturer in criminology, 1991-, director of graduate studies, reader in criminology, research officer, Green Templeton College, fellow. Writer. **Publications:** Negotiating Domestic Violence: Police, Criminal Justice and Victims, 1998; Proceed with Caution: An Evaluation of the Thames Valley Police Initiative in Restorative Cautioning, 2002; (ed. with R. Young) New Visions of Crime Victims, 2002; (with R. Hood) The Death Penalty: A Worldwide Perspective, 2008; (ed.) Restorative Justice: Critical Concepts in Criminology, 2009; (with C. Cunneen) Debating Restorative Justice, 2010; (ed. with M. Bosworth) What is Criminology?, 2011. Contributor to books and periodicals. **Address:** Centre for Criminology, Oxford University, Manor Rd., Oxford, OX OX1 3UQ, England. **Online address:** carolyn.hoyle@crim.ox.ac.uk

HOYLE, Geoffrey. British (born England), b. 1942. **Genres:** Science Fiction/Fantasy, Children's Fiction, Children's Non-fiction, Novels, Novellas/Short Stories. **Career:** Writer. **Publications:** Flight, 1984. WITH F. HOYLE: Fifth Planet, 1963; October the First is Too Late, 1966; Rockets in Ursa Major: A Novel, 1969; Seven Steps to the Sun, 1970; The Molecule Men, 1971; The Molecule Men: And The Monster of Loch Ness, 1971; The Inferno, 1973; Into Deepest Space, 1974; The Incandescent Ones, 1977; The Westminster Disaster, 1978; Commonsense in Nuclear Energy, 1980. PROFESSOR GAMMA SERIES WITH F. HOYLE: The Energy Pirate, 1982; The Frozen Planet of Azuron, 1982; The Giants of Universal Park, 1982; The Planet of Death, 1982. OTHERS: 2010: Living in the Future, 1975; Disaster, 1975; (with J. Robertson) Ask Me Why, 1976; 2011: Living In The Future, 2010. Contributor to periodicals. **Address:** West Wissett 8, Milner Rd., Bournemouth, DS PR4 OTJ, England.

HOYLE, Russ. American (born United States), b. 1947. **Genres:** Politics/Government. **Career:** Time Magazine, editor, senior editor; New Republic, editor, senior editor; New York Daily News, deputy sunday editor, editor, senior editor; Trinity College, visiting lecturer; The Daily Beast, writer. **Publications:** (Ed., contrib. and intro.) Gale Environmental Almanac, 1993; Going to War: How Misinformation, Disinformation and Arrogance Led America into Iraq, 2008. **Address:** Thomas Dunne Books, 175 5th Ave., New York, NY 10010, U.S.A.

HOYLE, Trevor. Also writes as Joseph Rance, Larry Milne. British (born

England), b. 1940. **Genres:** Novels, Mystery/Crime/Suspense, Science Fiction/Fantasy, Plays/Screenplays. **Career:** Actor, 1960-62; advertising copywriter, 1963-69; educator, 1975-. **Publications:** NOVELS: The Relatively Constant Copywriter, 1972; The Adulterer, 1972; Rule of Night, 1975, new ed., 2003; The Sexless Spy, 1977; Rock Fix, 1977; The Svengali Plot, 1978, The Man Who Travelled on Motorways, 1979; Earth Cult in US as This Sentient Earth, 1979; The Stigma, 1980; (as Joseph Rance with A. Kato) Bullet Train, 1980; Ultraworld, 1980; The Last Gasp: Crown, 1983, rev. ed., 1990; Vail, 1984; (as Larry Milne) Ghostbusters, 1985; (as Larry Milne) Biggles, 1986; (as Larry Milne) Hearts of Fire, 1987; K.I.D.S., 1987; Blind Needle, 1994; Soft Verges, 1999; Padroni Della Notte, 2006; Down the Figure 7, 2010. SCIENCE-FICTION THE Q SERIES: Seeking the Mythical Future, 1977; Through the Eye of Time, 1977; The Gods Look Down, 1978; Mirrorman, 1999. THE BLAKE'S SEVEN SERIES: Blake's Seven, 1977; Blake's Seven: Project Avalon, 1979; Blake's Seven: Scorpio Attack, 1981; Blake's Seven: Their First Adventure, 1988. MYSTERIES: Prime Suspect 2, 1992; Prime Suspect 3, 1993; The Governor, 1995. OTHER: Trevor Hoyle, forthcoming. **Address:** c/o Tanja Howarth, Tanja Howarth Literary Agency, 19 New Row, London, GL WC2N 4LA, England.

HOYNINGEN-HUENE, Paul. German/Swiss (born Switzerland), b. 1946. **Genres:** Philosophy. **Career:** University of Zurich, Institute of Theoretical Physics, teaching and research assistant, 1972-76, Seminar for Philosophy, teaching and research assistant, 1975-80, lecturer in philosophy of science, 1976-84, 1985-86, 1987, 1990-93; University of Bern, lecturer in philosophy of science, 1985-87, 1988-98; University of Pittsburgh, Center for the Philosophy of Science, senior visiting fellow, 1987-88; Swiss Federal Institute of Technology, lecturer in philosophy of science, 1987, 1988-92, senior research fellow for environmental sciences, 1989-90; University of Konstanz, professor of foundational theory and history of the sciences, 1990-97; Leibniz University, professor, 1997-, Center for Philosophy and Ethics of Science, director, 1997-, Institute of Philosophy, director, 2010-. Writer. **Publications:** (Ed. and intro.) Die Mathematisierung der Wissenschaften, 1983; (ed. with G. Hirsch and contrib.) Wozu Wissenschaftsphilosophie?, 1988; (ed. with F.M. Wuketits and contrib.) Reductionism and Systems Theory in the Life Sciences, 1989; Die Wissenschaftsphilosophie Thomas S. Kuhns: Rekonstruktion und Grundlagenprobleme, 1989; Reconstructing Scientic Revolutions, 1993; (ed. with M. Fischer and contrib.) Paradigmen, 1997; Formale Logik, 1998; (ed. with H. Sankey) Incommensurability and Related Matters, 2001; (ed. with M. Weber) Ethische Probleme in den Biowissenschaften, 2001; Formal Logic, 2004; (ed. with L. Soler and H. Sankey) Rethinking the Comparative Evaluation of Scientific Theories, 2008; (ed. with T.A.C. Reydon and H. Heit) Der universale Leibniz: Denker, Forscher, Erfinder, 2009. Works appear in anthologies. Contributor of articles to journals. **Address:** Institute of Philosophy, Leibniz University, Im Moore 21, Hannover, D-30167, Germany. **Online address:** hoyningen@ww.uni-hannover.de

HOYT, Elizabeth. (Julia Harper). American (born United States), b. 1970. **Genres:** Romance/Historical, Novels, Novellas/Short Stories. **Career:** Author. **Publications:** PRINCES TRILOGY SERIES: The Raven Prince, 2006; The Leopard Prince, 2007; The Serpent Prince, 2007; The Ice Princess, 2010. LEGEND OF THE FOUR SOLDIERS SERIES: To Taste Temptation, 2008; To Seduce a Sinner, 2008; To Beguile a Beast, 2009; To Desire a Devil, 2009. MAIDEN LANE SERIES: Wicked Intentions, 2010; Notorious Pleasures, 2011; Scandalous Desires, 2011; Thief of Shadows, 2012; Lord of Darkness, 2013. OTHERS: (as Julia Harper) Hot, 2008; (as Julia Harper) For the Love of Pete, 2009; Clever John, 2011. **Address:** PO Box 17134, Urbana, IL 61803, U.S.A. **Online address:** elizabeth@elizabethhoyt.com

HOZIC, Aida (A.). American (born Yugoslavia), b. 1963. **Genres:** Politics/Government, Economics. **Career:** University of Virginia, Department of Politics, teaching assistant, 1990-92, instructor, 1992-95, lecturer, 1998; Hobart and William Smith Colleges, Department of Political Science, visiting assistant professor, 1998-99; Ithaca College, Department of Politics, assistant professor, 1999-2000; Cornell University, Institute for European Studies, visiting fellow, 1999-2000, MacArthur fellow, 2000-01; University of Florida, Department of Political Science, assistant professor, 2001-, associate professor, undergraduate coordinator. Writer. **Publications:** Hollyworld: Space, Power, and Fantasy in the American Economy, 2001. **Address:** Department of Political Science, University of Florida, 234 Anderson Hall, PO Box 117325, Gainesville, FL 32611-7325, U.S.A. **Online address:** hozic@ufl.edu

HRIBAL, C. J. American (born United States), b. 1957?. **Genres:** Novellas/

Short Stories, Novels, Literary Criticism And History. **Career:** Warren Wilson College, MFA Program for Writers, faculty, 1989-; Marquette University, professor of English, 1990-. Writer. **Publications:** Matty's Heart (short stories), 1984; American Beauty (novel), 1987; (ed. and intro.) The Boundaries of Twilight: Czecho-Slovak Writing from the New World, 1991; The Clouds in Memphis (novellas and short stories), 2000; The Company Car, 2005. Contributor to periodicals. **Address:** Department of English, Marquette University, Coughlin Hall 261, PO Box 1881, Milwaukee, WI 53201, U.S.A. **Online address:** cj.hribal@mu.edu

HROMIC, Alma A. American/Yugoslav (born United States), b. 1963. **Genres:** Autobiography/Memoirs, Novels, Science Fiction/Fantasy, Biography, Literary Criticism And History. **Career:** Allergy Society, journal editor. **Publications:** Houses in Africa (autobiography), 1995; The Dolphin's Daughter and Other Stories, 1995; (with R.A. Deckert) Letters from the Fire, 1999; Changer of Days, vol. I, 2001, vol. II, 2002; The Hidden Queen, 2004; Jin-Shei, 2004; The Secrets of Jin-Shei, 2004, trans. as Le Parole Segrete di Jin-Shei, 2004; The Embers of Heaven, 2006; Gift of the Unmage, 2007; Spellspam, 2008; Cybermage, 2009; De gouden hemel. Contributor to periodicals. **Address:** c/o Author Mail, HarperCollins Publishers, 10 E 53rd St., 7th Fl., New York, NY 10022, U.S.A. **Online address:** anghara@vaxer.net

HRYCEJ, Tomas. German/Czech (born Czech Republic), b. 1954. **Genres:** Information Science/Computers, Technology, Education. **Career:** Institute for Financial and Insurance Mathematics, mathematician, 1981-85; PCS Computer Systems, software developer, 1985-90; Daimler Chrysler AG, senior scientist, team leader, 1990-2007, senior researcher, 1991-; ZF-Lenksysteme Gmbh, development engineer, 2009-. Writer. **Publications:** Modular Learning in Neural Networks: A Modularized Approach to Neural Network Classification, 1992; Neurocontrol: Towards An Industrial Control Methodology, 1997. **Address:** Research Center, DaimlerChrysler AG, Wilhelm-Runge-Strasse 11, PO Box 2360, Ulm, D-89013, Germany. **Online address:** tomas.hrycej@daimlerchrysler.com

HSIEH, Tony. American (born United States), b. 1973. **Genres:** Business/Trade/Industry. **Career:** Quincy House Grille, manager, 1990; Oracle, staff, 1990; LinkExchange, co-founder and director, 1996-98; Zappos, advisor and investor, 1999-2000, chief executive officer, 2000-; Venture Frogs, co-founder. Writer and entrepreneur. **Publications:** Delivering Happiness: A Path to Profits, Passion, and Purpose, 2010. **Address:** Las Vegas, NV, U.S.A. **Online address:** tony@deliveringhappinessbook.com

HSIUNG, Ping-Chen. Hong Kong/Taiwanese (born Taiwan), b. 1952. **Genres:** Popular Culture, Intellectual History. **Career:** Institute of Modern History, Academia Sinica, senior researcher, 1990-, associate director; Ming-Ch'ing Studies Group, founder, 1995-; National Central University, K.T. Li Chair, 2006-; China Medical University, School of Post-baccalaureate Chinese Medicine, Taiwan Joint Chair, 2008-; Chinese University of Hong Kong, Faculty of Arts, dean, 2009-, professor of history, 2009-, S.H. Ho College, founding college member, 2009-; Princeton University, Institute for Advanced Study, fellow; National Taiwan University, University of Medicine, Research Center for Medicine and Culture, founder; Fu Jeng Catholic University, adjunct professor of history; Freie Universität in Berlin, visiting faculty; école des Hautes Etudes en Sciences Sociale, visiting faculty; Keio University, visiting faculty; University of Southern California, visiting faculty; University of Michigan, visiting faculty; Harvard Medical School, visiting faculty; University of Chicago, visiting faculty. Writer and historian. **Publications:** Western Civilization, 1984; The Reminiscences of Dr. Huo-Yao Wei-Taiwan and Modern Health Care, Institute of Modern History, 1990; A Daily Chronicle of Health and Medicine in Modern China (1900-1937), 1991; The Reminiscences of Dr. Yang Wen-Ta-The Development of Military Medicine in Modern China, 1991; Yu-Yu: Infant Care in Traditional China, 1995; (with M.C. Poo) A History of Chinese Culture, 1997; (contrib.) Women and Man in Taiwan, 1998; In Peace or in Discomfort: Diseases and Health of Young Children in Late Imperial China, 1999; (contrib.) Imagining Boundaries: Changing Confucian Doctrines, 1999; (ed.) Neo-Confucian Orthodoxy and Human Desire in Ming-Ch'ing China, 1999; Reflections on Childhood in the Past-A History of Chinese Children, 2000; Tong nian yi wang: Zhongguo hai zi de li shi, 2000; (ed.) Let Proof Talk, 2001; A Tender Voyage: Children and Childhood in Late Imperial China, 2005; (ed. with C. Furth and J.T. Zeitlin) Thinking with Cases: Specialist Knowledge in Chinese Cultural History, 2007; (contrib.) The Quest for Gentility in China: Negotiations beyond Gender and Class, 2007. Contributor to books and periodicals. **Address:** Faculty of Arts, Chinese University of Hong Kong, Rm. 529, Fung King Hey Bldg., Shatin, 1, Hong Kong. **Online address:** mhpch@arts.cuhk.edu.hk

HSU, Albert Y. American (born United States), b. 1972?. **Genres:** Theology/Religion, Politics/Government. **Career:** Inter Varsity Press, promotional writer, 1994-, prints publicity manager, associate editor and developmental editor; Christian Church-Clarendon Hills, worship team pianist and church librarian. **Publications:** Singles at the Crossroads: A Fresh Perspective on Christian Singleness, 1997; Grieving a Suicide: A Loved One's Search for Comfort, Answers & Hope, 2002; The Suburban Christian: Finding Spiritual Vitality in the Land of Plenty, 2006. Contributor to periodicals. **Address:** InterVarsity Press, PO Box 1400, Downers Grove, IL 60515, U.S.A.

HSU, Carolyn L. American (born United States), b. 1969?. **Genres:** Social Sciences. **Career:** Jiangxi Institute of Finance and Economics, ESL instructor, 1991-93; University of California, teaching assistant, 1994-98; Williams College, visiting assistant professor, 1999-2000; Colgate University, associate professor of sociology and chair of sociology and anthropology, 2001-. Writer. **Publications:** Creating Market Socialism: How Ordinary People Are Shaping Class and Status in China, 2007. Contributor to books and periodicals. **Address:** Colgate University, 408 Alumni Hall, Hamilton, NY 13346, U.S.A. **Online address:** chsu@colgate.edu

HSU, Madeleine (DeMory). American (born United States), b. 1938. **Genres:** Music. **Career:** Professional pianist, 1952-; teacher, 1955-64; Ecole Magda Tagliaferro, private instructor, 1960-63; teacher, 1965-71; Bronx House Music School, piano instructor, 1968-70; Boise State University, professor of piano, 1971-, emeritus guild, Velma V. Morrison Center for the Performing Arts, professor emeritus of piano; Yale University, visiting Hendon fellow, 1996. Writer. **Publications:** Olivier Messiaen, the Musical Mediator: A Study of the Influence of Liszt, Debussy, and Bartok, 1996. Contributor to periodicals. **Address:** Velma V. Morrison Center for the Performing Arts, Boise State University, 1910 University Dr., Boise, ID 83725-1560, U.S.A.

HSUEH, Tien tung. (Xue Tiandong). Chinese/Taiwanese (born Taiwan), b. 1939. **Genres:** Economics, Social Commentary, Politics/Government. **Career:** National Taiwan University, instructor, 1965-69, associate professor of economics, 1969-71; Transportation Planning Board of Taiwan, head of economic section, 1970-71; Chinese University of Hong Kong, lecturer, 1971-80, senior lecturer, 1980-90, reader, 1990-95, professor of economics, 1995-99, United College, head of department, 1972-77, Hong Kong Institute of Asia-Pacific Studies, director of China's Reform and Development Programme, 1990-99; Harvard University, Harvard-Yenching Institute, research fellow, 1977-78; Asian Productivity Organization, consultant, 1980-; World Bank, consultant, 1981, 1982; Northeast University of Technology, lecturer, 1983-; Xiamen University, lecturer, 1984-; Peking University, educational expert in economics, 1985-86; Beijing Metallurgical Management Cadres Institute, lecturer, 1986-; Nagoya University, visiting research fellow in economics, 1993-; Zhongshan University, lecturer, 1994-; Tainan Theological College and Seminary, visiting professor, 1999-2000; National Cheng Kung University, professor of political economy, dean of College of Social Sciences and director of Taiwan Center of Asian Pacific Studies, 2000-03; Beijing Institute of Information and Control, lecturer; Chinese Academy of Social Sciences, lecturer; Xian Institute of Metallurgy and Construction Engineering, lecturer; Nankai University, lecturer; Huazhong University of Science and Technology, lecturer; Asian Development Bank, consultant. Writer. **Publications:** An Econometric Model for Taiwan Economic Development, 1971; (contrib.) Hong Kong: Economic, Social and Political Studies in Development, 1979; (with T. Woo) The Economics of Industrial Development in the People's Republic of China, 1991; (contrib.) Comparative Asian Economics, 1995; (with T.O. Woo) The Comparative Development Study of Taiwan, Japan and Mainland China, 2002. IN CHINESE: (trans. and contrib.) Foundations of Economic Analysis, 2 vols., 1974; Modern Western Public Finance, 1983; National Economic Management, 1983; (with T. Woo) Trade Between Hong Kong and China, 1984; Quantitative Economics, 1986; The Church Governance, 2004. EDITOR AND CONTRIBUTOR: (with S. Yun-Wing and Y. Jingyuan) Studies on Economic Reforms and Development in the People's Republic of China, 1993; (with L. Qiang. and L. Shucheng) China's Provincial Statistics, 1949-1989, 1993; (with K. Tsui and T.G. Rawski) Productivity, Efficiency and Reform in China's Economy, 1995; (with R.C.K. Chan and C. Luk) China's Regional Economic Development, 1996; (with Li Q.) China's National Income, 1952-1995, 1999. EDITOR AND CONTRIBUTOR IN CHINESE: (with Y. Jingyuan and S. Ruohua) Studies on Economic

Reforms and Development in the People's Republic of China, 1990; (with L. Jingwen and Z. Yuxin) Studies on China's Productivity Trend, 1993; (with Liu and Li) Studies on China's Regional Economic Development, 1994; (with L. Shucheng and L. Qiang) Studies on China's Regional Economic Development, 1994; (with Li Q.) China's Economic Development in Sectoral Analysis, 1998; (with Li) Sectoral Analysis of China's Economic Development: With a Series of Input-Output Tables Newly Compiled in Comparable Prices, 1998; The Future of Taiwan, 2002; (with C.F. Wang) International Comparisons of Taiwan and Japan, 2003. AS XUE TIANDONG: Xian dai xi fang cai zheng xue, 1983; (with H. Dun'ai) Xianggang yu nei di mao yi, 1984; (with Y. Jingyuan and S. Ruohua) Zhongguo jing ji gai ge yu fa zhan zhi yan jiu, 1990; (with L. Jingyuan and Z. Yuxin) Zhongguo sheng chan lü bian dong qu shi zhi yan jiu, 1993; (with L. Qiang and Z.B.L. Shucheng) Zhongguo di qu jing ji fa zhan yanjiu, 1994. Works appear in anthologies. Contributor to journals. **Address:** 7A Bl 2, Ravana, Garden, Shatin, New Territory, 1, Hong Kong. **Online address:** tthsueh@mail.ncku.edu.ty

HU, Xu-wei. Chinese (born China), b. 1928. **Genres:** Economics, Geography, Regional/Urban Planning, Architecture. **Career:** Institute of Geography, Chinese Academy of Sciences, assistant professor, 1954-78, associate professor, 1978-86, professor of geography, 1986-, director of branch economic geography, 1986-94, deputy director of academic committee, deputy director of experts committee for regional development research, 1991-95; Journal of Economic Geography, editor-in-chief, 1991-96; Association for China's Regional Sciences, vice president, 1992-; Association for China's Urban Planning, vice president, 1999-. **Publications:** (Co-author) East China Economic Geography, 1959; (co-author) Northwest China Economic Geography, 1963; Economic Regions: Planning and Organizing, 1994; Regional and Urban Study, 1998; (co-author) Studies on the Spatial Agglomeration and Dispersion in China's Coastal City-and-Town Concentrated Areas, 2000. EDITOR: The Distribution of Cities and Industries in Regional Study, 1986; (with Y. Yeung) China's Coastal Cities: Catalysts for Modernization, 1992; China's Coastal Zone: Social and Economic Survey, 1992. **Address:** Institute of Geography, Chinese Academy of Sciences, 52 Sanlihe Rd., Beijing, 100864, China.

HUA, Gu. American/Chinese (born China), b. 1942. **Genres:** Novels, Novellas/Short Stories. **Career:** Chengzhou Regional Agricultural Institute, farmer, 1962-75; Chengzhou Regional Song and Dance Ensemble, writer, 1975-79; Hunan Provincial Writers Association, professional writer, 1983-. **Publications:** Furongzhen, 1981; Paman Qingteng Oe Muwu, 1982; Gu Hua Zhongpian Xiaoshuoji, 1984, trans. as Collected Novellas of Gu Hua; Jiejie Zhai, 1984, trans. as Sisters' Village; Gu Hua Xiaoshud Xuan, 1985, trans. as Selected Novels of Gu Hua; Chen Neu, 1985; Xin ge jing, 1986. **Address:** 302 Bayi Lu, Changsha, Hunan, 410011, China.

HUANG, Ch. (Chun Ming Huang). Taiwanese (born Taiwan), b. 1939?. **Genres:** Novellas/Short Stories, Translations. **Career:** Short-story writer and folklorist. **Publications:** IN ENGLISH TRANSLATION: Lo (short stories), 1974. UNTRANSLATED WORKS: Er Zi Di Da Wan Ou, 1969; Sha-yu-na-la, Tsai Chien, 1974; Erh Tzu Ti Ta Wan Ou, 1974; Hsiao Kua Fu (short stories), 1975; Wo Ai Ma Li (short stories), 1975; Hsiang T'u Tsu Ch'u: T'aiwan Min Yao Ching Hsu An Chi (Chinese folk songs), 1977; Wo Ai Ma-li, 1979; Hsiao Shuo Tsi, 1980; Lo Han Shih Pa Shou (on martial arts), 1980; Shang Yeh Hsin Li Hsu, 1980; Luo, 1984; Hu Shan Tzu Men Shao Lin Lo Han Ch'uan, 1984; Ch'ing-fan Kung Ti Ku-shih, 1985; K'an Hai Ti Jih Tzu (short stories), 1985; Huang Ch'un-Ming Hsiao Shuo Chi (collected stories), 1985; (with C. Liu) Ai Tu Ti Ti Jen (biographical fiction), 1985; Teng Tai I To Hua Ti Ming Tzu, 1989; Wang Shan-Shou Yu Niu Chin, 1990; Hsiao t'o pei (juvenile fiction), 1993; Tuan Pi Hsiang (juvenile fiction), 1993; Wo Shih Mao Yeh (juvenile fiction), 1993; Ai ch'ih T'ang Ti Huang Ti (juvenile fiction), 1993; Hsiao Ma Ch'ueh, Tao Ts'ao Jen (juvenile fiction), 1993; Mao-Mao Yu Hua (juvenile fiction), 1993; Fang Sheng, 1999; Da bian lao shi, 2009; Jiu wan shi ba guai, 2009; Mei you shi ke de yue tai, 2009; Maomao you hua, 2010. **Address:** c/o Author Mail, Columbia University Press, 61 W 62nd St., New York, NY 10023, U.S.A.

HUANG, Chun-chieh. Taiwanese (born Taiwan), b. 1946. **Genres:** History, Area Studies, Education. **Career:** National Taiwan University, Department of History, lecturer, 1975-80, associate professor, 1980-84, professor, 1984-, distinguished professor of general education, 2006-, Institute for Advanced Studies in Humanities and Social Sciences, fellow, 2006-07, dean, 2008-, Commission for General Education, chairman, 2000-06, Program for East

Asian Classics and Cultures, director, 2006-; National Tsing Hua University, Department of History, professor, 1985-86; University of Washington, visiting professor of history, 1986-87; National Chung-cheng University, Department of History, professor, 1991-92; Institute of Chinese Literature and Philosophy, research fellow, 1998-; Chung-san University, visiting professor, 2000-; Wu-han University, visiting professor, 2001-; Hu-nan University, visiting professor, 2001-; Ministry of Education, Center-Program for East Asian Civilizations, principal investigator, 2002-05; Wu-han University of Science and Technology, visiting professor, 2003-; Kansai University, Society for Cultural Interaction, president, 2010-11. Writer. **Publications:** Inquiries into History, 1981; The Ancient Greek City-States and Democracy, 1981; History and Reality, 1982; Agricultural Construction in Mainland China and Taiwan: Retrospect and Prospect, 1983; The Confucian Tradition and Cultural Innovation, 1983; Development of Agricultural Policies in Postwar Taiwan: A Socio-Historical Analysis, 1986; The Dusk in Rural Taiwan, 1988; The Sino-American Commission Reconstruction and Taiwan Experience: 1949-79, 1991; Treatise on the History of Thoughts on the Mencius, vol. I, 1991, vol. II, 1997; Transformation of Farmers' Value Orientation in Postwar Taiwan, 1992; Education and Thought in Postwar Taiwan, 1992; Mencius, 1993; Reform of Track System: Theory, Practice and Strategies, 1996; Idea and Its Implementation of College General Education, 1999; Confucianism and Modern Taiwan, 2001; New Perspectives in the History of East Confucianism, 2001; Mencian Hermeneutics: A History of Interpretations in China, 2001; Inquiry into University General Education: Taiwan Experience and Its Lessons, 2002; New Interpretation of Mencius' Thought, 2002; New Challenges to College General Education in the Age of Globalization, 2004; Taiwan in Transformation: 1895-2005, 2006; A Study of the Tokugawa Confucians' Interpretations of the Analects, 2006; University General Education in Transformation: Ideas, Current States, and Prospects, 2006; The Postwar Taiwan Transformation and Its Prospect, 2006; Taiwanese Consciousness and Taiwanese Culture, 2007; East Asian Confucianism: The Dialectics between Classics and Interpretations, 2007. EDITOR: Essays on Historical Methodology, 1981; Dr. Shen Zonghan: Chronological Biography, 1981; The Way of Nature and the Way of Man, 1982; Ideals and Reality, 1982; Coping with the Challenge of History: Dr. Shen Zonghan and Modernization of Agriculture in China, 1984; Cultural History of China, vol. I, 1986; Teachers' Manual: Cultural History of China, vol. I-II, 1987; Selected Historical Materials of Sino-American Joint Commission on Rural Reconstruction, 1991; Development of Taiwan after the Second World War, 1991; Reminiscences of the Staffs of the Sino-American Joint Commission on Rural Reconstruction, 1992; (with E. Zuercher) Norms and the State in China, 1993; (with S. Harrell) Cultural Change in Postwar Taiwan, 1993; Imperial Rulership and Cultural Change in Traditional China, 1994; Collected Essays on the History and Culture of Kaohsiung vol. I, 1994, vol. II, 1995, vol. III, 1996, vol. IV, 1997; Historical Development of Mencius' Thought, 1995; (with E. Zuercher) Time and Space in Chinese Culture, 1995; Inquiries into East Asian Culture, 2 vols., 1997; Postwar Taiwan Experience in Historical Perspectives, 1998; The Idea of University and Presidential Search, 1999; Confucianism in Modern East Asia: Japan, 1999; The Fusion of Traditional Chinese Culture and Modern Values, 2 vols., 2001; Cultural Development in Taiwan: Some Reflections, 2003; Historical Knowledge and Historical Thinking, 2003; Hermeneutic Tradition in China: Introduction, 2004; (with J.B. Henderson) Notions of Time in Chinese Historical, 2006; Tasan Study and Korean Confucianism in the East Asian Perspective, 2006; Accords and Discords between East Asian Studies of Zhu Xi, 2006; (with G. Paul and H. Roetz) The Book of Mencius and Its Reception in China and Beyond, 2008. Contributor to books and journals. **Address:** Inst for Advanced Studies in Humanities & Soc Sci, National Taiwan University, Roosevelt Rd., Sec. 4, Ste. 1, Taipei, 10617, Taiwan. **Online address:** ccl0.huang@msa.hinet.net

HUANG, Chun Ming. See HUANG, Ch.

HUANG, Gregory T. American (born United States) **Genres:** Race Relations, Business/Trade/Industry, Economics, Marketing, Information Science/Computers. **Career:** Massachusetts Institute of Technology Lincoln Laboratory, research scientist, Artificial Intelligence Laboratory, biomedical engineering, research scientist, robotics, research scientist; Massachusetts Eye and Ear Infirmary, biomedical engineering, research scientist; New York Times, professional fellow; Xconomy, editor. **Publications:** (With R. Buderi) Guanxi (The Art of Relationships): Microsoft, China, and Bill Gates's Plan to Win the Road Ahead, 2006. **Address:** c/o Bridget Wagner, The Sagalyn Agency, 7201 Wisconsin Ave., Ste. 675, Bethesda, MD 20814, U.S.A. **Online address:** greg@guanxithebook.com

HUANG, Nicole. Chinese (born China) **Genres:** Cultural/Ethnic Topics, Intellectual History. **Career:** University of Wisconsin, associate professor of modern Chinese literature and culture; University of California, postdoctoral fellow. Writer. **Publications:** Women, War, Domesticity: Shanghai Literature and Popular Culture of the 1940s, 2005; (ed. and intro.) Eileen Chang, Written on Water, 2005. **Address:** Ctr. for Eastern Asian Studies, 333 Ingraham Hall, 1155 Observatory Dr., Madison, WI 53706-1397, U.S.A. **Online address:** nhuang@wismail.wisc.edu

HUBBARD, Bill. (William M. Hubbard). American (born United States), b. 1954. **Genres:** Documentaries/Reportage, Biography, Criminology/True Crime. **Career:** Lubbock Police Department, homicide sergeant, 1979-95; Women's Protective Services, vice-president, 1984-88; Red River Marshal's Office, deputy marshal, 1995-2000; Texas Commission on Law Enforcement, certified master peace officer, 1995; New Mexico Office of the Medical Investigator, deputy medical investigator, 1996-2000; New Mexico Department of Public Safety, certified executive peace officer, 1998; State of New Mexico, 8th District, attorney and chief investigator, 2000-. Writer. **Publications:** Substantial Evidence: A Whistleblower's True Tale of Corruption, Death and Justice, 1998; The Race Card, forthcoming; Texas Lawman, forthcoming. **Address:** PO Box 593, Red River, NM 87558-0593, U.S.A. **Online address:** rr4marsh@yahoo.com

HUBBARD, Charles M. American (born United States), b. 1939. **Genres:** History, Young Adult Non-fiction, Politics/Government. **Career:** Middle Tennessee State University, adjunct instructor in history, 1991-94; University of Mahasarakham, visiting professor, 1994; Cleveland State Community College, adjunct assistant professor, 1995; University of Tennessee, lecturer, 1995; Lincoln Memorial University, associate professor of history, director of Abraham Lincoln Library and Museum, and managing editor of Lincoln Herald, 1995-, professor of history, Abraham Lincoln historian; Brown University, John Nicholas Brown fellow, 1997; Lincoln Forum, director. Writer. **Publications:** (Ed. with T.R. Turner and S.K. Rogstad) The Many Faces of Lincoln, 1997; The Burden of Confederate Diplomacy, 1998; (ed.) Abraham Lincoln and His Contemporaries, 1999; Historical Reflections on U.S. Governance and Civil Society: Fulbright Lectures 2000-2001, 2001; (ed.) Lincoln Reshapes the Presidency, 2003; (with C.H. Davis, Jr.) Corregidor in Peace and War, 2006; Lincoln and the Struggle For Command, 2010. Contributor of articles to periodicals. **Address:** Abraham Lincoln Library and Museum, Lincoln Memorial University, 6965 Cumberland Gap Pkwy., Harrogate, TN 37752, U.S.A. **Online address:** charles.hubbard@lmunet.edu

HUBBARD, Christy. See HARRISON, C. C.

HUBBARD, Dolan. American (born United States), b. 1949. **Genres:** Literary Criticism And History, Social Sciences. **Career:** High school teacher, 1971-72; Frederick County Board of Education, teacher, 1971-72, 1974-76; Catawba College, minority counselor and admissions counselor, 1976-77; Winston-Salem State University, instructor, 1977-82; University of Cincinnati, assistant professor, 1988-89; University of Tennessee, assistant professor, 1989-94; University of Georgia, associate professor of English, 1994-98; College Language Association, president, 1994-96; Langston Hughes Review, editor, 1994-98; Morgan State University, Department of English and Language Arts, professor of English, chairperson, 1998-; Langston Hughes Society, president, 2000-; South Atlantic Association of Departments of English, president, 2001-02; George Mason University, Du Bois lecturer, 2002. Writer. **Publications:** The Sermon and the African American Literary Imagination, 1994. EDITOR: Recovered Writers/Recovered Texts: Race, Class, and Gender in Black Women's Literature, 1997; (and intro.) The Collected Works of Langston Hughes, 13 vols., 2001; (and intro.) The Souls of Black Folk: One Hundred Years Later, 2003; (with E.Y. Minor) The Library of Black America Collection of Black Sermons, 2004. Contributor to periodicals. **Address:** Department of English and Language Arts, Morgan State University, 202B HO, 202 Holmes Hall, 1700 E Cold Spring Ln., Baltimore, MD 21251-0002, U.S.A. **Online address:** dhubbard@morgan.edu

HUBBARD, Steve (Albert). American (born United States), b. 1957. **Genres:** Sports/Fitness, Biography, Theology/Religion. **Career:** Plain Dealer, intern, 1978; Springfield (Ohio) Daily News, sports writer, 1979; The (Springfield) Sun, sports editor, 1979-81; Delaware County Times, sports writer, 1981-86; The Pittsburgh Press, sports writer, 1986-92; X-Press Publishing, freelance writer, 1992-2001; Wells Fargo, IT communications staff, 2001-11. **Publications:** The 1993 Fantasy Football Insider, 1993; Great Running Backs: Football's Fearless Foot Soldiers, 1996; (with A. Robinson and F. Robinson) How to Raise an MVP: Most Valuable Person, 1996; David Robinson, 1996; Shark Among Dolphins: Inside Jimmy Johnson's Transformation of the Miami Dolphins, 1997; Faith in Sports: Athletes and Their Religion on and Off the Field, 1998; (with R. White) God's Playbook: The Bible's Game Plan for Life, 1998. Contributor to magazines. **Address:** 705 W Amberwood Dr., Phoenix, AZ 85045, U.S.A. **Online address:** sptwriter@cox.net

HUBBARD, Susan (S.). American (born United States), b. 1951. **Genres:** Novels, Novellas/Short Stories, Ethics. **Career:** Instructor Magazine, editorial intern, 1973; Evening Press, reporter, 1974-76, business columnist, 1974-75, general columnist, 1975-76; Evening Sentinel, reporter and columnist, 1976-78; Journal-Courier, investigative reporter, 1978; Herald-Journal, reporter, 1979-80; Syracuse University, instructor in English, 1984-88, Educational Resources Information Center, editor, 1986-87; State University of New York, College of Environmental Science and Forestry, instructor in English, 1988; Cornell University, senior lecturer, 1988-95, Cornell Engineer, faculty advisor, 1991-95; Pitzer College, visiting writer-in-residence, 1995; University of Central Florida, assistant professor, 1995-99, associate professor, 1999-2006, professor, 2006-; Florida College English Association, executive secretary, 1998-2000. **Publications:** SHORT STORY COLLECTIONS: Walking on Ice, 1990; Blue Money, 1999. NOVELS: Lisa Maria's Guide for the Perplexed, 2004; Lisa Maria Takes Off, 2005; The Society of S, 2007; The Year of Disappearances, 2008; The Season of Risks: An Ethical Vampire Novel, 2010. Contributor of articles to periodicals. **Address:** c/o Michelle Jasmine, Simon & Schuster, CNH417A, 1230 Ave. of the Americas, New York, NY 10020, U.S.A. **Online address:** thesocietyofs@yahoo.com

HUBBARD, Thomas K. American (born United States), b. 1956. **Genres:** Literary Criticism And History. **Career:** University of California, Regents' fellow, 1975-76; Bard College, visiting assistant professor of classics, 1980-81; Skidmore College, assistant professor of classical studies, 1982-84; University of Minnesota, visiting assistant professor of classical studies, 1984-85; University of Texas, visiting lecturer in classics, 1985-86, assistant professor of classics, 1988-93, associate professor, 1993-98, professor, 1998-, Latin coordinator; Cornell University, James Hutton assistant professor, 1986-87, visiting fellow, 1987-88. Writer. **Publications:** The Pindaric Mind: A Study of Logical Structure in Early Greek Poetry, 1985; The Mask of Comedy: Aristophanes and the Intertextual Parabasis, 1991; The Pipes of Pan: Intertextuality and Literary Filiation in the Pastoral Tradition from Theocritus to Milton, 1998; (ed.) Greek Love Considered, 2000; (ed.) Homosexuality in Greece and Rome: A Sourcebook of Basic Documents, 2003. **Address:** Department of Classics, University of Texas, WAG 9, 1 University Sta. C3400, Austin, TX 78712-1181, U.S.A. **Online address:** tkh@mail.utexas.edu

HUBBARD, William M. *See* **HUBBARD, Bill.**

HUBBARD, Woodleigh Marx. American (born United States) **Genres:** Children's Fiction, Illustrations, Young Adult Fiction, Food And Wine, Music, Art/Art History. **Career:** Writer and illustrator. **Publications:** SELF-ILLUSTRATED: C Is for Curious: An ABC of Feelings, 1990; 2 Is for Dancing: A 1, 2, 3 of Actions, 1991; The Friendship Book, 1993; C Is for Curious: An Emotional Address Book, 1993; Visual Feast Recipe Journal, 1995; Twelve Days of Christmas, 1996; All That You Are, 2000; Whoa, Jealousy, 2002; For the Love of a Pug, 2003; I Used to Be an Alphabet, forthcoming; The Birthday Book, forthcoming. Contributor to periodicals. **Address:** PO Box 10645, Bainbridge Island, WA 98110, U.S.A. **Online address:** art@woodleighhubbard.com

HUBER, Evelyne. (Evelyne Huber Stephens). American/Swiss (born Switzerland), b. 1950. **Genres:** Politics/Government, Area Studies, Social Sciences, Economics. **Career:** University of Rhode Island, visiting assistant professor of political science, 1977-78; University of Wisconsin-Milwaukee, lecturer in political science, 1978-79; College of the Holy Cross, assistant professor of political science, 1979-85, bachelor faculty fellow, 1980; University of California, assistant professor, 1985-86, associate professor of political science, 1986-87; Northwestern University, associate professor, 1986-90, professor of political science, 1990-92; University of North Carolina at Chapel Hill, Morehead Alumni distinguished professor of political science, 1992-, Institute of Latin American Studies, director and chairman, 1994-98, 2000-03. Writer. **Publications:** AS EVELYNE HUBER STEPHENS: Politics of Workers' Participation: The Peruvian Approach in Comparative Perspective, 1980; (ed. with P. Evans and D. Rueschemeyer) States Versus Markets in the

World System, 1985; (with J.D. Stephens) Democratic Socialism in Jamaica: The Political Movement and Social Transformation in Dependent Capitalism, 1986; (with J.D. Stephens and D. Rueschemeyer) Capitalist Development and Democracy, 1992. AS EVELYNE HUBER: (ed. with F. Safford) Agrarian Structure and Political Power: Landlord and Peasant in the Making of Latin America, 1995; (with J.D. Stephens) Political Economy of Pension Reform: Latin America in Comparative Perspective, 2000; (with D. Stephens) Development and Crisis of the Welfare State: Parties and Policies in Global Markets, 2001; (ed.) Models of Capitalism: Lessons for Latin America, 2002; (with J.D. Stephens) Democracy and the Left: Social Policy and Inequality in Latin America, 2012. Contributor to periodicals. **Address:** Department of Political Science, University of North Carolina at Chapel Hill, 361 Hamilton Hall, Chapel Hill, NC 27599-3265, U.S.A. **Online address:** ehuber@unc.edu

HUBER, Jeffrey T(odd). American (born United States), b. 1960. **Genres:** Medicine/Health, Food And Wine. **Career:** Huber Electric Company Inc., administrative assistant, 1983-86; New York Public Library, serials cataloger in research division, 1987-88; Brookdale Hospital Medical Center, Marie Smith Schwartz Medical Library, assistant librarian, 1988-89; Whitman-Walker Clinic, AIDS information specialist intern, 1990; Pennsylvania AIDS Education and Training Center, AIDS information specialist intern, 1990; University of Pittsburgh, library specialist on pneumonia patient outcomes research team, 1991-92, Department of Medicine, fellow of section of medical informatics, 1992-93, visiting lecturer in library science, 1992-93; Texas Woman's University, assistant professor of library and information studies, 1993-95, professor of library sciences; Vanderbilt University Medical Center, Eskind Biomedical Library, Active Digital Library, research information scientist, 1995-. Writer. **Publications:** Dictionary of AIDS Related Terminology, 1993; HIV/AIDS Community Information Services: Experiences in Serving Both at-Risk and HIV-Infected Populations, 1996; (with M.L. Gillaspy) HIV/AIDS and HIV/AIDS-Related Terminology, 1996; (with K. Riddlesperger) Eating Positive: A Nutrition Guide and Recipe Book for People with HIV/AIDS, 1998; (with M.L. Gillaspy) Encyclopedic Dictionary of AIDS-Related Terminology, 2000. EDITOR: How to Find Information about AIDS, 2nd ed., 1992; HIV/AIDS Internet Information Sources and Resources, 1998; (and comp. with J.A. Boorkman and F.W. Roper) Introduction to Reference Sources in the Health Sciences, 2004, (and comp. with J.A. Boorkman and J. Blackwell) 5th ed., 2008. Contributor to periodicals. **Address:** Active Digital Library, Eskind Biomedical Library, Vanderbilt University Medical Ctr., 2209 Garland Ave., Nashville, TN 37232, U.S.A. **Online address:** jhuber@mail.twu.edu

HUBER, Richard Miller. American (born United States), b. 1922. **Genres:** Education, Intellectual History, Race Relations, Biography, Social Sciences, Self Help. **Career:** Princeton Manor Construction Co., president, 1958-62; New Jersey Historical Series, co-editor, 1963-67; WHWH public affairs radio program, producer and moderator, 1965-67; channel 13 television, moderator, 1967-68; Oral History Project, director, 1969-; City University of New York, Hunter College, School of General Studies, dean, 1971-77, Division of Continuing Education, executive director, 1977-82; National Endowment for the Humanities, assistant director for TV and radio, 1983-84, special assistant to the chairman, 1984-85; Huber Associates, president, 1985-; Productions-in-Progress Inc., president, 1986-89; U.S. State Department, consultant on American studies, 1989-; Princeton University, faculty. **Publications:** Big All the Way Through: The Life of Van Santvoord Merle-Smith, 1952; (ed. with W.J. Lane) The New Jersey Historical Series, 31 vols., 1965; The American Idea of Success, 1971; How Professors Play the Cat Guarding the Cream: Why We're Paying More and Getting Less in Higher Education, 1992; (ed. with K. Gustavson and J. Ruitenbeek) Integrated Coastal Zone Management of Coral Reefs: Decision Support Modeling, 2000; No Race Left Behind: A Conversation with a Skeptical World about Racism in America, forthcoming; Yankee Go Home but Take Me with You: Answering Criticisms of American Society and Foreign Policy, forthcoming. Contributor to periodicals. **Address:** 2950 Van Ness St. NW, Ste. 926, Washington, DC 20008-1120, U.S.A. **Online address:** rmhuber2@aol.com

HUBER, Sonya. American (born United States), b. 1971. **Genres:** Novels, Autobiography/Memoirs. **Career:** Georgia Southern University, Department of Writing and Linguistics, assistant professor; Ashland University, MFA Program, faculty; Fairfield University, Department of English, assistant professor, Dogwood: A Journal of Poetry and Prose, editor. **Publications:** Opa Nobody (novel), 2008; The Backwards Research Guide for Writers: Using

Your Life for Reflection, Connection and Inspiration, 2010; Cover Me: A Health Insurance Memoir, 2010. **Address:** Department of English, Fairfield University, 1073 N Benson Rd., Fairfield, CT 06824, U.S.A. **Online address:** sonya@sonyahuber.com

HUBY, Pamela Margaret. British (born England), b. 1922. **Genres:** Classics, Philosophy, Biography, Autobiography/Memoirs, Young Adult Nonfiction, Psychology, History. **Career:** University of Reading, Department of Classics, assistant lecturer, 1944-45; Oxford University, St. Anne's College, lecturer in philosophy, 1947-49; University of Liverpool, assistant lecturer, 1949-52, lecturer, 1952-71, senior lecturer, 1971-83, reader in philosophy, 1983-87, now retired. Writer. **Publications:** (Contrib.) Critical History of Western Philosophy, 1964; Greek Ethics, 1967, rev. ed. as New Studies in Ethics, 1974; Plato and Modern Morality, 1972; Philosophy and Psychical Research, 1976; Stoic and Peripatetic Ethics, 1983; (ed. with W.W. Fortenbaugh and A.A. Long) Theophrastus of Eresus: On His Life and Work, 1985; Aristotle on Nature and Living Things, 1986; (ed. with G. Neal) The Criterion of Truth, 1989; Cicero's Knowledge of the Peripatos, 1989; The Human Embryo, 1990; Logical Foundations, 1991; The Pursuit of Mind, 1991; Aristotle and the Later Tradition, 1991; (intro.) Theophrastus of Eresus, 1991; The Divine Iamblichus, 1993; Infinity, 1993; Peripatetic Rhetoric after Aristotle, 1994; Historical Foundations of Informal Logic, 1997; (trans.) Priscian, On Theophrastus on Sense-Perception, 1997; Commentary on Theophrastus-Psychology, 1999; Dicaearchus of Messana, 2001; Eudemus of Rhodes, 2002. **Address:** 33A Barton Rd., Harlington, BD LU5 6LG, England. **Online address:** pamela-huby@lineone.net

HUCK, (Edwin) Arthur. Australian (born Australia), b. 1926?. **Genres:** International Relations/Current Affairs, Politics/Government, History, Anthropology/Ethnology, Cultural/Ethnic Topics, Social Sciences. **Career:** University of Melbourne, faculty, 1958-, dean faculty of arts, 1976-81, senior associate in political science, 1989-. Writer. **Publications:** The Chinese in Australia, 1968; The Security of China, 1970; The Assimilation of the Chinese in Australia, 1971; Kinas utrikespolitik; en analys av den kinesiska uppfattningen av. landets sükerhetsproblem, 1971. **Address:** Department of Political Science, School of Political Science, Criminology & Sociology, University of Melbourne, Parkvillie, VI 3010, Australia.

HUCKABEE, Mike Dale. American (born United States), b. 1955. **Genres:** How-to Books. **Career:** Baptist State Convention, president, 1989-91; State of Arkansas, lieutenant governor, 1993-96, governor, 1996-2007. Baptist pastor and writer. **Publications:** (With J. Perry) Character is the Issue: How People with Integrity Can Revolutionize America, 1997; Kids Who Kill: Confronting Our Culture of Violence, 1998; Living beyond Your Lifetime: How to Be Intentional about the Legacy You Leave, 2000; Quit Digging Your Grave with a Knife and Fork: A Twelve-Step Program to End Bad Habits and Begin a Healthy Lifestyle, 2005; From Hope to Higher Ground: 12 Stops to Restoring America's Greatness, 2007; Deja de cavar tu propia tumba con el cuchillo y el tenedor: 12 stops para acabar con los malos habitos y empezar a vivir de forma saludable, 2007; Do the Right Thing: Inside the Movement that's Bringing Common Sense Back to America, 2008; Simple Christmas: Twelve Stories that Celebrate the True Holiday Spirit, 2009; Can't Wait till Christmas, 2010; A Simple Government: Twelve Things We Really Need from Washington, 2010. **Address:** Sentinel HC, 375 Hudson St., New York, NY 10014-3657, U.S.A.

HUCKER, Hazel. British (born England), b. 1937. **Genres:** Novels, Novellas/Short Stories, Literary Criticism And History, Young Adult Fiction. **Career:** Winchester City Council, organization and methods officer, 1969-71; Hampshire County Schools, History and Economics, teacher, 1972-78. Writer. **Publications:** NOVELS: The Aftermath of Oliver, 1993; A Dangerous Happiness, 1994; Cousin Susannah, 1995; Trials of Friendship, 1996; The Real Claudia Charles, 1998; Changing Status, 2000. **Address:** MBA Literary Agents Ltd., 62 Grafton Way, London, GL W1P 5LD, England.

HUDAK, Michal. Swedish/Slovak (born Slovakia), b. 1956. **Genres:** Children's Fiction, Illustrations, Translations, Young Adult Non-fiction, Children's Non-fiction, Young Adult Fiction, Theology/Religion. **Career:** Lundquist & Carrier, architect, 1985-88; Glimåkra FHS, teacher, 1994-97. Writer, artist and illustrator. **Publications:** SELF-ILLUSTRATED: Vem Spelar i Natten?, 1981; Skeppet över Gamla Stan, 1988; Skeppet och Eldstenen, 1990; Herden och de 100 Fåren, 1998, trans. as The Shepherd and the 100 Sheep, 1999; Kalabaliken i Betlehem, 2001; trans. as The Uproar in Bethlehem, 2001; The

Shepherd's Book, 2004. **Address:** c/o Author Mail, Liturgical Press, Saint John's Abbey, PO Box 7500, Collegeville, MN 56321-7500, U.S.A. **Online address:** michal@michalhudak.se

HUDDLE, David. American (born United States), b. 1942. **Genres:** Novels, Novellas/Short Stories, Poetry, Writing/Journalism, Essays. **Career:** University of Vermont, assistant professor of English, emeritus professor of English, 1971-2009; Middlebury College, visiting professor, 1981-82, Bread Loaf School of English, faculty, 1979, 1985-; Hollins University, visiting distinguished professor of creative writing, 2009-. Writer. **Publications:** STORY COLLECTIONS: A Dream with No Stump Roots in It, 1975; Only the Little Bone, 1986; The High Spirits: Stories of Men and Women, 1989; Intimates, 1993; Not: A Trio-A Novella and Two Stories, 2000. POETRY: Paper Boy, 1979; Stopping by Home, 1988; The Nature of Yearning, 1992; Summer Lake: New and Selected Poems, 1999; Grayscale, 2004; Glory River, 2007. NOVELS: Tenorman: A Novella, 1995; The Story of a Million Years, 1999; La Tour Dreams of the Wolf Girl, 2002; Nothing Can Make Me Do This, 2011. OTHERS: The Writing Habit: Essays on Writing, 1994; A David Huddle Reader (poetry, fiction and essays), 1994; (ed. with G. Orth and A. Shepherd) About These Stories: Fiction for Fiction Writers and Readers, 1995. **Address:** Department of English, Hollins University, PO Box 9707, Roanoke, VT 24020-1707, U.S.A. **Online address:** david.huddle@uvm.edu

HUDDLESTON, Mark W. American (born United States), b. 1950. **Genres:** Public/Social Administration, Regional/Urban Planning, Adult Non-fiction, Business/Trade/Industry, Social Sciences, Politics/Government. **Career:** University of Wisconsin, instructor, 1976-77; State University of New York, assistant professor of political science, 1977-80; University of Delaware, Department of Political Science, assistant professor, 1980-84, associate professor, 1984-94, professor, 1994-2004, chair, 1999-2000, associate provost, 2000-01, College of Arts and Science, dean, 2001-04; Ohio Wesleyan University, president, 2004-07; University of New Hampshire, president, 2007-. Writer and consultant. **Publications:** Comparative Public Administration: An Annotated Bibliography, 1984; The Government's Managers: Report of the Twentieth Century Fund Task Force on the Senior Executive Service, 1987; The Public Administration Workbook, 1987, 6th ed., 2009; (with W.W. Boyer) The Higher Civil Service in the United States: Quest for Reform, 1996; Profiles in Excellence: Conversations with the Best of America's Career Executive Service, 1999. Contributor to journals. **Address:** University of New Hampshire, Thompson Hall, 105 Main St., Durham, NH 03824, U.S.A. **Online address:** presidents.office@unh.edu

HUDGENS, Dallas. American (born United States), b. 1964. **Genres:** Novels, Young Adult Fiction. **Career:** Writer. **Publications:** Drive Like Hell (novel), 2004; Season of Gene (novel), 2007. Contributor to periodicals. **Address:** Scribner, 1230 Ave. of the Americas, New York, NY 10020, U.S.A. **Online address:** fulmermail@aol.com

HUDLER, Ad. American (born United States), b. 1968. **Genres:** Novels. **Career:** The News-Press, features reporter. **Publications:** Househusband, 2002; Southern Living, 2003; All This Belongs to Me: A Novel, 2006; Man of the House: A Novel, 2008. **Address:** c/o Author Mail, Random House Inc., 1745 Broadway, New York, NY 10019, U.S.A. **Online address:** ad@adhudler.com

HUDNUT, Robert K. American (born United States), b. 1934. **Genres:** Theology/Religion. **Career:** Ordained presbyterian minister, 1959; Westminster Presbyterian Church, assistant pastor, 1959-62, pastor, 1975-; St. Luke Presbyterian Church, pastor, 1962-73; Princeton University, trustee, 1972-76; Minnesota Public Interest Research Group, executive director, 1973-75; Winnetka Presbyterian Church, pastor, 1975-94; Asheville School, trustee, 1978. Writer. **Publications:** Surprised by God: What It Means to Be a Minister in Middle-Class America Today, 1967; A Sensitive Man and the Christ, 1971; A Thinking Man and the Christ, 1971; The Sleeping Giant: Arousing Church Power in America, 1971; An Active Man and the Christ, 1972; Arousing the Sleeping Giant: How to Organize Your Church for Action, 1973; Church Growth Is Not the Point, 1975; The Bootstrap Fallacy: What the Self-Help Books Don't Tell You, 1978; This People, This Parish, 1986; Meeting God in the Darkness, 1989; The Aesthetics of Ralph Waldo Emerson: The Materials and Methods of His Poetry, 1996; Call Waiting: How to Hear God Speak, 1999. Contributor to books. **Address:** 7145 65th St. S, Cottage Grove, MN 55016, U.S.A.

HUDNUT-BEUMLER, James David. American (born United States), b.

1958. **Genres:** History, Theology/Religion. **Career:** Presbyterian Church of the United States of America, minister, 1987-; Princeton University, lecturer in international affairs, 1988-91; Lilly Endowment Inc., program officer, 1991-93; Columbia Theological Seminary, professor of religion and culture and dean, 1993-2000; Vanderbilt University, Divinity School, Anne Potter Wilson distinguished professor of American religious history and dean, 2000-. Writer. **Publications:** Looking for God in the Suburbs: The Religion of the American Dream and Its Critics, 1945-1965, 1994; Generous Saints: Congregations Rethinking Ethics and Money, 1999; (co-author) The History of the Riverside Church in the City of New York (Religion, Race, and Ethnicity), 2004; In Pursuit of the Almighty's Dollar: A History of Money and American Protestantism, 2007. **Address:** Vanderbilt University, 2201 W End Ave., Nashville, TN 37235, U.S.A. **Online address:** james.hudnut-beumler@vanderbilt.edu

HUDSON, Charles. (Charles M(elvin) Hudson). American (born United States), b. 1932. **Genres:** Anthropology/Ethnology, History. **Career:** University of Georgia, assistant professor, 1964-68, associate professor, 1968-77, professor of anthropology, 1977-, Franklin professor of anthropology and history emeritus; Newberry Library, Center for the History of the American Indian, senior fellow, 1977-78. Writer. **Publications:** The Catawba Nation, 1970; The Southeastern Indians, 1976; (contrib.) Of Sky and Earth, 1982; Elements of Southeastern Indian Religion, 1984; (with J.T. Milanich) Hernando de Soto and the Indians of Florida, 1993; Knights of Spain, Warriors of the Sun: Hernando de Soto and the South's Ancient Chiefdoms, 1997; Conversations with the High Priest of Coosa, 2003; (contrib.) Light on the Path: The Anthropology and History of the Southeastern Indians, 2006; Pack-horseman, 2009. EDITOR: Red, White, and Black, 1971; Four Centuries of Southern Indians, 1975; Black Drink: A Native American Tea, 1979; (and intro.) Ethnology of the Southeastern Indians: A Sourcebook, 1985; (with C.C. Tesser) The Forgotten Centuries, 1994; (with R. Ethridge) Transformation of the Southeastern Indians, 1540-1760, 2002; (with J.C. Guilds) Early and Strong Sympathy: The Indian Writings of William Gilmore Simms, 2003; (with R. Ethridge) Early Social History of the Southeastern Indians, forthcoming. **Address:** Department of Anthropology, University of Georgia, 250A Baldwin Hall, Jackson St., Athens, GA 30602-1619, U.S.A. **Online address:** chudson@mindspring.com

HUDSON, Charles M(elvin). *See* **HUDSON, Charles.**

HUDSON, John B. American (born United States), b. 1934. **Genres:** Sciences, Adult Non-fiction, Technology, Engineering. **Career:** General Electric Co., physical chemist, 1956-57, physical chemist research, 1957-60, senior research staff, 1960-63; Rensselaer Polytechnic Institute, research associate, 1963-65, assistant professor, 1965-67, associate professor, 1967-72, professor of materials engineering, 1972-, now professor emeritus; Writer and consultant. **Publications:** Surface Science: An Introduction, 1992, rev. ed., 1998; Thermodynamics of Materials: A Classical and Statistical Synthesis, 1996. **Address:** Department of Materials Science and Engineering, Rensselaer Polytechnic Institute, Rm. 104, Materials Research Ctr., 110 8th St., Troy, NY 12180-3590, U.S.A. **Online address:** hudsoj@rpi.edu

HUDSON, Maggie. *See* **PEMBERTON, Margaret.**

HUDSON, Margaret. *See* **SHUTER, Jane Margaret.**

HUDSON, Wade. American (born United States), b. 1946. **Genres:** Children's Non-fiction, Cartoons, Literary Criticism And History. **Career:** Just Us Books, founder and co-owner, 1987-, president and chief executive officer. Writer. **Publications:** (With V.W. Wesley) Afro-Bets Book of Black Heroes from A to Z: An Introduction to Important Black Achievers, 1988; Afro-Bets Alphabet Rap Song, 1990; Jamal's Busy Day, 1991; Afro-Bets Kids: I'm Gonna Be!, 1992; I Love My Family, 1993; (ed.) Pass It On: African-American Poetry for Children, 1993; Beebe's Lonely Saturday; (with C.W. Hudson) How Sweet the Sound: African-American Songs for Children, 1995; Five Brave Explorers, 1995; (with C.W. Hudson) Kids' Book of Wisdom, 1995; Five Notable Inventors, 1995; Black Olympic Champions: Book of Black Heroes, 1996; (with C.W. Hudson) In Praise of Our Fathers and Our Mothers: A Black Family Treasury by Outstanding Authors and Artists, 1997. FOR CHILDREN: Anthony's Big Surprise, 1998; Robo's Favorite Places, 1999; Five Bold Freedom Fighters, 2001; Book of Black Heroes, vol. III: Scientists, Healers and Inventors, 2002; God Smiles When, 2002; God Gave

Me, 2003; (ed.) Poetry from the Masters: The Pioneers: An Introduction to African-American Poets, 2003; Powerful Words: More Than 200 Years of Extraordinary Writing by African Americans, 2004; Two Tyrones, 2004; Underground Railroad, 2005; It's Church Going Time, 2008; Puddin', Jeffrey and Leah: Best Friends, 2008; Places I Love to Go, 2008. **Address:** Just Us Books, 356 Glenwood Ave., East Orange, NJ 07017, U.S.A. **Online address:** wade_hudson@justusbooks.com

HUFF, Toby E. American (born United States), b. 1942. **Genres:** Sciences, Social Sciences, Young Adult Non-fiction, History, Theology/Religion. **Career:** University of California, National Endowment for the Humanities, post-doctoral fellow, 1976-77; University of Massachusetts, chancellor professor of sociology, 1971-2005, chancellor professor emeritus, 2005-; Harvard University, Center for European Studies, research affiliate, 1988, Department of Astronomy, research associate, 2005-. Writer. **Publications:** Max Weber and the Methodology of the Social Sciences, 1984; The Rise of Early Modern Science, 1993, 2nd ed., 2003; Age of Science and Revolutions, 1600-1800, 2005; Intellectual Curiosity and the Scientific Revolution: A Global Perspective, 2010. EDITOR: On the Roads to Modernity, 1981; (with W. Schluchter) Max Weber and Islam, 1999. **Address:** Department of Policy Studies, University of Massachusetts, 285 Old Westport Rd., North Dartmouth, MA 02747-2300, U.S.A. **Online address:** thuff@umassd.edu

HUFFER, Lynne. American (born United States), b. 1960. **Genres:** Women's Studies And Issues, History. **Career:** University of Michigan, French and Women's Studies, graduate instructor, 1985-88; Yale University, assistant professor, 1989-95, French Department, director of undergraduate studies, 1990-92, associate professor of French literature and women's studies, 1995-98; Rice University, professor of French studies and women and gender studies, 1998-2005; Emory University, Department of Women's Studies, professor, 2005-, chair, 2007-. Writer. **Publications:** Another Colette: The Question of Gendered Writing, 1992; Maternal Pasts, Feminist Futures: Nostalgia and the Question of Difference, 1998; Mad for Foucault: Rethinking the Foundations of Queer Theory, 2009. **Address:** Department of Women's Studies, Emory University, 550 Asbury Cir., 128 Candler Library, Atlanta, GA 30322, U.S.A. **Online address:** lhuffer@emory.edu

HUFFINGTON, Arianna. Also writes as Arianna Stassinopoulos. Greek (born Greece), b. 1950. **Genres:** Social Commentary, Women's Studies And Issues, Biography. **Career:** Huffington Post, co-founder and editor-in-chief, 2005-; Center for Effective Compassion, co-founder. Journalist and educator. **Publications:** The Female Woman (nonfiction), 1973; (as Arianna Stassinopoulos) After Reason (nonfiction), 1978; (as Arianna Stassinopoulos) The Other Revolution, 1978; (as Arianna Stassinopoulos) Maria: Beyond the Callas Legend, 1980 as Maria Callas: The Woman behind the Legend, 1981; (as Arianna Stassinopoulos with R. Beny) The Gods of Greece, 1983; (as Arianna Stassinopoulos Huffington) Picasso: Creator and Destroyer, 1988; The Fourth Instinct: The Call of the Soul, 1994; Greetings from the Lincoln Bedroom, 1998; How to Overthrow the Government, 2000; Pigs at the Trough: How Corporate Greed and Political Corruption are Undermining America, 2003, rev. ed. 2009; Fanatics and Fools: The Game Plan for Winning Back America, 2004; On Becoming Fearless: In Love, Work, and Life, 2006; Right is Wrong: How the Lunatic Fringe Hijacked America, Shredded the Constitution, and Made Us All Less Safe, 2008; Third World America: How Our Politicians Are Abandoning The Middle Class and Betraying The American Dream, 2010. Contributor to periodicals. **Address:** Arianna Online, 1158 26th St., PO Box 428, Santa Monica, CA 90403, U.S.A. **Online address:** arianna@ariannaonline.com

HUFFMAN, Jennifer Lee. American (born United States), b. 1950. **Genres:** Adult Non-fiction, Economics, Money/Finance, Human Relations/Parenting, Law. **Career:** High school French teacher, 1973-75; City of Lansing Mayor's Office, clerk and receptionist, 1975-76; GMI Engineering and Management Institute, assistant director of financial aid, 1983-85; Rehabitat Systems of Michigan, director of administration and finance, 1986-96; Jennifer Lee Huffman Family Limited Partnership, general partner, 1989-; Torch Lake Publishing, owner; Bas de Laine Investment Club, president. Writer. **Publications:** (Co-author) What Fits You?, 1980; Money and Marriage: Choices, Rights and Responsibilities: A Guide to Financial Compatability for your Partnership, 1998. Contributor to newspapers. **Address:** Torch Lake Publishing, PO Box R, Petoskey, MI 49770-0918, U.S.A.

HUGDAHL, Kenneth. Norwegian/Swedish (born Sweden), b. 1948.

Genres: Psychology. **Career:** Uppsala University, senior lecturer in psychology, 1980-84; University of Bergen, professor of biological and medical psychology, 1984-. Writer. **Publications:** Psychophysiology: The Mind-Body Perspective, 1995. EDITOR: Handbook of Dichotic Listening, 1988; (with R.J. Davidson) Brain Asymmetry, 1995; Experimental Methods in Neuropsychology, 2003; (with R.J. Davidson) The Asymmetrical Brain, 2003; (with R. Westerhausen) The Two Halves of the Brain: Information Processing in the Cerebral Hemispheres, 2010. **Address:** Department of Biological and Medical Psychology, University of Bergen, Jonas Lies vei 91, PO Box 7800, Bergen, 5020, Norway. **Online address:** hugdahl@psybp.uib.no

HUGGETT, Frank Edward. British (born England), b. 1924. **Genres:** Plays/Screenplays, History, Local History/Rural Topics, Travel/Exploration, Humor/Satire. **Career:** Westminster Press Provincial Newspapers, reporter, 1949-52; Daily Telegraph, sub-editor, 1952-55; Look and Listen, editor, 1956-57; Polytechnic of Central London, visiting lecturer, 1957-65; Regent Street Polytechnic, lecturer in journalism, 1958-65; Ministry of Defense, lecturer, 1965-72. **Publications:** The Coal Miner, 1955; The True Book about Newspapers, 1955; South of Lisbon, 1960; Farming, 1963, 3rd ed., 1975; The Newspapers, 1969; Modern Belgium, 1969; A Short History of Farming, 1970; Nineteenth Century Reformers, 1971; The Modern Netherlands, 1971; How It Happened, 1972; What They've Said about Nineteenth Century Statesmen, 1972; A Day in the Life of a Victorian Farm Worker, 1972; Past, Present and Future of Travel and Communications, 1972; A Day in the Life of a Victorian Factory Worker, 1972; Nineteenth Century Statesmen, 1972; Travel and Communications, 1972; A Day in the Life of a Victorian Farm Worker, 1972; The Battle for Reform 1815-32, 1973; Factory Life and Work, 1973; The Battle for Reform 1815-32, 1973; A Day in the Life of a Victorian Factory Worker, 1973; Factory Life and Work, 1973; The Dutch Today, 1974, 2nd ed., 1977; A Dictionary of British History 1815-1973, 1975; The Land Question and European Society, 1975; Life and Work at Sea, 1975; Slavery and the Slave Trade, 1975; Life and Work at Sea, 1975; Farming in Britain, 1975, 3rd ed. as Framing, 1980; The Netherlands: The Land and Its People, 1976; Life below Stairs: Domestic Servants in England from Victorian Times, 1977; Victorian England as Seen by Punch, 1978; Carriages at Eight, 1979; Goodnight Sweetheart: Songs and Memories of the Second World War, 1979; Carriages at Eight: Horse-Drawn Society in Victorian and Edwardian Times, 1979; Cartoonists at War, 1981; The Dutch Connection, 1982; Teachers, 1986. Contributor to journals. **Address:** Dufour Editions Inc., PO Box 7, Chester Springs, PA 19425-0007, U.S.A. **Online address:** frankhuggett@aol.com

HUGGINS, Jackie. Australian (born Australia), b. 1956. **Genres:** Biography, History. **Career:** University of Melbourne, Australian Center, staff, 1992-93; National Inquiry into the Separation of Aboriginal and Torres Strait Islander Children from Their Families, commissioner, 1997; Inquiry into Release Policy and Practice in the Queensland Prison System, co-chair, 2004; Reconciliation Australia, co-chair; Telstra Foundation, director; University of Queensland, School of Social Work and Human Services, adjunct professor, Aboriginal and Torres Strait Islander Studies Unit, deputy director; Australian Journal of Indigenous Education, editor; Australian National University, Australian Centre for Indigenous History, director. Historian and activist. **Publications:** (With R. Huggins) Auntie Rita, 1994; If the Truth Be Known, 1998; Sister Girl: The Writings of Aboriginal Activist and Historian Jackie Huggins, 1998; (with L. Johnson and J. Jacobs) Placebound: Australian Feminist Geographies, 2000; Working the Walk: Activating Reconciliation, 2002; (foreword) Only Gammon: Three Plays from Kooemba Jdarra, 2002. **Address:** Aboriginal and Torres Strait Islander Studies Unit, University of Queensland, 32 Gordon Greenwood Bldg., 6th Fl., St. Lucia Campus, Brisbane, QL 4072, Australia. **Online address:** j.huggins@uq.edu.au

HUGHART, Barry. American (born United States), b. 1934. **Genres:** Novels, Plays/Screenplays, History. **Career:** United States Air Force, staff, 1956-60; TechTop, affiliater, 1960-65; Lenox Hill Book Shop, manager, 1965-70. Writer. **Publications:** Bridge of Birds: A Novel of an Ancient China that Never Was, 1984; The Story of the Stone (novel), 1988; Eight Skilled Gentlemen (novel), 1991; The Chronicles of Master Li and Number Ten Ox, 1998. Contributor to periodicals. **Address:** c/o Jane Butler, Jane Butler Literary & Art Agent, 212 3rd St., Milford, PA 18337, U.S.A. **Online address:** yrrab@spearnet.net

HUGHES, Colin Anfield. Australian/Bahamian (born Bahamas), b. 1930. **Genres:** Politics/Government, Public/Social Administration. **Career:** McKinney, Bancroft & Hughes (attorneys), counsel and attorney, 1954-56, 1959-

61; Australian National University, Australian Capital Territory, fellow, 1961-65, Institute of Advanced Studies, professorial fellow in political science, 1974-84, editor, 1975-77; University of Queensland, professor of political science, 1965-74, 1989-95, professor emeritus; Australian Electoral Commission, electoral commissioner, 1984-89; Queensland Constitution Review Commission, chair, 1999-2000. Writer. **Publications:** (With J.S. Western) The Prime Minister's Policy Speech: A Case Study in Televised Politics, 1966; Images and Issues: The Queensland State Elections of 1963 and 1966, 1969; (with J.S. Western) The Mass Media in Australia, 1971, 2nd ed., 1983; Voting for the Victorian Legislative Assembly, 1890-1964, 1975; Mr. Prime Minister: As 1901-1972, 1976; The Government of Queensland, 1980; Race and Politics in the Bahamas, 1981; Voting for the Australian State Lower Houses, 1965-1974, 1981; Handbook of Australian Government and Politics: 1975-1984, 1986; Voting for the Australian State Lower Houses, 1975-1984, 1987; Labour Rebuilt: The New Model Party, 1990; Handbook of Australian Government and Politics, 1985-1999, 2002. EDITOR: (with D.G. Bettison and P.W. van der Veur) The Papua New Guinea Elections 1964, 1965; Political Stability and Political Behaviour, 1968; Readings in Australian Government, 1968; (with B.D. Graham) A Handbook of Australian Government and Politics 1890-1964, 1968; (with D.J. Murphy and R.B. Joyce) Prelude to Power, 1970; (with I.F. Nicolson) Pacific Polities, 1972; (with B.D. Graham) Voting for the Australian House of Representatives 1901-1964, 1974; (with B.D. Graham) Voting for the Queensland Legislative Assembly 1890-1964, 1974; (with B.D. Graham) Voting for the New South Wales Legislative Assembly 1890-1964, 1975; (with B.D. Graham) Voting for the Victoria Legislative Assembly 1890-1964, 1975; (with B.D. Graham) Voting for the South Australian, Western Australian and Tasmanian Lower Houses 1890-1964, 1976; (with D.J. Murphy and R.B. Joyce) Labor in Power: The Labor Party in Queensland 1915-1957, 1980; (with B.J. Costar) Labor to Office: The Victorian State Election 1982, 1983; (with D. Aitkin) Voting for the Australian State Upper Houses 1890-1984, 1986; (with R. Whip) Political Crossroads: The 1989 Queensland Election, 1991; Voting for the Australian House of Representatives 1965-84, 1995. **Address:** School of Political Science &, International Studies, University of Queensland, Rm. 550, Bldg. 39 A, Brisbane, QL 4072, Australia. **Online address:** colin.hughes@uq.edu.au

HUGHES, Dean. American (born United States), b. 1943. **Genres:** Novels, Romance/Historical, Children's Fiction, Young Adult Fiction, Children's Non-fiction. **Career:** Roosevelt Hotel, bellman, 1967-72; Central Missouri State University, associate professor of English, 1972-80; Brigham Young University, faculty, part-time visiting professor, 1980-82, associate professor, 1998-2002; part-time editor and consultant, 1980-89, 2002-. **Publications:** MORMON HISTORICAL FICTION SERIES: Under the Same Stars, 1979, rev. ed., 2005; As Wide as the River, 1980, rev. ed., 2005; Facing the Enemy, 1982, rev. ed., 2005; Cornbread and Prayer, 1988. FOR YOUNG ADULTS FICTION: Nutty for President, 1981; Hooper Haller, 1981; Honestly, Myron, 1982; Switching Tracks, 1982; Jenny Haller, 1983; Millie Willenheimer and the Chestnut Corporation, 1983; Nutty and the Case of the Mastermind Thief, 1985; Nutty and the Case of the Ski-Slope Spy, 1985; Brothers, 1986; Nutty Can't Miss, 1987; Theo Zephyr, 1987; Nutty Knows All, 1988; Family Pose, 1989 as Family Picture, 1990; Jelly's Circus, 1989; Nutty the Movie Star, 1989; Nutty Knows All, 1991; End of the Race, 1993; Nutty's Ghost, 1993; Re-Elect Nutty!, 1994; The Trophy, 1994; Backup Soccer Star, 1995; Brad and Butter: Play Ball!, 1998; Search and Destroy, 2005; Saboteur: A Novel of Love and War, 2006; Before the Dawn, 2007; The Cost of Winning: Coming in First across the Wrong Finish Line, 2008. OTHERS: Romance and Psychological Realism in William Godwin's Novels, 1981; The Mormon Church: A Basic History, 1986; Jelly's Circus, 1989; (with T. Hughes) Baseball Tips (nonfiction), 1993; (with T. Hughes) Great Stories from Mormon History (nonfiction), 1995; (with T. Hughes) We'll Bring the World His Truth (nonfiction), 1995; Team Picture, 1996; Brad and Butter Play Ball, 1998; Igreja Mormon: Historia Basica, 2001; All Moms go to Heaven: Reflections, 2005; Promises to Keep: Diane's Story, 2008; Missing in Action, 2010. ANGEL PARK ALL-STARS SERIES: Making the Team, 1990; Big Base Hit, 1990; Winning Streak, 1990; What a Catch!, 1990; Rookie Star, 1990; Pressure Play, 1990; Line Drive, 1990; Championship Game, 1990; Superstar Team, 1991; Stroke of Luck, 1991; Safe at First, 1991; Up to Bat, 1991; Play-Off, 1991; All Together Now, 1991. LUCKY SERIES: Lucky Breaks Loose, 1990; Lucky's Crash Landing, 1990; Lucky's Gold Mine, 1990; Lucky Fights Back, 1991; Lucky's Mud Festival, 1991; Lucky the Detective, 1992; Lucky's Tricks, 1992; Lucky's Cool Club, 1993; Lucky in Love, 1993; Lucky Comes Home, 1994. ANGEL PARK SOCCER STARS SERIES: Kickoff Time, 1991; Defense!, 1991; Victory Goal, 1992; Psyched!, 1992; Backup Goalie, 1992;

Total Soccer, 1992; Shake Up, 1993; Quick Moves, 1993. NONFICTION: Lullaby and Goodnight, 1992. ANGEL PARK HOOP STARS SERIES: Nothing but Net, 1992; Point Guard, 1992; Go to the Hoop!, 1993; On the Line, 1993. ANGEL PARK KARATE STARS SERIES: Find the Power, 1994. ANGEL PARK FOOTBALL STARS SERIES: Quarterback Hero, 1994. FOR ADULTS. FICTION: Lullaby and Goodnight, 1992. CHILDREN OF THE PROMISE SERIES: Rumors of War, 1997; Since You Went Away, 1997; Far from Home, 1998; I'll Be Seeing You, 1999; When We Meet Again, 1999; As Long as I Have You, 2000; Midway to Heaven, 2004; So Much of Life Ahead: A Novel, 2005. SCRAPPERS SERIES: Play Ball!, 1999; Home Run Hero, 1999; Team Player, 1999; Now We're Talking, 1999; Bases Loaded, 1999; No Easy Out, 1999; Take Your Base, 1999; No Fear, 1999; Grand Slam, 1999; Soldier Boys, 2001. HEARTS OF THE CHILDREN SERIES: The Writing on the Wall, 2001; Troubled Waters, 2002; How Many Roads?, 2003; Take Me Home: A Novel, 2004. **Address:** 1161 N Warm Springs Rd., PO Box 307, Midway, UT 84049, U.S.A. **Online address:** dthughes@qwest.net

HUGHES, Declan. Irish (born Ireland), b. 1963?. **Genres:** Novels, Plays/Screenplays. **Career:** Rough Magic Theatre Co., co-founder, 1984-, artistic director, 1984-92, writer-in-residence, 1984-99. **Publications:** Digging for Fire: New Morning (play), 1991; Plays, 1, 1998; Shiver, 2003; The Wrong Kind of Blood (mystery novel), 2006; The Color of Blood, 2007; The Price of Blood in UK as The Dying Breed, 2008; All the Dead Voices, 2009; City of Lost Girls, 2010. **Address:** Rough Magic Theatre Co., 5/6 S Great George's St., Dublin, DU 2, Ireland. **Online address:** declan@declanhughesbooks.com

HUGHES, Gerard J. Scottish (born Scotland) **Genres:** Philosophy, Theology/Religion, Young Adult Non-fiction, Philosophy. **Career:** University of London, Heythorp College, Department of Philosophy, lecturer, 1970-98, head, 1974-95, vice-principal, 1983-98; British Province, vice-provincial, 1982-88; University of Santa Clara, visiting professor, 1988, 1992, 1996; Oxford University, Campion Hall, master, 1998-2006, tutor in philosophy, 2006-. Writer. **Publications:** Authority in Morals: An Essay in Christian Ethics, 1978; Moral Decisions, 1980; (ed.) The Philosophical Assessment of Theology: Essays in Honour of Frederick C. Copleston, 1987; The Nature of God, 1995; Routledge Philosophy Guidebook to Aristotle on Ethics, 2001; Is God to Blame?: The Problem of Evil Revisited, 2007; Fidelity without Fundamentalism: A Dialogue with Tradition, 2010. **Address:** Oxford University, Campion Hall, Brewer St., Oxford, OX OXI 1QS, England. **Online address:** gerard.hughes@campion-hall.oxford.ac.uk

HUGHES, Glenn. American (born United States), b. 1951. **Genres:** Philosophy, Poetry. **Career:** Simmons College, assistant professor of philosophy, 1988-90; Saint Mary's University, associate professor of philosophy, professor of philosophy, 1990-. Writer. **Publications:** Mystery and Myth in the Philosophy of Eric Voegelin, 1993; Transcendence and History: The Search for Ultimacy from Ancient Societies to Postmodernity, 2003; Sleeping at the Open Window (poetry chapbook), 2005. EDITOR: The Politics of the Soul: Eric Voegelin on Religious Experience, 1999; (ed. with S.A. McKnight and G.L. Price) Politics, Order and History: Themes in the Work of Eric Voegelin, 2001; Taos Mountain: Poems by Robert Sund, 2007. Contributor of poems to journals. **Address:** Department of Philosophy, St. Mary's University, Chaminade Twr. 516, 1 Camino Santa Maria, PO Box 66, San Antonio, TX 78228, U.S.A. **Online address:** ghughes@stmarytx.edu

HUGHES, James Raymond. British (born England), b. 1959. **Genres:** Economics, History. **Career:** London School of Economics and Political Science, lecturer, 1994-98, senior lecturer, 1998-2002, reader, 2002-07, professor of comparative politics, 2007-; European University Institute, Jean Monnet fellow, 2001-02. Writer. **Publications:** Stalin, Siberia, and the Crisis of the New Economic Policy, 1991; Stalinism in a Russian Province: A Study of Collectivization and Dekulakization in Siberia, 1996; (ed. with G. Sasse) Ethnicity and Territory in the Former Soviet Union: Regions in Conflict, 2002; (with G. Sasse and C. Gordon) Europeanization and Regionalization in the EU's Enlargement to Central and Eastern Europe: The Myth of Conditionality, 2004; Chechnya: From Nationalism to Jihad, 2007. Contributor to periodicals and journals. **Address:** London School of Economics and Political Science, Houghton St., London, GL WC2A 2AE, England. **Online address:** j.hughes@lse.ac.uk

HUGHES, Judith M(arkham). American (born United States), b. 1941. **Genres:** Intellectual History, Psychology, Psychiatry. **Career:** Harvard University, assistant professor of social studies, 1970-75; University of Califor-

nia, associate professor, 1975-84, professor of history, 1984-, adjunct professor of psychiatry, 2007-. Writer. **Publications:** To the Maginot Line: The Politics of French Military Preparation in the 1920's, 1971; Emotion and High Politics: Personal Relations at the Summit in Late Nineteenth-Century Britain and Germany, 1983; Reshaping the Psychoanalytic Domain: The Work of Melanie Klein, W.R.D. Fairbairn and D.W. Winnicott, 1989; From Freud's Consulting Room: The Unconscious in a Scientific Age, 1994; Freudian Analysts/Feminist Issues, 1999; From Obstacle to Ally: The Evolution of Psychoanalytic Practice, 2004; Guilt and Its Vicissitudes: Psychoanalytic Reflections on Morality, 2008; Interpeting the Holocaust: The Revival of Psychological History, forthcoming. **Address:** Department of History, University of California, H&SS 4085, 9500 Gilman Dr., PO Box 0104, La Jolla, CA 92093-0104, U.S.A. **Online address:** jhughes@ucsd.edu

HUGHES, Kevin L. American (born United States), b. 1969. **Genres:** Young Adult Non-fiction. **Career:** Saint Xavier University, adjunct instructor, 1995-96; Villanova University, assistant professor, 2000-05, associate professor of theology and religious studies, 2005-, director of theology graduate studies, 2002-04. Writer. **Publications:** NONFICTION: (ed. with K. Paffenroth and contrib.) Augustine and Liberal Education, 2000; (trans. and intro. with S.R. Cartwright) Second Thessalonians: Two Early Medieval Apocalyptic Commentaries, 2001; Church History: Faith Handed On, 2002; (ed. with J. Doody and K. Paffenroth) Augustine and Politics, 2005; Constructing Antichrist: Paul, Biblical Commentary and the Development of Doctrine in the Early Middle Ages, 2005. Contributor to books. **Address:** St. Augustine Ctr. for the Liberal Arts, Villanova University, Rm. 128, 800 Lancaster Ave., Villanova, PA 19085, U.S.A. **Online address:** kevin.hughes@villanova.edu

HUGHES, Matt. See **MATTHEWS, Jack.**

HUGHES, Matthew. (Hugh Matthews). Canadian/British (born England), b. 1949. **Genres:** Novellas/Short Stories, Adult Non-fiction, Novels. **Career:** Freelance corporate and political speechwriter, 1979-; Federation of British Columbia Writers, director. **Publications:** FILIDOR VESH SERIES: Fools Errant, 1994; Fool Me Twice, 2001; Gullible's Travels (omnibus), 2001. TALES OF HENGHIS HAPTHORN SERIES: Majestrum, 2006; The Spiral Labyrinth, 2007; Hespira, 2009. NOVELS: Downshift, 1997; Black Brillion, 2004; The Commons, 2007; (as Hugh Matthews) Wolverine: Lifeblood, 2007; Template, 2008; The Damned Busters, 2010; (as Hugh Matthews) Out of the Blue, 2011. OTHERS: (with L. Marchand) Breaking Trail (nonfiction), 2000; The Grist Hunter and Other Stories (collection), 2005; (ed. with K. Drushka) Mike Aspey, What's All This Got to Do with the Price of 2x4s? (nonfiction), 2006; Quartet and Triptych (novella), 2010. **Address:** BC , Canada. **Online address:** himself@archonate.com

HUGHES, Meirion. British/Welsh (born Wales), b. 1949. **Genres:** Archaeology/Antiquities, History, Music, Translations. **Career:** Teacher, 1979-97; University of Wales, Leverhulme research fellow in history and archaeology, 1990-91; St. David's Day, artistic director of opera, 1992; Yoga Plus, lecturer in ancient history and civilization, 1999-. Writer and historian. **Publications:** (With W. Evans) Rumours and Oddities from North Wales: A Selection of Folklore, Myths and Ghost Stories, 1986; (with R.A. Stradling) The English Musical Renaissance, 1860-1940: Construction and Deconstruction, 1993; (with R.A. Stradling) The English Musical Renaissance, 1840-1940: Constructing a National Music, 2001; The English Musical Renaissance and the Press, 1850-1914: Watchmen of Music, 2002; (trans., ed. and intro.) Liszt's Chopin, 2010. Contributor to books. **Address:** Yoga Plus, 177 Ditchling Rd., Brighton, ES BN1 6JB, England.

HUGHES, Phillip William. Australian (born Australia), b. 1926. **Genres:** Education, Mathematics/Statistics, Social Commentary, Young Adult Fiction. **Career:** Hobart Teachers College, principal, 1963-65; Education Department, deputy director general, 1965-69; Canberra College of Advanced Education, School of Education, head, 1970-80; University of Tasmania, professor of education, 1981-91, Centre for Education, dean, emeritus professor of education; Australian Prins Center, chief executive officer, 1995-97; Australian National University, visiting fellow and adjunct professor, 2006-. Consultant and writer. **Publications:** Academic Achievement at the University, 1960; Statistics of Academic Progress 1950-59, 1960; (with J.A. Pitman) An Introduction to Calculus, 1963; Mathematics for 20th Century Schools, 1964; (with K.A. Wilson) Explorations in Mathematics, 1965; An Introduction to Sets, 1966; (with K.A. Wilson) The World of Mathematics 1-4, 1966-67; (ed.) The Teacher's Role in Curriculum Design, 1973; A Design for the Governance and Organization of Education in the Australian Capital Territory, 1973; (with W. Mulford) The Development of an Independent Education Authority, 1977; (with C. Collins) Where Junior Secondary Schools Are Heading, 1982; (with D. Corson and B. Caldwell) Interface between Education and State Policy, Australia, 1985; Quality in Education, 1988; Identification and Development of Intellectual Ability, 1990; (ed.) Teachers' Professional Development, 1991; Assessment of the Value of Hospital Training for APs, 1993; Issues in Education in Asia and the Pacific, 1994; The Curriculum Redefined: Schooling for the 21st Century, 1994; Education for the 21st Century for Asia and the Pacific, 1998; Teachers Make a Difference, 2000; Monitoring Curriculum Reform, 2002; Reforming Secondary Education, 2003; How Do Teachers Influence People, 2004; Opening Doors to the Future: Stories of Prominent Australians and the Influence of Teachers, 2007. **Address:** The Australian National University, Canberra, AC 00120C, Australia. **Online address:** phillip.hughes@anu.edu.au

HUGHES, Rhys H(enry). Welsh (born Wales), b. 1966. **Genres:** Novellas/Short Stories, Novels. **Career:** Writer. **Publications:** NOVELS: The Percolated Stars, 2003; The Crystal Cosmos, 2007; Engelbrecht Again, 2008; Mister Gum, 2009; Twisthorn Bellow, 2010. COLLECTIONS: Worming the Harpy, 1995; Rawhead & Bloody Bones, 1998; The Smell of Telescopes, 2000; Stories From a Lost Anthology, 2002; Nowhere Near Milk Wood, 2002; Journeys Beyond Advice, 2002; A New Universal History of Infamy, 2004; At the Molehills of Madness, 2006; A Sereia de Curitiba, 2007; The Less Lonely Planet, 2008; The Postmodern Mariner, 2008; The Brothel Creeper, 2011; Link Arms With Toads!, 2011; Sangria in the Sangraal, 2011. OTHERS: Romance With Capsicum, 1995; Eyelidiad, 1996; In Praise of Ridicule (poetry), 2003; The Skeleton of Contention, 2004; The Fanny Fables, 2009; Plutonian Parodies, 2009; The Coanda Effect, 2010. **Address:** 133 Rhondda St., Swansea, WG SA1 6EU, Wales. **Online address:** rhysaurus@yahoo.co.uk

HUGHES, Richard (Edward). American (born United States), b. 1950. **Genres:** Novels, Young Adult Fiction, Literary Criticism And History. **Career:** American Samoa Community College, professor of English as a second language, 1984-86; Cambria English Institute, Instructor in English, 1986-88; freelance writer, 1988-. **Publications:** Isla Grande, 1994; Legends of the Heart, 1997. Contributor to magazines and periodicals. Works appear in anthologies. **Address:** Casilla 6572, Torres Sofer, Cochabamba, 28422, Bolivia.

HUGHES, Richard T(homas). American (born United States), b. 1943. **Genres:** Theology/Religion, History, Social Sciences. **Career:** Pepperdine University, assistant professor, 1971-76, professor of religion, 1988-94, acting chairperson of division, 1992-93, distinguished professor, 1994-2006, professor emeritus; Southwest Missouri State University, associate professor, professor of religious studies, 1977-82; University of Iowa, visiting associate professor, 1977; Institute for Christian Studies, Harrell lecturer, 1982; Abilene Christian University, professor of history, 1983-88, department head, 1984-86; Messiah College, distinguished professor of religion, 2006-. Writer. **Publications:** (With C.L. Allen and M.R. Weed) The Worldly Church: A Call for Biblical Renewal, 1988; (with C.L. Allen) Discovering Our Roots: The Ancestry of Churches of Christ, 1988; (with C.L. Allen) Illusions of Innocence: Protestant Primitivism in America, 1630-1875, 1988, 2nd ed., 2008; Reviving the Ancient Faith: The Story of Churches of Christ in America, 1996; (with A.L. Dunnavant and P.M. Blowers) Founding Vocation & Future Vision, 1999; (with N.O. Hatch and D.E. Harrell) American origins of Churches of Christ, 2000; (with R.L. Roberts) Churches of Christ, 2000; How Christian Faith Can Sustain the Life of the Mind, 2001; Reclaiming a Heritage: Reflections on the Heart, Soul & Future of Churches of Christ, 2002; Myths America Lives By, 2003; The Vocation of the Christian Scholar, 2005; Christian America and the Kingdom of God, 2009. EDITOR: The American Quest for the Primitive Church, 1988; The Primitive Church in the Modern World, 1995; (with T.F. Schlabach) Proclaim Peace: Christian Pacifism from Unexpected Quarters, 1997; (with W.B. Adrian) Models for Christian Higher Education: Strategies for Survival and Success in the 21st Century, 1997. Contributor to books and periodicals. **Address:** Religion Division, Messiah College, 1 College Ave., Grantham, PA 17027, U.S.A. **Online address:** rhughes@messiah.edu

HUGHES, Ryan. See OLTION, Jerry.

HUGHES, Shirley. British (born England), b. 1927. **Genres:** Children's Fiction, Autobiography/Memoirs, Picture/Board Books, Novels, Young Adult Non-fiction, inspirational/Motivational Literature, Young Adult Fiction. **Career:** Author and illustrator. **Publications:** SELF-ILLUSTRATED FOR CHILDREN: The Trouble with Jack, 1970; Sally's Secret; 1973; Helpers, 1975, rev. ed. as George the Babysitter, 1977; Dogger, 1977; It's Too Frightening for Me!, 1977; Haunted House, 1978; David and Dog, 1978; Moving Molly, 1978; Up and Up, 1979; (ed.) Over the Moon: A Book of Sayings, 1980; Chips and Jessie, 1985; Another Helping of Chips, 1986; Out and About, 1988; Stories by Firelight, 1993; Enchantment in the Garden, 1997; The Lion and the Unicorn, 1998; Let's Join In: Four Stories, 1999; Abel's Moon, 1999; The Shirley Hughes Collection, 2000; Things I Like: First Rhymes and Stories, 2001; Ella's Big Chance: A Jazz-Age Cinderella, 2003; Olly and Me, 2004 as Olly and Me 1, 2, 3, 2009; Jonadab and Rita, 2008; Bye Bye Birdie, 2009; Don't Want to Go!, 2010; The Christmas Eve Ghost, 2010; Bobbo Goes To School, 2012. LUCY AND TOM SERIES SELF- ILLUSTRATED: Lucy and Tom's Day, 1960; Lucy and Tom Go to School, 1973; Lucy and Tom at the Seaside, 1976; Lucy and Tom's Christmas, 1986; Lucy and Tom's ABC, 1986; Lucy and Tom's 1, 2, 3, 1987; Lucy and Tom's World, 1993; Lucy and Tom's 1, 2, 3 and ABC, 1999. CHARLIE MOON SERIES SELF-ILLUSTRATED: Here Comes Charlie Moon, 1980; Charlie Moon and the Big Bonanza Bust Up, 1982; The Charlie Moon Collection, 1998. ALFIE SERIES SELF-ILLUSTRATED: Alfie Gets in First, 1981; Alfie's Feet, 1982; Alfie Gives a Hand, 1983; An Evening at Alfie's, 1984; The Big Alfie and Annie Rose Story Book, 1989; The Big Alfie Out of Doors Story Book, 1992; The Alfie Treasury, 1993 as The Alfie Collection, 1993; Rhymes for Annie Rose, 1995; All about Alfie, 1997; Alfie and the Birthday Surprise, 1997; Alfie's ABC, 1998; Alfie's Numbers as Alfie's 1, 2, 3, 2000; Alfie Weather, 2002; Annie Rose is My Little Sister, 2003; Alfie Wins a Prize, 2006; Alfie's World: A Celebration, 2006; Alfie and the Big Boys, 2007. NURSERY COLLECTION SERIES SELF-ILLUSTRATED: Bathwater's Hot, 1976; When We Went to the Park, 1985; Noisy, 1985; All Shapes and Sizes, 1986; Colors, 1986; Two Shoes New Shoes, 1986; The Nursery Collection, 1993; Bouncing, 1993; Giving, 1993; Hiding, 1994; Chatting, 1994; Being Together, 1997; Playing, 1997; Helping, 1999; Keeping Busy, 1999. TROTTER STREET SERIES SELF- ILLUSTRATED: Angel Mae, 1989; The Big Concrete Lorry, 1989; The Snow Lady, 1990; Wheels, 1991; Tales of Trotter Street, 1997. NOVELS: Hero on a Bicycle, 2012. Illustrator of books by others. **Address:** c/o Author Mail, Random House, 61-63 Uxbridge Rd., Ealing, London, GL W5 5SA, England.

HUGHES, Steven C. American (born United States), b. 1949. **Genres:** Politics/Government. **Career:** University of Colorado, instructor and lecturer, 1982-95; Loyola University Maryland, Department of History, assistant professor, 1985-91, associate professor, 1991-96, professor of history, 1996-, chair. Writer and historian. **Publications:** Crime, Disorder, and the Risorgimento: The Politics of Policing in Bologna, 1994; Politics of the Sword: Dueling, Honor, and Masculinity in Modern Italy, 2007. Contributor to books, journals and periodicals. **Address:** Loyola University Maryland, Humanities 301, 4501 N Charles St., Baltimore, MD 21210, U.S.A. **Online address:** schughes@loyola.edu

HUGHES, Susan. Canadian (born Canada), b. 1960?. **Genres:** Young Adult Non-fiction. **Career:** Crabtree Publishing Co., editor researcher and writer. **Publications:** JUVENILE NONFICTION: (With B. Kalman) I Live in a City, 1986; The Environmental Detective Kit (with equipment), 1991, rev. ed., 1998; (with S. Cumbaa) Megalodon: The Prehistoric Shark, 1998; The Titanic Book and Submersible Model, 1999; Canada Invents, 2002; When Beep-Beep Came to Earth, 2002; Let's Call It Canada: Amazing Stories of Canadian Place Names, 2003; Lester B. Pearson, 2003; Coming to Canada: Building a Life in a New Land, 2005; (reteller) The Promise, 2005; Buses, Cars, and Trucks, 2005; Where Are the Bears?, 2005; (reteller) The Frog Prince, 2005; True or False: Finding Out about Newfoundland Dogs, 2005; Raise Your Voice, Lend a Hand, Change the World, 2006; Canadian Festivals, 2007; No Girls Allowed: Tales of Daring Women Dressed as Men for Love, Freedom, and Adventure, 2008; Canadian Sports, 2009; Canada's Birds, 2010; Case Closed? Nine Mysteries Unlocked by Modern Science, 2010. FICTION FOR CHILDREN: Anything Can Happen (middle-grade novel), 1992; The Not-Quite World Famous Scientist, 2002; Earth to Audrey (picture book), 2005; Virginia (young- adult novel), 2010. IN MY WORLD SERIES FOR CHILDREN: Animal Worlds, 1986; Time and the Seasons, 1986; The Food We Eat, 1986; People at Play, 1986; People at Work, 1986. HOLIDAYS AND FESTIVALS SERIES FOR CHILDREN: (with B. Kalman) We Celebrate Family Days, 1986; (with B. Kalman) We Celebrate Valentine's Day, 1986; We Celebrate Hanukkah, 1986; (with B. Kalman) We Celebrate the Harvest, 1986; (with B. Kalman) We Celebrate Winter, 1986. WILD PAWS CHAPTER-BOOK SERIES FOR CHILDREN: Bobcat Rescue, 2003; Lonely

Wolf Pup, 2003; Bunnies in Trouble, 2004; Orphaned Beluga, 2004; Cubs All Alone, 2004. LANDS, PEOPLES, AND CULTURES SERIES FOR CHILDREN: (with A. Fast) Cuba: The Culture, 2004; (with A. Fast) Cuba: The Land, 2004; (with A. Fast) Cuba: The People, 2004. Contributor to books. **Online address:** susanhughes@sympatico.ca

HUGHES, Tracy. *See* **BLACKSTOCK, Terri.**

HUGHES-HALLETT, Lucy. British (born England), b. 1951. **Genres:** Biography, History, Autobiography/Memoirs. **Career:** Vogue Magazine, writer, 1974-79; London Evening Standard, television critic, 1983-87; Sunday Times, Books Section, reviewer, 1987-. Historian. **Publications:** Cleopatra: Histories, Dreams, and Distortions, 1990; Heroes: Saviours, Traitors and Supermen, 2004; Heroes: A History of Hero Worship, 2006. Contributor to periodicals. **Address:** c/o Felicity Rubinstein, Lutyens & Rubinstein, 21 Kensington Park Rd., London, GL W11 2EU, England.

HUGHEY, Elizabeth. American (born United States), b. 1974?. **Genres:** Poetry. **Career:** Bateau Press, contributing editor; Johns Hopkins University, Center For Talented Youth, instructor, 2003-; University of Alabama, Spencer Honors House, lecturer in creative writing, 2009-; Desert Island Supply Co., co-founder. **Publications:** Sunday Houses the Sunday House (poems), 2007. Contributor to periodicals. **Address:** University of Iowa Press, 11030 S Langley Ave., Chicago, IL 60628, U.S.A. **Online address:** lizhughey@yahoo.com

HUGON, Anne. French (born France), b. 1965. **Genres:** History, Third World, Young Adult Fiction, Local History/Rural Topics, Translations. **Career:** University of Lyon, assistant lecturer in history, 1990-. Writer and translator. **Publications:** LAfrique des Explorateurs, 1991, trans. as The Exploration of Africa, 1993; (trans.) M. Kingsley, Une odyssee Africaine (title means: 'Travels in West Africa'), 1992; Tombouctou, 1994; Histoire des femmes en situation coloniale: Afrique et Asie, XXe siécle, 2004; Un protestantisme africain au XIXe siecle: Limplantation du methodisme en gold coast, Ghana, 1835-1874, 2007. **Address:** 23 rue Berthollet, Paris, 75005, France.

HUHNE, Christopher. British (born England), b. 1954. **Genres:** Economics, Politics/Government, Money/Finance. **Career:** Freelance journalist in India, 1975-76; Liverpool Daily Post and Echo, graduate trainee, 1976-77; Economist, correspondent, 1977-80; Guardian, economic leader writer, 1980-85; economic editor and weekly columnist, 1985-90; The Independent, business and economics editor and department head, 1990-94; The Independent on Sunday, business and economics editor and department head, 1990-94; IBCA Ltd., managing director and chief economist, 1994-99; European Parliament, member of parliament, 1999-2005; Liberal Democrats, member of parliament, 2005-, treasury chief secretary spokesman, 2005-06, environment, food and rural affairs spokesman, 2006-07, home affairs spokesman, 2007-10; Department of Energy & Climate, secretary of state, 2010-. Lecturer and writer. **Publications:** Issues in the 1984 European Parliamentary Elections, 1984; (with H. Lever) Debt and Danger: The World Financial Crisis, 1985, rev. ed., 1987; The Forces Shaping British Attitudes towards the European Community, 1985; Real World Economics: Essays on Imperfect Markets and Fallible Governments, 1990; (with M. Emerson) The ECU Report, 1991; (with J. Fordor) Both Sides of the Coin, 1999. Contributor to books and magazines. **Address:** European Parliament, 109a Leigh Rd., Rue Wiertz, Eastleigh, HB SO50 9DR, England. **Online address:** chrishuhne@cix.co.uk

HUISINGA, Roger. American (born United States), b. 1961. **Genres:** Poetry, Literary Criticism And History, Young Adult Fiction. **Career:** Monticello Agriculture Center, custom applicator. Poet. **Publications:** I Don't Know Jack: Poems in Search of Reason, 2005; Forty Acres of Thoughts: Poems from around the Bend, 2006. **Address:** Mayhaven Publishing Inc., PO Box 557, Mahomet, IL 61853-0557, U.S.A. **Online address:** rogerhuisinga@yahoo.com

HUIZENGA, John R(obert). American (born United States), b. 1921. **Genres:** Physics, Chemistry. **Career:** Manhattan Wartime Project, laboratory supervisor, 1944-46; Calvin College, instructor in chemistry, 1946-47; Argonne National Laboratory, associate scientist, 1949-57, senior scientist, 1958-67; University of Chicago, professorial lecturer, 1963-67; University of Rochester, professor of chemistry and physics, 1967-78, Tracy H. Harris professor of chemistry and physics, 1978-91, chair of chemistry department, 1983-88, Tracy H. Harris professor emeritus of chemistry and physics, 1991-. Writer. **Publications:** A Study of the Transference Properties of Polymeric Electrolytes Using Radioactive Tracers, 1949; (with R. Vandenbosch) Nucle-

ar Fission, 1973; (with W.U. Schroeder) Damped Nuclear Reactions, 1982; Cold Fusion: The Scientific Fiasco of the Century, 1992; Five Decades of Research in Nuclear Science, 2009. **Address:** Department of Chemistry, University of Rochester, 453 Hutchison Hall, 120 Trustee Rd., PO Box 270216, Rochester, NY 14627, U.S.A. **Online address:** hedges@chem.rochester.edu

HULL, Isabel V. American (born United States), b. 1949. **Genres:** History, Social Sciences. **Career:** Cornell University, Department of History, assistant professor, professor, 1977-, John Stambaugh professor of history, chair of the department. Writer. **Publications:** The Entourage of Kaiser Wilhelm III, 1888-1918, 1982; (ed. with C. Fink and M. Knox) German Nationalism and the European Response, 1890-1945, 1985; Sexuality, State and Civil Society in Germany, 1700-1815, 1996; Absolute Destruction: Military Culture and the Practices of War in Imperial Germany, 2005. **Address:** Department of History, Cornell University, 431 McGraw Hall, Ithaca, NY 14853, U.S.A. **Online address:** ivh1@cornell.edu

HULL, John M. British/Australian (born Australia), b. 1935. **Genres:** Education, Theology/Religion, Young Adult Non-fiction. **Career:** Teacher, 1957-59, 1962-66; Westhill College, lecturer, 1966-68; University of Birmingham, lecturer in religious education, 1968-78, senior lecturer, 1978-86, reader, 1986-89, professor of religious education, 1989-2002, professor emeritus, 2002-, Faculty of Education and Continuing Studies, dean, 1990-93; British Journal of Religious Education, editor, 1971-96; Queen's Foundation, honorary professor of practical theology, 2004-. **Publications:** Sense and Nonsense about God, 1974, 2nd ed., 1999; Hellenistic Magic and the Synoptic Tradition, 1974; School Worship: An Obituary, 1975; Studies in Religion and Education, 1984; What Prevents Christian Adults from Learning?, 1985; The Act Unpacked: The Meaning of the 1988 Education Reform Act for Religious Education, 1989; Touching the Rock: An Experience of Blindness, 1990, 2nd ed., 1992; God-Talk with Young Children: Notes for Parents and Teachers, 1991; (co-author) A Gift to the Child: Religious Education in the Primary School, 1991; Mish-Mash: Religious Education in Multi-Cultural Britain: A Study of Metaphor, 1991; On Sight & Insight: A Journey into the World of Blindness, 1997; Utopian Whispers: Moral, Religious & Spiritual Values in Schools, 1998; Glaube und Bildung, 2000; Gott und Geld, 2000; In the Beginning There Was Darkness: A Blind Person's Conversations with the Bible, 2002; Mission-Shaped Church: A Theological Response, 2006. EDITOR: The Child in the Church, 1976; (with M. Keys) Religion in Education and Learning for Living: Index 1934-78, 1979; Understanding Christian Nurture, 1981; (and intro.) New Directions in Religious Education, 1982. Works appear in anthologies. Contributor to books and journals. **Address:** The Queen's Foundation, Somerset Rd., Edgbaston, Birmingham, WM B15 2TT, England. **Online address:** j.hull@queens.ac.uk

HULL, Jonathan. American (born United States), b. 1960?. **Genres:** Novels. **Career:** Time magazine, correspondent, 1985-95, Los Angeles bureau staff, 1985-88, chief of Jerusalem bureau chief, 1988-91, chief of Chicago bureau, 1991-95. WereYouThere.com, founder and chief executive officer. Writer, 1995-. **Publications:** Losing Julia, 2000; The Distance from Normandy, 2003. **Address:** c/o Author Mail, St. Martins Press, 175 5th Ave., New York, NY 10010-7703, U.S.A. **Online address:** jonathan@jonathanhull.com

HULL, Nancy L. American (born United States), b. 1952. **Genres:** Children's Fiction, Children's Non-fiction, Military/Defense/Arms Control. **Career:** Rockford High School, English teacher, 1974-75; Grand Rapids Baptist College, adjunct instructor, 1980-85; Pace Group Inc., corporate reading/writing instructor, 1983-85; Calvin College, adjunct instructor, 1985-90, 1994-99, assistant professor of English, 1999-; Caledonia Middle School, teacher, 1990-94. Writer. **Publications:** On Rough Seas, 2008. **Address:** Calvin College, 1795 Knollcrest Cir., Grand Rapids, MI 49546, U.S.A. **Online address:** nhull@calvin.edu

HULL, William E(dward). American (born United States), b. 1930. **Genres:** Theology/Religion, Literary Criticism And History, Poetry. **Career:** Samford University, instructor, 1955-58, assistant professor, 1958-61, associate professor, 1961-67, professor, 1967-75, director of graduate studies, 1968-70, The School of Theology, dean, 1969-75, provost, 1972-75, provost and university professor, 1987-, research professor, now retired; National Association of Baptist Professors of Religion, president, 1967-68; First Baptist Church, pastor, 1975-87. Writer. **Publications:** The Gospel of John, 1964; The Broadman Bible, 1970; The Bible, 1974; Beyond the Barriers, 1981; Shreveport Sermons, vol. I, 1981, vol. II, 1982; Love in Four Dimensions, 1982; The

Christian Experience of Salvation, 1987; Southern Baptist Higher Education: Retrospect and Prospect, 2001; The Quest for Spiritual Maturity, 2004. The Four-Way Test: Core Values of the Rotary Movement, 2004; Strategic Preaching: The Role of the Pulpit in Pastoral Leadership, 2006; Harbingers of Hope: Claiming God's Promises in Today's World, 2007. Contributor to numerous periodicals. **Address:** 435 Vesclub Way, Birmingham, AL 35216, U.S.A. **Online address:** wehull@samford.edu

HULME, Ann. *See* **GRANGER, (Patricia) Ann.**

HULSE, James Warren. American (born United States), b. 1930. **Genres:** History, Social Sciences. **Career:** Nevada State Journal, journalist, 1954-59; Central Washington State College, assistant professor, 1961-62; University of Nevada, assistant professor, 1962-66, associate professor, 1966-70, professor of history, 1970, now professor emeritus of history. **Publications:** The Forming of the Communist International, 1964; The Nevada Adventure: A History, 1965, 6th ed., 1990; Revolutionists in London: A Study of Five Unorthodox Socialists, 1970; Lincoln County, Nevada: 1864-1909, 1971; The University of Nevada: A Centennial History, 1974; Forty Years in the Wilderness: Impressions of Nevada, 1940-1980, 1986; The Silver State: Nevada's History Reinterpreted, 1991, 3rd ed., 2004; The Reputations of Socrates, 1995; (with L.E. Goodall and J. Allen) Reinventing the System: Higher Education in Nevada, 1968-2000, 2002; Oases of Culture: A History of Public and Academic Libraries in Nevada, 2003; Nevada's Environmental Legacy: Progress or Plunder, 2009. **Address:** University of Nevada, 940 Grand View Ave., Reno, NV 89503, U.S.A.

HULSE, Michael (William). British (born England), b. 1955. **Genres:** Poetry, Literary Criticism And History, Translations, History. **Career:** University of Erlangen-Nürnberg, lecturer in English and drama, 1977-79; Catholic University of Eichstätt, lecturer in English and literature, 1981-83; University of Cologne, part-time lecturer, 1985-95; Deutsche Welle TV, translator, 1986-2000; Littlewood Arc, associate editor, 1992-98; University of Zurich, visiting lecturer, 1994; Leviathan, founder and editorial director, 2000-; Hippocrates Prize, co-founder, 2009-; Leviathan Quarterly, founder and editor; University of Warwick, Department of English and Comparative Literary Studies, lecturer, associate professor; Stand, editor. **Publications:** POETRY: Monochrome Blood, 1980; Dole Queue, 1981; Knowing and Forgetting, 1981; Propaganda, 1985; Eating Strawberries in the Necropolis, 1991; Mother of Battles, 1991; (ed. with D. Kennedy and D. Morley) New Poetry, 1993; Monteverdi's Photographs, 1995; Empires and Holy Lands: Poems 1976-2000, 2002; Charles Simic in Conversation with Michael Hulse, 2002. TRANSLATOR: Tumult, 1984; Matisse, 1987; Essays in Honor of Elias Canetti, 1987; Toulouse-Lautrec, 1987; Chagall, 1987; Prison Journal, 1987 in US as A Woman's Prison Journal, 1988; The Sorrows of Young Werther, 1989; Munch, 1989; Cézanne, 1989; Karl Lagerfeld, 1990; Chargesheimer, 1990; Dahmane, 1990; The Complete Paintingsof van Gogh, 2 vols., 1990; E. Jelinek, Wonderful, Wonderful Times, 1990; Salvador Dali, 1990; Wonderful Wonderful Times, 1990; Jan Lobel from Warsaw, 1991; The Idiot: Paraphrases of Dostoyevsky, 1991; Edward Hopper, 1991; Egon Schiele, 1991; Degas, 1992; Picasso, 2 vols., 1992; Gauguin in Tahiti, 1992; Helnwein, 1992; Japan Design, 1992; Casper Hauser, 1992; (trans.) Lust, 1992; Impressionism, 2 vols., 1993; Written in the Westm 1993; Best of Graphis, 8 vols., 1993; Rainer Maria Rilke, 1993; George Grosz, 1994; Guglielmo Plüschow, 1994; Desert: The Colour of Egypt, 1994; GDR Souvenirs, 1994; G. Néret, Salvador Dalí: The Paintings, 2 vols., 1994; Claude Monet, 1994; (with M. Chalmers) Night Drive, 1995; (co-author) Art of the Italian Renaissance, 1995; Egon Schiele, 1995; (trans.) The Emigrants, 1996; Ernst Ludwig Kirchner, 1996; (trans.) The Rings of Saturn, 1998; Unter Krahnehbäumen, 1998; (trans.) Vertigo, 1999; Seurat, 1999; (trans. with P. Boehm) The Appointment, 2001; (with M. Chalmers) A. Kluge, Devil's Blind Spot: Tales From the New Century, 2004; (and forward) A. Andersch, Cherries of Freedom: A Report, 2004. OTHER: Secret History, 2009. **Address:** Department of English and Comparative Literary, Studies, University of Warwick, Rm. H544, Humanities Bldg., Gibbet Hill Rd., Coventry, CV4 7AL, England. **Online address:** m.w.hulse@warwick.ac.uk

HULSMAN, John C. German/American (born United States), b. 1967?. **Genres:** Politics/Government. **Career:** University of St. Andrews, tutor and graduate lecturer in world politics and U.S. foreign policy, 1992-95; Center for Strategic and International Studies (CSIS), fellow in European studies, 1997; Heritage Foundation, senior research fellow European affairs/senior foreign policy analyst, 1999-2006; Johns Hopkins School of Advanced International Studies (SAIS), adjunct professor of European security studies, 2004; Hague

Centre for Strategic Studies, senior research fellow; The National Interest, contributing editor, 2005. Writer. **Publications:** Paradigm for the New World Order: A Schools of Thought Analysis of American Foreign Policy in the Post Cold War Era, 1997; (with A. Lieven) Ethical Realism: A Vision for America's Role in the World, 2006; To Begin the World Over Again: Lawrence of Arabia and the Invention of the Middle East, 2009, To Begin the World Over Again: Lawrence of Arabia from Damascus to Baghdad, 2009; (with A.W. Mitchell) Godfather Doctrine: A Foreign Policy Parable, 2009. Contributor to journals and periodicals. **Address:** German Council on Foreign Relations, Alfred von Oppenheim Ctr. for European Studies, Rauchstrasse 17/18, Berlin, 10787, Germany. **Online address:** info@john-hulsman.com

HULT, Karen. (Karen M. Hult). American (born United States), b. 1956. **Genres:** Institutions/Organizations, Politics/Government, Public/Social Administration, Biography. **Career:** U.S. Department of Health and Human Services, Office of Adolescent Pregnancy Programs, analyst, 1982; Pomona College, assistant professor, 1984-89, associate professor of government, 1990, Program in Public Policy Analysis, acting director, 1984-85, 1986-87, director, 1988-90; Claremont Graduate School, graduate faculty, 1986-90, Department of Psychology, faculty, 1989-90; Virginia Polytechnic Institute and State University, Department of Political Science, associate professor, 1990-98, professor, 1998-, Center for Public Administration and Policy, associate professor, 1994-98, professor, 1998-, director of graduate studies, School of Public and International Affairs, affiliated faculty, 2004-. Writer. **Publications:** Agency Merger and Bureaucratic Redesign, 1987; (with C. Walcott) Governing Public Organizations: Politics, Structures, and Institutional Design, 1990; (with C. Walcott) Governing the White House: From Hoover through LBJ, 1995; (with C. Walcott) Empowering the White House: Governance under Nixon, Ford, and Carter, 2004. Contributor of articles to journals. **Address:** Department of Political Science, Virginia Polytechnic Institute, 531 Major Williams, Blacksburg, VA 24061, U.S.A. **Online address:** khult@vt.edu

HULT, Karen M. *See* **HULT, Karen.**

HUME, John Robert. Scottish (born Scotland), b. 1939. **Genres:** Archaeology/Antiquities, Business/Trade/Industry, Travel/Exploration, Illustrations, History, Photography, Archaeology/Antiquities, Architecture, Architecture. **Career:** University of Strathclyde, assistant lecturer, senior lecturer in history, 1964-91; Scottish Industrial Archaeology Survey, director, 1978-85; Historic Scotland, on assignment to Historic Buildings and Monuments Commission, 1984-91, principal inspector of historic buildings, 1991-93, chief inspector of historic buildings, 1993; Royal Commission on the Ancient and Historical Monuments of Scotland, chairman, now retired; University of Glasgow, honorary professor in the faculty of arts; University of St. Andrews, honorary professor in the faculty of art. Writer. **Publications:** (Co-ed.) Transport History, 1968-75; (with J. Butt and I.L. Donnachie) Industrial History in Pictures: Scotland, 1968; (with B.F. Duckham) Steam Entertainment, 1974; The Industrial Archaeology of Glasgow, 1974; (intro. with M.S. Moss) Clyde Shipbuilding from Old Photographs, 1975; Glasgow As It Was, 1975; (contrib.) New and Splendid Edifice: The Architecture of the University of Glasgow, 1975; (with M. Moss) A Plumber's Pastime, 1975; Industrial Archaeology of Scotland: The Lowlands and the Borders, 1976; Industrial Archaeology of Scotland: The Highlands and the Islands, 1977; (with M.S. Moss) The Workshop of the British Empire: Engineering and Shipbuilding in the West of Scotland, 1977; (comp. with M. Moss) Glasgow at War, 1977; (with I. Donnachie and M. Moss) Historic Industrial Scenes: Scotland, 1977; (comp. with I. Donnachie and M. Moss) Scotland, 1977; (with C. Johnston) Glasgow Stations, 1979; (with M.S. Moss) Beardmore: The History of a Scottish Industrial Giant, 1979; (ed.) Early Days in a Dundee Mill, 1819-1823: Extracts from the Diary of William Brown, An Early Dundee Spinner, 1980; (comp. with M. Moss) Old Photographs from Scottish Country Houses, 1980; (with M. Moss) The Making of Scotch Whisky, 1981; (with M.S. Moss) Bed of Nails: The History of P. MacCallum & Sons Ltd of Greenock, 1781-1981, A Study in Survival, 1983; (with G.J. Douglas and M. Oglethorpe) Scottish Windmills: A Survey, 1984; (co-author) Scottish Brickmarks, 1985; (with M. Moss) Shipbuilders to the World: 125 Years of Harland and Wolff, Belfast 1861-1986, 1986; Scotland's Industrial Past, 1990; Dumfries and Galloway: An Illustrated Architectural Guide, 2000; Scotland's Best Churches, 2005; 1000 Churches to Visit in Scotland, 2006. **Address:** Royal Commission, Ancient and Historical Monuments of Scotland, John Sinclair House, 16 Bernard Terr., Edinburgh, EH8 9NX, Scotland.

HUME, Robert D. (Robert David Hume). American (born United States), b.

1944. **Genres:** Literary Criticism And History, Theatre, History, Biography. **Career:** Cornell University, assistant professor, 1969-74, associate professor of English, 1974-77; Pennsylvania State University, Department of of English, professor, 1977-90, distinguished professor, 1990-91, Edwin Erle Sparks professor, 1991-98, Evan Pugh professor, 1998-. Writer. **Publications:** Dryden's Criticism, 1970; The Development of English Drama in the Late Seventeenth Century, 1976; (ed. with A.H. Scouten) Country Gentleman, 1976; (ed.) The London Theatre World, 1660-1800, 1980; Vice Chamberlain Coke's Theatrical Papers 1706-1715, 1982; The Rakish Stage: Studies in English Drama, 1600-1800, 1983; (with J. Milhous) Producible Interpretation, 1985; (ed. with J. Milhous) Roscius Anglicanus, 1987; Henry Fielding and the London Theatre, 1988; A Register of English Theatrical Documents, 1660-1737, 2 vols., 1991; (with C. Price and J. Milhous) Impresario's Ten Commandments: Continental Recruitment for Italian Opera in London, 1763-64, 1992; (with C. Price and J. Milhous) Italian Opera in Late Eighteenth-Century London, vol. I: The King's Theater Haymarket, 1778-1791, 1995, vol. II: The Pantheon Opera and Its Aftermath, 1789-1795, 2001; Reconstructing Contexts: The Aims and Principles of Archaeo-Historicism, 1999; (ed. with H. Love) Plays, Poems, and Miscellaneous Writings associated with George Villiers, Second Duke of Buckingham, 2 vols. 2007. **Address:** Department of English, Pennsylvania State University, 31 Burrowes Bldg., University Park, PA 16802, U.S.A. **Online address:** rob-hume@psu.edu

HUME, Robert David. *See* **HUME, Robert D.**

HUMEZ, Nicholas (David). American (born United States), b. 1948. **Genres:** Adult Non-fiction, Politics/Government. **Career:** Composer of classical music, 1959-; cartoonist, 1967-; copy-writer and proofreader, 1974-; Portland (ME) Newspapers, music reviewer, 1990-97; Verbatim: The Language Quarterly, columnist, 1998-2008; Montclair State University, Department of Classics and General Humanities, adjunct professor of mythology, 1999-2005. **Publications:** (Co-author) The Boston Basin Bicycle Book, 1975; WITH A. HUMEZ: Latin for People/Latina pro Populo, 1976; Silversmithing: A Basic Manual, 1976; Alpha to Omega: The Life and Times of the Greek Alphabet, 1981; A.B.C Et Cetera: The Life and Times of the Roman Alphabet, 1985; (and J. Maguire) Zero to Lazy Eight: The Romance of Numbers, 1993; On the Dot: The Speck that Changed the World, 2008; (and R. Flynn) Short Cuts: A Guide to Oaths, Ring Tones, Ransom Notes, Famous Last Words, and Other Forms of Minimalist Communication, 2010. **Address:** David R. Godine, 15 Court Sq., Ste. 320, Boston, MA 02108-4715, U.S.A. **Online address:** spintrian@earthlink.net

HUMMEL, Jeffrey Rogers. American (born United States), b. 1949. **Genres:** Economics, History. **Career:** University of Texas, teaching assistant, 1975-76, 1979-80, assistant instructor in history, 1978-79; Libertarian Party of California, research director, 1982; Independent Institute, publications director, 1988-93; Golden Gate University, adjunct associate professor of economics and history, 1989-2001; Stanford University, Hoover Institution, national fellow, 2001-02; San Jose State University, assistant professor of economics, 2002-08, associate professor of economics, 2008-; Santa Clara University, adjunct faculty. Writer. **Publications:** Emancipating Slaves, Enslaving Free Men: A History of the American Civil War, 1996. Contributor to books and periodicals. **Address:** Department of Economics, San Jose State University, Hall 147, Dudley Moorhead, 1 Washington Sq., San Jose, CA 95192-0114, U.S.A. **Online address:** jhummel@gguol.ggu.edu

HUMMEL, Monte. Canadian (born Canada), b. 1946. **Genres:** Environmental Sciences/Ecology, Natural History. **Career:** Pollution Probe, co-founder, executive director and chairman, 1969-81; University of Toronto, Innis College, coordinator of environmental studies program, 1977-82; World Wildlife Fund Canada, builder, director, executive director, 1978-2004, president, 1985-2004, president emeritus, 2004-, executive head; Institute of Environmental Studies, associate; Order of Canada, officer, 2000. Writer. **Publications:** Arctic Wildlife, 1984; (ed. and contrib.) Endangered Spaces, 1989; (with S. Pettigrew) Wild Hunters: Predators in Peril, 1991; (ed.) Protecting Canada's Endangered Species: An Owner's Manual, 1995; Wintergreen: Reflections from Loon Lake, 1999; Caribou and the North: A Shared Future, 2008. Contributor to journals and magazines. **Address:** World Wildlife Fund Canada, 245 Eglinton Ave. E, Ste. 410, Toronto, ON M4P 3J1, Canada. **Online address:** mhummel@wwfcanada.org

HUMMER, T(erry) R(andolph). American (born United States), b. 1950. **Genres:** Poetry, Literary Criticism And History, Essays. **Career:** Oklahoma State University, assistant professor of English, 1980-84; Kenyon College, assistant professor of English, 1984-89; Middlebury College, assistant professor of English, 1989-93; New England Review, editor, 1989-93; University of Oregon, professor and director of creative writing, 1993-97; Virginia Commonwealth University, senior poet, 1997-2001; University of Georgia, professor of English, 2001-07, Georgia Review, editor, 2001-07; Arizona State University, College of Liberal Arts and Sciences, Department of English, professor, 2007-, Creative Writing Program, director, 2007-; Exeter College, visiting professor; University of California, writer-in-residence. **Publications:** Translation of Light, 1976; The Angelic Orders, 1982; The Passion of the Right-Angled Man, 1984; Lower-Class Heresy, 1987; The 18, 000-Ton Olympic Dream, 1990; Walt Whitman in Hell: Poems, 1996; Useless Virtues: Poems, 2001; The Infinity Sessions: Poems, 2005; The Muse in the Machine: Essays on Poetry and the Anatomy of the Body Politic, 2006; Ephemeron: Poems, 2011. EDITOR: (and intro. with B. Weigl) The Imagination as Glory: The Poetry of James Dickey, 1984; (with D. Jersild) The Unfeigned Word: Fifteen Years of New England Review, 1993. **Address:** Department of English, College of Liberal Arts and Sciences, Arizona State University, Rm. 542, 851 S Cady Mall, PO Box 870302, Tempe, AZ 85287-0302, U.S.A. **Online address:** trhummer@asu.edu

HUMPHREY, Carol Sue. American (born United States), b. 1956. **Genres:** History, Writing/Journalism, Communications/Media. **Career:** Oklahoma Baptist University, Shawnee, assistant professor, 1985-92, associate professor, 1992-98, professor of history, 1998-. Writer. **Publications:** This Popular Engine: The Role of New England Newspapers during the American Revolution, 1992; The Press of the Young Republic, 1783-1833, 1996; (comp.) The Revolutionary Era: Primary Documents on Events from 1776 to 1800, 2003; The Revolutionary War: U.S. Wars and the Media in Primary Documents Series, 2004; (with D. Copeland) The Greenwood Library of American War Reporting: The War of 1812, 2005; The Greenwood Library of American War Reporting: The Revolutionary War, 2005. Contributor of articles to books. **Address:** Department of History, Oklahoma Baptist University, Owens Hall 312, 500 W Univ., PO Box 61201, Shawnee, OK 74804, U.S.A. **Online address:** carol.humphrey@okbu.edu

HUMPHREY, Kate. *See* **FORSYTH, Kate.**

HUMPHREY, Sandra McLeod. American (born United States), b. 1936. **Genres:** Children's Fiction, Children's Non-fiction. **Career:** Anoka Metro Regional Treatment Center, clinical psychologist, 1961-92. Writer. **Publications:** FOR CHILDREN: A Dog Named Sleet, 1984; If You Had to Choose, What Would You Do?, 1995; It's Up to You, What Do You Do?, 1999; Keepin' It Real: A Young Teen Talks with God, 2003; More-If You Had to Choose, What Would You Do?, 2003; Dare to Dream!: 25 Extraordinary Lives, 2005; Hot Issues, Cool Choices!: Facing Bullies, Peer Pressure, Popularity and Put-downs, 2007; Me, Myself, and I: Youth Meditations for Grades 5-8, 2008; The No-Name Club's Not-So-Official Guide to Solving Your Problems, 2011; They Stood Alone!: 25 Men and Women Who Made a Difference, 2011. **Address:** 19 Westwood Rd., Minnetonka, MN 55305, U.S.A. **Online address:** sandra305@aol.com

HUMPHREY-KEEVER, Mary Ann. American (born United States), b. 1943?. **Genres:** Civil Liberties/Human Rights, Gay And Lesbian Issues, History, Military/Defense/Arms Control, Psychiatry, Psychology, Recreation, Sports/Fitness, Sports/Fitness. **Career:** Portland Community College, coordinator of physical education, 1973-, part-time instructor, instructor. Writer. **Publications:** My Country, My Right to Serve: Experiences of Gay Men and Women in the Military, World War II to the Present, 1990; Waterplay: Games and Activities for Everyone, 1990. **Address:** Portland Community College, RC 5 105, 17705 NW Springville Rd., PO Box 19000, Portland, OR 97229, U.S.A. **Online address:** mhumphre@pcc.edu

HUMPHREYS, Edward. *See* **BUSBY, Brian.**

HUMPHREYS, Emyr (Owen). Welsh/British (born England), b. 1919. **Genres:** Novels, Novellas/Short Stories, Plays/Screenplays, Poetry, Literary Criticism And History, Young Adult Fiction. **Career:** Wimbledon Technical College, teacher, 1948-51; Pwllheli Grammar School, teacher, 1951-55; BBC Radio, producer, 1955-58; BBC Television, drama producer, 1958-62; freelance writer and director, 1962-65; University College of North Wales, lecturer in drama, 1965-72, honorary professor, 1988; full-time writer, 1972-. **Publications:** The Little Kingdom, 1946; The Voice of a Stranger, 1949; A

Change of Heart, 1951; Hear and Forgive, 1952; A Man's Estate, 1955; The Italian Wife, 1957; Y Tri Llais, 1958; A Toy Epic, 1958; King's Daughter, 1959; The Gift, 1963; Outside the House of Baal, 1965; Natives (stories), 1968; Roman Dream (poetry), 1969; An Apple Tree and a Pig (poetry), 1969; (with W.S. Jones) Dinas, 1970; Ancestor Worship: A Cycle of 18 Poems, 1970; National Winner (novel), 1971; Cymod Cadarn, 1973; Flesh and Blood, 1974; The Best of Friends, 1978; Landscapes: A Sequence of Songs, 1979; (with J. Ormond and J. Tripp) Penguin Modern Poets 27, 1979; Theatr Saunders Lewis, 1979; Pwyll a Riannon, 1979; The Kingdom of Brân (poetry), 1979; The Anchor Tree, 1980; Miscellany Two, 1981; The Taliesin Tradition, 1983; Jones: A Novel, 1984; Salt of the Earth, 1985, rev. ed., 1999; An Absolute Hero, 1986; Open Secrets, 1988; The Triple Net: A Portrait of the Writer Kate Roberts 1891-1985, 1988; The Crucible of Myth: W.D. Thomas Memorial Lecture, 1990; Bonds of Attachment, 1991; Outside Time, 1991; Brodyr A Chwiorydd, 1994; Dwylo, 1994; Unconditional Surrender, 1996; The Gift of a Daughter, 1998; Collected Poems, 1999; Dal Pen Rheswm: Cyfweliadau Gydag Emyr Humphreys, 1999; Land of the Living, 2000; Ghosts and Strangers, 2001; Conversations and Reflections, 2002; Old People Are a Problem, 2003; Shop, 2005; The Rigours of Inspection, 2005; Woman at the Window, 2009. **Address:** Seren Books, 57 Nolton St., Bridgend, CF31 3AE, Wales.

HUMPHREYS, George G(ary). American (born United States), b. 1949. **Genres:** Politics/Government, History, Business/Trade/Industry, Economics, Social Sciences, Administration/Management. **Career:** Oklahoma House of Representatives, fiscal director, 1981-83, research director, 1985-2004; Oklahoma Department of Economic and Community Affairs, director of information services, 1983-85; Madisonville Community College, Muhlenberg County Campus, extended campus director, 2004-. Writer. **Publications:** Taylorism in France, 1904-1920: The Impact of Scientific Management on Factory Relations and Society, 1986; (with D.R. Morgan and R.E. England) Oklahoma Politics and Policies: Governing the Sooner State, 1991; A Century to Remember: A Historical Perspective on the Oklahoma House of Representatives, 2000. **Address:** Madisonville Community College, Muhlenberg County Campus, Rm. 102D, 406 W Everly Brothers Blvd., Central City, KY 42330, U.S.A. **Online address:** george.humphreys@kctcs.edu

HUMPHREYS, Helen (Caroline). (Catherine Brett). Canadian/British (born England), b. 1961. **Genres:** Poetry, Novels, Young Adult Fiction, Romance/Historical, Novellas/Short Stories. **Career:** Writer. **Publications:** POETRY: Gods and Other Mortals, 1986; Nuns Looking Anxious, Listening to Radios, 1990; The Perils of Geography, 1995; Anthem, 1999. NOVELS: Leaving Earth, 1997; Afterimage, 2000; The Lost Garden, 2002; Wild Dogs, 2004; The Reinvention of Love, 2011. OTHER: Ethel on Fire, 1991; The Frozen Thames, 2007; Coventry, 2008. AS CATHERINE BRETT: Things Just Aren't the Same, 1987; S.P. Likes A.D., 1989. Contributor of articles to periodicals. **Address:** 56 Chestnut St., Kingston, ON K7K 3W2, Canada. **Online address:** info@hhumphreys.com

HUMPHREYS, Margaret. (Margaret Warner). American (born United States), b. 1955. **Genres:** History, Medicine/Health. **Career:** Harvard University, instructor, 1983-84, lecturer, 1986-93, Fae Kass lecturer, 1987; Duke University, assistant professor of history and medicine, University Medical Center, physician (internal medicine), 1993-, Josiah Charles Trent professor, associate clinical professor of medicine; Francis Wood Institute, editorial consultant, 1993-. Writer. **Publications:** Yellow Fever and the South, 1992; Malaria: Poverty, Race and Public Health in the United States, 2001; Intensely Human: The Health of the Black Soldier in the American Civil War, 2008. Contributor to journals. **Address:** Department of History, Duke University, 206 Carr Bldg., PO Box 90719, Durham, NC 27710, U.S.A. **Online address:** meh@duke.edu

HUMPHRYS, Geoffrey. See HUMPHRYS, Leslie George.

HUMPHRYS, Leslie George. Also writes as Bruno Brack, B. Condray, Geoffrey Humphrys. British (born England), b. 1921. **Genres:** Children's Non-fiction, Writing/Journalism, Sciences. **Career:** Teacher, 1948-58; North Walsham County Primary School, headmaster, 1959-81, now retired; writer, 1981-. Freelance journalist. **Publications:** (As V. Brack) Odyssey in Space, 1954; (as Geoffrey Humphrys) Time to Live, 1959; Wonders of Life (Books 1-4), 1959; Weather in Britain, 1963; Your Body at Work, 1963; Men Learn to Fly, 1966; Life is Exciting, 1966; Science Through Experience (Books 1-3), 1967; Fruit and Fruit Growing, 1969; Drinks, 1970; Men Travel in Space, 1971; Glass and Glass Making, 1971; Tools, 1974; Motion and Power, 1974;

Machines, 1976. AS B. CONDRAY: Outer Beyond, 1954; Exile From Jupiter, 1954; Serving Two Worlds, 1954; The Dissentizens, 1955. **Address:** 27 Litester Close, North Walsham, NF NR28, England.

HUNDERT, E(dward) J. Canadian/American (born United States), b. 1940. **Genres:** History, Biography. **Career:** University of British Columbia, historian, professor, professor emeritus, 2000-. Writer. **Publications:** The Enlightenment's Fable: Bernard Mandeville and the Discovery of Society, 1994; (ed. and intro.) Fable of the Bees: And Other Writings, 1997. **Address:** Department of History, University of British Columbia, 1873 E Mall, Vancouver, BC V6T 1Z1, Canada. **Online address:** hundert@shaw.ca

HUNDERT, Edward M. American (born United States), b. 1956. **Genres:** Medicine/Health. **Career:** McLean Hospital, psychiatrist, 1984-; Harvard University, Harvard Medical School, associate professor of psychiatry and associate dean for student affairs, 1990-97, Center for Teaching and Learning, director, senior lecturer in medical ethics; University of Rochester, senior associate dean for medical education, 1997-2002, School of Medicine and Dentistry, dean, 2000-02; Case Western Reserve University, professor of biomedical ethics and professor of cognitive science, president, 2002-06; The Washington Advisory Group, director and consultant. Writer. **Publications:** Philosophy, Psychiatry, and Neuroscience: Three Approaches to the Mind: A Synthetic Analysis of the Varieties of Human Experience, 1989; Lessons from an Optical Illusion: On Nature and Nurture, Knowledge and Values, 1995. **Address:** Harvard Medical School, Division of Medical Ethics, FXB Bldg., 6th Fl., 641 Huntington Ave., Boston, MA 02115, U.S.A. **Online address:** edward_hundert@hms.harvard.edu

HUNDLEY, Jessica. American (born United States) **Genres:** Novels. **Career:** L.A. based production Co., co-founder and current consultant; Men's Magazine Complex, west coast editor; Boston Phoenix, arts contributor, 1992; Mommy and I Are One (magazine), founder and editor, 1992-2000. Journalist and filmmaker. **Publications:** (Ed. with J.A. Guzik) Horny? Los Angeles: A Sexy, Steamy, Downright Sleazy Handbook to the City, 2001; (with P. Parsons) Grievous Angel: An Intimate Biography of Gram Parsons, 2005; (with W. Hopps and T. Shafrazi) Dennis Hopper: Photographs, 1961-1967, 2009. Contributor to periodicals. **Address:** c/o Author Mail, Thunder's Mouth Press, 245 W 17th St., 11th Fl., New York, NY 10011-5300, U.S.A. **Online address:** jessiehundley@gmail.com

HUNDLEY, Norris C. American (born United States), b. 1935. **Genres:** History, Local History/Rural Topics, Social Commentary, Bibliography, Essays, Politics/Government. **Career:** University of Houston, instructor in American history, 1963-64; Latin American Center, director, 1990-94; Pacific Historical Review, managing editor, 1968-97; University of California, Department of History, assistant professor, 1964-69, associate professor, 1969-73, professor of history, 1973-94, emeritus professor of history, 1994-, chairman of university program on Mexico, 1981-94, Latin American Center, acting director, 1989-90. Writer. **Publications:** John Walton Caughey: A Bibliography of His Writings, 1961; Dividing the Waters: A Century of Controversy between the United States and Mexico, 1966; California History: A Teacher's Manual, 1970; Water and the West: The Colorado River Compact and the Politics of Water in the American West, 1975, 2nd ed., 2009; (coauthor) The California Water Atlas, 1979; (with J. Caughey) California: History of a Remarkable State, 1982; The Great Thirst: Californians and Water, 1770s-1990s, 1992, rev. ed. as The Great Thirst: Californians and Water: A History, 2001; Las aguas divididas: Un siglo decontroversia entre Mexico y Estados Unidos, 2000. EDITOR: (and intro. with J.A. Schutz) The American West, Frontier and Region: Interpretations, 1969; The American Indian: Essays from the Pacific Historical Review, 1975; The Chicano: Essays, 1975; The Asian American: The Historical Experience: Essays, 1976. Contributor to journals. **Address:** Department of History, University of California, 6265 Bunche Hall, PO Box 951473, Los Angeles, CA 90095-1473, U.S.A. **Online address:** hundley@history.ucla.edu

HUNG, Chang-tai. Hong Kong (born Hong Kong), b. 1949. **Genres:** History, Politics/Government, Popular Culture. **Career:** Carleton College, assistant professor, 1981-87, associate professor, 1987-92, professor of history, 1992-98, Jane and Raphael Bernstein professor of Asian studies, 1993-98; Hong Kong University of Science and Technology, Division of Humanities, instructor, visiting professor, 1994, professor, 1995-, chair professor, School of Humanities and Social Science, associate dean, 1999-2000, professor of history. Writer. **Publications:** Going to the People: Chinese Intellectuals and

Folk Literature, 1918-1937, 1985; War and Popular Culture: Resistance in Modern China, 1937-1945, 1994; The New Cultural History and Chinese Politics (in Chinese), 2003; Mao's New World: Political Culture in the Early People's Republic, 2011. **Address:** Division of Humanities, Hong Kong University of Science and Technology, Rm. 3345 Clearwater Bay, Kowloon, 852, Hong Kong. **Online address:** hmhung@ust.hk

HUNGERFORD, Rachael A. American (born United States) **Genres:** Education, Literary Criticism And History. **Career:** Lycoming College, assistant professor of education, 1989-, department chair, now assistant professor emeritus of education; Children's Literature Jubilee, director. Writer. **Publications:** (Ed. with K.E. Holland and S.B. Ernst) Journeying: Children Responding to Literature, 1993; Literacy and Working Class Women: Stories from a Two-Room Schoolhouse, forthcoming. **Address:** Lycoming College, 700 College Pl., Williamsport, PA 17701-5157, U.S.A. **Online address:** hunger@lycoming.edu

HUNKIN, Tim(othy) Mark Trelawney. British (born England), b. 1950. **Genres:** Children's Fiction, Children's Non-fiction, Science Fiction/Fantasy. **Career:** The Observer, cartoonist, 1973-87; Secret Life of Machines, writer and presenter, 1987-93. **Publications:** Mrs. Gronkwonk and the Post Office Tower, 1971; Rudiments of Wisdom, 1974; Almost Everything There Is to Know, 1988; Hunkin's Experiments, 2004. **Address:** Bulcamp House, Blythburgh, SU IP19 9LG, England. **Online address:** tim@timhunkin.com

HUNNER, Jon. American (born United States) **Genres:** History, Adult Non-fiction, Military/Defense/Arms Control. **Career:** New Mexico State University, Department of History, professor and head, Public History Program, director; New Mexico History Museum, consultant. Writer and public speaker. **Publications:** NONFICTION: (comp.) A Selective Bibliography of New Mexico History, 1992; (co-author) Santa Fe: An Historical Walking Tour, 2000; (co-author) Las Cruces: City of Crosses, 2003; (co-author) Time Traveling through New Mexico History: The Spanish Colonial Period, 2004; Inventing Los Alamos: The Growth of an Atomic Community, 2004; (contrib.) Atomic Culture: How We Learned to Stop Worrying and Love the Bomb, 2004; (contrib.) Western Lives: A Biographical History of the American West, 2004; (contrib.) Oppenheimer and the Manhattan Project, 2006; (co-author) The Mesilla Valley: An Oasis in the Desert, 2008; J. Robert Oppenheimer, The Cold War, and the Atomic West, 2009; (ed.) Senator Pete Domenici's Legacy: The Proceedings from the 2008 Pete V. Domenici Public Policy Conference, 2009. Contributor to periodicals. **Address:** Department of History, New Mexico State University, MSC 3H, 1780 E University Ave., PO Box 30001, Las Cruces, NM 88003-1229, U.S.A. **Online address:** jhunner@nmsu.edu

HUNNICUTT, Benjamin Kline. American (born United States), b. 1943. **Genres:** Recreation, History, Organized Labor, Humanities, Theology/Religion. **Career:** Iowa, Department of Leisure Studies, assistant professor, 1975-80, chairman, 1976-79, 1989-90, associate professor, 1981-88, professor of leisure studies, 1988-2011, College of Liberal Arts, Division of Physical Education, director, 1990-92. Writer. **Publications:** Work Without End: Abandoning Shorter Hours for the Right to Work, 1988; Kellogg's Six-Hour Day, 1996. **Address:** Department of Leisure Studies, University of Iowa, 342 FH, Iowa City, IA 52242, U.S.A. **Online address:** benjamin-hunnicutt@uiowa.edu

HUNT, Angela Elwell. American (born United States), b. 1957. **Genres:** Novels, Romance/Historical, Children's Fiction, Young Adult Fiction, Human Relations/Parenting/Memoirs, Autobiography/Memoirs, Picture/Board Books. **Career:** Teacher, through 1983; writer, 1983-; Young Writers' Institute, faculty; Angela Hunt Communications Inc., owner, 1994-. **Publications:** CASSIE PERKINS SERIES: No More Broken Promises, 1991; A Forever Friend, 1991; A Basket of Roses, 1991; A Dream to Cherish, 1992; The Much-Adored Sandy Shore, 1992; Love Burning Bright, 1992; Star Light, Star Bright, 1993; The Chance of a Lifetime, 1993; The Glory of Love, 1993. NICKI HOLLAND SERIES: The Case of the Mystery Mark, 1991; The Case of the Phantom Friend, 1991; The Case of the Teenage Terminator, 1991; Calico Bear, 1991; A Gift for Grandpa, 1991; The Case of the Terrified Track Star, 1992; The Case of the Counterfeit Cash, 1992; The Case of the Haunting of Lowell Lanes, 1992; The Case of the Birthday Bracelet, 1993; The Secret of Cravenhill Castle, 1993; The Riddle of Baby Rosalind, 1993. THEYN CHRONICLES SERIES: Afton of Margate Castle, 1993; The Troubadour's Quest, 1994; Ingram of the Irish, 1995. LEGACIES OF THE ANCIENT RIVER SERIES: Dreamers, 1996; Brothers, 1997; Journey, 1997. THE COLONIAL

CAPTIVES SERIES: Kimberly and the Captives, 1996; The Deadly Chase, 1996; The Pirates Revenge, 1996; Lost in the Fog, 1996. THE KEEPERS OF THE RING SERIES: Roanoke: The Lost Colony, 1996; Jamestown, 1996; Hartford, 1996; Rehoboth, 1997; Charleston, 1998. The Sleeping Rose, 1999; My Life as a Middle School Mom, 2000; YOUNG BELIEVERS SERIES (with S. Arterburn): Josiah, 2004; Liane, 2004; Noah, 2004; Paige, 2004; Shane, 2004; Taz, 2004. HEAVENLY DAZE SERIES (with L. Coopeland): The Island of Heavenly Daze, 2000; Grace in Autumn, 2001; Warmth in Winter, 2002; A Perfect Love, 2002; Pretzels by the Dozen, 2002; Hearts at Home, 2003. HEIRS OF CAHIRA O'CONNOR SERIES: The Silver Sword, 1998; The Golden Cross, 1998; The Velvet Shadow, 1999; The Emerald Isle, 1999. FAIRLAWN: Doesn't She Look Natural, 2007; She Always Wore Red, 2008; She's in a Better Place, 2009. OTHERS: (with G. Hunt) Surviving the Teenage Years, 1988, as Too Young to Drive, Too Old to Ride, 1993; If I Had Long, Long Hair, 1988; (with G. Hunt) Mom and Dad Don't Live Together Anymore, 1989; The Tale of Three Trees, 1989; The Adoption Option, 1989; (with G. Hunt) Now That You've Asked Her Out, 1989; (with G. Hunt) Now That He's Asked You Out, 1989; Calico Bear (picture book), 1991; A Gift for Grandpa, 1991; If God Is Real, Where on Earth Is He?, 1991; (with C. Dyer) The Rise of Babylon: Sign of the End Times, 1991; Loving Someone Else's Child, 1992; The Singing Shepherd, 1992; The True Princess, 1992; (with L.K. Calenberg) Beauty from the Inside Out: Becoming the Best You Can Be, 1993; Howie Hugemouth, 1993; When Your Parents Pull Apart, 1995; Where Dragons Dance, 1995; The Proposal, 1996; (with H. Whitestone) Listening with My Heart, 1997; Gentle Touch, 1997; (with G. Jeffrey) Flee the Darkness, 1998; (with G. Jeffrey) By Dawn's Early Light, 1999; The Truth Teller, 1999; (with G. Jeffrey) The Spear of Tyranny, 2000; My Life as a Middle School Mom: My Kids May Be Deductible, But They're Still Taxing!, 2000; The Immortal, 2000; The Note: A Story of Second Chances, 2001; (with R.L. Hatcher and D. Bedford) The Story Jar, 2001; (with B. Myers) Then Comes Marriage, 2001; The Justice, 2002; The Shadow Women, 2002; (with S. Arterburn) Flashpoints: Igniting the Hidden Passions of Your Soul, 2002; Pretzels by the Dozen: Truth and Inspiration with a Heart-Shaped Twist, 2002; The Pearl, 2003; The Canopy, 2003; (with H.W. McCallum) Let God Surprise You: Trust God with Your Dreams, 2003; The Awakening, 2004; (with H.W. McCallum) Heavenly Crowns: Striving for a Godly Life in the Midst of Daily Struggles, 2004; The Debt, 2004; Unspoken: If We Teach Her to Talk... Can She Trust Us to Listen?, 2005; Uncharted, 2006; A Time to Mend, 2006; The Nativity Story, 2006; The Novelist, 2006; Magdalene, 2006; (with S. Arterburn) Soul on Fire: Discover Your Life's Passion and Purpose, 2006; Idoleyes: My New Perspective on Faith, Fat & Fame, 2007; The Elevator, 2007; (with D. Favre) Don't Bet Against Me!: Beating the Odds Against Breast Cancer and in Life, 2007; The Face, 2008; Let Darkness Come, 2009; The Note II, 2009; (with G. Haggard) Why I Stayed, 2009; (with S. Morell and P. Morell) Misconception, 2010; The Fine Art of Insincerity, 2011; Five Miles South of Peculiar, 2012. Contributor to magazines. **Address:** c/o Danielle Egan-Miller, Browne & Miller Literary Associates, 410 S Michigan Ave., Ste. 460, Chicago, IL 60605-1390, U.S.A. **Online address:** angie@angelaelwellhunt.com

HUNT, Bruce J. American (born United States), b. 1956. **Genres:** History, Physics, Technology. **Career:** University of Texas, assistant professor of history, 1985-92, associate professor of history, 1992-. Writer. **Publications:** The Maxwellians, 1991; Pursuing Power and Light: Technology and Physics from James Watt to Albert Einstein, 2010. **Address:** Department of History, University of Texas, 2.106 Garrison Hall, 1 University Sta., Austin, TX 78712, U.S.A. **Online address:** bjhunt@mail.utexas.edu

HUNT, Courtney. American (born United States) **Genres:** History, Adult Non-fiction. **Career:** Writer and attorney. **Publications:** The History of Iraq (nonfiction), 2005. Contributor to magazines. **Address:** VA , U.S.A. **Online address:** courtneyhunt71@aol.com

HUNT, David. See BAYER, William.

HUNT, Edward H. British (born England), b. 1939?. **Genres:** History, Industrial Relations, Economics. **Career:** Queen's University of Belfast, assistant lecturer in economic history, 1966-69; London School of Economics, senior lecturer in economic history, 1969-; Economic History Review, book review editor, 1981-86. **Publications:** Regional Wage Variations in Britain 1850-1914, 1973; British Labour History 1815-1914, 1981. **Address:** London School of Economics and Political Science, Houghton St., London, GL WC2A 2AE, England. **Online address:** e.h.hunt@lse.ac.uk

HUNT, Janie Louise. British/Kenyan (born Kenya), b. 1963. **Genres:** Children's Fiction, Illustrations, Animals/Pets. **Career:** Templar Publishing Co., illustrator, 1986-, senior designer. Writer. **Publications:** Shapes: A Busy Fingers Book (Board book), 2004. SELF-ILLUSTRATED FOR CHILDREN: Big and Small: A Book of Opposites, 1997; Red and Yellow, 1997; One, Two, Three: A Through-the-Window Book of Counting, 1998; Round and Square: A Through-the-Window Book of Shapes, 1998. CONTRIBUTOR: Snappy Little Bugs, 1999; Super Snappy ABC, 2000; Super Snappy Words, 2002. **Address:** Templar Publishing Co., Pippbrook Mill, London Rd., Dorking, SR RH4 1JE, England.

HUNT, J. Timothy. Canadian/American (born United States), b. 1959. **Genres:** History, Biography. **Career:** Writer and journalist. **Publications:** The Politics of Bones: Dr. Owens Wiwa and the Struggle for Nigeria's Oil, 2006. Contributor of essays and articles to periodicals. **Address:** Toronto, ON , Canada. **Online address:** mail@jtimothyhunt.com

HUNT, Lynn (Avery). American/Panamanian (born Panama), b. 1945. **Genres:** Politics/Government, Sex, Theology/Religion. **Career:** University of California-Berkeley, assistant professor, 1974-79, associate professor, 1979-84, professor of history, 1984-87; University of Pennsylvania, Joe and Emily Lowe Foundation, term professor, 1987-98, Annenberg Professor, 1991-98; University of Utrecht, visiting professor, 1993; University of Amsterdam, visiting professor, 1993; University of California-Los Angeles, professor of history, 1999-, Eugene Weber professor of modern European history, 1999-. Writer. **Publications:** Revolution and Urban Politics in Provincial France: Troyes and Reims, 1786-1790, 1978; Politics, Culture and Class in the French Revolution, 1984, 20th ed., 2004; (ed. and intro.) The New Cultural History: Essays, 1989; (ed.) Eroticism and the Body Politic, 1991; The Family Romance of the French Revolution, 1992; (ed.) Invention of Pornography: Obscenity and the Origins of Modernity, 1500-1800, 1993; (with J. Appleby and M. Jacob) Telling the Truth about History, 1994; (ed. with J. Revel) Histories: French Constructions of the Past, 1995; (co-author) Challenge of the West: Peoples and Cultures from the Stone Age to the Global Age, 1995; (ed., trans. and intro.) French Revolution and Human Rights: A Brief Documentary History, 1996; (ed. and intro. with V.E. Bonnell) Beyond the Cultural Turn: New Directions in the Study of Society and Culture, 1999; (ed. with J.N. Wasserstrom and M.B. Young) Human Rights and Revolutions, 2000; (with J.R. Censer) Liberty, Equality, Fraternity: Exploring the French Revolution, 2001; (co-author) Making of the West: Peoples and Cultures: A Concise History, 2003, 3rd ed., 2010; Inventing Human Rights: A History, 2007; Measuring Time, Making History, 2008; (with M. Jacob and W. Mijnhardt) Book that Changed Europe: Picart and Bernard's Religious Ceremonies of the World, 2010; (ed. with M. Jacob and W. Mijnhardt) Bernard Picart and the First Global Vision of Religion, 2010. **Address:** Department of History, University of California, 6254 Bunche Hall, PO Box 951473, Los Angeles, CA 90095-1473, U.S.A. **Online address:** lhunt@history.ucla.edu

HUNT, Marjorie. American (born United States), b. 1954?. **Genres:** Art/Art History, Architecture, Film, Crafts. **Career:** Smithsonian Institution, Center for Folklife and Cultural Heritage, education specialist and curator of the building arts program. Writer. **Publications:** (With M. Hufford and S. Zeitlin) The Grand Generation: Memory, Mastery, Legacy, 1987; The Stone Carvers: Master Craftsmen of Washington National Cathedral, 1999. Contributor to periodicals. **Address:** Center for Folklife and Cultural Heritage, Smithsonian Institution, MRC 520, Capital Gallery Bldg.,, 600 Maryland Ave SW, Ste 2001, PO Box 37012, Washington, DC 20013-7012, U.S.A. **Online address:** huntm@si.edu

HUNT, Marvin W. American (born United States) **Genres:** Literary Criticism And History. **Career:** North Carolina State University, Department of English, lecturer. Writer. **Publications:** Looking for Hamlet, 2007. Contributor to periodicals. **Address:** Department of English, North Carolina State University, Tompkins Hall, PO Box 8105, Raleigh, NC 27695-8105, U.S.A. **Online address:** mhunt@unity.ncsu.edu

HUNT, Peter (Leonard). Welsh/British (born England), b. 1945. **Genres:** Children's Fiction, Literary Criticism And History. **Career:** University of Wales, Institute of Science and Technology, lecturer in English, 1969-88, senior lecturer, 1988-95, reader, 1995-96, professor of English, 1996-, now professor emeritus; University of Michigan, visiting professor, 1977, lecturer, 1978; Engineering Council, joint examiner, 1978-; John Kirkman Communication Consultancy, principal associate, 1981-; Massachusetts Institute of Technology, visiting lecturer, 1982, 1983, 1984, 1987, 1990; University of Wales, senior lecturer, 1988-95, reader, 1995, professor of English, 1996-2004, now professor emeritus, 2004-; San Diego State University, adjunct professor, 1990; University of Wollongong, visiting fellow, 1991; Cardiff University, professor, now professor emeritus. Writer. **Publications:** Children's Book Research in Britain, 1977, rev. ed., 1982; The Maps of Time, 1983; A Step Off the Path, 1985; Backtrack, 1986; Sue and the Honey Machine, 1989; Fay Cow and the Mystery of the Missing Milk, 1989; Going Up, 1989; Criticism, Theory and Children's Literature, 1991; Approaching Arthur Ransome, 1992; An Introduction to Children's Literature, 1994; The Wind in the Willows: A Fragmented Arcadia, 1994; (with M. Lenz) Alternative Worlds in Fantasy Fiction, 2003; The Norton Anthology of Children's Literature, 2005. EDITOR: Further Approaches to Research in Children's Literature, 1982; Bevis, 1989; Children's Book Research in Britain: Research in British Institutions of Higher Education on Children's Books and Related Subjects, 1977; (and intro.) Bevis, 1989; Children's Literature, 1989; Children's Literature, The Development of Criticism, 1990; Arthur Ransom, 1991; Literature for Children: Contemporary Criticism, 1992; Wind in the Willows: A Fragmented Arcadia, 1994; An Illustrated History of Children's Literature, 1995; International Companion Encyclopedia of Children's Literature, 1996, 2nd ed., 2004; Understanding Children's Literature, 1999, 2nd ed., 2005; Children's Literature: A Guide, 2001; Children's Literature: An Anthology 1801-1902, 2001; (and intro.) Alice's Adventures in Wonderland and Through the Looking-glass and what Alice Found There, 2009; (and intro.) Wind in the Willows, 2010; Treasure Island, 2011. Contributor of articles to periodicals. **Address:** Cardiff School of English, Communication, and Philosophy, Cardiff University, Humanities Bldg., Colum Dr., PO Box 94, Cardiff, CF10 3EU, Wales. **Online address:** huntp@cardiff.ac.uk

HUNT, Rameck. American (born United States), b. 1973. **Genres:** Biography, Autobiography/Memoirs. **Career:** Princeton Health Care Medical Associates, physician, 2006-; Robert Wood Johnson University Hospital, resident; University Medical Center, internist; Robert Wood Johnson Medical School, assistant professor of medicine; St. Peter's University Hospital, director of outpatient clinic; Three Doctors Foundation, co-founder. Writer. **Publications:** (With S. Davis, G. Jenkins and L.F. Page) The Pact: Three Young Men Make a Promise and Fulfill a Dream, 2002; (with S. Davis, G. Jenkins and S.M. Draper) We Beat the Street: How a Friendship Pact Helped Us Succeed, 2005; (with S. Davis, G. Jenkins and M. Bernstein) The Bond: Three Young Men Learn to Forgive and Reconnect with Their Fathers, 2007. **Address:** Three Doctors Foundation L.L.C., 65 Hazelwood Ave., Newark, NJ 07106, U.S.A. **Online address:** drhunt@threedoctors.com

HUNT, Richard (Patrick). British (born England), b. 1938. **Genres:** Mystery/Crime/Suspense, History, Military/Defense/Arms Control, Biography, Autobiography/Memoirs. **Career:** Packback Ltd., director. Writer. **Publications:** Murder in Ruins, 1991; Death Sounds Grand, 1991; The Death of a Merry Widow, 1992; Deadlocked, 1994; Murder Benign, 1995; Cure for Killers, 1996; The Mantrap, 1997; A Ring of Vultures, 1998; Dead Man's Shoes, 1999; Queen Boudicca's Battle of Britain, 2003. **Address:** Garden Bungalow, The Driftway, Wootton Rd., King's Lynn, NF NR20 3JU, England.

HUNT, Robert (William Gainer). (R. W. G. Hunt). British (born England), b. 1923. **Genres:** Photography, Art/Art History, Humanities. **Career:** Kodak Ltd., assistant director of research, 1947-82; Colour Group of Great Britain, chairman, 1961-63; City University, visiting professor of physiological optics, 1968-98; University of Derby, visiting professor of colour science, 1993-. Writer. **Publications:** AS R.W.G. HUNT: The Reproduction of Colour, 1957, 6th ed., 2004; (trans.) Y.L. Grand, Light, Colour and Vision, 1968; Measuring Colour, 1987, (with M. R. Pointer) 4th ed., 2011. **Address:** John Wiley & Sons Inc., 111 River St., Hoboken, NJ 07030-5774, U.S.A.

HUNT, R. W. G. *See* **HUNT, Robert (William Gainer).**

HUNT, Samantha (J.). American (born United States), b. 1971?. **Genres:** Novels, Young Adult Fiction, History. **Career:** Pratt Institute, Department of Humanities and Media Studies, associate professor, writing and bookmaking, teacher. Writer. **Publications:** The Seas, 2004; The Invention of Everything Else, 2008; (intro.) My inventions and other writings, 2012. Contributor to periodicals. Works appear in anthologies. **Address:** Pratt Institute, 3 DeKalb Hall, 200 Willoughby Ave., Brooklyn, NY 11205-3802, U.S.A. **Online address:** samanthajhunt@hotmail.com

HUNT, Tom. American (born United States), b. 1960?. **Genres:** Essays. **Career:** Kent School, teacher of English. head coach, 2003-. Writer. **Publications:** Tully's Trouble, 1996; (with S. Lee) At The Ballet; On Stage, Backstage, 1998; Portlaw, County Waterford: Portrait of an Industrial Village and its Cotton Industry, 1825-76, 2000; Cliffs of Despair: A Journey to Suicide's Edge, 2006; Port and Society in Victorian Ireland: The Case of Westmeath, 2007. Works appear in anthology. Contributor to periodicals. **Address:** Kent School, PO Box 2006, Kent, CT 06757, U.S.A.

HUNT, Tony. British (born England), b. 1944. **Genres:** History, Language/Linguistics, Literary Criticism And History, Medicine/Health. **Career:** University of St. Andrews, lecturer, 1968-79, reader, 1979-90; University of London, Westfield College, visiting professor of medieval studies, 1986-88; University of Oxford, St. Peter's College, lecturer and tutorial fellow, 1990-, Besse Fellow and tutor in French, now emeritus fellow, university faculty lecturer in French. Writer. **Publications:** (Ed.) Kalender, 1983; (ed.) Les Gius Partiz des Eschez: Two Anglo-Norman Chess Treatises, 1986; Chrétien de Troyes: Yvain (Le Chevalier auLion), 1986; (with R. Barber) Arthurian Literature, IX, 1989; Plant Names of Medieval England, 1989; Popular Medicine in Thirteenth-Century England: Introduction and Texts, 1990; Teaching and Learning Latin in Thirteenth-Century England, 1991; The Medieval Surgery, 1992; (ed.) Anglo-Norman Medicine, 1994; Villon's Last Will: Language and Authority in the Testament, 1996; (ed.) Les Cantiques Salemon: The Song of Songs in MS Paris BNF fr. 14966, 2006; Miraculous Rhymes: The Writing of Gautier De Coinci, 2007; (ed.) Les Proverbez d'Alain, 2007; (ed.) Old French Herbal, 2008; (ed. with J. Bliss and H. Leyser) Cher Alme: Texts of Anglo-Norman Piety, 2010; (ed.) Old French Medical Texts, 2011. Contributor to periodicals. **Address:** St. Peter's College, University of Oxford, New Inn Hall St., Oxford, OX OX1 2DL, England. **Online address:** anthony.hunt@spc.ox.ac.uk

HUNT, Tristram. British (born England), b. 1974. **Genres:** Administration/Management, History. **Career:** University of Cambridge, King's College, Centre for History and Economics, associate fellow; University of London, Queen Mary College, lecturer in history, 2002-; Stoke-on-Trent Central, member of parliament, 2010-. Writer and historian. **Publications:** The English Civil War: At First Hand, 2002; Building Jerusalem: The Rise and Fall of the Victorian City, 2005; Marx's General: The Revolutionary Life of Friedrich Engels, 2009; Frock-Coated Communist: The Life and Times of the Original Champagne Socialist, 2010. Contributor to periodicals. **Address:** School of History, Queen Mary College, University of London, Mile End Rd., London, GL E1 4NS, England. **Online address:** t.hunt@qmul.ac.uk

HUNT, Walter H. American (born United States), b. 1959?. **Genres:** Science Fiction/Fantasy, Novels, Literary Criticism And History. **Career:** Writer. **Publications:** DARK WING SERIES: The Dark Wing, 2001; The Dark Path, 2003; The Dark Ascent, 2004; The Dark Crusade, 2005. NOVELS: A Song in Stone, 2008; Madness in Harmony: A Novel of the Mists, 2009. **Address:** c/o Author Mail, Tor Books, 175 5th Ave., New York, NY 10010-7703, U.S.A. **Online address:** hotc@walterhunt.com

HUNTER, Chris. See **FLUKE, Joanne.**

HUNTER, Douglas. Canadian (born Canada), b. 1959?. **Genres:** Sports/Fitness, Business/Trade/Industry, History. **Career:** Freelance journalist, 1993-. **Publications:** Against the Odds, 1981; (with J. Boyd as Doug Hunter) Trials: Canada 1 and the 1983 America's Cup, 1984; Open Ice, 1994; A Breed Apart: An Illustrated History of Goaltending, 1995; War Games: Conn Smythe and Hockey's Fighting Men, 1996; Champions: The Illustrated History of Hockey's Greatest Dynasties, 1997; (with S. Killing) Yacht Design Explained: A Sailor's Guide to the Principles and Practice of Design, 1998; Scotty Bowman: A Life in Hockey, 1998; The Glory Barons: The Saga of the Edmonton Oilers, 1999; Molson: The Birth of a Business Empire, 2001; The Bubble and the Bear: How Nortel Burst the Canadian Dream, 2002; Yzerman: The Making of a Champion, 2004; (co-author) Building the Best: Inside Canada's Best Managed Companies, 2006; God's Mercies: Rivalry, Betrayal, and the Dream of Discovery, 2007; Half Moon: Henry Hudson and the Voyage That Redrew the Map of the New World, 2009. Contributor to newspapers. **Address:** c/o Jeff Gerecke, G Agency L.L.C., PO Box 374, Bronx, NY 10471, U.S.A. **Online address:** dwh5@mac.com

HUNTER, Eric J. British (born England), b. 1930?. **Genres:** Novels, Information Science/Computers, Librarianship, Education, Bibliography. **Career:** Liverpool John Moores University (formerly Liverpool Polytechnic), lecturer, 1969-76, senior lecturer, 1976-89, reader, 1989-92, head of information and library studies, 1992-94, Liverpool Business School, professor of information management, 1994-95, emeritus professor of information management, 1995-. Writer. **Publications:** John J. Ogle, 1966; Anglo-American Cataloguing Rules, 1967: An Introduction, 1972, 2nd ed., 1989; Examples Illustrating Anglo-American Cataloguing Rules, 1973, 3rd ed., 1989; Cataloguing: A Guidebook, 1974; Display for Librarians: A Handbook, 1975; AACR 2: An Introduction, 1979; Cataloguing; A Guidebook, 1979, 3rd ed., 1991; (with N.J. Fox) Examples Illustrating AACR2: Anglo-American Cataloguing Rules, 2nd ed., 1980; The ABC of BASIC: An Introduction to Programming for Librarians, 1982; (with K.G.B. Bakewell) Cataloguing, 2nd rev. ed., 1983; Computerized Cataloguing, 1985; Examples Illustrating AACR 2 1988 Revision, 1989; An Introduction to AACR 2: A Programmed Guide to the Second Edition of the Anglo-American Cataloguing Rules, 1988, rev. ed., 1989; Classification Made Simple, 1988, 3rd ed. as Classification Made Simple: An Introduction to Knowledge Organisation and Information Retrieval, 2009; A Guide to the Concise AACR 2, 1988, rev. ed. as A Programmed Introduction, 1994; The Bullet and the Ring (novel), 2009. Contributor to monographs, periodicals and conference proceedings. **Address:** 44 Cornwall Way, Ainsdale, Southport, MS PR8 3SH, England. **Online address:** e.j.hunter@livjm.ac.uk

HUNTER, Faith. See **HUNTER, Gwen.**

HUNTER, Gwen. (Faith Hunter). American (born United States) **Genres:** Mystery/Crime/Suspense, Westerns/Adventure. **Career:** Writer. **Publications:** SUSPENSE NOVELS: Betrayal, 1994; Stolen Children, 1994; False Truths, 1995; Ashes to Ashes, 1996; Law of the Wild, 1997; Delayed Diagnosis, 2001; Prescribed Danger, 2002; Deadly Remedy, 2003; Grave Concerns, 2004; Bloodstone, 2005; Shadow Valley, 2005; Blackwater Secrets, 2006; Sleep Softly, 2008; Rapid Descent, 2009; His Blood Like Tears, 2011. ADVENTURE NOVELS WITH G. LEVEILLE: Death Warrant, 1990; Death Sentence, 1992. URBAN FANTASY NOVELS AS FAITH HUNTER: Bloodring, 2008; Seraphs, 2008; Host, 2009; Skinwalker, 2009; Blood Cross, 2010; Mercy Blade, 2011; Rogue Mage World Book/Role Playing Game, 2011; Raven Cursed 2012. **Address:** U.S.A. **Online address:** gwen@gwenhunter.com

HUNTER, J(ames) Paul. American (born United States), b. 1934. **Genres:** Literary Criticism And History. **Career:** University of Florida, instructor in English, 1957-59; Williams College, instructor, 1962-64; University of California, assistant professor, 1964-66; Emory University, associate professor, 1966-68, professor of English, 1968-80, chairman of English, 1973-79; University of Rochester, College of Arts and Science, dean, 1981-86; University of Chicago, professor of English, 1987-90, Chester D. Tripp professor in the humanities, 1990-96, Barbara E. and Richard J. Franke professor in the humanities, 1996-2001, Barbara E. and Richard J. Franke professor emeritus, 2001-, Franke Institute for the Humanities, director; University of Virginia, professor of English, 2002-. Writer. **Publications:** The Reluctant Pilgrim: Defoe's Emblematic Method and Quest for Form in Robinson Crusoe, 1966; Occasional Form: Henry Fielding and the Chains of Circumstance, 1975; (co-author) The State of the Discipline, 1970s-1980s: A Special Issue of the ADE Bulletin, 1979; (with M.C. Battestin) Henry Fielding in His Time and Ours: Papers Presented at a Clark Library Seminar, 14 May 1983, 1987; Before Novels: The Cultural Contexts of Eighteenth-Century English Fiction, 1990; Sound Argument: A Cultural History of the Anglophone Couplet, forthcoming. EDITOR: Moll Flanders: A Critical Edition, 1970; (with C.E. Bain and J. Beaty) The Norton Introduction to Literature, 1973, (with A. Booth and K.J. Mays) 9th ed., 2005; Norton Introduction to Poetry, 1973, (with A. Booth and K.J. Mays) 9th ed., 2007; Poetry, 1973; (and intro.) The Plays of Edward Moore, 1982; (with J.D. Canfield) Rhetorics of Order/Ordering Rhetorics in English Neoclassical Literature, 1989; (with J. Beaty) New Worlds of Literature, 1989, 2nd ed. as New Worlds of Literature: Writings from America's Many Cultures, 1994; Moll Flanders, 1995; Frankenstein: The 1818 Text, Contexts, Nineteenth-Century Responses, Modern Criticism, 1996, 2nd ed. as Frankenstein: The 1818 Text, Contexts, Criticism, 2012. Contributor to journals. **Address:** Department of English, University of Chicago, 1115 E 58th St., Chicago, IL 60637-1511, U.S.A. **Online address:** jph7f@virginia.edu

HUNTER, Jessie Prichard. American (born United States), b. 1957?. **Genres:** Mystery/Crime/Suspense, Novels, Young Adult Fiction, Literary Criticism And History. **Career:** Lear's magazine, copy chief; Success magazine, copy editor. **Publications:** Blood Music, 1993; One, Two, Buckle My

Shoe, 1997. Contributor to periodicals. **Address:** c/o Jane Cushman, JCA Literary Agency, 174 Sullivan St., New York, NY 10012, U.S.A.

HUNTER, Matthew. *See* STONE, Rodney.

HUNTER, Michael (Cyril William). British (born England), b. 1949. **Genres:** Intellectual History, Biography, Art/Art History, Archaeology/Antiquities. **Career:** Oxford University, research fellow, 1972-75; Worcester College, research fellow, 1972-75; University of Reading, research fellow, 1975-76; University of London, Birkbeck College, lecturer, 1976-84, reader, 1984-92, professor of history, 1992-, professor emeritus of history. Writer. **Publications:** John Aubrey and the Realm of Learning, 1975; Science and Society in Restoration England, 1981; The Royal Society and Its Fellows 1660-1700: The Morphology of an Early Scientific Institution, 1982, rev. ed., 1994; (with A. Gregory) An Astrological Diary of the 17th Century, 1988; Establishing the New Science: The Experience of the Early Royal Society, 1989; (with S. Schaffer) Robert Hooke: New Studies, 1989; (with R. Thorne) Change at Kings Cross, 1990; (co-author) Avebury Reconsidered: From the 1600s to the 1990s, 1991; Letters and Papers of Robert Boyle, 1992; (with D. Wootton) Atheism from the Reformation to the Enlightenment, 1992; Robert Boyle Reconsidered, 1994; Robert Boyle by Himself and His Friends, 1994; Science and the Shape of Orthodoxy, 1995; (ed.) Preserving the Past: The Rise of Heritage in Modern Britain, 1996; (with E.B. Davis) A Free Enquiry into the Vulgarly Received Notion of Nature, 1996; Archives of the Scientific Revolution: The Formation and Exchange of Ideas in 17th Century Europe, 1998; (ed.) A Radicals Books: The Library Catalogue of Samule Jeake of Rye, 1623-90, 1999; (with E.B. Davis) The Works of Robert Boyle, 14 vols., 1999-2000; Robert Boyle (1627-91): Scrupulosity and Science, 2000; Robert Boyle, 1627-91: Scrupulosity and Science, 2000; (ed. with A. Clericuzio and L.M. Principe) The Correspondence of Robert Boyle, 6 vols., 2001; The Occult Laboratory: Magic Science and Second Sight in Late 17th-Century Scotland, 2001; (co-author) London's Leonardo: The Life and Work of Robert Hooke, 2003; (ed. with F. Harris) John Evelyn and His Milieu, 2003; (ed. with L. Gowing and M. Rubin) Love, Friendship and Faith in Europe, 1300-1800, 2005; (ed. with H. Knight) Unpublished Material Relating to Robert Boyles Memoirs for the Natural History of Human Blood, 2005; Robert Boyles Heads and Inquiries, 2005; (ed. with M. Cooper) Robert Hooke: Tercentennial Studies, 2006; Editing Early Modern Texts: An Introduction to Principles and Practice, 2006; Boyle Papers: Understanding the Manuscripts of Robert Boyle, 2007; (ed. with P. Anstey) The Text of Robert Boyles Design about Natural History, 2008; Boyle: Between God and Science, 2009; (ed.) Printed Images in Early Modern Britain: Essays in Interpretation, 2009; (with I. Avramov and H. Yoshimoto) Boyle's Books: The Evidence of His Citations, 2010; (contrib.) Francis Barlow: Painter of Birds & Beasts: Clandon Park, 10 May-24 July 2011, 2011; (ed.) Magic and Mental Disorder: Sir Hans Sloane's Memoir of John Beaumont, 2011. **Address:** School of History, Classics and Archaeology, Birkbeck College, University of London, Rm. 307, 26 Russell Sq., Malet St., London, GL WC1B 5DQ, England. **Online address:** m.hunter@bbk.ac.uk

HUNTER, Mollie. Scottish (born Scotland), b. 1922. **Genres:** Novels, Children's Fiction, Plays/Screenplays, History, Picture/Board Books, Young Adult Non-fiction, Ghost Writer, Mystery/Crime/Suspense, Children's Non-fiction, Criminology/True Crime. **Career:** Writer, 1953-; Dalhousie University, writer-in-residence, 1980, 1981; Aberlour Summer School for Gifted Children, teacher of creative writing, 1987, 1988. **Publications:** Stay for an Answer, 1962; Patrick Kentigern Keenan, 1963 in US as The Smartest Man in Ireland, 1965; Hi Johnny, 1963; The Spanish Letters, 1964; The Kelpie's Pearls, 1964; A Pistol in Greenyards, 1965; The Ghosts of Glencoe, 1966; Thomas and the Warlock, 1967; The Ferlie, 1968; The Bodach in US as The Walking Stones: A Story of Suspense, 1970; The Lothian Run, 1970; The Thirteenth Member: A Story of Suspense, 1971; A Sound of Chariots, 1972; The Haunted Mountain: A Story of Suspense, 1972; The Stronghold, 1974; A Stranger Came Ashore: A Story of Suspense, 1975; Talent is Not Enough: Mollie Hunter on Writing for Children, 1976; The Wicked One: A Story of Suspense, 1977; A Furl of Fairy Wind: Four Stories, 1977; The Third Eye, 1979; You Never Knew Her as I Did!, 1981; The Knight of the Golden Plain, 1983; The Dragonfly Years, 1983 in US as Hold on to Love, 1984; The Enchanted Whistle, 1985; The Three-Day Enchantment, 1985; I'll Go My Own Way in US as Cat, Herself, 1985; The Brownie, 1986; The Enchanted Boy, 1986; Flora MacDonald and Bonnie Prince Charlie, 1988; The Mermaid Summer, 1988, rev. ed., 2003; The Pied Piper Syndrome and Other Essays, 1992; The Day of the Unicorn, 1994; (reteller) Gilly Martin the Fox, 1994; The King's Swift Rider: A Novel

on Robert the Bruce, 1998; Escape from Loch Leven, 2003. Contributor of articles to newspapers and magazines. **Address:** A. M. Heath & Company Ltd., 6 Warwick Ct., Holborn, London, GL WC1R 5DJ, England.

HUNTER, R(ichard) L(awrence). British/Australian (born Australia), b. 1953. **Genres:** Classics, Language/Linguistics, Archaeology/Antiquities, Poetry. **Career:** University of Cambridge, Pembroke College, fellow, 1977-2001, director of studies in classics, 1979-99, university lecturer in classics, 1987-97, reader in Greek and Latin literature, 1997-2001, Regius professor of Greek, 2001-; Trinity College, fellow, 2001-. Writer. **Publications:** A Study of Daphnis and Chloe, 1983; The New Comedy of Greece and Rome, 1985; The Argonautica of Apollonius: Literary Studies, 1993; (trans., intro. and contrib.) Jason and the Golden Fleece: The Argonautica, 1993; Theocritus and the Archaeology of Greek Poetry, 1996; (with M. Fantuzzi) Muse eModelli: La Poesia Ellenistica da Alessandro Magno ad Augusto, 2002; (contrib. and intro.) Idylls, 2002; The Encomium for Ptolemy Philadelphus, 2003; Plato's Symposium, 2004; (with M. Fantuzzi) Tradition and Innovation in Hellenistic Poetry, 2004; The Shadow of Callimachus, 2006; On Coming After: Studies in Post-Classical Greek Literature and Its Reception, 2008; Critical Moments in Classical Literature: Studies in the Ancient View of Literature and Its Uses, 2009; (trans. and intro) Jason and the Golden Fleece, 2009; Plato and the Traditions of Ancient Literature: The Silent Stream, 2012. EDITOR: Eubulus: The Fragments, 1983; Argonautica: Book III/Apollonius of Rhodes, 1989; Theocritus, A Selection, 1999; The Hesiodic Catalogue of Women: Constructions and Reconstructions, 2005; (with I. Rutherford) Wandering Poets in Ancient Greek Culture: Travel, Locality and Pan-Hellenism, 2009; (with D. Russell) How to Study Poetry: De audiendis Poetis, 2011. Contributor to journals. **Address:** Faculty of Classics, University of Cambridge, Sidgwick Ave., Cambridge, CB CB3 9DA, England. **Online address:** rlh10@cam.ac.uk

HUNTER, Sara Hoagland. American (born United States), b. 1954. **Genres:** Children's Fiction, Songs/Lyrics And Libretti, Cartoons, Picture/Board Books. **Career:** Christian Science Monitor, writer and radio producer, 1976-80; Massachusetts Public School System, teacher of English, drama and public speaking, 1982-94; Sara Hunter Productions Inc. (producer of children's videos, books and music), founder and president, 1994-. Writer. **Publications:** Miss Piggy's Night Out, 1995; Rondo's Stuff, 1996; The Good, the Bad, and the Tweety, 1996; Beauty and the Feast, 1996; The Unbreakable Code, 1996; Chocolate Yak-A-Lot, 1997; Baby Bugs's Wacky Dress-Up, 1997; The Lighthouse Santa, 2011. **Address:** Sara Hunter Productions Inc., 8C Pleasant St., South Natick, MA 01760, U.S.A. **Online address:** sara@sarahunterproductions.com

HUNTER, Seb. British (born England), b. 1971. **Genres:** Music, Humor/Satire, Biography. **Career:** Musician and writer. **Publications:** Dated, 2001; Hell Bent for Leather: Confessions of a Heavy Metal Addict, 2004; Rock Me Amadeus: When Ignorance Meets High Art, Things Can Get Messy, 2006; How To Be a Better Person, 2008. **Address:** c/o Author Mail, Fourth Estate/HarperCollins, 10 E 53rd St., 7th Fl., New York, NY 10022-5244, U.S.A.

HUNTER, Shireen T. American/Iranian (born Iran), b. 1945. **Genres:** Politics/Government, Social Sciences. **Career:** Private secretary to the Iranian Foreign Minister, 1966-67; Iranian Embassy, third secretary, 1967-71; Intl. Organizations Department of the Iranian Ministry of Foreign Affairs, in-charge of economic affairs, assistant, 1971-74, second secretary, 1974-78; Harvard University, Center for Intl. Affairs, research fellow, 1979; Center for Strategic and Intl. Studies, Middle East Program, deputy director, 1983-93, senior associate, 1993-97, Islam Program, director, 1998-2005; George Mason University, adjunct professor, 1984; Mediterranean Program, visiting senior fellow and director of Centre for European Policy Studies, 1993-97; Centre for European Policy Studies, director, 1993-97; Harvard University, Belfer Center for Science and Intl. Affairs, associate, 1999-2002; RAND Corp., consultant, 2000-; Carnegie Corp., academic fellow, 2000-02; Georgetown University, Carnegie Project on Reformist Islam, director, 2005-, adjunct professor, 2006-07, Center for Muslim-Christian Understanding, visiting fellow, 2005-. Writer. **Publications:** (Ed.) The Gulf Cooperation Council: Problems and Prospects, 1984; OPEC and the Third World: The Politics of Aid, 1984; (ed.) PLO After Tripoli, 1984; (ed.) Political and Economic Trends in the Middle East, 1985; (ed.) Internal Developments in Iran, 1985; (with R.G. Neumann and F.W. Axelgard) Revitalizing U.S. Leadership in the Middle East, 1988; (ed.) The Politics of Islamic Revivalism: Diversity and Unity, 1988; Iran and the World: Continuity in a Revolutionary Decade, 1990; Iran after Khomeini, 1992; The Transcaucasus in Transition: Nation-building and

Conflict, 1994; Central Asia since Independence, 1996; The Future of Islam and the West: Clash of Civilizations or Peaceful Coexistence?, 1998; Iran, Between the Gulf and the Caspian Basin: Strategic and Economic Implications, 2000; (ed.) Islam, Europe's Second Religion: The New Social, Cultural and Political Landscape, 2002; (with J.L. Thomas and A. Melikishvili) Islam in Russia: The Politics of Identity and Security, 2004; (ed. with H. Malik) Modernization, Democracy and Islam, 2005; (ed. with H. Malik) Islam and Human Rights: Advancing a U.S. Muslim Dialogue, 2005; (with J.B. Alterman and A.L. Phillips) The Idea and Practice of Philanthropy in the Muslim World, 2005; (ed.) Reformist Voices of Islam: Mediating Islam and Modernity, 2009; Iran's Foreign Policy in the Post-Soviet Era: Resisting the New International Order, 2010. Contributor to periodicals. **Address:** Georgetown University, 37th and O St. NW, Washington, DC 20057, U.S.A. **Online address:** sth23@georgetown.edu

HUNTER, S. L. See **HAWKE, Simon.**

HUNTLEY, James Robert. American (born United States), b. 1923. **Genres:** International Relations/Current Affairs, Politics/Government, Young Adult Non-fiction, Social Sciences. **Career:** State of Washington Parks and Recreation Commission, staff and consultant on international affairs, 1949-51; U.S. Foreign Service, exchange-of-persons officer, 1952-54, U.S. Information Agency Information Center, director, 1954-55, U.S. Information Agency, European regional affairs officer, 1956-58, U.S. Mission to the European Communities, deputy public affairs officer, 1958-60; Atlantic Institute, founder and executive officer, 1960-63, director, 1963-65; Ford Foundation, International Affairs Division, program associate, 1965-67; Council of the Atlantic Colleges, secretary-general, 1967-68; freelance writer and lecturer, 1968-74; Battelle Memorial Institute, research fellow, 1974-83; Atlantic Council of the United States, president, 1983-85; Council for a Community of Democracies, founder and vice president. **Publications:** The NATO Story, 1965, rev. ed., 1969; (with W.R. Burgess) Europe and America-The Next Ten Years, 1970; Toward New Transatlantic Education Relationships, 1970; Man's Environment and the Atlantic Alliance, 1971, 2nd ed., 1972; Uniting the Democracies: Institutions of the Atlantic-Pacific System, 1980; Pax Democratica: A Strategy for the 21st Century, 1998; An Architect of Democracy: Building a Mosaic of Peace, 2006. EDITOR: The Atlantic Community, A Force for Peace, 1963; Teaching about the American Impact on Europe, 1970; Teaching about Collective Security and Conflict, 1972. **Address:** 1213 Towne Rd., Sequim, WA 98382-8849, U.S.A.

HUNTLEY, Paula (Bowlin). American (born United States), b. 1944. **Genres:** Adult Non-fiction, Autobiography/Memoirs, Biography. **Career:** English teacher, marketing consultant and Writer. **Publications:** (With H.B. Sugaya) Heritage and Tourism in California: Report, 1984; The Hemingway Book Club of Kosovo (memoir), 2003. **Address:** Lorraine Kisly, Cherry Hill Farm, 305 Cherry Hill, Shickshinny, PA 18655-2322, U.S.A. **Online address:** paula@bookclubofkosovo.com

HUPCHICK, Dennis P(aul). American (born United States), b. 1948. **Genres:** Area Studies, History, Cultural/Ethnic Topics. **Career:** Wilkes University, assistant professor of history, 1990-, professor of history. Writer. **Publications:** (Ed.) The Pen and the Sword: Studies in Bulgarian History, 1988; The Bulgarians in the Seventeenth Century: Slavic Orthodox Society and Culture under Ottoman Rule, 1993; Culture and History in Eastern Europe, 1994; Conflict and Chaos in Eastern Europe, 1995; (with H.E. Cox) A Concise Historical Atlas of Eastern Europe, 1996; (ed. with D.L. Dyer and intro.) Bulgaria Past and Present: Transitions and Turning Points, 1996; (ed. with R.W. Weisberger) Hungary's Historical Legacies, 2000; (with H.E. Cox) The Palgrave Concise Historical Atlas of the Balkans, 2001, French language ed. as Les Balkans: Atlas Historique, 2008; The Balkans: From Constantinople to Communism, 2002; (ed. with R.W. Weisberger and D.L. Anderson) Profiles of Revolutionaries in Atlantic History, 2007. **Address:** Department of Humanities and History, Wilkes University, 4222 Capin Hall, 84 W South St., PO Box 111, Wilkes-Barre, PA 18766, U.S.A. **Online address:** dennis.hupchick@wilkes.edu

HUR, Nam-lin. Canadian (born Canada), b. 1957. **Genres:** History, Theology/Religion. **Career:** University of British Columbia, professor. Writer. **Publications:** Prayer and Play in Late Tokugawa Japan: Asakusa Sensoji and Edo Society, 2000; Death and Social Order in Tokugawa Japan: Buddhism, Anti-Christianity, and the Danka System, 2007. Contributor to books and periodicals. **Address:** University of British Columbia, 2329 W Mall, Vancouver,

BC V6T 1Z4, Canada. **Online address:** namlin@interchange.ubc.ca

HUREWITZ, Daniel. American (born United States), b. 1966. **Genres:** Politics/Government. **Career:** City University of New York, Hunter College, assistant professor of history. Academic, historian and writer. **Publications:** Stepping Out: Nine Tours through New York City's Gay and Lesbian Past, 1997; Bohemian Los Angeles and the Making of Modern Politics, 2007. Contributor to periodicals and journals. **Address:** Department of History, Hunter College, City University of New York, 695 Park Ave., New York, NY 10065, U.S.A. **Online address:** daniel.hurewitz@hunter.cuny.edu

HURKA, Thomas. Canadian (born Canada), b. 1952. **Genres:** Ethics, Philosophy, Sciences. **Career:** University of Calgary, lecturer, 1978-79, assistant professor of philosophy, 1979-84, associate professor, 1984-92, professor, 1992-2002; Canadian Journal of Philosophy, executive editor, 1992-2002; University of Toronto, Department of philosophy, professor, 2002-, Chancellor Henry N.R. Jackman distinguished chair in philosophical studies, 2003-. **Publications:** Perfectionism, 1993 as Perfectionism and Neutrality: Essays in Liberal Theory, 2003; (ed. with H.G. Coward) The Greenhouse Effect: Ethics and Climate Change, 1993; Principles: Short Essays on Ethics, 1993; Virtue, Vice, and Value, 2001; The Best Things in Life: A Guide to What Really Matters, 2010; Drawing Morals: Essays in Ethical Theory, 2011; (ed.) Underivative Duty: British Moral Philosophers from Sidgwick to Ewing, 2011. Contributor to periodicals. **Address:** Department of Philosophy, University of Toronto, Rm. 430, 170 St. George St., 27 King's College Cir., Toronto, ON M5R 2M8, Canada. **Online address:** tom.hurka@utoronto.ca

HURLEY, Andrew. American (born United States), b. 1944. **Genres:** Translations, Novellas/Short Stories. **Career:** University of Puerto Rico, College of Humanities, Department of English, faculty, 1973, professor of English, now professor emeritus, Graduate Program in Translation, director. Writer and translator. **Publications:** TRANSLATOR: Legacies: Selected Poems by Heberto Padilla, 1982; H. Padilla, Heroes Are Grazing in My Garden, 1984; R. Arenas, Farewell to the Sea, 1985; Against All Hope: The Prison Memoirs of Armando Valladares, 1986; R. Arenas, The Ill-Fated Peregrinations of Fray Servando, 1987; F. Arrabal, The Compass-Stone, 1987; G. Sainz, The Princess of the Iron Palace, 1987; R. Arenas, Singing from the Well, 1987; R. Arenas, The Brightest Star (novella), 1989; R. Arenas, The Palace of the White Skunks, 1990; E. Sabato, The Angel of Darkness, 1991; F. Arrabal, El Greco and Fernando Arrabal, 1991; L. Lopez-Baralt, Islam and Spanish Literature, 1992; F. Arrabal, The Red Virgin, 1993; G.A. Baralt, Tradition into the Future: The First Hundred Years of the Banco Popular de Puerto Rico, 1993; J. Edwards, Persona Non Grata, 1993; R. Arenas, The Assault, 1994; A. Lydia Vega, True and False Romances, 1994; E. Rodriguez-Julia, The Renunciation, 1997; S. Puledda, On Being Human: Interpretations of Humanism from the Renaissance to the Present, 1997; J.L. Borges, Collected Fictions, 1998; R. Arenas, The Color of Summer, 2000; Z. Valdes, Dear First Love, 2002; C. Rivera-Garza, No One will See Me Cry: A Novel, 2003; A. Pérez-Reverte, Queen of the South, 2004; (and intro.) J.L. Borges, Aleph, 2004; (and intro.) J.L. Borges, Universal History of Iniquity, 2004; M. Glantz, Wake, 2005; (and intro.) J.L. Borges, Brodie's Report: Including the Prose Fiction from In Praise of Darkness, 2005; J.L. Borges, Book of Imaginary Beings, 2005; J.L. Borges, The Library of Babel, 2005; R. Darío, Selected Writings, 2005; J. Navarro, Brotherhood of the Holy Shroud, 2007; J. Navarro, Bible of clay, 2008; Fidel Castro: My Life, 2008. OTHER: (ed. with G. Guinness) Auctor Ludens, 1986. **Address:** Department of English, College of Humanities, University of Puerto Rico, Basement of Pedreira Bldg., Office 8, PO Box 23356, San Juan, PR 00931-3356, U.S.A. **Online address:** memail@libertypr.net

HURLEY, Valerie. American (born United States), b. 1943?. **Genres:** Novels, Mystery/Crime/Suspense, Literary Criticism And History. **Career:** Writer. **Publications:** St. Ursula's Girls Against the Atomic Bomb, 2003; The Thirty-One Rules of Love, forthcoming. Contributor to periodicals. **Address:** MacAdam Cage Publishing Inc., 155 Sansome St., Ste. 550, San Francisco, CA 94104-3615, U.S.A. **Online address:** readermail@valeriehurley.com

HURRELL, Andrew. British (born England), b. 1955. **Genres:** Politics/Government. **Career:** Christ Church, research fellow, 1983-86; Johns Hopkins University, School of Advanced International Studies, Bologna Center, assistant professor of international relations, 1986-89; University of São Paulo, visiting professor, 1994, 1997; Oxford University, Centre for International Studies, director, 1994-96, 2004-, director of graduate studies in international relations, 1996-98, 2000-03, director of research training in international relations, 1998-99, 2006, Balliol College, fellow, 2007-, Montague Burton Professor of International Relations, 2007-; New York University, Law School, global research fellow, 2003; University of Brasilia, San Tiago Dantas visiting professor of international relations, 2005; New York Institute, Straus fellow, 2009-10. Writer. **Publications:** (With E.A. Felder) The U.S.-Brazilian Informatics Dispute, 1988; (co-author) Estado, Mercado e Democracia: Política e Economia Comparadas, 1993; (afterword) The United States and Brazil: A Long Road of Unmet Expectations, 2005; On Global Order: Power, Values, and the Constitution of International Society, 2007. EDITOR: (with B. Kingsbury) The International Politics of the Environment: Actors, Interests, and Institutions, 1992; (with L. Fawcett) Regionalism in World Politics: Regional Organization and International Order, 1995; (co-ed.) Challenges: United Kingdom and Brazil, 1997; (with N. Woods) Inequality, Globalization, and World Politics, 1999; (and intro. with K. Alderson) Hedley Bull on International Society, 2000; (with R. Foot and J. Gaddis) Order and Justice in International Relations, 2003. Contributor to books and periodicals. **Address:** Balliol College, Oxford University, 53 Chalfont Rd., Oxford, OX OX2 6TJ, England. **Online address:** andrew.hurrell@balliol.ox.ac.uk

HURST, Frances. See **MAYHAR, Ardath (Hurst).**

HURT, Harry. American (born United States), b. 1951. **Genres:** Adult Nonfiction, Biography, Sports/Fitness, Essays. **Career:** Texas Monthly, senior editor, 1975-86; Newsweek, correspondent, 1988-90. **Publications:** Texas Rich: The Hunt Dynasty from the Early Oil Days through the Silver Crash, 1981; For All Mankind, 1988; Lost Tycoon: The Many Lives of Donald J. Trump, 1993; Chasing the Dream: A Mid-life Quest for Fame and Fortune on the Pro-Golf Circuit, 1997; How to Learn Golf, 2002; (with M. Spearman) A.I.M. of Golf: Visual-Imagery Lessons to Improve Every Aspect of Your Game, 2004; Hurt Yourself: In Executive Pursuit of Action, Danger and a Decent-Looking Pair of Swim Trunks, 2008. **Address:** c/o Bob Dattila, Phoenix Literary Agency, 216 S Yellowstone, Livingston, MT 59047, U.S.A.

HURTADO, Albert L. (Albert Leon Hurtado). American (born United States), b. 1946. **Genres:** History, Social Sciences. **Career:** University of California, Department of History, teaching assistant, 1975-77; California Department of Parks and Recreation, Office of Historic Preservation, park interpretive specialist, 1977-78; Theodoratus Cultural Research, senior staff historian, 1978-80; Public History Services Associates, consultant, 1980-83; Sierra College, Social Science Division, instructor, 1981-82; California Committee for the Promotion of History, chairman, 1981-82; Superior Court of the State of California, expert witness, 1982; National Council on Public History, director, 1982-85; Indiana University-Purdue University, Department of History, assistant professor, 1983-86; Arizona State University, Department of History, assistant professor, 1986-89, associate professor, 1990-98, director of graduate studies, 1992-98; University of Oklahoma, professor and Paul H. and Doris Eaton Travis chair in American history, 1998-. Writer. **Publications:** Indian Survival on the California Frontier, 1988; Intimate Frontiers: Sex, Gender and Culture in Old California, 1999; John Sutter: A Life on the North American Frontier, 2006. EDITOR: (with T.J. Karamanski and C. Davis) Public History Education in America: A Guide, 1986; (with P. Iverson) Major Problems in American Indian History, 1994, 2nd ed., 2001; Reflections on American Indian History: Honoring the Past, Building a Future, 2008; The American West, forthcoming. Contributor to history journals. **Address:** Department of History, University of Oklahoma, Rm. 403A, W Lindsey, Norman, OK 73019, U.S.A. **Online address:** ahurtado@ou.edu

HURTADO, Albert Leon. See **HURTADO, Albert L.**

HURTADO, Larry W. American/Canadian (born Canada), b. 1943. **Genres:** Theology/Religion, History. **Career:** Regent College, assistant professor of New Testament, 1975-78; University of Manitoba, professor of religion, 1978-96; University of Edinburgh, professor of New Testament language, literature and theology, 1996-2011, professor emeritus, 2011-. Writer. **Publications:** Text-Critical Methodology and the Pre-Caesarean Text: Codex W in the Gospel of Mark, 1981; One God, One Lord: Early Christian Devotion and Ancient Jewish Monotheism, 1988, 2nd ed., 1998; Mark: New International Biblical Commentary, 1989; At the Origins of Christian Worship: The Content and Character of Earliest Christian Devotion, 1999; Lord Jesus Christ: Devotion to Jesus in Earliest Christianity, 2003; How on Earth did Jesus Become a God? Historical Questions about Earliest Devotion to Jesus, 2005; The Earliest Christian Artifacts: Manuscripts and Christian Origins, 2006; God in New Testament Theology, 2010. EDITOR: Goddess in Religions and

Modern Debate, 1990; (with K. Klostermaier) Religious Studies: Issues, Prospects and Proposals, 1991; (with D.L. Jeffrey) A Dictionary of Biblical Tradition in English Literature, 1992; The Freer Biblical Manuscripts: Fresh Studies of an American Treasure Trove, 2006; (with P. Owen) Who is This Son of Man?': The Latest Scholarship on a Puzzling Expression of the Historical Jesus, 2011. Contributor to books and periodicals. **Address:** New College, University of Edinburgh, Mound Pl., Edinburgh, EH1 2LX, Scotland. **Online address:** l.hurtado@ed.ac.uk

HURTIG, Mel. Canadian (born Canada), b. 1932. **Genres:** Politics/Government, Autobiography/Memoirs, History, International Relations/Current Affairs. **Career:** Hurtig Publishers Ltd., owner, 1972-91, president, 1972-; National Party of Canada, founder and elected leader, 1992; Edmonton Art Gallery, president. Writer. **Publications:** The Betrayal of Canada, 1991; A New and Better Canada: Principles and Policies of a New Canadian Political Party, 1992; At Twilight in the Country, 1996; Pay the Rent or Feed the Kids: The Tragedy and Disgrace of Poverty in Canada, 1999; (ed.) True North Strong and Free? The Proceedings of a Public Inquiry into Canadian Defense Policy and Nuclear Arms, 2000; The Vanishing Country: Is It Too Late to Save Canada?, 2002; Rushing to Armageddon: The Shocking Truth About Canada, Missile Defence and Star Wars, 2004; The Truth About Canada: Some Important, Some Astonishing, Some Truly Appalling Things All Canadians Should Know About Our Country, 2008. **Address:** McClelland & Stewart Ltd., 481 University Ave., Ste. 900, Toronto, ON M5G 2E9, Canada. **Online address:** mhurtig@telusplanet.net

HURWITZ, David. American (born United States), b. 1961. **Genres:** Music, How-to Books, Humor/Satire, Photography. **Career:** ClassicsToday.com, founder, executive editor and advertising manager; Classical Internet Awards (formerly the Cannes Classical Awards), founder and chairman; Denon Records, Classics Exposed, producer; Ondine Records, Earquake, producer; National Public Radio's Performance Today, radio commentator; WNYC's Soundcheck, radio commentator. **Publications:** Beethoven or Bust: A Practical Guide to Understanding and Listening to Great Music, 1992; The Mahler Symphonies: An Owner's Manual, 2004; Dvorak: Romantic Music's Most Versatile Genius, 2005; Exploring Haydn: A Listener's Guide to Music's Boldest Innovator, 2005; Getting the Most out of Mozart: The Instrumental Works, 2005; Getting the Most out of Mozart: The Vocal Works, 2005; Shostakovich Symphonies and Concertos: An Owner's Manual, 2006; Sibelius: The Orchestral Works, An Owner's Manual, 2007; Beethoven's Fifth and Seventh Symphonies: A Closer Look, 2008; Brahms' Symphonies: A Closer Look, 2009; Bernstein's Orchestral Music: An Owner's Manual, 2011. **Address:** Continuum International Publishing Group, 80 Maiden Ln., Ste. 704, New York, NY 10038, U.S.A. **Online address:** dhurwitz@classicstoday.com

HURWITZ, Johanna (Frank). American (born United States), b. 1937. **Genres:** Children's Fiction, Children's Non-fiction, Young Adult Fiction, Education, Travel/Exploration, Literary Criticism And History. **Career:** New York Public Library, children's librarian, 1959-64; New York Public Library, visiting storyteller, 1964-67; City University of New York, Queen's College, lecturer in children's literature, 1965-68; Calhoun School, children's librarian, 1968-75; Manor Oaks School, children's librarian, 1975-77; Great Neck Public Library, children's librarian, 1978-92. Writer. **Publications:** Busybody Nora, 1976; Nora and Mrs. Mind-Your-Own-Business, 1977; The Law of Gravity, 1978; Much Ado About Aldo, 1978; Aldo Applesauce, 1979; New Neighbors for Nora, 1979; Once I Was a Plum Tree, 1980; Superduper Teddy, 1980; Aldo Ice Cream, 1981; Baseball Fever, 1981; The Rabbi's Girls, 1982; Tough-Luck Karen, 1982; What Goes up Must Come Down, 1983; Rip-Roaring Russell, 1983; De De Takes Charge!, 1984; The Hot and Cold Summer, 1985; The Adventures of Ali Baba Bernstein, 1985; Russell Rides Again, 1985; Hurricane Elaine, 1986; Yellow Blue Jay, 1986; Class Clown, 1987; Russell Sprouts, 1987; Bunk Mates, 1988; The Cold and Hot Winter, 1988; Teacher's Pet, 1988; Anne Frank: Life in Hiding, 1988; Hurray for Ali Baba Bernstein, 1989; Russell and Elisa, 1989; Astrid Lindgren: Storyteller to the World, 1989; Class President, 1990; Aldo Peanut Butter, 1990; E Is for Elisa, 1991; School's Out, 1991; Roz and Ozzie, 1992; Ali Baba Bernstein: Lost and Found, 1992; Make Room for Elisa, 1993; New Shoes for Silvia, 1993; The Up and Down Spring, 1993; Leonard Bernstein: A Passion for Music, 1993; School Spirit, 1994; A Word to the Wise: And Other Proverbs, 1994; A Llama in the Family, 1994; Elisa in the Middle, 1995; Ozzie on His Own, 1995; Even Stephen, 1996; The Down and Up Fall, 1996; Spring Break, 1997; Ever-Clever Elisa, 1997; Helen Keller: Courage in the Dark, 1997; Faraway Summer, 1998; Starting School, 1998; A Dream Come

True, 1998; A Llama in the Library, 1999; The Just Desserts Club: Stories and Snacks with Cricket and Lucas, 1999; Summer with Elisa, 2000; Pee Wee's Tale, 2000; One Small Dog, 2000; Lexi's Tale, 2001; Russell's Secret, 2001; Oh No, Noah!, 2002; Pee Wee & Plush, 2002; Dear Emma, 2002; Ethan Out and About, 2002; Elisa Michaels, Bigger & Better, 2003; Ethan at Home, 2003; Fourth Grade Fuss, 2004; Unsigned Valentine: And Other Events in the Life of Emma Meade, 2006; Mostly Monty, 2007; Squirrel World, 2007; Mighty Monty, 2008; Amazing Monty, 2010; (ed.) I Fooled You: Ten Stories of Tricks, Jokes and Switcheroos, 2010; Magical Monty, 2012. Contributor to periodicals. **Address:** 10 Spruce Pl., Great Neck, NY 11021, U.S.A. **Online address:** imhur@yahoo.com

HUSAIN, Shahrukh. British/Pakistani (born Pakistan), b. 1950. **Genres:** Children's Non-fiction, Children's Fiction, Young Adult Non-fiction, Young Adult Fiction. **Career:** Psychotherapist, folklorist, storyteller and writer. **Publications:** (With D.J. Matthews and C. Shackle) Urdu Literature, 1985; Demons, Gods and Holy Men from Indian Myths and Legends, 1987; Mecca, 1993; (ed.) The Virago Book of Witches, 1993; (ed.) Daughters of the Moon, 1994; What Do We Know about Islam?, 1995; Handsome Heroines: Women as Men in Folklore, 1996; The Goddess, 1997; The Virago Book of Temptresses, 1998; The Goddess: Power, Sexuality and the Feminine Divine, 2000; (ed.) The Virago Book of Erotic Myths and Legends, 2002; Egypt, 2005; Rome, 2005; The Vikings, 2005; Greece, 2005; (contrib.) The Barefoot Book of Stories from the Opera, 2006; (with B. Willey) Indian Myths, 2007; (with B. Willey) African Myths, 2007; (contrib.) Wise Fool, 2011. **Address:** Blake Friedmann Lit, Film & TV Agency, 122 Arlington Rd., London, GL NW1 7HP, England. **Online address:** info@shahrukh-husain.com

HUSER, Glen. Canadian (born Canada), b. 1943. **Genres:** Children's Fiction, Novels. **Career:** Rosslyn and Highlands Schools, teacher, 1962-65; McArthur School, teacher, 1967-69; Learning Resources, Edmonton Public Schools, consultant, 1988-96; Concordia College, student teaching advisor, 1997-98; University of Alberta, sessional instructor, 1997-98, 1999-2000, 2003-04; Oz NewMedia/Education-on-line, language arts resource writer, 2000-01; Mee-Yah-Noh Elementary School, writer-in-residence, 2001-02; Virginia Park Elementary School, writer-in-residence, 2003-04. **Publications:** Grace Lake (for adults), 1990; Touch of the Clown, 1999; Jeremy's Christmas Wish, 2000; Stitches, 2003; Skinnybones and the Wrinkle Queen, 2007. Contributor to periodicals. Works appear in anthologies. **Address:** 19-531 SW Marine Dr., Vancouver, BC V6P 5X9, Canada. **Online address:** glenhuser@shaw.ca

HUSKEY, Eugene. American (born United States), b. 1952. **Genres:** International Relations/Current Affairs, Politics/Government. **Career:** Colgate University, visiting instructor, 1981-83; Bowdoin College, assistant professor, 1983-89; Stetson University, associate professor, 1989-96, director of Russian studies, 1994-2000, 2005-; professor, 1996-99, William R. Kenan Jr. professor and chair of political science and Russian studies, 1999-. Writer. **Publications:** Russian Lawyers and the Soviet State, 1986; (ed.) Executive Power and Soviet Politics: The Rise and Decline of the Soviet State, 1992; Presidential Power in Russia, 1999; (co-ed.) Russian State and Bureaucracy, 2009. Contributor to books. **Address:** Department of Political Science, Stetson University, 421 N Woodland Blvd., Ste. 8301, DeLand, FL 32723, U.S.A. **Online address:** ehuskey@stetson.edu

HUSS, Sandy. American (born United States), b. 1953. **Genres:** Novellas/Short Stories, Young Adult Fiction. **Career:** Washington University, lecturer in fiction writing and exposition, 1987-88; University of Alabama, assistant professor of English, 1988-95, associate professor, 1995-, now professor emeritus. Writer. **Publications:** Labor for Love: Stories, 1992. Works appear in anthologies. **Address:** Department of English, University of Alabama, PO Box 870244, Tuscaloosa, AL 35487-0244, U.S.A. **Online address:** shuss@english.as.ua.edu

HUSSAIN, Nasser. American (born United States), b. 1965. **Genres:** Law. **Career:** Amherst College, professor. Writer. **Publications:** The Jurisprudence of Emergency: Colonialism and the Rule of Law, 2003; (ed. with A. Sarat) Forgiveness, Mercy, and Clemency, 2007. **Address:** Dept of Law, Jurisprudence & Social Thought, Amherst College, 74 College St., Amherst, MA 01002-5000, U.S.A. **Online address:** nhussain@amherst.edu

HUSSEY, Mark. American/British (born England), b. 1956. **Genres:** Humanities, Literary Criticism And History, Women's Studies And Issues, Au-tobiography/Memoirs. **Career:** Sussex Publications, English Tapes Program and Sussex Tapes, editor, 1976-82; Association of American Publishers, International Division and Professional and Scholarly Publishing Division, assistant, 1982-84; Pace University, adjunct assistant professor, 1984-88, Thinking and Learning Center, assistant, 1985-88, Department of English, assistant professor, 1988-, professor, 1988-, Feminist Research Group, coordinator, 1990-91; Sander Gallery, assistant, 1985-86; Northern Business Information, writing consultant, 1985-86; New School for Social Research, faculty, 1987-90. **Publications:** The Singing of the Real World: The Philosophy of Virginia Woolf's Fiction, 1986; Virginia Woolf A to Z, 1995; Masculinities: Interdisciplinary Readings, 2003; (intro.) To the Lighthouse, 2005. EDITOR: (intro.) Virginia Woolf and War: Fiction, Reality, and Myth, 1991; Virginia Woolf Miscellanies: Proceedings of the First Annual Conference on Virginia Woolf, 1992; Virginia Woolf: Themes and Variations, Selected Papers from the Second Annual Conference on Virginia Woolf, 1993; Virginia Woolf: Emerging Perspectives, Selected Papers from the Third Annual Conference on Virginia Woolf, 1994; Harcourt Annotated Edition of Virginia Woolf, 2005; The Waves, 2006; Orlando: A Biography, 2006; The Years, 2008; Jacob's Room, 2008; Between the Acts, 2008. **Address:** Department of English, Pace University, Rm 1510, 41 Park Row, New York, NY 10038, U.S.A. **Online address:** mhussey@pace.edu

HUSSEY, Patricia (Ann). American (born United States), b. 1949. **Genres:** Theology/Religion, Women's Studies And Issues, Cultural/Ethnic Topics. **Career:** St. Teresa's School, teacher, 1972-73; Long Lane School, youth service worker, 1973-76, recreation worker, 1977; Covenant House, co-director, 1981-. Writer. **Publications:** (With B. Ferraro and J. O'Reilly) No Turning Back: Two Nuns' Battle with the Vatican Over Women's Right to Choose, 1990. **Address:** Covenant House, 600 Shrewsbury St., Charleston, WV 25301-1211, U.S.A. **Online address:** phussey@wvcovenanthouse.org

HUSTON, James E(dward). American (born United States), b. 1930. **Genres:** Medicine/Health, Technology. **Career:** Family physician, 1959-69; Kaiser Foundation Hospital, resident in obstetrics and gynecology, 1969-72; American College of Obstetrics and Gynecology, life fellow; Rogue Valley Country Club, board director, 1998-2001. Writer. **Publications:** (With L.D. Lanka) Perimenopause: Changes in Women's Health after Thirty-Five, 1997, 2nd ed., 2001; Menopause: A Guide to Health and Happiness, 1998; (with L.C. Fujitsubo) PMDD: A Guide to Coping with Premenstrual Dysphoric Disorder, 2002. Contributor to journals. **Address:** 2424 London Cir., Medford, OR 97504, U.S.A. **Online address:** jhuston@mind.net

HUSTON, James W(ebb). American (born United States), b. 1953. **Genres:** Novels, Law, Reference. **Career:** Gray, Cary, Ames and Frye (now Gray, Cary, Ware and Freidenrich LLP), attorney, 1984-90, partner, 1990-; Morrison & Foerster, partner, 1990-, chairman. Writer. **Publications:** NOVELS: Balance of Power, 1998; The Price of Power, 1999; Flash Point, 2000; Fallout, 2001; The Shadows of Power, 2002; Secret Justice, 2003; (with A. Bashey and R. Abonour) 100 Questions & Answers About Myeloma, 2005, 2nd ed. 2009; Marine One, 2009; Falcon Seven, 2010. **Address:** The Gernert Co., 136 E 57th St., 18th Fl., New York, NY 10022, U.S.A. **Online address:** jwh@jameswhuston.com

HUSTON, Nancy. Also writes as Annécie Rosiers. French/Canadian (born Canada), b. 1953. **Genres:** Novels, Human Relations/Parenting, Young Adult Non-fiction, Novellas/Short Stories, Translations. **Career:** Académie Commerciale Internationale, professor of English, 1976-78; University of Columbia, instructor, 1976-, professor of French feminist theory, 1983-89, professor of composition and stylistics, 1990-91, professor of French literature, 1992-93; Institut Supérieur Libre des Carrières Artistiques, professor of French literature, 1977-78; Centre de Formation Permanente et de Perfectionnement, Ministère des Finances, professor of English, 1978-85; Sarah Lawrence College, professor of literature and semiology, 1983-86; American University, Women's Institute for Continuing Education, fiction writer-in-residence, 1989; University of Massachusetts, visiting professor, 1990; Harvard University, visiting professor, 1994; l'Abbaye de Royaumont, writer-in-residence, 1994. **Publications:** Jouer au papa et à l'amant: De l'amour des petites filles, 1979; Dire et interdire: Eléments de jurologie, 1980; Les Variations Goldberg, 1981; Mosaïque de la pornographie: Marie-Therese et les autres, 1982; (with S. Kinser) A l'amour comme à la guerre, 1984; (ed. with P. Magli) Le Donne e i segni: Scrittura, linguaggio, identità nel segno della differenza femminile, 1985; Histoire d'Omaya, 1985 as The Story of Omaya, 1987; (with L. Sebbar) Lettres parisiennes: Autopsie de l'exil, 1986; Trois fois septembre, 1989;

Journal de la création, 1990; (with L. Huston) Véra Veut la Vérité, 1992; Cantique des plaines, 1993; (with L. Huston) Dora demande des details, 1993; Plainsong, 1993; plaines La Virevolte, 1994; (trans.) J. Lazarre, Le Noeud Maternel, 1994; Lignes de Faille, 1994; Tombeau de Romain Gary, 1995; Désirs et réalités: textes choisis 1979-1993, 1995; Pour un Patriotisme de l'ambiguïté, 1995; Instruments des ténèbres, 1996; (trans.) F. Figes, Spectres, 1996; The Goldberg Variations, 1996; In Deo, 1997; Desirs et realites, 1997; L'Empreinte de l'ange, 1998; (trans.) E. Gorham, My Tailor is Rich, 1998; The Mark of the Angel, 1998; Prodige, 1999; Nord perdu, 1999; Limbes/Limbo: un homage a Samuel Beckett, 2000; (trans.) G. Tunstrnm, Un Prosateur à New York, 2000; Dolce agonia: Roman, 2001; Visages de l'aube, 2001; Chants Polaires, 2002; Losing North: Musings on Land, Tongue and Self, 2002; (with V. Grail) Angela et Marina: Tragicomeédie Musicale, 2002; (with T. Todorov) Des Duos et des Couples: Jean Arp et Sophie Taeuber, 2003; Une Adoration, 2003; Professeurs de Désespoir, 2004; Ames et Corps: Textes Choisis, 1981-2003, 2004; Longings and Belongings: Essays, 2005; Lignes de faille: roman, 2006; Passions d'Annie Leclerc, 2007; Jacques Noël: décors et dessins de théâtre, 2007; Fault Lines: A Novel, 2007; L'espèce fabulatrice, 2008; Jocaste reine: Théâtre, 2009; Tale-Tellers: A Short Study of Humankind, 2009; Infrarouge: Roman, 2010. **Address:** c/o Mary Kling, La Nouvelle Agence, 7 Corneille St., Paris, 75006, France.

HUSTVEDT, Siri. American (born United States), b. 1955. **Genres:** Novels, Poetry, Essays, Translations, Young Adult Non-fiction. **Career:** Writer. **Publications:** Reading to You (poems), 1983; (trans. with D. McDuff) G. Kjetsaa, Fyodor Dostoyevsky: A Writer's Life, 1987; Fragments for a History of the Human Body, 1989; The Blindfold (novel), 1992; The Enchantment of Lily Dahl: A Novel, 1996; Yonder: Essays, 1998; What I Loved: A Novel, 2003; Mysteries of the Rectangle: Essays on Painting, 2005; A Plea for Eros: Essays, 2006; Sorrows of an American: A Novel, 2008; (contrib.) Gerhard Richter, Fotografias Pintadas, 2009; The Shaking Woman, Or, A History of My Nerves, 2010; The Summer Without Men, 2011. Works appear in anthologies. Contributor to periodicals. **Address:** c/o Amanda Urban, International Creative Management Inc., 730 5th Ave., New York, NY 10019, U.S.A.

HUTCHEON, Linda. Canadian (born Canada), b. 1947. **Genres:** Humanities, Literary Criticism And History, Music. **Career:** McMaster University, assistant professor, 1976-82, associate professor, 1982-85, professor of English, 1985-88; University of Toronto, Center for Comparative Literature, adjunct professor, 1980, professor of English and comparative literature, 1988-96, university professor, 1996-2010, university professor emeritus, 2010-; York University, Robarts Chair of Canadian studies, 1988-89. Writer. **Publications:** (Trans.) F. Leclerc, Allegro, 1974; Narcissistic Narrative: The Metafictional Paradox, 1980; Formalism and the Freudian Aesthetic, 1984; A Theory of Parody: The Teachings of Twentieth-Century Art Forms, 1985; A Poetics of Postmodernism: History, Theory, Fiction, 1988; The Canadian Postmodern: A Study of Contemporary English-Canadian Fiction, 1989; The Politics of Postmodernism, 1989; (with M.A. Cheetham) Remembering Postmodernism: Trends in Recent Canadian Art, 1991; Splitting Images: Contemporary Canadian Ironies, 1991; Irony's Edge: The Theory and Politics of Irony, 1995; (with M. Hutcheon) Opera: Desire, Disease and Death, 1996; (with M. Hutcheon) Bodily Charm: Living Opera, 2000; (with M. Hutcheon) Opera: The Art of Dying, 2004; Theory of Adaption, 2006. EDITOR: Other Solitudes: Canadian Multicultural Fiction and Interviews, 1990; Double-Talking: Essays on Verbal and Visual Ironies in Contemporary Canadian Art and Literature, 1992; Likely Stories: A Postmodern Sampler, 1992; A Postmodern Reader, 1993; (with M.J. Valdes) Rethinking Literary History: A Dialogue on Theory, 2002. **Address:** Department of English, University of Toronto, 170 Saint George St., Jackman Humanities Bldg., Toronto, ON M5R 2M8, Canada. **Online address:** l.hutcheon@utoronto.ca

HUTCHEON, Michael. Canadian (born Canada), b. 1945. **Genres:** Music, Art/Art History, Social Sciences. **Career:** University of Toronto, head of respirology division, 1976-99, professor of medicine, 1999-; Toronto General Hospital, medical director, 1996-. Writer. **Publications:** (With L. Hutcheon) Opera: Desire, Disease, Death, 1996; (with L. Hutcheon) Bodily Charm: Living Opera, 2000; (with L. Hutcheon) Opera: The Art of Dying, 2004. **Address:** Department of Medicine, University of Toronto, 11C1196 New Clinical Services Bldg., 200 Elizabeth St., Toronto, ON M6R 1S9, Canada. **Online address:** michael.hutcheon@uhn.on.ca

HUTCHERSON, Hilda. American (born United States), b. 1955. **Genres:** Medicine/Health. **Career:** Columbia University, Diversity and Minority Affairs, associate dean, assistant professor of clinical obstetrics and gynecology, clinical professor of obstetrics and gynecology, New York Center for Women's Sexual Health, co-director; Pelham Family Service, staff, 1996-2000; Parents Magazine, online advisor; Glamour Magazine, online advisor. Writer and physician. **Publications:** (With M. Williams) Having Your Baby: A Guide for African-American Women, 1997; What Your Mother Never Told You about S.E.X., 2002; Pleasure: A Woman's Guide to Getting the Sex You Want, Need, and Deserve, 2006. **Address:** Department of Obstetrics and Gynecology, Columbia University Medical Center, 16 E 60th St., Ste. 480, New York, NY 10022, U.S.A. **Online address:** hilda@drhilda.com

HUTCHINGS, Stephen. British (born England), b. 1957. **Genres:** Literary Criticism And History, Young Adult Non-fiction. **Career:** University of Rochester, associate professor of Russian, 1990-96; University of Surrey, professor of cultural studies and Russian, 1996-2006; University of Manchester, School of Languages, Linguistics and Cultures, professor of Russian studies, 2006-. Writer. **Publications:** NONFICTION: A Semiotic Analysis of the Short Stories of Leonid Andreev, 1900-1909, 1990; Russian Modernism: The Transfiguration of the Everyday, 1997; Russian Literary Culture in the Camera Age: The Word as Image, 2004; (ed. with A. Vernitski) Russian and Soviet Film Adaptations of Literature, 1900-2001: Screening the Word, 2005; (ed. with B. Beumers and N. Rulyova) The Post-Soviet Russian Media: Conflicting Signals, 2008; Russia and Its Other(s) on Film: Screening Intercultural Dialogue, 2008; (with N. Rulyova) Television and Culture in Putin's Russia: Remote Control, 2009. Contributor of articles to books and journals. **Address:** School of Languages, Linguistics and Cultures, University of Manchester, Oxford Rd., Manchester, GM M13 9PL, England. **Online address:** stephen.hutchings@manchester.ac.uk

HUTCHINS, Hazel J. Canadian (born Canada), b. 1952. **Genres:** Novels, Children's Fiction, Picture/Board Books. **Career:** Writer. **Publications:** The Three and Many Wishes of Jason Reid, 1983; Anastasia Morningstar and the Crystal Butterfly, 1984; Leanna Builds a Genie Trap, 1986; Ben's Snow Song: A Winter Picnic, 1987; Casey Webber, The Great, 1988; Norman's Snowball, 1989; Nicholas at the Library, 1990; Katie's Babbling Brother, 1991; A Cat of Artimus Pride, 1991; And You Can Be a Cat, 1992; The Best of Arlie Zack, 1993; The Catfish Palace, 1993; Within a Painted Post, 1994; Believing Sophie, 1995; Tess, 1995; Yancy and Bear, 1996; The Prince of Tarn, 1997; Reach for the Moon Robyn, 1997; Shoot for the Moon, Robyn, 1997; It's Raining Yancy and Bear, 1998; Robyn's Want Ad, 1998; One Duck, 1999; Two So Small, 2000; Robyn Looks for Bears, 2000; The Wide World of Suzie Mallard, 2000; Robyn's Best Idea, 2001; One Dark Night, 2001; Robyn's Art Attack, 2002; T.J. and the Cats, 2002; I'd Know You Anywhere, 2002; TJ and the Haunted House, 2003; Robyn Makes the News, 2003; TJ and the Rockets, 2004; Skate, Robyn, Skate, 2004; A Second is a Hiccup, 2004; The Sidewalk Rescue, 2004; Beneath the Bridge, 2004; Robyn's Party-in-the-Park, 2005; T.J. and the Sports Fanatic, 2006; The List, 2007; TJ and the Quiz Kids, 2007; After, 2008; (with G. Herbert) Mattland, 2008; Together, 2009. **Address:** Annick Press, 15 Patricia Ave., Willowdale, ON M2M 1H9, Canada. **Online address:** hjhutch@telusplanet.net

HUTCHINS, J. C. American (born United States), b. 1975. **Genres:** Young Adult Fiction, Horror, Mystery/Crime/Suspense. **Career:** Writer and consultant. **Publications:** FICTION: 7th Son: Descent, 2009; (with J. Weisman) Personal Effects: Dark Art, 2009. **Address:** Lindstrom Literary Management L.L.C., 871 N Greenbrier St., Arlington, VA 22205, U.S.A.

HUTCHINS, Pat. British (born England), b. 1942. **Genres:** Children's Fiction, Poetry, Young Adult Fiction, Education, Picture/Board Books, inspirational/Motivational Literature, Illustrations, Animals/Pets, Animals/Pets. **Career:** J. Walter Thompson Agency, assistant art director, 1963-65; freelance writer and illustrator, 1965-. **Publications:** FOR CHILDREN: Rosie's Walk, 1967; Tom and Sam, 1968; The Surprise Party, 1969; Clocks and More Clocks, 1970; Changes, Changes, 1971; Titch, 1971; Good Night, Owl, 1972; The Wind Blew, 1974; The Silver Christmas Tree, 1974; The House That Sailed Away, 1975; Don't Forget the Bacon, 1976; Follow That Bus!, 1977; The Best Train Set Ever, 1978; Happy Birthday, Sam, 1978; Yom Huledet Sameah, 1978; One-eyed Jake, 1979; The Tale of Thomas Mead, 1980; The Mona Lisa Mystery, 1981; 1 Hunter, 1982; You'll Soon Grow into Them, Titch, 1983; King Henry's Palace, 1983; The Curse of the Egyptian Mummy, 1983; The Very Worst Monster, 1985; The Doorbell Rang, 1986; Where's the Baby?, 1988; Which Witch Is Which?, 1989; Rats!, 1989; What Games Shall We Play?, 1990; Tidy Titch, 1991; Silly Billy!, 1992; My Best Friend, 1993;

Little Pink Pig, 1994; Three-star Billy, 1994; Titch and Daisy, 1996; Shrinking Mouse, 1997; It's My Birthday!, 1998; Ten Red Apples, 2000; We're Going on a Picnic!, 2002; There's Only One of Me!, 2003; Don't Get Lost!, 2004; Bumpety Bump, 2006; Barn Dance!, 2007. **Address:** 75 Flask Walk, London, GL NW3 1ET, England. **Online address:** pat@titch.net

HUTCHINS, William. (William Maynard Hutchins). American (born United States), b. 1944. **Genres:** Translations, Literary Criticism And History. **Career:** Gerard Institute, instructor in English, 1964-65; Encyclopaedia Britannica, Middle East research editor, 1971-72; Northern Illinois University, instructor in Arabic, 1972-73; University of Chicago, Islamic civilization teaching fellow, 1971-72, visiting assistant professor of Arabic, 1973-74; University of Ghana, lecturer and head of Arabic studies, 1974-77; Harvard University, Center for Middle Eastern Studies, postdoctoral researcher, 1977-78; Appalachian State University, Department of philosophy and religion, assistant professor, 1978-79, 1980-81, associate professor, 1981-86, professor, 1986-; Bowdoin College, visiting assistant professor, 1979; ASU Loft Facility, director, 1983; American Research Center, fellow, 1984-85; American University of Cairo, Department of English and Comparative Literature, professor, 1991-93; University of Angers, exchange professor, 2002-03. **Publications:** TRANSLATOR: Plays, Prefaces and Postscripts of Tawfiq al-Hakim, 1981; Al-Mazini's Egypt, 1983; Come Back Tomorrow, 1985; Egyptian Tales and Short Stories of the 1970s and 1980s, 1987; Nine Essays of al-Jahiz, 1989; Palace Walk, 1990; Return of the Spirit: Tawfig al-Hakim's Classic Novel of the 1919 Revolution, 1990; Palace of Desire, 1991; Sugar Street, 1992; T. Al-Hakim, In the Tavern of Life and Other Stories, 1997; N. Mahfouz, The Cairo Trilogy, 2001; H. Nasr, Return to Dar al-Basha: A Novel, 2006; F. Al-Azzawi, Last of the Angels: A Novel, 2008; F. Al-Azzawi, Cell Block Five, 2008; N. Mahfouz, Cairo Modern: A Novel, 2009; (and intro.) Puppet, 2010; F. Al-Azzawi, Traveler and the Innkeeper, 2011. OTHERS: Tawfiq al-Hakim: A Reader's Guide, 2003. **Address:** Department of Philosophy and Religion, Appalachian State University, 215 I.G. Greer Hall, Boone, NC 28608, U.S.A. **Online address:** hutchwm@appstate.edu

HUTCHINS, William Maynard. *See* **HUTCHINS, William.**

HUTCHINSON, Allan C. Canadian/British (born England), b. 1951. **Genres:** Law, Education. **Career:** Called to the Bar at Gray's Inn, 1975; York University, Osgoode Hall Law School, lecturer in Law, 1978-80, assistant professor, 1982-84, associate professor, 1984-88, professor of law, 1988-, associate dean, 1994-96, 2003-, graduate studies and external relations, distinguished research professor, 2006-; University Newcastle-Upon-Tyne, lecturer in law, 1980-82; Cambridge University, lecturer, 1985, 1987; Monash University, visiting professor, 1986; University of Toronto, visiting professor, 1989-90; University of Western Australia, visiting professor, 1991; University of Sydney, Parsons professor, 1995; University of London, Institute of Advanced Legal Studies, 1997, senior research fellow, 2000-; University of Wales, Cardiff Law School, professorial research fellow, 2000-. Writer. **Publications:** (Ed. with P. Monahan) The Rule of Law: Ideal or Ideology, 1987; Dwelling on the Threshold: Critical Essays on Modern Legal Thought, 1988; (co-ed.) Canadian Civil Procedure, 3rd ed., 1988; (ed.) Critical Legal Studies, 1989; (ed. with L.J.M. Green) Law and the Community: The End of Individualism? 1989; (ed.) Access to Justice: Barriers and Bridges, 1990; (ed.) Access to Civil Justice, 1990; (co-ed.) Civil Litigation: Cases and Materials, 4th ed., 1991; Waiting for Coraf: A Critique of Law and Rights, 1995; The Law School Book: Succeeding at Law School, 1996, 3rd ed., 2009; (ed. with K. Peterson) Censorship in Canada, 1997; Professional Responsibilities, 1997; Legal Ethics and Professional Responsibility, 1998; (ed. with K. Petersen) Interpreting Censorship in Canada, 1999; It's All in the Game: A Non-foundationalist Account of Law and Adjudication, 2000; Evolution and the Common Law, 2005; Companies We Keep: Corporate Governance in a Democratic Society, 2005; If Plato Had Played Football: Playing a Different Game of Philosophy and Life, 2006; Province of Jurisprudence Democratized, 2009; Is Eating People Wrong?: Great Legal Cases and How They Shaped the World, 2011; Laughing at the Gods: Great Judges and How they Made the Common Law, 2012. Contributor to books and journals. **Address:** Osgoode Hall Law School, York University, Rm. 4025, Ignat Kaneff Bldg., 4700 Keele St., Toronto, ON M3J 1P3, Canada. **Online address:** ahutchinson@osgoode.yorku.ca

HUTCHINSON, Bill. American (born United States), b. 1947. **Genres:** History, Biography, Autobiography/Memoirs, Romance/Historical. **Career:** United Church of Christ, minister; United Way of the Bay Area, associate campaign director, 1974-81; Otter Hutchinson & Associates, partner, 1980;

Marin Interfaith Task Force on Central America, director, 1985-95; Hew Hope Church, founding minister, 1990-94; Hutchinson Consulting, co-owner, 1996-, principal, hospitality recruiter; Christians for Peace in El Salvador, president of board of directors, 1999-2000; United Way of Sonoma, director, 1996-2002. Writer. **Publications:** When the Dogs Ate Candles: A Time in El Salvador, 1998. **Address:** Hutchinson Consulting, 20735 5th St. E, Sonoma, CA 95476-7905, U.S.A. **Online address:** bill@hutchinsonconsulting.com

HUTCHINSON, Earl Ofari. American (born United States), b. 1945. **Genres:** Race Relations, Human Relations/Parenting, Social Commentary, Biography, Autobiography/Memoirs, Politics/Government, Social Sciences, Economics, Economics. **Career:** Monthly Review Publishers, editorial consultant, 1970-71; Mafundi Institute, instructor in journalism, 1972-; KPFK, public affairs director; National Alliance for Positive Action, president; New America Media, associate editor. **Publications:** (Ed.) Black Book, 1965; The Myth of Black Capitalism, 1970; Let Your Motto Be Resistance; The Life and Thought of Henry Highland Garnet, 1972; Crime: Why It Exists, What Can Be Done, 1986; From Black Fathers with Love, 1986; Crime, Drugs, and African Americans, 1987; The Mugging of Black America, 1990; Black Fatherhood: The Guide to Male Parenting, 1992; The Assassination of the Black Male Image, 1994; Black Fatherhood II: Black Women Talk about Their Men, 1994; Blacks and Reds: Race and Class in Conflict, 1919-1990, 1995; Betrayed: A History of Presidential Failure to Protect Black Lives, 1996; Beyond O.J.: Race, Sex and Class Lessons for America, 1996; The Crisis in Black and Black, 1998; The Disappearance of Black Leadership, 2000; (with E. Hutchison) A Colored Man's Journey Through Twentieth Century Segregated America, 2000; The Emerging Black GOP Majority, 2006; The Latino Challenge to Black America: Towards a Conversation Between African Americans and Hispanics, 2007; The Ethnic Presidency: How Race Decides the Race to the White House, 2008; How the GOP Can Keep the White House, How the Democrats Can Take it Back, 2008; How Obama Won, 2008. Contributor to periodicals. **Address:** Middle Passage Press, 5517 Secrest Dr., Los Angeles, CA 90043, U.S.A. **Online address:** hutchinsonreport@yahoo.com

HUTCHINSON, George B. American (born United States), b. 1953?. **Genres:** Cultural/Ethnic Topics, Race Relations, Biography, Adult Nonfiction, Education. **Career:** University of Tennessee, Kenneth Curry chair of English, 1982-2000, chairman of American studies program, 1987-2000; Indiana University, Booth Tarkington chair of literary studies, 2001-, Booth Tarkington professor of literary studies, Department of English, chairman, Department of African American and African Diaspora Studies, adjunct professor, adjunct professor of American studies. Writer. **Publications:** The Ecstatic Whitman: Literary Shamanism and the Crisis of the Union, 1986; The Harlem Renaissance in Black and White, 1995; In Search of Nella Larsen: A Biography of the Color Line, 2006; (ed.) The Cambridge Companion to the Harlem Renaissance, 2007; The Poetics of Democracy: Walt Whitman and Langston Hughes, forthcoming. Contributor to journals. **Address:** Department of English, Indiana University, 442 Ballantine Hall, 1020 E Kirkwood Ave., Bloomington, IN 47405-7103, U.S.A. **Online address:** gbhutchi@indiana.edu

HUTCHINSON, G(regory) O(wen). British (born England), b. 1957. **Genres:** Classics, Literary Criticism And History, Politics/Government. **Career:** Oxford University, Christ Church, research lecturer, 1981-84; Oxford University, Exeter College, fellow and tutor in classics, 1984-, professor of Greek and Latin languages and literature, 1998-, chairman of sub-faculty of languages and literature. Writer. **Publications:** (Ed. and intro.) Septem Contra Thebas, 1985, rev. ed. as Seven Against Thebes, 1994; Hellenistic Poetry, 1988; Latin Literature from Seneca to Juvenal: A Critical Study, 1993; Cicero's Correspondence: A Literary Study, 1998; Greek Lyric Poetry: A Commentary on Selected Larger Pieces: Alcman, Stesichorus, Sappho, Alcaeus, Ibycus, Anacreon, Simonides, Bacchylides, Pindar, Sophocles, Euripides, 2001; (ed.) Elegies, 2006; Talking Books: Readings in Hellenistic and Roman Books of. Poetry, 2008; (ed.) Politics and the Sublime in the Panegyricus, 2011; House Politics and City Politics in Aristophanes, 2011; (ed.) Space and Text Worlds, 2011. **Address:** Exeter College, Oxford University, Turl St., Oxford, OX OX1 3DP, England. **Online address:** gregory.hutchinson@exeter.ox.ac.uk

HUTCHINSON, Peter. American (born United States), b. 1949. **Genres:** Social Sciences, Politics/Government. **Career:** City of Minneapolis, deputy mayor, 1977-79; Dayton Hudson Corp., vice president, 1980; Dayton Hudson Foundation, vice president for external affairs, chair, 1981-90; State of Minnesota, commissioner of finance, through 1990; Public Strategies Group, founder, 1991-; Bush Foundation, president, 2007-. Writer. **Publications:**

(With D. Osborne) The Price of Government: Getting the Results We Need in an Age of Permanent Fiscal Crisis, 2004. **Address:** Public Strategies Group Inc., 325 Cedar St., Ste. 710, St. Paul, MN 55101-1012, U.S.A. **Online address:** bush_president@bushfoundation.org

HUTCHINSON, Robert. British (born England), b. 1948. **Genres:** Young Adult Non-fiction. **Career:** Press Association, night sub-editor, defence correspondent, 1976-83; Jane's Publishing Group, staff, 1983-; Jane's Information Group, publishing director, 1987-97; University of Sussex, Centre for Continuing Education, associate tutor in church archaeology. **Publications:** NONFICTION: (ed.) Jane's Warship Recognition Guide, 2nd ed., 1999; Jane's Submarines: War beneath the Waves: From 1776 to the Present Day, 2001; Weapons of Mass Destruction: The No-Nonsense Guide to Nuclear, Chemical and Biological Weapons Today, 2003; The Last Days of Henry VIII: Conspiracies, Treason and Heresy at the Court of the Dying Tyrant, 2005; Elizabeth's Spymaster: Francis Walsingham and the Secret War That Saved England, 2007; Thomas Cromwell: The Rise and Fall of Henry VIII's Most Notorious Minister, 2007; House of Treason, 2009. OTHER: Young Henry, 2011. **Address:** Andrew Lownie Literary Agency Ltd., 36 Great Smith St., London, GL SW1P 3BU, England.

HUTCHINSON, Ron. American/Irish (born Ireland), b. 1947?. **Genres:** Plays/Screenplays, Art/Art History. **Career:** Department of Health and Social Security, social worker and claims investigator; Royal Shakespeare Co., resident writer, 1978-79. **Publications:** Says I, Says He, 1980; Rat in the Skull, 1984; Connie, 1985; Flight, 1998; Burning Issues, 2000; Beau Brummell, 2001; Moonlight and Magnolias, 2005; Topless Mum, 2008. **Address:** Judy Daish Associates, 2 St. Charles Pl., London, GL W10 6EG, England.

HUTCHINSON, Samuel. French (born France), b. 1965?. **Genres:** Novels, History, Biography, Autobiography/Memoirs. **Career:** Moscoop (photographic press agency), director. Writer. **Publications:** (With I. Zbarsky) A l'ombre du mausolée, 1998. **Address:** c/o Author Mail, The Harvill Press Ltd., 2 Aztec Row, Berners Rd., London, GL N1 0PW, England.

HUTCHINSON, Timothy A. American (born United States), b. 1960. **Genres:** Adult Non-fiction, Autobiography/Memoirs, Biography. **Career:** Writer. **Publications:** Battle Scars (autobiography), 2003. **Address:** c/o Author Mail, Riverstone Publishing, PO Box 270852, St. Paul, MN 55127-0852, U.S.A. **Online address:** contact@americanyouth.net

HUTCHISON, Kay Bailey. (Kathryn Ann Bailey). American (born United States), b. 1943. **Genres:** Women's Studies And Issues, History. **Career:** KPRC-TV, political & legal correspondent, 1969-71; private law practice, 1969-74; Texas House of Representatives, representative, 1972-76; National Transportation Safety Board vice chair, 1976-78; University of Texas, assistant professor, 1978-79; Republic Bank Corp., senior vice president & general counsel, 1979-81; Fidelity National Bank of Dallas, cofounder; McCraw Candies Inc., owner; Boyd-Levinson Ltd., partner, 1981-91; Texas State Treasurer, 1991-93; U.S. Senate, senator, 1993-, deputy majority whip, 1995-, Senate GOP Regulatory Reform Task Force, co-chair, 1995, Republican Policy Committee, chair, 2007-. Writer. **Publications:** (co-author) Nine and Counting: The Women of the Senate, 2000; American Heroines: The Spirited Women Who Shaped Our Country, 2004; Leading Ladies: American Trailblazers, 2007. **Address:** 284 Russell Senate Office Bldg., Washington, DC 20510-4304, U.S.A. **Online address:** senator@hutchison.senate.gov

HUTCHISON, Linda Margaret. American/Canadian (born Canada), b. 1952. **Genres:** Children's Non-fiction. **Career:** End-of-Life Choices of California, newsletter editor; Mission Valley Diet Center, newsletter editor; Flavor Wear Clothing, copywriter; Los Angeles Times, community correspondent; Gardena Valley News, managing editor; Palos Verdes Peninsula News, feature and arts editor; Palos Verdes Estates, Peninsula Shopping Center, advertising copywriter; Wilson, Frank & Associates, advertising copywriter. **Publications:** Lebanon, 2003; Finland, 2004. Contributor to journals. **Address:** La Jolla, CA , U.S.A. **Online address:** linda@lindahutchison.com

HUTCHISSON, James M. American (born United States), b. 1961. **Genres:** Literary Criticism And History, Biography, History, Social Sciences. **Career:** Washington & Jefferson College, assistant professor of English, 1987-89; The Citadel, Department of English, assistant professor, 1989-94, associate professor, 1994-99, professor, 1999-, director of graduate studies; Charleston Post and Courier, book reviewer, 1992-; Charleston Collegiate School, trust-

ee, 2009-; University of Pennsylvania, editor. Writer. **Publications:** (Ed. and intro.) Babbit, 1995, 2nd ed., 2004; The Rise of Sinclair Lewis 1920-1930, 1996; (ed.) Sinclair Lewis: New Essays in Criticism, 1997; DuBose Heyward: A Charleston Gentleman and the World of Porgy and Bess, 2000; (ed. and intro.) A DuBose Heyward Reader, 2003; (ed. with H. Greene) Renaissance in Charleston: Art and Life in the Carolina Low Country, 1900-1940, 2003; Poe, 2005; (ed.) Edgar Allan Poe: Beyond Gothicism, 2011. Contributor to periodicals. **Address:** Department of English, The Citadel, 116 Capers Hall, 171 Moultrie St., Charleston, SC 29409, U.S.A. **Online address:** jim.hutchisson@citadel.edu

HUTSON, Lorna. Scottish/British (born England), b. 1958. **Genres:** Literary Criticism And History, Intellectual History. **Career:** University of London, Queen Mary and Westfield College, lecturer in English, 1986-; University of Hull, professor of English literature, 1998-2000; University of California, professor of English, 2000-04; University of St. Andrews, Berry professor of English literature, 2004-, School of English, head. Writer. **Publications:** Thomas Nashe in Context, 1989; The Usurer's Daughter: Male Friendship and Fictions of Women in Sixteenth-Century England, 1994; (ed.) Feminism and Renaissance Studies, 1999; (ed. with V. Kahn) Rhetoric and Law in Early Modern Europe, 2001; (ed. with E. Sheen) Literature, Politics, and Law in Renaissance England, 2005; The Invention of Suspicion: Law and Mimesis in Shakespeare and Renaissance Drama, 2007; (ed.) Discoveries, 2009; (ed. with D.T. Lochman and M. Lopez) Discourses and Representations of Friendship in Early Modern Europe, 1500-1700, 2010. **Address:** School of English, University of St. Andrews, Castle House, St. Andrews, FF KY16 9AR, Scotland. **Online address:** lmh10@st-andrews.ac.uk

HUTSON, Shaun P. Also writes as Nick Blake, Robert Neville, Wolf Kruger, Clive Harold, Mike Dickinson. British (born England), b. 1958?. **Genres:** Novels, Novellas/Short Stories, Young Adult Non-fiction, Horror, Mystery/Crime/Suspense, Adult Non-fiction. **Career:** Full-time writer, 1983-. **Publications:** HORROR AND GOTHIC NOVELS: (as Clive Harold) The Uninvited, 1979; Blood and Honour, 1982; Slugs, 1982; Kesslers Raid, 1982; The Skull, 1982; My Dad Doesnt Even Notice, 1982; Convoy of Steel, 1982; Sledgehammer, 1982; Sabres in the Snow, 1983; Spawn, 1983; My Brothers Silly, 1983; The Terminator, 1984; Men of Blood, 1984; Erebus, 1984; Chainsaw Massacre, 1984; The Uninvited II: The Visitation, 1984; The Rambling Rat, 1985; The Uninvited III: The Abduction, 1985; No Survivors, 1985; Shadows, 1985; Breeding Ground, 1985; Partners in Death, 1986; Track, 1986; Relics, 1986; Victims, 1987; Slugs, 1987; Spawn, 1988; Assassin, 1988; Erebus, 1988; The Skull, 1989; Nemesis, 1989; (as Robert Neville) Deathday, 1989, rev. ed., 1993; Shadows, 1990; Breeding Ground, 1990; Renegades, 1991; Captives, 1991; Heathen, 1992; White Ghost, 1994; Lucy's Child, 1995; Stolen Angels, 1996; Knife Edge, 1997; Purity, 1998; Warhol's Prophecy, 1999; Exit Wounds, 2000; Compulsion, 2001; Hybrid, 2002; Hell to Pay, 2003; Necessary Evil, 2004; Twisted Souls, 2005; Dying Words, 2006; Unmarked Graves, 2007, rev. ed., 2008; Body Count, 2008. SERIES: Slugs, 1982; Breeding Ground, 1985; The Visitation, 1984; The Abduction, 1985; Track, 1986; Partners In Death, 1986; Apache Gold, 1988. GENRE NOVELS: (as Clive Harold) The Uninvited, 1979; (as Stefan Rostov) Sabres in the Snow, 1983; (as Nick Blake) Chainsaw Massacre, 1984; The Terminator, 1984; (as Frank Taylor) The Uninvited II: The Visitation, 1984; No Survivors, 1985; (as Frank Taylor) The Uninvited III: The Abduction, 1985; (as Samuel P. Bishop) Track, 1986; (as Samuel P. Bishop) Partners in Death, 1986; Taken by Force, 1987; (as Samuel P. Bishop) Apache Gold, 1988; Swords of Vengeance, 1988; Last Rites, 2009; Epitaph, 2010. GENRE NOVELS AS WOLF KRUGER: Sledgehammer, 1982; Convoy of Steel, 1982; Kessler's Raid, 1982; Blood and Honour, 1982; Men of Blood, 1984. CHILDREN: My Dad Doesn't Even Notice, 1982; (as Mike Dickinson) My Brother's Silly, 1983; The Rambling Rat, 1985; (as Mike Dickinson) Smudge, 1987. NON-FICTION: Horror Film Quiz Book, 1991. SHORT STORIES: The Prize, 1988. OMNIBUS: Slugs/Spawn/Erebus, 1994; Abduction/Visitation/Come the Night, 1999; Lucy's Child/Slugs, 1999; No Survivors/Forgedin Fire/Taken By Force, 1999; Purity/Deadhead, 2004; Relics/Spawn/Shadows, 2004; Heathen/Nemesis, 2005; Erebus/Victims, 2007; Shadows/Nemesis, 2007; Heathen/Lucy's Child, 2008. OTHERS: (as Robert Neville) World of the Vatican, 1962; (comp.) Voices, 2005; (as Mike Dickinson) Science Project Helper, 2006; Dying Words, 2007; Unmarked Graves, 2007; Body Count, 2008. **Address:** Warner Books, 1271 Ave. of the Americas, New York, NY 10020, U.S.A.

HÜTTNER, Harry J. M. Dutch (born Netherlands), b. 1938. **Genres:** Social

Sciences, Reference. **Career:** Radboud University of Nijmegen (formerly Catholic University of Nijmegen), lecturer in research methodology, 1965-2002, Department of Social Sciences, professor. Writer. **Publications:** (With P.V.D. Eeden) Multi-Level Research, 1982; Multilevel Onderzoek: De Operationalisatie van Omgevingskenmerken (title means: 'Multilevel Research: The Operationalization of Collective Properties'), 1985; (with P.V.D. Eeden) The Multilevel Design: A Guide with an Annotated Bibliography, 1980-1993, 1995. CONTRIBUTOR: Education from the Multilevel Perspective: Models, Methodology and Empirical Findings, 1984; Social Network Research: Substantive Issues and Methodological Questions, 1990. EDITOR: (with H. Kleijer) Gezin En Onderwijs (title means: 'Family and Education'), 1990; (with P.V.D. Eeden) Onderzoeken Op Niveau: Toepassingen Van Multilevel Analyse (title means: 'Investigations on a High Level: Applications of Multilevel Analysis'), 1995; (with K. Renckstorf and F. Wester) Onderzoekstypen in De Communicatiewetenschap (title means: 'Designs in Communication Research'), 1995. Contributor to journals. **Address:** Department of Social Sciences, Research Methodology Division, Radboud University Nijmegen, Thomas Van Aquinostraat 4.01.57, PO Box 9104, Nijmegen, 6500, Netherlands. **Online address:** hjm.huttner@inter.n1.net

HUTTON, Barbara (Audrey). British (born England), b. 1920. **Genres:** Architecture, Homes/Gardens, History. **Career:** Cleveland Vernacular Buildings Study Group, chair, 1972-; York Georgian Society, buildings officer, 1973-77, vice president, 1981-85; University of Leeds, Workers' Educational Association, part-time teacher, 1975-84; writer, 1984-; Vernacular Architecture Group, president, 1986-89; Society of Antiquaries of London, fellow. **Publications:** (With G. Bailey) Crown Post Roofs in Hertfordshire, 1966; Clifton and Its People in the Nineteenth Century: A North Riding Township Now Part of York City, 1969; The Works in Architecture of John Carr, Sessions of York, 1973; (with B. Harrison) Vernacular Houses in North Yorkshire and Cleveland, 1984; (co-author) Horton-in-Ribblesdale: The Story of an Upland Parish, 1984; Historic Farmhouses Around Derby, 1991; Houses and Everyday Life in Weston on Trent, 1994. Contributor to periodicals. **Address:** 50 Daventry Close, Mickleover, DB DE3 5QT, England.

HUTTON, Drew. Australian (born Australia), b. 1947?. **Genres:** Area Studies, Environmental Sciences/Ecology, Social Sciences. **Career:** Queensland University of Technology, Department of Applied Ethics, lecturer; Australian Greens, founding member, social movement campaigner; National Council and National Conference, delegate; Queensland Greens, social movement campaigner, founding member and spokesperson. Writer. **Publications:** Green Politics in Australia: A Collection of Essays, 1987; (with L. Connors) A History of the Australian Environment Movement, 1999. Contributor to periodicals. **Address:** Queensland Greens, PO Box 5763, West End, QL 4101, Australia. **Online address:** drew.hutton@greens.org.au

HUTTON, Frankie. American (born United States) **Genres:** History, Communications/Media, Writing/Journalism, Literary Criticism And History. **Career:** Mitre Corp., senior technical editor, 1980-82; Lehigh University, assistant professor of journalism, 1988-94; Howard University, visiting lecturer, visiting professor of history, 1998-2000; Hampton University, associate professor of mass media studies, 1996-; Montclair State University, visiting associate professor, adjunct professor of history, 2001-. **Publications:** NONFICTION: The Early Black Press in America, 1827-1860, 1993; (with B.S. Reed) Outsiders in 19th-Century Press History: Multicultural Perspectives, 1995; Rose Lore: Essays in Cultural History and Semiotics, 2008; Greatest of My Dreams: Lore of African Americans in Diaspora, 2010. Contributor of articles to periodicals. **Address:** PO Box 649, Little Silver, NJ 07739, U.S.A. **Online address:** fhutton@aol.com

HUTTON, John (Harwood). Welsh/British (born England), b. 1928. **Genres:** Novels, Young Adult Fiction. **Career:** West Bromwich Education Authority, supply teacher, 1953; University College, assistant lecturer in English, 1953-54; Wigan and District Mining and Technical College, lecturer, 1954-58; Ruabon Girl's Grammar School, Department of English, head, 1959-67; Cartrefle College, North East Wales Institute, senior lecturer in English, 1967-85, now retired. **Publications:** 29 Herriott Street, 1979; Accidental Crimes, 1983. **Address:** Ty Mawr, Penmynydd, Llanfairpwll, Anglesey, LL61 5BX, Wales.

HUTTON, Paul Andrew. American (born United States), b. 1949. **Genres:** Plays/Screenplays, History, Biography, Military/Defense/Arms Control. **Career:** Western History Quarterly, assistant editor, 1977-79, associate editor, 1979-84; Utah State University, visiting instructor, 1977-80, assistant pro-

fessor of American history, 1980-84; New Mexico Historical Review, editor, 1984-; University of New Mexico, assistant professor, 1984-86, associate professor of American history, 1986-96, professor of American history, 1996-; New Mexico Historical Review, editor, 1985-91; Western History Association, executive director, 1991-2006; Western Writers of America, vice president, 2002-04; The Missing, historical consultant, 2003. **Publications:** Phil Sheridan and His Army, 1985; Soldiers West: Biographies from the Military Frontier, 1987, 2nd ed., 2009; (foreword) Sheridan's Troopers on the Borders, 1985; (intro.) Glory-Hunter: A Life of General Custer, 1988; (foreword) Without Quarter: The Wichita Expedition and the Fight on Crooked Creek, 1991; Phil Sheridan and His Army, 1999; (intro.) Wave High the Banner, 1999; Sunrise in His Pocket: The Life, Legend, and Legacy of Davy Crockett, 2007. EDITOR: Custer and His Times, 1981; Ten Days on the Plains, 1985; Soldiers West, 1987; A Narrative of the Life of David Crockett of the State of Tennessee, 1987; Civil War Memoirs: General Philip Sheridan, 1991; The Passing of Armies, by Joshua Chamberlain, 1992; Gettysburg, 1992; The Custer Reader, 1992; Eyewitness to the Civil War, 10 vols., 1992-93; (with R.C. Ritchie) Frontier and Region: Essays in Honor of Martin Ridge, 1997; Frontier and Region: Essays in Honor of Martin Ridge, 1997; Roundup!: Western Writers of America Presents Great Stories of the West from Today's Leading Western Writers, 2010. **Address:** Department of History, University of New Mexico, 1104 Mesa Vista Hall, MSC06 3760, 1 University of New Mexico, Albuquerque, NM 87131, U.S.A. **Online address:** hutton@unm.edu

HUTTON, Ronald. British/Indian (born India), b. 1953. **Genres:** History, Biography, Autobiography/Memoirs, Theology/Religion. **Career:** Home Civil Service, clerical officer, 1972-73; Guardian, editorial junior, 1974; Oxford University, Magdalen College, fellow, 1979-81, lecturer, 1981-89; Cornwall College, reader, 1985-94; University of Bristol, Department of History, reader in British history, 1989-96, professor of history, 1996-. Writer. **Publications:** The Royalist War Effort, 1642-1646, 1982, 2nd ed., 1999; The Restoration: A Political and Religious History of England and Wales, 1658-1667, 1985; Charles the Second: King of England, Scotland, and Ireland, 1989; The British Republic, 1649-1660, 1990, 2nd ed., 2000; The Pagan Religions of the Ancient British Isles, 1991; The Rise and Fall of Merry England: The Ritual Year, 1400-1700, 1994; The Stations of the Sun: A History of the Ritual Year in Britain, 1996; The Triumph of the Moon: A History of Modern Pagan Witchcraft, 1999; Shamans: Siberian Spirituality and the Western Imagination, 2001; Witches, Druids, and King Arthur, 2003; Debates in Stuart History, 2004; The Druids: A History, 2007; Blood and Mistletoe: The History of the Druids in Britain, 2009. Contributor to journals and periodicals. **Address:** Department of History, University of Bristol, Rm. 1.40, 13 Woodland Rd., Senate House, Tyndall Ave., Bristol, GL BS8 1TH, England. **Online address:** r.hutton@bristol.ac.uk

HUTTON, Sam. *See* **JONES, Allan Frewin.**

HUXLEY, George Leonard. Irish/British (born England), b. 1932. **Genres:** Classics, History, Literary Criticism And History. **Career:** Oxford University, All Souls College, fellow, 1955-61; British School of Archaeology at Athens, assistant director, 1956-58; Harvard University, visiting lecturer, 1958-59, 1961-62; Queen's University of Belfast, professor of Greek, 1962-83; Trinity College, honorary research associate, 1983-89, honorary professor of classics, 1989-; American School of Classical Studies, Gennadius Library, director, 1986-89; Royal Irish AcAademy, librarian, 1990-94, special envoy, 1994-97. Writer. **Publications:** Anthemius of Tralles, a Study of Later Greek Geometry, 1959; Achaeans and The Hittites, 1960; Crete and the Luwians, 1961; Early Sparta, 1962; The Interaction of Greek and Babylonian Astronomy, 1964; (contrib.) The Birth of Western Civilization: Greece and Rome, 1964; The Early Ionians, 1966; Minoans in Greek Sources, 1968; Greek Epic Poetry from Eumelos to Panyassis, 1969; (ed. with J.N. Coldstream) Kythera: Excavations and Studies, 1972; Pindar's Vision of the Past, 1975; On Aristotle and Greek Society, 1979; Monemvasia and the Slavs: A Lecture on Some Works of Historical Geography in the Gennadius Library of the American School of Classical Studies at Athens, 1982; Homer and the Travellers: A Lecture on Some Antiquarian and Topographical Books in the Gennadius Library of the American School of Classical Studies at Athens, 1988; Herodotos and the Epic: A Lecture, 1989. **Address:** Department of Classics, Trinity College, College Green, DU 2, Ireland.

HUYGHE, Patrick. American (born United States), b. 1952. **Genres:** History, Medicine/Health, Paranormal, Psychiatry, Psychology, Sciences, Biography. **Career:** University of Virginia, Department of Psychology, researcher, 1974; Public High schools, teacher, 1975; U.S. Magazine, columnist and staff editor, 1977-78; freelance writer, 1978-79; Newsweek, staff writer, 1980; WLSA-Radio, disc jockey, 1980; Hearst Magazines, contributing editor, 1981-84; National Public Radio, science reporter and producer, 1985; WGBH-FM Radio, science reporter and producer, 1985; Ten O'Clock News, staff producer, 1985; New England Science Gazette, staff producer, 1985; WGBH-TV, staff producer, 1985; Virginia Polytechnic Institute and State University, science writer-in-residence, 1986; WNET-TV-Innovation, associate producer, 1987, producer, 1988-90; Reeves Corporate Services, senior project writer, 1988; Liberty Science Center, label writer of environment, 1991-92; Petronas Project, senior exhibit writer, 1996-97; Omni Magazine Online, Edge, science editor, 1996-98; EPCOT, staff of biotechnology exhibit, 1999; Paraview Press, editor-in-chief, 2000-01; Simon & Schuster Inc., Paraview Pocket Books, editor-in-chief, 2002-05; Anomalist Books L.L.C., editor-in-chief, 2006-; ICRL Press, publisher, 2009-; The Anomalist, editor. **Publications:** (Ed.) Brief Psychotherapy in Medical and Health Practice, 1978; Glowing Birds: Stories from the Edge of Science, 1985; (ed.) Oceans, 1987; (ed.) The Mind, 1988; (with L.A. Frank) The Big Splash: A Scientific Discovery that Revolutionizes the Way We View the Origin of Life, the Water We Drink, the Death of the Dinosaurs, the Creation of the Oceans, the Nature of the Cosmos, and the Very Future of the Earth Itself, 1990; Columbus Was Last, 1992, 2nd ed. as Columbus Was Last: From 200, 000 b.c. to 1492, A Heretical History of Who Was First, 2003; The Field Guide to Extraterrestrials, 1996; (with L. Coleman) The Field Guide to Bigfoot, Yeti, and Other Mystery Primates Worldwide, 1999; (with H. Evans) The Field Guide to Ghosts and Other Apparitions, 2000; (with D. Stacy) The Field Guide to UFOs: A Classification of Various Unidentified Aerial Phenomena Based on Eyewitness Accounts, 2000; Swamp Gas Times, 2001; (with L. Coleman) The Field Guide to Lake Monsters, Sea Serpents and Other Mystery Denizens of the Deep, 2003; (ed. with J. Weber and M. Bober) An Illustrated Guide to The Lost Symbol, 2009. Contributor to books. **Address:** Anomalist Books L.L.C., 5150 Broadway, Ste. 108, San Antonio, TX 78209-5710, U.S.A. **Online address:** huyghe@anomalist.com

HUYLER, Frank. American (born United States), b. 1964. **Genres:** Medicine/Health, Young Adult Fiction. **Career:** University of New Mexico Hospitals, resident, 1993-96; physician, 1996-; University of New Mexico, emergency medicine, assistant professor and associate professor. Writer. **Publications:** The Blood of Strangers: Stories From Emergency Medicine, 1999; The Laws of Invisible Things, 2004; Right of Thirst, 2009. **Address:** Department of Emergency Medicine, University of New Mexico, MSC10 5560, 1 University of New Mexico, ACC 4th Fl., Albuquerque, NM 87102, U.S.A. **Online address:** fhuyler@salud.unm.edu

HVIDT, Niels Christian. Danish (born Denmark), b. 1969. **Genres:** Theology/Religion. **Career:** Kofoeds School, teacher, 1992-93; International Ecumenical Bridgettine Centre of Farfa, coordinator, 1999-2004; Vatican Radio, radio programmer, 2000-02; Pontifical Gregorian University, teacher and researcher, 2000-04; University of Southern Denmark, Research Unit: Health, Man and Society, Institute of Public Health, associate professor, 2006-; Danish Network for Research in Faith and Health, coordinator, 2007-, director, 2008-. Theologian and writer. **Publications:** The Problem of Christian Prophecy, 2001; Mirakler-Mder mellem Himmel og Jord, 2001; (ed. with C. Johansen) Kan Tro Flytte Bjerge?, 2003; Christian Prophecy: The Post-Biblical Tradition, 2007. Contributor of books to periodicals and journals. **Address:** Institute of Public Health, University of Southern Denmark, J.B. Winslows, Vej 9 B, 5000 C, Odense, 5000, Denmark. **Online address:** n.c@hvidt.com

HWANG, David Henry. American (born United States), b. 1957. **Genres:** Plays/Screenplays, Novels, Young Adult Non-fiction. **Career:** Menlo-Atherton High School, teacher of English and writing, 1980. Writer and lyricist. **Publications:** Broken Promises: Four Plays, 1983; The Sound of a Voice, 1984; M. Butterfly, 1988; The Dance and the Railroad and Family Devotions, 1989; FOB and Other plays, 1990; Golden Child, 1998; Trying to Find Chinatown: The Selected Plays, 2000; Flower Drum Song, 2003; (adapted with S. Müller) Peer Gynt: A Drama, 2006; Tibet Through the Red Box: A Drama for Young People, 2006; Yellow Face, 2009. **Address:** Steven Barclay Agency, 12 Western Ave., Petaluma, CA 94952, U.S.A.

HWANG, Jenny. American (born United States), b. 1980. **Genres:** Children's Fiction, Politics/Government. **Career:** World Relief, Refugee and Immigration Program, director of advocacy and policy. Writer. **Publications:**

(With M. Soerens), Welcoming the Stranger: Justice, Compassion, & Truth in the Immigration Debate, 2009. Contributor to periodicals. **Address:** World Relief, 7 E Baltimore St., Baltimore, MD 21202, U.S.A.

HWANG, Tong-gyu. Korean (born Korea (South)), b. 1938?. **Genres:** Poetry. **Career:** Seoul National University, Department of English Language and Literature, professor, 1968-2003, professor emeritus, 2003-; New York University, faculty, 1987; University of Iowa, International Creative Writing Program, faculty. Writer. **Publications:** ŏttŏn kaein nal, 1961; Piga, 1965; P'yŏnggyunnyul, 1968; Samnam e naerinŭn nun, 1974; Na nŭn pak'wirŭl pomyŏn kulligo sip'ojinda, 1978; Kyŏul norae: Hwang Tong-gyu sanmunjip, 1979; Hwang Tong-gyu Sisŏn: Yŏrha ilgi, 1982; P'ungjang, 1984; Agŏrŭl Chosim Harago: Hwang Tong-gyu Sijip, 1986; Hyŏndae Yŏng-Misi Yŏn'gu, 1986; Kyŏndilsu ŏpsi Kabyŏun Chonjaedŭl: Hwang Tong-gyu Sisŏn, 1988; Hae Chinŭn Tchok ŭro Kago Sipta: Pak Chŏng-Man sisŏn, 1989; K ege, 1991; Molundae Haeng: Hwang Tong-gyu Sijip, 1991; Mŏmurŭra Kŭdae Nŭn Kut'orok Arŭmdapta: Han'guk Chisŏng 50-in ŭi Chajŏnjŏk ŭmak Kobaengnok, 1991; Miriryŏng K'ŭn Param: Hwang Tong-gyu Sijip, 1993; Hwang Tong-gyu Si Chŏnjip, 1998; Posada de nubes y otros poemas, 1998; Bŏk'ŭlli P'ung ŭi Sarang Norae, 2000; Si Ka T'aeŏnanŭn Chari, 2001; Sam ŭi Hyanggi Myŏtchŏm: Hwang Tong-gyu Sanmunjip, 2008; (with Y. Kyŏng-su) Hong Sin-sŏn si chŏnjip. 2, P'yehŏ wa chŏnyul, 2008; (co-author) Abŏji, kŭriun tangsin, 2009; Sam ŭl sara naendanŭn kŏn, 2010. **Address:** Department of English Language and Literature, College of Humanities, Seoul National University, 599 Gwanak-ro, Gwanak-gu, Seoul, 151-745, Korea (South).

HYAM, Ronald. British (born England), b. 1936. **Genres:** History, Humanities. **Career:** Cambridge University, Magdalene College, lecturer in history, 1960-2002, fellow, 1962-, librarian, 1963-, admissions tutor, 1980-, president, 1996-98, university reader in British imperial history, 1996-99, university emeritus reader in British Imperial History; Institute of Commonwealth Studies, editor. **Publications:** Elgin and Churchill at the Colonial Office 1905-1908, 1968; A History of Isleworth Grammar School, 1969; The Failure of South African Expansion 1908-1948, 1972; (with G.W. Martin) Reappraisals in British Imperial History, 1975; Britain's Imperial Century 1815-1914: A Study of Empire and Expansion, 1976, 3rd ed., 2002; Empire and Sexuality: The British Experience, 1990; Godliness, Hunting and Quite Good Learning: The History of Magdalene College, 1792-1992, 1992; (with P.J. Henshaw) The Lion and the Springbok: Britain and South Africa since the Boer War, 2003; Britain's Declining Empire: The Road to Decolonisation, 1918-1968, 2006; Understanding the British Empire, 2010. EDITOR: The Labour Government and the End of Empire, 1945-1951, 1992; A History of Magdalene College, Cambridge, 1428-1988, 1994; (co-ed.) The Conservative Government and the End of Empire, 1957-64, 2 vols., 2000. **Address:** Magdalene College, Cambridge University, Magdalene St., Cambridge, CB3 0AG, England.

HYDE, Anthony. (Nicholas Chase). Canadian (born Canada), b. 1946. **Genres:** Novels, Mystery/Crime/Suspense, Literary Criticism And History. **Career:** Freelance writer, 1968-. **Publications:** (As Nicholas Chase) Locksley, 1983; The Red Fox, 1985; China Lake, 1992; (contrib.) Gulliver's Travels, 1994; Formosa Straits, 1995; Promises, Promises: Breaking Faith in Canadian Politics, 1997; Double Helix, 1999; Private House, 2007. Contributor to books and periodicals. **Address:** Lucinda Vardey Agency, 297 Seaton St., Toronto, ON M5A 2T6, Canada.

HYDE, Christopher. Also writes as Paul Christopher, A. J. Holt, Nicholas Chase. Canadian (born Canada), b. 1949. **Genres:** Novels, Adult Non-fiction. **Career:** Canadian Broadcasting Corp. (CBC), freelance broadcaster, 1966-69, 1973-75; CJOH-TV, freelance broadcaster, 1970-71; Canadian Television (CTV), freelance broadcaster; Ontario Educational Communications Authority (OECA), freelance broadcaster, 1971-72; full-time writer, 1977-; Ripping Yarns Inc., president; Nicholas Chase Productions, partner; Plain Brown Wrapper Puzzles, owner. **Publications:** Temple of the Winds, 1965; The Wave: A Novel, 1979; The Icarus Seal, 1982; Styx, 1982; The Tenth Crusade, 1983; (as Nicholas Chase) Locksley, 1983; Echo Drive, 1983; Maxwell's Train, 1985; Jericho Falls, 1986; Whisperland: A Chilling Tale of Dynastic Evil, 1986; Holy Ghost, 1987; Crestwood Heights, 1988; Egypt Green, 1989; White Lies, 1990; Hard Target, 1990; Abuse of Trust: The Career of Dr. James Tyhurst, 1991; Black Dragon: A Novel, 1992; The Paranoid's Handbook, 1993; A Gathering of Saints: A Novel, 1996; The Second Assassin, 2002; Wisdom of the Bones, 2003; The House of Special Purpose, 2004; An American Spy, 2005. AS PAUL CHRISTOPHER: Michelangelo's Notebook, 2005; The Lucifer Gospel, 2006; Rembrandt's Ghost, 2007; The Aztec Heresy, 2008;

The Sword of the Templars, 2009; The Templar Cross, 2010; The Templar Throne, 2010; The Templar Conspiracy, 2011; The Templar Legion, 2011; Red Templar, 2012; Valley of the Templars, 2012. AS A.J. HOLT: Watch Me, 1995; Unforgiven, 1996; Catch Me, 1999. **Address:** c/o Author Mail, Douglas & McIntyre Ltd., 2323 Quebec St., Ste. 201, Vancouver, BC V5T 4S7, Canada.

HYDE, Eleanor (M.). American (born United States) **Genres:** Novels, Mystery/Crime/Suspense, Plays/Screenplays. **Career:** American Institute of Physics, copy editor, 1960-65. **Publications:** Tudor Maid, 1972; Tudor Mayhem, 1973; Tudor Mystery, 1974; Tudor Mausoleum, 1977; Tudor Murder, 1977; Those Who Stayed Behind (novel), 1981; In Murder We Trust (mystery novel), 1995; Animal Instincts (mystery novel), 1996. Contributor to literary quarterlies and national magazines. **Address:** c/o Agnes Birnbaum, Bleecker St. Associates, 532 LaGuardia Pl., Ste. 617, New York, NY 10012, U.S.A. **Online address:** ehyde@msn.com

HYDE, Samuel C. American (born United States), b. 1958. **Genres:** History, Politics/Government, Military/Defense/Arms Control, Biography. **Career:** Southeastern Louisiana University, associate professor of history, 1992-, professor, Center for Southeast Louisiana Studies, director, 1997-, Leon Ford endowed chair in regional studies, 2000-. Writer. **Publications:** (Co-ed.) Two Hundred Years a Nation: Aspects of the American Experience, 1994; Pistols and Politics: The Dilemma of Democracy in Louisiana's Florida Parishes, 1810-1899, 1996; (ed. and contrib.) Plain Folk of the South Revisited, 1997; (co-ed.) An American Retrospective: People and Places from Our Nation's Past, 1997; (co-ed.) Carnivals and Conflicts: A Louisiana History, 2000; (ed.) Sunbelt Revolution: The Historical Progression of the Civil Rights Struggle in the Gulf South, 1866-2000, 2003; (ed. and contrib.) Economy, Ecology, War and Identity in a Southern Sub-region: Louisiana's Florida Parishes, 1699-2000, 2003; (ed.) Fierce and Fractious Frontier: The Curious Development of Louisiana's Florida Parishes, 1699-2000, 2004; (ed.) Wisconsin Yankee in Confederate Bayou Country: The Civil War Reminiscences of a Union General, 2009. Contributor of articles to journals. **Address:** Center for Southeast Louisiana Studies, Southeastern Louisiana University, Rm. 306, Linus A. Sims Memorial Library, 3rd Fl., 1211 SGA Dr., PO Box 10730, Hammond, LA 70402, U.S.A. **Online address:** shyde@selu.edu

HYDE, (W.) Lewis. American (born United States), b. 1945. **Genres:** Poetry, Cultural/Ethnic Topics, Literary Criticism And History, Translations. **Career:** University of Iowa, instructor in literature, 1969-71, teaching-research fellow, 1969-72; Cambridge Hospital, alcoholism counselor, 1974-76; Harvard University, researcher in the study of adult development, 1976-, lecturer in expository writing, 1983-85, Briggs-Copeland assistant professor of English, 1985-89, director of the creative writing, 1988-89, Berkman Center, visiting fellow; Centrum Foundation, writer-in-residence, 1984; Kenyon College, Henry R. Luce professor of art and politics, 1989-2001; Richard L. Thomas professor of creative writing, 2001-; Headlands Arts Center, artist-in-residence, 1990; The Exploratorium, Osher fellow; University of Southern California, Annenberg Center for Communication, non-resident fellow. **Publications:** (Trans. with D. Unger) Vicente Aleixandre, World Alone (poems), 1982; The Gift: Imagination and the Erotic Life of Property, 1983; Alcohol and Poetry: John Berryman and the Booze Talking, 1986 (pamphlet); This Error is the Sign of Love: Poems, 1988; (contrib.) Bill Viola, 1997; Trickster Makes This World, 1997; (with J.R. Gross) Lee Mingwei: The Living Room, 2000; Gift: Creativity and the Artist in the Modern World, 2007; Creative Commons, forthcoming. EDITOR: (trans. with R. Bly) Twenty Poems of Vicente Aleixandre, 1977; A Longing for the Light: Selected Poems of Vicente Aleixandre, 1979, 2nd ed., 2007; On the Poetry of Allen Ginsberg, 1984; The Essays of Henry D. Thoreau, 2002; Common as Air: Revolution, Art & Ownership, 2010. Contributor of poetry, translations, and essays to periodicals. **Address:** Department of English, Kenyon College, Rm. 11, Bailey House, 224 N Acland St., Gambier, OH 43022, U.S.A. **Online address:** hydel@kenyon.edu

HYDE-PRICE, Adrian. British (born England), b. 1957. **Genres:** International Relations/Current Affairs, Politics/Government. **Career:** Social Science Research Council, postgraduate research grant, 1979-82; University of Kent at Canterbury, Department of Politics, research assistant, 1984-86; University of Manchester, Department of Government, lecturer in government and politics, 1986-87; Royal Institute of International Affairs, International Security Programme, research fellow, 1987-90; Stockholm Institute of International Affairs, visiting research fellow; University of Southampton, Department of Politics, lecturer in politics and international relations, 1990-96; University of Birmingham, senior lecturer in international politics, 1996-2001; Swedish Institute of International Affairs, visiting research fellow, 1997; University of Leicester, director of postgraduate studies, 2001-03, professor of politics and international relations, 2001-07, head of department, 2003-06; University of Bath, Department of European Studies and Modern Languages, professor of international politics, 2007-. Writer. **Publications:** European Security beyond the Cold War, 1991; The New International Politics of East Central Europe, 1996; (ed. with L. Aggestam) Security and Identity in Europe: Exploring the New Agenda, 2000; (co-ed.) Europe's New Security Challenges, 2001; European Security in the Twenty-First Century: The Challenge of Multipolarity, 2007; (co-ed.) British Foreign Policy and the Anglican Church: Christian Engagement with the Contemporary World, 2008. **Address:** Dept. of European Studies & Modern Languages, University of Bath, 1 W N 4.37, Bath, LE BA2 7AY, England. **Online address:** a.g.v.hyde-price@bath.ac.uk

HYMAN, Harold M(elvin). American (born United States), b. 1924. **Genres:** History, Social Sciences, Politics/Government, Literary Criticism And History. **Career:** U.S. Veterans Administration, rehabilitation officer, 1946-48; City College (now City College of the City University of New York), instructor in modern history, 1950-52; Earlham College, assistant professor of history, 1952-55; University of California, visiting assistant professor of American history, 1955-56, professor of history, 1963-68; Rice University, William P. Hobby professor of history, 1968-97, chairman of history department, 1968-70, professor emeritus, 1997-, Center for the History of Leadership Institutions, director. Writer. **Publications:** Era of the Oath: Northern Loyalty Tests During the Civil War and Reconstruction, 1954; To Try Men's Souls: Loyalty Tests in American History, 1959; (with B.P. Thomas) Stanton: The Life and Times of Lincoln's Secretary of War, 1962; Soldiers and Spruce: The Loyal Legion of Loggers and Lumbermen, the Army's Labor Union of World War I, 1963; A More Perfect Union: The Impact of the Civil War and Reconstruction on the Constitution, 1973; Union and Confidence: The 1860s, 1976; With Malice Toward Some: Scholarship on the Lincoln Murder, 1978; Lincoln's Reconstruction: Neither Failure of Vision nor Vision of Failure, 1980; (with W. Wiecek) Equal Justice Under Law: Constitutional History, 1835-75, 1982; Quiet Past and Stormy Present?: War Powers in American History, 1986; American Singularity: The 1787 Northwest Ordinance, the 1862 Homestead-Morrill Acts, and the 1944 G.I. Bill, 1986; Oleander Odyssey: The Kempners of Galveston, Texas, 1854-1980s, 1990; The Reconstruction Justice of Salmon P. Chase: In Re Turner and Texas v. White, 1997; Craftsmanship and Character: A History of the Vinson & Elkins Law Firm of Houston, 1917-97, 1998. EDITOR: The Radical Republicans and Reconstruction Policy, 1861-70, 1966; New Frontiers of the American Reconstruction, 1966; (with L.W. Levy) Freedom and Reform: Essays in Honor of Henry Steele Commager, 1967; Heard Round the World: The Impact Abroad of the Civil War, 1969; (and intro.) The Casual Laborer and Other Essays, 1972; (and with F. Hyman) The Circuit Court Opinions of Salmon Portland Chase, 1972; (and intro.) The Trail of the Constitution, 1972; The Political History of the United States of America During the Great Rebellion, 1860-65, 1972; (with H.L. Trefousse) Handbook of Politics, 6 vols., 1972-73; (with Trefousse) The Political History of the United States of America During the Period of Reconstruction, 1973; (with K.L. Hall and L.V. Sigal) The Constitutional Converstion as an Amending Device, 1981. **Address:** Department of History, Rice University, Rm. 326, Humanities Bldg., 6100 Main St.-42, Houston, TX 77005-1827, U.S.A. **Online address:** hyman@rice.edu

HYMAN, Meryl. American (born United States), b. 1950. **Genres:** Anthropology/Ethnology, History. **Career:** Writer. **Publications:** Who is a Jew? Conversations, Not Conclusions, 1998. **Address:** c/o Jewish Lights Publishing, Sunset Farm Offices, Rte. 4, PO Box 237, Woodstock, VT 05091-0237, U.S.A.

HYMAN, Ronald T(erry). American (born United States), b. 1933. **Genres:** Education, Law. **Career:** Columbia University, research assistant, 1962-64; Queens College, City University of New York, assistant professor, 1964-66; Rutgers University, Graduate School of Education, associate professor, 1966-74, professor of education, 1974-, chair of department of science and humanities education, 1977-80; lawyer, 1986-; New Jersey School Development Council, executive director. Writer. **Publications:** The Principles of Contemporary Education, 1966; (with A.A. Bellack, H.M. Kliebard and F.L. Smith) The Language of the Classroom, 1966; Ways of Teaching, 1970, rev. ed., 1974; School Administrator's Handbook of Teacher Supervision and Evaluation Methods, 1975; (with A. Teplitsky) Walk in My Shoes, 1976; Paper, Pencils and Pennies: Games for Learning and Having Fun, 1977; (with A. Pessin) The Securities Industry, 1977; (with K. Goldstein-Jackson and N. Rudnick) Experiments with Everyday Objects: Science Activities for Children, Parents and Teachers, 1978; Simulation Gaming for Values Education: The Prisoner's Dilemma, 1978; Strategic Questioning, 1979; Improving Discussion Leadership, 1980; School Administrator's Faculty Supervision Handbook, 1986; School Administrator's Staff Development Activities Manual, 1986; Corporal Punishment in the Schools, 1993; The Principal's Decision on Corporal Punishment, 1993; Mandatory Community Service in High School, 1999. EDITOR: Teaching: Vantage Points for Study, 1968, 2nd ed., 1974; Contemporary Thought on Teaching, 1971; (with M. Hillson) Change and Innovation in Elementary and Secondary Organization, 2nd ed., 1971; Approaches in Curriculum, 1973; (with S.L. Baily) Perspectives on Latin America, 1974. Contributor to periodicals. **Address:** Graduate School of Education, Rutgers University, Rm. 222, 10 Seminary Pl., New Brunswick, NJ 08901-1183, U.S.A. **Online address:** rhyman@rci.rutgers.edu

HYMAN, Steven E(dward). American (born United States), b. 1952. **Genres:** Psychiatry, Medicine/Health, Education. **Career:** Massachusetts General Hospital, intern in medicine, 1980-81, clinical and research fellow in endocrinology and neurology, 1983-84, research fellow in molecular biology, 1984-88, supervisor of psychiatric residents, 1984-, assistant in psychiatry, 1989, assistant psychiatrist, 1990-, director of research in psychiatry, 1992-96; Harvard University, Medical School, clinical fellow in medicine, 1980-81, clinical fellow in psychiatry, 1981-84, research fellow in genetics, 1984-87, instructor, 1987-89, assistant professor, 1989-92, associate professor, 1993, professor of psychiatry, Division on Addictions, director, 1992-95, provost, 2001-, The Mind/Brain/Behavior Interfaculty Initiative, director, 1994-96; McLean Hospital, resident in psychiatry, 1981-84, chief resident, 1982; U.S. Department of Health and Human Services, The National Institute of Mental Health, director, 1996-2001. Writer. **Publications:** (Ed.) Manual of Psychiatric Emergencies, 1984, (ed. with G.E. Tesar) 3rd ed., 1994; (with G.W. Arana) Handbook of Psychiatric Drug Therapy, 1987, (with G.W. Arana and J.F. Rosenbaum) 3rd ed., 1995; (ed. with M.A. Jenike) Manual of Clinical Problems in Psychiatry: With Annotated Key References, 1990; (with E.J. Nestler) Molecular Foundations of Psychiatry, 1993; (ed. and intro.) Science of Mental Health, 2001; (with E.J. Nestler and R.C. Malenka) Molecular Neuropharmacology: A Foundation for Clinical Neuroscience, 2001, 2nd ed., 2009. Contributor of articles to journals. Works appear in anthologies. **Address:** The Office of the Provost, Harvard College, University Hall, Cambridge, MA 02138, U.S.A. **Online address:** steven_hyman@harvard.edu

HYMAN, Timothy. British (born England), b. 1946. **Genres:** Art/Art History, Sex. **Career:** Artscribe, contributing editor. **Publications:** (Ed.) Narrative Paintings: Figurative Art of Two Generations, 1980; Bonnard, 1998; Bhupen Khakhar, 1998; Carnivalesque, 2000; (ed. with P. Wright) Stanley Spencer, 2001; Sienese Painting: The Art of a City-Republic (1278-1477), 2003; (with A.C. Danto and M. Livingstone) Redgrooms, 2004; Fifty Drawings, 2010. Contributor to magazines and newspapers. **Address:** 62 Myddelton Sq., London, GL EC1R 1XX, England. **Online address:** timothy.hyman@virgin.net

HYNES, Charles J. American (born United States), b. 1935. **Genres:** Novels. **Career:** Legal Aid Society, associate attorney, 1963; New York State, special state prosecutor to investigate nursing home fraud, 1975, Commission of Investigation, commissioner, 1983-85; Kings County, assistant district attorney, 1969, Rackets Bureau, chief, 1971, special state prosecutor of criminal justice system, 1985, district attorney and special state prosecutor, 1990-; National Association of Medicaid Fraud Control Units, president, 1976; City of New York, Fire Department, fire commissioner, 1980-82; St. Johns University, St. Johns School of Law, instructor; Brooklyn Law School, instructor; Fordham University School of Law, instructor. Writer. **Publications:** (With B. Drury) Incident at Howard Beach: The Case for Murder, 1990; Triple Homicide, 2007. **Address:** 210 Joralemon St., Brooklyn, NY 11201-3745, U.S.A.

HYNES, Joel. Canadian (born Canada), b. 1976?. **Genres:** Novels, Literary Criticism And History, Young Adult Fiction. **Career:** Actor and writer. **Publications:** NOVELS: Down to the Dirt, 2004; Right Away Monday, 2006; (with S. White) The Devil You Don't Know, 2010. Contributor to periodicals. **Address:** Transatlantic Literary Agency, 72 Glengowan Rd., Toronto, ON M4N 1G4, Canada.

HYNES, Pat. Irish (born Ireland) **Genres:** Children's Fiction, Young Adult Fiction, Science Fiction/Fantasy. **Career:** Writer and educator. **Publications:** Land of Deep Shadow, 1993; Dawn Flight, 1994; Chase the Wind, 1996. Contributor to periodicals. **Address:** Castle Jordan, Tullamore, Birr, OF R420, Ireland.

HYNES, Samuel. American (born United States), b. 1924. **Genres:** Literary Criticism And History, Autobiography/Memoirs, Essays, Biography, History. **Career:** Swarthmore College, instructor, 1949-68, professor of English literature, 1965-68; Northwestern University, professor of English, 1968-76; Princeton University, professor of English, 1976-77, Woodrow Wilson professor of literature, 1977-90, Woodrow Wilson professor of literature emeritus, 1990-. Writer. **Publications:** (Ed.) Further Speculations, 1955; The Pattern of Hardy's Poetry, 1961; (ed.) English Literary Criticism: Restoration and Eighteenth Century, 1963; (ed. with D.G. Hoffman) English Literary Criticism: Romantic and Victorian, 1963, rev. ed., 1979; William Golding, 1964; (ed.) Great Short Works of Thomas Hardy, 1967; (ed.) The Author's Craft and Other Critical Writings of Arnold Bennett, 1968; The Edwardian Turn of Mind, 1968, rev. ed., 1991; (ed.) Romance and Realism: A Study in English Bourgeois Literature by Christopher Caudwell, 1970; (ed. and intro.) Twentieth-Century Interpretations of 1984: A Collection of Critical Essays, 1971; Edwardian Occasions: Essays on English Writing in the Early Twentieth Century, 1972; (ed.) Graham Greene: A Collection of Critical Essays, 1973; The Auden Generation: Literature and Politics in England in the 1930's, 1976; (intro.) Rebecca West, A Celebration: A Selection of Her Writings Chosen by Her Publisher and Rebecca West, 1977; (ed. with D.G. Hoffman) English Literary Criticism: Romantic and Victorian, 1979; (ed.) Complete Poetical Works of Thomas Hardy, vol. I, 1982, vol. II, 1984, vol. III, 1985, vol. IV, 1995; (ed.) Thomas Hardy, 1984; Flights of Passage: Reflections of a World War II Aviator, 1988, rev. ed., 2005; A War Imagined: The First World War and English Culture, 1991; (ed. and intro.) Complete Short Fiction of Joseph Conrad, vol. I-III, 1991, vol. IV, 1993; (ed. and intro.) Selected Poetry, 1996; The Soldiers' Tale: Bearing Witness to Modern War, 1997; (ed. and intro.) The Enormous Room, 1999; The Growing Seasons: An American Boyhood Before the War, 2003; (ed. and intro.) Selected poetry, 2009. **Address:** Department of English, Princeton University, 22 McCosh Hall, Princeton, NJ 08544-1006, U.S.A. **Online address:** shynes@princeton.edu

HYSON, Marilou. See **HYSON, Marion C.**

HYSON, Marion C. (Marilou Hyson). American (born United States), b. 1942. **Genres:** Education, How-to Books. **Career:** Teacher and director of programs for infants and preschool-age children, 1975-82; University of Delaware, assistant professor, 1983-88, associate professor, 1988-95, acting chairperson, 1991-92, 1994-95, professor of individual and family studies, 1995-, head of department, 1995-, chair of individual and family studies, 1995, Commission on the Status of Women, head, 1993-95; National Association for the Education of Young Children, associate executive director and senior consultant, editor, Early Childhood Research Quarterly, editor-in-chief, consulting editor. **Publications:** (With S. Hatoff and C. Byram) Teachers' Practical Guide to Educating Young Children: A Growing Program, 1981; (ed. with L. Rescorla and K. Hirsh-Pasek) Academic Instruction in Early Childhood: Challenge or Pressure? New Directions for Child Development, 1991; (as Marilou Hyson) The Emotional Development of Young Children: Building an Emotion-Centered Curriculum, 1994, 2nd ed., 2004; (ed. as Marilou Hyson) Preparing Early Childhood Professionals: NAEYC's Standards for Programs: NAEYC's Standards for Initial Licensure, Advanced and Associate Degree Programs, 2003; (as Marilou Hyson) Enthusiastic and Engaged Learners: Approaches to Learning in the Early Childhood Classroom, 2008. Contributor to books and journals. **Address:** National Association for the Education, of Young Children, 1313 L St. NW, Ste. 500, Washington, DC 20005, U.S.A. **Online address:** mhyson@naeyc.org

HYTREK, Gary J. American (born United States), b. 1963?. **Genres:** Social Sciences, Sociology. **Career:** California State University, Department of Sociology, associate professor, 2002-. Writer. **Publications:** (With K.M. Zentgraf) America Transformed: Globalization, Inequality and Power, 2008. Contributor to journals. **Address:** Department of Sociology, California State University, 1250 Bellflower Blvd., Long Beach, CA 90840, U.S.A. **Online address:** ghytrek@csulb.edu

HYZY, Julie. American (born United States) **Genres:** Mystery/Crime/Suspense, Young Adult Fiction. **Career:** Writer. **Publications:** Artistic License, 2004; Deadly Blessings: An Alex St. James Mystery, 2005; Deadly Interest: An Alex St. James Mystery, 2006; Dead Ringer: A Ron Shade and Alex St. James Mystery, 2008; State of the Onion: A White House Chef Mystery, 2008; Hail to the Chef: A White House Chef Mystery, 2008; Eggsecutive Orders: A White House Chef Mystery, 2010; Grace Under Pressure: A Manor House Mystery, 2010; Buffalo West Wing: A White House Chef Mystery, 2011; Grace Interrupted: A Manor House Mystery, 2011. **Address:** PO Box 3062, Orland Park, IL 60462, U.S.A. **Online address:** juliehyzy@gmail.com

I

IACCINO, James F(rancis). American (born United States), b. 1955. **Genres:** Psychology, Film, Psychiatry, Adult Non-fiction. **Career:** DePaul University, instructor in psychology, 1978-80; Rosary College, instructor in psychology, 1980; Benedictine University (formerly Illinois Benedictine College), assistant professor, 1981-84, associate professor, 1984-91, professor of psychology, 1991-2006, director of academic advising, 1987-95; The Chicago School of Professional Psychology, Department of Forensic Psychology, associate professor, 2007-. Writer. **Publications:** Left Brain-Right Brain Differences: Inquiries, Evidence, and New Approaches, 1993; Psychological Reflections on Cinematic Terror: Jungian Archetypes in Horror Films, 1994; Jungian Reflections within the Cinema: A Psychological Analysis of Sci-Fi and Fantasy Archetypes, 1998; The Saw Films: Putting the Pieces of Jigsaw Together, forthcoming. Contributor of articles to journals. **Address:** Department of Forensic Psychology, The Chicago School of Professional Psychology, Rm. 4024, 222 Merchandise Mart Plz., 325 N Wells St., Chicago, IL 60654-7024, U.S.A. **Online address:** jiaccino@thechicagoschool.cdu

IACOBONI, Marco. American/Italian (born Italy), b. 1960. **Genres:** Medicine/Health, Sciences, Sports/Fitness, Psychology. **Career:** University of Rome, La Sapienza Medical School, resident in neurology, 1987-89, clinical instructor, 1989-92; University of California, Experimental Neuropsychology Lab, post-graduate researcher, 1992-96, Brain Mapping Division, postgraduate researcher, 1993-96, assistant researcher, 1997-99, Semel Institute, professor in residence, 2008-, Department of Psychiatry and Biobehavioral Sciences, assistant professor in residence, 1999-2002, associate professor in residence, 2002-08, professor in residence, 2008-, Transcranial Magnetic Stimulation Lab, director, 1999-, Ahmanson Lovelace Brain Mapping Center, director, 1999-, David Geffen School of Medicine, director, 1999-. Writer. **Publications:** (Ed. with E. Zaidel) The Parallel Brain: The Cognitive Neuroscience of the Corpus Callosum, 2003; Mirroring People: The New Science of How We Connect with Others, 2008. Contributor to journals. **Address:** Ahmanson-Lovelace Brain Mapping Center, University of California, Rm. 105, 660 Charles E Young Dr. S, Los Angeles, CA 90095-8347, U.S.A. **Online address:** iacoboni@loni.ucla.edu

IACOVETTA, Franca. Canadian (born Canada), b. 1957?. **Genres:** History. **Career:** University of Toronto, professor of history. Writer and historian. **Publications:** (With M. Valverde) Gender Conflicts: New Essays in Women's History, 1992; Such Hardworking People: Italian Immigrants in Postwar Toronto, 1992; (with P. Draper and R. Ventresca) A Nation of Immigrants: Women, Workers and Communities in Canadian History, 1840s-1960s, 1998; (with W. Mitchinson) On the Case: Explorations in Social History, 1998; (ed. with R. Perin and A. Principe) Enemies Within: Italian and Other Internees in Canada and Abroad, 2000. (ed. with D.R. Gabaccia) Women, Gender, and Transnational Lives: Italian Workers of the World, 2002; (ed. with M. Epp and F. Swyripa) Sisters or Strangers: Immigrant, Ethnic and Racialized Women in Canadian History, 2004; Gatekeepers: Reshaping Immigrant Lives in Cold War Canada, 2006. Contributor to periodicals. **Online address:** f.iacovetta@utoronto.ca

IAGNEMMA, Karl. American (born United States), b. 1972. **Genres:** Novels, Novellas/Short Stories, Technology, Engineering. **Career:** Massachusetts Institute of Technology, Department of Mechanical Engineering, principal research scientist and lecturer; Robotic Mobility Group, principal investigator; National Science Foundation, research scientist; National Technical University, Athens, visiting researcher; National Aeronautics and Space Administration (NASA), Jet Propulsion Laboratory, visiting researcher. Writer. **Publications:** On the Nature of Human Romantic Interaction (short stories), 2003; (with S. Dubowsky) Mobile Robots in Rough Terrain: Estimation, Motion Planning, and Control with Application to Planetary Rovers, 2004; (ed. with M. Buehler and S. Singh) 2005 Darpa Grand Challenge: The Great Robot Race, 2007; The Expeditions (novel), 2008; (ed. with M. Buehler and S. Singh) The DARPA Urban Challenge: Autonomous Vehicles in City Traffic, 2009; (ed. with A. Howard and A. Kelly) Field and Service Robotics: Results of the 7th International Conference, 2010. **Address:** Department of Mechanical Engineering, Massachusetts Institute of Technology, Rm. 35-237a, 77 Massachusetts Ave., Cambridge, MA 02139, U.S.A. **Online address:** kdi@mit.edu

IAKOVOU, Judy. American (born United States) **Genres:** Mystery/Crime/Suspense. **Career:** Silver Screen Grill, co-proprietor; Checkered Cloth Cafe, co-proprietor; University of Georgia, faculty in creative writing, Department of English, faculty, 2001-, Franklin College of Arts and Sciences, Office of Academic Advising, academic advisor, 2006-. Writer. **Publications:** WITH T. IAKOVOU: So Dear to Wicked Men, 1996; Go Close Against the Enemy, 1998; There Lies a Hidden Scorpion, 1999. **Address:** c/o Author Mail, St. Martin's Press L.L.C., 175 5th Ave., New York, NY 10010-7703, U.S.A. **Online address:** jiakovou@uga.edu

IAKOVOU, Takis. American/Greek (born Greece) **Genres:** Mystery/Crime/Suspense, Novels, Children's Fiction, Young Adult Fiction. **Career:** Silver Screen Grill, co-proprietor; Checkered Cloth Cafe, co-proprietor. Writer. **Publications:** WITH J. IAKOVOU: So Dear to Wicked Men, 1996; Go Close Against the Enemy, 1998; There Lies a Hidden Scorpion, 1999. Contributor to periodicals. **Address:** c/o Author Mail, St. Martin's Press, 175 5th Ave., New York, NY 10010, U.S.A. **Online address:** iakovou@ibm.net

IANNUZZI, John Nicholas. American (born United States), b. 1935. **Genres:** Mystery/Crime/Suspense, Law, Novels, Business/Trade/Industry, Economics, Young Adult Fiction. **Career:** Iannuzzi, Russo & Iannuzzi, attorney specializing in criminal work, 1962-, owner; Fordham University School of Law, adjunct professor of trial advocacy, 1987-, law professor; Law Offices of Iannuzzi, senior partner. Writer. **Publications:** FICTION: What's Happening?, 1963; Part 35, 1970; Sicilian Defense, 1973; Courthouse, 1980; J. T., 1984; Condemned, 2006. LEGAL PUBLICATION: Cross Examination: The Mosaic Art, 1984, Handbook of Cross Examination: The Mosaic Art, 2nd ed., 1998; Trial Strategy and Psychology, 1992; Handbook of Trial Strategies, 2001. **Address:** Iannuzzi and Iannuzzi, 74 Trinity Pl., Rm. 1800, New York, NY 10006-2104, U.S.A. **Online address:** lawoffice@iannuzzi.net

IBATA-ARENS, Kathryn. American (born United States) **Genres:** Politics/Government, Business/Trade/Industry. **Career:** Rosary College (now Dominican University), lecturer, 1994; Northwestern University, research assistant, 1993-94, lecturer, 1995-2000; Hosei University, Department of Economics, foreign research fellow, 1997; University of Tokyo, Research Center for Advanced Science and Technology, Fulbright graduate research fellow, 1997-98, Japan Society for the Promotion of Science, post-doctoral research fellow, 2002; Osaka University, Osaka School of International Public Policy, Fulbright graduate research fellow, 1997-98; Social Science Research Council, fellow, 2000-02, Abe fellow, 2005-06; DePaul University, Department of Political Science, assistant professor, 2003-; Japan Foundation Center for Global Partnership, Abe fellow, 2005-06; Doshisha University, faculty, 2005-06. Political scientist and writer. **Publications:** Innovation and Entrepreneurship in Japan: Politics, Organizations, and High Technology Firms, 2005. **Address:** Department of Political Science, DePaul University, Rm. 2209, 990 W Fullerton Ave., Chicago, IL 60614-2458, U.S.A. **Online address:** kibataar@depaul.edu

IBBITSON, John Perrie. Canadian (born Canada), b. 1955. **Genres:** Young Adult Fiction, Plays/Screenplays, Politics/Government, Adult Non-fiction. **Career:** Writer/journalist, 1979-; Collier Macmillan, editorial secretary, 1984-86, junior editor, 1986-87; Ottawa Citizen, city reporter, columnist and feature writer, 1988-95, correspondent, 1995-96; Southam News, reporter, columnist, Queen's Park correspondent, 1996-; The Globe and Mail, columnist, 1999, Washington bureau, chief, 2001-, correspondent and columnist, Ottawa bureau chief, 2009-. **Publications:** YOUNG ADULT FICTION: Masque, 1974; The Wimp, 1985; The Wimp and the Jock, 1986; The Wimp and Easy Money, 1987; Starcrosser, 1990; The Big Story, 1990; 1812: Jeremy and the General, 1991; The Night Hazel Came to Town, 1993; Jeremy's War: 1812, 2000; Loyal no More: Ontario's Struggle for a Separate Destiny, 2001; The Polite Revolution: Perfecting the Canadian Dream, 2005; Open & Shut: Why America has Barack Obama and Canada has Stephen Harper, 2009. ADULT NONFICTION: (ed. and contrib.) Fair Play and Daylight: The Ottawa Citizen Essays, 1995; Promised Land: Inside the Mike Harris Revolution, 1997. PLAYS: Catalyst (one-act play), 1974; Mayonnaise (two-act comedy), 1980; Country Matters (two-act farce), 1982; (with E. Heeley) Mayonnaise, 1983. **Address:** The Globe & Mail, 444 Front St. W, Toronto, ON M5V 2S9, Canada. **Online address:** jibbitson@globeandmail.com

IBBOTSON, Roger G. American (born United States), b. 1943. **Genres:** Economics, Money/Finance. **Career:** First National City Bank of New York, security analyst, 1966; Nevada Garvey Ranches, administrative coordinator, 1967; Pfizer Intl., assistant to vice-president, 1967-68; Bank of Japan, economist, 1969; Tau Investments, Botswana, developer, 1970; University of Chicago, lecturer in finance, 1971-75, assistant professor, 1975-79, senior lecturer, 1979-84, professor in practice of finance, 1984-, Center for Research in Security Prices, executive director, 1979-84, Office of the Treasurer, bond portfolio manager, 1972-75, securities trading department, manager, 1974-75; Ibbotson Associates (financial and investment advisers), president and chair, 1977-2006; Yale University, professor in the practice of finance, 1984-; Williams and Associates, general partner, 1979-; DFA Investment Dimensions Group Inc., director, 1981-; JLS Industries Inc., director, 1983-; CAPM Corp., director, 1983-87; Constitution Capital Management Co., director, 1985-92; Institute for the Study of Security Markets, director, 1987-96, chair, 1993-96; BIRR Portfolio Analysis Inc., director and principal, 1989-; Hospital Foundation for Research and Education, director, 1991-; Zebra Capital Management L.L.C., chairman and CIO, 2001-; Ibbotson Associates and Morningstar Inc., advisor, 2006. Writer. **Publications:** Price Performance of Common Stock New Issues, 1975; (with R.A. Sinquefield) Stocks, Bonds, Bills, and Inflation: The Past (1926-1976) and the Future (1977-2000), 1977, 3rd ed., 1989; (with R.A. Sinquefield) Stocks, Bonds, Bills, and Inflation: Historical Returns, 1926-1978, 1979; (with G.P. Brinson) Investment Markets: Gaining the Performance Advantage, 1987; (with G.P. Brinson) Global Investing: A Professional's Guide to the World's Capital Markets, 1993; (with J. Francis) Investments: A Global Perspective, 2002; (with W.N. Goetzmann) The Equity Risk Premium: Essays and Explorations, 2006; (co-author) Lifetime Financial Advice: Human Capital, Asset Allocation, and Insurance, 2007; The Importance of Asset Allocation, 2010. Works appear in anthologies. Contributor to journals. **Address:** Yale School of Management, 135 Prospect St., PO Box 208200, New Haven, CT 06520-8200, U.S.A. **Online address:** roger.ibbotson@yale.edu

IBER, Jorge. American (born United States), b. 1961. **Genres:** History. **Career:** Salt Lake Community College, adjunct instructor, 1992-96; University of Utah, teaching assistant, 1993-95; Texas Tech University, assistant professor of history, associate professor of history, 1997-, professor of history, College of Arts and Sciences, associate dean, Department of History, chairman, Ethnic Studies Program, director. Writer. **Publications:** Hispanics in the Land of Zion, 1912-1999, 2000; (with A. De Leon) Hispanics in the Ameri-

can West, 2006; (ed. with S.O. Regalado) Mexican Americans and Sports: A Reader on Athletics and Barrio Life, 2007; (co-author) Latinos in U.S Sport: A History of Isolation, Cultural Identity, and Acceptance, 2011. Contributor of articles periodicals. **Address:** Department of History, Texas Tech University, 60 Holden Hall, PO Box 41013, Lubbock, TX 79409-1013, U.S.A. **Online address:** Jorge.Iber@ttu.edu

IBRAHIM, Raymond. American (born United States), b. 1973?. **Genres:** History. **Career:** Middle East Forum, associate director; Middle East Quarterly, deputy publisher; Library of Congress, reference assistant, 2003-09. Writer. **Publications:** The Battle of Yarmuk: An Assessment of the Immediate Factors Behind the Islamic Conquests, 2002; (ed. and trans.) The Al Qaeda Reader, 2007. Contributor to periodicals. **Address:** U.S.A. **Online address:** raymondmef@gmail.com

IDAMANNEL, Sudhamani. See **AMRITANANDAMAYI, Mataji.**

IDOL, John L(ane). American (born United States), b. 1932. **Genres:** Biography, Genealogy/Heraldry, History, Adult Non-fiction. **Career:** English teacher, 1958; Clemson University, English teacher, 1964-, professor emeritus, now retired; Clemson Area Arts Council, Friends of the Clemson Community Library, president; Thomas Wolfe Review, editor; The Nathaniel Hawthorne Review, editor. **Publications:** A Thomas Wolfe Companion, 1987; (with R.K. Gollin and S.K. Eisiminger) Prophetic Pictures: Nathaniel Hawthorne's Knowledge and Uses of the Visual Arts, 1991; Thomas Wolfe, 2001; Blue Ridge Heritage: An Informal History of Three Generations of the Family of John Nicholson Idol, 2005. EDITOR: (with S. Eisiminger) Why Can't They Write? A Symposium on the State of Written Communication, 1979; (and intro.) K-19: Salvaged Pieces, 1983; (with L.D. Rubin, Jr.) Mannerhouse, 1985; (and foreword) The Hound of Darkness, 1986; (co-ed.) Women's Effect on Hawthorne and Hawthorne's Effect on Women, 1993; (with B. Jones) Nathaniel Hawthorne: Contemporary Reviews, 1994; (and intro. with S. Stutman) Party at Jack's, 1995; (with M.M. Ponder) Hawthorne and Women: Engendering and Expanding the Hawthorne Tradition, 1999; (and foreword) The Medical Students, 2000. Contributor to magazines and newspapers. **Address:** 3723 Krystle Ct., PO Box 413, Hillsborough, NC 27278-8465, U.S.A.

IDOV, Michael. American (born United States), b. 1976?. **Genres:** Novels. **Career:** Soviet Youth, writer, 1990; Village Voice, music listings writer, 1998-2006; Pitchfork, reviewer, 1998-2006; Café Trotsky, co-owner, 2005; National Broadcasting Company Inc. (NBC), news producer; Russia!, editor-in-chief; New York Magazine, contributing editor. **Publications:** Ground Up (novel), 2009. Contributor to magazines. **Address:** U.S.A. **Online address:** michaelidov@yahoo.com

IFILL, Sherrilyn A. American (born United States) **Genres:** History, Young Adult Fiction, Social Sciences. **Career:** University of Maryland, School of Law, professor of law, 1993-; NAACP Legal Defense and Educational Fund Inc., assistant counsel; Re-entry of Ex-Offenders Clinic, co-founder; Open Society Institute, board director; Enoch Pratt Free Library, board director. Writer, attorney and consultant. **Publications:** On the Courthouse Lawn: Confronting the Legacy of Lynching in the Twenty-first Century, 2007. Contributor to periodicals. **Address:** School of Law, University of Maryland, Rm. 353, 500 W Baltimore St., Baltimore, MD 21201-1786, U.S.A. **Online address:** sifill@law.umaryland.edu

IGGERS, Georg G(erson). American/German (born Germany), b. 1926. **Genres:** History, Essays, Translations. **Career:** University of Akron, instructor in German and humanities, 1948-49; Philander Smith College, associate professor of history, 1950-57; University of Arkansas, visiting professor, 1956-57; Dillard University, associate professor, 1957-59, professor of history, 1959-63; Tulane University, visiting associate professor, 1958-60, 1963; Roosevelt University, associate professor of history, 1963-65; State University of New York at Buffalo, professor of history, distinguished professor, 1978, chairman of department, 1981-84, distinguished professor emeritus, 1997-; University of Rochester, visiting professor, 1970-71; Technische Hochschule Darmstadt, visiting professor, 1991; Universitaer Leipzig, visiting professor, 1992; Arhus University, visiting professor, 1998; Military and Draft Counseling Center of Buffalo, chairperson; University of New England, visiting professor. Writer. **Publications:** The Cult of Authority: The Political Philosophy of the Saint-Simonians, 1958; The German Conception of History: The National Tradition of Historical Thought from Herder to the Present, 1968;

New Directions in European Historiography: Four Essays, 1975; Geschichtswissenschaft im 20. Jahrhundert: ein kritischer Überblick im internationalen Zusammenhang, 1993; Historiography in the Twentieth Century: From Scientific Objectivity to the Postmodern Challenge, 1997; Deutsche Geschichtswissenschaft: EineKritik der Traditionellen Geschichtsauffassung von Herder bis zurGegenwart, 1997; DDR-Geschichtswissenschaft als Forschungsproblem, 1998; (with W. Iggers) Zwei Seiten einer Geschichte: Lebensbericht aus unruhigenZeiten, 2002; Hochschule, Geschichte, Stadt: Festschrift fur Helmut Bohme, 2004; Refugee Historians from Nazi Germany: Political Attitudes Towards Democracy, 2006; Two Lives In Uncertain Times: Facing the Challenges Of The 20th Century as Scholars and Citizens, 2006; (with Q.E. Wang and S. Mukherjee) A Global History of Modern Historiography, 2008. EDITOR: (and trans.) The Doctrine of Saint-Simon: An Exposition, 1958, 2nd ed., 1972; (intro. with K. von Moltke) The Theory and Practice of History, 1973; (intro.) Two Lectures in Modern German History, 1978; (with H.T. Parker) International Handbook of Historical Studies: Contemporary Research and Theory, 1979; The Social History of Politics: Critical Perspectives in West German Historical Writing since 1945, 1985; (with J. Powell) Leopold von Ranke and the Shaping of Historical Discipline, 1989; Ein Anderer historischer Blick: Beispiele ostdeutscher Sozialgeschichte, 1991; Marxist Historiography in Transformation: Historical Writings in East Germany in the 1980s, 1991; (co-ed.) Intellektuelle in der Weimarer Republik, 1996; Crossing Boundaries: German and American Experiences with the Exclusion and Inclusion of Minorities, 2001; (with Q.E. Wang) Turning Points in Historiography: A Cross-Cultural Perspective, 2002. **Address:** Department of History, State University of New York, 562 Park Hall, Buffalo, NY 14260-4130, U.S.A. **Online address:** iggers@buffalo.edu

IGNATIEFF, Michael. American/Canadian (born Canada), b. 1947. **Genres:** Novels, Civil Liberties/Human Rights, Ethics, History, Literary Criticism And History. **Career:** Globe and Mail, reporter, 1966-67; Harvard University, teaching fellow, 1971-74; University of British Columbia, assistant professor of history, 1976-78; King's College, senior research fellow, 1978-84; Ecole des Hautes Etudes, visiting professor, 1985; British Broadcasting Corporation Television, host, 1986-; Channel Four, host, 1986; BBC2, The Late Show, host, 1989-92; John F. Kennedy School of Government, Harvard University, Carr Center for Human Rights, director, 2000-05; University of Toronto, visiting professor in human rights policy, 2005-, Chancellor Jackman professor in human rights policy, Munk Centre for International Studies, senior fellow, 2005-; member of parliament, 2006-; Liberal Party of Canada, deputy leader, 2006, leader, 2008, head, 2009-; University of Cambridge, faculty; University of Oxford, faculty; Harvard University, faculty. **Publications:** A Just Measure of Pain: The Penitentiary in the Industrial Revolution, 1978; The Needs of Strangers, 1984; (with H. Brody) Nineteen Nineteen, 1985; Psychoanalysis, 1987; The Russian Album, 1987; Blood and Belonging: Journeys into the New Nationalism, 1994; Isaiah Berlin: A Life, 1998; Warrior's Honor: Ethnic War and the Modern Conscience, 1998; Virtual War: Kosovo and Beyond, 2000; The Rights Revolution, 2000, 2nd ed., 2007; Nationalism and Self-Determination: Is There an Alternative to Violence?, 2000; Human Rights as Politics and Idolatry, 2001; Empire Lite: Nationbuilding in Bosnia, Kosovo and Afghanistan (essays), 2003; The Lesser Evil: Political Ethics in an Age of Terror, 2004; True Patriot Love, 2009. EDITOR: (with J. Rose) Religion and International Affairs, 1968; (with I. Hont) Wealth and Virtue: The Shaping of Classical Political Economy in the Scottish Enlightenment, 1983; (with S. Chesterman and R. Thakur) Making States Work: State Failure and the Crisis of Governance, 2005; American Exceptionalism and Human Rights, 2005. NOVELS: Asya, 1991; Scar Tissue, 1994; Charlie Johnson in the Flames, 2003; After Paradise, 2007; True Patriot Love, 2009. **Address:** House of Commons, Rm. 435-S, Centre Block, 79 John F. Kennedy St., Ottawa, ON K1A 0A6, Canada. **Online address:** ignatm@parl.gc.ca

IGNATIEV, Noel. American (born United States), b. 1940. **Genres:** History, Race Relations. **Career:** Massachusetts College of Art and Design, Department of Liberal Arts, professor of history. Writer. **Publications:** How the Irish Became White, 1995; (ed. with J. Garvey) Race Traitor, 1996; The Lesson of the Hour, 2001; A New Notion, 2010. **Address:** Department of Liberal Arts, Massachusetts College of Art and Design, 621 Huntington Ave., Boston, MA 02115-5882, U.S.A. **Online address:** ignatiev@massart.edu

IGO, John (N.). American (born United States), b. 1927. **Genres:** Poetry, Literary Criticism And History, Mythology/Folklore, Biography. **Career:** Trinity University, instructor in English and acquisitions librarian, 1952-53;

San Antonio College, associate professor, professor of English, 1953-99; University of the Incarnate Word, faculty; Renegade Theater, founder, producer and director; Choice Magazine, staff reviewer, 1964-2002; International Biographical Centre, deputy director general, 1997; The John Igo Library, founder, 2007. Writer. **Publications:** God of Gardens, 1962; (ed.) Yanaguana: A Chapbook of College Poetry, 1963; A Chamber Faust, 1964; Igo on Poetry, 1965; The Tempted Monk, 1967; (and intro.) Los Pastores: A Triple Tradition, 1967; No Harbor, Else, 1972; Golgotha, 1973; Day of Elegies, 1974; Alien, 1977; San Antonio Remembers Will Rogers on the Centenary of His Birth, November 4th, 1879-1979, 1979; Tropic of Gemini, 1981; Coven, 1984; A Companion to 'Los Pastores', 1987; The Mitotes, 1989; The Third Temptation of St. John, 1992; Charco Martinez (poems), 1997; Oenone (drama), 1999; The Bozzetti (poems), 2001; On Poetry and Poetics (textbook), 2001; Lost Landscape, 2004; Stet, 2009; Karagoz, 2009; Huero, forthcoming. **Address:** John Igo Library, 13330 Kyle Seale Pkwy., San Antonio, TX 78249, U.S.A.

IGO, Sarah E. American (born United States), b. 1969. **Genres:** Social Work, History, Politics/Government, Social Sciences, Sociology. **Career:** Harvard College, Lighthouse Magazine, founder and editorial staff, 1990-92; Phillips Academy, instructor in history, 1992-95; Princeton University, Forbes College, staff and supervisor of upper class residential and minority affairs, 1997-99; University of Pennsylvania, assistant professor of history, 2001-07; Vanderbilt University, associate professor of history, associate professor of political science, associate professor of sociology. Writer. **Publications:** The Averaged American: Surveys, Citizens, and the Making of a Mass Public, 2007. **Address:** Department of History, Vanderbilt University, 201 Benson Hall, 2301 Vanderbilt Pl., PO Box 351802, Nashville, TN 37235-1802, U.S.A. **Online address:** sarah.igo@vanderbilt.edu

IGOE, James. See **IGOE, Jim Joseph.**

IGOE, Jim Joseph. (James Igoe). American (born United States), b. 1964. **Genres:** Young Adult Non-fiction, Science Fiction/Fantasy, Economics. **Career:** University of Colorado, Department of Anthropology, assistant professor, director of graduate program; Bridge for Indigenous Development and Grassroots Empowerment, founder. Writer. **Publications:** Conservation and Globalization: A Study of National Parks and Indigenous Communities from East Africa to South Dakota(nonfiction), 2004; (ed. with T. Kelsall) Between a Rock and a Hard Place: African NGOs, Donors and the State (nonfiction), 2005; (with D. Brockington and R. Duffy) Nature Unbound: Conservation, Capitalism and the Future of Protected Areas, 2008. Contributor to books. **Address:** Department of Anthropology, University of Colorado, Rm. 103, PO Box 173364, Denver, CO 80217-3364, U.S.A. **Online address:** james.igoe@cudenver.edu

IHDE, Don. American (born United States), b. 1934. **Genres:** Philosophy, History, Technology, Engineering. **Career:** Southern Illinois University, assistant professor, 1964-67, associate professor of philosophy, 1968-69; State University of New York, Department of Philosophy, associate professor, 1969-71, professor of philosophy, 1971-, distinguished professor of philosophy, director of the technoscience research. Writer. **Publications:** Hermeneutic Phenomenology, The Philosophy of Paul Ricoeur, 1971; (with R.M. Zaner) Phenomenology and Existentialism, 1973; Sense and Significance, 1973; Postphenomenology: Essays in the Postmodern Context, 1973; (ed. with R.M. Zaner) Dialogues in Phenomenology, 1975; Listening and Voice: A Phenomenology of Sound, 1976, 2nd ed., 2007; Experimental Phenomenology: An Introduction, 1977, 2nd ed. as Experimental Phenomenology: Multistabilities, 2012; (ed. with R.M. Zaner) Interdisciplinary Phenomenology, 1977; Technics and Praxis, 1979; Existential Technics, 1983; (ed. with H.J. Silverman) Hermeneutics & Deconstruction, 1985; (ed. with H.J. Silverman) Descriptions, 1985; Consequences of Phenomenology, 1986; Technology and the Lifeworld: From Garden to Earth, 1990; Instrumental Realism: The Interface Between Philosophy of Science and Philosophy of Technology, 1991; Philosophy of Technology: An Introduction, 1993; Expanding Hermeneutics: Visualism in Science, 1998; Bodies In Technology, 2002; (ed. with E. Selinger) Chasing Technoscience: Matrix for Materiality, 2003; (ed.) Conflict of Interpretations, 2007; (foreword) Freedom and Nature, new ed., 2007; (foreword) Nature and Freedom: The Voluntary and the Involuntary, 2007; Postphenomenology and Technoscience: The Peking University Lectures, 2009; Heidegger's Technologies: Postphenomenological Perspectives, 2010; Imaging Technologies: Plato Upside Down, forthcoming. Contributor to periodicals. **Address:** Department of Philosophy, State University of New York, 221 Harriman Hall, Stony Brook, NY 11794-3750, U.S.A. **Online address:** dihde@notes.cc.stonybrook.edu

IHEDURU, Obioma M. American/Nigerian (born Nigeria), b. 1950?. **Genres:** Politics/Government, Economics, Social Commentary, Business/Trade/Industry. **Career:** Fort Valley State University, Department of Political Science, associate professor, Center for Social Science Research, co-director. Writer. **Publications:** The Politics of Economic Restructuring and Democracy in Africa, 1999; (ed.) Contending Issues in African Development: Advances, Challenges, and the Future, 2001. **Address:** Department of Political Science, Fort Valley State University, 1005 State University Dr., Fort Valley, GA 31030-4313, U.S.A. **Online address:** iheduruo@mail.fvsu.edu

IHIMAERA, Witi. New Zealander (born New Zealand), b. 1944. **Genres:** Novels, Novellas/Short Stories, Young Adult Non-fiction. **Career:** Post Office Headquarters, journalist, 1968-72; Ministry of Foreign Affairs, information officer, 1973-74, third secretary, 1976-77, secretary, 1979-85; Otago University, Robert Burns fellow, 1975; New Zealand High Commissioner, second secretary, 1978; New Zealand Embassy, public affairs, counselor, 1989; University of Auckland, lecturer, 1990-95, associate professor of English, professor, 1996-, distinguished creative fellow in Maori literature, now professor emeritus. Writer. **Publications:** NOVELS: Tangi, 1973; Whanau, 1974; The Matriarch, 1986; The Whale Rider, 1987; Bulibasha, 1994; Nights in the Gardens of Spain, 1995; The Dream Swimmer, 1997; The Uncle's Story, 2000; Sky Dancer, 2003; Whanau II, 2004; Band of Angels, 2005; The Trowenna Sea, 2009. SHORT STORIES: Pounamu Pounamu, 1970; The New Net Goes Fishing, 1977; Dear Miss Mansfield: A Tribute to Kathleen Mansfield Beauchamp, 1989; Land, Sea & Sky, 1994; Kingfisher Come Home: The Complete Maori Stories, 1995; Ihimaera: His Best Stories, 2003. OTHER: Maori, 1975; (with T. Woollaston and A. Curnow) New Zealand through the Arts, 1982; Bulibasha: King of the Gypsies, 1994; New Zealand: First to See the Dawn, 1997; Beautiful New Zealand, 1998; Beautiful North Island of New Zealand, 1998; This Is New Zealand, 1998; Woman far Walking, 2000; Te Kaieke Tohora, 2002; Little Kowhai Tree, 2002; Whale Rider, 2002; Rope of Man, 2005; Ask the Posts of the House, 2007; Matriarch, 2009. EDITOR: (with D.S. Long) Into the World of Light, 1982; Te Ao Mārama: M: Contemporary Māori Writing, vol. I-IV, 1992-94; Vision Aotearoa: kaupapa New Zealand, 1994; Mataora: The Living Face: Contemporary Maori Art, 1996; Growing Up Māori, 1998; Where's Waari?: A History of the Maori Through the Short Story, 2000; Te Ata: Māori Art from the East Coast, New Zealand, 2002; Auckland: The City in Literature, 2003; (and intro.) Get on the Waka: Best Recent Māori Fiction, 2007. **Address:** Department of English, The University of Auckland, Rm. 529, 1-11 Short St., Auckland, 1020, New Zealand. **Online address:** w.ihimaera@auckland.ac.nz

IHONVBERE, Julius O. (Julius Omozuanvbo Ihonvbere). Nigerian (born Nigeria) **Genres:** Politics/Government, Economics, Philosophy. **Career:** Houston-Tillotson College, associate professor of political science, 1993; University of Ife, assistant lecturer in international relations; University of Port Harcourt, lecturer in political science; University of Toronto, visiting professor of political science; University of Texas, professor of government; Ford Foundation, program officer in governance and civil society. Writer. **Publications:** The Oil Industry in Nigeria: An Annotated Bibliography, 1983; (with T. Falola) The Rise and Fall of Nigeria's Second Republic, 1979-1984, 1985; The 1983 Elections and the Buhari Coup in Nigeria: Contradictions in a (Semi-)Peripheral Political Economy, 1985; (ed. with T. Falola) Nigeria and the International Capitalist System, 1988; (with T.M. Shaw) Towards a Political Economy of Nigeria: Petroleum and Politics at the (Semi)-Periphery, 1988; (ed.) The Political Economy of Crisis and Underdevelopment in Africa: Selected Works of Claude Ake, 1989; Nigeria: The Politics of Adjustment and Democracy, 1994; Economic Crisis, Civil Society, and Democratization: The Case of Zambia, 1996; (with T.M. Shaw) Illusions of Power: Nigeria in Transition, 1998; Labor, State, and Capital in Nigeria's Oil Industry, 1998; (ed. with J.M. Mbaku) Multiparty Democracy and Political Change: Constraints to Democratization in Africa, 1998; (with P.O. Agbese) Structural Adjustment and the Nigerian State, 1999; Africa and the New World Order, 2000; (ed. with J.M. Mbaku) Political Liberalization and Democratization in Africa: Lessons from Country Experiences, 2003; (ed. with J.M. Mbaku) The Transition to Democratic Governance in Africa: The Continuing Struggle, 2003; Corruption and Sustainable Democracy in Nigeria, 2004. **Address:**

c/o Author Mail, Praeger/Greenwood Publishing Group Inc., 88 Post Rd. W, Westport, CT 06880, U.S.A. **Online address:** julius@jeeves.la.utexas.edu

IHONVBERE, Julius Omozuanvbo. See IHONVBERE, Julius O.

IIDA, Deborah. American (born United States), b. 1956?. **Genres:** Novels, Social Sciences, Young Adult Fiction. **Career:** Writer. **Publications:** Middle Son, 1996. **Address:** 291 Mohalu St., Kahului, HI 96732, U.S.A.

IKE, Vincent Chukwuemeka. Nigerian (born Nigeria), b. 1931. **Genres:** Novels, Area Studies, Education, How-to Books, Writing/Journalism, Young Adult Fiction, Adult Non-fiction, Novellas/Short Stories, Novellas/Short Stories. **Career:** Teacher, 1950-51, 1955-56; University College, administrative assistant and assistant registrar, 1957-60; University of Nigeria, pioneer deputy registrar, 1960-63, registrar and secretary to council, 1963-71, chairman of planning and management committee and interim chief executive officer, 1970; Umuahia Province, provincial refugee officer, 1968-69; Nsukka Province, headquarters scout commissioner, 1970-71; West African Examinations Council, registrar and chief executive officer, 1971-79; Daily Times of Nigeria, director, 1971-87; Times Leisure Services Ltd., chair, 1977-79; University Press, director, 1978-2002; City and Guilds of London Institute of Publishers, honorary fellow, 1978; Emekike and Co., executive chair, 1979-81; University of Jos, visiting professor, 1983-85; University of Iowa, honorary fellow, 1987; University of Benin, pro-chancellor, 1990-91; Nigerian Book Foundation, chair, 1991-93, president/chief executive officer, 1993-; Anambra State University of Science and Technology, pro-chancellor, 2001-. Writer. **Publications:** FICTION: Toads for Supper, 1965; The Naked Gods, 1970; The Potter's Wheel, 1973; Sunset at Dawn, 1976; The Chicken Chasers, 1980; Expo '77, 1980; The Bottled Leopard, 1985; Our Children Are Coming!, 1990; The Search, 1991; To My Husband, from Iowa, 1996; Anu Ebu Nwa, 1999; Conspiracy of Silence, 2001; The Accra Riviera (short stories), 2001. NONFICTION: University Development in Africa: The Nigerian Experience, 1976; How to Become a Published Writer, 1991. EDITOR: (with E. Obiechina and J.A. Umeh) The University of Nigeria, 1960-1985, 1986; Creating a Conducive Environment for Book Publishing, 1996; Meeting the Book Needs of the Rural Family, 1998; Directory of Nigerian Book Development, 1998; Ndikelionwu and the Spread of Christianity, 2000; The Book in 21st Century Nigeria and Universal Basic Education, 2000; Creating and Sustaining a Reading Culture, 2000. OTHER: Toad for Ever, 2007. Contributor to books and periodicals. **Address:** Ndikelionwu Postal Agency, Chinwuba House, Orumba North L.G.A., Via Awka, AN 420001, Nigeria. **Online address:** nbkfound@infoweb.abs.net

IKE, Young. See EISENHOWER, John S(heldon) D(oud).

IKENBERRY, G. John. American (born United States), b. 1954. **Genres:** Economics, History, Politics/Government, International Relations/Current Affairs. **Career:** Princeton University, Woodrow Wilson School, assistant professor, 1984-92, Albert G. Milbank professor of politics and international affairs, 2004-, Department of Politics, faculty; Carnegie Endowment for International Peace, senior associate, 1992-93; University of Pennsylvania, professor, 1993-99, Lauder Institute, director, 1994-98, associate professor of political science; The Brookings Institute, non-resident senior fellow, 1997-2002; International Relations of the Asia Pacific, associate editor, 1999-2004, editor, 2004-; Georgetown University, Edmund A. Walsh School of Foreign Service, Peter F. Krogh professor of geopolitics and global justice, 2000-04. **Publications:** (Ed. with D.A. Lake and M. Mastanduno) The State and American Foreign Economic Policy, 1988; Reasons of State: Oil Politics and the Capacities of American Government, 1988; (with J.A. Hall) The State, 1989; (ed.) American Foreign Policy: Theoretical Essays, 1989, 6th ed., 2011; (with M.M. Nelson and R.B. Zoellick) Atlantic Frontiers, 1993; (ed. with M.W. Doyle) New Thinking in International Relations Theory, 1997; (ed. with M. Cox and T. Inoguchi) American Democracy Promotion: Impulses, Strategies and Impacts, 2000; After Victory: Institutions, Strategic Restraint and the Rebuilding of Order after Major Wars, 2001; (ed.) America Unrivaled: The Future of the Balance of Power, 2002; (ed. with M. Mastanduno) International Relations Theory and the Asia-Pacific, 2003; (ed. with T. Inoguchi) Reinventing the Alliance: U.S.-Japan Security Partnership in an Era of Change, 2003; (with J.M. Grieco) State Power and World Markets: The International Political Economy, 2003; (ed. with T.V. Paul and J.A. Hall) The Nation-State in Question, 2003; (ed. with T. Inoguchi) The Uses of Institutions: The U.S., Japan and Governance in East Asia, 2006; (with A. Slaughter) Forging a World of Liberty under Law, 2006; Liberal Order and Imperial Ambition:

American Power and International Order, 2006; (ed. with J. Anderson and T. Risse) The End of the West?: Crisis and Change in the Atlantic Order, 2008; (ed. with C. Moon) The United States and Northeast Asia: Debates, Issues and New Order, 2008; (ed.) The Crisis of American Foreign Policy: Wilsonianism in the Twenty-first Century, 2009; Liberal Leviathan: The Rise, Triumph, Crisis and Transformation of the American World Order, 2011; (ed. with T. Inoguchi and Y. Sato) The Alliance Constrained: The U.S.- Japan Security Alliance and Regional Multilateralism, 2011; (ed. with M. Mastanduno and W.C. Wohlforth) International Relations Theory and the Consequences of Unipolarity, 2011. **Address:** Woodrow Wilson School, Princeton University, 116 Bendheim Hall, Princeton, NJ 08544-1013, U.S.A. **Online address:** gji3@princeton.edu

IKENSON, Ben. American (born United States) **Genres:** Adult Non-fiction, Writing/Journalism, Social Sciences. **Career:** U.S. Fish and Wildlife Service, writer. **Publications:** Patents: Ingenious Inventions: How They Work and How They Came to Be, 2004; The Daredevil's Manual, 2004; The Blokes' Book of Bloody Terrifying Stuff, 2009. Contributor of articles to periodicals. **Address:** c/o Terry Rossignol, Attwater Prairie Chicken National Wildlife Refuge, PO Box 519, Eagle Lake, TX 77434-0519, U.S.A.

ILAHIANE, Hsain. American (born United States) **Genres:** Intellectual History, Information Science/Computers, Adult Non-fiction. **Career:** United States Agency for International Development, consultant, 1991; CARE/USA, consultant, 1998; University of Arizona, instructor in anthropology, 1998, research associate, 1999; Iowa State University, assistant professor, 1999-2005, associate professor of anthropology, 2005-09, African and Middle Eastern Studies, director; Intel Corp., visiting senior researcher, 2006-07; University of Kentucky, Department of Anthrology, associate professor, 2009-. Writer. **Publications:** (Contrib.) Canals and Communities: Small-Scale Irrigation Systems, 1996; (contrib.) Charting Memory: Recalling Medieval Spain, 1999; (contrib.) Natural Communities? Ethnicity, Gender, and the State in Community-Based Conservation, 2001; (contrib.) Islanders and Mainlanders: Prehistoric Context for the Southern California Bight, 2002; (contrib.) Connected for Development: Information Kiosks and Sustainability, 2003; Ethnicities, Community Making, and Agrarian Change: The Political Ecology of a Moroccan Oasis, 2004; The Historical Dictionary of the Berbers, 2006. Contributor to books and journals. **Address:** Department of Anthropology, University of Kentucky, 211A Lafferty Hall, Ames, IA 50011-1050, U.S.A. **Online address:** hsain@iastate.edu

ILES, Jane. British (born England), b. 1954. **Genres:** Crafts, Art/Art History, Homes/Gardens. **Career:** Freelance writer and designer, 1976-81, 1985-; teacher, 1982-86. **Publications:** (With S. De Leon and V. Skelton) Machine Embroidery, 1979; Old English Roses in Needlework, 1986; Learn Embroidery, 1987; The Needlework Garden: Inspiring Designs for Creative Embroidery, 1989; Wildflowers in Cross Stitch: Twenty-Three Creative Embroidery Designs, 1990; (ed.) Embroidery Projects Book, 1990; Needlework Magic: Over 25 Original Embroidery Projects for Your Home, 1993; Old English Roses in Embroidery, 1994; Cross Stitch Country Garden, 1996. Contributor to books and magazines. **Address:** c/o Jane Judd, Jane Judd Literary Agency, 18 Belitha Villas, Barnsbury, London, GL N1 1PD, England.

ILESANMI, Simeon O. American/Nigerian (born Nigeria), b. 1963?. **Genres:** Institutions/Organizations, History, Ethics, Politics/Government, Theology/Religion. **Career:** Wake Forest University, faculty, 1993-, assistant professor of religion, associate professor, professor, director of graduate studies, 2006-, Washington M. Wingate professor of religion; Princeton University, visiting fellow, 1999-2000; Journal of Religious Ethics, associate editor. **Publications:** Religious Pluralism and the Nigerian State, 1997. **Address:** Department of Religion, Wake Forest University, 208 Wingate, PO Box 7212, Reynolda Sta., Winston-Salem, NC 27109-7212, U.S.A. **Online address:** ilesanmi@wfu.edu

ILIE, Paul. American (born United States), b. 1932. **Genres:** Literary Criticism And History, Art/Art History, Intellectual History, Young Adult Fiction. **Career:** University of Michigan, instructor, 1959-62, assistant professor, 1962-64, associate professor, 1964-68, professor of Spanish and comparative literature, 1968-82; National Endowment for Humanities, director, 1973-76; University of Southern California, professor of Spanish and comparative literature, 1982, professor emeritus of Spanish and comparative literature, retired, 1997. Writer. **Publications:** La novelistica de Camilo Jose Cela, 1963, 3rd ed. 1978; Unamuno: An Existential View of Self and Society, 1967; The

Surrealistic Mode in Spanish Literature, 1968; (ed.) Documents of the Spanish Vanguard, 1969; Los surrealistas espanoles, 1974; Literature and Inner Exile, 1981; The Age of Minerva, vol. II, 1995; The Grotesque Aesthetic in Spanish Literature, from the Golden Age to Modernism, 2009. **Address:** Department of Spanish and Comparative Literature, University of Southern California, 3620 S Vermont Ave., Los Angeles, CA 90089, U.S.A. **Online address:** pilie@usc.edu

ILLOUZ, Eva. Israeli/Moroccan (born Morocco), b. 1961. **Genres:** Cultural/Ethnic Topics, Self Help. **Career:** Hebrew University, senior lecturer, 2000-04, associate professor, 2004-07, professor, 2007-; Northwestern University, visiting professor; Princeton University, visiting professor; School for Advanced Studies in the Social Sciences, visiting professor; Institute for Advanced Study, fellow. Writer. **Publications:** Consuming the Romantic Utopia: Love and the Cultural Contradictions of Capitalism, 1997; Oprah Winfrey and the Glamour of Misery: An Essay on Popular Culture, 2003; Cold Intimacies: The Making of Emotional Capitalism, 2007; Saving the Modern Soul: Therapy, Emotions, and the Culture of Self-Help, 2008. **Address:** Department of Sociology and Anthropology, Faculty of Social Sciences, Hebrew University, Mt. Scopus, Jerusalem, 91905, Israel. **Online address:** illouz@mscc.huji.ac.il

ILSLEY, George K. Canadian (born Canada), b. 1958?. **Genres:** Novels, Gay And Lesbian Issues. **Career:** Writer. **Publications:** Random Acts of Hatred (short stories), 2003; ManBug (novel), 2006. Works appear in anthologies. **Address:** Arsenal Pulp Press, 101 - 211 East Georgia St., Vancouver, BC V6A 1Z6, Canada. **Online address:** george@thatwriter.ca

IMBARRATO, Susan Clair. American (born United States), b. 1954?. **Genres:** Autobiography/Memoirs, Women's Studies And Issues, History. **Career:** Minnesota State University, professor of English. Writer. **Publications:** Declarations of Independency in Eighteenth-Century American Autobiography, 1998; Traveling Women: Narrative Visions of Early America, 2006; (ed.) Women Writing Home, 1700-1920: Female Correspondence across the British Empire, vol. VI, 2006; (ed.) Encyclopedia of American Literature, vol. I: Settlement to the New Republic (1607-1820), 2nd ed., 2008. **Address:** Minnesota State University, 1104 7th Ave. S, Moorhead, MN 56563-0001, U.S.A. **Online address:** simbarra@mnstate.edu

IMBROSCIO, David L. American (born United States) **Genres:** Politics/Government. **Career:** National Center for Economic and Security Alternatives, senior research associate, 1999-2000; University of Louisville, Department of Political Science, assistant professor, 1993-99, director of graduate studies, 1996-99, 2000-01, associate professor of political science, 1999-2005, professor of political science and public and urban affairs, 2005-, PhD Program Urban and Public Affairs, program faculty, 2003-. Writer. **Publications:** Reconstructing City Politics: Alternative Economic Development and Urban Regimes, 1997; (with T. Williamson and G. Alperovitz) Making a Place for Community: Local Democracy in a Global Era, 2002; (ed. with J.S. Davies) Theories of Urban Politics, 2009; Urban America Reconsidered: Alternatives for Governance and Policy, 2010; (ed. with J.S. Davies) Critical Urban Studies: New Directions, 2010; (ed. with J.S. Davies) Urban Politics, 2010. Contributor to periodicals. **Address:** Department of Political Science, University of Louisville, Rm. 107, Ford Hall, 1st Fl., Belknap Campus, Louisville, KY 40292, U.S.A. **Online address:** imbroscio@louisville.edu

IMES, Birney. American (born United States), b. 1951. **Genres:** Photography, History. **Career:** Columbus Commercial Dispatch, photographer, 1973-; Art Institute of Chicago, staff, 1987; independent photographer and author. **Publications:** Juke Joint: Photographs, 1990; Partial to Home (photographs), 1994; Whispering Pines (photographs), 1994. **Address:** Twentieth Century Photography Ltd., 315 E 62nd St., New York, NY 10021, U.S.A.

IMHOFF, Dan. See **IMHOFF, Daniel.**

IMHOFF, Daniel. (Dan Imhoff). American (born United States) **Genres:** Natural History. **Career:** Watershed Media, president & co-founder; Wild Farm Alliance national sustainable agricultural promotion organization, co-founder; Farm and Garden radio show, Mendocino County Public Broadcasting, co-host; Esprit International, communications director, 1990-95. Writer. **Publications:** Building with Vision: Optimizing and Finding Alternatives to Wood, 2001; (with R. Carra) Farming with the Wild: Enhancing Biodiversity on Farms and Ranches, 2003; Paper or Plastic: Searching for Solutions to an

Overpackaged World, 2005; (ed. with J.A. Baumgartner) Farming and the Fate of Wild Nature: Essays in Conservation-based Agriculture, 2006; Foodfight: The Citizen's Guide to a Food and Farm Bill, 2007. Contributor to periodicals. **Address:** Watershed Media, 451 Hudson St., Healdsburg, CA 95448, U.S.A. **Online address:** danimhoff@pacific.net

IMMELL, Myra H. American (born United States), b. 1941. **Genres:** Children's Non-fiction, Young Adult Non-fiction. **Career:** Merrill Publishing Co., foreign languages editorial staff, 1969-74, social studies editorial staff, 1976-85, managing editor of social studies, 1986-89, acting executive director of social studies, 1989-90; Quest Intl., director of high school programs, 1993-96; Meeks Heit Publishing Co., managing editor, 1996-97; L3Comm, director of projects, 1997-2000; USi, proposal writer, 2000-04; Redemtech Inc., business communications specialist, 2004-07, 2007-. **Publications:** Automobiles: Connecting People and Places, 1994; (with W.H. Immell) Tecumseh, 1997; Han Dynasty, 2003. EDITOR: (with M. Sader) The Young Adult Reader's Adviser, 1992; Readings on the Diary of a Young Girl, 1998; Eating Disorders, 1999; 1900s, 2000; Ethnic Violence, 2000; Teen Pregnancy, 2000; World War II, 2001; World Wars, 2002; Teens and Sex, 2002; The Han Dynasty, 2003; Homeschooling, 2009; Homeland Security, 2010; The Dissolution of the Soviet Union, 2010; The Cuban Missile Crisis, 2010; The Creation of the State of Israel, 2010; Israel, 2010; The McCarthy Era, 2011. **Address:** 5548 Brighton Hill Ln., Dublin, OH 43016, U.S.A. **Online address:** Immellm@columbus.rr.com

IMOUKHUEDE, Mabel. *See* **SEGUN, Mabel D.**

IMPEY, Chris. British/Scottish (born Scotland), b. 1956. **Genres:** Astronomy, Education. **Career:** University of Edinburgh and Royal Observatory, research assistant, 1977-81; University of Arizona, Steward Observatory, assistant professor, 1986-91, associate professor, 1991-96, professor, 1996-2000, distinguished professor, 2000-, associate director, NASA Space Grant, 1991-95, Department of Astronomy, deputy department head, 1999-; University of Washington, Department of Astronomy, visiting professor, 1995-96. Writer. **Publications:** (With W.K. Hartmann) Astronomy: The Cosmic Journey, 5th ed., 1994, 6th ed., 2002; (ed. with J.I. Davies and S. Phillipps) The Low Surface Brightness Universe: IAU Colloquium 171: Proceedings of an IAU Colloquium Held at Cardiff, Wales, 5-10 July, 1998, 1999; (with W.K. Hartmann) The Universe Revealed, 2000; The Living Cosmos: Our Search for Life in the Universe, 2007; Talking About Life: Conversations on Astrobiology, 2010; How It Ends: From You to the Universe, 2010; How it Began: A Time-Traveler's Guide to the Universe, 2012. **Address:** Department of Astronomy, University of Arizona, Main Office, 933 N Cherry Ave., Ste. N204, Tucson, AZ 85721-0065, U.S.A. **Online address:** cimpey@as.arizona.edu

IMPOLA, Richard A(arre). American (born United States), b. 1923. **Genres:** Translations, Literary Criticism And History, Novels. **Career:** Michigan Technological University, instructor, assistant professor, 1950-62; State University of New York College, assistant professor, associate professor, 1963-83, professor of English. Writer. **Publications:** TRANSLATOR: K. Paatalo, Our Daily Bread (novel), 1990; A. Kivi, Seven Brothers (novel), 1991; T. Yliruusi, Hand in Hand (novel), 1992; K. Paatalo, Storm Over the Land (novel), 1993; A. Tervasmaa, The Life and Times of an Ordinary Captain, 1994; E. Joenpelto, The Bride of Life (novel), 1995; E. Komulainen, A Grave in Karelia (novel), 1995; (comp.) Words of Wisdom and Magic from the Kalevala (poetry), 1998; J. Mattinen, The History of Thomson Township (local history), 2000; K. Paatalo, Before the Storm (novel), 2000; V. Linna, Under the North Star (novel), 2001; J. Rislakki, No Home for Us Here (history), 2002; L. Wilson, Sisu Mother (memoirs), 2002; K. Paatalo, After the Storm (novel), 2002; K. Paatalo, The Winter of the Black Snow (novel), 2002; V. Linna, Under the North Star: The Uprising (novel), 2002; V. Linna, Under the North Star: The Reconciliation (novel), 2003; J. Aho, Juha: A Novel, 2005; M. Canth, The Burglary; The House of Roinila: Two Early Plays, 2010. EDITOR: (with S. Stone) Texts in Translation: Kielikannas, 1992; (with K. Virtanen and T. Onnela) Finnish Literature in North America: Papers Presented at the First Two Symposia on Finnish Literature in North America, 1994. Contributor to periodicals. **Address:** Aspasia Books Inc., 25040 Maple Beach Rd., RR 1, Beaverton, ON L0K 1A0, Canada. **Online address:** impolar@newpaltz.edu

INCH, Morris Alton. American (born United States), b. 1925. **Genres:** Theology/Religion. **Career:** Gordon College, associate professor of Christian education, 1955-62, academic dean, 1959-62, dean of students, 1960-61;

Wheaton College, professor of theology, 1962-86, Department of Religious Studies, chairman, 1969-84, professor emeritus, 1986; Institute of Holy Land Studies, president, 1986-90; Institutul Biblique din Oradea Romania, visiting professor, 1991-93. Writer. **Publications:** Psychology in the Psalms, 1969; Christianity without Walls, 1972; Paced by God, 1973; Celebrating Jesus as Lord, 1974; (ed. with S.J. Schultz) Interpreting the Word of God, 1976; Understanding Bible Prophecy, 1977; The Evangelical Challenge, 1978; My Servant Job, 1979; (ed.) The Literature and Meaning of Scripture, 1981; Doing Theology across Cultures, 1982; (with R. Youngblood) Living and Active Word of God: Studies in Honor of Samuel J. Schultz, 1983; Saga of the Spirit: A Biblical, Systematic and Historical Theology of the Holy Spirit, 1985; Making the Good News Relevant: Keeping the Gospel Distinctive in Any Culture, 1986; Making the Gospel Relevant, 1986; Revelation across Cultures, 1995; Charting a Good Church Trip, 1995; Exhortations of Jesus According to Matthew, 1997; Up from the Depths: Mark as Tragedy, 1997; A Case for Christianity, 1997; Sage Sayings, 1997; Chaos Paradigm: A Theological Exploration, 1998; In Tune with God: A User-Friendly Theology, 1998; Man: The Perennial Question, 1999; Devotions with David, 2000; Demetrius the Disciple, 2000; Casey and Tonka, 2000; Scripture as Story, 2000; Two Gospel Motifs, 2001; The High God, 2001; Why Take the Bible Seriously?, 2001; Whispers of Heaven, 2002; 12 Who Changed the World, 2003; Why Take Jesus Seriously?, 2003; Two Mosaic Motifs, 2003; Elder Brother: A Christian Alternative to Anti-Semitism, 2005; Matthew in the Messianic Tradition, 2006; Why Take the Church Seriously?, 2006; Service Is As Service Does, 2006; In Christ & On Track, 2008; Potpourri: Common Sense & the Conspiracies, Covenant Echoes, Amos Still Speaks, 2008; Pain As a Means of Grace, 2009; Space/Time Odyssey, 2009; The Wonder of It All: Mystery and Meaning in Scripture, 2009; Thumbs Up For the Family, 2010; Enigma of Justice, 2010. **Address:** 349 Cagle Rock Cir., Russellville, AR 72802, U.S.A. **Online address:** minch@centurytel.net

INDIANA, Gary. American (born United States), b. 1950. **Genres:** Novels, Novellas/Short Stories, Essays, Plays/Screenplays, Young Adult Non-fiction, History, Social Sciences. **Career:** Village Voice, senior art critic, 1985-88. Novelist. **Publications:** FICTION: Scar Tissue (stories) 1987; White Trash Boulevard (stories), 1988; Last Seen Entering the Biltmore, 2008. NOVELS: Horse Crazy, 1989; Gone Tomorrow, 1993; Rent Boy, 1993; Resentment: A Comedy, 1997; Depraved Indifference, 2001; Do Everything in the Dark, 2003; The Shanghai Gesture: A Novel, 2009. OTHERS: Roberto Juarez (nonfiction), 1986; (contrib.) Hybrid Neutral: Modes of Abstraction and the Social, 1988; (ed.) Living with the Animals, 1994; Let It Bleed: Essays, 1985-1995, 1995; Front Pages, 1997; Three Month Fever: The Andrew Cunanan Story, 1999; Salò or the 120 Days of Sodom, 2000; Viridiana, 2004; Schwarzenegger Syndrome: Politics and Celebrity in the Age of Contempt, 2005; Taylor Mead, A Simple Country Girl, 2005; Utopia's Debris: Selected Essays (nonfiction), 2008; Dike Blair: Now and Again, 2009; Andy Warhol and the Can That Sold the World, 2010; Last Seen Entering the Biltmore: Selected Writings 1976-1994, forthcoming. Contributor to books and periodicals. **Address:** Doubleday Publishers, 1540 Broadway, New York, NY 10036-4039, U.S.A.

INDRIDASON, Arnaldur. Icelander (born Iceland), b. 1961. **Genres:** Criminology/True Crime, Novels. **Career:** Morgunblao, journalist, 1981-82, film critic, 1986-2001. **Publications:** CRIME FICTION: Synir duftsins, 1997; Sons of Dust, 1997; Dauoarósir, 1998; Silent Kill, 1998; Mýrin, 2000; Tainted Blood, 2000; Jar City, 2000; Grafarpögn, 2001; Silence of the Grave, 2001; Röddin, 2003; Voices, 2003; Kleifarvatn, 2004; The Draining Lake, 2004; Vetrarborgin, 2005; Arctic Chill, 2005; Harskafi, 2007; Hypothermia, 2007; Draining Lake, 2008; Myrká, 2008; Svörtuloft, 2009. NOVELS: Napóleonsskjölin, 1999; Bettý, 2003; Konungsbók, 2006; Operation Napolean, 2010; Outrage, 2011. **Address:** c/o Author Mail, Department of Publicity, St. Martin, 175 5th Ave., New York, NY 10010, U.S.A.

INEZ, Colette. American/Belgian (born Belgium), b. 1931. **Genres:** Poetry, Autobiography/Memoirs. **Career:** Writer and teacher, 1961-71; New York University, adult education teacher, 1962-63; National Academy of Ballet, instructor, 1963-64; Federal Title III Anti-poverty Program, instructor, 1964-70; Denison University, Beck lecturer in poetry, 1974; New School University, Poetry Workshop, instructor, 1974-83; State University of New York, Poetry Workshop, lecturer, 1975-76; Kalamazoo College, visiting professor, 1976, 1978, 1981, 1985, 1989, 1993; Hunter College, staff, 1979-80; Columbia University, School of the Arts, lecturer on poetry, 1983-; Ohio University, staff, 1990-91; Bucknell University, poet-in-residence, 1992; Colorado State University, staff, 1993; Cornell University, staff, 1998; Colgate University, staff, 2000; University of Tennessee, staff, 1996. **Publications:** The Woman Who Loved Worms and other Poems, 1972; Alive and Taking Names, and Other Poems, 1977; Eight Minutes from the Sun, 1983; Family Life: Poems, 1988; Getting Underway: New and Selected Poetry, 1992; Naming the Moons, 1994; For Reasons of Music, 1994; Clemency, 1998; (contrib.) The Way Home: On the Poetry of Colette Inez, 2003; Spinoza Doesn't Come Here Anymore: Poems, 2004; Secret of M. Dulong: A Memoir, 2005; Horseplay, 2011. Works appear in anthologies. Contributor to books and journals. **Address:** 5 W 86th St., Apt. 6E, New York, NY 10024, U.S.A. **Online address:** ci1@columbia.edu

ING, Dean. American (born United States), b. 1931. **Genres:** Novellas/Short Stories, Mystery/Crime/Suspense, Science Fiction/Fantasy, Air/Space Topics, Military/Defense/Arms Control, Novels. **Career:** Aerojet-General, engineer, 1957-62; Lockheed & United Technologies, senior engineer, 1962-70; Missouri State University, assistant professor of speech, psycholinguistics and media, 1974-77; freelance writer, 1977-. **Publications:** NOVELS: Soft Targets, 1979; Systemic Shock, 1981; Pulling Through, 1983; Single Combat, 1983; Wild Country, 1985; (with M. Reynolds) Deathwish World, 1986; Blood of Eagles, 1987; The Big Lifters, 1988; (with P. Anderson and L. Niven) Man-Kzin Wars II, 1989; The Ransom of Black Stealth One, 1989; Cathouse, 1989; The Nemesis Mission, 1991; Butcher Bird, 1993; Spooker, 1995; Flying to Pieces, 1997; The Skins of Dead Men, 1998; Loose Cannon, 2000; (with J. Pournelle and S.M. Sterling) Houses of the Kzinti, 2002; Rackham Files, 2004. NONFICTION: (with J. Pournelle) Mutual Assured Survival, 1984; (with L. Myrabo) The Future of Flight, 1985. STORIES: Anasazi, 1980; High Tension, 1982; Firefight 2000 (collection), 1987; The Chernobyl Syndrome (collection), 1987; The Rackham Files (collection), 2004. EDITED WITH M. REYNOLDS: The Lagrangists, 1983; Home Sweet Home 2010 A.D., 1984; Eternity, 1984. OTHERS: Why must They All Have My Face?, 1980; The Other Time, 1984; (with M. Reynolds) Trojan Orbit, 1985. Contributor of stories to magazines. **Address:** c/o Eleanor Wood, Spectrum Literary Agency, 320 Central Park W, Ste. 1-D, New York, NY 10025, U.S.A.

INGE, M. Thomas. American (born United States), b. 1936. **Genres:** Cultural/Ethnic Topics, Bibliography, Cartoons, Humor/Satire, Popular Culture, Graphic Novels, Film, Humanities, Literary Criticism And History. **Career:** Irby Studio, freelance commercial artist, 1953-55; Vanderbilt University, instructor of English, 1962-64; Michigan State University, assistant professor, associate professor of American thought and language, 1964-69; University of Salamanca, Fulbright lecturer, 1967-68; Virginia Commonwealth University, associate professor, 1969-73, professor of English, 1973-80, chair of the department, 1974-80; Moscow State University, Fulbright lecturer, 1979; University of Leningrad, Fulbright lecturer, 1979; Greenwood Press Reference Series on American Popular Culture, general editor, 1976-; Clemson University, professor of English and head of department, 1980-82; U.S. Information Agency, Summer Institute in American Studies for Foreign Scholars, director, 1993-95; Randolph-Macon College, Robert Emory Blackwell professor of humanities, 1984-; University of Helsinki, Fulbright lecturer, 1994; Odense University, Fulbright lecturer, 1994; University of Kiel, Fulbright lecturer, 1994. **Publications:** (With T.D. Young) Donald Davidson: An Essay and a Bibliography, 1965; (with T.D. Young) Donald Davidson, 1971; The American Comic Book, 1985; Comics in the Classroom, 1989; Comics as Culture; 1990; Great American Comics, 1990; Faulkner, Sut and Other Southerners, 1992; Perspectives on American Culture: Essays on Humor, Literature and the Popular Arts, 1994; Anything Can Happen in a Comic Strip, 1995; William Faulkner: Overlook Illustrated Lives, 2006; The Incredible Mr. Poe: Comic Book Adaptations of the Works of Edgar Allan Poe, 2008. EDITOR: Publications of the Faculty of the University College: A Bibliography, 1966; (with J.E. Caron) Sut Lovingood's Yarns, 1966; High Times and Hard Times: Sketches and Tales, 1967; Agrarianism in American Literature, 1969; Augustus Baldwin Longstreet: A Study of the Development of Culture in the South, 1969; (co-ed.) The Black Experience, 1969; Honors College Essays 1967-1968, 1969; Faulkner: A Rose for Emily, 1970; William Byrd of Westover, 1970; Studies in Light in August, 1971; Virginia Commonwealth University Self-Study, 1972; The Frontier Humorists, 1975; Ellen Glasgow: Centennial Essays, 1976; (with M. Duke and J.R. Bryer) Black American Writers: Bibliographical Essays, 2 vols., 1978; Bartleby the Inscrutable (collection of commentary on Melville story), 1979; Concise Histories of American Popular Culture, 1982; (with E.E. MacDonald) James Branch Cabell: Centennial Essays, 1983; (with M. Duke and J.R. Bryer) American Women Writers: Bibliographic Essays, 1983; Huck Finn among the Critics: A Centennial Selection, 1984; Sut Lovingood Yarns, 1987; Truman Capote:

Conversations, 1987; Handbook of American Popular Literature, 1988; Naming the Rose, 1988; A Nineteenth-Century American Reader, 1988; Handbook of American Popular Culture, 3 vols., 1978-81, 1989; C. Waugh, The Comics, 1991; (and intro.) Dark Laughter: The Satiric Art of Oliver W. Harrington, 1993; (and intro.) Why I Left America and Other Essays, 1993; (with S. Chakovsky) Russian Eyes on American Literature, 1993; William Faulkner: The Contemporary Reviews, 1994; (with J.E. Caron) Sut Lovingood's Natural Born Yarnspinner: Essays on George Washington Harris, 1996; (intro.) A Connecticut Yankee in King Arthur's Court, 1997; The Achievement of William Faulkner, 1998; Conversations with William Faulkner, 1999; (and intro.) Co. Aytch: Or, a Sideshow of the Big Show, 1999; Charles M. Schulz: Conversations, 2000; (with E. Piacentino) Humor of the Old South, 2001; (with D. Hall) The Greenwood Guide to American Popular Culture, 2002; (with D. Hall) Greenwood Guide to American Popular Culture, 4 vols., 2002; The New Encyclopedia of Southern Culture, vol. IX: Literature, 2008; (with E. Piacentino) Southern Frontier Humor: An Anthology, 2010; (ed. and intro.) My Life With Charlie Brown, 2010; Will Eisner, 2011. **Address:** Blackwell Chair in the Humanities, Randolph-Macon College, 202 Henry St., PO Box 5005, Ashland, VA 23005-5505, U.S.A. **Online address:** tinge@rmc.edu

INGERSOLL, Earl G(eorge). American (born United States), b. 1938. **Genres:** Literary Criticism And History, Novels. **Career:** State University of New York. The College at Brockport, instructor, 1964-71, assistant professor, 1971-87, associate professor, 1987-91, professor, 1991-96, distinguished teaching professor of English, 1996-2002, distinguished professor, 2002-, now distinguished professor emeritus. Writer. **Publications:** Representations of Science and Technology in British Literature since 1880, 1992; Engendered Trope in Joyce's Dubliners, 1996; D.H. Lawrence, Desire, and Narrative, 2001; Waiting for the End: Gender and Ending in the Contemporary Novel, 2007. EDITOR: (with J. Kitchen and S.S. Rubin) The Post-Confessionals: Conversations with American Poets of the Eighties, 1989; Margaret Atwood: Conversations, 1990; Conversations with May Sarton, 1991; Doris Lessing: Conversations, 1994; Putting the Questions Differently: Interviews with Doris Lessing, 1964-1994, 1996; Lawrence Durrell: Conversations, 1998; (with K. Cushman) D.H. Lawrence: New Worlds, 2003; Conversations with Rita Dove, 2003; Breaking the Alabaster Jar: Conversations with Li-Young Lee, 2006; Waltzing Again: New and Selected Conversations with Margaret Atwood, 2006; (with M.C. Ingersoll) Conversations with Anthony Burgess, 2008; (with V. Hyde) Windows to the Sun: D.H. Lawrence's Thought-Adventures, 2009; (with V. Hyde) Terra Incognita: D.H. Lawrence at the Frontiers, 2010. Contributor of articles to journals. **Address:** Department of English, State University of New York, 205 D Hartwell Hall, 350 New Campus Dr., Brockport, NY 14420-2968, U.S.A. **Online address:** eingersoll@brockport.edu

INGHAM, John N. Canadian/American (born United States), b. 1939. **Genres:** Biography, Business/Trade/Industry, Race Relations, Urban Studies. **Career:** Carnegie-Mellon University, lecturer in history, 1966-68; University of Bridgeport, instructor in history, 1968-70; State University of New York, assistant professor, associate professor of history, 1970-77; University of Toronto, associate professor, professor of history, 1977-. Writer. **Publications:** The Iron Barons: A Social Analysis of an American Urban Elite, 1978; Biographical Dictionary of American Business Leaders, 4 vols., 1983; The Rise of Popular Culture, 1985; (ed.) Assault on Victorianism: The Rise of Popular Culture in America, 1890-1945, 1987; (ed.) Sex 'n' Drugs 'n' Rock 'n' Roll: American Popular Culture since 1945, 1988; (with L.B. Feldman) Contemporary American Business Leaders, 1990; Making Iron and Steel, 1991; (with L.B. Feldman) African-American Business Leaders: A Biographical History, 1994. **Address:** Department of History, University of Toronto, 100 St. George St., Toronto, ON M5S 3G3, Canada. **Online address:** jningham@interlog.com

INGHAM, Kenneth. *See* Obituaries.

INGHAM, R(ichard) A(rnison). British (born England), b. 1935. **Genres:** Plays/Screenplays, Poetry, Education, Speech/Rhetoric, Novels. **Career:** Elland Finishing Co., trainee, manager, 1959-61; writer, 1961-63; teacher, 1963-68; Swaziland Broadcasting Service, writer, 1965-68; Hobbs Padgett Group, salesman, 1969-70; Ipswich Civic College, associate, 1970-75; Lewes Technical College, associate, 1975-76; Chippenham Technological College, lecturer in English and technical/management communications, 1977-, head of department, director of marketing, staff governor; Hebden Royd Urban District Council, councillor; wool trade, manager; Royal Air Force, officer;

Westgate Leaseholders Association, leaseholder, 1996-. Writer. **Publications:** Yoris: A Novel, 1974; (with J.M. Buffton) Making Contact, vol. I, 1979, vol. II, 1981; Fifteen from Twenty-Two (verse), 1979; Ski Whizz: A Comedy, 1990; France, 2000; Church Establishments Considered: Especially in Reference to the Church of England, 2007. **Address:** c/o Sheri Safran, 21 Ladbroke Gardens, London, GL W 11, England.

INGLE, Bob. American (born United States) **Genres:** Cultural/Ethnic Topics, History, Politics/Government. **Career:** Gannett Newspapers, Trenton bureau chief. Writer. **Publications:** (With S. McClure) The Soprano State: New Jersey's Culture of Corruption, 2008. **Address:** Daily Record, 800 Jefferson Rd., Parsippany, NJ 07054, U.S.A. **Online address:** bobingle@app.com

INGLIS, Janet. Canadian (born Canada), b. 1946. **Genres:** Novels, Literary Criticism And History, Young Adult Non-fiction. **Career:** Writer. **Publications:** NOVELS: Daddy's Girl, 1994; Father of Lies, 1995. NONFICTION: Food Technology, 1997; Collins Design and Technology Food Foundation Course, 1999; The Essentials of Gcse Design & Technology, 2002. OTHERS: Daddy, 1994; The Colour of Sin, 1998; Handling Holland: A Manual for International Women in the Netherlands, 2002. **Address:** David Higham Associates Ltd., 5-8 Lower John St., Golden Sq., London, GL W1F 9HA, England.

INGMAN, Nicholas. British (born England), b. 1948. **Genres:** Children's Non-fiction, Music, Young Adult Fiction. **Career:** Norrie Paramor's Independent Record Co., arranger and producer, 1969-75; Phonogram Records, featured conductor and arranger, 1976-; British Broadcasting Corp., musical director, Radio Orchestra, regular conductor, 1978; London Symphony Orchestra, staff; Royal Philharmonic Orchestra, staff; London Chamber Orchestra, staff. Writer. **Publications:** The Story of Music, 1972; What Instrument Shall I Play?, 1975; (with B. Brett) Gifted Children of Music: Lives of Great Musicians, 1978. **Address:** 10 The Gardens, East Dulwich, London, GL SE22 9QD, England.

INGRAM, Derek Thynne. British (born England), b. 1925. **Genres:** Politics/Government. **Career:** Daily Sketch, editorial assistant, 1942-43, 1946-47; Daily Express, sub-editor, 1947-49; Daily Mail, sub-editor, 1949-63, deputy editor, 1963-66; Gemini News Service, founder, editor, 1967-93; Commonwealth Institute, governor, 1972-88; Commonwealth Journal, editor, 1983-86; European Union Election Unit, media adviser, 1994; Commonwealth Journalists Association, co-founder and president; The Royal Commonwealth Society, vice president. **Publications:** Partners in Adventure, 1960; The Commonwealth Challenge, 1962; Commonwealth for a Colour-Blind World, 1965; The Commonwealth at Work, 1969; The Imperfect Commonwealth, 1977. Contributor to journals. **Address:** The Royal Commonwealth Society, 25 Northumberland Ave., London, GL WC2N 5AP, England. **Online address:** derekingram@gn.apc.org

INGRAM, Heather E(lizabeth). Canadian (born Canada), b. 1969?. **Genres:** Administration/Management, Biography. **Career:** Chatelech High School, teacher, 1994-99. Writer. **Publications:** Risking It All: My Student, My Lover, My Story, 2003. Contributor to periodicals. **Address:** c/o Author Mail, Greystone Books, Douglas & McIntyre Publishing Group, 2323 Quebec St., Ste. 201, Vancouver, BC V5T 4S7, Canada.

INGRAM, Paul O. American (born United States), b. 1939. **Genres:** Theology/Religion, Sciences, History. **Career:** University of California, faculty associate in religious studies, 1966; Simpson College, assistant professor, associate professor of religion, 1966-75; School of Theology, visiting professor of history of religions, 1973-74; Pacific Lutheran University, assistant professor, 1975-78, associate professor, 1978-89, professor of religion, 1989-, now professor emeritus. Writer. **Publications:** The Dharma of Faith, 1977; (ed. with F.J. Streng) Buddhist-Christian Dialogue: Mutual Renewal and Transformation, 1986; The Modern Buddhist-Christian Dialogue: Two Universalistic Religions in Transformation, 1988; Tibet: The Facts, 2nd rev. ed., 1990; Wrestling with the Ox: A Theology of Religious Experience, 1997; (ed.with S.B. King) The Sound of Liberating Truth: Buddhist-Christian Dialogues in Honor of Frederick J. Streng 1933-1993, 1999; Buddhist-Christian Dialogue in An Age of Science, 2007; Process of Buddhist-Christian Dialogue, 2009; Theological Reflections at the Boundaries, 2012. **Address:** Department of Religion Lecture, Pacific Lutheran University, Rm. 222, Hauge Administration Bldg., Tacoma, WA 98447, U.S.A. **Online address:** ingrampo@plu.edu

INGVES, Gunilla. Swedish (born Sweden), b. 1939. **Genres:** Children's

Fiction, Animals/Pets, Illustrations, Sciences, Natural History. **Career:** Oestgoeta Correspondenten, illustrator, 1962-74. Writer. **Publications:** Animals on the Farm, 1982; The Dandelion, 1983; The Fly, 1983; The Grasshopper, 1983; The Ladybird, 1983; The Mushroom, 1983; The Potato, 1985; The Ant, 1985. **Address:** Uttersbo, Vikingstad, 59050, Sweden.

IN-HO, Choi. Korean (born Korea (South)), b. 1945. **Genres:** Novels, Literary Criticism And History. **Career:** Yonsei University, Department of Life Science, professor and chair. Writer. **Publications:** Pyolt ur ui kohyang (title means: 'Stars' Hometown'), 1972; Cham chanun sinhwa: yonjak changp'yon, 1974; Ch'on'guk ui kyedan: changp'yon sosol, 1979; Kajok: yonjakchang p'yon (essays), 1979; Nuga ch'onjaerul chugyonnun'ga, 1979; Chiguin: ponkyok taeha sosol, 1980; Pulsae: changp'yon sosol, 1980; Todani ui kurim, 1981; (co-author) Kipko p'urun pam oe: '82 che 6-hoe Yi Sang Munhaksang susang chakp'umjip (title means: 'The Deep Blue Night'), 1982; Chokto ui kkot, 1982; Nae maum ui p'ungch'a; Kaemi ui t'ap oe 3-p'yon, 1982; Chollamhoe kurim: cham chanun sinhwa yonjak changp'yon, 1983; Kamyon mudoho, 1983; Korae sanyang, 1983; Mul wi ui sama, 1983; Songnyo wa angnyorul wihayo, 1983; Kyoul nagune: Ch'oe In-ho changp'yon sosol, 1984; T'ain ui pangg: Ch'oe In-ho susang chakp'umjip, (title means: 'The Stranger's Room'), 1984; Ch'oe In-ho munhak chonjip, 1984; Kajok: sosollo ssun chasojon (essays), 1984; Hwanghol yonsup: Ch'oe In-ho changp'yon sosol, 1985; Chilp'ung nodo: Ch'oe In-ho taeha yoksa sosol, 1986; Ch'oe In-ho, 1986; Hwang Chin-i: Ch'oe In-ho usu tanp'yon sonjip, 1986; Iroborin wangguk: Ch'oe In-ho taeha yoksa sosol, 1986; Pimil ui mun: Ch'oe In-ho taeha yoksa sosol, 1986; (with Y. Chong-jun and K. Won-il) Pam kwa an'gae ui tosi, 1986; Tasi mannal ttae kkaji, 1987; Sarang ui chongyom: Ch'oe In-ho changp'yon sarang sosol, 1987; Sin Paekcherul ch'ajaso, 1987; Sinario sonjip, 1987; Tosi ui sanyangkkun: Ch'oe In-ho changp'yon sarang sosol, 1987; Paekche yo, Paekche yo: Ch'oe In- ho taeha yoksa sosol, 1987; Tulkkot han songi to sarang in kot ul: sam kwa kodok kwa sarang ui sinjak esei, 1987; Annyong haseyo Hananim: Ch'oe In- ho changp'yon sosol, 1987; Ch'oe In-ho, 1987; Kkum kkunun noma: Ch'oe In-ho tonghwajip, 1987; Kodokhan pulkkot: Ch'oe In-ho changp'yon sarang sosol, 1987; O no nou: Ch'oe In-ho maenbal ro segye rul tolta=Oh, No No!, 1987; Sulkkun: Ch'oe In-ho taep'yo chakp'umson, 1987; Turebak ul ollyora: Ch'oe In-ho usu sosolchip, 1988; Toroun son: Ch'oe In-ho usu tanp'yon sonjip, 1988; Omoni ku kuriun irum iyo: Ch'oe In-ho omonirul wihan kul moumjip, 1988; Chamdulgi chon e kayahal mon kil: Ch'oe In-ho saero ssun insaengnon, 1988; Hwangdo ui norae, 1988; Hundullinun song: Ch'oe In-ho changp'yon sosol, 1989; Todani: Ch'oe In-ho tonghwajip, 1989; Cham chanun sinhwa: Ch'oe In-ho yonjak sosol, 1990; Ch'ossarang: Ch'oe In-ho changp'yon sosol, 1990; Omoni ka karuch'yo chun norae: Ch'oe In-ho yonjak sosol, 1991; Pukkuroum e kwanhan myongsang: Ch'oe In-ho saenggak hanun kul, 1991; Saramdul sai e som I itta: Ch'oe In-ho taep'yo esei, 1991; Lut, 1992; Sinario chonjip, 1992; Tol ui ch'osang, 1992; Hosuabi: Ch'oe In-ho changp'yon sosol, 1993; Kil omnun kil: Ch'oe In-ho changp'yon sosol, 1993; Wangdo ui pimil: Ch'oe In-ho changp'yon sosol, 1995; Ch'oe In-ho munhaksang susang chakp'umjip, 2000; Nalk'aroun ch'ot k'isu ui ch'uok: Ch'oe In-ho p'angse, 2000; Sangdo: Ch'oe In-ho changp'yon sosol, 2000; Talk'omhan insaeng: Ch'oe In- ho sosolchip, 2001; Tower of Ants, 2004; Hanul eso naeryo on ppang: Ch'oe In-ho ui muksang iyagi, 2005; Yurim, 2005; Che-4 ui cheguk: Ch'oe In-ho changp'yon sosol, 2006; Munjang: Ch'oe In-ho susangnok, 2006; Mojori k'ullop: Ch'oe In-ho changp'yon sosol, 2008; Sanjung ilgi: Ch'oe In-ho sondap esei, 2008; (with S.P. Chongha) Ch'oe In-ho ui inyon: Ch'oe In-ho esei, 2010. Contributor to periodicals. **Address:** Department of Life Science, Yonsei University, 262 Seongsanno, Seodaemun-gu, Seoul, 120-749, Korea (South). **Online address:** ichoi@dragon.yonsei.ac.kr

INIGO, Martin. *See* **MILES, Keith.**

INKPEN, Mick. British (born England), b. 1952. **Genres:** Children's Fiction, Young Adult Fiction, Theology/Religion, Animals/Pets, Illustrations. **Career:** Graphic designer, 1970-86; freelance writer and illustrator of children's books, 1986-. **Publications:** SELF-ILLUSTRATED WITH N. BUTTERWORTH: The Nativity Play, 1985; The House on the Rock, 1986; The Precious Pearl, 1986; The Lost Sheep, 1986; The Two Sons, 1986; Nice and Nasty: A Book of Opposites in US as Nice or Nasty: A Book of Opposites, 1987; I Wonder at the Zoo, 1987; I Wonder in the Garden, 1987: I Wonder in the Country, 1987; I Wonder at the Farm, 1987 in US as I Wonder on the Farm, 1994; Who Made...In the Country, 1987; Who Made the Garden, 1987; Sports Day, 1988; The Magpie's Story: Jesus and Bacchaeus, 1988; The Mouse's Story: Jesus and the Storm, 1988; The Cat's Story: Jesus at the

Wedding, 1988; The Fox's Story: Jesus Is Born, 1988; The Good Stranger, 1989; Just Like Jasper!, 1989; The Little Gate, 1989; The Rich Farmer, 1989; Ten Silver Coins, 1989; The School Trip, 1990; The Wonderful Earth, 1990; Field Day, 1991; Jasper's Beanstalk, 1992; Opposites, 1997; Stories Jesus Told, 2002; Animal Tales, 2002. SELF-ILLUSTRATED: One Bear at Bedtime: A Counting Book, 1987; If I Had a Pig, 1988; If I Had a Sheep, 1988; Jojo's Revenge, 1989; The Blue Balloon, 1989; Gumboot's Chocolatey Day, 1989; Threadbear, 1990; Billy's Beetle, 1991; Penguin Small, 1992; Anything Cuddly Will Do!, 1993; Crocodile!, 1993; The Very Good Dinosaur, 1993; This Troll, That Troll, 1993; Lullabyhullaballoo!, 1993; Don't Do That, 1996; Bear, 1997; Little Spotty Thing, 1997; Say Aaah!, 1997; Silly Billies, 1997; Nothing, 1998; The Great Pet Sale, 1999; Hissss!, 1999; In Wibbly's Garden, 2000; Meow!, 2000; Rocket, 2001; Skates, 2001; Inkpen Treasury, 2003; Blue Nose Island: Ploo and the Terrible Gnobbler, 2003; Blue Nose Island: Beachmoles and Bellvine, 2004. KIPPER SERIES: Kipper, 1991; Kipper's Toybox, 1992; Kipper's Birthday, 1993; Kipper's Book of Colours, 1994; Kipper's Book of Counting, 1994 in US as Kipper's Book of Numbers, 1995; Kipper's Book of Opposites, 1994; Kipper's Book of Weather, 1994; Where, Oh Where, Is Kipper's Bear: A Pop-Up Book with Light!, 1994; Kipper's Snowy Day, 1996; Kipper's Christmas Eve, 1999; Kipper's A to Z: An Alphabet Adventure, 2000; Kipper and Roly, 2001; Kipper and the Egg, 2001; Kipper's Rainy Day, 2001; Kipper's Sunny Day, 2001; Kipper's Sticky Paws, 2001; Kipper's Basket, 2002; Kipper's Kite, 2002; Kipper's Lost Ball, 2002; Kipper's Monster, 2002; Kipper's Tree House, 2002; Kipper's Surprise, 2002; Kipper's Balloon, 2002; Kipper's Beach Ball, 2003. LITTLE KIPPER SERIES: Arnold, 1998; Honk!, 1998; Sandcastle, 1998; Splosh!, 1998; Butterfly, 1999; Swing!, 2000; Picnic, 2001; Thing!, 2001; Miaow, 2007. WIBBLY PIG SERIES: Wibbly Pig Is Upset, 1995; Wibbly Pig Can Dance!, 1995; Wibbly Pig Can Make a Tent, 1995; Wibbly Pig Likes Bananas, 1995; Wibbly Pig Makes Pictures, 1995; Wibbly Pig Opens His Presents, 1995; Everyone Hide from Wibbly Pig, 1997; In Wibbly's Garden, 2000; Is It Bedtime Wibbly Pig?, 2004. OTHER: Wibbly Pig is Happy!, 2000. **Address:** Hodder & Stoughton Ltd., 338 Euston Rd., London, GL NW1 3BH, England.

INNES, Jean. *See* **SAUNDERS, Jean (Innes).**

INNESS, Sherrie A. American (born United States), b. 1965. **Genres:** Women's Studies And Issues, Psychology. **Career:** University of California, instructor in writing and in dimensions of culture, 1989-93; Miami University, assistant professor, 1993-94, associate professor of English, 1994-. Writer. **Publications:** Intimate Communities: Representation and Social Transformation in Women's College Fiction, 1895-1910, 1995; The Lesbian Menace: Ideology, Identity and the Representation of Lesbian Life, 1997; Tough Girls: Women Warriors and Wonder Women in Popular Culture, 1999; Dinner Roles: American Women and Culinary Culture, 2001; Secret Ingredients: Race, Gender and Class at the Dinner Table, 2006. EDITOR: (with D. Royer) Breaking Boundaries: New Perspectives on Women's Regional Writing, 1997; Nancy Drew and Company: Culture, Gender and Girls' Series, 1997; Delinquents and Debutantes: Twentieth-Century American Girls' Cultures, 1998; Millennium Girls: Today's Girls Around the World, 1998; Running For Their Lives: Girls, Cultural Identity and Stories of Survival, 2000; Cooking Lessons: The Politics of Gender And Food, 2001; Kitchen Culture in America: Popular Representations of Food, Gender and Race, 2001; Pilaf, Pozole and Pad Thai: American Women and Ethnic Food, 2001; Disco Divas: Women and Popular Culture in the 1970s, 2003; Action Chicks: New Images of Tough Women in Popular Culture, 2004; Geek Chic: Smart Women in Popular Culture, 2007. Contributor to books. Contributor to books and journals. **Address:** Department of English, Miami University, 227C Rentschler, 356 Bachelor Hall, Hamilton Campus, Hamilton, OH 45011, U.S.A. **Online address:** inness@muohio.edu

INNESS-BROWN, Elizabeth (Ann). American (born United States), b. 1954. **Genres:** Novels, Novellas/Short Stories, Literary Criticism And History. **Career:** University of Southern Mississippi, assistant professor of English, 1979-84, Center for Writers Graduate Program in Creative Writing, acting director, 1983, associate professor of English, 1985-86; St. Lawrence University, visiting assistant professor, 1984-85; University of Hartford, visiting writer, 1987-88; Norwich University, Vermont College, Graduate Program, field faculty, 1988-90, Adult Degree Program, adjunct faculty, 1988-90; St. Michael's College, English lecturer, 1988-90, Writing Center, director, 1988-, assistant professor of English, 1990-94, associate professor of English, 1994-, professor of English. **Publications:** STORIES: Satin Palms, 1981; Here, 1994. OTHER: Burning Marguerite (novel), 2002. Works represented in an-

thologies. Contributor to periodicals. **Address:** Department of English, St. Michael's College, St. Edmund's Hall 333, 1 Winooski Pk., PO Box 277, Colchester, VT 05439-1000, U.S.A. **Online address:** einness-brown@smcvt.edu

INNIS, Robert E(dward). American (born United States), b. 1941. **Genres:** Language/Linguistics, Philosophy, Humanities. **Career:** Fordham University, instructor in philosophy, 1968-69; University of Massachusetts, instructor, 1969-70, assistant professor, 1970-73, associate professor, 1973-77, professor of philosophy, 1977-, university professor, 1981-84; University of Copenhagen, Fulbright professor, 1990-91. Writer. **Publications:** (Trans. and intro.) G. Brand, The Central Texts of Ludwig Wittgenstein, 1979; Karl Buehler: Semiotic Foundations of Language Theory, 1982; (ed. and intro.) Semiotics: An Introductory Anthology, 1985; (ed. and intro.) Meaning and Context: An Introduction to the Psychology of Language, 1986; (trans.) J.C. Hoffbauer, Tentamina Semiologica (title means: 'Semiological Investigations, or Topics Pertaining to the General Theory of Signs'), 1991; Consciousness and the Play of Signs, 1994; Pragmatism and the Forms of Sense: Language, Perception, Technics, 2002; Susanne Langer in Focus: The Symbolic Mind, 2009. Contributor to journals. **Address:** Department of Philosophy, University of Massachusetts, Olney Hall 102C, 1 University Ave., Lowell, MA 01854, U.S.A. **Online address:** rinnis41@gmail.com

INTRATOR, Sam M. American (born United States) **Genres:** Novels, Essays, Adult Non-fiction, Literary Criticism And History, inspirational/Motivational Literature, Young Adult Fiction. **Career:** Smith College, Department of Education and Child Study and the Program in Urban Studies, assistant professor of education and child study, 1999-, professor of education and the program in urban studies, Urban Education Initiative, co-director; Project Coach, co-director. Writer. **Publications:** Stories of the Courage to Teach: Honoring the Teacher's Heart, 2002; (ed. with M. Scribner) Teaching with Fire: Poetry That Sustains the Courage to Teach, 2003; Tuned In and Fired Up: How Teaching Can Inspire Real Learning in the Classroom, 2003; Living the Questions: Essays Inspired by the Work and Life of Parker J. Palmer, 2005; (with M. Scribner) Leading from Within: Poetry that Sustains the Courage to Lead, 2007. **Address:** Department of Education & Child Study, Program in Urban Studies, Smith College, 101 Morgan Hall, 37 Prospect St., Northampton, MA 01060-2105, U.S.A. **Online address:** sintrato@email.smith.edu

IOFFE, Grigory. American/Russian (born Russia), b. 1951. **Genres:** Area Studies, Demography, Geography, History. **Career:** Institute for Rural Physical Planning, junior research associate, 1974-77, senior research associate, 1977-80; U.S.S.R. Academy of Sciences, Institute of Geography, junior research associate, 1980-86, senior research associate, 1986-88, department chair, 1987-89, department head, 1988-89; Radford University, assistant professor, 1990-94, associate professor, 1994-2000, professor of geography, 2000-. Writer. **Publications:** Selskoe khoziaistvo Nechernozem'i: territorial'nye problemy, 1990; (with O.V. Gritsai and A.I. Treivish) TSentr i periferiia v regional'nom razvitii, 1991; (with T. Nefedova) Continuity and Change in Rural Russia, 1997; (with T. Nefedova) Environs of Russian Cities, 1999; (with T. Nefedova and I. Zaslavsky) End of Peasantry?: The Disintegration of Rural Russia, 2006; Understanding Belarus and How Western Foreign Policy Misses the Mark, 2008; Russia and the Near Abroad, 2010. ENGLISH TITLES OF BOOKS PUBLISHED IN RUSSIAN: (with A. Igudina) Applications of the Factor Analysis in Physical Planning: Guidelines for Planners, 1980; Non-Chernozem Zone: Social Geography and Agriculture, 1986; Agriculture in the Non-Chernozem Zone: Regional Problems, 1990; (with O. Gritsai and A. Treivisch) Center and Periphery in Regional Development, 1991; (co-author) Territorial Structure of the Economy in the Regions of Old Colonization, 1995. EDITOR AND CONTRIBUTOR: Territorial Organization of the Economy as a Development Factor, 1987; (with G.J. Demko and Z. Zayonchkovskaya) Population under Duress: The Geodemography of Post-Soviet Russia, 1999. Contributor to journals. **Address:** Department of Geography, Radford University, Rm. 134, Cook Hall, PO Box 6938, Radford, VA 24142, U.S.A. **Online address:** gioffe@radford.edu

IONAZZI, Daniel A. American (born United States), b. 1951?. **Genres:** Theatre. **Career:** NBC Studios, production manager and technical manager; Sander Gossard and Associates, production manager and technical manager; Crawford Studios, production manager and technical manager; Macy's Parade Studio, production manager and technical manager; Colorado Music Hall, production manager and technical manager; Lincoln Center Institute, production manager and technical manager; Continental Theater Co., production manager and technical manager; Detroit Institute of Arts, production manager and technical manager; Juilliard School, assistant technical director, 1977-80; Denver Center Theater Co., technical director, 1980-81, production manager, 1981-84; Santa Fe Festival Theater, production manager, 1981-82; Colorado Stage Co., executive director, 1984-86; Denver Partnership, director of festivals and events, 1987-88; University of California, School of Theater, Film and Television, faculty, Department of Theater, director of production, 1988-, academic administrator; Geffen Playhouse, production manager, 1995-; Theatre Consultants Collaborative, consultant, 2009-. Writer. **Publications:** The Stage Management Handbook, 1992; The Stagecraft Handbook, 1996. **Address:** Department of Theater, School of Theater, Film and Television, University of California, 303C E Melnitz Hall, PO Box 951622, Los Angeles, CA 90095-1622, U.S.A. **Online address:** dionazzi@tft.ucla.edu

IONE, Carole. American (born United States), b. 1937. **Genres:** Poetry, Theatre, Plays/Screenplays. **Career:** Letters (now Live Letters), founder, 1974, editor, artistic director; Essence, contributing editor, 1981-83; Village Voice, poetry editor; Manhattan Theatre Club, director; Pauline Oliveros Foundation, co-artistic director; Renaissance House Inc., artistic director; Unison Learning Center, poetry curator; Jazzmobile Inc., poet-in-residence; Ministry of Maat Inc., director; Deep Listening Institute Ltd., artistic director. **Publications:** The Coffee Table Lover, 1973; Private Pages, 1987; Unsealedlips, 1990; Piramida Negro: Selected Poetry, 1973-1991, 1991; Pride of Family: Four Generations of American Women of Color, 1991. Contributor to periodicals. **Address:** Ministry of Maat Inc., 156 Hunter St., PO Box 1956, Kingston, NY 12401-1956, U.S.A. **Online address:** iodreams@deeplistening.org

IPSEN, David. *See* **IPSEN, D. C.**

IPSEN, D. C. (David Ipsen). American (born United States), b. 1921. **Genres:** Children's Non-fiction, Engineering, Young Adult Non-fiction, Adult Non-fiction, Sciences. **Career:** General Electric Co., teacher, research engineer at plants, 1942-49; University of California, Engineering Department, lecturer, 1950-53, assistant professor of mechanical engineering, 1953-57, Elementary School Science Project, assistant director, 1959-66, Biomedical Curriculum Project, consultant, 1970-75. Writer. **Publications:** Units, Dimensions and Dimensionless Numbers, 1960; The Riddle of the Stegosaurus, 1969; Rattlesnakes and Scientists, 1970; What Does a Bee See?, 1971; The Elusive Zebra, 1971; Eye of the Whirlwind: The Story of John Scopes, 1973; Isaac Newton: Reluctant Genius, 1985; Archimedes: Greatest Scientist of the Ancient World, 1988; Endeavour: Quest for the Distance of the Sun, 2004; Edmond Halley: More Than a Man with a Comet, 2004; (with R. Stebbins and G. Gillfillan) Animal Coloration: Activities on the Evolution of Concealment, 2008. **Address:** 655 Vistamont Ave., Berkeley, CA 94708, U.S.A. **Online address:** dcipsen@earthlink.net

IRELAND, David. (David Neil Ireland). Australian (born Australia), b. 1927. **Genres:** Novels, Plays/Screenplays, Animals/Pets, Young Adult Fiction. **Career:** Writer. **Publications:** Image in the Clay (play), 1962, 2nd ed., 1986; The Chantic Bird, 1968; The Unknown Industrial Prisoner, 1971; The Flesheaters, 1972; Burn, 1975; The Glass Canoe, 1976; A Woman of the Future, 1979; City of Women, 1981; Archimedes and the Seagle, 1984; Bloodfather, 1987; The Chosen, 1997. **Address:** Curtis Brown Private Ltd., 2 Boundary St., Level 1, PO Box 19, Paddington, NW 2021, Australia.

IRELAND, David Neil. *See* **IRELAND, David.**

IRELAND, Kevin (Mark). New Zealander (born New Zealand), b. 1933. **Genres:** Novels, Poetry, Autobiography/Memoirs, Adult Non-fiction. **Career:** Canterbury University, writer-in-residence, 1986; Auckland University, writer-in-residence, 1990; Mate Magazine, founding editor; Quote Unquote Magazine, assistant editor. **Publications:** POETRY: Face to Face, 1963; Educating the Body, 1968; A Letter from Amsterdam, 1972; Orchids, Hummingbirds, and Other Poems, 1974; A Grammar of Dreams, 1975; Literary Cartoons, 1978; The Dangers of Art: Poems 1975-1980, 1981; Practice Night in the Drill Hall, 1985; The Year of the Comet, 1986; Tiberius at the Beehive, 1990; Skinning a Fish, 1994; Anzac Day: Selected Poems, 1997; Fourteen Reasons for Writing, 2001; Walking the Land, 2003; Airports and Other Wasted Days, 2007; How to Survive the Morning, 2008, Table Talk, 2009. NOVELS: Blowing My Top, 1996; The Man Who Never Lived, 1997; The Craymore Affair, 2000; Getting Away With It, 2004; The Jigsaw Chronicles, 2008; Daisy Chains, 2010. OTHERS: Sleeping with the Angels (stories), 1995; Under the Bridge & Over the Moon: A Memoir, 1998; Backwards to Forwards: A Memoir, 2002; On Getting Old, 2005; How to Catch a Fish,

2005. **Address:** 3a Everest St., Devonport, Auckland, 0624, New Zealand. **Online address:** kireland@xtra.co.nz

IRELAND, Patrick R(ichard). American (born United States), b. 1961. **Genres:** Politics/Government, International Relations/Current Affairs, Medicine/Health, Gay And Lesbian Issues, Social Sciences, Urban Studies. **Career:** Commonwealth of Massachusetts, Commission on Indian Affairs, researcher, 1984; Massachusetts Urban Reinvestment Advisory Group, researcher, 1984-85; Connecticut College, assistant professor of government, 1989-92; University of Denver, associate professor of political science, 1992-2000; University of Bremen, Center for Social Policy Research, visiting fellow, 1992; Berlin Institute for Comparative Social Policy Research, visiting fellow, 1993; Georgia Institute of Technology, associate professor of political science, 2000-02; American University of Beirut, visiting associate professor of political studies and public administration, 2002-03, associate professor of political science, 2005-07; University of Houston, University of St. Thomas, visiting faculty, 2003-04; Illinois Institute of Technology, professor of political science, 2007-, Department of Social Sciences, chair, 2007-. Writer. **Publications:** The Policy Challenge of Ethnic Diversity: Immigrant Politics in France and Switzerland, 1994; Becoming Europe: Immigration, Integration and the Welfare State, 2004. Contributor to journals. **Address:** Departmentt of Social Sciences, College of Science & Letters, Illinois Instituite of Technology, Rm. 116A, Siegel Hall, 3301 S Dearborn St., Chicago, IL 60616, U.S.A. **Online address:** pireland@iit.edu

IRELAND, R. Duane. American (born United States), b. 1947?. **Genres:** Business/Trade/Industry, Economics. **Career:** Texas Tech University, teaching assistant of management, 1970-71, instructor of management, 1971-72, 1975-77, lecturer of management, 1974-75; South Plains Association of Governments, director of manpower planning, 1972-73; West Texas Health Systems Inc., program development specialist, 1973-74; Oklahoma State University, assistant professor of management, 1977-81, associate professor of management, 1981-83; Baylor University, Department of Management, associate professor of management, 1983-85, professor of management, 1985-2000, chairman, 1986-92, W.A. Mays professor of entrepreneurship and strategic management, 1983-87, Curtis Hankamer chair of entrepreneurship, 1987-2000, John F. Baugh Center for Entrepreneurship, research fellow, 1992-2000, associate dean for research, 1992-98; Entrepreneurship Theory and Practice, consulting editor, 1988-92; Academy of Management Executive, associate editor, 1989-92, 2004-07, editor, 2008-10; University of Richmond, professor of management and W. David Robbins chair in strategic management, 2000-04; Texas A&M University, Mays Business School, Department of Management, professor of business management, 2004-08, Foreman R. and Ruby S. Bennett chair in business, 2004-10, head, 2005-07, distinguished professor of management, 2008-, Conn chair in new ventures leadership, 2010-; Ohio University, visiting fellow, 2010-12. **Publications:** NONFICTION: (with A.J. DuBrin and J.C. Williams) Management & Organization, 1989, (with A.J. DuBrin) 2nd ed., 1993; (with R.E. Hoskisson and M.A. Hitt) Strategic Management: Competitiveness and Globalization, 1995, 9th ed. as Strategic Management: Competitiveness and Globalization: Concepts, 2011; (with M.A. Hitt and R.E. Hoskisson) Insights: Readings in Strategic Management, 2nd ed., 1997; (with M.A. Hitt and J.S. Harrison) Mergers and Acquisitions: A Guide to Creating Value for Stakeholders, 2001; (with R.E. Hoskisson and M.A. Hitt) Competing for Advantage, 2004; (ed. with M.A. Hitt) The Blackwell Encyclopedia of Management Entrepreneurship, 2005; (with M.A. Hitt and R.E. Hoskisson) Nihul astrategi, 2005; (with B.R. Barringer) Entrepreneurship: Successfully Launching New Ventures, 2006, 4th ed., 2012; (with R.E. Hoskisson and M.A. Hitt) Understanding Business Strategy: Concepts, 2006; (with R.E. Hoskisson and M.A. Hitt) Understanding Business Strategy: Concepts and Cases, 2006, 2nd ed., 2008; (with B.R. Barringer) What's Stopping You?: Shatter the 9 Most Common Myths Keeping You from Starting Your Own Business, 2008. **Address:** Mays Business School, Texas A&M University, Rm. 420U, 4113 Texas A&M University, College Station, TX 77843-4113, U.S.A. **Online address:** direland@mays.tamu.edu

IRION, Mary Jean. American (born United States), b. 1922. **Genres:** Poetry, Theology/Religion, Essays. **Career:** Lancaster Country Day Upper School, teacher of English literature, 1968-74, 1980-81; Countermeasure Poets Workshop, founder and coordinator, 1974-94; Franklin and Marshall College, Et Cetera Program, teacher, 1975; Chautauqua Institution, Chautauqua Writers' Center, founder, teacher of modern poetry, 1983-97, director, 1987-97; Lancaster Theological Seminary, visiting lecturer in theology and literature, 1983-90, 1985-; Society for the Arts, Religion and Contemporary Culture, fellow, 1990-; United Church Herald, columnist. Writer. **Publications:** From the Ashes of Christianity: A Post-Christian View, 1968; Yes, World: A Mosaic of Meditation, 1970; Holding On, 1984; She-fire: A Safari into the Human Animal (creative non-fiction), forthcoming. Contributor to periodicals. **Address:** Society for the Arts, Religion and Contemporary, Culture, 15811 Kutztown Rd., PO Box 15, Maxatawny, PA 19538, U.S.A. **Online address:** mjirion@aol.com

IRMSCHER, Christoph. German (born Germany), b. 1962. **Genres:** Literary Criticism And History, Adult Non-fiction, Natural History. **Career:** University of Bonn, lecturer in English, 1992-96; University of Tennessee, visiting assistant professor of English, 1993-94; Harvard University, lecturer in English and literature and history, 1998-2000; University of Maryland, assistant professor, 2000-03, professor of English, 2003; Indiana University, professor, curator. Writer. **Publications:** Masken der Moderne: literarische Selbststilisierung bei T.S. Eliot, Ezra Pound, Wallace Stevens und William Carlos Williams, 1992; The Poetics of Natural History: From John Bartram to William James, 1999; (ed.) Writings and Drawings, 1999; Longfellow Redux, 2006; Public Poet, Private Man: Henry Wadsworth Longfellow at 200, 2007; (ed. with A.C. Bradcock) A Keener Perception: Ecocritical Studies in American Art History, 2009. FORTHCOMING: Louis Agassiz: A Cultural Biography; The McIlwraith Family. Contributor to periodicals. **Address:** Department of English, Indiana University, 442 Ballantine Hall, 1020 E Kirkwood Ave., Bloomington, IN 47405-7103, U.S.A. **Online address:** christoph.irmscher@gmail.com

IRVINE, Amy. American (born United States) **Genres:** Novellas/Short Stories, Environmental Sciences/Ecology, Sciences. **Career:** Southern Utah Wilderness Alliance, development director. Writer, environmentalist and rock climber. **Publications:** Making a Difference: Stories of How Our Outdoor Industry and Individuals Are Working to Preserve America's Natural Places, 2001; Trespass: Living at the Edge of the Promised Land, 2008. **Address:** Faye Bender Literary Agency, 19 Cheever Pl., Brooklyn, NY 11231, U.S.A.

IRVINE, Angela. (Val Davis). American (born United States) **Genres:** Mystery/Crime/Suspense, Travel/Exploration, Young Adult Fiction. **Career:** Writer. **Publications:** WITH R. IRVINE AS VAL DAVIS: Track of the Scorpion, 1996; Flight of the Serpent, 1998; Wake of the Hornet, 2000; The Return of the Spanish Lady, 2001; Thread of the Spider, 2002. **Address:** c/o Author Mail, St. Martins Press, 175 5th Ave., New York, NY 10010, U.S.A.

IRVINE, William. (William Burriss III Irvine). American (born United States), b. 1958. **Genres:** Adult Non-fiction, Reference. **Career:** The Drawing Center, assistant to the director, 1982-84; Avenue, assistant editor, 1984-86; freelance writer and editor, 1986-91; House Beautiful, copy chief and staff writer, 1992-. **Publications:** Madam I'm Adam and Other Palindromes, 1987; If I Had a Hi-Fi and Other Palindromes, 1992. Contributor to periodicals. **Address:** House Beautiful, 1700 Broadway, New York, NY 10019, U.S.A.

IRVINE, William Burriss III. See **IRVINE, William.**

IRVING, John (Winslow). American (born United States), b. 1942. **Genres:** Novels, Autobiography/Memoirs, Literary Criticism And History, Young Adult Fiction, Biography, Animals/Pets. **Career:** Phillips Exeter Academy, assistant wrestling coach, 1964-65; Windham College, assistant professor of English, 1967-69, 1970-72; University of Iowa, writer-in-residence, 1972-75; Mount Holyoke College, assistant professor of English, 1975-78; Brandeis University, assistant professor of English, 1978-79; Northfield Mt. Hermon School, assistant wrestling coach, 1981-83; Fessenden School, assistant wrestling coach, 1984-86; Vermont Academy, head wrestling coach, 1987-89. **Publications:** Setting Free the Bears, 1969, 2nd ed., 2003; The Water-Method Man, 1972; The 158-Pound Marriage, 1974; The World According to Garp: A Novel, 1978; 3 by Irving, 1980; The Hotel New Hampshire, 1981; The Cider House Rules (novel), 1985; A Prayer for Owen Meany, 1989; A Son of the Circus, 1994; Trying to Save Piggy Sneed, 1996; The Imaginary Girlfriend: A Memoir (autobiography), 1996; A Widow for One Year, 1998; My Movie Business: A Memoir, 1999; The Fourth Hand: A Novel, 2001; A Sound like Someone Trying Not to Make a Sound: A Story, 2004; Until I Find You: A Novel, 2005; Last Night in Twisted River: A Novel, 2009; In One Person, 2012. **Address:** c/o Author Mail, Random House, 201 E 50th St., New York, NY 10022-7703, U.S.A.

IRVING, Shae (Lyn). American (born United States), b. 1966. **Genres:** Money/Finance. **Career:** Nolo Press, legal editor, 1994-; WillMaker, managing editor. **Publications:** (Ed.) Nolo's Little Law Book: Answers to Everyday Legal Questions, 1996; Nolo's Everyday Law Book: Answers to Your Most Frequently Asked Legal Questions, 1996, 8th ed., 2010; The Financial Power of Attorney Workbook: Who Will Handle Your Finances if You Can't, 1997; (with R. Leonard) Take Control of Your Student Loans, 1997; (with B.K. Repa, R. Warner and S. Elias) Willmaker, 1998; (ed.) How to Change Your Name in California, 8th ed., 1999; (with R. Leonard) Take Control of Your Student Loan Debt, 2nd ed., 1999; (ed.) Credit Repair, 4th ed., 2000; Medical Directives and Powers of Attorney for California, 2001, 2nd ed., 2004; (with K.E. Stoner) Prenuptial Agreements: How to Write a Fair and Lasting Contract, 2004, 3rd ed., 2008; (with M. Cullen) Get It Together: Organize Your Records So Your Family Won't Hve To, 2005, 4th ed., 2010; (ed. with B. Simmons) Quicken WillMaker: Estate Planning Essentials, 6th ed., 2009; Living Wills & Powers of Attorney for California, 3rd ed., 2009; Nolo's Encyclopedia of Everyday Law: Answers to Your Most Frequently Asked Legal Questions, 8th ed., 2011. **Address:** Nolo Press, 950 Parker St., Berkeley, CA 94710-2524, U.S.A. **Online address:** shae@california.com

IRVING, Stephanie (Jean). American (born United States), b. 1962. **Genres:** Travel/Exploration, History. **Career:** University of Washington, Academic Computer Center, technical writer, 1985-86; St. Martin's Press Inc., editorial assistant, 1986; Sasquatch Books, editorial assistant, senior acquisitions editor, 1987-96; Irving Ink, owner, 1996-; Skyline Hospital, marketing department, staff, The Skyline Foundation, executive director. **Publications:** Restaurants, Lodgings, and Touring in Washington, Oregon, and British Columbia, 1991, 1995. EDITOR: (with D. Brewster) Seattle Best Places: The Most Discriminating Guide to Seattle's Restaurants, Shops, Hotels, Nightlife, Sights, Outings, and Annual Events, 1990, 7th ed., 1996; (with K. Carlson) Portland Best Places: A Discriminating Guide to Portland's Restaurants, Lodgings, Shopping, Nightlife, Arts, Sights, and Outings, 1990, 3rd ed., 1995; (with K. Robinson) Seattle Cheap Eats: 300 Terrific Bargain Eateries, 1990, 5th ed., 1993; (with D. Brewster) Northwest Best Places, 1992-1993, 1991; Northwest Cheap Sleeps: Mountain Motels, Island Cabins, Ski Bunks, Beach Cottages, and Hundreds of Penny-Pinching Travel Ideas for the Adventurous Road Tripper, 1992; (with L. Hagar) Northern California Best Places, 1993-1994, 1995-1996: Restaurants, Lodgings, Touring, 1992; (with K. Wilson) Vancouver Best Places: the Most Discriminating Guide to Vancouver's Restaurants, Shops, Hotels, Nightlife, Sights, and Outings, 1994. Work appears in anthologies. Contributor to magazines. **Address:** The Skyline Foundation, Skyline Hospital, 211 Skyline Dr., White Salmon, WA 98672, U.S.A. **Online address:** sirving@gorge.net

IRWIN, Peter George. Australian (born Australia), b. 1925?. **Genres:** Geography, Social Sciences. **Career:** Newcastle Teachers College, staff, 1959-65; University of Newcastle, Department of Geography, lecturer, 1959-66, senior lecturer, 1966-74, associate professor, 1974-85, now retired; University of Sydney, part-time faculty. Writer. **Publications:** (With D.A.M. Lea) New Guinea: The Territory and Its People, 1967, 2nd ed., 1971; Equatorial and Tropical Rainforest, 1968; The Monsoon Asia, 1968; The Tropical Savanna, 1969; Human Geography, 1970; Cotton Systems of the Namoi Valley, 1972; Systems in Human Geography, 1973; (with J.C.R. Camm) Space, People, Place, 1979; (with J.C.R. Camm) Land, Man, Region, 1982; (with J.C.R. Camm) Skills for Senior School Geography, 1985; (with J.C.R. Camm) Australians in Their Environment, 1987; (with J.C.R. Camm) Resources, Settlement, Livelihood: Perspectives on a Changing World, 1989; (with R.E. Bernard and P.P. Courtenay) Australia's Neighbours A Geography for Senior School Students, 1990. **Address:** 16/16 Myall Rd., Waratah, NW 2298, Australia. **Online address:** vivalamusica@bigpond.com

IRWIN, Robert (Graham). British (born England), b. 1946. **Genres:** Novels, History, Literary Criticism And History, Adult Non-fiction. **Career:** University of St. Andrews, lecturer in medieval history, 1972-77; School of Oriental and African Studies, research associate; The Times Literary Supplement, Middle East editor, novelist, publisher, consultant editor. **Publications:** The Arabian Nightmare, 1983; The Middle East in the Middle Ages: The Early Mamluk Sultanate, 1250-1382, 1986; The Limits of Vision, 1986; Mysteries of Algiers, 1988; The Arabian Nights: A Companion, 1994; Exquisite Corpse, 1995; Satan Wants Me, 1997; Islamic Artin Context: Art, Architecture, and the Literary World, 1999; (ed.) Night and Horses and The Desert: An Anthology of Classical Arabic Literature, 2000; Prayer-Cushions of the Flesh, 2002; The Alhambra, 2004; For Lust of Knowing: The Orientalists and Their Enemies in US as Dangerous Knowledge: Orientalism and Its Discontents,

2006; For Lust of Knowing, 2007; The Art of Orientalism, 2011; Memoirs of a Dervish, 2011. Contributor to periodicals. **Address:** c/o Juri Gabriel, 35 Camberwell Grove, London, GL SE11 5AX, England.

ISAACS, Anne. American (born United States), b. 1949. **Genres:** Children's Fiction, Young Adult Fiction, Poetry, Novels, Humor/Satire, Literary Criticism And History. **Career:** Writer, 1983-. **Publications:** Swamp Angel, 1994; Treehouse Tales, 1997; Cat up a Tree: A Story in Poems, 1998; Torn Thread, 2000; Dust Devil, 2006; Pancakes for Supper!, 2006; The Ghosts of Luckless Gulch, 2008; Dust Devil, 2010; Meanwhile, Back at the Ranch, 2013; The Garden of Hesperus, 2013. **Address:** c/o Susan Cohen, Writers House Literary Agents, 21 W 26th St., New York, NY 10010, U.S.A. **Online address:** anne@anneisaacs.com

ISAACS, Arnold R. American (born United States), b. 1941. **Genres:** History, Military/Defense/Arms Control, E-books, Young Adult Non-fiction, Politics/Government. **Career:** Sun, reporter, 1962-78, Sunday features editor, 1978-81; free-lance writer, 1981-; Johns Hopkins University, visiting professor of communications, 1983-88; Towson State University, lecturer, 1984-2001; Northwest University, visiting lecturer, 1990-91; Odessa State Pedagogic Institute, visiting lecturer, 1991; Marie Curie-Sklodowska University, visiting lecturer, 1994; Caucasus School of Journalism and Media Management, visiting lecturer, 2002-05; The Georgian Institute of Public Affairs, English faculty; Fudan University, faculty; State Pedagogical Institute, faculty; Baltimore Sun, foreign and Washington correspondent. Writer. **Publications:** Without Honor: Defeat in Vietnam and Cambodia, 1983, 3rd ed., 1999; (co-author) Pawns of War: Cambodia and Laos, 1987; Vietnam Shadows: The War, Its Ghosts, and Its Legacy, 1997; Workplace Violence: Issues in Response, 2003. Contributor to periodicals. **Address:** The Georgian Institute of Public Affairs, 2 Marie Brosset St., Tbilisi, 0108, Georgia. **Online address:** isaacs@saber.towson.edu

ISAACS, Ronald (Howard). American/Canadian (born Canada), b. 1947. **Genres:** Theology/Religion, inspirational/Motivational Literature. **Career:** Voices Four (Hebrew liturgical folk-rock ensemble), co-founder and performer, 1969-73; Greenburgh Hebrew Center, principal and youth director, 1973-75; Temple Sholom, rabbi, 1975-, Temple Sholom Hebrew High School, co-director; Lovin' Co. (Hebrew liturgical folk-rock ensemble), founder and performer, 1980-82; Rutgers University, visiting lecturer, 1976-82; United Synagogue of Conservative Judaism, Kadima rabbi, 1982-92; WCTC-Radio, Jewish American Hour, host, 1990-94; Northern New Jersey Rabbinical Assembly, vice president, 1995-96; Jewish Theological Seminary of America, adjunct lecturer, 2002. Writer. **Publications:** Jewish Expressions: My Holiday Activity Book, 1986; The Jewish Instructional Games Book, 1986; Shabbat Delight: A Celebration in Stories, Songs and Games, 1987; The Jewish Family Game Book for the Sabbath and Festivals, 1989; Loving Companions: Memories of Our Wedding, 1991; A Jewish Mourner's Handbook, 1991; Sh'ma Kolaynu: A High Holy Day Youth Mahzor, 1992; Rites of Passage: A Guide to the Jewish Life Cycle, 1992; The Chain of Life: A Curricular Guide for Teaching About Death, Bereavement and the Jewish Way of Honoring the Dead, 1993; The Jewish Information Source Book: A Dictionary and Almanac, 1993; The How-To Handbook for Jewish Living, 1993; Shir Chadash: A Sabbath and Festival Prayerbook, 1994; Jewish Family Matters: A Leaders Guide, 1994; Sacred Celebrations: A Jewish Holiday Handbook, 1994; Doing Mitzvot: Mitzvah Projects for Bar/Bat Mitzvah, 1994; The Discovery Haggadah, 1994; Becoming Jewish: A Handbook for Conversion, 1994; (ed. with D. Pressman) Siddur Shir Chadash: For Youth and Family, 1994; Lively Student Prayer Services: A Handbook of Teaching Strategies, 1995; Sacred Moments: Tales from the Jewish Life Cycle, 1995; Derech Eretz: The Path to an Ethical Life, 1995; Critical Documents of Jewish History: A Sourcebook, 1995; Critical Jewish Issues: A Book for Teenagers, 1996; Words for the Soul: Jewish Wisdom for Life's Journey, 1996; Mitzvot: A Sourcebook for the 613 Commandments, 1996; The Second How-To Handbook for Jewish Living, 1996; A Glossary of Jewish Life, 1996; Madrich LeGabbai: A Gabbai's How-to Manual, 1996; Every Person's Guide to Shabbat, 1996; The Bride and Groom Handbook, 1996; Rediscovering Judaism: Bar and Bat Mitzvah for Adults, 1997; Sidrah Reflections: Guide to the Torah Portions and Haftarot, 1997; Sacred Seasons: A Sourcebook for the Jewish Holidays, 1997; The Jewish Book of Numbers, 1997; Jewish Music: Its History, People, and Song, 1997; Every Person's Guide to Jewish Prayer, 1997; Close Encounters: Jewish Views About God, 1997; Miracles: A Jewish Perspective, 1998; Messengers of God: A Jewish Prophets Who's Who, 1998; Judaism, Medicine, and Healing, 1998; Ascending Jacob's Ladder: Jewish Views of Angels, Demons, and Evil Spirits,

1998; Divination, Magic, and Healing: The Book of Jewish Folklore, 1998; The Jewish Sourcebook on the Environment and Ecology, 1998; The Jewish Book of Etiquette, 1998; Every Person's Guide to the High Holy Days, 1998; Every Person's Guide to the Book of Proverbs and Ecclesiastes, 1998; Every Person's Guide to Jewish Philosophy and Philosophers, 1999; Every Person's Guide to Shavuot, 1999; Exploring Jewish Ethics and Values, 1999; Reaching for Sinai: A Practical Handbook for Bar/Bat Mitzvah and Family, 1999; Every Person's Guide to Death and Dying in the Jewish Tradition, 1999; The Bible: Where Do You Find It and What Does It Say?, 1999; I Believe: The Thirteen Principles of Faith: A Confirmation Textbook, 1999; Beginnings/Raising a Jewish Child: Early Years, 2000; The Jewish Bible Almanac, 2000; Animals in Jewish Thought and Tradition, 2000; Every Person's Guide to Jewish Law, 2000; Every Person's Guide to Jewish Sexuality, 2000; Every Person's Guide to Sukkot, Shemini Atzeret, and Simchat Torah, 2000; Every Person's Guide to Purim, 2000; Understanding the Hebrew Prophets, 2001; Every Person's Guide to Passover, 2001; Every Person's Guide to Hanukkah, 2001; Entering the Biblical Text: Exploring Jewish Values in the Torah, 2001; Defending the Faith: Great Trials and Debates, 2001; Let My People Go: An Instant Lesson on World Slavery, 2002; Siddur Lev Chadash for Shabbat and Festivals, 2002; Legends of Biblical Heroes: A Sourcebook, 2002; The Third How-To Handbook for Jewish Living, 2002; The Jewish Traveler's Handbook, 2003; A Taste of Text: An Introduction to the Talmud and Midrash, 2003; Ask the Rabbi: The Who, What, When, Where, Why, and How of Being Jewish, 2003; Count Your Blessings: 100 Prayers For a Day, 2004; Life's Little Book of BIG Jewish Advice, 2004; Essential Judaism in a Nutshell, 2004; Amazing Jewish Facts and Curiosities, 2004; (with K.M. Olitzky) Complete How to Handbook for Jewish Living, 2004; Amazing Jewish Facts and Curiosities, Kosher Living: It's More Than Just the Food, 2005; A Taste of Torah: An Introduction to Thirteen Challenging Bible Stories, 2005; Questions Christians Ask the Rabbi, 2006; Kos Tanhumim: A Service of Comfort, 2007; Siddur Kabbalat Shabbat, 2007; Reflections: A Jewish Grandparents' Gift of Memories, 2007; Why Hebrew Goes from Right to Left: 201 Things You Never Knew About Judaism, 2008; Bubbe Meises: Jewish Myths, Jewish Realities, 2008; Have a Good Laugh: Jewish Jokes for the Soul, 2009; (with D. Pressman) Siddur Or Shalom for Shabbat and Festivals, 2010. Contributor to periodicals. **Address:** Temple Sholom, 594 N Bridge St., Bridgewater, NJ 08807-2124, U.S.A.

ISAACS, Susan. American (born United States), b. 1943. **Genres:** Novels, Mystery/Crime/Suspense, Plays/Screenplays, Film, Writing/Journalism, Young Adult Non-fiction, Literary Criticism And History, Young Adult Fiction. **Career:** Seventeen Magazine, assistant editor, senior editor, 1966-70; freelance writer, 1970-76; Mystery Writers of America, president. **Publications:** Compromising Positions, 1978; Close Relations, 1980; Almost Paradise, 1984; Shining Through, 1988; Magic Hour, 1991; After All These Years, 1993; Lily White: A Novel, 1996; Red, White and Blue, 1998; Brave Dames and Wimpettes: What Women Are Really Doing on Page and Screen, 1999; Long Time No See, 2001; Any Place I Hang My Hat, 2004; Past Perfect, 2007; As Husbands Go: A Novel, 2010. Contributor to newspapers and periodicals. **Address:** c/o Author Mail, Scribner, 1230 Ave. of the Americas, New York, NY 10020-1513, U.S.A.

ISADORA, Rachel. American (born United States), b. 1953?. **Genres:** Children's Fiction, Illustrations, Biography. **Career:** Boston Ballet Co., dancer. Author and illustrator of children's books. **Publications:** SELF-ILLUSTRATED FOR CHILDREN: Max, 1976; The Potter's Kitchen, 1977; Willaby, 1977; Ben's Trumpet, 1979; My Ballet Class, 1980; No, Agatha!, 1980; Jesse and Abe, 1981; City Seen from A to Z, 1983; Opening Night, 1984; I Hear, 1985; I See, 1985; I Touch, 1985; The Pirates of Bedford Street, 1988; Babies, 1990; Friends, 1990; At the Crossroads, 1991; Over the Green Hills, 1992; Lili at the Ballet, 1993; Lili On Stage, 1995; My Ballet Diary, 1995; Newsboy, 1995; Lili Backstage, 1997; A South African Night, 1998; Caribbean Dreams, 1998; ABC Pop!, 1999; Sophie Skates, 1999; 123 Pop!, 2000; Listen to the City, 2000; Nick Plays Baseball, 2001; Bring on That Beat, 2002; Peekaboo Morning, 2002; Mr. Moon, 2002; On Your Toes: A Ballet ABC, 2003; Not Just Tutus, 2003; In the Beginning, 2003; Luke Goes to Bat, 2005; What a Family!: A Fresh Look at Family Trees, 2006; Yo, Jo!, 2007; The Princess and the Pea, 2007; Uh-oh!, 2008; Peekaboo Bedtime, 2008; Happy Belly, Happy Smile, 2009; 12 Days of Christmas, 2010; Say Hello!, 2010. ADAPTATIONS AND RETELLINGS: The Nutcracker, 1981; The Little Match Girl, 1987; The Princess and the Frog, 1989; Swan Lake: A Ballet Story, 1989; Firebird, 1994; The Steadfast Tin Soldier, 1996. BIOGRAPHY:

Young Mozart, 1997; Isadora Dances, 1998. Contributor to periodicals. **Address:** c/o Author Mail, William Morrow & Co., 1350 Ave. of the Americas, New York, NY 10019, U.S.A.

ISBISTER, John. Canadian/American (born United States), b. 1942. **Genres:** Economics, Philosophy, Third World, Ethics. **Career:** University of California, Merrill College, assistant professor, 1968-72, associate professor, 1972-78, professor of economics, 1978-99, provost, 1984-99, professor emeritus, 1999-, fellow; Laurentian University, Department of Sociology, dean of social sciences and humanities, 2006-, senior researcher. Writer. **Publications:** Promises Not Kept: The Betrayal of Social Change in the Third World, 1991, 6th ed. as Promises Not Kept: Poverty and the Betrayal of Third World development, 2003, 7th ed., 2006; The Lending Performance of Community Development Credit Unions, 1992; Thin Cats: The Community Development Credit Union Movement in the United States, 1994; (with F. Leroi, M. Brusin and K. Salyer) Current Regional Issues: California, Hawaii, 1994; The Immigration Debate: Remaking America, 1996; Capitalism and Justice: Envisioning Social and Economic Fairness, 2001. **Address:** Dean of Humanities and Social Sciences, Laurentian University, 935 Ramsey Lake Rd., Sudbury, ON P3E 2C6, Canada. **Online address:** jisbister@laurentian.ca

ISEGAWA, Moses. Dutch/Ugandan (born Uganda), b. 1963. **Genres:** Novels, Young Adult Fiction, Translations. **Career:** Educator and writer. **Publications:** Abessijnse kronieken, 1998, trans. as Abyssinian Chronicles, 2000; Snakepit, 2004. **Address:** c/o Author Mail, Knopf/Random House, 1745 Broadway, New York, NY 10019-4368, U.S.A.

ISENBERG, Andrew C. American (born United States) **Genres:** History, Social Sciences. **Career:** Northwestern University, teaching assistant, 1987-88, senior teaching fellow, 1988-91, lecturer in history, 1991-92; St. Olaf College, visiting instructor, 1990; Concordia University, visiting instructor, 1991; School of the Art Institute of Chicago, visiting instructor, 1992; University of Puget Sound, assistant professor of history, 1992-94; Brown University, assistant professor of history, 1994-97; Princeton University, visiting fellow, 1996-97, Shelby Cullom Davis Center for historical studies, fellow, 1996-97, Christian Gauss Fund university preceptor, 2000-03, assistant professor of history, 1997-2004; Temple University, Department of History, associate professor, 2004-07, chair, 2006-09, professor of history, 2007-; Ludwig-Maximilians University, Rachel Carson Center for Environmental Studies, fellow, 2010. Writer. **Publications:** The Destruction of the Bison: An Environmental History 1750-1920, 2000; Mining California: An Ecological History, 2005; (ed.) The Nature of Cities: Culture, Landscape, and Urban Space, 2006. **Address:** Department of History, Temple University, 943 Gladfelter Hall, 1115 W Berks St., Philadelphia, PA 19122-6089, U.S.A. **Online address:** aisenber@temple.edu

ISENBERG, Barbara. American (born United States) **Genres:** Art/Art History, Theatre, Photography. **Career:** Business Week, assistant editor, 1964-67; McGraw-Hill World News, correspondent, 1967-69; Wall Street Journal, staff reporter, 1969-73; California Business, senior editor, 1973-75; Los Angeles Times, staff writer, 1976-95, coordinator and editor of festival, 1984; University of California, instructor in arts journalism, 1979-81, coordinator and moderator of evenings out with the critics, 1985-87; British Theatre Backstage (tour group), theater expert and host, 1983-; KUSC-FM Radio, host of live from trumps, 1987, visiting lecturer and host of Getty Center art matters series, 2000-; freelance writer, 1995-; University of Southern California, Institute for the Humanities, associate director, 2004-. **Publications:** (Ed.) California Theater Annual, 1981; Making It Big: The Diary of a Broadway Musical, 1996; State of the Arts: California Artists Talk About Their Work, 2000; (with F.O. Gehry) Conversations with Frank Gehr, 2009. Contributor to periodicals. **Address:** c/o Susan Ramer, Don Congdon Associates, 156 5th Ave., Ste. 625, New York, NY 10010, U.S.A.

ISENBERG, Joan P. (Joan Packer Isenberg). American (born United States), b. 1941. **Genres:** Education, How-to Books. **Career:** Kindergarten teacher, 1963-68; Beth-El Pre-School, director and teacher, 1968-69; preschool teacher, 1970-71; Rutgers College, instructor in education, 1978; George Mason University, assistant professor, 1978-84, associate professor, 1984-92, College of Education and Human Development, professor of education, 1992-97, Early Childhood Undergraduate and Graduate Programs, coordinator, 1978-97, director of advanced studies in teaching and learning, 1997-, Outreach and Professional Development Office, associate dean, Office of Education Services, associate dean. Writer. **Publications:** (With J. Jacobs) Playthings as

Learning Tools: A Parents' Guide, 1982; (with S. Snover) MAZE-0 (computer games for teaching spelling), 1985; (with L. Hoffman) About the Preschool Years: Book I, 1986; (with M.R. Jalongo) Creative Expression and Play in Early Childhood, 1993, 5th ed. as Creative Thinking and Arts-Based Learning: Preschool Through Fourth Grade, 2010; (with M.R. Jalongo) Teachers' Stories: From Personal Narrative to Professional Insight, 1995; (ed. with M.R. Jalongo) Major Trends and Issues in Early Childhood Education, 1997, 2nd ed., 2003; (with M.R. Jalongo) Exploring Your Role: A Practitioner's Introduction to Early Childhood Education, 2000, 4th ed. as Exploring Your Role in Early Childhood Education, 2012. Contributor to books and periodicals. **Address:** College of Education and Human Development, George Mason University, MS 6D2, West Bldg. 2201, 4400 University Dr., Fairfax, VA 22030, U.S.A. **Online address:** jisenber@gmu.edu

ISENBERG, Joan Packer. See ISENBERG, Joan P.

ISENBERG, Nancy G. American (born United States) **Genres:** Novels. **Career:** University of Tulsa, Mary Francis Barnard professor, Mary Frances Barnard chair in 19th Century American history, co-holder; University of Northern Iowa, assistant professor of history; Louisiana State University, professor of history. Writer. **Publications:** Sex and Citizenship in Antebellum America, 1998; (ed. with A. Burstein) Mortal Remains: Death in Early America, 2003; Fallen Founder: The Life of Aaron Burr, 2007; (ed. with M.S. Garbero and M. Pennacchia) Questioning Bodies in Shakespeare's Rome, 2010; (with A. Burstein) Madison and Jefferson, 2010. **Address:** Department of History, Louisiana State University, 225A Himes Hall, Baton Rouge, LA 70803, U.S.A. **Online address:** nisenberg@lsu.edu

ISENBERG, Sheila. American (born United States), b. 1943. **Genres:** Human Relations/Parenting, Biography, Novels. **Career:** The Daily Freeman, investigative staff reporter, 1983-88; New York State Assembly Task Force on Women's Issues, principal media coordinator, 1988-92; Marist College, visiting lecturer of English and humanities, adjunct professor of English. Writer and journalist. **Publications:** Women Who Love Men Who Kill, 1991; (with W.M. Kunstler) My Life As a Radical Lawyer, 1994; (with Tracey L. Brown) The Life and Times of Ron Brown, 1998; A Hero of Our Own: The Story of Varian Fry, 2001; Muriel's War: An American Heiress in the Nazi Resistance, 2010; Muriel's War, 2011; Her War, forthcoming. Contributor to periodicals. **Address:** c/o Will Lippincott, Lippincott Massie McQuilkin, 27 W 20th St., Ste. 305, New York, NY 10011, U.S.A. **Online address:** isenberg@hvc.rr.com

ISERSON, Kenneth Victor. American (born United States), b. 1949. **Genres:** Criminology/True Crime, Education, Humanities, History, Medicine/Health, Biography, Ethics. **Career:** Cincinnati General Hospital, emergency medicine residency, 1976-78, chief resident, 1977-78; Community Mercy Hospital, general practice, 1976; Texas A&M University College of Medicine, Division of Emergency Medicine, clinical associate professor and chairman, 1980-81; University of Arizona College of Medicine, Department of Emergency Medicine, emergency physician, 1981-, assistant professor, 1981-85, associate professor, 1985-92, professor, 1992-, now professor emeritus, Arizona Bioethics Program, director; University of Chicago, senior fellow in bioethics, 1990-91; Journal of Emergency Medicine, ethics section editor, 1990-; Cambridge Quarterly of Healthcare Ethics, abstract editor, 1991-; Medical Society of the United States and Mexico, vice president, 2002-04. **Publications:** (Co-ed.) Ethics in Emergency Medicine, 1986, (with A.B. Sanders and D.R. Mathieu) 2nd ed., 1995; Getting into a Residency: A Guide for Medical Students, 1988, 7th ed. as Iserson's Getting into a Residency: A Guide for Medical Students, 2006; (ed.) Wilderness Medical Society: Position Statements, 1989; Death to Dust: What Happens to Dead Bodies?, 1994, 2nd ed., 2001; Get into Medical School!: A Guide for the Perplexed, 1997, 2nd ed., 2004; Non-standard Medical Electives in the U.S. and Canada, 1997; Grave Words: Notifying Survivors about Sudden, Unexpected Deaths, 1999; Pocket Protocols, 1999; Demon Doctors: Physicians as Serial Killers, 2002; Dying to Know: A Compendium of the Mortal, Morbid, and Macabre, 2004; Improvised Medicine: Wilderness, Remote and Disaster Situations, 2009. **Address:** Department of Emergency Medicine, University of Arizona, 1609 N Warren Ave., Tucson, AZ 85719, U.S.A. **Online address:** kvi@u.arizona.edu

ISHERWOOD, Charles. American (born United States), b. 1964. **Genres:** Biography, Autobiography/Memoirs, Social Sciences. **Career:** L.A. Style, articles editor, 1989-93; Variety, senior editor and theater critic, 1993-; The New York Times, articles editor. **Publications:** Wonder Bread and Ecstasy:

The Life and Death of Joey Stefano, 1996. Contributor to periodicals. **Address:** Variety Magazine, 5900 Wilshire Blvd., Ste. 3100, Los Angeles, CA 90036, U.S.A.

ISHIGURO, Kazuo. British/Japanese (born Japan), b. 1954. **Genres:** Novels, Novellas/Short Stories, Music, Art/Art History. **Career:** Writer, 1982-. **Publications:** (Contrib.) Introduction 7: Stories by New Writers, 1981; A Pale View of Hills, 1982; An Artist of the Floating World, 1986; The Remains of the Day, 1989; The Unconsoled, 1995; When We Were Orphans, 2000; Never Let Me Go, 2005; Nocturnes: Five Stories Of Music and Nightfall, 2009. Contributor to journals. **Address:** Rogers, Coleridge & White Ltd., 20 Powis Mews, London, GL W11 1JN, England.

ISITT, Larry R. American (born United States), b. 1945. **Genres:** History, Theology/Religion, Humanities, Literary Criticism And History. **Career:** College of the Ozarks, associate professor of English, 1997-. Writer. **Publications:** All the Names in Heaven: A Reference Guide to Milton's Supernatural Names and Epic Similes, 2002. Contributor to periodicals. **Address:** Department of English, Eastern Washington University, Cheney, WA 99004, U.S.A. **Online address:** larry.isitt@gmail.com

ISLES, John A. American (born United States), b. 1961. **Genres:** Poetry. **Career:** Teacher, 2004-; City College of San Francisco, Department of English, faculty. Writer. **Publications:** Ark: Poems, 2003; Inverse Sky: Poems, 2008. Contributor to periodicals. **Address:** Department of English, City College of San Francisco, 50 Phelan Ave., San Francisco, CA 94112, U.S.A. **Online address:** jisles@ccsf.edu

ISOARDI, Steven L. American (born United States), b. 1949?. **Genres:** Music, History. **Career:** Oakwood School, social studies teacher. Writer. **Publications:** (Co-ed.) Central Avenue Sounds: Jazz in Los Angeles, 1999; (with B. Collete) Jazz Generations: A Life in American Music and Society, 2000; (ed.) Songs of the Unsung: The Musical and Social Journey of Horace Tapscott, 2001; The Dark Tree: Jazz and the Community Arts in Los Angeles, 2006. Contributor to periodicals. **Address:** Oakwood School, 11600 Magnolia Blvd., North Hollywood, CA 91601-3015, U.S.A.

ISRAEL, Betsy. American (born United States), b. 1959. **Genres:** Writing/Journalism, History, Women's Studies And Issues, Social Sciences. **Career:** Mademoiselle, editor; Mirabella Magazine, contributing writer; Glamour Magazine, columnist; Us Magazine, columnist; New York Woman, columnist. **Publications:** Grown-up Fast: A True Story of Teenage Life in Suburban America, 1988; Bachelor Girl: The Secret History of Single Women in the Twentieth Century, 2002; Bachelor Girl: 100 Years of Breaking the Rules-A Social History of Living Single, 2003. Contributor to periodicals. **Address:** c/o Author Mail, William Morrow/HarperCollins, 10 E 53rd St., 7th Fl., New York, NY 10022-5244, U.S.A.

ISRAEL, Charles A. American (born United States), b. 1973?. **Genres:** History, Education. **Career:** Auburn University, associate professor of history, 2005-. Writer. **Publications:** Before Scopes: Evangelicalism, Education, and Evolution in Tennessee, 1870-1925, 2004. **Address:** Department of History, Auburn University, 310 Thach Hall, Auburn, AL 36849, U.S.A.

ISRAEL, Lee. American (born United States), b. 1939. **Genres:** Biography, Humor/Satire, Literary Criticism And History, Autobiography/Memoirs. **Career:** WRVR-FM Radio, producer and broadcaster; Eros Magazine, associate editor; Virginia Kirkus Service (now Kirkus Reviews), book reviewer. **Publications:** Miss Tallulah Bankhead, 1972; Kilgallen, 1979; Estée Lauder: Beyond the Magic, 1985; Can You Ever Forgive Me?: Memoirs of a Literary Forger, 2008. Contributor to newspapers and magazines. **Address:** 98 Riverside Dr., New York, NY 10024-5323, U.S.A.

ISRAEL, Shel. American (born United States), b. 1944. **Genres:** Marketing. **Career:** Strategic Implementation of Public Relations, founder and chief executive officer, 1986-2000; Shel Israel Associates, chief executive officer, 2006-. Writer and consultant. **Publications:** (With R. Scoble) Naked Conversations: How Blogs are Changing the Way Businesses Talk with Customers, 2006; Twitterville: How Businesses Can Thrive in the New Global Neighborhoods, 2009. Contributor to magazines. **Address:** CA , U.S.A. **Online address:** shel@itseemstome.net

ITANO, Nicole. American (born United States) **Genres:** Social Commentary. **Career:** Writer. **Publications:** No Place Left to Bury the Dead: Denial, Despair, and Hope in the African AIDS Pandemic, 2007. Contributor to periodicals. **Address:** Athens, Greece. **Online address:** nicoleitano@yahoo.com

ITTMANN, John W. American (born United States) **Genres:** Art/Art History, Novels. **Career:** Philadelphia Museum of Art, curator of prints. Writer. **Publications:** Clock and Watch Designs: Three Centuries of Horological Design: Prints Drawings, Watches and Clocks, 1967; (co-author) The Forest of Fontainbleau Refuge of Reality: French Landscape 1800 to 1870, 1972; (co-auhtor) Regency to Empire: French Printmaking 1715-1814, 1984; Post-Impressionist Prints: Paris in the1890s, 1998; Dox Thrash: An African American Master Printmaker Rediscovered, 2001; (ed.) Mexico And Modern Printmaking: A Revolution In The Graphic Arts, 1920 To 1950, 2006. **Address:** Philadelphia Museum of Art, 26th St. and the Benjamin Franklin Pkwy., PO Box 7646, Philadelphia, PA 19130, U.S.A.

ITZKOFF, Seymour William. American (born United States), b. 1928. **Genres:** Education, Biography, Philosophy. **Career:** Hartford symphony orchestra, 1948-50; teacher, 1955-60; City University of New York, Hunter College, lecturer in education, 1960-65; Herbert Lehman College, faculty, 1960-65; Smith College, assistant professor, 1965-70, associate professor, 1970-75, professor of education, 1975-, professor emeritus; Campus School, director, 1968-71. Writer. **Publications:** Cultural Pluralism and American Education, 1969; Ernst Cassirer: Scientific Knowledge and the Concept of Man, 1971, 2nd ed., 1997; A New Public Education, 1976; Ernst Cassirer, Philosopher of Culture, 1977; Emanuel Feuermann: Virtuoso, 1979, 2nd ed., 1995; The Form of Man, 1983; Triumph of the Intelligent, 1985; How We Learn to Read, 1986; Why Humans Vary in Intelligence, 1987; The Making of the Civilized Mind, 1990; Human Intelligence and National Power, 1991; The Road To Equality, 1992; The Decline of Intelligence in America, 1994; Children Learning to Read, 1996; The Inevitable Domination by Man: An Evolutionary Detective Story, 2000; Intellectual Capital in Twenty-First-Century Politics, 2003; 2050: The Collapse of the Global Techno-Economy, 2003; Who are the Jews?, 2004; Rebuilding Western Civilization: Beyond the Twenty-First Century Collapse, 2005; Fatal Gift: Jewish Intelligence and Western Civilization, 2006; World Energy Crisis and the Task of Retrenchment: Reaching the Peak of Oil Production, 2008; End of Economic Growth: What Does it Mean for American Society?, 2009. Contributor of articals to periodicals. **Address:** Department of Education & Child Study, Smith College, Morgan Hall, 37 Prospect St., Northampton, MA 01063, U.S.A.

IVANOVA, Tatyana G(rigoryevna). American/Russian (born Russia) **Genres:** Biography, Autobiography/Memoirs, Adult Non-fiction, Social Sciences. **Career:** Presidium, vice chair, 1985-90; Saint Petersburg State Conservatory, lecturer, 1993; Institute of Russian Literature/Pushkin House, Manuscript Department, manager; Saint Petersburg State University, professor of folklore studies. Writer and folklorist. **Publications:** Russkiĭ folklor: bibliograficheskiĭ ukazatel, 1961; Problemy tekstologii fol'klora, 1991; Russkaia folkloristika nachala XX veka v biograficheskikh ocherkakh: E.V. Anichkov, A.V. Markov, B.M. i IU.M. Sokolovy, A.D. Grigorev, V.N. Anderson, D.K. Zelenin, N.E. Onchukov, O.E. Ozarovskaia, 1993; Velikorusskie skazki Permskoĭ gubernii: s prilozheniem dvenadtsati bashkirskikh skazok i odnoĭ meshcheriakskoĭ, 1997; (trans. and intro. with J. Bailey) An Anthology of Russian Folk Epics, 1998; Semeĭnaia zapis o Diagilevykh, 1998; (with N.N. Skatov) Izbrannye trudy i pis'ma, 1999; Malye ochagi severnorusskoĭ bylinnoĭ traditsii: issledovanie i teksty, 2001; (with S.N. Azbelev) Skomorokhi i fol'klor, 2001; Belomorskie stáriny i dukhovnye stikhi: sobranie A.V. Markova, 2002; Velikorusskie skazki Viatskoi gubernii: s prilozheniem shesti votiatskikh skazok, 2002; Lokal'nye tradit s ii v narodnoi kul'true Russkogo Severa, 2003; Rukopisnyĭ otdel Pushkinskogo Doma: istoricheskiĭ ocherk, 2006; Ri a bininskie chtenii a-2007, 2007; Riabinskie chteniia-2007: materialy V nauchnoĭ konferentsii po izucheniiu narodnoĭ kul'tury Russkogo Severa, 2007; Istoriia russkoĭ fol'kloristiki XX veka: 1900-pervaiá polovina 1941 gg, 2009; Skazki i predanii a Severnogo kraia, 2009. **Address:** c/o Author Mail, M.E. Sharpe Inc., 80 Business Park Dr., Armonk, NY 10504, U.S.A.

IVERSEN, Leslie. Also writes as L. L. Iversen, Leslie L. Iversen. British (born England), b. 1937. **Genres:** Medicine/Health. **Career:** National Institutes of Health, postdoctoral fellow, 1964-65; Harvard University, Medical School, postdoctoral fellow, 1965-66; University of Cambridge, Trinity College, research fellow, 1966-67, Locke research fellow, 1967-70, MRC Neurochemical Pharmacology Unit, director, 1970-83; U.K. Medical Research

Council, director, 1970-83; British Pharmacological Society, Gaddum Lecturer, 1971; Merck Sharp & Dohme Ltd., Neuroscience Research Centre, research director, 1983-95, Merck Research Labs, vice president, 1986-95; University of Wisconsin, Rennebohm Lecturer, 1984; Royal Society, Ferrier lecturer, 1984; Beijing Medical University, honoured professor, 1988; Oxford University, visiting professor, 1995-, King's College, Wolfson Centre for Age Related Diseases, director, 1999-2004; British Physiological Society, Hans Kosterlitz memorial lecturer, 2000. Writer. **Publications:** Uptake and Storage of Noradrenaline in Sympathetic Nerves, 1967; (with S.D. Iversen) Behavioral Pharmacology, 1970, 2nd ed., 1981; (ed. with P.R. Rose and B. Pearce) Biochemistry and Mental Illness, 1973; (ed. with S.D. Iversen and S.H. Snyder) Handbook of Psychopharmacology, 1975; (ed. with P.J. Roberts and G.N. Woodruff) Dopamine, 1978; (ed. with S.D. Iversen and S.H. Snyder) New Techniques in Psychopharmacology, 1982; (ed. with S.D. Iversen and S.H. Snyder) Neuropeptides, 1983; (ed. with S.D. Iversen and S.H. Snyder) Biochemical Studies of CNS Receptors, 1983; (ed. with S.D. Iversen and S.H. Snyder) Drugs, Neurotransmitters, and Behavior, 1984; (ed. with A. Iggo and F. Cervero) Nociception and Pain, 1985; (ed. with E.C. Goodman) Fast and Slow Chemical Signalling in the Nervous System, 1986; (ed. with S.D. Iversen and S.H. Snyder) New Directions in Behavioral Pharmacolgy, 1987; (ed. with S.D. Iversen and S.H. Snyder) Psychopharmacology of the Aging Nervous System, 1988; The Science of Marijuana, 2000, 2nd ed., 2008; Drugs: A Very Short Introduction, 2001; Speed, Ecstasy, Ritalin: The Science of Amphetamines, 2006; (co-author) Introduction to Neuropsychopharmacology, 2009; (co-ed.) Dopamine Handbook, 2010. **Address:** Oxford University, Wellington Sq., Oxford, OX OX1 2JD, England. **Online address:** les.iversen@pharm.ox.ac.uk

IVERSEN, Leslie L. *See* **IVERSEN, Leslie.**

IVERSEN, L. L. *See* **IVERSEN, Leslie.**

IVERSON, Eric G. *See* **TURTLEDOVE, Harry (Norman).**

IVES, John. *See* **GARFIELD, Brian (F. W.).**

IVORY, James (Francis). American (born United States), b. 1928. **Genres:** Plays/Screenplays, Film, Photography. **Career:** Film director and screenwriter, 1957-; Merchant Ivory Productions, partner, 1963-. **Publications:** Savages and Shakespeare Wallah, 1973; (comp.) Autobiography of a Princess: Also Being the Adventures of an American Film Director in the Land of the Maharajas, 1975. Contributor to books. **Address:** Merchant Ivory Productions, 250 W 57th St., Ste. 1825, New York, NY 10019, U.S.A. **Online address:** contact@merchantivory.com

IVORY, Judith. (Judy Cuevas). American (born United States) **Genres:** Romance/Historical, Novels. **Career:** Dade County Public Schools, teacher; University of Miami, instructor, professor; Young Men's Christian Association, Miami Writes Program, writing instructor; The Writers' Workshop Public Television Program, writing instructor. Writer. **Publications:** AS JUDY CUEVAS: Starlit Surrender, 1988; Black Silk, 1991; Bliss, 1995; Dance, 1996. AS JUDITH IVORY: Beast, 1997; Sleeping Beauty, 1998; The Proposition, 1999; The Indiscretion, 2001; Untie My Heart, 2002; Angel in a Red Dress, 2006. **Address:** Avon Books, 1350 Ave. of the Americas, 2nd Fl., New York, NY 10019-4703, U.S.A.

IWAJIN, Antony. *See* **STEINER, Evgeny.**

IWAO, Sumiko. Japanese (born Japan), b. 1935. **Genres:** Women's Studies And Issues. **Career:** Harvard University, instructor in psychology, 1962-63, visiting professor; Keio University, assistant professor, 1963-67, associate professor, 1967-75, professor of psychology, 1975-, now professor emeritus; Tokyo University of Education, Graduate School, visiting lecturer, 1976-78; International Group for the Study of Women, founder, 1977; UNESCO Center for East Asian Cultural Studies, research fellow, 1979-84; University of Tsukuba, visiting lecturer, 1979-80; University of Tokyo, visiting lecturer, through 1984; Institute of Statistical Mathematics, research fellow, 1985-86; Tokyo University of Foreign Languages, Asia-African Research Institute, research associate, 1987-89; Echo, editor-in-chief, 1997-; Musashi Institute of Technology, professor of social psychology; Cambridge University, King's College, visiting fellow. **Publications:** (With H.S. Cho) Ryūgakusei ga mita Nihon: 10-nenme no miryoku to hihan, 1987; (with H. Shigeru) Nihon de manabu ryūgakusei: shakai shinrigakuteki bunseki, 1988; (with T.N. Hen) Jōhō shakai o ikiruonnatachi: komyunikeshon no shiten kara, 1991; Japanese Women in Transition: Trends in the Early 1990s, 1992; The Japanese Woman: Traditional Image and Changing Reality, 1993; Key Words in Women's Studies, 1998; Gaikokujin Hanzaisha, 2007; Social Psychological Analysis

of Japanese TV Dramas 1977-1994, forthcoming. Works appear in anthologies. **Address:** Musashi Institute of Technology, 1-28-1 Tamazutsumi, Tokyo, 158-8557, Japan

IYENGAR, Sheena. American/Canadian (born Canada), b. 1969. **Genres:** Young Adult Non-fiction. **Career:** Columbia University, Business School, S.T. Lee Professor of Business, 1998-, Jerome A. Chazen Institute of International Business, research director, 1998-. Writer. **Publications:** The Art of Choosing (nonfiction), 2010. Contributor to books and journals. **Address:** Business School, Columbia University, Uris Hall, 3022 Broadway, Ste. 714, New York, NY 10027, U.S.A. **Online address:** ss957@columbia.edu

IYENGAR, Sujata. British (born England), b. 1970?. **Genres:** Literary Criticism And History, History, Medicine/Health. **Career:** University of Georgia, assistant professor, 1998-2005, associate professor of English, 2005-, undergraduate coordinator, 2008-11. Writer. **Publications:** Shades of Difference: Mythologies of Skin Color in the English Renaissance, 2004; Shakespeare's Medical Language: A Dictionary, 2011. Contributor to books and periodicals. **Address:** Department of English, University of Georgia, 254 Park Hall, Athens, GA 30602-6205, U.S.A. **Online address:** iyengar@uga.edu

IYER, Pico. Japanese/British (born England), b. 1957. **Genres:** Novels, Travel/Exploration, Essays, Young Adult Fiction, Biography, Autobiography/Memoirs. **Career:** Harvard University, teaching fellow, 1980-82; Time Magazine, writer, 1982-86; freelance writer, 1986-. **Publications:** The Recovery of Innocence, 1984; Cuba and the Night: A Novel, 1995; (contrib.) Buddha, the Living Way, 1998; Imagining Canada: An Outsider's Hope for a Global Future, 2001; Abandon: A Romance, 2003; (intro.) Living Faith: Windows Into the Sacred Life of India, 2004; The Open Road: The Global Journey of the Fourteenth Dalai Lama, 2008; (ed. and intro.) Skeptical Romancer, 2009; (foreword) Year of the Hare, 2010; Man Within My Head, 2012. TRAVEL: Video Night in Kathmandu: And Other Reports from the Not-So-Far East, 1988; The Lady and the Monk: Four Seasons in Kyoto, 1991; Falling off the Map: Some Lonely Places of the World, 1993; Tropical Classical: Essays from Several Directions, 1997; The Global Soul: Jet Lag, Shopping Malls, and the Search for Home, 2000; Sun After Dark: Flights into the Foreign, 2004; (ed. with J. Wilson) The Best American Travel Writing 2004, 2004; Falling Off the Top, 2004. Contributor to magazines. **Address:** Time Warner Book Group Inc., 1271 Ave. of the Americas, New York, NY 10020-1300, U.S.A.

IZAKSON, Miron C. Israeli (born Israel), b. 1956. **Genres:** Poetry. **Career:** Ben Gurion University of the Negev, creative writing teacher, 2004-05; Bar-Ilan University, creative writing teacher, 2004-05, lecturer in philosophy, 2005-06, professor of literature; Council of Art of Israel, Literature Section, head. Writer. **Publications:** (Ed.) Menachem Begin Album, 2001; Les femmes de Nathan (novel), 2001; Ne en Israel (poetry), 2003; Vitne, 2004; L'Homme Connaît Toute Nostalgie, 2008; L'Appartement rue du Roi-Salomon, 2008; The Toby Press, 2010; A Different Source: Selected Poems, 2011. **Address:** 119 Rothschild Blvd., Tel Aviv, 65271, Israel. **Online address:** management@amina.co.il

IZZI DIEN, Mawil. Welsh/British (born England), b. 1948?. **Genres:** Law, Theology/Religion. **Career:** Manchester University, Department of Near Eastern Studies, part-time Arabic lector, 1976-78; Lancaster University, Department of Islamic Studies, lecturer, 1978-79; King Abd al-Aziz University, Department of Islamic Studies, assistant professor, 1979-89, head, 1983-85; University of Vermont, supervisor Goddard programme, 1981-83; University of Wales, Department of Theology and Religious Studies, lecturer, senior lecturer of Islamic studies, 1989-2010, reader in Islamic studies and Arabic, senior lecturer in Islamic studies, 2010-; Institut Europeen des Sciences Humaines, president, 1993-98. Writer. **Publications:** Nisab al Ihtisab A Critical Study and Edition, 1983; Three Arabic Manuscripts in the John Rylands Library, 1991; Tafsir Surat al Baqara and al-Fatiha, 1995; The Theory and Practice of Market Law in Medieval Islam, 1997; The Environmental Dimensions of Islam, 2000; Islamic Law: From Historical Foundations to Contemporary Practice, 2004; (ed. with A. Khorshid and S.T. al Din) Islamic Economics in the contemporary World, forthcoming. **Address:** Department of Theology, Religion and Islamic Studies, University of Wales Trinity Saint David, Sheikh Khalifa Bldg., Lampeter, Ceredigion, SA48 7ED, Wales. **Online address:** izzidien@trinitysaintdavid.ac.uk

J

JABES, Sophie. French/Italian (born Italy), b. 1958?. **Genres:** Novels. **Career:** National Broadcasting Corp., staff; Grey Advertising, staff; French Alliance, event organizer; Chinese Women Association, event organizer. Author. **Publications:** Alice, la saucisse (novel), 2003, trans. as Alice, the Sausage, 2007; Caroline Assassine (novel), 2004; Clitomotrice (novel), 2005. **Address:** Paris, France. **Online address:** sophie.jabes@wanadoo.fr

JABINE, Thomas B(oyd). American (born United States), b. 1925. **Genres:** Mathematics/Statistics, Education. **Career:** U.S.Bureau of the Census, Population and Housing Division, mathematical statistician, 1949-52, Transportation Division, mathematical statistician, 1952-55, Statistical Research Division, mathematical statistician, 1960-63, Center for Research in Measurement Methods, mathematical statistician, 1965-66, special assistant to the deputy director, 1966-68, Office of the Associate Director for Research and Development, mathematical statistician, 1968-69, Statistical Research Division, chief, 1969-73; International Cooperation Administration, Brazil's Special Public Health Service, adviser in vital and health statistics, 1955-57, Brazilian Institute of Geography and Statistics, sampling adviser, 1957-60; Agency for International Development, National Statistical Office, sampling adviser, 1963-65, acting principal statistical adviser, 1963-64; Social Security Administration, Office of Research and Statistics, chief mathematical statistician, 1973-79; Energy Information Administration, Office of the Administrator, statistical policy expert, 1979-80; independent statistical consultant, 1980-, George Washington University, professorial lecturer, 1982-83. Consultant and writer. **Publications:** Pautas y recomendaciones para actividades experimentales y encuestas piloto, 1982; (co-author) The Comparability and Accuracy of Industry Codes in Different Data Systems, 1984; Reporting Chronic Conditions in the National Health Interview Survey: A Review of Tendencies from Evaluation Studies and Methodological Test, 1987; Quality Profile for SASS: Aspects of the Quality of Data in the Schools and Staffing Surveys, 1994. EDITOR: (co-ed.) Cognitive Aspects of Survey Methodology, 1984; (with R.P. Claude) Human Rights and Statistics, 1992; (with G.T. Duncan and V.A. Wolf) Private Lives and Public Policies: Confidentiality and Accessibility of Government Statistics, 1993; (with T.A. Louis and A.L. Schirm) Choosing the Right Formula, 2001; (with T.A. Louis and M.A. Gerstein) Statistical Issues in Allocating Funds by Formula, 2003. Works appear in anthologies. Contributor to periodicals. **Address:** 3231 Worthington St. NW, Washington, DC 20015-2362, U.S.A. **Online address:** tbjabine@starpower.net

JABLONSKI, Carla. American (born United States) **Genres:** Children's Fiction, Young Adult Fiction. **Career:** Author and consultant. **Publications:** CHILDREN'S AND YOUNG ADULT FICTION: Homer Sweet Homer, 1998; Legend of Sleepy Hollow, 1998; The Sorcerer's Apprentice, 1999; Twenty Thousand Wags under the Sea, 2000; (with A. Capeci and B. Strickland) The Wishbone Halloween Adventure, 2000; The Gypsy Enchantment, 2001; Esther Dyson: Web Guru (biography), 2002; Shadow of the Sphinx, 2003; Van Helsing: The Junior Novel, 2004; Thicker Than Water, 2006; Silent Echoes, 2007; Prince of Persia: To Right a Wrong, 2010; Prince of Persia: The Gaurdian's Path, 2010; Resistance (graphic novel), 2010; Defiance (graphic novel), 2011; Epic Mickey, 2011. BOOKS OF MAGIC SERIES: BASED ON GRAPHIC NOVEL SERIES BY NEIL GAIMAN AND JOHNBOLTON:

The Invitation, 2003; The Children's Crusade, 2003; Bindings, 2003; Consequences, 2004; Lost Places, 2004; Reckonings, 2004. **Address:** U.S.A. **Online address:** reader@carlajablonski.com

JACCARD, Mark. Canadian (born Canada), b. 1955. **Genres:** Sciences, Earth Sciences, Environmental Sciences/Ecology. **Career:** Simon Fraser University, professor of energy economics, 1986-, Energy and Materials Research Group, research director, Canadian Industrial Energy End-use Data and Analysis Centre, university research associate; M.K. Jaccard and Associates Inc., president, 1990-; British Columbia Utilities Commission, chair and chief executive officer, 1992-97; Royal Society of Canada, fellow, 2009. Writer. **Publications:** British Columbia Inquiry into Gasoline Pricing, 1996; (with M.R. Khan and J. Richards) Natural Gas Options for Bangladesh= Bāṃlādeśera prakrtika gyāsera sambhābya byabahāra, 2001; (with J. Nyboer and B. Sadownik) The Cost of Climate Policy, 2002; Sustainable Fossil Fuels: The Unusual Suspect in the Quest for Clean and Enduring Energy, 2005; (with M. Jaccard and N. Rivers) Hot Air: Meeting Canada's Climate Change Challenge, 2008. Contributor to periodicals. **Address:** Energy & Materials Research Group, School of Resource & Environmental Management, Simon Fraser University, 8888 University Dr., Burnaby, BC V5A 1S6, Canada. **Online address:** jaccard@sfu.ca

JACK, Andrew (.John). American/British (born England), b. 1967. **Genres:** Young Adult Non-fiction, Politics/Government, History. **Career:** Harvard University, Choate Memorial fellow, 1988-89; New York City Office of Business Development, employment manager, 1989-90; Financial Times, correspondent, 1990-94, journalist, 1991-, Paris correspondent, 1994-98, Moscow correspondent, chief of Moscow bureau, 1998-. Writer. **Publications:** Life at the Top, 1989; The French Exception: France-Still So Special?, 1999; Inside Putin's Russia: Can There Be Reform without Democracy?, 2004; Inside Putin's Russia, 2004. **Address:** Financial Times, 14 E 60th St., New York, NY 10022-1006, U.S.A.

JACK, Dana Crowley. American (born United States), b. 1945. **Genres:** Women's Studies And Issues, Psychology, Adult Non-fiction. **Career:** Department of Social and Health Services, case worker, 1968-70; Western Washington University, University Counseling Center, counselor, 1972-79, instructor, 1984-92, Fairhaven College, professor, 1984-; Whatcom Counseling and Psychiatric Counseling Clinic, therapist, 1973-74; Groton School, counselor, 1975-76; University of Washington, field supervisor, 1977-78; Northwest Women's Services, supervisor of staff counselors, 1985-87; Tribhuvan University, faculty. Writer. **Publications:** (With R. Jack) Moral Vision and Professional Decisions: The Changing Values of Women and Men Lawyers, 1989; Silencing the Self: Women and Depression, 1991; Behind the Mask: Destruction and Creativity in Women's Aggression, 1999; (ed. with A. Ali) Silencing the Self Across Cultures: Depression and Gender in the Social World, 2010; (ed. with A. Ali) Cultural Perspectives on Women's Depression: Self Silencing, Psychological Distress and Recovery, 2010. Contributor of articles to books and journals. **Address:** Fairhaven College of Interdisciplinary Studies, Western Washington University, FA 334, 516 High St., Bellingham, WA 98225-9118, U.S.A. **Online address:** dana.jack@wwu.edu

JACK, Malcolm Roy. British (born England), b. 1946. **Genres:** Biography,

History, Social Sciences, Reference. **Career:** House of Commons, clerk, 1967-, clerk of supply, 1989-91, House of Commons Commission, secretary 1995-2001, clerk of the journals, 2001-02, clerk of legislation, 2003. Writer. **Publications:** The Social and Political Thought of Bernard Mandeville, 1987; Corruption and Progress: The Eighteenth-Century Debate, 1989; (ed. with A. Desai) The Turkish Embassy Letters of Lady Mary Wortley Montagu, 1993; (ed. and intro.) Vathek and Other Stories: A William Beckford Reader, 1993; (ed.) Episodes of Vathek, 1994; William Beckford: An English Fidalgo, 1996; Sintra: A Glorious Eden, 2001; Lisbon, City of the Sea: A History, 2007. **Address:** Public Bill Office, House of Common, London, GL SW1A 0AA, England. **Online address:** malcolm.jack@btinternest.com

JACKALL, Robert. American (born United States) **Genres:** Business/Trade/Industry, Ethics, Money/Finance, Criminology/True Crime. **Career:** Teacher, 1964-66; Center for Economic Studies, research associate, 1976-80; Williams College, visiting lecturer, 1976-77, Department of Anthropology & Sociology, assistant professor, 1977-84, associate professor, 1984-87, professor, 1987-, Class of 1956 professor of sociology and Social Thought, department chairman, 1984-91, 1993, Willmott Family Third Century Professor of Sociology and Public Affairs, adjunct professor; NYU Stern School of Business, adjunct professor, 1989-92; Columbia University School of Business, adjunct professor, 1989-90. Writer. **Publications:** Workers in a Labyrinth: Jobs and Survival in a Bank Bureaucracy, 1978; Moral Mazes: The World of Corporate Managers, 1988; Wild Cowboys: Urban Marauders & the Forces of Order, 1997; (with J.M. Hirota) Image Makers: Advertising, Public Relations, and the Ethos of Advocacy, 2000; Street Stories: The World of Police Detectives, 2005. EDITOR and CONTRIBUTOR: (with H.M. Levin) Worker Cooperatives in America, 1984; Propaganda, 1995; With a Critical Eye: An Intellectual and His Times (2009). Contributor to articles and journals. **Address:** Department of Anthropology & Sociology, Williams College, Hollander Hall, 85 Mission Park Dr., Williamstown, MA 01267, U.S.A. **Online address:** robert.jackall@williams.edu

JACKER, Corinne. American (born United States), b. 1933. **Genres:** Plays/Screenplays, Children's Non-fiction, Information Science/Computers, Physics, Politics/Government. **Career:** Charles Scribner's Sons, assistant editor, 1950-51; Macmillan Co., associate editor, 1952-54; freelance writer, 1965-70; WNET, story editor and reader, 1970-73; New York University, instructor, 1976-78; Yale University, instructor, 1979. Writer. **Publications:** Man, Memory and Machines: An Introduction to Cybernetics, 1965; Window on the Unknown: A History of the Microscope, 1966; H.C. Wainwright & Co., 1868-1968: A Centennial, 1967; Inspirations of Modern Science, 1967; The Black Flag of Anarchy: Antistatism in the United States, 1968; A Little History of Cocoa, 1968-1868, 1968; The Biological Revolution: A Background Book on Making a New World, 1971; (with M. Barry) Chocolate Bar Burst, 1995. PLAYS: Pale Horse, Pale Rider, 1958; A Happy Ending, 1959; Seditious Acts, 1969; The Scientific Method, 1970; Project Omega: Lillian (musical), 1971; Bits and Pieces, 1973; Night Thoughts, 1973; Travellers, 1974; My Life, 1975; Harry Outside: A Play in Two Acts, 1975; The Other People's Tables, 1976; Night Thoughts and Terminal, 1977; Later, 1979; After the Season, 1979; In Place, 1980; Domestic Issues, 1981; Hedda Gabler (adaptation), 1986; Three Sisters (adaption), 1988; Let's Dance, 1988; Parties (adaptation), 1999. **Address:** c/o Lois Berman, 250 W 57th St., New York, NY 10019, U.S.A.

JACKMAN, Stuart (Brooke). British (born England), b. 1922. **Genres:** Mystery/Crime/Suspense, Plays/Screenplays, Theology/Religion, Young Adult Fiction, Novellas/Short Stories, Novels. **Career:** Congregational Council for World Mission, editor, 1965-71. Pastor and writer. **Publications:** MYSTERY NOVELS: Portrait in Two Colours, 1948; The Daybreak Boys, 1961; The Davidson Affair, 1966; The Golden Orphans, 1968; Guns Covered with Flowers, 1973; Slingshot, 1974; The Burning Men, 1976; Sandcatcher, 1980; Operation Catcher, 1980; A Game of Soldiers, 1981; Death Wish, 1999. OTHER: But They Won't Lie Down: Three Plays, 1954; The Numbered Days, 1954; Angels Unawares (play), 1956; One Finger for God, 1957; My Friend, My Brother (play), 1958; The Waters of Dinyanti, 1959; The Lazy T.V. and Other Stories (juvenile), 1961; This Desirable Property, 1966; The Davidson File, 1982; A Word in Season, 1995. **Address:** Curtis Brown Group Ltd., Haymarket House, 28-29 Haymarket, 5th Fl., London, GL SW1Y 4SP, England.

JACKMAN, Sydney Wayne. See Obituaries.

JACKONT, Amnon. Israeli (born Israel), b. 1948. **Genres:** Novels, History,

Biography. **Career:** Keter publishing Co., editor; Tel Aviv University, lecturer in history. Writer and historian. **Publications:** NOVELS: Peseḳ-Zeman, 1982; Borrowed Time, 1986; Ish Hasagrir, 1987; Aḥron Ha Me'ahavim Haḥakhamim, 1991; Malkodet Devash, 1994; Muchan La Chayim (title means: 'Prepared For Life'), 1999; Mukhan Le ḥayim: Sipurim, 2000; Mavo Le Ahava, 2001; Shin Kmo Sheker (title means: 'L for Lie'); Together with Varda Rasiel Jackont, 2004; Over Ya'Shav (English title: Resurgence), 2010; Hidath Moti (title means: The Mystery of My Death) 2010; Na le-hitnaheg behet em, 2011. **Address:** 15 King David Blvd., Tel Aviv, 64953, Israel. **Online address:** amjack@netvision.net.il

JACKSON, Angela. American (born United States), b. 1951. **Genres:** Poetry, Plays/Screenplays, Novels, Literary Criticism And History. **Career:** Organization of Black American Culture Workshop, chairperson, 1976-90; Stephens College, writer-in-residence, 1983-86; Coordinating Council of Literary Magazines, secretary, 1983, president, 1984, treasurer, 1985; Columbia College, instructor, 1986-88, writer-in-residence, 1988-92, Framingham State College, Christa MacCauliffe visiting professor of diversity, 1994; Howard University, visiting professor, 1994, professor of writing, 1995-97. **Publications:** POETRY: Voo Doo/Love Magic: Poems, 1974; The Greenville Club (chapbook), 1977; Solo in the Boxcar Third Floor E, 1985; The Man with the White Liver: Poems, 1987; Dark Legs and Silk Kisses: The Beatitudes of the Spinners, 1993; And All These Roads Be Luminous: Poems Selected and New, 1998. OTHERS: (intro.) How I Got Ovah: New and Selected Poems, 1975; Celebrate Life: Create The Life You Love to Live, 2004; Beyond The Battlefield, 2005; And Then Came God, 2006; Warm Earth, 2007; Where I Must Go, 2009. Contributor to periodicals. **Address:** Northwestern University Press, 629 Noyes St., Evanston, IL 60208-4210, U.S.A.

JACKSON, Anthony. Canadian/British (born England), b. 1926. **Genres:** Architecture, History, Politics/Government, Social Sciences. **Career:** Design Research Unit, designer, 1950-51; School of Architecture, assistant lecturer, 1951-56; Canadian Government Exhibition Commission, designer, 1957-59; The Canadian Architect, technical editor, 1959-61, managing editor, 1961-62; Technical University of Nova Scotia, associate professor, 1963-73, professor, 1973-91, professor emeritus, 1991-. **Publications:** The Politics of Architecture: A History of Modern Architecture in Britain, 1970; A Place Called Home: A History of Low-Cost Housing in Manhattan, 1976; The Democratization of Canadian Architecture, 1978; The Future of Canadian Architecture, 1979; Space in Canadian Architecture, 1981; The Symbol Stones of Scotland: A Social Anthropological Resolution of the Problem of the Picts, 1984; (with R. Macdonald) Built in Canada/Du Construction Canadienne (film), 1985; Reconstructing Architecture for the 21st Century: An Inquiry into the Architect's World, 1995. **Address:** Technical University of Nova Scotia, School of Architecture, Halifax, NS B3J 2X4, Canada. **Online address:** anthonyjackson@ns.sympatico.ca

JACKSON, Belle. See CARR, Margaret.

JACKSON, Ben. British (born England), b. 1975. **Genres:** History. **Career:** Oxford University, University College, lecturer and tutorial fellow. Writer. **Publications:** Equality and the British Left: A Study in Progressive Political Thought, 1900-64, 2007. Contributor to books and periodicals. **Address:** University College, Oxford University, Queen's Ln., Oxford, OX OX1 4AR, England. **Online address:** benjamin.jackson@univ.ox.ac.uk

JACKSON, Clare. American (born United States), b. 1972. **Genres:** History, Politics/Government. **Career:** University of Cambridge, Department of History, lecturer, director of studies; Historical Journal, co-editor, 2004-. **Publications:** Restoration Scotland, 1660-1690: Royalist Politics, Religion and Ideas, 2003; (contrib.) George Buchanan: Political Thought in Early Modern Europe, forthcoming; (contrib.) Religion, Culture and the National Community, forthcoming. Contributor of articles to books. **Address:** Department of History, Cambridge University, Trinity Hall, Cambridge, CB CB2 1TJ, England. **Online address:** jclj1@cam.ac.uk

JACKSON, David Cooper. (David Pingree Jackson). British (born England), b. 1931?. **Genres:** Law, Civil Liberties/Human Rights. **Career:** University of Singapore, senior lecturer in law, 1963-64; Monash University, senior lecturer, 1964-65, Sir John Latham professor of law, 1965-70; University of Southampton, professor of law, 1971-98, Institute of Maritime Law, director, 1987-90, emeritus professor of law, 1998-; United Nations Conference on Trade and Development, consultant. Writer. **Publications:** Principles of Property Law, 1967; Law and Public Policy, the English Connection: An Inaugural Lecture Delivered at the University, 23 October 1973, 1974; The Conflicts Process, 1975; World Shipping Laws, 1979; Enforcement of Maritime Claims, 1985, 4th ed., 2005; Maritime Claims: Jurisdiction and Judgements, 1987; Immigration: Law and Practice, 1996, 2nd ed., 1999. Contributor to journals. **Address:** Institute of Maritime Law, University of Southampton, University Rd., Southampton, HM SO17 1BJ, England.

JACKSON, David Pingree. *See* **JACKSON, David Cooper.**

JACKSON, Edwardo. American/Panamanian (born Panama), b. 1975. **Genres:** Novels, Plays/Screenplays, Young Adult Fiction. **Career:** JCM Entertainment L.L.C., co-president. Writer. **Publications:** NICK-JASMINE TRILOGY NOVELS: Ever After, 2001; Neva Hafta, 2002; I Do?, 2006. Contributor to periodicals. Works appear in anthologies. **Address:** JCM Entertainment L.L.C., 15228-B Hawthorne Blvd., Ste. 203, Lawndale, CA 90260, U.S.A. **Online address:** everafteranovel@aol.com

JACKSON, Eve. British/Welsh (born Wales), b. 1943. **Genres:** Psychology, Astronomy, Air/Space Topics, Theology/Religion. **Career:** Writer and educator. **Publications:** Jupiter: Astrological Anatomy of a Planet, 1986; Astrology: A Psychological Approach, 1987; Food and Transformation: Imagery and Symbolism of Eating, 1996. **Address:** Inner City Books, PO Box 1271, Sta. Q, Toronto, ON M4T 2P4, Canada. **Online address:** unus.mundus@bigfoot.com

JACKSON, Everatt. *See* **MUGGESON, Margaret Elizabeth.**

JACKSON, Gina. *See* **FLUKE, Joanne.**

JACKSON, G. Mark. (Kano Shinichi). American (born United States), b. 1952. **Genres:** Novels, Criminology/True Crime, Sports/Fitness, Art/Art History. **Career:** Jefferson Advertiser, writer, 1978-79; Southside News and Sentinel Star (now Orlando Sentinel), writer, 1979-81; freelance writer, 1981-. **Publications:** (As Kano Shinichi) Ninja: Men of Iga, 1989. Contributor of articles to journals. **Address:** 2043 SE Isabell Rd., Port St. Lucie, FL 34952, U.S.A.

JACKSON, James R. *See* **JACKSON, J. R. de J.**

JACKSON, Jane. Also writes as Jane Collier, Dana Mills. British (born England), b. 1944?. **Genres:** Romance/Historical, Novels. **Career:** Writer. **Publications:** AS JANE COLLIER: Deadly Feast, 1978. ROMANCE NOVELS AS DANA MILLS: Desert Flower, 1983; Dr. in New Guinea, 1983; Dr. in the Andes, 1984; Rough Waters, 1985; The Marati Legacy, 1986; The Eagle and the Sun, 1987; Heart of Glass, 1987; Tarik's Mountain, 1988; Pool of Dreaming, 1988; Love's Ransom, 1989; Snowfire, 1989; Dark Moon Rising, 1990; A Tempting Shore, 1991; Bay of Rainbows, 1993. ROMANCE NOVELS: Harlyn Tremayne: An Historical Romance, 1984; The Consul's Daughter, 1986; A Place of Birds, 1997; The Iron Road, 1999; Eye of the Wind, 2001; Tide of Fortune, 2004; The Chain Garden, 2006; Dangerous Waters, 2006; Devil's Prize, 2008; Heart of Stone, 2009; Bonded Heart, 2009. **Address:** England. **Online address:** postmaster@janejackson.net

JACKSON, Jeffrey H. American (born United States), b. 1971. **Genres:** Music, History. **Career:** Rhodes College, assistant professor, 2000-07, associate professor, 2007-, Environmental Studies Program, associate director, 2008-09, director of environmental studies and sciences, 2009-. Writer. **Publications:** Making Jazz French: Music and Modern Life in Interwar Paris, 2003; (ed. with S.C. Pelkey) Music and History: Bridging the Disciplines, 2005; Paris under Water: How the City of Light Survived the Great Flood of 1910, 2010. Works appear in anthologies. Contributor of articles to journals and periodicals. **Address:** Rhodes College, 2000 North Pkwy., Memphis, TN 38112-1690, U.S.A. **Online address:** jacksonj@rhodes.edu

JACKSON, Jesse. (Jesse Louis Jackson). American (born United States), b. 1965. **Genres:** Money/Finance, Young Adult Non-fiction, Social Sciences, Law. **Career:** Rainbow Coalition/Operation PUSH, national field director, 1993-95; United States House of Representatives, Illinois's 2nd Congressional District, representative, 1995-. Politician and author. **Publications:** WITH J. JACKSON SR.: Legal Lynching: Racism, Injustice, and the Death Penalty, 1996; (and M. Gotschall as Jesse L. Jackson, Jr.) It's about the Money!: The Fourth Movement of the Freedom Symphony: How to Build Wealth, Get Access to Capital, and Achieve Your Financial Dreams, 1999; (and B. Shapiro

as Jesse L. Jackson, Jr.) Legal Lynching: The Death Penalty and America's Future, 2001. OTHER: (with F.E. Watkins as Jesse L. Jackson, Jr.) A More Perfect Union: Advancing New American Rights, 2001. **Address:** 2nd Congressional District, United States House of Representatives, 17926 S Halsted, Homewood, IL 60430-2013, U.S.A.

JACKSON, Jesse Louis. *See* **JACKSON, Jesse.**

JACKSON, John A. American (born United States), b. 1943. **Genres:** Music, Literary Criticism And History, Social Sciences. **Career:** Farmingdale Public Schools, physical education teacher, 1966-98, retired, 1998; Rockin' 50s, columnist, 1986-87. **Publications:** Big Beat Legends: Rock and Roll's Evolution on Television, 1988; Big Beat Heat: Alan Freed and the Early Years of Rock and Roll, 1991; American Bandstand: Dick Clark and the Making of a Rock n Roll Empire, 1997; A House on Fire: The Rise and Fall of Philadelphia Soul, 2004. Contributor to periodicals. **Address:** Nancy Love Literary Agency, 250 E 65th St., New York, NY 10021-6614, U.S.A. **Online address:** beachrunner@tampabay.rr.com

JACKSON, John N. Canadian/British (born England), b. 1925. **Genres:** Geography, Regional/Urban Planning, Urban Studies. **Career:** Manchester University, lecturer in town and country planning, 1956-65; Brock University, professor of applied geography, 1965-91, head of department, 1965-70, professor emeritus, 1991-. Writer. **Publications:** Surveys for Town and Country Planning, 1963; Recreational Development and the Lake Erie Shore, 1967; The Industrial Structure of the Niagara Peninsula, 1971; The Urban Future, 1972; The Canadian City: Space, Form, Quality, 1973; (ed. with J. Forrester) Practical Geography: Strategies for Study, 1974; Welland and the Welland Canal: The Welland Canal By-Pass, 1975; St. Catharines, Ontario: Its Early Years, 1976; (with J. Burtniak) Railways in the Niagara Peninsula, 1978; (with F.A. Addis) The Welland Canals: A Comprehensive Guide, 1982; St. Catharines: The Contribution of the City to Two Hundred Years of Ontario Life, 1984; (with R.M. Styran and R.R. Taylor) The Welland Canals: The Growth of Mr. Merritt's Ditch, 1987; The Four Welland Canals, 1988; Names across Niagara, 1990; (with S.M. Wilson) St. Catharines: Canada's Canal City, 1992; The Welland Canals and Their Communities: Engineering, Industrial, and Urban Transformation, 1997; (with J. Burtniak and G.P. Stein) The Mighty Niagara: One River-Two Frontiers, 2003. **Address:** Brock University, 500 Glenridge Ave., St. Catharines, ON L2S 3A1, Canada.

JACKSON, John P. American (born United States), b. 1961. **Genres:** Sociology, Race Relations, Law, Education. **Career:** Macalester College, assistant debate coach, 1984-87; University of Minnesota, Program in History of Science and Technology, teaching/research assistant, 1991-93, Charles Babbage Institute for the History of Information Processing, teaching/research assistant, 1991-93; Florida State University, adjunct instructor, 1995-98; University of Colorado, Department of Ethnic Studies, instructor, 1999-2000, Department of History, instructor, 1999-2000, Department of Communication, instructor, 1999-2000, 2001-04, assistant professor, 2004-08, associate professor, 2008-, Center for the Study of Ethnicity and Race in the Americas, postdoctoral fellow, 2000-01, member of graduate faculty, 2002-. Writer. **Publications:** Social Scientists for Social Justice: Making the Case against Segregation, 2001; (ed.) Science, Race, and Ethnicity: Readings from Isis and Osiris, 2002; (with N.M. Weidman) Race, Racism, and Science: Social Impact and Interaction, 2004; Science for Segregation: Race, Law, and the Case against Brown v. Board of Education, 2005. Contributor to books, periodicals and journals. **Address:** Department of Communication, University of Colorado, Hellems 94, PO Box 270, Boulder, CO 80309-0270, U.S.A. **Online address:** john.p.jackson@colorado.edu

JACKSON, J. R. de J. Also writes as James R. Jackson. Canadian/Scottish (born Scotland), b. 1935. **Genres:** Literary Criticism And History, Bibliography. **Career:** McMaster University, assistant professor, 1963-64; University of Toronto, assistant professor, 1964-, professor, 1974-94, university professor, 1994-2001, university professor emeritus, 2001-; Guggenheim fellow, 1972-73; Killam research fellow, 1975-76, 1982-84; Connaught senior fellow, 1985-86. Writer. **Publications:** Method and Imagination in Coleridge's Criticism, 1969; Poetry of the Romantic Period, 1980; Annals of English Verse, 1770-1835, 1985; Historical Criticism and the Meaning of Texts, 1989; Romantic Poetry by Women: A Bibliography 1770-1835, 1993. EDITOR: The Critical Heritage, 1970, vol. II, 1991; Logic, 1981; (with H.J. Jackson) Shorter Works and Fragments, vol. II, 1995; Lectures 1818-1819 on the History of Philosophy, vol. II, 2000. **Address:** Department of English, University of Toronto, 7 King's College Cir., Toronto, ON M5S 3K1, Canada.

JACKSON, Kate. American/Canadian (born Canada), b. 1972. **Genres:** Animals/Pets, Sciences. **Career:** Whitman College, assistant professor of biology. Writer. **Publications:** Mean and Lowly Things: Snakes, Science, and Survival in the Congo, 2008. **Address:** Whitman College, 345 Boyer Ave., Walla Walla, WA 99362, U.S.A. **Online address:** jacksok@whitman.edu

JACKSON, Kathy Merlock. American (born United States), b. 1955. **Genres:** Film, Bibliography, Children's Fiction. **Career:** QPA Personnel Consultants, employment counselor, 1979; Tufts University, Office of Research and Development, researcher and writer, 1979-81; Smithsonian Institution, National Museum of American History, Division of Transportation, researcher, 1982; Virginia Wesleyan College, professor and coordinator of communications, 1984-, Batten professor, 2008-; Research Communications Ltd., research consultant, 1986-89; Port Folio Magazine, columnist. **Publications:** Images of Children in American Film: A Socio-Cultural Analysis, 1986; Walt Disney: A Bio-Bibliography, 1993; (ed.) Rituals and Patterns in Children's Lives, 2005; (ed.) Walt Disney: Conversations, 2006; (ed. with M.I. West) Disneyland and Culture: Essays on the Parks and their Influence, 2011. Works appear in anthologies. Contributor of articles to periodicals. **Address:** Department of Communications, Virginia Wesleyan College, Rm. 208, Birdsong Hall, 1584 Wesleyan Dr., Norfolk, VA 23502, U.S.A. **Online address:** kmjackson@vwc.edu

JACKSON, Kenneth T(erry). American (born United States), b. 1939. **Genres:** History, Regional/Urban Planning, Urban Studies, Reference. **Career:** Wittenberg University, lecturer in history, 1967-68; Columbia University, assistant professor, associate professor, 1968-76, professor of history, 1976-87, Mellon professor, 1987-90, Jacques Barzun professor of history and the social sciences, 1990-, Department of History, chairman, 1994-97, Herbert H. Lehman Center for American History, director; Princeton University, visiting professor, 1973-74; George Washington University, visiting professor, 1982-83; University of California-Los Angeles, visiting professor, 1986-87. Writer. **Publications:** The Chicago Council on Foreign Relations: A Record of Forty Years, 1963; The Ku Klux Klan in the City, 1915-1930, 1967, 2nd ed., 1992; (ed. with L. Dinnerstein) American Vistas, 2 vols., 1971, 7th ed., 1995; (ed. with S.K. Schultz) Cities in American History, 1972; Dictionary of American Biography, Supplement Three-(ten): With an Index Guide to the Supplements, 1973; (ed.) Atlas of American History, 1978, 2nd ed., 1984; Crabgrass Frontier: The Suburbanization of the United States, 1985; (with C.J. Vergara) Silent Cities: The Evolution of American Cemeteries, 1989; (ed.) The Encyclopedia of New York City, 1995; (intro.) The Neighborhoods of Brooklyn, 1998, 2nd ed., 2004; (intro.) The Past Revealed: Museum Collection Highlights from the New York Historical Society, 2000; (ed. with D.S. Dunbar) Empire City: New York through the Centuries, 2002; (ed.) The Scribner Encyclopedia of American Lives, 6 vols., 2003; Robert Moses and the Modern City: The Transformation of New York, 2007; (with F. Kameny) Almanac of New York City, 2008. Contributor to journals. **Address:** Department of History, Columbia University, 603 Fayerweather Hall, PO Box 2538, New York, NY 10027, U.S.A. **Online address:** ktj1@columbia.edu

JACKSON, Kevin. British (born England), b. 1955. **Genres:** Film, Plays/Screenplays. **Career:** Vanderbilt University, teaching fellow in English, 1980-82; British Broadcasting Corp., producer and director for radio and television, 1983-87; Independent, associate arts editor, 1987-; Alces Press, managing director; writer and presenter of documentary films; Royal College of Art, lecturer; Arena Magazine, contributing editor; University College London, visiting professor. **Publications:** The Language of Cinema, 1998; Invisible Forms: A Guide to Literary Curiosities, 2000; (with J. Stamp) Building the Great Pyramid, 2003; (with I. Sinclair) The Verbals, 2003; Withnail and I, 2004; Bite: A Vampire Handbook, 2009; Worlds of John Ruskin, 2010. EDITOR: Schrader on Schrader, 1990; The Humphrey Jennings Film Reader, 1993; The Oxford Book of Money, 1995; Selected Writings of Dylan Francis, 1995; (with R. Hackney) A Parent-Teacher's Guide to Children's Educational Software, 1996. Contributor to periodicals. **Address:** c/o Georgina Capel, Simpson-Fox Associates, 52 Shaftesbury Ave., London, GL W1V 7DE, England.

JACKSON, Lisa. American (born United States) **Genres:** Mystery/Crime/Suspense, Novels, Romance/Historical, Young Adult Fiction, Children's Fiction. **Career:** Writer. **Publications:** A Twist of Fate, 1983; Shadow of Time,

1984; Dark Side of the Moon, 1984; A Dangerous Precedent, 1985; Devils Gambit, 1985; Innocent by Association, 1985; Midnight Sun, 1985; Pirates Gold, 1985; Gypsy Wind, 1985; Yesterdays Lies, 1986; Zacharys Law, 1986; Summer Rain, 1987; Renegade Son, 1987; Snowbound, 1987; In Honors Shadow, 1988; Brass Ring, 1988; Hurricane Force, 1988; Tender Trap, 1989; Aftermath, 1989; His Bride to Be, 1989; With No Regrets, 1990; Double Exposure, 1990; Obsession, 1991; Mystery Man, 1991; Enchantress, 1991; Sail Away, 1992; Million Dollar Baby, 1992; A Husband to Remember, 1993; He's a Bad Boy, 1993; He's Just a Cowboy, 1993; He's the Rich Boy, 1993; Kiss of the Moon, 1994; A Is for Always, 1994; B is for Baby, 1994; C is for Cowboy, 1994; He's My Soldier Boy, 1994; Wishes, 1995; Whispers, 1995; Outlaw, 1995; Intimacies, 1995; D ss for Danis Baby, 1995; The Millionaire and the Cowgirl, 1996; New Years Daddy, 1996; (co-author) Tis the Season: Snowbound, 1997; Twice Kissed, 1998; A Fortunes Children Christmas: Angel Baby, 1998; A Family Kind of Gal, 1998; A Family Kind of Guy, 1998; Dark Ruby, 1998; A Family Kind of Wedding, 1999; Unspoken, 1999; Dark Emerald, 1999; If She Only Knew, 2000; The McCaffertys: Thorne, 2000; Love Letters, 2000; Lone Stallions Lady, 2000; Dark Sapphire, 2000; Slow Heat, 2001; The McCaffertys: Matt, 2001; Hot Blooded, 2001; Tears of Pride, 2002; Wild and Wicked, 2002; Cold Blooded, 2002; The McCaffertys: Slade, 2002; Santa Baby: A Baby for Christmas, 2002; Mystic, 2002; Impostress, 2003; Enchantress, 2003; The Night Before, 2003; Deck the Halls, 2004; Best Kept Lies: The McCaffertys: Randi, 2004; The Morning After, 2004; Kiss of the Moon, 2004; See How She Dies, 2004; Best-kept Lies, 2004; Dark Emerald, 2004; Deep Freeze, 2005; Temptress, 2005; Dark jewels, 2005; (with B. Boswell and L. Turner) A Fortune's Children Christmas, 2005; Strangers, 2005; Final Scream, 2005; Kiss Me Again, 2005; Shiver, 2006; Fatal Burn, 2006; Absolute fear, 2007; Sorceress, 2007; (with W.C. Staub and B. Barton) Most Likely to Die, 2007; Almost Dead, 2007; Lost Souls, 2008; Left To Die, 2008; Malice, 2009; Chosen To Die, 2009; (with L. Conrad and B. McCauley) Secrets and Desire, 2009; (with N. Bush) Wicked Game, 2009; Montana Fire, 2009; Risky Business, 2009; Without Mercy, 2010; Running Scared, 2010; Devious, 2011; Born to Die, 2011; Wicked Lies, 2011; (with R. Tramonto) Scars of a Chef: The Searing Story of a Top Chef Marked Forever by the Grit and Grace of Life in the Kitchen, 2011. **Address:** 333 S State St., PO Box 308, Lake Oswego, OR 97034, U.S.A. **Online address:** lisa@lisajackson.com

JACKSON, Maggie. American (born United States) **Genres:** Adult Nonfiction. **Career:** Associated Press, reporter, editor on foreign and business desks and national workplace columnist, 1995-2001, foreign correspondent; University of Maryland, journalism fellow in child and family policy, 2005-06; Center for Work-Life Policy, senior fellow. **Publications:** (With L.R. Helton) Social Work Practice with Families: A Diversity Model, 1997; What's Happening to Home?: Balancing Work, Life, and Refuge in the Information Age, 2002; Distracted: The Erosion of Attention and the Coming Dark Age, 2008. Contributor to Magazine. **Address:** Prometheus Books, 59 John Glenn Dr., Amherst, NY 14228-2197, U.S.A. **Online address:** maggie@maggie-jackson.com

JACKSON, Marian J. A. American (born United States), b. 1932. **Genres:** Mystery/Crime/Suspense, Criminology/True Crime, Literary Criticism And History. **Career:** Institute of Electrical and Electronics Engineers, manager of technical services department, 1970-78; freelance writer, 1985-. **Publications:** A MISS DANFORTH MYSTERY: The Punjat's Ruby, 1990; The Arabian Pearl, 1991; The Cat's Eye, 1991; Diamond Head, 1992; Sunken Treasure, 1994; (with J.T. Rogers) When Last Seen, 2001. **Address:** c/o Elizabeth Backman, Johnnycake Hollow Rd., PO Box 536, Pine Plains, NY 12567, U.S.A. **Online address:** marian@marianjackson.net

JACKSON, Mark. See KURZ, Ron.

JACKSON, Mark. British (born England), b. 1959?. **Genres:** Medicine/Health, Law, Biography, Humanities, History. **Career:** University of Leeds, researcher; University of Manchester, researcher; University of Exeter, professor of history of medicine, Centre for Medical History, director, staff. Writer. **Publications:** New-Born Child Murder: Women, Illegitimacy and the Courts in Eighteenth-Century England, 1996; (ed. with D. Atkinson and J. Walmsley) Forgotten Lives: Exploring the History of Learning Disability, 1997; The Borderland of Imbecility: Medicine, Society, and the Fabrication of the Feeble Mind in Late Victorian and Edwardian England, 2000; (ed.) Infanticide: Historical Perspectives on Child Murder and Concealment, 1550-2000, 2002; Allergy: The History of a Modern Malady, 2006; (ed.) Health and the Modern Home, 2007; Asthma: The Biography, 2009. Contributor to journals and periodicals. **Address:** Department of History, University of Exeter, Amory Bldg., Rennes Dr., Streatham Campus, Exeter, DN EX4 4RJ, England. **Online address:** m.a.jackson@exeter.ac.uk

JACKSON, Marni. Canadian (born Canada), b. 1946. **Genres:** Autobiography/Memoirs, Medicine/Health, Women's Studies And Issues, Writing/Journalism, Humor/Satire. **Career:** Ryerson University, Continuing Education, instructor, Walrus Magazine, senior editor, 2005-07; Banff Centre, Literary Journalism Program, Rogers chair, 2006-09, Mountain and Wilderness Writing Program, faculty, 2006-. Journalist. **Publications:** The Mother Zone: Love, Sex and Laundry in the Modern Family, 1992; Pain: The Fifth Vital Sign, 2002; Home Free: The Myth of the Empty Nest, 2010. Contributor to periodicals and newspapers. Works appear in anthologies. **Address:** c/o Samantha Haywood, Transatlantic Literary Agency, 2 Bloor St. E, Ste. 3500, Toronto, ON M4W 1A8, Canada. **Online address:** marnijackson@rogers.com

JACKSON, Michael (Derek). New Zealander (born New Zealand), b. 1940. **Genres:** Anthropology/Ethnology. **Career:** Massey University, Department of Anthropology and Maori Studies, senior lecturer, 1973-77, reader, 1977-82; Australian National University, Humanities Research Centre, visiting fellow, 1982, Department of Prehistory and Anthropology, part-time lecturer, 1984-85; Indiana University, Institute of Advance Study, visiting fellow, 1988-89, Department of Anthropology, professor, 1989-96; University of Sydney, Department of Anthropology, part-time lecturer, 1996-97; Victoria University, stout research fellow, 1998; University of Copenhagen, Institute of Anthropology, professor, 2003-05; Harvard Divinity School, distinguished visiting professor in world religions, 2005-. Writer. **Publications:** POETRY: The Kuranko: Dimensions of Social Reality in a West African Society, 1977; Allegories of the Wilderness: Ethics and Ambiguity in Kuranko Narratives, 1982; Barawa and the Ways Birds Fly in the Sky: An Ethnographic Novel, 1986; Paths toward a Clearing: Radical Empiricism and Ethnographic Inquiry, 1989; At Home in the World, 1995; The Blind Impress, 1997; Minima Ethnographica: Intersubjectivity and the Anthropological Project, 1998; The Politics of Storytelling: Violence, Transgression, and Intersubjectivity, 2002; In Sierra Leone, 2004; Existential Anthropology: Events, Exigencies, and Effects, 2004; Excursions, 2007; Palm at the End of the Mind: Relatedness, Religiosity, and the Real, 2009. Life Within Limits: Well-being in a World of Want, 2011; The Enigma of Anteriority: An Antipodean Journey, forthcoming. EDITOR: Personhood and Agency: The Experience of Self and Other in African Cultures, 1990; Things as They Are: New Directions in Phenomenological Anthropology, 1996. FICTION AND POEM: Latitudes of Exile: Poems, 1965-1975, 1976; Wall, 1980; Going On, 1985; Rainshadow: A Novel, 1988; Duty Free: Selected Poems, 1965-1988, 1989; Pieces of Music, 1994; Antipodes, 1996; Dead Reckoning, 2006; The Accidental Anthropologist: A Memoir, 2006. OTHERS: Between One and One Another, 2012; Road Markings: An Anthropologist in the Antipodes, 2012. **Address:** Center for the Study of World Religions, Harvard Divinity School, 45 Francis Ave., Cambridge, MA 02138, U.S.A. **Online address:** mjackson@hds.harvard.edu

JACKSON, Monica. (Monika Elaine). American (born United States) **Genres:** Novels, Romance/Historical. **Career:** Nurse and writer. **Publications:** Midnight Blue, 1997; Love's Celebration, 1998; Heart's Desire, 1998; The Look of Love, 1999; A Magical Moment, 1999; Never Too Late for Love, 2000; Too Hot to Handle, 2001; Gettin Merry: A Holiday Anthology, 2002; In My Dreams, 2004; Love's Potion, 2005; Mr. Right Now, 2005; Perfect Passion, 2006; Merry Christmas, Baby, 2006; Creepin, 2007. **Address:** Kensington Publishing Corp., 850 3rd Ave., New York, NY 10022-6222, U.S.A.

JACKSON, Richard D(ean) W(ells). New Zealander (born New Zealand), b. 1967. **Genres:** International Relations/Current Affairs, Military/Defense/Arms Control. **Career:** Critical Studies on Terrorism, founding editor and editor-in-chief; University of Otago, teaching fellow, 1996-2001, chairperson of foreign policy School, 1997-98, National Centre for Peace and Conflict, director; University of Canterbury, lecturer, 2002; University of Manchester, lecturer in government, 2003-05; Aberystwyth University, Department of International Politics, reader, 2005-; Centre for the Study of Radicalisation and Contemporary Political Violence, senior researcher, professor. Writer. **Publications:** (With J. Bercovitch) International Conflict: A Chronological Encyclopedia of Conflicts and Their Management, 1945-1995, 1997; (with J. Bercovitch) Conflict Resolution in the Twenty-First Century, 2003; (ed. and contrib.) Constructing Cultures of Violence and Peace, 2004; Writing the War on Terrorism: Language, Politics and Counterterrorism, 2005; Conflict Resolution in the Twenty-first Century: Principles, Methods, and Approaches,

2009; (ed. with M.B. Smyth and J. Gunning) Critical Terrorism Studies: A New Research Agenda, 2009; (ed. with E. Murphy and S. Poynting) Contemporary State Terrorism: Theory and Cases, 2010; (with M.B. Smyth, J. Gunning and L. Jarvis) Terrorism: A Critical Introduction, 2011; (ed. with S.J. Sinclair) Contemporary Debates on Terrorism, 2012. Contributor to journals. **Address:** National Centre for Peace and Conflict, University of Otago, 364 Leith Walk, Clocktower Bldg., Dunedin, 9016, New Zealand. **Online address:** richard.jackson@aber.ac.uk

JACKSON, Robert H. (Robert Howard Jackson). American (born United States), b. 1955. **Genres:** History, Social Sciences, Young Adult Non-fiction. **Career:** Gettysburg College, instructor in history, 1988; University of Minnesota, lecturer in history, 1989; University of Miami, visiting assistant professor of history, 1989-90; Texas Southern University, assistant professor of history, 1990-. Writer. **Publications:** (Ed. with E. Langer) The New Latin American Mission History, 1985; (ed. and intro.) The Spanish Missions of Baja California, 1991; Indian Population Decline, 1994; Regional Markets and Agrarian Transformation in Bolivia: Cocha-bamba, 1539-1960, 1994; (with E. Castillo) Indians, Franciscans and Spanish Colonization, 1995; (ed. with E. Langer) The New Latin American Mission History, 1995; (ed.) Liberals, the Church and Indian Peasants: Corporate. Lands and the Challenge of Reform in Nineteenth-Century Spanish America, 1997; (ed.) New Views of Borderlands History, 1998; Race, Caste and Status: Indians in Colonial Spanish America, 1999. **Address:** Department of History, Geography and Economics, Texas Southern University, 3100 Cleburne Ave., Houston, TX 77004, U.S.A.

JACKSON, Robert Howard. See **JACKSON, Robert H.**

JACKSON, Robert J. Canadian (born Canada), b. 1936. **Genres:** International Relations/Current Affairs, Politics/Government. **Career:** Carleton University, Department of Political Science, assistant professor, 1965-68, associate professor and supervisor of graduate studies, 1970-71, professor and chair, 1974-97; McGill University, associate professor, 1968-70; Office of the President of the Privy Council, legislative adviser and director of research, 1971-73; House of Commons, senior policy adviser, leader of the opposition, 1987-89; University of Redlands, Fletcher Jones professor of government and director of international relations, 1997-; University of Cambridge, visiting fellow; Griffith University, faculty fellow; Atlantic Institute of International Affairs, fellow; Australian National University, visitong fellow; University of New England, visiting fellow. Writer. **Publications:** Rebels and Whips: Dissensions, Discipline, and Cohesion in British Parties, 1968; (with M. Stein) Issues in Comparative Politics, 1971; (with M. Atkinson) Canadian Legislative System: Politicians and Policy-Making, 1974, 2nd ed., 1980; Continuity of Discord: Crises and Responses in the Altantic Community, 1985; (with D. Jackson, N. Baxter-Moore) Politics in Canada, 1985, 6th ed., 2004; (with M.P.C.M. van Schendelen) The Politicisation of Business in Western Europe, 1987; Contemporary Canadian Politics, 1987; (with D. Jackson)Stand Up for Canada: Leadership and the Canadian Political Crisis, 1992; (ed.) Europe in Transition: The Management of Security after the Cold War, 1992; Contemporary Government and Politics, 1993; Canadian Government in Transition, 1996; Politics in Canada, 1997; Comparative Government, 1997; (with D. Jackson) Comparative Introduction to Political Science, 1997; (ed. with P. Dutkiewicz) NATO looks East, 1998; (with D. Jackson) Politics in Canada: Culture, Institutions, Behaviour, and Public Policy, 1998; (J.C. Rea and G.S. Malher) Sistemas políticos de América del Norte en los noventa: desafíos y convergencias, 1999; (with J.C. Rea and G.S. Malher) Los sistemas políticos de América del Norte en los noventa, 1999; Introduction to Political Science, 2003; (co-author) North American Politics: Canada, USA, and Mexico in a Comparative Perspective, 2004; (with P. Towle) Temptations of Power: The United States in Global Politics After 9/11, 2006. **Address:** University of Redlands, Hall of Letters, Rm. 324, Redlands, CA 92373, U.S.A. **Online address:** robert-jackson@redlands.edu

JACKSON, Sheneska. American (born United States), b. 1970?. **Genres:** Novels, Literary Criticism And History, Young Adult Fiction. **Career:** University of California Extension Program, writing instructor; medical secretary, 1992-95. Writer. **Publications:** Caught up in the Rapture: A Novel, 1996; Li'l Mama's Rules, 1997; Blessings: A Novel, 1998. **Address:** c/o Simon & Schuster Children's Publishing, 1230 Ave. of the Americas, 10th Fl., New York, NY 10020, U.S.A.

JACKSON, Sherri L. American (born United States), b. 1962. **Genres:**

Psychology. **Career:** Jacksonville University, assistant professor, 1988-93, associate professor, 1993-98, professor of psychology, 1998-, faculty chair, 2002-03. Writer. **Publications:** (With R.A. Griggs) Study Guide to Accompany Invitation to Psychology, 1998, 2nd ed., 2002; Research Methods and Statistics: A Critical-Thinking Approach, 2003, 3rd ed., 2008; Statistics: Plain and Simple, 2005; Research Methods: A Modular Approach, 2008, 2nd ed., 2011. Contributor to periodicals. **Address:** Department of Psychology, Jacksonville University, 2800 University Blvd. N, Jacksonville, FL 32211, U.S.A.

JACKSON, Sid J. (C. C. Canby). American (born United States), b. 1937. **Genres:** Mystery/Crime/Suspense, Social Sciences, History. **Career:** Central Missouri University, teacher; Century College, professor, 1968-99, professor emeritus, 1999-; j-Press Publishing, owner and publisher. Writer. **Publications:** Sociological Science, 1997; (as C.C. Canby) Masks of Murder, 2003; (as C.C. Canby) Manitou Murder, 2009. **Address:** j-Press Publishing, 4796 N 126th St., White Bear Lake, MN 55110-5911, U.S.A. **Online address:** sidj1@nethere.com

JACKSON, Steve. American (born United States), b. 1955?. **Genres:** Criminology/True Crime, Adult Non-fiction. **Career:** Writer. **Publications:** NONFICTION: Monster, 1998; Rough Trade, 2001; Love Me to Death, 2002; No Stone Unturned: The Story of NecroSearch International, 2002; Lucky Lady: The World War II Heroics of the USS Santa Fe and Franklin, 2003; Partners in Evil, 2003. GHOST WRITER: To the Edge and Back: My Story from Organ Transplant Survivor to Olympic Snowboarder, 2004; Not Lost Forever: My Story of Survival, 2009. **Address:** CO , U.S.A. **Online address:** steve@stevejacksonauthor.com

JACKSON, Troy. American (born United States), b. 1968?. **Genres:** Biography, History. **Career:** University Christian Church, pastor, 1994-. Writer and historian. **Publications:** (Ed.) The Papers of Martin Luther King, Jr., vol. VI: Advocate of the Social Gospel, September 1948-March 1963, 2007; Becoming King: Martin Luther King, Jr. and the Making of a National Leader, 2008. **Address:** University Christian Church, 245 W McMillan, Cincinnati, OH 45219, U.S.A. **Online address:** ttjackson@yahoo.com

JACKSON, William J(oseph). American (born United States), b. 1943. **Genres:** Novels, History, Theology/Religion, Humanities, Novellas/Short Stories. **Career:** Indiana University-Purdue University, assistant professor, 1985-92, associate professor of religious studies, 1992-99, professor of religious studies, 1999-2008, professor emeritus, 2008-. Full-time writer, 2008-. **Publications:** Walk through a Hill Town: Being a Walk through Newark, Vermont, A Northeast Kingdom Hill Town: Or, A Poet's Rambling Account of an American Village, 1977; Sai Krishna Lila: Tales of the Li'l Butterthief: A Play in Verse Based Largely on Stories from Shri Sathya Sai Baba's Discourses, 1980; Tyagaraja-Life and Lyrics, 1991; (ed.) J.L. Mehta on Heidegger, Hermeneutics and Indian Tradition, 1992; Tyagaraja and the Renewal of Tradition: Translations and Reflections, 1994; (ed.) Power of the Sacred Name: V. Raghavan's Studies in Namasiddhanta and Indian Culture, 1994; Tyagaraja-Life and Legacy: Songs of Three Great South Indian Saints, 1998; Heaven's Fractal Net: Retrieving Lost Visions in the Humanities, 2004; Diving for Carlos, or Heroes' Welcome Blues, 2004; Soul Images in Hindu Traditions: Patterns East and West, 2004; Vijayanagara Voices: Exploring South Indian History and Hindu Literature, 2005; Vijayanagara Visions: Religious Experience and Cultural Creativity in a South Indian Empire, 2007; World Views Kaleidoscope (23 short stories), 2007; The Wisdom of Generosity: A Reader in American Philanthropy, 2008; (ed.) Kaveri's Children, 2008, (ed.) Power of the Sacred Name: Indian Spirituality Inspired by Mantras, 2011. **Address:** Department of Religious Studies, Indiana University-Purdue University, Cavanaugh Hall 335, 425 University Blvd., Indianapolis, IN 46202, U.S.A. **Online address:** wijackso@iupui.edu

JACKSON, William Keith. New Zealander (born New Zealand), b. 1928. **Genres:** Politics/Government. **Career:** J.&P. Coats, management trainee, 1954-55; Ministry of Defense, research officer, 1955-56; University of Otago, assistant lecturer, 1956-58, lecturer, 1959-62, senior lecturer in political science, 1963-67; University of Canterbury, head of department, 1967-80, professor of political science, 1968-94, emeritus professor, 1994-. Writer. **Publications:** (With A. Mitchell and R. Chapman) New Zealand Politics in Action, 1963; (with J. Harre) New Zealand, 1969; The New Zealand Legislative Council, 1972; New Zealand: Politics of Change, 1973; The Dilemma of Parliament, 1987; (with A. McRobie) Historical Dictionary of New Zealand, 1996, 2nd ed., 2005; (with A. McRobie) New Zealand Adopts Proportional

Representation: Accident? Design? Evolution?, 1998; (with A. McRobie) Historical and Political Dictionary of New Zealand, 2008. EDITOR: Fight for Life: New Zealand, Britain and the European Economic Community, 1972; (with J. Henderson and R. Kennaway) Beyond New Zealand: The Foreign Policy of a Small State, 1980. **Address:** Department of Political Science, University of Canterbury, PO Box 4800, Christchurch, 8140, New Zealand. **Online address:** keith.jackson@canterbury.ac.nz

JACKSON, William M. American (born United States), b. 1936. **Genres:** Chemistry, Sciences. **Career:** National Bureau of Standards, chemist, 1960-61, 1963-64; Martin-Marietta Aerospace Co., aerospace scientist, 1961-63; Goddard Space Flight Center, scientist, 1964-74; University of Pittsburgh, visiting associate professor, 1969-70; Howard University, professor of chemistry, 1974-85; University of California, professor of chemistry, 1985-, Miller professor, 1988, College of Letters and Sciences, associate dean for academic personnel, 1990-93, now professor emeritus; Miller fellow, 1989; Guggenheim fellow, 1989; Institute for Atomic and Molecular Science, distinguished visiting research professor, 1996. Writer. **Publications:** Methyl Radical Abstraction Reactions, Decomposition of the I-Butyl and T-Butyl Radicals, 1962; (ed. with A. Harvey) Lasers as Reactants and Probes, 1985; (ed. with B.J. Evans) Henry C. McBay: A Chemical Festschrift: Proceedings of a Symposium in Honor of the First Martin Luther King, Jr., Scholar at the Massachusetts Institute of Technology, 1994. **Address:** Department of Chemistry, University of California, Rm. 214, 1 Shields Ave., Davis, CA 95616, U.S.A. **Online address:** jackson@chem.ucdavis.edu

JACOB, Christian. French (born France), b. 1955?. **Genres:** Adult Nonfiction. **Career:** Centre National de la Recherche Scientifique, minister of public service, through 2007, director, research fellow and research professor. Writer and researcher. **Publications:** (Comp. with F. Lestringant) Arts et Légendes d'espaces: Figures du Voyage et Rhétoriques du Monde: Communications, 1981; Géographie et ethnographie en Grèce Ancienne, 1991; L'Empire Des Cartes: Approche Théorique de la Cartographie à Travers l'Histoire, 1992; (ed. with M. Baratin) Le Pouvoir des Bibliothèques: La Mémoire des Livres en Occident, 1996; (ed. with F. de Polignac) Alexandria, Third Century BC: The Knowledge of the World in a Single City, 2000; (ed. with L. Giard) Des Alexandries, vol. I, 2001; (contrib.) Les métamorphoses du livre, 2004; (ed. with J.M. Chatelain) Henri-Jean Martin, 2004; (ed.) Lieux de savoir, 2007. Contributor to periodicals. **Address:** Centre National de la Recherche Scientifique, 3 rue Michel-Ange, Paris, 75794, France. **Online address:** cjacob@ehess.fr

JACOB, James R. (J. R. Jacob). American (born United States), b. 1940. **Genres:** History, Sciences. **Career:** City University of New York, John Jay College of Criminal Justice, faculty, now retired. Writer. **Publications:** Robert Boyle and the English Revolution, 1977; Henry Stubbe: Radical Protestantism and the Early Enlightenment, 1983, rev. ed., 2002; (ed. with M.C. Jacob) The Origins of Anglo-American Radicalism, 1984; (with M. Perry and M. Jacob) Western Civilization: Ideas, Politics & Society, 1995; The Scientific Revolution: Aspirations and Achievements, 1500-1700, 1998. **Address:** Humanities Press International, Atlantic Highlands, NJ 08106, U.S.A.

JACOB, Joseph M. British (born England), b. 1943. **Genres:** Politics/Government. **Career:** University of London, London School of Economics and Political Science, Department of Law, faculty, 1970, reader in civil justice. Writer. **Publications:** Doctors & Rules: A Sociology of Professional Values, 1988, 2nd ed., 1998; Republican Crown: Lawyers and the Making of the State in Twentieth Century Britain, 1996; Civil Litigation, Practice and Procedure in a Shifting Culture, 2001; Civil Evidence for Practitioners, 2003; Civil Justice in the Age of Human Rights, 2006. **Address:** Ashgate Publishing, Wey Court E, Union Rd., Farnham, SR GU9 7PT, England. **Online address:** j.jacob@lse.ac.uk

JACOB, J. R. See **JACOB, James R.**

JACOB, Merle (Lynn). American (born United States), b. 1945. **Genres:** Literary Criticism And History, Bibliography, Librarianship, Reference, Humanities. **Career:** Chicago Historical Society Library, manuscript librarian, 1967; Academy of the Sacred Heart, Department of History, head, 1969-75; Park Ridge Public Library, reference librarian, 1976-78; Skokie Public Library, young adult librarian, 1978-80, Readers Advisory, head, 1980-86, coordinator of collection development, 1986-91; Chicago Public Library, adult materials selection specialist, 1991-, director of library collection development, now retired. Writer. **Publications:** (Comp.) Collection Development Plan: Skokie Public Library, 1990; (with H. Apple) To Be Continued: An Annotated Guide to Sequels, 1995, 2nd ed., 2000. Contributor to books and periodicals. **Address:** Oryx Press, 1434 E San Miguel Ave., Phoenix, AZ 85014-2422, U.S.A.

JACOB, Piers Anthony Dillingham. *See* **ANTHONY, Piers.**

JACOBS, Alan. American (born United States), b. 1958. **Genres:** Biography, Autobiography/Memoirs, Literary Criticism And History, Self Help, Theology/Religion. **Career:** Wheaton College, professor, 1984-, Clyde S. Kilby Chair Professor of English. Writer. **Publications:** What Became of Wystan: Change and Continuity in Auden's Poetry, 1998; A Visit to Vanity Fair: Moral Essays on the Present Age, 2001; A Theology of Reading: The Hermeneutics of Love, 2001; (ed. with K.R. Chase) Must Christianity Be Violent?: Reflections on History, Practice and Theology, 2003; Shaming the Devil: Essays in Truthtelling, 2004; The Narnian: The Life and Imagination of C.S. Lewis, 2005; Original Sin: A Cultural History, 2008; Looking Before and After: Testimony and the Christian Life, 2008; Wayfaring: Essays Pleasant and Unpleasant, 2010; (ed.) The Age of Anxiety: A Baroque Eclogue, 2011; The Pleasures of Reading in an Age of Distraction, 2011; Life Genres: The Personal Dimension of Narrative Theology, forthcoming. **Address:** Department of English, Wheaton College, 307 Blanchard Hall, 501 College Ave., Wheaton, IL 60187-5593, U.S.A. **Online address:** alan.jacobs@wheaton.edu

JACOBS, Andrew S. American (born United States), b. 1973?. **Genres:** Adult Non-fiction, Theology/Religion, Popular Culture. **Career:** University of California, assistant professor, 2001-05, undergraduate faculty advisor, 2002-05, associate professor, 2005-09, graduate advisor, 2005-08; Scripps College, Department of Religious Studies, associate professor, 2009-12, professor, 2012-. Writer. **Publications:** (Contrib.) Galilee through the Centuries: Confluence of Cultures, 1999; (contrib.) Watts Children's Dictionary of Religion, 2001; (ed. with B.D. Ehrman) Christianity in Late Antiquity, 300-450 C.E.: A Reader, 2003; Remains of the Jews: The Holy Land and Christian Empire in Late Antiquity, 2004; (contrib.) Religion and Law in Classical and Christian Rome, 2006; (contrib.) A Feminist Companion to the New Testament Apocrypha, 2006; Christ Circumcised: A Study in Early Christian History and Difference, 2012. Contributor to periodicals. **Address:** Department of Religious Studies, Scripps College, 110 Vita Nova Hall, 1030 Columbia Ave., Ste. 4005, Claremont, CA 91711-3905, U.S.A. **Online address:** andrew.jacobs@scrippscollege.edu

JACOBS, Anna. Also writes as Shannah Jay, Sherry-Anne Jacobs. Australian/British (born England), b. 1941?. **Genres:** Novels, Romance/Historical, Novels, How-to Books, Science Fiction/Fantasy. **Career:** Adult Technical College, lecturer. Writer. **Publications:** GIBSON FAMILY SERIES: Salem Street, 1995; High Street, 1995; Ridge Hill, 1996; Hallam Square, 1996; Spinner's Lake, 1997. KERSHAW SISTERS SERIES: Our Lizzie, 1999; Our Polly, 2001; Our Eva, 2003; Our Mary Ann, 2003. OTHERS: Jessie, 1998; Like No Other, 1999; Lancashire Lass, 2000; Crazy For You, 2000; Seasons of Love, 2000; A Forbidden Embrace, 2001; Lancashire Legacy, 2001; Replenish the Earth, 2001; Down Weavers Lane, 2002; Mistress of Marymoor, 2002; A Pennyworth of Sunshine, 2003; Change of Season, 2003; Twopenny Rainbows, 2004; The Wishing Well, 2004; Marrying Miss Martha, 2004; Three penny Dreams, 2004; An Independent Woman, 2005; Calico Road, 2005; The Corrigan Legacy, 2006. PRESTON SISTERS: Pride of Lancashire, 2005; Star of the North, 2006; Bright Day Dawning, 2006; Heart of the Town, 2006; Family Connections, 2007; Tomorrow's Promises, 2007; Kirsty's Vineyard, 2007; Yesterday's Girl, 2008; Freedom's Land, 2008; Saving Willowbrook, 2009; Farewell to Lancashire, 2009; In Focus, 2009; Beyond the Sunset, 2010; Licence to Dream, 2010, Cherry Tree Lane, 2010; Elm Tree Road, 2011; Destiny's Path, 2011; Moving On, 2011; Short and Sweet, 2011; The Trader's Wife, 2011; The Trader's Sister, 2012; Yew Tree Gardens, 2012; Winds of Change, 2012. AS SHERRY-ANNE JACOBS: Persons of Rank, 1992 as A Proper Match, 2000; An Introduction to Romance Writing, 1998; Plotting and Editing, 1998, 2nd ed., 2011. FANTASY FICTION AS SHANNAH JAY: Quest, 1993; Envoy, 1994; Lands of Nowhere, 1995; Shadow of the Serpent, 1995; The Price of Wisdom, 1996; (with K. Greenwood and L. Sussex) Alien Invasions, 2000; Tenebrak, 2010. Contributor to periodicals. **Address:** Wade & Doherty Literary Agency, 33 Cormorant Lodge, Thomas More St., London, GL E1W 1AU, England. **Online address:** anna@annajacobs.com

JACOBS, Barbara. Mexican (born Mexico), b. 1947. **Genres:** Novels, Novellas/Short Stories, Essays, Young Adult Fiction. **Career:** College of Mexico, investigator, professor, 1974-77; Stanford University, lecturer; New York University, lecturer. Writer. **Publications:** Un justo acuerdo, 1979; Doce cuentos en contra, 1982; Escrito en el tiempo, 1985; Las hojas muertas (novel), 1987, trans. as The Dead Leaves, 1993; Las siete fugas de Saab, alias El Rizos, 1992; Vida con mi amigo, 1994; Juego limpio: Ensayos y Apostillas, 1997; (comp.) Antologia del cuento triste, 1997; Adios humanidad, 2000; Carol dice y otros textos, 2000; Los mejores cuentos mexicanos, 2001; Atormentados, 2002; Florencia y Ruisenor, 2006; Vidas en vilo, 2007; Nin reir, 2009; Lunas, 2010. Contributor to periodicals. **Address:** International Editors' Co., Rambla de Cataluna 63, Barcelona, 08007, Spain. **Online address:** barjaco@nidr.com

JACOBS, Barry. American (born United States), b. 1950?. **Genres:** Young Adult Non-fiction. **Career:** WRAL-Radio, staff; WRAL SportsFan.com, staff. Writer. **Publications:** NONFICTION: Barry Jacobs' Fan's Guide to ACC Basketball, 1987, 14th ed., 1998; Three Paths to Glory: A Season on the Hardwood with Duke, N.C. State and North Carolina, 1993; The World according to Dean: Four Decades of Basketball as Seen by Dean Smith, 1998; Coach K's Little Blue Book: Lessons from College Basketball's Best Coach: The Message of Mike Krzyzewski, 2000, rev. ed., 2004; Golden Glory: The First 50 Years of the ACC, 2002; Across the Line: Profiles in Basketball Courage: Tales of the First Black Players in the ACC and SEC, 2008. **Address:** WRAL, PO Box 12000, Raleigh, NC 27605, U.S.A.

JACOBS, Bruce A. (Bruce Abel Jacobs). American (born United States), b. 1968. **Genres:** Social Sciences. **Career:** University of Missouri, assistant professor, 1994-2003; University of Texas, associate professor, 2003-, director of doctoral and master's degree program in criminology, 2007-. Writer and educator. **Publications:** Dealing Crack: The Social World of Streetcorner Selling, 1999; Robbing Drug Dealers: Violence beyond the Law, 2000; (ed.) Investigating Deviance: An Anthology, 2002; (with R. Wright) Street Justice: Retaliation in the Criminal Underworld, 2006. Contributor of articles to journals and books. **Address:** School of Economic, Political & Policy Sciences, University of Texas, 800 W Campbell Rd., PO Box GR31, Richardson, TX 75080-3021, U.S.A. **Online address:** bruce.jacobs@utdallas.edu

JACOBS, Bruce Abel. *See* **JACOBS, Bruce A.**

JACOBS, Dan(iel) N(orman). American (born United States), b. 1924. **Genres:** Politics/Government, History. **Career:** Hunter College (now Hunter College of the City University of New York), lecturer in political science, 1958-59; Miami University, assistant professor of political science, 1959-62, associate professor, 1962-65, professor, 1965-98, professor emeritus, 1998-. Writer. **Publications:** The New Communist Manifesto, 1961, 3rd ed., 1965; The Masks of Communism, 1963; (ed. with H.H. Baerwald) Chinese Communism, 1963; (ed.) The New Communisms, 1968; (co-author) Ideologies and Modern Politics, 1972; (ed.) From Marx to Mao and Marchais: Documents on the Development of Communist Variations, 1979; Borodin: Stalin's Man in China, 1981; (ed. with E.F. Paul) Studies of the Third Wave: Recent Migration of Soviet Jews to the United States, 1981; (co-author) Comparative Politics: An Introduction to the Politics of the United Kingdom, France, Germany, and the Soviet Union, 1983. **Address:** Department of Political Science, Miami University, 218 Harrison Hall, 501 E High St., Oxford, OH 45056, U.S.A. **Online address:** jacobsdn@muohio.edu

JACOBS, David. American (born United States), b. 1939. **Genres:** Politics/Government, Novels, Technology, Art/Art History, Humor/Satire. **Career:** Freelance writer, 1963-75; The Blue Knights, Columbia Broadcasting System (CBS), staff writer, 1976; Family, American Broadcasting Companies (ABC), story editor, 1977-78; CBS, executive story consultant and creator, 1978. **Publications:** NONFICTION, WITH THE EDITORS OF "HORIZON": Master Builders of the Middle Ages, 1969; Constantinople: The City on the Golden Horn, 1969; Beethoven, 1970; Constantinople and the Byzantine Empire, 1971. OTHERS: (with A.E. Neville) Bridges, Canals, and Tunnels, 1968; Master Painters of the Renaissance, 1968; An American Conscience: Woodrow Wilson's Search for World Peace, 1973; Architecture, 1974; Chaplin, the Movies, and Charlie, 1975; Disney's America on Parade: A History of the U.S.A. in a Dazzling, Fun-Filled Pageant, 1975; (with S.A. Friedman) Police!: A Precinct at Work, 1975; Me, Myself & Irene: A Novel, 2000. Contributor to periodicals. **Address:** c/o Author Mail, St. Martin's Press, 175 5th Ave., New York, NY 10010, U.S.A.

JACOBS, Francis G(eoffrey). British (born England), b. 1939. **Genres:** Law, Civil Liberties/Human Rights. **Career:** University of Glasgow, lecturer in jurisprudence, 1963-65; London School of Economics and Political Science, lecturer in law, 1965-69; Court of Justice of the European Communities, law clerk, 1972-74, advocate general, 1988-2006; University of London, professor of European law, 1974-88; King's College London, Centre of European Law, director, 1981-88, president, School of Law, professor of law, 2006-, Jean Monnet professor; University of Ghent, visiting Marcel Storme chair, 2005-06; College of Europe, Department of European Legal Studies, visiting professor, 2006-; Missing Children Europe, president, 2007-. Writer. **Publications:** Public International Law, 1968; Criminal Responsibility, 1971; (with A. Durand) References to the European Court: Practice and Procedure, 1975; European Convention on Human Rights, 1975, (with R.C.A. White and C. Ovey) 5th ed. as Jacobs, White and Ovey: The European Convention on Human Rights, 2010; (ed.) European Law and The Individual, 1976; (with L.N. Brown) The Court of Justice of the European Communities, 1977, 3rd ed., 1989; (ed. with F.M. Rowe and M.R. Joelson) Enterprise Law of the 80s: European and American Perspectives on Competition and Industrial Organization, 1980; (ed. with M. Hilf and E. Petersmann) European Community and GATT, 1986; The European Union Treaty, 1986; (ed. with S. Roberts) Effect of Treaties in Domestic Law, 1987; (ed.) Liber Amicorum Pierre Pescatore, 1987; (ed. with M. Andenas) European Community Law in the English Courts, 1998; The Sovereignty of Law: The European Way, 2007. **Address:** Centre of European Law, King's College London, Strand, London, GL WC2R 2LS, England. **Online address:** francis.jacobs@kcl.ac.uk

JACOBS, Jack L. American (born United States), b. 1953. **Genres:** Politics/Government, Sociology, Theology/Religion. **Career:** City University of New York, Queens College, adjunct lecturer, 1978, John Jay College of Criminal Justice, assistant professor, 1986-90, associate professor of government, 1991-, professor of government, Graduate School and University Center, Political Sciences Program, deputy executive officer, Hunter College, visiting associate professor, 1992; Marymount College, adjunct lecturer, 1979; Columbia University, preceptor, 1979-83, assistant professor, 1983-86, adjunct assistant professor, 1990; YIVO Institute for Jewish Research, Dr. Emanuel Patt Visiting Professor, 2003-04. Writer. **Publications:** On Socialists and the Jewish Question after Marx, 1992; (ed.) Jewish Politics in Eastern Europe: The Bund at 100, 2001; Bundist Counterculture in Interwar Poland, 2009. Works appear in anthologies. Contributor of articles to periodicals. **Address:** Department of Government, John Jay College of Criminal Justice, 3255 N Hall, 445 W 59th St., New York, NY 10019, U.S.A. **Online address:** jjacobs@gc.cuny.edu

JACOBS, Joanne. American (born United States), b. 1952. **Genres:** Education. **Career:** Suburban Newspapers, copy editor and reporter, 1974-76; Super 8 Filmmaker, associate editor, 1976-78; San Jose Mercury News, copywriter, 1978-80, editorial writer, 1980-84, columnist and editorial writer, 1984-2001; Stanford University, Hoover Institution, media fellow; Pacific Research Institute for Public Policy, media fellow; The Wednesday Report, co-editor-in-chief; Suburban Newspaper Publications Inc., staff. **Publications:** Our School: The Inspiring Story of Two Teachers, One Big Idea and the School That Beat the Odds, 2005. **Address:** c/o Author Mail, Palgrave Macmillan, 175 5th Ave., New York, NY 10010, U.S.A. **Online address:** joanne@joannejacobs.com

JACOBS, Jonnie. American (born United States) **Genres:** Mystery/Crime/Suspense, Novels, inspirational/Motivational Literature. **Career:** Full-time writer and attorney. **Publications:** MYSTERY NOVELS: Murder among Neighbors, 1994; Murder among Friends: A Kate Austen Mystery, 1995; Shadow of Doubt: A Kali O'Brien Mystery, 1996; Evidence of Guilt: A Kali O'Brien Mystery, 1997; Murder among Us: A Kate Austen Mystery, 1998; Motion to Dismiss, 1999; Murder among Strangers: A Kate Austen Mystery, 2000; Witness for the Defense, 2001; Cold Justice, 2002; Intent to Harm, 2003; The Only Suspect (stand-alone Suspense), 2005; The Next Victim, 2007; Paradise Falls, 2012. Works appear in anthologies. **Address:** c/o Deborah Schneider, Gelfman Schneider Literary Agency, 250 W 57th St., Ste. 2515, New York, NY 10017, U.S.A. **Online address:** jonnie@jonniejacobs.com

JACOBS, Kathryn. (Kathryn Elisabeth Jacobs). American/German (born Germany), b. 1957. **Genres:** Social Commentary, History, Literary Criticism And History. **Career:** Glassboro College (now Rowan College), assistant professor of English, 1984-89; New York University, adjunct professor, 1992; Texas A&M University-Commerce, Department of Literature and Languages, professor, 1993-. Writer. **Publications:** (As Kathryn Elisabeth Jacobs) Marriage Contracts from Chaucer to the Renaissance Stage, 2001. FORTHCOMING: Chaucer through Shakespeare's Eyes; Harry: Is That Potter, Percy, or Plantagenet? The Influence of Shakespeare's History Cycle on J.K. Rowling; In Transit. **Address:** Department of Literature and Languages, Texas A & M University-Commerce, HL 227, 2600 S Neal St., PO Box 3011, Commerce, TX 75429-3011, U.S.A. **Online address:** kathryn_jacobs@tamu-commerce.edu

JACOBS, Kathryn Elisabeth. See JACOBS, Kathryn.

JACOBS, Laura. American (born United States) **Genres:** Children's Fiction, Novels, Young Adult Fiction. **Career:** Stagebill, editor-in-chief, 1987-95; The New Criterion, dance critic, 1994-; Vanity Fair, contributing editor, 1995-; Chicago Reader, dance critic; Boston Phoenix, dance critic; The New Leader, dance critic. **Publications:** Barbie: In Fashion, 2nd ed., 1994, rev. ed. as Barbie: Four Decades in Fashion, 1998; Barbie: What a Doll!, 1994, 2nd ed., 1999; (contrib.) The Art of Haute Couture, 1995; Beauty and the Beene: A Modern Legend, 1999; Women about Town, 2002; (with G. Beene, M. Luther and P.A. Parmal) Beene by Beene, 2005; Landscape With Moving Figures: A Decade On Dance, 2006; The Bird Catcher, 2009. Contributor to periodicals. **Address:** c/o Author Mail, Viking Publicity, 375 Hudson St., New York, NY 10014, U.S.A.

JACOBS, Leah. See GELLIS, Roberta (Leah Jacobs).

JACOBS, Margaret (D.). American (born United States), b. 1963. **Genres:** History, Women's Studies And Issues. **Career:** Diablo Valley College, instructor, 1994; California State University, instructor, 1994-95; Pikes Peak Community College, instructor, 1996-97; New Mexico State University, Department of History, assistant professor and undergraduate advisor, 1997-2002, associate professor, 2002-04, director of graduate studies, 2002-03; University of Nebraska, Department of History, associate professor, 2004-09, professor, 2009-, Chancellor's professor of history, 2011-, Women's and Gender Studies Program, affiliate faculty, 2004-, director, 2006-, Center for Great Plains Studies, affiliate fellow, 2005-, affiliate faculty of Native American studies, 2007-. Writer. **Publications:** Engendered Encounters: Feminism and Pueblo Cultures, 1879-1934, 1999; White Mother to a Dark Race: Settler Colonialism, Maternalism and the Removal of Indigenous Children in the American West and Australia, 1880-1940, 2009. **Address:** Department of History, University of Nebraska Lincoln, 612 Oldfather Hall, Lincoln, NE 68588-0327, U.S.A. **Online address:** mjacobs3@unl.edu

JACOBS, Martha Moody. See MOODY, Martha.

JACOBS, Shannon K. American (born United States), b. 1947. **Genres:** Plays/Screenplays, Children's Fiction, Animals/Pets, Children's Non-fiction, Travel/Exploration. **Career:** Nurse, 1967-78; University of California, senior editor, 1978; Jeppesen Sanderson, technical writer, 1979-81; Colorado Business, news and feature writer, 1981-82; Craig Hospital, writer, 1983-85, patient-staff education coordinator, 1985-87; freelance writer, 1987-. **Publications:** Next of Kin, 1986; Song of the Giraffe, 1991; The Boy Who Loved Morning, 1993; Healers of the Wild: People Who Care for Injured and Orphaned Wildlife, 1998, 2nd ed. as Healers of the Wild: Rehabilitating Injured and Orphaned Wildlife, 2003. **Address:** Coyote Moon Press, PO Box 6867, Denver, CO 80206, U.S.A. **Online address:** wldlifewwriter@aol.com

JACOBS, Sherry-Anne. See JACOBS, Anna.

JACOBS, Steve. American/South African (born South Africa), b. 1955?. **Genres:** Novels, Novellas/Short Stories, Literary Criticism And History. **Career:** The Argus, sub-editor. Advocate. **Publications:** NOVELS: Light in a Stark Age, 1984; Diary of an Exile: And, Crystal Night, 1986; Under the Lion, 1988; The Enemy Within, 1995. Contributor to periodicals. **Address:** Heinemann Publishers, 88 Post Rd. W, PO Box 5007, Westport, CT 06880-4208, U.S.A.

JACOBS, Steven L(eonard). American (born United States), b. 1947. **Genres:** Theology/Religion. **Career:** Temple Emanu-El, assistant rabbi, 1974-76, rabbi, 1984-90, 2001-; Temple Shalom, associate rabbi of Jewish congregation and director of education, 1976-77; rabbi, 1977-2001; Herbert P. Feibelman Jr. Chautauqua professor of Jewish studies, 1978-; Spring Hill College, faculty, 1984; University of Alabama, adjunct instructor in history, 1986-; University of Alabama-Tuscaloosa, adjunct professor of religious studies, 1988-, Aaron Aronov endowed chair of Judaic studies, associate professor of religious studies, 2001-; Birmingham-Southern College, Jewish Chautauqua society instructor in Jewish studies, 1990; Samford University, visiting instructor of Jewish studies, 1990; Calhoun Community College, adjunct professor of religion, 2000; Martin Methodist College, adjunct professor of religion, 2000; University of Alabama-Birmingham, associate professor, 2001-, chair of Judaic studies. Writer. **Publications:** Shirot Bialik, 1987; (ed.) Rabbi Lemkin's Thoughts on Nazi Genocide, 1992; (ed.) Contemporary Christian and Jewish Religious Responses to the Shoah, 1993, (ed.) Contemporary Jewish Religious Responses to the Shoah, 1993; Rethinking Jewish Faith, 1994; (ed.) Holocaust Now: Contemporary Christian and Jewish Thought, 1996; Pioneers of Genocide Studies, 2002; Biblical Masorah and the Temple Scroll, 2002; Dismantling the Big Lie: The Protocols of the Elders of Zion, 2003; Post-Shoah Dialogues: Re-Thinking Our Texts Together, 2004; Teaching about the Holocaust: Essays by College and University Teachers, 2004; In Search of Yesterday: The Holocaust and the Quest for Meaning, 2005; (ed.) Maven in Blue Jeans: A Festschrift in Honor of Zev Garber, 2008; Judaism: A Brief History, 2008; (with P.R. Bartrop) Dictionary of Genocide, 2008; Confronting Genocide, 2009; Jewish Experience: An Introduction to Jewish History and Jewish Life, 2010; (with P.R. Bartrop) Fifty Key Thinkers on the Holocaust and Genocide, 2010. Contributor to articles to periodicals. **Address:** Department of Religious Studies, University of Alabama, 212 Manly Hall, PO Box 870264, Tuscaloosa, AL 35487-0264, U.S.A. **Online address:** sjacobs@bama.al.edu

JACOBSEN, David. American (born United States), b. 1977. **Genres:** Race Relations, Human Relations/Parenting, Theology/Religion. **Career:** Lindamood-Bell Learning Processes, tutor, 1999-2001; VCS School, teacher, 2001-03; Westmont College, instructor of English, 2007-; Kilns College, School of Theology and Mission, faculty. Writer. **Publications:** Rookie Dad: Thoughts on First-Time Fatherhood, 2007. **Address:** School of Theology & Mission, Kilns College, 550 SW Industrial Way, Ste. 180, PO Box 673, Bend, OR 97709-0673, U.S.A. **Online address:** djacobsen@westmont.edu

JACOBSEN, Douglas G. American (born United States), b. 1951. **Genres:** Theology/Religion, History. **Career:** University of Illinois, visiting lecturer in religious studies, 1981-82; College of St. Francis, adjunct professor of religion, 1983; Messiah College, assistant professor of church history and theology, 1984-88, associate professor of church history and theology, 1988-94, professor of church history and theology, 1994-2001, distinguished professor of church history and theology, 2001-. Writer. **Publications:** An Unprov'd Experiment: Religious Pluralism in Colonial New Jersey, 1991; (ed. with W.V. Trollinger, Jr.) Re-forming the Center: American Protestantism, 1900 to the Present, 1998; Thinking in the Spirit: Theologies of the Early Pentecostal Movement, 2003; (ed. with R.H. Jacobsen) Scholarship and Christian Faith: Enlarging the Conversation, 2004; (ed.) A Reader in Pentecostal Theology: Voices from the First Generation, 2006; (with R.J. Sawatsky) Gracious Christianity: Living the Love We Profess, 2006; (ed. with A.T. Thayer) Christ, Creeds and Life: Conversations About the Center of Our Faith, 2007; (ed. with R.H. Jacobsen) The American University in a Postsecular Age, 2008; The World's Christians: Who They Are, Where They Are, and How They Got There, 2011. **Address:** Department of Biblical & Religious Studies, Messiah College, PO Box 3053, Grantham, PA 17027, U.S.A. **Online address:** djacobse@messiah.edu

JACOBSON, Dan. British/South African (born South Africa), b. 1929. **Genres:** Novels, Novellas/Short Stories, Poetry, Literary Criticism And History, Travel/Exploration, Essays, Translations, Young Adult Non-fiction, Young Adult Non-fiction. **Career:** South African Jewish Board of Deputies, public relations assistant, 1951-52; Mills & Feeds Ltd., correspondence secretary, 1952-54; writer, 1954-; Syracuse University, visiting professor, 1965-66; University College London, lecturer, 1974-79, reader in English, 1979-86, professor of English, 1988-94, professor emeritus, 1994-, honorary fellow; Australian National University, Humanities Research Center, visiting fellow, 1980, fellow, 1981. **Publications:** The Trap: A Novel, 1955; A Dance in the Sun: A Novel, 1956; The Price of Diamonds, 1958; A Long Way from London, 1958; The Zulu and the Zeide, 1959; No Further West, 1959; The Evidence of Love, 1960; Time of Arrival, 1963; Beggar My Neighbour, 1964; The Beginners, 1966; Through the Wilderness, 1968; The Rape of Tamar, 1970; A Way of Life and other Stories, 1971; Inklings, 1973; The Wonder-Worker, 1973; The Confessions of Joseph Baisz, 1977; The Story of Stories: The Chosen People and Its God, 1982; Time and Time Again: Autobiographies, 1985; Her Story, 1987; Adult Pleasures: Essays on Writers and Read-

ers, 1988; Hidden in the Heart, 1991; The God-Fearer: A Novel, 1992; The Electronic Elephant, 1994; (ed. with D. Bar-Tal and A. Klieman) Security Concerns: Insights From the Israeli Experience, 1998; Heshel's Kingdom, 1998; (trans.) H. van Woerden, The Assassin: A Story of Race and Rage in the Land of Apartheid, 2001; All for Love: A Novel, 2005. Contributor to periodicals. **Address:** A.M. Heath & Company Ltd., 6 Warwick Ct., Holborn, London, GL WC1R 5DJ, England.

JACOBSON, Jennifer Richard. American (born United States), b. 1958?. **Genres:** Children's Fiction, Education, Young Adult Non-fiction, Reference. **Career:** Author and educational consultant. **Publications:** Mr. Lee, 1995; Getting to Know Sharks, 1997; (with D. Raymer) How is My Second Grader Doing in School?: What to Expect and How to Help, 1998; How is My First Grader Doing in School?: What to Expect and How to Help, 1998; A Net of Stars, 1998; The Big Book of Reproducible Graphic Organizers, 1999; How is My Third Grader Doing in School?: What to Expect and How to Help, 1999; Moon Sandwich Mom, 1999; (with D. Raymer) How is My Sixth Grader Doing In School?: What to Expect and How to Help, 2000; (with D. Raymer) How is My Fifth Grader Doing In School?: What to Expect and How to Help, 2000; (with D. Raymer) How is My Fourth Grader Doing In School?: What to Expect and How to Help, 2000; Winnie Dancing on Her Own, 2001; (with D. Raymer) Reading Renaissance Power Lessons: Literature-based Lessons to Teach Reading Skills, 2001; Truly Winnie, 2003; Stained, 2005; Winnie at Her Best, 2005; Andy Shane and the Very Bossy Dolores Starbuckle, 2005; Andy Shane and the Pumpkin Trick, 2006; Andy Shane and the Queen of Egypt, 2008; Andy Shane is Not in Love, 2008; Andy Shane and the Barn Sale Mystery, 2009; Andy Shane: Hero At Last!, 2010; No More I'm Done!: Fostering Independent Writing in the Primary Grades, 2010; Complete History of Why I Hate Her, 2010; Small as an Elephant, 2011. FOR PARENTS AND TEACHERS: (with E. Herman) Stones from the Muse, 1997; (with D. Raymer and N. Richard) How is My... Grader Doing in School?, 6 vols., 1998-2000; The Big Book of Reproducible Graphic Organizers, 1999; Easy Spelling Lessons For the Overhead, 2003; Easy Grammar Lessons For the Overhead, 2003; Great Games for the Overhead: Reading, 2003; Great Games for the Overhead: Math, 2003; Easy Word Family Lessons for the Overhead, 2004; Graphic Organizers for the Overhead: Reading and Writing, 2007; Trait-Based Writing, 2008; Reading Response for Fiction, 2008; Vocabulary, 2008; Reading Response for Nonfiction, 2008. **Address:** c/o Author Mail, Candlewick Press, 99 Dover St., Somerville, MA 02144, U.S.A. **Online address:** jennifer@jenniferjacobson.com

JACOBSON, Joanne. American (born United States), b. 1952. **Genres:** Literary Criticism And History, Area Studies, Autobiography/Memoirs. **Career:** University of Iowa, teaching assistant, 1975-79; University of Angers, American Literature and Civilization, Fulbright junior lecturer, 1979-80; Middlebury College, visiting instructor, 1981-82, assistant professor of American literature and civilization, 1982-90, American Civilization Program, director, 1983-90; Yeshiva University, associate professor of English, 1990-2005, English Department, chair, 2004-06, professor of English, 2005-, director of humanities, social sciences and Jewish studies, 2005-06, associate dean for academic affairs, 2006-09, Jay and Jeanie Schottenstein Honors Program, director, 2008-09. Writer. **Publications:** (With M.J. Meldman and M. Wellhasen) Occupational Therapy Manual, 1969; (with L. Card and K. Suttkus) WordPerfect 5.1 for Creative Writing, 1991; Authority and Alliance in the Letters of Henry Adams, 1992; Hunger Artist: A Suburban Childhood, 2007. Contributor of articles to periodicals. **Address:** Department of English, Yeshiva University, Belfer Hall, Rm. 514, 2495 Amsterdam Ave., New York, NY 10033, U.S.A. **Online address:** jacobson@yu.edu

JACOBSON, Judy. American (born United States), b. 1947. **Genres:** Adult Non-fiction, Reference, History. **Career:** Starkville Public Library, staff; Mississippi State University, Library, faculty; Oktibbeha County Heritage, museum curator. Writer. **Publications:** Southold Connections, 1991; Massachusetts Bay Connections: Historical and Biographical Sketches of the Towns and Communities of the Massachusetts Bay Colony, 1992; Detroit River Connections, 1994; A Genealogist's Refresher Course, 1995, 2nd ed., 1996; Alabama and Mississippi Connections, Historical and Biographical Sketches of Families Who Settled on Both Sides of the Tombigbee River, 1999; A Field Guide for Genealogists, 2001, 2nd ed., 2003; Norwegian Connections: From Arctic Fjord to American Prairie, 2002; History for Genealogists, 2009. **Address:** c/o Author Mail, Clearfield Company Inc., 200 E Eager St., Baltimore, MD 21202, U.S.A.

JACOBSON, Matthew Frye. American (born United States), b. 1958. **Genres:** History, Cultural/Ethnic Topics, Military/Defense/Arms Control. **Career:** State University of New York, assistant professor of history, 1992-95; Yale University, assistant professor of history, 1995-, associate professor of American studies, history and African American studies, professor of American studies and history, chair of American studies. Writer. **Publications:** Special Sorrows: The Diasporic Imagination of Irish, Polish, and Jewish Immigrants in the United States, 1995; Whiteness of a Different Color: European Immigrants and the Alchemy of Race, 1998; Barbarian Virtues: The United States Encounters Foreign Peoples at Home and Abroad, 1876-1917, 2000; (with G. González) What Have They Built You to Do?: The Manchurian Candidate and Cold War America, 2006; Roots Too: White Ethnic Revival in Post-Civil Rights America, 2006; Odetta's Voice and Other Weapons: The Civil Rights Era as Cultural History, forthcoming. **Address:** Department of History, Yale University, HGS 2675, 307 College Hall, 320 York St., New Haven, CT 06520-8324, U.S.A. **Online address:** matthew.jacobson@yale.edu

JACOBUS, Mary. British (born England), b. 1944. **Genres:** Literary Criticism And History. **Career:** Oxford University, Randall McIver research fellow, 1968-70, fellow and tutor in English, 1971-80, lecturer in English, 1972-80; Manchester University, Department of English, lecturer, 1970-71; Georgetown University, visiting professor, 1976; Cornell University, Department of English, associate professor, 1980-82, professor, 1982-90, John Wendell Anderson professor, 1990-2000; Lady Margaret Hall, honorary fellow, 2000-; University of Cambridge, Grace 2 professor of English, 2000-, Churchill College, fellow, 2000-, Center for Research in the Arts, Social Sciences and Humanities, director, 2006-. Writer. **Publications:** Tradition and Experiment in Wordsworth's Lyrical Ballads (1798), 1976; Reading Woman: Essays in Feminist Criticism, 1986; Romanticism, Writing and Sexual Difference: Essays on The Prelude, 1989; First Things: The Maternal Imaginary in Literature, Art, and Psychoanalysis, 1995; Psychoanalysis and the Scene of Reading, 1999; The Poetics of Psychoanalysis: In the Wake of Klein, 2005. EDITOR: Woman Writing and Writing about Women, 1979; (co-ed.) Body/Politics: Women and the Discourses of Science, 1990. **Address:** Churchill College, University of Cambridge, 17 Mill Ln., Cambridge, CB2 1RX, England. **Online address:** mlj25@cam.ac.uk

JACOBY, Karl. American (born United States), b. 1965. **Genres:** Environmental Sciences/Ecology, History. **Career:** Oberlin College, visiting assistant professor, 1998; Brown University, assistant professor, 1999-2001, Robert Carney assistant professor, 2001-03, associate professor, 2003-09, professor, 2009-. Writer and historian. **Publications:** Crimes against Nature: Squatters, Poachers, Thieves, and the Hidden History of American Conservation, 2001; Shadows at Dawn: A Borderlands Massacre and the Violence of History, 2008. Contributor of articles to books and journals. **Address:** Department of History, Brown University, 79 Brown St., PO Box N, Providence, RI 02912, U.S.A. **Online address:** karl_jacoby@brown.edu

JACOBY, Tamar. American (born United States), b. 1954. **Genres:** Race Relations, Sociology, History. **Career:** Hudson Research, writer and editor, 1976-77; The New York Review of Books, editorial staff, 1977-81; New York Times, department editor for Op-Ed page, 1981-87; Yale University, lecturer, 1986-90; Newsweek, senior editor, 1987-89, justice editor, 1988-89; Manhattan Institute, senior fellow, 1989-2007; New School for Social Research, instructor, 1991-; Immigration Works USA, president and chief executive officer. **Publications:** Someone Else's House: America's Unfinished Struggle for Integration, 1998; (ed.) Reinventing the Melting Pot: The New Immigrants and What It Means to be American, 2004. Contributor of articles to periodicals. **Address:** ImmigrationWorks USA, 737 8th St. SE, Ste. 201, PO Box 15471, Washington, DC 20003, U.S.A. **Online address:** tjacoby@immigrationworksusa.org

JACQ, Christian. Swiss/French (born France), b. 1947. **Genres:** Novels, Mystery/Crime/Suspense, Archaeology/Antiquities, History, Young Adult Non-fiction. **Career:** Writer, 1974-; French Radio, producer, 1979-83; Groupe de la Cité, literary director, 1983-88; Ramses Institute, co-founder and head, 1986. **Publications:** (With F. Brunier and M. Locquin) L'astrologie relativiste, 1970; Message spirituel de Saint Bertrand de Comminges, 1972; (with F. Brunier) Le message spirituel de Saint Just de Valcabrère, 1972; (with F. Brunier) Le message des bâtisseurs de cathédrales, 1974; La Franc-Maçonnerie, histoire et initiation, 1975; (with F. Brunier) Saint-Bertrand-de-Comminges, 1975; (with F. Brunier) Saint-Just-de-Valcabrère, 1975; Akhenaton et Néfertiti: le couple solaire, 1976; (with P. Delaperrière) De sable et

d'or: symbolique héraldique, l'honneur du nom, 1976; Le livre des deux chemins: symbolique du Puy-en-Velay, 1976; Le message des constructeurs de cathédrales, 1980; La conferrie des sages du nord, 1980; Lestrente-trois degrés de la sagesse, ou, comment vivre l'initiation en occident: dialogues avec Pierre Delœuvre, 1981, rev. ed. as Le voyage initiatique, ou, les trente-trois degrés de la sagesse: dialogues avec Pierre Delœuvre, 1986; (with P. de La Perrière) Les origines sacrées de la royauté française, 1981; L'Egypte des grands pharaons: l'histoire et la légende, 1981; Pouvoir et sagesse selon l'Egypte ancienne, 1981; La prodigieuse aventure du lama Dancing, 1982; Le monde magique de l'Egypte ancienne, 1983; Lemoine et le vénérable: roman, 1985; L'Egypte ancienne au jour le jour, 1985; Les grands monuments de l'Egypte ancienne, 1986; L'Empire du pape blanc, 1986; Le voyage dans l'autre monde selon l'Egypte ancienne: épreuves et métamorphoses du mort d'après les textes des pyramides et les textes des sarcophages, 1986; Champollion l'Egyptien: roman historique, 1987; Le voyage sur le Nil, 1987; La reine soleil: l'aimée de Toutankhamon: Roman, 1988; Lafiancée du Nil, 1988; Sur les pas de Champollion: l'Egypte des hiéroglyphes, 1988; Le voyage aux pyramides, 1989; Maître Hiram et le roi Salomon, 1989; Pour l'amour de Philae: Roman, 1990; Néfertiti et Akhénaton, le couple solaire, 1990; (with J. Pilarsky) Un espion pour l'éternité, 1990; Karnak et Louxor, 1990; L'affaire Toutankhamon: Roman, 1992; Lavallée des rois: histoire et découverte d'une demeure d'éternité, 1992; Le juge d' Egypte, vol. I: La pyramide assassinée, 1993, vol. II: La loi du désert, 1993, vol. III: La Justice du vizir, 1994; La vallee des rois, images et mysteres, 1993; Recherches sur les paradis de l'autre monde d'après les Textes des Pyramides et les Textes des Sarcophages, 1993; L'enseignement du sageégyptien Ptahhotep, le plus ancien livre du monde, 1993; Barrage sur le Nil: Roman, 1994; Initiation à l'égyptologie, 1994; Le petit Champollion illustré: Les hiéroglyphes à la portée de tousou comment devenir scribe amateur tout en s'amusant, 1994; (ed.) Le message initiatique des cathédrales, 1995; Voyage dans l'Egypte des pharaons, 1995; Ramses, vol. I: Le fils de la lumière: Roman, 1995, vol. II: Le temple des millions d'années: Roman, 1996, vol. III: le Bataille de Kadesh, 1996, vol. IV: La Dame d'Abou Simbel: Roman, 1996, vol. V: Sous l'acacia d'Occident, 1997; Contes et Légendes du temps des pyramides, 1996; Les Egyptiennes: portraits de femmes de l'Egypte pharaonique, 1996; Les pharoansracontés, 1996; Sur les pas de Ramsès, 1997; Fascinating Hieroglyphics, 1997; Le pharaon noir: roman, 1997; La sagesse vivante de l'égypte ancienne, 1998; La Tradition primordiale de l'Egypte ancienne: selon les Textes des pyramides, 1998; Magic and Mystery in Ancient Egypt, 1998; The Living Wisdom of Ancient Egypt, 1999; La Pierre delumiere, vol. I: Nefer le silencieux, 2000, trans. as Nefer the Silent, 2000, vol. II: La femme sage: roman, 2000, vol. III: Paneb l'ardent, 2000, trans. as Paneb the Ardent, 2001, vol. IV: la Place de vérité, 2000; The Wise Woman, 2000; La viequotidienne dans la place de vérité, 2000; The Stone of Light, 2000; La Reine Liberté: roman, vol. I: L'Empire des ténèbres, 2001, vol. II: La Guerre des couronnes, 2002, vol. III: L'Epée flamboyante, 2002; Voyage dans l'Egyptedes pharaons, 2002; Les Mystères d'Osiris: roman, vol. I: L'arbre devie, 2003, vol. II: La conspiration du Mal, 2003; Que la vie est douce à l'ombre des palmes: dernières nouvelles d'Egypte, 2005; La Vengeance des dieux: Roman, 2006; Mozart: roman, 2006; Mozart 4, L'aimé d'Isis: Roman, 2006; Mozart 2, Le fils de la lumière: Roman, 2006; Les grands sages de l'Egypte ancienne: d'Imhotep à Hermès, 2007; Toutânkhamon: l'ultime secret: roman, 2008; Procès de la momie: Roman, 2008; Tutânkhamon, 2008; The Judgement of the Mummy, 2009; Egypt, 2009; Et l'égypte s'éveilla, 2010; Imhotep, l'inventeur de l'éternité, 2010; Paysages et paradis de l'autre monde selon l'égypte ancienne, 2010. MOZART SERIES: The Great Magician, 2008; The Son of Enlightenment, 2010; The Brother of Fire, 2011; The Beloved of Isis, 2012. JUDGE OF EGYPT SERIES: Beneath the Pyramid, 2004; Secrets of the Desert, 2004; Shadow of the Sphinx, 2004. MYSTERIES OF OSIRIS SERIES: The Tree of Life, 2005; The Conspiracy of Evil, 2005; The Way of Fire, 2005; The Great Secret, 2005. VENGEANCE OF THE GODS SERIES: Manhunt, 2007; The Divine Worshipper, 2008. AS J.B. LIVINGSTONE: DOSSIERS DE SCOTLAND YARD SERIES: Meurtre au British Museum, 1984; Secret des Mac Gordon, 1985; Crime à Lindenbourne, 1985; Assassin de la Tour de Londres, 1986; Trois crimes de Noël, 1986; Meurtre à Cambridge, 1987; Meurtre chez les druides, 1987; Meurtre à quatre mains, 1988; Higgins mène l'enquête, 1989. **Address:** c/o Author Mail, Simon & Schuster Inc., 1230 Ave. of the Americas, New York, NY 10020-1513, U.S.A.

JACQUES, Martin. British (born England), b. 1945. **Genres:** History. **Career:** Marxism Today, editor, 1977-91; Sunday Times, columnist and essayist, 1988-94; Demos (think tank), co-founder, 1993; Independent, deputy editor, 1994-96; Observer, columnist, 1996-2008; Times, columnist, 1999-2001;

Guardian, columnist, 2002-; Ritsumeikan University, visiting professor; Renmin University, visiting professor, 2005-06; National University of Singapore, Asia Research Institute, visiting senior research fellow, 2006; Aichi University, International Centre for Chinese Studies, visiting professor, 2010; London School of Economics Asia Research Centre, visiting fellow, 2010; IDEAS, visiting senior fellow. **Publications:** When China Rules the World: The End of the Western World and the Birth of a New Global Order, 2009. EDITOR: (co-ed.) The Forward March of Labour Halted?, 1981; (with S. Hall) New Times: The Changing Face of Politics in the 1990s, 1990; (co-ed.) Tercera via o neoliberalismo?, 2000. **Address:** London, GL, England. **Online address:** martin@martinjacques.com

JAECK, Lois Marie. Canadian (born Canada), b. 1946. **Genres:** Literary Criticism And History, Language/Linguistics, Young Adult Fiction. **Career:** Teacher, 1970-77, 1985-86; St. Francis Xavier University, assistant professor of modern languages (French and Spanish), 1986-88; University of Saskatchewan, associate professor of Spanish and comparative literature, 1988-, Department of Art and Art History, acting head. Writer. **Publications:** Marcel Proust and the Text as Macrometaphor, 1990. Contributor to journals. **Address:** Department of Languages and Linguistics, University of Saskatchewan, Rm. 181.1, Murray Bldg., 9 Campus Dr., Saskatoon, SK S7N 5A5, Canada. **Online address:** lois.jaeck@usask.ca

JAFFARY, Nora E. Canadian (born Canada), b. 1968?. **Genres:** Adult Non-fiction, Race Relations. **Career:** Concordia University, assistant professor of history, associate professor of history, director of graduate program. Writer. **Publications:** False Mystics: Deviant Orthodoxy in Colonial Mexico, 2004; (ed.) Gender, Race and Religion in the Colonization of the Americas, 2007; (ed. with E.W. Osowski and S.S. Porter) Mexican History: A Primary Source Reader, 2010. **Address:** Department of History, Concordia University, Sir George Williams Campus, Rm. LB 1041.05, McConnell Bldg., 1400 de Maisonneuve Blvd. W, Montreal, QC H3G 1M8, Canada. **Online address:** njaffary@alcor.concordia.ca

JAFFE, Betsy. (Elizabeth Latimer Jaffe). American (born United States), b. 1935. **Genres:** Business/Trade/Industry, Young Adult Non-fiction. **Career:** Catalyst, director of corporate board resource and operations, 1977-82; Career Continuum (consultants), owner and president, 1982-98. Writer. **Publications:** Altered Ambitions: What's Next in Your Life?, 1991, rev. ed., 2000. Contributor to journals. **Address:** c/o Anne Edelstein, 510 W 110th St., Ste. 7E, New York, NY 10025-2012, U.S.A.

JAFFE, Elizabeth Latimer. See **JAFFE, Betsy.**

JAFFE, Mark. American (born United States), b. 1949?. **Genres:** Social Sciences, History. **Career:** Philadelphia Inquirer, science and environment writer. **Publications:** (With D. Drake and S. FitzGerald) Hard Choices: Health Care at What Cost?, 1993; And No Birds Sing: The Story of an Ecological Disaster in a Tropical Paradise as And No Birds Sing: A True Ecological Thriller Set in a Tropical Paradise, 1994; The Gilded Dinosaur: The Fossil War between E.D. Cope and O.C. Marsh and the Rise of American Science, 2000. **Address:** c/o Author Mail, Crown Publishing Group, 1745 Broadway, New York, NY 10019-4343, U.S.A.

JAFFEE, Al(lan). American (born United States), b. 1921. **Genres:** Humor/Satire, Cartoons, Criminology/True Crime. **Career:** Quality Comics, writer and artist for inferior man, 1941; Marvel Comics, humor feature writer, 1942-55; Trump and Humbug Magazines, writer and artist, 1955-58; Mad Magazine, writer and artist, 1955, 1958-; freelance advertising illustrator, 1958-; illustrator of children's books, 1960-. **Publications:** OTHERS: Ghastly Jokes, 1976; Mad's Al Jaffee Spews Out Still More Snappy Answers to Stupid Questions, 1976; Al Jaffee Blows a Fuse, 1979; The Ghoulish Book of Weird Records, 1979; Al Jaffee Meets His End, 1979; Al Jaffee Gets His Just Desserts, 1980; Willie Weirdie drives Al Jaffee to Distraction, 1984; An Overblown Collection: More Mad Snappy Answers to Stupid Questions, 1990; Holy Cow! Not another Mad Snappy Answers to Stupid Questions, 1992. SELF-ILLUSTRATED: Mad's Al Jaffee Spews Out Snappy Answers to Stupid Questions, 1968; Funny Jokes and Foxy Riddles, 1968; Witty Jokes and Wild Riddles, 1968; Al Jaffee's Mad (Yecch!) Monstrosities, 1974; Al Jaffee Gags, 1974; Al Jaffee Gags Again, 1975; Al Jaffee Blows His Mind, 1975; (with F. Jacobs) Sing Along with Mad, 1977; Al Jaffee Draws a Crowd, 1978; (with N. Meglin) Rotten Rhymes and Other Crimes, 1978; Al Jaffee Bombs Again, 1978; Al Jaffee Sinks to a New Low, 1978; Al Jaffee's Mad Inven-

tions, 1978; More Snappy Answers to Stupid Questions, 1979; Good Lord! Not Another Book of Snappy Answers to Stupid Questions, 1980; Al Jaffee: Dead or Alive, 1980; Al Jaffee Fowls His Nest, 1981; Al Jaffee Meets Willie Weirdie, 1981; Al Jaffee Hogs the Show, 1981; Al Jaffee Goes Bananas, 1982; Al Jaffee Shoots His Mouth Off, 1982; Mad's Al Jaffee Freaks Out, 1982; Willie Weirdie Zaps Al Jaffee, 1983; (contrib.) Mad's Vastly Overrated Al Jaffee, 1983; Snappy Answers to Stupid Questions, No.5, 1984; Mad Book of Puzzles, Games, and Lousy Jokes, 1986; Mad's Al Jaffee Sweats Out Another Book, 1988; Al Jaffee's Mad Book of Magic and Other Dirty Tricks, 1988; Snappy Answers to Stupid Questions, No. 7, 1989; Al Jaffee's Mad Rejects, 1990; Mad Fold This Book!: A Ridiculous Collection of Flod-ins, 1997. Illustrator of books by others. **Address:** Mad Magazine, E.C. Publications Inc., 1700 Broadway, New York, NY 10019, U.S.A.

JAFFEE, Annette Williams. American (born United States), b. 1945. **Genres:** Novels, Adult Non-fiction, Education, History, Young Adult Fiction. **Career:** Little, Brown & Co., editorial assistant, 1966-67. **Publications:** Adult Education, 1981; Recent History, 1988; The Dangerous Age: A Novel, 1999. Contributor to periodicals. **Address:** c/o Liz Darhansoff, Liz Darhansoff Literary Agency, 1220 Park Ave., New York, NY 10128-1733, U.S.A.

JAFFIN, David. German/American (born United States), b. 1937. **Genres:** Novellas/Short Stories, Poetry, Art/Art History, History, Theology/Religion, Humor/Satire. **Career:** Evangelilcal Church, pastor; New York University, graduate assistant, 1961-62; University of Maryland, European Division, lecturer in European history, 1966-71; Lutheran Church, minister, 1974-94. Writer. **Publications:** 18th and 19th Century Historical Interpretations of the Reign of James I of England, 1966; Conformed to Stone, 1968; Emptied Spaces, 1972; Late March, 1973; Objects, 1973; Opened, 1973; At the Gate, 1974; Of, 1974; Changes, 1975; In the Glass of Winter, 1975; As One, 1975; The Half of a Circle, 1977; Space Of, 1978; Preceptions, 1979; INRI, 1980; Die Welt und der Welt-ueberwinder, 1981; The Density for Color, 1982; For the Finger's Want of Sound, 1982; Selected Poems, 1982; Der Bringt viel Frucht, 1983; Die Heiligkeit Gottes in Jesus Christus, 1984; Jesus, Mein Herr und Befreier, 1985; Warum brauchen wir das Alte Testament, 1986; Der auferstandene Christus als unsere Seelsorger, 1986; Israel am Ende der Tage, 1987; Malmsheimer Predigten, 1988; Josua, 1989; Salomo, 1989; Wastl, die Geschichte eines Pfarrdackel, 1989; Juedische Feste/Christliche Deutung, 1990; Errinnerungen eines alterenden Pfarrdackel, 1990; Die Geheimnisvolle Gegenwart Gottes, zur Gemaelde von Casper David Fredrich, 1990; Alle Lande sind seine Ehre Voll, 1990; 74 New Poems, 1994; The Telling of Time, 1999; That Sense for Meaning, 2001; Into the Timeless Deep, 2002; A Birth in Sceing, 2003; Through Lost Silences, 2003; A Voiced Awakening, 2004; These Time-Shifting Thoughts, 2004; Die Urgeschichte der Menschheit/Unsere Geschichte, forthcoming; Ihr Fragt, Wastl Antwortet, forthcoming. Contributor to periodicals. **Address:** 88636 Ilmensee, Sonnenhalde, 9, Germany.

JAFFRELOT, Christophe. French (born France), b. 1964. **Genres:** History, Race Relations, Politics/Government, Adult Non-fiction. **Career:** National Center for Scientific Research (CNRS), researcher, 1991-; Center for International Studies and Research (CERI), director, 2000-; Critique Internationale, editor-in-chief and director. Writer. **Publications:** Les nationalistes hindous: Idéologie, implantation et mobilisation des années 1920 aux années 1990, 1993, trans. as The Hindu Nationalist Movement in India, 1996; Mouvements d'autodétermination et intervention des etats en asie du sud: une comparaison Inde-Pakistan, 1997; La démocratie en Inde: religion, caste et politique, 1998; Dr. Ambedkar: Leader intouchable et père de la constitution indienne, 2000; Tribus et basses castes: résistance et autonomie dans la société indienne, 2002; India's Silent Revolution: The Rise of the Lower Castes in North India, 2003; Dr. Ambedkar and Untouchability: Fighting the Indian Caste System, 2005; Inde, la démocratie par la caste: histoire d'une mutation socio-politique (1885-2005), 2005; Emerging States: The Wellspring of a New World Order, 2009. EDITOR: (with T.B. Hansen) The BJP and the Compulsions of Politics in India, 1998; Le Pakistan, carrefour de tensions régionales, 1999; Démocraties d'ailleurs: démocraties et démocratisations hors d'Occident, 2000; Le Pakistan, 2000; A History of Pakistan and Its Origins, 2002; Pakistan: Nationalism without a Nation?, 2002; The Sangh Parivar: A Reader, 2005; (with A. Dieckhoff) Repenser le nationalisme: théories et pratiques, 2006; (with P. van der Veer) Patterns of Middle Class Consumption in India and China, 2008; (with L. Gayer) Milices armées d'Asie du Sud: privatisation de la violence et implication des états, 2008; Religion, 2010; Religion, Caste and Politics in India, 2011; (ed. with L. Gayer) Muslims in Indian Cities: Trajectories of Marginalisation, 2011. Contributor to books. **Address:** Center for International

Studies and Research, 56 rue Jacob, Paris, 75006, France. **Online address:** jaffrelot@ceri-sciences-po.org

JAFREE, Mohammed Jawaid Iqbal. (Iqbal Geoffrey). American/Pakistani (born Pakistan), b. 1939. **Genres:** Law, Art/Art History, Human Relations/Parenting, History, Cultural/Ethnic Topics. **Career:** Geoffrey & Khitran (international law firm), partner and chairperson, 1960-; Pakistan Institute for Human Rights, general counsel, 1960-; United Nations, human rights officer, 1966-67; St. Mary's College, professor, 1967-68; British Lion Films, chief accountant, 1968-69; CWS University, professor, 1970-71; American University of Pakistan, founder, 1970; Cleveland State University, professor, 1971-72; Shahzadi Mumtaz Jehan Trust, general counsel, 1972-; State of Illinois, assistant attorney general, 1972-73; Embassy of Kuwait, chief accountant, 1974-75; special advisor to the President of Pakistan, 1980-84; Office of Ombudsman Order of Pakistan, founder, 1983; Hunerkada College of Art, distinguished visiting professor; University of Reading, Law Center, professor; Lahore Law College, distinguished visiting professor; Silver Jubilee University, distinguished visiting professor. Writer. **Publications:** AS IQBAL GEOFFREY: Iqbal Geoffrey: Paintings, Drawings, Watercolours, 1949-1963, 1963; Geoffrey: Power and the Image, 1969; (with Z. Haider, Sir H.E. Read) Iqbal Geoffrey Drawings and Collages, 1941-2008, 2008. OTHERS: Qose-Qizah, 1957; Justice Is the Absence of Dictatorial Prerogative, 1965; Human Rights in Pakistan, 1965; A Critical Study of Moral Dilemmas, Iconographical Confusions and Complicated Politics of Twentieth-Century Art, 1967; The Concept of Human Rights in Islam, 1980; (co-author) ABA: BLI Recognition and Enforcement of Money Judgments, 1994; (co-author) International Agency and Distribution Law, 1996; Implosion of Injustice, 2001. **Address:** Sul Sabeel, 128-E-1 Gulberg Main Blvd., Lahore, 54660, Pakistan. **Online address:** iqbaljafree@hotmail.com

JAGER, Eric. American (born United States), b. 1957. **Genres:** History, Humanities, Language/Linguistics, Literary Criticism And History. **Career:** Columbia University, instructor, professor of English and comparative literature; University of California, professor of medieval literature, 1996-. Writer. **Publications:** The Tempters Voice: Language and the Fall in Medieval Literature, 1993; The Book of the Heart, 2000; The Last Duel: A True Story of Crime, Scandal and Trial by Combat in Medieval France, 2004. **Address:** Department of English, University of California, Humanities 254, 149 Humanities Bldg., PO Box 951530, Los Angeles, CA 90095-1530, U.S.A. **Online address:** ejager@humnet.ucla.edu

JAGOSE, Annamarie. New Zealander/British (born England), b. 1965?. **Genres:** Film, Gay And Lesbian Issues, Sex, Philosophy. **Career:** University of Melbourne, lecturer in English, 1992-2002, associate professor and reader, 2002-; University of Auckland, associate professor of film, television and media studies, 2003-06, professor of film, television and media studies, 2007-, head. Writer. **Publications:** Lesbian Utopics, 1994; Queer Theory: An Introduction, 1996; Inconsequence: Lesbian Representation And The Logic Of Sexual Sequence, 2002. NOVELS: In Translation, 1995; Lulu: A Romance, 1998; Slow Water, 2003. **Address:** Department of Film, Television and Media Studies, University of Auckland, Rm. 400C, Arts 2 Bldg., 18 Symonds St., PO Box 92019, Auckland, 1020, New Zealand. **Online address:** a.jagose@auckland.ac.nz

JAHME, Carole. British (born England) **Genres:** Women's Studies And Issues, Literary Criticism And History. **Career:** Writer, documentary filmmaker and psychologist. **Publications:** Beauty and the Beasts: Woman, Ape and Evolution, 2000. Contributor to periodicals. **Address:** c/o Author Mail, Virago Press, Brettenham House, Lancaster Pl., London, GL WC2E 7EN, England.

JAHN-CLOUGH, Lisa. American (born United States), b. 1967. **Genres:** Illustrations. **Career:** Emerson College, teacher of writing and children's literature, 1994-2004; Maine College of Art, interim chair of illustration program, 2004-08; Hamline University, low-residency faculty in writing for children & young adults, 2007; Vermont College, teacher of writing for children and young adults. **Publications:** Country Girl, City Girl (young-adult novel), 2004; Me, Penelope (young adult novel), 2007; SELF-ILLUSTRATED: Alicia and Her Happy Way of Life, 1991; Alicia's Evil Side, 1992; Alicia Has a Bad Day, 1994; My Happy Birthday Book!, 1996; ABC Yummy, 1997; 1 2 3 Yippie, 1998; My Friend and I, 1999; Missing Molly, 2000; Simon and Molly plus Hester, 2001; Alicia's Best Friends, 2003; On the Hill, 2004; Little Dog, 2006; ILLUSTRATOR: Carol Snyder, We're Painting, 2002; (illus.) Laurie

Friedman, (illus.) A Big Bed for Jed, 2002. **Address:** U.S.A. **Online address:** jahnclough@atsaol.com

JAHODA, Gustav. Scottish/Austrian (born Austria), b. 1920. **Genres:** Anthropology/Ethnology, Psychology, Race Relations, Cultural/Ethnic Topics. **Career:** University of Manchester, lecturer in psychology, 1949-52; University College of Gold Coast (now University of Ghana), lecturer in psychology, 1952-56; University of Glasgow, senior lecturer in social psychology, 1956-64; University of Strathclyde, professor of psychology, 1964-86, professor emeritus, 1986-. Writer. **Publications:** White Man: A Study of the Attitudes of Africans to Europeans in Ghana before Independence, 1961; The Psychology of Superstition, 1969; (with J. Cramond) Children and Alcohol: A Developmental Study in Glasgow, 1972; Psychology and Anthropology: A Psychological Perspective, 1982; (with I.M. Lewis) Acquiring Culture, 1988; Crossroads Between Culture and Mind: Continuities and Change in Theories of Human Nature, 1993; Images of Savages: Ancient Roots of Modern Prejudice in Western Culture, 1999; A History of Social Psychology, 2007. Contributor to journals. **Address:** Department of Psychology, University of Strathclyde, 40 George St., Glasgow, G1 1QE, Scotland. **Online address:** g.jahoda@strath.ac.uk

JAIN, Anita. American/Indian (born India), b. 1972. **Genres:** Travel/Exploration, Biography, Autobiography/Memoirs. **Career:** Mohan Lal Sukhadia University, research associate, 2002, teacher, 2002; Vidhya Bhavan Rural Institute, teacher, 2000-02. Journalist and researcher. **Publications:** Marrying Anita: A Quest for Love in the New India, 2008. **Address:** c/o Esmond Harmsworth, Zachary Shuster Harmsworth, 1776 Broadway, Ste. 1405, New York, NY 10019, U.S.A. **Online address:** anita@anitajain.net

JAIN, Raj. American (born United States), b. 1951. **Genres:** Information Science/Computers, Mathematics/Statistics, Technology, Engineering. **Career:** Digital Equipment Corp., senior consulting engineer, 1978-94; Jain Center of Greater Boston, secretary, 1979-83; Massachusetts Institute of Technology, honorary lecturer, 1987; Ohio State University, professor, 1994-2002, Nayna Networks Inc., co-founder and chief technical officer, 2000-07; Washington University, professor of computer science and engineering, 2005-. Writer. **Publications:** Control-Theoretic Formulation of Operating Systems Resource Management Policies, 1979; The Art of Computer Systems Performance Analysis: Techniques for Experimental Design, Measurement, Simulation and Modeling, 1991; FDDI Handbook: High-Speed Networking Using Fiber and Other Media, 1994; High Performance TCP/IP Networking: Concepts, Issues and Solutions, 2004; Broadband Access Communication Technologies, 2006; Broadband Access Communication Technologies II, 2007; Broadband Access Communication Technologies III, 2009; Broadband Access Communication Technologies IV, 2010; Quality of Service Architectures for Wireless Networks: Performance Metrics and Management, 2010. **Address:** Department of Computer Science and Engineering, Washington University, CB 1045, 1 Brookings Dr., St. Louis, MO 63130, U.S.A. **Online address:** jain@acm.org

JAKES, John. Also writes as William Ard, Alan Payne, Jay Scotland. American (born United States), b. 1932. **Genres:** Novels, Mystery/Crime/Suspense, Romance/Historical, Science Fiction/Fantasy, Westerns/Adventure, Young Adult Fiction, Novellas/Short Stories, History, Literary Criticism And History. **Career:** Abbott Laboratories, copywriter, product promotion manager, 1954-60; Rumrill Co., copywriter, 1960-61; Kircher Helton & Collet Inc., senior copywriter, 1965-68; Oppenheim, Herminghausen, Clarke Inc., copywriter, vice president, 1968-70; Dancer-Fitzgerald-Sample Inc., creative director, 1970-71; University of South Carolina, Department History, research fellow, 1989-96. **Publications:** The Texans Ride North: The Story of the Cattle Trails (for children), 1952; Wear a Fast Gun, 1956; A Night for Treason, 1956; (as Alan Payne) Murder, He Says, 1958; (as Alan Payne) This Will Slay You, 1958; The Devil Has Four Faces, 1959; The Impostor, 1959; Johnny Havoc, 1960; (as William Ard) Make Mine Mavis, 1961; (as William Ard) and So to Bed, 1962; (as William Ard) Give Me This Woman, 1962; Johnny Havoc Meets Zelda, 1962, rev. ed. as Havoc for Sale, 1990; Johnny Havoc and the Doll Who Had It, 1963, rev. ed. as Holiday for Havoc, 1991; G.I. Girls, 1963; Arena, 1963; Tiros: Weather Eye in Space, 1966; When the Star Kings Die, 1967; Great War Correspondents, 1967; Famous Firsts in Sports, 1967; Making It Big, 1968, rev. ed. as Johnny Havoc and the Siren in Red, 1991; Great Women Reporters, 1969; Tonight We Steal the Stars, 1969; The Hybrid, 1969; The Last Magicians, 1969; Secrets of Stardeep, 1969; The Planet Wizard, 1969; The Asylum World, 1969; Mohawk: The Life of Joseph

Brant, 1969; Black in Time, 1970; Six-Gun Planet, 1970; Mask of Chaos, 1970; Monte Cristo 99, 1970; Master of the Dark Gate, 1970; Conquest of the Planet of the Apes, 1972; Time Gate, 1972; Witch of the Dark Gate, 1972; Mention My Name in Atlantis: Being, at Last, the True Account of the Calamitous Destruction of the Great Island Kingdom, Together with a Narrative of Its Wondrous Intercourses with a Superior Race of Other-Worldlings, as Transcribed from the Ms. of a Survivor, Hoptor the Vintner, for the Enlightenment of a Dubious Posterity, 1972; On Wheels, 1973; The Best of John Jakes, 1977; The Bastard Photostory, 1980; (with G. Kane) Excalibur!, 1982; Susanna of the Alamo: A True Story, 1986; California Gold, 1989; The Best Western Stories of John Jakes, 1991; Homeland, 1993; In the Big Country: The Best Western Stories of John Jakes, 1993; John Jakes' Mullkon Empire, 1995; Great Stories of the American West, 1995; American Dreams, 1998; On Secret Service (novel), 2000; The Bold Frontier, 2001; Crime Time: Mystery and Suspense Stories, 2001; Charleston: A Novel, 2002; Savannah; or A Gift for Mr. Lincoln, 2004. BRAK THE BARBARIAN SERIES: Brak the Barbarian, 1968; Brak the Barbarian versus the Sorceress, 1969; Brak the Barbarian versus the Mark of Demons, 1969; Brak: When the Idols Walked, 1978; Fortunes of Brak, 1980. AMERICAN BICENTENNIAL SERIES: ALSO PUBLISHED AS KENT FAMILY CHRONICLES SERIES: The Bastard, vol. I: Fortune's Whirlwind, 1975, vol. II: To an Unknown Shore, 1975; The Rebels, 1975; The Seekers, 1975; The Titans, 1976; The Furies, 1976; The Patriots, 1976; The Pioneers, 1976; The Warriors, 1977; The Lawless, 1978; The Americans, 1980. NORTH AND SOUTH TRILOGY: North and South, 1981; Love and War, 1984; Heaven and Hell, 1988. PLAYS: (contrib.) Dracula, Baby, 1970; (contrib.) Wind in the Willows, 1972; A Spell of Evil, 1972; Violence, 1972; Stranger with Roses, 1972; For I Am a Jealous People, 1972; Gaslight Girl, 1973; Pardon Me, Is This Planet Taken?, 1973; Doctor, Doctor!, 1973; (adapter) Charles Dickens's A Christmas Carol, 1997. AS JAY SCOTLAND: The Seventh Man, 1958; I, Barbarian, 1959; Strike the Black Flag, 1961; Sir Scoundrel, 1962; Veils of Salome, 1962; Traitors' Legion, 1963, rev. ed. as The Man from Cannae, 1977. OTHERS: (ed. with M.H. Greenberg) New Trails: Twenty-three Original Stories of the West from Western Writers of America, 1994; (ed.) A Century of Great Western Stories, 2000; (with E. Kelton and R.J. Randisi) The Funeral of Tanner Moody, 2004; The Gods of Newport: A Novel, 2006; Charles Dickens', A Christmas Carol: Touring Version, 2007; (intro.) Civil War, 2010. Contributor to magazines. **Address:** Rembar & Curtis, 19 W 44th St., Ste. 711, New York, NY 10036-5900, U.S.A. **Online address:** jjfiction@aol.com

JAKOBSON, Michael. American/Russian (born Russia), b. 1939. **Genres:** History, Music, Politics/Government, Social Sciences. **Career:** West Virginia University, assistant professor of history, 1989-91; University of Toledo, associate professor, 1991-98, professor of history, 1999-. Writer. **Publications:** (Comp.) Guide to the Boris I. Nicolaevsky Collection in The Hoover Institution Archives, 1989; Origins of the GULAG: The Soviet Prison Camp System, 1917-1934, 1993; Musical Folklore of the Gulag as Historical Source, 1917-1939, 1998; Musical Folklore of the Gulag as Historical Source, 1940-1991, 2001; Crime and Punishment in Russian Musical Folklore Before 1917, 2006. **Address:** Department of History, University of Toledo, Rm. 3122, Tucker Hall, 2801 W Bancroft St., PO Box 503, Toledo, OH 43606-3390, U.S.A. **Online address:** michael.jakobson@utoledo.edu

JAKSIĆ, Iván. Chilean (born Chile), b. 1954. **Genres:** History, Philosophy, International Relations/Current Affairs, Politics/Government, Literary Criticism And History. **Career:** University of California, Center for Latin American Studies, postdoctoral research associate, 1982-83, vice-chairperson, 1984-89, visiting lecturer, 1986-87; State University of New York, visiting assistant professor, 1983; Stanford University, consulting assistant professor, 1988, Stanford Program in Santiago, director, 2006-; University of Wisconsin, associate professor of history, 1989-94, Center for Latin America, director, 1989; University of Notre Dame, professor of history, 1994-2005; Pontificia Universidad Católica de Chile, professor of history, 2006-, visiting professor. Writer. **Publications:** (With J.R. Rogachevesky) Politics and the Novel in Latin America, 1980; (ed. with J.J.E. Gracia) Filosofía e identidad cultural en América Latina, 1988; Academic Rebels in Chile: The Role of Philosophy in Higher Education and Politics, 1989; (ed. with P.W. Drake) The Struggle for Democracy in Chile, 1982-1990, 1991, rev. ed., 1995; (co-ed.) El difícil camino hacia la democracia en Chile, 1982-1990, 1993; (co-ed. and contrib.) Sarmiento: Author of a Nation, 1994; (ed. and intro.) Selected Writings of Andrés Bello, 1997; Andrés Bello and the Problem of Order in Post-independence Spanish America, 1997; (ed. with P.W. Drake) El modelo chileno: democracia y desarrollo en los noventa, 1999; Andrés Bello: Scholar-

ship and Nation-building in Nineteenth-Century Latin America, 2001; Andrés Bello: La pasión por el orden, 2001; (ed. and contrib.) The Political Power of the Word: Press and Oratory in Nineteenth-Century Latin America, 2002; The Hispanic World and American Intellectual Life, 1820-1880, 2007; Ven conmigo a la España lejana, 2007; Bitácora de archivos, 2009; (ed. and intro.) Durante la Reconquista, 2010; (with I. Stavans) What Is La Hispanidad?: A Conversation, 2011. Works appear in anthologies. Contributor of articles to journals. **Address:** Stanford Program in Santiago, Stanford University, Rm. 202, Hernando de Aguirre 162, Providencia, Santiago, 751-0026, Chile. **Online address:** ijaksic@stanford.edu

JALAN, Edi Lee. *See* **STIVENDER, Ed.**

JALATA, Asafa. American/Ethiopian (born Ethiopia), b. 1954. **Genres:** Area Studies, Cultural/Ethnic Topics, International Relations/Current Affairs, Politics/Government, Race Relations, Sociology, Third World. **Career:** Horst Spingies High School, teacher, 1976-77; Socio-economic Study and Implementation Group of Forestry, research assistant, 1977; Wild Life Development Authority, research assistant, 1977; Swedish International Development Agency, research sociologist, 1978-80; Arssi Rural Development Project, regional development officer and researcher, 1978-79, teacher, 1978-80; University of California, research assistant, 1983-85; State University of New York, research assistant, 1985, adjunct professor, 1990-91; Journal of the Union of Oromo in North America, editor, 1986-88; Ithaca College, visiting professor of sociology and African-American studies, 1989-90; Clinton Community College, assistant professor of sociology, 1990-91; University of Tennessee, assistant professor, 1991-96, associate professor, 1997-2004, professor of sociology and African-American studies, 2004-; Journal of Oromo Studies, associate editor, 1992-96, editor, 1996-2000; Oromo Studies Association, president, 1992-94, board director, 2002-07; National Summit of Africa, chair, 1998-2001. **Publications:** Oromia and Ethiopia: State Formation and Ethnonational Conflict, 1868-1992, 1993; (ed.) Oromo Nationalism and the Ethiopian Discourse: The Search for Freedom and Democracy, 1998; Fighting against the Injustice of the State and Globalization: Comparing the African American and Oromo Movements, 2001; (ed.) State Crises, Globalisation, and National Movements in North-East Africa, 2004; Oromummaa: Oromo Culture, Identity, and Nationalism, 2007; Contending Nationalisms of Oromia and Ethiopia: Struggling for Statehood, Sovereignty, and Multinational Democracy, 2010. **Address:** Department of Sociology, Africana Studies Program, University of Tennessee, 901 McClung Twr., Knoxville, TN 37996, U.S.A. **Online address:** ajalata@utk.edu

JALLAND, Pat(ricia). Australian/British (born England), b. 1941. **Genres:** History, Women's Studies And Issues, Autobiography/Memoirs, Military/Defense/Arms Control, Politics/Government, Cultural/Ethnic Topics. **Career:** Cambridge University, Lucy Cavendish College, research fellow, 1973-76; University of London, lecturer in history, 1974-75; Curtin University, lecturer, 1976-81, senior lecturer in history, 1981-83; Australian National University, College of Arts and Social Sciences, Research School of Social Sciences, senior research fellow in history, 1983-86, 1991-92, professor of history, 1997-; Murdoch University, senior lecturer, 1986-88, associate professor of history, 1988-96. Writer. **Publications:** The Liberals and Ireland: The Ulster Question in British Politics to 1914, 1980; Women, Marriage, and Politics, 1860-1914, 1986; (ed. with J.P. Hooper) Women from Birth to Death: The Female Life Cycle in Britain, 1830-1914, 1986; Octavia Wilberforce: The Autobiography of a Pioneer Woman Doctor, 1989; Death in the Victorian Family, 1996; Australian Ways of Death: A Social and Cultural History, 1840-1918, 2002; Changing Ways of Death in Twentieth-Century Australia: War, Medicine, and the Funeral Business, 2006; Death in War and Peace: Loss and Grief in England, 1914-1970, 2010. Contributor to books and journals. **Address:** Research School of Social Sciences, College of Arts and Social Sciences, Australian National University, Coombs Bldg., Fellows Rd., Canberra, AC 0200, Australia. **Online address:** jalland@coombs.anu.edu.au

JALONGO, Mary Renck. American (born United States), b. 1950. **Genres:** Education. **Career:** Capac Local School, teacher, 1971-72; Cloverleaf Local School, teacher, 1972-75; University of Toledo, graduate assistant, 1975-77, instructor, 1977-78; Indiana University of Pennsylvania, assistant professor, 1978-82, associate professor, 1982-85, professor of education, 1985-, assistant chairperson, 1982-83, coordinator, 1983-87, elementary education coordinator, 1991-95, Doctoral Program, coordinator, 2002-. Writer. **Publications:** Young Children and Picture Books, 1988, 2nd ed., 2004; Creating Learning Communities: The Role of the Teacher in the Twenty-first Century,

1991; Early Childhood Language Arts, 1992, 5th ed., 2010; (with J.P. Isenberg) Creative Expression and Play in Early Childhood, 1993, 5th ed., 2010; (with J.P. Isenberg) Teacher's Stories: From Personal Narrative to Professional Insight, 1995; (with L.N. Stamp) The Arts in Young Children's Lives, 1997; (with J.B. McCracken) Writing about Teaching and Learning: A Guide for Aspiring and Experienced Authors, 1997; (with M.M. Twiest and G. Gerlach) College Learner: How to Survive and Thrive in an Academic Environment, 1996, 2nd ed., 1999; (with J.P. Isenberg) Exploring Your Role, 2000, 3rd ed., 2008; Writing for Professional Publication, 2002; (with S.A. Rieg and V.R. Helterbran) Planning for Learning: Collaborative Approaches To Lesson Design And Review, 2007; Learning to Listen, Listening to Learn: Building Essential Skills in Young Children, 2008. EDITOR/CO-EDITOR: (with J.P. Isenberg) Major Trends and Issues in Early Childhood, 1997, 2nd ed., 2003; Resisting the Pendulum Swing, 1999; (with G. Gerlach and W. Yan) Research Methods (annual), 2000; Annual Editions: Research Methods, 2000; The World's Children and Their Companion Animals, 2004. Contributor to journals. **Address:** Department of Professional Studies in Education, Indiana University of Pennsylvania, 122 Davis Hall, 570 S 11th St., Indiana, PA 15705-1087, U.S.A. **Online address:** mjalongo@iup.edu

JAMAIL, Dahr. American (born United States), b. 1968?. **Genres:** Social Sciences, Language/Linguistics, Military/Defense/Arms Control, International Relations/Current Affairs. **Career:** Democracy Now!, radio reporter; British Broadcasting Corp., radio reporter; National Public Radio, radio reporter. Journalist. **Publications:** Beyond the Green Zone: Dispatches from an Unembedded Journalist in Occupied Iraq, 2007; Will to Resist: Soldiers Who Refuse to Fight in Iraq and Afghanistan, 2009. Contributor to periodicals. **Online address:** mail@dahrjamailiraq.com

JAMES, Alan. British (born England), b. 1965. **Genres:** History, Politics/Government, Humanities. **Career:** University of Sheffield, Department of History, lecturer; University of Manchester, lecturer; King's College London, Department of War Studies, lecturer, 2002-07, senior lecturer, 2007-; Journal of Strategic Studies, reviews editor. **Publications:** The Navy and Government in Early Modern France, 1572-1661, 2004; The Origins of French Absolutism, 1598-1661, 2006. Contributor to books and journals. **Address:** Department of War Studies, King's College London, K6.23, Strand, London, GL WC2R 2LS, England. **Online address:** alan.2.james@kcl.ac.uk

JAMES, Bill. See TUCKER, (Allan) James.

JAMES, B. J. See JAMES, Brian.

JAMES, Brian. (B. J. James). American (born United States), b. 1976. **Genres:** Children's Fiction, Young Adult Fiction, Novels. **Career:** Writer. **Publications:** Pure Sunshine (novel), 2002; The Shark Who Was Afraid of Everything, 2002; The Spooky Hayride, 2003; Tomorrow, Maybe (novel), 2003; Everybody Hates School Dances, 2007; Everybody Hates Best Friends, 2007; Life is but a Dream, 2012. SUPERTWINS SERIES: (as B.J. James) The Supertwins meet the Bad Dogs from Space, 2003; The Supertwins: The Terrible Tooth Snatcher, 2003; (as B.J. James) The Supertwins and Tooth Trouble, 2003; The Supertwins: Meet the Dangerous Dinobots, 2003; (as B.J. James) The Supertwins: Meet the Sneaky, Slimy Bookworms, 2004; Perfect World (novel), 2004; The Easter Bunny's On His Way, 2005; Dirty Liar (novel), 2006; Ahoy! Ghost Ship Ahead, 2007; Attack on the High Seas!, 2007; Curse of Snake Island, 2007; Port of Spies, 2007; CatKid: I'm No Fraidy Cat, 2007; CatKid: The Fishy Field Trip, 2007; CatKid: Purrfect Princess, 2007; CatKid: Three's a Crowd, 2008; Camp Buccaneer, 2008; Treasure Trouble, 2008; Thief (novel), 2008; Zombie Blondes (novel), 2008; Yo-Ho-Ho, 2008; Shiver Me Shipwreck, 2009; The Heights (novel), 2009; The Code Breakers, 2009. **Address:** 26 Baker Rd., Phoenicia, NY 12464, U.S.A. **Online address:** brianjamespush@hotmail.com

JAMES, Caryn. American (born United States) **Genres:** Novels, Young Adult Fiction, Humanities. **Career:** New York Times, chief television critic, film critic and cultural reporter; The New York Times Book Review, film critic and editor; The Daily Beast, cultural critic. **Publications:** Glorie: A Novel, 1998; What Caroline Knew, 2006. Contributor to periodicals. **Address:** Arts/Culture Desk, New York Times, 229 W 43rd St., New York, NY 10036, U.S.A.

JAMES, Catherine. American (born United States), b. 1950. **Genres:** Biography, Autobiography/Memoirs. **Career:** Author. **Publications:** Dandelion: Memoir of a Free Spirit (memoir), 2007. **Address:** St. Martin's Press, 175 5th Ave., Ste. 1500, New York, NY 10010-7703, U.S.A. **Online address:** pinkshoes11@netzero.net

JAMES, Clive (Vivian Leopold). Australian (born Australia), b. 1939. **Genres:** Novels, Poetry, Literary Criticism And History, Autobiography/Memoirs, Humor/Satire, Young Adult Non-fiction, Biography. **Career:** Sydney Morning Herald, assistant editor, 1961; Observer, television reviewer, 1972-82, feature writer, 1972-; Cambridge University, president; Watchmaker Productions, founder, 1995-; Welcome Stranger, chairman of the internet enterprise. **Publications:** The Metropolitan Critic, 1974; Peregrine Prykke's Pilgrimage through the London Literary World, 1974, rev. ed., 1976; The Fate of Felicity Fark in the Land of the Media: A Moral Poem in Rhyming Couplets, 1975; Britannia Bright's Bewilderment in the Wilderness of Westminster: A Political Poem in Rhyming Couplets, 1976; Visions Before Midnight, 1977; Fan-Mail: Seven Verse Letters, 1977; At the Pillars of Hercules, 1979; First Reactions: Critical Essays, 1968-79, 1980; Unreliable Memoirs, 1980; The Crystal Bucket: Television Criticism from the Observer, 1976-79, 1981; Charles Charming's Challenges on the Pathway to the Throne: A Royal Poem in Rhyming Couplets, 1981; From the Land of Shadows, 1982; Glued to the Box: Television Criticism from the Observer, 1979-82, 1983; Brilliant Creatures: A First Novel, 1983; Poem of the Year, 1983; Flying Visits: Postcards from the Observer, 1976-83, 1984; Falling Towards England: Reliable Memoirs Continued in UK as Falling Towards England: Unreliable Memoirs II, 1985; Other Passports: Poems, 1958-85, 1986; The Remake, 1987; Snakecharmers in Texas: Essays 1980-87, 1988; May Week Was in June: Unreliable Memoirs Continued, 1990; Brrm! Brrm!, or, the Man from Japan, or, Perfume at Anchorage: A Novel, 1991 as The Man from Japan, 1993; The Dreaming Swimmer: Non-Fiction, 1987-92, 1992; Clive James on Television: Criticism from the Observer, 1972-82, 1993; Fame in the 20th Century, 1993; The Silver Castle (novel), 1996; Reliable Essays: The Best of Clive James, 2001; Even as We Speak: New Essays, 1993-2000, 2001; As of This Writing: The Essential Essays, 1968-2002, 2003; Book of My Enemy: Collected Verse, 1958-2003, 2003; The Meaning of Recognition: New Essays, 2001-2005, 2005; North Face of Soho: Unreliable Memoirs, vol. IV, 2006; Cultural Amnesia: Necessary Memories From History and the Arts, 2007; Opal Sunset: Selected Poems, 1958-2008, 2008; Angels over Elsinore: Collected Verse 2003-2008, 2008; Revolt of the Pendulum: Essays, 2005-2008, 2009; Blaze of Obscurity: Unreliable Memoirs V, 2009; A Point of View, 2011; Nefertiti in the Flak Tower, 2012. Contributor to periodicals. **Address:** United Agents, 12-26 Lexington St., London, GL W1F OLE, England.

JAMES, Cooper. See FLINT, James.

JAMES, (Darryl) Dean. Also writes as Honor Hartman, Jimmie Ruth Evans. American (born United States) **Genres:** Mystery/Crime/Suspense. **Career:** Houston Academy of Medicine, Texas Medical Center Library, librarian and director of cataloging; Murder by the Book (mystery book store), general manager, 1996-. Writer. **Publications:** SIMON KIRBY-JONES MYSTERY SERIES: Posted to Death: A Simon Kirby-Jones Mystery, 2002; Faked to Death: A Simon Kirby-Jones Mystery, 2003; Decorated to Death, 2004; Baked to Death: A Simon Kirby-Jones Mystery, 2005. WITH JEAN SWANSON: By a Woman's Hand: A Guide to Mystery Fiction by Women, 1991; Killer Books: A Reader's Guide to Exploring the Popular World of Mystery and Suspense, 1998; The Dick Francis Companion, 2003. OTHER: (ed. with J. Grape and E. Nehr) Deadly Women, 1998; Cruel as the Grave, 2000; Closer than the Bones, 2001; Death by Dissertation, 2004; (with E. Foxwell) Robert B. Parker Companion, 2005; Murder Past Due, 2010. AS JIMMIE RUTH EVANS: Flamingo Fatale, 2005; Murder Over Easy: a Trailer Park Mystery, 2006; Best Served Cold, 2007; Bring Your Own Poison, 2008; Leftover Dead, 2009. AS HONOR HARTMAN: On the Slam, 2007; The Unkindest Cut, 2008. Works appear in anthologies. Contributor to periodicals. **Address:** Murder by the Book, 2342 Bissonnet St., Houston, TX 77005, U.S.A.

JAMES, David Edward. British (born England), b. 1937. **Genres:** Education, Psychology, Sociology, Politics/Government. **Career:** City of Bath Technical College, Biology Section, head, 1961-63; St. Mary's College of Education, head of educational psychology, 1963-65; University of Surrey, lecturer in human biology, 1965-69, professor of educational studies, 1969-96, dean of associated institutions, 1996-. Writer. **Publications:** A Student's Guide to Efficient Study, 1966; Introduction to Psychology for Teachers, Nurses and

Other Social Workers, 1968, 2nd ed., 1970. Contributor to books and journals. **Address:** University of Surrey, Guildford, SR GU2 5XH, England.

JAMES, Deana. Also writes as Rachel Davis, Mona D. Sizer. American (born United States), b. 1934. **Genres:** Romance/Historical, History, Biography, Novels. **Career:** Brookhaven College, creative writing teacher, distinguished adjunct faculty. Novelist, biographer and historian. **Publications:** ROMANCE NOVELS: Lovestone, 1983; Lovespell, 1984; Lovefire, 1985; Texas Storm, 1986; Texas Tempest, 1986; Texas Star, 1987; Crimson Obsession, 1988; Hot December, 1988; Captive Angel, 1988; Angel's Caress, 1989; Masque of Sapphire, 1990; Texas Heart, 1990; Speak Only Love, 1991; Acts of Passion, 1992; Acts of Love, 1992; Seek Only Passion, 1993; Beloved Rogue, 1994; Duchess, 1995; My Lawman, 1998; Taggart's Lady, 2000. AS RACHEL DAVIS: Loving Enemies, 1996; My Outlaw, 1997. AS MONA D. SIZER: The King Ranch Story: Truth and Myth, 1999; Texas Heroes: A Dynasty of Courage, 2000; The Salt Cedars: Stories for My Daughter, 2000; Texas Justice, 2001; Texas Politicians: Good 'n' Bad, 2002; Texas Money: All the Law Allows (and Then Some), 2003; Texas Bandits: Real to Reel, 2004; Texas Disasters: Wind, Flood and Fire, 2005; Before the Wind: Poems out of My Life and Thought, 2006; (ed. and contrib.) Tales Told at Midnight along the Rio Grande, 2006; Outrageous Texans: Tales of the Rich and Infamous, 2008; Glory Guys: The Story of the U.S. Army Rangers, 2009. **Address:** c/o Maria Carvainis, Maria Carvainis Agency Inc., 1270 Ave. of the Americas, Ste. 2320, New York, NY 10020, U.S.A. **Online address:** monawriter@aol.com

JAMES, Emily. See STANDIFORD, Natalie.

JAMES, Frederick. See MARTIN, William.

JAMES, Jamie. Indonesian/American (born United States) **Genres:** Sciences, Novels, Theology/Religion, Adult Non-fiction. **Career:** New Yorker Magazine, staff art critic, 1994-99; Discover Magazine, staff; London Times, music critic. Writer. **Publications:** (With D. Soren) Kourion: The Search for a Lost Roman City, 1988; (with R. Ciochon and J. Olsen) Other Origins: The Search for the Giant Ape in Human Prehistory, 1990; The Music of the Spheres: Music, Sciences and the Natural Order of the Universe, 1993; (with D. Weeks) Eccentrics: A Study of Sanity and Strangeness, 1995; (ed.) Proceedings of the 1995 Meeting of Integrated Conservation and Development Projects in Papua New Guinea, Christensen Research Institute, Madang April 26-28, 1995, 1996; Pop Art, 1996; (with D. Weeks) Secrets of the Superyoung: The Scientific Reasons Some People Look Ten Years Younger Than They Really Are-And How You Can, Too, 1998; Andrew and Joey, 2002; Inspirational Thoughts of a Spiritual Patriot, 2002; Java Man: A Novel, 2004; The Snake Charmer: A Life and Death in Pursuit of Knowledge, 2008; Rimbaud in Java, 2011. Contributor to periodicals. **Address:** Hyperion Books, 114 5th Ave., New York, NY 10011, U.S.A.

JAMES, Julie. American (born United States), b. 1974. **Genres:** Novels. **Career:** United States Court of Appeals, clerk. Writer and attorney. **Publications:** Just the Sexiest Man Alive, 2008; Practice Makes Perfect (novel), 2009; Something about You (novel), 2010. **Address:** Chicago, IL , U.S.A. **Online address:** info@juliejamesbooks.com

JAMES, Kelvin Christopher. American/Trinidadian (born Trinidad and Tobago) **Genres:** Novels, Novellas/Short Stories, Mystery/Crime/Suspense, Horror, Science Fiction/Fantasy, Young Adult Fiction, Poetry. **Career:** Childhood, Trinidad, scientific research assistant, 1960-64; high school science teacher, 1968; Harlem Hospital, clinical technologist, 1973-79, lab technician; free-lance writer, 1980-. **Publications:** Jumping Ship and Other Stories, 1992; Secrets (novel), 1993; A Fling with a Demon Lover, 1996; The Sorcerer's Drum, 2009; Web of Freedom, 2011. Works appear in anthologies. **Address:** 1295 5th Ave., Ste. 32F, New York, NY 10029-3134, U.S.A. **Online address:** yokelvinc@kelvinchristopherjames.com

JAMES, Laura M. British (born England), b. 1978. **Genres:** Military/Defense/Arms Control, History, Autobiography/Memoirs. **Career:** Economist Intelligence Unit, Middle East analyst; Oxford University, lecturer. Writer, historian and consultant. **Publications:** Nasser at War: Arab Images of the Enemy, 2006. **Address:** Economist Intelligence Unit, 26 Red Lion Sq., London, GL WC1R 4HQ, England. **Online address:** laurajames@eiu.com

JAMES, Laurie. American (born United States), b. 1930. **Genres:** Adult Non-fiction, Literary Criticism And History, Plays/Screenplays, Women's Studies And Issues, Biography. **Career:** Pat Hart, manager; Actor and playwright. **Publications:** NONFICTION: (comp. and ed.) The Wit and Wisdom of Margaret Fuller Ossoli, 1988; Why Margaret Fuller Ossoli Is Forgotten, 1988; Outrageous Questions, Legacy of Bronson Alcott and America's One-Room Schools, 1993. BIOGRAPHIES: Men, Women and Margaret Fuller, 1990; How I Got to Harvard: Off and On Stage with Margaret Fuller, 1998. **Address:** 500 W 43rd St., Ste. 26J, New York, NY 10036, U.S.A. **Online address:** booking@lauriejames.net

JAMES, Livia. See REASONER, Livia Jane Washburn.

JAMES, Marlon. American/Jamaican (born Jamaica), b. 1970?. **Genres:** Novels. **Career:** Macalester College, assistant professor of literature and creative writing. Writer. **Publications:** John Crow's Devil (novel), 2005; The Book of Night Women (novel), 2009. Contributor to books and periodicals. Works appear in anthologies. **Address:** Macalester College, 1600 Grand Ave., St. Paul, MN 55105-1899, U.S.A. **Online address:** mjames1@macalester.edu

JAMES, Mary. See MEAKER, Marijane (Agnes).

JAMES, Michael Leonard. See HARTLAND, Michael.

JAMES, Oliver. British (born England), b. 1953?. **Genres:** Psychology, Medicine/Health. **Career:** Writer and television producer, 1987-. Psychologist. **Publications:** Juvenile Violence in a Winner-Loser Culture: Socioeconomic and Familial Origins of the Rise in Violence against the Person, 1995; Britain on the Couch: Why We're Unhappier Compared with 1950 Despite Being Richer-A Treatment for the Low-Serotonin Society, 1997; They F*** You Up: How to Survive Family Life, 2006; Affluenza: How to Be Successful and Stay Sane, 2007; Contented Dementia: 24-Hour Wraparound Care for Lifelong Well-Being, 2008; The Selfish Capitalist: Origins of Affluenza, 2008. **Address:** London, GL , England. **Online address:** oliver.james@eburypublishing.co.uk

JAMES, P. D. British (born England), b. 1920. **Genres:** Mystery/Crime/Suspense, Young Adult Non-fiction, Novels, Autobiography/Memoirs, Criminology/True Crime, Novellas/Short Stories. **Career:** North West Regional Hospital Board, principal administrative assistant, 1949-68; Department of Home Affairs, Police Department, principal administrative assistant, 1968-72; Criminal Policy Department, principal administrative assistant, 1972-79; full-time writer, 1979-; Downing College, associate fellow, 1986. **Publications:** Cover Her Face, 1962; A Mind to Murder, 1963; Unnatural Causes, 1967; Shroud for a Nightingale, 1971; (with T.A. Critchley) The Maul and the Pear Tree: The Ratcliffe Highway Murders, 1811 (non-fiction), 1971; An Unsuitable Job for a Woman, 1972; The Black Tower, 1975; Death of an Expert Witness, 1977; Crime Times Three: Three Complete Novels Featuring Adam Dalgliesh of Scotland Yard, 1979; (co-author) Nursing Stories, 1979; Innocent Blood, 1980; Murder in Triplicate: Three Complete Novels by the Queen of Crime, 1980; The Skull beneath the Skin, 1982; Trilogy of Death: The Three Complete Novels, 1984; A Taste for Death, 1986; In Murderous Company: Complete and Unabridged Novels by the Queen of Crime, 1988; Devices and Desires, 1989; The Children of Men, 1992; (foreword) 800 Years of Women's Letters, 1993; Original Sin, 1994, rev. ed., 2002; A Certain Justice, 1997; Time to Be in Earnest: A Fragment of Autobiography, 1999; Death in Holy Orders, 2001; (ed. with H.H. Wood) Sightlines, 2001; The Murder Room, 2003; The Lighthouse, 2005; (intro.) Father Brown: The Essential Tales, 2005; The Private Patient, 2008; Talking About Detective Fiction, 2009; Death Comes to Pemberley, 2011. **Address:** Greene & Heaton Ltd., 37 Goldhawk Rd., London, GL W12 8QQ, England.

JAMES, Peter. British (born England), b. 1948. **Genres:** Novels, Mystery/Crime/Suspense, Novellas/Short Stories, Horror. **Career:** Polka Dot Door, writer, 1970; Quadrant Films, film producer, 1971-78; Brighton Evening Argus, assistant; Pavilion Internet P.L.C., founder; novelist, 1980-. **Publications:** THRILLER NOVELS: Dead Letter Drop, 1981; Atom Bomb Angel, 1982; Billionaire, 1983; Travelling Man, 1984; Down Under, 1985; Possession, 1988; Dreamer, 1989; Sweet Heart, 1991; Twilight, 1991; Prophecy, 1992; Host, 1993; Ancient Inventions, 1994; Alchemist, 1995; Getting Wired!: A Techno Terrors Story, 1996; The Truth, 1997; Denial, 1998; Faith, 2000. DETECTIVE SUPERINTENDENT ROY GRACE SERIES: Dead Simple, 2005; Looking Good Dead, 2006; Not Dead Enough, 2007; Dead Man's Footsteps, 2008; Dead Tomorrow, 2009; Dead Like You, 2010; Dead Man's Grip, 2011; Not Dead Yet, 2012. OTHER NOVELS: Biggles: The Untold Story, 1986; The Perfect Murder, 2010; (co-author) No Rest for the Dead, 2011; Perfect People, 2011; Christmas is for the Kids, 2011. **Address:** c/o Carole Blake, Blake Friedmann Literary, Film & TV Agency, 122 Arlington Rd., London, GL NW1 7HP, England. **Online address:** scary@pavilion.co.uk

JAMES, Reina. British (born England), b. 1947?. **Genres:** Young Adult Fiction, Romance/Historical. **Career:** Writer. **Publications:** This Time of Dying, 2007; The Old Joke, 2009. **Address:** c/o Gillon Aitken, Aitken Alexander Associates, 18-21 Cavaye Pl., London, GL SW10 9PT, England.

JAMES, Rupert. *See* **SMITH, Rupert.**

JAMES, Russell. British (born England), b. 1942. **Genres:** Mystery/Crime/Suspense, History, Literary Criticism And History, Popular Culture, Biography, Essays, Reference, Novels, Adult Non-fiction, Art/Art History, Photography. **Career:** Writer, 1989-; Crime Writers Association, chairman, 2001-02. **Publications:** Underground, 1989; Daylight, 1990; Payback, 1993; (comp.) Proceedings of the Australian Marine Turtle Conservation Workshop, 1994; Slaughter Music, 1995; Count Me Out, 1996; Oh No, Not My Baby, 1999; Painting in the Dark, 2000; Pick Any Title, 2002; The Annex, 2002; No One Gets Hurt, 2003; The Maud Allan Affair, 2008; Great British Fictional Detectives, 2008; Great British Fictional Villains, 2009; Pocket Guide to Victorian Writers and Poets, 2010; V2, 2010; Pocket Guide to Victorian Artists and Their Models, 2011; Requiem for a Daughter, 2011. Contributor to journals. **Address:** c/o Jane Conway-Gordon, 38 Cromwell Grove, London, GL W6 7RG, England. **Online address:** findrj@lineone.net

JAMES, Sibyl. American (born United States), b. 1946. **Genres:** Novellas/Short Stories, Poetry, Essays, Travel/Exploration, Adult Non-fiction, Autobiography/Memoirs. **Career:** Teacher, 1971-; Highline Community College, instructor in English, 1982-, adjunct professor in humanities; University of Tunis, Fulbright professor, 1989-91; University of Abidjan, Fulbright professor, 1999-2000; Seattle City Light, editor and public relations specialist. **Publications:** The White Junk of Love, Again (poetry), 1986; Vallarta Street (poetry), 1988; In China with Harpo and Karl (creative nonfiction), 1990; The Adventures of Stout Mama (stories), 1993; The Bakery of the Three Whores (poetry), 1994; Ho CHi Minh's Motorbike (creative nonfiction), 2005; China Beats (poetry), 2006; Pistols and Hearts (poetry), 2009; The Last Woro Woro to Treichville (creative nonfiction). Works appear in anthologies. Contributor to periodicals. **Address:** 1712 22nd Ave. S, Seattle, WA 98144-4514, U.S.A. **Online address:** sibyljames@hotmail.com

JAMES, Stanlie. (Stanlie M. James). American (born United States) **Genres:** Novels, Social Sciences, Politics/Government. **Career:** University of Wisconsin, professor of women's studies, 1988-; professor and chair of Afro-American studies department, 2001-; Women's Studies Research Center, director, 1996-2000. Writer. **Publications:** (Ed. with A.P.A. Busia) Theorizing Black Feminisms: The Visionary Pragmatism of Black Women, 1993; (ed. with C.C. Robertson) Genital Cutting and Transnational Sisterhood: Disputing U.S. Polemics, 2002; (ed. with F.S. Foster and B. Guy-Sheftall) Still Brave: The Evolution of Black Womens Studies, 2009. Contributor to periodicals. **Address:** Department of Afro-American Studies, University of Wisconsin-Madison, 4141 Helen C White Hall, 600 N Park St., Madison, WI 53706, U.S.A. **Online address:** smjames@facstaff.wisc.edu

JAMES, Stanlie M. *See* **JAMES, Stanlie.**

JAMES, Syrie. American (born United States) **Genres:** Novels. **Career:** Writer. **Publications:** NOVEL: The Lost Memoirs of Jane Austen, 2008; The Secret Diaries of Charlotte Brontë, 2009; Dracula, My Love, 2010; Nocturne, 2011; Jane Austen Made Me Do It, (Short Story Anthology), 2011; Forbidden, 2012. **Address:** Los Angeles, CA , U.S.A. **Online address:** authorsyriejames@gmail.com

JAMES, Tania. American (born United States), b. 1980?. **Genres:** Literary Criticism And History. **Career:** Writer. **Publications:** Atlas of Unknowns, 2009. Contributor of articles to periodicals and newspapers. **Address:** New York, NY , U.S.A. **Online address:** tania.james@gmail.com

JAMES, Vanessa. *See* **BEAUMAN, Sally.**

JAMES, Warren A. American (born United States), b. 1960. **Genres:** Architecture, Art/Art History, Design, Essays, Translations. **Career:** Catalan Art and Architecture Archives, research assistant, 1982-84; Robert A.M. Stern Architects, designer and junior project architect, 1984-88; Ricardo Bofill/Taller de Arquitectura, designer and junior project architect, 1985-86; Arquitectura Magazine, U.S. correspondent, 1987-91; New Jersey Institute of Technology, instructor, 1987-89; James Warren & Associates, designer, principal and managing director, 1988-; Australian Koala Foundation, staff; Newcrest Mining Group, staff; Woodward Clyde Consultant, principle ecologist. Writer. **Publications:** Ricardo Bofill/Taller de Arquitectura: Buildings and Projects 1960-1985, 1988; (trans.) J. Larrea and Q. Capella, Designed by Architects in the '80s, 1989; (trans.) The Catalan Spirit: Gaudi and His Contemporaries (exhibition catalog), 1991; (trans.) Barragan: Armando Salas Portugal Photographs of the Architecture of Luis Barragan, 1992; (ed. and contrib.) Kohn Pedersen Fox: Architecture and Urbanism 1986-1992, 1993; (trans. with H. Salichs) A. Rossi: Architecture (Spanish ed.), 1994; Dream Houses: Three Latino Constructions (exhibition catalog), 1998. Contributor to periodicals. **Address:** c/o David A. Morton, Rizzoli International Publications Inc., 300 Park Ave. S, 3rd Fl., New York, NY 10010, U.S.A. **Online address:** warrenjames@juno.com

JAMES, (William) Louis (Gabriel). British (born England), b. 1933?. **Genres:** History, Literary Criticism And History, Novels, Politics/Government. **Career:** University of Hull, staff tutor in English, 1958-63; University of the West Indies, lecturer in English, 1963-66; University of South Carolina, assistant professor, 1969-70; University of Ibadan, fellow, 1973-74; University of Colorado, professor, 1978-80; University of Kent, Keynes College, reader in Victorian and modern literature, 1981, School of English, now professor emeritus. Writer. **Publications:** Fiction for the Working Man, 1830-1850: A Study of the Literature Produced for the Working Classes in Early Victorian Urban England, 1963; (ed. and intro.) The Islands in Between: Essays on West Indian Literature, 1968; (ed. and intro.) English Popular Literature, 1819-1851, 1976; (ed. and intro.) Print and the People 1819-1851, 1976; Jean Rhys, 1978; (ed. with D. Bradby and B. Sharratt) Performance and Politics in Popular Drama: Aspects of Popular Entertainment in Theatre, Film, and Television, 1800-1976, 1980; Writers from the Caribbean, 1990; Passport's Illustrated Travel Guide to Vienna, 1993, 2nd ed., 1997; Passport's Illustrated Travel Guide to Budapest, 1994; Up Close Vienna, 1996; Vienna, 2nd ed., 1996; Passport's Illustrated Travel Guide to Prague, 2nd ed., 1997; Caribbean Literature in English, 1999; (with D. West) Adults Only Travel: The Ultimate Guide to Romantic and Erotic Destinations, 2001; Victorian Novel, 2006; (ed. with A. Humpherys) G.W.M. Reynolds: Nineteenth-Century Fiction, Politics, and the Press, 2008. Contributor to journals. **Address:** Keynes College, School of English, University of Kent, 0 Canterbury Hill, Canterbury, KT CT2 7LX, England.

JAMES, W(illiam) Martin. American (born United States), b. 1952. **Genres:** Politics/Government, History, Documentaries/Reportage. **Career:** Foreign affairs research assistant, 1977-78; legislative and research assistant, 1978-83; Arkansas's Auditor of State, research director, 1983-88; Henderson State University, assistant professor, 1988-91, associate professor of political science, 1991-98, professor of political science, 1998-. Writer. **Publications:** (With J.P. Vanneman) Soviet Foreign Policy in Southern Africa: Problems and Prospects, 1983; A Political History of the Civil War in Angola, 1974-1990, 1991; Historical Dictionary of Angola, 2004. Contributor to journals. **Address:** Department of Political Science, Henderson State University, 1100 Henderson St., PO Box 7511, Arkadelphia, AR 71999, U.S.A. **Online address:** jamesm@hsu.edu

JAMES, Wilmot G. South African (born South Africa), b. 1953. **Genres:** Sociology, Biology. **Career:** University of the Western Cape, lecturer in politics, 1983-84; University of Cape Town, lecturer, associate professor of sociology, 1986-, professor, 1992-, dean of humanities, Division of Genetics, honorary professor; Indiana University, visting fellow, 1990; American Bar Foundation, vising fellow, 1992; Institute For Democracy in South Africa (IDASA), executive director, 1994-98; Cape Argus, associate editor, 2001; Human Sciences Research Council, executive director, 2001-04; California Institute of Technology, Moore distinguished visiting professor, 2003; University of Pretoria, Department of Sociology, honorary professor; Africa Genome Education Institute, executive director, 2005; Sanlam Ltd., director; Media24, director; Grape Co., director; Naspers, director. Writer. **Publications:** Our Precious Metal: African Labour in South Africa's Gold Industry, 1970-1990, 1992; Africa in the Age of Biology, 2004; Nature's Gifts: Why We Are The Way We Are, 2010; Grape: Stories of the Vineyards in South Africa, 2011. EDITOR: The State of Apartheid, 1987; (with J. Lever) Towards a Deracialised Labour

Force: Industrial Relations and the Abolition of the Job Colour Bar on the South African Gold Mines, 1987; (with M. Simons) The Angry Divide: The Social and Economic History of the Western Cape, 1989; (with M. Simons) Class, Caste, and Color: A Social and Economic History of the South African Western Cape, 1992; (with J. Crush) Crossing Boundaries: Mine Migrancy in a Democratic South Africa, 1995; (with D. Caliguire and K. Cullinan) Now That We are Free: Coloured Communities in a Democratic South Africa, 1996; (with M. Levy) Pulse. Passages in Democracy-Building: Assessing South Africa's Transition, 1998; (with L. Vijver) After the TRC: Reflections on Truth and Reconciliation in South Africa, 2001; (with L. Wilson) Architect and the Scaffold: Evolution and Education in South Africa, 2002; (with K. Asmal and D. Chidester) In his Own Words, 2003; (with K. Asmal and D. Chidester) Nelson Mandela: From Freedom to the Future: Tributes and Speeches, 2003; (with P. Dexter and D. Chideste) What Holds Us Together: Social Cohesion in South Africa, 2004; (with K. Asmal and D. Chidester) South Africa's Nobel Laureates: Peace, Literature and Science, 2004; (with J. Chataway) Biotechnology and Health: South Africa's Aspirations in Health-Related Biotechnology, 2007. **Address:** University of Cape Town, PO Box X3, Rondebosch, 7701, South Africa. **Online address:** wilmotjames@mweb.co.za

JAMESON, Marianna. American (born United States) **Genres:** Novels. **Career:** National Aeronautics and Space Administration, technical writer; Writer and educator. **Publications:** My Hero, 2005; Big Trouble, 2006; (with B. Evans) Category 7, 2007; (with B. Evans) Frozen Fire, 2009; (with B. Evans) Dry Ice, 2011. **Address:** Tom Doherty Associates L.L.C., 175 5th Ave., New York, NY 10010-7703, U.S.A. **Online address:** marianna@mariannajameson.com

JAMESON, W. C. American (born United States), b. 1942. **Genres:** Poetry, Area Studies, History, Travel/Exploration, Environmental Sciences/Ecology. **Career:** University of Central Arkansas, associate professor, professor of geography, through 1974, now retired; Western Writers of America Inc, president. Writer. **Publications:** Concepts in Biometeorology, 1970; (with B.M. Barker) Platt National Park: Environment and Ecology, 1975; Environmental Analysis Workbook, 1978; Buried Treasures of the American Southwest: Legends of Lost Mines, Hidden Payrolls and Spanish Gold, 1989; Buried Treasures of the Ozarks: Legends of Lost Gold, Hidden Silver and Forgotten Caches, 1990; Buried Treasures of the Appalachians: Legends of Homestead Caches, Indian Mines and Loot from Civil War Raids, 1991; Buried Treasures of Texas, Legends of Outlaw Loot, Pirate Hoards, Buried Mines, Ingots In Lakes and Santa Anna's Pack-Train Gold, 1991; A Sense of Place: Essays on the Ozarks, 1992; Buried Treasures of the South: Legends of Lost, Buried and Forgotten Treasures, from Tidewater Virginia and Coastal Carolina to Cajun Louisiana, 1992; Buried Treasures from America's Heartland, 1993; Buried Treasures of the Ozarks and Appalachians, 1993; I Missed the Train to Little Rock (poems), 1993; Buried Treasures of the Rocky Mountain West: Legends of Lost Mines, Train Robbery Gold, Caves of Forgotten Riches and Indians Buried Silver, 1993; The Guadalupe Mountains: Island in the Desert, 1994; (ed.) J. Hamilton, River of Used to Be, 1994; Buried Treasures of California: Legends from California's Mountains, Deserts, Beaches and Cities, 1995; Buried Treasures of the Pacific Northwest: Secret Indian Mines, Lost Outlaw Hoards and Stolen Payroll Coins, 1995; Tales of the Guadalupe Mountains, 1996; America's Buried Treasures, 1996; Buried Treasures of the Atlantic Coast: Legends of Sunken Pirate Treasures, Mysterious Caches, and Jinxed Ships, From Maine to Florida, 1998; Buried Treasures of New England States: Legends of Hidden Riches, Forgotten War Loots and Lost Ship Treasures, 1998; Buried Treasures of the Great Plains, 1998; Exploring Branson: A Family Guide, 1998; Bubba Speak: Texas Folk Sayings, 1998; Return of the Outlaw, Billy the Kid, 1998; Return of Assassin John Wilkes Booth, 1999; Unsolved Mysteries of the Old West, 1999; The Ultimate Chili Cookbook: History, Geography, Fact and Folklore of Chili, 1999; Buried Treasures of the Mid-Atlantic States: Legends of Island Treasure, Jewelry Caches, and Secret Tunnels, 2000; Colorado Treasure Tales, 2001; New Mexico Treasure Tales, 2003; Chili from the Southwest: Fixin's, Flavors and Folklore, 2005; Billy the Kid: Beyond The Grave, 2005; (ed.) Hot Coffee and Cold Truth: Living and Writing the West, 2006; Lost Treasures of American History, 2006; Beating the Devil, 2007; Legend and Lore of the Guadalupe Mountains, 2007; (ed. with L.W. Buyer) Open Range: Poetry of the Reimagined West, 2007; (ed.) Notes from Texas: On Writing in the Lone Star State, 2008; Lost Mines and Buried Treasures of Arizona, 2009; Treasure Hunter: A True Story of Caches, Curses and Deadly Confrontations, 2010; Lost Mines & Buried Treasures of Old Wyoming, 2010. Contributor to books. Contributor of articles to newspapers and periodicals. **Address:** 208 W College, Llano, TX 78643, U.S.A. **Online address:** jamesonwc@gmail.com

JAMIESON, Kathleen Hall. American (born United States), b. 1946. **Genres:** Communications/Media, Law, Social Sciences. **Career:** University of Maryland, professor of communications, 1971-86; University of Texas at Austin, professor of communications, 1986-89; University of Pennsylvania, professor of communications, 1989-, The Annenberg School of Communications, director, 1993, dean, 1993-; Annenberg Public Policy Center, Walter and Leonore Annenberg director, Elizabeth Ware Packard professor of communication. Writer. **Publications:** (Co-author) Debating Crime Control, 1967; (comp.) A Critical Anthology of Public Speeches, 1978; (with K.K. Campbell) The Interplay of Influence: Mass Media and Their Publics in News, Advertising and Politics, 1982, 6th ed. as The Interplay of Influence: News, Advertising, Politics and the Mass Media, 2006; Packaging the Presidency: A History and Criticism of Presidential Campaign Advertising, 1984, 3rd ed., 1996; Eloquence in an Electronic Age: The Transformation of Political Speechmaking, 1988; (with D.S. Birdsell) Presidential Debates: The Challenge of Creating an Informed Electorate, 1988; (with K.K. Campbell) Deeds Done in Words: Presidential Rhetoric and the Genres of Governance, 1990; Dirty Politics: Deception, Distraction and Democracy, 1992; (with K. Auletta and T.E. Patterson) 1-800-PRESIDENT: The Report of the Twentieth Century Fund Task Force on Television and the Campaign of 1992, 1993; Beyond the Double Bind: Women and Leadership, 1995; (with J. Cappella) Spiral of Cynicism: The Press and the Public Good, 1997; Incivility and Its Discontents: Lessons Learned from Studying Civility in the U.S. House of Representatives, 2000; Everything You Think You Know about Politics And Why You're Wrong, 2000; (with P. Waldman) The Press Effect: Politicians, Journalists and the Stories that Shape the Political World, 2003; (with R. Johnston and M.G. Hagen) The 2000 Presidential Election and the Foundations of Party Politics, 2004; (with B. Jackson) UnSpun: Finding Facts in a World of Disinformation, 2007; (with K.K. Campbell) Presidents Creating the Presidency: Deeds Done in Words, 2008. EDITOR: (with K.K. Campbell) Form and Genre: Shaping Rhetorical Action, 1978; Age Stereotyping and Television, 1978; Televised Advertising and the Elderly, 1978; (with P. Waldman) Electing the President, 2000: The Insiders' View, 2001; (with G. Overholser) The Press, 2005; Electing the President, 2004: The Insider's View, 2006; (with J.N. Cappella) Echo Chamber: Rush Limbaugh and the Conservative Media Establishment, 2008; Electing The President, 2008: The Insiders View, 2009; (with K. Kenski, B.W. Hardy) Obama Victory: How Media, Money and Message Shaped the 2008 Election, 2010. Contributor to periodicals journals. **Address:** Annenberg School of Communications, University of Pennsylvania, 3620 Walnut St., Ste. 200, Philadelphia, PA 19104-6220, U.S.A. **Online address:** kjamieson@asc.upenn.edu

JAMIESON, Perry D. American (born United States), b. 1947. **Genres:** Military/Defense/Arms Control, History. **Career:** Air Force History Support Office, historian, 1980-; U.S. Defense Department, Joint Military Intelligence College, lecturer; Grady McWhiney Research Foundation, fellow. Writer. **Publications:** (With G. McWhiney) Attack and Die: Civil War Military Tactics and the Southern Heritage, 1982; Crossing the Deadly Ground: United States Army Tactics, 1865-1899, 1994; Death in September: The Antietam Campaign, 1995; Air House: A History, 2001; Lucrative Targets: The U.S. Air Force in the Kuwaiti Theater of Operations, 2001; Winfield Scott Hancock: Gettysburg Hero, 2003; Khobar Towers: Tragedy and Response, 2008. **Address:** Air Force History Support Office, 3 Brookley Ave., Bolling AFB, PO Box 94, Washington, DC 20032, U.S.A.

JAMIOLKOWSKI, Raymond M. American (born United States), b. 1953. **Genres:** Education, Young Adult Non-fiction, Human Relations/Parenting, Medicine/Health. **Career:** Schaumburg School District No. 54, elementary teacher, 1975-80; Marion County Schools, guidance counselor and testing and research specialist, 1980-84; Naperville School District No. 203, guidance counselor, 1984-98; Naperville Central High School District No. 203, director of guidance, 1998-, assistant principal of operations. Writer. **Publications:** (With T. Dewing) I Get It! Critical Thinking for Kids, 1986; (with T. Dewing and D. Andre) The Inquiry Method of Teaching Science, 1988; Coping in a Dysfunctional Family, 1993, rev. ed., 1998; Coping with an Emotionally Distant Father, 1995, rev. ed., 1998; Drugs and Domestic Violence, 1995; A Baby Doesn't Make the Man: Alternative Sources of Power and Manhood for Young Men, 1997, rev. ed., 2001. **Address:** Naperville Central High School, 440 W Aurora Ave., Naperville, IL 60540-6298, U.S.A. **Online address:** rjamiolkowski@naperville203.org

JAMISON, Bill. American (born United States), b. 1942. **Genres:** Food And Wine. **Career:** Southwest Texas State University, professor of American history; British Airways, consultant; Honeywell, consultant. Writer. **Publications:** WITH C.A. JAMISON: The Insider's Guide to Santa Fe, 1987, 4th ed. as The Insider's Guide to Santa Fe, Taos, and Albuquerque, 1996; The Rancho de Chimayó Cookbook: The Traditional Cooking of New Mexico, 1991; Texas Home Cooking, 1993; Smoke and Spice, 1994, rev. ed. as Smoke & Spice: Cooking with Smoke, the Real Way to Barbecue, 2003; The Border Cookbook: Authentic Home Cooking from the American Southwest and Northern Mexico, 1995; Best Places to Stay in Mexico, 3rd ed., 1995; Best Places to Stay in Hawaii, 3rd ed., 1995; Sublime Smoke: Bold New Flavors Inspired by the Old Art of Barbecue, 1996; Best Places to Stay in the Caribbean, 4th ed., 1996; Born to Grill: An American Celebration, 1998; American Home Cooking: Over 300 Spirited Recipes Celebrating Our Rich Tradition of Home Cooking, 1999; A Real American Breakfast: The Best Meal of the Day, Anytime of the Day, 2002; Chicken on the Grill: 100 Surefire Ways to Grill Perfect Chicken Every Time, 2004; Grilling for Friends: Surefire, Fun Food for Great Grill Parties, 2006; The Big Book of Outdoor Cooking and Entertaining: Spirited Recipes and Expert Tips for Barbecuing, Charcoal and Gas Grilling, Rotisserie Roasting, Smoking, Deep-Frying, and Making Merry, 2006; Around the World in 80 Dinners: The Ultimate Culinary Adventure, 2008. OTHER: Santa Fe: An Intimate View, 1982. Contributor to periodicals. **Address:** PO Box 1804, Santa Fe, NM 87504-1804, U.S.A.

JAMISON, Cheryl Alters. American (born United States), b. 1953. **Genres:** Food And Wine, Travel/Exploration. **Career:** Writer. **Publications:** WITH B. JAMISON: Insider's Guide to Santa Fe, 1987 as The Insider's Guide to Santa Fe, Taos and Albuquerque, 4th ed., 1996; The Rancho de Chimayo Cookbook: The Traditional Cooking of New Mexico, 1991; Texas Home Cooking, 1993; Smoke and Spice, 1994 as Smoke & Spice: Cooking with Smoke, The Real Way to Barbecue, 2003; The Border Cookbook: Authentic Home Cooking from the American Southwest and Northern Mexico, 1995; Best Places to Stay in Mexico, 3rd ed., 1995; Best Places to Stay in Hawaii, 3rd ed., 1995; Sublime Smoke: Bold New Flavors Inspired by the Old Art of Barbecue, 1996; Best Places to Stay in the Caribbean, 4th ed., 1996; Born to Grill: An American Celebration, 1998; American Home Cooking: Over 300 Spirited Recipes Celebrating Our Rich Tradition of Home Cooking, 1999; A Real American Breakfast: The Best Meal of the Day, Anytime of the Day, 2002; Chicken on the Grill: 100 Surefire Ways to Grill Perfect Chicken Every Time, 2004; Good Times, Good Grilling: Surefire Recipes for Great Grill Parties, 2005; Grilling for Friends: Surefire, Fun Food for Great Grill Parties, 2006; The Big Book of Outdoor Cooking and Entertaining: Spirited Recipes and Expert Tips for Barbecuing, Charcoal and Gas Grilling, Rotisserie Roasting, Smoking, Deep-Frying and Making Merry, 2006; Around the World in 80 Dinners: The Ultimate Culinary Adventure, 2008; (with B. Jamison) Texas Home Cooking: 400 Terrific And Comforting Recipes Full Of Big, Bright Flavors And Loads Of Down-home Goodness, 2011; (with B. Jamison) Tasting New Mexico: Recipes Celebrating One Hundred Years Of Distinctive New Mexican Cooking, 2011. **Address:** PO Box 1804, Santa Fe, NM 87504, U.S.A. **Online address:** b-c-jamison@msn.com

JAMISON, Janelle. *See* **PETERSON, Tracie.**

JAMISON, Kay R(edfield). American (born United States), b. 1946. **Genres:** Medicine/Health, Psychology. **Career:** University of California Los Angeles, School of Medicine, Department of Psychiatry, research assistant, 1968-73, assistant professor, 1974-81, School of Medicine, director and co-founder, 1977-87, associate professor, 1981-87, Neuropsychiatric Institute, intern, 1973-74; National Institute of Mental Health, Clinical Psychobiology Branch, visiting scientist, 1981; University of Oxford, Merton College, visiting senior research fellow, 1982-83, Department of Psychiatry, visiting scientist, 1985-86, Litchfield Lecturer, 2003; Johns Hopkins University, School of Medicine, Department of Psychiatry, associate professor, 1987-93, professor, 1993-, co-director, 2005-, Mood Disorders and Artistic Creativity, project director, 1987-2001, Mood Disorders Center, Dalio Family Professor in Mood Disorders and co-director, 2005-; Manic-Depressive Illness Foundation, president, 1988-; American College of Neuropsychopharmacology, consultant, 1990; International Arts-Medicine Association, director, 1990-93; Dana Consortium on the Genetic Basis of Manic-Depressive Illness, clinical director, 1993-97; Depression and Related Affective, Disorders Association, director, 1994-2004; American Foundation for Suicide Prevention, director, 1994-; University of St. Andrews, School of English, honorary professor, 1997-; The Dana Foundation, senior scientific consultant, 2000-; Harvard University, distinguished lecturer, 2002; Friends of St. Andrews University Library, chair, 2008-. Writer. **Publications:** (With B.L. Baker and M.J. Gold-

stein) Abnormal Psychology: Experiences, Origins and Interventions, 1980, 2nd ed. 1986; (with F.K. Goodwin) Manic-Depressive Illness, 1990, 2nd ed. as Manic-Depressive Illness: Bipolar Disorders and Recurrent Depression, 2007; Touched with Fire: Manic-Depressive Illness and the Creative Temperament, 1993; An Unquiet Mind (memoir), 1995; Night Falls Fast, 1999; Exuberance: The Passion for Life, 2004; Nothing Was the Same: A Memoir, 2009. Contributor to articles. **Address:** Department of Psychiatry & Behavioral Sciences, Johns Hopkins Hospital, Meyer 3-181, 600 N Wolfe St., Baltimore, MD 21287, U.S.A.

JANCE, J. A. American (born United States), b. 1944. **Genres:** Mystery/Crime/Suspense, Children's Fiction, Novels, Poetry. **Career:** Pueblo High School, teacher, 1966-68; Indian Oasis Schools, librarian, 1968-73; Equitable Life Assurance Society, life insurance salesperson and district manager, 1974-84. Writer, 1985-. **Publications:** MYSTERY NOVELS: J.P. BEAUMONT SERIES: Until Proven Guilty, 1985; Injustice for All, 1986; Trial by Fury, 1987; Taking the Fifth, 1987; Improbable Cause, 1987; A More Perfect Union, 1988; Dismissed with Prejudice, 1989; Minor in Possession, 1990; Payment in Kind, 1991; Without Due Process, 1992; Failure to Appear, 1993; Lying in Wait, 1994; Name Withheld, 1995; Breach of Duty, 1999; Birds of Prey, 2001; Long Time Gone, 2005; Justice Denied, 2007; Fire and Ice, 2009; Betrayal of Trust, 2011. JOANNA BRADY SERIES: Desert Heat, 1993; Tombstone Courage, 1994; Shoot/Don't Shoot, 1995; Dead to Rights, 1997; Skeleton Canyon, 1997; Rattlesnake Crossing, 1998; Outlaw Mountain, 1999; Devil's Claw, 2000; Paradise Lost, 2001; Partner in Crime, 2002; Exit Wounds, 2003; Dead Wrong, 2006; Damage Control, 2008; Judgment Call, 2012. FOR CHILDREN: It's Not Your Fault, 1985; Dial Zero for Help: A Story of Parental Kidnapping, 1985; Welcome Home, Stranger: A Child's View of Family Alcoholism, 1986. OTHERS: Hour of the Hunter (novel), 1991; Kiss of the Bees (novel), 2000; (co-author) Naked Came the Phoenix, 2001; After the Fire, 2004; Day of the Dead, 2004; Sentenced to Die, 2005; Bark M for Murder, 2006; Edge of Evil, 2006; Hand of Evil: A Novel of Suspense, 2007; Web of Evil: A Novel of Suspense, 2007; Cruel Intent, 2008; Trial by Fire, 2009; Queen of the Night, 2010; Fatal Error, 2011; Left for Dead, 2012. **Address:** PO Box 766, Bellevue, WA 98009-0766, U.S.A. **Online address:** jajance@jajance.com

JANCOVICH, Mark. British (born England), b. 1960. **Genres:** Film, Literary Criticism And History, Popular Culture, Horror, Communications/Media, Young Adult Non-fiction. **Career:** Victoria University of Manchester, lecturer, 1990-93; University of Keele, lecturer, 1993-95; University of Nottingham, lecturer, professor in American studies, 1995-, leader, 2001-; University of East Anglia, professor of film and television studies, 2004-. Writer. **Publications:** Horror, 1992; The Cultural Politics of the New Criticism, 1993; American Horror from 1951 to the Present, 1994; (ed. with J. Hollows) Approaches to Popular Film, 1995; Rational Fears: American Horror in the 1950s, 1996; (ed. with J. Hollows and P. Hutchings) The Film Studies Reader, 2000; (co-author) The Place of the Audience: Cultural Geographies of Film Consumption, 2003; (ed.) Horror: The Film Reader, 2002; Quality Popular Television, 2003; (with L. Faire and S. Stubbings) The Place of the Audience, 2003; (co-ed.) Defining Cult Movies: The Cultural Politics of Oppositional Taste, 2003; (with P. Grainge and S. Monteith) Film Histories: An Introduction and Reader, 2007; (ed. with I. Gordon and M.P. McAlliser) Film and Comic Books, 2007; (ed. with L. Geraghty) Shifting Definitions of Genre: Essays on Labeling Films, Television Shows and Media, 2008. **Address:** Department of Film and Television Studies, University of East Anglia, 3.11 Registry And Council House, Norwich Research Pk., Norwich, NF NR4 7TJ, England. **Online address:** m.jancovich@uea.ac.uk

JANDREY, G. Davies. American (born United States), b. 1947. **Genres:** Homes/Gardens, Young Adult Fiction. **Career:** Educator and writer. **Publications:** A Garden of Aloes, 2008. **Address:** The Permanent Press, 4170 Noyac Rd., Sag Harbor, New York, NY 11963, U.S.A.

JANECZKO, Paul B(ryan). American (born United States), b. 1945. **Genres:** Young Adult Fiction, Poetry, History, Novellas/Short Stories, Adult Non-fiction. **Career:** High school English teacher, 1968-77; Gray-New Gloucester High School, teacher of language arts, 1977-90; visiting writer, 1990-. **Publications:** Loads of Codes and Secret Ciphers, 1984; Bridges to Cross, 1986; Brickyard Summer: Poems, 1989; Stardust Hotel: Poems, 1993; That Sweet Diamond: Baseball Poems, 1998; How to Write Poetry, 1999; (comp.) Seeing the Blue Between: Advice and Inspiration for Young Poets, 2002; Writing Winning Reports and Essays, 2003; Good for a Laugh: A Guide to Writing Amusing, Clever and Downright Funny Poems, 2003; Opening a Door: Reading Poetry in the Middle School Classroom, 2003; Worlds Afire, 2004; Top Secret: A Handbook of Codes, Ciphers and Secret Writing, 2004; How to Write Haiku and Other Short Poems, 2004; (with J.P. Lewis) Wing Nuts: Screwy Haiku, 2006; Birds on a Wire, or, A Jewel Tray of Stars, 2008; (with J.P. Lewis) Birds on a Wire: A Renga 'Round Town, 2008; (with C. Raschka) Foot in the Mouth: Poems to Speak, Sing and Shout, 2009; Dark Game: True Spy Stories from the Revolution to the 21st Century, 2010; Requiem: Poems of the Terezin Ghetto, 2011; Reading Poetry in the Middle Grades, 2011. EDITOR: The Crystal Image, 1977; Postcard Poems: A Collection of Poetry for Sharing, 1979; It's Elementary, 1981; Don't Forget to Fly: A Cycle of Modern Poems, 1981; Poetspeak: In their Work, about their Work: A Selection, 1983; Strings: A Gathering of Family Poems, 1984; Pocket Poems: Selected for a Journey, 1985; This Delicious Day: 65 Poems, 1987; Going over to Your Place: Poems for Each Other, 1987; The Music of What Happens: Poems that Tell Stories, 1988; The Place My Words Are Looking For: What Poets Say about and through Their Work, 1990; Preposterous: Poems of Youth, 1991; Looking for Your Name: A Collection of Contemporary Poems, 1993; Poetry from A to Z: A Guide for Young Writers, 1994; Wherever Home Begins: 100 Contemporary Poems, 1995; (with N.S. Nye) I Feel a Little Jumpy Around You: A Book of Her Poems & His Poems Collected in Pairs, 1996; Home on the Range: Cowboy Poetry, 1997; Very Best (almost) Friends: Poems of Friendship, 1999; Stone Bench in an Empty Park, 2000; Poke in the I, 2001; Dirty Laundry Pile: Poems in Different Voices, 2001; Blushing: Expressions of Love in Poems and Letters, 2004; Kick in the Head, 2005; (contrib.) Hey, You!: Poems to Skyscrapers, Mosquitoes and other Fun Things, 2007. Contributor to newspapers and magazines. **Address:** c/o Author Mail, Candlewick Press Inc., 99 Dover St., Somerville, MA 02144, U.S.A. **Online address:** poetguy@megalink.net

JANELLO, Amy (Elizabeth). American (born United States), b. 1962. **Genres:** Writing/Journalism, Autobiography/Memoirs. **Career:** New York Foundation for the Arts, program assistant, 1985-86; American Showcase, executive assistant, 1986; William Collins Publishers Inc., A Day in the Life of America, assistant managing editor, A Day in the Life of Spain, associate managing editor and editor, 1986-87; Jones and Janello, partner and editor, 1987-. American Showcase, executive assistant. **Publications:** (Co-ed.) The Wall: Images and Offerings from the Vietnam Veterans Memorial, 1987; (ed. with B. Jones and contrib.) The American Magazine, 1991; (ed. with Jones) USSR: The Collapse of an Empire, 1992; (ed. with Jones) Essential Liberty: First Amendment Battles for a Free Press, 1992; I Dream of Peace: Images of War by Children of Former Yugoslavia, 1994; Golf-The Greatest Game, 1994. **Address:** Jones and Janello, 267 5th Ave., Ste. 800, Bedford, NY 10506, U.S.A.

JANES, J(oseph) Robert. Canadian (born Canada), b. 1935. **Genres:** Novels, Novellas/Short Stories, Earth Sciences, Children's Fiction, Young Adult Fiction, Children's Non-fiction, Young Adult Non-fiction, Natural History, Natural History. **Career:** Mobil Oil of Canada, petroleum engineer, 1958-59; Ontario Research Foundation, research engineer in minerals benefication, 1959-64, field researcher in geology, 1966; teacher in Toronto, 1964-66; Brock University, lecturer in geology, 1966-67, 1968-70; Ontario Science Centre, earth scientist, 1967-68; consulting field geologist, 1968-70; writer, 1970-. **Publications:** Geology, 1966; NON-FICTION FOR YOUNG ADULTS: Rocks, Minerals and Fossils, 1973; Earth Science, 1974; Geology and the New Global Tectonics: An Introduction to Physical and Historical Geology, 1976; (co-author) Searching for Structure, 1977; The Great Canadian Outback, 1978; (with J.D. Mollard) Airphoto Interpretation and the Canadian Landscape, 1984. FICTION FOR YOUNG ADULTS: The Odd-Lot Boys and the Tree-Fort War, 1976; Theft of Gold, 1980; Danger on the River, 1982; Spies for Dinner, 1984; Murder in the Market, 1985. FICTION FOR ADULTS: The Toy Shop, 1981; The Watcher, 1982; The Third Story, 1983; The Hiding Place, 1984; The Alice Factor, 1991; Mayhem, 1992; Carousel, 1992; Kaleidoscope, 1993; Salamander, 1994; Mannequin, 1994; Dollmaker, 1995; Stonekiller, 1996; Sandman, 1996; Gypsy, 1997; Madrigal, 1999; Beekeeper, 2001; Flykiller, 2002. Contributor to magazines and newspapers. **Address:** Acacia House Publishing Services Ltd., 51 Acacia House Rd., Toronto, ON M4S 2K6, Canada. **Online address:** jrjanes@sympatico.ca

JANIS, Michael. American (born United States), b. 1968?. **Genres:** Philosophy. **Career:** Morehouse College, assistant professor of English; Morehouse African Film Society, founder and advisor. Writer. **Publications:** Africa after Modernism: Transitions in Literature, Media, and Philosophy, 2008. Contrib-

utor to journals and periodicals. **Address:** Department of English, Morehouse College, 830 Westview Dr. SW, Atlanta, GA 30314, U.S.A. **Online address:** mjanis@morehouse.edu

JANISCH, Heinz. Austrian (born Austria), b. 1960?. **Genres:** Novels. **Career:** Austrian Broadcasting, staff, 1982-; ORF Radio House, freelancer, 1982-, Menschenbilder, editor-in-chief. **Publications:** Vom Untergang der Sonne am frühen Morgen, 1989; Lobreden auf Dinge, 1990; Mario, der Tagmaler, 1989; Salbei & Brot: Ger'che der Kindheit, 1992; Gute Reise, Leo, 1993; Schon nähert sich das Meer, 1994; Ein Krokodil Zuviel, 1994; Nach Lissabon, 1994; Benni und die sieben Löwen, 1995; Sarah und der Wundervogel, 1996; Der rote Pirat und andere Rucksackgeschichten, 1996; Die Arche Noah, 1997; Josef ist im Büro oder der Wegnach Bethlehem, 1998; Der Sonntagsriese, 1998; Die Prinzessin auf dem K'rbis, 1998; Ich schenk dir einen Ton Aus Meinem Saxofon, 1999; Gesang, Um Den Schalf gef'gig zu machen, 1999; Heut Bin Ich Stark, 2000; Zack Bumm!, 2000; Es gibt so Tage..., 2001; Die Reise zu den Fliegenden Inseln, 2001; (reteller) Fire: An Ethiopian Folk Tale, 2002; Her Mit Den Prinzen!, 2002; Her mit den Prinzen!, 2002; Zu Haus, 2002; Bärenhunger, 2002; Ich Bin Noch Gar Nicht müde, 2003; Schenk mir Flügel, 2003; Her Mit Den Prinzen!, 2003; Einer f'r alle! Alle f'r einem!: eine Hasengeschichte, 2004; Ein ganz gewöhnlicher Montag, 2004; Katzensprung, 2004; Der Prinz im Pyjama, 2004; Herr Jemineh hat Glück, 2004; Bist Du Morgen Auch Noch da?, 2005; Cleo in der Klemme, 2005; Drei Birken, 2005; Heute Will Ich Langsam Sein, 2005; Rote Wangen, 2005; Ho ruck!, 2005; Morgennatz und Ringelstern: Gedichte von Christian Morgenstern und Joachim Ringelnatz, 2005; Die Kluge Katze: die schösten Tiermärchen aus aller Welt, 2006; Ein Haus am Meer, 2006; Ich bin Flonx, 2006; Der grosse Hu und die Farben der Menschen, 2006; über die Liebe, 2006; Der Stärske von allen!, 2006; Krone sucht König, 2006; Einfach du, 2006; Der Tod auf Urlaub: Wegen Urlaub Geschlossen!, 2006; Rittergeschichten, 2007; Wenn ich Nachts Nicht Schlafen Kann, 2007, trans. as. Good Night Giants, 2011; Zeppelin: ein Geschichte, 2007; Schatten, 2007; Lilli und die Dschunglebande, 2007; Eine Wolke in meinem Bett, 2007; Ich hab ein kleines Problem, sagte der Bär, 2007; Der grosze Gustav Und Die Kleinste Frau Der Welt, 2007; Ich Hab Ein Kleines Problem, Sagt Der Bär, 2007; Der kleine Nikolaus, 2007; Sieben schreckliche Seepiraten, 2008; Auch die Götter lieben Fubball, 2008; Guten Morgen, 2008; Enzos Traumtor, 2008; Frau Friedrich, 2008; (with L. Wolfsgruber) Wie war das am Anfang, 2009; Fantastic Adventures of Baron Munchausen: Traditional and Newly Discovered Tales of Karl Friedrich Hieronymus von Munchausen, 2010; Good Night Giants, 2011. **Address:** ORF Radio House, Editorial People Pictures, Argentinierstrasse 30a, Vienna, 1040, Austria. **Online address:** info@janisch-heinz.com

JANKEN, Kenneth Robert. American (born United States), b. 1956. **Genres:** Biography, History, Autobiography/Memoirs, Politics/Government. **Career:** University of North Carolina, assistant professor, 1991-97, associate professor, 1997-2004, adjunct professor of history, 1999-, Department of African and Afro-American studies, professor, 2004-, College of Arts and Sciences, Office of Experiential Education, director. Writer. **Publications:** Rayford W. Logan and the Dilemma of the African-American Intellectual, 1993; White: The Biography of Walter White, Mr. NAACP, 2003. Contributor of articles to journals. **Address:** Department of African and Afro-American Studies, University of North Carolina-Chapel Hill, 207 Battle Hall, PO Box 3395, Chapel Hill, NC 27599-3995, U.S.A. **Online address:** krjanken@email.unc.edu

JANKO, James. American (born United States), b. 1949?. **Genres:** Novels, Young Adult Fiction, Literary Criticism And History. **Career:** City College of San Francisco, instructor of English. Writer. **Publications:** Buffalo Boy and Geronimo, 2006. Contributor to periodicals. **Address:** c/o Author Mail, Curbstone Press, 321 Jackson St., Willimantic, CT 06226-1738, U.S.A.

JANKO, (Kathleen) Susan. (Goody-Jones). American (born United States), b. 1951. **Genres:** Human Relations/Parenting, Novellas/Short Stories, Self Help, Medicine/Health, Sciences. **Career:** University of Oregon, Center on Human Development, Early Intervention Program, head teacher, 1984-85, Early Intervention Program, assistant coordinator, 1985-87; Oregon State Children's Services Division, Lane County Relief Nursery, Therapeutic Daycare and Family Intervention Programs, program director, 1987-89; University of Oregon, Center on Human Development, outreach trainer, 1988-91; University of Washington, Child Development and Mental Retardation Center, High Priority Infant Tracking Program, coordinator, 1989-91; coordinator of evaluation and community outreach, 1991-93, University Affiliated Program, associate director, 1993-94; Washington State University, Early Childhood

Research Institute on Inclusion, research coordinator, 1994-95; University of Washington, Early Childhood Research Institute on Inclusion, assistant professor, 1995-. Writer. **Publications:** Vulnerable Children, Vulnerable Families: The Social Construction of Child Abuse, 1994; Running Away, forthcoming; Saint Epain Stories, forthcoming. Contributor to books and periodicals. **Address:** College of Education, University of Washington, PO Box 353600, Seattle, WA 98195, U.S.A. **Online address:** sjanko@u.washington.edu

JANKOWSKI, James P. American (born United States), b. 1937. **Genres:** History, Social Sciences, Young Adult Non-fiction, Politics/Government. **Career:** University of Colorado, Department of History, instructor, 1966-67, assistant professor, 1967-72, associate professor, 1972-77, professor, 1977-, now emeritus professor, department head, 1985-89, 1995. Writer. **Publications:** Egypt's Young Rebels: Young Egypt, 1933-1952, 1975; (with I. Gershoni) Egypt, Islam, and the Arabs, 1986; (with I. Gershoni) Redefining the Egyptian Nation, 1930-1945, 1995; (ed. with I. Gershoni) Rethinking Nationalism in the Arab Middle East, 1997; Nasser's Egypt, Arab Nationalism, and the United Arab Republic, 2001; (with I. Gershoni) Commemorating the Nation: Collective Memory, Public Commemoration and National Identity in Twentieth-Century Egypt, 2004; (with S. Longrigg) The Geography of the Middle East, 2nd ed., 2009; (with I. Gershoni) Confronting Fascism in Egypt: Dictatorship Versus Democracy in the 1930s, 2010. **Address:** Department of History, University of Colorado, PO Box 234, Boulder, CO 80309, U.S.A. **Online address:** james.jankowski@colorado.edu

JANNUZZI, Luigi. American/Italian (born Italy), b. 1952. **Genres:** Plays/Screenplays. **Career:** Immaculata High School, teacher of drama, creative writing and public speaking, 1978-2012. Playwright. **Publications:** PLAYS: A Bench at the Edge, 1982; The Barbarians Are Coming, 1986; The Appointment, 1996; With or Without You, 1997; Night of the Foolish Moon, 1999; For the Love of Juliet!: A Comedy, 2004; Exhibit This!: The Museum Comedies, 2008; All The King's Women, 2009. **Address:** c/o Author Mail, Samuel French Inc., 45 W 25th St., New York, NY 10010, U.S.A. **Online address:** ljannuzzi@hotmail.com

JANODA, Jeff. Canadian (born Canada), b. 1960?. **Genres:** Novels, Literary Criticism And History. **Career:** Educator and writer. **Publications:** Saga: A Novel of Medieval Iceland, 2005. Contributor to periodicals. **Address:** c/o Author Mail, Academy Chicago Publishers, 363 W Erie St., 7E, Chicago, IL 60610, U.S.A. **Online address:** jeff@jeffjanoda.com

JANOVER, Caroline (Davis). American (born United States), b. 1943. **Genres:** Children's Fiction, Young Adult Fiction, Young Adult Non-fiction. **Career:** Dalton School, teacher, 1968-77; Ridge School, learning disabilities teacher and consultant, 1979-2003. Writer. **Publications:** Josh: A Boy with Dyslexia, 1988; The Worst Speller in Junior High, 1995; Zipper: The Kid with ADHD, 1997; How Many Days until Tomorrow?, 2000; The Worst Speller: A One Act Comedic Drama, 2004. Contributor of articles. **Address:** PO Box 1300, Damariscotta, ME 04543, U.S.A. **Online address:** info@janover.com

JANOWITZ, Brenda. American (born United States) **Genres:** Romance/Historical, History, Literary Criticism And History. **Career:** Kaye Scholer LLP (law firm), associate attorney; Honorable Marilyn Dolan Go, United States Magistrate Judge for the Eastern District of New York, law clerk; Mediabistro, instructor in creative writing, novelist, lecturer, educator, career counselor and attorney. **Publications:** Scot on the Rocks: How I Survived My Ex-boyfriends Wedding with My Dignity Ever-so Slightly Intact, 2007; Jack With a Twist, 2008. Contributor to periodicals. **Address:** The Jean V. Naggar Literary Agency Inc., 216 E 75th St., Ste. 1E, New York, NY 10021-2921, U.S.A. **Online address:** brenda@brendajanowitz.com

JANOWITZ, Henry D. American (born United States), b. 1918. **Genres:** Medicine/Health, Psychology. **Career:** Mount Sinai Hospital, professor of medicine, 1958-83, Division of Gastroenterology, head, distinguished physician, clinical professor of medicine emeritus. Writer. **Publications:** (Ed.) Symposium on Gastroenterology for Internists, 1978; Inflammatory Bowel Disease: A Personal View, 1985; Your Gut Feelings: A Complete Guide to Living Better with Intestinal Problems, 1987, rev. ed., 1994; Indigestion: Living Better with Upper Intestinal Problems from Heartburn to Ulcers and Gallstones, 1992; Inflammatory Bowel Disease: A Clinical Approach, 1994; Good Food for Bad Stomachs, 1997. **Address:** Mount Sinai School of Medicine, 1 Gustave L Levy Pl., New York, NY 10029-6574, U.S.A.

JANOWITZ, Tama. American (born United States), b. 1957. **Genres:** Novels, Cultural/Ethnic Topics, Young Adult Fiction, Travel/Exploration, Young Adult Non-fiction, Novellas/Short Stories. **Career:** Fine Arts Work Center, writer-in-residence, 1981-82; freelance journalist, 1985-. **Publications:** American Dad, 1981; Slaves of New York: Stories, 1986; A Cannibal in Manhattan, 1987; The Male Cross-Dresser Support Group, 1992; By the Shores of Gitchee Gumee, 1996; A Certain Age: A Novel, 1999; Hear That?, 2001; Area Code 212, 2002; Peyton Amberg, 2003; Area Code 212 with 718, 646, 917, 516 and A Brief Foray to 518: New York Days, New York Nights, 2004; They Is Us, 2009. Contributor of articles to periodicals and newspapers. **Address:** c/o Betsy Lerner, The Gernert Co., 136 E 57th St., New York, NY 10022, U.S.A.

JANSEN, Jared. See CEBULASH, Mel.

JANSEN, Marc C. Dutch (born Netherlands), b. 1946. **Genres:** History, Biography, Romance/Historical. **Career:** University of Amsterdam, assistant professor, 1973-; Netherlands Organisation for Scientific Research, staff; University of Utrecht, faculty; International Institute of Social History, faculty. Writer. **Publications:** Showproces onder Lenin: het voorspel van de Grote Terreur, 1980; (ed. with N. Petrov) The Socialist-Revolutionary Party after October 1917, 1989; (with E.V. Ree) Russische schurken, 1992; (with N. Petrov) Stalin's Loyal Executioner, 2002; (with N. Petrov) Stalinskiĭ pitomets-Nikolaĭ Ezhov, 2008; (with J.W. Bezemer) Een geschiedenis van Rusland, 7th ed., 2008; Geschiedenis van Rusland: Van Rurik Tot Poetin, 2008; (with N. Petrov) Stalinskii pitomet, 2008. **Address:** University of Amsterdam, 652 Kamer, Spuistraat 134, Amsterdam, 1012 VB, Netherlands. **Online address:** m.c.jansen@uva.nl

JANSEN, Michael E(lin). Cypriot/American (born United States), b. 1940. **Genres:** Novels, International Relations/Current Affairs, History. **Career:** American University of Beirut, editor, 1964-67; writer and freelance journalist, 1967-; Jansen Partners, co-director. **Publications:** The United States and the Palestinian People, 1970; The Battle of Beirut: Why Israel Invaded Lebanon, 1982; The Aphrodite Plot, 1983; Ma'rakat Bayrūt: limādhā ghazat Isrā'īl Lubnān!?, 1986; Dissonance in Zion, 1987; War and Cultural Heritage: Cyprus After the 1974 Turkish Invasion, 2005. Contributor to newspapers. **Address:** Jansen Partners, 5 John Metaxas St., Ayios Dhometios, PO Box 7621, Nicosia, 94014, Cyprus.

JANSEN, Sharon L. American (born United States), b. 1951. **Genres:** Women's Studies And Issues, Literary Criticism And History. **Career:** Fort Steilacoom Community College, part-time instructor in English, 1975-79; Pacific Lutheran University, assistant professor, 1980-86, associate professor of English, 1986-94, professor of English, 1994-. Writer. **Publications:** Political Protest and Prophecy under Henry VIII, 1991; (with K. Jordan) The Welles Anthology (Ms. Rawlinson C.813): A Critical Edition, 1991; Dangerous Talk and Strange Behavior: Women and Popular Resistance to the Reforms of Henry VIII, 1996; The Monstrous Regiment of Women: Female Rulers in Early Modern Europe, 2002; Anne of France: Lessons for My Daughter, 2004; Debating Women, Politics, and Power in Early Modern Europe, 2008; Reading Women's Worlds from Christine De Pizan to Doris Lessing: A Guide to Six Centuries of Women Writers Imagining Rooms of Their Own, 2011. Works appear in anthologies. **Address:** 706 5th St., Steilacoom, WA 98388, U.S.A. **Online address:** jansensl@plu.edu

JANSSEN, Marian (L. M.). Dutch (born Netherlands), b. 1953. **Genres:** Literary Criticism And History, Biography, Reference. **Career:** Radboud University Nijmegen, research assistant, 1977-80, research fellow, 1980-84, instructor in American literature, 1985-86, coordinator of American studies program, 1986-95, postdoctoral research fellow, 1988-92, External Relations Office, director, 1995-, International Office, head; International Student Exchange Program, consultant; Catholic University of Nijmegen, affiliated. Writer. **Publications:** The Kenyon Review: 1939-1970: A Critical History, 1990. **Address:** External Relations Office, Radboud University Nijmegen, PO Box 9102, Nijmegen, 6500 HC, Netherlands. **Online address:** m.janssen@er.ru.nl

JANSSON, Bruce S. American (born United States) **Genres:** Social Commentary, Social Work. **Career:** University of Southern California, lecturer, 1973-75, assistant professor, 1975-79, associate professor, 1979-88, professor of social work, 1988-2000, Margaret W. Driscoll/Louise M. Clevenger professor of social policy and administration professor, 2001-, Ph.D. Program, director, COPA Concentration, chair, 1985-91; City University of New York Graduate Center, Moses professor, 1990. Writer. **Publications:** Theory and Practice of Social Welfare Policy: Analysis, Processes and Current Issues, 1984; The Reluctant Welfare State: A History of American Social Welfare Policies, 1988, 7th ed. as Reluctant Welfare State: Engaging History to Advance Social Work Practice in Contemporary Society, 2011; Social Welfare Policy: From Theory to Practice, 1990; Social Policy: From Theory to Policy Practice, 1994; Becoming an Effective Policy Advocate: From Policy Practice to Social Justice, 1999, 6th ed., 2011; The Sixteen-Trillion-Dollar Mistake: How the U.S. Bungled Its National Priorities from the New Deal to the Present, 2001; Improving Healthcare Through Advocacy: A Guide for the Health and Helping Professions, 2011. **Address:** School of Social Work, University of Southern California, Montgomery Ross Fisher Bldg., Los Angeles, CA 90089, U.S.A. **Online address:** jansson@usc.edu

JANZEN, David. American (born United States), b. 1968. **Genres:** Theology/Religion. **Career:** North Central College, assistant professor of philosophy and religious studies, associate professor. Writer. **Publications:** The Social Meanings of Sacrifice in the Hebrew Bible: A Study of Four Writings, 2004. **Address:** North Central College, H225 12, 30 N Brainard St., Naperville, IL 60540, U.S.A. **Online address:** djanzen@noctrl.edu

JANZEN, Lorraine. See **KOOISTRA, Lorraine Janzen.**

JANZEN, Tara. See **MCREYNOLDS, Glenna Jean.**

JARAMILLO, Stephan. American (born United States), b. 1970?. **Genres:** Novels, Literary Criticism And History, Young Adult Fiction. **Career:** Chef and writer. **Publications:** Going Postal, 1997; Chocolate Jesus, 1998; The Scoundrel, 1999. Contributor to periodicals. **Address:** c/o Berkley Publishing Group, 200 Madison Ave., New York, NY 10026, U.S.A.

JARAUSCH, Konrad H(ugo). American/German (born Germany), b. 1941. **Genres:** Area Studies, History, International Relations/Current Affairs, Humanities. **Career:** University of Wisconsin, instructor in history, 1965-68; University of Missouri, assistant professor, 1968-71, associate professor, 1971-78, professor of history, 1978-83; Princeton University, Shelby Cullom Davis Center for Historical Studies, visiting fellow, 1970-71; University of Saarbruecken, visiting professor, 1975-76; University of Goettingen, visiting professor; Woodrow Wilson Center for International Scholars, visiting fellow, 1979-80; University of North Carolina, Lurcy professor of European civilization, 1983-; Netherlands Institute for Advanced studies, fellow, 1986; Swedish Center for Advanced Studies, fellow, 1988, Duke Center for European Studies, co-director, 1994-98; Zentrum fuer Zeithistorische Studien, acting director and director, 1994-2006. Writer. **Publications:** The Four Power Pact, 1933, 1965; The Enigmatic Chancellor: Bethmann Hollweg and the Hubris of Imperial Germany, 1973; (contrib.) The University in Society, 1974; Students, Society and Politics in Imperial Germany: The Rise of Academic Illiberalism, 1982; Deutsche Studenten, 1800-1970 (title means: German Students, 1800-1970), 1984; (with G. Arminger and M. Thaller) Quantitative Methoden in der Geschichtswissenschaft: Eine Einfuerung (title means: Quantitative Methods in History: An Introduction), 1985; The Unfree Professions: German Lawyers, Teachers and Engineers, 1900-1950, 1990; (with K.A. Hardy) Quantitative Methods for Historians: An Introduction to Research, Data and Statistics, 1991; (with V. Gransow) Unititng Germany: Documents and Debates, 1994-1993, 1994; The Rush to German Unity, 1994; Die Unverhoffte Einheit 1989-1990, 1995. EDITOR: Quantifizierung in der Geschichtswissenschaft: Probleme und Moeglichkeiten (title means: 'Quantification in Historical Research: Problems and Possibilities'), 1976; The Transformation of Higher Learning, 1860-1930, 1982; (with W.H. Schroeder) Quantitative History of Society and Economy: Some International Studies, 1987; (with G. Cocks) German Professions, 1800-1950, 1990; (with L.E. Jones) In Search of a Liberal Germany: Essays on German Liberalism, 1990; (with V. Gransow) Die Deutsche Vereinigung: Dokumente zu Buergerbewegung, Annaeherung und Beitruitt, 1991; Zwischen Parteilichkeitund Professionalitaet: Bilanz der Geschichtswissenschafter der DDR, 1991; (with M. Middell) Nach dem Erdbeben, 1994; After Unity: Reconfiguring German Identities, 1997; (with M. Sabrow) Weg in den Untergang: Der Innere Zerfall der DDR, 1999; Dictatorship as Experience: Towards a Socio-cultural History of the GDR, 1999; The Conundrum of Complicity: German Professionals and the Final Solution, 2001; (with M. Sabrow)Verletztes Gedächtnis: Erinnerungskultur und Zeitgeschichte im Konflikt, 2002; (with H. Hertle and C. Klessmann) Mauerbau und Mauerfall: Ursachen, Verlauf, 2002; (with M. Sabrow) Die

Historische Meistererzählung: Deutungslinien der Deutschen Nationalgeschichte nach 1945, 2002; (with M. Geyer) Shattered Past: Reconstructing German Histories, 2003; Die Umkehr: Deutsche Wandlungen 1945-1995, 2004; After Hitler: Recivilizing Germans, 1945-1995, 2006; (with T. Lindenberger) Conflicted Memories: Europeanizing Contemporary Histories, 2007; Das stille Sterben: Feldpostbriefe von Konrad Jarausch aus Polen und Russland 1939-1942, 2008; (with K. Hagemann and C. Allemann-Ghionda) Children, Families, States: Time Policies of Childcare, Preschool and Primary Education in Europe, 2011. Contributor of articles to books, periodicals and journals. **Address:** Department of History, University of North Carolina, CB 3195, 502 Hamilton Hall, Chapel Hill, NC 27599-3195, U.S.A. **Online address:** jarausch@email.unc.edu

JARES, Joe. American (born United States), b. 1937. **Genres:** Sports/Fitness, Biography, Autobiography/Memoirs. **Career:** United Press Intl., staff writer, 1959; Los Angeles Herald-Express, sports writer, 1959-60; Los Angeles Times, staff writer, 1961-65; Sports Illustrated Magazine, staff writer, 1965-80; Los Angeles Daily News, sports editor, 1982-85, sports staff, 1985-2002. **Publications:** (With E. Lindop) White House Sportsmen, 1964; (with W. Frazier) Clyde, 1970; Basketball, The American Game, 1972; Whatever Happened to Gorgeous George? The Blood and Ballyhoo of Professional Wrestling, 1974; (with J. Robinson) Conquest: A Cavalcade of USC Football, 1981; (with K. Sprague) The Athlete's Body, 1981; (ed.) A Marmac Guide to Los Angeles, 1996; (with G. Toley) Golden Age of College Tennis: A Coach's Unique Influence on the Game, 2009. **Address:** 9701 Cresta Dr., Los Angeles, CA 90035, U.S.A. **Online address:** jfjares@hotmail.com

JARMAKANI, Amira. American (born United States), b. 1974. **Genres:** Cultural/Ethnic Topics. **Career:** Georgia State University, Women's Studies Institute, assistant professor. Writer. **Publications:** Imagining Arab Womanhood: The Cultural Mythology of Veils, Harems, and Belly Dancers in the U.S., 2008. Contributor to books and periodicals. **Address:** U.S.A. **Online address:** amira@gsu.edu

JARMAN, Julia. British (born England), b. 1946. **Genres:** Children's Fiction, Picture/Board Books, Animals/Pets. **Career:** Teacher of English and drama. author, 1983-. **Publications:** FOR CHILDREN: When Poppy Ran Away, 1985; Ollie and the Bogle, 1987; Poppy and the Vicarage Ghost, 1988; Squonk, 1989; The Ghost of Tantony Pig, 1990; Pippa and the Witch, 1990; Toby and the Space Cats, 1990; Not-So-Silly Billy, 1990; The Magic Carrot, 1990; Emily the Spy, 1990; Aunt Horrible and the Very Good Idea, 1990; James and the Dragon, 1990; The Rabbit Said Miaow, 1990; The Goat Is Eating Debbie!, 1990; Naughty Norman, 1990; Fat Cat, 1990; Lucy Calls the Fire Brigade, 1990; Babies Are Yuck!, 1990; There's a Monster, 1990; Upstarts Series; Paul and the Robber, 1990; Look at My Spots, 1990; Lucy the Tiger, 1990; (with D. Burnard) Georgie and the Dragon, 1991; Topher and the Time-Travelling Cat, 1992 as The Time-Travelling Cat and the Egyptian Goddess, 2001; (with D. Burnard) Georgie and the Planet Raider, 1993; Will There Be Polar Bears for Christmas?, 1994; The Jessame Stories, 1994; (with D. Burnard) Georgie and the Computer Bugs, 1995; Return of Squonk, 1995; (with J. Anderson) Gertie and the Bloop, 1996; The Crow Haunting, 1996; A Test for the Time-Travelling Cat, 1997 as The Time-Travelling Cat and the Tudor Treasure, 2001; More Jessame Stories, 1997; Little Mouse Grandma, 1997; Convict: A Tale of Criminals Sent to Australia, 1997; The Sewer Sleuth: A Tale of Victorian Cholera, 1997; Chillers: The Haunting of Nadia, 1998; Hangman, 1999; The Revenge of Tommy Bones, 2001; The Time-Travelling Cat and the Roman Eagle, 2001; Bully Bear; Rabbit's Birthday Surprise; Terrible Tiger; Rabbit Helps Out, 2003; Ghost Writer, 2003; Peace Weavers, 2004; Big Red Bath, 2004 in US as Big Red Tub, 2004; The Magic Backpack, 2004; Kangaroo's Cancan Cafe, 2004; Jack in a Box, 2004; Story Cat, 2006; Class Two at the Zoo, 2007; Class Three at Sea, 2008; Inside, 2010; Big Yellow Digger, 2011; Pillywiggins and the Tree Witch, 2011; Little Tiger and the Lost Fire, 2011; Pillywiggins and the Tree Witch, 2011; Ants in Your Pants!, 2011; Cinderella, 2011; Little Bad Riding Hood, 2011; King Midas's Golden Touch, 2011; When Baby Lost Bunny, 2012; Ghost Riter, forthcoming. ALL ABOARD SERIES: Sam and the Tadpoles, 1994; You Can't Scare Me, 1994; Detective Tilak, 1994; Mountain Rescue, 1994; The Great Lorenzo, 1994; Speedy's Day Out, 1994; Hiccups!, 1994; Big Sister Rosie, 1994; Clumsy Clara, 1994; Little Monster, 1994; Clouds, 1994; No, Sam!, 1994; The Terrible Fright, 1994; Computer Kate, 1994; Bobby's Bad Day, 1994; The Magic Smell, 1994; Rosie and the Dinosaurs, 1994; Nog's Dinner, 1994; Jabeen and the New Moon, 1994; Pancakes, 1994; Grandad's Balloon, 1994; Pandora and the Pirates, 1994; The Hot Pepper Queen and the Mango Babies, 1994; Fussy

Frieda, 1994; (reteller) The Ghost Next Door, 1994; Swan Rescue, 1994; The Parrot, 1994; (with M. Simon) All Aboard: Extended Stories for Reading Aloud, 1994; Something in the Fridge, 1994; The Giant Sandwich, 1994; The Ghost in the Castle, 1994; It's Not Fair, 1994; The Greedy Guinea-Pig, 1994; Lizzie and the Car Wash, 1994; Scat Cat!, 1994; The Fun Run, 1994; Naughty Nog, 1994; A Guinea-Pig for Rosie, 1994; (with M. Simon) Sam and Rosie's ABC, 1994; The Wizard, 1995; Dognapped? And Other Stories from Mulberry Green, 1995; Rosie's Photo Album, 1996; Jessame to the Rescue and Other Stories, 2008. TALES FROM THE WHISPERY WOODS SERIES: Flying Friends, 2002; Mole's Useful Day, 2002; Owl's Big Mistake, 2003; Always There, forthcoming. Contributor to periodicals. **Address:** c/o Caroline Walsh, David Higham Associates, 5-8 Lower John St., Golden Sq., London, GL W1F 9HA, England. **Online address:** juliajarman@btopenworld.com

JARMAN, Mark (F.). American (born United States), b. 1952. **Genres:** Poetry, Literary Criticism And History, Essays. **Career:** University of Iowa, teaching and writing fellow, 1974-76; Indiana State University, instructor in English, 1976-78; University of California, visiting lecturer, 1979-80; Murray State University, assistant professor, 1980-83; Vanderbilt University, assistant professor, 1983-86, associate professor, 1986-92, professor of English, 1992-2007, Centennial professor of English, 2007-; The Reaper (poetry journal), co-founder and editor, 1989; Story Line Press, co-founder; Creative Writing, director; The Hudson Review, advisory editor. **Publications:** POETRY: Tonight is the Night of the Prom (chapbook), 1974; North Sea, 1978; The Rote Walker, 1981; Far and Away, 1985; The Black Riviera, 1990; Iris, 1992; (ed. with D.Mason) Rebel Angels: 25 Poets of the New Formalism, 1996; Questions for Ecclesiastes: Poems, 1997; Unholy Sonnets: Poems, 2000; To the Green Man: Poems, 2004; Epistles: Poems, 2007; Bone Fires: New and Selected Poems, 2011. OTHERS: (with R. McDowell) The Reaper Essays, 1996; The Secret of Poetry: Essays, 2001; Body and Soul: Essays on Poetry, 2002; (ed. with J. Bednarik and R. McDowell) One-Man Boat: The George Hitchcock Reader: Poetry, Fiction and Drama, 2003. Contributor to periodicals. **Address:** Department of English, Vanderbilt University, 400 Benson Hall, PO Box 1654, Nashville, TN 37235, U.S.A. **Online address:** mark.jarman@vanderbilt.edu

JARMAN, Rosemary Hawley. Welsh/British (born England), b. 1935. **Genres:** Romance/Historical, Novels. **Career:** Worcestershire County Council, local government officer, 1962-68; Rural District Council, secretary, 1970. Writer. **Publications:** We Speak No Treason, 1971; The King's Grey Mare, 1973 in US as Crown of Glory, 1987; Crown in Candlelight, 1978; Crispin's Day: The Glory of Agincourt, 1979; The Courts of Illusion, 1983; The Captain's Witch, 2005; (contrib.) Lace and Blade. 2, 2009. WE SPEAK NO TREASON SERIES: Flowering of the Rose, 2006; White Rose Turned to Blood, 2006. Contributor to periodicals. **Address:** A M Heath & Company Ltd., 6 Warwick Ct., Holborn, London, GL WC1R 5DJ, England. **Online address:** rhjarman@sbcglobal.net

JAROFF, Leon Morton. American (born United States), b. 1927. **Genres:** Air/Space Topics, Astronomy, Biology, Communications/Media, Medicine/Health, Physics, Sciences, Technology, Technology. **Career:** Life Magazine, editorial trainee and reporter, 1951-54, correspondent, 1954-58; University of Michigan, cochairman; Michigan Daily, managing editor; Time, correspondent and senior editor, 1959-79, Detroit bureau chief, 1960-64, contributing editor, 1964-, associate editor, 1966-, senior editor, 1970-, science editor, 1985-87; Discover, founder and managing editor, 1980-84, now retired. **Publications:** The New Genetics: The Human Genome Project and its Impact on the Practice of Medicine, 1991. **Address:** Time, Time & Life Bldg., 1271 Ave. of the Americas, New York, NY 10020, U.S.A. **Online address:** neonleo@aol.com

JARRAR, Randa. American (born United States), b. 1978?. **Genres:** Novels, Translations. **Career:** Make/ Shift Magazine, columnist. Writer and translator. **Publications:** (trans.) H. Daoud, The Year of the Revolutionary New Bread-making Machine, 2007; A Map of Home: A Novel, 2008. Contributor to periodicals. **Address:** Ann Arbor, MI , U.S.A. **Online address:** randajarrar@gmail.com

JARROW, Gail. American (born United States), b. 1952. **Genres:** Children's Fiction, Children's Non-fiction, Biography, Young Adult Non-fiction, Animals/Pets, Zoology, History. **Career:** School teacher, 1974-79; freelance writer, 1983-; Institute of Children's Literature, instructor, 1991-. **Publications:** That Special Someone, 1985; If Phyllis Were Here, 1987; The Two-Ton

Secret, 1989; Beyond the Magic Sphere, 1994; Naked Mole-Rat Mystery: Scientific Sleuths At Work, 1996; Naked Mole-Rats, 1996; Animal Baby Sitters, 2001; Bears, 2003; Rhinos, 2003; Hookworms, 2004; Chiggers, 2004; Medieval Castle, 2005; The Printer's Trial: The Case of John Peter Zenger and the Fight for a Free Press, 2006; Robert H. Jackson: New Deal Lawyer, Supreme Court Justice, Nuremberg Prosecutor, 2008; Lincoln's Flying Spies: Thaddeus Lowe and the Civil War Balloon Corps, 2010; The Amazing Harry Kellar: Great American Magician, 2012. **Address:** Ithaca, NY , U.S.A. **Online address:** gailjarrow@gailjarrow.com

JARVIK, Laurence. American (born United States), b. 1956. **Genres:** Communications/Media. **Career:** University of California, Department of Film and Television, teaching assistant and teaching associate, 1986-88, teaching fellow, 1990-91; California State University, Department of Communication Studies, assistant professor, 1989-90; Comint: A Journal about Public Media, editor, 1992-96; Center for the Study of Popular Culture, director, 1992-96; Capital Research Center, cultural studies fellow, Culture Watch and Foundation Watch, editor, 1996-97; The Idler, proprietor, 2002-; Georgetown Theatre Co., board director. **Publications:** PBS: Behind the Screen, 1997; Masterpiece Theatre and the Politics of Quality, 1999. EDITOR: (with D. Horowitz) Public Broadcasting and the Public Trust, 1995; (with H.I. London and J.F. Cooper) The National Endowments: A Critical Symposium, 1995. Contributor to periodicals. **Address:** c/o Carol Mann, Carol Mann Agency, 55 5th Ave., 15th Fl., New York, NY 10003, U.S.A. **Online address:** lajarvik@erols.com

JARVIS, Brian. British (born England), b. 1966. **Genres:** Cultural/Ethnic Topics, Young Adult Non-fiction, Law. **Career:** Loughborough University, senior lecturer in American literature and film, 1991-, School of the Arts, English and Drama, associate dean for teaching; University of Southern Mississippi, faculty, 2002-03. Writer. **Publications:** NONFICTION: Postmodern Cartographies: The Geographical Imagination in Contemporary American Culture, 1998; Cruel and Unusual: Punishment and U.S. Culture, 2004; (with P. Jenner and A. Dix) The Contemporary American Novel in Context, 2011. **Address:** Department of English and Drama, Loughborough University, Rm. NN.0.11, Martin Hall Bldg. East Park, Loughborough, LE LE11 3TU, England. **Online address:** b.jarvis@lboro.ac.uk

JARVIS, Christina S. American (born United States) **Genres:** Military/Defense/Arms Control. **Career:** State University of New York at Fredonia (SUNY Fredonia), assistant professor, 2000-04, associate professor of English & director of American studies program, 2004-. Writer. **Publications:** The Male Body at War: American Masculinity during World War II, 2004. Contributor to books and journals. **Address:** State University of New York at Fredonia, Fenton Hall, Fredonia, NY 14063, U.S.A. **Online address:** christina.jarvis@fredonia.edu

JARVIS, Jeff. American (born United States), b. 1954. **Genres:** Business/Trade/Industry, Technology. **Career:** San Francisco Examiner, columnist, 1976-81; Advance.net, president and creative director, 1994-2005; Daylife (news service), consulting editor, 2005-, partner; Entertainment Weekly, creator and founding editor; New York Daily News, sunday editor and associate publisher; London Guardian, columnist, 2005-, Guardian News and Media, columnist and consultant, 2006-; consultant, 2005-; City University of New York, Graduate School of Journalism, associate professor and director of interactive journalism program, 2006-, Tow-Knight Center for Entrepreneurial Journalism, director. **Publications:** What Would Google Do?, 2009; Public Parts: How Sharing in the Digital Age Improves the Way We Work and Live, 2011. Contributor to periodicals. **Address:** Graduate School of Journalism, City University of New York, 219 W 40th St., New York, NY 10018, U.S.A. **Online address:** jeff@buzzmachine.com

JARVIS, Sharon E. American (born United States), b. 1969. **Genres:** Politics/Government, Language/Linguistics, Social Sciences. **Career:** University of Texas, assistant professor of communication studies, Annette Strauss Institute for Civic Participation, associate director, 2000-, Office of Survey Research, research director, 2004-. Writer. **Publications:** (With R.P. Hart, D.S. Howell and W.P. Jennings) Political Keywords: Using Language That Uses Us, 2004; The Talk of the Party: Political Labels, Symbolic Capital and American Life, 2005. Contributor to periodicals. **Address:** University of Texas at Austin, 1 University Sta. A1105, Austin, TX 78712-0119, U.S.A. **Online address:** sjarvis@mail.utexas.edu

JARVIS, William E. American (born United States), b. 1945. **Genres:** History, Humanities, Librarianship, Mythology/Folklore, Intellectual History, Philosophy, Popular Culture, Theology/Religion, E-books, Anthropology/Ethnology, Administration/Management. **Career:** Otisca Industries, corporate librarian, 1979-80; State University of New York College of Environmental Science and Forestry, Moon Library, archivist, 1981; Lehigh University, science reference librarian, 1982-84, collection and acquisitions librarian, 1984-90; Washington State University, head of library acquisitions, 1990-99, WSU Libraries, associate professor, 1996-, collection services librarian, 1999-2002, knowledge manager, 2002-06, professor emeritus, 2006-. Writer. **Publications:** (Ed.) Acquiring Online Management Reports, 2000; Time Capsules: A Cultural History, 2003. Contributor to library journals. **Address:** Washington State University, Libraries, Pullman, WA 99164, U.S.A. **Online address:** jarvis@wsu.edu

JASON *See* **Sæterøy, John Arne.**

JASON, Sonya. American (born United States), b. 1927. **Genres:** Novels, Plays/Screenplays, Adult Non-fiction, Young Adult Non-fiction, Essays, Social Sciences. **Career:** Los Angeles Welfare Department, social worker, 1963-66, deputy probation officer, 1966-76; writer, 1976-; American Citizens Together, president, 1986-90. **Publications:** Helper: Real Stories of Welfare and Probation, 1993. Contributor to periodicals. **Address:** 21165 Escondido St., Woodland Hills, CA 91364-5904, U.S.A.

JASPER, James M(acdonald). (Harry Green). American (born United States), b. 1957. **Genres:** Politics/Government, Sociology, Social Sciences. **Career:** Resources for the Future, research assistant, 1985-86; New York University, Department of Sociology, faculty, 1987-96; consultant, 1995-2000; Columbia University, Department of Sociology, visiting professor, 1997; Princeton University, Department of Sociology, visiting professor, 1997, 1999-2000, 2003-05; Social Science Research Council, research associate, 2004-05; Contexts Magazine, editor, 2005-07; New School for Social Research, visiting professor, 2006; CUNY Graduate Center, visiting professor, 2007-; University of California at Berkeley, acting instructor and research associate. **Publications:** Nuclear Politics: Energy and the State in the United States, Sweden and France, 1990; (with D. Nelkin) The Animal Rights Crusade: The Growth of a Moral Protest, 1992; The Art of Moral Protest: Culture, Biography and Creativity in Social Movements, 1997; Restless Nation: Starting over in America, 2000; (ed. with J. Goodwin and F. Polletta) Passionate Politics: Emotions and Social Movements, 2001; (ed. with J. Goodwin) The Social Movements Reader: Cases and Concepts, 2003, 2nd ed., 2009; (ed. with J. Goodwin) Rethinking Social Movements: Structure, Meaning and Emotion, 2004; Getting Your Way: Strategic Dilemmas in the Real World, 2006; (ed. with J. Goodwin) Social Movements: Critical Concepts in Sociology, 2006; (ed. with J. Goodwin) The Contexts Reader, 2008; (ed. with J. Goodwin) Contention in Context: Political Opportunities and the Emergence of Protest, 2012. Contributor to periodicals. **Address:** CUNY Graduate Center, Dept of Sociology, 365 5th Ave., New York, NY 10016-4309, U.S.A. **Online address:** jjasper@gc.cuny.edu

JASPER, Kenji (Nathaniel). American (born United States), b. 1976?. **Genres:** Novels, Autobiography/Memoirs, Young Adult Non-fiction. **Career:** The Armory, chief executive officer and editor. Journalist, novelist, web designer, photographer and radio commentator. **Publications:** Dark, 2001, 2nd ed. as Snow, 2007; Dakota Grand, 2002; Seeking Salamanca Mitchell, 2004; The House on Childress Street: A Memoir, 2005; (ed. with Y. Womack) Beats, Rhymes, and Life: What We Love and Hate About Hip-Hop, 2007; (with M. Brighthaupt) Baby Girl: My Life Protecting Anna Nicole Smith, 2007; (ed.) Got, 2007; Remembering Dark Streets. Contributor to periodicals. **Address:** c/o Author Mail, Broadway Books, 1745 Broadway, New York, NY 10019, U.S.A. **Online address:** youngjasper@kenjijasper.com

JASPER, Margaret C. American (born United States) **Genres:** Law. **Career:** Gold City Records/Jasper Stone Music, general counsel. Writer and lawyer. **Publications:** Estate Planning, 1994, rev. ed., 2001; Juvenile Justice and Children's Law, 1994, rev. ed., 2001; Law for the Small Business Owner, 1994, 2nd ed., 2001; Marriage and Divorce, 1994, 3rd ed., 2008; The Law of Contracts, 1995; The Law of Dispute Resolution: Arbitration and Alternative Dispute Resolution, 1995, 2nd ed., 2000; The Law of Personal Injury, 1995, 2nd ed., 2000; Real Estate Law for Homeowner & Broker, 1995, 2nd ed., 2000; AIDS Law, 1996, 3rd ed., 2008; Dictionary of Selected Legal Terms, 1996, 3rd ed., 2009; Elder Law, 1996, 2nd ed., 2001; The Law of Buying and Selling, 1996, 2nd ed., 2002; The Law of Immigration, 1996, 3rd ed., 2008;

The Law of Libel & Slander, 1996; The Law of Medical Malpractice, 1996, 2nd ed., 2001; The Law of No-Fault Insurance, 1996, 2nd ed., 2002; The Law of Obscenity and Pornography, 1996, 2nd ed., 2009; The Law of Product Liability, 1996, 2nd ed., 2001; The Right to Die, 1996, 2nd ed., 2000; Animal Rights Law, 1997, 2nd ed., 2002; Bankruptcy Law for the Individual Debtor, 1997; Consumer Rights Law, 1997, 2nd ed., 2007; Employee Rights in the Workplace, 1997, 2nd ed., 2003; Environmental Law, 1997, 2nd ed., 2002; The Law of Child Custody, 1997; The Law of Debt Collection, 1997, 2nd ed., 2001; Probate Law, 1997; Victim's Rights Law, 1997; Workers' Compensation Law, 1997, 2nd ed., 2008; The Americans with Disabilities Act, 1998, 2nd ed., 2008; Commercial Law, 1998; Education Law, 1998; Insurance Law, 1998; Labor Law, 1998, 2nd ed., 2002; Landlord/Tenant Law, 1998; The Law of Capital Punishment, 1998, 2nd ed., 2008; The Law of Violence against Women, 1998, rev. ed., 2007; Motor Vehicle Law, 1998; Religion and the Law, 1998; Drunk Driving Law, 1999; Employment Discrimination Law under Title VII, 1999, 2nd ed., 2008; Hospital Liability Law, 1999, 2nd ed., 2008; The Law of Speech and the First Amendment, 1999; Social Security Law, 1999, 2nd ed., 2004; Home Mortgage Law Primer, 3rd ed., 2009; The Law of Attachment and Garnishment, 2nd ed., 2000; The Law of Copyright, 2nd ed., 2000; The Law of Patents, 2nd ed., 2000; The Law of Premises Liability, 2000; The Law of Special Education, 2000; The Law of Trademarks, 2000, 2nd ed., 2004; More Everyday Legal Forms, 2nd ed., 2001; Harassment in the Workplace, 2002; Healthcare and Your Rights under the Law, 2002; Identity Theft and How to Protect Yourself, 2002, 2nd ed., 2006; Individual Bankruptcy and Restructuring, 2002, 2nd ed., 2006; Welfare: Your Rights and the Law, 2002; Executors and Personal Representatives: Rights and Responsibilities, 2003; International Adoption, 2003; Living Together: Practical Legal Issues, 2003; Nursing Home Negligence, 2003; Privacy and the Internet: Your Expectations and Rights under the Law, 2003, 2nd ed., 2009; Teenagers and Substance Abuse, 2003; What If It Happened to You: Violent Crimes and Victims' Rights, 2003; What If the Product Doesn't Work: Warranties and Guarantees, 2003; Your Child's Legal Rights: An Overview, 2003; Banks and Their Customers, 3rd ed., 2004; Buying and Selling Your Home, 2004; DWI, DUI and the Law, 2004; Auto Leasing, 2005; Becoming a Citizen, 2005; Co-ops and Condominiums: Your Rights and Obligations as an Owner, 2005; Hiring Household Help and Contractors: Your Obligations under the Law, 2005; How to Change Your Name, 2005; How to Protect Your Challenged Child, 2005; Injured on the Job: Employee Rights, Worker's Compensation and Disability, 2005; Lemon Laws, 2005; Prescription Drugs, 2005; Retirement Planning, 2005; Rights of Single Parents, 2005; Small Claims Courts, 2005; Your Rights in a Class Action Suit, 2005; Your Rights under the Family and Medical Leave Act, 2005; You've Been Fired: Your Rights and Remedies, 2005; Custodial Rights, 2006; How to Start Your Own Business, 2006; Missing and Exploited Children: How to Protect Your Child, 2006; Credit Cards and the Law, 3rd rev. ed., 2007; Dealing with Debt, 2007; Health Care Directives, 2007; How to Form a Limited Liability Company, 2007; Pet Law, 2007; Trouble Next Door: What to Do with Your Neighbor, 2007; Your Rights as a Tenant, 2007; Guardianship, Conservatorship, and the Law, 2008; Protecting Your Business: Disaster Preparation and the Law, 2008; The Law of Adoption, 2008; Veteran's Rights and Benefits, 2009; Transportation Law: Passenger Rights and Responsibilities, 2009. **Address:** Law Office of Margaret C. Jasper, 10 Deepwell Farms Rd., South Salem, NY 10590, U.S.A. **Online address:** jasperlaw@aol.com

JASPIN, Elliot. American (born United States), b. 1946. **Genres:** History, Adult Non-fiction, Social Sciences. **Career:** Pottsville Republican, general assignment reporter, investigative reporter, 1976-; Providence Journal-Bulletin, reporter; University of Missouri, associate professor of journalism, Missouri Institute for Computer-Assisted Reporting, director; Philadelphia Daily News, investigative reporter; Columbia University, Gannett Center for Media Studies, fellow, 1988-89; Cox Newspapers, system editor and journalist, 1992-. **Publications:** (Ed.) Jim Thorpe, Formerly, Mauch Chunk: Guide/History, 1977; Buried in the Bitter Waters: The Hidden History of Racial Cleansing in America, 2007. **Address:** Cox Newspapers, Washington Bureau, 400 N Capitol St. NW, Ste. 750, Washington, DC 20001-1536, U.S.A.

JAUNCEY, James. (Jamie Jauncey). Scottish (born Scotland), b. 1949. **Genres:** Novels, Young Adult Fiction, Mystery/Crime/Suspense. **Career:** Radio Heartland, governor. Writer and musician. **Publications:** NOVELS: The Albatross Conspiracy, 1990; The Mapmaker, 1994; The Crystal Keeper, 1996; The Witness, 2008; The Reckoning, 2008. **Address:** Society of Authors, 8 Briar Rd., Kirkin-Hilloch, Glasgow, G66 3SA, Scotland.

JAUNCEY, Jamie. *See* **JAUNCEY, James.**

JAUSS, David. American (born United States), b. 1951. **Genres:** Novellas/Short Stories, Poetry, Writing/Journalism, Essays. **Career:** Southwest State University, instructor in English, 1974-77; University of Arkansas, assistant professor, 1980-83, associate professor, 1983-88, professor of English and creative writing, 1988-, director of creative writing, 1980-; Crazyhorse, fiction editor, 1981-91; Vermont College of Fine Arts MFA in Writing Program, faculty, 1998-, chair, 2005-09. **Publications:** SHORT STORY COLLECTIONS: Crimes of Passion, 1983; Black Maps, 1996. POETRY COLLECTIONS: Improvising Rivers, 1995; You Are Not Here, 2002. OTHERS: Alone With All That Could Happen: Rethinking Conventional Wisdom About the Craft of Fiction, 2008; A Crack in Everything: How Writers and Artists Know What's Done Is Done, 2009; On Writing Fiction, 2011. EDITOR: (with P. Dacey) Strong Measures: Contemporary American Poetry in Traditional Forms, 1986; The Best of Crazyhorse, 1990; Words Overflown by Stars: Creative Writing Instruction and Insight from the Vermont College of Fine Arts MFA Program, 2009. Contributor of articles to periodicals. Works appear in anthologies. **Address:** Department of English, University of Arkansas, 2801 S University Ave., Little Rock, AR 72204, U.S.A. **Online address:** davidjauss@sbcglobal.net

JAVERNICK, Ellen. American (born United States), b. 1938. **Genres:** Education, Children's Fiction, Young Adult Fiction, Biography. **Career:** Loveland Preschool Inc., director, 1976-88; Garfield School, elementary teacher, 1988-. Writer. **Publications:** Christmas Bulletin Boards, Walls, Windows, Doors & More, 1986; Celebrate the Christian Family, 1987; Celebrate Me Made in God's Image, 1988; What If Everybody Did That?, 1990; Where's Brooke?, 1992; Double the Trouble, 1994; Time for Bed!, 1994; Ms. Pollywog's Problem-Solving Service, 1995; Patient Papas, 1996; Show and Tell, 1996; Crash, Flash, 1998; Allie's Plan, 1998; God's House, 1999; Concrete, 2001; Beatrix Potter, 2002; Fiesta, 2004; Birthday Pet, 2009; Animal Fathers, 2010; Patterned Spelling; Readiness for Preschool; Thunder and Lightening; Sorting It Out; Only A Dummy Would; Where Animals Sleep; I Go To Work. Contributor of articles to magazines and journals. **Address:** Chicago Review Press, 814 N Franklin St., Chicago, IL 60610, U.S.A. **Online address:** javernicke@aol.com

JAY, Antony (Rupert). British (born England), b. 1930. **Genres:** Administration/Management, Business/Trade/Industry, Politics/Government, Speech/Rhetoric. **Career:** British Broadcasting Corp., current affairs and documentary writer, director and producer, 1955-64, editor, 1962-63, head of talks features, 1963-64; freelance writer and consultant, 1964-; Video Arts Ltd., chairman, 1972-89. **Publications:** (Ed.) The Pick of the Rhubarb, 1965; (with D. Frost) To England with Love, 1967; (with D. Frost) English, 1967; Management and Machiavelli, 1967; Effective Presentation, 1970; Corporation Man, 1971; The Householder's Guide to Community Defence against Bureaucratic Aggression, 1972; (with J. Lynn) Yes, Minister, 3 vols., 1981-83; (ed. with J. Lynn) The Complete Yes, Minister: The Diaries of Cabinet Minister, 1984; (ed. with J. Lynn) Yes, Prime Minister, vol. I, 1986, vol. II, 1989; Elizabeth R.: The Role of the Monarchy Today, 1992; (ed.) Oxford Dictionary of Political Quotations, 1996, 4th ed., 2010; How to Beat Sir Humphrey, 1997; Not in Our Back Yard, 2005; How to Run a Meeting, 2008; Lend Me Your Ears, 4th ed., 2010. Play: (with Jonathan Lynn) Yes Prime Minister, 2010. **Address:** Alan Brodie Representation Ltd., Paddock Ste., The Courtyard, 55 Charterhouse St., London, GL ECIM 6HA, England. **Online address:** antony.jay@virgin.net

JAY, Peter. British (born England), b. 1937. **Genres:** Economics, International Relations/Current Affairs, Politics/Government, Business/Trade/Industry, Philosophy. **Career:** Her Majesty's Treasury, assistant principal, principal, 1961-67; The Times, economics editor, 1967-77; Times Business News, associate editor, 1969-77; Weekend World, TV programme, presenter, 1972-77; British ambassador to the United States, 1977-79; Intelligence Unit, director, 1979-83; Banking World, senior editorial consultant, 1983-84, editor, 1984-86, Mirror Group Newspapers, chief of staff, 1986-90; British Broadcasting Corp., economics editor, 1990-2001; Bank of England, non-executive director, 2003-. **Publications:** Currencies in Crisis: Out of the Bretton Woods, 1971; (ed.) The Budget: A Collection of Documents, 1972; (co-author) America and the World 1979, 1980; (ed.) Economy, Three Views, 1980; Crisis of Western Political Economy, 1981; Crisis for Western Political Economy and Other Essays, 1984; (with M. Stewart) Apocalypse 2000: Economic Breakdown and the Suicide of Democracy, 1987; The Road to Riches in UK as

The Wealth of Man, 2000. Contributor to periodicals. **Address:** Bank of England, Threadneedle St., London, GL EC2R 8AH, England. **Online address:** peter@jay.prestel.co.uk

JAY, Ricky. American (born United States), b. 1949?. **Genres:** Social Work, History, Trivia/Facts, Humor/Satire. **Career:** Magic historian, consultant, actor and writer. **Publications:** Cards as Weapons, 1977; Learned Pigs & Fireproof Women, 1986; Donald Sultan: Playing Cards, 1989; Many Mysteries Unraveled, or, Conjuring Literature in America, 1786-1874, 1990; The Magic Magic Book: An Inquiry into the Venerable History and Operation of the Oldest Trick-Conjuring Volumes, 1998; Jay's Journal of Anomalies: Conjurers, Cheats, Hustlers, Hoaxsters, Pranksters, Jokesters, Imposters, Pretenders, Sideshow Showmen, Armless Calligraphers, Mechanical Marvels, Popular Entertainments (originally published in Jay's Journal of Anomalies), 2001; Ricky Jay: On the Stem, (show), 2002; Dice: Deception, Fate & Rotten Luck, 2003; Extraordinary Exhibitions: The Wonderful Remains Of An Enormous Head, The Whimsiphusicon, & Death To The Savage Unitarians, 2005. Contributor to books. **Address:** W & V Dailey, 8216 Melrose Ave., Los Angeles, CA 90046, U.S.A.

JAY, Shannah. *See* **JACOBS, Anna.**

JEAL, (John Julian) Tim(othy). British (born England), b. 1945. **Genres:** Novels, Biography. **Career:** British Broadcasting Corp., producer of television documentaries, 1966-70; Writers' Guild of Great Britain, publishing negotiator, 1980-90. Writer. **Publications:** For Love or Money, 1967; Somewhere beyond Reproach, 1968; Livingstone, 1973; Cushing's Crusade, 1974; Until the Colors Fade: A Novel, 1976; A Marriage of Convenience, 1979; Carnforth's Creation, 1983; Baden-Powell, 1989, rev. ed., 2001 in US as The Boy-Man: The Life of Lord Baden-Powell, 1990; For God and Glory, 1996; Missionary's Wife, 1997; Deep Water, 2000; Baden-Powell, 2001; Swimming with My Father: A Memoir, 2004; Stanley: The Impossible Life of Africa's Greatest Explorer, 2007; Explorers of the Nile: The Triumph and Tragedy of a Great Victorian Adventure, 2011. **Address:** Yale University Press, PO Box 209040, New Haven, CT 06520-9040, U.S.A.

JEANS, Peter D(ouglas). Australian (born Australia), b. 1936. **Genres:** Language/Linguistics, Mythology/Folklore, Novels, Sciences. **Career:** University of Western Australia, Department of Education, secondary schoolteacher, 1958-, English teacher and department head, 1972-87. Writer. **Publications:** My Word, 1993; Ship to Shore: A Dictionary of Everyday Words and Phrases Derived from the Sea, 1993; The Long Road to London, 1995; An Ocean of Words: A Dictionary of Nautical Words and Phrases, 1998; Bodger, 2002; Stoker's Bay, 2003; Seafaring Lore and Legend: A Miscellany of Maritime Myth, Superstition, Fable and Fact, 2004; The Mirror Man, forthcoming. **Address:** c/o Christine Nagel, 7 Hartung St., Mundaring, Perth, WA 6073, Australia.

JECKS, Michael. British (born England), b. 1960. **Genres:** Mystery/Crime/Suspense, Novels. **Career:** Wordplex, Wang, and Xerox, computer salesperson. Writer. **Publications:** The Last Templar, 1995; The Merchant's Partner, 1995; A Moorland Hanging, 1996; The Crediton Killings, 1997; The Abbot's Gibbet, 1998; The Leper's Return, 1998; Squire Throwleigh's Heir, 1998; Belladonna at Belstone, 1999; The Traitor of St. Giles, 1999; The Boy-Bishop's Glovemaker, 2000; The Tournament of Blood, 2001; The Sticklepath Strangler, 2001; The Devil's Acolyte, 2002; The Mad Monk of Gidleigh, 2002; The Templar's Penance, 2003; The Outlaws of Ennor, 2003; The Tolls of Death, 2004; The Chapel of Bones, 2004; The Butcher of St Peter's, 2005; The Friar's Bloodfeud, 2005; The Death Ship of Dartmouth, 2006; The Malice of Unnatural Death, 2007; The Dispensation of Death, 2007; The Templar, the Queen and Her Lover, 2007; The Prophecy of Death, 2008; The King of Thieves, 2008; No Law in the Land, 2009; The Bishop Must Die, 2009; The Oath, 2010; King's Gold, 2011. THE MEDIEVAL MURDERERS: The Tainted Relic, 2005; Sword of Shame, 2006; House of Shadows, 2007; The Lost Prophecies, 2008; King Arthur's Bones, 2009. Works appear in anthologies. **Address:** The Bell Lomax Moreton Agency, Watergate House, 13/15 York Bldg., Ground Fl., London, GL WC2N 6JU, England. **Online address:** mail@michaeljecks.co.uk

JEEVES, Malcolm. (Malcolm A. Jeeves). Scottish/British (born England), b. 1926. **Genres:** Psychology, Sciences, Theology/Religion, Natural History. **Career:** University of Leeds, lecturer, 1956; University of Adelaide, Department of psychology, professor and head, 1959-69; University of St. Andrews, professor of psychology, 1969-, vice-principal, 1980-84, now professor emeritus of psychology; Royal Society of Edinburgh, president, 1996-99. Writer. **Publications:** (Co-author) Where Science and Faith Meet, 1955; Scientific Psychology and Christian Belief, 1965; (with Z.P. Dienes) Thinking in Structures, 1965; (with Z.P. Dienes) The Effects of Structural Relations on Transfer, 1968; The Scientific Enterprise and Christian Faith, 1968; Experimental Psychology: An Introduction for Biologists, 1974; Psychology and Christianity: The View Both Ways, 1976; Psychology Survey No. 3, 1980; (with G.B. Greer) Analysis of Structural Learning, 1983; Behavioral Sciences: A Christian Perspective, 1983; (with R.J. Berry and D. Atkinson) Free to be Different: Varieties of Human Behaviour, 1984; (ed.) Behavioural Sciences, 1984; (ed. with G. Baumgartner) Methods in Neuropsychology, 1986; (with D.G. Myers) Psychology Through the Eyes of Faith, 1987, rev. ed., 2002; Mind Fields, 1993; (ed. with M. Lassonde) Callosal Agenesis: A Natural Split Brain? 1994; Human Nature at the Millennium: Reflections on the Integration of Psychology and Christianity, 1997; (with R.J. Berry) Science, Life and Christian Belief: A Survey of Contemporary Issues, 1998; (ed.) From Cells to Souls and Beyond: Changing Portraits of Human Nature, 2004; (ed. and contrib.) Human Nature: Reflections on the Integration of Psychology and Christianity, 2005; (W.S. Brown) Neuroscience, Psychology and Religion, 2009; (ed.) Rethinking Human Nature: A Multidisciplinary Approach, 2010. **Address:** School of Psychology, University of St. Andrews, Saint Andrews, FF KY16 9AJ, Scotland. **Online address:** maj2@st-andrews.ac.uk

JEEVES, Malcolm A. *See* **JEEVES, Malcolm.**

JEFFERIES, Matthew (Martin). British (born England), b. 1962. **Genres:** History, Politics/Government, Social Sciences. **Career:** University of Warwick, lecturer in history, 1990-91; Victoria University of Manchester, lecturer in German history, 1991, senior lecturer and professor of German history; Sovereign Education, lecturer and consultant. Writer. **Publications:** Politics and Culture in Wilhelmine Germany: The Case of Industrial Architecture, 1995; Imperial Culture in Germany, 1871-1918, 2003; Contesting the German Empire 1871-1918, 2008; (with M. Tyldesley) Rolf Gardiner: Folk, Nature and Culture in Interwar Britain, 2011; Hamburg: A Cultural & Literary History, 2011. Contributor to books and periodicals. **Address:** School of Languages, Linguistics and Cultures, University of Manchester, Oxford Rd., Samuel Alexander Bldg., Manchester, GM M13 9PL, England. **Online address:** matt.jefferies@manchester.ac.uk

JEFFERIES, William. *See* **DEAVER, Jeffery Wilds.**

JEFFERS, Honorée Fanonne. American (born United States), b. 1967. **Genres:** Poetry. **Career:** University of Oklahoma, Department of English, assistant professor, 2002-07, associate professor, 2007-. Writer. **Publications:** POEMS: The Gospel of Barbecue: Poems, 2000; Outlandish Blues, 2003; Red Clay Suite, 2007. Works appear in anthologies. **Address:** Department of English, University of Oklahoma, 760 Van Vleet Oval, Gittinger Hall, Norman, OK 73019-2055, U.S.A. **Online address:** honoree.f.jeffers-1@ou.edu

JEFFERS, Thomas L. American (born United States), b. 1946. **Genres:** History, Language/Linguistics, Biography, Literary Criticism And History. **Career:** Cornell University, assistant professor of English, 1974-81; Harvard University, Mellon fellow, 1981-82; Marquette University, assistant professor, 1982-88, associate professor of English, 1989-, professor, 2005-. Writer. **Publications:** Samuel Butler Revalued, 1981; (ed.) The Norman Podhoretz Reader: A Selection of His Writings from the 1950s through the 1990s, 2004; Apprenticeships: The Bildungsroman from Goethe to Santayana, 2005; Norman Podhoretz, A Biography, 2010. **Address:** Department of English, Marquette University, 337 Coughlin Hall, Milwaukee, WI 53201-1881, U.S.A. **Online address:** tjeffers@wi.rr.com

JEFFERSON, Margo. American (born United States), b. 1947. **Genres:** History, Music. **Career:** Newsweek, associate editor, 1973-78; New York University, Department of Journalism and Mass Communication, assistant professor, 1979-83, 1989-91; Vogue, contributing editor, 1984-89; 7 Days, contributing editor, 1988-89; Columbia University, lecturer, assistant professor, 1991-93; New York Times, critic, 1993-, sunday theater critic, 1995-96, critic-at-large, 1996-; New School for Social Research, visiting lecturer; Eugene Lang College the New School for Liberal Arts, associate professor of writing. **Publications:** On Michael Jackson, 2006. Contributor to periodicals. **Address:** c/o Author Mail, Pantheon Books, 1745 Broadway, New York, NY 10019, U.S.A. **Online address:** jeffersm@newschool.edu

JEFFERY, Anthea J. South African (born South Africa) **Genres:** Politics/Government, History, Novels, Military/Defense/Arms Control. **Career:** South African Institute of Race Relations, research consultant. Author and attorney. **Publications:** (With S. Bekker) Local Government in Urban South Africa: A Normative Approach, 1989; Forum on Mass Mobilisation, 1991; Riot Policing in Perspective, 1991; Conflict at the Crossroads in Bophuthatswana, 1993; Bill of Rights Report 1996/97, 1997; The Natal Story: Sixteen Years of Conflict, 1997; The Truth about the Truth Commission, 1999; People's War: New Light on the Struggle for South Africa, 2009; Chasing the Rainbow: South Africa's Move from Mandela to Zuma, 2010. **Address:** South African Institute of Race Relations, PO Box 31044, Braamfontein, 2017, South Africa.

JEFFREY, Anna. *See* **MCCLANAHAN, Jeffery.**

JEFFREY, Francis. American (born United States), b. 1950?. **Genres:** Sciences, Biography, Psychology. **Career:** University of California, research associate, 1972-73; Institute for Advanced Computation, consultant, 1973-75; Scientific Applications Inc., consultant, 1973-75; Alive Systems Informational Sciences, consultant, 1978-87; Human-Dolphin Foundation, consultant, 1980-81, 1987-89; Esalen Institute, consultant, 1982-83; New Forum, co-founder, 1984; Great Whales Foundation, co-founder and director, 1986-; Alive Systems Inc., founder, president and chief executive officer, 1987-; Elfnet Inc., founder, president and chief executive officer, 1987-; Arthur C. Clarke Communicators, co-founder, 2000-. Writer and software developer. **Publications:** (Contrib.) Handbook of States of Consciousness (collection) 1986; (with J.C. Lilly) John Lilly, So Far..., 1990; (co-author) Voices from the Edge (collection), 1995. **Address:** PO Box 6844, Malibu, CA 90264-6844, U.S.A. **Online address:** francis@elfi.com

JEFFREY, Thomas E. American (born United States), b. 1947. **Genres:** Politics/Government, History. **Career:** Benjamin Henry Latrobe Papers, microfiche editor, 1972-77; Vanderbilt University, visiting assistant professor of history, 1977-79; Rutgers University, Thomas A. Edison Papers, senior editor, associate director and microfilm editor, 1979-. **Publications:** State Parties and National Politics: North Carolina, 1815-1861, 1989; Thomas Lanier Clingman: Fire Eater from the Carolina Mountains, 1998; (with T.A. Edison) From Phonographs to U-Boats: Edison and His Insomnia Squad in Peace and War, 1911-1919, 2008. Contributor to journals. **Address:** Thomas A. Edison Papers, Rutgers University, 44 Rd. 3, Piscataway, NJ 08854, U.S.A. **Online address:** tjeffrey@rci.rutgers.edu

JEFFREY, Zoey. *See* **BENNETT, Cherie.**

JEFFREYS, Derek S. American (born United States), b. 1964?. **Genres:** Politics/Government, Humanities, History, Theology/Religion, Philosophy. **Career:** University of Wisconsin, associate professor of humanistic studies and religion. Writer. **Publications:** Defending Human Dignity: John Paul II and Political Realism, 2004; Spirituality and the Ethics of Torture, 2009. **Address:** Department of Humanistic Studies, University of Wisconsin, 331 Theatre Hall, 2420 Nicolet Dr., Green Bay, WI 54311-7003, U.S.A. **Online address:** jeffreyd@uwgb.edu

JEFFREYS, Diarmuid. British (born England) **Genres:** Medicine/Health, Novels, History. **Career:** British Broadcasting Corporation Television, Channel 4, producer of public-affairs and documentary programming. Writer. **Publications:** The Bureau: Inside Today's FBI, 1994; Aspirin: The Remarkable Story of a Wonder Drug, 2004; Hell's Cartel: IG Farben and the Making of Hitler's War Machine, 2008. Contributor to periodicals. **Address:** c/o Anthony Sheil, Gillon Aitken Associates, 18-21 Cavaye Pl., London, GL SW10 9PT, England.

JEFFRIES, Don. American (born United States), b. 1940. **Genres:** Biography, Travel/Exploration, Theology/Religion. **Career:** Cargill, Wilson & Acree Advertising, copywriter, 1965-69; Garner & Associates Advertising, creative director, 1969-74; Ullman, Fouler & Jeffries Advertising, creative director, 1974-76; William Cook Advertising, copywriter, 1976-77; Newman, Saylor & Gregory, creative director, 1977-79; Wray Ward Advertising, vice president and creative director, 1979-95; Rebound Christian Rehabilitation Center, board director, 1984. Freelance writer, 1995-. **Publications:** Balm in Gilead: A Baptist Minister's Personal Journey through Drug Addiction, 1992; (with P. Stokkebye and S. Jeffries) Stokkebye: The Life and Good Times of a Tobacco Man, 2002. **Address:** 2001 Dugan Dr., Charlotte, NC 28270-9775, U.S.A.

JEFFRIES, Ian. Welsh (born Wales), b. 1942. **Genres:** Economics, International Relations/Current Affairs. **Career:** University of Wales, Swansea University, School of Business and Economics, lecturer in economics, 1966-, professor, honorary professor. Writer. **Publications:** Increasing Heterodoxy in Soviet Development Economics, 1978; A Guide to the Socialist Economies, 1990; Socialist Economies and the Transition to the Market: A Guide, 1993; A Guide to the Economies in Transition, 1996; (with R. Bideleux) A History of Eastern Europe: Crisis and Change, 1998, 2nd ed., 2007; Economies in Transition: A Guide to China, Cuba, Mongolia, North Korea and Vietnam at the Turn of the Twenty-First Century, 2001; The New Russia: A Handbook of Economic and Political Development, 2002; Eastern Europe at the Turn of the Twenty-First Century: A Guide to Economies in Transition, 2002; The Former Yugoslavia at the Turn of the Twenty-First Century: A Guide to Economies in Transition, 2002; The Caucasus and Central Asian Republics at the Turn of the Twenty-First Century: A Guide to Economies in Transition, 2003; The Former Soviet Union at the Turn of the Twenty-First Century: The Baltic and European States in Transition, 2004; Countries of the Former Soviet Union at the Turn of the Twenty-First Century: The Baltic and European States in Transition, 2004; North Korea: A Guide to Economic and Political Developments, 2006; China, 2006; (with R. Bideleux) Balkans: A Post-Communist History, 2006; Vietnam: A Guide to Economic and Political Developments, 2006; Mongolia: A Guide to Economic and Political Developments, 2007; Contemporary North Korea: A Guide to Economic and Political Developments, 2009; Political Developments in Contemporary China: A Guide, 2011; Economic Developments in Contemporary China: A Guide, 2011; Economic Developments in Contemporary Russia, 2011; Contemporary Vietnam: A Guide to Economic and Political Developments, 2011. EDITOR: The Industrial Enterprise in Eastern Europe, 1981; (with M. Melzer) The East German Economy, 1987; Industrial Reform in Socialist Countries: From Restructuring to Revolution, 1992; Problems of Economic and Political Transformation in the Balkans, 1996. **Address:** School of Business and Economics, Swansea University, Rm. 224, Singleton Pk., James Callaghan Bldg., Swansea, WG SA2 8PP, Wales. **Online address:** i.jeffries@swan.ac.uk

JEFFRIES, John C. American (born United States), b. 1948. **Genres:** Law, Biography. **Career:** University of Virginia, professor of law, 1973-86, Emerson Spies professor of law, 1986-2008, Horace W. Goldsmith research professor, 1992-, Arnold H. Leon professor, academic associate dean, 1994-99, School of Law, dean, 1999, 2001-08, Virginia Law Review, editor-in-chief, David and Mary Harrison distinguished professor of law, 2008-. **Publications:** Criminal Law: cases and materials, 1982, 3rd ed., 2009; (with P.W. Low) Federal Courts and the Law of Federal-State Relations, 1987, 6th ed. 2008; (with P.W. Low) Civil Rights Actions: Section 1983 and Related Statutes, 1988, 2nd ed. as Civil Rights Actions: Enforcing the Constitution, 2007; Justice Lewis F. Powell, Jr., 1994; (with R.J. Bonnie and P.W. Low) A Case Study in the Insanity Defense: The Trial of John W. Hinckley, Jr, 3rd ed., 2008. **Address:** School of Law, University of Virginia, Rm. WB179E, 580 Massie Rd., Charlottesville, VA 22903, U.S.A. **Online address:** jjeffries@virginia.edu

JEFFRIES, Judson L. American (born United States), b. 1965. **Genres:** Adult Non-fiction, Biography, History. **Career:** Purdue University, Department of Political Science, assistant professor, 1998-2002, associate professor, 2002-06, Homeland Security Institute, consultant, 2006-; Ohio State University, Department of African American and African Studies, professor, 2006-, Community Extension Center, director, 2006-. Writer. **Publications:** Virginia's Native Son: The Election and Administration of Governor L. Douglas Wilder, 2000; Huey P. Newton: The Radical Theorist, 2002; (with H. Hahn) Urban America and Its Police: From the Postcolonial Era through the Turbulent 1960s, 2003; (ed.) Black Power in the Belly of the Beast, 2006; (ed.) Comrades: A Local History of the Black Panther Party, 2007; (ed.) On the Ground: The Black Panther Party in Communities Across America, 2010. **Address:** Department of African American and African Studies, Ohio State University, 105 AAAS Extension Ctr., 905 Mount Vernon Ave., Columbus, OH 43203, U.S.A. **Online address:** jeffries.70@osu.edu

JEFFRIES, Roderic. Also writes as Graham Hastings, Hastings Draper, Peter Alding, Jeffrey Ashford, Roderic Graeme. Spanish/British (born England), b. 1926. **Genres:** Novels, Mystery/Crime/Suspense, Children's Fiction. **Career:** Writer, 1954-. Barrister. **Publications:** Evidence of the Accused, 1961; Exhibit No. Thirteen, 1962; Police and Detection, 1962; The Benefits of Death, 1963; An Embarrassing Death, 1964; Dead against the Lawyers, 1965; Police Dog, 1965; Death in the Coverts, 1966; A Deadly Marriage, 1967; Police Car, 1967; A Traitor's Crime, 1968; River Patrol, 1969; Dead Man's Bluff, 1970;

Police Patrol Boat, 1971; Trapped, 1972; The Riddle in the Parchment, 1976; The Boy Who Knew Too Much, 1977; Eighteen Desperate Hours, 1979; The Missing Man, 1980; Just Desserts, 1980; Voyage into Danger, 1981; Peril at Sea, 1983; Sunken Danger, 1985; Meeting Trouble, 1986; The Man Who Couldn't Be, 1987; Dead against the Lawyers, 2003; Murder, Majorcan Style, 2011. INSPECTOR ALVAREZ SERIES: Mistakenly in Mallorca, 1974; Two Faced Death, 1976; Troubled Deaths, 1977; Murder Begets Murder, 1979; Just Deserts, 1980; Unseemly End, 1982; Deadly Petard: An Inspector Alvarez Novel, 1984; Three and One Make Five, 1984; Layers of Deceit, 1985; Almost Murder, 1986; Relatively Dangerous, 1987; Death Trick, 1988; Dead Clever, 1989; Too Clever by Half, 1990; A Fatal Fleece, 1991; Murder's Long Memory, 1992; Murder Confounded, 1993; Death Takes Time, 1994; An Arcadian Death, 1996; Artistic Way to Go, 1996; A Maze of Murders, 1998; An Enigmatic Disappearance, 2000; Artful Death, 2000; The Ambiguity of Murder, 2001; Definitely Deceased, 2001; Seeing Is Deceiving: An Inspector Alvarez Mystery, 2002; An Intriguing Murder, 2003; An Air of Murder, 2003; A Sunny Disappearance, 2005; Murder Delayed, 2006; Murder Needs Imagination, 2007; An Instinctive Solution, 2008. AS PETER ALDING: The C.I.D. Room in US as All Leads Negative, 1967; Circle of Danger, 1968; Murder among Thieves, 1969; Guilt without Proof, 1970; Despite the Evidence, 1971; Call Back to Crime, 1972; Field of Fire, 1973; The Murder Line, 1974; Six Days to Death, 1975; Murder Is Suspected, 1977; Ransom Town, 1979; A Man Condemned, 1981; One Man's Justice, 1983; Betrayed by Death, 1984. AS JEFFREY ASHFORD: Counsel for the Defence, 1960; Investigations Are Proceeding, 1961 in US as The D.I., 1962; The Burden of Proof, 1962; Will Anyone Who Saw the Accident, 1963 in UK as Hit and Run, 1966; Enquiries Are Continuing, 1964 in US as The Superintendent's Room, 1965; The Hands of Innocence, 1965; Forget What You Saw, 1967; Grand Prix Monaco (children), 1968; Prisoner at the Bar, 1969; To Protect the Guilty, 1970; Grand Prix Germany (children), 1970; Grand Prix United States (children), 1971; Bent Cooper, 1971; A Man Will Be Kidnapped Tomorrow, 1972; The Double Run, 1973; Grand Prix Britain (children), 1973; Dick Knox at Le Mans (children), 1974; The Colour of Violence, 1974; Three Layers of Guilt, 1975; Slow Down the World, 1976; Hostage to Death, 1977; The Anger of Fear, 1978; A Recipe for Murder, 1980; The Loss of the Culion, 1981; Guilt with Honour, 1982; A Sense of Loyalty, 1983; Presumption of Guilt, 1984; An Ideal Crime, 1985; A Question of Principle, 1986; A Crime Remembered, 1987; The Honourable Detective, 1988; A Conflict of Interests, 1989; An Illegal Solution, 1991; Deadly Reunion, 1992; Twisted Justice, 1992; Judgement Deferred, 1993; The Bitter Bite, 1996; A Web of Circumstances, 1997; The Price of Failure, 1998; The Cost of Innocence, 1998; An Honest Betrayal, 1999; Loyal Disloyalty, 1999; Murder Will Out, 2000; Looking-Glass Justice, 2001; A Truthful Injustice, 2002; A Fair Exchange Is Robbery, 2002; Evidentially Guilty, 2004; Deadly Corruption, 2005; Illegal Guilt, 2007; Jigsaw Guilt, 2009. AS HASTINGS DRAPER: Wiggery Pokery (novel), 1956; Wigged and Gowned (novel), 1958; Brief Help, 1961. AS RODERIC GRAEME: Brandy Ahoy!, 1951; Concerning Blackshirt, 1952; Where's Brandy?, 1953; Blackshirt Wins the Trick, 1953; Blackshirt Passes By, 1953; Brandy Goes a Cruising, 1954; Salute to Blackshirt, 1954; The Amazing Mr. Blackshirt, 1955; Blackshirt Meets the Lady, 1956; Paging Blackshirt, 1957; Blackshirt Helps Himself, 1958; Double for Blackshirt, 1958; Blackshirt Sets the Pace, 1959; Blackshirt Sees It Through, 1960; Blackshirt Finds Trouble, 1961; Blackshirt Takes the Trail, 1962; Blackshirt on the Spot, 1963; Call for Blackshirt, 1963; Blackshirt Saves the Day, 1964; Danger for Blackshirt, 1965; Blackshirt at Large, 1966; Blackshirt in Peril, 1967; Blackshirt Stirs Things Up, 1969; A Question of Motive, 2010. AS GRAHAM HASTINGS: Twice Checked, 1959; Deadly Game, 1961. **Address:** HarperCollins Publishers Ltd., 77-85 Fulham Palace Rd., Hammersmith, GL W6 8JB, England. **Online address:** peter@chessvalleybooks.co.uk

JEFFRIES, Sabrina. Also writes as Deborah Nicholas, Deborah Martin. American (born United States) **Genres:** Novels. **Career:** Educator and writer. **Publications:** AS SABRINA JEFFRIES: LORD TRILOGY SERIES: The Pirate Lord, 1998; The Forbidden Lord, 1999; The Dangerous Lord, 2000. SWANLEA SPINSTERS SERIES: A Dangerous Love, 2000; A Notorious Love, 2001; After the Abduction, 2002; Dance of Seduction, 2003; Married to the Viscount, 2004. ROYAL BROTHERHOOD SERIES: In the Prince's Bed, 2004; To Pleasure a Prince, 2005; One Night with a Prince, 2005. SCHOOL FOR HEIRESSES SERIES: Never Seduce a Scoundrel, 2006; Only a Duke Will Do, 2006; Beware a Scot's Revenge, 2007; (co-author) The School for Heiresses, 2007; Let Sleeping Rogues Lie, 2008; (J. Feather and J. London) Snowy Night with a Stranger, 2008; Don't Bargain with the Devil, 2009; Wed Him Before You Bed Him, 2009. HELLIONS OF HALSTEAD HALL SE-

RIES: The Truth About Lord Stoneville, 2010; A Hellion in Her Bed, 2010; To Wed a Wild Lord, 2011; How to Woo a Reluctant Lady, 2011; A Lady Never Loses, 2012. AS DEBORAH MARTIN: Moonlight Enchantment, 1992; Creole Nights, 1992; By Love Unveiled, 1993; Dangerous Angel, 1994; Silver Deceptions, 1994; Storm Swept, 1995; (co-author) One Night with a Rogue, 1995; Windswept, 1996; Creole Bride, 1997; (co-author) A Dance with the Devil, 1997. AS DEBORAH NICHOLAS: Night Vision, 1993; Silent Sonata, 1994; Shattered Reflections, 1995. OTHERS: (co-author) Fantasy, 2002; (ed.) A Day in Mossy Creek, 2006; (co-author) At Home in Mossy Creek, 2007. **Address:** PO Box 3551, Cary, NC 27519, U.S.A. **Online address:** sabrinajeffries@me.com

JEFFS, Julian. British (born England), b. 1931. **Genres:** Food And Wine, Law, Education. **Career:** Wine and Food, editor, 1965-67; Faber's Wine Series, general editor, 1966-2002. **Publications:** Sherry, 1961, rev. ed., 2004; (ed. with R. Harling) Wine, 1966; (contrib.) Torts, 1969; The Wines of Europe, 1971; Little Dictionary of Drink, 1973; Little Dictionary of World Wines, Liqueurs and Other Drinks, 1975; (co-author) Encyclopedia of United Kingdom and European Patent Law, 1977; Vino de Jerez, 1994; The Wines of Spain, 1999, rev. ed., 2006; (ed. with J. Hillgarth) Maurice Baring: Letters, 2007. Contributor to books. **Address:** Church Farm House, East Ilsley, Newbury, BR RG20 7LP, England.

JEFFS, Rae. (Frances Rae Sebley). British (born England), b. 1921. **Genres:** Biography. **Career:** Air Ministry, Directorate of Bombing Operations, staff, 1940-42; Lambe and Robinson, advertising copywriter, 1947-50; Hutchinson and Company Ltd., publicity staff, 1950-57, Publicity Department, manager, 1957-63; Brendan Behan, editor and agent, 1960-64. Writer, 1964-. **Publications:** (Intro.) Confessions of An Irish Rebel, 1965; Brendan Behan: Man and Showman, 1966. EDITOR: Brendan Behan's Island, 1962; Hold Your Hour and Have Another, 1963; Brendan Behan's New York, 1964; The Scarperer, 1966. **Address:** Rotherfield Farmhouse, Newick, Lewes, Sussex, ES BN8 4JJ, England.

JELEN, Ted G. American (born United States), b. 1950. **Genres:** Politics/Government, Bibliography, Theology/Religion. **Career:** Ohio State University, instructor in political science, 1976-77; Lamar University, instructor of political science, 1978-79; Illinois State University, assistant professor of political science, 1979-80; University of Kentucky, assistant professor of political science, 1980-81; Illinois Benedictine College, assistant professor, professor of political science, 1981-90, 1991-93, department head, 1989-90, 1991-93; Georgetown University, visiting professor of political science, 1990-91; University of Nevada, Department of Political Science, professor and chair of political science; Journal for the Scientific Study of Religion, editor; Women and Politics, associate editor. **Publications:** (Ed.) Religion and Political Behavior in the United States, 1989; The Political Mobilization of Religious Beliefs, 1991; (with E.A. Cook and C. Wilcox) Between Two Absolutes: Public Opinion and the Politics of Abortion, 1992; The Political World of the Clergy, 1993; (ed. with M.A. Chandler) Abortion Politics in the United States and Canada: Studies in Public Opinion, 1994; The Religious Dimension of Political Behavior: A Critical Assessment and Annotated Bibliography, 1994; (with C. Wilcox) Public Attitudes Toward Church and State, 1995; (ed.) Perspectives on the Politics of Abortion, 1995; (with M.C. Segers) A Wall of Separation?: Debating the Public Role of Religion, 1998; (comp. with L.R. Olson) Religious Dimension of Political Behavior: A Critical Analysis and Annotated Bibliography, 1998; To Serve God and Mammon: Church-State Relations in American Politics, 2000, 2nd ed., 2010; (ed.) Ross for Boss: The Perot Phenomenon and Beyond, 2001; (ed. with C. Wilcox) Religion and Politics in Comparative Perspective: The One, the Few, and the Many, 2002; (ed.) Sacred Markets, Sacred Canopies: Essays on Religious Markets and Religious Pluralism, 2002. Works appear in anthologies. Contributor of articles to journals. **Address:** Department of Political Science, University of Nevada, B206 WRI, 4505 S Maryland Pkwy., PO Box 455029, Las Vegas, NV 89154-5029, U.S.A. **Online address:** jelent@unlv.nevada.edu

JELLICOE, Ann. (Patricia Ann Jellicoe). British (born England), b. 1927. **Genres:** Plays/Screenplays, Travel/Exploration, Songs/Lyrics And Libretti. **Career:** Writer and actress, 1947-51; Cockpit Theatre Club, founding director, 1950-53; Central School of Speech and Drama, lecturer and director, 1953-55; Royal Court Theatre, literary manager, 1973-75; Colway Theatre Trust, founding director, 1979-85, president, 1986. **Publications:** Rosmersholm, 1960; The Knack, 1962; The Knack: A Comedy in Three Acts, 1962; Two Plays: The Knack and The Sport of My Mad Mother, 1964; The Knack:

A Comedy, 1964; Shelley: or, The Idealist, 1966; Some Unconscious Influences in the Theatre, 1967; The Giveaway, 1970; (with R. Mayne) Devon, 1975; Sport of my Mad Mother, 1976; 3 Jelliplays, 1975; Community Plays: How to Put Them On, 1987. **Address:** Cassarotto Ramsay & Associates Ltd., Waverley House, 7-12 Noel St., London, GL W1F 8GQ, England.

JELLICOE, Patricia Ann. See **JELLICOE, Ann.**

JELLISON, Katherine. American (born United States), b. 1960. **Genres:** History, Social Sciences, Biography, Autobiography/Memoirs. **Career:** University of Iowa, visiting instructor in history, 1990; Memphis State University, assistant professor of history, 1991-93; Ohio University, assistant professor, 1993-96, associate professor of history, 1996-2008, professor of history, 2008-. Writer. **Publications:** Entitled to Power: Farm Women and Technology, 1913-1963, 1993; (intro.) Years of Struggle: The Farm Diary of Elmer G. Powers, 1931-1936, 1995; It's Our Day: America's Love Affair With the White Wedding, 1945-2005, 2008. Contributor to journals. **Address:** Department of History, Ohio University, 429 Bentley Annex, Athens, OH 45701, U.S.A. **Online address:** jellison@ohio.edu

JEN, Gish. American (born United States), b. 1956?. **Genres:** Novels, Novellas/Short Stories, Science Fiction/Fantasy, Young Adult Fiction. **Career:** Tufts University, lecturer in fiction writing, 1986; University of Massachusetts, visiting writer, 1990-91; Harvard University, Radcliffe Institute for Advanced Study, writer-in-residence; Brandeis University, Department of English and American Literature, professor and co-director of creative writing. **Publications:** NOVELS: Typical American, 1991; Mona in the Promised Land, 1996. STORIES: Who's Irish?: stories, 1999; Dian Xing De Meiguo Lao, 2000; The Love Wife, 2004; World and Town: A Novel, 2010. Works appear in anthologies. Contributor to books and periodicals. **Address:** c/o Melanie Jackson, Melanie Jackson Agency, 41 W 72nd St., Ste. 3F, New York, NY 10023, U.S.A. **Online address:** gjen@brandeis.edu

JENCKS, Charles (Alexander). American (born United States), b. 1939. **Genres:** Architecture, Art/Art History, History. **Career:** Architectural Association, senior lecturer in architectural history, 1968-88; University of California, adjunct professor of architecture to visiting professor, 1974-92. Writer. **Publications:** Architecture 2000, 1971; (with N. Silver) Adhocism: The Case for Improvisation, 1972; Modern Movements in Architecture, 1973; Le Corbusier and the Tragic View of Architecture, 1973, 2nd ed., 1987; The Language of Post-Modern Architecture, 1977, 7th ed. as The New Paradigm in Architecture, 2002; The Daydream Houses of Los Angeles, 1978; Bizarre Architecture, 1979; Late-Modern Architecture: Selected Essays, 1980; Skyscrapers-Skyprickers-Skycitics, 1980; Architecture Today, 1982; Kings of Infinite Space, 1983; Towards a Symbolic Architecture: The Thematic House, 1985; (with T. Farrell) Designing a House, 1986; What is Post-Modernism?, 1986, 4th ed., 1996; Post-Modernism: The New Classicism in Art and Architecture, 1987; Post-Modernism & Discontinuity, 1987; The Prince, the Architects and New Wave Monarchy, 1988; The New Moderns: From Late to Neo-Modernism, 1990; Language of Post-Modern Architecture, 1991; Heteropolis: Los Angeles, the Riots and Hetero-Architecture, 1993; The Architecture of the Jumping Universe: A Polemic: How Complexity Science is Changing Architecture and Culture, 1995, 2nd ed., 1997; Ecstatic Architecture: The Surprising Link: From a Debate of the Academy International Forum at the Royal Academy, 1999; Architecture 2000 and Beyond: Success in the Art of Prediction, 2000; Le Corbusier and the Continual Revolution in Architecture, 2000; (contrib.) Hopkins2, 2001; New Paradigm in Architecture: The Language of Post-Modern Architecture, 2002; The Garden of Cosmic Speculation, 2003; (contrib.) Chinese Garden: History, Art, and Architecture, 2003; Scottish Parliament, 2005; The Iconic Building, 2005. EDITOR: (with G. Baird) Meaning in Architecture, 1969; (with R. Bunt and G. Broadbent) Signs, Symbols and Architecture, 1980; Post-Modern Classicism: The New Synthesis, 1980; Free-Style Classicism, 1982; Abstract Representation, 1983; The Architecture of Democracy, 1987; Post-Modern Triumphs in London, 1991; The Post-Modern Reader, 1992; Frank O. Gehry: Individual Imagination and Cultural Conservatism, 1995; (with K. Kropf) Theories and Manifestos of Contemporary Architecture, 1997; (ed. with M. Toy) Millennium Architecture, 2000; (with K. Kropf) Theories and Manifestoes of Contemporary Architecture, 2006. **Address:** c/o Author Mail, Rizzoli/Universe International Publications, 30 Park Ave. S, 3rd Fl., New York, NY 10010, U.S.A.

JENIKE, Michael A. American/British/Scottish (born Scotland), b. 1945. **Genres:** Medicine/Health. **Career:** University of Oklahoma, intern in internal medicine, 1978-79; Massachusetts General Hospital, resident in psychiatry, 1979-81, chief resident and consultation-liaison, 1981-82, Ethel Dupont-Warren Research Fellow, 1982-83, assistant in psychiatry, 1982-84, assistant psychiatrist, 1984-88, associate psychiatrist, 1988-89, psychiatrist, 1989-; Harvard Medical School, clinical fellow in psychiatry, 1979-82, instructor in psychiatry, 1982-83, assistant professor of psychiatry, 1983-86, associate professor of psychiatry, 1987-94, professor of psychiatry, 1995-. Writer. **Publications:** Handbook of Geriatric Psychopharmacology, 1985; Geriatric Psychiatry and Psychopharmacology: A Clinical Approach, 1989; (with T.W. Murphy and E.E. Zine) Life in Rewind: The Story of a Young Courageous Man Who Persevered Over OCD and the Harvard Doctor Who Broke All the Rules to Help Him, 2009. EDITOR: (with L. Baer and W.E. Minichiello) Obsessive-Compulsive Disorders: Theory and Management, 1986, 3rd ed. as Obsessive-Compulsive Disorders: Practical Management, 1998; (with S.E. Hyman) Manual of Clinical Problems in Psychiatry: With Annotated Key References, 1990; (with M. Åsberg) Understanding Obsessive-Compulsive Disorder (OCD): An International Symposium Held during the VIIIth World Congress of Psychiatry, Athens, Greece, October 1989, 1991. Contributor to books and periodicals. **Address:** Department of Psychiatry, Massachusetts General Hospital, 9th Fl., 149 Bldg., 13th St., Charlestown, MA 02129, U.S.A. **Online address:** jenike@comcast.net

JENKINS, Amy. British (born England), b. 1966?. **Genres:** Mystery/Crime/Suspense, Novels, Romance/Historical, Young Adult Fiction. **Career:** Film producer and screenwriter. **Publications:** Honeymoon: A Romantic Rampage, 2000; Funny Valentine, 2002. Contributor to periodicals. **Address:** Little Brown & Co., 1271 Ave. of the Americas, New York, NY 10020, U.S.A.

JENKINS, Beverly. American (born United States), b. 1951. **Genres:** Novels, Romance/Historical. **Career:** Michigan State University, librarian, 1974-80. Writer. **Publications:** Night Song, 1994; Vivid, 1995; Indigo, 1996; Topaz, 1997; Through the Storm, 1998; The Taming of Jessi Rose, 1999; Always and Forever, 2000; Before the Dawn, 2001; Belle and the Beau, 2002; A Chance at Love, 2002; (with G. Guillaume, F. Ray and M. Jackson) Gettin' Merry: A Holiday Anthology, 2002; Josephine and the Soldier, 2003; The Edge of Dawn, 2004; The Edge of Midnight, 2004; Something Like Love, 2005; Black Lace, 2005; Sexy/Dangerous, 2006; Winds of the Storm, 2006; (co-author) Cuffed by Candlelight, 2007; Wild Sweet Love, 2007; Deadly Sexy, 2007; Jewel, 2008; Belle, 2009; Josephine, 2009; Captured, 2009; Bring on the Blessings, 2009; A Second Helping: A Blessings Novel, 2010; Midnight, 2010; (with A. Byrd and K.K. Terry) Once Upon a Holiday, 2010; (with E. Overton) Rhythms of Love, 2010; Something Old, Something New, 2011; Night Hawk, 2011; A Wish and a Prayer, 2012. **Address:** Avon Books, 10 E 53rd St., New York, NY 10022-5299, U.S.A. **Online address:** indigo@beverlyjenkins.net

JENKINS, Brian. See **JENKINS, Brian Michael.**

JENKINS, Brian M. See **JENKINS, Brian Michael.**

JENKINS, Brian Michael. Also writes as Brian Jenkins, Brian M. Jenkins. American (born United States), b. 1942. **Genres:** Politics/Government, History, International Relations/Current Affairs, Military/Defense/Arms Control. **Career:** Rand Corp., Political Science Department, chair, 1972-89, senior advisor to president; Long Commission, advisor, 1983; Kroll Associates, deputy chair, 1989-98; Mineta Transportation Institute, research associate, National Transportation Security Center, director; National Commission on Terrorism, advisor, 1999-2000. Writer. **Publications:** A People's Army for South Vietnam: A Vietnamese Solution, 1971; The Five Stages of Urban Guerrilla Warfare: Challenge of the 1970's, 1971; Why the North Vietnamese Will Keep Fighting, 1972; An Urban Strategy for Guerrillas and Governments, 1972; (as Brian Jenkins) The Seventh Son Leaves Hanoi for the Front, 1972; (as Brian M. Jenkins) The Unchangeable War, 1972; (as Brian Jenkins) A Route for the Enemy to Escape, Hanoi's View of the Ceasefire, 1973; (as Brian Jenkins) After the War, 1973; (as Brian M. Jenkins) International Terrorism: A New Kind of Warfare, 1974; (as Brian M. Jenkins) Terrorism and Kidnapping, 1974; (with J. Johnson) International Terrorism: A Chronology, 1968-1974: A Report Prepared for Department of State and Defense Advanced Research Projects Agency, 1975; High Technology Terrorism and Surrogate War: The Impact of New Technology on Low-Level Violence, 1975; (as Brian Jenkins) International Terrorism: A New Mode of Conflict, 1975; (as Brian M. Jenkins with J.A. Johnson) International Terrorism: A Chronology (1974 Supplement): A Report, 1976; (as Brian Jenkins with J. Johnson and D. Ronfeldt)

Numbered Lives: Some Statistical Observations from 77 International Hostage Episodes, 1977; (as Brian M. Jenkins with S.T. Hosmer and K. Kellen) The Fall of South Vietnam: Statements by Vietnamese Military and Civilian Leaders: Prepared for the Office of Secretary of Defense, Office of Historian, 1978; (as Brian M. Jenkins) Traditions and Patterns of Vietnamese History, 1979; (as Brian M. Jenkins with S.T. Hosmer and K. Kellen) The Fall of South Vietnam: Statements by Vietnamese Military and Civilian Leaders, 1980; Combatting Terrorism: Some Policy Implications, 1981; Embassies under Siege: A Review of 48 Embassy Takeovers, 1971-1980, 1981; Talking to Terrorists, 1982; (with S. Wildhorn and M.M. Lavin) Intelligence Constraints of the 1970s and Domestic Terrorism: Executive Summary, 1982; Diplomats on the Front Line, 1982; New Modes of Conflict, 1983; (with G. Bass) A Review of Recent Trends in International Terrorism and Nuclear Incidents Abroad, 1983; (ed.) Terrorism and Personal Protection, 1985; (as Brian M. Jenkins) International Terrorism: The Other World War, 1985; (as Brian M. Jenkins) A Conceptual Framework for Analyzing Terrorist Groups, 1985; (as Brian Jenkins with D. Ronfeldt) The Nicaraguan Resistance and U.S. Policy: Report on a May 1987 Conference, 1989; Terrorism: Policy Issues for the Bush Administration, 1989; (with A. Sassa) Gurōbaru Keiei Jidai No Kigy No Kiki Kanri (title means: 'Risk Wave Will Japan Sink or Swim'), 1994; (ed. with P. Wilkinson) Aviation Terrorism and Security, 1999; Terrorism: Current and Long Term Threats, 2001; Countering Al Qaeda: An Appreciation of the Situation and Suggestions for Strategy, 2002; (with P.K. Davis) Deterrence and Influence in Counterterrorism: A Component in the War on al Qaeda, 2002; Saving City Lifelines: Lessons Learned in the 9-11 Terrorist Attacks, 2003; Remarks before the National Commission on Terrorist Attacks upon the United States, 2003; Unconquerable Nation: Knowing Our Enemy, Strengthening Ourselves, 2006; Selective Screening of Rail Passengers, 2007; Will Terrorists Go Nuclear?, 2008; (with B.R. Butterworth and W.T. Poe) Potential Terrorist Uses of Highway-borne Hazardous Materials, 2009; (with B.R. Butterworth and J. Clair) The 1995 Attempted Derailing of the French TGV (high-speed train) and a Quantitative Analysis of 181 Rail Sabotage Attempts, 2010; (with B.R. Butterworth) Explosives and Incendiaries Used in Terrorist Attacks on Public Surface Transportation-A Preliminary Empirical Analysis, 2010; (with B.R. Butterworth) Federal Implementation and Development of Vehicle Tracking and Immobilization Technologies, 2010; (with B.R. Butterworth) Supplement to MTI Study on Selective Passenger Screening in the Mass Transit Rail Environment, 2010; (B.R. Butterworth and K.S. Shrum) Terrorist Attacks on Public Bus Transportation, 2010; Would-be Warriors: Incidents of Jihadist Terrorist Radicalization in the United States Since September 11, 2001, 2010; (ed. with J.P. Godges) The Long Shadow of 9/11, 2010; Stray Dogs and Virtual Armies, 2011; Al Qaeda in its Third Decade: Irreversible Decline or Imminent Victory?, 2012. Contributor to books and periodicals. **Address:** RAND Corp., 1776 Main St., Santa Monica, CA 90401-3208, U.S.A. **Online address:** brian_jenkins@rand.org

JENKINS, Carol. American (born United States), b. 1944. **Genres:** Biography. **Career:** WOR-TV, reporter, anchor and moderator on news program, 1970-72; ABC Network, correspondent, 1972; WNBC-TV, general reporter, Weekend News Channel 4, co-anchor, News Channel 4, co-anchor, 1972-; Fox 5/WNYW, Fox Midday News, co-anchor, Carol Jenkins Live, host, 1996-; Women's Media Center, co-founder and president, 2004-. Broadcaster. **Publications:** (With E.G. Hines) Black Titan: A.G. Gaston and the Making of a Black American Millionaire, 2004. Works appear in anthologies. Contributor to periodicals. **Address:** Women's Media Center, 320 W 37th St., 12A Fl., Ste. C, New York, NY 10018, U.S.A.

JENKINS, Catherine. Canadian (born Canada), b. 1962. **Genres:** Novels, Poetry, Adult Non-fiction. **Career:** Sam the Record Man, manager, 1984-93; freelance writer, 1993-99, 2008-; Solidus Communications, owner and operator, 1999-2008. **Publications:** POETRY: Submerge (chapbook), 1997; Blood, Love and Boomerangs, 1999. NOVELS: Swimming in the Ocean, 2002; Pairs & Artichoke Hearts, forthcoming. Works appear in anthologies. Contributor to periodicals. **Address:** Insomniac Press, 520 Princess Ave., London, ON N6B 2B8, Canada. **Online address:** solidus@sympatico.ca

JENKINS, Dafydd. Welsh/British (born England), b. 1911. **Genres:** History, Law. **Career:** Welsh Language Petition, organizing secretary, 1938-39; University of Wales, law teacher, 1962-65; Aberystwyth University, faculty, 1965-, professor of history and Welsh law and chair, 1975-78, professor emeritus, 1978-. Writer. **Publications:** Tân yn Llŷn, 1937; Thomas Johnes o'r Hafod, 1748-1816, 1948; Law for Co-Operatives, 1958; Llyfr Colan: Y Gyfraith Gymreig yn Ol Hanner Cyntaf Llawysgrif Peniarth 30, 1963; Gyfraith Hywel,

1970, 2nd ed., 1976; D. J. Williams, 1973; Damisciniau Colan, 1973; (ed. with M.E. Owen) The Welsh Law of Women: Studies Presented to Professor Daniel A. Binchy on His Eightieth Birthday, 3 June 1980, 1980; Lawyers and Laymen, 1986; (trans. and ed.) The Law of Hywel Dda: Law Texts of Medieval Wales, 1986, 2nd ed. as The Law of Hywel the Good, 1990; A Nation On Trial: Penyberth 1936, 1998. **Address:** Department of Law and Criminology, Aberystwyth University, Hugh Owen Bldg., Penglais, SY23 3DY, Wales.

JENKINS, David L. American (born United States), b. 1931. **Genres:** Theology/Religion, History, Cultural/Ethnic Topics. **Career:** Baptist minister. Writer. **Publications:** (With F.A. Craig and V. Harvey) Openings to Understandings, 1971; Find Yourself in Genesis, 1976; God's People: United for Conquest, 1977; Planning a Family Budget, 1981; Windows on the Gospel of John, 1988; Great Prayers of the Bible: A Guide for Individual or Group Study, 1990; A Sesquicentennial History: First Baptist Church, Gilmer, Texas, 1846-1996, 1998. Contributor to magazines. **Address:** First Baptist Church, 217 W Cass St., Gilmer, TX 75644, U.S.A.

JENKINS, Fred W(illiam). American (born United States), b. 1957. **Genres:** Bibliography, Classics, Reference, Archaeology/Antiquities, Literary Criticism And History. **Career:** University of Illinois, teaching and research assistant, 1979-85, research assistant, 1980-81, 1985-86; College of Physicians of Philadelphia, historical collections cataloger, 1986-87; University of Dayton, instructor, 1988-89, assistant professor, 1987-96, associate professor, 1996-2001, professor, 2001-, catalog specialist, 1987-96, rare book librarian, 1993-96, coordinator and head of collection management, 1996-2007, interim dean of libraries, 2004-05, associate dean of libraries, 2007-. Writer. **Publications:** Classical Studies: A Guide to the Reference Literature, 1996, 2nd ed., 2006. Contributor of articles to journals. **Address:** University of Dayton, 106a Roesch Library, 300 College Pk., Dayton, OH 45469-1360, U.S.A. **Online address:** fred.jenkins@udayton.edu

JENKINS, Garry. (Augustus Brown). British (born England) **Genres:** Biography, Animals/Pets, Ghost Writer. **Career:** Daily Mail, staff. Journalist. **Publications:** Daniel Day-Lewis: The Fire Within, 1995; Empire Building: The Remarkable Real-Life Story of Star Wars, 1997, rev. ed., 1999; Harrison Ford: Imperfect Hero, 1998; (with S. D'Antal) Kiri: Her Unsung Story, 1998; Colonel Cody and the Flying Cathedral: The Adventures of the Cowboy Who Conquered the Sky, 2000; The Wizard of Sun City: The Strange True Story of Charles Hatfield, The Rainmaker Who Drowned a City's Dreams, 2005. AS AUGUSTUS BROWN: Why Pandas Do Handstands: And Other Curious Truths About Animals, 2006; Play It Again Tom, 2009. **Address:** c/o Author Mail, Picador USA, 175 5th Ave., New York, NY 10010, U.S.A.

JENKINS, Gary W. American (born United States), b. 1961. **Genres:** History. **Career:** Eastern University, John H. Van Gorden professor in history. Writer. **Publications:** John Jewel and the English National Church: The Dilemmas of an Erastian Reformer, 2006. **Address:** Department of History, Eastern University, 1300 Eagle Rd., St. Davids, PA 19087-3696, U.S.A.

JENKINS, George. American (born United States), b. 1973. **Genres:** Biography, Autobiography/Memoirs, Young Adult Fiction, Young Adult Nonfiction, Children's Fiction. **Career:** University of Medicine and Dentistry of New Jersey, faculty in community health; Columbia University, assistant clinical professor of dentistry; Three Doctors Foundation, co-founder. Writer. **Publications:** (With S. Davis, R. Hunt and L.F. Page) The Pact: Three Young Men Make a Promise and Fulfill a Dream, 2002; (with S. Davis, R. Hunt and S.M. Draper) We Beat the Street: How a Friendship Pact Helped Us Succeed, 2005; (with S. Davis, R. Hunt and M. Bernstein) The Bond: Three Young Men Learn to Forgive and Reconnect with Their Fathers, 2007. **Address:** The Three Doctors Foundation Inc., 65 Hazelwood Ave., Newark, NJ 07106, U.S.A. **Online address:** drjenkins@threedoctorsfoundation.org

JENKINS, Jean. (Jean Loewer). American (born United States) **Genres:** Children's Fiction, Illustrations, Children's Non-fiction, Natural History, Picture/Board Books. **Career:** Freelance illustrator, 1972-; Asheville-Buncombe Library System, staff. Writer and educator. **Publications:** SELF-ILLUSTRATED: (with P. Loewer as Jean Loewer) The Moonflower, 1997. Illustrator of books by others. **Address:** Peachtree Publishers Ltd., 1700 Chattahoochee Ave. NW, Atlanta, GA 30318-2112, U.S.A.

JENKINS, Mark. American (born United States), b. 1958. **Genres:** Travel/Exploration. **Career:** Freelance writer, 1983-; Cross Country Skier Maga-

zine, managing editor, 1988-89; Adventure Travel, managing editor, 1988; Backpacker Magazine, Rocky mountain editor, 1989-96; Men's Health Magazine, investigative editor, 1997-. **Publications:** Off the Map: Bicycling Across Siberia, 1992; To Timbuktu: A Journey Down the Niger, 1997; The Hard Way: Stories of Danger, Survival and the Soul of Adventure, 2002; A Man's Life: Dispatches from Dangerous Places, 2007; To Timbuktu: A Journey Down the Niger, 2008. Contributor to periodicals. Works appear in anthologies. **Address:** 1102 Grand, Laramie, WY 82070, U.S.A. **Online address:** mark@globalcorrespondent.net

JENKINS, Michael (Romilly Heald). British (born England), b. 1936. **Genres:** Autobiography/Memoirs, Biography. **Career:** United Kingdom Diplomatic Service, staff, 1959; Commission of the European Communities, deputy secretary-general, 1981-83; Foreign and Commonwealth Office, assistant under-secretary of state, 1983-85; British Embassy, minister, 1985-87; British ambassador to the Netherlands, 1988-93; Dresdner Kleinwort Wasserstein, vice-chairman, 1993-; Dutch insurance group, staff, 1995-2001; British Group of the Trilateral Commission, staff, 1996-98; Boeing U.K., president, 2003-05; Aegon, non-executive director; GEOPARK, non-executive director, 2007-; Matra Petroleum Plc, chairman, 2008; Kleinwort Benson Ltd., senior advisor; Royal Hospital Chelsea, commissioner. Writer. **Publications:** Arakcheev: Grand Vizir of the Russian Empire, 1969; A House in Flanders, 1992. Contributor to magazines. **Address:** Deborah Rogers Ltd., 29 Goodge St., London, GL W1P 1FD, England.

JENKINS, Philip. British/Welsh (born Wales), b. 1952. **Genres:** Theology/Religion, History. **Career:** Pennsylvania State University, assistant professor of criminal justice, 1980-84, associate professor of criminal justice, 1984-89, professor of criminal justice and American studies, 1989-93, Religious Studies Program, director, 1992-98, professor of history and religious studies, 1993-97, distinguished professor of history and religious studies, 1997-2007, Edwin Erle Sparks professor of humanities, 2007-; Baylor University, Institute for Studies of Religion, distinguished senior fellow, 2009-; American Conservative, contributing editor, 2009-. **Publications:** The Making of a Ruling Class: The Glamorgan Gentry, 1640-1790, 1983; Crime and Justice: Issues and Ideas, 1984; (with G.W. Potter) The City and the Syndicate: Organizing Crime in Philadelphia, 1985; Intimate Enemies: Moral Panics in Contemporary Great Britain, 1992; A History of Modern Wales, 1536-1990, 1992; Using Murder: The Social Construction of Serial Homicide, 1994; Pedophiles and Priests: Anatomy of a Contemporary Crisis, 1996; Hoods and Shirts: The Extreme Right in Pennsylvania, 1925-1950, 1997; A History of the United States, 1997, 2nd ed., 2003; Moral Panic: Changing Concepts of the Child Molester in Modern America, 1998; The Cold War at Home: The Red Scare in Pennsylvania, 1945-1960, 1999; Synthetic Panics: The Symbolic Politics of Designer Drugs, 1999; Mystics and Messiahs: Cults and New Religions in American History, 2000; Beyond Tolerance: Child Pornography on the Internet, 2001; Hidden Gospels: How the Search for Jesus Lost Its Way, 2001; The Next Christendom: The Coming of Global Christianity, 2002, 3rd ed., 2011; Images of Terror: What We Can and Can't Know about Terrorism, 2003; New Anti-Catholicism: The Last Acceptable Prejudice, 2003; Xia yi ge Jidu wang guo, 2003; Dream Catchers: How Mainstream America Discovered Native Spirituality, 2004; Decade of Nightmares: The End of the Sixties and the Making of Eighties America, 2006; New Faces of Christianity: Believing the Bible in the Global South, 2006; God's Continent: Christianity, Islam, and Europe's Religious Ccrisis, 2007; Nuovi volti del cristianesimo, 2008; Lost history of Christianity, 2008; (foreword) Dayspring, 2009; Jesus Wars: How Four Patriarchs, Three Queens, and Two Emperors Decided What Christians Would Believe for the Next 1, 500 Years, 2010; Laying Down the Sword, 2011. EDITOR: (with E. Schuerer) B. Traven: Life and Work, 1987; (with E. Schuerer and M. Keune) The Berlin Wall: Representations and Perspectives, 1996. **Address:** Department of History & Religious Studies Program, Pennsylvania State University, 407 Weaver Bldg., University Park, PA 16802, U.S.A. **Online address:** jpj1@psu.edu

JENKINS, Sally. American (born United States), b. 1960. **Genres:** Sports/Fitness, Novels. **Career:** San Francisco Examiner, sports journalist, 1982-83; Los Angeles Herald Examiner, gossip columnist, 1983; San Francisco Chronicle, journalist, 1983-84; Washington Post, sports journalist, 1984-90, sports columnist and feature writer, 1996-; Sports Illustrated, journalist, 1990-96, senior writer; Conde Nast's Sports for Women, journalist, 1996. **Publications:** Men Will Be Boys: The Modern Woman Explains Football and Other Amusing Male Rituals, 1996; (with P. Summit) Reach for the Summit: The Definite Dozen System for Succeeding at Whatever You Do, 1998; (with P. Summit)

Raise the Roof: The Inspiring Inside Story of the Tennessee Lady Vols' Undefeated 1997-98 Season, 1998; (with D. Smith and J. Kilgo) A Coach's Life, 1999; (with L. Armstrong) It's Not About the Bike: My Journey Back to Life, 2000; (with M. Runyan) No Finish Line: My Life as I See It, 2001; (with L. Armstrong) Every Second Counts, 2003; (co-author) Funny Cide: How a Horse, a Trainer, a Jockey, and a Bunch of High School Buddies Took on the Sheiks and Blue Bloods and Won, 2004; Real all Americans: The Team that Changed a Game, a People, a Nation, 2007; (with J. Stauffer) The State of Jones, 2009; (with L. Anne and S. Tuohy) In a Heartbeat: Sharing the Power of Cheerful Giving, 2010. **Address:** Washington Post, 1150 15th St. NW, Washington, DC 20071, U.S.A. **Online address:** jenkinss@washpost.com

JENKINS, Simon. British (born England), b. 1943. **Genres:** Environmental Sciences/Ecology, Urban Studies, Writing/Journalism. **Career:** Country Life Magazine, editorial assistant, 1965; Times Educational Supplement, news editor, 1966-68; London Evening Standard, staff, 1968-74, features editor, 1972-74, deputy editor, 1976, editor, 1977-78, columnist; Sunday Times, insight editor, 1974-75, columnist, 1986-90, through 2008; British Railways, board director, 1979-90; The Economist, political editor, 1979-86; London Transport, director, 1984-86; Historic Buildings and Monuments Commission, deputy chairman, 1988-90, millennium commissioner, 1994-; The Times, editor, 1990-92, columnist, 1992-, commentator; The Guardian, journalist, columnist; Huffington Post, contributor, 2005-; National Trust, chair, 2008-. **Publications:** Conservatives and Comprehensives, 1967; (with B. van Straubenzee) Student Loans: Pros and Cons, 1968; Education and Labour's Axe, 1969; Putting the Goats with the Sheep, 1969; City at Risk, 1970; Here to Live: Study of Race Relations in an English Town, 1971; Landlords to London: The Story of a Capital and Its Growth, 1975; (ed.) Insight on Portugal, 1975; Newspapers: The Power and the Money, 1979; Images of Hampstead, 1982; (with M. Hastings) The Battle for the Falklands, 1983; Companion Guide to Outer London, 1984; (with A. Sloman) With Respect, Ambassador: An Inquiry into the Foreign Office, 1985; The Market for Glory: Fleet Street Ownership in the Twentieth Century, 1986; The Times Guide to English Style and Usage, 1992; The Selling of Mary Davies and Other Writings, 1993; Against the Grain: Writings of a Sceptical Optimist, 1994; Accountable to None: The Tory Nationalization of Britain, 1995; England's Thousand Best Churches, 2000; England's Thousand Best Houses, 2003; Big Bang Localism, 2004; Thatcher & Sons-A Revolution in Three Acts Penguin, 2006. **Address:** Th Guardian, 119 Farringdon Rd., London, GL EC1R 3ER, England. **Online address:** simon.jenkins@guardian.co.uk

JENKINS, Steven. (Steven W. Jenkins). American (born United States), b. 1950. **Genres:** Food And Wine. **Career:** Dean & Deluca, general manager, 1977-79; Fairway Market, general manager, 1980-88, partner, 1996-. Writer. **Publications:** Cheese Primer, 1996; The Food Life, 2008. **Address:** Fairway Markets, 2328 12th Ave., New York, NY 10027, U.S.A. **Online address:** steven.jenkins@fairwaymarket.com

JENKINS, Steven W. See **JENKINS, Steven.**

JENKINS, T(erence) A(ndrew). British (born England), b. 1958. **Genres:** History, Politics/Government, Young Adult Fiction, Adult Non-fiction. **Career:** Cambridge University, British Academy, postdoctoral fellow, 1987-90; University of East Anglia, lecturer, 1990-91; University of Exeter, lecturer, 1991-92; University of East Anglia, lecturer, 1992-94, 1995-96; University of Bristol, lecturer, 1996-97; History of Parliament, senior researcher officer, 1998-. Writer. **Publications:** Gladstone, Whiggery and the Liberal party, 1874-1886, 1988; The Liberal Ascendancy, 1830-1886, 1994; Disraeli and Victorian Conservatism, 1996; Parliament, Party and Politics in Victorian Britain, 1996; Disraeli and Victorian Conservatism, 1996; Sir Robert Peel, 1999; Britain: A Short History, 2001. EDITOR: The Parliamentary Diaries of Sir John Trelawny, 1858-1865, 1990; The Parliamentary Diaries of Sir John Trelawny, 1868-1873, 1994. Contributor to periodicals. **Address:** History of Parliament, Wedgwood House, 15 Woburn Sq., London, GL WC1H 0NS, England. **Online address:** tjenkins@histparl.ac.uk

JENKINS, Virginia Scott. American (born United States), b. 1948. **Genres:** Horticulture, Advertising/Public Relations, Cultural/Ethnic Topics, Environmental Sciences/Ecology, Food And Wine, History, Technology, Adult Non-fiction, Adult Non-fiction. **Career:** Harvard University Graduate School of Design, staff assistant to the registrar, 1973-75; Mount Auburn Hospital, planning assistant, staff assistant and assistant director of development, 1975-83; consultant, 1984-; George Washington University, teaching assistant and

university fellow of American studies program, 1986-89, university fellow of history department, 1988-89, American Studies Program, research associate, 1992-93; Henry Francis duPont Winterthur Museum and Library, research fellow, 1993; U.S. Department of Agriculture Graduate School, instructor in history, 1993; Catholic University of America, lecturer in history, 1995-; University of Maryland, visiting assistant professor in American studies, 1996-99; Chesapeake College, instructor in ESL, 2003-06; Dorchester County Department of Education, instructor in GED. Writer. **Publications:** The Lawn: A History of an American Obsession, 1994; Bananas: An American History, 2000. Contributor to books and periodicals. **Address:** 315 Oakley St., Cambridge, MD 21613, U.S.A. **Online address:** virginiajenkins@earthlink.net

JENKINSON, Bill. American (born United States), b. 1947?. **Genres:** Sports/Fitness. **Career:** The Baseball Hall of Fame, consultant; Major League Baseball, consultant; The Society for American Baseball Research, consultant; The Babe Ruth Museum, consultant; ESPN, consultant. Writer and Sports historian. **Publications:** The Year Babe Ruth Hit 104 Home Runs: Recrowning Baseball's Greatest Slugger, 2007; Baseball's Ultimate Power: Ranking the All-Time Greatest Distance Home Run Hitters, 2010. **Address:** James Fitzgerald Agency, 80 E 11th St., Ste. 301, New York, NY 10003-6000, U.S.A.

JENNAWAY, Megan. Australian (born Australia), b. 1958. **Genres:** Young Adult Non-fiction. **Career:** University of Queensland Medical School, Australian Centre for International and Tropical Health and Nutrition, casual lecturer, 1996-97; University of Queensland, School of Asian Languages and Studies, associate lecturer, 1998-2000, School of Languages and Comparative Cultural Studies, honorary research advisor, 2001-04, School of Population Health, Indigenous Health Program, lecturer, 2002; Queensland University of Technology, Creative Industries Research and Allocations Center, postdoctoral re-entry fellow, 2003-05, research fellow, 2005; University of Queensland, School of Population Health, lecturer, 2006-. Writer. **Publications:** Sisters and Lovers: Women and Desire in Bali (nonfiction), 2002. Contributor to books and journals. **Address:** School of Population Health, University of Queensland, Level 2, Public Health Bldg., Herston Rd., Herston, QL 4006, Australia. **Online address:** m.jennaway@sph.uq.edu.au

JENNINGS, Charles. British (born England), b. 1956?. **Genres:** Documentaries/Reportage, Humor/Satire. **Career:** Journalist. **Publications:** The Confidence Trick: The City's Progress from Big Bang to Great Crash, 1988; Up North: Travels Beyond the Watford Gap, 1995; (with P. York) Peter York's Eighties, 1995; Up North, 1996; People Like Us: A Season Among the Upper Classes, 1997; Greenwich: The Place Where Days Begin and End, 2001; Faintheart: An Englishman Ventures North of the Border, 2002; The Fast Set, 2005; Burning Rubber: The Extraordinary Story of Formula One, 2010. Contributor to periodicals. **Address:** Abacus/Little Brown, Brettenham House, Lancaster Pl., London, GL WC2E 7EN, England.

JENNINGS, Dana. See **JENNINGS, Dana Andrew.**

JENNINGS, Dana Andrew. (Dana Jennings). American (born United States), b. 1957. **Genres:** Novels, Children's Fiction. **Career:** Wall Street Journal, editor and writer, 1983-91; New York Times, editor and writer, 1993-. **Publications:** Mosquito Games, 1989; Women of Granite, 1992; Lonesome Standard Time, 1996; Me, Dad, and No. 6 (children's fiction), 1997; Sing Me Back Home: Love, Death, and Country Music, 2008; What a Difference a Dog Makes: Big Lessons on Life, Love and Healing from a Small Pooch, 2010. Contributor to periodicals. **Address:** The New York Times Co., 620 Eighth Ave., New York, NY 10018, U.S.A.

JENNINGS, Judith. American (born United States), b. 1947. **Genres:** History. **Career:** Kentucky Humanities Council, associate director; Appalshop Arts and Education Center, fundraiser; University of Louisville, founding director of the women's center; Kentucky Foundation for Women, executive director; Grant Makers in the Arts, board director. Writer. **Publications:** Why Work?, 1989; (ed.) The Business of Abolishing the British Slave Trade, 1783-1807, 1997; Gender, Religion, and Radicalism in the Long Eighteenth Century: The Ingenious Quaker and Her Connections, 2006. **Address:** U.S.A. **Online address:** judi@kfw.org

JENNINGS, Kate. American/Australian (born Australia), b. 1948. **Genres:** Novels, Novellas/Short Stories, Poetry, Essays, Biography, Animals/Pets, Homes/Gardens. **Career:** Writer. **Publications:** Come to Me My Melancholy

Baby (poetry), 1975; (ed.) Mother, I'm Rooted: An Anthology of Australian Women Poets, 1975; Save Me, Joe Louis (essays), 1988; Women Falling Down in the Street (short fiction), 1990; Cats, Dogs and Pitchforks (poems), 1993; Bad Manners (essays), 1993; Snake (novel), 1996; Moral Hazard, 2002; Stanley and Sophie, 2008. Contributor to periodicals. **Address:** c/o Author Mail, HarperCollins Publishers, 10 E 53rd St., 7th Fl., New York, NY 10022, U.S.A. **Online address:** kjennings@att.net

JENNINGS, Maureen. Canadian/British (born England) **Genres:** Novels, Young Adult Fiction, Literary Criticism And History. **Career:** Ryerson Polytechnical Institute, teacher of English, 1964-72; psychotherapist in private practice, 1972-. Writer. **Publications:** WILLIAM MURDOCH MYSTERY SERIES: Except the Dying, 1997; Under the Dragon's Tail, 1998; Poor Tom Is Cold, 2001; Let Loose the Dogs, 2003; Night's Child, 2005; Vices of My Blood, 2006; A Journeyman to Grief, 2007. CHRISTINE MORRIS MYSTERY SERIES: Does Your Mother Know?, 2006; K Hand Shape, 2008; Season of Darkness, 2011. OTHERS: The Map of Your Mind: Journeys Into Creative Expression, 2001. **Address:** The Cooke Agency Intl., 366 Adelaide St. E, Ste. 501, Toronto, ON M5A 3X9, Canada. **Online address:** jenford@sympatico.ca

JENNINGS, Patrick. American (born United States), b. 1962. **Genres:** Children's Fiction. **Career:** San Cristobal de las Casas, educator, 1991-96; Writer, 1991-; Copper Queen Library, library technician, 1994, library assistant. **Publications:** Faith and the Electric Dogs, 1996; Faith and the Rocket Cat, 1998; Putnam and Pennyroyal, 1999; The Beastly Arms, 2001; The Wolving Time, 2003; Out Standing in My Field, 2005; Friends, 2005; Wish Riders, 2006; Barb and Dingbat's Crybaby Hotline, 2007; We Can't All Be Rattlesnakes, 2009; Guinea Dog, 2010; Lucky Cap, 2011. IKE AND MEM: The Bird Shadow, 2001; The Tornado Watches, 2002; The Weeping Willow, 2002; The Lightning Bugs, 2003; The Ears of Corn, 2003; The Pup Tent, 2005. **Address:** PO Box 1527, Port Townsend, WA 98368, U.S.A. **Online address:** pjennings@patrickjennings.com

JENNINGS, Paul. Australian/British (born England), b. 1943. **Genres:** Young Adult Fiction, Young Adult Non-fiction, Children's Non-fiction, Children's Fiction, Picture/Board Books, Novels. **Career:** Speech pathologist and special education teacher, 1963-68; Australian Ministry of Education, speech pathologist, 1972-75; Burwood State College, lecturer in special education, 1976-78; Warrnambool Institute of Adult Education, senior lecturer, 1979-88; full-time writer, 1989-. **Publications:** Unbelievable! More Surprising Stories, 1986; Quirky Tails! More Oddball Stories, 1987; The Cabbage Patch Fib, 1988; The Paw Thing, 1989; Round the Twist, 1990; The Naked Ghost, Burp! and Blue Jam, 1991; Uncanny! Even More Surprising Stories, 1991; Unreal! Eight Surprising Stories, 1991; Unmentionable!: More Amazing Stories, 1993; Round the Twist 1: Featuring Pink Bow Tie and Nails, 1993; The Gizmo, 1994; The Gizmo Again, 1995; Undone! More Mad Endings, 1995; Unbearable! More Bizarre Stories, 1995; Uncovered!: Weird, Weird Stories, 1996; The Cabbage Patch War, 1996; Come Back Gizmo, 1996; Thirteen! Unpredictable Tales from Paul Jennings, 1996; Sink the Gizmo, 1997; (with M. Gleitzman) Wicked! A Novel in Six Parts, 1997; Singenpoo Strikes Again, 1998; Covered with Nails and Other Stories to Shock You Silly, 1998; Unseen!, 1998; Listen Ear and Other Stories to Shock You Silly, 1998; Singenpoo Shoots Through, 1999; (with Gleitzman) Totally Wicked!, 1999; Sucked In, 2000; The Paul Jennings Superdiary 2002, 2001; Singenpoo's Secret Weapon, 2001; Uncollected, 2002; Tongue-Tied, 2002; Spit it Out, 2004; How Hedley Hopkins Did a Dare, Robbed a Grave, Made a New Friend Who might Not Have Really been There at All and while He was at It Committed a Terrible Sin which Everyone was Doing even though He didn't Know It, 2005; Uncooked!: Three Stories, 2005; Funniest Stories, 2005; Deadly, 2005; Little Rascal to the Rescue, 2006; Rascal in Trouble, 2006; Rascal's Trick, 2007; Rascal the Dragon, 2007; Rascal Takes Off, 2007; Rascal and the Cheese, 2008; Rascal at the Show, 2008; Weirdest Stories, 2008; The Cabbage Patch Fibs, 2008; Spookiest Stories, 2008; Rascal and Little Flora, 2009; Rascal Plays Up, 2009; The Many Adventures of Singenpoo, 2009; Trickiest Stories, 2009; Trickiest Stories, 2009; Rascal and the Hot Air Balloon, 2009; Rascal and the Bad Smell, 2010; Rascal's Shadow, 2010; Rascal and the Bad Smell, 2010; The Fantastic and Amazing Gizmo, 2010; Rascal and the Monster, 2010; Rascal Goes Fishing, 2010; Rascal Runs Away, 2010; Rascal Bumps His Head, 2011; Rascal and the Dragon Droppings, 2011; Rascal Bumps His Head, 2011; The Nest, 2011; Rascal's Big Day, 2011. PICTURE BOOKS: Teacher Eater, 1991; Grandad's Gifts, 1992; The Fisherman and the Theefyspray, 1994. FUN WORD GAME BOOKS;

(with T. Greenwood and T. Denton) Spooner or Later, 1992; (with Greenwood and Denton) Duck for Cover, 1994; (with Greenwood and Denton) Freeze a Crowd, 1996. Works appear in anthologies. **Address:** c/o Author Mail, Penguin Group, 250 Camberwell Rd., Camberwell, VI 3124, Australia. **Online address:** bookshop@pauljennings.com.au

JENNINGS, Phillip E. American (born United States) **Genres:** Novels, Literary Criticism And History, Young Adult Fiction. **Career:** Mayfair Capital Partners, chief executive officer, 1984-; Teleres, founder and chief executive officer; Apartment and Commercial Technology (later Darwin Networks), founder and chief executive officer; Soufun.com, co-founder; Brazil Gold Corp., vice president of corporate development, president and chief operating officer; FirstForge Capital L.L.C., co-founder and managing director for business development. Writer. **Publications:** Nam-a-Rama, 2005; Goodbye Mexico, 2007; Politically Incorrect Guide to the Vietnam War, 2010. Contributor to periodicals. **Address:** c/o Author Mail, Forge Books, 175 5th Ave., New York, NY 10010-7703, U.S.A. **Online address:** pjennings@firstforgecapital.com

JENSEN, Arthur Robert. American (born United States), b. 1923. **Genres:** Education, Psychology, Adult Non-fiction, Medicine/Health, Sciences. **Career:** University of Maryland, Psychiatric Institute, assistant in medical psychology, 1955-56; University of London, Institute of Psychiatry, U.S. Public Health Service research fellow, 1956-58; University of California, Graduate School of Education, assistant professor, 1958-62, associate professor, 1962-66, professor of educational psychology, 1956-92, professor emeritus, 1992-, Institute of Human Learning, research psychologist, 1962-94. Writer. **Publications:** Aggression in Fantasy and Overt Behavior, 1957; (with P.M. Symonds) From Adolescent to Adult, 1961; Individual Differences in Learning: Interference Factor, 1964; (ed. with M. Deutsch and I. Katz) Social Class, Race and Psychological Development, 1968; Parent and Teacher Attitudes toward Integration and Busing, 1970; Genetics and Education, 1972; Educability and Group Differences, 1973; Educational Differences, 1973; (contrib.) The Psychologists, vol. II, 1974; Bias in Mental Testing, 1980; (contrib.) Cognitive Basis of the Intellect: A Response to Jensen's Bias in Mental Testing, 1981; Straight Talk about Mental Tests, 1981; (contrib.) Consensus and Controversy, 1987; The G Factor: The Science of Mental Ability, 1998; Intelligence, Race and Genetics: Conversations with Arthur R. Jensen, 2002; The Scientific Study of General Intelligence, 2003; Clocking the Mind: Mental Chronometry and Individual Differences, 2006. Contributor to journals. **Address:** Graduate School of Education, University of California, 4511 Tolman Hall, Berkeley, CA 94720-1670, U.S.A. **Online address:** jep@socrates.berkeley.edu

JENSEN, Clayne. American (born United States), b. 1930. **Genres:** Administration/Management, Recreation, Sports/Fitness, Adult Non-fiction. **Career:** Utah State University, instructor, associate professor of physical education, 1956-64; Utah Recreation and Parks Association, executive director, 1958-63; Utah Inter-Agency Council for Recreation and Parks, executive director, 1962-65; Brigham Young University, associate professor and coordinator of college programs, 1965-67, professor and associate dean, 1968-74, College of Physical Education/Athletics, dean, 1974-92, associate vice president, 1992-95, director of athletics, professor emeritus. Writer. **Publications:** (With V.S. Barney and C.C. Hirst) Conditioning Exercises: Exercises to Improve Body Form and Function, 1965, 3rd ed., 1972; (with M.B. Jensen) Beginning Folk Dancing, 1966; (with M.B. Jensen) Beginning Square Dance, 1966; (with G. Howard and K. Tucker) Skiing, 1968, 4th ed., 1983; (co-author) To Improve Body Form and Function, 1968, 3rd ed., 1977; (G.W. Schultz) Applied Kinesiology: The Scientific Study of Human Performance, 1970, 3rd ed., 1983; Outdoor Recreation in America: Trends, Problems and Opportunities, 1970, 6th ed., 2006; (co-author) Measurement and Statistics in Physical Education, 1971, 3rd ed., 1989; (with A.G. Fisher) Scientific Basis of Athletic Conditioning, 1972, 3rd ed., 1990; (comp. with C. Thorstenson) Issues in Outdoor Recreation, 1972; (with M.B. Jensen) Square Dancing, 1973; (with M.B. Jensen) Square Dance, 1973; (with M.B. Jensen) Folk Dancing, 1973; (with C. Robison) Modern Track and Field Coaching Technique, 1974; Recreation and Leisure Time Careers, 1976; Winter Touring: Cross-Country Skiing and Snowshoeing, 1977; Leisure and Recreation: Introduction and Overview, 1977; (with C.C. Hirst) Measurement in Physical Education and Athletics, 1980; (with C. Jensen) Backpacking for Fun & Fitness, 1981; (with G.W. Schultz and B.L. Bangerter) Applied Kinesiology and Biomechanics, 1983; (with J.H. Naylor) Opportunities in Recreation and Leisure Careers, 2000, rev. ed., 2005; Administrative Management of Physical Education and Athletic Programs, 1982, 4th ed. as Administration and Management of Physical Education and Athletic Programs, 2003. **Address:** Waveland Press Inc., 4180 IL, Rte. 83, Ste. 101, Long Grove, IL 60047, U.S.A.

JENSEN, David H. (David Hadley Jensen). American (born United States), b. 1968. **Genres:** Theology/Religion. **Career:** Manchester College, assistant professor of religion and philosophy, through 2001; Austin Presbyterian Theological Seminary, associate professor of constructive theology, 2001-. Theologian and writer. **Publications:** In the Company of Others: A Dialogical Christology, 2001; Graced Vulnerability: A Theology of Childhood, 2005; Responsive Labor: A Theology of Work, 2006; (ed.) The Lord and Giver of Life: Perspectives on Constructive Pneumatology, 2008. **Address:** Austin Presbyterian Theological Seminary, 100 E 27th St., Austin, TX 78705-5711, U.S.A. **Online address:** djensen@austinseminary.edu

JENSEN, David Hadley. See **JENSEN, David H.**

JENSEN, Derrick. American (born United States), b. 1960. **Genres:** Cultural/Ethnic Topics. **Career:** Writer, educator and activist. **Publications:** Listening to the Land: Conversations About Nature, Culture, and Eros, 1995; (with G. Draffan and J. Osborn) Railroads and Clearcuts: Legacy of Congress's 1864 Northern Pacific Railroad Land Grant, 1995; A Language Older than Words, 2000; The Culture of Make Believe, 2002; (with G. Draffan) Strangely Like War: The Global Assault on Forests, 2003; Walking on Water: Reading, Writing, and Revolution, 2004; (with G. Draffan) Welcome to the Machine: Science, Surveillance, and the Culture of Control, 2004; Endgame, 2006; Thought to Exist in the Wild, 2007; (with S. McMillan) As the World Burns: 50 Simple Things You Can Do to Stay in Denial, 2007; How Shall I Live My Life?: On Liberating the World from Civilization, 2008; (with A. McBay) What We Leave Behind, 2009; Songs of the Dead, 2009; Resistance Against Empire, 2010; Lives Less Valuable, 2010; (with S. McMillan) Mischief in the Forest, 2010; (with A. McBay and L. Keith) Deep Green Resistance, 2011; Dreams, 2011; Truths Among Us, 2011. **Address:** PO Box 903, Crescent City, CA 95531, U.S.A. **Online address:** derrick@derrickjensen.org

JENSEN, Ejner J. American (born United States), b. 1937. **Genres:** Literary Criticism And History. **Career:** University of Michigan, instructor, assistant professor, professor of English, 1964-2004, professor emeritus, 2004-, director, Sweetland Writing Center, director. Writer. **Publications:** John Marston, Dramatist: Themes and Imagery in the Plays, 1979; (ed.) The Future of Nineteen Eighty-Four, 1984; Ben Jonson's Comedies on the Modern Stage, 1985; Shakespeare and the Ends of Comedy, 1991. **Address:** Department of English Language & Literature, University of Michigan, 3187 Angell Hall, 435 S State St., Ann Arbor, MI 48109-1003, U.S.A. **Online address:** ejjensen@umich.edu

JENSEN, Emma. American (born United States) **Genres:** Romance/Historical, Novels, Young Adult Fiction, Novellas/Short Stories. **Career:** Writer. **Publications:** Choice Deceptions, 1996; Coup de Grace, 1996; Vivid Notions, 1996; What Chloe Wants, 1996; Entwined, 1997; Best Laid Schemes, 1998; His Grace Endures, 1998; The Irish Rogue, 1999; A Grand Design, 2000; Fallen, 2001; (co-author) Regency Christmas Spirits, 2001; Moonlit, 2002; (co-author) Regency Christmas Wishes: Five Stories, 2003; (co-author) A Homespun Regency Christmas, 2008. **Address:** c/o Author Mail, Ballantine Publishing Group, 1540 Broadway, New York, NY 10036, U.S.A.

JENSEN, Erik. American (born United States), b. 1970?. **Genres:** Plays/Screenplays, Law, Social Sciences. **Career:** Actor, producer and writer. **Publications:** WITH J. BLANK: The Exonerated (play), 2004; Living Justice: Love, Freedom, and the Making of the Exonerated, 2005. **Address:** c/o Author Mail, Atria Books, 1230 Ave. of the Americas, New York, NY 10020-1513, U.S.A. **Online address:** theexonerated@aol.com

JENSEN, Geoffrey. (Robert Geoffrey Jensen). American (born United States), b. 1965. **Genres:** Military/Defense/Arms Control, Technology, History. **Career:** Virginia Military Institute, John Biggs '30 Cincinnati Chair in Military History. Writer. **Publications:** (ed. with A. Wiest) War in the Age of Technology: Myriad Faces of Modern Armed Conflict, 2001; Irrational Triumph: Cultural Despair, Military Nationalism, and the Ideological Origins of Franco's Spain, 2002; Franco: Soldier, Commander, Dictator, 2005; (ed.) Warfare in Europe, 1919-1938, 2008. **Address:** Department of History, Virginia Military Institute, 536 Scott Shipp Hall, Lexington, VA 24450, U.S.A. **Online address:** jensenrg@vmi.edu

JENSEN, Kathryn. Also writes as Kathryn Mary Jensen, Nicole Davidson. American (born United States), b. 1949. **Genres:** Young Adult Fiction, Novels, Romance/Historical, Human Relations/Parenting. **Career:** Writer, 1975-; University of Pennsylvania, The Publishing Institute, instructor, 1988-89; Johns Hopkins University, lecturer and seminar leader, 1990-; Institute of Children's Literature, instructor, 1992-; Columbia Literary Associates Inc., part-time literary agent, 1992-. **Publications:** CHRISMA INC SERIES: Breathless, 1988; (with A. Leonhardt) Risky Venture, 1989; (with R. Glick) The Big Score, 1989; (with R. Glick) Nightstalker, 1989. LOOP SERIES: Getting a Life: Marissa, 1994; Getting Real: Christopher, 1994; Getting a Grip: Dig, 1995. AS NICOLE DAVIDSON: Crash Course, 1990; Winterkill, 1991; Demon's Beach, 1992; The Stalker, 1992; Fan Mail, 1993; Surprise Party, 1993; Night Terrors, 1994; Final Kiss, 1995; Kiss of Death, 1995; Farewell Kiss, 1995; Dying to Dance, 1996; Crash Landing, 1996. OTHERS: The Revenge of the Ghostosaurs, 1987; Select Circles, 1987; Pocket Change, 1989; Sing to Me, Saigon, 1994; Couples, 1995; Time and Again, 1995; Angel's Child, 1996; The Twelve-Month Marriage, 1997; (co-author) Be Mine, 1997; I Married a Prince, 1997; The Earl Takes a Bride, 2000; Mail-order Cinderella, 2000; The Earl's Secret, 2001; The American Earl, 2001; Just One Touch, 2001; The Secret Prince, 2002; Business or Pleasure?, 2002; Mail-Order Prince in Her Bed, 2003; The Royal and the Runaway Bride, 2003; The Secret Prince, 2003; Hot Pursuit, 2005; The Boss Man's Fortune, 2005; Her Last Defense, 2005; Seduced By a Prince, 2008; The Gentleman Poet, 2010. **Address:** c/o Linda Hayes, Columbia Literary Associates Inc., 7902 Nottingham Way, Ellicott City, MD 21043-6721, U.S.A. **Online address:**

JENSEN, Kathryn Mary. See **JENSEN, Kathryn.**

JENSEN, Kim. American (born United States), b. 1966?. **Genres:** Women's Studies And Issues, Literary Criticism And History. **Career:** Community College of Baltimore County, School of Liberal Arts, assistant professor of English, associate professor of English. Writer. **Publications:** The Woman I Left Behind: A Novel, 2006; Bread Alone, 2009. Contributor to periodicals. **Address:** Department of English, School of Liberal Arts, Community College of Baltimore County, E-326, 7201 Rossville Blvd., Baltimore, MD 21237-3855, U.S.A. **Online address:** jensenkim@msn.com

JENSEN, Muriel. American (born United States), b. 1945. **Genres:** Romance/Historical, Novels, Adult Non-fiction, Young Adult Fiction. **Career:** Writer. **Publications:** ROMANCE NOVELS: Winter's Bounty, 1984; Lovers Never Lose, 1985; Fantasies and Memories, 1987; Love and Lavender, 1987; The Mallory Touch, 1987; Strings, 1988; The Duck Shack Agreement, 1988; Carol Christmas, 1989; Side by Side, 1989; A Wild Iris, 1990; Everything, 1990; Trust a Hero, 1990; Bridge to Yesterday, 1991; Fantasies and Memories, Silhouette, 1991; The Miracle, 1991; Racing With the Moon, 1991; In Good Time, 1992; Middle of the Rainbow, 1992; Milky Way, 1992; Valentine Hearts and Flowers, 1992; The Unexpected Groom, 1993; Trust, 1993; Candy Kisses, 1994; Make-Believe Mom, 1994; Night Prince, 1994; The Wedding Gamble, 1994; A Bride for Adam, 1994; The Courtship of Dusty's Daddy, 1995; Make Way for Mommy, 1995; Merry Christmas, Mommy, 1995; Mommy on Board, 1995; The Comeback Mom, 1996; Husband in a Hurry, 1996; Christmas in the Country, 1997; Love by Chocolate, 1997; The Fraudulent Fiancee, 1997; The Heart of the Matter Yours Truly, 1997; Kids and Co., 1997; Hot Pursuit (Hometown Reunion), 1997; The Little Matchmaker, 1997; The Prince, the Lady and the Tower, 1997; Undercover Mom, 1997; One and One Makes Three, 1998; Gout de Passion, 1998; Daddy by Design, 1998; Daddy by Destiny, 1998; Gift-Wrapped Dad/Christmas Is for Kids, 1998; Knock Three Times, 1998; His Bodyguard, 1999; Countdown to Baby, 1999; The Third Wise Man, 1999; Home to You, 2000; Four Reasons for Fatherhood, 2000; Father Fever, 2000; Bride by Surprise, 2000; Father Formula, 2001; Billion Dollar Bride, 2001; Father Found, 2001; (with J. Arnold and B. Hutchinson) All Summer Long, 2001; Daddy to Be Determined, 2001; (with S. Cameron) Shadows/Daddy in Demand, 2001; Mommy and Me, 2001; (with J. Cresswell) Marriage on the Run/The Little Matchmaker, 2002; Man with a Message, 2002; Man with a Miracle, 2002; Man with a Mission, 2002; Daddy by Default: Who's the Daddy, 2003; Reinventing Julia, 2003; (with K. Rolofson and K. Gabriel) Date with Destiny, 2003; For the Love of Mike!, 2003; Jackpot Baby, 2003; That Summer in Maine, 2003; Man in a Million, 2003; (with A. Stuart and C. Addir) Date with a Devil: Better the Devil You Know, 2004; The Man She Married, 2004; His Baby, 2004; The Man Under the Mistletoe, 2004; His Wife, 2004; His Wedding, 2005; Season of Shadows, 2005; His Family, 2005. Contributor to books. **Address:** 659 15th St., Astoria, OR 97103, U.S.A. **Online address:** romance@pacifier.com

JENSEN, Nathan M. American (born United States), b. 1975. **Genres:** Economics, Business/Trade/Industry, Politics/Government. **Career:** Washington University, Center for Political Economy, fellow, 2002-, assistant professor of political science, 2002-08, associate professor of political science, 2008-, Weidenbaum Center, Program on Multinational Enterprises and the Global Economy, director and senior fellow, 2008-, associate professor in international and area studies, 2010-; University of California, fellow, 2005-06. Writer. **Publications:** Nation-States and the Multinational Corporation: A Political Economy of Foreign Direct Investment, 2006. Contributor to periodicals. **Address:** Department of Political Science, Washington University, 219 Eliot Hall, 1 Brookings Dr., St. Louis, MO 63130-4899, U.S.A. **Online address:** njensen@artsci.wustl.edu

JENSEN, Robert Geoffrey. See **JENSEN, Geoffrey.**

JENSEN, Ruby Jean. (R. J. Hendrickson). American (born United States) **Genres:** Horror, Novels, Young Adult Fiction. **Career:** Writer. **Publications:** NOVELS: The House That Samael Built, 1974; Seventh All Hallows' Eve, 1974; The Girl Who Didn't Die, 1975; House at River's Bend, 1975; Satan's Sister, 1978; Child of Satan House, 1978; Dark Angel, 1978; (as R.J. Hendrickson) Hear the Children Cry, 1981; Such a Good Baby, 1982; The Lake, 1983; Mama, 1983; Home Sweet Home, 1985; Best Friends, 1985; Wait and See, 1986; Annabelle, 1987; Chain Letter, 1987; Smoke, 1987; House of Illusions, 1988; Jump Rope, 1988; Pendulum, 1989; Death Stone, 1989; Vampire Child, 1990; Lost and Found, 1990; Victoria, 1990; Celia, 1991; Baby Dolly, 1991; The Reckoning, 1992; Living Doll, 1993; The Living Evil, 1993; The Haunting, 1994; Night Thunder, 1995. Contributor of articles to periodicals. **Address:** Publicity Director, Zebra Books, 850 3rd Ave., New York, NY 10022-6222, U.S.A.

JENSEN, Vickie (Dee). Canadian/American (born United States), b. 1946. **Genres:** Children's Non-fiction, Language/Linguistics, Technology, Social Sciences, History, Politics/Government. **Career:** English Valleys School District, English teacher, 1971-72; Sioux Falls Continuing Education Centre, instructor, 1971-72; Sioux Falls Public School System, English teacher, 1972; Vancouver Image Exploration Workshops, photography instructor, 1974-78, B.C. Photographer, contributing editor, 1974-76; Native Language Education Projects, author, photographer and curriculum designer, 1975-86; U'mista Cultural Centre and North Island Community College, instructor, 1983-85; Westcoast Mariner, editor, 1987-91; Simon Fraser University, Native Education Program, instructor, 1993. Writer. **Publications:** (With C. McLaren) Hunqum'i'num' for Kids: Books 1-3, 1975; (with C. McLaren) Quileute for Kids, vol. I-III, 1975-76; (with J. Powell) Quileute: An Introduction to the Indians of La Push, 1976; (with J. Powell) Gitksan for Kids, vol. I-VII, 1977-80; (with J. Powell) Let's Study Shuswap: Books1-2, 1979; (with J. Powell) Learning Shuswap, vol. I-II, 1980; (with J. Powell) Learning Gitksan, vol. I-IV, 1980; (with J. Powell) Learning Kwa'kwala, vol. I-XII, 1980-82; (with J. Powell) Gitksan Teachers Manual, 1981; (with J. Powell and J. Wild) Shuswap Teachers Manual, 1983; Where the People Gather: Carving a Totem Pole, 1992; Saltwater Women at Work: True-Life Accounts from Over 110 Women Mariners, 1995; Carving a Totem Pole (children's book), 1996; Working These Waters, 1996; (with H. Bohm) Build Your Own Underwater Robot and Other Wet Projects, 1997; Totem Pole Carving, 1999; (with T.A. McLaren) Ships of Steel: A British Columbia Shipbuilder's Story, 2000; Why Women Kill: Homicide and Gender Equality, 2001; (with H. Bohm) Introduction to Underwater Technology and Vehicle Design, 2002; Totem Pole Carving: Bringing a Log to Life, 2004; Totem Poles of Stanley Park, 2004. **Address:** 3036 Waterloo St., Vancouver, BC V6R 3J6, Canada.

JENSON-ELLIOTT, Cindy. See **JENSON-ELLIOTT, Cynthia L(ouise).**

JENSON-ELLIOTT, Cynthia L(ouise). (Cindy Jenson-Elliott). American (born United States), b. 1962. **Genres:** Children's Non-fiction, Natural History. **Career:** Cuyamaca Outdoor School, outdoor educator; Girl Scouts, education program coordinator. Writer. **Publications:** (With L.C. Wood) Cheetahs, 1991; East Africa, 2002; Southern Africa, 2003; Zombies, 2006; Weeds Find a Way, 2013. AS CINDY JENSON-ELLIOTT: Camping, 2012; Fly Fishing, 2012; Life under the Pirate Code, 2013; Most Famous Pirates, 2013; Pirates' Tools for Life at Sea, 2013; Pirate Ships Ahoy!, 2013. **Address:** c/o Author Mail, Lucent Books, 15822 Bernardo Center Dr., San Diego, CA 92127-2320, U.S.A. **Online address:** cjensonelliott@aol.com

JEPPSON, J. O. See **ASIMOV, Janet Jeppson.**

JEPSON, Bryan. American (born United States), b. 1967. **Genres:** Human Relations/Parenting, Medicine/Health. **Career:** Children's Biomedical Center, co-founder and physician, 2002-05; Thoughtful House Center for Children, physician, 2006-, director of medical center; Autism Research Institute, medical coordinator. Writer and researcher. **Publications:** (With J. Johnson) Changing the Course of Autism: A Scientific Approach for Parents and Physicians, 2007. **Address:** Thoughtful House Center for Children, 3001 Bee Caves Rd., Ste. 120, Austin, TX 78746-5590, U.S.A.

JEPSON, Jill. (Jill Christine Jepson). American (born United States), b. 1950. **Genres:** Novels, Essays, Writing/Journalism, Language/Linguistics, Theology/Religion, Cultural/Ethnic Topics, Local History/Rural Topics, Essays, Essays. **Career:** University of Minnesota, Center for Research in Human Learning, research fellow, 1986-87; American Institute of Indian Studies, senior fellow, 1987-88; University of California, Program in Medical Anthropology, research fellow, 1989-93; College of St. Catherine, Department of English, assistant professor, associate professor, 2001-; Writing the Whirlwind, writing and spirituality coach and president, 2007-. Writer. **Publications:** No Walls of Stone: An Anthology of Literature by Deaf and Hard of Hearing Writers, 1992; Writing as a Sacred Path: A Practical Guide to Writing With Passion and Purpose, 2008; Womens Concerns: Twelve Women Entrepreneurs of the Eighteenth and Nineteenth Centuries, 2009. Contributor to magazines and literary journals. **Address:** Department of English, College of St. Catherine, 2004 Randolph Ave., PO Box 4033, St. Paul, MN 55105, U.S.A. **Online address:** jcjepson@stkate.edu

JEPSON, Jill Christine. See **JEPSON, Jill.**

JERAM, Anita. British (born England), b. 1965. **Genres:** Children's Fiction, Illustrations, Animals/Pets. **Career:** Writer. **Publications:** CHILDREN'S BOOKS: Bill's Belly Button, 1991; It Was Jake!, 1991; The Most Obedient Dog in the World, 1994; Contrary Mary, 1995; Daisy Dare, 1995; Birthday Happy, Contrary Mary, 1998; All Together Now, 1999; Bunny, My Honey, 1999; I Love My Little Storybook, 2002; Bunny Love: Two Stories, 2003. Illustrator of books by others. **Address:** c/o Author Mail, Candlewick Press Inc., 2067 Massachusetts Ave., Ste. 5, Cambridge, MA 02140-1339, U.S.A.

JERICHO, Chris. American (born United States), b. 1970. **Genres:** Autobiography/Memoirs, Biography, Sports/Fitness. **Career:** Ash Records, founder. Writer and actor. **Publications:** A Lion's Tale: Around the World in Spandex, 2007; (with P.T. Fornatale) Undisputed: How to become the World Champion in 1,372 Easy Steps, 2011. **Address:** Tampa, FL , U.S.A. **Online address:** messagesforchris@gmail.com

JERMAN, Jerry. American (born United States), b. 1949. **Genres:** Young Adult Fiction, Children's Fiction. **Career:** Almar Bookstore, assistant manager, manager, 1972-74; Oklahoma City University, instructor, 1974-77; The Economy Co., writer/editor, 1978-81; Blue Cross and Blue Shield, technical writer, 1981-82; freelance writer and editor, 1981-89; University of Oklahoma Outreach, College of Liberal Studies, College of Continuing Education, interim director of marketing and communication, director of marketing and communication, promotion and information specialist, 1982-83, assistant to the vice provost, 1983-90, head of marketing, director of marketing, 1990-2002, director of development, 2002-adjunct instructor of humanities; Confluence Magazine, managing editor. **Publications:** THE JOURNEYS OF JESSIE LAND SERIES: The Long Way Home, 1995; My Father, the Horse Thief, 1995; Phantom of the Pueblo, 1995; Danger at Outlaw Creek, 1995; Calamity at the Circus, 1996; The Secret of Whispering Woods, 1996. **Address:** College of Continuing Education, College of Liberal Studies, University of Oklahoma Outreach, 1700 Asp Ave., Norman, OK 73072-6407, U.S.A. **Online address:** jjerman@ou.edu

JERNIGAN, Brenda K. American (born United States) **Genres:** Romance/Historical, Novels, Young Adult Fiction. **Career:** Novelist. **Publications:** HISTORICAL FICTION: The Duke's Lady, 1999; The Wicked Lady, 2000; Love Only Once, 2001; Every Good and Perfect Gift, 2001; Christmas in Camelot, 2002; Dance on the Wind, 2002; Until September, 2003; Whispers on the Wind, 2004; Southern Seduction, 2007; Black Magic, 2011. **Address:** NC , U.S.A. **Online address:** bkj1608@juno.com

JERNIGAN, Gisela (Evelyn). American (born United States), b. 1948.

Genres: Botany, Children's Non-fiction, Education. **Career:** Saint Francis Cabrini Church, lector and commentator, 1976-93, librarian, 1982-93; freelance writer, 1986-; Harbinger House Publishers, freelance editor, 1989-91; University of Arizona, instructor in language, reading and culture, 1993-. **Publications:** One Green Mesquite Tree, 1988; Agave Blooms Just Once, 1989; Sonoran Seasons: A Year in the Desert, 1994. **Address:** 2532 N Columbus Blvd., Tucson, AZ 85712, U.S.A. **Online address:** moundspirits@hotmail.com

JERSILD, Devon. American (born United States), b. 1958. **Genres:** Novellas/Short Stories, Self Help. **Career:** New England Review, associate editor, 1990-94; Middlebury College, Center for Counseling and Human Relations, administrative director, 1994-, counseling staff; Counseling Center of Addison County, psychotherapist. **Publications:** (Ed. with T.R. Hummer) The Unfeigned Word: Fifteen Years of New England Review, 1993; Happy Hours: Alcohol in a Woman's Life, 2001. Contributor of articles to periodicals. **Address:** 1641 Horse Farm Rd., Weybridge, VT 05753, U.S.A. **Online address:** jersild@middlebury.edu

JERVEY, Edward D(rewry). American (born United States), b. 1929. **Genres:** History. **Career:** Lambuth College, associate professor of history, 1958-61; Radford University, associate professor, 1961-63, professor of history, 1963-91, professor emeritus, 1991-. Writer. **Publications:** History of Methodism in Southern California and Arizona, 1960; (ed.) Prison Life among the Rebels: Recollections of a Union Chaplain, 1990. Contributor of articles to periodicals. **Address:** Department of History, Radford University, 801 E Main St., PO Box 6941, Radford, VA 24142, U.S.A. **Online address:** tjed1234@aol.com

JERVIS, Robert. American (born United States), b. 1940. **Genres:** International Relations/Current Affairs, Military/Defense/Arms Control, Politics/Government. **Career:** Harvard University, assistant professor, 1968-72, associate professor of government, 1972-74; Yale University, visiting associate professor of political science, 1974-75; University of California, professor of political science, 1974-80; Hebrew University of Jerusalem, visiting professor, 1977; Columbia University, Department of Political Science, professor of political science, 1980-, Adlai E. Stevenson professor of international politics, 1989-, deputy chair of the political science, School of International and Public Affairs, professor of international and public affairs, Adlai E. Stevenson professor of international affairs, 1989-. Writer. **Publications:** The Logic of Images in International Relations, 1970; (ed. with R.J. Art) International Politics: Anarchy, Force, Imperialism, 1973, 11th ed. as International Politics: Enduring Concepts and Contemporary Issues, 2012; Perception and Misperception in International Politics, 1976; Deterrence Theory Revisited, 1978; Deterrence and Perception, 1982; The Illogic of American Nuclear Strategy, 1984; (with R.N. Lebow and J.G. Stein) Psychology and Deterrence, 1985; The Symbolic Nature of Nuclear Politics, 1987; The Logic of Images in International Relations, 1989; The Meaning of the Nuclear Revolution: Statecraft and the Prospect of Armageddon, 1989; (ed. with S. Bialer) Soviet-American Relations after the Cold War, 1991; (ed. with J. Snyder) Dominoes and Bandwagons: Strategic Beliefs and Great Power Competition in the Eurasian Rimland, 1991; (ed. with J. Snyder) Coping with Complexity in the International System, 1993; System Effects: Complexity in Political and Social Life, 1997; (ed. with D.O. Sears and L. Huddy) Oxford Handbook of Political Psychology, 2003; (ed. and intro. with D. Wetzel and J.S. Levy) Systems, Stability, and Statecraft: Essays on the International History of Modern Europe, 2004; American Foreign Policy in a New Era, 2005; (ed. with L. Kando) Future of U.S. Foreign Policy, 2008; Why Intelligence Fails: Lessons from the Iranian Revolution and the Iraq War, 2010. Contributor to books and periodicals. **Address:** Department of Political Science, Columbia University, Rm. 1333, International Affairs Bldg., 420 W 118th St., 7th Fl., PO Box 3347, New York, NY 10027, U.S.A. **Online address:** rlj1@columbia.edu

JESCHKE, Wolfgang. German/Czech (born Czech Republic), b. 1936. **Genres:** Science Fiction/Fantasy, Novels, Young Adult Non-fiction. **Career:** Kindler Verlag, editor, 1960-69; Kindlers Literaturlexikon, editor, 1969-73; Wilhelm Heyne Verlag, editor, 1973-. **Publications:** Die Anderen, 1959; Der Zeiter (short stories), 1970; The King and the Dollmaker, 1970; A Little More Than Twelve Minutes, 1975; Yeti, 1980; Haike the Heretic's Writings, 1981; Der letzte Tag der Schöpfung (novel): Roman, 1981, trans. as The Last Day of Creation, 1982; Loitering at Death's Door, 1984; Midas (novel), 1987; Schlechte Nachrichten aus dem Vatikan (short stories and radio dramas), 1993; Partners for Life, 1996; Meamones Auge, 1997; Osiris Land, 1997;

Marsfieber, 2003. **Address:** Thomas Schluck Literary Agency, Hinter der Worth 12, Garbsen, 30827, Germany.

JETT, Stephen Clinton. American (born United States), b. 1938. **Genres:** Anthropology/Ethnology, Geography, History, Language/Linguistics, Travel/Exploration, Cultural/Ethnic Topics. **Career:** Ohio State University, instructor, 1963-64; University of California, assistant professor of geography, 1964-72, associate professor, 1972-79, chairman, 1978-82, 1987-89, professor of geography, 1979-2000, professor of textiles and clothing, 1996-2000, professor emeritus of textiles and clothing, 2000-. Writer and researcher. **Publications:** Tourism in the Navajo Country: Resources and Planning, 1966; (with P. Hyde) Navajo Wildlands: As Long as the Rivers Shall Run, 1967; (with D. Bohn) House of Three Turkeys: Anasazi Redoubt, 1977; (with V.E. Spencer) Navajo Architecture: Forms, History, Distributions, 1981; (comp.) A Bibliography of North American Geographers Works on Native Americans North of Mexico, 1917-1991, 1994; Navajo Placenames and Trails of the Canyon de Chelly System, Arizona, 2001; France, 2004. CONTRIBUTOR: Man Across the Sea: Problems of Pre-Columbian Contacts, 1971; Wajin mo Taiheiyo o Watatta: Korombus ijen no Amerika Hakken (The Japanese also Crossed the Pacific: The Discovery of America before Columbus), 1977; Ancient Native Americans, 1978; Navajo Religion and Culture, 1982; Ancient North Americans, 1983; Ancient South Americans, 1983; By Hands Un-known: Papers on Rock Art and Archaeology in Honor of James G. Bain, 1986; A Cultural Geography of North American Indians, 1987; To Build in a New Land: Ethnic Landscapes in North America, 1992; Why Museums Collect: Papers in Honor of Joe Ben Wheat, 1993; Artifacts, Shrines, and Pueblos: Papers in Honor of Gordon Page, 1994; Encyclopedia of Vernacular Architecture of the World, 1997; Baseball, Barns, and Bluegrass: A Geography of American Folklife, 1998; Across before Columbus? Evidence for Transoceanic Contact with the Americas Prior to 1492, 1998; Mormons, Scripture, and the Ancient World: Studies in Honor of John L. Sorenson, 1998; Diné Bíkéyah: Papers in Honor of David M. Brugge, 1998; Tourism and Gaming on American Indian Lands, 1998; After the Encounter: A Continuing Process: Selected Papers and Commenaries from the November 1992 Columbus Quincentenary Symposium, 1999; Homelands: A Geography of Culture and Place across America, 2002; Southwestern Interludes: Papers in Honor of Charlotte J. and Theodore R. Frisbie, 2006; Proceedings of the International Science Conference, Science in Archaeology, 2007; Flowing through Time: Exploring Archaeology through Humans and Their Aquatic Environment, 2008; Landscape in Language. Transdisciplinary Perspectives, 2011. Contributor to periodicals. **Address:** 333 Court St. NE, Abingdon, VA 24210-2921, U.S.A. **Online address:** scjett@hotmail.com

JHABVALA, Ruth Prawer. American/German (born Germany), b. 1927. **Genres:** Novels, Plays/Screenplays, Young Adult Fiction, inspirational/Motivational Literature, Novellas/Short Stories. **Career:** Novelist. **Publications:** Meet Yourself at the Doctor, 1949; To Whom She Will: A Novel, 1955 in US as Amrita: A Novel, 1956; The Nature of Passion: A Novel, 1956; Esmond in India: A Novel, 1958; The Householder, 1960; Get Ready for Battle, 1962; Like Birds, Like Fishes and Other Stories, 1963; A Backward Place, 1965; A Stronger Climate: 9 Stories, 1968; An Experience of India, 1972; A New Dominion, 1972 in US as Travelers, 1973; Heat and Dust, 1975; How I Became a Holy Mother and Other Stories, 1976; In Search of Love and Beauty, 1983; Silence, Exile and Cunning: The Fiction of Ruth Prawer Jhabvala, 1983; Out of India: Selected Stories, 1986; Three Continents, 1987; Poet and Dancer, 1993; Shards of Memory, 1995; East into Upper East: Plain Tales from New York and New Delhi (stories), 1998; My Nine Lives: Chapters of a Possible Past, 2004; A Lovesong For India: Tales from East and West, 2011. Contributor to periodicals. **Address:** 400 E 52nd St., New York, NY 10022-6404, U.S.A.

JIANG, Fuming. Australian/Chinese (born China), b. 1960. **Genres:** Business/Trade/Industry, Marketing. **Career:** Swinburne University of Technology, lecturer and tutor, 1999-2002; Charles Sturt University, faculty of commerce, lecturer in marketing, 2002-04; Australian National University, School of Management, Marketing and International Business, College of Business and Economics, lecturer in international business, 2004-06, senior lecturer, 2006-, deputy head and convenor for international business; University of South Australia, associate professor of strategy and international business, program director, 2009-, Centre for Asian Business, associate director, International Graduate School of Business, acting head; Zhejiang University, Centre for Regional Economic Opening and Development Research, adjunct professorial research fellow; Curtin University of Technology, Curtin Business School Intl., professor of international management, chair in international business and deputy head. Writer. **Publications:** (With G. Kunmo) Guan li jing ji xue, 1984; (with B.W. Stening) The Chinese Business Environment: An Annotated Bibliography, 2006; Foreign Pharmaceutical Firms' FDI Entry Strategies into China, 2006; (ed.) International Strategic Management, 2008; (with B.W. Stening) Doing Business in China: The Challenges for Foreign Firms, 2009. **Address:** Curtin Business School Intl., Curtin University of Technology, Rm. 408.3025, PO Box U1987, Perth, WA 6845, Australia. **Online address:** fuming.jiang@curtin.edu.au

JIANG, Ji li. American/Chinese (born China), b. 1954. **Genres:** Autobiography/Memoirs, History. **Career:** Aston Hotels and Resorts, corporate operations analyst, 1987-92; East West Exchange Inc., co-founder and president, 1992-; University Health System, budgeting director, 1995-96; Cultural Exchange Intl., founder, 2003-. Writer. **Publications:** Red Scarf Girl: A Memoir of the Cultural Revolution, 1997; (reteller) Magical Monkey King: Mischief in Heaven: Classic Chinese Tales, 2002; In My Grandmother's House, 2003. **Address:** East West Exchange Inc., 4 Commodore Dr., Ste. 442, Emeryville, CA 94608-1603, U.S.A. **Online address:** info@jilijiang.com

JIANG, Tao. American (born United States), b. 1969?. **Genres:** Theology/Religion. **Career:** Rutgers University, associate professor and chair of Buddhism and Chinese philosophy. Writer. **Publications:** Contexts and Dialogue: Yogacara Buddhism and Modern Psychology on the Subliminal Mind, 2006. Contributor to books and periodicals. **Address:** Department of Religion, School of Arts & Sciences, Rutgers University, Rm. 140, 70 Lipman Dr., Loree Bldg., New Brunswick, NJ 08901-8525, U.S.A. **Online address:** tjiang@rci.rutgers.edu

JIN, Ha. Also writes as Ha Jin Zhu. American/Chinese (born China), b. 1956. **Genres:** Novels, Poetry, Young Adult Fiction, Novellas/Short Stories. **Career:** Writer, 1990-; Emory University, assistant professor of creative writing, associate professor of creative writing, 1993-2002; Boston University, Department of English, professor, 2002-, Creative Writing Program, professor; American Academy of Arts and Sciences, fellow. **Publications:** POETRY: Between Silences: A Voice from China, 1990; Facing Shadows, 1996; Wreckage, 2001. FICTION: Ocean of Words: Army Stories, 1996; Under the Red Flag: Stories, 1997; Waiting, 1999; The Bridegroom: Stories, 2000; Deng dai, 2000; The Crazed, 2002. OTHERS: In the Pond: A Novel, 1998; (as Ha Jin Zhu) Guang tian hua ri: xiang cun de gu shi, 2001; War Trash, 2004; Free Life, 2007; Writer as Migrant, 2008; (as Ha Jin Zhu) A Good Fall, 2009; Nanjing Requiem, 2011. **Address:** Department of English, College of Arts & Sciences, Boston University, Rm. 221, 236 Bay State Rd., Boston, MA 02215, U.S.A. **Online address:** xjin@bu.edu

JIN, Jian-Ming. American (born United States), b. 1962. **Genres:** Engineering, Information Science/Computers, Technology, Sciences. **Career:** Nanjing University, research assistant, 1982-84, faculty, 1984-85; Summitec Corp., research engineer, 1991-92; University of Michigan, research assistant, 1985-89, research fellow, 1989-90, assistant research scientist, 1990-92; Otsuka Electronics (USA) Inc., senior scientist and mathematical modeler, 1992-93; University of Illinois, Department of Electrical and Computer Engineering, assistant professor, 1993-97, associate professor, 1997-2001, professor, 2001-, Y.T. Lo chair in electrical and computer engineering, Center for Computational Electromagnetics, associate director, 1995-; American Geophysical Union, Radio Science, associate editor, 1999-2002; Air Force Research Laboratory, distinguished visiting professor, 1999; City University of Hong Kong, visiting professor, 2000-01, 2008; Anhui University, adjunct professor, 2001; Peking University, adjunct professor, 2003; Nanjing University, adjunct professor, 2004; Shanghai Jiao Tong University, adjunct professor, 2007; University of Hong Kong, visiting professor, 2008. **Publications:** The Finite Element Method in Electromagnetics, 1993, 2nd ed., 2002; (with S. Zhang) Computation of Special Functions, 1996; Electromagnetic Analysis and Design in Magnetic Resonance Imaging, 1999; (ed. with W.C. Chew and E. Michielssen) Fast and Efficient Algorithms in Computational Electromagnetics, 2001; (with D.J. Riley) Finite Element Analysis of Antennas and Arrays, 2009; Theory and Computation of Electromagnetic Fields, 2010. **Address:** Department of Electrical and Computer Engineering, University of Illinois, 468 William L. Everitt Laboratory, MC-MC 702, 1406 W Green St., Urbana, IL 61801-2918, U.S.A. **Online address:** j-jin1@illinois.edu

JING, Li. See **LEE, Jennifer.**

JINKS, Catherine. Australian (born Australia), b. 1963. **Genres:** Children's Fiction, Novels, Young Adult Fiction. **Career:** Westpac Banking Corp., journalist, 1986-93; writer, 1993-. Illustrator and educator. **Publications:** This Way Out, 1991; Pagan's Crusade, 1992; The Future Trap, 1993; Pagan in Exile, 1994; Witch Bank, 1995; Pagan's Vows, 1995; Pagan's Scribe, 1996; An Evening with the Messiah (adult novel), 1996; Eye to Eye, 1997; Little White Secrets (adult novel), 1997; The Secret of Hermitage Isle (cartoon book), 1997; The Inquisitor, 1999; You'll Wake the Baby!, 2000; The Notary, 2000; The Rapture, 2001; Bella Vista, 2001; Daryl's Dinner, 2002; Gentleman's Garden, 2003; The Road, 2004; Evil Genius, 2005; The Secret Familiar, 2006; Eustace. 2007; Katie and Cleo Move In, 2007; Elysium, 2007; Eloise, 2007; Eglantine, 2007; Genius Squad, 2008; Babylonne, 2008; The Dark Mountain, 2008; The Reformed Vampire Support Group, 2009; Genius Wars, 2009; Living Hell, 2010; The Abused Werewolf Rescue Group, 2011. **Address:** c/o Margaret Connolly, 16 Winton St., Warrawee, Sydney, NW 2074, Australia.

JINPA, Geshe Thupten. See **JINPA, Thupten.**

JINPA, Thupten. (Geshe Thupten Jinpa). Canadian/Tibetan (born Tibet), b. 1958. **Genres:** Theology/Religion, Poetry, Self Help. **Career:** Gaden Shartse, lecturer, 1985-89; Office of the Dalai Lama, translator, 1986-; Girton College, Margaret Smith Research Fellow, 1996-99; The Library of Tibetan Classics, editor-in-cheif; Institute of Tibetan Classics, president; Amye Machen Institute, consultant. **Publications:** (Trans.) D. Lama and T. Gyatso, Union of Bliss and Emptiness: A Commentary on the Lama Choepa Guru Yoga Practice, 1988; (trans.) D. Lama and T. Gyatso, The Path to Bliss, 1989; Ran rigs blo gsar ba rnams la dam pa i chos kyi sñin po no sprod pa chos kyi snan ba gsar ba, 1994; (trans. and ed.) World of Tibetan Buddhism, 1995; (ed.) Collected Works of Kyabje Zemey Rinpoche: Journals of Teachings Received and Assorted Lecture Notes, 1997; (trans.) D. Lama, Healing Anger: The Power of Patience from a Buddhist Perspective, 1997; (ed.) Skyabs-rje Dze-Smad Rin-Po-Che i gsun Rtsom Gces Btus, 1997; (trans. with J. Elsner) Songs of Spiritual Experience: Tibetan Buddhist Poems of Insight and Awakening, 2000; (trans. with R. Barron) D. Lama, Dzogchen: The Heart Essence of the Great Perfection: Dzogchen Teachings Given in the West, 2000; (trans.) Dalai Lama's Book of Awakening, 2002; (ed. and trans.) D. Lama and T. Gyatso, Essence of the Heart Sutra: The Dalai Lama's Heart of Wisdom Teachings, 2002; Self, Reality and Reason in Tibetan Philosophy: Tsongkhapa's Quest for the Middle Way, 2002; (ed. and trans.) D. Lama, Lighting the Path: The Dalai Lama Teaches on Wisdom and Compassion, 2003; (ed. and trans.) D. Lama, Practicing Wisdom: The Perfection of Shantideva's Bodhisattva Way, 2004; (trans.) D. Lama, Lighting the Way, 2004; (contrib.) Ornament of Stainless Light, 2004; (ed. and trans.) D. Lama, Essence of the Heart Sutra: The Dalai Lama's Heart of Wisdom Teachings, 2005; (ed. and trans.) D. Lama, Art of Living: A Guide to Contentment, Joy, and Fulfillment, 2005; (ed. with G. Coleman) The Tibetan Book of the Dead, 2005; (ed. and trans.) Mind Training, 2006; (trans.) Book of Kadam, 2008; (trans.) D. Lama, Union of Bliss and Emptiness: Teachings on the Practice of Guru Yoga, 2009; (trans.) D. Lama, Middle Way: Faith Grounded in Reason, 2009; (contrib.) Meditations on Living, Dying, and Loss, 2009; (ed. and intro.) Essential Mind Training, 2011. **Address:** Institute of Tibetan Classics, 304 Aberdare Rd., Montreal, QC H3P 3K3, Canada. **Online address:** tjinpa@tibetanclassics.org

JIRGENS, Karl (E.). Canadian (born Canada), b. 1952. **Genres:** Novels, Novellas/Short Stories, Theatre, Literary Criticism And History, Humanities, Mythology/Folklore, Psychology, Politics/Government, Sciences, Biography, Poetry, Plays/Screenplays, Sports/Fitness. **Career:** Rampike Magazine, editor-in-chief, 1979-; York University, instructor of English, 1982-; Algoma University, assistant professor, Faculty Association, president, Department of English, chair, 1994-2004; University of Windsor, department head, 2004-09, associate professor, 2010-. Writer. **Publications:** Strappado: Elemental Tales, 1985; Bill Bissett and His Works, 1992; A Measure of Time, 1995; Christopher Dewdney and His Works, 1996; (ed.) Hymn to the Sun: Early Works of Jack Bush, 1997; (ed. and intro.) Children of the Outer Dark: The Poetry of Christopher Dewdney, 2007. Contributor to periodicals. **Address:** Department of English, University of Windsor, 401 Sunset Ave., Windsor, ON N9B 3P4, Canada. **Online address:** jirgens@uwindsor.ca

JO, Kyung-Ran. Korean (born Korea (South)), b. 1969?. **Genres:** Novels. **Career:** Writer. **Publications:** Tongue (novel), 2009. **Address:** Barbara J. Zitwer Agency, 525 W End Ave., Ste. 11H, New York, NY 10024, U.S.A.

JOAS, Hans. German (born Germany), b. 1948. **Genres:** Philosophy, Sociology, Theology/Religion. **Career:** Free University of Berlin, research and teaching fellow, 1973-77, professor of sociology, 1990-2002; Max-Planck-Institute for Human Development and Education, research fellow, 1979-83; University of Tübingen, visiting professor, 1980-81; University of Chicago, visiting professor of sociology, 1985, 2000-04, Department of Sociology, professor of sociology, 2000-; University of Erlangen, professor of sociology, 1987-90; University of Uppsala, visiting professor, 1992; John F. Kennedy Institute for North American Studies, executive director, 1993-95; Duke University, visiting professor, 1998; Swedish Collegium for Advanced Study in the Social Sciences, fellow, 1999-2000, Ernst Cassirer professor, 2004-05; University of Erfurt, Max Weber Center for Advanced Cultural and Social Studies, director, 2002-, dean and chair, Max Weber professor in sociology; Wissenschaftskolleg zu Berlin, fellow, 2005-06. Writer. **Publications:** Die Gegenwärtige Lage der Soziologischen Rollentheorie, 1973, 3rd ed., 1978; Praktische Intersubjektivität: d Entwicklung d Werkes von George Herbert Mead, 1980; (with A. Honneth) Soziales Handeln und Menschliche Natur: Anthropologische Grundlagen der Sozialwissenschaften, 1980; (with M. Bochow) Wissenschaft und Karriere: Der Berufliche Verbleib des Akasemischem Mittelbaus, 1987; Die Kreativiteat des Handelns, 1992; Pragmatism and Social Theory, 1993; Die Entstehung der Werte, 1997; Kriegeund Werte, 2000; Creatividad, Acción y valores: Hacia una Teoría Sociológica de la Contingencia, 2002; (with W. Knöbl) Sozialtheorie: Zwanzig Einführende Vorlesungen, 2004; Braucht Werterziehung Religion?, 2007; (with K. Wiegandt) Säkularisierung und die Weltreligionen, 2007; (with W. Knöbl) Kriegsverdrängung: Ein Problem in der Geschichte der Sozialtheorie, 2008; Do We Need Religion?, 2008; (with W. Knobl) Social Theory: Twenty Introductory Lectures, 2009; (with W. Knobl) War in Social Thought, 2013. EDITOR: Das Problem der Intersubjektivität: Neuere Beiträge zum Werk George Herbert Mead, 1985; (with A. Honneth) Kommunikatives Handeln: Beiträge zu Jürgen Habermas' Theorie des Kommunikativen Handelns, 1986; (with H. Steiner) Machtpolitischer Realismus und Pazifistische Utopi: Krieg und Frieden in der Geschichte der Sozialwissenschaften, 1989; (with M. Kohli) Der Zusammenbruch der DDR: Soziologische Analysen, 1993; (with W. Knöbl) Gewalt in den USA, 1994; Philosophie der Demokratie, 2000; Lehrbuch der Soziologie, 2001; (with J. Fischer) Kunst, Macht undInstitution: Studien zur Philosophischen Anthropologie, Soziologischen Theorie und Kultursoziologie der Moderne: Festschrift Für Karl-Siegbert Rehberg, 2003; (with C. Camic) Dialogical Turn: New Roles for Sociology in the Postdisciplinary Age, 2004; (with K. Wiegandt) Kulturellen Werte Europas, 2005; (with H.G. Kippenberg) Interdisziplinarität als Lernprozess: Erfahrungen mit Einem Handlungstheoretischen Forschungsprogramm, 2005; Die Zehn Gebote: Ein Widerspruchliches Erbe?, 2006; Von der Ursprünglichkeit der Gabe: Jean-Luc Marions Phänomenologie in der Diskussion, 2007; (with M. Gabel) Die Anthropologie von Macht und Glauben: Das Werk Wolfgang Reinhards in der Diskussion, 2008; (with B. Klein) Benefit of Broad Horizons, 2010. **Address:** Department of Sociology, University of Chicago, 307 Foster, 1126 E 59th St., Chicago, IL 60637-1580, U.S.A. **Online address:** hjoas@uchicago.edu

JOBLING, Curtis. British (born England), b. 1972. **Genres:** Children's Fiction, Animals/Pets, Illustrations. **Career:** HOT Animation, model maker and animator. Writer. **Publications:** SELF-ILLUSTRATED: My Daddy, 2004. OTHERS: Frankenstein's Cat, 2001; (with J. Emmett) Dinosaurs After Dark, 2001; Cheeky Monkey, 2006; Wereworld: Rise of the Wolf, 2011; Wereworld: Rage Of Lions, 2011. Illustrator of books by others. **Address:** Knight Hall Agency Ltd., 7 Mallow St., Lower Ground Fl., London, GL EC1Y 8RQ, England. **Online address:** enquiries@curtisjobling.com

JOBS, Daniel Steve. Also writes as Daniel Lyons, Fake Steve Jobs. Canadian (born Canada), b. 1960. **Genres:** Young Adult Fiction. **Career:** Forbes, senior editor, 1998-2008; Newsweek, technology columnist, 2008-; University of Michigan, faculty; University of Toledo, faculty. **Publications:** The Last Good Man, 1993; Dog Days, 1998; (as Fake Steve Jobs) Options: The Secret Life of Steve Jobs, A Parody, 2007. Contributor to magazines. **Address:** The Lavin Agency, 77 Peter St., 4th Fl., Toronto, ON M5V 2G4, Canada. **Online address:** dlyons@forbes.com

JOBS, Fake Steve. See JOBS, Daniel Steve.

JOCELYN, Ann Henning. See HENNING, Ann.

JOCELYN, Marthe. American/Canadian (born Canada), b. 1956?. **Genres:** Novels, Children's Fiction, Children's Non-fiction, Young Adult Fiction, Young Adult Non-fiction, Picture/Board Books. **Career:** Jesse Design (toy and clothing design firm), owner. Writer. **Publications:** EARLY CHAPTER BOOKS: The Invisible Day, 1997; The Invisible Harry, 1998; The Invisible Enemy, 2002. SELF-ILLUSTRATED PICTURE BOOKS: Hannah and the Seven Dresses, 1999; Hannah's Collections, 2000; A Day with Nellie, 2002; Mayfly, 2004. PICTURE BOOKS: One Some Many, 2004; Over Under, 2005; ABC x 3: English, Español, Français, 2005; Same Same, 2009; Which Way?, 2010; Ones and Twos, 2011. OTHERS: Earthly Astonishments, 2000; Mable Riley: A Reliable Record of Humdrum, Peril and Romance, 2004; Secrets, 2005; A Home for Foundlings, 2005; (ed.) First Times: Stories, 2007; How It Happened in Peach Hill, 2007; Ready for Spring, 2008; Ready for Winter, 2008; Would You, 2008; Ready for Summer, 2008; Ready for Autumn, 2008; Folly, 2010; Scribbling Women: True Tales of Astonishing Lives, 2011. **Address:** 552 Broadway, New York, NY 10012, U.S.A. **Online address:** marthe@marthejocelyn.com

JOENS, Michael R. American (born United States), b. 1951. **Genres:** Mystery/Crime/Suspense, Novels. **Career:** Stillwater Production Co., founder, 1987-; Columbia Broadcasting System Inc., director and producer for television programs; National Broadcasting Corp., director and producer for television programs; Hanna Barbera, cartoonist and illustrator; Warner Brothers, cartoonist and illustrator; Marvel Productions, cartoonist and illustrator. Writer. **Publications:** The Crimson Tapestry, 1995; The Shadows of Eden, 1995; The Dawn of Mercy: A Novel, 1996; Triumph of the Soul, 1999; An Animated Death in Burbank, 2004; Blood Reins: A Detective Sandra Cameron Mystery, 2005; Angels Descending, 2006. Contributor to periodicals. **Address:** Natasha Kern Literary Agency, PO Box 2908, Portland, OR 97208, U.S.A.

JOES, Anthony James. American (born United States), b. 1942. **Genres:** Social Sciences. **Career:** Saint Joseph's University, faculty member, 1969-, full professor of political science, 1980-, director of international relations program, 1972-2002, chair of department of political science, 1992-96; U.S. Army War College, Department of National Security and Strategy, visiting professor, 2001-03. Writer and educator. **Publications:** Fascism in the Contemporary World: Ideology, Evolution, Resurgence, 1978; Mussolini, 1982; From the Barrel of a Gun: Armies and Revolutions, 1986; The War for South Viet Nam, 1954- 1975, 2001; Modern Guerrilla Insurgency, 1992; Guerrilla Conflict before the Cold War, 1996; Guerrilla Warfare: A Historical, Biographical and Bibliographical Sourcebook, 1996; Saving Democracies: U.S. Intervention in Threatened Democratic States, 1999; America and Guerrilla Warfare, 2000; (ed. with M.G. Manwaring) Beyond Declaring Victory and Coming Home: The Challenges of Peace and Stability Operations, 2000; Resisting Rebellion: The History and Politics of Counterinsurgency, 2004; Urban Guerrilla Warfare, 2007. Contributor to books. **Address:** College of Arts & Sciences, St. Joseph's University, 5600 City Ave., Philadelphia, PA 19131-1395, U.S.A. **Online address:** ajoes@sju.edu

JOHANSEN, Iris. American (born United States), b. 1938. **Genres:** Mystery/Crime/Suspense, Romance/Historical, Novels, Criminology/True Crime, Young Adult Fiction. **Career:** Writer. **Publications:** DELANEYS OF KILLAROO SERIES: Matilda, the Adventuress, 1987; Wild Silver, 1988; Satin Ice, 1988. WILD DANCER TRILOGY: The Wind Dancer, 1991; Storm Winds, 1991; Reap the Wind, 1991. OTHER NOVELS: Stormy Vows, 1983; Tempest at Sea, 1983; The Reluctant Lark, 1983; The Bronzed Hawk, 1983; The Lady and the Unicorn, 1983; The Golden Valkyrie, 1984; The Trustworthy Redhead, 1984; Return to Santa Flores, 1984; No Red Roses, 1984; Capture the Rainbow, 1984; Touch the Horizon, 1984; The Forever Dream, 1985; White Satin, 1985; Blue Velvet, 1985; A Summer Smile, 1985; York, the Renegade, 1986; And the Desert Blooms, 1986; Always, 1986; Everlasting, 1986; Til the End of Time, 1986; Last Bridge Home, 1987; Across the River of Yesterday, 1987; The Spellbinder, 1987; Magnificent Folly, 1987; One Touch of Topaz, 1988; Star Light, Star Bright, 1988; This Fierce Splendor, 1988; Man from Half Moon Bay, 1988; Blue Skies and Shining Promises, 1988; Strong, Hot Winds, 1988; Notorious, 1990; The Golden Barbarian, 1990; Wicked Jake Darcy, 1990; A Tough Man to Tame, 1991; Tender Savage, 1991; The Tiger Prince, 1993; Star Spangled Bride, 1993; The Magnificent Rogue, 1993; The Beloved Scoundrel, 1994; Midnight Warrior, 1994; Dark Rider, 1995; Lion's Bride, 1996; The Ugly Duckling, 1996; Long After Midnight, 1996; The Face of Deception, 1998; And Then You Die, 1998; Killing Game, 1999; The Search, 2000; Final Target, 2001; Body of Lies, 2002; No One to Trust, 2002; Fatal Tide, 2003; Firestorm, 2003; Dead Aim, 2003; Blind Alley, 2004; Countdown, 2005; On the Run, 2005; An Unexpected Song, 2006; Stalemate, 2006; Killer Dreams, 2006; Pandora's Daughter, 2007; (with R. Johansen) Silent Thunder, 2008; Dark Summer, 2008; The Treasure, 2008; Quicksand,

2008; Deadlock, 2009; (with R. Johansen) Storm Cycle, 2009; Blood Game, 2009; (with R. Johansen) Shadow Zone, 2010; Chasing the Night, 2010; Eight Days to Live, 2010; Eve, 2011; Bonnie, 2011; Quinn, 2011; What Doesn't Kill You, 2012. Works appear in anthologies. **Address:** c/o Andrea Cirillo, Jane Rotrosen Agency, 318 E 51st St., New York, NY 10022-7803, U.S.A. **Online address:** mail@irisjohansen.com

JOHANSSON, M. Jane. American (born United States), b. 1963. **Genres:** History. **Career:** University of North Texas, teaching fellow, 1988-91; Tarrant County Junior College, adjunct instructor in history, 1993-94; Rogers University (now Rogers State University), adjunct instructor, 1994-97, Department of History and Political Science, adjunct instructor in history, 2000-01, assistant professor of history, 2001-06, associate professor, 2006-; Pryor Area Arts and Humanities Council, humanities project director, 1995-2001; Friends of the Pryor Public Library, secretary, 1996-99, 2001-05; Northeastern State University, adjunct instructor in history, 1997-2000. Writer. **Publications:** Peculiar Honor: A History of the 28th Texas Cavalry, 1862-1865, 1998; (ed.) Widows by the Thousand: The Civil War Letters of Theophilus and Harriet Perry, 1862-1864, 2000; (ed. with S.K. Gragert) The Papers of Will Rogers, vol. IV: From Broadway to the National Stage, September 1915-July 1928, 2005, vol. V: The Final Years, August 1928-August 1935, 2006. Contributor to periodicals. **Address:** Department of History and Political Science, Rogers State University, 421 S Elliott St., Pryor, OK 74361-6409, U.S.A. **Online address:** jjohansson@rsu.edu

JOHN, Antony. American/British (born England), b. 1972?. **Genres:** Novels. **Career:** Duke University, instructor; University of South Carolina, instructor. Writer. **Publications:** Busted: Confessions of an Accidental Player, 2008; Five Flavors of Dumb, 2010. **Address:** c/o Ted Malawer, Upstart Crow Literary L.L.C., PO Box 25404, Brooklyn, NY 11202, U.S.A. **Online address:** antony@antonyjohn.net

JOHN, Juliet. British (born England), b. 1967?. **Genres:** Literary Criticism And History, Bibliography. **Career:** University of Manchester, lecturer in English; University of Liverpool, faculty, 1994-96, reader in Victorian literature, 2002-, Gladstone Centre for Victorian Studies, director, professor of English Literature; University of Salford, senior lecturer in English, 1997-; Edge Hill University College, faculty. Writer. **Publications:** Dickens's Villains: Melodrama, Character, Popular Culture, 2001; Dickens and Mass Culture, 2010. EDITOR: (intro.) Cult Criminals: The Newgate Novels, 1830-1947, 1997; (with A. Jenkins) Rereading Victorian Fiction, 1999; (with A. Jenkins) Rethinking Victorian Culture, 2000; Charles Dickens's Oliver Twist: A Sourcebook, 2006; The Oxford (Online) Bibliography of Victorian Literature, 2010; Essays and Studies on Dickens and Modernity, 2012. Contributor to periodicals. **Address:** The School of English, The University of Liverpool, Cypress Bldg., Chatham St., Liverpool, L69 7ZR, England. **Online address:** j.john@liverpool.ac.uk

JOHNS, Derek. British (born England), b. 1948?. **Genres:** Mystery/Crime/Suspense. **Career:** Random House, editor, 1983-86; Harrap, publishing director, 1986-88; Bodley Head, managing director, 1988-89; Granta, managing director, 1990-92; A.P. Watt Ltd., director & literary agent, 1992-, joint managing director, 1996-. Editor, publisher and literary agent. **Publications:** The Beatrice Mystery, 1980; Wintering, 2007; Wakening, 2008. **Address:** A.P. Watt Ltd., 20 John St., London, WC1N 2DR, England. **Online address:** djohns@apwatt.co.uk

JOHNS, Jeremy. British (born England), b. 1954?. **Genres:** Administration/Management, Art/Art History, Photography. **Career:** Oxford University, university lecturer in Islamic archaeology, Division of Humanities, deputy chair, Faculty of Oriental Studies, chair, 2007-09; Khalili Research Center, director, professor of the art and archaeology of the Islamic Mediterranean. Writer. **Publications:** (Ed. with J. Raby) Bayt al-Maqdis: Abd al-Malik's Jerusalem, 1992; Arabic Administration in Norman Sicily: The Royal Diwan, 2002; (with E.J. Grube) The Painted Ceilings of the Cappella Palatina, 2005. Contributor to books, journals and periodicals. **Address:** Khalili Research Centre, 3 St. John St., Oxford, OX OX1 2LG, England. **Online address:** jeremy.johns@orinst.ox.ac.uk

JOHNS, Linda. Canadian (born Canada), b. 1945. **Genres:** Poetry, Animals/Pets, Natural History, Illustrations. **Career:** Professional artist, 1975-. Writer. **Publications:** Sharing a Robin's Life, 1993; In the Company of Birds, 1995. SELF-ILLUSTRATED: Touching Water, Touching Light (poems), 1990;

Spiritus (poems), 1992; The Eyes of the Elders (poem), 1995; For the Birds, 1999 in US as A Feathered Family: Nature Notes from a Woodland Studio, 1999; Wild and Woolly, 2000; Touchstone (poems), 2004; Birds of a Feather, 2005. Contributor to periodicals. **Address:** c/o Jeff Parker, Lyghtesome Gallery, 166 Main St., Antigonish, NS B2G 2B7, Canada.

JOHNS, Richard Alton. American (born United States), b. 1929. **Genres:** Novels, Novellas/Short Stories, Plays/Screenplays, Poetry, Advertising/Public Relations, History, Theology/Religion, Biography, Biography. **Career:** General Dynamics, illustrator and editor, 1951-61; Tyler Star, artist and columnist, 1961-. **Publications:** Thirteenth Apostle, 1966; Garden of the Okapi, 1968; Return to Heroism, 1969; (co-author) Everyday, Five Minutes with God, 1969; History of the Mental Health Mental Retardation Center, 1991; History of Jarvis Christian, 1993. **Address:** 912 W Camellia, Tyler, TX 75701, U.S.A.

JOHNSGARD, Paul A. American (born United States), b. 1931. **Genres:** Biology, Environmental Sciences/Ecology, Zoology, Natural History. **Career:** University of Nebraska, instructor, 1961-62, assistant professor, 1962-65, associate professor, 1965-68, School of Biological Sciences, professor of zoology, 1968-80, Foundation Regents professor of life sciences, 1980-2001, Foundation Regents professor emeritus, 2001-. Writer. **Publications:** SELF-ILLUSTRATED: Prairie Children, Mountain Dreams, 1985; Lewis and Clark on the Great Plains: A Natural History, 2003; Great Wildlife of the Great Plains, 2003; Wind through the Buffalo Grass: A Lakota Story Cycle, 2008. OTHERS: Handbook of Waterfowl Behavior, 1965; Animal Behavior, 1967; Waterfowl, Their Biology and Natural History, 1968; Grouse and Quails of North America, 1973; Song of the North Wind: A Story of the Snow Goose, 1974; American Game Birds of Upland and Shoreline, 1974; North American Game Birds of Upland Shoreline, 1975; Waterfowl of North America, 1975; (ed.) The Bird Decoy: An American Art Form: A Catalog of Carvings Exhibited at the Sheldon Memorial Art Gallery, Lincoln, Nebraska, 1976; Ducks, Geese and Swans of the World, 1978; A Guide to North American Waterfowl, 1979; Birds of the Great Plains: Breeding Species and Their Distribution, 1979; The Plovers, Sandpipers and Snipes of the World, 1981; Those of the Gray Wind: The Sandhill Cranes, 1981; Teton Wildlife: Observations of a Naturalist, 1982; (with K.L. Johnsgard) The Natural History of Dragons and Unicorns: A Natural History, 1982; Grouse of the World, 1983; Cranes of the World, 1983; Hummingbirds of North America, 1983, 2nd ed., 1997; The Platte: Channels in Time, 1984; The Pheasants of the World, 1986, 2nd ed. as The Pheasants of the World: Biology and Natural History, 1999; Birds of the Rocky Mountains: With Particular Reference to National Parks in the Northern Rocky Mountain Region, 1986; Quails, Partridges and Francolins of the World, 1987; Diving Birds of North America, 1987; The Waterfowl of North America: The Complete Ducks, Geese, and Swans, 1987; The Quails, Partridges, and Francolins of the World, 1988; North American Owls: Biology and Natural History, 1988, 2nd ed., 2002; Waterfowl of North America: The Paintings of Robin Hill, 1989; Hawks, Eagles & Falcons of North America: Biology and Natural History, 1990, 2nd ed., 2002; Bustards, Hemipodes and Sandgrouse: Birds of Dry Places, 1991; Crane Music: A Natural History of North American Cranes, 1991; Ducks in the Wild: Conserving Waterfowl and Their Habitats, 1992; Dragons and Unicorns: A Natural History, 1992; Ducks in the Wild: Conserving Waterfowl and their Habitats, 1992; Cormorants, Darters and Pelicans of the World, 1993; Arena Birds: Sexual Selection and Behavior, 1994; This Fragile Land: A Natural History of the Nebraska Sandhills, 1995; Ruddy Ducks & Other Stifftails: Their Behavior and Biology, 1996; The Avian Brood Parasites: Deception at the Nest, 1997; Earth, Water, and Sky: A Naturalist's Stories and Sketches, 1999; Trogons and Quetzals of the World, 2000; Prairie Birds: Fragile Splendor in the Great Plains, 2001; The Nature of Nebraska: Ecology and Biodiversity, 2001; The Nature of Nebraska, 2001; Grassland Grouse and Their Conservation, 2002; Faces of the Great Plains: Prairie Wildlife, 2003; Great Wildlife of the Great Plains, 2003; Prairie Dog Empire: A Saga of the Shortgrass Prairie, 2005; The Niobrara: A River Running through Time, 2007; Sandhill and Whooping Cranes: Ancient Voices Over America's Wetlands, 2011. Contributor of articles to journals. **Address:** School of Biological Sciences, University of Nebraska, 348 Manter Hall, 1400 R St. Lincoln NE, Lincoln, NE 68588-0118, U.S.A. **Online address:** pjohnsga@unlserve.unl.edu

JOHNSON, Adam. American (born United States), b. 1967. **Genres:** Novels. **Career:** Stanford University, Department of English, faculty, 1999-, Jones lecturer in creative writing and fiction, 2001-, associate professor. Writer. **Publications:** Emporium: Stories, 2002; Parasites Like Us, 2003; The

Orphan Master's Son: A Novel, 2012. Contributor to books and periodicals. **Address:** Department of English, Stanford University, Rm. 324, 460 Bldg., Margaret Jacks Hall, Stanford, CA 94305-2087, U.S.A. **Online address:** adamjohn@stanford.edu

JOHNSON, A. E. *See* **JOHNSON, Annabel (Jones).**

JOHNSON, Alaya Dawn. American (born United States), b. 1982?. **Genres:** Novels. **Career:** Novelist. **Publications:** SPIRIT BINDERS SERIES: Racing the Dark, 2008; The Burning City, 2010. OTHER NOVELS: The Goblin King, 2009; Moonshine: A Novel, 2010; Detective Frankenstein, 2011. Contributor to magazines. Works appear in anthologies. **Address:** New York, NY , U.S.A. **Online address:** alaya@alayadawnjohnson.com

JOHNSON, Alexandra. American (born United States), b. 1949. **Genres:** Literary Criticism And History, Language/Linguistics, Self Help. **Career:** Christian Science Monitor, writer and assistant literary editor, 1976-82; freelance writer, 1982-; WGBH-TV, writer, 1986; Harvard University, instructor in creative writing, 1990-98; Wellesley College, creative writing, senior lecturer. Writer. **Publications:** The Hidden Writer: Diaries and the Creative Life, 1997; Anchor Paper, 1998; Leaving a Trace: On Keeping a Journal: The Art of Transforming a Life into Stories, 2001. Contributor of articles to magazines and newspapers. **Address:** The Writing Program, Wellesley College, 106 Central St., Wellesley, MA 02481, U.S.A. **Online address:** ajohnso1@wellesley.edu

JOHNSON, Allan G. American (born United States), b. 1946. **Genres:** Race Relations, Social Commentary, Women's Studies And Issues, Novels, Sociology, Adult Non-fiction. **Career:** Wesleyan University, assistant professor, 1972-80; Hartford College for Women, professor, 1984-2003; Charles River Consulting Group, senior associate. Writer. **Publications:** Social Statistics Without Tears, 1977; Human Arrangements: An Introduction to Sociology, 1986, 4th ed., 1996; Statistics, 1988; The Forest for the Trees: An Introduction to Sociological Thinking, 1991; The Blackwell Dictionary of Sociology: A User's Guide to Sociological Language, 1995, 2nd ed., 2002; The Forest and the Trees: Sociology as Life, Practice and Promise, 1997, rev. ed., 2008; The Gender Knot: Unraveling Our Patriarchal Legacy, 1997, rev. ed., 2005; Privilege, Power and Difference, 2000, 2nd ed., 2005; The First Thing and the Last: A Novel, 2010; Nothing Left to Lose, 2011. **Address:** 8 Stone Meadow Ln., 1265 Asylum Ave., Collinsville, CT 06019-3733, U.S.A. **Online address:** agjohnson@comcast.net

JOHNSON, Andrew. British (born England), b. 1949. **Genres:** Agriculture/ Forestry, Economics, Local History/Rural Topics, Sciences, Earth Sciences. **Career:** School teacher, 1973-77; publisher, 1990-. Writer. **Publications:** Factory Farming, 1991; (with B. Dollery and L. Crase) Australian Local Government Economics, 2006. Contributor to periodicals. **Address:** UNSW Press, University of New South Wales, Sydney, NW 2052, Australia.

JOHNSON, Angela. American (born United States), b. 1961. **Genres:** Children's Fiction, Novels, Picture/Board Books, Poetry. **Career:** Volunteers in Service to America, child development worker, 1981-82; freelance writer of children's books, 1989-. **Publications:** FOR CHILDREN: Tell Me a Story, Mama, 1989; Do Like Kyla, 1990; When I Am Old with You, 1990; One of Three, 1991; The Leaving Morning, 1992; One of Three, 1992; Julius, 1993; The Girl Who Wore Snakes, 1993; Toning the Sweep, 1993; Shoes Like Miss Alice's, 1995; The Aunt in Our House, 1996; The Rolling Store, 1997; Daddy Calls Me Man, 1997; Wedding, 1999; Those Building Men, 1999; Maniac Monkeys on Magnolia Street, 1999; When Mules Flew on Magnolia Street, 2000; Casey Jones, 2000; Down the Winding Road, 2000; Running Back to Ludie, 2001; Those Building Men, 2001; Looking for Red, 2002; I Dream of Trains, 2003; The First Part Last, 2003; Cool Moonlight, 2003; Bird, 2004; Just like Josh Gibson, 2004; Violet's Music, 2004; Sweet Smell of Roses, 2005; Lily Brown's Paintings, 2007; Up, Up and a Ray, 2010; Sweet, Hereafter, 2010; Lottie Paris Lives Here, 2011. BOARD BOOKS: Joshua by the Sea, 1994; Mama Bird, Baby Birds, 1994; Joshua's Night Whispers, 1994; Rain Feet, 1994. NOVELS: Toning the Sweep, 1993; Humming Whispers, 1995; Songs of Faith, 1998; Heaven, 1998; Gone from Home, 1998. POETRY: The Other Side, 1998. OTHERS: The Day Ray got Away, 2010; Lottie Paris and Carl, 2013. **Address:** Orchard Books/Scholastic, 557 Broadway, Ste. 95G, New York, NY 10012-3958, U.S.A.

JOHNSON, Annabel (Jones). (A. E. Johnson). American (born United

States), b. 1921. **Genres:** Novels, Children's Fiction, Young Adult Fiction, Romance/Historical, Science Fiction/Fantasy, Literary Criticism And History. **Career:** Writer, 1957-. Librarian. **Publications:** As a Speckled Bird, 1956; I am Leaper, 1990; Last Days of a Toyshop, 2003; The Oxblood Effect, 2004; The Craft So Long to Lerne: An Author's Journey, 2004; The First Days of Chaos, 2006; One Man's War, 2008; A Time to Gather Stones, 2010. WITH E. JOHNSON: The Big Rock Candy, 1957; The Black Symbol, 1959; Torrie, 1960; The Bearcat, 1960; The Rescued Heart, 1961; Pickpocket Run, 1961; Wilderness Bride, 1962; A Golden Touch, 1963; The Grizzly, 1964; A Peculiar Magic, 1965; The Burning Glass, 1966; Count Me Gone, 1968; The Last Knife, 1971; Finders, Keepers, 1981; An Alien Music, 1982; The Danger Quotient, 1984; Prisoner of PSI, 1985; A Memory of Dragons, 1986; Gamebuster, 1990; Niner, 1994. WITH E. JOHNSON AS A.E. JOHNSON: The Secret Gift: A Novel, 1961; Come Closer: Selected Poems of A. E. Johnson, 1966; A Blues I Can Whistle, 1969. Contributor to periodicals. **Address:** 21 Leisure World, Mesa, AZ 85206-3102, U.S.A. **Online address:** annjite@cs.com

JOHNSON, Annette R. American (born United States), b. 1969. **Genres:** Novellas/Short Stories. **Career:** Decatur-Dekalb News, reporter and editor, 1994-96; Positive Publications, editor, 1998; Atlanta Bulletin, editor, 1998-99; Atlanta Metropolitan College, instructor in journalism, 2000; Georgia State University, instructor in journalism, 2001-; Allwrite Advertising and Publishing, founder and editor. **Publications:** What's Your Motivation?: Identifying and Understanding What Drives You, 2010. Contributor to periodicals. **Address:** Allwrite Advertising & Publishing, PO Box 1071, Atlanta, GA 30301-1071, U.S.A. **Online address:** editor@e-allwrite.com

JOHNSON, A. Ross. American (born United States), b. 1939?. **Genres:** International Relations/Current Affairs, Politics/Government. **Career:** Rand Corp., senior social scientist, 1969-88; Radio Free Europe, policy assistant, 1966-69, director, 1988-91, senior executive, 1988-2002; Foundation for Science and Politics, visiting RAND research fellow, 1983-85; Radio Free Europe/Radio Liberty Research Institute, director, 1991-94, acting president and counselor, adviser; Radio Free Europe/Radio Liberty Inc., counselor, 1994-2001; senior advisor, 2002-; Hoover Institution, research fellow, 2002-. Writer. **Publications:** The Transformation of Communist Ideology: The Yugoslav Case 1945-53, 1972; Yugoslavia: In the Twilight of Tito, 1974; (with A.L. Horelick and J.D. Steinbruner) The Study of Soviet Foreign Policy: Decision-Theory-Related Approaches, 1975; The Role of the Military in Communist Yugoslavia, 1978; (with R. Dean and A. Alexiev) East European Military Establishments: The Warsaw Pact Northern Tier, 1982; Poland in Crisis, 1982; Impressions of Post-Tito Yugoslavia, 1982; (with L. Dzirkals and T. Gustafson) The Media and Intra-Elite Communication in the USSR, 1982; (with J.L. Curry) The Media and Intra-Elite Communication in Poland, 1980; (with B. Kliszewski) The Polish Military after Martial Law, 1983; (with J.F. Brown) Challenges to Soviet Control in Eastern Europe, 1984; The Impact of Eastern Europe on Soviet Policy toward Western Europe, 1986; (with A. Alexiev) East European Military Reliability, 1986; United States Policy toward Poland, 1987; (ed.) Communicating with the World of Islam, 2008; (ed. with R. Eugene Parta) Cold War Broadcasting; Impact on the Soviet Union and Eastern Europe, 2010; Radio Free Europe and Radio Liberty: The CIA Years and Beyond, 2010. **Address:** Radio Free Europe/Radio Liberty, 1201 Connecticut Ave. NW, Washington, DC 20036, U.S.A. **Online address:** johnsonr@rferl.org

JOHNSON, Barb. American (born United States), b. 1957?. **Genres:** Novellas/Short Stories. **Career:** Writer. **Publications:** More of This World or Maybe Another (short stories), 2009. Contributor to magazines and journals. **Address:** New Orleans, LA , U.S.A. **Online address:** barbjohnson111@gmail.com

JOHNSON, Cait. American (born United States), b. 1952. **Genres:** Food And Wine, inspirational/Motivational Literature, Paranormal, Adult Non-fiction, Psychology, Human Relations/Parenting. **Career:** Care2.com, managing editor; Black Health Institute, fellow; Omega Institute, faculty. **Publications:** (With M.D. Shaw) Tarot Games: 45 Playful Ways to Explore Tarot Cards Together; A New Vision for the Circle of Community, 1994; (with M.D. Shaw) Celebrating the Great Mother: A Handbook of Earth-Honoring Activities for Parents and Children, 1995; Tarot for Every Day: Ideas and Activities for Bringing Tarot Wisdom into Your Daily Life, 1995; Cooking like a Goddess: Bringing Seasonal Magic into the Kitchen, 1997; (with E. Cunningham) Naked Masks, 1998; Witch in the Kitchen: Magical Cooking for All Seasons, 2001; Earth, Water, Fire and Air: Essential Ways of Connecting to Spirit,

2003. Contributor to periodicals. **Address:** Omega Institute, 150 Lake Dr., Rhinebeck, NY 12572, U.S.A. **Online address:** caitjohnson@hotmail.com

JOHNSON, Carla. American (born United States), b. 1944?. **Genres:** Writing/Journalism, Advertising/Public Relations, Business/Trade/Industry. **Career:** University of Notre Dame, teaching assistant, 1983-88, adjunct assistant professor, 1988-90; Saint Mary's College, assistant professor, 1990-2001, professional writing specialist, 2001-, now professional writing specialist emerita, assistant director for writing proficiency program, 2001-, Department of English, internship coordinator. Writer. **Publications:** (With M. Lee) Principles of Advertising: A Global Perspective, 1999, 2nd ed., 2005; 21st Century Feature Writing, 2004. **Address:** Saint Mary's College, Rm. 147K, 22 Madeleva, Notre Dame, IN 46556, U.S.A. **Online address:** ccjhnsn@sbcglobal.net

JOHNSON, Cathy Marie. American (born United States), b. 1956. **Genres:** Politics/Government. **Career:** Brookings Institution, fellow, 1984-85; University of Wisconsin, assistant professor of political science and public policy, 1986-90; State of Wisconsin, Department of Health and Social Services, program and planning analyst, 1990-91; Williams College, Department of Political Science, assistant professor, 1991-, professor. Writer. **Publications:** The Dynamics of Conflict Between Bureaucrats and Legislators, 1992; (with G. Duerst and N.H. Norton) Creating Gender: The Sexual Politics of Welfare Policy, 2007. **Address:** Department of Political Science, Williams College, Rm. 341, Hollander Hall, Stetson H-10, Williamstown, MA 01267, U.S.A. **Online address:** cathy.m.johnson@williams.edu

JOHNSON, Charles Floyd. *See* **ROBINSON, Peter (Mark).**

JOHNSON, Charles R(ichard). American (born United States), b. 1948. **Genres:** Novels, Plays/Screenplays, Literary Criticism And History, Humor/Satire, Novellas/Short Stories, Young Adult Fiction, Illustrations, History, History. **Career:** Chicago Tribune, cartoonist and reporter, 1969-70; University of Washington, assistant professor, 1976-79, associate professor, 1979-82, S. Wilson and Grace M. Pollock endowed professor of English, 1982-, now professor emeritus, director of creative writing program; Seattle Review, fiction editor, 1978-98. **Publications:** SELF-ILLUSTRATED: Black Humor, 1970; Half-Past Nation Time, 1972. NOVELS: Faith and the Good Thing, 1974; Oxherding Tale, 1982, new ed., 2005; Middle Passage, 1990; Dreamer, 1998. OTHER: The Sorcerer's Apprentice (short stories), 1986; Being and Race: Black Writing Since 1970, 1988; Olly Olly Oxen Free: A Farce in Three Acts, 1988; Pieces of Eight, 1989; All this and Moonlight, 1990; (with R. Chernow) In Search of a Voice, 1991; (foreword) Rites of Passage: Stories About Growing Up by Black Writers from around the World, 1993; (intro.) On Writers and Writing, 1994; (co-ed.) Black Men Speaking, 1997; (foreword) Northwest Passages, 1997; (co-author) Africans in America: America's Journey through Slavery, 1998; (co-author) I Call Myself an Artist: Writings by and about Charles Johnson, 1999; (foreword) A Treasury of North American Folktales, 1999; (ed. with Y. Taylor) I was Born a Slave: An Anthology of Classic Slave Narratives, 1999; (with J. Toomer and R.P. Byrd) Essentials, 2001; (co-author) King: The Photobiography of Martin Luther King, Jr., 2000; (ed. with M. Rodriguez and C. Taylor) Sacred Fire: The QBR 100 Essential Black Books, 2000; Soulcatcher and Other Stories, 2001; (intro.) Uncle Tom's Cabin, 2002; (foreword) Black Images in the Comics: A Visual History, 2003; Turning the Wheel: Essays on Buddhism and Writing, 2003; Dr. King's Refrigerator: And Other Bedtime Stories, 2005; (with B. Adelman) Mine Eyes Have Seen: Bearing Witness to the Struggle for Civil Rights, 2007; Remembering Martin Luther King, Jr: 40 Years Later, His Life and Crusade in Pictures, 2008; (with M. Boylan) Philosophy: An Innovative Introduction: Fictive Narrative, Primary Texts and Responsive Writing, 2010; (intro.) Photographs of Gordon Parks, 2011. Contributor to books, journals and periodicals. **Address:** Department of English, University of Washington, PDL A-406, PO Box 354330, Seattle, DC 98195-4330, U.S.A. **Online address:** chasjohn@u.washington.edu

JOHNSON, Chas Floyd. *See* **ROBINSON, Peter (Mark).**

JOHNSON, Cherry L(urae) F(lake). American (born United States), b. 1968. **Genres:** Novels, Young Adult Fiction. **Career:** Wake Technical Community College, English instructor. Writer. **Publications:** Half Moon Pocosin, 1997. **Address:** Academy Chicago Publishers, 363 W Erie St., 4W, Chicago, IL 60654, U.S.A.

JOHNSON, Chester L. American (born United States), b. 1951. **Genres:** Novels, Poetry, Young Adult Fiction, Literary Criticism And History, Mystery/Crime/Suspense. **Career:** KCMJ Radio (CBS 1010), announcer, operator and music director, 1974-77; KACE FM Radio, announcer and operator, 1977-82; KCMO/KC95 FM Radio, master control operator, announcer and writer, 1983-85; Naval Aviation Depot, security supervisor, 1985-95; Naval Aviation Depot, security supervisor, 1985-95; C.Johnson Enterprisesl.td.com (business consultants), chief executive officer and founder, 1995-. Entrepreneur, broadcaster and writer. **Publications:** Wisdom (poetry), 1998; White Man Brown, a Failure of the American Dream, 2001; White Man Brown, the Hip-Hop Godfather, 2002. **Address:** C. Johnson Enterprises Ltd.com, 440 29th St., Richmond, CA 94804, U.S.A. **Online address:** cbebee510@aol.com

JOHNSON, Clint. American (born United States), b. 1953. **Genres:** Politics/Government, History. **Career:** Writer, historian and journalist. **Publications:** Touring the Carolinas' Civil War Sites, 1996; Civil War Blunders, 1997; Touring Virginia's and West Virginia's Civil War Sites, 1999; In the Footsteps of Robert E. Lee, 2001; Bull's-eyes and Misfires: Fifty People Whose Obscure Efforts Shaped the American Civil War, 2002; In the Footsteps of Stonewall Jackson, 2002; In the Footsteps of J.E.B. Stuart, 2003; (with C.E. Gaines) They Call Me Big House, 2004; The Twenty-five Best Civil War Sites: The Ultimate Traveler's Guide to the Battlefields, Monuments, and Museums, 2005; The Politically Incorrect Guide to the South: And Why It Will Rise Again, 2006; Pursuit: The Chase, Capture, Persecution, and Surprising Release of Confederate President Jefferson Davis, 2008; A Vast and Fiendish Plot: The Confederate Attack on New York City, 2010. Contributor to books, newspapers and magazines. **Address:** NC , U.S.A. **Online address:** clintjohnson@skybest.com

JOHNSON, Colin. British (born England), b. 1939. **Genres:** Medicine/Health, Philosophy. **Career:** Writer. **Publications:** WITH ARABELLA MELVILLE: Cured to Death: The Effects of Prescription Drugs, 1983; Hayfever: No Need to Suffer, 1985; The Long-Life Heart: How to Avoid Heart Disease and Live a Longer Life, 1985; Persistent Fat and How to Lose It, 1986 in US as Fat Free Forever, 1987; Alternatives to Drugs: A Handbook to Health without Hazards, 1987 in US as Health without Drugs, 1990; Immunity Plus: How to Be Healthy in an Age of New Infections, 1988; The Complete Diet Book, 1989; Eat Yourself Thin, 1990. SOLE AUTHOR: (comp.) Green Dictionary, 1991. **Address:** David Grossman Literary Agency Ltd., 118B Holland Park Ave., London, GL W11 4UA, England. **Online address:** colcon@enterprise.net

JOHNSON, David K. American (born United States) **Genres:** Gay And Lesbian Issues. **Career:** Northwestern University, School of Continuing Studies, lecturer, 1999-2001; Roosevelt University, School of Liberal Studies, lecturer, 2002; University of South Florida, Department of History, visiting assistant professor, 2003-05, assistant professor, 2005-09, associate chair, 2009-, associate professor, 2009-, coordinator of graduate studies, 2010-. Writer. **Publications:** The Lavender Scare: The Cold War Persecution of Gays and Lesbians in the Federal Government, 2004; (ed. with R.P. Ingalls) The United States Since 1945: A Documentary Reader, 2009. Contributor of articles. **Address:** Department of History, University of South Florida, SCO 263, 4202 E Fowler Ave., Tampa, FL 33620-8100, U.S.A. **Online address:** djohnson@cas.usf.edu

JOHNSON, Diane. American (born United States), b. 1934. **Genres:** Novels, Biography, Young Adult Non-fiction, History, Art/Art History, Photography, Literary Criticism And History. **Career:** University of California, assistant professor, professor of English, 1968-87. Writer. **Publications:** Fair Game: A Novel, 1965; Loving Hands at Home, 1968; Burning, 1971, 2nd ed., 1998; Lesser Lives: The True History of the First Mrs. Meredith and Other Lesser Lives, 1972; The Shadow Knows, 1974; Lying Low, 1978; Terrorists and Novelists, 1982; Dashiell Hammett, A Life, 1983; Persian Nights, 1987; Health and Happiness, 1990; (intro.) Selected Tales, 1991; Natural Opium: Some Travelers' Tales, 1993; Le Divorce, 1997; Le Mariage, 2000; L'Affaire, 2003; Into a Paris Quartier: Reine Margot's Chapel and Other Haunts of St.-Germain, 2005; Lulu in Marrakech, 2008. OTHERS: Edwin Broun Fred: Scientist, Administrator, Gentleman, 1975; Dashiell Hammett: A Life, 1983; (intro. with P. Borhan and T. Mellins) Changing Paris: A Tour Along the Seine, 2000; American Symbolist Art: Nineteenth-century Poets in Paint Washington Allston, John La Farge, William Rimmer, George Inness and Albert Pinkham Ryder, 2004. Contributor to periodicals. **Address:** c/o Lynn Nesbit, Janklow & Nesbit Associates, 445 Park Ave., New York, NY 10022-2606, U.S.A.

JOHNSON, Dianne. (Dinah Johnson). American (born United States), b. 1960. **Genres:** Literary Criticism And History, Children's Non-fiction, Children's Fiction. **Career:** University of South Carolina, Department of English Language and Literature, associate professor of English, 1990-, professor, African-American Studies Program, interim director, 1998-2000. Writer. **Publications:** Telling Tales: The Pedagogy and Promise of African American Literature for Youth, 1990; Presenting Laurence Yep, 1995; (ed.) The Best of The Brownies' Book, 1996; (with I.M.G. Quimby) American Silver at Winterthur, 1997; Sacred Waters: The Story of the Blue Mountains Gully Traditional Owners, 2007. JUVENILE AS DINAH JOHNSON: All around Town: The Photographs of Richard Samuel Roberts, 1998; Sunday Week, 1999; Quinnie Blue, 2000; Sitting Pretty: A Celebration of Black Dolls (poetry), 2000; Hair Dance!, 2007; Black Magic, 2010. Works appear in anthologies. **Address:** Department of English Language and Literature, University of South Carolina, 507 Humanities Office Bldg., Columbia, SC 29208, U.S.A. **Online address:** dianne@sc.edu

JOHNSON, Dick. (Richard A. Johnson). American (born United States), b. 1955. **Genres:** Sports/Fitness. **Career:** Sports Museum, associate director and curator, 1982-; Florentine Films and Museum of Science, consultant. Writer. **Publications:** The Baseball Almanac, 1991; (ed. with G. Stout) Ted Williams: A Portrait in Words and Pictures, 1991; Twentieth Century Baseball Chronicle, 1991; Players of Cooperstown, 1992; (with F. Lewis) Young at Heart: The Story of Johnny Kelley, 1992; Soccer Zones, 1994; Treasury of Baseball, 1994; (contrib. and ed.) Boston Garden: Banner Years, 1994; (with G. Stout) DiMaggio: An Illustrated Life, 1995; (with G. Stout) Jackie Robinson: Between the Baselines, 1997; (with G. Stout) Red Sox Century: One Hundred Years of Red Sox Baseball, 2000; Century of Boston Sports, 2000; (ed. with L. Baldassaro) American Game: Baseball and Ethnicity, 2002; (ed.) Yankees Century: 100 Years of New York Yankees Baseball, 2002; (with B. Codagnone) Bruins in Black and White, 1924-1966, 2003; (with B. Codagnone) Bruins in Black & White: 1966 to the 21st Century, 2004; (with G. Stout) Red Sox Century: The Definitive History of Baseball's Most Storied Franchise, 2004; (with R.H. Johnson) Celtics in Black and White, 2006; (ed.) The Cubs: The Complete Story of Chicago Cubs Baseball, 2007; Field of Our Fathers: An Illustrated History of Fenway Park, 2011. **Address:** Sports Museum Of New England, 1 Fleet Ctr., Boston, MA 02114, U.S.A. **Online address:** djcurator@aol.com

JOHNSON, Dinah. See **JOHNSON, Dianne.**

JOHNSON, Dolores. American (born United States), b. 1949. **Genres:** Children's Non-fiction, Children's Fiction, Illustrations, Biography. **Career:** Author and illustrator. **Publications:** SELF-ILLUSTRATED: What Will Mommy Do When I'm at School?, 1990; What Kind of Baby-sitter is This?, 1991; The Best Bug to Be, 1992; Now Let Me Fly: The Story of a Slave Family, 1993; Your Dad was Just Like You, 1993; Seminole Diary: Remembrances of a Slave, 1994; Papa's Stories, 1994; The Children's Book of Kwanzaa: A Guide to Celebrating the Holiday, 1996; Grandma's Hands, 1998; My Mom is My Show-and-Tell, 1999. OTHERS: She Dared to Fly: Bessie Coleman, 1997; Onward: A Photo Biography of African-American Polar Explorer Matthew Henson, 2005; The Harlem Renaissance, 2008. Illustrator of books by others. **Address:** 7312 S St. Andrews Pl., Los Angeles, CA 90047, U.S.A. **Online address:** dolojo2@yahoo.com

JOHNSON, Donald Leslie. Australian (born Australia), b. 1930. **Genres:** Architecture, Humanities, Regional/Urban Planning, Bibliography. **Career:** C.V. Rueger and Associates (architects), drafter, 1956, 1958; Bassetti & Morse (architects), designer and drafter, 1957, 1961; Harbeson, Hough, Livingston & Larson (architects), designer and drafter, 1958-60; Grant, Copeland & Chervenak (architects), designer and drafter, 1960-61; Cain, Nelson & Wares (architects), design associate, 1965-67; architect, 1962-65; University of Pennsylvania, faculty, 1965-72; University of Arizona, faculty, 1965-72, Architecture Library, founder and librarian pro tem, 1962-67; University of Adelaide, faculty, 1965-72; Washington State University, faculty, 1965-72, Narrimore lecturer in architecture; Flinders University of South Australia, teacher of architectural history, 1972-88, retired, 1988; Australia Studies Program, founder, 1985, founding director; University of South Australia, Architecture Archives, founder, 1980-93, founding director, School of Art, Architecture and Design, Division of Education, Arts and Social Sciences, adjunct associate professor, 1995-, adjunct professor; Royal Australian Institute of Architects, honorary fellow, 2005. Writer. **Publications:** The Architecture of Walter Burley Griffin, 1977; Canberra and Walter Burley Griffin, 1979; Assessment

of 20th-Century Architecture, 1980; Australian Architecture, 1901-51, 1980, rev. ed., 2002; Canberra and Walter Burley Griffin: A Bibliography of 1876 to 1976 and a Guide to Published Sources, 1979; (with M.S. Fallon) 18th and 19th Century Architecture Books and Serials in South Australia, 1981; (with D. Langmead) The Adelaide City Plan, 1986; Frank Lloyd Wright versus America: The 1930s, 1990; (with D. Langmead) Makers of 20th Century Modern Architecture, 1997; (with D. Langmead) Architectural Excursions: Frank Lloyd Wright, Holland and Europe, 2000; The Fountainheads, Wright, Rand, the FBI, Hollywood, 2005; Parks for City People, 2011; Origins of Municipal Parks, 2011. Contributor to books and journals. **Address:** Division of Education, Arts & Social Sciences, School of Art, Architecture & Design, University of South Australia, Level 3, Kaurna Bldg., PO Box 2471, Adelaide, SA 5001, Australia. **Online address:** donald.johnson@unisa.edu.au

JOHNSON, Doug(las A.). American (born United States), b. 1952. **Genres:** Librarianship, Education, Technology. **Career:** Stuart-Menlo Schools, English teacher, 1976-78; West Branch Schools, English teacher and librarian, 1979-84; Aramco Schools, library media specialist, 1984-89; Saint Peter Schools, library media specialist, 1989-91; Minnesota State University-Mankato, adjunct faculty, 1990-; Mankato Area Public Schools, director of media and technology, 1991-. Writer. **Publications:** The Indispensable Librarian: Surviving (and Thriving) in School Media Centers in the Information Age, 1997; The Indispensable Teacher's Guide to Computer Skills, 2nd ed., 2002; Learning Right from Wrong in the Digital Age, 2003; Teaching Right from Wrong in the Digital Age, 2003; Machines Are the Easy Part; People are the Hard Part: Observations about Making Technology Work in Schools, 2004; School Libraries Head for the Edge: Rants, Raves and Reflections, 2009; The Classroom Teachers Survival Guide to Technology, forthcoming. **Address:** 46813 Cape Horn Rd., Cleveland, MN 56017, U.S.A. **Online address:** dougj@doug-johnson.com

JOHNSON, Elizabeth A. American (born United States), b. 1941. **Genres:** Theology/Religion. **Career:** Catholic University of America, professor of theology, 1981-91; Fordham University, distinguished professor of theology, 1991-. Writer. **Publications:** Consider Jesus: Waves of Renewal in Christology, 1990; She Who Is: The Mystery of God in Feminist Theological Discourse, 1992; Women, Earth and Creator Spirit, 1993; Friends of God and Prophets: A Feminist Theological Reading of the Communion of Saints, 1998; Truly Our Sister: A Theology of Mary in the Communion of Saints, 2003; Dangerous Memories: A Mosaic of Mary in Scripture, 2004; Quest for the Living God: Mapping Frontiers in Theology of God, 2007. Contributor to books and journals. **Address:** Department of Theology, Fordham University, 107Duane Library, 441 E Fordham Rd., Bronx, NY 10458, U.S.A. **Online address:** ejohnson@fordham.edu

JOHNSON, E. Patrick. American (born United States), b. 1967. **Genres:** Social Sciences. **Career:** Amherst College, visiting lecturer, 1994-96, assistant professor, 1995-2000; Louisiana State University, Pre-Doctoral Scholar's Institute, director, 1997-99; Northwestern University, Department of Performance Studies, assistant professor, 2000-03, professor of African American studies and performance studies, 2003-, chair; Columbia College, Ellen Stone Belic Institute for the Study of Women and Gender in the Arts and Media, fellow. Writer. **Publications:** Appropriating Blackness: Performance and the Politics of Authenticity, 2003; (with M.G. Henderson) Black Queer Studies: A Critical Anthology, 2005; Sweet Tea: Black Gay Men of the South, 2008. **Address:** Department of Performance Studies, Northwestern University, Annie May Swift Hall, 1920 Campus Dr., Ste. G08, Evanston, IL 60208, U.S.A. **Online address:** e-johnson10@northwestern.edu

JOHNSON, Fenton. American (born United States), b. 1953. **Genres:** Novels, Gay And Lesbian Issues, Intellectual History, Theology/Religion, Autobiography/Memoirs. **Career:** U.S. Representative Ron Mazzoli, legislative assistant and press secretary, 1975-77; Rockefeller Foundation, freelance consultant, writer and editor, 1987; San Francisco State University, adjunct faculty, 1988-96; Santa Clara University, visiting faculty, 1992; Knight Foundation, freelance consultant, writer and editor, 1993; Columbia University, Program in Writing, adjunct assistant professor, 1996-98; New York University, adjunct assistant professor, 1997-99; Sarah Lawrence College, adjunct assistant professor, 1999-2000; University of Arizona, associate professor, 2000-; University of California-Davis, visiting distinguished professor of creative writing, 2003, 2005; Guggenheim fellow, 2008-09. Writer. **Publications:** Crossing the River: A Novel, 1989; Scissors, Paper, Rock, 1993; Geography of the Heart: A Memoir, 1996; Keeping Faith: A Skeptic's Journey among Christian and Buddhist Monks, 2003. Contributor to books and periodicals. Works appear in anthologies. **Address:** Creative Writing Program, University of Arizona, PO Box 210067, Tucson, AZ 85721, U.S.A. **Online address:** johnfenton@aol.com

JOHNSON, Freddie Lee. American (born United States) **Genres:** Novels, Politics/Government, History, Theology/Religion. **Career:** General Motors, Packard Electric Division, production scheduler; Contel Page Telecommunications, operations specialist; Aircraft Braking Systems Corp., corporate trainer; Malone College, professor of history; Walsh University, professor of history; Hope College, assistant professor of American history, 2000-, associate professor, professor. Writer. **Publications:** Bittersweet, 2002; A Man Finds his Way, 2003; Other Men's Wives: A Novel, 2005; (with T.L. McQuillar) Tupac Shakur: The Life and Times of an American Icon, 2010; Eagle on the Continent: U.S. Foreign Policy in Africa, 1945-Present, forthcoming; Second Bachelorhood: A Man's Guide to Succeeding after Divorce, forthcoming; While We Were Sleeping: African Americans Since the End of the Civil Rights Movement, forthcoming. **Address:** Department of History, Hope College, 126 E 10th St., Holland, MI 49423, U.S.A. **Online address:** johnson@hope.edu

JOHNSON, Galen K. American (born United States), b. 1970. **Genres:** Theology/Religion, History, Education. **Career:** Davidson County Community College, adjunct instructor, 1996-98; McLennan Community College, adjunct instructor, 2000-02; Baylor University, instructor in religion and coordinator of teaching fellows program, 2001-02; John Brown University, assistant professor of biblical studies and assistant director of honors and faculty development, 2002-, secretary; Grace Cumberland Presbyterian Church, preacher, 2004-; Victory Baptist Church, pastor; Blue Ridge Baptist Church, pastor. Writer. **Publications:** Prisoner of Conscience: John Bunyan on Self, Community and Christian Faith, 2003; (with C.S. Pastoor) Historical Dictionary of the Puritans, 2007. Contributor to periodicals. **Address:** John Brown University, 802 Amanda Dr., Siloam Springs, AZ 72761, U.S.A. **Online address:** gjohnson@jbu.edu

JOHNSON, George (Laclede). American (born United States), b. 1952. **Genres:** Information Science/Computers, Politics/Government, Sciences, Social Commentary, Biography. **Career:** Albuquerque Journal, staff writer and copy editor, 1976-77, police reporter, 1977-78; Minneapolis Star, special assignment reporter, 1979-82; New York Times, editor, 1986-94, contract writer, 1994-. **Publications:** Architects of Fear: Conspiracy Theories and Paranoia in American Politics, 1984; Machinery of the Mind: Inside the New Science of Artificial Intelligence, 1986; In the Palaces of Memory: How We Build the Worlds Inside Our Heads, 1991; Fire in the Mind: Science, Faith, and the Search for Order, 1995; Strange Beauty: Murray Gell-Mann and the Revolution in Twentieth-Century Physics, 1999; A Shortcut through Time: The Path to the Quantum Computer, 2003; Miss Leavitt's Stars: The Untold Story of the Woman Who Discovered How to Measure the Universe, 2005; The Ten Most Beautiful Experiments, 2008. Works appear in anthologies. **Address:** c/o Esther Newberg, International Creative Management, 40 W 57th St., New York, NY 10019, U.S.A. **Online address:** johnson@nytimes.com

JOHNSON, George Lloyd. American (born United States), b. 1955. **Genres:** History, Travel/Exploration. **Career:** East Carolina University, teaching fellow, 1984-85; University of South Carolina, Department of History, teaching assistant, 1986-90, instructor in history, 1990-91; Campbell University, Department of Government and History, assistant professor, 1991-98, associate professor of history, 1998-2001, director of historical studies, 2003-, professor of history, 2005-, Department of Government, History and Justice, interim chair, 2006. Writer. **Publications:** The Frontier in the Colonial South: South Carolina Backcountry, 1736-1800, 1997. Contributor to books and journals. **Address:** Department of Government, History and Justice, Campbell University, Rm. 207, D. Rich Bldg., PO Box 356, Buies Creek, NC 27506-0356, U.S.A. **Online address:** johnson@campbell.edu

JOHNSON, Greg. American (born United States), b. 1953. **Genres:** Novels, Novellas/Short Stories, Poetry, Literary Criticism And History, Biography, Young Adult Fiction, Education, Reference, Reference. **Career:** Kennesaw State University, associate professor, 1989-95, professor of English, 1995-; Emory University, professor; University of Mississippi, professor. Writer. **Publications:** Emily Dickinson: Perception and the Poet's Quest, 1985; Understanding Joyce Carol Oates, 1987; Distant Friends: Stories, 1990; A Friendly Deceit: Short Stories, 1992; Pagan Babies, 1993; Aid and Com-

fort: Poems, 1993; Joyce Carol Oates: A Study of the Short Fiction, 1994; I Am Dangerous: Stories, 1996; Invisible Writer: A Biography of Joyce Carol Oates, 1998; Sticky Kisses: A Novel, 2001; (with T.R. Arp) Perrine's Sound and Sense: An Introduction to Poetry, 10th ed., 2001, 12th ed., 2007; (comp. with T.R. Arp) Perrine's Literature: Structure, Sound and Sense, 8th ed., 2002, 10th ed., 2009; (with T.R. Arp) Perrine's Story and Structure, 10th ed., 2002, 12th ed., 2009; Last Encounter with the Enemy: Stories, 2004; (ed.) Joyce Carol Oates: Conversations, 1970-2006, 2006; Women I've Known: New and Selected Stories, 2007; (ed.) The Journal of Joyce Carol Oates: 1973-1982, 2007. **Address:** Master of Arts in Professional Writing, Kennesaw State University, Rm. 217, English Bldg., 1000 Chastain Rd., PO Box 2701, Kennesaw, GA 30144-5591, U.S.A. **Online address:** gjohnson@kennesaw.edu

JOHNSON, James W. American (born United States), b. 1938. **Genres:** Young Adult Non-fiction. **Career:** University of Arizona, associate professor of journalism, 1979-2003, professor emeritus, 2003-; Oakland Tribune, journalist and editor; Philadelphia Enquirer, journalist and editor; Providence Journal, journalist and editor; Arizona Republic, journalist and editor; Arizona Daily Star, journalist and editor; Phoenix Gazette, journalist and editor. **Publications:** NONFICTION: (with G.B. Montgomery and P.G. Manolis) One Step from the White House: The Rise and Fall of Senator William F. Knowland, 1998; (with D.W. Carson) Mo: The Life and Times of Morris K. Udall, 2001; Arizona Politicians: The Noble and the Notorious, 2002; The Wow Boys: A Coach, a Team and a Turning Point in College Football, 2006; The Dandy Dons: Bill Russell, K.C. Jones, Phil Woolpert and One of College Basketball's Greatest and Most Innovative Teams, 2009; Double No-Hit: Johnny Vander Meer's Historic Night Under the Lights, 2012. **Address:** Department of Journalism, University of Arizona, Rm. 101M, Franklin Bldg., Tucson, AZ 85721-0001, U.S.A. **Online address:** jwj@email.arizona.edu

JOHNSON, Jason. British/Irish (born Ireland), b. 1969?. **Genres:** Novels. **Career:** Irish Sunday People, news editor, through 2004; writer, 2004-; Irish News, staff; Belfast Telegraph, staff. **Publications:** Wound Licker (novel), 2005; Alina (novel), 2006. **Address:** Blackstaff Press, 4c Heron Wharf, Sydenham Business Park, Belfast, BT3 9LE, England. **Online address:** woundlicker@gmail.com

JOHNSON, Jazz Voyd. See **ROBINSON, Peter (Mark).**

JOHNSON, Je'Caryous. American (born United States), b. 1977. **Genres:** Young Adult Fiction. **Career:** I'm Ready Productions, executive producer and chief executive officer. Playwright and director. **Publications:** Men, Money, and Gold Diggers, 2009. **Address:** I'm Ready Productions Inc., 515 N Sam Houston Pkwy. E, Ste. 215, Houston, TX 77060, U.S.A.

JOHNSON, Joan Marie. American (born United States), b. 1935. **Genres:** History, Women's Studies And Issues, Biography, Autobiography/Memoirs. **Career:** University of California, research assistant, 1992-95, reader, 1994, teaching assistant, 1994-95, Miami University, visiting assistant professor of history, 1996-98; University of Cincinnati, visiting assistant professor of history, 1999-2000, adjunct assistant professor, 1999; Northeastern Illinois University, lecturer in history, 2003-, Newberry Seminar on Women and Gender, co-founder and co-director, 2007-; Roosevelt University, adjunct professor of history, 2003; Lake Forest College, lecturer, 2005. Writer. **Publications:** (Ed.) Southern Women at Vassar: The Poppenheim Family Letters, 1882-1916, 2002; (contrib.) Warm Ashes: Issues in Southern History at the Dawn of the Twenty-first Century, 2003; Southern Ladies, New Women: Race, Region and Clubwomen in South Carolina, 1890-1930, 2004; Southern Women at the Seven Sister Colleges: Feminist Values and Social Activism, 1875-1915, 2008; (ed. with M. Spruill and V. Littlefield) South Carolina Women: Their Lives and Times, 2009. Contributor to journals. **Address:** Department of History, Northeastern Illinois University, 5500 N St. Louis Ave., Chicago, IL 60625, U.S.A. **Online address:** joanmjohnson@comcast.net

JOHNSON, John L. American (born United States), b. 1945. **Genres:** Theology/Religion, History. **Career:** U.S. Postal Service, staff. Writer. **Publications:** Per Capita Income of Kentucky Counties in 1952, 1952; (ed. with P. Knoblock) The Teaching-Learning Process in Educating Emotionally Disturbed Children, 1967; Confessions of an Assistant Treasurer: The Calling Officer's Handbook, 1991; The Black Biblical Heritage: Study Guide for Upper Elementary - Junior High: Four Thousand Years of Black Biblical History,

1993; God's Kinship with Dark Colors, 1994; 500 Astounding Questions and Answers Concerning the Black Presence in the Holy Bible, 1999. **Address:** 8312 Pepperidge Dr., Berkeley, MO 63134, U.S.A.

JOHNSON, John W. (John William Johnson). American (born United States), b. 1946. **Genres:** Law, Natural History, Meteorology/Atmospheric Sciences, Military/Defense/Arms Control. **Career:** University of Minnesota, teaching assistant, 1970-73; Skidmore College, instructor, assistant professor, 1973-76; Clemson University, assistant professor, professor, 1976-88; University of Northern Iowa, professor of history and head of department, 1988-; University of Wales, visiting faculty, 1999. Writer. **Publications:** American Legal Culture, 1908-1940, 1981; Insuring against Disaster: The Nuclear Industry on Trial, 1986; The Dimensions of Non-Legal Evidence in the American Judicial Process: The Supreme Court's Use of Extra-Legal Materials in the Twentieth Century, 1990; (ed.) Historic U.S. Court Cases, 1690-1990: An Encyclopedia, 1992, 2nd ed. as Historic U.S. Court Cases: An Encyclopedia, 2001; The Struggle for Student Rights: Tinker v. Des Moines and the 1960s, 1997; (contrib.) Constitutionalism and American Culture: Writing the New Constitutional History, 2002; Griswold v. Connecticut: Birth Control and the Constitutional Right of Privacy, 2005; (with R.P. Green) Affirmative Action, 2009. Contributor to periodicals. **Address:** Department of History, University of Northern Iowa, Seerley 209, PO Box 0701, Cedar Falls, IA 50614-0701, U.S.A. **Online address:** john.johnson@uni.edu

JOHNSON, John William. See **JOHNSON, John W.**

JOHNSON, Jory (F.). American (born United States), b. 1950. **Genres:** Architecture. **Career:** Hunter Reynolds Jewell, landscape architect, 1985-87; University of North Carolina, assistant professor of architecture, 1987-91; University of Illinois, Department of Landscape Architecture, assistant professor, 1991-. Writer. **Publications:** (With M.B. Reeve and M.R. Van Valkenburgh) Transforming the American Garden: 12 New Landscape Designs, 1986; Modern Landscape Architecture: Redefining the Garden, 1991. **Address:** Department of Landscape Architecture, University of Illinois Urbana Champaign, 214 Mumford Hall, Urbana, IL 61801, U.S.A.

JOHNSON, Kathleen Jeffrie. American (born United States), b. 1950?. **Genres:** Young Adult Fiction, Children's Fiction, Social Sciences. **Career:** Library technician and novelist. **Publications:** The Parallel Universe of Liars, 2002; Target, 2003; A Fast and Brutal Wing, 2004; Dumb Love, 2005; Gone, 2007. **Address:** Roaring Brook Press, 175 5th Ave., New York, NY 10010-7703, U.S.A. **Online address:** yak@kathleenjeffriejohnson.com

JOHNSON, K. C. See **JOHNSON, Robert David.**

JOHNSON, Kenneth C. American (born United States), b. 1942. **Genres:** Novels. **Career:** University of California, instructor; University of Southern California, Film School, instructor. Writer. **Publications:** NOVELS: V: The Second Generation, 2007; V: The Original Miniseries, 2008. **Address:** 4461 Vista Del Monte Ave., Sherman Oaks, CA 91403, U.S.A. **Online address:** kennycjohnson@aol.com

JOHNSON, Leland R(oss). American (born United States), b. 1937. **Genres:** Local History/Rural Topics, History, Military/Defense/Arms Control. **Career:** Rock Island Railroad, construction manager, 1955-57; Trunkline Gas Co., construction manager, 1956-57; teacher, 1957-63; Western Kentucky University, instructor in history, 1964-67; Clio Research Co., founder, 1967, owner, 1967-; Vanderbilt University, George Peabody College, instructor, 1967-70; U.S. Army, Corps of Engineers, historian and technical writer, 1978-79, senior historian, 1980-81; Sandia National Laboratories, corporate historian, 1994-96. Writer. **Publications:** The Building of Nashville, 1968; Falls City Engineers: A History of the Louisville District, Corps of Engineers, United States Army, 1974; Men, Mountains, and Rivers, 1977; From Memphis to Bristol: A Half Century of Highway Construction, 1978; Engineers on the Twin Rivers: A History of the Nashville District Corps of Engineers, United States Army, 1978; Headwaters District: A History of the Pittsburgh District, U.S. Army Corps of Engineers, 1979; The Tennessee Limestone Industry: A History of Its Association, 1982; Boys Will Be Men: Middle Tennessee Scouting Since 1910, 1983; Davis Island Lock and Dam, 1870-1922, 1985; The First Presbyterian Church of Nashville: A Documentary History, 1986; (with J.S. Minnotte) Headwaters District Roundtables, 1989; The Parthenon of Nashville, 1991; Ohio River Division, U.S. Army Corps of Engineers, 1992; Oak Ridge National Laboratory: The First Fifty Years, 1994;

(with C.E. Parrish) Engineering the Kentucky River: The Commonwealth's Waterway, 1999; (with C.E. Parrish) Triumph at the Falls: The Louisville and Portland Canal, 2007; Situation Desperate: U.S. Army Engineer Disaster Relief Operations, Origins to 1950, 2011. **Address:** 301 Lake Westmoreland Rd., Westmoreland, TN 37186-4812, U.S.A.

JOHNSON, LouAnne. American (born United States), b. 1953. **Genres:** Documentaries/Reportage, Adult Non-fiction, Novels. **Career:** Copley News Service, special sections editor, 1982-84; Xerox PARC, personal assistant to the corporate director of systems technology, 1984-87; Del Mar Publishing, assistant editor, editorial supervisor, staff writer, 1988-89; Carlmont High School, English teacher and department head, 1989-; Santa Fe Community College, assistant professor. **Publications:** Making Waves: A Woman in This Man's Navy, 1986; My Posse Don't Do Homework, 1992 as Dangerous Minds, 1995; Girls in the Back of the Class, 1995; School is not a Four Letter Word, 1997; Two Parts Text Book, One Part Love: A Recipe for Successful Teaching, 1998; Queen of Education: Rules for Making School Work, 2004; Teaching Outside the Box: How to Grab Your Students by Their Brains, 2005, 2nd ed., 2011; Vigilante Grandmas, 2005; Alternative Ed, 2007; Eddie Corazon, 2009; Muchacho: A Novel, 2009. Contributor to periodicals. **Address:** Macmillan Publishers Ltd., 175 5th Ave., New York, NY 10010, U.S.A. **Online address:** louannejo@yahoo.com

JOHNSON, Lynn Staley. See **STALEY, Lynn.**

JOHNSON, Marguerite Annie. See **ANGELOU, Maya.**

JOHNSON, Marilynn S. American (born United States), b. 1957. **Genres:** History. **Career:** Southern Methodist University, assistant professor of history, 1990-94; Legacies: A History Journal for Dallas and North Texas, editor, 1992-94; Pacific Historical Review, editor, 1993-96; Boston College, Department of History, assistant professor of history, 1995-97, associate professor, 1997-2005, graduate placement director, 1999-2006, professor, 2005-, chair, 2006-09; National Park Service, historical consultant, 2010-11. **Publications:** The Second Gold Rush: Oakland and the East Bay in World War II, 1993; (coauthor) America's History, 4th ed., 2000; Street Justice: A History of Police Violence in New York City, 2003; Violence in the West: The Johnson County Range War and the Ludlow Massacre, 2008. Contributor of articles to books, periodicals and journals. **Address:** Department of History, Boston College, Rm. 433, 21 Campanella Way, 140 Commonwealth Ave., Chestnut Hill, MA 02467-3859, U.S.A. **Online address:** marilynn.johnson@bc.edu

JOHNSON, Maureen. American (born United States), b. 1973. **Genres:** Novels, Young Adult Fiction, Romance/Historical. **Career:** Writer. **Publications:** The Key to the Golden Firebird, 2004; The Bermudez Triangle, 2004; 13 Little Blue Envelopes, 2005; Devilish, 2006; Girl at Sea, 2007; Suite Scarlett, 2008; (with J. Green and L. Myracle) Let it Snow: Three Holiday Romances, 2008; Scarlett Fever, 2010; The Last Little Blue Envelope, 2011; The Name of the Star, 2011. **Address:** HarperCollins Publishers, 10 E 53rd St., New York, NY 10022-5244, U.S.A. **Online address:** maureen@maureenjohnsonbooks.com

JOHNSON, Merri Lisa. American (born United States) **Genres:** Novels, Women's Studies And Issues. **Career:** Ohio University, teaching associate, 1994-96; State University of New York, graduate instructor, 1996-99; University of West Georgia, instructor of English, 1999-2000, visiting assistant professor of English, 2000-02; Lenoir-Rhyne College, visiting assistant professor of English and women's literature, 2002-03; Coastal Carolina University, assistant professor of English and cultural studies, 2003-06, Women's and Gender Studies Program, director, 2005-06; University of South Carolina Upstate, Center for Women's and Gender Studies, director, 2006-, assistant professor of languages, literature and composition, 2006-08, assistant professor of women's and gender studies, 2008-09, associate professor of women's & gender studies, 2010-, honors faculty, 2009-. Writer. **Publications:** (Ed.) Jane Sexes It Up: True Confessions of Feminist Desire, 2002; (ed. with R.D. Egan and K. Frank) Flesh for Fantasy: Producing and Consuming Exotic Dance, 2006; (ed.) Third Wave Feminism and Television: Jane Puts It in a Box, 2007; Girl in Need of a Tourniquet: Memoir of a Borderline Personality, 2010; Borderline Is, Borderline Ain't: Discourses of Stigma and the Dys/Regulation of Borderline Personality Disorder, forthcoming. Contributor of articles to books and periodicals. **Address:** Center for Women's and Gender Studies, University of South Carolina Upstate, 124 CASB, 800 University Way, Spartanburg, SC 29303, U.S.A. **Online address:** mjohnson@uscupstate.edu

JOHNSON, Michael P(aul). American (born United States), b. 1941. **Genres:** History, Essays, Cultural/Ethnic Topics. **Career:** LeMoyne College, assistant professor of history, 1967-68; San Jose State University, instructor in history, 1970-71; University of California, lecturer, 1971-73, assistant professor, 1973-76, associate professor, 1976-84, professor of history, 1984-94; Johns Hopkins University, department of history, professor, 1994-. Writer. **Publications:** Toward a Patriarchal Republic: The Secession of Georgia, 1977, (contrib.) From the Old South to the New: Essays on the Transitional South, 1981; (with J.L. Roark) Black Masters: A Free Family of Color in the Old South, 1984; (with J.L. Roark) No Chariot Let Down: Charleston's Free People of Color on the Eve of the Civil War, 1984; (co-author) The American Promise: A History of the United States, 1998; (ed.) Reading the American Past: Selected Historical Documents, 1998, 4th ed., 2009; (ed.) Abraham Lincoln, Slavery and the Civil War: Selected Writings and Speeches, 2001; The Making of a Slave Conspiracy, 2002. Contributor to journals and periodicals. **Address:** Department of History, Johns Hopkins University, 338E Gilman Hall, 3400 N Charles St., Baltimore, MD 21218, U.S.A. **Online address:** vze1vntz@verizon.net

JOHNSON, Mudrooroo. *See* **WOJAHN, David (Charles).**

JOHNSON, Neil L. American (born United States), b. 1954. **Genres:** Photography, Children's Non-fiction, How-to Books, History, inspirational/Motivational Literature, Military/Defense/Arms Control, Architecture, Children's Fiction, Adult Non-fiction, Geography, Humanities, Travel/Exploration. **Career:** Photo lab technician, 1976-80; photographer and writer, 1980-; Centenary College of Louisiana, photography instructor, 1981-2004. **Publications:** PHOTO-ILLUSTRATOR AND AUTHOR: Step into China, 1988; Born to Run: A Racehorse Grows Up, 1988; The Battle of Gettysburg, 1989; All in a Day's Work, 1989; Batter Up!, 1990; Fire and Silk: Flying in a Hot Air Balloon, 1991; The Battle of Lexington and Concord, 1992; Jack Creek Cowboy, 1993; Big-Top Circus, 1995; Shreveport and Bossier City, 1995; Ghost Night: An Adventure in 3-D, 1996; Louisiana Journey, 1997; National Geographic Photography Guide for Kids, 2001. Contributor of articles to periodicals. **Address:** 1301 Louisiana Ave., Shreveport, LA 71101, U.S.A. **Online address:** njohnson@njphoto.com

JOHNSON, Paul (Bede). British (born England), b. 1928. **Genres:** Architecture, History, Travel/Exploration, Biography, Essays. **Career:** Realité, assistant executive editor, 1952-55; New Statesman, assistant editor, 1955-60, deputy editor, 1960-64, director, 1965, editor, 1965-70; Iver Village Labour Party, chairman, 1966; American Enterprise Institute, DeWitt Wallace professor of communications, 1980. Writer. **Publications:** The Suez War, 1957; Journey into Chaos, 1958; Left of Center, 1960; Merrie England, 1964; Statesmen and Nations, 1971; The Offshore Islanders: From Roman Occupation to European Entry in US as The Offshore Islanders: England's People from Roman Occupation to the Present, 1972; (with G. Gale) The Highland Jaunt, 1973; The Life and Times of Edward III, 1973; A Place in History, 1974; Elizabeth I: A Study in Power and Intellect in US as Elizabeth I: A Biography, 1974; Pope John XXIII, 1974; A History of Christianity, 1976; Enemies of Society, 1977; (ed.) The Peripheral Circulation, 1978; The National Trust Book of British Castles, 1978, rev. ed., 1984; The Civilization of Ancient Egypt, 1978; Britain's Own Road to Serfdom (monograph), 1978; Civilizations of the Holy Land, 1979; A Tory Philosophy of Law, 1979; (contrib.) Will Capitalism Survive?: A Challenge by Paul Johnson With Twelve Responses, 1979; The Recovery of Freedom, 1980; British Cathedrals, 1980; (with I. Kristol and M. Novak) The Moral Basis of Democratic Capitalism: Three Essays, 1980; Ireland: Land of Troubles, 1980, new ed., as Ireland: A Concise History from the Twelfth Century to the Present Day, 1992; The Things That Are Not Caesar's, 1980; Pope John Paul II and the Catholic Restoration, 1982; A History of the Modern World from 1917 to the 1980's in US as Modern Times: The World from the Twenties to the Eighties, 1983, rev. ed. as Modern Times: The World from the Twenties to The Nineties, 1992; Aerofilms Book of London from the Air, 1984; The Pick of Paul Johnson, 1985; A History of the English People, 1985; Saving and Spending: The Working-Class Economy in Britain, 1870-1939, 1985; (ed.) Oxford Book of Political Anecdotes, 1986; (co-author) Unsecular America, 1986; A History of the Jews, 1987; Intellectuals, 1988; (ed. with E. Haimo) Stravinsky Retrospectives, 1988; Cathedrals of England, Scotland and Wales, 1990, rev. ed., 2000; (co-ed.) Workers versus Pensioners: Intergenerational Justice in an Ageing World, 1990; (co-ed.) American Government: People, Institutions and Policies, 2nd ed., 1990; The Birth of the Modern: World Society, 1815-1830, 1991; Wakes Up Britain!, 1994; The Quotable Paul Johnson: A Topical Compilation of His Wit, Wisdom, and Sat-ire, 1994; Offshore Islanders: A History of the English People, 1995; Paul Johnson in New Zealand, 1995; The Quest for God: A Personal Pilgrimage, 1996; Spring Address: What is a Conservative?, 1996; To Hell with Picasso, and Other Essays, 1996; A History of the American People, 1998; The Renaissance: A Short History, 2000; Napoleon, 2002; Art: A New History, 2003; Vanished Landscape: A 1930s Childhood in the Potteries, 2004; George Washington: The Founding Father, 2005; Creators: From Chaucer and Durer to Picasso and Disney, 2006; Heroes: From Alexander the Great and Julius Caesar to Churchill and de Gaulle, 2007; Churchill, 2009; Brief Lives, 2010; Humorists, 2010; Jesus: A Biography From a Believer, 2010; Socrates: A Man for Our Times, 2011. Contributor to books and periodicals. **Address:** New Statesman, 10 Great Turnstile, London, GL WC1V 7JU, England.

JOHNSON, Rebecca L. American (born United States), b. 1965. **Genres:** Novels, Human Relations/Parenting. **Career:** Writer. **Publications:** And Sometimes Why (novel), 2008. Contributor to periodicals and magazines. **Address:** NY , U.S.A. **Online address:** rebeccajohnsonauthor@yahoo.com

JOHNSON, Rebecca L. American (born United States), b. 1956. **Genres:** Natural History, Children's Non-fiction, Sciences, Illustrations, Young Adult Non-fiction, Adult Non-fiction. **Career:** Freelance writer and illustrator, 1982-; Great Plains Zoo and Delbridge Museum of Natural History, part-time instructor. **Publications:** FOR YOUNG ADULTS: The Secret Language: Pheromones in the Animal World, 1989; Diving into Darkness: A Submersible Explores the Sea, 1989; The Greenhouse Effect: Life on a Warmer Planet, Lerner, 1990; The Great Barrier Reef: A Living Laboratory, 1991; Investigating the Ozone Hole, 1993; Science on the Ice: An Antarctic Journal, 1995; Braving the Frozen Frontier: Women Working in Antarctica, 1997; What It Took: A History of the USGS EROS Data Center, 1998; A Walk in the Boreal Forest, 2001; A Walk in the Deciduous Forest, 2001; A Walk in the Desert, 2001; A Walk in the Prairie, 2001; A Walk in the Rain Forest, 2001; A Walk in the Tundra, 2001; Global Warming, 2002; Sylvia Earle: Protecting the Seas, 2002; Ernest Shackleton: Gripped by the Antarctic, 2003; Looking at Cells, 2003; You and Your Genes, 2003; The Magic of Light and Sound, 2003; (with P. Sereno) Paul Sereno: Digging for Dinosaurs, 2003; Robert Ballard: Discovering Underwater Treasures, 2003; Weather and Climate, 2003; Tracking Animal Migrators, 2003; Peering Into Darkness, 2003; Surviving Volcanoes and Glaciers, 2003; A Journey into a Lake, 2004; A Journey into a River, 2004; A Journey into a Wetland, 2004; A Journey into an Estuary, 2004; A Journey into the Ocean, 2004; Bones and Muscles, 2004; Respiration and Circulation, 2004; Chemical Changes, 2004; Puzzling Out Patterns, 2004; Acids and Bases, 2004; Sizing Up Shapes, 2004; Crunching Numbers, 2004; Decoding Data, 2004; Digestive System, 2005; Muscular System, 2005; Sistema Muscular, 2005; Eruption of Mount St. Helens, 2006; Tri-state Tornado, 2006; Machines: Simple and Compound, 2006; From Cells to Systems, 2006; Ocean Exploration, 2006; Plate Tectonics, 2006; San Francisco Earthquake, 2006; (with S. Foster) Desk Reference to Nature's Medicine, 2006; Genetics, 2006; Satellites, 2006; Nanotechnology, 2006; Aparato Digestivo, 2007; Carnivorous Plants, 2007; Atomic Structure, 2008; Ultra-Organized Cell Systems, 2008; Mighty Animal Cells, 2008; Powerful Plant Cells, 2008; Amazing DNA, 2008; Daring Cell Defenders, 2008; Understanding Global Warming, 2009; Investigating Climate Change: Scientists Search for Answers in a Warming World, 2009; (with S. Foster, T.L. Dog and D. Kiefer) National Geographic Guide to Medicinal Herbs: The World's Most Effective Healing Plants, 2010; Journey Into the Deep: Discovering New Ocean Creatures, 2010. OTHER: (with L.G. Johnson) Essentials of Biology (college text), 1986. **Address:** c/o Author Mail, Lerner Publications Co., 1251 Washington Ave. N, Minneapolis, MN 55401, U.S.A. **Online address:** rebeccajohnsonbooks@gmail.com

JOHNSON, Richard A. *See* **JOHNSON, Dick.**

JOHNSON, Rick. *See* **JOHNSON, Rick L.**

JOHNSON, Rick L. (Rick Johnson). American (born United States), b. 1954. **Genres:** Children's Non-fiction, Biography, Autobiography/Memoirs. **Career:** Concordia Blade-Empire, part-time reporter and photographer, 1972-75, sports editor, 1976-78, copy editor, 1978-81; Associated Press, wire editor, 1978-81; freelance writer, 1981-; Cloud County Community College, Travel/Tourism and Management Department, part-time assistant, 1981-82; Studentprofileservices.com, founder/owner, 2002-. **Publications:** Jim Abbott: Beating the Odds, 1991; Bo Jackson: Baseball/Football Superstar, 1991; Magic Johnson: Basketball's Smiling Superstar, 1992. Contributor of articles to periodicals. **Address:** Student Profile Services, PO Box 2875, Snowflake, AZ 85937, U.S.A. **Online address:** rljfw@frontiernet.net

JOHNSON, R. Kikuo. American (born United States), b. 1981?. **Genres:** Novels. **Career:** SPX: Small Press Expo, writer, 1998, 2003; Nickelodeon magazine, writer, 2006. **Publications:** Night Fisher (graphic novel), 2005; SPX: Small Press Expo, 1998; SPX 2003, 2003; Project: Superior, 2005. **Address:** Brooklyn, NY , U.S.A. **Online address:** rkikuo@seabread.com

JOHNSON, Rob. Australian/British (born England), b. 1927?. **Genres:** Poetry, Literary Criticism And History, Art/Art History, Young Adult Fiction. **Career:** University of New England, lecturer in English, 1954-58; University of Adelaide, lecturer, 1958-63, senior lecturer, 1963-70, reader, 1971-88. Writer. **Publications:** Walter Pater: A Study of His Critical Outlook and Achievement, 1961; Aestheticism, 1969; Caught on the Hop (poetry), 1984. **Address:** 3/63 Hackney Rd., Hackney, SA 5069, Australia. **Online address:** rhjohn@picknow1.com.au

JOHNSON, Robert David. (K. C. Johnson). American (born United States), b. 1967. **Genres:** History, Politics/Government. **Career:** Harvard University, lecturer, 1993-94; Arizona State University, assistant professor, 1994-95; Williams College, assistant professor, 1995-99; City University of New York, Brooklyn College, associate professor, 1999-2003, professor of history, 2003-, Graduate Center, associate professor of history, 2001-03, professor, 2003-. Writer. **Publications:** (Ed.) On Cultural Ground: Essays in International History, 1994; The Peace Progressives and American Foreign Relations, 1995; Ernest Gruening and the American Dissenting Tradition, 1998; (ed.) The Presidential Recordings: Lyndon B. Johnson, 2005; Congress and the Cold War, 2006; (ed. with E.R. May, P.D. Zelikow and K. Lundberg) Dealing with Dictators: Dilemmas of U.S. Diplomacy and Intelligence Analysis, 1945-1990, 2006; (as K.C. Johnson with S. Taylor, Jr.) Until Proven Innocent, 2007; Lyndon Johnson and Israel: The Secret Presidential Recordings, 2008; All the Way with LBJ: The 1964 Presidential Election, 2009. CONTRIBUTOR: Oxford Companion to American History, 2001; The Cultural Turn, 2002; Encyclopedia of American Foreign Policy, 2nd ed., 2002; Vietnam and the American Political Tradition: The Politics of Dissent, 2003; Looking Back at LBJ: White House Politics in a New Light, 2005; Lyndon B. Johnson: The Kennedy Assassination and the Transfer of Power, November 1963-January 1964, 2005. Contributor to journals. **Address:** Brooklyn College, City University of New York, 501 Whitehead Hall, 2900 Bedford Ave., Brooklyn, NY 11210, U.S.A. **Online address:** robertjohnson@brooklyn.cuny.edu

JOHNSON, R(odney) M(arcus). American (born United States), b. 1968. **Genres:** Novels, Young Adult Fiction. **Career:** Little Company of Mary Hospital, radiation therapist, x-ray technologist. Writer. **Publications:** The Harris Men, 1999; Father Found, 2000; The Harris Family, 2001; Love Frustration, 2002; Dating Games: A Novel, 2003; The Million Dollar Divorce: A Novel, 2004; Do You Take This Woman? A Novel, 2006; Stacie & Cole, 2007; The Million Dollar Deception, 2008; The Million Dollar Demise: A Novel, 2009; Why Men Fear Marriage, 2009; No One in the World, 2011. Works appear in anthologies. **Address:** c/o Warren Frazier, John Hawkins & Associates, 71 W 23rd St., Ste. 1600, New York, NY 10010-4185, U.S.A.

JOHNSON, Roger. American (born United States), b. 1942. **Genres:** Literary Criticism And History, Translations, History. **Career:** Writer. **Publications:** Molière and the Commonwealth of Letters (essays), 1975; (ed. with M.E. Clark) Curricular Reform: Narratives of Interdisciplinary Humanities Programs, 1991; (trans. with G. Fontecchio) Fifty Years of a Life in Music, 1905-1955, 1993. **Address:** Division of Literature & Languages, Lewis-Clark State College, 500 8th Ave., Lewiston, ID 83501, U.S.A.

JOHNSON, Sandy. American (born United States), b. 1934?. **Genres:** Information Science/Computers, Novels, Medicine/Health, Young Adult Fiction. **Career:** Writer. **Publications:** The CUPPI (novel), 1979; Walk a Winter Beach, 1982; Against the Law (nonfiction), 1986; The Book of Elders: The Life Stories of Great American Indians (nonfiction), 1994; The Book of Tibetan Elders: Life Stories and Spiritual Wisdom from the Great Spiritual Masters of Tibet (nonfiction), 1996; (with B. Glick and C. Pham) 1998 Oregon Domestic Violence Needs Assessment: A Report to the Oregon Governor's Council on Domestic Violence, 2nd ed., 2000; The Brazilian Healer with the Kitchen Knife: And Other Stories of Mystics, Shamans and Miracle-Makers, 2003. **Address:** c/o Publicity Department, Riverhead Books, 375 Hudson St., Ste. 4079, New York, NY 10014, U.S.A.

JOHNSON, Sara R. *See* **JOHNSON, Sara Raup.**

JOHNSON, Sara Raup. (Sara R. Johnson). American (born United States), b. 1966. **Genres:** History, Theology/Religion. **Career:** University of Rochester, visiting assistant professor, 1996-98; University of Connecticut, assistant professor, 1998-2004, associate professor, 2004-. Writer. **Publications:** Historical Fictions and Hellenistic Jewish Identity: Third Maccabees in Its Cultural Context, 2004. Contributor of articles to journals. **Address:** Department of Modern and Classical Languages, University of Connecticut, 228 J.H. Arjona Bldg., Storrs, CT 06269, U.S.A. **Online address:** sjohnson@uconnvm.uconn.edu

JOHNSON, Sherrie. American (born United States), b. 1948. **Genres:** Theology/Religion, Children's Fiction, inspirational/Motivational Literature, Novels. **Career:** Brigham Young University, Department of Ancient Scripture, instructor. Writer. **Publications:** Spiritually Centered Motherhood, 1983; Man, Woman and Deity, 1991; Abinadi, 1994; Nephi and Lehi in Prison, 1994; Alma at the Waters of Mormon, 1994; Ammon and the King, 1994; Broken Bow, 1994; Captain Moroni's Title of Liberty, 1994; The Gadianton Robbers, 1994; Jesus is Born, 1994; Jesus Visits the Nephites, 1995; Enos Prays, 1995; Jared and His Brother, 1995; A House with Wings: A Novel, 1995; Abish, 1996; Bible Treasury for LDS Children, 1999. **Address:** Department of Ancient Scripture, Brigham Young University, 316R JSB, Joseph Smith Bldg., Provo, UT 84602, U.S.A. **Online address:** smillsjo@aol.com

JOHNSON, Shoshana Nyree. American/Panamanian (born Panama), b. 1973. **Genres:** Biography, Military/Defense/Arms Control. **Career:** Writer and soldier. **Publications:** (With M.L. Doyle) I'm Still Standing: From Captive U.S. Soldier to Free Citizen-My Journey Home, 2010. **Address:** El Paso, TX , U.S.A. **Online address:** missshana@shoshanajohnson.com

JOHNSON, Stephen P. American (born United States), b. 1952?. **Genres:** Military/Defense/Arms Control, History. **Career:** Houston Chronicle, staff, 1979-. Journalist. **Publications:** The Complete Idiot's Guide to Sunken Ships and Treasures, 2000; (with R.T. Leon) Encyclopedia of Bridges and Tunnels, 2002; Silent Steel: The Mysterious Death of the Nuclear Attack Sub USS Scorpion, 2006. Contributor to periodicals. **Address:** c/o Author Mail, Wiley Books, 111 River St., Hoboken, NJ 07030-5774, U.S.A.

JOHNSON, Steven F(orrest). American (born United States), b. 1954. **Genres:** Local History/Rural Topics. **Career:** Lowell University, teacher of history, 1980-82; Lawrence Academy, adult education lecturer, 1981; teacher, 1982-84, 1985-86; DC Heath Publishing Co., salesperson, 1984-85; Marlborough High School, instructor in history, 1986-. Writer. **Publications:** New England Indians, 1980; Ninnuock (the People): The Algonkian People of New England, 1995, 2nd ed., 1997. **Address:** Marlborough High School, 431 Bolton St., Marlborough, MA 01752-3950, U.S.A. **Online address:** sjohnson@mps-edu.org

JOHNSON, Susan (M.). (Jill Barkin). American (born United States), b. 1939. **Genres:** Romance/Historical, Novels, Human Relations/Parenting. **Career:** Art historian and writer. **Publications:** Seized by Love, 1979; Lovestorm, 1981; Sweet Love, Survive, 1985; Blaze, 1986; The Play, 1987; Silver Flame, 1988; (as Jill Barkin) Hot Streak, 1990; Golden Paradise, 1990; Forbidden, 1991; Sinful, 1992; Blaze, 1992; Outlaw, 1993; Pure Sin, 1994; Brazen, 1995; Wicked, 1996; Taboo, 1997; A Touch of Sin, 1999; To Please a Lady, 1999; Legendary Lover, 2000; Temporary Mistress, 2000; Fascinated, 2000; Tempting, 2001; Seduction in Mind, 2001; Again and Again, 2002; Blond Heat, 2002; Delighted, 2002; Hot Pink, 2003; Force of Nature, 2003; (with T. Devine and K. O'Neal) Taken by Surprise, 2003; Hot Legs, 2004; Pure Silk, 2004; (with K. O'Neal and P. Rosenthal) Strangers in the Night, 2004; (with K. O'Neal and D. Whiteside) Not Just for Tonight, 2005; Twin Peaks, 2005; Hot Spot, 2005; French Kiss, 2006; When You Love Someone, 2006; When Someone Loves You, 2006; Wine, Tarts & Sex, 2007; (with S. Day and N. Mack) Perfect Kisses, 2007; Hot Property, 2008; At Her Service, 2008; Gorgeous as Sin, 2009; Sexy as Hell, 2010; (with T. Brisbin and M. Wine) Undone, 2010; Sweet as the Devil, 2011; Seductive as Flame, 2011. Works appear in anthologies. Contributor to periodicals. **Address:** Berkley Publicity, 375 Hudson St., New York, NY 10014, U.S.A. **Online address:** info@susanjohnsonauthor.com

JOHNSON, Susan (Ruth). British/Australian (born Australia), b. 1956. **Genres:** Novels, Adult Non-fiction, Young Adult Fiction, Essays, Romance/

Historical. **Career:** Courier-Mail, cadet journalist, 1975-77; Australian Women's Weekly, journalist, 1977-78; The Sun-Herald, journalist, 1980; The Sydney Morning Herald, feature writer, 1980-82; The National Times, correspondent, 1982-84; Novelist, 1984-; fiction writer, 1985-; Keesing Studio, resident, through 1992; The Age, journalist, 1999-2001; Agni Literary Magazine, contributing editor. **Publications:** FICTION: Messages from Chaos, 1987; Flying Lessons, 1990; A Big Life, 1993; Hungry Ghosts, 1996; The Broken Book, 2004, My Hundred Lovers, forthcoming. NONFICTION: A Better Woman: A Memoir, 1999; On Beauty, 2010. EDITOR: (with M. Roberts) Latitudes: New Writing from the North, 1986; Women Love Sex, 1996; Life in Seven Mistakes, 2010. Contributor of short stories to magazines. **Address:** Margaret Connolly & Associates, PO Box 945, Wahroonga, NW 2076, Australia. **Online address:** sjreaders@hotmail.com

JOHNSON, Todd. American (born United States), b. 1960. **Genres:** Novels, Literary Criticism And History. **Career:** Writer, musician and composer. **Publications:** The Sweet By and By (novel), 2009. Contributor to periodicals. **Address:** Wendy Sherman Associates, 450 7th Ave., Ste. 2307, New York, NY 10123, U.S.A.

JOHNSON, Victoria. American (born United States), b. 1958?. **Genres:** Dance/Ballet, Sports/Fitness, Medicine/Health, inspirational/Motivational Literature. **Career:** Victoria Johnson Intl., owner and president, 1994-. Writer, educator, entrepreneur, consultant and producer. **Publications:** (With M.V. Davis) Victoria Johnson's Attitude: An Inspirational Guide to Redefining Your Body, Your Health, and Your Outlook, 1993; Body Revival: Lose Weight, Feel Great, and Pump Up Your Faith, 2002. Contributor to periodicals. **Address:** Victoria Johnson Intl., PO Box 1744, Lake Oswego, OR 97035, U.S.A. **Online address:** info@victoriajohnson.com

JOHNSON, Whittington B. American (born United States), b. 1931. **Genres:** History, Race Relations. **Career:** Edward Waters College, instructor in social science, 1957-62; Savannah State College, assistant professor of social science, 1962-67; University of Miami, Department of History, associate professor, 1970-95, chair, 1976-77, 2000-02, professor of history, 1995-, now professor emeritus, Afro-American Studies Center, director, 1972-73; Civil Rights Museum, Savannah, board director. Writer. **Publications:** The Promising Years, 1750-1830: The Emergence of Black Labor and Business, 1993; Black Savannah, 1788-1864, 1996; Race Relations in the Bahamas, 1784-1834: The Nonviolent Transformation from a Slave to a Free Society, 2000; Post-Emancipation Race Relations in the Bahamas, 2006. Contributor of articles to books and periodicals. **Address:** Department of History, University of Miami, 619 Ashe Bldg., 1252 Memorial Dr., PO Box 248107, Coral Gables, FL 33146, U.S.A. **Online address:** wjohnson@miami.edu

JOHNSON, William Stacy. American (born United States), b. 1956. **Genres:** Theology/Religion, History. **Career:** WIOZ, radio announcer, 1973-74; attorney at law, 1981-85; Union Theological Seminary, teaching assistant and research assistant, 1987-88; Harvard University, teaching fellow, 1990-91; Austin Presbyterian Theological Seminary, assistant professor of systematic theology, 1992-96, associate professor of systematic theology, 1996-97, W.C. Brown associate professor of systematic theology, 1997-99; Westlake Hills Presbyterian Church, theologian-in-residence, 1995-99; Episcopal Seminary of the Southwest, visiting professor of theology, 1996-97; Princeton Theological Seminary, Arthur M. Adams associate professor of systematic theology, 1999-2009, Arthur M. Adams professor of systematic theology, 2009-, Arthur M. Adams chair of theology; First Presbyterian Church, theologian-in-residence. Writer. **Publications:** (Ed. with J.H. Leith) Reformed Reader: A Sourcebook in Christian Theology, 1993; (ed.) Theology, History and Culture: Major Unpublished Writings, 1996; The Mystery of God: Karl Barth and the Postmodern Foundations of Theology, 1997; A Time to Embrace: Same-Gender Relationships in Religion, Law and Politics, 2006; (ed. with P. Ochs) Crisis, Call and Leadership in the Abrahamic Traditions, 2009; John Calvin, Reformer for the 21st Century, 2009. **Address:** Department of Theology, Princeton Theological Seminary, 104 Hodge Hall, 64 Mercer St., PO Box 821, Princeton, NJ 08542-0821, U.S.A. **Online address:** stacy.johnson@ptsem.edu

JOHNSON-CARTEE, Karen S. American (born United States), b. 1956. **Genres:** Politics/Government, Adult Non-fiction, Advertising/Public Relations, Social Sciences. **Career:** University of Alabama-Birmingham, assistant professor, 1982-83; University of Alabama-Tuscaloosa, assistant professor, 1983-89, associate professor, 1989-96, professor of advertising and public re-

lations and communication studies, 1996-, College of Communication and Information Sciences, associate dean for undergraduate studies, 1991-95. Writer and political consultant. **Publications:** (Contrib.) New Perspectives on Political Advertising: The Political Communication Yearbook II, 1986; (with G.A. Copeland) Negative Political Advertising: Coming of Age, 1991; (with G.A. Copeland) Inside Political Campaigns: Theory and Practice, 1997; (with G.A. Copeland) Manipulation of the American Voter: Political Campaign Commercials, 1997; (with G.A. Copeland) Strategic Political Communication: Rethinking Social Influence, Persuasion, and Propaganda, 2004; News Narratives and News Framing: Constructing Political Reality, 2005. Contributor to periodicals and books. **Address:** College of Communication and Information Sciences, University of Alabama, 414-C Resse Phifer Hall, Tuscaloosa, AL 35487-0172, U.S.A. **Online address:** cartee@apr.ua.edu

JOHNSON-FREESE, Joan. American (born United States), b. 1952?. **Genres:** Mystery/Crime/Suspense. **Career:** University of Central Florida, Center for Space Policy & Law, director; Air War College, faculty; Asia Pacific Center for Security Studies, faculty; Harvard University, Summer and Extensions Schools, adjunct professor; Brown University, Watson Institute, adjunct professor; U.S. Naval War College, faculty, 2002-. CBS, consultant; CNN, consultant; BBC, consultant; Discovery Channel, consultant; ABC, consultant; New York Times, consultant; Washington Post, consultant; USA Today, consultant; Florida Today, consultant; Space News, consultant. Writer. **Publications:** (With R.L. Bledsoe and D.B. Slaughter) Legal Research Handbook: A Guide for Students and Laymen, 1985, Changing Patterns of International Cooperation in Space, 1990., Over the Pacific: Japanese Space Policy into the Twenty-first Century, 1993; (with R. Handberg) Space, the Dormant Frontier: Changing the Paradigm for the 21st Century, 1997; The Chinese Space Program: A Mystery within a Maze, 1998., The Viability of U.S. Anti-Satellite (ASAT) Policy: Moving Toward Space Control, 2000; Space as a Strategic Asset, 2007; Heavenly Ambitions: America's Quest to Dominate Space, 2009. Contributor to periodicals. **Address:** Center for Naval Warfare Studies, U.S. Naval War College, 686 Cushing Rd., Newport, RI 02841, U.S.A. **Online address:** johnsonj@usnwc.edu

JOHNSON-SMITH, Jan. British/American (born United States), b. 1963?. **Genres:** Sciences, Film. **Career:** Clark University, part-time teacher; Bournemouth University, Media School, faculty, 1995, senior lecturer in film and television, programme leader. Writer. **Publications:** American Science Fiction TV: Star Trek, Stargate, and Beyond, 2005. Contributor to journals. **Address:** Bournemouth Media School, Bournemouth University, Weymouth House, Talbot Campus, Fern Barrow, Poole, DS BH12 5BB, England. **Online address:** jjosmith@bournemouth.ac.uk

JOHNSTON, Alan (William). British (born England), b. 1942. **Genres:** Archaeology/Antiquities, History, Social Sciences. **Career:** National University of Ireland, assistant lecturer in classics, 1969-72; University of London, University College, lecturer and reader in classical archaeology, 1972-, professor of psychology, deputy director of Complex program, lecturer of Greek archaeology, 1992-, now emeritus reader in classical archaeology, Institute of Archaeology, Classical Archaeology Seminars, co-organiser. Writer. **Publications:** A Catalogue of Greek Vases in Public Collections in Ireland, 1973; The Emergence of Greece, 1976; Trademarks on Greek Vases, 1979; (with M. Pandolfini) Le Iscrizioni, 2000; Trademarks on Greek Vases: Addenda, 2006. Contributor to periodicals. **Address:** Institute of Archaeology, University College London, 31-34 Gordon Sq., London, GL WC1H 0PY, England. **Online address:** a.johnston@ucl.ac.uk

JOHNSTON, Anna. Australian (born Australia), b. 1972. **Genres:** Writing/Journalism, Travel/Exploration, History. **Career:** University of Tasmania, faculty member, deputy director of Centre for Colonialism and Its Aftermath. Writer. **Publications:** (ed. with H. Gilbert) In Transit: Travel, Text, Empire, 2002; Missionary Writing and Empire, 1800-1860, 2003. Contributor to books and periodicals. **Address:** Sch of English, Journalism & European Languages, University of Tasmania, PO Box 82, Hobart, TA 7001, Australia. **Online address:** anna.johnston@utas.edu.au

JOHNSTON, Barbara Rose. American (born United States), b. 1957. **Genres:** Environmental Sciences/Ecology, Politics/Government, History. **Career:** County of Santa Clara, environmental planner, 1978-80; California State University, lecturer in environmental studies, 1988-90; Simon Fraser University, adjunct professor and visiting lecturer in anthropology, 1990-91; Center for Political Ecology, research associate, 1991-, senior research fellow, 1991-; Society for Applied Anthropology Environmental Project, director. Writer, archaeologist and consultant. **Publications:** (Ed.) Who Pays the Price? The Sociocultural Context of Environmental Crisis, 1994; (ed.) Life and Death Matters: Human Rights and the Environment at the End of the Millennium, 1997, 2nd ed., 2010; (ed. with J.M. Donahue) Water, Culture, and Power: Local Struggles in a Global Context, 1998; (ed. with B.A. Brower) Disappearing Peoples?: Indigenous Groups and Ethnic Minorities in South and Central Asia, 2007; (ed.) Half-Lives and Half-Truths: Confronting the Radioactive Legacies of the Cold War, 2007; (with H.M. Barker) Consequential Damages of Nuclear War: The Rongelap Report, 2008; (ed. with S. Slyomovics) Waging War, Making Peace: Reparations and Human Rights, 2009; Water, Cultural Diversity and Global Environmental Change: Emerging Trends, Sustainable Futures?, 2011. Contributor of articles and reviews journals. **Address:** Center for Political Ecology, PO Box 8467, Santa Cruz, CA 95061, U.S.A. **Online address:** bjohnston@igc.org

JOHNSTON, Carolyn. *See* **JOHNSTON, Carolyn Ross.**

JOHNSTON, Carolyn Ross. (Carolyn Johnston). American (born United States), b. 1948?. **Genres:** History. **Career:** Colorado College, instructor, 1976-78; Eckerd College, assistant professor, 1978-83, associate professor, 1983-88, professor of American studies and history, 1988-, Women's and Gender Studies Program, director, 1990-2004; Florida Consortium, co-founder. Writer. **Publications:** Jack London: An American Radical?, 1984; (as Carolyn Johnston) Sexual Power: Feminism and the Family in America, 1992; Cherokee Women in Crisis: Trail of Tears, Civil War and Allotment, 1838-1907, 2003; My Father's War: Fighting with the Buffalo Soldiers in World War II, 2012. Contributor to books and periodicals. **Address:** Department of History, Eckerd College, 4200 54th Ave. S, Saint Petersburg, FL 33711, U.S.A. **Online address:** johnstc@eckerd.edu

JOHNSTON, Jennifer. Irish (born Ireland), b. 1930. **Genres:** Novels, Plays/Screenplays. **Career:** Writer. **Publications:** The Captains and the Kings, 1972; The Gates, 1973; How Many Miles to Babylon?, 1974; Shadows on Our Skin, 1977; The Old Jest, 1979; The Christmas Tree, 1981; The Railway Station Man, 1984; Fool's Sanctuary, 1987; The Invisible Worm, 1991; Three Monologues, 1995; The Illusionist (monologues), 1995; The Desert Lullaby: A Play in Two Acts, 1996; Two Moons, 1998; (contrib.) Finbar's Hotel, 1999; Gingerbread Woman, 2000; (contrib.) Great Irish Stories of Murder and Mystery, 2000; The Great Shark Escape, 2001; This is Not a Novel, 2002; Selected Short Plays, 2003; Grace and Truth, 2005; Foolish Mortals, 2007; Truth or Fiction, 2009; Shadowstory, 2011. **Address:** Headline Book Publishing Ltd., 338 Euston Rd., London, GL NW1 3BH, England.

JOHNSTON, Joan. American (born United States), b. 1948. **Genres:** Westerns/Adventure, Romance/Historical, Novels, inspirational/Motivational Literature, Young Adult Fiction. **Career:** Weekly Herald, news editor and drama critic, 1971-73; Southwest Texas Junior College, director of theater, 1973-77; Hunton & Williams, attorney, 1980-83; Squire, Sanders & Dempsey, attorney, 1983-85; Barry University, instructor, 1985-88; University of Miami, assistant professor, 1988-91. **Publications:** ROMANCE NOVELS: A Loving Defiance, 1985; Colter's Wife, 1986; Frontier Woman, 1988; Fit to Be Tied, 1988; Comanche Woman, 1989; Texas Woman, 1989; Marriage by the Book, 1989; Sweetwater Seduction, 1991; Never Teasea Wolf, 1991; A Wolf in Sheep's Clothing, 1991; The Barefoot Bride, 1992; A Little Time in Texas, 1992; Honey and the Hired Hand, 1992; Kid Calhoun, 1993; Outlaw's Bride, 1993; The Rancher and the Runaway Bride, 1993; The Cowboy and the Princess, 1993; Hawk's Way: Faron & Garth, 1993; The Wrangler and the Rich Girl, 1993; The Cowboy Takes a Wife, 1994; The Unforgiving Bride, 1994; The Headstrong Bride, 1994; The Inheritance, 1995; The Disobedient Bride, 1995; Maverick Heart, 1995; Captive, 1996; After the Kiss, 1997; Hawk's Way: The Virgin Groom, 1997; Hawk's Way: The Substitute Groom, 1998; The Bodyguard, 1998; The Bridegroom, 1999; Hawkes Way Bachelors, 2000; Hawkes Way Rogues, 2001; Hawkes Way Grooms, 2002; The Price, 2003; The Rivals, 2004; No Longer a Stranger, 2005; The Next Mrs. Blackthorne, 2005; The Diary, 2008; A Stranger's Game, 2008. NOVELS: The Cowboy, 2000; The Texan, 2001; The Loner, 2002; Sisters Found, 2002; Outcast, 2009; Shattered, 2010. OTHERS: (contrib.) Avon Books Presents, 1993; Invincible, 2010; Texas Bride, 2012. Works appear in anthologies. **Address:** Trident Media Group L.L.C., 41 Madison Ave., 36th Fl., PO Box 3368, New York, NY 10010, U.S.A. **Online address:** joan@joanjohnston.com

JOHNSTON, Joni E. American (born United States), b. 1960. **Genres:** Psy-

chology, How-to Books, Sports/Fitness, Medicine/Health. **Career:** West Side Veterans Administration Medical Center, intern in clinical psychology and neuropsychology, 1984-85; Hawthorne College, associate professor, 1984; Dallas Child Guidance Clinic, psychologist, 1985-87; Growth Co., founder, 1991, speaker and consultant, 1991-; Charter Hospital of Dallas, eating disorder coordinator, 1991; Work Relationships Inc., president and chief executive officer, 1991-; University of Texas, adjunct professor, 1992-; Mental Health Matters (cable television program), host and content producer, 1994-. Writer. **Publications:** Appearance Obsession: Learning to Love the Way You Look, 1994; Complete Idiot's Guide to Psychology, 2000, 4th ed., 2009; Complete Idiot's Guide To Controlling Anxiety, 2006; How Hearts Heal: Lessons of Hope and Courage Therapists Have Learned from Their Clients, forthcoming. Contributor to magazines. **Address:** WorkRelationships Inc, 1940 Seaview Ave., Del Mar, CA 92014-2228, U.S.A. **Online address:** jonij@workrelationships.com

JOHNSTON, Julie. Canadian (born Canada), b. 1941. **Genres:** Young Adult Fiction, Plays/Screenplays, Young Adult Non-fiction, Novels, History. **Career:** Therapist, 1963-65; Rehabilitation Centre, therapist, 1965-69; writer, 1980-; Peterborough Board of Education, Continuing Education Department, creative writing instructor, 1988-89. **Publications:** YOUNG ADULT NOVELS: Hero of Lesser Causes, 1992; Adam and Eve and Pinch-Me, 1994; The Only Outcast, 1998; In Spite of Killer Bees, 2001; As If By Accident, 2005; Very Fine Line, 2006. NONFICTION: (ed.) Love Ya Like a Sister: A Story of Friendship, 1999; Susanna's Quill, 2004. Contributor to periodicals. **Address:** c/o Author Mail, Tundra Books, 75 Sherbourne St., 5th Fl., Toronto, ON M5A 2P9, Canada. **Online address:** julie.johnston@sympatico.ca

JOHNSTON, Lyle. American (born United States), b. 1948. **Genres:** History, Biography, Autobiography/Memoirs. **Career:** United methodist minister, 1975-; United Methodist Church, Iowa Conference Archives and History North Central Commission, president, 1981-90; Kiwanis, president, 1998; St. Pauls' United Methodist Church, pastor. Writer. **Publications:** The Sioux City District: A History, 1978; The Dubuque District: A History, 1979; The Ottumwa District (church history), 1983; The Mason City District (church history), 1985; (ed.) Centennial Memories: Holbrook, AZ, 1993; Frank Waltron: Holbrook Lawman, 1996; Good Night, Chet: A Biography of Chet Huntley, 2003; Oratorical Genius: Gerald H. Kennedy, forthcoming. Contributor to periodicals. **Address:** St. Pauls' United Methodist Church, 141 N Hill St., Globe, AZ 85501-2105, U.S.A. **Online address:** tawanda_rev@yahoo.com

JOHNSTON, Marilyn. American (born United States), b. 1942. **Genres:** Education, Psychology, Young Adult Non-fiction, Reference. **Career:** University of Utah, Curriculum and Instruction, assistant professor, 1979-86, associate professor, 1986-88; Michigan State University, associate adjunct professor, 1987-88; Ohio State University, Integrated Teaching and Learning, assistant professor, 1988-91, associate professor, 1991-99, section head, 1998-2001, professor, 1999-2004; University of Illinois-Urbana-Champaign, Department of Curriculum and Instruction, head, 2005-06, professor, 2005-. Writer. **Publications:** Contradictions in Collaboration: New Thinking on School/University Partnerships, 1997; (contrib.) A Community of Learners, 1998; (co-ed. and contrib.) Collaborative Reform and Other Improbable Dreams: Professional Development Schools at the Ohio State University, 2000; Teaching Together: School/University Collaboration in the Social Studies, 2001; Constructing Ourselves: An Evolving Philosophy in the Open Classroom, 2001; Knowledge, Social Justice and Self Study, 2004; (co-author) Success Stories From a Failing School: Teachers Living Under the Shadow of NCLB, 2007. Contributor to books and journals. **Address:** Curriculum & Instruction, College of Education, University of Illinois, Urbana-Champaign, 319 Education Bldg., 1310 S 6th St., PO Box 708, Champaign, IL 61820, U.S.A. **Online address:** marilynj@illinois.edu

JOHNSTON, Michael. American (born United States), b. 1974?. **Genres:** Autobiography/Memoirs. **Career:** Colorado State Senate, legislator, 2009-, senator; New Leaders for New Schools, co-founder and policy advisor; University of Denver, adjunct professor of education. Writer. **Publications:** In the Deep Heart's Core, 2002. **Address:** Colorado General Assembly, 200 E Colfax Ave., Denver, CO 80203-1776, U.S.A. **Online address:** deepheartscore@hotmail.com

JOHNSTON, Richard. Canadian (born Canada), b. 1948. **Genres:** Politics/Government. **Career:** University of Toronto, assistant professor of political science, 1975-77, visiting professor, 1975-76; University of British Columbia, Department of Political Science, assistant professor, 1977-82, associate professor, 1982-88, professor, 1988-2006, 2009-, Canada Research Chair in Public Opinion, Elections, and Representation, European University Institute, Marie Curie research fellow; California Institute of Technology, visiting associate professor, 1985-86; Harvard University, Mackenzie King professor of Canadian studies, 1994-95; University of Pennsylvania, Department of Political Science, professor and research director, 2006-09. Writer. **Publications:** Bureaucrats and Elections, 1977; (contrib.) Two Political Worlds: Parties and Voting in British Columbia, 1985; Public Opinion and Public Policy in Canada: Questions of Confidence, 1986; (co-author) Letting the People Decide: Dynamics of a Canadian Election, 1992; (co-author) The Challenge of Direct Democracy: The 1992 Canadian Referendum, 1996; (with M.G. Hagen, K.H. Jamieson) 2000 Presidential Election and the Foundations of Party Politics, 2004; (ed. with P. Howe and A. Blais) Strengthening Canadian Democracy, 2005; (ed. with H.E. Brady) Capturing Campaign Effects, 2006; (with B.E. Shafer) End of Southern Exceptionalism: Class, Race, and Partisan Change in the Postwar South, 2006; (ed. with F.M. Kay) Social Capital, Diversity, and The Welfare State, 2007. **Address:** Department of Political Science, University of British Columbia, C424 Buchanan, C425-1866 Main Mall, Vancouver, BC V6T 1Z1, Canada. **Online address:** rjohnston@politics.ubc.ca

JOHNSTON, Ronald. (Mark Nelson). Scottish (born Scotland), b. 1926. **Genres:** Novels, Mystery/Crime/Suspense, Horror, Military/Defense/Arms Control. **Career:** Merchant Marine, master mariner, 1942-47, 1951-59, 1975-80; Chartered Insurance Institute, associate; Manufacturers Life Insurance of Canada, staff, 1947-51; Socony Mobil Oil Co., chief officer of marine transport service, 1952-58, Anglo-Dutch Cigar Company Ltd., salesman, general manager, director, 1959-63, part-time importers agent, 1963-65, full-time importers agent, 1963-65; Boston University, Mugar Memorial Library Special Collections, archival material, 1964; author, 1965-; Dunswood Products, managing partner, 1982-. **Publications:** Disaster at Dungeness, 1964 in US as Collision Ahead, 1965; Red Sky in the Morning, 1965 in US as Danger at Bravo Key, 1965; The Stowaway, 1966; The Wrecking of Offshore Five, 1967; The Angry Ocean, 1968; The Black Camels of Qahran in US as The Black Camels, 1969; Paradise Smith, 1972; The Eye of the Needle, 1975; (as Mark Nelson) The Crusoe Test, 1976; Sea Story, 1980; Flying Dutchman, 1983. **Address:** Manderston Mill, Berwickshire, Duns, TD11 3PP, Scotland.

JOHNSTON, R(onald) J(ohn). British (born England), b. 1941. **Genres:** Geography, History, Politics/Government. **Career:** Monash University, lecturer in geography, 1964-66; University of Canterbury, lecturer, 1967-69, senior lecturer, 1969-73, reader in geography, 1973-74; New Zealand Geographer, editor, 1969-74; University of Toronto, associate professor, 1972; University of Sheffield, professor of geography, 1972-92, department head, 1982-85, pro-vice-chancellor for academic affairs, 1989-92; University of the Witwatersrand, professor, 1976; Environment and Planning, co-editor, 1979-; Progress in Human Geography, co-editor and review editor, 1980-; Institute of British Geographers, secretary, 1982-85, president, 1990; University of Edinburgh, Wreford Watson memorial lecturer, 1992; University of Essex, vice-chancellor, 1992-95; University of Bristol, School of Geographical Sciences, professor of geographical sciences, 1995-; Macquarie University, visiting research fellow in earth sciences, 1998, adjunct professor of human geography, 1999; Royal Holloway-Bedford College, Gordon Manley lecturer, 1999; University of North Carolina, Frey distinguished visiting professor, 2001. **Publications:** (With P.J. Rimmer) Derelict Land in the City of Bendigo, 1966; (with P.J. Rimmer) Retailing in Melbourne, 1969; Urban Residential Patterns, 1971; (ed. with J.M. Soons) Proceedings of the Sixth New Zealand Geography Conference, 2 vols., 1971; (ed.) Urbanization in New Zealand: Geographical Essays, 1973; Spatial Structures: An Introduction to the Study of Spatial Systems in Human Geography, 1973; (ed.) Society and Environment in New Zealand, 1974; The World Trade System: Some Enquiries into Its Spatial Structure, 1976; The New Zealanders: How They Live and Work, 1976; (ed. with D.T. Herbert) Social Areas in Cities: Processes, Patterns, and Problems, 3 vols., 1976-78; (with B.E. Coates and P.L. Knox) Geography and Inequality, 1977; (ed.) People, Places and Votes: Essays on the Electoral Geography of Australia and New Zealand, 1977; Multivariate Statistical Analysis in Geography: A Primer on the General Linear Model, 1978; (ed. with D.T. Herbert) Geography and the Urban Environment (annual), 1978; (ed. with D.T. Herbert) Geography and Urban Environment: Progress in Research and Applications, 6 vols., 1978-84; (with P.J. Taylor) Geography of Elections, 1979; Political, Electoral and Spatial Systems, 1979; Geography and Geographers: Anglo-American Human Geography since 1945, 1979, (with J.D. Sidaway) 6th ed., 2004; The Geography of Federal Spending in

the United States, 1980; City and Society, 1980; (co-ed.) Dictionary of Human Geography, 1981, 4th ed., 2000; The American Urban System, 1981; (ed. with J.C. Doornkamp) The Changing Geography of the United Kingdom, 1982, rev. ed., 1991; (ed.) The Future of Geography, 1982; Geography and the State, 1982; (ed. with K.R. Cox) Conflict: Politics and the Urban Scene, 1982; (ed. with K.R. Cox) Conflict, Politics, and the Urban Scene, 1982; Philosophy and Human Geography, 1983, 2nd ed., 1989; Residential Segregation: The State and Constitutional Conflict in American Urban Areas, 1984; (ed. with P. Claval) Geography since the Second World War, 1984; The Geography of English Politics, 1985; On Human Geography, 1986; Bell Ringing: The English Art of Change Ringing, 1986; A Nation Dividing?: The Electoral Map of Great Britain, 1979-1987, 1988; (ed. with P.J. Taylor) A World in Crisis, 1986, 2nd ed., 1989; Environmental Problems, 1989; An Atlas of Bells, 1989; (ed. with F.M. Shelley and P.J. Taylor) Developments in Electoral Geography, 1990; A Question of Place, 1991; (ed.) The Challenge for Geography: A Changing World, a Changing Discipline, 1993; (co-ed.) Geographies of Global Change: Remapping the World in the Late Twentieth Century, 1995, (ed. with P.J. Taylor and M.J. Watts) 2nd ed., 2002; Nature, State, and Economy: A Political Economy of the Environment, 1996; (with D.J. Rossiter and C.J. Pattie) The Boundary Commissions: Redrawing the UK's Map of Parliamentary Constituencies, 1999, 2nd ed., 2009; (co-author) From Votes to Seats: The Operation of the UK Electoral System Since 1945, 2001; (ed. with M. Williams) Century of British Geography, 2003; (ed. with P. Cloke) Spaces of Geographical Thought: Deconstructing Human Geography's Binaries, 2005; (with C. Pattie) Putting Voters in their Place: Geography and Elections in Great Britain, 2006. Contributor of articles to books and journals. **Address:** School of Geographical Sciences, University of Bristol, Rm. 1.9s, University Rd., Bristol, GL BS8 1SS, England. **Online address:** r.johnston@bristol.ac.uk

JOHNSTON, Stanley H(oward). American (born United States), b. 1946. **Genres:** Bibliography, Horticulture, Sciences, Reference. **Career:** University of Western Ontario, assistant, 1972-73; Holden Arboretum, bibliographer for Cleveland herbals project, 1984-90, curator of rare books, 1989-, vice-president. Writer. **Publications:** The Cleveland Herbal, Botanical, and Horticultural Collections: A Descriptive Bibliography of Pre-1830 Works From The Libraries of the Holden Arboretum, the Cleveland Medical Library Association, and the Garden Center of Greater Cleveland, 1992; Cleveland's Treasures from the World of Botanical Literature, 1998. **Address:** The Holden Arboretum, 9500 Sperry Rd., Kirtland, OH 44094, U.S.A. **Online address:** sjohnston@holdenarb.org

JOHNSTON, William Murray. Australian/American (born United States), b. 1936. **Genres:** History, Theology/Religion. **Career:** University of Massachusetts, assistant professor, 1965-70, associate professor, 1970-75, professor of history, 1975-99, professor emeritus, 1999-; Yarra Theological Union, faculty associate in church history. Writer. **Publications:** The Formative Years of R.G. Collingwood, 1968; The Austrian Mind: An Intellectual and Social History 1848-1938, 1972; Vienna, Vienna: The Golden Age, 1815-1914, 1981; In Search of Italy: Foreign Writers in Northern Italy since 1800, 1987; Celebrations: The Cult of Anniversaries in Europe and the United States Today, 1991; (contrib.) Ein Stein für die Kunst, 1994; Recent Reference Books in Religion: A Guide for Students, Scholars, Researchers, Buyers and Readers, 1996; (ed.) The Encyclopedia of Monasticism, 2000; Der österreichische Mensch, 2010. **Address:** Yarra Theological Union, 98 Albion Rd., Box Hill, VI 3128, Australia. **Online address:** william@betterlink.com.au

JOHNSTONE, Bob. Australian/Scottish (born Scotland) **Genres:** Technology, Information Science/Computers, History. **Career:** New Scientist Magazine, Japan correspondent; Far Eastern Economic Review, technology correspondent. **Publications:** We Were Burning: Japanese Entrepreneurs and the Forging of the Electronic Age, 1999; Never Mind the Laptops: Kids, Computers, and the Transformation of Learning, 2003; I Have Computers in My Classroom-Now What?, 2006; Brilliant!: Shuji Nakamura and the Revolution in Lighting Technology, 2007; Switching to Solar: What We can Learn from Germany's Success in Harnessing Clean Energy, 2010. Contributor to periodicals. **Address:** c/o Author Mail, Basic Books, 387 Park Ave. S, New York, NY 10016, U.S.A.

JOHNSTONE, Nick. American (born United States), b. 1970. **Genres:** Autobiography/Memoirs, Novels, Young Adult Fiction. **Career:** University of Westminster, teacher of creative writing; Journalist and author. **Publications:** Radiohead: An Illustrated Biography, 1997; Patti Smith: A Biography, 1997;

The Melody Maker History of Twentieth-Century Popular Music, 1999; Abel Ferrara: The King of New York, 1999; Sean Penn: A Biography, 2000; A Head Full of Blue (autobiography), 2002; Lou Reed: Talking, 2006; Yoko Ono: Talking, 2006; Johnny Depp: The Illustrated Biography, 2006, 4th ed., 2010; A Brief History of Rock 'N' Roll, 2007; Amy, Amy, Amy, 2008; Apples in the Morning, forthcoming. **Address:** The Guardian, Kings Pl., 90 York Way, London, GL N1 9GU, England. **Online address:** nrjohnstone@googlemail.com

JOINER, Gary D. (Gary Dillard Joiner). American (born United States), b. 1951. **Genres:** Biography, History. **Career:** Petroleum Graphics/Precision Cartographics Inc., owner, 1981-; Bossier Parish Community College, instructor, 1991-95; Louisiana State University, adjunct instructor, 1995-97, instructor, 1997-2004, assistant professor, 2004-09, associate professor, 2009-; Red River Regional Studies Center, director, 1999-. Writer and historian. **Publications:** (With E. Brock) Red River Steamboats, 1999; (with M.R. Plummer) Historic Shreveport-Bossier: An Illustrated History of Shreveport and Bossier City, 2000; One Damn Blunder from Beginning to End: The Red River Campaign of 1864, 2003; (with M.S. Joiner and C.D. Cardin) No Pardons to Ask, nor Apologies to Make: The Journal of William Henry King, Gray's 28th Louisiana Infantry Regiment, 2006; Through the Howling Wilderness: The 1864 Red River Campaign and Union Failure in the West, 2006; (ed.) Little to Eat and Thin Mud to Drink: Letters, Diaries and Memoirs from the Red River Campaigns, 1863-1864, 2007; Mr. Lincoln's Brown Water Navy: The Mississippi Squadron, 2007; (with E. Roberston) Lost Shreveport: Vanishing Scenese from the Red River Valley, 2010; (with C.H. White) Historic Haunts of Shreveport, 2010. Contributor of articles to journals. **Address:** Department of History and Social Sciences, Louisiana State University in Shreveport, 1 University Pl., Shreveport, LA 71115-2399, U.S.A. **Online address:** gdjoiner@bellsouth.net

JOINER, Gary Dillard. See **JOINER, Gary D.**

JOJEAN See **HOLLAND, JoJean.**

JOKINEN, Tom. Canadian (born Canada), b. 1962?. **Genres:** Autobiography/Memoirs. **Career:** Canadian Broadcasting Corp., radio producer and video journalist. **Publications:** Curtains: Adventures of an Undertaker-in-Training, 2010. **Address:** Ottawa, ON , Canada. **Online address:** tom@tomjokinen.com

JOLAOSO, Mabel. See **SEGUN, Mabel D.**

JOLIN, Paula. American (born United States) **Genres:** Novels, Young Adult Fiction, Science Fiction/Fantasy. **Career:** Writer. **Publications:** In the Name of God, 2007; Three Witches, 2009. **Address:** c/o Author Mail, Roaring Brook Press, 175 5th Ave., New York, NY 10010-7703, U.S.A. **Online address:** pgj@paulajolin.com

JOLLES, Michael Adam. British (born England), b. 1951?. **Genres:** History, Biography, Autobiography/Memoirs, Social Sciences. **Career:** Dr. Mccollum and Partners, general practitioner. Writer. **Publications:** The Northampton Jewish Cemetery, 1994; A Short History of the Jews of Northampton, 1159-1996, 1996; Samuel Isaac, Saul Isaac and Nathaniel Isaacs, 1998; Report of the Discovery of a Medieval Decorated Stone Capital at Lochstadt, 1999; The Chatham Hebrew Society Synagogue Ledger, 1839-1865, 2000; Jews and the Carlton Club, 2002; A Directory of Distinguished British Jews, 1830-1930, 2002; (ed. with W.D. Rubinstein and H.L. Rubinstein) The Palgrave Dictionary of Anglo-Jewish History, 2011. **Address:** 78 Greenfield Gardens, London, GL NW2 1HY, England.

JOLLY, Roslyn. Australian (born Australia), b. 1963. **Genres:** Literary Criticism And History, Travel/Exploration, Biography. **Career:** University of Newcastle, lecturer in English, 1990-94; University of New South Wales, School of English, Media and Performing Arts, lecturer, 1994-96, senior lecturer in English, 1997-, associate professor. Writer. **Publications:** Henry James: History, Narrative, Fiction, 1993; (ed. and intro.) South Sea Tales, 1996; (ed.) The Cruise of the Janet Nichol among the South Sea Islands: A Diary, 2004; Robert Louis Stevenson in the Pacific: Travel, Empire, and the Author's Profession, 2009. Contributor to periodicals. **Address:** School of English, Media and Performing Arts, University of New South Wales, Rm. 204, Robert Webster Bldg., Sydney, NW 2052, Australia. **Online address:** r.jolly@unsw.edu.au

JOLOWICZ, J(ohn) A(nthony). British (born England), b. 1926. **Genres:** Law. **Career:** University of Cambridge, Trinity College, fellow, 1952, assistant lecturer, 1955-59, lecturer, 1959-72, reader, 1972-76, professor of comparative law, 1976-93, professor emeritus, 1993-; Journal of Society of Public Teachers of Law, editor, 1962-80, president, 1986-87; University of Paris, associate professor, 1976, faculty chair, 1982-84; Gray's Inn, bencher, 1978; Hebrew University, Lionel Cohen lecturer, 1983; International Academy of Comparative Law, vice-president, 1994. **Publications:** Winfield on Tort, 1963; (ed.) H.F. Jolowicz's Lectures on Jurisprudence, 1963; The Division and Classification of the Law: Papers Submitted to the Joint Seminar of the Society of Public Teachers of Law and the Law Commissions of England and Scotland, Birmingham, July, 1969, 1970; Winfield and Jolowicz on Tort, 1971; (with M. Cappelletti) Public Interest Parties and the Active Role of the Judge, 1975; Judicial Protection of Fundamental Rights Under English Law, 1980; (co-author) Droit Anglais, 1986, 2nd ed., 1992; (with M. Capelletti) Le contrôle juridictionnel des lois: actes du colloque de l Association internationale des sciences juridiques, Uppsala, 26-28 juin 1984, 1986; (with R. Bernherdt) International Enforcement of Human Rights: Reports Submitted to the Colloquium of the International Association of Legal Science, Heidelberg, 28-30 August 1985, 1987; (ed. with C.H. van Rhee) Recourse against Judgments in the European Union: Voies de recours dans l Union européenne, 1999; On Civil Procedure, 2000. Contributor to journals. **Address:** Trinity College, University of Cambridge, G3b Whewells Ct., 10 West Rd., Cambridge, CB CB3 9DZ, England. **Online address:** jaj1000@cam.ac.uk

JONAITIS, Aldona. American (born United States), b. 1948. **Genres:** Natural History, Art/Art History, Anthropology/Ethnology, Literary Criticism And History, Social Sciences, Young Adult Fiction. **Career:** State University of New York at Stony Brook, lecturer to professor of arts, 1973-89, associate provost, 1984-86, vice-provost for undergraduate studies, 1986-89; American Museum of Natural History, vice-president for public programs, 1989-93; Columbia University, adjunct professor of art history and archeology, 1990-93; University of Alaska Fairbanks, professor of anthropology, 1993-, director, now director emeritus; University of Alaska Museum, director, 1993-2009, director emeritus, 2009-; Stanford University, visiting distinguished professor of American art history, 2002. Writer. **Publications:** Tlingit Halibut Hooks: An Analysis of the Visual Symbols of a Rite of Passage, 1981; (comp. with Z.P. Mathews) Native North American Art History: Selected Readings, 1982; Art of the Northern Tlingit, 1986; (ed.) From the Land of the Totem Poles: The Northwest Coast Indian Art Collection at the American Museum of Natural History, 1988; (ed.) Chiefly Feasts: The Enduring Kwakiutl Potlatch, 1991; (contrib.) Robert Davidson: Eagle of the Dawn, 1993; (ed.) A Wealth of Thought: Franz Boas and Native American Art, 1995; (ed.) Looking North: Art from the University of Alaska Museum, 1998; The Yuquot Whaler's Shrine, 1999; The Mowachaht Whaler's Shrine, 1999; Art of the Northwest Coast, 2006; (with A. Glass) Totem Pole: An Intercultural History, 2010; (intro.) Primitive Art, 2010; Discovering Totem Poles, 2012. **Address:** University of Alaska Museum, PO Box 756960, Fairbanks, AK 99775-6960, U.S.A. **Online address:** ffaj@uaf.edu

JONAS, Ann. American (born United States), b. 1932. **Genres:** Children's Fiction, Children's Non-fiction. **Career:** Rudolph de Harak Inc., designer, 1959-62; Advertis Inc., designer, 1962-63; Donald & Ann Crews, designer, 1964-; author and illustrator of children's books, 1981-. **Publications:** SELF-ILLUSTRATED FOR CHILDREN: When You Were a Baby, 1982; Two Bear Cubs, 1982; Round Trip, 1983; Holes and Peeks, 1984; The Quilt, 1984; Trayecto, 1985; The Trek, 1985; Now We Can Go, 1986; Where Can It Be?, 1986; Reflections, 1987; Color Dance, 1989; Aardvarks, Disembark!, 1990; The 13th Clue, 1992; Splash!, 1995; Watch William Walk, 1997; Bird Talk, 1999. **Address:** Greenwillow Books, 1350 Ave. of the Americas, New York, NY 10019, U.S.A.

JONAS, Manfred. American/German (born Germany), b. 1927. **Genres:** History, International Relations/Current Affairs. **Career:** U.S. Department of Defense, intelligence analyst, 1950-53; Free University of Berlin, visiting assistant professor of American history, 1959-62; Widener University, Widener College, associate professor of history, 1962-63; Union College, assistant professor, 1963-64, associate professor, 1964-67, professor, 1967-81, chair, department of history, 1970-81, Washington Irving professor of modern literary and historical studies, 1981-86, John Bigelow professor of history, 1986-96, director of graduate program in American studies, 1964-74, director of transdisciplinary program in American studies, 1981-, now professor emeritus; Freedom Forum Inc., board director, 1966-77; Eotvos Loran University, Dr. Otto Salgo visiting professor of American studies, 1983-84. Writer. **Publications:** Die Unabhängigkeitserklarung der Vereinigten Staaten, 1964; Isolationism in America, 1935-1941, 1966; The United States and Germany: A Diplomatic History, 1984. EDITOR: American Foreign Relations in the Twentieth Century, 1967; (with F.L. Loewenheim and H.D. Langley) Roosevelt and Churchill: Their Secret Wartime Correspondence, 1975; (with R.V. Wells) New Opportunities in a New Nation: The Development of New York after the Revolution, 1982. Contributor to periodicals. **Address:** Department of History, Union College, 807 Union St., Schenectady, NY 12308, U.S.A. **Online address:** jonasm@union.edu

JONAS, Raymond. Also writes as Raymond Anthony Jonas, Raymond A. Jonas. American (born United States), b. 1954. **Genres:** Politics/Government, Cultural/Ethnic Topics. **Career:** University of Washington, professor; UniversitÉ de Nantes, lecturer; UniversitÉ de Montpellier, lecturer. Writer. **Publications:** Industry and Politics in Rural France: Peasants of the Iseère, 1870-1914, 1994; France and the Cult of the Sacred Heart: An Epic Tale for Modern Times, 2000; The Tragic Tale of Claire Ferchaud and the Great War, 2005. Contributor of articles to journals. **Address:** University of Washington, PO Box 353560, Seattle, WA 98195-3560, U.S.A. **Online address:** jonas@u.washington.edu

JONAS, Raymond A. *See* **JONAS, Raymond.**

JONAS, Raymond Anthony. *See* **JONAS, Raymond.**

JONAS, Susan. American (born United States), b. 1938. **Genres:** Antiques/Furnishings, Theatre, Adult Non-fiction, Psychology, Homes/Gardens. **Career:** Time Inc., secretary, deputy picture editor, picture editor of Discover, 1961-87; freelance writer. **Publications:** EDITOR: Ellis Island: Echoes from a Nation's Past; 1989; (with G.S. Proehl) Dramaturgy in American Theater: A Source Book. WITH M. NISSENSON: Cuff Links, 1991; The Ubiquitous Pig, 1992; Going, Going, Gone: Vanishing Americana, 1994, 2nd ed., 1998; Snake-Charm, 1995; Friends for Life: Enriching the Bond Between Mothers and Their Adult Daughters, 1997, 2nd ed., 2007; Jewelled Bugs and Butterflies, 2000. **Address:** c/o Pam Bernstein, 790 Madison Ave., New York, NY 10021, U.S.A. **Online address:** susmar6o@aol.com

JONASDOTTIR, Anna G(udrun). Swedish/Icelander (born Iceland), b. 1942. **Genres:** Politics/Government, Sociology, Women's Studies And Issues. **Career:** Orebro University, senior lecturer in politics, 1986-2000, associate professor of political science, professor of women's studies, 2000-, professor of gender studies, School of Humanities, Education and Social Sciences, researcher, now professor emeritus of women's studies; University of Gothenburg, Departments of Women's Studies and Political Science, affiliated. Writer. **Publications:** Love Power and Political Interests: Towards A Theory Of Patriarchy In Contemporary Western Societies, 1991; Why Women Are Oppressed, 1994. EDITOR: (with K.B. Jones) The Political Interests of Gender, 1988; (with D.V. der Fehr and B. Rosenbeck) Is There a Nordic Feminism?: Nordic Feminist Thought on Culture and Society, 1998; (with K.B. Jones) Political Interests of Gender Revisited: Redoing Theory and Research With a Feminist Face, 2009. **Address:** School of Humanities,, Education and Social Sciences, Orebro University, Rm. F2222, Orebro, SE-701 82, Sweden. **Online address:** anna.jonasdottir@sam.oru.se

JONELL, Lynne. American (born United States), b. 1956. **Genres:** Children's Fiction, Young Adult Fiction, Picture/Board Books, Novels. **Career:** Boulder Public Library, director of graphics, 1981-82; freelance artist and writer, 1983-; The Loft Literary Center, writing instructor, 1999-2011, master track advisor, 2006-08. **Publications:** SELF-ILLUSTRATED: Bravemole, 2002. JUVENILE FICTION: Mommy Go Away!, 1997; I Need a Snake, 1998; It's My Birthday, Too!, 1999; Let's Play Rough, 2000; Mom Pie, 2001; When Mommy was Mad, 2002; (with A. Kingsriter) Move, and I Will Move: How The Great Church Builder Taught Me Step By Step, 2006; Emmy and the Incredible Shrinking Rat, 2007; Emmy and the Home for Troubled Girls, 2008; The Secret of Zoom, 2009; Hamster Magic, 2010. OTHERS: Emmy and the Rats in the Belfry, 2011; Lawn Mower Magic, 2012; Grasshopper Magic, 2013. **Address:** Putnam Books, 375 Hudson St., New York, NY 10014, U.S.A. **Online address:** lj@lynnejonell.com

JONES, Alan Griffith. British/Welsh (born Wales), b. 1943. **Genres:** Language/Linguistics, Travel/Exploration, Social Sciences. **Career:** University of Hertfordshire, lecturer, 1968-72, senior lecturer, 1973-82, German Centre, head, 1973-89, principal lecturer, 1985-97; Treffpunkt, honorary editor, 1977-86; German Teaching, honorary editor, 1991-94; Parbeck Citizen's Advice Bureau, adviser, 1999-. **Publications:** 77 mal England. Panorama einer Insel, 1967; The Germans: An Englishman's Notebook, 1968; (comp. and trans.) Anglo-German Songbook, 1968; This is Germany, 1980; (with L. Lawlor) Practice in German Grammar, 1992, 2nd ed., 2001; Chapters in Open University German courses, 1998. EDITOR/CO-EDITOR: Deutsche Schuler in England, 1972; British Teenagers on the Rhine, 1975; A Handbook of Information for Teachers of German, 1979; German in the Classroom, 1984; Wende 89, 1992; Aspekte deutscher Gegenwart, 1999. **Address:** 17 Bay Cres., Swsanage, DS BH19 1RB, England.

JONES, Alex S. American (born United States), b. 1946. **Genres:** Writing/Journalism, Biography, Social Sciences. **Career:** Daily Post-Athenian, managing editor, 1974-78; Greeneville Sun, editor, 1978-83; New York Times, business reporter, 1983-92; WNYC-AM, New York City Public Radio, On the Media radio programming, host, 1993; Public Broadcasting System (PBS), Media Matters, host and executive editor, 1996-; Duke University, Eugene Patterson professorship of journalism, 1998-2000; Harvard University, John F. Kennedy School of Government, Laurence M. Lombard lecturer in the press and public policy, 2000-, Laurence M. Lombard chair in the press and public policy, Joan Shorenstein Center on the Press, Politics and Public Policy, director, 2000-; Appalshop, director; International Center for Journalists, director. Broadcaster. **Publications:** (With S.E. Tifft) The Patriarch: The Rise and Fall of the Bingham Dynasty, 1991; (with S.E. Tifft) The Trust: The Private and Powerful Family Behind the New York Times, 1999; Losing the News: The Future of the News That Feeds Democracy, 2009. Contributor to periodicals. **Address:** John F. Kennedy School of Government, Harvard University, 79 JFK St., Taubman-268, PO Box 113, Cambridge, MA 02138-5801, U.S.A. **Online address:** alex_jones@ksg.harvard.edu

JONES, Allan Frewin. Also writes as Michael Coleman, Fiona Kelly, Fiona Saunders, Steven Saunders, Sam Hutton. British (born England), b. 1954. **Genres:** Young Adult Fiction, Picture/Board Books, Novels. **Career:** Writer, 1992-. **Publications:** STACEY AND FRIENDS SERIES: The Great Sister War, 1998; Pippa's Problem Page, 1998; My Sister, My Slave, 1998; My Real Best Friend, 1998; Stacy the Matchmaker, 1998; The New Guy, 1998; Copycat, 1998; Party Time, 1998; Sneaking Out, 1998; Scary Sleepover, 1998; Sister Switch, 1999; Fern Flips, 1999; Full House, 1999; You Look Great!, 1999; Bad Boy, 1999; The New Stacy!, 1999; Pippa on Air, 1999; Dream Sister, 1999. THE HUNTER AND MOON MYSTERIES: The Weird Eyes File, 1997; The Alien Fire File, 1997; The Skull Stone File, 1997; The Time Traveller File, 1988; The Thunderbolt File, 1998; The Star Ship File, 1998. FOR CHILDREN: Anna's Birthday Adventure, 1997; Meerkat in Trouble, 1998. OTHER: (with L. Pollinger) Teach Yourself Writing Children's Books, 1997. AS FIONA KELLY THE MYSTERY CLUB SERIES: Secret Clues, 1993; Dangerous Tricks, 1993; Hide and Seek, 1994; Secret Treasure, 1994; Crossed Line, 1994; Crash Landing, 1994; Poison!, 1994; Out of Control, 1994; The Secret Room, 1994; Spy-Catchers, 1995; The Empty House, 1995; Blackmail!, 1996; Hostage!, 1996. THE MYSTERY KIDS SERIES: Spy-catchers, 1995; The Empty House, 1995; Blackmail!, 1996; Hostage!, 1996. AS MICHAEL COLEMAN: Virus Attack, 1997; Access Denied, 1997. AS STEVEN SAUNDERS: Dark Secrets, Red Ink, 1988; Kisschase, 1989; Blind Ally, 1989. SPECIAL AGENTS SERIES AS SAM HUTTON: Countdown, 2003; Deep End, 2003; Final Shot, 2003; Full Throttle, 2004; Kiss and Kill, 2004; Meltdown, 2005. FAERIE PATH SERIES: The Faerie Path, 2007; The Lost Queen, 2007; The Sorcerer King, 2008. AS ALLAN FREWIN JONES: The Mole and Beverley Miller, 1987; The Cost of Going Free, 1988; Rabbit Back and Doubled, 1989; Millions of Lisa, 1990; Bad Penny, 1990; The Half Good Samaritan, 1991; Tommy and the Sloth, 1992; Wishing Bird and Co., 1993; Burning Issues, 1994; (with L. Pollinger) Writing for Children and Getting Published, 1997; Anna's Birthday Adventure, 1997; The Wicker Man, 1998; The Plague Pit, 1998; Blood Stone, 1999; Unquiet Graves, 1999; The Wreckers, 1999; The Monk's Curse, 1999; Ghostlight, 1999; The Phantom Airman, 1999; (with A. Kennaway) Meerkat in Trouble, 1999; The Tears of Isis, 2005; The Amulet of Quilla, 2005; Elephant of Parvati, 2005; The Mooncake of Chang-O, 2005; Legend of the Pharaoh's Tomb, 2005; Legend of the Anaconda King, 2006; The Cat Lady, 2006; (with S. Jones) Shut Your Mouth/Nick Shadow, 2006; (with G. Chalk) Trundle's Quest, 2010; (with G. Chalk) Fair Wind to Widdershins, 2010; (with G. Chalk) Fire Over Swallowhaven, 2010; (with G. Chalk) The Ice Gate of Spyre, 2011; (with G. Chalk) Sargasso Skies, 2011; Full Circle, 2012. LITTLE SISTER SERIES AS ALLAN FREWIN JONES: Copy Cat, 1995; The Great Sister War, 1995; My Sister, My Slave, 1995; Stacy the Matchmaker, 1995; The New Stacy, 1996; Parent Trouble, 1996; Star Search, 1996; Summer Camp, 1996. STACY AND FRIENDS SERIES AS ALLAN FREWIN JONES: Sneaking Out, 1995; Sister Switch, 1995; Full House, 1996; Party Time!, Red 1998; Pippa's Problem Page, 1998; My Real Best Friend, 1998; You Look Great!, 1999; Bad Boy, 1999; Scary Sleepover, 1999; Pippa on Air, 1999; Dream Sister, 1999; Fern Flips, 1999. WARRIOR PRINCESS: Rhiannon Of The Spring, 2009; Destiny's Path, 2011; Merion of the Stones, 2012; Destiny's Path: Caradoc of the North Wind, 2012. **Address:** Pollinger Ltd., 9 Staple Inn, Holborn, GL WC1V 7QH, England. **Online address:** allanfrewin@tesco.net

JONES, Alun Arthur Gwynne. *See* **CHALFONT.**

JONES, Amelia. Canadian/American (born United States), b. 1961. **Genres:** Art/Art History. **Career:** Art Center College of Design, instructor and advisor, 1990-91; University of California, assistant professor 1991-96, associate professor of 20th-century art and theory, 1996-99, professor, 1999-2003; University of Southern California, instructor in art history, 1992; Framework, co-editor, 1995-98; SIGNS: A Journal of Women in Culture and Society, associate editor, 2001-05; California Museum of Photography, curator of exhibitions; Armand Hammer Museum of Art, curator of exhibitions; University of Manchester, Art History and Visual Studies, professor and Pilkington chair, 2003-10, department chair, 2004-06, postgraduate coordinator, 2009; McGill University, Department of Art History and Communication Studies, professor, visual culture, Grierson chair. **Publications:** Postmodernism and the En-Gendering of Marcel Duchamp, 1994; Body Art/Performing the Subject, 1998; (ed. with A. Stephenson) Performing the Body, Performing the Text, 1999; Paul McCarthy: Pinocchio, 2002; Irrational Modernism: A Neurasthenic History of New York Dada, 2004; (ed.) Companion to Contemporary Art Since 1945, 2006; Self Image: Technology, Representation, and the Contemporary Subject, 2006; (co-trans.) Name: Readymade, 2008. Works appear in anthologies. Contributor of articles to journals. **Address:** Dept. of Art History & Comm. Studies, McGill University, Rm. W285, Arts Bldg., 853 Sherbrooke St. W, Montreal, QC H3A 2T6, Canada. **Online address:** amelia.jones@mcgill.ca

JONES, Andrew. British (born England), b. 1973. **Genres:** Economics, Geography. **Career:** University of London, Birkbeck College, reader in human geography, Department of Geography, Environment and Development Studies, professor. Geographer. **Publications:** Management Consultancy and Banking in an Era of Globalization, 2003; Review of Gap Year Provision, 2004; Dictionary of Globalization, 2006; Globalization Key Thinkers, 2010; Human Geography: The Basics, 2012. **Address:** Department of Geography, Environment & Development, Studies, University of London, Rm.710, Malet St., Birkbeck, London, GL WC1E 7HX, England. **Online address:** a.jones@bbk.ac.uk

JONES, Ann (Maret). American (born United States), b. 1937. **Genres:** Criminology/True Crime, Travel/Exploration, Women's Studies And Issues, History, Adult Non-fiction, Social Sciences. **Career:** Black College, faculty; City College of New York, assistant professor of English, 1970-73; University of Massachusetts, assistant professor of English and coordinator of women's studies, 1973-75; freelance writer, 1975-; New York State Council for the Arts, literary panelist, 1982-86; University of Southern Maine, visiting professor, 1985; Lake George Arts Council, writer-in-residence, 1986; Manhattanville College, faculty, 1986, 1994, 1997, 2000-02; Mount Holyoke College, faculty, 1986-97; Boise State University, distinguished visiting writer, 1997; The Nation, contributor. **Publications:** Uncle Tom's Campus, 1973; Women Who Kill, 1980, rev. ed., 1981; Everyday Death: The Case of Bernadette Powell, 1985; (with S. Schechter) When Love Goes Wrong: What to Do When You Can't Do Anything Right, 1992; Next Time, She'll Be Dead: Battering and How to Stop It, 1994, rev. ed., 2000; Guide to America's Outdoors: Middle-Atlantic, 2001; Looking for Lovedu, 2001; Kabul in Winter: Life without Peace in Afghanistan, 2006; War Is Not Over When It's Over: Women Speak Out from the Ruins of War, 2010. Contributor to periodicals. **Address:** c/o Ellen Geiger, Frances Goldin Literary Agency, 57 E 11th St., Ste. 5B, New York, NY 10003, U.S.A. **Online address:** ann@annjonesonline.com

JONES, Bart. American (born United States) **Genres:** Novellas/Short Stories. **Career:** Newsday, reporter; Associated Press, foreign correspondent. Writer. **Publications:** Hugo! The Hugo Ch Avez Story from Mud Hut to Perpetual Revolution, 2007. **Address:** New York, NY , U.S.A. **Online address:** bart.jones@newsday.com

JONES, Ben Lewis. American (born United States), b. 1941. **Genres:** Biography, Autobiography/Memoirs. **Career:** U.S. House of Representatives, Georgia congressman, 1989-93. Actor, politician and writer. **Publications:** Redneck Boy in the Promised Land: The Confessions of Crazy Cooter, 2008. Contributor to periodicals. **Address:** VA , U.S.A. **Online address:** info@cootersplace.com

JONES, Bill. *See* **JONES, William B(ryan).**

JONES, Bobi. *See* **JONES, R(obert) M(aynard).**

JONES, Brian Jay. American (born United States), b. 1967?. **Genres:** Social Sciences. **Career:** Writer, biographer, speech writer, policy analyst and administrator. **Publications:** Washington Irving: An American Original, 2008. **Address:** c/o Jonathan Lyons, Lyons Literary, 16 W 23rd St., Ste. 500, New York, NY 10011, U.S.A. **Online address:** brian@brianjayjones.com

JONES, Bridget. British/Welsh (born Wales), b. 1955. **Genres:** Food And Wine, Cultural/Ethnic Topics. **Career:** Hamlyn Test Kitchen, assistant home economist, 1978-80, home economist, 1980-81; Hamlyn Publishing, staff in cookery editorial department, associate editor, 1981-84, deputy editor, 1984-85, cookery editor, 1985-88; freelance writer and editor, 1988-. **Publications:** Fred s Pastry Book, 1981; Contact Grill, 1982; Jams, Pickles and Chutneys, 1983; Gale's Honey Book, 1983; Meals in Minutes, 1984; Cooking with a Wok, 1985; Complete Mince Cookbook, 1985; Making the Most of Your Microwave, 1985; Seasonal Cookery, 1986; Combination Microwave Cookbook, 1987; High Speed Food (juvenile), 1987; Microwave Tips and Timings, 1989; Barbecue Tips and Timings, 1990; Recipes from a Polish Kitchen, 1990; Kid's Cookbook, 1990; Does It Freeze?, 1991; Cooking and Kitchen Skills, 1991; Stir Fry Cooking, 1992; Diabetic Cookbook, 1992; The Quilting and Patchwork Project Book, 1992; Fresh Pasta Cookbook, 1993; Encyclopedia of Pasta, 1994; Book of Claypot Cooking, 1996; Mrs. Beeton's Christmas Menus, 1997; Le Cordon Bleu Dessert Techniques, 1999; Farmer's Market Guide to Vegetables, 2001; The Ultimate Juices for Healthy Living, 2002. EDITOR: Hamlyn Microwave Cookery Course, 1989; Home Preservation of Fruit and Vegetables, 1989; Mrs Beeton's Traditional Cake Decorating, 1991; Mrs. Beeton's Book of Baking, 1991; Mrs. Beeton's Complete Book of Fish and Seafood Cookery, 1992; Mrs. Beeton's Main Course Cookbook, 1992; Mrs. Beeton's Pantry: Preserving, Freezing, Cooking Ahead and Tasty Meals From Store Cupboard Basics, 1992; The Book of Cookery and Household Management, 1992; Mrs. Beeton's Complete Book of Cakes & Biscuits, 1993; Mrs. Beeton's Complete Book of Puddings and Desserts, 1993; Easy Dishes for Entertaining, 1994; Easy Everyday Dishes, 1994; Making More of Vegetables, 1994; Mrs. Beeton's Book of Summer: A Celebration of Summer Living, with Simple Seasonal Cooking, Traditional Activities and Perfect Pastimes for Warm Days, 1994; Mrs. Beeton's Traditional Christmas: Recipes, Gifts, Customs and Games From a Bygone Era, 1994; Soups, Starters and Savouries, 1994; Mrs Beeton's Best of British Home Cooking, 1997; (comp.) The Concise Mrs. Beeton's Book of Cookery, 1998. Contributor to magazines. **Address:** 88 High View Rd., Guildford, SR GU2 5RY, England.

JONES, Bruce. American (born United States), b. 1944?. **Genres:** Novels. **Career:** Bruce Jones Associates, owner; actor; author and screenwriter. **Publications:** Sorcerers: A Collection of Fantasy Art, 1978; Amberstar: An Illustrated Comic Odyssey, 1980; Tarotown, 1982; Twisted Tales, 1987; In Deep, 1991; Maximum Velocity, 1996; Sprinter, 1998. AS BRUCE ELLIOT: Village, 1982; Still Life, 2001; Death Rites, 2002; Deadman, 2006; Batman, Two-Face and Scarecrow: Year One, 2009; Checkmate. Chimera, 2009; The War That Time Forgot, 2009; (contrib.) Star Wars. Episode IV, A New Hope, 2010. Contributor to periodicals. **Address:** Doubleday, 1745 Broadway, New York, NY 10019, U.S.A.

JONES, Bryan D(avidson). American (born United States), b. 1944. **Genres:** Politics/Government. **Career:** University of Houston, assistant professor of political science, 1970-71; Wayne State University, assistant professor, professor of political science, chair of department, 1972-85; Texas A&M University, professor of political science and head of department, 1985-96, Puryear professor of liberal arts, 1991; University of Washington, professor, 1996-, Donald R. Matthews distinguished professor of American politics,

Center for American Politics and Public Policy, director; University of Texas, professor and J.J. Jake Pickle regents chair in congressional studies. Writer. **Publications:** Service Delivery in the City: Citizen Demand and Bureaucratic Rules, 1980; Governing Urban America: A Policy Focus, 1983; Governing Buildings and Building Government: A New Perspective on the Old Party, 1985; (with L.W. Bachelor and C. Wilson) The Sustaining Hand: Community Leadership and Corporate Power, 1986, 2nd ed., 1993; (with F. Baumgartner) Agendas and Instability in American Politics, 1993, 2nd ed., 2009; Reconceiving Decision-Making in Democratic Politics: Attention, Choice, and Public Policy, 1994; Politics and the Architecture of Choice: Bounded Rationality and Governance, 2001; (ed. with F.R. Baumgartner) Politics of Attention: How Government Prioritizes Problems, 2005; (with W. Williams) Politics of Bad Ideas: The Great Tax Cut Delusion and the Decline of Good Government in America, 2008. EDITOR: Leadership and Politics: New Perspectives in Political Science, 1989; The New American Politics: Reflections on Political Change and the Clinton Administration, 1995; (ed. with F.R. Baumgartner) Policy Dynamics, 2002. **Address:** Department of Government, University of Texas, 1 University Sta., A 1800, Austin, TX 78723, U.S.A. **Online address:** bdjones@u.washington.edu

JONES, Caroly. American (born United States), b. 1941. **Genres:** Travel/Exploration, Transportation, Reference. **Career:** Writer and educator. **Publications:** Tips for Frugal Travelers, 1998; The Frugal Traveler: How to See More of the World for Less, 2001. Contributor to periodicals. **Address:** HC 61, PO Box 5040, Ramah, NM 87321, U.S.A.

JONES, Carrie. American (born United States), b. 1971. **Genres:** Novels, Young Adult Non-fiction. **Career:** Ellsworth Weekly, reporter and editor; Ellsworth American, reporter; Bar Harbor Times, reporter. **Publications:** NOVELS: Love (and Other Uses for Duct Tape), 2008; Girl, Hero, 2008. NEED PIXIES SERIES: Need, 2008; Captivate: Playaway Children, 2010; Entice, 2010. NON FICTION: Tips on Having a Gay (ex) Boyfriend, 2007; Cutting Up Playgirl: A Cheerful Memoir of Sexual Disappointment, 2008; Love Letters Great Men, 2008. OTHERS: Sarah Emma Edmonds was a Great Pretender: The True Story of a Civil War Spy, 2011; Moe Berg: The Spy Who Played Baseball, 2012. Contributor to periodicals. **Address:** c/o Edward Necarsulmer IV, McIntosh & Otis Inc., 353 Lexington Ave., New York, NY 10016-0941, U.S.A.

JONES, Charlotte Foltz. American (born United States), b. 1945. **Genres:** Young Adult Non-fiction, Children's Non-fiction, Technology, Food And Wine, History, Animals/Pets, Mystery/Crime/Suspense, Human Relations/Parenting, Human Relations/Parenting. **Career:** Boulder Valley Public Schools, secretary, 1966-75; freelance writer, 1976-, Boulder Valley Schools, Lifelong Learning Program, writing instructor, 1990-2000; Boulder Senior Center, writing instructor, 1991. **Publications:** Only Child-Clues for Coping, 1984; Mistakes That Worked: 40 Familiar Inventions and How They Came to Be, 1991; Colorado Wildflowers: A Beginner's Field Guide to the State's Most Common Flowers, 1994; Accidents May Happen: Fifty Inventions Discovered by Mistake, 1996; Fingerprints and Talking Bones: How Real-Life Crimes Are Solved, 1997; Yukon Gold: The Story of the Klondike Gold Rush, 1999; Eat Your Words: A Fascinating Look at the Language of Food, 1999; Westward Ho!: Eleven Explorers of the West, 2005; King Who Barked: Real Animals Who Ruled, 2009. Contributor to magazines. **Address:** 1620 Quince Ave., Boulder, CO 80304-1111, U.S.A.

JONES, Christopher S. American/British (born England), b. 1971. **Genres:** Young Adult Fiction. **Career:** Writer. **Publications:** Legacy, 2001; Conrad, 2003. **Address:** c/o Author Mail, Xlibris, 436 Walnut St., 11th Fl., Philadelphia, PA 19106-3703, U.S.A. **Online address:** chrisjones@starpower.net

JONES, Constance. American (born United States), b. 1961?. **Genres:** History, Theology/Religion. **Career:** University of California, Graduate Theological Union, Department of Religious Studies, faculty; Columbia Theological Seminary, faculty; Banaras Hindu University, faculty; Vasanta College, faculty; California Institute of Integral Studies, faculty, Transformative Studies, core faculty. Writer. **Publications:** (With M. Vinet) Social Services and Work, 1983; (with D.L. Raper and J.J. Sbrega) The American Experience: Documents and Notes, 1985; Beat the MBAs to the Top!, 1987; The 220 Best Franchises to Buy, 1987; Karen Horney, 1989; Pasta, 1990 as Pasta: Sauces and Fillings for All Shapes and Sizes, 1993; (with D.L. Rapper) A Goodly Heritage: The Episcopal Diocese of Southern Virginia, 1992; Africa, 1500-1900, 1993; The European Conquest of North America, 1995; Trailblazers:

The Men and Women Who Forged the West, 1995; Sexual Harassment, 1996; R.I.P.: The Complete Book of Death and Dying, 1997; 1001 Things Everyone Should Know about Women's History, 1998; G.I. Gurdjieff e la sua eredita, 2005; (with J.D. Ryan) Encyclopedia of Hinduism, 2007; Gurdjieff in Tiflis, 2008; (co-author) Taking Refuge: Research on the True Buddha School, forthcoming. **Address:** California Institute of Integral Studies, 1453 Mission St., San Francisco, CA 94103, U.S.A. **Online address:** cjones@ciis.cdu

JONES, Daryl (Emrys). American (born United States), b. 1946. **Genres:** Literary Criticism And History, Poetry, Young Adult Fiction. **Career:** Texas Tech University, assistant professor, 1973-79, associate professor, 1979-82, professor of English and chairman of department, 1982-86; Boise State University, College of Arts and Sciences, professor of English and dean, 1986-91, provost and vice president for academic affairs, 1991-2004, Interdisciplinary Studies Program, director; State of Idaho, writer-in-residence, 1992-93. **Publications:** The Dime Novel Western, 1978; Someone Going Home Late: Poems, 1990. Contributor of articles to magazines. **Address:** College of Arts and Sciences, Boise State University, 1910 University Dr., Education Bldg., Ste. 601, Boise, ID 83725-1500, U.S.A. **Online address:** aprjones@boisestate.edu

JONES, David. Canadian/American (born United States), b. 1956?. **Genres:** Novels, Young Adult Non-fiction. **Career:** Writer. **Publications:** NOVELS: Baboon, 2007; Monks in Space, 2008. NONFICTION: Eagles, 1996; Whales, 1998; Ducks, 1998; North American Wildlife, 1999; Mighty Robots: Mechanical Marvels That Fascinate and Frighten, 2005. Contributor of articles to journals. **Address:** 119 W Pender St., Ste. 205, Vancouver, BC V6B 1S5, Canada. **Online address:** baboonboy@telus.net

JONES, David (Erik) Hay. British/Swedish (born Sweden), b. 1959. **Genres:** Travel/Exploration, Business/Trade/Industry, Politics/Government, Education. **Career:** Go For It, editor, 1982-83; Big Sur, editor, 1984-85; Architectural Press, sub-editor, 1985-86; Surveyor, chief sub-editor, 1986-87; Athens Daily News, sub-editor, 1987; freelance writer, 1987-; True North Adventure Holidays, director; Lapland Picture Library, managing director; Survival and Outdoor Techniques Magazine, Scandinavian correspondent, 1991-; The Public Ledger, Scandinavian correspondent, 1994-; Wilderness News, editorial director; Swedish Conservative Party, chairman. Photographer. **Publications:** (Contrib.) Sunday Times Travel Book 1985, 1985; Night Times and Light Times: A Journey through Lapland, 1989; (contrib.) Göra upp eld, 1996; (ed.) Words of Fire, Spirit of Grace, 2003. Contributor to periodicals. **Address:** The Viking Press, 375 Hudson St., New York, NY 10014, U.S.A. **Online address:** dhayjones@yahoo.com

JONES, David Lee. American (born United States), b. 1948. **Genres:** Science Fiction/Fantasy, Novels, Young Adult Fiction. **Career:** Applied Magnetics, quality engineer, 1973-78; Hughes Delco, senior quality engineer, 1978-. Writer. **Publications:** FANTASY NOVELS: Unicorn Highway, 1992; Zeus and Co., 1993; Montezuma's Pearl, 1995; The Princess Frog, forthcoming. **Address:** Larsen Pomada Literary Agents, 1029 Jones St., San Francisco, CA 94109-5023, U.S.A.

JONES, David Martin. Australian/Welsh (born Wales), b. 1951. **Genres:** Politics/Government, History. **Career:** Teacher, 1975-77, 1988-90; University of London, London School of Economics and Political Science, tutor, 1978-84, teacher, 1984-90, King's College, Centre for Urban Education, researcher, 1987-90; Brent Educational Workshop, Truancy Project, coordinator, 1981-88; Open University, tutor, 1982-89; North East London Polytechnic, teacher fellow, 1986-87; National University of Singapore, Department of Political Science, lecturer in political science, 1989-95; University of Tasmania, School of Government, senior lecturer in political theory, 1995-2003; The University of Queensland, associate professor. Writer. **Publications:** (With D.A. Bell, D. Brown and K. Jayasuriya) Towards Illiberal Democracy in Pacific Asia, 1995; Political Development in Pacific Asia, 1997; Conscience and Allegiance in Seventeenth Century England: The Political Significance of Oaths and Engagements, 1999; Myths of the Meltdown: The Curious Case of the Developmental State in the Asia Pacific, 1999; The Image of China in Western Social and Political Thought, 2000; (with M.L. Smith) Reinventing Realism: Australia's Foreign and Defence Policy at the Millennium, 2000; (ed.) Globalisation and the New Terror: The Asia Pacific Dimension, 2004; (with M.L. Smith) ASEAN and East Asian International Relations: Regional Delusion, 2006; (ed. with K. Windschuttle and R. Evans) The Howard Era, 2009; (ed. with A. Lane and P. Schulte) Terrorism, Security and the Power of Informal Networks, 2010. Contributor of articles to books and journals. **Address:** Department of Political Science, The University of Queensland, Sir Fred Schonnell Dr., Brisbane, QL 4072, Australia. **Online address:** d.jones2@uq.edu.au

JONES, David W(yn). Welsh (born Wales), b. 1950. **Genres:** Music. **Career:** University College Cardiff, lecturer in music, 1974-98, senior lecturer in music, 1998-2002, reader in music, 2002, professorial chair, 2007-, professor, head of school, 2008; University of Wales, lecturer in music. Writer. **Publications:** (Ed.) Divertimento in G for Violin, Viola and Violone (double bass), 1982; (ed. with J. Haydn) Fifteen Scottish, Welsh and Irish Folksongs /Arranged for High Voice (two duets), Violin, Cello and Piano, 1984; (with H.C. Robbins) Haydn: His Life and Music, 1988; (ed. with H.C.R. Landon) Missa Sunt Bona Mixta Malis: Hob. XXII: 2, 1992; Beethoven Pastoral Symphony, 1995; (ed.) Music in Eighteenth-Century Austria, 1996; (ed. with O. Biba) Studies in Music History Presented to H.C. Robbins Landon on His 70th Birthday, 1996; The Life of Beethoven, 1998; (ed.) Music in Eighteenth-Century Britain, 2000; Haydn: Oxford Composer Companions, 2002; The Symphony in Beethoven's Vienna, 2006; Life of Haydn, 2009. **Address:** School of Music, Cardiff University, Rm. 1.05, 33 Corbett Rd., Cardiff, SG CF10 3EB, Wales. **Online address:** jonesdw@cardiff.ac.uk

JONES, Denice. American (born United States), b. 1965. **Genres:** Adult Non-fiction, Art/Art History. **Career:** Crestfield Convalescent Home, certified aide, 1981-85; Visiting Nurses of Manchester, certified health aide, 1990-93; Living in Fear Ends Foundation (LIFE Foundation), founder, 1992-. Writer. **Publications:** The Other Side: The True Story of the Boy Who Sees Ghosts, 2000. **Address:** LIFE Foundation Inc., PO Box 1112, Manchester, CT 06045-1112, U.S.A. **Online address:** dajones1315@aol.com

JONES, D(ouglas) G(ordon). Canadian (born Canada), b. 1929. **Genres:** Poetry, Literary Criticism And History, Translations, Young Adult Fiction. **Career:** Royal Military College of Canada, lecturer in English, 1954-55; Ontario Agricultural College, lecturer, assistant professor of English, 1955-61; Bishop's University, assistant professor of English, 1961-63; University of Sherbrooke, associate professor, professor of English, 1964-94; Ellipse (publisher of English and French poetry in translation), founder, 1969; University of Victoria, visiting professor, 1978; Universite Canadienne en France, visiting professor, 1987. Writer. **Publications:** POETRY: Frost on the Sun, 1957; The Sun Is Axeman, 1961; Phrases from Orpheus, 1967; Under the Thunder, the Flowers Light Up the Earth, 1977; A Throw of Particles: New and Selected Poems, 1983; Balthazar and Other Poems, 1988; A Thousand Wooded Eyes (poems), 1991; The Floating Garden, 1995; Wild Asterisks in Cloud, 1997; Grounding Sight, 1999; Terre D'Or, 2001; Les Roses, 2003; Satoshi Saito, Louise Doucet-Saito: Marebito: Sculpture, 2006. TRANSLATOR: P.M. Lapointe, The Terror of the Snows: Selected Poems, 1976; (with M. Plourde and intro.) G. Miron, Embers and Earth: Selected Poems, 1984; P.M. Lapointe, The Fifth Season, 1986; (and ed.) The March to Love: Selected Poems, 1986; N. de Bellefeuille, Categorics: One, Two and Three, 1992; G. Miron, Embers and Earth: Selected Poems, 1994; E. Martel, For Orchestra and Solo Poet, 1996. OTHER: Butterfly on Rock: A Study of Themes and Images in Canadian Literature, 1970; (ed. with L. Blouin and B. Pozier) Esprit de corps: Québec Poetry of the Late Twentieth Century in Translation, 1997. **Address:** Houghton St., PO Box 356, North Hatley, QC J0B 2C0, Canada.

JONES, Douglas Samuel. See **JONES, D. S.**

JONES, D. S. (Douglas Samuel Jones). Scottish/British (born England), b. 1922. **Genres:** Information Science/Computers, Physics, Mathematics/Statistics, Sciences. **Career:** Massachusetts Institute of Technology, fellow, 1947-48; Victoria University, assistant lecturer, senior lecturer, 1948-57; New York University, research professor, 1955, 1962-63; University of Keele, professor, 1957-64; Journal of the Institute of Mathematics and Its Applications, associate editor, 1964-; University of Dundee, Ivory professor of mathematics and computer science, 1965-92, professor emeritus, 1992-; Proceedings of the Royal Society of Edinburgh, associate editor, 1969-82; SIAM Journal of Applied Mathematics, associate editor, 1975-92; Applicable Analysis, associate editor, 1976-92; Mathematical Methods in the Applied Sciences, associate editor, 1977-2002; Proceedings of the Royal Society, associate editor, 1978-83; Quarterly Journal of Mechanics and Applied Mathematics, trustee, 1980-92; Methods and Applications of Analysis, associate editor, 1992-; Journal of Engineering Mathematics, associate editor, 1992-; Communications in Applied Analysis, associate editor, 1997-. **Publications:** Electrical and Me-

chanical Oscillations, 1961; Theory of Electromagnetism, 1964; Generalised Functions, 1966; (with D.W. Jordan) Introductory Analysis, vol. I, 1969, vol. II, 1970; Methods in Electromagnetic Wave Propagation, 1979, 2nd ed., 1994; Elementary Information Theory, 1979; The Theory of Generalised Functions, 1982; (with B.D. Sleeman) Differential Equations and Mathematical Biology, 1983; Acoustic and Electromagnetic Waves, 1986; Assembly Programming and the 8086 Microprocessor, 1988; 80x86 Assembly Programming, 1991; Introduction to Asymptotics, 1996. **Address:** Department of Mathematics, University of Dundee, Dundee, DD1 4HN, Scotland.

JONES, Eileen. British (born England), b. 1952. **Genres:** Biography, Travel/Exploration. **Career:** Yorkshire Post, staff reporter; Holland Herald, staff reporter; Hull Daily Mail, journalist and sub-editor; Lancashire Evening Post, journalist and sub-editor; Northside Magazine, editor; Higher Education Academy, fellow; University of Huddersfield, School of Music, Humanities and Media, senior lecturer. **Publications:** Neil Kinnock, 1994; (co-author) The Yorkshire Guide, 1994. **Address:** School of Music, Humanities and Media, University of Huddersfield, 2/08 Journalism and Media Bldg., Queensgate, Huddersfield, WY HD1 3DH, England. **Online address:** e.jones@hud.ac.uk

JONES, Eva. See **JONES, Evan (Lloyd).**

JONES, Evan (Lloyd). (Eva Jones). Australian (born Australia), b. 1931. **Genres:** Poetry, Literary Criticism And History, Biography, Young Adult Fiction. **Career:** University of Melbourne, tutor, senior tutor, 1955-58, lecturer in English, 1964, senior lecturer, 1965-89; associate of English, 1989-; Australian National University, lecturer in English, 1960-63. Writer. **Publications:** Inside the Whale: Poems, 1960; Understandings: Poems, 1967; Kenneth Mackenzie, 1969; (ed. with G. Little) The Poems of Kenneth Mackenzie, 1972; Recognitions: Poems, 1978; Left at the Post, 1984; Alone at Last!, 2010. **Address:** PO Box 122, North Carleton, VI 3054, Australia.

JONES, (Everett) LeRoi. See **BARAKA, Imamu Amiri.**

JONES, Frank Lancaster. Australian (born Australia), b. 1937. **Genres:** Race Relations, Sociology. **Career:** Australian National University, research assistant in demography, 1958, Australian Institute of Aboriginal Studies, research officer, 1962, research fellow in sociology, 1963-66, fellow in sociology, 1966-69, senior fellow in sociology, 1969-72, head of the department of sociology, 1972-89, professor of sociology, 1972-2001, Division of Demography and Sociology, head, 1990-96, head of sociology program, 1990-2000, Research School of Social Sciences, associate director, 1997, visiting fellow, 2001; University of Texas, visiting associate professor, 1967-68; Australian and New Zealand Journal of Sociology, editor, 1970-72; Oxford University, Nuffield College, visiting professor, 1974-75; University of Wisconsin-Madison, visiting professor, 1975; American Journal of Sociology, international consulting editor, 1979-82; University of Rome, visiting research professor, 1983; Australian Bureau of Statistics, senior principal research scientist, 1989-90; Ibaraki University, visiting professor, 1991; University of Queensland, School of Social Science, adjunct professor, 2001-. Writer. **Publications:** (Contrib.) The Study of Immigrants in Australia, 1960; A Demographic Survey of the Aboriginal Population of the Northern Territory, with Special Reference to Bathurst Island Mission, 1963; Dimensions of Urban Social Structure: The Social Areas of Melbourne, 1969; The Structure and Growth of Australia's Aboriginal Population, 1970; (with L. Broom) A Blanket a Year, 1973; (with L. Broom and J. Zubrzycki) Opportunity and Attainment in Australia, 1976; (co-author) Investigating Social Mobility, 1977; (co-author) The Inheritance of Inequality, 1980; Is It True What They Said About Women: The Census 1801-1911 and Women in the Economy, 1984; (with P. Davis) Models of Society: Class, Stratification and Gender in Australia and New Zealand, 1986; Ancestry Groups in Australia: A Descriptive Overview, 1991; Sex and Ethnicity in the Australian Labour Market: The Immigrant Experience, 1992. Contributor to journals. **Address:** School of Social Science, University of Queensland, Level 3, 9 Michie Bldg.,, St. Lucia, QL 4072, Australia. **Online address:** f.jones@uq.edu.au

JONES, Gayl. American (born United States), b. 1949. **Genres:** Novels, Novellas/Short Stories, Plays/Screenplays, Poetry, Social Sciences, Humanities, Literary Criticism And History, Young Adult Fiction, Essays. **Career:** Wellesley College, faculty; University of Michigan, Department of English and Afro-American and African Studies, assistant professor, professor, 1975-83. Writer. **Publications:** Chile Woman (play), 1974; Corregidora (novel), 1975; Eva's Man (novel), 1976; White Rat (short stories), 1977; Song for Anninho (poetry), 1981; The Hermit-Woman (poetry), 1983; Xarque and Other Poems, 1985; Liberating Voices: Oral Tradition in African American Literature, 1991; The Healing, 1998; Mosquito, 1999; Die Volgelfaengerin. Works appear in anthologies. Contributor to periodicals. **Address:** c/o Author Mail, Beacon Press, 25 Beacon St., Boston, MA 02108-2824, U.S.A.

JONES, Geraldine. *See* **MCCAUGHREAN, Geraldine (Jones).**

JONES, Gerard. American (born United States), b. 1957. **Genres:** Popular Culture, Plays/Screenplays, Humor/Satire, Children's Fiction. **Career:** Lemon Custard Comics, co-founder; Art and Story Workshops, founder. Writer. **Publications:** (With W. Jacobs) The Beaver Papers: The Story of the Lost Season, 1983; (with W. Jacobs) The Comic Book Heroes: From the Silver Age to the Present, 1985, rev. ed., 1997; Diablo, 1989; Green Lantern: The Road Back, 1992; Honey, I'm Home!: Sitcoms, Selling the American Dream, 1992; (with L. Strazewski) Prime Time, 1994; Oktane, 1996; The Comic Book Heroes, 1997; Batman: Fortunate Son, 1999; Killing Monsters: Why Children Need Fantasy and Make-believe Violence, 2002; (adapted) Dragon Ball, 2003; (with K. Giffen) Green Lantern, Emerald Dawn II, 2003; Men of Tomorrow: Geeks, Gangsters and the Birth of the Comic Book, 2004; Ginny Good, 2004; (with M. Badger) Networked: Carabella on the Run, 2010; The Undressing of America: How a Bodybuilder, a Swimming Queen and a Magician Created Reality Media, forthcoming. **Address:** c/o Author Mail, Carol Mann Agency, 55 5th Ave., New York, NY 10003, U.S.A. **Online address:** gerardjones@earthlink.net

JONES, Gwyneth A(nn). (Ann Halam). British (born England), b. 1952. **Genres:** Novels, Science Fiction/Fantasy, Children's Fiction, Novellas/Short Stories, Literary Criticism And History, Young Adult Fiction, Adult Nonfiction, Horror, Ghost Writer. **Career:** Manpower Services Commission, executive officer, 1975-77; writer, 1977-. **Publications:** NOVELS: Divine Endurance, 1984; Escape Plans, 1986; Kairos, 1988; White Queen, 1993; Identifying the Object (short stories), 1993; Flowerdust, 1995; Seven Tales and a Fable, 1995; North Wind, 1996; Phoenix Café, 1998; Deconstructing the Starships: Science, Fiction, and Reality, 1999; Bold as Love, 2001; Castles Made of Sand, 2002; Midnight Lamp, 2003; Life: A Novel, 2004; Band of Gypsys, 2005; Rainbow Bridge, 2006; Spirit: The Princess of Bois Dormant, 2008; Grazing the Long Acre, 2009. The Buonarotti Quartet, 2009; Imagination/Space, 2009; The Universe Of Things, forthcoming. CHILDREN'S FICTION: Water in the Air, 1977; The Influence of Ironwood, 1978; The Exchange, 1979; Dear Hill, 1980; The Hidden Ones 1988. CHILDREN'S FICTION AS ANN HALAM: Ally Ally, Aster, 1981; The Alder Tree, 1982; King Death's Garden, 1986; The Daymaker, 1987; Transformations, 1988; The Sky Breaker, 1990; Dinosaur Junction, 1992; The Haunting of Jessica Raven, 1994; The Fear Man, 1995; The Powerhouse, 1997; Crying in the Dark, 1998; The Nimrod Conspiracy, 1999; Don't Open Your Eyes, 2000; Dr. Franklin's Island, 2001; Taylor Five, 2002; Understanding the Author's Craft: Shadow on the Stairs, 2004; Siberia, 2005; The Visitor, 2006; Snakehead, 2007. OTHER: (contrib.) Year's Best SF 14, 2009. **Address:** David Higham Associates Ltd., 5-8 Lower John St., Golden Sq., London, GL W1R 4HA, England. **Online address:** gwyneth.jones@ntlworld.com

JONES, (Henry) John (Franklin). British (born England), b. 1924. **Genres:** Novels, Literary Criticism And History, Social Sciences, Reference. **Career:** Oxford University, Merton College, fellow and tutor in law, 1949-55, senior lecturer in English literature, 1956-63, fellow and tutor in English, 1962-79, professor of poetry, 1979-84; The Observer, football correspondent, 1956-59; Queen's University, Dill memorial lecturer, 1983. Writer. **Publications:** The Egotistical Sublime: A History of Wordsworth's Imagination, 1954, rev. ed., 1978; On Aristotle and Greek Tragedy, 1962, rev. ed., 1980; (ed.) The Study of Good Letters, 1963; John Keats's Dream of Truth, 1969, rev. ed., 1980; The Same God, 1971; Dostoevsky, 1983; Shakespeare at Work, 1995. Contributor to books and periodicals. **Address:** Garden Flat, 41 Buckland Cres., London, GL NW3 5DJ, England.

JONES, Jacqueline. American (born United States), b. 1948. **Genres:** Cultural/Ethnic Topics, History, Race Relations. **Career:** Wellesley College, Department of history, assistant professor, 1976-81, associate professor, 1981-86, professor, 1986-91, chair; Brandeis University, Department of History, Harry S. Truman professor, 1991-2008, chair, adjunct professor; Brown University, Clare Booth Luce visiting professor, 1988-90; University of Texas, Mastin Gentry White professor of southern history, 2008-, Walter Prescott Webb chair in history and ideas, 2008-. Writer. **Publications:** Soldiers of Light and

Love: Northern Teachers and Georgia Blacks 1865-1873, 1980; Labor of Love, Labor of Sorrow: Black Women, Work and the Family from Slavery to the Present, 1985; The Dispossessed: America's Underclasses from the Civil War to the Present, 1992; American Work: Four Centuries of Black and White Labor, 1998; A Social History of the Laboring Classes: From Colonial Times to the Present, 1999; Creek Walking: Growing up in Delaware in the 1950s, 2001; (co-author) Created Equal: A Social and Political History of the United States, 2003, 3rd ed., 2010; (ed.) Best American History Essays 2007, 2007; Saving Savannah: The City and the Civil War, 2008. **Address:** Department of History, University of Texas, GAR 2.109, 1 University Sta., PO Box 7000, Austin, TX 78712, U.S.A. **Online address:** jjones@mail.utexas.edu

JONES, Jason B. American (born United States), b. 1971?. **Genres:** Literary Criticism And History, History. **Career:** Central Connecticut State University, associate professor of English; Vanguard, book review editor. **Publications:** Lost Causes: Historical Consciousness in Victorian Literature, 2006. **Address:** Central Connecticut State University, 1615 Stanley St., New Britain, CT 06050-4010, U.S.A. **Online address:** jonesjason1@ccsu.edu

JONES, J. Barrie. British (born England), b. 1946. **Genres:** Music, Biography, Photography, Reference. **Career:** Cambridge University, Downing College, music supervisor, 1970-72; Open University, research assistant, 1972-75, research fellow, 1975-83, lecturer in music, 1983-; Trinity College, lector in music, 1983-84, Professor of astronomy. Writer. **Publications:** (Co-ed.) From Classical to Romantic Keyboard Music, 1974; (ed. and trans.) Gabriel Fauré: A Life in Letters, 1989; (ed.) The Hutchinson Concise Dictionary of Music, 1989; (trans. and intro.) Correspondence of Camille Saint-Saëns and Gabriel Fauré: Sixty Years of Friendship, 2004. Contributor of articles to periodicals and journals. **Address:** Department of Music, Open University, Walton Hall, Milton Keynes, MS MK7 6AA, England. **Online address:** b.jones@open.ac.uk

JONES, Jenny. American/Palestinian (born Palestine), b. 1946. **Genres:** Novels. **Career:** Image Foundation, founder, 1992; Jenny Jones, founder; Cover Girls, founder; Chicago Race for the Cure, Susan G. Komen Breast Cancer Foundation, honorary chair. Writer. **Publications:** (With P.B. Cox) Jenny Jones: My Story, 1997; Look Good, Feel Great Cookbook, 2006. Contributor to periodicals. **Address:** Andrews McMeel Publishing L.L.C., 1130 Walnut St., Kansas City, MO 64106, U.S.A. **Online address:** dearjenny@jennyjones.com

JONES, Jenny. British (born England), b. 1954?. **Genres:** Science Fiction/Fantasy, Novels, Children's Fiction. **Career:** Writer. **Publications:** FLIGHT OVER FIRE SERIES: Fly by Night, 1990; The Edge of Vengeance, 1991; Lies and Flames, 1992. FANTASY NOVELS: The Webbed Hand, 1994; The Blue Manor, 1995; Firefly Dreams, 1995; The House of Bird, 1996; The Carver, Scholastic Point, 1997; Where the Children Cry, 1998. DREAMTIME SERIES: Shadowsong, 1995. **Address:** c/o Gollancz, Wellington House, 125 Strand, London, GL WC2R 0BB, England.

JONES, Jerry W. American (born United States), b. 1964. **Genres:** History. **Career:** Northeast Texas Community College, instructor, 1992; University of North Texas, teaching fellow, 1993-95; Collin County Community College, faculty, 1995; University of Central Texas, assistant professor of history, 1996-99; Tarleton State University, assistant professor, associate professor of history, 1999-2009; Texas A&M University, Academy of Educator, faculty, 2001, associate professor of history, 2003, 2009-11, professor, 2011-. Writer. **Publications:** U.S. Battleship Operations in World War I, 1998. **Address:** Department of History, Texas A&M University Central Texas, North Campus Ste. 18, 1901 S Clear Creek Rd., Killeen, TX 76549, U.S.A. **Online address:** jjones@tarleton.edu

JONES, Jessie. *See* **BEAUMONT, Maria.**

JONES, J. Gwynfor. (John Gwynfor Jones). Welsh (born Wales), b. 1936. **Genres:** History, Politics/Government, Adult Non-fiction, Social Commentary. **Career:** University of Wales, senior lecturer, 1975-95, professor of Welsh history, 1997-; Cardiff University, School of History and Archaeology, now professor emeritus. Writer. **Publications:** (Ed.) Class, Community and Culture in Tudor Wales, 1989; (as John Gwynfor Jones) Patrymau Diwylliant A Moes Yn n heulu'r Wynniaid O Wedir, 1989; Wales and the Tudor State: Government, Religious Change and the Social Order, 1534-1603, 1534-1605, 1989; History of the Gwydir Family, and Memoirs, 1990; (ed.)The Memoirs of Sir John Wynn, 1990; Concepts of Order and Gentility in Wales, 1540-1640, 1992; Agweddau Ar Dwf Piwritaniaeth Yng Nghymru Yn Yr Ail Ganrif Ar Bymtheg, 1992; Early Modern Wales: 1525-1640, 1994; Morgan Family of Tredegar: Its Origins, Growth and Advancement c. 340-1674, 1995; Wynn Family of Gwydir: Origins, Growth and Development, c. 490-1674, 1995; (as John Gwynfor Jones) Law, Order and Government in Caernarfonshire, 1558-1640: Justices of the Peace and the Gentry, 1996; Welsh Gentry, 1536-1640: Images of Status, Honour and Authority, 1998; Conflict, Continuity and Change in Wales, 1500-1603: Essays and Studies, 1999. **Address:** School of History and Archaeology, Cardiff University, Humanities Bldg., Colum Dr., Cardiff, SG CF10 3XU, Wales. **Online address:** jonesjg1@cardiff.ac.uk

JONES, Jill. American (born United States), b. 1945. **Genres:** Romance/Historical, Novels, Young Adult Fiction, Mystery/Crime/Suspense. **Career:** Advertising copywriter. **Publications:** ROMANCE NOVELS: Emily's Secret, 1995; My Lady Caroline, 1996; The Scottish Rose, 1997; Essence of My Desire, 1998; Circle of the Lily, 1998; The Island, 1999. OTHERS: (with D. Silverman) Organizational Work: The Language of Grading, the Grading of Language, 1976; Bloodline, 2000; Remember Your Lies, 2001; Every Move You Make, 2002; (ed.) God Calling: 365 One Minute Meditations from the Life Changing Devotional Classic, 2008. Works appear in anthologies. **Address:** PO Box 696, Montreat, NC 28757-0696, U.S.A.

JONES, John Gwynfor. See **JONES, J. Gwynfor.**

JONES, John Henry. British (born England), b. 1942. **Genres:** Chemistry, History, Local History/Rural Topics, Genealogy/Heraldry. **Career:** Oxford University, Balliol College, junior research fellow in biological sciences, 1966-68, official fellow and tutor in organic chemistry, 1968-2008, university lecturer in organic chemistry, 1970-2008, dean, 1972-2002, fellow archivist, 1981-2009, vice-master, 2002-07, emeritus fellow 2009; Journal of Peptide Science, editor-in-chief, 1999-2007. **Publications:** Balliol College: A History, 1263-1939, 1988, 2nd ed., 1997; The Chemical Synthesis of Peptides, 1990; Amino Acid and Peptide Synthesis, 1992; The Records of Balliol College, Oxford, 1992; Core Carbonyl Chemistry, 1997, 2nd ed., 2002; The Dyson Perrins Laboratory and Oxford Organic Chemistry 1916-2004, 2008. **Address:** Balliol College, Oxford University, Oxford, OX1 3BJ, England. **Online address:** john.jones@balliol.ox.ac.uk

JONES, John Philip. American/Welsh (born Wales), b. 1930. **Genres:** Advertising/Public Relations, Marketing, History. **Career:** British Market Research Bureau, research officer, 1953-55; Colman, Prentis and Varley (advertising company), account executive, 1955-57; J. Walter Thompson Co. (advertising company), account executive, 1957-65, accounts director, 1965-80; Syracuse University, S.I. Newhouse School of Public Communications, professor of advertising, 1981-, chair of advertising, 1983-90, now professor emeritus; RGC Consulting Corp., president, 1986-. Writer. **Publications:** The Great Gray Spire, 1985; What's in a Name?: Advertising and the Concept of Brands, 1986, (with J.S. Slater) 2nd ed., 2003; Does It Pay to Advertise?: Cases Illustrating Successful Brand Advertising, 1989; How Much Is Enough?: Getting the Most from Your Advertising Dollar, 1992; When Ads Work: New Proof that Advertising Triggers Sales, 1995, 2nd ed., 2007; (ed.) How Advertising Works: The Role of Research, 1998; (ed.) How to Use Advertising to Build Strong Brands, 1999; (ed.) Advertising Business: Operations, Creativity, Media Planning, Integrated Communications, 1999; (ed.) International Advertising: Realities and Myths, 2000; Behind Powerful Brands: From Strategy to Campaign, 2000; (ed.) Advertising Organizations and Publications: A Resource Guide, 2000; The Ultimate Secrets of Advertising, 2002; Fables, Fashions, and Facts About Advertising, 2004; How To Turn Advertising Expenses Into Investments, 2005; Keynes's Vision: Why the Great Depression Did Not Return, 2008; Successes and Sacrifices of the British Army in 1914: Soldiers Marching, All to Die, 2009. Contributor of articles to periodicals. **Address:** S.I. Newhouse School of Public Communications, Syracuse University, Rm. 370, Newhouse 2, 215 University Pl., Syracuse, NY 13244-2100, U.S.A. **Online address:** jpjones@syr.edu

JONES, J(on) Sydney. American (born United States), b. 1948. **Genres:** Mystery/Crime/Suspense, Young Adult Fiction, Travel/Exploration, History, Biography. **Career:** Journalist, 1971-76; English as a second language and writing, instructor, 1977-. **Publications:** FOR ADULTS FICTION: Time of the Wolf, 1990; The Hero Game, 1992; Frankie, 1997; The Empty Mirror: A Viennese Mystery, 2009, Requiem in Vienna: A Viennese Mystery, 2010, The Silence: A Viennese Mystery, 2011. NONFICTION: Bike and Hike: Sixty Tours Around Great Britain and Ireland, 1977; Vienna Inside-Out: 16 Walking Tours, 1979; Hitler in Vienna, 1907-1913, 1983; Tramping in Europe: A Walking Guide, 1984; Viennawalks, 1985, rev. ed., 1994; The Crusades: Primary Sources, 2005; The Crusades: Biographies, 2005; (with M.J. O'Neal) World Religions Reference Library, 2 vols., 2006. **Address:** Severn House Publishers Ltd., 9-15 High St., Sutton, SR SM1 1DF, England. **Online address:** syd@jsydneyjones.com

JONES, Judith. See **TUCKER, (Allan) James.**

JONES, Julia. British (born England), b. 1923?. **Genres:** Novels. **Career:** Writer. **Publications:** The Navigators, 1987. **Address:** Jill Foster Ltd., 9 Barb Mews, Brook Green, London, GL W6 7PA, England.

JONES, J. V. American/British (born England), b. 1963?. **Genres:** Novels. **Career:** Writer, computer consultant and software developer. **Publications:** The Barbed Coil, 1997. THE BOOK OF WORDS SERIES: The Baker's Boy, 1995; A Man Betrayed, 1996; Master and Fool, 1996. SWORD OF SHADOWS SERIES: A Cavern of Black Ice, 1999; A Fortress of Grey Ice, 2003; A Sword from Red Ice, 2007. **Address:** San Diego, CA, U.S.A. **Online address:** julia@jvj.com

JONES, Kaylie (Ann). American/French (born France), b. 1960. **Genres:** Novels, Adult Non-fiction. **Career:** Poets and Writers Inc., grants coordinator, 1983-84, freelance worker, 1984-85, assistant, 1985-86; teacher and writer, 1989-; Long Island University, instructor, 1995-; Wilkes University, MFA Program in Professional Writing, instructor. **Publications:** As Soon as It Rains, 1986; Quite the Other Way, 1988; A Soldier's Daughter Never Cries, 1990; Celeste Ascending: A Novel, 2000; (intro.) The Ice-Cream Headache: And Other Stories, 2002; Speak Now, 2003; Lies My Mother Never Told Me: A Memoir, 2009. Contributor to periodicals. **Address:** c/o Trena Keating, Keating Literary L.L.C., 80 5th Ave., Ste. 1101, New York, NY 10011, U.S.A. **Online address:** kjones5@nyc.rr.com

JONES, Keith. American (born United States) **Genres:** Novels. **Career:** Writer. **Publications:** Calculation of Stress from Strain in Concrete, 1961; Reaching Port: A Montana Couple Sails Around the World, 1983; Sixty-Four Days of a Normandy Summer: With a Tank Unit After D-Day, 1990; Mayan Equinox, 2006; Mayan Key, 2007; Adam's Dream: Human Longings and the Love of God, 2007; (ed. with A.D. White) RICS Public Sector Asset Management Guidelines: A Guide to Best Practice, 2008; Suspicious Spouse, 2010; Regularized Fast Hartley Transform: Optimal Formulation of Real-Data Fast Fourier Transform for Silicon-Based Implementation in Resource-Constrained Environments, 2010. **Address:** Savlo Press, PO Box 9095, Bend, OR 97708, U.S.A. **Online address:** kjones@n2.net

JONES, K. F. American (born United States), b. 1946. **Genres:** Food And Wine. **Career:** Volo Del Corvo (winery), founder, 1995-; Westways, travel writer; Corvo Publications, founder. **Publications:** Waldo: An All-Too-True Dog Story, 2001; The Wrath of Grapes: How Not to Start a Winery, 2008. Contributor of articles to periodicals. **Address:** CA, U.S.A. **Online address:** corvo@redshift.com

JONES, Larry. American (born United States), b. 1940?. **Genres:** Autobiography/Memoirs, Young Adult Fiction, Novels. **Career:** Feed the Children, co-founder and president, 1979-2009; Southern Baptist Church, minister. Writer. **Publications:** (With C.A. Roberts) Hustler for the Lord, 1978; How to Make It to Friday, 1978; Practice to Win, 1982; How to Bend without Breaking, 1987; The Fifteen-Second Secret, 1991; (with K. Abraham) Life's Interruptions, God's Opportunities: Lessons from the Good Samaritan, 2002; Black Box (novel), 2004; Keep Walking: One Man's Journey to Feed the World One Child at a Time (memoir), 2007; The Virgin Cure, 2009. **Address:** Creation House, 600 Rinehart Rd., Lake Mary, FL 32746, U.S.A.

JONES, Laurie Beth. American (born United States), b. 1952. **Genres:** Theology/Religion, inspirational/Motivational Literature. **Career:** U.S. Congress, intern, 1970-71; Georgia State University, administrative assistant, 1974-75; YMCA0, public relations director, 1975-76; women's information director, 1976-81; Jones Group, founder and president. Writer. **Publications:** Jesus, CEO: Using Ancient Wisdom for Visionary Leadership, 1995; The Path: Creating Your Mission Statement for Work and for Life, 1996; Jesus in Blue Jeans: A Practical Guide to Everyday Spirituality, 1997; Grow Something Besides Old: Seeds for a Joyful Life, 1998; The Power of Positive

Prophecy: Finding the Hidden Potential in Everyday Life, 1999; Jesus, Inc.: The Visionary Path: An Entrepreneur's Guide to True Success, 2001; Teach Your Team to Fish: Using Ancient Wisdom for Inspired Teamwork, 2002; Jesus, Life Coach: Learn from the Best, 2004; Four Elements of Success: A Simple Personality Profile that will Transform Your Team, 2005; Personal Notes to the Graduate: 24 Values to Shape Your Destiny, 2006; Jesus, Career Counselor: How to Find (and keep) Your Perfect Work, 2010. **Address:** c/o Julie Castiglia, Castiglia Literary Agency, 1155 Camino del Mar, Ste. 510, Del Mar, CA 92014, U.S.A. **Online address:** ljones@elp.rr.com

JONES, Lawrence K. American (born United States), b. 1940. **Genres:** Education, Business/Trade/Industry, Administration/Management. **Career:** Tarsus Amerikan Koleji, secondary school teacher, 1963-66; Philadelphia Child Study Center, teacher, 1967; Britton Road Junior High School, school counselor, 1967-68; Ft. Roots VA Hospital, counseling psychology intern, 1970, Department of Psychology, instructor, 1970-71; Stephens College, department of psychology, instructor, 1970-71; North Carolina State University, assistant professor, 1971-76, associate professor, 1976-79, 1980-84, visiting associate professor, 1979-80, professor, 1984-95, acting head of department, 1976-84, professor emeritus, 1995-; Vanderbilt University, visiting associate professor, 1979-80. Writer. **Publications:** (Ed.) The Encyclopedia of Career Change and Work Issues, 1992; Job Skills for the 21st Century: A Guide for Students, 1996. Contributor of articles to books and journals. **Address:** North Carolina State College of Education, North Carolina State University, 208 Poe Hall, 2310 Stinson Dr., PO Box 7801, Raleigh, NC 27695-7801, U.S.A. **Online address:** larry_jones@ncsu.edu

JONES, Linda. See **JONES, Linda Winstead.**

JONES, Linda Winstead. Also writes as Linda Jones, Linda Fallon, Linda Devlin, Linda Winstead. American (born United States) **Genres:** Romance/Historical, Young Adult Fiction, Adult Non-fiction, Novels. **Career:** Writer. **Publications:** ROMANCE NOVELS: Bridger's Last Stand, 1999; Every Little Thing, 2000; Secret-Agent Sheikh, 2002; Fever, 2004; A Touch of the Beast, 2004; (with E. Vaughn and K. Whiddon) Beyond the Dark, 2005; (with B. McCauley) In His Bed, 2007; The Sheikh and I, 2006; Raintree: Haunted, 2007; (with M. Ferrarella) Romancing the Crown, 2008; (with L. Leigh, E. McCarthy and N. Singh) The Magical Christmas Cat, 2008; (with L. Childs and B. Vanak) Holiday with a Vampire III, 2009; Come to Me, 2010; Last of the Ravens, 2010; The Husband Recipe, 2011. EMPEROR'S BRIDE TRILOGY: Untouchable, 2008; 22 Nights, 2008; Bride By Command, 2009. SINCLAIR CONNECTION SERIES: Madigan's Wife, 2001; Hot on His Trail, 2001; Capturing Cleo, 2002; In Bed with Boone, 2002; Wilder Days, 2003; Clint's Wild Ride, 2003; On Dean's Watch, 2003. FYNE SISTERS TRILOGY: The Sun Witch, 2004; The Moon Witch, 2005; The Star Witch, 2006. LAST CHANCE HEROES SERIES: Running Scared, 2004; Truly, Madly, Dangerously, 2005; One Major Distraction, 2005; Lucky's Woman, 2006; The Guardian, 2008. CHILDREN OF THE SUN SERIES: Prince of Magic, 2007; Prince of Fire, 2007; Prince of Swords, 2007. AS LINDA WINSTEAD: No Angel's Grace, 1979; Guardian Angel, 1994; Chase the Lightning, 1995; West Wind, 1995; In Enemy Hands, 1996. AS LINDA JONES: Desperado's Gold, 1996; Big Bad Wolf, 1997; On a Wicked Wind, 1998; Cinderfella, 1998; The Indigo Blade, 1999; The Seduction of Roxanne, 2000; One Day, My Prince, 2000; Let Down Your Hair, 2001; Into the Woods, 2001; Debuty and the Beast, 2002; (with L. Howard) Blood Born, 2010; (with L. Howard) Warrior Rising, 2012. SHADES OF TWILIGHT SERIES AS LINDA FALLON: Shades of Scarlet, 2002; Shades of Midnight, 2003; Shades of Winter, 2003. ROCK CREEK SIX SERIES AS LINDA DEVLIN: Jed, 2001; Sullivan, 2001; Cash, 2002. **Address:** Harlequin Enterprises Ltd., PO Box 5190, Buffalo, NY 14240-5190, U.S.A. **Online address:** lindawjones@comcast.net

JONES, Lisa. American (born United States), b. 1959. **Genres:** Autobiography/Memoirs. **Career:** Writer. **Publications:** Broken: A Love Story-Horses, Humans, and Redemption on the Wind River Indian Reservation (memoir), 2009. Contributor to periodicals. **Address:** Boulder, CO , U.S.A. **Online address:** lisajoneswrites@gmail.com

JONES, Louis B. American (born United States), b. 1953. **Genres:** Novels. **Career:** College of Marin, tutor, 1980-92; Washington University, writer-in-residence, 1998; Wichita State University, distinguished visiting writer, 2000; St. Mary's College, writer-in-residence, 2002; Squaw Valley Community of Writers, fiction director. **Publications:** Ordinary Money (novel), 1990; Particles and Luck (novel), 1993; California's Over (novel), 1997; Radiance

(novel), 2011. Contributor to periodicals. Works appear in anthologies. **Address:** c/o Joy Harris, Joy Harris Literary Agency, 381 Park Ave. S, Ste. 428, New York, NY 10016, U.S.A. **Online address:** lbj@louisbjones.com

JONES, Madison. American (born United States), b. 1925. **Genres:** Novels, Mystery/Crime/Suspense, History, Young Adult Fiction, Humanities, Young Adult Non-fiction. **Career:** Miami University, instructor in English, 1953-54; University of Tennessee, instructor in English, 1955-56; Auburn University, assistant professor, 1956-68, alumni writer-in-residence, 1966-87, professor of English, 1968-87, distinguished faculty lecturer, 1980, professor emeritus, 1987-. Writer. **Publications:** NOVELS: The Innocent, 1957; Forest of the Night, 1960; A Buried Land, 1963; An Exile, 1967 in US as I Walk the Line, 1970; A Cry of Absence, 1971; Passage through Gehenna, 1978; Season of the Strangler, 1982; Last Things, 1989; To the Winds, 1996; Nashville 1864: The Dying of the Light, 1997; Herod's Wife, 2003; Adventures of Douglas Bragg: A Novel, 2008. OTHERS: The Guide and Other Stories, 1951; (with T.D. Dow) History of the Tennessee State Dental Association, 1958. **Address:** Department of English, Auburn University, Auburn, AL 36849-5203, U.S.A. **Online address:** m.p.jones@att.net

JONES, Malcolm. American (born United States), b. 1952. **Genres:** Autobiography/Memoirs. **Career:** Twin City Sentinel, staff; Winston-Salem Journal, staff; Daily News, editorial writer, 1978-83; St. Petersburg Times, book reviewer, 1983-89; Newsweek, book reviewer, Arts Section, general editor, Newsweek.com, editor, 1989-. **Publications:** (Adapted with V.D. Parks) Jump! The Adventures of Brer Rabbit, 1986; Little Boy Blues (memoir), 2010. Contributor to periodicals. **Address:** Croton, NY , U.S.A. **Online address:** jones@littleboybluesbook.com

JONES, Malcolm V(ince). British (born England), b. 1940. **Genres:** Intellectual History, Literary Criticism And History. **Career:** University of Sussex, School of European Studies, assistant lecturer, 1965-67; University of Nottingham, lecturer, 1967-73, senior lecturer, 1973-80, Faculty of Arts, vice dean, 1976-79, dean, 1982-85, Slavonic studies, professor, 1980-97, pro vice chancellor, 1987-91, emeritus professor, 1997-; Cambridge Studies in Russian Literature, general editor, 1985-96. **Publications:** Dostoevsky: The Novel of Discord, 1976; (ed.) New Essays on Tolstoy, 1978; (ed. G.M. Terry) New Essays on Dostoevsky, 1983; Dostoevsky after Bakhtin: Readings in Dostoyevsky's Fantastic Realism, 1990; (ed.) Dostoevsky and the Twentieth Century: The Ljubljana Papers, 1993; (ed. with R.F. Miller) The Cambridge Companion to the Classic Russian Novel, 1998; Dostoevskyposle Bakhtina, 1998; Dostoevsky and the Dynamics of Religious Experience, 2005; Slavianskiimir, The Story of Slavonic Studies at The University of Nottingham in the Twentieth Century, 2009. **Address:** Department of Russian & Slavonic Studies, University of Nottingham, University Pk., Nottingham, NT NG7 2RD, England. **Online address:** malcolmvjones@btinternet.com

JONES, Margaret C. (Margaret Catherine Jones). British (born England), b. 1949. **Genres:** Literary Criticism And History, Social Sciences, History, Psychology. **Career:** University of Alexandria, teacher, 1972-76; Goucher College, instructor, 1987-88; Central Washington University, assistant professor, 1990-92; University of the West of England, senior lecturer in humanities and coordinator of American studies, 1992-94. Writer. **Publications:** Prophets in Babylon: Five California Novelists in the 1930s, 1992; Heretics & Hellraisers: Women Contributors to The Masses, 1911-1917, 1993; (ed. and intro.) Elsie Clews Parsons, The Journal of a Feminist, 1994. **Address:** University of Texas Press, 2100 COMAL, PO Box 7819, Austin, TX 78722, U.S.A.

JONES, Margaret Catherine. See **JONES, Margaret C.**

JONES, Martin. British (born England), b. 1951. **Genres:** Biology, Sciences. **Career:** University of Cambridge, George Pitt-Rivers professor of archaeological science; Natural Environment Research Council, Ancient Biomolecule Initiative program, chair. Writer. **Publications:** (Ed. with G. Dimbleby) The Environment of Man: The Iron Age to the Anglo-Saxon Period, 1981; England before Domesday, 1986; The Molecule Hunt: Archaeology and the Search for Ancient DNA, 2001; (ed. with A.C. Fabian) Conflict, 2006; Feast: Why Humans Share Food, 2007. Contributor to periodicals. **Address:** Cambridge, England. **Online address:** mkj12@cam.ac.uk

JONES, Mary Voell. American (born United States), b. 1933. **Genres:** Children's Fiction, Songs/Lyrics And Libretti, Music, Literary Criticism And History. **Career:** Whitman Publishing Co., writer and editor, 1956-59; freelance writer, 1959-; Community Concerts Inc., secretary, 1963-66. **Publications:** Captain Kangaroo's Picnic, 1959; Huckleberry Hound Helps a Pal, 1960; Captain Kangaroo and Tick Tock Trouble, 1961; Yogi Bear's Secret, 1963; Little Red Riding Hood Retold, 1964; (with N.R. Knoche) What Do Mothers Do?, 1966; First Songs the Young Child Sings: A Picture-Activity-Songbook, 1976; Let's Make Music Today, 1977. **Address:** 2167 Mohawk Trl., Maitland, FL 32751, U.S.A.

JONES, Matthew F. American (born United States), b. 1956. **Genres:** Novels, Young Adult Fiction. **Career:** Lynchburg College, writer-in-residence, 1995; University of Virginia, workshop leader, 1996; Randolph-Macon Woman's College, writer-in-residence, 1997-98; Randolph College, visiting writer; Lynchburg College, visiting writer; University of Virginia, visiting writer. **Publications:** NOVELS: The Cooter Farm, 1991; The Elements of Hitting, 1994; A Single Shot, 1996; Blind Pursuit, 1997; Deepwater, 1999; Boot Tracks, 2006. **Address:** c/o Paul Bresnick, Paul Bresnick Literary Agency L.L.C., 115 W 29th St., 3rd Fl., New York, NY 10001, U.S.A.

JONES, Matthew L. American (born United States), b. 1972. **Genres:** History, Philosophy. **Career:** Columbia University, professor. Writer. **Publications:** The Good Life in the Scientific Revolution: Descartes, Pascal, Leibniz, and the Cultivation of Virtue, 2006. Contributor of articles to journals. **Address:** Department of History, Columbia University, MC2513, 523 Fayerweather Hall, 1180 Amsterdam Ave., New York, NY 10027-7039, U.S.A. **Online address:** mj340@columbia.edu

JONES, Merry Bloch. (Robert Llewellyn Jones). American (born United States), b. 1948. **Genres:** Adult Non-fiction, Humor/Satire, Mystery/Crime/Suspense. **Career:** Temple University, instructor; WKBS-TV, producer and director; Sun Co., staff communication consultant. Writer. **Publications:** (With J.A. Schiller) Stepmothers: Keeping it Together with Your Husband and His Kids, 1992; Birthmothers: Women Who Have Relinquished Babies for Adoption Tell Their Stories, 1993; (comp.) I Love Him, But-, 1995, rev. ed., 2005; (as Robert Llewellyn Jones) I Love Her, But-, 1996; Please Don't Kiss Me at the Bus Stop: Over 700 Things Parents Do That Drive Their Kids Crazy, 1997; If She Weren't My Best Friend, I'd Kill Her: Almost 600 Ways Women Drive Their Girlfriends Crazy, 1998; America's Dumbest Dates: Over 500 Tales of Fumbled Flirtations, 1998; The Nanny Murders, 2005; The River Killings, 2006; The Deadly Neighbors, 2007; Borrowed and Blue Murders, 2008; Summer Session, 2011; Behind the Walls, 2011. Contributor to magazines and newspapers. **Address:** c/o Rebecca Strauss, McIntosh & Otis Inc., 353 Lexington Ave., New York, NY 10016, U.S.A. **Online address:** merryddjones@gmail.com

JONES, Nancy L. See **HOLDER, Nancy L.**

JONES, Naomi Brooks. American (born United States), b. 1941. **Genres:** Poetry, Young Adult Fiction, Theology/Religion, Sociology, Children's Fiction. **Career:** Writer. **Publications:** Turn Back, Teenager, Turn Back (poem), 1959; Jessie's Table, 1993. **Address:** 1226 Duffy Way, Brentwood, CA 94513, U.S.A.

JONES, Norman (Leslie). American (born United States), b. 1951. **Genres:** History, Law, Humanities, Theology/Religion, Business/Trade/Industry, Biography. **Career:** Utah State University, Department of History, assistant professor, 1978-81, associate professor, 1981-87, professor of history, 1987-, assistant department head, 1987-94, Liberal Arts and Sciences Program, associate director, 1987-2001, acting director, 1993-94, 1997-98, head of department, 1994-, director of religious studies, 2002-08, 2010-, director of general education and curricular integration, 2010-; Harvard University, Mellon faculty fellow, 1982-83; The Huntington Library, Fletcher Jones fellow, 1991-92; Cambridge University, Clare College, visiting fellow, 1992; Oxford University, Jesus College, visiting senior research fellow, 2008-09. Writer. **Publications:** Faith by Statute: Parliament and the Settlement of Religion, 1559, 1982; God and the Moneylenders: Usury and Law in Early Modern England, 1989; (ed. with D.M. Dean) The Parliaments of Elizabethan England, 1990; The Birth of the Elizabethan Age: England in the 1560s, 1993; The English Reformation: Religion and Cultural Adaptation, 2002; (ed. with R. Tittler) A Companion to Tudor Britain, 2004; Local Identities in Early Modern England, 2007; (ed. with S. Doran) Elizabethan World, 2011. Works appear in

anthologies. Contributor to journals. **Address:** Department of History, Utah State University, 323 Old Main Hill, Logan, UT 84322-0710, U.S.A. **Online address:** norm.jones@usu.edu

JONES, Pamela M. American (born United States), b. 1953. **Genres:** Art/Art History. **Career:** National Museum of American Art, intern, 1977-78, sculpture, 1978-79; Franklin and Marshall College, visiting assistant professor of art history, 1985-86; University of Maine, visiting assistant professor of art history, 1987-88; University of Massachusetts, assistant professor, 1988-94, associate professor of art history, 1994-2006, Department of Art, chair, 1998-2001, professor of art history, 2006-; McMullen Museum of Art, co-curator, 1999. Writer. **Publications:** Federico Borromeo and the Ambrosiana: Art, Patronage, and Reform in Seventeenth-Century Milan, 1992; (ed. with T. Worcester) From Rome to Eternity: Catholicism and the Arts in Italy, ca. 1550-1650, 2002; Altarpieces and Their Viewers in the Churches of Rome from Caravaggio to Guido Reni, 2008; (intro.) Sacred Painting: Museum, 2010; Work represented in anthologies. Contributor to journals. **Address:** Department of Art, University of Massachusetts, McCormack 04-00447, 100 Morrissey Blvd., Boston, MA 02125-3393, U.S.A. **Online address:** pamela.jones@umb.edu

JONES, Patricia Spears. American (born United States), b. 1951. **Genres:** Poetry. **Career:** Coordinating Council of Literary Magazines, Grants program director, 1977-81; Heresies Collective, administrator, 1982-83; St. Mark's Church, Poetry Project, program coordinator, 1984-86; Massachusetts Council on the Arts and Humanities, program specialist, 1987-89; Film News Now Foundation, program director, 1990-91; consultant, 1996-; Bomb Magazine, contributing editor; Heliotrope, contributing editor; Mabou Mines, program coordinator; The Black Earth Institute, fellow, 2008, senior fellow. **Publications:** (Co-ed.) Ordinary Women: An Anthology of New York City Women Poets, 1978; Mythologizing Always, 1981; Mother, 1994; The Weather That Kills, 1995; Femme du Monde, 2006; Repuestas!, 2007; (comp. and ed.) Think: Poems for Aretha Franklin's Inauguration Day Hat, 2009; Painkiller, 2010. **Address:** 426 Sterling Pl., Apt. 1C, Brooklyn, NY 11238-4545, U.S.A. **Online address:** pksjones@hotmail.com

JONES, (R.) Dennis. (S. D. Tower). Canadian (born Canada), b. 1945?. **Genres:** Novels, Information Science/Computers, Technology, Sciences. **Career:** London Board of Education, office manager, 1971-85; technical writer. Full-time novelist, 1988-. **Publications:** NOVELS: Rubicon One: A Novel, 1983, rev. ed., 1984; Russian Spring, 1984; Barbarossa Red: A Novel, 1985; Winter Palace: A Novel, 1988; Concerto, 1989. HOUSE OF PANDRAGORE SERIES: The Stone and the Maiden, 1999; The Mask and the Sorceress, 2001. WITH N. RANDALL: Using Microsoft FrontPage, 1996; Using Microsoft FrontPage 97, 1997; Using Microsoft FrontPage 2000, 1999; Using Microsoft FrontPage 2002, 2001. OTHERS: Fenris Option, 1981; Concerto, 1989, The Minstrel Boy, 1990; Easy FrontPage 97, 1997; How To Do Everything with the Internet, 2001; (as S.D. Tower) The Assassins of Tamurin, 2003. **Address:** c/o Author Mail, HarperCollins Publishers, 10 E 53rd St., 7th Fl., New York, NY 10022-5244, U.S.A.

JONES, Richard Allan. Canadian/American (born United States), b. 1943. **Genres:** History, Social Commentary. **Career:** College Ste-Anne-de-la-Pocatiere, professor of history, 1966-68; Universite Laval, assistant professor, 1970-75, associate professor of history, 1975-, professor of Canadian history, through 2000. Writer. **Publications:** Community in Crisis: French-Canadian Nationalism in Perspective, 1967; Idéologie de L'Action catholique, 1974; (with J. Hamelin) Histoire du Quebec, 1976; Vers une hégémonie libérale: Apercu de la politique canadienne de Laurier King, 1980; Duplessis and the Union Nationale Administration, 1983; Origins, 1988; Destinies: Canadian History since Confederation, 1988, 4th ed., 2000; (with R. Bélanger and R. Jones) Marc Valliéres Les grands débats parlementaires, 1792-1992, 1994. **Address:** St. Cyrille-de-L'Islet, Quebec, QC G0R 2W0, Canada.

JONES, Richard Granville. American/British (born England), b. 1926. **Genres:** Theology/Religion, Medicine/Health. **Career:** Ordained methodist minister, 1954; minister of methodist churches in Sheffield, 1955-64, birkenhead, 1964-69; Victoria University of Manchester, lecturer in theology, 1962-82; Hartley Victoria College, tutor, 1969-73, principal, 1973-82; Methodist Church of East Anglia District, chairman, 1983-. Writer. **Publications:** (Ed.) Worship for Today: Suggestions and Ideas, 1968; (with A.J. Wesson) Towards a Radical Church, 1970; How Goes Christian Marriage?, 1978; Groundwork of Worship and Preaching, 1981; Groundwork of Christian Ethics, 1984; (ed.)

Silicon-Containing Polymers, 1995; (with B.R. Payne) Clinical Investigation and Statistics in Laboratory Medicine, 1997; What to Do?: Christians and Ethics, 1999; Thinking Things Through: What to Do? Christians and Ethics, 2000. **Address:** 24 Townsend Rd., Norwich, NF NR4 6RG, England.

JONES, Ricky L. American (born United States), b. 1967. **Genres:** Politics/Government, History, Education. **Career:** University of Kentucky, graduate assistant, 1994-96, Department of Political Science, instructor, 1995-96; University of Louisville, Department of Pan-African Studies, assistant professor, 1996-2002, associate professor, 2002-09, vice chair, 2002-03, chair, 2004-08, professor, 2009-, Center for the Study of Crime and Justice in Black Communities, director, 2007-. Writer. **Publications:** Black Haze: Violence, Sacrifice, and Manhood in Black Greek-Letter Fraternities, 2004; What's Wrong with Obamamania? Black America, Black Leadership, and the Death of Political Imagination, 2008. Contributor of articles to books and journals. **Address:** Department of Pan-African Studies, University of Louisville, 446 Strickler Hall, 4th Fl., E Wing, Louisville, KY 40292, U.S.A. **Online address:** ricky.jones@louisville.edu

JONES, Robert Llewellyn. See JONES, Merry Bloch.

JONES, R(obert) M(aynard). (Bobi Jones). Welsh (born Wales), b. 1929. **Genres:** Novellas/Short Stories, Poetry, Literary Criticism And History, Autobiography/Memoirs, Young Adult Fiction. **Career:** Trinity College, lecturer, 1956-58; University of Wales, University College of Wales, lecturer in education, 1959-66, lecturer in Welsh, 1966-80, professor, 1980-89, now professor emeritus. Writer. **Publications:** Highlights in Welsh Literature, 1969; System in Child Language, 1970; (with G. Thomas) The Dragon's Pen: A Brief history of Welsh Literature (criticism), 1986; The Christian Heritage of Welsh Education, 1986; (as Bobi Jones) Selected Poems, 1987; (as Bobi Jones) Language Regained, 1993. IN WELSH-CRITICISM: I'r Arch, 1959; Y Tair Rhamant, 1960; Llenyddiaeth Gymraeg yn Addysg Cymru, 1961; Guto'r Glyn a'i Gyfnod, 1963; Angau Ellis Wynne, 1968; (ed.) Kate Roberts, 1969; Pedwar Emynydd, 1970; Tafod y Llenor, 1974; Llenyddiaeth Gymraeg, 1936-1972, 1975; (ed.) Ym Marn Alwyn D. Rees, 1976; Llen Cymru a Chrefydd, 1977; Ann Griffiths, 1977; Llenyddiaeth Gymraeg, 1902-1936, 1987; Seiliau Beirniadaeth, vol. I, 1984, vol. II, 1986, vol. III, 1987, vol. IV, 1988; (ed.) Yr Hen Ganrif, 1991; (ed.) Detholiad o Gerddi W.J. Gruffydd, 1991; Cyfriniaeth Gymraeg, 1994; Crist a Chenedlaetholdeb, 1994; Ysbryd y Cwlwm: Delwedd y Genedl yn ein llenyddiaeth, 1998; Mawl a'i Gyfeillion, 2000; Mawl a Gelynion ei Elynion, 2002; Bairniadaeth Gyfansawdd, 2003. LINGUISTICS: Graddio Geirfa, 1962; Cymraeg i Oedolion, 1963; Cyflwyno'r Gymraeg, 1964; Cymraeg i Oedolion: I Nodiadau'r Dysgwyr, 1965, 2nd ed., 1966; Cymraeg i Oedolion: I Llyfr yr Athro, 1965, 2nd ed., 1966; Beirniadu Gwersi Ail Iaith, 1966; Cyfeiriadur i'r Athro, vols. I-II, 1974, vol. III, 1979; Cymraeg Drwy Ddamhegion, 1982; Gloywi Iaith, 3 vols., 1988; (ed.) Iaith Ifanc, 1994; Dysgu Cyfanswdd, 2002. POEMS: (ed.) Camre Cymru, 1952; Y Gan Gyntaf, 1957; Rhwng Taf a Thaf, 1960; Tyred Allan, 1965; Man Gwyn, 1965; Yr Wyl Ifori, 1967; Allor Wydn, 1971; Gwlad Llun, 1976; Hunllef Arthur, 1986; Bwyta'n Te, 1988; Casgliad o Gerddi, 1989; Canu Arnaf I, 1995; Canu Arnaf II, 1995. NOVELS: Nid yw Dwr yn Plygu, 1958; Bod yn Wraig, 1960; Epistol Serch ae Selsig, 1997. STORIES: Y Dyn na Ddaeth adref, 1966; Ci wrth y Drws, 1968; Daw'r Pasg i Bawb, 1969; Traed Prydferth, 1973; (ed.) Storiau Tramor, 1975; (ed.) Storiau Tramor III, 1976; Pwy Laddodd Miss Wales?, 1977; Crio Chwerthin, 1990; Dawn Gweddwon, 1992; Rhy Iach, 2004. JUVENILE: Ysgol yr Anifeiliaid, 1966; Gwiffred, 1966; Y Tri Mochyn Bach, 1966; Hugan Goch Fach, 1966; Tanwen, 1966. OTHER: Crwydro Mon (travel), 1957; Geiriadur Lluniau (dictionary), 1969; O'r Bedd i'r Crud (autobiography), 2000; Rhy Iach: storïau byrion, 2004. **Address:** Department of History & Welsh History, University of Wales, Aberystwyth, Ceredigion, SY23 3DY, Wales.

JONES, Rodney. American (born United States), b. 1950. **Genres:** Poetry. **Career:** Virginia Intermont College, writer-in-residence, 1978-84; Southern Illinois University, assistant professor of English, 1984-, professor of English. **Publications:** Going Ahead, Looking Back, 1977; The Story They Told Us of Light, 1980; The Unborn, 1985; Transparent Gestures, 1989; Apocalyptic Narrative and Other Poems, 1993; Things that Happen Once, 1996; Elegy for the Southern Drawl, 1999; Kingdom of the Instant, 2002; Salvation Blues: One Hundred Poems, 1985-2005, 2006; Twelve Fables Set in The Shawnee Hills, 2010; The Art of Heaven, 2011; Imaginary Logic, 2011. Contributor to magazines. **Address:** Department of English, Southern Illinois University, 2225 Faner Hall, 1000 Faner Dr., Carbondale, IL 62901, U.S.A. **Online address:** rodjones@siu.edu

JONES, Sabrina. American (born United States), b. 1960. **Genres:** Biography. **Career:** Writer. **Publications:** Isadora Duncan: A Graphic Biography, 2008. Contributor to books. **Address:** Brooklyn, NY , U.S.A. **Online address:** sabjonze@yahoo.com

JONES, Sally Roberts. (Sally Roberts). British (born England), b. 1935. **Genres:** Novellas/Short Stories, Poetry, Literary Criticism And History, Bibliography, Children's Fiction, Local History/Rural Topics. **Career:** Borough of Havering, Reference Library, senior assistant, 1964-67; Borough of Port Talbot, reference librarian, 1967-70; Alun Books, publisher, 1977-; Port Talbot Historical Society, general secretary, 1982-2002, chairman, 2009-; Swansea University, royal literary fund writing fellow, 1999-2009; Allen Raine Celebration Society, president, 2007-. Writer. **Publications:** AS SALLY ROBERTS: Turning Away: Collected Poems, 1952-1968, 1969; Romford in the Nineteenth Century, 1969. OTHERS: (ed.) About Welsh Literature, 1970; (comp.) Books of Welsh Interest: A Bibliography, 1977; The Forgotten Country, 1977; Elen and the Goblin, and Other Legends of Afan, 1977; Allen Raine, 1979; (ed.) Margam through the Ages, 1979; Welcome to Town: The Story of Pat Talbot's Inns, 1980; Relative Values, 1985; The History of Port Talbot, 1991; Pendaruis, 1992; Dic Penderyn: The Man and the Martyr, 1993; (ed. with P. Read) Over Milk Wood: Poems from Wales, 2000; Kiki is Not Well, 2004; Notes For A Life: New and Selected Poems, 2010. Contributor to magazines. **Address:** Alun Books, 3 Crown St., Port Talbot, WG SA13 1BG, Wales. **Online address:** srjones@alunbooks.co.uk

JONES, Seth G. American (born United States), b. 1972. **Genres:** Law. **Career:** RAND Corp., associate political scientist; Georgetown University, adjunct professor of security studies; Naval Postgraduate School, professor. Writer. **Publications:** America's Role in Nation-Building: From Germany to Japan, 2003; The UN's Role in Nation-Building: From Congo to Iraq, 2005. (co-author) Establishing Law and Order after Conflict, 2005; (with G.F. Treverton) Measuring National Power, 2005; (co-author) Securing Health: Lessons from Nation-Building Missions, 2006; (co-author) Securing Tyrants or Fostering Reform? U.S. Internal Security Assistance to Repressive and Transitioning Regimes, 2006. (with R.E. Hunter) Building a Successful Palestinian State: Security, 2006; The Rise of European Security Cooperation, 2007. (with J. Dobbins, K. Crane and B.C. DeGrasse) The Beginner's Guide to Nation- Building, 2007; Counterinsurgency in Afghanistan, 2008; (with M.C. Libicki) How Terrorist Groups End: Lessons for Countering Al Qa'ida, 2008; (contrib.) James Dobbins, Europe's Role in Nation-Building: From the Balkans to the Congo, 2008; (with C. Benard) Women and Nation-Building, 2008; (with D. Eberly, B. Runkle and S. Mohandas) Occupying Iraq: A History of the Coalition Provisional Authority, 2009; In the Graveyard of Empires: America's War in Afghanistan, 2009; (with C.C. Fair) Counterinsurgency in Pakistan, 2010. Contributor to periodicals and journals. **Address:** RAND Corporation, 1200 S Hayes St., Arlington, VA 22202-5050, U.S.A. **Online address:** seth_jones@rand.org

JONES, Shane. American (born United States), b. 1980. **Genres:** Children's Fiction. **Career:** Author. **Publications:** NOVELS: Light Boxes, 2009; The Failure Six, 2010. POETRY: Maybe Tomorrow, 2002; A Cake Appeared, 2010. SHORT STORIES AND CHAPBOOKS: I Will Unfold You with My Hairy Hands, 2008; Black Kids in Lemon Trees, 2009. Contributor to periodicals. **Address:** PO Box 7208, Cap. Stn., Albany, NY 12224, U.S.A. **Online address:** sejones85@gmail.com

JONES, Solomon. American (born United States), b. 1969. **Genres:** Novels, Novellas/Short Stories. **Career:** Philadelphia Tribune, reporter, 1993-94; Philadelphia Weekly, senior contributing editor, writer, 1996-2004; Salvation Army of Eastern PA and Delaware, director of public relations, 1997-98; City Council of Philadelphia, public affairs director, 2002-04; Temple University's College of Liberal Arts, adjunct professor, 2004-; Fattah for Mayor, communications director, 2006-07; Philadelphia Daily News, columnist, 2007-; Office of Congressman Chaka Fattah, community outreach director, 2007-. **Publications:** Pipe Dream, 2001; The Bridge, 2003; Ride Or Die, 2004; Keeping Up With The Jones: Marriage, Family and Life Unplugged, 2004; C.R.E.A.M., 2006; Payback: The Return of C.R.E.A.M, 2009; The Last Confession, 2010; Gravedigger's Ball: A Coletti Novel, 2011. **Address:** c/o Author Mail, St. Martin's Press, 175 5th Ave., New York, NY 10010, U.S.A. **Online address:** info@solomonjones.com

JONES, Star(let Marie). American (born United States), b. 1962. **Genres:** Essays. **Career:** Kings County District Attorney's Office, prosecution staff,

1986-91, senior assistant district attorney, 1991-92; TruTV (formerly Court TV), legal correspondent, 1991, executive editor, 2007-08, legal expert contributor, 2008-; NBC-TV, legal correspondent, 1992-93, The View (NBC-TV), co-host, 1997-2006; Jones & Jury, host and co-owner, 1994-; Inside Edition, senior correspondent, chief legal analyst, 1995; Brooklyn District Attorney, assistant, Homicide Division, senior assistant attorney; UPTOWN Magazine, editor-at-large. **Publications:** (With D. Paisner) You Have to Stand for Something, or You'll Fall for Anything, 1998; Shine!: A Physical, Emotional, and Spiritual Journey to Finding Love, 2006; Satan's Sisters: A Novel Work of Fiction, 2011. **Address:** TruTV, 600 3rd Ave., New York, NY 10016-1901, U.S.A.

JONES, Stephen. British (born England), b. 1953. **Genres:** Novellas/Short Stories, Horror, Science Fiction/Fantasy, Film, Reference. **Career:** Stephen Jones Media, owner, 1987-. Writer, film producer, film director, film publicist and consultant. **Publications:** The Illustrated Vampire Movie Guide, 1993; The Illustrated Dinosaur Movie Guide, 1993; The Illustrated Frankenstein Movie Guide, 1994; The Illustrated Werewolf Movie Guide, 1996; The Essential Monster Movie Guide, 1999; Creepshows, 2001; The Dead that Walk: Flesh-eating Stories, 2009; Zombie Apocalypse!, 2010; The Vampire 100: The Essential Guide to the Best Vampire Movies & TV Shows, 2010. EDITOR: (with K. Newman) Horror: 100 Best Books, 1988; (with J. Fletcher) Gaslight and Ghosts, 1988; (with C. Paget) Dark Voices: The Best from the Pan Book of Horror Stories, 1990; (with R. Campbell) Best New Horror, vols. I-VII, 1990-96; Clive Barker's The Nightbreed Chronicles, 1990; The Mammoth Book of Terror, 1991; Clive Barker's Shadows in Eden, 1991; James Herbert: By Horror Haunted, 1991; (with N. Gaiman) Now We Are Sick, 1991; (with Campbell) The Hellraiser Chronicles, 1992; The Mammoth Book of Vampire Stories, 1992, new ed., 2004; (with Campbell) The Giant Book of Best New Horror, 1993; The Mammoth Book of Zombies, 1993; (with D. Carson) H.P. Lovecraft's Book of Horror, 1993; The Mammoth Book of Werewolves, 1994; (with Campbell) The Giant Book of Terror, 1994; The Mammoth Book of Frankenstein, 1994; Shadows over Innsmouth, 1994; (comp.) Clive Barker's A-Z of Horror, 1997; The Mammoth Book of Dracula, 1997; Dancing with the Dark, 1997; The Mammoth Book of Best New Horror, vol. VIII-XXII, 1997-2011; Exorcisms and Ecstasies, 1997; The Vampire Stories of R. Chetwynd-Hayes, 1997; (with Fletcher) Secret City, 1997; Dark of the Night, 1997; White of the Moon, 1999; Dark Detectives, 1999; The Conan Chronicles, vol. I: The People of the Black Circle, 2000, vol. II: The Hour of the Dragon, 2001; Phantoms and Fiends, 2000; The Mammoth Book of Vampire Stories by Women, 2001; The Emperor of Dreams, 2002; Keep out the Night, 2002; Frights and Fancies, 2002; By Moonlight Only, 2003; Great Ghost Stories, 2004; The Mammoth Book of New Terror, 2004; Mammoth Book of Vampires, 2004; (with K. Newman) Horror: Another 100 Best Books, 2005; Weird Shadows over Innsmouth, 2005; H.P. Lovecraft's Book of the Supernatural, 2006; (and afterword) The Complete Chronicles of Conan, 2006; (with R. Chetwynd-Hayes) Tales to Freeze the Blood, 2006; Summer Chills: Strangers in Stranger Lands, 2007; (and afterword) Necronomicon: The Best Weird Tales of H.P. Lovecraft, 2008; (and comp.) Basil Copper: A Life in Books, 2008; The Mammoth Book of Monsters, 2008; (and afterword) Eldritch Tales: A Miscellany of the Macabre, 2011; Haunts: Reliquaries of the Dead, 2011; A Book of Horrors, 2011; (and intro.) Told Only at Midnight, 2011; The Best Short Stories of R. Chetwynd-Hayes: Ghosts And Ghouls, forthcoming. EDITOR WITH D. SUTTON: Fantasy Tales I-VII, 1988-91; The Best Horror from Fantasy Tales, 1988; Dark Voices, vols. II-VI, 1990-94; The Anthology of Fantasy and the Supernatural, 1994; Dark Terrors, vols. I-VI, 1995-2002; The Giant Book of Fantasy Tales, 1996. **Address:** c/o Dorothy Lumley, Dorian Literary Agency, Upper Thornehill, 27 Church Rd., St. Marychurch, Torquay, Torbay, DN TQ1 4QY, England.

JONES, Ted. American (born United States), b. 1937. **Genres:** History, Young Adult Fiction, Literary Criticism And History. **Career:** Boeing Military Aircraft Co., project administrator for development, 1984-85; Unified School District 434, superintendent of schools, 1991-94. Writer. **Publications:** Grant's War: A Novel of the Civil War, 1992; Hard Road to Gettysburg: A Novel, 1993; Fifth Conspiracy: A Novel, 1995; While God Slept: A Novel of World War II, 1996. **Address:** 2105 Hageman Ave., Salina, KS 67401, U.S.A.

JONES, Thai. American (born United States), b. 1977. **Genres:** Psychology, Human Relations/Parenting, History. **Career:** Writer. **Publications:** A Radical Line: From the Labor Movement to the Weather Underground, One Family's Century of Conscience, 2004; More Powerful Than Dynamite: Radicals,

Plutocrats, Progressives, and New York's Year of Anarchy, 2012. Contributor to periodicals. **Address:** c/o Author Mail, Free Press, 1230 Ave. of the Americas, New York, NY 10020-1513, U.S.A.

JONES, Thom. (Thom Douglas Jones). American (born United States), b. 1945. **Genres:** Novellas/Short Stories, Biography, Photography. **Career:** Writer. **Publications:** SHORT STORIES: The Pugilist at Rest: Stories, 1993; Cold Snap: Stories, 1995; Sonny Liston Was a Friend of Mine: Stories, 1999; Anna Gaskell: Stories, 2001. Contributor to periodicals. **Address:** Little, Brown & Co., 34 Beacon St., Boston, MA 02108-1415, U.S.A.

JONES, Thomas D. American (born United States), b. 1955. **Genres:** Air/Space Topics, Travel/Exploration. **Career:** Central Intelligence Agency (CIA), Office of Development and Engineering, program management engineer, 1989-90; Science Applications International Corp., senior scientist, 1990; National Aeronautics and Space Administration (NASA), Solar System Exploration Division, staff, 1990-, advanced program planner, 1991, astronaut, 1991-2001, commander, 1994, planetary scientist, consultant, through 2001, advisory council, staff; Florida Institute for Human & Machine Cognition, senior research scientist. Pilot and author. **Publications:** NONFICTION: (with J.A. English) Mission, Earth: Voyage to the Home Planet (young adult), 1996; (with J.A. English) Scholastic Encyclopedia of the United States at War (young adult), 1998, new ed., 2003; (with M. Benson) The Complete Idiot's Guide to NASA, 2002; Sky Walking: An Astronaut's Memoir, 2006; (with R.F. Dorr) Hell Hawks!: The Untold Story of the American Fliers who Savaged Hitler's Wehrmacht, 2008: (with T. Jones) Planetology: Unlocking the Secrets of the Solar System, 2008. Contributor to periodicals and journals. **Address:** HarperCollins Speakers Bureau, 10 E 53rd St., New York, NY 10022, U.S.A. **Online address:** skywalking1@gmail.com

JONES, Thom Douglas. See **JONES, Thom.**

JONES, Tobias. British (born England), b. 1972?. **Genres:** Air/Space Topics, Novels. **Career:** London Review of Books, member of editorial department; Independent on Sunday, staff writer; freelance journalist, 1999-. **Publications:** The Dark Heart of Italy: Travels through Time and Space across Italy in US as The Dark Heart of Italy: An Incisive Portrait of Europe's Most Beautiful, Most Disconcerting Country, 2004; (A. Andrea) Alessandro Rizzi: Vision from Another World, 2006; (E. Ghezzi) Made In Italy: CGIL 100, 2006; Utopian Dreams: In Search of the Good Life, 2007; Salati Case, 2009; White Death, 2011. Contributor of essays and articles to periodicals. **Address:** c/o Editorial Department, Faber & Faber Ltd., 3 Queen Sq., London, GL WC1N 3AU, England.

JONES, Tony H. American (born United States), b. 1968. **Genres:** Theology/Religion, Young Adult Non-fiction. **Career:** Pasadena Covenant Church, junior high director, 1990-93; Youth Works Missions, executive director, 1993-97; Colonial Church of Edina, minister, 1997-2003; Edina Police Department, police chaplain, 1999-2008; Emergent Village, national coordinator, 2005-08; Solomon's Porch, theologian-in-residence, 2008-; Andover Newton Theological School, adjunct professor, 2009-; Rochester College, visiting lecturer, 2010-; Fuller Theological Seminary, adjunct professor, 2011-; Augsburg-Fortress Press, Sparkhouse, senior acquisitions editor and contributor, 2012-. **Publications:** NONFICTION: Postmodern Youth Ministry: Exploring Cultural Shift, Creating Holistic Connections, Cultivating Authentic Community, 2001; Pray, 2003; Read, Think, Pray, Live, 2003; Soul Shaper: Exploring Spirituality and Contemplative Practices in Youth Ministry, 2003; The Sacred Way: Spiritual Practices for Everyday Life, 2004; Divine Intervention: Encountering God through the Ancient Practice of Lectio Divina, 2006; (intro.) The Most Difficult Journey You'll Ever Make: The Pilgrim's Progress, 2006; (ed. with D. Pagitt) An Emergent Manifesto of Hope, 2007; (intro.) Practicing the Presence of God: A Modernized Christian Classic, 2007; Ask, Seek, Knock: Prayers to Change Your Life, 2008; The New Christians: Dispatches from the Emergent Frontier, 2008; Teaching of the Twelve, 2009; The Church is Flat: The Relational Ecclesiology of the Emerging Church Movement, 2011. **Address:** Sparkhouse, Augsburg-Fortress Press, 2800 Lyndale Ave. S, Minneapolis, MN 55408, U.S.A. **Online address:** tj@tony.net

JONES, Webb. See **HENLEY, Arthur.**

JONES, William B(ryan). (Bill Jones). American (born United States), b. 1950. **Genres:** Plays/Screenplays, Humanities, Intellectual History, Literary Criticism And History. **Career:** Catholic High School for Boys, English teacher, 1975-78; Office of the Arkansas Attorney General, legal intern, 1980-81; Roman Catholic High School, English teacher, 1982-83; Arkansas Court of Appeals, attorney law clerk, 1984-88; Arkansas Supreme Court, attorney law clerk, 1989-95, reporter of decisions, 1995-2006. Writer. **Publications:** AS WILLIAM B. JONES JR.: Classics Illustrated: A Cultural History, 2002, 2nd ed., 2011; Author Biographies and Introductions for Classics Illustrated Junior Series, 2003. EDITOR: (as Bill Jones with P. Martin and S. Bucl) A Spectrum Reader: Five Years of Iconoclastic Reporting, Criticism, and Essays, 1991; Robert Louis Stevenson Reconsidered: New Critical Perspectives, 2003. Contributor to periodicals. **Address:** Arkansas Supreme Ct., 420 N McAdoo St., Justice Bldg., 625 Marshall St., Little Rock, AR 72205, U.S.A. **Online address:** bottleimp2000@yahoo.com

JONES, William P. (William Powell Jones). American (born United States), b. 1970. **Genres:** Adult Non-fiction, Economics, Social Sciences. **Career:** New Orleans Public School District, Carter G. Woodson Middle School, teacher, 1992-94; Southern Oral History Program, researcher, 1995-98; University of North Carolina, teaching assistant, 1994-99, instructor, 1999; Rutgers, the State University of New Jersey, assistant professor, 2000-02; University of Wisconsin-Milwaukee, assistant professor, 2002-05; University of Wisconsin-Madison, Department of History, assistant professor, associate professor, 2005-. Writer and historian. **Publications:** (Contrib.) W.E.B. Du Bois: An Encyclopedia, 2001; The Tribe of Black Ulysses: African American Lumber Workers in the Jim Crow South, 2005; (contrib.) The Black Worker: Race and Labor Activism since Emancipation, 2005; (contrib.) Black Milwaukee: The Making of an Industrial Proletariat, 1915-45, 2nd ed., 200; The New Color of Class: Race and Inequality in the Service Economy, forthcoming. Contributor to periodicals. **Address:** Department of History, University of Wisconsin, 3211 Mosse Humanities Bldg., 455 N Park St., PO Box 5006, Madison, WI 53706-1483, U.S.A. **Online address:** wpjones@uwm.edu

JONES, William Powell. See **JONES, William P.**

JONES CHALFONT, Arthur Gwynne. See **CHALFONT.**

JONG, Erica (Mann). American (born United States), b. 1942. **Genres:** Novels, Poetry, Children's Non-fiction, Essays, Adult Non-fiction, Plays/Screenplays, Sex, Romance/Historical, Social Sciences, Biography, Westerns/Adventure. **Career:** City University of New York, City College, lecturer in English, 1964-65; University of Maryland, Overseas Division, lecturer in English, 1966-69; Borough of Manhattan Community College, lecturer in English, 1969-70; YM/YWCA Poetry Center, instructor in poetry, 1971-73; Bread Loaf Writers Conference, instructor, 1981, Ben-Gurion University, visiting writer, 1998; Bennington College, associate faculty, 2003; Columbia University, instructor of masters degree classes, advisor to rare book library, 2007-. **Publications:** FICTION: Fear of Flying, 1973; How to Save Your Own Life, 1977; Fanny: Being the True History of the Adventures of Fanny Hackabout-Jones, 1980; Parachutes & Kisses, 1985; Shylock's Daughter, 1987; Any Woman's Blues, 1990; Inventing Memory: A Novel of Mothers and Daughters, 1997; Sappho's Leap, 2003. POETRY: Fruits & Vegetables, 1971; Half-Lives, 1973; Loveroot, 1975; Here Comes and Other Poems, 1975; The Poetry of Erica Jong, 1976; Selected Poetry, 1977; The Poetry Suit, 1978; At the Edge of the Body, 1979; Ordinary Miracles: New Poems, 1983; Becoming Light: New and Selected, 1991; Love Comes First, 2009. OTHER WORKS: (co-author) Four Visions of America, 1977; Witches, 1981; Megan's Two Houses: A Story of Adjustment, 1984; Serenissima, 1987; The Devil at Large: Erica Jong on Henry Miller, 1993; Fear of Fifty: A Midlife Memoir, 1994; Zipless: Songs of Abandon from the Erotic Poetry of Erica Jong, 1995; Megan's Two Houses: A Story of Adjustment, 1996; What Do Women Want?: Bread, Roses, Sex, Power, 1998; Conversations With Erica Jong, 2002; Seducing the Demon: Writing for My Life, 2006; (ed.) Sugar in my Bowl, 2011. Contributor of articles to newspapers and periodicals. **Address:** c/o Amy Berkower, Writers House Literary Agency, 21 W 26th St., New York, NY 10010-1003, U.S.A. **Online address:** queryjonglcur@rcn.com

JONGMAN, Mariken. Dutch (born Netherlands), b. 1965. **Genres:** Novels, Young Adult Fiction. **Career:** Youth-theater Productions, actor, singer and scriptwriter, 1997-. **Publications:** Rits (children's novel), 2008. **Address:** Front Street Inc., 862 Haywood Rd., Asheville, NC 28806, U.S.A. **Online address:** post@marikenjongman.nl

JONSSON, Lars O(ssian). Swedish (born Sweden), b. 1952. **Genres:** Art/Art History, Natural History. **Career:** Writer and artist, 1971-. **Publications:**

Birds of Lake, River, Marsh and Field, 1978; Birds of the Mediterranean and Alps, 1982; On: Bilder Från en Sandrevel, 1984; Birds of Europe: With North Africa and the Middle East, 1992; Dagrar, 2000; Lars Jonsson: Birds and Light, 2002; Lars Jonsson: fåglar och ljus, 2003; Lars Jonsson's Birds, 2009. **Address:** Norrgarde, Hamra, S-62010, Sweden.

JOOSSE, Barbara M(onnot). Amcrican (born United States), b. 1949. **Genres:** Children's Fiction, Biography, Essays, Picture/Board Books. **Career:** Stephan & Brady, associate, 1970-71; Waldbillig & Besteman, copywriter, 1971-74. **Publications:** The Thinking Place, 1982; Spiders in the Fruit Cellars, 1983; Fourth of July, 1985; Jam Day, 1987; Anna, The One and Only, 1988; Better with Two, 1988; Dinah's Mad, Bad Wishes, 1989; Pieces of the Picture, 1989; Mama, Do You Love Me?, 1991; The Pitiful Life of Simon Schultz, 1991; Anna and the Cat Lady, 1992; Nobody's Cat, 1992; Wild Willie and King Kyle, Detectives, 1993; The Losers Fight Back: A Wild Willie Mystery, 1994; The Morning Chair, 1995; Snow Day!, 1995; I Love You the Purplest, 1996; Nugget and Darling, 1997; Ghost Trap: A Wild Willie Mystery, 1998; Lewis and Papa: Adventure on the Santa Fe Trail, 1998; Alien Brain Fryout: A Wild Willie Mystery, 2000; Ghost Wings, 2001; A Houseful of Christmas, 2001; Stars in the Darkness, 2002; Bad Dog School, 2004; Hot City, 2004; Nikolai, the Only Bear, 2005; Papa Do You Love Me?, 2005; Dead Guys Talk: A Wild Willie Mystery, 2006; Wind-Wild Dog, 2006; Please is a Good Word to Say, 2007; Grandma Calls Me Beautiful, 2008; In the Night Garden, 2008; Love is a Good Thing to Feel, 2008; Roawr!, 2009; Higgledy-piggledy Chicks, 2010; Sleepover at Gramma's House, 2010; Friends (mostly), 2010; Dog Parade, 2012; Old Robert and the Sea-silly Cats, 2012. Contributor to periodicals. **Address:** c/o Scott Treimel NY, 434 Lafayette St., New York, WI 10003, U.S.A. **Online address:** bjoosse@barbarajoosse.com

JOOSTE, Pamela. South African (born South Africa), b. 1946?. **Genres:** Adult Non-fiction, Novels, Young Adult Fiction. **Career:** Howard Timmins publishers, staff; BP Southern Africa, Department of Communications, head. Writer. **Publications:** Dance with a Poor Man's Daughter, 1998; Frieda and Min, 1999; Like Water in Wild Places, 2000; People Like Ourselves, 2003; Star of the Morning, 2007. **Address:** c/o Author Mail, Doubleday, 1540 Broadway, New York, NY 10036-4094, U.S.A.

JOPPKE, Christian. Swiss/German (born Germany), b. 1959. **Genres:** Military/Defense/Arms Control, Sociology, History. **Career:** University of Southern California, Department of Sociology, assistant professor, 1990-94; Georgetown University, Center for German and European Studies, research associate, 1993-94, European University Institute, Department of Political and Social Sciences, Jean-Monnet Fellow, 1994, associate professor of sociology, 1995-2002; University of British Columbia, Department of Anthropology and Sociology, professor of sociology, 2003-04; International University, professor of sociology, 2004-06; American University of Paris, Graduate School of Government, professor of politics, 2006-; Central European University, Nationalism Studies Program, visiting professor, 2010; University of Bern, Department of Sociology, professor; Theory and Society, corresponding editor, 2011-. **Publications:** Mobilizing Against Nuclear Energy: A Comparison of Germany and the United States, 1993; East German Dissidents and the Revolution of 1989: Social Movement in a Leninist Regime, 1995; Immigration and the Nation-State: The United States, Germany, and Great Britain, 1999; Selecting by Origin: Ethnic Migration in the Liberal State, 2005; Veil: Mirror of Identity, 2009; Citizenship and Immigration, 2010. EDITOR: Challenge to the Nation-State: Immigration in Western Europe and the United States, 1998; (with S. Lukes) Multicultural Questions, 1999; (with V. Guiraudon) Controlling a New Migration World, 2001; (with E. Morawska) Toward Assimilation and Citizenship: Immigrants in Liberal Nation-states, 2003. Contributor of articles to journals. **Address:** Department of Sociology, University of Bern, Lerchenweg 36, Bern, CH-3012, Switzerland. **Online address:** christian.joppke@soz.unibe.ch

JORDAN, Alma. See **JORDAN, Alma Theodora.**

JORDAN, Alma Theodora. (Alma Jordan). Trinidadian (born Trinidad and Tobago), b. 1929. **Genres:** Librarianship, Bibliography, Language/Linguistics. **Career:** Carnegie Free Library, librarian, 1955-56; Industrial Development Corp., librarian, 1959-60; University of West Indies, campus librarian, 1960-89, University librarian, 1982-89. Writer. **Publications:** The Development of Library Service in the West Indies Through Inter-Library Cooperation, 1970; (ed.) Research Library Cooperation in the Caribbean, 1973; (with B. Comissiong) The English-speaking Caribbean: A Bibliography of Bibliographies, 1984; The Changing World of Librarianship, Or, Change on the Library Scene, Our Constant Companion: A Public Lecture, 1991. **Address:** 28 Gilwell Rd., Valsayn Pk., Curepe, 1426, Trinidad and Tobago.

JORDAN, Anne Devereaux. American (born United States), b. 1943. **Genres:** Novels, Novellas/Short Stories, Science Fiction/Fantasy, Children's Fiction, History, Literary Criticism And History, Ghost Writer, Poetry, Poetry. **Career:** Western Michigan University, instructor in English, 1970-73; University of Connecticut, instructor in English, 1973-74; Parousia Press, graphic and layout artist and camera person, 1977-80; Wesleyan University, artist-in-residence, 1977, visiting lecturer, 1990-; Magazine of Fantasy and Science Fiction, assistant editor, 1979-83, associate editor, 1984-85, managing editor, 1985-89; University of Hartford, adjunct faculty; 1980-87; Cowan, Liebowitz & Latman, literary consultant, 1986-; ghostwriter, 1986-; freelance writer and editor, 1989-; Weiss, David, Fross, Zelnick and Lehrman, literary consultant, 1990-; Teaching and Learning Literature and Young Adults, senior editor, 1994-98; David Wright Tremaine L.L.P., literary consultant, 1994-. **Publications:** (Comp. with F. Butler and R. Rotert) The Wide World All Around: A Creative Anthology of Children's Literature, 1986; The Seventh-Day Adventists: A History, 1988; (with J.M. Stifle) The Baptists, 1990; Following the Gleam: Teaching and Learning Genre with Children and Young Adults, 2 vols., 1997; Romancing the Book: Teaching and Learning Literary Elements with Children and Young Adults, 1997; Literature? Why Bother?, 1997; (with V. Schomp) The Civil War, 2006; (with V. Schomp) Slavery and Resistance, 2006. EDITOR: (with E.L. Ferman) The Best Horror Stories from the Magazine of Fantasy and Science Fiction, 1988; Fires of the Past: Thirteen Contemporary Fantasies about Hometowns, 1991. Contributor of articles to periodicals. **Address:** 117 Mansfield Hollow Rd., Ste. A4, Mansfield Center, CT 06250-1319, U.S.A.

JORDAN, Chris. See **PHILBRICK, (W.) Rodman.**

JORDAN, Constance. American (born United States) **Genres:** Literary Criticism And History, History. **Career:** Yale University, visiting lecturer in English, 1974, 1977; Bryn Mawr College, lecturer in comparative literature, 1977-78; Columbia University, assistant professor of English and comparative literature, 1978-87; National Endowment for the Humanities, fellow, 1984, 1985; Folger Institute, fellow, 1985; Newberry Library, fellow, 1987; Northwestern University, visiting associate professor of English, 1987-88; American Council of Learned Societies, fellow, 1988; Claremont Graduate University, associate professor, 1988-92, professor of English, 1993-, now professor emeritus; University of California, Center for Medieval and Renaissance Studies, associate, 1992-; Folger Library, fellow, 1994. Writer. **Publications:** Pulci's Morgante: Poetry and History in Fifteenth-Century Florence, 1986; Renaissance Feminism: Literary Texts and Political Models, 1990; Shakespeare's Monarchies: Ruler and Subject in Shakespeare's Romances, 1997; (ed.) Longman Anthology of British Literature, vol. I: Middle Ages, Early Modern, Restoration and Eighteenth Century, 1998; (ed.) William Shakespeare's Hamlet, Prince of Denmark, 2004, 2nd ed., 2005; (ed. with K. Cunningham) Law in Shakespeare, 2007. Contributor of articles to periodicals. **Address:** Department of English, Claremont Graduate University, 150 E 10th St., Claremont, CA 91711, U.S.A. **Online address:** constance.jordan@cgu.edu

JORDAN, Daniel P(orter). American (born United States), b. 1938. **Genres:** History. **Career:** University of Maryland, Overseas Division, instructor in history, 1963-65; University of Richmond, instructor in history, 1968-69; Virginia Commonwealth University, instructor, 1969-70, assistant professor, 1970-73, associate professor, 1973-80, professor of American history, 1980-84; Virginia Department of Historic Resources, vice chair, 1984-87, chair, 1987-90; Richmond Civilian Round Table, president, 1983; Thomas Jefferson Foundation, executive director, 1985-, president, 1991-; U.S. Secretary of the Interior, National Park System, chair, 1987-88; Arizona State University, distinguished visiting lecturer, 1995; Virginia State Penitentiary, teacher; Virginia Advisory Council on Libraries, director; Edgar Allan Poe Foundation, director; Thomas Jefferson Forum, director; Gilder-Lehrman Institute of American History, director; Central Virginia Educational Telecommunications Corp., director; National Endowment for the Humanities, consultant; Museum of the Confederacy, consultant; National Public Radio, producer; Little League, coach. Writer. **Publications:** Political Leadership in Jefferson's Virginia, 1983; (ed. and intro. with M. Duke) A Richmond Reader, 1733-1983, 1983; (with M. Duke) Tobacco Merchant: The Story of Universal Leaf Tobacco Company, 1995. Contributor to books. **Address:** Thomas Jefferson

Foundation, Ivy Business Pk., 556 Dettor Rd., Ste. 107, PO Box 316, Charlottesville, VA 22903, U.S.A. **Online address:** djordan@monticello.org

JORDAN, David C. American (born United States), b. 1935. **Genres:** Politics/Government, History, Adult Non-fiction. **Career:** University of Virginia, professor of government and foreign affairs, 1965-, department head, 1969-77; U.S. ambassador to Peru, 1984-86; New World Institute, president, 1993-. Writer. **Publications:** (With A.P. Whitaker) Nationalism in Contemporary Latin America, 1966; World Politics in Our Time, 1970; Spain, the Monarchy and the Atlantic Community (monograph), 1979; Revolutionary Cuba and the End of the Cold War, 1993; Drug Politics: Dirty Money and Democracies, 1999. EDITOR AND CONTRIBUTOR: A Strategy for Latin America in the Nineties (monograph), 1988; U.S. Latin American Policy for the Nineties (monograph), 1994. **Address:** Department of Politics, University of Virginia, S152 Gibson Hall, 1540 Jefferson Park Ave., PO Box 400787, Charlottesville, VA 22904, U.S.A. **Online address:** dcj2e@virginia.edu

JORDAN, Hillary. American (born United States), b. 1963. **Genres:** Novels. **Career:** Writer. **Publications:** Mudbound: A Novel, 2008. Contributor to periodicals. **Address:** Tivoli, NY , U.S.A. **Online address:** hj@hillaryjordan.com

JORDAN, James M. American (born United States), b. 1953?. **Genres:** Philosophy, Music. **Career:** Rider University, Westminster Choir College, associate professor of music, professor and senior conductor, Westminster Conducting Institute, artistic director; West Chester University, visiting professor of musical education. Writer. **Publications:** (With F. Haasemann) Group Vocal Technique, 1991; Evoking Sound: Fundamentals of Choral Conducting and Rehearsing, 1996; The Musician's Soul: A Journey Examining Spirituality for Performers, Teachers, Composers, Conductors and Music Educators, 1999; (with M. Mehaffey) Choral Ensemble Intonation: Method, Procedures and Exercises, 2001; The Musician's Spirit: Connecting to Others through Story, 2002; (with H. Buchanan) Evoking Sound: Body Mapping Principles and Basic Conducting Techniques, 2002; Evoking Sound: The Choral Warm-Up: Methods, Procedures, Planning and Core Vocal Exercises, 2005; Evoking Sound: The Choral Conductor's Aural Tutor, 2006; The Musician's Walk: An Ethical Labyrinth, 2006; (with T. O'Regan and E. Corporon) Evoking Sound: The Choral Rehearsal, 2007; (with M. Holt) The School Choral Program: Philosophy, Planning, Organizing and Teaching, 2008; The Conductor's Gesture: A Practical Application of Rudolf Von Laban's Movement Language, 2011. **Address:** Westminster Choir College, Rider University, 34 Williamson Hall, 101 Walnut Ln., Princeton, NJ 08540, U.S.A. **Online address:** jevoke@mac.com

JORDAN, Ken. American (born United States) **Genres:** Communications/ Media. **Career:** SonicNet.com, founding editorial director, 1995; Icon New Media, creative director, 1996; MediaChannel.org (global media Web portal), co-founder, 1999; Art and Culture Network, director. **Publications:** Unbalancing Acts: Foundations for a Theater, 1992; (ed. with R. Packer) Multimedia: From Wagner to Virtual Reality, 2001; (ed. with D. Pinchbeck) Toward 2012: Perspectives on the Next Age, 2009. **Address:** 258 W 22nd St., Ste. 3E, New York, NY 10011, U.S.A. **Online address:** ken@kenjordan.tv

JORDAN, Laura. See **BROWN, Sandra.**

JORDAN, Lee. See **SCHOLEFIELD, Alan (A. T.).**

JORDAN, Mark D. American (born United States), b. 1953. **Genres:** Philosophy, Theology/Religion, History. **Career:** University of Notre Dame, assistant professor, 1977-78, 1985-87, associate professor, 1987-95, professor, 1995-2000; Emory University, Asa Griggs Candler professor, 1999-2008; Harvard Divinity School, Richard Reinhold Niebuhr professor, 2009-. Writer. **Publications:** Ordering Wisdom: The Hierarchy of Philosophical Discourses in Aquinas, 1986; The Invention of Sodomy in Christian Theology, 1997; The Silence of Sodom: Homosexuality in Modern Catholicism, 2000; The Ethics of Sex, 2002; Telling Truths in Church: Scandal, Flesh, and Christian Speech, 2003; Blessing Same-Sex Unions: The Perils of Queer Romance and the Confusions of Christian Marriage, 2005; Rewritten Theology: Aquinas after His Readers, 2006; Recruiting Young Love: How Christians Talk about Homosexuality, 2011. EDITOR: (with K. Emery) Ad Litteram: Authoritative Texts and Their Medieval Readers, 1992; Authorizing Marriage? Canon, Tradition, and Critique in the Blessing of Same-Sex Unions, 2006; Alan Bray, The Friend, 2006. Contributor to books. **Address:** Harvard Divinity School,

45 Francis Ave., Cambridge, MA 02138-1911, U.S.A. **Online address:** mjordan@hds.harvard.edu

JORDAN, Michele Anna. American (born United States), b. 1949. **Genres:** Food And Wine, Travel/Exploration, Documentaries/Reportage, Essays. **Career:** Santa Rosa Junior College, adjunct culinary arts faculty, 1991-; San Francisco Chronicle, restaurant critic, 1993-2003; San Francisco Focus Magazine (now San Francisco Magazine), restaurant critic and contributing editor, 1995; KRCB-FM Radio, host, 1995-; Sonoma-Provence Exchange, founder, 1995-; Santa Rosa Press Democrat, columnist; Savor Wine County magazine, contributor; The Wine Enthusiast, contributor. **Publications:** A Cook's Tour of Sonoma, 1990; The Good Cook's Book of Oil and Vinegar, 1992; The Good Cook's Book of Mustard, 1994; The Good Cook's Book of Tomatoes, 1995; The Good Cook's Book of Days, 1995; Ravioli and Lasagne, 1996; Pasta with Sauces, 1996; Polenta: 100 Innovative Recipes from Appetizers to Desserts, 1997; California Home Cooking, 1997; Salt and Pepper: 135 Perfectly Seasoned Recipes for the Cook's Best Friends, 1999; Williams-Sonoma Complete Pasta Cookbook, 1999; (with J. Weir and K. Kidd) Complete Pasta Cookbook, 1999; San Francisco Seafood, 2000; Pasta Classics, 2000; The New Cook's Tour of Sonoma, 2000; BLT Cookbook: Our Favorite Sandwich, 2003; Veg Out!, 2004; (ed. with S. Brady) The World is a Kitchen: Cooking Your Way through Culture; Stories, Recipes, Resources, 2006; California Home Cooking: 400 Recipes That Celebrate The Abundance of Farm and Garden, Orchard and Vineyard, Land and Sea, 2011; Travelers' Tales: The World is a Kitchen, forthcoming; A Sensual Tour: A Reader's Bibliography to the Works of MFK Fisher, forthcoming. Works appear in anthologies. Contributor to periodicals. **Address:** Amy Rennert Agency, 98 Main St., Ste. 302, Tiburon, CA 94920, U.S.A. **Online address:** michele@micheleannajordan.com

JORDAN, Penny. Also writes as Melinda Wright, Lydia Hitchcock, Annie Groves, Caroline Courtney. British (born England), b. 1946. **Genres:** Romance/Historical, Novels, Science Fiction/Fantasy. **Career:** Writer, 1970-. **Publications:** AS ANNIE GROVES: Goodnight Sweetheart, 2006; Hettie of Hope Street, 2006; As Time Goes By, 2007; The Grafton Girls, 2007; Some Sunny Day, 2007; Elli Pride, 2009; Connies Courage, 2010. AS CAROLINE COURTNEY: Duchess in Disguise, 1979; A Wager for Love, 1979; Love Unmasked, 1979; Guardian of the Heart, 1979; Dangerous Engagement, 1979; Loves Masquerade, 1980; The Fortunes of Love, 1980; The Romantic Rivals, 1980; Heart of Honour, 1981; Destinys Duchess, 1981; The Masquerading Heart, 1981; Abandoned for Love, 1981; The Tempestuous Affair, 1981; Love of My Life, 1981; Love Triumphant, 1981; Lovers Victory, 1981; The Courier of Love, 1982; Love in Waiting, 1982; Libertine in Love, 1982; The Daring Heart, 1982; Forbidden Love, 1982; Hearts or Diamonds, 1985; Prisoner of Passion, 1985; Dual Enchantment, 1985; Conspiracy of Kisses, 1986. AS MELINDA WRIGHT: The Concorde Affair, 1981; Love at 30, 000 Feet, 1982; Flight into Ecstasy, 1983. AS LYDIA HITCHCOCK: The Ducetti Lair, 1981; The Geneva Touch, 1982. NOVELS: Falcon's Prey, 1981; Marriage without Love, 1981; Tiger Man, 1982; Northern Sunset, 1982; Blackmail, 1982; Bought with His Name, 1982; The Caged Tiger, 1982; Daughter of Hassan, 1982; Island of the Dawn, 1982; Long Cold Winter, 1982; Escape from Desire, 1982; Desire's Captive, 1982; An Unbroken Marriage, 1982; Passionate Protection, 1983; Forgotten Passion, 1983; Phantom Marriage, 1983; The Flawed Marriage, 1983; Rescue Operation, 1983; Man-Hater, 1983; A Sudden Engagement, 1983; Savage Atonement, 1983; Response, 1984; Shadow Marriage, 1984; Darker Side of Desire, 1984; The Inward Storm, 1984; The Friendship Barrier, 1984; Rules of the Game, 1984; Campaign for Loving, 1984; Wanting, 1985; Injured Innocent, 1985; The Hard Man, 1985; Permission to Love, 1985; Desire for Revenge, 1985; Exorcism, 1985; Fire with Fire, 1985; Time Fuse, 1985; The Six-Month Marriage, 1985; Taken Over, 1985; What You Made Me, 1985; You Owe Me, 1985; A Man Possessed, 1986; Stronger than Yearning, 1986; Capable of Feeling, 1986; Desire Never Changes, 1986; Return Match, 1986; A Reason for Marriage, 1986; Loving, 1986; Research into Marriage, 1987; Passionate Relations, 1987; For One Night, 1987; A Savage Adoration, 1987; Substitute Lover, 1987; Too Short a Blessing, 1987; Fight for Fight, 1988; Levelling the Score, 1988; Potential Danger, 1988; Without Trust, 1988; Special Treatment, 1988; Power Play, 1988; Love's Choices, 1988; Stronger than Yearning, 1988; Lovers Touch, 1988; So Close and No Closer, 1989; Valentine's Night, 1989; Power Play Sampler, 1989; Force of Feeling, 1989; Equal Opportunities, 1989; A Reason for Being, 1989; A Rekindled Passion, 1989; Beyond Compare, 1989; Bitter Betrayal, 1989; Free Spirit, 1989; Silver, 1989; An Expert Teacher, 1989; Payment in Kind, 1990; Unspoken Desire, 1990; Rival Attractions, 1990; Breaking Away, 1990; Time for Trust, 1990; Out of the Night, 1990; The Hidden Years, 1990; Game of Love, 1990; Second Time Loving, 1990; A Kind of Madness, 1990; A Time to Dream, 1991; A Cure for Love, 1991; Second-best Husband, 1991; Dangerous Interloper, 1991; A Forbidden Leaving, 1991; Payment Due, 1991; Stranger from the Past, 1991; Tug of Love, 1992; Lingering Shadows, 1992; Laws of Attraction, 1992; Lesson to Learn, 1992; A Matter of Trust, 1992; Mistaken Adversary, 1992; Past Passion, 1992; Yesterday's Echoes, 1993; Lingering Shadows, 1993; For Better, For Worse, 1993; French Leave, 1994; Cruel Legacy, 1995; Unwanted Wedding, 1995; An Unforgettable Man, 1996; Her Christmas Fantasy, 1996; Love's Choices, 1996; Power Games, 1996; Valentine's Night, 1996; The Trusting Game, 1996; Mistletoe Magic, 1996; Mission: Make-Over, 1997; Too Wise to Wed?, 1997; Woman to Wed?, 1997; Yours, Mine and Ours, 1997; Best Man to Wed?, 1997; A Perfect Family, 1998; Perfect Marriage Material, 1998; The Perfect Seduction, 1998; To Love, Honour and Betray, 1998; To Love, Honor and Betray, 1998; Fantasy for Two, 1998; Marriage Make Up, 1998; The Perfect Match?, 1998; Mission: Makeover, 1998; The Perfect Sinner, 1999; Lover by Deception, 1999; Wanting His Child, 1999; The Mistress Assignment, 1999; The Mistress Assignment: Society Weddings, 1999; The Perfect Lover, 1999; One Intimate Night, 1999; A Treacherous Seduction, 2000; The Marriage Resolution, 2000; Back in the Marriage Bed, 2000; The Ultimate Surrender, 2000; The Bride's Bouquet, 2000; Coming Home, 2000; A Perfect Night, 2000; The Demetrios Virgin, 2001; The Marriage Demand, 2001; The City-Girl Bride, 2001; The Tycoon's Virgin, 2002; Women and Love, 2002; Christmas Eve Wedding, 2002; (with D. Maguire) What Women Want!, 2002; (with S. Marton) For Love or Money, 2003; Now or Never 2003; Marco's Convenient Wife, 2003; Sheikh's Virgin Bride, 2003; Mistress Purchase, 2004; Response, 2005; Sweet Revenge, 2005; Bedding His Virgin Mistress, 2005; Expecting the Playboy's Heir, 2005; Blackmailing the Society Bride, 2005; Master of Pleasure, 2006; The Sheikh's Bride (collection), 2006; Her Lover Her Husband, 2006; The Italian Duke's Mistress, 2006; Master of Pleasure, 2006; Christmas Bride, 2006; Taken by the Sheikh, 2007; (with H. Brooks and C. Wood) It Happened at Christmas, 2007; Sheikh's Blackmailed Mistress, 2008; The Boss's Marriage Arrangement, 2008; Silk, 2008; Jet Set Wives, 2008; They're Wed Again, 2008; Virgin for the Billionaire's Taking, 2008; Captive At the Sicilian Billionaire's Command, 2009; The Sicilian Boss's Mistress, 2009; The Sicilian's Baby Bargain, 2009; Sins, 2009; Bride for his Majesty's Pleasure, 2009; Marriage: To Claim His Twins, 2010; The Reluctant Surrender, 2010; The Dutiful Wife, 2010; Scandalous Seductions, 2010; Giselle's Choice, 2011; Secret Heirs, 2011; A Stormy Spanish Summer, 2011; Scandals, 2011; Passion and the Prince, 2011; The Most Coveted Prize, 2011; The Power of Vasilii, 2011; Lords of the Desert, 2011; Pride, 2011; Nine Months, forthcoming. Works appear in anthologies. Contributor to periodicals. **Address:** Harlequin Mills & Boon Ltd., Eton House, 18-24 Paradise Rd., Richmond, SR TW9 1SR, England. **Online address:** penny@penny-jordan.com

JORDAN, Pete. American (born United States), b. 1967?. **Genres:** Biography, Travel/Exploration. **Career:** Writer. **Publications:** Dishwasher: One Man's Quest to Wash Dishes in All 50 States, 2007. Contributor to periodicals. **Address:** Dishwasher, PO Box 8213, Portland, OR 97207, U.S.A. **Online address:** pete@dishwasherpete.com

JORDAN, Richard Tyler. Also writes as R. T. Jordan, Ben Tyler. American (born United States), b. 1960. **Genres:** Novels, Gay And Lesbian Issues, History, Music, Popular Culture, Theatre, Mystery/Crime/Suspense, Humor/Satire, Humor/Satire. **Career:** Walt Disney Studios, senior publicist and writer, 1984-. **Publications:** But Darling, I'm Your Auntie Mame!: The Amazing History of the World's Favorite Aunt, 1998, rev. ed., 2004; Suffer Fools (novel), forthcoming. AS BEN TYLER: Tricks of the Trade, 2002; Hunk House, 2002; Gay Blades, 2004; One Night Stand, 2004. POLLY PEPPER MYSTERY SERIES AS R.T. JORDAN: Remains to be Scene, 2007; Final Curtain, 2008; A Talent for Murder, 2009; Set Sail For Murder, 2010. **Address:** Walt Disney Studios, 500 S Buena Vista St., Burbank, CA 91521-1770, U.S.A. **Online address:** rtylerjordan@aol.com

JORDAN, Robert B. Canadian (born Canada), b. 1939. **Genres:** Chemistry, Sciences, Mathematics/Statistics, Reference. **Career:** University of Alberta, Department of Chemistry, faculty, now professor emeritus. Writer. **Publications:** Oxygen Isotope Studies on Carboxylatopentaamine-Cobalt (III) Complexes, 1965; Reaction Mechanisms of Inorganic and Organometallic Systems, 1991, 3rd ed., 2007. Contributor to journals. **Address:** Department of Chemistry, University of Alberta, E4-52, Chemistry Ctr., 11227 Saskatchewan Dr., Edmonton, AB T6G 2G2, Canada. **Online address:** bob.jordan@ualberta.ca

JORDAN, Robert Smith. American (born United States), b. 1929. **Genres:** Institutions/Organizations, International Relations/Current Affairs, Military/Defense/Arms Control, Politics/Government, Biography, Essays. **Career:** U.S. Bureau of the Budget, Executive Office of the President, budget examiner, 1956; Princeton University, instructor in politics, 1956-57; University of Pittsburgh, assistant professor of public and international affairs, 1959-60; George Washington University, Army War College Center, assistant director, 1960-61, Air University Center, director, 1961-62, associate professor of political science and international affairs, 1962-70, assistant to the president, 1962-64, Program of Policy Studies, International Organization and International Security Studies, associate director, 1964-65, School of Public and International Affairs, Foreign Affairs Intern Program, director, 1968-70; University of Sierra Leone, Department of Political Science, Littauer visiting professor of political science, head, 1965-67, Faculty of Economics and Social Studies, dean, chairman; State University of New York, professor of political science, 1970-76, department chairman, 1970-74; UN Institute for Training and Research, senior research specialist and director of research, 1974-79; Columbia University, adjunct professor of political science, 1978-80; University of South Carolina, Dag Hammarskjoeld professor, 1979-; University of New Orleans, College of Urban and Public Affairs, professor of political science, university research professor of public and international affairs, 1980-2004, research professor emeritus of political science, 2004-; University of Lancaster, Centre for the Study of Arms Control and International Security, Fulbright professor, 1988; International Studies Association, vice president. Writer. **Publications:** The NATO International Staff/Secretariat, 1952-57: A Study in International Administration, 1967; Government and Power in West Africa, 1969; (with T.G. Weiss) The World Food Conference and Global Problem-Solving, 1976; (with M.W. Bloome) Political Leadership in NATO: A Study in Multinational Diplomacy, 1979; (with W. Feld and L. Hurwitz) International Organizations: A Comparative Approach, 1983, (with C. Archer, G.P. Granger and K. Ordes) 4th ed., 2001; (with W. Feld) Europe in the Balance: The Changing Context of European International Politics, 1986; Alliance Strategy and Navies: The Evolution and Scope of NATO's Maritime Dimension, 1990; Atlantic Relations and the new Europe: A Conference Report and Analysis, 1992; Norstad, Cold War NATO Supreme Commander, Airman, Strategist, Diplomat, 2000. EDITOR: (with H. Gibbs and A. Gyorgy) Problems in International Relations, 3rd ed., 1970; Europe and the Superpowers: Perceptions of European International Politics, 1971; International Administration: Its Evolution and Contemporary Applications, 1971; Multinational Cooperation: Economic, Social and Scientific Development, 1972; (with P. Toma and A. Gyorgy) Basic Issues in International Relations, 2nd ed., 1974; (with N. Graham) The International Civil Service: Changing Role and Concepts, 1980; Dag Hammarskjöld Revisited: The UN Secretary-General as a Force in World Politics, 1983; The U.S. and Multilateral Resource Management, 1985; The United States and Multilateral Resource Management, 1985; Generals in International Politics: NATO's Supreme Allied Commander, Europe, 1987; (with J. Hattendorf) Maritime Strategy and the Balance of Power: Britain and America in the Twentieth Century, 1989; Europe and the Super Powers: Essays on European International Politics, 1991. **Address:** College of Urban & Public Affairs, University of New Orleans, 2000 Lakeshore Dr., New Orleans, LA 70148, U.S.A. **Online address:** rjordan@uno.edu

JORDAN, Rosa. Canadian/American (born United States), b. 1939. **Genres:** Novels, Young Adult Non-fiction. **Career:** Writer. **Publications:** (With D. Choukalos) Rossland: The First 100 Years (history), 1996; Dangerous Places: Travels on the Edge (non-fiction), 1997; (with D. Choukalos) Lonely Planet Cycling Cuba (non-fiction), 2002; Lost Goat Lane (novel), 2004; The Goatnappers (novel), 2007; The Last Wild Place (novel), 2008; Far from Botany Bay (novel), 2008; Wild Spirits (novel), 2010. **Address:** Dundurn Press, 500-3 Church St., Toronto, ON M5E 1M2, Canada. **Online address:** rosaj@look.ca

JORDAN, R. T. See **JORDAN, Richard Tyler.**

JORDAN, Sherryl. New Zealander (born New Zealand), b. 1949. **Genres:** Children's Fiction, Young Adult Fiction. **Career:** University of Iowa, writer-in-residence, 1993. **Publications:** The Firewind and the Song, 1984; Matthew's Monsters, 1986; No Problem Pomperoy, 1988; Kittens (school reader), 1989; The Wobbly Tooth, 1989; Babysitter Bear, 1990; Rocco in US as A Time of Darkness, 1990; The Juniper Game, 1991; The Wednesday Wizard, 1991; Denzil's Dilemma, 1992; Winter of Fire, 1992; Rocco, 1992; Other Side of Midnight, 1993; Tanith in US as Wolf-woman, 1994; Sign of the Lion, 1995; Secret Sacrament, 1996; Denzil's Great Bear Burglary, 1997; The Raging Quiet, 1999; Secret Sacrament, 2000; The Wobbly Tooth: Safe and Sound,

2001; The Hunting of the Last Dragon, 2002; The Teeny Tiny Ghost and the Monster, 2004; Time of the Eagle, 2007. Contributor to periodicals. Illustrator of books by J. Cowley. **Address:** c/o Tracy Adams, McIntosh and Otis Inc., 353 Lexington Ave., New York, NY 10016, U.S.A.

JORDAN, Wendy A(dler). American (born United States) **Genres:** Homes/Gardens, Architecture, Air/Space Topics. **Career:** Washington Daily News, Women's Department, assistant, 1969-72; National Trust for Historic Preservation, magazine editor, 1972-77, director of programs for Preservation Press, 1977-79; Hanley-Wood Co., vice president, Builder Magazine, managing editor, 1979-82, Builder, executive editor, 1982-85; Remodeling Magazine, editor, 1985-96, vice president, 1990-96; SGC Horizons Inc., Professional Remodeler Magazine, senior contributing editor, 1996-; Washington Lawyer, editor, 1996-98; Wendy A. Jordan Co., owner, author, editor and editorial consultant, 1996-; Rails to Trails, editor, 1998-. **Publications:** By the Light of the Qulliq: Eskimo Life in the Canadian Arctic (for children), 1979; Lead Carpenter System: A Guide for Remodelers and Their Employees, 1999; (with E. Whitaker and C. Mahoney) Great Kitchens: At Home with America's Top Chefs, 1999, rev. ed. as Great Kitchens: Design Ideas from America's Top Chefs, 2001; (with L. Case and V. Downing) Mastering the Business of Design/Build Remodeling, 2001; The Kidspace Idea Book, 2001; (with W. Asdal) Paper Trail, 2002, 2nd ed., 2010; (with L. Hunter and M. Schoenherr) House Transformed, 2005; New Kidspace Idea Book, 2005; (with S. Stirling) Baby & Kidspace idea Book, 2006; Making Room: Finding Space in Unexpected Places, 2007; Universal Design for the Home, 2008. Contributor to magazines and journals. **Address:** Professional Remodeler Magazine, SGC Horizons Inc., 3030 W Salt Creek Ln., Ste. 201, Arlington Heights, IL 60005, U.S.A. **Online address:** wendyajordan@hotmail.com

JORDAN-LAKE, Joy. American (born United States), b. 1963. **Genres:** Young Adult Non-fiction, Young Adult Fiction. **Career:** Baylor University, adjunct professor, 2000-04; Belmont University, adjunct professor, 2005-09, part-time teacher; Harvard University, Baptist chaplain. Freelance journalist. **Publications:** FICTION: Grit & Grace: Portrait of a Woman's Life (short stories), 1997; Blue Hole Back Home: A Novel Inspired by a True Story, 2008. NONFICTION: Whitewashing Uncle Tom's Cabin: Nineteenth-Century Women Novelists Respond to Stowe, 2005; Why Jesus Makes Me Nervous: Top Ten Alarming Words of Faith, 2007; Working Families: Navigating the Demands and Delights of Marriage, Parenting, and Career, 2007. **Address:** Belmont University, 1900 Belmont Blvd., Nashville, TN 37212-3757, U.S.A. **Online address:** joyjordanlake@aol.com

JORGENSEN-EARP, Cheryl R(uth). American (born United States), b. 1952. **Genres:** Women's Studies And Issues, Biography. **Career:** Virginia Intermont College, instructor in speech and theater, 1980-81; John Umstead Psychiatric Hospital, instructor in speech and theater, 1982; Tacoma Community College, instructor in speech and theater, 1982-83, instructor in speech communication, 1983; Fort Steilacoom Community College, instructor in speech communication, 1983; University of Puget Sound, instructor in communication and theater arts, 1985-90; Lynchburg College, associate professor of communication studies, 1993-, professor of communication studies. Writer. **Publications:** The Transfiguring Sword: Reformist Terrorism and the Just War of the Women's Social and Political Union, 1997; (ed.) Speeches and Trials of the Militant Suffragettes: The Women's Social and Political Union, 1903-1918, 1998; In the Wake of Violence: Image and Social Reform, 2008. Contributor to journals. **Address:** Lynchburg College, Schewel 331, 1501 Lakeside Dr., Lynchburg, VA 24501, U.S.A. **Online address:** jorgensenearp@lynchburg.edu

JORGENSON, Ivar. See **SILVERBERG, Robert.**

JOSEPH, Diana. American (born United States), b. 1970. **Genres:** Biography, Essays, Literary Criticism And History. **Career:** Syracuse University, instructor, 1994-96; Mesa State College, Department of Languages, Literature, and Communication, instructor, 1996-2005; Minnesota State University, MFA Program, assistant professor of English and creative writing, 2005-. Writer. **Publications:** Happy or Otherwise, 2003; I'm Sorry You Feel That Way: The Astonishing but True Story of a Daughter, Sister, Slut, Wife, Mother and Friend to Man and Dog, 2009. **Address:** Department of English, Minnesota State University, 212D Armstrong Hall, Mankato, MN 56001, U.S.A. **Online address:** diana.joseph@mnsu.edu

JOSEPH, Henry. American (born United States), b. 1948. **Genres:** Novels,

Biography, Autobiography/Memoirs, Literary Criticism And History, Young Adult Fiction. **Career:** Writer. **Publications:** Bloodwork: The New Rugged Cross (novel), 1994; Dinosaur Heaven, 1997; The Well Spent Death of Eightball Barnett, 2000. Contributor to periodicals. **Address:** c/o John Hawkins & Associates, 71 W 23rd St., Ste. 1600, New York, NY 10010, U.S.A.

JOSEPH, Lawrence. American (born United States), b. 1948. **Genres:** Poetry, Novels, Literary Criticism And History, Law. **Career:** Office of Michigan Supreme Court Justice G. Mennen Williams, law clerk, 1976-78; University of Detroit, School of Law, associate professor, 1978-81; Shearman and Sterling, associate litigator, 1981-84; Hofstra University, School of Law, associate professor, 1984-87; St. John's University, School of Law, professor of law, 1987-, Tinnelly professor of law, 2003; Princeton University, Creative Writing Program, 1994. Writer and critic. **Publications:** BOOKS: POETRY: Shouting at No One, 1983; Curriculum Vitae, 1988; Before Our Eyes, 1993; Codes, Precepts, Biases, and Taboos: Poems 1973-1993, Poems, 2005; Into It: Poems, 2005. PROSE: Lawyerland, 1997; The Game Changed: Essays and Other Prose, 2011. **Address:** St. John's University School of Law, Belson Hall Rm. 4-16, 8000 Utopia Pkwy., Jamaica, NY 11439, U.S.A. **Online address:** josephl@stjohns.edu

JOSEPH DUDLEY. *See* **CHAPMAN, J. Dudley.**

JOSEPHS, Arthur. *See* **GOTTLIEB, Arthur.**

JOSHI, S(unand) T(ryambak). American/Indian (born India), b. 1958. **Genres:** Romance/Historical, Poetry, Literary Criticism And History, Bibliography. **Career:** Lovecraft Studies, founder and editor, 1979-; Chelsea House Publishers, associate editor, 1984-85, Literary Criticism Division, managing editor, 1985-89, senior editor, 1989-; Studies in Weird Fiction, founder and editor, 1986-. **Publications:** An Index to the Selected Letters of H.P. Lovecraft, 1980; (with M.A. Michaud) Lovecraft's Library: A Catalogue, 1980; Reader's Guide to H.P. Lovecraft, 1982; H.P. Lovecraft and Lovecraft Criticism: An Annotated Bibliography, 1981, Supplement, 1981-84, 1985; Selected Papers on Lovecraft, 1989; The Weird Tale, 1990; John Dickson Carr: A Critical Study, 1990; H.P. Lovecraft: The Decline of the West, 1990; An Index to the Fiction and Poetry of H.P. Lovecraft, 1992; (with D. Schweitzer) Lord Dunsany: A Bibliography, 1993; Lord Dunsany: Master of the Anglo-Irish Imagination, 1995; A Subtler Magick, 1996; H.P. Lovecraft: A Life, 1996; Ramsey Campbell and Modern Horror Fiction, 2001; Modern Weird Tale, 2001; (with D.E. Schultz) An H.P. Lovecraft Encyclopedia, 2001; Dreamer and a Visionary: H.P. Lovecraft in His Time, 2001; God's Defenders: What They Believe and Why They Are Wrong-William James, G.K. Chesterton, T.S. Eliot, William F. Buckley, Jerry Fallwell, Annie Dillard, C.S. Lewis, 2003; The Angry Right: Why Conservatives Keep Getting It Wrong, 2006; Gore Vidal: A Comprehensive Bibliography, 2007; H.P. Lovecraft: a Comprehensive Bibliography, 2009; H.L. Mencken: an Annotated Bibliography, 2009; (intro.) Savage Menace and Other Poems of Horror, 2010; I Am Providence: The Life and Times of H.P. Lovecraft, 2010; (with D. Hussey and D.E. Schultz) Ten Years of Hippocampus Press, 2010; The Unbelievers: The Evolution of Modern Atheism, 2011. EDITOR: (with M.A. Michaud) Uncollected Prose and Poetry, 3 vols., 1978-82; (with M.A. Michaud) H.P. Lovecraft in The Eyrie, 1979; (with S. Connors) Science versus Charlatanry: Essays on Astrology, 1979; H.P. Lovecraft: Four Decades of Criticism, 1980; Saturnalia and Other Poems, 1984; H.P. Lovecraft, Juvenilia, 1897-1905, 1984; The Dunwich Horror and Others, 1984; In Defence of Dagon, 1985; At the Mountains of Madness and Other Novels, 1985; Dagon and Other Macabre Tales, 1986; Uncollected Letters, 1986; Collected Poems, 1988; The Horror in the Museum and Other Revisions, 1989; The Conservative, 1990; (with D.E. Schultz) An Epicure in the Terrible, 1991; H.P. Lovecraft Centennial Conference Proceedings, 1991; On Lovecraft and Life, 1992; Autobiographical Writings, 1992; The Count of Thirty: A Tribute to Ramsey Campbell, 1993; (with D.E. Schultz) Letters to Richard F. Searight, 1992; The Fantastic Poetry, 1990, rev. ed., 1993; (with D.E. Schultz) Letters to Robert Bloch, 1993; H.P. Lovecraft in The Argosy, 1994; (with D.E. Schultz and W. Murray) The H.P. Lovecraft Dreambook, 1994; (with D.E. Schultz) The Shadow over Innsmouth, 1994; (with D.E. Schultz) Letters to Samuel Loveman and Vincent Starrett, 1994; Miscellaneous Writings, 1995; (with R. Dalby and S. Dziemianowicz) Best Ghost and Horror Stories, 1997; The Call of Cthulhu and Other Weird Stories, 1999; Documents of American Prejudice, 1999; Sixty Years of Arkham House, 1999; (with D.E. Schultz) Ambrose Bierce: An Annotated Bibliography of Sources, 1999; (with P.H. Cannon) More Annotated H.P. Lovecraft, 1999; (and intro.) Mark of the Beast and Other Horror

Tales, 2000; Lord of a Visible World, 2000; Atheism: A Reader, 2000; Civil War Memories, 2000; The Collected Fables of Ambrose Bierce, 2000; (with D.E. Schultz) The Unabridged Devil's Dictionary, 2000; The Fall of the Republic and Other Political Satires, 2000; Thing on the Doorstep and Other Weird Stories, 2001; The Ancient Track: The Complete Poetical Works of H.P. Lovecraft, 2001; Shadow out of Time, 2001; From Baltimore to Bohemia: The Letters of H.L. Mencken and George Sterling, 2001; H.L. Mencken on Religion, 2002; H.L. Mencken on American Literature, 2002; (and intro.) Ancient Sorceries and Other Weird Stories, 2002; Great Tales of Terror, 2002; Pleasures of a Futuroscope, 2003; Mencken's America, 2004; (and intro.) Dreams in the Witch House and Other Weird Stories, 2004; (and intro.) In the Land of Time and Other Fantasy Tales, 2004; Collected Essays, 2004; (and intro.) Count Magnus and Other Ghost Stories: The Complete Ghost Stories of M.R. James, 2005; Closing Arguments: Clarence Darrow on Religion, Law and Society, 2005; (with S. Dziemianowicz) Supernatural Literature of the World: An Encyclopedia, 2005; In Her Place: A Documentary History of Prejudice against Women, 2006; (with L.I. Berkove and D.E. Schultz) The Short Fiction of Ambrose Bierce: A Comprehensive Edition, 2006; Icons of Horror and the Supernatural: An Encyclopedia of Our Worst Nightmares, 2006; The Agnostic Reader, 2007; (and intro.) American Supernatural Tales, 2007; (with D.E. Schultz) O Fortunate Floridian: H.P. Lovecraft's Letters to R.H. Barlow, 2007; (with D.E. Schultz) The Complete Poetry and Translations, 2007; (and intro.) The Caves of Death and Other Stories, 2008; (ed.) Icons of Unbelief: Atheists, Agnostics and Secularists, 2008; Emperors of Dreams: Some Notes on Weird Poetry, 2008; (and intro.) What is Man? And Other Irreverent Essays, 2009; Mencken on Mencken: a New Collection of Autobiographical Writings, 2010; Case of Charles Dexter Ward, 2010; Encyclopedia of the Vampire: the Living Dead in Myth, Legend and Popular Culture, 2010; (and intro.) The White People and Other Weird Stories, 2011. Contributor to periodicals. **Address:** Chelsea House Publishers, 2080 Cabot Blvd., Ste. 201, Langhorne, PA 19047, U.S.A. **Online address:** stjoshi@cs.com

JOSIPOVICI, Gabriel (David). British/French (born France), b. 1940. **Genres:** Novels, Novellas/Short Stories, Plays/Screenplays, Literary Criticism And History, History. **Career:** University of Sussex, assistant lecturer, 1962-, professor of English, 1984-, research professor, 1997-98; University College, Northcliffe lecturer, 1980; University of Oxford, Weidenfeld visiting professor, 1996. Writer. **Publications:** NOVELS: The Inventory, 1968; Words: A Novel, 1971; The Present: A Novel, 1975; Migrations, 1977; The Echo Chamber, 1980; The Air We Breathe, 1981; Conversations in Another Room: A Novel, 1984; Contre-Jour: A Triptych after Pierre Bonnard, 1986; The Big Glass, 1991; In a Hotel Garden, 1993; Moo Pak: A Novel, 1994; Now, 1998; Goldberg: Variations, 2002; Only Joking, 2005; Everything Passes, 2006. CRITICISM: The World and the Book: A Study of Modern Fiction, 1971, 3rd ed., 1994; The Lessons of Modernism and Other Essays, 1977, 2nd ed., 1987; Writing and the Body: The Northcliffe Lectures 1981; The Mirror of Criticism: Selected Reviews, 1977-1982, 1983; The Book of God: A Response to the Bible, 1988; Text and Voice: Essays, 1981-1991, 1992; Touch, 1996; On Trust: Art and the Temptations of Suspicion, 1999. OTHERS: Mobius the Stripper: Stories and Short Plays, 1974; (ed.) The Modern English Novel: The Reader, The Writer and the Book, 1976; Four Stories, 1977; Vergil Dying (play), 1981; (ed. and intro.) Sirens' Song: Selected Essays of Maurice Blanchot, 1982; In the Fertile Land, 1987; Deuxième Personne à La Fenêtre: Suivi de, Introduction à Maurice Blanchot, 1988; Steps: Selected Fiction and Drama, 1990; (ed. and intro.) Collected Stories, 1993; (ed.) The Collected Aphorisms, 1994; (ed.) Molloy; Malone Dies; The Unnameable, 1997; A Life: Sacha Rabinovitch 1910-1996, 2001; Singer on the Shore: Essays, 1991-2004, 2006; Two Novels: After & Making Mistakes, 2009; Heart's Wings & Other Stories, 2010; (ed. with B. Cummings) Spirit of England: Selected Essays of Stephen Medcalf, 2010; What Ever Happened to Modernism?, 2010. Contributor to periodicals. **Address:** Johnson and Alcock Ltd., Clerkenwell House, 45/47 Clerkenwell Green, London, GL EC1R OHT, England.

JOSSELSON, Ruthellen (Lefkowitz). American (born United States), b. 1946. **Genres:** Psychology, Social Sciences. **Career:** Psychological Clinic, clinical psychology intern, 1968-70; Massachusetts Mental Health Center, clinical fellow in psychiatry, 1970-71, staff psychologist, 1971-72; University of Toledo, assistant professor of psychology, 1972-73; Johns Hopkins University, associate research scientist, 1973-75; Towson University, assistant professor, 1975-82, associate professor, 1982-89, professor of psychology, 1989-97, Clinical Concentration Program, director, 1975-97; University of Paris,

School of Medicine, researcher, 1982-83; Hebrew University, Fulbright professor, 1989-90, Forchheimer professor of psychology, 1993-94, Department of Psychology, professor, 1997-2005, Institute for Advanced Study, fellow, 2001-02; Harvard University, visiting professor, 1992-93; Fielding Graduate University, professor, 1995-; University of Cambridge, Newnham College, visiting bye-fellow, 2007. Writer. **Publications:** Finding Herself: Pathways to Identity Development in Women, 1987; The Space Between Us: Exploring the Dimensions of Human Relationships, 1992; (ed. with A. Lieblich) The Narrative Study of Lives: An Annual Review, 1993-96; Revising Herself: The Story of Women's Identity from College to Midlife, 1996; (co-author) Conversation as Method: Analyzing the Relational World of People Who Were Raised Communally, 1997; (with T. Apter) Best Friends: The Pleasures and Perils of Girls' and Women's Friendships, 1998; (ed. with A. Lieblich) Making Meaning of Narratives, 1999; (ed. with D.P. McAdams and A. Lieblich) Turns in the Road: Narrative Studies of Lives in Transition, 2001; (ed. with D.P. McAdams and A. Lieblich) Up Close and Personal: The Teaching and Learning of Narrative Research, 2003; (ed. with D.P. McAdams and A. Lieblich) Healing Plots: The Narrative Basis of Psychotherapy, 2004; (ed. with D.P. McAdams and A. Lieblich) Identity and Story: Creating Self in Narrative, 2006; Playing Pygmalion: How People Create One Another, 2007; (ed. with D.P. McAdams and A. Lieblich) The Meaning of Others: Narrative Studies of Relationships, 2007. Contributor to periodicals. **Address:** Fielding Graduate University, 2112 Santa Barbara St., Santa Barbara, CA 93105-3538, U.S.A. **Online address:** rjosselson@fielding.edu

JOURDAIN, Robert. American (born United States), b. 1950?. **Genres:** Information Science/Computers, Music, Photography. **Career:** Writer and musician. **Publications:** Programmer's Problem Solver for the IBM PC, XT and AT, 1985, 2nd ed., 1992; Turbo Pascal Express: 250 Ready-to-Run Assembly Language Routines (computer file), 1987, rev. 2nd ed., 1988; (with P. Norton) The Hard Disk Companion, 1988, 2nd ed., 1991; C Express: 250 Ready-to-Run Assembly Language Routines (computer file), 1989; Music, the Brain and Ecstasy: How Music Captures Our Imagination, 1997. **Address:** William Morrow & Company Inc., 1350 Ave. of the Americas, New York, NY 10019, U.S.A.

JOURDAN, Carolyn. American (born United States), b. 1955?. **Genres:** Autobiography/Memoirs, Biography. **Career:** Committee on Environment and Public Works and the Committee on Governmental Affairs (now Homeland Security and Governmental Affairs), U.S. senate counsel. Attorney and writer. **Publications:** Heart in the Right Place: A Memoir, 2007. **Address:** c/o Michael Taeckens, Algonquin Books, 127 Kingston Rd., Ste. 105, Chapel Hill, NC 27514-1650, U.S.A. **Online address:** carolynjourdan@att.net

JOUVE, Nicole Ward. British (born England) **Genres:** Literary Criticism And History, Autobiography/Memoirs. **Career:** University of York, Department of English and Related Literature, lecturer, professor of literature, now professor emeritus; Granta Magazine, contributor. Writer and literary critic. **Publications:** Spectre du Gris, 1977; Baudelaire: A Fire to Conquer Darkness, 1979; L'Entremise, 1980; Shades of Grey, 1981; Un Homme Nommé Zapolski, 1983; The Streetcleaner: The Yorkshire Ripper Case on Trial, 1986; Colette, 1987; White Woman Speaks with Forked Tongue: Criticism as Autobiography, 1991; (with M. Roberts, S. Roe and S. Sellers) The Semi-Transparent Envelope: Women Writing-Feminism and Fiction, 1994; Female Genesis: Creativity, Self, and Gender, 1998. **Address:** Department of English and Related Literature, University of York, Heslington, York, NY YO10 5DD, England.

JOVANOVIC, Rob. British (born England), b. 1969. **Genres:** Biography, Autobiography/Memoirs, Music. **Career:** Organic chemist, 1988-2001. Writer. **Publications:** Beck! On a Backwards River, 2000; (with T. Abbott) Adventures in Hi-Fi: The Complete REM, 2001; Nirvana, 2002; Official ISL Yearbook and Media Guide, 2002; Forest Giants: The Story of Nottingham Forest, 1975-80, 2003; Perfect Sound Forever: The Story of Pavement, 2004; Big Star: The Story of Rock's Forgotten Band, 2004; The Velvet Underground, 2004; Nirvana: The Complete Recording Sessions, 2004; George Michael: The Biography, 2008; The Velvet Underground Peeled, 2010. **Address:** c/o Author Mail, Piatkus Books, 100 Victoria Embankment, London, GL EC4Y 0DY, England. **Online address:** robj@innotts.co.uk

JOVANOVSKI, Meto. Macedonian (born Macedonia), b. 1928. **Genres:** Novels, Novellas/Short Stories, Children's Fiction, Mythology/Folklore,

Travel/Exploration, Translations, Literary Criticism And History, Reference, Reference. **Career:** Pirin Macedonia, teacher of Macedonian language and history; Makedonska Kniga (publishing house), editor, 1954-63; TV Skopje, head of foreign programming department, 1963-88; Forum for Human Rights of Macedonia, vice-president, 1989-. **Publications:** NOVELS: Slana vo cutot na bademite (title means: 'Frost in the Blossom of the Almondtree'), 1967; Zemja i tegoba (title means: 'Earth and Toil'), 1968; Svedoci (title means: 'Witnesses'), 1970; Budaletinki, 1973; Secho Sekula (novella), 1977; Orlovata dolina: Roman (title means: 'Valley of the Eagles'), 1979; Krlezi (title means: 'Ticks'), 1984; Balkan Book of the Death, 1992; Prodavnica zaljubopitnite (title means: 'Shop for the Curious'), 2003; Ljubovta na Grifonot, 2005; Pogubata na Pretsedatelot, 2007; Pisma do Sakanata, 2009. SHORT STORIES: Jadres: Raskazi (title means: 'Bloom'), 1952; Meni na mojata mesecina (title means: 'Changes on My Moon'), 1956; Nateznati dzvezdi, 1969; Prvite covekovi umiranja, 1971; Patot do osamata (title means: 'Road to Loneliness'), 1978; Krstopatot kon osamata (title means: 'The Crossroad to Serenity'); Krstopat kon spokojot, 1987; Faceless Men & Other Macedonian Stories, 1992. NOVELS FOR CHILDREN: Ljuman aramijata (title means: 'Ljuman the Robber'), 1954; Krstot, kambanata, znameto (title means: 'The Cross, the Bell, the Banner'), 1990. OTHER: Koj e koj, sto e sto: kratok literaturno-jazicen leksikon, 1963; (with K. Kamilov and S. Janevski) Temni khzuvanjh Sostavuvaci, 1967; Prva covjekova umiranja, 1967; Mal literaturen leksikon, 1971; (ed. and trans.) Edna druga Amerika (title means: 'Another America'; Anthology of Contemporary American Poetry), 1977; Klucevite na Manhatan: zapisi odzapadnite predeli (title means: 'The Keys to Manhattan'; travelogue), 1983; Balkanskakniga na umrenite, ili, Osloboduvanje preku zboruvanje; Secko Sekula: makedonska junacka povest, 1992; Zborovnik po Brajcinski: budalastini zaumni luǵe (title means: 'Talking in a Brajcino Way'), 1998. **Address:** St. Partenij Zografski 51, Skopje, 1000, Macedonia. **Online address:** metoj@mhc.org.mk

JOVEN, Enrique. Spanish (born Spain), b. 1964?. **Genres:** Literary Criticism And History, Mystery/Crime/Suspense. **Career:** Instituto de Astrofísica de Canarias, senior engineer, 1991-. Writer and physicist. **Publications:** El Castillo de las Estrellas, 2007. Contributor of articles to periodicals. **Address:** Instituto de Astrofísica de Canarias, C/Vía Láctea, s/ n La Laguna, Tenerife, E38205, Spain.

JOY, Camden. American (born United States), b. 1963?. **Genres:** Art/Art History, Novels, Biography, Autobiography/Memoirs. **Career:** Author. **Publications:** The Greatest Record Album Ever Told, 1995; The Greatest Record Album Singer That Ever Was, 1996; The Last Rock Star Book: Or: Liz Phair: A Rant (novel), 1998; Boy Island (novel), 2000; Hubcap Diamond Star Halo (novella), 2001; Camden Joy, 2002; (with C.B. Morton) Pan (novella), 2002; Lost Joy, 2002; Palm Tree 13 (novella), 2003. Contributor to periodicals. **Address:** c/o Author Mail, Highwater Books, 5944 Rue Waverly, Montreal, Montreal, QC H2T 2Y3, Canada.

JOY, David (Anthony Welton). British (born England), b. 1942. **Genres:** History, Transportation, Local History/Rural Topics, Travel/Exploration, Humor/Satire. **Career:** Yorkshire Post Newspaper, general reporter, 1962-65; Dalesman Publishing Company Ltd., editorial assistant, 1965-70, books editor, 1970-88, editor, 1988-. **Publications:** (With W.R. Mitchell) Settle-Carlisle Railway, 1966, 5th ed., 1979; Main Line Over Shap, 1967; Cumbrian Coast Railways, 1968; Whitby and Pickering Railway, 1969; Railways in the North, 1970; (with A.J. Peacock) Traction Engines in the North, 1970; George Hudson of York, 1971; Railways of the Lake Counties, 1973; Regional History of the Railways of Great Britain: South and West Yorkshire, 1975; (comp.) Railways in Lancashire: A Pictorial History, 1975; (comp. with W.R. Mitchell) Settle-Carlisle Centenary, 1975; Railways of Yorkshire: The West Riding, 1976; (with P. Williams) North Yorkshire Moors Railway: A Pictorial Survey, 1977; Steam on the North York Moors: A Guide to the Grosmont-Pickering Railway, 1978; (with A. Haigh) Yorkshire Railways, 1979; (comp.) Steam on the Settle and Carlisle, 1981; (comp. with W.R. Mitchell) Settle to Carlisle: A Railway over the Pennines, 1982; Yorkshire Dales Railway, 1983; Settle-Carlisle in Colour, 1983; Regional History of the Railways of Great Britain: The Lake Counties, 1984; Portrait of the Settle-Carlisle, 1985; The Dalesman: A Celebration of 50 Years, 1989; Life in the Yorkshire Coalfield, 1989; Settle-Carlisle Celebration, 1990; Uphill to Paradise, 1991; Yorkshire's Christmas, 1992; Best Yorkshire Tales, 1993; The Dalesman Bedside Books, 1993; Yorkshire's Farm Life, 1994; (with D. Pratt) Railways in Your Garden, 1994; St. Andrews & the Open Championship: The Official History, 1999; Fourth Dimension: Traveling the Realms of Discovery-Beyond the Rooms of AA, 2000; Discoveries: Exploration's Dawning, 2000; (with J. Hope) Discoveries II: Ascending into Insight, 2001; One Step Beyond: The First Year, 2002; (with J. Hope) Empty Words: Hungry Hearts in Search of the Kingdom, 2002; (with P. Lennon) Grand Memories: The Life and Times of the Grand Theatre and Opera House, Leeds, 2006; (with A. Singleton) Barns of the Yorkshire Dales, 2008. **Address:** Hole Bottom, Hebden, Skipton, NY BD23 5DI, England.

JOY, Donald Marvin. American (born United States), b. 1928. **Genres:** Education, Human Relations/Parenting, Psychology, Recreation, Theology/Religion, Women's Studies And Issues. **Career:** Cave Community Free Methodist Church, pastor, 1949-52; Rockwall Texas Free Methodist Church, pastor, 1954-58; Free Methodist Publishing House, executive editor, 1958-73; Light and Life Press, executive editor of Sunday school literature, 1960-72; Asbury Theological Seminary, associate professor of Christian education, 1971, professor of human development and family studies, 1971-98, adjunct professor, professor emeritus, 1998-; Center for the Study of the Family in Wilmore, director. **Publications:** Let's Teach, 1961; The Holy Spirit and You, 1965; Meaningful Learning in the Church, 1969; Family Life and Conscience Development, 1979; (ed.) Moral Development Foundations: Judeo-Christian Alternatives to Piaget/Kohlberg, 1983; Bonding: Relationships in the Image of God, 1985; Re-Bonding: Preventing and Restoring Broken Relationships, 1986; (with R. Joy) Lovers: Whatever Happened to Eden?, 1987; Parent, Kids and Sexual Integrity: Equipping Your Child for Healthy Relationships, 1988; Walk On!, 1988; Unfinished Business: How a Man Can Make Peace with His Past, 1989; Sex, Strength and the Secrets of Becoming A Man: A Celebration of Sexuality, Responsibility and the Christian Young Man, 1990; Becoming a Man, 1991; (with D. Hager) Women at Risk: The Real Truth About Sexually Transmitted Disease, 1993; Men under Construction, 1993; Celebrating the New Woman in Family, 1994; Risk-Proofing Your Family, 1995; (with S.F. Venable) How to Use Christian Camping Experiences in Religious Education: Transformation Through Christian Camping, 1998; Empower Your Kids to Be Adults: A Guide for Parents, Ministers and Other Mentors, 2000; (with R. Joy) Two Become One, 2002. **Address:** Asbury Theological Seminary, 204 N Lexington Ave., Wilmore, KY 40390-1129, U.S.A. **Online address:** don.joy@asburyseminary.edu

JOYA, Malalai. Afghani (born Afghanistan), b. 1978. **Genres:** Biography, Autobiography/Memoirs. **Career:** Politician, memoirist and writer. **Publications:** (With D. O'Keefe) A Woman among Warlords: The Extraordinary Story of an Afghan Who Dared to Raise Her Voice in Australia as Raising My Voice: The Extraordinary Story of the Afghan Woman Who Dares to Speak Out, 2009. **Address:** Kabul, Afghanistan. **Online address:** mj@malalaijoya.com

JOYAUX, Julia. See **KRISTEVA, Julia.**

JOYCE, B. D. See **JOYCE, Brenda.**

JOYCE, Brenda. (B. D. Joyce). American (born United States), b. 1963?. **Genres:** Romance/Historical, Novels. **Career:** Writer, 1988-. **Publications:** BRAGG SAGA SERIES: Innocent Fire, 1988; Firestorm, 1988; Violet Fire, 1989; Dark Fires, 1991; The Fires of Paradise, 1992; Scandalous Love, 1992; The Secrets, 1993. DE WARENNE DYNASTY SERIES: The Conqueror, 1990; Promise of the Rose, 1993; The Game, 1994; House of Dreams, 2000; The Prize, 2004; The Masquerade, 2005; The Stolen Bride, 2006; A Lady At Last, 2006; The Perfect Bride, 2007; A Dangerous Love, 2008; An Impossible Attraction, 2010; The Promise, 2010. DELANZAS SERIES: After Innocence, 1994. FRANCESCA CAHILL SERIES: (as B.D. Joyce) Deadly Love, 2001; Deadly Pleasure, 2002; Deadly Affairs, 2002; Deadly Desire, 2002; Deadly Caress, 2003; Deadly Promise, 2003; Deadly Illusions, 2005; Deadly Kisses, 2006; Deadly Vows, 2011. MASTERS OF TIME SERIES: Dark Rival, 2007; Dark Seduction, 2007; Dark Embrace, 2008; Dark Victory, 2009; Dark Lover, 2009. NOVELS: The Darkest Heart, 1989; Lovers and Liars, 1989; Captive, 1996; Splendor, 1997; The Rival, 1998; The Third Heiress, 1999; The Chase, 2002; Double Take, 2003. SAINT GEORGES SERIES: Beyond Scandal, 1995; The Finer Things, 1997. OTHERS: (with C. Brockway, C. Logan and S. Mittman) Outlaw Love, 1997; (with R. Becnel, J. Jones and B.D. Smith) Scandalous Weddings, 1998; (with K. Kane, J. O'Brien and D. Parr) Perfect Secrets, 1999. Works appear in anthologies. Contributor to periodicals. **Address:** St. Martin's Press, 175 5th Ave., New York, NY 10010, U.S.A. **Online address:** brenda@brendajoyce.com

JOYCE, Davis D. American (born United States), b. 1940. **Genres:** History,

Politics/Government. **Career:** University of Tulsa, assistant professor, associate professor of history, 1966-83; University of Keele, visiting professor of American studies, 1981; East Central University, associate professor, professor of history, 1987-2002, professor emeritus, 2002-; University of Debrecen, Soros professor of American studies, 1994-96; Rogers State University, professor. Writer. **Publications:** Edward Channing and the Great Work, 1974; History and Historians, 1983; (with M. Kraus) The Writing of American History, rev. ed., 1985; (with T. Glant) United States History: A Brief Introduction for Hungarian Students, 1996; (with P. Boeger) East Central University: The Wagner Years, 1969-1989, 2001; Howard Zinn: A Radical American Vision, 2003. EDITOR: A History of the United States, 1993; An Oklahoma I Had Never Seen Before: Alternative Views of Oklahoma History, 1994; Alternative Oklahoma: Contrarian Views of the Sooner State, 2007. Contributor to journals. **Address:** Department of History, East Central University, 1100 E 14th St., Ada, OK 74820, U.S.A. **Online address:** dcjoyce@sstelco.com

JOYCE, Graham. (Graham William Joyce). British (born England), b. 1954. **Genres:** Novels, Horror, Science Fiction/Fantasy, Autobiography/Memoirs, Mystery/Crime/Suspense, Young Adult Fiction. **Career:** Teacher, 1980-81; National Association of Youth Clubs, youth officer, 1980-88; freelance writer, 1988-; Nottingham Trent University, faculty of writing, 1995-. **Publications:** NOVELS: Dreamside (fantasy), 1991; Dark Sister (horror), 1992; House of Lost Dreams (horror/fantasy), 1993; Requiem (fantasy), 1995; The Tooth Fairy, 1996; Spiderbite, 1997; The Stormwatcher, 1998; Indigo, 2000; Smoking Poppy, 2002; The Facts of Life, 2003; The Limits of Enchantment, 2005; Do the Creepy Thing, 2006; The Devil's Ladder, 2009; The Silent land, 2010. OTHERS: Requiem, 1996; Leningrad Nights, 2000; TWOC: Taken Without Owner's Consent, 2007; Exchange, 2008; Memoirs of a Master Forger, 2008; Simple Goalkeeping Made Spectacular: A Riotous Footballing Memoir About the Loneliest Position on the Field, 2009. Works appear in anthologies. **Address:** c/o Luigi Bonomi, Luigi Bonomi Associates Ltd., 91 Great Russell St., London, GL WC1B 3PS, England. **Online address:** graham@grahamjoyce.net

JOYCE, Graham William. See **JOYCE, Graham.**

JOYCE, Joyce Ann. American (born United States), b. 1949. **Genres:** Literary Criticism And History, Essays, Social Sciences, Literary Criticism And History, Poetry, Reference. **Career:** Valdosta State College, instructor in English, 1972-74; University of Georgia, instructor in English, 1978-79; University of Maryland, assistant professor, 1979-86, associate professor of English, 1986-89; University of Nebraska, professor of English, 1989-92; Smithsonian Institution, lecturer; Chicago State University, professor of English, Gwendolyn Brooks Center, director, Black Studies Department, chair; Temple University, College of Liberal Arts, professor. Writer. **Publications:** Native Son: Richard Wrights Art of Tragedy, 1986; (ed. with A.P. Davis and J.S. Redding) Cavalcade: An Anthology of Afro-American Literature, 1991; (ed. with A.P. Davis and J.S. Redding) The New Cavalcade: An Anthology of Afro-American Literature, 1991; (En)gendering Knowledge: Feminists in Academe, 1991; Warriors, Conjurers and Priests: Defining African-Centered Literary Criticism, 1994; Ijala: Sonia Sanchez and the African Poetic Tradition, 1996; Black Studies as Human Studies: Critical Essays and Interviews, 2005; (ed.) Conversations with Sonia Sanchez, 2007; Women, Marriage, and Wealth: The Impact of Marital Status on the Economic Well-Being of Women through the Life Course, 2007. Contributor to periodicals. Works appear in anthologies. **Address:** Department of African American Studies, Temple University, 810 Gladfelter Hall, 1115 W Berks St., Philadelphia, PA 19122, U.S.A. **Online address:** jjoyce@temple.edu

JOYCE, Michael. American (born United States), b. 1945. **Genres:** Novels, Essays, Poetry, E-books. **Career:** Jackson Community College, associate professor of language and literature, Center for Narrative and Technology, coordinator, 1975-95; Vassar College, visiting professor in hypertext media, technology and culture, 1992-93, Randolph visiting distinguished professor of English and the library, 1993-, associate professor, 1994-2003, faculty director of media cloisters, 1994-, professor of English and media studies, 2003-. Writer. **Publications:** (Trans. with M. Cain) A. Chekhov, The Cherry Orchard (play), 1980; Of Two Minds: Hypertext Pedagogy and Poetics (essays), 1995; Othermindedness: The Emergence of Network Culture (essays), 2000; Moral Tales and Meditations: Technological Parables and Refractions, 2001. NOVELS: The War Outside Ireland, 1982; Afternoon, a Story 1987, rev. ed., 1993;

Liam's Going, 2002; Was: A Novel of Internet, 2007. Contributor to journals. **Address:** Department of English, Vassar College, PO Box 360, Poughkeepsie, NY 12604-0360, U.S.A. **Online address:** mijoyce@vassar.edu

JOYCE, Richard. British/Australian (born Australia), b. 1966. **Genres:** Philosophy, Psychology. **Career:** University of Sheffield, lecturer, 1997-2001; Australian National University, Research School of Social Sciences, research fellow, 2002-08; University of Sydney, international senior research fellow, associate professor, 2006-10; Victoria University of Wellington, professor, 2010-. Writer. **Publications:** The Myth of Morality, 2001; The Evolution of Morality, 2006. Contributor to journals. Works appear in anthologies. **Address:** Department of Philosophy, Victoria University of Wellington, Wellington, New Zealand. **Online address:** richard.joyce@vuw.ac.nz

JOYCE, Rosemary A. American (born United States), b. 1956. **Genres:** Anthropology/Ethnology, Archaeology/Antiquities, Cultural/Ethnic Topics, Art/Art History, Women's Studies And Issues, History. **Career:** Proyecto Arqueológico Valle de Sula, field crew director, 1979-87; Jackson Community College, Social Sciences Department, instructor, 1983-84; University of Illinois, Anthropology Department, lecturer, 1984-85; Harvard University, Peabody Museum of Archaeology and Ethnology, assistant curator of pre-Columbian archaeology, 1985-94, assistant director of the museum, 1986-89, lecturer at the university, 1986-89, assistant professor, 1989-91, associate professor of anthropology, 1991-94; Proyecto Arqueologico Cataguana y Oloman, Department of Yoro, co-director, 1988-93; Proyecto Arqueológico Valle Inferior del Río Ulúa, co-director, 1992-; University of California, associate professor, 1994-2001, Phoebe Hearst Museum of Anthropology, director, 1994-99, professor of anthropology, 2001-, Anthropology Department, chair, 2006-09; Proyecto Arqueológico Colonial de la Costa Norte, director, 2002-; Proyecto Arqueológico Los Naranjos, co-director, 2003-; American Anthropological Association, Archeology Division, distinguished lecturer, 2003. Writer. **Publications:** Cerro Palenque: Power and Identity on the Maya Periphery, 1991; (ed.) Maya History, 1993; (with S.A.M. Shumaker) Encounters with the Americas, 1995; (with C. Claassen) Women in Prehistory: North America and Mesoamerica, 1997; (with D. Grove) Social Patterns in Pre-Classic Mesoamerica, 1999; (ed. with S. Gillespie) Beyond Kinship: Social and Material Reproduction in House Societies, 2000; Gender and Power in Prehispanic Mesoamerica, 2001; The Languages of Archaeology: Dialogue, Narrative, and Writing, 2002; (with L. Meskell) Embodied Lives: Figuring Ancient Maya and Egyptian Experience' 2003; (ed. with J. Hendon) Mesoamerican Archaeology: Theory and Practice, 2004; Ancient Bodies, Ancient Lives: Sex, Gender, and Archaeology, 2008. **Address:** Department of Anthropology, University of California, Kroeber Hall, Ste. 3710, Berkeley, CA 94720-3710, U.S.A. **Online address:** rajoyce@berkeley.edu

JOYCE, William. American (born United States), b. 1957. **Genres:** Children's Fiction, Illustrations. **Career:** Centenary College of Louisiana, Centenary News Service, artist-in-residence; Aimesworth Amusements, founding partner; Moonbot Studios, co-founder. Screenwriter and illustrator. **Publications:** SELF-ILLUSTRATED FOR CHILDREN: George Shrinks, 1985; Dinosaur Bob and His Adventures with the Family Lazardo, 1988; A Day with Wilbur Robinson, 1990; Bently & Egg, 1992; Santa Calls, 1993; The Leaf Men and the Brave Good Bugs, 1996; Buddy, 1997; World of William Joyce Scrapbook, 1997; Dinosaur Bob, 1998; Life with Bob, 1998; Rolie Polie Olie, 1999; Baseball Bob, 1999; Little Spot of Color, 2000; Rolie Polie Olie: How Many Howdys?, 2000; Snowie Rolie, 2000; Rolie Polie Olie: Polka Dot! Polka Dot!, 2000; Be My Pal!, 2000; Spot, 2001; Billy, 2001; Sleepy Time Olie, 2001; Olie, 2001; Zowie, 2001; Big Time Olie, 2002; Rolie Polie Olie and Friends: Friendship Box, 2002; Rolie Polie Shapes, 2002; Peekaboo, you!, 2002; Rocket up, Rolie!, 2002; (intro.) Art of Robots, 2005; A Day with Wilbur Robinson, 2006; Man in the Moon, 2010. Contributor to books. Illustrator of books by others. **Address:** Centenary News Service, Centenary College of Louisiana, 2911 Centenary Blvd., PO Box 4188, Shreveport, LA 71134-1188, U.S.A. **Online address:** wjoyce@williamjoyce.com

JOYNER, Hannah. American (born United States) **Genres:** Novellas/Short Stories, Autobiography/Memoirs. **Career:** Author and historian. **Publications:** From Pity to Pride: Growing up Deaf in the Old South, 2004; (with S. Burch) Unspeakable: The Story of Junius Wilson, 2007. **Address:** University of North Carolina Press, 116 S Boundary St., Chapel Hill, NC 27514-3808, U.S.A. **Online address:** hrjoyner@gmail.com

JOYNER, Tim(othy). American (born United States), b. 1922. **Genres:** Marine Sciences/Oceanography, Travel/Exploration, Biography. **Career:** Texas Co., geophysicist, 1945-48; University of Washington, Laboratory of Radiation Biology, geochemist, 1957-62; National Marine Fisheries Service, oceanographer, 1962-75; United Nations Food and Agriculture Organization, director of marine aquaculture, 1975. Writer. **Publications:** Magellan, 1992. Contributor to journals and periodicals. **Address:** 3284 Rickey Rd. NE, Apt. D101, Bremerton, WA 98310-6633, U.S.A.

JUAREZ, Tina. American (born United States), b. 1942. **Genres:** Education, Young Adult Fiction. **Career:** Austin Independent School District, Stephen F. Austin High School, high school principal. University of Texas, Department of Educational Administration, adjunct professor. Novelist. **Publications:** (Ed. with J.A. Laska) Grading and Marking in American Schools: Two Centuries of Debate, 1992; Call No Man Master, 1995; South Wind Come, 1998. Contributor of articles on grading and assessment to educational journals. **Address:** c/o Arte Publico Press, University of Houston, Houston, TX 77203-2090, U.S.A.

JUBY, Susan. Canadian (born Canada), b. 1969?. **Genres:** Novels. **Career:** Editor, 1992-; writer, 1995-; Vancouver Island University, creative writing instructor; University of British Columbia, Writing Center, instructor. **Publications:** Alice, I Think, 2000; Miss Smithers, 2004; Alice Macleod Realist at Last, 2005; Another Kind of Cowboy, 2007; Getting the Girl: A Guide to Private Investigation, Surveillance and Cookery, 2008; Nice Recovery, 2010; Home to Woefield, 2011. **Address:** c/o Author Mail, HarperCollins Publishers, 11th Fl., 10 E 53rd St., New York, NY 10022, U.S.A. **Online address:** andfurthermore@shaw.ca

JUDAH, Aaron. British/Indian (born India), b. 1923. **Genres:** Novels, Children's Fiction, Literary Criticism And History. **Career:** Munitions factory in London, draftsman, 1945-46; part-time physiotherapist and writer, 1972-. **Publications:** Tommy with Hole in His Shoe, 1957; Tales of Teddy Bear, 1958; The Adventures of Henrietta Hen, 1958; Miss Hare and Mr. Tortoise, 1959; The Pot of Gold and Two Other Tales, 1959; Basil Chimpy Isn't Bright, 1959; Henrietta in the Snow, 1960; God and Mr. Sourpuss, 1960; Basil Chimpy's Comic Light, 1960; Anna Anaconda: The Swallowing Wonder, 1960; Henrietta In Love, 1961; The Elf's New House, 1962; The Careless Cuckoos, 1963; Clown of Bombay (Novel), 1963; Clown on Fire (Novel), 1965; On the Feast of Stephen, 1965; Cobweb Pennant (Novel), 1968; Lillian's Dam (Novel), 1970. **Address:** 6 Lower Denmark Rd., Ashford, KT TN23 7SU, England.

JUDD, Alan. (Holly Budd). British (born England), b. 1946?. **Genres:** Novels, History, Biography, Humor/Satire, Young Adult Fiction, Young Adult Non-fiction. **Career:** Royal Society of Literature, fellow, 1990; British Foreign Office, diplomat. Writer. **Publications:** NOVELS: A Breed of Heroes, 1981; Short of Glory, 1984; The Noonday Devil, 1987; Tango, 1989; The Devil's Own Work, 1991; Legacy, 2001; The Kaiser's Last Kiss, 2003; Dancing with Eva, 2006; Uncommon Enemy, 2012. OTHER: Ford Maddox Ford (biography), 1990; (as Holly Budd) The Office Life Little Instruction Book, 1996; (with D. Crane) First World War Poets (biography), 1997; The Quest for C: Mansfield Cumming and the Founding of the Secret Service (biography), 1999. Contributor of book to magazines. **Address:** David Higham Associates Ltd., 5-8 Lower John St., Golden Sq., Golden Sq., London, GL W1F 9HA, England.

JUDD, Denis. British (born England), b. 1938. **Genres:** Novels, Children's Fiction, History, Biography. **Career:** University of North London, lecturer, 1964-68, senior lecturer, 1968-72, principal lecturer, 1972-, head of history, 1975-, professor of British imperial and commonwealth history, 1990-, now professor emeritus; University of California, London Campus, visiting professor; New York University, London, professor of history. Historian and writer. **Publications:** Balfour and the British Empire: A Study in Imperial Evolution 1874-1932, 1968; The Victorian Empire, 1837-1901: A Pictorial History, 1970; Posters of World War Two, 1972; The British Raj, 1972; Livingstone in Africa, 1973; Someone has Blundered: Calamities of the British Army in the Victorian Age, 1973; The House of Windsor, 1973; The Life and Times of George V, 1973; The Royal Victorians: A Pictorial Biography, 1975; The Crimean War, 1975; Palmerston, 1975; Edward VII: A Pictorial Biography, 1975; Eclipse of Kings: European Monarchies in the Twentieth Century, 1976; Adventures of Long John Silver, 1977; The Boer War, 1977; Radical Joe: A Life of Joseph Chamberlain, 1977, rev. ed., 1993; Return to Treasure Island, 1979; Prince Philip: A Biography, 1980; Lord Reading, Rufus

Isaacs, First Marquess of Reading, Lord Chief Justice and Viceroy of India, 1860-1935, 1982; The Evolution of the Modern Commonwealth, 1982; King George VI, 1895-1952, 1983; Alison Uttley: The Life of a Country Child, 1884-1976: The Authorised Biography, 1986, 3rd ed. as Alison Uttley: Spinner of Tales: The Authorised Biography of the Creator of Little Grey Rabbit, 2010; Further Tales of Little Grey Rabbit, 1989; Jawaharlal Nehru, 1993; (intro.) A Traveller's History of Ireland, 1993; (ed.) A Traveller's History of Italy, 1993; Empire: The British Imperial Experience from 1765 to the Present, 1996; (ed.) British Tale of Indian and Foreign Service: The Memoirs of Sir Ian Scott, 1999; Someone has Blundered: Calamities of the British Army in the Victorian Age, 2000; Lion and the Tiger: The Rise and Fall of the British Raj, 1600-1947, 2004; (ed.) The Private Diaries of Alison Uttley, 2009. Contributor to periodicals. **Address:** c/o Andrew Gordon, David Higham Associates Ltd., 5-8 Lower John St., London, GL W1F 9HA, England. **Online address:** denisjudd@ntlworld.com

JUDD, Frank (Ashcroft). (Judd of Porrsea). British (born England), b. 1935. **Genres:** International Relations/Current Affairs, Politics/Government. **Career:** International Voluntary Service, secretary general, 1960-66; Portsmouth West, member of parliament, 1966-74; Portsmouth North, member of parliament, 1974-79; Parliamentary Under Secretary of State for Defense for the Royal Navy, staff, 1974-76; State for Overseas Development, minister 1976-77; State, Foreign and Commonwealth Office, minister 1977-79; International Defense and Aid Fund for Southern Africa, associate director, 1979-80; Voluntary Service Overseas, director, 1980-85; Centre for World Development Education, chairman, 1980-85; Oxfam, director, 1985-91; International Council of Voluntary Agencies, chairman, 1985-90; London School of Economics, member of court of governors, 1986-; World Economic Forum Conference on South Africa, chairman, 1990, 1991; Oxford Diocesan Board for Social Responsibility, chairman, 1992-94; National Tenants Resource Centre, director, 1992-95; Westminster College, governor, 1992-98; International Commission on Global Governance, 1992-2001; Selly Oak Colleges, chair, 1996-98; Lancaster University, member of council, 1996-2002, member of court, 2002-; Ruskin Foundation, trustee, 2002-; Saterworld, trustee, 2002-; University of Newcastle, member of court, 2004-; Royal Naval Museum, president; Council for National Parks, vice-president; Royal Society of Arts, fellow. Writer. **Publications:** CO-AUTHOR: Radical Future, 1967; Fabian International Essays, 1970; Purpose in Socialism, 1973; Imagining Tomorrow, 2000. **Address:** Newcastle University, Newcastle upon Tyne, NE1 7RU, England.

JUDD OF PORRSEA See **Judd, Frank (Ashcroft).**

JUDGE, Edward H. American (born United States), b. 1945. **Genres:** History. **Career:** Teacher, 1968-96; Ford Motor Co., quality control inspector, 1969-70; General Motors Corp., materials coordinator, 1970; University of Michigan, Residential College, lecturer in history, 1976; State University of New York at Plattsburgh, assistant professor of history, 1977-78, LeMoyne College, assistant professor, 1978-82, associate professor, 1982-92, department head, 1988-91, 1992-95, 2009-10, professor of history, 1992-, Joseph C. Georg distinguished professor, 1997-2000; Worldwide Marriage Encounter, coordinator and co-leader. Writer. **Publications:** Plehve: Repression and Reform in Imperial Russia, 1902-1904, 1983; Easterin in Kishinev: Anatomy of a Pogrom, 1993; (with J.W. Langdon) A Hard and Bitter Peace: A Global History of the Cold War, 1996, 2nd ed., 2010; (and comp, with J.W. Langdon) The Cold War: A History through Documents, 1998, 2nd ed., 2010; (with J.W. Langdon) Connections and Conflicts, 2008; (with J.W. Langdon) Connections: A World History, 2009, 2nd ed., 2012; (with J.W. Langdon) The Cold War: A History with Documents, 2011. EDITOR: (with J.Y. Simms, Jr. and contrib.) Modernization and Revolution: Dilemmas of Progress in Late Imperial Russia, 1993. Contributor to history journals. **Address:** Department of History, LeMoyne College, RH 404, 1419 Salt Springs Rd., Syracuse, NY 13214, U.S.A. **Online address:** judge@lemoyne.edu

JUDGE, Harry George. British (born England), b. 1928. **Genres:** Education, History, Humanities, Young Adult Non-fiction. **Career:** Cumberland Lodge, director of studies, 1959-62; Grammar school, headmaster, 1962-67, principal, 1967-73; Oxford University, Department of Educational Studies, director, 1973-88; Brasenose College, fellow, 1973-80, tutor for admissions, through 1980, senior research fellow, now emeritus fellow; Massachusetts Institute of Technology, visiting professor, 1977, 1980-82; School Broadcasting Council, chairman, 1977-81; Carnegie-Mellon University, visiting professor, 1984-86. Writer. **Publications:** Louis XIV, 1965; School is Not Yet Dead,

1974; Future of Secondary Education, 1976; American Graduate Schools of Education: A View From Abroad: A Report to the Ford Foundation, 1982; A Generation of Schooling: English Secondary Education since 1944, 1984; (ed.) Oxford Illustrated Encyclopedia, 1985; The University and the Teachers, 1994; Faith-Based Schools and the State: Catholics in America, France and England, 2002. **Address:** Brasenose College, Radcliffe Sq., Oxford, OX OX1 4AJ, England. **Online address:** harry.judge@bnc.ox.ac.uk

JUDIS, John B. American (born United States), b. 1941. **Genres:** Biography, History, Adult Non-fiction. **Career:** In These Times, Washington correspondent, 1982-; East Bay Voice, founder, 1975-; The New Republic, senior editor, 1984-; American Prospect, senior correspondent, 1999-. **Publications:** William F. Buckley, Jr: Patron Saint of the Conservatives, 1988; Grand Illusion: Critics and Champions of the American Century, 1992; The Paradox of American Democracy: Elites, Special Interests, and the Betrayal of Public Trust, 1999; (with R. Teixeira) The Emerging Democratic Majority, 2002; The Folly of Empire: What George W. Bush Could Learn from Theodore Roosevelt and Woodrow Wilson, 2004. **Address:** 1428 Winding Waye Ln., Silver Spring, MD 20902-1452, U.S.A. **Online address:** jjudis@ceip.org

JUDKINS, Phil(lip Edward). British (born England), b. 1947. **Genres:** Information Science/Computers, Law, Business/Trade/Industry, Economics, Technology. **Career:** City of Bradford Metropolitan Council, principal manpower services officer, 1975-77; Rank Xerox Ltd., Management Services, manager, 1977-87; Provincial Insurance PLC, director of resources, 1987-95; AXA Insurance, director, 1995-2002; U.K.'s Defence College, visiting fellow. Writer. **Publications:** (With D. West and J. Drew) Networking In Organisations: The Rank Xerox Experiment, 1985; (with B. Sherman) Glimpses of Heaven, Visions of Hell: Virtual Reality and Its Implications, 1993; (with B. Sherman) Licensed to Work, 1995. **Address:** c/o Watson, Little & Co., 12 Egbert St., London, GL NW1 8LJ, England. **Online address:** phil.judkins@axa-insurance.co.uk

JUDOVITZ, Dalia. American/Romanian (born Romania), b. 1951?. **Genres:** Art/Art History, Literary Criticism And History, Philosophy. **Career:** University of Pennsylvania, assistant professor of French, 1978-82; University of California, assistant professor of French, 1982-88; Emory University, associate professor of French, 1988-94, chair, 1988-, professor, 1994-2002, National Endowment for the Humanities professor of French and Italian, 2002-. Writer. **Publications:** Subjectivity and Representation in Descartes: The Origins of Modernity, 1988; (ed. with T. Flynn) Dialectic and Narrative, 1993; Unpacking Duchamp: Art in Transit, 1995; (trans.) Deplier Duchamp: Passages de l'art, 2000; The Culture of the Body: Genealogies of Modernity, 2001; Drawing on Art: Duchamp and Company, 2010. **Address:** Department of French and Italian, Emory University, N411 N Callaway Ctr., Callaway Bldg., 537 Kilgo Cir., Atlanta, GA 30322, U.S.A. **Online address:** djudovi@emory.edu

JUDSON, D. Daniel. American (born United States), b. 1962?. **Genres:** Novels, Young Adult Fiction. **Career:** Temple Beth David of the South Shore, rabbi, 1999-2008; Hebrew College, Rabbinical School, director of professional development and placement. Writer. **Publications:** NOVELS: The Bone Orchard, 2002; The Poisoned Rose, 2002; The Darkest Place, 2006; The Water's Edge, 2008; The Violet Hour, 2009; Voyeur, 2010. **Address:** Trident Media Group L.L.C., 41 Madison Ave., 36th Fl., New York, NY 10010, U.S.A.

JUDSON, John. American (born United States), b. 1930. **Genres:** Novellas/Short Stories, Plays/Screenplays, Poetry, Autobiography/Memoirs, Novels. **Career:** Northeast literary Magazine, editor, 1962-; Juniper Press, founder, 1963, editor; University of Wisconsin, assistant professor, 1965-, professor of English, now emeritus. **Publications:** (Co-author) Two from Where It Snows, 1963; Surreal Songs, 1968; Within Seasons, 1970; Finding Worlds in Winter, 1973; Ash Is the Candle's Wick, 1974; (ed.) Voyages to the Inland Sea, 6 vols., 1976; Roots from the Onion's Dark, 1978; A Purple Tale, 1978; North of Athens, 1980; Letters to Jirac, II, 1980; August on a Lone Bassoom, 1981; Reasons Why I Am Not Perfect, 1982; The Carrabassett, Street William, Was My River (autobiography), 1982; Suite for Drury Pond, 1989; Muse (SIC), 1992; The Inardo Poems, 1996; Three Years before the Braves Left Boston, 2000. **Address:** Department of English, University of Wisconsin, 1725 State St., La Crosse, WI 54601, U.S.A.

JUFFER, Jane. American (born United States), b. 1962. **Genres:** Social Sciences, Gay And Lesbian Issues, Social Sciences, Politics/Government.

Career: Pennsylvania State University, Department of English, assistant professor, 1999-2005, associate professor and director of Latina/o studies initiative, 2005-08; Cornell University, Department of English, associate professor, Program of Feminist, Gender and Sexuality Studies, associate professor, 2008-. Writer. **Publications:** At Home with Pornography: Women, Sex and Everyday Life, 1998; Single Mother: The Emergence of the Domestic Intellectual, 2006. **Address:** Department of English, Cornell University, 391 Uris Hall, 250 Goldwin Smith Hall, Ithaca, NY 14853-3201, U.S.A. **Online address:** jaj93@cornell.edu

JUHASZ, Anne McCreary. American/Canadian (born Canada), b. 1922. **Genres:** Education, Sociology, Psychology. **Career:** Canadian-Scandinavian research fellow, 1961-62; University of British Columbia, assistant professor, 1962-65, associate professor of education, 1965-67; Loyola University, associate professor, 1967-70, professor of educational foundations, 1970-, now professor emeritus. Writer. **Publications:** (Co-author) Gage Language Experience Reading Program, 1966, rev. ed., 1970; Effective Study, 1968; (with G.M. Szasz) Adolescents in Society: Selected Sources in Personal and Social Relationships, 1969; (ed.) Sexual Development and Behavior: Selected Readings, 1973; (with A. Ornstein and H. Talmage) A Paraprofessional's Handbook: A Guide for the Teacher Aide, 1975. Contributor to books and periodicals. **Address:** School of Education, Loyola University of Chicago, 820 N Michigan Ave., Lewis Twr., 11th Fl., Chicago, IL 60611, U.S.A.

JUKOFSKY, Diane. American (born United States) **Genres:** Environmental Sciences/Ecology. **Career:** Minnesota Conservation Federation, lobbyist and editor; National Wildlife Federation, public information officer; Prentice Hall, reporter; Scientists' Institute for Public Information, vice president; Rainforest Alliance, director of communications, marketing and education, 2002-, vice president of communications and education and neotropics communications, 2002-, Sustainable Agriculture Program, manager, Adopt-A-Rainforest Program, manager, Conservation Media Center, director; Eco-Index, manager, editor. **Publications:** (With C. Wille) Difundan su mensaje: guia para los lideres de grupos ambientales, 1993; Encyclopedia of Rainforests, 2001. Contributor to periodicals. **Address:** Rainforest Alliance, 665 Broadway, Ste. 500, New York, NY 10012, U.S.A.

JULIANI, Richard N. American (born United States), b. 1938. **Genres:** History, Social Sciences. **Career:** Villanova University, Department of Sociology and Criminal Justice, professor. Writer. **Publications:** The Social Organization of Immigration: The Italians in Philadelphia, 1980; (ed. with P.V. Cannistraro) Italian Americans: The Search for a Usable Past: Proceedings of the 19th Annual Conference of the American Italian Historical Association Philadelphia, Pa., November 14-15, 1986, 1986; (ed. with S.P. Juliani) New Explorations in Italian American Studies: Proceedings of the 25th Annual Conference of the American Italian Historical Association, Washington, DC, November 12-14, 1992, 1994; Building Little Italy: Philadelphia's Italians before Mass Migration, 1998; Priest, Parish, and People: Saving the Faith in Philadelphia's Little Italy, 2007. **Address:** St. Augustine Center for the Liberal Arts, Villanova University, Rm. 277, Sociology, 800 Lancaster Ave., Villanova, PA 19085, U.S.A. **Online address:** richard.juliani@villanova.edu

JULIEN, Eric Allan. See ALLAN, Von.

JULIUS, Anthony (Robert). British (born England), b. 1956. **Genres:** Art/Art History. **Career:** Mishcon de Reya, attorney, 1981-, partner, 1984-, head of litigation, 1987-, consultant, deputy chairman; Diana, Princess of Wales, Memorial Fund, trustee, 1997-, chairman, 1997-99, vice president, 2002-; Jewish Chronicle Newspaper, chairman; London Consortium, chairman; University College London, part-time law faculty; University of London, Birkbeck College, visiting professor. Writer. **Publications:** T.S. Eliot: Anti-Semitism and Literary Form, 1995; Idolizing Pictures: Idolatry, Iconoclasm and Jewish Art, 2001; Transgressions: The Offences of Art, 2002; (with R. Wulkan and O.S. Soltes) Komar and Melamid: Symbols of the Big Bang, 2002; Trials of the Diaspora: A History of Anti-Semitism in England, 2010. **Address:** Mishcon de Reya, Summit House, 12 Red Lion Sq., DX 37945 Kingsway, London, GL WC1R 4QD, England. **Online address:** anthony.julius@mishcon.co.uk

JUNG, Moon-Ho. American (born United States), b. 1969?. **Genres:** History, Business/Trade/Industry, Economics. **Career:** University of Washington, professor, 2001-. Writer. **Publications:** Coolies and Cane: Race, Labor, and Sugar in the Age of Emancipation, 2006. Contributor of articles to books and journals. **Address:** Department of History, University of Washington, 315 Smith, PO Box 353560, Seattle, WA 98195-3560, U.S.A. **Online address:** mhjung@u.washington.edu

JUNG, Patrick J. American (born United States), b. 1963. **Genres:** History. **Career:** Marquette University, adjunct professor; Legal Aid Society of Milwaukee, development officer; Milwaukee School of Engineering, associate professor of history. Writer. **Publications:** The Black Hawk War of 1832, 2007; (with N.O. Lurie) The Nicolet Corrigenda: New France Revisited, 2009. **Address:** Milwaukee School of Engineering, 1025 N Broadway, Milwaukee, WI 53202-3109, U.S.A.

JUNGER, Sebastian. American (born United States), b. 1962. **Genres:** Adult Non-fiction, Natural History, Sciences, Biography, Autobiography/Memoirs. **Career:** The Half King, owner. Freelance writer. **Publications:** The Perfect Storm: A True Story of Men Against the Sea, 1997; Fire, 2001; A Death in Belmont, 2006; War, 2010. Contributor of journals to periodicals. **Address:** The Half King, 505 W 23rd St., New York, NY 10011, U.S.A. **Online address:** sjunger@literati.net

JUNGMAN, Ann. British (born England) **Genres:** Cartoons, Children's Fiction, Novels, Picture/Board Books. **Career:** Barn Owl Books (publisher), founder and owner, 1999-. Writer and researcher for television. **Publications:** (With M. Shapiro) Igor the Friendly Ghost, 1973; Battle of Marathon, 1975; Battle of the Alamo, 1975; Battle on the Ice, 1975; Battles of Stamford Bridge and Hastings, 1975; Vlad the Drac, 1982; Max and the Moon Monsters, 1986; Lucy and the Big Bad Wolf, 1986; Fred and the Robot, 1987; Rundown on Robots, 1987; Big Max and the Satellite, 1987; Lucy and the Wolf in Sheeps Clothing, 1987; Big Max and the Oil Rig, 1987; (with D. Weir) Big Max goes to the moon, 1987; Robot Plays, 1987; I Don't Want to Live in a House, 1987; I Don't Want to Go to School, 1988; Vlad the Drac Down Under, 1989; I Don't Want to Go in a Car, 1989; Lucky Keeps the Wolf from the Door, 1989; The Little Dragon Steps Out, 1989; Dracula Play, 1989; Count Dracula and the Monster, 1989; Count Dracula and the Victim, 1989; Count Boris Bolescu and the Black Pudding, 1989; The Day Teddy Didn't Tidy Up, 1989; Day Teddy Didn't Clean Up, 1989; The Day Teddy Got Very Worried, 1989; The Day Teddy Made New Friends, 1989; The Day Teddy Wanted Grandad to Notice Him, 1989; Spine-Chiller, 1989; Count Dracula and the Ghost, 1989; Bold Bad Ben, 1989; Count Dracula Meets His Match, 1989; Broomstick Services, 1990; Count Boris Bolescu and the Transylvanian Tango, 1991; Leilas Magical Monster Party, 1991; Septimouse Supermouse, 1991; The Little Dragon Falls Out, 1991; There's a Troll at the Bottom of My Garden, 1991; When the People are Away, 1992; Rosie and the Royal Hunt, 1992; Cinderella and the Hot Air Balloon, 1992; Roland and the Green Knight, 1992; Honest Mum, I've Looked Everywhere, 1993; Picnic for a Tortoise, 1993; Little Luis and the Bad Bandit, 1993; The Little Dragon Nips Out, 1993; Vlad the Drac Superstar, 1993; Sally and the Booted Puss and Other Stories, 1994; Septimouse Big Cheese!, 1994; Count Boris Bolescu and the Midsummer Madness, 1994; Pete and the New Girl, 1995; Count Dracula and the Wedding, 1995; Count Dracula and the Witch, 1995; Count Dracula Gets a Shock, 1995; Count Dracula and the Vampire, 1995; Homes, 1995; Pete and the New Rucksack, 1995; Pete and the Figs, 1995; Schools Now and Then, 1995; Pete and the Bully, 1995; There's a Troll at the Bottom of Our Street, 1996; Frank N. Stein and the Monster in Love, 1996; The Monster Idea, 1996; The Missing Monster, 1996; Sasha and the Wolfcub, 1996; Count Draco down Under, 1996; Vlad the Drac Goes Travelling, 1996; Frank N. Stein and the Monster in Trouble, 1996; School for Dragons, 1997; The Big Book of Dragons, 1997; The Big Wicked Witch Book, 1997; Theres a Troll at the Top of Our Tip, 1998; Broomstick Baby, 1999; Broomstick Removals, 1999; Broomstick Rescues, 1999; Sasha and the Wolf Child, 1999; Dracula Is Backula, 1999; Leila's magical monsterparty, 2000; A Pack of Wolf Tales, 2000; (with B. Patten) The Walker Book of Funny Stories, 2000; The Musicians of Bremen, 2001; Tertius and the Horrible Hunt, 2001; Dragon Disasters, 2001; Resistance!, 2002; Clottus and the Ghostly Gladiator, 2002; Twitta and the Ferocious Fever, 2002; Bacillus and the Beastly Bath, 2002; Waiting for Elijah: A Story About Passover, 2002; Septimouse and the Cheese Party, 2004; The Most Magnificent Mosque, 2004; Vlad the Drac Returns, 2004; Seige!, 2005; Vlad the Drac Vampire, 2006; (with C. Wilcox) Bold Bad Ben the Beastly Bandit, 2006; (with S. Fowles) The Most Magnificent Mosque, 2006; The Footballing Frog, 14 vols., 2007; Betrayal, 2007; The Skeleton Bride: And Other Jewish Stories, 2007; The Prince Who Thought He was a Rooster: And Other Jewish Stories, 2008; Frank N. Stein and the Great Green Greedy Garbage Monster, 2008; Further Adventures of Frank N. Stein and the Great Green Greedy Garbage Monster, 2009; Matti's Miracle, 2009; Barmy Barney Barn Owl, 2010.

Address: Frances Lincoln Publishers, 4 Torriano Mews, Torriano Ave., London, GL NW5 2RZ, England. **Online address:** ann@barnowlbooks.com

JUNKER, Patricia. American (born United States), b. 1952. **Genres:** Art/Art History, Photography. **Career:** Toledo Museum of Art, fellow, 1976-77; Smith College, Art Museum, intern, 1978-80, curatorial assistant, 1980-82; University of Rochester, Memorial Art Gallery, curator of American art, chief curator, 1982-90; University of Wisconsin, Elvehjem Museum of Art, curator of collections, senior curator, 1990-92; Fine Arts Museums of San Francisco, assistant curator of American paintings, 1992-94, American art department, acting head, 1994-96, associate curator of American art, 1996-99; Amon Carter Museum, curator of paintings and sculpture, 1999-; Seattle Art Museum, curator of American art. Writer. **Publications:** The Course of Empire: The Erie Canal and the New York Landscape, 1825-1875, 1984; North Country Landscape: Gibson Gallery at the Brainerd Arts Complex, 1986; Winslow Homer in the 1890s: Prout's Neck Observed, 1990; (with M. Simpson) The Rockefeller Collection of American Art at the Fine Arts Museums of San Francisco, 1994; John Steuart Curry: Inventing the Middle West, 1998; (co-author) An American Collection: Works from the Amon Carter Museum, 2001; (with S. Burns) Winslow Homer, Artist and Angler, 2002; Edward Hopper: Women, 2008; Albert Bierstadt: Puget Sound on the Pacific Coast: A Superb Vision of Dreamland, 2011. Contributor to periodicals. **Address:** Seattle Art Museum, 1300 1st Ave., Golden Gate Pk., Seattle, WA 98101-2003, U.S.A. **Online address:** pjunker@famsf.org

JUNKINS, Donald (Arthur). American (born United States), b. 1931. **Genres:** Poetry, Novels. **Career:** Emerson College, instructor, 1961-62, assistant professor of English, 1962-63; Chico State College (now California State University), assistant professor of English, 1963-66; University of Massachusetts, assistant professor, 1966-69, associate professor, 1969-74, Master of Fine Arts Program in English, director, 1970-78, 1989-90, professor of English, 1974-95, professor emeritus, 1995-. Writer. **Publications:** POEMS: The Sunfish and the Partridge, 1965; The Graves of Scotland Parish, 1969; Walden, 100 Years after Thoreau, 1969; And Sandpipers She Said, 1970; (ed.) The Contemporary World Poets, 1976; The Uncle Harry Poems and Other Maine Reminiscences, 1977; Crossing by Ferry: Poems New and Selected, 1978; The Agamenticus Poems, 1984; Playing for Keeps: Poems, 1991; Journey to the Corrida (poems), 2000; Late at Night in the Rowboat: Poems, 2005. Contributor to periodicals. **Address:** Department of English, University of Massachusetts, 170 Bartlett Hall, PO Box 30515, Amherst, MA 01003-0515, U.S.A.

JUNNE, George H. American (born United States), b. 1953. **Genres:** History. **Career:** Washtenaw Community College, part-time instructor in photography, 1975-81; University of Colorado, instructor, 1988-2004; Museum of Paleontology, field assistant, 1991-; Institute for Multicultural Education, Department of Black Studies, interim chair and assistant professor, 1994-95, assistant professor of Africana studies and interim director, 1995-99; University of Northern Colorado, associate professor of Africana studies, 1999-2005, chair of Africana studies, 2003-, professor of Africana studies, 2005-, co-chair of black studies, 1997-. Writer. **Publications:** Afroamerican History: A Chronicle of People of African Descent in the United States, 1996; The Black American West: A Bibliography, 1998; Blacks in the American West and Beyond-America, Canada, and Mexico: A Selectively Annotated Bibliography, 2000; History of Blacks in Canada: A Selectively Annotated Bibliography, 2003; Massachusetts 54th, 2007; Neither Christian nor Heathen: African Muslim Slaves in the United States, 2007. **Address:** Department of Africana Studies, University of Northern Colorado, 924 20th St., PO Box 129, Greeley, CO 80639, U.S.A. **Online address:** george.junne@unco.edu

JURAGA, Dubravka. American (born Yugoslavia), b. 1956. **Genres:** Literary Criticism And History. **Career:** Workers University of Novi Sad, instructor, 1981-84; Institute of Neurology, Psychiatry, and Mental Health, medical translator and instructor, 1981-88; Dnevnik (daily newspaper), editor and translator, 1982-88; University of Arkansas, University of Arkansas Press, editorial assistant, 1988-89, Arkansas Traveler, copy editor and proof editor, 1988-89, editorial assistant for meteoritics and planetary science, 1996, instructor in English, 1997-99; Northeastern Oklahoma State University, adjunct instructor in English and in Russian language and culture, 1997-98; writer and translator, 1999-; Triton College, librarian. **Publications:** WITH M.K. BOOKER: Bakhtin, Stalin, and Modern Russian Fiction: Carnival, Dialogism, and History, 1995; The Caribbean Novel in English: An Introduction,

2001; (ed.) Socialist Cultures East and West: A Post-Cold War Reassessment, 2002; (ed.) Rereading Global Socialist Cultures after the Cold War: The Reassessment of a Tradition, 2002. Contributor of articles to books and periodicals. **Address:** Triton College, 2000 5th Ave., River Grove, IL 60171, U.S.A.

JURIS, Jeffrey S. American (born United States), b. 1971?. **Genres:** Social Sciences. **Career:** Hogar Nuevos Horizontes, project supervisor, 1993-94; Citizens Advice Bureau-Nelson Avenue Family Residence, case manager, 1994-95; Civil Society for Reproducible and Sustainable Rural Development, research project supervisor, 1995; Fruitvale Latino Employment Cooperative, facilitator and job coordinator, 1996-2000; Gaspar de Portola Catalonian Studies Program, research fellow, 1997; University of Southern California, postdoctoral research fellow, 2004-05; Arizona State University, assistant professor of anthropology, 2005-09; National Autonomous University of Mexico, visiting research fellow, 2008-09; Northeastern University, assistant professor of anthropology, 2009-. Academic, writer and anthropologist. **Publications:** Networking Futures: The Movements against Corporate Globalization, 2008. Contributor to periodicals and journals. **Address:** Department of of Sociology, Northeastern University, 500 Holmes Hall, 360 Huntington Ave., Boston, MA 02115, U.S.A. **Online address:** j.juris@neu.edu

JURMAIN, Suzanne. (Suzanne Tripp Jurmain). American (born United States), b. 1945?. **Genres:** Children's Fiction, Young Adult Fiction, History, Adult Non-fiction, Social Sciences. **Career:** Actress, 1949-; TV Guide, assistant editor, 1966; Legal Directories Publishing Co., editor, 1967; University of California, Museum of Cultural History, editor and public relations coordinator, 1968-77; freelance writer and editor, 1978-. **Publications:** The Adventures of King Saltagong, 1949; From Trunk to Tail: Elephants Legendary and Real (juvenile), 1989; Once upon a Horse: A History of Horses and How They Shaped Our History (juvenile), 1989; Freedom's Sons: The True Story of the Amistad Mutiny (juvenile), 1998; The Forbidden Schoolhouse: The True and Dramatic Story of Prudence Crandall and Her Students, 2005; George Did It, 2006; The Secret of the Yellow Death: A True Story of Medical Sleuthing, 2009; (as Suzanne Tripp Jurmain) The Worst of Friends: Thomas Jefferson, John Adams and the True Story of an American Feud, 2011. **Address:** c/o Tracey Adams, McIntosh & Otis Inc., 353 Lexington Ave., Fl. 15, New York, NY 10016, U.S.A.

JURMAIN, Suzanne Tripp. See **Jurmain, Suzanne.**

JUSSAWALLA, Feroza. (Feroza F. Jussawalla). American/Indian (born India), b. 1953. **Genres:** Literary Criticism And History. **Career:** University of Utah, graduate teaching fellow, 1974-79; University of Texas, Department of English, lecturer, 1980-83, assistant professor, 1983-90, associate professor, 1990-98, professor, 1998-2001; Border Book Festival, board director; University of New Mexico, Department of English, director of literature, 1996-98, professor, 2001-, instructor; National Endowment for the Humanities, panel reviewer, 2001; Modern Language Association, organizer, 2001; Prentice-Hall High School World Literature text, consultant. Writer. **Publications:** (As Feroza F. Jussawalla) Family Quarrels: Towards a Criticism of Indian Writing in English, 1985; Excellent Teaching: Essays in Honor of Kenneth Eble, 1990; (ed. with R.W. Dasenbrock) Interviews with Writers of the Post Colonial World, 1992; (ed.) Conversations with V.S. Naipaul, 1997; Chiffon Saris (poems), 2003. **Address:** Department of English Language & Literature, University of New Mexico, Humanities Bldg. 370, 1 University of New Mexico, Albuquerque, NM 87131-0001, U.S.A. **Online address:** fjussawa@unm.edu

JUSSAWALLA, Feroza F. See **JUSSAWALLA, Feroza.**

JUST, Ward. American (born United States), b. 1935. **Genres:** Novels, Novellas/Short Stories, Young Adult Fiction. **Career:** Waukegan News-Sun, reporter, 1957-59; Newsweek, reporter, 1959-62, London correspondent, 1963-65; Reporter, political reporter, 1962-63; Washington Post, correspondent, 1965-67, 1968-70; writer, 1970-; Phillips Academy, writer-in-residence, 1982-84. **Publications:** NOVELS: A Soldier of the Revolution, 1970; The Congressman Who Loved Flaubert and Other Washington Stories, 1973; Stringer, 1974; Nicholson at Large, 1975; A Family Trust, 1978; Honor, Power, Riches, Fame and the Love of Women, 1979; In the City of Fear, 1982; The American Blues, 1984; The American Ambassador, 1987; Jack Gance, 1989; Twenty-One: Selected Stories, 1990; The Translator, 1991; Ambition and Love, 1994; Echo House, 1997; Congressman Who Loved Flaubert: 21 Stories and Novellas, 1998; A Dangerous Friend, 1999; Lowell Limpett and Two Stories, 2001; The Weather in Berlin, 2002; An Unfinished Season, 2004; Forgetfulness, 2006; Exiles in the Garden, 2009; Rodin's Debutante, 2011. OTHERS: To What End: Report from Vietnam, 1968; Military Men, 1970. **Address:** c/o Lynn Nesbit, Janklow & Nesbit Associates, 445 Park Ave., New York, NY 10022-2606, U.S.A.

JUSTER, Norton. American (born United States), b. 1929. **Genres:** Children's Fiction, Women's Studies And Issues, Songs/Lyrics And Libretti, Architecture, Children's Non-fiction, Picture/Board Books, Humor/Satire, Adult Non-fiction, Homes/Gardens. **Career:** Juster & Gugliotta, architect, 1960-68; Pratt Institute, professor of environmental design, 1960-70; Juster Pope Frazier Associates, founder and architect, 1970-99; Hampshire College, professor of design, 1970-92, professor emeritus of architecture and environmental design, 1992-. Writer. **Publications:** The Phantom Tollbooth, 1961; The Dot and the Line: A Romance in Lower Mathematics, 1963; Alberic the Wise and Other Journeys, 1965; Otter Nonsense, 1982; (contrib.) A Colorful Symphony, 1988; As: A Surfeit of Similes, 1989; As Silly as Knees, as Busy as Bees: An Astounding Assortment of Similes, 1998; The Hello, Goodbye Window, 2005; Sourpuss and Sweetie Pie, 2008; The Odious Ogre, 2010; Neville, 2011; The Annotated Phantom Tollbooth, 2011. FOR ADULTS: Stark Naked: A Paranomastic Odyssey, 1970; (comp.) So Sweet to Labor: Rural Women in America, 1865-1895, 1979; (comp.) A Woman's Place: Yesterday's Rural Women in America, 1996. Contributor to periodicals. **Address:** Brandt & Hochman Literary Agents Inc., 1501 Broadway, New York, NY 10036-5601, U.S.A.

JUSTISS, Julia. American (born United States) **Genres:** Romance/Historical, Novels. **Career:** Journalist and educator. **Publications:** The Wedding Gamble, 1999; A Scandalous Proposal, 2000; (with M. Lovelace and D. Simmons) Officer's Bride, 2001; The Proper Wife, 2001; My Lady's Trust, 2002; My Lady's Pleasure, 2002; My Lady's Honor, 2002; Wicked Wager, 2003; (with H. Graham) Forbidden Stranger, 2003; The Courtesan, 2005; (with M.

Balogh and N. Cornick) Christmas Keepsakes, 2005; The Untamed Heiress, 2006; Rogue's Lady, 2007; A Most Unconventional Match, 2008; (with A. Burrows and T. Brisbin) One Candlelit Christmas, 2008; From Waif to Gentleman's Wife, 2009; The Smuggler and the Society Bride, 2010; Society's Most Disreputable Gentleman, 2011; Regency Secrets, 2011. **Address:** 179 County Rd., Ste. 4112, Daingerfield, TX 75638, U.S.A. **Online address:** julia@juliajustiss.com

JUSTMAN, Stewart. American (born United States), b. 1948. **Genres:** Psychology, Adult Non-fiction, Social Commentary, Medicine/Health. **Career:** University of Montana, professor of English, 1975-, Liberal Studies Program, director. Writer. **Publications:** The Hidden Text of Mill's Liberty, 1991; The Autonomous Male of Adam Smith, 1993; The Jewish Holocaust for Beginners, 1995; The Psychological Mystique: An Investigation of the Sources of Psychology's Influence over Our Way of Life, 1998; The Springs of Liberty: The Satiric Tradition and Freedom of Speech, 1999; Seeds of Mortality: The Public and Private Worlds of Cancer, 2003; Fool's Paradise: The Unreal World of Pop Psychology, 2005; Literature and Human Equality, 2006; Do No Harm: How a Magic Bullet for Prostate Cancer Became a Medical Quandary, 2008; Apple of Discord: Ten Tortured Marriages, 2009. **Address:** Liberal Studies Program, University of Montana, 101A Liberal Arts, 32 Campus Dr., Missoula, MT 59812-0003, U.S.A. **Online address:** stewart.justman@umontana.edu

JWEID, Rosann. American (born United States), b. 1933. **Genres:** Education, Literary Criticism And History, Social Sciences. **Career:** Elementary schoolteacher, 1954; Scotia-Glenville Central School, library media specialist, 1967-93, K-12 Library Department, head, 1982-92. Writer and consultant. **Publications:** WITH M. RIZZO: The Library Classroom Partnership: Teaching Library Media Skills in the Middle and Junior High Schools, 1988, 2nd ed., 1998; Building Character through Literature: A Guide for Middle School Readers, 2001; Building Character through Multicultural Literature: A Guide for Middle School Readers, 2004. **Address:** 707 Riverside Ave., Scotia, NY 12302, U.S.A.

K

KA, Olivier. French (born France), b. 1967. **Genres:** Autobiography/Memoirs, Young Adult Fiction. **Career:** Joystick, editor, 1990-; By Jove, founder, 1993-. **Publications:** Bioutifoul Weurld, 1995; Je suis venu te dire que je suis mort, 1997; Le Manteau du Père Noël, 2000; Y a pas plus trouillard qu'un vampire, 2001; Le Chien des Chnorglz, 2001; La Mariée était en bottes, 2002; Le Sourire de mémé, 2002; Avant le nuage, 2002; Monsieur Rouge entre en scène, 2002; Le Moustique qui voulait devenir célèbre, 2003; Monsieur Rouge fait ses valises, 2003; Magie noire et pommes pourries, 2003; Pleure pas, Batman!, 2003; Le Complot des Gluants, 2003; Amélie contre les parents, 2003; Monsieur Rouge contre Docteur Slip, 2004; (with Mélaka) Nénesse, Chien de vieux, 2004; Les Saucisses de l'archiduchesse, 2004; (with E. Richard and Charrette) C'est l'homme qui dit qu'y est!, 2004; (co-author) Case départ, 2004; Ce Monstre qui me ressemble, 2004; Tom chewing-gum, 2004; Histoires de Loups, 2004; L'Esprit, le fantôme et la vache, 2004; Garuel et l'elfe fou, 2005; Y a pas plus grognon qu'un fantôme!, 2005; Nos Vacances chez les Gz, 2005; Rien qu'un enfant, 2006; (with Mélaka) L'Ange ordinaire, 2006; (with Alfred) Why I Killed Peter (graphic memoir), 2008. **Address:** NBM Publishing Inc., 40 Exchange Pl., Ste. 1308, New York, NY 10005, U.S.A. **s:** olivierkaontheweb@free.fr

KAARTINEN, Marjo. (Marjo Tuulikki Kaartinen). Finnish (born Finland), b. 1964. **Genres:** Intellectual History, Theology/Religion, Popular Culture, History. **Career:** University of Turku, lecturer, 1991-95, assistant in cultural history, 1995-2001, 2000-07, senior assistant in cultural history, 2003, adjunct professor, 2003-, senior lecturer, 2004-05, associate professor of cultural history, professor; Academy of Finland, research fellow, 1997-99, senior research fellow, 2000-01, academy research fellow, 2005-10; University College London, Wellcome Trust Centre for the History of Medicine, honorary research fellow, 2005-06. Writer. **Publications:** (Ed. with A. Korhonen) Bodies in Evidence: Perspectives on the History of the Body in Early Modern Europe, 1997; Religious Life and English Culture in the Reformation, 2002. **Address:** Cultural History, University of Turku, Rm. 322, Turku, 20014, Finland. **Online address:** marjo.kaartinen@utu.fi

KAARTINEN, Marjo Tuulikki. See **KAARTINEN, Marjo.**

KABASERVICE, Geoffrey (M.). American (born United States), b. 1966. **Genres:** Young Adult Fiction, Biography, Autobiography/Memoirs, Education, History. **Career:** Advisory Board Co., manager, 2000-05; Yale University, lecturer, assistant professor, 2005-. Writer. **Publications:** (With W.S. Beinecke) Through Mem'ry's Haze: A Personal Memoir, 2000; The Guardians: Kingman Brewster, His Circle and the Rise of the Liberal Establishment, 2004; Rule and Ruin: The Downfall of Moderation and the Destruction of the Republican Party, from Eisenhower to the Tea Party, 2012. **Address:** Department of History, Yale University, PO Box 208324, New Haven, CT 06520-8324, U.S.A.

KABIRA, Wanjiku Mukabi. Kenyan (born Kenya), b. 1945?. **Genres:** Essays. **Career:** University of Nairobi, Department of Literature, lecturer, 1983-96, senior lecturer, 1996, associate professor, professor of oral literature; Collaborative Centre for Gender and Development, founding member; Kenya Constitutional Review Process, vice-chair. Editor and writer. **Publications:** The Oral Artist, 1983; (with K. Mũtahi) Gĩkũyũ Oral Literature, 1988; (with

A.N. Ngoru) Gender Sensitivity in Bamako Initiative in Kisumu District: An Evaluation Report, 1992; (comp. with M. Masinjila) Gender and Development: The Femnet Model for Gender Responsive Planning, Programming, Advocacy and Sensitization, 1993; (with M. Gachago) Gender and Development: A FEMNET Manual for Trainers, 1993; (with E.A. Nzioki) Celebrating Women's Resistance: A Case Study of Women's Groups Movement in Kenya, 1993; (comp. with M. Masinjila and W. Njau) Needs Assessment Rusinga Island, 1993; Agikuyu (nonfiction), 1995; (with M. Masinjila) ABC of Gender Analysis: A Framework of Analysis for the Education Sector, 1995; (with B.M. Gituto) Affirmative Action: The Promise of a New Dawn, 1998; (with A. Bukenya) Understanding Oral Literature, 2000; (with P. Wasamba) Reclaiming Women's Space in Politics, 1998; Letter to Mariama Ba, 2005. EDITOR: (with K. Adagala) Kenyan Oral Narratives: A Selection, 1985; (with A. Luvai and B. Muluka) Tender Memories, 1989; (with M. Karega and E. Nzioki) Our Secret Lives: An Anthology of Poems and Short Stories, 1991; (with A. Nzioki and M. Karega) They've Destroyed the Temple, 1992; (with J.A. Oduol and M. Nzomo) Democratic Change in Africa: Women's Perspective, 1993; (with M. Masinjila and W. Mbugua) Delusions: Essays on Social Construction of Gender, 1994; (with W. Muthoni) The Road to Empowerment, 1994; (with W. Mbugua) With a Song in Our Hearts: A Collection of Poems on Women and Girls, 1996; (with M. Masinjila and M. Obote) Contesting Social Death: Essays on Gender and Culture, 1997; (with M. Masinjila) Towards Gender Responsive Politics, 1997; (with P. Ngurukie) Our Mothers' Footsteps: Stories of Women in the Struggle for Freedom, 1997; (with P. Wasamba) Tilda: A Collection of Poems on Women and Girls, 1998; Reclaiming My Dreams: Oral Narratives by Wanjĩra wa Rũkenya, 2010. **Address:** Department of Literature, University of Nairobi, PO Box 30197, Nairobi, 00100, Kenya.

KACAPYR, Elia. American (born United States), b. 1956. **Genres:** Economics. **Career:** Georgia State University, teaching fellow, 1981-82, instructor, 1983; Bloomsburg University, instructor, 1983-84; Salisbury State College, instructor, 1984-85; Ithaca College, Department of Economics, assistant professor, 1985-89, associate professor, 1989-2003, professor of economics, 2003-, chair, 2001-; American Demographics, contributing editor, 1996-98; Educational Testing Service Corp., faculty consultant, 2001, 2008; New York State Economics Association, president, 2003-05; American Institute for Economic Research, visiting research fellow, 2006. **Publications:** Economic Forecasting: The State of the Art, 1996; (with F. Musgrave) Barron's How to Prepare for the AP Microeconomics/Macroeconomics Advanced Placement Examinations, 2001, 3rd ed. as How to Prepare for the Advanced Placement Examination In Economics, 2008; Introductory Econometrics for Undergraduates, 2011. **Address:** Department of Economics, Ithaca College, 426 Muller Ctr., 953 Danby Rd., Ithaca, NY 14850, U.S.A. **Online address:** kacapyr@ithaca.edu

KACHTICK, Keith. American (born United States) **Genres:** Novels, Young Adult Fiction, Literary Criticism And History. **Career:** Lineage Project, senior instructor. Writer. **Publications:** Hungry Ghost: A Novel, 2003; (ed.) You Are Not Here And Other Works Of Buddhist Fiction, 2006. Contributor to periodicals. **Address:** c/o Author Mail, HarperCollins Publishers, 10 E 53rd St., New York, NY 10022-5244, U.S.A.

KACHUR, Lewis. American (born United States) **Genres:** Art/Art History. **Career:** S.R. Guggenheim Museum, curatorial assistant, 1982-84; Kean University, Department of Fine Arts, assistant professor of art history, 1990-95, associate professor of art history, 1995-, art history coordinator. Writer. **Publications:** Stuart Davis: An American in Paris, 1988; (with K. Wilkin) The Drawings of Stuart Davis: The Amazing Continuity, 1992; Word-Image in Contemporary Art: Pour un art de l'ecriture, 1992; Myron Lechay, 1994; Displaying the Marvelous: Marcel Duchamp, Salvador Dali, and Surrealist Exhibition Installations, 2001. **Address:** Department of Fine Arts, Kean University, Rm. 422, Vaughn-Eames, 1000 Morris Ave., Union, NJ 07083, U.S.A. **Online address:** lkachur@kean.edu

KACOWICZ, Arie M. (Arie Marcelo Kacowicz). Israeli/Argentine (born Argentina), b. 1959. **Genres:** International Relations/Current Affairs, History, Military/Defense/Arms Control. **Career:** Hebrew University, lecturer, 1993-97, Department of International Relations, lecturer, 1993-97, senior lecturer, 1997-2006, chair, 2005-08, associate professor of international relations, 2006-, professor, Chaim Weizmann chair in international relations, Leonard Davis Institute for International Relations, director, 2003-04; Georgetown University, Goldman Israeli visiting professor, 2002-03; Notre Dame University, visiting professor; Joan B. Kroc Institute for International Peace Studies, fellow; Kellogg Institute for International Studies, fellow. Writer. **Publications:** (As Arie Marcelo Kacowicz) Peaceful Territorial Change, 1994; Latin America on the International Stage, 1996; Human Rights and Foreign Policy: The Argentine Case, 1976-1983, 1997; Zones of Peace in the Third World: South America and West Africa in Comparative Perspective, 1998; (with L. Gedalia) Identity Formation Processes in the Transition from War to Peace, 2000; (co-ed.) Stable Peace among Nations, 2000; Rashomon in Jerusalem: Mapping the Israeli Negotiators' Positions on the Israeli-Palestinian Peace Process, 1993-2001, 2004; The Impact of Norms in International Society: The Latin American Experience, 1881-2001, 2005; (co-author) Saḥar habenle'umi ki-meḳadem shalom ezori, 2006; (ed. with P. Lutomski) Population Resettlement in International Conflicts: A Comparative Study, 2007; Globalization and the Distribution of Wealth: The Latin American Experience, 1982-2008, forthcoming. Contributor to periodicals and journals. **Address:** Department of International Relations, Hebrew University, Rm. 5312, Mount Scopus, Jerusalem, 91905, Israel. **Online address:** mskaco@mscc.huji.ac.il

KACOWICZ, Arie Marcelo. *See* **KACOWICZ, Arie M.**

KADARE, Ismail. French (born France), b. 1936. **Genres:** Novels, Novellas/Short Stories, Poetry, Literary Criticism And History, Essays. **Career:** Novelist. **Publications:** NOVELS: Gjenerali i ushtrise se vdekur, 1963, trans. as The General of the Dead Army, 1971; Dasma, 1968, trans. as The Wedding, 1972; Keshtjella, 1970, trans. as The Castle, 1980; Kronike ne gur, 1971, trans. as Chronicle in Stone, 1987; Dimri i vetmise se madh, 1973, as Dimri i madh, 1981; Nentori i nje kryeqyti, 1975; Ura me tri harqe: triptik me nje intermexo, 1978, trans. as The Three-Arched Bridge, 1995; The Niche of Shame, 1978; Gjakftohtesia: Novela, 1980; Kush e solli Doruntinen, 1980, trans. as Doruntine, 1988; Viti I mbrapshte (The Dark Year), 1980; Krushqit jane te ngrire (The Wedding Procession Turned into Ice), 1980; Prilli I thyer, 1980, trans. as Broken April, 1990; Nenpunesi I pallatit te enderrave, 1980, trans. as The Palace of Dreams, 1993; Nje dosje per Homerin (also known as Dosja H), 1980, trans. as The File on H, 1998; Le crepuscule des dieux de la steppe (The Twilight of the Gods of the Steppe), 1981; La niche de la honte, trans., 1984; Nata me hene (A Moonlit Night), 1985; Koncert ne fund te dimrit, 1988, trans. as The Concert: A Novel, 1994; Perbindeshi (The Monster), 1991; Piramida, 1992, trans. as The Pyramid, 1996; Hija (The Shadow), 1994; Shkaba: Roman, 1996; Pyramid, 1996; La ville sans enseignes, 1996; Lulet e ftohta të marsit: Roman, 2000; Vie, jeu et maor de Lul Mazrek, 2002; La fille d'Agamemnon, 2003; Le Successeur, 2003; (trans.) D. Bellos, The Successor, 2005; Cështje të marrëzisë, Roman, 2005; Darka e gabuar: roman, 2008; Kadare ndryshe, 2009; E penguara: requiem për Linda B.: roman, 2009; Aksidenti: roman, 2010; The Accident, 2010. SHORT STORIES: Qyteti jugut, 1964; Sjellesi I fatkeqesise, 1980; Invitation a un concert officiel et autre recits, 1985; La Grande Muraille, suivi de Le firman aveugle, 1993; Les Adieux du mal, 1996; Le Concours de beaute masculine, 1998; Trois chants funetres pour le Kosovo, 1998; L'envol du migrante, 2001; Agamemnon's Daughter: A Novella and Stories, 2006. POETRY: Frymezimet djaloshare, 1954; Motive me diell: vjersha dhe poema, 1969; Koha: vjersha dhe poema, 1976; Poezi, 1979; Buzeqeshje mbi bote, 1980; Oeuvres: Tome onzième, 2002; Ca pika shiu rane mbi qel: dyzet poezi te zgjedhura, 2003; (with A. Podrimja) Eni vjen pej Camerie: antologji poetike, 2004; Kristal: 60 poezi të zgjedhura, 2004; Pa formë është qielli: 100 poezi dhe poema të zgjedhura, 2006; The Sixties;

Insufficient Time. CRITICISM AND ESSAYS: Autobiografia e popullit ne vargje, 1980, trans. as The Autobiography of the People in Verse, 1987; Eskili, ky humbes i madh, 1988; Ftese ne studio (Invitation to the Studio), 1990; Ardhja e Migjenit ne letersine shqipe (The Arrival of Migjeni in Albanian Literature), 1991; Pranvera shqiptare (The Albanian Spring), 1991; La legende des legendes (The Legend of Legends), 1995; Visage des Balkans (Visages of Balkans), 1995; Il a fallu ce deuil pour se retrouver, 2000; Poshtërimi në Ballkan: sprovë, 2004. OTHERS: Emblema e dikurshme: tregime e novela, 1977; Keshtjella dhe helmi: pjese teatrale, 1977; On the Lay of the Knights, 1979; Vepra letrare, 12 vols., 1981; Koha e shkrimeve: tregime, novela, pershkrime, 1986; Entretiens avec Eric Faye, 1991; Endrra mashtruese: tregime e novela, 1991; Spiritus: roman me kaos, zbulese dhe cmeers, 1996; Mauvaise saison sur l'Olympe (play), 1998; Lulet e ftohta te marsit, Froides flours d'avril, 2000; Unaza në kthetra, 2001; Përballë pasqyrës së një gruaje, 2001; (co-author) Shqiptarët në Ballkan, 2001; Princesha Argjiro, 2001; Qyteti pa reklama, 2001; Shqiptarët në kërkim të një fati të ri, 2001; Jeta, loja dhe vdekja e Lul Mazrekut, 2002; Stinë e mërzitshme në Olymp, 2002; (with D. Fernagrave) Les quatre interpregrave; tes, 2003; Pasardhësi, 2003; Kështjella, 2003; Vajza e Agamemnonit, 2003; (with G. Rapper) L'Albanie: entre la leacute; gende et l'histoire, 2004; Dantja i pashmangshëm ose nje histori e shkurtër e shqipërisë me Dante Aligierin: sprovë, 2005; Leteiorkeiombim me presidentin, 2005; Hamleti, princi i vështirë: sprovë, 2006; Identiteti evropian i shqiptarëve, 2006; Muzgu i perëndive të stepës, 2006; Works, 2007; Mosmarrëeshja, 2010. **Address:** Librairie Artheme Fayard, 75 rue des Saints-Peres, Paris, F-75006, France.

KADEL, Andrew. American (born United States), b. 1954. **Genres:** Bibliography, Adult Non-fiction. **Career:** Episcopal Church, curate, 1981-83, vicar, 1983-85; ordained Episcopal priest, 1982; Princeton University, bibliographic specialist, 1987-89; Mercy College, reference librarian, 1989-90; Episcopal Diocese of New York, assisting priest; Union Theological Seminary, librarian, 1990-, Burke Library, interim director; Wesley Theological Seminary, director of the library; General Theological Seminary, St. Mark's Library, director, 2003-11; Christoph Keller, Jr. Library, director, 2011-; Church of Holy Apostles, assisting priest. Writer. **Publications:** Matrology: A Bibliography of Writings by Christian Women from the First to the Fifteenth Centuries, 1995. Contributor to journals. **Address:** St. Mark's Library, General Theological Seminary, 175 9th Ave., New York, NY 10011-4977, U.S.A. **Online address:** kadel@gts.edu

KADIR, Djelal. American/Cypriot (born Cyprus), b. 1946. **Genres:** Literary Criticism And History. **Career:** Purdue University, professor of comparative literature and head of department, 1973-91; University of Oklahoma, distinguished professor of literature, 1991-94, Neustadt professor of comparative literature, 1995-97; The Pennsylvania State University, Edwin Erle Sparks professor of comparative literature; International American Studies Association, founding president; UNESCO Commission for Encyclopedia of Life Support Systems, vice president. Writer. **Publications:** Juan Carlos Onetti, 1977; Questing fictions: Latin America's Family Romance, 1987; Cultural De-liberations: States of Emergency, 1987; Columbus and the Ends of the Earth: Europe's Prophetic Rhetoric as Conquering Ideology, 1992; Other Writing: Postcolonial Essays in Latin America's Writing Culture, 1993. EDITOR: Triple espera: novelas cortas de Hispanoamérica, 1976; (ed.) J. Cabral Selected poetry, 1937-1990/João Cabral de Melo Neto, 1994; (with D. Löbbermann) Other Modernisms in an Age of Globalization, 2002; (ed. with M.J. Valdes) Literary Cultures of Latin America: A Comparative History, 2004; Memos from the Besieged City: Lifelines for Cultural Sustainability, 2011. **Address:** Department of Comparative Literature, The Pennsylvania State University, 436 Burrowes Bldg., University Park, PA 16802-6204, U.S.A. **Online address:** kadir@psu.edu

KADISH, Alon. Israeli/American (born United States), b. 1950. **Genres:** Economics, History, Military/Defense/Arms Control. **Career:** University of London, Institute of Historical Research, research fellow, 1978-79; Hebrew University of Jerusalem, Department of History, lecturer, 1980-84, senior lecturer in history, 1984-92, associate professor of history, 1992-, chairman, 1995-97, professor, academic coordinator, 1995-, Rechovet Programme, head, 1997-; University of Manchester, Simon senior research fellow, 1991-92, associate professor, 1992-2000, professor, 2000-; Israeli Defense Forces, Centre for the Study of Tactics and Force Employment, fellow. Writer. **Publications:** The Oxford Economists in the Late Nineteenth Century, 1982; Apostle Arnold: The Life and Death of Arnold Toynbee, 1852-1883, 1986; Historians, Economists, and Economic History, 1989; (ed. with K. Tribe) The Market for Political Economy: The Advent of Economics in British University Culture, 1850-1905, 1993; To Arms and Farms: The Hachsharot in the Palmach (Hebrew), 1995; La-meshek yela-neshek: ha-hakhsharot ha-meguyasot ba-Palmaḥ, 1995; (ed.) The Corn Laws: The Formation of Popular Economics in Britain, vol. VI, 1996; (with A. Sela and A. Golan) The Occupation of Lydda, July 1948 (Hebrew), 2000; (with A.S. Golan) Kibush Lod, Yuli 1948, 2000; Milḥemet ha-Atsma'ut, 708-709: diyun mehudash, 2004; (with B.Z. kedar) Me'aṭim mul rabim?, 2005; (ed.) The Few against Many?, 2006; kehilah ba-milḥamah: Yehude Tsefat ba-shanim 1947-1948, 2006; keravot Yevusi, 2008. Contributor of articles to books and journals. **Address:** Department of History, Hebrew University of Jerusalem, Rm. 6503, Givat Ram, Jerusalem, 91904, Israel. **Online address:** kadish@mscc.huji.ac.il

KADREY, Richard. American (born United States), b. 1957?. **Genres:** Graphic Novels, Novels, Young Adult Non-fiction. **Career:** San Francisco Chronicle, columnist. Writer, photographer and futurist. **Publications:** Accelerate (graphic novel), 2007. NONFICTION: Covert Culture Sourcebook, 1993; Covert Culture Sourcebook 2.0, 1994; From Myst to Riven: The Creations & Inspirations, 1997. NOVELS: Metrophage, 1988; Kamikaze L'Amour: A Novel of the Future, 1995; Butcher Bird, 2007; Sandman Slim, 2009; Kill the Dead, 2011. Works appear in anthologies. Contributor to magazines and periodicals. **Address:** 2440 16th St., Ste. 229, San Francisco, CA 94103-4211, U.S.A. **Online address:** kadrey@gmail.com

KADUK, Kevin. American (born United States), b. 1979?. **Genres:** Novels. **Career:** Kansas City Star, sportswriter and columnist, 2001-04; Northwest News Group, sports columnist; Northwest Herald, sports columnist. **Publications:** Wrigleyworld: A Season in Baseball's Best Neighborhood, 2006. Contributor to periodicals. **Address:** Northwest Herald Main Office, 7717 S Rte. 31, Crystal Lake, IL 60014, U.S.A. **Online address:** kkaduk@nwnewsgroup.com

KADUSHIN, Alfred. American (born United States), b. 1916. **Genres:** Sociology, Social Work, Human Relations/Parenting. **Career:** University of Wisconsin, School of Social Work, assistant professor, 1950-55, associate professor, 1955-58, Julia Lathrop professor of social work, 1959-90, Julia C. Lathrop distinguished professor, through 1986, Julia C. Lathrop distinguished professor emeritus of social work, 1991-; Groningeen School of Social Work, senior Fullbright lecturer, 1957-58; Hebrew University, Paul Baerwald School of Social Work, faculty, 1960-61; Tel Aviv University, School of Social Work, faculty, 1981; National Academy of Science, National Academies of Practice, distinguished scientist associate, 1983; Melbourne University, faculty, 1987; LaTrobe University, faculty, 1987. Writer. **Publications:** Child Welfare Services: A Research Source Book, 1967, (with J.A. Martin) 4th ed., 1988; Adopted When Older, 1970; Adopting Older Children, 1970; (with G. Kadushin) The Social Work Interview: A Guide for Human Service Professionals, 1972, 4th ed., 1997; (with D. Harkness) Supervision in Social Work, 1976, 4th ed., 2002; Consultation in Social Work, 1977; New Foster Parents, the First Experience, 1980; (with J.A. Martin and J. McGloin) Child Abuse: An Interactional Event, 1981; (with W.A. Berkan) Child Abuse and Neglect Prevention: A Resource and Planning Guide, 1993. **Address:** School of Social Work, University of Wisconsin, 1350 University Ave., Madison, WI 53706, U.S.A.

KAEMPFER, William H. American (born United States), b. 1951. **Genres:** Economics, Business/Trade/Industry. **Career:** Duke University, teaching assistant, 1973-78; College of Wooster, instructor, 1975-76; University of North Carolina, visiting assistant professor of economics, 1975-76; University of Washington, assistant professor of economics, 1979-81; University of Colorado, assistant professor, 1981-89, associate professor, 1989-94, professor, 1994-, department chair, 1995-97, associate vice chancellor for budget and planning, 1997-, vice provost, 2003-; Claremont McKenna College, visiting assistant professor, 1985-86, associate professor of economics, 1986-90; Claremont Graduate School, visiting assistant professor, 1985-86, visiting lecturer, 1986-88, 1991, associate professor of economics, 1986-90. Writer. **Publications:** (With A.D. Lowenberg) International Economic Sanctions: A Public Choice Perspective, 1992; (with J. Marlow, J. Melvin and K. Maskus) International Trade: Theory and Evidence, 1995; (with A.D. Lowenberg) Origins and Demise of South African Apartheid: A Public Choice Analysis, 1998. **Address:** Department of Economics, University of Colorado, 361 Regent Hall, PO Box 256, Boulder, CO 80309-0256, U.S.A. **Online address:** william.kaempfer@colorado.edu

KAFKA, Kimberly. American (born United States) **Genres:** Novels, Young Adult Fiction. **Career:** University of Wisconsin-Whitewater, faculty; University of Michigan, faculty; Bennington College, faculty; University of Southern Maine, faculty. Writer. **Publications:** True North, 2000; (co-author) Quentins, 2002; Miranda's Vines, 2004. Contributor to periodicals. **Address:** Dutton Children's Books, Division of Penguin Putnam Inc., 375 Hudson St., New York, NY 10014-3658, U.S.A.

KAFKA, Mitzi. *See* **PRELLER, James.**

KAFKA-GIBBONS, Paul. American (born United States) **Genres:** Novels, Adult Non-fiction. **Career:** Writer and dancer. **Publications:** Love Enter, 1993; Dupont Circle, 2001; Judiciary Square; Markie and Esperanto. **Address:** c/o Author Mail, Houghton Mifflin Co., Trade Division, 222 Berkeley St., Boston, MA 02116-3754, U.S.A. **Online address:** franznot@yahoo.com

KAGAN, Donald. American/Lithuanian (born Lithuania), b. 1932. **Genres:** Classics, History, Adult Non-fiction, Politics/Government. **Career:** Ohio State University, teaching assistant in history, 1956-58; Capital University, instructor in history, 1957-58; Pennsylvania State University, instructor in history, 1959-60; Cornell University, Department of History, assistant professor, 1960-63, associate professor, 1964-66, professor of ancient history, 1967-69; Yale University, professor of history and classics, 1969-, Classics Department, chairman, 1972-75, Timothy Dwight College, master, 1976-78, Richard M. Colgate professor of history and classics, 1979-90, Department of Classics, acting chairman, 1986-87, acting director of athletics, 1987-88, Yale College, dean, 1989-92, Bass professor of history, classics and western civilization, 1991-95, Hill House professor of history and classics, 1995-2002, Sterling professor of classics and history, 2002-. Writer. **Publications:** The Great Dialogue: A History of Greek Political Thought from Homer to Polybius, 1965, 2nd ed., 1986; The Outbreak of the Peloponnesian War, 1969; The Archidamian War, 1974, 2nd ed., 1990; (with S. Ozment and F. Turner) The Western Heritage, 1979, 10th ed. as The Western Heritage: Since 1300: AP version, 2010; The Peace of Nicias and the Sicilian Expedition, 1981; The Fall of the Athenian Empire, 1987; Pericles and the Triumph of Democracy, 1990; Pericles of Athens and the Birth of Democracy, 1991; On the Origins of War and the Preservation of Peace, 1995; (contrib.) Honor Among Nations: Intangible Interests and Foreign Policy, 1998; (with F.W. Kagan) While America Sleeps: Britain between the Wars and America after the Cold War, 2000; The Pelopommesian War, 2003; Thucydides: The Reinvention of History, 2009; (with G.F. Viggiano) Problems in the History of Ancient Greece: Sources and Interpretation, 2010. EDITOR: (and intro.) The Decline and Fall of the Roman Empire in the West, 1962, 3rd ed. as The End of the Roman Empire: Decline or Transformation?, 1992; Sources in Greek Political Thought: From Homer to Polybius, 1965; Readings in Greek Political Thought, 1965; Problems in Ancient History, 1966, 2nd ed., 1975; (with L.P. Williams and B. Teirney) Great Issues in Western Civilization, 1967, 4th ed., 1992; Botsford and Robinson's Hellenic History, 5th ed., 1969; Studies in the Greek Historians: In Memory of Adam Parry, 1975. OTHER: (comp.) Problems in Ancient History, 1966. Contributor to journals. **Address:** Department of History, Yale University, Hall of Graduate Studies 215, 320 York St., New Haven, CT 06520, U.S.A. **Online address:** donald.kagan@yale.edu

KAGAN, Elaine. American (born United States) **Genres:** Novels. **Career:** Writer and actor. **Publications:** NOVELS: The Girls, 1994; Blue Heaven, 1996; Somebody's Baby, 1998; No Good-Byes, 2000; Losing Mr. North, 2002. **Address:** c/o Virginia Barber, William Morris Endeavor L.L.C., 1325 Ave. of the Americas, New York, NY 10019-6026, U.S.A.

KAGAN, Frederick W. American (born United States), b. 1970. **Genres:** History, Military/Defense/Arms Control. **Career:** United States Military Academy, assistant professor, 1995-2001, associate professor of military history, 2001-05, professor of military history; American Enterprise Institute for Public Policy Research, Critical Threats Project, director. Writer and historian. **Publications:** The Military Reforms of Nicholas I: The Origins of the Modern Russian Army, 1999; (with D. Kagan) While America Sleeps: Self-Delusion, Military Weakness, and the Threat to Peace Today, 2000; (ed. and with R. Higham) The Military History of Tsarist Russia, 2002; (ed. with R. Higham) The Military History of the Soviet Union, 2002; (ed. with C. Kubik) Leaders in War: West Point Remembers the 1991 Gulf War, 2005; The End of the Old Order: Napoleon and Europe, 1801-1805, 2006; Finding the Target: The Transformation of American Military Policy, 2006; (with T. Donnelly) Ground Truth: The Future of U.S. Land Power, 2008; (ed. with T. Donnelly) Lessons for a Long War: How America can Win on New Battlefields, 2010.

Contributor to periodicals. **Address:** American Enterprise Institute for Public Policy, Research, 1150 17th St. NW, Washington, DC 20036, U.S.A. **Online address:** fkagan@aei.org

KAGAN, Jerome. American (born United States), b. 1929. **Genres:** Psychology. **Career:** Ohio State University, instructor in psychology, 1954-55; Fels Institute, researcher in developmental psychology, 1957-64; Antioch College, associate professor psychology, 1959-64; Harvard University, Department of Psychology, professor of psychology, 1964-2000, Mind/Brain Behavior Interfaculty Initiative, director, 1996-2000, research professor, 2000-05, Daniel and Amy Starch professor of psychology, professor emeritus, 2005-; Massachusetts General Hospital, Department of Pediatrics, consultant, 1965-; Harcourt, consulting editor, 1965-; American Psychological Association, Division of Developmental Psychology, president, 1966-67; American Academy of Arts and Sciences, fellow; Foundation to Improve Television, board director, 1969-; Foundation's Fund for Research in Psychiatry, board director, 1970-74; Eastern Psychological Association, board director, 1973-75, president, 1974-75. **Publications:** (Ed. with G.S. Lesser) Contemporary Issues in Thematic Apperceptive Methods, 1961; (with H. Moss) Birth to Maturity, 1962; (with P. Mussen, J. Conger and A. Huston) Child Development and Personality (text), 1963, 6th ed., 1984; (ed. with J.C. Wright) Basic Cognitive Processes in Children, 1963; (co-author) Information Processing in the Child: Significance of Analytic and Reflective Attitudes, 1964; (co-ed.) Readings in Child Development and Personality, 1965, 2nd ed., 1970; (co-author) Three Views of Human Development, 1967; (ed. and intro.) Creativity and Learning, 1967; (with J. Segal) Psychology: An Introduction (text), 1968, 8th ed., 1995; Change and Continuity in Infancy, 1971; Personality Development, 1971; (co-author) Behavioral Science in Pediatric Medicine, 1971; (co-ed.) Psychology: Adapted Readings, 1971; Understanding Children: Behavior, Motives, and Thought, 1971; Change and Continuity in Infancy, 1971; (ed. with R. Coles) Twelve to Sixteen: Early Adolescence, 1972; (co-ed.) Basic and Contemporary Issues in Developmental Psychology, 1975; (with R. Kearsley and P. Zelazo) Infancy: Its Place in Human Development, 1978; Growth of the Child, 1978; (with C. Lang) Psychology and Education: An Introduction, 1978; The Family, 1978; (ed.) Fundamental Statistics for Psychology, 1980; (ed.) Abnormal Behavior, 1980; (co-ed.) Readings in Child and Adolescent Psychology: Contemporary Perspectives, 1980; (with O.G. Brim) Constancy and Change in Human Development, 1980; The Second Year: The Emergence of Self-Awareness, 1981; Psychological Research on the Human Infant: An Evaluative Summary, 1982; The Nature of the Child, 1984, rev. ed., 1994; Power and Limitations of Parents, 1986; (ed.) Psychology of Human Development, 1986; (ed.) Adventures in Thinking, 1987; (ed. with S. Lamb) Emergence of Morality in Young Children, 1987; Rational Choice in An Uncertain World, 1988; Unstable Ideas: Temperament, Cognition, and Self, 1989; Unstable Ideas, 1989; (ed.) Cognitive Development, 1990; (co-author) Galen's Prophecy: Temperament in Human Nature, 1994; Three Seductive Ideas, 1998; (co-ed.) Methods and Models for Studying the Individual: Essays in Honor of Marian Radke-Yarrow, 1998; (ed.) Gale Encyclopedia of Childhood & Adolescence, 1998; (co-ed.) Infancy to Early Childhood: Genetic and Environmental Influences on Developmental Change, 2001; Surprise, Uncertainty, and Mental Structures, 2002; (with N. Snidman) Long Shadow of Temperament, 2004; (co-author) Kagan & Segal's Psychology: An Introduction, 2004; (with N. Herschkowitz) Young Mind in a Growing Brain, 2005; Argument for Mind, 2006; (ed. with L. Harrison) Developing Cultures: Essays on Cultural Change, 2006; What is Emotion?: History, Measures, and Meanings, 2007; Three Cultures: Natural Sciences, Social Sciences, and the Humanities in the 21st Century, 2009; Temperamental Thread: How Genes, Culture, Time and Luck Make Us Who We Are, 2010; Recalcitrant Ghosts: Psychology's Problems and Promises, 2012. Contributor to periodicals. **Address:** Department of Psychology, Harvard University, 806 William James Hall, 33 Kirkland, Cambridge, MA 02138, U.S.A. **Online address:** jk@wjh.harvard.edu

KAGAN, Shelly. American (born United States), b. 1954. **Genres:** Philosophy, Theology/Religion. **Career:** University of Pittsburgh, instructor; University of Illinois, instructor; Yale University, Henry R. Luce professor of social thought and ethics, 1995, Clark professor of philosophy. Writer. **Publications:** The Limits of Morality, 1989; Normative Ethics, 1998; Geometry of Desert, 2005; Death, 2012. Contributor to periodicals. **Address:** Department of Philosophy, Yale University, 204 CT Hall, PO Box 208306, New Haven, CT 06520-8306, U.S.A. **Online address:** shelly.kagan@yale.edu

KAGARLITSKY, Boris. Russian (born Russia), b. 1958. **Genres:** Area Studies, International Relations/Current Affairs, Politics/Government, Busi-

ness/Trade/Industry. **Career:** IMA Press News Agency, political observer and journalist, 1988-90; Moscow Soviet, deputy staff, 1990-93; Institute for Comparative Political Studies, Russian Academy of Sciences, TNI Global Crisis Project, coordinator, senior research fellow; Institute of Globalization Studies, director, 2002-06; Institute for Globalisation and Social Movements, director, 2007-. Writer. **Publications:** The Thinking Reed: Intellectuals and the Soviet State 1917 to the Present, 1988; The Dialectic of Hope, 1989; The Dialectic of Change, 1989; Farewell Perestroyka, 1990; The Disintegration of the Monolith, 1992; Kvadratnyekolesa, rev. ed. as The Square Wheels: How Russian Democracy Got Derailed, 1994; The Mirage of Modernization, 1995; The Restoration in Russia, 1995; Restavraëtisiëiia v Rossii, rev. ed. as Restoration in Russia: Why Capitalism Failed, 1995; (with R. Burback and O. Núñez) Globalization and Its Discontents: The Rise of Postmodern Socialisms, 1997; New Realism, New Barbarism: Socialist Theory in the Era of Globalization, 1999; The Twilight of Globalization: Property, State and Capitalism, 2000; The Return of Radicalism: Reshaping the Left Institutions, 2000; Restavratsiia v Rossii, 2000; Globalizatsiia I levye, 2001; Russia Under Yeltsin and Putin: Neo-liberal Autocracy, 2002; Vosstanie Srednego Klassa, 2003; Periferiïnaia imeriia: Rossiia imirosistema, 2003; (ed. with A. Freeman) Politics of Empire: Globalisation in Crisis, 2004; Upravli a emaia demokratiia, 2005; Marksizm: ne rekomendovano dliaobucheniia, 2005; The Revolt of the Middle class, 2006; Politologiiá revoliutsii, 2007; Empire of the Periphery: Russia and the World System, 2008; Ot imperiï, 2010. Contributor of periodicals. **Address:** 29 Krasnoarmeyskaya, 43 Flat, Moscow, 125319, Russia. **Online address:** kagarlitsky@narod.ru

KAGEL, John H(enry). American (born United States), b. 1942. **Genres:** Economics. **Career:** Purdue University, teaching assistant and instructor, 1966-68; Texas A&M University, assistant professor, professor of economics, 1969-82; Hoover Institution, national fellow, 1981-82; University of Houston, professor, 1982-88, Cullen professor of economics, 1987-88; University of Pittsburgh, professor of economics, 1988-99, Economics Laboratory, director, 1988-99, Center for Philosophy of Science, fellow, 1988-99, Graduate School of Business, professor of business administration, 1998-99; Ohio State University, chaired professor of applied microeconomics, 1999-, Economics Laboratory, director, 1999-. Writer. **Publications:** (Ed. with L. Green) Advances in Behavioral Economics, 1987, vol. III, 1996; (with R.C. Battalio and L. Green) Economic Choice Theory: An Experimental Analysis of Animal Behavior, 1995; (ed. with A.E. Roth) The Handbook of Experimental Economics, 1995; (with D. Levin) Common Value Auctions and the Winner's Curse, 2002. Contributor of articles to books and journals. **Address:** Department of Economics, Ohio State University, 473 Arps Hall, 1945 N High St., Columbus, OH 43210-1120, U.S.A. **Online address:** kagel@economics.sbs.ohio-state.edu

KAGURI, Twesigye Jackson. Ugandan (born Uganda), b. 1970?. **Genres:** Education, Biography. **Career:** Nyaka and Kutamba AIDS Orphans Schools, founder and director, 2003-; Michigan State University, interim senior director of development, through 2010. Writer. **Publications:** (With S.U. Linville) The Price of Stones: Building a School for My Village, 2010. **Address:** Uganda. **Online address:** info@thepriceofstones.com

KAHAN, Alan S. American/French (born France), b. 1959. **Genres:** History, Politics/Government, Travel/Exploration, Translations. **Career:** Journal of Modern History, editorial assistant, 1983-84; University of Chicago, lecturer in Western civilization, 1985, lecturer in social sciences, 1986-87; Rice University, Mellon assistant professor of history, 1988-92; Florida International University, assistant professor, 1992-95, associate professor, 1995-2003, professor, 2003-07, European Studies Program, director, 2003-05, Graduate Studies in History, director, 2003-06, professor emeritus, 2007-; freelance editor and copy editor, 2007-; Paris Herald, travel writer, 2008-; American Graduate School of International Relations and Diplomacy, teacher, adjunct professor, 2009-; SciencesPo, adjunct professor, 2010-; New York University, adjunct professor, 2010-. **Publications:** Aristocratic Liberalism: The Social and Political Thought of Jacob Burckhardt, John Stuart Mill, and Alexis de Tocqueville, 1992; (trans.) A. de Tocqueville, The Old Regime and the Revolution, vol. I, 1998, vol. II, 1999; (ed.) The Tocqueville Reader, 2002; Liberalism in Nineteenth-Century Europe: The Political Culture of Limited Suffrage, 2003; (ed. and intro.) On Liberty, 2008; Alexis de Tocqueville, 2009; Mind vs. Money: The War Between Intellectuals and Capitalism, 2010. **Address:** Department of History, Florida International University, DM 390, Modesto A. Maidique Campus, Miami, FL 33199, U.S.A. **Online address:** kahana@fiu.edu

KAHL, Jonathan. American (born United States), b. 1959. **Genres:** Meteorology/Atmospheric Sciences, Children's Fiction, Sciences. **Career:** National Oceanic and Atmospheric Administration, research associate, 1987-89; University of Colorado, Cooperative Institute for Research in Environmental Science (CIRES), research associate, 1989-90; University of Wisconsin, Department of Mathematical Sciences, assistant professor, 1990-94, associate professor, 1994-2000, professor of atmospheric science, 2000-; National Autonomous University of Nuevo Leon, Department of Chemical Sciences, affiliated professor, 2006-. Writer. **Publications:** Weatherwise: Learning about the Weather, 1992; Wet Weather: Rain Showers and Snowfall, 1992; Storm Warning: Tornadoes and Hurricanes, 1993; Thunderbolt: Learning about Lightning, 1993; Weather Watch: Forecasting the Weather, 1996; Hazy Skies: Weather and the Environment, 1998; National Audubon Society First Field Guide to Weather, 1998. **Address:** Department of Mathematical Sciences, University of Wisconsin-Milwaukee, EMS W435, 2200 E Kenwood Blvd., PO Box 413, Milwaukee, WI 53201-0413, U.S.A. **Online address:** kahl@uwm.edu

KAHLENBERG, Richard D. American (born United States), b. 1963. **Genres:** Education, Law, Politics/Government, Race Relations, Autobiography/Memoirs, Biography. **Career:** Office of Senator Charles S. Robb, legislative assistant, 1989-93; George Washington University, visiting associate professor, 1993-94; Center for National Policy, fellow, 1996-98; Century Foundation, senior fellow, 1998-. Writer. **Publications:** Broken Contract: A Memoir of Harvard Law School, 1992; The Remedy: Class, Race, and Affirmative Action, 1996; All Together Now: Creating Middle-Class Schools through Public School Choice, 2001; Tough Liberal: Albert Shanker and the Battles over Schools, Unions, Race and Democracy, 2007. EDITOR: A Notion at Risk: Preserving Public Education as an Engine for Social Mobility, 2000; Divided We Fail: Coming Together through Public School Choice, 2002; Public School Choice vs. Private School Vouchers, 2003; America's Untapped Resource: Low Income Students in Higher Education, 2004; Improving on No Child Left Behind: Getting Education Reform Back on Track, 2008; Rewarding Strivers: Helping Low-Income Students Succeed in College, 2010; Affirmative Action for the Rich: Legacy Preferences in College Admissions, 2010. **Address:** 1333 II St. NW, 10th Fl., Washington, DC 20005, U.S.A. **Online address:** kahlenberg@tcf.org

KAHN, David. American (born United States), b. 1930. **Genres:** Military/Defense/Arms Control, Biography, History, Translations. **Career:** Newsday, reporter, 1955-63, assistant viewpoints editor, 1979-94, assistant editor, 1996-99; St. Antony's College, senior associate, 1972-74; New York University, associate professor of journalism, 1975-79, adjunct professor of military intelligence, 1984, 1985-89; Cryptologia, co-editor, 1977-; State University of New York in Stony Brook, adjunct professor of journalism, 1991-94. **Publications:** Two Soviet Spy Ciphers, 1960; Plaintext in the New Unabridged, 1963; The Codebreakers: The Story of Secret Writing, 1967; Hitler's Spies: German Military Intelligence in World War II, 1978; Kahn on Codes: Secrets of the New Cryptology, 1983; (trans. and ed.) Clandestine Operations, 1983; (intro.) The Final Solution of the Abwehr, 1989; Seizing the Enigma: The Race to Break the German U-Boat Codes, 1939-1943, 1991; (intro.) The Story of MAGIC: Memoirs of an American Cryptologic Pioneer, 1998; The Reader of Gentlemen's Mail: Herbert O. Yardley and The Birth of American Codebreaking, 2004. Contributor to magazines. **Address:** 120 Wooleys Ln., Great Neck, NY 11023-2301, U.S.A. **Online address:** davidkahn1@aol.com

KAHN, Michael A. (Michael Baron). American (born United States), b. 1952. **Genres:** Mystery/Crime/Suspense, Novels, Young Adult Non-fiction, Criminology/True Crime. **Career:** Elementary school teacher, 1974-76; Reuben and Proctor, associate, 1975-85; Husch and Eppenberger, associate, 1985-87; Gallop, Johnson and Newman, partner, 1987-; Blackwell Sanders LLP, Partner, 2002-; Blackwell Sanders Peper Martin, trial attorney, 2003-. Writer. **Publications:** RACHEL GOLD MYSTERIES: The Canaan Legacy, 1988 in US as Grave Designs, 1992; Death Benefits: A Rachel Gold Mystery, 1992; Firm Ambitions: A Rachel Gold Mystery, 1994; Due Diligence: A Rachel Gold Mystery, 1995; Sheer Gall, 1996; Bearing Witness, 2000; Trophy Widow: A Rachel Gold Novel, 2002. OTHER: (as Michael Baron) The Mourning Sexton, 2005. **Address:** Blackwell Sanders Peper Martin L.L.P., 720 Olive St., Ste. 2400, St. Louis, MO 63101, U.S.A. **Online address:** mkahn@blackwellsanders.com

KAHN, Peggy. See KATZ, Bobbi.

KAHN, Sharon. American (born United States), b. 1934?. **Genres:** Children's Fiction, Children's Non-fiction, Mystery/Crime/Suspense, Novels. **Career:** Writer and attorney. **Publications:** Kacy and the Space Shuttle Secret: A Space Adventure for Young Readers, 1996; (with R. Weingarten) Brave Black Women: From Slavery to the Space Shuttle, 1997. RUBY, THE RABBI'S WIFE MYSTERY SERIES: Fax Me a Bagel, 1998; Never Nosh a Matzo Ball, 2000; Don't Cry for Me, Hot Pastrami, 2001; Hold the Cream Cheese, Kill the Lox, 2002; Which Big Giver Stole the Chopped Liver?, 2004; Out of the Frying Pan, Into the Choir, 2006. **Address:** c/o Author Mail, Simon & Schuster, 1230 Ave. of the Americas, New York, NY 10020, U.S.A.

KAHNE, Joseph. American (born United States), b. 1964. **Genres:** Education. **Career:** New York City Public Schools, social studies teacher, 1986-88; Stanford University, School of Education, research assistant in educational policy and administration, 1988-93; University of Illinois, assistant professor of education, 1993-98, associate professor of education, 1998-99; Mills College, associate professor of education, 1999-2002, professor of education, 2002-, John and Martha Davidson professor of education, 2002-, Abbie Valley professor of education, 2006-, Doctoral Program in Educational Leadership, founding director, 14999-2006, Institute for Civic Leadership, founding director, 2000-05, Kathryn P. Hannam professor of American studies, 2003-06, School of Education, dean, 2006-09, MacArthur Research Network on Youth and Participatory Politics, chair, John and Martha Davidson chair, Civic Engagement Research Group, research director. Writer. **Publications:** Reframing Educational Policy: Democracy, Community, and the Individual, 1996; (with E. Middaugh and C. Evans) The Civic Potential of Video Games, 2009. Contributor of articles to books and journals. **Address:** Department of Education, Mills College, Education 220, 5000 MacArthur Blvd., Oakland, CA 94613-1301, U.S.A. **Online address:** jkahne@mills.edu

KAHNEY, Leander. American/British (born England), b. 1965. **Genres:** Information Science/Computers, Technology. **Career:** Wired News, managing editor and senior reporter; Penguin Group, author, 2004-; Cultofmac.com, editor, 2009-. **Publications:** The Cult of Mac, 2004; The Cult of iPod, 2005; Inside Steve's Brain, 2008. Contributor to magazines. **Address:** Penguin Group (USA) Inc., 375 Hudson St., New York, NY 10014, U.S.A. **Online address:** leander@cultofmac.com

KAIMANN, Diane S. (Nana Diane). American (born United States), b. 1939. **Genres:** Novels, Children's Non-fiction, Social Sciences. **Career:** High school English teacher, 1960-64; Evelyn Wood Reading Dynamics, instructor, 1965-69; Wisconsin franchise, 1980-91; Milwaukee Holocaust Education Center, coordinator, 1994-99; Writer and business consultant, 1999-. **Publications:** Common Threads: Nine Widows Journeys through Love, Loss and Healing, 2002; (as Nana Diane) Chatterbox and Jessica and the Magic Pillow, forthcoming. Contributor to periodicals. **Address:** 1509 W Eastbrook Dr., Mequon, WI 53092, U.S.A. **Online address:** dskaimann@aol.com

KAIN, Philip J(oseph). American (born United States), b. 1943. **Genres:** Ethics, Philosophy, Politics/Government. **Career:** University of California, assistant professor of philosophy, 1974-82; Stanford University, Western Culture Program, lecturer, 1982-86; Stevenson College, visiting lecturer, 1986-88; Santa Clara University, associate professor, 1988-94, Department of Philosophy, chairman, 1991-97, 2008-, professor of philosophy, 1994-. Writer. **Publications:** Schiller, Hegel and Marx: State, Society and the Aesthetic Ideal of Ancient Greece, 1982; Marx, Method, Epistemology and Humanism: A Study in the Development of His Thought, 1986; Marx and Ethics, 1988; Marx and Modern Political Theory: From Hobbes to Contemporary Feminism, 1993; Hegel and the Other: A Study of the Phenomenology of Spirit, 2005; Nietzsche and the Horror of Existence, 2009. **Address:** Department of Philosophy, Santa Clara University, Santa Clara, CA 95053, U.S.A. **Online address:** pkain@scu.edu

KAIRYS, David. American (born United States), b. 1943. **Genres:** Law, Civil Liberties/Human Rights, Novels. **Career:** University of Pennsylvania, Community Law and Criminal Litigation, fellow, 1968-71, lecturer in urban studies, 1972-79, associate professor and lecturer, adjunct professor of sociology, 1980-90; National Emergency Civil Liberties Committee, Philadelphia counsel, 1971-90; Kairys and Rudovsky (law firm), partner, 1971-90, co-founder; University of California, lecturer, 1975; Temple University, professor of law, 1990-, James E. Beasley chair, 2001-07. Lawyer and writer. **Publications:** (Co-author) The Jury System: New Methods for Reducing Prejudice: A Manual for Lawyers, Legal Workers and Social Scientists, 1975; (ed. and contrib.) The Politics of Law: A Progressive Critique, 1982, 3rd ed., 1998; With Liberty and Justice for Some: A Critique of the Conservative Supreme Court, 1993; Philadelphia Freedom: Memoir of a Civil Rights Lawyer, 2008; (ed.) Why are Handguns So Accessible on Urban Streets?, 2008. Work appears in anthologies. Contributor of articles and reviews to law journals, popular magazines and newspapers. **Address:** Beasley School of Law, Temple University, Rm. 606, Klein Hall, 1719 N Broad St., Philadelphia, PA 19122, U.S.A. **Online address:** david.kairys@temple.edu

KAISER, David E. American (born United States), b. 1947. **Genres:** History, Politics/Government. **Career:** Williams College, faculty; Harvard University, lecturer and assistant professor of history, 1976-80; Carnegie-Mellon University, associate professor of history, 1980; Naval War College, Strategy and Policy Department, professor, William B. Pratt chair of military history strategy and policy. Writer. **Publications:** Economic Diplomacy and the Origins of the Second World War: Germany, Britain, France and Eastern Europe, 1930-1939, 1980; (with W. Young) Postmortem: New Evidence in the Case of Sacco and Vanzetti, 1985; Politics and War: European Conflict from Philip II to Hitler, 1990; Epic Season: The 1948 American League Pennant Race, 1998; American Tragedy: Kennedy, Johnson and the Origins of the Vietnam War, 2000; The Road to Dallas: The Assassination of John F. Kennedy, 2008. Contributor to periodicals. **Address:** Strategy and Policy Department, Naval War College, 686 Cushing Rd., Newport, RI 02841-1207, U.S.A. **Online address:** david.kaiser@usnwc.edu

KAISER, Ken. American (born United States), b. 1945. **Genres:** Adult Nonfiction, Sports/Fitness, Biography, Autobiography/Memoirs. **Career:** Western Carolinas League, minor league baseball umpire; American League, major league baseball umpire, 1977-99. Writer. **Publications:** (With D. Fisher) Planet of the Umps: A Baseball Life from behind the Plate, 2003; (ed. and intro. with M. Aubrey) In the Promised Land of Alberta's North: The Northern Journal of Katherine Hughes, Summer 1909, 2006. **Address:** St. Martin's Press, 175 5th Ave., New York, NY 10010-7703, U.S.A.

KAISER, Ward L(ouis). American/Canadian (born Canada), b. 1923. **Genres:** Education, Geography, Social Commentary, Theology/Religion, Earth Sciences, Politics/Government, Third World, Ethics, Translations. **Career:** United Church of Canada, minister, 1949-57; National Council of Churches, Friendship Press, associate editor, 1957-59, editor and senior editor, 1960-86, senior editor, executive director, 1978-86; Fair Housing Council, president, 1962-63. **Publications:** Focus: The Changing City, 1966; (with J.L.S. Shearman) Canada: A Study-Action Manual, 1966; Intersection: Where School and Faith Meet (student text and teacher's manual), 1969; The Challenge of a Closer Moon, 1969; Launching Pad: Literacy, 1970; (with C.P. Lutz) You and the Nation's Priorities, 1971; (ed.) People and Systems, 1975; (coauthor) Forum: Religious Faith Speaks to American Issues, 1976; (trans.) The New Cartography, 1983; (trans.) Space and Time, 1984; (trans.) The Peters Map, 1985; A New View of the World: A Handbook to the World Map: Peters Projection, 1987, rev. ed., 1993; Live by Faith, Live by Risk, 1989; (with D. Wood) Seeing through Maps: The Power of Images to Shape Our World View, 2001; (with B. Abramms and D. Wood) Seeing Through Maps: Many Ways to See the World, 2nd ed., 2005, 3rd ed., 2006; How Maps Change Things: A Conversation about Perspectives and How We Deal with the World, 2011. Contributor to magazines and journals. **Address:** 16630 Daeza Dr., Winter Garden, FL 34787-9335, U.S.A. **Online address:** newmapper@aol.com

KALAIDJIAN, Walter B. American (born United States), b. 1952?. **Genres:** Literary Criticism And History, Language/Linguistics. **Career:** Emory University, professor of English. Writer. **Publications:** Understanding Theodore Roethke, 1987; Languages of Liberation: The Social Text in Contemporary American Poetry, 1989; American Culture between the Wars: Revisionary Modernism and Postmodern Critique, 1993; (ed. with J. Roof and S. Watt) Understanding Literature: An Introduction to Reading and Writing, 2004; (ed.) The Cambridge Companion to American Modernism, 2005; Understanding Poetry, 2005; The Edge of Modernism: American Poetry and the Traumatic Past, 2006. **Address:** Emory University, N 302 Callaway Ctr., 537 Kilgo Cir., Atlanta, GA 30322, U.S.A. **Online address:** wkalaid@emory.edu

KALB, Jonathan. American (born United States), b. 1959. **Genres:** Theatre, Plays/Screenplays. **Career:** Hunter College, Graduate Center, professor of theater, 1992-, HotReview.org, founding editor; New York Press, theater critic, 1997-. Writer. **Publications:** Beckett in Performance, 1989; Free Admissions: Collected Theater Writings, 1993; The Theater of Heiner Muller,

1998, rev. ed., 2001; Play by Play: Theater Essays and Reviews, 1993-2002, 2003; Great Lengths: Seven Works of Marathon Theater, 2011. **Address:** Department of Theater, Hunter College, Rm. 520D HN, North Bldg., New York, NY 10021, U.S.A. **Online address:** jkalb@hunter.cuny.edu

KALBACKEN, Joan. American (born United States), b. 1925. **Genres:** Children's Fiction, Poetry, Children's Non-fiction, Animals/Pets, Food And Wine. **Career:** Lincoln Junior High School, mathematics teacher, 1947-48; Pekin Community High School, algebra teacher, 1958-60; McLean County Unit Five Schools, teacher of mathematics, French and foreign language supervisor, 1960-85, now retired. Writer, 1988-. **Publications:** (With E.U. Lepthien) Recycling, 1991; White-Tailed Deer, 1992; (with E.U. Lepthien) Wetlands, 1993; (with E.U. Lepthien) Foxes, 1993; The Menominee, 1994; Peacocks and Peahens, 1994; Isle Royale National Park, 1996; Badgers, 1996; Sheepskin and Morning Star, 1996; The Food Pyramid, 1998; Food Safety, 1998; Vitamins and Minerals, 1998. **Address:** 903 Ruston Ave., Normal, IL 61761, U.S.A. **Online address:** jokalb@earthlink.net

KALE, Steven D(avid). American (born United States), b. 1957. **Genres:** History. **Career:** Doane College, visiting assistant professor, 1987-88; Youngstown State University, assistant professor, 1988-91; Washington State University, Department of History, assistant professor, 1988-91, associate professor, 1996-2004, professor, 2004-. Writer. **Publications:** Legitimism and the Reconstruction of French Society, 1852-1883, 1992; French Salons: High Society and Political Sociability from the Old Regime to the Revolution of 1848, 2004. **Address:** Department of History, Washington State University, 338 Wilson-Short Hall, 1435 NW Deane St., PO Box 644030, Pullman, WA 99163, U.S.A. **Online address:** kale@wsu.edu

KALER, Anne K(atherine). American (born United States), b. 1935. **Genres:** Literary Criticism And History, Mythology/Folklore, Popular Culture, Writing/Journalism, Social Sciences, History. **Career:** Montgomery County Community College, part-time teacher, 1962-64; Saint Francis College, teacher, 1964-65; Gwynedd-Mercy College, professor of English, 1966-2004, now retired. Writer. **Publications:** The Picara: From Hera to Fantasy Heroine, 1991; (ed.) Cordially Yours, Brother Cadfael, 1998; (ed. with R.E. Johnson-Kurek) Romantic Conventions, 1999. Contributor of articles to magazines. **Address:** 27 Highland Ave., Lansdale, PA 19446-3249, U.S.A.

KALESNIKO, Mark G(aston). American/Canadian (born Canada), b. 1958. **Genres:** Graphic Novels, Communications/Media, Literary Criticism And History. **Career:** Writer. **Publications:** GRAPHIC NOVELS: S.O.S., 1992; Alex, 6 vols., 1994-95; Why Did Pete Duel Kill Himself?, 1997; Mail Order Bride, 2001; Freeway, 2011. **Address:** c/o Author Mail, Fantagraphics Books Inc., 7563 Lake City Way NE, Seattle, WA 98115-4218, U.S.A. **Online address:** kalesniko58@hotmail.com

KALETA, Kenneth C. American (born United States), b. 1948. **Genres:** Film, Biography, Autobiography/Memoirs. **Career:** Rowan University, Department of Radio, Television & Film, associate professor of cinema studies, professor of cinema studies, 1977-. Writer. **Publications:** Asphodel, 1989; Occasional Papers, 1993; David Lynch, 1993; Hanif Kureishi: Postcolonial Storyteller, 1998; (contrib.) True Fiction Pictures and Possible Films, 2008; With the Rich and Mighty: Emlen Etting of Philadelphia, 2008, 2nd ed., 2010; Dimly And In Flashes, forthcoming. **Address:** Department of Radio, Television & Film, Rowan University, 201 Mullica Hill Rd., Glassboro, NJ 08028, U.S.A. **Online address:** kaleta@rowan.edu

KALETSKI, Alexander. American/Russian (born Russia), b. 1946. **Genres:** Novels, Art/Art History. **Career:** Songwriter, musician, and language instructor, 1975-77; artist-illustrator, 1975-85; fabric designer, 1977-83. **Publications:** Cardboard People, 1996; Darkness of Light (novel), 2002. SELF ILLUSTRATOR: Metro: A Novel of the Moscow Underground, 1985. **Address:** 334 E 73rd St., Ste. 4C, New York, NY 10021, U.S.A. **Online address:** info@alexanderkalestski.coms

KALFATOVIC, Martin R. American (born United States), b. 1961. **Genres:** Archaeology/Antiquities, Art/Art History, Bibliography. **Career:** Library of Congress, collections assistant, 1983-86; Smithsonian Institution, National Portrait Gallery, National Museum of American Art and Library, librarian, 1986-93, information access coordinator for the libraries, 1993-98, digital projects librarian, 1998-, head of new media office, 2001-, Digital Services Division, assistant director. Writer. **Publications:** Nile Notes of a Howadji: A

Bibliography of Travelers' Tales from Egypt, from the Earliest Time to 1918, 1992; The New Deal Fine Arts Projects: A Bibliography, 1933-1992, 1994; Creating a Winning Online Exhibition: A Guide for Libraries, Archives, and Museums, 2002. Contributor of articles to book and periodicals. **Address:** Smithsonian Institution Libraries, Smithsonian Institution, Washington, DC 20560-0001, U.S.A. **Online address:** kalfatovicm@si.edu

KALIA, Ravi. American/Indian (born India), b. 1947. **Genres:** History. **Career:** City University of New York, City College, associate professor, 1993-, professor of history. Writer. **Publications:** Chandigarh: In Search of an Identity, 1987; Bhubaneswar: From a Temple Town to a Capital City, 1994; Chandigarh: The Making of an Indian City, 1999; Gandhinagar: Building National Identity in Postcolonial India, 2004; Imaging India in the Twentieth Century: An Architectural View, forthcoming. **Address:** Department of History, City College, City University of New York, NAC 5/131C, 160 Convent Ave., New York, NY 10031-9101, U.S.A. **Online address:** rkalia@ccny.cuny.edu

KALIAN, Cady. See **KALISH, Irma.**

KALIAN, Cady. See **GURIAN, Naomi.**

KALIN, Jim. American (born United States), b. 1959. **Genres:** Novels, Poetry, Young Adult Fiction, Criminology/True Crime. **Career:** Writer. **Publications:** One Worm (novel), 1998. Works appear in anthologies. **Address:** Russian Hill Press, 1250 17th St., Ste. 2, San Francisco, CA 94107, U.S.A.

KALISH, Irma. (Cady Kalian). American (born United States) **Genres:** Young Adult Fiction, Mystery/Crime/Suspense. **Career:** Writers Guild of America, vice president, 1981-85; Women in Film Foundation, president. Screenwriter and producer. **Publications:** MAGGIE MARS SERIES AS CADY KALIAN: As Dead As It Gets, 2005; A Few Good Murders, 2007. **Address:** c/o Author Mail, Forge Books, 175 5th Ave., New York, NY 10010-7703, U.S.A. **Online address:** cadykalian@gmail.com

KALLEN, Stuart A(rnold). American (born United States), b. 1955. **Genres:** Children's Fiction, Young Adult Fiction, Children's Non-fiction, Young Adult Non-fiction, Music, History, Civil Liberties/Human Rights, Environmental Sciences/Ecology, Biography, Ghost Writer, Adult Non-fiction. **Career:** Freelance writer and musician. **Publications:** NONFICTION FOR CHILDREN: Recycle It! Once Is Not Enough, 1990; Before the Communist Revolution: Russian History through 1919, 1992; The Brezhnev Era, 1964-1982, 1992; Exploring the Origins of the Universe, 1997; Egypt, 1999; The Rolling Stones, 1999; Rosie O'Donnell, 1999; The Salem Witch Trials, 1999; Witches, 2000; Leonardo Da Vinci, 2000; The War At Home, 2000; The Home Front: Americans Protest the War, 2001; The Mayans, 2001; Understanding the Catcher in the Rye, 2001; Striving into 2000, 2001; Alligators, 2002; Spiders, 2002; John Lennon, 2002; Dolphins and Porpoises, 2002; Pyramids, 2002; Shinto, 2002; The Kennedy Assassination, 2003; Life on an Ocean Shore, 2003; Native Americans of California, 2003; Primary Sources, 2003; Rhine, 2003; Travel Guide to California Gold Country, 2003; Arts and Entertainment, 2004; Deepest Canyon, 2004; Dreams, 2004; Fortune-telling, 2004; Ghosts, 2004; Harlem Jazz Era, 2004; Highest Waterfall, 2004; Life in a Desert, 2004; Life in a Pond, 2004; Political Activists of the 1960s, 2004; Shamans, 2004; Figures of the Salem Witch Trials, 2005; Medieval Merchant, 2005; Poltergeists, 2005; Possessions and Exorcisms, 2005; Voodoo, 2005; Roswell UFO Incident, 2006; Urban Legends, 2006. WITH P.M. BOEK-HOFF: Lasers, 2002; Dr. Seuss, 2002; Mercury, 2002; Tornadoes, 2003; Meteors, 2003; J.K. Rowling, 2003; Venus Williams, 2003; Comets, 2003; NSYNC, 2003; Mozart, 2004; Steve Irwin, 2004. THE HISTORY OF ROCK 'N ROLL SERIES: Roots of Rock, 1989; Renaissance of Rock: The British Invasion, 1989; Renaissance of Rock: The Sixties-Sounds of America, 1989; Revolution of Rock: The 1970s, 1989; Rock in Retrospect: The 1980s, 1989. THE BUILDING OF A NATION SERIES: Newcomers to America, 1400s-1600s, 1990; Life in the Thirteen Colonies, 1650-1750, 1990; The Road to Freedom, 1750-1783, 1990; A Nation United, 1780-1850, 1990; A Nation Divided, 1835-1900, 1990; A Modern Nation, 1880-1990, 1990. BLACK HISTORY AND THE CIVIL RIGHTS MOVEMENT SERIES: The Lost Kingdoms of Africa: Black Africa Before 1600, 1990; Days of Slavery: A History of Black People in America, 1619-1863, 1990; The Civil War and Reconstruction: History of Black People in America, 1830-1880, 1990; The Civil Rights Movement: The History of Black People in America, 1930-1980, 1990; The Twentieth Century and the Harlem Renaissance: A History of Black People in America, 1880-1930, 1990; The Struggle into the 1990s: A History of Black

People from 1968 to the Present, 1990. GHASTLY GHOST STORIES SERIES: How to Catch a Ghost, 1991; Haunted Hangouts, 1991; Phantoms of the Rich and Famous, 1991; Vampires, Werewolves and Zombies, 1991; Monsters, Dinosaurs, and Beasts, 1991; Ghosts of the Seven Seas, 1991; World of the Bizarre, 1991; Witches, Magic and Spells, 1991. THE WORLD RECORD LIBRARY SERIES: Human Oddities, 1991; Spectacular Sports Records, 1991; Incredible Animals, 1991, Awesome Entertainment Records, 1991; Super Structures of the World, 1991; Amazing Human Feats, 1991. THE SECOND REVOLUTION SERIES: Princes, Peasants and Revolution, 1992; The Lenin Era, 1900-1924, 1992; Stalin: Man of Steel, 1992; Khrushchev Era: 1953-1965, 1992; Brezhnev: Before the Dawn, 1992; Gorbachev-Yeltsin: The Fall of Communism, 1992. THE FABULOUS FUN LIBRARY SERIES: Ridiculous Riddles (Giggles, Gags and Groaners), 1992; Tricky Tricks (Simple Magic Tricks), 1992; Mad Scientist Experiments (Safe, Simple Science Experiments), 1992; Mathmagical Fun (Fun with Numbers), 1992; Puzzling Puzzles, 1992; Silly Stories, 1992; Funny Answers to Foolish Questions, 1992; The Giant Joke Book, 1992; Only the Funniest Joke Book, 1992. TARGET EARTH SERIES: If the Clouds Could Talk, 1993; If Trees Could Talk, 1993; If the Sky Could Talk, 1993; If the Waters Could Talk, 1993; If Animals Could Talk, 1993; Eco-Games, 1993; Precious Creatures A-Z, 1993; Eco-Fairs and Carnivals: A Complete Guide to Raising Funds for the Environment, 1993; Earth Keepers, 1993; Eco-Arts & Crafts, 1993. I HAVE A DREAM SERIES: Maya Angelou: Woman of Words, Deeds and Dreams, 1993; Arthur Ashe: Champion of Dreams and Motion, 1993; Martin Luther King Jr.: A Man and His Dream, 1993; Thurgood Marshall: A Dream of Justice for All, 1993; Quincy Jones, 1996. FAMOUS ILLUSTRATED SPEECHES AND DOCUMENTS SERIES: The Statue of Liberty: The New Colossus, 1994; The Gettysburg Address, 1994; Pledge of Allegiance, 1994; Star-Spangled Banner, 1994; Declaration of Independence, 1994. IF THE DINOSAURS COULD TALK SERIES: Brontosaurus, 1994; Stegosaurus: The Armored Dinosaur, 1994; Tyrannosaurus Rex, 1994; Pterandon, 1994; Plesiosaurus, 1994; Triceratops, 1994. THE HOLOCAUST SERIES: The History of a Hatred: 70 A.D. to 1932, 1994; The Nazis Seize Power: 1933-1939, 1994; The Holocaust: 1939-1945, 1994; Bearing Witness: Liberation and the Nuremberg Trials, 1994; Holocausts in Other Lands, 1994; The Faces of Resistance, 1994. DOGS SERIES: German Shepherds, 1995; Cocker Spaniels, 1996; Dalmatians, 1996; Golden Retrievers, 1996, rev. ed., 2002; Poodles, 1996; Labrador Retrievers, 1996; Mutts, 1996; Yorkshire Terriers, 1998; Beagles, 1998, rev. ed., 2002; Collies, 1998, rev. ed., 2002; Dachshunds, 1998; Old English Sheepdogs, 1998. CATS SERIES: Abyssinian Cats, 1995; Maine Coon Cats, 1996; Manx Cats, 1996; Persian Cats, 1996; Tabby Cats, 1996; Siamese Cats, 1996; American Curl Cats, 1998; Balinese Cats, 1998; Russian Blue Cats, 1998; Devon Rex Cats, 1998; Exotic Shorthair Cats, 1998; Oriental Shorthair Cats, 1998. BEARS SERIES: Black Bears, 1996; Alaskan Brown Bears, 1998; Giant Pandas, 1998; Grizzly Bears, 1998; Polar Bears, 1998; Sun Bears, 1998. GIANT LEAPS SERIES: The Apollo Moonwalkers, 1996; The Gemini Spacewalker, 1996; The Mercury Seven, 1996; The Race to Space, 1996; Space Shuttles, 1996; Space Stations, 1996. FIELD TRIPS SERIES: The Farm, 1997; The Museum, 1997; The Fire Station, 1997; The Police Station, 1997; The Airport, 1997; The Zoo, 1997. THE WAY PEOPLE LIVE SERIES: Life among the Pirates, 1999; Life on the American Frontier, 1999; Life in the Amazon Rain Forest, 1999; Life on the Underground Railroad, 2000; Life in America during the 1960s, 2001; Life in Tokyo, 2001; Life during the American Revolution, 2002. CULTURAL HISTORY OF THE UNITED STATES SERIES: The 1950s, 1999; The 1980s, 1999; The 1990s, 1999. HISTORY MAKERS SERIES: Native American Chiefs and Warriors, 1999; Great Composers, 2000; Great Male Comedians, 2000. INDIGENOUS PEOPLES OF NORTH AMERICA SERIES: Native Americans of the Northeast, 2000; Native Americans of the Southwest, 2000; The Pawnee, 2001. FOUNDING FATHERS SERIES: Alexander Hamilton, 2001; Benjamin Franklin, 2001; George Washington, 2001; James Madison, 2001; James Monroe, 2001; John Adams, 2001; John Hancock, 2001; John Jay, 2001; Thomas Jefferson, 2001; John Marshall, 2001; Patrick Henry, 2001; Samuel Adams, 2001. SEEDS OF A NATION SERIES WITH P.M. BOEKHOFF: California, 2002; New York, 2002; Illinois, 2002; Minnesota, 2002; Delaware, 2002; Indiana, 2002; Ohio, 2002; Washington, 2003; Oregon, 2004. LUCENT LIBRARY OF BLACK HISTORY SERIES: Marcus Garvey and the Back to Africa Movement, 2006; A History of Free Blacks in America, 2006. MUSIC LIBRARY SERIES: The Instruments of Music, 2003; The History of Rock n Roll, 2003; The History of Jazz, 2003; The History of Country Music, 2003; The History of Classical Music, 2003; The History of World Music, 2006; The History of Latin Music, 2006; The History of Reggae, 2006. DAILY LIFE SERIES WITH P.M. BOEKHOFF: A Plains Indian Village,

2002; The Gold Rush, 2002; The Underground Railroad, 2005.WOMEN IN HISTORY SERIES: Women of the 1960s, 2003; Women of the American Frontier, 2004; Women of the Civil Rights Movement, 2005. NORTH AMERICAN INDIANS SERIES WITH P.M. BOEKHOFF: Native Americans of the Great Lakes, 2004; The Navajo, 2004. WONDERS OF THE WORLD SERIES: Mummies, 2003; Icebergs, 2003; The Grand Canyon, 2003; Gems, 2003; (with P.M. Boekhoff) Geysers, 2003. FOR ADULTS: Beer Here: A Traveler's Guide to American Brewpubs and Microbreweries, 1995; The Fifty Greatest Beers of the World: An Expert's Ranking of the Very Best, 1997; The Complete Idiot's Guide to Beer, 1997. EDITOR: The 1950s, 2000; The 1990s, 2000; The 1400s, 2001; The 1700s, 2001; Sixties Counterculture, 2001; The Baby Boom, 2001; The Roaring Twenties, 2002; The Age of Revolution, 2002; Media Bias, 2004; What Energy Sources Should Be Pursued?, 2005; What Are the Most Serious Threats to National Security?, 2005; Nuclear and Toxic Waste, 2005; Managing America's Forests, 2005; How Should America's Wilderness Be Managed?, 2005; Food Safety, 2005; Rain Forests, 2006; Legalizing Drugs, 2006; Is Factory Farming Harming America, 2006; Indian Gaming, 2006; Biological and Chemical Weapons, 2006; Heroin, 2006; Are Privacy Rights Being Violated?, 2006; Are America's Wealthy too Powerful?, 2006; Are American Elections Fair?, 2006; Are Conspiracy Theories Valid?, 2007; Does Equality Exist in America?, 2007; The Wireless Society, 2007. OTHERS: Astrology, 2006; Photography, 2007; The Artist's Tools, 2007; Romanticism, 2007; Rigoberta Menchu, Indian Rights Activist, 2007; Twentieth-century Immigration to the United States, 2007; World Energy Crisis, 2007; Gas Crisis, 2007; National Security, 2008; Alien Abductions, 2008; Haunted Houses, 2008; Vampires, 2008; Renaissance Art, 2008; Angels: The Mysterious & Unknown, 2008; Spontaneous Human Combustion, 2009; Loch Ness Monster, 2009; Postmodern Art, 2009; Pablo Picasso, 2009; John F. Kennedy Assassination, 2009; Harlem Renaissance, 2009; Gwen Stefani, 2009; Graphic Design, 2009; Crop Circles, 2009; Claude Monet, 2009; Bono, 2009; Aftermath of the Sandinista Revolution, 2009; Hydrogen Power, 2010; How Should the World Respond to Global Warming?, 2010; Communication with the Dead, 2010; Werewolves, 2010; Time Travel, 2010; IPod and MP3 Players, 2011; Open the Jail Doors, 2011; Delano Grape Strike, 2011; Aliens, 2011; Atlantis, 2011; Beatles: British Pop Sensation, 2011; Information Revolution, 2011; Manga, 2011; Defiance Campaign, 2011; We are not Beasts of Burden, 2011; Vampire History and Lore, 2011; Search for Extraterrestrial Life, 2011; Toxic Waste, 2011; Renewable Energy Research, 2011; Ancient Egypt, 2012; Discovery of HIV, 2012; The History of Alternative Rock, 2012; History of American Pop, 2012; History of Rock and Roll, 2012; Prophecies and Soothsayers, 2012; Race to Discover the AIDS, 2012; Sorcery, 2012; Sphinx: Part of the Monsters and Mythical Creatures Series, 2012; Che Guevara, 2013; Pharaohs of Egypt, 2013. Contributor to magazines and periodicals. **Address:** 4601 30th Ave. S, Minneapolis, MN 55406-3734, U.S.A.

KALLEVIG, Christine Petrell. American (born United States), b. 1961. **Genres:** Children's Fiction, Adult Non-fiction. **Career:** Music therapist, 1978-84; special education teacher, 1981-84; Author, professional storyteller and origami artist, 1991-. **Publications:** Folding Stories: Storytelling and Origami Together as One, 1991; Holiday Folding Stories: Storytelling and Origami Together for Holiday Fun, 1992; All about Pockets: Storytime Activities for Early Childhood, 1993; Bible Folding Stories: Old Testament Stories and Paper folding Together as One, 1993; Carry Me Home Cuyahoga: An Historical Novel, 1996; Fold-along Stories: Quick and Easy Origami Tales for Beginners, 2001; Please Pass Grandmas Leg: The Case of the Sacked Potatoes, 2004; Our Sculptures Ourselves: A New Look At Public Art in Northeast Ohio, 2007; Nature Fold-Along Stories: Quick and Easy Origami Tales About Plants and Animals, 2009. **Address:** Storytime Ink Intl., PO Box 470505, Cleveland, OH 44147, U.S.A. **Online address:** foldalong@att.net

KALLEY, Jacqueline A(udrey). South African (born South Africa), b. 1945. **Genres:** Area Studies, Economics, Politics/Government. **Career:** History teacher, 1967-68, 1970; Natal Provincial Library Services, staff, 1972; University of the Witwatersrand, Jan Smuts Library, international affairs librarian, 1974-98, honorary research associate in politics, 1998-; Alexsan Library Centre, affiliate, 1991-; South African Research Documentation Information User Service, co-editor of database, 1996-98; Electoral Institute of Southern Africa, information coordinator, librarian and publications manager, 1998-. **Publications:** The Transkei Region of Southern Africa, 1877-1978: A Select and Annotated Bibliography, 1980; South Africa's Foreign Relations, 1980-1984: A Select and Annotated Bibliography, 1984; Jan Christian Smuts-a Bibliophile?, 1985; South Africa by Treaty, 1806-1986: A Chronological and Subject Index, 1987; South Africa under Apartheid: A Select and An-

notated Bibliography, 1987; Pressure on Pretoria: Sanctions, Boycotts, and the Divestment/Disinvestment Campaign against South Africa: A Select and Annotated Bibliography, 1988; South Africa's Road to Change, 1987-1990: A Select and Annotated Bibliography, 1991; Apartheid in South African Libraries: The Transvaal Experience, 2000; South Africa's Treaties in Theory and Practice, 1806-1998, 2001; (ed. with E. Schoeman and M. Burger) Indexing for Southern Africa: A Manual Compiled in Celebration of ASAIB's First Decade, 1994-2004, 2005; (ed. with D. Kadima and K. Matlosa) Election Update South Africa: Local Government Elections, 1 March 2006, 2006. COMPILER: Transkeian Bibliography, 1945 to Independence, 1976, 1976; Transkeian Bibliography: 1945 to Independence, 1976; Index to the Republic of South Africa Treaty Series, 1961-1975, 1976; Bophuthatswana Politics and the Economy: A Select and Annotated Bibliography, 1978; Index to the Union of South Africa Treaty Series, 1926-1960, 1978; (with E. Schoeman and J. Willers) Letters to Smuts: Correspondence relating to the Personal Library of General J.C. Smuts, 1902-1950, 1980; (with E. Schoeman and N. Musiker) Mandela's Five Years of Freedom: South African Politics and Economics, 1990-1995, 1996; (co-author) Southern African Political History of Chronology of the Political Events from Independence to Mid-1997, 1999. Contributor to books and articles to periodicals. **Address:** Electoral Institute of Southern Africa, 14 Park Rd., PO Box 740, Johannesburg, 2006, South Africa. **Online address:** jkalley@eisa.org.za

KALLGREN, Beverly Hayes. American (born United States), b. 1925. **Genres:** Novels, Poetry, Children's Non-fiction, History, Travel/Exploration, Literary Criticism And History, Young Adult Fiction. **Career:** School teacher, 1947-53, 1959-64; guidance counselor, 1965-84. Writer. **Publications:** (Ed. with J.L. Crouthamel) Dear Friend Anna: The Civil War Letters of a Common Soldier from Maine, 1992; Abial & Anna: The Life of a Civil War Veteran As Told in Family Letters, 1992; Merry Christmas-and Then Some (poetry), 1993; Indian Interlude, 1996; Ministry of the First Congregational Church of Litchfield, Connecticut 1723-1999, 1999; Queen Anne's Lace (poetry); The Last Trolley Home (poetry); Tuesday Poems and the Maine Collection, 2002; The House of Seven Secrets (novel), 2003; The Priest's Inn (novel), 2003; A Goose Named Duck (children's nonfiction), 2004. Contributor to local newspapers. **Address:** 49 Goodhouse Rd., Litchfield, CT 06759, U.S.A.

KALMAN, Laura. American (born United States), b. 1955. **Genres:** Biography, Law, Politics/Government, Biography. **Career:** University of California at Santa Barbara, professor of history. Writer and lawyer. **Publications:** Legal Realism at Yale, 1927-1960, 1986; Abe Fortas: A Biography, 1990; The Strange Career of Legal Liberalism, 1996; Yale Law School and the Sixties: Revolt and Reverberations, 2005; Right Star Rising: A New Politics, 1974-1980, 2010. **Address:** Department of History, University of California, HSSB 4258, Santa Barbara, CA 93106-9410, U.S.A. **Online address:** kalman@history.ucsb.edus

KALMAN, Maira. American/Israeli (born Israel), b. 1949?. **Genres:** Art/Art History, Children's Fiction, Illustrations, Young Adult Non-fiction. **Career:** M and Co., designer; artist, writer and illustrator of children's books, 1986-. **Publications:** SELF-ILLUSTRATED FOR CHILDREN: Stay Up Late, 1985; Hey Willy, See the Pyramids, 1988; Sayonara, Mrs. Kackleman, 1989; Max Makes a Million, 1990; Ooh-la-la (Max in Love), 1991; Max in Hollywood, Baby, 1992; Chicken Soup, Boots, 1993; Swami on Rye: Max in India, 1995; Max Doll, 1995; Max Deluxe, 1996; Next Stop, Grand Central, 1999; Where's That Hat? There's That Hat, 1999; (with K. Tibor) (un) Fashion, 2000; What Pete Ate from A-Z: Where We Explore the English Alphabet (in Its Entirety) in Which a Certain Dog Devours a Myriad of Items Which He Should Not, 2001; Fireboat: The Heroic Adventures of the John J. Harvey, 2002; Smartypants: Pete in School, 2003; Principles of Uncertainty, 2007. OTHERS: Roarr: Calder's Circus, 1991; (ed. with R. Peltason) Colors: Tibor Kalman, Issues 1-13, 2002; And the Pursuit of Happiness, 2010; Food Rules, 2011; Looking at Lincoln, 2012. Illustrator of book by others. **Address:** c/o Author Mail, Viking Children's Books, 375 Hudson St., New York, NY 10014, U.S.A. **Online address:** maira@mairakalman.com

KALMIN, Richard. American (born United States), b. 1953?. **Genres:** History. **Career:** Jewish Theological Seminary, faculty, 1982-, Theodore R. Racoosin chair of rabbinic literature; Yale University, visiting professor; Hebrew Union College, visiting professor; Union Theological Seminary, visiting professor; Hebrew University, faculty fellow; University of Michigan, faculty fellow and visiting professor. Writer. **Publications:** The Redaction of the Babylonian Talmud: Amoraic or Saboraic?, 1989; Sages, Stories, Authors, and Editors in Rabbinic Babylonia, 1994; The Sage in Jewish Society of Late Antiquity, 1999; (ed. with S. Schwartz) Jewish Culture and Society under the Christian Roman Empire, 2003; Jewish Babylonia between Persia and Roman Palestine, 2006. Contributor to periodicals. **Address:** Jewish Theological Seminary, 3080 Broadway, New York, NY 10027, U.S.A. **Online address:** rikalmin@jtsa.edu

KALPAKLI, Mehmet. Turkish (born Turkey), b. 1964. **Genres:** History. **Career:** Mimar Sinan University, lecturer, 1991-96; Bilkent University, assistant professor, 1996-, Center for Ottoman Studies, director, 2002-; University of Washington, Ottoman Text Editing Project, cofounder. Writer. **Publications:** (ed. and trans. with Walter G. Andrews and Najaat Black) Ottoman Lyric Poetry: An Anthology, 2006; Osmanli divan siiri uzerine metinler, 1999; (with W.G. Andrews) The Age of Beloveds: Love and the Beloved in Early-Modern Ottoman and European Culture and Society, 2005. Contributor of scholarly articles. **Address:** Department of History, Faculty of Economic, Admin. & Social Sci., Bilkent University, Ankara-Bilkent, 06800, Turkey. **Online address:** kalpakli@bilkent.edu.tr

KALSON, Albert E(ugene). American (born United States), b. 1932. **Genres:** Literary Criticism And History, Theatre, Humor/Satire. **Career:** Purdue University, instructor, 1963-65, assistant professor, 1965-72, associate professor of English, 1972-93, professor, 1993-95, professor emeritus, 1995-. Writer. **Publications:** (With A.A. DeVitis) J.B. Priestley, 1980; Laughter in the Dark: The Plays of Alan Ayckbourn, 1993. Contributor to journals. **Address:** Department of English, Purdue University, 500 Oval Dr., West Lafayette, IN 47907-2038, U.S.A.

KALTNER, John. American (born United States), b. 1954. **Genres:** Theology/Religion, Essays. **Career:** Rhodes College, Virginia Ballou McGehee professor of Muslim-Christian relations. Writer and theologian. **Publications:** The Use of Arabic in Biblical Hebrew Lexicography, 1996; Ishmael Instructs Isaac: An Introduction to the Qur'an for Bible Readers, 1999; (ed. with S.L. McKenzie) Beyond Babel: A Handbook for Biblical Hebrew and Related Languages, 2002; Inquiring of Joseph: Getting to Know a Biblical Character through the Qur'an, 2003; Islam: What Non-Muslims Should Know, 2003; (ed. with L. Stulman) Inspired Speech: Prophecy in the Ancient Near East: Essays in Honor of Herbert B. Huffmon, 2004; (with S.L. McKenzie) The Old Testament: Its Background, Growth and Content, 2007; (with H.R. Greenstein and K.G. Hotz) What Do Our Neighbors Believe? Questions and Answers about Judaism, Christianity, and Islam, 2007; (with S.L. McKenzie and J. Kilpatrick) The Uncensored Bible: The Bawdy and Naughty Bits of the Good Book, 2008. **Address:** Rhodes College, 2000 North Pkwy., Memphis, TN 38112-1690, U.S.A. **Online address:** kaltner@rhodes.edu

KALYN, Wayne. American (born United States), b. 1951. **Genres:** Homes/Gardens, Antiques/Furnishings, Architecture. **Career:** Family Health magazine, editor, 1976-76; World Tennis, executive editor, 1976-87; Vis a Vis, senior editor, 1987; Men's Journal, senior editor, Reader's Digest, editorial director of health books. **Publications:** Design Ideas for Basements, 2004, 2nd ed., 2008; 1001 Ideas for Trimwork, 2005; Guy Spaces, 2008. Contributor to periodicals. **Address:** c/o Author Mail, Creative Homeowner, 24 Park Way, PO Box 38, Upper Saddle River, NJ 07458, U.S.A.

KAMAKAHI, Jeffrey J(on). American (born United States), b. 1960. **Genres:** Cultural/Ethnic Topics, Sociology, Philosophy, Reference. **Career:** University of Hawaii, instructor in sociology, 1989-91; University of Central Arkansas, assistant professor of sociology, 1991-96; St. John's University, assistant professor of sociology, 1996-2002, associate professor of sociology, 2002-, professor; Tohoku University, Fulbright lecturer, 2003-04. Writer. **Publications:** (Ed. with D.B.K. Chang) Social Control in Health and Law, 1992; Uncovering Sociology: A Primer, 1996; (with E. Fox and S. Capek) Come Lovely and Soothing Death: The Right to Die Movement in the U.S., 1999; Sovereign Trusts: Unfulfilled Promises for Native Hawaiian Health, forthcoming; (ed.) Imua Kānaka Maoli: Navigating Native Hawaiian Identity, forthcoming. Contributor to books and periodicals. **Address:** Department of Sociology, St. John's University, 116 Simons Hall, 37 S College Ave., PO Box 2000, Collegeville, MN 56321, U.S.A. **Online address:** jkamakahi@csbsju.edu

KAMAKARIS, Tina. Canadian/Greek (born Greece), b. 1946. **Genres:** Novels, Education, Law. **Career:** George Brown College, professor of legal administration, 1973-74; Seneca College, professor of legal administration,

1974-75, program director, 1976-81, professor, 1981-85, professor of English, 1986-, now professor emeritus; Ontario College of Teachers, faculty. Writer. **Publications:** Legal Office Procedures, 1982, 5th ed., 2006; Legal Office Transcriptions Tapes and Guide, 1995, 5th ed., 2006. **Address:** Seneca College, 1750 Finch Ave. E, Toronto, ON M2J 2X5, Canada.

KAMAU, Kwadwo Agymah. American/Barbadian (born Barbados), b. 1960?. **Genres:** Novels, Horror, Young Adult Fiction. **Career:** New York City Office for Economic Development, research assistant, 1983-85; United Nations Secretariat, research assistant in international economic and social affairs, 1984; New York City Department of Investigation, statistician, 1985-86; New York State Department of Taxation and Finance, Office of Tax Policy Analysis, senior economist, 1986-89; Virginia Commonwealth University, adjunct professor, 1989-; New Virginia Review, editorial assistant, 1991-92; Richmond Free Press, copy editor, 1992-93; freelance copy editor and proofreader, 1993-94; writer, 1994-; University of Oklahoma, assistant professor of English, 2001-, associate professor. **Publications:** Flickering Shadows (novel), 1996; Pictures of a Dying Man (novel), 1999. Contributor of stories and articles to periodicals. **Address:** Department of English, University of Oklahoma, 660 Parrington Oval, Norman, OK 73019-0390, U.S.A. **Online address:** akamau@ou.edu

KAMBALU, Samson. British/Malawian (born Malawi), b. 1975?. **Genres:** Autobiography/Memoirs, Biography, Art/Art History. **Career:** Artist and writer. **Publications:** The Jive Talker: An Artist's Genesis: A Memoir, 2008. **Address:** c/o Laetitia Rutherford, Mulcahy Conway Associates, 15 Canning Passage, London, GL W8 5AA, England. **Online address:** info@holyballism.com

KAMBIL, Ajit. American (born United States) **Genres:** Business/Trade/Industry, Administration/Management. **Career:** New York University, Stern School of Business, assistant professor of information systems, 1992-99; Accenture Institute for Strategic Change, senior research fellow and associate partner, 1998-2003; Deloitte & Touche, Deloitte Research, global director of technology and innovation, 2003-08, global research director of CFO program; Journal of Business Strategy, columnist. Writer. **Publications:** (With E.V. Heck) Making Markets: How Firms Can Design and Profit from Online Auctions and Exchanges, 2002. Contributor to periodicals. **Address:** Deloitte Touche L.L.P., 200 Berkeley St., Boston, MA 02116-5022, U.S.A. **Online address:** akambil@yahoo.com

KAMEN, Henry. Spanish/American/British (born England), b. 1936. **Genres:** History, Translations. **Career:** University of Edinburgh, lecturer, 1963-66; University of Warwick, reader, 1966-90; Higher Council for Scientific Research, professor, 1991-2002, now professor emeritus. Writer. **Publications:** (Trans.) In the Interlude: Poems by Boris Pasternak 1945-1960, 1962; The Spanish Inquisition, 1965, rev. ed. as The Spanish Inquisition: A Historical Revision, 1998; Histoire de l'Inquisition espagnole, 1966; The Rise of Toleration, 1967; Age of Expansion: Europe and the World 1559-1660, 1968; The War of Succession in Spain 1700-1715, 1969; The Iron Century: Social Change in Europe 1550-1660, 1971, rev. ed., 1976; A Concise History of Spain, 1973; Spain in the Later Seventeenth Century 1665-1700, 1980; Spain, 1469-1714: A Society of Conflict, 1983, 3rd ed., 2005; European Society, 1500-1700, 1984; Golden Age Spain, 1988, 2nd ed., 2004; The Phoenix and the Flame: Catalonia and the Counter Reformation, 1993; Crisis and Change in Early Modern Spain, 1993; Philip of Spain, 1997; Early Modern European Society, 2000; Philip V of Spain: The King Who Reigned Twice, 2001; (ed. and contrib.) Who's Who in Europe, 1450-1750, 2000; Felipe V: el rey que reinó dos veces, 2000; Spain's Road to Empire, 2002 in US as Empire: How Spain Became a World Power, 1492-1763, 2003; Duke of Alba, 2004; The Disinherited: The Exiles who Created Spanish Culture in US as The Disinherited: Exile and the Making of Spanish Culture 1492-1975, 2007; Imagining Spain. Historical Myth and National identity, 2008; The Escorial: Myth and Power in the Renaissance, 2010. **Address:** Paseo de San Juan 48, Barcelona, 08010, Spain. **Online address:** henrykamen@hotmail.com

KAMENETZ, Anya. American (born United States), b. 1980. **Genres:** Young Adult Non-fiction, Business/Trade/Industry, Education. **Career:** Village Voice, staff, 2005-; Fast Co., senior writer. Research assistant and journalist. **Publications:** Generation Debt: Why Now Is a Terrible Time to Be Young, 2006; Generation Debt: How Our Future was Sold Out for Student Loans, Credit Cards, Bad Jobs, No Benefits and Tax Cuts for Rich Geezers-and How to Fight Back, 2007; DIY U: Edupunks, Edupreneurs and the Coming Transformation of Higher Education, 2010. Contributor to periodicals. **Address:** c/o Katinka Matson, Brockman Inc., 5 E 59th St., New York, NY 10022, U.S.A. **Online address:** akamenetz@villagevoice.com

KAMENSKY, Jane. American (born United States), b. 1963?. **Genres:** History, Novels. **Career:** Brandeis University, associate professor of American history, Harry S. Truman professor of American civilization, 1993-; Commonplace, co-founder, co-editor, 2000-04; National Endowment for the Humanities, fellow, 1996; History of American Religion, fellow, 1996. Writer. **Publications:** The Colonial Mosaic: American Women, 1600-1760, 1995; Governing the Tongue: The Politics of Speech in Early New England, 1997; The Exchange Artist: A Story of Paper, Bricks, and Ash in Early National America, 2008; The Exchange Artist: A Tale of High-Flying Speculation and America's First Banking Collapse, 2008; (with J. Lepore) Blindspot: By a Gentleman in Exile and a Lady in Disguise, 2008; (co-ed.) Oxford Handbook of The American Revolution, forthcoming. Contributor to periodicals. **Address:** Department of History, Brandeis University, 213 Olin-Sang, 415 S St., PO Box 9110, Waltham, MA 02454, U.S.A. **Online address:** kamensky@brandeis.edu

KAMERICK, Kathleen. American (born United States), b. 1953. **Genres:** Art/Art History, Humanities. **Career:** University of Iowa, Department of History, lecturer, 1992-. Writer. **Publications:** Popular Piety and Art in the Later Middle Ages: Image Worship and Idolatry in England, 1350-1500, 2002. **Address:** Department of History, University of Iowa, 172 Schaeffer Hall, Iowa City, IA 52242, U.S.A. **Online address:** kathleen-kamerick@uiowa.edu

KAMIENIECKI, Sheldon. American (born United States) **Genres:** Politics/Government, Business/Trade/Industry. **Career:** State University of New York, lecturer in environmental policy, 1977-78; California State University, assistant professor of public administration, 1978-81, Paralegal Studies Program, director, 1979-81; University of Southern California, assistant professor, 1981-86, associate professor, 1986-93, professor of global environmental issues and political attitudes and behavior, 1993-2006, Social Science Data Laboratory, director, 1981-87, Department of Political Science, vice-chair, 1989-92, Environmental Studies Program, director, 1992-2005, School of Policy, affiliated professor, 2002-, social sciences division, dean, 2005-; University of California-Santa Barbara, Donald Bren School of Environmental Science and Management, visiting professor, 2001-02; University of California-Santa Cruz, Division of Social Sciences, dean, 2006-. Writer. **Publications:** Public Representation in Environmental Policymaking: The Case of Water Quality Management, 1980; Party Identification, Political Behavior and the American Electorate, 1985; (ed. with R. O'Brien and M. Clarke and contrib.) Controversies in Environmental Policy, 1986; (with H. Hahn) Referendum Voting: Social Status and Policy Preferences, 1987; (with S. Cohen) Environmental Regulation Through Strategic Planning, 1991; (ed. and contrib.) Environmental Politics in the International Arena: Movements, Parties, Organizations and Policy, 1993; (ed. with G.A. Gonzalez and R.O. Vos) Flashpoints in Environmental Policymaking: Controversies in Achieving Sustainability, 1997; (with S. Cohen and M.A. Cahn) Strategic Planning in Environmental Regulation: A Policy Approach that Works, 2005; Corporate America and Environmental Policy: How Often Does Business Get Its Way?, 2006; (ed. with M.E. Kraft) Business and Environmental Policy: Corporate Interests in the American Political System, 2007; (with H. Hahn) The Politics of American Life, forthcoming. Contributor to journals. Works appear in anthologies. **Address:** Department of Social Sciences, University of California, Rm. 460, Humanities and Social Sciences Bldg., 1156 High St., Santa Cruz, CA 95064, U.S.A. **Online address:** sk1@ucsc.edu

KAMIL, Alan C(urtis). American (born United States), b. 1941. **Genres:** Psychology, Biology, Medicine/Health, Environmental Sciences/Ecology. **Career:** University of Massachusetts, assistant professor, 1967-72, associate professor, 1972-79, professor of psychology, 1979-91, professor emeritus, 1991-; University of California, visiting associate professor, 1976-77; University of Nebraska-Lincoln, professor of biological sciences and psychology, 1991-, School of Biological Sciences, director, George Homes professor of biological sciences and psychology. Writer. **Publications:** Mastering Psychology: A Guide to Brown-Herrnstein's Psychology, 1975. EDITOR: (with N.R. Simonson) Patterns of Psychology: Issues and Prospects, 1973; (with T.D. Sargent) Foraging Behavior: Ecological, Ethological and Psychological Approaches, 1981; (with J.R. Krebs and H.R. Pulliam) Foraging Behavior, 1987; (with R.P. Balda and I.M. Pepperberg) Animal Cognition in Nature: The Convergence of Psychology and Biology in Laboratory and Field, 1998;

(with J.A. French and D.W. Leger) Evolutionary Psychology and Motivation, 2001. **Address:** School of Biological Sciences, University of Nebraska-Lincoln, 348 Manter Hall, 1400 R St., Lincoln, NE 68588-0118, U.S.A. **Online address:** akamil@unlserve.unl.edu

KAMIL, Neil D. American (born United States), b. 1954?. **Genres:** Education, History, Theology/Religion, Social Sciences. **Career:** Johns Hopkins University, Department of History, World History Slide Project, Frederick Jackson Turner research fellow, 1984-85; Towson State University, Department of History, visiting instructor, 1985-86, senior visiting instructor, 1987-88; University of Maryland, Department of History, N.E.H. postdoctoral fellow in early American history and culture, 1988-90; Brandeis University, Department of History, lecturer in early American history, 1990-93; University of Texas, Department of History, assistant professor of early American history, 1993-2000, associate professor of early American history, 2000-. Writer. **Publications:** Fortress of the Soul: Violence, Metaphysics, and Material Life in the Huguenots' New World, 1517-1751, 2005. **Address:** Department of History, The University of Texas, 1 University Sta., B7000, Austin, TX 78712-0220, U.S.A. **Online address:** kamil@mail.utexas.edu

KAMIR, Orit. Israeli (born Israel), b. 1961. **Genres:** Law, Women's Studies And Issues, Social Sciences. **Career:** Supreme Court of Israel, law clerk, 1986-87; Israeli Parliament, legal advisor, 1989; Israeli Women's Network, legal advisor and director of legal department, 1990-91; Israeli Anti-Drug Authority, legal advisor, 1991; Hebrew University, teaching fellow, 1991-92, lecturer, 1996-2001, senior lecturer, 2001-09; University of Michigan, Law School, international visiting professor of law, 1999-2006; Tel Aviv University, visiting professor, 2003; Israeli Center for Human Dignity, co-founder and co-director, 2004-; Hartman Institute for Judaic Studies, research fellow, 2007-09; Peres Academic Center, staff, 2011-. Writer, researcher and activist. **Publications:** Kevod ha-ishah ye-shiyyonah, 1999; Every Breath You Take: Stalking Narratives and the Law, 2001; Feminizem, zekhuyot u-mishpaṭ, 2002; Feminism, Rights, and Law in Israel, 2002; Israeli Honor and Dignity: Social Norms, Gender Politics, and the Law, 2004; She' elah shel kavod, 2004; Framed: Women in Law and Film, 2006; Kevod Adam ye-Ḥayah, 2007; Human Dignity Feminism in Israel: A Socio-Legal Analysis, 2007. Contributor to books, periodicals and journals. **Address:** University of Michigan Press, 839 Greene St., Ann Arbor, MI 48104-3209, U.S.A. **Online address:** oritkami@umich.edu

KAMM, Henry. French/German (born Germany), b. 1925. **Genres:** International Relations/Current Affairs, History, Adult Non-fiction. **Career:** New York Times, correspondent, senior foreign correspondent, 1949-96. **Publications:** Dragon Ascending: Vietnam and the Vietnamese, 1996; Cambodia: Report from a Stricken Land, 1998. **Address:** Chemin du Riotord, Lagnes, 84800, France.

KAMMEN, Michael. (Michael G. Kammen). American (born United States), b. 1936. **Genres:** History, Politics/Government. **Career:** Harvard University, instructor, 1964-65; Cornell University, Department of History, assistant professor, 1965-67, associate professor, 1967-69, professor of American history, 1969-73, Newton C. Farr professor of American history and culture, 1973-2008, chair, 1974-76, Newton C. Farr professor emeritus of American history and culture, 2008-, Society for Humanities, director, 1977-80; John Hopkins University, Humanities Center, fellow, 1968-69; National Public Radio, host, 1975-76; Ecole des Hautes Etudes, visiting professor of American history, 1980-81; Princeton University, Center for Arts and Cultural Policy Studies, research affiliate. Writer. **Publications:** (Co-ed.) The Glorious Revolution in America: Documents on the Colonial Crisis of 1689, 1964, rev. ed., 1972; (ed. as Michael G. Kammen) Politics and Society in Colonial America: Democracy or Deference?, 1967, (comp.) 2nd ed., 1978; (as Michael G. Kammen) A Rope of Sand: The Colonial Agents, British Politics and the American Revolution, 1968; Deputyes and Libertyes: The Origins of Representative Government in Colonial America, 1969; Empire and Interest: The American Colonies and the Politics of Mercantilism, 1970; (ed.) The Contrapuntal Civilization: Essays toward a New Understanding of the American Experience, 1971; (ed.) The History of the Province of New-York, 1972; People of Paradox: An Inquiry Concerning the Origins of American Civilization, 1972; (ed.) What Is the Good of History? Selected Letters of Carl L. Becker, 1940-45, 1973; Colonial New York: A History, 1975; (with J.P. Greene and R.L. Bushman) Society, Freedom, and Conscience: The American Revolution in Virginia, Massachusetts, and New York, 1976; (with K.E. Boulding and S.M. Lipset) From Abundance to Scarcity: Implications for the American Tradition, 1977;

A Season of Youth: The American Revolution and the Historical Imagination, 1978; (ed.) The Past before Us: Contemporary Historical Writing in the United States, 1980; Spheres of Liberty: Changing Perceptions of Liberty in American Culture, 1986; A Machine That Would Go of Itself: The Constitution in American Culture, 1986; (ed. and intro.) The Origins of the American Constitution: A Documentary History, 1986; Selvages and Biases: The Fabric of History in American Culture, 1987; Constitutional Pluralism: Conflicting Interpretations of the Founder's Intentions, 1987; Sovereignty and Liberty: Constitutional Discourse in American Culture, 1988; (ed. with J.A. Henretta and S.N. Katz) The Transformation of Early American History: Society, Authority and Ideology, 1991; Mystic Chords of Memory: The Transformation of Tradition in American Culture, 1991; Meadows of Memory: Images of Time and Tradition in American Art and Culture, 1992; (ed.) Contested Values: Democracy and Diversity in American Culture, 1995; The Lively Arts: Gilbert Seldes and the Transformation of Cultural Criticism in the United States, 1996; In the Past Lane: Historical Perspectives on American Culture, 1997; Alexis de Tocqueville and Democracy in America, 1998; (contrib.) Carolyn Plochmann: Fantasies and Realities, 1998; (contrib.) Unknown Terrain: The Landscapes of Andrew Wyeth, 1998; American Culture, American Tastes: Social Change and the 20th Century, 1999; Robert Gwathmey: The Life and Art of a Passionate Observer, 1999; Spheres of Liberty: Changing Perceptions of Liberty in American Culture, 2001; A Time to Every Purpose: The Four Seasons in American Culture, 2004; Visual Shock: A History of Art Controversies in American Culture, 2006; (intro.) Democracy in America, 2008; Digging Up the Dead: A History of Notable American Reburials, 2010. Contributor to periodicals and journals. **Address:** Department of History, Cornell University, 450 McGraw Hall, Ithaca, NY 14853-4601, U.S.A. **Online address:** mgk5@cornell.edu

KAMMEN, Michael G. *See* **KAMMEN, Michael.**

KAMOIE, Laura Croghan. American (born United States), b. 1970. **Genres:** History, Business/Trade/Industry, Autobiography/Memoirs, Business/Trade/Industry. **Career:** Colonial Williamsburg Foundation, James River Institute for Archaeology, historical archaeologist, 1992-97; American University, visiting assistant professor, 2000-05; Historical Society of Washington, senior editor of Washington history, 2001-05; Adams Morgan Heritage Trail, project coordinator and historian, 2001-05; U.S. Naval Academy, assistant professor, 2005-. Writer. **Publications:** Neabsco and Occoquan: The Tayloe Family Iron Plantations, 1730-1830, 2003; Irons in the Fire: The Business History of the Tayloe Family and Virginia's Gentry, 1700-1860, 2007. **Address:** Department of History, U.S. Naval Academy, 107 Maryland Ave., Annapolis, MD 21402-1316, U.S.A. **Online address:** kamoie@usna.edu

KAMPFNER, John. British (born England), b. 1962. **Genres:** History, Politics/Government. **Career:** Reuters News Service, correspondent, 1984-89; Daily Telegraph, correspondent, 1989-91; Financial Times, correspondent; British Broadcasting Corp., correspondent; New Statesman, editor, 2005-08; Index on Censorship, chief executive, 2008-. **Publications:** Inside Yeltsin's Russia: Corruption, Conflict, Capitalism, 1994; Robin Cook, 1998, rev. ed., 1999; Blair's Wars, 2003; Freedom for Sale: Why the World Is Trading Democracy for Security, 2010. Contributor to periodicals. **Address:** London, GL , England. **Online address:** john@jkampfner.net

KAMPHOEFNER, Walter D. American (born United States), b. 1948. **Genres:** History. **Career:** University of Munster, Institute of Comparative Urban History, research associate, 1978-81; California Institute of Technology, Mellon postgraduate instructor, 1981-83; University of Miami, assistant professor, 1983-87, associate professor of history, 1987-88; Texas A&M University, assistant professor, 1988-90, associate professor of history, 1990-96, professor of history, 1996-. Writer. **Publications:** Westfalen in der Neuen Welt: Eine Sozialgeschichte der Auswanderung im 19.Jahrhundert, 1982, rev. ed. 2006; The Westfalians: From Germany to Missouri, 1987. EDITOR: (with W. Helbich and U. Sommer) Briefe aus Amerika: Deutsche Auswanderer Schreiben aus der Neuen Welt, 1830-1930, 1988; (with W. Helbich and U. Sommer) News from the Land of Freedom: German Immigrants Write Home, 1991; An Immigrant Miller Picks Texas: The Letters of Carl Hilmar Guenther, 2001; (with W. Helbich) Deutsche im Amerikanischen Bürgerkrieg: Briefe von Front und Farm, 1861-1865, 2002; (with W. Helbich) German-American Immigration and Ethnicity in Comparative Perspective, 2004; (with W. Helbich) Germans in the Civil War: The Letters They Wrote Home, 2006. **Address:** Department of History, Texas A & M University, 4236 TAMU, College Station, TX 77843-4236, U.S.A. **Online address:** waltkamp@tamu.edu

KAMRAVA, Mehran. American/Iranian (born Iran), b. 1964. **Genres:** Politics/Government, History. **Career:** Rand Corp., resident consultant, 1987-88; Institute of International Studies, research director, 1989-91; Rhodes College, assistant professor, 1991-95, associate professor, 1995-; California State University, professor of political science; Georgetown University, School of Foreign Service in Qatar, interim dean, professor, Center for International and Regional Studies, director. Writer. **Publications:** Revolution in Iran: The Roots of Turmoil, 1990; The Political History of Modern Iran: From Tribalism to Theocracy, 1992; Revolutionary Politics, 1992; Politics and Society in the Third World, 1993; Understanding Comparative Politics: A Framework for Analysis, 1996, 2nd ed., 2008; Democracy in the Balance: Culture and Society in the Middle East, 1998; Cultural Politics in the Third World, 1999; Politics and Society in the Developing World, 2nd ed., 2000; The Modern Middle East: A Political History since the First World War, 2005, 2nd ed., 2011; (ed.) The New Voices of Islam: Rethinking Politics and Modernity: A Reader, 2006; Iran's Intellectual Revolution, 2008; (ed. with M. Dorraj) Iran Today: An Encyclopedia of Life in the Islamic Republic, 2008; (ed.) Innovation in Islam: Traditions and Contributions, 2011; (ed.) International Politics of the Persian Gulf, 2011; (ed.) Political Economy of the Persian Gulf, 2012; (ed.) Nuclear Question in the Middle East, 2012; (ed. with Z. Babar) Migrant Labor in the Persian Gulf, 2012. Contributor to journals. **Address:** Center for International and Regional Studies, Georgetown University, Rm. 0A31, Georgetown University Bldg., PO Box 23689, Doha, 1, Qatar. **Online address:** mk556@georgetown.edu

KAN, Blossom. American (born United States) **Genres:** Novels. **Career:** Orrick, Herrington & Sutcliffe, associate; Akin Gump Strauss Hauer & Feld, staff, 2001-07; MetLife, senior counsel, 2007-; PALS Inc., board director. Writer. **Publications:** (With M. Yu) China Dolls, 2007; (with M. Yu) Young, Restless, and Broke: A Novel, 2010. **Address:** Thomas Dunne Books, 175 5th Ave., New York, NY 10010-7703, U.S.A. **Online address:** michelleandblossom@chinadollsnovel.com

KAN, Sergei. American (born United States), b. 1953. **Genres:** Anthropology/Ethnology, Translations, History. **Career:** Northeastern University, assistant professor of anthropology, 1981-83; University of Michigan, assistant professor of anthropology, 1983-89; Dartmouth College, assistant professor, 1989-92, associate professor of anthropology, 1992-98, professor of anthropology and Native American Studies, 1998-. Writer. **Publications:** (Trans.) A. Kamenskii, Tlingit Indians, 1985; Symbolic Immortality: The Tlingit Potlatch of the Nineteenth Century, 1989; Memory Eternal: Tlingit Culture and Russian Orthodox Christianity Through Two Centuries, 1999; (ed.) Strangers to Relatives, 2001; (co-ed.) Coming to Shore: Northwest Coast Ethnology, Traditions, and Visions, 2004; (co-ed.) New Perspectives on Native North America, 2006; Lev Shternberg: Anthropologist, Russian Socialist, Jewish Activist, 2009; (ed.) Sharing Our Knowledge: the Tlingit and Their Coastal Neighbors, 2012. **Address:** Department of Anthropology, Dartmouth College, Hanover, NH 03755, U.S.A. **Online address:** sergei.a.kan@dartmouth.edu

KANAANEH, Rhoda Ann. Italian (born Italy), b. 1970?. **Genres:** History. **Career:** European University Institute, Robert Schuman Center for Advanced Studies Jean Monnet Fellow. Writer. **Publications:** Birthing the Nation: Strategies of Palestinian Women in Israel, 2002; Surrounded: Palestinian Soldiers in the Israeli Military, 2009; (ed. with I. Nusair) Displaced at Home: Ethnicity and Gender among Palestinians in Israel, 2010. Works appear in anthologies. **Address:** Robert Schuman Centre for Advanced Studies, European University Institute, Via delle Fontanelle 19, San Domenico di Fiesole, I-50014, Italy.

KANAFANI, Deborah. American (born United States) **Genres:** Autobiography/Memoirs. **Career:** Palestinian Broadcasting Corp., director; Women in Film and Video, executive director; Oxygen Media, consultant; Just Vision, director. Writer, producer, administrator, media expert and consultant. **Publications:** Unveiled: How an American Woman Found Her Way through Politics, Love and Obedience in the Middle East (memoir), 2008. **Address:** New York, NY , U.S.A. **Online address:** deborah@deborahkanafani.com

KANAR, Stephen (Patrick). American (born United States), b. 1944. **Genres:** Law, Novels, Mystery/Crime/Suspense. **Career:** Fishback, partner, 1969-78; Troutman, Parrish & Kanar, senior partner, 1978-79; Kanar Law Firm, senior partner, 1979-; Embry-Riddle Aeronautical University, adjunct professor of aviation, 1983; U.S. Court of Appeals, attorney; U.S. Court of

Claims, attorney; U.S. Tax Court, attorney; U.S. Supreme Court, attorney. Writer. **Publications:** Aviation Law, 1983; The J Factor (novel), 2000. **Address:** 1200 Oakland Ln., PO Box 1818, Mount Dora, FL 32757, U.S.A. **Online address:** stephenkanar@aol.com

KANAZAWA, Satoshi. Japanese (born Japan), b. 1962. **Genres:** Novels. **Career:** University of Illinois, visiting assistant professor, 1988-99; Indiana University of Pennsylvania, assistant professor, 1999; Cornell University, assistant professor, 1994-98; London School of Economics and Political Science, 2003-. Writer. **Publications:** (with A. Miller) Order by Accident: The Origins and Consequences of Conformity in Contemporary Japan, 2000; (with A. Miller) Why Men Gamble and Women Buy Shoes: How Evolution Shaped the Way We Behave, 2007; (with A. Miller) Why Beautiful People Have More Daughters: From Dating, Shopping, and Praying to Going to War and Becoming a Billionaire'Two Evolutionary Psychologists Explain Why We Do What We Do, 2007. Contributed to scholarly journals. **Address:** London School of Economics & Political Science, Houghton St., London, WC2A 2AE, England. **Online address:** s.kanazawa@lse.ac.uk

KANCHIER, Carole. Canadian (born Canada) **Genres:** How-to Books, Psychology, Self Help. **Career:** Winnipeg Board of Parks and Recreation, director of arts and crafts; Royal Winnipeg Ballet, director of publicity; University of Calgary, instructor in educational psychology, 1980-82; psychologist, 1981-; University of California, lecturer; University of Alberta, instructor in educational psychology, 1983-92; University of Berkeley, lecturer; University of Santa Cruz, lecturer; Institute of Transpersonal Psychology, visiting fellow; National Career Development Association, chair. Writer. **Publications:** Questers: Dare to Change Your Job and Your Life, 1987, 5th ed. as Dare to Change Your Job and Your Life, 2009. Contributor to magazines and journals. **Address:** 1265 Burnaby St., Ste. 1201, Vancouver, BC V6G 1P8, Canada. **Online address:** carole@daretochange.com

KANDALL, Stephen R. American (born United States), b. 1940. **Genres:** Medicine/Health, Sciences. **Career:** Yeshiva University, Albert Einstein College of Medicine, Bronx Municipal Hospital Center, intern, 1965-66, assistant resident, 1966-67, senior resident, 1967-68, chief resident in pediatrics, 1968-69, assistant instructor at the medical college, 1968-69, Lincoln Hospital, assistant visiting pediatrician, 1969-76, assistant professor, 1972-76, lecturer in pediatrics, 1976-78, Albert Einstein Hospital, attending physician, 1972-76, Division of Neonatology, associate director and director of clinical neonatology, 1972-76, professor of pediatrics, 1994-, now professor emeritus; Tulane University, visiting scientist, 1969-71; University of California, Medical Center, research fellow in neonatology, 1971-72; City University of New York, Mount Sinai School of Medicine, assistant professor, 1976-77, associate professor, 1977-85, professor of clinical pediatrics, 1986-91, professor of pediatrics, 1991-94, assistant attending physician, 1976-85, attending physician, 1985-94; Beth Israel Medical Center, pediatrician, Division of Neonatology, chief, 1976-. Writer and consultant. **Publications:** Improving Treatment for Drug-Exposed Infants, 1993; (with J. Petrillo) Substance and Shadow: Women and Addiction in the United States, 1996. Contributor to journals. **Address:** Beth Israel Medical Center, 16th St., 1st Ave., New York, NY 10003, U.S.A.

KANDEL, Michael. American (born United States), b. 1941. **Genres:** Science Fiction/Fantasy, Children's Fiction, Translations, Novels, Novellas/Short Stories. **Career:** Modern Language Association, assistant editor, editor; Harcourt, consultant science fiction editor; Words Without Borders, contributor. **Publications:** Strange Invasion, 1989; In Between Dragons, 1991; Captain Jack Zodiac, 1992; Virtual Reality, 1993; Panda Ray, 1996; Acolytes, 1997. TRANSLATOR: (with E. Ford) P. Huelle, Who Was David Weiser?, 1994; S. Lem, Peace on Earth, 1994; P. Huelle, Moving House: Stories, 1995; S. Lem, Highcastle: A Remembrance, 1995; S. Lem, His Master's Voice, 1999; S. Lem, A Perfect Vacuum, 1999; (and ed.) A Polish Book of Monsters: Five Dark Tales from Contemporary Poland, 2010. Contributor to periodicals. **Address:** Modern Language Association, 26 Broadway, 3rd Fl., New York, NY 10004-1789, U.S.A. **Online address:** mkdw@nyc.rr.com

KANDEL, Susan. American (born United States), b. 1961. **Genres:** Mystery/Crime/Suspense, Young Adult Fiction, Novels. **Career:** University of California-Los Angeles, Art Center College of Design, faculty of art history and theory; University of California-Santa Barbara, teacher of art history and theory; Artext, editor. Art historian. **Publications:** I Dreamed I Married Perry Mason, 2004; Not a Girl Detective: A Cece Caruso Mystery, 2005; Shamus

in the Green Room, 2006; Christietown: A Cece Caruso Mystery, 2007; Dial H for Hitchcock, 2009. **Address:** c/o Author Mail, HarperCollins Publishers, 10 E 53rd St., 11th Fl., New York, NY 10022, U.S.A. **Online address:** susan@susankandel.com

KANE, Alex. *See* **LAZUTA, Gene.**

KANE, Gordon L. American (born United States), b. 1937. **Genres:** Physics, Sciences. **Career:** Johns Hopkins University, research associate in physics, 1963-65; University of Michigan, assistant professor, 1965-69, associate professor, 1969-75, professor of physics, 1975-, Victor Weisskopf collegiate professor of physics, 2002-, Michigan Center for Theoretical Physics, director, 2005-, School of Art and Design, adjunct professor. Writer. **Publications:** Modern Elementary Particle Physics, 1987; (co-author) Higgs Hunter's Guide, 1990; The Particle Garden, 1995; Supersymmetry: Unveiling the Ultimate Laws of Nature, 2000. EDITOR: Perspectives on Higgs Physics, 1992; Perspectives on Supersymmetry, 1998. **Address:** Department of Physics, University of Michigan, 3464 Randall Bldg., 450 Church St., Ann Arbor, MI 48109-1040, U.S.A. **Online address:** gkane@umich.edu

KANE, Jessica Francis. American (born United States), b. 1971. **Genres:** Novels, Novellas/Short Stories. **Career:** The Morning News, contributing writer. **Publications:** Bending Heaven: Stories, 2002; The Report, 2010. **Address:** New York, NY, U.S.A. **Online address:** jessica@themorningnews.org

KANE, John. American (born United States), b. 1946. **Genres:** Novels, Mystery/Crime/Suspense. **Career:** Solters & Roskin, film publicist, 1977-80; Home Box Office, director of publicity, 1983-90; independent film and television publicist, 1990-. Writer. **Publications:** Best Actress (novel), 1998; Der Mann aus Gold, 2000; The Politics of Moral Capital (Contemporary Political Theory), 2001; A Type Primer, 2002; Twisted Yoga, 2002; The Human Alphabet, 2005; Between Virtue and Power: The Persistent Moral Dilemma of U.S. Foreign Policy, 2008; The Final Sacrament: Hell's Gate is Heaven's Door, 2009; Dispersed Democratic Leadership: Origins, Dynamics, and Implications, 2009; (with W.H. Askwith) List of Officers of the Royal Regiment of Artillery from the Year 1716 to the Year 1899, 2010. **Address:** c/o B. J. Robbins, B. J. Robbins Literary Agency, 5130 Bellaire Ave., North Hollywood, CA 91607, U.S.A.

KANE, Kathleen. *See* **CHILD, Maureen.**

KANE, Larry. (Lawrence Kanowitz). American (born United States), b. 1942. **Genres:** History, Young Adult Non-fiction, Music. **Career:** WQAM, broadcast journalist; WAME, broadcast journalist; WFUN, broadcast journalist; WFIL Radio, anchor, 1966, general assignment reporter, 1966; WPVI, Action News, anchor, 1970; WABC-TV, Eyewitness News anchor, 1977-78; WCAU, primary anchor; KYW-TV, anchor, 1993-2002; Dynamic Images Inc., co-owner. Broadcast journalist. **Publications:** NONFICTION: Larry Kane's Philadelphia, 2000; Ticket to Ride: Inside the Beatles' 1964 & 1965 Tours That Changed the World, 2004; Lennon Revealed, 2005. Contributor to periodicals. **Address:** c/o Author Mail, Running Press, 2300 Chestnut St., Ste. 200, Philadelphia, PA 19103-4371, U.S.A. **Online address:** info@larrykane.com

KANE, Leslie. American (born United States), b. 1945. **Genres:** Theatre, Literary Criticism And History, Plays/Screenplays. **Career:** Westfield State College, assistant professor, 1979-84, associate professor, 1985-89, professor of English, 1989-, now professor emeritus; Massachusetts Institute of Technology, adjunct professor, 1983; Babson College, visiting lecturer, 1985-86. Writer. **Publications:** The Language of Silence: On the Unspoken and the Unspeakable in Modern Drama, 1984; (ed.) David Mamet: A Casebook, 1992; (ed.) Israel Horovitz: A Collection Of Critical Essays, 1994; (ed.) David Mamet's Glengarry Glen Ross: Text and Performance, 1996; Weasels and Wisemen: Ethics and Ethnicity in the Work of David Mamet, 1999; (ed.) David Mamet in Conversation, 2001; (ed. with C.C. Hudgins) Gender and Genre: Essays on David Mamet, 2001; (ed.) Art of Crime: The Plays and Films of Harold Pinter and David Mamet, 2004; (ed. with M. Tyler) Siddur Sha'ar Zahav, 2009. Works appear in anthologies. Contributor of articles to journals. **Address:** Department of English, Westfield State College, 577 Western Ave., Westfield, MA 01086-1630, U.S.A.

KANE, Penny. Australian/Kenyan (born Kenya), b. 1945. **Genres:** Demography, Women's Studies And Issues, Literary Criticism And History, Medicine/Health, History, Young Adult Fiction. **Career:** Freelance journalist, 1964-70; Family Planning Association, information officer, 1971-73; International Planned Parenthood Federation, press officer, 1973-75, deputy director, 1978-84, consultant on health and population, 1984-; University of Wales, University College, Department of Population Studies, information officer, 1975-78, Population Centre, visiting lecturer, 1980-92; Australian National University, Contemporary China Centre, associate, 1988-92, University of Melbourne, Office for Gender and Health, senior associate, 1994-97, associate professor, 1998-2006, now retired; Family Planning Federation of Australia, president, 1988-93. Writer. **Publications:** (With M. Smith) The Pill Off Prescription, 1976; (ed.) Food, Population and Politics, 1977; (ed.) Health, Nutrition and Population in Human Settlements, 1977; (ed.) The Decline in the Birthrate, 1978; (with B. Bewley and J. Cook) Choice Not Chance, 1978; The Which? Guide to Birth Control, 1983; A Decade of Partnership, 1974-1984, 1984; (with J. Porter) The Choice Guide to Birth Control, 1984, 2nd ed., 1988; (with S.S. Fader) Successfully Ever After, 1985; Famine in Selected Countries of the ESCAP Region, 1985; (ed. with D. Lucas) Asking Demographic Questions, 1985; (ed. with D. Davin and E. Croll) China's One-Child Family Policy, 1985; The Impact of Birth Spacing on Child Health, 1985; (ed. with L.T. Ruzicka) Tradition, Development and the Individual: A Study of Conflicts and Supports to Family Planning in Rural Bangladesh, 1986; (with M. Sparrow) Consumer Guide to Birth Control, 1986; (with L.T. Ruzicka) Mortality and Health Issues, 1987; (with L.T. Ruzicka) Australia's Population Trends and Their Social Implications, 1987; The Second Billion: People and Population in China, 1987; Ehkaisy (title means: 'Contraception'), 1988; Famine in China, 1959-1961: Demographic and Social Implications, 1988; (ed. with G. Wunsch and L.T. Ruzicka) Differential Mortality: Methodological Isuues and Biosocial Factors, 1989; Women's Health from Womb to Tomb, 1991, 2nd ed., 1993; Victorian Families in Fact and Fiction, 1995; Women and Occupational Health, 1999. Contributor to books. **Address:** The Old School, Major's Creek, Braidwood, NW 2622, Australia. **Online address:** pskane@braidwood.net.au

KANG, David C. American (born United States), b. 1965. **Genres:** Economics. **Career:** Dartmouth College, professor, 1996-2007; University of Southern California, School of International Relations, professor, 2009-, Marshall School of Business, professor, 2009-, Korean Studies Institute, director, 2009-; Stanford University, visiting professor; Yale University, visiting professor; Seoul National University, visiting professor; Korea University, visiting professor; University of Geneva, visiting professor. Writer. **Publications:** Crony Capitalism: Corruption and Development in South Korea and the Philippines, 2002; (with V.D. Cha) Nuclear North Korea: A Debate on Engagement Strategies, 2003; China Rising: Peace, Power, and Order in East Asia, 2007; (with S.C. Kim) Engagement with North Korea: A Viable Alternative, 2009; East Asia Before the West: Five Centuries of Trade and Tribute, 2010. Contributor of articles to journals. **Address:** Dartmouth College, HB 6108, 211 Silsby Hall, Hanover, NH 03755, U.S.A. **Online address:** kangdc@usc.edu

KANG, K. Connie. American/Korean (born Korea (South)), b. 1942. **Genres:** Novels, Autobiography/Memoirs, Biography, History, Social Sciences, Civil Liberties/Human Rights. **Career:** Democrat and Chronicle, reporter, 1964-; Korean Times, columnist, 1967-; Haukuk University, assistant professor of foreign studies, 1967-70; San Francisco Examiner, editorial writer, assistant metropolitan editor, reporter and foreign correspondent, 1975-92; San Francisco Chronicle, staff reporter, 1976; Los Angeles Times, staff writer, 1992-. **Publications:** Home Was the Land of Morning Calm: A Saga of a Korean-American Family, 1995. **Address:** Los Angeles Times, 202 W 1st St., Los Angeles, CA 90012-4105, U.S.A. **Online address:** connie.kang@latimes.com

KANIGEL, Robert. American (born United States), b. 1946. **Genres:** History, Literary Criticism And History, Sciences, Adult Non-fiction, Travel/Exploration, Writing/Journalism, Biography, Essays, Essays, Language/Linguistics, Mathematics/Statistics, Transportation, Classics, Regional/Urban Planning. **Career:** Bendix Corp., mechanical engineer, 1968-69; freelance writer, 1970-; Johns Hopkins University, instructor in writing, 1985-91; University of Baltimore, Yale Gordon College of Liberal Arts, professor of English, 1991-99, Institute for Language, Technology, and Publications Design, senior fellow, 1991-99; Massachusetts Institute of Technology, Program in Writing and Humanistic Studies, professor of science writing, 1999-, Graduate Program in Science Writing, director, 1999-2008. Writer. **Publications:** Apprentice to Genius: The Making of a Scientific Dynasty, 1986; The Man Who Knew Infinity: A Life of the Genius Ramanujan, 1991; The One Best Way: Frederick Winslow Taylor and the Enigma of Efficiency, 1997; Vintage

Reading: From Plato to Bradbury, A Personal Tour of Some of the World's Best Books, 1998; High Season: How One French Riviera Town has Seduced Travelers for Two Thousand Years, 2002; Faux Real: Genuine Leather and 200 Years of Inspired Fakes, 2007; On an Irish Island, 2012. Contributor to periodicals. **Address:** 2634 N Calvert St., Baltimore, MD 21218, U.S.A. **Online address:** kanigel@mit.edu

KANIPE, Jeff. American (born United States), b. 1953. **Genres:** Astronomy, Sciences, History, Mathematics/Statistics, Air/Space Topics. **Career:** Astronomy, editor; StarDate, editor; Space.com, skywatching columnist. Writer. **Publications:** NONFICTION: (co-author) Advanced Skywatching: The Backyard Astronomer's Guide to Starhopping and Exploring the Universe, 1997, 2nd ed. as Backyard Astronomy, 1999; A Skywatcher's Year, 1999; Star and Sky, 2000; (co-author) Astronomy: The Definitive Guide, 2003; Chasing Hubble's Shadows: The Search for Galaxies at the Edge of Time, 2006; (with D. Webb) The Arp Atlas of Peculiar Galaxies: A Chronicle and Observer's Guide, 2006; The Cosmic Connection: How Astronomical Events Impact Life on Earth, 2009. **Address:** Regula Noetzli Literary Agency, 2344 County, Rte. 83, Pine Plains, NY 12567, U.S.A. **Online address:** jeff.kanipe@comcast.net

KANN, Mark E. American (born United States), b. 1947. **Genres:** Politics/Government. **Career:** Chicago Public Schools, teacher, 1968-71; University of Wisconsin, graduate teaching assistant, 1972-75; University of Southern California, assistant professor, 1975-81, associate professor, 1981-88, professor of political science, 1988-, director of graduate affairs, 1979-81, associate dean of graduate studies, 1990-93, Center for Excellence in Teaching, founder and director, 1990-93, Henry Salvatori endowed chair of American studies, 1992-94, associate endowed chair in social science, 1995-, professor of political science and history, 2001-, Department of Political Science, chair, 2001-04, Academic Culture Initiative, Office of the Provost, director, 2001-07, Office of Residential Education, director of academic initiatives, 2007-08; Humanities in Society, associate editor, 1979-81, editor, 1981-84; Los Angeles Herald Examiner, monthly political columnist, 1985-87; Jefferson Center for Character Education, senior consultant, 1987-91, 1995, vice president, 1991-93. **Publications:** Thinking About Politics: Two Political Sciences, 1980; The American Left: Failures and Fortunes, 1982; Middle Class Radicalism in Santa Monica, 1986; On the Man Question: Gender and Civic Virtue in America, 1991; A Republic of Men: TGendering of American politicse and Patriarchial Politics, 1998; The Gendering of American Politics: Founding Mothers, Founding Fathers and Political Patriarchy, 1999; Punishment, Prisons and Patriarchy: Liberty and Power in the Early American Republic, 2005. EDITOR: (with J.P. Diggins) The Problem of Authority in America, 1981; The Future of American Democracy: Views From the Left, 1983; (with E. Chapple) The Road After 1984: High Technology and Human Freedom, 1984; (with M. Clarke and others) Controversies in Environmental Policy, 1984, 2nd ed., 1986; (with M. Zeitlin) Political Power and Social Theory: A Research Annual, vol. V, 1984. Contributor to books. **Address:** Department of Political Science, University of Southern California, 230B VKC, 699 Exposition Blvd., Los Angeles, CA 90089, U.S.A. **Online address:** mkann@usc.edu

KANNUS, (Veli) Pekka. Finnish (born Finland), b. 1959. **Genres:** Sports/Fitness, Medicine/Health, Sciences. **Career:** Research Center for Sports Medicine, resident physician, 1987-91; University of Vermont, research fellow, 1989-90, specialist in sports medicine, 1991-92, visiting professor, 1994; University of Jyvaskyla, associate professor, 1991-95; University of Tampere, UKK Institute, senior research fellow, 1992, Accident and Trauma Research Center, chief physician and head, 1993-, associate professor, 1995-99, professor of injury prevention, 2000-, senior physician; Australian Conference of Science and Medicine in Sport, Vince Higgings keynote lecturer, 1995; KPH Hip Protector, scientist. Writer. **Publications:** (With L.G. Józsa) Human Tendons: Anatomy, Physiology, and Pathology, 1997. Contributor to journals. **Address:** Accident and Trauma Research Center, UKK Institute, University of Tampere, Kaupinpuistonkatu 1, PO Box 30, Tampere, 33501, Finland. **Online address:** klpeka@uta.fi

KANON, Joseph A. American (born United States), b. 1946?. **Genres:** Novels, Mystery/Crime/Suspense. **Career:** Writer, 1995-; The Atlantic, reader; E.P. Dutton, editor-in-chief, president and chief executive officer; Houghton Mifflin Harcourt Publishing Co., editor-in-chief, president and chief executive officer, senior vice-president, Trade and Reference Publishing, head; The Saturday Review, staff; Little, Brown and Co., staff; Coward-McCann, staff; Trade and Reference Publishing, head, executive vice president, senior vice president. **Publications:** NOVELS: Los Alamos, 1997; The Prodigal Spy,

1998; The Good German, 2001; Alibi, 2005; Stardust, 2009. **Address:** c/o Robin Straus, Robin Straus Agency Inc., 229 E 79th St., Ste. 5A, New York, NY 10075, U.S.A.

KANOWITZ, Lawrence. *See* **KANE, Larry.**

KANTARIS, Sylvia (Mosley). British (born England), b. 1936. **Genres:** Poetry, Literary Criticism And History, Essays, Writing/Journalism, Essays. **Career:** Comprehensive School, teacher of English, 1958-59; Secondary Modern School, teacher of English, 1960-62; University of Queensland, tutor in French, 1963-66; writer, 1972-74, 1984-; Open University, tutor, 1974-84; University of Exeter, extramural lecturer, 1974-92; Cornwall, writer-in-residence, 1987. **Publications:** (As Sylvia Kantarizis) Time and Motion (poems), 1975; Stocking Up, 1981; The Tenth Muse, 1983; (with D.M. Thomas) News from the Front, 1983; The Sea at the Door, 1985; (with P. Gross) The Air Mines of Mistila, 1988; Dirty Washing: New and Selected Poems, 1989; (intro.) Before We Were Strangers, 1989; (contrib.) Delighting the Heart: A Notebook by Women Writers, 1989; Lad's Love, 1993; Lost Property, 1998. Contributor to books and periodicals. **Address:** 14 Osborne Parc, Helston, CW TR13 8PB, England. **Online address:** sylvia@kantaris.com

KANTER, Lynn. American (born United States), b. 1954. **Genres:** Novels, Young Adult Fiction. **Career:** Center for Community Change, writer, 1992-, chief writer, deputy director of development, writing director. **Publications:** NOVELS: On Lill Street, 1992; The Mayor of Heaven, 1997. Works appear in anthologies. **Address:** Center for Community Change, 1536 U St. NW, Washington, DC 20009-3912, U.S.A. **Online address:** lynnkanter@aol.com

KANTNER, Seth. American (born United States), b. 1965. **Genres:** Science Fiction/Fantasy, Novels, Young Adult Non-fiction. **Career:** Anchorage Daily News, columnist; Orion Magazine, columnist. Writer, educator and photographer. **Publications:** Ordinary Wolves, 2004; Shopping for Porcupine: A Life in Arctic Alaska, 2008. Works appear in anthologies. Contributor to periodicals. **Address:** c/o Jessica Deutsch, Milkweed Editions, Open Book Bldg., 1011 Washington Ave. S, Ste. 300, Minneapolis, MN 55415-1246, U.S.A. **Online address:** sethkantner@yahoo.com

KANTOR, Jean-Michel. French (born France), b. 1946. **Genres:** History. **Career:** Institut de Mathematiques de Jussieu, mathematician and historian of mathematics; National Museum of Science and Industry, curator of the mathematics section. Writer. **Publications:** Formes et opérateurs différentiels sur les espaces analytiques complexes, 1977; Mathématiques venues d'ailleurs: Divertissements mathématiques en U.R.S.S., 1982; Nodi: A cura di Marco Belpoliti, 1996; Ou en sont les mathématiques?, 2002; (with L. Graham) Naming Infinity: A True Story of Religious Mysticism and Mathematical Creativity, 2009. Contributor to journals. **Address:** Paris, France. **Online address:** kantor@math.jussieu.fr

KANTOR, Melissa. American (born United States), b. 1970?. **Genres:** Novels. **Career:** Writer and educator. **Publications:** Confessions of a Not It Girl, 2004; If I Have a Wicked Stepmother, Where's My Prince?, 2005; The Breakup Bible: A Novel, 2007; (with A. Valentino) Invisible I, 2009; Girlfriend Material, 2009; The Darlings Are Forever, 2011; The Darlings in Love, 2012. **Address:** c/o Author Mail, Hyperion Books for Children, 114 5th Ave., New York, NY 10011, U.S.A. **Online address:** melissa@melissakantor.com

KANUNGO, R(abindra) N. (Rabindra Nath Kanungo). Canadian/Indian (born India), b. 1935. **Genres:** Administration/Management, Cultural/Ethnic Topics, Social Sciences, Business/Trade/Industry, Institutions/Organizations, Ethics. **Career:** Ravenshaw College, lecturer, 1955-60; Indian Institute of Management, assistant professor, 1963-64, visiting professor, 1983-84; Indian Institute of Technology, assistant professor and head of social science division, 1964-65; Dalhousie University, research associate, assistant professor, associate professor, 1965-69; McGill University, associate professor, 1969-73, professor of management, 1974-, chair of department, 1988-, now professor emeritus; J Walter Thompson Co., consultant; Xerox Corporation of Canada, consultant; Clarion Advertising Services, consultant; Canadian Broadcasting Corp., consultant. Writer. **Publications:** (With P. Misra) Introduction to the Child's Mind, 1974; (with S. Dutta) Affect and Memory: A Reformulation, 1975; Biculturalism and Management, 1980; Work Alienation: An Integrative Approach, 1982; (with M. Mendonca) Compensation: Effective Reward Management, 1992; (with M. Mendonca) Introduction to Organizational Behavior, 5th ed., 1994; (with M. Mendonca) Ethical Dimensions

of Leadership, 1996; (with J.A. Conger) Charismatic Leadership in Organizations, 1998. EDITOR AND CONTRIBUTOR: (with H.C. Jain) Behavioral Issues in Management: The Canadian Context, 1977; (with M.D. Lee) Management of Work and Personal Life: Problems and Opportunities, 1984; South Asians in the Canadian Mosaic, 1984; (with J.A. Conger) Charismatic Leadership: The Elusive Factor in Organizational Effectiveness, 1988; (with A. Jaeger) Management in Developing Countries, 1992; (with R. Ghosh) South Asian Canadians, 1992; (with M. Mendonca) Work Motivation: Models for Developing Countries, 1994; Entrepreneurship and Innovation: Models for Development, 1998. Contributor to periodicals and journals. Works appear in anthologies. **Address:** Faculty of Management, McGill University, Bronfman Bldg., 1001 Sherbrooke St. W, Montreal, QC H3A 1G5, Canada. **Online address:** kanungo@management.mcgill.ca

KANUNGO, Rabindra Nath. *See* **KANUNGO, R(abindra) N.**

KAO, John J. American (born United States), b. 1950. **Genres:** Medicine/Health, Business/Trade/Industry, How-to Books. **Career:** Harvard University, Harvard Business School, senior lecturer, associate professor, 1982-96; The Idea Factory, founder and chief executive officer, 1997-2001; Kao & Company L.L.C., founder and chief executive officer; Massachusetts Institute of Technology, Media Lab, visiting professor, 1996; U.S. Naval Postgraduate School, distinguished visiting professor of innovation; Bay Area Science and Innovation Consortium, director; The Daily Beast, contributing editor; TwoFour54, director; Phylotech, director; Cisco System's Innovation Commission, founding member. Entrepreneur, consultant and film producer. **Publications:** (Comp. and trans. with F.F. Kao) Acupuncture Therapeutics: An Introductory Text, 1973; (ed. with F.F. Kao) Chinese Medicine-New Medicine, 1977; (ed. with F.F. Kao) Recent Advances in Acupuncture Research, 1979; Three Millennia of Chinese Psychiatry, 1979; (ed. with H.H. Stevenson) Entrepreneurship, What It Is and How to Teach It, 1985; Entrepreneurship, Creativity & Organization: Text, Cases & Readings, 1989; The Entrepreneur, 1991; The Entrepreneurial Organization, 1991; Managing Creativity, 1991; The New Business of Design: The Forty-fifth International Design Conference in Aspen, 1996; Jamming: The Art and Discipline of Business Creativity, 1996; (ed. with R.M. Kanter and F. Wiersema) Innovation: Breakthrough Ideas at 3M, DuPont, GE, Pfizer, and Rubbermaid, 1997; (ed. with E.L. Kao) Frederick F. Kao, A Life between Two Worlds: A Memoir, 2001; Innovation Nation: How America Is Losing Its Innovation Edge, Why It Matters, and What We Can Do to Get It Back, 2007. Contributor to periodicals. **Address:** The Harry Walker Agency, 355 Lexington Ave., 21st Fl., New York, NY 10024, U.S.A. **Online address:** john@jamming.com

KAPFERER, Jean-Noel. French (born France), b. 1948. **Genres:** Marketing, Administration/Management, Business/Trade/Industry. **Career:** Procter and Gamble, assistant product manager, 1970; H.E.C., professor of business administration, 1975-, Brigitte AZZARO, secretariat. Writer. **Publications:** Chemins de la Persuasion: Le Mode d'influence des Media et de la Publicité sur les Comportements, 1978; Enfant et la Publicité: Les Chemins de la Séduction, 1985; Rumeurs: Le Plus Vieux Média du Monde 1987; Rumors: Uses, Interpretations and Images, 1990; Strategic Brand Management: New Approaches to Creating and Evaluating Brand Equity, 1992, 4th ed., 2008; Re-marques: Les Marques à l'épreuve de la Pratique, 2000; Reinventing the Brand, 2001; Ce qui va Changer les Marques, 2005; (with V. Bastien) The Luxury Strategy: Break the Rules of Marketing to Build Luxury Brands, 2009; The New Strategic Brand Management: Advanced Insights and Strategic Thinking, 5th ed., 2012. **Address:** HEC Paris Graduate Business School, Bureau 417, 1 rue de la Liberation, Jouy-en-Josas, 78351, France. **Online address:** jnkapferer@kapferer.com

KAPLAN, Alice Yaeger. American (born United States), b. 1954. **Genres:** Literary Criticism And History, Translations, History. **Career:** Duke University, associate professor, professor of romance studies and literature, 1986-, Gilbert, Louis and Edward Lehrman professor of romance studies, 2003-, now professor emeritus, professor of literature and history, Center for French and Francophone Studies, founding director, 2000-; Yale University, Department of French, John M. Musser professor of French, 2009-. Writer. **Publications:** Reproductions of Banality: Fascism, Literature, and French Intellectual Life, 1986; Relevé des sources et citations dans Bagatelles pour un massacre, 1987; French Lessons: A Memoir, 1993; The Collaborator: The Trial and Execution of Robert Brasillach, 2000; The Interpreter, 2005; Dreaming in French, 2012. TRANSLATOR: R. Grenier, Another November, 1998; R. Grenier, The Difficulty of Being a Dog, 2000; (and intro.) R. Grenier, Piano

Music for Four Hands, 2001; (and intro.) L. Guilloux, OK, Joe, 2003; E. Bloch-Dano, Madame Proust: A Biography, 2007. Contributor to periodicals. **Address:** Department of French, Yale University, Rm. 324, 82-90 Wall St., 3rd Fl., PO Box 208251, New Haven, CT 06511, U.S.A. **Online address:** alice.kaplan@yale.edu

KAPLAN, Andrew S. American (born United States), b. 1960. **Genres:** Young Adult Non-fiction, Business/Trade/Industry, Education, Self Help, Mathematics/Statistics, Children's Fiction. **Career:** Curriculum Concepts, editor and writer, 1982-85; freelance writer and editor, 1985-. **Publications:** Scorpion, 1985; Dragonfire, 1987; War of the Raven, 1989; CONTRIBUTOR: Careers for Sports Fans, 1991; Careers for Computer Buffs, 1991; Careers for Artistic Types, 1991; Careers for Outdoor Types, 1991; Careers for Number Lovers, 1991; Careers for Wordsmiths, 1991. OTHER: Math on Call: A Mathematics Handbook, 2004; World of Good, 2004. **Address:** 25 Tudor City Pl., Apt. 1205, New York, NY 10017, U.S.A.

KAPLAN, Barbara Beigun. American (born United States), b. 1943. **Genres:** History. **Career:** University of Maryland, adjunct professor of history, 1981-, Center for Instructional Development and Evaluation, senior instructional designer, 1985-90, Program in Science, Technology and Society Studies, executive director, 1988-91, coordinator of faculty development, 1993-; Gaithersburg Gazette, journalist, 1984; Applied Science Associates Inc., instructional technologist, 1985-90; Montgomery College, Instructional Programs, associate dean, dean; Stevenson University, associate dean for academic affairs; American Public University System, Graduate History and Military Studies, program director; Villa Julie College, associate dean of academic affairs. **Publications:** Divulging of Useful Truths in Physick: The Medical Agenda of Robert Boyle, 1993; Land and Heritage in the Virginia Tidewater: A History of King and Queen County, 1993. Work represented in anthologies. Contributor of articles to academic journals. **Address:** American Public University System, 111 W Congress St., Charles Town, WV 25414, U.S.A.

KAPLAN, Beth. Canadian/American (born United States), b. 1950?. **Genres:** Biography, Autobiography/Memoirs. **Career:** Ryerson University, instructor in memoir and personal essay writing, 1995-; University of Toronto, faculty, 2007-, instructor. Writer. **Publications:** Finding the Jewish Shakespeare: The Life and Legacy of Jacob Gordin, 2007. Contributor to periodicals. **Address:** c/o Richard Curtis, Richard Curtis Associates, 171 E 74th St., Ste. 2, New York, NY 10021, U.S.A. **Online address:** beth@bethkaplan.ca

KAPLAN, Bruce Eric. American (born United States), b. 1964?. **Genres:** Cartoons, Graphic Novels, Humor/Satire, Animals/Pets. **Career:** Home Box Office, Six Feet Under, executive producer, 2001-. Writer and cartoonist. **Publications:** No One You Know: A Collection of Cartoons, 1999; The Cat That Changed My Life: Fifty Cats Talk Candidly about How They Became Who They Are, 2002; This Is a Bad Time: A Collection of Cartoons, 2004; Every Person on the Planet: An Only Somewhat Anxiety-Filled Tale for the Holidays, 2005; Edmund and Rosemary Go to Hell: A Story of Our Times with (Hopefully) Some Hope for Us All, 2007; Monsters Eat Whiny Children, 2010; I Love You, I Hate You, I'm Hungry, 2010; Everything Is Going to Be Okay: A Book for You Or Someone Like You, 2011. **Address:** c/o Camille McDuffie, Goldberg McDuffie Communicaions Inc., 444 Madison Ave., Ste. 3300, New York, NY 10022, U.S.A.

KAPLAN, Carter. American (born United States), b. 1960. **Genres:** Literary Criticism And History. **Career:** Yeshiva University, adjunct assistant professor, 1997; College of St. Elizabeth, assistant professor, 1998-99; Shippensburg University, assistant professor, 1999-2000; Mountain State University, associate professor of English, 2001-; Belmont Technical College, Department of English, professor. Writer. **Publications:** Critical Synoptics: Menippean Satire and the Analysis of Intellectual Mythology, 2000. **Address:** Department of English, Belmont Technical College, 120 Fox-Shannon Pl., St. Clairsville, OH 43950-8751, U.S.A. **Online address:** ckaplan@btc.edu

KAPLAN, Edward S. American (born United States), b. 1942. **Genres:** Economics, History, Politics/Government, Business/Trade/Industry, Money/Finance, Politics/Government, Social Sciences. **Career:** New York City College of Technology, School of Arts and Sciences, Department of Social Science, professor and coordinator of economics, 1971-, chair. Writer. **Publications:** (With T.W. Ryley) Prelude to Trade Wars: American Tariff Policy, 1890-1922, 1994; American Trade Policy, 1923-1995, 1996; U.S. Imperialism in Latin America: Bryan's Challenges and Contributions, 1900-1920, 1998; The Bank of the United States and the American Economy, 1999; Essentials of Macroeconomics, 2005. Contributor to journals. **Address:** Department of Social Science, New York City College of Technology, Rm. N-624, 300 Jay St., Brooklyn, NY 11201, U.S.A. **Online address:** ekaplan@citytech.cuny.edu

KAPLAN, Elizabeth (A.). American (born United States), b. 1956. **Genres:** Children's Non-fiction, Sciences, Geography, History. **Career:** Encyclopaedia Britannica, editorial indexer, 1980-82; Field Museum Discovery Program, lecturer, 1980-88; Scott, Foresman and Co., associate editor, 1982-85; Gareth Stevens Books, editor, 1990-91; Congregation Sinai, Family Center, co-coordinator. Freelance writer. **Publications:** (With I. Asimov) How Do Airplanes Fly?, 1993; (with I. Asimov) How Do Big Ships Float?, 1993; (with I. Asimov) How Does a TV Work?, 1993; (with I. Asimov) How is Paper Made?, 1993; (with I. Asimov) What Happens When I Flush the Toilet?, 1993. BIOMES SERIES: Tundra, 1995; Temperate Forest, 1996; Taiga, 1996. OTHER: (with D.P. Press) Jewish Americans, 1995; (with I. Asimov) Henry Hudson: Arctic Explorer and North American Adventurer, 1991; (with C. Price-Groff) Illinois, 2011; (with M.T. Brill) Minnesota, 2011. **Address:** 2626 N Farwell, Milwaukee, WI 53211, U.S.A.

KAPLAN, Ellen. American (born United States), b. 1936. **Genres:** Mathematics/Statistics, Illustrations, Education. **Career:** Commonwealth School, teacher, 1959-97; Educational Development Corp., constructed history curriculum staff, 1967-68; Harvard School of Public Health, faculty, 1989; The Math Circle, co-founder and co-director, 1994-; Sage School, chair of the board, 1995-98; New Jewish High School, Department of Mathematics, chair, 1997-2000. Writer. **Publications:** SELF-ILLUSTRATED: (with R. Kaplan) The Art of the Infinite: The Pleasures of Mathematics, 2003. OTHERS: (with M. Kaplan) Chances Are...: Adventures in Probability, 2006; (with R. Kaplan) Out of the Labyrinth: Setting Mathematics Free, 2007; (with M. Kaplan) Bozo Sapiens: Why to Err is Human, 2009; (with R. Kaplan) Hidden Harmonies: The Lives and Times of the Pythagorean Theorem, 2011. **Address:** The Math Circle, 27 East St., Southampton, MA 01073, U.S.A. **Online address:** kaplan@math.harvard.edu

KAPLAN, James. (James Andrew Kaplan). American (born United States), b. 1951. **Genres:** Novels, Novellas/Short Stories, Plays/Screenplays, Business/Trade/Industry, Film, Writing/Journalism, Autobiography/Memoirs, Biography, Essays. **Career:** New Yorker, editorial typist, 1974-76; freelance writer, 1976-82, 1987-; University of Southern Mississippi, assistant professor of English, 1978-79; United Research Co., editor and office manager, 1982-84; Warner Brothers, screenwriter, 1984-87; Manhattan Inc., contributing editor, 1985-89; United Artists, screenwriter, 1986-87; Vanity Fair Magazine, contributing editor, 1989-91; Entertainment Weekly Magazine, writer-at-large, 1991-93; New York Magazine, contributing editor, 1993-99; Premier, contributing editor and writer, 1997; Us Weekly Magazine, special correspondent, 2000-; Esquire Magazine, writer; The New York Times Magazine. **Publications:** Pearl's Progress (novel), 1989; The Airport: Terminal Nights and Runway Days at John F. Kennedy International, 1994; The Airport: Planes, People, Triumphs and Disasters at John F. Kennedy International, 1996; Two Guys from Verona: A Novel of Suburbia, 1998; (with J. McEnroe) You Cannot Be Serious, 2002; (with J. Lewis) Dean & Me: (A Love Story), 2005; Frank: The Voice, 2010, vol. II: Sinatra: The Chairman of the Board, 2014. Contributor of articles to magazines. **Address:** c/o Joy Harris, Joy Harris Literary Agency, 156 5th Ave., Ste. 617, New York, NY 10010-7787, U.S.A.

KAPLAN, James Andrew. See **KAPLAN, James.**

KAPLAN, Janet A(nn). American (born United States), b. 1945. **Genres:** Art/Art History, Communications/Media, Cultural/Ethnic Topics, Women's Studies And Issues, Social Commentary, Writing/Journalism, Biography. **Career:** University of Wisconsin, instructor in art history, 1975-76; Franconia College, faculty member and chair of art history department, 1976-78; University of New Hampshire, assistant professor of art history, 1978-79; Moore College of Art, assistant professor, 1980-86, associate professor, 1987-92, chair of liberal arts department, 1989-96, professor of art history, 1993-, program director curatorial studies; National Institute for Women and the Visual Arts, director, 1982-84; Vermont College MFA in Visual Arts, graduate faculty, 1992-; Art Journal, executive editor, 1996-2002; Metropolitan Museum of Art, researcher; National Museum of American Art, researcher. **Publications:** Unexpected Journeys: The Art and Life of Remedios Varo, 1988, 3rd ed., 2000; (contrib.) Philadelphia Art Now: Artists Choose Artists, 1991. Contributor to art catalogs and journals. **Address:** Moore College of Art & Design, 20th St. & The Pkwy., Philadelphia, PA 19103, U.S.A. **Online address:** jkaplan@moore.edu

KAPLAN, Jerry. American (born United States), b. 1952. **Genres:** Business/Trade/Industry, Sciences. **Career:** GO Corp., co-founder and chair, 1987-93; Stanford University, research associate in computer science; Lotus Development Corp., principal technologist; TeKnowledge, co-founder and vice president of business development; ONSALE, chief executive officer. Writer. **Publications:** Startup: A Silicon Valley Adventure, 1995. **Address:** c/o Kris Dahl, International Creative Management, 8942 Wilshire Blvd., Beverly Hills, CA 90211, U.S.A. **Online address:** support@onsale.com

KAPLAN, Jonathan. South African (born South Africa), b. 1954?. **Genres:** Autobiography/Memoirs, Medicine/Health, History, Biography, Young Adult Fiction. **Career:** Writer, physician, documentary filmmaker. **Publications:** The Dressing Station: A Surgeon's Chronicle of War and Medicine, 2002; Contact Wounds: A War Surgeon's Education, 2005. **Address:** c/o Author Mail, Grove/Atlantic Inc., 841 Broadway, Fl. 4, New York, NY 10003, U.S.A.

KAPLAN, Justin. American (born United States), b. 1925. **Genres:** Literary Criticism And History, Biography. **Career:** Simon & Schuster Inc., editor, 1954-59, senior editor; full-time writer, 1959-; Harvard University, lecturer, 1969-70, 1972-73, 1976, 1978; Griffith University, visiting lecturer, 1983; College of the Holy Cross, Jenks professor of contemporary letters, 1992-95. **Publications:** With Malice Toward Women: A Handbook for Women-haters Drawn from the Best Minds of All Time, 1952; Mr. Clemens and Mark Twain: A Biography, 1966; Mark Twain, a Profile, 1967; Lincoln Steffens: A Biography, 1974; Mark Twain and His World, 1974; Walt Whitman: A Life, 1980; Born to Trouble: One Hundred Years of Huckleberry Finn, 1985; (with A. Bernays) The Language of Names, 1997; (with A. Bernays) Back Then: Two Lives in 1950's New York, 2002; (foreword) Bartlett's Shakespeare Quotations, 2005; When the Astors Owned New York: Blue Bloods and Grand Hotels in a Gilded Age, 2006; (intro.) Life on the Mississippi, 2009. EDITOR: (and intro.) Dialogues of Plato, 1950; (and intro.) Great Short Works of Mark Twain, 1967; (and intro.) Great Short Works of Mark Twain, 1967; Best American Essays, 1990; Familiar Quotations: A Collection of Passages, Phrases, and Proverbs Traced to Their Sources in Ancient and Modern Literature, 16th ed., 1992 as Bartlett's Familiar Quotations: A Collection of Passages, Phrases, and Proverbs Traced to Their Sources in Ancient and Modern Literature, 17th ed., 2002; Bartlett's Bible Quotations, 2005; (and intro.) Signet Classic Book of Mark Twain's Short Stories, 2006. Contributor to periodicals. **Address:** Sterling Lord Literistic Inc., 65 Bleecker St., New York, NY 10012-2420, U.S.A.

KAPLAN, Kalman J. American (born United States), b. 1941. **Genres:** Medicine/Health, Psychology, Sciences. **Career:** Northwestern University, Department of Psychology, research assistant, 1962-63, 1965; University of Illinois, Department of Psychology, research assistant, 1963-64, 1966, teaching assistant, 1966, USPHS measurement trainee, 1964-66, College of Medicine, Chicago, adjunct professor, 1992-99, lecturer, 1995-99, clinical professor of psychology, 2000-, Program In Religion, Spirituality And Mental Health, director; Wayne State University, principal investigator, 1969, 1970-74, assistant professor, 1967-73, associate professor, 1973-83, professor of psychology, 1984-, chair of social psychology program, 1979-82, visiting professor, 1984-85, Institute of Gerontology, research associate, 1990; NSF Projects, co-director, 1970-74; Bell Laboratories, Special Communications Research Department, technical staff, 1973-74; Hebrew University of Jerusalem, Center for Cognitive Studies, visitor, 1975; Harvard University, research associate in psychology and social relations, 1977-78; Personal Growth Services, therapist, 1982-84; Jensen Counseling Associates, intern, 1986-88, psychotherapist, 1988-92; Midwestern Educational Resources Center, psychotherapist, 1987-89; Humana Michael Reese Hospital and Medical Center, attending clinical psychologist, 1990-, director of Suicide Research Center, 1994-; Joseph Counseling Services, clinical supervisor, 1990-92; North Shore Center for Behavioral Medicine, psychotherapist, 1992-93; Old Orchard Hospital, attending clinical psychologist, 1992-94; Highland Park Hospital, attending clinical psychologist, 1992-94; Psychological Assessments, co-director, 1994; Tel-Aviv University, visiting lecturer, 2005-06, Fulbright fellow, 2006-07. Writer. **Publications:** (With M.W. Schwartz and M.M. Kaplan) The Family: Biblical and Psychological Foundations, 1984; (contrib.) Metapsychology: Missing Links in Behavior, Mind & Science, 1990; (with M.B. Schwartz) A

Psychology of Hope: An Antidote to the Suicidal Pathology of Western Civilization, 1993; (co-author) Living with Schizophrenia, 1997; TILT: Teaching Individuals to Live Together, 1998; (with M.B. Schwartz) Biblical Stories for Psychotherapy and Counseling: A Sourcebook, 2004; (with M.B. Schwartz) The Seven Habits of the Good Life: How the Biblical Virtues Free Us from the Seven Deadly Sins, 2006; (with M.B. Schwartz) The Fruit of Her Hands: A Psychology of Biblical Woman, 2007; (with M.B. Schwartz) Psychology of Hope: A Biblical Response to Tragedy and Suicide, 2008. EDITOR: (with M.B. Schwartz) Jewish Approaches to Suicide, Martyrdom, and Euthanasia, 1998; Right to Die versus Sacredness of Life, 2000. Contributor to books and journals. **Address:** Department of Psychiatry, University of Illinois, 1601 W Taylor St., 71 W Warren Ave., PO Box 912, Chicago, IL 60612, U.S.A. **Online address:** kalkap@aol.com

KAPLAN, Louise J. American (born United States), b. 1929. **Genres:** Psychology, Adult Non-fiction, Social Sciences. **Career:** Psychoanalyst, 1966-68; Children's Day Treatment Center, chief psychologist, 1966-70; New York University, director of mother-infant research nursery, 1973-77; Margaret S. Mahler Research Foundation, Separation-Individuation Follow-up Study, research associate, 1975-; College of City University of New York, associate professor of psychology and director of child clinical services, 1977-80. Writer. **Publications:** Oneness and Separateness: From Infant to Individual, 1978; Adolescence: The Farewell to Childhhood, 1984; The Family Romance of the Impostor-Poet Thomas Chatterton, 1988; Female Perversions: The Temptations of Emma Bovary, 1991; No Voice Is Ever Wholly Lost, 1995; (ed.) Clinical and Social Realities, 1995; Cultures of Fetishism, 2006. **Address:** 175 W 12th St., New York, NY 10011, U.S.A.

KAPLAN, Marion A. American (born United States), b. 1946. **Genres:** History, Women's Studies And Issues, Translations. **Career:** City University of New York, Queens College, professor of history, 1985-2001; New York University, Skirball Department of Hebrew and Judaic Studies, Skirball professor of modern Jewish history, 2001-, professor of Hebrew and Judaic studies. Writer. **Publications:** Campaign for Women's Suffrage in the Jewish Community in Germany, 1976; Fellowship Guide to Western Europe, 1978; The Jewish Feminist Movement in Germany: The Campaigns of the Jüdischer Frauenbund, 1904-1938, 1979; (trans.) Die Juedische Frauenbewegung in Deutschland: Oganistation und Ziele des Juedischen Frauenbundes, 1904-1938, 1979; The Making of the Jewish Middle Class: Women, Family, and Identity in Imperial Germany, 1991; The Portuguese: The Land and Its People, 1992; Between Dignity and Despair: Jewish Life in Nazi Germany, 1998; Dominican Haven: The Jewish Refugee Settlement in Sosúa, 1940-1945, 2008. EDITOR: (with R. Bridenthal and A. Grossmann) When Biology Became Destiny: Women in Weimar and Nazi Germany, 1984; The Marriage Bargain: Women and Dowries in European History, 1985; (contrib.) Geschichte des Judischen Alltags in Deutschland: Vom 17. Jahrhundert bis, 1945, 2003; Jewish Daily Life in Germany, 1618-1945, 2005; (with B. Meyer and contrib.) Jüdische Welten: Juden in Deutschland vom 18, 2005; (with D.D. Moore) Gender and Jewish History, 2010. **Address:** Skirball Department of Hebrew and Judaic Studies, New York University, 101 Heyman Hall, 51 Washington Sq. S, New York, NY 10012-1075, U.S.A. **Online address:** marionkaplan@yahoo.com

KAPLAN, Mitchell James. American (born United States), b. 1958?. **Genres:** Novels. **Career:** Writer. **Publications:** By Fire, By Water (novel), 2010. **Address:** Mt. Lebanon, PA , U.S.A. **Online address:** mitchell.j.kaplan@mitchelljameskaplan.com

KAPLAN, Morton A. American (born United States), b. 1921. **Genres:** International Relations/Current Affairs, Philosophy, Politics/Government, History, Military/Defense/Arms Control, Social Sciences. **Career:** Ohio State University, instructor in political science, 1951-52; Haverford College, assistant professor of political science, 1953-54; Brookings Institution, Department of International Relations, staff, 1954-55; University of Chicago, assistant professor, 1956-61, associate professor, 1961-65, professor of political science, 1965, Center for Strategic and Foreign Policy Studies, director, 1976, now distinguished service professor emeritus; Princeton University, Center for International Studies, research associate, 1958-62; Yale University, visiting professor, 1961-62; Hudson Institute, consultant, 1961-80; Cetra Music Corp., president, 1962-; Columbia University, visiting professor, 1964, 1966; Braddock, Dunn & McDonald Inc., consultant, 1969, 1972; U.S. Information Agency, consultant, 1972; National Endowment for the Humanities, consultant, 1972-; Army War College, lecturer; Air War College, lecturer; Professors

World Peace Academy Intl., president; The World & I Magazine, publisher. Writer. **Publications:** (With W. Reitzel and C.G. Coblenz) United States Foreign Policy, 1945, 3rd ed. as United States Foreign Policy: 1945-55, 1956; System and Process in International Politics, 1957; Some Problems in the Strategic Analysis of International Politics, 1959; The Strategy of Limited Retaliation, 1959; The Communist Coup in Czechoslovakia, 1960; (with N. Katzenbach) Political Foundations of International Law, 1961; United States Foreign Policy in a Revolutionary Age, 1961; Modernes Völkerrecht: Form oder Mittel der Aussenpolitik, 1965; Macropolitics: Selected Essays on the Philosophy and Science of Politics, 1969, rev. ed., 2005; Dissent and the State in Peace and War: An Essay on the Grounds of Public Morality, 1970; On Historical and Political Knowing: An Inquiry into Some Problems of Universal Law and Human Freedom, 1971; Nixon Initiative and Chinese-American Relations, 1972; On Freedom and Human Dignity: The Importance of the Sacred in Politics, 1973; (co-author) Vietnam Settlement: Why 1973, Not 1969?, 1973; (comp.) Strategic Thinking and Its Moral Implications, 1973; The Rationale for NATO: European Collective Security-Past and Future, 1973; Justice, Human Nature and Political Obligation, 1976; The Life and Death of the Cold War: Selected Studies in Post-War Statecraft, 1976; Alienation and Identification, 1976; Towards Professionalism in International Theory: Macrosystem Analysis, 1979; Science, Language and the Human Condition, 1984; Ethics of Nuclear Strategy, 1984; Bun Senmei, Shisō to tōitsu undō, 1987; Law in a Democratic Society, 1993. EDITOR: (and contrib.) The Revolution in World Politics, 1962; (and contrib.) New Approaches to International Relations, 1968; (and contrib.) Great Issues of International Politics: The International System and National Policy, 1970, 2nd ed., 1974; (and contrib.) SALT: Problems and Prospects, 1973; (and contrib.) NATO and Dissuasion, 1974; (and contrib.) Isolation or Interdependence?: Today's Choices for Tomorrow's World, 1975; (with K. Mushakoji and contrib.) Japan, America, and the Future World Order, 1976; (and contrib.) The Many Faces of Communism, 1978; Japan at the Turning Point: Prospects for the Coming Decade, 1981; Global Policy, Challenge of the '80s, 1984; Consolidating Peace in Europe: A Dialogue between East and West, 1987; The Soviet Union and the Challenge of the Future, 1988-89; (with G.L. Anderson) Morality and Religion in Liberal Democratic Societies, 1992; (with C. Sheffield and M. Alonso) The World of 2044: Technological Development and the Future of Society, 1994; Character and Identity, vol. I, 1998, vol. II, 2000. Contributor to books. **Address:** Department of Political Science, University of Chicago, 406, Pick Hall, 5828 S University Ave., Chicago, IL 60637, U.S.A.

KAPLAN, Nelly. French/Argentine (born Argentina), b. 1936. **Genres:** Novels, Novellas/Short Stories, Plays/Screenplays, Film, Biography, History, Young Adult Fiction. **Career:** Cythere Films, assistant director, 1957-64, director, 1967-. Scriptwriter and actress. **Publications:** SHORT STORIES: Le Réservoir des Sens: Suivi de, La gardienne du temps; 1966; Le Collier de Ptyx, 1971; Un Manteau de Fou-Rire ou les Memoires d'une Liseuse de Draps, 1974; LaGardienne du Temps, 1995; Aux Orchidées Sauvage, 1998. OTHERS: Le Manifested'un Art Nouveau on Magirama, Le Sunlight d'Austerlitz, 1960; Abel Gance's Napoleon (film history), 1994; Ils furent une étrange comète, 2002; Cuisses de grenouille, 2005; Et Pandore en avait deux!: roman; Mon cygne, mon signe (correspondances Abel Gance-Nelly Kaplan), 2008; (with A.P. de Mandiargues) Correspondance, 1962-1991: écris-moi tes hauts faits et tes crimes, 2009. Contributor to periodicals. **Address:** Cythere Films, 34 Ave. des Champs Elysees, Paris, 75008, France.

KAPLAN, Rachel. French (born France) **Genres:** Travel/Exploration. **Career:** National Science Foundation, postdoctoral fellow, 1962-64; University of Michigan, Department of Psychology, lecturer, 1964-77, associate professor, 1977-87, professor of psychology, 1987-, School of Natural Resources and Environment, associate professor, 1973-78, professor, 1978-, Samuel T. Dana professor of environment and behavior, 2000-; Western Australia Forests Department, consultant, 1983; Brookfield Zoo, consultant, 1987; Toledo Museum of Art, consultant, 1990; University of Washington, College of Forest Resources, professor, 1997-; French Links (a tourism service), founder; Logan Simpson Design Inc., consultant, 2003-04. Writer. **Publications:** (Trans.) Manet: Painter of Modern Life, 1995; Little-known Museums in and Around Paris, 1996; Little-known Museums In and Around London, 1997; Little-known Museums In and Around Berlin, 1999; Little-known Museums In and Around Rome, 2000. WITH S. KAPLAN: (ed.) Humanscape: Environments for People, 1978; Cognition and Environment: Functioning in an Uncertain World, 1982; The Experience of Nature: A Psychological Perspective, 1989; (and R.L. Lyan) With People in Mind: Design And Management of Everyday Nature, 1998. Contributor to periodicals. **Address:** School of Natural Resources and Environment, University of Michigan, 3516 Dana Bldg., 440 Church St., Ann Arbor, MI 48109-1041, U.S.A. **Online address:** rkaplan@umich.edu

KAPLAN, Robert B. American (born United States), b. 1929. **Genres:** Language/Linguistics, Speech/Rhetoric. **Career:** University of Oregon, instructor in English, 1957-60; University of Southern California, English Communication Program for Foreign Students, instructor, 1961-62, co-ordinator of program, 1962-63, director of program, 1966-73, assistant professor of English, 1963-65, associate professor of English and linguistics, 1965-73, professor of applied linguistics, 1973-95, professor emeritus, 1995-, Department of Linguistics, chair, 1967-69, 1977-78, associate dean of continuing education, 1973-76, American Language Institute, director, 1986-91; National Association for Foreign Student Affairs, field service consultant, 1966-86, president, 1983-84; Association of Teachers of English as a Second Language, president, 1968; Annual Review of Applied Linguistics, founding editor, editor-in-chief, 1981-90; Meikai University, distinguished visiting professor of applied linguistics, 1998-2000; Current Issues in Language Planning, founding co-editor, 1999-. **Publications:** EDITOR: Reading and Rhetoric, 1963; On the Scope of Applied Linguistics, 1980; (with R.B. Baldauf, Jr.) Language Planning in Malawi, Mozambique and the Philippines, 1999; Oxford Handbook of Applied Linguistics, 2002, 2nd ed., 2010; (with R.B. Baldauf, Jr.) Language Planning and Policy in Africa, 2004; (ed. with R.B. Baldauf, Jr.) Language planning and Policy in Europe, 2005; (with R.B. Baldauf, Jr.) Language Planning and Policy in Latin America, 2007; (with R.B. Baldauf, Jr.) Language Planning and Policy in Asia, 2008. CO-AUTHOR: Transformational Grammar: A Guide for Teachers, 1968; English at Your Fingertips, 1969; Exploring Academic Discourse, 1983; Writing across Languages, 1987; Introduction to Applied Linguistics, 1991; Theory and Practice of Writing, 1996; Language Planning from Practice to Theory, 1997; Language and Language-in-Education Planning in the Pacific Basin, 2002; Africa, vol. I: Botswana, Malawi, Mozambique and South Africa, 2004, vol. II: Algeria, Cote d'Ivoire, Nigeria and Tunisia, 2007; Europe, vol. I: Hungary, Finland and Sweden, 2005, vol. II: The Czech Republic, the European Union and Northern Ireland, 2005, vol. III: The Baltic States, Ireland and Italy, 2007; Pacific, vol. I: Fiji, The Philippines and Vanuatu, 2006; Latin America, vol. I: Ecuador, Mexico and Paraguay, 2007; Asia, vol. I: Japan, Nepal and Taiwan and Chinese Characters, 2008; Language Planning in the Asia Pacific: Hong Kong, Timor-Leste and Sri Lanka, 2011. Contributor to journals. **Address:** PO Box 577, Port Angeles, WA 98362, U.S.A. **Online address:** rkaplan@olypen.com

KAPLAN, Robert S. American (born United States), b. 1940. **Genres:** Administration/Management, Business/Trade/Industry, Economics. **Career:** Carnegie-Mellon University, industrial administration faculty, 1968-84, Graduate School of Industrial Administration, dean, 1977-83; Harvard University, Harvard Business School, faculty, 1984-, Marvin Bower professor of leadership development, Baker Foundation professor. Writer. **Publications:** (With H.T. Johnson) Relevance Lost: The Rise and Fall of Management Accounting, 1991, (with A. Atkinson, E.M. Matsumura and M. Young) Management Accounting, 6th ed., 2011; (ed.) Measures for Manufacturing Excellence, 1992; Measuring Corporate Performance, 1994; (with D. Norton) The Balanced Scorecard: Translating Strategy into Action, 1996; (with R. Cooper) Cost and Effect: Using Integrated Cost Systems to Drive Profitability and Performance, 1998; (with W.J. Salmon and M.K. Dew) The Economics of Variety, 1999; (with D. Norton) The Strategy-Focused Organization: How Balanced Scorecard Companies Thrive in the New Business Environment, 2001; (with D.P. Norton) Strategy Maps: Converting Intangible Assets into Tangible Outcomes, 2004; (with D.P. Norton) Alignment: Using the Balanced Scorecard to Create Corporate Synergies, 2006; (with S.R. Anderson) Time-driven Activity-based Costing: A Simpler and More Powerful Path to Higher Profits, 2007; (with D.P. Norton) The Execution Premium, 2008. Contributor to journals. **Address:** Graduate School of Business Administration, Harvard University, 367 Morgan Hall, Boston, MA 02163, U.S.A. **Online address:** rkaplan@hbs.edu

KAPLAN, Steven L. American (born United States), b. 1943. **Genres:** History, Cultural/Ethnic Topics, Social Sciences, Young Adult Fiction. **Career:** Cornell University, Goldwin Smith Professor of European History; University of Versailles, visiting professor of modern history. Writer. **Publications:** Bread, Politics and Political Economy in the Reign of Louis XV, 1976; (ed. and intro.) La Bagarre: Galiani's Lost Parody, 1979; (ed. with D. LaCapra) Modern European Intellectual History: Reappraisals and New Perspectives, 1982; The Famine Plot Persuasion in Eighteenth-Century France, 1982; Provisioning Paris: Merchants and Millers in the Grain and Flour Trade during the Eighteenth Century, 1984; (ed.) Understanding Popular Culture: Europe from the Middle Ages to the Nineteenth Century, 1984; (ed. with C.J. Koepp) Work in France: Representations, Meaning, Organization and Practice, 1986; (with D. LaCapra) Geschichte Denken: Neubestimmungen und Perspektiven Moderner EuropAischer Geistesgeschichte, 1988; Farewell, Revolution: Disputed Legacies; France, 1789/1989, 1995; Farewell, Revolution: The Historians' Feud; France, 1789/1989, 1995; The Bakers of Paris and the Bread Question, 1700-1775, 1996; Le Meilleur Pain du monde: Les Boulangers de Paris au dix-huitieme siecle, 1996; (ed. with C.M. Couniham) Food and Gender: Identity and Power, 1998; La Fin des corporations, 2001; Le Retour du bon pain: Une Histoire contemporaine du pain, de ses techniques et de ses hommes, 2002; Cherchez le pain: Guide des meilleures boulangeries de Paris, 2004; (ed. with P. Minard) La France, malade du corporatisme? XVIIIe-XXe Siecles, 2004; Good Bread is Back: a Contemporary History of French Bread, the Way It Is Made and the People Who Make It, 2006; (ed. with B. De Munck and H. Soly) Learning on the Shop Floor: Historical Perspectives on Apprenticeship, 2007; Pain maudit: retour sur la France des années oubliées, 1945-1958, 2008; France et son pain: histoire d une passion, 2010. Contributor to books and periodicals. **Address:** Cornell University, 344 McGraw Hall, Ithaca, NY 14853, U.S.A. **Online address:** slk8@cornell.edu

KAPLAN-MAXFIELD, Thomas. American (born United States), b. 1952. **Genres:** Young Adult Fiction, Autobiography/Memoirs, Novels, Novellas/Short Stories. **Career:** KMH Contracting, owner and writer, 1985; Boston College, Department of English, instructor, 1985-, adjunct faculty; Tufts University, instructor; Wang Center for the Performing Arts, teacher of writer-in-residence, 1997-2002. Writer. **Publications:** Memoirs of a Shape-Shifter, 2005; Black Forest Love; The Scarab Chase; Hide & Seek; Brockton Tales; The UMass Murders, The Father, forthcoming. Contributor to periodicals. **Address:** Department of English, Boston College, Carney Hall 331, 140 Commonwealth Ave., Chestnut Hill, MA 02467, U.S.A. **Online address:** thomas.kaplan-maxfield.1@bc.edu

KAPLAR, Richard T. American (born United States), b. 1951. **Genres:** Writing/Journalism, Economics, Money/Finance, Politics/Government, Law, Ethics. **Career:** Writer. **Publications:** Economic Forecasts, Election Years and the Media: A Content Analysis of the Los Angeles Times, Newsweek and NBC News, 1984; The Financial Interest and Syndication Rules: Prime Time for Repeal, 1990; Advertising Rights, the Neglected Freedom: Toward a New Doctrine of Commercial Speech, 1991; (with P.D. Maines) The Government Factor: Undermining Journalistic Ethics in the Information Age, 1995; Cross Ownership at the Crossroads: The Case for Repealing the FCC's Newspaper/Broadcast Cross Ownership Ban, 1997. EDITOR: Beyond the Courtroom: Alternatives for Resolving Press Disputes, 1991; Bad Prescription for the First Amendment: FDA Censorship of Drug Advertising and Promotion, 1993; Speaking Freely: The Public Interest in Unfettered Speech, 1995; The First Amendment and the Media, 1997, rev. ed., 2003. Contributor to periodicals. **Address:** The Media Institute, 2300 Clarendon Blvd., Ste. 503, Arlington, VA 22201, U.S.A. **Online address:** kaplar@mediainstitute.org

KAPLOW, Louis. American (born United States), b. 1956. **Genres:** Economics. **Career:** U.S. Court of Appeals, Second Circuit, law clerk, 1981-82; Harvard University, Harvard Law School, assistant professor, 1982-87, professor, 1987-2004, associate dean for research, 1989-91, John M. Olin Center for Law, Economics, and Business, associate director, Finn M.W. Caspersen and Household International professor of law and Economics, 2004-; U.S. Department of Justice, Anti-trust Division, consultant; Federal Trade Commission, consultant; State of Israel, consultant; American Academy of Arts and Sciences, fellow; National Bureau of Economic Research, research associate. Writer. **Publications:** Antitrust Analysis: Problems, Text, Cases, 1988, 6th ed., 2004; Recovery of Pre-Enactment Basis Under a Consumption Tax: The USA Tax System, 1996; (with S. Shavell) Fairness Versus Welfare, 2002; On The(ir) Relevence of Distribution and Labor Supply Distortion of Government Policy, 2004; The Theory of Taxation and Public Economics, 2008. **Address:** Harvard Law School, Harvard University, Hauser 322, 1563 Massachusetts Ave., Cambridge, MA 02138-2903, U.S.A.

KAPLOW, Robert. American (born United States), b. 1954. **Genres:** Novels, Songs/Lyrics And Libretti, Romance/Historical. **Career:** Journalist and educator. **Publications:** Two in the City, 1979; Alex Icicle: A Romance in Ten Torrid Chapters, 1984; Alessandra in Love, 1989; Alessandra in Between, 1992; The Cat Who Killed Lilian Jackson Braun: A Parody, 2003; Me and Or-

son Welles: A Novel, 2003; Hot, Naked High-school Teachers, 2006; Who's Killing The Great Writers Of America? Who's Killing The Great Writers Of America?, 2007; Nobody's Heart: A Novel About Teachers, forthcoming. Contributor to periodicals. **Address:** Literary and Creative Artists Inc., 3543 Albemarle St. NW, Washington, DC 20008-4213, U.S.A. **Online address:** info.robertkaplow@gmail.com

KAPLOWITZ, Craig A. (Craig Allan Kaplowitz). American (born United States), b. 1970?. **Genres:** Public/Social Administration, Civil Liberties/Human Rights, History, Social Sciences. **Career:** Vanderbilt University, lecturer, 1997-98; Middle Tennessee State University, assistant professor, 1999-2002; Educational Testing Service, consultant, 2001-; Judson University, assistant professor, 2002-03, associate professor, 2004-, professor of history, The Honors Program, director. Writer. **Publications:** LULAC, Mexican Americans, and National Policy, 2005; (contrib.) The Encyclopedia of Activism and Social Justice, 2007. Contributor to journals. **Address:** Department of History, Judson University, 325 Lindner Twr., 1151 N State St., Elgin, IL 60123-1404, U.S.A. **Online address:** ckaplowitz@judsonu.edu

KAPLOWITZ, Craig Allan. See **KAPLOWITZ, Craig A.**

KAPPES, Marcianne. American (born United States), b. 1947. **Genres:** Theology/Religion, Young Adult Fiction. **Career:** Carmelite Sisters of Saint Therese, formation director, 1966-; school teacher, 1968-87; Oklahoma City University, teacher, 1981-84; St. Gregory's University, professor of theology. Writer. **Publications:** Track of the Mystic: The Spirituality of Jessica Powers, 1994. Contributor to periodicals. **Address:** Department of Theology, St. Gregory's University, BH 312 Benedictine, 1900 W MacArthur St., Shawnee, OK 74804, U.S.A. **Online address:** srmarcianne@stgregorys.edu

KAPSIS, Robert E. American (born United States), b. 1943. **Genres:** Film, Human Relations/Parenting, Art/Art History, Biography. **Career:** Brandeis University, assistant director of violence project, 1968-70; City University of New York, Queens College, assistant professor, 1973-78, director of neighborhood delinquency project, 1974-75, faculty retrenchment study, principal investigator, 1976-83, associate professor, 1979-92, Graduate Center, associate professor, 1992, professor, 1993, professor of sociology and film studies, 1993-; University of California, social and political researcher, 1975-77; Columbia University, social and political researcher, 1975-77; Long Island University, adjunct professor, 1992; New School for Social Research, adjunct professor, 1992. Writer. **Publications:** (Co-author) The Reconstruction of a Riot: A Case Study of Community Tensions and Civil Disorder, 1970; Hitchcock: The Making of a Reputation, 1992; (ed. with K. Coblentz) Clint Eastwood: Interviews, 1999; Alfred Hitchcock: A Profile, 1999; (ed. with K. Coblentz) Woody Allen: Interviews, 2006; (ed.) Jonathan Demme: Interviews, 2009; (ed.) Charles Burnett: Interviews, 2011. Contributor to journals. **Address:** Department of Sociology, Queens College, City University of New York, Powdermaker Hall 252H, Flushing, NY 11367, U.S.A. **Online address:** robert.kapsis@qc.cuny.edu

KAPSTEIN, Ethan B. American (born United States), b. 1953. **Genres:** Novels, Politics/Government. **Career:** DELTEC Management Corp., consultant, 1996-99; Harvard University, Cambridge, MA, lecturer in international business, 1984-94, Center for International Affairs, associate, 1984-, Bank of Boston, Boston, MA, Brazil officer, 1984-87; John M. Olin Institute, Economics and National Security Program, director, 1989-94, Leverett House, associate, 1992-; National Institute for Defense Studies, visiting professor, 1994-; Organization for Economic Cooperation and Development (OECD), principal administrator, 1994-95; Council on Foreign Relations, vice president, 1995- 96; University of Minnesota, Stassen professor of international peace, 1996-2001; INSEAD, Fontainebleau, Paul Dubrule professor of sustainable development, 2000-; French Institute for International Relations, research associate, 2001-; German Marshall Fund of the United States, transatlantic fellow, 2003-; Center for Global Development, visiting fellow, 2004-; United States Navy, commander. Writer. **Publications:** The Insecure Alliance: Energy Crises and Western Politics since 1944, 1990; Supervising International Banks: Origins and Implications of the Basle Accord, 1991; (as Ethan Barnaby Kapstein) The Political Economy of National Security: A Global Perspective, 1992; (ed.) Global Arms Production: Policy Dilemmas for the 1990s, 1992; (ed. with R. Vernon) Defense and Dependence in a Global Economy, 1992; (ed.) Downsizing Defense, 1993; Governing the Global Economy: International Finance and the State, 1994; (ed. with M. Mandelbaum) Sustaining the Transition: The Social Safety Net in Postcommunist Europe, 1997; Sharing the Wealth: Workers and the World Economy, 1999; (ed. with M. Mastanduno) Unipolar Politics: Realism and State Strategies after the Cold War, 1999; (with B. Milanovic) Dividing the Spoils: Pensions, Privatization, and Reform in Russia's Transition, 2000; (ed. with B. Milanovic) When Markets Fail: Social Policy and Economic Reform, 2002; (with B. Milanovic) Income and Influence: Social Policy in Emerging Market Economies, 2003; Architects of Stability? International Cooperation among Financial Supervisors, 2006; Economic Justice in an Unfair World: Toward a Level Playing Field, 2006; (with N. Converse) The Fate of Young Democracies, 2009. Contributor to books. **Address:** INSEAD, Boulevard de Constance, Fontainebleau Cedex, 77305, France. **Online address:** ethan.kapstein@insead.edu

KAPUR, Manju. Indian (born India), b. 1948?. **Genres:** Novels, Women's Studies And Issues. **Career:** Delhi University, instructor, Miranda House College, professor of English literature. Writer. **Publications:** Difficult Daughters, 1998; A Married Woman, 2002; Home, 2006; The Immigrant, 2008; Custody, 2011. **Address:** Publicity Department, Penguin Putnam, 375 Hudson St., New York, NY 10014, U.S.A.

KARAMITROGLOU, Fotios. Greek (born Greece), b. 1971. **Genres:** Language/Linguistics, Business/Trade/Industry. **Career:** University of Manchester, Institute of Science and Technology, teaching assistant, 1997-98; Hellenic Telecommunications Organization, English language teacher, 1998-99; National and Kapodistrian University of Athens, lecturer in translation methodology, 1998-2002; European Educational Organization, lecturer in translation theory and practice, 1999-2001; Deluxe Digital Studios, freelance subtitler, 2001-; Athens University of Economics and Business, lecturer in business terminology, 2002-; Aristotle University of Thessaloniki, lecturer in audiovisual translation, 2003-04. Writer. **Publications:** Towards a Methodology for the Investigation of Norms in Audiovisual Translation, 2000; Essential Business Terminology for Native Speakers of Greek, 2008. Contributor to periodicals. **Address:** Athens University of Economics and Business, Patission 76, Athens, 104 34, Greece. **Online address:** karamitr@aueb.gr

KARASIK, Paul. American (born United States), b. 1956?. **Genres:** Cartoons, Novels. **Career:** Packer Collegiate, School of Visual Arts, instructor in cartooning; Scuola de Comics, instructor in cartooning; Bad News, publisher; RAW Magazine, associate editor; Rhode Island School of Design, faculty; School of Visual Arts, faculty. Writer. **Publications:** (With D. Mazzucchelli) Paul Auster's City of Glass, 1994; The Ride Together: A Brother and Sister's Memoir of Autism in the Family, 2003; (ed. with J. Carlin and B. Walker) Masters of American Comics, 2005; (ed.) I Shall Destroy All the Civilized Planets, 2007. Illustrator of books by L. Treat. **Address:** c/o Author Mail, Picador Publishers, 175 5th Ave., New York, NY 10010, U.S.A. **Online address:** pkarasik@risd.edu

KARAYIANNI, Lori. (Tori Carrington). American (born United States) **Genres:** Romance/Historical, Novels. **Career:** Freelance writer, 1984-. **Publications:** NOVELS WITH T. KARAYIANNI AS TORI CARRINGTON: Constant Craving, 1998; License to Thrill, 1999; The P.I. Who Loved Her, 2000; For Her Eyes Only, 2000; Just Eight Months Old, 2000; The Woman for Dusty Conrad, 2001; You Only Love Once, 2001; Never Say Never Again, 2001; You Sexy Thing!, 2001; What a Woman Wants, 2002; Private Investigations, 2002; Skin Deep, 2002; A Stranger's Touch, 2002; Every Move You Make, 2002; Fire and Ice, 2002; Flavor of the Month, 2003; Red-Hot and Reckless, 2003; Just between Us, 2003; Going Too Far, 2003; Night Fever, 2003; Forbidden, 2004; (with R. Nelson) The Sex Diet, 2004; (with A. McAllister) Marry Me... Maybe?, 2004; Total Exposure, 2004; (with J. Wayne and J. Christenberry) Private Scandals, 2004; (with A. McCallister) By Request, 2004; (with S. Woods) Where You Least Expect It, 2004; Indecent, 2004; Wicked, 2004; (with J. Denison and L. Kelly) That's Amore, 2005; Sofie Metropolis, 2005; Possession, 2005; A Real McCoy, 2005; (co-author) More than Words, vol. III, 2006; (with J. Denison and L. Kelly) Wedding Fever, 2006; Dirty Laundry: A Sofie Metropolis Novel, 2006; Seducing McCoy, 2006; Submission, 2006; Obsession, 2006; Foul Play: A Sofie Metropolis Novel, 2007; Taken, 2007; Dangerous, 2007; Working Stiff: A Sofie Metropolis Novel, 2008; Shameless, 2008; Restless, 2008; Reckless, 2008; A Few Good Men, 2009; Branded, 2009; Unbridled, 2009; Private Affairs, 2010; Private Sessions, 2010; Love Bites, 2010. OTHERS: (with T. Weber) Blazing Bedtime Stories, vol. III, 2010; Reckless Pleasures, 2011; Wicked Pleasures, 2011; Undeniable Pleasures, 2011; Shiver, 2011; Red-Hot Santa, 2011. Contributor to periodicals. **Address:** c/o Robert Gottlieb, Trident Media Group L.L.C., 41 Madison Ave., 36th Fl., New York, NY 10010-2257, U.S.A. **Online address:** toricarrington@aol.com

KARAYIANNI, Tony. (Tori Carrington). American/Greek (born Greece) **Genres:** Novels, Romance/Historical. **Career:** Freelance writer, 1984-. **Publications:** NOVELS WITH L. KARAYIANNI AS TORI CARRINGTON: Constant Craving, 1999; License to Thrill, 1999; The P.I. Who Loved Her, 2000; For Her Eyes Only, 2000; Just Eight Months Old, 2000; The Woman for Dusty Conrad, 2001; You Only Love Once, 2001; Never Say Never Again, 2001; You Sexy Thing!, 2001; What a Woman Wants, 2002; Private Investigations, 2002; Skin Deep, 2002; A Stranger's Touch, 2002; Every Move You Make, 2002; Fire and Ice, 2002; Flavor of the Month, 2003; Red-Hot and Reckless, 2003; Just Between Us, 2003; Going Too Far, 2003; Night Fever, 2003; Forbidden, 2004; (with R. Nelson) The Sex Diet, 2004; Total Exposure, 2004; (with J. Wayne and J. Christenberry) Private Scandals, 2004; (with A. McCallister) By Request, 2004; Marry Me...Maybe?, 2004; Where You Least Expect It, 2004; (with J. Denison and L. Kelly) That's Amore, 2005; Sofie Metropolis, 2005; Wicked, 2004; Possession, 2005; A Real McCoy, 2005; From McCoy, with Love (includes The P.I. Who Loved Her and For Her Eyes Only), 2005; Indecent, 2004; (co-author) More than Words, vol. III, 2006; Dirty Laundry: A Sofie Metropolis Novel, 2006; Submission, 2006; Seducing McCoy (contains You Only Love Once and Never Say Never Again), 2006; Obsession, 2006; Foul Play: A Sofie Metropolis Novel, 2007; Taken, 2007; Dangerous, 2007; Working Stiff: A Sofie Metropolis Novel, 2008; Shameless, 2008; Restless, 2008; Reckless, 2008; A Few Good Men, 2009; Branded, 2009; Unbridled, 2009. OTHERS: (with T. Weber) Blazing Bedtime Stories, vol. III, 2010; Reckless Pleasures, 2011; Wicked Pleasures, 2011; Love Bites, 2011; Undeniable Pleasures, 2011; Shiver, 2011; Red-Hot Santa, 2011. **Address:** c/o Robert Gottlieb, Trident Media Group, 41 Madison Ave., 36th Fl., New York, NY 10010, U.S.A. **Online address:** karayianni@aol.com

KARCH, Andrew. American (born United States), b. 1975. **Genres:** Politics/Government, Social Sciences, International Relations/Current Affairs. **Career:** University of Texas, Department of Government, assistant professor, 2003-09, associate professor, 2009-10; University of Minnesota, Department of Political Science, Arleen C. Carlson associate professor, 2010-. Writer. **Publications:** Democratic Laboratories: Policy Diffusion among the American States, 2007. Contributor of articles to journals. **Address:** Department of Government, University of Texas, A1800, 1 University Sta., Austin, TX 78712-0119, U.S.A. **Online address:** akarch@mail.utexas.edu

KAREM, Jeff. American (born United States), b. 1973. **Genres:** Literary Criticism And History, Young Adult Fiction. **Career:** Cleveland State University, College of Liberal Arts and Social Sciences, Department of English, assistant professor of English, associate professor of English. Writer. **Publications:** The Romance of Authenticity: The Cultural Politics of Regional and Ethnic Literatures, 2004; The Purloined Islands: Caribbean-U.S. Crosscurrents in Literature and Culture, 1880-1959, 2011. **Address:** Department of English, College of Liberal Arts and Social Sciences, Cleveland State University, RT 1844, 2121 Euclid Ave., Cleveland, OH 44115-2214, U.S.A. **Online address:** f.karem@csuohio.edu

KARETZKY, Patricia E(ichenbaum). American (born United States), b. 1947. **Genres:** Art/Art History, Theology/Religion. **Career:** New York University, Washington Square College, adjunct lecturer, 1976-79, adjunct assistant professor of fine arts, 1979-87; Fordham University, lecturer, 1988; Bard College, Oskar Munsterberg lecturer in art history and Oskar Munsterberg chair of Asian art, 1988-, Graduate School of Decorative Arts, adjunct, 1997-98; Metropolitan Museum of Art, curatorial research assistant in Asian art, 1989-90; School of Visual Arts, lecturer, 1991; Journal of Chinese Religions, assistant editor, co-editor and editor, 1991-98; Sarah Lawrence College, faculty, 1992-93; City University of New York, Herbert H. Lehman College, adjunct professor of art history, 1994-. **Publications:** The Life of the Buddha: Ancient Scriptural and Pictorial Traditions, 1992; Court Art of the Tang, 1996; Arts of the Tang Court, 1996; Early Buddhist Narrative Art: Illustrations of the Life of the Buddha from Central Asia to China, Korea, and Japan, 2000; Chinese Buddhist Art, 2002; Guanyin, 2004. Contributor to journals. **Address:** Department of Asian Studies, Bard College, PO Box 5000, Annandale-on-Hudson, NY 12504-5000, U.S.A. **Online address:** karetzky@bard.edu

KARETZKY, Stephen. American (born United States), b. 1946. **Genres:** Librarianship, Writing/Journalism. **Career:** Brooklyn Public Library, librarian, 1969-70; State University of New York-Buffalo, assistant professor of library and information studies, 1974-76; State University of New York-Geneseo, assistant professor of library and information studies, 1977-78; Haifa University, associate professor of library and information studies, 1978-81; Shapolsky/Steimatzky Publishers, senior editor, 1981-82; San Jose State University, associate professor of library and information studies, 1982-85; Shapolsky Publishers, senior editor, 1985-86; Americans for a Safe Israel, executive director, 1985-86; Felician College, associate professor and director of library, 1986-, now professor emeritus. **Publications:** Reading Research and Librarianship: A History and Analysis, 1982; The Cannons of Journalism, 1984; Not Seeing Red: American Librarianship and the Soviet Union, 1917-1960, 2002. EDITOR: (with P.E. Goldman) The Media's War against Israel, 1986; (with N. Frankel) The Media's Coverage of the Arab-Israeli Conflict, 1989. Contributor of articles to periodicals. **Address:** Felician College, 262 S Main St., Lodi, NJ 07644-2117, U.S.A. **Online address:** karetzkys@felician.edu

KARI, Daven M(ichael). American (born United States), b. 1953. **Genres:** Poetry, Literary Criticism And History, Theology/Religion, Bibliography, Business/Trade/Industry. **Career:** Boys Brigade, founder and co-director, 1969-71; Linden First Baptist Church, assistant pastor, 1971; Baylor University, part-time faculty, 1978-79; Purdue University, part-time faculty, 1979-85; Calvary Baptist Church, founder and director of singles ministry, 1983-85; Spalding University, part-time faculty, 1986-90; University of Louisville, part-time faculty, 1986-90, assistant, 1988-89; Jefferson Community College, part-time faculty, 1986-90; Lindsey Wilson College, part-time faculty, 1989; Missouri Baptist College, assistant professor, 1991-; California Baptist University, professor, 1991-98, Christian Ministry Center, director, 1991-98, The Banner, co-faculty adviser, 1993-96; Magnolia Avenue Baptist Church, teacher, 1994; Washington Bible College, academic dean, 1998-2000; Baptist Christian School, administrator and principal, 2000-01; Westwood Technical College, part-time faculty, 2002; Chapman University, part-time faculty, 2002; Vanguard University, Department of English, professor of English, 2002-, chair, 2006-07; Golden Gate Baptist Theological Seminary, part-time faculty, 2005-. Writer. **Publications:** T.S. Eliot's Dramatic Pilgrimage: A Progress in Craft as an Expression of Christian Perspective, 1990; A Bibliography of Sources in Christianity and the Arts, 1995. EDITOR: (with D.M. Rayburn and D.G. Gwaltney) Baptist Reflections on Christianity and the Arts: Learning from Beauty, 1997. Contributor of articles to books and periodicals. **Address:** Department of English, Vanguard University, 55 Fair Dr., Costa Mesa, CA 92626-6597, U.S.A. **Online address:** dkari@vanguard.edu

KARIER, Thomas. American (born United States), b. 1956. **Genres:** Economics, History, Business/Trade/Industry. **Career:** Eastern Washington University, professor of economics, 1981-, associate dean, 1995-98; The Levy Economics Institute of Bard College Blithewood, research associate. **Publications:** Beyond Competition: The Economics of Mergers and Monopoly Power, 1993; Great Experiments in American Economic Policy: From Kennedy to Reagan, 1997; Intellectual Capital: Forty Years of The Nobel Prize in Economics, 2010. **Address:** Eastern Washington University, N 501 Riverpoint Blvd., Ste. 425, Spokane, WA 99202, U.S.A. **Online address:** thomas.karier@mail.ewu.edu

KARKALA, John A. (John B. Alphonso-Karkala). American/Indian (born India), b. 1923. **Genres:** Novels, Poetry, Genealogy/Heraldry, Literary Criticism And History, Bibliography, Biography. **Career:** Columbia University, teaching fellow, 1962-64, visiting professor of Oriental humanities, 1969-70; City University of New York, City College, visiting lecturer, 1963; State University of New York, assistant professor, 1964-65, associate professor, 1965-68, professor of literature, 1969-98, visiting professor, 1969-70, professor emeritus, 1999-; UNESCO Associated School and Colleges, curriculum consultant, 1976-77. Writer. **Publications:** AS JOHN B. ALPHONSO-KARKALA: Indo-English Literature in the Nineteenth Century, 1970; Comparative World Literature, 1974; Passions of the Nightless Nights (novel), 1974; Jawaharlal Nehru: A Literary Portrait, 1975; (with L. Karkala) Indo-English Literature: Essays, 1994. OTHERS: (with L. Karkala) Bibliography of Indo-English Literature: A Checklist of Works by Indian Authors in English, 1800-1966, 1974; Studies in Comparative Literature: Essays, 1974; (with L. Karkala) When Night Falls (verse), 1980; (with L. Karkala) Teisko Ancestry: Record of Six Generations (Finland), 2001; St. Joseph's Higher Primary School: Origin Chronology, 2005; Kurngaje Santan: Record of Six Generations (India), 2008. EDITOR: An Anthology of Indian Literature: Selections from Vedas to Tagore, 1971, rev. ed., 1987; Vedic Vision, 1980. Contributor of articles to journals. **Address:** Department of English and World Literature, State University of New York, 1 Hawk Dr., New Paltz, NY 12561, U.S.A. **Online address:** jakarkala@aol.com

KARKAZIS, Katrina. American (born United States), b. 1970?. **Genres:** Medicine/Health. **Career:** Writer. **Publications:** Fixing Sex: Intersex, Medical Authority, and Lived Experience, 2008. Contributor to periodicals. **Address:** Center for Biomedical Ethics, Stanford University, 701 Welch Rd., Ste. A1105, Palo Alto, CA 94304, U.S.A. **Online address:** karkazis@stanford.edu

KARL, M. S. See SHUMAN, Malcolm K.

KARLE, Hellmut (William Arthur). French/German (born Germany), b. 1932. **Genres:** Psychology, Biography. **Career:** Aycliffe Hospital, clinical psychologist, 1954-56; North Wales Child Guidance Service, clinical psychologist, 1956-60; East Sussex County Council, educational psychologist, 1960-70; Royal College of Midwives, visiting lecturer, 1963-78; Brighton Polytechnic, part-time lecturer, 1963-78; University of Sussex, field tutor, 1966-70; Lingfield Hospital School, educational psychologist, 1970-72; Medway and Maidstone College of Technology, part-time lecturer, 1970-76; Guy's Hospital, Department of Child and Adolescent Psychiatry, principal psychologist, 1972-90, Linbury Research Project, director, 1981-86, Child Psychology Services, acting head, 1990-91. Writer. **Publications:** (With J.H. Boys) Hypnotherapy: A Practical Handbook, 1987; Hypnosis and Hypnotherapy: A Patient's Guide, 1988; Thorson's Introductory Guide to Hypnotherapy: What It Is, How It Works, Where to Go for Hypnotherapy, 1992; The Filthy Lie: Discovering and Recovering from Childhood Sexual Abuse, 1992. Works appear in anthologies. **Address:** Free Association Books, 57 Warren St., London, GL W1T 5NR, England.

KARLEN, Neal (Stuart). American (born United States), b. 1959. **Genres:** Music, Songs/Lyrics And Libretti, Adult Non-fiction, Sports/Fitness, Ethics, History, Language/Linguistics, Philosophy, Popular Culture, Writing/Journalism, Adult Non-fiction. **Career:** Newsweek, staff writer and reporter, 1982-86; Rolling Stone, contributing editor, 1986-91; CBS News/America Tonight, on-air essayist, 1990; Minneapolis-St. Paul Magazine, columnist, 1990-; New York Times, contract writer, 1990-; University of Minnesota, School of Journalism and Mass Communications, instructor of writing and magazine production, 1997-2005. English, Literature and Language, teaching specialist; British Broadcasting Corp., documentary correspondent. **Publications:** (With H. Youngman) Take My Life, Please, 1991; Babes in Toyland: The Making and Selling of a Rock and Roll Band, 1994; (with N. Donnellan) The Babe in Boyland: The Fabulous Sports Babe, 1995; (with J. McCarthy) Jen-X: Jenny McCarthy's Open Book, 1997; Slouching Toward Fargo: A Two-Year Saga of Sinners and St. Paul Saints at the Bottom of the Bush Leagues with Bill Murray, Darryl Strawberry, Dakota Sadie and Me, 1999; Shanda: The Making and Breaking of a Self-Loathing Jew, 2004; The Story of Yiddish: How a Mish-mosh of Languages Saved the Jews, 2008. Works appear in anthologies. Contributor to periodicals. **Address:** 2315 Irving Ave., Ste. 8, Minneapolis, MN 55405, U.S.A. **Online address:** karle019@umn.edu

KARLIN, Daniel. British (born England), b. 1953. **Genres:** Literary Criticism And History, Biography, Young Adult Fiction. **Career:** Boston University, affiliate faculty, 2005-, university professor, professor of English. Writer. **Publications:** The Courtship of Robert Browning and Elizabeth Barrett, 1985; Browning's Hatreds, 1993; (with J. Woolford) Robert Browning, 1996; Proust's English, 2005. EDITOR: (intro.) The Jungle Books, 1987; Browning: Selected Poetry, 1989; Robert Browning and Elizabeth Barrett: The Courtship Correspondence, 1845-1846, 1989; The Courtship Correspondence 1845-1846, 1990; (with J. Woolford) The Poems of Robert Browning, 1991; (intro.) She, 1991; (intro.) Penguin Book of Victorian Verse, 1998; (intro.) Rudyard Kipling, 1999; (intro.) Robert Browning: The Major Works, 2005; (intro.) Rubáiyát of Omar Khayyám, 2009; (intro.) Major Works, 2009. Contributor of articles to periodicals. **Address:** University Professors, Boston University, 745 Commonwealth Ave., 1 Silber Way, Boston, MA 02215, U.S.A. **Online address:** dkarlin@bu.edu

KARLIN, Wayne (Stephen). American (born United States), b. 1945. **Genres:** Novels, Novellas/Short Stories, Autobiography/Memoirs, History, Travel/Exploration, Literary Criticism And History, Military/Defense/Arms Control. **Career:** Gannett Newspapers, reporter for the reporter dispatch, 1972; First Casualty Press, president and co-editor, 1972-73; American College, instructor in creative writing and director of student activities, 1973-75; Jewish Community Center, director of youth programs, 1976-77; Montgomery College, instructor in English, 1982-84; College of Southern Maryland, Department of Languages and Literature, professor, 1984-, coordinator, Connections Literary Readings Series, coordinator; University of Massachusetts, visiting writer and faculty of Joiner Center for the Study of War and Social Consequences, 1989-93; St. Mary's College, Literary Festival, fiction director, 1994-. Writer. **Publications:** NOVELS: Crossover, 1984; Lost Armies, 1988; The Extras, 1989; US, 1993; Prisoners, 1998; The Wished-For Country, 2002; Marble Mountain, 2008. NON-FICTION: Rumors and Stones: A Journey, 1996; War Movies: Scenes and Out-Takes, 2005; Wandering Souls: Journeys with the Dead and the Living in Viet Nam, 2009; (adaptor and intro.) Insignificant Family: A Novel, 2009. TRANSLATOR: (with P.T. Hao and C. Bacchi) Ho Anh Thai, Women on the Island: A Novel, 2000; (adaptor with P.T. Hao) Ma Van Khang, Against the Flood, 2000; (and adaptor with P.T. Hao) Nguyen Khai, Past Continuous, 2001; (co-author) The Cemetery of Chua Village and Other Stories, 2005. EDITOR: (co-ed. and contrib.) Free Fire Zone: Short Stories by Vietnam Veterans, 1973; (co-ed.and contrib.) The Other Side of Heaven: Postwar Fiction by Vietnamese and American Writers, 1995; The Stars, the Earth, the River: Short Fiction byLe Minh Khue, 1997; Behind the Red Mist: Fiction, 1998; (with H.A. Thai) Love after War: Contemporary Fiction from Vietnam, 2003. Works appear in anthologies. Contributor to journals. **Address:** Languages and Literature Division, College of Southern Maryland, Rm. C-313, 8730 Mitchell Rd., PO Box 910, La Plata, MD 20646-0910, U.S.A. **Online address:** waynek@csmd.edu

KARMILOFF-SMITH, Annette Dionne. British/French (born France), b. 1938. **Genres:** Language/Linguistics, Psychology, Education, Reference. **Career:** American University of Beirut, UNWRA/UNESCO Institute of Education, associate in psychology and research consultant, 1970-72; International Centre for Genetic Epistemology, research collaborator, 1972-79; Geneva University, director of studies, 1979-80; Max Planck Institute, research associate, 1979-82; University of Sussex, honorary professorial fellow in cognitive science, 1979-81; University of California, Sloan fellow in cognitive science, 1981; Medical Research Council, Cognitive Development Unit, senior scientist, 1982-98; Universite Libre de Bruxelles, visiting professor, 1985, Max-Planck Institute for Psychiatry, visiting professor, 1986; University of Chicago, visiting professor, 1987; University of Barcelona, visiting professor, 1988; Carnegie-Mellon University, visiting professor, 1991-92; University of Madrid, visiting professor, 1994; Institute of Child Health, professor and head of neurocognitive development Unit, 1998-2006; Academy of Medical Sciences, fellow, 1999; University of London, School of Psychology, Developmental Neurocognition Laboratory, professor, 2006-, Centre for Brain and Cognitive Development, professorial research fellow; British Museum, consultant; BBC-TV, consultant; Salk Institute for Biological Studies, consultant. Writer. **Publications:** A Functional Approach to Child Language: A Study of Determiners and Reference, 1979; (with W.M. Levelt and A. Mills) Child Language Research in ESF Countries, 1981; Beyond Modularity: A Developmental Perspective on Cognitive Science, 1992; Baby It's You, 1994; (with J. Elman and others) Rethinking Innateness; (with K. Karmiloff) Everything Your Baby Would Ask, if Only Heor She Could Talk, 1999; (with K. Karmiloff) Pathways to Language: From Fetus to Adolescent, 2001; (with T. Nazzi and A. Gopnik) Asynchrony in the Cognitive and Lexical Development of Young Children with Williams Syndrome, 2005; (with R. Mackinlay and T. Charman) High Functioning Children with Autistic Spectrum Disorder: A Novel Test of Multi-tasking, 2006; Modules, Genes and Evolution: What have We Learned from Atypical Development?, 2006; (with M. Elsabbagh) Modularity of Mind and Language, 2006; Ontogeny, Genetics and Evolution: A Perspective from Developmental Cognitive Neuroscience, 2006; The Tortuous Route from Genes to Behaviour: A Neuroconstructivist Approach, 2006.Contributor of articles to journals. Works appear in anthologies. **Address:** Centre for Brain and Cognitive Development, School of Psychology, University of London, Rm. 102, 32 Torrington Sq., Birkbeck, ES WC1E 7HX, England. **Online address:** a.karmiloff-smith@bbk.ac.uk

KARNICKY, Jeffrey. American (born United States) **Genres:** Adult Nonfiction, Literary Criticism And History. **Career:** Millersville University, Department of English, assistant professor; Drake University, College of Arts and Sciences, Department of English, visiting assistant professor of English, associate professor. Writer. **Publications:** (Contrib.) Charles Dickens' A Tale of Two Cities, 1994; Contemporary Fiction and the Ethics of Modern Culture, 2007. Contributor to periodicals. **Address:** Department of English, College of Arts and Sciences, Drake University, 316 Howard Hall, 2505 University Ave., Des Moines, IA 50311, U.S.A. **Online address:** jeffrey.karnicky@drake.edu

KARNOW, Stanley. American (born United States), b. 1925. **Genres:** History, Military/Defense/Arms Control, Photography, Translations, Biography, Autobiography/Memoirs. **Career:** Time Magazine, correspondent, 1950-57, chief correspondent, bureau chief-North Africa, 1958-59, Hong Kong bureau chief, 1959-62; Life Magazine, chief correspondent and bureau chief-North Africa, 1958-59, Hong Kong bureau chief, 1959-62; London Observer, correspondent, 1961-65; Time Inc., special correspondent, 1962-63; Saturday Evening Post, correspondent, 1963-65; Washington Post, correspondent, 1965-71, diplomatic correspondent, 1971-72; Harvard University, John F. Kennedy School of Government, Institute of Politics, fellow, 1970-71, East Asian Research Center, fellow, 1970-71; National Broadcasting Corp. (NBC), special correspondent, 1972-73; New Republic, associate editor, 1973-75; Register and Tribune Syndicate, syndicated columnist, 1974-85; King Features, columnist, 1975-87; correspondent for public television, 1975-; International Writers Service, editor-in-chief, 1975-86; Le Point, columnist, 1976-83; Newsweek Intl., columnist, 1978-85. **Publications:** Southeast Asia, 1962; Bitter Seeds: A Farmer's Story of the Revolution in China, 1964; Mao and China: From Revolution to Revolution, 1972, 3rd ed. as Mao and China: A Legacy of Turmoil, 1990; (trans. and intro.) Y. Ming-le, The Conspiracy and Death of Lin Biao, 1983; Vietnam: The War Nobody Won, 1983; Vietnam: A Television History, 1983; Vietnam: A History, 1983, rev. ed., 1997; In Our Image: America's Empire in the Philippines, 1989; (with N. Yoshihara) Asian Americans in Transition, 1992; Paris in the Fifties, 1997; (intro.) The First Time I Saw Paris: Photographs and Memories from the City of Light, 1999; (contrib.) Shaggy Six: Tribute to a Fallen Soldier, 2007. Contributor to periodicals. **Address:** Random House Inc., 201 E 50th St., New York, NY 10022-7703, U.S.A.

KARODIA, Farida. Canadian/South African (born South Africa), b. 1942?. **Genres:** Novels, Novellas/Short Stories, Young Adult Fiction, Mythology/Folklore. **Career:** Writer and educator. **Publications:** NOVELS: Daughters of the Twilight, 1986; A Shattering of Silence, 1993; Other Secrets, 2000; Boundaries, 2003; Tiger Moon, forthcoming. SHORT STORIES: Coming Home and Other Stories, 1988; Against an African Sky and Other Stories, 1995. Works appear in anthologies. **Address:** c/o Author Mail, Penguin Books, 24 Sturdee Ave., Rosebank, PO Box 9, Parklands, Johannesburg, 2196, South Africa. **Online address:** fklll@telkomsa.net

KARON, Jan. American (born United States), b. 1937. **Genres:** Novels, inspirational/Motivational Literature, Young Adult Fiction, Children's Fiction. **Career:** Copywriter and novelist. **Publications:** MITDFORD SERIES: At Home in Mitford, 1994, 2nd ed., 2005; A Light in the Window, 1995, 2nd ed., 2005; These High, Green Hills, 1996; Out to Canaan, 1997; A New Song, 1999; A Common Life: The Wedding Story, 2001; In This Mountain, 2002; Shepherds Abiding: A Mitford Christmas Story, 2003; Light from Heaven, 2005. MITFORD GIFT BOOKS: The Mitford Snowmen: A Christmas Story, 2001; Patches of Godlight: Father Tim's Favorite Quotes, 2001; Esther's Gift: A Mitford Christmas Story, 2002; The Trellis and the Seed: A Book of Encouragement for All Ages, 2003; The Mitford Cookbook and Kitchen Reader, 2004; (ed. with B. Furman) The Mitford Bedside Companion, 2006. NOVELS: Miss Fannie's Hat, 1998; Jeremy: The Tale of an Honest Bunny, 2000; The Wedding, 2005; Home to Holly Springs: The First of the Father Tim Novels, 2007. COLLECTIONS: (comp.) A Continual Feast: Words of Comfort and Celebration Collected by Father Tim, 2005; The Jan Karon Story Hour, 2005. OTHERs: (co-author) A Southern Style Christmas, 2000; The Mitford Years, 2001; Father Timothy A. Kavanaugh, 2001; (foreword) Never Let It End: Poems of a Lifelong Love, 2001; (comp. and contrib.) Cynthia Coppersmith's Violet Comes to Stay: A Mitford Storybook, 2006; In the Company of Others, 2010. Contributor to periodicals. **Address:** Viking Publicity, Penguin Group USA, 375 Hudson St., New York, NY 10014, U.S.A. **Online address:** support@mitfordbooks.com

KARP, David A(llen). American (born United States), b. 1944. **Genres:** Social Sciences, Psychology. **Career:** Boston College, assistant professor, 1971-76, associate professor, 1977-82, professor of sociology, 1983-, Department of Sociology, assistant chair, 1992-95, Undergraduate Honors Program, director. Writer. **Publications:** Being Urban: A Social Psychological View of City Life, 1977; (co-author) The Research Craft: An Introduction to Social-Science Methods, 1977; Symbols, Selves, and Society: Understanding Interaction, 1979; (with W.C. Yoels) Experiencing the Life Cycle: A Social Psychology of Aging, 1982; The Burden of Sympathy, 1984; Sociology and Everyday Life, 1986, 3rd ed., 2004; (with G.P. Stone and W.C. Yoels) Being Urban: A Sociology of City Life, 1991; Experiencing the Life Cycle: A Social Psychology of Aging, 1993; Speaking of Sadness: Depression, Disconnection, and the Meanings of Illness, 1996; The Burden of Sympathy: How Families Cope with Mental Illness, 2001; Is It Me Or My Meds?: Living with

Antidepressants, 2006; The Research Imagination: Qualitative And Quantitative Approaches, 2007; (ed. with G.E. Sisson) Voices from the Inside: Readings on the Experiences of Mental Illness, 2010. Contributor to periodicals. **Address:** Department of Sociology, Boston College, McGuinn Hall 426B, 140 Commonwealth Ave., Chestnut Hill, MA 02467, U.S.A. **Online address:** karp@bc.edu

KARP, Larry. American (born United States), b. 1939. **Genres:** Novels, Mystery/Crime/Suspense, Technology, History, Music, Medicine/Health, Race Relations, Adult Non-fiction, Antiques/Furnishings. **Career:** University of Washington, Prenatal Diagnosis Center, founder, 1972; Swedish Hospital, Department of Perinatal Medicine, founder, 1982; writer, 1995-. **Publications:** Genetic Engineering: Threat or Promise?, 1976; The View from the Vue, 1977; The Enchanted Ear: Or Lured into the Music Box Cosmos, 1996; The Music Box Murders, 1999; Scamming The Birdman, 2000; The Midnight Special, 2001; First, Do No Harm, 2004; The Ragtime Kid, 2006; The King of Ragtime, 2008; The Ragtime Fool, 2010; A Perilous Conception, 2011. **Address:** Poisoned Pen Press, 6962 E 1st Ave., Ste. 103, Scottsdale, AZ 85251, U.S.A. **Online address:** larry@larrykarp.com

KARPELES, Eric. American (born United States), b. 1955?. **Genres:** Art/Art History. **Career:** Writer, painter and art critic. **Publications:** Paintings in Proust: A Visual Companion to In Search of Lost Time, 2008. **Address:** Bolinas, CA , U.S.A. **Online address:** ek@paintingsinproust.com

KARR, Kathleen. American (born United States), b. 1946. **Genres:** Romance/Historical, Children's Fiction, Young Adult Fiction, Novels. **Career:** Barrington High School, English and speech teacher, 1968-69; Providence College, lecturer, 1969-70; Rhode Island Historical Society Film Archives, curator, 1970-71, faculty, 1971; American Film Institute, archives assistant, 1971-72, catalog staff, 1972-; University of Rhode Island, lecturer, 1971-; University of Maryland, lecturer, 1972-; Catholic University of America, lecturer, 1973-77; Washington Circle Theater Corp., general manager, 1973-78; New Line Presentations Lecture Bureau, lecturer, 1974-76; George Washington University, assistant professor, 1979-, 1980-81; Circle/Showcase Theaters, advertising director, 1979-83, director of public relations, 1984-88; American Film Institute, lecturer, 1979-80; Trinity College, lecturer, 1985-86, 1995-; Circle Management Co./Circle Releasing, public relations staff, 1988-93. Writer. **Publications:** EDITOR: The American Film Heritage: Views from the American Film Institute Collection, 1972. ROMANCE NOVELS FOR ADULTS: Light of My Heart, 1984; From This Day Forward, 1985; Chessie's King, 1986; Destiny's Dreamers, vol. I: Gone West, 1993, vol. II: The Promised Land, 1993. FICTION FOR CHILDREN: It Ain't Always Easy, 1990; Oh, Those Harper Girls!, Or Young and Dangerous, 1992; Gideon and the Mummy Professor, 1993; The Cave, 1994; In the Kaiser's Clutch, 1995; Spy in the Sky, 1997; The Great Turkey Walk, 1998; The Lighthouse Mermaid, 1998; Man of the Family, 1999; Skull Duggery, 2000; The Boxer, 2000; It Happened in the White House: Extraordinary Tales From America's Most Famous Home, 2000; Playing with Fire, 2001; Bone Dry, 2002; The 7th Knot, 2003; Gilbert & Sullivan Set Me Free, 2003; Exiled: Memoirs of a Camel, 2004; Worlds Apart, 2005; Mama Went to Jail for the Vote, 2005. PETTICOAT PARTY SERIES: Go West, Young Women!, 1996; Phoebe's Folly, 1996; Oregon, Sweet Oregon, 1998; Gold-Rush Phoebe, 1998. OTHERS: Born for Adventure, 2007; Fortune's Fool, 2008. Contributor to journals. **Address:** c/o Tracey Adams, Adams Literary, 7845 Colony Rd. C-4, Ste. 215, Charlotte, NC 28226, U.S.A. **Online address:** karr@bellatlantic.net

KARR, Mary. American (born United States), b. 1955. **Genres:** Poetry, Autobiography/Memoirs. **Career:** Harvard University, Radcliffe College, Bunting fellow; Syracuse University, faculty, 1991-, Jesse Truesdell Peck professor of literature; Tufts University, assistant professor; Emerson College, assistant professor; Harvard University, assistant professor; Sarah Lawrence College, assistant professor. Writer. **Publications:** POETRY: Abacus, 1987; The Devil's Tour, 1993; Viper Rum: With the afterword Against Decoration, 1998; Sinners Welcome, 2006. MEMOIRS: The Liars' Club, 1995; Cherry, 2000; Lit: A Memoir, 2009. Contributor to magazines and periodicals. **Address:** Department of English, Syracuse University, 434 Hall of Languages, Syracuse, NY 13244, U.S.A.

KARRAS, Ruth Mazo. American (born United States), b. 1957. **Genres:** Sex, Social Commentary, History, Cultural/Ethnic Topics. **Career:** University of Pennsylvania, assistant professor of history, 1985-93, University of Pennsylvania Press, general editor, 1995-; Common Knowledge, assistant editor, 1993-98, 2001-; Temple University, associate professor of history, 1993-96, professor of history, 1996-2000, Intellectual Heritage Program, director, 1999-2000, College of Liberal Arts, associate dean, 1999-2000, Provost's Task Force on Undergraduate Education, co-chair, 1999-2000; Delaware Valley Medieval Association, vice president, 1997-98, president, 1998-99; University of Minnesota, Department of History, professor of history, 2000-, director of graduate studies, 2003-04, 2005-06, 2007-08, Center for Medieval Studies, director; Journal of British Studies, associate editor, 2004-; Berkshire Conference on the History of Women, president, 2005-08. **Publications:** Slavery and Society in Medieval Scandinavia, 1988; Common Women: Prostitution and Sexuality in Medieval England, 1996; (contrib.) Desire and Discipline: Sex and Sexuality in the Premodern West, 1996; (contrib.) Obscenity: Social Control and Artistic Creation in the European Middle Ages, 1998; From Boys to Men: Formations of Masculinity in Late Medieval Europe, 2003; Sexuality in Medieval Europe: Doing unto Others, 2005; (contrib.) In the Garden of Evil: The Vices and Culture in the Middle Ages, 2005; (contrib.) The Boswell Thesis: Essays on Christianity, Social Tolerance, and Homosexuality, 2006; (ed. with J. Kaye and E.A. Matter) Law and the Illicit in Medieval Europe, 2008; (contrib.) Professing Gender, 2008. Contributor to journals. **Address:** Department of History, University of Minnesota, 737 Social Sciences Bldg., 267 19th Ave. S, Minneapolis, MN 55455, U.S.A. **Online address:** rmk@umn.edu

KARSH, Efraim. British (born England), b. 1953. **Genres:** Military/Defense/Arms Control. **Career:** King's College London, professor & head of the Mediterranean studies program; Harvard University, faculty; Columbia University, faculty; Helsinki University, faculty; Sorbonne, faculty; London School of Economics, faculty; Kennan Institute for Advanced Russian Studies, faculty; Tel Aviv University, Jaffee Center for Strategic Studies, faculty. Writer. **Publications:** Soviet Arms Transfers to the Middle East in the 1970s, 1983; The Cautious Bear: Soviet Military Engagement in Middle East Wars in the Post-1967 Era, 1985; (ed.) The Iran-Iraq War: Impact and Implications, Macmillan in association with the Jaffee Center for Strategic Studies, 1987; The Soviet Union and Syria: The Asad Years, 1988; Neutrality and Small States, 1988; Soviet Policy Towards Syria Since 1970, 1991; (with I. Rautsi) Saddam Hussein: A Political Biography, 2002; (with L. Freedman) The Gulf Conflict, 1990-1991: Diplomacy and War in the New World Order, 1993; (ed. with M.S. Navias and P. Sabin) Non-conventional-weapons Proliferation in the Middle East: Tackling the Spread of Nuclear, Chemical and Biological Capabilities, 1993; (ed.) Peace in the Middle East: The Challenge for Israel, 1994; (ed. with G. Mahler) Israel at the Crossroads: The Challenge of Peace, 1994; (ed.) Between War and Peace: Dilemmas of Israeli Security, 1996; Shikhtuv Ha-historyah Shel Yisrael, 1997; (ed.) From Rabin to Netanyahu: Israel's Troubled Agenda, 1997; Fabricating Israeli History: The New Historians, 1997, 2nd ed., 2000; (with I. Karsh) Empires of the Sand: The Struggle for Mastery in the Middle East, 17891923, 1999; (ed. with D. Urian) In Search of Identity: Jewish Aspects in Israeli Culture, 1999; (ed.) Israel: The First Hundred Years, vol. I: From Community to State, 1999; (ed.) Israel: The First Hundred Years, vol. II: From War to Peace?, 2000; (ed.) Israel: The First Hundred Years, vol. III: Problems of Collective Identity, 2002; The Iran-Iraq War, 1980-1988, 2002; Arafat's War: The Man and His Battle for Israeli Conquest, 2003; Milhemet Oslo: Anatomyah Shel Honaah Eatsmit, 2003; Rethinking the Middle East, 2003; (ed. with P.R. Kumaraswamy) Israel, the Hashemites and the Palestinians: The Fateful Triangle, 2003; (ed.) Israel: The First Hundred Years, vol. IV: Israel in the International Arena, 2004; Islamic Imperialism: A History, 2006; Arab Imperialism: The Tragedy of the Middle East, 2006; The Iran-Iraq War, 2009; The Arab-Israeli Conflict: The 1948 War, 2009. Contributor to periodicals. **Address:** Mediterranean Studies, King's College London, Strand, GL WC2R 2LS, England. **Online address:** efraim.karsh@kcl.ac.uk

KARTTUNEN, Frances. American (born United States), b. 1942. **Genres:** Anthropology/Ethnology, History, Language/Linguistics, Race Relations, Travel/Exploration, Women's Studies And Issues. **Career:** RAND Corp., Computational Linguistics, NSF research fellow, 1967-68; University of Texas, Department of Linguistics, research associate, 1968-71, linguist, 1968-, extension instructor, 1973-76, postdoctoral researcher, 1977-78, Linguistics Research Center, research scientist, 1978-2000, senior university research scientist 1987-, retired, 2000, Department of English, lecturer, 1981-82; University of Tampere, Fulbright senior lecturer in linguistics, 1972; University of Massachusetts, LSA Summer Institute, visiting assistant professor, 1974; University of Jyäskylä, visiting assistant professor, 1976; University of Helsinki, bicentennial professor of North American studies, 1977-78; International Business Machine (IBM) Corp., linguist, 1980; National Science Foundation, program director for linguistics, 1987-88; University of Umeå, Department of General Linguistics, visiting professor, 1999. Writer. **Publications:** Finnish Phonology; Form 1040 or Form 1040A, 1968; (with J. Lockhart) Nahuatl in the Middle Years, 1976; An Analytical Dictionary of Nahuatl, 1983; Nahuatl and Maya in Contact with Spanish, 1985; (ed. with J. Lockhart) The Art of Nahuatl Speech: The Bancroft Dialogues, 1987; (with R.J. Campbell) Foundation Course in Nahuatl Grammar, 1989; Between Worlds: Interpreters, Guides and Survivors, 1994; The Other Islanders, 2005. **Address:** Linguistics Research Center, University of Texas, Rm. 5.112, 1 University Sta. S5490, Austin, TX 78712-0791, U.S.A. **Online address:** karttu@nantucket.net

KASABOV, Nikola K(irilov). New Zealander (born New Zealand), b. 1948. **Genres:** Information Science/Computers, Sciences, Technology, Medicine/ Health, Engineering. **Career:** Technical University of Sofia, Department of Computer Science, research fellow, 1976-78, lecturer, senior lecturer, 1978-88, associate professor, 1988-89, International Graduate School in Artificial Intelligence, director, 1988-91; University of Essex, Department of Computer Science, research fellow and senior lecturer, 1989-91; University of Otago, Department of Information Science, senior lecturer, 1992-95, associate professor of information science, 1996-98, professor of information science and personal chair, 1999-2002, Knowledge Engineering/Discovery Laboratory, founding director, 1994-2002; Asia-Pacific Neural Network Assembly, co-founder, 1993-, president, 1997-2008; Auckland University, School of Computing and Mathematical Sciences, adjunct professor, professor and chair of knowledge engineering, 2002-, Knowledge Engineering and Discovery Research Institute, founding director, 2002-. Writer. **Publications:** (Ed.) 1993 the First New Zealand International Two-Stream Conference on Artificial Neural Networks and Expert Systems, November 24-26, 1993, Dunedin, New Zealand: Proceedings, 1993; (ed. with G. Coghill) 1995 Second New Zealand International Two-Stream Conference on Artificial Neural Networks and Expert Systems, November 20-23, 1995, Dunedin, New Zealand: Proceedings, 1995; (with R. Romanski) Computing, 1995; Foundations of Neural Networks, Fuzzy Systems, and Knowledge Engineering, 1996; (ed. with S. Amari) Brain-Like Computing and Intelligent Information Systems, 1998; (ed. with R. Kozma) Neuro-Fuzzy Techniques for Intelligent Information Systems, 1999; (ed.) Future Directions for Intelligent Systems and Information Sciences: The Future of Speech and Image Technologies, Brain Computers, WWW, and Bioinformatics, 2000; Evolving Connectionist Systems: Methods and Applications in Bioinformatics, Brain Study and Intelligent Machines, 2003, (ed. with M.W. Barley) Intelligent Agents and Multi-Agent Systems: 7th Pacific Rim International Workshop on Multi-Agents, PRIMA 2004, Auckland, New Zealand, August 8-13, 2004: Revised Selected Papers, 2005; (with L. Benuskova) Computational Neurogenetic Modeling, 2007; Evolving Connectionist Systems: The Knowledge Engineering Approach, 2007; (ed. with M. Köppen and G. Coghill) Advances in Neuro-information Processing, 2009; (with P. Angelov and D.P. Filev) Evolving Intelligent Systems: Methodology and Applications, 2009. Contributor to books and periodicals. **Address:** Knowledge Engineering and Discovery Research, Institute, Auckland University, Level 7, 350 Queen St., PO Box 92006, Auckland, 1010, New Zealand. **Online address:** nkasabov@aut.ac.nz

KASCHAK, Ellyn. American (born United States), b. 1943. **Genres:** Psychology, Women's Studies And Issues, Medicine/Health. **Career:** George Washington University, lecturer in psychology, 1965-66, Arthritis Research Institute, research assistant, 1968-69; District of Columbia General Hospital, psychology intern, 1966; school psychologist for public schools of Washington, 1967-69; National Institute of Mental Health, research assistant, 1967-68; University Hospital, psychology intern, 1969-70; Ohio State University, instructor in psychology, 1970-71; Veterans Administration Hospital, psychology intern, 1971-73; University of California, extension lecturer, 1972-74; San Francisco Women's Counseling Service, co-founder and coordinator, 1972; San Jose State University, assistant professor, 1974-78, professor of psychology, 1983-, director of Family Counseling Service, 1975-, chairperson of Marriage, Family and Child Counseling Program, 1985-; Inter-Accion (consultants in Latino/Chicano services), co-founder and coordinator, 1976; California State University, Hayward, administrative fellow, 1980-81; Pacific Graduate School, adjunct professor, 1983-85; Universidad Nacional de Costa Rica, senior research associate, 1985-88; Feminist Therapy Institute, national chair, 1990-92; Women & Therapy Journal, editor, 1998-. **Publications:** Engendered Lives: A New Psychology of Women's Experience, Basic Books,

1992. EDITOR: (with S. Sharratt) Assault on the Soul: Women in the Former Yugoslavia, 1999; (with M. Hill) Beyond the Rule Book: Moral Issues and Dilemmas in the Practice of Psychotherapy, 1999; (with Hill) For Love or Money: The Fee in Feminist Therapy, 1999; Intimate Betrayal: Domestic Violence in Lesbian Relationships, 2001; Minding the Body: Psychotherapy in Cases of Chronic and Life-Threatening Illness, 2001; The Next Generation: Third Wave Feminist Psychotherapy, 2001; (with L. Tiefer) A New View of Women's Sexual Problems, 2002; Women with Visible and Invisible Disabilities: Multiple Intersections, Multiple Issues, Multiple Therapies, 2003. Works appear in anthologies. Contributor to journals. **Address:** Department of Psychology, San Jose State University, 1 Washington Sq., San Jose, CA 95192, U.S.A. **Online address:** ekaschak@sbcglobal.net

KASDORF, Julia. (Julia Spicher Kasdorf). American (born United States), b. 1962. **Genres:** Poetry, Local History/Rural Topics, Essays. **Career:** Saint Anthonys Commercial High School, teacher of English, 1985-86; Pennsylvania Governors School for the Arts, instructor, 1984, 1985-87; St. Anthony's Commercial School, teacher, 1985-86; Institute of Fine Arts, slide library assistant, 1986-87; New York University, writer, 1987-89, instructor, 1989, 1993-95; Messiah College, Writing Center, director, 1996-99, assistant professor, Poetry and Fiction Reading Series, coordiinator, Minnemingo Review Literary Magazine, faculty advisor, 1996-2000; Oregon Extension of Eastern College, visiting faculty, 1999-; Pennsylvania State University, associate professor of English, 2000-01, associate professor of English and women's studies, 2001-, Master of Fine Arts Program in in Creative Writing, director, 2000-09, Institute for Arts and Humanities, fellow, 2007; Hathaway Brown School, poet-in-residence, 2000; Favorite Poem Project of State College, faculty advisor, 2001; Chrysostom Society, president, 2009-. **Publications:** (As Julia Spicher) Moss Lotus (chapbook), 1983; Sleeping Preacher (poems), 1992; Eve's Striptease, 1998; The Body and the Book: Writing from a Mennonite Life: Essays and Poems, 2001; Fixing Tradition: Joseph W. Yoder, Amish American, 2003; (ed. with M. Tyrell) Broken Land: Poems of Brooklyn, 2007; (ed. with J.R. Brown) Rosanna of the Amish, 2008; Sacrificial Figures, forthcoming; Poetry in America, forthcoming. Works appear in anthologies. Contributor to periodicals. **Address:** Department of English, Penn State University, 35A Burrowes Bldg., University Park, PA 16802-6202, U.S.A. **Online address:** jmk28@psu.edu

KASER, Michael Charles. British (born England), b. 1926. **Genres:** Area Studies, Economics. **Career:** H.M. Foreign Services, staff, 1947-51; U.N. Secretariat, economic affairs officer, 1951-63; Oxford University, faculty fellow, 1963-72, lecturer in Soviet economics, 1963-72, St. Antony's College, professorial fellow, 1972-83, reader in economics, 1972-83, Institute for Russian, Soviet and East European Studies, director, 1988-93; Birmingham University, Institute for German Studies, honorary professor, 1994-. Writer. **Publications:** Comecon, 1965, 2nd ed., 1967; Soviet Economics, 1970; (with J. Zielinski) Planning in East Europe, 1970; (with H. Hoehmann and K.C. Thalheim) Die Wirtschaftsordnungen Osteuropas im Wandel: Ergebnisse der Wirtschaftsreformen, 1972; Health Care in the Soviet Union and Eastern Europe, 1976; (with S. Mehrotra) The Central Asian Economies since Independence, 1992; Privatization in the CIS, 1995; The Economies of Kazakstan and Uzbekistan, 1997. EDITOR: Economic Development for Eastern Europe, 1958; Soviet Affairs No. 4, 1966; (with R. Portes) Planning and Market Relations, 1971; Soviet Economists of the Twenties: Names to Be Remembered, 1972; (with H. Hohmann and K. Thalheim) The New Economic Systems of East Europe, 1975; (with A. Brown) The Soviet Union since the Fall of Khrushchev, 1975; The Economic History of Eastern Europe 1919-1975, 3 vols., 1985-86; (co-ed.) The Cambridge Encyclopedia of Russia and the Soviet Union, 1982, 2nd ed., 1994; (with A. Brown) Soviet Policy for the 1980s, 1982; Reforms in Foreign Economic Relations of Eastern Europe and the Soviet Union, 1991; (with E.A.G. Robinson) Early Steps in Comparing East-West Economies: The Bursa Conference of 1958, 1992; (with D. Phillips) Education and Economic Change in Eastern Europe and the Former Soviet Union, 1992; (co-ed.) Cambridge Encyclopedia of Russia and the Former Soviet Union, 1994. **Address:** Department of Economics, University of Oxford, 62 Woodstock Rd., Oxford, OX OX2 6JF, England. **Online address:** michael.kaser@economics.ox.ac.uk

KASH, Don E. American (born United States), b. 1934. **Genres:** Politics/Government, Public/Social Administration, Sciences, Technology, Business/Trade/Industry. **Career:** Texas Tech University, instructor, 1960-61; Arizona State University, assistant professor of political science, 1963-65; University of Missouri, assistant professor of political science, 1965-66; Purdue University, associate professor of political science and director, 1966-70; University of Oklahoma, Program in Science and Public Policy, director, 1970-78, George Lynn Cross research professor of political science and research fellow in science and public policy, 1975-90; George Mason University, Hazel chair in public policy, 1991, School of Public Policy, now professor emeritus. Writer. **Publications:** The Politics of Space Cooperation, 1967; (co-author) North Sea Oil and Gas: Implications for Future United States Development, 1973; (co-author) Energy under the Oceans: A Technology Assessment of Outer Continental Shelf Oil and Gas Operations, 1973; (co-author) Energy Alternatives: A Comparative Analysis, 1975; (co-author) Our Energy Future: The Role of Research, Development and Demonstration in Reaching a National Consensus on Energy Supply, 1976; (co-author) Energy Policy-Making: A Selected Bibliography, 1977; (with R.W. Ryfrot) U.S. Energy Policy: Crisis and Complacency, 1984; Perpetual Innovation: The New World of Competition, 1989; (with R.W. Ryfrot) The Complexity Challenge: Technological Innovation for the 21st Century, 1999. Contributor to journals. **Address:** School of Public Policy, George Mason University, 3351 Fairfax Dr., Arlington, VA 22201, U.S.A. **Online address:** dkash@gmu.edu

KḎASHU, Sayed. *See* **KASHUA, Sayed.**

KASHUA, Sayed. (Sayed ḵashu). Israeli (born Israel), b. 1975?. **Genres:** Translations, Young Adult Fiction. **Career:** Journalist, 1995-. **Publications:** AS SAYED ḴASHU: Arvim roḵdim, 2002; Ya-yehi Boḵer, 2004; Guf sheni yaḥid, 2010. Contributor of periodicals. **Address:** Deborah Harris Agency, PO Box 8528, Jerusalem, 91083, Israel.

KASINITZ, Philip. American (born United States), b. 1957. **Genres:** Urban Studies, Social Sciences, Politics/Government. **Career:** New York University, instructor in metropolitan studies, 1986-87; Williams College, assistant professor of sociology, 1987-93; Hunter College, Graduate Center of CUNY, associate professor, 1993-98, professor of sociology, 1999-, chair, 2008-, Ph.D. Program in Sociology, executive officer, CUNY Center for Urban Research, associate director. Writer. **Publications:** Caribbean New York, 1992; (co-author) Inheriting the City: The Children of Immigrants Come of Age, 2008. EDITOR: Metropolis: Center and Symbol of Our Times, 1995; (with C. Hirschman and J. DeWind) The Handbook of International Migration: The American Experience, 1999; (with J.H. Mollenkopf and M.C. Waters) Becoming New Yorkers: Ethnographies of the New Second Generation, 2004. Contributor to periodicals. **Address:** Department of Sociology, Hunter College City University New York, Rm. 6112.04,365 5th Ave., New York, NY 10016, U.S.A. **Online address:** pkasinitz@gc.cuny.edu

KASISCHKE, Laura. American (born United States), b. 1961. **Genres:** Novels, Poetry. **Career:** South Plains College, writing instructor, 1987-88; University of Michigan, Department of creative writing and literature, visiting lecturer, 1989-90, associate professor, professor; Washtenaw Community College, instructor of creative writing and literature, 1990-; University of Nevada, professor, 1994-95. Writer. **Publications:** POETRY: Wild Brides, 1992; Housekeeping in a Dream, 1995; Fire and Flower, 1998; What It Wasn't, 2001; Dance and Disappear, 2002; Gardening in the Dark, 2004; Lilies Without, 2007. NOVELS: Suspicious River, 1996; White Bird in a Blizzard, 1998; Life Before Her Eyes, 2002; Boy Heaven, 2006; Be Mine, 2007; In a Perfect World, 2009; Sweet Things, 2011; The Raising 2011. OTHERS: Brides, Wives, and Widows, 1990; Feathered, 2008; Eden Springs, 2010; Space, in Chains; 2011; Ghost writers, 2011. Contributor to periodicals. **Address:** Department of English Language and Literature, University of Michigan, Rm. 4184AH 126TY EQ, 435 S State St., 3187 Angell Hall, Ann Arbor, MI 48109, U.S.A. **Online address:** laurakk@umich.edu

KASLIK, Ibi. *See* **KASLIK, Ibolya Emma.**

KASLIK, Ibolya Emma. (Ibi Kaslik). Canadian (born Canada), b. 1973. **Genres:** Novels. **Career:** Apropos, part-time teacher, 1999, 2005; teacher, 2000; Multi-Langues Services, teacher, 2000-01; Concordia University, teacher of creative writing, 2002-03; Banff Centre, writer-in-residence, 2004; Regina Public Library, writer-in-residence, 2007-08; University of Toronto, School of Continuing Studies, instructor. Writer. **Publications:** AS IBI KASLIK: Skinny, 2004; The Angel Riots, 2008. Contributor of articles to periodicals. **Address:** c/o Shaun Bradley, Transatlantic Literary Agency Inc., 2 Bloor St. E, Ste. 3500, Toronto, ON M4W 1A8, Canada. **Online address:** ibikas@hotmail.com

KASPAROV, Garry (Kimovich). Russian (born Russia), b. 1963. **Genres:** How-to Books, Autobiography/Memoirs, Biography. **Career:** Azerbaidzhan Champion chess player, 1975, U.S.S.R. Junior Champion, 1975, International Master, 1979, International Grandmaster, 1980, World Junior Champion, 1980, U.S.S.R. Champion, 1981, world champion, 1985-. Writer. **Publications:** (With R. Keene) Batsford Chess Openings, 1982; (with B. Wade) Fighting Chess: Kasparov's Games and Career, 1983; My Games, 1983; (with A. Nikitin) The Sicilian Scheveningen: Sicilian E6 and D6 Systems, 1983; (with A. Shakarov) Caro-Kann, 1984; Ispytanie vremenem, 1985; New World Chess Champion: All the Championship Games with Annotations, 1986; The Test of Time, 1986; Kasparov Teaches Chess, 1987; (with D. Trelford) Child of Change: The Autobiography of Garry Kasparov, 1987; London-Leningrad Championship Games: Rematch Championship Games with Annotations by the World Champion, 1987; (with D. Trelford) Unlimited Challenge (autobiography), 1990; (co-author) Kasparov v. Karpov 1990, 1991; (with Keene) Battle of the Titans: Kasparov-Karpov, 1991; (foreword) Secrets of Chess Training, 1991; (with R. Keene) Kasparov on the King's Indian, 1993; Learn Chess with Gary Kasparov, 1993; (with J. Speelman and B. Wade) Garry Kasparov's Fighting Chess, 1995; On My Great Predecessors, 2003; Moi Velikie Predshestvenniki: Noveishaia Istoriia Razvitiia Shakhmatnoi Igry, 2005; Pozitsiia, 2005; Learn From Garry Kasparov's Greatest Games, 2005; (with N. Belykh and M. Kasi) Kvartet: alternativa, 2006; (with M. Greengard) How Life Imitates Chess: Making the Right Moves, From the Board to the Boardroom, 2007; Velikoe protivostoianie: moi poedinki s Anatoliem Karpovym, 1975-1985, 2008; My sozdaëm v Rossii realnuiu oppozitsiiu, 2008; Shakhmaty kak model zhizni, 2008; (with M. Levchin and P. Thiel) The Blueprint: Reviving Innovation, Rediscovering Risk and Rescuing the Free Market, 2012. Contributor to periodicals. **Address:** c/o Owen Williams, The Kasparov Agency, 249 Peruvian Ave., Ste. F-2, Palm Beach, FL 33480, U.S.A. **Online address:** maiavia@dol.ru

KASSABOVA, Kapka. Scottish (born Scotland), b. 1973?. **Genres:** Young Adult Non-fiction, Novels, Poetry. **Career:** Strathclyde University, royal literary fund fellow; WhatsOnWhen.com, content writer and researcher. Poet and travel writer. **Publications:** NOVELS: Reconnaissance, 1999; Love in the Land of Midas, 2000. POETRY COLLECTIONS: All Roads Lead to the Sea, 1997; Dismemberment, 1998; Someone Else's Life, 2003; Geography for the Lost, 2007. NONFICTION: Delhi, Jaipur, and Agra, 2005; Bulgaria: Globetrotter Travel Pack, 2008; (with S. Ghose) The Best of Delhi: Globetrotter Best of Series), 2008; Street without a Name: Childhood and Other Misadventures in Bulgaria, 2008. Contributor to periodicals. **Address:** c/o Isobel Dixon, Blake Friedmann Agency, 122 Arlington Rd., London, GL NW1 7HP, England. **Online address:** kapka@kapka-kassabova.com

KASSELL, Lauren. British (born England) **Genres:** Young Adult Non-fiction. **Career:** Pembroke College, R.A. Butler fellow, 1998-2000; University of Cambridge, Department of History and Philosophy of Science, lecturer, 2000-, senior lecturer, part II manager. Writer. **Publications:** Medicine and Magic in Elizabethan London: Simon Forman, Astrologer, Alchemist and Physician, 2005. Contributor to periodicals. **Address:** Department of History & Philosophy of Science, University of Cambridge, Free School Ln., Cambridge, CB CB2 3RH, England. **Online address:** ltk21@cam.ac.uk

KASSIRER, Jerome P. American (born United States), b. 1932. **Genres:** Sciences, Medicine/Health. **Career:** Buffalo General Hospital, intern and assistant resident in medicine, 1957-59; New England Medical Center (now Tufts Medical Center), fellow in nephrology, 1959-61, senior resident in medicine, 1961-62, assistant physician, 1961-65, physician in renal services, 1969-74, associate physician-in-chief, 1971-91, acting physician-in-chief, 1976-77, Department of Medicine, House Staff Training, director, 1971-75; Tufts University, School of Medicine, Department of Medicine, instructor in medicine, 1961-65, assistant professor of medicine, 1965-69, associate professor of medicine, 1969-74, professor of medicine, 1974-, distinguished professor of medicine, acting chair, 1974-75, vice chairman, 1979-91, Sara Murray Jordan professor of medicine, 1987-91, special assistant, 2000-, senior assistant; Harvard University, lecturer in medicine, 1991-; New England Journal of Medicine, editor-in-chief, 1991-99; Yale University, School of Medicine, adjunct professor of medicine, 2000-05; Case Western Reserve University, School of Medicine, adjunct professor of medicine, 2005-06; Stanford University, visiting professor, 2007-. **Publications:** (With J.J. Cohen) Acid-Base, 1982; (ed. with J.J. Cohen and J.T. Harrington) Nephrology Forum, 1983; (with D.E. Hricik and J.J. Cohen) Repairing Body Fluids: Principles & Practice, 1989; (with R.I. Kopelman) Learning Clinical Reasoning, 1991; (with H.L. Greene,

II) Current Therapy in Adult Medicine, 1997; (with R.I. Kopelman) Learning Clinical Reasoning, 1999, (with J.B. Wong and R.I. Kopelman) 2nd ed., 2010; On the Take: How Medicine's Complicity with Big Business Can Endanger Your Health, 2005. Contributor to journals. **Address:** School of Medicine, Tufts University, 136 Harrison Ave., Boston, MA 02111-1817, U.S.A. **Online address:** jerome.kassirer@tufts.edu

KASSLER, Jamie C(roy). Australian/American (born United States), b. 1938. **Genres:** Intellectual History, Music, Sciences, Law. **Career:** University of Sydney, research fellow in music, 1975-77; University of New South Wales, research fellow in English, history and philosophy of science, 1979-93. Writer. **Publications:** The Science of Music in Britain, 1714-1830: A Catalogue of Writings, Lectures and Inventions, 2 vols., 1979; Inner Music: Hobbes, Hooke and North on Internal Character, 1995; Music, Science, Philosophy: Models in the Universe of Thought, 2001; Beginnings of The Modern Philosophy of Music In England: Francis North's A Philosophical Essay of Musick (1677) With Comments of Isaac Newton, Roger North And in the Philosophical Transactions, 2004. EDITOR and CONTRIBUTOR: (with J. Stubington) Problems and Solutions: Occasional Essays in Musicology Presented to Alice M. Moyle, 1984; (with M. Chan) Roger North's Cursory Notes of Musicke (c. 1698-c. 1703): A Physical, Psychological, and Critical Theory, 1986; (with M. Chan and intro.) Roger North, The Musical Grammarian 1728, 1990; Metaphor: A Musical Dimension, 1991; (with M. Chan) Roger North's Writings On Music c. 1704-c.1709: Digests of the Manuscripts, 1999; (with M. Chan and J.D. Hine) Roger North's Of Sounds and Prendcourt Tracts: Digests and Editions with and Analytical Index, 2000; Honourable Roger North (1651-1734): On Life, Morality, Law and Tradition, 2009. **Address:** 2/2 W Crescent St., McMahon's Point, New South Wales, NW 2060, Australia.

KASTEL-BLUM, Orli. See **CASTEL-BLOOM, Orly.**

KASTELY, James L. American (born United States), b. 1947. **Genres:** Literary Criticism And History, Philosophy. **Career:** University of Hawaii-Manoa, assistant professor, associate professor of English, 1980-93; University of Houston-Texas, associate professor of English, 1994, professor, Creative Writing Program, director. Writer. **Publications:** Rethinking the Rhetorical Tradition: From Plato to Postmodernism, 1997. **Address:** Department of English, University of Houston, 228 Roy Cullen Bldg., 4800 Calhoun Rd., Houston, TX 77004, U.S.A. **Online address:** jkastely@uh.edu

KASTER, Robert A. American (born United States), b. 1948. **Genres:** Social Sciences. **Career:** Harvard University, teaching fellow, 1972-73; Colby College, instructor in classics, 1973-74; University of Chicago, Department of Classical Languages and Literatures, assistant professor, 1975-82, associate professor, 1982-89, professor of classics, 1989-97, chair, 1994-97; Princeton University, Department of Classics, professor of classics and Kennedy Foundation professor of Latin, 1997-, chair, 2000-03, Old Dominion Professor, Council of Humanities, 2008-09; Oxford University, Oriel College, visiting fellow, 1999. Writer. **Publications:** Guardians of Language: The Grammarian and Society in Late Antiquity, 1988; The Tradition of the Text of the Aeneid in the Ninth Century, 1990; Studies on the Text of Suetonius: De grammaticis et rhetoribus, 1992; (ed., trans. and intro.) C. Suetonius Tranquillus, De grammaticis et rhetoribus, 1995; Emotion, Restraint and Community in Ancient Rome, 2005; (trans. and intro.) Marcus Tullius Cicero, Speech on Behalf of Publius Sestius, 2006. Contributor to books and journals. **Address:** Department of Classics, Princeton University, 155 E Pyne, Princeton, NJ 08544-5264, U.S.A. **Online address:** kaster@princeton.edu

KASZYNSKI, William. American (born United States), b. 1953. **Genres:** Travel/Exploration, Adult Non-fiction, History. **Career:** Attorney, 1981-99; freelance writer, 1997-; Waddell and Reed, financial advisor, 2001-. **Publications:** The American Highway: The History and Culture of Roads in the United States, 2000; Route 66: Images of America's Main Street, 2003. **Address:** 1132 E Magnolia Ave., St. Paul, MN 55106-3338, U.S.A.

KATAGIRI, Yasuhiro. Japanese (born Japan), b. 1960. **Genres:** Area Studies, Civil Liberties/Human Rights, History, Humanities, Local History/Rural Topics, Politics/Government, Race Relations, Social Sciences, Social Sciences. **Career:** Japan Travel Bureau, sales representative, 1984-89; Kyoritsu Women's University, research assistant, 1994-97; Tokai University, instructor of American studies, assistant professor of American history and government, 1997-2000, associate professor of American history and government, 2000-05, professor of American history and government, 2005-, chair of Ameri-

can civilization, 2007-09. Writer. **Publications:** (Co-author) Contemporary America, 1995; (co-author) Encyclopedia of Nations and Ethnic Relations, 1995, rev. ed., 2002; (co-author) One Hundred and One Important Figures in American History, 1997; The Mississippi State Sovereignty Commission: Civil Rights and States' Rights, 2001; (co-author) America: Perspectives on the U.S.-Iraq War, 2003; (co-author) Federalism in America: An Encyclopedia, 2006; (co-author) States' Rights, 2006; (co-author) Law and Politics, vol. X, 2008. Contributor to periodicals. **Address:** Tokai University, 4-1-1 Kitakaname, Hiratsuka-shi, Kanagawa, Tokyo, 259-1292, Japan. **Online address:** katagiris@aol.com

KATCHANOVSKI, Ivan. Canadian/Ukranian (born Ukraine), b. 1967. **Genres:** Adult Non-fiction, International Relations/Current Affairs, Politics/Government, Organized Labor, Social Sciences. **Career:** Volyn State University, lecturer, 1993-94; Institute for Humane Studies, John Olin Junior Faculty fellow, 1994, Humane Studies fellow, 1997-98; United States Institute of Peace, research assistant, 1996; George Mason University, research assistant, 1997-2001, adjunct professor, 2002-04; Smith College, research associate, 2001-; Library of Congress, Kluge postdoctoral fellow, 2002-03; University of Toronto, fellow, 2005-08; Franklin and Eleanor Roosevelt Institute, Lubin-Winant research fellow, 2005; State University of New York, visiting professor, 2008-09. Writer. **Publications:** (Co-author) The Paradox of American Unionism: Why Americans Like Unions More Than Canadians Do, but Join Much Less, 2004; (co-ed.) Development of the Mathematical Ideas of Mykhailo Kravchuk, 2004; Cleft Countries: Regional Political Divisions and Cultures in Post-Soviet Ukraine and Moldova, 2006. Contributor to periodicals and journals. **Address:** School of Political Studies, University of Ottawa, 55 Laurier Ave. E, Ottawa, ON K1N 6N5, Canada. **Online address:** ivan.katchanovski@utoronto.ca

KATCHER, Brian. American (born United States), b. 1975. **Genres:** Novels. **Career:** Author and librarian. **Publications:** YOUNG-ADULT NOVELS: Playing with Matches, 2008; Almost Perfect, 2009. **Address:** Centralia, MO , U.S.A. **Online address:** brian@briankatcher.com

KATHY. See **DE GRAVE, Kathleen.**

KATIN, Miriam. Israeli/American (born United States), b. 1942?. **Genres:** Young Adult Fiction, Children's Fiction, Art/Art History. **Career:** Israel Defense Forces, graphic artist, 1960-63, Ein Gedi Films, background designer, 1981-90; Jumbo Pictures, MTV Animation, Disney Studio, background designer, 1991-2001; children's book illustrator; comic book artist. Writer. **Publications:** (With S. Smith and C.A. Belcher) Exploring Habitats, 1999; We Are on Our Own. A Memoir, 2006. Works appear in anthologies. **Address:** New York, NY , U.S.A. **Online address:** miriamkatin@nyc.rr.com

KATOUZIAN, Homa. British/Iranian (born Iran), b. 1942. **Genres:** Area Studies, History, Economics, Politics/Government, Autobiography/Memoirs. **Career:** BBC Persian Service, contributor, 1963-64; University of Leeds, lecturer in economics, 1968-69; University of Kent, lecturer, 1969-82, senior lecturer, 1982-86; Phalavi University, visiting professor of economics, 1972; McMaster University, visiting associate professor of economics, 1977-78; Iranian Studies, editor, 1982-94; University of California in Los Angeles, visiting professor of economics, 1985; Comparative Economic Studies, editor, 1989-92; University of California in San Diego, visiting professor of sociology, 1990; University of Oxford, St. Anthony's College, visiting fellow, 1975-76, Iran Heritage Foundation, research fellow, associate faculty of Oriental studies, 1999-, teaching Persian literature and Iranian history, 1986-; Princeton University, Institute for Advanced Studies, School of Historical Studies, staff, 2001. Writer. **Publications:** Ideology and Method in Economics, 1980; The Political Economy of Modern Iran: Despotism and Pseudo-Modernism, 1926-1979, 1981; Iqtiṣ ād-isiyāsī-i īrān, 1987; (ed. and trans.) Musaddiq's Memoirs: The End of the British Empire in Iran, 1988; Musaddiq and the Struggle for Power in Iran, 1990, 2nd ed., 1999; Sadeq Hedayat: The Life and Literature of an Iranian Writer, 1991; Istibdād, dimūkrāsī va nahzat-imillī, 1994; Chahārdah Maqālah dar Adabīyāt, Ijtimā, Falsafah valqtiṣ ād, 1995; State and Society in Iran: The Eclipse of the Qajars and the Emergence of the Pahlavis, 2000; Iranian History and Politics: The Dialectic of State and Society in Iran, 2003; (with H. Shahidi) Iran in the 21st Century: Politics, Economics and Confrontation, 2007; (ed.) Sadeq Hedayat: His Work and His Wondrous World, 2008; Persians: Ancient, Mediaeval and Modern Iran, 2009. IN PERSIAN: International Economic Theory, 1973; Universities and Higher Education oday, 1974, 2nd ed., 1978; Adam Smith and the Wealth of Nations, 1979, 2nd ed., 2003; The Political Memoirs of Khalil Maleki, 1981, 2nd ed., 1988; Essays in Memory of Khalil Malek, 1991; Sadeq Hedayat and the Death of the Author, 1993, 4th ed., 2005; Khalil Maleki's The Contest of Ideas, 1995, 2nd ed., 1997; 14 Essays on Literature, Sociology, Philosophy and Economics, 1996; A Song of Innocence (poetry), 1997, 2nd ed., 2003; Ahmad Kasravi's The Revolt of Sheikh Mohammad Khiyabani, 1997, 3rd. ed., 2006; Hedayat's The Blind Owl, 2nd ed., 1998; Nine Essays on the Historical Sociology of Iran, 1998, 2nd ed., 2004; The Contradiction of State and Society in Iran, 2001; Arbitrary Rule, Democracy and the Popular Movement of Iran, 3rd ed., 2002; Satire and Irony in Hedayat, 2003; Jamalzadeh and His Literature, 2003; (ed. with A. Pichdad) Khalil Maleki's Letters, 2003; (ed.) Iran Nameh, 2003; Eight Essays on Contemporary History and Literature, 2006; Sa'di, the Poet of Life, Love and Compassion, 2006. Contributor to books and periodicals. **Address:** Middle East Centre, St. Antony's College, University of Oxford, 62 Woodstock Rd., Oxford, OX OX2 6JF, England. **Online address:** homa.katouzian@sant.ox.ac.uk

KATRAK, Ketu H. American/Indian (born India), b. 1952. **Genres:** Literary Criticism And History, Women's Studies And Issues. **Career:** Yale University, lecturer and researcher in Afro-American studies and English, 1982-84; University of Massachusetts, assistant professor of English, 1986-89, associate professor of English, 1989-93, professor of English, 1993-96; University of California-Los Angeles, visiting associate professor of English, 1991; University of California-Irvine, director of Asian-American Studies, professor of English and comparative literature, 1996-, Department of Asian American Studies, chair, 1996-2004. Writer. **Publications:** (Comp. with J. Gibbs and H.L. Gates, Jr.) Wole Soyinka: A Bibliography of Primary and Secondary Sources, 1986; Wole Soyinka and Modern Tragedy: A Study of Dramatic Theory and Practice, 1986; (ed. and contrib. with V. Clark, S.N. Garner and M. Higonnet) Antifeminism in the Academy, 1996; (ed. with P.A. Egejuru) Nwanyibu: Womanbeing & African Literature, 1997; Politics of the Female Body: Postcolonial Women Writers of the Third World, 2006. Contributor of articles to books and journals. **Address:** University of California, 300 Krieger Hall, PO Box 6900, Irvine, CA 92697, U.S.A. **Online address:** khkatrak@uci.edu

KATRITZKY, M. A. (Peg Katritzky). British (born England), b. 1953?. **Genres:** Art/Art History, Literary Criticism And History, Theatre. **Career:** University of Oxford, St. Catherine's College, research associate and graduate advisor, 2001-05; Open University, research fellow, 2001-, Barbara Wilkes Research Fellow in Theatre Studies. Writer and researcher. **Publications:** The Art of Commedia dell'Arte: A Study in the Commedia dell'Arte, 1560-1620, with Special Reference to the Visual Records, 2006; Women, Medicine, and Theatre, 1500-1750: Literary Mountebanks and Performing Quacks, 2007. Contributor of articles to books and journals. **Address:** Department of Literature, Open University, Walton Hall, Milton Keynes, BK MK7 6AA, England. **Online address:** m.a.katritzky@open.ac.uk

KATRITZKY, Peg. See **KATRITZKY, M. A.**

KATSH, M. Ethan. American (born United States), b. 1945. **Genres:** Law, Communications/Media, Information Science/Computers. **Career:** University of Massachusetts, assistant professor, 1970-76, Legal Studies Program, director, 1975-77, associate professor, 1976-88, adjunct professor of Judaic studies, 1986-, professor of legal studies, 1988-, now professor emeritus, Legal Studies Department, acting chair, chair, 1993-94, Mediation Project, co-founder, Online Ombuds Office, director, 1996-, Center for Information Technology and Dispute Resolution, co-founder and director, 1997-, Department of Computer Science, National Science Foundation Funded Project, co-principal investigator; Hampshire College, visiting professor, 1973; East-West Center Culture Learning Institute, fellow in law and society, 1977; Modern Media Institute, fellow, 1981; University of Haifa, Fulbright distinguished chair, 2010-11; Yale University, Yale Legislative Services, co-founder. Writer and consultant. **Publications:** (Ed. with J.J. Bonsignore) Before the Law, 1974, 6th ed., 1998; (ed. and intro.) Taking Sides: Clashing Views on Controversial Legal Issues, 1983, 8th ed., 1998; The Electronic Media and the Transformation of Law, 1989; Law in a Digital World, 1995; (with J. Rifkin) Online Dispute Resolution: Resolving Conflicts in Cyberspace, 2001. Contributor to books. **Address:** Department of Legal Studies, University of Massachusetts, 107 Gordon Hall, 200 Hicks Way, Amherst, MA 01003, U.S.A. **Online address:** katsh@legal.umass.edu

KATZ, Avner. Israeli (born Israel), b. 1939. **Genres:** Children's Fiction, Novels. **Career:** Bezalel Academy of Art and Design, staff, 1973-78, Avni Institute for Painting, Ha'mifrasha for Painting, instructor, 1976-79; Midrasha Art Teachers' Training College, staff, 1976-80; University of Haifa, Art Department, Fine Art Section, instructor, 1978-, senior lecturer, 1985-93, head, 1988-91, associate professor, 1993-2007, professor of fine arts, professor emeritus, 2007-. Artist, writer and illustrator. **Publications:** SELECTED TITLES FOR CHILDREN: SELF-ILLUSTRATED IN ENGLISH TRANSLATION: Mishehu Motse Keter, 1979; Ahavah Rishona, 1989; Tortoise Solves a Problem, 1993; The Little Pickpocket, 1996. IN HEBREW: Chamor Af, 1979; Mishehu Motse Perach, 1979; Mishehu Motse Keter, 1979; Shabtai Vehatsipor, 1985; Hutz Miprat Ze Oh Aher, Hacol Emet, 1986. OTHERS: Ha-Kayas Ha-Katòan, 1979; Itstrubalim: tsiyurim, pesalim va-ávodot al neyar, 1966-2007, 2008. Works appear in anthologies. **Address:** 12 She'erit Israel St., Ramat-Hasharon, 47201, Israel.

KATZ, Bernard S. American (born United States), b. 1932. **Genres:** Economics. **Career:** Lafayette College, professor of economics, 1967-91; Changchun University, Fulbright senior lecturer, 1991-93; Xiamen University, Fulbright senior lecturer, 1991-93; San Francisco State University, lecturer. Writer. **Publications:** (With R. Robbins) Modern Economic Classics: Evaluation through Time, 1988; Nobel Laureates in Economic Science, 1989; The Fountains of San Francisco, 1989. EDITOR: (with R. Sobel) Biographical Directory of the Council of Economic Advisors, 1988; (with R. Bukics) International Financial Management: A Handbook for Operation, Financial, and Treasury Professionals, 1990; Biographical Directory of the Governors of the Federal Reserve, 1991; (with S. Shojai) The Oil Market in the 1980's: A Decade of Decline, 1992; (with L. Rittenberg) The Economic Transformation of Eastern Europe: Problems and Prospects, 1992; (with R.A. Ahene) Privatization and Investment in Sub-Saharan Africa, 1992; (with D. Vencill) Biographical Dictionary of the United States Secretaries of the Treasury, 1789-1995, 1996. **Address:** 255 Shawnee Ave., Easton, PA 18042, U.S.A. **Online address:** katzbmee@yahoo.com

KATZ, Bobbi. Also writes as Della Maison, Ali Reich, Emily George, Barbara George, Peggy Kahn. American (born United States), b. 1933. **Genres:** Children's Fiction, Poetry, Children's Non-fiction, Biography. **Career:** Greater Newburgh Arts Council, executive director, 1968-71; Cornwall School Systems, creative writing consultant, 1970-78; freelance writer and editor of environmental and educational materials, 1977-82; Mount St. Mary's College, teacher of short story writing, 1977-78; Random House, juvenile division in-house writer and editor, 1982-; Harper and Row School Department, poetry consultant. **Publications:** Nothing But a Dog, 1972; I'll Build My Friend a Mountain, 1972; Upside Down and Inside Out: Poems for All Your Pockets, 1973; The Manifesto and Me-Meg, 1974; Rod-and-Reel Trouble, 1974; 1001 Words, 1975; Snow Bunny: Action on the Ice, 1976; Volleyball Jinx, 1977; (co-author) The Cousteau Almanac, 1980; (ed.) Birthday Bear's Book of Birthday Poems, 1983; (ed.) Bedtime Bear's Book of Bedtime Poems, 1983; Month by Month: A Care Bear Book of Poems, 1984; Play with the Care Bears, 1985; (ed.) Popple in Your Pocket and Other Funny Poems, 1986; Little Wrinkle's Surprise, 1987; Creepy, Crawly Book, 1989; Poems for Small Friends, 1989; Old Woman's Counting Book, 1989; Peekaboo Animals, 1989; (ed.) Ghosts and Goose Bumps: Poems to Chill Your Bones, 1991; (as Emily George) Profile of a Co-Addict, 1991; (as Emily George) The Womyn is Perfected, 1991; Teenage Mutant Ninja Turtles: Don't Do Drugs: A Rap Song, 1991; Care Bears and the Big Cleanup, 1991; A Family Hanukkah, 1992; Puddle Wonderful: Poems to Welcome Spring, 1992; Story of Hanukkah, 1995; Meet Nelson Mandela, 1995; Poems Just for Us, 1995; Story of Passover, 1996; Germs! Germs! Germs!, 1996; Could We Be Friends?: Poems for Pals, 1997; Truck Talk: Rhymes on Wheels, 1997; American History Poems, 1998; Lots of Lice, 1998; Make Way for Tooth Decay, 1999; We the People, 2000; A Rumpus of Rhymes: A Book of Noisy Poems, 2001; Grammar Poems, 2003; (ed.) Pocket Poems, 2004; Once Around the Sun, 2006; Trailblazers: Poems of Exploration, 2007; (ed.) More Pocket Poems, 2009; The Monsterologist: A Memoir in Rhyme, 2009. AS PEGGY KAHN: The Care Bears' Book of ABC's, 1983; Did You Ever Pet a Care Bear, 1983; Ten Little Care Bears Counting Book, 1983; The Care Bears' Circus of Shapes, 1984; Handy Girls Can Fix it, 1984; Care Bears help Santa, 1984; When Do You Snuzzle a Wuzzle?, 1985; The Wuzzle Book of Seasons, 1985; The Care Bears: Try, Try Again!, 1985; The Care Bears: Night before Christmas, 1985; Wuzzles Alphabet Book, 1986; Rub a Wuzzle's Tummy!, 1986; Popples and King Most, 1986; Popple Opposites, 1986; Popples' Vacation, 1987. AS ALI REICH: The Have-It-All Wuzzle, 1985; Meet the Wuzzles, 1985; The Wuzzles' Wishing Flower, 1985. OTHERS: (as Barbara George) The Wuzzles'

Fair, 1986; (as Don E. Plumme) The Wuzzles and the Creepasaurs, 1986; (as Gail George) The Popples' Pajama Party, 1986; (as Gail George) The Wuzzles and the Big Game, 1986; (as Don E. Plumme) Merry Christmas, Teddy Beddy Bear, 1987. Contributor to periodicals. **Address:** 82 Riverview, Port Ewen, NY 12466, U.S.A. **Online address:** bobbikatz@aol.com

KATZ, David. (David S. Katz). Israeli/American (born United States), b. 1953. **Genres:** History, Politics/Government, Theology/Religion, Cultural/Ethnic Topics, Reference. **Career:** Tel-Aviv University, Department of History, lecturer, 1978-82, senior lecturer, 1982-87, associate professor, 1987-90, professor, 1990-, Abraham Horodisch chair for the history of books, 1994-, chair, 2002-06, Goldstein-Goren Diaspora Research Center, director, 2005-06, Fred W. Lessing Institute for European History and Civilization, director, 2006-, Porter School of Environmental Studies, fellow. Writer. **Publications:** AS DAVID S. KATZ: Philo-Semitism and the Readmission of the Jews to England, 1603-1655, 1982; Sabbath and Sectarianism in Seventeenth-Century England, 1988; The Jews in the History of England, 1485-1850, 1994; (with R.H. Popkin) Messianic Revolution: Radical Religious Politics to the End of the Second Millennium, 1998; God's Last Words: Reading the English Bible from the Reformation to Fundamentalism, 2004; Occult Tradition: From the Renaissance to the Present Day, 2005. EDITOR: (with J.I. Israel) Sceptics, Millenarians and Jews, 1990; (with Y. Kaplan) Gerush ve-shivah: Yehude Angliyah be-Hilufe ha-Zemanim (title means: 'Exile and Return: Anglo-Jewry Through the Ages'), 1993; (with J.E. Force) Everything Connects: Essays in Honor of Richard H. Popkin, 1999. **Address:** Department of History, Tel-Aviv University, Ramat Aviv, 69978, Israel. **Online address:** dskatz@post.tau.ac.il

KATZ, David S. See **KATZ, David.**

KATZ, Elia (Jacob). American (born United States), b. 1948. **Genres:** Novels, Novellas/Short Stories, Plays/Screenplays. **Career:** Elia Katz Inc., president, 1984-; NetBack Inc., co-founder and president. Writer. **Publications:** Armed Love, 1971; Stengrow's Dad, 1994. **Address:** c/o Julie Popkin, Julie Popkin Literary Agency, 15340 Albright St., Ste. 204, Pacific Palisades, CA 90272, U.S.A. **Online address:** eliakatz@eliakatz.com

KATZ, Esther. American (born United States), b. 1948. **Genres:** Women's Studies And Issues, History, Humanities. **Career:** Drexel University, Garrison Papers, research assistant, 1972-74; New York University, Livingston Papers, editorial assistant, 1974-75; State University of New York College-Brockport, visiting instructor, 1976; Radcliffe College, WTUL Papers, research assistant, 1976-78; College of New Rochelle, instructor, 1981; Institute for Research in History, deputy director, 1982-87; New York University, adjunct assistant professor, 1983-93, adjunct associate professor of history, 1993-, NYU Program in Archival Management and Historical Editing, acting director, 1993-94; Margaret Sanger Papers Project, director and editor, 1986-; City University of New York, Center Lesbian and Gay Studies, board chair, 1991-94; Ford Foundation, consultant, 1997-98; Association for Documentary Editors, president, 2003-04; Committee on Research and Preservation of the Organization of American Historians, chair, 2004. **Publications:** (Ed. with A. Rapone and contrib.) Women's Experience in America: An Historical Anthology, 1980; Proceedings of the Conference on Women Surviving-the Holocaust, 1983; (ed. and intro.) Recent Work in Women's History, 1986; (comp. with J. Ringelheim) A Catalogue of Audio and Video Collections of Holocaust Testimony, 1986; (ed.) The Selected Letters and Writings of Margaret Sanger, vol. I: The Woman Rebel, 1900-1928, 2003, vol. II: Birth Control Comes of Age, 1928-1939, 2007, vol. III: The Politics of Planned Parenthood, 1939-1966, 2010, vol. IV: Round the World for Birth Control, 1920-1966, forthcoming; (co-ed.) Margaret Sanger and Japan for Women and Social Movements, 2010; (co-author) Teaching Digital Skills in an Archives and Public History Curriculum, forthcoming; (with C. Hajo and P. Wosh) Teaching Digital Skills in Archives Curriculum, forthcoming; Margaret Sanger: A Biography, forthcoming. **Address:** Sanger Papers Project, Department of History, New York University, 53 Washington Sq. S, New York, NY 10012, U.S.A. **Online address:** esther.katz@nyu.edu

KATZ, Jackson. American (born United States), b. 1960?. **Genres:** Self Help, Medicine/Health. **Career:** Mentors in Violence Prevention (MVP) Strategies, founder and director; Real Men (anti- sexist men's organization), organizer. Writer, educator, anti-sexist activist and filmmaker. **Publications:** The Macho Paradox: Why Some Men Hurt Women and How All Men Can Help, 2006;

(contrib.) Men Speak Out: Views on Gender, Sex and Power, 2008. **Address:** Los Angeles, CA , U.S.A. **Online address:** jacksonkatz@aol.com

KATZ, James Everett. American (born United States), b. 1948. **Genres:** Politics/Government, Social Sciences. **Career:** Clarkson College, associate professor, 1979-81; U.S. Senate, professional staff, 1981-83; University of Texas, LBJ School of Public Affairs, assistant professor, 1983-86; Bell Communication Research, researcher, 1986-, Rutgers, the State University of New Jersey, School of Communication and Information, Department of Communication, professor II and chair, Center for Mobile Communication Studies, director. Writer. **Publications:** (With I.L. Horowitz) Social Science and Public Policy in the United States, 1975; Presidential Politics and Science Policy, 1978; Congress and National Energy Policy, 1984; Connections: Social and Cultural Studies of the Telephone in American Life, 1999; Magic in the Air: Mobile Communication and the Transformation of Social Life, 2006. EDITOR: (with O.S. Marwah) Nuclear Power in Developing Countries: An Analysis of Decision Making, 1982; Arms Production in Developing Countries: An Analysis of Decision Making, 1984; People in Space: Perspectives for a Star Wars Century, 1985; The Implications of Third World Military Industrialization: Sowing the Serpents' Teeth, 1986; (with R.E. Rice) The Internet and Health Communication: Experiences and Expectations, 2001; (with M.A. Aakhus) Perpetual Contact: Mobile Communication, Private Talk, Public Performance, 2002; (co-ed.) Corpo futuro: il corpo umano tra tecnologie, comunicazione e moda, 2002; (R.E. Rice) Social Consequences of Internet Use: Access, Involvement, and Interaction, 2002; (with L. Fortunati and R. Riccini) Mediating the Human Body: Technology, Communication, and Fashion, 2003; Machines that Become Us: The Social Context of Personal Communication Technology, 2003; Handbook of Mobile Communication Studies, 2008; Mobile Communication: Dimensions of Social Policy, 2011. Contributor to journals. **Address:** Center for Mobile Communication Studies, School of Communication and Information, Rutgers, The State University of New Jersey, 4 Huntington St., New Brunswick, NJ 08901-1071, U.S.A. **Online address:** j.k@rutgers.edu

KATZ, Jesse. American (born United States), b. 1962?. **Genres:** Autobiography/Memoirs. **Career:** Los Angeles Magazine, senior writer; Los Angeles Times, journalist; University of California, visiting professor in literary journalism; Los Angeles Juvenile Halls, creative writing instructor; Inside Out Writers, writing instructor. **Publications:** The Opposite Field: A Memoir of Love and Little League, 2009. Contributor to books, magazines and periodicals. Works appear in anthologies. **Address:** Monterey Park, CA , U.S.A. **Online address:** jessekatz13@gmail.com

KATZ, Judith. American (born United States), b. 1951. **Genres:** Novels, Gay And Lesbian Issues, Young Adult Non-fiction. **Career:** At the Foot of the Mountain Theatre, arts administrator, 1983-85; Great Midwestern Book Show, arts administrator, 1985-86; University of Minnesota, adjunct faculty of women's studies, 1986-, Center for Jewish Studies, faculty, Gender, Women, and Sexuality Studies, staff; The Loft, writing teacher, 1988; Hamline University, MALS/MFA program, adjunct faculty, 1993-; Macalester College, visiting writer, 2002-03. **Publications:** NOVELS: Running Fiercely Toward a High Thin Sound, 1992; The Escape Artist, 1997. **Address:** Center for Jewish Studies, University of Minnesota, 150B Nicholson Hall, 216 Pillsbury Dr. SE, Minneapolis, MN 55455, U.S.A. **Online address:** jwst@umn.edu

KATZ, Lawrence S(anford). American (born United States), b. 1947?. **Genres:** Sports/Fitness, History. **Career:** Gerald M. Lorence, law clerk and associate, 1971-73; Weingarden & Hauer, associate, 1973-74; Goldstein & Raznick, associate, 1974-76; Goldstein, Raznick & Katz, partner, 1977-78; Attorney Grievance Commission, special investigator, 1977-80, special counsel, 1980-81; Macomb County Circuit Court, domestic relations mediator, 1986-2001; Civic Searchlight Inc., director, 1993-95. Writer. **Publications:** Baseball in 1939: The Watershed Season of the National Pastime, 1995. **Address:** 38850 Van Dyke Ave., Ste. 102, Sterling Heights, MI 48312-1142, U.S.A. **Online address:** greatunclelarry@aol.com

KATZ, Mark. American (born United States), b. 1970. **Genres:** Music, Adult Non-fiction. **Career:** Johns Hopkins University, Peabody Conservatory, instructor, 1999-2006; University of North Carolina, Department of Music, assistant professor, 2006-, associate professor. Musician, violinist and writer. **Publications:** (Contrib.) Reader's Guide to Music History, 1999; (contrib.) International Dictionary of Black Composers, 1999; (contrib.) I Sing the Body Electric: Music and Technology in the Twentieth Century, 2000;

(contrib.) The Harvard Dictionary of Music, 4th ed., 2003; Capturing Sound: How Technology Has Changed Music, 2004, rev. ed., 2010; The Violin: A Research and Information Guide, 2006; (with T. Taylor and A. Grajeda) Music, Sound, and Technology in America: A History in Documents, 2012; Groove Music: The Art and Culture of the Hip Hop DJ, 2012. Contributor to books, periodicals and journals. **Address:** Department of Music, University of North Carolina, 209 Hill Hall, Chapel Hill, NC 27599-3320, U.S.A. **Online address:** mkatz@email.unc.edu

KATZ, Marshall P. American (born United States), b. 1939. **Genres:** Art/Art History, History. **Career:** Papercraft Corp., chair and chief executive officer, 1962-91; Carnegie Institute, board director; Pittsburgh Cultural Trust, board director; Pittsburgh Symphony, board director; Pittsburgh Opera, board director; University of Pittsburgh, Joseph M. Katz Graduate School of Business, board director. Writer. **Publications:** 19th Century French Followers of Palissy, 1994; (with R. Lehr) Palissy Ware: Nineteenth-Century French Ceramists from Avisseau to Renoleau, 1996; Portuguese Palissy Ware, 1999. Contributor to magazines. **Address:** 4875 Ellsworth Ave., Pittsburgh, PA 15213-2843, U.S.A. **Online address:** palissy@bellatlantic.net

KATZ, Michael Ray. American (born United States), b. 1944. **Genres:** Literary Criticism And History, Translations. **Career:** Williams College, assistant professor, associate professor of Russian, 1972-83; University of Texas, professor of Russian, 1984-97, Slavic Languages Department, chairman, 1984-97; Middlebury College, dean of language schools and schools abroad, 1998-2004, C.V. Starr professor of Russian and East European studies, 2005-10. Writer. **Publications:** The Literary Ballad in Early 19th-Century Russian Literature, 1976; Dreams and the Unconscious in 19th-Century Russian Literature, 1984; (trans.) Herzen, Who is to Blame?, 1984; (trans.) N. Chernyshevsky, What is to Be Done?, 1989; (trans.) Dostoevsky, Notes from the Underground, 1989; (trans.) Tolstoy's Short Fiction, 1991; (trans.) Dostoevsky, Devils, 1992; (trans.) Druzhinin, Polinka Saks, 1992; N. Chernyshevsky, Prologue, 1995; Tur, Antonina, 1996; Artsybashev, Sanin, 2001; Jabotinsky, The Five, 2005; Pecherin, The First Russian Political Emigre, 2008; Shcheglov, The Dacha Husband 2009; S. An-sky, The Pioneers, 2011. **Address:** Middlebury College, FIC Freeman FR6, Middlebury, VT 05753, U.S.A. **Online address:** mkatz@middlebury.edu

KATZ, Molly. American (born United States) **Genres:** Mystery/Crime/Suspense, Humor/Satire, Novels, Romance/Historical. **Career:** Mystery novelist and stand-up comedian. **Publications:** No Reservations, 1985; Always Keep Him Laughing, 1985; Heights of Desire, 1986; Best Bet of His Life, 1986; Worth His Weight in Gold, 1987; Mischief-Make, 1987; When Sparks Fly, 1987; Jewish as a Second Language: How to Worry, How to Interrupt, How to Say the Opposite of What You Mean, 1991, 2nd ed., 2010; Nobody Believes Me, 1994; Love, Honour and Kill, 1999; New York as a Second Language: Haddabea Neyawka, 2004; 101 Reasons to Dump Your Man and get a Cat, 2006; No One Saw Anything, forthcoming; Presumed Guilty, forthcoming. **Address:** Andrews McMeel Publishing, 4520 Main St., Ste. 700, Kansas City, MO 64111, U.S.A.

KATZ, Paul R. (Paul Russell Katz). Taiwanese/American (born United States), b. 1961. **Genres:** Popular Culture, Adult Non-fiction. **Career:** University of California, fellow, 1990-91; National Chung Cheng University, associate professor, 1991-93; National Tsing-hua University, part-time associate professor, 1993-; Academia Sinica, Institute of History and Philology, visiting fellow, 1993-95, associate research fellow, 2002-, research fellow; National Central University, associate professor, 1995-2002, Language Center Preparatory Office, director, 2001-02, part-time associate professor, 2002-; University of Illinois, faculty, 1998; Chiang Ching-kuo Foundation for International Scholarly Exchange, program director. Historian, editor and writer. **Publications:** Demon Hordes and Burning Boats: The Cult of Marshal Wen in Late Imperial Chekiang, 1995; Taiwan De Wangye Xin Yang, 1998; Images of the Immortal: The Cult of Lu Dongbin at the Palace of Eternal Joy, 1999; (ed. and contrib. with M.A. Rubinstein) Religion and the Formation of Taiwanese Identities, 2003; When Valleys Turned Blood Red: The Ta-pa-ni Incident in Colonial Taiwan, 2005; Divine Justice: Religion And The Development Of Chinese Legal Culture, 2008; Cong di yu dao xian jing: Han ren min jian xin yang de duo yuan mian mao, 2009. CONTRIBUTOR: Encyclopedia of Taoism; Proceedings of the International Conference on Popular Beliefs and Chinese Culture, 1994; Society and Culture in Taiwan and Fukien, Chuang Ying-chang and P'an Ying-hai, 1994; Ritual, Temple, and Community-Taoism, Popular Religion, and Popular Culture, 1996; Unruly Gods: Divinity

and Society in China, 1996; Papers from the Seventh Conference on Chinese Maritime History, 1999; Ethnography in China Today: A Critical Assessment of Methods and Results, 2002; Searching for the Paradigm: New Perspectives on Taiwanese Religious Studies, 2003; Voices of the Voiceless (II): Women and Society in Modern China, 16001950, 2003; Religion in Modern Taiwan: Tradition and Innovation in a Changing Society, 2003; The Minor Arts of Daily Life: Popular Culture in Taiwan, 2004. Contributor to books and periodicals. **Address:** Academia Sinica, Institute of Modern History, 128 Academia Rd., Section 2, Nankang, Taipei, 11529, Taiwan. **Online address:** mhprkatz@gate.sinica.edu.tw

KATZ, Paul Russell. *See* **KATZ, Paul R.**

KATZ, Richard Stephen. American (born United States), b. 1947. **Genres:** Politics/Government, Art/Art History, Institutions/Organizations. **Career:** University of Michigan, Institute for Social Research, Summer Program of the Inter-University Consortium for Political Research, assistant research and programmer, 1967-69; Yale University, Department of Political Science, teaching fellow, teaching associate, 1971-72; City University of New York, assistant professor of political science, 1974-76; Johns Hopkins University, assistant professor, 1976-81, associate professor, 1981-85, professor of political science, 1985-, chair; International School of Political Science, lecturer, 1993; State University of New York, professor of political science and chair, 1995-96, graduate director. Writer. **Publications:** (With K.V. Mulcahy) American Votes: What You Should Know About Election Today, 1976; A Theory of Parties and Electoral Systems, 1980; Democracy and Elections, 1997; Political Institutions in the United States, 2007. EDITOR: (with M.C. Cummings, Jr.) The Patron State: Government and the Arts in Europe, North America and Japan, 1987; (with P. Mair) Party Organizations: A Data Handbook on Party in Western Democracies, 1960-90, 1992; (with P. Mair) How Parties Organize: Change and Adaptation in Party Organizations in Western Democracies, 1994; (with S. Bowler and D.M.Farrell) Party Discipline and Parliamentary Government, 1998; (with B. Wessels) The European Parliament, the National Parliaments and European Integration, 1999; (ed. with W.J. Crotty) Handbook of Party Politics, 2005; Political Institutions in the United States, 2007. Contributor to books. **Address:** Department of Political Science, Johns Hopkins University, 327 Megenthaler, 3400 N Charles St., Baltimore, MD 21218, U.S.A. **Online address:** richard.katz@jhu.edu

KATZ, Sanford N. American (born United States), b. 1933. **Genres:** Law, Social Sciences, Humanities. **Career:** Catholic University of America, instructor, 1959-60, assistant professor, 1960-62, associate professor of law, 1963-64; University of Florida, professor of law, 1964-68; Boston College, Law School, Newton Center, professor of law, 1968-2000, Darald & Juliet Libby professor of law, 2000-; Family Law Quarterly, editor-in-chief, 1971-84; U.S. Department of Health, law and child protection, education and welfare director, 1973-75; Oxford University, All Souls College, visiting fellow, 1997; Pembroke College, visiting fellow, 2006. **Publications:** When Parents Fail: The Law's Response to Family Breakdown, 1971; (ed. with M. McGrath) The Youngest Minority: Lawyers in Defense of Children, 1974; Creativity in Social Work: Selected Writings of Lydia Rapoport, 1975; Subsidized Adoption in America, 1976; (ed. with M. McGrath and R. Howe) Child Neglect Laws in America, 1976; (ed. with J.M. Eekelaar) Family Violence: An International and Interdisciplinary Study, 1978; (with Meezan and Reisso) Adoptions without Agencies: A Study of Independent Adoptions, 1978; (comp. with M.L. Inker and M. McGrath) Fathers, Husbands and Lovers: Legal Rights and Responsibilities, 1979; (ed. with J.M. Eekelaar) Marriage and Cohabitation in Contemporary Societies: Areas of Legal, Social and Ethical Change: An International and Interdisciplinary Study, 1980; Child Snatching: The Legal Response to the Abduction of Children, 1981; (with W.O. Weyrauch) American Family Law in Transition, 1983; (with Eekelaar) The Resolution of Family Conflict: Comparative Legal Perspectives, 1984; (ed.) Negotiating to Settlement in Divorces, 1985, rev. ed., 1987; (with W.O. Weyrauch and F. Olsen) Cases and Materials on Family Law: Legal Concepts and Changing Human Relationships, 1994; (with J. Eekelaar and M. Maclean) Cross Currents: Family Law and Policy in the United States and England, 2000; Family Law in America, 2003; Continuity of Relationships in Child Custody, 2004. **Address:** Boston College Law School, EW321, 885 Centre St., Newton, MA 02459, U.S.A. **Online address:** katzs@bc.edu

KATZ, Steve. Also writes as Stephanie Gatos. American (born United States), b. 1935. **Genres:** Novels, Novellas/Short Stories, Plays/Screenplays, Poetry, Literary Criticism And History, Young Adult Fiction. **Career:** English Language Institute, staff, 1960; University of Maryland Overseas, faculty, 1961-62; Cornell University, assistant professor of English, 1963-68; University of Iowa, lecturer at writer's workshop, 1969-70; Brooklyn College, writer-in-residence, 1970-71, Projects in Innovative Fiction, co-director, 1971-73; Queens College, assistant professor of English, 1971-75, adjunct assistant professor, 1973-75; University of Notre Dame, associate professor of English, 1976-78; University of Colorado, associate professor, 1978-, professor of English, 1978-2003, director of creative writing, 1978-81. Writer. **Publications:** The Lestriad (novel), 1962; The Weight of Antony (poetry), 1964; The Exagggerations of Peter Prince (novel), 1968; Creamy and Delicious: Eat My Words (in Other Words) (short stories), 1970; (as Stephanie Gatos) Posh (novel), 1971; Saw (novel), 1972; Cheyenne River Wild Track (poetry), 1973; Moving Parts (novel), 1977; Wier & Pouce (novel), 1984; Stolen Stories, 1984; Florry of Washington Heights (novel), 1987; Lestriad, 1987; Journalism (poetry), 1990; 43 Fictions (new and selected stories), 1991; Swanny's Ways, 1995; Antonello's Lion, 2005; Kissssss: A Miscellany, 2007; Time's Wallet, 2010. **Address:** 669 Washington St., Ste. 602, Denver, CO 80203, U.S.A. **Online address:** skatz@stevekatzwrites.com

KATZ, Steven T(heodore). American (born United States), b. 1944. **Genres:** Philosophy, Essays, Theology/Religion, Cultural/Ethnic Topics. **Career:** Hebrew University of Jerusalem, visiting research fellow, 1969-70, visiting faculty, 1971-73, visiting professor, 1976-77; Cambridge University, lecturer in Judaism and comparative religion, 1971-72; Rutgers University, Summer Institute, instructor, 1971, Department of religion, chairman, 1979-81; Dartmouth College, staff, 1972-84; University of Lancaster, visiting senior lecturer, 1974-75; University of Toronto, visiting professor, 1978; University of California, visiting professor, 1981; Yale University, visiting professor, 1982; College of William and Mary, Mason Visiting Professor, 1983; Cornell University, Department of Near Eastern studies, professor, 1984-96, chair, 1985-88, Jewish Studies Program, director, 1985-89; University of Pennsylvania, Meyerhoff professor of Jewish history, 1989-90; Yeshiva University, visiting university professor, 1995-96; Boston University, Elie Wiesel Center for Judaic Studies, director and professor of religion Judaica, holocaust studies, philosophy of religion and comparative mysticism, 1996-, Alvin J. and Shirley Slater chair in Jewish and Holocaust studies, 2007. Writer. **Publications:** (Contrib.) Christ, Faith and History, 1972; Post-Holocaust Dialogues: Critical Studies in Modern Jewish Thought, 1983; (contrib.) The Foundations of Ethics, 1983; The Cambridge History of Judaism, 1984; Historicism, the Holocaust and Zionism: Critical Studies in Modern Jewish Thought and History, 1992; The Holocaust in Historical Context, vol. I: The Holocaust and Mass Death before the Modern Age, 1994. EDITOR: (contrib.) Jewish Philosophers: A History, 1975; (contrib.) Jewish Ideas and Concepts, 1977; (contrib.) Mysticism and Philosophical Analysis, 1978; Maimonides: Selected Essays: An Original Anthology, 1980; Medieval Jewish Philosophy: An Original Anthology, 1980; Jewish Neo-Platonism: Selected Essays: An Original Anthology, 1980; Saadiah Gaon: Selected Essays: An Original Anthology, 1980; Collected Papers of Jacob Guttmann: An Original Anthology, 1980; Studies by Samuel Horodezky: An Original Anthology, 1980; Selected Writings of Julius Guttmann: An Original Anthology, 1980; (contrib.) Mysticism and Religious Traditions, 1983; (with S.L. Gilman) Anti-Semitism in Times of Crisis, 1991; Mysticism and Language, 1992; Frontiers of Jewish Thought, 1992; Interpreters of Judaism in the Late Twentieth Century, 1993; (contrib.) Essential Agus: The Writings of Jacob B. Agus, 1997; American Rabbi: The Life and Thought of Jacob B. Agus, 1997; Mysticism and Sacred Scripture, 2000; Comparative Mysticism: An Anthology of Original Sources, 2002; Impact of the Holocaust on Jewish Theology, 2005; (with A. Rosen) Obliged by Memory: Literature, Religion, Ethics, 2005; The Shtetl: New Evaluations, 2006; Shtetl: New Evaluations, 2007; (with S. Biderman and G. Greenberg) Wrestling with God: Jewish Responses During and After the Holocaust, 2007; American Jewry at 350, 2008; (ed. with R. Landes) The Paranoid Apocalypse, 2011. Contributor of articles to journals. **Address:** Department of Religion, Boston University, 147 Bay State Rd., Ste. 301, Boston, MA 02215, U.S.A. **Online address:** judaics@bu.edu

KATZ, Susan. American (born United States), b. 1945. **Genres:** Children's Non-fiction, Children's Fiction, Sciences. **Career:** Drexel University, adjunct instructor in English, 1970; Community College of Philadelphia, instructor and writing specialist, teacher in English. **Publications:** (With C. Berman) Yogurt Book: 100 Ways to Use Yogurt besides Eating It Out of a Container,

1977; Just Desserts: Fast But Fancy, 1978; Frampton!: An Unauthorized Biography, 1978; Superwomen of Rock, 1978; (with M. Klein, S. Zabar and S. Zabar) Zabar's Deli Book, 1979; Kristy and Jimmy: TV's Talented McNichols, 1979; Kristy and Jimmy McNichol: An Unauthorized Biography, 1978; (co-author) Glossary of Software Reuse Terms, 1994; Snowdrops for Cousin Ruth, 1998; Mrs. Brown on Exhibit: And Other Museum Poems, 2002; A Revolutionary Field Trip: Poems of Colonial America, 2004; Looking for Jaguar and Other Rainforest Poems, 2005; Oh, Theodore!: Guinea Pig Poems, 2007; (with C. Messinger) When the Shadbush Blooms, 2007; President's Stuck in the Bathtub, 2012. Contributor to periodicals. **Address:** Greenwillow Books, 1350 Ave. of the Americas, New York, NY 10019, U.S.A. **Online address:** katz@netaxs.com

KATZ, Welwyn Wilton. Canadian (born Canada), b. 1948. **Genres:** Novels, Children's Fiction, Young Adult Fiction, Science Fiction/Fantasy. **Career:** Writer. **Publications:** The Prophecy of Tau Ridoo, 1982; Witchery Hill, 1984; Sun God, Moon Witch, 1986; False Face, 1987; The Third Magic, 1988; Whalesinger, 1990; Come Like Shadows, 1993; Time Ghost, 1994; Out of the Dark, 1995; Beowulf, 1999; Come Like Shadows, 2000. **Address:** 33 Parkview Cres., Kitchener, ON N2A 1M1, Canada. **Online address:** booksbywelwyn@hotmail.ca

KATZEN, Mollie. American (born United States), b. 1950. **Genres:** Food And Wine. **Career:** Moosewood Restaurant, co-founder, 1973; Harvard University, Hospitality and Dining Services, consultant, 2003-; University of California, culinary advisor. Artist, musician, cook and writer. **Publications:** The Moosewood Cookbook, 1974, rev. ed., 1992; (ed. and comp.) The Moosewood Cookbook: Recipes from Moosewood Restaurant, 1977; The Enchanted Broccoli Forest: And Other Timeless Delicacies, 1982, rev. ed., 1995; Still Life With Menu: Fifty New Meatless Menus With Original Art, 1988; (with A. Henderson) Pretend Soup and Other Real Recipes: A Cookbook for Preschoolers and Up, 1994; Moosewood Cookbook Classics, 1996; Mollie Katzen's Vegetable Heaven, 1997; Honest Pretzels: And 64 Other Amazing Recipes for Cooks Ages 8 and Up, 1999; New Enchanted Broccoli Forest, 2000; New Moosewood Cookbook, 2000; Mollie Katzen's Sunlight Café, 2002; Salad People and More Real Recipes: A New Cookbook for Preschoolers and Up, 2005; (with W. Willett) Eat, Drink and Weigh Less: A Flexible and Delicious Way to Shrink Your Waist Without Going Hungry, 2006; Vegetable Dishes I can't Live Without, 2007; Mollie Katzen's Recipes: Soup, 2007; Mollie Katzen's Recipes: Salads, 2008; Mollie Katzen's Recipes: Desserts, 2009; Get Cooking: 150 Simple Recipes to Get You Started in the Kitchen, 2009. **Address:** Beth Shepard Communications, 32 Franklin Rd., Gill, MA 01376, U.S.A. **Online address:** mollie@molliekatzen.com

KATZENBACH, Jon R. American (born United States), b. 1932. **Genres:** Administration/Management, Business/Trade/Industry. **Career:** McKinsey & Co., director, 1959-98; Katzenbach Partners L.L.C., founder; Booz & Co., senior partner, 1998-. Writer. **Publications:** (With D. Smith) The Wisdom of Teams: Creating the High-Performance Organization, 1993; (co-author) Real Change Leaders: How You Can Create Growth and High Performance at Your Company, 1995; The Myth of the Top Management Team, 1997; Teams at the Top: Unleashing the Potential of Both Teams and Individual Leaders, 1998; (ed. and intro.) The Work of Teams, 1998; (with J. Santamaria) Firing Up the Front Line, 1999; Peak Performance: Aligning the Hearts and Minds of Your Employees, 2000; (with D. Smith) The Discipline of Teams: A Mindbook-Workbook for Delivering Small Group Performance, 2001, rev. ed. as The Discipline of Teams, 2008; (with D. Smith) Virtual Teaming, 2001; Why Pride Matters More than Money: The Power of the World's Greatest Motivational Force, 2003; Pride: A Strategic Asset, 2003; (with Z. Khan) Leading Outside the Lines, 2010. **Address:** Booz & Co., 101 Park Ave., 18th Fl., New York, NY 10178, U.S.A. **Online address:** jon.katzenbach@booz.com

KATZEW, Ilona. American (born United States), b. 1965. **Genres:** Art/Art History. **Career:** Los Angeles County Museum of Art, associate curator of Latin American art, curator and co-head of Latin American art. Writer. **Publications:** (Ed. with J.A. Farmer) A Hemispheric Venture: Thirty-five Years of Culture at the Americas Society, 1965-2000=Una Aventura Hemisferica: Treinta y Cinco Anos de Cultura en La Americas Society, 1965-2000, 2000; Casta Painting: Images of Race in Eighteenth-Century Mexico, 2004; Una Vision del Mexico del Siglo de Las Luces: La Codificacion de Joaquin Antonio de Basars: Origen, Costumbres y Estado Presente de Mexicanos y Filipinos, 2006; (ed. with S. Deans-Smith) Race and Classification: The Case of Mexican America, 2009. Contributor to periodicals. **Address:** Los Angeles County Museum of Art, 5905 Wilshire Blvd., Los Angeles, CA 90036, U.S.A.

KATZMAN, Melanie A. American (born United States), b. 1958. **Genres:** Psychology, Medicine/Health, Sports/Fitness. **Career:** Devereux Center, therapist, 1981-82; Good Samaritan Medical Center, therapist, 1982-83; Bulimia Therapy and Research Team, coordinator and consultant, 1983-84; New York University, Bellevue Medical Center, psychology intern, 1984-85; Institute for Behavior Therapy, part-time post-doctoral fellow, 1985-86; New York Hospital-White Plains, Weill-Cornell Medical School, Westchester Division, post-doctoral fellow, 1985-86; Regent Hospital, director of outpatient eating disorders services, 1986-87, Metropolitan Medical Group, clinical director of psychiatric outpatient services, 1988-89; Cornell University, Medical Center, clinical assistant professor of psychology, 1987-; New York Hospital-New York, assistant attending psychologist, 1987-; The Business Practice, Hong Kong, director of corporate consultations, 1994-95; University of London, Institute of Psychiatry, lecturer, 1995-; Leaders' Quest, partner; Henley Management College, School of Leadership, Change and HR, visiting tutor; Katzman Consulting, president. Writer. **Publications:** (With L. Weiss and S. Wolchik) Treating Bulimia: A Psychoeducational Approach, 1985; (with L. Weiss and S. Wolchik) You Can't Have Your Cake and Eat It Too: A Program for Controlling Bulimia, 1986; (ed. with P. Fallon and S.C. Wooley) Feminist Perspectives on Eating Disorders, 1994; (ed. with H.W. Hoek and J.L. Treasure) Neurobiology in the Treatment of Eating Disorders, 1998; (ed. with M. Nasser and R.A. Gordon) Eating Disorders and Cultures in Transition, 2001. Contributor of articles to books, journals and periodicals. **Address:** Katzman Consulting, 10 E 78th St., Ste. 4A, New York, NY 10075-1734, U.S.A. **Online address:** mkatzman@katzmanconsulting.com

KAUFFMAN, Bill. American (born United States), b. 1959. **Genres:** Novels, Politics/Government, Travel/Exploration, Social Sciences. **Career:** Legislative assistant for Senator Daniel Patrick Moynihan, 1981-83; Reason, assistant editor, 1985-88; The American Enterprise, associate editor, 1994-; Chronicles, contributing editor; Liberty, contributing editor; The American Conservative, columnist; First Principles, columnist. **Publications:** Every Man a King (novel), 1989; Country Towns of New York, 1994, 2nd ed. as Country Towns of New York: Charming Small Towns and Villages to Explore, 1999; America First!: Its History, Culture, and Politics, 1995; With Good Intentions?: Reflections on the Myth of Progress in America, 1998; Dispatches from the Muckdog Gazette: A Mostly Affectionate Account of a Small Town's Fight to Survive, 2003; (ed. and intro.) A Story of America First: The Men and Women Who Opposed U.S. Intervention in World War II, 2003; Look Homeward, America: In Search of Reactionary Radicals and Front-Porch Anarchists, 2006; Ain't My America: The Long, Noble History of Antiwar Conservatism and Middle American Anti-Imperialism, 2008; Forgotten Founder, Drunken Prophet: The Life of Luther Martin, 2008; Bye Bye, Miss American Empire: Neighborhood Patriots, Backcountry Rebels, and Their Underdog Crusades to Redraw America's Political Map, 2010. **Address:** c/o Kirsten Manges, Curtis Brown Ltd., 10 Astor Pl., New York, NY 10003, U.S.A.

KAUFFMAN, Donna. American (born United States), b. 1960?. **Genres:** Romance/Historical, Novels. **Career:** Writer. **Publications:** Illegal Motion, 1993; Black Satin, 1994; Tango in Paradise, 1994; Bounty Hunter, 1994; Wild Rain, 1995; Bayou Heat, 1996; Tease Me, 1998; Her Secret Thrill, 2001; Heat of the Night, 2001; Walk on the Wild Side, 2001; His Private Pleasure, 2002; Sean, 2003; (with L. Foster and J. Shalvis) Men of Courage, 2003; Jingle Bell Rock, 2003; The Big Bad Wolf Tells All, 2003; Against the Odds, 2003; (co-author) Merry Christmas Baby, 2004; Catch Me If You Can, 2004; (with L. Foster and J. Shalvis) Men of Courage II, 2005; Perfectly Plum, 2007; (with J. Shalvis and H. Dimon) To All a Good Night, 2008; Let Me In, 2009; A Great Kisser, 2009; Kissing Santa Claus, 2009; Here Comes Trouble, 2010; (with C. Eden and S. Fox) The Naughty List, 2010; Simon Says, 2011; Off Kilter, 2011; Sugar Rush, 2012; Sweet Stuff, 2012. THREE MUSKETEERS SERIES: Surrender the Dark, 1995; Born to Be Wild, 1996; Midnight Heat, 1996. DELGADO'S DIRTY DOZEN SERIES: Santerra's Sin, 1996; Silent Warrior, 1997; Light My Fire, 1997; Dark Knight, 1998. PARANORMAL NOVELS: The Legend MacKinnon, 1999; The Legend of the Sorcerer, 2000; Your Wish Is My Command, 2001; The Royal Hunter, 2001; The Charm Stone, 2002. CONTEMPORARY ROMANCE NOVELS: The Big Bad Wolf Tells All (formerly titled The Last Bridesmaid), 2003; The Cinderella Rules, 2003; Dear Prince Charming, 2004, Sleeping With Beauty, 2005; Not So Snow White, 2006; Bad Boys in Kilts, 2006; The Black Sheep

and The Princess, 2007; The Great Scot, 2007; The Black Sheep and the Hidden Beauty, 2008; The Black Sheep and the English Rose, 2008; Some Like It Scot, 2010. **Address:** PO Box 650533, Potomac Falls, VA 20165, U.S.A. **Online address:** donna@donnakauffman.com

KAUFFMAN, Janet. American (born United States), b. 1945. **Genres:** Novels, Novellas/Short Stories, Poetry, Young Adult Fiction, Adult Non-fiction, Literary Criticism And History. **Career:** Jackson Community College, professor, 1976-88; University of Michigan, visiting professor of English, 1984-85; Eastern Michigan University, professor, 1988-, MA Creative Writing Program, coordinator. Writer. **Publications:** POETRY: (with J. McCann) Writing Home, 1978; The Weather Book, 1981; Five on Fiction (poems), 2004. SHORT STORIES: Places in the World a Woman Could Walk, 1983; Obscene Gestures for Women, 1989; Characters on the Loose, 1997; Trespassing: Dirt Stories and Field Notes, 2008. NOVELS: Collaborators, 1986; The Body in Four Parts, 1993; Rot, 2001. Contributor to periodicals. **Address:** Department of English Language & Literature, Eastern Michigan University, 603 N Pray-Harrold, Ypsilanti, MI 48197, U.S.A. **Online address:** jkauffman@emich.edu

KAUFFMAN, Michael W. American (born United States) **Genres:** Writing/Journalism, History, Autobiography/Memoirs, Romance/Historical. **Career:** Writer and historian. **Publications:** (Ed.) Memoirs of a Lincoln Conspirator, 1995; American Brutus: John Wilkes Booth and the Lincoln Conspiracies, 2004. **Address:** c/o Author Mail, Random House Inc., 1745 Broadway, New York, NY 10019-4368, U.S.A.

KAUFFMAN, Stuart Alan. American (born United States), b. 1939. **Genres:** Biology, Sciences, Theology/Religion. **Career:** Cincinnati General Hospital, intern, 1969; University of Chicago, assistant professor of biophysics and theoretical biology, 1969-75, assistant professor of medicine, 1970-73; National Cancer Institute, Laboratory of Theoretical Biology, research associate, surgeon, 1973-75; University of Pennsylvania, College of Medicine, associate professor of biochemistry and biophysics, 1975-81, professor of biochemistry and biophysics, 1981-95, professor emeritus, 1995-; Los Alamos National Laboratory, consultant, 1985-89; Santa Fe Institute, professor, 1986-97, external professor, 1996-2005, faculty-in-residence, 1986-97; Genesys Molecular Inc., founder and president, 1990; Darwin Molecular Inc., co-founder, 1992, president, 1992-93; Bios Group Inc., owner, 1996-, founding general partner and chief scientific officer, 1996-2003, board director, 1996-; Genpathway, board director, 1997-2007, chairman, 2001-07; Investigations Group, chairman, 2000-; Gene Network Science, board director, 2001-03; University of New Mexico, School of Medicine, research professor of cell biology and physiology, 2003-05; Montana State University, affiliate, 2003-; George Mason University, Krasnow Institute, internal visiting professor, 2003-; NuTech Solutions, board director, 2003-07, senior fellow, 2007-; M.D. Anderson Cancer Center, Department of Pathology, adjunct professor, 2003-; Banff Centre, researcher-in-residence, 2004-; Genesis Molecular Discovery, co-founder, 2004; University of Calgary, Department of Biological Sciences and Physics and Astronomy, professor, 2004-09, The Institute for Biocomplexity and Informatics, founding director, 2005-09, adjunct professor of philosophy, iCORE chair in biocomplexity and informatics, 2005-, iCore visiting professor, chair, director; Tampere University of Technology, Department of Signal Processing, Finland distinguished professor, 2009-; University of Vermont, College of Medicine, Biochemistry CEMS, Department of Mathematics & Statistics, visiting distinguished research professor, 2010-, Complex Systems Center, senior researcher, 2010-. Writer. **Publications:** (Ed. with A.S. Perelson) Molecular Evolution On Rugged Landscapes: Proteins, RNA, and the Immune System: The Proceedings of the Workshop On Applied Molecular Evolution and the Maturation of the Immune Response, 1991; The Origins of Order: Self-Organization and Selection in Evolution, 1993; At Home in the Universe: The Search for Laws of Self-Organization and Complexity, 1995; Investigations, 2000; Reinventing the Sacred: A New View of Science, Reason and Religion, 2008. Contributor to books and periodicals. **Address:** Complex Systems Center, University of Vermont, 200C Farrell Hall, 210 Colchester Ave., 85 S Prospect St., Burlington, VT 05405, U.S.A. **Online address:** skauffman@ucalgary.ca

KAUFFMANN, Stanley. (Spranger Barry). American (born United States), b. 1916. **Genres:** Novels, Plays/Screenplays, Film, Literary Criticism And History, Autobiography/Memoirs, Young Adult Fiction. **Career:** Washington Square Players, actor and stage manager, 1931-41; Bantam Books, associate editor, 1949-52; Ballantine Books, editor-in-chief, 1952-56, consulting editor,

1957-59; New Republic, contributing editor and film critic, 1958-65, 1968, associate literary editor, 1966-67, theater critic, 1969-79; Alfred A. Knopf Inc., editor, 1959-60; Yale University, Morse College, honorary associate fellow, 1964; New York Times, drama critic, 1966; Yale School of Drama, visiting professor, 1967-73, 1977-86, 1995, 1997; York College of the City University of New York, distinguished professor, 1973-76, Graduate School and University Center, visiting professor, 1977-92; Saturday Review, theater critic, 1979-85; Hunter College, visiting professor of drama, 1993, Adelphi University, professor of performing arts, 1992-96, distinguished visiting professor, 1992-94. Actor, director and theater and film critic. **Publications:** The Red-Handkerchief Man, 1933; The Prince Who Shouldn't Have Shaved: A Frolic in One Act, 1934; How She Managed Her Marriage, 1935; The True Adventure, 1935; The Singer in Search of a King, 1935; Altogether Reformed, 1936; Father Spills the Beans, 1936; A Word from the Wise, for Three Women, 1937; Come Again, A South Seas Vignette in One Act, 1937; Coming of Age, 1937; Eleanor on the Hill: A One-Act Fantasia on Comic Themes, 1937; Right Under Her Nose, a Comedy in One Act, 1938; Mr. Flemington Sits Down, 1938; Cow Was in the Parlor, 1938; The Salvation of Mr. Song, 1939; (as Spranger Barry) Play Ball!, 1940; (as Spranger Barry) Close Courting, 1940; Bobino, His Adventures, 1941; Pig of My Dreams, 1942; The King of Proxy Street, 1941 in UK as The Bad Samaritan, 1943; Food for Freedom: A United Nations Play for Elementary School Children in One Act, 1944; This time Forever, 1945; The Hidden Hero, 1949; The Tightrope, 1952, as The Summing-Up by Justice Stable in the Trial for an Alleged Obscene Libel, 1954; A Change of Climate, 1954; Man of the World in UK as The Very Man, 1956; If It Be Love, 1960; A World on Film: Criticism and Comment, 1966; Figures of Light: Film Criticism and Comment, 1971; Living Images: Film Comment and Criticism, 1975; Persons of the Drama: Theater Criticism and Comment, 1976; (ed. with B. Henstell) American Film Criticism: From the Beginnings to Citizen Kane, 1972, 1979; Before My Eyes: Film Criticism and Comment, 1980; Albums of Early Life, 1980; Theater Criticisms, 1984; Field of View: Film Criticism and Comment, 1985; Distinguishing Features: Film Criticism and Comment, 1994; Regarding Film: Criticism and Comment, 2001; Conversations with Stanley Kauffmann, 2006; Albums of a Life, 2007; About the Theater, 2009. **Address:** Brandt & Hochman Literary Agents Inc., 1501 Broadway, New York, NY 10036, U.S.A.

KAUFMAN, Bel. American/Russian/German (born Germany), b. 1911. **Genres:** Novels, Education, Essays. **Career:** New School for Social Research, instructor in English, 1964; Borough of Manhattan Community College, assistant professor of English, 1964-; University of Rochester, lecturer; University of Florida, lecturer; Hunter College, adjunct professor. Writer. **Publications:** Up the Down Staircase, 1965; Love, Etc., 1979. **Address:** c/o Sidney J. Gluck, 202 W 40th St., New York, NY 10018, U.S.A. **Online address:** belkau@aol.com

KAUFMAN, Frederick L. American (born United States), b. 1961. **Genres:** Novels. **Career:** City University of New York and Graduate School of Journalism, professor of English. Writer. **Publications:** Forty-two Days and Nights on the Iberian Peninsula with Anis Ladron, Harcourt Brace Jovanovich (San Diego, CA), (Author of essay) Manuel Alvarez Bravo: Photographs and Memories, Aperture Foundation (New York, NY), A Short History of the American Stomach, Harcourt (Orlando, FL), Author of script for Fastpitch, a documentary about fast-pitch softball. Also author of the blog American Stomach. Contributor to books, including About Men: Reflections on the Male Experience, edited by Don Erickson, Poseidon Press, 1987; and Everything That Lives, Eats, Aperture, 1996. Contributor to periodicals, including Harpers, New Yorker, Gastronomica, Gourmet, and New York Times Magazine. Contributing editor, Harper's. **Address:** New York, NY , U.S.A. **Online address:** fredkaufman@verizon.net

KAUFMAN, Gerald (Bernard). British (born England), b. 1930. **Genres:** Politics/Government, Humor/Satire. **Career:** Balham and Tooting College of Commerce, governor, 1954-55; Fabian Society, assistant secretary, 1954-55; Daily Mirror, political staff, leader writer, 1955-64; New Statesman, political correspondent, journalist, 1964-65; British Labour Party, parliamentary press liaison officer, 1965-70; Ardwick Division of Manchester, member of parliament, 1970-83, Manchester Gorto, member of parliament, 1983-2010, government minister, junior minister, 1974-79; State Department of the Environment, under-secretary of state, 1974-75; Department of Industry, parliamentary under-secretary, 1975-79; Shadow Cabinet, shadow environment secretary, 1980-83, shadow home secretary, 1983-87, shadow foreign secretary, 1987-92. Writer. **Publications:** (With D. Frost, C. Booker and H. Sar-

gent) How to Live Under Labour, 1964; (ed. and intro.) The Left, 1966; To Build the Promised Land, 1973; How to Be a Minister, 1980; (ed.) Renewal, 1983; My Life in the Silver Screen, 1985; Inside the Promised Land: A Personal View of Today's Israel, 1986; The God of the Poor, 1993; Meet Me in St Louis, 1994; Tourism: The Hidden Giant and Foot and Mouth, Fourth Report Session 2000-01: Minutes of Evidence and Appendices, 2001; Closing The Gap, 2003. **Address:** House of Commons, London, GL SW1A 0AA, England. **Online address:** kaufmang@parliament.uk

KAUFMAN, Joyce P. American (born United States), b. 1949. **Genres:** History, Institutions/Organizations. **Career:** University of Michigan, Institute for Social Research, research assistant in the center for political studies, 1975-76; Department of Defense, foreign affairs specialist, Office of Nuclear Police, Office of the Assistant Secretary of Defense, staff, 1978-79; Open University, University of Maryland, faculty, 1978-84, Department of Government and Politics, visiting associate professor and associate director of Project ICONS, 1992-93; Pacific-Sierra Research Corp., national security analyst, 1979-82; Logistic Management Institute, research fellow, 1983-84; California State University, Department of Political Science, lecturer, 1984-85; Whittier College, assistant professor, 1985-90, associate professor, 1990-97, professor of political science, 1998-, director of the International Negotiation Project, 1987-, associate academic dean and director of the Whittier scholars program, 1997-; University of Southern California, visiting associate professor in the school of international relations, 1994-96; Immaculate Heart College Center, professor in the global studies department and vice president of the program development, 1994-96. Writer and political scientist. **Publications:** (Ed. and contrib. with L.P. Brady) NATO in the 1980s: Challenges and Responses, 1985; (co-author) Europe after the Cold War: An Instructional Guide for High Schools, 1994; NATO and the Former Yugoslavia: Crisis, Conflict and Atlantic Alliance, 2002; A Concise History of U.S. Foreign Policy, 2006; (with K.P. Williams) Women, the State and War: A Comparative Perspective on Citizenship and Nationalism, 2007. Contributor of articles to books and journals. **Address:** Whittier College, PO Box 634, Whittier, CA 90608, U.S.A. **Online address:** jkaufman@whittier.edu

KAUFMAN, Kenn. American (born United States), b. 1954?. **Genres:** Zoology, Animals/Pets. **Career:** American Birds, associate editor, 1984; Bird-Watching, columnist; Bird Watcher's Digest, columnist; WildBird, editorial consultant; Audubon Magazine, field editor. Artist and tour leader. **Publications:** (With L. Line and K.L. Garrett) The Audubon Society Book of Water Birds, 1987; (with J. Farrand) National Audubon Society Pocket Guide to Familiar Birds: Eastern Region, 1987; (with J. Farrand) National Audubon Society Pocket Guide to Familiar Birds: Western Region, 1987; Lives of North American Birds, 1996; (intro.) Vanishing Songbirds: The Sixth Order: Wood Warblers and Other Passerine Birds, 1996; Kingbird Highway: The Story of a Natural Obsession That Got a Little Out of Hand, 1997; (co-author) Birds of North America, 2000; (co-author) City Birding: True Tales of Birds and Birdwatching in Unexpected Places, 2003; (with J.P. Brock) Kaufman Field Guide to Butterflies of North America, 2003; (co-author) Kaufman Focus Guide to Mammals of North America, 2004; (with J.P. Brock) Kaufman Field Guide to Birds of North America, 2005; Kaufman Field Guide to Insects of North America, 2006; Kingbird Highway: The Biggest Year in the Life of an Extreme Birder, 2006; (foreword) Birding for Everyone: Encouraging People of Color to Become Birdwatchers, 2008; Flights Against the Sunset: Stories that Reunited a Mother and Son, 2008; Kaufman Field Guide to Advanced Birding: Understanding What You See and Hear, 2011. Contributor to periodicals. **Address:** Houghton Mifflin Co., 222 Berkeley St., Boston, MA 02116-3764, U.S.A.

KAUFMAN, Lynne. American (born United States) **Genres:** Law, Novels, Plays/Screenplays. **Career:** University of California-Berkeley, staff and director of travel study programs. Writer. **Publications:** PLAYS: Roshi, 1987; Speaking in Tongues, 1989; Our Lady of the Desert, 1991; Dottie and the Boys, 1991; Shooting Simone, 1994; Fifty/Fifty, 1994; Fakes, 1997; The Couch, 1998; The Last Game Show, 2000; The Next Marilyn, 2003; Daisy in the Dreamtime, 2003; Picasso, 2003; Shooting Simone, 2003; Magician's Choice, 2005, The Secret Museum, 2005; The Yellow House, 2006. OTHERS: Slow Hands, 2003; Wild Women's Weekend, 2004; Taking Flight, 2005. Contributor to periodicals. **Address:** c/o Gail Hochman, Brandt and Hochman Literary Agents Inc., 1501 Broadway, New York, NY 10036, U.S.A. **Online address:** lynnekaufman@comcast.net

KAUFMAN, Menahem. Israeli/German (born Germany), b. 1921. **Genres:** History, Politics/Government, Social Sciences. **Career:** Hebrew University of Jerusalem, The Institute of Contemporary Jewry, administrative director, 1972-88, researcher, 1980, senior researcher, professor emeritus, 1989-. Writer. **Publications:** Guide to America-Holy Land Studies, 1980; America-Jerusalem Policy, 1947-1948, 1982; Non-Zionists in America and the Struggle for Jewish Statehood (in Hebrew), 1984; Lo-Tsiyonim ba-Amerikah ba-maavak alha-medinah, 1939-1948, 1984; An Ambiguous Partnership: Non-Zionists and Zionists in America, 1939-48, 1991; Die hessischen Landjuden, 1933-45, 1991; Ha-Umah ha-Amerikanit ve-Erets-Yiśrael: Yesodot kishre ha-gomlinha-meyuḥadim, 1996; (intro.) The Magnes-Philby Negotiations, 1929: The Historical Record, 1998. EDITOR: (with M. Levine) Guide to America-Holy Land Studies, 1620-1948, vol. IV: Resource Material in British, Israeli and Turkish Repositories, 1984; America and the Holy Land, the Foundation of a Special Relationship (in Hebrew), 1996. **Address:** The Avraham Harman Institute of Contemporary Jewry, The Hebrew University, Mount Scopus, Jerusalem, 91905, Israel.

KAUFMAN, Robert G. (Robert Gordon Kaufman). American (born United States) **Genres:** Politics/Government, Biography, Military/Defense/Arms Control. **Career:** Colgate University, faculty; Naval War College, faculty; University of Vermont, faculty; Pepperdine University, School of Public Policy, professor of public policy. Writer and scientist. **Publications:** (As Robert Gordon Kaufman) Arms Control During the Pre-Nuclear Era: The United States and Naval Limitation Between the Two World Wars, 1990; Henry M. Jackson: A Life in Politics, 2000; In Defense of the Bush Doctrine, 2007. Contributor to periodicals. **Address:** School of Public Policy, Pepperdine University, 24255 Pacific Coast Hwy., Malibu, CA 90263-7493, U.S.A. **Online address:** robert.kaufman@pepperdine.edu

KAUFMAN, Robert Gordon. See **KAUFMAN, Robert G.**

KAUFMAN, Scott S. (Victor Scott Kaufman). American (born United States), b. 1969. **Genres:** Children's Fiction. **Career:** Francis Marion University, associate professor, 2001-. Writer. **Publications:** (As Victor S. Kaufman) Confronting Communism: U.S. and British Policies toward China, 2001; The Pig War: The United States, Britain, and the Balance of Power in the Pacific Northwest, 1846-72, 2004; (with B.I. Kaufman) The Presidency of James Earl Carter, Jr., 2nd ed., 2006; Francis Marion: Swamp Fox of South Carolina (children's book), 2007; Rosalynn Carter: Equal Partner in the White House, 2007; Plans Unraveled: The Foreign Policy of the Carter Administration, 2008; (ed. with A. Warters) The United Nations: Past, Present, and Future: Proceedings of the 2007 Francis Marion University UN Symposium, 2009. Contributor to books. **Address:** Francis Marion University, PO Box 100547, Florence, SC 29502, U.S.A. **Online address:** vkaufman@fmarion.edu

KAUFMAN, Suzanne K. American (born United States), b. 1965. **Genres:** History, Cultural/Ethnic Topics. **Career:** Loyola University, graduate programs director. Writer, administrator, academic and historian. **Publications:** Consuming Visions: Mass Culture and the Lourdes Shrine, 2005. Contributor to books and journals. **Address:** Department of History, Loyola University, Crown Ctr., 6525 N Sheridan Rd., 5th Fl., Chicago, IL 60626-5761, U.S.A. **Online address:** skaufma@luc.edu

KAUFMAN, Victor Scott. See **KAUFMAN, Scott S.**

KAUFMAN, Victor S(cott). American (born United States), b. 1969. **Genres:** History. **Career:** Ohio University, instructor in history, 1997; Virginia Polytechnic Institute and State University, instructor in history, 1997-98; Kennesaw State University, instructor in history, 1998-99; Georgia State University, instructor, 1998-99; Southwest Missouri State University, lecturer in history, 1999-2001; Francis Marion University, assistant professor of history, 2001-, associate professor of history. Writer. **Publications:** Confronting Communism: U.S. and British Policies toward China, 2001; Pig War: The United States, Britain and the Balance of Power in the Pacific Northwest, 1846-72, 2003; (with B.I. Kaufman) Presidency of James Earl Carter, Jr., 2nd ed., 2006; Francis Marion: Swamp Fox of South Carolina, 2007; Rosalynn Carter: Equal Partner in the White House, 2007; Plans Unraveled: The Foreign Policy of the Carter Administration, 2008. Contributor to periodicals. **Address:** Department of History, Francis Marion University, 4822 E Palmetto St., PO Box 100547, Florence, SC 29506-4530, U.S.A. **Online address:** vkaufman@fmarion.edu

KAUFMAN, Will. British/American (born United States), b. 1958. **Genres:** Literary Criticism And History, History, Cultural/Ethnic Topics, Politics/Government. **Career:** North Staffordshire Polytechnic, lecturer in English and American literature, 1986-88; Crewe and Alsager College of Higher Education, lecturer, 1987-88; Sriwijaya University, lecturer in English language and literature, 1988-90; Lancashire Polytechnic, lecturer in English and American studies, 1991-93; University of Central Lancashire, Department of Humanities, senior lecturer in English and American studies, 1993-, School of Journalism, Media and Communication, professor of American literature and culture, reader in English and American studies; British Association for American Studies, vice chair; Maastricht University, Centre for Transatlantic Studies, co-founder. Writer. **Publications:** (Contrib.) Mark Twain: A Sumptuous Variety, 1985; (contrib.) Matthew Arnold: Between Two Worlds, 1986; The Comedian as Confidence Man: Studies in Irony Fatigue, 1997; Civil War in American Culture, 2006; American Culture in the 1970s, 2009; Woody Guthrie, American Radical, 2011. EDITOR WITH H.S. MACPHERSON: Transatlantic Studies, 2000; New Perspectives in Transatlantic Studies, 2001; Britain and the Americas: Culture, Politics, and History: A Multidisciplinary Encyclopedia, 2005. Contributor to periodicals. **Address:** Department of Humanities, University of Central Lancashire, Fylde 427, Preston, LC PR1 2HE, England. **Online address:** wkaufman@uclan.ac.uk

KAUFMANN, Dovid Yisroel Ber. American (born United States), b. 1951. **Genres:** Novels, Young Adult Fiction, Adult Non-fiction, History, Ethics, Biography, Theology/Religion. **Career:** Tulane University, instructor in English, 1985-89, adjunct assistant professor of Hebrew and Israeli studies, 1994-96, postdoctoral teaching fellow; Chabad House (Jewish student center), coordinator and teacher, 1985-. Writer. **Publications:** The Silent Witness (novel), 1996; (with S. Zakar) Judaism OnLine: Confronting Spirituality on the Internet, 1998; (ed. and trans. with H. Greenberg) Besuros He Geuloh, 1998. Contributor to periodicals. **Address:** Department of English, Tulane University, Rm. 235, Norman Mayer, New Orleans, LA 70118, U.S.A. **Online address:** kaufmann@tulane.edu

KAUFMAN-OSBORN, Timothy. American (born United States), b. 1953. **Genres:** Politics/Government, Law. **Career:** Whitman College, Department of Politics, assistant professor, 1982-85, chair, 1984-87, 1989-90, 1991-92, 1994, 1998, 2001, associate professor, 1985-92, professor, 1992-96, Baker Ferguson professor of politics and leadership, 1996-2009, Baker Ferguson professor emeritus of politics and leadership, 2009-, Baker Ferguson chair of politics and leadership, Women's Resource Center, faculty advisor, 1986-90, Whitman Civil Liberties Union, faculty advisor, 1992-, Division of Social Sciences, chair, 2004-06, interim dean of the faculty, 2006-07, chair of the faculty, 2008-09, provost and dean of the faculty, 2009-; Princeton University, Department of Politics, visiting research fellow, 1985-86; American Civil Liberties Union of Washington, board director, 1991-2006, vice president, 1998-2002, president, 2002-06; Tau Kappa Epsilon, faculty advisor, 1996-2000; Western Political Science Association, vice president, 2000-01, president, 2001-03. Writer. **Publications:** Politics/Sense/Experience: A Pragmatic Inquiry into the Promise of Democracy, 1991; Creatures of Prometheus: Gender and the Politics of Technology, 1997; From Noose to Needle: Capital Punishment and the Late Liberal State, 2002. Contributor to journals. **Address:** Department of Politics, Whitman College, Rm. 308, Memorial Bldg., 345 Boyer Ave., Walla Walla, WA 99362, U.S.A. **Online address:** kaufmatv@whitman.edu

KAVANAGH, Julie. British/South African (born South Africa), b. 1952. **Genres:** Biography, Theology/Religion. **Career:** British Vogue, staff; Women's Wear Daily, London editor; Harper's and Queen, arts editor, 1980-90; Spectator, dance critic; Vanity Fair, London editor, 1990-93; New Yorker, London editor, 1993-97. **Publications:** Secret Muses: The Life of Frederick Ashton (biography), 1996; Nureyev: The Life (biography), 2007; (with M. Mahon) A Welcome for Your Child: A Guide to Baptism for Parents, 2008. Contributor to periodicals. **Address:** Veritas, 7-8 Lower Abbey St., Dublin, DU 1, Ireland.

KAVANAGH, P(atrick) J(oseph). British (born England), b. 1931. **Genres:** Novels, Children's Fiction, Young Adult Fiction, Plays/Screenplays, Poetry, Autobiography/Memoirs, Essays, Travel/Exploration, Travel/Exploration. **Career:** University of Indonesia, lecturer, 1957-58; actor, 1959-70; The Spectator, columnist, 1983-96; The Times Literary Supplement, columnist, 1996-2002. Writer. **Publications:** POETRY: One and One: Poems, 1959; On the Way to the Depot, 1967; About Time, 1970; Edward Thomas in Heaven,

1974; Life before Death, 1979; Selected Poems, 1982; Presences: New and Selected Poems, 1987; An Enchantment, 1991; Collected Poems, 1992; More Poetry Please! B.B.C. Radio4 Program: Everyman's Poetry, 1997. NOVELS: A Song and Dance, 1968; A Happy Man, 1972; People and Weather, 1978; Only By Mistake, 1986. FOR CHILDREN: Scarf Jack, 1978 in US as The Irish Captain, 1979 in UK as Rebel for Good, 1980. OTHERS: The Perfect Stranger (autobiography), 1966; Autobiography, 1974; People and Places (essays), 1988; Finding Connections (travel), 1990; Voices in Ireland: A Traveller's Literary Companion, 1994; A Kind of Journal, 1987-2002 (essays), 2003; Something About, 2004. EDITOR: (and intro.) Collected Poems of Ivor Gurney, 1982, rev. ed. as Selected Poems of Ivor Gurney, 1990; (with J. Michie) The Oxford Book of Short Poems, 1985; The Bodley Head G.K. Chesterton, 1985; The Essential G.K. Chesterton, 1985; A Book of Consolations, 1992. Contributor of articles to periodicals and journals. **Address:** Peters Fraser and Dunlop Group Ltd., Drury House, 34-43 Russell St., London, GL WC2B 5HA, England.

KAVANAGH, Paul. See **BLOCK, Lawrence.**

KAVANAUGH, Andrea L(ee). American (born United States), b. 1951. **Genres:** Technology, Sociology, Information Science/Computers, Politics/ Government, Regional/Urban Planning, Reference, Social Sciences. **Career:** French American Bilingual School, instructor, administrative assistant, 1974-77; U.S. Department of Commerce, research assistant, 1984-85; Virginia Tech, Communications Network Services, research assistant, 1985-87; Hollins College, instructor in communications studies, 1989; Virginia Polytechnic Institute and State University, fellow, 1991, Blacksburg Electronic Village, director of research, 1993-2001, Communication Studies, adjunct professor, 1997-98, Center for Human-Computer Interaction, assistant director, associate director, senior research scientist, 2002-, fellow. Writer. **Publications:** (Contrib.) Television and Adult Education, 1984; (ed. with A. Cohill) Community Networks: Lessons from Blacksburg, Virginia, 1997, 2nd ed., 2000; The Social Control of Technology in North Africa: Information in the Global Economy, 1998; (contrib.) Telecommunications in Africa, 1998; (ed. with J. Turow) The Wired Homestead: An MIT Press Sourcebook on the Internet and the Family, 2003. **Address:** Center for Human-Computer Interaction, Department of Computer Science, Virginia Polytech Institute and State University, 1116 KWII, 2202 Kraft Dr., Blacksburg, VA 24060, U.S.A. **Online address:** kavan@vt.edu

KAVENEY, Roz J. American (born United States), b. 1949. **Genres:** Novellas/Short Stories, Sciences. **Career:** Writer. **Publications:** (With N. Gaiman and M. Gentle) The Weerde (short stories), vol. I, 1992, vol. II, 1993; From Alien to The Matrix: Reading Science Fiction Film, 2005; Teen Dreams: Reading Teen Film from Heathers to Veronica Mars, 2006; Superheroes! Capes and Crusaders in Comics and Films, 2008. EDITOR: Tales from the Forbidden Planet (short stories), 1987; More Tales from the Forbidden Planet (short stories), 1990; (with M. Gentle) Mary Gentle and Neil Gaiman, Villains! (short stories), 1992; Reading the Vampire Slayer: An Unofficial Critical Companion to Buffy and Angel, 2002. **Online address:** rkaveney@gmail.com

KAVENNA, Joanna. British (born England), b. 1974?. **Genres:** Novels, Travel/Exploration, Autobiography/Memoirs. **Career:** St Peter's College, writer-in-residence. **Publications:** The Ice Museum: In Search of the Lost Land of Thule, 2005; Inglorious, 2007; The Birth of Love: A Novel, 2010. Contributor to periodicals. **Address:** Rogers, Coleridge and White Ltd., 20 Powis Mews, London, GL W11 1JN, England. **Online address:** jk@joannakavenna.com

KAWAKAMI, Barbara Fusako. American/Japanese (born Japan), b. 1921. **Genres:** Cultural/Ethnic Topics, History, Local History/Rural Topics, Biography, Documentaries/Reportage, Translations, Adult Non-fiction. **Career:** Leeward Community College, community services program, sewing instructor, 1975-78; University of Hawaii, community services program, sewing instructor, 1978; Hawaii Public Television ARCHIVE Project, researcher, writer, associate producer, interviewer, translator and costumer, 1985-89; Everlasting Reflection, contributing scriptwriter, director, costume coordinator, 1990; Japanese American National Museum, Discover Nikkei, manager, 1990-. **Publications:** Japanese Immigrant Clothing in Hawaii, 1885-1941, 1993. Contributor to periodicals and journals. **Address:** Discover Nikkei, Japanese American National Museum, 369 E 1st St., Los Angeles, CA 90012, U.S.A.

KAWATSKI, Deanna. Also writes as Deanna Barnhardt, Deanna Barnhardt. Canadian (born Canada), b. 1951. **Genres:** Poetry, Autobiography/Memoirs. **Career:** Freelance writer. **Publications:** AS DEANNA BARNHARDT: Bird, Bubble, and Stream (poems), 1980; Wilderness Mother, 1994; Clara and Me: The Story of an Unexpected Friendship, 1996; (ed.) A Pocketful of Muse, 2001; Stalking the Wild Heart, 2010. FORTHCOMING: Burning Man, Slaying Dragon. Contributor to periodicals. **Address:** 2508 Garland Rd., Celista, BC V0E 1M6, Canada. **Online address:** deemay@mail.ocis.net

KAWIN, Bruce F. American (born United States), b. 1945. **Genres:** Plays/ Screenplays, Poetry, Film, Literary Criticism And History. **Career:** Columbia Review, editor, 1966-67; Wells College, part-time instructor, 1969-70, assistant professor of English, 1970-73, director of film program, 1970-73, director creative writing program 1971-73; University of California, lecturer in English and film, 1973-75; University of Colorado, professor of English and film, 1975-. **Publications:** Slides (poetry), 1970; Telling It Again and Again: Repetition in Literature and Film, 1972; Faulkner and Film, 1977; Mindscreen: Bergman, Godard, and First-Person Film, 1978; To Have and Have Not, 1980; The Mind of the Novel: Reflexive Fiction and the Ineffable, 1982; Faulkner's MGM Screenplays, 1982; How Movies Work, 1987; (with G. Mast) A Short History of the Movies, 11th ed., 2010; Love If We Can Stand It, 2012. **Address:** Department of English, University of Colorado, 226 UCB, Hellems 101, Boulder, CO 80309-0226, U.S.A. **Online address:** bruce.kawin@colorado.edu

KAY, Alan N. American (born United States), b. 1965. **Genres:** Novels, Young Adult Non-fiction, Children's Fiction. **Career:** Lake Taylor Middle School, civics teacher, 1989-92; Booker T. Washington High School, history teacher, 1992-93; Horace Mann Junior High School, history teacher, 1993-94; Media Projects Inc., consultant, 1993; King High International Baccalaureate School, advanced history teacher, 1994-97; Dunedin High School, social studies teacher, 1997-; Pinellas County, history day coordinator, 1997-; East Lake High School, teacher. Writer. **Publications:** YOUNG HEROES OF HISTORY SERIES: Send 'Em South, 2000; On the Trail of John Brown's Body, 2001; Off to Fight, 2002; Nowhere to Turn, 2002; No Girls Allowed, 2003; Crossroads at Gettysburg, 2005; Ten, forthcoming. OTHER: I Love History But I Hated It in School. Contributor to periodicals. **Address:** 5471 Stallion Lake Dr., Palm Harbor, FL 34685, U.S.A. **Online address:** akay@youngheroesofhistory.com

KAY, Betty Carlson. American (born United States), b. 1949. **Genres:** Young Adult Non-fiction, Children's Non-fiction, History, Young Adult Fiction, Children's Fiction, Literary Criticism And History. **Career:** Teacher, 1970-74; Springfield School District 186, teacher, 1974-2004, retired, 2004. Writer. **Publications:** Americans of Character, 5 vols., 1997; (with G.J. Barwick) Jacksonville, Illinois: The Traditions Continue, 1999; Cicero: The First Suburb West, 2000; Illinois from A to Z, 2000; What Did Lincoln Do... In 1832? In 1842? In 1862?, 2005; Lincolns from A to Z, 2008; The Civil War from A to Z: Two Points of View, 2010. **Address:** 14 Catalina Ct., Jacksonville, IL 62650-3615, U.S.A. **Online address:** bckay@mchsi.com

KAY, Cameron. See **VIDAL, Gore.**

KAY, Elizabeth. British (born England), b. 1949. **Genres:** Children's Fiction, Novellas/Short Stories, Young Adult Fiction. **Career:** Writer and illustrator. **Publications:** The Spirit Collection, 2000; The Divide, 2003; Back to the Divide, 2004; The Jinx on the Divide, 2005; Fury, 2008; Hunted, 2009; Missing Link, 2009; The Tree Devil, 2010; Lost in the Desert, 2011. **Address:** c/o Author Mail, The Chicken House, 2 Palmer St., Frome, Somerset, BA11 1DS, England. **Online address:** divide2@elizabethkay.co.uk

KAY, George. British (born England), b. 1936. **Genres:** Geography, Third World, Recreation, History, Social Sciences. **Career:** Rhodes-Livingstone Institute, research officer, 1959-62; University of Hull, Leverhulme Fellow in Commonwealth Studies and lecturer in geography, 1962-67; University of Zimbabwe, professor of geography, 1968-74; University of Rhodesia, professor of geography and head of department, 1968-74, Faculty of Arts, dean, 1969-71; Staffordshire University, professor of geography, 1976-2000. Writer. **Publications:** A Social and Economic Study of Fort Rosebery Township and Peri-urban Area, 1960; Chief Kalaba's Village: A Preliminary Survey of Economic Life in an Ushi Village, Northern Rhodesia, 1964; Changing Patterns of Settlement and Land Use in the Eastern Province of Northern Rhodesia, 1965; Maps of the Distribution and Density of African Population in Zambia, 1967;

Social Aspects of Village Regrouping in Zambia, 1967; A Social Geography of Zambia: A Survey of Population Patterns in a Developing Country, 1967; Rhodesia: A Human Geography, 1970; Rhodesia, African Population Density as at April-May 1969, 1971; Distribution and Density of African Population in Rhodesia, 1972; (with M. Smout) Salisbury: A Geographical Survey of the Capital of Rhodesia, 1976; Access for Countryside Walking, 2002. **Address:** 1 Hoober St., Wath-on-Dearne, SY S63 6AX, England.

KAY, Guy Gavriel. Canadian (born Canada), b. 1954. **Genres:** Science Fiction/Fantasy, Novels, History, Poetry, Science Fiction/Fantasy. **Career:** Editorial consultant, 1974-75; Canadian Broadcasting Corp. (CBC-Radio), Drama Department, writer and associate producer, 1982-89. Writer. **Publications:** FANTASIES: The Summer Tree, 1984; The Wandering Fire, 1986; The Darkest Road, 1986; Tigana, 1990; A Song for Arbonne, 1992; The Lions of Al-Rassan, 1995; Sailing to Sarantium, 1998; Lord of Emperors, 2000; Beyond This Dark House (poems), 2003; The Last Light of the Sun, 2004; Ysabel, 2007; Under Heaven, 2010. **Address:** Westwood Creative Artists, 94 Harbord St., Toronto, ON M5S 1G6, Canada.

KAY, Jackie. (Jacqueline Margaret Kay). British/Scottish (born Scotland), b. 1961. **Genres:** Poetry, Novels. **Career:** Wingfield Arts, poet-in-the-schools; University of Newcastle, Newcastle upon Tyne, instructor, professor of creative writing. Poet and writer. **Publications:** FOR CHILDREN: Two's Company (poetry), 1992; Three Has Gone (poetry), 1994; The Frog Who Dreamed She Was an Opera Singer, 1998; Strawgirl, 2002; Number Parade: Number Poems from 0-100, 2002. ADULT POETRY: Chiaroscuro, 1986; The Adoption Papers, 1991; That Distance Apart (chapbook), 1991; Other Lovers, 1993; Christian Sanderson: A Poem, 1996; Off Colour, 1998; Sick Bag, 1998; Life Mask, 2005; Darling: New & Selected Poems, 2007. OTHER: Bessie Smith (biography), 1997; Trumpet (novel), 1998; Why Don't You Stop Talking (short stories), 2002; Wish I Was Here (short stories), 2006; Lamplighter, 2008; Red Dust Road, 2010; Fiere, 2011. **Address:** School of English Literature, Language and Linguistics, Newcastle University, Claremont Rd., Tyne and Wear, TW NE1 7RU, England. **Online address:** jackie.kay@ncl.ac.uk

KAY, Jacqueline Margaret. *See* **KAY, Jackie.**

KAY, John (A.). British/Scottish (born Scotland), b. 1948. **Genres:** Business/Trade/Industry, Economics, Psychology. **Career:** Oxford University, St John's College, fellow in economics, 1970-, lecturer in economics, 1971-78, head of business school, 1996-99; Said Business School, Peter Moores, director, 1997-99; Institute for Fiscal Studies, research director, 1979-81, director, 1981-86; Border and Southern Stockholders Trust, board director, 1982; London School of Business, professor, 1986-96, Centre for Business Strategy, director, 1986-91; London School of Economics, founding chair in business strategy. Writer. **Publications:** (With L. Hannah) Concentration in Modern Industry, 1977; (with M.A. King) The British Tax System, 1978, 5th ed., 1990; (with A.W. Dilnot and C.N. Morris) The Reform of Social Security, 1984; (with Mayer and J. Edwards) The Economic Analysis of Accounting Profitability, 1987; Foundations of Corporate Success, 1993; Why Firms Succeed, 1995; The Business of Economics, 1996; The Truth about Markets, 2003; Culture and Prosperity, 2004; Everlasting Lightbulbs, 2004; The Hare & the Tortoise, 2006; Obliquity: Why Our Goals are Best Achieved Indirectly, 2010. EDITOR: The 1982 Budget, 1982; The Economy and the 1983 Budget, 1983; The Economy and the 1985 Budget, 1985; (with C.P. Mayer and D.J. Thompson) Privatisation and Regulation: The U.K. Experience, 1986; (with J.A. Fairburn) Mergers and Merger Policy, 1989; (with M. Bishop) European Mergers and Merger Policy, 1993; (with Bishop and Mayer) Privatisation and Economic Performance, 1994; (with Bishop and Mayer) The Regulatory Challenge, 1995. Contributor to books and journals. **Address:** PO Box 4026, London, GL W1A 6N2, England. **Online address:** johnkay@johnkay.com

KAYE, Barrington. Also writes as Tom Kaye, Henry Cooper. Fijian (born Fiji), b. 1924?. **Genres:** Novels, Poetry, Education, Sociology, Philosophy, History, Anthropology/Ethnology, Travel/Exploration, Travel/Exploration, Romance/Historical. **Career:** University of Malaya, lecturer in education, 1951-54, social research fellow, 1955-56; University of the Gold Coast, senior lecturer in education, 1956-62; Redland College, Department of Education, head, 1962-72; Unesco, chief technical adviser, 1972-75; Bristol Polytechnic, Department of Education Studies, head, 1975-80; University of the South Pacific, reader, 1980-83, professor of education, 1983-. Writer. **Publications:** The Song of my Beloved and Other Poems, 1949; Manifesto for Education in Malaya, 1955; Bugis Street Blues (poetry), 1960; The De-

velopment of the Architectural Profession in Britain, 1960; Upper Nankin Street, Singapore; A Sociological Study of Chinese Households Living in a Densely Populated Area, 1960; It Had Been a Mild, Delicate Night (novel), 1960; Bringing Up Children in Ghana, an Impressionistic Survey, 1962; (with I. Rogers) Group Work in Secondary Schools and the Training of Teachers in Its Methods, 1968; Participation in Learning: A Progress Report on Some Experiments in the Training of Teachers, 1970; Tom Kaye's Love Poems, 1983; (as Henry Cooper) Upcountry (novel), 1985; Tom Kaye's Other Love Poems, 1988. AS TOM KAYE: Natten Hade Varit Mild Och Om (novel), 1959; Une Nuit, Douce, Fragile... (novel), 1960; Bugis Street Blues (poetry), 1960; David, From Where He was Lying (novel), 1961; Dar David lag (novel), 1962; How I Write My Novels, chapter in After Narrative, 1990. **Address:** PO Box 4267, Samabula, 1, Fiji.

KAYE, Elizabeth. American (born United States), b. 1945. **Genres:** Biography, Dance/Ballet, History, Sports/Fitness. **Career:** Writer. **Publications:** Mid-Life: Notes from the Halfway Mark, 1995; The American Ballet Theatre: A 25-Year Retrospective, 1999; Ain't No Tomorrow: Kobe, Shaq, and the Making of a Lakers Dynasty, 2002. Contributor to periodicals. **Address:** 241 W 23rd St., New York, NY 10011-2328, U.S.A.

KAYE, Geraldine. British (born England), b. 1925. **Genres:** Children's Fiction, Young Adult Fiction, History, Novellas/Short Stories, Transportation, Animals/Pets, Children's Non-fiction. **Career:** Malayan Film Unit, scriptwriter, 1951-52; teacher, 1952-54; Mitford Colmer School, teacher, 1962-64. **Publications:** Tales for Malayan Children, 1956; The Boy Who Wanted to Go Fishing, 1960; The Creek Near Kwarme's Village and Other Stories, 1961; Kwaku and the Bush Baby, 1961; Kwaku Goes Shopping, 1961; Kwasi and the Parrot and Other Stories, 1961; Susie and Sophie and Other Stories, 1961; Great Day in Ghana: Kwasi Goes to Town, 1962; Nii-Ofrang and His Garden and Other Stories, 1962; Kofi and the Eagle, 1963; Annan and the Grass Village, 1965; Kwabena and the Leopard, 1966; Oh, Essie!, 1966; The Raffle Pony, 1966; Tail of the Siamese Cat, 1966; Chik and the Bottle-House, 1966; Koto and the Lagoon, 1967; Yaa Goes South, 1967; The Blue Rabbit, 1967; The Sea Monkey: A Picture Story from Malaysia, 1968; Tawno, Gypsy Boy, 1968; Bonfire Night, 1969; Eight Days to Christmas, 1970; Runaway Boy, 1971; Nowhere to Go, 1971; Red Shoes, 1971; In the Park, 1971; The Tin Soldier, 1971; Nowhere to Stop, 1972; Donkey Boy, 1972; Ginger, 1972; The London Adventure, 1973; Kofi and the Eagle, 1973; Marie Alone, 1973; The Children of the Brown Family, 1973; Joanna All Alone, 1974; A Mad, Skipping Cat, 1974; Scrap's Club, 1974; Billy Boy, 1975; Pegs and Flowers, 1975; To Catch a Thief, 1975; Christmas Is a Baby, 1975; Adventure in London and Another Adventure in London, 2 vols., 1975-78; The Yellow Pom-Pom Hat, 1976; A Nail, a Stick and a Lid, 1976; The Rotten Old Car, 1976; Goodbye, Ruby Red, 1976; Children of the Turnpike, 1976; Tim and the Red Indian Head-dress, 1976; A Different Sort of Christmas, 1976; In Portobello Road, 1976; In the New Forest, 1976; Penny Black, 1976; Where Is Fred?, 1977; Joey's Room, 1978; A Life of Her Own, 1978; Week Out, 1978; King of the Knockdown Gingers, 1979; The Beautiful Take-Away Palace, 1980; The Day after Yesterday, 1981; The Plum Tree Party, 1981; The Birthday Ball, 1982; The Sky-Blue Dragon, 1983; Frangipani Summer, 1983; The Donkey Strike, 1984; Comfort Herself, 1984, rev. ed., 1997; The Biggest Bonfire in the World, 1985; The Call of the Wild Wood, 1986; The School Pool Gang, 1986; A Breath of Fresh Air, 1987; The Rabbit Minders, 1987; The Donkey Christmas, 1988; Great Comfort, 1988; Summer in Small Street, 1989; A Dog Called Dog, 1990; The Babysitting Gang, 1990; Winter in Small Street, 1990; A Piece of Cake, 1991; Snowgirl, 1992; Stone Boy, 1992; Someone Else's Baby, 1992; Hands Off My Sister, 1993; Birthdays in Small Street, 1993; Kelso's Carnival, 1994; Forests of the Night, 1995; Night at the Zoo, 1995; The Dragon Upstairs, 1997; Late in the Day (adult fiction), 1997; Between Us (adult fiction), 1998; My Second Best Friend, 1998. **Address:** A M Heath & Company Ltd., 6 Warwick Ct., Holborn, GL WC1R 5DJ, England.

KAYE, Marvin. American (born United States), b. 1938. **Genres:** Novels, Novellas/Short Stories, Mystery/Crime/Suspense, Horror, Science Fiction/Fantasy, Plays/Screenplays, Recreation. **Career:** GRIT Newspaper, reporter, 1963-65, New York correspondent, 1970-; Toys Magazine, senior editor, 1966-70; H.P. Lovecraft's Magazine, editor, 2004-09; Sherlock Holmes Mystery Magazine, editor, 2008-; Weird Tales Magazine, co-publisher and editor, 2011-; New York University, adjunct professor of creative writing. **Publications:** The Histrionic Holmes: An Analysis and Dissertation on the Impersonatory Genius of Sherlock Holmes, with Technical Notes and a Compendium of His Performances, 1971; A Lively Game of Death, 1972; A Toy

Is Born, 1973; The Handbook of Magic, 1973; Stein and Day Handbook of Magic, 1973; The Grand Ole Opry Murders, 1974; The Handbook of Mental Magic, 1975; Bullets for Macbeth, 1976; Catalog of Magic, 1977; My Son, the Druggist, 1977; The Laurel and Hardy Murders: A Hilary Quayle Mystery Novel, 1977; (with P. Godwin) The Masters of Solitude, 1978; The Incredible Umbrella, 1979; My Brother, the Druggist, 1979; The Possession of Immanuel Wolf and Other Improbable Tales, 1981; The Amorous Umbrella, 1981; (with P. Godwin) Wintermind, 1982; The Soap Opera Slaughters, 1982; (with P. Godwin) A Cold Blue Light, 1983; Ghosts of Night and Morning, 1987; Fantastique (novel), 1993; The Last Christmas of Ebenezer Scrooge, 2003; The Passion of Frankenstein (novel), 2010. EDITOR: (and contrib.) Fiends and Creatures, 1974; (and contrib.) Brother Theodore's Chamber of Horrors, 1974; (and contrib.) Ghosts: A Treasury of Chilling Tales Old and New, 1981; Masterpieces of Terror and the Supernatural: A Treasury of Spellbinding Tales Old & New, 1985; Devils and Demons: A Treasury of Fiendish Tales Old & New, 1987; Weird Tales, the Magazine That Never Dies, 1988; Witches and Warlocks, 1989; 13 Plays of Ghosts and the Supernatural, 1990; Haunted America, 1990; Lovers and Other Monsters, 1992; Sweet Revenge, 1993; Frantic Comedy, 1993; Masterpieces of Terror and the Unknown, 1993; Angels of Darkness: Tales of Troubled and Troubling Women, 1995; Readers Theatre: What It is and How to Stage It and Four Award-Winning Scripts, 1995; The Game Is Afoot: Parodies, Pastiches and Ponderings of Sherlock Holmes, 1995; Page to Stage, 1996; The Definitive Dracula, 1997; The Resurrected Holmes: New Cases from the Notes of John H. Watson, M.D., 1996; The Confidential Casebook of Sherlock Holmes, 1998; Don't Open this Book!, 1998; The Vampire Sextette, 2000; Incisions, 2000; The Ultimate Halloween, 2001; The Dragon Quintet, 2004; The Fair Folk, 2005; Forbidden Planets, 2006; The Ghost Quartet, 2008; A Book of Wizards, 2008. **Address:** The Open Book, 525 W End Ave., 12 E, New York, NY 10024-3207, U.S.A. **Online address:** marvinnkaye@yahoo.com

KAYE, Peggy. American (born United States), b. 1948. **Genres:** Education, Young Adult Non-fiction, Sciences. **Career:** Writer. **Publications:** SELF-ILLUSTRATED: Games for Reading: Playful Ways to Help Your Child Read, 1984; Games for Math: Playful Ways to Help Your Child Learn Math from Kindergarten to Third Grade, 1987; Homework: Math, 6 vols., 1989; Homework: Reading, 1990; Games for Learning: Ten Minutes a Day to Help Your Child Do Well in School-from Kindergarten to Third Grade, 1991; Games for Writing: Playful Ways to Help Your Child Learn to Write, 1995; Afterwards: Folk and Fairy Tales with Mathematica Ever Alters, 2 vols., 1996-1997; Games with Books: Twenty-eight of the Best Children's Books and How to Use Them to Help Your Child Learn, from Preschool to Third Grade, 2002. Contributor to periodicals. **Address:** 55 W 86th St., New York, NY 10024, U.S.A. **Online address:** yggep1@me.com

KAYE, Tom. See KAYE, Barrington.

KAYE-KANTROWITZ, Melanie. American (born United States), b. 1945. **Genres:** Novels, Cultural/Ethnic Topics. **Career:** Harlem Education Project, instructor and director of remedial reading project, 1963-65; University of California, instructor, 1971-72; Portland State University, assistant professor, 1972-76, instructor, 1977-79; Portland Women's Crisis Center, community educator, counselor and organizer, 1977-78; Goddard College, adjunct professor, 1978-81; University of New Mexico, adjunct faculty, 1981; Johnson State College, adjunct faculty, 1981; Norwich University, Vermont College, adjunct professor, 1981-85, assistant professor, 1985-89, associate professor, 1989-92; University of Maine, Rockland Extension, adjunct faculty, 1983; Sinister Wisdom Books, editor and publisher, 1984-88; Jews for Racial and Economic Justice, founding director, 1990-95; Hamilton College, visiting distinguished professor, 1995-97, distinguished chair; City University of New York, Brooklyn College, visiting distinguished professor, 1997-98, distinguished chair, Queens College, Worker Education Extension, director, 1999-2004, adjunct professor, 2005-; Bard College Prison Initiative, teacher; WBAI, Beyond the Pale, co-founder. **Publications:** We Speak in Code: Poems and Other Writings, 1980; My Jewish Face and Other Stories, 1990; The Issue Is Power: Essays on Women, Jews, Violence and Resistance, 1992; The Colors of Jews: Racial Politics and Radical Diasporism, 2007. EDITOR AND CONTRIBUTOR: (with I. Klepfisz) The Tribe of Dina: A Jewish Women's Anthology, 1986, rev. ed., 1989; (with Eber and I. Klepfisz) Action and Awareness: Handbook on Anti-Semitism, 1991. Works appear in anthologies. Contributor of articles to periodicals. **Address:** Department of Comparative Literature, Queens College, The City University of New York, PH 352J, 65-30 Kissena Blvd., Flushing, NY 11367, U.S.A. **Online address:** melaniekk@diasporism.net

KAYLIN, Lucy. American (born United States) **Genres:** Young Adult Non-fiction, Human Relations/Parenting, History, Medicine/Health. **Career:** GQ Magazine, senior writer, through 2006; Marie Claire Magazine, executive editor, 2006. **Publications:** For the Love of God: The Faith and Future of the American Nun, 2000; The Perfect Stranger: The Truth about Mothers and Nannies, 2007. **Address:** Marie Claire Magazine, 300 W 57th St., 34th Fl., New York, NY 10019-1497, U.S.A.

KAYNAK, Erdener. American/Turkish (born Turkey), b. 1947. **Genres:** Marketing, Business/Trade/Industry. **Career:** Hacettepe University, assistant professor, 1975-78; Army Staff College, adjunct assistant professor of management, 1976-78; Turkish Consumer Protection Association, vice president, 1977-78; Acadia University, assistant professor, 1978-79; Mount Saint Vincent University, associate professor, 1979-84, professor of marketing, 1984-86, head; Canadian Turkish Cultural Association, vice president, 1982-83; Tomarket International Ltd., vice president of research and development, 1982-83; Academy of Marketing Science, director of international programs, 1983-86; Chinese University of Hong Kong, visiting professor, 1985-86; Pennsylvania State University, Capital College, professor of marketing, 1986-; Bilkent University, visiting professor, 1989, 1991; The Malibu Center for International Research, Associate, 1991-; Helsinki School of Economics and Business Administration, visiting professor, 1992; Norwegian School of Management, visiting professor, 1993; University of Hawaii-Manoa, visiting professor; Curtin University of Technology, visiting professor; University of Botswana, visiting professor; University of the South Pacific, visiting professor; Akdeniz University, visiting professor; Turku School of Economics, visiting professor; Lingnan University, visiting professor; Cross-Cultural Marketing Services Inc., founder and president; International Journal of Commerce and Management, adviser; Haworth Press Inc., senior editor; International Management Development Association, director and executive vice-president, 1987-; International Business Press, executive editor. **Publications:** Food Retailing Systems in a Developing Economy, 1975; Marketing in the Third World, 1982; (with R. Savitt) Comparative Marketing Systems, 1984; (ed.) International Marketing Management, 1984; The Global Perspective in Marketing, 1985; (ed.) World Food Marketing Systems, 1986; International Business in the Middle East, 1986; Marketing and Economic Development, 1986; Service Industries in Developing Countries, 1986; (ed.) Transnational Retailing, 1988; (ed. with K.H. Lee) Global Business: Asia-Pacific Dimensions, 1989; The Management of International Advertising, 1989; Socio-Political Aspects of International Marketing, 1991; The Global Business: Four Key Marketing Strategies, 1993; (with F. Karakaya) Utilizing New Information Technology in the Teaching of International Business, 1993; (with P.N. Ghauri) Euromarketing, 1994; (ed. with S.S. Hassan) The Globalization of Consumer Markets, 1994; (ed.) International Business Teaching, 1995; (with R. Baran and Y. Pan) International Joint Ventures in East Asia, 1996; (ed. with D.M. Johnson) Marketing in the Third World, 1996; Guide to Publishing Opportunities in Business, Administration and Management, 1995; (ed. with F. Karakaya) How to Utilize New Information Technology in the Global Marketplace: A Basic Guide, 1995; (ed.) International Marketing, 1996; Cross-National and Cross-Cultural Issues in Food Marketing, 1999; (ed. with J.R. Schermerhorn) Teaching and Program Variations in International Business, 1999; (ed.) Strategic Global Marketing: Issues and Trends, 2002; (ed. with F. Jallat) Marketing Issues in Western Europe: Changes and Developments, 2004; (ed.) European Perspectives in Marketing, 2004; (with V.H. Kirpalani and L. Garbarski) Successfully Doing Business/Marketing in Eastern Europe, 2009. Contributor to books and journals. **Address:** School of Business Administration, Pennsylvania State University, E-355 Olmsted Bldg., 777 W Harrisburg Pike, Middletown, PA 17057, U.S.A. **Online address:** k9x@psu.edu

KAYS, Scott A. (Scott Anthony Kays). American (born United States), b. 1960. **Genres:** Money/Finance, Business/Trade/Industry, Economics. **Career:** Kays Financial Advisory Corp., founder, president and chief executive officer, 1985-; Lockheed Martin Corp., staff, through 1986; Scott Kays Ministries Inc., founder, 1992. Writer. **Publications:** Achieving Your Financial Potential: A Comprehensive Guide to Applying Biblical Principles of Financial Success, 1999; 5 Key Lessons from Top Managers, 2005. **Address:** Kays Financial Advisory Corp., 200 Galleria Pkwy., Ste. 1150, Atlanta, GA 30339-3185, U.S.A. **Online address:** skays@scottkays.com

KAYS, Scott Anthony. See KAYS, Scott A.

KAYSEN, Susanna. American (born United States), b. 1948. **Genres:** Novels, Autobiography/Memoirs, Biography, Education. **Career:** Writer. **Publications:** NOVELS: Asa, as I Knew Him, 1987; Far Afield, 1990; Girl, Interrupted, 1993; The Camera My Mother Gave Me, 2001. Contributor to periodicals. **Address:** c/o Jonathan Matson, Harold Matson Company Inc., 276 5th Ave., New York, NY 10001-4509, U.S.A.

KAYYEM, Juliette N. American (born United States), b. 1970?. **Genres:** Social Sciences. **Career:** State of Massachusetts, Homeland Security chief, 2007-; Harvard University, John F. Kennedy School of Government, Program of Domestic Preparedness, director, Belfer Center for Science and International Affairs, resident scholar & lecturer in public policy, acting executive director for research & instructor in law and national security, 2001-07; National Commission on Terrorism, appointee, 1999-2000; Dubai School of Government, Dubai Initiative, co-faculty chair; NBC News, security analyst; U.S. Department of Justice, trial lawyer; U.S. Attorney General Janet Reno, legal advisor; Human Rights First, director; Third Way organization, trustee. Writer, educator and attorney. **Publications:** (ed. with R.L. Pangi) First to Arrive: State and Local Responses to Terrorism, 2003; (with P.B. Heymann) Protecting Liberty in an Age of Terror, 2005. Contributor to periodicals and journals. **Address:** Harvard University, John F. Kennedy School of Government, 79 JFK St., PO Box 53, Cambridge, MA 02138, U.S.A. **Online address:** juliette_kayyem@ksg.harvard.edu

KAZA, Stephanie. American (born United States), b. 1947. **Genres:** Essays, Environmental Sciences/Ecology. **Career:** Teacher, 1969-76; University of California-Santa Cruz, teaching assistant, 1976-79, lecturer in environmental studies, 1979-82; Point Reyes Bird Observatory, educational director, 1982-87; University of California-Berkeley, lecturer, 1988-89, Botanical Garden, educational coordinator, 1988-90; Starr King School for the Ministry, instructor, 1989-90; University of Vermont, Rubenstein School of Environment and Natural Resources, assistant professor, 1991-97, associate professor, 1997-2005, professor, 2005-, Environmental Studies Program, director; Institute of Deep Ecology, faculty, 1993-98; American Academy of Religion and ecology group, co-chair, 1995-99. Writer. **Publications:** The Attentive Heart: Conversations with Trees (essays), 1993; Mindfully Green: A Personal and Spiritual Guide to Whole Earth Thinking, 2008. EDITOR: (with B.J. Le Boeuf) The Natural History of Ano Nuevo, 1981; (with K. Kraft) Dharma Rain: Sources of Buddhist Environmentalism, 2000; Hooked!: Buddhist Writings on Greed, Desire and the Urge to Consume, 2005. Contributor to periodicals. **Address:** Environmental Studies Program, University of Vermont, 153 S Prospect St., Burlington, VT 05401, U.S.A. **Online address:** stephanie.kaza@uvm.edu

KAZANTZIS, Judith. British (born England), b. 1940. **Genres:** Novels, Poetry, Translations, Young Adult Fiction, inspirational/Motivational Literature. **Career:** Poet, short fiction writer, novelist. **Publications:** (Comp.) The Gordon Riots: A Collection of Contemporary Documents, 1967; (comp.) Women in Revolt: The Fight for Emancipation: A Collection of Contemporary Documents, 1968. POETRY: Minefield, 1977; The Wicked Queen: Poems, 1980; (with M. Roberts and M. Wandor) Touch Papers, 1982; Let's Pretend, 1984; A Poem for Guatemala, 1988; Flame Tree, 1988; The Rabbit Magician Plate, 1992; Selected Poems 1977-92, 1995; Swimming through the Grand Hotel: Poems 1993-1996, 1997; The Odysseus Poems: Fictions on the Odyssey of Homer, 1999, 2nd ed., 2010; (trans.) In Cyclops Cave, 2002; Just after Midnight: Poems, 1997-2003, 2004. NOVEL: Of Love and Terror, 2002. **Address:** PO Box 1671, Key West, FL 33041, U.S.A. **Online address:** judith@judithkazantzis.com

KAZER, Meredith Wallace. *See* **WALLACE, Meredith.**

KEAHEY, John. American (born United States), b. 1945. **Genres:** Travel/Exploration, Natural History, History. **Career:** The Salt Lake Tribune, news editor, reporter, 1989-. **Publications:** A Sweet and Glorious Land: Revisiting the Ionian Sea, 2000; Venice Against the Sea: A City Besieged, 2002; Seeking Sicily: A Cultural Journey through Myth and Reality in the Heart of the Mediterranean, 2011. **Address:** The Salt Lake Tribune, 90 South 400 West, Ste. 700, Salt Lake City, UT 84101, U.S.A. **Online address:** jkeahey@comcast.net

KEAL, Jenny. British (born England), b. 1951. **Genres:** Art/Art History. **Career:** Paul Reeves Photography, director, 1984-90; artist, 1990-. Freelance writer. **Publications:** Learn to Paint: Landscapes in Pastel, 2003; Painting with Pastels, 2011. **Address:** Clockwork Penguin, Maesmawr, Aberedw, Builth Wells, PW LD2 3UW, Wales. **Online address:** jenny@davidbellamy.co.uk

KEALEY, Edward J. American (born United States), b. 1936. **Genres:** History, Technology, Biography, Engineering, Science Fiction/Fantasy. **Career:** College of the Holy Cross, advisor for graduate studies, 1964-69, assistant professor, 1962-66, associate professor, 1966-73, professor of history, 1973-86, chairman, 1980-83; University of Massachusetts, Labor Relations Research Center, lecturer, 1969-75; ordained Catholic priest, 1989-; St. Sylvester Church, co-pastor, 1996; Writer. **Publications:** Roger of Salisbury, Viceroy of England, 1972; Medieval Medicus: A Social History of Anglo-Norman Medicine, 1981; Harvesting the Air: Windmill Pioneers in Twelfth Century England, 1987. Contributor to periodicals. **Address:** c/o St. Sylvester, 68 Ohio Ave., Medford, NY 11763-2613, U.S.A.

KEANE, John. Australian (born Australia), b. 1949. **Genres:** History, Politics/Government. **Career:** University of Westminster, professor of politics and founder of Centre for the Study of Democracy, 1989-, Karl Deutsch professor; Institute for Public Policy Research, fellow; European Civil Society Network, CSD coordinator; University of Leiden, United Nations and the Evolution of Global Values project, consultant; University of Sydney, professor of politics; Berlin Social Science Research Center, visiting professor. Writer. **Publications:** Public Life and Late Capitalism: Toward a Socialist Theory of Democracy, 1984; (with J. Owens) After Full Employment, 1986; Democracy and Civil Society: On the Predicaments of European Socialism, the Prospects for Democracy and the Problem of Controlling Social and Political Power, 1988; The Media and Democracy, 1991; Tom Paine: A Political Life, 1995; Reflections on Violence, 1996; Civil Society: Old Images, New Visions, 1998; Václav Havel: A Political Tragedy in Six Acts, 1999; On Communicative Abundance, 2000; Whatever Happened to Democracy?, 2002; Global Civil Society?, 2003; Violence and Democracy, 2004; Life and Death of Democracy, 2009. EDITOR: Contradictions of the Welfare State, 1984; Disorganized Capitalism: Contemporary Transformations of Work and Politics, 1985; The Power of the Powerless: Citizens Against the State in Central-Eastern Europe, 1985; Civil Society and the State: New European Perspectives, 1988; (with P. Mier) Nomads of the Present: Social Movements and Individual Needs in Contemporary Society, 1989; (with T. Inoguchi and E. Newman) The Changing Nature of Democracy, 1998; Civil Society: Berlin Perspectives, 2006; (with M. Podunavac and C. Sparks) Politika I strah, 2008; (with S. Alonso and W. Merkel) The Future of Representative Democracy, 2010. **Address:** Department of Government and International, Relations, University of Sydney, Rm. S505, A14 Quadrangle Bldg., Sydney, NW 2006, Australia. **Online address:** jk@johnkeane.net

KEANE, Nancy J. American (born United States), b. 1951. **Genres:** Children's Fiction, Education. **Career:** University of Vermont, associate professor, 1979-90; Trinity College, visiting assistant librarian, 1987-88, director of libraries, 1990-92; Rundlett Middle School, library media specialist, 1992-; New Hampshire Technical Institute, adjunct computer faculty, 1998-; Plymouth State University, Graduate Library Media Program, adjunct faculty and library media specialist. Writer. **Publications:** Booktalks and Beyond: Thematic Learning Activities for Grades K-6, 2001; Booktalking Tie-ins: Science Literature in the 4-6 Classroom, 2002; Booktalking across the Curriculum: The Middle Years, 2002; (with C.L. Wait) Teaching Social Studies through Literature: Grades 6-8, 2002; (with C.L. Wait) Teaching Reading and Writing Through Literature: Grades 6-8, 2002; (with C.L. Wait) Teaching Science through Literature: Grades 6-8, 2002; Teaching Science Through Literature: Grades 4-6, 2002; (with C.L. Wait) Teaching Language Arts through Literature: Grades 6-8, 2002; Teaching Social Studies through Literature: Grades 4-6, 2002; Teaching Language Arts through Literature: Grades 4-6, 2002; Using Literature in the Middle School Classroom, 2005; Middle School Pathfinders: Guiding Student Research, 2005; The Big Book of Children's Reading Lists: 100 Great, Ready-to-Use Book Lists for Educators, Librarians, Parents, and Children, 2006; The Big Book of Teen Reading Lists: 100 Great, Ready-to-Use Book Lists for Educators, Librarians, Parents, and Teens, 2006; (with T.W. Cavanaugh) Tech-savvy Booktalker: A Guide for 21st-Century Educators, 2008. Contributor to magazines. **Address:** c/o Debby LaBoon, ABC-CLIO, 23851 E Phillips Pl., Aurora, CO 80016, U.S.A. **Online address:** nancy@nancykeane.com

KEANE, Webb. American (born United States), b. 1955. **Genres:** Adult Non-fiction. **Career:** University of Pennsylvania, faculty; University of Michigan, faculty, 1997-, professor and director of graduate studies; anthropologist; University of Michigan Society of Fellows, senior fellow. Writer.

Publications: Signs of Recognition: Powers and Hazards of Representation in an Indonesian Society, 1997; (co-ed.) Handbook of Material Culture, 2006; Christian Moderns: Freedom and Fetish in the Mission Encounter, 2007. Contributor to books and periodicals. **Address:** Department of Anthropology, University of Michigan, 101 West Hall, 1085 S University Ave., Ann Arbor, MI 48109-1107, U.S.A. **Online address:** wkeane@umich.edu

KEANEY, Brian. British/Irish (born Ireland), b. 1954. **Genres:** Young Adult Fiction, Young Adult Non-fiction, Science Fiction/Fantasy, Children's Fiction, Novels, Education, Children's Non-fiction, Theatre, Theatre. **Career:** Teacher, 1976-86; University of London, Goldsmiths College, royal literary fellow, 2001-02, 2007-08, 2011-; London College of Fashion, London Institute, royal literary fellow, 2002-03; University of Surrey, St. Mary's College, royal literary fellow, 2003-05; City and Guilds of London School of Art, royal literary fellow, 2005-07; freelance writer, 2008-10. **Publications:** NOVELS: Don't Hang About, 1986; Some People Never Learn, 1986; No Need for Heroes, 1989; If This is the Real World, 1991; Limited Damage, 1991; Boys Don't Write Love Stories, 1993; Family Secrets, 1997; The Private Life of Georgia Brown, 1998; Bitter Fruit, 1999; Balloon House, 2000; No Stone Unturned, 2001; Falling for Joshua, 2001; Where Mermaids Sing, 2004; Jacob's Ladder, 2005; The Hollow People, 2006; The Gallowglass, 2007; The Haunting of Nathaniel Wolfe, 2008; Nathaniel Wolfe and the Body Snatchers, 2009; The Magical Detectives, 2011; The Magical Detectives and the Forbidden Spell, 2011. NON-FICTION: Making Sense of English, 1987; Talking Sense, 1987; (ed. with B. Lucas) Girls' Talk Boys' Talk, 1989; (ed. with B. Lucas) Family Matters, 1990; (ed. with B. Lucas) Class Rules, 1990; (with B. Lucas) A Kiss From France, 1990; (with B. Lucas) Boycott, 1990; (with B. Lucas) The Fat of The Land, 1990; A Question of Courage, 1990; (with B. Lucas) Between Two Shores, 1991; (with B. Lucas) Taking Sides, 1991; Presenting Ideas, 1992; (ed.) Bright Ideas in the Outside Classroom, 1992; English in the School Grounds, 1993; (with C. Vorderman) The Way to Pass National Curriculum English: The Easy Way to Learn and Revise: 11-13 Years Level 5 (the Way to Pass), 1994; (with C. Vorderman) The Way to Pass National Curriculum English Level 6, 1994. OPPORTUNITIES SERIES: (with B. Lucas) Sharing Experience, 1991; (with B. Lucas) Taking Shape, 1991. OTHERS: (with B. Lucas) Poetry in Practice, 1993; (with B. Lucas) Looking at Language, 1994; Arts in the School Grounds, 1996. **Address:** 111 Drakefell Rd., London, GL SE4 2DT, England. **Online address:** brian@briankeaney.co.uk

KEAR, Lynn. American (born United States), b. 1957. **Genres:** Film, Gay And Lesbian Issues, Paranormal, Theatre, Biography, Novels, Mystery/Crime/Suspense. **Career:** Writer. **Publications:** Agnes Moorehead: A Bio-Bibliography, 1992; Reincarnation, 1996; We're Here: An Investigation into Gay Reincarnation, 1999; Kay Francis: A Passionate Life and Career, 2006; The Complete Kay Francis Career Record: All Film, Stage, Radio and Television Appearances, 2008; (with J. King) Evelyn Brent: The Life and Films of Hollywood's Lady Crook, 2009; Laurette Taylor, American Stage Legend, 2010; Murder in a Buckhead Garden, 2010; Guilty Truth, forthcoming; Black Hearted Bitch, forthcoming. **Address:** 2162 Colonial Oak Way, Stone Mountain, GA 30087, U.S.A. **Online address:** lynnkear@yahoo.com

KEARNEY, Richard Marius. American/Irish (born Ireland), b. 1954. **Genres:** Philosophy, Politics/Government. **Career:** University College Dublin, lecturer, 1980-90, personal chair of philosophy, 1990-2001, rotating head of philosophy department, 1993-98, co-founder of Irish film school, 1993-99, chair of Irish film school, 1993-2005, visiting professor; Boston College, visiting professor, 1986-2001, Charles Seelig professor in philosophy, 2001-, Charles B. Seelig chair of philosophy; University of Warwick, external examiner, 1993-97; National University, Irish Film School, co-founder and chair of Board of Studies, 1994-; Louvain and Lisbon University, l'Institut Catholique de Paris, EU Erasmus exchange professor, 1994-99; University of Paris, visiting professor, 1997, 1999; University of Nice-Sophia Antipolis, visiting professor, 1999, 2001-; University of Paris, visiting professor. Writer. **Publications:** (Ed.)The Black Book, 1977; (ed. with J.S. O'Leary) Heidegger et la Question de Dieu, 1980; (ed.) The Crane Bag Book of Irish Studies, vol. I, 1982, vol. II, 1987; Poetique du Possible: Phenomenologie Hermeneutique de la Figuration, 1984; Dialogues with Contemporary Continental Thinkers: The Phenomenological Heritage: Paul Ricoeur, Emmanuel Levinas, Herbert Marcuse, Stanislas Breton, Jacques Derrida, 1984; The Irish Mind: Exploring Intellectual Traditions, 1985; (ed.) Jeremy Madden Simpson, The No Word Image, 1986; Modern Movements in European Philosophy, 1987, 2nd ed., 1994; The Wake of Imagination: Toward a Postmodern Culture, 1988; (ed.) Across the Frontiers: Ireland in the 1990s: Cultural, Political, Economic,

1988; Transitions: Narratives in Modern Irish Culture, 1988; (ed.) Migrations: The Irish at Home & Abroad, 1990; (ed. with J. Greisch) Paul Ricoeur, Les Metamorphoses de la Raison Hermeneutique: Actes du Colloque de Cerisy-la-Salle, 1er-11 out 1988, 1991 in US as Paul Ricoeur: The Hermeneutics of Action, 1996; Angel of Patrick's Hill, 1991; Poetics of Imagining: From Husserl to Lyotard, 1991; Visions of Europe: Conversations on the Legacy and Future of Europe, 1992; (ed.) Twentieth- Century Continental Philosophy, 1994; States of Mind: Dialogues with Contemporary Thinkers, 1995; Poetics of Modernity: Toward a Hermeneutic Imagination, 1995; Sam's Fall, 1995; (ed. with M. Rainwater) The Continental Philosophy Reader, 1996; Postnationalist Ireland: Politics, Culture, Philosophy, 1997; (ed. with P. McGuinness and A. Harrison) John Toland, John Toland's Christianity Not Mysterious: Text, Associated Works, and Critical Essays, 1997; Poetics of Imagining: Modern to Post-modern, 1998; (ed. with M. Dooley) Questioning Ethics: Contemporary Debates in Philosophy, 1999; (ed. with D. Rasmussen) Continental Aesthetics: Romanticism to Postmodernism: An Anthology, 2001; The God Who May Be: A Hermeneutics of Religion, 2001; On Stories, 2002; (ed. with L. Gibbons and W. Murphy) Encyclopedia of Contemporary Irish Literature, 2002; Strangers, Gods and Monsters: Interpreting Otherness, 2003; On Paul Ricoeur: The Owl of Minerva, 2004; Debates in Continental Philosophy: Conversations with Contemporary Thinkers, 2004; Navigations: Collected Irish Essays, 1976-2006, 2006; (foreword) Traversing the Imaginary: Richard Kearney and the Postmodern Challenge, 2007; (ed.) The Inter-Religious Imagination, 2008; Anatheism, 2010; (ed. with E. Rizo-Patron) Traversing the Heart, 2010; (ed. with J. Taylor) Hosting the Stranger, 2011; (with K. Semonovitch) Phenomenologies of the Stranger, 2011. Contributor to journals. **Address:** Department of Philosophy, Boston College, Rm. 389, Maloney Hall, 140 Commonwealth Ave., 21 Campanella Way, Chestnut Hill, MA 02467-3800, U.S.A. **Online address:** kearneyr@bc.edu

KEARNS, Doris. See **GOODWIN, Doris (Helen) Kearns.**

KEARNS, Josie. American (born United States), b. 1954. **Genres:** Poetry, Adult Non-fiction, Humanities. **Career:** University of Michigan, lecturer, professor, 1994-; Ragdale Foundation, writer-in-residence, 1995-2002. **Publications:** (With D.L. Rendleman, C.S. Russell) Industrial strength poetry, 1984; Life after the Line (nonfiction), 1990; New Numbers (poetry chapbook), 2000; (ed.) New Poems from the Third Coast: Contemporary Michigan Poetry, 2000; The Theory of Everything (poetry), 2009; Alphabet of the Ocean (chapbook), 2009; Stealing: Theft and Consequence, forthcoming; Pink Noise, forthcoming. Contributor to journals. **Address:** Department of English Language and Literature, University of Michigan, 3262 Angell Hall, 435 S State St., Ann Arbor, MI 48109-1003, U.S.A. **Online address:** jakearns@umich.edu

KEARNS, Lionel (John). Canadian (born Canada), b. 1937. **Genres:** Poetry, Autobiography/Memoirs, Bibliography, Essays, History, Theology/Religion. **Career:** University of British Columbia, teaching assistant and lecturer in English, 1961-64, Creative Writing Program, visiting professor; Simon Fraser University, Department of English, assistant professor, 1966-, associate professor, through 1986; Concordia University, writer-in-residence, 1981-82. **Publications:** Songs of Circumstance, 1963; Listen George, 1965; Pointing, 1967; By the Light of the Silvery McLune: Media Parables, Poems, Signs, Gestures, and Other Assaults on the Interface, 1970; About Time, 1974; The Birth of God, 1974; Negotiating a New Canadian Constitution, 1975; Two Poems for a Manitoulin Island Canada Day, 1976; Practicing Up to Be Human, 1978; Ignoring the Bomb: Poems New and Selected, 1982; Loops and Chains: Selected Poems, 1982; Convergences, 1984; A Few Words Will Do, 2007; Victoria Day, 2007. **Address:** 1616 Charles St., Vancouver, BC V5L 2T3, Canada.

KEARNS, Sheila M. American (born United States), b. 1955. **Genres:** Literary Criticism And History. **Career:** University of Texas, assistant professor of English, 1985-94, Innovation, Creativity and Capital Institute, research associate, 1994-; Vermont Department of Libraries, system administrator, IT manager. Writer and consultant. **Publications:** Coleridge, Wordsworth and Romantic Autobiography (literary criticism), 1995. **Address:** Vermont Department of Libraries, 109 State St., Montpelier, VT 05609, U.S.A. **Online address:** sheila.kearns@dol.state.vt.us

KEATES, Jonathan. British/French (born France), b. 1946. **Genres:** Novellas/Short Stories, Music, Biography, Travel/Exploration, History. **Career:** City of London School, teacher of English literature. Travel and short story writer. **Publications:** The Companion Guide to the Shakespeare Country, 1979; (with A. Hornak) Historic London, 1979; (with A. Hornak) Canterbury Cathedral, 1980; The Love of Italy, 1980; Drawings and Sketches of Oxford, 1983; Allegro Postillions (short stories), 1983; Handel: The Man and His Music, 1985; Strangers Gallery, 1987; Tuscany, 1988; Italian Journeys, 1991; Umbria, 1991; Stendahl, 1994; Venice, 1994; Purcell: A Biography, 1995; Soon to Be a Major Motion Picture (short stories), 1997; Smile Please, 2001; Short Stories, 2001; The Rough Guide History of Italy, 2003; The Siege of Venice, 2005. Contributor to periodicals. **Address:** c/o Author Mail, Chatto & Windus, Random House Group Ltd., 20 Vauxhall Bridge Rd., London, GL SW1V 2SA, England.

KEATING, AnaLouise. (AnnLouise Keating). American (born United States), b. 1961. **Genres:** Literary Criticism And History, Intellectual History, Women's Studies And Issues, Race Relations, Gay And Lesbian Issues, Cultural/Ethnic Topics, Humanities, inspirational/Motivational Literature, Paranormal, Social Sciences, Women's Studies And Issues. **Career:** Eastern New Mexico University, assistant professor, 1990-94, associate professor, 1994-99; Aquinas College, associate professor, 1999-2001; Texas Woman's University, professor of Women's Studies, 2001-. Writer. **Publications:** Women Reading Women Writing: Self-Invention in Paula Gunn Allen, Gloria Anzaldua, and Audre Lorde, 1996; Perspectives: Gender Studies, 1999; (ed.) Interviews/Entrevistas, 2000; (ed. with Gloria Anzaldua) This Bridge We Call Home: Radical Visions for Transformation, 2002; (ed.) Entre Mundos/Among Worlds: New Perspectives on Gloria E. Anzaldua, 2005; Teaching Transformation: Transcultural Classroom Dialogues, 2007; The Gloria Anzaldua Reader, 2009. Bridging: How and Why Gloria Anzaldua's Life and Work Transformed Our Own, 2011 Contributor to books and journals. **Address:** The Department of Women's Studies, Texas Woman's University, Human Development Bldg., Ste. 307K, PO Box 425557, Denton, TX 76204-5557, U.S.A. **Online address:** akeating@twu.edu

KEATING, AnnLouise. See **KEATING, AnaLouise.**

KEATING, Frank. American (born United States), b. 1944. **Genres:** Biography, Children's Fiction, Humor/Satire, Education. **Career:** Federal Bureau of Investigation, special agent, 1969-; State of Oklahoma, member of House of Representatives, 1972-74, governor, 1995-2003; U.S. attorney for the northern district of Oklahoma, 1981-85; U.S. Department of the Treasury, assistant secretary, 1985-; American Council of Life Insurers, president and chief executive officer, 2003-; U.S. Department of Justice, associate attorney general; U.S. Department of Housing and Urban Development, general counsel and acting deputy secretary. Writer. **Publications:** Will Rogers: An American Legend, 2002; Theodore, 2006; The Trial of Standing Bear, 2008. Contributor to periodicals. **Address:** American Council of Life Insurers, 101 Constitution Ave. NW, Washington, DC 20001, U.S.A.

KEATON, Corey. See **THOMPSON, Vicki Lewis.**

KEATS-ROHAN, K. S. B. British/American (born United States), b. 1957. **Genres:** Politics/Government, Poetry. **Career:** Oxford University, Linacre College, Linacre Unit for Prosopographical Research, founder director and faculty, European Humanities Research Centre, fellow, 1997-; University of London, School of History, research fellow. Writer and historian. **Publications:** (Ed. with D.E. Thornton) Domesday Names: An Index of Latin Personal and Place Names in Domesday Book, 1997; (ed.) Family Trees and the Roots of Politics: The Prosopography of Britain and France from the Tenth to the Twelfth Century, 1997; Domesday People: A Prosopography of Persons Occurring in English Documents, 1066-1166, 1999; Domesday Descendants: A Prosopography of Persons Occurring in English Documents, 1066-1166, 1999; (ed.) Resourcing Sources, 2002; (ed.) The Cartulary of the Abbey of Mont-Saint-Michel, 2006; (ed.) Prosopography Approaches and Applications: A Handbook, 2007. POETRY: Beautiful Contortions: And other Poems, 1982; Before Follows After, 1983; Woman of Shadows, 1984. **Address:** Faculty of History, Linacre College, Oxford University, George St., Oxford, OX OX1 2RL, England.

KEAY, John. Scottish/British (born England), b. 1941. **Genres:** Travel/Exploration, History. **Career:** Economist Magazine, staff, political correspondent, 1965-71; freelance writer, journalist, and editor, 1972-; BBC Radio, writer and presenter. Historian. **Publications:** Into India, 1973; When Men and Mountains Meet: The Explorers of the Western Himalayas 1820-75, 1977;

The Gilgit Game: The Explorers of the Western Himalayas, 1865-95, 1979; India Discovered: The Achievement of the British Raj, 1981; Eccentric Travellers, 1982; Highland Drove, 1984; Explorers Extraordinary, 1985; Banaras, City of Shiva, 1987; The Honourable Company: A History of the English East India Company, 1991; Indonesia: From Sabang to Merauke, 1995; Last Post: The End of Empire in the Far East, 1997; Empire's End: A History of the Far East from High Colonialism to Hong Kong, 1997; Ann Arbor, 1999; India: A History, 2000; The Great Arc: The Dramatic Tale of How India was Mapped and Everest was Named, 2000; Sowing the Wind: The Seeds of Conflict in the Middle East, 2003; Mad about the Mekong: Exploration and Empire in South-East Asia, 2005; The Spice Route: A History, 2005; China: A History, 2008; The Mammoth Book of Travel in Dangerous Places, 2010; (contrib.) Ladakh 1974-2008, 2010. EDITOR: The Royal Geographical Society's History of World Exploration, 1991; (with J. Keay) Collins Encyclopedia of Scotland, 1994, 2nd ed., 2000; Mammoth Book of Explorers, 2002. **Address:** c/o Bruce Hunter, David Higham & Associates Ltd., 5-8 Lower John St., Golden Sq., London, GL W1F 4HA, England. **Online address:** john@johnkeay.com

KEE, Robert. British/Indian (born India), b. 1919. **Genres:** Novels, History, Autobiography/Memoirs, Social Sciences, Adult Non-fiction. **Career:** Picture Post magazine, staff, 1948-52, journalist, 1948-51; World Health Organization, picture editor, 1953; Observer, special correspondent, journalist, 1956-57; Spectator, literary editor, 1957; The Sunday Times, special correspondent, journalist, 1957-58; British Broadcasting Corp., staff, 1953, affiliate, 1958-62, 1978-82; Television Reporters Intl., presenter, affiliate, 1962-64; Independent Television, broadcaster, 1964-76; Yorkshire Television, broadcaster, 1976-78, 1984-89; TV-AM, co-founder, 1983-92, presenter, 1983-92, associate, 1983, co-presenter, 1984. **Publications:** A Crowd is not Company, 1947, 2nd ed., 1982; The Impossible Shore, 1949; (ed. with R. Mortimer and C. Connolly) Memories, 1953; A Sign of the Times, 1955; Broadstrop in Season, 1959; Refugee World, 1959; The Green Flag: A History of Irish Nationalism, 1972; The Green Flag: The Turbulent History of the Irish National Movement, 1972; General Strike Report ..., 1976; Ireland: A History, 1980, rev. ed., 1995; 1939: In the Shadow of War, 1984; (intro.) We'll Meet Again, 1984; The World We Left Behind, 1984; 1945: The World We Fought For, 1985; (contrib.) A Journalist's Odyssey, 1985; Trial and Error: The Maguires, the Guildford Pub Bombings and British Justice, 1986; Munich: The Eleventh Hour, 1988; Picture Post Album, 1989; The Laurel and the Ivy: The Story of Parnell and Irish Nationalism, 1993; (with A. Huth) Another Kind of Cinderella, 1997; (trans.) H.H. Kirst, Officer Factory, 2002. Contributor to books. **Address:** Roger Coleridge and White, 20 Powis Mews, London, GL W11 1JN, England.

KEEBLE, Neil H(oward). Scottish/British (born England), b. 1944. **Genres:** History, Literary Criticism And History, Theology/Religion, Women's Studies And Issues, Biography, Autobiography/Memoirs, Travel/Exploration, Cultural/Ethnic Topics, Cultural/Ethnic Topics. **Career:** University of Aarhus, lecturer in English, 1969-74; University of Stirling, lecturer, 1974-88, reader in English, 1988-95, professor of English, 1995-, deputy principal, 2001-, senior deputy principal, 2003-10, now professor emeritus. Writer. **Publications:** Richard Baxter: Puritan Man of Letters, 1982; The Literary Culture of Nonconformity in Later Seventeenth-Century England, 1987; (with G.F. Nuttall) Calendar of the Correspondence of Richard Baxter, 2 vols., 1991; Loving and Free Converse: Richard Baxter in His Letters, 1991; The Restoration: England in the 1660s, 2002. EDITOR: (intro.) The Autobiography of Richard Baxter: Abridged by J.M. Lloyd Thomas, 1974; Handbook of English and Celtic Studies in the United Kingdom and the Republic of Ireland, 1988; John Bunyan: Conventicle and Parnassus: Tercentenary Essays, 1988; (comp.) The Cultural Identity of Seventeenth-Century Woman: A Reader, 1994; (intro.) The Pilgrim's Progress, 1984, rev. ed., 1998; Memoirs of the Life of Colonel Hutchinson, 2000; Cambridge Companion to Writing of the English Revolution, 2001; Writings on Travel, Discovery, and History, 2001; John Bunyan: Reading Dissenting Writing, 2002; Memoirs of the Church of Scotland, 2002; Remarks upon a Late Disingenuous Discourse, 2003. **Address:** Department of English Studies, University of Stirling, Cottrell 4B16, Stirling, FK9 4LA, Scotland. **Online address:** n.h.keeble@stir.ac.uk

KEECH, Thomas (Walton). American (born United States), b. 1946. **Genres:** Novels, Law, Young Adult Fiction. **Career:** Maryland Department of Juvenile Services, juvenile probation officer, 1969-72; Legal Aid Bureau of Baltimore Inc., staff attorney, 1975-81; Maryland Department of Economic and Employment Development, Board of Appeals, chair, 1981-94; Baltimore City Office of the Attorney General, assistant attorney general, 1994-. Writer. **Publications:** (Co-author) Unemployment Insurance Benefits, 1990; The Crawlspace Conspiracy (novel), 1995. **Address:** Department of Health & Mental Hygiene, Office of the Attorney General, 300 W Preston St., Ste. 302, 2nd & 3rd Fl., Baltimore, MD 21201-2301, U.S.A. **Online address:** tkeech@oag.state.md.us

KEEFAUVER, Larry. American (born United States) **Genres:** Theology/ Religion, inspirational/Motivational Literature, Young Adult Fiction. **Career:** Ministries Today, senior advisory editor, 2001-, senior editor; Your Ministries Consultation Services, executive director; Charisma Magazine, editor. Pastor. **Publications:** (With J.D. Stone) Friend to Friend: How You Can Help a Friend through a Problem, 1983; Starting a Youth Ministry, 1984; Friends & Faith: Friendship Evangelism in Youth Ministry, 1986; Faith in the Workplace: A Four-Week Course to Help Adults Discover How to Live out Their Faith at Work, 1993; (with R. Cherry) The Doctor and the Word, 1996; Prayer and the Bible, 1996; Praying with Smith Wigglesworth, 1996; Welcoming the Presence of the Spirit, 1997; Receiving the Anointing of the Spirit, 1997; Blazing with the Fire of the Spirit, 1997; Hearing the Voice of the Spirit, 1997; Living the Spirit-Led Life, 1997; Operating in the Power of the Holy Spirit, 1997; Lord, I Wish My Husband Would Pray with Me, 1998; Carlton Pearson's Azuza Street Revival, 1998; Hugs for Grandparents: Stories, Sayings and Scriptures to Encourage and Inspire, 1998; Lord, I Wish My Teenager would Talk with Me, 1999; (with L. Mintle) Kids Killing Kids, 1999; When God Doesn't Heal Now: How to Walk by Faith, Facing Pain, Suffering and Death, 2000; Lord, I Wish My Family Would Get Saved, 2000; Experiencing the Holy Spirit: Transformed by His Presence, 2000; 77 Irrefutable Truths of Parenting: Foundations for Godly Parenting, 2001; Commanding Angels: Invoking the Standing Orders, 2001; (with J. Keefauver) Seventy-Seven Irrefutable Truths of Marriage, 2002; I'm Praying for You, Mom: Prayers and Inspiration for All You Encounter in Life, 2002; Hugs for Heroes: Stories, Sayings and Scriptures to Encourage and Inspire, 2002; (with T. Gill) Prophetic Giving: Sowing for Your Harvest, 2003; Inviting God's Presence: An Interactive Guide, 2003; Seventy-Seven Irrefutable Truths of Prayer, 2003; Angels On Command: Invoking the Standing Orders, 2004. EDITOR: (and comp.) Smith Wigglesworth on Faith: A Thirty-Day Devotional, 1996; (and comp.) Smith Wigglesworth on Healing: A Thirty-Day Devotional, 1996; The Original Smith Wigglesworth Devotional, 1997; The Original Azusa Street Revival Devotional, 1997; Healing Words, 1997; The Original John G. Lake Devotional, 1997; The Original Maria Woodworth-Etter Devotional, 1997; From the Oval Office, Prayers of the Presidents, 2003. **Address:** c/o Author Mail, Thomas Nelson Inc., 501 Nelson Pl., PO Box 141000, Nashville, TN 37214, U.S.A. **Online address:** drlarry@powerhouseuniversity.com

KEEFE, Patrick Radden. American (born United States), b. 1976?. **Genres:** Novels, Autobiography/Memoirs, Social Sciences. **Career:** World Policy Institute, project leader; Century Foundation, fellow; New York Public Library, writers fellow, 2003. **Publications:** Chatter: Dispatches from the Secret World of Global Eavesdropping, 2005; Chatter: Uncovering the Echelon Surveillance Network and the Secret World of Global Eavesdropping, 2006; The Snakehead: An Epic Tale of the Chinatown Underworld and the American Dream, 2009. Contributor to periodicals. **Address:** c/o Tina Bennett, Janklow & Nesbit, 445 Park Ave., New York, NY 10022, U.S.A. **Online address:** patrick@patrickraddenkeefe.com

KEEFE, Richard S.E. American (born United States), b. 1958. **Genres:** Psychology, Medicine/Health. **Career:** Princeton University, research assistant, 1979-80; Schizophrenia Biological Research Center, research coordinator, 1983-85, assistant research psychologist, 1985-89; City University of New York, Mount Sinai School of Medicine, Mount Sinai Medical Center, research coordinator, 1983-85, assistant research psychologist, 1985-89, assistant professor, 1990-95, Mount Sinai and Bronx VA Medical Centers, Cognition Studies, director, 1990-95; Beth Israel Medical Center, neuropsychology extern, 1987-88; Yale University, Yale-New Haven Hospital, clinical psychology intern, 1989-90, Kidd Laboratory, visiting scientist, 1990-92; Elmhurst Hospital, director of diagnostic assessment service, 1990-95; Kraepelinian Schizophrenia Research Project, Neurocognitive Laboratories, director, 1990-95; University of Utrecht, lecturer, 1994; Duke University, Medical Center, assistant professor, 1995-97, associate professor, 1997-2007, Department of Psychiatry and Behavioral Sciences, Division of Medical Psychology, School of Medicine, director, professor, 2007-, Department of Psychology and Neuroscience, professor, 2007-10, National University of Singapore, adjunct professor, 2007-10; University of North Carolina, School of Medicine, De-

partment of Psychiatry, adjunct research associate professor, 2001-, adjunct professor, 2008-. Writer. **Publications:** (With P.D. Harvey) Understanding Schizophrenia: A Guide to the New Research on Causes and Treatment, 1994; (ed. with J.P. McEvoy) Negative Symptom and Cognitive Deficit Treatment Response in Schizophrenia, 2000; On the Sweet Spot: Stalking the Effortless Present, 2003. Contributor of articles to books and journals. **Address:** Department of Psychiatry and Behavioral Sciences, Duke University Medicine Center, Rm. 3270, 3425 Hospital S, Durham, NC 27710, U.S.A. **Online address:** richard.keefe@duke.edu

KEEGAN, John E. American (born United States), b. 1943. **Genres:** Novels, Law, Young Adult Fiction, Literary Criticism And History. **Career:** U.S. Department of Housing and Urban Development, attorney, 1968-70; Office of the Prosecuting Attorney of King County, deputy prosecutor, 1972-79; Davis Wright Tremaine LLP, partner. Writer. **Publications:** NOVELS: Clearwater Summer, 1994; Piper, 2001; LAW: A Good Divorce, 2003. Contributor to periodicals and journals. **Address:** Davis Wright Tremaine L.L.P., 1201 3rd Ave., Ste. 2200, Seattle, WA 98101-3045, U.S.A. **Online address:** johnkeegan@dwt.com

KEEGAN, Marcia. American (born United States), b. 1943?. **Genres:** Area Studies, Cultural/Ethnic Topics, History, Photography. **Career:** Albuquerque Tribune, journalist and photographer, 1963-64; Albuquerque Journal, editor, 1964-68; freelance photographer, 1969-88; Clear Light Publishers, co-founder, 1988, president and book designer, 1988-. **Publications:** Taos Pueblo and Its Sacred Blue Lake, 1972, 2nd ed., 2010; Taos Indians and Their Sacred Blue Lake, 1972; Mother Earth, Father Sky: Navajo and Pueblo Indians of the Southwest, 1974, rev. ed. as Mother Earth, Father Sky: Pueblo and Navajo Indians of the Southwest, 1988; We Can Still Hear Them Clapping, 1975; Pueblo and Navajo Cookery, 1977; Oklahoma, 1979; The Dalai Lama's Historic Visit to North America, 1981; (ed.) Teachings of His Holiness the Dalai Lama, 1981; New Mexico, 1986; Southwest Indian Cookbook, 1987; Enduring Culture: A Century of Photography of the Southwest Indians, 1990; Pueblo Boy: Growing up in Two Worlds, 1991; Ancient Wisdom, Living Tradition, 1998; Pueblo People: Ancient Traditions, Modern Lives, 1999; Pueblo Girls: Growing up in Two Worlds, 1999; (contrib.) Female Buddhas: Women of Enlightenment in Tibetan Mystical Art, 2002. Contributor to books and magazines. **Address:** 823 Don Diego, Santa Fe, NM 87501, U.S.A. **Online address:** marcia@clearlightbooks.com

KEEGAN, William (James Gregory). British (born England), b. 1938. **Genres:** Novels, Politics/Government, Economics, Business/Trade/Industry. **Career:** Financial Times, economics correspondent, 1967-76; Bank of England, assistant to governor, 1976-77; Observer, economics editor, 1977-, assistant editor and business editor, 1981-83, associate editor, 1983-, senior economics commentator; Sheffield University, visiting professor of journalism, 1989, honorary residential fellow, 1990. **Publications:** FICTION: Consulting Father Wintergreen, 1974; A Real Killing: A Novel, 1977. NONFICTION: (with R. Pennant-Rea) Who Runs the Economy?: Control and Influence in British Economic Policy, 1979; Mrs. Thatcher's Economic Experiment, 1984; Britain without Oil, 1985; Mr. Lawson's Gamble, 1989; The Spectre of Capitalism: The Future of the World Economy after the Fall of Communism, 1992; 2066-and All That, 2000; Prudence of Mr. Gordon Brown, 2003. Contributor to journals. **Address:** Observer, 119 Farringdon Rd., London, GL EC1R 3ER, England.

KEELE, Alan (Frank). American (born United States), b. 1942. **Genres:** Humanities, Language/Linguistics, Translations. **Career:** Mormon Missionary in Germany, 1962-64; Brigham Young University, professor of Germanic and Slavic languages, P.A. Christensen memorial lecturer, 1976, Karl G. Maeser professor, 1996, Department of Germanic and Slavic Languages, associate chair, chair, associate dean of honors and general education, professor emeritus, 2010. Writer. **Publications:** Paul Schallueck and the Postwar German Don Quixote: A Case History Prolegomenon to the Literature of the Federal Republic, 1976; (with M.H. Folsom) Learn German series, 1978; A German-English, English-German Glossary for Missionaries, 1982, (with M.H. Folsom) 2nd ed., 1983; The Apocalyptic Vision: A Thematic Exploration of Postwar German Literature, 1983; (with M.H. Folsom) German Core Vocabulary in Context: A Pedagogical Dictionary for Beginning Students of German, 1983; (with K.H. Schnibbe and D.F. Tobler) The Price: The True Story of a Mormon Who Defied Hitler, 1984; Understanding Guenter Grass, 1988; (with R.L. Jones and F.J. Goertz) Wortindex zur Blechtrommel von Guenter Grass, 1990; (with Schnibbe and B. Holmes) Jugendliche gegen Hitler: Die Helmuth

Huebener Gruppe in Hamburg, 1941-42, 1991; (with B. Holmes) When Truth Was Treason: German Youth against Hitler, 1995; In Search of the Supernal: Pre-Existence, Eternal Marriage, and Apotheosis in German Literary, Operatic, and Cinematic Texts, 2003. TRANSLATOR: (with L. Norris) R.M. Rilke, Sonnets to Orpheus; (with N. Davis and G. Davis) W. Kempowski, Dog Days, 1991; (with L. Norris) Rilke, Duino Elegies, 1993. EDITOR: (with M.H. Folsom) P.P. Ashworth and C. Vigo, Learn Spanish, 1980; (with M.H. Folsom) C.W. Griggs and R. Stewart, Learn Greek, 1981, 2nd ed. (with M.F. Shelley), 1984; (with M.H. Folsom) M. Watabe, Learn Japanese, 1984. Contributor to books. Contributor of articles and reviews to journals. **Address:** Department of Germanic & Slavic Languages, Brigham Young University, 3105 JSFB, Provo, UT 84602, U.S.A. **Online address:** alan_keele@byu.edu

KEELER, Robert F. American (born United States), b. 1944. **Genres:** Writing/Journalism, Theology/Religion. **Career:** New York Herald Tribune, editorial assistant, 1965; Waterbury Republican, journalist, 1969; Staten Island Advance, journalist, 1969-71; Newsday, reporter, 1971-, Albany bureau chief, 1978-81, editor, 1982-83, state editor, 1984, reporter on religion, ethics and values, 1993-2001, editorial writer, 2001-, columnist. **Publications:** Newsday: A Candid History of the Respectable Tabloid, 1990; Parish!: The Pulitzer Prize-winning Story of a Vibrant Catholic Community, 1997; (with P. Moses) Days of Intense Emotion: Praying with Pope John Paul II in the Holy Land, 2001. **Address:** Newsday, 235 Pinelawn Rd., Melville, NY 11747, U.S.A. **Online address:** bob.keeler@newsday.com

KEELEY, Edmund. American/Syrian (born Syrian Arab Republic), b. 1928. **Genres:** Novels, Novellas/Short Stories, History, Literary Criticism And History, Travel/Exploration, Translations, Adult Non-fiction. **Career:** American Farm School, Fulbright teacher of English, 1949-50; Brown University, instructor of English, 1952-53; Salonika University, professor of English and American literature and Fulbright lecturer, 1953-54; Princeton University, instructor, 1954-57, assistant professor, 1957-62, associate professor, 1963-70, professor of English and creative writing, 1970-94, Charles Barnwell Straut Class of 1923 Professor of English, 1992-94, Charles Barnwell Straut Professor Emeritus, 1994-, co-director of comparative literature program, 1964-65, director of creative arts program, 1966-71, 1974-81, director of creative writing and theater, 1971-74, director, program in Hellenic Studies, 1985-94; U.S. Information Agency, lecturer, 1954; Oxford University, lecturer, 1960; University of Iowa, Writers Workshop, lecturer, 1962-63; Knox College, writer-in-residence, 1963; New School for Social Research, visiting professor, 1980; Columbia University, School of the Arts, visiting professor, 1981; Athens University, Fulbright lecturer, 1985; University of Thessaloniki, Fulbright lecturer; University of Crete, Fulbright lecturer, 1986; King's College, London University, visiting professor, 1996; Virginia Center for the Creative Arts, resident. Writer. **Publications:** The Libation, 1958; The Gold-Hatted Lover, a Novel, 1961; The Impostor, 1970; Voyage to a Dark Island, 1972; Cavafy's Alexandria: Study of a Myth in Progress, 1976; Modern Greek Poetry: Voice and Myth, 1983; A Wilderness Called Peace, 1985; The Salonika Bay Murder, 1989; School for Pagan Lovers, 1993; Albanian Journal, 1996; George Seferis and Edmund Keeley: Correspondence, 1951-1971, 1997; Inventing Paradise: The Greek Journey, 1937-47, 1999; On Translation: Reflections and Conversations, 2000; Some Wine for Remembrance, 2001; Low Crimes and Misdemeanors in High Places: John Mitchell and Watergate, 2004; Borderlines: A Memoir, 2005. EDITOR: (with P. Bien) Modern Greek Writers, 1972; (with E.T. Cone and J. Frank) The Legacy of R.P. Blackmur: Essays, Memoirs, Texts, 1987; (with P. Bien, P. Constantine and K.V. Dyck) A Century of Greek Poetry, 2004, (with P. Constantine, R. Hadas and K.V. Dyck) Greek Poets: Homer to the Present, 2010. TRANSLATIONS: (with P. Sherrard) Six Poets of Modern Greece, 1960; (with M. Keeley) V. Vassilikos, The Plant, The Well, The Angel, 1964; (with P. Sherrard) Four Greek Poets, 1966; (with P. Sherrard) George Seferis: Collected Poems, 1924-1955, 1967; (with G. Savidis) C.P. Cavafy: Passions and Ancient Days, 1971; (with P. Sherrard) C.P. Cavafy: Selected Poems, 1972; (with G. Savidis) Odysseus Elytis: The Axion Esti, 1974; (with P. Sherrard) C.P. Cavafy: Collected Poems, 1975; Ritsos in Parentheses, 1979; (with P. Sherrard) Angelos Sikelianos: Selected Poems, 1979; (with P. Sherrard) Odysseus Elytis: Selected Poems, 1981; (and ed. with P. Sherrard) Cavafy, Voices of Modern Greece, 1981; (with P. Sherrard) The Dark Crystal: An Anthology of Modern Greek Poetry, 1982, as A Greek Quintet, 1992; Y. Ritsos, Return & Other Poems, 1983; Yannis Ritsos: Exile and Return, Selected Poems 1967-1974, 1985; Yannis Ritsos: Repetitions, Testimonies, Parentheses, 1991; (and intro.) The Essential Cavafy, 1995. **Address:** Department of English, Princeton University, 22 McCosh Hall, Princeton, NJ 08544-1014, U.S.A. **Online address:** keeley@princeton.edu

KEELING, Kara. American (born United States), b. 1971. **Genres:** Film, History. **Career:** University of Southern California, School of Cinematic Arts, assistant professor. Writer. **Publications:** (with C. MacCabe and C. West) Racist Traces and Other Writings: European Pedigrees/African Contagions, 2003; The Witch's Flight: The Cinematic, the Black Femme, and the Image of Common Sense, 2007. **Address:** School of Cinematic Arts, University of Southern California, SCA 222, University Pk., Los Angeles, CA 90089-2211, U.S.A. **Online address:** kkeeling@cinema.usc.edu

KEEN, Ernest. American (born United States), b. 1937. **Genres:** Psychology, Medicine/Health. **Career:** Bucknell University, assistant professor, 1964-69, associate professor, 1969-74, professor, 1974-2000, professor emeritus, 2000-; Pennsylvania Bureau of Vocational Rehabilitation, psychological consultant, 1964-74; Federal Penitentiary, psychological consultant, 1965-68; Capital District Psychiatric Center, clinical psychologist, 1971-72; Yale University, National Humanities Institute, fellow, 1976-77. Writer. **Publications:** Three Faces of Being: Toward an Existential Clinical Psychology, 1970; Psychology and the New Consciousness, 1972; Primer in Phenomenological Psychology, 1975; Emotion, 1977; Drugs, Therapy, and Professional Power, 1998; Chemicals for the Mind, 2000; Ultimacy and Triviality in Psychotherapy, 2000; A History of Ideas in American Psychology, 2001; Depression: Self-Consciousness, Pretending, and Guilt, 2002. Contributor to periodicals. **Address:** Department of Psychology, Bucknell University, 203 O'Leary, Lewisburg, PA 17837, U.S.A. **Online address:** keen@bucknell.edu

KEEN, Sam. American (born United States), b. 1931?. **Genres:** Human Relations/Parenting, Philosophy, Psychology, Theology/Religion, Geography, Self Help. **Career:** Boston University, lecturer in religion, 1956-58; Douglas College, lecturer in religion, 1959-60; Louisville Presbyterian Theological Seminary, professor of philosophy of religion, 1962-68; Princeton Seminary, lecturer in philosophy of religion; Psychology Today, contributing editor, 1969-86; Western Behavioral Science Institute, National Institute of Mental Health postdoctoral fellow, 1969-70; Prescott College, professor of philosophy, 1970-71; Humanistic Psychology Institute, professor, 1972; University of Florida Medical School, visiting professor of medical ethics, 1983; Spirituality and Health, contributing editor, 2001-. **Publications:** Gabriel Marcel, 1966; Apology for Wonder, 1969; To a Dancing God, 1970; (with A.V. Fox) Telling Your Story, 1973; Voices and Visions, 1974; Beginnings without End, 1975; (with J. Fowler) Life-Maps: Conversations on the Journey of Faith, 1978; What to Do When You're Bored and Blue, 1980; Auf den Spuren Carlos Castanedas, 1981; The Passionate Life: Stages of Loving, 1983; Faces of the Enemy: Reflections of the Hostile Imagination, 1986; (with A.V. Fox) Your Mythic Journey, 1989; Fire in the Belly: On Being a Man, 1991; Inward Bound: Exploring the Geography of Your Emotions, 1992; Hymns to an Unknown God: Awakening the Spirit in Everyday Life, 1994; To Love and Be Loved, 1997; Learning to Fly: Trapeze--Reflections on Fear, Trust and the Joy off Letting Go, 1999; Sightings: Extraordinary Encounters with Ordinary Birds, 2007; In the Absence of God, 2010. Contributor of articles to magazines and journals. **Address:** 16331 Norrbom Rd., Sonoma, CA 95476, U.S.A. **Online address:** sam@samkeen.com

KEENAN, Brian. Irish (born Ireland), b. 1950. **Genres:** Novels, Plays/Screenplays, Travel/Exploration, Biography, Politics/Government. **Career:** Orangefield Boys School, teacher, 1975-77; Belfast City Council, community development officer, 1977-84; American University, instructor in English, 1985-86; Trinity College, writer-in-resident, 1993-. **Publications:** An Evil Cradling: The Five-Year Ordeal of a Hostage, 1992; Between Extremes (travel), 1999; Turlough (novel), 2000; Four Quarters of Light: A Journey through Alaska, 2004; I'll Tell Me Ma, 2010. **Address:** Department of English, Trinity College, Dublin, 1, Ireland.

KEENAN, Sheila. American (born United States), b. 1953. **Genres:** Children's Fiction, Children's Non-fiction, History. **Career:** Children's Express (extracurricular journalism program), program director, 1986-89; Scholastic Inc., editorial supervisor, 1989-93, senior editor, 1999-; writer, 1993-99. **Publications:** Good Morning, Monday, 1994; Frederick Douglass: Portrait of a Freedom Fighter, 1995; The History of Moviemaking, 1995; (adaptor) The Story of Flight: Early Flying Machines, Balloons, Blimps, Gliders, Warplanes and Jets, 1995; The World of Theater, 1995; What the Painter Sees, 1996; The Art of Making Books, 1996; The Scholastic Encyclopedia of Women in the United States, 1996, rev. ed., 2002; The Biggest Fish, 1996; More or Less a Mess!, 1997; The World of Insects, 1997; Bikes, Cars, Trucks, and Trains, 1997; What Time Is It?: A Book of Math Riddles, 1999; What's Up with that Cup?, 2000; Gods, Goddesses and Monsters: An Encyclopedia of World Mythology, 2000; Lizzy's Dizzy Day, 2001; The Trouble with Pets, 2001; Scholastic Book of Outstanding Americans, 2003; O, Say Can You See?: America's Symbols and Landmarks, 2004; Looking for Leprechauns, 2005; (ed.) Scary Summer, 2007; Animals in the House: A History of Pets and People, 2007; Greetings from the 50 States: How They Got Their Names, 2008; Dogs of War, 2012; Down, Boy!: A History of Pets and People, forthcoming. **Address:** 75 Abbott Ave., Ocean Grove, NJ 07756, U.S.A. **Online address:** asktheauthor@aol.com

KEENE, Ann T(odd). American (born United States), b. 1940. **Genres:** Young Adult Non-fiction, Children's Fiction, Natural History, Science Fiction/Fantasy, Reference. **Career:** Bloomington Montessori Association, founder, 1968; Bloomington Montessori School, co-founder, 1969; Indiana University, instructor/adjunct professor, 1974-79; Business Horizons (magazine), managing editor, 1977-79; President's Select Commission on Immigration, chief writer and editor, 1979-81; George Mason University, adjunct professor of writing, 1982-83; E.P. Dutton, managing editor, 1984-85; freelance writer, 1986-. **Publications:** NONFICTION FOR YOUNG ADULTS: (ed.) Encyclopedia of Psychoactive Drugs, rev. ed., 1992; Earthkeepers: Observers and Protectors of Nature, 1994; Willa Cather, 1994; (contrib.) Young Oxford History of Women in the United States, 1994; Racism, 1995; Peacemakers: Winners of the Nobel Peace Prize, 1996; (ed.) Oxford American Children's Encyclopedia, 2002. OTHERS: Another Time, Another Place, 2010; Will's Girl, 2012. Contributor to books. **Address:** Oxford University Press, 198 Madison Ave., New York, NY 10016, U.S.A.

KEENE, Donald. American/Japanese (born Japan), b. 1922. **Genres:** Area Studies, Literary Criticism And History, Translations, History, Essays. **Career:** Cambridge University, lecturer, 1949-55; Columbia University, assistant professor, 1955-60, associate professor, 1960-, Shincho professor of Japanese literature, 1986-92, university professor, 1989-92, Shincho professor emeritus of Japanese literature and university professor emeritus, 1992, Donald Keene Foundation for Japanese Culture, president, 1999-. Writer. **Publications:** The Battles of Coxinga: Chikamatsu's Puppet Play, Its Background and Importance, 1951; The Japanese Discovery of Europe: Honda Toshiaki and Other Discoverers, 1720-1798, 1952, rev. ed. 1969; Japanese Literature; An Introduction for Western Readers, 1953; Modern Japanese Literature, An Anthology, 1956; Modern Japanese Novels and the West, 1961; Bunraku: The Art of the Japanese Puppet Theatre, 1965; Nō: The Classical Theatre of Japan, 1966; La Literatura Japonesa Entre Oriente y Occidente, 1969; Landscapes and Portraits, Appreciations of Japanese Culture, 1971; 30 Things Japanese, 1978; Some Japanese Portraits, 1978; Meeting with Japan, 1978; Appreciations of Japanese Culture, 1981; Tsui Saki no Utagoe Wa, 1981; Nihonjin no Shitsumon, 1983; Dawn to the West: Japanese Literature of the Modern Era, 1984; Hyakudai no Kakaku, 1984; Futatsu no Bokoku Nilkite, 1987; The Pleasures of Japanese Literature, 1988; Travelers of a Hundred Ages, 1989; Koten O Tanoshimu: Watakushi No Nihon Bungaku, 1990; Seeds in the Heart: Japanese Literature From Earliest Times to the Late Sixteenth Century, 1993; On Familiar Terms: A Journey Across Cultures, 1994; Modern Japanese Diaries: The Japanese at Home and Abroad As Revealed Through Their Diaries, 1995; The blue-eyed tarōkaja, 1996; On Familiar Terms: To Japan and Back, a Lifetime Across Cultures, 1996; Seeds in the Heart: Japanese Literature From Earliest Times to the Late Sixteenth Century, 1999; World Within Walls: Japanese Literature of The Pre-Modern Era, 1600-1867, 1999; Japan At The Dawn of the Modern Age: Woodblock Prints From the Meiji Era, 2001; Emperor of Japan: Meiji and His World, 1852-1912, 2002; Five Modern Japanese Novelists, 2003; Les Journaux Intimes Dans La Litteirature Japonaise, 2003; Yoshimasa and the Silver Pavilion: The Creation of the Soul of Japan, 2003; Meiji Tennō o Kataru, 2003; Frog in the Well: Portraits of Japan by Watanabe Kazan, 1793-1841, 2006; Chronicles of My Life: An American in the Heart of Japan, 2008; Sakka no nikki o yomu, Nihonjin no sensō, 2009; So Lovely a Country Will Never Perish: Wartime Diaries of Japanese Writers, 2010. EDITOR: Anthology of Japanese Literature, From the Earliest Era to the Mid-Nineteenth Century, 1955; Anthology of Chinese Literature, 1965; Twenty Plays of the Nō Theatre, 1970. TRANSLATOR: Four Major Plays, 1961; The Old Woman, The Wife and the Archer; Three Modern Japanese Short Novels, 1961; The Treasury of Loyal Retainers, 1971; The Man Who Turned into a Stick, 1975; An Account of My Hut: The Hojoki of Kamo no Chomei, 1976; World Within Walls: Japanese Literature of the Pre-Modern Era, 1600-1867, 1976; The Narrow Road to Oku, 1996; Four Major Plays of Chikamatsu, 1998; Essays in Idleness, 1998; The Breaking Jewel, 2003; Y.

Mishima, Five modern Nō plays, 2009. **Address:** Donald Keene Center of Japanese Culture, Columbia University, 507 Kent Hall, MC 3920, New York, NY 10027, U.S.A.

KEENE, John (R.). American (born United States), b. 1965. **Genres:** Novels, Poetry, Translations, Gay And Lesbian Issues, History. **Career:** Massachusetts Institute of Technology, Laboratory for Manufacturing and Productivity Collegium, librarian and assistant, 1991-93, assistant director of collegium affairs, 1992-93; University of Virginia, lecturer, Callaloo, managing editor, 1992-94, Global Studies for Teachers Program, board director, 1993-95; New York Times, fellow, 1995-96; East Side Community High School, creative writing teacher, 1995-96; New York University, Wagner School, lecturer, 1997-2001; Northwestern University, Weinberg College of Arts & Sciences, Department of English, assistant professor, 2002-05, associate professor of English and African American studies, 2005-. **Publications:** Annotations, 1995; Seismosis (cross-genre/poetry), 2006. Works aopear in anthologies. Contributor to magazines and periodicals. **Address:** Department of English, Weinberg College of Arts & Sciences, Northwestern University, Rm. 413, University Hall, 1897 Sheridan Rd., Evanston, IL 60208-2240, U.S.A. **Online address:** j-keene@northwestern.edu

KEENE, Raymond D(ennis). (R. D. Keene). British (born England), b. 1948. **Genres:** Recreation, Sports/Fitness, Humor/Satire. **Career:** Freelance author, 1968-; Spectator, chess correspondent, 1977; Times, chess correspondent, 1985-; The British Monarchy, Order of the British Empire, officer, 1985; Sunday Times, chess correspondent, 1997; Hardinge/Simpole Publishing, co-founder, 2001; Intl. Herald Tribune, chess correspondent, 2002-. **Publications:** NON-FICTION: (as R.D. Keene) Flank Openings: A Study Of Reti's Opening, The Catalan, English and King's Indian Attack Complex, 1967, rev. ed., 1970; (as R.D. Keene with L.W. Barden and W.R. Hartston) The King's Indian Defence, 1969, 2nd ed., 1973; Yugoslav Attack, Dragon Variation, Sicilian Defence, 1969; (with D.N. Levy) Siegen Chess Olympiad, September 5th to September 26th 1970, 1970; (as R.D. Keene with G.S. Botterill) The Modern Defence: 1... P-KN3: A Universal Reply to IP-K4, 1 P-Q4 or IP-QB4, 1972; (with D. Levy) Chess Olympiad, 1972; (with D. Levy) Chess Olympiad, Skopje 1972; (with D. Levy) Chess Olympiad 1972; (as R.D. Keene with G.S. Botterill) The Pirc Defence, 1973; Aron Nimzowitsch, 1886-1935: Areappraisal, 1974; (as R.D. Keene with W.G. Raines and A.K. Crombleholme) The European Team Championship, 1974; (as R.D. Keene with W.R. Hartston) Karpov-Korchnoi 1974, 1974; (with Levy) How to Play the Opening in Chess, 1974, 2nd ed., 1980; (ed. with R. Edwards) The Chess Player's Bedside Book, 1975; (ed.) Learn from the Grandmasters, 1975; Beginner's Guide to Chess, 1975; (with D. Levy) Chess Olympiad Nice 1974: World Team Championship, 1975; Leonid Stein: Master of Attack, 1976; (ed. with R.G. Wade and K.J. O'Connel) Contemporary Approach to the Middle Game, 1976; (as R.D. Keene) How to Play the King's Indian, Saemisch Variation, 1976; (with D. Levy) An Opening Repertoire for the Attacking Club Player, 1976 in US as An Opening Repertoire for the Attacking Player, 1977, 1st ed., 1994; (as R.D. Keene with D. Levy) Haifa Chess Olympiad, 1976, 1977; Nimzowitsch/Larsen Attack, 1977; Becoming a Grandmaster, 1977; The Chess Combination from Philidor to Karpov, 1977; Korchnoi vs. Spassky, 1978; World Chess Championship: Korchnoi vs. Karpov in UK as Karpov-Korchnoi 1978, 1978; (with B. Ivkov and J. Kaplan) Nimzo-Indian Defence 1, 1979; (comp. with J.D.M. Nunn and R.G. Wade) 46th U.S.S.R. Chess Championships, 1978, 1979; The Openings in Modern Theory and Practice, 1979; (co-author) Caro-Kann Defence, 1980; (with S. Taulbut) French Defence: Tarrasch Variation, 1980; (with M. Chandler and L. Barden) English Chess Explosion: From Miles to Short, 1981; Karpov Korchnoi: Massacre in Merano, 1981; How to Play the Nimzo-Indian, 1982; (with G. Kasparov) Batsford Chess Openings, 1982; Dynamic Chess Openings, 1982; (with A. Whiteley) Ray Keene's Good Move Guide, 1982; London 1927, 1983; (with D. Goodman and R. Wade) U.S.S.R. v Rest of the World Challenge Match, 1984; An Opening Repertoire for White, 1984, (with B. Jacobs) new ed., 1995; The Evolution of Chess Opening Theory, 1985; (with D. Goodman) Maneuvers in Moscow: Karpov-Kasparov II, 1985; (ed. with B. Kazic and L.K. Ann) The Official Laws of Chess and Other FIDE Regulations, 1985; (with R.G. Wade and A.J. Whiteley) The World Chess Championship: Botvinnik to Kasparov, 1986; (with D. Goodman) The Centenary Match Kasparov-Karpov III, 1986; Speed Chess Challenge Kasparov v. Short: 1987, 1987; (with J. Plaskett and J. Tisdall) The English Defence, 1987; (with Taulbut) How to Play the Caro-Kann Defense, 1988; (with D. Goodman and D. Spanier) Showdown in Seville: Kasparov-Karpov IV, 1988; Kingfisher Pocket Book of Chess, 1988; The Simon & Schuster Pocket Book of Chess (juvenile), 1988; (with

Kasparov) Batsford Chess Openings 2, 1989; (with N. Divinsky) Warriors of the Mind: A Quest for the Supreme Genius of The Chess Board, 1989; Chess: An Illustrated History, 1990; Battle of the Titans: Kasparov-Karpov, 1991; Duels of the Mind: The Twelve Best Games of Chess, 1991; How to Beat Gary Kasparov, 1991; Winning Moves, 1991; Fischer-Spassky II: The Return Of The Legend, 1992; Discover Your Chess Strength, 1992; (with J. Speelman) Essential Chess Openings, 1992; (with G. Kasparov) Kasparov on the King's Indian, 1993; Gary Kasparov's Best Games, 1993; Nigel Short: World Chess Challenger, 1993; Nigel Short's Best Games, 1993; Chess for Absolute Beginners, 1993; The Complete Book of Gambits, 1993; Kasparov v. Short 1993, 1993; (with E. Schiller) Winning with the Hypermodern, 1994; The Young Pretenders, 1994; (with T. Buzan) Buzan's Book of Genius, 1994; World Chess Championship: Kasparov v Anand, 1995; How to Win at Chess, 1995; (with Buzan) The Age Heresy, 1996; Winning Moves 2, 1996; (with M.J. Gelb) Samurai Chess: Mastering Strategic Thinking Through the Martial Art of the Mind, 1997; (with Buzan) Buzan's Book of Mental World Records, 1997; (with D. Goodman) Man Versus Machine: Kasparov Versus Deep Blue, 1997; (with E. Schiller) World Champion Combinations, 1998; Brain Games World Championship, 2000; (with N. Stewart) Learn Chess Fast: The Fun Way To Start Smart and Master the Game, 2001; Grandmaster Strategey, 2002; Complete Book of Beginning Chess, 2003; (with E. Schiller and L. Shamkovich) Killer Chess Tactics, 2003; Kasparov's Sicilian Strategies: Thirty Nine Steps from the Art of Counterattack in Chess Opening Play, 2006; England's Chess Gladiator, 2006; (with B. Martin and C. Davey) Staunton's City: Chess in London and Simpson's and The Savoy, 2006; (N. Divinsky and J. Sonas) Who Was the Strongest?: Warriors of the Mind II, 2006; Grandmaster Tactics, 2008. **Address:** 86 Clapham Common N Side, London, GL SW4 9SE, England. **Online address:** rdkobe@aol.com

KEENE, R. D. See **KEENE, Raymond D(ennis).**

KEENS-DOUGLAS, Richardo. Canadian/West Indian (born British West Indies), b. 1953. **Genres:** Children's Fiction, Theatre, Young Adult Fiction. **Career:** Children's Theatre Montreal, choreographer, 1974-77; Children's Theatre, movement teacher, 1974-77; CBC-Radio host; CBC-TV, Sunday Arts Entertainment, host; Cloud 9, host. Playwright and actor. **Publications:** The Nutmeg Princess, 1992; El misterio de la isla de las especias, 1992; Le mystère de l'île aux épices. 1992; La Diablesse and the Baby, 1994; Freedom Child of the Sea, 1995; Grandpa's Visit, 1996; The Miss Meow Pageant, 1998; Mama God, Papa God: A Caribbean Tale, 1999; The Trial of the Stone, 2000; Anancy and the Haunted House, 2002; Tales from the Isle of Spice: A Collection of New Caribbean Folktales, 2004. Works appears in anthologies. **Address:** c/o Author Mail, Annick Press, 15 Patricia Ave., Toronto, ON M2M 1H9, Canada. **Online address:** rkd38@hotmail.com

KEERY, James. British/Irish (born Ireland), b. 1958. **Genres:** Poetry, Literary Criticism And History. **Career:** High school English teacher, 1980-86; Fred Longworth High School, English teacher, 1986-95, English Department, head, 1995-; Warrington District Council for the Protection of Rural England, chair person, 1990-97. Writer. **Publications:** That Stranger, the Blues (poems), 1996; (ed.) Burns Singer: Collected Poems, 2001; A Study of J.H. Prynne, forthcoming. Works appear in anthologies. Contributor to books and periodicals. **Address:** Fred Longworth High School, Printshop Ln., Tyldesley, Manchester, GM M29 8JN, England.

KEETER, (Charles) Scott. American (born United States), b. 1951. **Genres:** Politics/Government, Social Sciences. **Career:** Union College, visiting assistant professor of political science, 1978-79; Rutgers University, assistant professor of political science, 1979-85; Virginia Commonwealth University, Department of Political Science and Public Administration, assistant professor, 1986-88, associate professor, 1988-95, professor of political science and head, 1995-98, director of survey research laboratory, 1988-91; George Mason University, Department of Public and International Affairs, professor and chairman, 1998-2002; Pew Research Center, director of survey research, 2007-. Writer. **Publications:** (With C. Zukin) Uninformed Choice: The Failure of the New Presidential Nominating System, 1983; (with M.X.D. Carpini) What Americans Know about Politics and Why It Matters, 1996; (with J.C. Green and R.C. Toth) The Diminishing Divide: Religion's Changing Role in American Politics, 2000; (co-author) A New Engagement? Political Participation, Civic Life and the Changing American Citizen, 2006; The Diminishing Divide: Religion and Politics at the End of the Century, forthcoming. CONTRIBUTOR: The President and the Public, 1982; The Election of 1984, 1985; Public Opinion, the Press and Public Policy, 1992; Realignment in the

American States, 1992; The Election of 1996, 1997. Contributor of articles to journals. **Address:** Pew Research Center, 1615 L St. NW, Ste. 700, Washington, DC 20036, U.S.A. **Online address:** skeeter@pewresearch.org

KEETON, Morris Teuton. American (born United States), b. 1917. **Genres:** Education, Philosophy. **Career:** Southern Methodist University, instructor in philosophy and social science, 1938-41; Antioch College, pastor of college, 1947-60, professor of philosophy and religion, 1956-77, dean of the faculty, 1963-66, chief academic officer, 1963-77, academic vice-president, 1966-77, vice-president and provost, 1972-77, chief administrator and acting president, 1975-76; American Association for Higher Education, president, 1972-73; Council for the Advancement of Experimental Learning, executive director, 1977-79; Council for Adult and Experiential Learning, founding president, 1980-90, president emeritus, 1990-, editor; University of Maryland, University College, Institute for Research on Adults in Higher Education, director, 1990-97. **Publications:** The Philosophy of Edmund Montgomery, 1950; Values Men Live By, 1960; Journey through a Wall, 1964; (with H.H. Titus) Range of Ethics; Introductory Readings, 1966; (with H.H. Titus) Ethics for Today, 5th ed., 1973; (with C. Hilberry) Struggle and Promise: Future for Colleges, 1969; Models and Mavericks: A Profile of Private Liberal Arts Colleges, 1971; (co-author) Shared Authority on Campus, 1971; (co-author) Experiential Learning, 1976; (ed. with P.J. Tate) Learning by Experience: What, Why, How?, 1978; (ed.) Defining and Assuring Quality in Experiential Learning, 1980; Employability in a High Performance Economy, Cael, 1993; (ed.) Perspectives on Experiential Learning, 1994; (with B.G. Sheckley) Improving Employee Development, 1997; (with J.K. Griggs and B.G. Sheckley) Effectiveness and Efficiency in Higher Education for Adults, 2002. Contributor of articles to journals. **Address:** University College, University of Maryland, 3501 University Blvd. E, Adelphi, MD 20783, U.S.A. **Online address:** mkeeton@umuc.edu

KEEVAK, Michael. Taiwanese/American (born United States), b. 1962. **Genres:** Novels, History, Young Adult Non-fiction. **Career:** National Taiwan University, professor of foreign languages, 1993-. Writer. **Publications:** Sexual Shakespeare: Forgery Authorship Portraiture, 2001; The Pretended Asian: George Psalmanazars Eighteenth-Century Formosan Hoax, 2004; The Story of a Stele: China's Nestorian Monument and its Reception in the West, 1625-1916, 2008; Becoming Yellow: A Short History of Racial Thinking, 2011. **Address:** Department of Foreign Languages, National Taiwan University, Roosevelt Rd., Section 4, Taipei, 106, Taiwan. **Online address:** keevak@ccms.ntu.edu.tw

KEEVERS, Thomas J. American (born United States) **Genres:** Novels, Mystery/Crime/Suspense. **Career:** Chicago Police Department, homicide detective. Writer and lawyer. **Publications:** Music across the Wall, 2003; What the Hyena Knows, 2005; The Chainsaw Ballet, 2007. Contributor to periodicals. **Address:** Five Star Publishing, 10 Water St., Ste. 310, Waterville, ME 04901, U.S.A. **Online address:** tkeevers@tamblum.com

KEFALA, Antigone. Australian/Romanian (born Romania), b. 1935. **Genres:** Novels, Novellas/Short Stories, Poetry, Children's Fiction, Cultural/Ethnic Topics, Art/Art History. **Career:** University of New South Wales, Department of Education, teacher of English, 1961-65, administrative assistant, 1966-67; Australia Council for the Arts, arts administrator, 1971-87. Writer. **Publications:** POETRY: The Alien, 1973; Thirsty Weather, 1978; European Notebook, 1988; Absence: New and Selected Poems, 1992, 2nd ed., 1998; Nepritomnost-Absence, 1998; Poems, 2000. NOVELS: The First Journey, 1975; The Island, 1984. OTHER: Alexia: A Tale of Two Cultures (for children), 1984; Summer Visit (novellas), 2002; Sydney Journals: Reflections, 1970-2000, 2008. EDITOR: Multiculturalism and the Arts, 1986. **Address:** 12 Rose St., Annandale, NW 2038, Australia.

KEGAN, Robert G. American (born United States), b. 1946. **Genres:** Philosophy, Psychology, inspirational/Motivational Literature, Adult Non-fiction, Business/Trade/Industry. **Career:** Junior and senior high school teacher, 1968-71; Emmanuel College, visiting faculty, 1972-77; Harvard University, instructor, 1975-76, Bureau of Study Counsel, senior counselor, 1976-79, lecturer, 1977-90, Spencer research fellow, 1982-83, Institute for Management and Leadership in Education, educational chair, 1983-, senior lecturer, 1990-98, Harvard-Macy Institute for the Reform of Medical Education, co-director, 1994-, chair of the learning and teaching area, 1996-2001, professor of education, 1998-, William and Miriam Meehan professor of adult learning and professional development, 2000-, Change Leadership Group, co-director, 2000-;

Massachusetts School of Professional Psychology, teaching faculty, 1977-99. Writer. **Publications:** The Sweeter Welcome, Voices for a Vision of Affirmation: Malamud, Bellow and Martin Buber, 1976; The Evolving Self: Problem and Process in Human Development, 1982; In Over Our Heads: The Mental Demands of Modern Life, 1994; (with L. Lahey) How the Way We Talk Can Change the Way We Work: Seven Languages for Transformation, 2001; Toward a New Pluralism in ABE/ESOL Classrooms: Teaching to Multiple Cultures of Mind, 2001; (with T. Wagner) Change Leadership: A Practical Guide to Transforming Our Schools, 2006; Immunity to Change: How to Overcome It and Unlock Potential in Yourself and Your Organization, 2009. Contributor to journals and periodicals. **Address:** Harvard Graduate School of Education, Harvard University, 205 Longfellow Hall, Cambridge, MA 02138, U.S.A. **Online address:** robert_kegan@gse.harvard.edu

KEHDE, Ned. American (born United States), b. 1940. **Genres:** Recreation, Politics/Government. **Career:** Freelance writer, 1967-; University of Kansas, acting assistant regional history librarian and archivist, 1970-, acting assistant archivist, 1971-73, Reference Department, acting assistant reference librarian, 1972, associate archivist, 1973-, librarian III, 1978-, emeritus associate archivist, 2003, now retired. **Publications:** (Ed. and comp.) The American Left, 1955-1970: A National Union Catalog of Pamphlets Published in the United States and Canada, 1976; Dictionary of Contemporary Quotations, 1976; Index to The Sporting News, 1992. Contributor to periodicals. **Address:** The University of Kansas Libraries, 1450 Jayhawk Blvd., Lawrence, KS 66045, U.S.A. **Online address:** nkehde@ku.edu

KEHLER, Dorothea. American (born United States), b. 1936. **Genres:** Literary Criticism And History. **Career:** Mac Murray College, instructor in English literature, 1964-65; Ohio University, lecturer, 1966-68; San Diego State University, lecturer, professor of English literature, 1970-2001, professor emerita, 2006-. Writer. **Publications:** Problems in Literary Research: A Guide to Selected Reference, 1975, 4th ed., 1997; (with J. Devlin and C.H. Curran) Studies in Anglo-Irish Fiction and Balladry, 1994; Shakespeare's Widows, 2009. EDITOR AND CONTRIBUTOR: (with S. Baker) In Another Country: Feminist Perspectives on Renaissance Drama, 1991; A Midsummer Night's Dream: Critical Essays, 1998; (with L. Amtower) The Single Woman in Medieval and Early Modern England, 2003. Contributor to articles to books and journals. **Address:** Department of English and Comparative Literature, San Diego State University, 5500 Campanile Dr., San Diego, CA 92182-6020, U.S.A. **Online address:** kehler@mail.sdsu.edu

KEIL, Charles. American (born United States), b. 1939. **Genres:** Poetry, Anthropology/Ethnology, Cultural/Ethnic Topics, Education, Music, Sociology, Urban Studies. **Career:** State University of New York, Upward Bound Program, instructor, 1968, Henry Adams Fellow, 1968-70, assistant professor, 1970-71, associate professor, 1971-83, professor of American studies, 1983-, director of graduate studies, 1970-77, 1979-82, acting chair of American studies department, 1978-79, 1992, director of undergraduate studies, 1986-89; Central Community School, co-founder, 1970; Trent University, visiting lecturer, 1982, 1983; WBFO FM, co-host, 1989-91; Musicians United for Superior Education Inc., president and director, 1990-99. Consultant and writer. **Publications:** Urban Blues, 1966, rev. ed., 1992; Tiv Song, 1979; (with A. Keil and D. Blau) Polka Happiness, 1992; (ed. with S.D. Crafts and D. Cavicchi) My Music, 1993; (with S. Feld) Music Grooves, 1994, 2nd ed., 2005; (with A. Keil, R. Blau and S. Feld) Bright Balkan Morning, 2002; (with P. Campbell) Born to Groove, 2005. Contributor of articles to books and periodicals. **Address:** State University of New York, Department of American Studies, 732 Clemens Hall, PO Box 604680, Buffalo, NY 14260-4680, U.S.A. **Online address:** charleskeil@sbcglobal.net

KEIL, Roger. Canadian (born Canada), b. 1957?. **Genres:** Adult Non-fiction, Politics/Government, Humanities, Social Sciences. **Career:** York University, The City Institute, associate professor, professor in the faculty of environmental studies, 1992-, director; environmental scientist. Writer. **Publications:** Weltstadt, Stadt der Welt: Internationalisierung Und Lokale Politik in Los Angeles, 1993; (ed. with D.V.J. Bell and G. Wekerle) Human Society and the Natural World: Perspectives on Sustainable Futures, 1994; (ed. with G.R. Wekerle and D.V.J. Bell) Local Places in the Age of the Global City, 1996; (ed. with D.V.J. Bell, L. Fawcett and P. Penz) Political Ecology: Global and Local, 1998; Los Angeles: Globalization, Urbanization and Social Struggles, 1998; (contrib.) Changing Canada: Political Economy as Transformation, 2003; (contrib.) State/Space: A Reader, 2003; (contrib.) Contested Metropolis, 2004; (with G. Desfor) Nature and the City: Making Environmental Policy

in Toronto and Los Angeles, 2004; (contrib.) Metropolitan Governance in the 21st Century: Governing Capacity, Democracy and the Dynamics of Place, 2005; (contrib.) Contested Urban Futures: Neoliberalisms and Their Discontents, 2006; (contrib.) In the Nature of Cities: Urban Political Ecology, 2006; (ed. with N. Brenner) The Global Cities Reader, 2006; (ed. with S.H. Ali) Networked Disease: Emerging Infections in the Global City, 2008; (ed. with R. Mahon) Leviathan Undone?: Towards a Political Economy of Scale, 2009; (with J. Anne Boudreau and D. Young) Changing Toronto: Governing Urban Neoliberalism, 2009; (ed. with D. Young and P.B. Wood) In-Between Infrastructure: Urban Connectivity in an Age of Vulnerability, 2011. Contributor to periodicals. **Address:** York University, 109 Health, Nursing & Environmental Studies Bldg, 4700 Keele St., Toronto, ON M3J 1P3, Canada. **Online address:** rkeil@yorku.ca

KEILEN, Sean. American (born United States), b. 1970. **Genres:** Literary Criticism And History, Essays. **Career:** University of Pennsylvania, assistant professor, 2000-; National Humanities Center, fellow. Writer. **Publications:** Vulgar Eloquence: On the Renaissance Invention of English Literature, 2006. EDITOR: (and intro. with S. Orgel) Postmodern Shakespeare, 1999; (and intro. with S. Orgel) Shakespeare in the Theatre, 1999; (and intro. with S. Orgel) Shakespeare's Poems, 1999; (and intro. with S. Orgel) Political Shakespeare, 1999; (and intro. with S. Orgel) Shakespeare and History, 1999; (and intro. with S. Orgel) Shakespeare and Gender, 1999; (and intro. with S. Orgel) Shakespeare and the Editorial Tradition, 1999; (and intro. with S. Orgel) Shakespeare and the Arts, 1999; (and intro. with S. Orgel) Shakespeare and the Interpretive Tradition, 1999; (and intro. with S. Orgel) Shakespeare and the Literary Tradition, 1999; (with L. Barkan and B. Cormack) The Forms of Renaissance Thought: New Essays on Literature and Culture, 2008. **Address:** Department of English, University of Pennsylvania, Fisher-Bennett Hall, 3340 Walnut St., Ste. 127, Philadelphia, PA 19104-6273, U.S.A. **Online address:** skeilen@princeton.edu

KEILER, Allan Ronald. American (born United States), b. 1938. **Genres:** Music, Bibliography. **Career:** University of Michigan, instructor, 1962-63, assistant professor of linguistics, 1963-66, associate professor of linguistics, 1967-73, psycholinguistics program chair, 1970-72; Association de Française de Linguistics, visiting lecturer, 1966; University of Washington, visiting assistant professor, 1966-67; Brandeis University, professor of music. Writer. **Publications:** Marian Anderson: A Singer's Journey, 2000. **Address:** Department of Music, Brandeis University, Slosberg Hall 220, 415 South St., Waltham, MA 02453, U.S.A. **Online address:** keiler@brandeis.edu

KEILLOR, Garrison (Edward). American (born United States), b. 1942. **Genres:** Novels, Novellas/Short Stories, Humor/Satire, Young Adult Non-fiction, Picture/Board Books, inspirational/Motivational Literature, Literary Criticism And History. **Career:** KUOM-Radio, staff announcer, 1963-68; Minnesota Public Radio, producer and announcer, 1971-74, host and principal writer for weekly program, 1974-87, 1993-; American Radio Company of the Air, host, 1989-93; Writer's Almanac, host, 1995-; Common Good Books, owner, 2006-. Actor. **Publications:** G.K. the DJ, 1977; The Selected Verse of Margaret Haskins Durber, 1979; Happy to Be Here: Stories and Comic Pieces, 1982; Lake Wobegon Days, 1985; Leaving Home: A Collection of Lake Wobegon Stories, 1987; We are Still Married: Stories & Letters, 1989; Stories from Lake Wobegon: Advance Listening and Conversation Skills, 1990; News from Lake Wobegon, 1991; WLT: A Radio Romance, 1991; (co-author) Late Harvest: Rural American Writing, 1992; The Book of Guys: Stories, 1993; Cat, You Better Come Home, 1995; The Old Man Who Loved Cheese, 1996; (with J.L. Nilsson) The Sandy Bottom Orchestra, 1996; Wobegon Boy, 1997; (ed. with K. Kenison) The Best American Short Stories: 1998, 1998; A Prairie Home Companion Commonplace Book: 25 Years on the Air, 1999; Me: By Jimmy (Big Boy) Valente, 1999; (intro.) Pretty Good Joke Book, 2000, 4th ed., 2005; In Search of Lake Wobegon, 2001; Lake Wobegon Summer 1956, 2001; (comp. and intro.) Good Poems, 2002; Love Me, 2003; Homegrown Democrat: A Few Plain Thoughts from the Heart of America, 2004, rev. ed., 2006; The Writer's Almanac: 2005 Engagement Calendar, 2004; Daddy's Girl, 2005; (comp. and intro.) Good Poems for Hard Times, 2005; (foreword) Misunderestimated & Overunderappreciated, 2007; Pontoon: A Lake Wobegon Novel, 2007; Prairie Home Christmas, 2007; Liberty: A Lake Wobegon Novel, 2008; Pilgrims: A Wobegon Romance, 2009; Even More Pretty Good Jokes, 2009; The Keillor Reader, 2009; 77 Love Sonnets, 2009; Life among the Lutherans, 2009; A Christmas Blizzard, 2009; (comp.

and intro.) Good Poems, American Places, 2011; Guy Noir and the Straight Skinny, 2012. Contributor to periodicals. **Address:** Prairie Home Productions L.L.C., 611 Frontenac Pl., St. Paul, MN 55104-4947, U.S.A.

KEILLOR, Steven J(ames). American (born United States), b. 1948. **Genres:** History, Essays, Biography, Autobiography/Memoirs. **Career:** Minnesota Historical Society, consultant for political campaign exhibit, 1994-; Iowa State University, assistant professor, 1995-96; Minnesota State University, adjunct professor; Northwestern College, adjunct professor; Bethel University, adjunct professor; Normandale Community College, instructor. Writer. **Publications:** Hjalmar Petersen of Minnesota: The Politics of Provincial Independence, 1987; Prisoners of Hope: Sundry Sunday Essays, 1992; (with M.L. Gieske) Norwegian Yankee: Knute Nelson and the Failure of American Politics, 1860-1923, 1995; This Rebellious House: American History and the Truth of Christianity, 1996; Cooperative Commonwealth: Co-ops in Rural Minnesota, 1859-1939, 2000; Erik Ramstad and the Empire Builder, 2002; Grand Excursion: Antebellum America Discovers the Upper Mississippi, 2004; God's Judgments: Interpreting History and the Christian Faith, 2007; Transforming the World: Rochester at 150, 2007; The Basis of Belief: A Century of Drama and Debate at the University of Minnesota, 2008; Shaping Minnesota's Identity: 150 Years of State History, 2008; Premodern, Modern, Postmodern: A History of Ideas and a Case Study of Christianity and Secularization at One State University, 1869-1984, forthcoming. EDITOR: No More Gallant a Deed: A Civil War Memoir of the First Minnesota Volunteers, 2001. Contributor to journals. **Address:** Pogo Press, 8075 215th St. W, Lakeville, MN 55044, U.S.A. **Online address:** skeillor@ecenet.com

KEIN, Sybil. American (born United States), b. 1939. **Genres:** Plays/Screenplays, Poetry, Language/Linguistics, Social Sciences. **Career:** Louisiana State University, instructor in public speaking, 1970-72; Upward Bound, instructor in communications skills, 1971; University of Michigan, instructor in English and theater, 1972-75, assistant professor, 1975-78, associate professor, 1979-88, professor of English, 1988-2000, now professor emeritus; Children's Theater Touring Co., director, 1972-74; McCree Theater, consultant, 1976-79. Writer. **Publications:** Visions from the Rainbow, 1979; Gombo People: Poésies Créole de la Nouvelle Orléans, 1981, rev. ed. as Gumbo People, 1999; Delta Dancer: New and Selected Poems, 1984; An American South: Poems, 1996; Creole Journal: The Louisiana Poems, 1999; (ed.) Creole: The History and Legacy of Louisiana's Free People of Color, 2000. FORTHCOMING: Images of Earth; Digging up the Dead; The Creole Cowboys: A Short History. Works appear in anthologies. Contributor to journals. **Address:** Department of English, University of Michigan, 326 French Hall, 303 E Kearsley St., Flint, MI 48502, U.S.A. **Online address:** sybkein@aol.com

KEITH, Caroline H(elen). American (born United States), b. 1940. **Genres:** Biography, Novellas/Short Stories, Autobiography/Memoirs, History. **Career:** Richter McBride Productions Inc., researcher and writer, 1968-69; University of Maryland, editor, 1977-79, speech writer and author of editorials, 1988-89; U.S. Senator Jacob K. Javits, researcher, 1980; freelance writer, 1980-. **Publications:** For Hell and a Brown Mule: The Biography of Senator Millard E. Tydings, 1991. Works appear in anthologies. **Address:** 4816 Broad Brook Dr., Bethesda, MD 20814-3906, U.S.A.

KEITH, Julie (Houghton). Canadian/American (born United States), b. 1940. **Genres:** Novellas/Short Stories, Novels, Young Adult Fiction, Mystery/Crime/Suspense. **Career:** Writer. **Publications:** The Jaguar Temple and Other Stories, 1994; The Devil Out There: A Novella and Stories, 2000. Works appear in anthologies. Contributor to periodicals. **Address:** 87 Arlington Ave., Westmount, QC H3Y 2W5, Canada.

KEITH, William H(enry). Also writes as Ian Douglas, H. Jay Riker, Keith William Andrews, Robert Cain. American (born United States), b. 1950. **Genres:** Novels, Science Fiction/Fantasy, Ghost Writer, Novellas/Short Stories, Mystery/Crime/Suspense, Westerns/Adventure, Paranormal, Technology, E-books. **Career:** Writer. **Publications:** NOVELS: DR. WHO SERIES: Dr. Who & the Vortex Crystal, 1986; Dr. Who & the Rebel's Gamble, 1986. BATTLETECH SERIES: Decision at Thunder Rift, 1986; Mercenary's Star, 1987; The Price of Glory, 1987; (with J.A. Keith) Blood of Heroe, 1993; Tactics of Duty, 1995; Operation Excalibur, 1996. RENEGADE LEGION: Renegade's Honor, 1988. FREEDOM'S RANGERS SERIES: (with J.A. Keith as Keith William Andrews) Freedom's Rangers, 1989; Raiders of the Revolution, 1989; Search and Destroy, 1990; Treason in Time, 1990; Sink the Armada!, 1990; Snow Kill, 1991. CARRIER SERIES: (as Keith Douglass)

Carrier, 1991; Viper Strike, 1991; Armageddon Model, 1992; Flame-Out, 1992; Maelstrom, 1993; Countdown, 1994; Afterburn, 1996. CYBERNARC SERIES: (as Robert Cain) Cybernarc, 1991; Gold Dragon, 1991; Island Kill, 1992; Capo's Revenge, 1992; Shark Bait, 1992; End Game, 1993. BUCK ROGERS IN THE XXVTH CENTURY SERIES: Nomads of the Sky, 1992; Warlords of Jupiter, 1993. SHARUQ/STINGRAY: (as Bill Keith) Sharuq, 1993; Stingray, 1994. WARSTRIDER SERIES: Warstrider, 1993; Rebellion, 1993; Jackers, 1994; Symbionts, 1995; Netlink, 1995; Battlemind, 1996. SEALS, THE WARRIOR BREED SERIES: (as H. Jay Riker) Silver Star, 1993; Purple Heart, 1994; Bronze Star, 1995; Navy Cross, 1996; Medal of Honor, 1997; Marks of Valor, 1998; In Harm's Way, 1999; Duty's Call, 2000; Casualties of War, 2003; Enduring Freedom, 2005; Iraqi Freedom, 2007. SEAL TEAM SEVEN SERIES: (as Keith Douglass) SEAL Team Seven, 1994; Specter, 1995; Nucflash, 1995. BOLOS: Bolo Brigade, 1997; Bolo Rising, 1998; Bolo Strike, 2001. DIPLOMATIC ACT: (with P. Jurasik) Diplomatic Act, 1998. IN THE STAR*DRIVE UNIVERSE: Two of Minds, 1999. FRONTIER EARTH: Frontier Earth: Ghostwritten for Bruce Boxleitner, 1999; Frontier Earth: Searcher, 2001. THE SILENT SERVICE SERIES: (as H. Jay Riker) Greyback Class, 2000; Los Angeles Class, 2001; Seawolf Class, 2002; Virginia Class, 2004; Ohio Class, 2006. RETIEF'S PEACE: Retief's Peace, 2005. GALACTIC MARINES SERIES AS IAN DOUGLAS: HERITAGE TRILOGY: Semper Mars, 1998; Luna Marine, 1999; Europa Strike, 2000. LEGACY TRILOGY: Star Corps, 2003; Battlespace, 2006; Star Marines, 2007. INHERITANCE TRILOGY: Star Strike, 2008; Galactic Corps, 2008; Semper Human, 2009. STEPHEN COONTS' DEEP BLACK SERIES: (with S. Coonts) Arctic Gold, 2009; Sea of Terror, 2010; Death Wave, 2011. STAR CARRIER SERIES AS IAN DOUGLAS: Earth Strike, 2010; Center of Gravity, 2011; Singularity, 2012. ANDROID SERIES: Free Fall, 2011. STAR CORPSMAN SERIES: Bloodstar, 2012. NON-FICTION: CD-ROM GAME GUIDES: (with N. Barton) Toonstruck, 1996; Titanic: Adventure out of Time, 1996; Spycraft: the Great Game, 1997; Riven Hints & Solutions, 1997; Riven Official Solutions, 1997; Fallout, 1997; Lands of Lore: Guardians of Destiny, 1997; Riven Player's Guide, 1997; Baldur's Gate, 1998. CRAFT: The Science of the Craft, 2005. SHORT STORIES: Dance of Vengeance, in Shrapnel: Fragments from the Inner Sphere, 1989; Hold Until Relieved, in Bolos IV: Last Stand, 1997; Fossils, in Asimov's Science Fiction, 1999; The Scent of Evil, in Starfall, 1999; (as H. Jay Riker) UNODIR in First to Fight, 1999; A Place to Stand, in Civil War Fantastic, 2000; A Show of Force, in Guardsmen of Tomorrow, 2000; Worldmakers, 2001; A Terrible Resolve, in A Date Which Will Live in Infamy, 2001; Brothers, in Bolos V: Old Guard, 2001; (as H. Jay Riker) Friendly Fire in First to Fight II, 2001; Iterations, in Past Imperfect, 2001; Power Play, in Silicon Dreams, 2001; In the Bubble, in Alternate Gettysburgs, 2002; Los Ninos, in Future Wars, 2003; Silent Company, in Crash Dive: First to Fight III, 2003; Partnership, in Man vs. Machine, 2007; The Weapon, in Future Weapons of War, 2007; Americans Landing at Normandy Beach, in Men at War, 2009; Starfire, in Battletech, 2009; Dead Names, in Spells & Chrome, 2010; Best of the Bolos: Their Finest Hour, 2010. **Address:** Ethan Ellenberg Agency, 548 Broadway, Ste. 5E, New York, NY 10012, U.S.A. **Online address:** bill_keith@comcast.net

KELBAUGH, Gretchen. (Gretchen Wilson). Canadian/American (born United States), b. 1956. **Genres:** Children's Fiction, Plays/Screenplays, Biography, Young Adult Fiction, Poetry. **Career:** High school science teacher, 1980-87. Film maker and writer. **Publications:** With All Her Might: The Life of Gertrude Harding, Militant Suffragette, 1998; Lollipopsicles (children's poetry), 2000; Can You Catch It Like a Cold?: A Story to Help Children Understand a Parent's Depression, 2002. **Address:** Story First Productions, 277 Model Farm Rd., Quispamsis, NB E2E 4Z8, Canada. **Online address:** gretchk@rogers.com

KELEMEN, Julie. American (born United States), b. 1959. **Genres:** Theology/Religion, Children's Non-fiction. **Career:** Central Institute for the Deaf, technical writer and editor, 1986-87; Liguori Publications, Book And Pamphlet Department, associate editor, 1987-90, Parish Education Products, associate editor, 1990-93; St. Louis Community College, adjunct English instructor, 1993-95; Suburban Journals, copy editor, 1997-2003; University of Wisconsin, associate lecturer, 2004-. Chronotype, proof reader, copy editor and journalist. **Publications:** Lent Is for Children, 1987, rev. ed., 1993; Advent Is for Children, 1988; Prayer is for Children: Stories, Prayers, Activities, 1992, rev. ed. as Learning to Pray: A Guide for Young People, 2000. **Address:** Department of English, University of Wisconsin, 1800 College Dr., Rice Lake, WI 54868, U.S.A. **Online address:** jkelemen@uwc.edu

KELLEHER, Victor Michael Kitchener. Australian/British (born England), b. 1939. **Genres:** Novels, Children's Fiction, Young Adult Fiction, Novellas/Short Stories, Horror, Politics/Government, Mystery/Crime/Suspense. **Career:** University of Witwatersrand, junior lecturer in English, 1969; University of South Africa, lecturer, 1970-71, senior lecturer in English, 1972-73; Massey University, lecturer in English, 1973-76, senior lecturer, 1976-83; University of New England, lecturer, 1976-79, senior lecturer, 1980-83, associate professor of English, 1984-87. Writer. **Publications:** YOUNG ADULT FICTION: Forbidden Paths of Thual, 1979; The Hunting of Shadroth, 1981; Master of the Grove, 1982; Papio, 1984; The Green Piper, 1984; Taronga, 1986; The Makers, 1987; Baily's Bones, 1988; The Red King, 1989; Brother Night, 1990; Del-Del, 1991; To the Dark Tower, 1992; Rescue!, 1992; Where the Whales Sing, 1994; Slow Burn, 1997; The Ivory Trail, 1999; Beyond the Dusk, 2000; Red Heart, 2001; The Other, 2001; The Gorilla Suit, 2002; Dogboy, 2006. NOVELS: Voices from the River, 1979; The Beast of Heaven, 1984; EM's Story, 1988; Wintering, 1990; Micky Darlin', 1992; Into the Dark, 1998. HORROR: Double God, 1993; The House That Jack Built, 1994; Storyman, 1996. OTHERS: Africa and After (short stories), 1983 as The Traveller, 1987; Johnny Wombat (children's fiction), 1996; Collected Stories, 1999. PARKLAND SERIES: Parkland, 1994; Earthsong, 1995; Fire Dancer, 1996. GIBBLEWORT THE GOBLIN SERIES: Goblin at the Zoo, 2005; Gibblewort the Goblin, 2008; Goblin at the Beach, 2008; (with S.M. King) Goblin in the Bush, 2008; Goblin in the City, 2008; Goblin in the Rainforest, 2008; Goblin in the Snow, 2008; (with S.M. King) Goblin on the Reef, 2008; (with S.M. King) The Return of Gibblewort the Goblin, 2008. **Address:** c/o Margaret Connolly, PO Box 945, Wahroonga, NW 2076, Australia.

KELLENBERGER, J(ames). American (born United States), b. 1938. **Genres:** Philosophy, Theology/Religion, Young Adult Non-fiction. **Career:** Cameroon College of Arts and Science, lecturer in logic, 1962-64; California State University, assistant professor, 1967-71, associate professor, 1971-75, professor of philosophy, 1975-; Albion College, visiting professor, 1971-72; Claremont Graduate School, adjunct professor of religion, 1991. Writer. **Publications:** Religious Discovery, Faith and Knowledge, 1972; The Cognitivity of Religion: Three Perspectives, 1985; God-Relationships with and without God, 1989; (ed.) Inter-Religious Models and Criteria, 1993; Relationship Morality, 1995; Kierkegaard and Nietzsche: Faith and Eternal Acceptance, 1997; Moral Relativism, Moral Diversity and Human Relationships, 2001; (ed.) Introduction to Philosophy of Religion: Readings, 2007; Moral Relativism: A Dialogue, 2008. Contributor to books. **Address:** Department of Philosophy, California State University, 18111 Nordhoff St., Northridge, CA 91330, U.S.A.

KELLER, Catherine., b. 1953. **Genres:** Women's Studies And Issues. **Career:** Xavier University, assistant professor, 1984-86; Drew University, professor of constructive theology, 1986-. Theologian, educator and writer. **Publications:** From a Broken Web: Separation, Sexism and Self, 1986; Apocalypse Now and Then: A Feminist Guide to the End of the World, 1996; (ed. and contrib. with A. Daniell) Process and Difference: Between Cosmological and Poststructuralist Postmodernisms, 2002; Face of the Deep: A Theology of Becoming, 2003; (ed. with M. Nausner and M. Rivera) Postcolonial Theologies: Divinity and Empire, 2004; God and Power: Counter- Apocalyptic Journeys, 2005; (ed. and contrib. with V. Burrus) Toward a Theology of Eros: Transfiguring Passion at the Limits of Discipline, 2006; (ed. and contrib. with D.R Griffin, J.B. Cobb and R.A. Falk) The American Empire and the Commonwealth of God: A Political, Economic, Religious Statement, 2006; (ed. and contrib. with L. Kearns) Ecospirit: Religions and Philosophies for the Earth, 2007; (ed.) On the Mystery: Discerning Divinity in Process, 2008. Contributor to books and periodicals. **Online address:** ckeller@drew.edu

KELLER, Debra. American (born United States), b. 1958. **Genres:** Children's Fiction, Animals/Pets. **Career:** Advertising copywriter, 1984-90; freelance copywriter, 1990-. **Publications:** The Trouble with Mister, 1995; Snake Food, 2000. Contributor to periodicals. **Address:** 1220 H St., Ste. 102, Sacramento, CA 95814-1931, U.S.A. **Online address:** junedoe@sbcglobal.net

KELLER, Ed. See **KELLER, Edward B.**

KELLER, Edward B. (Ed Keller). American (born United States), b. 1955. **Genres:** Marketing. **Career:** Yankelovich, Skelly and White Inc., research associate, 1979-80, senior associate, 1980-82, vice president, 1982-86, executive; ASK Associates, partner, 1984-86; Roper ASW, president, senior vice president, 1986-94, chief operating officer, 1994-2001, chief executive officer, 2001-05; GFK NOP, chief executive officer, 2004-; Keller Fay Group L.L.C., founder, chief executive officer, 2004-; Market Research Council, president; Word of Mouth Marketing Association, treasurer; University of Pennsylvania, Annenberg School for Communication, lecturer, 2006. Writer. **Publications:** (As Ed Keller with J. Berry) The Influentials: One American in Ten Tells the Other Nine How to Vote, Where to Eat and What to Buy, 2003. Contributor of articles to journals, magazines and newspapers. **Address:** Keller Fay Group, 65 Church St., 3rd Fl., New Brunswick, NJ 08901, U.S.A. **Online address:** ekeller@kellerfay.com

KELLER, Emily. American (born United States) **Genres:** Biography, Education, History. **Career:** High school English teacher, 1960-90; Math Association of America, editorial assistant, chief copy editor, 1977-84; Erie County Community College, instructor, 1989-91; Niagara County Community College, writing instructor, 1990-91; American Legion Auxiliary, president, 1992-93; Echo Society of Niagara Falls, director, 1997. **Publications:** Margaret Bourke-White: A Photographer's Life, 1996; Frances Perkins: First Woman Cabinet Member, 2006. Works appear in anthologies. **Address:** 9354 Rivershore Dr., Niagara Falls, NY 14304, U.S.A. **Online address:** emilykeller@verizon.net

KELLER, Holly. American (born United States), b. 1942?. **Genres:** Humor/Satire, Children's Non-fiction, Cartoons, Illustrations, Picture/Board Books, Children's Fiction, Animals/Pets, Humor/Satire, Humor/Satire. **Career:** Writer. **Publications:** SELF-ILLUSTRATED: Geraldine's Blanket, 1984. OTHERS: Cromwell's Glasses, 1982; Ten Sleepy Sheep, 1983; Too Big, 1983; Will It Rain?, 1984; Henry's Fourth of July, 1985; When Francie Was Sick, 1985; A Bear for Christmas, 1986; Goodbye, Max, 1987; Lizzie's Invitation, 1987; Geraldine's Big Snow, 1988; Snakes Are Hunters, 1988; Shooting Stars, 1989; Maxine in the Middle, 1989; The Best Present, 1989; Henry's Happy Birthday, 1990; What Alvin Wanted, 1990; Horace, 1991; The New Boy, 1991; Furry, 1992; Island Baby, 1992; Harry and Tuck, 1993; Geraldine's Baby Brother, 1994; Grandfather's Dream, 1994; Rosata, 1995; Geraldine First, 1996; I Am Angela, 1997; Merry Christmas, Geraldine, 1997; Angela's Top-Secret Computer Club, 1998; Brave Horace, 1998; A Bed Full of Cats, 1999; Jacob's Tree, 1999; What I See, 1999; Geraldine and Mrs. Duffy, 2000; That's Mine, Horace, 2000; Cecil's Garden, 2002; Farfallina & Marcel, 2002; What a Hat!, 2003; The Hat, 2005; Pearl's New Skates, 2005; Sophie's Window, 2005; Nosy Rosie, 2006; Help!: A Story of Friendship, 2007; The Van, 2008; Miranda's Beach Day, 2009. **Address:** c/o Author Mail, Greenwillow Books, HarperCollins, 10 E 53rd St., 7th Fl., New York, NY 10022, U.S.A.

KELLER, Joe. American (born United States), b. 1963. **Genres:** Antiques/Furnishings, Art/Art History, Engineering. **Career:** Writer. **Publications:** WITH D. ROSS: Jadite: An Identification and Price Guide, 1999, 3rd ed., 2003; Russel Wright: Dinnerware, Pottery and More: An Identification and Price Guide, 2000; Delphite and Jadite: A Pocket Guide, 2002; Fire-King: An Information and Price Guide, 2002; (with M. Gibbs) English Transferware: Popular 20th Century Patterns, 2005. **Address:** PO Box 783, Melrose, MA 02176, U.S.A. **Online address:** jk3434@aol.com

KELLER, Laurent. Swiss (born Switzerland), b. 1961. **Genres:** Zoology. **Career:** University of Lausanne, Department of Zoology and Animal Ecology, research assistant in zoology, 1983-85, Museum of Comparative Zoology, postdoctoral research associate, 1989-90, postdoctoral research fellow, 1990-92, private docent, 1994-96, associate professor of ecology, 1996-2000, Institute of Ecology, head, 1998-2000, professor of evolutionary ecology and head of department of ecology and evolution, 2000-; University Paul-Sabatier, Laboratory of Entomology, research associate, 1985-87; Harvard University, Museum of Comparative Zoology, postdoctoral research fellow, 1990-92. Writer. **Publications:** (Ed.) Queen Number and Sociality in Insects, 1993; (ed.) Levels of Selection in Evolution, 1999; Les Clés De La Motivation Au Travail, 2007; (with E. Gordon) The Lives of Ants, 2009. **Address:** Department of Ecology and Evolution, University of Lausanne, Rm. 3121, Batiment de biologie, Lausanne, 1015, Switzerland. **Online address:** laurent.keller@unil.ch

KELLER, Marian Jean. American (born United States), b. 1953. **Genres:** Education, Gerontology/Senior Issues, Recreation, Social Sciences, Sports/Fitness. **Career:** Florida State University, program administrator, 1975-78; Indiana University, visiting lecturer, 1978-79; University of Georgia, Gerontology Center, public service assistant and project director, 1979-84, Institute of Community and Area Development, public service associate, adjunct associate professor, 1984-89, acting department head, 1987-89; Grayson Community College, instructor, 1989-93; University of North Texas, associate professor, 1989-92, professor of kinesiology, health promotion and recreation, 1992-, associate dean of academic affairs, 1993-97, College of Education, dean, 1997-. Writer. **Publications:** Planning Social Group Activities for Older Adults, 1981; (co-author) Helping Older Adults Develop Active Leisure Lifestyles, 1987; Activity Programming in Long-Term Health Care Facilities, 1989; (with B. Wilshite) Therapeutic Recreation, 1992, 2nd ed., 2000. EDITOR: Leisure Activities, 1985; Leisure Programming with Senior Citizens, 1985; (with N.J. Osgood) Dynamic Leisure Programming with Older Adults, 1987; Activities with Developmentally Disabled Elderly and Older Adults, 1991; Caregiving-Leisure and Aging, 1999. Contributor to books and professional journals. **Address:** College of Education, University of North Texas, Dean's Office, 214 Matthews Hall, PO Box 311337, Denton, TX 76203-1337, U.S.A. **Online address:** JKeller@unt.edu

KELLER, Richard C. American (born United States), b. 1969?. **Genres:** Psychiatry. **Career:** Rutgers University, excellence fellow, 1996-2000, Center for Historical Analysis, graduate fellow, 1999-2000; Columbia University, Council for European Studies, pre-dissertation fellow, 1998; Pratt Institute, visiting assistant professor, 2000; Washington University, Andrew W. Mellon postdoctoral fellow, 2001-02; University of Wisconsin, assistant professor, 2002-08, associate professor of medical history and the history of science, 2008-; Institut de Recherche Interdisciplinaire sur les Enjeux Sociaux, residential fellow, 2007. Writer. **Publications:** Colonial Madness: Psychiatry in French North Africa, 2007. Contributor of articles to books and journals. **Address:** University of Wisconsin, Rm. 1135, 1300 University Ave., Madison, WI 53706-1532, U.S.A. **Online address:** rckeller@wisc.edu

KELLER, Timothy. (Timothy J. Keller). American (born United States), b. 1950. **Genres:** Theology/Religion. **Career:** West Hopewell Presbyterian Church, pastor; Redeemer Presbyterian Church, founder and senior pastor, 1989-. Writer and speaker. **Publications:** (As Timothy J. Keller) Ministries of Mercy: The Call of the Jericho Road, 1989, 2nd ed., 1997; The Prodigal God: Recovering the Heart of the Christian Faith, 2008; The Reason for God: Belief in an Age of Skepticism, 2008; Counterfeit Gods: The Empty Promises of Money, Sex, and Power, and the Only Hope that Matters, 2009; Generous Justice: How God's Grace Makes us Just, 2010; Gospel in Life. Study Guide, 2010; King's Cross: The Story of the World in the Life of Jesus, 2011; Meaning of Marriage: Facing the Complexities of Commitment with the Wisdom of God, 2011; (contrib. and co-author) Sunday's Best, 2011; (contrib. and co-author) Is Hell for Real or Does Everyone go to Heaven?, 2011; (ed. with D.A. Carson) Gospel as Center: Renewing our Faith and Reforming our Ministry Practices, 2012. **Address:** Redeemer Presbyterian Church, 1359 Broadway, 4th Fl., New York, NY 10018, U.S.A. **Online address:** andi@redeemer.com

KELLER, Timothy J. See **KELLER, Timothy.**

KELLER, William W(alton). American (born United States), b. 1950. **Genres:** International Relations/Current Affairs, Politics/Government, History. **Career:** Massachusetts Institute of Technology, Center for International Studies, executive director, research director of Japan program and principal research scientist, 1997-2002; Congressional Office of Technology Assessment, senior analyst and project director, 1986-95; University of Pittsburgh, Graduate School of Public and International Affairs, Wesley W. Posvar chair and director of Matthew B. Ridgway Center for International Security Studies, 2002-11; University of Georgia, professor of international affairs, Center for International Trade and Security, Gary Bertsch director, 2011-. Writer. **Publications:** The Liberals and J. Edgar Hoover: Rise and Fall of a Domestic Intelligence State, 1989; Arm in Arm: The Political Economy of the Global Arms Trade, 1995; (with P.N. Duremus, L.W. Pauly and S. Reich) The Myth of the Global Corporation, 1999; (ed. with R.J. Samuels) Crisis and Innovation in Asian Technology, 2003; (ed. with G.R. Mitchell) Hitting First: Preventive Force in U.S. Security Strategy, 2006; (ed. with T.G. Rawski) China's Rise and the Balance of Influence in Asia, 2007. **Address:** Center for International Trade and Security, University of Georgia, 328 Candler Hall, 120 Holmes/Hunter Bldg., Athens, GA 30602, U.S.A. **Online address:** bkeller@pitt.edu

KELLERMAN, Jesse. American (born United States), b. 1978. **Genres:** Plays/Screenplays, Science Fiction/Fantasy, Novels, Human Relations/Parenting. **Career:** Playwright and novelist. **Publications:** SELF-ILLUSTRATED: (with J. Kellerman) Daddy, Daddy, Can You Touch the Sky? (juvenile; short verses), 1994. OTHERS: Things Beyond Our Control, 1999;

Sunstroke, 2006; Trouble, 2007; Genius in UK as The Brutal Art, 2008; Executor, 2010. **Address:** c/o Author Mail, G. P. Putnam's Sons, Penguin Group, 375 Hudson St., New York, NY 10014-3657, U.S.A. **Online address:** websubmit@jessekellerman.com

KELLERMAN, Jonathan. American (born United States), b. 1949. **Genres:** Mystery/Crime/Suspense, Psychology, Novels, Adult Non-fiction, Medicine/Health. **Career:** Freelance illustrator, 1966-72; University of California, Daily Bruin, editorial cartoonist, columnist, editor and political satirist, 1967-71; Children's Hospital of Los Angeles, staff psychologist, 1975-81, Psychosocial Program, director, 1976-81, post-doctoral HEW fellow; University of Southern California, Keck School of Medicine, assistant clinical professor, 1978-79, clinical associate professor, 1979-97, clinical professor, 1998-; Jonathan Kellerman Ph.D. and Associates, head, 1981-88. **Publications:** (Ed.) Psychological Aspects of Childhood Cancer, 1980; Helping the Fearful Child: A Parent's Guide to Everyday and Problem Anxieties, 1981; When the Bough Breaks, 1985; Blood Test, 1986; Over the Edge, 1987; The Butcher's Theatre, 1988; Silent Partner, 1989; Time Bomb, 1990; Private Eyes, 1992; Devil's Waltz, 1993; Bad Love, 1994; Daddy, Daddy, Can You Touch the Sky?, 1994; Jonathan Kellerman's ABC of Weird Creatures, 1995; Self-Defense, 1995; The Web, 1996; The Clinic, 1996; Survival of the Fittest, 1997; Billy Straight, 1998; Billy Straight, 1998; Monster, 1999; Savage Spawn: Reflections on Violent Children, 1999; (ed.) Diagnosis Dead: A Mystery Writers of America Anthology, 1999; Dr. Death, 2000; Flesh and Blood, 2001; The Murder Book, 2002; The Conspiracy Club, 2003; A Cold Heart, 2003; Therapy, 2004; (with F. Kellerman) Double Homicide, 2004; Twisted, 2004; Rage, 2005; Gone, 2006; (with F. Kellerman) Capital Crimes, 2006; Obsession: An Alex Delaware Novel, 2007; Bones, 2008; Compulsion, 2008; With Strings Attached: The Art and Beauty of Vintage Guitars, 2008; True Detectives: A Novel, 2009; Evidence, 2009; Deception, 2010; Mystery, 2011; Victims, 2012. Work appears in anthologies. Contributor to periodicals. **Address:** Karpfinger Agency, 357 W 20th St., New York, NY 10011-3379, U.S.A. **Online address:** email@jonathankellerman.com

KELLERT, Stephen R. American (born United States), b. 1944. **Genres:** Ethics, Animals/Pets, Biology, Bibliography. **Career:** Yale University, School of Medicine, Behavioral Sciences Study Center, research associate, 1971-77, School of Forestry and Environmental Studies, senior research associate and lecturer, 1977-80, associate professor, 1980-87, director of admissions, 1987-91, professor, 1988-, associate dean, 1990-92, Tweedy/Ordway Professor of Social Ecology, 2001-, now Tweedy/Ordway Emeritus Professor of Social Ecology; Hixon Center for Urban Ecology, co-director, 2002-; Environmental Capital Partners, partner, 2007-09, senior consultant, 2009-; Bio-Logical Capital, executive chairman, 2009-. Writer. **Publications:** Policy Implications of a National Study of American Attitudes and Behavioral Relations to Animals, 1978; (with M.O. Westervelt) Trends in Animal Use and Perception in 20th Century America, 1981; (with J.K. Berry) Knowledge, Affection and Basic Attitudes Toward Animals in American Society, 1982; (with J.K. Berry) Activities of the American Public Relating to Animals, 1982; Public Attitudes Toward Critical Wildlife and Natural Habit Issues, 1982; Children's Attitudes, Knowledge and Behaviors Toward Animals, 1983; (with J.K. Berry) Bibliography of Human/Animal Relations, 1985; (ed. with F.H. Bormann) Ecology, Economics, Ethics: The Broken Circle, 1991; (ed. with E.O. Wilson) The Biophilia Hypothesis, 1993; The Value of Life: Biological Diversity and Human Society, 1996; (ed. with M. Black and R. Haley) Macmillan Encyclopedia of the Environment, 1997; Kinship to Mastery: Biophilia in Human Evolution and Development, 1997; (ed.) Encyclopedia of the Environment, 1999; (with T. Farnham) The Good in Nature and Humanity: Connecting Science, Religion and Spirituality with the Natural World, 2002; (with P. Kahn) Children and Nature: Psychological, Sociocultural and Evolutionary Investigations, 2002; Building for Life: Designing and Understanding the Human-Nature Connection, 2005; Biophilia, 2006; Biophilic Design, 2006; Biodiversity, Quality of Life and Evolutionary Psychology, 2006; Building for Life: Designing and Understanding the Human-nature Connection, 2006; Connecting with Creation: The Convergence of Nature, Religion, Science and Culture, 2007; (ed. with J.H. Heewagen and M.L. Mador) Implementing Biophilic Design: The Theory, Science and Practice of Bringing Buildings to Life, 2008; (ed. with J.G. Speth) The Coming Transformation: Values to Sustain Human and Natural Communities, 2009; Nature and Humanity: Values, Culture and Biology, 2010; (ed. with J. Dunlap) Companions in Wonder: Children and Adults Exploring Nature Together, 2012. **Address:** School of Forestry and Environmental Studies, Yale University, Rm. 120, Kroon Hall, 205 Prospect St., New Haven, CT 06511, U.S.A. **Online address:** stephen.kellert@yale.edu

KELLEY, Alec E. *See* **KELLEY, Alec E(rvin).**

KELLEY, Alec E(rvin). (Alec E. Kelley). American (born United States), b. 1923. **Genres:** Novellas/Short Stories, Poetry, Autobiography/Memoirs, Translations. **Career:** Manhattan Project, chemist, 1944-46; University of Arizona, assistant professor of chemistry, professor of chemistry, 1952-86, professor emeritus, 1987-; Wesleyan University, professor, 1967-68; Pennsylvania State University, professor, 1993. Writer. **Publications:** (Trans. with A. Kelley) José Promis, The Identity of Hispanoamerica, 1991; Take Me Away to Dreamland, 2001; The Road to the NBA, vol. I, 2005; The Eye At The Center, 2005. **Address:** Department of Chemistry and Biochemistry, The University of Arizona, Rm. 221, 1306 East University Blvd., PO Box 210041, Tucson, AZ 85721-0041, U.S.A. **Online address:** kak7@psu.edu

KELLEY, Alexia. (Alexia K. Kelley). American (born United States), b. 1966. **Genres:** Theology/Religion. **Career:** Catholics in Alliance for the Common Good, co-founder and executive director, 2005-09; United States Department of Health and Human Services, Center for Faith-based and Community Initiatives, director, 2009-; Catholic Campaign for Human Development, staff; Environmental Resources Trust, staff. Writer. **Publications:** (Ed. with K.M. Weigert) Living the Catholic Social Tradition: Cases and Commentary, 2005; (with C. Korzen) A Nation for All: How the Catholic Vision of the Common Good Can Save America from the Politics of Division, 2008. **Address:** Center for Faith-Based and Neighborhood, Partnerships (CFBNP), U.S. Department of Health & Human Services, 200 Independence Ave., Washington, DC 20201, U.S.A. **Online address:** partnerships@hhs.gov

KELLEY, Alexia K. *See* **KELLEY, Alexia.**

KELLEY, Ann. British (born England), b. 1941. **Genres:** Poetry. **Career:** Novelist, educator and photographer. **Publications:** GUSSIE YOUNG-ADULT NOVEL SERIES: The Burying Beatle, 2005; The Bower Bird, 2007; Inchworm, 2008; A Snail's Broken Shell, 2010. OTHERS: Born and Bred (photography), 1988; The Poetry Remedy (poetry), 1999; Paper Whites (poetry), 2001; Sea Front (photography), 2005; Because We Have Reached That Place (poetry), 2006; Koh Tabu (young- adult novel), 2010; (co-author) The Light at St. Ives (photography), 2010. **Address:** St. Ives, CW , England. : annkelley@blue-earth.co.uk

KELLEY, Douglas. American (born United States), b. 1957?. **Genres:** Novels, Young Adult Fiction. **Career:** Pilot and writer. **Publications:** The Captain's Wife, 2001. **Address:** c/o Author Mail, Dutton Publishing, 345 Hudson St., New York, NY 10014-4502, U.S.A.

KELLEY, (Kathleen) Alita. (C. A. de Lomellini). American/British (born England), b. 1932. **Genres:** Poetry, Literary Criticism And History, Translations, Novellas/Short Stories. **Career:** Teacher of English, 1962-68; U.S. Embassy, teacher of Italian, 1967-68; Wiesman and Co., commercial translator and office manager, 1970-92; Humanist Community of Tucson, program coordinator, 1970-92; Pennsylvania State University, assistant professor, 1992-98, associate professor of Spanish and French, 1998-, now associate professor emeritus of Spanish and French. Writer. **Publications:** (Trans. with A.E. Kelley) Jose Promis, The Identity of Hispanoamerica, 1991; (ed.) New Chicana/Chicano Writing 2, 1992; (trans. with E. Grossman) Julio Ortega, Goodbye, Ayacucho and Moscow Gold (stories), 1994. AS C.A. DE LOMELLINI (POEMS): (trans.) J. Radcliffe, Lima Rooftops, 1978; Shared Images, 1981; Dreams of Samarkand' 1982; Ineffable Joys, 1983; Antimacassars, 1984; Target Practice, 1994; (trans. with D. Tipton) Path through the Canefields, 1997; Northern Paranoia and Southern Comfort, 2003; (trans.) R.H. Espejo, Obstinaćin, 2009. Contributor of articles to periodicals. **Address:** Department of Spanish & French, Pennsylvania State University, 25 Yearsley Mill Rd., Media, PA 19063, U.S.A. **Online address:** kak7@psu.edu

KELLEY, Liam C. American (born United States), b. 1966. **Genres:** Poetry, Literary Criticism And History, History, Politics/Government. **Career:** University of Hawaii, Department of History, associate professor. Historian and writer. **Publications:** Beyond the Bronze Pillars: Envoy Poetry and the Sino-Vietnamese Relationship, 2005. Contributor to periodicals. **Address:** Department of History, University of Hawaii at Manoa, B408 Sakamaki Hall, 2530 Dole St., Honolulu, HI 96822-2283, U.S.A. **Online address:** liam@hawaii.edu

KELLEY, Tom. American (born United States), b. 1955?. **Genres:** inspira-tional/Motivational Literature. **Career:** IDEO (design firm), general manager, 1987-; Towers Perrin, management consultant. Writer. **Publications:** (With J. Littman) Art of Innovation: Lessons in Creativity from IDEO, America's Leading Design Firm, 2001; (with J. Littman) Ten Faces of Innovation: IDEO's Strategies for Beating the Devil's Advocate & Driving Creativity throughout Your Organization, 2005. **Address:** c/o Author Mail, Knopf Doubleday Publishing Group, 1745 Broadway, New York, NY 10019-4368, U.S.A. **Online address:** tom@tenfacesofinnovation.com

KELLING, Hans Wilhelm. American/German (born Germany), b. 1932. **Genres:** History, Literary Criticism And History, Translations, Poetry, Humanities. **Career:** Brigham Young University, assistant professor, 1962-67, associate professor, 1967-72, professor of German, 1972-, chairman of department, 1977-84, Foreign Language Housing and Summer Language Institute, director, 1985-, European Internship Program, director, 1986-, European Studies Program, director, 1992-; German South Mission, Church of Jesus Christ of Latter-day Saints, president, 1973-76. Writer. **Publications:** (With M.H. Folsom) Deutsche Aufsatzhilfe, 1967, rev. ed., 1969; The Idolatry of Poetic Genius in German Goethe Criticism, 1970; (with M.H. Folsom) Deutsch-Wie man's sagt und schreibt, 1972; Deutsche Kulturgeschichte, 1974, rev. ed., 2002; (with C. Gellinek) Avenues Toward Christianity, 2001. TRANSLATOR: Mormon Doctrine, 1992; Kirchengeschichte, 1998. EDITOR: From Vergil to Akhmatova: A Collection of Essays by Members of the Language Departments and the Department of Humanities, Classics, and Comparative Literature at Brigham Young University, 1983. **Address:** Department of German Studies and Slavic Languages, Brigham Young University, 3107 JFSB, Provo, UT 84602, U.S.A. **Online address:** hans-wilhelm_kelling@byu.edu

KELLNER, Bruce. American (born United States), b. 1930. **Genres:** Gerontology/Senior Issues, Literary Criticism And History, Bibliography, Biography, Popular Culture, Art/Art History, Plays/Screenplays, Art/Art History, Art/Art History. **Career:** Coe College, faculty, 1956-60; Hartwick College, faculty, 1960-69; Millersville University, professor of English, 1969-91, professor emeritus, 1991-. Writer. **Publications:** Carl Van Vechten and the Irreverent Decades, 1968; A Bibliography of the Work of Carl Van Vechten, 1980; Friends and Mentors: Richmond's Carl Van Vechten and Mark Lutz, 1980; (co-author) American Literature: Second Supplement to the University of Minnesota Monographs, 1981; The Harlem Renaissance: A Historical Dictionary for the Era, 1984, rev. ed., 1987; A Gertrude Stein Companion: Content with the Example, 1988; Donald Windham: A Bio-Bibliography, 1991; The Last Dandy: Ralph Barton, American Artist, 1991; Kiss Me Again: An Invitation to a Group of Noble Dames, 2002. EDITOR: Keep a-Inchin' Along: Selected Writings about Black Arts and Letters, 1979; Letters of Carl Van Vechten, 1987; The Major Works of Gertrude Stein, 16 vols., 1993; Early Modern African American Writers, 1892-1922, 25 vols., 1998; Letters of Charles Demuth, American Artist, 1883-1935, 2000; The Splendid Drunken Twenties: Selections from the Day Books, 1922-1930, 2003; What's For Dinner Also Breakfast Lunch and In Between, 2005; Winter Ridge: A Love Story, 2008; Caruso's Mustache Off and Other Writings about Music and Musicians, 2010; The Prettiest Girls in Euphoria, 2010. Contributor to books and periodicals. **Address:** Department of English, Millersville University, 1 S George St., PO Box 1002, Millersville, PA 17551, U.S.A. **Online address:** brucekellnerb@aol.com

KELLNER, Menachem. (Menachem Marc Kellner). Israeli/American (born United States), b. 1946. **Genres:** Philosophy, Theology/Religion, Translations. **Career:** University of Virginia, acting assistant professor of religious studies, 1972-73, assistant professor, 1975-80; College of William and Mary, lecturer in religious studies, 1973-75; University of Haifa, visiting senior lecturer, 1978-79, senior lecturer, 1980-, associate professor, 1987, Department of Maritime Civilizations chair, 1988-91, Sir Isaac and Lady Edith Wolfson Chair of Jewish Religious Thought, 1990-2005, dean of students, 1994-97, professor of Jewish history, 1995-; Ecole Pratique des Hautes Etudes, visiting professor, 1992-93; Northwestern University, visiting professor, 1992. University of Haifa Press, editor, 1999-2003. Translator and educator. **Publications:** (ed. as Menachem Marc Kellner) Contemporary Jewish Ethics, 1978; (comp. as Menachem Marc Kellner) Register of Work in Progress in the Fields of Jewish Philosophy, Thought, and Mysticism, 1978; (trans. and intro. as Menachem Marc Kellner) I. Abravanel, Principles of Faith, 1982; Dogma in Medieval Jewish Thought: From Maimonides to Abravanel, 1986; (ed.) The Pursuit of the Ideal: Jewish Writings of Steven Schwarzschild, 1990; Maimonides on Human Perfection, 1990; Maimonides on Judaism and the Jewish People, 1991; Maimonides on the Decline of the Generations and the Nature of Rabbinic Authority, 1996; (ed. with C.H. Manekin) Freedom and Moral Responsibility: General and Jewish Perspectives, 1997; (trans. and intro.) L. ben Gershom, Commentary on Song of Songs, 1998; Must a Jew Believe Anything?, 1999, 2nd ed., 2006; (trans.) The Code of Maimonides: Book Two, the Book of Love, 2004; Maimonides' Confrontation with Mysticism, 2006. Contributor to books, periodicals and journals. **Address:** University of Haifa, Haifa, 31905, Israel. **Online address:** kellner@research.haifa.ac.il

KELLNER, Menachem Marc. See **KELLNER, Menachem.**

KELLOGG, Frederick. American (born United States), b. 1929. **Genres:** History. **Career:** Boise State University, instructor, 1962-64, assistant professor, 1964-65, associate professor of history, 1966-67; Idaho Historical Conference, founder, 1964; University of Idaho, visiting assistant professor, 1965; University of Arizona, instructor, 1967-68, assistant professor, 1969-71, associate professor of history, 1971-, now professor emeritus; The Laws of Romania Series, editor-in-chief; Southeastern Europe/L' Europe du sudest, managing editor, 1974-. Writer. **Publications:** (Ed.) The Romanians' Struggle for Unification, 1834-1849, 1970; A History of Romanian Historical Writing (monograph), 1990; The Road to Romanian Independence, 1995; O Istorie a Istoriografiei Romane, 1996; Drumul Romaniei Spre Independenta Lasi, 2002. Contributor to books and journals. **Address:** Department of History, University of Arizona, Rm. 215, Social Sciences Bldg., 1145 SE Campus Dr., PO Box 210027, Tucson, AZ 85721-0027, U.S.A. **Online address:** kellogg@u.arizona.edu

KELLOGG, Marjorie Bradley. (M. Bradley Kellogg). American (born United States), b. 1946. **Genres:** Novels, Science Fiction/Fantasy, Plays/Screenplays, Theatre. **Career:** Princeton University, visiting professor, 1983-84, 1985-86; National Actors Theatre, resident designer, 1992-93; Columbia University, adjunct professor, 1993-95; Colgate University, associate professor of design and scene designer, 1995-. Writer. **Publications:** NOVELS: A Rumor of Angels, 1983; Lear's Daughters (science fiction), vol. I: The Wave and the Flame, 1986, vol. II: Reign of Fire, 1986, rev. ed., 2008; Harmony, 1991; The Book of Earth, 1995; The Book of Water, 1997; The Book of Fire, 2000; The Book of Air, 2003. OTHER: A Wrinkle in Time, 1991; Livin' in the Garden, 1997. Contributor to magazines. Works appear in anthologies. **Address:** Charles Dana Arts Center, Colgate University, 303 University Theater, 13 Oak Dr., Hamilton, NY 13346, U.S.A. **Online address:** mkellogg@colgate.edu

KELLOGG, Marne Davis. American (born United States), b. 1946. **Genres:** Mystery/Crime/Suspense, Novels, Young Adult Fiction, Humor/Satire. **Career:** Denver Center for the Performing Arts, director of communications, 1976-78; The Kellogg Organization Inc., executive vice-president, 1981-; King Resources Intl., interpreter; Frontier Airlines, regional sales manager; People/Time Inc., assistant Rocky Mountain bureau chief. Writer. **Publications:** HUMOROUS MYSTERY NOVELS: Bad Manners, 1996; Curtsey, 1996; Tramp, 1997; Nothing But Gossip, 1999; Birthday Party, 1999; Insatiable, 2001; Brilliant, 2003; Priceless, 2004; Perfect, 2005; Friends in High Places, 2007; The Real Thing, forthcoming. **Address:** The Kellogg Organization Inc., 825 E Speer Blvd., Ste. 100D, Denver, CO 80218, U.S.A. **Online address:** author@marnedaviskellogg.com

KELLOGG, M. Bradley. See **KELLOGG, Marjorie Bradley.**

KELLOGG, Steven. American (born United States), b. 1941. **Genres:** Children's Fiction, Illustrations, Picture/Board Books, Young Adult Fiction, Humor/Satire, Social Sciences. **Career:** American University, instructor in sketching, 1966; National Children's Book and Literacy, vice president. Writer and illustrator of children's books. **Publications:** SELF-ILLUSTRATED FOR CHILDREN: The Wicked Kings of Bloon, 1970; Can I Keep Him?, 1971; The Mystery Beast of Ostergeest, 1971; The Orchard Cat, 1972; Won't Somebody Play with Me?, 1972; The Island of the Skog, 1973; Much Bigger Than Martin, 1976; (and contrib.) The Mysterious Tadpole, 1977; Pinkerton, Behave!, 1979; A Rose for Pinkerton, 1981; The Mystery of the Stolen Blue Paint, 1982; Tallyho, Pinkerton!, 1982; Ralph's Secret Weapon, 1983; Best Friends: Story and Pictures, 1986; Aster Aardvark's Alphabet Adventures, 1987; Prehistoric Pinkerton, 1987; (reteller) Johnny Appleseed: A Tall Tale, 1988; (reteller) Jack and the Beanstalk, 1991; (reteller) Mike Fink: A Tall Tale, 1992; The Christmas Witch, 1992; Sally Ann Thunder Ann Whirlwind Crockett: A Tall Tale, 1995; (reteller) Three Little Pigs, 1997; A-hunting We will Go!, 1998; Three Sillies, 1999; (with B. Martin) Beasty Story, 1999; The

Missing Mitten Mystery, 2000; Give the Dog a Bone, 2000; A Penguin Pup for Pinkerton, 2001; Pinkerton & Friends: A Steven Kellogg Treasury, 2004; Pied Piper's Magic, 2009. COLOR STORIES: The Mystery of the Missing Red Mitten, 1974; The Mystery of the Magic Green Ball, 1978; There was an Old Woman, 1980; The Mystery of the Flying Orange Pumpkin, 1980. **Address:** c/o Author Mail, HarperCollins Children's Books, 10 E 53rd St., New York, NY 10022-5244, U.S.A.

KELLOUGH, J. Edward. American (born United States), b. 1954. **Genres:** Politics/Government, Civil Liberties/Human Rights, Education. **Career:** Miami University, Department of Political Science, teaching assistant, 1981-85, visiting instructor, 1985-86; Texas A&M University, Department of Political Science, assistant professor, 1986-88; University of Georgia, Department of Political Science, assistant professor, 1988-94, associate professor, 1994-2002, associate professor in the department of public administration and policy, 2002-06, professor in the department of public administration and policy, 2006-, Ph.D. program director, 1999-2008, graduate coordinator and MPA program director, 2002-08, head of the department of public administration and policy, 2008-. Writer. **Publications:** Federal Equal Employment Opportunity Policy and Numerical Goals and Timetables: An Impact Assessment, 1989; (ed. with L.G. Nigro) Civil Service Reform in the States: Personnel Policy and Politics at the Subnational Level, 2006; Understanding Affirmative Action: Politics, Discrimination and the Search for Justice, 2006; (with L.G. Nigro and F.A. Nigro) The New Public Personnel Administration, 6th ed., 2007. Contributor to books and journals. **Address:** Department of Public Administration & Policy, University of Georgia, 204 Baldwin Hall, 355 South Jackson St., Athens, GA 30602-1615, U.S.A. **Online address:** kellough@uga.edu

KELLY, Brian. American (born United States), b. 1954. **Genres:** Area Studies, Documentaries/Reportage, Adult Non-fiction, Economics. **Career:** Georgetown Voice, editor-in-chief, 1974-75; Daily Register, reporter, 1975-76; Chicago Sun-Times, reporter, 1976-84; freelance writer, 1984-; Regardie's Business Magazine, editor, 1985-92; Outlook, Sunday Opinion Section, deputy editor, 1985-92; Washington Post, congressional editor, 1992-98; U.S. News & World Report, assistant managing editor, 1998-, executive editor, 2003-07, editor, 2007-. **Publications:** NONFICTION: (with M. London) Amazon, 1983; (with London) The Four Little Dragons: Inside Korea, Taiwan, Hong Kong, and Singapore at the Dawn of the Pacific Century, 1989; Adventures in Porkland: How Washington Wastes Your Money and Why They Won't Stop, 1992; (with M. London) The Last Forest: The Amazon in the Age of Globalization, 2007. **Address:** U.S. News & World Report, 1050 Thomas Jefferson St. NW, Washington, DC 20007, U.S.A.

KELLY, Catriona. British (born England), b. 1959. **Genres:** Literary Criticism And History, Translations, Biography, History. **Career:** Oxford University, Christ Church, research fellow, 1987-93; University of London, London School of Slavonic and East European Studies, lecturer in Russian, 1993-96; Oxford University, lecturer, 1996-97, reader, 1997-2002, professor, 2002-, New College, lecturer. Writer. **Publications:** Petrushka: The Russian Carnival Puppet Theatre, 1990; (trans.) E. Shvarts, Paradise, 1993; A History of Russian Women's Writing, 1820-1992, 1994; (trans.) O. Sedakova, Poems and Elegies, 2003; Children's World: Growing up in Russia, 1890-1991, 2007. EDITOR: (with M. Makin and D. Shepherd) Discontinuous Discourses in Modern Russian Literature, 1989; An Anthology of Russian Women's Writing, 1777-1992, 1994; (ed. with D. Shepherd) Constructing Russian Culture in the Age of Revolution, 1998; An Introduction to Russian Cultural Studies: An Introduction, 1998; Utopias: Russian Modernist Texts 1905-1940, 1999; Russian Literature: A Very Short Introduction, 2001; Refining Russia: Advice Literature, Polite Culture, and Gender from Catherine to Yeltsin, 2001; Comrade Pavlik: The Rise and Fall of a Soviet Boy Hero, 2005; Children's World: Growing Up in Russia, 1890-1991, 2008. Contributor to periodicals. **Address:** New College, Oxford University, Holywell St., Oxford, OX OX1 3BN, England. **Online address:** catriona.kelly@new.ox.ac.uk

KELLY, Chris. British (born England), b. 1940. **Genres:** Novels. **Career:** Anglia Television, continuity announcer, 1963-; Granada Television, producer, 1965-70; Central Television, producer, 1989-92; Carlton Productions, producer, 1992-; Midsummer House Ltd., chairperson; River Court Films Ltd., director. Writer. **Publications:** NOVELS: The War of Covent Garden, 1989; The Forest of the Night, 1991; Taking Leave, 1995; (with S. Kelly) Herstory: Lisa Marie's Wedding Diary, 1996; A Suit of Lights, 2000. **Address:** c/o Leah Schmidt, The Agency Ltd., 24 Pottery Ln., Holland Pk., London, GL W11 4LZ, England.

KELLY, Christopher. British (born England), b. 1964. **Genres:** History. **Career:** University of Cambridge, professor of ancient history, Corpus Christi College, fellow. Academic, writer and classicist. **Publications:** Ruling the Later Roman Empire, 2004; The Roman Empire: A Very Short Introduction, 2006; Attila the Hun: Barbarian Terror and the Fall of the Roman Empire, 2008 in US as The End of Empire: Attila the Hun and the Fall of Rome, 2009. **Address:** Faculty of Classics, University of Cambridge, Sidgwick Ave., Cambridge, CB CB3 9DA, England. **Online address:** cmk11@cam.ac.uk

KELLY, C. L. See **KELLY, Clint.**

KELLY, Clint. (C. L. Kelly). American (born United States), b. 1950. **Genres:** Novels, inspirational/Motivational Literature, Adult Non-fiction, Young Adult Fiction, Children's Non-fiction, Children's Fiction, Young Adult Non-fiction. **Career:** Seattle Pacific University, communications specialist, 1988-. Journalist. **Publications:** FICTION: The Landing Place, 1993; The Lost Kingdom, 1994; The Aryan, 1995; Deliver Us from Evil, 1998; The Power and the Glory, 1999; Escape Underground (juvenile novel), 2001. NONFICTION: The Fame Game: How You, Too, Can Become the Greatest, 1984; (with C. Bottemiller) The Everett Cartoon and Trivia Book, 1985; (with J.H. Hampsch) The Key to Inner Peace, 1985; Me Parent, You Kid!: Taming the Family Zoo, 1993; How to Win Grins and Influence Little People, 1996; Dare to Raise Exceptional Children: Give Your Kids a Sense of Purpose, a Sense of Adventure, and a Sense of Humor, 2001; (with C. Patterson) Carly Patterson: Be Strong, 2006. AS C.L. KELLY: Scent: A Dark Secret Hidden in Petals of Pink, 2006; Echo: A Silent Plea to be Heard, A Desperate Cry to be Found, 2007; Delicacy, 2008. Works appear in anthologies. Contributor to periodicals. **Address:** c/o Author Mail, Zondervan, 5300 Patterson SE, Grand Rapids, MI 49530, U.S.A. **Online address:** ckelly@spu.edu

KELLY, Deirdre. Canadian (born Canada), b. 1960?. **Genres:** Autobiography/Memoirs. **Career:** Globe and Mail, dance critic, investigative reporter, fashion columnist, 2000-06, features writer, 2006-. **Publications:** Paris Times Eight: Finding Myself in the City of Dreams (memoir), 2009. Contributor to magazines. **Address:** Globe and Mail, 444 Front St. W, Toronto, ON M5V 2S9, Canada. **Online address:** dkelly@globeandmail.com

KELLY, Deirdre M. Canadian/American (born United States), b. 1959. **Genres:** Education, Sociology, Women's Studies And Issues. **Career:** High school music appreciation teacher, 1988-89; University of British Columbia, assistant professor of sociology of schooling, 1991-96, professor of sociology of education, 1996-. Writer. **Publications:** Hard Work, Hard Choices: A Survey of Women in St. Lucia's Export-Oriented Electronics Factories, 1987; Last Chance High: How Girls and Boys Drop in and out of Alternative Schools, 1993; (co-author) Balancing Diversity and Community: A Large, Urban High School Adopts the Mini-School Approach: Exemplary Schools Project, Case Study of Vancouver Technical Secondary School, 1995; Four Roads to Dublin: A History of Rathmines, Ranelagh and Leeson Street, 1995; (ed. with J. Gaskell) Debating Dropouts: Critical Policy and Research Perspectives on School Leaving, 1996; (ed.) Internet @Home: Internet Activities for Everyone in the Family: Ages 4 to Adult, 2000; Pregnant with Meaning: Teen Mothers and the Politics of Inclusive Schooling, 2000; Ten Quick and Fun Internet Field Trips: Instant Activity Sheets that Guide Kids on Internet Learning Journeys: From Ellis Island to Mars: And Enhance the Topics You Teach, 2001; Teaching for Social Justice, 2004; (with D.H. Currie, S. Pomerantz) Girl Power: Girls Reinventing Girlhood, 2009. Works appear in anthologies. Contributor to periodicals. **Address:** Department of Sociology, University of British Columbia, 3129 ANSO, 6303 NW Marine Dr., Vancouver, BC V6T 1Z1, Canada. **Online address:** deirdre.kelly@ubc.ca

KELLY, Elizabeth M. See **KELLY, Liz.**

KELLY, Fiona. See **COLEMAN, Michael.**

KELLY, Fiona. See **JONES, Allan Frewin.**

KELLY, Franklin (Wood). American (born United States), b. 1953. **Genres:** Art/Art History, Photography. **Career:** Virginia Museum of Fine Arts, art-mobile curator, 1975-76, curatorial assistant, 1976-77; Clark Art Institute, curatorial assistant, 1978-79; National Gallery of Art, intern, 1980, Center for Advanced Study in the Visual Arts, Samuel H. Kress fellow, 1981-83, Department of American art, assistant curator, 1985-87, curator, 1987-88, deputy director and chief curator, American and British Painting, senior curator; University of Delaware, lecturer, 1981; Minneapolis Institute of Arts, associate curator of paintings, 1983-85; George Mason University, lecturer, 1986; Rutgers University, lecturer, 1987; Corcoran Gallery of Art, curator of collections, 1988-90; Rhodes College, Moss lecturer, 1988; University of Maryland, visiting professor, 1990, adjunct associate professor, 1991-, professor; Princeton University, visiting professor, 1991. Writer. **Publications:** America: Art and the West, 1986; (with G.L. Carr) The Early Landscapes of Frederic Edwin Church, 1845-1854, 1987; Frederic Edwin Church and the National Landscape, 1988; (with J.A. Ryan, S.J. Gould and D. Rindge) Frederic Edwin Church, 1989; (co-author) The Paintings of George Bellows, 1992; Thomas Cole's Paintings of Eden, 1994; (co-ed.) American Paintings from the Manoogian Collection, 1989; (co-author) Winslow Homer, 1995; (co-author) American Paintings of the Nineteenth Century, 1996; (ed. with K.J. Avery) Hudson River School Visions: The Landscapes of Sanford R. Gifford, 2003; American Masters from Bingham to Eakins: The John Wilmerding Collection, 2004; (with L. Warrell) J.M.W. Turner, 2007. Works appears in anthologies. Contributor to art journals. **Address:** Department of American and British Painting, National Gallery of Art, 4th and Constitution Ave. NW, Washington, DC 20565, U.S.A. **Online address:** f-kelly@nga.gov

KELLY, Ian. British (born England), b. 1966. **Genres:** Biography, Autobiography/Memoirs, Food And Wine. **Career:** Writer. **Publications:** Cooking for Kings: The Life of Antonin Carême, the First Celebrity Chef, 2003; Beau Brummell: The Ultimate Dandy, 2005 in US as Beau Brummell: The Ultimate Man of Style, 2006; Casanova: Actor, Lover, Priest, Spy, 2008. **Address:** c/o Ivan Mulcahy, Mulcahy & Viney Ltd., 15 Canning Passage, Kensington, London, GL W8 5AA, England.

KELLY, James Patrick. American (born United States), b. 1951. **Genres:** Science Fiction/Fantasy. **Career:** C.E. Maguire Inc., Architects, Engineers, and Planners, proposal writer, coordinator of public relations, 1972-77; part-time consultant, 1977-79; New England Foundation for the Arts, director, 1999-2005; New Hampshire State Council on the Arts, chair, 2003-06, councilor; University of Southern Maine, Stonecoast MFA in Creative Writing, faculty, 2004-; Clarion Foundation, vice chair. Writer. **Publications:** Planet of Whispers, 1984; (with J. Kessel) Freedom Beach, 1985; Look into the Sun, 1989; Heroines, 1991; Wildlife, 1994; Think Like a Dinosaur and Other Stories, 1997; Solstice, 1999; (with J. Kessel and J. Lethem) Ninety Percent of Everything, 2001; Strange But Not a Stranger (stories), 2002; Burn, 2005; Feeling Very Strange, 2006; Wreck of the Godspeed, 2008. **Address:** University of Southern Maine, 222 Deering Ave., PO Box 9300, Portland, ME 04102, U.S.A. **Online address:** jim@jimkelly.net

KELLY, Jim. British (born England), b. 1957. **Genres:** Criminology/True Crime, Novels, Mystery/Crime/Suspense. **Career:** Bedfordshire Times, reporter, 1979-83; Yorkshire Evening Press, reporter, deputy news editor, 1983-88; Financial Times, journalist and education correspondent, 1988-2003. **Publications:** PHILIP DRYDEN SERIES: The Water Clock, 2002; The Fire Baby, 2004; The Moon Tunnel, 2005; The Coldest Blood, 2006; The Skeleton Man, 2007. DI PETER SHAW AND DS GEORGE VALENTINE SERIES: Death Wore White, 2009; Death Watch, 2010; Death Toll: A Mystery, 2011. Contributor to periodicals. **Address:** Financial Times, 1 Southwark Bridge, London, GL SE1 9HL, England.

KELLY, Joanne (W.). American (born United States), b. 1934. **Genres:** Librarianship, Bibliography, Children's Fiction, Reference. **Career:** Thomas Paine Elementary School, librarian, 1967; Urbana School District, elementary librarian, 1968-92, coordinator of libraries, 1984-92; The Regional Office of Education in Rantoul, librarian; Unit 4 Champaign Early Childhood School, consultant. Writer. **Publications:** The Battle of Books: K-8, 1990; (with M. Pat and K.V. Grabow) Rebuses for Readers, 1992; On Location: Settings from Famous Children's Books, 1992; Newbery Authors of the Eastern Seaboard: Integrating Social Studies and Literature, Grades 5-8, 1994; The Beverly Cleary Handbook, 1996. **Address:** 2110 Galen Dr., Champaign, IL 61821-6525, U.S.A. **Online address:** jkelly@roe9.k12.il.us

KELLY, Judith. American/British (born England), b. 1943?. **Genres:** Novels, Biography, Autobiography/Memoirs. **Career:** TV-am, staff; Reuters, staff; BSkyB, staff; television producer. Writer. **Publications:** Rock Me Gently: A True Story of a Convent Childhood, 2005. Contributor to periodicals.

Address: Bloomsbury Publishing Plc, 36 Soho Sq., London, GL W1D 3QY, England. **Online address:** info@judithkelly.co.uk

KELLY, Kevin (J.). American (born United States), b. 1952. **Genres:** Documentaries/Reportage, Economics. **Career:** Walking! Journal, editor and publisher, 1982-84; Nomadic Books, founder, 1982; Whole Earth Review, editor and publisher, 1984-90; Point Foundation, director, 1985; Wired Magazine, founding executive editor, 1992-99, executive director, 1994, editor, 1999-; Whole Earth Catalog, editor, editor in chief and publisher; All Species Foundation, co-founder. **Publications:** (Ed.) Signal: Communication Tools for the Information Age, 1988; Out of Control: The Rise of Neo-Biological Civilization, 1994; Out of Control: The New Biology of Machines, Social Systems and the Economic World, 1995; New Rules for the New Economy, 1998; What Technology Wants, 2010. Contributor to periodicals. **Address:** 149 Amapola Ave., Pacifica, CA 94044-3102, U.S.A.

KELLY, Lauren. See OATES, Joyce Carol.

KELLY, Linda. British (born England), b. 1936. **Genres:** Literary Criticism And History, Theatre, Biography, Art/Art History. **Career:** Vogue Magazine, copy writer, 1957-60, travel editor, 1960-63; writer, 1963-; Royal Society of Literature, fellow. **Publications:** The Marvellous Boy: The Life and Myth of Thomas Chatterton, 1971; The Young Romantics: Paris 1827-1837 in US as The Young Romantics: Victor Hugo, Sainte-Beuve, Vigny, Dumas, Musset and George Sand and their Friendships, Feuds and Loves in the French Romantic Revolution, 1976; The Kemble Era: John Philip Kemble, Sarah Siddons and the London Stage, 1980; Women of the French Revolution, 1987; (ed. with Christopher Bland) Feasts, 1987; (with L. Kelly) Proposals, 1989; Juniper Hall: An English Refuge from the French Revolution, 1991; Richard Brinsley Sheridan: A Life, 1997; Susanna, the Captain and the Castrato, 2004; Ireland's Minstrel: A Life of Tom Moore: Poet, Patriot and Byron's Friend, 2006. **Address:** 44 Ladbroke Grove, London, GL W11 2PA, England.

KELLY, Liz. (Elizabeth M. Kelly). American (born United States), b. 1967?. **Genres:** History. **Career:** University of Alaska Jazz Faculty Ensemble, featured vocalist, 1991-94; University of Alaska Theatre, vocal coach, 1993; Watkins Film Institute/Watkins School of Art and Design, writing teacher; Harvard University, endowment office staff; University of St. Thomas, fellow, adjunct professor of Catholic studies. Writer. **Publications:** The Seeker's Guide to the Rosary, 2001; The Rosary: A Path into Prayer, 2004; May Crowning, Masses and Merton: 50 Reasons to Love Being Catholic, 2006; Heaven in You and You in Heaven: Unveiling Eternity on Earth, 2008. Contributor to periodicals. **Address:** c/o Author Mail, Loyola Press Inc., 3441 N Ashland Ave., Chicago, IL 60657, U.S.A. **Online address:** emkelly1@stthomas.edu

KELLY, Louis Gerard. British/New Zealander (born New Zealand), b. 1935. **Genres:** Novellas/Short Stories, Language/Linguistics, Literary Criticism And History, Translations, Essays. **Career:** Teacher, 1960, 1961-63; Laval University, lecturer in phonetics and English, 1963-65; Royal Commission on Bilingualism and Biculturalism, research associate, 1965-67; University of Ottawa, assistant professor, 1967-68, associate professor, 1969-78, professor of linguistics, 1978, now retired; University of Cambridge, Darwin College, faculty. Writer and consultant. **Publications:** Twenty-Five Centuries of Language Teaching: An Inquiry Into the Science, Art and Development of Language Teaching Methodology, 500 B.C, 1969; The Best Method of Translating: A Translation of St. Jerome's Letter to Pammachius, 1976; (trans.) Quaestiones Alberti de Modis Significanti, 1977; (contrib.) La Grammaire desmodistes aux ideologues, 1977; The True Interpreter: A History of Translation Theory and Practice in the West, 1979; Prorsus Taliter: The Latin Text of Kipling's Just-So Stories 1980; (contrib.) Aufsteig und Niedergang der Roemischen Welt, 1983; Basil Valentine his Triumphant Chariot of Antimony, 1990; (intro.) Summa de Modis Significandi, 1995; The Mirror of Grammar: Theology, Philosophy and the Modistae, 2002. EDITOR: (with L.W.A. Crawley and contrib.) Essays Presented to E.M. Blaiklock, 1958; Descriptions and Measurement of Bilingualism: An International Seminar, University of Moncton, June 6-14, 1967, 1969; (ed. with H. Aarsleff and H. Niederehe) Papers in the History of Linguistics: Proceedings of the Third International Conference on the History of the Language Sciences (IChoLS III), Princeton, 19-23 August 1984, 1987; Basil Valentine: His Triumphant Chariot of Antimony: With Annotations of Theodore Kirkringius (1678), 1990. Contributor to journals. **Address:** 308 Cherry Hinton Rd., Cambridge, CB CB1 4AU, England.

KELLY, Maeve. Irish (born Ireland), b. 1930?. **Genres:** Novels, Poetry, Humor/Satire, Literary Criticism And History. **Career:** Shelter for Victims of Domestic Violence, founder, 1978; Residential Center for Victims of Domestic Violence, administrator. Writer. **Publications:** A Life of Her Own, and Other Stories, 1976; Necessary Treasons (novel), 1985; Resolution (poems), 1986; Florrie's Girls, 1989; Orange Horses, 1991; Alice in Thunderland, 1993. Works appear in anthologies. Contributor to periodicals. **Address:** c/o Mic Cheetham, Sheil Land Associates Ltd., 43 Doughty St., London, GL WC1N 2LF, England.

KELLY, Mij. British/Scottish (born Scotland) **Genres:** Children's Non-fiction. **Career:** Writer. **Publications:** (Ed. with T. Edensor) Moving Worlds, 1989; 48 Hours With Franklin, 1993; Franklin Falls Apart, 1995; I Hate Everyone, 2000; William and The Night Train, 2001; One More Sheep, 2004; Sweet Pea and Boogaloo, 2004; Where's My Darling Daughter?, 2005; Potty Thieves, 2006; Mi raah et ha-sir shel Shir?, 2007; Giants, 2007; Have You Seen My Potty?, 2007; The Bump, 2008; The Happiest Man in the World, 2008; Baby Blue Egg, 2008 as I Want My Mummy, 2009; Atchoo!: Good Manners For Complete Animals, 2009; Where Giants Hide, 2009; Bed of Your Own, 2011. **Address:** PFD, Drury House, 34-43 Russell St., London, GL WC2B 5HA, England. **Online address:** mij@mijkelly.com

KELLY, Nataly E. American (born United States), b. 1975. **Genres:** Adult Non-fiction, Language/Linguistics, Reference. **Career:** Language Line Services, senior language specialist, 1996-2001; freelance consultant, interpreter and translator, 2002-04; LogiLing Inc., co-founder and principal, 2004-05; Network Omni Multilingual Communications, director of product development, 2005-07; Common Sense Advisory Inc., cultural communications strategist, senior analyst and chief research officer; independent consultant, 2007-, chief research officer. Writer. **Publications:** Telephone Interpreting: A Comprehensive Guide to the Profession, 2008; (ed.) From Our Lips to Your Ears: How Interpreters Are Changing the World, forthcoming. Contributor to periodicals. **Address:** Common Sense Advisory Inc., 100 Merrimack St., Ste. 301, Lowell, MA 01852-1708, U.S.A. **Online address:** natalyekelly@yahoo.com

KELLY, Robert. American (born United States), b. 1935. **Genres:** Novels, Novellas/Short Stories, Poetry, Novellas/Short Stories. **Career:** Continental Translation Service, translator, 1955-58; Chelsea Review (now Chelsea), co-founder, ed. 1957-60; Wagner College, lecturer in English, 1960-61; Trobar, co-editor, 1960-65; Bard College, assistant professor of English, 1961-68, professor of English, 1974-, Asher B. Edelman professor of literature, 1986-, Division of Languages and Literature, The Writing Program, co-director; Matter, editor, 1963-; State University of New York, assistant professor of English, 1964; Tufts University, visiting professor in modern poetry, 1966-67; Caterpillar, contributing editor, 1968-72; California Institute of Technology, poet-in-residence, 1971-72; Milton Avery Graduate School of the Arts, co-director of writing program, 1974-; University of Kansas, poet-in-residence, 1975; Naropa Institute, lecturer, 1977-; Alcheringa Ethnopoetics, contributing editor, 1977-80; Milton Avery Graduate School, director of the writing program, 1980-93; Sulfur, contributing editor, 1980-81; Conjunctions, contributing editor, 1990; Poetry Intl., contributing editor, 1996; Yale University, poet-in-residence; Cal Tech, poet-in-residence; Dickinson College, poet-in-residence; University of Southern California, poet-in-residence; California Institute of the Arts, poet-in-residence. Writer. **Publications:** Armed Descent, 1961; Her Body Against Time, 1963; Round Dances, 1964; Tabula, 1964; Enstasy, 1964; Matter/Fact/Sheet/1, 1964; Matter/Fact/Sheet/2, 1964; The Well Wherein a Deer's Head Bleeds (play), 1964; Lunes, 1964; Lectiones, 1965; (ed. with P. Leary) A Controversy of Poets: An Anthology of Contemporary American Poetry, 1965; Words in Service, 1966; Weeks, 1966; Songs XXIV, 1967; Twenty Poems, 1967; Devotions, 1967; Axon Dendron Tree, 1967; Crooked Bridge Love Society, 1967; A Joining: A Sequence for H.D., 1967; The Scorpions (novel), 1967; Alpha, 1968; Finding the Measure, 1968; Songs I-XXX, 1968; Sonnets, 1968; From the Common Shore, Book 5, 1968; Statement, 1968; We Are the Arbiters of Beast Desire, 1969; A California Journal, 1969; The Common Shore, Books I-V: A Long Poem about American in Time, 1969; Kali Yuga, 1970; In Time (essays), 1971; Eros and Psyche (chamber opera), 1971; Cities (novels), 1971; Flesh: Dream: Book, 1971; Ralegh, 1972; The Pastorals, 1972; Reading Her Notes, 1972; Sulphur, 1972; The Tears of Edmund Burke, 1973; Whaler Frigate Clippership, 1973; The Mill of Particulars, 1973; A Line of Sight, 1974; The Loom, 1975; Sixteen Odes, 1976; The Lady of, 1977; The Convections, 1978; Wheres, 1978; The Book of Persephone, 1978; The Cruise of the Pnyx, 1978; Kill the Messenger Who Brings Bad News, 1979; Sentence, 1980; Spiritual Exercises, 1981;

The Alchemist to Mercury, 1982; Russian Tales, 1982; Mulberry Women, 1982; Under Words, 1983; Thor's Thrush, 1984; A Transparent Tree (short stories), 1985; Not This Island Music (poetry), 1987; The Flowers of Unceasing Coincidence (long poem), 1988; Doctor of Silence (short stories), 1988; Oahu (travel notation poems), 1988; Cat Scratch Fever (stories), 1991; Ariadne (long poem), 1991; A Strange Market (poetry), 1992; Queen of Terrors (stories), 1994; Mont Blanc (poem), 1994; Red Actions: Selected Poems 1960-1993, 1995, (with J. Roubaud and Schuldt) Abziehbilder, Heimgeholt, 1995; Time of Voice: Poems, 1994-1996, 1998; Lapis: Poems, 2005; (with B. Kempker) Shame/Scham: A Collaboration, 2005; Book from the Sky: A Novel, 2008; Logic of the World and Other Fictions, 2010; Uncertainties, 2011. Contributor of literary magazines. **Address:** Department of English, Bard College, PO Box 5000, Annandale-On-Hudson, NY 12504, U.S.A. **Online address:** kelly@bard.edu

KELLY, Robert J. American (born United States), b. 1938. **Genres:** Criminology/True Crime, Sociology, Cultural/Ethnic Topics, Biography. **Career:** City University of New York, Brooklyn College, professor of social science, 1968-, now Broeklundian professor emeritus, Graduate Center, professor of sociology and criminology; New York Police Department, consultant; Pennsylvania Crime Commission, consultant; New Jersey State Police, consultant; Robert Kelly Associates Inc., president; Edward Sagarin Institute for the Study of Social Problems, president. Writer. **Publications:** (Ed.) Organized Crime: A Global Perspective, 1986; (ed. with D.E. MacNamara) Perspectives on Deviance: Dominance, Degradation, and Denigration, 1991; (ed. and intro.) Bias Crime: American Law Enforcement and Legal Responses, 1993; (ed. with K. Chin and R. Schatzberg) Handbook of Organized Crime in the United States, 1994; (with R. Schatzberg) African-American Organized Crime: A Social History, 1996; (ed. with J. Maghan) Hate Crime: The Global Politics of Polarization, 1998; The Upperworld and the Underworld: Case Studies of Racketeering and Business Infiltrations in the United States, 1999; Encyclopedia of Organized Crime in the United States: From Capone's Chicago to the New Urban Underworld, 2000; Notorious: A Biographical Dictionary, 2002; (with R.W. Rieber) Terrorism, Organized Crime and Social Distress: The New World Order, 2003; (with J. Maghan and J.D. Serio) Illicit Trafficking: A Reference Handbook, 2005. Contributor to periodicals. **Address:** Brooklyn College, City University of New York, 2211B Boylan Hall, 2900 Bedford Ave., Brooklyn, NY 11210, U.S.A. **Online address:** rkelly@brooklyn.cuny.edu

KELLY, Ronald. Also writes as Ron Spicer. American (born United States), b. 1959. **Genres:** Novels, Novellas/Short Stories, Mystery/Crime/Suspense, Horror, Science Fiction/Fantasy, Young Adult Fiction. **Career:** Writer, 1986-. **Publications:** NOVELS: Hindsight, 1990; Pitfall, 1990; Something Out There, 1991; Moon of the Werewolf, 1991; Father's Little Helper, 1992; (contrib.) Slocum and the Nightriders, 1993; The Possession, 1993; Fear, 1994; (contrib.) Slocum and the Gold Slaves, 1994; Blood Kin, 1996; Midnight Grinding and Other Twilight Terrors, 2009; A Dark & Bloody Ground, 2010; Hell Hollow, 2009; Timber Gray, forthcoming. OTHERS: The Sick Stuff, 2009; After the Burn, 2010. Works appear in anthologies. Contributor to magazines. **Address:** c/o Joshua Bilmes, Jabberwocky Literary Agency, PO Box 4558, Sunnyside, NY 11104-0558, U.S.A. **Online address:** ron@ronaldkelly.com

KELLY, Saul. British/American (born United States), b. 1957?. **Genres:** History, Military/Defense/Arms Control. **Career:** University of Durham, International Boundaries Research Unit, research associate; University of Westminster, research fellow, Department of Defence Studies, reader, 2001-; King's College London, Defence Studies Department, lecturer, reader, 2001-. Writer. **Publications:** (Ed. with A. Gorst) Whitehall and the Suez Crisis, 2000; (with C. Douglas-Home) Dignified and Efficient: The British Monarchy in the Twentieth Century, 2000; Cold War in the Desert: Britain, the United States and the Italian Colonies, 1945-52, 2000; The Hunt for Zerzura: The Lost Oasis and the Desert War, 2002; The Lost Oasis: The Desert War and the Hunt for Zerzura, 2002; Westview, 2003; (with M.F. Hopkins and J.W. Young) The Washington Embassy: British Ambassadors to the United States, 1939-77, 2009; War & Politics in the Desert, 2010. Contributor of articles to books. **Address:** Department of Defence Studies, King's College London, Joint Services Command and Staff College, Rm. 150, Faringdon Rd., Shrivenham, WT SN6 8TS, England. **Online address:** skelly.jscsc@defenceacademy.mod.uk

KELMAN, Herbert C. American/Austrian (born Austria), b. 1927. **Genres:** Ethics, International Relations/Current Affairs, Psychology, Social Sciences. **Career:** Johns Hopkins University, Social Science Research Council, post-doctoral research training fellow, 1951-52, U.S. Public Health Service, postdoctoral research fellow, 1952-54; Baltimore College of Commerce, instructor in psychology, 1952-54; Congress of Racial Equality, field representative, 1954-60; Center for Advanced Study in the Behavioral Sciences, fellow, 1954-55; National Institute of Mental Health, research psychologist, 1955-57; Harvard University, lecturer on social psychology, 1957-62; Oslo Institute for Social Research, U.S. Public Health Service, special research fellow, 1960-61, Richard Clarke Cabot professor of social ethics, 1968-99, Program on International Conflict Analysis and Resolution, Weatherhead Center for International Affairs, director, 1993-2003, Doctoral Program in Social Psychology, chair, 1994-97, Center for Middle Eastern Studies, faculty, Joint Working Group on Israeli-Palestinian Relations, co-chair, 1994-2000, Richard Clarke Cabot Research professor of social ethics, 1999-2004, Richard Clarke Cabot professor emeritus, 2004-, faculty associate emeritus, 2004-; Sociometry, editorial consultant, 1959-62; Journal of Abnormal and Social Psychology, consulting editor, 1962-64; University of Michigan, Center for Research on Conflict Resolution, professor of psychology and research psychologist, 1962-69, Doctoral Program in Social Psychology, chair, 1966-67; Journal of Personality and Social Psychology, consulting editor, 1965-67; Journal of Applied Behavioral Science, consulting editor, 1965-70; Society for the Psychological Study of Social Issues, president, 1964-65; Institute of Society, Ethics and the Life Sciences, fellow, 1969-89, board director, 1970-72; Battelle Seattle Research Center, fellow, 1972-73; International Studies Association, vice president, 1972-73, president, 1977-78; Peace Science Society, president, 1975-76; Interamerican Society of Psychology, president, 1976-79; Fellowship in Israel for Arab-Jewish Youth, board director, 1977-96; Woodrow Wilson International Center for Scholars, fellow, 1980-81; International Society of Political Psychology, president, 1985-86; Psychologists for Social Responsibility, president, 1990-92; National Peace Foundation, board director, 1992-95; Society of Experimental Social Psychology, founding member. **Publications:** (Ed. and contrib.) International Behavior: A Social Psychological Analysis, 1965; (ed. with E. Converse and E.L. Vandenberg) Alternative Perspectives on Vietnam, 1966; A Time to Speak: On Human Values and Social Research, 1968; (with R.S. Ezekiel) Cross-National Encounters, 1970; (ed. with G. Bermant and D.P. Warwick) The Ethics of Social Intervention, 1978; Understanding Arafat, 1983; (with V.L. Hamilton) Crimes of Obedience: Toward a Social Psychology of Authority and Responsibility, 1989; (contrib.) The Social Psychology of Group Identity and Social Conflict, 2004. **Address:** Department of Psychology, Harvard University, Rm. 1304, William James Hall, 33 Kirkland St., Cambridge, MA 02138, U.S.A. **Online address:** hck@watsjh.harvard.edu

KELMAN, James. Scottish/British (born England), b. 1946. **Genres:** Novels, Novellas/Short Stories, Plays/Screenplays, Literary Criticism And History, Young Adult Fiction. **Career:** Writer. **Publications:** NOVELS: The Busconductor Hines, 1984; A Chancer, 1985; A Disaffection, 1989; How Late It Was, How Late, 1994 (Booker Prize); Translated Accounts, 2001; You Have to Be Careful in the Land of the Free, 2004. SHORT STORIES: An Old Pub Near the Angel, 1973; (with T. Leonard and A. Hamilton) Three Glasgow Writers, 1976; Short Tales from the Nightshift, 1978; Not Not While the Giro and Other Stories, 1983; (with A. Gray and A. Owens) Lean Tales, 1985; Greyhound for Breakfast, 1987; The Burn, 1991; Busted Scotch, 1997; The Good Times, 1998. OTHER: (ed.) An East End Anthology, 1988; Some Recent Attacks: Essays Clutural and Political, 1992; (with B. Zephaniah) Inna Liverpool, 1993; Tantalising Twinkles: Some Thoughts On a First Order Radical Thinker of European Standing, 1997; And the Judges Said: Essays, 2002; (intro.) Born up a Close: Memoirs of a Brigton Boy, 2006; Kieron Smith, Boy, 2009; If It Is Your Life, 2010. Contributor to periodicals. **Address:** c/o Rogers, Coleridge & White Ltd., 20 Powis Mews, London, GL W11 1JN, England.

KELMAN, Judith (Ann). American (born United States), b. 1945. **Genres:** Mystery/Crime/Suspense, Young Adult Fiction, Medicine/Health, Sports/Fitness, inspirational/Motivational Literature, Adult Non-fiction. **Career:** Valley Stream Public Schools, teacher of mentally handicapped students, 1968-71; Camp A.N.C.H.O.R., recreation supervisor of extracurricular activities for handicapped children, 1968-71; Touch Inc., founder, 1975, president, 1975-76; freelance writer, 1981-. **Publications:** MYSTERY/CRIME/SUSPENSE NOVELS: Prime Evil, 1986; Where Shadows Fall, 1988; While Angels Sleep, 1990; Hush Little Darlings, 1991; Someone's Watching, 1992; The House on the Hill, 1993; If I Should Die, 1993; One Last Kiss, 1995; More Than You Know, 1996; Fly Away Home, 1997; After the Fall, 1999; Summer of Storms, 2001; Every Step You Take, 2003; The Session, 2006; Backward in High Heels, 2006; The First Stone, 2007. OTHER: (with P.T. Scardino) Dr. Peter Scardino's Prostate Book: The Complete Guide to Overcoming Prostate Cancer, Prostatitis, and BPH, 2005. Works appear in anthologies. Contributor to periodicals. **Address:** Putnam Publicity, 375 Hudson St., New York, NY 10014, U.S.A. **Online address:** jkelman@jkelman.com

KELNER, Toni L. P. American (born United States) **Genres:** Mystery/Crime/Suspense. **Career:** Writer. **Publications:** LAURA FLEMING MYSTERY NOVELS: Down Home Murder, 1993; Dead Ringer, 1994; (co-author) Murder Most Merry, 1994; Trouble Looking for a Place to Happen, 1995; Country Comes to Town, 1996; Tight as a Tick, 1998; Death of a Damn Yankee, 1999; Mad as the Dickens, 2001; Wed and Buried, 2003; Many Bloody Returns, 2007; Without Mercy, 2008; (ed. with C. Harris) Wolfsbane and Mistletoe, 2008; Curse of the Kissing Cousins, 2009; Who Killed the Pinup Queen?, 2010; (ed. with C. Harris) Death's Excellent Vacation, 2010; (ed. with C. Harris) Home Improvement, 2011; Blast from the Past, 2011. Work appears in anthologies. Contributor of short stories to magazines. **Address:** Joan Brandt Agency, 788 Wesley Dr. NW, Atlanta, GA 30305, U.S.A. **Online address:** info@tonilpkelner.com

KELSAY, John. American (born United States), b. 1953?. **Genres:** Military/Defense/Arms Control, Cultural/Ethnic Topics, History, Social Sciences. **Career:** University of Virginia, instructor, 1985-87; James Madison University, instructor, 1986-87; Florida State University, assistant professor, 1987-91, associate professor, 1991-96, department chair, 1996-2006, Richard L. Rubenstein professor, 2001-, distinguished research professor, 2006-, College of Arts and Sciences, associate dean, 2008-, Bristol distinguished professor of religion and ethics, 2009-; Journal of Religious Ethics, co-editor, 2002-. **Publications:** (With D. Little and A.A. Sachedina) Human Rights and the Conflict of Cultures: Western and Islamic Perspectives on Religious Liberty, 1988; (ed. with J.T. Johnson) Cross, Crescent, and Sword: The Justification and Limitation of War in Western and Islamic Tradition, 1990; (ed. with J.T. Johnson) Just War and Jihad: Historical and Theoretical Perspectives on War and Peace in Western and Islamic Traditions, 1991; Islam and War: A Study in Comparative Ethics, 1993; (with L.S. Cunningham) The Sacred Quest: An Invitation to the Study of Religion, 2002, 5th ed., 2010; Arguing the Just War in Islam, 2007; (ed.) Politics and Religion in France and the United States, 2007. **Address:** Florida State University, M05 Dodd Hall, Tallahassee, FL 32306, U.S.A. **Online address:** jkelsay@fsu.edu

KELSAY, Michael. American (born United States), b. 1957. **Genres:** Novels, Sports/Fitness, Young Adult Fiction, Children's Fiction. **Career:** McNeese State University, graduate assistant, 1990-93; Bluegrass Community and Technical College, instructor, 1999-; Florida Atlantic University, visiting writer, 2002; University of Kentucky, creative writing and faculty, 2003. Writer. **Publications:** Too Close to Call (novel), 2001; Hardwood Heaven, 2003. Contributor to periodicals. **Address:** Witherspoon & Associates Inc., 235 E 31st St., New York, NY 10016-6302, U.S.A. **Online address:** michael.kelsay@gmail.com

KELSEY, Elin. American/Canadian (born Canada), b. 1961. **Genres:** Environmental Sciences/Ecology, Animals/Pets. **Career:** Canadian Museum of Nature, manager of chief of science education; Vancouver Aquarium, director of exhibits and interpretation; Calgary Zoo, manager of interpretive services; Elin Kelsey & Co. (specializing in environmental education and community involvement), founder; Monterey Institute of International Studies, adjunct instructor; Royal Roads University, School of Environment and Sustainability, adjunct instructor, associate faculty; Monterey Bay Aquarium, consultant. Writer. **Publications:** Owls, 1985; Beavers, 1985; Bees, 1986; Elephants, 1986. NATURE'S CHILDREN SERIES: (with L. Ham) Learning About Biodiversity: A First Look at the Theory and Practice of Biodiversity Education, Awareness, and Training in Canada, 1998; Saving Sea Otters: Stories of Survival, 1999; Finding Out About Dinosaurs, 2000; Canadian Dinosaurs, 2003; Strange New Species: Astonishing Discoveries of Life on Earth, 2005; The Sea of Cortez: An Ecological Odyssey, 2006; Watching Giants: The Secret Lives Of Whales, 2009; Not Your Typical Book About The Environment, 2010; (with S. Kim) You are Stardust, 2012. **Address:** Elin Kelsey and Co., 762 Laurel Ave., Pacific Grove, CA 93950, U.S.A. **Online address:** elin@elinkelseyandcompany.com

KELTY, Christopher M. American (born United States), b. 1972. **Genres:** Information Science/Computers. **Career:** Rice University, assistant professor, 2001-08, associate professor of anthropology, 2008; Harvard University,

visiting assistant professor of the history of science, 2007-08; University of California, Department of Information Studies, associate professor of information studies, 2008-, Center for Society and Genetics, faculty, 2008-. Writer. **Publications:** Two Bits: The Cultural Significance of Free Software, 2008. Contributor of articles to periodicals. **Address:** Department of Information Studies, University of California, 1315 Rolfe Hall, 405 Hilgard Ave., PO Box 951521, Los Angeles, CA 90095-1521, U.S.A. **Online address:** ckelty@socgen.ucla.edu

KEMMIS, Daniel (Orra). American (born United States), b. 1945. **Genres:** Urban Studies, Regional/Urban Planning. **Career:** Montana House of Representatives, state representative, 1975-84, minority leader, 1981-82, speaker, 1983-84; Morrison, Jonkel, Kemmis and Rossbach, partner, 1978-84; Northern Lights Research and Education Institute, senior fellow and project director, 1985-89; Bitterroot Resource Conservation and Development District, Hamilton, economic and community development specialist, 1985-88; KUFM, radio program developer, 1986-88; University of Montana, adjunct professor, 1988-89, Center for the Rocky Mountain West, director, 1996-, senior fellow; Missoula City Council, Missoula, councilman, 1988-89; City of Missoula, mayor, 1990-96; Dallas Institute for Humanities and Culture, fellow, 1994-; Charles F. Kettering Foundation, associate; Center for Natural Resources and Environmental Policy, senior fellow. Writer. **Publications:** Community and the Politics of Place, 1990; The Good City and the Good Life, 1995; (intro.) Across the Great Divide: Explorations In Collaborative Conservation and the American West, 2000; This Sovereign Land: A New Vision for Governing the West, 2001. Contributor to professional journals. **Address:** 521 Hartman Ct., Ste. 10, Missoula, MT 59802, U.S.A. **Online address:** dkemmis@bresnan.net

KEMP, (Bernard) Peter. British (born England), b. 1942. **Genres:** Literary Criticism And History, Young Adult Fiction. **Career:** Middlesex Polytechnic, Department of English, lecturer, 1968-74, senior lecturer, 1974-88; The Sunday Times, fiction editor and chief fiction reviewer. Writer. **Publications:** Muriel Spark, 1974; H.G. Wells and the Culminating Ape, 1982; (ed.) The Oxford Dictionary of Literary Quotations, 1997, 2nd ed., 2003. Contributor to newspapers. **Address:** The Sunday Times, 3 Thomas More Sq., London, GL E98 1RL, England.

KEMP, Gene. British (born England), b. 1926. **Genres:** Children's Fiction, Animals/Pets, Novels, inspirational/Motivational Literature, Science Fiction/Fantasy, Novellas/Short Stories. **Career:** Saint Sidwell's School, teacher, 1963-77; Rolle College, lecturer, 1974-75. Writer. **Publications:** The Prime of Tamworth Pig, 1972; Tamworth Pig Saves the Trees, 1973; Tamworth Pig and the Litter, 1975; Christmas with Tamworth Pig, 1977; The Turbulent Term of Tyke Tiler, 1977; Gowie Corby Plays Chicken, 1979; Dog Days and Cat Naps, 1980; The Clock Tower Ghost, 1981; No Place Like, 1983; Charlie Lewis Plays for Time, 1984; The Well, 1984; Jason Bodger and the Priory Ghost, 1985; Mr. Magus is Waiting For You, 1986; Juniper: A Mystery, 1986; Crocodile Dog, 1987; I Can't Stand Losing, 1987; Tamworth Pig Stories, 1987; The Room with No Windows, 1989; Just Ferret, 1990; Matty's Midnight Monster, 1991; The Mink War, 1992; Tamworth Pig Rides Again, 1992; Wanting a Little Black Gerbil, 1992; Roundabout (stories), 1993; The Wacky World of Wesley Baker, 1994; Zowey Corby's Story, 1995; (comp.) Ghosts, Ghouls and Other Nightmares: Spooky Stories, 1995; Dog's Journey, 1996; Rebel Rebel, 1997; Zowey Corby and the Black Cat Tunnel, 1997; Tyke Tiler Terrible Joke Book, 1997; The Wishing Tower, 1998; The Hairy Hands, 1999; Bluebeard's Castle, 2000; Snaggletooth's Mystery, 2000; The Haunted Piccolo, 2004; Nothing Scares Me, 2006; No Way Out, 2010. EDITOR: Ducks and Dragons: Poems For Children, 1980; The Puffin Book of Ghosts and Ghouls, 1992. **Address:** Pollinger Ltd., 9 Staple Inn, Holborn, London, GL WC1V 7QH, England. **Online address:** genekemp6@aol.com

KEMP, Kenny. American (born United States), b. 1955. **Genres:** Romance/Historical, Plays/Screenplays, Essays, Novels. **Career:** Attorney, 1984-; building contractor. Writer. **Publications:** 3/4 Inch Marine Ply (essay), 1996; I Hated Heaven (romance fiction), 1998; Dad Was a Carpenter: A Memoir, 2001; The Welcoming Door (historical fiction), 2002; City on a Hill, 2004; Oki's Island: A Hero's Journey, 2006; Lightland: A Supernatural Thriller, 2008; The Wise Man Returns, 2011. **Address:** 3292 E Bengal Blvd., Salt Lake City, UT 84121, U.S.A. **Online address:** kenny@kennykemp.com

KEMP, Martin (John). Scottish (born Scotland), b. 1942. **Genres:** Art/Art History, Sciences. **Career:** Dalhousie University, lecturer in history of art,

1965-66; University of Glasgow, lecturer in history of art, 1966-81; University of St. Andrews, Faculty of the Arts, professor of fine arts, 1981-90, professor of the history and theology of art, 1990-95; Princeton University, Institute of Advanced Study, fellow, 1984-85; University of Cambridge, Slade Professor of Fine Art, 1987-88; New York University Institute of Fine Arts, Benjamin Sonenberg Visiting Professor, 1988; St. Leonard's College, provost, 1991-94; University of North Carolina, Dorothy Ford Wiley Visiting Professor in Renaissance Culture, 1993; British Academy, Wolfson Research Professor, 1993-98; Centre for Visual Studies, founder, 1999; Oxford University, professor of art history, 1995-2003, emeritus professor of the history of art, 2003-; University of Chicago, Brosse Professor, 2000. Writer. **Publications:** Dr. William Hunter at the Royal Academy of Arts, 1975; Leonardo da Vinci: The Marvellous Works of Nature and Man, 1981, rev. ed., 2006; Geometrical Perspective from Brunelleschi to Desargues: Pictorial Means Oran Intellectual End?, 1985; (intro.) Leonardo da Vinci, 1988; (ed.) Leonardo on Painting: An Anthology of Writings, 1989; The Science of Art, 1990; (ed. with P. Humfrey) The Altarpiece in the Renaissance, 1990; The Science of Art: Optical Themes in Western Art from Brunelleschi to Seurat, 1990; (contrib.) Beauty of Another Order: Photography in Science, 1997; Behind the Picture: Art and Evidence in the Italian Renaissance, 1997; Imagine Everità. Per Una Storia dei Rapporti Fra Arte e Scienza, 1999; (contrib.) New Paintings, 1999; (contrib.) Liquid Form, 1985-99, 2000; (ed. and contrib.) The Oxford History of Western Art, 2000; (contrib.) Spectacular Bodies: The Art and Science of the Human Body from Leonardo to Now, 2000; Visualizations: The Nature Book of Art and Science, 2000; Leonardo, 2004; Seen/Unseen: Art, Science, and Intuition from Leonardo to the Hubble Telescope, 2006; Leonardo Da Vinci: Experience, Experiment and Design, 2006; The Human Animal in Western Art and Science, 2007; (contrib.) Leonardo Da Vinci and the Art of Sculpture, 2009; (contrib.) Acts of Seeing: Artists, Scientists and the History of the Visual: A Volume Dedicated to Martin Kemp, 2009; Christ to COKE, 2012; The Human Animal, forthcoming. Contributor to periodicals. **Address:** Department of the History of Art, University of Oxford, Littlegate House, Oxford, OX OX1 1PT, England. **Online address:** martin.kemp@trinity.ox.ac.uk

KEMP, Penn. (Penny Chalmers). Canadian (born Canada), b. 1944. **Genres:** Novellas/Short Stories, Plays/Screenplays, Poetry, Education, Theology/Religion, Cartoons, Women's Studies And Issues, Translations, Translations. **Career:** Educator, 1966-; Ontario Arts Council, writer in the schools, 1981-; University of Western Ontario, writer-in-residence, 2009-10; City of London Poet Laureate, 2010-11. **Publications:** POETRY: Clearing, 1977; Toad Tales, 1980; Animus, 1983; Some Talk Magic, 1984; Binding Twine, 1984; Traveling Light, 1984; Eidolons, 1988; Throo, 1990; Vocal Braiding, 2001; Sarasvati Scapes, 2001; Poem for Peace in Many Voices, vol. II, 2003; Incrementally, 2004; Gathering Voice, 2004; C'Loud, 2004; Sound Spoke, 2004; Pinceladas, 2005; Trance Form, 2006. POEMS AS PENNY CHALMERS: Bearing Down, 1972; Tranceform, 1976; Changing Place, 1978. **Address:** Pendas Productions, 525 Canterbury Rd., London, ON N6G 2N5, Canada. **Online address:** pendas@pennkemp.ca

KEMP, Roger L. American (born United States), b. 1946. **Genres:** Administration/Management, Institutions/Organizations, Politics/Government, Public/Social Administration, Regional/Urban Planning, Urban Studies. **Career:** City of Oakland, assistant, 1978-79; City of Seaside, city manager, 1979-83; City of Placentia, city administrator, 1983-87; City of Clifton, city manager, 1987-93; City of Meriden, city manager, 1993-2005; City of Vallejo, city manager, 2005-06; private consultant, 2006-; Town of Berlin, town manager, 2007-; University of California, visiting lecturer; California State University, lecturer, adjunct professor; Golden Gate University, professorial lecturer; University of Connecticut, adjunct professor; Rutgers University, adjunct professor, lecturer; Fairleigh Dickinson University, adjunct professor; Central Connecticut State University, adjunct professor; ICMA University, legacy leader instructor; University of New Haven, lecturer; Kemp Consulting L.L.C., president; Clifton Center for Strategic Planning, consultant. Writer. **Publications:** Coping with Proposition 13, 1980; Strategies for Hard Times, 1988; City Manager Eases Transition with Formal Plan, 2005. EDITOR: America's Infrastructure: Problems and Prospects, 1986; America's Cities: Strategic Planning for the Future, 1988; Privatization: The Provision of Public Services by the Private Sector, 1991; Strategic Planning in Local Government: A Casebook, 1992; Strategic Planning for Local Government: A Handbook for Officials and Citizens, 1993; America's Cities: Problems and Prospects, 1995; Economic Development in Local Government: A Handbook for Public Officials and Citizens, 1995; Urban Economic Development: Successful Case Studies from American Cities, 1995; Handbook of Strategic Planning,

1995; Managing America's Cities: A Handbook for Local Government Productivity, 1997; Local Government Election Practices: A Handbook for Public Officials and Citizens, 1999; Forms of Local Government: A Handbook on City, County, and Regional Options, 1999; Main Street Renewal: A Handbook for Citizens and Public Officials, 2000; The Inner City: A Handbook for Renewal, 2001; How American Governments Work: A Handbook for City, County, Regional, State and Federal Operations, 2002; Regional Government Innovations: A Handbook for Citizens and Public Officials, 2003; Community Renewal through Municipal Investment: A Handbook for Citizens and Public Officials, 2003; Model Government Charters: A City, County, Regional, State, and Federal Handbook, 2003; Homeland Security: Best Practices for Local Government, 2003, 2nd ed., 2010; Cities and the Arts: A Handbook for Renewal, 2004; Cities and Nature: A Handbook for Renewal, 2006; Homeland Security Handbook for Citizens and Public Officials, 2006; Homeland Security for the Private Sector: A Handbook, 2007; Cities and Cars: A Handbook of Best Practices, 2007; Museums, Libraries and Urban Vitality: A Handbook, 2008; Cities and Growth: A Policy Handbook, 2008; Cities and Sports Stadiums: A Planning Handbook, 2009; Cities and Adult Businesses: A Regulatory Planning Handbook, 2010; Documents of American Democracy: A Collection of Essential Works, 2010. Contributor to books and journals. **Address:** Kemp Consulting L.L.C., PO Box 342, Meriden, CT 06450-0342, U.S.A. **Online address:** rlkbsr@snet.net

KEMPE, Frederick. (Frederick Schumann Kempe). American (born United States), b. 1954. **Genres:** Politics/Government, International Relations/Current Affairs. **Career:** Associated Press-Dow Jones, Federal Republic of Germany, bureau chief, 1978-79; Newsweek, Federal Republic of Germany, correspondent, 1979-81; Wall Street Journal, editor, associate publisher, columnist, roving correspondent, 1981-83; bureau chief, 1984-86; chief diplomatic correspondent, 1986-; Wall Street Journal Europe, editor and associate publisher, 1992-97; Global Wall Street Journal, European editor, 2002-05; Atlantic Council, president and chief executive offcer, 2006-; Oxford University, Said School of Business, visiting fellow; Central European Economic Review, founder; Bloomberg News, columnist; Columbia University School of Journalism, international fellow. **Publications:** Divorcing the Dictator: America's Bungled Affair with Noriega, 1990; Siberian Odyssey: A Voyage into the Russian Soul, 1992; Father/Land: A Personal Search for the New Germany, 1999; Berlin 1961: Kennedy, Khrushchev and the Most Dangerous Place on Earth, 2011. Contributor to periodicals. **Address:** Atlantic Council, 1101 15th St. NW, 11th Fl., Washington, DC 20005, U.S.A.

KEMPE, Frederick Schumann. See **KEMPE, Frederick.**

KEMPER, Steve. American (born United States), b. 1951. **Genres:** Business/Trade/Industry, Engineering. **Career:** University of Connecticut, faculty, 1980. Writer and educator. **Publications:** Goarles Darwin: Working for the Love of Science, 1998; Code Name Ginger: The Story Behind Segway and Dean Kamen's Quest to Invent a New World, 2003; Reinventing the Wheel: A Story of Genius, Innovation, and Grand Ambition, 2005; A Labyrinth of Kingdoms: 10000 Miles Through Islamic Africa, forthcoming. Contributor to periodicals. **Address:** c/o Author Mail, Harvard Business School, 60 Harvard Way, Boston, MA 02163, U.S.A. **Online address:** email@stevekemper.net

KEMPRECOS, Paul. American (born United States) **Genres:** Mystery/Crime/Suspense, Novels, Young Adult Fiction. **Career:** The Cape Codder Newspaper, reporter and managing editor; Cape Cod Business Journal, editor. **Publications:** ARISTOTLE SOCARIDES MYSTERY NOVELS: Cool Blue Tomb, 1991; Neptune's Eye, 1991; Death in Deep Water, 1992; Feeding Frenzy: An Aristotle 'Soc' Socarides Mystery, 1993; The Mayflower Murder, 1996; Bluefin Blues, 1997. NUMA FILES SERIES WITH C. CUSSLER: Serpent, 1999; Blue Gold, 2000; Fire Ice: A Novel, 2002; White Death: A Novel, 2003; Lost City: A Novel, 2004; Polar Shift, 2004; The Navigator: A Novel, 2007; Medusa: A Novel, 2009. **Address:** St. Martin's Press, 175 5th Ave., New York, NY 10010, U.S.A.

KEMSKE, Floyd. American (born United States), b. 1947. **Genres:** Novels, Advertising/Public Relations, Writing/Journalism, Young Adult Non-fiction. **Career:** Weingarten Publications, editor and editorial director, 1980-92; freelance writer and graphic designer, 1992-99; Novel Enterprises (writing workshops), general partner, 1996-97; Kaplan College Online Education, editorial director, 2000-01. **Publications:** NOVELS: Lifetime Employment,

1992; The Virtual Boss, 1993; Human Resources, 1995; The Third Lion, 1997; Labor Day: A Corporate Nightmare, 2000. OTHERS: Letters of the Alien Publisher, 1991; (with D.B. Stein) Write on Target (nonfiction), 1997. **Address:** 69 Shirley St., Pepperell, MA 01463, U.S.A. **Online address:** fkemske@thirdlion.com

KEMSLEY, Deen. American (born United States), b. 1957. **Genres:** Theology/Religion. **Career:** Morgan Stanley, accounting consultant, 1999-; Tulane University, professor of accounting, 2004-; Lehman Brothers, accounting consultant, 2006-. Writer. **Publications:** Trust in the Lord: Reflections of Jesus Christ, 2008. Contributor of articles to periodicals. **Address:** A.B. Freeman School of Business, Tulane University, 14 Merlins Ln., Newtown, CT 06470, U.S.A. **Online address:** dkemsley@tulane.edu

KENAAN, Hagi. Israeli (born Israel) **Genres:** Philosophy, Adult Non-fiction. **Career:** Tel Aviv University, senior lecturer in philosophy; philosopher. Writer. **Publications:** (Contrib.) The Craft of Judgment, 1999; One Day, Philosophy, 2000; (contrib.) Eye and Mind, 2004; (contrib.) The Blind Spot, 2005; (contrib.) The Present Personal: Philosophy and the Hidden Face of Language, 2005; Panimdibur: Li-re'ot Aheret Be- 'Ik' Vot 'Imanu' El Levinas, 2008; Philosophy's Moods: The Affective Grounds of Thinking, 2011. Contributor of essays and articles to periodicals. **Address:** Department of Philosophy, Tel Aviv University, Ramat-Aviv, 69978, Israel. **Online address:** kenaan@post.tau.ac.il

KENAN, Randall (G.). American (born United States), b. 1963. **Genres:** Novels, Novellas/Short Stories, Literary Criticism And History, Women's Studies And Issues. **Career:** Alfred A. Knopf Inc., editorial staff, 1985-89; Sarah Lawrence College, lecturer, 1989-96; Columbia University, lecturer, 1990-96; Vassar College, lecturer and faculty of urban literature, 1990; Duke University, William Blackburn visiting professor of creative writing, 1994; University of North Carolina, Edourd Morot-Sir visiting professor of creating writing, 1995, Department of English and Comparative literature, associate professor, 2004-; University of Mississippi, John and Renee Grisham writer-in-residence, 1997-98; University of Memphis, visiting professor of creative writing, 1998-2002. **Publications:** A Visitation of Spirits (novel), 1989; Let the Dead Bury Their Dead and Other Stories, 1992; James Baldwin, 1994; A Time Not Here, 1997; Walking on Water: Black American Lives at the Turn of the Twenty-First Century, 1999; (with A. Sickels) James Baldwin, 2005; The Fire This Time, 2007; (ed. and intro.) Cross of Redemption: Uncollected Writings of James Baldwin, 2010. **Address:** Department of English and Comparative Literature, University of North Carolina, Greenlaw Hall, CB Ste. 3520, Chapel Hill, NC 27599-3520, U.S.A. **Online address:** rkenan@email.unc.edu

KENAZ, Yehoshua. Israeli (born Israel), b. 1937. **Genres:** Novels, Novellas/Short Stories, Essays. **Career:** Writer. **Publications:** Ahare ha-hagim, 1964; Ha-Isha ha-gedolah min ha-halomot, 1973, rev. ed., 1986; Moment Musikali: Sipurim, 1980, trans. as Musical Moment and Other Stories, 1995; Hitganvut yehidim, 1986; (contrib.) ha-Ishah ha-gedolah min ha-halomot, 1986; Ba-derekh el ha-hatulim, 1991; Hitganvut yehidim, 1986; Sefer ha-Arets, 1996; Mahazir ahavot kodmot, 1997; (co-author) keshet, 1998; Nof 'im sheloshah 'etsim: shete novelot, 2000; Ben lailah u-ven shahar, 2000; Dirah 'im kenisah ba-hatser, 2008. **Address:** c/o Author Mail, Steerforth Press, PO Box 70, South Royalton, VT 05068, U.S.A.

KENDA, Margaret. American (born United States), b. 1942. **Genres:** Mathematics/Statistics, Education. **Career:** University of Maine, professor of English, 1967-77. Writer. **Publications:** WITH PHYLLIS S. WILLIAMS: The Natural Baby Food Cookbook, 1972, rev. ed., 1982; Cooking Wizardry for Kids, 1990; Math Wizardry for Kids, 1995; Geography Wizardry for Kids, 1997. OTHER: Crime Prevention Manual for Business Owners and Managers, 1982; Science Wizardry for Kids, 1992, 2nd ed., 2009; (with R.K. Ullman and W. Kenda) Word Wizardry, 1999; Big Book of Cool Inventions: 77 Inventions, Experiments, and Mind-Bending Games, 2001; Whole Foods for Babies & Toddlers, 2001. **Address:** Barron's Educational Series Inc., 250 Wireless Rd., Hauppauge, NY 11788, U.S.A. **Online address:** margaretkenda@aol.com

KENDALL, Carol. American (born United States), b. 1917. **Genres:** Novels, Children's Fiction, Translations, Novellas/Short Stories, Young Adult Fiction, Mystery/Crime/Suspense, Young Adult Non-fiction. **Career:** Writer. **Publications:** The Black Seven, 1946; The Baby Snatcher, 1952; The Other

Side of the Tunnel, 1957; (with E. Blegvad) The Gammage Cup: A Novel of the Minnipins, 1959; The Big Splash, 1960; The Whisper of Glocken, 1965; (with Y. Li) Sweet and Sour: Tales from China, 1979; The Firelings, 1981; Haunting Tales from Japan, 1985; (with Li) Cinnamon Moon: Tales from China, 1987; The Wedding of the Rat Family, 1988. **Address:** 928 Holiday Dr., Lawrence, KS 66044, U.S.A.

KENDALL, Diana. American (born United States) **Genres:** Sociology. **Career:** University of Texas-Arlington, Department of Sociology, instructor, 1970-73; Austin Community College, professor of sociology, 1977-97, Division of Social and Behavioral Sciences, chair, 1981-97; St. David's Hospital Health Care System Foundation, director, 1987-2002; Austin Symphony Orchestra Society, director, 1987-98; University of Texas-Austin, Department of Sociology, senior lecturer, 1988-89; St. Edward's University, New College, adjunct faculty, 1991-92; American Sociological Association, Section on Teaching and Learning, council officer, 1995-98; Baylor University, Department of Sociology, assistant professor, 1997-2000, associate professor, 2001-05, professor, 2005-. Writer. **Publications:** Sociology in Our Times, 1996, 8th ed., 2011; (ed.) Race, Class and Gender in a Diverse Society, 1997; Sociology in Our Times: The Essentials, 1998, 7th ed., 2010; Social Problems in a Diverse Society, 1998, 5th ed., 2012; The Power of Good Deeds: Privileged Women and the Social Reproduction of the Upper Class, 2002; Framing Class: Media Representations of Wealth and Poverty in America, 2005; Members Only: Elite Clubs and the Process of Exclusion, 2008. **Address:** Department of Sociology, Baylor University, 1 Bear Pl., PO Box 97326, Waco, TX 76798-7326, U.S.A. **Online address:** diana_kendall@baylor.edu

KENDALL, Jane (F.). American (born United States), b. 1952. **Genres:** Children's Fiction, Illustrations. **Career:** Freelance illustrator of children's books, 1983-; feature writer and columnist, 1985-; Greenwich Magazine, senior writer, 1992-; Bruce Museum, costume history and design consultant. **Publications:** SELF-ILLUSTRATED FOR CHILDREN: (with L. Marcus) Petrouchka: A Ballet Cut-Out Book, 1983; Miranda and the Movies, 1989; Miranda Goes to Hollywood: Adventures in the Land of Palm Trees, Cowboys, and Moving Pictures, 1999. OTHER: Maestoso Petra, 2010. Illustrator of books by others. **Address:** Greenwich Magazine, 39 Lewis St., Ste. 8, Greenwich, CT 06830-5558, U.S.A. **Online address:** jkendl@discovernet.net

KENDALL, Joshua. American (born United States), b. 1960?. **Genres:** Psychology. **Career:** Journalist and freelance writer. **Publications:** (ed. with P.A. Curtis and G. Dale) The Foster Care Crisis: Translating Research into Policy and Practice, 1999; (with P.T. Stien) Psychological Trauma and the Developing Brain: Neurologically Based Interventions for Troubled Children, 2004; The Man Who Made Lists: Love, Death, Madness and the Creation of Roget's Thesaurus, 2008. Contributor to books and periodicals. **Address:** Boston, MA , U.S.A. **Online address:** joshuakendall@themanwhomadelists.com

KENDRICK, Beth. (Beth Killian). American (born United States) **Genres:** Novels, Young Adult Fiction. **Career:** Writer. **Publications:** NOVELS: My Favorite Mistake, 2004; Exes and Ohs, 2005; Fashionably Late, 2006; Nearlyweds, 2006; In One Year and Out the Other: A New Year's Story Collection, 2006; Everything I Needed to Know About Being a Girl I Learned form Judy Blume, 2007; Grey's Anatomy, 2007; Pre-nup, 2008; Second Time Around, 2010; Bake-Off, 2011. THE 310 SERIES: YOUNG ADULT NOVELS; UNDER PSEUDONYM BETH KILLIAN: Life As a Poser, 2006; Everything She Wants, 2006. **Address:** c/o Author Mail, Downtown Press, 1230 Ave. of the Americas, New York, NY 10020, U.S.A. **Online address:** beth@bethkendrick.com

KENDRICK, Christopher. American (born United States), b. 1953. **Genres:** History, Essays, Humor/Satire. **Career:** Loyola University, professor of English. Writer. **Publications:** Milton: A Study in Ideology and Form, 1986; (ed.) Critical Essays on John Milton, 1995; Utopia, Carnival, and Commonwealth in Renaissance England, 2004. Contributor to books and periodicals. **Address:** Department of English, Crown Center for the Humanities, Loyola University, 1032 W Sheridan Rd., Chicago, IL 60660-1537, U.S.A. **Online address:** ckendri@luc.edu

KENDRICK, Paul Calvert. American (born United States), b. 1983. **Genres:** Social Sciences, Politics/Government, Biography. **Career:** George Washington University, Department of Government International and Corporate Affairs, presidential administrative fellow. Historian and writer. **Publications:** (With S. Kendrick) Sarah's Long Walk: The Free Blacks of Boston and

How Their Struggle for Equality Changed America, 2004; (with S. Kendrick) Douglass and Lincoln: How a Revolutionary Black Leader and a Reluctant Liberator Struggled to End Slavery and Save the Union, 2008. Contributor to periodicals. **Online address:** pkendrick@hcz.org

KENDRICK, Stephen. American (born United States), b. 1954?. **Genres:** Mystery/Crime/Suspense, Theology/Religion, Adult Non-fiction, Film. **Career:** Sherwood Baptist Church, senior associate pastor, 2001-; Kendrick Brothers Productions, staff. Writer. **Publications:** (With A. Kendrick and L. Kimbrough) The Love Dare, 2008; (with A. Kendrick and L. Kimbrough) The Love Dare, Day by Day: A Year of Devotions for Couples, 2009; (with A. Kendrick and M. Catt) The Love Dare Bible Study, 2009; (with A. Kendrick and R. Alcorn) The Resolution for Men, 2011. **Address:** Sherwood Baptist Church, 2201 Whispering Pines Rd., Albany, GA 31707-2421, U.S.A. **Online address:** stephenkendrick@sherwoodpictures.com

KENDYL, Sharice. *See* **MICHELS, Sharry C.**

KENEALLY, Thomas (Michael). (William Coyle). Australian (born Australia), b. 1935. **Genres:** Novels, Children's Fiction, Plays/Screenplays, Adult Non-fiction, Writing/Journalism, Young Adult Non-fiction, History. **Career:** Teacher, 1960-64; University of New England, lecturer in drama, 1968-70; University of California, School of Writing, visiting professor, 1985, distinguished professor, 1991-95; New York University, Berg professor of English, 1988. Writer. **Publications:** FICTION: The Place at Whitton, 1964; The Fear, 1965; Bring Larks and Heroes, 1967; Three Cheers for the Paraclete, 1968; The Survivor, 1969; A Dutiful Daughter, 1971; The Chant of Jimmie Blacksmith, 1972; Blood Red, Sister Rose: A Novel of the Maid of Orleans, 1974; Moses the Lawgiver, 1975; Gossip from the Forest, 1975; Season in Purgatory, 1976; A Victim of the Aurora, 1977, 2nd ed., 2001; Ned Kelly and the City of the Bees, 1978; Passenger, 1979; Confederates, 1979; The Cut-Rate Kingdom, 1980; Bullie's House, 1981; Schindler's List in UK as Schindler's Ark, 1982; A Family Madness, 1986; The Playmaker, 1987; To Asmara: A Novel of Africa in UK as Towards Asmara, 1989; By the Line, 1989; Flying Hero Class, 1991; Woman of the Inner Sea, 1992; Jacko: The Great Intruder, 1993; A River Town, 1995; Bettany's Book, 2000; An Angel in Australia, 2002; The Office of Innocence: A Novel, 2002; The Tyrant's Novel, 2004; (ed. with R. Scott) Another Country, 2005; The Widow and Her Hero, 2007; The People's Train, 2009; The Daughters of Mars, 2012. NONFICTION: Outback, 1983; (with P. Adam-Smith and R. Davidson) Australia: Beyond the Dreamtime, 1987; With Yellow Shoes, 1992; Now and in Time to Be: Ireland and the Irish, 1992; The Place Where Souls Are Born: A Journey into the Southwest in UK as The Place Where Souls Are Born: A Journey into the American Southwest, 1992; Memoirs from a Young Republic, 1993; The Utility Player: The Des Hasler Story, 1993; Our Republic, 1995; Homebush Boy: A Memoir, 1995; The Great Shame: A Story of the Irish in the Old World and the New, 1998 in US as The Great Shame: And the Triumph of the Irish in the English-speaking World, 1999; American Scoundrel: The Life of the Notorious Civil War General Dan Sickles, 2002; Abraham Lincoln, 2003; A Commonwealth of Thieves: The Improbable Birth of Australia, 2005; Searching for Schindler: A Memoir, 2008; Australians, vol. I: Origins to Eureka, 2009, vol. II: Eureka to the Diggers, 2012; Three Famines, 2011. PLAYS: Halloran's Little Boat, 1975; Bullies House, 1981. AS WILLIAM COYLE: Act of Grace, 1988; Firestorm, 1988; Chief of Staff: A Novel, 1991. Contributor to periodicals. **Address:** c/o Author Mail, Random House, 100 Pacific Hwy., Level 3, Sydney, NW 2060, Australia.

KENISON, Katrina. American (born United States), b. 1958. **Genres:** Novellas/Short Stories, Novels, Biography, Autobiography/Memoirs. **Career:** Houghton Mifflin Co., editor, 1981-88, series editor, 1990-2006. **Publications:** (Contrib.) Leaving Cold Sassy: The Unfinished Sequel to Cold Sassy Tree, 1992; (ed. and intro. with K. Hirsch) Mothers: Twenty Stories of Contemporary Motherhood, 1996; (ed. with J. Updike) The Best American Short Stories of the Century, 1999; Mitten Strings for God: Reflections for Mothers in a Hurry, 2000; (with R. Gates) Meditations from the Mat: Daily Reflections on the Path of Yoga, 2002; Gift of an Ordinary Day: A Mother's Memoir, 2009. **Address:** Grand Central Publishing, 3 Center Plz., Boston, MA 02108, U.S.A.

KENJO, Takashi. American/Japanese (born Japan), b. 1940. **Genres:** Administration/Management, Engineering, Business/Trade/Industry. **Career:** TEAC Corp., researcher, 1964-65; Polytechnic University of Japan, lecturer, 1965-71, associate professor, 1971-81, professor of electric motors and their controls, 1981-2005; University of Industrial Technology, lecturer, 1965-71; associate professor, 1971-81; professor of electric motors and their controls, 1981; NIDEC Motor Engineering Research Laboratory, founding director emeritus. Writer. **Publications:** (With A. Sugawara) Stepping Motors and Their Microprocessor Controls, 1984, 2nd ed., 1994; (with S. Nagamori) Permanent-Magnet and Brushless DC Motors, 1985; Power Electronics for the Microprocessor Age, 1990; Electric Motors and Their Controls: An Introduction, 1991; (with T. Sashida) An Introduction to Ultrasonic Motors, 1993; (with J. Lorriman) Japan's Winning Margins: Management, Training and Education, 1994, 2nd ed., 1996. **Address:** 3-4-17 Maehara-cho, Koganei, Tokyo, 184, Japan. **Online address:** kenjo@uitec.ac.jp

KENNARD, David. British (born England) **Genres:** Biography, Autobiography/Memoirs, Animals/Pets. **Career:** Farmer, filmmaker and writer. **Publications:** A Shepherd's Watch: Through the Seasons with One Man and His Dogs, 2004; The Dogs of Windcutter Down: One Shepherd's Struggle for Survival, 2005. Contributor to periodicals. **Address:** North Devon, England. **Online address:** djkennards@aol.com

KENNEALY, Jerry. Also writes as James Brant, Paul Boray. American (born United States), b. 1938. **Genres:** Mystery/Crime/Suspense, Young Adult Fiction. **Career:** San Francisco Police Department, police officer, 1961-65. Writer. **Publications:** Nobody Wins, 1977; The Conductor, 1995; The Forger, 1996; The Suspect, 1997; The Hunted, 1999; The Other Eye, 2000; (as Paul Boray) Cash Out, 2001; (as James Brant) Vatican Connection, 2003; (as James Brant) Chasing the Devil, 2004; Jigsaw, 2007; Still Shot, 2008. NICK POLO MYSTERIES: Polo Solo, 1987; Polo, Anyone?, 1988; Polo's Ponies, 1988; Polo in the Rough, 1989; Polo's Wild Card, 1990; Green with Envy, 1991; Special Delivery, 1992; Vintage Polo, 1993; Beggar's Choice, 1994; All That Glitters, 1997. **Address:** c/o Dominick Abel, Dominick Abel Literary Agency, 146 W 82nd St., Ste. 1B, New York, NY 10024, U.S.A. **Online address:** jerrykennealy@hotmail.com

KENNEDY, Adrienne. American (born United States), b. 1931. **Genres:** Plays/Screenplays, Autobiography/Memoirs. **Career:** Yale University, lecturer, 1972-74, visiting lecturer; School of Drama, CBS fellow, 1973; Princeton University, visiting lecturer, 1977; Brown University, visiting lecturer, visiting associate professor, 1979-80; University of California-Berkeley, chancellor's distinguished lecturer, 1980, 1986, visiting lecturer; Harvard University, visiting lecturer, 1990-91; Signature Theater Co., playwright-in-residence, 1995-96; University of California-Davis, lecturer. Playwright. **Publications:** The Owl Answers, 1963; A Lesson in a Dead Language, 1964; A Rat's Mass, 1966; (with J. Lennon and V. Spinetti) The Lennon Play: In His Own Write, 1968; Sun: A Poem for Malcolm X Inspired by His Murder, 1968; Funnyhouse of a Negro, 1969; Cities in Bezique: 2 One-Act Plays: The Owl Answers and A Beast's Story, 1969; Boats, 1969; An Evening with Dead Essex, 1973; A Movie Star Has to Star in Black and White, 1976; A Lancashire Lad, 1980; Orestes and Electra, 1980; Black Children's Day, 1980; People Who Led to My Plays (memoirs), 1986; Diary of Lights, 1987; Adrienne Kennedy in One Act (collected works) 1988; Deadly Triplets: A Theater Mystery and Journal, 1990; The Alexander Plays (collected works), 1992; Intersecting Boundaries: The Theatre of Adrienne Kennedy, 1992; Letter to My Students, Kenyon Review, 1993; (with A.P. Kennedy) Sleep Deprivation Chamber: A Theater Piece, 1996; The Adrienne Kennedy Reader, 2001. Works appear in anthologies. **Address:** c/o Buddy Thomas, International Creative Management, 730 5th Ave., New York, NY 10019, U.S.A. **Online address:** adriennekennedy1@yahoo.com

KENNEDY, A(lison) L. Scottish (born Scotland), b. 1965. **Genres:** Novels, Novellas/Short Stories, Young Adult Fiction. **Career:** Clydebank & District, community arts worker, 1988-89; Hamilton & East Kilbride Social Work Department, writer-in-residence, 1989-95; Project Ability, coordinator of creative writing, 1989-94; SAC/Strathclyde Regional Social Work Department, writer-in-residence, 1990-92; Copenhagen University, writer-in-residence, 1995; University of St. Andrews, instructor in creative writing; University of Warwick, associate professor in creative writing; Department 5, staff. **Publications:** SHORT STORY COLLECTIONS: Night Geometry and the Garscadden Trains, 1991; Now That You're Back, 1994; Original Bliss, 1997; Absolutely Nothing, 1998; Indelible Acts: Stories, 2002. NOVELS: Looking for the Possible Dance, 1993; So I am Glad, 1995; Everything You Need, 1999; Paradise, 2004; Day, 2007; The Blue Book, 2011. OTHERS: (ed. with H. White and M. Bateman) The Ghost of Liberace, 1993; (ed. with J. McGonigal and M. Bateman) A Sort of Hot Scotland, 1994; The Life and Death of Colonel Blimp (non-fiction), 1997; On Bullfighting (non-fiction), 1999; (co-author) Crimespotting, 2009; (co-author) Ox-Tales: Air, 2009; What Becomes, 2009. Contributor to books, newspapers and periodicals. **Address:** Department 5, 355 Byres Rd., Glasgow, G12 8QZ, Scotland. **Online address:** info@a-l-kennedy.co.uk

KENNEDY, Dan. American (born United States), b. 1967. **Genres:** Autobiography/Memoirs, Humor/Satire. **Career:** Atlantic Records, director of creative development, 2002-03. Writer. **Publications:** Loser Goes First: My Thirty-Something Years of Dumb Luck and Minor Humiliation (memoir), 2003; Rock On: An Office Power Ballad, 2008. Contributor to periodicals. Works appear in anthologies. **Address:** Atlantic Records, 1290 6th Ave. NYC, New York, NY 10104, U.S.A. **Online address:** dskmail@earthlink.net

KENNEDY, David Michael. American (born United States), b. 1941. **Genres:** History, Language/Linguistics, Literary Criticism And History, Economics, Social Sciences, Politics/Government. **Career:** Stanford University, assistant professor, 1967-72, associate professor, 1972-80, professor of history, 1980-, Program in International Relations, chair, 1977-80, School of Humanities and Sciences, associate dean, 1981-, Donald J. McLachlan professor of history, 1992-, now emeritus; National Public Radio, chief humanities consultant, 1975-76; University of Florence, visiting professor, 1976-77; International Communications Agency, lecturer, 1976-77, 1980; Oxford University, Harmsworth professor, 1995-96; American Academy of Arts and Sciences, fellow; American Philosophical Society, fellow. Writer. **Publications:** Birth Control in America: The Career of Margaret Sanger, 1970; (with T.A. Bailey) The American Pageant, 6th ed., 1979, 14th ed. (with L. Cohen and T.A. Bailey), 2010; Over Here: The First World War and American Society, 1980, rev. ed., 2005; Over Here: The First World War and American Society, 1980; Freedom from Fear: The American People in Depression and War, 1929-1945, 1999. EDITOR: (with P.A. Robinson) Social Thought in America and Europe, 1970; Progressivism: The Critical Issues, 1971; American People in Depression, 1973; American People in the Age of Kennedy, 1973; (intro. with T.A. Bailey) The American Spirit: United States History as Seen by Contemporaries, 1984, 12th ed., 2010; (with M.E. Parrish) Power and Responsibility: Case Studies in American Leadership, 1986; (intro.) The Library of Congress World War II Companion, 2007; (with L. Cohen and M. Piehl) The Brief American Pageant: A History of the Republic, 2011. Contributor to periodicals. **Address:** Department of History, Stanford University, 450 Serra Mall, Bldg. 200, Stanford, CA 94305-2024, U.S.A. **Online address:** dmk@stanford.edu

KENNEDY, Emmet. See **KENNEDY, Robert Emmet.**

KENNEDY, Gavin. Scottish/British (born England), b. 1940. **Genres:** Biography, Military/Defense/Arms Control, Business/Trade/Industry. **Career:** Brunel University, lecturer in economics, 1970-72; University of Strathclyde, faculty, 1972, senior lecturer in economics, 1974-, professor of economics, through 1982; Heriot-Watt University, Edinburgh Business School, Esmee Fair Research Center, Department of Accounting and Finance, faculty, 1982, professor of defence finance, professorial fellow, 1988-, now professor emeritus, 2005-; Negotiate Ltd., founder, chairman, managing director, 1987- ; Blair, Kennedy & Associates, director. Writer. **Publications:** The Military in the Third World, 1974; The Economics of Defence, 1975; The Death of Captain Cook, 1978; Bligh, 1978; Burden Sharing in NATO, 1979; (with J. Benson and J. McMillan) Managing Negotiations, 1980, rev. ed., 1982; Mathematics for Innumerate Economists, 1982; Everything Is Negotiable!: How to Get a Better Deal, 1982, 4th ed., 2008; Defense Economics, 1982; Invitation to Statistics, 1983; Doing Business Abroad, 1985; Negotiate Anywhere, 1985; Superdeal, 1986; Macroeconomics, 1987; The Pocket Negotiator, 1987; Captain Bligh: The Man and His Mutinies, 1989; Negotiation, 1991; The Perfect Negotiation, 1992; Kennedy's Simulations for Negotiation Training, 1993, (with F. Kennedy) 3rd ed., 2007; Field Guide to Negotiation: A Glossary of Essential Tools and Concepts for Today's Manager, 1994; Kennedy on Negotiation, 1997; New Negotiating Edge, 1998; Profitable Negotiation, 1999; Influencing for Results, 2000; Essential Negotiation, 2004, 2nd ed., 2009; Adam Smith's Lost Legacy, 2005; (with F. Kennedy) Kennedy's Simulations for Negotiation Training, 2007; Strategic Negotiation, 2007; Adam Smith: A Moral Philosopher and His Political Economy, 2008; Myopic Visionaries, forthcoming. EDITOR: The Radical Approach, 1976; R.T. Gould's Captain Cook, 1978; Mutiny of the Bounty, 1980; A Book of the Bounty, 1981. **Address:** Negotiate Ltd., 5 Kilmaurs Rd., Edinburgh, EH16 5DA, Scotland. **Online address:** gavin@negotiate.demon.co.uk

KENNEDY, Holly. Canadian (born Canada) **Genres:** Novels, Mystery/Crime/Suspense. **Career:** Writer. **Publications:** NOVELS: The Tin Box, 2005; The Penny Tree, 2007; The Silver Compass, 2008; Keeper of the Pond, forthcoming. **Address:** c/o Liza Dawson, Liza Dawson Associates, 350 7th Ave., Ste. 2003, New York, NY 10001-1930, U.S.A. **Online address:** holly@hollykennedy.com

KENNEDY, James. See **LUSBY, Jim.**

KENNEDY, John C. (John Charles Kennedy). American/Canadian (born Canada), b. 1943. **Genres:** Anthropology/Ethnology, History. **Career:** Memorial University of Newfoundland, professor of anthropology, 1973-, now retired; University of Bergen, exchange professor, 1995. Writer. **Publications:** Holding the Line, 1982; People of the Bays and Headlands: Anthropological History and the Fate of the Communities in the Unknown Labrador, 1995; Labrador Village, 1996. **Address:** Waveland Press, 404 N Wheeling Rd., Prospect Heights, IL 60070, U.S.A.

KENNEDY, John Charles. See **KENNEDY, John C.**

KENNEDY, Kelly S. American (born United States), b. 1970. **Genres:** History. **Career:** Ogden Standard-Examiner, reporter, 1997-98; Salt Lake Tribune, reporter, 1998-2000; Oregonian, reporter, 2000-01; Chicago Tribune, reporter, 2005; Army Times, reporter, 2005-07; Times News Service, reporter, 2007-; Dart Center, Ochberg fellow, 2008; USA Today, reporter, 2011-; University of Northern Colorado, lecturer; University of Colorado, lecturer. **Publications:** They Fought for Each Other: The Triumph and Tragedy of the Hardest Hit Unit in Iraq, 2010. **Address:** Alexandria, VA , U.S.A. **Online address:** kellyskennedy@yahoo.com

KENNEDY, Kieran A. Irish (born Ireland), b. 1935. **Genres:** Economics, Sociology, Young Adult Non-fiction. **Career:** Office of the Comptroller and Auditor General, executive officer, 1954-55; Irish Civil Service, Department of Industry and Commerce, executive officer, 1954-58, Department of Finance, administrative officer, 1958-65, assistant principal officer, 1965-70; University College, lecturer, 1965-; Economic and Social Research Institute, senior research officer, 1968-71, director, 1971-96, research professor, 1996-; Central Bank of Ireland, economic consultant, 1970-71; client services commissioner. Writer. **Publications:** Productivity and Industrial Growth: The Irish Experience, 1971; (with R. Bruton) The Irish Economy, 1975; (with B.R. Dowling) Economic Growth in Ireland: The Experience since 1947, 1975; (comp.) The ESRI Research Plan, 1976-80 and Background Analysis, 1976; (comp.) The ESRI Research Plan, 1981-85 and Background Analysis, 1981; (ed. with D. Conniffe) Employment and Unemployment Policy for Ireland, 1984; (with T. Healy) Small-Scale Manufacturing Industry in Ireland, 1985; (ed.) Ireland in Transition, 1986; (comp.) The ESRI Research Plan, 1986-1990 and Background Analysis, 1986; (with T. Giblin and D. McHugh) The Economic Development of Ireland in the Twentieth Century, 1988; (with E. O'Malley and R. O'Donnell) Report to the Industrial Policy Review Group on the Impact of the Industrial Development Agencies, 1992; Facing the Unemployment Crisis in Ireland, 1993; (ed. with M. Littleton) From Famine to Feast: Economic and Social Change in Ireland 1847-1997, 1998; (contrib.) Final Report of the Social Welfare Benchmarking and Indexation Group, 2001. **Address:** The Economic & Social Research Institute, Whitaker Sq., Sir John Rogerson's Quay, Dublin, DU 2, Ireland.

KENNEDY, Lawrence W. American (born United States), b. 1952. **Genres:** History, Regional/Urban Planning, Urban Studies. **Career:** St. Sebastian's Country Day School, teacher, 1975-76; Boston College, High School, teacher, 1976-85, lecturer, 1987-92; Boston Redevelopment Authority, consultant, 1987-92; University of Scranton, assistant professor, 1992-98, associate professor of history, 1998-2004, professor of history, 2004-. Writer. **Publications:** Planning the City upon a Hill: Boston since 1630, 1992; (with W.M. Whitehill) Boston: A Topographical History, 3rd ed., 2000. **Address:** Department of History, University of Scranton, 800 Linden St., Scranton, PA 18510, U.S.A. **Online address:** lawrence.kennedy@scranton.edu

KENNEDY, Leigh. British/American (born United States), b. 1951. **Genres:** Novels, Novellas/Short Stories, Science Fiction/Fantasy. **Career:** Rose Memorial Hospital, clerk, 1971-80; Austin Community College, typist, 1981-85; writer, 1985-. **Publications:** The Journal of Nicholas the American, 1986; Faces (stories), 1987; Saint Hiroshima, 1987; (co-author) Custer's Last Jump and Other Collaborations, 2003; Wind Angels, 2011. Contributor to periodicals. **Address:** Maggie Noach Literary Agency, 22 Dorville Cres., London, GL W6 OHJ, England.

KENNEDY, Liv. Canadian (born Canada), b. 1934. **Genres:** Travel/Exploration. **Career:** Dalcraft Ltd., commercial artist, 1950-55; Grouse Mountain Resorts Ltd., ski instructor, 1955-63; freelance writer and photographer, 1968-; Strasser Travel, professional tour escort and travel consultant, 1973-; Jib Set Sailing School, sailing instructor, 1974-78; Maritime Museum of Vancouver, coordinator, 1976-; Canadian Broadcasting Corp., yachting correspondent, 1977-; Good Morning Radio, broadcaster, 1977-; Malaspina College, photojournalism teacher, 1992. Writer. **Publications:** (Co-author) Vancouver Once upon a Time, 1974; Coastal Villages, 1991. **Address:** 3600 Outrigger Rd., PO Box 14, Nanoose Bay, BC V9P 9H3, Canada. **Online address:** kennmac@island.net

KENNEDY, Marlane. American (born United States), b. 1962. **Genres:** Novels, Literary Criticism And History. **Career:** Writer. **Publications:** Me and the Pumpkin Queen (middle-grade novel), 2007; The Dog Days of Charlotte Hayes (middle-grade novel), 2009. **Address:** Greenwillow Books, 1350 Ave. of the Americas, New York, NY 10019, U.S.A. **Online address:** marlane@marlanekennedy.com

KENNEDY, Michael. British (born England), b. 1926. **Genres:** Music, Biography, Autobiography/Memoirs. **Career:** Daily Telegraph, music critic, 1941-58, assistant northern editor to northern editor, 1958-86, chief music critic, 1989-2005; Sunday Telegraph, chief music critic, 1989-2005. **Publications:** The Hallé Tradition: A Century of Music, 1960; The Works of Ralph Vaughan Williams, 1964; Portrait of Elgar, 1968, 4th ed., 1993; Portrait of Manchester, 1970; Elgar Orchestral Works, 1970, 2nd ed., 1971; History of the Royal Manchester College of Music, 1971; Barbirolli: Conductor Laureate, 1971, 2nd ed., 1982; Mahler, 1974, rev. ed., 2000; Richard Strauss, 1976, rev. ed., 1995; (contrib.) William Walton: A Thematic Catalogue of His Musical Works, 1977; Hallé, 1858-1976: A Brief Survey of The Orchestra's History Travels and Acheivements, 1977; Concise Oxford Dictionary of Music, 1980, (with J.B. Kennedy) 5th ed., 2007; Britten, 1981, rev. ed., 2001; Catalogue of the Works of Ralph Vaughan Williams, 1982, 2nd ed., 1996; The Hallé: 1858-1983: A History of The Orchestra, 1982; Strauss Tone Poems, 1984; Adrian Boult, 1987; Portrait of Walton, 1989; Music Enriches All: 21 Years of the Royal Northern College of Music, 1994; Richard Strauss, Man, Musician, Enigma, 1999; The Life of Elgar, 2004; Buxton: An English Festival, 2004. EDITOR: (intro.) Autobiography of Charles Hallé, With Correspondence and Diaries, 1981; Oxford Dictionary of Music, 1985, 2nd rev. ed., 2006; Who's Who in Opera: A Guide to Opera Characters, 1998. **Address:** The Bungalow, 62 Edilom Rd., Manchester, GM M8 4HZ, England.

KENNEDY, Michael P. J. Canadian (born Canada), b. 1947. **Genres:** Sports/Fitness, Recreation, History. **Career:** University of Ottawa, part-time instructor, 1971-75; Concordia University, Loyola College, instructor, 1973-75; University of Regina, special lecturer, 1975-76; Saskatchewan Institute, Kelsey Campus, Canadian literature and communication arts instructor, 1976-; University of Saskatchewan, College of Arts and Science, Department of English, lecturer, 1991-, College of Agriculture and Bioresources, faculty, 1994-98. Writer. **Publications:** (Ed.) Words on Ice: A Collection of Hockey Prose, 2003; (ed.) Going Top Shelf: An Anthology of Canadian Hockey Poetry, 2005; Dogs on Ice: A History of Hockey at University of Saskatchewan, 2006. Contributor to periodicals and journals. **Address:** Department of English, University of Saskatchewan, 257.5 Arts Bldg., 9 Campus Dr., Saskatoon, SK S7N 5A5, Canada. **Online address:** mpk104@mail.usask.ca

KENNEDY, Pagan. (Pamela Kennedy). American (born United States), b. 1962. **Genres:** Novels, Novellas/Short Stories, Horticulture, Young Adult Fiction, Literary Criticism And History, Sex, Young Adult Non-fiction. **Career:** Pagans Head magazine, publisher, 1988-93; Village Voice, columnist, 1990-93; Voice Literary Supplement, columnist, 1991-; Boston College, adjunct instructor, 1995-; PC Week, copy editor; Dartmouth College, visiting writer of nonfiction, 2009; Warren Wilson College, Warren Wilson MFA program, writing instructor; Johns Hopkins University, writing instructor. **Publications:** Stripping and Other Stories, 1994; Platforms: A Microwaved Cultural Chronicle of the 1970s, 1994; Spinsters (novel), 1995; Zine: How I Spent Six Years of My Life in the Underground and Finally Found Myself-I Think, 1995; Exes, 1998; Black Livingstone: A True Tale of Adventure in the Nineteenth-Century Congo, 2002; Confessions of a Memory Eater: A Novel, 2006; First Man-Made Man: The Story of Two Sex Changes, One Love Af-

fair, and a Twentieth-Century Medical Revolution, 2007; Dangerous Joy of Dr. Sex and Other True Stories, 2008. Contributor to periodicals. **Address:** c/o Kim Witherspoon, InkWell Management, 521 5th Ave., 26th Fl., New York, NY 10175, U.S.A. **Online address:** paganken@gmail.com

KENNEDY, Pamela. *See* **KENNEDY, Pagan.**

KENNEDY, Paul Michael. American/British (born England), b. 1945. **Genres:** History, International Relations/Current Affairs, Military/Defense/Arms Control, Social Commentary, Economics, Adult Non-fiction, Politics/Government. **Career:** Sir Basil Liddell Hart, research assistant, 1966-70; University of Oxford, Theodor Heuss Research fellow, 1968-69; University of East Anglia, lecturer, 1970-75, reader in history, 1975-82, professor of history, 1982-83; The Alexander Von Humboldt Foundation, fellow, 1972; Institute for Advanced Study, visiting fellow, 1978-79; Yale University, J. Richardson Dilworth professor of history, 1983-, The United Nations In Its Second Half Century, co-director, 1993-96, International Security Studies, director; The Lehrman Institute, visiting fellow, 1984; St. Antonys College, supernumerary fellow. Writer. **Publications:** Pacific Onslaught, 7th December, 1941 to 7th February, 1943, Ballantine, 1972; Pacific Victory, 1973; The Samoan Tangle: A Study in Anglo-German-American Relations 1878-1900, 1974; The Rise and Fall of British Naval Mastery, 1976; The Rise of the Anglo-German Antagonism, 1860-1914, 1980; The Realities Behind Diplomacy: Background Influences on British External Policy, 1865-1980, 1981; Strategy and Diplomacy, 1870-1945: Eight Essays, 1985; Lessons from the Fall and Rise of Nations: The Future for America, 1987; The Rise and Fall of the Great Powers: Economic Change and Military Conflict from 1500 to 2000, 1988; Preparing for the Twenty-First Century, 1994; (with R. Cohen) Global Sociology, 2000, 2nd ed., 2007; Zhan Zheng Yu He Ping De Da Zhan Lüe/ Grand Strategies in War and Peace, 2005; The Parliament of Man: The Past, Present and Future of the United Nations, 2006; (co-author) Fronteiras do pensamento: retratos de um mundo complexo, 2008; (contrib.) Power Shifts and Global Governance Challenges: Perspectives From South and North, 2009. EDITOR: (with J.A. Moses) Germany in the Pacific and Far East, 1870-1914, 1977; The War Plans of the Great Powers 1880-1914, 1979; The Rise of Anglo-German Antagonism 1860-1914, 1980; (with A. Nicholls) Nationalist and Racialist Movements in Britain and Germany Before 1914, 1981; Grand Strategies in War and Peace, 1991; Global Trends, 1994; To Make Another World: Studies in Protest and Collective Action, 1996; To Make Another World: Studies in Protest and Collective Action, 1996; The Pivotal States: A New Framework for U.S. Policy in the Developing World, 1999; From War to Peace: Altered Strategic Landscapes in the Twentieth Century, 2000. Contributor to books and periodicals. **Address:** Department of History, Yale University, PO Box 208353, New Haven, CT 06520-8324, U.S.A. **Online address:** paul_kennedy@yale.edu

KENNEDY, Philip F. British (born England) **Genres:** Literary Criticism And History. **Career:** New York University-New York, Middle Eastern Studies, associate professor; New York University-Abu Dhabi, Abu Dhabi Institute, faculty director. Writer. **Publications:** The Wine Song in Classical Arabic Poetry: Abū Nuwās and the Literary Tradition, 1997; (ed. with R.G. Hoyland) Islamic Reflections, Arabic Musings: Studies in Honour of Professor Alan Jones, 2004; (ed.) On Fiction and Adab in Medieval Arabic Literature, 2005; (ed. with M. Lawrence) Recognition: The Poetics of Narrative: Interdisciplinary Studies on Anagnorisis, 2009. Contributor to journals. **Address:** Department of Middle Eastern & Islamic Studies, New York University, 50 Washington Sq. S, New York, NY 10012, U.S.A. **Online address:** philip.kennedy@nyu.edu

KENNEDY, Randall L. American (born United States), b. 1954. **Genres:** Law, Social Commentary, Young Adult Non-fiction, Essays. **Career:** U.S. Court of Appeals, law clerk, 1982-83; U.S. Supreme Court, law clerk, 1983-84; Harvard University, assistant professor of law, 1984-85, associate professor, 1985-89, professor, 1989-2005, Michael R. Klein professor of law, 2005-. Writer. **Publications:** Race, Crime and the Law, 1997; Nigger: The Strange Career of a Troublesome Word, 2002; Interracial Intimacies: Sex, Marriage, Identity and Adoption, 2003; Sellout: The Politics of Racial Betrayal, 2008; (ed.) Best African American Essays, 2010; Persistence of the Color Line: Racial Politics and the Obama Presidency, 2011. Contributor to journals. **Address:** Harvard Law School, Harvard University, Areeda 228, 1563 Massachusetts Ave., Cambridge, MA 02138, U.S.A. **Online address:** rkennedy@law.harvard.edu

KENNEDY, **Rick**. Japanese/American (born United States), b. 1935. **Genres:** Travel/Exploration, Essays, Music, Young Adult Non-fiction, Social Sciences, Writing/Journalism. **Career:** Random House, editor, 1970-79; Sony Corp., editor, 1979-; Metropolis, columnist. **Publications:** Good Tokyo Restaurants, 1985, 3rd ed., 1992; Home, Sweet Tokyo (essays): Life in a Weird and Wonderful City, 1988; Little Adventures in Tokyo: 39 Thrills for the Urban Explorer (nonfiction), 1992, rev. ed., 1998; Jelly Roll, Bix and Hoagy: Gennett Studios and the Birth of Recorded Jazz, 1994; The Tokyo Q Guide to Tokyo, 1999; (with R. McNutt and A. Kooper) Little Labels-Big Sound: Small Record Companies and the Rise of American Music, 1999. **Address:** 5-7-7 Takada Nishi, Kohoku-ku, Yokohama, 223-0066, Japan. **Online address:** rok@ba2.so-net.ne.jp

KENNEDY, **Robert Emmet**. (Emmet Kennedy). American (born United States), b. 1941?. **Genres:** History, Philosophy. **Career:** Merrimack College, instructor in history, 1964-66; Brandeis University, Department of the History of Ideas, teaching assistant, 1968; Kent State University, instructor, 1968-69; University of Toulouse-le-Mirail, instructor in history, 1969-73; George Washington University, assistant professor, 1973-77, associate professor, 1977-82, professor of European history, 1982-. Writer. **Publications:** (Ed. with J. Friguglietti) The Shaping of Modern France: Writings on French History since 1715, 1969; A Philosopher in the Age of Revolution: Destutt de Tracy and the Origins of Ideology, 1978; A Cultural History of the French Revolution, 1989; (with M.L. Netter, J.P. McGregor and M.V. Olsen) Theatre, Opera and Audiences in Revolutionary Paris, Analysis and Repertory, 1996; Secularism and its Opponents from Augustine to Solzhenitsyn, 2006. Contributor to periodicals. **Address:** Department of History, George Washington University, 801 22nd St. NW, Washington, DC 20052, U.S.A. **Online address:** ekennedy@gwu.edu

KENNEDY, **Sarah**. American (born United States), b. 1960. **Genres:** Poetry. **Career:** Mary Baldwin College, faculty. Poet. **Publications:** POEMS: From the Midland Plain: Poems, 1999; (ed. with R.T. Smith) Common Wealth: Contemporary Poets of Virginia, 2003; Double Exposure, 2003; Consider the Lilies, 2004; A Witch's Dictionary, 2007; Home Remedies: Poems, 2009. Contributor to magazines. **Address:** Mary Baldwin College, 201 E Frederick St., Staunton, VA 24401-3610, U.S.A. **Online address:** skennedy@mbc.edu

KENNEDY, **Scott**. American (born United States), b. 1967. **Genres:** Business/Trade/Industry, Economics, History. **Career:** Woodrow Wilson Center, Cold War International History Project, research assistant, 1992-93; Brookings Institution, research assistant in foreign policy studies program, 1993-97; Indiana University, lecturer, 2000-02, assistant professor, 2002-06, associate professor of political science, 2006-, Research Center for Chinese Politics and Business, director, 2007-. Writer. **Publications:** (Ed.) China Cross Talk: The American Debate over China Policy since Normalization: A Reader, 2003; The Business of Lobbying in China, 2005; Beyond the Middle Kingdom: Comparative Perspectives on China's Capitalist Transformation, 2011; Mandarins Playing Capitalist Games, forthcoming; The Politics of Lobbying in China, forthcoming; Capitalism with Chinese Characteristics, forthcoming. Contributor to periodicals. **Address:** Department of East Asian Languages and Cultures, Indiana University, 205 Goodbody Hall, 1011 E 3rd St., Bloomington, IN 47405-7005, U.S.A. **Online address:** kennedys@indiana.edu

KENNEDY, **Sheila Suess**. American (born United States), b. 1941. **Genres:** Humor/Satire. **Career:** Baker & Daniels, attorney, 1975- 77; corporation counsel, 1977-80; Kennedy & Eichholtz, partner, 1980-86; Kennedy Development Services, 1987-92; Indiana Civil Liberties Union, executive director, 1992-98; School of Public and Environmental Affairs, adjunct professor, 1996-98, assistant professor, 1998- 2003, associate professor, 2003-08, professor, 2008-; Indiana University, philanthropic studies faculty & adjunct faculty in political science 1999-; Center for Urban Policy and Environment, faculty fellow, 2000-; Tobias Center for Leadership, faculty fellow, 2004-; Center for Religion and American Culture, research fellow, 2005-. Writer. **Publications:** What's a Nice Republican Girl like Me Doing in the ACLU?, 1997; Free Expression in America: A Documentary History, 1999; (ed. with I. Ritchie) To Market, to Market: Reinventing Indianapolis, 2001; Charitable Choice: First Results from Three States, 2003; (with W. Bielefeld) Charitable Choice at Work: Evaluating Faith-based Job Programs in the States, 2006; God and Country: America in Red and Blue, 2007. Contributor to journals and periodicals. **Address:** Indianapolis, IN , U.S.A. **Online address:** shekenne@iupui.edu

KENNEDY, **Thomas E.** Danish/American (born United States), b. 1944. **Genres:** Young Adult Non-fiction, Young Adult Fiction. **Career:** Fairleigh Dickinson University, lecturer; Copenhagen's Rehabilitation Centre for Torture Victims, translator. Writer. **Publications:** COPENHAGEN QUARTET SERIES: Kerrigan's Copenhagen, A Love Story, 2002; Bluett's Blue Hours, 2003; Greene's Summer, 2004 in US as In the Company of Angels: A Novel, 2010; Danish Fall, 2005 in US as Falling Sideways: A Novel, 2011. FICTION: Crossing Borders: A Novel, 1990; A Weather of the Eye, 1996; Unreal City: Stories, 1996; The Book of Angels, 1997; Drive Dive Dance & Fight: Stories, 1997; Cast upon the Day: Stories, 2007; A Passion in the Desert, 2007; (trans. and intro.) D. Turéll, Last Walk Through the City, 2010. NONFICTION: Andre Dubus: A Study of the Short Fiction, 1988; (ed. with H. Specht) The American Short Story Today: Proceedings of a Seminar, 1990; Robert Coover: A Study of the Short Fiction, 1992; Index to American Short Story Award Collections, 1970-90, 1993; Realism & Other Illusions: Essays on the Craft of Fiction, 2002; (with W. Cummins) The Literary Traveler, 2005. (trans. and intro.) The Meeting with Evil: Inge Genefke's Fight against Torture, 2008; Riding the Dog: A Look Back at America, 2008; (ed. with W. Cummins) Writers on the Job: Tales of the Non-writing Life, 2008; Last Night My Bed a Boat of Whiskey Going Down, 2010; (ed. with W. Cummins) The Book of Worst Meals, 2010; (ed. with W. Cummins) The Girl with Red Hair, 2010. **Address:** c/o Nat Sobel, Sobel Weber Associates Inc., 146 E 19th St., New York, NY 10003-2404, U.S.A. **Online address:** info@thomasekennedy.com

KENNEDY, **William (Joseph)**. American (born United States), b. 1928. **Genres:** Novels, Plays/Screenplays, Young Adult Non-fiction, Children's Fiction, History. **Career:** Post Star, assistant sports editor and columnist, 1949-50; Times-Union, reporter, 1952-56, special writer, 1963-70, film critic, 1968-70; Puerto Rico World Journal, assistant managing editor and columnist, 1956; Miami Herald, reporter, 1957; Time-Life, correspondent, 1957-59; Dorvillier, reporter, 1957-59; Knight Newspaper, reporter, 1957-59; San Juan Star, founding managing editor, 1959-61; writer, 1961-; State University of New York, instructor creative writing and journalism, 1974-82, professor of English, 1983-; Writers Institute, founder, 1983, executive director, 1984-; Cornell University, visiting professor of English, 1982-83; University of Oregon, Kritikos Professor, 2001-02. **Publications:** The Ink Truck (novel), 1969; Legs (novel), 1975; Billy Phelan's Greatest Game (novel), 1978; (contrib.) Gabriel Garcia Marquez, 1982; Ironweed (novel), 1983; O Albany!: Improbable City of Political Wizards, Fearless Ethnics, Spectacular Aristocrats, Splendid Nobodies, and Underrated Scoundrels (non-fiction), 1983; (with B. Kennedy) Charlie Malarkey and The Belley-Button Machine (children's book), 1986; Quinn's Book, 1988; Very Old Bones, 1992; Riding The Yellow Trolley Car (non-fiction), 1993; (with B. Kennedy) Charlie Malarkey and the Singing Moose, 1994; An Albany Trio: Three Novels from the Albany Cycle, 1996; The Flaming Corsage, 1996; Roscoe, 2002; Roscoe and Me: The Specific and The Impossible, 2003; Chango's beads and two-tone shoes, 2011. Contributor to journals. **Address:** New York State Writers Institute, State University of New York, SL 320, Science Library, 1400 Washington Ave., Albany, NY 12222-0001, U.S.A. **Online address:** writers@uamail.albany.edu

KENNEDY, **X. J.** American (born United States), b. 1929. **Genres:** Children's Fiction, Poetry, Literary Criticism And History, Translations. **Career:** University of Michigan, teaching fellow, 1956-60, instructor in English, 1960-62; University of North Carolina, lecturer in English, 1962-63; Paris Review, poetry editor, 1962-64; Tufts University, assistant professor, 1963-67, associate professor, 1967-73, professor of English, 1973-79; Wellesley College, visiting lecturer, 1964; University of California, visiting lecturer, 1966-67, visiting professor, 1978; Counter/Measures, co-editor, 1972-74; Leeds University, Bruern fellow, 1974-75, visiting professor, 1978; Spectator Amateur Press Association, co-founder; University of Michigan, faculty; freelance writer, 1978-; Wellesley University, visiting professor. Writer. **Publications:** Nude Descending a Staircase, 1961, 2nd ed., 1994; An Introduction to Poetry, 1966, (with D. Gioia) 12th ed., 2007; Growing into Love, 1969; Breaking and Entering, 1972; Emily Dickinson in Southern California, 1974; One Winter Night in August, 1975; (with J.E. Camp and K. Waldrop) Three Tenors, One Vehicle, 1975; An Introduction to Fiction, 1976, (with D. Gioia) 10th ed., 2007; Literature, 1976, (with D. Gioia) 9th ed., 2005; The Phantom Ice Cream Man, 1979; Did Adam Name the Vinegarroon?, 1982; (with D.M. Kennedy) Knock at a Star: A Child's Introduction to Poetry, 1982, rev. ed., 1999; (with D.M. Kennedy) The Bedford Reader, 1982, (with D.M. Kennedy and J.E. Aaron) 11th ed., 2011; Missing Link, 1983; French Leave: Translations, 1984; Hangover Mass, 1984; The Forgetful Wishing Well: Poems for Young People,

1985; Cross Ties: Selected Poems, 1985; Brats, 1986; (with D.M. Kennedy) The Bedford Guide for College Writers, 1987, (with D.M. Kennedy, M.F. Muth and S.A. Holladay) 7th ed., 2005; Ghastlies, Goops and Pincushions, 1989; Winter Thunder, 1990; Fresh Brats, 1990; The Kite That Braved Old Orchard Beach, 1991; (with D.M. Kennedy) Talking Like the Rain: A First Book of Poetry, 1992; The Beasts of Bethlehem, 1992; Dark Horses: New Poems, 1992; Drat These Brats!, 1993; The Minimus Poems, 1996; Uncle Switch, 1997; The Eagle as Wide as the World, 1997; Compact Bedford Guide for College Writers, 1997; Elympics, 1999; Elefantina's Dream, 2002; Exploding Gravy: Poems to make you Laugh, 2002; The Purpose of Time, 2002; The Lords of Misrule: Poems, 1992-2001, 2002; Exploding Gravy: Poems to Make You Laugh, 2002; (intro.) Cartwheel to the Moon: My Sicilian Childhood: Poems, 2003; Owlstone Crown, 2005; (with D. Gioia and M. Bauerlein) Handbook of Literary Terms, 2005, 2 nd ed., 2009; (with D. Gioia and M. Bauerlein) Longman Dictionary of Literary Terms: Vocabulary for the Informed Reader, 2006; (with D. Gioia) Backpack Literature: An Introduction to Fiction, Poetry, Drama, and Writing, 2006, 11th ed., 2010; (with D.M. Kennedy and M.F. Muth) Writing and Revising: A Portable Guide, 2007; Peeping Tom's Cabin: Comic Verse, 1928-2008, 2007; In a Prominent Bar in Secaucus: New and Selected Poems, 1955-2007, 2007; (with D.M. Kennedy and J.E. Aaron) Brief Bedford Reader, 2008, 11th ed., 2011; EDITOR: (with J.E. Camp) Mark Twain's Frontier, 1963; (with J.E. Camp and K. Waldrop) Pegasus Descending, 1971, 2nd ed., 2004; Messages: A Thematic Anthology of Poetry, 1973; Tygers of Wrath, 1981; (with D.M. Kennedy and J.E. Aaron) Notes and Resources for Teaching the Bedford Reader, 1997; (with D.M. Kennedy and M.F. Muth) Bedford Guide for College Writers with Reader, Research Manual and Handbook, 2007, 9th ed., 2010; (trans. and contrib.) G. Apollinaire, The Bestiary, or, Procession of Orpheus, 2011. Contributor to periodicals. **Address:** 22 Revere St., Lexington, MA 02420-4424, U.S.A.

KENNEDY-ANDREWS, Elmer. *See* **ANDREWS, Elmer.**

KENNEFICK, Daniel. American/Irish (born Ireland), b. 1966. **Genres:** Sciences, History, Biography. **Career:** University College Cork, instructor, 1985-89; California Institute of Technology, teaching assistant for freshman physics lab, 1989-96, faculty of history of science course on Einstein and the history of modern physics, 2001-03, senior research fellow, 2001-04; Cardiff University, research associate, 1997-2000; University of Arkansas, Department of Physics, visiting assistant professor, 2000, assistant professor, 2004-, faculty of physics and human affairs, 2004, physics faculty, 2004-08; Princeton University Press, Einstein Papers Project, editor, 2004-. **Publications:** Traveling at the Speed of Thought: Einstein and the Quest for Gravitational Waves, 2007. **Address:** Arkansas Center for Space & Planetary Sciences, University of Arkansas, 202 Old Museum Bldg., Fayetteville, AZ 72701, U.S.A. **Online address:** danielk@uark.edu

KENNELL, Nigel M. Canadian/British (born England), b. 1955. **Genres:** Classics, History. **Career:** Brock University, lecturer in classics, 1985-86; Memorial University, assistant professor, 1986-92, associate professor of classics, 1992-; Institute for Advanced Study, research assistant, 1992-93; College de France, research associate, 1993; Canadian Archaeological Institute, director, 2000-02. Writer. **Publications:** The Gymnasium of Virtue: Education & Culture in Ancient Sparta, 1995; Spartans: A New History, 2010. Contributor to periodicals. **Address:** Department of Classics, Memorial University of Newfoundland, St. John's, NL A1C 5S7, Canada. **Online address:** nkennell@morgan.ucs.mun.ca

KENNELLY, (Timothy) Brendan. Irish (born Ireland), b. 1936. **Genres:** Novels, Poetry, Literary Criticism And History. **Career:** Trinity College, junior lecturer, 1963-66, lecturer, 1966-69, associate professor, 1969-73, Department of English, chairman, 1973-76, professor of modern literature, 1973-2005, professor emeritus, 2005; Barnard College, Guildersleeve professor, 1971; Swarthmore College, Cornell professor of literature, 1971-72; Boston College, Burns visiting professor, 2007. Writer. **Publications:** (With R. Holzapfel) Cast a Cold Eye, 1959; (with R. Holzapfel) The Rain, the Moon, 1961; (with R. Holzapfel) The Dark about Our Loves, 1962; (with R. Holzapfel) Green Townlands: Poems, 1963; Let Fall No Burning Leaf, 1963; The Crooked Cross (novel), 1963; My Dark Fathers, 1964; Up and At It, 1965; Collection One: Getting Up Early, 1966; Good Souls to Survive: Poems, 1967; The Florentines (novel), 1967; Dream of a Black Fox, 1968; A Drinking Cup: Poems from the Irish, 1970; Bread, 1971; Selected Poems, 1972; Salvation, The Stranger, 1972; Love Cry, 1972; The Voices: A Sequence of Poems, 1973; A Kind of Trust, 1975; New and Selected Poems, 1976; Island-

man: A Poem, 1977; Shelley in Dublin, 1977; The Visitor: Poems, 1978; A Small Light: Ten Songs of OConnor of Carrigafoyle, 1979; In Spite of the Wise, 1979; The Boats Are Home, 1980; The House That Jack Didn't Build: Poems, 1982; Cromwell: A Poem, 1983; Moloney Up and at It, 1984; Selected Poems, 1985; Real Ireland: People & Landscape: Photographs, 1988; (contrib.) Love of Ireland: Poems From The Irish, 1989; (with T. Kinsella and J. Montague) Myth, History, and Literary Tradition, 1989; A Time for Voices: Selected Poems 1960-1990, 1990; The Book of Judas: A Poem, 1991; Euripides Medea: A New Version, 1991; Breathing Spaces: Early Poems, 1992; Joycechoyce: The Poems in Verse and Prose of James Joyce, 1992; Euripides The Trojan Women, 1993; Journey into Joy: Selected Prose, 1994; Irelands Women: Writings Past and Present, 1994; Poetry My Arse: A Poem, 1995; Sophocles Antigone: A New Version, 1996; Blood Wedding: (Bodas de sangre), 1996; Words for Women (poems), 1997; Singing Tree, 1998; Man Made of Rain, 1998; Begin, 1999; Glimpses, 2001; Little Book of Judas, 2002; Between Innocence and Peace, 2002; Martial Art, 2003; Familiar Strangers: New & Selected Poems, 1960-2004, 2004; Now, 2006; When Then Is Now: Three Greek Tragedies, 2006; Reservoir Voices, 2009; Essential Brendan Kennelly, 2011. EDITOR: (intro.) The Penguin Book of Irish Verse, 1970, 2nd ed., 1981; Ireland Past and Present, 1986; Treasury of Irish Religious Verse, 1986; Landmarks of Irish Drama, 1988; Between Innocence and Peace: Favourite Poems of Ireland, 1993; (with K. Donovan and Jeffares) Irelands Women: Writings Past and Present, 1994; (with K. Donovan) Dublines, 1996. Contributor to periodicals. **Address:** Department of English, Trinity College, Dublin, 2, Ireland. **Online address:** tknnelly@tcd.ie

KENNEMORE, Tim. British (born England), b. 1957. **Genres:** Novellas/ Short Stories, Children's Fiction, Young Adult Fiction, Sports/Fitness, Science Fiction/Fantasy, Literary Criticism And History. **Career:** Writer. **Publications:** The Middle of the Sandwich, 1981; The Fortunate Few, 1981; Wall of Words, 1982; Here Tomorrow, Gone Today, 1983; Changing Times, 1984; Alice's Birthday Pig, 1995; Alice's World Record, 1996; Circle of Doom, 2001; Sabine, 2003; Alice's Shooting Star, 2008. **Address:** Andersen Press Ltd., 20 Vauxhall Bridge Rd., London, GL SW1V 2SA, England.

KENNER, Julie. American (born United States) **Genres:** Novels, Horror. **Career:** Writer, 2004-. Attorney. **Publications:** Nobody Does It Better, 2000; The Cat's Fancy, 2000; Reckless, 2000; Undercover Lovers, 2002; Silent Desires, 2003; Silent Confessions, 2003; (contrib.) Manhunting in Mississippi, 2003; Nobody but You, 2003; The Spy Who Loves Me, 2004; Stolen Kisses, 2004; (with S. Forster) Beyond Suspicion, 2004; (with S. Kearney and J.E. Leto) Essence of Midnight, 2004; First Love, 2005; (with J. D'Allesandro and S. Kearney) The Hope Chest, 2005; Night Moves, 2005; The Perfect Score, 2006; (with N. Warren and J. Leigh) Perfect Timing, 2006; (with K. O'Reilly and D. Davis) Hell with the Ladies, 2006; (with K. O'Reilly and D. Davis) Hell on Heels, 2007; (with J. Edwards and S. Robar) Fendi, Ferragamo and Fangs, 2007; (with N. Warren and Jo Leigh) Night We Met, 2007; The Good Ghouls' Guide to Getting Even, 2007; Good Ghouls Do, 2007; (co-author) Everything I Needed to Know About Being a Girl I Learned from Judy Blume, 2007; Tainted, 2009; Torn, 2009; Starstruck, 2009; (with K. Anders and J. Monroe) Endless Summer, 2009; (with K. O'Reilly) Just Fooling Around, 2010; Turned, 2010; Moonstruck, 2010; Holiday Hideout, 2011. PROTECTOR SERIES: Aphrodite's Kiss, 2001; Aphrodite's Passion, 2002; Aphrodite's Secret, 2003; Aphrodite's Flame, 2004. DEMON-HUNTING SOCCER MOM SERIES: Carpe Demon: Adventures of a Demon-Hunting Soccer Mom, 2005; California Demon: The Secret Life of a Demon-Hunting Soccer Mom, 2006; Demons Are Forever: Confessions of a Demon-Hunting Soccer Mom, 2007; Deja Demon: The Days and Nights of a Demon-hunting Soccer Mom, 2008; Demon Ex Machina: Tales of a Demon-hunting Soccer Mom, 2009. CODE-BREAKING SERIES: The Givenchy Code, 2005; The Manolo Matrix, 2006; The Prada Paradox, 2007. **Address:** PO Box 923, Goshen, IN 46527-0923, U.S.A. **Online address:** juliekenner@gmail.com

KENNEY, Catherine (McGehee). American (born United States), b. 1948. **Genres:** Novels, Literary Criticism And History, Women's Studies And Issues. **Career:** Thornton Community College, lecturer in English, 1974-76; Harper College, lecturer, 1974-75; Mundelein College, assistant professor, 1976-81, chair of department, 1978-85, associate professor of English, 1981-91; Newberry Library, Lyceum Seminars, director, 1981-; American National Bank, consultant. Writer. **Publications:** Thurber's Anatomy of Confusion, 1984; The Remarkable Case of Dorothy L. Sayers, 1990. Contributor of articles to journals, magazines and newspapers. **Address:** 228 Stanley Ave., Park Ridge, IL 60068-4942, U.S.A.

KENNEY, Charles. American (born United States), b. 1950. **Genres:** Documentaries/Reportage, Novels, Mystery/Crime/Suspense, Theology/Religion. **Career:** Boston Globe, reporter and editor, 1978-94; Blue Cross Blue Shield, consultant. **Publications:** (With R.L. Turner) Dukakis: An American Odyssey, 1988; Riding the Runaway Horse: The Rise and Decline of Wang Labs, 1992; Hammurabi's Code (novel), 1995 as Code of Vengeance, 1997; The Son of John Devlin (novel), 1999; John F. Kennedy: The Presidential Portfolio: History as Told Through the Collection of the John F. Kennedy Library and Museum, 2000; The Last Man (novel), 2001; (with J.E. Muller) Keep the Faith, Change the Church: The Battle by Catholics for the Soul of Their Church, 2004; Rescue Men, 2007; The Best Practice: How the New Quality Movement is Transforming Medicine, 2008; A Memoir of Michael William Balfe, 2010; The Gates of the East, 2010; Transforming Health Care: Virginia Mason Medical Center's Pursuit of the Perfect Patient Experience, 2011. Contributor to books and periodicals. **Address:** c/o Phillipa Brophy, Sterling Lord Literistic Inc., 65 Bleecker St., New York, NY 10012-2420, U.S.A.

KENNEY, Jeffrey T. American (born United States), b. 1954. **Genres:** Theology/Religion, Politics/Government, Sociology. **Career:** DePauw University, Nancy Shelly Schaenen fellow, 2002-05, professor of religious studies, university professor, 2010-. Writer. **Publications:** Muslim Rebels: Kharijites and the Politics of Extremism in Egypt, 2006. **Address:** Department of Religious Studies, Emison Museum, DePauw University, 204 E Seminary St., PO Box 37, Greencastle, IN 46135-0037, U.S.A. **Online address:** jkenney@depauw.edu

KENNEY, Michael. (Michael C. Kenney). American (born United States), b. 1967. **Genres:** Politics/Government, History, Military/Defense/Arms Control. **Career:** Pennsylvania State University, assistant professor of public policy and political science; Stanford University, CISAC (Center for International Security and Cooperation), postdoctoral fellow in organizational learning for homeland security, 2004-05. Political scientist and writer. **Publications:** (ed. with M.L. Brown and M. Zarkin) Organizational Learning in the Global Context, 2006; From Pablo to Osama: Trafficking and Terrorist Networks, Government Bureaucracies, and Competitive Adaptation, 2007. Contributor to books and periodicals. **Address:** Pennsylvania State University, W-160 G Olmsted Bldg., 777 W Harrisburg Pke., Middletown, PA 17057-4846, U.S.A. **Online address:** mck14@psu.edu

KENNEY, Michael C. See **KENNEY, Michael.**

KENNEY, Padraic (Jeremiah). American (born United States), b. 1963. **Genres:** Law, History, Humanities. **Career:** University of Colorado, Department of History, assistant professor, 1992-99, associate professor, 1999-2003, professor, 2003-, associate chair, Undergraduate Studies, director; Indiana University, Department of History, professor. Writer. **Publications:** A Carnival of Revolution: Central Europe, 1989; (editor, with Gerd-Rainer Horn) Transnational Moments of Change: Europe 1945, 1968, 1989; Rebuilding Poland: Workers and Communists, 1945-1950, 1997; Carnival of Revolution-Central Europe 1989, 2002; (ed. with G. Horn) Transnational Moments of Change: Europe 1945, 1968, 1989, 2004; Rewolucyjny Karnawal: Europa Srodkowa 1989, 2005; (with M.P. Friedman) Partisan Histories: The Past in Contemporary Global Politics, 2005; Burdens of History: Eastern Europe Since 1989, 2006; 1989: Democratic Revolutions at the Cold War's End: A Brief History with Documents, 2009. Contributor of articles to journals. **Address:** Department of History, Indiana University, Rm. 716, Ballantine Hall, 1020 E Kirkwood Ave., Bloomington, IN 47405-7103, U.S.A. **Online address:** pjkenney@indiana.edu

KENNEY, Richard (L.). American (born United States), b. 1948. **Genres:** Poetry. **Career:** University of Washington, assistant professor of English, 1989-, professor of English. Writer. **Publications:** The Evolution of the Flightless Bird (poetry), 1984; Orrery (poetry), 1985; The Invention of the Zero, (poetry), 1993; One-Strand River, 2008. **Address:** Department of English, University of Washington, Rm. PDL B-437, PO Box 354330, Seattle, WA 98195-4330, U.S.A. **Online address:** rk@u.washington.edu

KENNEY, William Howland. American (born United States), b. 1940. **Genres:** Music, History, Literary Criticism And History, Humor/Satire. **Career:** Kent State University, assistant professor, 1966-, associate professor,

professor of American history and studies, through 1976, instructor, professor emeritus of American history and studies, 1976-. Writer. **Publications:** Chicago Jazz: A Cultural History, 1904-1930, 1993; Recorded Music in American Life: The Phonograph and Popular Memory, 1890-1945, 1999; Jazz on the River, 2005. EDITOR: Laughter in the Wilderness: Early American Humor to 1783, 1976; (with S. Deveaux) The Music of James Scott, 1993. Contributor to books and journals. **Address:** Department of History, Kent State University, 305 Bowman Hall, PO Box 5190, Kent, OH 44242-0001, U.S.A. **Online address:** wkenney@kent.edu

KENNY, Anthony (John Patrick). British (born England), b. 1931. **Genres:** Intellectual History, Philosophy, Business/Trade/Industry. **Career:** Roman Catholic church, curate, 1959-63; University of Liverpool, assistant lecturer, 1961-63; University of Oxford, Exeter College, lecturer, 1963-64; Trinity College, lecturer, 1963-64; Balliol College, fellow, 1964-78, Wilde lecturer on Natural Religion, 1969-72, senior tutor, 1971-72, 1976-78, master, 1978-89, honorary fellow, pro-vice-chancellor for development, 1984-2001, retired, 2001; University of Edinburgh, Joint Gifford lecturer, 1972-73; Oxford Magazine, editor, 1972-73; University Edinburgh, Gifford lecturer, 1972-73; University Cambridge, Stanton lecturer, 1980-83; Bodleian Library, curator, 1985-88; delegate; University of Glasgow, Gifford lecturer, 1988; Rhodes House, warden, 1989-2002; British Academy, president, 1989-93; British Library, chairman, 1993-97; Harris Manchester College, honorary fellow, 1996-; University of London, School of Advanced Study, 2002, senior distinguished fellow, 2002-03; Royal Institute of Philosophy, president; Stanford University, visiting professor; Rockefeller University, visiting professor; University of Chicago, visiting professor; University of Washington, visiting professor; University of Michigan, visiting professor; Cornell University, visiting professor; St John's College, fellow emeritus. **Publications:** Action, Emotion and Will, 1963; Descartes, 1968; Aquinas, 1969; The Five Ways, 1969; (trans.) Descartes: Philosophical Letters, 1969; (ed. with P.T. Geach as A.J.P. Kenny) Objects of Thought, 1971; (co-author) The Nature of the Mind, 1972; The Development of Mind, 1973; Wittgenstein, 1973; Will, Freedom and Power, 1975; The Aristotelian Ethics, 1978; Freewill and Responsibility, 1978; Aristotle's Theory of the Will, 1979; The God of the Philosophers, 1979; Aquinas, 1980; Thomas More, 1983; Faith and Reason, 1983; Wyclif, 1985; The Legacy of Wittgenstein, 1984; The Ivory Tower, 1985; The Logic of Deterrence, 1985; Path From Rome, 1985; (ed. And intro.) Rationalism, Empiricism and Idealism, 1986; A Stylometric Study of the New Testament, 1986; The Road to Hillsborough, 1986; Reason and Religion, 1987; The Heritage of Wisdom, 1987; God and Two Poets, 1988; The Self, 1988; The Metaphysics of Mind, 1989; Managing Software: The Businessman's Guide to Software Development, 1989; The Oxford Diaries of Arthur Hugh Clough, 1990; Aristotle on the Perfect Life, 1992; What is Faith?: Essays in the Philosophy of Religion, 1992; Aquinas on Mind, 1993; Frege, 1995; A Life in Oxford, 1997; A Brief History of Western Philosophy, 1998; Essays on the Aristotelian Tradition, 2001; The History of the Rhodes Trust, 1902-1999, 2001; Aquinas on Being, 2002; The Unknown God, 2004; Ancient Philosophy: A New History of Western Philosophy, 2004; Arthur Hugh Clough: A Poet's Life, 2005; Medieval Philosophy, 2005; The Unknown God, 2004; (with C. Kenny) Life, Liberty and the Pursuit of Utility, 2006; An Illustrated Brief History of Western Philosophy, 2006; What I Believe, 2006; The Rise of Modern Philosophy, 2006; The Wittgenstein Reader, 2nd ed., 2006; Philosophy in the Modern World, 2007; Can Oxford be Improved?, 2007; From Empedocles to Wittgenstein: Historical Essays in Philosophy, 2008. **Address:** St John's College, St. Giles, Oxford, OX OX1 3JP, England.

KENNY, Lorraine Delia. American (born United States), b. 1961. **Genres:** Social Sciences, Women's Studies And Issues, Human Relations/Parenting. **Career:** Visual Studies Workshop, intern, 1984-85, assistant editor, 1985-86, subscriptions coordinator, 1985-87, associate editor, 1987-89; Afterimage, assistant editor, 1985-86, associate editor, 1987-89; University of California, instructor, 1992, 1993; Socialist Review, managing editor, 1993; National Council for Research on Women, coordinating editor, 1994-96; freelance copy editor and proofreader, 1996-97; Sarah Lawrence College, anthropology faculty, 1997-2000; LaGuardia Community College, adjunct assistant professor, 1996, 1997; New School for Social Research, Eugene Lang College, adjunct assistant professor, 1997; American Civil Liberties Union, Reproductive Freedom Project, public education coordinator, 2000-. Writer. **Publications:** Daughters of Suburbia: Growing Up White, Middle Class, and Female, 2000. Contributor of articles to books and periodicals. **Address:** American Civil Liberties Union, 125 Broad St., 18th Fl., New York, NY 10004, U.S.A. **Online address:** lkenny@aclu.org

KENNY, Maurice (Francis). American (born United States), b. 1929. **Genres:** Novellas/Short Stories, Poetry, Literary Criticism And History. **Career:** Paul Smith's College, associate professor; University of Victoria, faculty; North Country Community College, faculty; University of Oklahoma, visiting professor; State University of New York, writer-in-residence. **Publications:** Dead Letters Sent, and Other Poems, 1958; With Love to Lesbia, 1959; And Grieve, Lesbia; Poems, 1960; North: Poems of Home, 1977; Dancing Back Strong the Nation: Poems, 1979; I Am the Sun: A Lakota Chant, 1979; Only as Far as Brooklyn, 1979; Kneading the Blood, 1981, rev. ed., 1987; Blackrobe: Isaac Jogues, b. March 11, 1607, d. October 18, 1646: Poems, 1982; The Smell of Slaughter, 1982; Boston Tea Party, 1982; The Mama Poems, 1984; Rain and Other Fictions (short stories), 1985, rev. ed., 1990; Is Summer This Bear, 1985; Between Two Rivers: Selected Poems, 1987; Humors and/or Not So Humorous, 1987; Greyhounding This America: Poems and Dialog, 1988; Selections: Poems, 1988; The Short and the Long of It, 1990; Last Mornings in Brooklyn (chapbook), 1991; Tekonwatonti: Molly Brant 1735-1795: Poems of War, 1992, rev. ed., 2002; On Second Thought, 1995; Backward to Forward (essay), 1997; Tortured Skins and Other Fictions (short stories), 2000; In the Time of the Present (poetry), 2000; Carving Hawk: New & Selected Poems, 1953-2000, 2002. EDITOR: (and intro.) Wounds beneath the Flesh, 1983; (with J. Bruchac and Karoniaktatie) New Voices from the Longhouse, 1989; Stories for a Winter's Night: Native American Fictions (short stories), 2000; Connotations, 2008; Feeding Bears, 2010; (with N. Burlick) Being There, North Country Essays, 2012. Contributor to periodicals. **Address:** State University of New York, 44 Pierrepont Ave., Potsdam, NY 13676-2200, U.S.A. **Online address:** kennymf@potsdam.edu

KENRICK, Tony. American/Australian (born Australia), b. 1935. **Genres:** Mystery/Crime/Suspense, Novels, Film, Literary Criticism And History. **Career:** Farmer's Advertising Department, associate, 1953-56; Notley's, copywriter, 1956-57; McClaren's, advertising copywriter, 1957-60; Doyle Dane Bernbach, advertising copywriter, 1960-62; Johnson & Lewis, advertising copywriter, 1962-65; C.D.P, advertising copywriter, 1968-72; freelance writer, 1972-. **Publications:** The Only Good Body's a Dead One, 1970; A Tough One to Lose, 1972; Two for the Price of One, 1974; Stealing Lillian, 1975 in UK as The Kidnap Kid, 1976; The Seven Day Soldiers, 1976; The Chicago Girl, 1976; Two Lucky People, 1978; The Night-time Guy, 1979; The 81st Site, 1980; Faraday's Flowers, 1985; China White, 1986; Neon Tough, 1988; Glitterbug, 1991; (with D. Lemoine) Implants d'enfer, 1993; Up Against the House, 1995. **Address:** Bill Berger Associates Inc., 535 E 72nd St., Ste. 2-a, New York, NY 10021, U.S.A.

KENSLEA, Timothy. American (born United States), b. 1954. **Genres:** Biography, History, Women's Studies And Issues, Autobiography/Memoirs, Social Sciences. **Career:** Little, Brown & Co., editor, 1978-82; Ginn & Co. (became Silver Burdett Ginn), senior editor, 1984-87, managing editor, 1987-88; Norwell High School, history and English teacher, 1995-2006; Needham High School, history teacher, 2006-. Historian. **Publications:** The Sedgwicks in Love: Courtship, Engagement, and Marriage in the Early Republic, 2006. **Address:** Needham High School, 609 Webster St., Needham, MA 02494-1111, U.S.A. **Online address:** timkens@aya.yale.edu

KENT, Alexander. See REEMAN, Douglas (Edward).

KENT, Carol. American (born United States), b. 1947?. **Genres:** How-to Books, inspirational/Motivational Literature, Human Relations/Parenting, Self Help, Speech/Rhetoric, Theology/Religion, Autobiography/Memoirs, E-books, Illustrations. **Career:** Public speaker and author; Speak up Speaker Services, founder and president; Speak Up for Hope, founder. **Publications:** Speak up with Confidence!: A Step-by-Step Guide to Successful Public Speaking, 1987; Secret Passions of the Christian Woman, 1990; Tame Your Fears and Transform Them into Faith, Confidence and Action: Women Reveal What They Fear Most, 1993; Tame Your Fears and Transform Them into Faith, Confidence and Action: A Small Group Discussion Guide, 1994; Detours, Tow Trucks and Angels in Disguise: Finding Humor and Hope in Unexpected Places, 1996; Mothers Have Angel Wings: A Tribute to the Tears and Triumphs of Being a Mom, 1997; Speak up with confidence: A Step-by-Step Guide for Speakers and Leaders, 1997; Becoming a Woman of Influence: Making a Lasting Impact on Others, 2002; Secret Longings of the Heart: Overcoming Deep Disappointment and Unfulfilled Expectations, 2003; When I Lay My Isaac Down: Unshakable Faith in Unthinkable Circumstances, 2004; (ed.) Kisses of Sunshine for Sisters, 2005; (ed. with T. Wells) Kisses of Sunshine for Women, 2005; (with G. Malone) Kisses of Sunshine for Grand-

mas; (with V. Caruana) Kisses of Sunshine for Teachers; (ed.) Kisses of Sunsine for Moms; A New Kind of Normal, 2007; Between a Rock and a Grace Place: Divine Surprises in the Tight Spots of Life, 2010; (with J.A. Dimkoff) Miracle on Hope Hill: and Other True Stories of God's Love, 2011. Contributor to periodicals. **Address:** Speak Up Speaker Services, 3141 Winged Foot Dr., Lakeland, FL 33803, U.S.A. **Online address:** speakupinc@aol.coms

KENT, Christobel. British (born England), b. 1962. **Genres:** Novels. **Career:** Andre Deutsch Publishing Agency, publicity director. Writer and educator. **Publications:** NOVELS: A Party in San Niccolo, 2003; Late Season, 2004; The Summer House, 2005; A Florentine Revenge, 2006; A Murder in Tuscany, 2011. SANDRO CELLINI SERIES: NOVELS: A Time of Mourning, 2009 in US as The Drowning River: A Mystery in Florence, 2010; A Fine and Private Place, 2010. **Address:** c/o Victoria Hobbs, A M Heath & Company Ltd., 6 Warwick Ct., Holborn, London, GL WC1R 5DJ, England.

KENT, Cromwell. See SPARSHOTT, Francis (Edward).

KENT, Eliza F. American (born United States), b. 1966. **Genres:** Women's Studies And Issues, History, Theology/Religion. **Career:** American Theological Library Association, index analyst, 2001-02; Colgate University, Department of Philosophy and Religion, assistant professor, associate professor, 2003-. Writer. **Publications:** Converting Women: Gender and Protestant Christianity in Colonial South India, 2004. Contributor to journals. **Address:** Colgate University, 13 Oak Dr., Hamilton, NY 13346-1338, U.S.A. **Online address:** ekent@mail.colgate.edu

KENT, Gordon. See CAMERON, Christian.

KENT, Homer Austin. American (born United States), b. 1926. **Genres:** Theology/Religion, History. **Career:** Grace Theological Seminary and Grace College, professor of Greek and New Testament, 1949-99, dean, 1962-76, president, 1976-86, now retired. Writer. **Publications:** The Pastoral Epistles: Studies in 1 and 2 Timothy and Titus, 1958, rev. ed., 1982; Ephesians: The Glory of the Church: Studies in Ephesians, 1971, rev. ed., 2005; Jerusalem to Rome, 1972; Epistle to the Hebrews: An Expository Commentary, 1972; Light in the Darkness: Studies in the Gospel of John, 1974, 2nd ed., 2005; The Freedom of God's Sons, 1976; Treasures of Wisdom: Studies in Colossians & Philemon, 1978, rev. ed., 2006; A Heart Opened Wide: Studies in 2 Corinthians, 1982, rev. ed., 2006; Faith That Works: Studies in the Epistle of James, 1986, rev. ed., 2005; Mark: The Beginning of the Gospel of Jesus Christ, 2005. **Address:** Zondervan, 5300 Patterson SE, Grand Rapids, MI 49530, U.S.A.

KENT, James M. American (born United States), b. 1956. **Genres:** Marine Sciences/Oceanography, Engineering, Environmental Sciences/Ecology, Sciences, Earth Sciences, Architecture, Natural History, Sociology, Sociology. **Career:** The Daily News, editor, 1979-80; Litchfield County Times, reporter, 1980-82; The Advocate, reporter, 1982-83; Patient Care, associate editor, 1983-85; freelance writer, 1985-; Schlumberger-Doll Research, Oilfield Review, senior editor, 1985-97; Schlumberger Ltd., editor, 1997-2000, executive editor, 1998-2000; The Thomson Corp., director of communications, 2000-02; Woods Hole Oceanogrpahic Institution, director of communications, 2002-; Thornton Tomasetti, chief marketing and communications officer. **Publications:** (With P.C. Patton) A Moveable Shore: The Fate of the Connecticut Coast, 1992. Contributor to periodicals. **Address:** Thornton Tomasetti, 51 Madison Ave., New York, NY 10010, U.S.A. **Online address:** jimkent99@hotmail.com

KENT, Joseph (P.). American (born United States), b. 1940. **Genres:** Poetry. **Career:** Writer. **Publications:** POETRY: White Wind, 1989; Streams, 1996; Flowers of the Sun, 2007. Contributor to books and periodicals. **Address:** PO Box 640545, San Francisco, CA 94109, U.S.A. **Online address:** sunli8@msn.com

KENT, Kathleen. American (born United States), b. 1953?. **Genres:** Novels. **Career:** Writer. **Publications:** The Heretic's Daughter: A Novel, 2008. **Address:** Dallas, TX , U.S.A. **Online address:** hereticsdaughter@yahoo.com

KENT, Peter C. Canadian (born Canada), b. 1938. **Genres:** History, Theology/Religion. **Career:** Oromocto School Board, teacher, 1961-62; Protestant School Board of Greater Montreal, teacher, 1962-65; University of New

Brunswick, lecturer, 1965-80, professor of history, chair of history department, 1980-86, dean of faculty of arts, 1988-89, professor and dean emeritus, 1989-2005, professor emeritus in history and dean emeritus, 2005-. Writer. **Publications:** The Pope and the Duce: The International Impact of the Lateran Agreements, 1981; (ed. with J.F. Pollard) Papal Diplomacy in the Modern Age, 1994; The Lonely Cold War of Pope Pius XII: The Roman Catholic Church and the Division of Europe, 1943-1950, 2002. Contributor to periodicals. **Address:** Department of History, University of New Brunswick, PO Box 4400, Fredericton, NB E3B 5A3, Canada. **Online address:** kent@unb.ca

KENT, Richard G. American (born United States), b. 1951. **Genres:** Law, Sports/Fitness. **Career:** Meyers, Breiner and Kent, attorney and partner. Writer. **Publications:** (With J. Steinbreder) Fighting for Your Children: A Father's Guide to Custody, 1998; (ed.) Inside Women's College Basketball: Anatomy of a Season, 2000, rev. ed. as Inside Women's College Basketball: Anatomy of Two Seasons, 2002; (with J. Steinbreder) Solomon's Choice: A Guide to Custody for Ex-Husbands, Spurned Partners and Forgotten Grandparents, 2006. **Address:** Meyers Breiner & Kent, L.L.P., 55 Walls Dr., Ste. 204, Fairfield, CT 06824, U.S.A. **Online address:** rkent@mbnllp.com

KENT, Timothy J. American/French/Greek (born Greece), b. 1949. **Genres:** Local History/Rural Topics, History, Travel/Exploration. **Career:** Silver Fox Enterprises, writer and publisher. **Publications:** Birchbark Canoes of the Fur Trade, 2 vols., 1997; Tahquamenon Tales: Experiences of an Early French Trader and His Native Family, 1998; Ft. Pontchartrain at Detroit: A Guide to the Daily Lives of Fur Traders, Military Personnel, Settlers and Missionaries at French Posts, 2 vols., 2001; Paddling Across the Peninsula: An Important Cross-Michigan Canoe Route During the French Regime, 2003; Rendezvous at the Straits: Fur Trade and Military Activity at Fort de Buade and Fort Michilimackinac, 1669-1781, 2 vols., 2004; Within the Sphere of the Master: My Recollections as a Student and Long Time Colleague of Adolph Herseth, Trumpeter Supreme of the Chicago Symphony Orchestra, 2006; A Modern-Day Voyageur Family; Paddling the 3000 Mile Fur Trade Canoe Route Across the U.S. and Canada, 2009. **Address:** Silver Fox Enterprises, 11504 U.S. 23 S, PO Box 176, Ossineke, MI 49766, U.S.A.

KENTFIELD, John A. C. *See* **KENTFIELD, J(ohn) A(lan) C.**

KENTFIELD, J(ohn) A(lan) C. (John A. C. Kentfield). Canadian/British (born England), b. 1930. **Genres:** Engineering, Sciences, Earth Sciences. **Career:** C.V.A. Kearney and Trecker Ltd., trainee, 1950-52; Ricardo and Company Ltd., assistant tester, 1952-56; University of London, Imperial College of Science and Technology, assistant lecturer in mechanical engineering, 1952-53, lecturer in mechanical engineering, 1966-70; Curtiss-Wright Corp., project engineer, 1963-66; University of Calgary, associate professor, 1970-78, professor of mechanical engineering, 1978-, Killam resident fellow, 1980, now professor emeritus of mechanical and manufacturing engineering; Swiss Federal Institute of Technology, visiting professor, 1974-75; Naval Postgraduate School, visiting professor, 1990. Writer. **Publications:** (As John A.C. Kentfield) Nonsteady, One-Dimensional, Internal, Compressible Flows, 1993; (as J.A.C. Kentfield) The Fundamentals of Wind-Driven Water Pumpers, 1996. Contributor to scientific journals. **Address:** Department of Mechanical Engineering, University of Calgary, 2500 University Dr. NW, Calgary, AB T2N 1N4, Canada.

KENTON, Warren. (Zev ben Shimon Halevi). British (born England), b. 1933. **Genres:** Novels, Paranormal, Theatre, Theology/Religion, Young Adult Fiction. **Career:** Royal Academy of Dramatic Art, lecturer, 1963-78; Architectural Association, School of Architecture, tutor, 1966-71; Wrekin Trust, lecturer; Temenos Academy, fellow; International Kabbalah Society, principal tutor, 1971-, director of tutors. Freelance writer. **Publications:** Stage Properties and How to Make Them, 1964, 2nd ed., 1978; As Above So Below: A Study in Cosmic Progression, 1969; Introducing Stagecraft in UK as The Play Begins: A Documentary-Novel Upon The Mounting of a Play, 1971; Astrology: The Celestial Mirror, 1974. AS Z'EV BEN SHIMON HALEVI: An Introduction to the Cabala: Tree of Life in UK as Tree of Life: An Introduction to the Cabala, 1972; Adam and the Kabbalistic Tree, 1974; The Way of Kabbalah, 1976; Kabbalah: Tradition of Hidden Knowledge, 1979; Kabbalah and Exodus, 1980; The Work of the Kabbalist, 1984; The School of Kabbalah, 1985; Kabbalah and Psychology, 1986; The Anointed: A Kabbalistic Novel, 1987; A Kabbalistic Universe, 1988; Kabbalah: The Divine Plan, 1996; The Anointed: A Kabbalistic Novel: A Story Of Spiritual Courage Against The Inquisition, 2001. OTHERS: The Anatomy of Fate: Kabbalistic Astrology,

1978; Astrology and Kabbalah, 2001. **Address:** Kabbalah Society, 56 Torbay Rd., London, GL NW6 7DZ, England.

KENWARD, Jean. British (born England), b. 1920. **Genres:** Children's Fiction, Poetry, Novellas/Short Stories, Science Fiction/Fantasy, Literary Criticism And History. **Career:** Harrow School of Art, part-time lecturer in creative writing, 1969-. Writer. **Publications:** Rain: A Volume of Poems by Jean Kenward, 1946; Rain: A Flight of Words, 1966; The Forest, 1972; Sing for Christmas, 1973; Old Mister Hotch Potch, 1974; Ragdolly Anna Stories, 1979; Clutterby Hogg, 1980; Theme and Variations, 1981; Three Cheers for Ragdolly Anna, 1985; (adaptor) Aesop's Fables, 1986; The Hotchpotch Horse, 1987; Ragdolly Anna's Circus, 1987; The Odd Job Man and the Thousand Mile Boots, 1988; A Kettle Full of Magic, 1988; Seasons, 1989; Ragdolly Anna's Treasure Hunt, 1989; A Book of Rhymes. **Address:** 15 Shire Ln., Chorley Wood, HF WD3 5NQ, England.

KENWORTHY, Brian J(ohn). Scottish/British (born England), b. 1920. **Genres:** Literary Criticism And History, Translations, Plays/Screenplays. **Career:** Teacher, 1943-46; Control Commission for Germany, interpreter and translator, 1946-47; University of Aberdeen, assistant lecturer, 1947-52, lecturer, 1952-68, senior lecturer, 1968-81. Writer. **Publications:** Georg Kaiser, 1957; (co-trans.) W. Braunbek, The Drama of the Atom, 1958; (co-author) A Manual of German Prose Composition for Advanced Students, 1966; (ed. and intro.) Die Koralle, Gas I and II, 1968; (ed.) Litauische Geschichten, 1971; (contrib. of trans.) Kaiser, Five Plays, 1971; (contrib., trans. and intro.) Kaiser, Plays, 1981; (ed.) George Kaiser: Plays, vol. II, 1982. Contributor to books and journals. **Address:** 22 Upper Cranbrook Rd., Redland, Bristol, SM BS6 7UN, England.

KENYON, Cory. *See* **THOMPSON, Vicki Lewis.**

KENYON, Nate. American (born United States) **Genres:** Novels, Horror, Novellas/Short Stories, Mystery/Crime/Suspense, Science Fiction/Fantasy. **Career:** Brookline Public Library, staff; Boston College Law School, director of marketing and communications. Writer. **Publications:** Bloodstone, 2006; The Reach, 2008; The Bone Factory, 2009; Prime, 2009; Sparrow Rock, 2010; When the Night Comes Down, 2010; Star Craft Ghost: Spectres, 2011; Diablo, forthcoming. **Address:** Boston College Law School, Stuart House M305, 885 Center St., Newton Center, MA 02459-1100, U.S.A. **Online address:** nate@natekenyon.com

KEOGH, Pamela Clarke. American/German (born Germany) **Genres:** Biography, Reference. **Career:** Spy Magazine, receptionist; Vogue Magazine, journalist; freelance writer, 1999-; US Magazine, editor. **Publications:** Audrey Style, 1999; Jackie Style, 2001; Elvis Presley: The Man the Life the Style, 2004; What Would Audrey Do?: Timeless Lessons for Living With Grace and Style, 2008; Are You a Jackie or a Marilyn?: Timeless Lessons on Love, Power and Style, 2010. Contributor to periodicals. **Address:** The Linda Chester Agency, 630 5th Ave., Ste. 2306, New York, NY 10111, U.S.A. **Online address:** info@pamelakeogh.com

KEOHANE, Dan. British/Irish (born Ireland), b. 1941. **Genres:** International Relations/Current Affairs, Politics/Government, History, Military/Defense/Arms Control, Social Sciences. **Career:** University of Keele, Department of International Relations, lecturer, 1977-95, senior lecturer, 1995-. Writer. **Publications:** Labour Party Defence Policy since 1945, 1993; (ed. with A. Danchev) International Perspectives on the Gulf Conflict, 1990-1991, 1994; Security in British Politics, 1945-99, 2000. **Address:** School of Politics, International Relations and the Environment, University of Keele, Keele, ST ST5 5BG, England. **Online address:** d.j.keohane@keele.ac.uk

KEOWN, Tim. American (born United States) **Genres:** Sports/Fitness, Young Adult Non-fiction, Biography. **Career:** San Francisco Chronicle, sports reporter; ESPN magazine, senior writer. **Publications:** Skyline: One Season One Team One City, 1994; (with D. Rodman) Bad as I Wanna Be, 1996; (with B. Waugh) Hunting the Jackal: A CIA Ground Soldiers Fifty-Year Career Hunting Americas Enemies, 2004; (with J. Hamilton) Beyond Belief: Finding the Strength to Come Back, 2010; (with R. Harrison) License to Pawn: Deals, Steals, and My Life at the Gold & Silver, 2011. **Address:** ESPN the Magazine, 19 E 34th St., New York, NY 10016-4304, U.S.A. **Online address:** tim.keown@espnmag.com

KEPLINGER, David. American (born United States), b. 1968. **Genres:** Poetry, Translations. **Career:** American University, Department of Literature, director of creative writing and associate professor of literature; Colorado State University, undergraduate creative writing program, director. Writer. **Publications:** POETRY: The Rose Inside: Poems, 1999; The Clearing, 2005; The Prayers of Others, 2006; (trans.) C.R. Nielsen, The World Cut Out with Crooked Scissors: Selected Prose Poems, 2007; House Inspections: Prose Poems, 2011. Works appear in anthologies. Contributor to periodicals. **Address:** Department of Literature, American University, 233 Battelle-Tompkins, 4400 Massachusetts Ave. NW, Washington, DC 20016, U.S.A. **Online address:** keplinge@american.edu

KER, A. M. *See* **KERR,** Alexander McBride.

KER, Ian (Turnbull). British/Indian (born India), b. 1942. **Genres:** History, Literary Criticism And History, Theology/Religion, Biography, Essays. **Career:** University of Oxford, university professor. Writer. **Publications:** John Henry Newman: A Biography, 1988; The Achievement of John Henry Newman, 1990; Newman on Being a Christian, 1990; Healing the Wound of Humanity: The Spirituality of John Henry Newman, 1993; The Catholic Revival in English Literature, 1845-1961: Newman, Hopkins, Belloc, Chesterton, Greene, Waugh, 2003; Mere Catholicism, 2006; (contrib.) Newman's Second Spring, 2010; G.K. Chesterton, 2011. EDITOR: (intro. and contrib.) The Idea of a University: Defined and Illustrated, 1976; (ed. with T. Gornall) The Letters and Diaries of John Henry Newman, vol. I-IV, 1978-80; (and intro.) An Essay in Aid of a Grammar of Assent, 1985; (and intro.) The Genius of John Henry Newman: Selections from His Writings, 1989; An Essay on the Development o Christian Doctrine, 1989; (with A.G. Hill) Newman after a Hundred Years, 1990; Newman the Theologian, 1990; Apologia pro vita sua, 1994; (and intro.) Selected Sermons: John Henry Newman, 1994; Newman and Conversion, 1997; (with T. Merrigan and contrib.) Newman and the Word, 2000; (with T. Merrigan and contrib.) Newman and Faith, 2004; (with T. Merrigan and contrib.) Newman and Truth, 2008; (with T. Merrigan and contrib.) Cambridge Companion to John Henry Newman, 2009; (and intro.) Meditations and Devotions, 2010; (and intro.) The Everyman Chesterton, 2011. **Address:** University Office, University of Oxford, St. Benet's Hall, Wellington Sq., Oxford, OX OX1 2JD, England. **Online address:** ian.ker@theology.ox.ac.uk

KER, James. American (born United States), b. 1970. **Genres:** Humanities, Education. **Career:** University of Pennsylvania, associate professor, 2002-. Writer. **Publications:** The Deaths of Seneca, 2009; A Seneca Reader: Selections from Prose and Tragedy, 2011. Contributor of articles to periodicals. **Address:** PA, U.S.A. **Online address:** jker@sas.upenn.edu

KERASOTE, Ted. American (born United States), b. 1950. **Genres:** Animals/Pets. **Career:** Writer and naturalist. **Publications:** Navigations: One Man Explores the Americas and Discovers Himself, 1986; Bloodties: Nature, Culture and the Hunt, 1993; Heart of Home: People, Wildlife, Place, 1997; Return of the Wild: The Future of Our Natural Lands, 2001; Out There: In the Wild in a Wired Age, 2004; Merle's Door: Lessons from a Freethinking Dog, 2007; Pukka: The Pup After Merle, 2010; Why Dogs Die Young, 2011. Contributor to periodicals. **Address:** Houghton Mifflin Harcourt, 222 Berkeley St., Boston, MA 02116, U.S.A. **Online address:** ted@kerasote.com

KERBEL, Matthew Robert. American (born United States), b. 1958. **Genres:** Politics/Government, Communications/Media, Social Sciences, History. **Career:** WNET/13 Public Television, news writer, 1980-82; University of Michigan, research assistant, 1983-85, teaching assistant, 1983-87, lecturer, 1987-88; Eastern Michigan University, visiting assistant professor, 1987-88; Villanova University, College of Liberal Arts and Sciences, Department of Political Science, assistant professor, 1988-95, associate professor, 1995-99, professor, 1999-; Bryn Mawr College, visiting associate professor, 1995. **Publications:** Beyond Persuasion: Organizational Efficiency and Presidential Power, 1991; Edited for Television: CNN, ABC, and the 1992 Presidential Campaign, 1994, 2nd ed., 1998; Remote and Controlled: Media Politics in a Cynical Age, 1995, 2nd ed., 1999; If It Bleeds, It Leads: An Anatomy of Television News, 2000; American Government: Your Voice, Your Future, 2006, 4th ed., 2011; (ed.) Get This Party Started: How Progressives Can Fight Back and Win, 2006; Netroots: Online Progressives and the Transformation of American Politics, 2009; (with J.K. White) Party On!: Political Parties from Hamilton and Jefferson to Today's Networked Age, 2012. Contributor of articles to journals. **Address:** Department of Political Science, College of Liberal Arts and Sciences, Villanova University, St. Augustine Ctr., 800 Lancaster Ave., Villanova, PA 19085-1699, U.S.A. **Online address:** matthew.kerbel@villanova.edu

KERBER, Linda K(aufman). American (born United States), b. 1940. **Genres:** History, Women's Studies And Issues. **Career:** Yeshiva University, Stern College for Women, lecturer, 1963-67, assistant professor, 1968; Barnard College, Alumnae fellow, 1965; Danforth Foundation, Kent fellow, 1966-68; San Jose State College, assistant professor, 1969-70; Stanford University, visiting assistant professor, 1970-71; University of Iowa, associate professor, 1971-75, professor of history, 1975-85, May Brodbeck professor of liberal arts, 1985-, chairman, 2003-06; American Studies Association, president, 1988; University of Chicago, visiting professor, 1991-92; Organization of American Historians, president, 1996-97; American Historical Association, president, 2006; Oxford University, Harold Vyvyan Harmsworth visiting professor of American history, 2006-07; American Academy of Arts and Sciences, fellow. Writer. **Publications:** Federalists in Dissent: Imagery and Ideology in Jeffersonian America, 1970; Women of the Republic: Intellect and Ideology in Revolutionary America, 1980; (contrib.) Women and Society in the Eighteenth Century, 1983; History will do it no Justice, 1987; Toward an Intellectual History of Women: Essays, 1997; No Constitutional Right to Be Ladies: Women and the Obligations of Citizenship, 1998. EDITOR: (with J. De Hart) Women's America: Refocusing the Past, 1982, (with J. De Hart and C.H. Dayton) 7th ed., 2010; (with A. Kessler-Harris and K.K. Sklar) U.S. History as Women's History: New Feminist Essays, 1995. Contributor to journals. **Address:** Department of History, University of Iowa, 117 Schaeffer Hall, Iowa City, IA 52242-1409, U.S.A. **Online address:** linda-kerber@uiowa.edu

KERBY, Mona. American (born United States), b. 1951. **Genres:** Children's Fiction, Children's Non-fiction, Librarianship, History, Animals/Pets. **Career:** J.B. Little Elementary School, librarian, 1978-93; Texas Woman's University, adjunct professor in library and information science, 1989-94; McDaniel College, school library media program, associate professor, professor of library science, 2008-, coordinator, 1994-. Writer. **Publications:** Investigating the Effectiveness of School Library Instruction, 1984; Friendly Bees, Ferocious Bees, 1987; 38 Weeks till Summer Vacation, 1989; Asthma, 1989; Beverly Sills: America's Own Opera Star, 1989; Cockroaches, 1989; Amelia Earhart: Courage in the Sky, 1990; Samuel Morse, 1991; Frederick Douglass, 1994; Yearbooks in Science 1950-59, 1995; Robert E. Lee: Southern Hero of the Civil War, 1997; Reading Fun: Quick and Easy Activities for the School Library Media Center, 1998; School Library Media Collection Development: A Practical Guide, 2006; Owney, the Mail Pouch Pooch, 2008. **Address:** School Library Media Program, McDaniel College, Academic Hall, 2 College Hill, Westminster, MD 21157-4390, U.S.A. **Online address:** rkerby@mcdaniel.edu

KERESZTY, Roch A. American/Hungarian (born Hungary), b. 1933. **Genres:** Theology/Religion, Adult Non-fiction. **Career:** University of Dallas, lecturer in theology, 1963-65, chaplain, 1963-65, Department of Theology, assistant professor of theology, 1965-70, associate professor, 1970-78, adjunct professor of theology, 1978-; Cistercian Preparatory School, instructor, 1969-, Department of Theology, chairman, 1970-; Cistercian Abbey Our Lady of Dallas, novice master, 1975-. Writer. **Publications:** God Seekers for a New Age: From Crisis Theology to Christian Atheism, 1970; Krisztus, 1977; (with W.R. Farmer) Peter and Paul in the Church of Rome: The Ecumenical Potential of a Forgotten Perspective, 1990; Jesus Christ, Fundamentals of Christology, 1991, rev. ed., 2002; Bevezetés az Egyhaz teologiajaba, 1998; If Today You Hear His Voice, 1998; (ed.) Rediscovering the Eucharist: Ecumenical Conversations, 2002; Wedding Feast of the Lamb: Eucharistic Theology from a Historical, Biblical and Systematic Perspective, 2004; Christianity Among Other Religions: Apologetics in a Contemporary Context, 2006. **Address:** Department of Theology, University of Dallas, 1845 E Northgate Dr., Irving, TX 75062-4736, U.S.A. **Online address:** fr-roch@cistercian.org

KERET, Etgar. Israeli (born Israel), b. 1967. **Genres:** Novels, Novellas/Short Stories. **Career:** Tel Aviv University School of Film, lecturer; University of Iowa, writer-in-residence, 2001. Author, journalist and filmmaker. **Publications:** IN HEBREW: Tsinorot, 1992; Ga'gu'ai le-Kising'er, 1994; (with R. Modan) Lo banu le-henot, 1996; (with A. Hanuka) Simta'ot ha-za'am, 1997; Ha-Kaitanah shel Kneler, 1998; Pizzeria Kamikaze, 2004. IN ENGLISH TRANSLATION: Ga'gu'ai le-Kising'er, 1994; How to Make a Good Script Great, 1996; Jetlag, 1998; Selected Stories, 1998; The Bus Driver Who Wanted to Be God and Other Stories, 2001; Anihu, 2002; Dad Runs Away with the Circus, 2004; (with S. El-Youssef) Gaza Blues: Different Stories,

2004; One Last Story and That's It, 2005. OTHERS: Pitseriyah ḳamiḳazeh: 'al-pi ha-ḳaiṭanah shel ḳneler me-et Etgar ḳeret, 2004; The Nimrod flip-out, 2005; Tselaliyot: 11 sipurim, 2005; Jetlag: Five Graphic Novellas, 2006; The Girl on the Fridge, 2008; Pit'om defiḳah ba-delet, 2010; Hitnahaguyot hisṭeriyot, 2010. **Address:** c/o Atar Dekel, Kneller Artist Agency, 169 Hayar-kon St., Tel-Aviv, 63453, Israel.

KERKHOFF, Blair. American (born United States), b. 1959?. **Genres:** Sports/Fitness, Biography, History. **Career:** Times & World-News, reporter, 1981-89; Kansas City Star, reporter, 1989-. **Publications:** Phog Allen: The Father of Basketball Coaching, 1996; A Century of Jayhawk Triumphs: The 100 Greatest Victories in the History of Kansas Basketball, 1997; The Greatest Book of College Basketball, 1998; Upon Further Review: Controversy in Sports Officiating, 2000. Contributor to periodicals. **Address:** Kansas City Star, 1729 Grand Blvd., Kansas City, MO 64108, U.S.A. **Online address:** bkerkhoff@kcstar.com

KERLEY, Jack. American (born United States), b. 1952?. **Genres:** Novels. **Career:** Writer and advertising director. **Publications:** The Hundredth Man, 2004; The Death Collectors, 2005; A Garden of Vipers, 2006; Little Girls Lost, 2007; Blood Brother, 2008; In the Blood, 2009; Buried Alive, 2010; Her Last Scream, 2011. **Address:** The Aaron M. Priest Literary Agency, 708 3rd Ave., 23rd Fl., New York, NY 10017-4201, U.S.A. **Online address:** jack@jackkerley.com

KERMAN, Joseph. (Joseph Wilfred Kerman). American/British (born England), b. 1924. **Genres:** Music, Essays. **Career:** Westminster Choir College, director of graduate studies, 1949-51; University of California, Department of Music, associate professor, 1956-60, professor, 1960-, chair, 1961-64, now professor emeritus; All Souls College, visiting fellow, 1966-67; Cornell University, visiting fellow, 1971; Oxford University, Heather professor of music, 1972-74. Writer. **Publications:** Opera as Drama, 1956, rev. ed., 1988; The Elizabethan Madrigal, 1962; The Beethoven Quartets, 1967; (with H.W. Janson and D.J. Janson) A History of Art and Music, 1968; (ed.) Beethoven: Autograph Miscellany (the Kafka Sketchbook), 1970; (with V. Kerman) Listen, 1972, 7th ed., 2012; The Masses and Motets of William Byrd, 1981; (with A. Tyson) The New Grove Beethoven, 1983; Contemplating Music: Challenges to Musicology, 1985; (ed.) Music at the Turn of Century: A 19th-Century Music Reader, 1990; Write All These Down: Essays on Music, 1994; Concerto Conversations, 1999; The Art of Fugue: Bach Fugues for Keyboard, 1715-1750, 2005; (ed. with D. Moroney) William Byrd and his Contemporaries: Essays and a Monograph, 2007; Opera and the Morbidity of Music, 2008. **Address:** Department of Music, University of California, 104 Morrison Hall, Ste. 1200, Berkeley, CA 94720-1200, U.S.A. **Online address:** jokerm@socrates.berkeley.edu

KERMAN, Joseph Wilfred. See **KERMAN, Joseph.**

KERN, E. R. See **KERNER, Fred.**

KERNER, Elizabeth. American (born United States), b. 1958?. **Genres:** Science Fiction/Fantasy, Young Adult Non-fiction, Romance/Historical. **Career:** Writer. **Publications:** Song in the Silence: The Tale of Lanen Kaelar, 1997; The Lesser Kindred, 2001; Redeeming the Lost, 2004. Contributor to periodicals. **Address:** c/o Author Mail, Tor Books, 175 5th Ave., New York, NY 10010, U.S.A. **Online address:** elizabeth@elizabethKerner.com

KERNER, Fred. Also writes as E. R. Kern, M. N. Thaler. Canadian (born Canada), b. 1921. **Genres:** Novellas/Short Stories, Songs/Lyrics And Libretti, Children's Non-fiction, Food And Wine, History, How-to Books, inspirational/Motivational Literature, Medicine/Health, Medicine/Health, Medicine/Health, Psychology, Self Help, Writing/Journalism, Humor/Satire, Reference. **Career:** Newsman and foreign correspondent, 1942-56; Saskatoon Star, editorial writer, 1942; Montreal Gazette, assistant sports editor, 1942-44; Canadian Press, editor, 1944-50; Associated Press, editor, 1950-56; Prentice-Hall, senior editor, 1957-59; Hawthorn Books, editor, 1957-58, president and editor-in-chief, 1964-68; Fawcett World Library, editor-in-chief, 1959-64; Hall House Inc., editor, 1963-64; Centaur House Publishers Inc., president and editor-in-chief, 1964-75; Publishing Projects Inc., president, 1964-; Reader's Digest Association (Canada) Ltd., Book and Educational Division, editorial director, 1968-75; Long Island University, lecturer, 1968; Communications Unlimited, president, 1969-; Harlequin Enterprises Ltd., vice-president of publishing, 1975-85, editor emeritus and senior consulting editor, 1985-.

Publications: (With L. Kotkin) Eat, Think and Be Slender, 1954; (with W. Germain) The Magic Power of Your Mind, 1956; (with J. Brothers) Ten Days to a Successful Memory, 1957; Love Is a Man's Affair, 1958; Stress and Your Heart, 1961; (as Frederick Kerr) Watch Your Weight Go Down, 1962; (with W. Germain) Secrets of Your Supraconscious, 1965; A Treasury of Lincoln Quotations, 1965; (with D. Goodman) What's Best for Your Child and You, 1966; (with J. Reid) Buy High, Sell Higher!, 1966; (as M.N. Thaler) It's Fun to Fondue, 1968; (with I. Grumenza) Nadia, 1976; (ed.) The Canadian Writer's Guide, 9th ed., 1985, 11th ed., 1991; Mad about Fondue, 1986; Folles, Folles, Les Fondues, 1987; (with A. Willman) Prospering through the Coming Depression, 1988; The Home Emergency Handbook, 1990; Fabulous Fondues, 2000; Don't Count Calories, 2000; Los Mejores Fondues, 2000; 1001 Ways to Have Good Luck; Public Speaking for Fun and Profit, forthcoming. **Address:** Publishing Projects Inc., 1555 Finch Ave. E, Ste. 1405, Toronto, ON M2J 4X9, Canada. **Online address:** fkerner@pubproj.com

KERNFELD, Barry (Dean). American (born United States), b. 1950. **Genres:** Music, Songs/Lyrics And Libretti. **Career:** Hamilton College, part-time lecturer, 1981-82; Cornell University, lecturer, 1983-84; part-time saxophonist, 1980-84, 1994-; freelance writer, 1984-; Pennsylvania State University, staff archivist and lecturer, 2005-. **Publications:** What to Listen for in Jazz, 1995; The Story of Fake Books: Bootlegging Songs to Musicians, 2006; Pop Song Piracy: Disobedient Music Distribution Since 1929, 2011. EDITOR: (and contrib.) The New Grove Dictionary of Jazz, 1988, 2nd ed., 2002; The Blackwell Guide to Recorded Jazz, 1991, 2nd ed., 1995. Contributor to periodicals. **Address:** Historical Collections and Labor Archives, Pennsylvania State University, 104 Paterno Library, University Park, PA 16802-1808, U.S.A. **Online address:** bdk4@psu.edu

KERNS, Daniel R. See **LICHTENBERG, Jacqueline.**

KERNS, Thomas A. American (born United States), b. 1942. **Genres:** Ethics, Social Sciences, Sciences, History. **Career:** St. Ambrose College, instructor in philosophy, 1967-69; University of Portland, assistant professor of philosophy, 1970-71; Marquette University, part-time teacher, 1972-73; Alverno College, part-time teacher, 1972-73; University of Wisconsin, part-time teacher, 1973; St. Martin's College, assistant professor of philosophy and social science, 1973-76; North Seattle Community College, professor of philosophy, 1976-; Seattle University, adjunct associate professor of philosophy, 1991-; Chemical Injury Council, secretary, 1996-97. Writer. **Publications:** Ethical Issues in HIV Vaccine Trials, 1997; Jenner on Trial: An Ethical Examination of Vaccine Research in the Age of Smallpox and the Age of AIDS, 1997; Environmentally Induced Illnesses: Ethics, Risk Assessment and Human Rights, 2001. Contributor to journals. **Address:** Department of Philosophy, North Seattle Community College, 9600 College Way N, Seattle, WA 98103, U.S.A. **Online address:** tkerns@sccd.ctc.edu

KERR, Alex. See **KERR, Alexander McBride.**

KERR, Alex. Japanese/American (born United States), b. 1952. **Genres:** Novels, Translations. **Career:** Oomoto Foundation, International Department, staff, 1977-97; Trammell Crow Art Collection Co., consultant, 1984-93, Japan representative, 1986-93; Chiiori Ltd., founder, 1984-; Chiiori Company Ltd.-Thailand, president, 1997-2004; IORI Corp., chairman and founding director, 2004-; ORIGIN Asia Company Ltd., founder and president, 2005-. Writer. **Publications:** (Trans. and ed.) C. Karhu, Kyoto Rediscovered: A Portfolio of Woodblock Prints, 1980; Immortal Images, 1989; Utsukushiki Nihon no Zanzō, 1993, trans. as Lost Japan, 1996; Inu to Oni, trans. as Dogs and Demons: Tales from the Dark Side of Japan, 2001; Nihon Burando De Iko, 2003; Living in Japan, 2006; Bangkok Found: Reflections on the City, 2010; Alex Kerr's Kyoto, forthcoming. **Address:** Chiiori Company Ltd., Yada-Tenmangu Mubanchi, Higashi-Kakiuchi, Kamiyada-cho, Kameoka-shi, Kyōto-fu, 621-0856, Japan. **Online address:** nemoglassman@gmail.com

KERR, Alexander McBride. Also writes as A. M. Ker, Alex Kerr. Australian (born Australia), b. 1921. **Genres:** Economics, Business/Trade/Industry. **Career:** University of Western Australia, lecturer, 1952-53, senior research fellow, 1954-55, senior lecturer, 1956-63, reader, 1964-71, associate professor of economics, 1971-74; Murdoch University, professor of economics, 1975-; Challenge Bank, director; Vincent Corp., director; Nusantaqua Pte., director; National Oil N.L., director; Atlas Pacific Ltd., director; P.T. Cendana Pearls, director; P.T. Daya Sakti Baruna Nusantara Biomanagement Systems Pty, director; Development Analysis Pty, director. Writer. **Publications:** Personal

Income of Western Australia, 1949, new ed., 1951; Resources and Development of the South West Region of Western Australia, 1955; Personal South West Revisited, A Comparative Study of the South West Region of Western Australia, 1960; Northwestern Australia, 1962; State and Regional Income Estimation: Theory and Practice, 1963; The South-West Region of Western Australia, 1965; Australia's North-West, 1967; The Texas Reef Shell Industry, 1967; Regional Income Estimation in Indonesia: Historical Development, 1973; New Horizons for Economics, 1977. EDITOR: The Indian Ocean Region: Resources and Development, 1981; We Flew, We Fell, We Survived, 1991. **Address:** 146 Alderbury St., Floreat, WA 6014, Australia.

KERR, Andrea Moore. American (born United States), b. 1940. **Genres:** Biography, Women's Studies And Issues, History, Social Sciences, Young Adult Non-fiction. **Career:** Lorton Correctional Facility, Literacy Project, director, 1974-76. Copywriter, freelance journalist and teacher. **Publications:** Lucy Stone: Speaking Out for Equality, 1992. Contributor to books. **Address:** c/o Gail Ross, 1666 Connecticut Ave. NW, Washington, DC 20009, U.S.A.

KERR, Ann. See **KERR, Ann Zwicker.**

KERR, (Anne) Judith. British/German (born Germany), b. 1923. **Genres:** Children's Fiction, Illustrations. **Career:** Red Cross, secretary, 1941-45; teacher and textile designer, 1946-53; BBC-TV, reader, script editor and script writer, 1953-58. **Publications:** SELF-ILLUSTRATED: The Tiger Who Came to Tea, 1968; When Hitler Stole Pink Rabbit, 1971; Mog the Forgetful Cat, 1972; When Willy Went to the Wedding, 1973. OTHERS: The Other Way Round, 1975; Mog's Christmas, 1976; A Small Person Far Away, 1978; Mog and the Baby, 1980; Mog in the Dark, 1983; Mog and Me, 1984; Mog's Family of Cats, 1985; Baby Animals, 1985; Favorite Things, 1985; My Home, 1985, Mog's Amazing Birthday Caper, 1986, rev. ed., 2009; Mog and Bunny, 1988; Look Out Mog! in UK as Mog and Barnaby, 1991; How Mrs. Monkey Missed the Ark, 1992; The Adventures of Mog, 1993; Mog on Fox Night, 1993; Mog in The Garden, 1994; Mog's Kittens, 1994; Mog and the Granny, 1995; Mog and the VeeEe Tee, 1996; The Big Mog Book, 1997; Birdie Halleluyah!, 1998; Hog's Bad Thing, 2000; Goodbye Mog, 2002; Other Goose, 2002; Twinkles, Arthur and Puss, 2007; Mog and the V.e.t, 2009; One Night in the Zoo, 2010. **Address:** HarperCollins Publishers, 77-85 Fulham Palace Rd., London, GL W6 8JB, England.

KERR, Ann Zwicker. (Ann Kerr). American (born United States), b. 1934. **Genres:** Autobiography/Memoirs. **Career:** American University-Beirut, instructor of English language and communications, 1983-84; American University-Cairo, instructor of English language and communications, 1984-89; University of California, Visiting Fulbright Scholar Enrichment Program, Fulbright coordinator, 1990-. Writer and speaker. **Publications:** Come with Me from Lebanon: An American Family Odyssey, 1994; Painting the Middle East, 2002. **Address:** University of California-Los Angeles International, 11347 Bunche Hall, Los Angeles, CA 90095-1487, U.S.A. **Online address:** akerr@international.ucla.edu

KERR, Audrey Elisa. American (born United States), b. 1969. **Genres:** Young Adult Non-fiction. **Career:** Washington Review of the Arts, arts critic, 1994-97; Washington Citizen News, arts critic and book columnist, 1995-96; Montgomery College, instructor, 1995-97; University of Maryland, instructor, 1995-97; Simon's Rock College, assistant professor, 1997; Southern Connecticut State University, professor; Leeway Inc., chaplain. Writer. **Publications:** The Paper Bag Principle: Class, Colorism and Rumor and the Case of Black Washington, D.C., 2006. Contributor of articles to periodicals and professional journals. **Address:** Department of English, Southern Connecticut State University, 501 Crescent St., New Haven, CT 06510, U.S.A. **Online address:** audreyelisa@aol.com

KERR, Carole. See **CARR, Margaret.**

KERR, Graham. American/British (born England), b. 1934. **Genres:** Food And Wine. **Career:** Royal Ascot Hotel, manager, 1957-58; Royal New Zealand Air Force, chief catering adviser, 1958-63; Cornell University's School of Hotel Administration, adjunct professor, 1973; director of food services of youth with a mission, 1978-80; Kerr Corp., founder, chairman; Culinary Institute of America, visiting professor, 1996; Art Institute of Seattle, visiting professor, 1997; Johnson & Wales University, visiting professor, 2003;

Bastyr University, visiting lecturer, 2008. Writer. **Publications:** Entertaining with Kerr, 1963; Graham Kerr Cookbook, 1966; (with L. Evans) The Galloping Gourmet, 1967; Television Cookbook Series, 1968-74; The Graham Kerr Cookbook by the Galloping Gourmet, 1970; Complete Galloping Gourmet Cookbook, 1972; The New Seasoning, 1976; The Love Feast: How Good, Natural, Wholesome Food can Create a Warm and Lasting Christian Family, 1978; (with T. Kerr) The Graham Kerr Step by Step Cookbook, 1982; Graham Kerr's Smart Cooking, 1991; Graham Kerr's Minimax Cookbook: Illustrated Step-by-Step Techniques, Plus 150 All-New Minimax Recipes to Guarantee Minimum Risk and Maximum Flavor in Everything You Cook, 1992; Graham Kerr's Creative Choices Cookbook, 1993; Graham Kerr's Kitchen, 1994; Graham Kerr's Best: A Low-Fat, Heart-Healthy Cookbook, 1995; Graham Kerr's Swiftly Seasoned, 1997; Gathering Place: Informal International Menus that will Bring Family and Friends Back to the Table, 1997; (with T. Kerr) Charting a Course to Wellness, 2004; (with T. Kerr and C. Hanson) My Personal Path to Wellness: A Journal for Living Creatively with Chronic Illness, 2004; (with S. Butler) Graham Kerr's Simply Splenda Cookbook, 2004; (with T. Kerr) Recipe for Life: How to Change Habits that Harm into Resources that Heal, 2006; Day-by-day Gourmet Cookbook: Eat Better, Live Smarter, Help Others, 2007; Growing at the Speed of Life: A Year in the Life of My First Kitchen Garden, 2011. **Address:** Kerr Corp., 1020 N Sunset Dr., Camano Island, WA 98282-6665, U.S.A. **Online address:** graham@grahamkerr.com

KERR, Katharine. American (born United States), b. 1944. **Genres:** Science Fiction/Fantasy, Novels. **Career:** TSR Inc., fantasy game designer; Dragon magazine, contributing editor. **Publications:** FANTASY NOVELS-DEVERRY SERIES: Daggerspell, 1986, rev. ed., 1993; Darkspell, 1987, rev. ed., 1994; The Bristling Wood, 1989; The Dragon Revenant, 1990; A Time of Exile, 1991; A Time of Omens, 1992; Days of Blood and Fire, 1993; Days of Air and Darkness, 1994; (ed.) Shimmering Door, 1996; The Red Wyvern, 1997; The Black Raven, 1999; The Fire Dragon, 2001; The Gold Falcon, 2006; The Spirit Stone, 2007; The Shadow Isle, 2008; The Silver Mage, 2009. OTHER NOVELS: Polar City Blues, 1991; Resurrection, 1992; (with M.H. Greenberg) Weird Tales from Shakespeare, 1994; (with M.H. Greenberg) Enchanted Forests, 1995; Freeze Frames, 1995; (with M.A. Kreighbaum) Palace, 1996; Polar City Nightmare, 2000; Snare, 2003; License to Ensorcell, 2011. Works appear in anthologies. Contributor to periodicals. **Address:** c/o Elizabeth Pomada, Larsen-Pomada Literary Agency, 1029 Jones St., San Francisco, CA 94109, U.S.A. **Online address:** kathkerr@ix.netcom.com

KERR, K. Austin. American (born United States), b. 1938. **Genres:** History, Politics/Government. **Career:** Ohio State University, instructor, 1965-68, assistant professor, 1968-71, associate professor, 1971-84, professor of history, 1984-, now professor emeritus; University of Tokyo, visiting lecturer, 1973; Waseda University, visiting lecturer, 1973; H-Business, founding editor; Ohio Academy of History, president, 2003-04; The Business History Conference, president; Alcohol and Drugs History Society, president. **Publications:** American Railroad Politics, 1914-1920, 1968; (ed.) The Politics of Moral Behavior: Prohibition and Drug Abuse, 1973; Organized for Prohibition: A New History of the Anti-Saloon League, 1985; (with M.G. Blackford) Business Enterprise in American History, 1986, 3rd ed., 1994; (with A.J. Loveday and M.G. Blackford) Local Businesses: Exploring Their History, 1990; (with M.G. Blackford) BF Goodrich, Tradition and Transformation, 1870-1995, 1996. **Address:** Department of History, Ohio State University, 106 Dulles Hall, 230 W 17th Ave., Columbus, OH 43210-1367, U.S.A. **Online address:** kerr.6@osu.edu

KERR, Margaret (H.). Canadian (born Canada), b. 1954. **Genres:** Law. **Career:** Centennial College, part-time professor, 1994-98; Seneca College, part-time professor, 1994-98; York University, executive officer, research projects facilitator, 1998-. Writer. **Publications:** (With J. Kurtz and L.M. Olivo) Canadian Tort Law in a Nutshell, 1997; (with J. Kurtz) The Complete Guide to Buying, Owning, and Selling a Home in Canada, 1997, 2nd ed., 2001; (with J. Kurtz) Make It Legal: What Every Canadian Entrepreneur Needs to Know about the Law, 1998; Legal Research: Step by Step, 1998, 3rd ed., 2009; (with J. Kurtz) Facing a Death in the Family, 1999; (with J. Kurtz) Wills and Estates for Canadians for Dummies, 2000; (with J. Kurtz) Canadian Small Business Kit for Dummies, 2002. Contributor to books and periodicals. **Address:** York University, 4700 Keele St., Toronto, ON M3J 1P3, Canada. **Online address:** mhkerr@sympatico.com

KERR, M. E. See **MEAKER, Marijane (Agnes).**

KERR, Steven. American (born United States), b. 1941. **Genres:** Administration/Management, Business/Trade/Industry. **Career:** Ohio State University, College of Administrative Science, assistant professor, 1970-74, associate professor, 1974-77; University of Southern California, School of Business Administration, professor of organizational behavior, 1977-82, chair, 1979-82, associate dean, 1982-85, professor of management and organization, 1982-92, director of Ph.D. program, 1985-88, dean of faculty, 1985-89, interim director entrepreneur program, 1988-89; General Electric Co., vice president of leadership development and chief learning officer, 1994-2001; The Goldman Sachs Group Inc., chief learning officer, 2001-06, senior advisor. Writer. **Publications:** (Co-author) Managerial Process and Organizational Behavior, 1976; (co-ed.) Organizational Behavior, 1979; (co-ed.) The Boundaryless Organization, 1995; (ed. and intro.) Ultimate Rewards: What Really Motivates People to Achieve, 1997; (co-author) The GE Work-Out: How to Implement GE's Revolutionary Method for Busting Bureaucracy and Attacking Organizational Problems-Fast!, 2002; Reward Systems: Does Yours Measure Up?, 2009. Contributor to periodicals. **Address:** Goldman, Sachs & Co., 85 Broad St., 17th Fl., New York, NY 10004, U.S.A.

KERRISON, Catherine M. American (born United States), b. 1953. **Genres:** Women's Studies And Issues, History. **Career:** Villanova University, assistant professor, 1999-2005, associate professor of history, 2005-. Writer. **Publications:** Claiming the Pen: Women and Intellectual Life in the Early American South, 2006. **Address:** Villanova University, St. Augustine Ctr., Liberal Arts Rm. 436, 800 Lancaster Ave., Villanova, PA 19085-1603, U.S.A. **Online address:** catherine.kerrison@villanova.edu

KERRY, Lois. See DUNCAN, Lois.

KERSAUDY, François. French (born France), b. 1948. **Genres:** History, Military/Defense/Arms Control, Translations. **Career:** Oxford University, international relations faculty; University of Paris, professor of international relations, 1981-. Writer. **Publications:** Stratèges Et Norvège 1940: Les Jeux De La guerre Et Du Hasard, 1977; Churchill and De Gaulle, 1981; De Gaulle Et Churchill, 1982; LaGuerre Du Fer 1940, 1987 in UK as Norway 1940, 1990, rev. ed., 1991; Vistoler på England, 1939-1949, 1991; Winston Churchill, Le Pouvoir Del'imagination, 2000; Churchill Contre Hitler: Norvège 1940, Lavictoire Fatale, 2002; Churchill Et Monaco, 2002; De Gaulle Et Roosevelt: Le Duel Au Sommet, 2004; Affaire Cicéron, 2005; Lord Mountbatten: L'ètoffe Des Hèros, 2006; Hermann Goering: le deuxième homme du IIIe Reich, 2009; Hitler, 2011. Contributor to periodicals. **Address:** University of Paris 1 - Pantheon - Sorbonne, 12 place du pantheon, Paris, 75231, France. **Online address:** francois.kersaudy@univ-paris1.fr

KERSCH, Ken I. American (born United States), b. 1964. **Genres:** Civil Liberties/Human Rights, Law, Politics/Government. **Career:** Wiley, Rein & Fielding (law firm), lawyer, 1991-93; Cornell University, Department of Government, head teaching assistant trainer, 1996-99, Department of Government, Professional Development Workshops, organizer, 1997-99; Lehigh University, Department of Political Science, assistant professor of political science, 1999-2002, pre-law advisor, 1999-2003; Princeton University, James Madison Program in American Ideals and Institutions, Ann and Herbert W. Vaughan fellow, 2001-02, assistant professor of politics, 2003-07, Program in Law and Public Affairs, faculty associate, 2003-07, Public Law Colloquium, director, 2004-05, Forbes College, faculty advisor and faculty fellow, 2003-07; Boston College, Department of Political Science, associate professor, 2007-, Clough Center for the Study of Constitutional Democracy, founding director, 2008-10. Writer. **Publications:** NONFICTION: Freedom of Speech: Rights and Liberties under the Law, 2003; (contrib.) Rehnquist Justice: Understanding the Court Dynamic, 2003; Constructing Civil Liberties: Discontinuities in the Development of American Constitutional Law, 2004; (ed. with R. Kahn) The Supreme Court and American Political Development, 2006; (contrib.) Supreme Court Justices: A Biographical Dictionary, 2006; (contrib.) The Bill of Rights in Modern America, 2008. Contributor to periodicals. **Address:** Department of Political Science, Boston College, 219 McGuinn Hall, 140 Commonwealth Ave., Chestnut Hill, MA 02467-3807, U.S.A. **Online address:** kenneth.kersch.1@bc.edu

KERSENBOOM, Saskia. (Saskia C. Kersenboom-Story). Dutch (born Netherlands), b. 1953. **Genres:** Anthropology/Ethnology, Dance/Ballet, Music. **Career:** University of Utrecht, Liberal Arts Program, faculty, 1986-87; Royal Academy of Arts and Sciences, fellow, 1987-90, researcher; University of Amsterdam, associate professor of linguistic anthropology, 1990-2006, associate professor of theatre studies, 2005-, Faculty of Humanities, lecturer; Faculty of Social and Behavioural Sciences, lecturer; Paramparai, founder and director, 1994-; Rietberg Museum, research consultant, 2006-. Writer. **Publications:** (As Saskia C. Kersenboom-Story) Nityasumangali: Devadasi Tradition in South India, 1987, 3rd ed., 2002; Word, Sound, Image: The Life of the Tamil Text, 1995; (contrib.) Shiva Nataraja: der kosmische Tänzer, 2008. Contributor to books and periodicals. **Address:** Faculty of Humanities, University of Amsterdam, Rm. 006, Nieuwe Doelenstraat 16, Amsterdam, 1012 CP, Netherlands. **Online address:** s.c.kersenboom@uva.nl

KERSENBOOM-STORY, Saskia C. See KERSENBOOM, Saskia.

KERSHAW, Alex. American/British (born England) **Genres:** Biography, Politics/Government, Novels. **Career:** Journalist and screenwriter. **Publications:** (Intro.) The Call of the Wild and Selected Stories, 1998; Jack London: A Life, 1998; Blood and Champagne: The Life and Times of Robert Capa, 2002; The Bedford Boys: One Small Town's D-Day Sacrifice in US as The Bedford Boys: One American Town's Ultimate D-Day Sacrifice, 2003; The Longest Winter: The Battle of the Bulge and the Epic Story of World War II's Most Decorated Platoon, 2004; The Few: American Knights of the Air Who Risked Everything to Fight in the Battle of Britain, 2006; Escape from the Deep: The Epic Story of a Legendary Submarine and Her Courageous Crew, 2008; Envoy: The Epic Rescue of the Last Jews of Europe in the Desperate Closing Months of World War II, 2010; Envoy's Briefcase: Raoul Wallenberg and the Epic Rescue of the Jews of Budapest, 2010. **Address:** St. Martin's Press, 175 5th Ave., New York, NY 10010-7703, U.S.A. **Online address:** akers78451@aol.com

KERSHAW, Ian. British (born England), b. 1943. **Genres:** History, Politics/Government. **Career:** University of Manchester, assistant lecturer, 1968-, lecturer in medieval history, 1970, senior lecturer, 1979-87, reader elect in modern history, 1987; Ruhr-Universitaet Bochum, visiting professor of contemporary European history, 1983-84; University of Nottingham, professor and chair of modern history, 1987-89; University of Sheffield, professor and chair of modern history, 1989-2008, now professor emeritus; University of Oxford, Merton College, fellow. Writer. **Publications:** Bolton Priory Rentals and Ministers' Accounts, 1473-1539, 1970; Bolton Priory: The Economy of a Northern Monastery, 1286-1325, 1973; Der Hitler-Mythos: Volksmeinung und Propaganda im Dritten Reich, 1980 in UK as The Hitler Myth: Image and Reality in the Third Reich, 1987; Popular Opinion and Political Dissent in the Third Reich: Bavaria: 1933-1945, 1983, new ed., 2002; The Nazi Dictatorship: Problems and Perspectives of Interpretation, 1985, 4th ed., 2000; Hitler: A Profile in Power, 1991; Germany's Present, Germany's Past, 1992; Hitler, 1889-1936, 1998; Hitler, 1936-45: Nemesis, 2000; Making Friends with Hitler: Lord Londonderry, the Nazis, and the Road to War, 2004; Fateful Choices. Ten Decisions that Changed the World, 1940-1941, 2007; Hitler, the Germans, and the Final Solution, 2008; (intro.) Heydrich Et La Solution Finale, 2008; Hitler: A Biography, 2008; End: The Defiance and Destruction of Hitler's Germany, 1944-1945, 2011. EDITOR: Weimar: Why Did German Democracy Fail?, 1990; (with M. Lewin) Stalinism and Nazism: Dictatorships in Comparison, 1997; (with D.M. Smith and T.N. Cooper) The Bolton Priory Compotus, 1286-1325, 2000. **Address:** Department of History, University of Sheffield, Jessop West, 1 Upper Hanover St., Sheffield, SY S3 7RA, England. **Online address:** b.eaton@sheffield.ac.uk

KERSHAW, Peter. See LUCIE-SMITH, (John) Edward (McKenzie).

KERSHEN, (L.) Michael. American (born United States), b. 1982. **Genres:** Young Adult Fiction, Children's Fiction. **Career:** Writer. **Publications:** Why Buffalo Roam, 1993. **Address:** 1000 Elmwood St., Norman, OK 73072-6113, U.S.A. **Online address:** lmkershen@ou.edu

KERTES, Joseph. Canadian (born Canada), b. 1951?. **Genres:** Novels, Children's Fiction, Human Relations/Parenting. **Career:** Humber College, Humber School for Writers, director, Humber's School of Creative and Performing Arts, dean. Writer. **Publications:** NOVELS: Winter Tulips, 1988; Boardwalk, 1998; Gratitude, 2008. CHILDREN'S FICTION: The Gift, 1996; The Red Corduroy Shirt, 1998. **Address:** School of Creative & Performing Arts, Humber College, 3199 Lakeshore Blvd. W, Toronto, ON M8V 1K8, Canada. **Online address:** info@josephkertes.com

KERTESS, Klaus. American (born United States), b. 1940. **Genres:** Art/Art History, Essays, Photography. **Career:** Bykert Gallery Inc., founder and director, 1966-75; Parrish Art Museum, Robert Lehman Curator, 1983-89; Whitney Museum of American Art, adjunct curator of drawing, 1989-95, curator, 1993-95; School of Visual Arts, graduate seminar instructor, 1997-. Writer and art critic. **Publications:** Roses Are Read, 1982; Marin in Oil, 1987; (contrib.) Terry Winters, 1991; Brice Marden: Paintings and Drawings, 1992; Desire by Numbers, 1994; Shaman as Artist, the Artist as Shaman, 1994; 1995 Biennial Exhibition, 1995; Jane Wilson: Paintings, 1985-1995, 1996; South Brooklyn Casket Company (short stories), 1997; Joan Mitchell, 1997; Alfonso Ossorio: Congregations, 1997; Sea Change: 1998; (with A. Philbin) Willem de Kooning: Drawing Seeing/Seeing Drawing, 1998; John O'Reilly: Assemblies of Magic, 2002; Fabulism: Carrol Dunham, Ellen Gallagher, Chris Ofili, Neo Rauch, Matthew Ritchie, 2004; Jane Freilicher, 2004; (co-author) Matthew Ritchie: More than the Eye, 2008; Lee Friedlander: Recent Western Landscape, 2010; Seen, Written: Selected Essays, 2010; Salle: Works from the 1980s, 2010. Contributor to periodicals. **Address:** 4 E 8th St., New York, NY 10003-5913, U.S.A.

KERTSCHER, Kevin M. American (born United States), b. 1964. **Genres:** Travel/Exploration. **Career:** Ken Burns/Florentine Films, documentary editor, 1994-96; independent documentary producer, 1997-. **Publications:** Africa Solo: A Journey Across the Sahara, Sahel, and Congo, 1998. Contributor to periodicals. **Address:** c/o Steerforth Press, 105-106 Chelsea St., PO Box 70, South Royalton, VT 05068, U.S.A.

KERVEN, Rosalind. British (born England), b. 1954. **Genres:** Children's Fiction, Children's Non-fiction, Mythology/Folklore, Social Sciences. **Career:** Talking Stone (publisher), founder, 2000-. Author. **Publications:** FOR CHILDREN FICTION: The Reindeer and the Drum, 1980; Mysteries of the Seals, 1981; Treasure of Bird Island, 1983; The Sea Is Singing, 1986; Who Ever Heard of a Vegetarian Fox?, 1988; Wild!, 1991; Sorcery and Gold, 1998. NON-FICTION: Equal Rights for Animals, 1992; Saving Planet Earth, 1992; The Man Who Found America, 1999; Journeys to Other Worlds, 1999. MYTHS, LEGENDS, AND FOLK TALES: Legends of the Animal World, 1986; The Slaying of the Dragon, 1987; The Tree in the Moon and Other Legends of Plants and Trees, 1989; King Leopard's Gift and Other Animal Legends, 1990; Earth Magic, Sky Magic, 1991; The Woman Who Went to Fairyland, 1992; In the Court of the Jade Emperor, 1993; The Rain Forest Storybook, 1994; Feather-Snake, 1995; Fire, 1995; Coyote Girl, 1996; Kintu's Mistake: Myths and Legends, 1996; Volcano Woman, 1996; The Weather Drum, 1996; The Mythical Quest, 1996; Ramadan and Id-ul-Fitr, 1997; Enchanted Kingdoms, 1997; The Giant King, 1998; King Arthur, 1998; The Enchanted Forest, 1999; How Did the World Begin, 2001; Do You Believe in Fairies?, 2003; The Flying Head, 2006; Snow King, 2007; The Sparrow, the Crow, and the Pearl, 2007; Grim Gruesome, 2008. FOR ADULTS: Aladdin: And other Tales from the Arabian Nights, 1998; Traditional Stories: A Practical Guide for People Sharing Books with Children, 2000; The Fairy Spotter's Handbook, 2003; Spellbinding!, 2003; Northumberland Folk Tales, 2005; Secret World of Magic, 2005; English Fairy Tales and Legends, 2008; Arthurian Legends, 2011. GRIM GRUESOME VIKING VILLAIN SERIES: The Cursed Sword, 2008; The Queen's Poison, 2008; Trolls' Treasure, 2010; The Rings of Doom, 2011. **Address:** Swindonburn Cottage W, Sharperton, Morpeth, NM NE65 7AP, England. **Online address:** roskerven@hotmail.com

KESHAVARZ, Fatemeh. American/Iranian (born Iran), b. 1952?. **Genres:** Theology/Religion, History. **Career:** National Iranian Radio Television, writer, producer and moderator, 1976-79; Institute of Ismaili Studies, cataloger, 1982-87, lecturer, 1983-87; Washington University, Department of Asian and Near Eastern Languages and Literatures, Islamic studies librarian and lecturer in Persian language and literature, 1988-90, visiting assistant professor, 1990-91, assistant professor, 1991-97, associate professor of Persian and comparative literature, 1997-2006, professor of Persian and comparative literature, 2006-, Near Eastern Section, head, 1993-99, Association of Women Faculty, president, 1998-99, Graduate Program in Jewish, director, 2000-04, Mentoring Task Force, chair, 2000-04, university faculty senate, 2003-05, chair, 2004. Writer. **Publications:** Talashi dar aghaz, 1976; A Descriptive and Analytical Catalogue of Persian Manuscripts in the Library of the Wellcome Institute for the History of Medicine, 1986; Reading Mystical Lyric: The Case of Jalal Al-Din Rumi, 1998; Recite in the Name of the Red Rose: Poetic Sacred Making in Twentieth-Century Iran, 2006; Jasmine and Stars: Reading More Than Lolita in Tehran, 2007. Contributor to periodicals. **Address:** Department of Asian and Near Eastern Languages and, Literatures, Washington

University, Busch 114A, PO Box 1111, St. Louis, MO 63130-0899, U.S.A. **Online address:** fatemeh@wustl.edu

KESSEL, Brent. American (born United States), b. 1969?. **Genres:** Money/Finance. **Career:** Abacus Wealth Management (now Abacus Wealth Partners), president, founder and chief executive officer, 1996-; Abacus Portfolios, chief executive officer, 1998-; Yoga Journal, columnist. **Publications:** It's Not about the Money: Unlock Your Money Type to Achieve Spiritual and Financial Abundance, 2008. Contributor to journals and periodicals. **Address:** Abacus Portfolios, 17383 Sunset Blvd., Ste. A360, Pacific Palisades, CA 90272, U.S.A.

KESSELER, Rob. British (born England), b. 1951?. **Genres:** Botany, Art/Art History, Biology, Design. **Career:** Holy Trinity School, artist-in-residence, 1984; NESTA Kew, fellow, 2001-04; University of the Arts London, Central Saint Martin's College of Art and Design, professor of ceramic art and design, 2005-; Gulbenkian Science Institute Portugal, fellow, 2010. Writer. **Publications:** Pollinate: Encounters with Lakeland Flowers, 2001; Botanizing the Library, 2004; (with W. Stuppy) Seeds: Time Capsules of Life, 2006; (with M. Harley) Pollen: The Hidden Sexuality of Flowers, 2006, 3rd ed., 2009; (with W. Stuppy) Fruit: Edible, Inedible, Incredible, 2008; (with W. Stuppy) Seeds: Time Capsules of Life, 2009; (with W. Stuppy and M. Harley) Bizarre and Incredible World of Plants, 2009; Up Close, 2010; Rob Kesseler Up Close, 2010. **Address:** Papadakis Publisher, Kimber Studio, Winterbourne, BR RG20 8AN, England. **Online address:** info@zen.co.uk

KESSELMAN, Wendy. American (born United States), b. 1940?. **Genres:** Novels, Plays/Screenplays, Literary Criticism And History. **Career:** Bryn Mawr College, teaching fellow, 1987. Writer. **Publications:** Franz Tovey and the Rare Animals, 1968; Angelita, 1970; Slash: An Alligator's Story, 1971; Joey, 1972; Little Salt, 1975; Time for Jody, 1975; Maine Is a Million Miles Away, 1976; Emma, 1980; Merry-Go-Round, 1981; There's a Train Going by My Window, 1982; My Sister in This House, 1982; Flick: A novel, 1983; The Juniper Tree: A Tragic Household Tale, 1985, rev. ed., 2004; Maggie Magalita, 1987; Cinderella in a Mirror, 1987; Becca, 1988; I Love You, I Love You Not, 1988, rev. ed., 1996; The Griffin and the Minor Cannon, 1988; A Tale of Two Cities, 1992; The Butcher's Daughter, 1993; Sand in My Shoes, 1995; Sister My Sister, 1995; The Diary of Anne Frank, 1997; Mad or In Love, 2000; The Bridge, 2002; A Separate Peace, 2004; The Notebook, 2004. **Address:** William Morris Agency, 1325 Ave. of the Americas, George Ln., New York, NY 10019, U.S.A.

KESSLER, Andy. American (born United States), b. 1958. **Genres:** Business/Trade/Industry, Money/Finance, Technology, Economics. **Career:** AT&T Bell Labs, chip designer and programmer, through 1985; Paine Webber, researcher and analyst, 1985-89; Morgan Stanley, semiconductor analyst, 1989-93; Unterberg Harris, fund manager, 1993-; Velocity Capital Management, co-founder and president, 1996-2001. Writer. **Publications:** Wall Street Meat: Jack Grubman, Frank Quattrone, Mary Meeker, Henry Blodget and Me, 2003; Running Money: Hedge Fund Honchos, Monster Markets, and My Hunt for the Big Score, 2004; Wall Street Meat: My Narrow Escape from the Stock Market Grinder, 2004; How We Got Here: A Slightly Irreverent History of Technology and Markets, 2005; The End of Medicine: How Silicon Valley (and Naked Mice) Will Reboot Your Doctor, 2006; Grumby, 2010; Eat People: Unapologetic Rules for Entrepreneurial Success, 2011. Contributor to periodicals. **Address:** Portfolio, Penguin Group Inc., 375 Hudson St., New York, NY 10014-3657, U.S.A. **Online address:** akessler@velcap.com

KESSLER, Brad. American (born United States), b. 1963. **Genres:** Novels, Children's Fiction, Philosophy. **Career:** New School University, teacher; Antioch University, teacher. Writer. **Publications:** (Contrib.) Dona Ann McAdams: The Garden of Eden: November 7-December 31, 1997, 1997; Goat Song: A Seasonal Life, a Short History of Herding, and the Art of Making Cheese, 2009. CHILDREN'S BOOKS: John Henry, 1995; Moses the Lawgiver, 1996; The Firebird, 1996; Brer Rabbit and Boss Lion, 1996; Moses in Egypt, 1997; The Woodcutter's Christmas, 2001. NOVELS: Lick Creek, 2001; Birds in Fall, 2006. Contributor to periodicals. **Address:** c/o Author Mail, Scribner, 1230 Ave. of the Americas, New York, NY 10020, U.S.A.

KESSLER, David A. American (born United States), b. 1951. **Genres:** Medicine/Health, Business/Trade/Industry, Law. **Career:** Montefiore Medical Center, special assistant to the president, 1982-84; Albert Einstein College of Medicine, University Hospital, medical director and instructor, 1984-90; Columbia University, School of Law, instructor, 1986-90; U.S. Food and Drug Administration, commissioner, 1990-97; Yale University, School of Medicine, dean, 1997-2003; University of California, School of Medicine, dean and vice chancellor for medical affairs, 2003-07, professor, 2007-. Writer and lawyer. **Publications:** (Ed. with C. Eisdorfer and A.N. Spector) Caring for the Elderly: Reshaping Health Policy, 1989; A Question of Intent: A Great American Battle with a Deadly Industry, 2001; The End of Overeating: Taking Control of the Insatiable American Appetite, 2009. **Address:** CA , U.S.A. **Online address:** kesslerd@medsch.ucsf.edu

KESSLER, Edward. (Edward David Kessler). British (born England), b. 1963. **Genres:** Theology/Religion, Essays, Biography. **Career:** Woolf Institute of Abrahamic Faiths, co-founder and executive director, Centre for the Study of Jewish-Christian Relations (CJCR), founder and executive director, 1998, Centre for the Study of Muslim-Jewish Relations (CMJR), founder and executive director, 2006; St. Edmund's College, fellow. Writer and radio broadcaster. **Publications:** (Ed. and intro.) An English Jew: The Life and Writings of Claude Montefiore, 2002; (ed. with D.J. Goldberg) Aspects of Liberal Judaism: Essays in Honour of John D. Rayner, 2004; (ed. and intro.) A Reader of Early Liberal Judaism: The Writings of Israel Abrahams, Claude Montefiore, Lily Montagu and Israel Mattuck, 2004; Bound by the Bible: Jews, Christians, and the Sacrifice of Isaac, 2004; (ed. with N. Wenborn) A Dictionary of Jewish-Christian Relations, 2005; (ed. with J.K. Aitken) Challenges in Jewish-Christian Relations, 2006; Introduction to Jewish-Christian Relations, 2010. Contributor to periodicals. **Address:** Centre for the Study of Muslim-Jewish Relations, Wesley House, Jesus Ln., Cambridge, CB CB5 8BJ, England. **Online address:** ed.kessler@woolfinstitute.cam.ac.uk

KESSLER, Edward David. See **KESSLER, Edward.**

KESSLER, Glenn. American (born United States), b. 1959. **Genres:** Autobiography/Memoirs, Biography, Social Sciences, Politics/Government. **Career:** Corporate Financing Week and Wall Street Letter, managing editor; Investment Dealers Digest, editor; Newsday, reporter, 1987-98; Washington Post, national business editor, 1998-2000, reporter, 2000-02, diplomatic correspondent, 2002-. **Publications:** The Confidante: Condoleezza Rice and the Creation of the Bush Legacy, 2007. Contributor to periodicals. **Address:** Washington Post, 1150 15 St. NW, Washington, DC 20071, U.S.A.

KESSLER, Jackie H. American (born United States), b. 1971?. **Genres:** Science Fiction/Fantasy. **Career:** Wild Child Publishing, fantasy editor. **Publications:** HELL ON EARTH SERIES: Hell's Belles, 2007; The Road to Hell, 2007; Hotter Than Hell, 2008. THE ICARUS PROJECT SERIES: (with C. Kittredge) Black and White, 2009; (with C. Kittredge) Shades of Gray, 2010. Works appear in anthologies. **Address:** c/o Miriam Kriss, Irene Goodman Literary Agency, 27 W 24th St., New York, NY 10010, U.S.A. **Online address:** jax@jackiekessler.com

KESSLER, Jascha (Frederick). American (born United States), b. 1929. **Genres:** Novels, Novellas/Short Stories, Plays/Screenplays, Poetry, Songs/Lyrics And Libretti, Translations, Literary Criticism And History. **Career:** University of Michigan, instructor, 1951-54; New York University, instructor in English, 1954-55; Hunter College, assistant professor, 1955-56; Harcourt, Brace and Company Inc., educational research director, 1956-57; Hamilton College, assistant professor of English, 1957-61; University of California, assistant professor, 1961-64, associate professor, 1964-70, professor of English and modern literature, 1961-, Institute of Government and Public Affairs, director of research project, 1967-68, now professor emeritus; Centro di Studi Americani, Fulbright professor of American literature and director of American studies seminar, 1970; University of Urbino, seminar professor of American literature, 1970; PEN, lecturer and translator of contemporary poetry, 1972, 1974, 1977, 1979; U.S. Department of State, lecturer, 1974; KUSC-FM Radio, reviewer, 1979-85; City of Santa Monica, arts commissioner, 1990-96; Bellagio Study Center, Rockefeller fellow. Writer. **Publications:** An Egyptian Bondage and Other Stories, 1967, rev. ed., 2000; Lee Mullican: Selected Works, 1948-1980, 1980; Death Comes for the Behaviorist: 4 Long Stories, 1983; Classical Illusions: 28 Stories, 1985; Siren Songs & Classical Illusions: 50 Stories, 1992; Christmas Carols & Other Plays, 1999; Rapid Transit-1948: An Unsentimental Education, 2000. POETRY: (ed. and contrib.) American Poems: A Contemporary Collection, 1964; Whatever Love Declares: Poems, 1969; After the Armies Have Passed, 1970; In Memory of the Future, 1976; Bearing Gifts: Two Mythologems, 1979; Transmigrations: 18 Mythologems, 1985; Collected Poems, 1998. TRANSLATOR: (with C.

Rogers) The Magician's Garden: 24 Stories, 1980; (with A. Banani) Bride of Acacias: Selected Poems of Forugh Farrokhzad, 1982; (with C. Rogers) G. Csaath, Opium and Other Stories, 1983; (with G. Olujic) Rose of Mother-of-Pearl: A Fairytale, 1983; (with A. Shurbanov) N. Kantchev, Time as Seen from Above and Other Poems, 1984; Under Gemini: A Prose Memoir and Selected Poetry, 1985; (with A. Shurbanov) Medusa: The Selected Poetry of Nicolai Kantchev, 1986; The Face of Creation: 23 Contemporary Hungarian Poets, 1988; (with M. Korosy) S. Rakos, Catullan Games, 1989; (with A. Banani) Look! The Guiding Dawn: Selected Poetry of Taaheraeh, 1993; King Oedipus, 1999; (with G. Olujic and contrib.) Tataga's Children: The Fairy Tales of Grozdana Olujic, 2000; (and contrib.) Our Bearings at Sea: A Novel in Poems, 2001; (with K. Simonsuuri) Traveling Light: Selected Poems of Kirsti Simonsuuri, 2001; (contrib.) Táhirih: A Portrait in Poetry: Selected Poems of Qurratu'l-'Ayn, Poet, Mystic, Scholar, Activist, Martyr, Woman of Iran, 2004. **Address:** Department English and Modern Literature, University of California, Humanities 211, Los Angeles, CA 90095-1530, U.S.A. **Online address:** jkessler@ucla.edu

KESSLER, Judy. American (born United States), b. 1947. **Genres:** Communications/Media, Documentaries/Reportage, Biography, Art/Art History. **Career:** People Magazine, writer, 1974-80; The Today Show, producer, 1980-84; Entertainment Tonight, producer, senior producer, 1984-86; Gorillas in the Mist (film), co-producer, 1987-88; Time Inc. Ventures, vice-president. Writer. **Publications:** Inside Today: The Battle for the Morning, 1992; Inside People: The Stories behind the Stories, 1994; (with D. Bryant) Beyond Integration: One Multiple's Journey, 1996; Affair to Remember: Recipes, Menus and Home-Entertaining Tips from Hollywood's Leading Caterers, 1998. **Address:** Time Inc. Ventures, 11100 Santa Monica Blvd., Ste. 300, Los Angeles, CA 90025, U.S.A. **Online address:** jude001@aol.com

KESSLER, Julia Braun. (Julia Barrett). American (born United States), b. 1926. **Genres:** Novels, Romance/Historical, Young Adult Fiction, Gerontology/Senior Issues, Ghost Writer. **Career:** Encyclopedia Americana, research editor, 1949-50; University of Michigan, Institute for Social Research, editor, 1951-54; Seventeen, features editor, 1954-57; University of California, adjunct associate professor of humanities, 1964-69; University of Southern California, Ethel Percy Andrus Gerontology Center, editorial consultant, 1971-74; Freelance writer, 1974-. **Publications:** Getting Even with Getting Old, 1980. AS JULIA BARRETT: (with G. Donnelly) Presumption: An Entertainment, 1993; The Third Sister: A Continuation of Jane Austen's Sense and Sensibility, 1996; Charlotte: A Completion of Jane Austen's Last Work, 2000. Contributor of articles to magazines and newspapers. **Address:** 218 16th St., Santa Monica, CA 90402-2216, U.S.A. **Online address:** jbraun@ucla.edu

KESSLER, Liz. British (born England), b. 1966?. **Genres:** Young Adult Non-fiction. **Career:** Cornerstones (advisory and editorial service), Children's Division, managing editor. Educator. **Publications:** EMILY WINDSNAP SERIES: The Tail of Emily Windsnap, 2003; Emily Windsnap and the Monster from the Deep, 2004; Emily Windsnap and the Castle in the Mist, 2006; Emily Windsnap's Friendship Book, 2008. PHILIPPA FISHER SERIES: Philippa Fisher's Fairy Godsister, 2007; Philippa Fisher and the Dream-maker's Daughter, 2009. OTHER: Philippa Fisher and the Fairy's Promise, 2010; Year without Autumn, 2011. **Address:** c/o Catherine Clarke, Felicity Bryan Agency, 2A N Parade Ave., Oxford, OX OX2 6LX, England. **Online address:** lizkesslerweb@hotmail.co.uk

KESSLER, Suzanne J. American (born United States), b. 1946. **Genres:** Psychology, Women's Studies And Issues. **Career:** City University of New York, Hunter College, lecturer in psychology, 1970-73; State University of New York, Purchase College, assistant professor, 1972-81, associate professor, 1981-95, Children's Center, president, 1986-89, Psychology Program, chair, 1986-89, 1991-95, Bedford Hills Correctional Facility, AIDS Education and Counseling Program, coordinator, 1990, professor of psychology, 1996-, School of Natural and Social Sciences, dean, 2004-, vice provost for academic affairs. Writer. **Publications:** (With W. McKenna) Gender: An Ethnomethodological Approach, 1978; Lessons from the Intersexed, 1998. Contributor of articles and reviews to periodicals. **Address:** Purchase College, State University of New York, Rm. 2013, Social Sciences Bldg., 735 Anderson Hill Rd., Purchase, NY 10577-1400, U.S.A. **Online address:** suzanne.kessler@purchase.edu

KESSNER, Thomas. American/German (born Germany), b. 1946. **Genres:** Novellas/Short Stories, Cultural/Ethnic Topics, History, Biography. **Career:**

City University of New York, The Graduate Center, instructor, professor of history, distinguished professor; Kingsborough Community College, Graduate School, University Center, instructor, associate professor of history, 1971-, associate director of graduate program in history and humanities, 1980-83; Brooklyn College, visiting associate professor, 1980-81; City University of New York, La Guardia Community College, The Fiorello H. La Guardia Archives, director, 1982-83; National Endowment for the Humanities, fellow, 1983-84. Writer. **Publications:** The Golden Door: Italian and Jewish Immigrant Mobility in New York City, 1880-1915, 1977; (with B. Caroli) Ethnic Heritage: A Teacher's Manual, 1979; (ed. with R. Hirt.) Issues in Teaching the Holocaust: A Guide, 1981; (with B.B. Caroli) Today's Immigrants, Their Stories: A New Look at the Newest Americans, 1981; (contrib.) The American Experience: Contemporary Immigrant Artists, 1985; Fiorello H. La Guardia and the Making of Modern New York, 1989; (contrib.) The Encyclopedia of the City of New York, 1991; Capital City: New York City and the Men behind America's Rise to Economic Dominance, 1860-1900, 2003; The Flight of the Century: Charles Lindbergh and the Rise of American Aviation, 2010. Contributor to books. **Address:** PhD Program in History, City University of New York Graduate Ctr., Rm. 5111, 365 5th Ave., New York, NY 10016-4309, U.S.A. **Online address:** tkessner@gc.cuny.edu

KETCHAM, Ralph Louis. American (born United States), b. 1927. **Genres:** History, Biography. **Career:** Syracuse University, graduate fellow and instructor in citizenship, 1951-56, Maxwell School, Department of American studies and public affairs, professor, 1963-97, Maxwell distinguished professor, 1994-97, Maxwell professor emeritus, 1997-; University of Chicago, research associate in political science, 1956-60; Yale University, lecturer in American studies and history, 1961-63; University of Leiden, Fulbright lecturer, 1987; Rochester Institute of Technology, Gannett lecturer, 1989-90. Writer. **Publications:** Benjamin Franklin, 1965; James Madison: A Biography, 1971; From Colony to Country: The Revolution in American Thought, 1750-1820, 1974; From Independence to Interdependence, 1976; Presidents Above Party: The First American Presidency 1789-1829, 1984; Anti-federalist Papers, 1986; Individualism and Public Life: A Modern Dilemma, 1987; (co-author) Participation in Government, 1988; Framed for Posterity: The Enduring Philosophy of the Constitution, 1993; The Idea of Democracy in the Modern Era, 2004; Madisons at Montpelier: Reflections on the Founding Couple, 2009. EDITOR: (with W. Hutchinson and W.M.E. Rachal) The Papers of James Madison, vol. I-II, 1962; (with L.W. Labaree) The Papers of Benjamin Franklin, vol. VI-VII, 1963; (with L.W. Labaree) The Autobiography of Benjamin Franklin, 1964; The Political Thought of Benjamin Franklin, 1965; (intro.) Selected Writings of James Madison, 2006. **Address:** Maxwell School, Syracuse University, 145 Eggers Hall, Syracuse, NY 13244, U.S.A. **Online address:** rketcham@syr.edu

KETCHUM, Richard M. American (born United States), b. 1922. **Genres:** History, Biography, Military/Defense/Arms Control. **Career:** Charles F. Orvis Co., assistant, 1946-48; Vermonters Ltd., partner, 1948-51; American Heritage Publishing Company Inc., Book Division, editor, 1956-64, editorial director, 1964-67, managing director, vice-president and director, 1967-74; Blair & Ketchum's Country Journal, editor and co-founder, 1974-84. **Publications:** What Is Communism?, 1955; Male Husbandry, 1956; American Heritage Book of Great Historic Places, 1957; The Battle for Bunker Hill, 1962; Faces from the Past, 1970; The Secret Life of the Forest, 1970; The Winter Soldiers: The Battles for Trenton and Princeton, 1973; Will Rogers, His Life and Times, 1973; The World of George Washington, 1974; Decisive Day: The Battle for Bunker Hill, 1974; Second Cutting: Letters from the Country, 1981; The Borrowed Years, 1938-1941: America on the Way to War, 1989; The Borrowed Years, 1938-1941: America on the Way to War, 1991; The Winter Soldiers, 1991; The Winter Soldiers: The Battles for Trenton and Princeton, 1991; Saratoga: Turning Point of the American Revolutionary War, 1997; Divided Loyalties: How the American Revolution Came to New York, 2002; Victory at Yorktown: The Campaign that Won the Revolution, 2004. EDITOR: What Is Democracy?, 1955; American Heritage Book of the Revolution, 1958; American Heritage Book of the Pioneer Spirit, 1959; American Heritage Picture History of the Civil War, 1960; The Horizon Book of the Renaissance, 1961; Four Days, 1964; American Heritage Cookbook and Illustrated History of American Eating and Drinking, 1964; The Original Water-Color Paintings for the Birds of America, 1966; (with I. Glusker) American Testament: Fifty Great Documents of American History, 1971; (with J.H. Plumb and B. Lancaster) American Heritage History of the American Revolution, 1984. **Address:** Brandt and Hochman, 1501 Broadway, Ste. 2310, New York, NY 10036-5689, U.S.A.

KETCHUM, William C. (William C(larence) Ketchum). American (born United States), b. 1931. **Genres:** Antiques/Furnishings, Art/Art History, Crafts, Education. **Career:** Attorney, 1960-74; New School for Social Research, instructor in collecting American antiques, 1971-88, instructor in fine arts, 1974-78; New York University, instructor in art and art editor, 1984-86, 1989-; Museum of American Folk Art, curator of special projects, 1984-89, faculty, 1986-87, 1990-; Marymount College, instructor in antiques, 1986-92; Folk Art Institute, faculty, 1990-. **Publications:** Early Potters and Potteries of New York State, 1970, 2nd ed. as Potters and Potteries of New York State, 1650-1900, 1987; The Pottery and Porcelain Collector's Handbook: A Guide to Early American Ceramics from Maine to California, 1971; American Basketry and Woodenware, 1974; A Treasury of American Bottles, 1975; Hooked Rugs: A Historical And Collector's Guide: How to Make Your Own, 1976; A Catalog of American Antiques, 1977; The Family Treasury of Antiques, 1978; Early American Crafts, 1979; A Collector's Book of American Folk Crafts, 1979; The Catalog of American Collectibles, 1979; Western Memorabilia: Collectibles of Old West, 1980; The New and Revised Catalog of American Antiques, 1980; Collecting American Craft Antiques, 1980; Auction: The Guide to Bidding, Buying, Bargaining, Selling, Exhibiting & Making a Profit, 1980; The Catalog of World Antiques, 1981; Furniture 2: Neoclassic to the Present, 1981; Toys & Games, 1981; Boxes, 1982; American Furniture: Cupboards, Chests and Related Pieces, 1982; Pottery & Porcelain, 1983; American Folk Art of 20th Century, 1983; Collecting American Bottles for Fun and Profit, 1985; Collecting American Toys, 1985; Collecting Sport Memorabilia, 1985; Collecting Toys for Fun & Profit, 1985; Collecting Bottles for Fun & Profit, 1985; Sports Collectibles for Fun & Profit, 1985; 40's & 50's Collectibles for Fun & Profit 1985; All American: Folk Art and Crafts, 1986; All-American Folk Arts and Crafts, 1986; American Country Pottery: Yellowware and Spongeware, 1987; Holiday Collectibles, 1989; How to Run an Antiques Business, 1990; Holiday Ornaments and Antiques, 1990; How to Make a Living in Antiques, 1990; American Redware, 1991; American Stoneware, 1991; Country Wreaths & Baskets, 1991; Collecting the West, 1992; Western Memorabilia Identification and Price Guide, 1993; American Pottery and Porcelain, 1994; Marked American Furniture, 1995; American Folk Art, 1995; American Cabinetmakers: Marked American Furniture, 1640-1940, 1995; Grandma Moses: An American Original, 1996; Simple Beauty: The Shakers in America, 1996; Art of the Golden West, 1996; Native American Art, 1997; Remington & Russell: Artists of the West, 1997. **Address:** 241 Grace Church St., Rye, NY 10580-4217, U.S.A.

KETCHUM, William C(larence). See KETCHUM, William C.

KETNER, Kenneth Laine. American (born United States), b. 1939. **Genres:** History, Humanities, Philosophy, Biography, Essays, Autobiography/Memoirs, Sciences. **Career:** Texas Tech University, Institute for Studies In Pragmaticism, professor and director, 1971-, Charles Sanders Peirce interdisciplinary professor, 1981-99, Paul Whitfield Horn professor, 1999-. Writer. **Publications:** An Emendation of R.G. Collingwood's Doctrine of Absolute Presuppositions, 1973; Elements of Logic: An Introduction to Peirce's Existential Graphs, 1990; Thief of Peirce: The Letters of Kenneth Laine Ketner and Walker Percy, 1995; His Glassy Essence: An Autobiography of Charles Sanders Peirce, 1998; (with R.G. Beil) A Triadic Theory of Elementary Particle Interactions and Quantum Computation, 2006. EDITOR: (co-ed.) Comprehensive Bibliography and Index of the Published Works of Charles Sanders Peirce with a Bibliography of Secondary Studies, 1977; (co-ed.) Proceedings of the C.S. Peirce Bicentennial International Congress, 1981, 2nd ed., 1986; (with C.J.W. Kloesel) Peirce, Semeiotic and Pragmatism: Essays, 1986; (intro. with H. Putnam) Reasoning and the Logic of Things: The Cambridge Conferences Lectures of 1898, 1992; Peirce and Contemporary Thought: Philosophical Inquiries, 1995. Contributor of articles to books and journals. **Address:** Institute for Studies in Pragmaticism, Texas Tech University, PO Box 40002, Lubbock, TX 79409-0002, U.S.A. **Online address:** kenneth.ketner@ttu.edu

KETRON, Larry. American (born United States), b. 1947. **Genres:** Plays/Screenplays. **Career:** Writer, 1972-74; screen writer, 1983-; Workshop of the Players Art Theater (WPA), playwright, 1979-86. **Publications:** Patrick Henry Lake Liquors, 1977; Quail Southwest, 1977; Rib Cage, 1978; Character Lines, 1980; The Trading Post, 1981; Ghosts of the Loyal Oaks, 1982; Asian Shade, 1983; Eudora Welty's The Hitch-Hikers, 1986; Fresh Horses, 1986. **Address:** c/o David Saunders, APA/Agency, 9000 Sunset Blvd., Ste. 1200, Los Angeles, CA 90069, U.S.A. **Online address:** lketron@sc.rr.com

KETTELKAMP, Larry Dale. American (born United States), b. 1933. **Genres:** Children's Non-fiction, Music, Paranormal, Psychology, Sciences, Sports/Fitness, Biography, Novels, History. **Career:** Garrard Publishing, art director, 1959-60; Highlights for Children, layout and staff artist, 1962-67; Cranbury School, art teacher, 1968-70; Summy-Birchard Music, director of publications, 1981-82; Bookarts Associates, director, 1982-; Rider University, instructor of graphic design, 1986-90; Cranbury United Methodist Church, organist and choir director, 1989-. Writer and musician. **Publications:** The Sun, 1953; Parrakeets, 1953; Spooky Magic, 1955; The Magic of Sound, 1956; Shadows, 1957; Singing Strings, 1958; Kites, 1959; Drums, Rattles and Bells, 1960; Gliders, 1961; Flutes, Whistles and Reeds, 1962; Puzzle Patterns, 1963; Spirals, 1964; Horns, 1964; Spinning Tops, 1966; Song, Speech and Ventriloquism, 1967; Dreams, 1968; Haunted Houses, 1969; Sixth Sense, 1970; Investigating UFOs, 1971; Religions East and West, 1972; Astrology, Wisdom of the Stars, 1973; Hypnosis: The Wakeful Sleep, 1975; The Dreaming Mind, 1975; A Partnership of Mind and Body: Biofeedback, 1976; Tricks of Eye and Mind, 1976; Investigating Psychics, 1977; The Healing Arts, 1978; Lasers, 1979; Mischievous Ghosts, 1980; Your Marvelous Mind, 1980; Electronic Musical Instruments, 1984; Starter Solos for Classical Guitar, 1984; Intermediate Etudes for Classical Guitar, 1984; The Human Brain, 1986; Modern Sports Science, 1986; Bill Cosby, 1987; Computer Graphics: How it Works, What it Does, 1989; High Tech for the Handicapped: New Ways to Hear, See, Talk and Walk, 1991; Living in Space, 1993; Ets and UFOs: Are They Real, 1996. Illustrator of books by others. **Address:** 26 Labaw Dr., Cranbury, NJ 08512, U.S.A. **Online address:** bookartsandmusic@comcast.net

KETTELL, Steven. British (born England), b. 1973. **Genres:** Politics/Government, Economics. **Career:** University of Birmingham, lecturer in British politics, 2003-05; University of Warwick, associate professor of political science, 2005-. Writer. **Publications:** The Political Economy of Exchange Rate Policy-Making: From the Gold Standard to the Euro, 2004; Dirty Politics? New Labour, British Democracy and the Invasion of Iraq, 2006. **Address:** Department of Politics and International Studies, University of Warwick, Coventry, WM CV4 7AL, England. **Online address:** s.kettell@warwick.ac.uk

KEVANE, Bridget. American/Italian (born Italy), b. 1963?. **Genres:** Language/Linguistics, Race Relations, Ethics. **Career:** Montana State University, Department of Modern Languages and Literatures, professor of Latin American and Latino Studies and chair; The Forward, contributing writer; Tablet, contributing writer. **Publications:** (With J. Heredia) Latina Self-Portraits: Interviews with Contemporary Women Writers, 2000; Latino Literature in America, 2003; Literature as Windows to World Literature: U.S. Latino/Literature, 2003; Profane & Sacred: Latino/American Writers Reveal the Interplay of the Secular and the Religious, 2008; The Anxiety of Social Identities: Jewish Latino Voices in the 21st Century, forthcoming. **Address:** Department of Modern Languages and Literatures, College of Letters & Science, Montana State University, 117A Gaines Hall, PO Box 172980, Bozeman, MT 59717-2980, U.S.A. **Online address:** umlbk@montana.edu

KEVILL-DAVIES, Sally. British (born England), b. 1945. **Genres:** Antiques/Furnishings, Medicine/Health, History, Children's Fiction. **Career:** Sotheby's, cataloger and ceramics expert, 1965-74; Fitzwilliam Museum, staff. Writer. **Publications:** Price Guide to Eighteenth Century English Pottery, 1972; Antique Pocket Guides: Jelly Moulds, 1983; Yesterday's Children: The Antiques and History of Childcare, 1991. Works appear in anthologies. Contributor to periodicals. **Address:** Maggie Noach Literary Agency, 21 Redan St., London, GL W14 0AB, England.

KEVLES, Bettyann Holtzmann. American (born United States), b. 1938. **Genres:** Animals/Pets, Art/Art History, Biology, Natural History, Travel/Exploration, Bibliography, Medicine/Health, Essays, Essays. **Career:** Sunbeam, editor, writer, 1967-69; Westridge School, history instructor, 1970-76; Los Angeles Times, columnist, book reviewer, 1982-96; University of California Press, sponsoring editor, 1984-87, science editor, 1993-97; Stanford University Press, consulting editor, 1988-90; Art Center College, instructor, 1989-2001; Yale University, department of history, senior lecturer, 2001-. **Publications:** Watching the Wild Apes: The Primate Studies of Goodall, Fossey, and Galdikas, 1976; (contrib.) Cassandra Rising: Science Fiction by Women, 1978; Thinking Gorillas: Testing and Teaching the Greatest Ape, 1980; Listening In, 1981; Females of the Species: Sex and Survival in the Animal Kingdom, 1986; Naked to the Bone: Medical Imaging in the Twentieth Century, 1997; Gary Schneider, Genetic Self-Portrait, a Portrait Without the Camera Face at the Santa Barbara Museum of Art, 1999; (with M. Nissenson) Pictur-

ing DNA: An Essay on Art, Science, and the Human Genome, 2000; Almost Heaven: The Story of Women in Space, 2003; Tomorrow: An American Place and Time, forthcoming. **Address:** Department of History, Yale University, SHM L-218, PO Box 208324, New Haven, CT 06520-8324, U.S.A. **Online address:** bettyann.kevles@yale.edu

KEVLES, Daniel J. American (born United States), b. 1939. **Genres:** History, Sciences, Horticulture, Law, Physics, Politics/Government, Technology, Environmental Sciences/Ecology, Environmental Sciences/Ecology. **Career:** California Institute of Technology, Division of Humanities and Social Sciences, professor of the humanities, 1964-; Yale University, Department of History, faculty, 2000-; NY Public Library, Cullman Center for Scholars and Writers, fellow, 2008-09. Writer. **Publications:** The Physicists: The History of a Scientific Community in Modern America, 1978; In the Name of Eugenics: Genetics and the Uses of Human Heredity, 1985; (co-ed.) The Code of Codes: Scientific and Social Issues in the Human Genome Project, 1992; The Baltimore Case: A Trial of Politics, Science, and Character, 1998; (co-author) Inventing America: A History of the United States, 2002, 2nd ed., 2006; (co-ed.) Le Scienze Biologiche e la Medicina, in Storia di Scienza, vol. VIII, 2004; (co-ed) Living Properties: Making Knowledge and Controlling Ownership in the History of Biology, 2009. **Address:** Department of History, Yale University, PO Box 208324, New Haven, CT 06520-8324, U.S.A. **Online address:** daniel.kevles@yale.edu

KEVORKIAN, Martin. American (born United States), b. 1968?. **Genres:** Technology, Information Science/Computers, History. **Career:** University of Texas, Department of English, assistant professor, 2002-06, associate professor, 2006-, associate chair, 2007-. Writer. **Publications:** Color Monitors: The Black Face of Technology in America, 2006. Contributor to journals. **Address:** Department of English, University of Texas, PAR 325, B5000, 1 University Sta., Austin, TX 78712-0803, U.S.A. **Online address:** mkevorkian@mail.utexas.edu

KEYES, Daniel. American (born United States), b. 1927. **Genres:** Novels, Mystery/Crime/Suspense, Science Fiction/Fantasy, Adult Non-fiction, Young Adult Fiction, Autobiography/Memoirs. **Career:** Stadium Publishing Co., associate fiction editor, 1950-52; Pulp Magazine, editor, 1950; Fenko & Keyes Photography Inc., co-owner, 1953; Wayne State University, instructor in English, 1962-66; Ohio University, lecturer, 1966-72, professor of English, 1972-2000, professor emeritus, 2000-, Creative Writing Center, director, 1973-74, 1977-78. **Publications:** Flowers for Algernon, 1966; The Touch, 1968 in UK as The Contaminated Man, 1973; The Fifth Sally, 1980; The Minds of Billy Milligan (non-fiction), 1981, rev. ed., 1982; Charlie and Algernon, 1981; Unveiling Claudia: A True Story of a Serial Murder (non-fiction), 1986; Daniel Keyes Collected Stories, 1993; The Milligan Wars (non-fiction), 1993; Daniel Keyes Reader, 1994; Until Death Do Us Part: The Sleeping Princess (fiction), 1998; Algernon, Charlie and I: A Writer's Journey (non-fiction), 1999; The Asylum Prophecies (novel), 2009. **Address:** c/o Marcy Posner, William Morris Agency, 1325 Ave. of the Americas, New York, NY 10019, U.S.A.

KEYNES, Randal. American/British (born England), b. 1948. **Genres:** Biography, Sciences, Biology. **Career:** Writer. **Publications:** Annie's Box: Charles Darwin, His Daughter and Human Evolution, 2001 in UK as Darwin, His Daughter and Human Evolution, 2002. **Address:** c/o Author Mail, Riverhead Books, 375 Hudson St., New York, NY 10014, U.S.A.

KEYNES, Simon. British (born England), b. 1952. **Genres:** History, Bibliography. **Career:** University of Cambridge, Trinity College, fellow, 1976-, Department of Anglo-Saxon, Norse, and Celtic, lecturer in Anglo-Saxon history, 1978-92, reader in Anglo-Saxon history, 1992-99, Elrington and Bosworth professor of Anglo-Saxon history, 1999-; Oxford Dictionary of National Biography, associate editor, 2003-2004; Anglo-Saxon England, co-editor. **Publications:** HISTORY: The Diplomas of King Aethelred The Unready (978-1016): A Study in Their Use as Historical Evidence, 1980; (trans. and intro. with M. Lapidge) Alfred the Great: Asser's Life of King Alfred and Other Contemporary Sources, 1983; The Liber Vitae of the New Minster and Hyde Abbey Winchester, 1996; (intro.) Encomium Emmae Reginae, 1998; Anglo-Saxon History: A Select Bibliography, 1998; A Handlist of Anglo-Saxon Charters, 2001. EDITOR: (with D. Dumville) The Anglo-Saxon Chronicle: A Collaborative Edition, 1983; Facsimiles of Anglo-Saxon Charters, 1991; Quentin Keynes, 2004; (with A.P. Smyth) Anglo-Saxons: Studies Presented to Cyril Roy Hart, 2006. **Address:** Department of Anglo-Saxon, Norse, and Celtic, University of Cambridge, 9 West Rd., Cambridge, CB CB3 9DP, England. **Online address:** sdk13@cam.ac.uk

KEYS, David. British (born England) **Genres:** Archaeology/Antiquities, Sciences, History. **Career:** The Independent, archaeology correspondent. Writer. **Publications:** (With G. Allen and A. Sharples) Thatcher's Britain: A Guide to the Ruins, 1983; Catastrophe: An Investigation into the Origins of the Modern World, 2000. Contributor to periodicals. **Address:** The Independent, Independent House, 191 Marsh Wall, London, GL E14 9RS, England.

KEYS, Kerry Shawn. (Gopiah). American (born United States), b. 1946. **Genres:** Novellas/Short Stories, Plays/Screenplays, Poetry, Songs/Lyrics And Libretti, Translations. **Career:** Pennsylvania State University, Mont Alto Campus, instructor in English literature, 1973, Language Laboratory, teacher of English and coordinator, 1974-77; Pine Press, editor and publisher, 1977-; Harrisburg Area Community College, instructor in English literature, 1979-84; Dickinson College, instructor in English literature, 1980, associate fellow in English, 1981-; Vilnius University, Fulbright associate professor of English, 1998-2000. Writer. **Publications:** POETRY: Swallowtails Gather These Stones, 1973; Jade Water, 1974; O Pintore o Poeta: The Painter and the Poet, Jose Paulo Moreira da Fonseca, 1976; Loose Leaves Fall: Selected Poems, 1977; Quingumbo: Nova Poesia Norte-Americana, 1980; Seams, 1985; A Gathering of Smoke: Gopiah's South Indian Prose-Poem Journals, 1986; The Hearing, 1992; Fingerlings, 1993; Decoy's Desire, 1993; Fingerlings 2, 1994; Selected Poems, 1994; Tao Te ching Meditations, Bones & Buzzards, 2003; Conversations with Tertium Quid: And 27 Books of Poems and Prose, 2003; Blue Rose Fusion, 2004; Broken Circle, 2005; Burning Mirror, 2008; Book of Beasts, 2009; Transporting, a Cloak of Rhapsodies, 2010. TRANSLATOR: A Knife All Blade (poem), 1982; In the Tracks of the Dead (poems), 1993; Landsend, 1998; S. Geda, Biopsy of Winter, 2002; A Selection, 2002; Six Young Lithuanian Poets: Laurynas Katkus, Tomas S. Butkus, Marius Burokas, Jurgita Butkytė, Agnė Žagrakalytė, Giedrė Kazlauskaitė, 2002; J. Jackevicius, (with J. Glauberzonaite) The Yellow Insect, 2005; J. Jackevicius, (with J. Glauberzonaite) A Bug In The Brain, 2007. OTHER: Warm Springs, 1995; Flamenco Songs, 1995; Blues in Green, 1996; (with J. Burns) The Nearing Notebooks, 1996; Narrow Passage to the Deep Light, 1996; Ratoons, 1996; Krishna's Karma, 1997; Turning the Mask, 1997; Ch'antscapes, 1998; Moon Shining the Millennium, 1997; Sorrows of an Old Worder, 1998; The Festival of Familiar Light, 1998; Menulio smukle, 1999; Inclusions, 2002; Law of Returns, 2004; Land of People, 2007. Contributor to periodicals. **Address:** Zemaitijas 3-15, Vilnius, 2001, Lithuania. **Online address:** kkeys@post.omnitcl.nct

KEYS, Mary M. American (born United States), b. 1966. **Genres:** Young Adult Fiction. **Career:** University of Notre Dame, Department of Government and International Studies (now the Department of Political Science), visiting instructor and adjunct instructor, 1994-96, instructor, 1996-98, assistant professor, 1998-2005, associate professor of political science, 2005-, director of graduate studies, 2008-09, Erasmus Institute, junior faculty fellow, 2000-01, Medieval Institute, fellow, Nanovic Institute for European Studies, fellow; University of Chicago, The Martin Marty Center, senior research fellow, 2003-04. Writer and political scientist. **Publications:** Aquinas, Aristotle, and the Promise of the Common Good, 2006. Contributor to periodicals. **Address:** Department of Political Science, University of Notre Dame, 352 Decio, 217 O'Shaughnessy Hall, 400 Main Bldg., Notre Dame, IN 46556-5639, U.S.A. **Online address:** mkeys1@nd.edu

KEYSER, James D. American (born United States), b. 1950. **Genres:** Anthropology/Ethnology, Art/Art History, Biography, Social Sciences, Photography. **Career:** Field archaeologist, 1973-76; State University of New York, assistant professor of anthropology, 1976-77; University of Tulsa, assistant professor of anthropology, 1977-78; U.S. Forest Service, Minerals and Geology Group, archaeologist, 1978-80, Pacific Northwest Region, regional archaeologist, 1980-; Plains Anthropological Conference, director, 1985-88; Portland State University, lecturer, 1999-2000; Walking Softly Adventures, European rock art tour leader, 1999-2001. Writer. **Publications:** (With J.A. Farley) Little Caney River Prehistory: 1977 Field Season, 1979; Rock Art of Western South Dakota, 1984; Indian Rock Art of the Columbia Plateau, 1992; Indian Petroglyphs of the Columbia Gorge: The Jeanne Hillis Rubbings, 1994; The Five Crows Ledger: Biographic Warrior Art of the Flathead Indians, 2000; (with M.A. Klassen) Plains Indian Rock Art, 2001; Art of the Warriors: Rock art of the American Plains, 2004; (ed. with G. Poetschat and

M.W. Taylor) Talking with the Past: The Ethnography of Rock Art, 2006. Contributor to books. **Address:** University of Utah Press, Rm. 252, 260 S Central Campus Dr., Salt Lake City, UT 84112-9153, U.S.A.

KEYSERLINGK, Robert H. *See* Obituaries.

KHADIVI, Laleh. American/Iranian (born Iran), b. 1977?. **Genres:** Novels. **Career:** Documentary filmmaker, 1998-; University of Wisconsin, Carl Djerassi fellow in creative writing; Emory University, creative writing fellow in fiction, 2007-09. Writer. **Publications:** The Age of Orphans (novel), 2009. Contributor to magazines. **Address:** Creative Writing Program, Emory University, N110 Callaway Ctr., 537 Kilgo Cir., Atlanta, GA 30322, U.S.A. **Online address:** lkhadiv@emory.edu

KHADRA, Yasmina. *See* **MOULESSEHOUL, Mohammed.**

KHAKPOUR, Porochista. American/Iranian (born Iran), b. 1978. **Genres:** Novels. **Career:** Fairfield University, low-residency MFA Program, faculty. Freelance writer. **Publications:** Sons and Other Flammable Objects (novel), 2007. **Address:** c/o Seth Fishman, The Gernert Company, 136 E 57th St., New York, NY 10022, U.S.A. **Online address:** flammableobjects@gmail.com

KHALID, Mansour. British (born England), b. 1931. **Genres:** Area Studies, International Relations/Current Affairs, Politics/Government. **Career:** Attorney, 1957-59; United Nations (UN), legal officer, 1962-63, deputy resident representative in Algeria, 1964-65, UN Security Council, president, 1971-75, special consultant on coordination of UN information system, 1982; Government of Sudan, minister of youth and social affairs, 1969-71, UN General Assembly, chair of delegation of Sudan, special consultant and personal representative of UNESCO director-general for United Nations WRA fund-raising mission, 1970, permanent representative of Sudan to UN, 1971, minister of foreign affairs, 1971-75, 1977, minister of education, 1975-77, assistant, 1976-77; University of Colorado, visiting professor, 1968; University of Khartoum, 1982; Office of the President, special adviser, 2006-07; Ministry of Foreign Trade, staff, 2007-08; United Nations Environmental Program, senior advisor to the executive director; African Center for Resources and the Environment, chair. Writer. **Publications:** NON FICTION: Private Law in Sudan, 1970; The Nile Basin, Present and Future, 1971; Solution of the Southern Problem and its African Implications, 1972; The Decision-Making Process in Foreign Policy, 1973; Sudan Experiment With Unity, 1973; Diplomacy and Development, 1974; ḥiwār ma a al-safwah, 1974; The Socio-Cultural Determinants of Arab Diplomacy, 1974; World Food Crisis: What After Rome?, 1975; La khayr fī-nā in lam naqulhā, 1980; Nimeiri and the Revolution of Dis-May, 1985; Fajr al-kādhib: Numayrii, wa-taḥrīif al-sharī'ah, 1986; (ed. and intro.) John Garang Speaks, 1987; The Government They Deserve: The Role of the Elite in Sudan's Political Evolution, 1990; (ed. and intro.) The Call for Democracy in Sudan, 1992; Al-Nukhbah al-Sūdānīyah wa-idmān al-fashal, 1993; Al-Thulāthīyah al-Mājidīyah, 1997; Janūb al-Sūdān fī al-mukhayyalah al-Arabīyah, 2000; (ed. and intro.) Africa through the Eyes of a Patriot: A Tribute to General Olusegun Obasanjo, 2001; War and Peace in Sudan: A Tale of Two Countries, 2002; Takāthur al-zâEāizi' wa-tanāqus al-awtād, 2010. **Address:** 9 Jubilee Palace, London, GL SW3 3TD, England.

KHALVATI, Mimi. British/Iranian (born Iran), b. 1944. **Genres:** Poetry, Anthropology/Ethnology. **Career:** The Poetry School, coordinator, 1997-2004; Slade Poetry School, director; Manchester University, Poetry Centre, faculty; Theatre Workshop, actress and director; Theatre in Exile, co-founder; University of London, Goldsmiths College, visiting lecturer; London Poetry School, director; Arvon Foundation, tutor; Royal Mail, poet-in-residence. **Publications:** I Know a Place, 1985; Persian Miniatures/A Belfast Kiss, 1990; In White Ink, 1991; Mirrorwork, 1995; Entries on Light, 1997; Selected Poems, 2000; The Chine, 2002; Plant Care: A Festschrift for Mimi Khalvati, 2004; The Meanest Flower, 2007; (trans. with C. Hardi) K. Ahmad, Poems, 2008. EDITOR: (with P. Petit) Tying the Song: A First Anthology fro the Poetry School, 1997-2000, 2000; (with G. Fawcett) Entering the Tapestry: A Second Anthology from the Poetry School, 2001-2003, 2003; Poetry to Calm Your Soul, 2005; (with K. Green) This Little Stretch of Life, 2006; (with S. Knight) I am Twenty People!: A Third Anthology from the Poetry School, 2004-2006, 2007; Saudade: An Anthology of Fado Poetry, 2010. **Address:** Carcanet Press Ltd., Alliance House, Cross St., 4th Fl., Manchester, GM M2 7AP, England. **Online address:** mk@mimikhalvati.co.uk

KHAN, Adib. Australian/Bangladeshi (born Bangladesh), b. 1949. **Genres:**

Literary Criticism And History, Novels, Young Adult Fiction. **Career:** Ballarat Grammar School, teacher. Writer. **Publications:** Poetry Examined, 1984; Seasonal Adjustments, 1994; Solitude of Illusions, 1996; The Storyteller, 2000; Homecoming, 2003; Spiral Road, 2007. Contributor to periodicals and journals. **Address:** Allen & Unwin Ltd., 83 Alexander St., PO Box 8500, Crows Nest, NW 2065, Australia.

KHAN, Aisha. American (born United States), b. 1955. **Genres:** Theology/Religion, Race Relations, History, Anthropology/Ethnology, Social Sciences. **Career:** New York University, Department of Anthropology, associate professor, director of undergraduate studies. Writer. **Publications:** Callaloo Nation: Metaphors of Race and Religious Identity among South Asians in Trinidad, 2004; (ed. with G. Baca and S. Palmié) Empirical Futures: anthropologists and Historians Engage the Work of Sidney W. Mintz, 2009. Contributor to journals. **Address:** Department of Anthropology, New York University, Rufus D. Smith Hall, 25 Waverly Pl., New York, NY 10003-6701, U.S.A. **Online address:** ak105@nyu.edu

KHAN, Badrul H(uda). American/Bangladeshi (born Bangladesh), b. 1958. **Genres:** Education, Business/Trade/Industry, Economics, Information Science/Computers. **Career:** Indiana University, Indianapolis, University Computing Services, computer consultant, 1988-90, Medical Educational Resources Program, instructional systems developer and evaluation specialist, 1993-94; National Science Foundation, research associate, 1990-92; Indiana University-Purdue University, School of Education, research assistant, 1993; University of Texas, assistant professor of educational technology and founding director of graduate program in educational technology, 1994-97; George Washington University, associate professor of educational technology and founding program director of educational technology leadership cohort program, 1997-2006; e-TQM College, chief e-learning advisor, 2003-; Granato Group, chief learning consultant, 2004-, chief learning officer; independent consultant, 2006-; Elsevier Inc., branded learning portal expert, 2006-; Asian Virtual University, BooksToRead.com, founder, WebCourseReview.com, founder; George Mason University, Instructional Technology Program, adjunct professor, 2008-; Educational Technology, editor; International Review of Research, consulting editor; McWeadon Education, founder and president. Writer. **Publications:** (Ed.) Web-Based Instruction, 1997; Instructional Multimedia Presentation with PowerPoint: A Practical Guide, 1997; (ed.) Web-Based Training, 2001; E-Learning Strategies, 2002; E-Learning Checklist, 2002; Web-Based Learning, 2003; E-learning QUICK Checklist, 2005; E-learning: Design, Delivery and Evaluation, 2005; Managing e-learning: Design, Delivery, Implementation, and Evaluations, 2005; (ed.) Flexible Learning in an Information Society, 2006; (ed.) User Interface Design for Virtual Environments, 2012. Contributor to periodicals. **Address:** George Mason University, MS4F3, 4400 University Dr., Fairfax, VA 22030-4422, U.S.A. **Online address:** khanb@bookstoread.com

KHAN, Hasan-Uddin. American/Indian (born India), b. 1947. **Genres:** Architecture, Theology/Religion. **Career:** Payette Associates Inc., assistant architect, 1972-73; Gerald Shenstone and Partners, project architect, 1973-74; Unit 4 Architects and Planners, partner, 1974-76; Aga Khan Award for Architecture (now Aga Khan Trust for Culture), assistant convenor, 1977-79, convenor, 1980, director of special projects and public education, 1991-94; Mimar: Architecture in Development, founder and editor-in-chief, 1980-83; Concept Media Ltd., board director, 1981-87; Secretariat of the Aga Khan, head of architectural activities, 1984-91; Zamana Gallery Ltd., board director, 1985-92; Massachusetts Institute of Technology, Department of Architecture, visiting associate professor, 1994-2000, visiting professor of architecture; Roger Williams University, distinguished professor of architecture and historic preservation, 1999-, International Fellows Program, director, 1999; Rockefeller Foundation, consultant. Writer. **Publications:** Charles Correa: Architect in India, 1987; (ed. with M. Frishman) The Mosque: History, Architectural Development & Regional Diversity, 1994; Contemporary Asian Architects (trilingual in English, French, and German), 1995; (with R. Holod) Contemporary Mosques: Architects, Clients, and Designs since the 1950s (monograph), 1997; Modernities and Memories: Recent Works from the Islamic World, 1997; (with R. Holod) The Mosque and the Modern World: Architects, Patrons and Designs Since the 1950s, 1997; International Style: Modernist Architecture from 1925 to 1965, 1998; The Middle East, 2001; The Architecture of Habib Fida Ali: Buildings and Projects, 1965-2009, 2010; (ed.) Le Corbusier: Chandigarh and the Modern City, 2010. Contributor of ar-

ticles to journals and books. **Address:** School of Architecture, Art & History, Roger Williams University, 1 Old Ferry Rd., Bristol, RI 02809-2921, U.S.A. **Online address:** hkhan@rwu.edu

KHAN, Mahmood H(asan). Canadian/Pakistani (born Pakistan), b. 1937. **Genres:** Economics, Agriculture/Forestry, Business/Trade/Industry, History. **Career:** Simon Fraser University, assistant professor, 1966-68, associate professor, 1969-79, professor of economics, 1980-, now professor emeritus. Consultant and writer. **Publications:** Role of Agriculture in Economic Development: A Case Study of Pakistan, 1966; Economics of the Green Revolution in Pakistan, 1975; Underdevelopment and Agrarian Structure in Pakistan, 1981; Lectures on Agrarian Transformation in Pakistan, 1985; (ed. with S.N.H. Naqvi and M.G. Chaudhry) Land Reforms in Pakistan: A Historical Perspective, 1987; (with S.N.H. Naqvi and M.G. Chaudhry) Structural Change in Pakistan's Agriculture, 1989; (with S.S. Khan) Rural Change in the Third World: Pakistan and the Aga Khan Rural Support Program, 1992; (ed. with M.A. Faris) Third World Sustainable Agriculture in Egypt, 1993; (with M.A. Faris) Egyptian Women in Agricultural Development, 1994; (with M.A. Faris) Structural Adjustment Policies and Changes in the Agricultural Research System in Egypt, 1995; Climbing the Development Ladder with NGO Support: Experiences of Rural People in Pakistan, 1998; Public Policy and the Rural Economy of Pakistan: Experiences of Rural People in Pakistan, 1998; Community Organizations and Rural Development: Experience in Pakistan, 2001; Methods of Assessment of Rural Poverty, Projects and Programme Impact: A Handbook for Practitioners in Rural Support Programmers, 2004; Agriculture in Pakistan: Change and Progress 1947-2005, 2006; Agricultural Growth in Irrigated Punjab: Some Issues and Policies, 2008; Rural Support Programmes in Pakistan: Methods for Assessment of Cost and Impact, 2009; Participatory Rural Development in Pakistan: Experience of Rural Support Programmes, 2009. **Address:** Department of Economics, Simon Fraser University, WMX 2688, 8888 University Dr., Burnaby, BC V5A 1S6, Canada. **Online address:** mkhan@sfu.ca

KHAN, Rukhsana. Canadian (born Canada), b. 1962. **Genres:** Young Adult Fiction, Novels, Race Relations, Picture/Board Books, Third World, Children's Fiction. **Career:** Writer and storyteller. **Publications:** Bedtime Ba-a-a-lk, 1998; The Roses in My Carpets, 1998; Muslim Child: A Collection of Short Stories and Poems, 1999 as Muslim Child: Understanding Islam through Stories and Poems, 2002; Dahling If You Luv Me Would You Please Please Smile, 1999; King of the Skies, 2001; Ruler of the Courtyard, 2003; Silly Chicken, 2005; Many Windows: Six Kids, Five Faiths, One Community, 2008; A New Life, 2009; Wanting Mor, 2009; Big Red Lollipop, 2010. **Address:** Sterling Lord Literistic Inc., 65 Bleecker St., New York, NY 10012, U.S.A. **Online address:** rukhsana@rukhsanakhan.com

KHAN, Uzma Aslam. Pakistani/American (born United States), b. 1969?. **Genres:** Novels. **Career:** Beaconhouse National University, faculty; University of Arizona, faculty; University of Hawai'i, visiting writer, Department of English, assistant professor, 2008-. **Publications:** The Story of Noble Rot, 2001; Trespassing, 2003; Geometry of God, 2008; The Anatomy of God, forthcoming. **Address:** Department of English, University of Hawai'i, 713 Kuykendall Hall, 1733 Donaghho Rd., Honolulu, HI 96822, U.S.A. **Online address:** uakhan@hawaii.edu

KHAN, Yasmin. British (born England), b. 1977. **Genres:** History. **Career:** University of London, Department of Politics and International Relations, lecturer in politics, senior lecturer, deputy admissions tutor, 2012-. Writer. **Publications:** The Great Partition: The Making of India and Pakistan, 2007. Contributor of articles to periodicals. **Address:** Department of Politics and International Relations, University of London, Rm. FW120, Royal Holloway, Egham, SR TW20 0EX, England. **Online address:** yasmin.khan@rhul.ac.uk

KHANNA, Parag. Indian (born India), b. 1977?. **Genres:** Social Sciences. **Career:** World Economic Forum, scenario & risk planner, 2000-02; Brookings Institution, Global Governance Fellow, 2002-05; United States Special Operations Forces, senior geopolitical advisor, 2007; New America Foundation, Global Governance Initiative, director, American Strategy Program, senior research fellow, 2007-; Observer Research Foundation, visiting fellow, 2004; Georgetown University, Institute for the Study of Diplomacy, non-resident associate, 2004-05; Lee Kwan Yew School of Public Policy, visiting fellow, 2006; American Assembly, Next Generation Fellow, 2007-08; Council on Foreign Relations, research associate. Writer and geopolitical advisor. **Publications:** America's Interests in the United Nations: A U.S. Response to the Report of the UN Secretary General's High-Level Panel on Threats, Challenges and Change, 2005; The Second World: Empires and Influence in the New Global Order, 2008. Contributor to periodicals and magazines. **Online address:** paragkhanna@gmail.com

KHARE, R(avindra) S. American/Indian (born India) **Genres:** Anthropology/Ethnology, Intellectual History, Literary Criticism And History, Theology/Religion, Essays. **Career:** University of Wisconsin, faculty; University of Virginia, professor of anthropology, Center on Critical Human Survival Issues, director. Writer. **Publications:** The Changing Brahmans: Associations and Elites among the Kanya-Kubjas of North India, 1970; Culture and Reality: Essays on the Hindu System of Managing Foods, 1976; The Hindu Hearth and Home, 1976; Normative Culture and Kinship: Essays on Hindu Categories, Processes and Perspectives, 1983; The Untouchable as Himself: Ideology, Identity, and Pragmatism among the Lucknow Chamars, 1984; Culture and Democracy: Anthropological Reflections on Modern India, 1985; Cultural Diversity and Social Discontent: Anthropological Studies on Contemporary India, 1998; Dalits' Changing Challenges: Progressive Social Discourses and New Communication Strategies, 2005. EDITOR: (with J.W. Kolka and C.A. Pollis) Environmental Quality and Social Responsibility, 1972; (with D. Little) Leadership: Interdisciplinary Reflections, 1984; (with M.S.A. Rao) Food, Society, and Culture: Aspects in South Asian Food Systems, 1986; Perspectives on Islamic Law, Justice, and Society, 1987; The Eternal Food: Gastronomic Ideas and Experiences of Hindu and Buddhists, 1992; On and About the Postmodern Crisis: Writing/Rewriting, 1994; Caste, Hierarchy, and Individualism: Indian Critiques of Louis Dumont's Contributions, 2006; (with D.S. Babu) Caste in Life: Experiencing Inequalities, 2011. **Address:** Department of Anthropology, University of Virginia, 305 Brooks Hall, PO Box 400120, Charlottesville, VA 22904-4120, U.S.A. **Online address:** vsk3m@virginia.edu

KHAZANOV, Anatoly M. (Anatoly Michailovich Khazanov). American/Russian (born Russia), b. 1937. **Genres:** Anthropology/Ethnology, Social Sciences. **Career:** Academy of Sciences of the U.S.S.R., Institute of Ethnography, senior assistant, 1960-67; Moscow State University, senior lecturer, 1974, 1975, visiting professor, 1978, 1979; Chernigov Pedagogical Institute, senior lecturer, 1975; Kiev State University, visiting professor, 1976, 1979; Leningrad State University, visiting professor, 1977; The Hebrew University of Jerusalem, visiting professor, 1985-86, 2003-04, professor of sociology and social anthropology, 1985-90; Trenton State College, distinguished visiting professor, 1988-89; University of Manchester, honorary Lord Simon visiting professor, 1990; University of Wisconsin-Madison, professor of anthropology, 1990-97, Ernest Gellner Professor of Anthropology, 1997-, Institute for Research in the Humanities, fellow, 1992; Centre for the Study of Nationalis, co-director, 1996; International Institute for Asian Studies, fellow, 1998; Institute for Advanced Studies, fellow, 2000; Max Plank Institute for Social Anthropology, fellow, 2002, 2005. Writer. **Publications:** (Ed. with S. Payne) Perpetrators, Accomplices and Victims in Twentieth-Century Politics. Reconing with the Past, 2009; (ed. with A. Wink) Nomads in the Sedentary World, 2001; Nomads and the Outside World, 1984, 2nd ed., 1994; Krymchaks: A Vanishing Group in the Soviet Union, 1989; Soviet Nationality Policy During Perestroika, 1991; (ed. with O. Bar-Iosef and intro.) Pastoralism in the Levant: Archaeological Materials in Anthropological Perspectives, 1992; (with I. Peev) Vostochnoe Sredizemnomor'e: mezhdunarodnye otnosheniia v 80-e gody, 1992; After the U.S.S.R.: Ethnicity, Nationalism and Politics in the Commonwealth of Independent States, 1995; (ed. with V. Naumkin and K. Shapiro) Pastoralism in Central Asia, 1997; (ed. with J. Ginat) Changing Nomads in a Changing World, 1998; (ed. with G. Schlee) Who Owns The Stock?: Collective And Multiple Forms of Property in Animals, 2012. IN RUSSIAN: Kochevniki i vneshnii mir, 2000; Essay on the History of the Sarmatian Military Act, 1971, rev. ed., 2008; (with V.P. Alexeev and L.A. Fainberg) Primitive Society: Main Problems of Evolution, 1975; The Gold of the Scythians, 1975; The Social History of the Scythians: Main Problems of Development of the Ancient Nomads of the Eurasian Steppes, 1975; (with A.I. Pershits and L.E. Koubel) The Primitive Periphery of Class Societies, 1978. Contributor of articals to books and journals. **Address:** Department of Anthropology, University of Wisconsin-Madison, 5408 Sewell Social Science Bldg., 1180 Observatory Dr., Madison, WI 53706, U.S.A. **Online address:** khazanov@wisc.edu

KHAZANOV, Anatoly Michailovich. See **KHAZANOV, Anatoly M.**

KHEDAIRI, Betool. Jordanian/Iraqi (born Iraq), b. 1965. **Genres:** Novels.

Career: Writer and consultant. **Publications:** Kam Badat Al Sama Qareeba (novel), 1999, 3rd ed., 2003; Ghayeb (novel), 2004. Contributor to periodicals. **Address:** PO Box 500, Wadi Es-Seir, Amman, 11810, Jordan. **Online address:** betool@betoolkhedairi.com

KHEIRABADI, Masoud. American/Iranian (born Iran), b. 1951. **Genres:** Environmental Sciences/Ecology, Geography, Humanities, International Relations/Current Affairs. **Career:** University of Oregon, adjunct professor of geography, 1987-89; Lewis and Clark College, adjunct instructor, 1987-93; Lane Community College, Adult Education Center, adjunct instructor, 1988-89; Portland State University, adjunct professor of international studies, 1989-; Marylhurst University, adjunct professor, 1990-. Writer. **Publications:** Iranian Cities, 1991, rev. ed., 2000; Iran (Modern World Nations), 2003, 2nd ed., 2011; Islam (Religions of the World), 2004; Sri Satya Sai Baba (Spritual Leaders and Thinkers), 2005. Contributor to journals. **Address:** International Studies Program, Portland State University, Rm. 316, Eastern Hall, Portland, OR 97207, U.S.A. **Online address:** kheirabadim@pdx.edu

KHERDIAN, David. American (born United States), b. 1931. **Genres:** Novels, Children's Fiction, Poetry, Literary Criticism And History, Bibliography, Biography, Young Adult Fiction, Theatre, Theatre. **Career:** The Book House, manager, 1962-63; Northwestern University, literary consultant, 1965; Giligia Press, founder and editor, 1966-73; Institute of American Indian Arts, poetry judge, 1968; Ararat Magazine, editor, 1970-71; State of New Hampshire, poet-in-the-schools, 1971; Two Rivers Press, founder and editor, 1978-86; Forkroads Magazine, editor, 1995-96; Stopinder, editor, 2000-. **Publications:** FICTION: It Started with Old Man Bean, 1980; Beyond Two Rivers, 1981; The Song in the Walnut Grove, 1982; Asking the River: A Novel, 1993. JUVENILE FICTION: (with N. Hogrogian) Right Now; 1983; The Mystery of the Diamond in the Wood, 1983; (with N. Hogrogian) The Animal, 1984; A Song for Uncle Harry, 1989; (with N. Hogrogian) The Cat's Midsummer Jamboree, 1990; The Great Fishing Contest, 1991; By Myself, 1993; Juna's Journey, 1993; Lullaby for Emily, 1995; The Rose's Smile: Farizad of the Arabian Nights, 1997. NON-FICTION: The Road from Home: The Story of an Armenian Girl, 1979; Finding Home, 1981; Root River Run, 1984; Bridger: The Story of a Mountain Man, 1987; On a Spaceship with Beelzebub: By A Grandson Of Gurdjieff, 1991; I Called It Home, 1997; The Revelations of Alvin Tolliver, 2001. TRANSLATOR: The Pearl: Hymn of the Robe of Glory, 1979; Pigs Never See the Stars, 1982; W. Ch'eng-en, Monkey: A Journey to the West, 1992; The Song of the Stork: Early and Ancient Armenian Songs, 2004. EDITOR: (with J. Baloian) Down at the Santa Fe Depot: 20 Fresno Poets, 1970; Poems Here and Now, 1976; The Dog Writes on the Window with His Nose and Other Poems, 1977; Traveling America with Today's Poets, 1977; If Dragon Flies Made Honey: Poems, 1977; I Sing the Song of Myself: An Anthology of Autobiographical Poems, 1978; Beat Voices: An Anthology of Beat Poetry, 1995; (with J. Baloian) Forgotten Bread: First-generation Armenian American Writers, 2007; Armenian Cilicia, 2008. AUTHOR OF INTRODUCTION: The Shivurrus Plant of Mopant, 1968; Father Me Home, Winds, 1975; William Saroyan, Births, 1983; Themes III, 1984. BROADSIDES: Letter to Virginia in Florence from Larkspur, California, 1966; Mother's Day, 1967; Kato's Poem, 1967; Christmas, 1968; My Mother Takes My Wife's Side, 1969; O Kentucky, 1969; Outside the Library, 1969; Root River, 1970; Bird in Suet, 1971; Of Husbands and Wives, 1971; Hey Nonny, 1972; Poem for Nonny, 1973; Onions from New Hampshire, 1973; In the Tradition, 1974; 16: IV: 73, 1975; Anniversary Song, 1975; Remembering Mihran, 1975; The Toy Soldier, 1975; Melkon, 1976; Dafje Vartan, 1978; October 31, 1980, 1980; Letter to Charles J. Hardy from David Kherdian, 1981; Solstice, 1983; The Press at Butternut Creek, 1987. OTHERS: David Meltzer: A Sketch From Memory and Descriptive Checklist, 1965; A Bibliography of William Saroyan: 1934-1965, 1965; A Biographical Sketch and Descriptive Checklist Of Gary Snyder, 1965; Six Poets of the San Francisco Renaissance: Portraits And Checklists, 1967; Six San Francisco Poets, 1969; On the Death of My Father, 1970; Homage to Adana, 1970; Looking Over Hills, 1972; Visions of America By the Poets of Our Time, 1973; Feathers and Tails, 1992; Seeds of Light: Poems from a Gurdjieff Community, 2002; The Buddha: The Story of an Awakened Life, 2004; Letters To My Father: Poems, 2004; Gatherings: Selected and Uncollected Writings, 2011; David of Sassoun, 2012. Contributor to periodicals. **Address:** 5082 County, Rte. 7, Chatham, NY 12037-2604, U.S.A. **Online address:** tavit@earthlink.net

KHILNANI, Sunil. American/Indian (born India), b. 1960. **Genres:** Politics/Government, Literary Criticism And History. **Career:** Cambridge University, Christ's College, fellow, 1987-89; University of London, senior lecturer in politics, 1989-; Seikei University, visiting professor, 1993-94; John Hopkins University, Starr Foundation Professor and director of the South Asia studies program. Writer. **Publications:** Arguing Revolution: The Intellectual Left in Post-War France, 1993; (ed. with P.Hirst) Reinventing Democracy, 1996; The Idea of India, 1998, 3rd ed., 2003; (ed. with S. Kaviraj) Civil Society: History and Possibilities, 2001. Contributor to books. **Address:** Paul H. Nitze School of Advanced International, Studies, John Hopkins University, Rm. 722, 1619 Massachusetts Ave. NW, Washington, DC 20036, U.S.A. **Online address:** khilnani@jhu.edu

KHLENTZOS, Drew M. Australian (born Australia), b. 1952. **Genres:** Philosophy, Sports/Fitness, Medicine/Health. **Career:** University of New England, senior lecturer in philosophy, 1998-, senior lecturer in psychology, 2007-, Language and Cognition Research Centre, faculty. Writer. **Publications:** Fundamentals of logic, 2001; Naturalistic Realism and the Antirealist Challenge, 2004; (ed. with A.C. Schalley) Mental States, vol. I: Evolution, Function, Nature, vol. II: Language and Cognitive Structure, 2007. **Address:** School of Social Science, University of New England, S6 Rm. E11, Armidale, NW 2451, Australia. **Online address:** dkhlentz@une.edu.au

KHLEVNIUK, Oleg V. Russian/Ukranian (born Ukraine), b. 1959. **Genres:** Politics/Government, History, Social Sciences. **Career:** U.S.S.R. Academy of Sciences, Institute of History of the U.S.S.R., affiliate, 1985-87; Kommunist/Svobodnaia mysl' (journal), editorial assistant, 1987-96; State Archive of the Russian Federation, senior researcher fellow, 1996-. **Publications:** NONFICTION AS O.V. KHLEVNIUK: (with V.A. Kozlov) Nachinaetsia s cheloveka: Chelovecheskii faktor v sotsialisticheskom stroitel'stve: Itogi i uroki 30-kh godov, 1988; (with V.A. Kozlov, G.A. Bordiugov and E.Y. Zubkova) Istoricheskii opyt I perestroika: Chelovecheskii faktor v sotsial'no-ekonomicheskom razvitii SSSR, 1989; (with S.S. Khizhniakov) XVIII part-konferentsiia: Vremia, problemy, resheniia, 1990; 1937-i: Stalin, NKVD I sovetskoe obshchestvo, 1992; Stalin I Ordzhonikidze: Konflikty v Politbiuro v 30-e gody, 1993; (ed.) Stalinskoe Politbiuro v 30-e gody: Sbornik dokumentov (Dokumenty sovetskii istorii series), 1995; (contrib.) Soviet History, 1917-53: Essays in Honour of R.W. Davies, 1995; (ed. with L.T. Lih and O.V. Naumov) Pis'ma I.V. Stalina V.M. Molotovu, 1925-1936 gg., 1995; Politbiuro: Mekhanizmy politicheskoi vlasti v 1930-e gody, 1996; (ed. with A.V. Kvashonkin, L.P. Kosheleva and L.A. Rogovaia) Bol'shevistskoe rukovodstvo. Perepiska, 1912-1927 (Dokumenty sovetskii istorii series), 1996; (ed. with V.P. Danilov and A.IU. Vatlin) Kak lomali NE?P: Stenogrammy plenumov TSK VKP(b) 1928-1929, 2000; (ed. with G.S. Sagatelian and B.S. Ilizarov) Stalin, stalinizm, sovetskoe obshchestvo: Sbornik statei, 2000; (ed. with R.W. Davies and E.A. Rees) Stalin I Kaganovich: Perepiska 1931-1936, 2001; (ed. with A.I.A. Livshin and I.B. Orlov) Pis'ma vo vlast', 1928-1939: Zaiavleniia, zhaloby, donosy, pis'ma v gosudarstvennye struktury I sovetskim vozhdiam (Dokumenty sovetskii istorii series), 2002; (contrib.) Central-Local Relations in the Stalinist State, 1928-1941, 2002; (co-author) Politbiuro TSK VKP(b) I Sovet Ministrov SSSR, 1945-1953, 2002; (contrib.) Stalin's Terror: High Politics and Mass Repression in the Soviet Union, 2003; (co-ed.) The History of Stalin's Gulag: Collected Documents, 2004; (contrib.) The Nature of Stalin's Dictatorship: The Politburo, 1924-1953, 2004; (ed. with L.I. Borodkin and P. Gregori) Gulag: E?konomika prinuditel'nogo truda (title means: 'Gulag: Economics of Forced Labor'), 2005; (co-ed.) Stenograms of the TsK RKP(b)-VKP(b) Politburo Meetings, 1923-1938, 2007; Zakliuchennye na stroi?kakh kommunizma, 2008; Master of the House: Stalin and His Inner Circle, 2009; Regional' naià politika N.S. Khrushcheva, 2009; Khòan: Stalin I Utverzhdenie stalinskódiktatury, 2010; (with L. Gorlitskii?) Kholodnyi? mir, 2011. AS OLEG V. KHLEVNIUK: The History of the Gulag: From Collectivization to the Great Terror, 2004; (with Y. Gorlizki) Cold Peace: Stalin and the Soviet Ruling Circle, 1945-1953, 2004. Contributor to periodicals. **Address:** State Archive of the Russian Federation, B. Pirogovskaia 17, Moscow, 119992, Russia.

KHOO, Gaik Cheng. Australian (born Australia), b. 1969?. **Genres:** Literary Criticism And History. **Career:** National University of Singapore, post-doctoral fellow; Australian National University, Australian Capital Territory, lecturer; University of British Columbia, faculty; Simon Fraser University, faculty; University of Victoria, faculty. Academic and writer. **Publications:** Reclaiming Adat: Contemporary Malaysian Film and Literature, 2006. Contributor to periodicals and journals. **Address:** School of Humanities, Australian National University, A.D. Hope Bldg., Canberra, 0200, Australia. **Online address:** gaikcheng.khoo@anu.edu.au

KHOROCHE, Peter (Andrew). British (born England), b. 1947. **Genres:** Art/Art History, Theology/Religion, Translations, Photography, Biography, History. **Career:** University of London, lecturer in Sanskrit, 1970-74. Writer. **Publications:** Towards a New Edition of ārya-Sūra's Jātakamālā, 1978; (trans.) A. Sura, Once the Buddha Was a Monkey, 1989; Ivon Hitchens, 1990; Ben Nicholson: Drawings and Painted Reliefs, 2002; Ivon Hitchens, 2007; (trans. and intro. with H. Tieken) Poems on Life and Love in Ancient India, 2009. Contributor to periodicals. **Address:** 20 Orchard St., Cambridge, CB1 1JS, England.

KHOSLA, Dhillon. American/Belgian (born Belgium) **Genres:** Autobiography/Memoirs. **Career:** California Supreme Court, judicial staff attorney; Ninth Circuit Court of Appeals, judicial staff attorney. Musician and writer. **Publications:** Both Sides Now: One Man's Journey through Womanhood (memoir), 2006. **Address:** c/o Tony Colao, MasterMedia Speakers Bureau, 14 Laurel Dr., Easthampton, MA 01027, U.S.A. **Online address:** dhillon@dhillonkhosla.com

KHOURI, Elias. See **KHOURY, Elias.**

KHOURY, Elias. Also writes as Ilyas Khuri, Elias Khouri. Lebanese/Lebanese (born Lebanon), b. 1948. **Genres:** Novels, Novels. **Career:** Palestinian Liberation Organization Research Center, staff, 1973-79; Shu'un Filastin, editor, 1975-79; Al-Safir, editor for literature, 1979-91, Cultural Section, editorial director, 1983-90; Al-Karmel, editorial director, 1981-82; Al-Nahar, editor-in-chief, 1992-, Al-Mulhaq, editor; Columbia University, faculty; New York University, faculty; American University of Beirut, faculty; Lebanese University, faculty; Lebanese American University, faculty. Journalist, literary critic and playwright. **Publications:** AS ILYAS KHURI: (with I. Abbas and F. al-Naqib) Ghassān Kanafāni, 1974; Tajribat al-baḥth an ufuq, 1974; An alaqat al-da irah, 1975; Jabal al-ṣ aghīr, 1977; Dirāsāt fi naqd al-shir, 1979; Abwāb al madīnah, 1981; Wujūh al-bayḍ ā, 1981; Dhākirah al-mafqūdah, 1982; Mubtadā wa-al-khabar, 1984; Zaman al-iḥtilāl, 1985; Riḥlat Ghāndī al-ṣ aghīr, 1989; Mamlakat al-ghurabā, 1993; Majma' al asrar 1994; Bāb al-shams, 1998; Raihat al saboon, 2000; Yalo, 2002; Kaanaha naoma 2007; Sinalcol, 2012. **Address:** c/o Author Mail, Archipelago Books, 25 Jay St., Ste. 203, Brooklyn, NY 11201-8325, U.S.A. **Online address:** ek47@nyu.edu

KHOURY, Raymond. British/Lebanese (born Lebanon), b. 1960?. **Genres:** Novels. **Career:** British Broadcasting Corp. (BBC), staff writer, producer. **Publications:** The Last Templar, 2006; The Sanctuary, 2007; The Sign, 2009; The Templar Salvation, 2010; The Devil's Elixir, 2011. **Address:** c/o Aaron Kaplan, William Morris Agency, 1 William Morris Pl., Beverly Hills, CA 90212, U.S.A.

KHOURY-GHATA, Vénus. French/Lebanese (born Lebanon), b. 1937?. **Genres:** Novels, Poetry, Young Adult Fiction, Literary Criticism And History. **Career:** Poet and novelist. **Publications:** Les inadaptés, 1971; Dialogue à propos d'un Christ ou d'un acrobate, 1975; Au sud du silence, 1975; Alma cousue main: ou le Voyage immobile, 1977; Les ombres et leurs cris: poèmes, 1979; Le fils empaillé, 1980; Qui parle au nom du Jasmin, 1980; Un faux pas du soleil, 1982; Vacarme pour une lune morte, 1983; Les morts n'avaient pas d'ombre, 1984; Mortemaison, 1986; Monologue du mort, 1986; Bayarmine, 1988; Les fugues d'Olympia, 1989; (trans.) Bagiarmin, 1991; Fables pour un peuple d'argilie, 1992; La maîtresse du notable, 1992; Mon anthologie, 1993; Les fiancées du cap Téns, 1995; Le maestra, 1996; Baalbek, 1997; Anthologie Personnelle: poésie, 1997; Une maison au bord des larmes, 1998; Elle dit; suivi de Les sept brins de chvrefeuille de la sagesse: pomes, 1999; La voix des arbres, 1999; Compassion des pierres: pomes, 2001; Here There Was Once a Country, 2001; Privilège des morts, 2001; Le fleuve, 2001; Le moine l'Ottoman et la femme du grand argentier, 2003; Quelle est la nuit parmi les nuits, 2004; Maison aux orties: Roman, 2006; Sept pierres pour la femme adultère, 2007; Obscurcis, 2008; Revenante, 2009; Alphabets of Sand, 2009; Fille Qui Marchait Dans le Désert: Roman, 2010. Contributor to periodicals. **Address:** Graywolf Press, 2402 University Ave., Ste. 203, Saint Paul, MN 55114, U.S.A.

KHURI, Ilyas. See **KHOURY, Elias.**

KHUSH, Gurdev S. American/Indian (born India), b. 1935. **Genres:** Agriculture/Forestry, Horticulture, Sciences. **Career:** University of California, research assistant, 1957-60, assistant geneticist, 1960-67, adjunct professor, now professor emeritus; International Rice Research Institute (IRRI), plant breeder, 1967-72, principle plant breeder, Division of Plant Breeding Genetics and Biochemistry, head, 1972-2002. Writer. **Publications:** Cytogenetics of Aneuploids, 1973; (ed. with G.H. Toenniessen) Rice Biotechnology, 1991; (ed. with J. Bennett) Nodulation and Nitrogen Fixation in Rice: Potential and Prospects, 1992; (with N. Panda) Host Plant Resistance to Insects, 1995; (with P.S. Virk) IR Varieties and Their Impact, 2005. Contributor to journals and periodicals. **Address:** Department of Vegetable Crops, University of California, 1135 PRB, 1 Shields Ave., Davis, CA 95616, U.S.A. **Online address:** gurdev@khush.org

KHWAJA, Waqas. (Waqas Ahmad Khwaja). American (born United States), b. 1952. **Genres:** Poetry, Translations, Literary Criticism And History, Politics/Government, Law, Novellas/Short Stories. **Career:** High Court, lawyer/advocate, 1983-93; Writers Group, co-founder, 1984, convener and general editor of publications, 1984-92; Quaid-e-Azam Law College, visiting professor, 1988-91; Punjab Law College, visiting professor, 1988-92; Lahore College for Arts and Sciences, visiting faculty, 1989-90; Punjab University, visiting faculty, 1990-91; Income Tax directorate of Training, visiting faculty, 1992-93; Emory University, visiting instructor, 1995, 1996; Agnes Scott College, Department of English, visiting professor of English, 1995-2000, assistant professor of English, 2001-04, chair, 2004-07, associate professor of English, 2004-10, full professor, 2010-. **Publications:** POETRY: Six Geese from a Tomb at Medum (poems), 1987; (as Waqas Ahmad Khwaja) Writers and Landscapes, 1991; (as Waqas Ahmad Khwaja) Miriam's Lament and Other Poems, 1992; No One Waits for the Train, 2007. EDITOR AND TRANSLATOR: (as Waqas Ahmad Khwaja) Cactus: An Anthology of Recent Pakistani Literature, 1984; (as Waqas Ahmad Khwaja) Mornings in the Wilderness(prose and poems), 1988; Short Stories from Pakistan, 1992; (as Waqas Ahmad Khwaja) Modern Poetry of Pakistan, 2010; Dalkey Archive Press, 2011. **Address:** Department of English, Agnes Scott College, 141 E College Ave., Decatur, GA 30030, U.S.A. **Online address:** wkhwaja@agnesscott.edu

KHWAJA, Waqas Ahmad. *See* **KHWAJA, Waqas.**

KIAROSTAMI, Abbas. Iranian (born Iran), b. 1940. **Genres:** Plays/Screenplays. **Career:** Institute for the Intellectual Development of Children and Young Adults, Filmmaking Department, co-founder. Scriptwriter and director. **Publications:** Harfhāi bā Abbās Kiyārustami bih bahānah-yi namāyish-i Zir-i dirakhtān-i zaytun dar ālmān, 1995; Abbas Kiarostami, 1997; La Lettre du Cinema, 1997; Avec le vent, 2002; Mondo dal finestrino: il cinema di Abbas Kiarostami, 2002; Le vent nous emportera, 2002; Durushkah chi, 2004; Hāfiz bih rivāyat-i Abbās Kiyarustami, 2007; Victor Erice, Abbas Kiarostami: Correspondances: Exposition-Installation, Galerie Sud, 2007; Sadi az dast-i khvishtan faryād, 2007; (contrib.) Abbas Kiarostami: Le Cinema a Lepreuve du Rel, 2008; Sa'dī az dast-i khvīshtan faryād, 2008; Pluie et Vent, 2008; (foreword and contrib.) Inside Iran, 2008. **Address:** Zeitgeist Films, 247 Centre St., 2nd Fl., New York, NY 10013, U.S.A.

KIBERD, Declan. American/Irish (born Ireland), b. 1951. **Genres:** Literary Criticism And History, Essays. **Career:** University of Kent, English teacher, lecturer, 1976-77; Trinity College, Irish teacher, 1977-79; University College, Anglo-Irish literature, lecturer, 1979-97, Anglo-Irish Literature and Drama, chair, 1997-2011; RTE Arts programme, presenter, 1984-86; Irish Times, columnist, 1985-87; Yeats International Summer School, director, 1985-87; Irish Press, columnist, 1987-93; Patron of the Dublin Shaw Society, director, 1995-2000; University of Notre Dame, Donald and Marilyn Keough Professor of Irish Studies, 2011-, professor of English. Writer. **Publications:** LITERARY CRITICISM: Synge and the Irish Language, 1979; Men and Feminism in Modern Literature, 1985; Idir Dha Chultur, 1993; Samuel Beckett, 1994; Inventing Ireland: The Literature of the Modern Nation, 1996; Irish Classics, 2001; (with E. Longley) Multi-Culturalism: The View from the Two Irelands, 2001; Irish Writer and the World, 2005; Ulysses and Us: The Art of Everyday Life in Joyce's Masterpiece, 2009. EDITOR: (with S. Dick) Omnium Gatherum: Essays for Richard Ellmann, 1989; (with G. Fitzmaurice) An Crann Faoi Bhláth The Flowering Tree: Contemporary Irish Poetry with Verse Translations, 1991; The Student's Annotated Ulysses, 1992. Contributor to periodicals. **Address:** Department of English, University of Notre Dame, 515 Flanner Hall, 356 O'Shaughnessy, Notre Dame, IN 46556, U.S.A. **Online address:** dkiberd@nd.edu

KIBLER, M. Alison. American (born United States) **Genres:** Theatre, Cultural/Ethnic Topics. **Career:** University of Wisconsin, women's studies faculty; Franklin & Marshall College, assistant professor of American studies, 2001-, department chair, associate professor of american studies, associate professor of women's and gender studies. Writer. **Publications:** Rank Ladies: Gender and Cultural Hierarchy in American Vaudeville, 1999. **Address:** Department of American Studies, Franklin & Marshall College, 317 Stager Hall, 415 Harrisburg Ave., PO Box 3003, Lancaster, PA 17604-3003, U.S.A. **Online address:** alison.kibler@fandm.edu

KIBLINGER, Kristin Beise. American (born United States), b. 1972. **Genres:** Theology/Religion. **Career:** Thiel College, faculty; Winthrop University, Department of Religion, faculty, 2005-, assistant professor, associate professor of religious studies, International Studies Minor, director. Writer. **Publications:** Buddhist Inclusivism: Attitudes towards Religious Others, 2005. **Address:** Department of Philosophy and Religious Studies, Winthrop University, 326 Kinard Hall, 701 Oakland Ave., Rock Hill, SC 29733, U.S.A. **Online address:** kiblingerw@winthrop.edu

KIBRIA, Nazli. American/Bangladeshi (born Bangladesh), b. 1961. **Genres:** Novels, Social Sciences. **Career:** Wellesley College, Department of Sociology, adjunct professor, 1987-89; Tufts University, Department of Sociology, adjunct professor, 1989-90; University of Southern California, Department of Sociology, assistant professor, 1991-93; Boston University, Women's Studies Program, director, 1996-97, Department of Sociology, assistant professor, 1994-2001, associate professor, 2001-, acting chair, 2010-11, Graduate Programs in Sociology, director, 2009-10. **Publications:** Family Tightrope: The Changing Lives of Vietnamese Americans, 1993; Becoming Asian American: Second-Generation Chinese and Korean American Identities, 2002; Muslims in Motion: Islam and National Identity in the Bangladeshi Diaspora, 2011; Islam and Identity in the Bangladeshi Diaspora, forthcoming; Muslims in Diaspora: Bangladeshis at Home and Abroad, forthcoming. Contributor to periodicals. **Address:** Department of Sociology, Boston University, Rm. 273 Sociology, 96-100 Cummington St., Boston, MA 02215, U.S.A. **Online address:** nkibria@bu.edu

KIBUISHI, Kazu. American/Japanese (born Japan), b. 1978?. **Genres:** Novels. **Career:** Writer, art director and animator. **Publications:** (Illus.) Daisy Kutter: The Last Train (graphic novel), 2006; (illus.) Amulet: The Stonekeeper (graphic novel), 2008; Amulet Book Three: The Cloud Searchers, 2010; Amulet Book Four: The Last Council, 2011. FLIGHT SERIES: (ed. and contrib.) Flight: vol, I, 2004; (ed. and contrib.) Flight: vol. II, 2005; (ed. and contrib.) Flight: vol. III, 2006; (ed. and contrib.) Flight: vol. IV, 2007; Flight: Explorer, 2008. **Address:** Bolt City Productions L.L.C., 210 E Main St., Alhambra, CA 91801, U.S.A. **Online address:** info@boltcity.com

KIDD, Charles (William). British (born England), b. 1952. **Genres:** Genealogy/Heraldry, Biography, History. **Career:** Burke's Peerage Ltd., assistant editor, 1972-77; Debrett's Peerage Ltd., assistant editor, 1977-80, editor, 1980-. **Publications:** (With P. Montague-Smith) Debrett's Book of Royal Children, 1982; Debrett Goes to Hollywood, 1986; (ed. with D. Williamson) Debrett's Peerage and Baronetage, 1985, rev. ed., 2003. **Address:** Debrett's Ltd., 18-20 Hill Rise, Richmond, SR TW10 6UA, England. **Online address:** peerage@debretts.co.uk

KIDD, Chip. American (born United States), b. 1964. **Genres:** Cartoons, Design. **Career:** Alfred A. Knopf, junior assistant, book designer, 1986-, associate art director; Paris Review, consultant, 1995-; Pantheon, Comics Division, associate editor, editor-at-large; School of Visual Arts, teacher; Cooper-Hewitt Museum's, staff, 2006-. Writer. **Publications:** Batman Collected, 1996; (with P. Dini) Batman Animated, 1998; (with L. Daniels) Superman, the Complete History, 1998; (ed.) Peanuts: The Art of Charles M. Schulz, 2001; (with A. Spiegelman) Jack Cole and Plastic Man: Forms Stretched to Their Limits, 2001; The Cheese Monkeys: A Novel in Two Semesters, 2001; Mythology: The DC Comics Art of Alex Ross, 2003, vol. I, 2005; (ed.) Golden Age of DC Comics: 365 Days, 2004; Chip Kidd: Book One: Work 1986-2006, 2005; Learners: A Novel, 2008; (with D. Gibbons and M. Essl) Watching the Watchmen, 2008; (with G. Spear) Shazam!: The Golden Age of the World's Mightiest Mortal, 2010; (with L. Birnbach) True Prep: It's a Whole New Old World, 2010; Batman: Death By Design, 2012. Contributor to periodicals. **Address:** Department of Design, Alfred A. Knopf Inc., 201 E 50th St., New York, NY 10022-7703, U.S.A.

KIDD, Colin. Scottish/British (born England), b. 1964. **Genres:** History. **Career:** University of Glasgow, School of Historical Studies, Department of

History, faculty, reader, professor of modern history, 2003-, department deputy head and chair of modern history; Queen's University, professor of intellectual history and history of political thought, 2010-; All Souls College, fellow. Writer. **Publications:** Subverting Scotland's Past: Scottish Whig Historians and the Creation of an Anglo-British Identity, 1689-1830, 1993; British Identities Before Nationalism: Ethnicity and Nationhood in the Atlantic World, 1600-1800, 1999; The Forging of Races: Race and Scripture in the Protestant Atlantic World, 1600-2000, 2006; Union and Unionisms: Political Thought in Scotland, 1500-2000, 2008. Contributor to books and journals. **Address:** Department of History, University of Glasgow, 9 University Gardens, Glasgow, G12 8QQ, Scotland. **Online address:** c.kidd@history.arts.gla.ac.uk

KIDD, I(an) G(ray). Scottish/Indian (born India), b. 1922. **Genres:** Classics, History, Philosophy, Essays, Social Sciences. **Career:** University of St. Andrews, lecturer, 1949-65, senior lecturer, 1965-73, professor of ancient philosophy, 1973-76, professor of Greek, 1976-87, emeritus professor of Greek, 1987-; University of Texas, Austin, visiting professor, 1965-66; Institute for Advanced Study, faculty, 1971-72, 1979-80; St. Leonard's College, provost, 1978-83; University Court, chancellor's assessor, 1989-98; Institute for Research in Classical Philosophy and Science, fellow, 1989-; Hon. D Litt St. Andrews, staff, 2001. Writer. **Publications:** (Ed.) Posidonius, Works: vol. I, (with L. Edelstein) The Fragments, 1972, 2nd ed., 1989, vol. II: (i) and (ii), The Commentary, 1988, vol. III: The Translation of the Fragments, 1999; (ed.) Essays, 1992. CONTRIBUTIONS: (ed. with P. Edwards) Concise Encyclopedia of Western Philosophy and Philosophers, 1960; The Encyclopedia of Philosophy, 1967; Problems in Stoicism, 1971; The Stoics, 1978; Les Stoiciens et leur Logique, 1978; Stoic and Peripatetic Ethics, 1983; Aspects de la Philosophie Hellenistique, 1986; The Criterion of Truth, 1989; Philosophia Togata, 1989; Owls to Athens, 1990; Handbook of Metaphysics and Ontology, 1991; Theophrastus, 1992; Socratic Questions, 1992; Philosophen der Antike, 1996; The Oxford Classical Dictionary, 1996; Polyhistor: Studies in the History of Ancient Philosophy, 1996; Collecting Fragments, 1997; Fragments ammlungen philosophischer Texte der Antike, 1998; The Philosophy of Zeno, 2002. Contibutor of articles to journals. **Address:** School of Classics, University of St. Andrews, Swallowgate, St. Andrews, FF KY16 9AL, Scotland. **Online address:** igk@st-andrews.ac.uk

KIDD, Paul. Australian (born Australia), b. 1963. **Genres:** Cartoons, Science Fiction/Fantasy, Design, Novels, Young Adult Fiction, Novellas/Short Stories, Travel/Exploration, Adult Non-fiction, Adult Non-fiction, Horror, Humor/Satire. **Career:** Melbourne House/Beam, senior designer of computer games, 1985-92; freelance scriptwriter for computer games, 1994-. **Publications:** How to Play Lord of the Rings, 1987; Cyberswine, Sega Australia, 1995; Expedition to the Barrier Peaks, 2000; Red Sails in the Fallout, 2011. NOVELS: Neue Europa, 1991; Fangs of K'aath; Mus of Kerbridge, 1995; Petal Storm, 1995; Diskworld, Perfect Ten, 1995; Council of Blades, 1996; Lilith, 1996; The White Plume Mountain, 1999; Whisper of Wings, 1999; Descent into the Depths of the Earth, 2000; The Rats of Acomar: Book One of Takes from the Mornmist, 2000; Queen of the Demonweb Pits, 2001; Dreamscape, 2005; Fey, 2005; Fangs of K'aath 2: Guardians of Light, 2006; Hoo Boy, forthcoming. COMICS: Princess Karanam, 1993; Genus, 1993; Wild Kingdom, 1993; Zu, 1995; Tank Vixens, 1994-96; Cyberkitties, 1996-; Wild Side, 1998-99; Third Eye Private Eyes, forthcoming; Oceana, forthcoming; Hive, forthcoming. Contributor to periodicals. **Address:** E Victoria Pk., PO Box 1472, Perth, WA 6981, Australia. **Online address:** paul@purehubris.com

KIDD, Sue Monk. American (born United States), b. 1948. **Genres:** Novels, inspirational/Motivational Literature, Adult Non-fiction, Essays, Biography, Autobiography/Memoirs. **Career:** Saint Joseph's Hospital, nurse and instructor in nursing; Medical College of Georgia, instructor of creative writing, speaker and lecturer; Phoebe Pember House, writer-in-residence. **Publications:** NON FICTION: God's Joyful Surprise, 1987; All Things Are Possible, 1988; When the Heart Waits: Spiritual Direction for Life's Sacred Questions, 1990; Love's Hidden Blessings: God Can Touch Your Life When You Least Expect It, 1990; The Dance of the Dissident Daughter: A Woman's Journey from Christian Tradition to the Sacred Feminine, 1996; A Luminous Presence: One Woman's Awakening to the Inner Life, 2005; Firstlight: Early Inspirational Writings, 2006. NOVELS: The Secret Life of Bees, 2002; The Mermaid Chair, 2005; (with A.K. Taylor) Traveling With Pomegranates: A Mother-Daughter Story, 2009. Works appear in anthologies. Contributor to periodicals. **Address:** c/o Miriam Feuerle, Lyceum Agency L.L.C., 915 SE 35th Ave., Ste. 205, Portland, OR 97214-4381, U.S.A.

KIDD, Thomas S. American (born United States), b. 1971?. **Genres:** History, Theology/Religion. **Career:** Baylor University, Institute for Studies of Religion, senior fellow, College of Arts and Sciences, Department of History, assistant professor, 2002-07, associate professor, 2007-. Writer and columnist. **Publications:** The Protestant Interest: New England after Puritanism, 2004; The Great Awakening: The Roots of Evangelical Christianity in Colonial America, 2007; American Christians and Islam: Evangelical Culture and Muslims from the Colonial Period to the Age of Terrorism, 2009; God of Liberty: A Religious History of the American Revolution, 2010; Founding Fathers and The Debate Over Religion in Revolutionary America: A History in Documents, 2010; Patrick Henry: First among Patriots, 2011. Contributor to books and journals. **Address:** Department of History, Baylor University, B08 Tidwell Bible Bldg., 2nd Fl., 1 Bear Pl., PO Box 97306, Waco, TX 76798-7306, U.S.A. **Online address:** thomas_kidd@baylor.edu

KIDDER, Tracy. American (born United States), b. 1945. **Genres:** Novellas/Short Stories, Adult Non-fiction, Autobiography/Memoirs, Documentaries/Reportage, Social Sciences, Criminology/True Crime, History, Biography. **Career:** Writer, 1974-; Atlantic Monthly, contributing editor, 1982-; Smith College, visiting lecturer, 1985, 1986; Northwestern University, writer-in-residence, 1995. **Publications:** The Road to Yuba City: A Journey into the Juan Corona Murders, 1974; The Soul of a New Machine, 1981; House, 1985; Among Schoolchildren, 1989; Old Friends, 1993; Home Town, 1999; Mountains Beyond Mountains: The Quest of Dr. Paul Farmer, A Man Who Could Cure the World, 2003; My Detachment: A Memoir, 2005; Strength in What Remains: A Journey of Remembrance and Forgetting, 2009. Contributor to journals and magazines. **Address:** c/o London King, Random House Inc., 1745 Broadway, 3rd Fl., New York, NY 10019-4368, U.S.A.

KIDDY, Elizabeth W. American (born United States), b. 1957. **Genres:** History, Biography, Autobiography/Memoirs. **Career:** Albright College, associate professor of history and director of Latin American and Caribbean studies. Writer. **Publications:** Blacks of the Rosary: Memory and History in Minas Gerais, Brazil, 2005. **Address:** Albright College, 1800 N 13th St., Reading, PA 19612, U.S.A. **Online address:** ekiddy@alb.edu

KIDMAN, Fiona (Judith). New Zealander (born New Zealand), b. 1940. **Genres:** Novels, Novellas/Short Stories, Poetry, Social Sciences, Travel/Exploration, History. **Career:** Librarian, 1961-62; writer, 1962-. **Publications:** NOVELS: A Breed of Women, 1979; Mandarin Summer, 1981; Paddy's Puzzle, 1983 in US as In the Clear Light, 1985; The Book of Secrets, 1987; True Stars, 1990; Ricochet Baby, 1996; The House Within, 1997; Songs from the Violet Cafe, 2003; The Captive Wife, 2005; At the End of Darwin Road: A Memoir, 2008; Beside the Dark Pool, 2009. SHORT STORIES: Mrs. Dixon and Friends, 1982; Unsuitable Friends, 1988; The Foreign Woman, 1993; The Best of Fiona Kidman's Short Stories, 1998; (ed.) New Zealand Love Stories, an Oxford Anthology, 1999; A Needle in the Heart, 2002; (ed.) The Best New Zealand Fiction, 2004. POETRY: Honey and Bitters, 1975; On the Tightrope, 1978; Going to the Chathams, Poems: 1977-1984, 1985; Wakeful Nights: Poems Selected and New, 1991. OTHERS: (with J. Ussher) Gone North (travel), 1984; (with G. Sheehan) Wellington, 1989; Palm Prints (biographical sketches), 1994; Where Your Left Hand Rests, 2010. Contributor to periodicals. **Address:** 28 Rakau Rd., Hataitai, Wellington, 3, New Zealand. **Online address:** fionakidman@yahoo.com

KIDWELL, Carol (Evelyn Beryl). (Carol Maddison). French/Canadian (born Canada), b. 1923. **Genres:** Literary Criticism And History, Biography, Philosophy. **Career:** University of New Brunswick, assistant professor of classics, 1946-49; American College (now University), Humanities Division, chairman and professor of English, 1963-66, dean, 1966-78, dean emeritus, 1978-. Writer. **Publications:** Marullus: Soldier Poet of the Renaissance, 1989; Pontano: Poet and Prime Minister, 1991; Sannazaro and Arcadia, 1993; Pietro Bembo, Lover, Linguist, Cardinal, 2004. AS CAROL MADDISON: Apollo and the Nine: A History of the Ode, 1960; Marcantonio Flaminio: Poet, Humanist and Philosopher, 1965. Works appear in anthologies. **Address:** American University of Paris, 31, Ave. Bosquet, Paris, 75007, France.

KIDWELL, Clara Sue. American (born United States), b. 1941. **Genres:** History, Bibliography, Theology/Religion. **Career:** Kansas City Art Institute, instructor in history, 1968-69; University of Washington, Experimental Education Unit, coordinator of publications, 1970; Haskell Indian Junior College, instructor in social sciences and chairperson of division, 1970-72; University of Minnesota, assistant professor of American Indian studies, 1972-74;

University of California, associate professor, professor of Native American studies, 1974-96, Department of Ethnic Studies, head, 1974-75, 1978-79; Dartmouth College, visiting associate professor, 1980; Council of Graduate Schools, dean-in-residence, 1988-89; National Museum of the American Indian, assistant director for cultural resources, 1993-95; University of Oklahoma, professor of history and director of Native American studies, 1995-; VOVA, board director. Writer. **Publications:** (With C. Roberts) The Choctaws: A Critical Bibliography, 1980; A Helsinki Record: Native American Rights, 1980; Choctaws and Missionaries in Mississippi, 1818-1918, 1995; (co-author) Treasures of the National Museum of the American Indian: Smithsonian Institution, 1996; (with H. Noley and G.E. Tinker) A Native American Theology, 2001; (with A. Velie) Native American Studies, 2005; (with A. Velie) The Choctaw Nation in Oklahoma: From Tribe to Nation, 1855-1970, 2007. Contributor to books. **Address:** Department of History, University of Oklahoma, ELLH 216, 660 Parrington Oval, Norman, OK 73019, U.S.A. **Online address:** cskidwell@ou.edu

KIEFER, Louis. American (born United States), b. 1936. **Genres:** Self Help, Law. **Career:** U.S. Army Officers' Infantry School, staff, 1961; Allstate Insurance Co., claims adjuster, 1961; University of Virginia, Advocate General School, judge, 1962; Office of the Judge Advocate General, Claims and Litigation Division, chief, 1962-63, Litigation Branch, Public Utility Division, staff, 1963-64; Aetna Insurance Co., trial counsel, 1965-66; Superior Court, assistant temporary clerk, 1967-71; Resolute Insurance Co., general counsel, 1966-67; Kiefer and Holtman, partner, 1967-70. Writer. **Publications:** How to Win Custody, 1982. Contributor to journals. **Address:** Raines & Raines, 71 Park Ave., Ste. 4A, New York, NY 10016, U.S.A. **Online address:** lkiefer1@hotmail.com

KIELY, Robert (James). American (born United States), b. 1931. **Genres:** Literary Criticism And History, Adult Non-fiction, Novels, Romance/Historical. **Career:** Harvard University, Faculty of Arts and Sciences, Department of English, instructor, 1962, assistant professor, 1964-66, associate professor, 1966-68, professor of English, 1968-85, Loker professor of English, 1985-2001, chairman, 1987-90, emeritus professor, 2001-, associate dean, 1972-75, Adams House, master, 1973-99, I Tatti Center for Italian Renaissance Studies, visiting professor, 1999, 2009; Sichuan University, visiting professor, 1982; Hebrew University, visiting professor, 1983; Providence College, Randall visiting professor, 2008. Writer. **Publications:** Robert Louis Stevenson and the Fiction of Adventure, 1964; Literature for Composition on the Theme of Man and Nature, 1966; The Romantic Novel in England, 1972; Beyond Egotism: The Fiction of James Joyce, Virginia Woolf and D.H. Lawrence, 1980; Reverse Tradition: Postmodern Fictions and the Nineteenth-Century Novel, 1993; Still Learning, 1999; Blessed and Beautiful: Picturing the Saints, 2010. EDITOR: Man and Nature, 1966; (with J. Hildebidle) Modernism Reconsidered, 1983; (and intro.) The Good Heart: A Buddhist Perspective on the Teachings of Jesus, 1996. Contributor of articles to magazines and newspapers. **Address:** Department of English, Harvard University, Barker Ctr., 12 Quincy St., Cambridge, MA 02138, U.S.A. **Online address:** rkiely@fas.harvard.edu

KIERNAN, Ben. Australian (born Australia), b. 1953. **Genres:** History, Essays. **Career:** University of New South Wales, tutor in history, 1975-77; University of Wollongong, senior lecturer in history, 1986-89; Yale University, associate professor, 1990-97, director of Cambodian genocide program, 1994-99, professor of history, 1997-99, director of genocide studies program, 1998-, A. Whitney Griswold professor of history, 1999-, professor of international and area studies, Council on Southeast Asia Studies, chair. Writer. **Publications:** The Samlaut Rebellion and Its Aftermath, 1967-70, 1975; Social Cohesion in Revolutionary Cambodia, 1976; (with D.P. Chandler and M.H. Lim) Early Phase of Liberation in Northwestern Cambodia, 1977; (with S. Thion) Khmers Rouges!, 1981; How Pol Pot Came to Power, 1985, 2nd ed., 2004; Cambodia: The Eastern Zone Massacres, 1986; The Pol Pot Regime, 1996, 3rd ed., 2008; Le genocide au Cambodge, 1998; Blood and Soil: A World History of Genocide and Extermination from Sparta to Darfur, 2007; Genocide and Resistance in Southeast Asia: Documentation, Denial & Justice in Cambodia & East Timor, 2008. EDITOR: (with C. Boua) Peasants and Politics in Kampuchea, 1942-81, 1982; (with D.P. Chandler) Revolution and Its Aftermath in Kampuchea: Eight Essays, 1983; Burchett: Reporting the Other Side of the World, 1939-83, 1986; (and trans. with D.P. Chandler and C. Boua) Pol Pot Plans the Future, 1988; (and intro.) Genocide and Democracy in Cambodia, 1993; Conflict and Change in Cambodia, 2002; (with R.

Gellately) The Specter of Genocide, 2003. **Address:** Department of History, Yale University, 326 HGS, 500 College St., PO Box 208324, New Haven, CT 06511-8962, U.S.A. **Online address:** ben.kiernan@yale.edu

KIERNAN, Brian. Australian (born Australia), b. 1937. **Genres:** Literary Criticism And History, Essays. **Career:** Freelance writer, 1964-72; University of Sydney, lecturer, 1972-76, senior lecturer in English, 1976-, associate professor, honorary associate. **Publications:** Images of Society and Nature: Seven Essays on Australian Novels, 1971; Criticism, 1974; (intro.) Responses: Selected Writings, 1979; Patrick White, 1980; David Williamson: A Writer's Career, 1990; Studies in Australian Literary History, 1997. EDITOR: (and intro.) The Portable Henry Lawson, 1976; Considerations: New Essays on Kenneth Slessor, Judith Wright and Douglas Stewart, 1977; Douglas Stewart, 1977; The Most Beautiful Lies, 1977; The Essential Henry Lawson, 1982; (with D. Brooks) Running Wild, 2004. Contributor to journals. **Address:** Department of English, University of Sydney, A20 John Woolley Bldg., Sydney, NW 2006, Australia. **Online address:** brian.kiernan@arts.usyd.edu.au

KIERNAN, Caitlín R(ebekah). Irish (born Ireland), b. 1964. **Genres:** Romance/Historical, Novels, Science Fiction/Fantasy, Horror. **Career:** Red Mountain Museum, associate paleontologist, 1985-86; San Diego State University, research associate, 1986-88. Writer. **Publications:** Candles for Elizabeth, 1998; Silk, 1998; (with P. Hogan and J. Nicholson) The Dreaming: Through the Gates of Horn and Ivory, 1999; Tales of Pain and Wonder, 2000; A Study for Estate, 2000; Threshold: A Novel of Deep Time, 2001; (with P.Z. Brite) Wrong Things, 2001; On the Road to Jefferson, 2002; From Weird and Distant Shores, 2002; In the Garden of Poisonous Flowers, 2002; Embrace the Mutation, 2003; Trilobite: The Writing of Threshold, 2003; Waycross, 2003; The Five of Cups, 2003; Low Red Moon, 2003; Murder of Angels, 2004; The Dry Salvages, 2004; To Charles Fort, with Love, 2005; Frog Toes and Tentacles, 2005; Alabaster, 2006; (contrib.) Beowulf, 2007; Daughter of Hounds, 2007; Red Tree, 2009; A is for Alien, 2009; (contrib.) The Mammoth Book of Vampire Romance 2, 2009; The Ammonite Violin & Others, 2010; Confessions of a Five-Chambered Heart, 2010; Two Worlds and in Between, 2011; Drowning Girl, 2012. Contributor to books and journals. **Address:** c/o Merrilee Heifetz, Writers House, 21 W 26th St., New York, NY 10010, U.S.A. **Online address:** greygirlbeast@gmail.com

KIERNAN, Pauline. British (born England) **Genres:** Theatre, Plays/Screenplays, Young Adult Fiction. **Career:** University of Reading, Leverhulme research fellow, 1995-98. Writer. **Publications:** Shakespeare's Theory of Drama, 1996; Staging Shakespeare at the New Globe, 1999; Filthy Shakespeare: Shakespeare's Most Outrageous Sexual Puns, 2007; Screenwriting They Can't Resist, 2011. **Address:** The School of English & American Literature, White Knights, PO Box 218, Reading, BR RG6 6AA, England.

KIERNER, Cynthia A. American (born United States), b. 1958?. **Genres:** History, Politics/Government, Women's Studies And Issues, Business/Trade/Industry. **Career:** University of North Carolina, associate professor of history; George Mason University, professor of history. Writer. **Publications:** Traders and Gentlefolk: The Livingstons of New York, 1675-1790, 1992; Beyond the Household: Women's Place in the Early South, 1700-1835, 1998; (ed.) Southern Women in Revolution, 1776-1800: Personal and Political Narratives, 1998; Revolutionary America, 1750-1815: Sources and Interpretation, 2003; Scandal at Bizarre: Rumor and Reputation in Jefferson's America, 2004; The Contrast: Manners, Morals, and Authority in the Early American Republic, 2007. **Address:** Department of History and Art History, George Mason University, Robinson B-359, MSN 3G1, 4400 University Dr., Fairfax, VA 22030-4422, U.S.A. **Online address:** ckierner@gmu.edu

KIESSLING, Nicolas K. American (born United States), b. 1936. **Genres:** Literary Criticism And History. **Career:** Washington State University, professor of English, 1967-2000, now emeritus; Abdelmalek Essaadi University, faculty. Writer. **Publications:** The Incubus in English Literature: Provenance and Progeny, 1977; The Library of Robert Burton, 1988; (co-ed.) The Anatomy of Melancholy, vol. I, 1989, vol. II, 1990, vol. III, 1994; The Legacy of Democritas Junior, Robert Burton: An Exhibition to Commemorate the 350th Anniversary of the Death of Robert Burton (1577-1640), 1990; The Library of Anthony Wood, 2002; The Life of Anthony Wood in His Own Words, 2009. **Address:** Department of English, Washington State University, PO Box 642630, Pullman, WA 99164-2630, U.S.A. **Online address:** kiesslin@wsu.edu

KIEVES, Tama J. American (born United States), b. 1961. **Genres:** Novels. **Career:** Sherman & Howard (law firm), attorney, 1985-86; writer and speaker, 1989-; Awakening Artistry, founder, 2000. **Publications:** This Time I Dance! Trusting the Journey of Creating the Work You Love, 2002; Inspired and Unstoppable: Wildly Succeeding in Your Life's Work, 2012. Works appear in anthologies. **Address:** PO Box 9040, Denver, CO 80209-9040, U.S.A. **Online address:** contact@awakeningartistry.com

KIEWE, Amos. American/Israeli (born Israel), b. 1954. **Genres:** Politics/Government. **Career:** Syracuse University, assistant professor of speech communication and professor of communication and rhetorical studies, professor, chair of communication and rhetorical studies department, 2001-07, 2010-. Writer. **Publications:** (With D.W. Houck) A Shining City on a Hill: Ronald Reagan's Economic Rhetoric, 1951-1989, 1991; (ed. with D.W. Houck) Actor, Ideologue, Politician: The Public Speeches of Ronald Reagan, 1993; (ed.) The Modern Presidency and Crisis Rhetoric, 1994; (with D.W. Houck) FDR's Body Politics: The Rhetoric of Disability, 2003; FDR's First Fireside Chat: Public Confidence and the Banking Crisis, 2007. Contributor to books and periodicals. **Address:** Syracuse University, 900 S Crouse Ave., Syracuse, NY 13244, U.S.A. **Online address:** akiewe@syr.edu

KIGER, Patrick J. American (born United States), b. 1957. **Genres:** Business/Trade/Industry, Social Sciences. **Career:** Pittsburgh (magazine), staff writer and assistant editor, 1981-84; Pittsburgh Press, reporter, 1984-89; Orange County Register, reporter, 1984-89; Baltimore (magazine), senior writer, 1989-93. Journalist. **Publications:** (With M.J. Smith) Poplorica: A Popular History of the Fads, Mavericks, Inventions, and Lore That Shaped Modern America, 2004; (with M.J. Smith) Oops: 20 Life Lessons from the Fiascos That Shaped America, 2006. **Address:** c/o Susan Ginsburg, Writers House Inc., 21 W 26th St., New York, NY 10010, U.S.A. **Online address:** patrickjkiger@gmail.com

KIGHTLINGER, Laura. American (born United States), b. 1964. **Genres:** Adult Non-fiction, Humor/Satire. **Career:** Writer. **Publications:** Quick Shots of False Hope: A Rejection Collection, 1999. **Address:** Supreme Talent Intl., 210 Summit Ave., Montvale, NJ 07645, U.S.A.

KIHN, Greg. American (born United States), b. 1952?. **Genres:** Science Fiction/Fantasy, Biography, Literary Criticism And History, Young Adult Fiction. **Career:** Musician and writer. **Publications:** Horror Show, 1996; Shade of Pale, 1997; Big Rock Beat, 1998; Mojo Hand, 1999; (ed.) Storyteller: Short Stories by Rock Stars, 2001; (ed.) Carved in Rock: Short Stories by Musicians, 2003. Contributor to periodicals. **Address:** Tom Doherty Associates, 175 5th Ave., New York, NY 10010-7703, U.S.A.

KIJEWSKI, Karen. (Karen J. Kijewski). American (born United States), b. 1943?. **Genres:** Mystery/Crime/Suspense, Novels. **Career:** High school English teacher, 1970-80; bartender, 1980-91. Writer. **Publications:** MYSTERY NOVELS: Katwalk, 1989; Katapult, 1990; Kat's Cradle, 1992; Copy Kat, 1992; Wild Kat, 1994; Alley Kat Blues, 1995; Honky Tonk Kat, 1996; Kat Scratch Fever, 1997; Stray Kat Waltz, 1998. Contributor to anthologies. **Address:** c/o Deborah Schneider, Gelfman Schneider Literary Agents Inc., 250 W 57th St., New York, NY 10107, U.S.A.

KIJEWSKI, Karen J. See **KIJEWSKI, Karen.**

KILDUFF, Peter. American (born United States), b. 1941. **Genres:** Autobiography/Memoirs, Biography. **Career:** Hartford Times, staff member; Front magazine, editor; American Cross & Cockade Journal, editor; Central Connecticut State University, director of university relations; now emeritus. **Publications:** That's My Bloody Plane: The World War I Experiences of Major Cecil Montgomery-Moore, 1975; Germany's Last Knight of the Air: The Memoirs of Major Carl Degelow, 1979; (trans.) Manfred von Richthoven, The Red Baron Manfred Freiherr von Richthoven (memoir), 1980; U.S. Carriers at War, 1981, 2nd ed., 1997; Douglas A-4 Skyhawk, 1983; Germany's First Air Force, 1914-1918, 1991; Richthofen: Beyond the Legend of the Red Baron, 1993; The Red Baron Combat Wing: Jagdgeschwader Richthofen in Battle, 1997; The Red Baron: Beyond the Legend, 1999; The Illustrated Red Baron: The Life and Times of Manfred von Richthofen, 1999; Talking with the Red Baron: Interviews with Manfred von Richthofen, 2003; Black Fokker Leader: Carl Degelow, the First World War's Last Airfighter Knight, 2009;

Hermann Göring: Fighter Ace-the World War I Career of Germany's Most Infamous Airman, 2010. Contributor to periodicals. **Address:** Central Connecticut State University, 1615 Stanley St., New Britain, CT 06050, U.S.A.

KILEY, David. American (born United States), b. 1963. **Genres:** Business/Trade/Industry. **Career:** Nightline, consultant and analyst; CNBC, consultant and analyst; CNN, consultant and analyst; The Today Show, consultant and analyst; USA Today, Detroit bureau chief, 2000-. Writer. **Publications:** Getting the Bugs Out: The Rise, Fall, and Comeback of Volkswagen in America, 2002; Driven: Inside BMW, the Most Admired Car Company in the World, 2004. Contributor to periodicals. **Address:** c/o Author Mail, Wiley, 111 River St., Hoboken, NJ 07030-5774, U.S.A. **Online address:** kiley@davidkiley.com

KILGORE, Evan. American (born United States), b. 1983. **Genres:** Novels, Mystery/Crime/Suspense. **Career:** Software designer, entertainment industry story analyst, film and television assistant, online games designer, novelist and screenwriter. **Publications:** Who Is Shayla Hacker?, 2007; The Children of Black Valley, 2008. **Address:** c/o Anthony Mattero, Renaissance Literary & Talent Agency, 8523 Sunset Blvd., Los Angeles, CA 90069, U.S.A. **Online address:** evan@evankilgore.com

KILHAM, Benjamin. American (born United States), b. 1953?. **Genres:** Zoology, Animals/Pets, Biology, Sciences. **Career:** Abercrombie & Fitch, gunsmith, 1976; Griffin & Howe, gunsmith, 1976; Austin Behler Pistolsmith Union, pistolsmith, 1977; Paul Jaeger Inc., manager/gunsmith, 1978-80; Colt Firearms, product engineer, 1980-82; Kilham & Co., owner, 1982-. Writer, naturalist and wildlife rehabilitator. **Publications:** (With E. Gray) Among the Bears: Raising Orphan Cubs in the Wild, 2002. Contributor to periodicals. **Address:** c/o Author Mail, Henry Holt and Co., 175 5th Ave, New York, NY 10010, U.S.A. **Online address:** benjamin.kilham@valley.net

KILLAN, Gerald. Canadian/British (born England), b. 1945. **Genres:** History, Local History/Rural Topics, Biography, Social Sciences. **Career:** University of Western Ontario, King's University College, assistant professor of history, 1973-77, associate professor of history, 1977-82, chairperson, 1982-87, professor of history, 1984-92, academic dean, 1992-97, principal, 1997-2009, St. Joseph's Health Care London, chair; Ontario Conservation Review Board, chair, 1997-2000; Universities of Canada, president; Association of Catholic Colleges, president; Ontario Historical Society, president. Writer. **Publications:** Preserving Ontario's Heritage: A History of the Ontario Historical Society, 1975; (ed.) The Ontario Heritage Act: Present Problems, Future Prospects: Minutes and Proceedings of the Ontario Historical Society Conference on Preservation Legislation in Ontario, 1977; David Boyle: From Artisan to Archaeologist, 1983; Protected Places: A History of Ontario's Provincial Parks System, 1993. **Address:** St. Joseph's Health Care London, University of Western Ontario, 268 Grosvenor St., London, ON N6A 4V2, Canada. **Online address:** gkillan@julian.uwo.ca

KILLDEER, John. See **MAYHAR, Ardath (Hurst).**

KILLEEN, Jarlath. Irish (born Ireland), b. 1976. **Genres:** Literary Criticism And History, Horror. **Career:** Keele University, lecturer in victorian English, 2004-05; Trinity College, School of English, lecturer and head of junior freshmen, Oscar Wilde Center, assistant professor. Writer. **Publications:** The Faiths of Oscar Wilde: Catholicism, Folklore and Ireland, 2005; Gothic Ireland: Horror and the Irish Anglican Imagination in the Long Eighteenth Century, 2005; The Fairy Tales of Oscar Wilde, 2007; Gothic Literature, 1825-1914, 2009. **Address:** School of English, Trinity College, University of Dublin, Rm. 4005, Arts Bldg., College Green, DU 2, Ireland. **Online address:** killeej@tcd.ie

KILLEN, Andreas. American (born United States) **Genres:** History. **Career:** City University of New York, City College of New York, assistant professor of history, associate professor of history, MA advisor. Writer. **Publications:** 1973 Nervous Breakdown: Watergate, Warhol, and the Birth of Post-Sixties America, 2006; Berlin Electropolis: Shock, Nerves, and German Modernity, 2006. Contributor to periodicals. **Address:** Department of History, City College of New York, City University of New York, NAC 5/128A, 160 Convent Ave., New York, NY 10031-9101, U.S.A. **Online address:** akillen@ccny.cuny.edu

KILLHAM, Edward L(eo). American (born United States), b. 1926.

Genres: International Relations/Current Affairs, Young Adult Non-fiction. **Career:** U.S. Department of State, U.S. Foreign Service, minister/counselor, 1952-87; Department of Treasury, executive secretary, 1961-63, North Atlantic Treaty Organization (NATO), deputy assistant secretary general, 1974-77; U.S. Delegation, special adviser, 1977-78, deputy chairperson, 1985; ACDA representative, 1978-79; U.S. Embassy, deputy chief of mission, 1979-82, deputy chairperson, 1982-83; Naval War College, state department adviser, 1983-85; Central African affairs, director, 1985-87; Killham Associates Consulting, president, 1987-; Copenhagen University, Fulbright professor, 1996. Writer. **Publications:** The Nordic Way: A Path to Baltic Equilibrium, 1993. Contributor of articles to newspapers and journals. **Address:** Killham Associates Consulting, 3615 Winfield Ln. NW, Washington, DC 20007-2368, U.S.A.

KILLIAN, Beth. *See* **KENDRICK, Beth.**

KILLOUGH, (Karen) Lee. American (born United States), b. 1942. **Genres:** Mystery/Crime/Suspense, Science Fiction/Fantasy. **Career:** St. Joseph Hospital, radiologic technician, 1964-65; St. Mary Hospital, radiologic technician, 1965-67, 1969-71; Morris Cafritz Memorial Hospital, radiologic technician, 1967-69; Kansas State University, KSU Veterinary Medical Teaching Hospital, chief radiologic technologist, 1971-2000. Writer. **Publications:** BRILL AND MAXWELL: The Doppelganger Gambit, 1979; Spider Play, 1986; Dragon's Teeth, 1990; Bridling Chaos, 1998. BLOOD HUNT: Blood Hunt, 1987; Bloodlinks, 1988; Bloodwalk, 1997; Blood Games, 2001. NOVELS: A Voice Out of Ramah, 1978; The Monitor, The Miners and the Shree, 1980; Deadly Silents, 1981; Liberty's World, 1985; The Leopard's Daughter, 1987; Wilding Nights, 2002; Killer Karma, 2005. OTHERS: Aventine, 1981; Checking on Culture: An Aid to Building Story Backgrounds, 2nd ed., 2007. Works appear in anthologies. Contributor to periodicals. **Address:** 2426 Galloway Dr., PO Box 1167, Manhattan, KS 66505-1167, U.S.A. **Online address:** klkillo@flinthills.com

KILMER, Nicholas (John). American (born United States), b. 1941. **Genres:** Mystery/Crime/Suspense, Art/Art History, Plays/Screenplays, Poetry, Translations. **Career:** Teacher, 1960-62, 1967-70; Action for Boston Community Development, Department of Planning and Evaluation, writer, 1966-67; Swain School of Design, associate professor of liberal arts, 1970-82, dean, 1979-82; Art Research of Cambridge, affiliate, 1984-88; Nicholas Kilmer Fine Art, founder, 1988-. Writer. **Publications:** CRIME NOVELS: Harmony in Flesh and Black, 1995; Man with a Squirrel, 1996; O Sacred Head, 1997; Dirty Linen, 1999; Lazarus, Arise, 2001; Madonna of the Apes, 2005; Butterfly in Flame, 2010. POETRY TRANSLATIONS: (intro. and ed.) Poems of Pierre de Ronsard, 1979; F. Petrarch: Songs and Sonnets, 1981; Rime, 1981; Dante's Comedy: The Inferno, 1986. OTHERS: (contrib.) Thomas Buford Meteyard, 1865-1928, 1989; A Place in Normandy (memoir), 1996; Frederick Carl Frieseke: The Evolution of an American Impressionist, 2001; Paradise for Fools, 2011. Contributor to periodicals. **Address:** 14A Eliot St., Cambridge, MA 02138, U.S.A. **Online address:** nickkilmer@aol.com

KILPATRICK, Alan Edwin. American (born United States) **Genres:** Anthropology/Ethnology, Young Adult Fiction. **Career:** University of California, Oakes College, lecturer, 1989-91; University of California, extension lecturer in archaeology, 1989-90; University of Minnesota, American Indian Studies, assistant professor of 1991-93, McKnight Land Grant professor, 1993; San Diego State University, American Indian Studies, associate professor, professor, 1993-, department head, 1997; Museum of Man, director, 1994-. Writer. **Publications:** The Night Has a Naked Soul: Witchcraft and Sorcery among the Western Cherokee, 1997. Contributor of articles and reviews to periodicals. **Address:** Department of American Indian Studies, San Diego State University, AL-327, 5500 Campanile Dr., San Diego, CA 92182-5500, U.S.A. **Online address:** akilpatr@mail.sdsu.edu

KILPATRICK, Andrew. American (born United States), b. 1943. **Genres:** Money/Finance, Biography, History. **Career:** Raleigh News and Observer, copy editor, 1971-72; Birmingham News, reporter, 1972-84; Birmingham Post-Herald, business reporter, 1984-92; Prudential Securities Inc., stockbroker, 1992-; Wells Fargo Advisors, stockbroker, 1992-. **Publications:** Warren Buffett: The Good Guy of Wall Street, 1992; Of Permanent Value: The Story of Warren Buffett, 1994, vol. I, 2002, vol. III: A Trilogy, 2004; A Legacy of Leadership: The History of AmSouth Bank, 1996. **Address:** 2850 Cahara Rd., Ste. 210, Birmingham, AL 35223-2344, U.S.A. **Online address:** andyakpe@aol.com

KILPATRICK, Nancy. Also writes as Desiree Knight, Amarantha Knight. Canadian/American (born United States), b. 1946. **Genres:** Horror, Novellas/Short Stories, Novels. **Career:** George Brown College, part-time writing teacher, 1985-. Writer. **Publications:** NOVELS: Near Death, 1994; Child of the Night, 1996; As One Dead, 1996; Reborn, 1998; Dracul, 1998; Bloodlover, 2000; Eternal City, 2003; Mercedez: Day of the Dead, 2005; Jason X: Planet of the Beast, 2005; Jason X: To the Third Power, 2006; Transformation, 2012. NON FICTION: The Goth Bible: A Compendium for the Darkly Inclined, 2004. COLLECTIONS: Sex and the Single Vampire, 1994; Endorphins, 1997; The Vampire Stories of Nancy Kilpatrick, 2000; Cold Comfort, 2001; Vampyric Variations 2012. AS AMARANTHA KNIGHT: DARKER PASSIONS SERIES: Dracula, 1993; Dr. Jekyll and Mr. Hyde, 1995; Frankenstein, 1995; The Fall of the House of Usher, 1995; The Portrait of Dorian Gray, 1996; Carmilla, 1997; The Pit and the Pendulum, 1998. AS AMARANTHA KNIGHT: COLLECTIONS: The Darker Passions Reader, 1996; The Amarantha Knight Reader, 1996. AS DESIREE KNIGHT: Hunted, 2007. EDITOR: Love Bites, 1995; Flesh Fantastic, 1995; Seductive Spectres, 1996; Sex Macabre, 1996; Demon Sex 1998; In The Shadow of the Gargoyle, 1998; Graven Images, 2000; Outsiders, 2005; Tesseracts Thirteen, 2009; Evolve: Vampire Stories of the New Undead, 2010, vol. II: Vampire Stories of the Future Undead, 2011; Danse Macabre, 2012; Expiry Date, 2013. Works appear in anthologies. Contributor to magazines and newspapers. **Address:** c/o Ian Drury, Sheil Land Associates Ltd., 52 Doughty St., London, GL WC1N 2LS, England. **Online address:** nancy.kilpatrick@sympatico.ca

KILROY, Thomas. Irish (born Ireland), b. 1934. **Genres:** Novels, Plays/Screenplays, Novellas/Short Stories, Young Adult Fiction. **Career:** Stanford College, headmaster, 1959-64; University of Notre Dame, visiting professor, 1962-63; Vanderbilt University, visiting professor, 1964-65; University of Dublin, University College, assistant lecturer in English, senior lecturer, 1965-73, visiting professor, 1977-78; School of Irish Studies, lecturer, 1972-73; Sir George Williams University, visiting professor, 1973; McGill University, visiting professor, 1973; National University of Ireland, University College-Galway, visiting professor, 1975-76, 1979, professor of English, 1977-89; Dartmouth College, visiting professor, 1976; Abbey Theatre, play editor, 1977; Trinity College, examiner in modern English, 1983, honorary fellow; Thomond College, examiner in modern English, 1983; Bamberg University, visiting professor, 1984; Field Day Theatre Co., director, 1988. **Publications:** The Death and Resurrection of Mr. Roche, 1969, rev. ed., 2002; The O'Neill, 1969; The Big Chapel, 1971; Sean O'Casey: A Collection of Critical Essays, 1974; Tea and Sex and Shakespeare, 1976; Talbot's Box, 1979; Double Cross, 1986; That Man, Bracken, 1986; The Madam MacAdam Travelling Theatre, 1991; Seagull: After Chekhov, 1993; Gold in the Streets, 1993; The Secret Fall of Constance Wilde, 1997; Illusions comiques à l'irlandaise, 1998; Tea and Sex and Shakespeare, 1998; Ghosts: After Ibsen, 2002; The Shape of Metal, 2003; My Scandalous Life, 2004; Blake, 2004; Pirandellos, 2007; Henry, 2007; Christ Deliver Us: After Wedekind's Spring Awakening, 2010. **Address:** Alan Brodie Representation Ltd., The Courtyard, 55 Charterhouse St., Paddock Ste., London, GL EC1M 6HA, England.

KILSON, Marion D. de B. American (born United States), b. 1936. **Genres:** Anthropology/Ethnology, Human Relations/Parenting, Social Sciences, Medicine/Health. **Career:** University of Massachusetts, instructor, 1966-67, assistant professor of anthropology, 1967-68; Simmons College, associate professor of sociology, 1969-73; Newton College, professor of sociology and chair of department, 1973-75; Radcliffe Institute, director of research, 1975-77, director of institute, 1977-80. Writer. **Publications:** Kpele Lala: Ga Religious Songs and Symbols, 1971; African Urban Kinsmen: The Ga of Central Accra, 1974; (comp.) Royal Antelope and Spider: West African Mende Tales, 1976; Mary Jane Forbes Greene (1895-1910), Mother of the Japan Mission: An Anthropological Portrait, 1991; Claiming Place: Biracial Young Adults of the Post-Civil Rights Era, 2001; (with F. Ladd) Is That Your Child?: Mothers Talk about Rearing Biracial Children, 2009. **Address:** 4 Eliot Rd., Lexington, MA 02421, U.S.A. **Online address:** marionkilson@worldnet.att.nct

KILWORTH, Garry. Also writes as Garry Douglas Kilworth, F. K. Salwood. British (born England), b. 1941. **Genres:** Novels, Novellas/Short Stories, Romance/Historical, Science Fiction/Fantasy, Children's Fiction, Children's Non-fiction, Young Adult Fiction, Adult Non-fiction, Adult Non-fiction. **Career:** Cable and Wireless, senior executive, 1974-82; writer, 1977-. **Publications:** In Solitary, 1977; The Night of Kadar, 1978; Split Second, 1979; Gemini God, 1981; A Theatre of Timesmiths, 1984; Witchwater Country, 1986; Spiral Winds, 1987; The Wizard of Woodworld, 1987; The Voyage of the Vigilance, 1988; Cloudrock, 1988; Abandonati, 1988; The Rain Ghost, 1989; Hunter's Moon, 1989; Midnight's Sun, 1990; The Third Dragon, 1991; The Drowners, 1991; Standing on Shamsan, 1992; Frost Dancers, 1992; Angel, 1993; Billy Pink's Private Detective Agency, 1993; Archangel, 1994; The Phantom Piper, 1994; The Electric Kid, 1994; The Bronte Girls, 1995; House of Tribes, 1995; The Roof of Voyaging, 1996; Cybercats, 1996; The Raiders, 1996; A Midsummer's Nightmare, 1996; Thunder Oak, 1997; The Princely Flower, 1997; The Gargoyle, 1997; Land-of-Mists, 1998; Drummer Boy, 1998; Castle Storm, 1998; The Lantern Fox, 1998; (with M. Oliver) Heavenly Hosts versus Hell United, 1998; Shadow-Hawk, 1999; Windjammer Run, 1999; Hey, New Kid!, 1999; Icehouse Boy, 2001; Gaslight Geezers, 2001; Soldier's Son, 2001; Vampire Voles, 2002; The Winter Soldiers, 2002; Nightdancers, 2002; Spiggot's Quest, 2002; (with S. Anderson) Monster School, 2002; Heastward Ho!, 2003; Mallmoc's Castle, 2003; Attack on the Redan, 2003; Brothers of the Blade, 2004; Boggart and Fen, 2004; Attica, 2006; The Silver Claw, 2006; Jigsaw, 2007; The Rogue Officer, 2007; The Hundred-towered City, 2008; Kiwi Wars, 2008; Scarlet Sash: A Novel of the Zulu Wars, 2010; Dragoons, 2011; Poems, Peoms and Other Atrocities, 2011. SHORT STORIES: Hogfoot Right and Bird-Hands, 1984; The Songbirds of Pain, 1985; Trivial Tales, 1988; In the Hollow of the Deep-Sea Wave, 1989; Dark Hills, Hollow Clocks, 1990; (co-author) Haunting Christmas Tales, 1991; In the Country of Tattooed Men, 1993; (co-author) Thirteen More Tales of Horror, 1994; Moby Jack and Other Tall Tales, 2005; Tales from the Fragrant Harbour, 2010; (co-author) Infinities, 2011. AS GARRY DOUGLAS: Highlander, 1986; The Street, 1987; The Devil's Own, 1997; The Valley of Death, 1998; Soldiers in the Mist, 1999. AS F.K. SALWOOD: The Oystercatcher's Cry, 1993; The Saffron Fields, 1994; The Ragged School, 1995. Contributor to periodicals. **Address:** 16 Chedworth Pl., Church Rd, Tattingstone, IP9 2ND, England. **Online address:** wychwater@tinyworld.co.uk

KILWORTH, Garry Douglas. See **KILWORTH, Garry.**

KIM, Byoung-lo Philo. Korean (born Korea (South)), b. 1960. **Genres:** Politics/Government, Language/Linguistics, Social Sciences. **Career:** Writer. **Publications:** Two Koreas in Development: A Comparative Study of Principles and Strategies of Capitalist and Communist Third World Development, 1992; (with J. Suh) Prospects for Change in Kim Jong-il Regime, 1994. WORKS IN KOREAN: The Bibliographical Explanation of the Work of Kim Il Sung, 1993; The Bibliographical Explanation of the Work of Kim Jong Il, 1993; Analysis on the Internalization of Juche Ideology, 1994; Kim Chŏng-il Chŏngkwŏn ŭi Inkwŏn Chŏngchaek Pyŏnhwa Chŏnmang, 1995; Pukhan ŭi Chiyŏk Charip Cheje, 1999; Pukhan Sahoe ŭi Chonggyosŏng: Chuche Sasang kwa Kidokkyo ŭi Chonggyo Yangsik Pigyo, 2000; Pukhan Chonggyo Chŏngchaek ŭi pyŏnhwa wa Chonggyo Siltae, 2002; (co-author) 2007 t'ongil ŭisik chosa, 2007; (co-author) Pukhan-Chungguk kan sahoe, kyŏngjejŏkyŏn'gyŏlmang ŭi hyŏngsŏng kwa kujo, 2008; 7.1 kyŏngje kwalli kaesŏn choch'i ihu Pukhan kyŏngje wa sahoe, 2009. **Address:** Korea Institute for National Unification, SL Tobong, PO Box 22, Seoul, 142-600, Korea (South). **Online address:** philo@ku.kinu.or.kr

KIM, Chi-Ha. Korean (born Korea (South)), b. 1941. **Genres:** Novels, Poetry, Translations. **Career:** Writer and activist. **Publications:** ENGLISH TRANSLATIONS: Yellow Earth Road, 1970; Cry of the People and Other Poems, 1974; The Gold-Crowned Jesus and Other Writings, 1978; The Middle Hour: Selected Poems of Kim Chi Ha, 1980; Susan, 1984; Heart's Agony: Selected Poems, 1998; (ed. and trans.) Cracking the Shell, 2006. IN KOREAN: Shin'ya, 1976; Kim Chi-ha chakpum sŏnjip: Namjosŏn aeguk siin (selections), 1982; T'anŭn mok marŭm ŭro: Kim Chi-ha sisŏnjip, 1982; Minjok ŭi norae minjung ŭi norae, 1984; Taesŏl nam, 1984; (co-author) Tong-yang chŏngsin kwa ijil munhwa kan ŭi taehwa, 1984; Pap, 1984; Namnyŏk ttang paennorae, 1985; Aerin, 1986; Kŏmŭn san hayan pang, 1986; Sallim, 1987; Ojŏk, 1987; Na ŭi ŏmŏni, 1988; I kamun nal e pi kurŭm, 1988; (co-author) Nunmul ŭl samk'imyŏ, 1988; Han'guk munhak p'irhwa chakp'umjip, 1989; Pyŏl pat ŭl urŏrŭmyŏ, 1989; (co-author) 70, 80-yŏndae kongyŏn kŭmji hŭigok sŏnjip, 1990; Malttugi ippal un palman sachon-kae, (works), 1991; T'anŭn mok marŭm esŏ saengmyŏng ŭi pada ro, 1991; Ttongttakki ttongttak, 1991; Han sarang i taeonamuro, 1991; Igot kurigo chogot, 1991; Mungchimyŏn chukko hechimyon sanda, (works), 1991; Saengmyong, i challanhan chongche (works), 1991; Moro nuun tol puchŏ, 1992; Saengmyŏng, 1992; Kyŏlchŏngbon Kim Chi-ha si chŏnjip, 1993; Ongchi kyŏk, 1993; Pam nara, 1993; Tonghak iyagi, 1994; Chungsim ŭi koeroum, 1994; Nim: yojŭm sesang e taehayŏ, 1995; Pin san: Kim Chi-ha sijip, 1996; Sasang kihaeng, 1999; Mi ŭi yŏjŏng, Kim Chi-ha ŭi mungnan, 2001; Hwagae, 2002; Chŏl,

kŭ ŏnjŏri: Kim Chi ha sumuk sihwach'ŏp, 2003; Kim Chi-ha ŭi hwadu: pulgŭn angma wa ch'otpul, 2003; Talchum ŭi minjok mihak, 2004; Yumok kwa ŭndun, 2004; Pidankil, 2006; Kim Chi-ha ŭi yegam, 2007; Hŭin kŭnŭl ŭi kil, 2008; Pangk'ok ŭi net'ŭwŏk'ŭ, 2009; Sae sidae ŭi yullyŏ, p'umba p'umba tŭrŏ kanda, 2009; Tijitŏl saengtaehak, 2009; Ch'otpul, hwaetpul, sutpul, 2009; Monnan sidŭl, 2009; Sanal morankkot, 2010; Si sambaek, 2010; Hŭin kŭnŭl ŭi sanal sosik kwa sanal ŭi hŭin kŭnŭl norae, 2010. Contributor to books. **Address:** c/o Author Mail, White Pine Press, PO Box 236, Buffalo, NY 14213-0230, U.S.A.

KIM, Elaine H(aikyung). American (born United States), b. 1942. **Genres:** Literary Criticism And History, Social Commentary, Adult Non-fiction, Art/Art History, Photography. **Career:** Ewha University, instructor in English, 1966-67; Institute of Modern Languages, teacher of English as a second language, 1967-68; Washington Concentrated Employment Program, teacher of adult education topics, 1967-68; University of California, lecturer, 1969-74, acting assistant professor, 1974-76, assistant professor, 1976-81, associate professor, 1981, professor of Asian American studies, coordinator of Asian American studies, 1984-87, Coordinating Council on the Status of Women, chair, 1991-94, Ethnic Studies Department, chair, 1995-97, Graduate Division, acting associate dean, 1998-99, associate dean, 2000-05, Asian American Studies program, head, 2009-; North Peralto Community College, instructor, 1971-72; KTVU-TV, producer and host of Asians Now, 1975-81; Laney College, instructor, 1976-77; Korean Community Center, co-founder, 1977; Western Public Radio, associate producer of crosscurrents, 1981; University of Michigan, Lora Hutchins lecturer, 1989; Pomona College, Spaulding lecturer, 1991; University of Chicago, Kilmok lecturer, 1994; State University of New York, Gail Paradise Kelly Memorial lecturer, 1996; Rutgers University, distinguished lecturer, 1998. Writer. **Publications:** Asian American Literature: An Introduction to the Writings and Their Social Context, 1982; (with J. Otani) With Silk Wings: Asian American Women at Work, 1983; (with I. Hong) Aedul Ttaemune, 1987; (co-ed.) Making Waves: Writings by and About Asian American Women, 1989; (ed. with N. Alarcon and contrib.) Writing Self, Writing Nation: Four Essays on Theresa Hak Kyung Cha's DICTEE, 1994; (ed. with N. Alarcón) Writing Self, Writing Nation: A Collection of Essays on Dictée by Theresa Hak Kyung Cha, 1994; (co-ed.) New Visions in Asian American Studies: Diversity, Community and Power, 1994; (ed. with E.Y. Yu) East to America: Korean American Life Stories, 1996; (co-ed.) Making More Waves: New Writing by Asian American Women, 1997; (co-ed.) New Formations, New Questions: Asian American Studies, 1997; (ed. with C. Choi) Dangerous Women: Gender and Korean Nationalism, 1998; (ed. with L.H.Y. Kang) Echoes upon Echoes: New Korean American Writings, 2002; (co-author) Fresh Talk, Daring Gazes: Conversations on Asian American Art, 2003; (co-ed.) Invasion: Asian Sisters Represent, 2003; (with M. Machida and M. Sharon) Fresh Talk/Daring Gazes: Conversations on Asian American Art, 2005. Contributor to books and periodicals. **Address:** Department of Comparative Ethnic Studies, University of California, 594 Barrows Hall, Ste. 2570, Berkeley, CA 94720-2570, U.S.A. **Online address:** ehkim@berkeley.edu

KIM, Hakjoon. Korean (born Korea (South)), b. 1943. **Genres:** International Relations/Current Affairs, History, Adult Non-fiction. **Career:** Seoul National University, Department of Political Science, assistant professor, professor of political science, 1973-89, department head; Office of the South Korean President for Policy Research, chief assistant, 1989-91; Office of the South Korean President for the Press, chief secretary, 1991-93; University of Inchon, president; Stanford University, Freeman Spogli Institute for International Studies, Center for East Asian Studies, distinguished practitioner, 2008-09; Dong-A Ilbo, chairman, president and publisher; Korea Advanced Institute of Science and Technology, distinguished visiting professor. Writer. **Publications:** Unification Policy of South and North Korea: A Comparative Study, 1977, 3rd ed. as Unification Policies of South and North Korea, 1945-1991, 1992; (ed. with C. Chung) Korean Unification Problems in the 1970s, 1980; Panoese ŭi tongil iron: chŏngchi palchŏn ŭi hyŏn tangye, 1980; Rŏsia hyŏngmyŏngsa, 1980; Hanguk munje wa kukchechŏngchi, 1980; Soryŏn oegyoron sŏsŏl, 1981; HyŏndaeSoryŏn ŭi haebu, 1981; Pan oese ŭi tongil nolli: chŏngchipalchŏn ŭi hyŏndangye, 1983; Hanguk chŏngchiron: yŏnguŭi hyŏnhwang kwa panghyang, 1983; Marŭkŭsijŭm ŭiihae: Soryŏn kwa che-3 segye Marŭkŭsijŭm ŭi ppuri, 1983; Kangdaeguk kwangye wa Hanbando, 1983; Hanguk minjokchuŭi ŭitongil nolli, 1983; Chōsen Hantō no bundan kōzō, 1984; Soryŏn oegyoron sŏsoHCKI, 1985; Nam-Pukhan kwangye ŭikaltŭng kwa palchŏn, 1985; Sino-North Korean Relations, 1945-1984, 1985; Nambuk ŭi saenghwalsang: kŭ sam ŭi hyŏnjuso, 1986; Nam-Pukhan chŏngchi tonghap kwa kukche kwangye, 1986; Yi Tong-hwapyŏngjŏn: han minju sahoejuŭija ŭi saengae, 1987; Hyŏngmyŏnggadŭl ŭi hangil hoesang: Kim Sŏng-suk, ChangKŏn-sang, Chŏng Hwa-am, Yi Kang-hun, 1988; Kain Kim Pyŏng-nopyŏngjŏn: minjokchuŭijŏk pŏmnyulga, chŏngchigaŭi saengae, 1988; Democratization Under the Sixth Republic, 1989; Hanguk chŏnjaeng: wŏnin, kwajŏng, hyujŏn, yŏnghyang, 1989; Pulgŭn yŏngungdŭl ŭi sam kwa isang: Soryŏn kwaTong-Yurŏp kongsanjuŭijadŭl ŭi palchachwi, 1990; Hangukchŏngchiron sajŏn, 1990; Hanguk chŏnjaeng 40-yŏn kwaHanbando anbo wising, 1990; Koha Song Chin-u pyŏngjŏn: minjokminjujuŭi ŏllonin, chŏngchiga ŭi saengae, 1990; Hangukmunje wa kukche chŏngchl, 1990; Minjuhwa ro kanŭn kil: 6.29 sŏnŏn ihu ŭi pyŏnhwa wa kwaje, 1991; Rŏsia sa, 1991; Shwipke p'urŏ ssŭn Rŏsia-sa: kodae Lusi ro put'ŏ Tongnip Kukka Yŏnhap (CIS) ŭi ch'ulbŏm kkaji, 1992; Korea's Relations with Her Neighbors in a Changing World, 1993; Chŏngwadae taebyŏnini nunmul ro ssŭn sarang hanŭn na ŭi pumonim kwa ŭnsanim, 1993; Sŏnjin Hanguk ŭi mosaek: Che-6 Konghwaguk chŏngchaekpyŏngka, 1993; Chŏnhwangi Hanguk oegyo ŭi siryŏn kwakŭkpok: 60-yŏndae chŏngchibu kija ŭi chŭngŏn, 1993; Haek sidae, Hanguk ŭi mirae: han kŭlcha ŭi chŏngchl, 1994; Pukhan 50-yŏnsa: uri ka ttŏ anaya hal pantchok ŭi uriyŏksa, 1995; Kim Chŏng-il kwa koka kolla: Kim Hak-chunkallŏm-chip, 1995; Tokto nŭn uri ttang, 1996, 2nd ed., 2003; Haebang konggan ŭi chuyŏktŭl, 1996; Whither Path for the TwoKoreas in the 21st Century: War, Peace or Unification?, 1998; Hanmalŭi sŏyang chŏngchihak suyong yŏngu: Yu Kil-chun, AnKuk-sŏn, Yi Sŭng-man ŭl chungsim ŭro, 2000; Tokto nŭnuri ttang, 2003; Hanguk chŏnjaeng: wŏnin, kwajŏng, hyujŏn, yŏnghyang, 2003; (ed. with G-K. Kindermann) New International Order and Future of Divided Nations, 2003; North and South Korea: Internal Politics and External Relations Since, 1988, 2006; (with H. Yuji) Dokuto, 2007; Mi-So naengjon kwa Soryon kunjong arae soui Choson Minjujuui Inmin Konghwaguk konguk: 1946-yon 1-wol - 1948-yon 9-wol, 2008; Kangdaeguk kwollyok chongchi arae soui Hanbando punhal kwa Soryon ui Pukhan kunjong kaesi: 1863-yon - 1946-yon 1-wol, 2008; Hangil pulkkot uro sanhwahan Maehon Yun Pong-gil, 2008; Domestic Politics of Korean Unification: Debates on the North in the South, 1948-2008, 2010; T'ongil ihu t'ongil ul saenggak handa: Nambuk t'ongil, 2011. **Address:** 97 Nonhyon-dong Kangnam-ku, Seoul, 135-010, Korea (South). **Online address:** hkim3@stanford.edu

KIM, In S(oo). Korean (born Korea (South)), b. 1943. **Genres:** History, Theology/Religion. **Career:** Presbyterian College and Theological Seminary, Graduate School of Ministry, professor of church history and director of museum, 1982-, dean, 2000-02, now retired. Writer. **Publications:** Hanguk Kidok kyohoesa, 1994; Protestants and the Formation of Modern Korean Nationalism: A Study of the Contributions of Horace G. Underwood and Sun Chu Kil, 1996; History of the Christian Church in Korea, 1997; Pyŏngsindo wa kyohoe hakkyo kyosa rŭl wihan kanchurin Hanguk kyohoe ŭi yŏksa, 1998; Brief History of the Christian Church in Korea, 1998; History of 100 Years of the Presbyterian College and Presbyterian Theological Seminary, 2002; Saryo Hanguk sinhak sasangsa, 2003; Ilche ŭi Hanguk kyohoe pakhaesa, 2006. **Address:** University of Michigan Press, 839 Greene St., Ann Arbor, MI 48104-3209, U.S.A. **Online address:** iskim@pcts.ac.kr

KIM, Kyu Hyun. American/Korean (born Korea (South)), b. 1963?. **Genres:** History. **Career:** Harvard University, Edwin O. Reischauer Institute of Japanese Studies, postdoctoral fellow, 1996-97; University of California at Davis, associate professor of Japanese and Korean history and Japanese popular culture. Writer. **Publications:** The Age of Visions and Arguments: Parliamentarianism and the National Public Sphere in Early Meiji Japan, 2007. Contributor to books and periodicals. **Address:** University of California, 1 Shields Ave., 4213 Social Sciences & Humanities, Davis, CA 95616, U.S.A. **Online address:** kyukim@ucdavis.edu

KIM, Myung Mi. American/Korean (born Korea (South)), b. 1957. **Genres:** Poetry. **Career:** Chinatown Manpower Project, English teacher, 1981-82; Stuyvesant High School, English teacher, 1983-84; University of Iowa, teaching-writing fellow, 1984-86; Luther College, director of student support services, 1987-91; San Francisco State University, assistant professor, 1991-, professor of creative writing; State University of New York, University at Buffalo, professor of English. Poet. **Publications:** POETRY: Under Flag, 1991; The Bounty, 1996; Dura, 1998; Spelt, 2000; Commons, 2002; River Antes, 2006; Penury, 2009. Works appear in anthologies. Contributor to journals. **Address:** Department of English, University at Buffalo, State University of New York, 505 Clemens Hall, Buffalo, NY 14260-4600, U.S.A. **Online address:** mmkim@buffalo.edu

KIM, Rebecca Y. American/Korean (born Korea (South)), b. 1974. **Genres:** Theology/Religion, Social Sciences. **Career:** Pepperdine University, associate professor of sociology, Ethnic Studies Program, director, Social Science Division, senior fellow, 2004-06. Writer and sociologist. **Publications:** God's New Whiz Kids?: Korean American Evangelicals on Campus, 2006. Contributor to books and journals. **Address:** Pepperdine University, 24255 Pacific Coast Hwy., Malibu, CA 90263, U.S.A. **Online address:** rebecca.y.kim@pepperdine.edu

KIM, Thomas P. American (born United States), b. 1969. **Genres:** Politics/Government, Race Relations. **Career:** Scripps College, associate professor of politics and international relations; Korea Policy Institute, executive director; Claremont Colleges, Intercollegiate Department of Asian American Studies, core faculty. Writer. **Publications:** The Racial Logic of Politics: Asian Americans and Party Competition, 2007. Contributor of articles to periodicals. **Address:** Korea Policy Institute, 3465 W 8th St., 2nd Fl., Los Angeles, CA 90005-2519, U.S.A. **Online address:** thomas.kim@scrippscollege.edu

KIM, Young (Hum). American/Korean (born Korea (South)), b. 1920. **Genres:** History, International Relations/Current Affairs, Human Relations/Parenting. **Career:** United States International University, assistant professor, 1961-64, associate professor, 1964-66, professor of history and political science, 1966-; U.S. Embassy, assistant secretary. Writer. **Publications:** East Asia's Turbulent Century, 1966; Patterns of Competitive Coexistence: USA vs. USSR, 1966; Twenty Years of Crises: The Cold War Era, 1968; Toward Rational View of China: The Vietnam War in Struggle Against History: U.S. Foreign Policy in an Age of Revolution, 1968; The Central Intelligence Agency: Problems of Secrecy in a Democracy, 1981; America's Frontier Activities in Asia: U.S. Diplomatic History in Asia in the Twentieth Century, 1981; The War of No Return, vol. I, 1988, vol. II, 1989; Woman's Liberation Issue in Korea, 1989; United States-Asian Relations in the 20th Century, 1996. **Address:** 3001 Conner Way, San Diego, CA 92117, U.S.A. **Online address:** ykim6@yahoo.com

KIMBALL, Cheryl. American (born United States), b. 1957. **Genres:** Howto Books, Self Help, Homes/Gardens. **Career:** Heinemann (publisher), publisher in trade division, 1990-96; Chronimed Publishing, publishing director, 1996-98; Adams Media Corp., acquisitions editor, 1998-2000; freelance writer and editor, 2000-. **Publications:** The Everything Horse Book: Buying, Riding and Caring for Your Equine Companion, 2002; The Everything Get-out-of-Debt Book: Evaluate Your Options, Determine Your Course of Action and Make a Fresh Start, 2002; Mindful Horsemanship: Increasing Your Awareness One Day at a Time, 2002; (with S.R. Turlington and C.A. Shea) The Everything Kid's Monsters Book: From Ghosts, Goblins and Gremlins to Vampires, Werewolves and Zombies: Puzzles, Games and Trivia Guaranteed to Keep You up at Night, 2002; The Everything Home Decorating Book, 2003; (with M. Hammerly) What to Do When the Doctor Says It's PCOS, 2003; (with T. Lyons) What to Do When the Doctor Says It's Endometriosis: Everything You Need to Know to Stop the Pain and Heal Your Fertility, 2003; Outwitting Ants: 101 Truly Ingenious Methods and Proven Techniques to Prevent Ants from Devouring Your Garden and Destroying Your Home, 2003; Start your Own Pet Sitting Business: Your Step-by-Step Guide to Success, 2004; Horse Wise: Thinking Outside the Stall and other Lessons I Learned from my Horse, 2004; Horse Showing for Kids: Everything a Young Rider Needs to Know to Prepare, Train and Compete in English or Western Events, 2004; The Everything Horseback Riding Book: Step-by-Step Instruction for Riding like a Pro, 2005; Start your own Florist Shop and other Floral Businesses: Your Step-by-Step Guide to Success, 2006; The Complete Horse: An Entertaining History of Horses, 2006; (with J.V. Gelder) Entrepreneur Magazine's Ultimate Book of Sales Letters, 2007; Start your Health Care Career, 2007; (with J.V. Gelder) Ultimate Book of Business Letters, 2007; Start your Own Pet-Sitting Business and More: Doggie Day Care, Grooming, Walking, 2nd ed., 2007; Start your Own Home Inspection Service: Your Step-by-Step Guide to Success, 2nd ed., 2007; Start your Own Bed & Breakfast: Your Step-By-Step Guide to Success, 2nd ed., 2008; Start Your Own Gift Basket Business and More: Special Events, Holiday, Real Estate, Corporate, 2nd ed., 2008; 55 Surefire Homebased Businesses you can Start for under $5, 000, 2008; The Field Guide to Goats, 2009; Design and Launch an Online Gift Business in a Week, 2009; 55 Surefire Food-Related Businesses You can Start for under $5, 000, 2009; (co-author) Start Your Own Pet Business and More: Pet Sitting, Dog Walking, Training, Grooming, Food/Treats, Upscale Pet Products, 2009; Start Your Own Event Planning Business, 3rd ed., 2011; Wisdom I Learned from My Horses, forthcoming. **Address:** c/o Author Mail,

Adams Media Corp., 57 Littlefield St., Avon, MA 02322, U.S.A. **Online address:** ckimball@worldpath.net

KIMBALL, John (Ward). American (born United States), b. 1931. **Genres:** Biology, Sciences, Medicine/Health. **Career:** Noble and Greenough School, instructor in science, 1953-54; Phillips Academy, instructor in biology, 1956-69; Tufts University, assistant professor, 1972-77, associate professor of biology, 1977-81; Harvard University, visiting lecturer, 1982-86, 1990-91, now retired. Writer. **Publications:** Biology, 1965, 6th ed., 1994; Cell Biology, 1970, 3rd ed., 1984; Man and Nature: Principles of Human and Environmental Biology, 1975; Introduction to Immunology, 1983, 3rd ed., 1990. Contributor to scientific journals. **Address:** Addison Wesley Publishing Company, 75 Arlington St., Ste. 300, Boston, MA 02116, U.S.A. **Online address:** jkimball@mcb.harvard.edu

KIMBALL, Meredith M. Canadian/American (born United States), b. 1944. **Genres:** Psychology, Women's Studies And Issues. **Career:** University of Minnesota, research assistant, 1964-66; University of British Columbia, assistant professor of psychology, 1970-76; Simon Fraser University, assistant professor, 1976-82, associate professor, 1982-96, Department of Women's Studies, head, 1991-93, professor of psychology and women's studies, 1996-, now professor emeritus. Writer. **Publications:** (With E.M. Gee) Women and Aging, 1987; Feminist Visions of Gender Similarities and Differences, 1995. Contributor of articles to books and journals. **Address:** Department of Psychology, Simon Fraser University, RCB 5246, 8888 University Dr., Burnaby, BC V5A 1S6, Canada. **Online address:** kimball@sfu.ca

KIMBALL, Robert (Eric). American (born United States), b. 1939. **Genres:** Music, Theatre, Poetry. **Career:** Yale University, Yale Collection of Literature and American Musical Theatre, curator, 1967-71; lecturer, 1970, 1974, 1980-81; New York Post, music and dance reviewer, 1973-87, chief classical music critic, 1987-88; City University of New York, Brooklyn College, Institute for Studies in American Music, senior research fellow and visiting professor of music, 1974-75; New York University, lecturer in drama, 1979-80; Roxbury Records, president, 1988-. Writer. **Publications:** (With W. Bolcom) Reminiscing with Sissle and Blake, 1973; (with A. Simon) The Gershwins, 1973; (with T. Krasker) Catalog of the American Musical: Musicals of Irving Berlin, George and Ira Gershwin, Cole Porter, Richard Rodgers and Lorenz Hart, 1988; (with W. Bolcom) Reminiscing with Noble Sissle and Eubie Blake. EDITOR: Cole, 1971; The Unpublished Cole Porter, 1975; The Complete Lyrics of Cole Porter, 1983; (with D. Hart) The Complete Lyrics of Lorenz Hart, 1986; The Complete Lyrics of Ira Gershwin, 1993; Complete Lyrics of Irving Berlin, 2000; (intro. with R. Gottlieb) Reading Lyrics, 2000; (with S. Nelson) Complete Lyrics of Frank Loesser, 2003; Selected Lyrics: Cole Porter, 2006; The Complete Lyrics of Johnny Mercer, 2009; Ira Gershwin: Selected Lyrics, 2009. Contributor to periodicals. **Address:** 180 W 58th St., New York, NY 10019, U.S.A.

KIMBALL, Roger. American (born United States), b. 1953. **Genres:** Education, Cultural/Ethnic Topics, Literary Criticism And History. **Career:** New Criterion, editor and publisher; Encounter Books, president and publisher; Spectator, art critic; Yale University, teacher; Connecticut College, teacher. **Publications:** Tenured Radicals: How Politics Has Corrupted Our Higher Education, 1990, 3rd ed., 2008; (ed. with H. Kramer) Against the Grain: The New Criterion of Art and Intellect at the End of the Twentieth Century, 1995; (ed. and intro. with H. Kramer) The Future of the European Past, 1997; (intro. and contrib.) Physics and Politics, or, Thoughts on the Application of the Principles of Natural Selection and Inheritance to Political Society, 1999; (ed. and intro. with H. Kramer) The Betrayal of Liberalism: How the Disciples of Freedom and Equality Helped Foster the Illiberal Politics of Coercion and Control, 1999; (ed. and intro.) Against the Idols of the Age, 1999; The Long March: How the Cultural Revolution of the 1960s Changed America, 2000; Experiments Against Reality: The Fate of Culture in the Postmodern Age, 2000; Lives of the Mind: The Use and Abuse of Intelligence from Hegel to Wodehouse, 2002; (ed. and intro. with H. Kramer) The Survival of Culture: Permanent Values in a Virtual Age, 2002; Art's Prospect: The Challenge of Tradition in an Age of Celebrity, 2003; (ed. and intro. with H. Kramer) Lengthened Shadows: America and Its Institutions in the Twenty-First Century, 2004; The Rape of the Masters: How Political Correctness Sabotages Art, 2004; (ed.) Diversions and Animadversions: Essays from The New Criterion, 2005; (ed. and intro. with H. Kramer) Counterpoints: Twenty-five Years of the New Criterion on Culture and the Arts, 2007; Retaking the University: A Battle Plan, 2009; (ed. and intro.) Athwart History: Half a Century of Polemics, Animadversions

and Illuminations, 2010. Contributor to periodicals. **Address:** New Criterion, Foundation for Cultural Review, 900 Broadway, Ste. 602, New York, NY 10003, U.S.A. **Online address:** letters@newcriterion.com

KIMBRIEL, Katharine Eliska. American (born United States), b. 1956?. **Genres:** Science Fiction/Fantasy, Mystery/Crime/Suspense, Young Adult Fiction. **Career:** Book View Cafe, founding member. Science fiction and fantasy writer. **Publications:** NOVELS-NUALA SERIES: Fire Sanctuary, 1986; Fires of Nuala, 1988; Hidden Fires, 1991. ALFREDA SORENSSON SERIES: Night Calls, 1996; Kindred Rites, 1997; Wings of Morning, 2005. Contributor to books. **Address:** c/o Jonathan Matson, Harold Matson Company Inc., 276 5th Ave., New York, NY 10001, U.S.A. **Online address:** alfreda89@ke-kimbriel.com

KIMBROUGH, S. T. American (born United States), b. 1936. **Genres:** Music, Theology/Religion. **Career:** United Methodist Church, General Board of Global Ministries, GBGMusik, founder, Global Praise Program, founder, associate general secretary for mission evangelism, 1990-98; Charles Wesley Society, founding president; writer, researcher, and singer, 1993-. **Publications:** Israelite Religion in Sociological Perspective: The Work of Antonin Causse, 1978; Lost in Wonder: Charles Wesley, The Meaning of His Hymns Today, 1987; Resistless Love: Christian Witness in the New Millennium, 1987; Charles Wesley: Poet and Theologian, 1992; A Heart to Praise My God: Wesley Hymns for Today, 1996; Who are the People Called Methodists, 2000; Anna Eklund: A Methodist Saint in Russia, 2001; The Lyrical Theology of Charles Wesley, 2011. EDITOR: (with O.A. Breckerlegge) The Unpublished Poetry of Charles Wesley, vol. I, 1988, vol. II: Hymns and Poems on Holy Scripture, 1990, vol. III: Hymns and Poems for Church and World, 1992; (with J.C. Holbert and C.R. Young) Psalms for Praise and Worship: A Complete Liturgical Psalter, 1992; Charles Wesley: Poet and Theologian, 1992; Methodism in Russia and the Baltic States: History and Renewal, 1995; Global Praise 1, 1997, rev. ed. 2000; A Song for the Poor, 1997; Global Praise, 1997; Africa Praise Songbook: Songs from Africa, 1998; Songs for the World: Hymns, 2001; Orthodox and Wesleyan Spirituality, 2002; Songs of Love and Praise: Hymns by John Wesley, 2003; Farther Along: The Gospel Collection, 2003; We Offer Them Christ, 2004; Orthodox and Wesleyan Scriptural Understanding and Practice, 2005; Companion to Global Praise 1 and 2 Songbooks: Worship Leader's Guide, 2005; Exaltation: Songs of Women: Sacred Solos, 2006; Beams of Heaven: Hymns of Charles Albert Tindley, 2006; (with C.R. Young) Sing the Wondrous Love of Jesus: Women Hymn Writers and their Songs, 2006(with C.R. Young) God's Mission, God's Song, 2006; Orthodox and Wesleyan Ecclesiology, 2007; (with K.G.C. Newport) The Manuscript Journal of the Reverend Charles Wesley, M.A, 2008. **Address:** General Board of Global Ministries, 475 Riverside Dr., New York, NY 10115, U.S.A. **Online address:** stkimbrough@stkimbrough.com

KIMES, Martha. American (born United States) **Genres:** Law. **Career:** Lawyer; litigation associate. Writer. **Publications:** Ivy Briefs: A Privileged and Confidential Law School Story, 2007. Contributor to periodicals. **Address:** c/o Yona Deshommes, Simon & Schuster Inc., 1230 Ave. of the Americas, New York, NY 10020, U.S.A. **Online address:** martha@marthakimes.com

KIMMEL, Allan J. French/American (born United States), b. 1952. **Genres:** Adult Non-fiction, Ethics, Reference. **Career:** Moravian College, Department of Psychology, assistant professor and director of human resources administration certificate program, 1982-86; Fitchburg State College, Behavioral Sciences Department, instructor, 1986-, coordinator, 1990-91, professor of psychology, 1993-96; Ecole Superieure des Sciences Economiques et Commerciales, Graduate School of Management, visiting profesor, 1993-99, lecturer, 2003; University of Paris IX Dauphine, DMSP Research Center, DEA Marketing et Strategie, CMI Master Program, visiting professor, 1994-2007; ESCP-EAP/European School of Management, professor of marketing, 1995-, Marketing Option-English Track, director, 1995-; The American University of Paris, Department of International Business Administration, adjunct assistant professor, 1995-98; Université Libre de Bruxelles, Solvay Business School, visiting professor, 2001; TEC de Monterrey Business School, The Graduate School of Business Administration, visiting professor, 2004-06; Universidad de San Andrés, Marketing Department, visiting professor, 2007; University of Vaasa, Marketing Department, visiting professor, 2009; Turku School of Economics, Marketing Department, visiting professor, 2009. Writer. **Publications:** (Ed.) Ethics of Human Subject Research, 1981; Ethics and Values in Applied Social Research, 1988; Ethical Issues in Behavioral Research, 1996, 2nd ed., 2007; Rumors and Rumor Control: A Manager's Guide to Understanding and Combatting Rumors, 2004; (ed.) Marketing Communication: New Approaches, Technologies and Styles, 2005; Connecting With Consumers: Marketing for New Marketplace Realities, 2010. Contributor to journals. **Address:** ESCP-EAP European School of Management, 79 Ave. de la Republique, Paris, 75543, France. **Online address:** kimmel@escpeurope.eu

KIMMEL, Daniel M. American (born United States), b. 1955. **Genres:** Film, Romance/Historical, Humor/Satire, Young Adult Fiction. **Career:** Barron and Stadfeld (law firm), associate, 1980-81; Docktor Pet Centers Inc., associate counsel, 1981-83; freelance writer, 1983-; Worcester Telegram & Gazette, film reviewer, 1984-2009; Emerson College, instructor, 1985-98; Boston Center for Adult Education, faculty, 1984; Variety, Boston correspondent, 1986-; Boston University, faculty, 1990; Suffolk University, faculty, 1998- . Lawyer; Boston Business Journal, contributing editor; Boston Society of Film Critics, president. **Publications:** (With N. Segaloff) Love Stories: Hollywood's Most Romantic Movies, 1992; (with N. Segaloff) Isn't It Romantic, 1992; The Fourth Network: How Fox Broke the Rules and Reinvented Television, 2004; (ed.) Work and Worth, 2005; Dream Team: The Rise and Fall of Dream Works: Lessons from the New Hollywood, 2006; I'll Have What She's Having: Behind the Scenes of the Great Romantic Comedies, 2008; Jar Jar Binks Must Die, forthcoming. Contributor to periodicals. **Address:** c/o Alison J. Picard, PO Box 2000, Cotuit, MA 02635, U.S.A. **Online address:** daniel.kimmel@rcn.com

KIMMEL, Elizabeth Cody. American (born United States), b. 1964. **Genres:** Young Adult Fiction, Young Adult Non-fiction, Novels. **Career:** Children's book writer. **Publications:** FICTION: In the Stone Circle, 1998; Balto and the Great Race, 1999; Visiting Miss Caples, 2000; To the Frontier (Adventures of Young Buffalo Bill series), 2001; One Sky above Us (Adventures of Young Buffalo Bill series), 2002; My Wagon Will Take Me Anywhere, 2002; What Do You Dream?, 2003; In the Eye of the Storm (Adventures of Young Buffalo Bill series), 2003; Before Columbus: The Leif Eriksson Expedition, 2003; West on the Wagon Train (Adventures of Young Buffalo Bill Series), 2003; Lily B. on the Brink of Cool, 2003; My Penguin Osbert, 2004; Lily B. on the Brink of Love, 2005; Ladies First: 40 Daring American Women Who Were Second to None, 2005; Lily B. on the Brink of Paris, 2006; Dinosaur Bone War: Cope and Marsh's Fossil Feud, 2006; Top Job, 2007; Mary Ingalls on Her Own, 2008; School Spirit, 2008; Glamsters, 2008; Osbert in Love, 2008; Spin the Bottle, 2008; Unhappy Medium, 2009; My penguin Osbert in Love, 2009; Scaredy Kat, 2009; Reinvention of Moxie Roosevelt, 2010; Crossing Over, 2010. NONFICTION: Ice Story: Shackleton's Lost Expedition, 1999; Before Columbus: The Leif Eriksson Exped, 2003; As Far As the Eye Can Reach: Lewis and Clark's ward Quest, 2003; The Look-It-Up Book of Explorers, 2004; Boy on the Lion Throne: The Story of the 14th Dalai Lama, 2009; The Best American Sports Writing 2009, 2009. OTHERS: Got Issues?, 2011; What's with the Drama?, 2012; Forever Four, 2012. Contributor to periodicals. **Address:** c/o Author Mail, HarperCollins, 10 E 53rd St., 7th Fl., New York, NY 10022, U.S.A. **Online address:** ecodykimmel@gmail.com

KIMMEL, Eric A. American (born United States), b. 1946. **Genres:** Novels, Novellas/Short Stories, Children's Fiction. **Career:** Indiana University, assistant professor of education, 1973-78; Portland State University, professor of education, 1978-93, professor emeritus of education, 1993-; Shearwater Books Ltd., president, 1993-; writer, 1993-. Librarian. **Publications:** The Tartar's Sword, 1974; Mishka, Pishka and Fishka, 1976; Why Worry?, 1979; Nicanor's Gate, 1980; Hershel of Ostropol, 1981; (with R. Zar) In the Mouth of the Wolf, 1983; Anansi and the Moss-Covered Rock, 1988; The Chanukah Tree, 1988; Charlie Drives the Stage, 1989; Hershel and the Hanukkah Goblins, 1989; I Took My Frog to the Library, 1989; The Chanukah Guest, 1990; Nanny Goat and the Seven Kids, 1990; Four Dollars and Fifty Cents, 1990; Baba Yaga, 1991; Days of Awe, 1991; Bearhead, 1991; The Greatest of All, 1991; The Four Gallant Sisters, 1992; The Old Woman and Her Pig; Anansi Goes Fishing, 1992; Boots and His Brothers, 1992; The Spotted Pony and Other Stories, 1992; The Tale of Aladdin and the Wonderful Lamp, 1992; The Gingerbread Man, 1993; Three Sacks of Truth, 1993; Asher and the Capmakers, 1993; The Witch's Face, 1993; I Know Not What, I Know Not Where, 1994; The Three Princes, 1994; Anansi and the Talking Melon, 1994; One Good Tern Deserves Another, 1994; Iron John, 1994; Bernal and Floridia, 1994; Bar Mitzvah, 1995; Count Silvernose, 1996; The Magic Dreidels, 1996; Billy Lazroe and the King of the Sea, 1996; Ali Baba and the Forty Thieves, 1996; One Eye, Two Eyes, and Three Eyes, 1996; Squash It, 1997; Sirko and the Wolf, 1997; Ten Suns, 1998; Easy Work, 1998; When Mindy Saved Hanukkah, 1998; A Hanukkah Treasury, 1998; Seven at One Blow, 1998; The

Birds' Gift, 1999; Sword of the Samurai, 1999; The Rooster's Antlers, 1999; The Two Mountains, 2000; Montezuma and the Fall of the Aztecs, 2000; Grizz!, 2000; The Jar of Fools, 2000; The Runaway Tortilla, 2000; Gershon's Monster, 2000; Pumpkinhead, 2001; A Cloak for the Moon, 2001; Robin Hook, Pirate Hunter, 2001; Website of the Warped Wizard, 2001; Zigazak!, 2001; Website of the Cracked Cookies, 2001; Anansi and the Magic Stick, 2001; Why the Snake Crawls on Its Belly, 2001; The Brass Serpent, 2002; The Erie Canal Pirates, 2002; Three Samurai Cats, 2003; Brother Wolf, Sister Sparrow (stories), 2003; (adapter) Don Quixote and the Windmills, 2004; Wonders and Miracles, 2004; Cactus Soup, 2004; Castle of the Cats, 2004; Hayyim's Ghost, 2004; (adapter) The Hero Beowulf, 2005; Tuning Up, 2005; A Horn for Louis, 2005; Blackbeard's Last Fight, 2006; Three Cabritos, 2007; Sopa de cactus, 2007; Picture for Marc, 2007; Great Texas Hamster Drive, 2007; (adapter) Rip Van Winkle's Return, 2007; Stormy's Hat: Just Right for a Railroad Man, 2008; Mysterious Guests: A Sukkoth Story, 2008; McElderry Book of Greek Myths, 2008; Little Britches and the Rattlers, 2008; Anansi's Party Time, 2008; (adapter) The Fisherman and the Turtle, 2008; Three Little Tamales, 2009; (adapter) Even Higher!, 2009; Spotlight for Harry, 2009; (adapter) Medio Pollito: A Spanish Tale, 2010; (adapter) Joha makes a Wish, 2010; Joseph and the Sabbath Fish, 2011; The Golem's Latkes, 2011; Jack and the Giant Barbecue, 2012. **Address:** c/o Christopher Schelling, Ralph M. Vincinanza Ltd., 303 W 18th St., New York, NY 10011-4440, U.S.A. **Online address:** kimmels@comcast.net

KIMMEL, Haven (Koontz). American (born United States), b. 1965?. **Genres:** Novellas/Short Stories, Novels, Children's Fiction. **Career:** Writer. **Publications:** A Girl Named Zippy: Growing up Small in Mooreland, Indiana, 2001; The Solace of Leaving Early, 2002; Orville: A Dog Story, 2003; Something Rising (Light and Swift), 2004; Killing the Buddha: A Heretic's Bible, 2004; She Got up Off the Couch: And Other Heroic Acts from Mooreland, Indiana, 2006; The Used World: A Novel, 2007; Kaline Klattermaster's Tree House, 2008; Iodine, 2008. Contributor to periodicals. **Address:** Broadway Books Publicity, 1745 Broadway, New York, NY 10019, U.S.A. **Online address:** hkwebmaster@mac.com

KIMMEL, Jordan L. American (born United States), b. 1958. **Genres:** Money/Finance, Information Science/Computers, Business/Trade/Industry. **Career:** Office of Management and Budget, staff, 1981-86; A.G. Edwards Inc., vice president of investments, 1988-91; Paine Webber, vice president of investments, 1991-94; Morgan Stanley Dean Witter, vice president for investment, 1994-97; First Montauk Securities, market strategist, principal and branch manager, 1997-2003; Red Bank, principal and branch manager, 1997-2003; Magnet Fund L.P., president and portfolio manager, 1997-2007; Brookstreet Securities Corp., principal and branch manager, 2003-05; National Securities Corp., market strategist, principal and branch manager, 2006-07, 2009-; Magnet Investment Group L.L.C., president and portfolio manager, 2007-, managing director; National Asset Management, investment advisor. Writer. **Publications:** Magnet Investing: Build a Portfolio and Pick Winning Stocks Using Your Home Computer, 1999; Magnet Method of Investing: Find, Trade, and Profit from Exceptional Stocks, 2009. **Address:** Magnet Investment Group L.L.C., 1201 Sussex Tpke., 2nd Fl., Randolph, NJ 07869-2974, U.S.A.

KIMMEL, Michael S(cott). American (born United States), b. 1951. **Genres:** Sociology, Politics/Government. **Career:** Bryant College, instructor in sociology, 1973; State University of New York College-Oneonta, instructor in sociology, 1973-74; University of California-Berkeley, instructor in sociology, 1974-76, visiting professor, 1990-94; School of Law, research assistant, 1976-77; University of California-Santa Cruz, visiting lecturer, 1977-81; Rutgers University, assistant professor of sociology, 1982-86; New York University, visiting assistant professor of sociology, 1984-85; State University of New York-Stony Brook, assistant professor, 1987-90, associate professor, 1990-95, professor of sociology, 1995-. Writer. **Publications:** Absolutism and Its Discontent: State and Society in Seventeenth-Century France and England, 1988; (intro.) Mundus Foppensis/The Levellers, 1988; (comp. with M.A. Messner) Men's Lives, 1989, 8th ed., 2010; Revolution: A Sociological Interpretation, 1990; Manhood in America: A Cultural History, 1996, 2nd ed., 2006; The Gendered Society, 2000, 4th ed., 2011; The Invisible Sex: Masculinity in Contemporary America, 2003; The History of Masculinity: Essays, 2003; The History of Men: Essays in the History of American and British Masculinities, 2005; The Gender of Desire: Essays on Male Sexuality, 2005; (with A. Aronson) Sociology Now, 2008; Guyland: The Perilous World Where Boys Become Men, 2008; Misframing Men, 2010; (with A.

Aronson) Sociology Now: The Essentials, 2011; Gendered Society, 2011; (with M. Kaufman) The Guy's Guide to Feminism, 2011. EDITOR: Changing Men: New Directions in Research on Men and Masculinity, 1987; Love Letters Between a Certain Late Nobleman and the Famous Mr. Wilson, 1990; Men Confront Pornography, 1990; (with T.E. Mosmiller) Against the Tide: Pro-Feminist Men in the United States, 1776-1990, a Documentary History, 1992; The Politics of Manhood: Profeminist Men Respond to the Mythopoetic Men's Movement (and Mythopoetic Leaders Answer), 1995; (with C. Stephen) Social and Political Theory: Classical Readings, 1998; (intro.) Gay Macho: The Life and Death of the Homosexual Clone, 1998; (with A. Aronson) Gendered Society Reader, 2000, 4th ed., (ed. with A. Aronson), 2011; (with R. Plante) Sexualities: Identities, Behaviors and Society, 2004; (with A. Aronson) Men and Masculinities: A Social, Cultural and Historical Encyclopedia, 2004; (with J. Jearn and R.W. Cornwell) Handbook of Studies on Men and Masculinities, 2005; (with M. Mahler) Classical Sociological Theory, 2007; The Sexual Self: The Construction of Sexual Scripts, 2007; (with Y. Besen) The Jessie Bernard Reader, 2008; (with A.E. Travor) Women, Family and Class: The Lillian Rubin Reader, 2009; (with A.L. Ferber) Privilege: A Reader, 2010. Contributor of articles to journals. **Address:** Department of Sociology, State University of New York, SBS S406 Social & Behavioral Sciences, Stony Brook, NY 11794-4356, U.S.A. **Online address:** michael.kimmel@sunysb.edu

KIMMELMAN, Michael Simon. American (born United States), b. 1958. **Genres:** Art/Art History, Photography. **Career:** Harvard University, teaching fellow, 1982-84; Atlanta Journal-Constitution, art critic, 1984; Philadelphia Inquirer, art critic, 1985-87; U.S. News and World Report, culture editor, 1987; New York Times, art critic, 1988-90, chief art critic, 1990-. **Publications:** Portraits: Talking with Artists at the Met, the Modern, the Louvre, and Elsewhere, 1998; The Accidental Masterpiece: On the Art of Life, and Vice Versa, 2005; Oscar Niemeyer, 2009; (intro.) More Things Like This, 2009; (foreword) Playing Piano for Pleasure: The Classic Guide to Improving Skills Through Practice and Discipline, 2011. Contributor to periodicals. **Address:** New York Times, 229 W 43rd St., New York, NY 10036, U.S.A.

KIMURA, Margaret. American/Japanese (born Japan), b. 1965. **Genres:** Fash Ion/Costume, inspirational/Motivational Literature, How-to Books, Marketing, Photography, Popular Culture, Self Help, Women's Studies And Issues, Autobiography/Memoirs, Film, Business/Trade/Industry, Education, Cultural/Ethnic Topics, Advertising/Public Relations, Art/Art History, Reference, Urban Studies. **Career:** Margaret Kimura Cosmetics, MKC Distributions, owner and chief executive officer; MKC Beauty Academy Inc., founder and head; I NUOVI Professional Cosmetics, creative director. Writer and makeup artist. **Publications:** Asian Beauty, 2001. **Address:** MKC Beauty Academy Inc., 3603 Seneca Ave., Los Angeles, CA 90039-1820, U.S.A. **Online address:** mk@margaretkimura.com

KINCAID, Jamaica. American (born United States), b. 1949. **Genres:** Novels, Novellas/Short Stories, Essays, inspirational/Motivational Literature, Homes/Gardens. **Career:** New Yorker, staff writer, 1976-95; Harvard University, visiting professor. **Publications:** At the Bottom of the River (short stories), 1983; Annie John (novel), 1985; A Small Place (essays), 1988; (with E. Fischi) Annie, Gwen, Lilly, Pam and Tulip, 1989; Lucy (novel), 1990; The Autobiography of My Mother, 1995; My Brother, 1997; (intro.) Generations of Women: In Their Own Words, 1998; (ed. and intro.) My Favorite Plant: Writers and Gardeners on the Plants They Love, 1998; Poetics of Place (essay), 1998; My Garden (Book), 1999; Talk Stories, 2000; Mr. Potter, 2002; Among Flowers: A Walk in the Himalaya, 2005; (ed.) The Best American Travel Writing 2005; Losfantabulosos vuelos: Antologiia de relatos de autoras caribenpas, 2005. **Address:** Department of African and African American Studies, Harvard University, 12 Quincy St., Cambridge, MA 02138, U.S.A. **Online address:** jkincaid@fas.harvard.edu

KINCHER, Jonni. American (born United States), b. 1949. **Genres:** Children's Non-fiction, Psychology, Social Sciences, Medicine/Health. **Career:** Inklusions, founder. Author and educator. **Publications:** Dreams Can Help, 1988; Psychology for Kids, 1990, rev. ed., 2008; The First Honest Book about Lies, 1992; More Psychology for Kids, 1995. **Address:** Inklusions, PO Box 435, North Bend, OR 97459, U.S.A. **Online address:** jonnikincher@aol.com

KINDER, R. M. (Rose Marie Kinder). American (born United States) **Genres:** Novels. **Career:** University of Central Missouri, faculty, editor of Pleiades & developer of the creative writing program now professor emerita.

Publications: Sweet Angel Band & Other Stories, 1991; (co-ed.) Murder, Mystery, Madness, Magic, and Mayhem II: Triskaideka: Thirteen Selections from the Second Cave Hollow Press Anthology Contest, 2005; A Near-perfect Gift (stories), 2005; An Absolute Gentleman (novel), 2007. Contributor to journals and periodicals. **Address:** Mollie Glick, Jean V. Naggar Literary Agency, 216 E 75th St., New York, NY 10021, U.S.A. **Online address:** rmkinder@sprintmail.com

KINDER, Rose Marie. See **KINDER, R. M.**

KINDL, Patrice. American (born United States), b. 1951. **Genres:** Novels, Young Adult Fiction. **Career:** Writer. **Publications:** YOUNG ADULT FANTASY: Owl in Love, 1993; The Woman in the Wall, 1997; Goose Chase, 2001; Lost in the Labyrinth: A Novel, 2002; Keeping the Castle, 2012. **Address:** 116 Middlefort Rd., Middleburgh, NY 12122-9601, U.S.A. **Online address:** patricekindl@nycap.rr.com

KINDRED, Dave. American (born United States) **Genres:** Sports/Fitness, Autobiography/Memoirs, Education. **Career:** Washington Post, sports writer; Atlanta Journal-Constitution, sports writer. **Publications:** Basketball, the Dream Game in Kentucky, 1975; (with J. Theismann) Theismann, 1987; Heroes, Fools & Other Dreamers: A Sportswriter's Gallery of Extraordinary People, 1988; (with T. Callahan) Around the World in Eighteen Holes (memoir), 1994; The Colorado Silver Bullets: For the Love of the Game: Women Who Go Toe-to-Toe with the Men, 1995; (co-author) Celebrating 70: Mark McGwire's Historic Season, 1998; Sound and Fury: Two Powerful Lives, One Fateful Friendship (biography/memoir), 2006; Morning Miracle, 2010. Contributor to periodicals. **Address:** c/o Author Mail, Simon & Schuster, 1230 Ave. of the Americas, New York, NY 10020, U.S.A.

KINEALY, Christine. British/American (born United States), b. 1956. **Genres:** History, Social Sciences. **Career:** Macquarie University, researcher for australian government, 1984-85; People's College, lecturer, 1985-88; Ulster Historical Foundation, deputy director, 1988-90; University of Liverpool, Joint Education Programme, deputy director, 1990-92, honorary fellow, 1991-; Edge Hill University College, associate lecturer, 1993-97; University of Central Lancashire, senior lecturer, 1998-2000, reader, 2000-02, professor of history, 2002-07; Drew University, visiting professor, 2003-07, Caspersen School of Graduate Studies, professor, 2007-. Writer. **Publications:** (Ed. with C. Gallagher and T. Parkhill) Making Sense of Irish History: Evidence in Ireland for the Young Historian, 1990; Tracing your Irish Roots, 1991; Migration and Settlement: A Multi-Cultural Approach, 1992; The Glorious Revolution in Ireland, 1992; This Great Calamity: The Irish Famine, 1845-52, 1994; (ed. with T. Parkhill) Famine in Ulster: The Regional Impact, 1997; Death-dealing Famine: The Great Hunger in Ireland, 1997; Disunited Kingdom?: England, Ireland, Scotland, and Wales, 1800-1949, 1999; (with G. MacAtasney) Hidden Famine: Poverty, Hunger, and Sectarianism in Belfast, 1840-50, 2000; (with S. Sexton) The Irish: A Photohistory, 1840-1940, 2002; The Great Famine in Ireland: Impact, Ideology and Rebellion, 2002; The Great Irish Famine: Impact, Ideology, and Rebellion, 2002; (ed. with D.A. Valone) Ireland's Great Hunger: Silence, Memory, and Commemoration, 2002; New History of Ireland, 2004; (with G. Timmins and K. Vernon) Teaching and Learning History, 2005; (ed. with R. Swift) Politics and Power in Victorian Ireland, 2006; (ed. with K. Boardman) 1848, The Year the World Turned?, 2007; Repeal and Revolution: 1848 in Ireland, 2009; War and Peace, 2010; The Saddest People the Sun Sees, 2011. Contributor to books and journals. **Address:** Caspersen School of Graduate Studies, Drew University, 36 Madison Ave., Madison, NJ 07940, U.S.A. **Online address:** ckinealy@drew.edu

KING, Alison. See **MARTINI, Teri.**

KING, Anthony. British/Canadian (born Canada), b. 1934. **Genres:** Politics/Government, Social Commentary, Local History/Rural Topics. **Career:** Oxford University, Magdalen College, fellow, 1961-65; Columbia University, American Council of Learned Societies fellow in American studies, 1962-63; University of Essex, senior lecturer, 1966-67, reader-in-government, 1967-69, department chair, 1968-71, 1985-86, professor of government, 1969-99, pro-vice-chancellor, 1986-89, Essex County Council Millennium professor of British government, 1999-; University of Wisconsin, visiting professor, 1966; British Journal of Political Science, editor, 1972-77, co-editor, 1984-87, 1989-92; Center for Advanced Study in the Behavioral Sciences, fellow, 1977-78; Politics Association, president, 1981-84; Princeton University, Woodrow Wilson School, visiting professor of public and international affairs, 1984; Institute for Government, associate, 2009. Writer. **Publications:** Yoruba Sacred Music From Ekiti, 1961, (with D.E. Butler) British General Election of 1964, 1965; (contrib.) European Politics, 1966; (with D.E. Butler) British General Election of 1966, 1966; (with A. Sloman) Westminster and Beyond: Based on the B.B.C. Radio Series Talking Politics, 1973; British Members of Parliament: A Self-Portrait, 1974; (contrib.) Handbook of Political Science, 1975; (co-author) Why is Britain Becoming Harder to Govern?, 1976; (with R. Downey and G. Soffe) The Roman Temple on Hayling Island, First Interim Report on Excavations, 1976; Britain Says Yes: The 1975 Referendum on the Common Market, 1977; (with R. Downey and G. Soffe) Roman Temple on Hayling Island, Second Interim Report on Excavations 1977, 1978; The Archaeology of Ancient Rome, 1981; Roman Gaul and Germany, 1990; (co-author) Britain at the Polls, 1992, 1993; (comp.) British and Irish Archaeology: A Bibliographical Guide, 1994; (with I. Crewe) SDP: The Birth, Life and Death of the Social Democratic Party, 1995; Running Scared: Why America's Politicians Campaign Too Much and Govern Too Little, 1997; Does the United Kingdom Still have a Constitution?, 2001; (co-author) Britain at the Polls, 2001, 2002; British Constitution, 2007; The Founding Fathers v. the People: Paradoxes of American Democracy, 2011. EDITOR: (and intro.) British Politics: People, Parties and Parliament, 1966; (and intro.) British Prime Minister: A Reader, 1969, rev. ed., 1985; The New American Political System, 1978, rev. ed., 1990; Both Ends of the Avenue: The Presidency, the Executive Branch and Congress in the 1980s, 1983; (with T.F.C. Blagg) Military and Civilian In Roman Britain: Cultural Relationships in a Frontier Province, 1984; New Labour Triumphs: Britain at the Polls, 1998; British Political Opinion, 1937-2000: The Gallup Polls, 2001; Leaders' Personalities and the Outcomes of Democratic Elections, 2002; (with J. Bartle) Britain at the Polls 2005, 2006. **Address:** Department of Government, University of Essex, Rm. 5.022, Wivenhoe Pk., Colchester, EX CO4 3SQ, England. **Online address:** kinga@essex.ac.uk

KING, A. S. American (born United States), b. 1970?. **Genres:** Young Adult Fiction. **Career:** Author and educator. **Publications:** The Dust of 100 Dogs, 2009; Please Ignore Vera Dietz, 2010. Contributor to periodicals. **Address:** PA , U.S.A. **Online address:** asking@as-king.com

KING, Barbara J. American (born United States) **Genres:** Social Sciences, Animals/Pets, Anthropology/Ethnology, Theology/Religion. **Career:** College of William and Mary, Department of Anthropology, professor, chancellor professor. Writer. **Publications:** The Information Continuum: Evolution of Social Information Transfer in Monkeys, Apes, and Hominids, 1994; (ed.) The Origins of Language: What Nonhuman Primates Can Tell Us, 1999; (ed. with R.G. Fox) Anthropology beyond Culture, 2002; The Dynamic Dance: Nonvocal Communication in African Great Apes, 2004; Evolving God: A Provocative View of the Origins of Religion, 2007; (with A. Fogel and S.G. Shanker) Human Development in the Twenty-first Century: Visionary Ideas from Systems Scientists, 2008; Being With Animals: Why We Are Obsessed with the Furry, Scaly, Feathered Creatures Who Populate Our World, 2010. Contributor to journals. **Address:** Department of Anthropology, College of William & Mary, Rm. 102, Washington Hall, PO Box 8795, Williamsburg, VA 23187-8795, U.S.A. **Online address:** bjking@wm.edu

KING, Brian. (Brian R. King). British (born England) **Genres:** Sciences, Poetry, History. **Career:** Journalist and producer. **Publications:** The Lying Ape: An Honest Guide to a World of Deception, 2006; (with M. Plimmer) Beyond Coincidence: Stories of Amazing Coincidence and the Mystery and Mathematics behind Them, 2006; I'm An Aspie, 2008; Thank You Sammy, 2008. Contributor to periodicals. **Address:** c/o Author Mail, St. Martin's Press, 175 5th Ave., New York, NY 10010, U.S.A.

KING, Brian R. See **KING, Brian.**

KING, Bruce (Alvin). American (born United States), b. 1933. **Genres:** Intellectual History, Literary Criticism And History, Biography. **Career:** University of Ibadan, lecturer in English, 1962-65; University of Bristol, lecturer in English, 1965-67; University of Lagos, professor of English and head of department, 1967-69; University of Windsor, professor of English, 1970-73; Ahmadu Bello University, professor of English and head of department, 1973-77; University of Paris III, visiting professor of English, 1977-78; University of Stirling, visiting professor of English, 1979; University of Canterbury, professor of English, 1979-83; University of North Alabama, distinguished professor of English, 1983-86; Ben Gurion University, professor of English, 1987-89; University of Paris, visiting professor of English, 1990-99;

University of Angers, visiting professor of English, 1995. Writer. **Publications:** Dryden's Major Plays, 1966; Marvell's Allegorical Poetry, 1977; The New English Literatures, 1980; Ibsen's A Doll's House, 1980; G.B. Shaw's Arms and the Man, 1980; Fielding's Joseph Andrews, 1981; History of 17th-Century English Literature, 1982; Modern Indian Poetry in English, 1987, rev. ed., 2004; (contrib.) Demon Shield, 1989; Coriolanus, 1989; Three Indian Poets: Ezekiel, Ramanujan and Moraes, 1991, 2nd ed., 2005; V.S. Naipaul, 1993, 2nd ed., 2003; Derek Walcott and West Indian Drama, 1995; Derek Walcott: A Caribbean Life, 2000; The Internationalization of English Literature 1948-2000, 2004; (trans. with A. King) P. Delacourcelle, Spiced: Recipes from Le Pre Verre, 2007; Robert Graves: A Biography, 2008. EDITOR: 20th Century Interpretations of All for Love, 1968; Dryden's Mind and Art, 1969; Introduction to Nigerian Literature, 1971; Literatures of the World in English, 1974; (co-ed.) A Celebration of Black and African Writing, 1976; West Indian Literature, 1979, 2nd ed., 1995; Contemporary American Theatre, 1991; The Commonwealth Novel since 1960, 1991; Post-Colonial English Drama, 1992; The Later Fiction of Nadine Gordimer, 1993; New National and Post-Colonial Literatures, 1996. **Address:** 145 Quai de Valmy, Paris, 75010, France. **Online address:** king.adele@wanadoo.fr

KING, Carol Soucek. American (born United States), b. 1943. **Genres:** Architecture, Design, Homes/Gardens, inspirational/Motivational Literature. **Career:** Santa Monica Evening Outlook, drama critic; Los Angeles Herald Examiner, Lifestyle Section, editor; Designers West, editor-in-chief, 1978-93; Designers World, editor-in-chief, 1991-93; Interior Expressions magazine, editor, 1998-99; Institute of Philosophy and the Arts and Its Salon on the Spiritually Creative Life, 1996-, founder; University of Southern California, lecturer in contemporary theater; California Institute of the Arts, project director; Nichi Bei Fujin Kai, president, 2006-08; Tuesday Reading Group, president, 2005-07. **Publications:** At Home and at Work, 1993; Furniture: Architect's and Designer's Originals, 1994; The Creative Touch: Designing with Wood, 1995; The Creative Touch: Designing with Tile, Stone and Brick, 1995; The Creative Touch: Designing with Fabrics, 1996; The Creative Touch: Designing with Glass, 1996; Empowered Gardens: Architects and Designers at Home, 1997; Gardenscapes: Designs for Outdoor Living, 1997; Designing with Light: The Creative Touch, 1997; Natural Light, 1998; Light Styling, 1999; Feng Shui at Home, 1999; Designing with Spirituality, 2000; Unique Homes: Personalize Your Home With Good Design, 2006. **Address:** 60 El Circulo Dr., Pasadena, CA 91105, U.S.A. **Online address:** kingcarol@saol.com

KING, Cassandra. (Sandra King Ray). American (born United States), b. 1944. **Genres:** Novels, Novellas/Short Stories, Romance/Historical. **Career:** Journalist and educator. **Publications:** Making Waves in Zion, 1995, rev. ed. as Making Waves, 2003; The Sunday Wife, 2002; The Same Sweet Girls, 2005; Queen of Broken Hearts, 2007. Works appear in anthologies. Contributor to journals and periodicals. **Address:** c/o Author Mail, Hyperion Books, 11th Fl., 77 W 66th St., New York, NY 10023-6201, U.S.A.

KING, Cynthia. American (born United States), b. 1925. **Genres:** Novels, Novellas/Short Stories, Children's Fiction, Young Adult Fiction. **Career:** Hillman Periodicals, associate editor, 1946-51; Fawcett Publications, managing editor, 1951-55; Milam School, teacher and tutor of creative writing, 1970-72; Awty School, teacher of creative writing, 1973-75; Michigan Council for the Arts, Creative Writers in the Schools Program, writer-in-residence, 1976-83; Seminars on Book Proposals, coordinator, 1981-; Detroit Public Library, director of seminars, 1981-85; Short Story Symposium, director, 1985-. **Publications:** In the Morning of Time: The Story of the Norse God Balder, 1970; The Year of Mr. Nobody, 1978; Beggars and Choosers, 1980; Sailing Home, 1982; (with S. Sayre) Entertainment and Society: Influences, Impacts, and Innovations, 2010. Contributor to newspapers. **Address:** 228 River St., Bethel, VT 05032-9487, U.S.A. **Online address:** tonibking@adelphia.net

KING, Daniel (John). British (born England), b. 1963. **Genres:** Recreation, Sports/Fitness, How-to Books, Children's Fiction. **Career:** Guardian Newspaper, columnist, 1996-; ChessBase Magazine, columnist, 1996-. Journalist. **Publications:** Winning with the Najdorf, 1992; How Good Is Your Chess?, 1993; (with D. Trelford) World Chess Championship, Kasparov v. Short, 1993; Learn Chess With Nigel Short, 1993; (with P. Ponzetto) Mastering the Spanish, 1994; How to Win at Chess: The Ten Golden Rules, 1995; World Chess Championship 1995, Kasparov vs Anand, 1995; (with P. Dove) Choose the Right Move, 1995; Kasparov v. Deeper Blue: The Ultimate Man vs. Machine Challenge, 1997; The Closed Sicilian, 1997; (with C. Duncan) Choose the Right Move, 1998; The English Defence, 1999; (with G. Kasparov) Kasparov Against the World, 2000; Chess: From First Moves to Checkmate, 2000; Games: Learn to Play, Play to Win, 2003; Games: From Backgammon to Blackjack, 2003; Test Your Chess With Daniel King, 2004; How to Play Chess, 2009. Contributor to journals. **Address:** Kingfisher Publications P.LC., New Penderel House, 283-288 High Holbom, London, GL WC1V 7HZ, England. **Online address:** danieljohnking@compuserve.com

KING, Daren. British (born England), b. 1972?. **Genres:** Young Adult Fiction, Children's Fiction, Young Adult Non-fiction, Children's Non-fiction, Ghost Writer, Humor/Satire, Animals/Pets. **Career:** Writer. **Publications:** FOR CHILDREN: Smally the Mouse and Friends (Who Don't Like Him) In: Smally's Party, 2005; Mouse Noses on Toast, 2006; Sensible Hare and the Case of Carrots, 2007; Peter the Penguin Pioneer, 2008; The Frightfully Friendly Ghosts, 2009. FOR ADULTS: Boxy an Star, 1999; Jim Giraffe: A Ghost Story about a Ghost Giraffe, 2004; Tom Boler, 2005; Manual, 2008. Works appear in anthologies. Contributor to magazines. **Address:** 375 Hudson St., New York, NY 10014, U.S.A. **Online address:** hello@darenking.co.uk

KING, Dave. American (born United States), b. 1955?. **Genres:** Novels, Poetry. **Career:** Columbia University, Literary Journal, editor-in-chief, 1998-99; Dynaflow Studios Inc., founder; The Little Book Room, editor; City University of New York, Baruch College, Department of English, adjunct lecturer; New York University, Gallatin School of Interdisciplinary Studies, staff. **Publications:** The Ha-Ha, 2005. Contributor to journals. **Address:** Brooklyn, NY , U.S.A. **Online address:** davekingwriter@gmail.com

KING, David. British/South African (born South Africa), b. 1939. **Genres:** Environmental Sciences/Ecology, Natural History, Sciences. **Career:** Imperial College, lecturer in chemical physics UEA, 1966-74; University of Liverpool, Brunner professor of physical chemistry, 1974-88, Leverhulme Centre for Innovative Catalysis, founder, 1987; St. John's College, fellow, 1988-95; University of Cambridge, 1920 professor of physical chemistry, 1988-2005, head of department of chemistry, 1993-2000, Downing College, master, 1995-2000, director of research, 2005-, Queens' College, fellow, 2001-; United Kingdom Government, chief scientific advisor, Office of Science and Technology, head, 2000-07; UBS, senior scientific advisor; University of Oxford, Smith School of Enterprise and the Environment, director, 2008-. Writer. **Publications:** (Ed. with D.P. Woodruff) Interdisciplinary Surface Science: Proceedings of the Third Interdisciplinary Surface Science Conference University of York, England, 27-30 March, 1977, 1977; (ed. with D.P. Woodruff) The Chemical Physics of Solid Surfaces and Heterogeneous Catalysis, 1981; (ed. with N.V. Richardson and S. Holloway) Vibrations at Surfaces 1985: Proceedings of the Fourth International Conference, Bowness-on-Windermere, United Kingdom, 15-19 September 1985, 1986; (ed. with N.P. Weatherill and M.J. Marchant) Multiblock Grid Generation: Results of the EC/BRITE-EURAM Project EUROMESH, 1990-1992, 1993; (with G. Walker) The Hot Topic: What We Can Do about Global Warming, 2008; The Hot Topic: How to Tackle Global Warming and Still Keep the Lights On, 2008. **Address:** Department of Chemistry, Cambridge University, Lensfield Rd., Cambridge, CB CB2 1EW, England. **Online address:** dak10@cam.ac.uk

KING, David. American/British (born England), b. 1943?. **Genres:** Art/Art History, Photography, Reference. **Career:** Writer, photohistorian, art historian and designer. **Publications:** NONFICTION: (with F. Wyndham) Trotsky: A Documentary, 1972; (comp.) I Am King: A Photographic Biography of Muhammad Ali, 1975; (with C. Porter) Images of Revolution: Graphic Art from 1905 Russia, 1983 in UK (with C. Porter) as Blood & Laughter: Caricatures from the 1905 Revolution, 1983; Trotsky: A Photographic Biography, 1986; (ed. with F. Wyndham) Far Journeys: Photographs and Notebooks, 1993; (with K. Campbell) Ten Years of Uzbekistan, 1994; The Commissar Vanishes: The Falsification of Photographs and Art in Stalin's Russia, 1997. OTHER: Red Star over Russia, 2009. **Address:** Henry Holt & Co., 115 W 18th St., New York, NY 10011, U.S.A.

KING, Deja. *See* **KING, Joy.**

KING, Donna. *See* **OLDFIELD, Jenny.**

KING, Don W. American (born United States), b. 1951. **Genres:** Biography. **Career:** Montreat College, faculty, 1974-, associate professor, 1992-2000,

professor of English, 2000-, chair of humanities division, 1986-88, associate dean of academic affairs, 1988-92, dean of academic affairs, 1992-93, vice president and dean of academics, 1993-2000, interim president, 2003-04; Asheville Christian Academy, board director, 1985-91, board secretary, 1988-90, board president, 1990-91; Western North Carolina C.S. Lewis Society, founder and director, 1985-93; Mythopoeic Society, board director; Christian Scholar's Review, editor, 1999-. **Publications:** C.S. Lewis, Poet: The Legacy of His Poetic Impulse, 2001; Hunting the Unicorn: A Critical Biography of Ruth Pitter, 2008; (ed. and intro.) Out of My Bone: The Letters of Joy Davidman, 2009. Contributor to books and periodicals. **Online address:** dking@montreat.edu

KING, Doreen. British (born England), b. 1952?. **Genres:** Animals/Pets, Homes/Gardens, Zoology. **Career:** Institute of Biomedical Science, fellow and chartered chemist; London Hospital, organ transplant researcher; King's College London, visiting research associate and research fellow; Time Haiku, editor; British Haiku Society, general secretary. **Publications:** First Aid and Nursing for Wild Birds, 1994; Hedgehog in Your Garden, 1996; Squirrels in Your Garden, 1997; Fox in Your Garden, 2000; The Katsura Tree, 2004; Bedford Square, 2006. **Address:** British Haiku Society, 2 Clifton Lawns, Flat 4, Ramsgate, KT CT11 9PB, England.

KING, Francis P(aul). American (born United States), b. 1922. **Genres:** Economics, Education, Money/Finance, Adult Non-fiction, Social Sciences. **Career:** Teachers Insurance and Annuity Association, research officer, 1955-69, senior research officer, 1969-98; College Retirement Equities Fund, staff, 1955-; TIAA-CREF, 1953--, research officer, 1955-69, senior research officer, 1969-; Tuition Exchange Inc., chair. Writer. **Publications:** Financing the College Education of Faculty Children, 1954; (with W.C. Greenough) Retirement and Insurance Plans in American Colleges, 1959; (with W.C. Greenough) Benefit Plans in American Colleges, 1971; Benefit Plans in Junior Colleges, 1971; (with W.C. Greenough) Pension Plans and Public Policy, 1976; (with T.J. Cook) Benefit Plans in Higher Education, 1980. **Address:** TIAA-CREF, 730 3rd Ave., New York, NY 10017, U.S.A.

KING, Gary C. American (born United States) **Genres:** Mystery/Crime/Suspense, Novels, Horror. **Career:** Writer and educator. **Publications:** Blood Lust: Portrait of a Serial Sex Killer, 1992; Driven to Kill, 1993; Web of Deceit, 1994; Blind Rage, 1995; (with D. Lasseter) Savage Vengeance, 1996; The Texas 7: A True Story of Murder and a Daring Escape, 2001; Murder in Hollywood: The Secret Life and Mysterious Death of Bonny Lee Bakley, 2001; An Early Grave, 2001; Angels of Death, 2003; The Good Neighbor, 2004; Stolen in the Night, 2007; Love, Lies, and Murder, 2007; An Almost Perfect Murder, 2008; Butcher, 2009; Rage, 2010. Contributor to magazines. **Address:** c/o Peter Miller, PMA Literary & Film Management Inc., 45 W 21st St., Ste. 4SW, PO Box 1817, Old Chelsea Sta., New York, NY 10010-6865, U.S.A. **Online address:** garycking@earthlink.net

KING, Geoff. British (born England), b. 1960?. **Genres:** Film, Plays/Screenplays, Art/Art History, Information Science/Computers. **Career:** London Times, journalist and researcher; Brunel University, School of Arts, lecturer in film and television studies, 1998-, professor of film and television studies, Screen Media Research Centre, director and subject leader. **Publications:** Mapping Reality: An Exploration of Cultural Cartographies, 1996; Spectacular Narratives: Hollywood in the Age of the Blockbuster, 2000; (with T. Krzywinska) Science Fiction Cinema: From Outerspace to Cyberspace, 2000; New Hollywood Cinema: An Introduction, 2002; Film Comedy, 2002; (ed. with T. Krzywinska) Screen Play: Cinema/Videogame Interfaces, 2002; (ed.) Spectacle of the Real: From Hollywood to Reality TV and Beyond, 2005; American Independent Cinema, 2005; (with T. Krzywinska) Tomb Raiders and Space Invaders: Videogame Forms and Contexts, 2006; Indiewood, USA: Where Hollywood Meets Independent Cinema, 2009; Lost in Translation, 2010; Indie 2.0: American Independent Cinema Since 2000, 2012; Indie 2.0: Change and Continuity in Contemporary American Indie Film, 2012. Contributor to periodicals. **Address:** School of Arts, Brunel University, 111 Gaskell Bldg., Kingston Ln., Uxbridge, UB8 3PH, England. **Online address:** geoff.king@brunel.ac.uk

KING, Gilbert. (Gilbert King). American (born United States), b. 1962. **Genres:** History, Photography. **Career:** Writer and photographer. **Publications:** The Art of Golf Antiques: An Illustrated History of Clubs, Balls, and Accessories, 2001; The Bicycle: Boneshakers, Highwheelers, and Other Celebrated Cycles, 2002; The Execution of Willie Francis: Race, Murder, and the Search for Justice in the American South, 2008; Devil in the Grove: Thurgood Marshall, The Groveland Boys, and the Dawn of a New America, 2012. Contributor to newspapers and magazines. **Address:** New York, NY , U.S.A. **Online address:** gilbertking@mac.com

KING, Gilbert. *See* **KING, Gilbert.**

KING, Heather Donnellan. American (born United States), b. 1952. **Genres:** Novels. **Career:** Writer. **Publications:** Parched (memoir), 2005; Redeemed: A Spiritual Misfit Stumbles toward God, Marginal Sanity, and the Peace That Passes All Understanding (memoir), 2008. Contributor to books and anthologies. **Address:** Laurie Liss, Sterling Lord Literistic, Inc., 65 Bleecker St., New York, NY 10013, U.S.A. **Online address:** hdking719@aol.com

KING, Iain. British (born England), b. 1971. **Genres:** History, Humanities. **Career:** United Nations Mission in Kosovo (UNMIK), staff, 2000-03, head of planning for mission in Kosovo, 2003; Westminster Foundation for Democracy, director of programs, 2004. Writer. **Publications:** (With W. Mason) Peace at Any Price: How the World Failed Kosovo, 2006; (with B. Ferguson) Blue: The Life and Times of Barry Ferguson, 2007; How to Make Good Decisions and be Right all the Time: Solving the Riddle of Right and Wrong, 2008; (with A. Goram) Goalie, 2009. Contributor to periodicals. **Address:** Westminster Foundation for Democracy, Artillery House, 11/19 Artillery Row, London, GL SW1P 1RT, England.

KING, James. American (born United States), b. 1955. **Genres:** Novels. **Career:** Freelance writer. **Publications:** Bill Warrington's Last Chance (novel), 2010. **Address:** Wilton, CT , U.S.A. **Online address:** jamesking.writer@gmail.com

KING, Jeanette (Margaret). New Zealander (born New Zealand), b. 1959. **Genres:** Poetry, Literary Criticism And History. **Career:** Avonside Girls' High School, teacher, 1982-87; University of Canterbury, tutor, 1988-92, Department of Maori, lecturer, 1993, senior lecturer, associate professor, School of Languages, Cultures and Linguistics, senior lecturer in indigenous language revitalisation. Writer. **Publications:** E Pirangi Ana Koe?, 1994; E Haere Mai Ana Nga Manuhiri, 1994; One Sleepy Day, 1998; Te Pu Harakeke, 1998; Maramara (poems), 1999. Contributor to periodicals. Works appear in anthologies. **Address:** School of Maori and Indigenous Studies, University of Canterbury, 158 Hikuraki, English Bldg., Te Whare Wananga O Waitaha, PO Box 4800, Christchurch, 64033, New Zealand. **Online address:** j.king@canterbury.ac.nz

KING, Jerry P. American (born United States), b. 1935. **Genres:** Mathematics/Statistics. **Career:** Lehigh University, assistant professor, associate professor, 1962-68, professor of mathematics, 1968-, College of Arts and Sciences, associate dean, 1979-81, Graduate School, dean, 1981-87, now dean emeritus, now professor emeritus. Writer. **Publications:** The Art of Mathematics, 1992; Mathematics in 10 Lessons: The Grand Tour, 2009. **Address:** Department of Mathematics, Lehigh University, Christmas-Saucon Hall, 14 E Packer Ave., 27 Memorial Dr. W, Bethlehem, PA 18015-3175, U.S.A. **Online address:** jpk2@lehigh.edu

KING, John. New Zealander (born New Zealand), b. 1944. **Genres:** Air/Space Topics, Technology, Engineering, History. **Career:** Auster Productions, writer, photographer and pilot. **Publications:** Vintage Aeroplanes in New Zealand, 1986; New Zealand Warbirds, 1989; On the Road, 1995; Aviation Accidents and Disasters, 1995; Famous New Zealand Aviators, 1996; Wings over New Zealand, 1996; Warbirds around the World, 1999; The Whole Nine Yards: The Story of an Anzac P-40, 2002; All Their Own Wings, 2007. **Address:** Auster Productions, 29 Fairclough Rd., PO Box 66-041, Beach Haven, 0626, New Zealand. **Online address:** king.jdm@xtra.co.nz

KING, Jonathon. American (born United States) **Genres:** Mystery/Crime/Suspense, Novels. **Career:** Philadelphia Daily News, police and court reporter; South Florida Sun-Sentinel, police and court reporter and feature writer. Journalist. **Publications:** MAX FREEMAN CRIME SERIES: The Blue Edge of Midnight, 2002; A Visible Darkness, 2003; Shadow Men, 2004; A Killing Night, 2005; Acts of Nature, 2007; Midnight Guardians, 2010. SHORT STORY: The Burning of the Styx, 2005. NOVELS: Eye of Vengeance, 2006; The Styx, 2009. Contributer to periodicals. **Address:** Dutton Books, 375 Hudson St., New York, NY 10014-3657, U.S.A. **Online address:** jon@jonathonking.com

KING, Jonny. American (born United States), b. 1965. **Genres:** Music. **Career:** Jazz pianist, 1980-; Cowan, Liebowitz & Latman, intellectual property attorney, 1994-. Writer and musical composer. **Publications:** What Jazz Is: An Insider's Guide to Understanding and Listening to Jazz, 1997. **Address:** Walker & Co., 175 5th Ave., New York, NY 10010-7703, U.S.A. **Online address:** jonnyking@jazzcorner.com

KING, Joy. Also writes as Deja King. American (born United States), b. 1978. **Genres:** Novels, Young Adult Fiction, Sex, Romance/Historical. **Career:** Click Radio, Hip Hop Artist Relations, director; Young Diamond Books, co-founder, publisher and owner; A King Production, founder and owner. Writer. **Publications:** Dirty Little Secrets, 2006; Hooker to Housewife, 2007; (co-author) These are My Confessions, 2007; Superstar, 2008; Stackin' Paper, 2008. AS DEJA KING: Bitch, 2004; Ride wit' Me, 2006; Bitch Reloaded, 2007; The Bitch is Back: Part 3, 2008, Queen Bitch, 2008; (contrib.) Diamond Playgirls, 2008; Last Bitch Standing, 2009; Trife Life 2 Lavish, 2009; Bitch A New Beginning, 2011; Rich or Famous...: Rich Because You Can Buy Fame, 2011. Works appear in anthologies. **Address:** A King Production, PO Box 912, Collierville, TN 38027-0912, U.S.A. **Online address:** jk@joykingonline.com

KING, Karen L. American (born United States), b. 1954. **Genres:** Novels, Theology/Religion. **Career:** Occidental College, professor of religious studies, 1984-97, chair of religious studies department, 1991-94, 1995, chair of womens studies program, 1989-90, 1991-93; Harvard Divinity School, professor of New Testament studies and the history of ancient Christianity, 1997-, Department of New Testament studies, chair, 1999-2001, Winn professor of ecclesiastical history, 2003-09, Hollis professor of divinity, 2009-. Writer. **Publications:** (Ed.) Images of the Feminine in Agnosticism, 1988; Revelation of the Unknowable God: With Text, Translation and Notes to NHC XI, 3 Allogenes, 1995; (ed.) Women and Goddess Traditions: In Antiquity and Today, 1997; The Gospel of Mary of Magdala: Jesus and the First Woman Apostle, 2003; What is Gnosticism?, 2003; The Secret Revelation of John, 2006; (with E. Pagels) Reading Judas: The Gospel of Judas and the Shaping of Christianity, 2007. **Address:** Harvard Divinity School, Andover 503, 45 Francis Ave., Cambridge, MA 02138, U.S.A. **Online address:** karen_king@harvard.cdu

KING, Kathryn R. American (born United States) **Genres:** Literary Criticism And History, Adult Non-fiction. **Career:** University of Montevallo, faculty, 1988, associate professor of English language and literature, professor of English language and literature, learning communities coordinator. Writer. **Publications:** Jane Barker, Exile: A Literary Career, 1675-1725, 2000. EDITOR: (and intro.) Wessex Tales, 1991; The Poems of Jane Barker: The Magdalen Manuscript, 1998; (with A. Pettit) The Female Spectator, 2vols., 2001. **Address:** Department of English and Foreign Languages, University of Montevallo, Comer Hall, Highland Ave., Sta. 6420, Montevallo, AL 35115, U.S.A. **Online address:** kingk@montevallo.edu

KING, Laurie R. (Leigh Richards). American (born United States), b. 1952. **Genres:** Mystery/Crime/Suspense, Science Fiction/Fantasy. **Career:** Writer, 1993-; La Leche League Intl., counselor. **Publications:** KATE MARTINELLI SERIES: A Grave Talent, 1993; To Play the Fool, 1995; With Child, 1996; Night Work: A Kate Martinelli Mystery, 2000; The Art of Detection, 2006. MARY RUSSELL SERIES: The Beekeeper's Apprentice, or, On the Segregation of the Queen, 1994; A Monstrous Regiment of Women, 1995; A Letter of Mary: A Mary Russell Novel, 1997; The Moor, 1998; O Jerusalem, 1999; Justice Hall, 2002; The Game, 2004; Locked Rooms, 2005; The Language of Bees, 2009. SHORT STORIES: Mrs. Hudson's Case, 1997; Paleta Man, 1999; Weaving the Dark, 2004; The Salt Pond, 2004; (contrib.) Murder at the Foul Line, 2006. OTHER NOVELS: A Darker Place in UK as Birth of a New Moon, 1999; Folly, 2001; (intro.) The Hound of the Baskervilles, 2002; (intro.) The Past is a Foreign Country, 2002; (intro.) Criminal Kabbalah, 2002; Keeping Watch, 2003; (as Leigh Richards) Califia's Daughter, 2004; Touchstone, 2007; The God of the Hive: A Novel of Suspense Featuring Mary Russell and Sherlock Holmes, 2010; Pirate King: A Novel of Suspense Featuring Mary Russell and Sherlock Holmes, 2011; Garment of Shadows, 2012. Contributor to books and periodicals. **Address:** c/o Linda Allen, Linda Allen Literary Agency, 1949 Green St., Ste. 5, San Francisco, CA 94123, U.S.A. **Online address:** info@laurierking.com

KING, Martha. American (born United States), b. 1937. **Genres:** Poetry, Novels. **Career:** Writer. **Publications:** Weather (poetry), 1978; Seventeen Walking Sticks (poetry and memoir), 1998; Little Tales of Family and War,

1990-1999 (fiction), 2000; (co-author) Separate Parts: Six Memory Pieces, 2002; Imperfect Fit: Selected Poems, 2004; North & South, 2006. Contributor to magazines. **Address:** 326-A 4th St., Brooklyn, NY 11215, U.S.A. **Online address:** gpwitd@aol.com

KING, Mia Hsu. (Darien Gee). American (born United States), b. 1968?. **Genres:** Novels, Young Adult Fiction. **Career:** Writer. **Publications:** Good Things, 2007; Sweet Life, 2008; Table Manners, 2009; (as Darien Gee) Friendship Bread, 2011. **Address:** c/o Dorian Karchmar, William Morris Endeavor Entertainment, 1325 Ave. of the Americas, New York, NY 10019-6026, U.S.A. **Online address:** mia@miaking.com

KING, Nicholas. British (born England), b. 1947. **Genres:** Theology/Religion. **Career:** St. Joseph's Theological Institute, dean of Biblical studies, 1989-96; St. John Vianney Seminary, spiritual director and lecturer; University of Oxford, Worcester College, alumini secretary and lecturer. Writer. **Publications:** (Trans.) J. Osuna, Friends in the Lord: A Study in the Origins and Growth of Community in the Society of Jesus from St. Ignatius' Conversion to the Earliest Texts of the Constitutions (1521-1541), 1974; What Is a Gospel?, 1981; Setting the Gospel Free, 1995; Jesuit Companions, 1997; Whispers of Liberation: Feminist Perspectives on the New Testament, 1998; Thirsting for God, 2003; The New Testament Freshly Translated, 2005; Strangest Gospel, 2006; The Rosary, 2007; Stations of the Cross, 2009; Not that Man!, 2009; The Psalms, 2009; The Old Testament vol. I: The Pentateuch, 2010, vol. II: The Historical Books, 2012, vol. III: The Wisdom Literature, 2008, vol. IV: Isaiah to Malachi, 2013. Contributor of articles to periodicals. **Address:** Department of Theology, Worcester College, University of Oxford, Campion Hall, Walton St., Oxford, OX OX1 2HB, England. **Online address:** nicholas.king@theology.ox.ac.uk

KING, Peter. British (born England), b. 1949. **Genres:** Law, Criminology/True Crime. **Career:** University College, professor of social history. Writer and historian. **Publications:** (Ed. with T. Hitchcock and P. Sharpe) Chronicling Poverty: The Voices and Strategies of the English Poor, 1640-1840, 1997; Crime, Justice, and Discretion in England, 1740-1820, 2000; Crime and Law in England, 1750-1840: Remaking Justice from the Margins, 2006. **Address:** England. **Online address:** p.j.r.king@open.ac.uk

KING, Philip J. American (born United States), b. 1925. **Genres:** Theology/Religion, Archaeology/Antiquities. **Career:** W.F. Albright Institute of Archaeological Research, president, 1972-76; Boston College, Department of Theology, professor of biblical studies, 1974-2001, faculty fellow, 1989, now professor emeritus; Catholic Biblical Quarterly, associate editor, 1974-77; American Schools of Oriental Research, president, 1976-82, honorary trustee, 1991-; Archaeology and Biblical Studies Series, editor, 1985-91; Cambridge University, visiting fellow, 1989; Harvard University, Shelby White-Leon Levy Program for Archaeological Publications, director. **Publications:** A Study of Psalm 45, 1959; The Book of Judges, 1960; The Book of Psalms, Two Parts, 1962; The Book of Numbers, 1966; American Archaeology in the Mideast: A History of the American Schools of Oriental Research, 1983; Amos, Hosea, Micah: An Archaeological Commentary, 1988; (ed.) Studies on the Mesha Inscriptions and Moab, 1989; Jeremiah: An Archaeological Companion, 1993; (contrib.) Scripture and Other Artifacts: Essays on the Bible and Archaeology in Honor of Philip J. King, 1994; A Parable of Hell, 1995; (with L.E. Stager) Life in Biblical Israel, 2001; Bible is for Living: A Scholar's Spiritual Journey, 2008. Contributor to journals. **Address:** Department of Theology, Boston College, 140 Commonwealth Ave., Chestnut Hill, MA 02467-3800, U.S.A.

KING, Poppy Cybele. American/Australian (born Australia), b. 1972. **Genres:** Fash Ion/Costume. **Career:** Writer. **Publications:** Lessons of a Lipstick Queen: Finding and Developing the Great Idea That Can Change Your Life, 2008. **Address:** New York, NY , U.S.A. **Online address:** poppy@lipstickqueen.com

KING, R. Alan. American (born United States), b. 1963. **Genres:** Military/Defense/Arms Control. **Career:** Writer. **Publications:** Twice Armed: An American Soldier's Battle for Hearts and Minds in Iraq, 2006. **Address:** Zenith Press, 400 1st Ave. N, Ste. 300, Minneapolis, MN 55401, U.S.A.

KING, Robert C(harles). American (born United States), b. 1928. **Genres:** Biology, Sciences, Reference. **Career:** Brookhaven National Laboratory, sci-entist, 1951-55; Northwestern University, assistant professor, 1956-59, associate professor, 1959-64, professor of biology and acting chair of department, 1964-65, professor emeritus, 1965-; Rockefeller Institute, visiting investigator and fellow, 1959. Writer. **Publications:** Genetics, 1962, 2nd ed., 1965; A Dictionary of Genetics, 1968, (with W.D. Stansfield and P.K. Mulligan) 8th ed., 2012; Ovarian Development in Drosophila Melanogaster, 1970; (ed.) Plants, Plant Viruses, and Protists, 1974; (ed.) Bacteria, Bacteriophages, and Fungi, 1974; (ed.) Handbook of Genetics, vol. I-V, 1974-76; (ed.) Vertebrates of Genetic Interest, 1975; (ed.) Invertebrates of Genetic Interest, 1975; (ed.) Molecular Genetics, 1976; (ed. with H. Akai and S. Morohoshi) Ultrastructure and Functioning of Insect Cells: Proceedings of the International Conference Held at Sapporo, Japan, Aug. 3-6, 1982, 1982; (ed. with H. Akai) Insect Ultrastructure, vol. I, 1982, vol. II, 1984; (with W.D. Stansfield) Encyclopedic Dictionary of Genetics: With German Term Equivalents and Extensive German/English Index, 1990. Contributor to journals. **Address:** Department of Molecular Biosciences, Northwestern University, 2205 Tech Dr., Hogan 2100, Evanston, IL 60208, U.S.A.

KING, Roger (Frank Graham). (Leonard Frank). American/British (born England), b. 1947. **Genres:** Novels, Novellas/Short Stories, Plays/Screenplays, International Relations/Current Affairs. **Career:** Ahmadu Bello University, lecturer and research fellow in agricultural economics and rural development, 1972-74; University of Reading, research officer in rural development, 1975-79; Eastern Washington University, visiting professor of English, 1990-91; San Francisco State University, associate professor of creative writing, 1994-97; Amherst College, Copeland Fellow, 2010-11; United Nations Research Institute for Social Development, advisor; University of New Mexico, faculty of creative writing; Warren Wilson College, MFA Program, faculty; The MacDowell Colony, fellow; The Corporation of Yaddo, fellow; Virginia Center for the Creative Arts, fellow. Writer and consultant. **Publications:** NOVELS: Horizontal Hotel, 1983; Written on a Stranger's Map, 1987; Sea Level, 1992; Jacques Cousteau and the Undersea World, 2001; A Girl from Zanzibar, 2002; Love and Fatigue in America, forthcoming. OTHER: Farmers Cooperatives in Northern Nigeria, 1976. **Address:** 154 Shutesbury Rd., Leverett, MA 01054-9703, U.S.A. **Online address:** roger@rogerking.org

KING, Ross James. Australian (born Australia), b. 1936. **Genres:** Architecture, Geography. **Career:** University of Melbourne, professor, 1995-2002, Faculty of Architecture Building and Planning, dean of faculty, 1995-2002, professorial fellow. Writer. **Publications:** (Ed.) Collected Papers: Architecture Research Seminars 1970, 1970; (with R.V. Cardew) Housing in Metropolitan Areas, Selected Aspects: A Statistical Description of Characteristics of Private Dwellings and of Their Occupants in Australian Metropolitan Areas and in Local Government Areas in Sydney, 1970; Yass, NSW: Residential Quality of a Country Town, 1972; Sydney Housing Study: Outline, 1972; (with J. Mors) Sydney Housing Study: Residential Densities, 1974; (with T.J. Brown, R.M. Itami) Procedures for Landscape Assessment and Management, 1980; Emancipating Space: Geography, Architecture, and Urban Design, 1996; (ed. with R. Camacho and A. Srinivasan) Inductive Logic Programming: 14th International Conference, ILP 2004, Porto, Portugal, September 6-8, 2004: Proceedings, 2004; Kuala Lumpur and Putrajaya: Negotiating Urban Space in Malaysia, 2008. Contributor to books and journals. **Address:** Australia. **Online address:** rossjk@unimelb.edu.au

KING, Sallie B. (Sallie Behn King). American (born United States), b. 1952. **Genres:** Autobiography/Memoirs, History, Theology/Religion. **Career:** State University of New York, lecturer, 1979-80; Colby College, assistant professor, 1981-82; Bates College, assistant professor, 1982-83; Southern Illinois University, assistant professor, associate professor, 1983-89, director of undergraduate studies, 1985-89; James Madison University, associate professor, professor, 1992-, department head, 1992-97. Writer. **Publications:** (trans.) S. Myodo, Passionate Journey: The Spiritual Autobiography of Satomi Myodo, 1987; Buddha Nature, 1991; (ed. with C.S. Queen) Engaged Buddhism: Buddhist Liberation Movements in Asia, 1996; (ed. with P.O. Ingram) The Sound of Liberating Truth: Buddhist-Christian Dialogues in Honor of Frederick J. Streng, 1999; Being Benevolence: The Social Ethics of Engaged Buddhism, 2005; Socially Engaged Buddhism, 2009. **Address:** Department of Philosophy and Religion, James Madison University, MSC 8006, Harrisonburg, VA 22807, U.S.A. **Online address:** kingsb@jmu.edu

KING, Sallie Behn. See **KING, Sallie B.**

KING, Sarah Belk. American (born United States) **Genres:** Food And Wine.

Career: House Beautiful, senior editor; House and Garden, associate food editor; Bon Apetit magazine, project manager, contributing editor, senior editor, style director; Big Sky Journal, western style editor; stylist; producer; recipe developer. **Publications:** The Hungry Traveler, France: Menu Translator and Food Guide, 1997; The Foster's Market Cookbook: Favorite Recipes for Morning, Noon and Night, 2002; (with E.R. Scarpetta) Eleanora's Kitchen: 125 Fabulous Authentic Italian-American Recipes, 2004. Contributor to periodicals. **Address:** Sarah Belk King Productions Inc., PO Box 1680, Bozeman, MT 59771, U.S.A. **Online address:** sally@sbkproductions.com

KING, Sorrel McElroy. American (born United States), b. 1964?. **Genres:** Medicine/Health, Autobiography/Memoirs. **Career:** Josie King Foundation, co-founder, 2001-; Patient Safety Group, co-founder. Writer. **Publications:** Josie's Story: A Mother's Inspiring Crusade to Make Medical Care Safe, 2009. **Address:** Fletcher and Co., 78 5th Ave., 3rd Fl., New York, NY 10011, U.S.A. **Online address:** sking@josieking.org

KING, Stephen. (Richard Bachman). American (born United States), b. 1947. **Genres:** Novels, Novellas/Short Stories, Plays/Screenplays, Mystery/Crime/Suspense, Young Adult Non-fiction, Science Fiction/Fantasy. **Career:** Hampden Academy, instructor, 1971-74; University of Maine, writer-in-residence, 1978-79; Philtrum Press, owner; WZON-AM, owner. Writer. **Publications:** NOVELS: Carrie, 1974; Salem's Lot, 1975; The Shining, 1977; The Stand, 1978; The Dead Zone, 1979; Firestarter, 1980; Cujo, 1981; Pet Sematary, 1983; Christine, 1983; Cycle of the Werewolf, 1985; It, 1986; The Eyes of the Dragon, 1987; Misery, 1987; The Tommyknockers, 1987; The Dark Half, 1989; The Stand: The Complete & Uncut Edition, 1990; Needful Things, 1991; Gerald's Game, 1992; Dolores Claiborne, 1993; Insomnia, 1994; Rose Madder, 1995; Green Mile: The Complete Serial Novel, 1996; Desperation, 1996; Bag of Bones, 1998; The Girl Who Loved Tom Gordon, 1999; Plant: Zenith Rising, 2000; Dreamcatcher, 2001; (with P. Straub) Black House, 2001; From a Buick 8, 2002; The Colorado Kid, 2005; Cell, 2006; Lisey's Story: A Novel, 2006; Duma Key, 2008; Under the Dome, 2009; 11/22/63, 2011. GREEN MILE SERIES: The Two Dead Girls, 1996; The Mouse on the Mile, 1996; Coffey's Hands, 1996; The Bad Death of Eduard Delacroix, 1996; Night Journey, 1996; Coffey on the Mile, 1996. DARK TOWER SERIES: The Gunslinger, 1982; The Drawing of the Three, 1987; The Waste Lands, 1991; The Dark Tower Trilogy, 1993; Wizard and Glass, 1997; Wolves of the Calla, 2003; The Song of Susannah, 2004; The Dark Tower: The Gunslinger Born, 2004; (with P. David, R. Furth and R. Isanove) The Long Road Home, 2008. NON-FICTION: Danse Macabre, 1980; Nightmares in the Sky, 1988; Mid-Life Confidential: The Rock Bottom Remainders Tour America With Three Chords and an Attitude, 1994; On Writing: A Memoir of the Craft (non-fiction), 2000; Secret Windows: Essays and Fiction on the Craft of Writing, 2000; (with S. O'Nan) Faithful: Two Diehard Boston Red Sox Fans Chronicle the Historic 2004 Season, 2004. SHORT STORY COLLECTIONS: The Star Invaders, 1964; Night Shift, 1978; Different Seasons, 1982; Skeleton Crew, 1985; (with B. Kruger) My Pretty Pony, 1988; Nightmares and Dreamscapes, 1993; Lunch at the Gotham Cafe, 1995; Hearts in Atlantis, 1999; Everything's Eventual: 14 Dark Tales, 2002; The Secretary of Dreams, 2006; Just After Sunset, 2008; Stephen King Goes to the Movies, 2009; Full Dark, No Stars, 2010. AS RICHARD BACHMAN: Rage, 1977; The Long Walk, 1979; Roadwork: A Novel of the First Energy Crisis, 1981; The Running Man, 1982; Thinner, 1984; The Regulators, 1996; Blaze, 2007. NOVELLAS: The Breathing Method, 1984; The Langoliers, 1990; Four Past Midnight, 1990; Secret Window, Secret Garden, 1991; The Body, 1994; The Shawshank Redemption, 1994; Two Past Midnight: Secret Window, 1994; Riding the Bullet, 2000; Stationary Bike, 2006; The Gingerbread Girl, 2008; Blockade Billy, 2010; Ur, 2010; Mile 81, 2011. OTHERS: Creepshow, 1982; Dolan's Cadillac, 1989; (foreword) Ideal, Genuine Man, 1989; Storm of the Century, 1999; (ed.) Ridley Pearson, The Diary of Ellen Rimbauer: My Life As Rose Red, 2001; Dreamcatcher: The Shooting Script, 2003; (intro.) The Best American Short Stories 2007, 2007; (foreword) Blaze, 2007; (comic book with P. Straub) The Talisman, vol. I: The Road of Trials, 2010; (with R. Albuquerque and S. Snyder) American Vampire, vol. I, 2010; (with P. Straub) The Talisman, vol. I: The Road of Trials, 2010; 11/22/63: A Novel, 2011; Wind Through the Keyhole, 2012. Works appear in anthologies. Contributor to periodicals. **Address:** Penguin Group USA Inc., 375 Hudson St., New York, NY 10014-3658, U.S.A.

KING, Thomas. (Hartley GoodWeather). Canadian/American (born United States), b. 1943. **Genres:** Novels, Children's Fiction, Literary Criticism And History. **Career:** University of Utah, director of native studies, 1971-73, California State University, associate dean for student services, 1973-77; Indians of the Americas Program, coordinator of history, 1977-79; University of Lethbridge, assistant professor of native studies, 1979-89; University of Minnesota-Twin Cities, associate professor of American and native studies, 1989, chair of native studies; University of Guelph, associate professor, professor of English, 2003-. Novelist and editor. **Publications:** (Ed. with C. Calver and H. Hoy) The Native in Literature, 1987; Medicine River, 1990; (ed. and intro.) All My Relations: An Anthology of Contemporary Canadian Native Fiction, 1992; One Good Story, That One: Stories, 1993; Green Grass, Running Water, 1993; Truth & Bright Water, 1999; Coyote Sings to the Moon, 2001; A Coyote Columbus Story, 2002; The Truth about Stories: A Native Narrative, 2003; Coyote's New Suit, 2004; A Short History of Indians in Canada: Stories, 2005. AS HARTLEY GOODWEATHER: Dreadful Water Shows Up, 2002; The Red Power Murders: A Dreadful Water Mystery, 2006. Contributor to periodicals. **Address:** University of Guelph, 50 Stone Rd. E, Guelph, ON N1G 2W1, Canada. **Online address:** thking@uoguelph.ca

KING, William Davies. American (born United States), b. 1955. **Genres:** Autobiography/Memoirs, Biography. **Career:** University of California, Department of Theater and Dance, professor. Writer. **Publications:** (As W.D. King) Henry Irving's Waterloo: Theatrical Engagements with Arthur Conan Doyle, George Bernard Shaw, Ellen Terry, Edward Gordon Craig: Late-Victorian Culture, Assorted Ghosts, Old Men, War, and History, 1993; (as W.D. King) Writing Wrongs: The Work of Wallace Shawn, 1997; (ed. and intro.) A Wind Is Rising: The Correspondence of Agnes Boulton and Eugene O'Neill, 2000; Collections of Nothing (memoir), 2008; Another Part of a Long Story: Literary Traces of Eugene O'Neill and Agnes Boulton, 2010. Contributor to books. **Address:** Department of Theater and Dance, University of California, Rm. 2513, TD West, Santa Barbara, CA 93106-7060, U.S.A. **Online address:** king@theaterdance.ucsb.edu

KING, (William) Dennis. American (born United States), b. 1941. **Genres:** How-to Books, Writing/Journalism, Marine Sciences/Oceanography, Zoology, Politics/Government. **Career:** Our Town, journalist, 1978-81. Freelance writer. **Publications:** Lyndon LaRouche and the New American Fascism, 1989; Get the Facts on Anyone, 1992, 3rd ed., 1999; Reef Fishes & Corals: East Coast of Southern Africa, 1996; Fight Back, 1997; (with V. Fraser) More Reef Fishes & Nudibranchs: East and South Coast of Southern Africa, 2001. **Address:** Nancy Love, 250 E 65th St., New York, NY 10021, U.S.A. **Online address:** wdennisking@cs.com

KING, William Richard. American (born United States), b. 1938. **Genres:** Administration/Management, Business/Trade/Industry, Information Science/Computers, Marketing. **Career:** Case Western Reserve University, assistant professor of operations research, 1964-65; U.S. Air Force Institute of Technology, assistant professor of statistics and operations research, 1965-67; University of Pittsburgh, associate professor, 1967-69, professor of business administration, 1969-85, doctoral program, director, 1971-74, Strategic Management Institute, director, 1980-84, professor of business administration, 1986-; Cleland-King Inc., vice-president, director, 1969-86; Management Science, associate editor, 1974-; Management Information Systems Quarterly, associate editor, 1977-82, senior editor, 1982, International Journal of Policy and Information, associate editor, 1982, editor-in-chief; Institute of Management Sciences, president, 1989-90; Nanyang Technological University, university professor of business administration. **Publications:** Quantitative Analysis for Marketing Management, 1967; Probability for Management Decisions, 1968; (with D.I. Cleland) Systems Analysis and Project Management, 1968; (with D.I. Cleland) Systems, Organizations, Analysis, Management: A Book of Readings, 1969; (with D.I. Cleland) Management: A Systems Approach, 1972; (with D. Dellinger) Defense Officer Personnel Management: An Analysis: A Study Prepared for the Committee on Armed Services, United States Senate, 1975; (with D.I. Cleland) Systems Analysis and Project Management, 1975; Marketing Management Information Systems, 1977; (with D.I. Cleland) Strategic Planning and Policy, 1978; (ed. with G. Zaltman) Marketing Scientific and Technical Information, 1979; (with J.H. Grant) The Logic of Strategic Planning, 1982; (with W.R. King) Systems Analysis and Project Management, 1983; (ed. with W.R. King) Systems Analysis and Project Management, 1983; (ed. with W.R. King) Project Management Handbook, 1983, 2nd ed., 1988; (ed. with V. Sethi) Organizational Transformation through Business Process Reengineering: Applying the Lessons Learned, 1998; (ed.) Knowledge Management and Organizational Learning, 2009. Contributor to journals. **Address:** Joseph M. Katz Graduate School of Business, College of Business Administration, University of

Pittsburgh, 222 Mervis Hall, Pittsburgh, PA 15260, U.S.A. **Online address:** wking115@yahoo.com

KING, Wilma. American (born United States), b. 1942. **Genres:** History, Women's Studies And Issues, Children's Fiction, Young Adult Fiction. **Career:** Hampton University, associate professor, 1973-85; National Endowment for the Humanities, principal investigator and co-director, 1984; U.S. Department of Interior, principal investigator and director, 1985; Indiana University, professor, 1985-91; public speaker, 1986-; Michigan State University, professor of history, 1991-99; University of Missouri, Arvarh E. Strickland professor of African American history, 1999-, Arvarh E. Strickland Distinguished Professor. Writer. **Publications:** (Ed.) A Northern Woman in the Plantation South: Letters of Tryphena Blanche Holder Fox, 1856-1876, 1993; (ed. with D.C. Hine and L. Reed) We Specialize in the Wholly Impossible: A Reader in Black Women's History, 1995; Toward the Promised Land, 1851-1861: From Uncle Tom's Cabin to the Onset of the Civil War, 1995; Stolen Childhood: Slave Youth in Nineteenth-Century America, 1995, 2nd ed., 2011; Children of the Emancipation (children's), 2000; African American Childhoods: Historical Perspectives from Slavery to Civil Rights, 2005; The Essence of Liberty: Free Black Women During the Slave Era, 2006. Contributor to periodicals. **Address:** Department of History, University of Missouri, 203 Read Hall, Columbia, MO 65211, U.S.A. **Online address:** kingw@missouri.edu

KING-HELE, Desmond. British (born England), b. 1927. **Genres:** Poetry, Air/Space Topics, Earth Sciences, Literary Criticism And History, Meteorology/Atmospheric Sciences, Sciences, Biography, Autobiography/Memoirs, Autobiography/Memoirs. **Career:** Royal Aircraft Establishment, scientific research staff, 1948-, deputy chief scientific officer, 1968-88; Royal Society, Bakerian lecturer, 1974, editor, 1989-96; Woilkins lecturer, 1997; Oxford University, Halley lecturer, 1974, Milne lecturer, 1984. **Publications:** Shelley: His Thought and Work, 1960, 3rd ed., 1984; Satellites and Scientific Research, 1960; Shelley, the Man and the Poet, 1960; Erasmus Darwin, 1963; Theory of Satellite Orbits in an Atmosphere, 1964; Observing Earth Satellites, 1966; The End of the Twentieth Century?, 1970; Poems and Trixies, 1972; Doctor of Revolution: The Life and Genius of Erasmus Darwin, 1977; Animal Spirits (poems), 1983; Erasmus Darwin and the Romantic Poets, 1986; Satellite Orbits in an Atmosphere: Theory and Applications, 1987; A Tapestry of Orbits, 1992; Erasmus Darwin: A Life of Unequalled Achievement, 1999; Antic and Romantic (poems), 2000. EDITOR: Essential Writings of Erasmus Darwin, 1968; Letters of Erasmus Darwin, 1981; The RAE Table of Earth Satellites 1957-80, 1981, 3rd ed., 1987; John Herschel, 1992; The Life of Erasmus Darwin, 2003; Collected Letters of Erasmus Darwin, 2007. **Address:** 7 Hilltops Ct., 65 North Ln., Buriton, GU31 5RS, England.

KINGMA, Daphne Rose. American (born United States), b. 1942. **Genres:** Human Relations/Parenting, Romance/Historical, Self Help. **Career:** Writer and educator. **Publications:** Coming Apart: Why Relationships End and How to Live through the Ending of Yours, 1987; Weddings from the Heart: Ceremonies for an Unforgettable Wedding, 1991; True Love: How to Make your Relationship Sweeter, Deeper, and More Passionate, 1991; Garland of Love: Daily Reflections on the Magic and Meaning of Love, 1992; The Men We Never Knew: Women's Role in the Evolution of a Gender, 1993; Weddings from the Heart: Contemporary and Traditional Ceremonies for an Unforgettable Wedding, 1995; Heart and Soul: Living the Joy, Truth, and Beauty of Your Intimate Relationship, 1995; Finding True Love: The Four Essential Keys to Discovering the Love of Your Life, 1996; To Have and to Hold: A Wedding Keepsake, 1997; The Future of Love: The Power of the Soul in Intimate Relationships, 1998; A Lifetime of Love: How to Bring More Depth, Meaning and Intimacy into Your Relationship, 1998; The Nine Types of Lovers: Why We Love the People We Do and How They Drive Us Crazy, 1999; The Book of Love, 2001; 365 Days of Love, 2002; Loving Yourself: Four Steps to a Happier You, 2004; 101 Ways to have True Love in Your Life, 2006; The Ten Things To Do When Your Life Falls Apart, 2010. **Address:** PO Box 5244, Santa Barbara, CA 93150-5244, U.S.A. **Online address:** daphne@daphnekingma.com

KINGMAN, (Mary) Lee. American (born United States), b. 1919. **Genres:** Children's Fiction, Literary Criticism And History. **Career:** Houghton Mifflin Co., editorial assistant, 1943-44, juvenile editor, 1945-46, children's book editor; Sawyer Free Library, board director; The Horn Book Inc., director. **Publications:** Pierre Pidgeon, 1943; Ilenka, 1945; The Rocky Summer, 1948; The Best Christmas, 1949; Philippe's Hill, 1950; The Quarry Adventure in UK as Lauri's Surprising Summer, 1951; Kathy and the Mysterious Statue,

1953; Peter's Long Walk, 1953; Mikko's Fortune, 1955; The Magic Christmas Tree, 1956; The Village Band Mystery, 1956; Flivver, the Heroic Horse, 1958; The House of the Blue Horse, 1960; The Saturday Gang, 1961; Peter's Pony, 1963; Sheep Ahoy!, 1963; Private Eyes, 1964; The Year of the Raccoon, 1966; The Secret of the Silver Reindeer, 1968; The Peter Pan Bag, 1970; Georgina and the Dragon, 1971; The Meeting Post: A Story of Lapland, 1972; Escape from the Evil Prophecy, 1973; Break a Leg, Betsy Maybe!, 1976; Head over Wheels, 1978; The Refiner's Fire, 1981; The Luck of the Miss L, 1986; Catch the Baby!, 1990. EDITOR: Newbery and Caldecott Medal Books: 1956-1965, 1965; (with J. Foster and R.G. Lontoft) Illustrators of Children's Books: 1957-1966, 1968; Newbery and Caldecott Medal Books 1966-1975, 1975; (with G. Hogarth and H. Quimby) Illustrators of Children's Books 1967-1976, 1978; The Illustrator's Notebook, 1978; Newbery and Caldecott Medal Books: 1976-1985, 1986. **Address:** The Horn Book Inc., 56 Roland St., Ste. 200, Boston, MA 02129, U.S.A.

KINGSBURY, Donald (Macdonald). Canadian/American (born United States), b. 1929. **Genres:** Science Fiction/Fantasy, Novels, Novellas/Short Stories, Young Adult Fiction. **Career:** McGill University, lecturer in mathematics, 1956-86, retired, 1986; writer, 1986-. **Publications:** Analog Science Fiction/Science Fact, 1979, rev. ed. as The Moon Goddess and the Son, 1986; Courtship Rite (science-fiction novel), 1982 in UK as Geta, 1984; (with M.O. Martin, G. Benford and L. Niven) Man-Kzin Wars IV, 1991; The Heroic Myth of Lieutenant Nora Argamentine, 1994; Man-Kzin Wars VI, 1995; Psychohistorical Crisis, 2001. Works appear in anthologies. **Address:** c/o Eleanor Wood, Spectrum Literary Agency, 320 Central Pk. W, Ste. 1-D, New York, NY 10033, U.S.A. **Online address:** donaldkingsbury@sympatico.ca

KINGSEED, Cole C. American (born United States), b. 1949. **Genres:** History, Military/Defense/Arms Control. **Career:** United States Military Academy, professor of history, chief of military history, now professor emeritus; Brecourt Leadership Experience, president; Battlefield Leadership, founder, partner. Writer. **Publications:** Eisenhower and the Suez Crisis of 1956, 1995; The American Civil War, 2004; (ed.) From Omaha Beach to Dawson's Ridge: The Combat Journal of Captain Joe Dawson, 2005; (with D. Winters) Beyond Band of Brothers: The War Memoirs of Major Dick Winters, 2006; Old Glory Stories: American Combat Leadership in World War II, 2006. **Address:** Brecourt Leadership Experience, 1 Braden Pl., Cornwall on Hudson, NY 12520, U.S.A. **Online address:** ckingseed@hotmail.com

KINGSLAND, Rosemary. British/Indian (born India), b. 1941?. **Genres:** Film, Novels, Mystery/Crime/Suspense. **Career:** Writer. **Publications:** Just a Gigolo (film novelization), 1979; A Saint among Savages, 1980; Hussy (film novelization), 1980; Treasure Islands, 1980; After the Ball Was Over, 1985; Cassata, 1987; Savage Seas, 1999; Hold Back the Night: Memoirs of a Lost Childhood, a Warring Family, and a Secret Affair with Richard Burton, 2003; The Secret Life of a Schoolgirl, 2003; (with T. Bramwell) Magical Mystery Tours: My Life With the Beatles, 2005. **Address:** c/o Author Mail, Crown Publishers, 299 Park Ave., New York, NY 10171, U.S.A. **Online address:** rosekingsland@aol.com

KINGSLEY, April. American (born United States), b. 1941. **Genres:** Art/Art History. **Career:** Park Place Gallery, assistant director, 1965-66; Museum of Modern Art, curatorial assistant, 1969-71; Pasadena Art Museum, associate curator, 1971-72; School of Visual Arts, instructor, 1973-91, teacher of art history; Sculpture Center, curator, 1980-89; City University of New York, adjunct professor, 1985-87, Queens College, adjunct professor, 1985; Franz Kline Catalogue Raisonne, project director, 1986-; American Craft Museum, curator, 1993-97; Michigan State University, Kresge Art Museum, curator, 1999-; City College of New York, teacher of art history, QC Queens college, teacher of art history; Rhode Island School of Design, teacher of art history. Writer. **Publications:** Afro-American Abstraction, 1981; Emotional Impact: New York School Figurative Expressionism, 1984; Adolph Gottlieb: Works on Paper, 1985; The Turning Point: The Abstract Expressionists and the Transformation of American Art, 1992; Lisa Bradley: February 3-February 27, 1993, 1993; Jean Miotte: Abstract Expressionist, 2000; The Paintings of Alice Dalton Brown, 2002. **Address:** Kresge Art Museum, Michigan State University, East Lansing, MI 48824-1119, U.S.A. **Online address:** akingsle@msu.edu

KINGSLEY, G. Thomas. American (born United States), b. 1936. **Genres:** Urban Studies, Social Sciences. **Career:** City planning consultant to the San Francisco, 1961-62; Arthur D. Little Inc., urban planner and economist, 1962-

65; Ford Foundation, Calcutta Metropolitan Planning Organization, assistant chief physical planner for advisory planning group, 1965-67, Urban Opportunity Program, co-director; University of Southern California, assistant professor of urban and regional planning, 1967-68; Rand Institute, senior program analyst, 1968-69; New York City Housing and Development Administration, assistant administrator for fiscal and administrative services, 1969-73; Rand Corp., Housing Studies Program, deputy director, Housing Assistance Supply Experiment, manager of field and program operations, 1973-78, Housing and Urban Policy Program, director, 1978-82; United Nations Center for Human Settlements, Indonesia's National Urban Development Strategy Project, chief adviser, 1982-85; Urban Institute, principal research associate, 1986-87, 1998-, Center for Public Finance and Housing, director, 1986-97, Metropolitan Housing & Communities Policy Center, senior fellow, National Neighborhood Indicators Partnership, director. Writer. **Publications:** (Ed. with I. Katagiri) Housing Allowance Office Handbook: Housing Assistance Supply Experiment, 1980; (with W.E. Rizor and S.N. Kirby) Housing Allowance Program Administration: Findings from the Supply Experiment, 1982; (with A.S. Gurwitz) The Cleveland Metropolitan Economy, 1982; (with J.P. Telgarsky, I. Jackson and M.N. Kennett) Urbanization in the Caribbean: Prospects and Management Priorities, 1990; (with Telgarsky and G.E. Peterson) Urban Economies and National Development, 1991; (ed. with M.A. Turner) Housing Markets and Residential Mobility, 1993; (co-author) Managing Urban Environmental Quality in Asia, 1994; (with J. McNeely and J.O. Gibson) Community Building: Coming of Age, 1997. Contributor to books and journals. **Address:** The Urban Institute, 2100 M St. NW, Washington, DC 20037, U.S.A. **Online address:** tkingsley@urban.org

KINGSLEY, Sean A. British (born England) **Genres:** History, Biography, Social Sciences. **Career:** Minerva, managing editor; Reading University, Research Centre for Late Antique and Byzantine Studies, visiting fellow. Archaeologist. **Publications:** (With K. Raveh) The Ancient Harbour and Anchorage at Dor, Israel: Results of the Underwater Surveys, 1976-1991, 1996; (ed. with M. Decker) Economy and Exchange in the East Mediterranean during Late Antiquity: Proceedings of a Conference at Somerville College, Oxford, 29th May, 1999, 2001; A Sixth-Century AD Shipwreck off the Carmel Coast, Israel: Dor D and Holy Land Wine Trade, 2002; Shipwreck Archaeology of the Holy Land: Processes and Parameters, 2004; God's Gold: A Quest for the Lost Temple Treasures of Jerusalem, 2007; (ed. with G. Stemm) Oceans' Odyssey, 2010; Oceans Odyssey 2: Underwater Heritage Management & Deep-Sea Shipwrecks in the English Channel & Atlantic Ocean, 2011. **Address:** Oxbow Books, David Brown Book Company, 28 Main St., PO Box 511, Oakville, CT 06779, U.S.A. **Online address:** editorial@minervamagazine.com

KINGSOLVER, Barbara. American (born United States), b. 1955. **Genres:** Novels, Novellas/Short Stories, Poetry, Natural History, Essays, Young Adult Fiction, Young Adult Non-fiction. **Career:** University of Arizona, Department of Physiology, research assistant, 1977-79, Office of Arid Lands Studies, technical writer, 1981-85; freelance journalist, 1985-87; full-time writer, 1987-. **Publications:** NOVELS: The Bean Trees: A Novel, 1988; Animal Dreams: A Novel, 1990; Pigs in Heaven: A Novel, 1993; The Poisonwood Bible: A Novel, 1998; Prodigal Summer: A Novel, 2000; The Lacuna, 2009; Flight Behavior, 2012. OTHERS: Homeland and Other Stories, 1989; (co-author) Mid-life Confidential, 1994; High Tide in Tucson: Essays from Now or Never, 1995; Cerdos en el cielo, 1995; Holding the Line: Women in the Great Arizona Mine Strike of 1983 (nonfiction), 1996; (intro.) Of the Beaten Path: Stories Place, 1998; Barbara Kingsolver: In Conversation, 1998; (ed. with K. Kenison and intro.) The Best American Short Stories, 2001; Small Wonder (essays), 2002; Last Stand: America's Virgin Lands (non-fiction), 2002; (intro.) The Essential Agrarian Reader, 2003; The Bean Trees, With Related Readings, 2004; (with S.L. Hopp and C. Kingsolver) Animal, Vegetable, Miracle: A Year of Food Life, 2007; Laguna, 2011. Contributor to books and periodicals. **Address:** HarperCollins Publishers, 10 E 53rd St., New York, NY 10022-5244, U.S.A.

KINGSTON, Beverley. (Beverley Rhonda Kingston). Australian (born Australia), b. 1941. **Genres:** History, Human Relations/Parenting, Women's Studies And Issues. **Career:** University of New South Wales, lecturer, associate professor of history, 1969-99, retired, 1999, School of History, honorary research fellow, 1999-. Writer. **Publications:** My Wife, My Daughter, and Poor Mary Ann: Women and Work in Australia, 1975; (ed.) The World Moves Slowly: A Documentary History of Australian Women, 1977; Elizabeth Macarthur, 1984; The Oxford History of Australia, 1860-1900: Glad, Confident Morning, vol. III, 1993; Basket, Bag, and Trolley: A History of Shopping

in Australia, 1994; (ed. with J. Roberts) Maybanke, a Woman's Voice: The Collected Work of Maybanke Anderson, 1845-1927, 2001; A History of New South Wales, 2006. **Address:** School of History, University of New South Wales, Rm. 309B, Morven Brown Bldg., Sydney, NW 2052, Australia. **Online address:** bevkingston@optusnet.com.au

KINGSTON, Beverley Rhonda. *See* **KINGSTON, Beverley.**

KINGSTON, Christina. (Christina Cordaire). American (born United States) **Genres:** Romance/Historical, Novels, Young Adult Fiction, Children's Fiction, Travel/Exploration. **Career:** Novelist, 1992-. **Publications:** Ride for the Roses, 2000; The Night the Stars Fell, 2001; Ride the Winter Wind, 2002; Ride the Wind Home, 2003. ROMANCES AS CHRISTINA CORDAIRE: Heart's Deception, 1992; Love's Triumph, 1993; Pride's Folly, 1993; Daring Illusion, 1994; Forgiving Hearts, 1994; Beloved Stranger, 1995; Loving Honor, 1995; Winter Longing, 1996; The Quilting Circle, 1996; Spring Enchantment, 1996; Loving a Lowly Stranger, 1998. Works appear in anthologies. **Address:** PO Box 111, Violet Hill, AR 72584, U.S.A. **Online address:** chriscordaire@centurytel.net

KINGSTON, Maxine Hong. American (born United States), b. 1940. **Genres:** Novels, Poetry, Autobiography/Memoirs, Essays, Mythology/Folklore, Biography, Young Adult Non-fiction, History, Literary Criticism And History, Travel/Exploration. **Career:** Sunset High School, teacher, 1965-67; Kahuku High School, teacher, 1967; Kahaluu Drop-In School, teacher, 1968; Kailua High School, teacher, 1969; Honolulu Business College, teacher, 1969; Mid-Pacific Institute, teacher, 1970-77; University of Hawaii, teacher, 1976-77, visiting associate professor of English, 1977; Eastern Michigan University, Thelma McCandless Professor, 1986; University of California, chancellor's distinguished professor, 1990-2003, chancellor's distinguished professor emeritus, 2003-, Institute of East Asian Studies, senior lecturer. Writer. **Publications:** The Woman Warrior: Memoirs of a Girlhood Among Ghosts, 1976; China Men, 1980; Jinshan Hua ren, 1985; Hawai'i One Summer, 1987; Through the Black Curtain, 1987; Tripmaster Monkey: His Fake Book, 1988; Nü Yong Shi, 1998; Sun Xing Zhe, 1998; Conversations with Maxine Hong Kingston, 1998; (ed.) The Literature of California, 2000; To Be the Poet, 2002; The Fifth Book of Peace, 2003; The Woman Warrior: China Men, 2005; (ed.) Veterans of War Veterans of Peace, 2006; I Love a Broad Margin to My Life, 2011. Contributor to magazines and periodicals. **Address:** Department of English, University of California, 322 Wheeler Hall, Berkeley, CA 94720-1030, U.S.A. **Online address:** yinglan@berkeley.edu

KINGSTONE, Peter R. American (born United States), b. 1964?. **Genres:** Politics/Government, History. **Career:** University of Vermont, assistant professor, 1994-99; University of Connecticut, Department of Political Science, associate professor and director of the Center for Latin American and Caribbean Studies. Writer. **Publications:** Crafting Coalitions for Reform: Business Preferences, Political Institutions, and Neoliberal Reform in Brazil, 1999; (ed. with T.J. Power) Democratic Brazil: Actors, Institutions, and Processes, 2000; (comp.) Readings in Latin American Politics: Challenges to Democratization, 2006; (ed. with T.J. Power) Democratic Brazil Revisited, 2008; The Political Economy of Latin America: Reflections on Neoliberalism and Development, 2011; (ed. with D. Yashar) The Handbook of Latin American Politics, forthcoming. Contributor to books and periodicals. **Address:** Department of Political Science, University of Connecticut, U-1024, 341 Mansfield Rd., Storrs, CT 06269-1024, U.S.A. **Online address:** kingston@uconnvm.uconn.edu

KINGWELL, Mark. Canadian (born Canada), b. 1963. **Genres:** Novels, History. **Career:** National Post, columnist; Toro, drinks columnist; Saturday Night, contributing editor; Harper's Magazine, contributing editor; Globe and Mail, contributing editor; Cambridge University, visiting professor, 1999; University of California, visiting professor, 2000; City University of New York, visiting professor, 2002; University of Toronto, Department of Philosophy, professor of philosophy and senior fellow of Massey College, associate chair, Jackman research fellow, 2011-, Trinity College, fellow; Royal Ontario Museum, Institute for Contemporary Culture, chair. **Publications:** A Civil Tongue: Justice, Dialogue and the Politics of Pluralism, 1995; Dreams of Millennium: Report from a Culture on the Brink, 1997; Better Living: In Pursuit of Happiness from Plato to Prozac, 1998; Our Century: 100 Voices 500 Visions, 1999; Marginalia: A Cultural Reader, 1999; The World We Want: Virtue, Vice and the Good Citizen, 2000; The World We Want: Restoring Citizenship In A Fractured Age, 2001; Practical Judgments: Essays in Culture, Politics and Interpretation, 2002; Catch & Release: Trout Fishing and the

Meaning of Life, 2004; Nearest Thing To Heaven: The Empire State Building And American Dreams, 2006; Bliss Express: Illustrating Happiness, 2007; Concrete Reveries: Consciousness and the City, 2008. Contributor to journals and periodicals. **Address:** Department of Philosophy, Trinity College, University of Toronto, Rm. 309, Gerald Larkin Bldg., 15 Devonshire Pl., Toronto, ON M5S 1H8, Canada. **Online address:** mark.kingwell@utoronto.ca

KINKADE, Thomas. American (born United States), b. 1958. **Genres:** Art/Art History, inspirational/Motivational Literature, Novels. **Career:** Lightpost Publishing (now Thomas Kinkade Co.), co-founder; Thomas Kinkade Foundation, founder. Artist and author. **Publications:** (With J. Gurney) The Artist's Guide to Sketching, 1982; (with P. Reed) Thomas Kinkade: Paintings of Radiant Light, 1995; (with A.C. Buchanan) Simpler Times, 1996; (with P. Kinkade) Chasing the Horizon: Our Adventures through the British Isles and France, 1997; Beyond the Garden Gate, 1997; Romantic Hideaways, 1997; I'll Be Home for Christmas, 1997; Spirit of America, 1998; Glory of Creation, 1998; Home Is Where the Heart Is, 1998; Every Day Light: Daily Inspirations, 1998; Hometown Memories, 1998; Seasons of Light, 1998; (with C. Miller) With Wings like Eagles: A Devotional, 1998; (with C. Miller) A Village Christmas: Personal Family Memories and Holiday Traditions, 1999; Child's Garden of Verses: A Collection of Scriptures, Prayers & Poems Featuring the Works of Robert Louis Stevenson, with the Artwork of Thomas Kinkade, 1999; Child's Christmas at St. Nicholas Circle, 199; (with A.C. Buchanan and D. Klingsporn) Christ, the Light of the World: A Devotional, 1999; (with A.C. Buchanan) Lightposts for Living: The Art of Choosing a Joyful Life, 1999; The Home You Made for Me: Celebrating a Mother's Love, 2000; Thomas Kinkade: Masterworks of Light, 2000; A Child's Garden of Prayers: A Collection of Classic Prayers ad Timeless Blessings, 2000; Beside Still Waters, 2000; Garden of Friendship, 2000; My Father's World: Masterpieces and Memories of the Great Outdoors, 2000; (with A.C. Buchanan) Let Your Light Shine, 2001; Shapes, 2001; Off the Beaten Path: Devotionals, 2001; (with A.C. Buchanan) Warmth from the Windows, 2001; Window Box Collection, 2001; Animals, 2001; Thomas Kinkade: Romantic Europe, 2001; Thomas Kinkade's Sea to Shining Sea, 2001; Favorite Bible Verses, 2001; It is Well with My Soul, 2001; Bedtime Prayers, 2001; Classic Prayers, 2001; Perfect Peace and Rest, 2001; Colors, 2001; Numbers, 2001; Blessings, 2001; A Book of Joy, 2002; Friends for Life, 2002; Joy of Fatherhood, 2002; Joy of Motherhood, 2002; Life's Little Blessings, 2002; (with A.C. Buchanan) Simple Little Pleasures, 2002; (with A.C. Buchanan) Finding a Peaceful Place, 2002; (with A.C. Buchanan) Just around the Bend, 2002; (with K. Spencer) Cape Light, 2002; Places in the Heart, 2002; Voice of Creation, 2002; Welcome Home for Christmas, 2002; (with K. Spencer) Home Song: A Cape Light Novel, 2002; Land that I Love, 2002; The Light of Christmas, 2002; (with N. Kinkade and L. Libby) The Many Loves of Marriage, 2002; Mealtime Memories: Sharing the Warmth of Family Traditions, 2002; Off the Beaten Path, 2002; Best Friends: A Collection of Classic Stories, 2002; Along the Lighted Path, 2002; (intro.) The Artist in Nature: Thomas Kinkade and the Plein Air Tradition, 2002; Christmas Traditions, 2002; The End of a Perfect Day, 2002; Family Traditions, 2002; A Mother's Timeless Wisdom: Inspiration for Your Journey, 2003; A Sister Knows Your Heart, 2003; The Thomas Kinkade Story: A 20-year Chronology of the Artist, 2003; (comp.) Prayers of Hope and Light, 2003; (with R.C. Larson) Touched by the Light: Inspirational Reflections from the Artist and His Friends, 2003; A Child is a Gift, 2003; A Christmas Celebration, 2003; The Garden of Prayer, 2003; (with K. Spencer) A Gathering Place: A Cape Light Novel, 2003; Let Freedom Ring, 2003; The Lights of Liberty, 2003; (with N. Kinkade and L. Libby) The Many Loves of Christmas, 2003; (with N. Kinkade and L. Libby) The Many Loves of Parenting, 2003; Beacons of Light, 2004; (with K. Spencer) Christmas Promise: A Cape Light Novel, 2004; (with K. Spencer) A New Leaf: A Cape Light Novel, 2004; (with D. Jeremiah) The Secret of the Light, 2004; (with P. Proctor) The Art of Creative Living: Making Every Day a Radiant Masterpiece, 2005; (with K. Spencer) The Christmas Angel: A Cape Light Novel, 2005; Silent Night, 2006; (with R. Goodwin and P. Proctor) Points of Light: A Celebration of the American Spirit of Giving, 2006; (with K. Spencer) A Christmas to Remember: A Cape Light Novel, 2006; Thomas Kinkade's Christmas Cottage, 2007; (with K. Spencer) A Christmas Visitor, 2007; (with K. Spencer) Christmas Star: A Cape Light Novel, 2008; Thomas Kinkade: Twenty-five Years of Light, 2008; (with K. Spencer) A Wish for Christmas, 2009; (with K. Spencer) On Christmas Eve, 2010; (with K. Spencer) The Inn at Angel Island, 2010; (with K. Spencer) The Wedding Promise, 2011; (with K. Spencer) Christmas Treasures, 2011; (with K. Spencer) Wandering Heart, 2012; Illustrator of books by others. Contributor to periodicals. **Address:** Thomas Kinkade Co., 900 Lightpost Way, Morgan Hill, CA 95037-2869, U.S.A.

KINNAMAN, David. American (born United States), b. 1973?. **Genres:** Theology/Religion. **Career:** Barna Group, owner and president, 1995-. Writer. **Publications:** (With A. Lyons) Unchristian: What a New Generation Really Thinks about Christianity and Why It Matters, 2007; (with A. Hawkins) You Lost Me: Why Young Christians are Leaving Church and Rethinking Faith, 2011. **Address:** Barna Group, 2368 Eastman Ave., Ste. 12, Ventura, CA 93003, U.S.A. **Online address:** dk@barna.org

KINNAMAN, Gary D. American (born United States) **Genres:** Theology/Religion, Psychology. **Career:** Word of Grace Church, senior minister, 1982-2008, pastor-at-large; Ottawa University, staff, 1985-87, director of studies in religion, 1985-88; Alberto Mottesi Evangelistic Association, chairman, 1990-; North Hills Church of God, interim senior pastor, 2009; Pastors In Covenant, founder; Grace Association of Churches, Ministers, and Ministries, founder and president; Hope Chapel, board director; BridgeBuilders, board director; Save the Family Foundation of Arizona, board director; Leaders that Last, board director; Grace Unlimited Inc., staff. Writer. **Publications:** And Signs Shall Follow, 1987; Overcoming the Dominion of Darkness, 1990; Angels Dark and Light, 1994; My Companion through Grief: Comfort for Your Darkest Hours, 1996; Learning to Love the One You Marry: Advice to Young Couples about Commitment, Intimacy, Sex, Money, Work, and Much More, 1997; How to Overcome the Darkness: Personal Strategies for Spiritual Warfare, 1999; Dumb Things Smart Christians Believe: Ten Misbeliefs That Keep Us from Experiencing God's Grace, 1999; (with A.H. Ells) Leaders That Last: How Covenant Friendships Can Help Pastors Thrive, 2003; The Beginner's Guide to Praise and Worship, 2003; Winning Your Spiritual Battles: How to Use the Full Armor of God, 2003; Experiencing the Power of the Cross: How It Changes Everything, 2005; (with R. Jacobs) Seeing in the Dark: Getting the Facts on Depression & Finding Hope Again, 2006. **Address:** Word of Grace Church, 655 E University Dr., Mesa, AZ 85203, U.S.A. **Online address:** garyk@garykinnaman.com

KINNEAR, Mary. Canadian (born Canada), b. 1942. **Genres:** Women's Studies And Issues, History, Biography, Social Sciences. **Career:** University of Manitoba, Department of History, head, professor. Writer. **Publications:** Daughters of Time: Women in the Western Tradition, 1982; First Days, Fighting Days: Women in Manitoba History, 1987; Planting the Garden: An Annotated Archival Bibliography of the History of Women in Manitoba, 1987; Margaret McWilliams: An Interwar Feminist, 1991; In Subordination: Professional Women, 1870-1970, 1995; A Female Economy: Women's Work in a Prairie Province, 1870-1970, 1998; Woman of the World: Mary McGeachy and International Cooperation, 2004. **Address:** Department of History, St. John's College, University of Manitoba, 314 Fletcher Argue Bldg., Dysart Rd, Winnipeg, MB R3T 5V5, Canada. **Online address:** mary_kinnear@umanitoba.ca

KINNELL, Galway. American (born United States), b. 1927. **Genres:** Novels, Poetry, Literary Criticism And History, Translations, Young Adult Fiction, History. **Career:** Poet and translator, 1949-; Alfred University, instructor in English, 1949-51; University of Chicago, supervisor of liberal arts program, 1951-55; University of Grenoble, American lecturer, 1956-57; University of Iran, Fullbright lecturer, 1959-60; Juniata College, poet-in-residence, 1964; Reed College, faculty, 1966-67; Colorado State University, faculty, 1968; University of Washington, faculty, 1968; University of California, faculty, 1968-69; Deya Institute, resident writer, 1969-70; University of Iowa, faculty, 1970; City University of New York, Queens College, visiting professor, 1971; Sarah Lawrence College, visiting poet, 1972-78; Columbia University, adjunct associate professor, 1972, adjunct professor, 1974, 1976; Brandeis University, faculty, 1974; Skidmore College, faculty, 1975; University of Hawaii, faculty, 1976, Citizens' professor, 1979-81; Princeton University, faculty, 1976; Holy Cross College, faculty, 1977; University of Delaware, faculty, 1978; Squaw Valley Community of Writers, director, 1979-; Macquarie University, visiting writer, 1979; New York University, director of writing program, 1981-84, Samuel F.B. Morse professor of arts and sciences, Erich Maria Remarque professor of creative writing, now retired; American Academy of Poets, chancellor, 2001-07. **Publications:** (With A. Ostroff and W.T. Scott) 3 Self-Evaluations, 1953; What a Kingdom It Was, 1960, rev. ed., 2002; Flower Herding on Mount Monadnock, 1964, rev. ed., 2002; (trans. and intro.) Poems, 1965; Black Light (novel), 1966; Poems of Night, 1968; Body Rags, 1968; The Poetics of the Physical World, 1969; The Hen Flower, 1969; First Poems, 1946-1954, 1970; The Book of Nightmares, 1971; The Shoes of Wandering, 1971; Body Rags, 1973; The Avenue Bearing the Initial of Christ into the New World: Poems 1946-1964, 1974; Saint Francis and the

Sow, 1976; Three Poems, 1976; Walking Down The Stairs: Selections from Interviews, 1978; Two Poems, 1979; Fergus Falling, 1979; There Are Things I Tell to No One, 1979; Mortal Acts, Mortal Words, 1980; The Last Hiding Place of Snow, 1980; Selected Poems, 1982; How the Alligator Missed Breakfast (for children), 1982; Thoughts Occasioned by the Most Insignificant of Human Events, 1982; The Fundamental Project of Technology, 1983; Remarks on Accepting the American Book Award for Poetry, 1984; (contrib.) Paul Zweig, Eternity's Woods, 1985; The Geese, 1985; The Seekonk Woods, 1985; The Past, 1985; (ed. and intro.) The Essential Whitman, 1987; When One Has Lived a Long Time Alone, 1990; Three Books: Body Rags: Mortal Acts, Mortal Words: The Past, 1993; Imperfect Thirst, 1994; A New Selected Poems, 2000; When the Towers Fell, 2005; Strong is Your Hold, 2006; (contrib.) Bloodaxe Poetry Introductions 3, 2007. TRANSLATOR: R. Hardy, Bitter Victory, 1956; H. Lehmann, Pre-Columbian Ceramics, 1962; Y. Bonnefoy, On the Motion and Immobility of Douve, 1968; Y. Goll, The Lackawanna Elegy, 1970; (intro.) The Poems of François Villon, 1977, new ed., 1982; (with R. Pevear) Y. Bonnefoy, Early Poems, 1947-1959, 1991; (and ed. with H. Liebmann) The Essential Rilke, 1999. Contributor to periodicals. **Address:** c/o Alison Granucci, Blue Flower Arts L.L.C., PO Box 1361, Millbrook, NY 12545-1361, U.S.A. **Online address:** gk1@nyu.edu

KINNEY, Arthur F. American (born United States), b. 1933. **Genres:** History, Literary Criticism And History, Humanities. **Career:** Yale University, instructor, 1963-66; University of Massachusetts, assistant professor, 1966-68, associate professor, 1968-73, professor of English, 1973-86, Thomas W. Copeland professor of literary history, 1986-, Center for Renaissance Studies, director, 1998-; Clark University, affiliate professor of English, 1971-, adjunct professor of English; English Literary Renaissance, editor, 1971-; Huntington Library, fellow, 1973-74, 1983; Twayne English Author-Renaissance Books, editor, 1973-; Massachusetts Studies in Early Modern Culture, editor, 1991-; New York University, adjunct professor of English, 1991-. Writer. **Publications:** On Seven Shakespearean Tragedies, 1968; On Seven Shakespearean Comedies, 1969; Titled Elizabethans: A Directory of Elizabethan State and Church Officers and Knights, with Peers of England, Scotland and Ireland, 1558-1603, 1973; Elizabethan Backgrounds: Historical Documents of the Age of Elizabeth I, 1975; Faulkner's Narrative Poetics: Style as Vision, 1978; Dorothy Parker, 1978; Rhetoric and Poetic in Thomas Mores Utopia, 1979; The Compson Family, 1982; Nicholas Hilliard's Art of Limning, 1983; Flannery O'Connor's Library: Resources of Being, 1985; The Sartoris Family, 1985; Humanist Poetics: Thought, Rhetoric and Fiction in Sixteenth-Century England, 1986; Essential Articles for the Study of Sir Philip Sidney, 1986; John Skelton: Priest as Poet: Seasons of Discovery, 1987; Continental Humanist Poetics: Studies in Erasmus, Castiglione, Marguerite de Navarre, Rabelais and Cervantes, 1989; The Coast of Illyria by Dorothy Parker and Ross Evans, 1990; The Birds and Beasts of Shakespeare, 1990; Go Down, Moses: The Miscegenation of Time, 1996; Dorothy Parker Revisited, 1997; Lies Like Truth: Shakespeare, Macbeth and The Cultural Moment, 2001; Shakespeare by Stages: An Historical Introduction, 2003; Shakespeare's Webs: Networks of Meaning in Renaissance Drama, 2004; Shakespeare and Cognition: Aristotle's Legacy and Shakespearean Drama, 2006; Renaissance Historicisms: Essays in Honor of Arthur F. Kinney, 2008. EDITOR: (with F.L. Utley and L.Z. Bloom) Bear, Man & God: Seven Approaches to William Faulkner's The Bear, 1964, 2nd ed. as Bear, Man and God: Eight Approaches to William Faulkner's The Bear, 1971; H.R. Mythomystes, 1972; Markets of Bawdrie: The Dramatic Criticism of Stephen Gosson, 1974; Critical Essays on William Faulkner: The Compson Family, 1982; Sir Philip Sidney in Retrospect, 1986; Sidney in Retrospect: Selections from English Literary Renaissance, 1988; Rogues, Vagabonds and Sturdy Beggars: A New Gallery of Tudor and Early Stuart Rogue Literature Exposing the Lives, Times and Cozening Tricks of The Elizabethan Underworld, 1990; Critical Essays on William Faulkner: The McCaslin Family, 1990; Approaches to Teaching Faulkner's The Sound and the Fury, 1996; Critical Essays on William Faulkner: The Sutpen Family, 1996; Classical, Renaissance and Postmodernist Acts of the Imagination, 1996; Renaissance Drama: An Anthology of Plays and Entertainment, 1999, 2nd ed., 2004; Cambridge Companion to English Literature 1500-1600, 2000; Hamlet: New Critical Essays, 2001; A Companion to Renaissance Drama, 2002; (with H. Craig) Shakespeare, Computers and the Mystery of Authorship, 2009; (ed.) Elizabethan and Jacobean England: Sources and Documents of the English Renaissance, 2009. CO-EDITOR: Symposium, 1969; Symposium on Love, 1970; 1576: Sir Philip Sidney and the Making of a Legend, 1986; Sir Philip Sidney: 1586 and The Creation of A Legend, 1986; Renaissance Historicism: Selections from English Literary Renaissance, 1987; Sir Philip Sidney's Achievement, 1990; Women in the Renaissance:

Selections from English Literary Renaissance, 1990; Shakespeare: Text and Performance, 1999; Tudor England: An Encyclopedia, 2001; Challenging Humanism: Essays in Honor of Dominic Baker-Smith, 2005. Contributor to periodicals. **Address:** Department of English, University of Massachusetts, 255 Bartlett Hall, PO Box 30515, Amherst, MA 01003-0515, U.S.A. **Online address:** afkinney@english.umass.edu

KINNEY, Jeff. American (born United States), b. 1971. **Genres:** Young Adult Fiction, Children's Fiction. **Career:** Internet publishing Co., design director. Author and illustrator. **Publications:** Diary of a Wimpy Kid: Greg Heffley's Journal, 2007; Diary of a Wimpy Kid: Rodrick Rules, 2008; Diary of a Wimpy Kid: The Last Straw, 2009; Diary of a Wimpy Kid: Dog Days, 2009; Diary of a Wimpy Kid: The Ugly Truth, 2010; Wimpy Kid Movie Diary: How Greg Heffley Went Hollywood, 2010. **Address:** Amulet Books, 115 W 18th St., New York, NY 10011, U.S.A.

KINSELLA, Sophie. (Madeleine Wickham). British (born England), b. 1969. **Genres:** Novels. **Career:** Journalist. **Publications:** (With M. Cabot and J. Weiner) Girls Night In, 2004; Can You Keep A Secret?, 2004; Undomestic Goddess, 2005; Remember Me?, 2008; Twenties Girl, 2009, I've Got Your Number: A Novel, 2011. SHOPAHOLIC SERIES: The Secret Dreamworld of a Shopaholic, 2000 in US as Confessions of a Shopaholic, 2001; Shopaholic Abroad, 2001 in US as Shopaholic Takes Manhattan, 2002; Shopaholic Ties the Knot, 2002; Shopaholic & Sister, 2004; Shopaholic & Baby, 2007; Mini-shopaholic, 2010. AS MADELEINE WICKHAM: The Tennis Party, 1995; A Desirable Residence, 1996; Swimming Pool Sunday, 1997; The Gatecrasher, 1998; Wedding Girl, 1999; Cocktails for Three, 2000; Sleeping Arrangements, 2001. **Address:** c/o Author Mail, Random House Group Ltd., 20 Vauxhall Bridge Rd., London, GL SW1V 2SA, England.

KINSELLA, T. E. See **KINSELLA, Thomas.**

KINSELLA, Thomas. (T. E. Kinsella). Irish/American (born United States), b. 1928. **Genres:** Poetry, Literary Criticism And History, Translations, inspirational/Motivational Literature, Essays. **Career:** Irish Land Commission, junior executive officer, 1946-50, Department of Finance, administrative officer, 1950-60, assistant principal officer, 1960-65; Southern Illinois University, writer-in-residence, 1965-67, professor of English, 1967-70; Temple University-Philadelphia, professor of English, 1970-90, professor emeritus, 1990-; Peppercanister Press, founding director, 1972-; Temple University-Dublin, Irish Tradition Program, founding director, 1976-; Dolmen Press Ltd., director; Cuala Press Ltd., director. **Publications:** The Starlit Eye, 1952; Three Legendary Sonnets, 1952; Per Imaginem, 1953; The Breastplate of St. Patrick, 1954; (trans.) Longes Mac n-Usnig, Being the Exile and Death of the Sons of Usnech, 1954; (trans.) Thirty Three Triads, 1955; The Death of a Queen, 1956; Poems, 1956; Another September, 1958; Moralities, 1960; Poems and Translations, 1961; (with J. Montague and R. Murphy) Three Irish Poets, 1961; (ed.) The Dolmen Miscellany of Irish Writing, 1962; Downstream, 1962; Wormwood, 1966; Nightwalker, 1967; Nightwalker and Other Poems, 1967; (with D. Livingstone and A. Sexton) Poems, 1968; (trans.) The Táin, 1969; Tear, 1969; (with W.B. Yeats) Davis, Mangan, Ferguson?: Tradition and the Irish Writer, 1970; Finistere, 1972; Butcher's Dozen, 1972; A Selected Life, 1972; Notes from the Land of the Dead and Other Poems, 1973; New Poems 1973; Selected Poems 1956-1968, 1973; Vertical Man: A Sequel to A Selected Life, 1973; The Good Fight, 1973; One, 1974; A Technical Supplement, 1976; (ed. and intro.) Selected Poems, 1976; Song of the Night and Other Poems, 1978; The Messenger, 1978; Fifteen Dead, 1979; One and Other Poems, 1979; Peppercanister Poems 1972-1978, 1979; Poems 1956-1973, 1979; Poems, 1956-76, 1980; One Fond Embrace, 1981; (ed.) Our Musical Heritage, 1981; Songs of the Psyche, 1985; Her Vertical Smile, 1985; (ed. and trans.) The New Oxford Book of Irish Verse, 1986; Out of Ireland, 1987; St. Catherine's Clock, 1987; (with J. Montague and B. Kennelly) Myth, History, and Literary Tradition, 1989; Blood and Family, 1989; Selected Poems, 1962-1989, 1989; Poems from Centre City, 1990; Personal Places, 1990; Madonna and Other Poems, 1991; Open Court, 1991; From Centre City, 1994; The Dual Tradition: An Essay on Poetry and Politics in Ireland, 1995; Collected Poems, 1956-1994, 1996; The Pen Shop, 1997; The Familiar, 1999; Godhead, 1999; Citizen of the World, 2000; Littlebody, 2000; Collected Poems: 1956-2001, 2006; Dublin Documentary, 2006; Marginal Economy, 2006; Readings in Poetry, 2006; Belief and Unbelief, 2007; Man of War, 2007; Selected Poems, 2007; Prose Occasions: 1951-2006, 2009; (intro. as T.E. Kinsella) The Pursuit of Diarmuid and Grainne, 2009; Fat Master, 2011; Love Joy Peace, 2011. **Address:** Department of English, College of Liberal Arts, Temple University, 1038 Anderson Hall, 1114 Polett Walk, Philadelphia, PA 19122-6090, U.S.A.

KINSELLA, W(illiam) P(atrick). Canadian (born Canada), b. 1935. **Genres:** Novels, Novellas/Short Stories, Sports/Fitness, Young Adult Fiction, Literary Criticism And History. **Career:** Government of Alberta, clerk, 1954-56; Retail Credit Co., manager, 1956-61; City of Edmonton, account executive, 1961-67; Caesar's Italian Village (restaurant), owner, 1967-72; University of Iowa, instructor, 1976-78; University of Calgary, assistant professor of English and creative writing, 1978-83, professor of English. Writer. **Publications:** Dance Me Outside, 1977 in US as Dance Me Outside: More Tales from the Ermineskin Reserve, 1986; Scars: Stories, 1978; Shoeless Joe Jackson Comes to Iowa, 1980; Born Indian, 1981; Shoeless Joe, 1982; The Ballad of the Public Trustee, 1982; The Moccasin Telegraph and Other Indian Tales, 1983; The Thrill of the Grass, 1984; The Alligator Report, 1985; The Iowa Baseball Confederacy, 1986; The Fencepost Chronicles, 1986; Five Stories, 1986; Red Wolf, Red Wolf, 1987; The Further Adventures of Slugger McBatt: Baseball Stories, 1988; (with A. Knight) The Rainbow Warehouse, 1989; Two Spirits Soar: The Art of Allen Sapp: The Inspiration of Allan Gonor, 1990; The Miss Hobbema Pageant, 1990; The First and Last Annual Six Towns Area Old Timers' Baseball Game, 1991; Box Socials, 1992; (with F. Bisher and D. Perkins) A Series for the World: Baseball's First International Fall Classic, 1992; The Dixon Cornbelt League and Other Baseball Stories, 1993; (with A. Knight) Even at This Distance, 1994; Brother Frank's Gospel Hour and Other Stories, 1994; (intro.) When the Gaints Were Gaints: Bill Terry and the Golden Age of New York Baseball, 1994; Go the Distance: Baseball Stories, 1995; The Winter Helen Dropped By (novel), 1995; If Wishes Were Horses, 1996; The Secret of the Northern Lights (stories), 1998; Magic Time (novel), 1998; The Silas Stories, 1998; (ed. and intro.) Baseball Fantastic: Stories, 2000; Japanese Baseball, and Other Stories, 2000; Butterfly Winter, 2011. Works appear in anthologies. Contributor to magazines. **Address:** c/o Carolyn Swayze, Carolyn Swayze Literary Agency Ltd., RPO White Rock, PO Box 39588, Surrey, BC V4A 0A9, Canada. **Online address:** buzzard2_99@yahoo.com

KINZIE, Mary. American (born United States), b. 1944. **Genres:** Poetry, Literary Criticism And History, Adult Non-fiction. **Career:** Northwestern University, Department of English, professor of English, 1975-, Undergraduate Creative Writing Program, director, 1979-, director of English major in writing, Martin J. and Patricia Koldyke outstanding teaching professor, 1990-92. Writer. **Publications:** POETRY: The Threshold of the Year, 1982; Summers of Vietnam and Other Poems, 1990; Masked Woman, 1990; Autumn Eros and Other Poems, 1991; Ghost Ship, 1996; Drift, 2003; California Sorrow, 2007. CRITICISM: The Cure of Poetry in an Age of Prose: Moral Essays on the Poet's Calling, 1993; The Judge Is Fury: Dislocation and Form in Poetry, 1994; A Poet's Guide to Poetry, 1999. EDITOR: (with C. Newman and N.T. di Giovanni) Prose for Borges, 1972; (with E. Anderson) The Little Magazine in America: A Modern Documentary History, 1978; The Tales of Arturo Vivante, 1990; (and intro.) A Poet's Prose: Selected Writings of Louise Bogan, 2005. Contributor to periodicals. **Address:** Department of English, Northwestern University, Rm. 224, University Hall, 1897 Sheridan Rd., Evanston, IL 60208-2240, U.S.A. **Online address:** mkinzie@northwestern.edu

KIPNIS, Aaron R. American (born United States), b. 1948. **Genres:** Human Relations/Parenting, Psychology, Social Commentary, Sociology, Medicine/Health, Economics. **Career:** Sweetwater Gardens Holistic Health Center, founder and director, 1983-86; Institute for Gender Studies, founder and director, 1986-2000; Gender Relations Institute, director, 1988-2005; The Fatherhood Coalition, president, 1997-2001; University of California, instructor, 1997; Pacifica Graduate Institute, adjunct faculty, 1997-99, core faculty, 1999-. Writer. **Publications:** Knights Without Armor: A Practical Guide for Men in Quest of Masculine Soul, 1991; (with E. Herron) Gender War, Gender Peace: The Quest for Love and Justice between Women and Men, 1994, rev. ed. as What Women and Men Really Want: Creating Deeper Understanding and Love in Our Relationships, 1995; Angry Young Men: How Parents, Teachers and Counselors Can Help Bad Boys Become Good Men, 1999; The Midas Complex, 2012. Contributor to books and journals. **Address:** 19726 Horseshoe Dr., Topanga, CA 90290, U.S.A. **Online address:** akipnis@pacifica.edu

KIPP, Rita Smith. American (born United States), b. 1948. **Genres:** Anthropology/Ethnology, Women's Studies And Issues, Area Studies. **Career:** University of Pittsburgh, instructor, 1971-72; Kenyon College, professor of anthropology, 1976-2004, Oden professor of anthropology and associate provost, 2003; Archaeological Tours, lecturer, 1987-90; Sewanee: The University of the South, professor of anthropology, dean of the college of arts and sciences, 2004-07; Marietta College, provost and dean, 2007-11; Georgian Court University, dean of arts and sciences. Writer. **Publications:** (Ed. with R.D. Kipp) Beyond Samosir: Recent Studies of the Batak Peoples of Sumatra, 1983; (ed. with S. Rodgers) Indonesian Religions in Transition, 1987; The Early Years of a Dutch Colonial Mission: The Karo Field, 1990; Dissociated Identities: Ethnicity, Religion and Class in an Indonesian Society, 1993; (comp. and ed.) International Directory of Indonesianists, 2nd ed., 1994. **Address:** 900 Lakewood Ave., Lakewood, NJ 08701, U.S.A. **Online address:** ritaskipp@gmail.com

KIPPAX, Frank. See NEEDLE, Jan.

KIRALY, Marie. See BERGSTROM, Elaine.

KIRALY, Sherwood. American (born United States), b. 1949. **Genres:** Novels, Humor/Satire, Literary Criticism And History. **Career:** National newspaper syndicate, Comics editor and managing editor; syndicate editor, 1984. **Publications:** NOVELS: California Rush, 1990; Diminished Capacity, 1995; Big Babies, 1996; Who's Hot Who's Not, 1998. Contributor of articles and newspapers. **Address:** 2954 Alta Laguna Blvd., Laguna Beach, CA 92651-2066, U.S.A.

KIRAS, James D. American (born United States) **Genres:** Social Sciences, History. **Career:** U.S. Air Force School of Advanced Air and Space Studies, associate professor. Writer and educator. **Publications:** (ed. with A. Morrison) UN Peace Operations and the Role of Japan, 1996; Special Operations and Strategy from World War II to the War on Terrorism, 2006. **Address:** School of Advanced Air & Space Studies, 600 Chennault Cir., Montgomery, AL 36112, U.S.A.

KIRBY, David Peter. Welsh/British (born England), b. 1936. **Genres:** History, Adult Non-fiction, Reference. **Career:** University of Liverpool, assistant lecturer, 1962-64, lecturer in medieval history, 1964-66; University College of Wales, lecturer, 1966-69, senior lecturer, 1969-73, reader, 1973-93, professor in history, 1993-96. Writer. **Publications:** The Making of Early England, 1967; (ed.) Saint Wilfrid at Hexham, 1974; The Earliest English Kings, 1991; (with A. Williams and A.P. Smyth) A Biographical Dictionary of Dark Age Britain: England, Scotland and Wales, 1991; Bede's Historia Ecclesiastica Gentis Anglorum: Its Contemporary Setting, Jarrow Lecture, 1992; (contrib.) Cardiganshire County History, 1993; (ed. with J.L. Davies) The County History of Cardiganshire, 1994; The Earliest English Kings, rev. ed., 2000. **Address:** The Villa, The Launches, W Lulworth, Wareham, DS BH20 5SF, England.

KIRBY, John R. Canadian (born Canada), b. 1951. **Genres:** Education, Psychology, Reference. **Career:** University of Newcastle, lecturer, associate professor, 1976-87; Queen's University, Faculty of Education, associate professor, 1987-, professor of educational psychology, Centre for Neuroscience Studies, faculty, Literacy Centre, coordinator. Writer. **Publications:** (With J.P. Das and R.F. Jarman) Simultaneous and Successive Cognitive Processes, 1979; (ed. with J.B. Biggs) Cognition, Development, and Instruction, 1980; (ed.) Cognitive Strategies and Educational Performance, 1984; (with N.H. Williams) Learning Problems: A Cognitive Approach, 1991; (with J.P. Das and J.A. Naglieri) Assessment of Cognitive Processes: The PASS Theory of Intelligence, 1994. Contributor to journals. **Address:** Faculty of Education, Queen's University, Rm. A220, Duncan McArthur Hall, 511 Union St., Kingston, ON K7L 3N6, Canada. **Online address:** john.kirby@queensu.ca

KIRBY, Michael Roger. British (born England), b. 1957?. **Genres:** Plays/Screenplays, Education, Philosophy, Social Sciences, Sex, Sociology, Social Sciences, Theology/Religion, Theology/Religion. **Career:** Dramatist and teacher. Editor, 1985-. **Publications:** Society Today: Pack A (Citizenship/social science/RE), 1992; Education for Citizenship, 1993; Rights and Responsibilities, 1993; Sex Education in Schools, 1994; Philosophy, Religion and Ethics, 1995; Issues in Science, 1995; Art, Culture and Aesthetics, 1995; Street Smarts: Activities that Help Teenagers Take Care of Themselves, 1995; Understanding Democracy, 1997; Religious Studies Handbook, 1999; New

Plays, 1999; Radio and Television Plays, 2001; Sociology in Perspective, 2002; Science and Technology Today, 2002; Sociology Explained, 2003; Collected Short Stories, 2003. **Address:** Penley House, Ellesmere Ln., Shropshire, AV SY12 0NG, England.

KIRBY, Susan E. American (born United States), b. 1949. **Genres:** Novels, Children's Fiction, Young Adult Non-fiction. **Career:** Writer. **Publications:** FOR CHILDREN: Ike and Porker, 1983; Culligan Man Can, 1988; Shadow Boy, 1991; Tear Jerkers: Once in a Blue Moon, 1997. MAIN STREET SERIES FOR CHILDREN: Home for Christmas, 1994; Lemonade Days, 1994; Home Front Hero, 1994; Goodbye, Desert Rose, 1995. ROMANCE NOVELS: The Maple Princess, 1982; Lessons for the Heart, 1982; Blizzard of the Heart, 1982; Chasing a Dream, 1982; Love's Welcome Home, 1983; Reach for Heaven, 1983; One Whispering Voice, 1984; Love's Secret Game, 1985; Heart Aflame, 1986; (as Suzanne Stephens) The Proud Heart, 1986; Butterscotch Moon, 1986; Cries the Wilderness Wind, 1987; Love, Special Delivery, 1987; In Perfect Harmony, 1988; Leah's Love Song, 1990; Too Good to Be True, 1991; (as Suzanne Wade) Candy Kisses, 1991; Partners in Love, 1993; My Secret Heart, 1993; Ike and Porker Perfect, 1993; The Field, 1995; Blue Moon, 1997; When the Lilacs Bloom, 1997; Prairie Rose, 1997; As the Lily Grows, 1997; Your Dream and Mine, 1999. AMERICAN QUILT SERIES FOR CHILDREN: Ellen's Story, 2000; Daniel's Story, 2000; Hattie's Story, 2000; Ida Lou's Story, 2001. Love Sign, 2001; Love Knot, 2004; No-Fuss Christmas, 2010. OTHERS: Chronicler's Tales or The PM Saga, book XII, 1989; Main Street: Lemonade Days, 1994. Contributor of articles to periodicals. Works appear in anthologies. **Address:** c/o Author Mail, Aladdin Publicity Department, Simon & Schuster Inc., 1230 Ave. of the Americas, New York, NY 10020, U.S.A.

KIRCH, Patrick V(inton). American (born United States), b. 1950. **Genres:** Archaeology/Antiquities, History. **Career:** Bernice P. Bishop Museum, associate anthropologist, 1974-75, anthropologist, 1975-84, Division of Archaeology, head, 1983-84, research associate, 1984-; University of Hawaii, faculty, 1979-, associate professor of anthropology, 1982-84; Burke Museum, director, 1984; University of Washington, associate professor, 1985-87, professor of anthropology, 1987-89, Thomas Burke Memorial Washington State Museum, director, 1984-89; University of California, professor of anthropology, 1989-, Class of 1954 professor of anthropology, 1995-, Hearst Museum of Anthropology, curator of oceanic archaeology 1989-, director, 1999-2002, Archaeological Research Facility, director, 1992-94, Oceanic Archaeology Laboratory, director. Writer. **Publications:** Marine Exploitation in Prehistoric Hawai'i, 1979; (with D.E. Yen) Tikopia: The Prehistory and Ecology of a Polynesian Outlier, 1982; The Evolution of the Polynesian Chiefdoms, 1984; Feathered Gods and Fishhooks, 1985; Niuatoputapu: The Prehistory of a Polynesian Chiefdom, 1988; (with M. Sahlins) Anahulu: The Anthropology of History in the Kingdom of Hawaii, vol. I: Historical Ethnography, vol. II: The Archaeology of History, 1992; The Wet and the Dry, 1994; Legacy of the Landscape: An Illustrated Guide to Hawaiian Archaeological Sites, 1996; The Lapita Peoples, 1997; On the Road of the Winds, 2000; (with R.C. Green) Hawaiki: Ancestral Polynesia, 2001; How Chiefs Became Kings, 2010. EDITOR: (with M. Kelly) Prehistory and Ecology in a Windward Hawaiian Valley, 1975; (with J.T. Clark) Archaeological Investigations of the Mudlane-Waimea-Kawaihae Road Corridor, Island of Hawai'i, 1983; Island Societies, 1986; (with T.L. Hunt) Archaeology of the Lapita Cultural Complex, 1988; Prehistoric Hawaiian Occupation in the Anahulu Valley, O'ahu Island, 1989; (with T.L. Hunt) To'aga Site: Three Millennia of Polynesian Occupation in the Manu'a Islands, American Samoa, 1993; (with T.L. Hunt) Historical Ecology in the Pacific Islands, 1997; Lapita and Its Transformations in Near Oceania, 2001; (with J. Rallu) Growth and Collapse of Pacific Island Societies: Archaeological and Demographic Perspectives, 2007; Roots of Conflict, 2010. Contributor to journals. **Address:** Archaeological Research Facility, University of California, Rm. 206, 2251 College Ave., Berkeley, CA 94720-1071, U.S.A. **Online address:** kirch@berkeley.edu

KIRCHNER, Bharti. American/Indian (born India), b. 1940. **Genres:** Novels, Food And Wine, Young Adult Fiction. **Career:** Bank of America, systems manager, 1980-84; IBM, advisory systems engineer, 1984-89; The Seattle Times, freelance book reviewer; freelance writer, 1989-. **Publications:** NONFICTION: The Healthy Cuisine of India: Recipes from the Bengal Region, 1992; Indian Inspired: A New Cuisine for the International Table, 1993; The Bold Vegetarian: One Hundred Fifty Inspired International Recipes, 1995; Vegetarian Burgers, 1996. NOVELS: Shiva Dancing, 1998; Sharmila's Book, 1999; Darjeeling, 2002; Pastries: A Novel of Desserts and Discoveries, 2003.

OTHER: Flavors of India: 175 Naturally Healthy, Savory and Authentic Recipes from the Bengal Region, 1995. **Address:** Liza Dawson Associates, 240 W 35th St., Ste. 500, New York, NY 10001, U.S.A. **Online address:** bhartik@aol.com

KIRCHNER, Emil J(oseph). German (born Germany), b. 1942. **Genres:** Politics/Government. **Career:** University of Essex, lecturer, 1974-76, Centre for European Studies, director, 1990-97, lecturer, professor, 1992-, Jean Monet professor of European integration, Jean Monnet European Centre of Excellence, coordinator, 1999-; European Institute for European Community Policy Making, director, 1981-86; European University Institute, Jean Monnet fellow, 1985-86; University of Connecticut, visiting professor, 1986-87; Charles University, Centre for Economic Research and Graduate Education, visiting professor, 1997, 1998; Journal of European Integration, executive editor, 1997-. **Publications:** Trade Unions as a Pressure Group in the European Community, 1977; European Interest Groups and Their Relations with the Economic and Social Committee, 1980; (with K. Schweiger) The Role of Interest Groups in the European Community, 1981; (with K. Schwaiger) Rolle der europäischen Interessenverbände: eine Bestandsaufnahme der europäischen Verbandswirklichkeit, 1981; The European Parliament: Performance and Prospects, 1984; (with N. Hewlett and F. Sobirey) Report on the Social Implications of Introducing New Technology in the Banking Sector, 1984; Decision Making in the European Community: The Council Presidency and European Integration, 1992; (with I. Budge and K. Newton) The Politics of the New Europe, 1998; (with J. Sperling) EU Security Governance, 2007. EDITOR: (and contrib.) Public Service Unions and the European Community, 1983; (and contrib.) Liberal Parties in Western Europe, 1988; (with J. Sperling) The Federal Republic and NATO, 1949-1989, 1992; (with C. Bluthand and J. Sperling) The Future of European Security, 1994; (with J. Sperling) Recasting the European Order: Security Architechtures and Economic Cooperation, 1997; Decentralisation and Transition: The Visegrad Countries, 1999; (with T. Christiansen) Committee Governance in the European Union, 2000; (co-ed.) Studies on Policies and Policy Processes of the European Union, 2003; (with J. Sperling) Global Security Governance: Competing Perceptions of Security in the 21st Century, 2007; (with J. Sperling) National Security Cultures: Patterns of Global Governance, 2010. **Address:** Jean Monnet European Centre of Excellence, University of Essex, Wivenhoe Pk., Colchester, EX CO4 3SQ, England. **Online address:** emil@essex.ac.uk

KIRK, Andrew G. American (born United States), b. 1964. **Genres:** Environmental Sciences/Ecology, Natural History. **Career:** Syracuse University, visiting assistant professor of environmental and western history, 1998-99; University of Nevada, associate professor, professor, 1999-, Public History Program, director, 1999-, Preserve Nevada, founding director, 2000-. Writer and historian. **Publications:** The Gentle Science: A History of the Conservation Library, 1995; (ed. with J.P. Herron) Human/Nature: Biology, Culture, and Environmental History, 1999; Collecting Nature: The American Environmental Movement and the Conservation Library, 2001; Counterculture Green: The Whole Earth Catalog and American Environmentalism, 2007. Contributor of articles to books and journals. **Address:** Department of History, University of Nevada, 4505 Maryland Pkwy., PO Box 455020, Las Vegas, NV 89154-5020, U.S.A. **Online address:** andy.kirk@unlv.edu

KIRK, Donald. American (born United States), b. 1938. **Genres:** International Relations/Current Affairs, History. **Career:** Reporter, 1960-64; correspondent, 1965-74; Chicago Tribune, far eastern correspondent, 1971-74, New York and United Nations correspondent, 1975-76; Council on Foreign Relations, Murrow fellow, 1974-75; International Herald Tribune, Seoul correspondent, 1997-2003. Writer. **Publications:** Wider War: The Struggle for Cambodia, Thailand and Laos, 1971; Tell It to the Dead: Memories of a War, 1975 as Tell It to the Dead: Stories of a War, 1996; Korean Dynasty: Hyundai and Chung Ju Yung, 1994; (ed.) The Business Guide to the Philippines, 1998; Looted: The Philippines after the Bases, 1998; Korean Crisis, Unraveling of the Miracle in the IMF Era, 2000; Philippines In Crisis: U.S. Power Versus Local Revolt, 2005; (ed. with C.S. Hun) Korea Witness: 135 Years of War, Crisis and News in the Land of the Morning Calm, 2006; Korea Betrayed: Kim Dae Jung and Sunshine, 2009. CONTRIBUTOR: Fodors Japan and East Asia (annual travel guide), 1968-72; Fodors Southeast Asia (annual travel guide), 1973-78; Electoral Politics in Vietnam, 1974; Communism in Indo China: New Perspectives, 1975; Kim Tae-jung sinhwa: 30-yŏn kyŏngnyŏk ŭi Sŏul tŭkpawŏn i ssŭn DJ ŭi sam kwa haetpyŏt chŏngchaek=Korea Betrayed, 2010. **Address:** 4343 Davenport St. NW, Washington, DC 20016, U.S.A. **Online address:** kirkdon@attglobal.net

KIRK, Paul. American (born United States), b. 1941?. **Genres:** Food And Wine, How-to Books. **Career:** School of Pitmasters, Traveling Course, owner and instructor, 1990-; Kansas City Barbecue Society, board director. Writer and restaurant chef. **Publications:** Paul Kirk's Championship Barbecue Sauces: 175 Make-Your-Own Sauces, Marinades, Dry Rubs, Wet Rubs, Mops, and Salsas, 1998; Smoke It!: Over 80 Succulent Recipes to Revolutionize Your Cooking, 2001; The Big Grill, 2003; (with B. Lyon) Paul Kirk's Championship Barbecue: BBQ Your Way to Greatness with 575 Lip-Smackin' Recipes from the Baron of Barbecue, 2004; 500 Barbecue Dishes: The Only Barbecue Compendium You'll Ever Need, 2008; (with A.A. Davis) America's Best BBQ: 100 Recipes from America's Best Smokehouses, Pits, Shacks, Rib Joints, Roadhouses, and Restaurants, 2009. **Address:** c/o Author Mail, The Harvard Common Press, 535 Albany St., Boston, MA 02118-2500, U.S.A. **Online address:** bbqbaron@hotmail.com

KIRK, Pauline (M.). British (born England), b. 1942. **Genres:** Novels, Poetry, Literary Criticism And History. **Career:** Methodist Ladies College, teacher, 1965-66; Universities of London, tutor in adult education, 1969-89; Open University, tutor, counselor and assistant senior counselor, 1969-89; Department of Social Services, senior officer and voluntary resource coordinator for city council, 1988-95; Fighting Cock Press, partner; writer, 1995-. **Publications:** POETRY: Scorpion Days, 1982, 2nd ed., 1986; Red Marl and Brick, 1985; Rights of Way, 1990; Travelling Solo, 1995; Return to Dreamtime, 1996; No Cure in Tears, 1997; Owlstone, 2002; Walking to Snailbeach: Selected and New Poems, 2004; Envying the Wild, 2008. NOVELS: Waters of Time, 1988; The Keepers, 1996. OTHER: (intro.) Scathed Earth: The Collected Poems of Mabel Ferrett, 1996. Blackthorn, forthcoming; Ellahnah, forthcoming. Work represented in anthologies. Contributor of poems and articles to magazines and newspapers. **Address:** Fighting Cock Press, 45 Middlethorpe Dr., 118b Holland Park Ave., York, NY YO24 1NA, England. **Online address:** pmk@pkirk304.force9.co.uk

KIRK, Thomas Allison. Italian (born Italy), b. 1962?. **Genres:** History, Politics/Government. **Career:** New York University in Florence, adjunct professor of medieval and renaissance studies; University of Siena, instructor in English and academic writing in the faculty of letters. Scholar, educator and writer. **Publications:** Genoa and the Sea: Policy and Power in an Early Modern Maritime Republic, 1559-1684, 2005. **Address:** New York University in Florence, Via Bolognese, 120, Firenze, 50139, Italy. **Online address:** tak2010@nyu.edu

KIRKBRIGHT, Suzanne. British (born England) **Genres:** Biography, Literary Criticism And History, Young Adult Fiction. **Career:** Aston University, lecturer, professor, 1995-2007. Writer and translator. **Publications:** Border and Border Experience: Investigations into the Philosophical and Literary Understanding of a German Motif, 1997; (ed. with R. von GoUMLrner) Nachdenken über Grenzen, 1999; (ed.) Cosmopolitans in the Modern World: Studies on a Theme in German and Austrian Literary Culture, 2000; Karl Jaspers: A Biography: Navigations in Truth, 2004; (ed.) Italienbriefe 1902, 2006. **Address:** c/o TriLiteral, Yale University Press, 100 Maple Ridge Dr., Cumberland, RI 02864-1769, U.S.A. **Online address:** suzkirkbright@yahoo.de

KIRK-GREENE, Anthony. British (born England), b. 1925. **Genres:** Area Studies, History, Politics/Government, Social Sciences. **Career:** British Colonial Administrative Service, district officer, 1950-57; Institute of Administration, senior lecturer in government, 1957-60; Ahmadu Bello University, associate professor of government and head of department, 1961-66; Oxford University, St. Antony's College, senior research fellow in African studies, 1967-81, director, 1980-84, university lecturer in the modern history of Africa, 1982-92, director of foreign service program, 1986-90, emeritus fellow, 1992-; Stanford University Center, adjunct professor, 1992-. Writer. **Publications:** (Foreword) This is Northern Nigeria: Background to an Invitation, 1956; Maiduguri and the Capitals of Bornu: Maiduguri da manyan biranen da no Barno, 1958; Adamawa Past and Present: An Historical Approach to the Development of a Northern Cameroons Province, 1958; (with C. Sassoon) The Cattle People of Nigeria, 1959; Northern Nigeria's Administrative Service Training Course: A Note on Its History & Curriculum, 1960; The Niger, 1961; Barth's Travels in Nigeria, 1962; (ed. and intro.) Principles of Native Administration in Nigeria: Selected Documents, 1900-1947, 1965; (with S.J. Hogben) The Emirates of Northern Nigeria: A Preliminary Survey of Their Historical Traditions, 1966; (trans.) Hausa Ba Dabo Ba Ne: A Collection of 500 Proverbs, 1966; (with Y. Aliyu) A Modern Hausa Reader, 1967; Crisis and Conflict in Nigeria: A Documentary Sourcebook, 1971; (trans. with P.

Newman) West African Travels and Adventures: Two Autobiographical Narratives from Northern Nigeria, 1971; (with C.H. Kraft) Teach Yourself Hausa, 1973, 9th ed., 1990; Mutumin Kirii: The Concept of the Good Man in Hausa, 1974; The Genesis of the Nigerian Civil War and the Theory of Fear, 1975; (with P. Ryan) Faces North: Some Peoples of Nigeria, 1975; A Biographical Dictionary of the British Colonial Governor, 1980; Stand by Your Radios, 1980; Stay by Your Radios: Documentation for a Study of Military Government in Tropical Africa, 1981; (with D. Rimmer) Nigeria since 1970: A Political and Economic Outline, 1981; The Sudan Political Service: A Profile in the Sociology of Empire, 1982; The Literature on Francophone Africa in English, 1989; A Short Story of the Corona Club, 1990; (comp. and intro.) A Biographical Dictionary of the British Colonial Service, 1939-66, 1991; Nationalism and Arcadianism in the Sudan, 1993; Diplomatic Initiative: A Jubilee History of the Foreign Service Programme, 1994; (with D. Bach) State and Society in Francophone Africa Since Independence, 1994; (with Vaughan) Hamman Yaji: Diary of a Nigerian Chief, Indiana, 1994; (ed. and intro. with J.H. Vaughan) The Diary of Hamman Yaji: Chronicle of a West African Muslim Ruler, 1995; On Crown Service: A History of HM Colonial and Overseas Civil Services, 1837-1997, 1999; Britain's Imperial Administrators, 1858-1966, 2000; Glimpses of Empire: A Corona Anthology, 2001; Symbol of Authority: The British District Officer in Africa, 2006. EDITOR: The Making of Northern Nigeria, 1965; Language and People of Bornu, 1968; Lugard and the Amalgamation of Nigeria: A Documentary Record; Being a Reprint of the Report by Sir F.D. Lugard On The Amalgamation of Northern And Southern Nigeria And Administration 1912-1919, 1968; Gazetteers of Northern Provinces Nigeria, 1972, rev. ed. as vol. I: The Hausa Emirates, vol. II: The Eastern Kingdoms, vol. III: The Central Kingdoms, vol. IV: The Highland Chieftaincies, 1972; The Transfer of Power: The African Administrator in the Age of Decolonization, 1979; (intro.) West African Passage: A Journey through Nigeria, Chad, and the Cameroons, 1931-1932, 1983; (with J. Stone) Ethnicity Empire and Race Relations, 1986; Pastoralists of the Western Savanna, 1986; (intro.) Pacific Prelude: A Journey to Samoa and Australasia, 1929, 1988; The Evolution of African History at British Universities, 1994; The Emergence of African History at British Universities: An Autobiographical Approach, 1995; (with D. Rimmer) The British Intellectual Engagement with Africa in the Twentieth Century, 2000. INTRO: The Making of Northern Nigeria, 2nd ed., 1965; Travels and Discoveries in North and Central Africa, 1965; Government and Mission Education in Northern Nigeria, 1966; The Languages and People of Bornu, 1968; The Vocabularies of Central African Languages, 1970; Political Memoranda, 1971; History of the Emirates of Northern Nigeria, 1973; Native Administration and Political Development in British Tropical Africa, 1979; Tales from the Dark Continent, 1979; African Studies: Into the 80s, 1981; Letters and Sketches from N. Nigeria (1910), 1992. **Address:** St. Antony's College, Oxford University, 62 Woodstock Rd., Oxford, OX OX2 6JF, England.

KIRK-GREENE, Christopher. (C. W. E. Kirk-Greene). British (born England), b. 1926. **Genres:** Language/Linguistics, History, Young Adult Fiction. **Career:** Lycee Berthollet, assistant in English, 1948-49; Eastbourne College, assistant master, 1949-86, Modern Languages Department, head, 1962-78. Writer. **Publications:** An Advanced French Vocabulary, 1958; Sixty Modern French Unseens, 1963; Les Mots Amis et Les Faux Amis, 1968; Lisez! Regardez! Repondez!, 1973; A First Book of French Idioms, 1973; Lectures Modernes, 1975; French False Friends, 1981; Modern French Passages for Translation, 1984; NTC's Dictionary of Faux Amis, 1990; Colloquial French, 1992; French Idioms and Expressions, 1997; Headlines: Colloquial English in Action, 2004; More Fluent French, 2008. **Address:** 7 S Cliff, Eastbourne, ES BN20 7AF, England.

KIRK-GREENE, C. W. E. *See* **KIRK-GREENE, Christopher.**

KIRKHAM, E. Bruce. American (born United States), b. 1938. **Genres:** Literary Criticism And History, Biology. **Career:** Ball State University, assistant professor, 1968-74, associate professor, 1974-80, professor of English, 1980, professor emeritus of English, Friends of the Alexander M. Bracken Library, founder, executive secretary, 1976-2000, Forum of Ball State University, editor. **Publications:** (Comp. with J.W. Fink) Indices to American Literary Annuals and Gift Books: 1825-1865, 1975; The Building of Uncle Tom's Cabin, 1977; (comp. and ed.) A Concordance to the Plymouth Collection of Hymns and Tunes 1885, 1984; (co-author) The Handbook of Biological Therapy, 2009. **Address:** Department of English, Ball State University, 2000 W University Ave., Muncie, IN 47306, U.S.A.

KIRKLAND, J. Russell. *See* **KIRKLAND, Russell.**

KIRKLAND, Martha. American (born United States) **Genres:** Romance/Historical, Novels, Young Adult Fiction. **Career:** Effective Leadership Bermuda, founder and director; Bermuda College, Adult and Continuing Education, assistant director. Writer, tutor and literacy advocate. **Publications:** ROMANCE NOVELS: (with J.A. Butler and T. Kirkland) Leading Older Children's Choirs, 1985; (ed. and comp. with S. Lyon) Pedalpoint Organist, 1990; The Message, 1993; The Marrying Season, 1995; The Secret Nabob, 1996; The Ruby Necklace, 1996; The Honorable Thief, 1996; The Gallant Gambler, 1997; Pratt's Landing, 1997; (contrib.) Seductive and Scandalous, 1997; The Righteous Rogue, 1997; Three for Brighton, 1998; The Artful Heir, 1998; The Noble Nephew, 1998; Magnolia Tree, 1998; (with D. Donley and C. Quinto) For Mother, with Love, 1998; (with J. Bennett and V. King) Summer Kittens, 1999; The Seductive Spy, 1999; To Catch a Scoundrel, 1999; Gentleman's Deception, 1999; That Scandalous Heiress, 2000; Uncommon Courtship, 2000; Miss Maitland's Letters, 2000; His Lordship's Swan, 2001; Mr. Montgomery's Quest, 2001; Rake's Fiancée, 2001; Miss Wilson's Reputation, 2002; Inconvenient Heir, 2003; Secret Diary, 2003; A Perfect Scoundrel, 2004. Works appear in anthologies. **Address:** c/o Author Mail, Signet Books, 375 Hudson St., New York, NY 10014-3657, U.S.A. **Online address:** mkirkland@rakehell.com

KIRKLAND, Russell. (J. Russell Kirkland). American (born United States), b. 1955. **Genres:** History, Theology/Religion. **Career:** Ming Studies, associate editor, 1985-88; Religious Studies Review, sub-editor, 1988-2001, area editor, 2001-; Journal of Chinese Religions, book review editor, 1990-2002; University of Georgia, associate professor of religion; Stanford University, faculty; University of Rochester, faculty; University of Missouri, faculty; Oberlin College, faculty; Macalester College, faculty. **Publications:** Taoism: The Enduring Tradition, 2004. Contributor to books and periodicals. **Address:** Department of Religion, University of Georgia, Peabody Hall, Athens, GA 30602-1625, U.S.A. **Online address:** kirkland@uga.edu

KIRKLEY, Evelyn A(nne). American (born United States), b. 1961. **Genres:** Theology/Religion, Adult Non-fiction, History, Social Sciences. **Career:** University of San Diego, assistant professor, 1995-2001, associate professor of theology, 2001-, co-director of the gender studies program, director of the faculty and curriculum development program. Writer. **Publications:** Rational Mothers and Infidel Gentlemen: Gender in American Atheism, 1865-1915, 2000. Contributor to journals. **Address:** Department of Theology and Religious Studies, University of San Diego, 291 Maher Hall, 5998 Alcala Pk., San Diego, CA 92110-2492, U.S.A. **Online address:** ekirkley@sandiego.edu

KIRKMAN, William Patrick. British/Indian (born India), b. 1932. **Genres:** International Relations/Current Affairs, History, Social Commentary, Adult Non-fiction. **Career:** Express & Star, editorial staff, 1955-57; Times, editorial staff, 1957-64, Commonwealth staff, 1960-64, Africa correspondent, 1962-64; Oxford University, careers adviser, 1964-68; Cambridge University, head of careers service, 1968-92, American Friends of Cambridge University, Cambridge administrator, 2000-01; Wolfson College, vice-president, 1980-84, emeritus fellow; The Hindu, columnist, 1993-; Magazine of the Cambridge Society, editor. **Publications:** Unscrambling an Empire: A Critique of British Colonial Policy, 1956-1966, 1966; Karriereplanung und Probleme des Beruflichen Einsatzes von Hochschulabsolventen: Tagungsbericht Mit erganzendem Material, 1982. **Address:** 14 George St., Willingham, Cambridge, CB CB4 5LJ, England. **Online address:** wpk1000@cam.ac.uk

KIRKPATRICK, Jane. American (born United States), b. 1946. **Genres:** Novels, Young Adult Non-fiction. **Career:** Eschutes County, director of a mental health program; Warm Springs Indian Reservation, mental health and educational consultant. Writer. **Publications:** NONFICTION: Homestead, 1991; A Sweetness to the Soul, 1995; Love to Water My Soul, 1996; A Gathering of Finches: A Novel, 1997; Mystic Sweet Communion, 1998; A Burden Shared: Words to Encourage Your Days, 1998; All Together in One Place: A Novel of Kinship, Courage, and Faith, 2000; No Eye Can See: A Novel of Kinship, Courage, and Faith, 2001; When the Stars Danced, 2001; What Once We Loved: A Sisterhood of Friendship and Faith, 2001; A Name of Her Own, 2002; A Simple Gift of Comfort, 2002; Every Fixed Star, 2003; Hold Tight the Thread, 2004; A Land of Sheltered Promise: A Novel Inspired by True Stories of the Big Muddy Ranch, 2005; Clearing in the Wild: A Novel, 2006; Tendering in the Storm: A Novel, 2007; Mending at the Edge: A Novel, 2008; Love to Water my Soul: A Novel, 2008; Sweetness to the Soul: A Novel, 2008; Au-

rora: An American Experience in Quilt, Community, and Craft, 2008; Flickering Light, 2009; An Absence So Great, 2010; The Daughter's Walk, 2011; Barcelona Calling, 2011. **Address:** c/o Author Mail, Waterbrook Press, 2375 Telstar Dr., Ste. 160, Colorado Springs, CO 80920, U.S.A. **Online address:** jane@jkbooks.com

KIRKPATRICK, Rob. American (born United States), b. 1968. **Genres:** Biography. **Career:** Thomas Dunne Books, senior editor, 2007-; Lyons Press, staff. **Publications:** BIOGRAPHIES: Alexi Lalas: Soccer Sensation, 2000; Cobi Jones: Soccer Star, 2000; Dale Earnhardt, Jr.: NASCAR Road Racer, 2000; Doug Flutie: International Football Star, 2000; Evander Holyfield: Heavyweight Champion, 2000; Grant Hill: Basketball All-Star, 2000; Jeff Gordon: NASCAR Champion, 2000; Kobe Bryant: Slam Dunk Champion, 2000; Mark McGwire: Record Breaker, 2000; Oscar De La Hoya: Gold- Medal Boxer, 2000; Sammy Sosa: Home-Run Hitter, 2000; Terrell Davis: Super Bowl Running Back, 2000; Florence Griffith Joyner: Olympic Runner, 2001; Mia Hamm, Soccer Star, 2001; Michael Jordan, Basketball Superstar, 2001; Wayne Gretzky, Hockey All- Star, 2001; Bob Cousy, 2002; Cecil Travis of the Washington Senators: The War-Torn Career of an All-Star Shortstop, 2005; The Words and Music of Bruce Springsteen, 2007. OTHERS: Trading Cards, 2000; (ed.) The Quotable Sixties, 2006; 1969: The Year Everything Changed, 2009. **Online address:** rob@robkirkpatrick.com

KIRKWOOD, Annie. American (born United States), b. 1937. **Genres:** Theology/Religion, inspirational/Motivational Literature, Human Relations/Parenting. **Career:** B&A Products, founder and owner, 1992-. Writer. **Publications:** (With B. Kirkwood) Messages to Our Family: From the Brotherhood, Mother Mary, and Jesus, 1994; Mary's Message of Hope, vol. I, 1995, vol. II, 2002; (with B. Kirkwood) Instructions for the Soul: Prayers, Affirmations, and Meditations for Daily Living as Compiled from Messages to Our Family, 1997; (contrib.) Mary's Message of Love: As Sent by Mary, the Mother of Jesus, 1999. **Address:** c/o Author Mail, Blue Dolphin Publishing, PO Box 8, Nevada City, CA 95959-0008, U.S.A.

KIRKWOOD, Catherine Mary. American (born United States), b. 1964. **Genres:** Novels. **Career:** Writer and cancer researcher. **Publications:** Leaving Abusive Partners: From the Scars of Survival to the Wisdom for Change, 1993; Cut Away: A Novel, 2009. Works appear in anthologies. **Address:** Seattle, WA , U.S.A. **Online address:** catkirk@catherinekirkwood.net

KIRKWOOD, Dianna. American (born United States), b. 1946?. **Genres:** Self Help, Medicine/Health. **Career:** Mercy Health Center, director of marketing, 1988-. Writer. **Publications:** (With J. Clemen, B. Schell and D. Myerson) The Town That Lost a Ton: How One Town Used the Buddy System to Lose 3998 Pounds-and How You Can Too!, 2002. **Address:** Mercy Medical Center, 250 Mercy Dr., Dubuque, IA 52001, U.S.A. **Online address:** kirkwood@trinity-health.org

KIRKWOOD, Kathryn. *See* **FLUKE, Joanne.**

KIRSCH, George B(enson). American (born United States), b. 1945. **Genres:** History, Sports/Fitness, Urban Studies. **Career:** Manhattan College, assistant professor, 1972-80, associate professor, 1980-88, department head, 1984-2001, professor of history, 1988-; American Studies Program, director, 1975-85. Writer. **Publications:** Jeremy Belknap: A Biography, 1982; The Creation of American Team Sports: Baseball and Cricket, 1838-72, 1989; Sports in North America: A Documentary History, 1992, vol. III: 1841-1860, 1992, vol. IV: Sport in War, Revival, and Expansion, 1860-1880, 1995; Voices from the Garden State: Documents in New Jersey History, 1993; (comp.) Glen Ridge Country Club: Centennial, 1894-1994, 1995; (co-author) The West in Global Context: From 1500 to Present, 1997; (ed. with O. Harris and C.E. Nolte) Encyclopedia of Ethnicity and Sports in the United States, 2000; Baseball in Blue and Gray: The National Pastime During the Civil War, 2003; Golf in America, 2009; Six Guys From Hackensack: Coming of Age in the Real New Jersey, forthcoming. **Address:** Department of History, Manhattan College, 411 Miguel Hall, Manhattan College Pkwy., Riverdale, NY 10471, U.S.A. **Online address:** george.kirsch@manhattan.edu

KIRSCH, Jonathan. American (born United States), b. 1949. **Genres:** Novels, Biography, Law, History. **Career:** Los Angeles Times Book Review, book reviewer, 1968-; California Magazine (formerly New West), senior editor, 1977-83; Newsweek, west coast correspondent, 1979-80; Kirsch & Mitchell, attorney, 1988-; Santa Cruz Sentinel, reporter; Jewish Journal, legal counsel;

Center for Media Literacy, legal counsel; California Lawyers for the Arts, legal counsel; Independent Book Publishers Association, general counsel; New York University Professional Publishing Institute, adjunct professor. Writer. **Publications:** NOVELS: Bad Moon Rising, 1977; Lovers in a Winter Circle, 1978. NONFICTION: Kirsch's Handbook of Publishing Law: For Authors, Publishers, Editors and Agents, 1995; The Harlot by the Side of the Road: Forbidden Tales of the Bible, 1997; Moses: A Life, 1998; King David: The Real Life of the Man Who Ruled Israel, 2000; The Woman Who Laughed at God: The Untold History of the Jewish people, 2001; God against the Gods: The History of the War between Monotheism and Polytheism, 2004; A History of the End of the World: How the Most Controversial Book in the Bible Changed the Source of Western Civilization, 2006; Grand Inquisitor's Manual: A History of Terror in the Name of God, 2008. Contributor to newspapers and magazines. **Address:** c/o Laurie Fox, Linda Chester Literary Agency, Rockefeller Ctr., 630 5th Ave., New York, CA 10111, U.S.A. **Online address:** jk@jonathankirsch.com

KIRSCHNER, Marc. *See* **KIRSCHNER, Marc W.**

KIRSCHNER, Marc W. Also writes as Marc Kirschner. American (born United States), b. 1945. **Genres:** Biology. **Career:** Princeton University, assistant professor of biochemistry, 1972-78; University of California, professor of biochemistry, 1978-93; Harvard University, Harvard Medical School, professor and chair of cell biology, 1993-2003, Department of Systems Biology, professor and founding chair, 2003-, John Franklin Enders university professor of systems biology, Carl W. Walter professor of systems biology; American Society for Cell Biology, president. Writer. **Publications:** (With J.C. Gerhart) Cells, Embryos and Evolution: Toward a Cellular and Developmental Understanding of Phenotypic Variation and Evolutionary Adaptability, 1997; (with J.C. Gerhart) The Plausibility of Life: Resolving Darwin's Dilemma, 2005. Contributor to periodicals. **Address:** Department of Systems Biology, Harvard Medical School, 200 Longwood Ave., Warren Alpert Bldg., Boston, MA 02115, U.S.A. **Online address:** marc@hms.harvard.edu

KIRSHNER, Jonathan. American (born United States), b. 1964. **Genres:** Politics/Government, Economics. **Career:** Cornell University, Department of Government, assistant professor, 1992-98, associate professor, 1998-2006, director of graduate studies, 2000-03, professor of government, 2006-, Einaudi Center of International Studies, International Political Economy Program, director, 1999-2008, Peace Studies Program, director, 2008-; Harvard University, John M. Olin Institute for Strategic Studies, WCFIA, Economics and National Security Program, director, 2000-04; Cornell University Press, series founding co-editor. **Publications:** Currency and Coercion: The Political Economy of International Monetary Power, 1995; Political Economy in Security Studies after the Cold War (pamphlet), 1997; (co-author) Iraq and Beyond: The New U.S. National Security Strategy (pamphlet), 2003; (ed.) Monetary Orders: Ambiguous Economics, Ubiquitous Politics, 2003; (ed.) Globalization and National Security, 2006; Appeasing Bankers: Financial Caution on the Road to War, 2007; (ed. with E. Helleiner) The Future of the Dollar, 2009. Contributor of articles to books and journals. **Address:** Ithaca, NY, U.S.A. **Online address:** jdk5@cornell.edu

KIRSHNER, Mia. Canadian (born Canada), b. 1976. **Genres:** Young Adult Non-fiction. **Career:** I Live Here Foundation, founder, 2001. Writer. **Publications:** (with J.B. MacKinnon, M. Simons and P. Shoebridge) I Live Here (nonfiction), 2008. **Address:** Brillstein-Grey Entertainment, 9150 Wilshire Blvd., Ste. 350, Beverly Hills, CA 90212-3453, U.S.A.

KIRSNER, Kim. Australian (born Australia), b. 1941. **Genres:** Psychology, History, Language/Linguistics, Sciences. **Career:** University of Toronto, postdoctoral research fellow, 1971; University of Western Australia, School of Psychology, lecturer, 1972-80, senior lecturer, 1980-86, associate professor, 1986-97, professor of psychology, 1997-, School of Animal Biology, senior research fellow; West Australian Museum, honorary associate, 1995-, researcher. Writer. **Publications:** (With J. Coney) Hemispheric Processes in Short Term Memory, 1976; (contrib.) Echanisms of Attention and Performance, 1985; (contrib.) Language Processing in Bilinguals: Psycholinguistic and Neuropsychological Perspectives, 1985; (contrib.) The Psychology of Reading, 1987; (co-ed. and contrib.) Implicit Memory: Theoretical Issues, 1989; (contrib.) Readings in Australian Psychology, 1991; (contrib.) Warship 1992, 1992; (contrib.) Theories of Memory, 1993; (contrib.) Implicit and Explicit Learning of Languages, 1994; (co-ed. and contrib.) Implicit Processes in Psychological Science: Theory and Practice, 1998; (co-ed.) Implicit and

Explicit Mental Processes, 1998; (with C.P. Speelman) Beyond the Learning Curve: The Construction of Mind, 2005. Contributor to books and journals. **Address:** School of Psychology, University of Western Australia, Rm. M304, 35 Stirling Hwy., Crawley, Perth, WA 6009, Australia. **Online address:** pkirsmer@bigpond.net.au

KISER, John W. American (born United States), b. 1942?. **Genres:** Military/Defense/Arms Control, Theology/Religion, History, Economics. **Career:** U.S. Department of State, private consultant, 1975-81; Kiser Research Inc., president, 1981-94. Writer and consultant. **Publications:** Report on the Potential for Technology Transfer from the Soviet Union to the United States, 1977; Commercial Technology Transfer from Eastern Europe to the United States and Western Europe, 1980; Communist Entrepreneurs: Unknown Innovators in the Global Economy, 1989; Stefan Zweig, Death of a Modern Man, 1998; The Monks of Tibhirine: Faith, Love, and Terror in Algeria, 2002; Commander of the Faithful: The Life and Times of Emir Abd El-Kader, 2008. Contributor of articles to magazines and journals. **Address:** Sperryville, VA, U.S.A. **Online address:** jwk@copper.net

KISLY, Lorraine. American (born United States) **Genres:** Adult Non-fiction, Theology/Religion. **Career:** Tricycle: The Buddhist Review, founding publisher, Tricycle Books, editor; Parabola Magazine, editor, editor-in-chief; Pilgrim Press, publisher. **Publications:** (Ed.) Ordinary Graces: Christian Teachings on the Interior Life, 2000; (ed.) Watch and Pray: Christian Teachings on the Practice of Prayer, 2002; The Prayer of Fire: Experiencing the Lord's Prayer, 2004; (ed.) Inner Journey: Views from the Christian Tradition, 2006; (ed.) Christian Teachings on the Practice of Prayer: From the Early Church to the Present, 2006. **Address:** Morning Light Press, 10881 N Boyer Rd., Sandpoint, ID 83864-5072, U.S.A.

KISSEL, Susan S. (Susan S. Adams). American (born United States), b. 1943. **Genres:** Literary Criticism And History, History, Social Sciences. **Career:** University of Cincinnati, instructor, 1967-69, adjunct instructor, 1975-78, lecturer in English, 1977-82; Northern Kentucky University, adjunct instructor, 1975-78, assistant professor, 1978-83, associate professor, 1984-92, professor of English, 1993-2003, director of women's studies, 1981-85, Student Media Board, chair, 1982-88, emeritus professor, 2004-; National Endowment for the Humanities, fellow, 1979; National Science Foundation, Chautauqua fellow, 1981. Writer. **Publications:** (Ed. with M. Rouse) The Story of the Pewter Basin and Other Occasional Writings: Collected in Southern Ohio and Northern Kentucky, 1981; In Common Cause: The Conservative Frances Trollope and the Radical Frances Wright, 1993; Moving On: The Heroines of Shirley Ann Grau, Anne Tyler, and Gail Godwin, 1996; The Slipping Down World of Anne Tyler's Novels, forthcoming. Contributor of articles to journals. **Address:** Department of Literature and Language, Northern Kentucky University, Nunn Dr., Highland Heights, KY 41099, U.S.A. **Online address:** adamsss@nku.edu

KISSELOFF, Jeff. American (born United States), b. 1955?. **Genres:** History, Children's Fiction, Biography, Sports/Fitness. **Career:** Alger Hiss Story Web Site, managing editor; The Nation, archivist. **Publications:** You Must Remember This: An Oral History of Manhattan from the 1890s to World War II, 1989; The Box: An Oral History of Television, 1920-1961, 1995; Who is Baseball's Greatest Hitter?, 2000, rev. ed., 2001; Who is Baseball's Greatest Pitcher?, 2003; Generation on Fire: Voices of Protest from the 1960s: An Oral History, 2007. **Address:** The University Press of Kentucky, 663 S Limestone St., Lexington, KY 40508-4008, U.S.A. **Online address:** jeffismee@yahoo.com

KISSING, Steve. American (born United States), b. 1963?. **Genres:** Advertising/Public Relations, Young Adult Fiction, Poetry. **Career:** HSR Business to Business (advertising firm), associate creative director; Barefoot Advertising, vice president, creative director; Cincinnati Magazine, contributing editor; Barefoot Proximity, creative director, copywriter, vice president. **Publications:** Running from the Devil: A Memoir of a Boy Possessed, 2003; Survival of the Fittest, 2004. Contributor to periodicals. **Address:** Barefoot Proximity, 700 W Pete Rose Way, Cincinnati, OH 45203, U.S.A. **Online address:** stevekissing@yahoo.com

KISSINGER, Henry (Alfred). American/German (born Germany), b. 1923. **Genres:** History, International Relations/Current Affairs, Politics/Government, Autobiography/Memoirs, Military/Defense/Arms Control, Social Sciences. **Career:** Operations Research Office, director, 1951; Harvard University, executive director of international studies seminar, 1951-69, instructor, 1954-55, Center for International Affairs, faculty, 1954-69, lecturer, 1957-59, Defense Studies Program, director, 1958-71, associate professor, 1959-62, professor of government, 1962-69; United States Arms Control and Disarmament Agency, consultant, 1961-68; Rand Corp., consultant, 1961-68; United States Government, National Security Council, consultant, 1961-62, director, 1969-75, secretary of state, 1973-77; Department of State, consultant, 1965-68; Georgetown University, School of Foreign Service, professor of diplomacy, 1977-; Kissinger Associates Inc., chairman, 1977-; National Bipartisan Commission, chair, 1983-85. Writer. **Publications:** Confluence, 1952; A World Restored: Castlereagh, Metternich and the Restoration of Peace, 1812-22, 1957; Nuclear Weapons and Foreign Policy, 1957; Amerikanische Aussenpolitik im Atomzeitalter, 1959; The Necessity for Choice: Prospects of American Foreign Policy, 1961; The Troubled Partnership: A Reappraisal of the Atlantic Alliance, 1965; (ed.) Problems of National Strategy: A Book of Readings, 1965; (with B. Brodie) Bureaucracy, Politics, and Strategy, 1965; American Foreign Policy: Three Essays, 1969, 3rd ed., 1977; Documentation on the Viet-Nam Agreement, 1973; Kissinger, l'homme et sa Pensée, 1976; White House Years, 1979; For the Record: Selected Statements, 1977-80, 1981; Years of Upheaval, 1982; American Foreign Policy: A Global View, 1982; Three Address of Foreign Policy, 1982; Report of the National Bipartisan Commission on Central America, 1984; Necessity for Choice: Prospects of American Foreign Policy, 1984; Observations: Selected Speeches and Essays, 1982-84, 1985; (with M. Bundy) The Dimensions of Diplomacy, 1989; Relazioni Est-ovest Negi anni '90, 1990; Diplomacy, 1994; (contrib.) Nova América Latina, 1996; United States and Middle Eastern Policy in a Changing Global Arena, 1997; Years of Renewal, 1999; Does America Need a Foreign Policy?: Toward a Diplomacy for the 21st Century, 2001; Reflections, October 2001: A Lecture Delivered at the Library of Congress on October 10, 2001, 2002; Ending the Vietnam War: A History of America's Involvement in and Extrication from the Vietnam War, 2003; Crisis: The Anatomy of Two Major Foreign Policy Crises, 2003; (with L.H. Summers and C.A. Kupchan) Renewing the Atlantic Partnership: Report of an Independent Task Force Sponsored by the Council on Foreign Relations, 2004; (foreword with A. Dobrynin) Soviet-American Relations: The Détente Years, 1969-1972, 2007; On China, 2011. **Address:** Penguin Group Inc., 375 Hudson St., New York, NY 10014-3657, U.S.A. **Online address:** info@henryakissinger.com

KISUBI, Alfred T(aligoola). American/Ugandan (born Uganda), b. 1949. **Genres:** Poetry, Social Sciences, Education. **Career:** Uganda Ministry of Information, Nakasero Ministry of Information Headquarters, research officer, 1981-82; World Bank, research assistant in Uganda, 1981-82; Johnson County Community College, instructor, 1985-86; University of Missouri, instructor, 1986-90; Penn Valley Community College, instructor, 1989-92; University of Wisconsin, associate professor of multicultural education and human services, 1992-, professor, distinguished professor; Pioneer College, teacher; Oshkosh Senior Center, Creative Writing Group, director; Brown Mackie College, teacher. Writer. **Publications:** POETRY: Time Winds, 1988; Maybe It's a Dream, 1991; Storms: Poems of Azania, 1990; Hi, 1992. OTHERS: (ed. with M.A. Burayidi) Race and Ethnic Relations in the First Person, 1998; My Sister's Drums: A Soliloquy, forthcoming. Work represented in anthologies. Contributor of poems to periodicals. **Address:** College of Education and Human Services, University of Wisconsin, N/E 509, 800 Algoma Blvd., Oshkosh, WI 54901, U.S.A. **Online address:** kisubi@uwosh.edu

KITA, Joe. American (born United States) **Genres:** Medicine/Health, Sports/Fitness, How-to Books. **Career:** Rodale Inc., vice-president of editorial, Men's Health Magazine, executive writer, Bicycle Magazine, editor-in-chief; Core Performance Center, contributing writer. Full-time freelance journalist, motivational speaker and consultant. **Publications:** (Ed.) Bicycling Magazine's Training for Fitness and Endurance, 1990; (comp. and ed.) Wisdom of Our Fathers: Timeless Life Lessons on Health, Wealth, God, Golf, Fear, Fishing, Sex, Serenity, Laughter and Hope, 1999; The Father's Guide to the Meaning of Life: What Being a Dad Has Taught Me about Hope, Love, Patience, Pride and Everyday Wonder, 2000; Another Shot: How I Relived My Life in Less than a Year, 2001; Accidental Courage: Finding out I'm a Bit Brave after All, 2002; Guy Q: 1305 Totally Essential Secrets You Either Know, or You Don't, 2003; (ed.) Weight-Free Workout, 2005; (ed.) Turn Fat into Muscle, 2005; (ed.) Sports Injuries Handbook, 2005. **Address:** Rodale Press, 33 E Minor St., Emmaus, PA 18098, U.S.A. **Online address:** jkita1@gmail.com

KITAJ, Karma. American (born United States), b. 1943. **Genres:** Biography, Autobiography/Memoirs, Art/Art History, Sports/Fitness. **Career:** Huckle Hill Press, chief executive officer, 2001-09; Life Spring Coaching, chief executive officer, 2005-. Psychotherapist and writer. **Publications:** Women Who could... and Did: Lives of 26 Exemplary Artists and Scientists, 2001; Women Riders Who Could-and Did: Life Stories of Top Level Equestriennes, 2010. **Address:** Life Spring Coaching, PO Box 67273, Chestnut Hill, MA 02467, U.S.A. **Online address:** karma@lifespringcoaching.com

KITCH, Sally L. American (born United States), b. 1946. **Genres:** Women's Studies And Issues, History, Race Relations, Humanities, Intellectual History. **Career:** Wichita State University, assistant professor, 1978-87, associate professor of women's studies, 1987-92, Master of Arts in Liberal Studies, graduate coordinator, 1986-88, Center for Women's Studies, director, 1988-92; Ohio State University, Department of Women's Studies, professor, 1992-2006, professor emeritus, 2006-, professor of comparative studies, 1992-95, Center for Women's Studies, director, 1992-96, chair, 1996-2000, vice chair, 2004-06; Arizona State University, Institute for Humanities Research, founding director, 2006-, professor of women's and gender studies, 2006-, Regents' professor, 2010-. Writer. **Publications:** (Co-ed. and contrib.) Design for Equity: Women and Leadership in Higher Education, 1980; (with C. Konek and F. Majors) The Source Book: An Inductive Approach to Composition, 1981; Chaste Liberation: Celibacy and Female Cultural Status, 1989; This Strange Society of Women: Reading the Letters and Lives of the Woman's Commonwealth, 1993; (ed. with C.W. Konek) Women and Careers: Issues and Challenges, 1994; Higher Ground: From Utopianism to Realism in American Feminist Thought and Theory, 2000; Specter of Sex: Gendered Foundations of Racial Formation in the United States, 2009; The Sex Factor: Gendered Foundations of Race and Strategies of Resistance, 2009. Contributor of articles to periodicals. **Address:** Institute for Humanities Research, Arizona State University, 107 Social Sciences Bldg., 951 S Cady Mall, PO Box 876505, Tempe, AZ 85287, U.S.A. **Online address:** sally.kitch@asu.edu

KITCHEN, Bert. (Herbert Thomas Kitchen). British (born England), b. 1940. **Genres:** Children's Fiction, Children's Non-fiction, Young Adult Fiction, Biology, Young Adult Non-fiction. **Career:** London Central School of Arts and Crafts, visiting lecturer in drawing and design, 1961-64; Edinburgh Weavers, freelance textile designer, 1961-63; City of London Polytechnic, visiting lecturer in drawing and design, 1964; Private Eye Magazine, illustrator, 1969-; British Broadcasting Corp., artist, 1975-88; London Weekend Television, artist, 1975-88; author and illustrator of children's books, 1983-. **Publications:** SELF-ILLUSTRATED FOR CHILDREN: Animal Alphabet, 1984; Mythical Creatures, 1986; Animal Numbers, 1987; Tenrec's Twigs, 1989; Gorilla Chinchilla and Other Animal Rhymes, 1990; Pig in a Barrow (poems), 1991; Somewhere Today, 1992; And So They Build, 1993; When Hunger Calls, 1994. Illustrator of books by others. **Address:** David Higham Associates, 5-8 Lower John St., Golden Sq., London, GL W1F 9HA, England.

KITCHEN, Herbert Thomas. See **KITCHEN, Bert.**

KITCHEN, Judith. American (born United States), b. 1941. **Genres:** Poetry, Literary Criticism And History, Essays. **Career:** State University of New York College, lecturer in English, 1983-97, writer-in-residence, 1998-2003; University of Rochester, Eastman School of Music, Aesthetic Education Institute, artist, 1983-90; Wells College, writer-in-residence, 1986-87; Chautauqua Institution, Writers' Center, writer-in-residence, 1992, 1994, 1999. Writer. **Publications:** Upstairs Window (poetry chapbook), 1983; Perennials (poems), 1986; Understanding William Stafford, 1989; Only the Dance: Essays on Time and Memory, 1994; Writing the World: Understanding William Stafford, 1998; Distance and Direction, 2002; The House on Eccles Road, 2002. EDITOR: (with P. Janus) Apple: An Anthology of Upstate New York Poets, 1979; Chapbook Series, 1981-; (with S.S. Rubin and E. Ingersoll) The Post-Confessionals: Conversations with Poets of the Eighties, 1989; The State Street Reader: An Anthology, 10 Years, 1990; In Short: A Collection of Brief Creative Nonfiction, 1996; In Brief: Short Takes on the Personal, 1999; Short Takes: Brief Encounters with Contemporary Nonfiction, 2005; (with T. Kooser) The Poets Guide to the Birds, 2009. Contributor to periodicals. **Address:** Department of English, State University of New York, Brockport, NY 14420, U.S.A.

KITCHEN, Martin. Canadian/British (born England), b. 1936. **Genres:** History, Military/Defense/Arms Control, International Relations/Current Affairs, Adult Non-fiction. **Career:** Simon Fraser University, assistant professor, 1966-69, associate professor, 1969-74, professor of history, 1974-, now professor emeritus, research professor, 1983-84; Cambridge University, faculty. Writer. **Publications:** The German Officer Corps 1890-1914, 1968; A Military History of Germany: From the Eighteenth Century to the Present Day, 1974; Fascism, 1976; The Silent Dictatorship: The Politics of the German High Command under Hindenburg and Ludendorff, 1976; The Political Economy of Germany 1815-1914, 1978; The Coming of Austrian Fascism, 1980; (ed. with V.R. Berghahn) Germany in the Age of Total War, 1981; British Policy towards the Soviet Union during the Second World War, 1986; (with L. Aronsen) The Origins of the Cold War in Comparative Perspective: American, British and Canadian Relations with the Soviet Union, 1941-48, 1987; Europe between the Wars: A Political History, 1988, 2nd ed., 2006; World in Flames: A Short History of the Second World War in Europe and Asia, 1939-1945, 1990; Empire and After: A Short History of the British Empire and Commonwealth, 1994; A World in Flames: A Concise History of the British Empire and the Commonwealth, 1994; Nazi Germany at War, 1994; The Cambridge Illustrated History of Germany, 1996; The British Empire and Commonwealth, 1996; Kaspar Hauser: Europe's Child, 2001; The German Offensives of 1918, 2001; History of Modern Germany, 1800-2000, 2006, 2nd ed. as A History of Modern Germany, 1800 to the Present, 2012; Third Reich: Charisma and Community, 2008; Rommel's Desert War: Waging World War II in North Africa, 1941-1943, 2009. Contributor to periodicals. **Address:** Department of History, Simon Fraser University, AQ 6230, 8888 University Dr., Burnaby, BC V5A 1S6, Canada. **Online address:** kitchen@sfu.ca

KITELEY, Brian. American (born United States), b. 1956. **Genres:** Novels, Sciences, Autobiography/Memoirs, Travel/Exploration, Young Adult Fiction. **Career:** City University of New York, City College, instructor in English, 1986-87; McGraw-Hill Publishing Co., 1986-87; American University in Cairo, instructor in English composition, 1987-89; Ohio University, assistant professor of English and creative writing, 1992-94; University of Denver, Department of English, assistant professor, 1994-98, Creative Writing Program, director, 1995-97, 2003-07, associate professor of English and creative writing, 1998-2007, professor of English literature and creative writing, 2007-, associate department chair. Writer. **Publications:** Still Life with Insects, 1989; I Know Many Songs, but I Cannot Sing, 1996; 3 A.M. Epiphany: Uncommon Writing Exercises that Transform Your Fiction, 2005; 4 a.m. Breakthrough: Unconventional Writing Exercises that Transform Your Fiction, 2008; River Gods, 2009. **Address:** Department of English, University of Denver, 487C Sturm Hall, 2000 E Asbury, Denver, CO 80208, U.S.A. **Online address:** bkiteley@du.edu

KITFIELD, James C. American (born United States), b. 1956. **Genres:** Documentaries/Reportage, Military/Defense/Arms Control, History, Politics/Government. **Career:** Stars and Stripes, European Edition, intern; Overseas!, editor; National Journal Group Inc., associate editor, 1989-, reporter and staff correspondent, national security and foreign affairs correspondent, senior correspondent. **Publications:** (With W. Walker) The Whole Europe Escape Manual: Germany, Austria, Switzerland, 1985; Prodigal Soldiers: How The Generation of Officers Born of Vietnam Revolutionized the American Style of War, 1995; (co-author) Ski Snowboard Europe, 2003; War and Destiny: How the Bush Revolution in Foreign and Military Affairs Redefined American Power, 2005. Contributor to periodicals. **Address:** National Journal Group Inc., The Watergate, 600 New Hampshire Ave. NW, Washington, DC 20037-2403, U.S.A. **Online address:** jkitfield@nationaljournal.com

KITH, Trystam. *See* **YARBRO, Chelsea Quinn.**

KITT, Sandra (E.). American (born United States) **Genres:** Novellas/Short Stories, Romance/Historical, Librarianship, Illustrations. **Career:** Philip Gips Studios Inc., art assistant, 1970-72; New York City Board of Education, Cloisters Workshop Program, teacher, 1972-73; Museum of Contemporary Arts, assistant registrar; Children's Art Center, assistant coordinator, 1972-73; New York City Office of Cultural Affairs, printmaking workshop, teacher, 1974-80; Information Specialist, librarian, 1974-92; American Museum of Natural History, Richard S. Perkin Library, manager of library services, 1992-. Writer. **Publications:** ROMANCE NOVELS: Rites of Spring, 1984; Adam and Eva, 1984; All Good Things, 1984; Perfect Combination, 1985; Only with the Heart, 1985; With Open Arms, 1987; An Innocent Man, 1989; The Way Home, 1990; Someone's Baby, 1991; Love Everlasting, 1993; Love Is Thanks Enough as Friends, Families and Lovers, 1993; Serenade, 1994; Sincerely, 1995; Significant Others, 1996; Between Friends, 1997; Family Affairs, 1998; Close Encounters, 2000; She's the One, 2001; Southern Comfort, 2004; The Next Best Things, 2005; Celluloid Memories, 2007; For All We Know, 2008. OTHERS: The Color of Love (novel), 1995; Back in Your Arms, 2006; Rsvp

with Love, 2009; Promises in Paradise, 2010. Contributor of articles to books and journals. **Address:** Aaron Priest Literary Agency Inc., 708 3rd Ave., 23rd Fl., New York, NY 10017, U.S.A. **Online address:** sandikitt@hotmail.com

KITTERMAN, Barry. American (born United States), b. 1953. **Genres:** Novels, Novellas/Short Stories. **Career:** Indiana University East, faculty of writing and literature; Miami University, faculty; Austin Peay State University, professor of English and creative writing, 1994-; Truman State University, The Green Hills Literary Lantern, associate editor; Zone 3 Magazine, editor. **Publications:** The Baker's Boy: A Novel, 2008; From the San Joaquin: Stories, 2011. Contributor to periodicals. **Address:** Department of Languages and Literature, Austin Peay State University, 601 College St., PO Box 4487, Clarksville, TN 37044, U.S.A. **Online address:** kittermanb@apsu.edu

KITTINGER, Jo S(usenbach). American (born United States), b. 1955. **Genres:** Children's Fiction, Natural History, Picture/Board Books, Biography, Children's Non-fiction, History. **Career:** Wood and the Works (fine crafts gallery), co-owner and resident potter, 1977-80; freelance crafts designer, 1978-91; The Flicker Children's Magazine, editorial assistant; Society of Children's Book Writers and Illustrators, Southern Breeze Region, assistant regional adviser, 1999-2002, co-regional advisor, 2002-; Shades Valley Community Church, Servant Leadership Team, staff. Writer. **Publications:** Dead Log Alive!, 1996; A Look at Rocks: From Coal to Kimberlite, 1997; A Look at Minerals: From Galena to Gold, 1998; Stories in Stone: The World of Animal Fossils, 1998; The Joy of Cats, 1999; Birds of North America East, 2001; Birds of North America West, 2001; Going to the Beach, 2002; Moving Day, 2003; Un Almeuro Con Ponche, 2003; A Lunch with Punch, 2003; When I Grow Up, 2004; Jane Goodall, 2005; George Washington Carver, 2005; Rosa's Bus: The Ride to Civil Rights, 2010; Lindy Lee Loves Pink, 2011; David Drew Likes Blue, 2011; A Perfect Princess, 2011; The House on Dirty-Third Street, 2012; A Breath of Hope, 2012. Contributor to periodicals. **Address:** c/o Author Mail, Calkins Creek Books, 815 Church St., Honesdale, PA 18431, U.S.A. **Online address:** jskittinger@gmail.com

KITTREDGE, William. (Owen Rountree). American (born United States), b. 1932. **Genres:** Novels, Novellas/Short Stories, Westerns/Adventure, Essays, Literary Criticism And History, Young Adult Fiction. **Career:** McRanch, cattle rancher and ranch manager, 1957-67; Northwest Review, assistant editor and consulting editor, 1968-70; University of Montana, assistant professor, 1969-74, associate professor, 1974-80, professor of English, 1980-87; Rocky Mountain Magazine, consulting editor, 1979-83; Pacific Northwest Magazine, consulting editor, 1979-86; Outside, consulting editor. **Publications:** EDITOR: (with S.M. Krauzer) Great Action Stories, 1977; (intro. with S.M. Krauzer) The Great American Detective, 1978; (with S.M. Krauzer) Stories into Film, 1979; (with J. Smart) Montana Spaces: Essays and Photographs in Celebration of Montana, 1988; (with A. Smith) The Last Best Place: A Montana Anthology, 1988; The Portable Western Reader, 1997; (with A.M. Jones) The Best of Montana's Short Fiction, 2004. SHORT STORIES: The Van Gogh Field and Other Stories, 1978; We Are Not in This Together, 1984; Phantom Silver, 1987. CORD SERIES AS OWEN ROUNTREE (with S.M. Krauzer): Cord, 1982; The Nevada War, 1982; Black Hills Gold, 1982; Gunman Winter, 1983; Hunt the Man Down, 1984; King of Colorado, 1984; Gunsmoke River, 1985; Paradise Valley, 1986; Brimstone Basin, 1986. ESSAYS: Owning It All: Essays, 1987; Hole in the Sky: A Memoir, 1992; (contrib.) Robert Helm, 1981-1993, 1994; The WPA Guide to 1930s Montana, 1994; Who Owns the West, 1996; Big Sky Country: Best of Montana, North Dakota, Wyoming and Idaho, 1996; (co-author) Waste Land: Meditations on a Ravaged Landscape, 1997; Taking Care: Thoughts on Storytelling and Belief, 1999; Balancing Water: Restoring the Klamath Basin, 2000; The Nature of Generosity, 2000; Southwestern Homelands, 2002; The Best Stories of William Kittredge, 2003; (intro.) America's 100th Meridian: A Plains Journey, 2005; The Willow Field, 2006; The Next Rodeo: New and Selected Essays, 2007. OTHERS: The Best Short Stories of William Kittredge, 2003. Contributor to periodicals. **Address:** c/o Amanda Urban, International Creative Management, 40 W 57th St., New York, NY 10019, U.S.A.

KITTS, Kenneth. American (born United States), b. 1964. **Genres:** Adult Non-fiction, Politics/Government, Military/Defense/Arms Control, History. **Career:** Francis Marion University, instructor, 1987, professor of political science, 2005, associate provost of Academic Affairs and director of graduate programs, 2002, leader of graduate programs, associate provost for enrollment management, 2007, Department of Political Science and Geography, chair, Office of Academic Affairs, provost and vice chancellor, chief academic officer; University of North Carolina Pembroke, Office of the Chancellor, provost and vice president of Academic Affairs, 2011-. Writer. **Publications:** Presidential Commissions and National Security: The Politics of Damage Control (nonfiction), 2006. **Address:** Office of the Chancellor, University of North Carolina Pembroke, PO Box 1510, Pembroke, NC 28372-1510, U.S.A. **Online address:** ken.kitts@uncp.edu

KITTS, Thomas M(ichael). American (born United States), b. 1955. **Genres:** Music, Popular Culture, Literary Criticism And History, Plays/Screenplays. **Career:** St. Peter's College, adjunct assistant professor of English, 1980; St. John's University, adjunct instructor, 1980-91, assistant professor, 1991-97, associate professor of English, 1997-2002, professor of English, 2002-, assistant director of alumni relations, 1980-83, director, 1983-91, Division of English and Speech, chair, 2000-; Mid-Atlantic Almanack, editor, 2007-; Popular Music and Society, co-editor. **Publications:** The Theatrical Life of George Henry Boker, 1994; Gypsies: An East Village Opera, 1994; Instructor's Manual to Accompany Literature: Reading Fiction, Poetry, Drama, and the Essay, 6th ed. 2004; Instructor's Manual to Accompany The American Tradition in Literature, 11th ed., 2005; (ed. with M.J. Kraus) Living on a Thin Line: Crossing Aesthetic Borders with the Kinks, 2002; Ray Davies: Not Life Everybody Else, 2008; Instructor's Manual to Accompany Literature: Craft and Voice, 2010; (ed.) Literature and Work, 2011. Contributor of books to periodicals. **Address:** St. John's University, Division of English/Speech, 8000 Utopia Pkwy., Queens, NY 11439, U.S.A. **Online address:** kittst@stjohns.edu

KITZINGER, Sheila. British (born England), b. 1929. **Genres:** Medicine/Health, Social Sciences, Women's Studies And Issues, Sex, Human Relations/Parenting. **Career:** University of Edinburgh, researcher, 1951-53; Open University, lecturer; Thames Valley University, honorary professor. Social anthropologist and writer. **Publications:** The Experience of Childbirth, 1962, 5th ed., 1984; Giving Birth: The Parent's Emotions in Childbirth, 1971, rev. ed., 1987; (ed.) Episiotomy: Physical and Emotional Aspects, 1972; Education and Counselling for Childbirth, 1977; Women as Mothers, 1978 as Ourselves as Mothers: The Universal Experience of Motherhood, 1994; Birth at Home, 1979, rev. ed., 1980; The Good Birth Guide, 1979; The Experience of Breastfeeding, 1979; (ed. with J.A. Davis) The Place of Birth: a Study of the Environment in Which Birth Takes Place with Special Reference to Home Confinements, 1978; Pregnancy and Childbirth, 1980 as The Complete Book of Pregnancy and Childbirth, 1996, 4th ed., 2004; (with J. Dorfman and H. Schuchman) Well-being: An Introduction to Health, 1980; Some Women's Experience of Episiotomy, 1981; The New Good Birth Guide, 1983; Woman's Experience of Sex, 1983; (ed.) Episiotomy and the Second Stage of Labor, 1984; Birth Over Thirty, 1985, rev. ed., 1994; Being Born, 1986; Freedom and Choice in Childbirth in US as Your Baby Your Way, 1987; Some Women's Experiences of Epidurals, 1987; (intro.) Generations: A Universal Family Album, 1987; The Midwife Challenge, 1988; Giving Birth: How it Really Feels, 1989; The Crying Baby, 1989; Breastfeeding Your Baby, 1989, as Breastfeeding, 1998; (with C. Kitzinger) Talking with Children about Things that Matter, 1989, 2nd ed., 1999 in US as Tough Questions: Talking Straigth with Your Kids about the Real World, 1991; (with V. Bailey) Pregnancy Day by Day, 1990, 2nd ed., 1998; Home Birth and Other Alternatives to Hospital, 1991; Homebirth: The Essential Guide to Giving Birth Outside of the Hospital, 1991; The Year after Childbirth: Surviving and enjoying the First Year of Motherhood, 1994; Becoming a Grandmother: A Life Transition, 1997; Rediscovering Birth, 2000; Birth Your Way, 2002; New Pregnancy and Childbirth, 2003; The New Experience of Childbirth, 2004; Politics of Birth, 2005; Understanding Your Crying Baby, 2005; Birth Crisis, 2006. **Address:** c/o Hilary Rubinstein, A. P. Watt & Son, 26/28 Bedford Row, London, GL WC1R 4HL, England.

KITZINGER, Uwe. (Uwe W. Kitzinger). American/British (born England), b. 1928. **Genres:** Economics, International Relations/Current Affairs, Politics/Government, Essays. **Career:** University of the Saar, lecturer, 1955-56; Oxford University, Nuffield College, fellow, 1956-, research fellow, 1958-62, official fellow and investment bursar, 1962-76, emeritus fellow, 1976-, Worcester College, Keble College, lecturer in politics, 1960-64; Harvard University, The Minda de Gunzburg Center for European Studies, staff, visiting professor, 1969-70; University of Paris, visiting professor, 1970-73; Journal of Common Market Studies, founding editor, 1962; University of West Indies, visiting professor of international relations, 1964-65; Commission of the European Communities, adviser to Sir Christopher Soames, vice-president, 1973-75; Fontainebleau, European Institute of Business Administration, dean, 1976-80; Oxford Centre for Management Studies, director, 1980-84;

Templeton College, founding president, 1984-91, fellow, 2001. Political analyst. **Publications:** (As U.W. Kitzinger) The Economics of the Saar Question, 1958; German Electoral Politics: A Study of the 1957 Campaign, 1960; (as U.W. Kitzinger) The Challenge of the Common Market, 1961, rev. ed. as The Politics and Economics of European Integration: Britain, Europe and the United States, 1963; Grossbritannien, 1963; Britain, Europe and Beyond: Essays in European Politics, 1964; The Background to Jamaica's Foreign Policy, 1965; The European Common Market and Community, 1967; Commitment and Identity: Inaugural Kathleen Freeman Memorial Lecture Delivered in the Grand Committee Room in the Palace of Westminster, 14 March 1968, 1968; The Second Try, 1969; Diplomacy and Persuasion: How Britain Joined the EEC, 1973; Europe's Wider Horizons, 1975; (with D. Butler) The 1975 Referendum, 1976, 2nd ed., 1996; (with E. Frankel) Macro-Engineering and the Earth, 1998. Contributor of articles to journals. **Address:** The Minda de Gunzburg Center for European Studies, Harvard University, 27 Kirkland St., Cambridge, MA 02138, U.S.A. **Online address:** kitzing@fas.harvard.edu

KITZINGER, Uwe W. See **KITZINGER, Uwe.**

KIVELSON, Valerie. American (born United States), b. 1957. **Genres:** History. **Career:** University of Michigan, professor. Writer. **Publications:** Autocracy in the Provinces: The Muscovite Gentry and Political Culture in the Seventeenth Century, 1996; (ed. with R.H. Greene) Orthodox Russia: Belief and Practice under the Tsars, 2003; Cartographies of Tsardom: The Land and Its Meanings in Seventeenth-Century Russia, 2006; (ed. with J. Neuberger) Picturing Russia: Explorations in Visual Culture, 2008; (ed.) The New Muscovite Cultural History: A Collection in Honor of Daniel B. Rowland, 2009. Contributor of articles to books and journals. **Address:** University of Michigan, 2743 Haven Hall, Ann Arbor, MI 48109, U.S.A. **Online address:** vkivelso@umich.edu

KIZAKI, Satoko. See **HARADA, Masako.**

KIZER, Amber. American (born United States) **Genres:** Human Relations/Parenting, Science Fiction/Fantasy. **Career:** Writer and educator. **Publications:** Gert Garibaldi's Rants and Raves: One Butt Cheek at a Time, 2007; Seven Kinds of Ordinary Catastrophes, 2008; Meridian, 2009; Wildcat Fireflies, 2011; Speed of Light, 2012; Counting Tens (forthcoming); Echoes of 1492 (forthcoming). **Address:** Delacorte Press Books for Young Readers, 1745 Broadway, New York, NY 10019, U.S.A. **Online address:** amber@amberkizer.com

KIZER, Carolyn. American (born United States), b. 1925. **Genres:** Poetry, Literary Criticism And History. **Career:** Poetry Northwest, founding editor, 1959-65; U.S. State Department, specialist in literature, 1965-66; National Endowment for the Arts, director of literary programs, 1966-70; University of North Carolina, professor, 1970-74, poet-in-residence; Washington University, visiting professor, Fannie Hurst professor of literature, 1971; Columbia University, Barnard College, visiting professor, acting director of graduate writing program, 1972; Ohio University, McGuffey Lecturer and poet-in-residence, 1975; University of Iowa, Iowa Writer's Workshop, professor of poetry, 1976; University of Maryland, professor, 1976-77; University of Iowa, visiting professor; University of Cincinnati, visiting professor; University of Louisville, visiting professor; State University of New York, visiting professor; Stanford University, visiting professor; University of Arizona, visiting professor, 1989, 1990; University of California, visiting professor, 1991; University of Alabama, coal royalty chair, 1995; National Endowment for the Arts, director of literary programs; Princeton University, visiting professor; Kinnaird College for Women, faculty; Seattle Community Psychiatric Clinic, founding board director; Association of Literary Magazines of America, founding member; Academy of American Poets, chancellor. **Publications:** The Ungrateful Garden, 1961; Knock upon Silence, 1965; Midnight Was My Cry: New and Selected Poems, 1971; YIN: New Poems, 1984; Mermaids in the Basement: Poems for Women, 1984; The Nearness of You, 1986; Carrying Over: Translations from Various Tongues, 1988; (with D. Finkel) Splintered Mirror (modern Chinese translations), 1991; Proses: Essays on Poets and Poetry, 1993; Picking and Choosing: Essays, 1995; Harping On: Poems 1985-1995, 1996; Pro Femina, 2000; Cool, Calm and Collected Poems, 2000. EDITOR: Leaving Taos, 1981; The Essential Clare, 1993; 100 Great Poems by Women, 1995; (intro.) American Spirituals, 1998. Contributor to periodicals. **Address:** 19772 8th St. E, Sonoma, CA 95476, U.S.A.

KLADSTRUP, Kristin. American (born United States), b. 1961. **Genres:**

Novels, Children's Fiction. **Career:** Writer. **Publications:** The Book of Story Beginnings (novel), 2006; The Gingerbread Pirates, 2009; A Night in Santa's Great Big Bag, 2010. **Address:** Viking Press, 375 Hudson St., New York, NY 10014, U.S.A. **Online address:** kristin.kladstrup@rcn.com

KLAHR, David. American (born United States), b. 1939?. **Genres:** Novels. **Career:** Wolf Research and Development Corp., designer, 1960-61; North American Air Defense Command Headquarters, developer of systems programs, 1961-62; Carnegie Mellon University, Carnegie Institute of Technology, Department of Mathematics, instructor in mathematics, 1964-66, Graduate School of Industrial Administration, associate professor, 1969-76, Department of Psychology, associate professor, 1969-76, professor of psychology, 1976-, head, 1983-93, Walter van Dyke Bingham professor of cognitive eevelopment and education sciences, Literacy in Science Center, director, 1988-96, Graduate Program, acting director, 2000-01, Program in Interdisciplinary Education Research, training director, 2005-; University of Chicago, Graduate School of Business, instructor in business, 1966-67, assistant professor of behavioral and information sciences, 1967-69; University of Stirling, visiting research fellow in education, 1968; University of London, London Graduate School of Business Studies, visiting Fulbright lecturer, 1969. Writer. **Publications:** (With J.G. Wallace) Cognitive Development: An Information-processing View, 1976; (ed.) Cognition and Instruction, 1976; (ed. with P. Langley and R. Neches) Production System Models of Learning and Development, 1987; (ed. with K. Kotovsky) Complex Information Processing: The Impact of Herbert A. Simon, 1989; (co-author) Exploring Science: The Cognition and Development of Discovery Processes, 2000; (ed. with S.M. Carver) Cognition and Instruction: Twenty-Five Years of Progress, 2001. **Address:** Department of Psychology, Carnegie Mellon University, 354M Baker Hall, 5000 Forbes Ave., Pittsburgh, PA 15213-3890, U.S.A. **Online address:** klahr@cmu.edu

KLAM, Julie. American (born United States) **Genres:** History. **Career:** Freelance writer. **Publications:** (With C. Claro) Comedy Central: The Essential Guide to Comedy (Because There Is a Fine Line between Clever and Stupid), 1997; Europe in Flames, 2003; The War at Home, 2003; From D-Day to V-E Day, 2003; Victory in the Pacific, 2003; (with D.J. Zimmerman) Air War!, 2003; (with D.J. Zimmerman) The Rise of Japan and Pearl Harbor, 2003; Please Excuse My Daughter, 2008; You Had Me at Woof: How Dogs Taught Me the Secrets of Happiness, 2010; Love at First Bark: How Saving a Dog Can Sometimes Help You Save Yourself, 2011. Contributor to periodicals. **Address:** c/o Ester Newberg, International Creative Management, 825 8th Ave., New York, NY 10019, U.S.A. **Online address:** jk@julieklam.com

KLAM, Matthew. American (born United States), b. 1964?. **Genres:** Novellas/Short Stories, Young Adult Fiction. **Career:** St. Albans School, teacher of creative writing; American University, teacher of creative writing; Stockholm University, teacher of creative writing; The New York Times Magazine, contributing writer; The Johns Hopkins University, visiting assistant professor. **Publications:** Sam the Cat and Other Stories, 2000. Contributor to periodicals. **Address:** c/o Author Mail, Random House Inc., 1745 Broadway, New York, NY 10019, U.S.A. **Online address:** mattklam@gmail.com

KLAMMER, Martin (P.). American (born United States), b. 1957. **Genres:** Literary Criticism And History. **Career:** Lutheran Council in the U.S.A., news and feature writer, 1983-84; University of Iowa, instructor in rhetoric and literature, 1984-90; Business and Professional People for the Public Interest, legal intern, 1990; Luther College, assistant professor of English and Africana studies, 1991-, associate professor of English, chair, Africana Studies Department, chair, professor of English and Africana studies, 2004-. Writer. **Publications:** Whitman, Slavery and the Emergence of Leaves of Grass, 1995; (with B.L. Guma) In the Dark with My Dress on Fire, 2010. Contributor to books and periodicals. **Address:** Department of Africana Studies, Luther College, Main 401, Koren Bldg., 700 College Dr., Decorah, IA 52101, U.S.A. **Online address:** klammerm@luther.edu

KLAPPERT, Peter. American (born United States), b. 1942. **Genres:** Poetry, Literary Criticism And History, Gay And Lesbian Issues, Autobiography/Memoirs, Humanities. **Career:** Rollins College, instructor in English, 1968-71; Harvard University, Briggs-Copeland lecturer in English and general education, 1971-74; New College, lecturer, 1972; College of William and Mary, writer-in-residence, 1976-77, assistant professor, 1977-78; George Mason University, assistant professor, 1978-81, director of writing program, 1979-80, 1985-88, associate professor, 1981-91, professor, 1991-2007, Master of Fine Arts Program in Poetry, director, 1995-98. Writer. **Publications:** Lugging Vegetables to Nantucket, 1971; Circular Stairs, Distress in the Mirrors, 1975; Non Sequitur O'Connor, 1977; The Idiot Princess of the Last Dynasty, 1984; '52 Pick-Up: Scenes from the Conspiracy, A Documentary, 1984; Chokecherries: New and Selected Poems, 1966-99, 2000; Circular Stairs, Distress in the Mirrors, 2008. Contributor to periodicals. **Address:** Department of English, George Mason University, 4400 University Dr., Fairfax, VA 22030, U.S.A. **Online address:** peterklappert@comcast.net

KLARE, Michael T(homas). American (born United States), b. 1942. **Genres:** International Relations/Current Affairs, Military/Defense/Arms Control, Politics/Government, History, Business/Trade/Industry. **Career:** Parsons School of Design, instructor in art history, 1967-70; North American Congress on Latin America, research director, 1970-76; Tufts University Experimental College, visiting instructor, 1973; Princeton University, Center of International Studies, visiting fellow, 1976-77; Institute for Policy Studies, fellow and co-director of program on national security, 1977-84; University of California, Institute for International Studies, associate research analyst, 1983; Hampshire College, Five College Professor of Peace and World Security Studies, 1985-, Five College Program in Peace and World Security Studies, director, 1985-; Wellesley College, professor of peace studies, visiting associate, 1992-93; Nation, defense correspondent. Writer. **Publications:** (Comp.) University-Military-Police Complex: A Directory and Related Documents, 1970; War without End: American Planning for the Next Vietnams, 1972; (with C. Arnson, D. Miller and D. Volman) Supplying Repression: U.S. Support for Authoritarian Regimes Abroad, 1978, rev. ed., 1981; (with N. Stein) Armas y poder en América Latina, 1978; Beyond the Vietnam Syndrome: U.S. Interventionism in the 1980s, 1981; American Arms Supermarket, 1984; Rogue States and Nuclear Outlaws, 1995; (with D. Anderson) A Scourge of Guns: The Diffusion of Small Arms and Light Weapons in Latin America, 1996; Scourge of Small Arms, 1999; Resource Wars: The New Landscape of Global Conflict, 2001; Blood and Oil: The Dangers and Consequences of America's Growing Petroleum Dependency, 2004; Rising Powers, Shrinking Planet: The New Geopolitics of Energy, 2008; The Race for What's Left: The Global Scramble for the World's Last Resources, 2011. EDITOR: (with P. Kornbluh) Low Intensity Warfare: Counterinsurgency, Proinsurgency, and Antiterrorism in the Eighties, 1988; (with D.C. Thomas) Peace and World Order Studies: A Curriculum Guide, 5th ed., 1989; Peace and World Security Studies: A Curriculum Guide, 6th ed., 1993; (with D.C. Thomas) World Security: Trends and Challenges, 1991, 3rd ed., (with Y. Chandrani), 1998; (with J. Boutwell and L.W. Reed) Lethal Commerce: The Global Trade in Small Arms and Light Weapons: A Collection of Essays from a Project of the American Academy of Arts and Sciences, 1995; (with J. Boutwell) Light Weapons and Civil Conflict, 1999. Contributor to books. **Address:** Peace and World Security Studies, Hampshire College, G8 Franklin Patterson Hall, 893 West St., Amherst, MA 01002, U.S.A. **Online address:** mtkss@hampshire.edu

KLARMAN, Michael Joseph. American (born United States), b. 1959. **Genres:** Social Sciences. **Career:** U.S. Court of Appeals, law clerk to Judge Ruth Bader Ginsburg, 1983-84; University of Virginia, assistant professor, 1987-92, professor, 1992-98, research professor of law, 1993-96, F. Palmer Weber research professor of civil liberties and human rights, 1997-2000, professor of history, 2003, James Monroe distinguished professor of law, 2003-, Elizabeth D. and Richard A. Merrill fesearch professor, 2003-; Harvard University, Ralph S. Tyler, Jr. visiting professor of law, 2006, Kirkland and Ellis professor of law, 2008. Writer. **Publications:** From Jim Crow to Civil Rights: The Supreme Court and the Struggle for Racial Equality, 2004; Unfinished Business: Racial Equality in American History, 2007. contribuot of articles to books, journals and periodicals. **Address:** School of Law, University of Virginia, 580 Massie Rd., Charlottesville, VA 22901-1789, U.S.A. **Online address:** mklarman@law.harvard.edu

KLASS, David. American (born United States), b. 1960. **Genres:** Science Fiction/Fantasy, Novels. **Career:** Writer and educator. **Publications:** The Atami Dragons, 1984; Breakaway Run, 1986; A Different Season, 1988; Wrestling with Honor, 1989; Night of the Tyger, 1990; Samurai Inc., 1992; California Blue, 1994; Danger Zone, 1995; Screen Test, 1997; (with R. Tine) Desperate Measures, 1998; You Don't Know Me, 2001; Home of the Braves, 2002; You Don't Know Me: A Novel, 2002; Dark Angel, 2005; Firestorm,

2006; Whirlwind, 2008; Timelock, 2009; Stuck on Earth, 2010. **Address:** Aaron M. Priest Literary Agency Inc., 708 3rd Ave., 23rd Fl., New York, NY 10017-4201, U.S.A.

KLASS, Perri (Elizabeth). American (born United States), b. 1958. **Genres:** Novels, Autobiography/Memoirs, Novellas/Short Stories, Essays, Medicine/Health, Autobiography/Memoirs. **Career:** Boston's Children's Hospital, resident in pediatrics, 1986-89; Dorchester House, pediatrician, 1993-2006; Reach Out and Read, national medical director; New York University, professor of journalism and pediatrics. Writer. **Publications:** Recombinations, 1985; I Am Having an Adventure, 1986; A Not Entirely Benign Procedure: Four Years as a Medical Student, 1987; Other Women's Children, 1990; Baby Doctor: A Pediatrician's Training, 1992, rev. ed., 2010; Taking Care of Your Own, 1992; Love and Modern Medicine, 2001; (with E. Costello) Quirky Kids: Understanding and Helping Your Child Who Doesn't Fit In, When to Worry and When Not to Worry, 2003; The Mystery of Breathing, 2004; Two Sweaters for My Father: Writing About Knitting, 2004; (with S.S. Klass) Every Mother Is A Daughter: The Never ending Quest for Success, Inner Peace and a Really Clean Kitchen, 2006; Treatment Kind and Fair: Letters to a Young Doctor, 2007; The Mercy Rule, 2008; (ed.) Real Life of a Pediatrician, 2009. **Address:** Arthur L. Carter Journalism Institute, 20 Cooper Sq., New York, NY 10003, U.S.A. **Online address:** perri.klass@nyu.edu

KLASS, Sheila Solomon. American (born United States), b. 1927. **Genres:** Novels, Autobiography/Memoirs, Children's Fiction, Young Adult Fiction. **Career:** Julia Ward Howe School, English teacher, 1951-57; writer, 1964-; City University of New York, Borough of Manhattan Community College, Department of English, lecturer, 1965-67, instructor, 1967-68, assistant professor, 1968-73, associate professor, 1973-82, professor of English, 1982-99, professor emeritus, 2000-. **Publications:** Come Back on Monday, 1960; Everyone in This House Makes Babies, 1964; Bahadur Means Hero, 1969; A Perpetual Surprise, 1981; Nobody Knows Me in Miami, 1981; To See My Mother Dance, 1981; Alive & Starting Over, 1983; The Bennington Stitch, 1985; Page Four, 1986; Credit Card Carole, 1987; Kool Ada, 1991; Rhino, 1993; Next Stop: Nowhere, 1995; A Shooting Star: A Novel about Annie Oakley, 1996; In a Cold Open Field, 1997; The Uncivil War, 1997; Little Women Next Door, 2000; (with P. Klass) Every Mother is a Daughter: The Never Ending Quest for Success, Inner Peace and A Really Clean Kitchen, 2006; Soldier's Secret: The Secret Story of Deborah Sampson, 2009; (contrib.) Mother Daughter, 2009; The Marble Princess, forthcoming. **Address:** Borough of Manhattan Community College, City University of New York, 199 Chambers St., New York, NY 10007, U.S.A. **Online address:** shkla3@aol.com

KLAUCK, Hans-Josef. American/German (born Germany), b. 1946. **Genres:** Theology/Religion. **Career:** Bayrische Ludwig Maximilians University, Institute of Biblical Exegesis, research assistant, 1975-77, assistant professor, 1978-81; Rheinische Friedrich Wilhelm University, Catholic Theological School, professor, 1981-82; Bayrische Julius Maximilians University, Catholic Theological School, professor of New Testament exegesis, 1982-97; Westfälische Wilhelms University, Catholic Thelogical School, professor of New Testament, 1992; Bayrische Ludwig Maximilians University, Catholic-Theological School, professor of New Testament exegesis, 1997-2001; University of Pretoria, Dutch Reformed Theological School, honorary professor of New Testament exegesis, 1999-2003; University of Chicago, Divinity School, professor of New Testament and early Christian literature, 2001-, Department of New Testament and Early Christian Literature in the Humanities Division, professor, 2001-, Naomi Shenstone Donnelley professor of New Testament and early Christian literature, 2006-. Writer. **Publications:** Allegorie und Allegorese in Synoptischen Gleichnixtexten, 1978; Hausgemeinde und Hauskirche im frühen Christentum, 1981; Herrenmahl und hellenistischer Kult: Eine Religionsgeschichtliche Untersuchung Zumersten Korintherbrief, 1982; Judas, Ein Jünger des Herrn, 1987, rev. ed. as Judas, un Disciple de Jésus: Exégèse et Répercussions Historiques, 2006; Dererste Johannesbriefe, 1991; Der zweite und dritte Johannesbrief, 1992; Alte Welt und Neucr Glaube: Beiträge zur Religiongeschichte, Forschungsgeschichte und Theologie des Neuen Testaments, 1994; Die Interpretation der Bibel in der Kirche: Das Dokumentder Päpstlichen Bibelkommission vom 23.4.1993, 1995; Die Religiose Umwelt des Urchristentums, 2 vols., 1995-1996; Magie und Heidentum in der Apostelgeschichte des Lukas, 1996; Vorspiel im Himmel?: Erzähltechnik und Theologie im Markusprolog, 1997; Die Antike Briefliteratur und das Neue Testament, 1998, rev. ed. as (with D.P. Bailey) Ancient Letters and the New Testament: A Guide to Context and Exegesis, 2006; Dion von Prusa: Olympischerere, 2000; Olympikos, 2000; Apokryphe Evangelien

eine Eintührung, 2002; Religion und Gesellschaft im Frühen Christentum: Neutestamentliche Studien, 2003; Die Apokryphe Bibel: Ein Anderer Zugang zum frühen Christentum, 2008; The Apocryphal Acts of the Apostles: An Introduction, 2008. EDITOR: Monotheismus und Christologie: Zur Gottesfrage im Hellenistischen Judentumund im Urchristentum, 1992; Weltgericht und Weltvollendung: Zukunftsbilderim Testament, 1994; (co-ed.) Encyclopedia of the Bible and Its Reception, 2009. Contributor to periodicals. **Address:** University of Chicago Divinity School, 306 D Swift Hall, 1025 E 58th St., Chicago, IL 60637, U.S.A. **Online address:** klauck@midway.uchicago.edu

KLAUSE, Annette Curtis. American/British (born England), b. 1953. **Genres:** Science Fiction/Fantasy. **Career:** Department of Public Libraries, staff, 1981-; substitute librarian, 1981-82; Silver Spring Community Library, children's librarian I, 1981; Montgomery County Department of Public Libraries, substitute librarian, 1981-82; Kensington Park Community Library, part-time children's librarian, 1982-84; Bethesda Regional Library, full-time children's librarian I, 1984-89; Olney Community Library, head of children's services, 1989-91; Kensington Park Community Library, head of children's services, 1991-92; Aspen Hill Community Library, head of children's services, 1992-. Writer. **Publications:** The Silver Kiss, 1990; Alien Secrets, 1993; Blood and Chocolate, 1997; Freaks: Alive, on the Inside!, 2006; Restless Dead: Ten Original Stories of the Supernatural, 2007. Contributor of articles to journals. **Address:** Margaret K. McElderry Books, Simon & Schuster Children's Publishing Division, 1230 Ave. of the Americas, New York, NY 10020-1586, U.S.A. **Online address:** human_oddity@juno.com

KLAUSEN, Jytte. American/Danish (born Denmark), b. 1954. **Genres:** History, Women's Studies And Issues, Social Sciences, Politics/Government, Economics. **Career:** University of Aarhus, assistant professor, 1986-88; Brandeis University, assistant professor, 1992-98, associate professor of political science, 1998, director of graduate studies in politics, professor, 2006, Lawrence A. Wien professor of international cooperation, 2009; Harvard University, Radcliffe College, Mary Ingraham Bunting Institute, fellow, 1996-97; Nuffield College, British academy visiting professor, 2003; American Academy, Berlin, fellow, 2004. Writer. **Publications:** Mocambique: Socialisme i Afrika, 1978; (ed. with L.A. Tilly) European Integration in a Social and Historical Perspective: 1850 to the Present, 1997; War and Welfare: Europe and the United States 1945 to the Present, 1998; (ed. with C.S. Maier) Has Liberalism Failed Women?: Assuring Equal Representation in Europe and the United States, 2001; Islamic Challenge: Politics and Religion in Western Europe, 2005; Europas muslimische Eliten, 2006; Cartoons that Shook the World, 2009; Western Jihadism, forthcoming. Contributor to books. **Address:** Department of Politics, Brandeis University, MS 058 415 South St., Olin-Sang, 110, PO Box 549110, Waltham, MA 02454-9110, U.S.A. **Online address:** klausen@brandeis.edu

KLAVAN, Andrew. Also writes as Margaret Tracy, Keith R. Peterson. American (born United States), b. 1954. **Genres:** Novels, Adult Non-fiction, Young Adult Fiction, Mystery/Crime/Suspense. **Career:** Manhattan Institute, City Journal, contributing editor; WOR Radio, news writer; ABC Radio Network, news writer. Journalist. **Publications:** NOVELS: Face of the Earth: A Novel, 1980; Darling Clementine, 1988; Son of Man, 1988; Don't Say a Word, 1991; The Animal Hour, 1993; Corruption, 1993; True Crime: The Novel, 1995; The Uncanny, 1998; Hunting Down Amanda, 1999; Man and Wife, 2001; Dynamite Road, 2003; Shotgun Alley, 2004; Damnation Street, 2006; Empire of Lies, 2008; Last Thing I Remember, 2009; Identity Man, 2010; Long Way Home, 2010; The Truth of the Matter, 2010; The Final Hour: The Last Homelanders Novel, 2011. NOVELS AS KEITH PETERSON: Eleanora, My Love, 1988; The Rain, 1988; There Fell a Shadow, 1988; The Trapdoor, 1988; Rough Justice, 1989; The Scarred Man, 1990. NOVELS AS MARGARET TRACY: Mrs. White, 1983. **Address:** Crown Publishing, 201 E 50th St., New York, NY 10022, U.S.A. **Online address:** andrew@andrewklavan.com

KLAVENESS, Jan O'Donnell. (Jan O'Donnell). American (born United States), b. 1939. **Genres:** Children's Fiction, Mystery/Crime/Suspense, Young Adult Fiction. **Career:** University of Michigan, assistant director of student organizations, 1963-65; Hofstra University, assistant director of financial aid, 1979-82. Writer. **Publications:** (As Jan O'Donnell) A Funny Girl Like Me, 1980; The Griffin Legacy, 1983; Ghost Island, 1985; Keeper of the Light, 1990; Beyond the Cellar Door, 1991. Contributor to periodicals. **Address:** 41 Vliet Dr., Hillsborough, NJ 08844-2238, U.S.A.

KLEBANOFF, Arthur. American (born United States), b. 1951?. **Genres:**

Business/Trade/Industry, Autobiography/Memoirs. **Career:** Morton L. Janklow Associates Inc., co-founder; Janklow, Traum & Klebanoff, partner; International Management Group, vice president and head of publishing division, 1991; Scott Meredith Literary Agency, owner and president, 1993-; Rosetta Books L.L.C. (electronic publishing company), co-founder and chief executive officer, 2001-. Writer. **Publications:** The Agent: Personalities, Politics, and Publishing, 2002. **Address:** The Scott Meredith Literary Agency, 200 W 57th St., Ste. 904, New York, NY 10019-3211, U.S.A. **Online address:** aklebanoff@rosettabooks.com

KLECK, Gary. American (born United States), b. 1951. **Genres:** Criminology/True Crime. **Career:** Florida State University, School of Criminology, instructor, 1978-79, assistant professor, 1979-84, associate professor, 1984-91, College of Criminology and Criminal Justice, professor, 1991-, David J. Bordua professor of criminology, College of Law, Courtesy professor of law, Graduate Student Association, faculty adviser, 2001-, Honors Programs, director, 2002-. Writer. **Publications:** Point Blank: Guns and Violence in America, 1991; (with D.B. Kates) The Great American Gun Debate: Essays on Firearms & Violence, 1997; Targeting Guns: Firearms and Their Controls, 1997; (with D.B. Kates) Armed: New Perspectives on Gun Control, 2001. Contributor to periodicals. **Address:** College of Criminology and Criminal Justice, Florida State University, 306 Hecht House, 634 W Call St., Tallahassee, FL 32306-1127, U.S.A. **Online address:** gkleck@fsu.edu

KLEH, Cindy (L.). American (born United States), b. 1959. **Genres:** Sports/Fitness, How-to Books, Marine Sciences/Oceanography, Natural History, Photography, Children's Non-fiction, Writing/Journalism, Young Adult Nonfiction, Zoology, Autobiography/Memoirs, Humor/Satire, Adult Non-fiction, Homes/Gardens, Ghost Writer, Dance/Ballet, Environmental Sciences/Ecology, Crafts, Novels. **Career:** Summit Outdoors, columnist, 1993-98; Mountain Gazette Magazine, editor, 1999-; Ten Mile Times, writer, 1999-2001; freelance writer, 2000-; Alpenglow Magazine, writer, 2004-06; Winter Park Manifest, associate editor, 2005-06; Grand County Living Magazine, editor, 2006-; Nordic Ski Colorado, editor, 2010-; National Sports Center for the Disabled, snowboard and horseback riding instructor; Winter Park Resort, snowboard instructor. **Publications:** Snowboarding Skills: The Back-to-Basic Essentials for All Levels, 2002; Get Outdoors: Skiing, 2010; Be A Pro Snowboarder, 2012. Contributor to magazines and newspapers. **Address:** Rm. 34, 9921 Hwy., Ste. 12, Grand Lake, CO 80447, U.S.A. **Online address:** ckleh63193@aol.com

KLEHR, Harvey. American (born United States), b. 1945. **Genres:** History, Politics/Government. **Career:** University of North Carolina, NDEA Title IV Fellow, 1967-70, teaching assistant, 1968-71; Emory University, assistant professor, 1971-76, associate professor, 1977-82, professor, 1983-85, Samuel Candler Dobbs professor of politics, 1985-96, professor of history, 1986-, chairman, 1989-95, Andrew W. Mellon professor of politics and history, 1996-, director of undergraduate studies, 1975-77, 1988-89, The Bill and Carol Fox Center for Humanistic Inquiry, senior fellow, 2007-08, Program in Democracy and Citizenship, director, 2009-; Journal of Politics, acting news and notes editor, 1974-75; Historians of American Communism, vice president, 1983, president, 1985-86; Phi Beta Kappa Society, vice president, 1984, president, 1985; Healey Inc., staff, 1986-89; League for Industrial Democracy, board director, 1986-92; Atlanta YAD, vice president, 1993-96. **Publications:** Communist Cadre: The Social Background of the American Communist Party Elite, 1978; The Heyday of American Communism: The Depression Decade, 1984; (ed. with B.K. Johnpoll) Biographical Dictionary of the American Left, 1986; Far Left of Center: The American Radical Left Today, 1988; The American Communist Movement: Storming Heaven Itself, 1992; (foreword) It Had to be Revolution, 1993; (with R. Radosh) The Amerasia Spy Case, 1996; (with J.E. Haynes and K.M. Anderson) The Soviet World of American Communism, 1998; (with J.E. Haynes) Venona: Decoding Soviet Espionage in America, 1999; (with J.E. Haynes) In Denial: Historians, Communism & Espionage, 2003; (with J.E. Haynes) Early Cold War Spies: The Espionage Trials that Shaped American Politics, 2006; (with J.E. Haynes and A. Vassiliev) Spies: The Rise and Fall of the KGB in America, 2009; Communist Experience in America: A Political and Social History, 2010. Contributor to journals. **Address:** Department of Political Science, Emory University, 305 Tarbutton Hall, 1555 Dickey Dr., Atlanta, GA 30322, U.S.A. **Online address:** polshk@emory.edu

KLEIMAN, Ed. Canadian (born Canada), b. 1932. **Genres:** Novellas/Short Stories, Literary Criticism And History, Young Adult Fiction, Children's Fiction. **Career:** University of Manitoba, lecturer, associate professor of English, 1961-96, Department of English Film and Theatre, now faculty emeritus. Writer. **Publications:** Leonard Cohen: Blossom Show in The Artist and His Critics (casebook), 1976; The Immortals (stories), 1980; A New-Found Ecstasy (stories), 1988; The World Beaters (stories), 1998. Works appear in anthologies. **Address:** Department of English Film and Theatre, University of Manitoba, 66 Chancellors Cir., Winnipeg, MB R3T 2N2, Canada. **Online address:** EdKleiman@shaw.ca

KLEIMAN, Mark A. R. American (born United States), b. 1951. **Genres:** Education, Social Work, Reference. **Career:** U.S. House of Representatives, legislative assistant, 1974-75; Polaroid Corp., special assistant, 1975-76; City of Boston, Office of Management and Budget, director of program analysis, 1977-78, deputy director for management, 1978-79; U.S. Department of Justice, Criminal Division, Office of Policy and Management Analysis, associate director for drug enforcement programs, 1979-82, director, 1982-83; University of Rochester, visiting senior lecturer in public policy, 1985-86; Harvard University, John F. Kennedy School of Government, lecturer, 1987-92, associate professor of public policy, 1992-96, research fellow; University of California, School of Public Affairs, professor of policy studies, 1996-, Drug Policy Analysis Program, director, Jacob Marschak Interdisciplinary Colloquium on Mathematics in the Social Sciences, co-director; Pew Charitable Trust, consultant. Writer. **Publications:** Risks and Prices: An Economic Analysis of Drug Enforcement, 1986; AIDS, Vice and Public Policy, 1988; With This Test I Thee Wed: Evaluating Premarital AIDS Testing, 1988; (contrib.) Street-Level Drug Enforcement, 1988; Marijuana: Costs of Abuse, Costs of Control, 1989; The Optimal Design of Drug Control Laws, 1991; Neither Prohibition Nor Legalization: Grudging Toleration in Drug Control Policy, 1992; Against Excess: Drug Policy for Results, 1992; (with A.L. Chalsma, D. Boyum and J. Nambiar) Marijuana Situation Assessment, 1994; Opportunities and Barriers in Probation Reform: A Case Study of Drug Testing and Sanctions, 2003; Political Philosophy: Religiosity, Piety, Humility and Democracy, 2005; Dueling Failures: Comparative Institutional Analysis and the Logic of Policy Choice, 2006; Alcohol as a Drug: A Moral Revolution, 2007; Dopey, Boozy, Smokey and Stupid, 2007; Fixing the Parole System, 2008; Jail Break, 2009; The Dynamics of Deterrence, 2009; When Brute Force Fails: How to Have Less Crime and Less Punishment, 2009; Drug Policy: Advice for the New Drug Czar, 2009; (with J.P. Caulkins and A. Hawken) Drugs and Drug Policy: What Everyone Needs to Know, 2011; (ed. with J.E. Hawdon) Encyclopedia of Drug Policy, 2011. **Address:** Department of Policy Studies, School of Public Affairs, University of California Los Angeles, 3250 Public Affairs Bldg., Los Angeles, CA 90095-1656, U.S.A. **Online address:** kleiman@ucla.edu

KLEIN, Adam. British (born England) **Genres:** Art/Art History, Young Adult Fiction, Novellas/Short Stories. **Career:** Writer. **Publications:** The Medicine Burns, 1995; (with T. Avena) Jerome: After the Pageant, 1996; Tiny Ladies, 2003. Contributor to journals and magazines. **Address:** c/o Author Mail, Serpent, 4 Black Stock Mews, London, GL N4 2BT, England.

KLEIN, Alan M. American (born United States), b. 1946?. **Genres:** Sports/Fitness. **Career:** Pacific Lutheran University, visiting assistant professor of anthropology, 1975-77; The Evergreen State College, visiting assistant professor of anthropology, 1977-78; Northeastern University, assistant professor of sociology and anthropology, 1979-85, associate professor of sociology and anthropology, 1986-92, professor of sociology and anthropology, 1992-; California State University, visiting assistant professor of anthropology, 1981-82; Wheaton College, William Cole professor of anthropology, 2009. Writer. **Publications:** Sugarball: The American Game, The Dominican Dream, 1991; Little Big Men: Bodybuilding Subculture and Gender Construction, 1993; Baseball on the Border: A Tale of Two Laredos, 1997; Growing the Game: The Globalization of Major League Baseball, 2006; Sport, Culture and Politics, 2006; New Pride, Old Prejudice: The Second Coming of Dominican Baseball, forthcoming. **Address:** Department of Sociology and Anthropology, Northeastern University, 517 Holmes Hall, 400 Huntington Ave., Boston, MA 02115, U.S.A. **Online address:** a.klein@neu.edu

KLEIN, Alec. American (born United States), b. 1967. **Genres:** Novels. **Career:** Washington Post, journalist, 2000, investigative business reporter; University of Wisconsin, business writer-in-residence; American University, faculty; Georgetown University, faculty; Virginian-Pilot, reporter; Baltimore Sun, reporter; Wall Street Journal, reporter; Northwestern University, Medill School, professor. **Publications:** Stealing Time: Steve Case Jerry Levin and the Collapse of AOL Time Warner, 2003; Beast of Love, 2006; A Class Apart: Prodigies, Pressure and Passion Inside One of America's Best High Schools, 2007. **Address:** Medill School Northwestern University, 1845 Sheridan Rd., Fisk 201B, Evanston, IL 60208-2101, U.S.A. **Online address:** alec-klein@northwestern.edu

KLEIN, Allen. American (born United States), b. 1938. **Genres:** Medicine/Health, Psychology, Self Help, Humor/Satire, Reference. **Career:** CBS-TV, scenic designer, 1962-71; San Francisco Opera, scenic artist, 1971-72; WORKS Silkscreen Studio, owner, 1972-78; Holistic Life Institute, director and teacher, 1979-82; speaker and writer, 1983-; The Association for Applied and Therapeutic Humor, president, 2005-06. **Publications:** The Healing Power of Humor, 1989; (comp.) Quotations to Cheer You Up When the World is Getting You Down, 1991; Wing Tips: How to Deal with Airline Delays, Cursed Cancellations, Lamentably Lost Luggage and Any Unexpected Adversity and Still Keep Smiling, 1996; The Courage to Laugh: Humor, Hope, and Healing in the Face of Death and Dying, 1998; (comp.) Up Words for Down Days, 1998; (comp.) The Change-Your-Life Quote Book, 2000; (comp.) The Lift-Your-Spirits Quote Book, 2001; Winning Words, 2002; (comp.) The Celebrate-Your-LIfe Quote Book: Over 500 Wise and Wonderful Quotes to Increase Your Joy in Living, 2005; (comp.) The Simplify-Your-Life Quote Book: Over 500 Inspiring Quotations to Help You Relax, Refocus, and Renew, 2005; (comp.) Wise and Witty Quote Book, 2005; (comp.) The Love and Kisses Quote Book, 2006; (comp.) Reflections on Life: Why We're Here and How to Enjoy the Journey, 2006; (comp.) Teacherlaughs: Quips, Quotes, and Anecdotes about the Classroom, 2006; (comp.) Parentlaughs, 2006; (comp.) Worklaughs: Quips, Quotes, and Anecdotes about Making a Buck, 2006; (comp.) Change Your LIfe!: A Little Book of Big Ideas, 2010; (comp.) Inspiration for a Lifetime, 2010; Learning to Laugh When You Feel Like Crying, 2011. **Address:** c/o Michael Larsen, Larsen Pomada Literary Agents, 1029 Jones St., San Francisco, CA 94109, U.S.A. **Online address:** info@allenklein.com

KLEIN, Anne Carolyn. American (born United States), b. 1947?. **Genres:** Theology/Religion, Humanities, Women's Studies And Issues, Area Studies, Translations, Social Sciences. **Career:** Mary Washington College, instructor in classics, philosophy and religion, 1981; University of Virginia, lecturer in religious studies, 1981-82; Harvard University, research associate in women's studies, 1982-83, Harvard Divinity School, research associate history of religion, 1982-83; Stanford University, lecturer, 1984-86, Jing Lyman lecturer, 1986, acting assistant professor of religious studies, 1986-89; Rice University, assistant professor, 1989-91, associate professor, 1989-95, professor of religious studies and head of department, 1995-, chair; Fairfield University, annual visiting lecturer, 1991; Namgyal Monastery, Institute of Buddhist Studies, adjunct faculty, 1992-; University of Hawaii, Numata distinguished professor lecturer, 1995; Dawn Mountain Tibetan Temple, co-founder, Community Center and Research Institute, faculty, 1996-. Writer. **Publications:** (Contrib.) The Buddhism of Tibet and the Key to the Middle Way, 1975; (contrib.) The Precious Garland and the Song of the Four Mindfulnesses, 1975; (contrib.) Compassion in Tibetan Buddhism, 1980; (ed. with Hopkins) Tantric Practice in Nyingma, 1982; (ed.) The Tantric Distinction: A Buddhist's Reflection on Compassion and Emptiness, 1984, rev. ed., 1999; Knowledge & Liberation: Tibetan Buddhist Epistemology in Support of Transformative Religious Experience, 1986, 2nd ed., 1992; (trans. and intro.) Knowing, Naming, and Negation: A Sourcebook on Tibetan Sautrāntika, 1991; (ed. with L. Zahler) Walking Through Walls: A Presentation of Tibetan Meditation, 1992; (trans, ed. and intro.) Path to the Middle: Oral Mādhyamika Philosophy in Tibet, the Spoken Scholarship of Kensur Yeshey Tupden, 1994; Meeting the Great Bliss Queen: Buddhists, Feminists, and the Art of the Self, 1994; (ed. with L. Zahler) Calm Abiding & Special Insight: Achieving Spiritual Transformation Through Meditation, 1998; (with G.T.W. Rinpoche) Unbounded Wholeness: Dzogchen, Bon, and the Logic of the Nonconceptual, 2006; Heart Essence of the Vast Expanse: A Story of Transmission, 2009. Contributor of articles to books and journals. **Address:** Department of Religious Studies, Rice University, 221 Humanities Bldg., 6100 Main St., MS-15, PO Box 1892, Houston, TX 77005-1892, U.S.A. **Online address:** ack@rice.edu

KLEIN, Cornelis. American (born United States), b. 1937. **Genres:** Earth Sciences, Sciences. **Career:** Harvard University, lecturer, 1965-69, Leverett House, Allston Burr senior tutor, 1966-70, associate professor of mineralogy, 1969-72; Indiana University-Bloomington, professor of mineralogy, 1972-84; University of New Mexico, professor of geology, through 2002, now profes-

sor emeritus and presidential teaching fellow. Writer. **Publications:** Minerals and Rocks: Exercises in Crystallography, Mineralogy, and Hand Specimen Petrology, 1989, 3rd ed. as Minerals and Rocks: Exercises in Crystal Chemistry and Mineral Chemistry, Crystallography, X-ray Powder Diffraction, Mineral and Rock Identification, and Ore Mineralogy, 2007; (co-ed.) The Proterozoic Biosphere, 1992; (co-author) UN: Jungtines Tautosir Lietuva, means The United Nations and Lithuania, 1997; (with C.S. Hurlbut) Manual of Mineralogy, 23rd ed., 2008; (with T. Philpotts) Earth Materials, 2012. **Address:** Department of Earth and Planetary Sciences, University of New Mexico, Rm. 212, Northrop Hall, 1 University of New Mexico, PO Box 03 2040, Albuquerque, NM 87131-0001, U.S.A. **Online address:** cklein@unm.edu

KLEIN, Donald F. American (born United States), b. 1928. **Genres:** Medicine/Health, Psychology, Reference. **Career:** U.S. Public Health Service Hospital, rotating intern, 1952-53; Creedmoor State Hospital, resident in psychiatry, 1953-54, 1956-58; Creedmoor Institute for Psychobiologic Studies, research associate, 1957-59; Hillside Hospital, research associate, 1959-64, senior staff psychiatrist, 1965, director of research, 1965-70, medical director for evaluation, 1970-71; Queens College of the City University of New York, adjunct professor, 1969-92; Queens Hospital Center, psychiatrist in chief, 1970-71, full attending psychiatrist, 1972-85; Long Island Jewish-Hillside Medical Center, director of research and evaluation in psychiatry, 1972-76; State University of New York, Stony Brook, professor of psychiatry, 1972-76; University of Auckland, visiting professor, 1975; Columbia University, department of therapeutics, director, 1976-, New York State Psychiatric Institute, director, 1976-, lecturer, 1976-78, professor of psychiatry, 1978, now professor emeritus; Yeshiva University, Albert Einstein College of Medicine, visiting professor, 1976-; New York Presbyterian Hospital, attending psychiatrist, 1977-, attending physician; University of Hawaii at Manoa, visiting professor, 1977, 1985, 1986; New York State Psychiatric Mental Health Clinical Research Center, director, 1978-; National Foundation for Depressive Illness, president, 1983-; Montefiore Medical Center, psychiatrist, 1995-; Nathan S Kline Institute for Psychiatric, research psychiatrist; New York University, Langone Medical Center, Department of Child and Adolescent Psychiatry, research professor; The Council for Scientific Medicine and Mental Health, fellow, 2003-; Consumer Reports Best Buy Drugs Project, reviewer, 2005-; The Scientific Review of Alternative Medicine, research fellow, 2005-. Writer. **Publications:** (With J.M. Davis) Diagnosis and Drug Treatment of Psychiatric Disorders, 1969, (with R. Gittelman, F. Quitkin and A. Rifkin) 2nd ed. as Diagnosis and Drug Treatment of Psychiatric Disorders: Adults and Children, 1980; Psychiatric Case Studies: Treatment, Drugs and Outcome, 1972; The Physicians Handbook on Depression, 1977; (with P.H. Wender) Mind, Mood and Medicine: A Guide to the New Biopsychiatry, 1981; Sexual Aversion, Sexual Phobias and Panic Disorder, 1987; (with P.H. Wender) Do You Have a Depressive Illness?: How to Tell, What to Do, 1988; (with P.H. Wender) Understanding Depression: A Complete Guide to its Diagnosis and Treatment, 1993; Current Neurologic Drugs, 2nd ed., 1998. EDITOR: (with R. Gittelman-Klein and contrib.) Progress in Psychiatric Drug Treatment, vol. I, 1975, vol. II, 1976; (ed. with R.L. Spitzer and contrib.) Evaluation of Psychological Therapies: Psychotherapies, Behavior Therapies, Drug Therapies and Their Interactions, 1976; (with R.L. Spitzer and contrib.) Critical Issues in Psychiatric Diagnosis, 1978; (with J.G. Rabkin and contrib.) Anxiety: New Research and Changing Concepts, 1981; (with M.R. Liebowitz, A.J. Fyer and J.M. Gorman) Modern Problems of Pharmacopsychiatry, vol. XXII: Anxiety, 1987. Contributor of articles to journals. **Address:** Columbia University, 1051 Riverside Dr., Ste. 22, New York, NY 10032, U.S.A. **Online address:** donaldk737@aol.com

KLEIN, George. Swedish/Hungarian (born Hungary), b. 1925. **Genres:** Medicine/Health, Sciences. **Career:** Budapest University, instructor in histology, 1945, instructor in pathology, 1946; Karolinska Institute, research fellow, 1947-49, assistant professor of cell research, 1951-57, Department of Tumor Biology, professor of tumor biology and head, 1957-93, Microbiology and Tumor Biology Center, active research group leader, 1993-, now professor emeritus; Stanford University, visiting professor, 1961; Harvard University, Dunham Lecturer, 1966; American Association of Cancer Research, Clowes Memorial Lecturer, 1967; Swedish Medical Association, Lennander Lecturer, 1967; Hebrew University, Hadassah Medical School, visiting professor, 1973-93; University of Arizona, Donald Wae Waddel Lecturer, 1991. Writer. **Publications:** I stället för Hemland: Memoarer, 1984; Ateisten och den Heliga Staden: Möten och Tankar, 1987; Tumor Suppressor Genes, 1990; (with P. Ahlmark) Motstaandet, 1991; Pietà, 1992; Utvagen, 1992; (with L. Gyllensten) Hack i häl på Minerva: ett Brevsamtal om Vetenskap, 1993; Den Sjunde

Djävulen, 1995; Live Now: Inspiring Accounts of Overcoming Adversity, 1997; Korpens Blick: Essäer om Vetenskap och Moral, 1998; (with P. Ahlmark) Motståndet-med Mera: Tjugo Brev omdöd och liv, 2001; Skapelsens fullkomlighet; 2005; Meteorer, 2008; Jag återvänder aldrig, 2011. EDITOR: Viral Oncology, 1980; Advances in Viral Oncology, 1982; Oncogene Studies, 1982; The Transformation-Associated Cellular p53 Protein, 1982; DNA-Virus Oncogenes and Their Action, 1983; Viral Oncology, 1984; Mechanisms of Neoplastic Transformation at the Cellular Level, 1984; Viruses as the Causative Agents of Naturally Occurring Tumors, 1985; Analysis of Multistep Scenarios in the Natural History of Human or Animal Cancer, 1987; Experimental Approaches to Multifactorial Interactions in Tumor Development, 1987; Cellular Oncogene Activation, 1988; Tumorigenic DNA Viruses, 1989; Tumor Suppressor Genes, 1990. Contributor to periodicals. **Address:** Microbiology and Tumor Biology Center, Karolinska Institute, PO Box 280, Stockholm, 171 77, Sweden. **Online address:** georg.klein@ki.se

KLEIN, Josephine (F. H.). British/German (born Germany), b. 1926. **Genres:** Psychiatry, Sociology, Theology/Religion, Psychology. **Career:** University of Birmingham, assistant lecturer, lecturer in social psychology, 1949-62; University of Oxford, Nuffield College, research fellow, 1962-65; University of Sussex, senior research fellow, 1965-66, reader in social relations, 1966-70; University of London, Goldsmiths College, Community and Youth Work Training, director, 1970-74. Psychotherapist and writer. **Publications:** The Study of Groups, 1956; Working with Groups: The Social Psychology of Discussion and Decision, 1961; Samples from English Cultures, vol. I: Three Preliminary Studies-Aspects of Adult Life in England, 1965, vol. II: Child-Rearing Practices, 1965; Social Class, 1968; Training for the New Helping Professions-Community and Youth Work, 1973; Our Need for Others and Its Roots in Infancy, 1987; Doubts and Certainties in the Practice of Psychology, 1995; Jacob's Ladder: Essays on Experiences of the Ineffable in the Context of Psychotherapy, 2003. **Address:** 58 Roupell St., London, GL SE1 STB, England.

KLEIN, Kathleen Gregory. American (born United States), b. 1946. **Genres:** Women's Studies And Issues, Literary Criticism And History, Mystery/Crime/Suspense. **Career:** Purdue University, assistant professor, 1976-80, associate professor of English and women's studies, 1980-88, Women's Studies Program, coordinator, 1978-82; Southern Connecticut State University, chairperson of department, 1988-91, professor of English, 1991-2002, professor emeritus, 2002-. Writer. **Publications:** The Woman Detective: Gender and Genre, 1988, 2nd ed., 1995; (ed.) Great Women Mystery Writers: Classic to Contemporary, 1994; (ed.) Women Times Three: Writers, Detectives, Readers, 1995; Diversity and Detective Fiction: Race, Gender, Ethnicity, 1999; Deadly Garden Tour, 2004. **Address:** Department of English, Southern Connecticut State University, D265A Engleman Hall, 501 Crescent St., New Haven, CT 06515, U.S.A. **Online address:** kleinrkr@tsaol.com

KLEIN, Lisa M. American (born United States) **Genres:** Novels, Young Adult Non-fiction. **Career:** Ohio State University, assistant professor of English literature, 1989-98, director of writing for children conference, 1998-2000. Writer. **Publications:** NOVELS: Ophelia, 2006; Two Girls of Gettysburg, 2008; Lady MacBeth's Daughter, 2009. NONFICTION: The Exemplary Sidney and the Elizabethan Sonneteer (dissertation), 1998; Be It Remembered: The Story of Trinity Episcopal Church on Capitol Square, 2003. **Address:** Department of English, Ohio State University, 421 Denney Hall, 164 W 17th Ave., Columbus, OH 43210-1370, U.S.A. **Online address:** lisamklein@columbus.rr.com

KLEIN, Marcus. (William Klein). American (born United States), b. 1928. **Genres:** Novellas/Short Stories, Literary Criticism And History, History, Novels, Young Adult Fiction. **Career:** Barnard College, assistant professor, 1952-65, associate professor, 1965-68, professor of English, 1968-; State University of New York, Department of English, chair, 1968-, professor, now professor emeritus. Writer. **Publications:** After Alienation: American Novels in Mid-Century, 1964; American Novel since World War II, 1969; Foreigners: The Making of Modern American Literature 1900-1940, 1981; Easterns, Westerns and Private Eyes: American Matters 1870-1900, 1994. EDITOR: (with R. Pack) Literature for Composition on the Theme of Innocence and Experiences, 1966; (with R. Pack) Innocence and Experience, 1966; (with R. Pack) Short Stories: Classic, Modern, Contemporary, 1967; The American Novel since World War II, 1969. **Address:** Department of English, University at Buffalo, State University of New York, 306 Clemens Hall, Buffalo, NY 14260, U.S.A.

KLEIN, Matthew. American (born United States), b. 1968?. **Genres:** Young Adult Fiction, Novels, Literary Criticism And History. **Career:** Release Software Corp., founder; Tech Planet Inc. (technology firms), founder; Collective 2, founder. Writer. **Publications:** Switchback, 2006; Con Ed, 2007; (with M.T. Loriente) Mentes En Blanco, 2007. Contributor to periodicals. **Address:** Philip G. Spitzer Literary Agency, 50 Talmage Farm Ln., East Hampton, NY 11937, U.S.A.

KLEIN, Norman M. American (born United States), b. 1945. **Genres:** Art/Art History, History, Politics/Government. **Career:** California Institute of the Arts, professor in European studies, popular culture and writing, 1974-; KCET, Los Angeles History Project, series advisor, 1989-90; Art Issues, contributing editor, 1989-; Smithsonian Institute, associate curator, 1994. **Publications:** (Contrib.) Helter Skelter: L.A. Art in the 1990s, 1992; Seven Minutes: The Life and Death of the American Animated Cartoon, 1993; The History of Forgetting: Los Angeles and the Erasure of Memory, 1998; (with P. Noever) Martin Kippenberger: The Last Stop West, 1999; (with R. Comella) Norman Klein: Bleeding Through-Layers of Los Angeles, 1920-1986, 2003; Vatican to Vegas: A History of Special Effects, 2004; (with L. Woods and P. Noever) Architectural Resistance: Contemporary Architects Face Schindler Today, 2004; Rosson Crow, Night At The Palomino 2007, 2007. EDITOR: (with R. Hertz) 20th Century Art Theory: Urbanism, Politics, Mass Culture, 1990; (with M.J. Schiesl) 20th Century Los Angeles: Power, Promotion and Social Conflict, 1990. **Address:** School of Critical Studies, California Institute of the Arts, 24700 McBean Pkwy., Rm. E118, Valencia, CA 91355, U.S.A. **Online address:** nklein@calarts.edu

KLEIN, Philip Alexander. See Obituaries.

KLEIN, Rachel S. American (born United States), b. 1953. **Genres:** Art/Art History, History, Young Adult Fiction, Social Sciences. **Career:** Writer. **Publications:** (With L. Rexer) One-Hundred-Twenty-Five Years of Expedition and Discovery: The American Museum of Natural History, 1995; (with G. Aiken) Moonlight and Music (juvenile art book), 1997; The Moth Diaries: A Novel, 2003. Contributor to periodicals. **Address:** 112 Park Pl., Brooklyn, NY 11217, U.S.A.

KLEIN, Richard. American (born United States), b. 1941?. **Genres:** Food And Wine, Novels. **Career:** Yale University, instructor, 1966-68; Johns Hopkins University, assistant professor, 1968-74, director of the graduate program, 1973-74; Cornell University, Department of Romance Studies, associate professor, 1974-87, Cornell in Paris Program, director, 1986-87, 1990-91, professor of French literature, 1988-, Cornell Abroad, 1990-91, director of graduate studies, 2001; Diacritics, editor, 1990-95. Writer. **Publications:** Cigarettes Are Sublime, 1993; Eat Fat, 1996; Jewelry Talks: A Novel Thesis, 2001. Contributor of articles to periodicals and journals. **Address:** Department of Romance Studies, Cornell University, Rm. 323A, 303 Morrill Hall, Ithaca, NY 14853-0001, U.S.A. **Online address:** rjk11@cornell.edu

KLEIN, Robin (McMaugh). Australian (born Australia), b. 1936. **Genres:** Children's Fiction, Novellas/Short Stories, Literary Criticism And History, Philosophy, History, Education. **Career:** Writer, 1981-. **Publications:** The Giraffe in Pepperell Street, 1978; Honoured Guest, 1979, rev. ed., 1989; Thing, 1982; Sprung!, 1982; Junk Castle, 1983; Penny Pollard's Diary, 1983; Oodoolay, 1983; People Might Hear You, 1983; Hating Alison Ashley, 1984; Brock and the Dragon, 1984; Thalia the Failure, 1984; Thingnapped!, 1984; Penny Pollard's Letters, 1984; Ratbags and Rascals, 1984; The Tomb Comb, 1984; Halfway Across the Galaxy and Turn Left, 1985; Annabel's Ghost, 1985; Separate Places, 1985; Separate Places, 1985; Snakes and Ladders: Poems about the Ups and Downs of Life, 1985; Penny Pollard in Print, 1986; The Princess Who Hated It, 1986; Boss of the Pool, 1986; Games, 1986; (with M. Dann) The Lonely Hearts Club, 1987; Brik the Berseker, 1987; Robin Klein's Crookbook, 1987; Get Lost, 1987; The Last Pirate, 1987; Parker-Hamilton, 1987; Christmas, 1987; I Shot an Arrow, 1987; Don't Tell Lucy, 1987; How Writers Write, 1987; The Inside Story: Creating Children's Books, 1987; The Story Makers, 1987; Birk the Berserker, 1987; Into Books: Literature Pack No.3, 1988; Stanley's Smile, 1988; Annabel's Party, 1988; Irritating Irma, 1988; The Kidnapping of Clarissa Montgomery, 1988; Jane's Mansion, 1988; Laurie Loved Me Best, 1988; Penny Pollard's Passport, 1988; Dear Robin: Letters to Robin Klein, 1988; Coming out from Under: Contemporary Australian Women Writers, 1988; Against the Odds, 1989; Enemies, 1989; The Ghost in Abigail Terrace, 1989; Penny Pollard's Guide to Modern Manners, 1989; Came Back to Show You I Could Fly, 1989; Boris and Borsch,

1990; Tearaways: Stories to Make You Think Twice, 1990; All in the Blue Unclouded Weather, 1991; Amy's Bed, 1992; Dresses of Red and Gold, 1992; Seeing Things, 1993; The Proof of the Puddin: Australian Children's Literature, 1970-90, 1993; Turn Right for Zyrgon, 1994; The Sky in Silver Lace, 1995; Thing's Concert, 1996; Thing's Birthday, 1996; Thing Finds a Job, 1996; Thing it is, 1996; The Listmaker, 1997; Bedtime Stories, 1997; Gabby's Fair, 1998; The Goddess, 1998; Penny Pollard's Scrapbook, 1999; Juegos/Games, 2000; I Came Back to Demostrate That I Could Fly, 2003; Te Odio Alison, Por Que Seras tan perfecta?/Hating Alison Ashley, 2005; Jocs, 2007. **Address:** c/o Author Mail, Curtis Brown Pty Ltd., PO Box 19, Paddington, NW 2021, Australia.

KLEIN, Sherwin. American (born United States), b. 1932. **Genres:** Ethics, Medicine/Health. **Career:** Rutgers University, adjunct instructor in philosophy, 1960-64; Fairleigh Dickinson University, Edward Williams College, assistant professor, 1965-75, associate professor, 1975-82, professor, 1982-; Bergen Community College, faculty; City University of New York, Brooklyn College, faculty; Long Island University, part-time faculty; Montclair State College, part-time faculty; Seton Hall University, part-time faculty. Writer. **Publications:** Business Ethics: Reflections from a Platonic Point of View, 1993, reprinted, 1995; Endoxic Method and Ethical Inquiry: An Analysis and Defense of a Method for Justifying Fundamental Ethical Principles, 2000; Ethical Business Leadership: Balancing Theory and Practice, 2002. Contributor to philosophy and business ethics journals. **Address:** Edward Williams College, Fairleigh Dickinson University, 150 Kotte Pl., Hackensack, NJ 07601, U.S.A.

KLEIN, William. See **KLEIN, Marcus.**

KLEIN, Zachary. American (born United States), b. 1948. **Genres:** Novels, Young Adult Fiction. **Career:** Writer. **Publications:** NOVELS: Still Among the Living: A Novel of Suspense, 1990; Two Way Toll: A Matt Jacob Novel of Suspense, 1991; No Saving Grace: A Matt Jacob Novel, 1994. **Address:** c/o Herb Katz, 151 E 83rd St., New York, NY 10028, U.S.A. **Online address:** mail@zachklein.com

KLEIN, Zoe. American (born United States), b. 1971. **Genres:** Children's Fiction, Theology/Religion. **Career:** Rabbi, Ordained rabbi, 1998; Temple Shalom, rabbi; Temple Isaiah, rabbi and spiritual leader, 2000-. Writer. **Publications:** Drawing in the Dust, 2009; The Scroll of Anatiya, 2009. Contributor to periodicals. **Address:** Temple Isaia, 10345 W Pico Blvd., Los Angeles, CA 90064, U.S.A. **Online address:** zoe@zoeklien.com

KLEINBERG, Ethan. American (born United States), b. 1967. **Genres:** Philosophy, History. **Career:** Wesleyan University, associate professor, chair of letters. Writer. **Publications:** Generation Existential: Heidegger's Philosophy in France, 1927-1961, 2005. **Address:** Department of History, Wesleyan University, 238 Church St., Middletown, CT 06459-3139, U.S.A. **Online address:** ekleinberg@wesleyan.edu

KLEINBERG, Jay. See **KLEINBERG, S. J.**

KLEINBERG, S. J. (Jay Kleinberg). British (born England), b. 1947. **Genres:** Women's Studies And Issues, Economics, History, Politics/Government. **Career:** University of California, acting assistant professor of history and urban and rural studies, 1972-75; Miami University, Western College, assistant professor of interdisciplinary studies, 1975-77; University of Tennessee, assistant professor of history, 1977-80; independent historian and researcher, 1980-82; University of Essex, ESRC Data Archive, senior research officer, 1983-84; London School of Economics, lecturer in economic history, 1984-86; West London Institute of Higher Education, senior lecturer and head of American studies, 1987-92, principal lecturer, 1993; Brunel University College, reader in American studies, 1996, department head, 1997-2001, professor of American studies and history, 1998, Faculty of Arts and Social Sciences, associate dean, 2002-04; Journal of American Studies, associate editor, 1996-2001, editor, 2001-06; Brunel Business School, Politics and History Section, professor of history, 2004-; Centre for American, Transatlantic and Caribbean History, director, 2005-. **Publications:** (ed.) Retrieving Women's History: Changing Perceptions of the Role of Women in Politics and Society, 1988; The Shadow of the Mills: Working-Class Families in Pittsburgh, 1870-1907, 1989; Women in American Society, 1820-1920, 1990; Women in the United States, 1830-1945, 1999; Widows and Orphans First: The Family Economy and Social Welfare Policy, 1880-1939, 2005; (ed. with E. Boris and V.L. Ruiz) The Practice of U.S. Women's History: Narratives, Intersections, and Dialogues, 2007. **Address:** Brunel University, West London, Uxbridge, UB8 3PH, England. **Online address:** jay.kleinberg@brunel.ac.uk

KLEINER, Diana E. E. American (born United States), b. 1947. **Genres:** Art/Art History. **Career:** University of Virginia, lecturer, 1975-76, assistant professor of classics, 1976-78, University of Massachusetts, visiting assistant professor of classics, 1979; Harvard University, Mellon faculty fellow, 1979-80; Yale University, assistant professor, 1980-82, associate professor, 1982-89, Whitney Humanities Center, fellow, 1984-87, Pierson College, master, 1986-87, director of graduate studies, 1986-95, professor of the history of art classics, 1989-, Department of Classics, chair, 1994-95, deputy provost for the arts, 1995-2003, Dunham professor of classics and history of art, 1995-, Open Yale Courses, principal investigator, 2006-. Writer. **Publications:** Roman Group Portraiture: The Funerary Reliefs of the Late Republic and Early Empire, 1977; The Monument of Philopappos in Athens, 1983; Roman Imperial Funerary Altars with Portraits, 1987; Roman Sculpture, 1992; Cleopatra and Rome, 2005. EDITOR: (with S.B. Matheson) I, Claudia: Women in Ancient Rome, 1996; (with S.B. Matheson) I, Claudia II: Women in Roman Art and Society, 2000. Contributor to periodicals. **Address:** Department of the History of Art, Yale University, Loria 554, 190 York St., PO Box 208272, New Haven, CT 06520-8272, U.S.A. **Online address:** diana.kleiner@yale.edu

KLEINER, Fred S. American (born United States), b. 1948. **Genres:** Art/Art History, Archaeology/Antiquities. **Career:** American School of Classical Studies, Agora Fellow, 1973-75; University of Virginia, assistant professor, 1975-78; Boston University, assistant professor, 1978-81, director of graduate studies, 1979-81, associate professor, 1981-86, Department of History of Art and Architecture, chair, 1981-85, 2005-, professor of history of art and archaeology, 1986-; American Journal of Archaeology, editor-in-chief, 1985-98. **Publications:** Greek and Roman Coins in the Athenian Agora, 1975; (with S.P. Noe) The Early Cistophoric Coinage, 1977; Mediaeval and Modern Coins in the Athenian Agora, 1978; The Arch of Nero in Rome, 1985; Gardner's Art through the Ages: A Concise Global History, 2005, 13th ed., 2010; A History of Roman Art, 2006, rev. ed., 2010. Contributor of articles to journals. **Address:** Department of History of Art and Architecture, Boston University, 725 Commonwealth Ave., Rm. 302E, Boston, MA 02215, U.S.A. **Online address:** fsk@bu.edu

KLEINKNECHT, William. American (born United States), b. 1960. **Genres:** Criminology/True Crime, Autobiography/Memoirs, History. **Career:** New York Daily News, staff; Star-Ledger, crime correspondent. Writer. **Publications:** The New Ethnic Mobs: The Changing Face of Organized Crime in America, 1996; The Man Who Sold the World: Ronald Reagan and the Betrayal of Main Street America, 2009. Contributor to journals and newspapers. **Address:** Star-Ledger, 1 Star Ledger Plz., Newark, NJ 07102, U.S.A. **Online address:** bkleinknecht@starledger.com

KLEINSASSER, Lois. Also writes as Cait London, Cait Logan. American (born United States) **Genres:** Romance/Historical, Novels, Adult Non-fiction. **Career:** Novelist. **Publications:** AS CAIT LOGAN: Lady on the Line, 1986; Rugged Glory, 1986; Gambler's Lady, 1987; Lady's Choice, 1988; Lady's Desire, 1988; Tame the Fury, 1990; Wild Dawn, 1992; Night Fire, 1994; Delilah, 1995; The Wedding Gamble, 1996; Be Mine, 1997; (with B. Joyce and C. Brockway) Outlaw love, 1997; Lady Desperado, 1997. AS CAIT LONDON: The Loving Season, 1989; Angel Versus Maclean, 1990; The Pendragon Virus, 1990; The Daddy Candidate, 1991; Midnight Rider, 1992; The Cowboy, 1993; Maybe No, Maybe Yes, 1993; The Seduction of Jake Tallman, 1993; The Bride Says No, 1994; Fusion, 1994; Lightfoot and Loving, 1994; Every Girl's Guide To ..., 1995; Miracles and Mistletoe, 1995; Mr. Easy, 1995; Every Groom's Guide To ..., 1996; The Perfect Fit, 1998; Rafe Palladin: Man of Secrets, 1998; Scent of a Woman, 1998; Three Kisses, 1998; Blaylock's Bride, 1999; Typical Male, 1999; Sleepless in Montana, 1999; Rio: Man of Destiny, 1999; Un Hombre y sus secretos, 1999; Last Dance, 2000; It Happened at Midnight, 2000; Slow Fever, 2000; Do You Take This Cowboy, 2000; Gabriel's Gift, 2001; A Loving Man, 2001; Leaving Lonely Town, 2001; Mr. Temptation, 2002; When Night Falls, 2002; (with L. Paige) Forbidden Attraction, 2002; Instinctive Male, 2003; With Her Last Breath, 2003; Stuck on You, 2004; Hold Me Tight, 2004; (with S. Mallery) Lassoed Hearts, 2004; What Memories Remain, 2004; Taking Her Time, 2004; Flashback, 2005; Hidden Secrets, 2005; Total Package, 2005; Silence the Whispers, 2006; Sugarplums and Scandal, 2006; At the Edge, 2007; For Her Eyes Only, 2008; Stranger's Touch, 2008. TALLCHIEF SERIES AS CAIT LONDON: The

Cowboy and the Cradle, 1996; Tallchief's Bride, 1996; The Groom Candidate, 1997; Tallchief for Keeps, 1997; The Seduction of Fiona Tallchief, 1998; The Homecoming, 2000; A Tallchief Celebration, 2001; The Hunter, 2002. Contributor to books and periodicals. **Address:** Silhouette Books, 300 E 42nd St., New York, NY 10017, U.S.A. **Online address:** cait@caitlondon.com

KLEINSMITH, Bruce John. *See* **NUTZLE, Futzie.**

KLEMM, Barry. Australian (born Australia), b. 1945. **Genres:** Novels, Animals/Pets, Young Adult Fiction. **Career:** Writer. **Publications:** NOVELS: The Tenth Hero, 1997; Last Voyage of the Albatross, 1998; Running Dogs, 2000; The Stone Age, 2010; The War of Immensities, 2010; Aesop's Solon, 2010; A 1000 1000 Slimy Things, 2010; Being Jarvis Kreeg, 2010; Pythagoras Dreaming, 2010; The Lake Mulga Mob, 2010; Boss Gull, 2010; Wandering At Large, 2011; ShadowRider, 2011; The World Beneath Their Feet, 2011. **Address:** The Clocktower, Ste. 20, 255 Drummond St., Carlton, VI 3053, Australia. **Online address:** barry@barryklemm.com

KLEMPNER, Joseph T(eller). American (born United States), b. 1940. **Genres:** Mystery/Crime/Suspense, Novels, Literary Criticism And History, Young Adult Fiction. **Career:** U.S. Treasury Department, Bureau of Narcotics, narcotics agent, 1964-66; Legal Aid Society, criminal defense attorney, 1966-68; self-employed criminal defense attorney, 1968-. Writer. **Publications:** NOVELS: Felony Murder, 1995; Shoot the Moon, 1997; Change of Course, 1998; Flat Lake in Winter, 1999; Irreparable Damage, 2002; Fogbound, 2003; The Tenth Case, 2008; Bronx Justice, 2009; Depraved Indifference, 2009; Overkill, 2010. **Address:** c/o Robert G. Diforio, D4EO Literary Agency, 7 Indian Valley Rd., Weston, CT 06883, U.S.A. **Online address:** sandjklempner@taconic.net

KLEMPNER, Mark. American (born United States), b. 1955?. **Genres:** History, Humanities, Mythology/Folklore, Social Commentary, Theology/Religion, Young Adult Non-fiction, Writing/Journalism, E-books, Essays, Film, Environmental Sciences/Ecology, Communications/Media, Civil Liberties/Human Rights, International Relations/Current Affairs, Autobiography/Memoirs. **Career:** Folklorist, historian, social commentator and journalist. **Publications:** The Heart Has Reasons: Holocaust Rescuers and Their Stories of Courage, 2006. **Address:** PO Box 025331, Miami, FL 33102-5331, U.S.A. **Online address:** klempner@hearthasreasons.com

KLERKX, Greg. American (born United States), b. 1963. **Genres:** Science Fiction/Fantasy, History, Air/Space Topics, Politics/Government, Popular Culture, Sciences. **Career:** Orange Coast Daily Pilot, staff journalist, 1986-90; California Academy of Mathematics and Science, director of development, 1992-94; University of California, associate director, 1994-97; SETI Institute, director of development, 1997-2002; journalist and consultant, 2002-; Nimble Fish, co-founder and partner, 2006-. **Publications:** Lost in Space: The Fall of NASA and the Dream of a New Space Age, 2004. **Address:** c/o Author Mail, Pantheon Press, 1745 Broadway, New York, NY 10019-4368, U.S.A. **Online address:** gremlin120@yahoo.com

KLEVEN, Elisa. (Elisa Schneider). American (born United States), b. 1958. **Genres:** Children's Fiction, Illustrations, Animals/Pets. **Career:** Berkeley Hills Nursery School, nursery school teacher, 1978-80; Prospect School, fourth-grade teacher and art teacher, 1984-86. Writer. **Publications:** SELF-ILLUSTRATED: The Lion and the Little Red Bird, 1992; The Paper Princess, 1994; The Apple Doll, 2007. OTHERS: (as Elisa Schneider) The Merry-Go-Round Dog, 1988; Ernst, 1989; Hooray! A Piñata!, 1996; Puddle Pail, 1997; Monster in the House, 1998; Sun Bread, 2001; Dancing Deer and the Foolish Hunter, 2002; The Paper Princess Finds Her Way, 2003; Paper Princess Flies Again: With Her Dog!, 2005; Wishing Ball, 2006; Carousel Tale, 2009; Welcome Home, Mouse, 2010; Friends for Foley, 2011; The Friendship Wish, 2011. Illustrator of books by others. **Address:** Dutton Children's Books, 345 Hudson St., New York, NY 10014, U.S.A. **Online address:** elisakleven7@gmail.com

KLIEM, Ralph L. American (born United States), b. 1951. **Genres:** Business/Trade/Industry, Economics. **Career:** Safeco Insurance, methods analyst, 1983-85; Boeing, senior program manager, 1985-; City University of Seattle, faculty; Seattle Pacific University, faculty; Bellevue Community College, instructor; LeanPM L.L.C., president, project manager, consultant and trainer, 2009-; Practical Creative Solutions Inc., president. Writer. **Publications:** Secrets of Successful Project Management, 1986; (with I.S. Ludin) The People

Side of Project Management, 1992; (with I.S. Ludin) Data Processing Manager's Model Reports and Formats, 1992; (with I.S. Ludin) The Noah Project: The Secrets of Practical Project Management, 1993; (with I.S. Ludin) Just-in-Time Systems for Computing Environments, 1994; (with I.S. Ludin) Stand and Deliver: The Fine Art of Presentation, 1995; (with I.S. Ludin and K.L. Robertson) Project Management Methodology: A Practical Guide for the Next Millennium, 1997; (with I.S. Ludin) Reducing Project Risk, 1997; (with I.S. Ludin) Project Management Practitioner's Handbook, 1998; (with I.S. Ludin) Managing Change in the Workplace: A 12-Step Program for Success, 1998; (with I.S. Ludin) Tools and Tips for Today's Project Manager, 1999; The Project Manager's Emergency Kit, 2003; (with H.B. Anderson) The Organizational Engineering Approach to Project Management: The Revolution in Building and Managing Effective Teams, 2003; Leading High-Performance Projects, 2004; Effective Communications for Project Management, 2008; Ethics and Project Management, 2011; Managing Projects in Trouble, 2011. Contributor of articles to periodicals. **Address:** CRC Press, 6000 Broken Sound Pkwy. NW, Ste. 300, Boca Raton, FL 33487, U.S.A. **Online address:** ralph.kliem@verizon.net

KLIMAN, Bernice W. *See* Obituaries.

KLINE, David. American (born United States), b. 1950?. **Genres:** Biography, Information Science/Computers, Business/Trade/Industry. **Career:** Wired (magazine), columnist; Upside (magazine), columnist; Waterside Associates, founder; New York Times, reporter; Christian Science Monitor, reporter; Atlantic, reporter; NBC News, reporter; CBS News, reporter; Rolling Stone, reporter. Journalist and business consultant. **Publications:** NONFICTION: (with D. Burstein) Road Warriors: Dreams and Nightmares along the Information Highway, 1995; (with K.G. Rivette) Rembrandts in the Attic: Unlocking the Hidden Value of Patents, 2000; Great Possessions, 2001; (with D. Burstein) Blog! How the Newest Media Revolution Is Changing Politics, Business and Culture, 2005; (with M. Phelps) Burning the Ships: Intellectual Property and the Transformation of Microsoft, 2009; (with H.P. Nothhaft) Great Again: Revitalizing America's Entrepreneurial Leadership, 2011. Contributor to periodicals. **Address:** c/o Author Mail, Macmillan, 175 5th Ave., New York, NY 10010, U.S.A. **Online address:** dkline@well.com

KLINE, Lisa Williams. American (born United States), b. 1954. **Genres:** Novels, Children's Fiction. **Career:** UNC-TV, writer and researcher, 1976-78; Arthur Andersen Video Training, video training writer, 1978-81; freelance writer, 1981-. **Publications:** Eleanor Hill, 1999; The Princesses of Atlantis, 2002; Floods, 2003; (ed.) Only Connect: The Charlotte Writers' Club Anthology, 2007; Write Before Your Eyes, 2008; Take Me and Other Stories, 2010; Summer of the Wolves, 2012; Wild Horse Spring, 2012. Contributor to periodicals. **Address:** c/o Caryn Wiseman, Andrea Brown Literary Agency Inc., 1076 Eagle Dr., Salinas, CA 93905, U.S.A. **Online address:** lisa73154@aol.com

KLINE, Michael. (Michael Joseph Kline). American (born United States), b. 1958. **Genres:** Biography, History, Politics/Government. **Career:** Coca-Cola Co., senior patent counsel, 1999-; Journal of Law and Commerce, editor. **Publications:** (Ed.) Introduction to Corporate Law, 1978; The Baltimore Plot: The First Conspiracy to Assassinate Abraham Lincoln, 2008. Contributor to periodicals. **Address:** Coca-Cola Co., PO Box 1734, Atlanta, GA 30301, U.S.A.

KLINE, Michael Joseph. *See* **KLINE, Michael.**

KLINE, Ronald R. American (born United States), b. 1947. **Genres:** History, Intellectual History, Biography. **Career:** General Electric Ordnance Systems, field service and systems engineer, 1969-77; University of Wisconsin, Technical Communications, lecturer and teaching assistant, 1978-84; Institute of Electrical and Electronics Engineers, Center for History of Electric Engineering, director, 1984-87; Cooper Union, adjunct assistant professor of history, 1985-87; Cornell University, assistant professor, 1987-93, associate professor, 1993-2000, professor of history of technology, 2001-03, Sue G. and Harry E. Bovay, Jr., professor in history and ethics of engineering, 2003-; Istanbul Technical University, Social Sciences Institute, visiting professor, 2000. **Publications:** Steinmetz: Engineer and Socialist, 1992; Consumers in the Country: Technology and Social Change in Rural America, 2000. **Address:** Cornell University, 394 Rhodes Hall, Ithaca, NY 14850, U.S.A. **Online address:** rrk1@cornell.edu

KLING, Christine. American (born United States), b. 1954. **Genres:** Marine Sciences/Oceanography, Mystery/Crime/Suspense, Novels. **Career:** Broward Community College, adjunct professor of English, 2004-, assistant professor, professor of English, through 2011; Broward County School System, coordinator of magnet programs. Writer, 2011-. **Publications:** Surface Tension, 2002; Cross Current, 2004; Bitter End, 2005; Wrecker's Key, 2007. Contributor to periodicals. **Address:** c/o Author Mail, Random House Inc., 1745 Broadway, New York, NY 10019-4368, U.S.A. **Online address:** ck@christinekling.com

KLING, David W. American (born United States), b. 1950. **Genres:** Theology/Religion. **Career:** Palm Beach Atlantic College, assistant professor of history, 1982-86; St. Vincent de Paul Theological Seminary, part-time visiting professor, 1986-91; University of Miami, assistant, 1986-89, administrator, 1986-93, assistant, 1989-93, Office of Admissions, director of publications, 1991-93, Department of Religious Studies, assistant professor, 1993-96, associate professor, 1996-2006, professor, 2006-. Writer and historian. **Publications:** A Field of Divine Wonders: The New Divinity and Village Revivals in Northwestern Connecticut, 1792-1822, 1993; (ed. with D.A. Sweeney) Jonathan Edwards at Home and Abroad: Historical Memories, Cultural Movements, Global Horizons, 2003; The Bible in History: How the Texts Have Shaped the Times, 2004. Contributor to books and periodicals. **Address:** Department of Religious Studies, University of Miami, PO Box 248264, Coral Gables, FL 33124, U.S.A. **Online address:** dkling@miami.edu

KLINGBERG, Torkel. Swedish (born Sweden), b. 1967?. **Genres:** Sciences, Psychology. **Career:** Stockholm Brain Institute, Karolinska Institute, professor of cognitive neuroscience, Developmental Cognitive Neuroscience Lab, department head; Cogmed, co-founder. Writer. **Publications:** The Overflowing Brain: Information Overload and the Limits of Working Memory, 2009. Contributor to journals. **Address:** Karolinska Institutet, Stockholm, SE-171 77, Sweden. **Online address:** torkel.klingberg@ki.se

KLINGENSTEIN, Susanne. American/German (born Germany), b. 1959. **Genres:** Intellectual History, Humanities, Literary Criticism And History, Writing/Journalism, Essays, Medicine/Health, Biography. **Career:** Astronomisches Rechen-Institut, proofreader, 1983-85; University of Mannheim, assistant professor of English, 1986-87; Harvard University, instructor, 1989-90, lecturer in English and American literature, 1990-92; Massachusetts Institute of Technology, assistant professor, 1993-96, associate professor of writing and humanistic studies, 1997-2001; Frankfurter Allgemeine Zeitung, writer and journalist, cultural correspondent, 2000-; Harvard University, Harvard-MIT Division of Health Sciences and Technology, lecturer, 2001-10; Brandeis University, visiting professor of German literature, 2009-. **Publications:** Jews in the American Academy, 1900-1940: The Dynamics of Intellectual Assimilation, 1991; Enlarging America: The Cultural Work of Jewish Literary Scholars, 1930-1990, 1998. Contributor to periodicals. Works appear in anthologies. **Address:** Harvard-MIT Health Sciences and Technology, Massachusetts Institute of Technology, E25-519, 77 Massachusetts Ave., Cambridge, MA 02139, U.S.A. **Online address:** sklingenstein@rcn.com

KLINGER, Eric. American/Austrian (born Austria), b. 1933. **Genres:** Psychology. **Career:** Association of American Medical Colleges, research associate, 1957-60; Hines VAH and the Mental Hygiene Clinic Service, clinical psychology trainee, 1957-60; University of Wisconsin, instructor in psychology, 1960-62; University of Minnesota, assistant professor, 1962-63, coordinator of psychology discipline, 1962-2006, associate professor, 1963-69, professor of psychology, 1969-2006, alumni distinguished teaching professor emeritus of psychology, 2006-; University of Minnesota-Twin Cities, adjunct professor of psychology, 1978-2006, adjunct professor emeritus of psychology, 2006-; Ruhr University, professor of psychology, 1983-84; University of Konstanz, visiting professor, 1995; Institute of Transpersonal Psychology, specialized research faculty, 2008-. Writer. **Publications:** Structure and Functions of Fantasy, 1971; Meaning and Void: Inner Experience and the Incentives in People's Lives, 1977; Daydreaming, 1990. EDITOR: Imagery: vol. II: Concepts, Results and Applications, 1981; (with W.M. Cox) Handbook of Motivational Counseling: Concepts, Approaches and Assessment, 2004, 2nd ed. as Handbook of Motivational Counseling: Goal-Based Approaches to Assessment and Intervention with Addiction and Other Problems, 2011. Contributor to books and periodicals. **Address:** Division of Social Sciences, University of Minnesota, 206 Imholte Hall, 600 E 4th St., Morris, MN 56267, U.S.A. **Online address:** klinger@morris.umn.edu

KLITZMAN, Robert (L.). American (born United States), b. 1958. **Genres:** Gay And Lesbian Issues, Medicine/Health, Psychiatry, Sciences, Travel/Exploration, Sports/Fitness, Social Work. **Career:** National Institutes of Health, research aide, 1980-81; Cornell University Medical Center, assistant unit chief, 1988, 1989; New York State Psychiatric Institute, fellow, 1989-93, Ethics and Policy Core, HIV Center for Clinical and Behavioral Studies, director, 2004-; Columbia Presbyterian Medical Center, fellow, 1989-93, mentor, 1994-95, assistant professor of clinical psychiatry, 1996-2003, Mailman School of Public Health, assistant professor, 2000-03, Center for Bioethics, co-director, 2001-06, associate professor of clinical psychiatry in sociomedical sciences, 2003-, Ethics and Policy Core, HIV Center for Clinical and Behavioral Studies, director, 2004, Masters of Bioethics Program, director; University of Pennsylvania, Leonard Davis Institute of Health Economics, adjunct senior fellow, 1993-. Writer. **Publications:** A Year-Long Night: Tales of a Medical Internship, 1989; In a House of Dreams and Glass: Becoming a Psychiatrist, 1995; Being Positive: The Lives of Men and Women with HIV, 1997; The Trembling Mountain: A Personal Account of Kuru, Cannibals and Mad Cow Disease, 1998; (with R. Bayer) Mortal Secrets: Truth and Lies in the Age of AIDS, 2003; When Doctors Become Patients, 2007; Am I My Genes?: Confronting Fate and Family Secrets in the Age of Genetic Testing, 2012. Contributor of articles to journals. **Address:** c/o Kristine Dahl, International Creative Management, 40 W 57th St., New York, NY 10019, U.S.A. **Online address:** rlk2@columbia.edu

KLUGER, Ruth. American/Austrian (born Austria), b. 1931. **Genres:** Autobiography/Memoirs, Poetry, Biography, History, Literary Criticism And History. **Career:** California State College (now California State University), assistant professor of German, 1965-66; Case Western Reserve University, assistant professor, associate professor, 1966-70; University of Kansas, associate professor of German, 1970-73; University of Cincinnati, visiting professor, 1972-73; University of Virginia, associate professor of German, 1973-76, chairman of department, 1974-76; Princeton University, professor, chair of German department; University of California, professor of German, faculty, 1976-94, now professor emeritus. Writer. **Publications:** Early German Epigram: A Study in Baroque Poetry, 1971; Weiter Leben: Eine Jugend, 1992; Frauen Lesen Anders?, 1994, rev. ed., 1996; Von Hoher Und Niedriger Literatur, 1996; Knigges Umgang mit Menschen, 1996; Still Alive: A Holocaust Girlhood Remembered, 2001; Landscapes of Memory: A Holocaust Girlhood Remembered, 2003; Gelesene Wirklichkeit: Fakten und Fiktionen inder Literatur, 2006. Contributor to periodicals. **Address:** German School of Humanities, University of California, 400A Murray Krieger Hall, PO Box 3150, Irvine, CA 92697-3150, U.S.A. **Online address:** rkluger@uci.edu

KLUGER, Steve. American (born United States), b. 1952. **Genres:** Novels, Plays/Screenplays, Adult Non-fiction, History, Young Adult Fiction, Gay And Lesbian Issues. **Career:** Author. **Publications:** FICTION: Changing Pitches, 1984; Last Days of Summer, 1998; Almost Like Being in Love, 2004; My Most Excellent Year, 2008. NON-FICTION: Yank: World War II from the Guys Who Brought You Victory, 1991. **Address:** c/o Gail Hochman, Brandt & Hochman Literary Agents, 1501 Broadway, Ste. 2310, New York, NY 10036, U.S.A. **Online address:** redsoxkid@stevekluger.com

KLYZA, Christopher McGrory. American (born United States), b. 1959. **Genres:** Agriculture/Forestry, Politics/Government, Environmental Sciences/Ecology, Natural History, Cultural/Ethnic Topics, Business/Trade/Industry, Economics. **Career:** Duke University, Center for Resource and Environmental Policy, teaching assistant, research associate, 1982-83; University of Minnesota, Department of Political Science, instructor in political science, 1986-88; University of Vermont, Department of Political Science, visiting instructor in political science, 1988-90; Middlebury College, assistant professor of political science, 1990-95, associate professor of political science, 1995-98, associate professor of political science and environmental studies, 1998-2000, professor of political science and environmental studies, 2000-, Stafford professor of public policy, political science and environmental studies, Program in Environmental Studies, director, 1994-97, 2000-03, 2007-08, Robert '35 and Helen '38 Stafford professor in public policy, 2003-. Writer. **Publications:** (Ed. with S.C. Trombulak) The Future of the Northern Forest, 1994; Who Controls Public Lands?: Mining, Forestry, and Grazing Policies, 1870-1990, 1996; (with S.C. Trombulak) The Story of Vermont: A Natural and Cultural History, 1999; (ed.) Wilderness Comes Home: Rewilding the Northeast, 2001; (with D.J. Sousa) American Environmental Policy, 1990-2006: Beyond Gridlock, 2008. Contributor of articles to books and journals. **Address:** Department of Political Science, Middlebury College, Franklin Environmental Ctr., 206 Hillcrest, 427 College St., Middlebury, VT 05753-1049, U.S.A. **Online address:** klyza@middlebury.edu

KNAPP, Edward. *See* **KUNHARDT**, Edith.

KNAPP, Raymond. American (born United States), b. 1952. **Genres:** Music. **Career:** University of California, professor of musicology, 1989-, chair of the musicology department, 2006-09, General Education Governance, chair, 2004-07, Faculty of the College of Letters and Science, chair, 2009-; Santa Monica Symphony, violinist. Writer. **Publications:** Brahms and the Challenge of the Symphony, 1997; Symphonic Metamorphoses: Subjectivity and Alienation in Mahler's Re-cycled Songs, 2003; The American Musical and the Formation of National Identity, 2005; The American Musical and the Performance of Personal Identity, 2006; (ed. with S. Baur and J. Warwick) Musicological Identities: Essays in Honor of Susan McClary, 2008. **Address:** Department of Musicology, University of California, 2443 Schoenberg Music Bldg., 445 Charles E Young Dr. E, PO Box 951623, Los Angeles, CA 90095-1623, U.S.A. **Online address:** knapp@humnet.ucla.edu

KNAPP, Sara D. American (born United States), b. 1936. **Genres:** Librarianship, Information Science/Computers. **Career:** Albany Medical Center, social case work aide, 1958-63; New York State Library, Division of Library Development, assistant library supervisor, 1964-67; First Unitarian Church of Albany, Channing Bookstore, chairperson, 1966-68 and 1970-71; State University of New York, assistant librarian, 1967-70, associate librarian, 1970-79, librarian, 1979-, cataloger, 1967-68, Periodicals Section, head, 1968-69, Serials and Bindery Department, head, 1969-71, reference librarian, 1971-72, Bibliographic Services Unit, head, 1972, Computer Search Service Unit, coordinator, 1972-, University at Albany, University Library, Online Search Service, coordinator; Capital District Library Council, staff, 1969-; Wheels to Independence, vice-president, 1974; Online Users Group, Computer Based Reference Services Committee, chairperson, 1975-76; Bibliographic Retrieval Services Inc., BRS/TERM, editor, 1983-89; Medical Reliance Co., consultant; Bancroft Group, consultant. **Publications:** BRS Training Workbook: An Introduction to Searching on the BRS System With Practice Exercises From the ERIC Database, Bibliographic Retrieval Services, 1979, rev. ed., 1981; (ed. and comp.) The Contemporary Thesaurus of Social Science Terms and Synonyms: A Guide for Natural Language Computer Searching, 1993, 2nd ed. as Contemporary Thesaurus of Search Terms and Synonyms: A Guide for Natural Language Computer Searching, 2000. Contributor of articles to journals. **Address:** University Library, State University of New York, 1400 Washington Ave., Albany, NY 12222, U.S.A.

KNAUFT, Bruce M. American (born United States), b. 1954. **Genres:** Anthropology/Ethnology, Social Sciences, Cultural/Ethnic Topics. **Career:** University of California, postdoctoral research fellow, 1983-85; Emory University, Department of Anthropology, assistant professor, 1985-90, associate professor, 1990-95, professor, 1995-2001, Women's Studies, associated faculty, 1995-, Winship distinguished researcher, 1998-2000, Samuel Candler Dobbs professor of anthropology, 2001-, Institute of the Liberal Arts, faculty, 2002-, Institute of Critical International Studies, executive director, 2004-09, States at Regional Risk Project, director, 2008-11, Vernacular Modernities Program, director; Stanford University, Center for Advanced Studies in the Behavioral Sciences, fellow, 1991-92; Ecole des Hautes Etudes en Sciences Sociales, fellow, 1994. Writer. **Publications:** Good Company and Violence: Sorcery and Social Action in a Lowland New Guinea Society, 1985; South Coast New Guinea Cultures: History, Comparison, Dialectic, 1993; Genealogies for the Present in Cultural Anthropology, 1996; From Primitive to Postcolonial in Melanesia and Anthropology, 1999; Exchanging the Past: A Rainforest World of Before and After, 2002; (ed.) Critically Modern: Alternatives, Alterities, Anthropologies, 2002; Gebusi: Lives Transformed in a Rainforest World, 2005, 2nd ed., 2010. Works appear in anthologies. Contributor to books and journals. **Address:** Department of Anthropology, Emory University, Rm. 213, Anthropology Bldg., 1557 Dickey Dr., Atlanta, GA 30322, U.S.A. **Online address:** bruce.knauft@emory.edu

KNECHT, Heidi Katz. American (born United States), b. 1961. **Genres:** Anthropology/Ethnology, Archaeology/Antiquities, Social Sciences, Sociology. **Career:** University of Miami, Department of Anthropology, adjunct assistant professor, 1991-96; Thinking Strings L.L.C., associate, 1998-. Writer. **Publications:** Upper Paleolithic Burins: Type, Form, and Function, 1988; (contrib.) From Bones to Behavior, 1993; (ed. with A. Pike-Tay and R. White) Before Lascaux: The Complex Record of the Early Upper Paleolithic, 1993;

(ed.) Projectile Technology, 1997. Contributor to books and journals. **Address:** Thinking Strings L.L.C., 37 Barnsdale Rd., PO Box 334, Short Hills, NJ 07078, U.S.A. **Online address:** hknecht@thinkingstrings.com

KNECHT, R. J. *See* **KNECHT**, Robert Jean.

KNECHT, Robert Jean. (R. J. Knecht). British (born England), b. 1926. **Genres:** History, Essays, Young Adult Fiction, Social Sciences. **Career:** History of Parliament Trust and Victoria County History, research assistant, 1954; Richard Lonsdale-Hands Associates, research assistant, 1954-56; University of Birmingham, assistant lecturer, 1956-59, lecturer, 1959-68, senior lecturer in modern history, 1969-78, reader, 1978-85, professor of French history, 1985-92, emeritus professor and honorary senior research fellow, 1992-; Wroxall Abbey School, chairman, 1984-92; Ecole des Hautes Etudes en Sciences Sociales, directeur d'etudes associe, 1994. Writer. **Publications:** AS R.J. KNECHT: (ed. and intro.) The Voyage of Sir Nicholas Carewe to the Emperor Charles V in the Year 1529, 1959; Francis I and Absolute Monarchy, 1969; Renaissance and Reformation, 1969; The Fronde, 1975; (ed. with E.W. Ives and J.J. Scarisbrick) Wealth and Power in Tudor England: Essays Presented to S. T. Bindoff, 1978; Francis I, 1982, rev. ed. as Renaissance Warrior and Patron: The Reign of Francis I, 1994; French Renaissance Monarchy: Francis I and Henry II, 1984, 2nd ed., 1996; French Wars of Religion, 1559-1598, 1989, 3rd ed., 2010; The Rise and Fall of Renaissance France: 1483-1610, 1996, 2nd ed., 2001; Un Prince De La Renaissance: Francois Let Et Son Royaume, 1998; Catherine De' Medici, 1998; The French Civil Wars, 1562-1598, 2000. (as Robert Knecht) Richelieu, 1991. OTHERS: The French Religious Wars, 1562-1598, 2002; Valois: Kings of France, 1328-1589, 2004; The French Renaissance Court, 1483-1589, 2008. Contributor to books, journals and newspapers. **Address:** Departement of History, University of Birmingham, Arts Bldg., Edgbaston, Birmingham, WM B15 2TT, England.

KNEECE, Mark. American (born United States), b. 1964?. **Genres:** Graphic Novels, Horror. **Career:** Savannah College of Art & Design, Department of Sequential Art, co-founder, 1993, chair, professor of sequential art, graduate coordinator, assessment coordinator; Trident Technical College, composition instructor; University of South Carolina, composition and literature instructor. Writer and artist. **Publications:** (With B. Hampton) Verdilak, 1996; (with S. Hampton) Batman: Other Realms, 1998; (with B. Pendarvis) The Bristol Board Jungle, 2004; (with J. Collins-Rousseau) Trailers, 2005; (contrib.) Working Methods, 2007; (adaptor) The Twilight Zone: The After Hours, 2008; (adaptor) The Twilight Zone: Walking Distance, 2008; (adaptor) Deaths-Head Revisited, 2009; (adaptor) Rod Serling's The Twilight Zone: The Midnight Sun, 2009; (adaptor) The Twilight Zone: The Monsters Are Due on Maple Street, 2009; (adaptor) The Twilight Zone: The Odyssey of Flight 33, 2009; (adaptor) The Twilight Zone: Will the Real Martian Please Stand Up, 2009; (adaptor) The Twilight Zone: The Big Tall Wish, 2009. **Address:** Savannah College of Art & Design, 342 Bull St., PO Box 3146, Savannah, GA 31402-3146, U.S.A.

KNEELAND, Timothy (W.). American (born United States), b. 1962. **Genres:** History, Politics/Government. **Career:** Oklahoma Junior College, social and behavior science chair, 1989-93; Greenville College, assistant professor of history, 1996-2000; Nazareth College, assistant professor of history, 2000-06, associate professor of history and political science, 2006-11, professor of history and political science, 2011-, Center for Public History, director, 2010-; State and Science Study, researcher. Writer. **Publications:** Presidents and Radio in Presidents and Popular Culture, 2005; (with C.A.B. Warren) Push Button Psychiatry: A Cultural History of Electroshock in America, rev. ed., 2008; A Companion to Franklin D. Roosevelt, 2011. Contributor to periodicals. **Address:** Department of History and Political Science, Nazareth College, 4245 E Ave., Rochester, NY 14618, U.S.A. **Online address:** tkneela8@naz.edu

KNEVITT, Charles. *See* **KNEVITT**, Charles (Philip Paul).

KNEVITT, Charles (Philip Paul). (Charles Knevitt). British/American (born United States), b. 1952. **Genres:** Architecture, History. **Career:** Freelance architectural journalist, 1974-78; Sunday Telegraph, architecture correspondent, 1980-84; Royal Institute of British Architects, London Region Yearbook, editor, 1980-82; Thames Television News, consultant, 1983-; Times, architecture correspondent, 1984-. **Publications:** Manikata: The Making of a

Church, 1980; Connections: The Architecture of Richard England, 1964-84, 1984; Space on Earth: Architecture, People and Buildings, 1985; Monstrous Carbuncles: A Cartoon Guide to Architecture, 1985; (with N. Wates) Community Architecture: How People Can Shape Their Own Environment, 1986; (ed.) Perspectives: An Anthology of 1001 Architectural Quotations, Lund, 1986; (comp.) From Pecksniff to the Prince of Wales: 150 Years of Punch on Architecture, Planning & Development, 1840-1991, 1990; Shelter: Human Habitats from Around the World, 1996. Contributor to journals. **Address:** Times, 200 Gray's Inn Rd., PO Box 7, London, GL WC1X 8EZ, England.

KNIGHT, Alanna (Cleet). (Margaret Hope). Scottish/British (born England) **Genres:** Mystery/Crime/Suspense, Romance/Historical, Biography, Novels, Young Adult Fiction, Young Adult Non-fiction, Plays/Screenplays. **Career:** Writer. **Publications:** Legend of the Loch, 1969; The October Witch, 1971; This Outward Angel, 1972; Castle Clodha, 1972; Lament for Lost Lovers, 1972; The White Rose, 1974; A Stranger Came By, 1974; The Passionate Kindness: The Love Story of Robert Louis Stevenson and Fanny Osbourne, 1974; A Drink for the Bridge: A Novel of the Tay Bridge Disaster, 1976; So you Want to Write, 1976; The Wicked Wynsleys, 1977; The Black Duchess: A Novel, 1980; Castle of Foxes, 1981; Colla's Children, 1982; Private Life of Robert Louis Stevenson: One Act Play, 1983; The Clan, 1985; (comp.) The Robert Louis Stevenson Treasury, 1985; Estella, 1986; (intro. and ed.) R.L.S. in the South Seas: An Intimate Photographic Record 1986; Enter Second Murderer: An Inspector Faro Novel, 1988; Blood Line: An Inspector Faro Novel, 1989; Deadly Beloved: An Inspector Faro Mystery, 1990; A Quiet Death, 1991; Killing Cousins: An Inspector Faro Mystery, 1992; To Kill a Queen, 1992; The Sweet Cheat Gone, 1992; This Outward Angel, 1993; Strathblair: A Novel, 1994; (comp. and ed. with E.S. Warfel) Robert Louis Stevenson: Bright Ring of Words, 1994; The Missing Duchess, 1994; The Bull Slayers, 1995; Murder by Appointment, 1996; The Coffin Lane Murders: A Case for Inspector Faro, 1998; Angel Eyes, 1998; The Royal Park Murder, 1998; The Monster in the Loch, 1998; Dead Beckoning, 1999; The Inspector's Daughter, 2000; The Dagger in the Crown, 2001; Edinburgh's Murder Mile: True Crime, 2002; Dangerous Pursuits, 2002; The Final Enemy: An Inspector Faro Mystery, 2002; Close and Deadly: Chilling Murders in the Heart of Edinburgh, 2002; An Orkney Murder, 2003; The Gowrie Conspiracy, 2003; Unholy Trinity, 2004; Ghost Walk, 2004; The Stuart Sapphire, 2005; Faro and the Royals, 2005; Burke and Hare, 2007; Miss Havisham's Revenge, 2007; Destroying Angel, 2007; Murder in Paradise, 2008; Quest for a Killer, 2010; The Seal King Murders, 2011. AS MARGARET HOPE: The Queen's Captain, 1978; Hostage Most Royal, 1979; The Shadow Queen, 1979; Perilous Voyage, 1983. Works appear in anthologies. Contributor of articles to magazines and newspapers. **Address:** 24 March Hall Cres., Edinburgh, EH16 5HL, Scotland. **Online address:** alanna.knight@virgin.net

KNIGHT, Amarantha. See KILPATRICK, Nancy.

KNIGHT, Angela. American (born United States), b. 1961?. **Genres:** Romance/Historical, Horror, Novels. **Career:** Writer. **Publications:** (With D. Whiteside) Captive Dreams, 2006; Jane's Warlord, 2004; Master of the Night, 2004; The Forever Kiss, 2004; Master of the Moon, 2005; Mercenaries, 2005; (with S. Gilmorea and M. Hawke) Hard Candy, 2005; (with M.J. Davidson and C. Anthony) Romance at the Edge: In Other Worlds, 2005; Master of Wolves, 2006; Master of Swords, 2006; Warlord, 2007; Passionate Ink: A Guide to Writing Erotic Romance, 2007; (co-author) Beyond the Dark, 2007; (with M.J. Davidson, V. Kantra, Sunny) Over the Moon, 2007; Master of Dragons, 2007; (with L. Leigh, A. Day and V. Kantra) Shifter, 2008; Warrior, 2008; Hot for the Holiday, 2009; Guardian: the Time Hunters, 2009; Master of Fire, 2010; Burning Up, 2010; The Dhampir, 2010; Master of Smoke, 2011; Master of Shadows, 2011; Chain of Kisses, forthcoming; Enforcer, forthcoming. **Address:** c/o Author Mail, Berkeley Sensation Publicity, Penguin Group, 375 Hudson St., New York, NY 10014, U.S.A. **Online address:** angela@angelasknights.com

KNIGHT, Bernard. (Bernard Picton). Welsh (born Wales), b. 1931. **Genres:** Mystery/Crime/Suspense, Plays/Screenplays, Medicine/Health. **Career:** University of London, lecturer in forensic medicine, 1959-62; Medicine, Science and the Law, medical editor, 1960-63; Welsh National School of Medicine (later University of Wales College of Medicine), lecturer, 1962-65, senior lecturer, 1965-76, reader, 1976, professor in forensic pathology, 1989-96, emeritus professor of forensic pathology; University of Newcastle, senior lecturer in forensic pathology, 1965-68; Forensic Science Intl., editor, 1984-

93. **Publications:** Lion Rampant: The Story of Owain and Nest, 1972; Legal Aspects of Medical Practice, 1972, 5th ed., 1992; Edyfyn Brau, 1973; (with M. Helpern) Autopsy: The Memoirs of Milton Helpern, the World's Greatest Medical Detective, 1977; Madoc, Prince of America, 1977; Discovering the Human Body: How Pioneers of Medicine Solved the Mysteries of Anatomy and Physiology, 1980; Forensic Radiology, 1981; Lawyer's Guide to Forensic Medicine: Handbook for Court and Chambers, 1982, rev. ed., 1998; Sudden Death in Infancy: The Cot Death Syndrome, 1983; The Coroner's Autopsy: A Guide to Non-Criminal Autopsies for the General Pathologist, 1983; Post-Mortem Technicians Handbook, 1984; Pocket Guide to Forensic Medicine, 1985; (co-author) Essentials of Forensic Medicine, 1985; Forensic Medicine, 9th ed. (with K. Simpson), 1985, 11th ed. as Simpson's Forensic Medicine, 1997; Forensic Pathology, 1991, 3rd ed., 2004; The Sanctuary Seeker, 1997; The Poisoned Chalice, 1998; Crowner's Quest, 1999; The Awful Secret, 2000; The Tinner's Corpse, 2001; The Grim Reaper, 2002; The Estimation of the Time Since Death in the Early Postmortem Period, 2002; Fear in the Forest, 2003; Brennan, 2003; The Witch Hunters, 2004; The Tainted Relic, 2005; Figure of Hate, 2005; The Elixir of Death, 2006; The Noble Outlaw, 2007; (co-author) Sword of Shame: A Historical Mystery, 2007; (co-author) House Of Shadows: A Historical Mystery, 2007; The Manor of Death, 2008; Crowner Royal, 2009; Where Death Delights, 2010; A Plague of Heretics, 2010; (co-author) The Sacred Stone, 2010; Grounds for Appeal, 2011; Dead in the Dog, 2012. AS BERNARD PICTON: The Lately Deceased, 1963; The Thread of Evidence, 1965; Mistress Murder, 1966; Russian Roulette, 1968; Policeman's Progress, 1969; Tiger at Bay, 1971; Murder, Suicide or Accident: The Forensic Pathologist at Work (nonfiction), 1971; The Expert, 1976. **Address:** Oxford University Press, 198 Madison Ave., New York, NY 10016, U.S.A. **Online address:** knight.j4@sky.com

KNIGHT, D(avid) M(arcus). British (born England), b. 1936. **Genres:** Intellectual History, Natural History, Sciences, Theology/Religion, Biography. **Career:** University of Durham, lecturer in the history of science, 1964-, Department of Philosophy, professor in the history and philosophy of science, now emeritus professor in the history and philosophy of science. Writer. **Publications:** Atoms and Elements: A Study of Theories of Matter in England in the 19th Century, 1967; (ed.) Classical Scientific Paper: Chemistry, 1968; Natural Science Book in English 1600-1900, 1972; Sources for the History of Science 1660-1914, 1975; The Nature of Science: The History of Science in Western Culture since 1600, 1976; Zoological Illustrations: An Essay towards a History of Printed Zoological Pictures, 1977; The Transcendental Part of Chemistry, 1978; Ordering the World: A History of Classifying Man, 1981; The Age of Science, 1986; A Companion to the Physical Sciences, 1989; Ideas in Chemistry: A History of the Science, 1992; Humphry Davy: Science and Power, 1992; Science in the Romantic Era, 1998; (ed.) Development of Chemistry, 1789-1914, 1998; (ed. with H. Kragh) Making of the Chemist: The Social History of Chemistry in Europe, 1789-1914, 1998; Science and Spirituality: The Volatile Connection, 2004; (ed. with M. Eddy) Science and Beliefs: From Natural Philosophy to Natural Science, 1700-1900, 2005; Public Understanding of Science: A History of Communicating Scientific Ideas, 2006; (ed. and intro.) Natural Theology: Or, Evidence of the Existence and Attributes of the Deity, Collected from the Appearances of Nature, 2006; Making of Modern Science: Science, Technology, Medicine and Modernity: 1789-1914, 2009. **Address:** Department of Philosophy, University of Durham, 50 Old Elvet, Durham, DU DH1 3HN, England. **Online address:** d.m.knight@durham.ac.uk

KNIGHT, Desiree. See KILPATRICK, Nancy.

KNIGHT, E. E. American (born United States), b. 1965. **Genres:** Science Fiction/Fantasy, Young Adult Fiction, Novels. **Career:** Harper College, faculty of fiction writing. Journalist. **Publications:** VAMPIRE EARTH SERIES: Way of the Wolf, 2003; Lara Croft: Tomb Raider: The Lost Cult, 2004; Choice of the Cat, 2004; Dragon Champion, 2005; Valentine's Rising, 2005; Tale of the Thunderbolt, 2005; Dragon Avenger, 2006; Valentine's Exile, 2006; Valentine's Resolve, 2007; Fall with Honor, 2008; Winter Duty, 2009; March in Country, 2010. AGE OF FIRE SERIES: Dragon Champion, 2005; Dragon Avenger, 2006; Dragon Outcast, 2007; Dragon Strike, 2008; Dragon Rule, 2009; Dragon Fate, 2010. Work appears in anthologies. **Address:** c/o Author Mail, Penguin Group (USA) Inc., 375 Hudson St., New York, NY 10014, U.S.A. **Online address:** eeknight@vampjac.com

KNIGHT, Gareth. See WILBY, Basil Leslie.

KNIGHT, Kathryn Lasky. *See* LASKY, Kathryn.

KNIGHT, **Louise W.** American (born United States), b. 1949. **Genres:** History, Speech/Rhetoric, Biography, Intellectual History, Women's Studies And Issues. **Career:** Learning Magazine, research assistant, 1973; Addison-Wesley, marketing editor, 1973-74; Fund for the Improvement of Post secondary Education, annual report editor, 1974-75; Education Funding Research Council, editor, 1975-78; Duke University, Office of General Counsel, federal relations coordinator, 1978-80, Office of Research Support, director, 1980-86; Wesleyan University, director, 1979-82; Durham Dispute Settlement, cofounder, 1981-85; Wheaton College, Foundation and Corporation Relations, director, 1986-91; Boston Women's Fund, director, 1988-89; United South End Settlements, director of development, 1991-92; Grantsmanship Center, trainer and consultant, 1993-96; Knight Consulting, principal, 1993-; Northwestern University, adjunct professor, 1998-. **Publications:** Citizen: Jane Addams and the Struggle for Democracy, 2005; Jane Addams: Spirit in Action, 2010. **Address:** 2634 Prairie Ave., Evanston, IL 60201-5742, U.S.A. **Online address:** lwk@louisewknight.com

KNIGHT, **Lynne.** American (born United States), b. 1943. **Genres:** Novels, Poetry, Young Adult Fiction. **Career:** Lowville Academy, English teacher and department head, 1970-90; Solano College, part-time English instructor, professor of English; Contra Costa College, part-time English instructor, professor of English, 1990. Writer. **Publications:** Dissolving Borders, 1996; Snow Effects, 2000; The Book of Common Betrayals, 2002; Deer in Berkeley, 2004; Night in the Shape of a Mirror: Poems, 2006; Again, 2009; Mother Less, forthcoming. Contributor of poetry to journals. **Address:** 1724 La Vereda Rd., Berkeley, CA 94709, U.S.A. **Online address:** lynneknight@yahoo.com

KNIGHT, **Mark J.** British (born England), b. 1972?. **Genres:** Theology/Religion. **Career:** Roehampton University, reader in English literature. Writer. **Publications:** Chesterton and Evil, 2004; (ed.) Sensation and Detection: Mary Cecil Hay, Old Myddelton's Money (1874), 2004; (ed. with T. Woodman) Biblical Religion and the Novel, 1700-2000, 2006; (with E. Mason) Nineteenth-Century Religion and Literature: An Introduction, 2006; An Introduction to Religion and Literature, 2009; (ed. with L. Lee) Religion, Literature and the Imagination: Sacred Worlds, 2009. Contributor to books and periodicals. **Address:** Roehampton University, Digby Stuart College, School of Arts, Fincham 304, Roehampton Ln., London, GL SW15 5PH, England. **Online address:** m.knight@roehampton.ac.uk

KNIGHT, **Michael.** American (born United States), b. 1969. **Genres:** Novels, Novellas/Short Stories. **Career:** University of Tennessee, associate professor & creative writing program director. Writer. **Publications:** Divining Rod (novel), 1998; Dogfight, and Other Stories (short stories), 1998; Goodnight, Nobody (short stories), 2003; The Holiday Season (novellas), 2008. Contributor of stories. **Address:** Department of English, University of Tennessee, 301 McClung Tower, Knoxville, TN 37996-0430, U.S.A. **Online address:** mknight@utk.edu

KNIGHT, **Roger.** British (born England), b. 1944. **Genres:** Young Adult Fiction, Essays, History. **Career:** Greenwich Maritime Institute, visiting professor; National Maritime Museum, deputy director; British Commission for Maritime History, staff. Writer. **Publications:** Edwin Muir: An Introduction to His Work, 1980; Valuing English: Reflections on the National Curriculum, 1996; (ed. with P. Ahluwalia and B. Ashcroft) White and Deadly: Sugar and Colonialism, 1999; The Pursuit of Victory: The Life and Achievement of Horatio Nelson, 2005. **Address:** Greenwich Maritime Institute, Old Royal Naval College, University of Greenwich, Park Row, Greenwich, London, GL SE10 9LS, England.

KNIGHTLEY, **Phillip (George).** British/Australian (born Australia), b. 1929. **Genres:** History, Biography. **Career:** The Northern Star, cadet reporter, 1946-47; The Oceania Daily News, copra trader and reporter, 1947-48; The Melbourne Herald, reporter, 1948-50; The Daily Mirror, reporter, 1950-54, foreign correspondent, special correspondent, 1956-60; Imprint, editor, 1960-62; The Sunday Times, special correspondent, 1965-85; University of Lincoln, visiting professor of journalism. **Publications:** (With B. Page and D. Leitch) Philby: The Spy Who Betrayed a Generation, 1968, rev. ed., 1977; (with B. Page and D. Leitch) Philby Conspiracy, 1968, rev. ed., 1969; (with H. Atkinson) The Games, 1968; (with C. Simpson) The Secret Lives of Lawrence of Arabia, 1969; (with H. Hobson and L. Russell) The Pearl of Days, 1972; The First Casualty: From the Crimea to Vietnam: The War Correspondent as Hero, Propagandist, and Myth Maker, 1975, 3rd ed. as The First Casualty: The War Correspondent as Hero and Myth-maker from the Crimea to Iraq, 2004; Lawrence of Arabia, 1976; (with S. Fay) The Death of Venice, 1976; (ed.) Suffer the Children, 1979; The Vestey Affair, 1981; The Second Oldest Profession: The Spy as Bureaucrat, Patriot, Fantasist, and Whore, 1986 in US as The Second Oldest Profession: Spies and Spying in the Twentieth Century, 1986; (with C. Kennedy) An Affair of State: The Profumo Case and the Framing of Stephen Ward, 1987; Philby: The Life and Views of the K.G.B. Masterspy, 1988; Master Spy: The Story of Kim Philby, 1989; Rise and Fall of the House of Vestey: The True Story of How Britain's Richest Family Beat the Taxman and Came to Grief, 1993; (ed. and intro.) Philby Files: The Secret Life of Master Spy Kim Philby, 1994; A Hack's Progress, 1997; Australia: A Biography of a Nation, 2000; (contrib.) The Eye of War: Words and Photographs from the Front Line, 2003. **Address:** c/o Rachel Calder, The Sayle Literary Agency, 8B King's Parade, Cambridge, GL CB2 1SJ, England. **Online address:** phillipgk@aol.com

KNIGHTON, **Ryan.** Canadian (born Canada), b. 1972. **Genres:** Poetry, Autobiography/Memoirs. **Career:** Capilano College, faculty of English, instructor in literature and creative writing, 1997-. Journalist and editor. **Publications:** Swing in the Hollow (poems), 2001; (with G. Bowering) Cars, 2002; Cockeyed: A Memoir, 2006; C'mon Papa: Dispatches from a Dad in the Dark, 2010. Contributor to periodicals and magazines. **Address:** c/o Denise Bukowski, The Bukowski Agency, 14 Prince Arthur Ave., Ste. 202, Toronto, ON M5R 1A9, Canada. **Online address:** ryan@ryanknighton.com

KNISLEY, **Lucy.** American (born United States), b. 1985?. **Genres:** Food And Wine. **Career:** FNews Magazine, editor and contributor. Educator and comic artist. **Publications:** French Milk, 2007. **Address:** c/o Holly Bemiss, Susan Rabiner Literary Agency, 315 W 39th St., Ste. 1501, New York, NY 10018, U.S.A. **Online address:** lucylou@gmail.com

KNOEPFLE, **John.** American (born United States), b. 1923. **Genres:** Poetry, Translations. **Career:** WCET Educational Television, producer-director, 1953-55; College of Music, lecturer, 1954-55; Ohio State University, assistant instructor, 1956-57; Southern Illinois University, instructor, 1957-61; Saint Louis University High School, instructor, 1961-62; Maryville College, assistant professor, 1961-65; Washington University College, assistant professor, 1963-66; Saint Louis University, associate professor, 1966-70, associate professor and director for creative writing, 1970-72; University of Illinois, professor of literature, 1972-91, professor emeritus of literature, 1991-. Writer. **Publications:** (Trans. with R. Bly and J. Wright) Twenty Poems of Cesar Vallejo, 1961; Poets at the Gate, 1965; Rivers into Islands: A Book of Poems, 1965; After Gray Days and Other Poems, 1967; Songs for Gail Guidry's Guitar, 1969; An Affair of Culture and Other Poems, 1969; The Intricate Land: A Book of Poems, 1970; (with L. Mueller and D. Etter) Voyages to the Inland Sea: Essays and Poems, 1971; Dogs and Cats and Things Like That: A Book of Poems for Children, 1971; The Ten-Fifteen Community Poems, 1971; (trans. with R. Bly and J. Wright) Neruda and Vallejo: Selected Poems, 1971; Our Street Feels Good (for children), 1972; Whetstone: A Book of Poems, 1972; Deep Winter Poems, 1972; (co-author) Regional Perspectives, 1973; Thinking of Offerings: Poems 1970-1973, 1975; A Gathering of Voices, 1978; (ed. with D. Jaffe) Frontier Literature: Images of the American West, 1979; A Box of Sandalwood: Love Poems, 1979; Poems for the Hours, 1979; Selected Poems, 1985; Poems from the Sangamon, 1985; (trans. with W. Shou-yi) T'ang Dynasty Poems, 1985; (trans. with W. Shou-yi) Song Dynasty Poems, 1985; Dim Tales, 1987; Begging an Amnesty, 1994; The Chinkapin Oak Poems 1993-95, 1995; The One Instant and Forever, 2001; Prayer Against Famine and Other Irish Poems, 2004; I Look Around for My Life: An Autobiography, 2008; Walking in Snow, 2008. **Address:** University of Illinois, 1 University Plz., Springfield, IL 62703, U.S.A. **Online address:** jackjohn@springnet1.com

KNOPP, **Lisa.** American (born United States), b. 1956. **Genres:** Writing/Journalism, Essays, Natural History, Social Commentary, Local History/Rural Topics, Philosophy, Homes/Gardens, Theology/Religion, Theology/Religion, History, Homes/Gardens. **Career:** Westside High School, English teacher, 1981-84; Western Illinois University, teaching assistant, 1984-86; Valley High School, English teacher, 1986-88; University of Nebraska-Lincoln, teaching assistant, 1988-93, lecturer, 1994-95; Southern Illinois University, assistant professor, 1995-98; Goucher College (Low-residency

M.F.A. Program in Creative Nonfiction), 1998-2005; University of Nebraska-Omaha, associate professor 2005-, Jefferis Chair, 2008-11. Writer. **Publications:** Field of Vision (essays), 1996; Flight Dreams: A Life in the Midwestern Landscape, 1998; Nature of Home: A Lexicon and Essays, 2002; Interior Places (essays), 2008; Three Rivers: Journey at Home and Beyond (essays), forthcoming. **Address:** Department of English, University of Nebraska-Omaha, ASH 189 C, 6001 Dodge St., Omaha, NE 68182, U.S.A. **Online address:** lknopp@unomaha.edu

KNOPPER, Steve Aaron. American (born United States), b. 1969. **Genres:** Music. **Career:** Rolling Stone Magazine, business correspondent; Fox News, on-air technology correspondent; Yahoo! Internet Life Magazine, Daily Net Buzz, columnist, 1999-2002; Post-Tribune, staff; Daily Camera, pop music critic and feature writer; Richmond News Leader, staff. **Publications:** (Ed.) MusicHound Lounge: The Essential Album Guide to Martini Music and Easy Listening, 1998; (ed.) MusicHound Swing! The Essential Album Guide, 1999; (with M. Bliesener) The Complete Idiot's Guide to Starting a Band, 2004; Colorado, 6th ed., 2006; Colorado Ski Towns, 2009; Appetite for Self-destruction: The Spectacular Crash of the Record Industry in the Digital Age, 2009. Contributor to periodicals. **Address:** Denver, CO , U.S.A. **Online address:** steveknopper@yahoo.com

KNOWLES, Elizabeth. British (born England), b. 1947. **Genres:** Language/Linguistics. **Career:** Oxford University Press, staff, senior editor of English dictionary, 1983-93, Oxford Quotations Dictionaries, publishing manager and managing editor, 1993-. **Publications:** (Comp.) Howard Hodgkin: Prints, 1977 to 1983, 1985; Quotations for Occasions, 2008; How to Read a Word, 2010. EDITOR: Concise Oxford Dictionary of Phrase and Fable, 1994; Terry Frost, 1994; (with J. Elliott) Oxford Dictionary of New Words, 1997; Oxford Dictionary of Phrase, Saying, and Quotation, 1997; Oxford Dictionary of Twentieth Century Quotations, 1998; Oxford Dictionary of Quotations, 1999, 2nd ed., 2004; Oxford Dictionary of Phrase and Fable, 2000; Concise Oxford Dictionary of Quotations, 2001, 7th ed., 2009; Oxford Dictionary of Modern Quotations, 2002, 3rd ed., 2008; What They Didn' Say: A Book of Misquotations, 2006; Trevor Bell, 2009; Little Oxford Dictionary of Proverbs, 2009. **Address:** Oxford University Press, Great Clarendon St., Oxford, OX OX2 6DP, England. **Online address:** elizabeth.knowles@oup.com

KNOWLES, Harry (Jay). American (born United States), b. 1971. **Genres:** Autobiography/Memoirs, Photography. **Career:** Ain't It Cool Inc., Ain't It Cool News, founder, 1996-. Writer. **Publications:** (With P. Cullum and M. Ebner) Ain't It Cool?: Hollywood's Redheaded Stepchild Speaks Out, 2002. **Address:** Ain't It Cool News, PO Box 180011, Austin, TX 78718-0011, U.S.A. **Online address:** harry@aintitcool.com

KNOWLES, Helen. American (born United States), b. 1973?. **Genres:** Law, Politics/Government. **Career:** State University of New York, assistant professor, 2006-; Whitman College, visiting professor, 2010-. Writer. **Publications:** The Tie Goes to Freedom: Justice Anthony M. Kennedy on Liberty, 2009. Contributor to journals and periodicals. **Address:** Whitman College, 345 Boyer Ave., Walla Walla, WA 99362, U.S.A. **Online address:** knowlehj@whitman.edu

KNOWLES, Jo. American (born United States), b. 1970?. **Genres:** Novels, Young Adult Non-fiction, Young Adult Fiction. **Career:** Simmons College, Center for the Study of Children's Literature, MFA Program, writing instructor. Writer. **Publications:** Huntington's Disease (nonfiction), 2006; Lessons from a Dead Girl, 2007; Junior Drug Awareness: Over-the-Counter Drugs (nonfiction), 2008; Jumping off Swings, 2009; Pearl, 2011, See You At Harry's, forthcoming. **Address:** Simmons College, 300 The Fenway, Boston, MA 02115, U.S.A. **Online address:** jo@joknowles.com

KNOX, Calvin M. See **SILVERBERG, Robert.**

KNOX, Elizabeth (Fiona). New Zealander (born New Zealand), b. 1959. **Genres:** Novels, Plays/Screenplays, Essays, Social Sciences, Young Adult Fiction, Biography, Autobiography/Memoirs. **Career:** Sport Magazine, assistant editor, 1988-93; Victoria University, tutor in film studies, 1989-95, writer-in-residence, 1997. **Publications:** HIGH JUMP SERIES: Paremata, 1989; Pomare, 1994; Tawa, 1998; The High Jump: A New Zealand Childhood, 2000. DREAM HUNTER DUET SERIES: Dream Hunter: Book One of the Dream hunter Duet, 2006; Dream Quake: Book Two of the Dream Hunter Duet, 2007. NOVELS: After Z-Hour, 1987; Treasure, 1992; Glamour and the Sea, 1996; The Vintner's Luck, 1998; Black Oxen, 2001; Billie's Kiss, 2002; Daylight, 2003; The Angel's Cut, 2009. OTHERS: (contrib.) Cherries on a Plate: New Zealand Writers Talk About Their Sisters, 1996; New Zealand Television: A Reader, 2002; Essays, 2004; The Love School: Personal Essays, 2009. Contributor to books and periodicals. **Address:** c/o Natasha Fairweather, A.P. Watt Ltd., 20 John St., London, GL WC1N 2DR, England. **Online address:** knoxbarrowman@paradise.net.nz

KNOX, George. British (born England), b. 1922. **Genres:** Art/Art History, Theatre, History, Humanities. **Career:** University of British Columbia, professor of history of art, 1970-87, professor emeritus, 1987-. Writer. **Publications:** Catalogue of the Tiepolo Drawings in the Victoria and Albert Museum, 1960; Tiepolo Drawings in the Victoria and Albert Museum, 1960, 2nd ed., 1975; Domenico Tiepolo: Raccolta di Teste, 1970; Tiepolo, A Bicentenary Exhibition, 1770-1970: Drawings, Mainly from American Collections, by Giambattista Tiepolo and the Members of His Circle, 1970; Tiepolo, 1971; Un Quaderno di Vedute di Giambattista e Domenico Tiepolo, 1974; (comp.) Etchings by the Tiepolos: Domenico Tiepolo's Collection of the Family Etchings: Eaux-Fortes des Tiepolo: Recueil de Domenico Tiepolo Rassemblantles Eaux-Fortes de sa Famille, 1976; Tiepolo: Tecnica e Immaginazione: Venezia, Palazzo Ducale, Luglio-Settembre 1979, 1979; Giambattista and Domenico Tiepolo: A Study and Catalogue Raisonne of the Chalk Drawings, 1980; Piazzetta: A Tercentenary Exhibition of Drawings, Prints and Books, 1983; (with J.B. Shaw) The Robert Lehman Collection, vol. VI: Italian Eighteenth-Century Drawings, 1988; 18th Century Venetian Art in Canadian Collections: L'art vénitien du dix-huitième siècledans les Collections Canadiennes, 1989; Giambattista Piazzetta, 1682-1754, 1992; Antonio Pellegrini, 1675-1741, 1995; (with A.M. Gealt) Domenico Tiepolo: Master Draftsman, 1996; (contrib.) The Mask of Venice: Masking, Theater and Identity in the Art of Tiepolo and His Time, 1996; (with A.M. Gealt) Giandomenico Tiepolo: Maestria e Gioco: Disegni dal Mondo, 1996; (with A.M. Gealt) Giandomenico Tiepolo: Scene di vita Quotidiana a Venezia e Nella Terraferma, 2005. Works appear in anthologies. **Address:** Art History, Visual Art and Theory, University of British Columbia, 2329 West Mall, Vancouver, BC V6T 1Z4, Canada. **Online address:** gknox@interchange.ubc.cc

KNOX, Melissa. (Melissa Gill Knox). American (born United States), b. 1957. **Genres:** Biography. **Career:** St. Peter's College, associate professor of English, 1992-; Barnard College, faculty; University of Duisburg, faculty. Writer. **Publications:** Oscar Wilde: A Long and Lovely Suicide, 1994; Oscar Wilde in the 1990s: the critic as creator, 2001; (ed. with B. James) Visions of Aggieland, 2008. **Address:** Department of Anglophone Studies, University of Duisburg, R12 S04 H22, Essen, 45141, Germany. **Online address:** melissa.knox-raab@uni-due.de

KNOX, Melissa Gill. See **KNOX, Melissa.**

KNOX-JOHNSTON, Robin. British (born England), b. 1939. **Genres:** Recreation, Sports/Fitness. **Career:** Writer. **Publications:** A World of My Own: The Singlehanded, Non-Stop Circumnavigation of the World in Suhaili, 1969; Robin Round the World: The Singlehanded, Non-Stop Circumnavigation of the World in Suhaili, 1970; Sailing, 1977; Last But Not Least, 1978; Twilight of Sail, 1978; Bunk Side Companion, 1982; Seamanship, 1986; The Boc Challenge, 1986; The Cape of Good Hope: A Maritime History, 1989; Yachting: The History of a Passion, 1990; The Columbus Venture, 1991; (with C. Bonington) Sea, Ice, Rock, 1993; Cape Horn, 1994; Beyond Jules Verne, 1995; Force of Nature, 2007. **Address:** 1 Tower St., Portsmouth, HM PO1 2JR, England. **Online address:** rknoxjohnston@clipper-ventures.com

KNUDSEN, Greta. See **KNUDSEN, Margrethe June.**

KNUDSEN, Margrethe June. (Greta Knudsen). Australian/Welsh (born Wales), b. 1934?. **Genres:** Gerontology/Senior Issues, Travel/Exploration. **Career:** William Balmain College, faculty, 1966-73; Australian Catholic University, lecturer in English and education, 1974-97. Writer. **Publications:** (Ed. with V. Aked) Quicksilver: A Modern Poetry Anthology, 1965; (as Greta Knudsen with E.S. Knudsen) Goldseekers, 1969. **Address:** 9 Best Rd., Middle Dural, NW 2158, Australia. **Online address:** margrethe.knudsen@uts.edu.au

KNUDSON, Danny Alan. New Zealander (born New Zealand), b. 1940. **Genres:** Education, History, Travel/Exploration, Art/Art History. **Career:**

Teacher, 1962-65; Otago Education Board, deputy principal, 1971-78, principal, 1978-; Green Island School, deputy principal, 1973-77; New Zealand Educational Institute, editor, 1973-74; Dunedin Teacher's College, lecturer, 1974, 1976; Reid Park School, Mosgiel, principal, 1978-80; Fairfield School, principal, 1980-81; George Street Normal School, principal, 1982-. **Publications:** The Story of Wakatipu, 1968; Goldfields Wonderland, 1974; The Road to Skippers, 1974; (ed. with M.E. Fleming and R.H. Jarratt) The Creative Arts, 1976; Goldtown School, 1976; Standard V, 1892, 1982. Contributor to journals. **Address:** George Street Normal School, George St., Dunedin, 1, New Zealand.

KNUTH, Donald E. American (born United States), b. 1938. **Genres:** Information Science/Computers, Mathematics/Statistics, Theology/Religion, Education, Sciences. **Career:** Burroughs Corp., consultant, 1960-68; California Institute of Technology, assistant professor of mathematics, 1963-68; ACM publications, Programming Languages, editor, 1964-67; Stanford University, professor of computer science, 1968-92, professor emeritus, 1993-; Guggenheim Foundation, fellow; Oxford University, visiting professor, 2002-06. Computer scientist, mathematician and writer. **Publications:** The Art of Computer Programming, vol. I: Fundamental Algorithms, 1968, vol. II: Seminumerical Algorithms, 1969, vol. III: Sorting and Searching, 1973, vol. IV: Combinatorial Algorithms, 1977, vol. V: Syntactic Algorithms, forthcoming; Surreal Numbers: How Two Ex-Students Turned on to Pure Mathematics and Found Total Happiness: A Mathematical Novelette, 1974; Mariages Stables Et Leurs Relations Avec D'autres Problèmes Combinatoires: Introduction à L'analyse Mathématique Des Algorithms, 1976; Tau Epsilon Chi: A System for Technical Text, 1979; TEX and METAFONT: New Directions in Typesetting, 1979; (ed. with A.P. Ershov) Algorithms in Modern Mathematics and Computer Science: Proceedings, Urgench, Uzbek SSR, September 16-22, 1979, 1981; (with D.H. Greene) Mathematics for the Analysis of Algorithms, 1981, 3rd ed., 1990; (ed. with A.P. Ershov) Algoritmy v Sovremennoï Matematike i ee Prilozheniiakh: Materialy Mezhdunarodnogo Simpoziuma Urgench, UzSSR, 16-22 Sentiabria 1979 g, 1982; The TeXbook, 1984; Computer Modern Typefaces, 1986; TEX: The Program, 1986; METAFONT: The Program, 1986; The METAFONT Book, 1986; TEXware, 1986; Torture Test for METAFONT, 1986; Computers and Typesetting, 5 vols., 1986; (with T. Larrabee and P.M. Roberts) Mathematical Writing, 1989; (with R.L. Graham and O. Patashnik) Concrete Mathematics: A Foundation for Computer Science, 1989, 2nd ed., 1994; 3: 16: Bible Texts Illuminated, 1991; Axioms and Hulls, 1992; Literate Programming, 1992; The Stanford Graph Base: A Platform for Combinatorial Computing, 1993; (with S. Levy) The CWEB System of Structured Documentation: Version 3.0, 1994; Selected Papers on Computer Science, 1996; Stable Marriage and Its Relation to Other Combinatorial Problems: An Introduction to the Mathematical Analysis of Algorithms, 1997; Digital Typography, 1999; MMIXware: A RISC Computer for the Third Millenium, 1999; Selected Papers on Analysis of Algorithms, 2000; Things a Computer Scientist Rarely Talks About, 2001; Selected Papers on Computer Languages, 2003; Selected Papers on Discrete Mathematics, 2003; Selected Papers on Design of Algorithms, 2010; Selected Papers on Fun and Games, 2010; éléments Pour une histoire de l'informatique, 2011; Algorithmes, 2011; Companion to the papers of Donald Knuth, 2011. **Address:** Department of Computer Science, Stanford University, 4B Gates Bldg., 353 Serra Mall, Stanford, CA 94305-9025, U.S.A.

KO, Dorothy. American (born United States), b. 1957?. **Genres:** History. **Career:** Rutgers University, faculty, Center for Critical Analysis of Contemporary Culture, fellow, 1999-2000; University of California, faculty; Columbia University, Barnard College, faculty, 2001-, professor of history. Writer. **Publications:** Teachers of the Inner Chambers: Women and Culture in Seventeenth-Century China, 1994; Every Step a Lotus: Shoes for Bound Feet, 2001; (ed. with J.K. Haboush and J.R. Piggott) Women and Confucian Cultures in Premodern China, Korea, and Japan, 2003; (with G.Y. Zhu and L.Z. Yi) Gui Shu Shi: Ming Mo Qing chu Jiang Nan de Cai n¨ Wen Hua, 2005; Cinderella's Sisters: A Revisionist History of Footbinding, 2005; (ed. with W. Zheng) Translating Feminisms in China, 2007; Chan Zu: Jin Lian Chong Bai Sheng Ji Er Shuai De Yan Bian, 2007. **Address:** Department of History, Barnard College, Columbia University, Rm. 416D, Lehman Hall, 3009 Broadway, New York, NY 10027, U.S.A. **Online address:** dko@barnard.edu

KO, Tanya Hyonhye. American/Korean (born Korea (South)), b. 1964. **Genres:** Poetry, Medicine/Health, Children's Non-fiction. **Career:** Young Women's Christian Association of the Greater Los Angeles Area, specialist with women's program, 1994-97; freelance writer, 1996-; Living Tree Con-

ference, artist-in-residence. **Publications:** Mrs Fox & Mrs Stork Korean, 1993; Mother's Diary from Generation 1.5, 2002; Yellow Flowers on a Rainy Day, 2003. Contributor to periodicals. **Address:** c/o Author Mail, Oma Books of the Pacific, PO Box 9095, San Pedro, CA 90734, U.S.A. **Online address:** tanyako@cox.net

KOBEL, Peter. American (born United States) **Genres:** Cultural/Ethnic Topics, Humor/Satire. **Career:** Premiere magazine, managing editor; Entertainment Weekly, editor; ARTnews, editor; NYTimes, editor. **Publications:** (Co-ed.) Bill Condon, Chicago: The Movie and Lyrics, 2003; Silent Movies: The Birth of Film and the Triumph of Movie Culture, 2007. Contributor to periodicals. **Address:** Little Brown, and Company, 3 Center Plaza, Boston, MA 02108, U.S.A. **Online address:** peter.kobel@gmail.com

KOCH, Ebba. Austrian (born Austria), b. 1944. **Genres:** History, Architecture, Theology/Religion. **Career:** University of Vienna, docent, 1992-2001, professor of Asian art, 2001-; American University in Cairo, distinguished visiting professor, 1998; Taj Mahal Conservation Collaborative, global advisor, 2001-; Harvard University, Aga Khan Program for the Study of Islamic Architecture, fellow, 2002, visiting professor, 2008; Institute of Art History, professor; Oxford University, visiting professor. Writer and art historian. **Publications:** Shah Jahan and Orpheus: The Pietre Dure Decoration and the Programme of the Throne in the Hall of Public Audiences at the Red Fort of Delhi, 1988; Mughal Architecture: An Outline of Its History and Development, 1526-1858, 1991, 2nd ed., 2002; (with M.C. Beach) King of the World: The Padshahnama: An Imperial Mughal Manuscript from the Royal Library, Windsor Castle, 1997; Dara-Shikoh Shooting Nilgais: Hunt and Landscape in Mughal Painting, 1998; Mughal Art and Imperial Ideology: Collected Essays, 2001; The Complete Taj Mahal and the Riverfront Gardens of Agra, 2006; Die Welt des Orients: Kunst und Kultur des Islam, 2006. **Address:** Institut für Kunstgeschichte, Universität Wien, Universitätscampus Hof 9, Spitalgasse 2, Wien, A-1090, Austria. **Online address:** kunstgeschichte@univie.ac.at

KOCH, Edward I(rving). American (born United States), b. 1924. **Genres:** Politics/Government, Autobiography/Memoirs, Biography, History. **Career:** Koch, Lankenau, Schwartz & Kovener (law firm), co-founder and senior partner, 1963-68; district leader, 1963-66; city council, 1966-68; mayor, 1978-89; Robinson, Silverman, Pearce, Aronsohn & Berman, partner, 1990-; Bryan Cave LLP, partner; New York University, College of Arts and Sciences, adjunct professor; Brandeis University, adjunct professor; City University of New York, Baruch College, adjunct professor; New York Congressional Delegation, secretary. Writer. **Publications:** The Mandate Millstone, 1980; How'm I Doing: The Wit and Wisdom of Ed Koch, 1981; (with W. Rauch) Mayor, 1984; (with W. Rauch) Politics, 1985; Mayor: The Musical, 1987; (with J.C. O'Connor) His Eminence and Hizzoner: A Candid Exchange, 1989; (with L.T. Jones) All the Best: Letters from a Feisty Mayor, 1990; (with D. Paisner) Citizen Koch: An Autobiography, 1992; Ed Koch on Everything: Movies, Politics, Personalities, Food, and Other Stuff, 1994; (with H. Resnicow) Murder at City Hall, 1995; (with W.C. Staub) Murder on Broadway, 1996; (with W.C. Staub) Murder on 34th Street, 1997; (with W.C. Staub) The Senator Must Die, 1998; (intro.) Giuliani: A Nasty Man, 1999; New York: A State of Mind, 1999; (with D. Paisner) I'm Not Done Yet!: Keeping at It, Remaining Relevant, and Having the Time of My Life, 2000; The Story of the Clancy Brothers and Tommy Makem, 2003; (with P.K. Thaler) Eddie: Harold's Little Brother, 2004; (with P.K. Thaler) Eddie's Little Sister Makes a Splash, 2007; (with C. Heady) Buzz: How To Create It and Win With It, 2007; The Koch Papers: My Fight Against Anti-Semitism, 2008. **Address:** Bryan Cave L.L.P., 161 N Clark St., Ste. 4300, 1290 Ave. of the Americas, Chicago, IL 60601-3315, U.S.A. **Online address:** eikoch@bryancave.com

KOCH, Peter O. American (born United States), b. 1953. **Genres:** Novels, Biography, Autobiography/Memoirs, History, Adult Non-fiction. **Career:** First American Bank, assistant branch manager, 1977-86; Virginia Alcoholic Beverage Control, Tysons Corner, warehouse worker, 1990-2000; Harris Tecter, accountant, 2000-. Writer. **Publications:** To the Ends of the Earth: The Age of the European Explorers, 2003; The Aztecs, the Conquistadors and the Making of Mexican Culture, 2006; Spanish Conquest of the Inca Empire, 2008; Imaginary Cities of Gold: The Spanish Quest for Treasure in North America, 2009. **Address:** 6200 Everglades Dr., Alexandria, VA 22312, U.S.A.

KOCH, Phyllis McCallum. American (born United States), b. 1911?. **Genres:** Plays/Screenplays, Poetry, Children's Fiction. **Career:** San Jose Junior Theatre Advisory Board, president; Greater San Jose Area Council of

Arts, vice-president; National League of American Pen Women, president; Waterford Readers Theater, producer. Writer. **Publications:** PLAYS FOR CHILDREN: The Pale Pink Dragon, 1966; The Uniform Unicorn, 1967; The Tough and Tender Troll, 1967; The Grateful Griffin, 1968; The Vanilla Viking, 1969; Hansel and Gretel and the Golden Petticoat, 1973; Crumple, Rumpelstiltskin, 1974; Jack and the Beanstalk, 1976; The Dignified Donkey of New Almaden, 1976; The Twelve Dancing Princesses, 1978; The Swiss Family Robinson (musical), 1978; Christmas with Little Women, 1980. PLAYS FOR ADULTS: Ho, Ho, Tyranny, 1991; The Mystery Guest, 1992. **Address:** 1860 Tice Creek Dr., Ste. 1311, Walnut Creek, CA 94595, U.S.A.

KOCHALKA, James. American (born United States), b. 1967. **Genres:** Graphic Novels, Humor/Satire. **Career:** Writer and artist. **Publications:** Magic Boy and Girlfriend, 1991; Paradise Sucks, 1997; Tiny Bubbles, 1998; Quit Your Job, 1998; Kissers, 1999; The Perfect Planet and Other Stories, 1999; Monkey vs. Robot, 2000; (editor, with others) Expo 2000, 2000; Sunburn, 2001; Pinky & Stinky, 2002; Fantastic Butterflies, 2002; Monkey vs. Robot and the Crystal of Power, 2003; Magic Boy and the Robot Elf, 2003; Fancy Froglin's Sexy Forest, 2003; Peanut Butter & Jeremy's Best Book Ever, 2003; American Elf: James Kochalka's Collected Sketchbook Diaries, 2004; The Cute Manifesto, 2005; Squirrelly Gray, 2007; Johnny Boo: The Best Little Ghost in the World, 2008; Super F*ckers, 2010. Work appears in anthologies. Contributor to books and magazines. **Address:** PO Box 8321, Burlington, VT 05402-8321, U.S.A. **Online address:** jks@indyworld.com

KOCHAN, Miriam (Louise). British (born England), b. 1929. **Genres:** History, Translations, Military/Defense/Arms Control. **Career:** Reuters Economic Services, sub-editor, 1950-54; freelance writer, 1954-77; Oxford, assistant sub-editor, 1977-80. **Publications:** (Ed. and intro. with L. Kochan) Russian Themes: A Selection of Articles from History Today, 1967; Life in Russia Under Catherine the Great, 1969; (with L. Kochan) Lenin, 1974; (ed. with L. Kochan) The Jewish Family Album: The Life of a People in Photographs, 1975; Catherine the Great, 1976; The Last Days of Imperial Russia, 1976; Prisoners of England, 1980; Britain's Internees in the Second World War, 1983. TRANSLATIONS: J. and G. Roux, Greece, 1958; M. Aubert, Gothic Cathedrals of France, 1959; P. Rivet, Maya Cities, 1960; M. Brion, The World of Archaeology, 1961; G. Picard, Carthage, 1964; P. Leveque, The Greek Adventure, 1968; P. Akamatsu, Meiji 1868, 1972; F. Braudel, Capitalism and Material Life, 1973; L. Poliakov, History of Anti-Semitism vol. III, 1975; L. Poliakov, The Jewish Bankers and The Holy Sea, 1977; (with P. Engel) P. Engel, The Norm of Truth, 1991; P. Birnbaum, Anti-Semitism in France, 1992; C. Charle, A Social History of France in the 19th Century, 1994; E. Benbassa, Haim Nahun, 1995; (with L. Kochan) Islam and Dhimmitude: Where Civilizations Collide, 2002; Fashion Under the Occupation, 2002; The History of Anti-Semitism: From Voltaire to Wagner, 2003. **Address:** Fairleigh Dickinson University Press, M-GH2-01, 285 Madison Ave., Madison, NJ 07940, U.S.A.

KOCKA, Jürgen. German (born Germany), b. 1941. **Genres:** History, Social Commentary. **Career:** University of Münster, assistant professor of history, 1968-73; University of Bielefeld, professor of history, 1973-88, Center for Interdisciplinary Research, director, 1983-88; Free University of Berlin, professor of history, 1988-2009, chair of the history of the industrial world, 1988-2009, Center for Comparative Social History, head, 1993-97, School for Comparative European History, director, 2004-; Wissenschaftskolleg zu Berlin, permanent fellow, 1991-2000, Social Science Research Center, president, 2001-07, research professor in historical science, 2007-09; Development and Management of the Research Area for the Study of Contemporary History, staff, 1992-96, senior fellow, 2009-; Centre for Contemporary History, founding director and senior fellow, 1992-96; Berlin-Brandenburg Academy of Sciences, vice president, 2009-; Humboldt University Berlin, director, 2004-, senior advisor, 2009-; Center for Research on Contemporary History, senior fellow, 2009-. Writer. **Publications:** Unternehmensverwaltung und Angestellten schaft am Beispiel Siemens 1847-1914, 1969; Klassengesellschaft im Krieg: dt. Sozialgeschichte1914-1918, 1973; Soziale Schichtung und Mobilität in Deutschland im19. und 20. Jahrhundert, 1975; Unternehmer in der deutschen Industrialisierung, 1975; Theorien in der Praxis des Historikers: Forschungsbeispiele u. ihre Diskussion, 1977; Angestellte zwischenFaschismus und Demokratie: zur polit Sozialgeschichte d. Angestellten, USA1890-1940 im internat Vergleich, 1977; Klassengesellschaft im Krieg: dtSozialgeschichte 1914-1918, 1978; Recht und Entwicklung derGrossunternehmen im 19. und frühen 20 Jahrhundert: wirtschafts-, sozial- u rechtshistor Unters zur Industrialisierung in Deutschland, Frankreich, England u.d.

U.S.A.: Law and the Formation of the Big Enterprisesin The 19th and Early 20th Centuries, 1979; Kapitalismus, Klassenstruktur und Probleme der Demokratie in Deutschland 1910-1940, 1979; White Collar Workers in America, 1890-1940: A Social-Political History In International Perspective, 1980; Die Angestellten in der deutschen Geschichte 1850-1980: vom Privatbeamten zum Angestellten Arbeitnehmer, 1981; Lohnarbeit und Klassenbildung: Arbeiter und Arbeiterbewegung in Deutschland 1800-1875, 1983; (trans.) Facing Total War: German society, 1914-1918, 1984; Bildungsbürgertum im 19. Jahrhundert, 1985; (with G. Ránki) Economic Theory and History, 1985; Sozialgeschichte: Begriff, Entwicklung, Probleme, 1986; Bürger und Bürgerlichkeit im 19. Jahrhundert, 1987; Interdisziplinarität: Praxis, Herausforderung, Ideologie, 1987; Max Weber, ein Symposion, 1988; Geschichte und Aufklärung: Aufsätze, 1989; Arbeitsverhältnisse und Arbeiterexistenzen: Grundlagen der Klassenbildung im 19. Jahrhundert, 1990; Weder Stand noch Klasse: Unterschichten um 1800, 1990; (ed. with A. Mitchell) Bourgeois society in Nineteenth-Century Europe, 1993; Historische DDR-Forschung: Aufsätze und Studien, 1993; (with M. Sabrow) Die DDR als Geschichte, 1994; Vereinigungskrise: zur Geschichte der Gegenwart, 1995; (with H.G. Haupt) Geschichte und Vergleich, 1996; Wissenschaft und Wiedervereinigung: Disziplinen im Umbruch, 1998; Parteien im Wandel: vom Kaiserreich zur Weimarer Republik: Rekrutierung, Qualifizierung, Karrieren, 1999; Industrial Culture and Bourgeois Society: Business, Labor and Bureaucracy in Modern Germany, 1999; (with D. Dowe and H.A. Winkler) Parteien im Wandel, 1999; (with M. Hildermeier and C. Conrad) Europäische Zivilgesellschaft in Ost und West, 2000; (with C. Offe) Geschichte und Zukunft der Arbeit, 2000; Interventionen, 2001; (with C. Conrad) Staatsbürgerschaft in Europa, 2001; (co-ed.) Progressive Governance for the XXI Century, 2002; (co-author) Geschichte als Last und Chance, 2003; Mehr Last als Lust: Arbeit und Arbeitsgesellschaft in DerEuropaischen Geschichte, 2006; Zukunftsfähigkeit Deutschlands: sozialwissenschaftliche Essays, 2008; (ed.) Work in a Modern Society: The German Historical Experience in Comparative Perspective, 2009; (ed. with H. Haupt) Comparative History and the Quest for Transnationality: Central European Approaches and New Perspectives, 2009; Civil Society and Dictatorship in Modern German History, 2010; Arbeiten an der Geschichte, 2011. **Address:** History of the Industrial World, Rm. 314, GoBlerstr 2-4, Berlin, D-14195, Germany. **Online address:** prokocka@zedat.fu-berlin.de

KODAS, Michael. American (born United States) **Genres:** History. **Career:** Hartford Courant, journalist & photographer, 1987-. Writer and adventurer. **Publications:** Hikes in Northern New England: New Hampshire, Maine, 1999; High Crimes: The Fate of Everest in an Age of Greed, 2008. Contributor to books and periodicals. **Online address:** mk@michaelkodas.com

KODIS, Michelle R. American/German (born Germany), b. 1968. **Genres:** Food And Wine, Medicine/Health, Architecture. **Career:** Gillette News-Record, reporter and feature writer, 1990; Colley Associates, health writer and editor, 1990; Willamette Falls Hospital, public relations coordinator and health writer, 1991-93; freelance writer and editor, 1992-; Buzzworm's Earth Journal, assistant editor, 1993-94; Telluride Historical Museum, public relations and graphics coordinator, 1994; Healthy Communities, editor; Telluride Mountain Film Festival, public relations and media director. **Publications:** The Telluride Cookbook: Recipes and Profiles of Telluride's Finest Restaurants and Caterers, 1995; Reach for Health: Regional, Environmental and Community Health Guide, 1996; (with D. Moran and D. Hony) Love Scents: How Your Natural Pheromones Influence Your Relationships, Your Moods and Who You Love, 1998; Blueprint Small: Creative Ways to Live with Less, 2003; Blueprint Affordable: How to Build a Beautiful House without Breaking the Bank, 2004; Blueprint Remodel: Tract Home Transformations that Turn Everyday to Extraordinary, 2004; Ultimate Outdoor Kitchens: Inspirational Designs and Plans, 2006; Ultimate Backyard: Inspired Ideas for Outdoor Living, 2006; Modern Cabin: New Designs for an American Icon, 2007; Turn Me On: 100 Easy Ways to Use Solar Energy, 2009. Contributor to periodicals. **Address:** PO Box 458, Telluride, CO 81435-0458, U.S.A. **Online address:** michellekodis@yahoo.com

KOEGLER, Hans Herbert. American/German (born Germany), b. 1960. **Genres:** Literary Criticism And History, Cultural/Ethnic Topics, Philosophy. **Career:** University of Frankfurt, research fellow, 1986-87; University of California, research fellow, 1989-90; The New School for Social Research, research fellow, 1989-90; Northwestern University, research fellow, 1989-90; University of Illinois at Urbana-Champaign, assistant professor of European philosophy, 1991-97, Programs in Arms Control, Disarmament and International Security, faculty associate, 1994, Unit for Criticism and Interpretive

Theory, assistant professor, 1994; University of Catamarca, honorary professor, 1996; University of North Florida, Department of History and Philosophy, assistant professor of language, 1997, Department of Philosophy, associate professor, 1999, professor and chair, 2007-, Office for Faculty Enhancement, faculty fellow, 2000-01, coordinator of graduate studies, 2005. Writer. **Publications:** Die Macht des Dialogs: Kritische Hermeneutik nach Gadamer, Foucault und Rorty, 1992; Michel Foucault: Ein Anti-Humanistischer Aufklaerer, 1994; (contrib.) Cultural Studies, 1998; (ed. with K.R. Stueber) Empathy and Agency: The Problem of Understanding in the Human Sciences, 2000; Kultura, Kritika, Dialog, 2006; Autonomie und Identität: Kritische Theorie und hermeneutische Kritik des Subjekts, forthcoming. Contributor of articles to journals. **Address:** Department of Philosophy, University of North Florida, Rm. 2337, Bldg. 10, 1 University of North Florida Dr., Jacksonville, FL 32224-2645, U.S.A. **Online address:** hkoegler@unf.edu

KOEHLER, **Cheryl Angelina.** American (born United States) **Genres:** Travel/Exploration, Local History/Rural Topics, Reference. **Career:** Edible East Bay Magazine, publisher and editor. **Publications:** Touring the Sierra Nevada, 2007. Contributor to periodicals. **Address:** Edible East Bay Magazine, 4200 Park Blvd., Ste. 267, Oakland, CA 94602, U.S.A. **Online address:** editor@edibleeastbay.com

KOEHLINGER, **Amy L.** American (born United States) **Genres:** History, Women's Studies And Issues. **Career:** Florida State University, assistant professor of North American religious history, 2002-08, associate professor of American religious history, 2009-; Princeton University, Center for the Study of Religion, visiting fellow, 2003-04; Indiana University-Purdue University, Center for the Study of Religion and American Culture, seminar fellow, 2003-05; The Sisters of Selma film documentary for the Public Broadcasting Service (PBS), historical consultant, 2004. Writer. **Publications:** The New Nuns: Racial Justice and Religious Reform in the 1960s, 2007; (contrib.) Women and Religion in America: Reimagining the Past, 2007. Contributor to periodicals. **Address:** Department of Religion, Florida State University, 120D Dodd Hall, 641 University Way, PO Box 3061520, Tallahassee, FL 32306-1520, U.S.A. **Online address:** akoehlin@mailer.fsu.edu

KOEHN, **Peter H.** American (born United States), b. 1944. **Genres:** International Relations/Current Affairs, Social Sciences, Social Commentary, Adult Non-fiction, Politics/Government, Public/Social Administration, Medicine/Health, Humanities, Third World, Environmental Sciences/Ecology, Sociology. **Career:** Haile Selassie I University (now Addis Ababa University), lecturer in public administration, 1970-72; University of Montana, instructor, 1972-73, assistant professor, 1973-77, associate professor, 1977-81, professor of political science, 1981-, founding director of international programs, 1987-96; Ahmadu Bello University, principal research fellow, 1978-80, Fulbright lecturer, 1979-80; University of Namibia, visiting professor of public administration, 1991; Shanghai International Studies University, exchange professor of English, 1996-97; Chinese University of Hong Kong, Hong Kong-America Center, visiting professor, director of research and development, 1997-98. Writer. **Publications:** (With L.S. McKinsey) Lake County, Montana: Growth of a Small Government, Bureau of Government Research, 1975; (with J. Konigsberg) Conduct of Local Government Review in Missoula, Montana: Dynamics of a City-County Consolidation Proposal, Bureau of Government Research, 1976; (with J.J. Lopach) Profile of Montana Local Government Study Commissioners, Bureau of Government Research, 1976; (with J.J. Lopach) Montana Local Government Review: An Analysis and Summary, Bureau of Government Research, 1977; (with S.R. Waldron) Afocha: A Link between Community and Administration in Harar, Ethiopia, 1978; (with J.M. Cohen) Ethiopian Provincial and Municipal Government: Imperial Patterns and Post-Revolution Changes (monograph), 1980; (ed. with E.A.O. Oyeyipo and L. Joye) Cases in Post Reform Nigerian Administration, 1982; (with A.Y. Aliyu) Local Autonomy and Inter-Governmental Relations in Nigeria: The Case of the Northern States in the Immediate Post Local Government Reform Period (1976-79), 1982; (with G. Negash) Resettled Refugees and Asylum Applicants: Implications of the Case of Migrants from Ethiopia for United States Policy (monograph), 1987; Public Policy and Administration in Africa: Lessons from Nigeria, 1990; Refugees from Revolution: U.S. Policy and Third-World Migration, 1991; (ed. with O.J.B. Ojo and contrib.) Making Aid Work: Innovative Approaches for Africa at the Turn of the Century, 1999; (ed. with J.Y.S. Cheng and contrib.) The Outlook for U.S.-China Relations following the 1997-1998 Summits: Chinese and American Perspectives on Security, Trade and Cultural Exchange, 1999; (ed. with J.Y.S. Cheng) 1997-1998 FenghuiHou Zhongmei Guanxi Zhi Fazhan, 1999;

(ed. with X. Yin and contrib.) The Expanding Roles of Chinese Americans in U.S.-China Relations: Transnational Networks and Trans-Pacific Interactions, 2002; (with J.N. Rosenau) Transnational Competence: Empowering Professional Curricula for Horizon-Rising Challenges, 2010. **Address:** Department of Political Science, University of Montana, LA 416, Missoula, MT 59812, U.S.A. **Online address:** peter.koehn@umontana.edu

KOELB, **Clayton T.** American (born United States), b. 1942. **Genres:** Literary Criticism And History. **Career:** University of Chicago, assistant professor, associate professor, professor of German, 1969-81; University of North Carolina, Guy B. Johnson distinguished professor of German and comparative literature, 1991-. Writer. **Publications:** Thomas Mann's Goethe and Tolstoy: Notes and Sources, 1984; The Incredulous Reader: Literature and the Function of Disbelief, 1984; Inventions of Reading: Rhetoric and the Literary Imagination, 1988; Kafka'a Rhetoric: The Passion of Reading, 1989; Legendary Figures: Ancient History in Modern Novels, 1998; Revivifying Word: Literature, Philosophy, and the Theory of Life in Europe's Romantic Age, 2008. EDITOR: (with V. Lokke) The Current in Criticism: Essays on the Present and Future of Literary Theory, 1987; (with S. Noakes) The Comparative Perspective on Literature: Approaches to Theory and Practice, 1988; Nietzsche as Postmodernist: Essays Pro and Contra, 1990; (and trans.) T. Mann, Death in Venice, 1994; (with E. Downing) German Literature of the Nineteenth Century, 1832-1899, 2005; (with R. Gray, R. Gross and R. Goebel) A Franz Kafka Encyclopedia, 2005; The Revivifying Word: Literature, Philosophy, and the Theory of Life in Europe's Romantic Age, 2008; Kafka: A Guide for the Perplexed, 2010. **Address:** Department of Germanic and Slavic Languages and Li, University of North Carolina, 443 Dey Hall, CB 3160, Chapel Hill, NC 27599-3160, U.S.A. **Online address:** ckoelb@email.unc.edu

KOENIG, **Harold G.** American (born United States), b. 1951. **Genres:** Medicine/Health, Human Relations/Parenting. **Career:** Duke University Medical Center, clinical assistant professor, 1992-93, assistant professor, 1993-96, associate professor of psychiatry, 1996-2001, associate professor of medicine, 1998-, associate professor, 2001-04, professor psychiatry and behavioral sciences, 2004-, Aging Center, senior fellow, 1992-, Center for the Study of Religion/Spirituality and Health, director and founder, 1998-2006, Center for Spirituality, Theology and Health, co-director, 2007-10, director, 2010-; Federal Correctional Center, research psychiatrist, 1992-93; Geriatric Evaluation and Treatment Clinic, director of psychiatric services; Dukes Center for Spirituality, co-director. Writer. **Publications:** (With M. Smiley and J.A.P. Gonzales) Religion, Health, and Aging: A Review and Theoretical Integration, 1988; Aging and God: Spiritual Paths to Mental Health in Midlife and Later Years, 1994; Research on Religion and Aging: An Annotated Bibliography, 1995; (with A.J. Weaver) Handbook of Religion and Mental Health: A Handbook for Pastors and Religious Caregivers, 1997; (with T. Lamar and B. Lamar) A Gospel for the Mature Years: Finding Fulfillment by Knowing and Using Your Gift, 1997; Is Religion Good for Your Health? The Effects of Religion on Physical and Mental Health, 1997; (with A.J. Weaver) Pastoral Care of Older Adults: Creative Pastoral Care and Counseling, 1998; (ed. with A.J. Weaver and P.C. Roe) Reflections on Aging and Spiritual Growth, 1998; (ed.) Handbook of Religion and Mental Health, 1998; (with M. McConnell) The Healing Power of Faith: Science Explores Medicine's Last Great Frontier, 1999; (with G. Lewis) Healing Connection: A World-Renowned Medical Scientist Discovers the Powerful Link between Christian Faith and Health, 2000; Purpose and Power in Retirement: New Opportunities for Mand Significance, 2002; (ed. with H.J. Cohen) Link between Religion and Health: Psychoneuroimmunology and the Faith Factor, 2002; (with A.J. Weaver and L.A. Revilla) Counseling Families across the Stages of Life: A Handbook for Pastors and Other Helping Professionals, 2002; (with V.B. Carson) Parish Nursing: Stories of Service and Care, 2002; Spirituality in Patient Care: Why, How, When, and What, 2002; Chronic Pain: Biomedical and Spiritual Approaches, 2003; (with W.D. Hale) Healing Bodies and Souls: A Practical Guide for Congregations, 2003; (with V.B. Carson) Spiritual Caregiving: Healthcare as a Ministry, 2004; (with D.M. Lawson and M. McConnell) Faith in the Future: Healthcare, Aging, and the Role of Religion, 2004; (with D.B. Biebel) New Light on Depression: Help, Hope & Answers for the Depressed & Those Who Love Them, 2004; (ed. with J. Levin) Faith, Medicine, and Science: A Festschrift in Honor of Dr. David B. Larson, 2005; Faith and Mental Health: Religious Resources for Healing, 2005; (with D.B. Biebel) Simple Health, 2005; In the Wake of Disaster: Religious Responses to Terrorism & Catastrophe, 2006; Kindness and Joy: Expressing the Gentle Love, 2006; (with A.J. Weaver and C.A. Hosenfeld) Counseling Persons with Addictions and Compulsions: A Handbook for Clergy and Other Helping Professionals, 2007; Medicine, Religion, and Health: Where Science & Spirituality Meet, 2008; (ed. with V.B. Carson) Spiritual Dimensions of Nursing Practice, 2008; (with A.J. Weaver) Pastoral Care of Alcohol Abusers, 2009; (with V.B. Carson) Parish Nursing: Stories of Service and Care, 2011; Spirituality and Health Research: Methods, Measurements, Statistics, and Resources, 2011; Handbook of Religion and Health, 2nd ed., 2011. Contributor to books and magazines. **Address:** Department of Psychiatry & Behavioral Sciences, Duke University, PO Box 3400, Durham, NC 27710, U.S.A.

KOENIG, Karl P. American (born United States), b. 1938. **Genres:** Anthropology/Ethnology, Photography, Art/Art History, Reference. **Career:** Stanford University, professor of psychology, 1964-66; University of New Mexico, professor of psychology, 1966-75, professor of psychiatry, 1975-81; private practice of psychology, Albuquerque, 1981-. Writer and photographic artist, 1990-. **Publications:** Gumoil Photographic Printing, 1994, rev. ed., 1999; (with N. Shapiro) Match Safe Masterpieces, 2008; (with R. Franklin and K. Jameson) Fragments: Architecture of The Holocaust, 2011. Contributor to journals. **Address:** 6435 Nabor Rd. NW, Los Ranchos, NM 87107, U.S.A. **Online address:** kpkoe@swcp.com

KOENIGSBERGER, Helmut Georg. British/German (born Germany), b. 1918. **Genres:** History. **Career:** Queen's University, lecturer in economic history, 1948-51; University of Manchester, senior lecturer, 1951-60; International Commission for the History of Representative and Parliamentary Institutions, secretary general, 1955-75, vice president, 1975-80, president, 1980; City University of New York, visiting professor, 1957; University of Wisconsin, visiting professor, 1958; University of Nottingham, professor of modern history, 1960-66; Columbia University, visiting professor, 1962; Cambridge University, visiting professor, 1963; Washington University, visiting professor, 1964; British Academy, fellow; Cornell University, professor of European history, 1966-73; University of London, Kings College, professor of history, 1973-84, professor emeritus, 1984-; Royal Historical Society, fellow, vice president, 1982-85; Historisches College, fellow, 1984-85, vice president, 1975-80, president, 1980-85; fellow, 1999. Writer. **Publications:** The Government of Sicily under Philip II of Spain: A Study in the Practice of Empire, 1951; Decadence or Shift?, 1960; (with G.L. Mosse and G.Q. Bowler) Europe in the Sixteenth Century, 1968; Estates and Revolutions: Essays in Modern European History, 1971; The Habsburgs and Europe 1516-1660, 1971; Politicians and Virtuosi: Essays in Early Modern History, 1986; Medieval Europe 400-1500, 1987; Early Modern Europe 1500-1789, 1987; Monarchies, States Generals and Parliaments, 2001. EDITOR: (with J.H. Elliott) The Diversity of History, 1970; Luther: A Profile, 1972; (with B. Oestreich) Neostoicism and the Early Modern State, 1982; A History of Europe, vol. I: Medieval Europe, 400-1500, vol. II: Early Modern Europe, 1500-1789, 1987; Republiken und Republikanismus im Europa der fruhen Neuzeit, 1988; (ed.) Sicilia e Spagna, 1998. Contributor to periodicals. **Address:** King's College, Strand, London, GL WC2R 2LS, England.

KOERNER, Joseph Leo. American (born United States), b. 1958. **Genres:** Art/Art History, Adult Non-fiction, Essays, Humanities. **Career:** Yale University, research assistant, 1976-80; University of California, teaching associate, 1985; Harvard University, assistant professor of fine art, 1989-91, professor of history of art and architecture, 1991-2000, Victor S. Thomas professor of the history of art and architecture and director of undergraduate studies, 2007-, senior fellow, 2008-; University of Frankfurt, Institute of Art History, professor of modern art history, 1999-2000, Ordinarius professor of modern art history, 2000-01; University College London, Department of History of Art, professor, 2000-04; Cambridge University, Slade Professor of Fine Art, 2002-03; University of London, professor in the history of art, 2004-07. Writer. **Publications:** Die Suche nach dem Labyrinth: Der Mythos von Daedalus und Ikarus, 1983; Henry Koerner, from Vienna to the U.S.A.: A Retrospective Exhibition, Paintings, Watercolors and Drawings: Selected Works 1930 to 1986, May 3 to 24, 1986, ACA Galleries, 1986; Caspar David Friedrich and the Subject of Landscape, 1990; (with R. Crone) Paul Klee: Legends of the Sign, 1991; The Moment of Self-Portraiture in German Renaissance Art, 1993; (with B. Butts) The Printed World of Pieter Bruegel, the Elder, 1995; Unheimliche Heimat: Henry Koerner, 1915-1991, 1997; (contrib.) Albrecht Dürer and His Legacy: The Graphic Work of a Renaissance Artist, 2002; The Reformation of the Image, 2004; (contrib.) Self Portrait: Renaissance to Contemporary, 2006; Dürer's Hands, 2006; (with M. Koster) Adam Fuss: At Home in the World, 2010; (contrib.) Hans van Aachen (1552-1612), 2010. FORTHCOMING: Parallel Worlds: Hieronymus Bosch and Pieter Bruegel; Hieronymus Bosch: Enemy Painting; The Family Portrait. **Address:** Depart-

ment of History of Art & Architecture, Arthur M. Sackler Museum, Harvard University, 485 Broadway, Cambridge, MA 02138, U.S.A. **Online address:** koerner@fas.harvard.edu

KOERNER, Lisbet. (Lisbet Rausing). British/American/Swedish (born Sweden), b. 1960?. **Genres:** Adult Non-fiction, Autobiography/Memoirs, History, Science Fiction/Fantasy. **Career:** Harvard University, Department of the History of Science, assistant professor; University of London, senior research investigator; Imperial College, Centre for the History of Science, Technology and Medicine, senior research investigator, senior research fellow, 2002-. Writer. **Publications:** (With D.B. Dick) Corrour, A History of a Sporting Estate, 1998; Linnaeus: Nature and Nation (biography), 1999. Contributor to books and journals. **Address:** Deparment of Humanities, Imperial College, South Kensington Campus, 446 Sherfield Bldg., London, GL SW7 2AZ, England. **Online address:** l.koerner@imperial.ac.uk

KOERTGE, Ron(ald). American (born United States), b. 1940. **Genres:** Young Adult Fiction, Poetry. **Career:** Writer, 1962-; Pasadena City College, professor of English, 1965-2002, now retired. **Publications:** FOR YOUNG ADULTS FICTION: Where the Kissing Never Stops, 1987, 2nd ed., 2005; The Arizona Kid, 1988; The Boy in the Moon, 1990; Mariposa Blues, 1991; The Harmony Arms, 1992; Tiger, Tiger, Burning Bright, 1994; Confess-O-Rama, 1996; The Heart of the City, 1998; The Brimstone Journals, 2001; Stoner and Spaz, 2002; Shakespeare Bats Cleanup, 2003; Margaux with an X, 2004; Boy Girl Boy, 2005; Strays, 2007; Deadville, 2008; Shakespeare Makes the Playoffs, 2010. POETRY: Meat: Cherry's Market Diary, 1973; The Father Poems, 1974; The Hired Nose, 1974; My Summer Vacation, 1975; Men under Fire, 1976; Twelve Photographs of Yellowstone, 1976; How to Live on Five Dollars a Day, 1976; Cheap Thrills, 1976; Sex Object, 1979; The Jockey Poems, 1980; Diary Cows, 1982; Life on the Edge of the Continent: Selected Poems, 1982; High School Dirty Poems, 1991; Making Love to Roget's Wife, 1997; Geography of the Forehead, 2000; Indigo, 2009. FOR ADULTS: The Boogeyman (novel), 1980; Now Playing, 2011. Contributor to periodicals. **Address:** c/o William Reiss, John Hawkins & Associates, 71 W 23rd St., Ste. 1600, New York, NY 10010, U.S.A. **Online address:** ronkoe@earthlink.net

KOESTENBAUM, Wayne. American (born United States), b. 1958. **Genres:** Poetry, Literary Criticism And History, Gay And Lesbian Issues, Popular Culture, Music, Novels. **Career:** Yale University, assistant professor, 1988-93, associate professor of English, 1993-96; City University of New York, Graduate School, visiting associate professor, 1996-97, professor, 1997-2007, distinguished professor of English, 2007-; Columbia University, adjunct assistant professor, 2002. Writer. **Publications:** Double Talk: The Erotics of Male Literary Collaboration, 1989; Ode to Anna Moffo and Other Poems, 1990; The Queen's Throat: Opera, Homosexuality, and the Mystery of Desire, 1993; Rhapsodies of a Repeat Offender, 1994; Jackie under My Skin: Interpreting an Icon, 1995; The Milk of Inquiry, 1999; Cleavage: Essays on Sex, Stars, and Aesthetics, 2000; Andy Warhol, 2001; Moira Orfei in Aigues-Mortes, 2004; Model Homes, 2004; Best-Selling Jewish Porn Films, 2006; Hotel Theory, 2007; Humiliation, 2011; Blue Stranger with Mosaic Background, 2012; The Anatomy of Harpo Marx, 2012. **Address:** Graduate Center, City University of New York, 365 5th Ave., New York, NY 10016, U.S.A. **Online address:** wkoestenbaum@aol.com

KOESTLER-GRACK, Rachel. American (born United States), b. 1973. **Genres:** Novels, Young Adult Non-fiction, Children's Non-fiction. **Career:** Capstone Press, acquisition editor and author, 1999-2001. **Publications:** Going to School during the Civil Rights Movement, 2002; Osceola 1804-1838, 2003; Tecumseh 1768-1813, 2003; The Sioux: Nomadic Buffalo Hunters, 2003; Daily Life in a Southwestern Settlement: San Antonio, 2003; Northern Colonial Town: Plymouth, 2003; The Iroquois: Longhouse Builders, 2003; The Seminole: Patchworkers of the Everglades, 2003; Eddie Rickenbacker, 2003; Chief John Ross, 2004; The Space Shuttle Columbia Disaster, 2004; The Story of Anne Frank, 2004; The Story of Clara Barton, 2004; Mary Baker Eddy, 2004; The Choctaw: Stickball Players of the South, 2004; Sacagawea, 2004; The Story of Harriet Tubman, 2004; The Story of Helen Keller, 2004; Kim II Sung and Kim Jong II, 2004; The Story of Eleanor Roosevelt, 2004; The Inuit: Ivory Carvers of the Far North, 2004; Chief Joseph, 2004; The Story of Mother Jones, 2004; Spirit of St. Louis, 2005; The Kent State Tragedy, 2005; Moon Landing, 2005; Mount Rushmore, 2005; The Pilgrims, 2005; The Assassination of Robert F. Kennedy, 2005; Eleanor of Aquitaine: Heroine of the Middle Ages, 2006; Hernando Cortes and the Fall of the Aztecs, 2006; Leonardo da Vinci: Artist, Inventor, and Renaissance Man, 2006; Molly Pitcher: Heroine of the War for Independence, 2006; Nathan Hale: Courageous Spy, 2006; Vasco da Gama and the Sea Route to India, 2006; Queen Latifah, 2007; Michelle Kwan, 2007; Kofi Annan: Guiding the United Nations, 2007; Kirby Puckett, 2007; The House of Representatives, 2007; The Department of Homeland Security, 2007; Bruce Lee, 2007; Brett Favre, 2008; Tom Brady, 2008; Ben Roethlisberger, 2008; Johnstown Flood of 1889, 2008; Katie Couric, Groundbreaking TV Journalist, 2008; William Tecumseh Sherman, 2009; Abraham Lincoln, 2009; Elie Wiesel: Witness for Humanity, 2009; Ferdinand Magellan, 2009; Helen Keller: Activist, 2009; Marie Curie: Scientist, 2009; Stonewall Jackson, 2009; Annie Oakley, 2010; Neil Armstrong, 2010; Spain, 2011; France, 2011; Sweden, 2011; American Paint Horse, 2012; American Saddlebred Horse, 2012. **Address:** 21 N Payne, New Ulm, MN 56073, U.S.A. **Online address:** rgrack@hotmail.com

KOETZSCH, Ronald E. American (born United States), b. 1944. **Genres:** Food And Wine, Education, Medicine/Health, Education. **Career:** Association of Waldorf Schools of North America, editor, 1991-. **Publications:** Macrobiotics Yesterday and Today, 1985; Macrobiotics beyond Food: A Guide to Health and Well-Being, 1988; The Parents' Guide to Alternatives in Education, 1997. **Address:** Association of Waldorf Schools of North America, 3901 Bannister Rd., Fair Oaks, CA 95628, U.S.A.

KOFF, Richard M. American (born United States), b. 1926. **Genres:** Novels, Sciences, Technology, Engineering, Children's Fiction. **Career:** American Hydromath Corp., design engineer, 1949-55; McGraw-Hill Publishing Co., associate editor, 1955-58, senior associate editor, 1958-60, managing editor of product engineering, 1960-66; Playboy, administrative editor, 1966-71, assistant publisher, 1972-77, Playboy Enterprises, New Publications Division, manager, 1971-74, director of new publications, 1974-76, vice-president, 1974-77, business manager, 1976-77; Oasis, board director, 1976-79; management consultant, 1977-. **Publications:** (With J.J. Pippinger) Fluid Power Controls, 1958; How Does It Work?, 1961; Home Computers: A Manual of Possibilities, 1979; (comp.) The Whole Home Electronics Catalog, 1979; The Home Electronics Catalog, 1979; Strategic Planning for Magazine Executives, 1981; Christopher (novel), 1981; Using Small Computers to Make Your Business Strategy Work, 1984; (with E.M. Lerner) Increasing Your Wealth in Good Times and Bad, 1985; Business Simulation: IBM-PC Version, 1985; Strategic Planning for Magazine Executives: How to Take the Guesswork out of Magazine Publishing Decisions, 1987; Allocating and Managing Your Investment Assets, 1989. **Address:** 1600 Ben Crenshaw Way, Austin, TX 78746, U.S.A. **Online address:** rkoff@austin.rr.com

KOGAWA, Joy Nozomi. Canadian (born Canada), b. 1935. **Genres:** Novels, Poetry, Young Adult Fiction, Children's Fiction. **Career:** Office of the Prime Minister, staff writer, 1974-76; University of Ottawa, writer-in-residence, 1978; freelance writer, 1978-. **Publications:** The Splintered Moon, 1967; A Choice of Dreams, 1974; Jericho Road, 1977; Six Poems, 1980; Obasan (novel), 1981; Woman in the Woods, 1985; Naomi's Road, 1986; Naomi no Michi, 1988; Itsuka (novel), 1992; The Rain Ascends (novel), 1995; A Song of Lilith, 2000; A Garden of Anchors, 2003. **Address:** 25 The Esplanade, Ste. 1418, Toronto, ON M5E 1W5, Canada.

KOGER, Lisa (Jan). American (born United States), b. 1953. **Genres:** Novels, Novellas/Short Stories. **Career:** Hillcrest West Nursing Home, teacher of writing workshops, 1978; freelance writer, 1980-; Hopkins Elementary School, teacher of writing workshops, 1987; Glenville State College, teacher of writing workshops, 1987; Pulaski County Library System, teacher of writing workshops, 1987, University of Iowa, teacher of writing workshops, 1988-89, Augustana College Graduate Studies Center, teacher of writing workshops, 1989; Kennesaw College, teacher of writing workshops, 1990; Mississippi State University, visiting lecturer in fiction and poetry writing, 1990-91. **Publications:** Farlanburg Stories, 1990. **Address:** c/o Jane Gelfman, Gelfman Schneider Literary Agents Inc., 250 W 57th St., Ste. 2515, New York, NY 10107, U.S.A. **Online address:** hamlet@kih.net

KOHEN, Arnold. (Arnold S. Kohen). American (born United States) **Genres:** Biography, History. **Career:** National Broadcasting Co., investigative reporter; Writer. **Publications:** (With J. Taylor) An Act of Genocide: Indonesia's Invasion of East Timor, 1979; From the Place of the Dead: A Biography of Bishop Carlos Ximenes Belo, 1996; From the Place of the Dead: The Epic Struggles of Bishop Belo of East Timor, 1999. **Address:** c/o Author Mail, St. Martin's Press, 175 5th Ave., New York, NY 10010-7703, U.S.A. **Online address:** askohen@aol.com

KOHEN, Arnold S. See **KOHEN, Arnold.**

KOHL, MaryAnn F(aubion). American (born United States), b. 1947. **Genres:** Art/Art History, Education, Crafts. **Career:** Author, 1985-; Bright Ring Publishing Inc., founder and owner, 1985-. Educator and consultant. **Publications:** Mudworks: Creative Clay, Dough, and Modeling Experiences, 1989; (with C. Gainer) Good Earth Art: Environmental Art for Kids, 1991; (with J. Potter) Science Arts: Discovering Science through Art Experiences, 1993; Preschool Art: It's the Process, Not the Product, 1994; (with C. Gainer) Math Arts: Exploring Math through Art for 3 to 6 Year Olds, 1996; (with J. Potter) Cooking Art: Easy Edible Art for Young Children, 1997; (with K. Solga) Discovering Great Artists: Hands-on-Art for Children in the Styles of the Masters, 1997; (with J. Potter) Global Art: Activities, Projects and Inventions from around the World, 1998; Making Make-Believe: Fun Props, Costumes, and Creative Play Ideas, 1999; The Big Messy Art Book: But Easy to Clean Up, 2000; (with J. Potter) Snacktivities!: 50 Edible Activities for Parents and Young Children, 2001; Mudworks Bilingual Edition Edicion Bilingue, 2002; (with J. Potter) Storybook Art: Hands-on Art for Children in the Styles of 100 Great Picture Book Illustrators, 2002; First Art: Art Experiences for Toddlers and Twos, 2002; Primary Art: It's the Process, Not the Product, 2005; (with K. Solga) Great American Artists for Kids: Hands-On Art Experiences in the Styles of Great American Masters, 2008; Art with Anything: 52 Weeks of Fun Using Everyday Stuff, 2010. OTHERS: Scribble Cookies and Other Independent Creative Art Experiences for Children, 1985, rev. ed. as Scribble Art: Independent Creative Art Experiences for Children, 1994. Works appear in anthologies. Contributor to periodicals. **Address:** Bright Ring Publishing Inc., PO Box 31338, Bellingham, WA 98228-3338, U.S.A. **Online address:** maryann@brightring.com

KOHLER, Dean Ellis. American (born United States), b. 1947. **Genres:** Music, Autobiography/Memoirs. **Career:** Dean and the Mustangs, musician; Electric Banana, musician; Satellites, musician; Spectrum, musician; Mad Wax, musician; Mousey Brown, musician; Big Bubba and the Blockbusters, musician. Author and copywriter. **Publications:** (With S. VanHecke) Rock 'n' Roll Soldier: A Memoir, 2009. **Address:** Hampton, VA , U.S.A. **Online address:** musicmill1@aol.com

KOHLER, Robert E. American (born United States), b. 1937?. **Genres:** Sciences, Biology, Natural History, Environmental Sciences/Ecology. **Career:** Harvard University, Harvard Medical School, Department of Microbiology, research fellow, 1965-68, Department of History of Science, research fellow, 1968-70; Burndy Library, assistant director, 1970-73; University of Pennsylvania, assistant professor, 1973-, professor, 1988-2005, professor emeritus of history and the sociology of science, 2005-. Writer. **Publications:** From Medical Chemistry to Biochemistry: The Making of a Biomedical Discipline, 1982; Partners in Science: Foundations and Natural Scientists, 1900-1945, 1991; Lords of the Fly: Drosophila Genetics and the Experimental Life, 1994; Landscapes & Labscapes: Exploring the Lab-Field Border in Biology, 2002; All Creatures: Naturalists, Collectors, and Biodiversity, 1850-1950, 2006. Contributor to periodicals and journals. **Address:** Department of History and Sociology of Science, University of Pennsylvania, 303 Claudia Cohen Hall, 3451 Walnut St., Philadelphia, PA 19104-6304, U.S.A. **Online address:** rkohler@sas.upenn.edu

KOHLER, Sandra. American (born United States), b. 1940. **Genres:** Poetry. **Career:** Prince of Wales College, instructor in English, 1967-68; Bryn Mawr College, instructor, 1969-70, lecturer, 1970-72, assistant professor of English, 1972-77; The Curtis Institute, instructor in literature, 1981, 1991-92; Main Line School Night, instructor in literature and writing, 1981-91; Susquehanna University, Department of English, faculty, 1994-99, Writers Institute, faculty, 1994-99, adjunct lecturer in creative writing. Poet. **Publications:** The Country of Women: Poetry, 1995; The Ceremonies of Longing, 2003. Contributor to periodicals. **Address:** University of Pittsburgh Press, Eureka Bldg., 3400 Forbes Ave., 5th Fl., Pittsburgh, PA 15260, U.S.A. **Online address:** kohler@susqu.edu

KOHN, Alan J(acobs). American (born United States), b. 1931. **Genres:** Zoology, Biology, Sciences. **Career:** Hopkins Marine Station, laboratory assistant, 1951; Narragansett Marine Laboratory, junior assistant in marine biology, 1952; Marine Biological Laboratory, technician, 1953; Hawaii Marine Laboratory, associate in research, 1954, visiting collaborator, 1955-56; Yale University, Bingham Oceanographic Laboratory, W.W. Anderson fellow, 1958; Florida State University, assistant professor of zoology, 1958-61;

University of Washington, assistant professor, 1961-63, associate professor, 1963-67, professor of zoology, 1967-98, professor emeritus of biology, 1998-, Quaternary Research Center, adjunct professor, 1986-; Thomas Burke Memorial Washington State Museum, affiliate curator of malacology, 1965-70, adjunct curator, 1971-; Smithsonian Institution, National Research Council, senior postdoctoral research associate, 1967, National Museum of Natural History, research associate, 1985-, senior fellow of the museum, 1990; University of Hawaii, visiting professor, 1968. Writer. **Publications:** A Chronological Taxonomy of Conus, 1758-1840, 1992; (ed. with F.W. Harrison) Microscopic Anatomy of Invertebrates, vol. V: Mollusca I, 1994; (with F.E. Perron) Life History and Biogeography: Patterns in Conus, 1994; (with D. Röckel and W. Korn) Manual of the Living Conidae, 1995. Contributor to scientific journals. **Address:** Department of Biology, University of Washington, Rm. KIN 434, PO Box 351800, Seattle, WA 98195, U.S.A. **Online address:** kohn@u.washington.edu

KOHN, Edward P. Turkish (born Turkey), b. 1968?. **Genres:** History, Politics/Government. **Career:** McGill University, assistant professor, 2000-03; Bilkent University, assistant professor of American history and chair of department of American culture and literature. Writer. **Publications:** This Kindred People: Canadian-American Relations and the Anglo-Saxon Idea, 1895-1903, 2004; Hot Time in the Old Town: The Great Heat Wave of 1896 and the Making of Theodore Roosevelt, 2010. Contributor of articles to periodicals. **Address:** Ankara, Turkey. **Online address:** kohn@bilkent.edu.tr

KOHN, Livia. American/German (born Germany), b. 1956. **Genres:** Theology/Religion. **Career:** Kyoto University, Research Institute for Humanistic Studies, research fellow, 1981-86; International Kyoto Zen Symposium, assistant organizer, 1983-86; Zen Buddhism Today, assistant editor, 1983-86; Institut du Hobogirin, research and editorial assistant, 1985-86; University of Michigan, Center for Chinese Studies, research fellow, 1986-87, adjunct lecturer in religious studies, 1987, Department of Asian Languages and Cultures, visiting assistant professor, 1987-88; Boston University, Department of Religion, assistant professor, 1988-92, associate professor in Religion, 1992-99, professor, 1999-2006, professor emeritus, 2006-, director of online certificate, 2006-08; Goettingen University, visiting assistant professor, 1988; Harvard University, John King Fairbank Center for East Asian Studies, research associate, 1988-91; Stanford University, Stanford Center, visiting associate professor, 1997; Eötvös Lorand University, adjunct professor, 2000-06; Union Institute, adjunct professor, 2003-07; Shandong University, adjunct professor, 2004-; San Francisco State University, visiting professor, 2007. **Publications:** Leben und Legende des Ch'en T'uan, 1981; Seven Steps to the Tao: Sima Chengzhen's Zuowanglun, 1987; Taoist Mystical Philosophy: The Scripture of Western Ascension, 1991; Early Chinese Mysticism: Philosophy and Soteriology in the Taoist Tradition, 1992; The Taoist Experience (anthology), 1993; (trans.) Laughing at the Tao: Debates among Buddhists and Taoists in Medieval China, 1994; God and the Dao, 1998; Daoism and Chinese Culture, 2001; Monastic Life in Medieval Daoism, 2003; (with C. Despeux) Women in Daoism, 2003; The Daoist Monastic Manual: A Translation of the Fengdao Kejie, 2004; Cosmos and Community: The Ethical Dimension of Daoism, 2004; Health and Long Life, 2005; Chinese Healing Exercises: The Tradition of Daoyin, 2008; Introducing Daoism, 2008; Meditation Works: In The Daoist, Buddhist, and Hindu Traditions, 2008; Internal Alchemy: Self, Society, and the Quest for Immortality, 2009. EDITOR/CO-EDITOR: Taoist Meditation and Longevity Techniques, 1989; Lao-tzu and the Teo-te-ching, 1998; Daoism Handbook, 2000; (with H.D. Roth) Daoist Identity: History, Lineage, and Ritual, 2002; Daoist Body Cultivation: Traditional Models and Contemporary Practices, 2006; Meditation Works, 2008; Chinese Healing Exercises, 2008; Internal Alchemy, 2009; Daoist Dietetics, 2010; Sitting in Oblivion, 2010. **Address:** Department of Religion, Boston University, 145 Bay State Rd., Boston, MA 02215, U.S.A. **Online address:** lkohn@bu.edu

KOHUT, Thomas A. American (born United States), b. 1950. **Genres:** History. **Career:** University of Cincinnati, assistant clinical professor of psychiatry, 1982-84; Williams College, assistant professor, 1984-90, associate professor of history, 1990-96, Sue and Edgar Wachenheim III professor of history, 1996-. Writer. **Publications:** Wilhelm II and the Germans: A Study in Leadership, 1991; A German Generation: An Experiential History of the Twentieth Century, 2012. Work appear in anthologies. Contributor to periodicals. **Address:** Department of History, Williams College, Mather House, 85 Mission Park Dr., Williamstown, MA 01267, U.S.A. **Online address:** thomas.a.kohut@williams.edu

KOJA, Kathe. American (born United States), b. 1960?. **Genres:** Novels, Young Adult Fiction, Theatre, Gay And Lesbian Issues. **Career:** Writer. **Publications:** The Cipher, 1991; Bad Brains, 1992; Skin, 1993; Strange Angels, 1994; Kink: A Novel, 1996; Extremities: Stories, 1998; Straydog, 2002; Buddha Boy, 2003; The Blue Mirror, 2004; Talk, 2005; Going Under, 2006; Kissing the Bee, 2007; Headlong, 2008; Under the Poppy, 2010. **Address:** c/o Christopher Schelling, Selectric Artists, 56 Planetarium Sta., New York, NY 10024, U.S.A. **Online address:** kathe@kathekoja.com

KOKORIS, Jim. American (born United States), b. 1958. **Genres:** Essays, Romance/Historical, Novels. **Career:** Golin/Harris Communications Inc., vice president, 1990-, senior vice president. Writer. **Publications:** The Rich Part of Life, 2001; Sister North, 2003; The Pursuit of Other Interests: A Novel, 2009. Contributor to books. **Address:** St. Martin's Press, 175 5th Ave., New York, NY 10010, U.S.A. **Online address:** jim@jsha.com

KOLATA, Gina. American (born United States), b. 1948. **Genres:** Medicine/Health, Sciences, Sports/Fitness, Sex. **Career:** Science Magazine, research news writer, 1973-74, senior writer, 1974-87; Bild der Wissenschaft, columnist, 1984-87; Journal of Investigative Dermatology, columnist, 1985-87; New York Times, medical reporter, 1987-. **Publications:** (With J.L. Marx) Combating the Number One Killer: The Scientific Report on Heart Disease, 1978; (with E.D. Freis) The High Blood Pressure Book: A Guide for Patients and their Families, 1979; The Baby Doctors: Probing the Limits of Fetal Medicine, 1990; (with R.T. Michael, J.H. Gagnon and E.O. Laumann) Sex in America: A Definitive Study, 1995; Clone: The Road to Dolly, and the Path Ahead, 1998; Flu: The Story of the Great Influenza Pandemic of 1918 and the Search for the Virus that Caused It, 1999; Ultimate Fitness: The Quest for Truth About Exercise and Health, 2003; Rethinking Thin: The New Science of Weight Loss-And the Myths and Realities of Dieting, 2007. Contributor to periodicals, newspapers and magazines. **Address:** New York Times, 620 8th Ave., New York, NY 10018-1405, U.S.A. **Online address:** kolata@nytimes.com

KOLBABA, Ginger. American (born United States), b. 1967?. **Genres:** Novels, Young Adult Non-fiction, Young Adult Fiction. **Career:** Marriage Partnership (magazine), editor; Journal Leadership, editorial staff; Preaching Today, assistant editor; Today's Christian Woman, associate editor; Kyria.com, founding editor. **Publications:** (With B. Birdwell and M. Birdwell) Refined by Fire: A Family's Triumph of Love and Faith: A Soldier's Story of 9-11, 2004; Dazzled to Frazzled and Back Again: The Bride's Survival Guide, 2004; Surprised by Remarriage: A Guide to the Happily-Even-After, 2006; (with G. Rosberg and B. Rosberg) The 5 Sex Needs of Men and Women, 2006; Katt's in the Cradle, 2009; (with L. Tomlinson and P. Britton) LT & Me, 2009. SECRETS OF LULU'S CAFE SERIES (NOVELS) WITH CHRISTY SCANNELL: Desperate Pastors' Wives, 2007; A Matter of Wife and Death, 2008. **Address:** PO Box 990, West Dundee, IL 60118-0990, U.S.A.

KOLBERT, Elizabeth. American (born United States), b. 1961. **Genres:** Mystery/Crime/Suspense, Environmental Sciences/Ecology, Politics/Government. **Career:** New York Times, stringer, 1984, reporter, 1984-99, staff of metro desk, 1985, Albany bureau chief, 1988-91, columnist, political and media reporter, 1992-97; The New Yorker, staff writer, 1999-, observer, commentator. **Publications:** The Prophet of Love: And Other Tales of Power and Deceit, 2004; Field Notes From a Catastrophe: Man, Nature, and Climate Change, 2006; Vor uns die Sintflut: Depeschen von der Klimafront, 2006; Ends of the Earth: An Anthology of the Finest Writing on the Arctic and the Antarctic, 2007. Contributor to magazines. **Address:** The New Yorker, 4 Times Sq., 17th Fl., New York, NY 10036, U.S.A.

KOLINSKY, Martin. British/Canadian (born Canada), b. 1936. **Genres:** International Relations/Current Affairs, Politics/Government, History. **Career:** University of Birmingham, lecturer in sociology, 1966-70, senior lecturer in political science and international studies, 1972-; Hebrew University of Jerusalem, lecturer in sociology, 1970-72. Writer. **Publications:** Aspects of Social Structure with Special Reference to France, 1967; Emergence of German State Power, 1969; Germany from War to War, 1970; Sociological Analysis of Fascism, 1972; Continuity and Change in European Society: German, France, and Italy Since 1870, 1974; (with M. Vaughan and P. Sheriff) Social Change in France, 1980; Law, Order and Riots in Mandatory Palestine, 1928-35, 1993; Britain's War in the Middle East: 1936-1942, 1999. EDITOR: (with W.E. Paterson) Social and Political Movements in Western Europe, 1976; Divided Loyalties, 1978; (with M.J. Cohen) Britain and the Middle East in the

1930s: Security Problems 1935-39, 1992; (with M.J. Cohen) Demise of the British Empire in the Middle East: Britain's Responses to Nationalist Movements, 1943-55, 1998. **Address:** Department of Political Science and, International Studies, University of Birmingham, PO Box 363, Birmingham, B15 2TT, England.

KOLKO, Joyce. Dutch/Canadian/American (born United States), b. 1933. **Genres:** Economics, History, Politics/Government, Money/Finance, Business/Trade/Industry. **Career:** Writer. **Publications:** (With G. Kolko) The Limits of Power: The World and United States Foreign Policy, 1945-1954, 1972; America and the Crisis of World Capitalism, 1974; Restructuring the World Economy, 1988. **Address:** Wittenburgergracht 53, Amsterdam, 1018 MX, Netherlands.

KOLLER, Jackie French. American (born United States), b. 1948. **Genres:** Children's Fiction, Young Adult Fiction, Social Sciences, Humor/Satire. **Career:** Writer. **Publications:** FOR CHILDREN: Impy for Always, 1989; The Dragonling, 1990; Mole and Shrew, 1991; Fish Fry Tonight!, 1992; Mole and Shrew Step Out, 1992; A Dragon in the Family, 1996; No Such Thing, 1997; Dragon Quest, 1997; Mole and Shrew, All Year Through, 1997; Dragons of Krad, 1997; Dragon Trouble, 1997; Dragons and Kings, 1998; Bouncing on the Bed, 1999; One Monkey Too Many, 1999; Nickommoh!, 1999; Mole and Shrew Are Two, 2000; Mole and Shrew Have Jobs to Do, 2001; Mole and Shrew Find a Clue, 2001; Baby for Sale, 2002; Baby for Sale, 2002; Horace the Horrible: A Knight Meets His Match, 2003; Seven Spunky Monkeys, 2005; Peter Spit a Seed at Sue, 2008. FOR YOUNG ADULTS: Nothing to Fear, 1991; If I Had One Wish..., 1991; The Last Voyage of the Misty Day, 1992; The Primrose Way, 1992; A Place to Call Home, 1995; The Falcon, 1998; The Promise, 1999; Someday, 2002. KEEPERS SERIES: A Wizard Named Nell, 2003; The Wizard's Apprentice, 2003; The Wizard's Scepter, 2004. Works appear in anthologies. **Address:** Curtis Brown Ltd., 10 Astor Pl., New York, NY 10003, U.S.A. **Online address:** jackiek@aol.com

KOLLER, James. American (born United States), b. 1936. **Genres:** Novels, Poetry, Essays, Natural History, Literary Criticism And History. **Career:** Coyote's Journal, editor, 1964-. **Publications:** POETRY: Two Hands, 1959-1961, 1965; Brainard & Washington Street Poems, 1965; Some Cows: Poems of Civilization and Domestic Life, 1965; The Dogs & Other Dark Woods, 1966; I Went to See My True Love, 1967; California Poems, 1971; Messages, 1972; Dark Woman, Who Lay with the Sun, 1972; Bureau Creek, 1975; Poems for the Blue Sky, 1976; (ed. and contrib.) Andiamo: Selected Poems by James Koller, Franco Beltrametti and Harry Hoogstraten, 1978; O, Didn't He Ramble/O Ware Er Nicht Umhergezogen, 1980; Back River, 1981; One Day at a Time, 1981; (ed.) Coyote's journal, 1982; Great Things Are Happening, 1984; Give the Dog a Bone, 1986; Openings, 1987; Fortune, 1987; (with F. Beltrametti) Graffiti Lyriques, 1987; Begin with the Women Sitting, 1988; (co-author) A Gang of Four, 1989; Roses Love Sunshine, 1989; This Is What He Said, 1991; Dans la Gueule du Loup, 1992; Grandfather Had Come a Long Way, 1993; A Dream, Starring Bill Brown, 1994; The Bone Show, 1999; Iron Bells, 1999; Close to the Ground, 2000; Crows Talk to Him, 2003; Looking for His Horses, 2003; Snows Gone By: New & Uncollected Poems, 1964-2002, 2004. NOVELS: If You Don't Like Me You Can Leave Me Alone, 1974; Shannon, Who Was Lost Before, 1975; (with F. Beltrametti) The Possible Movie, 1997. OTHER: Messages, 1972; Working Notes, 1985; Gebt Dem Alten Hund'nen Knochen, 1986; The Natural Order (essays), 1990; Like It Was, 2000; (trans. with J. Monod and M. Cyprys) J. Monod, The Man Who Knows, 2003. **Address:** Coyote Books, PO Box 629, Brunswick, ME 04011, U.S.A.

KOLLIN, Dani. American (born United States), b. 1964. **Genres:** Novels, Children's Fiction. **Career:** Writer. **Publications:** What's in a Name? (children's book), 1994; My Very Own Dreidel: A Pop-Up Hanukkah Celebration!, 2007; (with E. Kollin) The Unincorporated Man, 2009; (with E. Kollin) The Unincorporated War, 2010; (with E. Kollin) The Unincorporated Woman, 2011; (with E. Kollin) The Unincorporated Feature, 2012. **Address:** Tor Books, 175 5th Ave., 14th Fl., New York, NY 10010, U.S.A. **Online address:** dani@theunincorporatedman.com

KOLLIN, Eytan. American (born United States), b. 1964?. **Genres:** Literary Criticism And History, Young Adult Fiction. **Career:** Writer and educator. **Publications:** (With D. Kollin) The Unincorporated Man, 2009. Contributor to periodicals. **Address:** Pasadena, CA , U.S.A. **Online address:** eytan@theunincorporatedman.com

KOLLMANN, Dana D. American (born United States) **Genres:** Criminology/True Crime. **Career:** Maryland-National Capital Park and Planning Commission, archaeologist; Arlington County Police Department, intern; Baltimore County Police Department, forensic services technician, 1995-2004; Towson University, adjunct faculty, 1998-2006, lecturer, 2006-08, assistant professor. Writer. **Publications:** Never Suck a Dead Man's Hand: Curious Adventures of a CSI, 2007. **Address:** Department of Sociology, Anthropology, and Criminal Justice, Towson University, Rm. 3333, Liberal Arts, 8000 York Rd., Towson, MD 21252-0001, U.S.A. **Online address:** csi@danakollmann.com

KOLODNY, Nancy J. American (born United States), b. 1946. **Genres:** Self Help, Sex, Social Work, Young Adult Non-fiction, Medicine/Health, Social Sciences, Psychiatry. **Career:** University City High School, English teacher, 1967-69; South Boston High School, English teacher, 1970-71; Clayton High School, English teacher, 1971-72; Bulimia Anorexia Self Help, psychiatric social worker and eating disorder therapist, 1981-83; Barnard College, class correspondent, 1982-87; Behavioral Medicine Institute, psychiatric social worker and eating disorder therapist, 1983-; Keats Press, editor, 1997-99; Silver Hill Hospital, therapist, 1999-2000; Renfrew Center, therapist, 2000-03; Healthy Living Center of Greenwich Hospital, group therapist, 2004-. Consultant. **Publications:** (With M. Schwartz) Instructor's Manual for Human Sexuality by Masters, Johnson, Kolodny, 1982, 3rd ed., 1988; (with F.E.F. Larocca) Anorexia and Bulimia Facilitator's Training Manual: A Primer, the BASH Approach, 1983; (co-author) How to Survive Your Adolescent's Adolescence, 1984; (with R.C. Kolodny and T.E. Bratter) Smart Choices: A Guide to Surviving at Home and in School, Dating and Sex, Dealing with Crises, Applying to College and More, 1986; When Food's a Foe: How to Confront and Conquer Your Eating Disorder, 1987, rev. ed., 1998; Cuando la Comida Es Tu Enemiga: Como Enfrentarse y Vencer a los Trastornos Alimentarios, 2000; The Beginner's Guide to Eating Disorders Recovery, 2004. Contributor to books and periodicals. **Address:** 157 Silvermine Ave., Norwalk, CT 06850-1611, U.S.A. **Online address:** njkolodny@aol.com

KOLOSOV, Jacqueline. Also writes as Jacqueline A. Kolosov, Jacqueline McLean. American (born United States), b. 1967?. **Genres:** Novels, Young Adult Non-fiction, Poetry. **Career:** Texas Tech University, associate professor of English and creative writing. Writer and educator. **Publications:** FOR YOUNG READERS: (as Jacqueline McLean) Victoria Woodhull: First Woman Presidential Candidate (nonfiction), 2000; (as Jacqueline McLean) Women with Wings (nonfiction), 2001; (as Jacqueline McLean) Women of Adventure (nonfiction), 2003; (as Jacqueline A. Kolosov) Grace from China (middle-grade novel), 2004; The Red Queen's Daughter (young-adult novel), 2007. OTHERS: Danish Ocean (chapbook), 2003; Fabergé (chapbook), 2003; Why Plant Bougainvillea (chapbook), 2005; (ed. with L.H. Rodenberger and L.P. Butler) Writing on the Wind: An Anthology of West Texas Women Writers, 2005; Souvenir, Modigliani (chapbook), 2005; Vago (poetry), 2007; (ed. with K.S. Lunstrum) The Sincerest Form of Flattery: Contemporary Women Writers on Forerunners in Fiction, 2008. Contributor to periodicals. **Address:** TX , U.S.A. **Online address:** poppiesbloom@usa.net

KOLOSOV, Jacqueline A. *See* **KOLOSOV, Jacqueline.**

KOLP, John (Gilman). American (born United States), b. 1943?. **Genres:** History, Adult Non-fiction. **Career:** U.S. Naval Academy, assistant professor of history, professor, now retired; Augustana College, U.S. History, instructor. Writer and historian. **Publications:** Gentlemen and Freeholders: Electoral Politics in Colonial Virginia, 1998. **Address:** Department of History, Augustana College, 639 38th St., Rock Island, IL 61201, U.S.A. **Online address:** johnkolp@augustana.edu

KOLPAN, Steven. American (born United States) **Genres:** Food And Wine. **Career:** The Culinary Institute of America, Learning Resources Center, senior producer and writer, The Charmer Sunbelt Group endowed chair in wine and spirits and professor of wine studies and gastronomy; Ulster County Community College, faculty; State University of New York, faculty; Ramapo College of New Jersey, faculty; Ulster County Council for the Arts, executive director; Olive Oil: A Guide for Culinary Professionals, editor and project director; Salon.com, wine columnist; The Valley Table, wine consultant and contributing editor; Wine & Spirits, contributing writer; Wine from Spain News: International Cookbook Revue, contributing writer; The National Culinary Review, contributing writer; The Daily Freeman, wine and food critic; Up River/Down River Magazine, food and culture writer; The Woodstock Times, art and media critic. Food consultant. **Publications:** (With B.H. Smith and M.A. Weiss) Exploring Wine: The Culinary Institute of America's Complete Guide to Wines of the World, 1996, 3rd ed., 2010; A Sense of Place: An Intimate Portrait of the Niebaum-Coppola Winery and the Napa Valley, 1999; (with B.H. Smith and M.A. Weiss) Winewise, 2008; (with G. Scappin and A. Vanoli) Italian Cooking at Home: With the Culinary Institute of America, 2011. Contributor of articles to magazines and periodicals. **Address:** The Culinary Institute of America, 1946 Campus Dr., Hyde Park, NY 12538-1499, U.S.A. **Online address:** s_kolpan@culinary.edu

KOLPAS, Norman. American (born United States) **Genres:** Food And Wine, How-to Books, Food And Wine. **Career:** Time-Life Books, editorial staff; Knapp Communications, The Knapp Press, editor; Weldon Owen Publishing, consulting editor; Williams-Sonoma Publishing, consulting editor, 1991-2001; University of California, Writer's Program, nonfiction and cook-book-writing teacher; Wolfgang Puck Worldwide Inc., senior vice president of content, 2001-03. **Publications:** The Chocolate Lover's Companion, 1977; The Coffee Lover's Companion, 1977; Coffee, 1979; Mao, 1981; Abraham Lincoln, 1981; The Gourmet's Lexicon, 1982; (with J.R. Sedlar) Modern Southwest Cuisine, 1986; Britain: The Queen, Cricket, Sherlock Holmes and Other Things Indubitably British, 1987; Breakfast and Brunch Book, 1988 as Breakfast and Brunch: Over Seventy Ideas and Menus for Starting the Day, 1993; Pasta Presto: One Hundred Fast and Fabulous Pasta Sauces, 1988; Pizza California Style: More than Eighty Fast and Easy Recipes for Delicious Gourmet Pizza, 1989; (with M. McCarty) Michael's Cookbook, 1989; Hors d'oeuvre: Festive and Elegant Party Menus, 1990; The Big Little Peanut Butter Cookbook: Fifty Recipes for Delicious, Easy-to-Make Desserts, Snacks and Sandwiches, 1990; Pasta Light: Eighty Low-Fat, Low-Calorie, Fast and Fabulous Pasta Sauces, 1990; Sweet Indulgences, 1990 as Sweet Indulgences: Desserts for Every Occasion, 1993; (with G. Mahaffey) The Bel-Air Book of Southern California Food and Entertaining, 1991; The Chili Cookbook, 1991; Whole Meal Salads: One Hundred Fresh, Delectable Recipes for Easy One-Course Entrees, 1992; The World's Best Noodles, 1993; Pasta Menus, 1993; A Cup of Coffee: From Plantation to Pot, a Coffee Lover's Guide to the Perfect Brew, 1993; Gourmet Sandwiches, 1993; (recipes) Soups, 1993; Southwest the Beautiful Cookbook: Recipes from America's Southwest, 1994; Pasta Gusto: Fabulous Sauces and Flavored Pastas, 1994; More Pasta Light: Eighty Delicious, Low-Fat Sauces, 1995; Pizza Presto: Eighty Fast and Fabulous Recipes, 1996; Festive Desserts, 1996; Finger Food, 1996; Breakfast and Brunches, 1997; More Pasta Presto: One Hundred Fast and Fabulous Pasta Sauces, 1998; Main Dish Salads, 1998; Buongiorno! Breakfast and Brunch, Italian Style, 2001; The Quick Grill Artist: Fast and Fabulous Recipes for Cooking with Fire, 2002; Pottey Barn: Cocktails Style Recipes, 2005; (with K. Kolpas) Practically Useless Information, 2005; Food Made Fast: Slow Cooker, 2006; Cocktails: Style Recipes, 2008. EDITOR: (and comp.) Comforting Foods, 1996; Dinner Parties, 1996; Celebrating the Pleasure of Cooking, 1997. Contributor to periodicals. **Address:** c/o Author Mail, Random House/Clarkson Potter, 1540 Broadway, New York, NY 10036, U.S.A.

KOLPEN, Jana (Fayne). American (born United States), b. 1958. **Genres:** Romance/Historical, Food And Wine, Illustrations, inspirational/Motivational Literature, Art/Art History, Young Adult Fiction. **Career:** Writer. **Publications:** SELF-ILLUSTRATED: The Secrets of Pistoulet: A Fable of Food, Magic & Love (fiction), 1996. OTHERS: (with M. Tiegreen) The Legend of the Villa della Luna: Sequel to the Secrets of Pistoulet, 1997 as Dancing with the Moon: A Story of Love at the Villa della Luna (fiction), 2004; (with M. Tiegreen) The Circle of Kindness: An Irish Journey of the Heart, 2006. **Address:** 1749 Narrows Hill Rd., Upper Black Eddy, PA 18972, U.S.A. **Online address:** jana@janakolpen.com

KOMAIKO, Leah. American (born United States), b. 1954. **Genres:** Children's Fiction, Picture/Board Books, Adult Non-fiction, Picture/Board Books. **Career:** UCLA, teacher of writing. Writer. **Publications:** SELF-ILLUSTRATED: A Million Moms and Mine, 1992. PICTURE BOOKS: I Like the Music, 1987; Annie Bananie, 1987; Earl's Too Cool for Me, 1988; My Perfect Neighborhood, 1990; Leonora O'Grady, 1992; Aunt Elaine Does the Dance from Spain, 1992; Shoeshine Shirley, 1993; Broadway Banjo Bill, 1993; Where Can Daniel Be?, 1994; Great-Aunt Ida and Her Great Dane, Doc, 1994; Just My Dad and Me, 1995; Fritzi Fox Flew in from Florida, 1995; On Sally Perry's Farm, 1996. EASY-READERS: Annie Bananie Moves to Barry Avenue, 1996; Annie Bananie: Best Friends to the End, 1997; Annie Bananie and the People's Court, 1998; Annie Bananie and the Pain Sisters, 1998. OTHERS: Am I Old Yet?: The Story of Two Women, Generations Apart, Growing Up and Growing Young in a Timeless Friendship, 1999; Malibu Carmie, 2005. Contributer to periodicals. **Address:** 13525 Huston St., Sherman Oaks, CA 91423-1401, U.S.A. **Online address:** lkomaiko@hotmail.com

KOMAN, Aleta. American (born United States), b. 1954?. **Genres:** How-to Books, Self Help. **Career:** Families First, parent educator; Workplace Connections, parent educator; Wheelock College Center for Parenting Studies and Graduate School of Education, adjunct professor in psychology and professional studies; CBS-TV, on-air expert for family and parenting issues; Lawline.com, faculty; therapist and writer. **Publications:** How to Mend a Broken Heart: Letting Go and Moving On, 1997. WITH E. MYERS: The Parenting Survival Kit: How to Make It through the Parenting Years with Your Family, Sanity, and Wallet Intact, 2000; Who's the Boss: How to Regain and Maintain Your Parental Authority When Kids Rule the Roost, 2002; My Ex Is Driving Me Crazy, 2008. **Address:** Adams Media Corp., 57 Littlefield St., Avon, MA 02322, U.S.A.

KOMARNICKI, Todd. American (born United States), b. 1965. **Genres:** Novels. **Career:** Guy Walks into a Bar, president, founder, principal partner. Screenwriter and playwright. **Publications:** Free (novel), 1993; Famine (novel), 1997; War (novel), 2008. **Address:** Guy Walks into a Bar, 7421 Beverly Blvd., Ste. 4, Los Angeles, CA 90036, U.S.A.

KOMP, Diane M. American (born United States), b. 1940. **Genres:** Medicine/Health, inspirational/Motivational Literature. **Career:** Kings County Hospital, pediatric residency, 1965-67; University of Virginia, School of Medicine, assistant professor, 1969-73, associate professor, 1973-76, professor of pediatrics, 1976-78, chief of hematology/oncology, 1970-78; American Academy of Pediatrics, fellow, 1971; Yale University, School of Medicine, chief of hematology/oncology, 1978-85, professor of pediatrics, 1978-2000, professor emeritus, 2000-. Writer. **Publications:** A Window to Heaven: When Children See Life in Death, 1992; A Child Shall Lead Them: Lessons in Hope from Children with Cancer, 1993; Hope Springs from Mended Places: Images of Grace in the Shadows of Life, 1994; Children Are Images of Grace: A Pediatrician's Trilogy of Faith, Hope and Love, 1996; Breakfast for the Heart: Meditations to Nourish the Soul, 1996; Anatomy of a Lie: The Truth about Lies and Why Good People Tell Them, 1998; Bedtime Snacks for the Soul: Meditations to Sweeten Your Dreams, 2000; Why Me?: A Doctor Examines the Book of Job, 2001; Healer's Heart: A Modern Novel of the Life of St. Luke, 2006. Works appear in anthologies. Contributor of articles to journals. **Address:** Yale University School of Medicine, 333 Cedar St., New Haven, CT 06510-3206, U.S.A. **Online address:** doktordi@aol.com

KOMPORALY, Jozefina. British (born England), b. 1969. **Genres:** Adult Non-fiction, Humanities. **Career:** University of Warwick, tutor in English and drama, 1997-2002; University of London, Goldsmiths College, faculty; University of Hull, Centre for Performance Translation and Dramaturgy, post doctoral researcher; University of Hertfordshire, faculty; De Montfort University, School of English, Performance and Historical Studies, Department of Performance and Digital Arts, senior lecturer of drama, 2005-; Soros Foundation for an Open Society, interpreter, teacher of English and program coordinator. Writer. **Publications:** (Contrib.) Representing the Troubles, 2004; Staging Motherhood: British Women Playwrights, 1956 to the Present, 2006; (contrib.) Loving against the Odds: Women's Writing in a European Framework, 2006. Contributor to periodicals. **Address:** Faculty of Humanities, Department of Performance and Digital Arts, De Montfort University, Rm. CL 2.06A, Clephan Bldg., Leicester, LE LE1 9BH, England. **Online address:** jkomporaly@dmu.ac.uk

KOMPRIDIS, Nikolas. Australian/Canadian (born Canada) **Genres:** Adult Non-fiction. **Career:** Sound Pressure, founder and director, 1986-90; University of Frankfurt, fellow, 1992-94; Concordia University, assistant professor of philosophy, 1994-95; New School for Social Research, visiting professor, 1995-96; Wilfrid Laurier University, sessional assistant professor, 1996-98; University of Dundee, lecturer in philosophy, 1998-2002; York University, assistant professor of philosophy, 2003-; University of Western Sydney, College of Arts, Centre for Citizenship and Public Policy, professor and professorial fellow. Writer and philosopher. **Publications:** (Contrib.) The Transformation of Modernity, 2001; (ed.) Philosophical Romanticism, 2006;

Critique and Disclosure: Critical Theory Between Past and Future, 2006. Contributor to books and journals. **Address:** Centre for Citizenship and Public Policy, University of Western Sydney, Rm. 1.1.190, 4 Main Bldg., Bankstown Campus, PO Box 1797, Penrith, NW 2751, Australia. **Online address:** n.kompridis@uws.edu.au

KOMUNYAKAA, Yusef. American (born United States), b. 1947. **Genres:** Poetry. **Career:** University of Colorado, editor, contributor, 1973; Colorado State University, associate instructor of English composition, 1976-78; University of California, teaching assistant in poetry, writing instructor for remedial English composition, 1980; University of New Orleans-Lakefront, instructor in English and poetry, 1982-84; Indiana University at Bloomington, visiting assistant professor of English, 1985-86, associate professor of English and African American studies, 1986-93, Ruth Lilly professor, 1989-90, professor of English and African American studies, 1993-98; New Orleans Public Schools, elementary teacher; Princeton University, professor of creative writing and counsel in the humanities, 1997-; New York University, Creative Writing Program, humanities professor, senior distinguished poet, senior faculty, global distinguished professor of English. **Publications:** POETRY: Dedications and Other Darkhorses, 1977; Lost in the Bonewheel Factory, 1979; Copacetic, 1984; I Apologize for the Eyes in My Head, 1986; Dien Cai Dau, 1988; (ed. with S. Feinstein) The Jazz Poetry Anthology, 1991; Magic City, 1992; Neon Vernacular: New and Selected Poems, 1993; Thieves of Paradise, 1998; Talking Dirty to the Gods, 2000; Blue Notes: Essays, Interviews and Commentaries, 2000; Talking Dirty to the Gods, 2000; Pleasure Dome: New and Collected Poems, 2001; Taboo, 2004; Gilgamesh: A Verse Play, 2006; (contrib.) Covenant: Scenes from an African American Church, 2007; Warhorses, 2008; Chameleon Couch: Poems, 2011. Works appear in anthologies. **Address:** Creative Writing Program, Council of Humanities, New York University, Lillian Vernon Creative Writers House, 58 W 10th St., New York, NY 10011, U.S.A. **Online address:** yk24@nyu.edu

KONIG, Susan. American (born United States), b. 1963?. **Genres:** Young Adult Fiction, Animals/Pets. **Career:** Washington Post, Style section, staff writer; Seventeen, editor; Style magazine, fashion editor, 1980; New York Post, columnist, 1990; Catholic Channel, Speak Now (radio show), co-host; Catholic Digest, columnist; National Review Online, columnist. Freelance journalist and author. **Publications:** Why Animals Sleep So Close to the Road: And Other Lies I Tell My Children, 2005; I Wear the Maternity Pants in This Family, 2007. Contributor to periodicals and magazines. **Address:** Macmillan, 175 5th Ave., New York, NY 10010, U.S.A. **Online address:** susan@susankonig.com

KONIGSBERG, Allan Stewart. *See* **ALLEN, Woody.**

KONIGSBERG, Bill. American (born United States), b. 1970?. **Genres:** Young Adult Fiction, Sports/Fitness. **Career:** ESPN.com, assistant editor, 2001; Associated Press, sports writer and editor, 2005-08. **Publications:** Out of the Pocket, 2008. Contributor to periodicals. **Address:** c/o Caryn Wiseman, Andrea Brown Literary Agency Inc., 1076 Eagle Dr., Salinas, CA 93905, U.S.A. **Online address:** bkonigsberg@gmail.com

KONIGSBURG, E(laine) L(obl). American (born United States), b. 1930. **Genres:** Children's Fiction, Children's Non-fiction, Adult Non-fiction, Young Adult Non-fiction, Novels, Picture/Board Books. **Career:** Shenango Valley Provision Co., bookkeeper, 1947-48; Bartram School, science teacher, 1954-55, 1960-62; University of Pittsburgh, research assistant. Writer. **Publications:** SELF-ILLUSTRATED: Jennifer, Hecate, Macbeth, William McKinley, and Me, Elizabeth, 1967, 3rd ed., 2007; From the Mixed-Up Files of Mrs. Basil E. Frankweiler, 1967; About the B'nai Bagels, 1969, 2nd ed., 2008; George, 1970; A Proud Taste for Scarlet and Miniver, 1973; The Dragon in the Ghetto Caper, 1974; Samuel Todd's Book of Great Colors, 1990; Samuel Todd's Book of Great Inventions, 1991; Amy Elizabeth Explores Bloomingdale's, 1992. OTHERS: Altogether, One at a Time, 1971, 3rd ed., 2008; The Second Mrs. Gioconda, 1975; Father's Arcane Daughter, 1976; Throwing Shadows, 1979, 3rd ed., 2007; Journey to an 800 Number, 1982 in UK as Journey by First Class Camel, 1983; Up from Jericho Tel, 1986; The Mask Beneath the Face: Reading about and with, Writing about and for Children, 1990; T-Backs, T-Shirts, Coat, and Suit, 1993, 2nd ed., 2008; Talk, Talk: A Children's Book Author Speaks to Grown-Ups, 1995; The View from Saturday, 1996; Pages and Stages: The Art of E.L. Konigsburg, 1999; Silent to the Bone, 2000; The Outcasts of 19 Schuyler Place, 2004; The Mysterious Edge

of the Heroic World, 2007; My Father's Daughter, 2008. Contributor to books and periodicals. **Address:** c/o Author Mail, Thorndike Press, 10 Water St., Ste. 310, Waterville, ME 04901, U.S.A.

KONING, (Angela) Christina. British (born England), b. 1954. **Genres:** Novels, Young Adult Fiction, Poetry, Psychology. **Career:** Tate Gallery, publications assistant, 1978; Transworld Publishers Ltd., export sales assistant, 1978-81; The Guardian, columnist, 1987-89, book reviewer; freelance writer and reviewer; University of Greenwich, lecturer, 1993-94, lecturer in creative writing; Universidad Católica Andres Bello, lecturer, 1994; Universidad Simon Bolívar, lecturer, 1994; Birkbeck College, lecturer in creative writing, 1999, 2002-03; American Institute for Foreign Study, lecturer; University of Oxford, lecturer in creative writing; The Times, editor. **Publications:** A Mild Suicide (novel), 1992; (ed. and contrib.) The Oxford Guide to Twentieth Century Literature, 1996; The Good Reading Guide to Children's Books, 1997; Undiscovered Country (novel), 1998; Fabulous Time (novel), 2000; The Dark Tower, 2010; Variable Stars, 2011. Works appear in anthologies. Contributor to magazines and newspapers. **Address:** c/o Derek Johns, A. P. Watt Ltd., 20 John St., London, GL WC1N 2DR, England.

KONKLE, Marsena. American (born United States), b. 1970. **Genres:** Novels, Mystery/Crime/Suspense. **Career:** Writer. **Publications:** A Dark Oval Stone, 2006. **Address:** c/o Author Mail, Paraclete Press, PO Box 1568, Orleans, MA 02653-1568, U.S.A.

KONSTANTINOU, Lee. American (born United States), b. 1978. **Genres:** Novels. **Career:** Oracle Corp., technical writer, 2000-02. **Publications:** Pop Apocalypse: A Possible Satire (novel), 2009. Contributor to books and periodicals. **Address:** San Francisco, CA , U.S.A. **Online address:** lee.konstantinou@gmail.com

KONZAK, Burt. Canadian/American (born United States), b. 1946. **Genres:** Children's Fiction, Sports/Fitness, Literary Criticism And History. **Career:** State University of New York-Binghamton, Center for Comparative Political Research, research associate, 1969-70; Harvard University, research assistant, 1970; Toronto Academy of Karate, director and founder, 1970-; University of Toronto, School of Physical and Health Education, assistant professor, 1973-94, instructor of Zen Buddhism and the martial arts, 1974-77; University of Guelph, instructor in sociology, 1980-81. Writer. **Publications:** Noguchi the Samurai, 1994; Girl Power: Self-Defense for Teens, 1999; Samurai Spirit: Ancient Wisdom for Modern Life, 2002. Contributor of articles to journals and periodicals. **Address:** Toronto Academy Of Karate, 50 Poplar Plains Cres., Toronto, ON M4V 1E8, Canada. **Online address:** boudreau@glendon.yorku.ca

KOOISTRA, Lorraine Janzen. (Lorraine Janzen). Canadian (born Canada), b. 1953. **Genres:** Poetry, Illustrations. **Career:** Lincoln County Board of Education, primary school teacher, 1973-79; University of Toronto, SSHRC postdoctoral fellow, 1992-94, Book History and Print Culture Program, associate faculty; McMaster University, Department of English, faculty; Nipissing University, assistant professor, 1994-98, associate professor, 1998-2002, professor, 2002-05; Ryerson University, Department of English, professor, 2005-. Writer. **Publications:** The Artist as Critic: Bitextuality in Fin-de-siecle Illustrated Books, 1995; (ed. with M. Arseneau and A.H. Harrison) The Culture of Christina Rossetti: Female Poetics and Victorian Contexts, 1999; Christina Rossetti and Illustration: A Publishing History, 2002; (as Lorraine Janzen) Learning to See in the Dark, 2003; Poetry, Pictures, and Popular Publishing: The Illustrated Gift Book and Victorian Visual Culture 1855-1875, 2011. **Address:** Department of English, Ryerson University, 1011 Jorgenson Hall, 380 Victoria St., Toronto, ON M5B 2K3, Canada. **Online address:** ljanzen@ryerson.ca

KOOLHAAS, Rem. Dutch (born Netherlands), b. 1944. **Genres:** Archaeology/Antiquities, Architecture. **Career:** Office for Metropolitan Architecture, co-founder, principal, 1975-; Institute for Architecture and Urban Studies, teacher, 1975; University of California, Los Angeles, School of Architecture, teacher, 1975; Architectural Association, teacher, 1976; Technical University, professor of architecture, 1988-89; Rice University, professor of architecture, 1991-92; Harvard University, Graduate School of Design, Arthur Rotch adjunct professor of architecture, 1990-95, professor in practice of architecture and urban design, 1995-. Architect and writer. **Publications:** Delirious New York: A Retroactive Manifesto for Manhattan, 1978, new ed., 1994; Rem

Koolhaas: Conversations with Students, 1991, 2nd ed., 1996; (with B. Mau) Small, Medium, Large, Extra-Large: Office for Metropolitan Architecture, 1995, 2nd ed., 1998; (contrib.) Suburban City, 1996; (with B. Mau) Netherlands Embassy in Berlin, 1999; OMA Rem Koolhaas: Living, Vivre, Leben, 1999; OMA 30: 30 Colours, 1999; Colours, 2001; (co-author) Mutations, 2001; (intro.) Projects for Prada Part 1, 2001; (intro.) Harvard Design School Guide to Shopping, 2002; (co-author) Great Leap Forward, Harvard Design School Project on the City no. 1, 2002; Content: Triumph of Realization, 2004; Post-Occupancy, 2006. UNTRANSLATED WORKS: (co-author) Hoe Modern is de Nederlandse Architectuur?, 1990; Lille, 1990; OMA-Rem Koolhaas: Pour une Culture de La Congestion, 1990; Rem Koolhaas: Projectes Urbans (1985-1990), 1990; Six Projets/O.M.A., 1990; (ed.) OMA-Rem Koolhaas: Pour une Culture de la Congestion, 1990; Rem Koolhaas: Trasparenze Metropolitane, 1997; (co-ed.) Prada, 2001; Rem Koolhaas/OMA, 2002; Métropoles en Europe, 2004. OTHERS: (with G. Celant)Unveiling The Prada Foundation / Fondazione Prada, OMA, 2008. **Address:** Graduate School of Design, Harvard University, 48 Quincy St., Cambridge, MA 02138, U.S.A. **Online address:** rkoolhaas@gsd.harvard.edu

KOONS, Carolyn. (Carolyn A. Koons). American (born United States), b. 1942?. **Genres:** Adult Non-fiction. **Career:** Azusa Pacific University, faculty, 1962-, Institute for Outreach Ministries, founder, executive director, professor of religion; Fuller Theological Seminary, adjunct professor; Biola University, adjunct professor. Writer. **Publications:** AS CAROLYN A. KOONS: Tony, Our Journey Together, 1984; Beyond Betrayal: Healing My Broken Past, 1986; (with M.J. Anthony) Single Adult Passages, Uncharted Territories, 1991; Unstuck: Hope for Anyone Who Feels Stuck Between the Pain of the Past and the Promise of the Future, 1993; Unstuck, Risking Change In Adult Life Passages, 1993. Contributor to magazines. **Address:** Institute for Outreach Ministries, Azusa Pacific University, 901 E Alosta Ave., PO Box 7000, Azusa, CA 91702-7000, U.S.A. **Online address:** ckoons@apu.edu

KOONS, Carolyn A. See **KOONS, Carolyn.**

KOONS, James. See **PERNU, Dennis.**

KOONTZ, Dean R(ay). Also writes as Leigh Nichols, K. R. Dwyer, Brian Coffey, Deanna Dwyer, Owen West. American (born United States), b. 1945. **Genres:** Novels, Novellas/Short Stories, Horror, Science Fiction/Fantasy, Social Commentary, Writing/Journalism, Picture/Board Books, Graphic Novels, Graphic Novels. **Career:** Teacher, 1966-69; freelance writer, 1969-. **Publications:** Star Quest, 1968; The Fall of the Dream Machine, 1969; The Dark Symphony, 1970; Hell's Gate, 1970; Dark of the Woods, 1970; Beastchild, 1970; Anti-Man, 1970; Soft Come the Dragons (SF short stories), 1970; (with G. Koontz) The Pig Society (non-fiction), 1970; (with G. Koontz) The Underground Lifestyles Handbook (non-fiction), 1970; The Crimson Witch, 1971; The Flesh in the Furnace, 1972; A Darkness in My Soul, 1972; Time Thieves, 1972; Warlock, 1972; Starblood, 1972; Demon Seed, 1973; A Werewolf Among Us, 1973; Hanging On, 1973; The Haunted Earth, 1973; Writing Popular Fiction (non-fiction), 1973; After the Last Race, 1975; Nightmare Journey, 1975; Night Chills, 1976; The Vision, 1977; Whispers, 1980; How To Write Best-Selling Fiction, 1981; Phantoms, 1983; Darkness Comes in US as Darkfall, 1984; Strangers, 1986; Watchers, 1987; Twilight Eyes, 1987; Lightning, 1988; Oddkins: A Fable for All Ages, 1988; Stalkers: All New Tales of Terror and Suspense, 1989; Midnight, 1989; The Bad Place, 1990; Cold Fire, 1991; Obsessions, 1991; Three Complete Novels, 1991; Dean R. Koontz: A New Collection, 1992; Hideaway, 1992; Trapped, 1993; Dragon Tears, 1993; Mr. Murder, 1993; Dark Rivers of the Heart, 1994; Winter Moon, 1994; Strange Highways, 1995; Intensity: A Novel, 1995; Santa's Twin, 1996; Beautiful Death: Art of the Cemetery, 1996; Sole Survivor, 1997; Tick-Tock, 1997; Fear Nothing, 1998; Sieze the Night, 1999; False Memory, 1999; From the Corner of His Eye, 2001; One Door Away from Heaven, 2001; The Paper Doorway: Funny Verse and Nothing Worse, 2001; By the Light of the Moon, 2002; Face, 2003; Everyday's a Holiday: Amusing Rhymes for Happy Times, 2003; Life Expectancy, 2004; (ed.) Life is Good!: Lessons in Joyful Living, 2004; Odd Thomas, 2004; Robot Santa: The Further Adventures of Santa's Twin, 2004; The Taking, 2004; (ed.) Christmas is Good!: Trixie Treats & Holiday Wisdom, 2005; (with K.J. Anderson) Prodigal Son, 2005; City of Night, 2005; Forever Odd, 2005; Velocity, 2005; Brother Odd, 2006; The Husband, 2006; The Darkest Evening of The Year, 2007; The Good Guy, 2007; In Odd We Trust, 2008; Odd Hours, 2008; Breathless, 2009; Your Heart Belongs to Me, 2009; Trixie, Who is Dog, 2009; Dead and Alive, 2009; Relentless, 2009; A Big Little Life, 2009; (with K. Champagne) Nevermore,

2009; Trixie and Jinx, 2010; Lost Souls, 2010; (with F. van Lente) Odd Is on Our Side, 2010; What the Night Knows, 2010; Frankenstein, 2010; Shadowfires, 2010; 77 Shadow Street, 2011; Moonlit Mind, 2011; House of Odd, 2012; Odd Apocalypse, 2012. AS DAVID AXTON: Prison of Ice (novel), 1976, rev. ed. as Icebound: A Novel, 1995; Stolen Thunder, 1993. AS LEIGH NICHOLS: The Key to Midnight, 1979; The Eyes of Darkness, 1981; The House of Thunder, 1982; Servants of Twilight, 1984; Shadow Fires, 1987. AS RICHARD PAIGE: The Door to December, 1985, rev. ed., 2002. AS OWEN WEST: The Funhouse, 1980; The Mask, 1981. AS BRIAN COFFEY: Blood Risk, 1973; Surrounded, 1974; The Wall of Masks, 1975; The Face of Fear, 1977; The Voice of the Night, 1980. AS AARON WOLFE: Invasion, 1975. AS K.R. DWYER: Chase, 1972; Shattered, 1973; Dragonfly, 1975. AS JOHN HILL: The Long Sleep, 1975. AS ANTHONY NORTH: Strike Deep, 1974. AS DEANNA DWYER: Demon Child, 1971; Legacy of Terror, 1971; Children of the Storm, 1972; The Dark Summer, 1972; Dance with the Devil, 1972. **Address:** c/o Robert Gottlieb, Trident Media Group L.L.C., 41 Madison Ave., 36th Fl., New York, NY 10010-2257, U.S.A. **Online address:** dean@deankoontz.com

KOONTZ, Robin. Also writes as Robin Michal Koontz. American (born United States), b. 1954. **Genres:** Children's Fiction, Novellas/Short Stories, Picture/Board Books, Illustrations, Children's Non-fiction, Photography, Writing/Journalism, Novels, Novels. **Career:** Monterey Bay Publishing Co., typesetter, 1976-77; Express Press Printing, typesetter, 1978-84; freelance advertising production artist, 1984-85; freelance illustrator and writer, 1985-; Robin's Light-Arted Design Co., owner; SCBWI, Oregon regional advisor, 1994, newsletter editor, website manager, conference co-chair, retreat chairperson. **Publications:** Dinosaur Dream, 1988; Chicago and the Cat: A Little Chapter Book, 1992; I See Something You Don't See: A Riddle-Me Picture Book, 1992; Why a Dog? By a Cat, 2000; How is a Moose Like a Goose?, 2002; Up All Night Counting, 2006; Creepy Crawly Colors, 2006; Composting: Nature's Recyclers, 2007; Erosion: Changing Earth's Surface, 2007; Jewelry Making for Fun!, 2008; Tai Chi for Fun!, 2008; Butterfly Spring, 2009; The Case of the Haunted House, 2009; The Case of the Garden Club Caper, 2009; The Case of the Shifting Stacks, 2010; The Case of the Missing Goldfish, 2010; The Case of the Grumpy Chicken, 2010; Pick a Perfect Pumpkin; Learning About Pumpkin Harvests, 2010; The Case of the Mystery Museum, 2010; The Case of the Community Garden, 2010; Apples, Apples Everywhere!: Learning About Apple Harvests, 2010; What's the Difference Between a Butterfly and a Moth?, 2010; Vermont: The Green Mountain State, 2011; Water Goes Round: The Water Cycle, 2011; New Hampshire: The Granite State, 2011; West Virginia: The Mountain State, 2011; Rhode Island: The Ocean State, 2011; Connecticut: The Constitution State, 2011; Maine: The Pine Tree State, 2011; Hide and Seek Moon: The Moon Phases, 2011; Leaps and Creeps: How Animals Move to Survive, 2012; Sniffs and Stinks: How Animals Use Odor to Survive, 2012; Spits and Squirts: How Animals Squirt to Survive, 2012; Screams and Songs: How Animals Communicate to Survive, 2012; Movers and Makers, 2012. SELF-ILLUSTRATED: (and comp.) Pussycat Ate the Dumplings, 1987; Chicago and the Cat: The Camping Trip, 1994; Chicago and the Cat: The Halloween Party, 1994; Chicago and the Cat: The Family Reunion, 1996; Chicago and the Cat at the Country Fair, 1998; Complete Backyard Nature Activity Book, 1998. **Address:** PO Box 336, Noti, OR 97461, U.S.A. **Online address:** robink@robinkoontz.com

KOONTZ, Robin Michal. See **KOONTZ, Robin.**

KOONTZ, Tomas M. American (born United States), b. 1967?. **Genres:** Environmental Sciences/Ecology. **Career:** U.S. General Accounting Office, intern evaluator, 1992; Indiana University, School of Public and Environmental Affairs, teaching assistant, 1991-92, Center for the Study of Institutions, Population and Environmental Change, research assistant, 1994-96, post-doctoral research associate, 1997-98; Ohio State University, School of Environment and Natural Resources, assistant professor, 1998-2004, associate professor, 2004-, professor, academic coordinator, 2003-, Teaching Assistant Workshop, faculty co-facilitator, 2001-04, 2008, 2009, John Glenn School of Public Affairs, associate professor, 2005-, College of Food, Agricultural and Environmental Sciences, Environmental Working Group, leader, 2005-; Journal of Forestry, associate editor, 2005-10; Texas A&M University, Department of Ecosystem Science and Management, curriculum consultant, 2009. Writer. **Publications:** Federalism in the Forest: National versus State Natural Resource Policy, 2002; (co-author) Collaborative Environmental Management:

What Roles for Government?, 2004. **Address:** School of Natural Resources, Ohio State University, 316B Kottman Hall, 2021 Coffey Rd., Columbus, OH 43210, U.S.A. **Online address:** koontz.31@osu.edu

KOOPERMAN, Evelyn L. American (born United States), b. 1945. **Genres:** Local History/Rural Topics, Social Sciences. **Career:** San Diego Public Library, librarian, 1972-. Writer. **Publications:** San Diego Trivia, 1989; San Diego Trivia 2, 1993. **Address:** San Diego Public Library, 820 E St., San Diego, CA 92101, U.S.A.

KOOSER, Ted. (Theodore Kooser). American (born United States), b. 1939. **Genres:** Poetry, Adult Non-fiction. **Career:** Teacher, 1962-63; correspondent, 1964-65; underwriter, 1965-73; Bankers Life Nebraska, underwriter, 1964, senior underwriter, 1973-80, associate vice-president, 1980-94, vice president, 1994-98, now retired; University of Nebraska, professor of writing, 1970-95, visiting professor, 2000-, presidential professor; Lincoln Benefit Life Co., part-time instructor in creative writing, underwriter, 1973-84, vice president, 1984-99. **Publications:** Official Entry Blank, 1969; Grass County, 1971; Twenty Poems, 1973; A Local Habitation, and A Name, 1974; Shooting a Farmhouse; So This is Nebraska, 1973; Not Coming to Be Barked At, 1976; Hatcher, 1978; Old Marriage and New, 1978; (with W. Kloefkorn) Cottonwood County, 1979; Sure Signs: New and Selected Poems, 1980; (ed.) The Windflower Home Almanac of Poetry, 1980; One World at a Time, 1985; The Blizzard Voices, 1986; Weather Central, 1994; Winter Morning Walks: 100 Postcards to Jim Harrison, 2000; Local Wonders: Seasons in the Bohemian Alps, 2002; Braided Creek, 2003; Delights & Shadows, 2004; The Poetry Home Repair Manual, 2005; Flying at Night, 2005; Writing Brave and Free, 2006; Out of that Moment: Twenty-one Years of Valentines, 1986-2006, 2006; Valentines, 2007; Lights on a Ground of Darkness, 2009; Bag in the Wind, 2010. **Address:** 1820 Branched Oak Rd., Garland, NE 68360, U.S.A. **Online address:** kr84428@windstream.net

KOOSER, Theodore. See **KOOSER, Ted.**

KOPINAK, Kathryn. Canadian (born Canada) **Genres:** Sociology, Local History/Rural Topics. **Career:** University of Western Ontario, King's University College, Department of Social Sciences, assistant professor, 1978-82, Department of Sociology, associate professor, 1983-95, professor, 1996-; University of California-San Diego, Center for U.S.-Mexican Studies, visiting research fellow, 1990-91, Center for Comparative Immigration Studies, senior fellow, 2005-; York University, Centre for Research on Latin America and the Caribbean, associate fellow, 1993-; El Colegio de la Frontera Norte, visiting research fellow, 1997-99. Writer. **Publications:** Desert Capitalism: Maquiladoras in North America's Western Industrial Corridor, 1996 in Canada as Desert Capitalism: What Are Maquiladoras?, 1997; (ed.) The Social Costs of Industrial Growth in Northern Mexico, 2004. **Address:** Department of Sociology, King's University College, University of Western Ontario, FB101, 266 Epworth Ave., London, ON N6A 2M3, Canada. **Online address:** kopinak@uwo.ca

KOPIT, Arthur. American (born United States), b. 1937. **Genres:** Plays/ Screenplays, Songs/Lyrics And Libretti, Literary Criticism And History. **Career:** Wesleyan University, Center for Humanities, fellow, 1974-75, playwright-in-residence, 1975-76; Yale University, CBS fellow, 1976-77, adjunct professor of playwrighting, 1977-80; City College of New York (now the City University of New York), adjunct professor of playwrighting, 1981-. Director. **Publications:** (Contrib.) Oh Dad, Poor Dad, Mamma's Hung You in the Closet and I'm Feelin' so Sad, 1960; Symposium: Avante-garde Theatre, real or far out?, 1962; Day the Whores Came Out To Play Tennis, and Other Plays, 1965; Chamber Music and Other Plays, 1969; Indians: A Play, 1969; Wings: A Play, 1978; Good Help Is Hard to Find: A Play in One Act, 1982; Nine: The Musical, 1983; End of the World: A Play, 1984; (trans.) H. Ibsen, Ghosts: A Drama, 1984; End Of The World With Symposium To Follow: A Play in Three Acts, 1987; Road to Nirvana, 1991; Three Plays, 1997; Y2K, 2000. Works appear in anthologies. Contributor to periodicals. **Address:** William Morris Agency, 1325 Ave. of the Americas, 15th Fl., New York, NY 10019-6067, U.S.A.

KOPLEWICZ, Harold S. (Harold Samuel Koplewicz). American (born United States), b. 1953. **Genres:** Human Relations/Parenting. **Career:** Nathan S. Kline Institute for Psychiatric Research, founder, 1952-director, 2006-11; Bronx Municipal Hospital Center, internship in pediatrics, 1978-79; New York Hospital, Westchester Division, residency in psychiatry, 1979-81; Columbia Presbyterian Medical Center, director of general residency training

in child psychiatry, 1985-86; New York State Psychiatric Institute, NIMH research fellowship, 1983-85; Long Island Jewish Medical Center, chief of division of child and adolescent psychiatry, 1986-96; Dalton School, consultant, 1990-95; Jewish Child Care Association, consultant, 1990-95; New York State Commission, Youth Crime and Violence, commissioner, 1993-95; Violence and Reform of the Juvenile Justice System, commissioner, 1993-95; Our Children's Foundation, consultant, 1995-; New York University, Langone Medical Center, vice chair of department of psychiatry, 1996-, director of division of child and adolescent psychiatry, 1996-, senior vice president and vice dean for external affairs, 1997-, School of Medicine, professor of clinical psychiatry, 1996-2000, Child Study Center, director, 1997-, Arnold and Debbie Simon professor of child and adolescent psychiatry, 2000-, chair, 2006; Journal of Child and Adolescent Psychopharmacology, editor-in-chief, 1997-; NYU Child Study Center, editor, 1996, founder, 1997; Community Mainstreaming Association, director, 1988; National Foundation for Depressive Illnesses, director, 1990-; Child Mind Institute, founding president, 2009-. **Publications:** (Ed. with E. Klass) Depression in Children and Adolescents, 1993; It's Nobody's Fault: New Hope and Help for Difficult Children and Their Parents, 1996; Childhood Revealed: Art Expressing Pain, Discovery and Hope, 1999; Turbulent Times, Prophetic Dreams: Art of Palestinian and Israeli Children, 2000; More Than Moody: Recognizing and Treating Adolescent Depression, 2002. Contributor of articles to journals. **Address:** The Child Mind Institute, 909 3rd Ave., 5th Fl., New York, NY 10022, U.S.A. **Online address:** harold.koplewicz@nyumc.org

KOPLEWICZ, Harold Samuel. See **KOPLEWICZ, Harold S.**

KOPLOW, David A. American (born United States), b. 1951. **Genres:** Law. **Career:** U.S. Arms Control and Disarmament Agency, attorney and advisor, special assistant to the director, 1978-81; Georgetown University Law Center, professor of law, 1981-, Center for Applied Legal Studies, director; U.S. Department of Defense, deputy general counsel for international affairs, 1997-99, special counsel for arms control. Writer. **Publications:** Testing a Nuclear Test Ban: What Should Be Prohibited by a Comprehensive Treaty?, 1996; By Fire and Ice: Dismantling Chemical Weapons while Preserving the Environment, 1997; Smallpox: The Fight to Eradicate a Global Scourge, 2003; Non-Lethal Weapons: The Law and Policy of Revolutionary Technologies for the Military and Law Enforcement, 2006; Death by Moderation: The U.S. Military's Quest for Useable Weapons, 2010. Contributor to books. **Address:** Georgetown University Law Center, 332 McDonough, 600 New Jersey Ave. NW, Washington, DC 20001, U.S.A. **Online address:** koplow@law.georgetown.edu

KOPPEL, Tom. Canadian (born Canada) **Genres:** Young Adult Non-fiction, Cultural/Ethnic Topics, Sciences, History, Earth Sciences. **Career:** Journalist, 1985-; Rabochaya Gazeta, visiting staff, 1989-90. **Publications:** Kanaka: The Untold Story of Hawaiian Pioneers in British Columbia and the Pacific Northwest, 1995; Powering the Future: The Ballard Fuel Cell and the Race to Change the World, 1999; Lost World: Rewriting Prehistory: How New Science Is Tracing America's Ice Age Mariners, 2003; Ebb and Flow: Tides and Life on Our Once and Future Planet, 2007. Contributor of articles to periodicals. **Address:** 193 Richard Flack Rd., Salt Spring Island, BC V8K 1N4, Canada. **Online address:** koppel@saltspring.com

KOPPER, Lisa (Esther). British/American (born United States), b. 1950. **Genres:** Children's Fiction, Illustrations, Animals/Pets. **Career:** Writer and illustrator. **Publications:** SELF-ILLUSTRATED FOR CHILDREN: Daisy Thinks She Is a Baby, 1993; I'm a Baby, You're a Baby, 1994; My Pony Ride, 1995; Daisy Is a Mummy, 1996 in US as Daisy Is a Mommy, 1997; Daisy Knows Best, 1998; Daisy's Babies, 2000; Good Dog, Daisy!, 2001. BABY SHAPE BOARD BOOKS AND WITH T. BRADMAN: The Baby's Bumper Book, 1987; Bedtime, 1987; The Cuddle, 1987; Our Cat, 1987. OTHER: (with H. Lewin) An Elephant Came to Swim, 1985. WITH K. PETTY: What's that Taste?, 1986; What's that Number?, 1986; What's that Noise?, 1986; What's that Color?, 1986; Starting School, 1987; The New Baby, 1987; Moving House, 1987; Going to the Doctor, 1987; What's that Smell?, 1987; What's that Size?, 1987; What's that Shape?, 1987; What's that Feel?, 1987; Staying Overnight, 1988; Splitting Up, 1988; Going to the Dentist, 1988; Being Careful with Strangers, 1988. Contributor to periodicals. Illustrator of books by others. **Address:** 1 Peary Pl., London, GL E2 0QW, England.

KORB, Scott. American (born United States), b. 1977?. **Genres:** Theology/ Religion, History. **Career:** Gallatin School of Individualized Study, Newyork

University, part-time faculty. Writer. **Publications:** (With P. Bebergal) The Faith between Us: A Jew and a Catholic Search for the Meaning of God, 2007; Life in Year One: What the World Was Like in First-Century Palestine, 2010. Contributor to periodicals. **Address:** Gallatin School of Individualized Study, Newyork University, Rm. 503, 1 Wash Pl., New York, NY 10003, U.S.A. **Online address:** smkorb@gmail.com

KORBEL, Kathleen. *See* **DREYER**, Eileen.

KORD, Susanne. Also writes as Susanne Theresia Kord. British/German (born Germany), b. 1959. **Genres:** Essays, Women's Studies And Issues. **Career:** Dartmouth College, visiting lecturer, 1988-90; University of Cincinnati, assistant professor, 1990-93; Georgetown University, assistant professor, George M. Roth distinguished professor of German, 1993-2003, professor, 1993-2004, head of the department, 2001-04; University College London, Department of German, professor, 2004-, head, 2006-10, chair of German. Writer. **Publications:** Thalias Daughters: German Women Dramatists from the Eighteenth Century to the Present Women Writers in German-speaking Countries; Ein Blick hinter die Kulissen: Deutschsprachige Dramatikerinnen im 18. und 19. Jahrhundert, 1992; The Lessing Yearbook XXVI, 1994; Sich einen Namen machen: Anonymität und weibliche Autorschaft 1700-1900, 1996; (ed. with F. Eigler) The Feminist Encyclopedia of German Literature, 1997; Charlotte von Stein: Dramen Gesamtausgabe, 1998; (ed. with B. Henke and S. Richter) Unwrapping Goethes Weimar: Essays in Cultural Studies and Local Knowledge, 2000; Little Detours: The Letters and Plays of Luise Gottsched (1713-1762), 2000; Women Peasant Poets in Eighteenth-Century England Scotland and Germany: Milkmaids on Parnassus, 2003; (trans.) E. Bernstein, Dämmerung (title means: 'Twilight: A Drama in Five Acts'), 2003; (with E. Krimmer) Hollywood Divas Indie Queens and TV Heroines: Contemporary Screen Images of Women, 2005; Murderesses in German Writing, 1720-1860: Heroines of Horror, 2009; (with E. Krimmer) Contemporary Hollywood Masculinities, 2011. **Address:** Department of German, University College London, 17 Gordon Sq., Ste. 105, Gower St., London, GL WC1E 6BT, England. **Online address:** susanne.kord@ucl.ac.uk

KORD, Susanne Theresia. *See* **KORD**, Susanne.

KORDA, Michael (Vincent). American/British (born England), b. 1933. **Genres:** Novels, Biography, Autobiography/Memoirs, History. **Career:** Columbia Broadcasting System Inc. (CBS-TV), script reader, 1957; Simon & Schuster Inc. (publishers), editorial assistant, 1958-2005, editor-in-chief. Writer. **Publications:** OTHERS: Male Chauvinism! How It Works, 1973; Power!: How to Get It, How to Use It, 1975 in UK as Power in the Office, 1976; Success! How Every Man and Woman Can Achieve It, 1977; Charmed Lives: A Family Romance (biography of the Korda brothers), 1979; Man to Man: Surviving Prostate Cancer, 1996; Another Life: A Memoir of Other People, 1999; Country Matters: The Pleasures and Tribulations of Moving from a Big City to an Old Country Farmhouse, 2001; Making the List: A Cultural History of the American Bestseller, 1900-1999, 2001; Ulysses S. Grant: The Unlikely Hero, 2004; Marking Time: Collecting Watches and Thinking About Time, 2004; (with Margaret) Cat People, 2005; (with Margaret) Horse Housekeeping: Everything You Need to Know to Keep a Horse at Home, 2005; Arise, Magyars!: A Personal History of the Hungarian Revolution of 1956, 2006; Journey to a Revolution: A Personal History of the Hungarian Revolution of 1956, 2006; Ike: An American Hero, 2007; With Wings like Eagles: A History of the Battle of Britain, 2009; Hero: The Life and Legend of Lawrence of Arabia, 2010. NOVELS: Worldly Goods, 1982; Queenie, 1985; The Fortune, 1989; Curtain: A Novel, 1991; The Immortals: A Novel, 1992. SELF-ILLUSTRATOR: Horse People: Scenes from the Riding Life, 2003. Contributor to periodicals. **Address:** HarperCollins Publishers, 10 E 53rd St., New York, NY 10022, U.S.A.

KORDER, Howard. American (born United States), b. 1957. **Genres:** Plays/Screenplays, Literary Criticism And History. **Career:** Columbia Broadcasting System Inc. (CBS), story editor. **Publications:** PLAYS: Middle Kingdom (one act), 1985 as Middle Kingdom; and Lip Service: Two Short Plays, 1986; Episode 26: A Comedy in Two Acts, 1985; Fun (one act), 1987 as Fun and Nobody: Two Short Plays, 1988. BOOKS: Boys' Life: A Comedy, 1988; The Pope's Nose: Short Plays and Sketches, 1991; Search and Destroy: A Play, 1992; The Lights, 1994; Night Manuever, 1995; The Hollow Lands, 2000; Sea of Tranquility, 2004. Contributor to periodicals. **Address:** Dramatists Play Service Inc., 440 Park Ave. S, New York, NY 10016-8012, U.S.A.

KORELITZ, Jean Hanff. American (born United States), b. 1961. **Genres:** Novels, Poetry, Young Adult Fiction. **Career:** Farrar, Straus & Giroux Inc., editorial assistant, 1987-88; University of Massachusetts, Division of Continuing Education, instructor, 1990-. **Publications:** The Properties of Breath (poems), 1988; A Jury of Her Peers, 1996; The Sabbathday River (novel), 1999; Interference Powder, 2003; The White Rose, 2004; Admission, 2009. Contributor of articles and essays to magazines and periodicals. **Address:** c/o Alison Granucci, Blue Flower Arts L.L.C., PO Box 1361, Millbrook, NY 12545, U.S.A. **Online address:** sgasst@wmeentertainment.com

KOREN, Yehuda. American/Israeli (born Israel) **Genres:** Novels, Biography, Autobiography/Memoirs, Social Sciences, History. **Career:** IBA, documentary editor, producer and director; journalist; historical consultant; British Broadcasting Corp., director. **Publications:** In Our Hearts We Were Giants: The Remarkable Story of the Lilliput Troupe-A Dwarf Family's Survival of the Holocaust, 2004; (with E. Negev) Lover of Unreason: The Life and Tragic Death of Assia Wevill, 2006; Lover of Unreason: Assia Wevill, Sylvia Plath's Rival and Ted Hughes's Doomed Love, 2007; The First Lady of Fleet Street: The Life of Rachel Beer: Crusading Heiress and Newspaper Pioneer, 2011. Contributor to periodicals. **Address:** c/o Author Mail, Carroll & Graf Publishers, 245 W 17th St., 11th Fl., New York, NY 10038, U.S.A.

KORG, Jacob. American (born United States), b. 1922. **Genres:** Literary Criticism And History, Biography, Poetry, Art/Art History. **Career:** Bard College, instructor in English, 1947-49; City College of New York (now City College of the City University of New York), instructor, 1951-55; University of Washington, assistant professor, associate professor, 1955-65, professor of English, 1970-, now professor emeritus of English; National Taiwan University, exchange professor, 1960; University of Maryland, professor of English, 1968-70. Writer. **Publications:** An Introduction to Poetry, 1959; London in Dickens' Day, 1960; Commonplace Book: A Manuscript in the Berg Collection of the New York Public Library, 1962; George Gissing: A Critical Biography, 1963; Dylan Thomas, 1965, 2nd ed., 1992; The Force of Few Words, 1966; Language in Modern Literature: Innovation and Experiment, 1979; Browning and Italy, 1983; Ritual and Experiment in Modern Poetry, 1995; Winter Love: Ezra Pound and H.D., 2003. EDITOR: (with S.F. Anderson) Westward to Oregon, 1958; (with R.S. Beal) Thought in Prose, 1958, 3rd ed., 1966; (with R.S. Beal) The Complete Reader, 1961, 2nd ed., 1967; George Gissing's Commonplace Book, 1962; Twentieth Century Interpretations of Bleak House, 1968; The Poetry of Robert Browning, 1971; Thyrza, 1974; The Unclassed, 1976; (and intro. With C. Korg) George Gissing on Fiction, 1978; George Gissing's Essay on Robert Burns: A Previously Unpublished Manuscript, 1992. **Address:** Department of English, University of Washington, PO Box 354330, Seattle, WA 98195-4330, U.S.A. **Online address:** korg@u.washington.edu

KORMAN, Bernice. Canadian (born Canada), b. 1937. **Genres:** Children's Fiction, Poetry, Sports/Fitness, Young Adult Fiction. **Career:** Suburban (weekly newspaper), columnist, 1964-81; Teleterm Inc., executive assistant, 1980-99; writer, 1999-. **Publications:** (With G. Korman) The D-Poems of Jeremy Bloom: A Collection of Poems about School, Homework and Life, 1992; (with G. Korman) The Last-Place Sports Poems of Jeremy Bloom: A Collection of Poems about Winning Losing and being a Good Sport, 1996. **Address:** Curtis Brown Ltd., 10 Astor Pl., New York, NY 10003, U.S.A.

KORMAN, Gordon (Richard). American/Canadian (born Canada), b. 1963. **Genres:** Children's Fiction, Novels. **Career:** Writer, 1975-. **Publications:** CHILDREN'S FICTION: This Can't Be Happening at Macdonald Hall!, 1977; Go Jump in the Pool!, 1979; Beware the Fish!, 1980; Who is Bugs Potter?, 1980; I Want to Go Home!, 1981; Our Man Weston, 1982; The War with Mr. Wizzle, 1982; Bugs Potter: Live at Nickaninny, 1983; No Coins, Please, 1984; Don't Care High, 1985; Son of Interflux, 1986; A Semester in the Life of a Garbage Bag, 1987; The Zucchini Warriors, 1988; Radio Fifth Grade, 1989; Losing Joe's Place, 1990; Macdonald Hall Goes Hollywood, 1991; (with B. Korman) The D-Poems of Jeremy Bloom, 1992; The Twinkie Squad, 1992; The Toilet Paper Tigers, 1993; Why Did the Underwear Cross the Road?, 1994; Something Fishy at Macdonald Hall, 1995; (with B. Korman) The Last Place Sports Poems of Jeremy Bloom, 1996; The Chicken Doesn't Skate, 1996; Liar, Liar, Pants on Fire, 1997; The Sixth-Grade Nickname Game, 1998; No More Dead Dogs, 2001; Son of the Mob, 2002; Maxx Comedy: The Funniest Kid in America, 2003; Jake, Reinvented, 2003; Great Gatsby Novel, 2003; (with K. Burkett) Clue Me In! The Detective Work of Ethan Flask and Professor Von Offel, 2003; Born to Rock, 2006; The Ultimate

Nose Pickers Collection, 2006; (with R.L. Stine and K.A. Applegate) Tales of Suspense for Boys, 2006; Schooled, 2007; The Juvie Three, 2008; Swindle, 2008; One False Note, 2008; The 39 Clues: Book Two, 2009; Pop, 2009; Zoobreak, 2009; Framed, 2010; The Emperor's Code, 2010; (with P. Lerangis, R. Riordan and J. Watson) Vespers Rising, 2011. MONDAY NIGHT FOOTBALL CLUB SERIES: Quarterback Exchange: I Was John Elway, 1997; Running Back Conversion: I Was Barry Sanders, 1997; Super Bowl Switch: I Was Dan Marino 1997; Heavy Artillery: I Was Junior Seau, 1997; Ultimate Scoring Machine: I Was Jerry Rice, 1998; (with J. Buckley, Jr. and B.C. Peterson) NFL Rules: Bloopers, Pranks, Upsets, and Touchdowns, 1998. SLAPSHOT SERIES: The Stars from Mars, 1999; The All-Mars All-Stars, 1999; The Face-Off Phony, 2000; Cup Crazy, 2000. NOSEPICKERS SERIES: Nosepickers from Outer Space, 1999; Planet of the Nosepickers, 2000; Your Mummy Is a Nosepicker, 2000; Invasion of the Nosepickers, 2001. ISLAND SERIES: Shipwreck, 2001; Survival, 2001; Escape, 2001. EVEREST SERIES: The Contest, 2003; The Climb, 2003; The Summit, 2003. DIVE SERIES: The Discover, 2003; The Deep, 2003; The Danger, 2003. ON THE RUN SERIES: Chasing the Falconers, 2005; The Fugitive Factor, 2005; Now You See Them, Now You Don't, 2005; The Stowaway Solution, 2005; Public Enemies, 2005; Hunting the Hunter, 2005. JERSEY SERIES: This Rocks, 2001; The Team Player, 2001; Head over Heels, 2001; Fight for Your Right, 2001; Need for Speed, 2001. KIDNAPPED TRILOGY: The Abduction, 2006; The Search, 2006; The Rescue, 2006. OTHERS: Invasion of the Nose Pickers, 2001; Island Trilogy, 2005; Cahills vs. Vespers, 2011. Contributor to periodicals. **Address:** Scholastic Inc., 557 Broadway, New York, NY 10012, U.S.A. **Online address:** info@gordonkorman.com

KORMONDY, Edward J(ohn). American (born United States), b. 1926. **Genres:** Biology, Environmental Sciences/Ecology, Sciences, Adult Non-fiction, Education, Reference. **Career:** University of Michigan, instructor in zoology, 1955-57, Museum of Zoology, curator of insects, 1956-57; Oberlin College, assistant professor, 1957-63, College of Arts and Sciences, associate professor, 1963-67, acting associate dean, 1966-67, professor of biology, 1967-69; University of Pittsburgh, visiting summer professor, 1960-62; American Institute of Biological Sciences, Commission of Undergraduate Education, director, 1968-71; Evergreen State College, faculty, 1971-79, academic dean, 1972-73, vice-president and provost, 1973-78; National Science Foundation, senior professional associate, 1979; University of Southern Maine, provost and professor of biology, 1979-82; California State University, vice-president of academic affairs and professor of biology, 1982-86; University of Hawaii, senior vice president, chancellor and professor of biology, 1986-93; University of West Los Angeles, president, 1995-97; Pacific Oaks College, special assistant, 2001-; Universidad Simon Bolivar, curriculum consultant. Writer. **Publications:** Catalogue of the Odonata of Michigan, 1958; The Systematics of Tetragoneuria, Based On Ecological, Life History, and Morphological Evidence, 1959; Introduction to Genetics: A Program for Self-Instruction, 1964; Concepts of Ecology, 1969, 4th ed., 1996; (with J.L. Aldrich) Environmental Education: Academia's Response, 1972; (with T. Sherman) Biology: The Natural History and Integrity of Organisms, 1977; (with B.J. Nebel) Environmental Science: The Way the World Works, 1981, 2nd ed., 1987; (with B. Essenfeld) Biology, 1984; International Handbook of Pollution Control, 1989; (with P. Corcoran) Environmental Education, 1997; (with D.E. Brown) Fundamentals of Human Ecology, 1998; The University of Hawaii-West Oahu: The First Forty Years, 1966-2006, 2010. EDITOR: Readings in Ecology, 1965; (comp.) General Biology, 2 vols., 1966; (with R. Leisner) Population, 1971; (with R. Leisner) Pollution, 1971; (with R. Leisner) Ecology, 1971; (with J.F. McCormick) Handbook of Contemporary Developments in World Ecology, 1981; (with F.T. Inouye) University of Hawaii-Hilo: A College in the Making, 2001; (with K.M. Keith) Nine University Presidents Who Saved Their Institutions: The Difference in Effective Administration, 2008. **Address:** Pacific Oaks College and Children's School, Westmoreland Pl., Pasadena, CA 91103, U.S.A. **Online address:** ekor@aol.com

KORNBLATT, Judith Deutsch. American (born United States), b. 1955. **Genres:** Mythology/Folklore, Cultural/Ethnic Topics, Literary Criticism And History, Philosophy, Intellectual History, Theology/Religion, History, Social Commentary, Social Commentary. **Career:** Columbia University, preceptor, 1982-85; Williams College, visiting lecturer, 1984; Indiana University, visiting assistant professor, 1986-87; University of Wisconsin, Department of Slavic Languages and Literature, visiting assistant professor, 1987-88, assistant professor, 1988-93, associate professor, 1993-98, professor, 1998-, Humanities Graduate School, associate dean, 1998-2006, senior associate dean for graduate education, 2007-10, associate chair. Writer. **Publications:** The

Cossack Hero in Russian Literature: A Study in Cultural Mythology, 1992; (ed. with R.F. Gustafson) Russian Religious Thought, 1996; Doubly Chosen: Jewish Identity, the Soviet Intelligentsia and the Russian Orthodox Church, 2004; (ed.) Divine Sophia: The Wisdom Writings Of Vladimir Solovyov, 2009. Works appear in anthologies. Contributor to periodicals. **Address:** Department of Slavic Languages and Literature, University of Wisconsin-Madison, 1432 Van Hise Hall, 1220 Linden Dr., Madison, WI 53706, U.S.A. **Online address:** jkornblatt@bascom.wisc.edu

KORNBLATT, Marc. American (born United States), b. 1954. **Genres:** Children's Fiction, Plays/Screenplays. **Career:** Children's book author, playwright, filmmaker and educator. **Publications:** Flame of the Inquisition, 1986; (with S. Nanus) Mission to World War II, 1986; Paul Revere and the Boston Tea Party, 1987. PICTURE BOOKS: The Search for Sidney's Smile, 1993; Eli and the Dimplemeyers, 1994. CHILDREN'S NOVELS: Understanding Buddy, 2001; Izzy's Place, 2003. Contributor of articles to periodicals. **Address:** 711 Orchard St., Madison, WI 53715, U.S.A. **Online address:** mkornblatt@charter.net

KORNBLITH, Hilary. (Hilary (Stuart) Kornblith). American (born United States), b. 1954. **Genres:** Philosophy. **Career:** University of Vermont, Department of philosophy, professor, 1979-, chair, 1991-97; University of Massachusetts, professor of philosophy, 2003-, head. Writer. **Publications:** (Ed.) Naturalizing Epistemology, 1985, 2nd ed. 1994; Inductive Inference and Its Natural Ground, 1993; (ed.) Epistemology: Internalism and Externalism, 2001; Knowledge and Its Place in Nature, 2002. Contributor to books. **Address:** Department of Philosophy, University of Massachusetts, 360 Bartlett Hall, 130 Hicks Way, Amherst, MA 01003-9269, U.S.A. **Online address:** kornblith@philos.umass.edu

KORNBLITH, Hilary (Stuart). *See* **KORNBLITH, Hilary.**

KORNBLUH, Peter. American (born United States), b. 1956?. **Genres:** International Relations/Current Affairs, Local History/Rural Topics, Adult Non-fiction, Politics/Government. **Career:** George Washington University, National Security Archive, senior analyst, 1986-, Cuba and Chile documentation projects, manager, 1990-99, director; Iran-contra documentation project, co-director; Columbia University, adjunct professor of international and public affairs, 1990-99. Writer. **Publications:** Nicaragua, the Price of Intervention: Reagan's Wars against the Sandinistas, 1987; (ed. with M.T. Klare) Low-Intensity Warfare: Counterinsurgency, Proinsurgency and Antiterrorism in the Eighties, 1988; Nicaragua: The Making of U.S. Policy, 1978-1990, 1991; (ed. with M. Byrne) The Iran-Contra Affair: The Making of a Scandal, 1983-1988, 1992; (ed.with M. Byrne) The Iran-Contra Affair: A National Security Archive Documents Reader, 1992; (ed. with L. Chang) The Cuban Missile Crisis, 1962: A National Security Archive Documents Reader, 1992; (ed. with M. Byrne) The Iran-Contra Scandal: The Declassified History, 1993; (with J.G. Blight) Politics of Illusion: The Bay of Pigs Invasion Reexamined, 1998; (ed.) Bay of Pigs Declassified: The Secret CIA Report on the Invasion of Cuba, 1998; (ed. with L. Chang) Cuban Missile Crisis, 1962: Including Recently Declassified Documents, 1998; The Pinochet File: A Declassified Dossier on Atrocity and Accountability, 2003; EEUU y el Derrocamiento De Allende: Una Historia Desclasificada, 2003. Contributor to periodicals. **Address:** The National Security Archive, George Washington University, The Gelman Library, 2130 H St. NW, Ste. 701, Washington, DC 20037, U.S.A. **Online address:** pkorn@gwis2.circ.gwu.edu

KORNFIELD, Jack. American (born United States), b. 1945?. **Genres:** inspirational/Motivational Literature, Theology/Religion. **Career:** Meditation teacher, 1974-; Spirit Rock Meditation Center, founding teacher, 1974-, Spiritwalk Foundation, instructor; Insight Meditation Society, co-founder, 1975-. Writer. **Publications:** Living Buddhist Masters, 1977; (with S. Bhikkhu) A Brief Guide to Meditation Temples of Thailand, 1978; (with J. Goldstein) Seeking the Heart of Wisdom: The Path of Insight Meditation, 1987; A Path with Heart: A Guide through the Perils and Promises of Spiritual Life, 1993; Buddha's Little Instruction Book, 1994; (with J. Goldstein) Path of Insight Meditation, 1995; Living Dharma: Teachings of Twelve Buddhist Masters, 1996; (co-author) Buddhism in the West: Spiritual Wisdom for the Twenty-First Century, 1998; After the Ecstasy, the Laundry, 2000; Art of Forgiveness, Lovingkindness, and Peace, 2002; Wise Heart: A Guide to the Universal Teachings of Buddhist Psychology, 2008; Living Dharma: Teachings and Meditation Instructions from Twelve Theravada Masters, 2010; Bringing Home the Dharma, 2011; Lamp in the Darkness, 2011. EDITOR: (and comp.

with P. Breiter) A Still Forest Pool: The Insight Meditation of Achaan Chah, 1985; (with C. Feldman) Stories of the Spirit, Stories of the Heart: Parables of the Spiritual Path from Around the World, 1991; (with G. Fronsdal) Teachings of the Buddha, 1993, rev. ed., 1996; (with C. Feldman) Soul Food: Stories to Nourish the Spirit and the Heart, 1996; (with N. Oxenhandler) The Buddha is Still Teaching: Contemporary Buddhist Wisdom, 2010. **Address:** Spirit Rock Meditation Center, 5000 Sir Francis Drake Blvd., PO Box 169, Woodacre, CA 94973, U.S.A.

KORNGOLD, Jamie S. American (born United States), b. 1966?. **Genres:** Theology/Religion, Environmental Sciences/Ecology. **Career:** Rockdale Temple, teacher, 1995-97, assistant youth group advisor, 1995-98; B'nai Mitzvah tutor, 1997-99; Congregation B'nai Vail, rabbinical intern, 1995-97; Cincinnati Reform Jewish High School, teacher, 1996-97; Jewish Hospital, chaplain intern, 1997-98; B'nai Tikvah, Calgary, rabbi, 1999-2001; Adventure Rabbi: Synagogue Without Walls, founder and rabbi, 2001-, executive director, senior rabbi and lead guide; Har HaShem, interim rabbi, 2002-03, rabbi, 2003-07; Ohr Shalom, rabbi, 2002-; Florence Melton Mini School Colorado Agency for Jewish Education, teacher, 2002-04. Writer. **Publications:** God in the Wilderness: Rediscovering the Spirituality of the Great Outdoors with the Adventure Rabbi, 2007. **Address:** Adventure Rabbi, 5353 Manhattan Cir., Ste. 103, Boulder, CO 80303, U.S.A.

KORNHEISER, Tony. American (born United States), b. 1948. **Genres:** Adult Non-fiction, Sports/Fitness, Biography. **Career:** Newsday, reporter, 1970-76; New York Times, reporter, 1976-79; The Washington Post, reporter/columnist, 1979-, sports columnist, 1984-; WMAL-Radio, cohost, 1988-90; WTEM-AM, staff, 1992-; ESPN, radio staff, 1997, Monday Night Football, analyst, 2006-. Radio and television commentator. **Publications:** The Baby Chase, 1983; Pumping Irony: Working Out the Angst of a Lifetime, 1995; Bald As I Wanna Be, 1997; I'm Back for More Cash: A Tony Collection (Because You Can't Take Two Hundred Newspapers into the Bathroom), 2002. Contributor to periodicals. **Address:** c/o Esther Newburg, International Creative Management, 730 5th Ave., New York, NY 10019, U.S.A.

KORNWOLF, James D. American (born United States) **Genres:** History, Architecture, Art/Art History. **Career:** New Jersey Institute of Technology, Rollins College, instructor; College of William and Mary, professor of art history, 1968-2002, emeritus, 2002-. Writer. **Publications:** A History of American Dwellings, 1967; M.H. Ballie Scott and the Arts and Crafts Movement: Pioneers of Modern Design, 1972; Modernism in America 1937-1941: A Catalog and Exhibition of Four Architectural Competitions, 1985; So Good a Design: The Colonial Campus of the College of William and Mary: Its History, Background, and Legacy, 1989; (with G.W. Kornwolf) Architecture and Town Planning in Colonial North America, vol. III, 2002. Contributor of articles to periodicals. **Address:** Department of Art & Art History, College of William & Mary, PO Box 8795, Williamsburg, VA 23187, U.S.A. **Online address:** jdkorn@wm.edu

KOROBKIN, Laura Hanft. American (born United States) **Genres:** Literary Criticism And History, Adult Non-fiction, History. **Career:** Brown University, Pembroke Center for Research, fellow, 1993-94; Bunting Institute, fellow, 1994-95; Rothermere American Institute, fellow, 2001; Boston University, assistant professor of English, associate professor of English, director of graduate studies; Catholic University of Leuven, Fulbright lecturer, 2009. Writer. **Publications:** Criminal Conversations: Sentimentality and Nineteenth-Century Legal Stories of Adultery, 1998. Contributor to books and journals. **Address:** Department of English, Boston University, Rm. 345, 236 Bay State Rd., Boston, MA 02215-1403, U.S.A. **Online address:** korobkin@bu.edu

KORT, Wesley A. American (born United States), b. 1935. **Genres:** Literary Criticism And History, Theology/Religion. **Career:** University of Chicago, Divinity School, Humanities Division, assistant, 1961-63; Princeton University, Department of Religion, instructor, 1963-65; Duke University, Department of Religion, assistant professor, 1965-70, associate professor, 1970-77, professor, 1977-, chair, 2002-06, Graduate Faculty of Religion, staff, 1965-, Graduate School, assistant dean, 1970-71, assistant provost, 1973-74, Cooperative Program in Humanities, co-chair, 1970-72; University of North Carolina, Cooperative Program in Humanities, co-chair, 1970-72; University of Notre Dame, Erasmus Institute, senior fellow, 1999-2000. Writer. **Publications:** Shriven Selves: Religious Problems in Recent American Fiction, 1972; Narrative Elements and Religious Meaning, 1975; Moral Fiber: Character

and Belief in Recent American Fiction, 1982; Modern Fiction and Human Time: A Study in Narrative and Belief, 1985; Story, Text and Scripture: Literary Interests in Biblical Narratives, 1988; Bound to Differ: The Dynamics of Theological Discourses, 1992; Take, Read: Scripture, Textuality and Cultural Practice, 1996; C.S. Lewis Then and Now, 2001: Place and Space in Modern Fiction, 2004. **Address:** Department of Religion, Duke University, 328 Gray Bldg., PO Box 90964, Durham, NC 27708, U.S.A. **Online address:** wkort@duke.edu

KORTH, Philip A. American (born United States), b. 1936. **Genres:** Organized Labor, Local History/Rural Topics, Anthropology/Ethnology, Politics/Government, Social Sciences. **Career:** Michigan State University, associate professor, professor, 1967-, College of Arts and Letters, associate dean, now professor emeritus; Xibei Daxue, foreign expert, 1984-85. Writer. **Publications:** (With M. Beegle) I Remember Like Today: The Auto-Lite Strike of 1934, 1988; Michigan: Visions of Our Past, 1990; Craftsmanship and the Michigan Union Carpenters, 1991; The Minneapolis Teamster's Strike of 1934, 1995. Contributor to periodicals. **Address:** Department of Writing Rhetoric and American, Cultures, Michigan State University, 235 Bessey Hall, East Lansing, MI 48824-1033, U.S.A. **Online address:** korth@msu.edu

KORYTA, Michael J. American (born United States), b. 1983?. **Genres:** Novels. **Career:** Herald-Times, reporter. Writer. **Publications:** Tonight I Said Goodbye, 2004; Sorrow's Anthem, 2006; A Welcome Grave, 2007; Envy the Night, 2008; Silent Hour, 2009; So Cold the River, 2010; Cypress House, 2011; The Ridge, 2011. **Address:** c/o David Hale Smith, DHS Literary Inc., 10711 Preston Rd., Ste. 100, Dallas, TX 75230, U.S.A. **Online address:** michael@michaelkoryta.com

KORZEN, Chris. American (born United States), b. 1976. **Genres:** Theology/Religion. **Career:** Catholic Voting Project (now Catholics United), co-founder and executive director, 2004-11; Maine's Majority L.L.C., co-founder and director, 2011-; Catholic Democracy Institute, executive director; Pax Christi USA, activist. Writer. **Publications:** (With A. Kelley) A Nation for All: How the Catholic Vision of the Common Good Can Save America from the Politics of Division, 2008. **Address:** Jossey-Bass, 1 Montgomery St., Ste. 1200, San Francisco, CA 94104, U.S.A. **Online address:** info@catholicsinalliance.org

KORZENIK, Diana. American (born United States), b. 1941. **Genres:** Art/Art History, Education, Sociology. **Career:** Massachusetts College of Art, Department of Art Education, professor of art education, 1972-, chairperson, 1972-87, now professor emeritus; Harvard University, visiting lecturer; The Friends of the Longfellow House, founder and president. Writer and consultant. **Publications:** (Ed. and contrib.) Feelings, Conflict, People, Change, Groups, Prejudice, 1972; Drawn to Art: A Nineteenth-Century American Dream, 1985; (with M. Brown) Art Making and Education, 1993; (ed. with G.B. Barnhill and C.F. Sloat) The Cultivation of Artists in Nineteenth-Century America, 1997; Objects of American Art Education: Highlights from the Diana Korzenik Collection, 2004. Contributor to books, journals and periodicals. **Address:** Friends of the Longfellow House, 105 Brattle St., Cambridge, MA 02138-3407, U.S.A.

KOSAK, Wendy. *See* **SPENCER, Wen.**

KOSAR, Kevin R. American (born United States), b. 1970. **Genres:** Education, History, Politics/Government. **Career:** Chess-in-the-Schools, program associate, 1996-97; Bully magazine, founder, 1998; AlcoholReviews.com, founder, 1998-; New York Press, faculty; New York University, lecturer in public service; Manhattan Institute and Hudson Institute, researcher; Metropolitan College of New York, special assistant, 2002, lecturer in public affairs and administration; Library of Congress, Congressional Research Service, researcher and analyst; Presidential Management Fellows Program, fellow. Writer. **Publications:** (Ed.) Bridging the Gap: Higher Education and Career-Centered Welfare Reform, 2003; Failing Grades: The Federal Politics of Education Standards, 2005; Quasi Government Organizations, 2009; Whiskey: A Global History, 2010. Contributor to periodicals and journals. **Address:** AlcoholReviews.com, Apt. 8FG, 3900A Watson Pl. NW, Washington, DC 20016, U.S.A. **Online address:** kevinkosar@gmail.com

KOSCIELNIAK, Bruce. American (born United States), b. 1947. **Genres:** Children's Fiction, Illustrations, Sciences, Technology. **Career:** U.S. Postal Service, clerk, 1977-91. Writer and illustrator. **Publications:** FOR CHIL-

DREN SELF-ILLUSTRATED: Hector and Prudence, 1990; Hector and Prudence-All Aboard!, 1990; Euclid Bunny Delivers the Mail, 1991; Bear and Bunny Grow Tomatoes, 1993; Geoffrey Groundhog Predicts the Weather, 1995; The Fabulous Four Skunks, 1996; Hear, Hear, Mr. Shakespeare: Story, Illustrations, and Selections from Shakespeare's Plays, 1998; The Story of the Incredible Orchestra, 2000; Johann Gutenberg and the Amazing Printing Press, 2003; About Time: A First Look at Time and Clocks, 2004; Looking At Glass Through The Ages, 2006. **Address:** 36 Summer St., Adams, MA 01220, U.S.A.

KOSHIRO, Yukiko. Japanese/American (born United States) **Genres:** Race Relations, History, Social Sciences. **Career:** Vassar College, Department of History, adjunct lecturer, 1989; University of Notre Dame, associate professor of history, 1992-2000; Williams College, visiting assistant professor and researcher, faculty of Asian studies, 2000-02; Bates College, Department of History, visiting associate professor, 2002-03; Colgate University, Department of History, visiting associate professor, 2003-04; American University, Department of History, visiting assistant professor, 2004-05; Nihon University, College of International Relations, Department of Global Exchange Studies, professor of international relations, 2006-, now professor emeritus; American-East Asian Relations, associate editor. **Publications:** Trans-Pacific Racisms and the U.S. Occupation of Japan, 1999. **Address:** Department of Global Exchange Studies, Nihon University, 2-31-145, Bunkyo-cho, Mishima-shi, Shizuoka, 411-8555, Japan. **Online address:** koshiro.yukiko@nihon-u.ac.jp

KOSITSKY, Lynne. Canadian (born Canada), b. 1947. **Genres:** Novels, Young Adult Fiction, Poetry, Literary Criticism And History. **Career:** University of Toronto, educator. Poet. **Publications:** PCB Jam, 1981; Candles, 1998; Rebecca's Flame, 1998; A Question of Will, 2000; Rachel: A Mighty Big Imagining, 2001; Rachel: The Maybe House, 2002; Rachel: Certificate of Freedom, 2003; Rachel: An Elephant Tree Christmas, 2004; The Thought of High Windows, 2004; Claire by Moonlight, 2005; Minerva's Voyage, 2009. Contributor of articles to periodicals. **Address:** Kids Can Press Ltd., 25 Dockside Dr., Toronto, ON M5A 0B5, Canada. **Online address:** lynnekositsky@sympatico.ca

KOSKI, Mary B(ernadette). American (born United States), b. 1951. **Genres:** Children's Fiction, Young Adult Fiction, Human Relations/Parenting. **Career:** Welcome Home, administrator, 1975-77; University of Minnesota, instructor in accounting, 1981-82; Mesabi Community College, instructor in accounting, 1982-92, acting vice-provost, 1985-87; Duluth Community College, director and executive dean, 1992-95; Lake Superior College, accounting and economics faculty, 1997-98, Lake Superior College Foundation, director, 1999-2001; Trellis Publishing Inc., president, 1998-2005; Minnesota State Community and Technical College, dean of academics and student services, 2005-; Vermilion Community College, provost and academic dean, 2006-. Writer. **Publications:** FOR CHILDREN: Impatient Pamela Calls 9-1-1, 1998, 2nd ed., 2004; Pamela Asks: Why are My Feet so Huge?, 1999; Impatient Pamela Wants a Bigger Family, 2002; Color, Color, Where are You, Color?, 2004. **Address:** Vermilion Community College, 1900 E Camp St., Ely, MN 55731-1918, U.S.A. **Online address:** m.dubois@vcc.edu

KOSLOW, Sally. American (born United States) **Genres:** Novels, Literary Criticism And History, Young Adult Fiction. **Career:** Mademoiselle Magazine, writer; McCalls, editor-in-chief, 1994-2001; Rosie magazine, corporate editor, 2001-02; Lifetime magazine, editor-in-chief, 2002-04; Sarah Lawrence College, faculty. **Publications:** Little Pink Slips, 2007; Late, Lamented Molly Marx: A Novel, 2009; With Friends Like These: A Novel, 2010. Contributor to periodicals. **Address:** Fletcher & Co., 78 5th Ave., New York, NY 10013, U.S.A.

KOSLOW, Tony. American/Australian (born Australia), b. 1947?. **Genres:** Adult Non-fiction, Environmental Sciences/Ecology. **Career:** Dalhousie University, Oceanography Department, fisheries oceanographer; Commonwealth Scientific and Industrial Research Organisation Marine and Atmospheric Research (CSIRO), senior principal research scientist, 1989-, principal investigator and chief scientist; University of California, Scripps Institution of Oceanography, research oceanographer, California Cooperative Oceanic Fisheries Investigations Program, director. Writer. **Publications:** The Silent Deep: The Discovery, Ecology and Conservation of the Deep Sea, 2007. **Address:** Scripps Institution of Oceanography, University of California, 9500 Gilman Dr., La Jolla, CA 92093, U.S.A. **Online address:** jkoslow@ucsd.edu

KOSS-CHIOINO, Joan D. American (born United States), b. 1935. **Genres:** Anthropology/Ethnology, Psychiatry, Psychology. **Career:** Eastern Pennsylvania Psychiatric Institute, research assistant, 1957; University of Pennsylvania, instructor, 1964, lecturer in anthropology, 1964-65, lecturer in nursing, 1965-67; Temple University, lecturer and assistant professor, 1965-66, adjunct assistant professor, 1966-67; University of Puerto Rico, associate professor of anthropology, 1967-69, lecturer in ecological sciences, 1972-74; Inter American University, visiting professor and head of social sciences division, 1971-73; University of California, lecturer in psychiatry and postdoctoral fellow in international health, 1974-76, adjunct professor, 1975-87; Government of Puerto Rico, Department of Health, program director and researcher, 1976-79; California State University, professor of anthropology, 1977-80; University of New Mexico, associate professor, 1980-89, professor of psychiatry, 1989-92; Tulane University, adjunct professor and visiting professor, 1989-; Arizona State University, department of human evolution and social change, professor of anthropology and women's studies, 1992-, now professor emeritus; George Washington University, research professor. Consultant and writer. **Publications:** Women as Healers, Women as Patients: Mental Health Care and Traditional Healing in Puerto Rico, 1991; (ed. with L.A. Vargas) Working with Culture: Psychotherapeutic Interventions with Ethnic Minority Children and Adolescents, 1992; (with L.A. Vargas) Working with Latino Youth: Culture, Development and Context, 1999; (ed. with T. Leatherman and C. Greenway) Medical Pluralism in the Andes, 2002; (ed. with P. Hefner) Spiritual Transformation and Healing: Anthropological, Theological, Neuroscientific and Clinical Perspectives, 2006. Contributor of articles to journals. **Address:** School of Human Evolution and Social Change, Arizona State University, PO Box 872402, Tempe, AZ 85287-2402, U.S.A. **Online address:** joan.koss@asu.edu

KOSSMAN, Nina. American/Russian (born Russia), b. 1959. **Genres:** Poetry, Autobiography/Memoirs, Translations, Biography, Young Adult Nonfiction, Social Sciences, Young Adult Fiction. **Career:** Language instructor in colleges, 1980-98. Writer, art therapist and translator. **Publications:** (Trans.) M. Tsvetayeva, In the Inmost Hour of the Soul, 1989; Pereboi (title means: 'Syncopated Rhythms'), 1990; Behind the Border: Memories of a Russian Childhood, 1994; Po Pravuyu Ruku Sna, 1996; (trans. with A. Newcomb) M. Tsvetaeva, Poem of the End: Selected Lyrical & Narrative Poetry, 1998; (ed.) Gods and Mortals: Modern Poems on Classical Myths (anthology), 2001. Contributor to periodicals. **Address:** Oxford University Press, 2001 Evans Rd., Cary, NC 27513, U.S.A. **Online address:** nina@ninakossman.com

KOSTELANETZ, Richard (Cory). American (born United States), b. 1940. **Genres:** Novels, Novellas/Short Stories, Poetry, Art/Art History, Communications/Media, Dance/Ballet, Literary Criticism And History, Music, Music, History, Humanities. **Career:** Assembling Press, co-founder and president, 1970-82; City University of New York, John Jay College, Thematic Studies Program, program associate, 1972-73; Future Press, literary director, 1976-; Precisely, co-editor and publisher, 1977-; University of Texas, visiting professor of American studies and English, 1977; Archae Editions, sole proprietor, 1978-; American Writing Today, coordinator, 1979-81; Atlantic Center for the Arts, master artist, 2001. **Publications:** Music of Today, 1967; The Theatre of Mixed Means, 1968; Master Minds, 1969; And So Forth, 1969; Visual Language, 1970; The End of Intelligent Writing, 1974; I Articulations/Short Fictions, 1974; Recyclings: A Literary Autobiography, vol. I, 1974; Number One, 1974; Come Here, 1975; Extrapolate, 1975; Modulations, 1975; Word Prints, 1975; Portraits from Memory, 1975; Openings and Closings, 1975; Rain Rains Rain, 1976; Numbers: Poems and Stories, 1976; Constructs, 1976; Illuminations, 1977; Foreshortenings and Other Stories, 1978; Words and, 1978; Constructs Two, 1978; Grants and the Future of Literature, 1978; Tabula Rasa, 1978; Inexistencies, 1978; Twenties in the Sixties: Previously Uncollected Critical Essays, 1979; The End Appendix/The End Essentials, 1979; Metamorphosis in the Arts, 1980; More Short Fictions, 1980; Exhaustive Parallel Intervals, 1980; Autobiographies, 1981; The Old Poetries and the New, 1981; Reincarnations, 1981; Turfs/Arenas/Fields/Pitches, 1983; Epiphanies, 1983; American Imaginations, 1983; Recycling, 1984; The Old Fictions and the New, 1987; After Texts/Prose Pieces, 1987; The Grants-Fix, 1987; Conversing with Cage, 1988, 2nd ed., 2002; On Innovative Music(ian)s, 1989; Unfinished Business, 1990; The New Poetries and Some Old, 1991; Politics in the African-American Novel, 1991; Word Works: Poems New and Selected, 1993; A Dictionary of the Avant-Gardes, 1993, 2nd ed., 2000; Minimal Fictions, 1994; On Innovative Performance(s), 1994; Morepartitions, 1994; Fillmore East: Recollections of Rock Theater, 1995; Crimes of Culture, 1995; An ABC of Contemporary Reading, 1995; One Million Words of Booknotes,

1996; John Cage (Ex)plain(ed), 1996; 30 Years of Critical Engagements with John Cage, 1996; Vocal Shorts: Collected Performance Texts, 1998; Political Essays, 1998; 3-Element Stories, 1998; 3 Canadian Geniuses, 2001; So Ho: The Rise and Fall of an Artists' Colony, 2003; More Openings and Closings, 2003; Autobiographies at 50, 2004; 35 Years of Visible Writing: A Memoir, 2004; Autobiographies at 50, 2005; Film and Video: Alternative Views, 2005; Kaddish and Other Audio Writings, 2005; Seven Jewish Short Fictions, 2006. NOVELS: In the Beginning, 1971; One Night Stood, 1977. EDITOR/CO-EDITOR: On Contemporary Literature, 1964; (and contrib.) The New American Arts, 1965; Twelve from the Sixties, 1967; The Young American Writers, 1967; Beyond Left and Right, 1968; Assembling: A Collection of Otherwise Unpublishable Manuscripts, 10 vols., 1970-81; Imaged Words and Worded Images, 1970; Possibilities of Poetry, 1970; Moholy-Nagy, 1970; John Cage, 1970; Social Speculations: Visions for Us Now, 1971; Young Writers in North America, 1971; Future's Fictions, 1971; Human Alternatives, 1971; Seeing through Shuck, 1972; In Youth, 1972; Breakthrough Fictioneers, 1973; The Edge of Adaptation, 1973; Essaying Essays, 1975; Language and Structure, 1975; Younger Critics in North America, 1976; Esthetics Contemporary, 1978, rev. ed., 1989; Assembling Assembling, 1978; Visual Literature Criticism, 1979; A Critical Assembling, 1979; Text-Sound Texts, 1980; Scenarios, 1980; Aural Literature Criticism, 1981; The Avant-Garde Tradition in Literature, 1982; American Writing Today, 1982; Pilot Proposals, 1982; Gertrude Stein Advanced, 1991; On Innovative Art(ist)s, Merce Cunningham: Dancing in Time and Space, 1992; John Cage, Writer, 1993; Writings about John Cage, 1993; Nicolas Slonimsky: The First 100 Years, 1994; A Portable Baker's Biographical Dictionary of Musicians, 1995; Classic Essays on 20th Century Music, 1996; A B.B. King Companion, 1997, rev. ed., 2005; A Frank Zappa Companion, 1997; Writings on Glass, 1997; An Other E.E. Cummings, 1998; A Gertrude Stein Reader, 2002; Virgil Thomson: A Reader, 2002; Conceptual Dance; Aaron Copland Reader, 2003. Works appear in anthologies. **Address:** 1600 Norman St., Ridgewood, NY 11385-5751, U.S.A. **Online address:** richkostelanetz@aol.com

KOSTELNIUK, James. Canadian (born Canada), b. 1946. **Genres:** Autobiography/Memoirs, Mystery/Crime/Suspense, Adult Non-fiction, Criminology/True Crime. **Career:** Winnipeg Transit, bus operator, 1980-2001, retired, 2001. Writer. **Publications:** Wolves among Sheep: The True Story of Murder in a Jehovah's Witness Community, 2000; Last Child on the Prairies: When Children were Still Connected to Nature, 2012; Bad Moon Rising, forthcoming; A Parody of Ernest Hemingway's Life and Works, forthcoming. **Address:** 788 Scotland Ave., Winnipeg, MB R3M 1X6, Canada.

KOSTERS, Marvin H(oward). American (born United States), b. 1933. **Genres:** Economics, Money/Finance. **Career:** RAND Corp., economist, 1965-69; University of California-Los Angeles, lecturer, 1966-69; President's Council of Economic Advisers, senior economist, 1969-71; U.S. Department of Labor, associate manpower administrator for policy, evaluation, and research, 1971; U.S. Cost of Living Council, associate director for economic policy and assistant director for economic planning and analysis, 1971-74; White House, Office of the Assistant to the President for Economic Affairs, staff, 1974-75; U.S. Department of the Treasury, consultant, 1975-77; American Enterprise Institute for Public Policy Research, Center for the Study of Government Regulation, director, 1976-86, director of economic policy studies, 1987-; Virginia Polytechnic Institute and State University, adjunct professor, 1994-2000. Writer. **Publications:** Income and Substitution Effects in a Family Labor Supply Model, 1966; (with D.H. Greenberg) Income Guarantees and the Working Poor, 1970; (with J.D. Ahalt) Controls and Inflation: The Economic Stabilization Program in Retrospect, 1975; (with M.N. Ross) Quality of Jobs: Evidence from Distributions of Annual Earnings and Hourly Wages, 1988; Wage Levels and Inequality: Measuring and Interpreting the Trends, 1998; (co-author) Measuring Prices in a Dynamic Economy: Re-Examining the CPI, 1999; (with B.D. Mast) Closing the Education Achievement Gap: Is Title I Working?, 2003. EDITOR: (with T.B. Clark and J.C. Miller III) Reforming Regulation, 1980; Workers and their Wages: Changing Patterns in the United States, 1991; (with A.H. Meltzer) International Competitiveness in Financial Services: A Special Issue of the Journal of Financial Services Research, 1991; Personal Saving, Consumption, and Tax Policy, 1992; Fiscal Politics and the Budget Enforcement Act, 1992; (with J. Bhagwati) Trade and Wages: Leveling Wages Down?, 1994; Effects of the Minimum Wage on Employment, 1996; Financing College Tuition: Government Policies and Educational Priorities, 1999. Works appears in anthologies. Contributor to periodicals. **Address:** American Enterprise Institute for Public Policy, Research, 1150 17th St. NW, Washington, DC 20036, U.S.A. **Online address:** mkosters@aei.org

KOSTMAN, Joel. American (born United States) **Genres:** Novels, Biography, Autobiography/Memoirs. **Career:** Writer. **Publications:** Keys to the City: Tales of a New York City Locksmith, 1997. Contributor to periodicals. **Address:** c/o Author Mail, DK Publishing Publicity, 375 Hudson St., New York, NY 10014, U.S.A.

KOSTOFF, Lynn. American (born United States), b. 1954?. **Genres:** Novels, Mystery/Crime/Suspense. **Career:** Francis Marion University, Department of English, professor of English, writer-in-residence, 1985-; Indiana State University, faculty; University of Alabama, faculty; Bowling Green State University, MFA Fiction, faculty. Writer. **Publications:** A Choice of Nightmares (novel), 1991; The Long Fall (novel), 2003; Late Rain (novel), 2010. **Address:** Department of English, Francis Marion University, Founders Hall, PO Box 100547, florence, SC 29501-0547, U.S.A. **Online address:** lkostoff@fmarion.edu

KOSTOVA, Elizabeth. American (born United States), b. 1964. **Genres:** Novels, Horror. **Career:** Elizabeth Kostova Foundation, founder, 2007; Writer and educator. **Publications:** The Historian: A Novel, 2005; (with B. Stoker) Dracula, 2005; Swan Thieves: A Novel, 2010. **Address:** c/o Author Mail, Little Brown and Co., 1271 Ave. of the Americas, New York, NY 10020, U.S.A.

KOTERBA, Jeffrey. American (born United States), b. 1961. **Genres:** Autobiography/Memoirs. **Career:** Omaha World-Herald, editorial cartoonist, 1989; Prairie Cats, singer, guitarist and songwriter. **Publications:** Inklings (memoir), 2009. **Address:** c/o Amy Moore-Benson, AMB Literary Management, 92 Willcocks St., Toronto, ON M5S 1C8, Canada. **Online address:** jeff@jeffreykoterba.com

KOTKER, Zane. American (born United States), b. 1934. **Genres:** Novels, History, Novellas/Short Stories, Adult Non-fiction, Literary Criticism And History. **Career:** Waterbury Republican-American, reporter, 1957-58; A New England Review, co-editor and publisher, 1960-63; Silver Burdett Co., editor, 1963-66; Harcourt Brace Jovanovich Inc., department head, 1966-69; writer, 1969-; Mount Holyoke College, associate professor, 1983; University of Massachusetts, MFA Program, professor, 1983; Smith College, visiting writer, 1990-91. **Publications:** Bodies in Motion, 1972; A Certain Man, 1976; White Rising: A Novel, 1981; Try to Remember: A Novel, 1997. Contributor of articles to periodicals. **Address:** Random House, 1745 Broadway, 3rd Fl., New York, NY 10019, U.S.A. **Online address:** zane@crocker.com

KOTKIN, Stephen Mark. American (born United States), b. 1959?. **Genres:** History. **Career:** Princeton University, assistant professor, 1989-95, associate professor, 1995-2001, professor, 2000-, director of program in Russian and Eurasian studies, 1996-2009; Columbia University, adjunct assistant professor, 1990-91; New York Times, Sunday Business Section, book reviewer, 2006-. Writer. **Publications:** (Ed.) Behind the Urals: An American Worker in Russia's City of Steel, 1989; Steeltown, USSR: Soviet Society in the Gorbachev Era, 1991; Soviet Society and Culture in the 1920-30s, 1993; (ed. with D. Wolff) Rediscovering Russia in Asia: Siberia and the Russian Far East, 1995; Magnetic Mountain: Stalinism as a Civilization, 1995; (ed. with B.A. Elleman) Mongolia in the Twentieth Century: Landlocked Cosmopolitan, 1999; Armageddon Averted: The Soviet Collapse, 1970-2000, 2001; (ed. with A. Sajoá) Political Corruption in Transition: A Skeptic's Handbook, 2002; (ed. with C. Evtuhov) The Cultural Gradient: The Transmission of Ideas in Europe, 1789-1991, 2003; (ed. with C.K. Armstrong, G. Rozman and S.S. Kim) Korea at the Center: Dynamics of Regionalism in Northeast Asia, 2005; Uncivil Society: 1989 and the Implosion of the Communist Establishment, 2009; (ed. with B.A. Elleman) Manchurian Railways and the Opening of China: An International History, 2010. **Address:** Princeton University, 228 Dickinson Hall, Princeton, NJ 08542, U.S.A. **Online address:** kotkin@princeton.edu

KOTLER, Neil G. American (born United States), b. 1941. **Genres:** History, Marketing, Business/Trade/Industry. **Career:** De Paul University, instructor in American government and political science, 1967-71; Dartmouth College, instructor in American government and political science, 1971-73; University of Texas, instructor, 1974-75; U.S. House of Representatives, legislative assistant, legislative director, 1975-84; Georgetown University, instructor, 1979; Smithsonian Institution, special assistant and program specialist, 1986-; Kotler Museum and Cultural Marketing Consultants, founder and president. Writer. **Publications:** Axum, Ethiopia, 1971; (with P. Kotler) Museum Strategy and Marketing: Designing Missions, Building Audiences, Generating Revenue and Resources, 1998, (with P. Kotler and W.I. Kotler) 2nd ed. as Museum Marketing and Strategy: Designing Missions, Building Audiences, Generating Revenue and Resources, 2008. EDITOR: Social Marketing: Strategies for Changing Public Behavior, 1989; (with P.M. Hirschoff) Completing the Food Chain: Strategies for Combating Hunger and Malnutrition, 1989; Sharing Innovation: Global Perspectives on Food, Agriculture, and Rural Development, 1990; Frontiers of Nutrition and Food Security in Asia, Africa, and Latin America, 1992; (with W.S. Dillon) The Statue of Liberty Revisited: Making a Universal Symbol, 1994. **Address:** Jossey-Bass, 111 River St., Hoboken, NJ 07030-5774, U.S.A. **Online address:** nkotler@museummarketing.net

KOTLER, Philip. American (born United States), b. 1931. **Genres:** Marketing, Social Sciences, Business/Trade/Industry, Economics. **Career:** Westinghouse Corp., management trainee, 1953; Roosevelt University, assistant professor, 1957-58, associate professor of economics, 1959-60; Northwestern University, Kellogg School of Management, assistant professor of marketing, 1962-64, associate professor of marketing, 1965-68, Montgomery Ward professor of marketing, 1969-72, Harold T. Martin professor of marketing, 1973-87, S.C. Johnson & Son distinguished professor of international marketing, 1988-; School of the Art Institute of Chicago, director; American Marketing Association, director; Kotler Marketing Group Inc., principal; Institute of Management Sciences, College of Marketing, chairman; MAC Group, director. Writer. **Publications:** (With R.E. Turner) Marketing Management: Analysis, Planning and Control, 1967, (with K.L. Keller) 14th ed., 2012; (with G.L. Lilien and K.S. Moorthy) Marketing Models, 1971, 3rd ed., 1992; Marketing Decision Making: A Model Building Approach, 1971; (ed. with K.K. Cox) Readings in Marketing Management, 1971; Simulation en Marketing, 1971; (ed. with G. Zaltman and I. Kaufman) Creating Social Change, 1972; (ed. with H. Guetzkow and R.L. Schultz) Simulation in the Social and Administrative Sciences, 1972; (with A.R. Andreasen) Strategic Marketing for Nonprofit Organizations, 1975, 7th ed., 2007; (with G. Armstrong) Principles of Marketing, 1980, 13th ed., 2010; (ed. with O.C. Ferrell and C. Lamb) Cases and Readings for Marketing for Nonprofit Organizations, 1983; Marketing Essentials, 1984; (with P.N. Bloom) Marketing Professional Services, 1984, (with P.N. Bloom and T. Hayes) 2nd ed., 2002; (with L. Fahey and S. Jatusripitak) The New Competition, 1985; (with K.F.A. Fox) Strategic Marketing for Educational Institutions, 1985, 2nd ed., 1994; (with G. Armstrong) Marketing: An Introduction, 1987, 10th ed., 2011; Marketing for Health Care Organizations, 1987; (with I.J. Rein and M.R. Stoller) High Visibility, 1987; (with E.L. Roberto) Social Marketing: Strategies for Changing Public Behavior, 1989, (with N.R. Lee) 3rd ed. as Social Marketing: Influencing Behaviors for Good, 2008; Marketing for Congregations: Serving People More Effectively, 1992; Marketing Places: Attracting Investment, Industry, and Tourism to Cities, States and Nations, 1993; (with J.T. Bowen and J.C. Makens) Marketing for Hospitality and Tourism, 1996, 5th ed., 2010; Standing Room Only: Strategies for Marketing the Performing Arts, 1996; The Marketing of Nations, 1997; (with N. Kotler) Museum Strategy and Marketing, 1998, (with N.G. Kotler and W.I. Kotler) 2nd ed. as Museum Marketing and Strategy, 2008; Kotler on Marketing, 1999; (with H. Kartajaya) Repositioning Asia: From Bubble to Sustainable Economy, 2000; Framework for Marketing Management, 2001, (with K.L. Keller) 5th ed., 2012; (with D.C. Jain and S. Maesincee) Marketing Moves: A New Approach to Profits, Growth, and Renewal, 2002; (co-author) Marketing Asian Places, 2002; (with F. Simon) Building Global Biobrands: Taking Biotechnology to Market, 2003; Marketing Insights from A to Z: 80 Concepts Every Manager Needs to Know, 2003; (with F.T. de Bes) Lateral Marketing: New Techniques for Finding Breakthrough Ideas, 2003; Rethinking Marketing: Sustainable Market-ing Enterprise in Asia: Text and Cases, 2003; (co-author) Marketing Management: An Asian Perspective, 3rd ed., 2003, 4th ed., 2006; Ten Deadly Marketing Sins: Signs and Solutions, 2004; (with H. Kartajaya and S.D. Young) Attracting Investors: A Marketing Approach to Finding Funds for Your Business, 2004; (with N. Lee) Corporate Social Responsibility: Doing the Most Good for Your Company and Your Cause, 2005; According to Kotler: The World's Foremost Authority on Marketing Answers Your Questions, 2005; (with I. Rein and B. Shields) Elusive Fan: Reinventing Sports in a Crowded Marketplace, 2006; (with W. Pfoertsch) B2B Brand Management, 2006; (with N. Lee) Marketing in the Public Sector: A Roadmap for Improved

Performance, 2007; (with J. Shalowitz and R.J. Stevens) Strategic Marketing for Health Care Orgaizations: Building a Customer-Driven Health System, 2008; (with N.R. Lee) Up and Out of Poverty: The Social Marketing Solution, 2009; (with J.A. Caslione) Chaotics: The Business of Managing and Marketing in the Age of Turbulence, 2009; (with W. Pfoertsch) Ingredient Branding, 2010; (with B. Wrenn and N. Shawchuck) Building Strong Congregations: Attracting, Serving and Developing Your Membership, 2010; (with R. Berger and N. Bickhoff) The Quintessence of Strategic Management: What You Really Need to Know to Survive in Business, 2010; (with H. Kartajaya and I. Setiawan) Marketing 3.0: From Products to Customers to the Human Spirit, 2010; (ed. with H. Cheng and N.R. Lee) Social Marketing for Public Health: Global Trends and Success Stories, 2011; (with H. Kartajaya and H.D. Huan) Merebut pasar ASEAN!, 2011. Contributor to journals. **Address:** Kotler Marketing Group Inc., 925 15th St. NW, 4th Fl., Washington, DC 20005, U.S.A. **Online address:** p-kotler@kellogg.northwestern.edu

KOTLIKOFF, Laurence J. American (born United States) **Genres:** Environmental Sciences/Ecology. **Career:** University of California, faculty, 1977-83; Yale University, faculty, 1977-83; Boston University, professor of economics; President's Council of Economic Advisors, senior economist, 1981-82; National Bureau of Economic Research, research associate; Economic Security Planning Inc. (a financial software company), president; International Monetary Fund, consultant; World Bank, consultant; Senate Finance Committee, consultant. Writer, economist, consultant, entrepreneur, public speaker and educator. **Publications:** (with D.E. Smith) Pensions in the American Economy, 1983; (with A.J. Auerbach) Dynamic Fiscal Policy, 1987; What Determines Savings?, 1989; (with D.A. Wise) The Wage Carrot and the Pension Stick: Retirement Benefits and Labor Force Participation, 1989; Generational Accounting: Knowing Who Pays and When, for What We Spend, 1992; (with A.J. Auerbach) Macroeconomics: An Integrated Approach, 1995, 2nd ed., 1998; (ed. with A.J. Auerbach and W. Leibfritz) Generational Accounting around the World, 1999; Essays on Saving, Bequests, Altruism and Life-Cycle Planning, 2001; Generational Policy, 2003; (with S. Burns) The Coming Generational Storm: What You Need to Know about America's Economic Future, 2004; (with H. Fehr and S. Jokisch) Will China Eat Our Lunch or Take Us out to Dinner? Simulating the Transition Paths of the U.S., EU, Japan and China, 2005; (with D. Rapson) Would the Fairtax Raise or Lower Marginal and Average Tax Rates?, 2005; (with D. Rapson) Comparing Average and Marginal Tax Rates under the Fairtax and the Current System of Federal Taxation, 2006; (with B. Marx and P. Rizza) Americans' Dependency on Social Security, 2006; (with J. Green) On the General Relativity of Fiscal Language, 2006; The Healthcare Fix: Universal Insurance for All Americans, 2007; (with B. Marx and D. Rapson) To Roth or Not?'That Is the Question, 2008; (with F.J. Gomes and L.M. Viceira) Optimal Life-Cycle Investing with Flexible Labor Supply: A Welfare Analysis of Life-Cycle Funds, 2008; (with S. Burns) Spend til the End: The Revolutionary Guide to Raising Your Living Standard Today and When You Retire, 2008. Contributor to books and periodicals. **Address:** Department of Economics, Boston University, 270 Bay State Rd., Boston, MA 02215, U.S.A. **Online address:** kotlikoff@bu.edu

KOTLOWITZ, Alex. American (born United States), b. 1955. **Genres:** Social Commentary, Documentaries/Reportage, Documentaries/Reportage. **Career:** MacNeil/Lehrer News Hour, producer; Bureau of Wall Street Journal, staff writer; The New York Times Magazine, contributor; The New Yorker, staff writer; This American Life, contributor; Northwestern University, Center for the Writing Arts, senior lecturer, writer-in-residence; University of Notre Dame, visiting professor; University of Chicago, writer-in-residence; Dartmouth College, Montgomery fellow. **Publications:** There Are No Children Here: The Story of Two Boys Growing up in the Other America, 1991; The Other Side of the River, 1998; Never a City So Real, 2004. **Address:** Ctr. for the Writing Arts, Northwestern University, Crowe Hall, Rm. 5-155, 1860 Campus Dr., Evanston, IL 60208-2215, U.S.A. **Online address:** alex@alexkotlowitz.com

KOTTER, John P(aul). American (born United States), b. 1947. **Genres:** Administration/Management, Business/Trade/Industry, Economics. **Career:** Harvard University Business School, research fellow, 1972-73, assistant professor, 1973-77, associate professor, 1977-81, professor, 1981-90, Konosuke Matsushita professor of leadership, 1990-2002, now Konosuke Matsushita professor of leadership emeritus; Kotter Associates, owner; Kotter Intl., creator and co-founder, chief innovation officer. Writer and management consultant. **Publications:** (With P.R. Lawrence) Mayors in Action: Five Approaches to Urban Governance, 1974; (with V.A. Faux and C. McArthur) Self-Assessment and Career Development, 1978, (co-author) 2nd ed., 1985; Organizational Dynamics: Diagnosis and Intervention, 1978; (with L. Schlesinger and V. Sathe) Organization: Text, Cases, and Readings on the Management of Organizational Design and Change, 3rd ed., 1979; Power in Management: How to Understand, Acquire, and Use It, 1979, 3rd ed., 1992; The General Managers, 1982, rev. ed., 1986; Power and Influence: Beyond Formal Authority, 1985; The Leadership Factor, 1988; A Force for Change: How Leadership Differs from Management, 1990; (with J.L. Heskett) Corporate Culture and Performance, 1992; The New Rules: How to Succeed in Today's Post-Corporate World, 1995; Leading Change, 1996; Matsushita Leadership: Lessons from the Twentieth Century's Most Remarkable Entrepreneur, 1997; John P. Kotter on What Leaders Really Do, 1999; (with D.S. Cohen) The Heart of Change: Real-Life Stories of How People Change Their Organizations, 2002; (ed. with M. Warner) International Encyclopedia of Business and Management, 2nd ed., 2002; Ling Dao Ren de Bian Ge Fa Ze: Zu Zhi Zhuan Xing Cheng Gong ba bu Zhou, 2004; Our Iceberg is Melting, 2006; (with J.J. Gabarro) Managing Your Boss, 2008; Sense of Urgency, 2008; (with L.A. Whitehead) Buy-in: Saving Your Good Idea From Being Shot Down, 2010; Leading Change: Why Transformation Efforts Fail, 2010. **Address:** Kotter International Inc., 1000 2nd Ave., Ste. 3300, Seattle, WA 98104, U.S.A. **Online address:** john@kotterinternational.com

KOTTLER, Jeffrey (A.). American (born United States), b. 1951. **Genres:** Self Help, Psychology, Education, inspirational/Motivational Literature, How-to Books. **Career:** University of North Alabama, assistant professor, 1976-81; Oakland University, adjunct professor, 1982-90; The Citadel, associate professor of counseling, 1990-91; University of Nevada, professor of counseling, 1991-2000; California State University, professor and chair of counseling, 2001-; Empower Nepali Girls Foundation, president. Writer. **Publications:** (With W. Van Hoose) Ethical and Legal Issues in Counseling and Psychotherapy, 1977; Mouthing Off, 1980; Pragmatic Group Leadership, 1983; (with R. Brown) Introduction to Therapeutic Counseling, 1985, (with D.S. Shepard) 7th ed. as Introduction to Counseling: Voices from the Field, 2011; On Being a Therapist, 1987, 4th ed., 2010; (with D. Blau) The Imperfect Therapist: Learning from Failure in Therapeutic Practice, 1989; Private Moments, Secret Selves, 1990; The Compleat Therapist, 1991; Compassionate Therapy: Working with Difficult Clients, 1992; (with S. Zehm) On Being a Teacher, 1993, (with S.J. Zehm and E. Kottler) 3rd ed., 2005; (with E. Kottler) Teacher as Counselor, 1993; (with R.J. Hazler) The Emerging Professional Counselor: Student Dreams to Professional Realities, 1994, 2nd ed., 2005; Beyond Blame: A New Way of Resolveing Conflict in Relationships, 1994; (with T. Sexton and S. Whiston) Heart of Healing: Relationships in Therapy, 1994, (with R. Powell and S. Zehm) Classrooms under the Influence: Counteracting Problems of Addiction, 1995; Growing a Therapist, 1995; The Language of Tears, 1996; (with R. Hazler) What You Never Learned in Graduate School, 1997; What's Really Said in the Teachers Lounge: Provocative Ideas About Cultures and Classrooms, 1997; Travel That Can Change Your Life, 1997; (with E. Kottler and C. Kottler) Secrets for Secondary School Teachers, 1998, 2nd ed., 2004; (with J. Moss) The Last Victim: A True-Life Journey into the Mind of the Serial Killer, 1999; Exploring and Treating Acquisitive Desire, 1999; (with E. Kottler) Counseling Skills for Teachers, 2000, 2nd ed., 2007; Doing Good: Passion and Commitment for Helping Others, 2000; Learning Group Leadership, 2001, (with M. Englar-Carlson) 2nd ed., 2010; Making Changes Last, 2001; (with J. Carlson) Bad Therapy, 2002; (with E. Kottler) Children with Limited English: Teaching Strategies for the Regular Classroom, 2nd ed., 2002, (with C. Street and E. Kottler) 3rd ed. as English Language Learners in Your Classroom: Strategies That Work, 2008; Theories in Counseling and Therapy, 2002, (with M.J. Montgomery) 2nd ed., 2011; Students Who Drive You Crazy, 2002, (with E. Kottler) 2nd ed., 2008; (with L. Brew) One Life at a Time: Helping Skills and Interventions, 2003; (with J. Carlson and B. Keeney) An American Shaman, 2004; (with J. Carlson) Their Finest Hour, 2004, 2nd ed., 2008; (with W.P. Jones) Understanding Research: Becoming a Competent and Critical Consumer, 2005; (with J. Carlson) The Client Who Changed Me, 2005; Divine Madness: Ten Stories of Creative Struggle, 2006; (with J. Carlson) Moved by the Spirit, 2007; (with D. Chen) Stress Management and Prevention, 2008, 2nd ed., 2011; A Brief Primer of Helping Skills, 2008; (with L. Brew) Applied Helping Skills: Transforming Lives, 2008; (with J. Carlson) Creative Breakthroughs in Therapy, 2009; (with M. Marriner) Changing People's Lives While Transforming Your Own, 2009; Lust for Blood, 2010; The Assassin and the Therapist: An Exploration of Truth in Psychotherapy and in Life, 2010; Excelling in College: Strategies for Student Success and Reducing Stress, 2011. EDITOR: Finding Your Way as a Counselor, 1996; (with H. Forester-Miller) Issues and Challenges

in Group Work, 1997; Nuts and Bolts of Helping, 2000; Counselors Finding Their Way, 2001; (with J. Carlson) The Mummy at the Dining Room Table, 2003; (with W.P. Jones) Doing Better: Improving Clinical Skills and Professional Competence, 2003; (with V. Minichiello) Qualitative Journeys: Student and Mentor Experiences With Research, 2009; (with J. Carlson) Duped, 2010. **Address:** Department of Counseling, California State University, Rm. 105, Education Classroom Bldg., PO Box 6868, Fullerton, CA 92834-6868, U.S.A. **Online address:** jk@jeffreykottler.com

KOTZWINKLE, William. American (born United States), b. 1938. **Genres:** Novels, Science Fiction/Fantasy, Children's Fiction, Novellas/Short Stories, Animals/Pets. **Career:** Freelance writer. **Publications:** SCIENCE FICTION: Elephant Bangs Train (short stories), 1971; Hermes 3000, 1972; Doctor Rat, 1976; E.T.: The Extra-Terrestrial (novelization of screenplay), 1982; Superman III (novelization of screenplay), 1983; E.T.: The Book of the Green Planet, 1985; Jewel of the Moon (stories), 1985. NOVELS: Hermes 3000, 1972; The Fan Man, 1974; Night-Book, 1974; Swimmer in the Secret Sea, 1975; Fata Morgana, 1977; Herr Nightingale and the Satin Woman, 1978; Jack in the Box, 1980; Book of Love, 1980; Christmas at Fontaine's 1982; Queen of Swords, 1983; Exile, 1987; Hot Jazz Trio, 1989; Midnight Examiner, 1989; The Game of Thirty, 1994; The Amphora Project, 2005, The Game of 30, 2007. FOR CHILDREN: The Fireman, 1969; The Ship That Came Down the Gutter, 1970; Elephant Boy: A Story of the Stone Age, 1970; The Day the Gang Got Rich, 1970; The Oldest Man and Other Timeless Stories, 1971; Return of Crazy Horse, 1971; The Supreme, Superb, Exalted and Delightful, One and Only Magic Building, 1973; Up the Alley with Jack and Joe, 1974; The Leopard's Tooth, 1976; The Ants Who Took Away Time, 1978; Dream of Dark Harbor, 1979; The Nap Master, 1979; The Extra Terrestrial Storybook, 1982; Great World Circus, 1983; Trouble in Bugland: A Collection of Inspector Mantis Mysteries, 1983; Seduction in Berlin, 1985; The Book of the Green Plant, 1985; Hearts of Wood and Other Timeless Tales, 1986; The World Is Big and I'm So Small, 1986; The Empty Notebook, 1990. OTHERS: The Million Dollar Bear, 1995; Tales from the Empty Notebook, 1995; The Bear Went Over the Mountain, 1996; (with G. Murray) Walter, the Farting Dog, 2001; (with G. Murray) Walter, the Farting Dog: Trouble at the Yard Sale, 2004; Walter, Canis Inflatus, 2004; (with G. Murray and E. Gundy) Rough Weather Ahead for Walter the Farting Dog, 2005; Walter the Farting Dog Farts Again, 2005; Walter the Farting Dog and the Windy Day, 2006; (with G. Murray and E. Gundy) Walter the Farting Dog Goes on a Cruise, 2006; (with G. Murray and E. Gundy) Walter the Farting Dog: Banned from the Beach, 2007. Contributor to books, magazines, newspapers and periodicals. **Address:** Doubleday, 1540 Broadway, New York, NY 10036-4039, U.S.A.

KOUPAL, Nancy Tystad. American (born United States), b. 1947. **Genres:** History, Literary Criticism And History, Women's Studies And Issues, Bibliography, Biography, Children's Fiction, Children's Non-fiction. **Career:** Morehead State University, teacher of composition, 1971-72; University of Wisconsin, teacher of American literature, 1972-74; South Dakota Department of Social Services, writer and editor, 1975-78; South Dakota State Library, library technician, 1978; freelance writer, 1978-79; South Dakota State Historical Society, South Dakota History, editor, 1979-, South Dakota State Historical Society Press, director, 1997-. **Publications:** South Dakota Women, 1850-1919: A Bibliography, 1975; Dakota Women, 1978; (contrib.) Encyclopedia of the Great Plains, 2002; (comp.) The Prairie-Dog Prince, 2008. EDITOR: The Woman Suffrage Movement in South Dakota, 2nd ed., 1975; The Way They Saw Us: The South Dakota State Historical Society Collection of Images from the Nineteenth-Century Illustrated Press, 1989; Our Landlady, 1996; (ed.) Baum's Road to Oz: The Dakota Years, 2000; (with J.P. Ronda) Finding Lewis and Clark: Old Trails, New Directions, 2004. Contributor to periodicals. Works appear in anthologies. **Address:** South Dakota State Historical Society Press, South Dakota State Historical Society, 900 Governors Dr., Pierre, SD 57501-2217, U.S.A. **Online address:** nancy.koupal@state.sd.us

KOURILSKY, Françoise. French (born France), b. 1933. **Genres:** Plays/Screenplays, Theatre, Young Adult Fiction. **Career:** University of Paris, associate professor of theater, 1968-74, Studies at the School of Law and Management, second director; City University of New York, Queens College, visiting professor of theater, 1974-75; State University of New York at Stony Brook, visiting professor of theater, 1975-76; New York University, professor of theater, 1976-78; Center for Theater Practice, co-founder, 1977, co-director, 1977-79; World Theatre Festival, director, 1981-82; Ubu Repertory Theater, founder, 1982, artistic director, 1982-2002; Francoise Kourilsky Associates, scientific advisor. Stage director and Writer. **Publications:** Théâtre aux états-Unis, 1967; Le Bread and Puppet Theatre, 1971. EDITOR: Afrique: New Plays, 1987; The Paris Stage: Recent Plays, 1988; (with C. Temerson) Plays by Women, 1989; Gay Plays: An International Anthology, 1989; Theater and Politics, 1990; Afrique II, 1991; Ubu Repertory Theater, 1982-1992, 1992; New French-Language Plays, 1993; Plays by Women II, 1994; Monologues: Plays from Martinique, France, Algeria, and Quebec, 1995; Plays by Women III, 1996; Playwrights of Exile, 1997; Du Désir au plaisir de changer: Le coaching du changement, 2004. Contributor to journals. **Address:** 924 W End Ave., Apt. 102, New York, NY 10025, U.S.A. **Online address:** frkourilsky@aol.com

KOVACH, Gay Haff. American (born United States), b. 1956. **Genres:** Children's Fiction, Art/Art History, Children's Non-fiction, Illustrations, Novels, History. **Career:** Sweet Art, artist and illustrator, 1988-. Writer. **Publications:** Coastal Colors, 1995. Illustrator of books by I. Bodie. **Address:** Sweet Art, 221 1st Creek Rd., Gaston, SC 29053, U.S.A. **Online address:** happytrailsfarmk@aol.com

KOVACS, Deborah. American (born United States), b. 1954. **Genres:** Children's Fiction, Children's Non-fiction. **Career:** Children's Television Workshop, staff, 1975-80; Sesame Street, toy, game and record developer; Children's Television Workshop, editor, 1978-80; Sesame Street Magazine, editor, 1978-80; Scholastic Inc., editor, 1980-81, magazine editor, 1980-85, Software Publishing Group, creative director, 1982-85; freelance writer for book, magazine and computer software publishers; Woods Hole Oceanographic Institution, Ocean Explorer, editor, 1991-; Turnstone Publishing Group, vice president, editor-in-chief, 1997-2001; Walden Media, senior vice president, editorial director, 2001-. **Publications:** (Ed.) Baby Strawberry Book of Baby Farm Animals, 1980; (ed.) Baby Strawberry Book of Pets, 1980; (ed.) Country Cat, 1980; Frazzle's Fantastic Day: Featuring Jim Henson's Sesame Street Muppets, 1980; When Is Saturday?, 1981; (adapter) Battle of the Bands, 1986; A Day Underwater, 1987; The Hottest Group in Town, 1987; Moondreamers: The Evening Song, 1987; Woody's First Dictionary, 1988; Disney's Chip 'n Dale Rescue Rangers: The Big Cheese Caper, 1991; (with J. Preller) Meet the Authors and Illustrators: 60 Creators of Favorite Children's Books Talk About their Work, vol. I, 1991, vol. II, 1993; Brewster's Courage, 1992; (adapter) Home for Little Turtle, 1992; (adapter) Little Bear's New Friend, 1992; Tooth Fairy Book: Text, 1992; Moonlight on the River, 1993; Ernie's Neighborhood, 1993; All About Dolphins, 1994; Whales: Activities Based on Research from the Center for Coastal Studies, 1994; All About Whales!, 1994; (with K. Madin) Beneath Blue Waters: Meetings with Remarkable Deep-Sea Creatures, 1996; Meet the Authors: 25 Writers of Upper Elementary and Middle School Books Talk About their Work, 1996; Very First Things to Know About Bears, 1997; Dive to the Deep Ocean: Voyages of Exploration and Discovery, 1999; Off to Sea: An Inside Look at a Research Cruise, 2000; Noises in the Night: The Habits of Bats, 2001; Catie Copley, 2007; Catie Copley's Great Escape, 2009; Catie Copley en voyage à Québec, 2009. **Address:** Theron Raines, Raines & Raines, 71 Park Ave., New York, NY 10016, U.S.A.

KOVALSKI, Maryann. Canadian/American (born United States), b. 1951. **Genres:** Children's Fiction, Illustrations. **Career:** Vickers and Benson Advertising, art director, 1974-75; freelance editorial illustrator, 1975-84; Dinsmore Gallery, co-owner, 1984-85. **Publications:** SELF-ILLUSTRATED FOR CHILDREN: Brenda and Edward, 1984; The Wheels on the Bus, 1987; Jingle Bells, 1988; Frank and Zelda, 1990 in US as Pizza for Breakfast, 1991; (with J.F. Green) Junk-pile Jennifer, 1991; Take Me Out to the Ball Game, 1992; Queen Nadine, 1998; Omar on Ice, 1999; Rain, Rain, 1999; Omar on Board, 2005; Omar's Halloween, 2006. Illustrator of books by others. **Address:** 80 Belmont St., Toronto, ON M5R 1P8, Canada. **Online address:** maryannkovalski@rcn.com

KOVEL, Joel. American (born United States), b. 1936. **Genres:** Environmental Sciences/Ecology, Social Commentary, Theology/Religion, Philosophy. **Career:** Albert Einstein College of Medicine, chief resident in psychiatry, 1964-65, instructor, 1967-69, assistant professor, 1969-74, associate professor, 1974-79, Department of Psychiatry, director of residency training, 1977-83, professor of psychiatry, 1979-86; New School for Social Research, adjunct professor of anthropology, 1980-85; University of California, visiting professor of political science and communications, 1986-87; Bard College, Alger Hiss professor of social studies, 1988-2003; Great Small Works Theatre, director, 1998-; San Diego State University, distinguished professor of social studies, 2003-09; Capitalism Nature Socialism, editor-in-chief,

2003-; Socialist Resistance, advisory editor. **Publications:** White Racism: A Psychohistory, 1970; A Complete Guide to Therapy, 1976; The Age of Desire, 1981; Against the State of Nuclear Terror, 1984; The Radical Spirit (essays), 1988; In Nicaragua, 1988; History and Spirit, 1991; Red Hunting in the Promised Land, 1994; The Enemy of Nature: The End of Capitalism or the End of the World?, 2001, 2nd ed., 2007; Overcoming Zionism: Creating a Single Democratic State in Israel/Palestine, 2007. Contributor to books and periodicals. **Address:** PO Box 89, Willow, NY 12495, U.S.A. **Online address:** jskovel@earthlink.net

KOVEL, Terry Horvitz. American (born United States), b. 1928. **Genres:** Plays/Screenplays, Antiques/Furnishings. **Career:** Kovels Antiques Inc., founder. Writer. **Publications:** WITH R. KOVEL: Kovels' Dictionary of Marks: Pottery and Porcelain, 1953, rev. ed., 1995; A Directory of American Silver, Pewter, and Silver Plate, 1961; American Country Furniture, 1780-1875, 1965; Know Your Antiques, 1967, rev. ed., 1993; Kovels' Antiques and Collectibles Price List, Annual, 1968; The Official Bottles Price List, 1971, 13th ed., 2006; Kovels' Price Guide for Collector Plates, Figurines, Paperweights and Other Limited Editions, 1974; Kovels' Collector's Guide to Limited Editions, 1974; Kovels' Complete Antiques Price List, 1974; Kovels' Collector's Guide to American Art Pottery, 1974; Kovels' Organizer for Collectors, 1978, rev. ed., 1983; Kovels' Illustrated Price Guide to Royal Doulton, 1980, 2nd ed., 1984; Kovels' Depression Glass and Dinnerware, 1980, 8th ed., 2004; Kovels' Know Your Collectibles, 1981, 2nd ed., 1992; The Kovels' Book of Antique Labels: Historic Packaging Designs for Decoration & Appreciation, 1982; Kovels' Collector's Source Book, 1983; Kovels' New Dictionary of Marks, Pottery and Porcelain, 1850-1985, 1986; Kovels' Advertising Collectibles Price List, 1986; Kovels' Guide to Selling Your Antiques and Collectibles, 1987, 2nd ed., 1990; Kovels' American Silver Marks: 1650 to the Present, 1989; Kovels' Antiques and Collectibles Fix-It Source Book, 1990; Kovels' American Art Pottery, 1993; Kovels' Guide to Selling, Buying and Fixing Your Antiques and Collectibles, 1995; Kovels' Quick Tips: 799 Helpful Hints on How to Care for Your Collectibles, 1995; The Label Made Me Buy It, 1998; Kovels' Yellow Pages: A Collector's Directory of Names, Addresses, Telephone and Fax Numbers, E-mail and Internet Addresses to Make Selling, Fixing, and Pricing your Antiques and Collectibles Easy, 1999, 2nd ed., 2003; Kovels' Bid, Buy and Sell Online: Basic Auction Information and Tricks of the Trade, 2001; Kovels' American Antiques, 1750-1900, 2004; Kovels' American Collectibles, 1900-2000, 2007. Contributor to periodicals. **Address:** Kovels Antiques Inc., PO Box 22192, Beachwood, OH 44122, U.S.A.

KÖVES, András. Hungarian (born Hungary), b. 1938. **Genres:** Economics. **Career:** Hungarian Ministry of Foreign Affairs, Soviet desk officer and embassy in Moscow, 1960-73; Hungarian Academy of Sciences, senior research fellow in economics, 1973-78; Kopint Institute for Economic and Market Research, head of research department for international economics, 1978-87; Kopint-Datorg, deputy general director of research, 1987-2002, adviser. 2002-07, now retired. Writer. **Publications:** The CMEA Countries in the World Economy: Turning Inwards or Turning Outwards, 1985; Foreign Economic Liberalization: Transformations in Socialist and Market Economies, 1991 (ed. with P. Marer) Central and East European Economies in Transition: The International Dimension, 1992; Some Aspects of Medium Term Development in Central and Eastern Europe, 2000. **Address:** 52 Emod St., Budapest, H-1031, Hungary. **Online address:** koves@mail.datanet.hu

KOWALESKI, Maryanne. American (born United States), b. 1952. **Genres:** History. **Career:** Université d'Aix-Marseille, exchange fellow, 1972-73; Fordham University, Department of History, assistant professor, 1982-88, associate professor, 1988-96, professor, 1996-2005, director of graduate studies in history, 1988-93, head of department, 1993-, chair, 1993-96, Women's Studies Program, co-director, 1998-99, Center for Medieval Studies, acting director, 1985, 1989, director, 1998-2001, 2002-05, 2006-, Joseph Fitzpatrick S.J. distinguished professor, 2005-; Royal Historical Society, fellow, 1994; University of Exeter, Centre for South West Historical Studies, honorary visiting professor, 1999-2001; Medieval Academy of America, fellow, 2005, second vice-president, 2010-; Memorial University, Henrietta Harvey Lecturer, 2011. Writer. **Publications:** Local Markets and Regional Trade in Medieval Exeter, 1995. EDITOR: (with M. Erler) Women and Power in the Middle Ages, 1988; (trans. and intro.) The Local Customs Accounts of the Port of Exeter, 1266-1321, 1993; (with M.C. Erler) Gendering the Master Narrative: Women and Power in the Middle Ages, 2003; Medieval Towns: A Reader, 2006; (with P.J.P. Goldberg) Medieval Domesticity: Home, Housing and Household in Medieval England, 2008. Contributor of articles to journals. **Address:** Department of History, Fordham University, 405A Faculty Memorial Hall, Rose Hill Campus, Bronx, NY 10458, U.S.A. **Online address:** kowaleski@fordham.edu

KOWALEWSKI, Michael (John). American (born United States), b. 1956. **Genres:** Film, Literary Criticism And History, Local History/Rural Topics, Natural History, Travel/Exploration. **Career:** Princeton University, assistant professor of English, 1986-91; Carleton College, Department of English, assistant professor of English, 1991-95, associate professor, 1995-2001, professor of English, 2001-08, chair, 2007-10, McBride professor of English and environmental studies, 2008-, Americaqn Studies Program, director, 2001-04. Writer. **Publications:** Deadly Musings: Violence and Verbal Form in American Fiction, 1993; Popular Classics of American Literature, 1996. EDITOR: Temperamental Journeys: Essays on the Modern Literature of Travel, 1992; Reading the West: New Essays on the Literature of the American West, 1996; Gold Rush: A Literary Exploration, 1997. **Address:** Department of English, Carleton College, Laird Hall, 1 N College St., Northfield, MN 55057, U.S.A. **Online address:** mkowalew@carleton.edu

KOWALKE, Kim H. American (born United States), b. 1948. **Genres:** Plays/Screenplays, Music, Theatre, Essays. **Career:** 102nd National Guard Band, conductor, 1971-77; Neighborhood Music School, orchestra teacher, 1973-75; Yale Dramat, musical director, 1973-74; Yale Cabaret, musical director, 1973-74; Greater New Haven Youth Symphony, conductor, 1973-75; College Light Opera Co., principal conductor, 1974, 1975, 1977, 1979; Occidental College, assistant professor, 1978-82, associate professor of music, 1982-86, Collegiate Symphony Orchestra and Collegiate Symphony Orchestra, conductor, 1977-83; Kurt Weill Foundation, Board of Trustees, president, 1981-; University of Rochester, Department of Musicology, professor of music and chairman of music program, 1986-, Richard L. Turner professor in humanities, Eastman School of Music, professor of musicology; California Institute of Technology, Occidental Faculty Players and Collegiate Symphony Orchestra, conductor, 1977-83. Writer. **Publications:** Kurt Weill in Europe, 1979; Makers of Modern Culture: Kurt Weill, 1980; (with L. Symonette) The Papers of Kurt Weill and Lotte Lenya: Yale University Music Library, archival collection MSS 30, 1984. EDITOR: A New Orpheus: Essays on Kurt Weill, 1986; (H. Edler) A Stranger Here Myself: Kurt Weill Studien, 1993; (and trans. with L. Symonette) Speak Low (The Letters of Kurt Weill and Lotte Lenya), 1996. **Address:** Eastman School of Music, University of Rochester, 210 Todd Union, 26 Gibbs St., Rochester, NY 14604, U.S.A. **Online address:** kim.kowalke@rochester.edu

KOWALSKI, Gary A. American (born United States), b. 1953?. **Genres:** inspirational/Motivational Literature, Theology/Religion, Animals/Pets. **Career:** First Unitarian Universalist Society, minister, 1989-, senior minister. Writer. **Publications:** The Souls of Animals, 1991, 2nd ed., 2007; Goodbye, Friend: Healing Wisdom for Anyone Who Has Ever Lost a Pet, 1997; Green Mountain Spring and Other Leaps of Faith, 1997; Bible According to Noah: Theology as if Animals Mattered, 2001; Science and the Search for God, 2003; Revolutionary Spirits: The Enlightened Faith of America's Founding Fathers, 2008; Earth Day: An Alphabet Book, 2009. **Address:** First Unitarian Universalist Society, 152 Pearl St., Burlington, VT 05401, U.S.A. **Online address:** gary@uusociety.org

KOWALSKI, Kathiann M. American (born United States), b. 1955. **Genres:** Politics/Government, Children's Non-fiction, Law, Social Sciences, Sciences, Environmental Sciences/Ecology, Young Adult Non-fiction. **Career:** Squire, Sanders and Dempsey (law firm), associate, 1979-88, partner, 1988-94; Writer, 1994-. **Publications:** Hazardous Waste Sites, 1996; Alternative Medicine: Is It for You?, 1998; Teen Rights: At Home, at School, Online, 2000; Campaign Politics: What's Fair? What's Foul?, 2000; The Everything Kids Nature Book, 2000; The Everything Kids Space Book, 2000; The Debate Over Genetically Engineered Foods: Healthy or Harmful?, 2002; Poverty in America: Causes and Issues, 2003; Global Warming: Open for Debate, 2004; A Balancing Act: A Look at Checks and Balances, 2004; Order in the Court: A Look at the Judicial Branch, 2004; Lemon Kurtzman and the Separation of Church and State Debate, 2005; Attack of the Superbugs: The Crisis of Drug-Resistant Diseases, 2005; Salvadorans in America, 2005; Earls Case and the Student Drug Testing Debate: Debating Supreme Court Decisions, 2006; Taxes: Open for Debate, 2006; Board of Education Earls and the Student Drug Testing Debate, 2006; Affirmative Action: Open for Debate, 2007; Free Trade, 2008; Pro/con Look at Homeland Security: Safety Liberty

after 9/11, 2008; National Health Care, 2009; Evolution on Trial: From the Scopes Monkey Case to Inherit the Wind, 2009; Alternative Energy Sources, 2010; Judges and courts: A Look at the Judicial Branch, 2012. Contributor of articles to magazines. **Address:** c/o Author Mail, Lerner Publishing Group, 1251 Washington Ave. N, Minneapolis, MN 55401, U.S.A. **Online address:** kowalskikm@yahoo.com

KOYA, Tatsuhito. American/Japanese (born Japan), b. 1964. **Genres:** Technology, Engineering, Mathematics/Statistics. **Career:** Reynolds Metals Co, staff. Writer. **Publications:** (With T. Mura) Variational Methods in Mechanics, 1992. **Address:** Reynolds Metals Co., 4th and Canal Sts., Richmond, VA 23261-7003, U.S.A.

KOZAMEH, Alicia. Argentine/American (born United States), b. 1953. **Genres:** Novels, Translations. **Career:** Monóculo Literary Workshops, founder, 1988; Santa Monica College's Emeritus College, English literature and creative writing instructor; Chapman University, Department of English, assistant professor of English, 2010-. Writer. **Publications:** Pasos Bajo el Agua, 1987; Steps under water, 1996; (co-author) Redes De La Memoria: Escritoras Exdetenidas: Testimonio y FicciOn, 2000; 259 Saltos, Uno Inmortal, 2001; Patas de Avestruz, 2003; Ofrenda De Propia Piel, 2004; (ed. and intro.) Caleidoscopio: La mujer en la mira, 2005; Caleidoscopio 2: Inmigrantes en la mira, 2006; (contrib.) Nosotras, Presas PolIticas, 1974-1983, 2006; Basse danse, 2007; Fragmento de Cantata, 2007; 259 Leaps, 2007; Mano en vuelo, 2009. Works appear in anthologies. Contributor to magazines. **Address:** Department of English, Chapman University, 1 University Dr., Orange, CA 92866, U.S.A. **Online address:** kozameh@chapman.edu

KOZLOSKI, Lillian D. American (born United States), b. 1934. **Genres:** Air/Space Topics, Local History/Rural Topics, History, Sciences. **Career:** National Air and Space Museum, museum specialist, 1977-95; James Monroe Museum, interpreter; Mary Washington House, interpreter; Mercer Apothecary Shop, interpreter. Writer. **Publications:** U.S. Space Gear: Outfitting the Astronaut, 1994. Contributor of articles to periodicals. **Address:** 5035 Ridge Rd., Spotsylvania, VA 22553-6334, U.S.A. **Online address:** lillkoz@rcn.com

KOZOL, Jonathan. American (born United States), b. 1936. **Genres:** Education, Social Commentary, Medicine/Health. **Career:** Boston Public Schools, teacher, 1964-65; U.S. Office of Economic Opportunity, consultant, 1965, 1966; Newton Public Schools, teacher, 1966-68; U.S. Office of Education, Curriculum Development, consultant, 1966-68; Storefront Learning Center, educational director and trustee, 1968-74; Yale University, visiting instructor, 1969; Center for Intercultural Documentation, instructor, 1969, 1970, 1974; University of Massachusetts, visiting instructor, 1978-79; South Boston High School, remedial writing and reading instructor, 1979; Trinity College, visiting instructor, 1980; New School for Children, trustee; Los Angeles Times, correspondent, 1982-83; USA Today, correspondent, 1982-83; New Yorker, reporter-at-large, 1988; The Nation, frequent contributor, 1990-2001; Education Action, founder. Writer. **Publications:** The Fume of Poppies, 1958; Death at an Early Age: The Destruction of the Hearts and Minds of Negro Children in the Boston Public Schools, 1967; Free Schools, 1972, rev. ed. as Alternative Schools: A Guide for Educators and Parents, 1982; The Night Is Dark and I Am Far from Home, 1975, rev. ed., 1990; Children of the Revolution: A Yankee Teacher inthe Cuban Schools, 1978; Prisoners of Silence: Breaking the Bonds of Adult Illiteracy in the United States, 1980; On Being a Teacher, 1981; Illiterate America, 1985; Rachel and Her Children: Homeless Families in America, 1988; Savage Inequalities: Children in America's Schools, 1991; Amazing Grace: The Lives of Children and the Conscience of a Nation, 1995; Ordinary Resurrections: Children in the Years of Hope, 2000; The Shame of the Nation: The Restoration of Apartheid Schooling in America, 2005; Letters to a Young Teacher, 2007. OTHER: (foreword) W.E. Mouradian, Children Our Future: Ethics, Health Policy, Medical/Dental Care for Children, 1998; (with D. Heier) Will Standards Save Public Education?, 2000. Contributor to books and periodicals. **Address:** Janklow and Nesbit, 445 Park Ave., Fl. 13, New York, NY 10022-2606, U.S.A.

KRAEUTER, David W. American (born United States), b. 1941. **Genres:** Technology, Bibliography, Sciences, Essays. **Career:** Washington and Jefferson College, assistant librarian, 1968-92, associate librarian, 1992, now retired, culture of teaching and learning, researcher; Pittsburgh Oscillator Journal of the Pittsburgh Antique Radio Society, editor, 1986-95. Writer. **Pub-**

lications: Photograph and Street Address Locater for Boyd Crumrine's Art Work of Washington Co., Pennsylvania: Derived from the RL Polk Washington Directories and Other Sources, 1986; (comp.) Preliminary Bibliography of Frank Conrad, 1988, (comp.) U.S. Patents of Reginald A. Fessenden: A List of Titles, Numbers, and Dates with a Title Index, 1990; (comp.) Bibliography of Frank Conrad, 1990; Radio and Television Pioneers: A Patent Bibliography, 1992; British Radio and Television Pioneers: A Patent Bibliography, 1993; (comp.) Reginald A. Fessenden Bibliography, 1993; (comp.) New Bibliography of Reginald A. Fessenden, 1993; Radio and Electronics Pioneers: A Patent Bibliography, 1994; Radio and Electronics Index to Patents, 1995; Electronic Essays, 1996, 2nd ed., 2000; Numerical Index to Radio and Electronics Patents, 1997; (ed.) Radio and Television Reminiscences: Raymond M. Bell in the Pittsburgh Oscillator, 1998; (comp.) U.S. Patents of Harold S. Black, Jack S. Kilby and Robert N. Noyce, 1999; (comp.) U.S. Patents of Stuart W. Seeley, 2000; Radio Patent Lists and Index, 1830-1980, 2001; Ten Patents from Radio History, 2007. Contributor to periodicals. **Address:** Washington and Jefferson College, 60 S Lincoln St., Washington, PA 15301, U.S.A. **Online address:** kraeuter@sgi.net

KRAFT, Erik. *See* **KRAFT, Erik P.**

KRAFT, Erik P. (Erik Kraft). American (born United States) **Genres:** Novels. **Career:** Columbia University, adjunct assistant professor. Writer. **Publications:** Chocolatina, 1998; (illus.) Lenny and Mel, 2002; (illus.) Lenny and Mel's Summer Vacation, Simon & Schuster, 2003; (illus.) Lenny and Mel: Afterschool Confidential, 2004; Miracle Wimp (youngadult novel). **Address:** PO Box 230508, Astor Sta., Boston, MA 02123, U.S.A. **Online address:** erik@erikpcraft.com

KRAFT, Robert A(lan). American (born United States), b. 1934. **Genres:** History, Humanities, Theology/Religion. **Career:** Harvard University, teaching fellow, 1959-61; University of Manchester, assistant lecturer in New Testament studies, 1961-63; University of Pennsylvania, Department of Religious Studies, assistant professor, 1963-68, associate professor, 1968-76, professor, 1976-2003, emeritus professor, 2003-, chairperson of department, 1977-, Berg chair of religious studies, 1992-2003; Lutheran Theological Seminary, visiting lecturer, 1965-66; Philadelphia Seminar on Christian Origins, coordinator. Writer. **Publications:** The Apostolic Fathers: A New Translation and Commentary, vol. III: Barnabas and the Didache, 1965; (with A. Tripolitis) Some Uncatalogued Papyri of Theological and Other Interest in the John Rylands Library, 1968; (with P. Prigent) épître de Barnabé: Introduction, Traduction et notes par Pierre Prigent Text grec établi etprésenté par, 1971; (trans. and ed. with G. Krodel) Orthodoxy and Heresy in Earliest Christianity, 1971; (ed.) 1972 Proceedings, 1972; (ed.) Septuagintal Lexicography, 1972, rev. ed., 1975; (ed. and trans. with A.E. Purintun) Paraleipomena Jeremiou, 1972; (co-ed.) Testament of Job, According to the SV Text, 1974; Studies on the Testament of Abraham, 1976; (ed. with G.W.E. Nickelsburg) Early Judaism and Its Modern Interpreters, 1986; (with E. Tov) Computer Assisted Tools for Septuagint Studies (CATSS), 1986; (contrib.) The Greek Minor Prophets Scroll from Nahal Hever: 8 Hev XII gr, 1990; Multiform Heritage: Studies on Early Judaism and Christianity in Honor of Robert A. Kraft, 1999; Exploring the Scripturesque: Jewish Texts and Their Christian Contexts, 2009. Contributor of articles. **Address:** Department of Religious Studies, School of Arts and Sciences, University of Pennsylvania, 201 Logan Hall, Philadelphia, PA 19104-6304, U.S.A. **Online address:** kraft@ccat.sas.upenn.edu

KRAFT, William F. American (born United States), b. 1938. **Genres:** Psychology, Self Help, Medicine/Health, Theology/Religion. **Career:** Atascadero State Hospital, psychology intern, 1964-65; Somerset State Hospital, director of psychological services, 1965-67; Dixmont State Hospital, director, 1967-69; Carlow University, associate professor, professor of psychology, 1969-; Duquesne University, adjunct professor, 1985-90. Psychologist and writer. **Publications:** The Search for the Holy, 1971; A Psychology of Nothingness, 1974; Normal Modes of Madness: Hurdles in the Path to Growth, 1978; Sexual Dimensions of the Celibate Life, 1979; Achieving Promises: A Spiritual Guide for the Transitions of Life, 1981; A Whole & Holy Sexuality, 1989; The Normal Alcoholic, 1999; Ways of the Desert: Becoming Holy Through Difficult Times, 2000; When Someone You Love Drinks Too Much, 2002; When You Love a Functional Alcoholic, 2011. Contributor of articles to journals and magazines. **Address:** 8072 Brittany Pl., Pittsburgh, PA 15237-6357, U.S.A. **Online address:** kraftwf@carlow.edu

KRAHN, Betina. American (born United States) **Genres:** Romance/Histori-

cal, Young Adult Fiction, Novels. **Career:** Writer and educator. **Publications:** Rapture's Ransom, 1983; Passion's Storm, 1985; Hidden Fires, 1988; Love's Brazen Fire, 1989; Midnight Magic, 1990; Caught in the Act, 1990; Christmas Romance: Love Stories, 1990; Behind Closed Doors, 1991; My Warrior's Heart, 1992; The Princess and the Barbarian, 1993; The Last Bachelor, 1994; The Perfect Mistress, 1995; Hidden Fires, 1995; The Unlikely Angel, 1996; Rebel Passion, 1996; The Mermaid, 1997; Passion's Treasure, 1998; The Soft Touch, 1999; Sweet Talking Man, 2000; Sweet-Talking Man, 2000; The Husband Test, 2001; Luck Be a Lady, 2002; Just Say Yes, 2002; Passion's Ransom, 2002; The Wife Test, 2003; The Paradise Bargain, 2003; The Marriage Test, 2004; Not Quite Married, 2004; Book of the Seven Delights, 2005; The Enchantment, 2005; The Book of True Desires, 2006; Make Me Yours, 2009; Manhunting, 2010; A Harlequin Christmas Carol, 2010. Works appear in anthologies. **Address:** Bantam Dell Publishing Group, Random House Inc., 1540 Broadway St., New York, NY 10036, U.S.A. **Online address:** betina@betinakrahn.com

KRAINZ, Thomas A. American (born United States), b. 1965. **Genres:** History, Social Sciences, International Relations/Current Affairs, Politics/Government. **Career:** Framingham State College, assistant professor of history. Writer. **Publications:** Delivering Aid: Implementing Progressive Era Welfare in the American West, 2005. Contributor to periodicals. **Address:** Department of History, Framingham State College, 100 State St., PO Box 9101, Framingham, MA 01701-9101, U.S.A. **Online address:** tkrainz@frc.mass.edu

KRAMER, Alan. Irish (born Ireland), b. 1954?. **Genres:** History. **Career:** Trinity College Dublin, senior lecturer, professor of European history. Writer. **Publications:** Die Britische Demontagepolitik am Beispiel Hamburgs, 1945-1950, 1991; The West German Economy: 1945-1955, 1991; (with J. Horne) German Atrocities, 1914: A History of Denial, 2001; Dynamic of Destruction: Culture and Mass Killing in the First World War, 2007. **Address:** Trinity College Dublin, College Green, Dublin, 2, Ireland. **Online address:** alkramer@tcd.ie

KRAMER, Dale. American (born United States), b. 1936. **Genres:** Literary Criticism And History, Bibliography, Biography, Essays. **Career:** Ohio University, instructor, 1962-63, assistant professor of English, 1963-65; University of Illinois, assistant professor, 1965-67; associate professor, 1967-71, professor of English, 1971-96, College of Arts and Sciences, associate dean, 1992-95, professor emeritus, 1996-; University of Oregon, courtesy professor of English, 1997-. Writer. **Publications:** Charles Robert Maturin, 1973; Thomas Hardy: The Forms of Tragedy, 1975; Thomas Hardy: Tess of the d'Urbervilles, 1991. EDITOR: Critical Approaches to the Fiction of Thomas Hardy, 1979; The Woodlanders, 1981; (intro.) The Mayor of Casterbridge, 1987, new ed., 2004; Critical Essays on Thomas Hardy: The Novels, 1990; The Cambridge Companion to Thomas Hardy, 1999. **Address:** Department of English, University of Illinois, 608 S Wright St., Urbana, IL 61801, U.S.A. **Online address:** dalek@uoregon.edu

KRAMER, Fritz W. German (born Germany), b. 1941. **Genres:** Novels, Anthropology/Ethnology, Education. **Career:** Free University of Berlin, assistant professor, 1974-77, professor of anthropology, 1979-83; freelance writer, 1983-89; Hochschulefür bildende Künste, professor of art theory, 1989-; College of Fine Arts-Hamburg, faculty. **Publications:** Literature Among the Cuna Indians, 1970; Verkehrte Welten: Zurimaginären Ethnographie d. 19. Jh., 1977; Gesellschaften Ohne Staat, 1978; Bikini, Oder, Die Bombardierung Der Engel: Auch Eine Ethnographie, 1983; Rote Fes: über Besessenheit und Kunst in Afrika, 1987; Sudanesische Marginalien: Ein Ethnographisches Programm, 1991; Zeitmarken: Die Feste Von Dimodonko, 1993; Bikini: Atomares Testgebiet im Pazifik, 2000. Contributor to magazines and newspapers. **Address:** Hochschule für bildende Künste, Finkenau 35, Hamburg, 22081, Germany.

KRAMER, Helen. American (born United States), b. 1946. **Genres:** Psychology. **Career:** Gestalt Associates, founder, 1975, supervisor, 1975-85; REAL Solutions, founder, 1990, director, 1990-; Personal Change System, co-founder and co-director. Writer. **Publications:** Liberating the Adult Within: Moving from Childish Responses to Authentic Adulthood, 1994. **Address:** 222 Park Ave. S, Ste. 29, New York, NY 10003, U.S.A. **Online address:** helen@pcs100.com

KRAMER, Hilton. American (born United States), b. 1928. **Genres:** Art/Art History, Politics/Government, Cultural/Ethnic Topics. **Career:** Arts Digest, associate editor and features editor, 1954-55; Arts Magazine, managing editor, 1955-58, editor, 1958-61; Nation, art critic, 1962-63; New Leader, art critic and associate editor, 1964-65; New York Times, art news editor, 1965-82; Yale University School of Drama, visiting professor of criticism, 1973-74; New Criterion, founding editor and publisher, 1982-; The New York Post, columnist, 1993-97; Indiana University, faculty; Bennington College, faculty; University of Colorado, faculty; Yale University, faculty. **Publications:** (Intro.) Paintings, 1930-1960, 1962; The Sculpture of Gaston Lachaise, 1967; The Age of the Avant-Garde: An Art Chronicle of 1956-1972, 1973; (contrib.) Richard Lindner, 1975; Brâncusi, the Sculptor as Photographer, 1979; The Revenge of the Philistines: Art and Culture, 1972-84, 1985; Joan Miró i La Mort de la Pintura: Dos Excursos, 1991; (with M. D'Estout) Julius Hatofsky, 1996; Gaston Lachaise: Sculpture and Drawings, 1998; The Twilight of the Intellectuals: Culture and Politics in the Era of the Cold War, 1999; William Scharf: Paintings, 1984-2000: The Phillips Collection, Washington, D.C. November 18, 2000-January 21, 2001, 2000; The Triumph of Modernism: The Art World, 1987-2005, 2006. EDITOR: Perspectives on the Arts, 1961; The New Criterion Reader: The First Five Years, 1988; (with R. Kimball) Against the Grain: The New Criterion on Art and Intellect at the End of the Twentieth Century, 1995; (and intro. with R. Kimball) The Future of the European Past, 1997; (and intro. with R. Kimball) The Betrayal of Liberalism: How the Disciples of Freedom and Equality Helped Foster the illiberal Politics of Coercion and Control, 1999; (and intro. with R. Kimball) Survival of Culture: Permanent Values in a Virtual Age, 2002; (and intro. with R. Kimball) Lengthened Shadows: America and Its Institutions in the Twenty-First Century, 2004; (and intro. with R. Kimball) Counterpoints: Twenty-five Years of the New Criterion on Culture and the Arts, 2007. **Address:** New Criterion, 900 Broadway, Ste. 602, PO Box 5194, FDR Sta., New York, NY 10003, U.S.A.

KRAMER, Joel P. American (born United States), b. 1976?. **Genres:** Travel/Exploration, History, Natural History. **Career:** Photographer and writer. **Publications:** Beyond Fear: A Journey Across New Guinea, 1995; Beyond Fear: A Harrowing Journey Across New Guinea through Rivers, Swamps, Jungle, and the Most Remote Mountains in the World, 2001. **Address:** c/o Author Mail, Globe Pequot Press Inc., 246 Goose Ln., PO Box 480, Guilford, CT 06437-2186, U.S.A.

KRAMER, Linda Konheim. American (born United States), b. 1939. **Genres:** Art/Art History, Photography, History, Biography. **Career:** Solomon R. Guggenheim Museum, curator and administrator, 1963-79; Sotheby Parke-Bernet, part-time cataloger of modern drawings, 1980-81; Sotheby's New York, expert in modern drawings, 1981-85; Brooklyn Museum, curator of prints and drawings, 1985-94; independent curator and freelance writer, 1994-96; Nancy Graves Foundation, executive director emeritus, 1996-. Writer. **Publications:** Selected Sculpture and Works on Paper, 1969; Prints from the Guggenheim Museum Collection, 1978; Milton Avery in Black and White: Drawings 1929-59, 1990; (with S. Faunce and K. Zieve) French Nineteenth-Century Drawings and Watercolors at the Brooklyn Museum, 1993; The Graphic Works of Philip Pearlstein, 1978-94, 1995; The Pictographs of Adolph Gottlieb, 1995; The Prints of Janet Fish: A Catalogue Raisonne, 1997; (with M. Bonesteel) Prints of John Himmelfarb: A Catalogue Raisonné, 1967-2004, 2005. Contributor to periodicals. **Address:** Nancy Graves Foundation, 450 W 31st St., 2nd Fl., New York, NY 10001, U.S.A. **Online address:** lkramer561@aol.com

KRAMER, Lloyd S. American (born United States), b. 1949. **Genres:** History. **Career:** Stanford University, lecturer in history, 1983-84; Northwestern University, Mellon assistant professor of history, 1984-86; University of North Carolina, assistant professor, 1986-89, associate professor, 1989-95, professor of history, 1995-, chair, Dean Smith distinguished term professor; School of Historical Studies, Institute for Advanced Study, faculty, 1991-92. Writer. **Publications:** Threshold of a New World: Intellectuals and the Exile Experience in Paris, 1830-1848, 1988; Lafayette in Two Worlds: Public Cultures and Personal Identities in an Age of Revolutions, 1996; Nationalism: Political Cultures in Europe and America, 1775-1865, 1998; (with R.R. Palmer and J. Colton) A History of the Modern World, 10th ed., 2007; Nationalism in Europe and America: Politics, Cultures and Identities Since 1775, 2011. EDITOR: (and intro.) Paine and Jefferson on Liberty, 1988; French-American Connection: 200 Years of Cultural and Intellectual Interaction, 1994; (with D. Reid and W. Barney) Learning History in America: Schools, Cultures, and Politics, 1994; (with S. Maza) A Companion to Western Historical Thought,

2002. **Address:** Department of History, University of North Carolina, 507 Hamilton Hall, 200 E Cameron Ave., PO Box 3195, Chapel Hill, NC 27599, U.S.A. **Online address:** lkramer@unc.edu

KRAMER, Lotte. British/German (born Germany), b. 1923. **Genres:** Poetry, History, Young Adult Fiction. **Career:** Writer and painter. **Publications:** Scrolls, 1979; Ice-Break, 1980; Family Arrivals, 1981, 2nd ed., 1992; A Lifelong House, 1983; The Shoemaker's Wife and Other Poems, 1987; The Desecration of Trees, 1994; Earthquake and Other Poems, 1994; Selected and New Poems, 1997; Bilingual (German/English) Selection of Poems, 1999; The Phantom Lane, 2000; Black Over Red, 2005; Kindertransport, Before and After: Elegy and Celebration: Sixty Poems, 1980-2007, 2007; Turning the Key, 2009. **Address:** 4 Apsley Way, Longthorpe, Peterborough, CB PE3 9NE, England.

KRAMER, Martin. Israeli/American (born United States), b. 1954. **Genres:** International Relations/Current Affairs, History, Theology/Religion, Politics/Government. **Career:** Tel Aviv University, research associate, 1981-85, senior research associate, 1985-95, Moshe Dayan Center for Middle Eastern and African Studies, associate director, 1987-95, director of the center, 1995-2001, principal research associate, 1995-2005, principal research associate emeritus, 2005-; Cornell University, visiting professor, 1984; George Mason University, Department of Government and Public Affairs, visiting associate professor, 1986-87; University of Chicago, visiting professor, 1990-91; Georgetown University, visiting professor, 1994-95; The Washington Institute for Near East Policy, Wexler-Fromer fellow, 2002-; Adelson Institute for Strategic Studies, Shalem Center, senior fellow, 2006-; Harvard University, Olin Institute for Strategic Studies, senior fellow, 2007-; Middle East Strategy, co-convener, 2007-; Brandeis University, visiting professor; Shalem college, president. Writer. **Publications:** An Introduction to World Islamic Conferences, 1978; Political Islam, 1980; Meḥa'ah u mahpekhah ba-Islam ha-Shi'i, 1985; Islam Assembled: The Advent of the Muslim Congresses, 1986; The Moral Logic of Hizballah, 1987; (ed.) Shi'ism, Resistance and Revolution, 1987; (ed.) Protest and Revolution in Shi'i Islam, 1987; Hezbollah's Vision of the West, 1989; (ed.) Middle Eastern Lives: The Practice of Biography and Self-Narrative, 1991; Arab Awakening and Islamic Revival: The Politics of Ideas in the Middle East, 1996, 2nd ed., 2008; (ed.) The Islamism Debate, 1997; Fadlallah: Ha-Matspen Shel Hizballah, 1998; (ed.) The Jewish Discovery of Islam: Studies in Honor of Bernard Lewis, 1999; Ivory Towers and Sand: The Failure of Middle Eastern Studies in America, 2000; Ivory Towers on Sand: The Failure of Middle Eastern Studies in America, 2001. Contributor of articles to journals. **Address:** Shalem Center, Adelson Institute of Strategic Studies, 13 Yehoshua Bin-Nun St., Jerusalem, 93102, Israel. **Online address:** kramerm@ccsg.tau.ac.il

KRAMER, Peter (D.). American (born United States), b. 1948. **Genres:** Novels, Psychiatry. **Career:** Alcohol, Drug Abuse and Mental Health Administration, Division of Science, Department of Health and Human Services, acting deputy director and acting director, 1980-81; George Washington University, instructor, 1980, assistant clinical professor of psychiatry, 1981-82; Brown University, assistant professor, 1982-85, Outpatient Psychiatry, director, 1982-85, assistant clinical professor, 1985-91, associate clinical professor, 1991-95, clinical professor of psychiatry, 1995-. Writer. **Publications:** Moments of Engagement: Intimate Psychotherapy in a Technological Age, 1989; Listening to Prozac: A Psychiatrist Explores Mood-Altering Drugs and the Meaning of the Self, 1993, rev. ed., 1997; Should You Leave?, 1997; Spectacular Happiness: A Novel, 2001; Against Depression, 2005; Freud: Inventor of the Modern Mind, 2006. Contributor to books and journals. **Address:** Department of Psychiatry & Human Behavior, Brown University, PO Box G-BH, Providence, RI 02912, U.S.A. **Online address:** peter_kramer@brown.edu

KRAMER, Reinhold. Canadian (born Canada), b. 1959?. **Genres:** History. **Career:** Brandon University, professor. Writer. **Publications:** Scatology and Civility in the English-Canadian Novel, 1997; (with T. Mitchell) Walk towards the Gallows: The Tragedy of Hilda Blake, Hanged 1899, 2002; Mordecai Richler: Leaving St. Urbain, 2008; When the State Trembled: How A.J. Andrews and the Citizens' Committee Broke the Winnipeg General Strike, 2010. **Address:** Department of English, Brandon University, 270-18th St., Brandon, MB R7A 6A9, Canada. **Online address:** kramer@brandonu.ca

KRAMNICK, Isaac. American (born United States), b. 1938. **Genres:** Politics/Government, Social Sciences. **Career:** Harvard University, teaching fellow, 1963-65, instructor in government, 1965-66, director of graduate studies, 1965-66; Brandeis University, Department of Politics, assistant professor, 1966-68, director of graduate studies, 1967-68; Antheneum Publishing Co., editorial consultant, 1968-, Yale University, Department of Political Science, assistant professor, 1968-71, associate professor, 1971-72, director, 1970; Cornell University, Department of Government, associate professor, 1972-74, professor, 1975-83, 2005-, Richard J. Schwartz professor, 1983-, director of graduate studies, 1973-77, acting chair, 1978-79, chair, 1981-85, 1996-, university senate, 1973-74, 1996-, director of undergraduate studies, 2008-10, College of Arts and Sciences, associate dean, 1986-89, senior sexual harassment officer, 1993-94, vice provost for undergraduate education, 2001-05, Cornell Labor College, consultant, 1973-74. Writer. **Publications:** Bolingbroke and His Circle: The Politics of Nostalgia in the Age of Walpole, 1968; The Rage of Edmund Burke, 1978; (with F.M. Watkins) The Age of Ideology: Political Thought, 1750 to the Present, 2nd ed., 1979; Republicanism and Bourgeois Radicalism: Political Ideology in Late Eighteenth-Century England and America, 1990; Harold Laski-A Life on the Left, 1993; (with R.L. Moore) The Godless Constitution: The Case Against Religious Correctness, 1996, rev. ed., 2005; (with G.C. Altschuler and R.L. Moore) 100 Most Notable Cornellians, 2003. EDITOR: Political Writings, 1970; Enquiry Concerning Political Justice, 1976; (and intro.) Is Britain Dying?: Perspectives on the Current Crisis, 1979; (with M. Foot) The Thomas Paine Reader, 1987; James Madison et al., The Federalist Papers, 1987; Portable Enlightenment Reader, 1995; (and intro.) Portable Edmund Burke, 1999; Democracy in America: An Annotated Text Backgrounds Interpretations, 2007; (with T.J. Lowi) American Political Thought: A Norton Anthology, 2009; Tocqueville's Writings on America, forthcoming. **Address:** Department of Government, Cornell University, 311 White Hall, Ithaca, NY 14853, U.S.A. **Online address:** ik15@cornell.edu

KRAMON, Justin. American (born United States), b. 1980. **Genres:** Novels. **Career:** Writer. **Publications:** Finny: A Novel, 2010. Contributor of articles to periodicals. **Address:** Philadelphia, PA , U.S.A. **Online address:** justin@justinkramon.com

KRAMP, Michael. American (born United States) **Genres:** Young Adult Fiction, Literary Criticism And History, Social Sciences, Humanities. **Career:** Washington State University, graduate instructor, 1995-2000, Blackburn Fellow, 2000-01; University of Northern Colorado, assistant professor of English, associate professor of English and director of cultural studies, 2001-. Writer. **Publications:** Disciplining Love: Austen and the Modern Man, 2007. Contributor to periodicals. **Address:** Department of English, University of Northern Colorado, Cultural Studies Minor, 1190A Ross Hall, 501 20th St., Greeley, CO 80639, U.S.A. **Online address:** michael.kramp@unco.edu

KRANE, Jim. British/American (born United States), b. 1964?. **Genres:** Business/Trade/Industry, Economics. **Career:** Laredo Morning Times, staff, 1991-; Newark Star-Ledger, staff; New Jersey News, staff; APBNews.com, staff; Newhouse Newspapers, staff; Associated Press, business writer, 2000-03, foreign correspondent, 2003-07. Dubai School of Government, visiting fellow, 2007-09. **Publications:** City of Gold: Dubai and the Dream of Capitalism in UK as Dubai: The Story of the World's Fastest City, 2009. Contributor to periodicals. **Address:** Cambridge, England. **Online address:** jim@jimkrane.com

KRANENDONK, Anke. Dutch (born Netherlands), b. 1959. **Genres:** Novels, Children's Fiction, Children's Non-fiction, Young Adult Non-fiction. **Career:** Dear Jan (theater company), founder. Wrietr. **Publications:** Van Huilen Krijg Je Dorst, 1993; Wat Een Verjaardag, 1994; Een Opa Voor Opa, 1994; Opa Voor Opa, 1997; Hoe Gaat Het? Goed, 1997; Leuk Wordt Het Nooit, 1997; Ik Kom Zo, 1998; Just a Minute!, 1998; Voor Rosa, Van Sonja, 2001; Dag Boet, 2001; Zeilen in De Nacht, 2002; Ties En Tos Verliefd, 2003; Liever Een Hond, 2003; Meneer De Haan, 2003; De Bruiloft Van Ties En Tos, 2004; Ik Word Nooit Normaal, 2004; Peer En De Pirates, 2004; Van Pen Voor Roos, 2004; De straatspeeldag, 2004; De Rode Tas, 2004; Pak Die Man!, 2004; Mi Mono, Mijn Aapje, 2004; Bep Maakt Een Hut, 2004; Ties En Tos Op Reis, 2004; Willem In De Boom, 2004; De Twee Kunstenaars, 2004; Uitverkoop, 2004; Een Boef Op Zolder, 2004; Bij De Kapper, 2004; Naar Opa; De Brief Van Sjim, 2004; Het Mooiste Huis, 2004; Met Poes Soes Naar Oom Mik, 2004; Wat Hangt Daar in De Lucht?, 2005; Peer Op Een Paard, 2005; Peer in De Scrum, 2005; De Kerstbengel, 2005; Kapot!, 2005; Pas Op! Hier Komt Ramona!, 2005; Miljonair Helpt Fancy Fair, 2006; Ties En Tos Naar Het Strand, 2006; Peer is Er Weer!, 2006; Muis En Snot, 2006; Boender, Waar Ben Je?, 2006; Daar Zwemt Roef, 2006; Hoe Was Het Op School, Samme?,

2006; Poes Leert Ook, 2006; Peer In De Sneeuw, 2006; Een Rare Agent, 2006; Stern is Het Zat, 2007; Wat Klopt Daar in De Nacht?, 2007; Feest, 2007; Ik Rijm Voor Piet, 2007; Stern is het zat!, 2007; Waar is het geld?, 2007; Dubbel Verliefd, 2007; Feest!, 2007; Waar Is Het Geld, 2007; Met Pim Naar Tim, 2008; Een Linke Wedstrijd, 2008; Mijn Eerste Zoen, 2008; Poesjes in nood!, 2008; Vriend; Alles Voor De Hond, 2008; Alles is Weg, 2008; Dat Doe Je Niet, 2008; Poesjes In Nood, 2008; Boelie: Over Hockey, 2008; Een Hond Als Behanger; Visite in Bad, 2009; Een Nijlpaard Voor De Juf, 2009; Waar Zijn De Spatjes?, 2009; Daar Gaan We Weer, 2009; Dokter, Mijn Hart Klopt Zo Snel; Verdwaald in Amsterdam, 2010; Gestolen!, 2010; Vuur, 2010; Ellende in de klas, 2011. **Address:** Front Street Inc., 862 Haywood Rd., Asheville, NC 28806, U.S.A. **Online address:** info@ankekranendonk.nl

KRANISH, Michael. American (born United States), b. 1957?. **Genres:** Biography, History, Politics/Government. **Career:** The Lakeland Ledger, staff reporter, 1979-80; The Miami Herald, staff reporter, 1980-83; Boston Globe, staff reporter, 1984-, New England correspondent, Washington Bureau, correspondent, assistant Washington editor, deputy chief. **Publications:** (With B.C. Mooney and N.J. Easton) John F. Kerry: The Complete Biography by the Boston Globe Reporters Who Know Him Best, 2004; Flight from Monticello: Thomas Jefferson at War, 2010; (with S. Helman) Real Romney, 2012. **Address:** Boston Globe, 1130 Connecticut Ave. NW, Ste. 520, Washington, DC 20036, U.S.A. **Online address:** kranish@globe.com

KRANTZ, Hazel. (Hazel (Newman) Krantz). American (born United States) **Genres:** Novels, Children's Fiction, Children's Non-fiction, Social Sciences. **Career:** McGreevey, Werring and Howell, home-furnishings coordinator, 1942-43; Felix Lilienthal, fashion coordinator, 1944-45; Nassau County Schools, elementary school teacher, 1957-68; True Frontier Magazine, editor, 1969-71; Sound Engineering Magazine, copy editor, 1973-78. **Publications:** 100 Pounds of Popcorn, 1961; Freestyle for Michael, 1964; The Secret Raft, 1965; Tippy, 1968; A Pad of Your Own, 1973; The Complete Guide to Happiness and Success, 1980; Pink and White Striped Summer, 1982; None But the Brave, 1986; Daughter of My People: Henrietta Szold and Hadassah, 1987; For Love of Jeremy, 1990; Look to the Hills, 1995; Walks In Beauty, 1997. **Address:** 1306 Stoney Hill Dr., Fort Collins, CO 80525, U.S.A. **Online address:** hkrantz600@aol.com

KRANTZ, Hazel (Newman). See **KRANTZ, Hazel.**

KRANTZ, Steven G. American (born United States), b. 1951. **Genres:** Mathematics/Statistics, Education, Reference. **Career:** University of California, assistant professor of mathematics, 1974-81; Universite de Paris-Sud, visiting professor, 1977; Princeton University, visiting professor, 1980; Institute for Advanced Study, visiting fellow, 1981; Pennsylvania State University, associate professor, 1981-84, professor of mathematics, 1984-87; Uppsala University, visiting professor, 1984; Beijing University, visiting professor, 1984; University of Umeå, visiting professor, 1986; University Autonoma de Madrid, visiting professor, 1986; Washington University, Department of Mathematics, professor of mathematics, 1986-, chairman, 1999-2004, Natural Sciences Division, head, 2002-; Mittag-Leffler Institute, visiting professor, 1988; Universite Paul Sabatier, visiting professor, 1988; Politecnico Torino, visiting professor, 1993; Australian National University, Richardson Fellow, 1995; Mathematical Sciences Research Institute, visiting professor, 1995-96; Stanford University, visiting professor, 1997; University of South Florida, Nagle Memorial Lecturer, 1998; Journal of Mathematical Analysis and Applications, editor-in-chief, 2000-; Allegheny College, distinguished lecturer, 2001; Mathematical Association of America, court lecturer, 2002; Bowdoin College, distinguished lecturer, 2003; Natoli Engineering, software consultant. **Publications:** (Co-author) Freshman Calculus, 1971; (with R.A. Bonic and E. Basor) Exercises and Sample Exams for Freshman Calculus, 1971; Function Theory of Several Complex Variables, 1982, 2nd ed., 1992; Complex Analysis: The Geometric Viewpoint, 1990, 2nd ed., 2004; Real Analysis and Foundations, 1991; Partial Differential Equations and Complex Analysis, 1992; (with H.R. Parks) A Primer of Real Analytic Functions, 1992, 2nd ed., 2002; Geometric Analysis and Function Spaces, 1993; How to Teach Mathematics, 1993; (with S. Sawyer) TEX Primer for Scientists, 1994; The Elements of Advanced Mathematics, 1995, 2nd ed., 2005; Techniques of Problem Solving, 1996; A Primer of Mathematical Writing: Being a Disquisition on Having Your Ideas Recorded, Typeset, Published, Read and Appreciated, 1997; (with R.E. Greene) Function Theory of One Complex Variable, 1997, 3rd ed., 2006; (with E. Gavosto and W. McCallum) Issues in Modern Mathematics Education, 1998; (with L. Fontana and M.M. Peloso) Hodge Theory in the Sobolev Topology for the de Rham Complex, 1998; Handbook of Complex Variables, 1999; A Panorama of Harmonic Analysis, 1999; (with H.R. Parks) The Geometry of Domains in Space, 1999; Handbook of Typography for the Mathematical Sciences, 2001; (with H.R. Parks) The Implicit Function Theorem: History, Function, and Applications, 2002; Handbook of Logic and Proof Techniques of Computer Science, 2002; Mathematical Apocrypha, Stories and Anecdotes of Mathematicians and Mathematical, 2002; Calculus Demystified, 2003, 2nd ed., 2010; A Mathematician's Survival Guide: Graduate School and Early Career Development, 2003; (co-author) Explorations in Complex and Reimannian Geometry: A Volume Dedicated to Robert E. Greene, 2003; A Handbook of Real Variables: With Applications to Differential Equations and Fourier Analysis, 2004; Mathematical Apocrypha Redux, 2005; Differential Equations Demystified, 2005; Geometric Function Theory: Explorations in Complex Analysis, 2005; Mathematical Publishing: A Guidebook, 2005; (with B.E. Blank) Calculus Multivariable, 2006, (with B.E. Blank) 2nd ed., 2010; (with B.E. Blank) Calculus, Single Variable, 2006; (with R.E. Green) Function Theory of One Complex Variable, 2006; Geometric Function Theory: Explorations in Complex Analysis, 2006; (with G.F. Simmons) Differential Equations: Theory, Technique, and Practice, 2007; Complex Variables: A Physical Approach With Applications and Matlab, 2008; (with H.R. Parks) Geometric Integration Theory, 2008; Survival of a Mathematician, 2009; Explorations in Harmonic Analysis, 2009; A Guide to Real Variables, 2009; A Guide to Topology, 2010; Discrete Mathematics Demystified, 2009; Essentials of Topology with Applications, 2010; Calculus: Single & Multivariable, (with B.E. Blank) 2nd ed., 2011. EDITOR: Complex Analysis Seminar, 1987; (with E.Bedford, J. D'Angelo and R.E. Greene) Several Complex Variables and Complex Geometry, 1991; (with K. Rosen and D. Zwillinger) The Standard Book of Tables and Formulas, 1995; (with E.A. Gavosto and W. McCallum) Contemporary Issues in Mathematics Education, 1999; (with K. Kim) Complex Geometric Analysis in Pohang: POSTECH-BSRI SNU-GARC International Conference on Several Complex Variables, 1999; Dictionary of Algebra, Arithmetic, and Trigonometry, 2000; (with G.R. Jensen) 150 Years of Mathematics at Washington University in St. Louis: Sesquicentennial of Mathematics at Washington University, October 3-5, 2003, Washington University, St. Louis, Missouri, 2006. Contributor of articles to journals. **Address:** Department of Mathematics, Washington University, Rm. 103, Cupples I, 1 Brookings Dr., PO Box 1146, St. Louis, MO 63130, U.S.A. **Online address:** sk@math.wustl.edu

KRASHEN, Stephen D. American (born United States), b. 1941. **Genres:** Language/Linguistics, Writing/Journalism, Literary Criticism And History, Education, Reference. **Career:** University of California, Neuropsychiatric Institute, postdoctoral fellow, 1972-73; City University of New York, Queens College, assistant professor of linguistics, 1973-75; University of Southern California, College of Letters, Arts and Sciences, Department of Linguistics, associate professor, 1975-81, professor of linguistics, 1981-, now professor emeritus, Rossier School of Education, Division of Learning and Instruction, professor of education, 1993-, now professor emeritus. Writer. **Publications:** (Ed. with R.C. Scarcella) Research in Second Language Acquisition, 1980; Second Language Acquisition and Second Language Learning, 1981; Principles and Practice in Second Language Acquisition, 1982; (ed. with R.C. Scarcella and M.H. Long) Child-adult Differences in Second Language Acquisition, 1982; (with H. Dulay and M. Burt) Language Two, 1982; (with T.D. Terrell) The Natural Approach: Language Acquisition in the Classroom, 1983; Writing: Research, Theory and Application, 1984; The Input Hypothesis: Issues and Implications, 1985; Inquiries and Insights: Essays in Language Teaching, Bilingual Education and Literacy, 1985; (with D. Biber) On Course: Bilingual Education's Success in California, 1988; (ed. with R.C. Scarcella and E.S. Andersen) Developing Communicative Competence in a Second Language, 1990; Fundamentals of Language Education, 1991; Foundations of Language Education, 1992; The Power of Reading: Insights from the Research, 1993, 2nd ed., 2004; Under Attack, 1996; (with J. McQuillan) The Case for Late Intervention: Once A Good Reader Always A Good Reader, 1996; Every Person A Reader, 1996; Foreign Language Education the Easy Way, 1997; (co-ed.) Heritage Language Development, 1998; Condemned Without a Trial: Bogus Arguments Against Bilingual Education, 1999; Three Arguments Against Whole Language and Why They Are Wrong, 1999; Explorations in Language Acquisition and Use, 2003; (with J. Crawford) English Learners in American Classrooms: 101 Questions, 101 Answers, 2007; (with F.H. Shin) Summer Reading: Program and Evidence, 2008; Free Voluntary Reading, 2011. Contributor to periodicals. **Address:** Department of Linguistics, University of Southern California, 301 Grace Ford Salvatori, ADM 304, 3551 Trousdale Pkwy, Los Angeles, CA 90089-1693, U.S.A. **Online address:** krashen@usc.edu

KRASILOVSKY, Phyllis. American (born United States), b. 1926. **Genres:** Children's Fiction, Travel/Exploration, Novellas/Short Stories, Children's Non-fiction, Picture/Board Books, Novels, Politics/Government, Social Sciences, Social Sciences. **Career:** Marymount College, teacher of children's literature, 1969-70; Katonah Library, teacher of creative writing, 1970-72; Westchester and Long Island Magazine, travel editor, 1975-. **Publications:** The Man Who Didn't Wash His Dishes, 1950; The Very Little Girl, 1953; The Cow Who Fell in the Canal, 1957; Scaredy Cat, 1959; Benny's Flag, 1960; The Very Little Boy, 1961; Susan Sometimes, 1962; The Girl Who Was a Cowboy, 1965; The Very Tall Little Girl, 1969; The Shy Little Girl, 1970; The Popular Girls Club, 1972; L.C. is the Greatest, 1975; The Man Who Tried to Save Time, 1979; The Man Who Entered a Contest, 1980; The Man Who Cooked for Himself, 1981; The First Tulips in Holland, 1982; The Happy Times Story Book, 1987; The Christmas Tree that Grew, 1987; The Man Who Was Too Lazy to Fix Things, 1992; The Woman Who Saved Things, 1993. Contributor to periodicals. **Address:** 235 Dolphin Cove Quay, Stamford, CT 06902-7751, U.S.A.

KRASNOW, Iris. American (born United States), b. 1954?. **Genres:** Essays, Self Help. **Career:** Dallas Times Herald, fashion writer; United Press International (UPI), feature writer, 1984-; American University, assistant professor of journalism, journalism professor, writer-in-residence, academic director; Fox Morning News, relationship correspondent. **Publications:** Surrendering to Motherhood: Losing Your Mind, Finding Your Soul, 1997; Surrendering to Marriage: Husbands, Wives, and Other Imperfections, 2001; Surrendering to Yourself: You are Your Own Soul Mate, 2003; I am My Mother's Daughter: Making Peace with Mom Before It's Too Late, 2007; The Secret Lives of Wives, 2011. Contributor to periodicals. **Address:** 47 Riverside Ave., PO Box 591, Westport, CT 06880, U.S.A. **Online address:** iris@iriskrasnow.com

KRASS, Peter. American (born United States), b. 1965?. **Genres:** Biography, Business/Trade/Industry, History. **Career:** Dun & Bradstreet, marketing manager; British Broadcasting Corp., script consultant, 2002-03; Best American Essays, managing editor. Journalist. **Publications:** Sojourner Truth, 1988, rev. ed. as Sojourner Truth: Antislavery Activist, 2004; Carnegie, 2002; Blood and Whiskey: The Life and Times of Jack Daniel, an American Legend, 2004; Portrait of War: The U.S. Army's First Combat Artists and The Doughboys' Experience in WWI, 2007; Ignorance, Confidence, and Filthy Rich Friends: The Business Adventures of Mark Twain, Chronic Speculator and Entrepreneur, 2007. EDITOR: The Book of Business Wisdom: Classic Writings by the Legends of Commerce and Industry, 1997; The Book of Leadership Wisdom: Classic Writings by Legendary Business Leaders, 1998; The Book of Entrepreneurs' Wisdom, 1999; The Book of Investing Wisdom: Classic Writings by Great Stock-Pickers and Legends of Wall Street, 1999; The Book of Management Wisdom: Classic Writings by Legendary Managers, 2000; The Conference Board Challenge to Business: Industry Leaders Speak Their Minds, 2000; The Little Book of Business Wisdom: Rules of Success from More than 50 Business Legends, 2001. **Address:** c/o Author Mail, John Wiley & Sons Inc., 111 River St., Hoboken, NJ 07030-5774, U.S.A. **Online address:** pete@petekrass.com

KRATZ, Martin P. J. Canadian (born Canada), b. 1955. **Genres:** Law, Information Science/Computers, Biology, Engineering, Chemistry. **Career:** Celanese Canada Ltd., chemical operator, 1974-76; Pitney Bowes Canada Ltd., service representative, 1976-77; Texaco Exploration, engineering trainee, 1978; University of Stuttgart, Institute fuer Thermodynamik und Warmetechnik, research assistant, 1979; Alberta Oil Sands Technology and Research Authority, engineer, 1980; Canadian Association of Fire Chiefs, consulting engineer, 1981; Alberta Science and Technology Leadership Awards Foundation, vice-president and board director, 1982-; Alberta Court of Appeal and Court of Queen's Bench, law clerk, 1984-85; Ogilvie and Co., barrister and solicitor, 1985-88; University of Alberta, law lecturer, 1986-2005; University of Calgary, assistant professor of law, 1987-2005, associate professor, professor of law; Cruickshank Karvellas, barrister and solicitor, 1988-89, partner, 1988-91; Bennett Jones L.L.P., lawyer and partner, 1991-; NeuroSpheres Ltd., acting president, 1993-; Osgoode Hall Law School, adjunct professor of law, 1999-; Concordia University College of Alberta, adjunct professor, 2000-. Writer. **Publications:** (With P.E. Fites and A.F. Brebner) Control and Security of Computer Information Systems, 1988; (with P.E. Fites and P. Johnston)

The Computer Virus Crisis, 1989, 2nd ed., 1992; (with P.E. Fites) Information Systems Security, 1994, 2nd ed., 2003; Protection of Copyright and Industrial Design, 1994, 2nd ed., 1999; Protecting Copyright and Industrial Design, 1995; Obtaining Patents, 1995, 2nd ed., 1999; Canadian Intellectual Property Law, 1998, 2nd ed., 2010; (with A.M. Gahtan and J.F. Mann) Internet Law: A Practical Guide for Legal and Business Professionals, 1998; Canada's Intellectual Property Law in a Nutshell, 1998; Trademarks and Industrial Designs, 2002; Electronic Commerce Law, 2003; (with S. Burns) Data Protection in Canada, 2006; Licensing, 2007; (with D. Card) Outsourcing, 2010. Contributor to journals. **Address:** Bennett Jones L.L.P., 4500 Bankers Hall E, 855 2nd St. SW, Calgary, AB T2P 4K7, Canada. **Online address:** kratzm@bennettjones.com

KRAUS, Caroline. American (born United States) **Genres:** Autobiography/Memoirs, Biography, Social Sciences. **Career:** Encyclopedia Britannica, staff; Scientific Learning Corp., staff; Northwestern University, staff; PBS, staff. Writer. **Publications:** Borderlines: A Memoir, 2004. **Address:** Broadway Books, The Doubleday Broadway Publishing Group, Rm. 2226, 1745 Broadway, New York, NY 10019, U.S.A. **Online address:** letters@carolinekraus.com

KRAUS, Joanna H. American (born United States), b. 1937. **Genres:** Novellas/Short Stories, Children's Fiction, Plays/Screenplays, Writing/Journalism, Young Adult Fiction. **Career:** Children's Theatre Association, associate director and creative drama teacher, 1960-61, secretary, 1982-84; New Rochelle Academy, director of drama program, 1962-63; Children's Theatre Showcase, chairperson, 1963-65; Clark Center for Performing Arts, assistant director, supervisor of performance program, 1963-65; Young Men's and Young Women's Hebrew Association (YM-YWHA), creative drama teacher, 1965-70; New York City Community College, instructor, 1966-69; Columbia University Teachers College, instructor, 1970-71; State University of New York-Purchase, instructor in theatre and drama, 1970-72; State University of New York College-New Paltz, lecturer, 1972-73, assistant professor, 1973-79; State University of New York, The College at Brockport, associate professor, 1979-86, Arts for Children, coordinator, 1981-90, professor of theatre, 1986-95, graduate coordinator, 1990-95, professor emeritus, 1995-; The Sunday Times, columnist. **Publications:** PLAYS: The Ice Wolf, 1967; Vasalisa, 1968; The Dragon Hammer and Oniroku: Two Plays from the Far East, 1977; Circus Home, 1979; The Last Baron of Arizona, 1985; Kimchi Kid, 1987; The Shaggy Dog Murder Trial: A Play for Young Audiences Based on New York's Barge Canal History, 1988; Remember My Name: A Story of Survival in Wartime France, 1989; Plays Plus, 1990; (co-author) Tenure Track, 1993; Angel in the Night, 1996; Ms. Courageous: Women of Science, 1997; Sunday Gold: A Playing Two Acts, 1998; Women of Courage: Five Plays, 2000; Secrets, 2005. OTHERS: Seven Sound and Motion Stories, 1971; The Great American Train Ride, 1975; Tall Boy's Journey, 1992; A Night of Tamales and Roses, 2007; Blue Toboggan, forthcoming. Contributor to books, periodicals and newspapers. **Address:** Department of Theatre, The College at Brockport, State University of New York, 350 New Campus Dr., Brockport, NY 14420, U.S.A. **Online address:** tjkraushouse@hotmail.com

KRAUSE, Jill A. See **STEANS, Jill A.**

KRAUSHAR, Peter Maximilian. British (born England), b. 1934?. **Genres:** Marketing, Administration/Management, Business/Trade/Industry, Economics. **Career:** D.F. Marketing Development Ltd., managing director, 1966-69; KAE Group Ltd., chairman, 1969-89, KAE Development Ltd., president and chairman; Kraushar and Ramsay Intl., partner; Mintel International Group, chairman; Institute of Marketing, staff. Writer. **Publications:** New Products and Diversification, 1969, 2nd ed., 1977; Practical Business Development: What Works, What Does Not?, 1985. **Address:** 2 Lauradale Rd., London, GL N2 9LU, England.

KRAUSS, Clifford. American (born United States), b. 1953. **Genres:** Area Studies, Politics/Government. **Career:** United Press Intl., night editor, 1977-79, reporter, 1979-80; Cox Newspapers, Latin American correspondent, 1981-84; Wall Street Journal, Central American correspondent, 1984-87, foreign correspondent; New York Times, State Department correspondent, 1990-91, congressional correspondent, 1991-94, Houston national business correspondent, Buenos Aires bureau chief, 1998-, Toronto bureau chief, 2002-; New York City Police Department Bureau, chief, 1992-93, 1994-97. **Publications:** Inside Central America: Its People, Politics and History, 1991. Contributor to

periodicals. **Address:** The New York Times, 229 W 43rd St., New York, NY 10036-3959, U.S.A.

KRAUSS, Lawrence M. American (born United States), b. 1954. **Genres:** Astronomy, Physics, Sciences, History, Education, Communications/Media. **Career:** Harvard University, Harvard Society of Fellows, junior research fellow, 1982-85, associate in physics, 1987-95; Yale University, junior fellow, 1982-85, assistant professor, 1985-88, associate professor of physics and astronomy, 1988-93; Boston University and Smithsonian Astrophysical Observatory, visiting scientist, 1985-86; Harvard-Smithsonian Center for Astrophysics, visiting scientist, 1986-89; Carleton University, Nesbitt lecturer, 1988, Chesley lecturer, 1998; University of Chicago, visiting researcher, 1989; Case Western Reserve University, Ambrose Swasey professor of physics, 1993-2008, Department of Physics, chair, 1993-2005, Center of Education & Research in Cosmology and Astrophysics, director, 2002, Office of Science, Public Policy and Bio-Entrepreneurship School of Medicine, director, 2005; Catholic University, Herzfeld lecturer, 1998; American Physical Society, Centennial lecturer, 1999; McMaster University, Origins Institute, Hooker distinguished visiting professor, 2005; Vanderbilt University, visiting professor, 2006-07; Arizona State University, School of Earth and Space Exploration, Department of Physics and Beyond Center, foundation professor and director of Origins Project, 2008-. Writer. **Publications:** The Fifth Essence: The Search for Dark Matter in the Universe, 1989; Fear of Physics: A Guide for the Perplexed, 1993; The Physics of Star Trek, 1995, rev. ed., 2007; Beyond Star Trek, 1997; Quintessence: The Mystery of Missing Mass in the Universe, 2000; Atom: An Odyssey from the Big Bang to Life on Earth-and Beyond, 2003; Hiding behind the Mirror: The Mysterious Allure of Extra Dimensions, 2005; Quantum Man: Richard Feynman's Life in Science, 2011. EDITOR: (with F. Accetta) Cosmic Strings: The Current Status, 1988; (with S.J. Rey) Baryon Number Violation at the Electroweak Scale, 1992; Cosmic Microwave Background Anisotropies Two Years after COBE, 1994. Contributor of articles to journals. **Address:** School of Earth and Space Exploration, Arizona State University, PO Box 871404, Tempe, AZ 85287-1404, U.S.A. **Online address:** krauss@asu.edu

KRAUSS, Nicole. American (born United States), b. 1974. **Genres:** Novels, Psychology, Young Adult Fiction. **Career:** Poet and writer. **Publications:** NOVEL: Man Walks into a Room, 2002; The History of Love, 2005; Great House, 2010. **Address:** c/o Author Mail, Random House, 299 Park Ave., New York, NY 10171-0002, U.S.A.

KRAUSZ, Ernest. Israeli/Romanian (born Romania), b. 1931. **Genres:** Race Relations, Social Sciences, Sociology, Philosophy. **Career:** Central London Polytechnic, lecturer in sociology, 1959-64; Nuffield Foundation, senior fellow, 1961-64; The City University, North-East London Polytechnic, lecturer, 1967-70, senior lecturer, 1970-72, reader in sociology, 1971-72; Bar-Ilan University, associate professor, 1972-73, chair of sociology, 1972-, professor of sociology, 1973-, dean of faculty of social science, 1974-76, rector, 1986-89, acting president, 1989, now emeritus; University of Newcastle, visiting professor, 1976-77; Studies of Israeli Society, editor, 1980-2002; Netanya Academic College, School of Behavioural Sciences, professor. **Publications:** Leeds Jewry: Its History and Social Structure, 1964; Sociology in Britain: A Survey of Research, 1969; Ethnic Minorities in Britain, 1971; The Making of a Community: The Ethnic Factor, 1972; (with S.H. Miller) Social Research Design, 1974; (ed. with S. Poll) On Ethnic and Religious Diversity in Israel, 1975; Sociological Research: A Philosophy of Science Perspective, 1986; (ed. with G. Tulea) Jewish Survival: The Identity Problem at the Close of the Twentieth Century, 1998; The Limits of Science, 2000; (ed. with G. Tulea) Starting the 21st Century, 2002; Exploring Reality and Its Uncertainties, 2010. **Address:** Department of Sociology, Bar-Ilan University, Ramat-Gan, 52900, Israel.

KRAUT, Richard. American (born United States), b. 1944. **Genres:** Philosophy, Ethics, History. **Career:** University of Illinois, professor of philosophy, 1969-95; Central Division of the American Philosophical Association, president, 1993-94, vice chair, 2002-04; Northwestern University, professor, 1995-, Charles and Emma Morrison professor in humanities. Writer. **Publications:** Socrates and the State, 1984; Aristotle on the Human Good, 1989; (ed.) Cambridge Companion to Plato, 1992; (ed.) Plato's Republic, 1997; (trans.) Aristotle Politics Books VII and VIII, 1997; Aristotle: Political Philosophy, 2002; (ed. with S. Skultety) Aristotle's Politics, 2005; (ed.) Blackwell Guide to Aristotle's Nicomachean Ethics, 2006; What is Good and Why: The Ethics of Well-Being, 2007; How to Read Plato, 2008; Against Absolute Goodness,

2011. **Address:** Department of Philosophy, Northwestern University, Kresge Rm. 3-205, 1880 Campus Dr., Evanston, IL 60208-2214, U.S.A. **Online address:** rkraut1@northwestern.edu

KRAVITZ, Lee. American (born United States), b. 1953?. **Genres:** Business/Trade/Industry. **Career:** Scholastic, editorial director, 1987-95; React magazine, founding editor, 1995-2000; Parade magazine, editor-in-chief, 2000-07. **Publications:** For All Time: A Pictorial Celebration of America, 2000; Unfinished Business: One Man's Extraordinary Year of Trying to Do the Right Things, 2010. Contributor to periodicals. **Address:** New York, NY , U.S.A.

KREBS, Nina. See **KREBS, Nina Boyd.**

KREBS, Nina Boyd. Also writes as Nina Krebs. American (born United States), b. 1938. **Genres:** Psychology, Race Relations, Art/Art History. **Career:** California State University, counseling psychologist, 1971-76; Counseling Center, director, 1973-75; Consulting, 1974-89, 1975-76, 1979-88; Center for Family, Individual and Organizational Development, partner, 1976-83; California State Board of Medical Quality Assurance, psychology examiner, 1978-93; U.S. Bureau of Reclamation, independent contractor, 1979-; Sacramento Valley Psychological Association, president, 1991-92. Writer. **Publications:** AS NINA KREBS: (with R.D. Allen) Psychotheatrics: The New Art of Self-Transformation, 1979; (with R. Allen) Dramatic Psychological Storytelling: Using Expressive Arts and Psychotheatrics, 2007. AS NINA BOYD KREBS: Changing Woman, Changing Work, 1993; Edgewalkers: Defusing Cultural Boundaries on the New Global Frontier, 1999. **Address:** 4651 Breuner Ave., Sacramento, CA 95819, U.S.A. **Online address:** nbkrebs@surewest.net

KREBS, Ronald R. American (born United States), b. 1974. **Genres:** Politics/Government, Military/Defense/Arms Control, History. **Career:** Foreign Affairs Magazine, assistant editor; University of Minnesota, associate professor of political science, McKnight Land-Grant Professor, 2006-08. **Publications:** Dueling Visions: U.S. Strategy toward Eastern Europe under Eisenhower, 2001; Fighting for Rights: Military Service and the Politics of Citizenship, 2006. Contributor to periodicals. **Address:** Department of Political Science, University of Minnesota, 1233 Social Sciences Bldg., 267 19th Ave. S, Minneapolis, MN 55455-0499, U.S.A. **Online address:** rkrebs@umn.edu

KREININ, Mordechai. American/Israeli (born Israel), b. 1930. **Genres:** Economics, Essays. **Career:** University of Michigan, part-time research assistant, 1952-53, Survey Research Center, assistant study director, 1954-55, study director, 1955-57, lecturer in economics, 1956-57; Michigan State University, assistant professor, 1957-59, associate professor, 1959-61, professor, 1961-89, acting department chairperson, 1967-68, University distinguished professor of economics, 1990-, Department Hospitality Business, adjunct professor; Monash University, visiting professor, 1987-88; Copenhagen Business School, visiting professor, 1994-95; Johns Hopkins University, visiting professor, 2002. Writer. **Publications:** Israel and Africa: A Study in Technical Cooperation, 1964; Alternative Commercial Policies: Their Effects on the American Economy, 1967; (co-author) Studies in Trade Liberalization: Problems and Prospects for the Industrial Countries, 1967; Israel and the European Community, 1969; International Economics: A Policy Approach, 1971, 10th ed., 2006; Trade Relations of the EEC: An Empirical Investigation, 1974; (L.H. Officer) The Monetary Approach to the Balance of Payments: A Survey, 1978; Economics, An Introductory Text, 1983, rev. ed., 1990; Can Australia Adjust?, 1988; (ed.) International Commercial Policy: Issues for the 1990s, 1993; (ed.) Contemporary Issues in Commercial Policy, 1995; (ed. with M.G. Plummer and S. Abe) Asia-Pacific Economic Linkages, 1999; (ed.) Building a Partnership: The Canada-United States Free Trade Agreement, 2000; (with Plummer) Economic Integration and Asia: The Dynamics of Regionalism in Europe, North American and the Asia-Pacific, 2000; Economic Integration and Development: Has Regionalism Delivered for Developing Countries?, 2002; (ed.) Empirical Methods in International Trade: Essays in Honor of Mordechai Kreinin, 2004. Contributor to journals. **Address:** Department of Economics, Michigan State University, 120C Marshall-Adams Hall, East Lansing, MI 48824-1038, U.S.A. **Online address:** kreinin@msu.edu

KREIT, Carol. American (born United States), b. 1936. **Genres:** Adult Nonfiction. **Career:** Henry Dunay Designs Inc., vice president, 1973-92; Plumb

Club of New York State Inc., executive director, 1982-95; Literacy Volunteers of America, educator. Writer. **Publications:** First Wives' Tool Kit: A Survival Manual, 2001. **Address:** 90 Chestnut St., Englewood, NJ 07631-3045, U.S.A.

KREITNER, Kenneth. American (born United States), b. 1956. **Genres:** Music, Biography, Bibliography, History. **Career:** University of Memphis, Rudi E. Scheidt School of Music, professor of musicology, assistant director for graduate curriculum and advising, Collegium Musicum, director of campus musical group. Writer. **Publications:** Robert Ward: A Bio-bibliography, 1988; Discoursing Sweet Music: Town Bands and Community Life in Turn-of-the-Century Pennsylvania, 1990; The Church Music of Fifteenth-Century Spain, 2004; (ed.) Renaissance Music, 2011. Contributor to periodicals and journals. **Address:** Rudi E. Scheidt School of Music, University of Memphis, Rm. 123, Music Bldg., 3775 Central Ave., Memphis, TN 38152-3160, U.S.A. **Online address:** kkreitnr@memphis.edu

KREJČÍ, Jaroslav. British/Czech (born Czech Republic), b. 1916. **Genres:** International Relations/Current Affairs, Social Sciences, Autobiography/Memoirs. **Career:** Central Union of Commerce, in charge of trade law, 1940-45; State Planning Office, Department of National Accounting, secretary, 1945-48; Graduate School of Political and Social Sciences, external associate professor, 1948-50; Technological University, external associate professor, 1950-52; State Bank, research worker, 1950-53; Czechoslovak Academy of Sciences, research worker, 1968; Lancaster University (formerly University of Lancaster), research fellow, 1969-70, visiting lecturer, 1970-72, lecturer, 1972-73, senior lecturer, 1973-76, School of European studies, professor, 1976-83, professor emeritus, 1983-; Institute of Philosophy of the Academy of Sciences, Center for Research into Socio-Cultural Pluralism, 1994-; Josef Hlavka Economic Institute, honorary chairperson, 1994; Palacký University, Department of Politics and European Studies, visiting professor, 1993-99; Charles university, Department of Constitutional Law, visiting professor, 1995-. Writer. **Publications:** Social Change and Stratification in Postwar Czechoslovakia, 1972; Social Structure in Divided Germany, 1976; (ed.) Sozialdemokratie Und Systemwandel, 1978; (with V. Velímsky) Ethnic and Political Nations in Europe, 1981; National Income and Outlay in Czechoslovakia, Poland, and Yugoslavia, 1982; Great Revolutions Compared: The Search for a Theory, 1983, 2nd ed. as Great Revolutions Compared, the Outline of a Theory, 1994; Before the European Challenge: The Great Civilizations of Asia and the Middle East, 1990; Czechoslovakia at the Crossroads of European History, 1990; The Human Predicament: Its Changing Image; A Study in Comparative Religion and History 1993; Society in a Global Perspective, 1993; (with P. Machonin) Czechoslovakia 1918-92, A Laboratory for Social Change, 1996; (ed.) Human Rights and Responsibilities in a Divided World, 1996; Between Democracy and Dictatorship (memoirs in Czech), 1998; Mezi demokrací a Diktaturou: Domov a Exil, 1998; Ceské křižovatky: Osm Pohledu Na Nase Proplouvaní Perejemisoudobych Dejin, 2001; Intelligible Currents of History (in Czech), 2002; (ed.) Kontrastní hodnoty a Multikulturní společnost: Sborník z Mezinárodní Konference 19. Až 22. září 2001 v Praze = Contrasting Values and Multicultural Society: International Workshop Conference, Prague, September 2001: Selected Proceedings, 2002; Postižitelné Proudy Dějin: Civilizace a Sociální Formace, Struktury a Procesy, Kultura a Politika, Revoluce a Renesance, Náboženství, Národy a StátyThe Paths of Civilization: Understanding the Currents of History, 2004. **Address:** Lonsdale College, Lancaster University, Bailrigg, Lancaster, ES LA1 4YW, England. **Online address:** a.taylor@lancaster.ac.uk

KREMENYUK, Victor (A.). Russian (born Russia), b. 1940. **Genres:** International Relations/Current Affairs, Human Relations/Parenting, Politics/Government. **Career:** Russian Academy of Sciences, Institute for the USA and Canada, professor and deputy director, 1970-, Vienna Diplomacy Academy, professor; Marshall Center, professor; International Institute for Applied Systems Analysis (IIASA), research associate; University for Humanitarian Sciences, Department of World Politics and International Relations, head. Writer. **Publications:** Politika SShA v razvivaiushchikhsia stranakh, 1977; Politika SShA v Azii, 1977; SShA i konflikty v strannakh Azii-70-e gg. XX v., 1979; (with V.P. Lukina and I.B. Bulaia) SShA I Problemy Tikhogo Okeana: Mezhdunar.-polit. aspekty, 1979; Global' naiavneshnepoliticheskaia strategiia SShA i razvivaiushchiesia strany, konets1960-kh-1970-e gody, 1981; SShA i Razvivaiushchiesia strany, 70-e gody, 1981; SShA, borba protiv natsionalno-osvoboditelnogo dvizheniia: istoriiai sovremennost, 1983; SShA i razvivaiushchiesia Strany: Kritikakontseptsii Vzaimozavisimosti, 1984; Borba Vashingtona protiv revoliutsiiv Irane, 1984; SShA v Mezhdunarodnykh Krizisakh:

Politiko-Psikhologicheskie Aspekty, 1988; (with V. Lukin and M. Nosov) U.S. Policy toward the Pacific, 1989; (co-author) SSHA i regionalnyekonflikty: 80-e gody (title means: 'The USA and Regional Conflicts'), 1990; Conflicts in and around Russia: Nation-Building in Difficult Times, 1994; (co-author) Rossiya I SSHA posle kholodnoy voyny (title means: 'Russia and the USA after the Cold War'), 1999; Voina v Irake--amerikanskie instituty vlasti i obshchestvo, 2006; (with T. A. Shakleina) Problemy transatlanticheskikh otnoshenii v nachale XXI veka, 2007. EDITOR AND CONTRIBUTOR: Rossiia I SShA posle kholodnoi voiny, 1979; International Negotiation: Analysis, Approaches, Issues, 1991, 2nd ed., 2002; Polozhenie Rossii I ee natsionalnye interesy, 1993; (with I.W. Zartman) Cooperative Security: Reducing Third World Wars, 1995; (with S. Cross, I.A. Zevelev and V.M. Gevorgian) Global Security beyond the Millennium: American and Russian Perspectives, 1999; (with G. Sjostedt) International Economic Negotiation: Models versus Reality, 2000; (with R. Avenhaus and G. Sjostedt) Containing the Atom: International Negotiations on Nuclear Security and Safety, 2002; Peace Versus Justice: Negotiating Forward and Backward Looking Outcomes, 2005; (with J. Bercovitch and I.W. Zartman) Sage Handbook of Conflict Resolution, 2008. Contributor to books. **Address:** Institute for the USA and Canada, Russian Academy of Sciences, 2/3 Khlebny per., Moscow, 123995, Russia. **Online address:** vkremenyuk@yahoo.com

KREMER, Marcie. *See* **SORENSON, Margo.**

KREML, William P. American (born United States), b. 1941. **Genres:** Philosophy, Politics/Government, Psychology, Young Adult Non-fiction, Law. **Career:** Northern Illinois University, assistant professor of business law, 1965-66; University of Tennessee, assistant professor of business law, 1966-68; University of South Carolina, Department of Political Science, assistant professor, 1971-77, associate professor, 1977-84, professor of government and international studies, 1984-96, vice-chair of department, 1991-93, interim chair of department, 1993, distinguished professor emeritus, 1996-; University of Peking, visiting professor, 1994, 1997; Concord Coalition, coordinator, 1995-; Mars Hill College, adjunct professor, 1998. Writer. **Publications:** The Anti-Authoritarian Personality, 1977; The Middle Class Burden, 1979, rev. ed. as America's Middle Class: From Subsidy to Abandonment, 1997; Relativism and the Natural Left, 1984; A Model of Politics, 1985; Psychology, Relativism, and Politics, 1991; Losing Balance: The De-Democratization of America, 1991; The Constitutional Divide: The Private and Public Sectors in American Law, 1997; The Twenty-First Century Left, 2005, 2nd ed., 2006. Contributor of articles. **Address:** Department of Political Science, University of South Carolina, 817 Henderson St., Columbia, SC 29208, U.S.A. **Online address:** kreml@mindspring.com

KREMMER, Christopher. Australian (born Australia), b. 1958?. **Genres:** Area Studies, Travel/Exploration. **Career:** Australian Broadcasting Corp., writer. **Publications:** Stalking the Elephant Kings: In Search of Laos, 1997; The Carpet Wars: From Kabul to Baghdad: A Ten-Year Journey Along Ancient Trade Routes, 2002; Bamboo Palace: Discovering the Lost Dynasty of Laos, 2003; Inhaling the Mahatma, 2006; The Chase, 2011. **Address:** c/o Author Mail, HarperCollins Publishers, 10 E 53rd St., 7th Fl., New York, NY 10022, U.S.A.

KRENTZ, Edgar Martin. American (born United States), b. 1928. **Genres:** Archaeology/Antiquities, Theology/Religion. **Career:** Concordia Seminary, instructor, 1953-54, assistant professor, 1955-64, librarian, 1955-64, associate professor, 1964-69, professor of New Testament, 1969-75; Foundation for Reformation Research, board director, 1957-59; Christ Seminary-Seminex, professor of New Testament, 1975-83; Lutheran School of Theology, professor of New Testament, 1983-98, Christ Seminary-Seminex professor, professor emeritus, 1998-; University of Chicago, Divinity School, Pacific Lutheran Theological Seminary, visiting professor; Yale Divinity School, visiting professor; Catholic Theological Union, adjunct professor of new testament. Writer. **Publications:** Biblical Studies Today, 1966; The Historical-Critical Method, 1975; (ed.) Historical Investigation and New Testament Faith, 1983; Galatians, Augsburg New Testament Commentary, 1985. **Address:** Lutheran School of Theology, 1100 E 55th St., Chicago, IL 60615-5112, U.S.A. **Online address:** ekrentz@lstc.edu

KRESS, Adrienne. Canadian (born Canada), b. 1980?. **Genres:** Novels, Children's Fiction. **Career:** Tempest Theatre Group, staff; Writer. **Publi-**cations: Alex and the Ironic Gentleman (novel), 2007; Timothy and the Dragon's Gate (novel), 2008. **Address:** Darley Anderson Literary Film & TV Agency, Estelle House, 11 Eustace Rd., London, GL SW6 1JB, England. **Online address:** adriennekress@gmail.com

KRESSEL, Neil J. American (born United States), b. 1957. **Genres:** Law, Adult Non-fiction, Politics/Government, Theology/Religion, Social Sciences. **Career:** Harvard University, tutor and instructor, 1979-83; private practice consultant, 1983-; William Paterson University of New Jersey, assistant professor, associate professor of psychology, 1984-, chair of department, 1992-95, professor of psychology, director of the honors program in the social sciences; New York University, adjunct assistant professor, 1989-91; Stevens Institute of Technology, adjunct associate professor, 1989-94; Institute for Rational-Emotive Therapy, clinical psychologist, 1993-94; Yale University, Yale Initiative for the Interdisciplinary Study of Antisemitism, visiting associate professor, 2008-09. Writer. **Publications:** (Ed.) Political Psychology: Classic and Contemporary Readings, 1993; Mass Hate: The Global Rise of Genocide and Terror, 1996, rev. ed., 2002; (with D.F. Kressel) Stack and Sway: The New Science of Jury Consulting, 2001; Bad Faith: The Danger of Religious Extremism, 2007. Contributor of articles to magazines and newspapers. **Address:** Department of Psychology, William Paterson University, Science E 2039, 300 Pompton Rd., Wayne, NJ 07470, U.S.A. **Online address:** kresseln@wpunj.edu

KRICH, Rochelle Majer. American/German (born Germany), b. 1947?. **Genres:** Mystery/Crime/Suspense, Novels, Literary Criticism And History. **Career:** Department of English, Yeshiva High School, chair and teacher. Writer. **Publications:** MYSTERY NOVELS: Where's Mommy Now?, 1990; Till Death Do Us Part, 1992; Nowhere to Run, 1994; Speak No Evil, 1996; Fertile Ground, 1998: First Blume, 2002; Grave Endings: A Novel of Suspense: 2004; Now You See Me: A Novel of Suspence, 2005. JESSIE DRAKE MYSTERY NOVELS: Fair Game, 1993; Angel of Death, 1994; (as Rochelle Krich) Blood Money, 1999; (as Rochelle Krich) Dead Air, 2000; (as Rochelle Krich) Shadows of Sin, 2001. Contributor to periodicals. **Address:** Avon Books, 1350 Ave. of the Americas, New York, NY 10019, U.S.A. **Online address:** rochellekrich@aol.com

KRICHER, John C. American (born United States), b. 1944. **Genres:** Environmental Sciences/Ecology, Natural History, Children's Non-fiction, Sciences, Philosophy. **Career:** Wheaton College, assistant professor, associate professor, 1970-80, professor of biology, 1980-, Meneely professor of biology, Brojan Harlan Jennings chair in the natural sciences and mathematics. Writer and ecologist. **Publications:** A Field Guide to Eastern Forests, North America, 1988; A Neotropical Companion: An Introduction to the Animals, Plants and Ecosystems of the New World Tropics, 1989, 2nd ed., 1997; Peterson First Guide to Dinosaurs, 1990; Peterson First Guide to Seashores, 1992; A Field Guide to the Ecology of Western Forests, 1993; A Field Guide to California and Pacific Northwest Forests, 1993, rev. ed., 1998; A Field Guide to Rocky Mountain and Southwest Forests, 1993; Peterson First Guide to Forests, 1994; Galàpagos, 2002; Tropical Forest Animal Communities, 2007; Balance of Nature: Ecology's Enduring Myth, 2009; Tropical Ecology, 2010. **Address:** Department of Biology, Wheaton College, Mars 2137, 156A, Science Ctr., Norton, MA 02766, U.S.A. **Online address:** jkricher@wheatoncollege.edu

KRICK, Robert K. (Robert Kenneth Krick). American (born United States), b. 1943. **Genres:** History, Military/Defense/Arms Control. **Career:** Fort McHenry National Monument, chief historian, 1967-69; Fort Necessity National Battlefield, superintendent, 1969-72; Fredericksburg and Spotsylvania National Military Park, chief historian, 1972-2002, now retired; Association for the Preservation of Civil War Sites, vice president, 1987-93; Company of Military Historians, fellow. Writer. **Publications:** Parker's Virginia Battery, C.S.A., 1975, 2nd ed., 1989; Neale Books: An Annotated Bibliography, 1976; Lee's Colonels: A Biographical Register of the Field Officers of the Army of Northern Virginia, 1979, 5th ed., 2005; (co-author) An Index-Guide to the Southern Historical Society Papers, 1876-1982, 2 vols., 1980; The Gettysburg Death Register, 1981, 4th ed., 2004; The 9th Virginia Cavalry, 1982, 4th ed., 1988; (co-author) Wildcat Cavalry, 1982; The 30th Virginia Infantry, 1983, 4th ed., 1991; A Virginia Marine on Iwo Jima, 1987; (co-author) Military Bibliography of the Civil War, 1987; The Fredericksburg Artillery, 1987; (co-author) Antietam: Essays on the 1862 Maryland Campaign, 1989; Stonewall Jackson at Cedar Mountain, 1990, 3rd ed., 1997; (co-author) Struggle for the Shenandoah: Essays on the 1864 Valley Campaign, 1991; (co-author) Gettysburg: The First Day, 1991; (co-author) Gettysburg: The Second Day, 1993; (co-author) Gettysburg: The Third Day, 1994; Conquering the Valley: Stonewall Jackson at Port Republic, 1996; (co-author) Chancellorsville: The Battle and Its Aftermath, 1996; The Wilderness Campaign, 1997; (co-author) The Spotsylvania Campaign, 1998; (co-author) The Antietam Campaign, 1999; (co-author) The Richmond Campaign of 1862, 2000; The American Civil War: The War in the East, 1863-1865, 2001; The Smoothbore Volley That Doomed the Confederacy: The Death of Stonewall Jackson and Other Chapters on the Army of Northern Virginia, 2002; (co-author) The Shenandoah Valley Campaign of 1862, 2003; (co-author) The Shenandoah Valley Campaign of 1864, 2006; (co-author) In Taller Cotton, 2006; Civil War Weather in Virginia, 2007; The 14th South Carolina Infantry Regiment, of the Gregg-McGowan Brigade, Army of Northern Virginia, 2008; (with R. O'Neill) The Civil War: Gettysburg and Other Eastern Battles, 1863-1865, 2011. FORTHCOMING: Ten Generals in Lee's Army; Eight Days in May: Stonewall Jackson's Last Battle and Death. Contributor of articles to periodicals and books. **Address:** PO Box 1327, Fredericksburg, VA 22402-1327, U.S.A.

KRICK, Robert Kenneth. See **KRICK, Robert K.**

KRICORIAN, Nancy. American (born United States), b. 1960. **Genres:** Novels, Romance/Historical, Young Adult Fiction. **Career:** City University of New York, Queens College, lecturer in English, 1987-90; Barnard College, instructor in English and women's studies, 1988; Rutgers University, visiting lecturer, 1988; European publishers, literary scout, 1989-; Yale University, visiting lecturer, 1989, 1991; Columbia University, faculty; CODEPINK NYC, coordinator. Writer. **Publications:** NOVELS: Zabelle, 1998; Dreams of Bread and Fire, 2003. Contributor of poetry and fiction to literary journals. **Address:** Atlantic Monthly Press, 841 Broadway, 4th Fl., New York, NY 10003-4793, U.S.A.

KRIEG, Joann P(eck). American (born United States), b. 1932. **Genres:** Biography, Local History/Rural Topics, Education, Autobiography/Memoirs, Literary Criticism And History. **Career:** Hofstra University, associate professor of English, 1978-, professor, now professor emeritus. Writer. **Publications:** Long Island and Literature (monograph), 1989; Epidemics in the Modern World, 1992; A Whitman Chronology, 1998; Whitman and the Irish, 2000. EDITOR: Walt Whitman, Here and Now, 1985; To Know the Place: Teaching Local History, 1986; Dwight D. Eisenhower: Soldier, President, Statesman, 1987; Evoking a Sense of Place, 1988; (with P. Harper) John F. Kennedy, The Promise Revisited, 1988; Robert Moses: Single-Minded Genius, 1989; Long Island Architecture, 1991; (with N.A. Naylor) To Know the Place: Exploring Long Island History, 1995; Nassau County: From Rural Hinterland to Suburban Metropolis, 2000. **Address:** Department of English, Hofstra University, Rm. 116 Mason Hall, Hempstead, NY 11550, U.S.A. **Online address:** joann.p.krieg@hofstra.edu

KRIEG, Robert Anthony. American (born United States), b. 1946. **Genres:** Theology/Religion, Biography, Autobiography/Memoirs. **Career:** Congregation of the Holy Cross, 1966, ordained Roman Catholic priest, 1973-2000, laicized, 2002; King's College, assistant professor of theology, 1975-77; University of Notre Dame, assistant professor, 1977-85, associate professor of theology, 1985-97, professor of theology, 1997-, director of field education for the ministry, 1978-84, Master's of Divinity Program, director, 1985-91, director of doctoral program, 1995-97. Writer. **Publications:** Story-Shaped Christology, 1988; Karl Adam: Catholicism in German Culture, 1992; (ed.) Romano Guardini: Proclaiming the Sacred in a Modern World, 1995; Romano Guardini: A Precursor of Vatican II, 1997; Catholic Theologians in Nazi Germany, 2004; (trans. and intro.) Romano Guardini: Spiritual Writings, 2005; (trans.) Letters and Writings from Prison, 2009; The Paschal Mystery of Jesus Christ, forthcoming. Contributor to journals. Works appear in anthologies. **Address:** Department of Theology, University of Notre Dame, 433 Malloy Hall, Notre Dame, IN 46556-4619, U.S.A. **Online address:** robert.a.krieg.1@nd.edu

KRIEGEL, Leonard. American (born United States), b. 1933. **Genres:** Novels, Autobiography/Memoirs, Essays, Sports/Fitness, Literary Criticism And History. **Career:** Long Island University, assistant professor of English, 1960-61; City University of New York, City College, assistant professor, professor of English, 1961-, now professor emeritus; University of Leiden, Fulbright lecturer, 1964-65; University of Groningen, Fulbright lecturer, 1968-69; University of Paris, Fulbright lecturer, 1981. Writer. **Publications:** The Long Walk Home, 1964; The Essential Works of the Founding Fathers, 1964;

(ed. with A.H. Lass) Masters of the Short Story, 1971; Edmund Wilson, 1971; Working Through: A Teacher's Journey in the Urban University, 1972; Working Through: An Autobiographical Journey in the Urban University, 1973; (ed. with A.H. Lass) Stories of the American Experience, 1973; Notes for the Two-Dollar Window: Portraits from an American Neighborhood, 1976; (ed.) The Myth of American Manhood, 1978; On Men and Manhood, 1979; Quitting Time: A Novel, 1982; Falling into Life: Essays, 1991; Flying Solo: Reimagining Manhood, Courage, and Loss (memoir), 1998; Handicapping the Crippled, 2002; Wrestling with Augie March, 2003. **Address:** Elaine Markson Literary Agency, 44 Greenwich Ave., New York, NY 10011-8347, U.S.A.

KRIEGER, Martin H. American (born United States), b. 1944. **Genres:** Business/Trade/Industry, Economics, Physics, Education. **Career:** University of California, Lawrence Radiation Laboratory, physicist, 1968-69, Institute of Urban and Regional Development, assistant research planner, 1969-72, College of Environmental Design, lecturer in environmental policy, 1970-73; Center for Advanced Study in the Behavioral Sciences, fellow, 1973-74; University of Minnesota-Twin Cities, Hubert H. Humphrey Institute of Public Affairs, assistant professor, 1974-80; Massachusetts Institute of Technology, Department of Urban Studies and Planning, visiting assistant professor and lecturer, 1980-82, Program in Science, Technology, and Society, research associate and lecturer, 1981-84; University of Southern California, associate professor of planning, 1984-91, professor of planning, 1991-, Center for Religion and Civic Culture, faculty research associate, vice chair, 2003-, Social Sciences Panel, chair, 2003-; University of Michigan, visiting associate professor of business administration and Zell-Lurie fellow, 1990-91; The Gallery, Ralph and Goldy Lewis Hall, curator. Writer. **Publications:** Poverty of Policy for the Environment: A Working Paper, 1970; Social Reporting for a City: A Perspective and Some Problems, 1971; Advice and Planning, 1981; Marginalism and Discontinuity: Tools for the Craft of Knowledge and Decision, 1989; Doing Physics: How Physicists Take Hold of the World, 1992; Constitutions of Matter: Mathematically Modeling the Most Everyday of Physical Phenomena, 1996; Entrepreneurial Vocations: Learning from the Callings of Augustine, Moses, Mothers, Antigone, Oedipus and Prospero, 1996; What's Wrong with Plastic Trees?, 2000; Doing Mathematics: Convention, Subject, Calculation, Analogy, 2003; Urban Tomographies, 2011. **Address:** School of Policy, Planning and Development, University of Southern California, 317 Ralph and Goldy Lewis Hall, Los Angeles, CA 90089-0626, U.S.A. **Online address:** krieger@usc.edu

KRIEGER, Melanie. (Melanie Jacobs Krieger). American (born United States), b. 1944?. **Genres:** Education, Mathematics/Statistics. **Career:** Ward Melville High School, teacher, 1979-86, academic teams coordinator, 1985-, West Prep, research director, 1986-; Stony Brook University, adjunct professor, 1984-96, Stony Brook High School Summer Research Institute, codirector, 1984-96, creator of mentor program linking high school students with college professors, 1984-96; Technion University, Summer Research Program, American representative, 1992-, Science Olympieda Competition, American representative, 1992-. Writer. **Publications:** AS MELANIE JACOBS KRIEGER: How to Excel in Science Competitions, 1991, rev. ed., 1999; Means and Probabilities: Using Statistics in Science Projects, 1996; How to Create an Independent Research Program, 1999; Using Statistics in Science Projects, Internet Enhanced, 2002. **Address:** Ward Melville High School, 380 Old Town Rd., East Setauket, NY 11733-3499, U.S.A.

KRIEGER, Melanie Jacobs. See **KRIEGER, Melanie.**

KRIEGER, Michael J. American (born United States), b. 1940. **Genres:** Travel/Exploration, Transportation, History, Young Adult Non-fiction, Westerns/Adventure. **Career:** International Building Products Inc., owner, 1964-69; Consolidated Foods Corp., European manager, 1969-74; journalist and travel writer, 1974-. **Publications:** Tramp: Sagas of High Adventure in the Vanishing World of the Old Tramp Freighters, 1986; Conversations with the Cannibals: The End of the Old South Pacific, 1994; Where Rails Meet the Sea: America's Connections between Ships and Trains, 1998; All the Men in the Sea: The Untold Story of One of the Greatest Rescues in History, 2002. Contributor of articles to periodicals. **Address:** c/o Jane Dystel, Dystel & Goderich Literary Management, 1 Union Sq. W, Ste. 904, New York, NY 10003, U.S.A.

KRIER, Léon. British/French (born France), b. 1946. **Genres:** Architecture.

Career: James Stirling, assistant, 1968-70, 1973-74; J.P. Kleihues, project partner, 1971-72; Architectural Association School, professor, 1974-76; Royal College of Arts, professor of architecture, 1974-76; Princeton University, professor of architecture, 1977; University of Virginia, Jefferson professor of architecture, 1982; His Royal Highness, Charles, the Prince of Wales, consultant, 1988-; Yale University, Davenport professor, 1990-91, Eero Saarinen professor, 2002; Prince of Wales Summer School and Architecture Institute, faculty, 1990-93; art director and designer, 1990-; New School for Traditional Architecture & Urbanism, founding trustee. Writer. **Publications:** Léon Krier: La Ricostruzione della Città Europea, 1980; Léon Krier, Houses, Palaces, Cities, 1984; (ed.) Albert Speer: Architecture, 1932-1942, 1987; Leon Krier: Galerie Der Stadt Stuttgart 27.2.-13.3.1988, 1988; Atlantis: Centre International Culturel, Scientifique, Politique, Etéconomique à Tenerife, Islas Canarias as Atlantis: International Centre for Culture, the Sciences, Politics, and Economics at Tenerife, Islas Canarias, 1988; Completar Santurce: Estudio Preliminar Para El Plan Maestro De Un Barrio, 1992; Leon Krier: Architecture and Urban Design, 1967-1992, 1992; Architecture: Choix Ou Fatalité, 1996 as Architecture: Choice or Fate, 1998; (with M. Culot and L. Boegly) Pier Carlo Bontempi: Piazza Nuova: Place de Toscane, Val d'Europe, Marne-la-Vallée, France, 2007; (with M. Cusato, B. Pentreath and R. Sammons) Get Your House Right: Architectural Elements to Use & Avoid, 2008; (contrib.) Trelles Cabarrocas Architects, 2008; Architecture of Community, 2009; Drawing for Architecture, 2009. Contributor of articles to journals and periodicals. **Address:** 16 Belsize Pk., London, GL NW3 4ES, England.

KRIESBERG, Louis. American (born United States), b. 1926. **Genres:** International Relations/Current Affairs, Sociology, Social Sciences. **Career:** Columbia University, School of General Studies, Department of Sociology, instructor, 1953-56; University of Chicago, Department of Sociology, senior fellow in law and the behavioral sciences, 1957-58, research associate, 1958-62, National Opinion Research Center, senior study director, 1958-62; Syracuse University, Youth Development Center, Department of Sociology, associate professor of sociology and research associate, 1962-67, professor of sociology, 1967-97, chair, 1974-77, Program on the Analysis and Resolution of Conflicts, director, 1986-94, program associate, Maxwell professor of social conflict Studies, 1994-97, professor emeritus of sociology, 1997-. Writer. **Publications:** Mothers in Poverty: A Study of Fatherless Families, 1970; Sociology of Social Conflicts, 1973, 2nd ed., 1982; Social Inequality, 1979; International Conflict Resolution: The U.S.-U.S.S.R. and Middle East Cases, 1992; Constructive Conflicts: From Escalation to Resolution, 1998, 3rd ed., 2007. EDITOR: Social Processes in International Relations, 1968; (with S. Thorsen and T. Northrup) Intractable Conflicts and Their Transformation, 1989; (with S. Thorson) Timing the De-Escalation of International Conflicts, 1991; Research in Social Movements, Conflicts and Change, 14 vols., 1992; (with B.W. Dayton) Conflict Transformation and Peacebuilding: Moving from Violence to Sustainable Peace, 2009. Contributor to periodicals. **Address:** Program on Analysis & Resolution of Conflicts, Syracuse University, 400 Eggers, Syracuse, NY 13244, U.S.A. **Online address:** lkriesbe@maxwell.syr.edu

KRIM, Arthur J. American (born United States), b. 1943?. **Genres:** History. **Career:** Writer and geographer. **Publications:** Northwest Cambridge: Survey of Architectural History in Cambridge, 1977; Roger Reed and Greer Hardwicke, Carriage House to Auto House: A Guide to Brookline's Transportation Buildings to 1940, 2002; Route 66: Iconography of the American Highway, 2006. **Address:** Cambridge, MA, U.S.A.

KRIMSKY, George A. American (born United States), b. 1942. **Genres:** Writing/Journalism, History, Social Sciences, Ethics. **Career:** Waterbury Republican-American, reporter, 1966-69; Associated Press, correspondent and editor, 1969-85, news chief; International Center for Journalists, president, 1985-96, co-founder; International Media Services, president. Writer. **Publications:** (With J.M. Hamilton) Hold the Press: The Inside Story on Newspapers, 1996; (with C.B. Saint) Making Freedom: The Extraordinary Life of Venture Smith, 2009; A Mount Olympus Syndrome, forthcoming. Contributor of articles to periodicals. **Address:** International Center For Journalists, 1616 H St. NW, 3rd Fl., Washington, DC 20006, U.S.A. **Online address:** gkrimsky@epo.com

KRIN, Sylvie. See FANTONI, Barry (Ernest).

KRINARD, Susan. American (born United States) **Genres:** Romance/Historical, Science Fiction/Fantasy, Novels, Novellas/Short Stories, Young Adult Fiction. **Career:** Writer, 1992-. **Publications:** Prince of Wolves, 1994; Prince of Dreams, 1995; Star Crossed, 1995; Prince of Shadows, 1996; Twice a Hero, 1997; Bewitched, 1997; Body and Soul, 1998; Touch of the Wolf, 1999; Once a Wolf, 2000; Secret of the Wolf, 2001; Kinsman, 2001; The Forest Lord, 2002; To Catch a Wolf, 2003; (with E. Vaughn and T. Lee) When Darkness Falls, 2003; Kinsman's Oath, 2004; Shield of the Sky, 2004; To Tame a Wolf, 2005; Lord of The Beasts, 2006; Hammer of the Earth, 2006; Call of the Wolf, 2006; (co-author) My Big Fat Supernatural Wedding, 2006; Chasing Midnight, 2007; Dark of the Moon, 2008; Come The Night, 2008; Lord of Legends, 2009; Lord of Sin, 2009; (co-author) Bespelling Jane Austen, 2010; Bride of the Wolf, 2010; Luck of the Wolf, 2010; Code of the Wolf, 2011. Contributor to books. **Address:** PO Box 51924, Albuquerque, NM 87181, U.S.A. **Online address:** susankrinard@comcast.net

KRINSKY, Natalie. American (born United States), b. 1982?. **Genres:** Novels, Young Adult Fiction, Literary Criticism And History. **Career:** Writer. **Publications:** Chloe Does Yale, 2005. Contributor to periodicals. **Address:** c/o Joni Evans, William Morris Agency, 1325 Ave. of the Americas, New York, NY 10019, U.S.A.

KRIPAL, Jeffrey J. American (born United States), b. 1962?. **Genres:** Theology/Religion, History, Sex. **Career:** Rice University, Department of Religious Studies, Lynette Autry associate professor of religious studies, 2002-, chair, J. Newton Rayzor chair in philosophy and religious thought and J. Newton Rayzor professor of religious studies, 2004-. Writer. **Publications:** Kāli's Child: The Mystical and the Erotic in the Life and Teachings of Ramakrishna, 1995, 2nd ed., 1998; (ed. with T.G. Vaidyanathan) Vishnu on Freud's Desk: A Reader in Psychoanalysis and Hinduism, 1999; Roads of Excess, Palaces of Wisdom: Eroticism & Reflexivity in the Study of Mysticism, 2001; (ed. with G.W. Barnard) Crossing Boundaries: Essays on the Ethical Status of Mysticism, 2002; (ed. with R.F. McDermott) Encountering Kali: In the Margins, at the Center, in the West, 2003; (ed. with G.W. Shuck) On the Edge of the Future: Esalen and the Evolution of American Culture, 2005; The Serpent's Gift: Gnostic Reflections on the Study of Religion, 2007; Esalen: America and the Religion of No Religion, 2007; (ed. with W.J. Hanegraaff) Hidden Intercourse: Eros and Sexuality in the History of Western Esotericism, 2008; Authors of the Impossible: The Paranormal and the Sacred, 2010; Mutants and Mystics: Science Fiction, Superhero Comics, and the Paranormal, 2011. Contributor to books and periodicals. **Address:** Department of Religious Studies, Rice University, MS-15, 6100 Main St., PO Box 1892, Houston, TX 77005-1827, U.S.A. **Online address:** jjkripal@rice.edu

KRISE, Thomas W(arren). American (born United States), b. 1961. **Genres:** Literary Criticism And History. **Career:** U.S. Air Force Academy, instructor in English, 1989-91, assistant professor of English, 1991-92, 1997-99, associate professor, 1999-2002, professor, 2002-05, Air Force Humanities Institute, founding director; University of Central Florida, Department of English, chair, 2005-07, professor of English, 2005-08; University of the Pacific, College of the Pacific, dean, 2008-, Department of English, professor; National Defense University, Institute for National Strategic Studies, senior military fellow, National Defense University Press, vice director. Writer. **Publications:** (Ed. and intro.) Caribbeana: An Anthology of English Literature of the West Indies, 1657-1777, 1999. Contributor to periodicals. **Address:** College of the Pacific, University of the Pacific, WPC 110, 3601 Pacific Ave., Stockton, CA 95211-0110, U.S.A. **Online address:** tkrise@mail.ucf.edu

KRISHER, Trudy (B.). American (born United States), b. 1946. **Genres:** Young Adult Fiction, Novels, Children's Non-fiction, Adult Non-fiction, Young Adult Non-fiction, Writing/Journalism. **Career:** University of Dayton, assistant professor and campus writing center coordinator, 1985-2001; Sinclair Community College, professor, 2001-. Writer. **Publications:** Kathy's Hats: A Story of Hope, 1990; Spite Fences, 1994; Writing for a Reader: Peers, Process, and Progress in the Writing Classroom, 1995; Kinship, 1997; Uncommon Faith, 2003; Fallout, 2006. Contributor to periodicals. Works appear in anthologies. **Address:** c/o Danielle Egan-Miller, Browne & Miller Literary Associates, 410 S Michigan Ave., Ste. 460, Chicago, IL 60605-1465, U.S.A. **Online address:** trudy.krisher@sinclair.edu

KRISHNA, K. R. Indian (born India), b. 1954. **Genres:** Agriculture/Forestry, Environmental Sciences/Ecology. **Career:** Indian Institute of Horticultural

Research, senior technical assistant, 1977-78; International Crops Research Institute for the Semi-Arid Tropics, scientist in cereals, 1981-88, scientist in microbiology and cell biology, 1988-89, scientist in crop physiology and agronomy, 1989-92; University of Florida, visiting professor, 1994-96. Writer. **Publications:** (With G. Hunsigi) The Science of Field Crop Production, 1998; (ed.) Soil Fertility and Crop Production, 2002; Agrosphere: Nutrient Dynamics, Ecology, and Productivity, 2003; Mycorrhizas: A Molecular Analysis, 2005; Peanut Agroecosystem: Nutrient Dynamcis and Productivity, 2008; Agroecosystems of South India: Nutrient Dynamics, Ecology and Productivity, 2010. **Address:** 211/7 9th Cross, J. P. Nagar 2nd Phase, Bangalore, KA 560078, India. **Online address:** krkrish007@rediffmail.com

KRISHNASWAMI, Uma. American/Indian (born India), b. 1956. **Genres:** Children's Fiction, Mythology/Folklore, Children's Non-fiction, Novels, Picture/Board Books. **Career:** Freelance writer, 1997-; Vermont College of Fine Arts, MFA Program in Writing for Children and Young Adults, faculty, 2006-. **Publications:** RETELLER: Stories of the Flood, 1994; The Broken Tusk: Stories of the Hindu God Ganesha, 1996; Shower of Gold: Girls and Women in the Stories of India, 1999. NONFICTION: Beyond the Field Trip: Teaching and Learning in Public Places (for teachers), 2001. PICTURE BOOKS: Yoga Class, 2000; Hello Flower, 2002; Chachaji's Cup, 2003; Monsoon, 2003; Holi, 2003; The Closet Ghosts, 2005; The Happiest Tree: A Yoga Story, 2005; Bringing Asha Home, 2006; Remembering Grandpa, 2007; Out of the Way! Out of the Way!, 2010. NOVELS: Naming Maya, 2004; The Grand Plan to Fix Everything, 2011. OTHER: (with R. Khan and E. Carbone) Many Windows, 2007. Contributor to magazines. **Address:** c/o Anna Webman, Curtis Brown Ltd., 10 Astor Pl., New York, NY 10003, U.S.A. **Online address:** uma@umakrishnaswami.com

KRISKA, Laura J. American (born United States) **Genres:** Novels, Women's Studies And Issues, Economics. **Career:** Honda Motor Co., trainee and factory worker. Writer. **Publications:** The Accidental Office Lady, 1997; The Accidental Office Lady: An American Woman in Corporate Japan, 2011. **Address:** Charles E. Tuttle Co., Airport Industrial Pk., RR1, PO Box 231-5, North Clarendon, VT 05759, U.S.A.

KRISLOV, Samuel. American (born United States), b. 1929. **Genres:** Social Sciences, Politics/Government. **Career:** University of Vermont, instructor in political science, 1955; Hunter College, instructor in political science, 1955-56; University of Oklahoma, Department of Political Science, assistant professor, 1956-60, associate professor, 1960-61; Michigan State University, visiting assistant professor, 1959-61, associate professor of political science, 1961-, School of Labor and Industrial Relations, research associate, 1961-64; University of Minnesota, Department of Political Science and Law, associate professor, 1964-65, professor, 1965-, chairman, 1969-72, 1975-78, 1984-85; Columbia University, visiting professor of political science, 1966; Brandeis University, visiting professor, 1978-79; University of California, Boalt Hall Law School, visiting professor; Fudan University, Law Schools, visiting professor; Marie Curie University, visiting professor; Bogazici University, visiting professor; Law and Society Association, president; Midwest Political Science Association, president. Writer. **Publications:** The Supreme Court in the Political Process, 1965; The Negro in the Federal Employment, 1967; (with R. Dixon, A.S. Miller and L. Huston) Roles of the Attorney General of the U.S., 1968; The Supreme Court and the Political Process, 1968; The Supreme Court and Political Freedom, 1968; (with M. Feeley and S. White) The Judicial Process and Constitutional Law (lab manual), 1972; Representative Bureaucracy, 1974; Rise of Consumerism in the U.S. Courts, 1980; Representative Bureaucracy and the American Political System, 1981; American Constitutional Law, 1984; (with M. Feeley) Constitutional Law, 1985, 2nd ed., 1990; How Nations Choose Product Standards, 1997. EDITOR: (with R.L. Lee and J.A. Burkhart) American Government: The Clash of Issues, 1960, 9th ed., 1989; (with L.D. Musolf) The Politics of Regulation, 1964; (with K. Boyum, R. Schaffer and S. White) Compliance and the Law: A Multi-Disciplinary Approach, 1972; (co-ed.) Clash of Issues: Readings and Problems in American Government, 1976, 9th ed., 1989; (co-ed.) Understanding Crime, 1977; (with K.O. Boyum) Forecasting the Impact of Legislation on Courts, 1980. Contributor to periodicals. **Address:** Department of Political Science, University of Minnesota, Rm. 1414, Social Sciences Bldg., 229-19th Ave. S, Minneapolis, MN 55455, U.S.A. **Online address:** krisl001@umn.edu

KRIST, Gary (Michael). American (born United States), b. 1957. **Genres:** Novels, Novellas/Short Stories, Travel/Exploration, Adult Non-fiction, Histo-

ry. **Career:** Writer and historian. **Publications:** STORIES: The Garden State, 1988; Bone by Bone, 1994. NOVELS: Bad Chemistry, 1997; Chaos Theory, 2000; Extravagance, 2002. NONFICTION: The White Cascade: The Great Northern Railway Disaster and America's Deadliest Avalanche, 2007; City of Scoundrels: The 12 Days of Disaster that Gave Birth to Modern Chicago, 2012. **Address:** 4225 Sleaford Rd , Bethesda, MD 20814, U.S.A. **Online address:** gary@garykrist.com

KRISTAL, Efrain. American (born United States), b. 1959?. **Genres:** Literary Criticism And History. **Career:** University of California, Department of Comparative Literature, professor of Spanish and comparative literature, chair. Writer. **Publications:** The Andes Viewed from the City: Literary and Political Discourse on the Indian in Peru, 1848-1930, 1987; Temptation of the Word: The Novels of Mario Vargas Llosa, 1998; Invisible Work: Borges and Translation, 2002; (ed.) The Cambridge Companion to the Latin American Novel, 2005; Introduction to The Complete Poetry of Cãesar Vallejo, 2007; (ed. and intro.) Poems of the Night, 2010; (ed. with P.M. Logan, O. George and S. Hegeman) Encyclopedia of the Novel, 2011; (ed. with J. King) The Cambridge companion to Mario Vargas Llosa, 2012; Peter Sloterdijk and literature, forthcoming; Art and Literature in the Liquid Modern Age, forthcoming. **Address:** Department of Comparative Literature, University of California, Humanities 350A, 350 Humanities Bldg., Los Angeles, CA 90095, U.S.A. **Online address:** kristal@ucla.edu

KRISTEVA, Julia. (Julia Joyaux). French (born France), b. 1941. **Genres:** Novels, Language/Linguistics, Literary Criticism And History. **Career:** Laboratoire d'anthropologie sociale, research assistant, 1967-73; University of Paris VII, instructor, 1972, professor of linguistics, 1973-99, professeur classe exceptionelle, 1999-; Columbia University, visiting professor, 1974-; University of Toronto, visiting professor, 1992; linguist; literary theorist. Writer. **Publications:** NONFICTION: Semeiotike, Recherce pour une semanalyse, 1969, trans. as Desire in Language, 1980; (as Julia Joyaux) Le Langage, cet inconnu, 1969, trans. as Language: The Unknown, 1989; Le Texte du roman, 1970; Lapu Revolution du langage poetique, 1974, trans. as Revolution in Poetic Language, 1984; Des Chinoises, 1974; (co-author) La Traversee des signes, 1975; Polylogue, 1977; About Chinese Women, 1977; (with J.M. Ribettes) Folle Verite, verite et vraisemblance du texte psychotique, 1980; Pouvoirs de l'horreur, 1980; Histoires d'amour, 1983; Au commencement etait l'amour: psychanalyse et foi, 1985; A Kristeva Reader, 1986; In the Beginning Was Love: Psychoanalysis and Faith, 1987; Soleil noir: dépression et mélancolie, 1987, trans. as Black Sun, 1989; Etrangers à nous-mêmes, 1988; Lettre ouverte à Harlem Désir, 1990; Strangers to Ourselves, 1991; The Samurai: A Novel, 1992; Les Nouvelles Maladies de l'ame, 1993; Nations without Nationalism, 1993; The Old Man and the Wolves, 1994; Le Temps sensible, Proust et l'Experience litteraire, 1994; Sens et non-sens de la revolte, 1996; La Revolte intime, 1997; Contre la depression nationale: Conversation avec Philippe Petit, 1997; L'avenir d'une revolte, 1998; Visions capitales, 1998; (with C. Clement) Le Feminin et le Sacre, 1998; Le Genie feminin, vol. I: Hannah Arendt, 1999, vol. II: Melanie Klein, 2000, vol. III: Colette, 2002; Crisis of the European Subject, 2000; Female Genius: Life, Madness, Words: Hannah Arendt, Melanie Klein, Colette, 2001; Lettre au prèsident de la Rèpublique sur les citoyens en situation de handicap, 2003; Meurtre a Byzance, 2004; La cruauté au féminine, 2004; L'amour de soi et ses avatars: Demesure et limites de la sublimation, 2005; La haine et le pardon, 2005; Handicap, le temps des engagements: Premiers états generaux, 2006; Diversité et culture, 2007; (contrib.) Europe des cultures et culture européenne: communauté et diversité, 2008; (contrib.) Guerre et paix des sexes, 2009; Hatred and Forgiveness, 2010; The Severed Head: Capital Visions, 2011; This Incredible Need to Believe, 2011; (with J. Vanier) Leur regard perce nos ombres: échange, 2011. NOVELS: Les Samourais, 1990; Le Vieil Homme et les loups, 1991; Possessions, 1996; Murder in Byzantium, 2006; Thérèse mon amour, 2008. EDITOR: (with T. Sebeok) Approaches to Semiotics, vol. I, 1969; (with J.R. Debove and D.J. Umiker) Essays in Semiotics, 1971; Epistemologie de la linguistique. Hommage a Emile Benveniste, 1971; (with J.C. Milner and N. Ruwet) Langue, discours, societe: pour Emile Benveniste, 1975. Contributor to periodicals. **Address:** Universite de Paris VII-Denis Diderot, UFR de Sciences des Textes et Documents, 2 Pl. Jussieu, Paris, 75251, France. **Online address:** kristeva@paris7.jussieu.fr

KRITZ, Mary M. American (born United States) **Genres:** Demography, Sociology. **Career:** Wellesley College, Leadership Institute for Latin American, group facilitator; University of Wisconsin, teaching assistant; Purdue University, assistant professor of sociology and anthropology, 1972-74; Rockefeller Foundation, program associate, 1974, assistant director of social sciences, 1975-78, assistant director of population sciences, 1979-82, associate director of population sciences, 1983-89; Cornell University, associate professor of rural sociology, 1989-97, Population and Development Program, associate director, 1989-, senior research associate, 1997-2009, New York Census Research Data Center, special sworn status researcher, 2007-, research adjunct, 2009-; Population Association of America, board director, 1989-92; World Health Organization, consultant, 1992-93; Fordham University, Department of Sociology and Anthropology, consultant. Writer. **Publications:** EDITOR: Migraciones internacionales en las Americas, 1980; (with C.B. Keely and S.M. Tomasi) Global Trends in Migration: Theory and Research on International Population Movements, 1981; U.S. Immigration and Refugee Policy: Global and Domestic Issues, 1983; (with L.L. Lim and H. Zlotnik and contrib.) International Migration Systems: A Global Approach, 1992; (with D. Gurak) Immigration and a Changing America, 2004. OTHERS: The New American Mosaic: Immigrant Group Diversity in Settlement and Integration, forthcoming; U.S. Internal Migration, Immigrants and New Destinations, forthcoming; Implications of Globalisation and Tertiary Education Trends for International Student Mobility and Brain Drain, forthcoming; Elderly Immigrants in Rural America: Trends and Characteristics, forthcoming; International Student Mobility and Tertiary Education Capacity in Africa, forthcoming; African International Student Mobility: Country Differences in Numbers and Destinations, forthcoming. **Address:** Department of Development Sociology, Cornell University, 221 Warren Hall, Ithaca, NY 14853-7801, U.S.A. **Online address:** mmk5@cornell.edu

KRITZER, Amelia Howe. American (born United States), b. 1947. **Genres:** Theatre, Women's Studies And Issues. **Career:** University of Wisconsin-Madison, research and editorial assistant for Theatre Journal, 1984-85, lecturer in English, 1989-90; University of Wisconsin-Milwaukee, lecturer in theater and dance, 1989; Indiana University-Bloomington, visiting assistant professor of theater and drama, 1990-91; West Virginia University, assistant professor of theater, 1991-95; University of St. Thomas, professor of English and theater, 1997-, chair of theater department, 1998-. **Publications:** The Plays of Caryl Churchill: Theatre of Empowerment, 1991; (ed.) Plays by Early American Women, 1775-1850, 1994; Political Theatre in Post-Thatcher Britain: New Writing, 1995-2005, 2008; (contrib.) Ethnicity and Identity: Global Performance, 2005. Works appear in anthologies. Contributor of articles to journals. **Address:** Department of Theater, University of St. Thomas, CSC 209 Speech/Theater Bldg., LOR 210A, 2115 Summit Ave., St. Paul, MN 55105, U.S.A. **Online address:** ahkritzer@stthomas.edu

KRITZLER, Ed. Jamaican/American (born United States), b. 1941?. **Genres:** History, Theology/Religion. **Career:** Jamaican Tourist Board, travel writer; Government of Jamaica, film liaison officer. Historian. **Publications:** Jewish Pirates of the Caribbean: How a Generation of Swashbuckling Jews Carved Out an Empire in the New World in Their Quest for Treasure, Religious Freedom and Revenge, 2008. **Address:** Kingston, Jamaica. **Online address:** edkritzler@yahoo.com

KRIVICH, Mikhail. Russian (born Russia) **Genres:** Criminology/True Crime, Mystery/Crime/Suspense. **Career:** Writer. **Publications:** (Co-author) Chikatilo i ego zhertvy, 1996. **Address:** Barricade Books Inc., 185 Bridge Plz. N, Ste. 309, Fort Lee, NJ 07024, U.S.A.

KRIZAN, Kim. American (born United States), b. 1961. **Genres:** Film, Plays/Screenplays, Young Adult Fiction. **Career:** Writer and actor. **Publications:** (With R. Linklater and G. Brandenstein) Before Sunrise: A Film, 1995; Before Sunset, 2005. **Address:** Vintage Publicity, 1745 Broadway, New York, NY 10019, U.S.A.

KROEGER, Brooke. American (born United States), b. 1949. **Genres:** Biography, Sociology, Communications/Media. **Career:** United Press Intl., reporter-Chicago, 1973-76, correspondent-Brussels, 1977, correspondent-London, 1978-79, correspondent-Tel Aviv, 1979-80, bureau chief-Tel Aviv, 1981-83, editor-Europe, the Middle East and Africa, 1983-84; Newsday-New York, United Nations correspondent and deputy metropolitan editor, 1984-87; New York University, professor of journalism, 1998-, department chair, 2005-11, Arthur L. Carter Journalism Institute, director, 2008-11, Global and Joint Program Studies, director; New York Times Co., Local East Village, faculty liaison. Writer. **Publications:** Nellie Bly: Daredevil, Reporter,

Feminist, 1994; Fannie: The Talent for Success of Writer Fannie Hurst, 1999; Passing: When People Can't Be Who They Are, 2003; Undercover Reporting: The Truth About Deception, 2012. Contributor to magazines and newspapers. **Address:** Arthur L. Carter Journalism Institute, New York University, 20 Cooper Sq., 6th Fl., New York, NY 10003, U.S.A. **Online address:** brooke.kroeger@nyu.edu

KROHN, Claus-Dieter. German (born Germany), b. 1941. **Genres:** History, Biography, Social Sciences. **Career:** Free University of Berlin, assistant professor, 1973-76; Leuphana University Luneburg, professor of modern history, 1977-2007, now retired. Writer. **Publications:** Stabilisierung und Oekonomische Juteressen, 1974; Wirtschaftstheorien als Politische Interessen, 1981; Wissenschaft im Exil, 1987; Der Philosophische Oekonom: Zur Intellektuellen Biographie Adolph Lowes, 1996; (co-author) Rueckkehr und Aufbau nach 1945: Deutsche Remigranten im Offentlichen Leben Nachkriegsdeutschlands, 1997; (co-author) Handbuch der Deutschsprachigen Emigration 1933-1945, 1998, 2nd ed. 2008; (co-author) Biographisches Handbuch der Deutschsprachigen Wirtschaftswissenschaftlichen Emigration nach 1933, 1999; (with M. Schumacher) Exil und Neuordnung: Beitraege zur Verfassungspolitischen Entwicklung in Deutschland nach 1945, 2000; Philipp Scheidemann. Das historische Versagen der SPD: Schriften aus dem Exil, 2002; (with A. Schildt) Zwischen den Stuehlen?: Remigranten und Remigration in der Deutschen Medienoeffentlichkeit der Nachkriegszeit, 2002; (with I. von der Luehe) Fremdes Heimatland: Remigration und literarisches Leben nach 1945, 2005; Arnold Brecht, 1884-1977: Demokratischer Beamter und Politischer Wissenschaftler in Berlin und New York, 2006. **Address:** Scheideweg 28, Hamburg, D-20253, Germany. **Online address:** cdkrohn@web.de

KROHN, Katherine E(lizabeth). American/German (born Germany), b. 1961. **Genres:** Children's Fiction, Children's Non-fiction, Biography, Graphic Novels. **Career:** Writer, 1991-. **Publications:** BIOGRAPHIES FOR CHILDREN: Lucille Ball: Pioneer of Comedy, 1992; Roseanne Arnold: Comedy's Queen Bee, 1993; Elvis Presley: The King, 1994; Marilyn Monroe: Norma Jean's Dream, 1996; Marcia Clark: Voice for the Victims, 1996; Princess Diana, 1999; Rosie O'Donnell, 1999; Women of the Wild West, 2000; Ella Fitzgerald: First Lady of Song, 2001; Oprah Winfrey, 2002; Sojourner Truth, 2006; Madam C.J. Walker, 2006; Wild West Women, 2006; Jane Goodall, 2006; Jonas Salk and the Polio Vaccine, 2007; Evelyn Cisneros: Prima Ballerina, 2007; Gwen Stefani, 2008; Michael Jackson: Ultimate Music Legend, 2010; Stephenie Meyer: Dreaming of Twilight, 2011. OTHER: Everything You Need to Know about Birth Order, 2000; Everything You Need to Know about Living on Your Own, 2000; You and Your Parents' Divorce, 2001; Is This Funny or What? (Full House Michelle and Friends), 2001; Haunted Houses, 2006; Jane Goodall: Animal Scientist, 2006; Vera Wang, 2007; Shakira, 2008; The Earth-Shaking Facts about Earthquakes with Max Axiom, Super Scientist, 2008; 1918 Flu Pandemic, 2008; Fortune Telling, 2009; Refreshing Look at Renewable Energy with Max Axiom, Super Scientist, 2010; Whirlwind World of Hurricanes with Max Axiom, Super Scientist, 2011. **Address:** Lerner Publications, 241 1st Ave. N, Minneapolis, MN 55401, U.S.A. **Online address:** author@katherinekrohn.com

KROKER, Arthur (W.). Canadian (born Canada), b. 1945. **Genres:** Art/Art History, Communications/Media, Information Science/Computers, Literary Criticism And History, Politics/Government. **Career:** University of Winnipeg, assistant professor, 1975-80, director of Canadian studies, 1979-80, associate professor of political science, 1980-81; Concordia University, associate professor, 1981-87, professor of political science, 1987-; Simone de Beauvoir Institute, associate fellow, 1984-85, Concordia Centre for Broadcasting Studies, research fellow, 1984-86; Detroit Institute of Arts, writer-in-residence, 1989; University of Victoria, Department of Political Science, Canada research chair, professor of political science, Pacific Centre for Technology and Culture, director. Writer. **Publications:** Technology and the Canadian Mind: Innis, McLuhan, and Grant, 1984, 2nd ed., 1987, 1985; (with D. Cook) The Postmodern Scene: Excremental Culture and Hyper-Aesthetics, 1986, 2nd ed., 1987; (with D. Cook and M. Kroker) Panic Encyclopedia: The Definitive Guide to the Postmodern Scene, 1989; The Possessed Individual: Technology and the French Postmodern, 1992; Spasm: Virtual Reality, Android Music, and Electric Flesh, 1993; (with M.A. Weinstein) Data Trash: The Theory of the Virtual Class, 1994; (with M. Kroker) Hacking the Future: Stories for the Flesh-Eating 90s, 1996; Will to Technology and the Culture of Nihilism: Heidegger, Nietzsche and Marx, 2004. EDITOR: (co-ed.) Feminism Now: Theory and Practice, 1985; (with M. Kroker and intro.) Body Invaders: Panic Sex in America, 1987; (with M. Kroker) The Hysterical Male: New Feminist

Theory, 1991; (with M. Kroker) Ideology and Power in the Age of Lenin in Ruins, 1991; (with M. Kroker) The Last Sex: Feminism and Outlaw Bodies, 1993; (with M. Kroker) Digital Delirium, St. Martin's, 1997; (with M. Kroker) Critical Digital Studies, 2008. Work appears in anthologies. Contributor to periodicals. **Address:** Department of Political Science, University of Victoria, 3800 Finnerty Rd., SSM A333, PO Box 3050, Victoria, BC V8P 5C2, Canada. **Online address:** akroker@uvic.ca

KROLL, Jerome. American (born United States), b. 1935?. **Genres:** Medicine/Health, Psychology, Theology/Religion. **Career:** Cornell Medical College, instructor in psychiatry, 1966-67, assistant professor, 1969-72; Rockland State Hospital, director of training, 1972-76; University of Minnesota, Department of Psychiatry, associate professor, 1976-87, professor, 1987-, Community-University Health Care Center, staff psychiatrist. Writer. **Publications:** (With M. Roth) The Reality of Mental Illness, 1986; The Challenge of the Borderline Patient: Competency in Diagnosis and Treatment, 1988; PTSD/Borderlines in Therapy: Finding the Balance, 1993; (with B. Bachrach) The Mystic Mind: The Psychology of Medieval Mystics and Ascetics, 2005. **Address:** Department of Psychiatry, University of Minnesota, F282/2A W, 2450 Riverside Ave. S, Minneapolis, MN 55454, U.S.A. **Online address:** kroll001@umn.edu

KROLL, Mark. American (born United States), b. 1946. **Genres:** Music, History, Biology. **Career:** University of California, lecturer in music, 1971-74; Emerson College, lecturer in music, 1976-78; Boston University, professor of music, Department of Historical Performance, chairman, 1978-2002, professor emeritus, 2002-; Boston Early Music Festival, founder and program chairman, 1981-83; Zagreb Musical Academy, visiting professor, 1989; Belgrade Music Academy, visiting professor, 1989; Würzburg Conservatory, visiting professor, 1993; Northeastern University, visiting professor, 2005; WBUR-FM Radio, music critic; Opera New England, artistic director. Writer. **Publications:** (ed.) Mozart's Haffner and Linz Symphonies, 2000; (ed.) Twelve Select Overtures, 2003; (ed. with L. Lockwood) The Beethoven Violin Sonatas: History, Criticism, Performance, 2004; Playing the Harpsichord Expressively: A Practical and Historical Guide, 2004; Johann Nepomuk Hummel: A Musician's Life and World, 2007. Contributor to periodicals. **Address:** Brookline, MA , U.S.A. **Online address:** m-kroll@rcn.com

KROLL, Virginia L(ouise). Also writes as Louisa Fox, Melrose Cooper. American (born United States), b. 1948. **Genres:** Children's Fiction, Children's Non-fiction, Picture/Board Books, Young Adult Fiction, Writing/Journalism. **Career:** Teacher, 1968-69, 1980-81; Hamburg Memorial Youth Center, recreation assistant, 1978-80; writer, 1984-; Medaille College, college instructor, 1993; Institute of Children's Literature, instructor, 1999-. **Publications:** PICTURE BOOKS: Helen the Fish, 1992; Wood-hoopoe Willie, 1992; My Sister, Then and Now, 1992; Masai and I, 1992; Naomi Knows It's Springtime, 1993; Africa Brothers and Sisters, 1993; A Carp for Kimiko, 1993; When Will We Be Sisters?, 1993; Jaha and Jamil went Down the Hill, 1994; Hats Off to Hair!, 1994; I Wanted to Know All about God, 1994; Beginnings, 1994; Pink Paper Swans, 1994; Sweet Magnolia, 1994; The Seasons and Someone, 1994; New Friends, True Friends, Stuck-Like-Glue Friends, 1994; Fireflies, Peach Pies and Lullabies, 1995; Shelter Folks, 1995; Can You Dance, Dalila?, 1996; Christmas Cow, 1996; Butterfly Boy, 1997; Hands!, 1997; Motherlove, 1998; With Love, to Earth's Endangered Peoples, 1998; The Making of Angels, 1998; Faraway Drums, 1998; When God Made the Tree, 1999; Lunching and Munching, 1999; Cat!, 1999; She Is Born!, 1999; Girl, You're Amazing, 2001; Kingston's Flowering Forest, 2001; Bluffy's Mighty Mountain, 2001; Flurry's Frozen Tundra, 2001; Especially Heroes, 2003; Busy, Busy Mouse, 2003; Boy, You're Amazing!, 2004; Marta and the Manger Straw, 2005; Equal, Shmequal, 2005; Jason Takes Responsibility, 2005; Forgiving a Friend, 2005; Brianna Breathes Easy: A Story about Asthma, 2005; Really Rabbits, 2006; Selvakumar Knew Better, 2006; Uno dos Tres Posada: Let's Celebrate Christmas, 2006; Cristina Keeps a Promise, 2006; Good Neighbor Nicholas, 2006; Honest Ashley, 2006; Let there be llamas!, 2006; On the Way to Kindergarten, 2006; Ryan Respects, 2006; Everybody has a Teddy Bear, 2007; Good Citizen Sarah, 2007; Makayla Cares about Others, 2007; Thanksgiving Bowl, 2007; Easter Eggs for Anya: A Ukrainian Celebration of New Life in Christ, 2007; Saying Grace: A Prayer of Thanksgiving, 2009; Luisa's Christmas Piñata: A Celebration of the Journey to Bethlehem, 2010; Mosquito, 2011. AS MELROSE COOPER: I Got a Family, 1993; Life Riddles, 1993; I Got Community, 1995; Life Magic, 1996; Gettin' through Thursday, 1998; Pets!, 1998; The Seven Days of Kwanzaa, 2007. AS LOUISA FOX: Every Monday in the Mailbox, 1995. Contributor

to periodicals. **Address:** c/o Publicity Director, Simon & Schuster Children's Publishing, 1230 Ave. of the Americas, New York, NY 10020, U.S.A.

KRONDL, Michael. American (born United States) **Genres:** Food And Wine. **Career:** Food journalist, 1985-. **Publications:** (trans.) Alain Senderens, The Table Beckons: Thoughts and Recipes from the Kitchen of Alain Senderens, 1993; Around the American Table: Treasured Recipes and Food Traditions from the American Cookery Collections of the New York Public Library, 1995; The Great Little Pumpkin Cookbook, 1998; The Taste of Conquest: The Rise and Fall of the Three Great Cities of Spice, 2007. Contributor to periodicals. **Address:** New York, NY , U.S.A. **Online address:** michael@spicehistory.net

KRONDORFER, Björn. American/German (born Germany), b. 1959. **Genres:** Theology/Religion, History, Social Sciences. **Career:** Jewish-German Dance Theatre, co-founder, 1985-89; Lehigh University, adjunct lecturer in religion and history, 1990; St. Marys College, visiting assistant professor, associate professor of religious studies, 1992-, Department for Philosophy and Religious Studies, professor, chair, Faculty Senate, vice president; Oxford University Press, Cultural Criticism Series, series editor, 1998-2003; Men, Masculinities and Spiritualities, book review editor; American Academy of Religion, Mens Studies in Religion Group, co-chair. **Publications:** Remembrance and Reconciliation: Encounters between Young Jews and Germans, 1995; (with K. von Kellenbach and N. Reck) Mit Blick auf die Täter: Fragen an die deutsche Theologie nach 1945, 2006; Men and Masculinities in Christianity and Judaism: A Critical Reader, 2009; Male Confessions: Intimate Revelations and the Religious Imagination, 2010. EDITOR: Body and Bible: Interpreting and Experiencing Biblical Narratives, 1992; Men's Bodies, Men's Gods: Male Identities in a (Post) Christian Culture, 1996; (and afterword) My Father's Testament: Memoir of a Jewish Teenager, 1938-1945, 2000; (with K. von Kellenbach and N. Reck) Von Gott reden im Land der Tater: Theologische Stimmen der dritten Generation seit der Shoah, 2001; (with B. Huhnke) Das Vermächtnis Annehmen: Kulturelle und Biographische Zugange zum Holocaust, 2002. Contributor to books and periodicals. **Address:** Department of Philosophy & Religious Studies, St. Mary's College of Maryland, Rm. 110-A, Anne Arundel Hall, 18952 E Fisher Rd., St. Marys City, MD 20686-3001, U.S.A. **Online address:** bhkrondorfer@smcm.edu

KRONEN, Steve. American (born United States), b. 1953. **Genres:** Poetry. **Career:** Miami Dade College, librarian. Writer. **Publications:** Empirical Evidence: Poems, 1992; Splendor, 2006. **Address:** Miami Dade College, Rm. 1128, 3800 NW 115th Ave., Doral, FL 33178, U.S.A. **Online address:** skronen@gmail.com

KRONENFELD, Jennie J(acobs). American (born United States), b. 1949. **Genres:** Medicine/Health, Social Sciences. **Career:** Brown University, teaching assistant, 1972-73; University of Alabama, assistant professor, 1975-80, associate professor, 1980-, Multi-purpose Arthritis Center, scientist, 1980; University of South Carolina, associate professor, 1980-85, professor of public health, 1985-90, Department of Health Education, adjunct associate professor, 1985-90, Department of Health Administration, director of doctoral programs, 1985-90; Arizona State University, professor of health administration and policy, 1990-99, professor of sociology, 1999-2006, Department of Sociology, interim chair, 2004-06, Program in Sociology, School of Social and Family Dynamics, professor, 2006-, Women's Studies Program, affiliate professor, 2006-. Writer. **Publications:** (Contrib.) Monitoring Health Status and Medical Care, 1976; (ed. with E.D. Charles, Jr.) The Social and Economic Impacts of Coronary Artery Disease, 1980; (with M.L. Whicker) U.S. National Health Policy: An Analysis of the Federal Role, 1984; (with Whicker) Sex Role Changes: Technology, Politics, and Policy, 1986; (with Whicker) Captive Populations: Caring for the Young, the Sick, the Imprisoned, and the Elderly, 1990; Controversial Issues in Health Care Policy, 1993; (with Whicker and R.A. Strickland) Getting Tenure, 1993; (with Whicker) Confronting Ethical Dilemmas in Research and Technology, 1994; (with M.L. Whicker) Dealing With Ethical Dilemmas on Campus, 1994; The Changing Federal Role in U.S. Health Care Policy, 1997; (with M.L. Whicker) Job Strategies: Getting An Academic Job, 1997; (ed.) Health Care Providers, Institutions, and Patients: Changing Patterns of Care Provision and Care Delivery, 2000; Schools and the Health of Children: Protecting Our Future, 2000; (ed.) Social Inequalities, Health and Health Care Delivery, 2002; Health Care Policy: Issues and Trends, 2002; (with M.R. Kronenfeld) Healthcare Reform in America: A Reference Handbook, 2004; Expansion of Publicly Funded Health Insurance in the United States: The Children's Health Insurance Program and Its Implications, 2006; Medicare, 2011. Works appear in anthologies. Contributor to journals. **Address:** Department of Sociology, Arizona State University, 120C COWDN, 699 S Mill Ave., PO Box 3701, Tempe, AZ 85281, U.S.A. **Online address:** jennie.kronenfeld@asu.edu

KRONINGER, Stephen. American (born United States) **Genres:** Art/Art History, Illustrations, Young Adult Fiction, Children's Fiction, Poetry. **Career:** East Village Eye, staff; National Lampoon, staff; Esquire, staff; New York Times, staff. Writer, graphic artist and educator. **Publications:** Nuclear Warheads: Artists Draw the Line, 1983; What the Songs Look Like: Contemporary Artists Interpret Talking Heads Lyrics, 1987; Album Cover/Album 5: The Fifth Book of Record Jackets, 1989; The Savage Mirror: The Art of Contemporary Caricature, 1992; Angry Graphics, 1992; Go Naked No. 1, 1993. SELF-ILLUSTRATED: If I Crossed the Road, 1997. Illustrator of books by others. **Address:** c/o Author Mail, Simon & Schuster Inc., 1230 Ave. of the Americas, New York, NY 10020, U.S.A. **Online address:** skron@nyc.rr.com

KROODSMA, Donald E. American (born United States), b. 1946. **Genres:** Novels, Animals/Pets. **Career:** University of Massachusetts, professor of biology, professor emeritus, 2004-. Ornithologist, writer. **Publications:** (Ed. with E.H. Miller and H. Ouellet) Acoustic Communication in Birds, 1982; (ed. with E.H. Miller) Ecology and Evolution of Acoustic Communication in Birds, 1996; The Singing Life of Birds: The Art and Science of Listening to Birdsong, 2005; The Backyard Birdsong Guide: Western North America: A Guide to Listening, 2008; Birdsong by the Seasons: A Year of Listening to Birds, 2009. Contributor of articles to periodicals. **Address:** Department of Biology, University of Massachusetts, 221 Morrill Science Ctr., 611 N Pleasant St., Amherst, MA 01003, U.S.A. **Online address:** kroodsma@bio.umass.edu

KROOTH, Richard. American (born United States), b. 1935. **Genres:** Earth Sciences, History, Law, Organized Labor, Politics/Government, Sociology. **Career:** Constitutional attorney, 1962-77; Law and Labor Research Group, director, 1978-79; University of California, professor, 1980-82, research associate, 1989, 1993-; Riverside County Criminal Youth Division, Diversion Team, academic director, 1980-82; Madison Area Technical College, visiting professor, 1983-84; California Institute of Management, professor, 1985-89, research associate, 1987-89; San Francisco State University, lecturer, 1990; Sonoma State University, lecturer, 1991-92; Golden Gate University, adjunct professor, 1993-; Harvest Publishers, editor and publisher. **Publications:** Empire: A Bicentennial Appraisal, 1975; Japan: 5 Stages of Development, 1976; The Great Social Struggle and the Foundations of Social Theory, 3 vols., 1980; Arms and Empire: Imperial Patterns before World War II, 1980; The Struggle for Grenada, 1984; The Dynamics of Enterprise in the American Milieu, vol. I: Socio-Economic Contours, 1985, vol. II: Legal Dimensions, 1988; Common Destiny: Japan and the America in the Global Age, 1990; (with H. Fukurai and E.W. Butler) Race and the Jury, 1993; (with B. Vladimirovitz) The Quest for Freedom, 1993; (with M. Moallem) The Middle East: A Geopolitical Study of the Region in the New Global Era, 1994; Mexico, NAFTA and the Hardships of Progress: Historical Patterns and Shifting Methods of Oppression, 1995; (co-author) Anatomy of the McMartin Child Molestation Trial, 2000; (with H. Fukurai) Race in Jury Box, 2003; Gaia and the Fate of Midas, vol. I, 2003, vol. II, 2004; A Century Passing: Carnegie, Steel and the Fate of Homestead, 2002; (with R. Krooth) Race in the Jury Box: Affirmative Action in Jury Selection, 2003; Gaia and the Fate of Midas: Wrenching Planet Earth, 2009; Blood River: Death on the Sixth of July, A Film Production of the 1892 Homestead Strike, 2010. Contributor to academic journals. Works appera in anthologies. **Address:** PO Box 9515, Berkeley, CA 94709, U.S.A. **Online address:** krooth@yahoo.com

KROPP, Paul. Canadian/American (born United States), b. 1948. **Genres:** Children's Fiction, Young Adult Fiction, Adult Non-fiction, Literary Criticism And History. **Career:** Teacher, 1972-94; writer and editor, 1994-. **Publications:** YOUNG ADULTS NOVELS: Wilted: A Novel, 1980, rev. ed. as You've Seen Enough, 1992; Getting Even, 1986; Moonkid and Liberty, 1988; The Rock, 1989; Ellen, Elena, Luna, 1992; Moonkid and Prometheus, 1997; The Countess and Me, 2002; Running the Bases: Definitely not a Book about Baseball, 2005; Homerun: Another Book Not About Baseball, 2006; (with L. Jamison) HIP Readers Theater Plays, 2007. JUVENILE NOVELS: Fast Times with Fred, 1986; Cottage Crazy, 1988; Ski Stooges, 1992; System Crash, 1998. CANADA ENCOUNTER SERIES: Burn Out, 1982; Dead On, 1982; Dirt Bike, 1982; Fair Play, 1982; No Way, 1982; Runaway, 1982; Hot Cars, 1982; Dope Deal, 1982; Baby, Baby, 1983; Gang War, 1983; Snow Ghost, 1983; Wild One, 1983; Amy's Wish, 1986; Micro Man, 1986; Take

Off, 1986; Get Lost, 1986; Head Lock, 1986; Tough Stuff, 1986; Split Up, 1986. SERIES 2000: Death Ride, 1986; Not Only Me, 1987; Under Cover, 1987; Baby Blues, 1989; Jo's Search, 1989; We Both Have Scars, 1990; The Victim Was Me, 1991; Riot on the Street, 1993; Blizzard, 1995. FOR CHILDREN: Justin, Jay-Jay and the Juvenile Dinkent, 1986; What a Story!, 2002. ADULTS NON-FICTION: The Reading Solution: Make Your Child a Reader, 1993 in US as Raising a Reader: Make Your Child a Reader for Life, 1996, rev. ed. as How to Make Your Child a Reader for Life, 2000; (with L. Hodson) The School Solution: Getting Canada's Schools to Work for Your Children, 1995; I'll Be the Parent, You Be the Kid, 1998; The Write Genre, 2004. JUVENILE AND YOUNG ADULT NOVELS: Tag Team, 2002; Terror 911, 2002; Scarface, 2002; Street Scene, 2002; Hitting the Road, 2002; My Broken Family, 2002; Ghost House, 2003; Show Off, 2003; Playing Chicken, 2003; Caught in the Blizzard, 2003; Student Narc, 2004; The Kid is Lost!, 2004; Against All Odds, 2004; Avalanche, 2005; One Crazy Night, 2005; Juvie, 2006; Foul Shot, 2007. JUNIOR NOVELS: The Crash, 2005; Three Feet Under, 2005; Shooting the Rapids, 2006; I Didn't Do It!, 2007; Winner, 2007. MONSTER BY MISTAKE SERIES: The Big Dog, 2002; (with A. Kapila) Billy Caves In, 2002; (with D. Jarvis) Fossel Remains, 2002; Just Desserts, 2002; Tracy's Magic Show, 2002; Jungle land, 2002; One Big Sneeze, 2002. **Address:** 391 Wellesley St. E, Toronto, ON M4X 1H5, Canada. **Online address:** paul-kropp@sympatico.ca

KROUSE, Erika Dawn. American (born United States), b. 1969. **Genres:** Poetry, Novellas/Short Stories, Young Adult Fiction. **Career:** University of Colorado, English instructor, 1994-96; Sniper Logic, editor, 1995-96; Cencorp, technical publications writer, 1996; Physician Reimbursement Systems, technical writer. **Publications:** Calamity Jane (poetry), 1996; Come up and See Me Sometime (short stories), 2001. Contributor of short stories to periodicals. **Address:** c/o Mary Evans, Mary Evans Inc., 242 E 5th St., New York, NY 10003, U.S.A. **Online address:** erika111@juno.com

KROVATIN, Christopher. American (born United States), b. 1985. **Genres:** Novels, Young Adult Fiction, Literary Criticism And History. **Career:** Revolver Magazine, editor, 2008-. **Publications:** (Ed.) The Best Ghost Stories Ever, 2003; Heavy Metal and You, 2005; Venomous, 2008. Contributor to periodicals. **Address:** c/o Author Mail, Push/Scholastic Inc., 557 Broadway, New York, NY 10012, U.S.A.

KRUCKEBERG, Arthur R(ice). American (born United States), b. 1920. **Genres:** Homes/Gardens, Natural History, Botany, Biology. **Career:** University of Washington, professor of botany, 1950-89, chairman of department, 1971-77, professor emeritus, 1989-; Kruckeberg Botanic Garden, founder, 1958-; Washington Native Plant Society, co-founder; State and Federal Agencies, environmental consultant. Writer. **Publications:** Study of the Perennial Species of Sidalcea, 1957; Gardening with Native Plants of the Pacific Northwest: An Illustrated Guide, 1982, 2nd ed., 1996; California Serpentines: Flora, Vegetation, Geology, Soils and Management Problems, 1984; Natural History of Puget Sound Country, 1991; Natural History of Puget Sound Country, 1991; (ed. with A.E. Leviton and R.B. Walker) Genecology and Ecogeographic Races: Papers in the Biological Sciences, 1995; Geology and Plant Life: The Effects of Landforms and Rock Types on Plants, 2002; (with K. Sykes and C. Romano) Best Wildflower Hikes, Washington, 2004; Introduction to California Soils and Plants: Serpentine, Vernal Pools, and Other Geobotanical Wonders, 2006. Contributor to journals and magazines. **Address:** Department of Biology, University of Washington, 106 Kincaid Hall, PO Box 351800, Seattle, WA 98195-1800, U.S.A. **Online address:** ark@u.washington.edu

KRUEGER, Arnd. *See* KRUGER, Arnd.

KRUEGER, Lesley. Canadian (born Canada) **Genres:** Novels, Travel/Exploration, Young Adult Fiction. **Career:** Ryerson University, faculty; Tasmanian Writers Centre, writer-in-residence; Varuna Writers Centre, writer-in-residence; PEN Canada, director. **Publications:** (With D.J. French and R. Mistry) Coming Attractions, 1986; Hard Travel, 1989; Poor Player, 1993; Drink the Sky, 1999; Foreign Correspondences: A Traveler's Tales, 2000; The Corner Garden, 2003. **Address:** c/o Author Mail, Penguin Books Canada Ltd., 10 Alcorn Ave., Ste. 300, Toronto, ON M4V 3B2, Canada.

KRUG, Manfred. (Manfred G. Krug). German (born Germany), b. 1966. **Genres:** Language/Linguistics. **Career:** Freiburg University, Department of English, staff, 1996-99, assistant professor, 1999-2004, academic assistant professor, 2004-05; Portland State University, visiting professor, 2002; University of Mannheim, professor and chair of English and historical linguistics, 2005-06; University of Bamberg, Department of English, professor, 2005-, head, 2006-11, chair, 2006-, head of the language centre, 2009-. Writer. **Publications:** (As Manfred G. Krug)Emerging English Modals: A Corpus-Based Study of Grammaticalization, 2000; (ed. with R. Facchinetti and F. Palmer) Modality in Contemporary English, 2003; (ed. with J. Schlueter) Research Methods in Language Variation and Change, forthcoming. **Address:** Department of English, University of Bamberg, An der Universität 9, Bamberg, 96045, Germany. **Online address:** manfred.krug@uni-bamberg.de

KRUG, Manfred G. See **KRUG, Manfred.**

KRUGER, Arnd. (Arnd Krueger). German (born Germany), b. 1944. **Genres:** Sports/Fitness, History, Marketing, Popular Culture, Social Sciences. **Career:** German Sports Federation, Germany, managing editor, 1971-74; University of Hambu Training College, university assistant, 1974-78; University of Hamburg, associate professor, 1978-80; University of Goettingen, professor, department head, 1980-2009, School of Social Science, dean, Department of Physical Education, chair; Lower Saxony Institute of Sport History (NISH), President, 2000-; American Academy of Kinesiology and Physical Education, international fellow; European College of Sport History, fellow; Willibald-Gebhardt Institute for Sport and Society, fellow. **Publications:** Sport und Politik, 1975; Theodor Lewald, 1975; Sport und Gesellschaft, 1980; Beitraege zur niedersaechsischen Sportgeschichte: Der Dr.-Bernhard-Zimmermann-Preis, 1984; (with L. Wieser and I. Bartsch) Informationseinrichtungen im Sport, 1991; Ritual and Record, 1990; The Story of Worker Sport, 1996; Nazi Olympics: Sport, Politics, and Appeasement in the 1930s; 2003. Contributor to journals. **Address:** University of Goettingen, 2 Sprangerweg, Raum 412, Goettingen, 37075, Germany. **Online address:** akruege1@gwdg.de

KRÜGER, Michael. German (born Germany), b. 1943. **Genres:** Poetry, Young Adult Fiction. **Career:** Carl Hanser Verlag, reader, 1968-86, chief reader, 1986-; Tintenfisch, editor, 1968-; Akzente, editor, 1976-. **Publications:** POETRY: Kommt, Kinder, wischt die Augen aus, es gibt hier was zu sehen: Die schönsten deutschen Kindergedichte, 1974; Reginapoly: Gedichte, 1976; Was alles hat Platz in einem Gedicht?, 1977; Diderots Katze: Gedichte, 1978; Kunert lesen, 1979; Vaterland, Muttersprache: Deutsche Schriftsteller und ihr Stät seit 1945: Ein Nachlesebuch für die Oberstufe, 1979; Bienek lesen, 1980; Lidas Taschenmuseum: Gedichte, 1981; Aus der Ebene, 1982; Wiederholungen: Gedichte, 1983; Gemütlich summt das Vaterland, 1984; Was tun?: Eine altmodische Geschichte, 1984; Wieso ich?: Eine deutsche Geschichte, 1987; Bausteine zu einer Poetik der Moderne: Festschrift für Walter Höllerer, 1987; Henri Michaux: Bilder, Aquarelle, Zeichnungen, Gedichte, Aphorismen, 1942-1984, 1987; Welt im Wort: Aufsätze und Rezensionen, 1987; Die Dronte: Gedichte, 1988; Warum Peking?: Eine chinesische Geschichte, 1989; Idyllen und Illusionen: Tagebuchgedichte, 1989; Das Ende des Romans: eine Novelle, 1990, trans. as The End of the Novel: A Novella, 1992; The Man in the Tower: A Novel, 1993; Himmelfarb: Roman, 1993, trans. as Der Mann im Turm: Roman, 1994; Brief nach Hause: Gedichte, 1993; Diderot's Cat: Selected Poems, 1994; Nachts, unter Bäumen, 1996; Wettervorhersage: Gedichte, 1998; Aus dem Leben eines Erfolgsschriftstellers: Geschichten, 1998; At Night, Beneath Trees: Selected Poems, 1998; Das Schaf im Schafspelz und andere Satiren aus der Bücherwelt, 2000; Die Cellospielerin: Roman, 2000; Wer das Mondlicht fängt: Bilder und Gedichte, 2001; Das falsche Haus: eine Novelle, 2002; Vorworte, Zwischenbemerkungen, Nachrufe, 2003; Kurz vor dem Gewitter: Gedichte, 2003; Candida Höfer: Monographie, 2003; Cello Player, 2004; (intro.) Candida Höfer: A Monograph, 2004; Turiner Komödie: Bericht eines Nachlassverwalters, 2005, trans. as Executor: A Comedy of Letters, 2006; Unter freiem Himmel: Gedichte, 2007; Schritte, Schatten, Tage, Grenzen, 2008. Contributor to periodicals. **Address:** c/o Author Mail, Harcourt, 6277 Sea Harbor Dr., Orlando, FL 32887, U.S.A.

KRUGER, Wolf. See **HUTSON, Shaun P.**

KRUGLER, David F. American (born United States), b. 1969. **Genres:** Novels. **Career:** University of Illinois at Urbana-Champaign, Department of History, teaching assistant, 1992-95, research assistant, 1992-97, graduate assistant to general education board, 1996-97; University of Wisconsin, assistant professor, 1997-2002, associate professor of history, 2002-. Writer. **Publications:** The Voice of America and the Domestic Propaganda Battles, 1945-1953, 2000; This Is Only a Test: How Washington, D.C. Prepared for Nuclear War, 2006. Contributor to journals and periodicals. **Address:** Social

Sciences Department, University of Wisconsin, 324 Warner Hall, Platteville, WI 53818, U.S.A. **Online address:** kruglerd@uwplatt.edu

KRUGLER, John D. American (born United States), b. 1940. **Genres:** History, Language/Linguistics. **Career:** Marquette University, Department of History, faculty, 1969-71, assistant professor, 1971-77, associate professor, 1977-2007, professor, 2007-, assistant chair, 1979-93, College of Arts and Sciences, associate dean, 1993-96; College of William and Mary, visiting associate professor, 1989, The William and Mary Quarterly, visiting editor, 1989; Historic St. Mary's City Commission, commissioner, 1997-. Historian. **Publications:** English and Catholic: The Lords Baltimore in the Seventeenth Century, 2004. Contributor to books. **Address:** Marquette University, PO Box 1881, Milwaukee, WI 53201-1881, U.S.A. **Online address:** john.krugler@marquette.edu

KRUH, David. American (born United States), b. 1956. **Genres:** History, Local History/Rural Topics, Travel/Exploration, Novels, Plays/Screenplays, Songs/Lyrics And Libretti. **Career:** WRAN-Radio, reporter and copywriter, 1978-80; WVNHRadio, reporter and copywriter, 1980-81; WPIX-FM Radio, copywriter, 1981; WRKO/WROR-FM Radio, staff engineer, 1981-87; Otocom Systems, product manager, 1987-91; WEEI Radio, producer and writer, 1991-92; First Data Technology, business writer, 1992-93; Central Artery Tunnel Project, writer, spokesperson and webmaster, 1994-97; Analog Devices, marketing communications manager, 1997-. **Publications:** Always Something Doing: A History of Boston's Infamous Scollay Square, 1990, 2nd ed., 1999; (with L. Kruh) Presidential Landmarks, 1992; Scollay Square, 2004; Riverbank: The Trail of William Shakespeare, 2005; (with Y. Tsipis) Building Route 128, 2005; Further Fenway Fiction, 2007. Contributor to periodicals. **Address:** Eldridge Publishing Company, PO BOX 14367, Tallahassee, FL 32317, U.S.A. **Online address:** davekruh@comcast.net

KRUMAN, Marc W. (Marc Wayne Kruman). American (born United States), b. 1949. **Genres:** History, Local History/Rural Topics. **Career:** Wayne State University, College of Liberal Arts and Sciences, Department of History, professor of history and chair, 1975-, Center for the Study of Citizenship, director; University of Rome, Fulbright senior lecturer, 1999. Writer. **Publications:** Parties and Politics in North Carolina, 1836-1865, 1983; Between Authority and Liberty: State Constitution Making In Revolutionary America, 1997. **Address:** Department of History, College of Liberal Arts & Sciences, Wayne State University, 3089 Faculty Administration Bldg., 656 W Kirby St., Detroit, MI 48202-3622, U.S.A. **Online address:** m.kruman@wayne.edu

KRUMAN, Marc Wayne. See **KRUMAN, Marc W.**

KRUPNICK, Karen. American (born United States), b. 1947. **Genres:** Children's Non-fiction, Technology, Information Science/Computers. **Career:** Litel Elementary School, teacher, through 1984; Newman Elementary School, teacher. Writer. **Publications:** The Great Race to Nome (for children), 1995; Kids@School.on.the.net, 1997; Teaching K-5 Social Studies Using the Internet, 2000. **Address:** Newman Elementary School, 4150 Walnut Ave., Chino, CA 91710, U.S.A. **Online address:** kkrupnic@cyberg8t.com

KRUPP, Robin Rector. American (born United States), b. 1946. **Genres:** Children's Fiction, Illustrations, Art/Art History, Travel/Exploration, Children's Non-fiction, Picture/Board Books, Young Adult Non-fiction, Literary Criticism And History, Literary Criticism And History. **Career:** Pierce College, instructor in art, 1971-85, 1988-93, 2001-02; Fashion Institute of Design and Merchandising, instructor in art, 1979-88; California State University, instructor in writing and illustrating children's books, 1987-89; Metropolitan Cooperative Library System, artist for the summer reading program, 1988, 1990. Writer. **Publications:** The Moon and You, 1993; Let's Go Traveling in Mexico, 1996; The Rainbow and You, 2000. SELF-ILLUSTRATED JUVENILE: The Comet and You, 1985; Get Set to Wreck!, 1988; The Big Dipper and You, 1989; Let's Go Traveling, 1992; Let's Go Traveling in Mexico, 1996. Contributor to periodicals. **Address:** Fine Artists Factory, 474 S Raymond Ave., Ste. 110, Pasadena, CA 91105, U.S.A. **Online address:** rrkrupp@hotmail.com

KRUSE, Kevin M. American (born United States), b. 1972?. **Genres:** Adult Non-fiction, Social Commentary. **Career:** Princeton University, Department of History, assistant professor, 2000-06, David L. Rike university preceptor of history, 2003-06, associate professor of history, 2006-, associate chair, 2006-.

Writer. **Publications:** Rechtstreue und lauterer Wettbewerb: das Verhältnis von Rechtswidrigkeit und Sittenwidrigkeit im Deutschen Wettbewerbsrecht, 2003; White Flight: Atlanta and the Making of Modern Conservatism, 2005; (contrib.) Massive Resistance: Southern Opposition to the Second Reconstruction, 2005; (ed. with T.J. Sugrue and contrib.) The New Suburban History, 2006; (ed. with G. Prakash) The Spaces of the Modern City: Imaginaries, Politics, and Everyday Life, 2008; One Nation Under God: Cold War Christianity and the Origins of the Religious Right, forthcoming; (ed. with S.G.N. Tuck) Mobilizing the Movement: Civil Rights and the Second World War, forthcoming. Contributor to periodicals and books. **Address:** Department of History, Princeton University, 129 Dickinson Hall, Princeton, NJ 08544, U.S.A. **Online address:** kkruse@princeton.edu

KRUSOE, Jim. American (born United States), b. 1942. **Genres:** Young Adult Fiction. **Career:** Santa Monica College, faculty; Antioch University, faculty. Poet. **Publications:** Blood Lake and Other Stories, 1997; Iceland, 2002; Girl Factory, 2008; Erased, 2009. Contributor to magazines and newspapers. **Address:** Los Angeles, CA, U.S.A. **Online address:** krusoe_james@smc.edu

KRYSTAL, Arthur. American (born United States) **Genres:** Essays, Literary Criticism And History, Humanities. **Career:** Literary critic and editor. **Publications:** (Ed.) The Culture We Deserve, 1989; (ed. and intro.) A Company of Readers: Uncollected Writings of W.H. Auden, Jacques Barzun, and Lionel Trilling from the Readers' Subscription and Mid Century Book Clubs, 2001; Agitations: Essays on Life and Literature, 2002; Half-life of an American Essayist: Essays, 2007; Except When I Write, 2011. **Address:** c/o Author Mail, Yale University Press, PO Box 209040, New Haven, CT 06520-9040, U.S.A.

KRYZA, Frank T. American (born United States), b. 1950. **Genres:** Novels, History, Sciences. **Career:** New Haven Journal Courier, staff reporter, 1972-73; Plainville News, editor, 1974-75; Hospice Inc., director of public information, 1975-77; Big Brothers/Big Sisters of South Central Connecticut Inc., executive director, 1977-79; ARCO International Oil & Gas Co., financial consultant, 1982-86, senior planning advisor, 1986-88, finance manager, 1988-92, director of international relations and external affairs, 1992-97. **Publications:** The Power of Light: The Epic Story of Man's Quest to Harness the Sun, 2003; The Race for Timbuktu: In Search of Africa's City of Gold, 2006. **Address:** c/o Christy Fletcher, Fletcher & Parry L.L.C., 78 5th Ave., New York, NY 10011, U.S.A. **Online address:** ftk@aya.yale.edu

KRZYZEWSKI, Mike. American (born United States), b. 1947. **Genres:** Sports/Fitness. **Career:** U.S. Military Academy Prep School, head basketball coach, 1974-76; Duke University, head basketball coach, 1980-; United States Men's National Basketball Team, coach. Writer. **Publications:** (With B. Brill) A Season Is a Lifetime: The Inside Story of the Duke Blue Devils and Their Championship Seasons, 1993; (with D.T. Phillips) Leading with the Heart: Coach K's Successful Strategies for Basketball, Business, and Life, 2000; (with D.T. Phillips) Five-Point Play: Duke's Journey to the 2001 National Championship, 2001; (with J.K. Spatola) Beyond Basketball: Coach K's Keywords for Success, 2006; (with J.K. Spatola) The Gold Standard: Building a World-Class Team, 2009. **Address:** Duke University, Durham, NC 27708, U.S.A.

KUBAN, Ron. Canadian (born Canada), b. 1953?. **Genres:** History. **Career:** Federal Public Service of Canada, staff, 1983-88; Albertas Public Service, manager, 1988-94; Pegasus Emergency Management Consortium, president, 1994, chief executive officer; International Federation of Red Cross and Red Crescent, delegate, 1995, 1996; Red Cross Regional Council, president; Emergency Management, publisher; Safe Guard, president; Edmonton Federation of Community Leagues, president; Edmonton Police Commission, commissioner, 2004; Edmonton Regional Crime Prevention Network, president; Mill Woods Presidents Council, chair; Alberta Association of Police Governance, chair; Canada's Department of National Defence, staff; Provincial Government of Alberta, staff; The Federal Government, staff. Writer. **Publications:** Crisis Management in Canada: A Study of Its Practice, 1995; (ed.) The Canadian Fire Officer's Guide to Emergency Management, 1996; Edmonton's Urban Villages: The Community League Movement, 2005. **Address:** Pegasus Emergency Management Consortium Corp., 3116 - 36B Ave., Edmonton, AB T6T 1H4, Canada. **Online address:** rkuban@compusmart.ab.ca

KUBERSKI, Philip. American (born United States), b. 1952. **Genres:** Literary Criticism And History, Autobiography/Memoirs, Sciences, Young Adult

Fiction. **Career:** Carnegie Mellon University, instructor, 1981-89; University of California, instructor, 1981-89; University of California, instructor, 1981-89; Wake Forest University, professor of English, 1989-. Writer. **Publications:** The Persistence of Memory: Organism, Myth, Text, 1992; A Calculus of Ezra Pound: Vocations of the American Sign, 1992; Chaosmos: Literature, Science and Theory, 1994. Contributor to periodicals. **Address:** Department of English, Wake Forest University, C105 Tribble Hall, PO Box 7387, Winston-Salem, NC 27109, U.S.A. **Online address:** kuberspf@wfu.edu

KUBEY, Robert W(illiam). American (born United States), b. 1952. **Genres:** Communications/Media, Adult Non-fiction. **Career:** University of Wisconsin-Madison, Department of Psychology, lecturer, 1980-81; University of Chicago, Office of Continuing Education, lecturer, 1984; University of California, visiting lecturer in social ecology, 1984-85; Rutgers University, Rutgers College, fellow, 1985-, assistant professor of communication, 1985-91, associate professor of communication, 1991-99, Center for the Critical Analysis of Contemporary Culture, fellow, 1986-87, Research Media Education Laboratory, director, 1995-97, director of master's program in communication and information studies, 1997-2000, Center for Media Studies, director, 1999-, Department of Journalism and Media Studies, associate professor, 1999-2004, professor, 2004-; Stanford University, visiting associate professor, 1995-96; University College, fellow, 1998-. Writer. **Publications:** (Contrib.) Television and the American Family, 1990; (with M. Csikszentmihalyi) Television and the Quality of Life: How Viewing Shapes Everyday Experience, 1990; (contrib.) The Audience and Its Landscape, 1996; (contrib.) Tunning in to Young Viewers: Social Science Perspectives on Television, 1996; (ed. and contrib.) Media Literacy in the Information Age: Current Perspectives, 1997; Creating Television: Conversations with the People behind 50 Years of American TV, 2004. Contributor of articles to journals and newspapers. **Address:** Department of Journalism and Media Studies, Rutgers University, SDW 301, 4 Huntington St., New Brunswick, NJ 08901-1071, U.S.A. **Online address:** kubey@scils.rutgers.edu

KUBLICKI, Nicolas M. American (born United States), b. 1966?. **Genres:** Documentaries/Reportage, Novels, Mystery/Crime/Suspense. **Career:** Office of Policy Development, assistant to deputy director, 1992-93; U.S. Department of Justice, assistant to senior trial attorneys of environmental enforcement section, 1993-94; Buchalter, Nemer, Fields and Younger Law Offices, associate, 1994-97; Good Shepherd Church, president, 1997-; Ervin, Cohen and Jessup L.L.P., associate, 1997-2002, partner, 2002-03. Pepperdine University, School of Law, adjunct professor, 2002-; Holmby Hills Park, vice president, 2006-; Sotheby's International Realty, broker associate, 2007-. Writer. **Publications:** The Diamond Conspiracy, 2002 in German as Das Monopol, 2004 in Portuguese as Conspiração Diamante, 2005; The Tesla Formula, forthcoming; The Secret Bankers, forthcoming. Author of articles to publications. **Address:** School of Law, Pepperdine University, 24255 Pacific Coast Hwy., 9th Fl., Malibu, CA 90263, U.S.A. **Online address:** patcarlton@earthlink.net

KUCHAR, Gary. Canadian (born Canada), b. 1974. **Genres:** Poetry, History, Theology/Religion. **Career:** University of Victoria, assistant professor, 2004-08, associate professor of English, 2008-. Writer and educator. **Publications:** Divine Subjection: The Rhetoric of Sacramental Devotion in Early Modern England, 2005; The Poetry of Religious Sorrow in Early Modern England, 2008. Contributor to books, periodicals and journals. **Address:** Department of English, University of Victoria, Stn CSC, PO Box 3070, Victoria, BC V8W 3W1, Canada.

KUCZKIR, Mary. (Fern Michaels). American (born United States), b. 1933. **Genres:** Novels, Romance/Historical, Humor/Satire, Young Adult Fiction, Children's Fiction. **Career:** Writer. **Publications:** My Dish Towel Flies at Half Mast, 1979. ROMANCE NOVELS WITH R. ANDERSON AS FERN MICHAELS: Pride and Passion, 1975, rev. ed., 2001; Vixen in Velvet, 1976; Captive Passions, 1977; Valentina, 1978; Captive Embraces, 1979; Captive Splendors, 1980; The Delta Ladies, 1980; Sea Gypsy, 1981; Beyond Tomorrow, 1981, rev. ed., 2001; Captive Innocence, 1981; Without Warning, 1981; Nightstar, 1982; Paint Me Rainbows, 1982; Wild Honey, 1982, rev. ed., 2000; All She Can Be, 1983, rev. ed., 1996; Tender Warrior, 1983; Whisper My Name, 1984; Cinders to Satin, 1984; Texas Rich, 1985, rev. ed., 2001; Golden Lasso, 1985; Free Spirit, 1986; Ever the Empire, 1986; Texas Heat, 1986; To Taste the Wine, 1988; Texas Fury, 1989; Sins of Omission, 1989; Sins of the Flesh, 1990; For All Their Lives, 1991; Captive Innocence, 1991; Texas Sunrise, 1993; Desperate Measures, 1994; Serendipity, 1994; Seasons of Her Life, 1994; To Have and to Hold, 1994; A Gift Of Joy, 1995; Dear

Emily, 1995; A Joyous Season, 1996; Vegas Rich, 1996; Wish List, 1996; Vegas Heat, 1997; Vegas Sunrise, 1997; White Fire, 1997; (co-author) Heart of the Home, 1998; Finders Keepers, 1998; Sara's Song, 1998; Yesterday, 1999; Split Second, 1999; Celebration, 1999; Annie's Rainbow, 1999; Guest List, 2000; Listen to Your Heart, 2000; What You Wish For, 2000; Plain Jane, 2001; Kentucky Rich, 2001; Charming Lily, 2001; Late Bloomer, 2002; Kentucky Sunrise, 2002; Kentucky Heat, 2002; No Place like Home, 2002; Shattered Night, 2002. OTHER: Panda Bear is Critical (novel), 1982; Maybe this Time, 2003; Crown Jewel, 2003; About Face, 2003; Trading Places, 2003; Jingle all the Way, 2004; Real Deal, 2004; Family Blessings, 2005; Picture Perfect, 2005; Nosy Neighbor, 2005; Pretty Woman, 2005; Payback: The Second Book in the Revenge of the Sisterhood Series, 2006; Vendetta, 2006; Sweet Revenge, 2006; Weekend Warriors: The First Book in the Revenge of the Sisterhood Series, 2006; Sugar and Spice, 2006; Fool Me Once, 2006; Hey, Good Looking, 2006; Jury, 2006; Lethal Justice, 2006; Marriage Game, 2006; Free Fall, 2006; Comfort and Joy, 2007; Hide and Seek, 2007; Hokus Pokus, 2007; Up Close and Personal, 2007; Fast Track, 2008; Silver Bells, 2008; Collateral Damage, 2008; Final Justice, 2008; Under the Radar, 2009; Scoop, 2009; Mr. and Miss Anonymous, 2009; Snow Angels, 2009; Betrayal, 2009; Deadly Deals, 2009; Vanishing Act, 2009; Razor Sharp, 2009; Game Over, 2010; Exclusive, 2010; Return To Sender, 2010; (co-author) Holiday Magic, 2010; Wildflowers, 2010; Cross Roads, 2010; Déjàvu, 2010; I'll Be Home For Christmas, 2010; Late Edition, 2010; Home Free, 2011. Contributor to books. **Address:** Kensington Publishing Corp., 119 W 40th St., New York, NY 10018, U.S.A. **Online address:** fernmichaels@fernmichaels.com

KUCZMARSKI, Susan Smith. American (born United States), b. 1951. **Genres:** Education, Adult Non-fiction, Anthropology/Ethnology, Social Sciences, Business/Trade/Industry. **Career:** University of Illinois at Chicago, instructor, 1976-77; Dominican University, lecturer, 1977-78; Concordia University, assistant professor, 1977-79; Constitutional Rights Foundation, educational director, 1979-81; Northwestern University, associate director of development and instructor, 1981-84; Kuczmarski & Associates, executive vice president, 1984-; Edward Lowe Foundation, adviser, 1984-94; National Louis University, instructor, 1986-88; Northwestern University, Kellogg School of Management, lecturer, 2009-. Writer. **Publications:** Youth and Society: Rights and Responsibilities, 2nd ed., 1980; (with T.D. Kuczmarski) Values-Based Leadership: Rebuilding Employee Commitment, Performance, and Productivity, 1995; The Family Bond: Inspiring Tips for Creating a Closer Family, 2000; (with T.D. Kuczmarski) Apples are Square: Thinking Differently about Leadership, 2007. **Address:** Kuczmarski & Associates Inc., 2001 N Halsted St., Ste. 201, Chicago, IL 60614, U.S.A. **Online address:** skuczmarski@sacredflight.com

KUCZMARSKI, Thomas D(ale). American (born United States), b. 1951. **Genres:** Administration/Management, Business/Trade/Industry, Economics, Marketing. **Career:** Quaker Oats, brand manager; Booz, Allen & Hamilton (international consulting firm), principal; Kuczmarski & Associates Inc. (consulting firm), founder, senior partner and president, 1984-; Northwestern University, Kellogg Graduate School of Management, adjunct professor and lecturer; University of Chicago, Graduate School of Business, adjunct professor and lecturer of executive program; School of the Art Institute of Chicago, founding member, 1988-92; Norcross Footwear Inc., director, 1990-; Kaytee Products Inc., director, 1991-. Writer. **Publications:** Managing New Products: Competing through Excellence, 1988, 3rd ed. as Managing New Products: Using the MAP System to Accelerate Growth, 2000; (with S.S. Kuczmarski) Values-Based Leadership: Rebuilding Employee Commitment, Performance and Productivity, 1995; Innovation: Leadership Strategies for the Competitive Edge, 1996; (with A. Middlebrooks and J. Swaddling) Innovating the Corporation: Creating Value for Customers and Shareholders, 2001; (with S.S. Kuczmarski) Apples are Square: Thinking Differently about Leadership, 2007. **Address:** Kuczmarski & Associates Inc., 2001 N Halsted St., Ste. 201, Chicago, IL 60614-4365, U.S.A. **Online address:** tkuczmarski@kuczmarski.com

KUDLINSKI, Kathleen V. American (born United States), b. 1950. **Genres:** Children's Non-fiction, Picture/Board Books, Children's Fiction. **Career:** New Haven Register, columnist, 1988-. Educator and writer. **Publications:** Rachel Carson: Pioneer of Ecology, 1988; Helen Keller, A Light for the Blind, 1989; Juliette Gordon Low, America's First Girl Scout, 1989, Hero over Here: A Story of World War I, 1990; Pearl Harbor is Burning: A Story of World War II, 1990; Animal Tracks and Traces, 1991; Night Bird: A Story of the Seminole Indians, 1993; Earthquake!: A Story of Old San Francisco,

1993; Lone Star: A Story of the Texas Rangers, 1994; Facing West: A Story of the Oregon Trail, 1994; Marie: An Invitation to Dance, 1996; Shannon: A Chinatown Adventure, 1996; Shannon, Lost and Found, 1997; Shannon: The Schoolmarm Mysteries, San Francisco, 1880, 1997; Popcorn Plants, 1998; Venus Flytraps, 1998; Dandelions, 1999; My Tree, 2000; My Body is Changing: Now What Do I Do?, 2000; Rosa Parks, Young Rebel, 2001; Harriet Tubman, Freedom's Trailblazer, 2002; How Plants Survive, 2003; Food for Life!, 2003; Sojourner Truth, Voice of Freedom, 2003; Franklin Delano Roosevelt, Champion of Freedom, 2003; The Spirit Catchers, 2004; What Do Roots Do?, 2005; Dr. Seuss, Young Artist and Author, 2005; Boy, Were We Wrong about Dinosaurs!, 2005; The Sunset Switch, 2005; Christopher Columbus, Young Explorer, 2005; Mother Teresa, Friend t the Poor, 2006, My Lady, Pocahontas, 2006; Gandhi, Young Revolutionary, 2006; Christopher Reeve, Young Movie Star, 2007; The Seaside Switch, 2007; Joan of Arc, 2008; Boy, Were We Wrong about the Solar System!, 2008; Horse Indian Wolf: The Hidden Pictures of Judy Larson, 2010; American Museum of Natural History Easy Readers, 2011. **Address:** c/o Susan Cohen, Writers House, 21 W 26th St., New York, NY 10010, U.S.A. **Online address:** kathkud@aol.com

KUEFLER, Mathew. American (born United States) **Genres:** Theology/Religion. **Career:** Red Deer College, instructor, 1988-90; Grant MacEwan Community College, instructor, 1989-91; University of Alberta, visiting lecturer, 1991-92; University of British Columbia, visiting lecturer, 1993; Yale University, teaching fellow, 1992-95, lecturer, 1995-96, visiting lecturer, 1997-98; Rice University, visiting lecturer, 1997-98; San Diego State University, assistant professor, 1998-2002, associate professor, 2002-; Rice University, National Endowment for the Humanities Summer Institute, assistant director. Historian, educator and writer. **Publications:** The Manly Eunuch: Masculinity, Gender Ambiguity and Christian Ideology in Late Antiquity, 2001; (ed. and contrib.) The Boswell Thesis: Essays on Christianity, Social Tolerance and Homosexuality, 2006; (ed.) The History of Sexuality Sourcebook, 2007. Contributor of articles to books and periodicals. **Address:** Department of History, San Diego State University, 5500 Campanile Dr., San Diego, CA 92182-8147, U.S.A. **Online address:** mkuefler@mail.sdsu.edu

KUEHN, Paul. See **GRANT, Pete.**

KUEHNERT, Stephanie. American (born United States), b. 1979?. **Genres:** Children's Fiction. **Career:** Forest Park Review, columnist. Author. **Publications:** I Wanna Be Your Jocy Ramone, 2008; Ballads of Suburbia, 2009. Contributor to periodicals. **Address:** Forest Park, IL , U.S.A. **Online address:** stephanie@stephaniekuehnert.com

KUFFEL, Frances. American (born United States), b. 1956. **Genres:** Women's Studies And Issues, Medicine/Health. **Career:** Jean V. Naggar Literary Agency, literary agent; Maria Carvainis Agency (literary agency), executive vice president; Fredrica S. Friedman and Co., literary agent at large. Writer. **Publications:** Passing for Thin: Losing Half My Weight and Finding My Self (memoir), 2004; Angry Fat Girls: 5 Women, 500 Pounds and a Year of Losing It-- Again, 2010. **Address:** c/o Fredrica Friedman, Fredrica S. Friedman and Company Inc., 136 E 57th St., 14th Fl., New York, NY 10022, U.S.A.

KUGLE, Scott. (Scott Alan Kugle). American (born United States), b. 1969?. **Genres:** Theology/Religion, Translations, History. **Career:** Swarthmore College, assistant professor; University of Leiden, Institute for the Study of Islam in the Modern World, research fellow. Writer. **Publications:** (trans. and intro.) Mubahisah-i Alamgiri: Mahdawi Debates with Emperor Aurangzeb, 1999; (trans. and intro.) Kitab al-tanwir fi isqat al-tadbir = The Book of Illumination, 2005; Rebel between Spirit and Law: Ahmad Zarruq, Sainthood, and Authority in Islam, 2006; Sufis and Saints' Bodies: Mysticism, Corporeality, and Sacred Power in Islam, 2007. Contributor to books and periodicals. **Address:** Department of Religion, Swarthmore College, Pearson 211, 500 College Ave., Swarthmore, PA 19081-1397, U.S.A.

KUGLE, Scott Alan. See **KUGLE, Scott.**

KUGLER, Anne. American (born United States), b. 1964. **Genres:** Biography. **Career:** John Carroll University, associate professor of French and English history and chair of department, Center for Faculty Development, director. Writer. **Publications:** Errant Plagiary: The Life and Writing of Lady Sarah Cowper, 1644-1720, 2002. **Address:** Department of History, John Carroll University, 20700 N Park Blvd., University Heights, OH 44118, U.S.A. **Online address:** akugler@jcu.edu

KUH, Patric. American/French (born France), b. 1964?. **Genres:** Young Adult Non-fiction, Food And Wine, Novels. **Career:** Writer and chef, 1990-; Los Angeles Magazine, contributing writer. **Publications:** An Available Man: A Novel, 1990; The Last Days of Haute Cuisine: America's Culinary Revolution, 2001; (ed. with D. Hamilton) Chef's Story: 27 Chefs Talk About What Got Them into the Kitchen, 2007. Contributor to periodicals. **Address:** c/o Author Mail, Penguin Group, 375 Hudson St., New York, NY 10014, U.S.A. **Online address:** letters@lamag.com

KUH, Richard H. (Richard Henry Kuh). American (born United States), b. 1921. **Genres:** Law. **Career:** Cahill, Gordon, Reindel & Ohl, associate, 1948-53; New York County, assistant district attorney, 1953-64, district attorney, 1974; Criminal Court Bureau, chief, 1956-64; New York University, lecturer in criminal procedure, 1958-64; New York State Combined Council of Law Enforcement Officials, coordinator, 1964-66; Kuh, Shapiro, Goldman, Cooperman & Levitt, partner, 1975-; Warshaw Burstein Cohen Schlesinger & Kuh L.L.P., partner and of counsel, 1978-. Writer. **Publications:** Foolish Figleaves? Pornography in and Out of Court, 1967. Contributor to journals. **Address:** Warshaw Burstein Cohen Schlesinger & Kuh L.L.P., 555 5th Ave., New York, NY 10017-2416, U.S.A. **Online address:** rkuh@wbcsk.com

KUH, Richard Henry. *See* KUH, Richard H.

KUHL, Stefan. German (born Germany), b. 1966. **Genres:** History, Politics/Government, Young Adult Non-fiction, Social Sciences, Sociology. **Career:** Independent consultant, 1990-94; Helmut-Schmidt-Universitat, Institut Gesellschaftswissenschaften, lecturer, professor, 2004-07; University of Bielefeld, professor, 2007-; Venice International University, visiting professor; University of Hamburg, visiting professor. Writer. **Publications:** The Nazi Connection: Eugenics, American Racism and German National Socialism, 1994; Die Internationale der Rassisten: Aufstieg und Niedergang der Internationalen Bewegung für Eugenik und Rassenhygiene im 20, 1997. **Address:** Department of Sociology, Universität Bielefeld, Rm. U3-216, PO Box 100131, Bielefeld, D-33501, Germany. **Online address:** stefan.kuehl@uni-bielefeld.de

KUHN, Robert Lawrence. American (born United States), b. 1944. **Genres:** Money/Finance, How-to Books, Business/Trade/Industry, History, Humanities. **Career:** Consultant, 1980; New York University, Graduate School of Business Administration, adjunct professor, 1981-89; IC2 Institute, University of Texas, research fellow in creative and innovative management, 1986; University of Southern California, executive-in-residence, 1990; Geneva Companies, co-owner and president, 1991-2002, vice chairman, 2002; Salomon Smith Barney, managing director, 2001; Kuhn Media Group and Pacvia Communications, chair; Closer to Truth, creator and host of television series; Public Broadcasting Service, In Search of China, producer; Massachusetts Institute of Technology, psychology faculty; University of California, anatomy faculty; Citigroup, senior advisor; State Science and Technology Commission, staff; Ministry of Science and Technology, staff; Chinese Academy of Engineering, staff; State Council Information Office, staff; State Administration of Radio, Film and Television, staff; China Central Television, staff; Ministry of Culture, staff; State Property Bureau, staff. State Council Research Office, staff; Chinese Academy of Social Sciences, staff; Beijing Institute for Frontier Science, vice-chairman; CCTV-IMG, partner. Writer. **Publications:** Mid-Sized Firms: Success Strategies and Methodology, 1982; (with G.T. Geis) The Firm Bond: Linking Meaning and Mission in Business and Religion, 1984; (ed. with R.W. Smilor) Corporate Creativity: Robust Companies and the Entrepreneurial Spirit, 1984; (ed.) Commercializing Defense Related Technology, 1984; (ed. with E.B. Konecci) Technology Venturing: American Innovation and Risk-Taking, 1985; (ed. with M.N. Maxey) Regulatory Reform: New Vision or Old Curse?, 1985; (ed.) Frontiers in Creative and Innovative Management, 1985; To Flourish among Giants: Creative Management for Mid-sized Firms, 1985; (ed. with R.W. Smilor) Managing Take-Off in Fast Growth Companies: Innovations in Entrepreneurial Firms, 1986; (ed. with S. Nozette) Commercializing SDI Technologies, 1987; (with G.T. Geis) Micromanaging: Transforming Business Leaders with Personal Computers, 1987; (ed.) Frontiers of Medical Information Sciences, 1988; (with A. Lavie) Industrial Research and Development in Israel: Patterns and Portents, 1988; Dealmaker: All the Negotiating Skills and Secrets You Need, 1988; (ed.) Handbook for Creative and Innovative Managers, 1988; (ed. with Y.

Ijiri) New Directions in Creative and Innovative Management: Bridging Theory and Practice, 1988; Creativity and Strategy in Mid-sized Firms, 1989; (with R.D. Gamach) The Creativity Infusion: How Managers Can Start and Sustain Creativity and Innovation, 1989; (ed.) Capital Raising and Financial Structure, 1990; (ed.) Index to the Library of Investment Banking, 1990; Investment Banking: The Art and Science of High-Stakes Dealmaking, 1990; (ed.) Corporate and Municipal Securities, 1990; (ed.) International Finance and Investing, 1990; (ed.) Investing and Risk Management, 1990; (ed.) Mortgage and Asset Securitization, 1990; (ed.) Mergers, Acquisitions, and Leveraged Buyouts, 1990; (ed.) Generating Creativity and Innovation in Large Bureaucracies, 1993; (ed.) Closer to Truth: Challenging Current Belief, 2000; The Man Who Changed China: The Life and Legacy of Jiang Zemin, 2004; Closer to Truth: Science, Meaning and the Future, 2007; How Chinas Leaders Think: The Inside Story of Chinas Reform and What This Means for the Future, 2010. **Address:** John Wiley & Sons, 111 River St., Hoboken, NJ 07030, U.S.A. **Online address:** rlkuhn@earthlink.net

KUHNS, Elizabeth. American (born United States) **Genres:** Novels, Art/Art History, Adult Non-fiction, Theology/Religion. **Career:** New Hampshire Humanities Council, staff. Journalist. **Publications:** The Habit: A History of the Clothing of Catholic Nuns, 2003. Contributor to magazines. **Address:** c/o Author Mail, Random House, 1745 Broadway, New York, NY 10019, U.S.A.

KUHRE, W. Lee. American (born United States), b. 1947. **Genres:** Technology, Information Science/Computers, Environmental Sciences/Ecology, Business/Trade/Industry, Marketing. **Career:** Anschutz Corp., environmental and safety manager, 1971-77; Kaiser Engineers, environmental and safety project manager, 1978-83; Pacific Bell, environmental and safety manager, 1984-90; University of San Francisco, senior lecturer, 1988-; Seagate Technology, executive director of environmental health and safety, 1991-, senior corporate director of environmental, health, safety and security. Writer. **Publications:** Practical Management of Chemicals and Hazardous Wastes: An Environmental and Safety Professional's Guide, 1995; ISO 14001 Certification: Environmental Management Systems: A Practical Guide for Preparing Effective Environmental Management Systems, 1995; ISO 14010s-Environmental Auditing: Tools and Techniques for Passing or Performing Environmental Audits, 1996; ISO 14020s Environmental Labelling-Marketing: Efficient and Accurate Environmental Marketing Procedures, 1997; ISO 14031-Environmental Performance Evaluation (EPE): Practical Tools and Techniques for Conducting An Environmental Performance Evaluation, 1998. **Address:** Seagate Technology, 920 Disc Dr., PO Box 66360, Scotts Valley, CA 95066, U.S.A.

KUITENBROUWER, Kathryn (Ann Frances). Canadian (born Canada), b. 1965. **Genres:** Novels, Graphic Novels, Novellas/Short Stories. **Career:** Freelance writer, 1995-; University of Toronto, School of Continuing Studies, instructor. **Publications:** Way Up, 2003; The Nettle Spinner, 2005; Perfecting, 2009; Foreign Beds, forthcoming. **Address:** c/o Hilary McMahon, Westwood Creative Artists, 94 Harbord St., Toronto, ON M5S 1G6, Canada. **Online address:** kathryn@kathrynkuitenbrouwer.com

KUJOORY, Parvin. American/Iranian (born Iran), b. 1936. **Genres:** Race Relations, Bibliography, Literary Criticism And History, Librarianship. **Career:** University of Shiraz, assistant professor, associate professor of English, 1967-83; Farsi Translation Bureau, director, 1983-85; Texas A&M University System, reference librarian, 1985-87, assistant professor of media, 1987-89; Choice, book reviewer, 1986-; University of the District of Columbia, assistant professor, associate professor, 1990-97; Southern Methodist University, lecturer in English, 1998-99; Wheaton Public Library, advisor; Plano Public Library System, director, 2004-06; Dallas County College District, adjunct professor of English, 2004-08; Collin County Community College District, adjunct professor of English, 2003-, professor of English, Writing Center, consultant, 2007-. Writer. **Publications:** Methods of Research, 1982; Black Slavery in America: An Annotated Mediagraphy, 1995; Shakespeare and Minorities: An Annotated Bibliography, 1970-2000, 2001. EDITOR: Readings in English: A Freshman English Textbook, 1974; Who's Who of the Nobel Prize Winners, 1986, 3rd ed., 1996. Contributor to periodicals. **Address:** Writing Center, Collin College, Rm. D-224, 2800 E Spring Creek Pkwy., Writing Ctr., Plano, TX 75074, U.S.A. **Online address:** pkujoory@cccd.edu

KUKLIN, Susan. American (born United States), b. 1941. **Genres:** Children's Non-fiction, Young Adult Non-fiction, Photography, Art/Art History. **Career:** New York City Public Schools, English teacher, 1965-74; New York

City Board of Education, curriculum developer, 1970-74; University of Tennessee, teacher of film studies, 1974-76. Photojournalist, 1974-. Writer. **Publications:** FOR YOUNG PEOPLE: Mine for a Year, 1984; (contrib.) Thinking Big: The Story of Young Dwarf, 1986; Reaching for Dreams: A Ballet from Rehearsal to Opening Night, 1987; When I See My Doctor, 1988; When I See My Dentist, 1988; Taking My Cat to the Vet, 1988; Taking My Dog to the Vet, 1988; Fighting Back: What Some People are Doing about AIDS, 1988; Going to My Ballet Class, 1989; Going to My Nursery School, 1990; Going to My Gymnastics Class, 1991; What Do I Do Now? Teenagers Talk about Sex and Pregnancy, 1991; How My Family Lives in America, 1992; Fighting Fires, 1993; Speaking Out: Teenagers Take on Race, Sex and Identity, 1993; From Head to Toe: How a Doll is Made, 1994; After a Suicide: Young People Speak Up, 1994; Kodomo: Children of Japan, 1995; Fireworks: The Science, the Art, and the Magic, 1996; Irrepressible Spirit: Conversations with Human Rights Activists, 1996; Iqbal Masih and the Crusaders against Child Slavery, 1998; Trail: The Inside Story, 2001; Hoops with Swoopes, 2001; Trial, 2001; (with D. Byrd) The Harlem Nutcracker: Based on the Ballet, 2001; From Wall to Wall, 2002; All Aboard!: A True Train Story, 2003; Families, 2006; No Choirboy: Murder, Violence, and Teenagers on Death Row, 2008. Contributor of essays to periodicals. **Address:** c/o Dina Sherman, Hyperion Books for Children, 114 5th Ave., 14th Fl., New York, NY 10011-5604, U.S.A. **Online address:** susan@susankuklin.com

KUKREJA, Veena. Indian (born India), b. 1960. **Genres:** Politics/Government. **Career:** University of Delhi, Shivaji College, lecturer, 1979-80; Janki Devi Mahavidyalaya, lecturer, Janaki Devi College, lecturer, 1981-89, lecturer of political science, 1989-93, associate professor of political science, 1993-. Writer. **Publications:** Military Intervention in Politics: A Case Study of Pakistan, 1985; (ed. with R. Basu and M.P. Singh) Congress Century, 1988; Civil-military Relations in South Asia: Pakistan, Bangladesh and India, 1991; Contemporary Pakistan: Political Processes, Conflicts, and Crises, 2003; (ed. with M.P. Singh) Pakistan: Democracy, Development and Security Issues, 2005; (ed. with M.P. Singh) Democracy, Development and Discontent in South Asia, 2008. Contributor of articles to journals. **Address:** Department of Political Science, University of Delhi, Arts Faculty Extension Bldg., Benito Juarez Marg, Near Dhaula Kuan, Benito Juarez Rd., New Delhi, DH 110 007, India. **Online address:** kukreja_veena@rediffmail.com

KULA, Irwin. American (born United States), b. 1957. **Genres:** Adult Nonfiction. **Career:** Congregation of the Old City, rabbi, 1980-81; Congregation B'nai Amoona, rabbi, 1982-88; Jewish Federation, St. Louis, board director, 1986-88; Wexner Heritage Foundation, faculty, 1988-; CLAL: The National Jewish Center for Learning and Leadership (formerly Center for Learning and Leadership), director of education, 1988-, co-president, president, 2002-; Bronfman Foundation, consultant, 1991; Center for Jewish Living, founder and consultant, 1993; Public Broadcasting Service, host, 2003; appeared on numerous television and radio programs; consultant. Writer. **Publications:** (With D.M. Elcott) Renewing the Covenant in the Face of Unbearable Pain, 1995; (ed. with V.L. Ochs) The Book of Jewish Sacred Practices: CLAL's Guide to Everyday & Holiday Rituals & Blessings, 2001; (with L. Loewenthal) Yearnings: Embracing the Sacred Messiness of Life, 2006. **Address:** National Jewish Center for Learning and Leadership, 440 Park Ave. S 4th Fl., New York, NY 10016, U.S.A. **Online address:** ikula@clal.org

KULISH, Nicholas. American (born United States), b. 1975?. **Genres:** Novels. **Career:** Wall Street Journal, Washington Bureau, staff reporter; New York Times, editorial writer, 2005-07, Berlin bureau chief, 2007-. **Publications:** Last One In (novel), 2007. **Address:** c/o Marly Russoff & Associates Inc., PO Box 524, Bronxville, NY 10708, U.S.A.

KULKA, Richard A. American (born United States), b. 1945. **Genres:** Psychiatry, Psychology, Medicine/Health, History. **Career:** University of Michigan, Institute for Social Research, Survey Research Center, assistant study director, 1973-75, assistant research scientist and study director, 1975-80, lecturer, 1979-80; Research Triangle Institute, senior survey methodologist, 1980-88, chief scientist, 1980, research vice president, 1994-2000, senior research vice president, 2000-; University of North Carolina, research associate professor, 1981-88; University of Chicago, National Opinion Research Center, associate director, 1989-93, senior vice president, 1994; Abt Associates, senior vice president for strategic business development, 2005-, group vice president for survey research. Writer. **Publications:** (Contrib.) Psychology and Women: In Transition, 1979; (contrib.) New Directions for Methodology of Behavioral Science: Methods for Studying Person-Situation Interactions,

1979; (contrib.) Violence and Crime in the Schools: Theoretical Perspectives, 1980; (with J. Veroff and E. Douvan) The Inner American: Life, Work and Mental Health from 1957 to 1976, 1981; (with J. Veroff and E. Douvan) The Inner American: A Self-Portrait from 1957 to 1976, 1981; (with J. Veroff and E. Douvan) Mental Health in America: Patterns of Help-Seeking from 1957 to 1976, 1981; (with J.E. McGrath and J. Martin) Judgment Calls in Research, 1982; (co-author) Trauma and the Vietnam War Generation: Report of Findings from the National Vietnam Veterans Readjustment Study, 1990; (co-author) The National Vietnam Veterans Readjustment Study: Tables of Findings and Technical Appendices, 1990; (ed. with M.L. Cynamon) Seventh Conference on Health Survey Research Methods, 2001. Contributor to periodicals and journals. **Address:** Abt Associates, 55 Wheeler St., Cambridge, MA 02138-1168, U.S.A. **Online address:** richard_kulka@abtassociates.com

KULL, Andrew. (A. Stoddard Kull). American (born United States), b. 1947. **Genres:** Law, Botany, Travel/Exploration, History. **Career:** Paul, Weiss, Rifkind, Wharton & Garrison, attorney, 1977-80; Cleary, Gottlieb, Steen & Hamilton, attorney, 1980-87; Emory University, associate professor of law, professor of law, 1987-2002, Robert T. Thompson professor of law; Restitution Law Review, U.S. regional editor, 1994-; The American Law Institute, Third Restatement of Restitution and Unjust Enrichment, reporter, 1997-; Boston University, School of Law, professor of law, 2002-, Austin B. Fletcher professor of law. Writer. **Publications:** (As A.S. Kull) Secrets of Flowers, 1966, rev. ed., 1976; New England Cemeteries: A Collector's Guide, 1975; The Color-Blind Constitution, 1992; Restatement of the Law Third, Restitution and Unjust Enrichment, 2011. **Address:** School of Law, Boston University, Rm. 1134C, 765 Commonwealth Ave., Boston, MA 02215, U.S.A. **Online address:** akull@bu.edu

KULL, A. Stoddard. *See* **KULL, Andrew.**

KULL, Robert. Canadian/American (born United States), b. 1946. **Genres:** Autobiography/Memoirs. **Career:** Royal Roads University, professor. Writer and photographer. **Publications:** Solitude: Seeking Wisdom in Extremes: A Year Alone in the Patagonia Wilderness (memoir), 2008. **Address:** Vancouver, BC , Canada. **Online address:** bobkull@bobkull.org

KULLING, Monica. Canadian (born Canada), b. 1952. **Genres:** Children's Fiction, Poetry, Children's Non-fiction. **Career:** Scholastic Canada, researcher and developer of anthologies, 1983-87; Ginn Publishing Canada, researcher and developer of anthologies, 1987-90; Houghton Mifflin Canada, researcher and developer of anthologies, 1990-92; Prentice-Hall, researcher and developer of anthologies, 1992-. Writer. **Publications:** FICTION FOR CHILDREN: Little Peanut at the Zoo, 1983; I Hate You, Marmalade!, 1992; Waiting for Amos, 1992; Go-Cart Getaway, 1993; (adaptor) Little Women, 1994; (adaptor) Les Misérables, 1995; (adaptor) The Adventures of Tom Sawyer, 1995; (adaptor) Great Expectations, 1996; Marmee's Surprise: A Little Women Story, 1996; Edgar Badger's Balloon Day, 1996; Fairy Tale: A True Story (movie storybook), 1997; Edgar Badger's Fix-It Day, 1997; (adaptor) The Body Snatcher, 1998; Edgar Badger's Fishing Day, 1999; Edgar Badger's Butterfly Day, 1999; Horses, 2001; Go, Stitch, Go!, 2002. NONFICTION: Vanished! The Mysterious Disappearance of Amelia Earhart, 1996; Bears: Life in the Wild, 1998; Eleanor Everywhere: The Life of Eleanor Roosevelt, 1999; The Great Houdini: World-Famous Magician and Escape Artist, 1999; Sea of Ice: The Wreck of the Endurance, 1999; Star Wars, Episode I. Queen in Disguise, 2000; Elephants, 2000; Escape North! The Story of Harriet Tubman, 2000; Alligators: Life in the Wild, 2000; Eat My Dust! Henry Ford's First Car Race, 2002; Listen Up!: Alexander Graham Bell's Talking Machine, 2007; (with N. Walker) Messiest Room on the Planet, 2009; It's a Snap!: George Eastman's First Photograph, 2009; All Aboard! Elijah Mccoy's Steam Engine, 2010; In the Bag!, 2011; Merci Mister Dash!, 2011. Contributor to magazines. Works appear in anthologies. **Address:** Random House, 1745 Broadway, New York, NY 10019, U.S.A. **Online address:** kulling@rogers.com

KULTERMANN, Udo. American/German (born Germany), b. 1927. **Genres:** Architecture, Art/Art History, History. **Career:** Museum Schloss Morsbroich, director, 1959-64; Washington University, Sam Fox School of Design & Visual Arts, professor, 1967-94, Ruth and Norman Moore professor of architecture, 1986-94, professor emeritus, 1994-. Writer. **Publications:** Hans und Wassili Luckhardt: Bauten und Entwuerfe, 1958; Architecture of Today, 1959; Dynamische Architektur, 1959; New Japanese Architecture,

1961; Der Schlüessel zur Architektur von heute, 1963; Neues Bauen in Afrika, 1963; Junge deutsche Bildhauer, 1963; History of Art History, 1966, rev. ed., 2002; Architektur der Gegenwart: Kunst der Welt, 1967; Gabriel Grupello, 1968; Kenzo Tange: Architecture and Urban Design, 1970; Art and Life, 1971; New Realism, 1972; Ernest Trova, 1977; Die Architektur im 20. Jahrhundert, 1977, 2nd ed., 1980; I Contemporanei (vol. XIV of Storia della Scultura del Mondo), 1979; Architecture in the Seventies, 1980; Architekten der Dritten Welt, 1980; Zeitgenöessische Architektur in Osteuropa, 1985; Kleine Geschichte der Kunsttheorie, 1987; Visible Cities-Invisible Cities, 1988; Geschichte der Kunstgeschichte: der Weg einer Wissenschaft, 1990; Kunst und Wirklichkeit, von Fiedler bis Derrida, 1991; Architecture in the 20th Century, 1993; Die Maxentius-Basilika-Ein Schlüesselwerk spaetantiker Architektur, 1996; Contemporary Architecture in the Arab States-Renaissance of a Region, 1999; (ed.) World Architecture: A Critical Mosaic, Beijing and Vienna, vol. VI: Architecture in Central and Southern Africa, 1900-2000, 2000; (ed.) St. James Modern Masterpieces, 1945, 1998; (with L. Hoptman and A. Tatehata) Yayoi Kusama, 2000; Thirty Years After, 2002; Architecture and Revolution, 2002; (with P. Antonelli and S.V. Dyk) Exit to Tomorrow, 2007. Contributor to books. **Address:** Sam Fox School of Design & Visual Arts, Washington University, 1 Brookings Dr., PO Box 1143, St. Louis, MO 63130-4862, U.S.A.

KUMAGAI, Fumie. Japanese (born Japan), b. 1943. **Genres:** Sociology. **Career:** University of New Hampshire, instructor, 1974-76; Hartwick College, assistant professor of sociology, 1976-78; Sophia University, lecturer of sociology, 1978-81; University of British Columbia, visiting associate professor of home economics, 1982-83, Ohira Commemorative Research Program, fellow, 1982-83; International University of Japan, associate professor of sociology, 1983-87; University of Michigan, Fulbright senior researcher and visiting professor of sociology, 1987-88; Kyorin University, professor of sociology, 1988-. Writer. **Publications:** America no Kateinai Boryoku: Kodomo, Otto, Tsuma, Oya Gyakutai no Jittai, 1983; Marginalization no Seishun, 1985; Kaso to Kamitsu ni Ikiru San-Sedaino Hinonjin, 1987; Kokusaikajidai no Katei Kyoiku, 1988; Nihonteki Seisann Shisutemu in Yu-Esu-Ei: Masatsu kara Sogorikaihe, 1996; Unmasking Japan Today: The Impact of Traditional Values on Modern Japanese Society, 1996; Degitaru Shakai no Shoyoso: Shakaigaku no Aratana Tenkai, 1999; 21-Seiki Amerika no Shakaimondai, 2004; Amerika no Kateinai Bouryoku to Gyakutai: Shakaigakuteki Shiten de Himotoku Ningenkankei, 2005; Families in Japan: Changes, Continuities, and Regional Variations, 2008; Jyukunenn Rikon Saiko, 2010; (with K. Fumie, Y. Hirotoshi and I. Taeko) Chienn to Chiikiryoku: Chiiki no Kizuna Kouchikuhemukete, 2011. Contributor to books, journals and newspapers. **Address:** Department of Foreign Studies, Kyorin University, 476 Miyashita-cho, Hachioji, Tokyo, 192-8504, Japan. **Online address:** fkumagai@ks.kyorin-u.ac.jp

KUMAR, Alok. American/Indian (born India), b. 1954. **Genres:** Physics, Sciences, History, Translations. **Career:** California State University, lecturer in physics, 1980-92; Indian Institute of Technology, science officer, 1984-85; Institut fur Kernphysik, Alexander von Humboldt fellow, 1985-86; State University of New York, Department of Physics, assistant professor of physics, 1992-93, associate professor, 1993-2000, professor of physics, 2000-, chair, 2005-11. Writer. **Publications:** (Trans. and ed. with S.I. Salem) S. Al-Andalusī, Science in the Medieval World: Book of the Categories of Nations, 1991; Laboratory Manual for College Physics, 2 vols., 2004. Works appear in anthologies. Contributor of articles to journals. **Address:** Department of Physics, State University of New York, 227 Snygg Hall, 7060 Rte. 104, Oswego, NY 13126-3599, U.S.A. **Online address:** alok.kumar@oswego.edu

KUMAR, Martha Joynt. American (born United States), b. 1941. **Genres:** Politics/Government, Communications/Media. **Career:** National Broadcasting Co., News Department Election Unit, researcher, 1965-66; Tennessee State University, instructor, 1967; University of Maryland, instructor, 1970-71; Towson State University, instructor, 1971-72, assistant professor, 1972-75, associate professor, 1975-81, professor of political science, 1981-. Writer. **Publications:** (With M.B. Grossman) Portraying the President: The White House and the News Media, 1981; (ed. with R.Y. Shapiro and L.R. Jacobs) Presidential Power: Forging the Presidency for the Twenty-first Century, 2000; (ed. with T. Sullivan) The White House World: Transitions, Organization, and Office Operations, 2003; Managing the President's Message: The White House Communications Operation, 2007. Contributor of articles to journals. **Address:** Department of Political Science, Towson University, Baltimore, MD 21204, U.S.A. **Online address:** mkumar@towson.edu

KUMIN, Maxine. American (born United States), b. 1925. **Genres:** Novels, Novellas/Short Stories, Children's Fiction, Young Adult Fiction, Poetry, Literary Criticism And History, Essays. **Career:** Tufts University, instructor in English, 1958-61, lecturer in English, 1965-68; Newton College, lecturer in English, 1971-72; University of Massachusetts, visiting lecturer in English, 1973; University of Massachusetts, visiting lecturer, 1973; Columbia University, adjunct professor of writing, 1975; Brandeis University, Fannie Hurst Professor of Literature, 1975; Washington University, Fannie Hurst Professor of Literature, 1977; Princeton University, visiting senior fellow, 1977, visiting lecturer, 1977, 1979, 1981-82; Bucknell University, poet-in-residence, 1983; Massachusetts Institute of Technology, visiting professor, 1984; Atlantic Center for the Arts, master artist, 1984; The Council of Independent Colleges, Woodrow Wilson Visiting Fellow, 1991-94; University of Miami, visiting professor, 1995; Pitzer College, visiting professor, 1996; Davidson College, McGee Professor of Writing, 1997; Florida International University, visiting professor, 1998-2000; Mary Baldwin College, Doenges Professor, 2002; New England College, distinguished poet-in-residence, 2003-05. **Publications:** POETRY: Halfway, 1961; The Privilege, 1965; The Nightmare Factory, 1970; Up Country: Poems of New England, New and Selected, 1972; House, Bridge, Fountain, Gate, 1975; Progress Report, 1976; The Retrieval System, 1978; Our Ground Time Here Will Be Brief: New and Selected Poems, 1982; Closing the Ring: Selected Poems, 1984; The Long Approach, 1985; Nurture, 1989; Looking for Luck, 1992; Connecting the Dots: Poems, 1996; Selected Poems, 1960-1990, 1997; The Long Marriage, 2001; Bringing Together: Uncollected Early Poems, 1958-1988, 2003; Jack and Other New Poems, 2005; Still to Mow: Poems, 2007; Where I Live: New & Selected Poems, 1990-2010, 2010. FICTION: Through Dooms of Love, 1965 in UK as A Daughter and Her Loves, 1965; The Passions of Uxport, 1968; The Abduction, 1971; The Designated Heir, 1974; Why Can't We Live Together like Civilized Human Beings?, 1982; Quit Monks or Die!: A Novel, 1999. FOR CHILDREN: Sebastian and the Dragon, 1960; Spring Things, 1961; A Summer Story, 1961; Follow the Fall, 1961; A Winter Friend, 1961; Mittens in May, 1962; No One Writes a Letter to the Snail, 1962; Eggs of Things, 1963; Archibald the Traveling Poodle, 1963; (with A. Sexton) More Eggs of Things, 1964; Speedy Digs Downside Up, 1964; The Beach before Breakfast, 1964; Paul Bunyan, 1966; Faraway Farm, 1967; The Wonderful Babies of 1809 and Other Years, 1968; When Grandmother Was Young, 1969; When Mother Was Young, 1970; When Great-Grandmother Was Young, 1971; (with A. Sexton) Joey and the Birthday Present 1971; (with A. Sexton) The Wizard's Tears, 1975; What Color Is Caesar? 1978; The Microscope, 1984; Mites to Mastodons: A Book of Animal Poems, Small and Large, 2006; Oh, Harry!, 2011. OTHERS: (intro.) The Loneliness Factor, 1979; To Make a Prairie: Essays on Poets, Poetry, and Country Living, 1979; (ed. and intro.) Rain, 1985; In Deep: Country Essays, 1987; Women, Animals, and Vegetables: Essays and Stories, 1994; Always Beginning: Essays on a Life in Poetry, 2000; Inside the Halo and Beyond: The Anatomy of a Recovery, 2000; (ed. with D. Brown and A. Finch) Lofty Dogmas: Poets on Poetics, 2005; Roots of Things: Essays, 2010. **Address:** c/o Giles Anderson, The Anderson Literary Agency, 435 Convent Ave., Ste. 5, New York, NY 10031-3624, U.S.A. **Online address:** montwid@aol.com

KUNDA, Gideon. American/Israeli (born Israel), b. 1952?. **Genres:** Engineering, Administration/Management, Anthropology/Ethnology, Sociology. **Career:** Bell Communications Research, consultant, 1984-87; Massachusetts Institute of Technology, Sloan School of Management, postdoctoral research fellow, 1987-88; Tel Aviv University, lecturer, 1988-92, director of institute for social research, 1992-95, Department of Labor Studies, senior lecturer, 1992-, chair, 1995-97, 2000-02, associate professor; Cornell University, School of Industrial and Labor Relations, visiting assistant professor, 1988-89; Israeli Kibbutz Movement, consultant, 1989-91; Stanford University, visiting professor, 1997-99, Stanford Advanced Project Management, faculty; Gothenburg University, visiting professor of management, 2009-; MIT Enterprise Forum of Israel, advisor. Writer. **Publications:** Engineering Culture: Control and Commitment in a High-Tech Corporation, 1992, rev. ed., 2006; Scenes From a Marriage: Work and Family In Corporate Drama, 1996; (with S.R. Barley) Gurus, Hired Guns, and Warm Bodies: Itinerant Experts in a Knowlege Economy, 2004. Works appear in anthologies. Contributor of articles to journals. **Address:** Stanford Center for Professional Development, Stanford Advanced Project Management, Stanford University, 496 Lomita Mall, Durand Bldg., 3rd Fl., Stanford, CA 94305, U.S.A. **Online address:** kunda@post.tau.ac.il

KUNHARDT, Edith. Also writes as Johnson Hill, Jessie Smith, Edward

Knapp. American (born United States), b. 1937. **Genres:** Children's Fiction, Children's Non-fiction, Illustrations, Education. **Career:** Golden Books, assistant editor, 1974-76, associate editor, 1976-80, editor, 1980-83, senior editor, 1983-86; freelance writer, 1986-. **Publications:** SELF- ILLUSTRATED: Pat the Cat, 1984; Danny's Birthday, 1986; Where's Peter?, 1988. FOR CHILDREN: The Mouse Family's New Home, 1981; (as Edward Knapp) What! No Spinach? A Popeye Story, 1981; Ned's Number Book, 1981; Martha's House, 1982; The Race to Pearl Peak: A Popeye Adventure, 1982; Animal Quiz Book, 1983; All Kinds of Trucks, 1984; Giant Sea Creatures, 1984; Grandma and Grandpa Smith, 1985; (as Johnson Hill) The Puppy Who Couldn't Remember (Pound Puppy story), 1986; Summer Vacation, 1986; (as Jessie Smith) Big Bird's Busy Day, 1987; (as Edward Knapp) How Speedy Is a Cheetah? Fascinating Facts about Animals (All Aboard Books series), 1987; The Airplane Book, 1987; Kittens, Kittens, Kittens, 1987; Danny's Mystery Valentine, 1987; Pompeii: Buried Alive!, 1987; (as Jessie Smith) Grover's Day at the Beach: A Counting Story, 1988; (as Jessie Smith) Going Places: Featuring Jim Henson's Sesame Street Muppets, 1988; Trick or Treat, Danny!, 1988; Danny and the Easter Egg, 1989; I Want to Be a Farmer (On the Job series), 1989; I Want to Be a Fire Fighter (On the Job series), 1989; Which One Would You Choose?, 1989; Danny's Christmas Star, 1989; Which Pig Would You Choose?, 1990; Red Day, Green Day, 1992; Pat the Puppy, 1993; Honest Abe, 1993; I'm Going to Be a Police Officer, 1995; I'm Going to Be a Farmer, 1996; I'm Going to Be a Vet, 1996; Pat the Christmas Bunny, 1999; Mummies, 2000; Tickle the Pig, 2001; Say Please, Bunny, 2002; Daddy's Scratchy Face, 2005; Judy's Flower Bed, 2005. **Address:** c/o Marilyn E. Marlow, Curtis Brown Ltd., 10 Astor Pl., New York, NY 10003, U.S.A.

KUNICH, John Charles. American (born United States), b. 1953. **Genres:** Sciences, Business/Trade/Industry, Economics, Law, Politics/Government, Social Sciences. **Career:** Roger Williams University, associate professor of law, 1999-2005, Fulbright senior specialist; Appalachian School of Law, associate professor, professor of law, 2005-. Writer. **Publications:** (With B. Greenberg) Entomology and the Law: Flies As Forensic Indicators, 2002; (with R. Lester) Survival Kit for Leaders, 2003; Naked Clone: How Cloning Bans Threaten Our Personal Rights, 2003; Ark of the Broken Covenant: Protecting the World's Biodiversity Hotspots, 2003; Killing Our Oceans: Dealing with the Mass Extinction of Marine Life, 2006. **Address:** School of Law, Roger Williams University, 10 Metacom Ave., Bristol, RI 02809-5171, U.S.A. **Online address:** jkunich@asl.edu

KUNIN, Aaron. American (born United States), b. 1973. **Genres:** Novels, Poetry. **Career:** Pomona College, assistant professor of English; Wesleyan University, visiting assistant professor. Writer. **Publications:** Folding Ruler Star: Poems, 2005; The Mandarin (novel), 2008; The Sore Throat and Other Poems, 2010. Contributor to periodicals. **Address:** Pomona College, Crookshank Hall, 140 W 6th St., Claremont, CA 91711-6335, U.S.A. **Online address:** aaron.kunin@pomona.edu

KUNTZ, Jerry. American (born United States), b. 1956. **Genres:** Information Science/Computers, History, Popular Culture, Sports/Fitness, Air/Space Topics, Autobiography/Memoirs. **Career:** Morris County Library, systems librarian, 1984-89; Finger Lakes Library System, automation manager, 1989-94; Ramapo Catskill Library System, electronic resources librarian, 1995-. Writer. **Publications:** (Ed.) Library Technology Consortia: Case Studies in Design and Cooperation, 1994; The Kids Click!: Web Searching Skills Guide with CD-ROM, 2001; Baseball Fiends and Flying Machines: The Many Lives and Outrageous Times of George and Al Lawson, 2009; A Pair of Shootists: The Wild West Story of S.F. Cody and Maud Lee, 2010. **Address:** Ramapo Catskill Library System, 619 Rte. 17M, Middletown, NY 10940-4395, U.S.A. **Online address:** jkuntz@rcls.org

KUNTZ, John Kenneth. American (born United States), b. 1934. **Genres:** Theology/Religion, History, Archaeology/Antiquities, Social Sciences. **Career:** United Methodist Chruch, ordained minister, 1959; Union Theological Seminary, tutor in old testament, 1961-63; Wellesley College, instructor in biblical history, 1963-65, assistant professor, 1965-67; University of Iowa, Department of Religious Studies, assistant professor, 1967-70, associate professor, 1970-76, professor of religion, 1976-, professor emeritus; Phi Beta Kappa, president of local chapter, 1977-78. Writer. **Publications:** The Self-Revelation of God, 1967; The World of the Old Testament, 1968, 4th ed., 1988; The World of the New Testament, 1968, rev. ed., 1996; The People of Ancient Israel: An Introduction to Old Testament Literature, History and Thought, 1974; Religion and Women: Images of Women in the Bible, 1978,

rev. ed., 1995; Biblical Archaeology: Scratching the Surface in the Holy Land, 1982, rev. ed., 1995; Prophecy in Biblical Israel, 1991. Contributor to books. **Address:** School of Religion, University of Iowa, Iowa City, IA 52242, U.S.A. **Online address:** ken-kuntz@uiowa.edu

KUNZE, Michael. Czech (born Czech Republic), b. 1943. **Genres:** Adult Non-fiction, History, Politics/Government, Social Sciences. **Career:** Lyric writer, record producer, playwright, librettist and translator of musicals; historian, 1980-. **Publications:** Der Prozess Pappenheimer, 1981; Strasse ins Feuer: vom Leben und Sterbenin in der Zeit des Hexenwahns, 1982; Warum ich Pazifist bin, 1983; Highroad to the Stake: A Tale of Witchcraft (nonfiction), 1987; Der Freiheit eine Gasse, 1990. **Address:** c/o Richard Roemer, Cavalier Entertainment Corp., 205 W End Ave., Ste. 11M, New York, NY 10023, U.S.A. **Online address:** drkunze@ix.netcom.com

KUNZRU, Hari. American/British (born England), b. 1969?. **Genres:** Novels, Young Adult Fiction. **Career:** Wired U.K., staff, 1995-97; Mute, contributing editor, 1995-; journalist, 1998-; Wallpaper, music editor, 1999-2004; Time Out, correspondent; English PEN, deputy President; freelance journalist. **Publications:** The Impressionist (novel), 2002; Transmission: A Novel, 2004; Noise, 2005; My Revolutions: A Novel, 2007; Gods Without Men, 2011. Contributor to periodicals. **Address:** c/o Melissa Pimentel, Curtis Brown Group Ltd., Haymarket House, 28-29 Haymarket, London, GL SW1Y 4SP, England. **Online address:** hari@dircon.co.uk

KUPCHAN, Charles A. American (born United States) **Genres:** Politics/Government. **Career:** University of Oxford, instructor, 1983-84; Harvard University, tutor, instructor, 1984-86; Princeton University, assistant professor of politics, 1986-93; United States Department of State, policy planning staff, 1992; The White House, National Security Council, director for European affairs, 1993-94; Georgetown University, Department of Government, associate professor, professor of international affairs, 1994-, Edmund A. Walsh School of Foreign Service, professor, Mortara Center for International Studies, director, 2004-05. Writer. **Publications:** The Persian Gulf and the West: The Dilemmas of Security, 1987; The Vulnerability of Empire, 1994; (ed.) Nationalism and Nationalities in the New Europe, 1995; (ed.) Atlantic Security: Contending Visions, 1998; (ed. with J. Janning and D. Rumberg) Civic Engagement in the Atlantic Community, 1999; (co-author) Power in Transition: The Peaceful Change of International Order, 2001; The End of the American Era: U.S. Foreign Policy and the Geopolitics of the Twenty-First Century, 2002; (contrib.) Renewing the Atlantic Partnership, 2004; The US and Europe in the Middle East and Beyond: Partners or Rivals?, 2007; How Enemies Become Friends: The Sources of Stable Peace, 2010; No One's World: The West, the Rising Rest, and the Coming Global Turn, 2012. Contributor to periodicals. **Address:** Department of Government, Georgetown University, 807 Intercultural Ctr., PO Box 571034, Washington, DC 20057-1034, U.S.A. **Online address:** kupchanc@georgetown.edu

KUPER, Adam (Jonathan). British/South African (born South Africa), b. 1941. **Genres:** Anthropology/Ethnology, Social Sciences, Humanities. **Career:** Makerere University, lecturer, 1967-70; University College of London, lecturer, 1970-76; University of Leiden, professor of African cultural anthropology, 1976-85; Brunel University, professor of social anthropology, Department of Human Sciences, head, Department of Anthropology, head, 1985-2008, retired, 2008-. Writer. **Publications:** Kalahari Village Politics: An African Democracy, 1970; (co-ed.) Councils in Action, 1971; Anthropologists and Anthropology: The British School 1922-1972, 1973, 3rd ed., 1996; Changing Jamaica, 1976; (ed.) The Social Anthropology of Radcliffe-Brown, 1977; Wives for Cattle: Bridewealth and Marriage in Southern Africa, 1982; (co-ed.) The Social Science Encyclopedia, 1985, rev. ed., 1989; (with A. Kouwenhoven) Contributions to Mauritian Ethnography, 1985; South Africa and the Anthropologist, 1987; The Invention of Primitive Society: Transformations of an Illusion, 1988; Ortodoxia y Tabú: apuntes criiticos sobre la teoríaantropológica, 1989; (ed.) Conceptualizing Society, 1992; The Chosen Primate: Human Nature and Cultural Variation, 1994; Culture: The Anthropologists' Account, 1999; Among the Anthropologists: History and Context in Anthropology, 1999; The Reinvention of Primitive Society: Transformations of a Myth, 2005; Incest and Influence: The Private Life of Bourgeois England, 2009. **Address:** 16 Muswell Rd., London, GL N10 2BG, England. **Online address:** adam.kuper@gmail.com

KUPER, Jenny Riva. British/American (born United States), b. 1948. **Genres:** Law, Civil Liberties/Human Rights. **Career:** B.M. Birnberg and Co., articled clerk, 1975-77; Camden Community Law Centre, solicitor, 1978-83; Children's Legal Centre, solicitor, 1983-93; British Red Cross, researcher on customary international humanitarian law, 1997; freelance legal researcher and consultant, 1998-99; University of Sussex, Royal College of Paediatrics and Child Health, lecturer, 1998-99; University of London, London School of Economics and Political Science, research fellow, 1999-; UNICEF, consultant. Writer. **Publications:** International Law Concerning Child Civilians in Armed Conflict, 1997; (contrib.) Human Rights as General Norms and a State's Right to Opt Out: Reservations and Objections to Human Rights Conventions, 1997; Children in Armed Conflict: The Law and Its Uses, 2000; Children and Armed Conflict: Some Issues of Law and Policy, 2000; Military Training Concerning Children in Armed Conflict, 2004; Military Training and Children in Armed Conflict: Law, Policy and Practice, 2005; Bridging the Gap: Military Training and International Accountability Regarding Children, 2006. Contributor of articles to periodicals. **Address:** Department of Law and Development Studies, London School of Economics and Political Science, University of London, Houghton St., London, GL WC2A 2AE, England. **Online address:** j.kuper@lse.ac.uk

KUPER, Peter. American (born United States), b. 1958. **Genres:** Cartoons, Illustrations, Graphic Novels. **Career:** World War 3 Illustrated Magazine, co-founder, 1979; School of Visual Arts, instructor, 1987-. Writer. **Publications:** (With S. Tobocman) World War 3 Illustrated: 1980-1988, 1989; Peter Kuper's Comic Strips: A Journal of Travels through Africa and Southeast Asia, 1992; (co-author) World War 3 Illustrated: Confrontational Comics, 1995; Stripped, 1995; The System, 1997; Topsy Turvy, 2000; Speechless, 2000; Mind's Eye: An Eye of the Beholder Collection, 2001; Comic Strip, 2003; Sticks and Stones, 2004; Theo and the Blue Note, 2006; Stop Forgetting to Remember, 2007; Diario De Oaxaca, 2009; Drawn to New York; 2011. Illustrator of books by others. **Address:** 235 W 102nd St., Ste. 11J, New York, NY 10025, U.S.A. **Online address:** pkuperart@gmail.com

KUPFER, Allen C. American (born United States) **Genres:** Novels, Horror, Young Adult Fiction. **Career:** Long Island University, assistant professor of English; Nassau Community College, professor of film and literature studies, vice president academic affairs. Writer. **Publications:** The Journal of Professor Abraham Van Helsing, 2004; (with J.R. Gannascoli) A Meal to Die For: A Culinary Novel of Crime, 2006. **Address:** Department of English, Nassau Community College, 210 Bradley Hall, 1 Education Dr., Garden City, NY 11530, U.S.A. **Online address:** allen.kupfer@ncc.edu

KUPFER, Marcia. *See* **KUPFER, Marcia A.**

KUPFER, Marcia A. Also writes as Marcia Kupfer. American (born United States), b. 1954. **Genres:** Art/Art History, Politics/Government, Novellas/Short Stories. **Career:** Johns Hopkins University, instructor, Washington Humanities Program, director; Ohio State University, College of Arts and Sciences, Department of History of Art, visiting associate professor, instructor of studies in medieval art. Writer. **Publications:** Romanesque Wall Painting in Central France: The Politics of Narrative, 1993; The Art of Healing: Painting for the Sick and the Sinner in a Medieval Town, 2003; (ed.) The Passion Story: From Visual Representation to Social Drama, 2008. Contributor of articles to books, periodicals and journals. **Address:** Department of History of Art, Ohio State University, 3180 Smith Lab, 174 W 18th, Columbus, OH 43210-1318, U.S.A. **Online address:** kupfer.6@osu.edu

KUPFERBERG, Feiwel. Danish/Swedish/German (born Germany), b. 1946. **Genres:** History, Politics/Government. **Career:** University of Aalborg, assistant professor, associate professor, 1975-2002; Berlin Institute for Social Research, visiting professor, 1994; Max Planck Institute for Human Development, visiting professor, 1996-97; University of California, Center for German and European Studies, visiting professor, 1997-98; Danish University of Education (now Aarhus University, Department of Education), professor of educational sociology, 2002-. Writer. **Publications:** Klassförhållandena i Sovjetunionen, 1975; Marxistisk sovjetforskning, 1978; Paternalistiska andan, 1980; (with J. Adolphsen and S. Keldorff) Kære Bertel: en bog om universiteter og planlægning, 1985; Creative Chaos in Project Work, 1996; The Break-up of Communism in East Germany and Eastern Europe, 1999; Calling or Profession: Becoming a Nurse, 1999; The Rise and Fall of the German Democratic Republic, 2002. **Address:** Department of Education, Aarhus University, Tuborgvej 164, Copenhagen, 2400, Denmark. **Online address:** feiwel@dpu.dk

KUPPNER, Frank. Scottish (born Scotland), b. 1951?. **Genres:** Poetry, Novels, History, Young Adult Fiction, Young Adult Non-fiction. **Career:** University of Glasgow, writer-in-residence; Strathclyde University, writer-in-residence. Engineer. **Publications:** POETRY: A Bad Day for the Sung Dynasty, 1984; The Intelligent Observation of Naked Women, 1987; Everything Is Strange, 1994; Second Best Moments in Chinese History, 1997; What? Again?: Selected Poems, 2000; Arioflotga, 2008. NOVELS: Ridiculous! Absurd! Disgusting!, 1989; A Very Quiet Street, 1989; A Concussed History of Scotland, 1990; Something Very Like Murder, 1994; Life on a Dead Planet, 1997; In the Beginning There was Physics, 1999; A God's Breakfast, 2004. **Address:** Polygon Books, 22 George Sq., Edinburgh, EH8 9LF, Scotland.

KURASAWA, Fuyuki. Canadian (born Canada), b. 1972. **Genres:** Civil Liberties/Human Rights, Cultural/Ethnic Topics. **Career:** Arbetslivscentrum (Swedish Centre for Working Life), visiting research fellow, 1994; La Trobe University, lecturer, 1997-99; Carleton University, visiting fellow, 1999-2000; York University, assistant professor, 2001-06, professor, 2006-; New York University, visiting fellow, 2003-04; Yale University, visiting fellow, 2003-04; École des hautes Études en sciences sociales, visiting professor, 2007. Writer. **Publications:** The Ethnological Imagination: A Cross-Cultural Critique of Modernity, 2004; The Work of Global Justice: Human Rights as Practices, 2007. Contributor of articles to periodicals. **Address:** Department of Sociology, Faculty of Arts, York University, 2088 Vari Hall, 4700 Keele St., Toronto, ON M3J 1P3, Canada. **Online address:** kurasawa@yorku.ca

KUREISHI, Hanif. (Antonia French). British (born England), b. 1954. **Genres:** Novels, Plays/Screenplays, Adult Non-fiction, Novellas/Short Stories, Autobiography/Memoirs. **Career:** Royal Court Theatre, writer-in-residence, 1982, 1985-86. Film director and playwright. **Publications:** NOVELS: The Buddha of Suburbia, 1990; The Black Album, 1995; Intimacy, 1998; My Son, the Fanatic, 1998; Gabriel's Gift, 2001; The Body, 2002; The Mother, 2003; When the Night Begins, 2004; Something to Tell You, 2008. OTHER: Outskirts, The King and Me, Tomorrow-Today!, 1983; Birds of Passage, 1983; My Beautiful Laundrette, 1986; Sammy and Rosie Get Laid, 1988; London Kills Me, 1991; (ed. with J. Savage) The Faber Book of Pop, 1995; Love in a Blue Time (stories), 1997; Sleep with Me, 1999; Midnight All Day (stories), 1999; Plays One, 1999; Dreaming and Scheming: Reflections on Writing and Politics, 2002; My Ear at His Heart, 2004; Word and the Bomb, 2005; Venus, 2006; (co-author) War With No End, 2007; Ox-Tales: Earth, 2009; Collected Stories, 2010; Collected Essays, 2011. **Address:** c/o Stephen Durbridge, The Agency, 24 Pottery Ln., Holland Pk., Holland Pk., London, GL W11 4LZ, England.

KURIAN, George Thomas. American (born United States), b. 1931. **Genres:** Theology/Religion, Adult Non-fiction. **Career:** George Kurian Reference Books, president, 1972-; United Nations Studies Forum, director. Writer. **Publications:** Dictionary of Indian English, 1966; Children's Literary Almanac, 1973; Directory of American Book Publishing, 1975; Historical and Cultural Dictionary of India, 1976; Worldwide Markets for English-Language Books, 1977; Encyclopedia of the Third World, 3 vols., 1978, 4th ed., 1991; The Illustrated Book of World Rankings, 1979, 4th ed., 1996; Laurel Dictionary of Biography, 1980; World Press Encyclopedia, 2 vols., 1982; New American Gazetteer, 1984; Geo-Data: World Almanac Gazetteer, 1984; World Data, 1984; What's What in American Business, 1985; Sourcebook of Global Statistics, 1986; World Encyclopedia of Police Forces and Penal Systems, 1987; Yearbook of American Universities and Colleges, 1987; Global Guide to Medical Information, 1987; Handbook of Business Quotations, 1987; World Education Encyclopedia, 3 vols., 1988; Geo-Data: World Geographical Encyclopedia, 1989; Glossary of the Third World, 1989; (ed.) Teachers as Writers, 1989; Encyclopedia of the First World, 2 vols., 1990; The Benelux Countries, 1990; British Isles, 1990; North America, 1990; Scandinavia, 1990; Japan, 1990; Australia and New Zealand, 1990; Encyclopedia of the Second World, 1991; World Encyclopedia of Cities, 2 vols., 1993; Datapedia of the United States, 1993; Atlas of the Third World, 2nd ed., 1993; (with G.T.T. Molitor) Encyclopedia of the Future, 2 vols., 1995; Encyclopedia of Medical Media and Communications, 1996; Encyclopedia of the Democratic Party, 2 vols., 1996; Encyclopedia of the Republican Party, 2 vols., 1996; Timenglish, 1996; Global Data Locator, 1997; World Encyclopedia of Parliaments and Legislatures, 2 vols., 1997; The Dictionary of America, 1997; The World as It Should Be, 1997; Historical Guide to U.S. Government, 1998; (with J.D. Schultz) The Political Market Place, 1998; (with J.Y. Cole) Encyclopedia of the Library of Congress, 1999; (with G.T.T. Molitor) Compendium of the 21st Century, 1999; (with J.D. Schultz) The Chronicles of Christianity, 1999; The Nobel Scientists, 1999; (with D.B. Barrett and T.M. Johnson) World Christian Encyclopedia, 2 vols., 2000; Datapedia of the United States, 1790-2005: America Year by Year, 2001; Timetables of World Literature, 2002; (ed.) Nelson's New Christian Dictionary: The Authoritative Resource on the Christian World, 2001; (ed.) Datapedia of the United States: American History in Numbers, 2004; (ed.) Testament Christian Dictionary: The Authoritative Compendium of Christian Terms, 2005; (ed.) World Encyclopedia of Police Forces and Correctional Systems, 2006; (ed.) Encyclopedia of the World's Nations and Culture, 2007; (ed.) Encyclopedia of Christian Civilization, 4 vols., 2009; (ed.) Encyclopedia of Political Science, 5 vols., 2010; (ed. with J. Smith) Encyclopedia of Christian Literature, 2 vols., 2010; (ed. with S.C. Day) Baker Handbook of Denominations and Ministries, 2011. **Address:** George Kurian Reference Books, PO Box 519, Baldwin Place, NY 10505, U.S.A. **Online address:** gtkurian@aol.com

KURIANSKY, Judith (Anne Brodsky). American (born United States), b. 1947. **Genres:** How-to Books, Psychology, Self Help, Sex. **Career:** New York State Psychiatric Institute, senior research scientist, 1970-78; Columbia University, College of Physicians and Surgeons, faculty, 1975-87, professor of clinical psychology, Teachers College, adjunct professor of psychology; National Institute for Psychotherapies, sex therapy coordinator, 1977-79; Quezon Corp., vice-president, 1978; St. Luke's Hospital, intern in psychology, 1978-79; Institutes of Religion and Health, lecturer, 1979-81; WABC-Radio, host, 1981-84; CBS-TV, reporter, 1982-86; Center for Marital and Family Therapy, therapist, 1987-; WPIX-TV, reporter, 1987-89; NBC (Consumer News and Business Channel), reporter and host, 1989-92. **Publications:** Sex: Now That I've Got Your Attention, Let Me Answer Your Questions!, 1984; How to Love a Nice Guy, 1990; Generation Sex: America's Hottest Sex Therapist Answers the Hottest Questions about Sex, 1995; The Complete Idiot's Guide to Dating, 1996, 3rd ed., 2003; Goodbye My Troubles, Hello My Happiness, 1997; The Complete Idiot's Guide to a Healthy Relationship, 1998, 2nd ed., 2002; China Reproductive Health Hotline Professionals Solve Problems on Sex and Emotions, 2001; The Complete Idiot's Guide to Tantric Sex, 2002, 2nd ed., 2004; (ed.) Terror in the Holy Land: Inside the Anguish of the Israeli-Palestinian Conflict, 2006; (ed.) Beyond Bullets and Bombs: Grassroots Peacebuilding between Israelis and Palestinians, 2007; (ed. with E. Schroeder) Sexuality Education: Past, Present, and Future, 2009; (with E. Hand) 31 Things to Raise A Child's Self-esteem, 2010. Contributor to periodicals and journals. **Address:** Turner Publishing Co., 200 4th Ave. N, Ste. 950, Nashville, TN 37219, U.S.A. **Online address:** drjudyk@aol.com

KURIEN, Christopher (Thomas). Indian (born India), b. 1931. **Genres:** Economics, Sociology, Business/Trade/Industry. **Career:** Madras Christian College, Department of Economics, tutor, 1953-54, lecturer in economics, 1954-62, professor and head, 1962-78; Madras Institute of Development Studies, director, 1978-88, professor, 1978-91, professor emeritus, 1991-, chairman, 1997-2003; Indian Council of Social Science Research, national fellow, 1992-94. Writer. **Publications:** Our Five Year Plans, 1966; (ed. with S.V. Anantakrishnan, C.T.K. Chari and S. Rajiva) India Today, 1967; Indian Economic Crisis: Diagnostic Study, 1969; A Theoretical Approach to the Indian Economy, 1970; (ed.) A Guide to Research in Economics, 1973; Poverty and Development, 1974; Poverty, Planning, and Social Transformation, 1978; (with J. James) Economic Change in Tamil Nadu, 1960-1970: A Regionally and Functionally Disaggregated Analysis, 1979; Dynamics of Rural Transformation: A Study of Tamil Nadu, 1950-1975, 1981; Mission and Proclamation: The Church in India Today and Other Pieces, 1981; Tamilaka Kirāmappura Mārutalkal, 1987; (ed. with E.R. Prabhakar and S. Gopal) Economy, Society, and Development: Essays and Reflections in Honour of Malcolm S. Adiseshiah, 1991; The Economy: An Interpretive Introduction, 1992; Growth and Justice: Aspects of India's Development Experience, 1992; On Markets in Economic Theory and Policy, 1993; Global Capitalism and the Indian Economy, 1994; Rethinking Economics: Reflections Based on a Study of the Indian Economy, 1996; Trade and Markets in the Context of Modern Development, forthcoming. **Address:** Madras Institute of Development Studies, 79 2nd Main Rd., Gandhinagar, Adyar, Chennai, TN 600 020, India.

KURKJIAN, Tim Bell. American (born United States), b. 1956. **Genres:** Sports/Fitness, Biography, Autobiography/Memoirs. **Career:** Washington Star, staff, 1978-; Baltimore News American, staff, 1981; Dallas Morning News, writer, 1981-85; Baltimore Orioles, staff, 1986-; Baltimore Sun, staff, 1986-; Sports Illustrated, senior writer, 1989-97; CNN Sports Illustrated, reporter, 1996-97; ESPN, senior writer and reporter, 1998-. **Publications:** America's Game, 2000; (foreword) Major League Baseball Hometown Heroes,

2006; Is This a Great Game, or What?: From A-Rod's Heart to Zim's Head-My 25 Years in Baseball, 2007. **Address:** St. Martin's Press, 175 5th Ave., New York, NY 10010, U.S.A. **Online address:** tim.kurkjian@espnmag.com

KURLAND, Geoffrey. American (born United States), b. 1947?. **Genres:** Autobiography/Memoirs, Medicine/Health. **Career:** Stanford University Medical Center, Children's Hospital, fellow, 1976-81; University of California, School of Medicine, assistant professor and director of pediatric pulmonology, 1981-88; University of Pittsburgh, School of Medicine, professor of pediatrics, 1988-, director of pediatric flexible bronchoscopy service, 1990-, director of pediatric pulmonary transplant program and director of pediatric pulmonology fellowship, 1992-, Pediatric Heart and Lung Transplantation, medical director. Writer. **Publications:** My Own Medicine: A Doctor's Life as a Patient, 2002. Contributor of articles to journals. **Address:** Division of Pediatric Pulmonology, Children's Hospital of Pittsburgh, University of Pittsburgh, 4401 Penn Ave., 3rd Fl., Pittsburgh, PA 15224-1334, U.S.A. **Online address:** geoffrey.kurland@chp.edu

KURLAND, Lynn. American (born United States) **Genres:** Novels. **Career:** Writer. **Publications:** A Dance through Time, 1996; (co-author) The Christmas Cat, 1996; Stardust of Yesterday, 1996; (co-author) Christmas Spirits, 1997; This is all I Ask, 1998; Another Chance to Dream, 1998; The Very Thought of You, 1998; (co-author) Veils of Time, 1999; The More I See You, 1999; If I Had You, 2000; (co-author) Opposites Attract, 2000; My Heart Stood Still, 2001; Love Came Just in Time, 2001; (co-author) A Knight's Vow, 2001; From This Moment On, 2002; (co-author) Tapestry, 2002; A Garden in the Rain, 2003; (with P.A. McKillip, C. Delacroix and S. Shinn) To Weave a Web of Magic, 2004; Dreams of Stardust, 2005; Star of the Morning, 2006; Much Ado in the Moonlight, 2006; (with S. Shinn, C. Delacroix and S. Monette) The Queen in Winter, 2006; When I Fall in Love, 2007; With Every Breath, 2008; The Mage's Daughter, 2008; Princess of the Sword, 2009; Till There was You, 2009; Tapestry of Spells, 2010; A Time for Love, 2010; One Enchanted Evening, 2010; Spellweaver, 2011; One Magic Moment, 2011; Gift of Magic, 2012. **Address:** Berkley Books, Penguin Group Publicity, 375 Hudson St., New York, NY 10014, U.S.A. **Online address:** lynn@lynnkurland.com

KURLAND, Michael (Joseph). (Jennifer Plum). American (born United States), b. 1938. **Genres:** Novels, Novellas/Short Stories, Mystery/Crime/Suspense, Science Fiction/Fantasy, Plays/Screenplays, Ghost Writer. **Career:** Full-time writer, 1963-; KPFK-Radio, news editor, 1966; Happy Valley School, teacher of English, 1967; Crawdaddy Magazine, managing editor, 1969; Pennyfarthing Press, editor, 1976-80. **Publications:** (With C. Anderson) Ten Years to Doomsday, 1964; Mission: Third Force (suspense), 1967; Mission: Tank War (suspense), 1968; A Plague of Spies (suspense), 1969; Police Action, 1969; The Unicorn Girl, 1969; Transmission Error, 1970; (as Jennifer Plum) The Secret of Benjamin Square (suspense), 1972; The Whenabouts of Burr, 1975; Pluribus, 1975; Tomorrow Knight, 1976; The Princes of Earth (juvenile), 1978; The Infernal Device (suspense), 1979; (with S.W. Barton) The Last President, 1980; Psi Hunt, 1980; (with H.B. Piper) First Cycle, 1982; Death by Gaslight, 1982; Star Griffin, 1987; Ten Little Wizards, 1988; The Spymaster's Handbook, 1988; A Study in Sorcery, 1989; Perchance, 1989; Button Bright, 1990; Encyclopedia of Horrifica, 1992; A Gallery of Rogues (true crime), 1993; How to Solve a Murder: The Forensic Handbook, 1995; Too Soon Dead (mystery), 1997; How to Try a Murder: The Handbook for Armchair Lawyers, 1997; Girls in the High-Heeled Shoes, 1998; The Complete Idiot's Guide to Extraterrestrial Intelligence, 1999; (with R.A. Lupoff) The Complete Idiot's Guide to Improving Your Memory, 1999; (with L. Robertson) Complete Idiot's Guide to Unsolved Mysteries, 2000; Encyclopedia of World Espionage, 2000; Great Game, 2001; Empress of India, 2006; Irrefutable Evidence: Adventures in the History of Forensic Science, 2009; Who Thinks Evil, forthcoming. EDITOR: The Redward Edward Papers, by Avram Davidson, 1978; The Best of Avram Davidson, 1979; My Sherlock Holmes: Untold Stories of the Great Detective, 2003; Sherlock Holmes: The Hidden Years, 2004; Sherlock Holmes: The American Years, 2010. **Address:** PO Box 2005, Petaluma, CA 94953-2005, U.S.A. **Online address:** michael@michaelkurland.com

KURLANSKY, Mark. American (born United States), b. 1948. **Genres:** Documentaries/Reportage, Biography, Children's Fiction, Young Adult Nonfiction, History. **Career:** Chicago Tribune, foreign correspondent; Miami Herald, foreign correspondent; Philadelphia Inquirer, foreign correspondent; Brooklyn College, playwright-in-residence. **Publications:** A Continent of Islands: Searching for the Caribbean Destiny, 1992; A Chosen Few: The Resurrection of European Jewry, 1994; Cod: A Biography of the Fish That Changed the World, 1997; The Basque History of the World, 1999; The White Man in the Tree and Other Stories, 2000; The Cod's Tale, 2001; Salt: A World History, 2002; A Chosen Few: The Resurrection of European Jewry, 2002; (ed.) Choice Cuts, A Savory Selection of Food Writing From Around the World and Throughout History, 2002; 1968: The Year that Rocked the World, 2004; Boogaloo on 2nd Avenue: A Novel of Pastry, Guilt and Music, 2005; Girl Who Swam to Euskadi: Euskadiraino Igerian Joan zen Neska, 2005; The Big Oyster: New York on the Half Shell, 2006; Yiddish Bugaloo, 2006; The Story of Salt, 2006; Nonviolence: Twenty-five Lessons From the History of a Dangerous Idea, 2006; Last Fish Tale: The Fate of the Atlantic and Survival in Gloucester, America's Oldest Fishing Port and Most Original Town, 2008; (ed.) Food of a Younger Land: A Portrait of American Food before the National Highway System, before Chain Restaurants and before Frozen Food, when the Nation's Food was Seasonal, Regional and Traditional: From the Lost WPA Files, 2009; (intro. and trans.) E. Ziola, Belly of Paris, 2009; Eastern Stars: How Baseball Changed the Dominican Town of San Pedro de Macors, 2010; Hank Greenberg: The Hero Who Didn't Want to Be One, 2010; Edible stories: A Novel in Sixteen Parts, 2010; What?: Are These the Twenty Most Important Questions in Human History, or, is this a Game of Twenty Questions?, 2011; Battle Fatigue, 2011; (with F. Stockton) The World Without Fish; A Biography of Jewish Baseball Great Hank Greenberg, 2011; Birdseye: The Adventures of a Curious Man, 2012. Contributor to periodicals. Works appear in anthologies. **Address:** c/o Charlotte Sheedy, Charlotte Sheedy Literary Agency, 19h, 240 E39th St., New York, NY 10012, U.S.A.

KURLANTZICK, Joshua. American (born United States), b. 1976?. **Genres:** Politics/Government. **Career:** Time, columnist; New Republic, foreign editor, special correspondent; Pacific Council on International Policy, fellow; University of Southern California, School of Public Diplomacy and the Pacific Council on International Policy, fellow; Council on Foreign Relations, fellow; The Economist, staff, Economics correspondent. **Publications:** Charm Offensive: How China's Soft Power Is Transforming the World, 2007; The Biography of Jim Thompson, forthcoming. Contributor to periodicals and journals. **Address:** Annenberg School, Center on Public Diplomacy, University of South California, 3502 Watt Way, Ste. G4, Los Angeles, CA 90089-0281, U.S.A. **Online address:** jkurlantzick@carnegieendowment.org

KUROKAWA, Mitsuhiro. Japanese (born Japan), b. 1954. **Genres:** Children's Fiction, Illustrations. **Career:** Author and illustrator. **Publications:** SELF-ILLUSTRATED: Kyoryu-tachi, 1987; Pompocoya-ai, 1988; Wa-a Kyoryu-da!, 1990; Kyoryu no Tani, 1991; Kyoryu Little Horn to Kyodai Yokuryu, 1992; Tatakac Kyoryu Torikeratopus, 1992; Kyoryu-tte Nandarou, 1992; Dinosaur Valley, 1992; Daibouken Kyoryu-jima Mogura Hakase wo Sukue!, 1993; Kyoryu Torikeratopus to Kyodai Wani, 1993; Chibi-chibi-saur to Kyofu no Tyrannosaur, 1994; Genshi-jidai no Zetsumetsu Dobutsu, 1994; Kaettekonai Kyoryu-tachi, 1994; Horobiyuku Nihon no Dobutsu tachi, 1995; Sekai no Zetsumetsu Dobutsu, 1995; Kyoryu Torikeratopus to Tyranosaur, 1995; Horobiyuku Sekai no Kyoryu-tachi, 1996; Nihon no Zetsumetsu Dobutsu, 1996; Kyoryu Torikeratopus to Kyodai-game, 1996. Contributor to periodicals. **Address:** Japan Foreign-Rights Centre, 27-8- 804, Naka Ochiai 2-chome, Shinjuku-ku, Tokyo, 161, Japan.

KUROMIYA, Hiroaki. American (born United States), b. 1953?. **Genres:** Social Sciences. **Career:** University of Indiana, professor of history. Writer. **Publications:** Stalin's Industrial Revolution: Politics and Workers, 1928-1932, 1988; Freedom and Terror in the Donbas: A Ukrainian-Russian Borderland, 1870s-1990s, 1998; Stalin, 2005; The Voices of the Dead: Stalin's Great Terror in the 1930s, 2007; (with A. Pepłoński) Miedzy Warszawa a Tokio: polsko-japońska współpraca wywiadowcza 1904-1944, 2009. **Address:** Department of History, Indiana University, 742 Ballantine Hall, 1020 E Kirkwood Ave., Bloomington, IN 47405-7103, U.S.A. **Online address:** hkuromiy@indiana.edu

KURSON, Ken. American (born United States), b. 1969?. **Genres:** Money/Finance, Business/Trade/Industry. **Career:** Worth, staff writer; Source, money columnist; Money, staff; Esquire, money columnist and contributing editor; Green, founder and editor-in-chief; CNN, Take It Personally (weekly program), commentator; National Public Radio Marketplace (program), regular commentator; GreenMagazine.com, editor; journalist. **Publications:** The Green Magazine Guide to Personal Finance: A No B.S. Book for Your Twenties and Thirties, 1998; (with D. Faber) The Faber Report: CNBC's The Brain Tells You How Wall Street Really Works and How You Can Make It Work for You, 2002; (with R.W. Giuliani) Leadership, 2002; (with J.F. Crowley) Chasing Miracles: The Crowley Family Journey of Strength, Hope, and Joy, 2010. **Address:** c/o Author Mail, Little Brown & Co., 1271 Ave. of the Americas, New York, NY 10020, U.S.A.

KURTZ, Don. American (born United States), b. 1951. **Genres:** Novels, Travel/Exploration. **Career:** New Mexico State University, assistant professor of Spanish, 1981, Department of Foreign Studies Program, coordinator, now retired; The Reuel Group Inc., Rio associate. Writer. **Publications:** (With W.D. Goran) Trails of the Guadalupes: A Hiker's Guide to the Trials of Guadalupe Mountains National Park (guidebook), 1978, 2nd ed., 1982; South of the Big Four (novel), 1995; Churchgoers, 2007. **Address:** c/o Deborah Schneider, 250 W 57th St., Ste. 2515, New York, NY 10107, U.S.A. **Online address:** donkurtz7@gmail.com

KURTZ, Donn M. American (born United States) **Genres:** Politics/Government. **Career:** Duquesne University, African Institute, fellow, 1967; University of Louisiana, faculty, 1969-2007, Department of Political Science, head, 1974-81, 1999-2006, Crocker professor of political science, 1989-99, retired, 2007; Louisiana Political Science Association, president, 1972-73, 1986-87. Writer. **Publications:** (Ed. and contrib.) The American Political Family, 1993; Kinship and Politics: The Justices of the United States and Louisiana Supreme Courts, 1997. Contributor to books. **Address:** PO Box 425, Grand Coteau, LA 70541, U.S.A. **Online address:** donnkurtz@netscape.net

KURTZ, Howard. American (born United States), b. 1953. **Genres:** Social Commentary, Adult Non-fiction, Business/Trade/Industry, Essays. **Career:** Washington Star, reporter, 1978-81; Washington Post, reporter, 1981-; CNN, host. **Publications:** (With F. Denton) Reinventing the Newspaper: Essays, 1993; Media Circus: The Trouble with America's Newspapers, 1993; Hot Air: All Talk, all the Time, 1996; Spin Cycle: Inside the Clinton Propaganda Machine, 1998; Spin Cycle: How the White House and the Media Manipulate the News, 1998; Fortune Tellers: Inside Wall Street's Game of Money, Media and Manipulation, 2000; Reality Show: Inside the Last Great Television News War, 2007. Contributor to periodicals. **Address:** The Washington Post, 1150 15th St. NW, Washington, DC 20071, U.S.A. **Online address:** kurtzh@washpost.com

KURTZ, Jane. American (born United States), b. 1952. **Genres:** Novels, Local History/Rural Topics. **Career:** Carbondale New School, teacher and director, 1975-81; Trinidad Catholic High School, teacher, 1984-89; University of North Dakota, senior lecturer, 1995-2002. Writer. **Publications:** FICTION: I'm Calling Molly, 1990; Fire on the Mountain, 1994; Pulling the Lion's Tail, 1995; Miro in the Kingdom of the Sun, 1996; (with C. Kurtz) Only a Pigeon, 1997; Trouble, 1997; The Storyteller's Beads, 1998; Faraway Home, 1999; I'm Sorry, Almira Ann, 1999; River Friendly, River Wild, 2000; Jakarta Missing, 2001; Saba: Under the Hyena's Foot, 2003; Bicycle Madness, 2003; The Feverbird's Claw, 2004; (ed.) Memories of Sun: Stories of Africa and America, 2004; In the Small, Small Night, 2005; Do Kangaroos Wear Seat Belts?, 2005; The Oregon Trail: Chasing the Dream, 2007; What Columbus Found: It Was Orange, It Was Round, 2007. PICTURE BOOKS: Water Hole Waiting, 2001; Rain Romp, 2002. NONFICTION: Ethiopia: The Roof of Africa, 1991; The American Southwest Resource Book: The People, 1996; Terrific Connections with Authors, Illustrators, and Storytellers, 1999; 35 Best Books for Teaching U.S. Regions, 2002; Johnny Appleseed, 2004; Mister Bones: Dinosaur Hunter, 2004; Jane Kurtz and You, 2007; Martin's Dream, 2008; Lanie, 2010; Lanie's Real Adventures, 2010; Lemon Sand, 2011. Contributor to journals and periodicals. **Address:** 1633 Vermont St., Ste. 4, Lawrence, KS 66044, U.S.A. **Online address:** jane@janekurtz.com

KURTZ, Katherine. American (born United States), b. 1944. **Genres:** Novels, Romance/Historical, Science Fiction/Fantasy. **Career:** Los Angeles Police Department, instructional technologist, 1969-81. Writer. **Publications:** Deryni Rising, 1970, rev. ed., 2004; Deryni Checkmate, 1972, rev. ed., 2005; High Deryni, 1973, rev. ed., 2007; Camber of Culdi, 1976; Saint Camber, 1978; Camber the Heretic, 1981; Lammas Night, 1983; The Bishop's Heir, 1984; The King's Justice, 1985; The Quest for Saint Camber, 1986; The Deryni Archives, 1986; The Legacy of Lehr, 1986; The Harrowing of Gwynedd, 1989; Deryni Magic: A Grimoire, 1991; King Javan's Year, 1992; The Bastard Prince, 1994; (ed.) Tales of the Knights Templar, 1995; Two Crowns for America, 1996; (ed.) On Crusade, 1998; King Kelson's Bride, 2000; St. Patrick's Gargoyle, 2001; Venture in Vain, 2001; (ed.) Deryni Tales: An Anthology, 2002; In the King's Service, 2003; Childe Morgan, 2006. ADEPT SERIES (with D.T. Harris): The Adept, 1991; The Lodge of The Lynx, 1992; The Templar Treasure, 1993; Dagger Magic, 1995; Death of an Adept, 1996; The Temple and the Stone, 1998; The Temple and the Crown, 2001. Contributor to periodicals. **Address:** Edge Hill, 1417 N Augusta St., Staunton, VA 24401, U.S.A. **Online address:** kkurtz@iol.ie

KURZ, Ron. (Mark Jackson). American (born United States), b. 1940. **Genres:** Novels, Plays/Screenplays, Cartoons, Young Adult Fiction. **Career:** Maryland Department of Corrections, correctional officer, 1963-69; freelance writer, 1975-. **Publications:** Lethal Gas, 1974; Black Rococo, 1975. Contributor to journals. **Address:** Robert Eisenbach Inc., 6072 Franklin Ave., Ste. 203, Los Angeles, CA 90028, U.S.A.

KURZMAN, Charles. American (born United States), b. 1963. **Genres:** Theology/Religion. **Career:** University of California, postdoctoral fellow, 1993; Georgia State University, assistant professor of sociology, 1994-97; University of North Carolina, assistant professor of sociology, 1998-2004, associate professor of sociology, 2004-08, professor of sociology, 2008-; Carolina Center for the Study of the Middle East and Muslim Civilizations, associate director, 2003-06. Writer and sociologist. **Publications:** (Ed.) Liberal Islam: A Source Book, 1998; (ed.) Modernist Islam, 1840-1940: A Sourcebook, 2002; (ed. and contrib. with M. Browers) An Islamic Reformation?, 2004; The Unthinkable Revolution in Iran, 2004; Democracy Denied, 1905- 1915: Intellectuals and the Fate of Democracy, 2008; The Missing Martyrs: Why There Are So Few Muslim Terrorists, 2011. Contributor of articles to books and periodicals. **Address:** Department of Sociology, University of North Carolina, 155 Hamilton Hall, PO Box 3210, Chapel Hill, NC 27599-3210, U.S.A. **Online address:** kurzman@unc.edu

KURZWEIL, Allen. American (born United States), b. 1960. **Genres:** Novels, Young Adult Non-fiction, Children's Non-fiction. **Career:** Yale University, visiting lecturer; Brown University, John Nicholas Brown Center, visiting fellow. Freelance journalist. **Publications:** NOVELS: A Case of Curiosities, 1992; The Grand Complication, 2001. LEON SERIES: Leon and the Spitting Image, 2003; Leon and the Champion Chip, 2005. NON-FICTION: Potato Chip Science: 29 Incredible Experiments, 2010. Contributor to periodicals. **Address:** c/o Liz Darhansoff, Darhansoff Verrill Feldman Literary Agents, 236 W 26th St., Ste. 802, New York, NY 10001-6736, U.S.A. **Online address:** allen@allenkurzweil.net

KURZYDŁOWSKI, Krzysztof Jan. Polish (born Poland), b. 1954. **Genres:** Engineering, Sciences. **Career:** University of Manitoba, research associate, 1986-88; Warsaw University of Technology, associate dean, 1990-93, professor of materials science and engineering and vice rector for student affairs, 1993-99, professor of technical sciences, 1995-, dean of faculty of materials engineering, 1999-2003, deputy rector, 1999-2003; Brunel University, researcher, 1994; Minister of Science and Higher Education, under secretary of state. Writer. **Publications:** Theory of Dislocations (in Polish), 1984; Geometryczne Aspekty Odkształcenia Plastycznego PolikryształÅ'ów o Sieci Regularnej, 1989; Mechanics of Materials (in Polish), 1992; (with B. Ralph) The Quantitative Description of the Microstructure of Materials, 1995; (ed. with Z. Pakieła) Bulk and Graded Nanometals: Proceedings of Symposium G: European Materials Research Society Fall Meeting 2003: Warsaw University of Technology, 15th-19th September 2003, 2005; (ed. with B. Major and P. Zięba) Foundation of Materials Design, 2006, 2006. **Address:** Faculty of Materials Science and Engineering, Warsaw University of Technology, Woloska 141, Bldg. IM, Warsaw, 02-507, Poland. **Online address:** kjk@inmat.pw.edu.pl

KUSHLAN, James A. American (born United States), b. 1947. **Genres:** Biology, Environmental Sciences/Ecology, Natural History. **Career:** Everglades National Park, research biologist, 1975-84; East Texas State University, Department of Commerce, associate professor, 1984-87, professor of biology, 1987-88, Center for Water Resources Studies, director, 1986-88; University of Mississippi, professor of biology and chair of department, 1988-; Patuxent Wildlife Research Center, director, 1994-2001; Smithsonian Institution, research associate, 1999-; U.S. Geological Survey, senior science adviser, 2001-02. Writer. **Publications:** Ecological Study of an Alligator Pond in the Big Cypress Swamp of Southern Florida, 1972; (with J. Hancock) The Herons Handbook, 1984; (with W.F. Loftus) Freshwater Fishes of Souther Florida, 1987; (with J. Hancock and M.P. Kahl) Storks, Ibises and Spoonbills of the World, 1992; (ed. with H. Hafner) Heron Conservation, 2000; Waterbird Con-

servation for the Americas, 2002; (with J. Hancock) The Herons, 2005. Works appear in anthologies. Contributor to journals. **Address:** 260 Crandon Blvd., Ste. 32-223, PO Box 2008, Key Biscayne, FL 33149-1536, U.S.A. **Online address:** jkushlan@earthlink.net

KUSHNER, Barak. British (born England), b. 1968. **Genres:** History, Adult Non-fiction, Cultural/Ethnic Topics. **Career:** Bernard Zell Day School, teacher, 1990-92; National Institute for Research Advancement, translator and editor, 1995-96; Davidson College, assistant professor of East Asian history, 2002-05; U.S. Department of State, political officer for East Asian affairs, 2005-06; University of Cambridge, university senior lecturer in modern Japanese history, 2006-, Emmanuel College, lecturer in modern Japanese history and fellow, Corpus Christi College, fellow; Japan Society, historical consultant. **Publications:** (Contrib.) America's War in Asia: A Cultural Approach to History and Memory, 1997; The Thought War: Japanese Imperial Propaganda, 2006; (contrib.) Propaganda and Mass Persuasion: A Historical Encyclopedia, 2003; (contrib.) The Role of Japan in Lian Qichao's Introduction of Modern Western Civilization to China, 2004; (contrib.) In Godzilla's Footsteps, 2006; Slurp!: A Culinary and Social History of Ramen, 2012. Contributor to periodicals. **Address:** Faculty of Asian & Middle Eastern Studies, University of Cambridge, Sidgwick Ave., Cambridge, CB CB3 9DA, England. **Online address:** bk284@cam.ac.uk

KUSHNER, Ellen (Ruth). American (born United States), b. 1955. **Genres:** Science Fiction/Fantasy, Children's Fiction, Plays/Screenplays, Poetry. **Career:** Ace Books, editorial assistant, 1977-79; Pocket Books, associate editor, 1979-80; copywriter, reviewer and artist's representative, 1980-87; WGBH Radio, producer/host, 1987-; Sound and Spirit Public Radio Show, host and producer, 1996-. **Publications:** FANTASY NOVELS: Swordspoint: A Melodrama of Manners, 1987; Thomas the Rhymer, 1990; (with D. Sherman) The Fall of the Kings, 2002; The Privilege of the Sword, 2006; Swords of Riverside, 2006; Golden Dreydl, 2007; The Man With the Knives, 2010. NOVELS FOR CHILDREN: Outlaws of Sherwood Forest, 1985; The Enchanted Kingdom, 1986; Statue of Liberty Adventure, 1986; The Mystery of the Secret Room, 1986; Knights of the Round Table, 1988; St. Nicholas and the Valley Beyond, 1994. EDITOR: Basilisk, 1980; (ed. with D.G. Keller and D. Sherman) The Horns of Elfland, 1997; (with H. Black) Welcome to Bordertown, 2011. **Address:** WGBH, 125 Western Ave., Boston, MA 02134, U.S.A. **Online address:** kushner.ellen@gmail.com

KUSHNER, Harold S. American (born United States), b. 1935. **Genres:** Theology/Religion. **Career:** Temple Israel-Great Neck, assistant rabbi, 1962-66; Temple Israel-Natick, rabbi, 1966-90, leader, 1990-, rabbi laureate, rabbi emeritus; Rabbinical Assembly, president, 1972-74; Clark University, visiting lecturer in Jewish literature, 1972-75; Clergy Association of Natick, president, 1976-78; Conservative Judaism Magazine, editor, 1980-84. **Publications:** When Children Ask about God, 1972, rev. ed., 1989; Commanded to Live (collected sermons), 1973; High Holy Day Sermons: Tishrei 5739, October 1978, 1978; When Bad Things Happen to Good People, 1981, 2nd ed., 1989; When Bad Things Happen to Good People: December 6, 1982, 1982; When All You've Ever Wanted Isn't Enough: The Search for a Life That Matters, 1986; Giving Meaning to Life: Proceedings of a Seminar on Adding Meaning to Our Lives in an Unfair World, 1988; Who Needs God, 1989; To Life!: A Celebration of Jewish Being and Thinking, 1993; How Good Do We Have to Be?: A New Understanding of Guilt and Forgiveness, 1996; Living a Life That Matters: Resolving the Conflict Between Conscience and Success, 2001; The Lord Is My Shepherd: Healing Wisdom of the Twenty-third Psalm, 2003; Overcoming Life's Disappointments, 2006; Faith & Family: Favorite Sermons of Rabbi Harold S. Kushner, 2007; Conquering Fear: Living Boldly in an Uncertain World, 2009; The Book of Job: When Bad Things Happened to a Good Person, 2012. **Address:** Temple Israel, 145 Hartford St., Natick, MA 01760-3125, U.S.A.

KUSHNER, James A(lan). American (born United States), b. 1945. **Genres:** Demography, Ethics, Law, Politics/Government, Regional/Urban Planning, Social Commentary, Transportation, Urban Studies, Urban Studies. **Career:** Office of Economic Opportunity, director of housing, 1969-70; Legal Aid of Western, Law Reform Project, managing attorney, 1970-73; University of California, National Housing and Economic Development Law Project, project attorney, 1973-75; Southwestern University, School of Law, professor of law, 1975-, Buchalter and Rosenberg professor, visiting professor; Los Angeles County Superior Court, temporary judge, 1981-86; university of Virginia School of Architecture, visiting professor; Dortmund University, School of Regional Planning, visiting professor; University of Utrecht, visiting professor; Saxion University, visiting professor; Fair Housing Congress of Southern California, president. Writer. **Publications:** Apartheid in America, 1980; Housing and Community Development, 1981, 3rd ed., 1999; Fair Housing: Discrimination in Real Estate, Community Development, and Revitalization, 1983, 2nd ed., 1995; Government Discrimination: Equal Protection Law and Litigation, 1988; Subdivision Law and Growth Management, 1991, 2nd ed., 2001; Land Use Regulation: Cases and Materials, 1999, 3rd ed., 2008; Comparative Urban Planning Law: An Introduction to Urban Land Development Law in the United States through the Lens of Comparing the Experience of Other Nations, 2003; The Post-Automobile City: Legal Mechanisms to Establish the Pedestrian-Friendly City, 2004; Healthy Cities: The Intersection of Urban Planning, Law and Health, 2007; Global Climate Change and the Road to Extinction, 2008. **Address:** School of Law, Southwestern University, Rm. BW343, 3050 Wilshire Blvd., Los Angeles, CA 90010-1106, U.S.A. **Online address:** jkushner@swlaw.edu

KUSHNER, Lawrence. American (born United States), b. 1943?. **Genres:** Theology/Religion, Young Adult Fiction. **Career:** Congregation Solel, rabbinic fellow-in-residence, 1969-71; Congregation Beth El, Sudbury, rabbi, 1971-; Hebrew Union College, Jewish Institute of Religion, rabbi-in-residence, instructor, 1986-; Jewish Spirituality at the Graduate Theological University in Berkeley, visiting professor; Reform Judaism s Commission on Religious Living, Rabbinic chairman; N.P.R s All Things Considered, commentator; Congregation Beth El in Sudbury, rabbi. Teacher and author of books on Jewish spirituality. **Publications:** Sefer Otiyot: The Book of Letters: A Mystical Alef-Bait, 1975, 2nd ed., 1990; Honey from the Rock: (Devash mi-sela): Visions of Jewish Mystical Renewal, 1977, rev. ed. as Honey from the Rock: (Devash mi-sela): An Introduction to Jewish Mysticism, 1990; The River of Light: Spirituality, Judaism and the Evolution of Consciousness, 1981; (with D. Kerdeman) The Invisible Chariot: An Introduction to Kabbalah and Jewish Spirituality, 1986; The Book of Miracles: A Young Person's Guide to Jewish Spiritual Awareness: For Parents to Read to Their Children, for Children to Read to Their Parents, 1987, 10th ed., 1997; River of Light: Spirituality, Judaism, Consciousness, 1990; God Was in This Place and I, I Did Not Know: Finding Self, Spirituality and Ultimate Meaning, 1991; (K.M. Olitsky) Sparks Beneath the Surface: A Spiritual Commentary on the Torah, 1993; The Book of Words: (Sefer shel devarim): Sefer Shel Devarim: Talking Spiritual Life, Living Spiritual Talk, 1994; Invisible Lines of Connection: Sacred Stories of the Ordinary, 1996; Eyes Remade for Wonder: A Lawrence Kushner Reader, 1999; Kabbalah: The Way of Light, 1999; (with K. Kushner) Because Nothing Looks like God, 2000; The River of Light: Jewish Mystical Awareness, 2000; (with K. Kushner) Where Is God?, 2000; (with K. Kushner) What Does God Look Like?, 2001; (with K. Kushner) How Does God Make Things Happen?, 2001; The Way into Jewish Mystical Tradition, 2001; Jewish Spirituality: A Brief Introduction for Christians, 2001; (with D. Mamet) Five Cities of Refuge: Weekly Reflections on Genesis, Exodus, Leviticus, Numbers, and Deuteronomy, 2003; (with N. Polen) Filling Words with Light: Hasidic and Mystical Reflections on Jewish Prayer, 2004; (with G. Schmidt) In God's Hands, 2005; Kabbalah: A Love Story, 2006; I'm God, You're Not: Observations On Organized Religion and Other Disguises of the Ego, 2010. **Address:** The Congregation Emanu-El, 2 Lake St., San Francisco, CA 94118, U.S.A. **Online address:** csimona@emanuelsf.org

KUSHNER, Malcolm. (Malcolm L. Kushner). American (born United States), b. 1952. **Genres:** Business/Trade/Industry, Humor/Satire, Food And Wine, Economics, Communications/Media. **Career:** California Workers Compensation Appeals Board, staff attorney, 1980-81; Graham & James (law firm), associate, 1981-82; Malcolm Kushner & Associates, president, 1982-; San Francisco Sheriff's Department, humor instructor; Stanford University, lecturer; University of Santa Clara, lecturer; University of California, lecturer. Writer. **Publications:** (As Malcolm L. Kushner) The Light Touch: How to Use Humor for Business Success, 1990; (with R. Anthony) High Octane Selling: Boost Your Creative Power to Close More Sales, 1995; Successful Presentations for Dummies, 1996; Jest for Success: How to Win with Wit, 1999; Public Speaking for Dummies, 1999, 2nd ed., 2004; Vintage Humor for Wine Lovers, 2002; Presentations for Dummies, 2004; California Squisine: Healthy Food that's Fast and Fun for Kids, 2006; The Little Book of Humorous Quotes, 2011; The Official Book of Mob Humor, 2012. Contributor to perioidcals. **Address:** Malcolm Kushner and Associates, PO Box 668, Menasha, WI 54952, U.S.A. **Online address:** mk@kushnergroup.com

KUSHNER, Malcolm L. *See* **KUSHNER, Malcolm.**

KUSHNER, Rachel. American (born United States), b. 1968?. **Genres:** Novels, Essays. **Career:** Grand Street Magazine, editor; BOMB Magazine, editor; Soft Targets, editor. **Publications:** Telex from Cuba (novel), 2008. Contributor to books. **Address:** Simon & Schuster Inc., 1230 Ave. of America, New York, NY 10020, U.S.A. **Online address:** rk@telexfromcuba.com

KUSHNER, Tony. American (born United States), b. 1956. **Genres:** Plays/Screenplays, History. **Career:** United Nations Plaza Hotel, switchboard operator, 1979-85; Saint Louis Repertory Theater, assistant director, 1985-86; New York Theater Workshop, artistic director, 1987-88; Theater Communication Group, director of literary services, 1990-91; Juilliard School of Drama, playwright-in-residence, 1990-92. Writer. **Publications:** PLAYS: Three Plays for Young Audiences, 1987; Yes, Yes, No, No, 1985; Stella, 1987; A Bright Room Called Day, 1987, 1991; Hydriotaphia, 1987; The Illusion L'Illusion Comique, 1991; Widows, 1991; Angels in America: A Gay Fantasia on National Themes, vol. I: Millennium Approaches, 1992, vol. II: Perestroika, 1992; Meditation from Angels in America, 1994; Thinking about the Longstanding Problems of Virtue and Happiness, 1995; A Dybbuk; Or, Between Two Worlds, 1997; The Good Person of Szechuan, 1997; (co-author) Love's Fire: Seven New Plays Inspired by Seven Shakespearean Sonnets, 1998; Henry Box Brown or the Mirror of Slavery, 1998; Death & Taxes: Hydriotaphia, and Other Plays, 2000; Homebody/Kabul, 2002, rev. ed., 2004; Caroline or Change, 2004. OTHER: A Meditation from Angels in America, 1994; Tony Kushner in Conversation, 1997; Death and Taxes: Hydriotaphia and Other Plays, 2000; (adapter) Brundibar, 2002, rev. ed., 2006; Art of Maurice Sendak: 1980 to the Present, 2003; (with Grove and A.Solomon) Wrestling with Zion: Progressive Jewish-American Responses to the Israeli-Palestinian Conflict, 2003; (ed. with N. Valman) Philosemitism, Antisemitism and the Jews: Perspectives from the Middle Ages to the Twentieth Century, 2004; Holocaust: Critical Historical Approaches, 2005; But the Giraffe!: A Curtain Raiser for Hans Krása's Brundibár, 2008; (trans.) Mother Courage and her Children: A Chronicle of the Thirty Years War, 2009. **Address:** Steven Barclay Agency, 12 Western Ave., Petaluma, CA 94952, U.S.A.

KUSHNICK, Louis. American (born United States), b. 1938. **Genres:** Race Relations, Administration/Management, Social Commentary, Adult Nonfiction, Business/Trade/Industry. **Career:** University of Manchester, Ahmed Iqbal Ullah Race Relations Resource Center, director, senior lecturer, honorary professorial fellow, professor of race relations, through 2007, now professor emeritus, 2007-. Sociologist and writer. **Publications:** The Role of Management: Nondiscrimination or Affirmative Action?, 1968; Race, Class and Struggle: Essays on Racism and Inequality in Britain, the United States and Western Europe, 1998. EDITOR: (with J. Jennings) A New Introduction to Poverty: The Role of Race, Power and Politics, 1999; (with B.P. Bowser and P. Grant) Against the Odds: Scholars Who Challenged Racism in the Twentieth Century, 2002. Contributor to books. **Address:** Ahmed Iqbal Ullah Race Relations Resource Centre, The University of Manchester, University Precinct Ctr., Oxford Rd., Manchester, GM M13 3PL, England. **Online address:** lou.kushnick@man.ac.uk

KUSUGAK, Michael (Arvaarluk). Canadian (born Canada), b. 1948. **Genres:** Children's Fiction, Children's Non-fiction, Mythology/Folklore, Picture/Board Books, Cultural/Ethnic Topics. **Career:** Nunavut Arctic College, educational administrator. Writer and storyteller. **Publications:** FOR CHILDREN FICTION: (with R. Munsch) A Promise Is a Promise, 1988; Hide and Sneak, 1992; Northern Lights: The Soccer Trails, 1993; My Arctic 1,2,3, 1996; Arctic Stories, 1998; Who Wants Rocks?, 1999; The Curse of the Shaman: A Marble Island Story, 2006; The Littlest Sled Dog, 2008. NON-FICTION: Baseball Bats for Christmas, 1990. **Address:** 234 Fern Rd. W, Qualicum Beach, BC V9K 1S4, Canada. **Online address:** storyteller@michaelkusugak.com

KUTTNER, Robert (Louis). American (born United States), b. 1943. **Genres:** Economics, Politics/Government. **Career:** Pacifica Radio, correspondent and program director, 1968-71; Village Voice, editor, 1971-73; More, contributing editor, 1973-78; Washington Post, national staff writer, 1974-75; National Commission on Neighborhoods, executive director, 1978; Boston University, visiting professor, 1980-82; Working Papers, editor, 1980-83; New Republic, economics writer and editor, 1983-91, economics editor; Business Week, columnist, 1984, contributing columnist; Boston Globe, columnist, 1985-; Washington Post Syndicate, columnist, 1985-; Economic

Policy Institute, co-founder, 1986, board director; University of Massachusetts, visiting professor, 1987-88; Families USA, board director, 1989-96; The American Prospect Inc., co-founder and co-editor, 1989-; Brandeis University, visiting professor, 1991-92, 2003; Working Papers for a New Society, editor-in-chief; Harvard University, John F. Kennedy Institute of Politics, visiting professor; Demos, distinguished senior fellow. **Publications:** NON-FICTION: Revolt of the Haves: Tax Rebellions and Hard Times, 1980; The Economic Illusion: False Choices between Prosperity and Social Justice, 1984; The Life of the Party: Democratic Prospects in 1988 and Beyond, 1987; Managed Trade and Economic Sovereignty, 1989; The End of Laissez-Faire: National Purpose and the Global Economy after the Cold War, 1991; Export Controls: Industrial Policy in Reverse, 1991; (ed.) Ticking Time Bombs: The New Conservative Assaults on Democracy, 1996; Everything for Sale: The Virtues and Limits of Markets, 1997; (with S. Trotter) Family Re-Union: Reconnecting Parents and Children in Adulthood, 2002; (ed.) Making Work Pay: America after Welfare: A Reader from The American Prospect, 2002; (with J.L. Brown and T. Shapiro) Building a Real Ownership Society, 2005; Squandering of America: How the Failure of Our Politics Undermines Our Prosperity, 2007; Obama's Challenge: America's Economic Crisis and the Power of a Transformative Presidency, 2008; A Presidency in Peril: The Inside Story of Obama's Promise, Wall Street's Power, and the Struggle to Control Our Economic Future, 2010. Contributor of articles to periodicals. **Address:** The American Prospect Inc., 1710 Rhode Island Ave. NW, 12th Fl., Washington, DC 20036, U.S.A. **Online address:** kuttner@prospect.org

KUUSISTO, Stephen. American (born United States), b. 1955. **Genres:** Poetry. **Career:** University of Iowa, instructor, 1983-85; Hobart and William Smith Colleges, adjunct assistant professor and assistant dean, 1985-93; Ohio State University, Moritz College of Law, Center for Interdisciplinary Law and Policy Studies, fellow, 1985-93, Department of English, assistant professor, 2000-06, associate professor, 2006-07, professor, 2007-, Program in Disability Studies, co-director, 2000-07, M.F.A. Program, visiting writers coordinator, 2002-04, University of Iowa Hospitals and Clinics, Carver Center for Macular Degeneration, professor of ophthalmology, 2007-; Guiding Eyes for the Blind, director of student services, 1995-2000. Writer. **Publications:** (Ed. with D. Tall and D. Weiss) Taking Note: From Poets' Notebooks, 1991; (ed. with D. Tall and D. Weiss) The Poet's Notebook: Excerpts from the Notebooks of Contemporary American Poets, 1995; Planet of the Blind, 1998; Only Bread, Only Light: Poems, 2000; Eavesdropping: A Life by Ear, 2006; Do Not Interrupt: A Playful Take on the Art of Conversation, 2010. Contributor to periodicals and journals. **Address:** Irene Skolnick Literary Agency, 22 W 23rd St., 5th Fl., New York, NY 10010-5240, U.S.A. **Online address:** stephen-kuusisto@uiowa.edu

KUVSHINOFF, Boris W. American (born United States), b. 1922. **Genres:** Novels, Young Adult Fiction, Poetry, Sciences, Translations, Meteorology/Atmospheric Sciences. **Career:** Johns Hopkins University, Applied Physics Laboratory, translator of foreign scientific and technical literature, 1958-60, supervisor of document library, 1960-70, information section supervisor of fire problems program, 1971-79, technical documentation analyst, 1980-85, U.S. Air Force Logistics Command Automated Warehouse Acquisition, program manager, 1986-87, APL Business Systems Documentation, manager, 1988-93; Fire Technology Abstracts, managing editor, 1977-79; McClure Center Magazine, managing editor, 1989-91; writer, 1993-. **Publications:** (Trans.) K.I. Shchelkin and Y.K. Troshin, Gas Dynamics of Combustion, 1965; (ed. and trans.) R.I. Soloukhin, Shock Waves and Detonations in Gases, 1965; (comp. and ed.) Fire Sciences Dictionary, 1977; (with R.A. Henle) Desktop Computers: In Perspective, 1992; Curse of the Firebirds Feather, forthcoming; The Tanana River Icebreakers, forthcoming. Work represented in anthologies. Contributor to professional journals. **Address:** 1103 Starway Ct., Baltimore, MD 21228-2728, U.S.A. **Online address:** b-kuvshinoff@worldnet.att.net

KUYPER, Sjoerd. Dutch (born Netherlands), b. 1952. **Genres:** Children's Fiction, Novels, Children's Non-fiction, Poetry. **Career:** Author. **Publications:** Mooie Gedichten, 1974; Ik herinner mij Klaas Kristiaan (poems), 1974; Handboek voor overleden knaagdieren, 1975; Dagen uit het leven, 1977; (ed.) Ontmoet de dichters, 1977; (with J.J. Diepstraten) Het nieuwe proza: interviews met jonge nederlandse schrijvers, 1978; Een kleine jongen en z'n beer, 1978; De glazen kamer: verhalen, 1979; (with J.J. Diepstraten) Dichters: interviews, 1980; Ratten en flamingo's, 1982; Een reisgenoot, 1985; (with J.J. Diepstraten) De verborgen steeg, 1986; De ogen van het paard, 1987; Het zand: verhalen, 1987; Majesteit, Uw ontbijt (juvenile), 1988; Nachtkind, 1992; Het zakmes, 1992; Robin en Suze, 1993; Zeepziederij de adelaar, 1994;

Het eiland Klaasje (juvenile), 1995; Robin en God, 1997; (with A. van Häringen) Malmok, 1999; Hoofden uit de mist: Over de moderne jeugdliteratuur, 2004; The Swan's Child, 2006; September, 2009; De heks in je hoofd, 2011. **Address:** c/o Author Mail, Uitgeverig Leopold BV, PO Box 3879, Amsterdam, 1001 AR, Netherlands.

KUZNESKI, Chris. American (born United States), b. 1969. **Genres:** Mystery/Crime/Suspense, Novels. **Career:** Pitt News, sportswriter, 1988-91; Indiana Gazette, sportswriter, 1991-93; Pittsburgh Post-Gazette, staff, 1992-98; Franklin Area School District, English teacher and football coach, 1993-98. Journalist. **Publications:** PAYNE AND JONES SERIES: The Plantation, 2000; Sign of the Cross, 2006; Sword of God, 2007; The Lost Throne, 2008; The Prophecy, 2009; The Secret Crown, 2010; The Death Relic, 2011. **Address:** c/o Scott Miller, Trident Media Group L.L.C., 41 Madison Ave., 36th Fl., New York, NY 10010-2257, U.S.A. **Online address:** chris@chriskuzneski.com

KUZNETSOV, Nickolaj. (Nickolaj Yu Kuznetsov). Ukranian (born Ukraine), b. 1955?. **Genres:** Mathematics/Statistics, Information Science/Computers, Engineering. **Career:** Institute of Cybernetics, junior researcher, 1979-84, senior researcher, 1984-89, leading researcher, 1989-. Writer. **Publications:** (With I.N. Kovalenko and V.M. Shurnkov) Random Processes, 1983; (with I.N. Kovalenko and V.M. Shurenkov) Sluchaïnye Protséssy: Spravochnik, 1983; (with Kovalenko) Methods for the Evolution of Highly Reliable Systems, 1988; (with I.N. Kovalenko) Metody Rascheta Vysokonadezhnykh Sistem, 1988; (with I.N. Kovalenko and V.M. Shurenkov) Models Of Random Processes A Handbook For Mathematicians And Engineers, 1996; (with I.N. Kovalenko and P.A. Pegg) The Mathematical Theory of Reliability of Time-Dependant Systems, with Practical Applications, 1997. **Address:** Institute of Cybernetics, Prospect Glushkova 40, Kiev, 252207, Ukraine.

KUZNETSOV, Nickolaj Yu. See **KUZNETSOV, Nickolaj.**

KVASNOSKY, Laura McGee. American (born United States), b. 1951. **Genres:** Children's Fiction, Illustrations, Humor/Satire. **Career:** Graphic Designer, 1980-95; Vermont College, MFA in Writing for Childrenand Young People program, faculty, 2000-. **Publications:** Pink, Red, Blue, What are You?, 1994; One, Two, Three, Play with Me, 1994; See You Later, Alligator, 1995; Mr. Chips!, 1996; What Shall I Dream?, 1996; Zelda and Ivy 1998; Zelda and Ivyand the Boy Next Door, 1999; Zelda and Ivy One Christmas, 2000; Frank and Izzy Set Sail, 2004; Zelda and Ivy, the Runaways, 2006; Zelda and Ivy: Keeping Secrets, 2009; Zelda and Ivy: The Big Picture, 2010. OTHER: One Lucky Summer (middlegrades novel), 2002; Really Truly Bingo, 2008. Illustrator of books by others. **Address:** c/o Author Mail, Candlewick Press Inc., 2067 Massachusetts Ave., Cambridge, MA 02140-1338, U.S.A. **Online address:** laura@lmkbooks.com

KWON, O. Yul. Australian/Korean (born Korea (South)), b. 1936. **Genres:** Economics, Business/Trade/Industry. **Career:** Bank of Korea, economist, 1962-64; McMaster University, instructor, 1968-69; Canadian Department of Finance, tax policy officer, 1971-75; University of Regina, associate professor, professor, 1975-95; Korea University, Business School, adjunct professor; Net Five Telecom, vice president, 1991-95; Korea Exchange Bank of Canada, board director, 1992-95; Saskatchewan Chamber of Commerce, board director, 1993-95; Griffith University, professor, 1996-, Australian Centre for Korean Studies, director, Korean Studies, Korean foundation chair. Writer. **Publications:** The Korean Mineral Market: Opportunities and Marketing Strategies for Canada, 1987; International Privatization: Global Trends, Policies, Processes, and Experiences, 1990; Korea's Mineral Trade with China and Russia: Challenges for Canada, 1994; (ed. with W. Shepherd) Korea's Economic Prospects: From Financial Crisis to Prosperity, 2001; (with I. Oh) Korean Direct Investment in Australia: Issues and Prospects, 2001; (with S. Jwa and K. Lee) Korea's New Economic Strategy in the Globalization Era, 2003; Australian Direct Investment in Korea: Issues and Prospects, 2003; International Business in Korea: The Evolution of the Market in the Globalization Era, 2008; The Korean Economy in Transition: An Institutional Perspective, 2010. **Address:** Griffith University, 170 Kessels Rd., Brisbane, QL 4111, Australia. **Online address:** y.kwon@griffith.edu.au

KWONG, Julia C. Canadian/Hong Kong (born Hong Kong), b. 1946. **Genres:** Education. **Career:** St. Francois Canossian College, teacher, 1967-69; University of Toronto, lecturer, 1975, visiting professor, 1976; St. Mary's University, professor of sociology, 1975-76; University of Manitoba, assistant professor, 1976-84, associate professor, 1984-89, professor of sociology, 1989-, distinguished professor, 2004, distinguished professor emeritus, 2006-; Harvard University, research associate, 1980-81, corresponding research associate, 1992-93; Royal Society of Canada, fellow, 2003. Writer. **Publications:** (With G. Baureiss) The History of the Chinese Community of Winnipeg, 1979; Chinese Education in Transition: Prelude to the Cultural Revolution, 1979; Sociolgy of Education, 1986; Cultural Revolution in China's Schools, 1988; (with I. Huffman) The Dream of Gold Mountain, 1989; The Political Economy of Corruption in China, 1997; (ed. with M. Wanhua) Chinese Women and the Teaching Profession, 2004. Contributor of articles to journals. **Address:** Department of Sociology, University of Manitoba, Isbister Bldg., 318-183 Dafoe Rd., Winnipeg, MB R3T 2N2, Canada. **Online address:** jkwong@cc.umanitoba.ca

KWONG, Peter. American (born United States), b. 1936. **Genres:** Cultural/Ethnic Topics, History, Social Sciences. **Career:** State University of New York, College at Old Westbury, assistant professor, 1972-79, associate professor, 1979-90, professor, 1990-93; Columbia University, Department of History, adjunct professor, 1991-94; Yale University, Cardozo visiting professor in United States history, 1992-93; City University of New York, Hunter College, Asian American Studies Program, director, 1993-2001, Department of Urban Affairs and Planning, professor, 1993-, Graduate Center, professor of sociology, 1994-. Writer. **Publications:** Chinatown, New York: Labor and Politics, 1930-1950, 1979, rev. ed., 2001; New Chinatown, 1987, rev. ed., 1996; Forbidden Workers: Illegal Chinese Immigrants and American Labor, 1997; (co-ed.) The Portable Lower East Side: New Asia, 1990; (with D. Miscević) Chinese America: The Untold Story of America's Oldest New Community, 2005. **Address:** Department of Urban Affairs and Planning, Hunter College, City University of New York, 1616 HW, West Bldg., 695 Park Ave., New York, NY 10065-5024, U.S.A. **Online address:** pkwong@hunter.cuny.edu

KYDD, Andrew H. American (born United States), b. 1963?. **Genres:** Adult Non-fiction, International Relations/Current Affairs, Politics/Government, Psychology. **Career:** University of California, faculty; Harvard University, faculty; University of Wisconsin-Madison, associate professor of political science, 2007-. Writer. **Publications:** Trust and Mistrust in International Relations, 2005. Contributor to periodicals. **Address:** Department of Political Science, University of Wisconsin-Madison, 322c North Hall, 1050 Bascom Mall, Madison, WI 53706, U.S.A. **Online address:** kydd@wisc.edu

KYLE, Donald G. American (born United States), b. 1950. **Genres:** Sports/Fitness. **Career:** McMaster University, lecturer in history, 1980; University of Winnipeg, lecturer in classics, 1980-81; University of Saskatchewan, visiting assistant professor, 1981-84, Museum of Antiquities, administrator, 1982-84; University of Texas at Arlington, assistant professor, 1984-89, associate professor, 1989-98, professor of history and classical studies, 1998-, assistant department chair, 1987-94, chair of history department, 1999-2006, Academy of Distinguished Teachers, distinguished teaching professor, 1999-; Southern Methodist University, adjunct professor of history, 1993; University of Queensland, School of History, Philosophy, Religion and Classics, R.D. Milns visiting professor, 2009. Writer. **Publications:** Athletics in Ancient Athens, 1987, 2nd rev. ed., 1993; (ed. with G.D. Stark) Essays on Sport History and Sport Mythology, 1990; Spectacles of Death in Ancient Rome, 1998; Sport and Spectacle in the Ancient World, 2007; (ed. with R.B. Fairbanks) Baseball in America and America in Baseball, 2008. Contributor to books. **Address:** Department of History, University of Texas at Arlington, PO Box 19529, Arlington, TX 76019-0529, U.S.A. **Online address:** kyle@uta.edu

KYLE, Susan S(paeth). Also writes as Katy Currie, Diana Palmer, Diana Blayne. American (born United States), b. 1946. **Genres:** Novels, Romance/Historical, Science Fiction/Fantasy, Novellas/Short Stories, History. **Career:** Times, district staff reporter, 1969-84; Tri-County Advertiser, staff reporter, 1972-82; novelist, 1979-. **Publications:** NOVELS AS SUSAN KYLE: The Morcai Battalion (science fiction), 1980, rev. ed., 2007; Diamond Spur, 1988; Fire Brand, 1989; True Colors, 1991; Escapade, 1992; After Midnight, 1993; All that Glitters, 1995; The Recruit, 2009. NOVELS AS DIANA PALMER: Now and Forever, 1979; Storm over the Lake, 1979; To Have and to Hold, 1979; To Love and Cherish, 1980; Sweet Enemy, 1980; Bound by a Promise, 1980; Dream's End, 1980; Love on Trial, 1980; If Winter Comes, 1981; At Winter's End, 1981; The Cowboy and the Lady, 1982; Heather's Song, 1982; Friends and Lovers, 1983; Fire and Ice, 1983; Snow Kisses, 1983; Darling Enemy, 1983; Diamond Girl, 1984; The Rawhide Man, 1984; Lady Love, 1984; Roomful of Roses, 1984; Heart of Ice, 1984; Passion Flower, 1984; Cattleman's Choice, 1985; Love by Proxy, 1985; The Australian, 1985; Eye of the Tiger, 1986; Loveplay, 1986; Rawhide and Lace, 1986; Champagne

Girl, 1986; After the Music, 1986; Unlikely Lover, 1986; Rage of Passion, 1986; Fit for a King, 1987; Betrayed by Love, 1987; Woman Hater, 1987; Hoodwinked, 1989; His Girl Friday, 1989; Night Fever, 1990; Sweet Enemy/Love on Trial, 1990; Storm over the Lake/To Love and Cherish, 1990; If Winter Comes/Now and Forever, 1990; After the Music/Dream's End, 1990; Bound by a Promise/Passion Flower, 1990; To Have and to Hold/The Cowboy and the Lady, 1990; Lacy (historical), 1991; Trilby (historical), 1993; Amelia (historical), 1993; King's Ransom, 1993; Calamity Mom, 1993; Secret Agent Man, 1993; (with D. Macomber and J. Duncan) To Mother with Love (stories); Nora, 1994; Noelle, 1995; Magnolia, 1996; Savage Heart, 1997; Once in Paris, 1998; Midnight Rider, 1998; Paper Rose, 1999; Callaghan's Bride, 1999; Beloved, 1999; Love with a Long, Tall Texan (short stories), 1999; Mercenary's Woman, 2000; Matt Caldwell, 2000; Lord of the Desert, 2000; Circle Of Gold, 2000; The Wedding in White, 2000; The Winter Soldier, 2001; The Last Mercenary, 2001; The Texas Rose, 2001; After the Music, 2001; A Man of Means, 2002; Lionhearted, 2002; Desperado, 2002; (with J. Blake and H. Graham) With a Suthern Touch, 2002; (with L. Worth and L. Lough) Blessings in Disguise, 2003; (foreword) The Black Moth, 2003; Lawless, 2003; Man in Control, 2003; Texas Ranger, 2004; Carrera's Bride, 2004; Renegade, 2004; Cattleman's Pride, 2004; Before Sunrise, 2005; Boss Man, 2005; Outsider, 2006; Heart of Winter, 2006; Lacy, 2006; Tycoon Lovers, 2006; Heartbreaker, 2006; Winter Roses, 2007; Lawman, 2007; Iron Cowboy, 2008; Man Of The Hour, 2008; Heart of Stone, 2008; Fearless, 2008; (foreword) Black Moth, 2009; Miss Greenhorn, 2009; Diamond in the Rough, 2009; Heartless, 2009; The Winterman, 2009; The Maverick, 2009; Rogue Stallion, 2010, Will of Steel, 2010; Tough to Tame, 2010; Innocence Protected, 2010; Dangerous, 2010; Merciless, 2011, A Man For All Seasons, 2011; True Blue, 2011; (with S. Mallery) Montana Mavericks Weddings, 2011; Wyoming Tough, 2011; Courageous, 2012. MERCENARY SERIES AS DIANA PALMER: The Tender Stranger, 1985; Soldier of Fortune, 1985; Enamoured, 1988. LONG TALL TEXAN SERIES AS DIANA PALMER: Calhoun, 1988; Justin, 1988; Tyler, 1988; Sutton's Way, 1989; Ethan, 1990; Connal, 1990; Harden, 1991; Evan, 1991; Donovan, 1992; Emmett, 1993. MAN OF THE MONTH SERIES AS DIANA PALMER: Reluctant Father, 1989; Hunter, 1990; Nelson's Brand, 1991; The Best Is Yet to Come, 1991; Night of Love, 1993. MOST WANTED TRILOGY AS DIANA PALMER: The Case of the Mesmerizing Boss, 1992; The Case of the Confirmed Bachelor, 1992; The Case of the Missing Secretary, 1992. CANDLELIGHT ECSTASY SERIES AS DIANA BLAYNE: A Waiting Game, 1982; A Loving Arrangement, 1983; White Sand Wild Sea, 1983; Dark Surrender, 1983. NOVELS AS DIANA BLAYNE: Color Love Blue, 1984; Tangled Destinies, 1986; Denim and Lace, 1990. AS KATY CURRIE: Blind Promises, 1984. Works appear in anthologies. Contributor to periodicals. **Address:** c/o Maureen Walters, Curtis Brown Ltd., 10 Astor Pl., New York, GA 10003, U.S.A. **Online address:** diana@dianapalmer.com

KYNASTON, David. British (born England), b. 1951. **Genres:** History, Money/Finance, Biography, Business/Trade/Industry, Education, Reference. **Career:** Kingston University, research fellow in history, research fellow, visiting professor, 2001. Writer. **Publications:** King Labour: The British Working Class, 1850-1914, 1976; The Secretary of State, 1978; The Chancellor of the Exchequer, 1980; Bobby Abel: Professional Batsman 1857-1936, 1982; Archie's Last Stand: M.C.C. in New Zealand, 1922-23: Being an Account of Mr. A.C. MacLaren's Tour and His Last Stand, 1984; The Financial Times: A Centenary History, 1988; WG's Birthday Party, 1990; The City of London, vol. I: A World of Its Own 1815-90, 1994, vol. II: Golden Years 1890-1914, 1995, vol. IV: A Club No More, 1945-2000, 2001; (ed. with R. Roberts) The Bank of England: Money, Power and Influence 1694-1994, 1995; City State: How the Markets Came to Rule the World, 2001; Austerity Britain, 1945-51, 2007; Family Britain 1951-1957, 2009. **Address:** Faculty of Arts and Social Sciences, Kingston University, Penrhyn Rd., Kingston upon Thames, SR KT1 2EE, England. **Online address:** d.kynaston@kingston.ac.uk

KYNOCH, Gary. Canadian (born Canada), b. 1962?. **Genres:** Women's Studies And Issues, History. **Career:** Dalhousie University, associate professor of history, 2002-. Writer. **Publications:** From Ninevite to Comtsotsi: Township Gangs, Divided Communities, and Urban Violence in Twentieth Century South Africa, 1998; (co-author) Cross- Border Raiding and Community Conflict in the Lesotho-South African Border Zone, 2001; We Are Fighting the World: A History of the Marashea Gangs in South Africa, 1947-1999, 2005. Contributor of articles to periodicals. **Address:** Department of History, Faculty of Arts & Social Sciences, Dalhousie University, Rm. 1158, 6135 University Ave., Halifax, NS B3H 4P9, Canada. **Online address:** gary.kynoch@dal.ca

L

LAAS, Virginia J(eans). American (born United States), b. 1943. **Genres:** History, Adult Non-fiction, Social Commentary, Biography, Autobiography/ Memoirs. **Career:** Teacher, 1964-65; Pittsburg State University, lecturer in history, 1981-88; Missouri Southern State University, lecturer, 1984-88, instructor, 1988-92, assistant professor, 1992-97, associate professor of history, 1997-2002, professor of history, 2003-, now professor emeritus; University of Wisconsin, intern, 1986. Writer. **Publications:** (With R.Stewart and D. Stewart) An Introduction to the Tri-State Mineral Museum, 1986; (with D.T. Cornish) Lincoln's Lee: The Life of Rear Admiral Samuel Phillips Lee, 1986; Love and Power in the 19th Century: The Marriage of Violet Blair, 1998. EDITOR: Guidebook to the Tri-State Mineral Museum, 1986; Wartime Washington: The Civil War Letters of Elizabeth Blair Lee, 1991; Bridging Two Eras: The Autobiography of Emily Newell Blair, 1977-1951, 1999. Contributor of reviews and articles to periodicals. **Address:** School of Arts and Sciences, Missouri Southern State University, WH-244, 3950 E Newman Rd., Joplin, MO 64801-1595, U.S.A. **Online address:** laas-v@mssu.edu

LABAND, John (Paul Clow). Canadian/South African (born South Africa), b. 1947. **Genres:** History, Third World. **Career:** University of Natal, lecturer, 1972-73, 1974-81, senior lecturer, 1982-89, associate professor, 1990-95, professor of history, 1996-, Department of Historical Studies, head, 1996-; Wilfrid Laurier University, Department of War and Society Studies, professor, Laurier Centre for Military Strategic and Disarmament Studies, associate, Department of History, chair. Writer. **Publications:** (With J. Wright) King Cetshwayo kaMpande, 1980; Fight Us in the Open: The Anglo-Zulu War through Zulu Eyes, 1985; The Battle of Ulundi, 1988; (intro.) Moodie's Zulu War, 1988; (with J. Mathews) Isandlwana, 1992; Kingdom in Crisis: The Zulu Response to the British Invasion of 1879, 1992; Rope of Sand: The Rise and Fall of the Zulu Kingdom in the Nineteenth Century, 1995 in US as The Rise and Fall of the Zulu Nation, 1997; (with I. Knight) The War Correspondents: The Anglo-Zulu War, 1996; The Atlas of the Later Zulu Wars: 1883-1888, 2001; The Transvaal Rebellion: The First Boer War, 1880-1881, 2005; Historical Dictionary of the Zulu Wars, 2009. WITH P.S. THOMPSON: A Field Guide to the War in Zululand 1879, 1979; War Comes to Umvoti: The Natal-Zululand Border, 1878-9, 1980; Field Guide to the War in Zululand and the Defense of Natal 1879, 1983; The Buffalo Border 1879: The Anglo-Zulu War in Northern Natal, 1983; Kingdom and Colony at War: Sixteen Studies on the Anglo-Zulu War of 1879, 1990; The Illustrated Guide to the Anglo-Zulu War, 2000. EDITOR: (with R. Haswell) Pietermaritzburg 1838-1988: A New Portrait of an African City, 1988; (with M. Ashe and Captain E.V. Wyatt-Edgell) The Story of the Zulu Campaign, 1989; Lord Chelmsford's Zululand Campaign, 1878-1879, 1994; Daily Lives of Civilians in Wartime Africa: From Slavery Days to Rwandan Genocide, 2007; (with B. Carton and J. Sithole) Zulu Identities: Being Zulu, Past and Present, 2008. **Address:** Department of War & Society Studies, Wilfrid Laurier University, DAWB 4-152, Leupold 118, 75 University Ave. W, Waterloo, ON N2L 3C5, Canada. **Online address:** jlaband@wlu.ca

LABANYI, Jo. British (born England), b. 1946. **Genres:** Literary Criticism And History, Social Sciences, History, Art/Art History. **Career:** University of London, Birkbeck College, professor of modern Spanish literature and cultural studies, 1971-, Institute of Romance Studies, honorary senior research fellow; University of Southampton, professor; British Academy, fellow. Writer. **Publications:** Ironía e historia en Tiempo de silencio, 1985; Myth and History in the Contemporary Spanish Novel, 1989; Gender and Modernization in the Spanish Realist Novel, 2000. EDITOR: Galdós, 1993; (with L.C. Deutsch) Culture and Gender in Nineteenth Century Spain, 1995; (with H. Graham) Introduction to Spanish Cultural Studies: The Struggle for Modernity, 1995; Constructing Identity in Contemporary Spain: Theoretical Debates and Cultural Practice, 2002; Spanish Literature: A Very Short Introduction, 2010. Translator of Latin American novels and short stories. Contributor of articles and translations to literature and cinema journals. **Address:** University of Southampton, Avenue Campus, 3031 Level 3, Southampton, SO17 1BJ, England. **Online address:** j.labanyi@soton.ac.uk

LA BERGE, Ann F. American (born United States), b. 1944. **Genres:** Sciences, Medicine/Health. **Career:** Virginia Polytechnic Institute and State University, visiting assistant professor, 1979-81, Center for the Study of Science in Society, assistant director, 1981-85, program coordinator, 1985-86, visiting assistant professor of history, 1986-88, assistant professor, 1991, Center for Programs in the Humanities, assistant professor, 1989-, Science and Technology Studies, associate professor, 1994-. Writer. **Publications:** Mission and Method: The Early Nineteenth-Century French Public Health Movement, 1992. EDITOR: (with A. Donovan) Working Papers in Science and Technology Studies: Ethics in Engineering, 1982; (with D. Zallen) Readings in Humanities, Science, and Technology, 1992, 2nd ed., 1995; (with M. Feingold) French Medical Culture in the Nineteenth Century, 1994. Contributor to history journals. **Address:** center for the Study of Science in Society, Virginia Polytechnic Institute, 220 Major Williams, 333 Lane Hall, Blacksburg, VA 24061, U.S.A. **Online address:** alaberge@vt.edu

LABRIE, Ross. Canadian (born Canada), b. 1936. **Genres:** Literary Criticism And History. **Career:** University of Saskatchewan, instructor in English, 1962-63; University of British Columbia, professor of English, 1963-2001, professor emeritus of English, 2001-, professor in arts one, 2002-. Writer. **Publications:** The Art of Thomas Merton, 1979; Howard Nemerov, 1980; James Merrill, 1982; The Writings of Daniel Berrigan, 1989; The Catholic Imagination in American Literature, 1997; Thomas Merton and the Inclusive Imagination, 2001. Contributor to periodicals. **Address:** Department of English, University of British Columbia, 397-1873 E Mall, Buchanan Twr., Vancouver, BC V6T 1Z1, Canada. **Online address:** labrie@interchange.ubc.ca

LABRO, Philippe (Christian). French (born France), b. 1936. **Genres:** Novels, Plays/Screenplays. **Career:** Marie-France, journalist, 1958-59; France-Soir, journalist, 1959-; Sunday Journal, columnist, 1965-72; RTL, director, 1985-2000, vice president, 1992, 1996-2001, managing director, 1985, chief executive officer, 1996-2001; Artmedia, director. **Publications:** Un Americain peu Tranquille, 1960; Des Feux Mal éteints (Poorly Extinguished Fires), 1967; Ce n'est qu'un Debut, 1968, trans. as This is Only a Beginning, 1969; Les Barricades de Mai (The Barricades of May), 1968; L'héritier, 1973; Tous Célèbres, 1979; Des Bateaux dans la Nuit, 1982; étudiant étranger: Roman, 1986; Un été dans l'Ouest, 1988; Le petit Garcon, 1990; Quinze Ans (Fifteen Years), 1992; Un Début ä Paris, 1994; La Traversée, 1996; Rendez-vous au Colorado, 1998; Manuella, 1999; (with O. Barrot) Lettres d'Amerique, 2001; Je Connais Gens de Toutes Sortes, 2002; Tomber sept Fois, se Relever huit,

2003; Franz et Clara: Roman, 2006; Les Gens: Roman, 2009; 7500 Signes: Chroniques, 2010. **Address:** Art-Media, 20 Ave. Rapp, Paris, 75007, France.

LABUTE, Neil. American (born United States), b. 1963. **Genres:** Plays/ Screenplays, Novels, Film, Literary Criticism And History. **Career:** Playwright, director and producer. **Publications:** In the Company of Men, 1997; Your Friends & Neighbors, 1999; Bash: Latterday Plays, 1999; Bash: Three Plays, 2001; Bash: A Gaggle of Saints, 2001; The Shape of Things, 2001; The Distance from Here: A Play, 2003; The Mercy Seat: A Play, 2003; Fat Pig: A Play, 2004; Seconds of Pleasure: Stories, 2004; This Is How It Goes: A Play, 2005; Autobahn: A Short-Play Cycle, 2005; Some Girl(s), 2005; Wrecks and Other Plays, 2007; In A Dark, Dark House, 2007; Reasons to be Pretty, 2008; Land of the Dead & Helter Skelter, 2008; Filthy Talk for Troubled Times, 2010; The Break of Noon, 2010. **Address:** Faber and Faber Ltd., 3 Queen Sq., London, GL WC1N 3AU, England.

LACEFIELD, Lori. American (born United States) **Genres:** Mystery/Crime/ Suspense, Young Adult Fiction. **Career:** Noel-Levitz Inc., product support manager, technical product support director. Writer and data analyst. **Publications:** The Seventh Survivor, 2006; 99 Truths, 2010. **Address:** Noel-Levitz Inc., 6300 S Syracuse Way, Ste. 645, Centennial, CO 80111-7307, U.S.A. **Online address:** writer@lorilacefield.com

LACEY, Andrew. British (born England), b. 1960. **Genres:** History. **Career:** Cambridge University, librarian, 1994-2005, senior library assistant & member of faculty of architecture and history of art. Educator and writer. **Publications:** The Cult of King Charles the Martyr, 2003. **Address:** Cambridge & Special Collections Library, Leicester University, Leicester, LE LE1 7RH, England. **Online address:** acl28@cam.ac.uk

LACEY, Josh. (Joshua Doder). British (born England) **Genres:** Children's Fiction. **Career:** Author and journalist. **Publications:** AS JOSHUA DODER: FOR CHILDREN: The Timetraveller's Guide to Shakespeare's London, 2004; The Timetraveller's Guide to Saxon and Viking London, 2004; A Dog Called Grk, 2005; Grk and the Pelotti Gang, 2006; Grk and the Hotdog Trail, 2006; The Duke of Wellington ("Who Was...?" series), 2006; Grk: Operation Tortoise, 2007; Grk Smells a Rat, 2008; Grk Takes Revenge, 2009; Grk Down Under, 2010. AS JOSH LACEY: God is Brazilian: Charles Miller, the Man Who Brought Football to Brazil, 2005. FOR CHILDREN: Bearkeeper, 2008; The One That Got Away, 2009; Two Tigers on a String, 2009; Three Diamonds and a Donkey, 2010; The Island of Thieves, 2011. Contributor of articles to periodicals. **Address:** c/o Nicola Barr, Greene & Heaton, 37 Goldhawk Rd., London, GL W12 8QQ, England. **Online address:** josh@joshlacey.com

LACEY, Nicola. British (born England), b. 1958. **Genres:** Criminology/ True Crime, Law, Women's Studies And Issues, Essays. **Career:** University of London, lecturer in law, 1981-84, Oxford and CUF lecturer, 1984-95, Birkbeck College, professor of law, 1995-97; Oxford University, fellow, tutor in law, 1984-95; London School of Economics, professor of criminal law and legal theory, 1998-2010, chair, 1998-; London School of Economics, professor of criminal law and legal theory, 1999-2010; New York University School of Law, Global Law School Faculty, 2001-03; Australian National University, Research School of Social Science, Social and Political Theory Program, adjunct professor, 2002-06; New College, honorary fellow, 2007; University of Oxford, All Souls College, senior research fellow, 2010-; University College, honorary fellow, 2010. Writer. **Publications:** State Punishment: Political Principles and Community Values, 1988; (with C. Wells and D. Meure.) Reconstructing Criminal Law: Critical Perspectives on Crime and the Criminal Process, 1990, (with C. Wells and O. Quick) 3rd ed. as Reconstructing Criminal Law: Text and Materials, 2003; (with E. Frazer) Politics of Community: A Feminist Critique of the Liberal-Communitarian Debate, 1993; (ed.) Criminal Justice, 1994; Unspeakable Subjects, Impossible Rights: Feminism, Sex and Criminal Law, 1997; Unspeakable Subjects: Feminist Essays in Legal and Social Theory, 1998; A Life of H.L.A. Hart: The Nightmare and the Noble Dream, 2004; (co-author) Regulating Law, 2004; The Prisoners' Dilemma: Political Economy and Punishment in Contemporary Democracies, 2008; Women, Crime and Character: From Moll Flanders to Tess of the D'urbervilles, 2008. **Address:** All Souls College, University of Oxford, 27 High St., City Ctr., Oxford, OX OX1 4AL, England. **Online address:** nicola.lacey@all-souls.ox.ac.uk

LACEY, Robert. Saudi/British (born England), b. 1944. **Genres:** History, Biography, Intellectual History. **Career:** Illustrated London News, writer,

1968, journalist; Sunday Times Magazine, journalist, assistant editor, 1969-73, Look! pages, editor, 1973-74; Cover Magazine, co-founder and co-editor, 1997-99. **Publications:** (And ed.) The French Revolution, 2 vols., 1968; (and ed.) The Rise of Napoleon, 1969; (and ed.) The Peninsular War, 1969; (and ed.) 1812: The Retreat from Moscow, 1812, 1969; The Pallisers: A Full Guide to the Serial, 1971; Robert, Earl of Essex: An Elizabethan Icarus, 1971; War and Peace: A Full Guide to the Serial, 1972; The Life and Times of Henry VIII, 1972; The Queens of the North Atlantic, 1973; Sir Walter Raleigh, 1973; (and ed.) Sir Francis Drake and the Golden Hinde, 1975; (ed. and contrib.) Heritage of Britain, 1975; Majesty: Elizabeth II and the House of Windsor, 1977; Elizabeth II: The Work of the Queen, 1977; The Kingdom: Arabia and the House of Saud, 1981; Princess, 1982; Aristocrats, 1983; Ford: The Men and the Machine, 1986; Queen Mother, 1987; God Bless Her, 1987; Little Man: Meyer Lansky and the Gangster Life, 1991; Grace, 1994; Sotheby's: Bidding for Class, 1998; The Queen Mother's Century, 1999; (with D. Danziger) The Year 1000, 1999; Monarch, 2002; Royal: Her Majesty Queen Elizabeth II, 2002; Great Tales from English History: Cheddar Man to the Peasants' Revolt, 2003; Chaucer to the Glorious Evolution, 2004; Great Tales from English History: Joan of Arc, the Princes in the Tower, Bloody Mary, Oliver Cromwell, Sir Isaac Newton, and More, 2005; Great Tales from English History: Captain Cook, Samuel Johnson, Queen Victoria, Charles Darwin, Edward the Abdicator, and More, 2006; Great Tales from English History: A Treasury of True Stories about the Extraordinary People, Knights and Knaves, Rebels and Heroes, Queens and Commoners, Who made Britain Great, 2007; Inside the Kingdom: Kings, Clerics, Modernists, Terrorists and the Struggle for Saudi Arabia, 2009. **Address:** Curtis Brown Ltd., Haymarket House, 28/29 Haymarket, London, GL SW1Y 4SP, England. **Online address:** robert@robertlacey.com

LACHMAN, Barbara. American (born United States), b. 1938. **Genres:** Music, Art/Art History, Autobiography/Memoirs. **Career:** Womens Chamber and Sight-Reading Chorus, conductor, 1972-82; Alexander Technique, teacher, 1982-92; Western Michigan University, annual lecturer, 1984-88; Greater Hartford Academy for the Performing Arts, liaison counselor, 1986-87; La Casa del Libro, associate director, 1988-92; University of Puerto Rico and Sacred Heart University, teacher, 1988-92; College of Notre Dame, Women's Institute, teacher, 1993-97; Johns Hopkins University, Peabody Conservatory of Music, teacher, 1993-97; Calvert School, editor for home instruction department, 1993-96; Baltimore Curriculum Project, writer, 1996-; Virginia Military Institute, world history teacher and tutor. Writer. **Publications:** The Journal of Hildegard of Bingen: A Novel, 1993; Hildegard, The Last Year, 1997; Voices for Catherine Blake: A Gathering, 2000. Contributor of articles to periodicals and books. Works appear in anthologies. **Address:** American Society for the Alexander Technique, 407 Spring Valley Rd., Lexington, VA 24450, U.S.A. **Online address:** blaclach@rockbridge.net

LACHMAN, Charles. American (born United States), b. 1952. **Genres:** Biography. **Career:** White Plains Reporter-Dispatch, reporter, 1974-78; Fort Lauderdale News, staff reporter, 1979-81; New York Post, staff reporter, 1981-88; A Current Affair, producer, 1988; WNYW-TV (Fox), managing editor; American Journal, senior producer and co-executive producer; Inside Edition, managing editor, 1989-95, co-executive producer, 1995-98, executive producer, 1998-. **Publications:** In the Name of the Law, 1988; The Last Lincolns: The Rise and Fall of a Great American Family, 2008; A Secret Life: The Lies and Scandals of President Grover Cleveland, 2011. Contributor to periodicals. **Address:** Inside Edition, PO Box 1323, Radio City Sta., New York, NY 10101, U.S.A.

LACHMAN, Seymour P. American (born United States), b. 1933. **Genres:** Education, Cultural/Ethnic Topics, Theology/Religion, Politics/Government, Social Sciences. **Career:** City University of New York, Kingsborough Community College, dean and professor of history, 1963-69, Graduate School and University Center, professor of education, 1974-80, Baruch College, dean of community development, 1980-96; New York City Board of Education, president, 1969-74; National Collaborative Public and Non-Public Schools, founder and chair, 1988; New York State Senate, senator from 22nd district, 1996-2004; Adelphi University, distinguished visiting professor, 2004; Wagner College, distinguished professor-in-residence, 2006-, Hugh L. Carey Center for Government Reform Carey Center, director. Writer. **Publications:** (With D. Bresnick and M. Polner) Black, White, Green, Red: The Politics of Education in Ethnic America, 1978; (with B.A. Kosmin) One Nation Under God: Religion in Contemporary American Society, 1993; (with R. Polner) Three Men in a Room: The Inside Story of Power and Betrayal in an American Statehouse, 2006; (with R. Polner) The Man Who Saved New York, 2010. Contributor to periodicals. **Address:** Wagner College, Campus Hall, 3rd Fl., Staten Island, NY 10301, U.S.A. **Online address:** seymour.lachman@wagner.edu

LACHNER, Dorothea. Austrian (born Austria), b. 1951. **Genres:** Children's Fiction, Sports/Fitness, Natural History, Young Adult Fiction. **Career:** Educator for mentally and physically impaired, 1972-95. Writer. **Publications:** Das grune Pferd im Himbeerbusch, 1995; Andrew's Angry Words, 1995; Geschenk vom Nikolaus, 1995; Ganz besondre Ostergeschenk, 1996; Hexenfest für Merrilu, 1997; Zauberspuk bei Merrilu, 2000; Eigentlich wollte er böse sein!, 2000; Muensteraner autorenpreis fur Kinder-u-Jugend Theater, 2001; UA, 2003; Hexenschule für Merrilu, 2003; Tonio und Giss Lif aus Leeds, 2005; Sab ein Ungeheuer auf dem Dach, 2011. Works appear in anthologies. **Address:** Badgasse 2/A-2721, Bad Fischau, AT 2721, Austria. **Online address:** dorla@utanet.at

LACHNIT, Carroll. American (born United States), b. 1954?. **Genres:** Mystery/Crime/Suspense, Novels. **Career:** Orange County Register, staff writer, 1984-92; Orange Coast Magazine, managing editor, 1999-, contributing writer. **Publications:** HANNAH BARLOW SERIES: Murder in Brief, 1995; A Blessed Death, 1996; Akin to Death, 1998; Janie's Law, 1999. Contributor to periodicals. **Address:** Berkley Prime Crime, 375 Hudson St., New York, NY 10014-3658, U.S.A.

LACHS, John. American (born United States), b. 1934. **Genres:** Philosophy, Ethics, Poetry, Bibliography. **Career:** College of William and Mary, assistant professor, 1959-62, associate professor, 1962-66, professor, 1966-67; Vanderbilt University, professor of philosophy, 1967-93, Centennial professor of philosophy, 1993-, faculty adviser of young Americans for liberty. Writer. **Publications:** (Ed.) Animal Faith and Spiritual Life: Previously Unpublished and Uncollected Works of George Santayana with Critical Essays on His Thought, 1967; Marxist Philosophy: A Bibliographical Guide, 1967; (ed. with S.M. Lachs) Physical Order and Moral Liberty: Previously Unpublished Essays of George Santayana, 1969; The Ties of Time (poetry), 1970; (ed. and trans. with P. Heath) Fichte's Science of Knowledge (Wissenschaftslehre 1794), 1970; Intermediate Man, 1981; (ed. with C.E. Scott) The Human Search: An Introduction to Philosophy, 1981; (ed. and trans. with P. Heath) The Science of Knowledge, 1982; Mind and Philosophers, 1987; George Santayana, 1988; The Relevance of Philosophy to Life, 1995; In Love with Life: Reflections on the Joy of Living and Why We Hate to Die, 1998; (with M. Hodges) Thinking in the Ruins: Wittgenstien and Santayana on Contingency, 2000; A Community of Individuals, 2003; (ed. with D.M. Hester) William Ernest Hocking Reader, 2004; On Santayana, 2006; (ed. with R. Talisse) American Philosophy: An Encyclopedia, 2007; (ed. with M.C. Flamm and K.P. Skowronski) American and European Values: Contemporary Philosophical Perspectives, 2008; Stoic Pragmatism, 2012. **Address:** Department of Philosophy, Vanderbilt University, 111 Furman Hall, Nashville, TN 37240, U.S.A. **Online address:** john.lachs@vanderbilt.edu

LACKEY, Kris. American (born United States), b. 1953. **Genres:** Literary Criticism And History, Young Adult Fiction. **Career:** University of New Mexico, instructor in English, 1982; University of Texas, visiting assistant professor of English, 1983; Auburn University, instructor in English, 1983-86; University of New Orleans, assistant professor, 1986-90, associate professor, 1990-97, associate chairperson of department, 1990-92, professor of English, 1997-. Writer. **Publications:** Roadframes: The American Highway Narrative, 1997. Contributor of articles, stories, and reviews to periodicals. **Address:** Department of English, University of New Orleans, Liberal Arts Bldg., 201E, 2000 Lakeshore Dr., New Orleans, LA 70148, U.S.A. **Online address:** klackey@uno.edu

LACKEY, Mercedes R. American (born United States), b. 1950. **Genres:** Young Adult Fiction, Novels, Novellas/Short Stories, Science Fiction/Fantasy. **Career:** Associates Data Processing, computer programmer, 1979-82; CAIRS, surveyor, layout designer, and analyst, 1981-82; American Airlines, computer programmer, 1982-. Writer. **Publications:** NOVELS FOR YOUNG ADULTS: Arrows of the Queen, 1987; Arrow's Flight, 1987; Arrow's Fall, 1988; Oathbound, 1988; Burning Water, 1989; Oathbreakers, 1989; Magic's Pawn, 1989; Reap the Whirlwind, 1989; (with E. Guon) A Knight of Ghosts and Shadows, 1990; Magic's Promise, 1990; Magic's Price, 1990; By the Sword, 1991; (with A. Norton) The Elvenbane: An Epic High Fantasy of the Halfblood Chronicles, 1991; Jinx High, 1991; Winds of Fate, 1991; Bardic Voices: The Lark and the Wren, 1992; (with L. Dixon) Born to Run, 1992; Children of the Night, 1992; (with E. Guon) Freedom Flight, 1992; (with

Guon) Summoned to Tourney, 1992; Winds of Change, 1992; Winds of Fury, 1993; (with L. Dixon) The Black Gryphon, 1993; (with R. Emerson) Fortress of Frost and Fire: The Bard's Tale II, 1993; (with P. Anthony) If I Pay Thee Not in Gold, 1993; (with M.Z. Bradley) Rediscovery: A Novel of Darkover, 1993; (with A. McCaffrey) The Ship Who Searched, 1993; (with H. Lisle) When the Bough Breaks, 1993; The Robin and the Kestrel, 1993; Sacred Ground, 1994; Cast of Corbies, 1994; Storm Warning, 1994; Chrome Circle, 1994; (with A. Norton) Elvenblood: An Epic High Fantasy, 1994; (with L. Dixon) The White Gryphon, 1994; (with M.Z. Bradley and A. Norton) Tiger Burning Bright, 1995; The Eagle & the Nightingales, 1995; The Fire Rose, 1995; Storm Rising, 1995; Firebird, 1996; (with L. Dixon) The Silver Gryphon, 1996; Storm Breaking, 1996; Four and Twenty Blackbirds, 1997; The Free Bards, 1997; Owlflight, 1997; Sword of Ice and Other Tales of Valdemar, 1997; Black Swan, 1999; Chrome Borne, 1999; Otherworld, 1999; Flights of Fantasy, 1999; Owlknight, 1999; River's Gift, 1999; Werehunter, 1999; Brightly Burning, 2000; Beyond World's End, 2001; Serpent's Shadow, 2001; Spirits White as Lightning, 2001; Take a Thief, 2001; Elvenborn, 2002; Exile's Honor: A Novel of Valdemar, 2002; Gates of Sleep, 2002; Shadow of the Lion, 2002; Joust, 2003; Mad Maudlin, 2003; Spirits White as Lightning, 2003; Exile's Honor, 2003; The Outstretched Shadow, 2003; Charmed Destinies, 2003; Exile's Valor, 2003; (ed.) Sun in Glory and Other Tales of Valdemar, 2003; (co-author) This Rough Magic, 2003; Alta, the Sequel to Joust, 2004; (with R. Gellis) This Scepter'd Isle, 2004; The Fairy Godmother, 2004; (with E. Flint and D. Freer) Wizard of Karres, 2004; Exile's Valor Paperback, 2004; Phoenyx and Ashes, 2004; (with J. Mallory) To Light a Candle, 2004; Sword of Knowledge, 2004; Phoenix and Ashes, 2004; Burning Water: A Diana TrTegarde Investigation, 2005; (with R. Gellis) Ill Met by Moonlight, 2005; (with T. Lee and C.E. Murphy) Winter Moon, 2005; Alta, 2005; Sanctuary, 2005; Rough Magic, 2005; Stars, 2005; Serenity, 2005; (ed. with R. Edghill) Bedlam's Edge, 2005; Children of the Night: A Diana Tregarde Investigation, 2005; (with R. Edghill) Music to My Sorrow, 2005; Sanctuary, 2005; Wizard of London, 2005; Aerie, 2006; Jinx High: A Diana Tregarde investigation, 2006; (ed.) Mapping the World of Harry Potter: Science Fiction and Fantasy Writers Explore the Best Selling Fantasy Series of all Time, 2006; One Good Knight, 2006; When Darkness Falls, 2006; Phoenix Unchained, 2007; Fortune's Fool, 2007; Reserved for the Cat, 2007; (with R. Gellis) By Slanderous Tongues, 2007; Snow Queen, 2007; Phoenix Endangered, 2008; Moving Targets: And Other Stories of Valdemar, 2008; And Less than Kind, 2008; Phoenix Transformed, 2009; Foundation, 2008; Gwenhwyfar, 2009; Changing the World: All New Tales of Valdemar, 2009; (with E. Flint and D. Freer) Much Fall of Blood, 2010; Trio of Sorcery, 2010; Sleeping Beauty, 2010; Balance, 2010; (ed.) Finding the Way: And Other Tales of Valdemar, 2010; Dragons Teeth, 2010; (with R. Edghill) Legacies, 2010; Intrigues, 2010; (with M. Sagara and C. Haley) Harvest Moon, 2010; (with S. Libbey) Invasion, 2011; Unnatural Issue, 2011; Beauty and the Werewolf, 2011; Changes, 2011; (with R. Edghill) Conspiracies, 2011; Home From the Sea, 2012; World Divided, 2012; Dead Reckoning, 2012. FORTHCOMING: Queen of Air and Darkness; (with E. Flint and D. Freer) Great Doom's Shadow; Shadow Hunt. **Address:** c/o Author Mail, DAW Books, 375 Hudson St., New York, NY 10014, U.S.A.

LACKEY, Michael. American (born United States) **Genres:** Literary Criticism And History, Intellectual History, Humanities. **Career:** University of Minnesota, associate professor of English. Writer. **Publications:** African American Atheists and Political Liberation: A Study of the Sociocultural Dynamics of Faith, 2007; Modernist God States: A Literary Study of the Theological Origins of Hitler and the Nazis, forthcoming. Contributor to periodicals. **Address:** Department of English, University of Minnesota, Hum 212, 600 E 4th St., Morris, MN 56267, U.S.A. **Online address:** lacke010@umn.edu

LACOUR, Nina. American (born United States), b. 1982. **Genres:** Novels. **Career:** Maybeck High School, English teacher. Writer. **Publications:** Hold Still (novel), 2009. Contributor to periodicals. **Address:** Maybeck High School, 2727 College Ave., Berkeley, CA 94705, U.S.A. **Online address:** nina@ninalacour.com

LA CROIX, I(sobyl) F. Scottish (born Scotland), b. 1933. **Genres:** Botany, Horticulture. **Career:** The Orchid Review Magazine, editor; The RHS Orchid Journal, editor. **Publications:** Rhododendrons and Azaleas, 1973; Gardening in the Shade, 1978; Malawi Orchids: Epiphytes, 1983; Growing Scented Plants in Southern Africa, 1984; (co-author) Orchids of Malawi, 1991; (with E. la Croix) African Orchids in the Wild and in Cultivation, 1997; Flora's Orchids, 2005; New Encyclopedia of Orchids: 1500 Species in Cultivation,

2008. Contributor to journals. **Address:** 9 Port Henderson, Gairloch, Gairloch, IV21 2AS, Scotland. **Online address:** i.la_croix@virgin.net

LACY, Allen. American (born United States), b. 1935. **Genres:** Homes/Gardens, Horticulture. **Career:** Clemson College, instructor in English, 1961-62; James Madison University, assistant professor, 1962-65, associate professor of philosophy and English, 1965-66; Michigan State University, assistant professor of humanities, 1966-68; Kirkland College, assistant professor, 1968-69, associate professor of philosophy and humanities, 1969-71; Richard Stockton College of New Jersey, Department of Philosophy, associate professor, 1971-72, professor, 1972-99, professor emeritus, 1999-; Wall Street Journal, gardening columnist, 1979-85; New York Times, gardening columnist, 1987-93; Allen Lacy's Home Ground (quarterly journal), founding editor, 1993-; Linwood Arboretum, curator, 2009-. **Publications:** Miguel de Unamuno: The Rhetoric of Existence (philosophy), 1967; (trans. with M. Nozick and A. Kerrigan and intro.) Peace in War, 1983; Home Ground: A Gardener's Miscellany, 1984; Farther Afield: A Gardener's Excursions, 1986; The Garden in Autumn, 1990; (contrib.) The Glory of Roses, 1990; The Gardener's Eye and Other Essays, 1992; Gardening with Groundcovers and Vines, 1993; The Inviting Garden: Gardening for the Senses, Mind and Spirit, 1998; In a Green Shade: Writings from Homeground, 2000; (with N. Goodwin) A Year in Our Gardens, 2001. EDITOR: (and co-trans.) The Private World, 1984; (and intro.) Gardening for Love: The Market Bulletins, 1987; (and intro.) The American Gardener: A Sampler, 1988; (with N. Goodwin) A Rock Garden in the South, 1990. Contributor of articles to periodicals. **Address:** School of Arts and Humanities, Richard Stockton College of New Jersey, 101 Vera King Farris Dr., PO Box 195, Pomona, NJ 08205, U.S.A. **Online address:** dalthird@mac.com

LACY, Tira. See **ESTRADA, Rita Clay.**

LADD, Brian. American (born United States), b. 1957. **Genres:** History, Urban Studies, Social Commentary. **Career:** Free University, postdoctoral fellow, 1986-88; University of Rhode Island, lecturer in history, 1988-90; Oglethorpe University, assistant professor of history, 1990-92; Rensselaer Polytechnic Institute, visiting assistant professor, 1992-98; American Academy in Berlin, fellow, 1998-99; State University of New York, lecturer and adjunct research associate, 1999-. Writer. **Publications:** Urban Planning and Civic Order in Germany, 1860-1914, 1990; Ghosts of Berlin: Confronting German History in the Urban Landscape, 1997; Companion Guide to Berlin, 2004; Autophobia: Love and Hate in the Automotive Age, 2008. **Address:** Department of History, University at Albany, State University of New York, 105 Ten Broeck, 1400 Washington Ave., Albany, NY 12222-0001, U.S.A. **Online address:** ladd@albany.edu

LADD, Linda. American (born United States) **Genres:** Science Fiction/Fantasy, Romance/Historical, Mystery/Crime/Suspense, Young Adult Fiction. **Career:** Writer. **Publications:** Wildstar, 1984; Moonspell, 1985; Fireglow, 1986; Silverswept, 1987; Dreamsong, 1988; Frost Fire, 1990; Midnight Fire, 1991; Dragon Fire, 1992; White Lily, 1993; White Rose, 1994; White Orchid, 1995; Lilacs on Lace, 1996; Forever My Love, 1997; A Love So Splendid, 1997; A Love So Fine, 1999; Running Scared, 2000; Head to Head, 2006; Dark Places, 2007; Die Smiling, 2008; Enter Evil, 2009. **Address:** c/o Author Mail, Doubleday Book Club, 401 Franklin Ave., Garden City, NY 11530, U.S.A. **Online address:** lindaladd@swbell.net

LADD, Louise. American (born United States), b. 1943. **Genres:** Children's Fiction, Young Adult Fiction, Biography, Ghost Writer, Autobiography/Memoirs, Essays, Ghost Writer, Novels, Novels. **Career:** Witer 1982-; Book Doctor 1993-; Fairfield University, Writers' Workshop, teacher, 1990-2010; Connecticut Center Acting Ensemble, producer and actress, 1974-93. **Publications:** CHILDREN'S FICTION: A Whole Summer of Weird Susan, 1987; The Double Fudge Dare, 1989. THE ANYWHERE RING SERIES: Miracle Island, 1995; Castle in Time, 1995; Lost Valley, 1996; Cherry Blossom Moon, 1996. THE DIAMOND DUDE RANCH SERIES: The Wrangler's Secret, 1997; Prize-Winning Horse-Maybe, 1997; Home for Christmas, 1997; Me, My Mare and the Movie, 1997; Rodeo!, 1997; Belle's Foal, 1997; The Perfect Horse, 1998; Call Me Just Plain Chris, 1998. OTHER: (ed. with D. Taylor) Sandy Dennis: A Personal Memoir (biography), 1997. Contributor to periodicals. **Address:** 27 Bloomfield Dr., Fairfield, CT 06825-3713, U.S.A. **Online address:** louiseld@optonline.net

LADD-TAYLOR, Molly. Canadian/American (born United States), b. 1955?. **Genres:** History, Social Sciences, Women's Studies And Issues. **Career:** York University, associate professor of history, undergraduate program director of history. Writer. **Publications:** Mother-Work: Women, Child Welfare and the State, 1890-1930, 1994. EDITOR: Raising a Baby the Government Way: Mothers' Letters to the Children's Bureau, 1915-1932, 1986; (co-ed.) Root of Bitterness: Documents of the Social History of American Women, 1996; (with L. Umansky) Bad Mothers: The Politics of Blame in Twentieth-Century America, 1998; (with K. McPherson, A. Li and G. Feldberg) Women, Health and Nation: Canada and the United States Since 1945, 2003; Eugenics and Social Welfare in New Deal Minnesota, in 100 Years of Eugenics, 2010. **Address:** Department of History, York University, 2136 Vari Hall, 4700 Keele St., Toronto, ON M3J 1P3, Canada. **Online address:** mltaylor@yorku.ca

LADELL, John L. (John Lindsay). Canadian/Thai (born Thailand), b. 1924. **Genres:** Local History/Rural Topics, Agriculture/Forestry, Sociology, Technology, Engineering, Astronomy. **Career:** Forest Products Laboratory, technical officer, 1950-67; Ontario Research Foundation, senior research scientist, 1961-72. Writer, 1972-. **Publications:** (With M. Ladell) Inheritance: Ontario's Century Farms, Past and Present, 1979; (with Ladell) A Farm in the Family: The Many Faces of Ontario Agriculture Over the Centuries, 1985; They Left Their Mark: Surveyors and Their Role in the Settlement of Ontario, 1993. Contributor to scientific journals. **Address:** 4276 Henderson Rd., Milton, ON L9T 2X5, Canada.

LADEN, Anthony. See **LYDEN, Jacki.**

LADNER, Kurt. See **DEMILLE, Nelson (Richard).**

LADOW, Beth. American (born United States), b. 1957?. **Genres:** History, Medicine/Health, Humanities. **Career:** Brandeis University, instructor of American history; Harvard University, faculty of writing; National Public Radio, WBUR-FM, commentator. Writer and historian. **Publications:** The Medicine Line: Life and Death on a North American Borderland, 2001. Contributor to books and periodicals. **Address:** 22 Lakeview Rd., Winchester, MA 01890-3857, U.S.A.

LADUKE, Betty. American (born United States), b. 1933. **Genres:** Art/Art History, Women's Studies And Issues, Cultural/Ethnic Topics, Social Sciences. **Career:** Southern Oregon State College, professor of art, 1964-96, professor emeritus, 1996-. Writer. **Publications:** Compañeras: Women, Art, and Social Change in Latin America, 1985; Africa Through the Eyes of Women Artists, 1991; Women Artists: Multi-Cultural Visions, 1992; Multi-Cultural Celebrations: The Paintings of Betty La Duke, 1972-1992, 1993; Africa: Women's Art, Women's Lives, 1997; Women Against Hunger: A Sketchbook Journey, 1997. **Address:** Africa World Press Inc., 541 West Ingham Ave., Ste. B, Trenton, NJ 08638, U.S.A. **Online address:** bladuke@jeffnet.org

LADUKE, Winona. American (born United States), b. 1959?. **Genres:** Novels, Environmental Sciences/Ecology. **Career:** White Earth Land Recovery Project, founder, 1988, campaign director, executive director; Indigenous Women's Network, founder and co-chair, 1994; Honor the Earth, executive director. Environmentalist, economist and writer. **Publications:** (Contrib.) Toxic Struggles: The Theory and Practice of Environmental Justice, 1993; (intro.) Ward Churchill, Struggle for the Land: Indigenous Resistance to Genocide, Ecocide, and Expropriation in Contemporary North America, 1993; (intro.) Al Gedicks, The New Resource Wars: Native and Environmental Struggles against Multinational Corporations, 1993; (intro.) Rick Whaley and Walter Bresette, Walleye Warriors: An Effective Alliance against Racism and for the Earth, 1994; Last Standing Woman, 1997; All Our Relations: Native Struggles for Land and Life, 1999; (with W. Kapashesit) The Sugar Bush, 1999; Winona LaDuke Reader: A Collection of Essential Writings, 2002; Recovering the Sacred: The Power of Naming and Claiming, 2005. Contributor to books and periodicals. **Address:** White Earth Land Recovery Project, PO Box 327, White Earth, MN 56591, U.S.A.

LAFAVOR, Carole S. American (born United States), b. 1948?. **Genres:** Mystery/Crime/Suspense, Novels. **Career:** Minnesota American Indian AIDS Task Force, nurse consultant, 1996-; Positively Native, founding member. Novelist. **Publications:** NOVELS: Along the Journey River: A Mystery, 1996; Evil Dead Center: A Mystery, 1997. Contributor to periodicals. Works appear in anthologies. **Address:** 3932 Oakland Ave. S, Minneapolis, MN 55407-2515, U.S.A. **Online address:** cslaf@aol.com

LAFAYE, A(lexandria R. T.). American (born United States), b. 1970. **Genres:** Young Adult Fiction, Novels, Children's Fiction. **Career:** Roanoke College, instructor in English, 1997-98; Plattsburgh State University, visiting assistant professor of English, 1998-2000; California State University, San Bernardino, associate professor of English, 2000-06; Hollins University, visiting assistant professor of English, 2001-; California State University, Fresno, Summer Arts Program, visiting assistant professor of English, 2002, 2004; Hamline University, visiting assistant professor of English, 2007-10; Lee University, assistant professor of English, 2010-. Writer. **Publications:** The Year of the Sawdust Man (juvenile historical novel), 1998; Edith Shay (young adult historical novel), 1998; Strawberry Hill (juvenile historical novel), 1999; Nissa's Place (juvenile historical novel), 1999; Dad, in Spirit, 2001; The Strength of Saints, 2002; Worth, 2004; Upriver, 2006; Stella Stands Alone, 2008; Water Steps, 2009; Keening, 2010; Walking Home to Rosie Lee, 2011. **Address:** c/o Marcia Wernick, Sheldon Fogelman Agency, 10 E 40th St., New York, NY 10016, U.S.A. **Online address:** alafayebooks@aol.com

LAFEBER, Walter Frederick. American (born United States), b. 1933. **Genres:** History, International Relations/Current Affairs, Politics/Government. **Career:** Cornell University, Department of History, assistant professor of history, 1959-63, associate professor, 1963-67, professor, 1967-68, Marie Underhill Noll professor of American history, 1968-2001, Andrew H. and James S. Tisch distinguished university professor, 2002-05, Marie Underhill Noll professor emeritus of American history, 2005-, Tisch distinguished university professor of American history, Andrew H. and James S. Tisch distinguished iniversity history professor emeritus and Stephen H. Weiss presidential teaching fellow; University of London, commonwealth lecturer, 1973; University of Aberdeen, Callander lecturer, 1987; Johns Hopkins University, Shaw lecturer, 1989; American University, Landmark professor, 1992; University of California, Jefferson lecturer, 1992. Writer. **Publications:** The New Empire: An Interpretation of American Expansion, 1860-1898, 1963; America, Russia, and the Cold War, 1945-1966, 1967, 10th ed. as America, Russia, and the Cold War, 1945-2006, 2008; America in the Cold War: Twenty Years of Revolutions and Response, 1947-1967, 1969; (with L.C. Gardner and T.J. McCormick) Creation of the American Empire, 1973, 2nd ed., 1976; Dynamics of World Power: A Documentary History of United States Foreign Policy, 1945-1973, 1973; (with R. Polenberg and N. Woloch) The American Century: A History of the United States since the 1890s, 1975, 6th ed. as American Century: A History of the United States since 1941, 2008; The Panama Canal: The Crisis in Historical Perspective, 1978; The Third Cold War, 1981; Inevitable Revolutions: The United States in Central America, 1983, 2nd ed., 1993; The American Age: United States Foreign Policy at Home and Abroad since 1750, 1989, 2nd ed., 1994; Revoluciones Inevitables, 1989; (contrib.) The American Search for Opportunity, 1865-1913, vol. II: The Cambridge History of American Foreign Relations, 1993; The Clash: U.S.-Japanese Relations throughout History, 1997; Michael Jordan and the New Global Capitalism, 1999, new ed., 2002; (contrib.) Jianqiao Meiguo Dui Wai Guan Xi shi, 2004; The Deadly Bet: LBJ, Vietnam, and the 1968 Election, 2005. EDITOR: John Quincy Adams and American Continental Empire, 1965; Origins of the Cold War, 1941-1947: A Historical Problem with Interpretations and Documents, 1971; (co-ed.) America in Vietnam, 1985; (with T.J. McCormick) Behind the Throne: Servants of Power to Imperial Presidents, 1898-1968, 1993. Contributor of articles to books and journals. **Address:** Department of History, Cornell University, 450 McGraw Hall, Ithaca, NY 14853-4601, U.S.A. **Online address:** wfl3@cornell.edu

LAFEMINA, Gerry. American (born United States), b. 1968?. **Genres:** Novellas/Short Stories, Poetry. **Career:** Kirtland Community College, teacher; West Virginia University, teacher; Wheeling Jesuit University, teacher; Sarah Lawrence College, teacher; Grand Valley State University, teacher; Frostburg State University, distinguished poet-in-residence, Department of English, assistant professor of English, associate professor, Frostburg Center for Creative Writing, director; Highbrow Magazine, columnist. **Publications:** Rest Stops, 1990; 23 Below, 1994; The City of Jazz and Punk, 1995; A Print of Wildflowers (poetry), 1996; Shattered Hours: Poems 1988-94, 1997; Zarathustra in Love, 2001; (trans. with S. Toprak) A. Yüce, Voice Lock Puppet: Poems, 2002; Graffiti Heart, 2003; A Garment Sewn from Night Itself, 2003; The Window Facing Winter, 2004; The Parakeets of Brooklyn: Poems, 2005; Wish List: Stories, 2009; Vanishing Horizon: Poems, 2011. Contributor to journals. **Address:** Department of English, Frostburg State University, 301-B Dunkle Hall, 101 Braddock Rd., Frostburg, MD 21532-2303, U.S.A. **Online address:** glafemina@frostburg.edu

LAFERRIÈRE, Dany. Canadian/Haitian (born Haiti), b. 1953. **Genres:** Novels, Translations. **Career:** Journalist. **Publications:** Comment Faire l'Amour Avec Un Nègre Sans Se Fatiguer: Roman, 1985; éroshima: Roman, 1987; L'odeur Du Café: Récit, 1991; Le Gout Des Jeunes Filles: Roman, 1992; Cette Grenade Dans La Main Du Jeune Nègre Est-elle Une Arme Ou Un Fruit?: Roman, 1993, new ed., 2002; Chronique De La Dérive Douce, 1994; Pays Sans Chapeau, 1996; La Chair Du Maître, 1997; Le Charme Des Après-midi Sans Fin, 1997; J'écris Comme Je Vis, 2000; Le Cri des Oiseaux Fous: Roman, 2000; Je Suis Fatigué, 2001, rev. ed., 2005; Comment Conquérir l'Amérique En Une Nuit: Scénario, 2004; Les Années 80 Dans Ma vieille Ford, 2005; Je suis fou de Vava, 2005; Vers Le Sud: Roman, 2006; Je Suis Un écrivain Japonais: Roman, 2008; énigme Du Retour: Roman, 2009; La fête des morts, 2009; Tout bouge autour de moi, 2010; Art presque perdu de ne rien faire, 2011. **Address:** 4625 rue Cornwall, Saint-Hubert, QC J3Y 2S7, Canada.

LAFEVERS, Stephen. American (born United States), b. 1943. **Genres:** Psychology, Medicine/Health, Sports/Fitness. **Career:** Trans Alaska Pipeline, medic, 1985-90; Ozarks Medical Center Clinics, primary care nurse practitioner; Alaska EMS Provider News, editor and creator. Writer and nurse. **Publications:** (With L. Marshall) Prehospital Care for the EMT-Intermediate: Assessment and Intervention, (textbook), 1984; Dreams of April Ten, 2005; Hypnosis In Healthcare, 2006; Dark Moon: Hypnosis and Health Care, forthcoming, The Last Guardian, forthcoming. Contributor to magazines. **Address:** c/o Author Mail, Whiskey Creek Press, PO Box 51052, Casper, WY 82605-1052, U.S.A. **Online address:** stevelafevers@yahoo.com

LAFFEY, Steve. American (born United States), b. 1962?. **Genres:** History, Politics/Government, Biography, International Relations/Current Affairs. **Career:** Morgan Keegan (investment banking firm), president and chief operating officer; City of Cranston, mayor, 2002-06. Writer. **Publications:** Primary Mistake: How the Washington Republican Establishment Lost Everything in 2006, 2007. **Address:** Cranston, RI , U.S.A. **Online address:** slaffey21@yahoo.com

LAFLEUR, Suzanne. American (born United States), b. 1983?. **Genres:** Children's Fiction. **Career:** Author and educator. **Publications:** Love, Aubrey, 2009. **Address:** Curtis Brown Ltd., 10 Astor Pl., New York, NY 10003, U.S.A. **Online address:** suzlafleur@gmail.com

LAFOREST, Gerard V. (J.). Canadian (born Canada), b. 1926. **Genres:** Law. **Career:** University of New Brunswick, associate professor of law, 1956-63, professor, 1963-68; University of Alberta, dean of law, 1968-70; Department of Justice, assistant deputy attorney general, 1970-74; University of Ottawa, professor of law, 1971-79, Common Law Section, professor and director, 1979-81; McGill University, professor of law, 1972, 1977; Law Reform Commission of Canada, commissioner, 1974-79; Kouchibouguac National Park, chairman of the special enquiry, 1980-81; New Brunswick Court of Appeal, judge, 1981-85; Supreme Court of Canada, judge, 1985-97. Writer. **Publications:** Disallowance and Reservation of Provincial Legislation, 1955; Extradition to and from Canada, 1961, 3rd ed., 1991; The Allocation of Taxing Power under the Canadian Constitution, 1967, 2nd ed., 1981; Natural Resources and Public Property Under the Canadian Constitution, 1969; (coauthor) Le Territoire Quebecois, 1970; Water Law in Canada: The Atlantic Provinces, 1973; Promoting Equality: A New Vision, 2000. **Address:** 320 University Ave., Fredricton, NB E3B 4J1, Canada.

LAFOREST, Guy. Canadian (born Canada), b. 1955. **Genres:** History, Politics/Government, Social Sciences. **Career:** Universite Laval, Department of Political Science assistant professor, 1988-92, associate professor, 1992-96, professor, 1996-, head, 1997-2000, director; Canadian Journal of Political Science, co-editor, 1993-96; Action démocratique du Québec, president, 2002-04. **Publications:** Trudeau et la fin d'un rêve canadien, 1992; (contrib.) Rapprocher les solitudes: écrits sur le fédéralisme et le nationalisme au Canada, 1992; De la prudence, 1993; De l'urgence, 1995; Depasser la Conquete, 1995; Trudeau and the End of a Canadian Dream, 1995; The Mirage of Recognition, 1995; Pour la liberté d'une société distincte, 2004; La gran paradoja canadiense=Kanadako paradoxa handia, 2008. EDITOR: (with L. Balthazar and V. Lemieux) Le Québec et la restructuration du Canada, 1980-1992: Enjeux et perspectives, 1991; Reconciling the Solitudes, 1992;

(with D.M. Brown) Integration and Fragmentation: The Paradox of the Late Twentieth Century, 1994; (with F. Blais and D. Lamoureux) Libéralismes et nationalismes: philosophie et politique, 1995; (with M. Elbaz and A. Fortin) Les frontiéres de l'identité: modernité et postmodernisme au Québec, 1996; (with R. Gibbins) Beyond the Impasse: toward Reconciliation, 1998; Sortir de l'impasse: les voies de la reconciliation, 1998; (with P.D. Lara) Charles Taylor et l'interprétation de l'identité moderne, 1998; (ed. with S. Kelly) Débates sur la fondation du Canada, 2004. Contributor to books and journals. **Address:** Department of Political Science, Universite Laval, Rm. 4411, House Charles-With Koninck, 1030 Ave. of the Humanities, Ste-Foy, QC G1K 7P4, Canada. **Online address:** guy.laforest@pol.ulaval.ca

LA FORTUNE, Knolly Stephen. British (born England), b. 1920?. **Genres:** Novels, Poetry, Novellas/Short Stories, Education, Young Adult Fiction. **Career:** A.T.C. Goldsmith's College, London University, staff, 1954-56; San Juan District Teacher's Association, secretary, 1954-55; I.L.E.A., schoolmaster, 1958-; Trinidad and Tobago Association, education officer, 1967-68; St. Paul's Roman Catholic School Library, teacher in charge, 1968-69. Writer. **Publications:** Moments of Inspiration, 1947; Legend of T-Marie, 1968; Anthology of Caribbean Poets, 1969; Caribbean Folk-Lore, 1975-77; The Schoolmaster Remembers: Colonial Trinidad 1930, 1979; Trouble Make Monkey Eat Pepper (novel), 1984; Word Print, Longman's Caribbean Anthologies, 1990-92; Manzanilla, 1999; Parnassus of World Poets, 1994. **Address:** 68 Arthurdon Rd., Brockley, London, GL SE4 1JU, England.

LAFOY, Leslie. American (born United States) **Genres:** Romance/Historical, Novellas/Short Stories, Young Adult Fiction. **Career:** Educator and writer. **Publications:** It Happened One Night, 1997; Lady Reckless, 1998; Daring the Devil, 1999; Maddie's Justice, 2000; Dangereuse Alliance, 2001; Jackson's Way, 2001; Come What May, 2002; The Perfect Seduction, 2003; The Perfect Temptation, 2004; (with S. Laurens, C. Dodd and C. Bradley) My Scandalous Bride, 2004; The Perfect Desire, 2005; Grin and Bear It, 2005; Blindsided, 2005; The Rogue's Bride, 2006; Her Scandalous Marriage, 2006; The Duke's Proposal, 2007; Money Man's Seduction, 2008. **Address:** c/o Author Mail, St. Martins Press, 175 5th Ave., New York, NY 10010, U.S.A. **Online address:** leslie@leslielafoy.com

LAGASSE, Emeril. American (born United States), b. 1959. **Genres:** Food And Wine. **Career:** Commander's Palace, executive chef, 1983-90; Emeril's New Orleans, owner, 1990-; NOLA, owner, 1992-; Emeril's New Orleans Fish House, owner, 1995-; Emeril's Delmonico, owner, 1998-; Good Morning America, food correspondent, 1998-; Emeril's Orlando, owner, 1999-; Delmonico Steakhouse, owner, 1999-; Emeril's Tchoup Chop, owner, 2002-; Emeril's Atlanta, owner, 2003-; Emeril's Miami Beach, owner, 2003-; restaurateur; Emeril Lagasse Foundation, founder. Writer. **Publications:** (With J. Tirsch) Emeril's New New Orleans Cooking, 1993; (with M. Bienvenu) Louisiana Real and Rustic, 1996; (with M. Avellar) Provincetown Portuguese Cookbook: With Recipes from Provincetown's Finest Cooks and Restaurants and Featuring Recipes from the Kitchens of Molly O'Neill and Emeril Lagasse, 1997; (with M. Bienvenu) Emeril's Creole Christmas, 1997; (with M. Bienvenu and F. Willett) Emeril's TV Dinners, 1998; (with M. Bienvenu and F. Willett) Every Day's a Party: Louisiana Recipes for Celebrating with Family and Friends, 1999; Prime Time Emeril: More TV Dinners from America's Favorite Chef, 2001; Emeril's There's a Chef in My Soup: Recipes for the Kid in Everyone (for children), 2002; From Emeril's Kitchens: Favorite Recipes from Emeril's Restaurants, 2003; Emeril's There's a Chef in My Family: Recipes to Get Everybody Cooking (for children), 2004; Emeril's Potluck: Comfort Food with a Kicked-Up Attitude, 2004; Emeril's Delmonico: A New Orleans Restaurant with a Past, 2005; Emeril's There's a Chef in My World: Recipes That Take You Places (for children), 2006; Emeril at the Grill: A Cookbook for All Season, 2009; Emeril 20-40-60: Fresh Food Fast, 2009; Farm to Fork: Cooking Local, Cooking Fresh, 2010; Sizzling Skillets and Other One-Pot Wonders, 2011. Contributor to periodicals. **Address:** Emeril, 829 St. Charles Ave., New Orleans, LA 70130, U.S.A.

LAGATREE, Kirsten M. American (born United States), b. 1948. **Genres:** Homes/Gardens, How-to Books, Sex. **Career:** Los Angeles Times, columnist. Writer and public speaker. **Publications:** Feng Shui: Arranging Your Home to Change Your Life, 1996; (with A. Bredin) The Home Office Solution: How to Balance Your Professional and Personal Lives while Working at Home, 1998; Feng Shui at Work: Arranging Your Work Space for Peak Performance and Maximum Profit, 1998; Checklists for Life, 1999; Sizzling Sex: 242 Sure-Fire Ways to Heat up Your Love Life, 2002; Keep It Together: 200+

Tips, Tricks, Lists, and Solutions for Everyday Life, 2006. **Address:** c/o Eric Lupfer, William Morris Endeavor L.L.C., 1325 Ave. of the Americas, New York, NY 10019-6026, U.S.A. **Online address:** kmlagatree@comcast.net

LAGRAND, Louis E. American (born United States), b. 1935. **Genres:** Education, Human Relations/Parenting, Paranormal, Psychology. **Career:** Columbia University, instructor in physical education, 1958-62; State University of New York, assistant professor, 1962-65, associate professor of health and physical education, 1965-70, professor of health and science, 1970-90, distinguished service professor emeritus, 1990-, head basketball coach, 1962-, varsity tennis coach, 1970-, director of health and physical education, 1970; Institute of Alcohol Problems, director, 1976; Suffolk Community College, adjunct professor of health careers, 1995-; Loss Education Associates, director, 1997-. Writer. **Publications:** (Contrib.) The Best of Basketball from the Coaching Clinic, 1966; Coach's Complete Guide to Winning Basketball, 1967; Discipline in the Secondary School, 1969; (contrib.) The Best in Basketball from Scholastic Coach, 1970; Hatha Yoga in Health and Physical Education, 1974; (contrib.) Encyclopedia of Physical Education, 1977; Coping with Separation and Loss as a Young Adult: Theoretical and Practical Realities, 1986; Changing Patterns of Human Existence: Assumptions, Beliefs and Coping with the Stress of Change, 1988; After Death Communication: Final Farewells, 1997; Messages and Miracles: Extraordinary Experiences of the Bereaved, 1999; Gifts from the Unknown: Using Extraordinary Experiences to Cope With Loss and Change, 2001; Mensajes De Alivio: Comunicacion Depues De La Muerte, 2001; Love Lives On: Learning from the Extraordinary Encounters of the Bereaved, 2006; Healing Grief, Finding Peace: 101 Ways to Cope with the Death of Your Loved One, 2011. Contributor to journals. **Address:** Loss Education Associates, 450 Fairway Isles Dr., Venice, FL 34285-5659, U.S.A. **Online address:** louislagrand@msn.com

LA GRECA, Annette M(arie). American (born United States), b. 1950. **Genres:** Psychology, Medicine/Health, Human Relations/Parenting. **Career:** Catholic Home Bureau, Foster Care Division, caseworker, 1972-73; Tippecanoe School Corp., school psychologist, 1974-75; De Pauw University, vocational and educational counselor, 1976-77; St. Elizabeth's Hospital and Arnette Medical Clinic, pediatric psychology intern, 1976-77; University of North Carolina, clinical intern in pediatric and clinical child psychology, 1977-78; University of Miami, Department of Psychology, assistant professor of psychology and pediatrics, 1978-82, associate professor of psychology and pediatrics, 1982-86, professor of psychology and pediatrics, 1986-, coordinator of clinical child and pediatric training, 1982-86, Clinical-Child/Pediatric Health Programs, director, 1982-2000, Mailman Center for Child Development, Department of Pediatrics, director of clinical psychology, 1984-86, Child Psychology Division, director, 1987-2000, Diabetes, Metabolic, and Lipid Disorders Unit, research consultant, 1988-, Hecht Center, fellow, 1991-, director of clinical training, 2000-, Cooper fellow, 2007-09; Montanari Residential Treatment Center, research consultant, 1979-82; Washington University, visiting professor, 1990; Journal of Consulting and Clinical Psychology, editor. **Publications:** (With S.W. Levin and E.L. Sevin) After the Storm: A Guide to Help Children Cope with the Psychological Effects of a Hurricane, 2005. EDITOR: Through the Eyes of the Child: Obtaining Self-Reports from Children and Adolescents, 1990; Stress and Coping in Child Health, 1992; Handbook of Psychological Services for Children and Adolescents, 2001; Helping Children Cope with Disasters and Terrorism, 2002; Parents' Guide to Psychological First Aid: Helping Children and Adolescents Cope with Predictable Life Crises, 2011. **Address:** Department of Psychology, University of Miami, PO Box 249229, Coral Gables, FL 33124-0721, U.S.A. **Online address:** alagreca@miami.edu

LAGUNA, Sofie. Australian (born Australia), b. 1968?. **Genres:** Children's Fiction, Animals/Pets, Theatre, Mystery/Crime/Suspense. **Career:** Writer and actor. **Publications:** FICTION FOR CHILDREN: My Yellow Blanky, 2002; Bill's Best Day, 2002; Too Loud Lily, 2002; Bad Buster, 2003; Surviving Aunt Marsha, 2003; On Our Way to the Beach, 2004; Big Ned's Bushwalk, 2005; Bird and Sugar Boy, 2006; One Foot Wrong, 2008. OTHERS: Difficult to Grow, 2000. **Address:** Booked Out Arts and Literature Agency, PO Box 2321, Prahran, VI 3181, Australia.

LAHIRI, Jhumpa. American/British (born England), b. 1967. **Genres:** Adult Non-fiction, Novels, Literary Criticism And History. **Career:** Boston University, professor of creative writing; Rhode Island School of Design, professor of creative writing. Writer. **Publications:** Interpreter of Maladies: Stories, 1999; (intro.) India Holy Song (photography collection), 2000; The

Namesake (novel), 2003; Unaccustomed Earth, 2008. **Address:** c/o Author Mail, Houghton Mifflin, 222 Berkeley St., Boston, MA 02116-3764, U.S.A.

LAHOOD, Marvin J(ohn). American (born United States), b. 1933. **Genres:** Literary Criticism And History, History, Essays. **Career:** Niagara University, instructor, 1960-61, associate professor of English, 1962-64; State University of New York College, associate professor, 1964-67, professor of English, 1967-68, professor of individual study, 1968-69, associate for academic development, 1969-71, distinguished teaching professor of English, 1978-, now distinguished teaching professor emeritus of English; College Misericordia, academic dean, 1971-72; Salem State College, academic dean and professor of English, 1972-75; D'Youville College, dean of faculty and professor of English, 1975-78. Writer. **Publications:** (Ed. with A. Rubulis) Latvian Literature, 1964; (ed.) Tender is the Night: Essays in Criticism, 1969; Conrad Richter's America, 1975; State University College at Buffalo: A History 1946-1972, 1980. Contributor to journals. **Address:** Department of English, Buffalo State University, 308 Ketchum Hall, 1300 Elmwood Ave., Buffalo, NY 14222, U.S.A. **Online address:** lahoodmj@buffalostate.edu

LAHR, John (Henry). British/American (born United States), b. 1941. **Genres:** Novels, Plays/Screenplays, Theatre, Biography, Adult Non-fiction, Essays, Photography. **Career:** City University of New York, Hunter College, instructor in dramatic literature, 1967-68; Minnesota Theatre Co., literary manager, 1968; Repertory Theatre of Lincoln Center, literary adviser, 1969-71; Grove Press, general theater editor, 1969-71; National Endowment for the Arts in experimental theater, consultant, 1970-73; New Yorker, senior theater critic and profile writer, 1992-. **Publications:** Notes on a Cowardly Lion: The Biography of Bert Lahr, 1969; Up against the Fourth Wall, 1970; Acting Out America: Essays on Modern Theatre, 1972; Astonish Me, Adventures in Contemporary Theater, 1973; (with J. Price) Life-Show: How to See Theatre in Life and Life in Theatre, 1973; The Autograph Hound, 1973; Hot to Trot (novel), 1974; Prick Up Your Ears: The Biography of Joe Orton, 1978; The Business of Rainbows: The Life and Lyrics of E. Y. Harburg, 1978; Coward: The Playwright, 1982; Automatic Vaudeville: Essays on Star Turns, 1984; Diary of a Somebody: Based on the Orton Diaries (play), 1989; The Manchurian Candidate (play), 1990; Dame Edna Everage and The Rise of Western Civilization, 1992; Light Fantastic: Adventures in Theatre, 1996; Frank Sinatra: The Artist and the Man, 1998; Show and Tell: New Yorker Profiles, 2000; Honky Tonk Parade: New Yorker Profiles of Show People, 2005; Tennessee Williams Biography, forthcoming. EDITOR: Showcase I, 1969; Showcase 1: Plays from Eugene O'Neill Memorial Foundation, 1969; (with A. Lahr) Casebook on Harold Pinter's The Homecoming, 1971; (with J. Price) The Great American Life Show: Nine Plays from the Avant-Garde Theatre, 1974; Grove Press Modern Drama: Six Plays, 1975; The Complete Plays of Joe Orton, 1975; The Orton Diaries: Including the Correspondence of Edna Welthorpe and Others, 1986; The Diaries of Kenneth Tynan, 2001. Contributor to periodicals. **Address:** Georges Borchardt Inc., 136 E 57th St., New York, NY 10022, U.S.A.

LAHUTSKY, John. American/Russian (born Russia), b. 1990. **Genres:** Biography, Autobiography/Memoirs. **Career:** Writer. **Publications:** (With A. Philps) The Boy from Baby House 10: From the Nightmare of a Russian Orphanage to a New Life in America, 2009. **Address:** Bethlehem, PA, U.S.A. **Online address:** john@johnlahutsky.com

LAI, David Chuenyan. Canadian/Chinese (born China), b. 1937?. **Genres:** Geography, Politics/Government, Social Sciences. **Career:** University of Hong Kong, tutor, 1960-64, lecturer in geography, 1967-68; University of Victoria, visiting lecturer, 1968-69, assistant professor, 1969-73, associate professor, 1973-88, professor of geography, 1988-2003, professor emeritus of geography, 2003-, Department of Pacific and Asian Studies, adjunct professor, 2003, Centre on Aging, research affiliate, 2003; Simon Fraser University, David See-Chai Lam Centre for International Communication, adjunct professor, 2010-. Writer. **Publications:** Arches in British Columbia, 1982; Chinatowns: Towns within Cities in Canada, 1988; The Forbidden City within Victoria: Myth, Symbol and Streetscape of Canada's Earliest Chinatown, 1991; Land of Genghis Khan: The Rise and Fall of Nation-States in Chinese Northern Frontiers, 1995; (with P. Madoff) Building and Rebuilding Harmony: The Gateway to Victoria's Chinatown, 1996; Canadian Steel, Chinese Government: No Chinese Labor, No Railway, 1998; (ed. with H.D. Foster and N. Zhou) Dragon's Head: Shanghai, China's Emerging Megacity, 1998; Chinese Community Leadership: Case Study of Victoria in Canada, 2010. **Address:** Department of Geography, University of Victoria, Rm. B203, Social Sciences

& Mathematics Bldg., 3800 Finnerty Rd., PO Box 3060 STN CSC, Victoria, BC V8P 5C2, Canada. **Online address:** dclai@uvic.ca

LAI, Larissa. Canadian/American (born United States), b. 1967. **Genres:** Novels, Biography. **Career:** CITR-Radio, host and producer, 1989; On Edge Productions, assistant curator, 1990; SAW Video Cooperative, coordinator, 1991; Banff Centre for the Arts, Department of Media Arts, television and video associate, 1992; Top Dollar Sisters, production manager, 1992; Western Front Society, editor, 1994-95; Vancouver Art Gallery, gallery animateur, 1996-97; University of Calgary, Markin Flanagan distinguished writer-in-residence, 1997-98; University of British Columbia, assistant professor in English; Simon Fraser University, writer-in-residence, 2006. **Publications:** NOVELS: (with P. Wong) Chinaman's Peak, Walking the Mountain, 1993; When Fox Is a Thousand, 1995; Salt Fish Girl, 2002; Automaton Biographies, 2009. Works appear in anthologies. Contributor to magazines. **Address:** Department of English, University of British Columbia, Rm. BuTo 526, 397 - 1873 East Mall, Vancouver, BC V6T 1Z1, Canada. **Online address:** lalai@ucalgary.ca

LAIMO, Michael. American (born United States), b. 1966. **Genres:** Adult Non-fiction, Novels, Novellas/Short Stories, Horror. **Career:** Swimwear Co., sales representative; Space and Time Magazine, assistant fiction editor, associate editor. **Publications:** The Twilight Garden (chapbook), 1998; Demons, Freaks, and Other Abnormalities (short stories), 1999; Within the Darkness, Golden Eyes (chapbook), 1999; Dregs of Society (short stories), 2001; (ed.) Bloodtype, 2001; Atmosphere (novel), 2002; Sleepwalker, 2004; Deep in the Darkness (novel), 2004; The Demonologist, 2005; Dead Souls, 2007; Fires Rising, 2008. Contributor to periodicals. **Address:** c/o Author Mail, Leisure Books, 200 Madison Ave., Ste. 2000, New York, NY 10016, U.S.A. **Online address:** michael@laimo.com

LAIN, Anna. See **LAMB, Nancy.**

LAIN, Douglas. American (born United States), b. 1970?. **Genres:** Novels, Young Adult Fiction. **Career:** Writer. **Publications:** Last Week's Apocalypse (short-story collection), 2006; Billy Moon: 1968, 2011; Thirty and Counting, forthcoming; The Brainwash Brand, forthcoming. Contributor of articles to magazines. Works appear in anthologies. **Address:** c/o Author Mail, Night Shade Books, 1661 Tennessee St., Ste. 3H, San Francisco, CA 94107-3578, U.S.A. **Online address:** douglain@hevanet.com

LAIRD, Holly A. American (born United States), b. 1953?. **Genres:** Poetry, Social Sciences, Gay And Lesbian Issues, History, Young Adult Fiction. **Career:** Princeton University, assistant in instruction, 1979-80; University of Virginia, assistant professor, 1981-88; University of Tulsa, Henry Kendall College of Arts and Sciences, Tulsa Studies in Women's Literature, executive editor, 1988-2005, Department of English, professor of English, chairman, 2000-03, Frances W. O'Hornett professor of literature. Writer. **Publications:** Self and Sequence: The Poetry of D.H. Lawrence, 1988; Women Coauthors, 2000. **Address:** Department of English, Henry Kendall College of Arts and Sciences, University of Tulsa, Zink Hall 344, 800 S Tucker Dr., Tulsa, OK 74104-9700, U.S.A. **Online address:** holly-laird@utulsa.edu

LAIRD, Nick. British/Irish (born Ireland), b. 1975?. **Genres:** Young Adult Fiction, Poetry, Novels, Criminology/True Crime. **Career:** Harvard University, visiting fellow; Columbia University, adjunct professor. Lawyer and writer. **Publications:** Utterly Monkey, 2005; To a Fault, 2005; On Purpose (poetry), 2007; Glover's Mistake (novel), 2009. Contributor to journals. Works appear in anthologies. **Address:** c/o Author Mail, HarperCollins Publishers, 10 E 53rd St., New York, NY 10022, U.S.A.

LAIRD, Ross. Australian (born Australia), b. 1947. **Genres:** Communications/Media, Music, Dance/Ballet, Photography. **Career:** Librarian, 1965-87; National Film and Sound Archive, librarian and consultant, 1988-91, sound archivist, 1997-; Wharf Cable Television, senior manager of video library system, 1992-94; Ernst and Young, manager of information and research unit, 1994-96; Screen Sound, sound archivist. Writer. **Publications:** A Discography of Popular Music Recorded in Australia, 1924-50, 1982; Tantalizing Tingles: A Discography of Early Ragtime, Jazz, and Novelty Syncopated Piano recordings, 1995; Moanin' Low: A Discography of Female Popular Vocal Recordings, 1920-33, 1996; The First Wave: Australian Rock and Pop Recordings, 1955-63, 1998; Sound Beginnings: The Early Record Industry in Australia, 1999; Brunswick Records: A Discography of Recordings, 1919-31 as

Brunswick Records: A Discography of Recordings Made by the Brunswick-Balke-Collender Company, Its Subsidiaries, and the Subsequent Corporate Entity, 2001; Currency Companion to Music and Dance in Australia, 2003; (with B. Rust) Discography of Okeh Records, 1918-1934, 2004. Contributor to books. **Address:** PO Box 22, Canberra, AC 2601, Australia. **Online address:** scarcesounds@hotmail.com

LAIRD, Thomas (Calvin). American (born United States), b. 1953?. **Genres:** Area Studies, Architecture, Adult Non-fiction, History, Photography, Art/Art History. **Career:** Asiaweek, reporter, 1991-2002. Journalist and photographer. **Publications:** The Dalai Lama's Secret Temple, 2000; Into Tibet: The CIA's First Atomic Spy and His Secret Expedition to Lhasa, 2002; The Story of Tibet: Conversations with the Dalai Lama, 2006; Murals of Tibet, 2012. Contributor to periodicals. **Address:** New Orleans, LA 70114, U.S.A. **Online address:** laird100@yahoo.com

LAJE, Zilia L. American/Cuban (born Cuba), b. 1941. **Genres:** Novels, Novellas/Short Stories, Food And Wine, Genealogy/Heraldry. **Career:** Pittsburgh Plate Glass Intl., export documentation assistant, 1959-60; Southeast Bank, corporate banking assistant, 1978-90; writer, 1995-. **Publications:** La cortina de bagazo (historical novel), 1995, trans. as The Sugar Cane Curtain, 2000; Cartas son cartas (novel), 2001, trans. as Love Letters in the Sand, 2002; Divagaciones: El premio y otros cuentos, 2003; 100 Recetas de cocina tradicionales, 2004; Genealogia-Laje (genealogy), 2005. Contributor to periodicals. **Address:** Escritores Cubanos de Miami, PO Box 45-1732, Shenandoah Sta., Miami, FL 33245-1732, U.S.A. **Online address:** ziliallaje@comcast.net

LAKE, David (John). Australian/Indian (born India), b. 1929. **Genres:** Science Fiction/Fantasy, Poetry, Literary Criticism And History. **Career:** Sherrardswood School, assistant master, 1953-58; St. Albans Boys Grammar School, assistant master, 1958-59; Saigon University, teacher of English, 1959-61; Thai Government, teacher of English, 1961-63; Chiswick Polytechnic, teacher of English, 1963-64; Jadavpore University, reader in English and teacher, 1965-67; University of Queensland, School of English, Media Studies and Art History, lecturer, 1967-72, senior lecturer, 1973-76, reader in English, 1977-, honorary research consultant, adviser, fellow. Writer. **Publications:** John Milton: Paradise Lost, 1967; Greek Tragedy, 1969; Style and Meaning, 1971; Hornpipes and Funerals (poems): Forty-Two Poems and Six Odes of Horace, 1973; The Canon of Thomas Middleton's Plays: Internal Evidence for the Major Problems of Authorship, 1975. SCIENCE FICTION NOVELS: Walkers on the Sky, 1976, rev. ed., 1978; The Right Hand of Dextra, 1977; The Wildings of Westron, 1977; The Gods of Xuma or Barsoom Revisited, 1978; The Fourth Hemisphere, 1980; The Man Who Loved Morlocks: A Sequel to the Time Machine as Narrated by the Time Traveller, 1981; The Ring of Truth, 1982; Warlords of Xuma, 1983. FANTASY NOVELS: The Changelings of Chaan, 1985; West of the Moon, 1988. EDITOR: (and intro.) The First Men in the Moon, 1995; The Invisible Man, 1996. Contributor to books. **Address:** School of English, Media Studies and Art History, University of Queensland, 9 Michie Bldg., E227 Forgan Smith Bldg., Saint Lucia, QL 4072, Australia.

LAKE, Deryn. See **LAMPITT, Dinah.**

LAKE, Jo Anne. Canadian (born Canada), b. 1941. **Genres:** Children's Nonfiction, Education, Sciences. **Career:** Elementary school teacher, 1961-65; University of Western Ontario, instructor in mathematics, 1965, board consultant, administrator; Durham District Board of Education, consultant, 1986-90, administrator, 1991-2000; Lakehead University, faculty of education, P/J Math in the Pre-Service Program, instructor; Niagara University, Faculty of Education, supervisor, instructor and coordinator. Writer and educational consultant. **Publications:** Imagine, 1993; Life Long Learning, 1997; Literature and Science Breakthroughs: Connecting Language and Science Skills in the Elementary Classroom, 2000; Math Memories You Can Count On: A Literature-based Approach to Teaching Mathematics in the Primary Classrooms, 2009. Contributor to journals. **Address:** c/o Author Mail, Stenhouse Publishers, 480 Congress St., Portland, ME 04101-3400, U.S.A. **Online address:** jlake@lakeheadu.ca

LAKE, Marilyn. Australian (born Australia), b. 1949?. **Genres:** Military/Defense/Arms Control, History. **Career:** La Trobe University, Charles La Trobe professor of history; Harvard University, chair in Australian studies, 2001-02; Stockholm University, visiting professor; University of Western Australia, visiting professor; Australian National University, visiting professor; University of Sydney, visiting professor. Writer. **Publications:** A Divided Society: Tasmania during World War I, 1975; The Limits of Hope: Soldier Settlement in Victoria, 1915-38, 1987; (ed. with C. Fox) Australians at Work: Commentaries and Sources, 1990; (with P. Grimshaw, A. McGrath and M. Quartly) Creating a Nation, 1994; (ed. with J. Damousi) Gender and War: Australians at War in the Twentieth Century, 1995; Getting Equal: The History of Australian Feminism, 1999; (with P. Grimshaw and K. Holmes) Women's Rights and Human Rights: International Historical Perspectives, 2001; Faith: Faith Bandler, Gentle Activist, 2002; (ed.) Memory, Monuments and Museums: The Past in the Present, 2006; (with H. Reynolds) Drawing the Global Colour Line: White Men's Countries and the International Challenge of Racial Equality in Australia as Drawing the Global Colour Line: White Men's Countries and the Question of Racial Equality, 2008; (with H. Reynolds, M. McKenna and J. Damousi) What's Wrong with ANZAC? The Militarisation of Australian History, 2010. **Address:** Australia. **Online address:** m.lake@latrobe.edu.au

LAKE, M. D. American (born United States), b. 1934?. **Genres:** Mystery/Crime/Suspense, Novels, Children's Fiction, Young Adult Fiction, Horror, Criminology/True Crime. **Career:** University of Minnesota, professor of Scandinavian languages and literature; The Minnesota Daily, humor columnist. **Publications:** PEGGY O'NEILL MYSTERY NOVELS: Amends for Murder, 1989; Cold Comfort, 1990; A Gift for Murder, 1992; Poisoned Ivy, 1992; Murder by Mail, 1993; Grave Choices, 1995; Once Upon a Crime, 1995; Flirting with Death, 1996; Ties of Blood, 1997; Midsummer Malice, 1997; Death Calls the Tune, 1999. **Address:** c/o Author Mail, Avon Books, 10 E 53rd St., New York, NY 10022, U.S.A. **Online address:** mdlake1234@aol.com

LAKE, Paul. American (born United States), b. 1951. **Genres:** Novels, Literary Criticism And History. **Career:** Arkansas Tech University, professor of English and creative writing. Writer and poet. **Publications:** Another Kind of Travel, 1988; Among the Immortals: A Novel, 1994; Walking Backward: Poems, 1999; Cry Wolf: A Political Fable, 2008. Contributor to journals and periodicals. **Address:** Department of English, Arkansas Tech University, Witherspoon 144, 1605 Coliseum Dr., Russellville, AR 72801, U.S.A. **Online address:** plake@atu.edu

LAKELAND, Paul. Canadian/Belgian (born Belgium), b. 1946. **Genres:** Sociology, Area Studies, International Relations/Current Affairs, Local History/Rural Topics, Cartoons, Third World, Women's Studies And Issues. **Career:** Fairfield University, assistant professor, 1981-84, associate professor, 1984-88, professor of religious studies, 1988-, Aloysius P. Kelley, S.J., professor of Catholic studies, Center for Catholic Studies Department, chair, 2004, director; Religious Studies Review, network editor. **Publications:** Can Women Be Priests?, 1975; The Politics of Salvation: The Hegelian Idea of the State, 1984; Freedom in Christ: An Introduction to Political Theology, 2nd ed., 1986; Theology and Critical Theory: The Discourse of the Church, 1990; Postmodernity: Christian Identity in a Fragmented Age, 1997; The Liberation of the Laity: In Search of an Accountable Church, 2003; (ed. with S. Jones) Constructive Theology, 2005; Catholicism at the Crossroads: How the Laity Can Save the Church, 2007; Church: Living Communion, 2009; (ed. and intro.) Essential Writings, 2010. Contributor to journals. **Address:** Department of Religious Studies, Fairfield University, 1073 N Benson Rd., Fairfield, CT 06824, U.S.A. **Online address:** plfakeland@fair1.fairfield.edu

LAKER, Rosalind. See **ØVSTEDAL, Barbara.**

LAKHOUS, Amara. Italian (born Italy), b. 1970?. **Genres:** Novels. **Career:** AdnKronos International (news agency), staff, 2003-. Journalist. **Publications:** Le cimici e il pirata, 1999; Scontro di civiltà per un ascensore a Piazza Vittorio: romanzo (novel), 2008. **Address:** Rome, Italy. **Online address:** amaralakhous@yahoo.it

LAKOS, Amos. American/Romanian (born Romania), b. 1946. **Genres:** International Relations/Current Affairs, Bibliography, History, Autobiography/Memoirs. **Career:** University of Waterloo, reference and collections development librarian, 1977-94, co-ordinator management information services, 1994-2002; University of California, Young Research Library, head of reference and instructional services, 2002-04, Anderson School of Management, librarian, 2004-07. Writer. **Publications:** Terrorism, 1970-1978: A Bibliography, 1979; (comp.) Comparative Provincial Politics of Canada: A Bibliography of Select Periodical Articles, 1970-1977, 1979; (with A. Kapur) Aspects of Negotiations Between States: A Select Bibliography, 1981; American Diplomatic Memoirs, 1985; Modern Diplomacy, 1985; International Terrorism: A Bibliography, 1986; Polish Crisis-Solidarity and Martial Law, 1987; International Negotiations: A Bibliography, 1988; Terrorism, 1980-1990: A Bibliography, 1991. **Address:** Rosenfeld Management Library, University of California, 110 Westwood Plz., PO Box 951460, Los Angeles, CA 90095-1460, U.S.A. **Online address:** aalakos@library.ucla.cdu

LAL, Brij V. Australian/Fijian (born Fiji), b. 1952. **Genres:** History, Politics/ Government, Local History/Rural Topics, Education, Humanities. **Career:** University of the South Pacific, lecturer, 1976-83; University of Hawaii, assistant professor, associate professor, 1983-91; Australian National University, senior research fellow, 1990-93, senior fellow, 1993-97, professor, 1997-, Center for the Contemporary Pacific, founding editor, director, 1998-. **Publications:** The Girmitiyas: The Origins of the Fiji Indians, 1983; Power and Prejudice: The Making of the Fiji Crisis, 1988; Broken Waves: A History of Fiji in the Twentieth Century, 1992; (with P. Reeves and T.R. Vakatora) Fiji Islands: Towards a United Future: Report of the Fiji Constitution Review Commission, 1996, 1996; (with T.R. Vakatora) Fiji and the World, 1997; A Vision for Change: AD Patel and the Politics of Fiji, 1997; Another Way: The Politics of Constitutional Reform in Post-Coup Fiji, 1998; Time to Change: The Fiji General Elections of 1999, 1999; Chalo Jahaji: On a Journey Through Indenture in Fiji, 2000; Fiji before the Storm: Elections and the Politics of Development, 2000; Mr. Tulsis Store: A Fijian Journey, 2001; On the Other Side of Midnight: A Fijian Journey, 2005; Islands of Turmoil: Elections and Politics in Fiji, 2006; Turnings: Fiji Factions, 2007. EDITOR: (with J. McGuire and M. Borthwick) Problems and Methods of Enquiry in South Asian History, 1984; (with J. McGuire and M. Borthwick) ACCTEST Problems and Methods of Enquiry in South Asian History, 1984; Politics in Fiji: Studies in Contemporary History, 1986; Pacific Islands History: Journeys and Transformations, 1992; (with D. Munro and E.D. Beechert) Plantation Workers: Resistance and Accommodation, 1993; (with K.R. Howe and R.C. Kiste) Tides of History: The Pacific Islands in the Twentieth Century, 1994; (with P. Larmour) Electoral Systems in Divided Societies: The Fiji Constitution Review, 1997; (with R.R. Vakatora) Fijiin Transition, 1997; (with K. Fortune) The Pacific Islands: An Encyclopedia, 2000; (with P. Hempenstall) Pacific Lives, Pacific Places: Bursting Boundaries in Pacific History, 2001; (with M. Pretes) Coup: Reflections on the Political Crisis in Fiji, 2001; Pacific Places, Pacific Histories: Essays in Honor of Robert C. Kiste, 2004; Bittersweet: The Indo-Fijian Experience, 2004; (with D. Munro) Texts and Contexts: Reflections in Pacific Islands Historiography, 2006; (with P. Reeves and R. Rai) Encyclopedia of the Indian Diaspora, 2006; (with A. Ley) Coombs: A House of Memories, 2006; (with G. Chand and V. Naidu) 1987: Fiji Twenty Years On, 2008; (with W. Safran and A.K. Sahoo) Transnational Migrations: The Indian Diaspora, 2009. **Address:** Research School of Pacific & Asian Studies, Australian National University, H.C. Coombs Bldg. 009, Canberra, AC 0200, Australia. **Online address:** brij.lal@anu.edu.au

LALICKI, Tom. (Tom L. Matthews). American (born United States), b. 1949?. **Genres:** History, Biography, Art/Art History, Novels, Mystery/Crime/ Suspense, Adult Non-fiction, Young Adult Fiction. **Career:** Writer. **Publications:** HOUDINI AND NATE MYSTERY SERIES: Danger in the Dark, 2006; Shots at Sea, 2007; Frame-up on the Bowery, 2009. NONFICTION: Spellbinder: The Life of Harry Houdini, 2000; Grierson's Raid: A Daring Cavalry Strike through the Heart of the Confederacy, 2004. AS TOM L. MATTHEWS: Light Shining through the Mist: A Photobiography of Dian Fossey, 1998; Always Inventing: A Photobiography of Alexander Graham Bell, 1999. **Address:** Farrar, Straus and Giroux, 175 5th Ave., New York, NY 10010-7703, U.S.A. **Online address:** tom.lalicki@gmail.com

LALITA, K. (Ke Lalita). Indian (born India), b. 1953. **Genres:** Women's Studies And Issues. **Career:** Administrative College of India, research associate, 1977-80; Rural Development Advisory Service, director of women's programs, 1980-84; Osmania University, Anveshi Research Centre for Women's Studies, founder, coordinator, 1986-95; ThinkSoft Consultants, co-founder-director, 1993-, Progressive Organisation of Women, founder-president; Royal Tropical Institute, Gender, Citizenship, Governance, South Asia coordinator, 1999-2002; Stree Shakti Sangatana, founder. Writer. **Publications:** Indian Women in Subsistence and Agricultural Labour, 1986; (co-ed.) Manaku Teliyani Mana Caritra, 1986, rev. ed., 2003; (co-author) We Were Making History: Life Histories of Women in the Telangana People's Struggle, 1989; (ed. with S. Tharu) Women Writing in India, vol. I: 600 B.C. to the Early Twentieth Century, 1991, vol. II: The Twentieth Century, 1990-1993;

(co-ed.) Savālakṣ a Sandehālu: Strīlu-āarōgyaṃ, Samskrit, Rājakīyālu, 2006. **Address:** Thinksoft Consultants Private Ltd., 3-4-142/6, Barkatpura, Hyderabad, AP 500 027, India. **Online address:** vithal2@hd1.vsnl.net.in

LALITA, Ke. *See* **LALITA, K.**

LAM, Truong Buu. American (born United States), b. 1933. **Genres:** History. **Career:** Institute of Historical Research, director, 1957-64; State University of New York, associate professor of history, 1968-71; University of Hawaii, associate professor of history, 1971-2000, professor, 2001-02, now retired. Writer. **Publications:** Patterns of Vietnamese Response to Foreign Intervention, 1967; New Lamps for Old: The Transformation of the Vietnamese Administrative Elite, 1982; (with M. Lâm) Resistance, Rebellion, Revolution in Vietnamese History, 1984; A Bibliographic Index, 1984; (ed.) Borrowings and Adaptations in Vietnamese Culture, 1987; Colonialism Experienced, 2000; A Story of Vietnam, 2010. **Address:** 189 Polihale Pl., Honolulu, HI 96825, U.S.A. **Online address:** lamb@hawaii.edu

LAM, Vincent. Canadian (born Canada), b. 1974. **Genres:** Adult Non-fiction, Novels. **Career:** Toronto East General Hospital, emergency room physician; University of Toronto, Department of Family and Community Medicine, lecturer. Writer. **Publications:** Bloodletting & Miraculous Cures: Stories, 2005; (with C.Lee) The Flu Pandemic and You: A Canadian Guide, 2006; Extraordinary Canadians: Tommy Douglas, 2011. Contributor to periodicals. **Address:** Anne McDermid & Associates, 64 Bloem Ave., Toronto, ON M6E 1S1, Canada. **Online address:** contact@vincentlam.ca

LAMAR, Howard Roberts. American (born United States), b. 1923. **Genres:** History, Reference, Politics/Government. **Career:** University of Massachusetts, instructor in history, 1945-46; Wesleyan University, instructor, 1948-49; Yale University, Department of History, instructor, 1949-54, assistant professor, 1954-57, associate professor, 1957-64, chair, 1962-63, 1967-70, professor of history, 1964-98, Sterling professor emeritus of history, 1998-, director of graduate studies in history, 1964-67, Humanities Division, director, 1972-74, Yale College, dean, 1979-85, president, 1992-93. Writer. **Publications:** Dakota Territory, 1861-1889: A Study of Frontier Politics, 1956, rev. ed., 1997; The Far Southwest, 1850-1912: A Political History of the Territories of Arizona, Colorado, New Mexico and Utah, 1966, rev. ed., 2000; Far Southwest, 1846-1912: A Territorial History, 1966, rev. ed., 2000; Trader on the American Frontier, 1977; Texas Crossings: The Lone Star State and the American Far West, 1991; Voices of the New Republic: Connecticut Towns, 1800-1832, 2003; Charlie Siringo's West: An Interpretive Biography, 2005. EDITOR: The Cruise of the Portsmouth, 1845-1847: A Sailor's View of the Naval Conquest of California, 1958; Party Politics and Public Action, 1877-1917, 1960; Reader's Encyclopedia of the American West, 1975; (with L. Thompson) The Frontier in History: North America and Southern Africa Compared, 1981; (and intro.) Gold Seeker: Adventures of a Belgian Argonaut During the Gold Rush Years, 1985; New Encyclopedia of the American West, 1998. **Address:** Department of History, Yale University, SML 313, Hall of Graduate Studies, 320 York St., PO Box 208324, New Haven, CT 06520-8324, U.S.A.

LAMAY, Craig L. American (born United States) **Genres:** Communications/Media, Social Sciences. **Career:** Columbia University, Freedom Forum Media Studies Center, director, staff; American Academy of Arts and Sciences, Public Service Television Project, associate director; Northwestern University, Medill School of Journalism, assistant professor, associate professor, associate dean, Institute for Policy Research, faculty associate, School of Law, adjunct professor; Media Studies Journal, editor. **Publications:** (With N.N. Minow) Abandoned in the Wasteland: Children, Television and the First Amendment, 1995; Exporting Press Freedom: Economic and Editorial Dilemmas in International Media Assistance, 2007; (with N.N. Minow) Inside the Presidential Debates: Their Improbable Past and Promising Future, 2008. EDITOR: (with E.E. Dennis) Media and the Environment, 1991; (with E.E. Dennis) America's Schools and the Mass Media, 1993; (with E.E. Dennis) Higher Education in the Information Age, 1993; (with E.E. Dennis) The Culture of Crime, 1995; (with E.E. Dennis and E.C. Pease) Publishing Books, 1997; (with E. Mickiewicz and C. Firestone) Television Autonomy and the State, 1999; Journalism and the Debate Over Privacy, 2003. Contributor to books. **Address:** Medill School, Northwestern University, Rm. Fisk 214, 1845 Sheridan Rd., Evanston, IL 60208-2101, U.S.A. **Online address:** clamay@northwestern.edu

LAMB, Andrew (Martin). British (born England), b. 1942. **Genres:** Music, History, Theatre. **Career:** Cooperative Insurance Society Ltd., actuarial student, 1963-69; Smiths Industries Ltd., investment manager, 1969-73; Lloyds Bank Ltd., investment manager, 1973; Philips Industries, assistant investment manager, 1973-76; MGM Assurance, assistant general manager, 1976-88; Friends Provident Life Office, chief investment manager, 1988-98; Friends Ivory & Sime plc, director, 1998-2000. Writer. **Publications:** (Comp.) A catalogue of the works of the Strauss family composed or arranged for their visits to Great Britain, 1969; Emile Waldteufel [1837-1915], 1979; Jerome Kern in Edwardian London, 1981; (with K. Ganzl) Ganzl's Book of the Musical Theatre, 1988; Skaters' Waltz: The Story of the Waldteufels, 1995; An Offenbach Family Album, 1997; Shirley House to Trinity School, 1999; 150 Years of Popular Musical Theatre, 2000; Leslie Stuart: Composer of Florodora, 2002; (with J. Myerscough) Fragson: The Triumphs and the Tragedy, 2004; The Merry Widow at 100, 2005; A Life on the Ocean Wave: The Story of Henry Russell, 2007. EDITOR: The Moulin Rouge, 1990; Light Music from Austria, 1992; Unterhaltungsmusik aus Österreich, 1992; Leslie Stuart: My Bohemian Life, 2003. Contributor to periodicals. **Address:** 12 Fullers Wood, Croydon, Surrey, CR0 8HZ, England. **Online address:** andrew-lamb@light-music.net

LAMB, Brian. American (born United States), b. 1941. **Genres:** Documentaries/Reportage, Communications/Media, History, Biography, Politics/Government. **Career:** United Press Intl., radio reporter; P.H. Dominick, U.S. Senator for Colorado, press secretary; White House Office of Telecommunications Policy, assistant, 1971-74; Media Reports, editor and cablevision Washington bureau chief; Cable-Satellite Public Affairs Network (C-SPAN), founder, chairman and chief executive officer, 1977-. **Publications:** America's Town Hall: C-SPAN, 1988; Booknotes: Writers and Their Stories from C-SPAN's Author Interviews, 1997; (comp.) Booknotes: America's Finest Authors on Reading, Writing, and the Power of Ideas, 1997; (comp.) Booknotes: Life Stories: Notable Biographers on the People Who Shaped America, 1999; Who's Buried in Grant's Tomb?: A Tour of Presidential Gravesites, 1999; Booknotes: Stories from American History, 2001; (comp.) Booknotes: On American Character, 2004; (ed. with S. Swain) Abraham Lincoln: Great American Historians on Our Sixteenth President, 2009; (ed. with S. Swain and M. Farkas) Supreme Court, 2010. **Address:** C-SPAN, 400 N Capitol St. NW, Ste. 650, Washington, DC 20001, U.S.A.

LAMB, Connie. American (born United States), b. 1947. **Genres:** Genealogy/Heraldry, Librarianship, Bibliography. **Career:** University of Utah, Air Pollution Laboratory, technician, 1972-73; Utah State Library Commission, reference librarian and information retrieval specialist, 1977-79; Brigham Young University, Computer-Assisted Research Services Department, chair, 1979-87, Jerusalem Center, librarian, 1987-88, Department of History and Religion, reference specialist, 1988-2000, Social Science/Education Department, reference specialist, 2000-, adjunct curator, Harold B. Lee Library, librarian. Writer. **Publications:** (Comp. with R.D. Jensen and N.M. Smith) Agricultural and Animal Sciences Journals and Serials: An Analytical Guide, 1986; (with G.L. Cronin and B.H. Hall) Jewish American Fiction Writers: An Annotated Bibliography, 1991; (ed. with A. Targowski) Civilizational Futures, 2010. Contributor to periodicals. **Address:** Harold B. Lee Library, Brigham Young University, 1202 HBLL, PO Box 26800, Provo, UT 84602-6800, U.S.A. **Online address:** connie_lamb@byu.edu

LAMB, Karl A(llen). American (born United States), b. 1933. **Genres:** Novels, Novellas/Short Stories, Politics/Government, Biography, Autobiography/Memoirs, History. **Career:** University of Michigan, assistant professor of political science, 1958-63; Michigan Citizenship Clearing House, director, 1959-61; University of California, assistant professor, professor of politics, 1963-85; Cowell College, fellow, 1965-85, associate professor of government, 1966-69, professor of politics, 1970-85, associate dean of graduate division, 1966-69, acting provost, 1978-79; U.S. Naval Academy, dean and professor, 1985-99, now professor emeritus. Writer. **Publications:** (Contrib.) The Politics of Reapportionment, 1962; (contrib.) Inside Politics: The National Conventions, 1962; (with J. Pierce and J.P. White) Apportionment and Representative Institutions: The Michigan Experience, 1963; (with N.C. Thomas) Congress: Politics and Practice, 1964; (with P.A. Smith) Campaign Decision-Making: The Presidential Election of 1964, 1968; (ed.) Democracy, Liberalism and Revolution: Reflections upon the Issues that Divide America and the Institutions which Confront those Issues, 1971; People, Maybe: Seeking Democracy in America, 1971, 3rd ed., 1978; As Orange Goes: Twelve California Families and the Future of American Politics, 1974; The Guardians: Leadership Values and the American Tradition, 1982; Reasonable Dis-

agreement: Two U.S. Senators and the Choices They Make, 1998. Contributor to professional journals. **Address:** Office of the Academic Dean and Provost, United States Naval Academy, 121 Blake Rd., Annapolis, MD 21402-5000, U.S.A. **Online address:** lamb.arnold@verizon.net

LAMB, Marion J. British (born England), b. 1939. **Genres:** Biology, Sciences, Zoology, Humanities. **Career:** Medical Research Council, Radiation Biology Unit, scientist, 1964-66; University of London, Birkbeck College, Department of Biological Sciences, lecturer, 1966-, senior lecturer, through 1994, retired, 1994. Writer. **Publications:** Biology of Ageing, 1977; (with E. Jablonka) Epigenetic Inheritance and Evolution: The Lamarckian Dimension, 1995; (with E. Jablonka) Evolution in Four Dimensions: Genetic, Epigenetic, Behavioral, and Symbolic Variation in the History of Life, 2005. **Address:** 11 Fernwood, Clarence Rd., London, GL N22 8QE, England. **Online address:** marionlamb@btinternet.com

LAMB, Nancy. Also writes as Anna Lain, Pamela Ryder, R. G. Austin. American (born United States), b. 1939. **Genres:** Novels, Mystery/Crime/Suspense, Children's Fiction, Young Adult Fiction, Poetry, Children's Nonfiction, Essays, Adult Non-fiction, Adult Non-fiction. **Career:** University of Georgia, Hariette Austin Writing Program, faculty; Big Sur Writing Workshop, faculty; Media Development Authority, faculty. Freelance writer and editor. **Publications:** (With R.G. Gelman) Vampires and Other Creatures of the Night (nonfiction), 1991; The Great Mosquito, Bull and Coffin Caper, 1992; (with M. Singer) The World's Greatest Toe Show, 1994; One April Morning: Children Remember the Oklahoma City Bombing, 1995; Alison Goes for the Gold, 1995; (with M. Singer) Vampires Went Thataway!, 1995. WHICH WAY BOOKS AS R.G. AUSTIN: The Castle of No Return, 1982; Vampires, Spies and Alien Beings, 1982; The Spell of the Black Raven, 1982; Famous and Rich, 1982; Lost in a Strange Land, 1982; The Curse of the Sunken Treasure, 1982; Cosmic Encounters, 1982; Creatures of the Dark, 1982; Invasion of the Black Slime and Other Tales of Horror, 1983; Trapped in the Black Box, 1983; Poltergeists, Ghosts and Psychic Encounters, 1984; The Shadow Stealers, 1984; Islands of Terror, 1985; Ten-Ton Monster, 1985. SECRETDOOR BOOKS AS R.G. AUSTIN: Wow! You Can Fly!, 1983; Giants, Elves and Scary Monsters, 1983; The Haunted Castle, 1983; The Secret Life of Toys, 1983; The Visitors from Outer Space, 1983; The Inch-High Kid, 1983; The Magic Carpet, 1983; Happy Birthday to You, 1983; The Monster Family, 1984; Brontosaurus Moves In, 1984; The Enchanted Forest, 1984; Crazy Computers, 1984. FOR ADULTS: Gentlemen Callers, 1978; The End of Summer, 1981; (as Pamela Ryder) Dakin Field, 1984; (as Anna Lain) Prism, 1988; (with C. Brod) The Creative Revolution and the Future of Japan (nonfiction), 1993; The Writers Guide to Crafting Stories for Children, 2001; The Art and Craft of Storytelling: A Comprehensive Guide to Classic Writing Techniques, 2008. **Address:** c/o Andrea Brown, Andrea Brown Literary Agency, 1076 Eagle Dr., Salinas, CA 93905, U.S.A. **Online address:** nancy@nancylamb.com

LAMB, Patricia Clare. American (born United States), b. 1935. **Genres:** Poetry, Natural History. **Career:** Writer. **Publications:** POETRY: Why Horatio, 1985; Dwelling, 1988; All Men by Nature, 1993; The Long Love: New and Collected Poems, 1957-1998, 1998; Happy the Man, 2003; A Loss for Words, 2009. Contributor to journals. **Address:** 1341 Castle Ct., Ste. 107, Houston, TX 77006-5753, U.S.A. **Online address:** harbottle@aol.com

LAMB, Ramdas. American (born United States), b. 1945. **Genres:** Theology/Religion, Anthropology/Ethnology. **Career:** University of Hawaii, associate professor of religion, 1989-. Writer. **Publications:** Rapt in the Name: The Ramnamis, Ramnam and Untouchable Religion in Central India, 2002. Contributor of articles to books and journals. **Address:** Department of Religion, University of Hawaii, 2530 Dole St., Honolulu, HI 96822-2309, U.S.A. **Online address:** ramdas@hawaii.edu

LAMB, Sharon. American (born United States), b. 1955. **Genres:** Psychology, Women's Studies And Issues, Social Sciences, Human Relations/Parenting. **Career:** Melrose-Mindoro High School, English teacher, 1977-78; Greater Lawrence Mental Health Center, intern, 1980; Greenhouse Inc., intern, 1980-81; Cambridgeport Problem Center, psychotherapist, 1981; Massachusetts General Hospital, clinical fellow and evaluator, 1982-88; Mt. Ida Junior College, lecturer, 1984-85; Judge Baker Children's Center, psychologist, 1988-89; Boston Institute for Psychotherapy, instructor, 1989; Bryn Mawr College, Clinical Developmental Psychology Program, assistant professor of psychology, 1989-96; Child Study Institute, psychologist, 1989-96; Network of Victim Assistance, consulting psychologist, 1993-; St. Michael's College, Department of Psychology, professor, 1996-2009; University of Massachusetts, Department of Counseling and School Psychology, distinguished professor of mental health and chair, 2009-, Professor, College of Education and Human Development, department chair, Mental Health Program, director, Family Therapy Program, co-director. Writer. **Publications:** The Trouble with Blame: Victims, Perpetrators, and Responsibility, 1996; The Secret Lives of Girls: What Good Girls Really Do--Sex Play, Aggression, and Their Guilt, 2001; Sex, Therapy, and Kids: Addressing Their Concerns Through Talk and Play, 2006; (with L.M. Brown) Packaging Girlhood: Rescuing Our Daughters from Marketers' Schemes, 2006; (with L.M. Brown and M. Tappan) Packaging Boyhood: Saving Our Sons from Superheroes, Slackers, and other Media Stereotypes, 2009. EDITOR: (with J. Kagan) The Emergence of Morality in Young Children, 1987; New Versions of Victims: Feminists Struggle with the Concept, 1999; (with J.G. Murphy) Before Forgiving: Cautionary Views of Forgiveness in Psychotherapy, 2002. Contributor of articles to newspapers and journals. **Address:** Department of Counseling and School Psychology, University of Massachusetts, 100 Morrissey Blvd., Boston, MA 02125-3393, U.S.A. **Online address:** sharon.lamb@umb.edu

LAMB, Wally. American (born United States), b. 1950. **Genres:** Novels, Poetry, Humanities. **Career:** Norwich Free Academy, English teacher, 1972-88, Writing Center, director, 1989-98; Fresh Air Fund, host parent, 1982-; University of Connecticut, director of creative writing, associate professor, 1997-99; Union Institute & University, writer-in-residence, 2006. **Publications:** NOVELS: She's Come Undone, 1992; I Know This Much Is True, 1998; The Hour I First Believed, 2008; Wishin' and Hopin': A Christmas Story, 2009. EDITOR: Always Begin Where You Are (poetry textbook), 1979; Couldn't Keep It to Myself: Testimonies from Our Imprisoned Sisters, 2003; (intro.) I'll Fly Away: Further Testimonies from the Women of York Prison, 2007. Contributor to periodicals. **Address:** Department of English, University of Connecticut, 215 Glenbrook Rd., Ste. 4025, Storrs, CT 06269-4025, U.S.A.

LAMBA, Marie. American (born United States) **Genres:** Novels, Young Adult Fiction, Romance/Historical, Essays, Novellas/Short Stories. **Career:** Freelance writer. **Publications:** What I Meant, 2007; Call Me Okaasan, 2009; Over My Head, 2011; Liar Liar, 2011; Drawn, 2012. Works appear in anthologies. Contributor to periodicals. **Address:** Lamba Associates Inc., PO Box 415, Doylestown, PA 18901, U.S.A. **Online address:** marielamba@hotmail.com

LAMBDIN, Dewey (W.). American (born United States), b. 1945. **Genres:** Romance/Historical, Novels, Westerns/Adventure. **Career:** WMC-TV 5, assistant director, 1969-72, producer and director, 1972-81; WPTY-TV 24, production manager, 1981-84; freelance director, 1984-87; Admark Advertising, writer and producer, 1987. **Publications:** ALAN LEWRIE NAVAL ADVENTURE SERIES: The King's Coat: A Novel, 1989; The French Admiral, 1990; The King's Commission, 1991; The King's Privateer, 1992; The Gun Ketch, 1993; For King and Country, 1994; H.M.S. Cockerel, 1995; A King's Commander, 1997; Jester's Fortune, 1999; The King's Captain, 2000; Sea of Grey, 2002; Havoc's Sword, 2003; The Captain's Vengeance, 2004; A King's Trade, 2006; Troubled Waters, 2008; The Baltic Gambit, 2009; King, Ship, and Sword, 2010; The Invasion Year, 2011; Reefs and Shoals, 2012. NOVEL: What Lies Buried: A Novel of Old Cape Fear, 2005. Contributor to books. **Address:** Harold Ober Associates Inc., 425 Madison Ave., New York, NY 10017, U.S.A.

LAMBERSON, Gregory. American (born United States), b. 1964. **Genres:** Novels. **Career:** Fear Zone.com, creator and editor. Director and producer. **Publications:** Cheap Scares! Low Budget Horror Filmmakers Share Their Secrets, 2008; Johnny Gruesome (novel), 2008; The Frenzy Way (novel), 2010. JAKE HELMAN FILES SERIES: Personal Demons, 2009; Desperate Souls, 2010. **Address:** Buffalo, NY , U.S.A. **Online address:** glamberson@verizon.net

LAMBERT, Andrew D. British (born England), b. 1956. **Genres:** History. **Career:** Bristol Polytechnic (now University of West of England), lecturer in modern international history, 1983-87; Royal Naval College, Department of History and International Affairs, consultant, 1987-89, Royal Military Academy, senior lecturer in war studies, 1989-91; King's College, lecturer, 1991-96, senior lecturer in war studies, 1996-, professor of naval history, 1999-2001, Laughton professor of naval history, 2001-, Laughton Naval History Unit, director. Writer. **Publications:** NONFICTION: Battleships in Transition: The Creation of the Steam Battlefleet, 1815-1860, 1984; Warrior: The World's First

Ironclad, Then and Now, 1987; The Crimean War: British Grand Strategy, 1853-1856, 1990; The Last Sailing Battlefleet: Maintaining Naval Mastery, 1815-1850, 1991; (with S. Badsey) The Crimean War, 1994; The Foundations of Naval History: Sir John Laughton, the Royal Navy and the Historical Profession, 1998; (with D. Griffiths and F. Walker) Brunel's Ships, 1999; War at Sea in the Age of the Sail: 1650-1850, 2000; Trincomalee: The Last of Nelson's Frigates, 2002; (ed.) Letters and Papers of Professor Sir John Knox Laughton, 1830-1915, 2002; Nelson: Britannia's God of War, 2005; (ed.) Naval History 1850-present, 2 vols., 2006; Admirals: The Men Who Made Britain Great, 2008; The Gates of Hell: Sir John Franklin's Tragic Search for the North Wert Passage, 2009; Franklin: Tragic Hero of Polar Navigation, 2009; (ed. with R. Blyth and J. Rüger) Dreadnought and the Edwardian Age, 2011. **Address:** Department of War Studies, King's College, Rm. K7.10, Strand, GL WC2R 2LS, England. **Online address:** andrew.lambert@kcl.ac.uk

LAMBERT, Frank T. American (born United States), b. 1943. **Genres:** Theology/Religion. **Career:** Pittsburgh Steelers, professional football player, 1965-66; IBM Corp., account manager, 1967-69; University Computing Co., national sales manager, 1969-71; Kentucky Country Day School, upper school head, 1971- 79; Humana, Inc., director of physician services, 1979-82; Rogers, Lambert & Co., partner, 1982-84; Belknap, Inc., president and chief executive officer, 1984-86; Northwestern University, visiting professor, 1990-91, 2001; Purdue University, assistant professor, 1991-95, associate professor, 1995-2000, professor, 2000-. Writer. **Publications:** Pedlar in Divinity: George Whitefield and the Transatlantic Revivals, 1737- 1770, 1994; Inventing the Great Awakening, 1999; The Founding Fathers and the Place of Religion in America, 2003; James Habersham: Loyalty, Politics, and Commerce in Colonial Georgia, 2005; The Barbary Wars: American Independence in the Atlantic World, 2005; Religion in American Politics: A Short History, 2008; The Battle of Ole Miss: Civil Rights v. States' Rights, 2009. Contributor to books. **Online address:** falamber@purdue.edu

LAMBERT, Josiah Bartlett. American (born United States), b. 1954. **Genres:** Politics/Government, Young Adult Non-fiction, International Relations/Current Affairs. **Career:** St. Bonaventure University, assistant professor, associate professor of political science. Writer. **Publications:** If the Workers Took a Notion: The Right to Strike and American Political Development (nonfiction), 2005. **Address:** St. Bonaventure University, 3261 W State Rd., St. Bonaventure, NY 14778-9800, U.S.A. **Online address:** jlambert@sbu.edu

LAMBERT, Katherine. British/American (born United States) **Genres:** Environmental Sciences/Ecology, Biography, History. **Career:** Good Gardens Guide, managing editor; World Expeditionary Association's Expedition magazine, editor. **Publications:** (With R. Verey) American Man's Garden, 1990; (ed. with R. Verey) Secret Gardens: Revealed by Their Owners, 1994; Hell With a Capital H, 2002 as The Longest Winter: The Incredible Survival of Captain Scott's Lost Party, 2004; (with P. King) Good Gardens Guide 2005, 2004. **Address:** c/o Author Mail, Smithsonian Institution Press, 22883 LEnfant Plz., Ste. 7100, Washington, DC 20560-0950, U.S.A.

LAMBERT, Page. American (born United States), b. 1952. **Genres:** Natural History, Women's Studies And Issues, Autobiography/Memoirs, Environmental Sciences/Ecology, Novels, Mythology/Folklore, Humanities, inspirational/Motivational Literature, Essays, Writing/Journalism, Literary Criticism And History. **Career:** Writer. **Publications:** In Search of Kinship: Modern Pioneering on the Western Landscape, 1996; Shifting Stars: A Novel of the West, 1997; Writing Down the River: Into the Heart of the Grand Canyon, 1998; Home Land, 2008; Pilgrimage, 2010. Contributor to magazines and newspapers. **Address:** 26037 Mountain View Rd., Golden, CO 80401, U.S.A. **Online address:** page@pagelambert.com

LAMBERTZEN, Gerret. See TERPENING, Ron.

LAMBRECHT, William. American (born United States), b. 1950?. **Genres:** Politics/Government, Environmental Sciences/Ecology, Novels. **Career:** St. Louis Post-Dispatch, Washington bureau chief; Bay Weekly Newspaper, co-founder. Writer. **Publications:** Dinner at the New Gene café: How Genetic Engineering is Changing What We Eat, How We Live and the Global Politics of Food, 2001; Big Muddy Blues: True Tales and Twisted Politics Along Lewis and Clark's Missouri River, 2005. Contributor to periodicals. **Address:** 236 Maryland Ave. NE, Washington, DC 20002, U.S.A. **Online address:** william.lambrecht@gmail.com

LAMBRICHS, Louise L. French (born France), b. 1952. **Genres:** Novels, Translations, Young Adult Fiction. **Career:** J. Vrin, assistant editor, 1973-75; University of Paris, professor, 1975-79; Belin, editor, 1980-85; Harpo/Pauvert, editor, 1985-86; freelance journalist, 1981-; Penser la Médecine, consulting editor, 1983-. **Publications:** Le cercle des sorcières, 1987; (with H. Warner) Le livre dont le héros se tient debout, 1987; (with C. Mérieux) Le virus de la découverte, 1988; La dyslexie en question, 1989; Journal d'Hannah, 1993; La vérité médicale: Claude Bernard, Louis Pasteur, Sigmund Freud, légendes et réalités de notre médecine, 1993; (with Jean-Pierre Relier) L'aimer avant qu'il naisse: le lien mère-enfant avant la naissance, 1993; (with B. Schwartz) Moderniser sans exclure, 1994; (with M. Szejer and R. Stewart) Ces neuf mois-là: une approche psychanalytique de la grossesse et de la naissance, 1994; Le livre de Pierre: psychisme et cancer, 1995; Le jeu du roman, 1995; A Ton Image, 1998; (with M. Drazen Grmek) Les révoltés de Villefranche: mutinerie d'un bataillon de Waffen-SS à Villefranche-de-Rouergue, septembre 1943, 1998; Hannah's Diary, 1998; (with M. Szejer) Le bébé face à labandon, 2000; (trans. and intro.) M.D. Grmek, La vie, les maladies et l'histoire, 2001; (intro.) M.D. Grmek, La guerre comme maladie sociale et autres textes politiques, 2001; Aloïs ou la nuit devant nous: Suivi de ce que je puis dire de la naissance d'un roman, et de celui-ci en particulier, 2002; Nous ne verrons jamais Vukovar, 2005; L'Invention sociale, 2006; L'effet Papillon, 2007; Puisqu'ils n'en diront rie, 2009. **Address:** c/o Author Mail, éditions Philippe Rey, 15, rue de la Banque, Paris, 75002, France.

LAMBSHEAD, John. British (born England), b. 1952?. **Genres:** Young Adult Fiction, Science Fiction/Fantasy, Novels. **Career:** Natural History Museum, Department of Zoology, researcher, 1978-2005, Deep Sea Group, head, 1987-90, Nematode & Poychaete Group, head, 1990-98, Nematode Research Group, head, 1998-, senior research scientist in marine biodiversity; Southampton University, School of Ocean and Earth Sciences, honorary visiting fellow, 1999-, National Oceanography Centre, visiting chair; University of California, regent's lecturer. Writer. **Publications:** (With L. Newsom) Fall of the West, 2000; The Hammer's Slammers Handbook: Vehicle Designs and Technical Specifications Plus an Easy Play Gaming System, 2004; Lucy's Blade, 2007; (with D. Drake) Into the Hinterlands, 2011. Contributor to periodicals. **Address:** Baen Books, PO Box 1403, Riverdale, NY 10471, U.S.A. **Online address:** docjohn@uk.medwaytowns.com

LAMBUR, Joan. Canadian (born Canada) **Genres:** Autobiography/Memoirs, Biography. **Career:** Lambur & Associates, president, 2002-07; Lenz Entertainment, president of on-screen entertainment, 2007-; The Itsy Bitsy Entertainment Co., president of on-screen entertainment. Writer. **Publications:** (With M. Lambur) Grabbing at Water: A Mother-Daughter Memoir, 2008. Contributor to periodicals. **Address:** Lenz Entertainment, 1 William Morgan Dr., Toronto, ON M4H 1N6, Canada.

LAMM, Leonard Jonathan. American (born United States), b. 1945. **Genres:** Psychology. **Career:** Clinical psychologist, Spunk Fund Inc., executive vice president and writer. **Publications:** The Idea of the Past: History, Science and Practice in American Psychoanalysis, 1993. **Address:** Spunk Fund Inc., 780 3rd Ave., 24th Fl., New York, NY 10017-2024, U.S.A.

LAMMERS, Wayne P. American (born United States), b. 1951. **Genres:** Language/Linguistics, Literary Criticism And History, Translations, Language/Linguistics. **Career:** Iwate University, foreign language instructor, 1982-83; University of Wisconsin-Madison, assistant professor of Japanese language and literature, 1984-90; Lewis and Clark College, assistant professor of Japanese, 1990-92; Mangajin magazine, translations editor, 1991-97; Japan Related magazine, advising editor, 1994-95; freelance translator, 1992-. **Publications:** TRANSLATOR: The Tale of Matsura: Fujiwara Teika's Experiment in Fiction, 1992; Junzo Shono, Still Life and Other Stories, 1992; Shohei Ooka, Taken Captive: A Japanese POW's Story, 1996; Junzo Shono, Evening Clouds, 2000; Taichi Yamada, Strangers, 2003; Shintaro Ishihara, Undercurrents: Episodes From A Life on the Edge, 2005; Mitsuyo Kakuta, Woman on the Other Shore, 2007; Aska Mochizuki, Spinning Tropics, 2009; Takashi Otoda, Yamihiko, 2010. OTHER: Japanese the Manga Way: An Illustrated Guide to Grammar and Structure, 2005. **Address:** PO Box 8208, Berkeley, CA 94707, U.S.A. **Online address:** wlammers@mac.com

LAMMING, George (Eric). American/British/Barbadian (born Barbados), b. 1927. **Genres:** Novels, Travel/Exploration, Social Sciences, History, Young Adult Fiction. **Career:** Teacher, 1946-50; University of the West Indies, writer-in-residence, 1967-68, Creative Arts Centre, lecturer, 1967-68; Department of Education, lecturer, 1967-68; University of Texas, visiting professor, 1977; University of Pennsylvania, visiting professor; City University of New York, visiting professor and writer-in-residence; Duke University, distinguished visiting professor; Brown University, Department of Africana Studies, visiting professor of Africana studies, Literary Arts Program, visiting professor, writer-in-residence of Africana studies and creative writing. **Publications:** In the Castle of My Skin, 1953; The Emigrants, 1954; Of Age and Innocence, 1958; Season of Adventure, 1960; The Pleasures of Exile, 1960; Water with Berries, 1972; Natives of My Person, 1972; (with H. Bangou and R. Depestre) Influencia del Africa en las Literaturas Antillanas; 1972; Cannon Shot and Glass Beads: Modern Black Writing, 1974; En el Castillo de mi Piel, 1979; George Lamming in Suriname, 1980; (with K. Drayton) The Most Important People, 1981; New World Quarterly, 1990; Conversations: Essays, Addresses and Interviews 1953-1990, 1992; Coming, Coming Home: Conversations II: Western Education and the Caribbean Intellectual: Coming, Coming, Coming Home, 1995; Sovereignty of the Imagination, 2004; Sovereignty of the Imagination: Conversations III, 2009. EDITOR: (with M. Carter) New World: Guyana Independence Issue, 1966; On the Canvas of the World, 1999; Enterprise of the Indies, 1999. Contributor to journals and periodicals. **Address:** Literary Arts Program, Brown University, Churchill House, 155 Angell St., PO Box 1923, Providence, RI 02912-9003, U.S.A. **Online address:** george_lamming@brown.edu

LAMMON, Martin. American (born United States), b. 1958. **Genres:** Poetry, Travel/Exploration, Autobiography/Memoirs. **Career:** Juniata College, visiting instructor in English, 1988-91; Fairmont State College, assistant professor, associate professor of English, 1991-97; Kestrel: A Journal of Literature and Art, co-founder and co-editor, 1992-97; Georgia College and State University, professor of English, Fuller E. Callaway endowed Flannery O'Connor chair in creative writing, 1997-, MFA program, graduate coordinator; Ohio University, faculty; Pennsylvania State University, faculty; Allied Arts, board director, 1998-; Arts and Letters Journal of Contemporary Culture, founding editor, 1998-; Association of Writers and Writing Programs, president, 2000-02. **Publications:** (Ed.) Written in Water, Written in Stone: Twenty Years of Poets on Poetry, 1996; News from Where I Live: Poems, 1998; Nine Degrees North: A Costa Rica Memoir, forthcoming. Contributor of articles to periodicals. **Address:** Department of English and Rhetoric, Georgia College and State University, PO Box 44, Milledgeville, GA 31061, U.S.A. **Online address:** mfa@gcsu.edu

LAMONT, Michèle. American/Canadian (born Canada), b. 1957. **Genres:** Sociology, Business/Trade/Industry, Education, Politics/Government. **Career:** Stanford University, postdoctoral research fellow in sociology, 1983-85; University of Texas, assistant professor of sociology, 1985-87; Princeton University, assistant professor, 1987-92, associate professor of sociology, 1993, professor, 2000-03; Canadian Institute for Advanced Research, director, 2002-; Harvard University, Department of Sociology, professor, 2003-, Center for European Studies, faculty, 2003-, Kennedy School of Government, director, 2004, professor of African and African American studies, 2005-, Robert I. Goldman professor of European studies, 2006-, faculty of arts and sciences, senior adviser on faculty development and diversity, 2009-10. Writer. **Publications:** (Ed. with M. Fournier) Cultivating Differences: Symbolic Boundaries and the Making of Inequality, 1992; Money, Morals, and Manners: The Culture of the French and the American Upper-Middle Class, 1992; (ed. and intro.) Cultural Territories of Race: Black and White Boundaries, 1999; (ed. with L. Thevenot) Rethinking Comparative Cultural Sociology: Repertoires of Evaluation in France and the United States, 2000; Dignity of Working Men: Morality and the Boundaries of Race, Class, and Immigration, 2000; How Professors Think: Inside the Curious World of Academic Judgment, 2009; (ed. with P.A. Hall) Successful Societies: How Institutions and Culture Affect Health, 2009; (ed. with C. Camic and N. Gross) Social Knowledge in the Making, 2011. **Address:** Department of Sociology, Harvard University, 510 William James Hall, 33 Kirkland St., Cambridge, MA 02138, U.S.A. **Online address:** mlamont@wjh.harvard.edu

LAMONT-BROWN, Raymond. Scottish/British (born England), b. 1939. **Genres:** History, Local History/Rural Topics, Mythology/Folklore, Paranormal, Travel/Exploration, Biography, Autobiography/Memoirs, Mystery/Crime/Suspense, Mystery/Crime/Suspense. **Career:** Yorkshire Electricity Board, staff in commercial and accounting departments, 1963-65; freelance writer, 1965-; Japan Research Projects, founder, 1965-; M.B. Publications Ltd., editor, 1967-69; University of St. Andrews, Continuing Education Department, lecturer, 1978-98; Writer's Monthly, managing editor, 1984-86;

University of Dundee, lecturer, 1988-98. Writer. **Publications:** The History of St. Mark's Church, Dewsbury 1865-1965, 1965; Book of Epitaphs, 1967; The Rural District of Doncaster Official Guide and Industrial Handbook, 1968; Clarinda: The Intimate Story of Robert Burns and Agnes Maclehose, 1968; Sir Walter Scott's Letters on Demonology and Witchcraft, 1968; Robert Burns's Commonplace Book 1783-85, 1969; A Book of Superstitions, 1970; A Book of Proverbs, 1970, 2nd ed., 1983; A Book of Witchcraft, 1971; Charles Kirkpatrick Sharpe's Historical Account of the Belief of Witchcraft in Scotland, 1972; Phantoms of the Sea, 1972; The Magic Oracles of Japan, 1972; Phantoms, Legends, Customs and Superstitions of the Sea, 1972; General Trade in Berwick on Tweed 1894, 1972; (ed.) Robert Burns's Tour of the Borders, 1972; (ed.) Robert Burns's Tours of the Highlands and Stirlingshire, 1973; A New Book of Epitaphs, 1974; Casebook of Military Mystery, 1974; Phantom Soldiers, 1975; Epitaph Hunting, 1976; (comp.) Scottish Epitaphs, 1977; Phantoms of the Theatre, 1978; Growing Up with the Highland Clans, 1979; Lothian and Border Walks for Motorists, 1980; East Anglian Epitaphs, 1980; My Fun Book of Scotland, 1980; Victorian and Edwardian Fife from Old Photographs, 1980; The Victorian and Edwardian Borderland from Rare Photographs, 1980; Victorian and Edwardian Dundee, 1981; Mary, Queen of Scots, 1982; Mysteries and Legends, 1982; Drives around Edinburgh, 1983; Drives around Glasgow, 1983; Mothers-in-Law, 1983; A Visitor's Guide to St. Andrews, 1984; St. Andrews: City of Change, 1984; A Book of British Eccentrics, 1984; Victorian and Edwardian Perthshire, 1984; Victorian and Edwardian Angus, 1985; Irish Grave Humour, 1987; Discovering Fife, 1988; The Life and Times of Berwick-upon-Tweed, 1988; The Life and Times of St. Andrews, 1989; Scottish Superstitions, 1990; Royal Murder Mysteries, 1990; Scottish Traditions and Festivals, 1991; Famous Scots, 1992; Scottish Witchcraft, 1994; Scottish Folklore, 1996; Kamikaze: Japan's Suicide Samurai, 1997; Scotland of 100 Years Ago, 1997; Kempeitai, 1998; Edward VII's Last Loves, 1998; Tutor to the Dragon Emperor: The Life of Sir Reginald Fleming, 1999; John Brown, 2000; Ships from Hell, 2002; Royal Poxes & Potions: The Lives of Court Physicians, Surgeons & Apothecaries, 2002; Fife in History and Legend, 2002; The Villages of Fife, 2002; Humphry Davy, 2004; Carnegie: The Richest Man in the World, 2005; St. Andrews: City by the Northern Sea, 2006; How Fat was Henry VIII?: And 101 Other Questions on Royal History, 2008; Royal Poxes & Potions: Royal Doctors and Their Secrets, 2009. **Address:** 11 Seabourne Gardens, Broughty Ferry, Dundee, DD5 2RT, Scotland.

LAMOTT, Anne. American (born United States), b. 1954. **Genres:** Food And Wine, Novels, Young Adult Non-fiction, Children's Non-fiction. **Career:** Women Sports, staff writer, 1974-75; writer, 1980-; California Magazine, food reviewer, 1988-91; Mademoiselle Magazine, book review columnist, 1990-92; University of California, faculty. **Publications:** NOVELS: Hard Laughter: A Novel, 1980; Rosie: A Novel, 1983; Joe Jones: A Novel, 1985; All New People: A Novel, 1989; Crooked Little Heart, 1997; Blue Shoe, 2002. NON-FICTION: Operating Instructions: A Journal of My Son's First Year, 1993; Home and Other Stories: Catherine Wagner, 1993; Bird by Bird: Some Instructions on Writing and Life, 1994; Traveling Mercies: Some Thoughts on Faith, 1999; Plan B: Further Thoughts on Faith, 2005; Grace (Eventually): Thoughts on Faith, 2007; Imperfect Birds, 2010; Some Assembly Required, 2012. Contributor to periodicals. **Address:** Steven Barclay Agency, 12 Western Ave., Petaluma, CA 94952-2907, U.S.A.

LAMPANELLI, Lisa. American (born United States), b. 1961. **Genres:** Autobiography/Memoirs. **Career:** Writer, comedian and actor. **Publications:** Chocolate, Please: My Adventures in Food, Fat, and Freaks (memoir), 2009. **Address:** c/o Nick Nuciforo, Creative Artists Agency, 2000 Ave. of the Stars, Los Angeles, CA 90067, U.S.A. **Online address:** lisa@insultcomic.com

LAMPERT, Ada. Israeli (born Israel), b. 1942. **Genres:** Psychology. **Career:** Ruppin Institute, professor of psychology, 1984-2010. Writer. **Publications:** Gof Vanefesh, 1993; Ha-Evolutsyah Shel ha-ahavah, 1994; The Evolution of Love, 1997; Nefesh Arumah: masa' mada'i-ishi el nefesh ha-adam, 2007. **Address:** Kibbutz Maabarot, 40230, Israel. **Online address:** alampert@ruppin.ac.il

LAMPHEAR, John. American (born United States), b. 1941. **Genres:** History, Humanities, Theology/Religion. **Career:** Ohio University, visiting assistant professor, 1972-73; De Pauw University, director of African studies, 1973-79; University of Illinois, visiting assistant professor, 1979-80; University of Texas, Department of History, professor, 1980-, now professor emeritus. Writer. **Publications:** The Traditional History of the Jie of Uganda, 1976;

The Scattering Time: Turkana Responses to Colonial Rule, 1992; Sub-Saharan African Warfare, 2003; (ed.) African Military History, 2007; (ed.) Pre-Colonial African Military History, 2007. **Address:** Department of History, College of Liberal Arts, University of Texas, 1 University Sta., PO Box B7000, Austin, TX 78712, U.S.A. **Online address:** lamphear@mail.utexas.edu

LAMPITT, Dinah. (Deryn Lake). British (born England), b. 1937. **Genres:** Novels, Romance/Historical, Mystery/Crime/Suspense, Literary Criticism And History, Young Adult Fiction. **Career:** Woman Magazine, junior writer; London Times, assistant news editor; London Evening News, assistant fiction editor. **Publications:** Sutton Place, 1983; The Silver Swan, 1984; Fortune's Soldier, 1985; To Sleep No More, 1987; Pour the Dark Wine, 1989; The King's Women, 1992; As Shadows Haunting, 1993; Banishment, 1994. HISTORICAL CRIME SERIES: Death in the Dark Walk, 1994; Death at the Beggar's Opera, 1995; Death at the Devil's Tavern, 1996; Death on the Romney Marsh, 1997; Death in the Peerless Pool, 1999. **Address:** c/o Darley Anderson, Estelle House, 11 Eustace Rd., London, GL SW6 1JB, England. **Online address:** deryn@derynlake.com

LAMPLUGH, Lois. British (born England), b. 1921. **Genres:** Children's Fiction, Poetry, History, Autobiography/Memoirs, Biography, Local History/Rural Topics, Photography, Mystery/Crime/Suspense, Mystery/Crime/Suspense. **Career:** Auxiliary Territorial Service, staff, 1939-43; Jonathan Cape Ltd., editorial staff, 1947-57. Educator. **Publications:** The Stream Way (autobiography), 1948; The Old Navigator 1967; The Quarry Hare (adult verse), 1976; Barnstaple: Town on the Taw (history), 1983; A History of Ilfracombe, 1984; Minehead with Dunster (history), 1987; Take off from Chivenor (history), 1990; A Shadowed Man: Henry Williamson 1895-1977 (biography), 1991; Lundy: Island without Equal (history), 1993; A Look at the Past of Swimbridge, 1993; Parson Jack Russell of Swimbridge, 1994; A Book of Georgeham and the Northwest Corner of Devon, 1995; Ilfracombe in Old Photographs, 1996; Two Rivers Meeting, 1998. FOR CHILDREN: The Pigeongram Puzzle, 1955; Nine Bright Shiners, 1955; Vagabonds' Castle, 1957; Rockets in the Dunes, 1958; The Sixpenny Runner, 1960; Midsummer Mountains, 1961; The Rifle House Friends, 1965; The Linhay on Hunter's Hill, 1966; The Fur Princess and the Fir Prince, 1969; Sean's Leap, 1979; The Winter Donkey, 1980; Falcon's Tor, 1984; Sandrabbit, 1991. **Address:** AP Watt Ltd., 20 John St., London, GL WC1N 2DR, England.

LAMPPA, William R. American (born United States), b. 1928. **Genres:** Poetry, History, Young Adult Fiction. **Career:** Saint Louis County, Department of Welfare, social worker, 1958-64; Hennepin County Community Services, Department of Welfare, social worker, 1964-87. Writer and educator. **Publications:** POEMS: The Crucial Point and Other Poems, 1971; In Familiar Fields with Old Friends, 1972; The Ancient Chariot and Other Poems, 1973. Works appear in anthologies. Contributor to journals, magazines and newspapers. **Address:** PO Box 81, Embarrass, MN 55732-0081, U.S.A.

LAMPTON, David M. American (born United States), b. 1946. **Genres:** Politics/Government, Money/Finance, Economics. **Career:** American Enterprise Institute, China Policy Program, director; Ohio State University, associate professor of political science; Nixon Center, director of Chinese studies; Johns Hopkins University, Paul H. Nitze School of Advanced International Studies (SAIS), George and Sadie Hyman professor of China studies, dean of faculty and director of China studies program. Writer. **Publications:** Health, Conflict, and the Chinese Political System, 1974; The Politics of Medicine in China: The Policy Process, 1949-1977, 1977; (with J.A. Madancy and K.M. Williams) A Relationship Restored: Trends in U.S.-China Educational Exchanges, 1978-1984, 1986; (with Y. Sai-cheung) Paths to Power: Elite Mobility in Contemporary China, 1986; (ed.) Policy Implementation in Post-Mao China, 1987; (ed. with C.H. Keyser) China's Global Presence: Economics, Politics, and Security, 1988; (ed. with K.G. Lieberthal) Bureaucracy, Politics, and Decision Making in Post-Mao China, 1992; United States and China Relations at a Crossroads, 1995; (ed.) The Making of Chinese Foreign and Security Policy in the Era of Reform, 1978-2000, 2001; Same Bed, Different Dreams: Managing U.S.-China Relations, 1989-2000, 2001; (ed.) Major Power Relations in Northeast Asia: Win-Win or Zero-Sum Game, 2001; The Three Faces of Chinese Power: Might, Money, and Minds, 2008. **Address:** Paul H. Nitze School of Advanced International, Studies, Johns Hopkins University, Nitze Bldg., 1740 Massachusetts Ave. NW, Washington, DC 20036, U.S.A. **Online address:** dmlampton@jhu.edu

LAMS, Victor. (Victor J. Lams). American (born United States), b. 1935.

Genres: Theology/Religion, Literary Criticism And History, Young Adult Fiction. **Career:** California State University, professor of English, 1965-96, emeritus professor, 1996-. Writer. **Publications:** Anger, Guilt, and the Psychology of the Self in Clarissa, 1999; Clarissa's Narrators, 2001; Newman's Anglican Georgic: Parochial Sermons, 2004; Newman's Visionary Georgic: A Reading of Parochial Sermons, 2006; Rhetoric of Newman's Apologia Pro Catholica, 1845-1864, 2007; Robertson Davies's Cornish Trilogy, 2008; Aspects of Robertson Davies's Novels, 2009. **Address:** Department of English, California State University, Taylor Hall 209, Chico, CA 95929-0830, U.S.A. **Online address:** vlams1@aol.com

LAMS, Victor J. See **LAMS, Victor.**

LAMSTER, Mark. American (born United States), b. 1969?. **Genres:** Art/Art History. **Career:** George Braziller Inc., staff, 1994-95; Princeton Architectural Press, editor, 1995-2008; YFSF.org, co-founder, 2003. **Publications:** Architecture and Film, 2000; Spalding's World Tour: The Epic Adventure That Took Baseball around the Globe'and Made It America's Game, 2006; Master of Shadows: The Secret Diplomatic Career of the Painter Peter Paul Rubens, 2009. Contributor to magazines and periodicals. **Address:** New York, NY , U.S.A. **Online address:** mdlamster@yahoo.com

LAN, David. British/South African (born South Africa), b. 1952. **Genres:** Plays/Screenplays, Anthropology/Ethnology, Translations, Adult Non-fiction. **Career:** Playwright, 1974-; University of Zimbabwe, research associate, 1980-82; Royal Court Theatre, writer-in-residence, 1995-97; Young Vic, artistic director, 2000-. **Publications:** Painting a Wall, 1974; Bird Child, 1974; Homage to Been Soup, 1975; Paradise, 1975; Red Earth, 1976; The Winter Dancers, 1977; Sergeant Ola, 1979; Guns and Rain: Spirit Mediums and Guerrillas in Zimbabwe (non-fiction), 1985; (with C. Churchill) A Mouthful of Birds, 1986; Flight, 1986; Desire and Other Plays, 1990; The Ends of the Earth, 1996; Collected Plays One, 1999; (contrib.) Tobias and the Angel, 2000. **Address:** Young Vic, 66 The Cut, Waterloo, GL SE1 8LZ, England.

LAN, Hai. See **YUAN, Gao.**

LANAGAN, Margo. Also writes as Belinda Hayes, Gilly Lockwood, Mandy McBride, Melanie Carter. Australian (born Australia), b. 1960?. **Genres:** Novellas/Short Stories, Young Adult Fiction, Novels. **Career:** Writer. **Publications:** (As Mandy McBride) Temper, Temper, 1990; Wild Game, 1991; (as Belinda Hayes) Star of the Show, 1991; (as Belinda Hayes) The Girl in the Mirror, 1991; (as Melanie Carter) The Cappuccino Kid, 1991; (as Gilly Lockwood) Nowhere Girl, 1992; (as Mandy McBride) New Girl, 1992; (as Mandy McBride) Cover Girl, 1992; The Tankermen, 1992; (as Gilly Lockwood) Misty Blues, 1993; (as Gilly Lockwood) On the Wildside, 1993; The Best Thing, 1995; Touching Earth Lightly, 1996; Walking through Albert, 1998; Black Juice, 2004; Treasure Hunters of Quentaris, 2004; White Time, 2006; Red Spikes, 2007; Tender Morsels, 2008; Yellowcake, 2011; Sea Hearts, 2012. **Address:** Allen & Unwin, 83 Alexander St., Crows Nest, NW 2065, Australia.

LANCASHIRE, Anne Begor. Canadian (born Canada), b. 1941. **Genres:** Art/Art History, Young Adult Fiction. **Career:** University of Toronto, lecturer, 1965-67, assistant professor, 1967-71, associate professor, 1971-76, professor of English, 1976-, undergraduate instructor, chair of English department, 1983-84, faculty of cinema studies and drama. Writer. **Publications:** (Ed.) Gallathea and Midas, 1969; (ed.) Editing Renaissance Dramatic Texts, English, Italian and Spanish: Papers Given at the Eleventh Annual Conference on Editorial Problems, 1976; (ed.) The Second Maiden's Tragedy, 1978; (ed.) Christopher Marlowe: Poet for the Stage, 1986; London Civic Theatre: City Drama and Pageantry from Roman Times to 1558, 2002. Contributor to periodicals. **Address:** University College, University of Toronto, Rm. 277, 15 King's College Cir., Toronto, ON M5S 1A1, Canada. **Online address:** anne@chass.utoronto.ca

LANCASTER, Carol J. American (born United States), b. 1942. **Genres:** Politics/Government, Social Sciences. **Career:** Kingston Polytechnic (now Kingston University), lecturer, 1968-72; Office of Management and Budget, Executive Office of the President, budget examiner, 1972-76; U.S. Congress, congressional fellow, 1976-77; U.S. Department of State, member of policy planning staff, 1977-80, Bureau of African Affairs, deputy assistant secretary, 1980-81; Georgetown University, research professor, 1981-89, director of African Studies, 1981-89, 2004-05, School of Foreign Service, assistant pro-

fessor, 1989-93, 1996-98, associate professor, 1999-2005, professor, 2005-, director of M.S. program in foreign service, 1998-2002, director of Mortara Center for International Studies, 2005-; U.S. Agency for International Development, deputy administrator, 1993-96. Writer. **Publications:** (contrib.) Careers in International Affairs, 1982; (ed. with J. Williamson) African Debt and Financing, 1986; U.S. Aid to Sub-Saharan Africa: Challenges, Constraints and Choices, 1988; African Economic Reform: The External Dimension, 1991; United States and Africa: Into the Twenty-first Century, 1993; Aid to Africa: So Much to Do, So Little Done, 1999; (with S. Wangwe) Managing a Smooth Transition from Aid Dependence in Africa, 2000; Transforming Foreign Aid: United States Assistance in the 21st Century, 2000; (co-author) Equity and Growth: The Role of Civil Society in Sustainable Development, 2003; (with A.V. Dusen) Organizing U.S. Foreign Aid: Confronting Challenges of the Twenty-first Century, 2005; Foreign Aid: Diplomacy, Development, Domestic Politics, 2007; George Bush's Foreign Aid: Transformation or Chaos?, 2008. Contributor of articles to periodicals. **Address:** School of Foreign Service, Georgetown University, Washington, DC 20057, U.S.A. **Online address:** lancastc@georgetown.edu

LANCASTER, Michael (L.). British (born England), b. 1928. **Genres:** Architecture, Homes/Gardens, Art/Art History, Design, Photography. **Career:** British Rail, assistant architect, 1948-57; architect, 1957-58; Fry, Drew, Drake and Lasdun, resident architect, 1958-61, architect, 1961-63; Derek Lovejoy and Partners, Colombo plan adviser, 1963-65; Gloucestershire College of Art and Design, senior lecturer, principal lecturer in landscape architecture, 1967-70; Thames Polytechnic, principal lecturer in landscape architecture and head of the division, 1970-91; Michael Lancaster Associates, principal, 1970-81, 1983-; Flora and Lancaster, partner, 1981-83; Thames Landscape Group, principal, 1985-. Writer. **Publications:** Britain in View: Colour and the Landscape, 1984; (ed. with G. Jellicoe, S. Jellicoe and P. Goode) The Oxford Companion to Gardens, 1986; (contrib.) Reflections on Landscape: The Lives and Work of Six British Landscape Architects, 1987; The Colour Eye No. 5, 1990; The Earth Dwellers Guide No. 3, 1991; The New European Landscape, 1994; Colourscape, 1996; Coloured Places, forthcoming. Contributor to books and periodicals. **Address:** 297 Lonsdale Rd., London, GL SW13 9QB, England.

LANCASTER, Roger N(elson). American (born United States), b. 1959. **Genres:** Anthropology/Ethnology, Sex, Cultural/Ethnic Topics, History, Politics/Government, Economics, Sciences. **Career:** University of California, Department of Anthropology, teaching assistant, 1983-87; Evergreen State College, Program in Central American Studies, visiting faculty, 1987-88; George Mason University, Department of Sociology and Anthropology, assistant professor, 1988-93, Department of Anthropology, associate professor, 1993-95, Department of Anthropology and Cultural Studies, associate professor, 1995-, professor, 2003-, Cultural Studies Program, director, 1999-; Anthropological Quarterly, book review editor, 1992-93; Columbia University, associate professor of anthropology, 1993-95; Society for Latin American Anthropology, editorial board, 1998-2002; American Anthropological Association, fellow. **Publications:** Thanks to God and the Revolution: Popular Religion and Class Consciousness in the New Nicaragua, 1988; Life is Hard: Machismo, Danger and the Intimacy of Power in Nicaragua, 1992; (ed. with M. Di Leonardo) The Gender/Sexuality Reader: Culture, History, Political Economy, 1997; The Trouble with Nature: Sex in Science and Popular Culture, 2003; Sex Panic and the Punitive State, 2011. Contributor to periodicals and collections. **Address:** Program in Cultural Studies, George Mason University, MSN 5E4, 4400 University Dr., Fairfax, VA 22030-4444, U.S.A. **Online address:** rlancast@gmu.edu

LANCASTER BROWN, Peter. British (born England), b. 1927. **Genres:** Novels, Archaeology/Antiquities, Astronomy, Geography, Travel/Exploration, Social Sciences, Sciences, Natural History, Natural History. **Career:** Writer. **Publications:** Twelve Came Back, 1957; Call of the Outback, 1970; What Star is That?, 1971; Astronomy in Colour, 1972, 5th ed. 1983; Coast of Coral and Pearl, 1972; (with C.F. Hickling) The Seas and Oceans in Colour, 1973; Comets, Meteorites and Men, 1973; Star and Planet Spotting, 1974, 1981; Australia's Coast of Coral and Pearl, 1974; (ed. and co-author) The Lore of Sport Fishing, 1974; Megaliths, Myths and Men, 1976; The Planet Earth in Colour, 1976; Megaliths and Masterminds, 1979; Travellers in the Outback, 1980; Fjord of Silent Men, 1982; Close Encounter Objects, 1983; The High Tatra Affair, 1983; Astronomy (Colour Library of Science), 1984; Halley and His Comet, 1985; Halley's Comet and the Principia, 1986; Caught Deep, 1986; The Comet Man: Memoirs of Edmond Halley, 1987; The Man I Might Have Been: A Creative Autobiography of Jack London, 1988; Sky-watch, 1993; Akywatch: Eyes-on Activities for Getting to Know the Stars, Planets, and Galaxies, 1993. **Address:** 10A St. Peter, Aldeburgh, SU IP15 5, England.

LANCE, James Waldo. Australian (born Australia), b. 1926. **Genres:** Medicine/Health. **Career:** Royal Prince Alfred Hospital, resident medical officer, 1950-51; University of Sydney, NHMRC research fellow, 1952-53, St. Paul's College, tutor in physiology and medicine, 1952-53, 1956-90, visiting lecturer in physiology, 1956-62; Hammersmith Hospital, house physician, 1954; National Hospital, assistant house physician, 1955; Northcott Neurological Centre, superintendent, 1956-57; Sydney Hospital, honorary assistant physician, 1956-61; St. Luke's Hospital, honorary assistant physician, 1957-61; Massachusetts General Hospital, Lilly Foreign Education Fellow, 1960-61; University of New South Wales, senior lecturer in medicine, 1961-63, associate professor of medicine, 1964-74, professor of neurology, 1975-92, professor emeritus, 1992-; Prince Henry Hospital, Department of neurology, chair, 1961-92; The Prince of Wales Hospital, Institute of Neurological Sciences, director, 1990-91, consultant neurologist; Order of Australia, officer, 1991. Writer. **Publications:** The Mechanism and Management of Headache, 1969, 7th ed., 2005; A Physiological Approach to Clinical Neurology, 1970, 3rd ed., 1981; Headache: Understanding, Alleviation, 1975; The Golden Trout, 1977; (with J.G. McLeod) Introductory Neurology, 1983, (co-author) 3rd ed., 1995; Migraine and Other Headaches, 1986. **Address:** University of New South Wales, Gate 9, High St., Kensington, Sydney, NW 2052, Australia.

LANCE, Peter. American (born United States) **Genres:** Mystery/Crime/Suspense. **Career:** Daily News, reporter; WNET, producer and reporter; Manhattan District Attorney's Office, trial preparation assistant; American Broadcast Co. (ABC), field producer, 1978-81, chief investigative correspondent, 1981-87; CBS TV, co-executive producer, 1989; National Broadcasting Co., writer and consulting producer; WABC-TV, writer and producer. **Publications:** First Degree Burn, 1997; Stingray: The Lethal Tactics of the Sole Survivor, 2000; 1000 Years for Revenge: International Terrorism and the FBI, 2004; Cover Up: What the Government Is Still Hiding about the War on Terror, 2004; Triple Cross: How Bin Laden's Master Spy Penetrated the CIA, the Green Berets and the FBI-and Why Patrick Fitzgerald Failed to Stop Him, 2006; SIX SIX SIX, 2011. **Address:** Berkley Publishing Group, 200 Madison Ave., New York, NY 10016, U.S.A. **Online address:** pl@cinema21group.com

LANCELOTTA, Victoria. American (born United States), b. 1969. **Genres:** Novels, Novellas/Short Stories. **Career:** Mississippi Review, associate fiction editor; Georgetown Review, editor. **Publications:** Here in the World (stories), 2000; Far (novel), 2003. Contributor to periodicals and journals. **Address:** Georgetown Review, 400 E College St., PO Box 227, Georgetown, KY 40324, U.S.A.

LANCILLOTTO, Mamurio. *See* **COTRONEO, Roberto.**

LANCTOT, Neil J. American (born United States), b. 1966. **Genres:** History. **Career:** University of Pennsylvania, faculty; University of Delaware, faculty. Historian and writer. **Publications:** Fair Dealing and Clean Playing: The Hilldale Club and the Development of Black Professional Baseball, 1910-1932, 1994; Negro League Baseball: The Rise and Ruin of a Black Institution, 2004. Contributor to periodicals and journals. Works appear in anthologies. **Address:** Philadelphia, PA , U.S.A. **Online address:** nlanctot@juno.com

LAND, Brad. American (born United States), b. 1976?. **Genres:** Novels, Young Adult Fiction, Literary Criticism And History. **Career:** Third Coast, editor. **Publications:** Goat: A Memoir, 2004; Pilgrims upon the Earth: A Novel, 2007. **Address:** Random House, 1745 Broadway, New York, NY 10019, U.S.A. **Online address:** bradland@goatthebook.com

LANDAU, Paul Stuart. American (born United States), b. 1962. **Genres:** History, Social Sciences. **Career:** University of New Hampshire, assistant professor of African history, 1992-95; Yale University, assistant professor of African history, 1995-98, associate professor, 1998-99; University of Maryland, associate professor of history, 1999-. Writer. **Publications:** The Realm of the Word: Language, Gender, and Christianity in a Southern African Kingdom, 1995; (ed. with D.D. Kaspin) Images and Empires: Visuality in Colonial and Postcolonial Africa, 2002; Popular Politics in the History of South Africa, 1400-1948, 2010. **Address:** Department of History, University of Maryland, 2115 Francis Scott Key, College Park, MD 20742, U.S.A. **Online address:** pl84@umail.umd.edu

LANDAU, Susan. American (born United States), b. 1954. **Genres:** Information Science/Computers. **Career:** Wesleyan University, assistant professor, 1983-89; University of Massachusetts, research associate, professor of computer science, 1989-99; Sun Microsystems, senior staff engineer, 1999-2005, distinguished engineer, 2005-10; Harvard University, Radcliffe Institute For Advanced Study, Elizabeth S. and Richard M. Cashin fellow, 2010-. Writer. **Publications:** (With W. Diffie) Privacy on the Line: The Politics of Wiretapping and Encryption, 1998; Surveillance or Security?: The Risks Posed by New Wiretapping Technologies, 2011. **Address:** Radcliffe Institute for Advanced Study, Harvard University, 10 Garden St., Cambridge, MA 02138-3630, U.S.A. **Online address:** susan.landau@privacyink.org

LANDER, Ernest McPherson. American (born United States), b. 1915. **Genres:** History, Autobiography/Memoirs. **Career:** Teacher and coach, 1937-40; Reinhardt College, professor of social sciences and coach, 1940-41; Clemson University, instructor, alumni professor of history, 1941-81, alumni professor emeritus of history, 1981-; Western Carolina University, visiting professor, 1954, 1957; University of South Carolina, visiting professor, 1958; University of Idaho, visiting professor, 1963; Jadavpur University, Fulbright lecturer, 1966-67; University of Lagos, Fulbright lecturer, 1970-71; University of North Carolina, visiting professor, 1974. Writer. **Publications:** A History of South Carolina, 1865-1960, 1960, 2nd. ed., 1970; (ed. with C.M. McGee) A Rebel Came Home: The (Civil War) Diary of Florida Clemson, 1961; (intro.) Sectionalism and Representation in South Carolina, 1968; The Textile Industry in Antebellum South Carolina, 1969; South Carolina: The Palmetto State, 1970; (ed. with R.K. Ackerman) Perspectives in South Carolina History: The First 300 Years, 1973; (ed. with R.J. Calhoun) Two Decades of Change: The South since the Supreme Court's Desegregation Decision, 1975; Reluctant Imperialists: Calhoun, the South Carolinians, and the Mexican War, 1980; The Calhoun Family and Thomas Green Clemson: The Decline of a Southern Patriarchy, 1983; South Carolina: An Illustrated History of the Palmetto State, 1988; Tales of Calhoun Falls, 1991; From Clemson College to India in World War II, by a GI Who Never Saw the Enemy, 1992; The Life and Times of Ella Lorton, A Pendleton SC Confederate, 1996; Few Would Listen: A Clemson Professor's Memoir of Dissent, 1997. Contributor to books and journals. **Address:** Department of History, Clemson University, 126 Hardin Hall, 801 University Union, Clemson, SC 29634, U.S.A.

LANDER, Jack Robert. (J. R. Lander). Canadian/British (born England), b. 1921. **Genres:** History, Politics/Government. **Career:** University of Ghana, senior lecturer in history, 1950-63; Dalhousie University, associate professor, 1963-65; University of Western Ontario, professor of history, 1965-69, J.B. Smallman professor, 1969-, now professor emeritus; Ghana Monuments and Relics Commission, assistant secretary and treasurer, 1952-60; Ghana Museums, director, 1956-63. Writer. **Publications:** AS J.R. LANDER: The Wars of the Roses, 1965; Conflict and Stability in Fifteenth-century England, 1969, 3rd ed., 1977; Ancient and Medieval England: Beginnings to 1509, 1973; Crown and Nobility, 1450-1509, 1976; Government and Community: England, 1450-1509, 1980; The Limitations of English Monarchy in the Later Middle Ages, 1989; English Justices of the Peace, 1461-1509, 1989; (ed. with P. Fleming and A. Gross) Regionalism and Revision: The Crown and Its Provinces in England, 1200-1650, 1998. Contributor to journals. **Address:** Department of History, University of Western Ontario, Rm. 4328, Social Science Ctr., London, ON N6A 5C2, Canada.

LANDER, J. R. *See* **LANDER, Jack Robert.**

LANDERS, John. British (born England), b. 1952?. **Genres:** History, Biology, Social Sciences. **Career:** Shell UK Ltd., oil demand analyst, 1979-80; University College London, lecturer in biological anthropology, 1980-90; University of Oxford, lecturer in historical demography, 1991-2005, assessor, 1994-95, All Souls College, fellow, through 2005, Quondam fellow, Hertford College, principal, 2005-11, senior research fellow. Writer. **Publications:** (Ed. with V. Reynolds) Fertility and Resources: 31st Symposium Volume of the Society for the Study of Human Biology, 1990; Death and the Metropolis: Studies in the Demographic History of London 1670-1830, 1993; (ed.) Historical Epidemiology and the Health Transition, 1993; The Field and the Forge: Population, Production, and Power in the Pre-Industrial West, 2003. **Address:** Hertford College, University of Oxford, Catte St., Oxford, OX OX1 3BW, England. **Online address:** john.landers@hertford.ox.ac.uk

LANDERS, Scott. American (born United States), b. 1952?. **Genres:** Novels, Young Adult Fiction, Literary Criticism And History. **Career:** Writer.

Publications: Coswell's Guide to Tambralinga: A Novel, 2004. Contributor to periodicals. **Address:** c/o Author Mail, Farrar, Straus & Giroux, 19 Union Sq. W, New York, NY 10001, U.S.A.

LANDES, Richard. American (born United States), b. 1949. **Genres:** History. **Career:** Columbia University, Mellon postdoctoral fellow, 1984-86; University of Pittsburgh, assistant professor of history, 1986-90; Boston University, assistant professor of history, 1990-97, associate professor of history, 1997-, Center for Millennial Studies, director, 1996-, co-founder. Writer. **Publications:** (With C. Paupert) Naissance d'Apotre: Les origines de la Vita prolixior de Saint Martial de Limoges au XIe siecle, 1991; Relics, Apocalypse, and the Deceits of History: Ademar of Chabannes, 989-1034, 1995; While God Tarried: Modernity as Frankenstein's Millennium, 2007; Heaven on Earth: The Varieties of the Millennial Experience, 2011. EDITOR: (with T. Head) The Peace of God: Social Violence and Religious Response in France Around the Year 1000, 1992; (with P. Bourgain and G. Pon) Ademari Cabannensis Chronicon, 1999; Encyclopedia of Millennialism And Millennial Movements, 2000; (with A. Gow and D.C. Van Meter) The Apocalyptic Year 1000, 2003; (with S.T. Katz) The Paranoid Apocalypse: A Hundred-Year Retrospective on The Protocols of the Elders of Zion, 2011. **Address:** Department of History, Boston University, Rm. 507, 226 Bay State Rd., Boston, MA 02215, U.S.A. **Online address:** rlandes@bu.edu

LANDESMAN, Peter. American (born United States), b. 1965. **Genres:** Novels, Mystery/Crime/Suspense, Young Adult Fiction. **Career:** New York Times Magazine, investigative staff journalist. Painter. **Publications:** NOVELS: The Raven, 1995; Two-For-One Christmas Fun (Full House Stephanie), 1995; Ten Ways to Wreck a Date (Full House Stephanie), 1996; Meereswunden, 1997; Blood Acre, 1999; (with A. Landesman) Spacemazes, 2002. Contributor to periodicals. **Address:** c/o Sloan Harris, International Creative Management, 730 5th Ave., New York, NY 10019, U.S.A.

LANDIS, Catherine. American (born United States), b. 1956?. **Genres:** Novels. **Career:** Writer and educator. **Publications:** NOVELS: Some Days There's Pie, 2002; Harvest, 2004. Contributor to periodicals. **Address:** c/o Author Mail, St. Martins Press, 175 5th Ave., New York, NY 10010-7703, U.S.A.

LANDIS, Dylan. American (born United States), b. 1956. **Genres:** Novellas/Short Stories. **Career:** Times-Picayune, reporter covering; Chicago Tribune, reporter. **Publications:** Checklist for Your New Baby, 1991, rev. ed., 1997; Designing for Small Homes, 1996; Elegant and Easy Rooms: 250 Trade Secrets for Decorating Your Home, 1997; Metropolitan Home American Style, 1999; Elegant and Easy Bedrooms: 100 Trade Secrets for Designing with Style, 2000; Elegant and Easy Living Rooms: 100 Trade Secrets for Designing with Style, 2000; Elegant and Easy Foyers, Halls, and Stairs: 100 Trade Secrets for Designing with Style, 2000; Normal People Don't Live like This (short stories), 2009. Contributor to periodicals. **Address:** Washington, DC, U.S.A. **Online address:** dylan@dylanlandis.com

LANDIS, Geoffrey A(lan). American (born United States), b. 1955. **Genres:** Science Fiction/Fantasy, Air/Space Topics, Sciences. **Career:** Spire Corp., staff scientist, 1977-82; Solar Energy Research Institute, research associate, 1986-87; National Aeronautics and Space Administration (NASA), Lewis Research Center, research associate, 1988-90, John Glenn Research Center, physicist, 1999-; aerospace engineer, Institute for Advanced Concepts, fellow; Ohio Aerospace Institute, adjunct professor, 1990-92, senior research associate, 1995-2000, senior scientist, 2000-; Sverdup Technology, physicist, 1994-95; NYMA Inc., senior engineer, 1994-95. Writer. **Publications:** Myths, Legends, and True History, 1991; (ed.) Vision-21, Space Travel For The Next Millennium: Proceedings of A Symposium Held At The NASA Lewis Research Center, Cleveland, Ohio, April 3-4, 1990, 1991; Mars Crossing (novel), 2000; Impact Parameter and Other Quantum Realities, 2001. Works appear in anthologies. Contributor of articles to journals. **Address:** John Glenn Research Center, National Aeronautics and Space Administration, 21000 Brookpark Rd., Cleveland, OH 44135, U.S.A. **Online address:** geoffrey.landis@sff.net

LANDIS, Jill Marie. American (born United States), b. 1948. **Genres:** Romance/Historical, Novels. **Career:** Writer and educator. **Publications:** Sunflower, 1988; Wildflower, 1989; Rose, 1990; Jade, 1991; Come Spring, 1992; Past Promises, 1993; (co-author) Sweet Hearts, 1993; Until Tomorrow, 1994;

After All, 1995; Last Chance, 1995; Day Dreamer, 1996; Just Once, 1997; Glass Beach, 1998; Blue Moon, 1999; The Orchid Hunter, 2000; Summer Moon, 2001; (with S. Cameron) Tell Me Why, 2001; Magnolia Creek, 2002; Lover's Lane, 2003; Heat Wave, 2004; Heartbreak Hotel: A Novel, 2005; Homecoming, 2008; (with J. Leigh and J. Braun) Destination: Marriage, 2008; Accidental Lawman, 2009; Heart of Stone: A Novel, 2010; Heart of Lies, 2011; Mai Tai One on, 2011; Heart of Glass, 2012. **Address:** Penguin Putnam Publishing, 375 Hudson St., New York, NY 10014, U.S.A.

LANDMAN, Jessica C. American (born United States), b. 1955. **Genres:** Environmental Sciences/Ecology, Natural History, Zoology. **Career:** U.S. House of Representatives, legislative aide, 1977-80; U.S. Department of Transportation, honors attorney, 1984-86; Natural Resources Defense Council, attorney, 1986-99, senior counsel, 2001-; Pew Oceans Commission, director of publications, 2000-01; Pew Institute for Ocean Science, Pew Fellows Program in Marine Conservation, fellow, 2001-; WWF European Policy Office, researcher, advisor, senior marine policy advisor; Clean Water Network, co-chair. Writer. **Publications:** (Contrib.) Poison Runoff: A Guide to State and Local Control of Nonpoint Source Water Pollution, 1989; (with R.W. Adler and D.M. Cameron) The Clean Water Act 20 Years Later, 1993; Prescription for Clean Water, 1997. Contributor to books. **Address:** Pew Fellows Program in Marine Conservation, Pew Institute for Ocean Science, 4600 Rickenbacker Causeway, Collier Bldg., Miami, FL 33149, U.S.A. **Online address:** jlandman@nrdc.org

LANDON, Lucinda. American (born United States), b. 1950. **Genres:** Children's Fiction, Illustrations. **Career:** Boston Center for the Arts, advertising assistant, 1974-75; teacher, 1975-76; Visualizations, artist, 1978-; writer and illustrator, 1978-. **Publications:** American History Mysteries, 1999. MEG MACKINTOSH SERIES: SELF ILLUSTRATED: Meg Mackintosh and the Case of the Missing Babe Ruth Baseball, 1986; Meg Mackintosh and the Case of the Curious Whale Watch, 1987; Meg Mackintosh and the Mystery at the Medieval Castle, 1989; Meg Mackintosh and the Mystery at Camp Creepy, 1990; Meg Mackintosh and the Mystery in the Locked Library, 1993; Meg Mackintosh and the Mystery at the Soccer Match: A Solve-It-Yourself Mystery, 1997; Meg Mackintosh and the Mystery on Main Street: A Solve-It-Yourself Mystery, 2000; Meg Mackintosh and the Stage Fright Secret: A Solve-It-Yourself Mystery, 2004; Meg Mackintosh Solves Seven American History Mysteries: A Solve-It-Yourself Mystery, 2008. **Address:** Independent Publishers Group, 814 N Franklin St., Chicago, IL 60610-3813, U.S.A.

LANDRUM, Gene N. American (born United States), b. 1935. **Genres:** Novels, Intellectual History, Psychology, Self Help, Writing/Journalism, Social Sciences, inspirational/Motivational Literature. **Career:** Condyne Technology, president, 1993-; Chuck E. Cheese, founder; Hodges University, Kenneth Oscar Johnson School of Business, administration Program, faculty, 1995-, now professor emeritus. Writer and entrepreneur. **Publications:** Profiles of Genius: Thirteen Creative Men Who Changed the World, 1993; Profiles of Female Genius: Thirteen Creative Women Who Changed the World, 1994; Profiles of Power and Success: Fourteen Geniuses Who Broke the Rules, 1996; Profiles of Black Success: Thirteen Creative Geniuses Who Changed the World, 1997; Prometheus 2000, 1997; Eight Keys to Greatness: How to Unlock Your Hidden Potential, 1999; Literary Genius, 2000; Sybaritic Genius, 2001; Entrepreneurial Genius, 2004; The Superman Syndrome, 2005; Empowerment, 2006; Paranoia and Power: Fear and Fame of Entertainment Icons!, 2007; The Innovative Mind, 2008; Cover Your Assets and Become Your Own Liability, 2009; Sex at Pelican Place, 2011; Warriors Who Win, 2011. **Address:** Hodges University, 2655 Northbrooke Dr., Naples, FL 34119, U.S.A. **Online address:** info@genelandrum.com

LANDRY, Donna. British/American (born United States), b. 1954?. **Genres:** Literary Criticism And History, Cultural/Ethnic Topics, Politics/Government. **Career:** Princeton University, assistant professor, 1982-83; University of Michigan, assistant professor, 1983-85; University of Southern California, assistant professor, 1985; University of Kent, professor. Writer. **Publications:** The Muses of Resistance: Laboring-class Women's Poetry in Britain, 1739-1796, 1990; Materialist Feminisms, 1993; (ed.) The Spivak Reader: Selected Works of Gayatri Chakravorty Spivak, 1996; (ed. with G. MacLean and J.P. Ward) The Country and the City Revisited: England and the Politics of Culture, 1550-1850, 1999; The Invention of the Countryside: Hunting, Walking, and Ecology in English Literature, 1671-1831, 2001; Noble Brutes: How Eastern Horses Transformed English Culture, 2008. Contributor to books and periodicals. **Address:** England. **Online address:** d.e.landry@kent.ac.uk

LANDSBERG, Brian K. American (born United States), b. 1937. **Genres:** Law. **Career:** U.S. Department of Justice, Civil Rights Division, trial attorney and supervisory attorney, 1964-69, chief of education section, 1969-74, Appellate Section, chief, 1974-86, acting deputy assistant attorney general, 1993-94; Georgetown University, adjunct professor, 1981-84; University of the Pacific, visiting professor, 1984-85, McGeorge School of Law, professor of law, 1986-, associate dean for academic affairs, 2001-02, distinguished professor, 2008-; University of California, visiting professor, 1995, 1997; United States Agency for International Development, program director, 2006-; International Law Institute, visiting professor, 2006; Zhejiang Gongshang University Law School, visiting professor, 2009. Writer. **Publications:** Enforcing Civil Rights: Race Discrimination and the Civil Rights Division, 1997; (ed.) Major Acts of Congress, 2004; Free At Last to Vote: The Alabama Origins of the 1965 Voting Rights Act, 2007; (with L.G. Jacobs) Global Issues in Constitutional Law, 2007; (with S. Estreicher) Global Issues in Employment Discrimination Law, 2008. Contributor of articles to periodicals. **Address:** McGeorge School of Law, University of the Pacific, 3200 5th Ave., Sacramento, CA 95817, U.S.A. **Online address:** blandsberg@pacific.edu

LANDSBERG, Melvin. American (born United States), b. 1926. **Genres:** Literary Criticism And History, Biography, Essays, Young Adult Fiction, Autobiography/Memoirs. **Career:** University of Kansas, faculty, 1961-, professor of English, professor emeritus. Writer. **Publications:** Dos Passos' Path to U.S.A.: A Political Biography, 1912-1936, 1972; (ed.) John Dos Passos' Correspondence with Arthur K. McComb, or, Learn to Sing the Carmagnole, 1991. **Address:** Department of English, University of Kansas, Rm. 3001, 1445 Jayhawk Blvd., Lawrence, KS 66045, U.S.A. **Online address:** melvinl@ku.edu

LANDSBURG, Steven E(lliot). American (born United States), b. 1954. **Genres:** Economics, Social Commentary. **Career:** University of Iowa, assistant professor, 1981-85; Cornell University, visiting assistant professor, 1983; University of Rochester, visiting assistant professor, 1986-88; Queens University, research associate, 1986; Institute for Definitive Analysis, research associate, 1987; Colorado State University, associate professor, 1989-95; University of Rochester, visiting associate professor, 1991-, professor of economics; Slate magazine, columnist; Hutchinson Technology, board director. Writer. **Publications:** Alegebraic Fiber Bundles, 1979; Price Theory and Applications, 1989, 7th ed., 2008; The Armchair Economist: Economics and Everyday Life, 1993; (with L.J. Feinstone) Macroeconomics, 1997; Fair Play: What Your Child Can Teach You About Economics, Values, and the Meaning of Life, 1997; More Sex is Safer Sex: The Unconventional Wisdom of Economics, 2007; The Big Questions: Tackling the Problems of Philosophy with Ideas from Mathematics, Economics, and Physics, 2009; Armchair Economist: Economics for Everyday Life, 2012; A Mathematical Introduction to General Relativity and Cosmology, forthcoming. Contributor to journals. **Address:** Department of Economics, University of Rochester, Harkness Hall 225, Rochester, NY 14627, U.S.A. **Online address:** steven@landsburg.com

LANDY, Joshua. American (born United States), b. 1965?. **Genres:** Philosophy, Language/Linguistics, Philosophy. **Career:** Princeton University, lecturer, 1995-96; Stanford University, Undergraduate Studies in French, director, 1998-99, 2000-02, 2003-05, Division of Literatures, Cultures and Languages, Philosophy and Literature Project, co-chair, 2002-05, Philosophical Reading Group, co-director, 2002-07, Philosophy and Literature Initiative, co-director and co-founder, 2004-, Aesthetics Project, co-chair, 2005-, Graduate Studies in French, director, 2005-06, Department of French and Italian, associate professor, 2005-, Department of English, associate professor, 2007-. **Publications:** (Ed. with C. Bremond and T. Pavel) Thematics: New Approaches, 1995; Philosophy As Fiction: Self, Deception, and Knowledge in Proust, 2004. (ed. with M. Saler) The Re-Enchantment of the World: Secular Magic in a Rational Age, 2009; How To Do Things With Fictions, forthcoming. Contributor to books and journals. **Address:** Division of Literatures, Cultures, and Languages, Stanford University, 104 Pigott Hall, Bldg. 260, 450 Serra Mall, Stanford, CA 94305-2005, U.S.A. **Online address:** landy@stanford.edu

LANDY, Marcia. American (born United States), b. 1931. **Genres:** Film, Literary Criticism And History, History, Popular Culture. **Career:** University of Pittsburgh, assistant professor, professor of English and film studies, 1967-, distinguished professor of English and film studies. Writer. **Publications:** Fascism in Film: The Italian Commercial Cinema, 1931-1943, 1986; British Genres: Cinema and Society, 1930-1960, 1991; (ed.) Imitations of Life: A

Reader on Film & Television Melodrama, 1991; Film, Politics, and Gramsci, 1994; Queen Christina, 1995; Cinematic Uses of the Past, 1996; The Folklore of Consensus: Theatricality in the Italian Cinema, 1930-1943, 1998; Italian Film, 2000; The Historical Film: History and Memory in Cinema, 2001; (ed. with L. Fischer) Stars: The Film Reader, 2004; Monty Python's Flying Circus, 2005; Stardom, Italian Style: Screen Performance and Personality in Italian Cinema, 2008. Works appear in anthologies. **Address:** Department of English, University of Pittsburgh, CL 443, Pittsburgh, PA 15260, U.S.A. **Online address:** mlandy@pitt.edu

LANE, Abbe. (Abigail Francine Lassman). American (born United States), b. 1932. **Genres:** Romance/Historical, Novels, Biography. **Career:** Writer. **Publications:** But Where Is Love?, 1993. **Address:** 444 N Faring Rd., Los Angeles, CA 90077, U.S.A.

LANE, Alcyee. See **LANE, Dakota.**

LANE, Connie. See **LAUX, Constance.**

LANE, Dakota. (Alcyee Lane). American (born United States), b. 1959. **Genres:** Young Adult Fiction, Novels, Mystery/Crime/Suspense. **Career:** Freelance writer, 1996-. **Publications:** Johnny Voodoo (juvenile novel), 1996; The Orpheus Obsession (juvenile novel), 2005; The Secret Life of It Girls, 2007; Gothic Lolita, 2008. Contributor to periodicals. **Address:** PO Box 591, Woodstock, NY 12498, U.S.A. **Online address:** dakotastories@yahoo.com

LANE, Dixie. See **SALAZAR, Dixie.**

LANE, George. American (born United States), b. 1952. **Genres:** History, Social Sciences. **Career:** University of London, School of Oriental and African Studies, Department of History, senior teaching fellow, research associate, International Foundation Courses and English Language Studies, English language teacher. Writer. **Publications:** Early Mongol Rule in Thirteenth-Century Iran: A Persian Renaissance, 2003; Genghis Khan and Mongol Rule, 2004; Daily Life in the Mongol Empire, 2006; Silk Roads and Steppe Empires, forthcoming. Contributor of article to periodicals. **Address:** School of Oriental and African Studies, University of London, 303 Thornhaugh St., Russell Sq., London, GL WC1H 0XG, England. **Online address:** gl1@soas.ac.uk

LANE, Harlan. (Harlan (Lawson) Lane). American (born United States), b. 1936. **Genres:** Intellectual History, Psychology, Language/Linguistics, Translations, Education. **Career:** University of Michigan, assistant professor, 1960-64, associate professor, 1964-67, professor of psychology, 1967-71, Center for Research on Language and Language Behavior, founder and director, 1965-69; University of Paris, professor of linguistics, 1969-73, visiting professor, 1989; University of California, visiting professor of linguistics, 1973-74; Northeastern University, Department of Psychology, professor, 1974-88, chairman, 1974-79, university distinguished professor, 1988-, Center for Research in Hearing, Speech and Language, founder, 1986, Matthews distinguished university professor; Massachusetts Eye and Ear Infirmary, research associate, 1985-93; Centre National de la Recherche Scientifique, research associate, 1985-86; Massachusetts Institute of Technology, Research Laboratory of Electronics, research affiliate, 1986-; Harvard Medical School, lecturer, 1988-93. Writer. **Publications:** Psychophysical Parameters of Vowel Preception, 1963; (with D. Bem) A Laboratory Manual for the Control and Analysis of Behavior, 1964; (with G. Capelle) The World's Research in Language Learning, 1969; Introduction a l'aetude du langage, 1972; The Wild Boy of Aveyron: A History of the Education of Retarded, Deaf and Hearing Children, 1976; (with R. Pillard) The Wild Boy of Burundi: Psychological Catastrophies of Childhood, 1978; (with R. Pillard) The Wild Boy of Burundi: A Study of an Outcast Child, 1978; (trans. with F. Philip) Major Philosophical Works of Etienne Bonnot de Condillac, 1982; When the Mind Hears: A History of the Deaf, 1984; The Mask of Benevolence: Disabling the Deaf Community, 1992, new ed., 1999; (with R. Hoffmeister and B. Bahan) A Journey into the Deaf-World, 1996; (with C. Wayser) Make Every Minute Count: More than 700 Tips and Strategies that Will Revolutionize How You Manage Your Time, 2000; Deaf Artist in Early America: The Worlds of John Brewster, Jr., 2004; (with R. Pillard and U. Hedberg) People of the Eye: Deaf Ethnicity and Ancestry, 2011. EDITOR: (with F. Grosjean) Recent Perspectives on American Sign Language, 1980; The Deaf Experience: Classics in Language and Education, 1984; (with C. Carroll) Diary of a Deaf Boy: The Youth of Laurent Clerc, 1991; (with R. Fischer) Looking Back: A Reader on the History of Deaf Communities and Their Sign Languages, 1993; Education and Access for Deaf People in France and the United States, 1994, (with K. Emmoery) The Signs of Language Revisited, 2000. **Address:** Department of Psychology, Northeastern University, 125 Nightingale Hall, 360 Huntington Ave., Boston, MA 02115-5000, U.S.A. **Online address:** lane@neu.edu

LANE, Harlan (Lawson). *See* **LANE, Harlan.**

LANE, John. American (born United States), b. 1954. **Genres:** Art/Art History, Essays, Adult Non-fiction, Poetry, Plays/Screenplays. **Career:** Wofford College, associate professor of English and environment studies and writing, 1988-, Goodall Environmental Studies Center, director; Hub City Writers Project, project director; Holocene Publications, editor; Resurgence, art editor. Writer. **Publications:** Quarries, 1984; As the World around Us Sleeps, 1992; Weed Time: Essays from the Edge of a Country Yard, 1993; Against Information and Other Poems, 1995; The Pheasant Cage (one-act play), 1995; The Dead Father Poems, 2000; Waist Deep in Black Water (essays), 2002; Chattooga: Descending into the Myth of Deliverance River (personal narrative), 2004; Circling Home, 2007; Best of the Kudzu Telegraph, 2008; The Old Rob Poems, 2009; Abandoned Quarry: New and Selected Poems, 2011; My Paddle to the Sea: Eleven Days on the River of the Carolinas, 2011. EDITOR AND CONTRIBUTOR: Usumacinta Journey-a Collaborative Journal from Mexico, 1992; (with B.W. Teter) Hub City Anthology: Spartanburg Writers & Artists (essays), 1996; (with B.W. Teter) Hub City Christmas: 32 Spartanburg Writers Trim the Literary Tree (essays), 1998; (with G. Thurmond) The Woods Stretched for Miles: New Nature Writing from the South (essays), 1999; (with J. Jones) The Once-Again Wilderness: Following Wendell Berry into Kentucky's Red River Gorge, 2000. **Address:** Wofford College, 326-A Main Bldg., 429 N Church St., Spartanburg, SC 29303-3663, U.S.A. **Online address:** laneje@wofford.edu

LANE, Nancy. American (born United States), b. 1947. **Genres:** Literary Criticism And History, How-to Books, Librarianship. **Career:** Indiana University, associate instructor in French, 1969-76; University of South Carolina, assistant professor, 1977-88, coordinator of French division, 1984-88, associate professor of French, 1988-, graduate director, 1995-, now CPLT professor emeritus, now distinguished professor emeritus; Haverford College, visiting assistant professor, 1985. Writer. **Publications:** Understanding Eugène Ionesco, 1994. Contributor of articles to journals. **Address:** Department of Languages, Literatures, and Cultures, University of South Carolina, 817 Humanities Office Bldg., 1620 College St., Columbia, SC 29208, U.S.A. **Online address:** lane@mailbox.sc.edu

LANE, Nick. British (born England), b. 1967. **Genres:** History. **Career:** MRC Clinical Research Centre, scientific officer, 1988-91; Oxford Clinical Communications, medical writer, 1995-96; MediCine Intl., senior writer/producer, 1996-99; University College London, honorary research fellow, 1997-2006, UCL Medical School, honorary reader, 2006-, Department of Genetics, provost's venture research fellow; Adelphi Medi Cine, strategic director, 1999-2002; science writer, freelance communications consultant, musician and researcher. **Publications:** Oxygen: The Molecule That Made the World, 2002; (ed. with E. Benson and B.J. Fuller) Life in the Frozen State, 2004; Power, Sex, Suicide: Mitochondria and the Meaning of Life, 2006; Life Ascending: The Ten Great Inventions of Evolution, 2009. Contributor to periodicals. **Address:** Caroline Dawnay, Peters Fraser and Dunlop Drury House, 34-43 Russell St., London, GL WC2B 5HA, England. **Online address:** nick.lane@ucl.ac.uk

LANE, Simon. British (born England), b. 1957. **Genres:** Novels, Novellas/Short Stories, Art/Art History, Essays. **Career:** Writer. **Publications:** May, In New York, and The Clipper Seamen's Bride (trilogy), 1985; The Hostage Returns, 1989; Le Veilleur, 1990; Still Life With Books: A Novel, 1993; Fear: A Novel, 1998; Boca a Boca, 2002; The Real Illusion, 2009; Twist, 2010. **Address:** Bridge Works Publishing Co., PO Box 1798, Bridgehampton, NY 11932, U.S.A. **Online address:** oliversimonlane@gmail.com

LANE, Terry. Australian (born Australia), b. 1939. **Genres:** Novels, Adult Non-fiction, Theatre, Biography, Humor/Satire. **Career:** Australia Broadcasting Corp., Religious Department, broadcaster, 1977, 1982-93, 1995-2005; Methodist Department of Christian Education, teacher; The Sunday Age, columnist, 2003-. Writer. **Publications:** Famous Leaders Through the Ages (juvenile), 1966; As the Twig is Bent, 1979; GOD: The Interview, 1993; Hectic (novel), 1993; Tit for Tat, 1994; Sparrow's Fall (novel), 1995; From Great White Nation to Arse End of the World in a Single Lifetime, 1997; The Full Round: The Several Lives and Theatrical Legacy of Stephen Joseph, 2006; Side by Side: The Traverse Theatre-Before and After, 2007. **Address:** Pan Macmillan Australia, 25/1 Market St., Sydney, NW 2000, Australia. **Online address:** lanet@alexia.net.au

LANG, Anthony E. Canadian (born Canada), b. 1951?. **Genres:** Medicine/Health. **Career:** University Health Network, Toronto Western Research Institute, senior scientist, 1985-; Toronto Western Hospital, Morton and Gloria Shulman Movement Disorder Clinic, director, 1993-; University of Toronto, Jack Clark chair for Parkinson's disease research and professor of medicine and neurology, 2000-, Department of Neurology, division director. Writer. **Publications:** WITH W.J. WEINER: Movement Disorders: A Comprehensive Survey, 1989; (with L. Shulman) Parkinson's Disease: A Complete Guide for Patients and Families, 2001, 2nd ed., 2007. EDITOR WITH W.J. WEINER: Drug-Induced Movement Disorders, 1992, 2nd ed., 2005; Behavioral Neurology of Movement Disorders, 1995, 2nd ed., 2005. OTHERS: (ed. with I. Litvan and C.G. Goetz) Corticobasal Degeneration and Related Disorders, 2000; (ed. with M.F. Beal and A.C. Ludolph) Neurodegenerative Diseases: Neurobiology, Pathogenesis and Therapeutics, 2005; (ed. with A.H.V. Schapira and S. Fahn) Movement Disorders 4, 2010. Contributor to books and periodicals. **Address:** Toronto Western Research Institute, University Health Network, Rm. 7-403, 7th Fl., 399 Bathhurst St., McLaughlin Pavilion, Toronto, ON M5T 2S8, Canada. **Online address:** lang@uhnres.utoronto.ca

LANG, Gladys Engel. American (born United States), b. 1919?. **Genres:** Communications/Media, Sociology, Politics/Government, Psychology. **Career:** Office of War Information, staff, 1942; State University of New York, professor of sociology, 1970-84; University of Washington, teaching assistant, professor of communications, political science and sociology, 1984-90, emeritus, 1990-, chair, 2006-07. Writer. **Publications:** (Ed.) Mental Health, 1958; Canada, 1959; (with K. Lang) Collective Dynamics, 1961; (ed.) Old Age in America, 1961; (with K. Lang) Politics and Television, 1968; (with K. Lang) Voting and Nonvoting: Implications of Broadcasting Returns Before Polls are Closed, 1968; (with K. Lang) The Battle for Public Opinion: The President, The Press and the Polls During Watergate, 1983; (with K. Lang) Politics and Television Re-Viewed, 1984; (with K. Lang) Etched in Memory: The Building and Survival of Artistic Reputation, 1990; (with K. Lang) Television and Politics, 2002. **Address:** University of Washington, 1249 20th Ave. E, Seattle, WA 98112-3530, U.S.A. **Online address:** gladyslang@comcast.net

LANG, Jenifer Harvey. American (born United States), b. 1951. **Genres:** Children's Non-fiction, Food And Wine, Reference. **Career:** 21 Club Restaurant, cook, 1976-78; Nathans, chef, 1978-; Cafe des Artistes, managing director, 1992-2009; Columbia Broadcasting System, journalist; Network News, journalist; Family Circle magazine, journalist. **Publications:** Tastings: The Best from Ketchup to Caviar, 1986; (ed.) Larousse Gastronomique, 1988, 3rd ed., 2001; Jenifer Lang Cooks for Kids: 153 Recipes and Ideas for Good Food that Kids Love to Eat, 1991; Best of Kitchen Basics, 1996. **Address:** Cafe des Artistes, 1 W 67th St., New York, NY 10023, U.S.A.

LANG, Judith. British/Egyptian (born Egypt), b. 1939. **Genres:** Theology/Religion, History, Biography. **Career:** Writer. **Publications:** Ministers of Grace, 1989; (ed. with L. de Bruin) M. Casey, A Net in Water, 1994; The Angels of God: Understanding the Bible, 1997; They Looked at God, 2006. **Address:** Redwood, Colebatch, Bishop's Castle, Shropshire, SY9 5JY, England.

LANG, Kurt. American (born United States), b. 1924. **Genres:** Art/Art History, Communications/Media, Sociology, Politics/Government. **Career:** CBC, research sociologist, 1954-56; City University of New York, Queens College, instructor, 1956-59, assistant professor, 1959-62, associate professor of sociology and chairman, 1963-64; State University of New York, professor of sociology, 1964-84; University of Washington, professor of sociology and communication, 1984-93, professor emeritus, 1993-. Writer. **Publications:** (With G.E. Lang) Collective Dynamics, 1961; (with G.E. Lang) Voting and Nonvoting: Implications of Broadcasting Returns before Polls are Closed, 1968; (with G.E. Lang) Politics and Television, 1968; Military Institutions and Sociology of War, 1972; (with G.E. Lang) The Battle for Public Opinion: The President, the Press, and the Polls during Watergate, 1983; (with G.E. Lang) Politics and Television Re-Viewed, 1984; (with G.E. Lang) Etched in Memory: The Building and Survival of Artistic Reputation, 1990, rev. ed., 2001. **Address:** Department of Sociology, University of Washington, PO Box 353340, Seattle, WA 98195-3340, U.S.A. **Online address:** lang@uw.edu

LANG, Lang. American/Chinese (born China), b. 1982. **Genres:** Autobiography/Memoirs, Biography. **Career:** Writer and pianist. **Publications:** (With M. French) Lang Lang: Playing with Flying Keys, 2008; (with D. Ritz) Journey of a Thousand Miles: My Story, 2008. **Address:** New York, NY , U.S.A. **Online address:** langlang@aligneg.com

LANG, Paul. American (born United States), b. 1948. **Genres:** Adult Nonfiction, Biography, Language/Linguistics, Art/Art History. **Career:** Model High School, instructor, 1977-78; freelance writer, 1991-. **Publications:** (With S.S. Lang) Censorship, 1993; (with S.S. Lang) Teen Fathers, 1995; The English Language Debate: One Nation, One Language?, 1995; Maria Tallchief: Native American Ballerina, 1997. **Address:** 1844 Commonwealth Ave., Ste. 8, Brighton, MA 02135-5524, U.S.A.

LANG, Susan S. American (born United States), b. 1950. **Genres:** Medicine/ Health, Psychology, How-to Books, Adult Non-fiction, Self Help. **Career:** Post-Star, reporter and photographer, 1975-77; Cornell University, research assistant to Carl Sagan, 1977-79, Ezra Magazine, senior editor; Cornell News Service, staff writer, senior science writer, 1980-86, 1991-2008; Cornell Chronicle Publications, managing editor, 2008-. **Publications:** Women without Children: Reasons, Rewards, Regrets, 1991; Extremist Groups in America, 1990; Teen Violence, 1991; Going Buggy!, 1991; Invisible Bugs and Other Creepy Creatures that Live With You, 1991; (with P. Lang) Censorship, 1993; (with R. Patt) You Don't Have to Suffer: A Complete Guide to Relieving Cancer Pain for Patients and Their Families, 1994; Nature in Your Backyard, 1994; (with P. Lang) Teen Fathers, 1995; (with L. Robbins) Headache Help: A Complete Guide to Understanding Headaches and the Medicines that Relieve Them, 1995; Teens and Tobacco, 1996; More Nature in Your Backyard, 1999; (with R. Patt) The Complete Guide to Relieving Cancer Pain and Suffering, 2004; (with M.E. Thase) Beating the Blues, 2004. **Address:** Cornell University, 312 College Ave., Ithaca, NY 14850, U.S.A. **Online address:** ssl4@cornell.edu

LANG, William L. American (born United States), b. 1942. **Genres:** Local History/Rural Topics, History, Essays. **Career:** Carroll College, associate professor, 1970-78; Montana Historical Society, executive editor, 1978-89; Center for Columbia River History, director, 1990-94; Portland State University, professor of history, 1994-. Writer. **Publications:** (With R.C. Myers) Montana Our Land and People, 1979, 2nd ed., 1989; (with M.P. Malone and R.B. Roeder) Montana: A History of Two Centuries, rev. ed., 1991; (ed.) Centennial West: Essays on the Northern Tier States, 1991; (ed.) Stories from an Open Country: Essays on the Yellowstone River Valley, 1995; Confederacy of Ambition: William Winlock Miller and the Making of Washington Territory, 1996; (ed. with R.C. Carriker) Great River of the West: Essays on the Columbia River, 1999; John McLoughlin, 2000; (intro.) Smoke Wars: Anaconda Copper, Montana Air Pollution, and the Courts, 1890-1924, 2000; (with C. Abbott) Two Centuries of Lewis and Clark: Reflections on the Voyage of Discovery, 2004; (intro.) Puget's Sound: A Narrative of Early Tacoma and the Southern Sound, 2003; (foreword) Cayuse Indians: Imperial Tribesmen of Old Oregon, 2005; (foreword) The Battle for Butte: Mining and Politics on the Northern Frontier, 1864-1906, 2006. **Address:** Department of History, Portland State University, CH 441-P, PO Box 751, Portland, OR 97207-0751, U.S.A. **Online address:** langw@pdx.edu

LANGA, Mandla. South African (born South Africa), b. 1950?. **Genres:** Novels, Novellas/Short Stories, Poetry, Young Adult Fiction, Children's Fiction, Literary Criticism And History. **Career:** African National Congress, cultural attache, 1995-; Independent Communications Authority of SA, chairperson, 1999-2005; Leadership Magazine, editor-at-large; Sunday Independent, columnist; South African Broadcasting Corp., program director for television; Contemporary African Music and Arts, director. **Publications:** NOVELS: Tenderness of Blood, 1987; A Rainbow on the Paper Sky, 1989; The Memory of Stones, 2000. SHORT STORIES: The Naked Song and Other Stories, 1996; (intro.) Moving in Time: Images of Life in a Democratic South Africa, 2004. OTHER: Lost Colours of the Chameleon, 2008. Works appear in anthologies. **Address:** David Philip Publishers, 208 Werdmuller Ctr., Newry St., PO Box 23408, Cape Town, 7700, South Africa. **Online address:** mlanga@icon.co.za

LANGAN, John P. American (born United States), b. 1969. **Genres:** Horror, Novels, Science Fiction/Fantasy. **Career:** Erebos Publications, editor; Dead Reckonings, staff reviewer; State University of New York, Department of English, adjunct professor. **Publications:** Mr. Gaunt and Other Uneasy Encounters, 2008; House of Windows (horror novel), 2009. Works appear in anthologies. Contributor to periodicals. **Address:** Department of English, State University of New York, 600 Hawk Dr., 820 JFT, New Paltz, NY 12561, U.S.A. **Online address:** langanj@newpaltz.edu

LANGAN, Mike. American (born United States), b. 1968?. **Genres:** Novels. **Career:** Piper Rudnick (law firm), criminal defense attorney, 1998-2001; Bond, Schoeneck & King PLLC (law firm), civil litigation attorney, 2001-04; federal law clerk, 2004-; George Mason University, instructor in composition and American literature; Syracuse University, Whitman School of Management, instructor in consumer law & premises liability. Writer. **Publications:** Dark Horse, 2008; Ready for the Defense, 2008. Contributor of fiction to magazines. **Address:** Fayetteville, NY, U.S.A. **Online address:** mike@mikelangan.com

LANGBAUM, Robert (Woodrow). American (born United States), b. 1924. **Genres:** Literary Criticism And History. **Career:** Cornell University, instructor in English, 1950-55, assistant professor, 1955-60; University of Virginia, associate professor, 1960-63, professor, 1963-67, James Branch Cabell professor of English and American literature, 1967-99, James Branch Cabell professor emeritus, 1999-, professor emeritus of English; Center for Advanced Study, Ford Foundation fellow, 1961-62; Columbia University, visiting professor, 1965-66. Writer. **Publications:** The Poetry of Experience: The Dramatic Monologue in Modern Literary Tradition, 1957; The Gayety of Vision: A Study of Isak Dinesen's Art, 1965; The Modern Spirit: Essays on the Continuity of Nineteenth and Twentieth Century Literature, 1970; The Mysteries of Identity: A Theme in Modern Literature, 1977; The Word from Below: Essays on Modern Literature and Culture, 1987; Thomas Hardy in Our Time, 1995. EDITOR: The Tempest, by Shakespeare, 1964; The Victorian Age: Essays in History and in Social and Literary Criticism, 1967. Contributor to periodicals. **Address:** Department of English, University of Virginia, 219 Bryan Hall, PO Box 400121, Charlottesville, VA 22904, U.S.A. **Online address:** rwl8v@virginia.edu

LANGBEIN, John Harriss. American (born United States), b. 1941. **Genres:** History, Law, Criminology/True Crime. **Career:** Max Planck Institute for European Legal History, Frankfurt, visiting fellow, 1969-70, 1977; University of Chicago Law School, assistant professor, 1971-73, associate professor, 1973-74, professor, 1974-80, Max Pam professor of American and foreign law, 1980-90; Max Planck Institute for Criminal Law, Freiburg, Alexander Von Humboldt-Stiftung fellow, 1973; University of Michigan Law School, visiting professor, 1976; All Soul's College, visiting fellow, 1977; Stanford Law School, visiting professor, 1985-86; American Law Institute, advisor, 1987-, associate reporter; Yale Law School, faculty, visiting professor, 1989-90; Yale University, Chancellor Kent professor of law and legal history, 1990-2001, Sterling professor of law and legal history, 2001-; Cambridge University, Arthur Goodhart professor in legal science, 1997-98; Trinity Hall, visiting fellow, 1997-98; New York University Law School, visiting professor, 2010. Writer. **Publications:** Prosecuting Crime in the Renaissance: England, Germany, France, 1974; Torture and the Law of Proof: Europe and England in the Ancient Regime, 1977; Comparative Criminal Procedure: Germany, 1977; (with L. Waggoner) Selected Statutes on Trusts and Estates, 1987, 2001; (with B. Walker) Pension and Employee Benefit Law, 1990, 5th ed., 2010; (with R.H. Helmholz et al.) The Privilege against Self-Incrimination, 1997; Pension and Employee Benefit Statutes and Regulations: Selected Sections, 2002; Origins of Adversary Criminal Trial, 2003; History of the Yale Law School: The Tercentennial Lectures, 2004; (with R.L. Lerner and B.P. Smith) History of the common Law: The Development of Anglo-American Legal Institutions, 2009. Contributor of articles to books and periodicals. **Address:** Yale Law School, Rm. 325, 127 Wall St., PO Box 208215, New Haven, CT 06511, U.S.A. **Online address:** john.langbein@yale.edu

LANGDON, E(sther) Jean Matteson. Brazilian/American (born United States), b. 1944. **Genres:** Anthropology/Ethnology, Theology/Religion, Social Sciences. **Career:** Indiana University, research associate, 1964-65; Universidad del Cauca, part-time professor, 1973; City University of New York, John Jay College of Criminal Justice, adjunct professor of anthropology, 1974-76; Cedar Crest College, associate professor, 1976-84; Universidade Federal de Santa Catarina, professor of social anthropology, 1983-, Pos-Graduacao de Ciencias Sociais, vice coordinator, 1986-88, 1996-98; Indiana University, research associate; Brazil's National Foundation of Health, consultant; CAPES, fellow, 1993-94. Writer. **Publications:** (Ed. with G. Baer and contrib.) Portals of Power: South American Shamanism, 1992; (co-ed. and contrib.) Muerte Y El Mas Alla En Las Culturas Indígenas Latinoamericanas: 47. Congreso Internacional de Americanistas (New Orleans 1991), 1992; Xamanismo No Brasil: Novas Perspectivas, 1994, rev. ed., 1996. Contributor to journals. **Address:** Pos-Graduacao em Antropologia, Universityersidade Federal de Santa Catarina, Florianopolis, Florianopolis, SC 888040-970, Brazil. **Online address:** jean@cfh.ufsc.br

LANGDON, Gabrielle. Irish (born Ireland) **Genres:** Women's Studies And Issues, Art/Art History, History. **Career:** Writer. **Publications:** Medici Women: Portraits of Power, Love and Betrayal from the Court of Duke Cosimo I, 2006. Contributor to books and journals. **Address:** Kilcandra Cottage, Kilmacurra, Redcross, WI 2, Ireland. **Online address:** gabriellelangdon@hotmail.com

LANGDON, Philip. (Philip Alan Langdon). American (born United States), b. 1947. **Genres:** Architecture, Regional/Urban Planning. **Career:** Franklin News-Herald, reporter, 1968; Meadville Tribune, campus reporter, 1968-69; Harrisburg News-Patriot, reporter, 1969-71; Buffalo Evening News, reporter, columnist and architecture critic, 1973-82; freelance writer on architecture and design, 1982-94, 1998-; Progressive Architecture Magazine, senior editor, 1994-96; Connecticut Conference of Municipalities, writer and editor, 1996-99; American Enterprise Magazine, associate editor, 1997-2000, contributing writer, 2000-; New Urban News, associate editor, 2002-03, senior editor, 2003-. **Publications:** Orange Roofs, Golden Arches: The Architecture of American Chain Restaurants, 1986; American Houses, 1987; (with R.G. Shibley and P. Welch) Urban Excellence, 1990; (with S. Thomas) This Old House Kitchens: A Guide to Design and Renovation, 1992; (with S. Thomas) This Old House Bathrooms: A Guide to Design and Renovation, 1993; A Better Place to Live: Reshaping the American Suburbs, 1994; Good Home: Interiors and Exteriors, 2001; (ed. with J. King) The CRS Team and the Business of Architecture, 2002; Designing the Good Home, 2003; Good House Hunting: 20 Steps to Your Dream Home, 2005. **Address:** New Urban News Publications, 202 E State St., PO Box 6515, Ithaca, NY 14850, U.S.A.

LANGDON, Philip Alan. *See* **LANGDON, Philip.**

LANGE, Arthur D. American (born United States), b. 1952?. **Genres:** Literary Criticism And History, Poetry, Essays, Music. **Career:** Brilliant Corners: A Magazine of the Arts, publisher and editor, 1975-77; Chicago Council on Fine Arts, artist-in-residence, 1977-78; Columbia College, instructor, 1979-, adjunct faculty; Chicago International Film Festival, judge, 1988-. **Publications:** Evidence, 1981; (ed. with N. Mackey and contrib.) Moment's Notice: Jazz in Poetry & Prose, 1993; (with A. Ellis) How to Keep People from Pushing Your Buttons, 1994. POETRY: The Monk Poems, 1977; Glee: Song, 1977; Needles at Midnight, 1986; Postmodern American Poetry, 1994. **Address:** Department of English, Columbia College of Chicago, 5th Fl., 33 E Congress, 600 S Michigan Ave., Chicago, IL 60605, U.S.A. **Online address:** alange@colum.edu

LANGE, James E(dward) T(homas). American (born United States) **Genres:** Criminology/True Crime, History, Law. **Career:** Montgomery County, chief judge of election, 1976-. Writer. **Publications:** (With K. DeWitt, Jr.) Chappaquiddick: The Real Story, 1993. Contributor to periodicals. **Address:** 10221 Menlo Ave., Silver Spring, MD 20910-1057, U.S.A. **Online address:** langejameset@aol.com

LANGENDOEN, Donald Terence. American (born United States), b. 1939. **Genres:** Language/Linguistics, Education, Humanities. **Career:** Hartford Theological Seminary, Kennedy School of Missions, lecturer in linguistics, 1963-64; Ohio State University, Department of Linguistics, assistant professor, 1964-68, associate professor of linguistics, 1968-69; Rockefeller University, visiting associate professor, 1968-69; City University of New York, Brooklyn College, Department of English, professor, 1969-87, Graduate Center, Programs in English and Linguistics, professor, 1969-88, executive officer of linguistics, 1971-78, Linguistics Program, associate director, 1977-82, director, 1982-87; University of Arizona, Department of Linguistics, professor of linguistics, 1988-2005, professor emeritus, 2005-, head, 1988-97; National Science Foundation, Division of Behavioral and Cognitive Sciences, linguistics program director, 2006-08, Division of Information and Intelligent Systems, expert, 2008-. Writer. **Publications:** London School of Linguistics: A Study of the Linguistic Theories of B. Malinowski and J.R. Firth, 1968; Study of Syntax: The Generative-Transformational Approach to the Structure

of American English, 1969; Essentials of English Grammar, 1970; (with P.M. Postal) The Vastness of Natural Languages, 1984. EDITOR: (with C.J. Fillmore) Studies in Linguistic Semantics, 1971; (with T.G. Bever and J.J. Katz) An Integrated Theory of Linguistic Ability, 1976; (with D.B. Archangeli) Optimality Theory: An Overview, 1997. Contributor to journals. **Address:** National Science Foundation, Rm. 1125 S, 4201 Wilson Blvd., Arlington, VA 22230, U.S.A. **Online address:** dlangend@nsf.gov

LANGER, Erick D. American (born United States), b. 1955. **Genres:** History, Theology/Religion. **Career:** Carnegie Mellon University, assistant professor of history, 1984-90, associate professor of history, 1990-98, adjunct associate professor of modern languages, 1994-98; University of Pittsburgh, adjunct associate professor of history, 1990-98; Georgetown University, associate professor of history and core faculty, 1999-2010, professor of history, 2010-, Center for Latin American Studies, acting director, 2009-11, director, 2011-; Universidad Nacional Tres De Febrero, visiting professor, 2007. Writer. **Publications:** (Co-ed.) Historia de Tarija: Corpus Documental, 1988; Economic Change and Rural Resistance in Southern Bolivia, 1880-1930, 1989; (ed. with R.H. Jackson) The New Latin American Mission History, 1995; (co-author) Experiencing World History, 2000; (ed. with E. Muñoz) Contemporary Indigenous Movements in Latin America, 2003; (ed.) Encyclopedia of Latin American History and Culture, 2008; Expecting Pears from an Elm Tree: Franciscan Missions on the Chiriguano Frontier in the Heart of South America, 2009. Contributor to periodicals. **Address:** Department of History, Georgetown University, 484 ICC, 600 Intercultural Ctr., 3700 O St., NW, PO Box 571035, Washington, DC 20057-1035, U.S.A. **Online address:** langere@georgetown.edu

LANGER, Maria. American (born United States), b. 1961. **Genres:** Information Science/Computers. **Career:** Flying M Air, owner and operator; Automatic Data Processing, auditor and financial analyst; Macintosh Tips & Tricks (newsletter), publisher. Writer. **Publications:** The Mac Shareware Emporium, 1992; Mac Power Toolkit, 1993; Murphys Laws of Macs, 1993; File Maker Pro 2.0 for the Mac in a Nutshell, 1993; Excel 5 for Macintosh: Visual Quick Start Guide, 1995; The Macintosh Bible Guide to Word 6: Visual Quick Start Guide, 1995; The Macintosh Bible Guide to Excel 5: Visual Quick Start Guide, 1996; Page Mill for Macintosh: Visual Quick Start Guide, 1996; Mac OS 8: Visual Quick Start Guide, 1997; Page Mill 2 for Windows, 1997; Page Mill 2 for Macintosh: Visual Quick Start Guide, 1997; America Online 3 for Macintosh: Visual Quick Start Guide, 1997; America Online 3 for Windows 95: Visual Quick Start Guide, 1997; Claris Home Page Companion, 1997; Word 98 for Macintosh: Visual Quick Start Guide, 1998; File Maker Pro 4 Companion, 1998; Mac OS 8.5: Visual Quick Start Guide, 1998; Quicken 99: The Official Guide, 1998; Excel 98 for Macintosh: Visual Quick Start Guide, 1998; Database Publishing with File Maker Pro on the Web, 1998; Excel 2000 for Windows: Visual Quick Start Guide, 1999; Word 2000 for Windows: Visual Quick Start Guide, 1999; Quicken 2000: The Official Guide, 1999; Mac OS 8.6: Visual Quick Start Guide, 1999; Page Mill 3 for Macintosh Windows: Visual Quick Start Guide, 1999; File Maker Pro 5 Companion, 2000; Putting Your Small Business on the Web, 2000; Quicken 2001: The Official Guide, 2000; Mac OS 9: Visual Quick Start Guide, 2000; Online Investing with Quicken 2000: The Official Guide, 2000; Quicken 2000 for the Mac: The Official Guide, 2000; Word 2001 for Macintosh: Visual Quick Start Guide, 2001; Word 2002 for Windows: Visual Quick Start Guide, 2001; Excel 2001 for Macintosh: Visual Quick Start Guide, 2001; Mac OS X: Visual Quick Start Guide, 2001; Quicken 2001 Deluxe for Macintosh: The Official Guide, 2001; Quicken 2002: The Official Guide, 2001; Quicken 2002 Deluxe for Macintosh: The Official Guide, 2001; Mac OS 9.1: Visual Quick Start Guide, 2001; Word X for Mac OS X: Visual Quick Start Guide, 2002; Quicken 2003: The Official Guide, 2002; Mac OS X 10.1: Visual Quick Start Guide, 2002; Excel X for Mac OS X: Visual Quick Start Guide, 2002; Excel 2002 for Windows: Visual Quick Start Guide, 2002; Mac OS X: Visual Quick Start Guide, 2002; Quicken 2004: The Official Guide, 2003; Microsoft Word 2001/X Advanced for Macintosh, 2003; Mac OS X 10.3 Panther: Visual Quick Start Guide, 2003; Mac OS X 10.2: Visual Quick Start Guide, 2003; Mac OS X 10.2 Advanced: Visual Quick Project Guide, 2003; Microsoft Office Excel 2003 for Windows: Visual Quick Start Guide, 2004; Quicken 2005: The Official Guide, 2004; Microsoft Office Word 2003 for Windows: Visual Quick Start Guide, 2004; Quick Books Pro 6 for Macintosh: Visual Quick Start Guide, 2004; Quicken 2006: The Official Guide, 2005; Mac OS X 10.4 Tiger: Visual Quick Start Guide, 2005; Microsoft Word 2004 for Mac OS X: Visual Quick Start Guide, 2005; Creating Spreadsheets and Charts in Excel: Visual Quick Project Guide, 2005; Creating Resumes Letters Business Cards and Flyers in Word: Visual Quick Project Guide, 2005; Quick Books Pro 2006 for Macintosh, 2006; Quicken 2007: The Official Guide, 2007; Microsoft Office Excel 2007 for Windows, 2007; Creating Spreadsheets and Charts in Microsoft Office Excel 2007 for Windows, 2007; Quicken 2008: The Official Guide, 2008; Mac OS X 10.5 Leopard, 2008; Quicken 2009: The Official Guide, 2009; Quicken 2010: the Official Guide, 2010; Mac OS X 10.6 Snow Leopard, 2010. Contributor to periodicals. **Address:** Flying M Air L.L.C., 32655 Homestead Dr., Wickenburg, AZ 85390, U.S.A. **Online address:** mlanger@theflyingm.com

LANGFIELD, Martin. American/British (born England), b. 1962?. **Genres:** Mystery/Crime/Suspense. **Career:** Reuters, east coast bureau chief, 1987-. Writer and educator. **Publications:** The Malice Box, 2007; The Secret Fire, 2009. Contributor to periodicals. **Address:** New York, NY , U.S.A.

LANGFIELD, Valerie. British (born England), b. 1951. **Genres:** Music. **Career:** British Broadcasting Corp., senior systems analyst; University of Manchester, Centre for Continuing Education, tutor. Writer and musician. **Publications:** Roger Quilter: His Life and Music, 2002. Contributor of articles to journals. **Address:** CH , England. **Online address:** rcq@minuet.demon.co.uk

LANGFORD, David. British (born England), b. 1953. **Genres:** Science Fiction/Fantasy, Literary Criticism And History, Sciences. **Career:** Atomic Research Establishment, weapons physicist, 1975-80; Ansible Newsletter, editor/publisher 1979-; freelance writer, 1980-; Ansible Information, managing director, 1987-; Interzone, New York Review of SF, SFX and Fortean Times, columnist. **Publications:** SCIENCE FICTION NOVELS: The Space Eater, 1982; The Leaky Establishment, 1984; (with J. Grant) Earthdoom!, 1987; (with J. Grant) Guts, 2001. STORY COLLECTIONS: The Dragonhiker's Guide to Battlefield Covenant at Dune's Edge: Odyssey Two, 1988; Irrational Numbers, 1994; (ed.) Maps: The Uncollected John Sladek (stories), 2002; He Do the Time Police in Different Voices (stories), 2003; Different Kinds of Darkness (stories), 2004. OTHER GENRES: (co-author) The Necronomicon, 1978; War in 2080: The Future of Military Technology, 1979; An Account of a Meeting with Denizens of Another World 1871, 1979; (with C. Morgan) Facts and Fallacies: A Book of Definitive Mistakes and Misguided Predictions, 1981; (with P. Nicholls and B.M. Stableford) The Science in Science Fiction, 1983; (with C. Platt) Micromania: The Whole Truth about Home Computers, 1984 in US as The Whole Truth Home Computer Handbook, 1984; (with B.M. Stableford) The Third Millennium: The History of the World AD 2000-3000, 1985; The Unseen University Challenge, 1996; (ed. with J. Clute and J. Grant) The Encyclopedia of Fantasy, 1997; (with J. Kirby) A Cosmic Cornucopia, 1999; The Wyrdest Link, 2002; The End of Harry Potter?, 2007. NON-FICTION COLLECTIONS: Critical Assembly, 1987; Critical Assembly II, 1992; Let's Hear It for the Deaf Man, 1992; The Silence of the Langford, 1996; Pieces of Langford, 1998; The Complete Critical Assembly, 2001; (ed.) Wrath of the Fanglord, 1998; Up through an Empty House of Stars, 2003; The SEX Column and Other Misprints, 2005; The Apricot Files, 2007; The Limbo Files, 2009; Starcombing, 2009. **Address:** Ansible Information Ltd., 94 London Rd., Reading, BR RG1 5AU, England. **Online address:** drl@ansible.co.uk

LANGFORD, Gary R(aymond). Australian/New Zealander (born New Zealand), b. 1947?. **Genres:** Novels, Plays/Screenplays, Poetry, Novellas/Short Stories. **Career:** Edge, co-editor, 1970-72; Super-box, editor, 1971; Shard, editor, 1972; teacher, 1974-76; Macarthur Institute of Higher Education, lecturer in theater, 1977-86; Ironbark, editor, 1977-83; Playhouse Theatre, director, 1982-86; University of Western Sydney, senior lecturer in creative writing, 1986-, founder and coordinator in creative writing. Writer. **Publications:** POETRY: The Family, 1972; Four Ships, 1981; The Pest Exterminator's Shakespeare, 1984; Bushido, 1987; Strange City, 1988; Love at the Traffic Lights, 1990; Jesus the Galilee Hitch-Hiker, 1991; Confessions of a Nude Revolutionary, 2000; Lunch at the Storyteller's Restaurant, 2002. NOVELS: Death of the Early Morning Hero, 1976; Players in the Bailgame, 1979; The Adventures of Dreaded Ned, 1980; The Last Giants, 1982; Vanities, 1984; Pillbox, 1986; A Classical Pianist in a Rock 'n Roll Band, 1989; Newlands, 1990; The Politics of Dancing, 1994; Friday Always Wanted to Be Tuesday, 1997. PLAYS: Lovers, 1977; Getting On, 1977; Reversals, 1978. EDITOR: Superbox, 1971; Shard, 1972. OTHER: The Writer's Dictionary (textbook), 1999. Contributor to magazines. **Address:** University of Western Sydney, PO Box 1797, Penrith South DC, NW 1797, Australia. **Online address:** g.langford@uws.edu.au

LANGLEY, Andrew. British (born England), b. 1949. **Genres:** Children's Non-fiction, Novels, History, Biography. **Career:** Penguin Books, marketing assistant, 1974-78. Children's book author. **Publications:** FOR CHILDREN: Explorers on the Nile, 1981; Working in the Army: A Guide for Young People, 1983; The Superpowers, 1983; The First Men Round the World, 1983; Ian Botham (biography), 1983; Cleopatra and the Egyptians, 1985; Doctor, 1985; Energy, 1985; Passport to Great Britain, 1985; John F. Kennedy (biography), 1985; Librarian, 1985; The Making of the Living Planet, 1985; Peoples of the World, 1985; The Army, 1986; Combat Pilot, 1986; A Family in the Fifties, 1986; The Search for Riches, 1986; The Royal Air Force, 1986; The Royal Navy, 1986; Sailor, 1986; Airports, 1987; Cars, 1987; Genghis Kahn and the Mongols, 1987; Travel Games for Kids, 1987; The World of Sharks, 1987; Twenty Names in Pop Music, 1987; Travel Quizzes for Kids, 1988; Twenty Explorers, 1988; Twenty Names in Crime, 1988; (with M. Butterfield) People, 1989; Sport, 1989; Sport and Politics, 1989; (co-author) World Issues, 2 vols., 1990; Trucks and Trailers, 1991; Young Sailor, 1993; Grasslands, 1993; The Illustrated Book of Questions and Answers, 1993; Wetlands, 1993; The Industrial Revolution, 1994; The Age of Industry, 1994; Medieval Life, 1996, rev. ed., 2004; (with P. de Souza) The Roman News, 1996; Victorian Factories, 1996; Victorian Railways, 1996; (with G. Wood) Life in a Victorian Steamship, 1997; Tudor Palaces, 1997; Food and Farming, 1997; Alexander the Great: The Greatest Ruler of the Ancient World, 1997; Amelia Earhart: The Pioneering Pilot, 1997; Oxford First Encyclopedia, 1998; Hans Christian Andersen: The Dreamer of Fairy Tales, 1998; Trade and Transport, 1998; Castle at War: The Story of a Siege, 1998; Renaissance, 1999; (with A. Brown) What I Believe: A Young Person's Guide to the Religions of the World, 1999; Leonardo, 1999, rev. ed., 2001; Shakespeare's Theater, 1999; Shakespeare and the Elizabethan Age, 2000; You Wouldn't Want to Be a Viking Explorer: Voyages You'd Rather Not Make, 2001; 100 Things You Should Know about the Wild West, 2001; (with F. Macdonald and J. Walker) 100 Things You Should Know about History, 2001; First Fun Atlas, 2001; Pirates, 2002; Barbara Hepworth, 2002; Mikhail Gorbachev, 2003; Pablo Picasso, 2003; 100 Things You Should Know about Pirates, 2003; Michelangelo, 2003; An International Rugby Union Star, 2004. BEHIND THE SCENES SERIES: Radio Station, 1983; Hotel, 1983; Car Ferry, 1983; Football Club, 1983; Supermarket, 1983; Police Station, 1983; Post Office, 1985; Newspapers, 1985. ORIGINS SERIES: A Cup of Tea, 1982; The Meat in Your Hamburger, 1982; The Paper in Your Home, 1982. TOPICS SERIES: Great Disasters, 1985; Under the Ground, 1985; Television, 1986; Jungles, 1986. FOCUS ON SERIES: Focus on Wool, 1985; Focus on Vegetables, 1985; Focus on Timber, 1986 in US as Spotlight on Timber, 1987. SPOTLIGHT ON SERIES: Spotlight on Airports, 1987; Spotlight on Aircraft, 1987 in US as Aircraft, 1989; Spotlight on Dinosaurs, 1987; Spotlight on Spacecraft, 1987; Spotlight on the Moon, 1987 in US as The Moon, 1988; Spotlight on Trees, 1987. LET'S LOOK AT SERIES: Let's Look at Bikes, 1988 in US as Bikes and Motorcycles, 1989; Let's Look at Trucks, 1988 in US as Trucks, 1989; Let's Look at Circuses, 1989; Let's Look at Aircraft in US as Aircraft, 1989; Let's Look at Trains in US as Trains, 1989; Let's Look at Racing Cars in US as Racing Cars, 1990; Let's Look at Monster Machines in US as Monster Machines, 1990. THE STORY OF SERIES: (with S. Alcantara and J.D. Hofilena) The Story of the Philippines, 1989; The Story of Singapore, 1990; (with G. Bailey) The Story of India, 1990. RESOURCES SERIES: Copper, 1981; Paper, 1991; Steel, 1992; Wool, 2009; Wood, 2009; Plastic, 2009; Paper products, 2009; Metal, 2009; Glass, 2009. HISTORY OF BRITAIN SERIES: The Tudors, 1485 to 1603, 1993; The Stuarts, 1603 to 1714, 1993; Georgian Britain 1714 to 1837, 1994; Victorian Britain, 1837 to 1901, 1994; Modern Britain: 1901 to the 1990s, 1994; Queen Victoria, 1995; The Blitz, 1939-1945, 1995; The Home Front, 1995; Elizabeth I, 1996; Shakespeare and the Theater, 1996. GREAT EXPLORERS SERIES: Discovering the New World: The Voyages of Christopher Columbus, 1994; Exploring the Pacific: The Expeditions of Captain Cook, 1994; The Great Polar Adventure: The Journeys of Roald Amundsen, 1994; Journey into Space: The Missions of Neil Armstrong, 1994. 100 GREATEST SERIES: 100 Greatest Tyrants, 1996; 100 Greatest Inventions, 1997; 100 Greatest Men, 1997; 100 Greatest Women, 1997; 100 Greatest Sports Champions, 1997; 100 Greatest Man made Wonders, 1997; 100 Greatest Medical Discoveries, 1997; 100 Greatest Explorers, 1997; 100 Greatest Disasters, 1997; 100 Greatest Natural Wonders, 1997; 100 Greatest Amazing Animals, 1997; 100 Archaeological Discoveries, 1997. TIME TOURS SERIES: Medieval Castle, 1998; Spanish Galleon, 1998; Egyptian Tomb, 1999; Roman Arena, 1999. OXFORD FIRST ENCYCLOPEDIA SERIES: Oxford First Encyclopedia, 1998; Earth and the Universe, 1999; Science and Technology, 1999; People and Places, 1999; My Body, 1999; Animals and Plants, 1999; Oxford First Book of Space, 1999. HISTORY IN ART SERIES: Ancient Egypt, 2005; Victorian Britain, 2005;

Ancient Greece, 2005. GREAT CITIES OF THE WORLD SERIES: Cape Town, 2005; St. Petersburg, 2005; Athens, 2005. LIVE ACTION SERIES: Swimming, 2004; Running, 2004; Walking, 2004. OTHERS: (ed. with J. Utting)The Village on the Hill: Aspects of Colerne History, 1990; Glenfiddich: Made without Compromise since 1887, 1995; London Pride: 150 Years of Fuller, Smith, and Turner, 1845-1995, 1995; (with A. Hargreaves) Mr. Mean's Guide to Management, 2000; (with A. Hargreaves) Mr. Lazy's Guide to Fitness, 2000; (with A. Hargreaves) Mr. Greedy's Guide to Food, 2000; Rupert Murdoch: An Unauthorized Biography, 2001; Leonardo da Vinci and the Renaissance, 2001; Jumping, 2004; September 11: Attack on America, 2006; Hurricanes, Tsunamis, and Other Natural Disasters, 2006; Hiroshima and Nagasaki: Fire from the Sky, 2006; Da Vinci & His Times, rev. ed., 2006; Should We Eat Animals?, 2007; KFK Natural Disasters, 2007; The Collapse of the Soviet Union: The End of an Empire, 2007; The Cultural Revolution: Years of Chaos in China, 2008; Is Organic Food Better?, 2008; How Much should Immigration be Restricted?, 2008; World War II, 2009; Hundred Days Offensive, 2009; Tiananmen Square: Massacre Crushes China's Democracy Movement, 2009; Are Girls Smarter than Boys?, 2009; Wartime Spies, 2010; Codes and Codebreaking, 2010; Helicopters, 2011; Avoiding Hunger and Finding Water, 2011; Planes, 2011; Submarines, 2011; Diggers, 2011; Bridging the Energy Gap, 2011; Pakistan in Our World, 2012; Israel in Our World, 2012; The Plains Indian Wars 1864-1890, 2012; Ancient Medicine, 2013. **Address:** c/o Author Mail, Raintree Publishers, Halley Ct., Jordan Hill, Oxford, OX OX2 8EJ, England.

LANGLEY, Charles P(itman). American (born United States), b. 1949. **Genres:** Children's Fiction, Novellas/Short Stories, Natural History. **Career:** Shelby Medical Associates, physician (internal medicine), 1979-, president. Writer. **Publications:** Catherine and Geku: The Adventure Begins, 1996; Catherine, Anna, and Geku Go to the Beach, 1997; North, East, South, West: Catherine, Anna, and Geku Take a Long Trip, 2001. **Address:** Shelby Medical Associates, 711 N DeKalb St., Shelby, NC 28150, U.S.A. **Online address:** cplffarms@aol.com

LANGLEY, Lester D(anny). American (born United States), b. 1940. **Genres:** History, Politics/Government, Adult Non-fiction, Humanities. **Career:** Texas A&M University, assistant professor of history, 1965-67; Central Washington State College, assistant professor of history, 1967-70; University of Georgia, associate professor, 1970-81, professor of history, 1981-, research professor, 1988-, now professor emeritus, university press, editor. **Publications:** The Cuban Policy of the United States: A Brief History, 1968; Struggle for the American Mediterranean: United States-European Rivalry in the Gulf Caribbean, 1776-1904, 1976; The United States and the Caribbean 1900-1970, 1980; The United States and the Caribbean in the Twentieth Century, 1982, 4th ed., 1989; The Banana Wars: An Inner History of American Empire 1900-1934, 1983; Central America: The Real Stakes, 1985; The Banana Wars: United States Intervention in the Caribbean, 1898-1934, rev. ed., 1985; Mex-America: Two Countries, One Future, 1988; America and the Americas: The United States in the Western Hemisphere, 1989, 2nd ed., 2010; Mexico and the United States: The Fragile Relationship, 1991; (with T. Schoonover) The Banana Men: American Mercenaries and Entrepreneurs in Central America, 1880-1930, 1995; The Americas in the Age of Revolution, 1750-1850, 1996; The Americas in the Modern Age, 2003; Simón Bolívar: Venezuelan Rebel, American Revolutionary, 2009. EDITOR: (and intro.) The United States, Cuba and the Cold War: American Failure or Communist Conspiracy, 1970; (with E.T. Glauert) The United States and Latin America, 1971; (with D. Bushnell) Simón Bolívar: Essays on the Life and Legacy of the Liberator, 2008. **Address:** Department of History, Franklin College of Arts & Sciences, University of Georgia, Old College, Athens, GA 30602, U.S.A. **Online address:** lesterd.langley@suddenlink.net

LANGLEY, Wanda. American (born United States) **Genres:** Air/Space Topics, Military/Defense/Arms Control, Business/Trade/Industry, Children's Fiction, Education. **Career:** U.S. Department of Defense, Department of the Air Force, Discharge Review Board, chief. Author and educator. **Publications:** The Air Force in Action, 2001; Flying Higher: The Women Airforce Service Pilots of World War II, 2002; Women of the Wind: Early Women Aviators, 2006; Business Leaders: The Faces Behind Beauty, 2008. Contributor to periodicals. **Address:** c/o Author Mail, Morgan Reynolds Publishing, 620 S Elm St., Ste. 223, Greensboro, NC 27406-1466, U.S.A.

LANGMEAD, Donald. *See* Obituaries.

LANGSTON, Cynthia. American (born United States), b. 1977?. **Genres:** Humor/Satire. **Career:** Consumer Dig, founder and market researcher, 1999-. Writer. **Publications:** Bicoastal Babe, 2006. Contributor to periodicals. **Address:** c/o Lissy Peace, Blanco & Peace Enterprises Ltd., 359 W Chicago Ave., Chicago, IL 60610, U.S.A. **Online address:** cynthia@cynthialangstonauthor.com

LANGSTON, Douglas C. American (born United States), b. 1950. **Genres:** Philosophy. **Career:** Harvard University, Mellon fellow, 1980-81; University of Helsinki, Fulbright fellow, 1989; New College of Florida, professor of philosophy and religion, 1977-. Writer. **Publications:** God's Willing Knowledge, 1986; Conscience and Other Virtues: From Bonaventure to MacIntyre, 2001. (ed.) The Consolation of Philosophy, 2010. **Address:** Division of Humanities, New College of Florida, 5800 Bay Shore Rd., Palmer Bldg. E 216, Sarasota, FL 34243-2197, U.S.A. **Online address:** langston@ncf.edu

LANGSTON, Laura. Canadian (born Canada), b. 1958. **Genres:** Children's Fiction, Picture/Board Books, Young Adult Fiction. **Career:** Canadian Broadcasting Corp., journalist; radio broadcaster. **Publications:** JUVENILE: No Such Thing as Far Away, 1994; Pay Dirt! The Search for Goldin British Columbia, 1994; The Magic Ear, 1995; The Fox's Kettle, 1998; A Taste of Perfection, 2002; Lesia's Dream, 2003; Mile-High Apple Pie, 2004 as Remember, Grandma?, 2004; Chan Hon Goh: Prima Ballerina, 2005; Rosemary Brown: Political Pioneer, 2005; Exit Point, 2006; Finding Cassidy, 2006; Perfect Blue, 2008; The Trouble with Cupid, 2008; Hannah's Touch, 2009; Last Ride, 2011. OTHER: Your Guide to Herb Gardening: Cooking, Crafts and Medicinal Herbs, Garden and Container Cultivation, Recipes and Instructions, 1999. **Address:** Victoria, BC , Canada. **Online address:** info@lauralangston.com

LANGTON, Jane. American (born United States), b. 1922. **Genres:** Mystery/Crime/Suspense, Children's Fiction, Novels, Picture/Board Books, Illustrations, Reference, Young Adult Fiction. **Career:** Simmons College, Graduate Center for the Study of Children's Literature, teacher of writing, 1979-80; Salem State College, Eastern Writers' Conference, teacher of writing, 1979-80. **Publications:** SELF-ILLUSTRATED: The Majesty of Grace, 1961 as Her Majesty, Grace Jones, 1974. OTHERS: The Diamond in the Window, 1962; The Transcendental Murder, 1964; The Swing in the Summer House, 1967; The Astonishing Stereoscope, 1971; The Boyhood of Grace Jones, 1972; Dark Nantucket Noon, 1975; Paper Chains, 1977; The Memorial Hall Murder, 1978; The Fledgling, 1980; Natural Enemy, 1982; Emily Dickinson Is Dead: A Novel of Suspense, 1984; The Fragile Flag, 1984; The Hedgehog Boy: A Latvian Folktale, 1985; Good and Dead, 1986; Murder at the Gardner, 1988; The Dante Game, 1991; God in Concord, 1992; Salt, 1992; Divine Inspiration: A Homer Kelly Mystery, 1993; The String of Pearls, 1994; The Queen's Necklace: A Swedish Folktale, 1994; The Shortest Day: Murder at the Revels, 1995; Dead as a Dodo: A Homer Kelly Mystery, 1996; The Face on the Wall, 1998; The Thief of Venice, 1999; The Time Bike, 2000; Murder at Monticello: A Homer Kelly Mystery, 2001; The Escher Twist: A Homer Kelly Mystery, 2002; The Deserter: Murder at Gettysburg, 2003; The Mysterious Circus, 2005; Steeplechase, 2005; Saint Francis and the Wolf, 2007; The Dragon Tree, 2008; The Thurber Murder, forthcoming. Contributor to magazines. **Address:** 9 Baker Farm Rd., Lincoln, MA 01773-3005, U.S.A. **Online address:** jlangton@earthlink.net

LANGUM, David J. American (born United States), b. 1940. **Genres:** History, Biography, Psychology. **Career:** San Francisco Law School, adjunct professor, 1966-67; Dunne, Phelps & Mills, associate, 1966-68; Lincoln University, School of Law, adjunct professor, 1968-78; Detroit College of Law, professor, 1978-83; Nevada School of Law, professor, 1983-85, dean, 1983-84; Samford University, Cumberland School of Law, professor of law and research professor, 1985-, Rushton Distinguished Lectureship Program, chairman, 1990-91, Doctoral Program in Law, Religion, and Culture, chairman, 1994-, Cumberland Colloquium on American Legal History, co-chairman, 1995-; Georgia State University, School of Law, visiting professor, 2008. Writer. **Publications:** (Ed.) Law in the West, 1985; Law and Community on the Mexican California Frontier: Anglo-American Expatriates and the Clash of Legal Traditions, 1821-1846, 1987, 2nd ed., 2006; (with H. Hague) Thomas O. Larkin: A Life of Profit and Patriotism in Old California, 1990; Crossing over the Line: Legislating Morality and the Mann Act, 1994; (with H.P. Walthall) From Maverick to Mainstream: Cumberland School of Law, 1847-1997, 1997; William M. Kunstler: The Most Hated Lawyer in America, 1999; Antonio De Mattos and The Protestant Portuguese Community in Antebellum Illinois, 2006. Contributor of articles to journals. **Address:** Cumberland School of Law, 800 Lakeshore Dr., Birmingham, AL 35229-0001, U.S.A. **Online address:** langumtrust@gmail.com

LANHAM, Richard Alan. American (born United States), b. 1936. **Genres:** Literary Criticism And History, Writing/Journalism. **Career:** Dartmouth College, Department of English, instructor, 1962-64, assistant professor, 1964-65; University of California, Department of English, assistant professor, 1965-69, associate professor, 1969-72, professor, 1972-94, vice chair for composition, 1980-86, emeritus professor of English, 1994-, Writing Program, director, 1979-82, executive director, 1982-86; University of Michigan, Institute for the Humanities, Norman Freehling visiting professor, 1994; Rhetorica Inc., president; Tulane University, Andrew W. Mellon professor, 1995. Writer. **Publications:** Sidney's Old Arcadia, 1965; A Handlist of Rhetorical Terms: A Guide for Students of English Literature, 1968, 2nd ed., 1991; Tristram Shandy: The Games of Pleasure, 1973; Style: An Anti-Textbook, 1974; The Motives of Eloquence: Literary Rhetoric in the Renaissance, 1976; Official Style: A Prose Paramedic for Bureaucrats, 1979; Revising Prose, 1979, 5th ed., 2007; Revising Business Prose, 1981, 4th ed., 2000; Analyzing Prose, 1983, 2nd ed., 2003; Literacy and the Survival of Humanism, 1983; (with M.E. Cohen) User's Manual for HOMER: A Computerized Revision Tool, 1984; The Electronic Word: Democracy, Technology and the Arts, 1993; Teflon Dad, 2005; Longman Guide to Revising Prose: A Quick and Easy Method for Turning Good Writing into Great Writing, 2006; Turning into Teflon, 2006; Teflon Teen, 2006; Economics of Attention: Style and Substance in the Age of Information, 2006; Style: An Anti-Textbook, 2007. **Address:** Department of English, University of California, 405 Hilgard Ave., Los Angeles, CA 90095-1530, U.S.A. **Online address:** lanham@ucla.edu

LANIER, Carlotta Walls. American (born United States), b. 1942. **Genres:** Autobiography/Memoirs. **Career:** LaNier and Co. (real estate brokerage company), founder; Little Rock Nine Foundation (scholarship organization), president. Writer. **Publications:** (With L.F. Page) A Mighty Long Way: My Journey to Justice at Little Rock Central High School, 2009. **Address:** U.S.A. **Online address:** carlottawallslanier@amightylongway.com

LANIER, Drew Noble. American (born United States), b. 1962. **Genres:** Novels, Law. **Career:** DePaul University, College of Law, legal research and writing teaching assistant, 1988-89; Hughes, Watters & Askanase L.L.P., associate attorney, 1990-92; University of North Texas, university pre-law advisor, 1993-97, graduate research assistant, 1994-97, teaching fellow, 1994-97; University of Central Florida, Department of Political Science, assistant professor of political science, 1997-2003, associate professor of political science, 2003-, Lou Frey Institute of Politics and Government, director, 2003-06, associate director, 2006-, fellow, 2009-. Writer. **Publications:** Of Time and Judicial Behavior: United States Supreme Court Agenda Setting and Decision-Making, 1888-1997, 2003; (with M.S. Hurwitz) The State of Judicial Selection, 2006. Contributor to books. **Address:** Department of Political Science, University of Central Florida, 3020 Howard Phillips Hall, 4000 Central Florida Blvd., PO Box 161356, Orlando, FL 32816-1356, U.S.A. **Online address:** drew.lanier@ucf.edu

LANIER, Jaron Zepel. American (born United States), b. 1960. **Genres:** Information Science/Computers. **Career:** Independent video game developer, 1980-83; Atari Labs, researcher, 1983-84; VPL Research, chief executive officer, 1984-90; New York University, Interactive Telecommunications Program, visiting artist, 1996-2001; National Tele-Immersion Initiative, lead scientist, 1997-2000; Advanced Network and Services, chief scientist, 1997-2001; Eyematic Interfaces, chief scientist, 1999-2002; Dartmouth College, visiting faculty, 2002-; University of Pennsylvania, Wharton School, Jones Center fellow, 2002-04; Silicon Graphics, visiting scientist, 2003-05; International Computer Science Institute, fellow, 2004-; Microsoft, partner architect, 2009-; University of Southern California, innovator-in-residence, 2010-; Wired Magazine, founding contributing editor. Composer and artist. **Publications:** (Co-author) Truth, Technology, and the Visual/Virtual World, 2006; You Are Not a Gadget: A Manifesto, 2010. Contributor to magazines. **Address:** U.S.A. **Online address:** hello@jaronlanier.com

LANKFORD, Mary D. American (born United States), b. 1932. **Genres:** Children's Fiction, Children's Non-fiction, Literary Criticism And History. **Career:** Elementary school librarian, 1962-63; Walker Air Force Base, media services librarian, 1965-66; Irving Independent School District, director of library and media services, 1966-; University of North Texas, adjunct professor; Texas Education Agency, assistant director of libraries. Writer. **Publi-**

cations: Is It Dark? Is It Light?, 1991; Hopscotch around the World, 1992; Films for Learning, Thinking, and Doing, 1992; Educational Fieldtrips, 1992; Successful Field Trips, 1992; Christmas Customs around the World, 1993; The Quinceanera, 1994; Christmas Around the World, 1995; Celebrating with Piñatas, 1996; Jacks around the World, 1996; Dominoes around the World, 1998; Birthdays around the World, 2002; Christmas USA, 2006; Leadership and the School Librarian: Essays from Leaders in the Field, 2006; Mazes Around the World, 2008. **Address:** 820 O'Connor Rd., Irving, TX 75061, U.S.A. **Online address:** mlankf2191@aol.com

LANKFORD, Nelson D. American (born United States), b. 1948. **Genres:** History, Biography, Social Sciences. **Career:** American Historical Review, book review editor, 1978-83; Indiana University, Budget Office, reports officer, 1983-84; Virginia Historical Society, editor, 1984-, assistant director, 1990-, director of publications and scholarship. **Publications:** (Comp.) Guide to the Manuscript Collections of the Virginia Historical Society, 1985; (ed.) Irishman in Dixie: Thomas Conolly's Diary of the Fall of the Confederacy, 1988; (ed.) OSS Against the Reich: The World War II Diaries of Colonel David K.E. Bruce, 1991; The Last American Aristocrat: The Biography of David K.E. Bruce, 1898-1977, 1996; (ed. with C.F. Bryan, Jr.) Eye of the Storm: A Civil War Odyssey, 2000; (ed. with C.F. Bryan, Jr. and J.C. Kelly) Images from the Storm: 300 Civil War Images by the Author of Eye of the Storm, 2001; Richmond Burning: The Last Days of the Confederate Capitol, 2002; Cry Havoc!: The Crooked Road to Civil War, 1861, 2007. Contributor to periodicals. **Address:** Virginia Historical Society, 428 N Blvd., PO Box 7311, Richmond, VA 23221-0311, U.S.A. **Online address:** nlankford@vahistorical.org

LANKFORD, Terrill Lee. Also writes as Roger Wade, Roger Wade. American (born United States) **Genres:** Novels, Mystery/Crime/Suspense. **Career:** Mysteries, Movies and Mayhem (bookstore), owner. Novelist and film maker. **Publications:** Angry Moon, 1997; Shooters, 1997; Earthquake Weather, 2004; Blonde Lightning, 2005. **Address:** c/o Author Mail, Ballantine Publishing Group, 201 E 50th St., New York, NY 10022, U.S.A. **Online address:** lankford2000@earthlink.net

LAN'KOV, Andreĭ N(ikolaevich). Russian/Australian (born Australia), b. 1963. **Genres:** History, Social Sciences. **Career:** Leningrad State University, assistant professor, 1990-92; Chungang University, lecturer, 1992-94; Osan College, lecturer, 1995-96; Australian National University, lecturer in Chinese and Korean studies, 1996-2004; Kookmin University, professor, 2004-. Writer. **Publications:** Pyŏngyang ŭi chibung mit: Soryŏn Leningradŭtae-Lankopŭ Kyosu ŭi Pukhan saenghwal chehŏmgi, 1991; Soryŏnŭi charyo ro pon Pukhan hyŏndae chŏngchisa, 1995; Politicheskaia borba v Koree XVI-XVIII vv., 1995; Severnaia Koreia: vcherai segodnia, 1995; Koreia: budni i prazdniki, 2000; From Stalin to Kim Il Sung: The Formation of North Korea, 1945-1960, 2002; Crisis in North Korea: The Failure of De Stalinization, 1956, 2004; KNDR vcherai segodnia: ne formalnaia istoriia Severnoĭ Korei, 2005; North of the DMZ: Essays on Daily Life in North Korea, 2007; Dawn of Modern Korea: The Transformation in Life and Cityscape, 2007; Avgust, 1956 God: Krizis v Severnoĭ Koree, 2009. **Address:** College of Social Science, Kookmin University, 861-2 Cheongneung-dong, Seongbuk-ku, Seoul, 136-702, Korea (South). **Online address:** andreilankov@gmail.com

LANOUETTE, William (John). American (born United States), b. 1940. **Genres:** Communications/Media, History, Military/Defense/Arms Control, Physics, Politics/Government, Writing/Journalism, Biography, Technology, Reference. **Career:** Newsweek, researcher and reporter, 1961-64; WVOX Radio, news editor, 1964; Hansard Society for Parliamentary Government, American lecturer, 1965-66, 1970-71; U.S. House of Representatives, legislative assistant, 1967-68; National Observer, staff writer, 1969-70, 1972-77; National Journal, staff correspondent, 1977-82, contributing editor, 1982-83; World Resources Institute, communications director, 1983-85, senior associate, 1985; Bulletin of the Atomic Scientists, Washington correspondent, 1989-90; U.S. General Accounting Office, senior analyst for energy and science issues, 1991-2006; The Atlantic Journal, writer and public policy analyst. **Publications:** The Atom, Politics and The Press, 1989; (with B. Silard) Genius in the Shadows: A Biography of Leo Szilard, the Man behind the Bomb, 1992; Odd Couple and the Bomb, 2000; Scientific American, 2000. Contributor to periodicals. **Address:** c/o F. Joseph Spieler, The Spieler Agency, Rm. 135, 154 W 57th St., New York, NY 10019, U.S.A. **Online address:** lanouette@erols.com

LANSDALE, Joe R(ichard). American (born United States), b. 1951.

Genres: Novellas/Short Stories, Mystery/Crime/Suspense, Horror, Science Fiction/Fantasy, Westerns/Adventure, Novels, Young Adult Fiction. **Career:** Goodwill Industries, transportation manager, 1973-75; Stephen F. Austin State University, custodian, 1976-80, writer-in-residence; LaBorde Custodial Services, foreman, 1980-81; full-time writer, 1981-; Shen Chuan: Martial Science, founder. **Publications:** Stories by Mama Lansdale's Youngest Boy, 1975; Act of Love, 1980; The Nightrunners, 1983; Texas Night Riders (novel), 1983; The Good, the Bad & the Indifferent (stories), 1983; Dead in the West, 1983; The Long Ones, 1985; Bestsellers Guaranteed, 1986; The Magic Wagon, 1986; By Bizarre Hands: Stories, 1987; The Drive-In: A B-Movie with Blood and Popcorn, 1988; On the Far Side of the Cadillac Desert with the Dead Folks, 1988; Tight Little Stitches on a Dead Man's Back, 1988; Cold in July, 1989; The Drive-In 2: Not Just One of Them Sequels, 1989; Savage Season, 1990; Lansdale's Limited Edition, 1990; The Steel Valentine, 1991; Batman: Captured by the Engines, 1991; Batman in Terror on the High Skies, 1992; Steppin' Out, 1992; (with G. Gianni) Drive-By, 1993; (with A.H. Vachss) Drive-By, Crossroads, 1993; Writer of the Purple Rage, 1994; Mucho MoJo, 1994; The Two-Bear Mambo, 1995; Electric Gumbo (stories), 1994; Jonah Hex: Two-Gun Mo (graphic novel), 1994; Fist Full of Stories, 1996; Bad Chili, 1997; High Cotton: Selected Stories of Joe R. Lansdale, 1997; (with L. Shiner) Private Eye Action as You Like It (stories), 1998; Rumble Tumble, 1998; The Boar, 1998; Freezer Burn, 1999; Waltz of Shadows, 1999; Something Lumber This Way Comes, 1999; The Bottoms, 2000; Blood Dance, 2000; The Big Blow, 2000; Selected Stories by Joe R. Lansdale, 2001; Captains Outrageous, 2001; Zeppelins West, 2001; For a Few Stories More, 2002; A Fine Dark Line, 2002; Bubba Ho-Tep, 2003; Bumper Crop, 2004; Dead Folks, 2004; Sunset and Sawdust, 2004; Flaming London, 2004; Mad Dog Summer and Other Stories, 2004; The King and Other Stories, 2005; Lost Echoes: A Novel, 2006; The Night They Missed the Horror Show, 2006; The God of the Razor, 2007; The Shadows, Kith and Kin, 2007; Conan and the Songs of the Dead, 2007; The Horror Hall of Fame The Stoker Winners, 2007; Leather Maiden, 2008; Vanilla Ride, 2009; Pigeons From Hell, 2009; Sanctified and Chicken-fried, 2009; Unchained and Unhinged, 2009; (with R. Bloch, K. Colden and J.L. Lansdale) Yours Truly, Jack the Ripper, 2010; The Best of Joe R. Lansdale, 2010; Deadman's Road, 2010; Dread Island: A Classics Mutilated Tale, 2011; Devil Red, 2011; Hyenas, 2011; All the Earth, Thrown to the Sky, 2011; Edge of Dark Water, 2012. EDITOR: The Best of the West, 1986; New Frontier: The Best of Todays Western Fiction, 1989; (with P. LoBrutto) Razored Saddles, 1989; Dark at Heart: All New Tales of Dark Suspense, 1992; (with T.W. Knowles) The West That Was, 1994; (with T.W. Knowles) The Wild West Show!, 1994; Tarzan: The Lost Adventure, 1994; (with R. Klaw) Weird Business, 1995; Atomic Chili: The Illustrated Joe R. Lansdale (comic-strip adaptations), 1996; A Fistful of Stories, 1997. Works appear in anthologies. Contributor of articles to magazines. **Address:** James C. Vines, The Vines Agency Inc., 648 Broadway, Ste. 901, New York, NY 10012-2348, U.S.A. **Online address:** wegotyourbackcovered@tenangrypitbulls.com

LANTHIER, Jennifer. Canadian (born Canada), b. 1964. **Genres:** Children's Fiction, Novels. **Career:** United Press Intl., reporter; Ottawa Citizen, journalist; Financial Post, journalist. **Publications:** The Mystery of the Martello Tower, 2006; The Legend of the Lost Jewels, 2008. Contributor to periodicals. **Address:** HarperCollins Publishers, 10 E 53rd St., New York, NY 10022, U.S.A. **Online address:** jennifer@jenniferlanthier.com

LANTIER, Patricia. American (born United States), b. 1952. **Genres:** Children's Non-fiction, Young Adult Non-fiction. **Career:** Teacher, 1973-82; Marquette University, instructor in English, 1982-89; Gareth Stevens Publishing, managing editor and director of creative department, 1990-2001; freelance writer and editor, 2001-02; Kalmbach Publishing Co., Astronomy Magazine, managing editor, 2002-. **Publications:** Take Me Out to the Ball Game, 1994; (with W. MacPherson) The Wonder of Cheetahs, 2001; (with A.D. Fredericks) The Wonder of Elephants, 2001; (K. Feeney) The Wonder of Pandas, 2001; (with J. Schuler) The Wonder of Fox, 2001; (K. Feeney) The Wonder of Koalas, 2001; (with J.L. Lehne) The Wonder of Kangaroos, 2001; Frederick Douglass, 2003; Kentucky, 2006; Arkansas, 2006; Louisiana, 2006; Tennessee, 2006; Wisconsin, 2006; Rachel Carson: Fighting Pesticides and Other Chemical Pollutants, 2009; Harriet Tubman: Conductor on the Underground Railroad, 2010. ADAPTER: The Wonder of Loons, 1992; The Wonder of Whitetails, 1992; The Wonder of Wolves, 1992; Hurricane: The Rage of Hurricane Andrew, 1993; Guatemala is My Home, 1993; Little Lost Fox Cub, 1993. THE ADVENTURES OF BUSTER THE PUPPY SERIES (picture books): Buster Catches a Cold, 1991 in Japan as Ame No Hi No Korowan;

Buster and the Little Kitten, 1991 in Japan as Korowan Wa Oniichan; Buster and the Dandelions, 1991 in Japan as Korowan To Fuwafuwa; Buster's First Snow, 1991 in Japan as Yuki No Hi No Korowan; Buster's Blustery Day, 1991 in Japan as Kaze No Hi No Korowan; Buster's First Thunderstorm, 1991 in Japan as Korowan To Gorogoro. PEOPLE WHO MAKE A DIFFERENCE SERIES (abridger): (with J. Bentley) Albert Schweitzer: The Doctor Who Devoted His Life to Africa's Sick, 1991; (with D. Winner) Desmond Tutu: Religious Leader Devoted to Freedom, 1991; (with B. Birch) Louis Braille: Bringer of Hope to the Blind, 1991. WINGS SERIES: Airplanes, 1994; Birds, 1994; Flying Animals, 1994; Flying Insects, 1994. **Address:** Gareth Stevens Publishing, 1555 N River Center Dr., Ste. 201, Milwaukee, WI 53212, U.S.A.

LANTIGUA, John. American (born United States), b. 1947. **Genres:** Novels, Young Adult Fiction, Mystery/Crime/Suspense, Biography. **Career:** Hartford Courant, reporter; Chicago Tribune, reporter; Washington Post, reporter; United Press Intl., reporter; Miami Herald, reporter, 1993-98; Palm Beach Post, investigative reporter, 2002-07, general assignment reporter. **Publications:** NOVELS: Heat Lightning, 1987; Burn Season, 1989; Twister, 1992; Player's Vendetta: A Little Havana Mystery, 1999; The Ultimate Havana, 2001; The Lady from Buenos Aires: A Willie Cuesta Mystery, 2007. OTHER: On Hallowed Ground, 2011. Contributor to periodicals. **Address:** Palm Beach Post, 2751 S Dixie Hwy., PO Box 24700, West Palm Beach, FL 33405, U.S.A. **Online address:** john_lantigua@pbpost.com

LANYON, Anna. Australian (born Australia) **Genres:** Novels, Social Sciences. **Career:** La Trobe University, Humanities and Social Sciences, honorary research associate. Writer and translator. **Publications:** Malinche's Conquest, 1999; The New World of Martin Cortes, 2003; Fire and Song, 2011. Contributor to periodicals. **Address:** c/o Author Mail, Allen and Unwin, PO Box 8500, St. Leonards, NW 1590, Australia.

LANZA, Joseph. American (born United States), b. 1955. **Genres:** Music, Film, Biography. **Career:** Writer. **Publications:** Fragile Geometry: The Films, Philosophy and Misadventures of Nicolas Roeg, 1989; Elevator Music: A Surreal History of Muzak, Easy-Listening, and Other Moodsong, 1994, rev. ed., 2004; The Cocktail: The Influence of Spirits on the American Psyche, 1995; Gravity: Tilted Perspectives on Rocketships, Rollercoasters, Earthquakes, and Angel Food, 1997; Russ Columbo and the Crooner Mystique, 2002; Vanilla Pop: Sweet Sounds from Frankie Avalon to ABBA, 2005; Phallic Frenzy: Ken Russell And His Films, 2007. Contributor to periodicals. **Address:** St. Martin's Press, 175 5th Ave., New York, NY 10010, U.S.A.

LANZMANN, Claude. French (born France), b. 1925. **Genres:** Cultural/Ethnic Topics, Film, History, Literary Criticism And History, Biography, History. **Career:** Free University of Berlin, lecturer for French literature and philosophy; European Graduate School, Media and Communication Division, professor of documentary film. Writer, director and filmmaker. **Publications:** (Ed.) The Bird Has No Wings: Letters of Peter Schwiefert, 1976; Shoah: An Oral History of the Holocaust, 1985; Shoah: The Complete Text of the Acclaimed Holocaust Film, 1995; Un vivant qui passe: Auschwitz 1943-Theresienstadt 1944, 1997; (comp. and ed.) Ruin's Traces: Young People's Diaries of the Holocaust, 2001; Sobibor: 14 Octobre 1943, 16 Heures, 2001; Le lièvre de Patagonie: mémoires, 2009; Patagonian Hare: A Memoir, 2012. Contributor to periodicals. **Address:** Media and Communication Division, European Graduate School, 151 1st Ave., Ste. 14, New York, NY 10003, U.S.A. **Online address:** clanzmann1@noos.fr

LAPCHAROENSAP, Rattawut. American (born United States), b. 1979?. **Genres:** Novellas/Short Stories, Young Adult Fiction, Literary Criticism And History. **Career:** Writer and teacher. **Publications:** Sightseeing: Stories, 2005. Contributor to periodicals. **Address:** c/o Author Mail, Grove Press, 841 Broadway, New York, NY 10003, U.S.A.

LAPE, Noreen Groover. American (born United States), b. 1966. **Genres:** Novels, Literary Criticism And History, Young Adult Fiction, Social Sciences, Politics/Government. **Career:** West Chester University, English instructor, 1992-94, 1995-97; Columbus State University, assistant professor, associate professor of language and literature, 1997-, Writing Center, director. Writer. **Publications:** West of the Border: The Multicultural Literature of the Western American Frontiers, 2000; (intro.) One-Smoke Stories, 2003. Contributor to periodicals and books. **Address:** Department of Language and Literature, Columbus State University, 4225 University Ave., Columbus, GA 31907, U.S.A. **Online address:** lape_noreen@colstate.edu

LAPHAM, Heather A. American (born United States), b. 1969. **Genres:** Young Adult Non-fiction, Natural History. **Career:** Southern Illinois University, Center for Archaeological Investigations, curator, assistant scientist, adjunct assistant professor of anthropology. Writer. **Publications:** Hunting for Hides: Deerskins, Status and Cultural Change in the Protohistoric Appalachians, 2005. Contributor of articles to periodicals and professional journals. **Address:** Center for Archaeological Investigations, Southern Illinois University, Faner 3479, 1000 Faner Dr., PO Box 4527, Carbondale, IL 62901, U.S.A. **Online address:** hlapham@siu.edu

LAPIERRE, Laurier L. Canadian (born Canada), b. 1929. **Genres:** Plays/Screenplays, History, Business/Trade/Industry, Economics. **Career:** University of Western Ontario, lecturer, 1960-62; McGill University, lecturer, 1963-64, associate professor of history, 1965-, French-Canadian Studies Program, director; University of Regina, School of Journalism, Bell professor of journalism; Order of Canada, officer, 1994; Telefilm Canada, chair, through 2000; Canadian Senate, senator, 2000-04, retired, 2004. Writer. **Publications:** 1759: The Battle for Canada, 1990; Canada, My Canada: What Happened?, 1992; Sir Wilfrid Laurier and the Romance of Canada, 1996; Quebec: A Tale of Love, 2001; Vancouver: A Tale of a City, forthcoming; The Spinning Wheel: The War of the Iroquois from the Founding of Quebec to the American Revolution, forthcoming. EDITOR: Four O'clock Lectures: French-Canadian Thinkers of the Nineteenth and Twentieth Centuries, 1966; Quebec: Hier et aujourd'hui, 1967; Essays on the Left: Essays in Honor of T.C. Douglas, 1971; If You Love this Country: Facts and Feelings on Free Trade, 1987. **Address:** Westwood Creative Artists, 94 Harbord St., Toronto, ON M5S 1G6, Canada. **Online address:** laurier.lapierre@sympatico.ca

LA PLANTE, Lynda. British (born England), b. 1943. **Genres:** Plays/Screenplays, Novels. **Career:** National Theatre and Royal Shakespeare Co., actor; La Plante Productions and Cougar Films, owner and producer. Television screenwriter, producer and novelist. **Publications:** DOLLY RAWLINS SERIES: Widows, 1983; Widows II, 1985; She's Out, 1995. LEGACY SERIES: The Legacy, 1987; The Talisman, 1987. JANE TENNISON SERIES: Prime Suspect, 1991; Prime Suspect 2, 1992; Prime Suspect 3, 1993. LORRAINE PAGE SERIES: Cold Shoulder, 1994; Cold Blood, 1996; Cold Heart, 1998. TRIAL AND RETRIBUTION SERIES: Trial and Retribution, 1997; Trial and Retribution II, 1998; Trial and Retribution III, 1999; Trial and Retribution IV, 2000; Trial and Retribution V, 2002; Trial and Retribution VI, 2002. ANNA TRAVIS SERIES: Above Suspicion, 2004; The Red Dahlia, 2007; Clean Cut, 2008; Deadly Intent, 2009; Silent Scream, 2010; Blind Fury, 2010; Bloodline, 2011. NOVELS: Bella Mafia, 1991; Civvies, 1992; Entwined, 1992; Framed, 1992; Seekers, 1993; The Governor, 1995; Sleeping Cruelty, 2001; Royal Flush, 2002; Royal Heist, 2004; The Little One, 2012. Contributor to periodicals. **Address:** La Plante Productions, Ground Fl., 4 Bourlet Cl., London, GL W1W 7BJ, England. **Online address:** info@laplantebooks.co.uk

LAPONCE, Jean. Canadian/French (born France), b. 1925. **Genres:** Politics/Government. **Career:** University of Santa Clara, instructor in political science, 1956; University of British Columbia, assistant professor, 1956-61, associate professor, 1961-66, professor of political science, 1966-92, emeritus professor of political science, 1992-; University of Ottawa, Institute of Interethnic Relations, director, 1993-2001. Writer. **Publications:** The Protection of Minorities, 1960; The Government of the Fifth Republic: French Political Parties and the Constitution, 1961; People vs. Politics, A Study of Opinions, Attitudes and Perceptions in Vancouver-Burrard, 1963-1965, 1969; (ed. with P. Smoker) Experimentation and Simulation in Political Science, 1972; Left and Right: The Topography of Political Perceptions, 1981; Langue et Territoire, 1984; (ed. with J. Meisel) Debating the Constitution, 1994; (ed. with J. Berry) Ethnicity and Culture in Canada: The Research Landscape, 1994; (ed. with W. Safran) Ethnicity and Citizenship: The Canadian Case, 1995; Loi de Babel et autres regularites des rapports ente langue et politique, 2006; Le référendum de souveraineté, 2010. **Address:** Department of Political Science, University of British Columbia, C472-1866 Main Mall, Vancouver, BC V6T 1Z1, Canada. **Online address:** jlaponce@interchange.ubc.ca

LAPPÉ, Frances Moore. American (born United States), b. 1944. **Genres:** Agriculture/Forestry, Economics, Education, Food And Wine, Human Relations/Parenting, International Relations/Current Affairs, Politics/Government, Race Relations, Social Commentary, Social Work, Urban Studies, Writing/Journalism. **Career:** Philadelphia Neighborhood Renewal Program, community organizer, 1967-69; Institute for Food and Development Policy,

founder and staff, 1975-90; Center for Living Democracy, founder and president, 1990-; Center's American News Service, founding editor, 1995-2001; Small Planet Institute, co-founder, 2001; Schumacher College, faculty, 2004; World Future Council, founding councilor, 2006; Food First: The Institute for Food and Development Policy, co-founder; People-Centered Development Forum, director; Suffolk University, visiting professor, 2006, 2008. **Publications:** Diet for a Small Planet, 1971, rev. ed., 1975; Great Meatless Meals, 1976; (with J. Collins) Food First: Beyond the Myth of Scarcity, 1977; (with J. Collins) El hambre en el mundo, 1979; (with J. Collins) Bhūk kyūn?, 1979; (with J. Collins) World Hunger: Ten Myths, 1979, 4th ed., 1982; (with A.N. Beccar-Varela) Mozambique and Tanzania, 1980; (J. Collins and D. Kinley) Aid as Obstacle, 1980; (with W. Valentine) What Can We Do?: A Food, Land, Hunger Action Guide, 1980; (co-author) Casting New Molds, 1980; (with J. Collins) Now We Can Speak, 1982; (with J. Collins and N. Allen) What Difference Could a Revolution Make? 1982; What to Do After You Turn Off the TV, 1985; (with J. Collins and P. Rosset) World Hunger: Twelve Myths, 1986, rev. ed., 1998; (with R. Schurman and K. Danaher) Betraying the National Interest, 1987; Rediscovering America's Values, 1989; (with R. Schurman) Taking Population Seriously, 1990; (with P.M. Dubois) The Quickening of America, 1994; (with A. Lappé) Hope's Edge: The Next Diet for a Small Planet, 1982; (with J. Perkins) You Have the Power: Choosing Courage in a Culture of Fear, 2004; (with R. Burton, A. Lappé and H. Richardson) Democracy's Edge: Choosing to Save Our Country by Bringing Democracy to Life, 2006; Getting A Grip: Clarity, Creativity and Courage in a World Gone Mad, 2007; Getting a Grip 2: Clarity, Creativity, and Courage for the World We Really Want, 2010; (foreword) Little House on a Small Planet: Simple Homes, Cozy Retreats and Energy Efficient Possibilities, 2nd ed., 2010; Eco-Mind: Changing the Way We Think, to Create the World We Want, 2011. **Address:** The Small Planet Institute, 25 Mt. Auburn St., Ste. 203, Cambridge, MA 02138, U.S.A. **Online address:** flappe@americannews.com

LAPPING, Brian (Michael). British (born England), b. 1937. **Genres:** Politics/Government, Public/Social Administration, Social Commentary, History, Social Sciences. **Career:** Daily Mirror, reporter, 1959-61; Guardian, reporter and deputy commonwealth correspondent, 1961-67; The Financial Times, feature writer, 1967-68; New Society, deputy editor, 1968-70; freelance television producer, writer and journalist, 1970-; Brian Lapping Associates, chief executive officer, 1988-97; Brook Lapping Productions, director, chairman, 2003-, executive producer, Teachers TV, chairman, 2003-. **Publications:** (Contrib.) Economic Sanctions Against South Africa, 1965; (ed. with G. Radice) More Power to the People: Young Fabian Essays on Democracy in Britain, 1968; The Labour Government 1964-70, 1970; (contrib.) The Future of the Social Services, 1971; (ed.) The State of the Nation: Parliament, 1973; (ed.) The State of the Nation: The Bounds of Freedom, 1980; End of Empire, 1985; Apartheid: A History, 1987, rev. ed., 1989. **Address:** Brook Lapping Productions, 6 Anglers Ln., London, GL NW5 3DG, England.

LAQUEUR, Thomas Walter. American/Turkish (born Turkey), b. 1945. **Genres:** History, Psychology, Gay And Lesbian Issues, Sex. **Career:** Concord College, instructor in social sciences, 1968-69; University of California, assistant, associate, full professor of history, Fawcett endowed professor, 1973-, Helen Fawcett professor, Doreen B. Townsend Center for the Humanities, director, 1992-95, acting director, 2003-04; University of Melbourne, lecturer, 1993. Writer. **Publications:** Religion and Respectability: Sunday Schools and Working Class Culture, 1780-1850, 1976; (ed. and intro. with C. Gallagher) The Making of the Modern Body: Sexuality and Society in the Nineteenth Century, 1987; Making Sex: Body and Gender from the Greeks to Freud, 1990; (contrib.) Corporal Politics, 1992; (contrib.) Hiding in Plain Sight, 1993; Solitary Sex: A Cultural History of Masturbation, 2003. Contributor to periodicals. **Address:** Department of History, University of California, 3123 Dwinelle Hall, Berkeley, CA 94720, U.S.A. **Online address:** tlaqueur@berkeley.edu

LAQUEUR, Walter. American/German (born Germany), b. 1921. **Genres:** History, Politics/Government. **Career:** Journalist, 1944-53; Survey, founder and editor, 1955-65; Johns Hopkins University, visiting professor of history and government, 1957; University of Chicago, visiting professor of history and government, 1958, Harvard Russian Research Center, fellow, Middle East Research Center, fellow; Institute of Contemporary History, Wiener Library, director, 1964-93; Brandeis University, professor of history of ideas and politics, 1967-72; Washington Papers, founder, 1969-2001; Washington Quarterly, founder, 1969-2001; Tel Aviv University, visiting professor, 1972-82; Georgetown University, Center for Strategic and International Studies,

International Research Council, chair, 1973-, university professor of government, 1977-91; Harvard University, visiting professor of history and government, 1976-77; Georgetown University, university professor, 1980-91. **Publications:** Ha-Neft yeha-Mizraḥ ha-Tikhon, 1950; Communism and Nationalism in the Middle East, 1956; The Soviet Union and the Middle East, 1959; Young Germany, 1962; Russia and Germany, 1965; The Fate of the Revolution, 1967; The Road to War, 1967 in US as The Road to Jerusalem, 1968; The Struggle for the Middle East, 1969; Out of the Ruins of Europe, 1971; A History of Zionism, 1972; Neo-Isolationism and the World of the Seventies, 1972; Confrontation: The Middle East War and World Politics, 1974; Weimar, 1974; Guerrilla, 1976; Terrorism, 1977; First News of the Holocaust, 1979; Continent Astray: Europe, 1970-1978, 1979; Terrible Secret, 1980; The Missing Years: A Novel, 1980; Political Psychology of Appeasement: Finlandization and Other Unpopular Essays, 1980; Farewell to Europe, 1981; Europe since Hitler, 1982 in US as Rebirth of Europe, 1970; America, Europe and the Soviet Union: Selected Essays, 1983; Black Hundred: The Rise of the Extreme Right in Russia, 1983; Young Germany: A History of the German Youth Movement, 1984; Germany Today, 1985; World of Secrets: The Uses and Limits of Intelligence, 1985; (with R. Breitman) Breaking the Silence, 1986; Age of Terrorism, 1987; The Long Road to Freedom, 1989; Stalin-the Glasnost Revelations, 1990; (co-author) Soviet Union 2000: Reform or Revolution?, 1990; Soviet Realities: Culture and Politics from Stalin to Gorbachev, 1990; Russia and Germany: A Century of Conflict, 1990; (with L. Sloss) European Security in the 1990s: Deterrence and Defense after the INF Treaty, 1990; Thursday's Child has Far to Go: A Memoir of the Journeying Years, 1992; Europe in Our Time: A History, 1945-1992, 1992; Uses and Limits of Intelligence, 1993; The Dream That Failed, 1994; Fascism, 1996; Fin de siècle and Other Essays on America & Europe, 1997; Guerrilla Warfare: A Historical & Critical Study, 1998; New Terrorism: Fanaticism and the Arms of Mass Destruction, 1999; History of Terrorism, 2001; Generation Exodus: the Fate of Young Jewish Refugees from Nazi Germany, 2001; No End to War: Terrorism in the Twenty-First Century, 2003; Dying for Jerusalem: The Past, Present and Future of the Holiest City, 2006; Changing Face of Antisemitism: From Ancient Times to the Present Day, 2006; Last Days of Europe: Epitaph for an Old Continent, 2007; Best of Times, Worst of Times: Memoirs of a Political Education, 2009; Harvest of a Decade: Disraelia and Other Essays, 2011. EDITOR: The Middle East in Transition: Studies in Contemporary History, 1958; Soviet Cultural Scene, 1956-1957, 1958; (with L. Labedz) Polycentrism, the New Factor in International Communism, 1962; (with L. Labedz) Future of Communist Society, 1962; Socialism and War, 1966; Left Wing Intellectuals between the Wars, 1919-1939, 1966; (co-ed.) International Fascism 1920-1945, 1966; 1914: The Coming of the First World War, 1966; Literature and Society, 1967; (with G.L. Mosse) Literature and Politics in the Twentieth Century, 1967; (co-ed.) History Today in USA, Britain, France, Italy, Germany, Poland, India, Czechoslovakia, Spain, Holland, Sweden, 1967; (with G.L. Mosse) Education and Social Structure in the Twentieth Century, 1967; (co-ed.) Reappraisals: A New Look at History, 1968; (co-ed.) The Middle East, 1968; The Israel-Arab Reader, 1969, 7th ed., 2008; (co-ed.) Urbanism: The City in History, 1969; (with G.L. Mosse) Great Depression, 1969; (co-ed.) Generations in Conflict, 1970; A Dictionary of Politics, 1971; A Readers Guide to Contemporary History, 1972; (with B. Krikler) Reader's Guide to Contemporary History, 1972; (with G.L. Mosse) Historians in Politics, 1974; Guerrilla Reader: A Historical Anthology, 1977; Terrorism Reader: A Historical Anthology, 1978; Fascism: A Reader's Guide, 1978; (with B. Rubin) Human Rights Reader, 1979, rev. ed., 1990; Second World War: Essays in Military and Political History, 1982; Pattern of Soviet Conduct in the Third World, 1983; (with D.M. Abshire) Looking Forward, Looking Back: A Decade of World Politics, 1983; (with R. Hunter) European Peace Movements and the Future of the Western Alliance, 1985; (with B. Roberts) America in the World, 1962-1987: A Strategic and Political Reader, 1987; Holocaust Encyclopedia, 2001; Voices of Terror: Manifestos, Writings and Manuals of Al Qaeda, Hamas and Other Terrorists from around the World and throughout the Ages, 2004. Contributor to periodicals. **Address:** Center for Strategic & International Studies, Georgetown University, 1800 K St. NW, Washington, DC 20006, U.S.A. **Online address:** laqueurw@csi.com

LARA, Adair. American (born United States), b. 1952. **Genres:** Essays, Novels, Autobiography/Memoirs, Adult Non-fiction, Humor/Satire. **Career:** Reader College of Marin, faculty, 1976-83; freelance editor, 1983-86; San Francisco Focus Magazine, managing editor, 1986-89; San Francisco Magazine, executive editor, 1988-89; San Francisco Chronicle, columnist, 1989-2002, reporter, 2002-04; educator and freelance writer, 2004-. **Publications:** Welcome to Earth, Mom, 1992; Slowing Down in a Speeded-Up World, 1994;

At Adair's House: More Columns from America's Favorite Former Single Mom, 1995; Hold Me Close, Let Me Go: A Mother, a Daughter, and an Adolescence Survived, 2001; Hanging Out the Wash: And Other Ways to Find More in Less, 2003; Normal is Just a Setting on the Dryer: And Other Lessons from the Real, Real World, 2003; Oopsie! Ouchie!, 2004; Bigger the Sign, the Worse the Garage Sale, 2007; You Know You're a Writer When, 2007; Granny Diaries, 2008; Naked, Drunk, and Writing, 2010. **Address:** 97 Scott St., San Francisco, CA 94117, U.S.A. **Online address:** adair.lara@gmail.com

LARA, Jaime. American (born United States), b. 1947?. **Genres:** Architecture. **Career:** Northeast Hispanic Catholic Center, Office of Liturgy and Cultural Affairs, director, 1985-90; Yale Divinity School, doctoral fellow, adjunct professor, 1995-96, visiting lecturer, 1996-97, assistant professor of Christian art and architecture, 1998-2003, Yale University Divinity School & Yale Institute of Sacred Music, associate professor & chair of the Program in Religion and the Arts, 2003-; California State University, assistant professor of art history, 1997-98; Universidad Nacional de Colombia, visiting professor of arts and humanities. Writer. **Publications:** City, Temple, Stage: Eschatological Architecture and Liturgical Theatrics in New Spain, 2004; Christian Texts for Aztecs: Art and Liturgy in Colonial Mexico, 2008. Contributor of articles to books. **Address:** Yale Divinity School, 409 Prospect St., New Haven, CA 06511, U.S.A. **Online address:** jaime.lara@yale.edu

LARA, Maria Pia. Mexican (born Mexico), b. 1954. **Genres:** Philosophy, Social Sciences, Sociology. **Career:** Universidad Autonoma Metropolitana, Department of Philosophy, professor; Stanford University, New School for Social Research, faculty. Writer. **Publications:** La democracia como proyecto de identidad ética, 1992; Moral Textures: Feminist Narratives in the Public Sphere, 1998; (ed.) Rethinking Evil: Contemporary Perspectives, 2001; Narrating Evil: A Postmetaphysical Theory of Reflective Judgment, 2007; Narrar el mal: Una Teoría Posmetafísica del Juicio Reflexionante, 2009. Contributor to periodicals. **Address:** Department of Philosophy, Universidad Autonoma Metropolitana, Av. San Rafael Atlixco 186, Col. Vicentina, Iztapalapa, 09340, Mexico.

LARCENET, Emmanuel. See **LARCENET, Manu.**

LARCENET, Manu. (Emmanuel Larcenet). French (born France), b. 1969. **Genres:** Astronomy. **Career:** Writer. **Publications:** (with L. Trondheim) Astronauts of the Future, 2003; Ordinary Victories, 2005; (with J. Sfar and L. Trondheim) Dungeon Parade, 2006. **Address:** NY , U.S.A.

LARDNER, Kate. American (born United States) **Genres:** Autobiography/ Memoirs, Autobiography/Memoirs. **Career:** Writer. **Publications:** Shut Up He Explained: The Memoir of a Blacklisted Kid, 2004. **Address:** c/o Liz Darhansoff, Daransoff & Verrill, 236 West 26th St., Ste. 802, New York, NY 10019, U.S.A. **Online address:** klardner@earthlink.net

LARDY, Nicholas R. American (born United States), b. 1946. **Genres:** Economics, International Relations/Current Affairs. **Career:** Yale University, assistant professor, associate professor of economics, 1975-83, Economic Growth Center, assistant director, 1979-82, School of Management, Frederick Frank adjunct professor of international trade and finance, 1997-2000; University of Washington, associate professor, 1983-85, professor of international studies, 1985-96, China Program, chair, 1984-89, Henry M. Jackson School of International Studies, director, 1991-95; Brookings Institution, senior fellow, 1995-2003; Peterson Institute for International Economics, senior fellow, 2003-09, Anthony M. Solomon senior fellow, 2010-. Writer. **Publications:** Economic Growth and Distribution in China, 1978; Agriculture in China's Modern Economic Development, 1983; Agricultural Prices in China, 1983; Foreign Trade and Economic Reform in China, 1978-1990, 1992; China in the World Economy, 1994; China's Unfinished Economic Revolution, 1998; Integrating China into the Global Economy, 2002; (with D. Rosen) Prospects for a U.S.-Taiwan Free Trade Agreement, 2004; (co-author) China: The Balance Sheet, 2006; (co-author) China's Rise: Challenges and Opportunities, 2008; (co-author) The Future of China's Exchange Rate Policy, 2009. EDITOR: (and intro.) Chinese Economic Planning: Translations from Ching-Chi Yen-Chiu, 1978; (with K.R. Lieberthal and intro.) Chen Yun's Strategy for China's Development: A Non-Maoist Alternative, 1983; (with M. Goldstein) Debating China's Exchange Rate Policy, 2008. **Address:** Peterson Institute for International Economics, 1750 Massachusetts Ave. NW, Washington, DC 20036-1903, U.S.A. **Online address:** nlardy@iie.com

LARIOS, Julie Hofstrand. American (born United States), b. 1949. **Genres:** Poetry, Young Adult Non-fiction, Mystery/Crime/Suspense. **Career:** University of Washington, creative writing instructor; Vermont College of Fine Arts, MFA-Writing for Children & Young Adults Program, faculty. Contributing editor. **Publications:** On the Stairs, 1999; Have You Ever Done That?, 2001; Yellow Elephant: A Bright Bestiary, 2006; Imaginary Menagerie: A Book of Curious Creatures, 2008. Works appear in anthologies. Contributor to books and journals. **Address:** Vermont College of Fine Arts, 36 College St., Montpelier, VT 05602, U.S.A. **Online address:** jlarios2007@gmail.com

LARKIN, Edward. (Edward J. Larkin). American (born United States), b. 1968?. **Genres:** Literary Criticism And History. **Career:** University of Richmond, assistant professor of English, American Studies Program, co-ordinator; University of Delaware, assistant professor of English, Center for Material Studies, faculty member. Writer. **Publications:** (ed.) Common Sense, 2004; Thomas Paine and the Literature of Revolution (nonfiction), 2005. Contributor of articles to journals. **Address:** Department of English, University of Delaware, 212 Memorial Hall, Newark, DE 19716, U.S.A. **Online address:** elarkin@udel.edu

LARKIN, Edward J. See **LARKIN, Edward.**

LARKIN, Joan. American (born United States), b. 1939. **Genres:** Women's Studies And Issues, Poetry, Gay And Lesbian Issues, inspirational/Motivational Literature, Women's Studies And Issues. **Career:** City University of New York, Brooklyn College, assistant professor of English, 1969-94, MFA Writing Program, adjunct professor, 1997; Goddard College, MFA Program in Writing, faculty, 1994-96, 2002; New England College, MFA Program in Poetry Writing, core faculty, 2002-08; Bloom, poetry editor, 2003-06; Drew University, MFA Program in Poetry and Poetry in Translation, faculty 2009-; University of Wisconsin Press, co-editor. **Publications:** POETRY: Housework, 1975; A Long Sound, 1986; Cold River, 1997; (trans. with J. Manrique) Sor Juana's Love Poems, 1997; My Body: New and Selected Poems, 2007. OTHERS: Glad Day: Daily Meditations for Gay, Lesbian, Bisexual and Transgender People, 1998; If You Want What We Have: Sponsorship Meditations, 1998. EDITOR: (with E. Bulkin) Amazon Poetry, 1975; (with E. Bulkin) Lesbian Poetry, 1981; (with C. Morse) Gay and Lesbian Poetry in Our Time, 1988; A Woman Like That: Lesbian and Bisexual Writers Tell Their Coming Out Stories, 1999. **Address:** Frances Goldin Agency, 57 E 11th St., Ste. 5B, PO Box 176, New York, NY 10003, U.S.A. **Online address:** larkin7@earthlink.net

LAROCCA, Roger T. American (born United States) **Genres:** Politics/Government, Social Sciences, History, International Relations/Current Affairs. **Career:** Purdue University, assistant professor, 1998-2005; University of Chicago, research fellow, 1999; Oakland University, assistant professor, 2005-, associate professor and internship director, 2009-. Writer. **Publications:** The Presidential Agenda: Sources of Executive Influence in Congress, 2006. Contributor to periodicals. **Address:** Department of Political Science, Oakland University, 418 Varner Hall, Rochester, MI 48309-4488, U.S.A. **Online address:** larocca@oakland.edu

LAROCHE, Loretta. American (born United States), b. 1939?. **Genres:** Medicine/Health, How-to Books, Humanities, Social Sciences. **Career:** Loretta LaRoche and Co., founder, The Humor Potential Inc., founder and president; Harvard Medical School, Behavior Institute of Medicine, adjunct faculty. Writer, television commentator and host. **Publications:** Relax: You May Only Have a Few Minutes Left: How to Use the Power of Humor to Defeat Stress in Your Life and Work, 1998, rev. ed., 2008; Life Is Not a Stress Rehearsal: Bringing Yesterday's Sane Wisdom into Today's Insane World, 2001; Life is Short-Wear Your Party Pants: Ten Simple Truths that Lead to An Amazing Life, 2003; Squeeze the Day: 365 Ways to Bring Joy and Juice Into Your Life, 2006; Kick Up Your Heels-Before You're Too Short to Wear Them: How to Live a Long, Healthy, Juicy Life, 2007; Juicy Living, Juicy Aging: Kick Up Your Heels-Before You're Too Short to Wear Them, 2009; Lighten Up!: The Authentic and Fun Way to Lose Your Weight and Your Worries, 2009. Contributor to magazines and newspapers. **Address:** Humor Potential Inc., 50 Court St., Plymouth, MA 02360, U.S.A. **Online address:** loretta@lorettalaroche.com

LAROQUE, Francois G. French (born France), b. 1948. **Genres:** Literary Criticism And History. **Career:** Oxford University, reader, 1969-70; University of Picardie, lecturer, 1972-73; Universite Paul Valery, faculty, 1974,

assistant professor, 1980, associate professor, 1980-88, professor of English, 1989, lecturer, 1984; LAFMA, staff, 1975; University of Texas, visiting lecturer, 1977; Universite de Paris III (Sorbonne Nouvelle), professor of English, 1991-; National Center for Scientific Research, deputy director, 1994-95, director, 2000-03; Institut du Monde Anglophone, creator and head, 1996, Committee of Specialists, chairman, 1998-2001; Directorate of Research, consultant, 1999-2001; League of Anglicists Higher Education, vice president, 1999; Commission of Experts, chairman, 2001-03; PRISMS, head, 2007. Writer. **Publications:** (Ed. with J. Fuzier) All's Well that Ends Well: Nouvelles Perspectives, 1986; Shakespeare et la fête, 1988; (with A. Morvan and A. Topia) Anthologie de la litterature anglaise, 1991; Shakespeare comme il vous plaira, 1991; (ed.) Show Within: Dramatic and Other Insets: English Renaissance Drama (1550-1642): Proceedings of the International Conference held in Montpellier, 22-25 November 1990, 1992; (with A. Morvan and F. Regard) Histoire de la litterature anglaise, 1997; Histoire et secret a la Renaissance: etudes sur la representation de la vie publique, la memoire et l'intimate dans l'Angleterre et l'Europe des XVIe et XVIIe siecles, 1997; (trans.) C. Marlowe, Doctor Faustus, 1997; (with F. Lessay) Figures de la royaute en Angleterre: de Shakespeare a la Glorieuse Revolution, 1999; Enfers et délices à la Renaissance, 2003; (ed. with P. Iselin and S. Alatorre) And that's True Too: New Essays on King Lear, 2009. **Address:** Institut du Monde Anglophone, Universite de Paris III, Sorbonne Nouvelle, 5 rue de l'Ecole-de-Medecine, Paris, 75006, France. **Online address:** flaroque@club-internet.fr

LA ROSA, Pablo. American/Cuban (born Cuba), b. 1944. **Genres:** Novellas/Short Stories, Novels. **Career:** Graceland College, associate professor, 1972-78; Lowell H. Listrom Co., margins analyst, 1983-88; Kansas State University, visiting instructor, 1988-89; Baker University, assistant professor of Spanish, 1989, now professor emeritus. Writer. **Publications:** Forbidden Fruit, and Other Stories, 1996. **Address:** Department of Language & Literature, Baker University, PO Box 65, Baldwin City, KS 66006, U.S.A. **Online address:** pablo.larosa@bakeru.edu

LAROSE, Lawrence. American (born United States), b. 1964?. **Genres:** Novels, Human Relations/Parenting, Homes/Gardens. **Career:** Writer. **Publications:** (With N. Penn) The Code: Time-tested Secrets for Getting What You Want from Women-Without Marrying Them!, 1996; Gutted: Down to the Studs in My House, My Marriage, My Entire Life, 2004. Contributor to periodicals. **Address:** c/o Author Mail, Bloomsbury Publishing Plc., 36 Soho Sq., London, GL W1D 3HB, England.

LARS, Max. See **CHWIN, Stefan.**

LARSEN, Clark Spencer. American (born United States), b. 1952. **Genres:** Anthropology/Ethnology, History. **Career:** Smithsonian Institution, National Museum of Natural History, Department of Anthropology, fellow-in-residence, 1978-79; University of Massachusetts, Department of Sociology and Anthropology, assistant professor, 1979-83; American Museum of Natural History, research associate, 1980-; La Florida Bioarchaeology Project, director, 1982-; Northern Illinois University, Department of Anthropology, assistant professor, 1983-85, associate professor, 1985-89, chair, 1987-89, The Anthropology Museum, director, 1983-89; Purdue University, Department of Anthropology, associate professor, 1989-91, professor of biological anthropology, 1991-93, School of Liberal Arts, Center for Social and Behavioral Sciences, fellow, 1992; University of North Carolina, Research Laboratories of Archaeology, research associate, 1993-2001, Department of Anthropology, associate professor, 1993-95, professor of biological anthropology, 1995-99, Amos Hawley Distinguished Professor, 1999-2001, adjunct professor, 2005-07; American Journal of Physical Anthropology, associate editor, 1994-98; Duke University, Department of Evolutionary Anthropology, adjunct professor, 1995-2001; University of California, Department of Anthropology, visiting professor, 1999; Journal of Archaeological Research, contributing editor, 1999-; Ohio State University, Department of Anthropology, distinguished professor of social and behavioral sciences and chair, 2001-, Bioarchaeology Research Laboratory, director, 2001-, Department of History, adjunct professor, 2004-, Department of Ecology, Evolution and Organismal Biology, adjunct professor, 2004-; East Carolina University, Department of Anthropology, adjunct professor, 2001-02; American Journal of Physical Anthropology, editor-in-chief, 2001-07; International Journal of Paleopathology, associate editor, 2010-. Anthropologist. **Publications:** (With D.H. Thomas and S. South) Rich Man, Poor Men: Observations on Three Antebellum Burials from the Georgia Coast, 1977; (with D.H. Thomas) The Anthropology of St. Catherines Island, 1979, vol. V, 1986; (ed. and intro.) The Antiquity and Origin of

Native North Americans, 1985; The Archeology of Mission Santa Catalina de Guale, vol. II: Biocultural Interpretations of a Population in Transition, 1990; (ed. with M.A. Kelley) Advances in Dental Anthropology, 1991; (with R.M. Matter and D.L. Gebo) Human Origins: The Fossil Record, 2nd ed., 1991; (ed. and intro.) Native American Demography in the Spanish Borderlands, 1991; (ed. with G.R. Milner) In the Wake of Contact, 1994; (with R.L. Kelly) Bioarchaeology of the Stillwater Marsh: Prehistoric Human Adaptation in the Western Great Basin, 1995; Bioarchaeology: Interpreting Behavior from the Human Skeleton, 1997; (ed. with B.E. Hemphill) Prehistoric Lifeways in the Great Basin Wetlands: Bioarchaeological Reconstruction and Interpretation, 1999; Skeletons in Our Closet: Revealing Our Past through Bioarchaeology, 2000; (ed.) Bioarchaeology of Spanish Florida: The Impact of Colonialism, 2001; Bioarchaeology of the Late Prehistoric Guale: South End Mound I, St. Catherines Island, Georgia, 2002; Our Origins: Discovering Physical Anthropology, 2008, 2nd ed., 2011; Essentials of Physical Anthropology, 2010; (ed.) Companion to Biological Anthropology, 2010. Contributor to journals and periodicals. **Address:** Department of Anthropology, Ohio State University, 4034 Smith Laboratory, 174 W 18th Ave., Columbus, OH 43210-1106, U.S.A. **Online address:** larsen.53@osu.edu

LARSEN, Jeanne (Louise). American (born United States), b. 1950. **Genres:** Poetry, Translations, Novels. **Career:** Tunghai University, Department of Western Languages and Literature, lecturer, 1972-74; Mitsubishi Shipyard, instructor of English as a second language, 1978-80; Hollins University, Department of English, assistant professor, 1980-86, associate professor, 1986-92, professor of English 1992-, Master of Fine Arts in Creative Writing, director, 2004-08, Susan Gager Jackson professor of creative writing. Writer. **Publications:** POETRY: James Cook in Search of Terra Incognita: A Book of Poems, 1979; (trans.) Brocade River Poems: Selected Works of the Tang Dynasty Courtesan Xue Tao, 1987; (trans.) Willow, Wine, Mirror, Moon: Women's Poems from Tang China, 2005; Why We Make Gardens, 2010. NOVELS: Silk Road: A Novel of Eighth-Century China, 1989; (co-ed.) Engendering the Word: Feminist Essays in Psychosexual Poetics, 1990; Bronze Mirror, 1991; Manchu Palaces, 1996. Works appear in anthologies. Contributor to periodicals. **Address:** Hollins University, 7900 Old York Rd., PO Box 9542, Roanoke, VA 24020, U.S.A. **Online address:** jlarsen@hollins.edu

LARSEN, Timothy. American (born United States), b. 1967. **Genres:** Politics/Government, Theology/Religion, History, Biography. **Career:** Wheaton College, Carolyn and Fred McManis professor of Christian thought, Carolyn and Fred McManis chair of Christian thought, 2002-; Trinity College, visiting fellow commoner, 2007. Writer. **Publications:** Friends of Religious Equality: Nonconformist Politics in Mid-Victorian England, 1999; Christabel Pankhurst: Fundamentalism and Feminism in Coalition, 2002; (with J. Vickery) For Christ in Canada: A History of Tyndale Seminary, 2004; Contested Christianity: The Political and Social Contexts of Victorian Theology, 2004; Crisis of Doubt: Honest Faith in Nineteenth-Century England, 2006; People of One Book, 2011. EDITOR (with D. Bebbington) Modern Christianity and Cultural Aspirations, 2003; Biographical Dictionary of Evangelicals, 2003; (with J.P. Greenman) Reading Romans through the Centuries: From the Early Church to Karl Barth, 2005; (with J.P. Greenman and S.R. Spencer) The Sermon on the Mount through the Centuries, 2007; (with D.J. Treier) The Cambridge Companion to Evangelical Theology, 2007; (with M. Husbands) Women, Ministry and the Gospel: Exploring New Paradigms, 2007. **Address:** Wheaton College, 284 BGC, 501 College Ave., Wheaton, IL 60187-5593, U.S.A. **Online address:** timothy.larsen@wheaton.edu

LARSEN, Torben B. Danish/British (born England), b. 1944. **Genres:** Zoology, Sciences, Animals/Pets, Natural History. **Career:** International Planned Parenthood Federation, family planning specialist, 1970-84; Danish International Development Agency, family planning specialist, 1984-86; University of Florida, research associate; freelance researcher and writer, 1986-. **Publications:** Indiens Kamp Mod Befolkningseksplosionen, 1969; Butterflies of Lebanon, 1974; (contrib.) The Butterflies of Oman, 1980; The Butterflies of the Yemen Arab Republic, 1982; The Butterflies of Saudi Arabia and Its Neighbours, 1984; The Butterflies of Egypt, 1990; The Butterflies of Kenya and Their Natural History, 1991; Butterflies of Bangladesh: An Annotated Checklist, 2004; Hazards of Butterfly Collecting, 2004; The Butterflies of West Africa, vol. I-II, 2005. **Address:** 358 Coldharbour Ln., London, GL SW9 8PL, England. **Online address:** torbenlarsen@compuserve.com

LARSGAARD, Chris. American (born United States), b. 1967?. **Genres:** Novels, Mystery/Crime/Suspense, Young Adult Fiction. **Career:** Private investigator, 1990-. Writer. **Publications:** The Heir Hunter (crime novel), 2000. **Address:** c/o Author Mail, Delacorte Press, 1745 Broadway, New York, NY 10019, U.S.A.

LARSON, Edward J(ohn). American (born United States), b. 1953. **Genres:** Biology, History, Law, Medicine/Health, Politics/Government, Biography, Travel/Exploration. **Career:** Davis, Wright & Tremaine (law firm), attorney, 1979-83; U.S. House of Representatives, associate counsel, 1983-89; University of Georgia, Richard B. Russell professor of American history, 1987, Herman E. Talmadge chair of law; Pepperdine University, professor in history, Hugh & Hazel Darling professor of law, 2007, university professor. Writer. **Publications:** Trial and Error: The American Controversy over Creation and Evolution, 1985, 3rd. ed., 2003; Sex, Race, and Science: Eugenics in the Deep South, 1995; Summer for the Gods: The Scopes Trial and America's Continuing Debate over Science and Religion, 1997; (with B. Spring) Euthanasia, 1998; (with D.W. Amundsen) Different Death, 1998; (ed.) History of Science and Religion in the Western Tradition, 2000; Evolution's Workshop: God and Science on the Galapagos Islands, 2001; Evolution: The Remarkable History of a Scientific Theory, 2004; (with M.P. Winship) Constitutional Convention: A Narrative History: From the Notes of James Madison, 2005; (ed. and intro. with J. Marshall) Essential Words and Writings of Clarence Darrow, 2007; Creation-Evolution Debate: Historical Perspectives, 2007; Magnificent Catastrophe: The Tumultuous Election of 1800, America's First Presidential Campaign, 2007; An Empire of Ice: Scott, Shackleton and the Heroic Age of Antarctic Science, 2011; Church, States, and Original Intent, forthcoming; The Deadlocked Election of 1800, forthcoming; Segregation's Science, forthcoming. Contributor to periodicals. **Address:** School of Law, Pepperdine University, 24255 Pacific Coast Hwy., Malibu, CA 90263, U.S.A. **Online address:** edlarson@uga.edu

LARSON, Gary. American (born United States), b. 1950. **Genres:** Humor/Satire, Cartoons, Literary Criticism And History. **Career:** Pacific Search, editor; syndicated cartoonist, 1978-95. **Publications:** The Far Side, 1982; Beyond the Far Side, 1983; In Search of the Far Side, 1984; The Far Side Gallery, 1984; Bride of the Far Side, 1984; Valley of the Far Side, 1985; It Came from the Far Side, 1986; The Far Side Gallery II, 1986; The Far Side Observer, 1987; Hound of the Far Side, 1987; Night of the Crash-Test Dummies: A Far Side Collection, 1988; The Far Side Gallery III, 1988; Pre-History of the Far Side: A Tenth Anniversary Exhibit, 1989; Wildlife Preserves: A Far Side Collection, 1989; Weiner Dog Art: The Far Side Collection, 1990; Unnatural Selections: A Far Side Collection, 1991; Cow of Our Planet: A Far Side Collection, 1992; The Chickens Are Restless: A Far Side Collection, 1993; The Far Side Gallery 4, 1993; The Curse of Madame C, 1994; The Far Side Gallery 5, 1995; Last Chapter and Worse: A Far Side Collection, 1996; There's a Hair in my Dirt! A Worm's Story, 1998; Humour Libre, 1998; Gary Larson 5, 2002; Complete Far Side, 2003. Contributor to periodicals. **Address:** Creators Syndicate, 5777 W Century Blvd., Ste. 700, Los Angeles, CA 90045, U.S.A.

LARSON, Hope. American (born United States), b. 1982. **Genres:** Children's Fiction, Novels, Illustrations. **Career:** Tulip Tree Press, founder. Cartoonist, writer and illustrator. **Publications:** SELF-ILLUSTRATED: Salamander Dream, 2005; Gray Horses/Chevaux gris, 2006; Chiggers, 2008; Mercury, 2010. Works appear in anthologies. **Address:** Asheville, NC , U.S.A. **Online address:** hope@hopelarson.com

LARSON, Ingrid D(ana). American (born United States), b. 1965. **Genres:** Children's Fiction, Young Adult Fiction, Novels, Human Relations/Parenting. **Career:** Writer. **Publications:** The Adventures of Herman and Hurby, 1995; The Adventures of Herman and Hurby and Family, 1997; Herman and Hurby, 2000. Works appear in anthologies. **Address:** 486 W Union St., East Bridgewater, MA 02333-1721, U.S.A. **Online address:** idanalarson@aol.com

LARSON, Jennifer. (Jennifer Lynn Larson). American (born United States), b. 1965. **Genres:** Classics, History. **Career:** Kent State University, Department of Modern and Classical Language Studies, assistant professor of classics, 1992-93, 1993-94, 1994-99, associate professor of classics, 1999-2005, professor of classics, 2005-. Writer. **Publications:** Greek Heroine Cults, 1995; Greek Nymphs: Myth, Cult, Lore, 2001; Ancient Greek Cults: A Guide, 2007. **Address:** Department of Modern and, Classical Language Studies, Kent State University, 109 Satterfield Hall, Kent, OH 44242, U.S.A. **Online address:** jlarson@kent.edu

LARSON, Jennifer Lynn. *See* **LARSON, Jennifer.**

LARSON, Kate Clifford. American (born United States) **Genres:** Biography. **Career:** National Park Service, Harriet Tubman Special Resource Study, consultant; Simmons College, adjunct professor, 1998-, lecturer; consultant, 2001-; Wheelock College, adjunct professor, 2007-. Writer. **Publications:** Bound for the Promised Land: Harriet Tubman, Portrait of an American Hero, 2004; Assassin's Accomplice: Mary Surratt and the Plot to Kill Abraham Lincoln, 2008. **Address:** Ballantine Books, 1745 Broadway, 10th Fl., New York, NY 10019-4368, U.S.A. **Online address:** kate.larson@simmons.edu

LARSON, Kirby. American (born United States), b. 1954. **Genres:** Children's Fiction, Young Adult Fiction, Children's Non-fiction. **Career:** Author. **Publications:** Second-Grade Pig Pals, 1994; Cody and Quinn, Sitting in a Tree, 1996; The Magic Kerchief, 2000. SWEET VALLEY KIDS BOOKS: Scaredy-Cat Elizabeth, 1995; Elizabeth Hatches an Egg, 1996; Hattie Big Sky, 2006; Two Bobbies: A True Story of Hurricane Katrina, Friendship and Survival, 2008; Nubs: The True Story of a Mutt, a Marine and a Miracle, 2009; The Fences Between Us (Dear America), 2010; The Friendship Doll, 2011. **Address:** 8523 NE 147th Pl., Kenmore, WA 98028, U.S.A. **Online address:** kirby@kirbylarson.com

LARSON, Sidner J. American (born United States), b. 1949. **Genres:** Literary Criticism And History. **Career:** Kessler Law Office, attorney, 1985-88; University of Arizona, instructor in English, 1989-92; Lewis-Clark State College, director of American Indian studies, 1992-95; University of Oregon, associate professor of American Indian literature, 1995-; Iowa State University, director of American Indian studies, associate professor of English, program director for American Indian Studies. Writer. **Publications:** NONFICTION: Catch Colt, 1995; (intro.) Indian Old-Man Stories: More Sparks from War Eagle's Lodge-Fire, 1996; (intro.) Indian Why Stories: Sparks from War Eagle's Lodge-Fire, 1996; Captured in the Middle: Tradition and Experience in Contemporary Native American Writing, 2000. Contributor to journals. **Address:** Department of English, Iowa State University, 435 Ross Hall, Ames, IA 50011-1201, U.S.A. **Online address:** sidner@iastate.edu

LARSON, Stephanie Greco. American (born United States), b. 1960. **Genres:** Politics/Government, Communications/Media, Women's Studies And Issues. **Career:** George Washington University, assistant professor of political science, 1986-92; Dickinson College, assistant professor of political science, 1992-94; associate professor, 1994-. Writer. **Publications:** Creating Consent of the Governed: A Member of Congress and the Local Media, 1992; Public Opinion: Using MicroCase ExplorIt, 2003; Media and Minorities: The Politics of Race in News and Entertainment, 2006. Works appear in anthologies. Contributor to periodicals. **Address:** Department of Political Science, Dickinson College, 312 Denny Hall, Carlisle, PA 17013, U.S.A. **Online address:** larson@dickinson.edu

LARSON, Wendy. American (born United States) **Genres:** Literary Criticism And History, Cultural/Ethnic Topics. **Career:** University of Oregon, associate professor, Department of East Asian languages and literatures, professor of modern Chinese literature and film, vice provost of Portland programs. Writer. **Publications:** (Trans. and intro.) Bolshevik Salute: A Modernist Chinese Novel, 1989; Literary Authority and the Modern Chinese Writer: Ambivalence and Autobiography, 1991; (ed. with A. Wedell-Wedellsborg) Inside Out: Modernism and Postmodernism in Chinese Literary Culture, 1993; Women and Writing in Modern China, 1998; (ed. with B. Goodman) Gender in Motion: Divisions of Labor and Cultural Change in Late Imperial and Modern China, 2005; From Ah Q to Lei Feng: Freud and Revolutionary Spirit in 20th Century China, 2009. **Address:** Department of East Asian Languages and Literatures, University of Oregon, 70 NW Couch Ave., Portland, OR 97209, U.S.A. **Online address:** walarson@uoregon.edu

LARUE, L. H. American (born United States), b. 1938. **Genres:** Law, Adult Non-fiction. **Career:** Washington and Lee University, assistant professor of law, 1967-70, associate professor of law, 1970-74, professor of law, 1974-85, Frances Lewis Law Center, director, professor of law, 1985-88, professor of law, 1988-90, Class of 1958 alumni professor, 1990-, professor of law, 1990-2005, professor emeritus, 2005-. Writer. **Publications:** A Student's Guide to the Study of Law, 1987, 2nd ed., 2001; Political Discourse: A Case Study of the Watergate Affair, 1988; (ed. with W. Holt) Rewriting the History of the Judiciary Act of 1789: Exposing Myths, Challenging Premises and Using New Evidence, 1990; Constitutional Law as Fiction: Narrative in the Rhetoric

of Authority, 1995; (with D.S. Caudill) No Magic Wand: The Idealization of Science in Law, 2006. **Address:** School of Law, Washington and Lee University, 450E Sydney Lewis Hall, Lexington, VA 24450, U.S.A. **Online address:** laruel@wlu.edu

LARZELERE, Alex. (Alex R. Larzelere). American (born United States), b. 1936. **Genres:** Military/Defense/Arms Control. **Career:** U.S. Coast Guard, career officer; U.S. Department of Energy, Advanced Modeling and Simulation, director, 2008-. Writer. **Publications:** The 1980 Cuban Boatlift, 1988; The Coast Guard at War: Vietnam, 1965-1975, 1997; (as Alex R. Larzelere) The Coast Guard in World War I: An Untold Story, 2003; (as Alex R. Larzelere) Witness to History: White House Diary of a Military Aide to President Richard Nixon, 2009. **Address:** 5904 Mount Eagle Dr., Alexandria, VA 22303, U.S.A. **Online address:** alex.larzelere@nuclear.energy.gov

LARZELERE, Alex R. *See* **LARZELERE, Alex.**

LA SALLE, Peter. American (born United States), b. 1947. **Genres:** Novels, Novellas/Short Stories, Young Adult Fiction. **Career:** Johnson State College, lecturer in creative writing, 1974-76; University of Texas, visiting assistant professor of creative writing, 1976-77, assistant professor, 1980-86, associate professor, 1986-94, professor of English, 1994-, Department of English, The College of Liberal Arts, Susan Taylor McDaniel Regents professor in creative writing; Iowa State University, assistant professor of English, 1977-80. Writer. **Publications:** The Graves of Famous Writers and Other Stories, 1980; Strange Sunlight (novel), 1984; Hockey Sur Glace: Stories, 1996; Tell Borges If You See Him: Tales of Contemporary Somnambulism, 2007; Mariposa's Song, forthcoming. Works appear in anthologies. Contributor of articles and magazines. **Address:** Department of English, College of Liberal Arts, University of Texas, PAR 24, 1 University Sta., PO Box B5000, Austin, TX 78712-0803, U.S.A.

LA SALLE, Victor. *See* **FANTHORPE, R(obert) Lionel.**

LASANSKY, D. Medina. (Medina Lasansky). American (born United States) **Genres:** Architecture. **Career:** Cornell University, Department of Architecture, associate professor. Historian, educator and writer. **Publications:** (ed. with B. McLaren) Architecture and Tourism: Perception, Performance and Place, 2004; The Renaissance Perfected: Architecture, Spectacle and Tourism in Fascist Italy, 2004. Contributor to books and periodicals. **Address:** College of Architecture, Art & Planning, Cornell University, 129 Sibley Dome, Ithaca, NY 14853, U.S.A. **Online address:** dml34@cornell.edu

LASANSKY, Medina. *See* **LASANSKY, D. Medina.**

LASENBY, Jack. New Zealander (born New Zealand), b. 1931. **Genres:** Novels, Children's Fiction, Novellas/Short Stories, Cartoons. **Career:** Teacher, 1950-68; New Zealand Department of Education, editor of school journal, 1969-75; Wellington Teacher's College, senior lecturer in English, 1975-87; writer, 1987-; New Zealand School Journal, editor. **Publications:** CHILDREN'S FICTION: Charlie the Cheeky Kea, 1976; Rewi the Red Deer, 1976. NOVELS: Lost and Found, 1970; Over Makara, 1971; Two Grandfathers, 1972; The Chatham Islands, 1973; The Lake, 1987; The Mangrove Summer, 1989; The Conjuror (young adult), 1992; Harry Wakatipu, 1993; Dead Man's Head, 1994; The Waterfall, 1995; The Battle of Poole Island, 1996; Because We Were the Travellers (young adult), 1997; Taur (young adult), 1998; The Shaman and the Droll, 1999; The Lies of Harry Wakatipu, 2000; Kalik, 2001; Aunt Effie, 2002; Harry Wakatipu Comes the Mong, 2003; Aunt Effie's Ark, 2003; Aunt Effie and the Island that Sank, 2004; Mr Bluenose, 2005; The Tears of Harry Wakatipu, 2006; When Mum Went Funny, 2006; Aunt Effie and Mrs. Grizzle, 2008. SHORT STORIES: Uncle Trev, 1991; Uncle Trev and the Great South Island Plan, 1991; Uncle Trev and the Treaty of Waitangi, 1992; Uncle Trev's Teeth, 1997. OTHERS: What Makes a Teacher?, 2004. Contributor to periodicals. **Address:** 137 Aro St., Wellington, 6006, New Zealand. **Online address:** jacklasenby@mac.com

LASH, Batton. American (born United States), b. 1953. **Genres:** Graphic Novels. **Career:** National Law Journal, creator, 1983-87; Exhibit A Press, cofounder and publisher, 1994-. Cartoonist and writer. **Publications:** GRAPHIC NOVELS: (with J. Wheelock and D. David) Panorama #2, 1991; Wolff & Byrd, Counselors of the Macabre: Supernatural Law, 1992; (with J. Valentino and R. Queen) Shadowhawk #14, 1994; Wolff & Byrd, Counselors of the Macabre #1, 1994; Wolff & Byrd, Counselors of the Macabre #3, 1994;

Wolff & Byrd, Counselors of the Macabre #4, 1994; Wolff & Byrd, Counselors of the Macabre #6, 1995; Wolff & Byrd, Counselors of the Macabre #7, 1995; Wolff & Byrd, Counselors of the Macabre: Case Files, 1995-98; Wolff & Byrd, Counselors of the Macabre: Fright Court, 1995; Wolff & Byrd, Counselors of the Macabre: Greatest Writs, 1997; Wolff & Byrd's Secretary Mavis Number 1, 1998; Sonovawitch! And Other Tales of Supernatural Law, 2000; The Vampire Brat: And Other Tales of Supernatural Law, 2001; Mr. Negativity: And Other Tales of Supernatural Law, 2004; (with J. Ho and B. Morrison) Radioactive Man: The Official Movie Adaptation, 2004; Tales of Supernatural Law, 2005; The Soddyssey, 2008; (with B. Galvan) The High School Chronicles: Archie Freshman Year, 2009. OTHERS: (with S. Franklin) The Penguin's Put-downs, Jokes, and Riddles, 1992; (co-author) Topps Kirby-Verse, 1993; (with N. Cuti and G. Gabner) Madraven Halloween Special October, 1995; (with Bill Galvan and Jesse Leon McCann) The Scrapyard Detectives Collected Cases, vol. I, 2007; (with J. Dyer, D. Haspiel and L. Pien) APE 2009, 2009. Works appear in anthologies. Contributor to books and journals. **Address:** Exhibit A Press, 4657 Cajon Way, San Diego, CA 92115, U.S.A. **Online address:** mail@exhibitapress.com

LASH, Nicholas. *See* **LASH, N. L. A.**

LASH, N. L. A. (Nicholas Lash). British/Indian (born India), b. 1934. **Genres:** Theology/Religion, Humanities. **Career:** Ordained Roman Catholic priest, 1963; assistant priest, 1963-68; Cambridge University, fellow, 1969-85, St. Edmund's House, dean, 1971-75, assistant lecturer, 1974-78, Norris-Hulse professor of divinity, 1978-99, Norris-Hulse professor emeritus of divinity, 1999-, Clare Hall, fellow, 1988-. Writer. **Publications:** AS NICHOLAS LASH: (ed.) Doctrinal Development and Christian Unity, 1967; His Presence in the World: A Study in Eucharistic Worship and Theology, 1968; Until He Comes: A Study in the Progress Toward Christian Unity, 1968; (ed. with J. Rhymer) Christian Priesthood, 1970; Luke, 1971; Change in Focus: A Study of Doctrinal Change and Continuity, 1973; Newman on Development: The Search for an Explanation in History, 1975; Voices of Authority, 1976; An Essay in Aid of a Grammar of Assent, 1979; Theology on Dover Beach, 1979; A Matter of Hope: A Theologian's Reflections on the Thought of Karl Marx, 1981; (ed. with D. Tracy) Cosmology and Theology, 1983; Theology on the Way to Emmaus, 1986; Easter in Ordinary: Reflections on Human Experience and the Knowledge of God, 1988; Believing Three Ways in One God: A Reading of the Apostles' Creed, 1992; The Beginning and End of Religion, 1996; (ed. with S. Freyne) Is the World Ending?, 1998; Holiness, Speech, and Silence: Reflections on the Question of God, 2004; Seeing in the Dark: University Sermons, 2005; Theology for Pilgrims, 2008. Contributor to periodicals. **Address:** Faculty of Divinity, University of Cambridge, West Rd., Cambridge, CM CB3 9BS, England.

LASKAS, Jeanne Marie. American (born United States), b. 1958?. **Genres:** Biography. **Career:** Life, contributing editor, 1989-92; Washington Post Magazine, syndicated columnist, 1994-2008; Esquire, columnist, 1995-2000, contributing editor; GQ, correspondent, 2000-; University of Pittsburgh, assistant professor of English, associate professor of English. Journalist. **Publications:** The Balloon Lady and Other People I Know, 1996; We Remember: Women Born at the Turn of the Century Tell the Stories of Their Lives in Words and Pictures, 1999; Fifty Acres and a Poodle: A Story of Love Livestock and Finding Myself on a Farm, 2000; The Exact Same Moon: Fifty Acres and a Family, 2003; Growing Girls: The Mother of All Adventures, 2006; Hidden America: The Unseen World of People Who Make Everything Work, forthcoming. **Address:** Department of English, University of Pittsburgh, CL 628-E, 4200 5th Ave., Pittsburgh, PA 15260, U.S.A. **Online address:** mail@jmlaskas.com

LASKIER, Michael M. Israeli (born Israel), b. 1949. **Genres:** History, International Relations/Current Affairs, Humanities. **Career:** American Friends of the Alliance Israelite Universelle, associate director, 1978-80; Tel-Aviv University, Diaspora Research Institute, lecturer, 1980-88; Ben-Gurion University, visiting lecturer, 1980-82, History Department, teacher, 1998-2000; Herzliyya Military College, teacher, 1983-87; University of Judaism, visiting associate professor, 1988-90, visiting professor, 1993-; Spertus College, Louis Susman associate professor of Jewish and Middle Eastern history, 1990-92, Louis Susman Graduate Management-Base Jewish Communal Studies Program, founder and director; University of Chicago, associate of center for Middle Eastern studies, 1990-94; World Sephardic Educational Center, ex-

ecutive director, 1992-94; University of Judaism, visiting professor, 1993-94; Bar-Ilan University, Ashqelon College, associate professor, 1994-, head of political science department, 1998-2002, Ramat-Gan, Political Science Department, teacher, 1998-2001, Department of Middle Eastern history, faculty, 2001-. Writer. **Publications:** The Alliance Israelite Universelle and the Jewish Communities of Morocco, 1862-1962, 1983; North African Jewry in the Shadow of Vichy France and the Swastika (in Hebrew), 1992; The Jews of Egypt, 1920-1970: In the Midst of Zionism, Anti-Semitism, and the Arab-Israeli Conflict, 1992; Yehude ha-Magreb be-tsel Vishi u-tselav ha-ḳeres, 1992; North African Jewry in the Twentieth Century: A Political History of the Jews in Morocco, Tunisia, and Algeria, 1994, 2nd ed., 1997; (ed. with R.S. Simon and S. Reguer) The Jews of the Middle East and North Africa in Modern Times, 2003; Israel and the Maghreb: From Statehood to Oslo, 2004; Yiśrael veha-aliyah mi-Tsefon Afrikah: 1948-1970, 2006. Contributor to periodicals. **Address:** Bar-Ilan University, Rm. 109, Bldg. 217, Ramat Gan, 52900, Israel. **Online address:** michael_1949@barak-online.net

LASKIN, David. American (born United States), b. 1953. **Genres:** Horticulture, Humanities, Meteorology/Atmospheric Sciences, Biography, Social Work, History, Children's Non-fiction. **Career:** Bantam Books, editor, freelance writer, 1979-. **Publications:** (Co-author) Esquire Wine and Liquor Handbook, 1984; Herman Melville's Billy Budd and Typee, 1984; Getting into Advertising, 1986; The Parents Book for New Fathers, 1988; Eastern Islands: Accessible Islands of the East Coast, 1990; Parents Book of Child Safety, 1991; (with K. O'Neill) The Little Girl Book: Everything You Need to Know to Raise a Daughter Today, 1992; A Common Life: Four Generations of American Literary Friendship and Influence, 1994; (with H. Hughes) Reading Group Book: The Complete Guide to Starting and Sustaining a Reading Group, with Annotated Lists of 250 Titles for Provocative Discussion, 1995; Braving the Elements: The Stormy History of American Weather, 1996; Rains All the Time: A Connoisseur's History of Weather in the Pacific Northwest, 1997; Partisans: Marriage, Politics, and Betrayal among the New York Intellectuals, 2000; Artists in Their Gardens, 2001; Children's Blizzard, 2004; Long Way Home: An Immigrant Generation and the Crucible of War, 2010. **Address:** 18757 Ridgefield Rd. NW, Seattle, WA 98177, U.S.A. **Online address:** d.laskin@verizon.net

LASKIN, Pamela L. American (born United States), b. 1954. **Genres:** Children's Non-fiction, Poetry, Young Adult Fiction, Literary Criticism And History. **Career:** Lopez Publications, assistant editor, 1977-78; McGraw-Hill Publishing Co., editor, 1978-81; Bryant High School, faculty, 1981; City University of New York, City College, adjunct instructor in English, 1981-2005, 2006-; New York University, faculty, 1982-90; Pratt Institute, adjunct instructor in creative writing and children's literature, 1989-93; Kingsborough Community College, faculty, 1995-97; Gotham Writer's Workshop, instructor of children's writing, 2001-05. **Publications:** A Little off the Top, 1985; Music from the Heart, 1989; (with A.A. Moskowitz) Wish upon a Star: A Story for Children with a Parent Who Is Mentally Ill, 1991; Heroic Horses, 1997; The Buried Treasure, 1997; Till Death Do Us Part, 2001; Trick or Treat, 2001; the Great Garden of Space, 2003; Getting to Know You, 2003; Other Stations, 2004; Grand Central Station, 2004; (ed.) The Heroic Young Woman, 2006; Remembering Fireflies, 2007; Ghosts, Goblins, Gods And Geodes, 2008; Secrets of Sheets, 2009; Van Gogh's Ear, 2009; Visitation Rites, 2011. Contributor to periodicals. **Address:** 414 5th St., Brooklyn, NY 11215, U.S.A. **Online address:** bigapplepoetpam@aol.com

LASKY, Kathryn. Also writes as Kathryn Lasky Knight, E. L. Swann. American (born United States), b. 1944. **Genres:** Young Adult Fiction, Young Adult Non-fiction, Picture/Board Books. **Career:** Writer. **Publications:** YOUNG ADULTS FICTION: The Night Journey, 1981; Beyond the Divide, 1983; Prank, 1984; Home Free, 1985; Pageant, 1986; The Bone Wars, 1988; Double Trouble Squared, 1991; Shadows in the Water, 1992; Voice in the Wind, 1993; Beyond the Burning Time, 1994; Memories of a Bookbat, 1994; A Journey to the New World: The Diary of Remember Patience Whipple, 1996; True North: A Novel of the Underground Railroad, 1996; Dreams of the Golden Country: The Diary of Zipporah Felman, 1998; (as E.L. Swann) Night Gardening, 1998. CHILDREN. FICTION: (with L. Floyd) Agatha's Alphabet, 1975; I Have Four Names for My Grandfather, 1976; Tugboats Never Sleep, 1977; My Island Grandma, 1979; Jem's Island, 1982; Sea Swan, 1988; Fourth of July Bear, 1991; I Have an Aunt on Marlborough Street, 1992; The Tantrum, 1993; Cloud Eyes, 1994; The Solo, 1994; Pond Year, 1995; The Gates of the Wind, 1995; She's Wearing a Dead Bird on Her Head, 1995; Lunch Bunnies, 1996; Grace the Pirate, 1997; Marven of the Great North

Woods, 1997; Hercules: The Man, the Myth, the Hero, 1997; Alice Rose and Sam, 1998. NONFICTION: Tall Ships, 1978; The Weaver's Gift, 1980; Dollmaker: The Eyelight and the Shadow, 1981; Sugaring Time, 1983; A Baby for Max, 1984; Puppeteer, 1985; Traces of Life: The Origins of Humankind, 1989; Dinosaur Dig, 1990; Surtsey: The Newest Place on Earth, 1992; Think Like an Eagle: At Work with a Wildlife Photographer, 1992; Monarchs, 1993; (with M. Knight) Searching for Laura Ingalls: A Reader's Journey, 1993; Days of the Dead, 1994; The Librarian Who Measured the Earth, 1994; The Most Beautiful Roof in the World: Exploring the Rainforest Canopy, 1997; Shadows in the Dawn: The Lemurs of Madagascar, 1998; A Brilliant Streak: The Making of Mark Twain, 1998; Vision of Beauty, 2001. NOVELS AS KATHRYN LASKY KNIGHT: Atlantic Circle, 1985; Trace Elements, 1986; The Widow of Oz, 1989; Mortal Words, 1990; Mumbo Jumbo, 1991; Dark Swan, 1994. OTHERS: Alice Rose & Sam: A Novel, 1998; Brilliant Streak: the Making of Mark Twain, 1998; Dreams in the Golden Country: The Diary of Zipporah Feldman, A Jewish Immigrant Girl, 1998; Robin Hood: The Boy who Became a Legend, 1998; Shadows in the Dawn: the Lemurs of Madagascar, 1998; Sophie and Rose, 1998; Show and Tell Bunnies, 1998; Elizabeth I, Red Rose of the House of Tudor, 1999; Emperor's Old Clothes, 1999; Star split, 1999; Lucille's Snowsuit, 2000; Marie Antoinette, Princess of Versailles, 2000; Science Fair Bunnies, 2000; Vision of Beauty: The Story of Sarah Breedlove Walker, 2000; First Painter, 2000; Born in the Breezes: The Seafaring Life of Joshua Slocum, 2001; Christmas After All: The Great Depression Diary of Minnie Swift, 2001; Interrupted Journey: Saving Endangered Sea Turtles, 2001; Starring Lucille, 2001; Mommy's Hands, 2002; Porkenstein, 2002; Time for Courage: The Suffragette Diary of Kathleen Bowen, 2002; Mary, Queen of Scots, Queen without a Country, 2002; Jahanara, Princess of Princesses, 2002; Lucille Camps In, 2003; The Man who Made Time Travel, 2003; Voice of Her Own: The Story of Phillis Wheatley, Slave Poet, 2003; Capture, 2003; Home at Last, 2003; Hope in My Heart, 2003; Before I was Your Mother, 2003; Love that Baby!: A Book about Babies for New Brothers, Sisters, Cousins and Friends, 2004; Rescue, 2004; Shattering, 2004; Siege, 2004; American Spring, 2004; Blood Secret, 2004; Burning, 2004; Humphrey, Albert and the Flying, 2004; Kazunomiya: Prisoner of Heaven, 2004; Hatchling, 2005; The Night Journey, 2005; Outcast, 2005; Tumble Bunnies, 2005; Dancing through Fire, 2005; Broken Song, 2005; To be a King, 2006; Pirate Bob, 2006; John Muir: America's First Environmentalist, 2006; Born to Rule, 2006; Coming of Hoole, 2006; First Collier, 2006; Georgia Rises, 2006; (contrib.) A Guide Book to the Great Tree, 2007; River of Wind, 2007; Unicorns?, Get Real!, 2007; Last Girls of Pompeii, 2007; Journey, 2007; Golden Tree, 2007; Poodle and Hound, 2009; Exile, 2008; War of the Ember, 2008; Yossel's Journey, 2008; One Beetle Too Many: The Extraordinary Adventures of Charles Darwin, 2009; Two Bad Pilgrims, 2009; Hannah, 2009; Georgia Rises: a Day in the Life of Georgia O'Keeffe, 2009; Shadow Wolf, 2010; (contrib.) Lost Tales of Ga'Hoole, 2010; Lone Wolf, 2010; Hawksmaid: The Untold Story of Robin Hood and Maid Marian, 2010; Felix Takes the Stage, 2010; Chasing Orion, 2010; Ashes, 2010; May, 2011; Watch Wolf, 2011; Silk & Venom, 2011; Spiders on the Case, 2011. Contributor to periodicals. **Address:** Scholastic Inc., 557 Broadway, New York, NY 10012, U.S.A. **Online address:** kathryn@kathrynlasky.com

LASS, Roger. South African/Scottish/American (born United States), b. 1937. **Genres:** Language/Linguistics, How-to Books, Literary Criticism And History. **Career:** Indiana University, lecturer, 1964-65, assistant professor, 1965-66, associate professor of English and linguistics, 1967-73; University of Edinburgh, visiting lecturer, 1969-70, lecturer, 1973-78, reader in linguistics, 1978-82, honorary professorial fellow; University of Cape Town, visiting lecturer, 1982, professor of linguistics, 1983-2002, honorary research fellow in linguistics, professor emeritus, 2002-; University College of North Wales, lecturer; University of Wales, lecturer. Writer. **Publications:** Approaches to English Historical Linguistics, 1969; (with J.M. Anderson) Old English Phonology, 1975; English Phonology and Phonological Theory: Synchronic and Diachronic Studies, 1976; (trans.) D. Wunderlich, Foundations of Linguistics, 1979; On Explaining Language Change, 1980; Phonology: An Introduction to Basic Concepts, 1984; The Shape of English, 1987; (ed.) The Cambridge History of the English Language, 1992; Old English: A Historical Linguistic Companion, 1994; Historical Linguistics and Language Change, 1997; (ed. with M. Dossena) Methods and Data in English Historical Dialectology, 2004; (ed. with M. Dossena) Studies in English and European Historical Dialectology, 2009. Contributor to journals. **Address:** University of Cape Town, PO Box X3, Rondebosch, 7701, South Africa. **Online address:** lass@iafrica.com

LASSALLE, Caroline. See CAVE, Emma.

LASSERRE, Philippe. Singaporean/French (born France), b. 1939. **Genres:** Business/Trade/Industry, Social Sciences. **Career:** French Foundation for Management Education, vice-general secretary, 1962-72; SNECMA, controller, 1963-69; INSEAD, professor, 1975-, now emeritus professor of strategy and Asian business; National University of Singapore, visiting professor; China Europe Management Institute, visiting professor; University of Texas, visiting professor; Curtin University, visiting professor; China Europe International Business School (CEIBS), visiting professor; Thunderbird University, visiting professor. Writer. **Publications:** (With M. Boisot) Strategies and Practices of Transfer of Technology from European to ASEAN Enterprises: Some Major Findings & Their Implications, 1980; (with M. Boisot) Transfer of Technology from European to ASEAN Enterprises: Strategies and Practices in the Chemical and Pharmaceutical Sectors, 1980; Export Generating Long Term Collaborative Agreements in Developing Countries, 1988; (with J. Putti) Business Strategy and Management: Text & Cases for Managers in Asia, 1990; (with H. Schütte) Strategies for Asia Pacific, 1995, 3rd ed. as Strategies for Asia Pacific: Meeting New Challenges, 2006; Global Strategic Management, 2002, 2nd ed., 2007. **Address:** INSEAD, 1 Ayer Rajah Ave., Singapore, 138676, Singapore. **Online address:** philippe.lasserre@insead.edu

LASSEZ, Sarah. Canadian/American (born United States) **Genres:** Young Adult Fiction, Biography, Autobiography/Memoirs, Art/Art History. **Career:** Actress and writer. **Publications:** (With G. Sardar) Psychic Junkie: A Memoir, 2006. **Address:** c/o Dan Strone, Trident Media Group, 41 Madison Ave., 36th Fl., New York, NY 10010, U.S.A. **Online address:** sarah@sarahlassez.com

LASSITER, Mary. See HOFFMAN, Mary (Margaret).

LASSITER, Matthew D. American (born United States), b. 1970. **Genres:** Politics/Government, Social Commentary, History. **Career:** Bowdoin College, visiting instructor and assistant professor of history, 1998-2000; University of Michigan, Department of History, assistant professor, 2000-06, associate professor and director of graduate studies, 2006-, associate professor of urban and regional planning, 2007-. Writer. **Publications:** (Ed. with A.B. Lewis) The Moderates' Dilemma: Massive Resistance to School Desegregation in Virginia, 1998; The Silent Majority: Suburban Politics in the Sunbelt South, 2006; (ed. with J. Crespino) The Myth of Southern Exceptionalism, 2010. Contributor of articles to books and journals. **Address:** Department of History, University of Michigan, 1029 Tisch Hall, Ann Arbor, MI 48109, U.S.A. **Online address:** mlassite@umich.edu

LASSITER, Rhiannon. British (born England), b. 1977. **Genres:** Children's Fiction, Novels, Young Adult Non-fiction, Ghost Writer, Novellas/Short Stories, Science Fiction/Fantasy, Mystery/Crime/Suspense. **Career:** Writer. **Publications:** FOR YOUNG ADULTS: White Walls, 1997; Hex, 1998; The Supernatural, 1999; Walking the Wire, 1999; Ghosts, 2001; Waking Dream, 2002; Shadows, 2002; Outland, 2003; (ed. with M. Hoffman) Lines in the Sand: New Writing on War and Peace, 2003; Borderland, 2004; Shadowland, 2005; Super Zeroes, 2005; Roundabout, 2006; Bad Blood, 2007; Ghost of a Chance, 2011. **Address:** Rogers, Coleridge & White Ltd., 20 Powis Mews, London, W11 1JN, United Kingdom. **Online address:** rhiannon@rhiannonlassiter.com

LASSMAN, Abigail Francine. See LANE, Abbe.

LASSNER, Phyllis. American (born United States), b. 1936. **Genres:** Autobiography/Memoirs. **Career:** Ben-Gurion University, visiting professor, 1992; Northwestern University, professor, 1993-. Writer. **Publications:** Elizabeth Bowen: A Feminist Study, 1990; Elizabeth Bowen: A Study of the Short Fiction, 1991; British Women Writers of World War II: Battlegrounds of Their Own, 1998; Colonial Strangers: Women Writing the End of the British Empire, 2004; Anglo-Jewish Women Writing the Holocaust: Displaced Witnesses, 2008; (ed. with L. Trubowitz) Antisemitism and Philosemitism in the Twentieth and Twenty-First Centuries: Representing Jews, Jewishness, and Modern Culture, 2008; A Tempered Wind: An Autobiography, 2009; (ed. with L.Le-Guilcher) Rumer Godden: International and Intermodern Storyteller, 2010. Contributor to journals and periodicals. **Address:** Northwestern University, 2111 Orrington Ave., Evanston, IL 60201, U.S.A. **Online address:** phyllisl@northwestern.edu

LASSON, Kenneth (Lee). American (born United States), b. 1943. **Genres:**

Law, Social Commentary, Biography, Essays. **Career:** Constitutional Convention Commission of Maryland, research assistant, 1966; Maryland School Law Revision Commission, executive secretary, 1966-67; Johns Hopkins University, teaching fellow and lecturer, 1966-68; University of Maryland-Baltimore, School of Law, assistant to dean, 1967-69; Ralph Nader's Center for the Study of Responsive Law, editorial and administrative consultant, 1969-72; Goucher College, lecturer in English, 1970-72, assistant to president, 1970-71; Loyola College, assistant professor of political science and communication arts, 1972-78, affirmative action officer, 1977-79; University of Baltimore, School of Law, professor of law, 1976-; Haifa Summer Law Institute, director, 1999-. **Publications:** The Workers: Portraits of Nine American Job-holders, 1971; Proudly We Hail: Profiles of Public Citizens in Action, 1975; Private Lives of Public Servants, 1978; Your Rights and the Draft, 1980; Your Rights as a Vet, 1981; (with W. Cohen) Getting the Most Out of Washington, 1982; Representing Yourself: What You Can Do without a Lawyer, 1983; Mousetraps and Muffling Cups: 1000 Brilliant and Bizarre U.S. Patriots, 1986; (with S. Margulies) Learning Law: The Mastery of Legal Logic, 1992; (with A.B. Morrison) Representing Yourself: What You Can Do without a Lawyer, 1995; Trembling in the Ivory Tower, 2003. **Address:** School of Law, University of Baltimore, Rm. LC 309, 1420 N Charles St., Baltimore, MD 21201-5779, U.S.A. **Online address:** klasson@ubalt.edu

LASSWELL, Marcia. (Marcia E. Lasswell). American (born United States), b. 1927. **Genres:** Human Relations/Parenting, Psychology, Medicine/Health. **Career:** Pepperdine College, lecturer, 1952-54, assistant professor, 1959-60; marriage and family counselor, 1959-; California State University, assistant professor, 1960-63, associate professor, 1963-68, professor of psychology, 1968-, Department of Behavioral Sciences, head, 1964-69; Occidental College, visiting professor, 1971-72. Writer. **Publications:** College Teaching of General Psychology, 1967; (as Marcia E. Lasswell with T.E. Lasswell) Love, Marriage and Family (textbook), 1973; (with N.M. Lobsenz) No-Fault Marriage: The New Technique of Self-Counseling and What it Can Help You Do, 1976; (contrib.) Encounter With Family Realities, 1977; (with N.M. Lobsenz) Styles of Loving, 1980; (with T.E. Lasswell) Marriage and the Family, 1982, 3rd ed., 1991; (with N.M. Lobsenz) Equal Time: The New Way of Living, Loving and Working Together, 1983; Time for Me, Time for You, Time for Us: A Guide to Personal Time Management, 1999. **Address:** Claremont Behavioral Studies Institute, 250 W 1st St., Claremont, CA 91711, U.S.A. **Online address:** mlass@aol.com

LASSWELL, Marcia E. See **LASSWELL, Marcia.**

LAST, Cynthia G. American (born United States) **Genres:** Psychology. **Career:** University of Pittsburgh School of Medicine, assistant professor of child psychiatry, 1984-88, associate professor of child psychiatry, 1988-89, adjunct associate professor of psychiatry, 1990-95, adjunct professor of psychiatry, 2001-08, Child and Adolescent Anxiety Disorder Programs, director, Child and Adolescent Anxiety Clinic, director, 1985-89; Nova Southeastern University, Child and Adolescent Anxiety Disorder Programs, director, Anxiety Treatment Center, director, 1989-99, Center for Psychological Studies, professor of psychology, 1989-2001; Health Professions Division, professor of behavioral sciences, 1999-2001. Writer. **Publications:** (Ed. with M. Hersen) Behavior Therapy Casebook, 1985; (ed. with M. Hersen) Issues in Diagnostic Research, 1987; (ed. with M. Hersen) Handbook of Anxiety Disorders, 1988; (ed. with M. Hersen) Child Behavior Therapy Casebook, 1988; (with R.G. Klein) Anxiety Disorders in Children, 1989; (ed. with M. Hersen) Handbook of Child Psychiatric Diagnosis, 1989; (ed. with M. Hersen) Handbook of Child and Adult Psychopathology: A Longitudinal Perspective, 1990; (ed. with R.T. Ammerman and M. Hersen) Handbook of Prescriptive Treatments for Children and Adolescents, 1993, 2nd ed., 1999; (ed.) Anxiety across the Lifespan: A Developmental Perspective, 1993; (ed. with M. Hersen) Adult Behavior Therapy Casebook, 1994; The 5 Reasons Why We Overeat: How to Develop a Long-term Weight-Control Plan That's Right for You, 1999; Help for Worried Kids: How Your Child Can Conquer Anxiety and Fear, 2006; When Someone You Love is Bipolar: Help and Support for You and Your Partner, 2009. **Address:** Glades St. Andrews Professional Center, 2499 Glades Rd., Ste. 205A, Boca Raton, FL 33431, U.S.A. **Online address:** info@drcynthialast.com

LASZLO, Pierre. French (born France), b. 1938. **Genres:** Chemistry, Biology, History. **Career:** Princeton University, research associate, 1962-63, assistant professor, 1966-70; University of Paris, instructor, 1963-68; University of Liége, professor, 1970-90, professor emeritus, 1999-; école Polytechnique,

professor, 1986-99, professor emeritus, 1999-; University of Connecticut, visiting professor; University of Kansas, visiting professor; University of California, visiting professor; University of Colorado, visiting professor; University of Chicago, visiting professor; Cornell University, visiting professor; Johns Hopkins University, visiting professor; University of Lausanne, visiting professor; University of Hamburg, visiting professor; University of Toulouse, visiting professor. Writer. **Publications:** ENGLISH LANGUAGE: GENERAL INTEREST: Salt: Grain of Life, 2001; Communicating Science: A Practical Guide, 2006; Citrus: A History, 2007. ENGLISH LANGUAGE: TECHNICAL: (with P.J. Stang) Organic Spectroscopy; Principles and Applications, 1977. (ed.) Protons and Ions Involved in Fast Dynamic Phenomena: Proceedings of the 30th International Meeting of the Société de Chimie Physique, Thiais, 28 November-2 December, 1977, 1978. (ed.) NMR of Newly Accessible Nuclei, 1983. (ed.) Molecular Correlates of Biological Concepts, 1986; (ed.) Preparative Chemistry Using Supported Reagents, 1987; (with M. Balogh) Organic Chemistry Using Clays, 1993; Organic Reactions, Simplicity and Logic, 1995; FRENCH LANGUAGE: (with R. Halleux) Représentations anciennes du savoir chimique et alchimique: catalogue, 1980; Cours de chimie organique, 1984; Logique de la synthése organique, 1993; La parole des choses, ou, le langage de la chimie, 1993; Résonances de la synthése organique: exemples et illustrations, 1993; La vulgarisation scientifique, 1993; La leon de choses, 1995; Qu'est-ce que l'alchimie?, 1996; (with S. Riviere) Sciences du parfum, 1997; Abrege de chimie industrielle, 1998; Chemins et savoirs du sel, 1998; Le savoir des plantes, 1999; Quelques concepts directeurs de la chimie organique, 2000; Terre et eau, air et feu, 2000; Miroir de la chimie, 2000; L'architecture du vivant, 2002; Peut-on doire l'eau du Robinet, 2002; Pourquoi la mer est-elle bleue?, 2002; Le phénix et la salamandre: histoires de sciences, 2004; Copal, Benjoin, Colophane ..., 2007. Works appear in anthologies. Contributor to periodicals. **Address:** France. **Online address:** pierre@pierrelaszlo.net

LATEEF, Tolen S. See **SANDERS, Clinton R.**

LATEINER, Donald. American (born United States), b. 1944. **Genres:** Classics, Communications/Media, Industrial Relations, Language/Linguistics, Literary Criticism And History, Romance/Historical, Military/Defense/Arms Control. **Career:** University of Pennsylvania, assistant professor of classical studies, 1972-79; Ohio Wesleyan University, assistant professor, associate professor, 1979-87, professor of humanities-classics, 1987-92, John R. Wright professor of Greek, 1992-; Lateiner Publishing, editor, 1985-. **Publications:** (Ed. with S.A. Stephens) Selected Papers of Lionel Pearson, 1983; The Historical Method of Herodotus, 1989; Sardonic Smile: Nonverbal Behavior in Homeric Epic, 1995; (ed.) The Histories of Herodotus, 2004; (ed.) The History of the Peloponnesian War, 2006. Contributor to periodicals. **Address:** Department of Humanities-Classics, Ohio Wesleyan University, 216 Sturges Hall, 61 S Sandusky St., Delaware, OH 43015-2333, U.S.A. **Online address:** dglatein@owu.edu

LATELL, Brian. American (born United States), b. 1941. **Genres:** History, Politics/Government. **Career:** Georgetown University, adjunct professor, 1978-; National Intelligence Council, national intelligence officer for Latin America, 1990-94; Center for the Study of Intelligence, director, 1994-98; Center for Strategic and International Studies, senior associate. Writer. **Publications:** Mexico at the Crossroads: The Many Crises of the Political System, 1986; (ed. with D.A. Day and J.M. Logsdon) Eye in the Sky: The Story of the Corona Spy Satellites, 1998; The Cuban Military and Transition Dynamics, 2003; After Fidel: The Inside Story of Castro's Regime and Cuba's Next Leader, 2005. **Address:** Center for Strategic and International Studies, 1800 K St. NW, Washington, DC 20006, U.S.A.

LATHAM, Alison. American (born United States) **Genres:** Music, Reference. **Career:** Royal Opera House, editor. **Publications:** (Ed. with S. Sadie) Stanley Sadie's Brief Guide to Music, 1986, 3rd ed., 1993; (ed. with S. Sadie) The Norton/Grove Concise Encyclopedia of Music, 1988; An End and a New Beginning, 1995; (ed. with R. Parker) Verdi in Performance, 2001; (ed. with S. Sadie) The Cambridge Music Guide, 2001; (ed.) The Oxford Companion to Music, 2002; (ed.) Sing, Ariel: Essays and Thoughts for Alexander Goehr's Seventieth Birthday, 2003; (ed.) The Oxford Dictionary of Musical Works, 2004; (ed.) Oxford Dictionary of Musical Terms, 2004. **Address:** c/o Author Mail, Oxford University Press, 198 Madison Ave., New York, NY 10016, U.S.A.

LATHER, Patti. American (born United States), b. 1948. **Genres:** Women's Studies And Issues, Education, Sciences. **Career:** Crawfordsville School System, high school teacher in English, history and American Studies, 1973-77; Indiana University, Department of Curriculum, teaching assistant, 1979-83; Mankato State University, associate professor in women's studies, 1983-88, Women's Studies Department, acting chair, 1985, 1986-87; The Ohio State University, assistant professor, 1988-97, professor of education, 1997-, Division of Comparative Studies, associated faculty, Women's Studies Graduate Faculty, associate; University of British Columbia, visiting professor, 1994; University of Goteberg, visiting professor, 1997; York University, visiting professor; Danish Pedagogy Institute, visiting professor. Writer. **Publications:** Getting Smart: Feminist Research and Pedagogy with/in the Postmodern, 1991; Feminist Research in Education: Within/Against, 1991; (with L. Richardson and L. Daisi) Big Talk: Academic Writing and Feminist Survival, 1991; (with C. Smithies) Troubling the Angels: Women Living with HIV/AIDS, 1997; Getting Lost: Feminist Efforts Toward a Double(d) Science, 2007; Engaging Science Policy: From The Side Of The Messy, 2010. Contributor to books and professional journals. **Address:** College of Education & Human Ecology, Ohio State University, 101B Ramseyer Hall, 29 W Woodruff, Bldg. 090, Columbus, OH 43210, U.S.A. **Online address:** lather.1@osu.edu

LATHEY, Gillian. British (born England), b. 1949. **Genres:** Literary Criticism And History, Young Adult Fiction. **Career:** Roehampton University, teacher trainer, 1989, senior lecturer in language in education, 1990-99, National Centre for Research in Children's Literature, deputy director, 1999-2004, reader in children's literature, 2003-, director, 2004-; Marsh Award for Children's Literature in Translation, administrator. Writer. **Publications:** The Impossible Legacy: Identity and Purpose in Autobiographical Children's Literature Set in the Third Reich and the Second World War, 1999; (ed.) The Translation of Children's Literature: A Reader, 2006; Role of Translators in Children's Literature: Invisible Storytellers, 2010. Contributor to books and professional journals. **Address:** National Centre for Research, in Children's Literature, School of Arts, Roehampton University, Fincham 101, Roehampton Ln., London, GL SW15 5PJ, England. **Online address:** g.lathey@roehampton.ac.uk

LATHROP, Douglas A. American (born United States), b. 1971. **Genres:** Politics/Government, Writing/Journalism, International Relations/Current Affairs, Public/Social Administration. **Career:** American Legislative Exchange Council, director of tax policy, 1999-2001; U.S. House of Representatives, senior legislative assistant, 2001-03, legislative director, 2003-; George Washington University, assistant professorial lecturer of entitlements policy, congressional ethics, Graduate School of Political Management, adjunct professor; New York Life Insurance Co., Office of Government Affairs, corporate vice president. Writer. **Publications:** The Campaign Continues: How Political Consultants and Campaign Tactics Affect Public Policy, 2003. **Address:** The George Washington University, The Graduate School of Political Management, 805 21St St. NW, Ste. 401, Washington, DC 20052, U.S.A. **Online address:** doug.lathrop@mail.house.gov

LATHROP, John. See **LATHROP, John P.**

LATHROP, John P. (John Lathrop). British/Canadian (born Canada), b. 1951. **Genres:** Novels. **Career:** Operations trainer for government ministries and writer. **Publications:** The Desert Contract: A Novel, 2008. **Address:** David Higham Associates, 5-8 Lower John St., Golden Sq., London, GL W1F 9HA, England.

LATKO, David W. American (born United States) **Genres:** Economics, Young Adult Non-fiction, Business/Trade/Industry. **Career:** Latko Wealth Management Ltd., founder and president, 1980-. Writer. **Publications:** NONFICTION: Financial Strategies for Today's Widow: Coping with the Economic Challenges of Losing a Spouse, 2003; Everybody Wants Your Money: The Straight-talking Guide to Protecting (and Growing) the Wealth You Worked So Hard to Earn, 2006. **Address:** Latko Wealth Management Ltd., 45 E Colorado Ave., Frankfort, IL 60423, U.S.A. **Online address:** david.latko@lpl.com

LATOURELLE, René. Canadian (born Canada), b. 1918. **Genres:** Theology/Religion, Social Sciences, History. **Career:** Ordained Roman catholic priest, 1950; University of Montreal, professor of fundamental theology, 1956-59; Pontifical Gregorian University, professor of fundamental theology,

1959-89, dean of faculty of theology, 1961-64, 1970-76, 1981-84. Writer. **Publications:** étude sur les écrits de Saint Jean de Brébeuf, 1952; Theology of Revelation, 1966; Théologie, Science su Salut, 1968; Christ et l'église, Signes du Salut, 1971; Accès à Jésus par les évangiles: Histoire et Herméneutique, 1978; Homme et ses problèmes dans la lumière du Christ, 1981; Miracles de Jésus et théologie du miracle, 1986; Jean de Brébeuf, 1993; Du Protege au Miracle, 1995; Pierre-Joseph-Marie Chaumonot: Compagnon des Martyrs Canadiens, 1998; François-Joseph Bressani: Missionnaire et Humaniste, 1999; Quel Avenir pour le Christianisme?, 2000; L'Infini du Sens: Jesus Christ, 2000; Seigneur Jesus: Montre Nous ton Visage, 2001; A la Recherche du Sens Perdu: Temoins du Sens Revele, 2004. EDITOR: (with G. O'Collins) Problems and Perspectives of Fundamental Theology, 1982; Gesú Rivelatore: Teologia Fondamentale, 1988; Vatican II, Assessment and Perspectives: Twenty-five Years After (1962-1987), 3 vols., 1989; (with R. Fisichella) Dictionary of Fundamental Theology, 1994. Contributor to periodicals. **Address:** Center of Vimont, 3200 Chemin de la Cote, Ste. Catherine, Montreal, QC H3T 1C1, Canada.

LATREILLE, Stanley. American (born United States) **Genres:** Law, Young Adult Fiction. **Career:** 44th Circuit Ct., chief justice, retired. Writer. **Publications:** Perjury, 1998. **Address:** 204 S Highlander Way, Ste. 5, Howell, MI 48843, U.S.A.

LATTIMORE, Jessie. See **FONTES, Montserrat.**

LATTIMORE, Jessie. See **DRESSER, Norine.**

LATTIN, Don. American (born United States), b. 1953. **Genres:** Theology/Religion, Biography. **Career:** San Francisco Chronicle, staff; News21, managing editor; University of California, Graduate School of Journalism, religious writing instructor, lecturer. Writer, consultant and commentator. **Publications:** (With R. Cimino) Shopping for Faith: American Religion in the New Millennium, 1998, rev. ed., 2002; Following Our Bliss: How the Spiritual Ideals of the Sixties Shape Our Lives Today, 2003; Jesus Freaks: A True Story of Murder and Madness on the Evangelical Edge, 2007; The Harvard Psychedelic Club: How Timothy Leary, Andrew Weil, Ram Dass and Huston Smith Killed the Fifties and Ushered in a New Age for America, 2010. Contributor to periodicals. **Address:** c/o Amy Rennert, The Amy Rennert Agency Inc., 1550 Tiburon Blvd., Ste. 302, Tiburon, CA 94920, U.S.A. **Online address:** don@donlattin.com

LATTIS, James M. American (born United States), b. 1954. **Genres:** Astronomy, History, Sciences, Theology/Religion. **Career:** University of Wisconsin, Space Astronomy Laboratory, faculty associate, Space Place, co-founder and director. Writer. **Publications:** Between Copernicus and Galileo, 1994; (comp. with J. Tedeschi) The Italian Reformation of the Sixteenth Century and the Diffusion of Renaissance Culture, 2000. **Address:** Space Astronomy Laboratory, University of Wisconsin, 2514 Sterling Hall, 1150 University Ave., Madison, WI 53706-1302, U.S.A. **Online address:** lattis@sal.wisc.edu

LATUCHIE, Karen. American (born United States), b. 1954?. **Genres:** Novels, Young Adult Fiction. **Career:** Alfred A. Knopf, editor, 1977-. Writer. **Publications:** The Honey Wall, 2004. **Address:** c/o Author Mail, W. W. Norton Co. Inc., 500 5th Ave., New York, NY 10110-0002, U.S.A.

LATYNIN, Leonid (Aleksandrovich). Russian (born Russia), b. 1938?. **Genres:** Design, Novels, Poetry, Translations, Adult Non-fiction, Literary Criticism And History. **Career:** Khudozhestvennaya Literatura Publishing House, Youth Magazine, Poetry Division, radio commentator, 1962-74; Central Asian poetry, translator, 1980. Writer. **Publications:** Patriarshie prudy, 1977; V chuzhom gorode: Grimer i Muza: Roman, 1988; Obriad: Stikhotvoreniia, 1965-1991, 1993; Spiashchii vo vremia zhatvy (novel), 1993, trans. as Sleeper at Harvest Time, 1994; Stavr and Sara, 1994; Glas 21: The Face-Maker and the Muse, 1999; Foneticheskiĭ shum. Evgenii Vitkovskiĭ: Dialogi, 2002; Russkaya Pravda, 2003; Dom Vrat: Kniga Stikhotvorenii, 2008; Prazdnyĭ dnevnik, 2010. **Address:** Russian Press Service, 1805 Crain St., Evanston, IL 60202, U.S.A. **Online address:** mail@latynin.ru

LATZER, Barry. American (born United States), b. 1945?. **Genres:** Criminology/True Crime, Law. **Career:** City University of New York, John Jay College of Criminal Justice, Department of Government (now Department of Political Science), professor of law, 1978-, Graduate Center, professor, 1978-; Fordham University, lecturer, 1984-; Universita degli Studi di Trento, lecturer, 1996-. Writer. **Publications:** State Constitutions and Criminal Justice, 1991; State Constitutional Criminal Law, 1995; (contrib.) Constitutional Politics in the States, 1996; (contrib.) Crime and Justice in New York City, 1998; Death Penalty Cases: Leading U.S. Supreme Court Cases on Capital Punishment, 1998, 3rd ed., 2011. Contributor of articles to books and journals. **Address:** Department of Government, John Jay College of Criminal Justice, City University of New York, Rm. 3246N, 445 W 59th St., New York, NY 10019, U.S.A. **Online address:** blatzer@jjay.cuny.edu

LAUBACH, David C. American/German (born Germany), b. 1939. **Genres:** Literary Criticism And History, Novels, Mythology/Folklore, Young Adult Non-fiction. **Career:** Loyalsock Township High School, Department of English, head, 1960-69; Lycoming College, adjunct teacher, 1964-69; Williamsport Community College, drama instructor, 1966-69; Hampshire Lodge, teacher in humanities, 1967-68; St. Nicholas Grammar School, English teacher, 1969-70; Westfield School District, Department of English, director, 1970-85; Maxwell Vacation School, director, 1971-77; University of Massachusetts, adjunct teacher in writing, 1977-85; Colonial School District, director of language arts and reading, 1985-87; Kutztown University, associate professor of English, 1988-. Writer. **Publications:** Introduction to Folklore (nonfiction), 1980; Growing Up Amish (novel), 1998. Contributor of articles to books and periodicals. **Address:** English Department, Kutztown University, 241 Lytle Hall, Kutztown, PA 19530, U.S.A. **Online address:** laubach@kutztown.edu

LAUBENBACHER, Reinhard C. German (born Germany), b. 1954. **Genres:** Mathematics/Statistics. **Career:** New Mexico State University, assistant professor, 1985-90, associate professor, 1990-96, professor of mathematics, 1996-2001; Cornell University, visiting associate professor, 1990, 1993; Los Alamos National Laboratories, visiting faculty, 1999-; Virginia Tech, Virginia Bioinformatics Institute, research professor, 2001-, director, Department of Mathematics, professor, 2001-, Wake Forest University, School of Biomedical Engineering and Sciences, affiliate faculty; Wake Forest University, Department of Cancer Biology, adjunct professor. **Publications:** (Trans.) Theory of Algebraic Invariants, 1993; (with D. Pengelley) Mathematical Expeditions: Chronicles by the Explorers, 1999; (ed.) Modeling and Simulation of Biological Networks, 2007. **Address:** Department of Mathematics, Virginia Bioinformatics Institute, Virginia Tech, Washington St., Blacksburg, VA 24061-0477, U.S.A. **Online address:** reinhard@vbi.vt.edu

LAUBER, Volkmar. Austrian (born Austria), b. 1944. **Genres:** Economics, Environmental Sciences/Ecology, Politics/Government, Business/Trade/Industry, Engineering. **Career:** University of South Florida, visiting instructor in political science, 1976-77; West Virginia Wesleyan College, Department of Government, assistant professor of government and chair, 1977-82; Johns Hopkins University, Bologna Center, assistant professor of European studies, 1979-80; University of Salzburg, professor of political science, 1982-, chairman of department, 1985-90. Writer. **Publications:** (Contrib.) The Fifth Republic at Twenty, 1981; (contrib.) After the Second Oil Crisis, 1982; The Political Economy of France from Pompidou to Mitterrand, 1983; The Politics of Economic Policy: France, 1976-1982, 1983. EDITOR: (co-ed. and contrib.) Hand buch des Politischen Systems Osterreichs, 1991; Contemporary Austrian Politics, 1996; (with A. Mol and D. Liefferink) Voluntary Approach to Environmental Policy: Joint Environmental Policy-making in Europe, 2000; Switching to Renewable Power: A Framework for the 21st Century, 2005. Works appear in anthologies. Contributor to journals. **Address:** Department of Political Science, University of Salzburg, Rm. 2033, Rudolfskai 42, Politikwissenschaft, Salzburg, 5020, Austria. **Online address:** volkmar.lauber@sbg.ac.at

LAUCK, Jon K. American (born United States), b. 1971. **Genres:** Agriculture/Forestry, Politics/Government. **Career:** University of Iowa, instructor, 1995-96; Davenport, Evans, Hurwitz and Smith LLP (law firm), associate, 2000-; South Dakota State University, adjunct professor, 2001, 2002; senior advisor and counselor. Writer. **Publications:** American Agriculture and the Problem of Monopoly: The Political Economy of Grain Belt Farming, 1953-1980, 2000; Daschle vs. Thune: Anatomy of a High-Plains Senate Race, 2007; Prairie Republic: The Political Culture of Dakota Territory, 1879-1889, 2010; (ed. with J.E. Miller and D.C. Simmons) Plains Political Tradition: Essays on South Dakota Political Culture, 2011. **Address:** Davenport, Evans, Hurwitz and Smith L.L.P., 206 W 14th St., PO Box 1030, Sioux Falls, SD 57101-1030, U.S.A. **Online address:** jlauck@hotmail.com

LAUDER, Robert E(dward). American (born United States), b. 1934. **Genres:** Philosophy, Theology/Religion. **Career:** Ordained Roman Catholic priest; Cathedral College of the Immaculate Conception, instructor in philosophy, 1967-85; St. John's University, professor of philosophy, 1985-. Writer. **Publications:** Loneliness Is for Loving, 1978, rev. ed., 1988; The Love Explosion: Human Experience and the Christian Mystery, 1979; Hope, the Christian Response to Chicken Little, 1980; The Priest as a Person: A Philosophy of Priestly Existence, 1981; Becoming a Christian Person, 1984; Rediscovering Myself and Others in God: The Never-Ending Dialogue, 1987; God, Death, Art and Love: The Philosophical Vision of Ingmar Bergman, 1989; Nothing but Love Health and Holiness Through Intimacy With God, 1993; Walker Percy: Prophetic, Existentialist, Catholic Storyteller, 1996; Your Sacred Story: How Relationships, Sexuality and Spirituality Shape Us, 1998; Magnetized by God: Religious Encounters Through Film, Theater, Literature and Art, 2004; Love and Hope: Pope Benedict's Spirituality of Communion, 2010. **Address:** Department of Philosophy, St. John's University, Rm. B30-13, St. John Hall, 8000 Utopia Pkwy., Queens, NY 11439, U.S.A. **Online address:** lauderr@stjohns.edu

LAUGHLAND, John. French/British (born England), b. 1963. **Genres:** Politics/Government, History, Social Sciences. **Career:** Sorbonne Centre for the History of Central Europe, researcher; Institute of Democracy and Cooperation, director of studies, 2008-; Institut d'etudes Politiques de Paris, lecturer; European Foundation (a think tank), European director. Writer. **Publications:** The Death of Politics: France under Mitterand, 1994; Tainted Source: The Undemocratic Origins of the European Idea, 1998; Le Tribunal Pénal International: Gardien du nouvel ordre mondial, 2003; (ed. with M. Korinman) The Long March to the West: Twenty-first Century Migration in Europe and the Greater Mediterranean Area, 2007; (ed. with M. Korinman) Shia Power: Next Target Iran? 2007; Schelling Versus Hegel: From German Idealism to Christian Metaphysics, 2007; Travesty: The Trial of Slobodan Milosević and the Corruption of International Justice, 2007; A History of Political Trials: From Charles I to Saddam Hussein, 2008; (ed. with M. Korinman) Israel on Israel, 2008; (ed. with M. Korinman) Russia: A New Cold War? 2008. Contributor to magazines. **Address:** Institute of Democracy and Cooperation, 63 bis, Rue de Varenne, Paris, 75007, France.

LAUGHTON, Bruce (Kyle Blake). Canadian/British (born England), b. 1928. **Genres:** Art/Art History. **Career:** Birmingham City Art Gallery, assistant, 1954-56; University of London, Courtauld Institute of Art, teaching collection librarian, 1958-71; Courtauld Institute of Art, teaching collection librarian 1960-71; Queen's University, professor of art history, 1971-93; head of department, 1983-89, emeritus professor, 1993-; Royal Society of Arts, fellow. Writer. **Publications:** Philip Wilson Steer, 1860-1942, 1971; (co-author) The James Carling Illustrations to Edgar Allan Poe's The Raven, 1982; The Euston Road School: A Study in Objective Painting, 1986; The Drawings of Daumier and Millet, 1991; Honor Daumier, 1996; William Coldstream 1908-1987, 2004. Contributor to books and periodicals. **Address:** Department of Art, Queen's University, Rm. 211, Ontario Hall, 67 University Ave., Kingston, ON K7L 3N6, Canada. **Online address:** bl5@queensu.ca

LAUNER, Donald. American (born United States), b. 1926. **Genres:** Marine Sciences/Oceanography. **Career:** American Broadcasting Co., television master control engineer, engineering supervisor; Good Old Boat Magazine, contributing editor; Waterway Guide, field editor. **Publications:** A Cruising Guide to New Jersey Waters, 1995, rev. ed., 2004; Dictionary of Nautical Acronyms and Abbreviations, 2006; Lessons from My Good Old Boat, 2007; Navigation Through the Ages, 2009; The Galley-How Things Work: Plus Upgrading Ideas, 2009. Contributor of articles to magazines. **Address:** 842 Spar Dr., Forked River, NJ 08731-3028, U.S.A. **Online address:** launerdm@aol.com

LAUNIUS, Roger D. American (born United States), b. 1954. **Genres:** Air/Space Topics, History. **Career:** Camp Moore State Commemorative Area, museum manager, 1982; Military Airlift Command, Scott Air Force Base, historian, 1982-84; McKendree College, instructor, 1983-84; Ogden Air Logistics Center, Hill Air Force Base, Office of History, chief, 1984-86; Weber State College, adjunct professor, 1985-86; Air Force Systems Command, Andrews Air Force Base, deputy command historian, 1986-87; Military Airlift Command, command historian, 1987-90; National Aeronautics and Space Administration, faculty, chief historian, 1990-2002; Graceland College, adjunct professor, 1990-95; Florida Institute of Technology, Krieger lecturer, 1993; University of Alabama, honors lecturer, 1994; Anne Arundel Community College, adjunct professor, 1995-; Loyola College, History of Technology, lecturer, 1995; Smithsonian Institution, National Air and Space Museum, Division of Space History, Planetary Exploration Programs, curator, senior curator, chair. Writer. **Publications:** EDITOR: (with F.M. McKiernan) An Early Latter Day Saint History: The Book of John Whitmer, 1980; John Whitmer Historical Association Monograph Series, 1989; (with McKiernan and contrib.) Missouri Folk Heroes of the Nineteenth Century, 1989; New Series in NASA History, 1990; (with W.B. Spillman) Let Contention Cease: The Dynamics of Dissent in the Reorganized Church of Jesus Christ of Latter Day Saints, 1991, 2nd ed., 1993; (with L. Thatcher) Differing Visions: Dissenters in Mormon History, 1994; History of Rocketry and Astronautics, 1994; (with L.J. Lear) Exploring the unknown: Selected Documents in the History of the U.S. Civil Space Program, 1995; Organizing for the Use of Space: Historical Perspectives on a Persistent Issue, 1995; (with J.E. Hallwas) Cultures in Conflict: A Documentary History of the Mormon War in Illinois, 1995; (with J.E. Hallwas) Kingdom on the Mississippi Revisited: Nauvoo in Mormon History, 1996; (H.E. McCurdy) Spaceflight and the Myth of Presidential Leadership, 1997; Frontiers of Space Exploration, 1998; Innovation and the Development of Flight, 1999; (and intro.) U.S. Space Program and American Society, 1999; (with D.R. Jenkins) To Reach the High Frontier: A History of U.S. Launch Vehicles, 2002; (with J.M. Logsdon and R.W. Smith) Reconsidering Sputnik: Forty Years Since the Soviet Satellite, 2002; (with J. Coopersmith) Taking Off: A Century of Manned Flight, 2003; (with S.J. Dick) Critical Issues in the History of Spaceflight, 2006; (with S.J. Dick) Societal Impact of Spaceflight, 2007; (with A.K. Johnston) Smithsonian Atlas of Space Exploration, 2009; (with J.R. Fleming and D.H. Devorkin) Globalizing Polar Science: Reconsidering the International Polar and Geophysical Years, 2010; (with G.M. Green) Charlie Finley: The Outrageous Story of Baseball's Super Showman, 2010. MORMON HISTORY: Zion's Camp: Expedition to Missouri, 1834, 1984; The Kirtland Temple: A Narrative History, 1986, 2nd ed., 1990; (with L.E. Braby) The Restoration: Themes of a Growing Faith, 1987; Invisible Saints: A History of Black Americans in the Reorganized Church, 1988; Joseph Smith III: Pragmatic Prophet, 1988; Father Figure: Joseph Smith III and the Creation of the Reorganized Church, 1990. AEROSPACE HISTORY NASA: A History of the U.S. Civil Space Program, 1994. OTHERS: (with J.W. Leland) Interview with Colonel Gail S. Halvorsen, 1988; The Military Airlift Command: A Short History, 1941-1988, 1989; (with C.F. Cross) MAC and the Legacy of the Berlin Airlift, 1989; (with J.D. Hunley) An Annotated Bibliography of the Apollo Program, 1994; Apollo: A Retrospective Analysis, 1994; Alexander William Doniphan: Portrait of a Missouri Moderate, 1997; (with B. Ulrich) NASA & the Exploration of Space: With Works from the NASA Art Collection, 1998; (with J.K. Matheews) General Duane H. Cassidy, Commander in Chief United States Transportation Command and Commander in Chief Military Airlift Command, 1998; (with H.E. McCurdy) Imagining Space: Achievements, Predictions, Possibilities: 1950-2050, 2001; (with B.J. Dvorscak) C-5 Galaxy History: Crushing Setbacks, Decisive Achievements, 2001; Seasons in the Sun: The Story of Big League Baseball in Missouri, 2002; Space Stations: Base Camps to the Stars, 2003; Frontiers of Space Exploration, 2004; (with H.E. McCurdy) Robots in Space: Technology, Evolution and Interplanetary Travel, 2008. Contributor to books and magazines. **Address:** Division of Space History, National Air and Space Museum, Smithsonian Institution, NASM Rm. 3560, MRC 311, PO Box 37012, Washington, DC 20013-7102, U.S.A. **Online address:** launiusr@nasm.si.edu

LAURANT, Guillaume. French (born France) **Genres:** Novels, History. **Career:** Montorgueil Theatre, affiliater, 1988-92. Writer. **Publications:** NOVELS: Les annees porte fenetres, 2003; Un long dimanche de fiancailles, 2005; Happy Hand: Roman, 2006. Contributor to periodicals. **Address:** Catherine Winckelmuller, Agents Associes, 201 FBG Saint Honore, Paris, 75008, France.

LAUREN, Jillian. American (born United States), b. 1973?. **Genres:** Autobiography/Memoirs. **Career:** Writer and actor. **Publications:** Some Girls: My Life in a Harem (memoir), 2010. Contributor to books, magazines and periodicals. **Address:** Los Angeles, CA , U.S.A. **Online address:** jillianlauren@me.com

LAURENCE, Charles. American/British (born England), b. 1950. **Genres:** Social Sciences. **Career:** Daily Telegraph, foreign correspondent. Journalist and memoirist. **Publications:** The Social Agent: A True Intrigue of Sex, Spies, and Heartbreak behind the Iron Curtain, 2010. Contributor to newspapers and magazines. **Address:** c/o Rob McQuilkin, Lippincott Massie McQuilkin, 27 W 20th St., Ste. 305, New York, NY 10011, U.S.A.

LAURENCE, Janet. British (born England), b. 1937. **Genres:** Mystery/Crime/Suspense, Food And Wine, Novels, History, Criminology/True Crime. **Career:** J. Walter Thompson (advertising agency), secretary, 1956-59; Max Wilson (travel entrepreneur), personal assistant, 1960-65; Nielson, McCarthy (public relations firm), executive, 1965-70; Daily Telegraph, columnist; freelance public relations consultant. Writer. **Publications:** DARINA LISLE CRIME NOVELS: A Deepe Coffyn, 1989; A Tasty Way to Die, 1990; Hotel Morgue, 1991; Recipe for Death, 1993; Death and the Epicure, 1993; Death à la Provencale, 1995; Diet for Death, 1996; Death at the Table, 1997; Appetite for Death, 1998; The Mermaid's Feast, 2001. HISTORICAL CRIME NOVELS: Canaletto and the Case of Westminster Bridge, 1997; Canaletto and the Case of the Westminster Bridge, 1998; Canaletto and the Case of the Privy Garden, 1999; Canaletto and the Case of Bonnie Prince Charlie, 2002. COOKBOOKS: A Little French Cookbook, 1989; A Little Scandinavian Cookbook, 1990; A Little Coffee Cookbook, 1992; Just for Two, 1992; To Kill The Past (suspense novel), 1994; Simply Delicious, 2001; The Food and Cooking of Norway, 2007. OTHERS: A Taste of Somerset Guide to Good Food and Drink, 1989; AS JULIA LISLE: The Changing Years, 1993; A Perfect Match, 1996; Journeys from Home, 1997. Works appear in anthologies. **Address:** Conifers, Mayfield Close, Galhampton, Yeovil, SM BA22 7AX, England. **Online address:** janetlaurence@compuserve.com

LAURENCE, Ray. British (born England), b. 1963?. **Genres:** History. **Career:** University of Reading, lecturer, through 2005; University of Birmingham, research fellow and senior lecturer; University of Kent, Roman History and Archaeology, professor, Classical and Archaeological Studies, head, 2010-; Canterbury Heritage, chair. Archaeologist and writer. **Publications:** NONFICTION: Roman Pompeii: Space and Society, 1994, 2nd ed., 2006; (ed. with A. Wallace-Hadrill) Domestic Space in the Roman World: Pompeii and Beyond, 1997; (ed. with J. Berry) Cultural Identity in the Roman Empire, 1998; The Roads of Roman Italy: Mobility and Cultural Change, 1999; (ed. with C. Adams) Travel and Geography in the Roman Empire, 2001; (with M. Harlow) Growing Up and Growing Old in Ancient Rome: A Life Course Approach, 2002; (with A. Butterworth) Pompeii: The Living City, 2005; (ed. with M. Harlow) Age and Ageing in the Roman Empire, 2007; Roman Passions: A History of Pleasure in Imperial Rome, 2009; A Cultural History of Childhood and Family, 2010; (with S.E. Cleary and G. Sears) The City in the Roman West, c.250 BC-c.AD 250, 2011. Contributor to books. **Address:** Classical and Archaeological Studies, University of Kent, Rm. 160, Canterbury, KT CT2 7NF, England. **Online address:** r.laurence@kent.ac.uk

LAURENS, Jeannine. Belgian (born Belgium), b. 1950. **Genres:** History, Young Adult Non-fiction. **Career:** Provinciebestuur Oost-Vlaanderen, teacher, 1985-. Writer. **Publications:** (With R. Stallaerts) Historical Dictionary of the Republic of Croatia, 1995, 2nd ed., 2003. **Address:** The Scarecrow Press Inc., 4501 Forbes Blvd., Ste. 200, Lanham, MD 20706, U.S.A.

LAURENT, John (Angus). Australian (born Australia), b. 1947. **Genres:** Biology, Business/Trade/Industry. **Career:** Griffith University, School of Science, lecturer in history of science and technology. Writer. **Publications:** (With M. Campbell) The Eye of Reason: Charles Darwin in Australasia, 1987; (ed. and intro.) Tom Mann's Social and Economic Writing: A Pre-Syndicalist Selection, 1988; (with C. Illert) Toxic Red-Tides: A Plain English Report Upon Possible Sewage-Poisoning of the Entire South-West Pacific Ocean, 1990; (ed. with P.C. Candy) Pioneering Culture: Mechanics Institutes and School of Art in Australia, 1994; (co-author) Science Technology and Society: An Introduction, 1998; Cooperation: The Missing Word in Economics Text Books, 2000; (ed. with J. Nightingale) Darwinism and Evolutionary Economics, 2001; (ed.) Evolutionary Economics and Human Nature, 2003; (ed.) Henry George's Legacy in Economic Thought, 2005; (ed. with G. Cockfield and A. Firth) New Perspectives on Adam Smith's The Theory of Moral Sentiments, 2007. **Address:** School of Science, Griffith University, 170 Kessels Rd., Nathan, QL 4111, Australia.

LAURER, Joanie. See CHYNA.

LAURIE, Clayton D. American (born United States), b. 1954. **Genres:** History, Military/Defense/Arms Control. **Career:** American University, adjunct lecturer, 1984-90; U.S. Army Center of Military History, military historian, 1986-; University of Maryland, Department of History, lecturer in history, 1991-, adjunct associate professor; Center for the Study of Intelligence, Central Intelligence Agency, historian; National Reconnaissance Office, deputy and chief historian. Writer. **Publications:** The Propaganda Warriors: America's Crusade Against Nazi Germany, 1996; (with R.H. Cole) The Role of Federal Military Forces in Domestic Disorders, 1877-1945, 1997; (ed.) Industrialists in Olive Drab: The Emergency Operation of Private Industries During World War II, 1999; (ed. with R.C. Hall) Early Cold War Overflights, 1950-1956: Symposium Proceedings, 2003; The United States Army and Psychological Warfare Operations, 1918-1945, forthcoming; (ed.) The Emergency Operation of Industrial Facilities by the War Department During World War II, 1940-1945, forthcoming. Contributor of articles to journals. **Address:** Department of History, University of Maryland, Administration Bldg., 7th Fl., 1000 Hilltop Cir., Baltimore, MD 21250-0001, U.S.A. **Online address:** clalauri@umbc.edu

LAURIE, Edward James. American (born United States), b. 1925. **Genres:** Mystery/Crime/Suspense, Information Science/Computers, Literary Criticism And History. **Career:** San Jose State University, assistant professor, 1956-59, associate professor, 1959-63, professor of management, 1964-70, professor of marketing, 1971-, chairman of marketing/quantitative studies, 1971-, associate dean of academic studies, 1974-81, dean, 1981; International Business Machines, Systems Research Institute, faculty research fellow, 1962-63; School of Business, professor emeritus of marketing and quantitative studies, 1991-; Oregon State University, instructor; Washington State University, instructor; University of California, instructor; Colorado State University, instructor. Writer. **Publications:** Computer Systems in the United States, 1960; Computers and How They Work: IBM 1620, IBM 1401, IBM 650, 1963; Computer and Computer Languages, 1966; Modern Computer Concepts: The IBM 360 Series, 1970; Computer, Automation and Society, 1979; Today's Electronic Data Processing for Business, 1983; The Borgia Blade, 2001; A Little Pinch of Death, 2001; The Detective Club, 2001; A Ladder of Death, 2001; The Seven Keys of Sara Seldon, 2001; One Murder for Money, 2002. Contributor to journals. **Address:** School of Business, San Jose State University, San Jose, CA 95192, U.S.A.

LAURIE, Hugh. British (born England), b. 1959. **Genres:** Novels, Plays/Screenplays, Young Adult Non-fiction, Literary Criticism And History. **Career:** Writer and director. **Publications:** The Gun Seller (novel), 1996; The Paper Soldier, 2009. FRY AND LAURIE SERIES WITH S. FRY: A Bit More Fry and Laurie, 1991; A Bit of Fry and Laurie, 1992; Three Bits of Fry and Laurie, 1992; Fry and Laurie Bit No. 4, 1995. NON FICTION: (with I. Jackman) House M.D.: The Official Guide to the Hit Medical Drama, 2010. **Address:** The Gersh Agency, 232 N Canon Dr., Ste. 201, Beverly Hills, CA 90210-5302, U.S.A. **Online address:** hughlaurie.net@gmail.com

LAURIE, Peter. British (born England), b. 1937. **Genres:** Adult Non-fiction, Politics/Government, Information Science/Computers. **Career:** Sunday Times, freelance journalist for Vogue and other publications, 1962-79; Practical Computing, editor, 1979-82; Southdata Ltd. (software publishers), managing director, 1980-. Journalist and software publisher. **Publications:** Teenage Revolution, 1965; Drugs: Medical, Psychological and Social Facts, 1967, 2nd ed., 1971; Beneath the City Streets: A Private Enquiry into the Nuclear Preoccupation of Government, 1970, rev. ed. as Beneath the City Streets: A Private Enquiry into Government Preparations for National Emergency, 1979; Scotland Yard: A Personal Inquiry in US as Scotland Yard: A Study of the Metropolitan Police, 1970; Meet Your Friendly Social System, 1974; Electronics Explained: A Handbook for the Layman, 1980; The Micro Revolution: Living with Computers, 1981; The Computer Book, 1982; (with R. Bradbeer and P. De Bono) The Beginner's Guide to Computers, 1982; Joy of Computers, 1983; Databases: How to Manage Information on Your Micro, 1985; (with B. Laurie) Apache: The Definitive Guide, 1997, 3rd ed., 2002. **Address:** Southdata Ltd., 166 Portobello Rd., London, GL W11 2EB, England.

LAURIMORE, Jill Frances. American (born United States), b. 1947. **Genres:** Novels, Plays/Screenplays. **Career:** Writer. **Publications:** NOVELS: Going to Pot, 1999; Dinosaur Days, 1999; The Bloody English Women of the Maison Puce, 2000; Cherry Ice, 2003. Works appear in anthologies. **Address:** c/o Harvey Unna, Harvey Unna & Stephen Durbridge Ltd., 14 Beaumont Mews, Marylebone High St., London, GL W1N 4HE, England.

LAURSEN, John Christian. American (born United States), b. 1952?. **Genres:** Politics/Government, Theology/Religion, Law. **Career:** University of California, professor of political science, 1991-; University of Valencia, chair. Writer. **Publications:** The Politics of Skepticism in the Ancients, Montaigne, Hume and Kant, 1992. EDITOR: New Essays on the Political Thought of the Huguenots of the Refuge, 1995; (with C.J. Nederman) Difference and

Dissent: Religious Toleration in Medieval and Early Modern Europe, 1996; (with C.J. Nederman) Beyond the Persecuting Society: Religious Toleration before the Enlightenment, 1998; Religious Toleration: The Variety of Rites from Cyrus to Defoe, 1999; (trans. and intro.) The Edict of Religion and History and Diary of My Imprisonment, 2000; Millenarianism and Messianism in Early Modern European Culture, vol. IV: Continental Millenarians, 2001; Histories of Heresy in Early Modern Europe, 2002: Early French and German Defenses of Freedom of the Press, 2003; (with J. Zande) Early French and German Defenses of Freedom of the Press: Elie Luzac's Essay on Freedom of Expression, 1749 and Carl Friedrich Bahrdt's On freedom of the Press and Its Limits, 1787 in English Translation, 2003; (with I. Hunter and C.J. Nederman) Heresy in Transition: Transforming Ideas of Heresy in Medieval and Early Modern Europe, 2005; (and intro. with C. Masroori) The History of the Sevarambians: A Utopian Novel, 2006; (with H. Blom and L. Simonutti) Monarchisms in the Age of Enlightenment: Liberty, Patriotism and the Common Good, 2007; (with J.R.M. Neto and G. Paganini) Skepticism in the Modern Age: Building on the Work of Richard Popkin, 2009. **Address:** Department of Political Science, University of California, 2224 Watkins Hall, 900 University Ave., Riverside, CA 92521, U.S.A. **Online address:** johnl@ucr.edu

LAUSE, Mark A. American (born United States), b. 1950?. **Genres:** Social Sciences. **Career:** University of Illinois, teaching assistant, 1977-82; Columbia College, faculty, 1982-86; University of Cincinnati, McMicken College of Arts and Sciences, Department of Humanities and Social Sciences, faculty, 1989-95, visiting assistant professor, 1995-96, assistant professor, 1996-2003, Department of History, associate professor, 2003-08, professor, 2008-, Honors Program, faculty, 1992, 1997, College of Evening and Continuing Education, faculty, 1992-. Writer and historian. **Publications:** Some Degree of Power: From Hired Hand to Union Craftsman in the Preindustrial American Printing Trades, 1778-1815, 1991; The Civil War's Last Campaign: James B. Weaver, the Greenback-Labor Party & the Politics of Race & Section, 2001; Young America: Land, Labor and the Republican Community, 2005; Antebellum Crisis & America's First Bohemians, 2009; Race and Radicalism In The Union Army, 2009; Secret Society History of the Civil War, 2011. **Address:** McMicken College of Arts & Sciences, University of Cincinnati, 322 McMicken Hall, Cincinnati, OH 45221-0373, U.S.A. **Online address:** mark.lause@uc.edu

LAUTERBACH, Ann. American (born United States), b. 1942. **Genres:** Poetry, Art/Art History. **Career:** Thames & Hudson Publishers, editor, 1967-73; Saint Martin's School of Art, teacher, 1967-73; Institute of Contemporary Art, director of literature program, 1967-73; Rosa Esman Gallery, consultant, 1974-84; The Washburn Gallery, assistant director, 1984-86; Brooklyn College, assistant professor, 1985-86; City University of New York, City College, Theodore Goodman professor of creative writing, 1989-98; Princeton University, lecturer, 1989-90; Graduate Center of the University of New York, English professor, 1993-; Bard College, teacher and co-director of writing faculty, 1991-, David and Ruth Schwab II professor of language and literature, 1998-, Milton Avery Graduate School of the Arts, writing, co-chair, director, 1998-, M.F.A. Program, Writing Division, co-director; Columbia University, faculty; Princeton University, faculty; University of Iowa, faculty; Max Protetch Gallery, staff; Art Latitude Gallery, staff; Yale Graduate School of the Arts, visiting core critic. Writer. **Publications:** Vertical, Horizontal, 1971; Book One, 1975; Many Times, But Then, 1979; Later That Evening, 1981; Closing Hours, 1983; Sacred Weather, 1984; (with B. Boice) Greeks, 1985; Before Recollection, 1987; How Things Bear Their Telling, 1990; Clamor, 1991; And for Example, 1994; A Clown, Some Colors, a Doll, Her Stories, a Song, a Moonlit Cove, 1996; On a Stair, 1997; (with J. Brainard) Thripsis, 1998; (contrib.) David Smith: Ink Drawings from 1957, 2000; If in Time: Selected Poems, 1975-2000, 2001; Hum, 2005; Night Sky: Writings on the Poetics of Experience, 2005; Or to Begin Again, 2009; Given and the Chosen, 2011. **Address:** Department of English, Bard College, PO Box 5000, Annandale-On-Hudson, NY 12504-5000, U.S.A. **Online address:** lauterba@bard.edu

LAUTERBORN, Robert F. American (born United States), b. 1936. **Genres:** Marketing, Advertising/Public Relations, Business/Trade/Industry. **Career:** Syracuse Herald Journal, advertising sales representative, 1957-60; General Electric Co., staff, 1960-76; International Paper, director of marketing communications and corporate advertising, 1976-86; University of North Carolina at Chapel Hill, School of Journalism and Mass Communication, James L. Knight Professor of Advertising, 1986-, now professor emeritus; Morgan, Anderson and Consulting, principal; Hong Kong Baptist University, university fellow, 2009. **Publications:** (With D.E. Schultz and S.I. Tannenbaum)

Integrated Marketing Communications: Pulling It Together And Making It Work, 1992; (with D.E. Schultz and S.I. Tannenbaum) The New Marketing Paradigm, 1994; (with R. Hines) Print Matters: How to Write Great Advertising, 2008. **Address:** School of Journalism and Mass Communication, University of North Carolina at Chapel Hill, Carroll Hall 375, CB 3365, PO Box 3365, Chapel Hill, NC 27599, U.S.A. **Online address:** lauter@email.unc.edu

LAUTERSTEIN, Ingeborg. American/Austrian (born Austria), b. 1935. **Genres:** Novels. **Career:** Boston Author's Club, director, 1983-. Educator and writer. **Publications:** The Water Castle, 1980; Vienna Girl, 1986; Shoreland, 2005. Contributor to periodicals. **Address:** Lightning Source Inc., 1246 Heil Quaker Blvd., La Vergne, TN 37086-3515, U.S.A.

LAUTURE, Denizé. American/Haitian (born United States), b. 1946. **Genres:** Children's Fiction, Poetry, Picture/Board Books, Literary Criticism And History. **Career:** St. Thomas Aquinas College, assistant professor of French and Haitian culture, 1980-; children's book writer, 1980-. **Publications:** POETRY: The Blues of the Lightning Metamorphosis (in Creole), 1987; When the Denizen Weeps, 1989; The Black Warrior and Other Poems, 2006. PICTURE BOOKS: Father and Son, 1992; Running the Road to ABC, 1996; Mother and Twin Daughters, 2004. OTHERS: Madichon Sanba Dlo Nan Rivye Sensèa, 2004. Contributor to periodicals. **Address:** St. Thomas Aquinas College, M136, 125 Rte. 340, Sparkill, NY 10976-1050, U.S.A. **Online address:** dlauture@stac.edu

LAUX, Constance. Also writes as Connie Daniels, Connie Lane, Connie Deka. American (born United States), b. 1952. **Genres:** Young Adult Fiction, Romance/Historical, Horror, Novels, Literary Criticism And History. **Career:** Writer. **Publications:** ROMANCE NOVELS: Twilight Secrets, 1992; (as Connie Deka) Bright Promise, 1993; Moonlight Whispers, 1993; Earthly Delights, 1995; Touched by Magic, 1996; Devil's Diamond, 1998; Diamond Rain, 1999; Diamonds and Desire, 2000. ROMANCE NOVELS (as Connie Lane): Reinventing Romeo, 2000; Romancing Riley, 2002; Stranded at Cupid's Hideaway, 2002; Guilty Little Secrets, 2003; Christmas at Cupid's Hideaway, 2003; The Visount's Bawdy Bargain, 2003; Dirtly Little Lies, 2004; The Duke's Scandalous Secret, 2004; Sarah's Guide to Life, Love & Gardening, 2005; Knit Two Together, 2007. YOUNG ADULT HORROR: (as Zoe Daniels) Year of the Cat (trilogy) vol. I: The Dream, vol. II: The Hunt, vol. III: The Amulet, 1995; Blood Moon (trilogy), vol. I: The Curse, 1995, vol. II: The Fortune Teller, 1995, vol. III: The Reckoning, 1996; R.L. Stine's Ghosts of Fear Street, vol. VII: Fright Knight, 1996. Work appears in anthologies. **Address:** Writer's House, 21 W 26th St., New York, NY 10010, U.S.A. **Online address:** ctlaux@aol.com

LAVENDER, Abraham D(onald). American (born United States), b. 1940. **Genres:** Anthropology/Ethnology, Cultural/Ethnic Topics, Genealogy/Heraldry, Local History/Rural Topics, Politics/Government, Sex, Sociology, Sports/Fitness, Sports/Fitness. **Career:** University of Maryland, European Division, lecturer in psychology, 1967-68; St. Mary's College of Maryland, lecturer, 1972-73, assistant professor, 1973-74; University of Maryland-College Park, visiting assistant professor of sociology, 1974-77; University of Miami, assistant professor, 1977-79, associate professor of sociology, 1979-83, adjunct faculty, 1986-88; St. Thomas University, adjunct faculty, 1985-87; Florida International University, adjunct professor, 1986-91, assistant professor, 1991-92, associate professor, 1992-97, professor of sociology and anthropology, 1997-, President Navon Program for the Study of Sephardic and Oriental Jewry, professor, 2004-; Society for Crypto Judaic Studies, president, 2003-07; Journal for the Study of Sephardic and Mizrahi Jewry, book review editor, 2006-; HaLapid: Journal of Crypto-Judaic Studies, co-editor for academics, 2007-08; Journal of Spanish, Portuguese, and Italian Crypto Jews, founding editor-in-chief, 2008-. **Publications:** Ethnic Women and Feminist Values: Toward a New Value System, 1986; French Huguenots: From Mediterranean Catholics to White Anglo-Saxon Protestants, 1990; (with C.B. Steinberg) Jewish Farmers of the Catskills: A Century of Survival, 1995; Miami Beach 1920: The Making of a Winter Resort, 2002; Social Life in Early Miami Beach: From Mangroves and Mosquitoes to Mansions and Millionaires, forthcoming. EDITOR: (and comp.) A Coat of Many Colors: Jewish Subcommunities in the United States, 1977; (with A.S. Newson) Black Communities in Transition: Voices from South Florida, 1996. Contributor to books and periodicals. **Address:** Department of Sociology and Anthropology, Florida International University, Rm. 334, SIPA Bldg., University Pk. Campus, Miami, FL 33199, U.S.A. **Online address:** lavender@fiu.edu

LAVENDER, Will Ross. American (born United States), b. 1977. **Genres:** Novels. **Career:** Jefferson Community College, instructor in creative writing. Writer and academic. **Publications:** Obedience (novel), 2008. **Address:** Louisville, KY , U.S.A. **Online address:** willrlavender@gmail.com

LA VERE, David. American (born United States), b. 1957. **Genres:** History. **Career:** Northwestern State University, lecturer, 1989; Blinn Junior College, lecturer, 1990-93; Texas A&M University, lecturer, 1992; University of North Carolina, professor of history, 1993-. Writer. **Publications:** Life among the Texas Indians: The WPA Narratives, 1998; The Caddo Chiefdoms: Caddo Economics and Politics, 700-1835, 1998; Contrary Neighbors: Southern Plains and Removed Indians in Indian Territory, 2000; The Texas Indians, 2004; North Carolina's Shining Hour: Images and Voices from World War II, 2005; Looting Spiro Mounds: An American King Tut's Tomb, 2007. Contributor to periodicals and journals. **Address:** Department of History, University of North Carolina, 601 S College Rd., Wilmington, NC 28403, U.S.A. **Online address:** lavered@uncw.edu

LAVERY, Bryony. (Bryony Mary Lavery). British (born England), b. 1947. **Genres:** Plays/Screenplays, Art/Art History. **Career:** Les Oeufs Malades, artistic director, 1976-78; Extraordinary Productions, artistic director, 1979-80; Female Trouble, artistic director, 1981-83; Unicorn Theatre for Young People, resident dramatist, 1986-88; Gay Sweatshop, artistic director, 1989-91; Birmingham University, M.A. Playwriting, tutor, 1989-92; The Unicorn Theatre for Children, writer-in-residence. **Publications:** Wedding Story, 2000; More Light, 2001; Frozen, 2004; Plays One, 2007; Last Easter, 2007; (adapted) Bloody Chamber, 2008; The Wicked Lady, 2009; Beautiful Burnout, 2010. **Address:** c/o St. John Donald, PFD, Drury House, 34-43 Russell St., London, GL WC2B 5HA, England.

LAVERY, Bryony Mary. See **LAVERY, Bryony.**

LAVERY, David. American (born United States), b. 1949. **Genres:** Communications/Media, Film, Literary Criticism And History, Art/Art History. **Career:** College of St. Benedict, instructor in English, 1975-76; University of Florida, teaching assistant, 1978; University of North Florida, adjunct assistant professor of English, 1979-80; Seattle University, visiting assistant professor of English, 1980-81; East China Normal University, foreign expert in English, 1981; University of Alabama, interim assistant professor of English, 1981-83; Northern Kentucky University, assistant professor, 1983-88, associate professor of English, 1987-88, director of freshman English, 1986-88; University of Memphis, associate professor of communication and film studies, 1988-93; Middle Tennessee State University, professor of English, 1993-2006, 2008-, department head, 1993-97; Brunel University, School of Arts, professor and chair of film and television studies, 2006-08. Writer. **Publications:** Late for the Sky: The Mentality of the Space Age, 1992; Re-Weaving the Rainbow: The Thought of Owen Barfield, 2003; How to Gut a Book: Essay on Imagination and the Evolution of Consciousness, 2004; The Encyclopedia of Native American Literature, 2005; Investigating Angel, 2005; Nineteenth-Century American Fiction on Screen: An Anthology of Critical Essays, 2005; (with L. Porter) Unlocking the Meaning of Lost: An Unauthorized Guide, 2006, rev. ed., 2007; (with L. Porter and H. Robson) Lost's Buried Treasures: The Unofficial Guide to Everything Lost Fans Need to Know, 2007; (with L. Porter and H. Robson) Saving the World: A Guide to Heroes, 2007; American Television, 2008; The Essential Cult Television Reader, 2008; Screwball Television: The Gilmore Girls, 2008; Joss Whedon: A Creative Portrait, 2008; (with L. Porter and H. Robson) Finding Battlestar Galactica: An Unauthorized Guide, 2008. EDITOR AND CONTRIBUTOR: Full of Secrets: Critical Approaches to Twin Peaks, 1995; (with A. Hague and M. Cartwright) Deny All Knowledge: Reading the X-Files, 1996; This Thing of Ours: Investigating the Sopranos, 2002; (with A. Hague) Teleparody: Predicting/Preventing the TV Discourse of Tomorrow, 2002; (with R.V. Wilcox) Fighting the Forces: What's at Stake in Buffy the Vampire Slayer, 2002; (with S.L. Dunne) Seinfeld, Master of Its Domain: Revisiting Television's Greatest Sitcom, 2006; Reading Deadwood: A Western to Swear by, 2006; Reading The Sopranos: Hit TV from HBO, 2006; (with M. Byers) Dear Angela: Remembering Myso-called Life, 2007; Essential Cult TV Reader, 2010; (with D.S. Diffrient) Screwball Television: Critical Perspectives on Gilmore Girls, 2010; (with C. Burkhead) Joss Whedon: Conversations, 2011. Contributor of articles to books and periodicals. **Address:** Department of English, Middle Tennessee State University, 372 Peck Hall, 1301 E Main St., PO Box 70, Murfreesboro, TN 37132-0001, U.S.A. **Online address:** david.lavery@gmail.com

LAVIGNE, Louis-Dominique. Canadian (born Canada), b. 1949. **Genres:** Plays/Screenplays, Theatre. **Career:** Theatre de Quartier, founding member, co-artistic director; University of Quebec, teacher of creative writing. Screenwriter, director and actor. **Publications:** Après de Serge Mercier. Ti-Jésus, bonjour de Jean Frigon. As-tu peur des voleurs?, 1977; On est capable, 1981; (with D. Meilleur) Parasol, 1988; Le sous-sol des anges, 1991; Les 2 s'urs: théâtre, 2001; Glouglou, 2008; Coeur de la tempête: théâtre, 2010. **Address:** Theatre Department, University of Quebec, Case Postale 8888, Succursale Centre-Ville, Montreal, QC H3C 3P8, Canada.

LAVIN, Irving. American (born United States), b. 1927. **Genres:** Art/Art History, Essays. **Career:** Columbia University, Matthews Lecturer, 1957; Dumbarton Oaks, fellow, 1957-59; Vassar College, lecturer in art history, 1959-61; New York University, associate professor of art history, professor, 1963-73; Institute for Advanced Study, professor of historical studies, 1973-2001, professor emeritus, 2001-; Princeton University, Department of Art and Archeology, advisory council, 1973-; Pierpont Morgan Library, Franklin Jasper Walls lecturer, 1975; College Art Association, director, 1976-. Writer. **Publications:** Bernini and the Crossing of St. Peter's, 1968; Bernini and the Unity of the Visual Arts, 2 vol., 1980; (co-author) Drawings by Gianlorenzo Bernini: From the Museum der Bildenden: Exhibition and Catalogue, 1981; Bernin et l'Art de la Satire Social, 1987; Past-Present: Essays on Historicism in Art from Donatello to Picasso, 1993; Caravaggio e La Tour: La Luce Occulta di Dio, 2000; Visible Spirit: The Art of Gianlorenzo Bernini, 2007; (with M.A. Lavin) Rome, Italy, Renaissance: Essays in Art History Honoring Irving Lavin on his Sixtieth Birthday, 2008. EDITOR: (with J. Plummer) Studies in Late Medieval and Renaissance Painting in Honor of Millard Meiss, 2 vols., 1978; Gianlorenzo Bernini: New Aspects of His Art and Thought: A Commemorative Volume, 1985; World Art: Themes of Unity in Diversity: Acts of the XXVI the International Congress of the History of Art, 1986; (with W. Tronzo) Studies on Art and Archeology in Honor of Ernst Kitzinger on his Seventy-Fifth Birthday, 1987; (with M.A. Lavin) IL 60: Essays Honoring Irving Lavin on His Sixtieth Birthday, 1990; Meaning in the Visual Arts: Views from the Outside: A Centennial Commemoration of Erwin Panofsky (1892-1968), 1995; (with E. Panofsky) Three Essays on Style, 1995; Bernini e il Salvatore: La Buona Morte Nella Roma del Seicento, 1998; Santa Maria del Fiore: il Duomo di Firenze e laVergine Incinta, 1999. Contributor to books and periodicals. **Address:** School of Historical Studies, Institute for Advanced Study, Einstein Dr., Princeton, NJ 08540, U.S.A. **Online address:** lavin@ias.edu

LAVIN, Maud. American (born United States), b. 1954. **Genres:** Design, History, Photography, Women's Studies And Issues. **Career:** New York University, faculty; Yale University, faculty; City University of New York, Hunter College, faculty, 1981-; School of the Art Institute of Chicago, Department of Art History, Theory and Criticism, associate professor, professor, 1998-, graduate director, Department of Visual and Critical Studies, professor, 1998-, chair. Writer. **Publications:** Cut with the Kitchen Knife: The Weimar Photomontages of Hannah Höch, 1993; Clean New World: Culture, Politics, and Graphic Design, 2001; (ed.) The Business of Holidays, 2004; (ed.) The Oldest We've Ever Been: Seven True Stories of Midlife Transitions, 2008; Push Comes to Shove: New Images of Aggressive Women, 2010. Contributor to periodicals. **Address:** Department of Art History, Theory and Criticism, School of the Art Institute of Chicago, Rm. 605, MacLean Bldg., 112 S Michigan Ave., 6th Fl., Chicago, IL 60603-6105, U.S.A. **Online address:** mlavin@saic.edu

LAW, Clara. Australian/Chinese (born China), b. 1957. **Genres:** Plays/Screenplays, Film. **Career:** Director and writer. **Publications:** (With E.L. Fong) Floating Life, 1996. **Address:** Southern Star Film Sales, 8 W St., Level 10, North Sydney, NW 2060, Australia.

LAW, Ingrid. American (born United States), b. 1970. **Genres:** Novels. **Career:** Writer. **Publications:** Savvy (young adult novel), 2008. **Address:** Lafayette, CO , U.S.A. **Online address:** ingrid@ingridlaw.com

LAW, John. British (born England), b. 1946. **Genres:** Anthropology/Ethnology, Sociology, Humanities. **Career:** University of Keele, professor of sociology, social anthropology, 1973-98; Lancaster University, Department of Sociology, professor, 1998-2010, Centre for Science Studies, director; Open University, Faculty of Social Sciences, Department of Sociology, professor, 2010-, Centre for Research on Socio-cultural Change, co-director, 2010-. Writer. **Publications:** (With P. Lodge) Science for Social Scientists, 1984; (ed.) Power, Action, and Belief: A New Sociology of Knowledge?, 1986; (with G. Fyfe) Picturing Power: Visual Depiction and Social Relations, 1988; (ed.) A Sociology of Monsters, 1991; (ed. with W.E. Bijker) Shaping Technology/Building Society: Studies in Sociotechnical Change, 1992; Organizing Modernity, 1994; (ed. with J. Hassard) Actor Network Theory and After, 1999; (ed. with A. Mol) Complexities: Social Studies of Knowledge Practices, 2002; Aircraft Stories: Decentering the Object in Technoscience, 2002; After Method: Mess in Social Science Research, 2004. **Address:** Department of Sociology, Faculty of Social Sciences, Open University, Walton Hall, Milton Keynes, BK MK7 6AA, England. **Online address:** j.law@open.ac.uk

LAWDAY, David. French/British (born England), b. 1938?. **Genres:** Biography, Autobiography/Memoirs, History. **Career:** Reuters News Agency, journalist; U.S. News & World Report, Europe correspondent; The Economist, correspondent. **Publications:** Napoleon's Master: A Life of Prince Talleyrand, 2006; Danton: The Gentle Giant of Terror, 2009; The Giant of the French Revolution: Danton, A Life, 2nd ed., 2009. Contributor to journals. **Address:** A.M. Heath & Company Ltd., 6 Warwick Ct., Holborn, London, GL WC1R 5DJ, England.

LAWLER, Jennifer. American (born United States), b. 1965. **Genres:** Novels, Novellas/Short Stories. **Career:** National Writers Union, co-chair; instructor; University of California, faculty. Writer. **Publications:** The Martial Arts Encyclopedia, 1996; Songs of Life: The Meaning of Country Music, 1996; Weight Training for Martial Arts, 1998; The Curmudgeon's Guide To-Child-Free Travel: Exactly How and Precisely Where to Enjoy Idyllic Grownup Getaways, 1998; Martial Arts for Women: A Practical Guide, 1998; Drug Legalization: A Pro/Con Issue, 1999; The Secrets of Tae Kwon Do: Principles and Techniques for Beginners, 1999; Coaching Women in the Martial Arts, 1999; (with W.J. Jung) Freestyle Sparring, 2000; Cyberdanger and Internet Safety: A Hot Issue, 2000; Small-Business Ownership for Creative People, 2000; Small Business Ownership for Creative People, 2000; Drug Testing in Schools: A Pro/Con Issue, 2000; Tae Kwon Do for Women, 2001; Encyclopedia of Women in the Middle Ages, 2001; Punch!: Why Women Participate in Violent Sports, 2002; Kickboxing for Women, 2002; Martial Arts for Dummies, 2003; Dojo Wisdom: 100 Simple Ways to Become a Stronger Calmer More Courageous Person, 2003; (with H. Ziegler) Feng Shui Your Workspace for Dummies, 2003; (with J. Lawler) ASVAB for Dummies, 2003, 2nd ed., 2007; Dojo Wisdom for Writers: 100 Simple Ways to Become a More Inspired Successful and Fearless Writer, 2004; Feng Shui Your Garden for Dummies, 2004; Encyclopedia of the Byzantine Empire, 2004; Dojo Wisdom for Mothers: 100 Simple Ways to Become a Calmer Happier More Loving Parent, 2005; Then Will Come Night and Darkness, 2006; (with L. Kamienski) Training Women in the Martial Arts: A Special Journey, 2007; (with L.E. Shapiro) The Complete Idiot's Guide to Baby Brain Games, 2008. Contributor to periodicals. **Address:** PO Box 4147, Lawrence, KS 66046, U.S.A.

LAWLER, Nancy Ellen. Welsh/American (born United States) **Genres:** Bibliography, Military/Defense/Arms Control, History. **Career:** Oakton Community College, professor of economics and history, professor emeritus of economics and history. Writer. **Publications:** Soldiers of Misfortune: Ivoirien Tirailleurs of World War II, 1992; (ed. with J.O. Hunwick) The Cloth of Many Colored Silks: Papers on History and Society, Ghanaian and Islamic, in Honor of Ivor Wilks, 1996; Soldiers, Airmen, Spies, and Whisperers: The Gold Coast in World War II, 2001. Contributor to periodicals. **Address:** c/o Author Mail, Ohio University Press, Scott Quadrangle, 1 Ohio University, Athens, OH 45701-2979, U.S.A.

LAWLER, Patrick. American (born United States), b. 1948. **Genres:** Plays/Screenplays, Poetry. **Career:** Syracuse University, teaching assistant and instructor of writing courses, 1977-78, 1982-90; Onondaga Community College, tutor and adjunct instructor, 1978-; Community Writers' Project, director, 1988-89; State University of New York, College of Environmental Science and Forestry, assistant professor of technical communications and writing project coordinator, 1990-, associate professor of environmental studies, writing program, director, now professor emeritus; Le Moyne College, adjunct professor of English. Writer. **Publications:** POETRY: A Drowning Man Is Never Tall Enough, 1990; Reading a Burning Book, 1994; Feeding the Fear of the Earth, 2006. FORTHCOMING: Breathe a Word of It; e(vaporating)-mail; House Dancing; Depth Finder: The Voices of the Loon Lake. Works appear in anthologies. **Address:** College of Environmental Science and Forestry, State University of New York, B5 Marshall Hall, 1 Forestry Dr., Syracuse, NY 13210, U.S.A. **Online address:** pjlawler@esf.edu

LAWLER, Peter Augustine. American (born United States), b. 1951. **Genres:** Politics/Government, History, Philosophy, Social Sciences. **Career:** Florida Southern College, assistant professor of political science, 1978-79; Berry College, assistant professor, 1979-83, associate professor of political science, 1983-, Dana professor of government and chair of the of government and international studies; Heritage Foundation, Salvatori fellow, 1991-93; American Political Science Association, chair, 1997-98; American Founding Society, George Washington Distinguished Professor; Perspectives on Political Science, executive editor. Writer. **Publications:** The Restless Mind: Alexis de Tocqueville on the Origin and Perpetuation of Human Liberty, 1993; Under God with Liberty: The Religious Dimension of the American Idea of Liberty, 1994; A Question of Values: John Galtungs Peace Research, 1995; American Views of Liberty, 1997; Postmodernism Rightly Understood: The Return to Realism in American Thought, 1999; Aliens in America: The Strange Truth about Our Souls, 2002; (intro.) American Republic: Its Constitution, Tendencies, and Destiny, 2003; Stuck with Virtue: The American Individual and Our Biotechnological Future, 2005; Homeless and At Home in America, 2007; Modern and American Dignity: Who We are As Persons and What that Means for Our Future, 2010. EDITOR: American Political Rhetoric: A Reader, 1982, (with R.M. Schaefer) 6th ed. as American Political Rhetoric: Essential Speeches and Writings on Founding Principles and Contemporary Controversies, 2010; (with J. Alulis) Tocqueville's Defense of Human Liberty: Current Essays, 1993; (with R.M. Schaefer) The American Experiment: Essays on the Theory and Practice of Liberty, 1994; (with J.M. Knippenberg) Poets, Princes, and Private Citizens, 1996; (with R.M. Schaefer and D.L. Schaefer) Active Duty: Public Administration As Democratic Statesmanship, 1998; (with D. McConkey) Community and Political Thought Today, 1998; (with D. Coates) New Labour in Power, 2000; (with D. McConkey) Social Structures, Social Capital, and Personal Freedom, 2000; (with D. McConkey) Faith, Reason, and Political Life Today, 2001; (with D. McConkey) Faith, Morality and Civil Society, 2003; Democracy and Its Friendly Critics: Tocqueville and Political Life Today, 2004; (with E.K. Busch) Democracy Reconsidered, 2009. **Address:** Department of Government and International Studies, Berry College, Evans 115, 2277 Martha Berry Hwy., NW, PO Box 5010, Mt. Berry, GA 30149-5010, U.S.A. **Online address:** plawler@berry.edu

LAWLESS, Jennifer L. American (born United States), b. 1975. **Genres:** Politics/Government. **Career:** Women's Housing and Economic Development Corp., staff, 1998; Brown University, assistant professor of political science and public policy, 2003-09; American University, Department of Government, associate professor, Women & Politics Institute, director, Politics & Gender, editor. Writer, academic and political scientist. **Publications:** (With R.L. Fox) It Takes a Candidate: Why Women Don't Run for Office, 2005, rev. ed., 2010; Becoming a Candidate: Political Ambition and the Decision to Run for Office, 2011. Contributor to journals. **Address:** Department of Government, American University, Ward - 213, 4400 Massachusetts Ave., Washington, DC 20016, U.S.A. **Online address:** lawless@american.edu

LAWLESS, John. See **BEST, Don(ald M.).**

LAWLOR, Clark. British (born England), b. 1965. **Genres:** Literary Criticism And History, Writing/Journalism. **Career:** Northumbria University, reader in eighteenth-century and romantic English literature, Northumbria Academy of English Language and Literature, director. Writer. **Publications:** (Contrib.) The European Spectator, vol. VI, 2003; (contrib.) Literature and Science 1660-1834, vol. II, 2003; (contrib.) Blackwell Companion to Eighteenth- Century Poetry, 2006; (contrib.) Laurence Sterne's Tristram Shandy: A Casebook, Casebooks in Criticism Series, 2006; Consumption and Literature: The Making of the Romantic Disease, 2007. Contributor to periodicals. **Address:** School of Arts & Social Sciences, Northumbria University, Rm. 410, Lipman Bldg., Newcastle upon Tyne, NM NE1 8ST, England. **Online address:** clark.lawlor@unn.ac.uk

LAWRENCE, Bruce B. American (born United States), b. 1941. **Genres:** Theology/Religion. **Career:** Duke University, Department of Religion, adjunct faculty, assistant professor, 1971-73, associate professor, 1973-79, professor of Islamic studies, 1979-, Inaugural Nancy and Jeffrey Marcus humanities professor of religion, acting chair, 1987-88, 1990-91, chair, 1996-2002, Program in Comparative Studies on Southern Asia, chair, 1976-78, Graduate Program in Religion, acting director, 1982-83, Comparative Area Studies Program, director, 1992-97, Duke Islamic Studies Center, inaugural director, 2004-; Rockefeller Foundation, Program, co-director; Carolina South Asian Center, interim director, 2005-; University of North Carolina Press, co-editor.

Religious Historian. **Publications:** RELIGIOUS HISTORY: Shahrastānī on the Indian Religions, 1976; An Overview of Sufi Literature in the Sultanate Period, 1206-1526 A.D., 1979; Defenders of God: The Fundamentalist Revolt against the Modern Age, 1989; (trans.) Nizam ad-din Awliya: Morals for the Heart: Conversations of Shaykh Nizam ad-din Awliya Recorded by Amir Hasan Sijzi, 1992; Shattering the Myth: Islam beyond Violence, 1998. EDITOR: Ibn Khaldun and Islamic Ideology, 1984; (with D. Gilmartin) Beyond Turk and Hindu: Rethinking Religions Ideologies in Islamicate South Asia, 2000; (with M. Cooke) Muslim Networks from Hajj to Hip Hop, 2005; (and intro.) Messages to the World: The Statements of Osama Bin Laden, 2005; (with A. Karim) On Violence: A Reader, 2007; (with L. Jones and R.M. Baum) Prophecy and Power, 2012. OTHERS: Notes from a Distant Flute, 1978; The Rose and the Rock, 1979; The Complete Idiot's Guide to Religions Online, 2000; New Faiths, Old Icons: Muslims and Other Asian Immigrants in American Religious Life, 2002; (with C.W. Ernst) Sufi Martyrs of Love: Chishti Sufism in South Asia and Beyond, 2002; (intro.) The Muqaddimah: An Introduction to History, 2005; Qur'an: A Biography, 2006. **Address:** Department of Religion, Duke University, 118 Gray Bldg., PO Box 90964, Durham, NC 27708, U.S.A. **Online address:** bbl@duke.edu

LAWRENCE, Caroline. British (born England), b. 1954. **Genres:** Mystery/Crime/Suspense, Young Adult Fiction. **Career:** Writer and teacher. **Publications:** ROMAN MYSTERIES SERIES: The Thieves of Ostia, 2001; The Secrets of Vesuvius, 2001; The Pirates of Pompeii, 2002; The Assassins of Rome, 2002; The Dolphins of Laurentum, 2003; The Twelve Tasks of Flavia Gemina, 2003; The Enemies of Jupiter, 2003; The Gladiators from Capua, 2004; The Colossus of Rhodes, 2005; The Fugitive from Corinth, 2005; The Sirens of Surrentum, 2006; The Charioteer of Delphi, 2006; Roman Mysteries Treasury, 2007; The Code of Romulus, 2007; The Slave-Girl from Jerusalem, 2007; Trimalchio's Feast and Other Mini-Mysteries, 2007; The Beggar of Volubilis, 2007; The First Roman Mysteries Quiz Book, 2007; The Second Roman Mysteries Quiz Book, 2007; From Ostia to Alexandra with Flavia Gemina, 2008; The Scribes from Alexandria, 2008; The Prophet from Ephesus, 2009; Man from Pomegranate Street, 2009. OTHERS: Legionary from Londinium and Other Mini-Mysteries, 2010; Case of the Deadly Desperados, 2012. **Address:** Orion Children's Books, Orion House, 5 Upper St. Martin's Ln., London, GL WC2H 9EA, England. **Online address:** caroline@romanmysteries.com

LAWRENCE, C(lifford) H(ugh). British (born England), b. 1921. **Genres:** History, Theology/Religion, Biography, Autobiography/Memoirs, Theology/Religion. **Career:** University of London, Bedford College, lecturer, 1951-62, reader, 1962-70, professor of medieval history, 1970-87, head of department, 1980-85, professor emeritus, 1987-; Heythrop College, vice-chairman, 1987-95. Writer. **Publications:** St. Edmund of Abingdon: A Study of History and Hagiography, 1960; The Medieval Idea of a University: An Inaugural Lecture, 1972; Medieval Monasticism: Forms of Religious Life in Western Europe in the Middle Ages, 1984, 3rd ed., 2001; The Friars: The Impact of the Early Mendicant Movement on Western Society, 1994. EDITOR: The English Church and the Papacy, 1965, 2nd ed., 1999; (and trans.) M. Paris, The Life of St. Edmund, 1996; (and trans.) The Letters of Adam Marsh, 2006. **Address:** University of London, Senate House, Malet St., London, GL WC1E 7HU, England.

LAWRENCE, David. Also writes as David Pascoe. British (born England), b. 1942. **Genres:** Novels, Mystery/Crime/Suspense, Young Adult Fiction. **Career:** Writer. **Publications:** The Dead Sit Round in a Ring, 2002; Nothing Like the Night, 2003; Cold Kill: A Detective Stella Mooney Novel, 2005; Down into Darkness, 2007. **Address:** c/o Charles Walker, PFD, Drury House, 34-43 Russell St., London, GL WC2B 5HA, England.

LAWRENCE, Kathleen Rockwell. American (born United States), b. 1945. **Genres:** Novels, Novellas/Short Stories, Essays, Young Adult Fiction. **Career:** Hunter College High School, teacher; Baruch College, Department of English, faculty, professor. Writer. **Publications:** Maud Gone (novel), 1986; The Last Room in Manhattan (novel), 1988; The Boys I Didn't Kiss and Other Essays, 1990. Contributor to periodicals. **Address:** Department of English, Baruch College, Rm. 7-290L, 55 LEX-Newman Vertical Campus, 7th Fl., PO Box B7-240, New York, NY 10010, U.S.A. **Online address:** kathleen.lawrence@baruch.cuny.edu

LAWRENCE, Louise. Irish/British (born England), b. 1943. **Genres:** Science Fiction/Fantasy, Young Adult Fiction, Novels. **Career:** Gloucestershire County Library, assistant librarian, 1960-64; Forest of Dean Branches, assistant librarian, 1969-71. Writer. **Publications:** Andra, 1971; Power of Stars, 1972; The Wyndcliffe, 1974; Sing and Scatter Daisies, 1977; Star Lord, 1978; Cat Call, 1980; The Earth Witch, 1981; Calling B for Butterfly, 1982; The Dram Road, 1983; Children of the Dust, 1985; Moonwind, 1986; The Warriors of Taan, 1988; Extinction is Forever and Other Stories, 1990; Satsuma, 1991; Ben-Harren's Castle in US as The Keeper of the Universe, 1992; The Disinherited in US as The Patchwork People, 1994; Journey through Llandor, 1995; The Road to Irriyan, 1995; The Shadow of Mordican, 1996; Dreamweaver, 1996; The Crowlings, 1999; The Parting of the Ways, 2000. **Address:** A M Heath & Company Ltd., 79 St. Martin's Ln., London, GL WC2N 4AA, England.

LAWRENCE, Mark Atwood. American (born United States), b. 1965. **Genres:** Military/Defense/Arms Control, History. **Career:** New York Times, staff; Associated Press, correspondent; Yale University, lecturer, 1998-2000; University of Texas, assistant professor, associate professor of history. Writer. **Publications:** (Ed.) The New York Times Twentieth Century in Review: The Vietnam War, 2002; Assuming the Burden: Europe and the American Commitment to War in Vietnam, 2005; (ed. with F. Logevall) The First Vietnam War: Colonial Conflict and Cold War Crisis, 2007; The Vietnam War: A Concise International History, 2008. **Address:** Department of History, University of Texas, 1 University Station, Mail Code B7000, Austin, TX 78712-0220, U.S.A. **Online address:** malawrence@mail.utexas.edu

LAWRENCE, Martha C. American (born United States), b. 1956. **Genres:** Mystery/Crime/Suspense, Crafts, Homes/Gardens. **Career:** Simon & Schuster, assistant editor, 1981-83; Harcourt Brace, acquisitions editor, 1983-87; The San Diego Union-Tribune, reviewer, 1987-95. **Publications:** Lightship Baskets of Nantucket, 1990; Scrimshaw: The Whaler's Legacy, 1993; Murder in Scorpio: A Mystery, 1995; The Cold Heart of Capricorn: A Mystery, 1997; Aquarius Descending, 1999; Pisces Rising, 2000; Ashes of Aries, 2001; Feathers Brush My Heart. Contributor to magazines. **Address:** Gina Maccoby Literary Agency, PO Box 60, Chappaqua, NY 10514, U.S.A. **Online address:** mysmartha@marthalawrence.com

LAWRENCE, Michael. British (born England), b. 1943. **Genres:** Children's Fiction, Poetry, Young Adult Fiction, Novels, Picture/Board Books. **Career:** Writer. **Publications:** A Stone in the Eye of the Sun: Selected Poems, 1967; Nudes and Victims (poetry collection), 1993; (adapter) The Strange Case of Dr. Jekyll and Mr. Hyde, 1997; Finella Minella, 1998; Jack and the Giant Kille, 2009; Jack and the Broomstick/From a Jack to a King, 2009; Jack-in-the-box/Tall-Tale Jack, 2009; Jack of the Gorgons/Jack Four's Jackdaws, 2009. NOVELS: When the Snow Falls, 1995; (with R. Ingpen) The Poppy Kettle Papers, 1999; Young Dracula, 2002; Young Monsters, 2003; (with D. Roberts) Where's Widdershins?, 2005; The Griffin and Oliver Pie, 2006; Areola Scratz, 2006; Juby's Rook, 2007; Young Wizards, 2008; Young Blackbeard, 2010; Milking the Novelty: A Tale of Two Cities and One Madhouse, 2011. JIGGY MCCUE SERIES: The Poltergoose, 1999; The Killer Underpants, 2000; The Toilet of Doom, 2001; Maggot Pie, 2002; The Snottle, 2003; Nudie Dudie, 2004; Neville the Devil, 2005; Ryan's Brain, 2006; The Iron, the Switch and the Broom Cupboard, 2007; Kid Swap, 2008; The Meanest Genie, 2009; One for All and All for Lunch!, 2009; Jiggy's Magic Balls: Jiggy's Genes, 2010; Rudie Dudie, 2010; Jiggy and the Witchfinder: Jiggy's Genes, 2011; Jiggy the Vampire Slayer: Jiggy's Genes, 2011; Murder and Chips, 2012. PICTURE BOOKS: Baby Loves, 1999; The Caterpillar That Roared, 2000; Baby Loves Hugs and Kisses, 2000; Baby Loves Visiting, 2002; Baby Christmas, 2006. ALDOUS LEXICON SERIES: A Crack in the Line, 2003; Small Eternities, 2004; The Underwood See, 2006. Works appear in anthologies. **Address:** c/o Author Mail, Dutton Children's Books, Penguin Group USA, 345 Hudson St., New York, NY 10014, U.S.A. **Online address:** ml@wordybug.com

LAWRENCE, Sara. British (born England), b. 1979. **Genres:** Young Adult Fiction. **Career:** Journalist. **Publications:** THOSE GIRLS SERIES: Those Girls, 2007; Crushworthy, 2008. Contributor to periodicals. **Address:** c/o Robert Caskie, Peters Fraser & Dunlop, Drury House, 34-43 Russell St., London, GL WC2B 5HA, England.

LAWRENCE, Starling. American (born United States) **Genres:** Novels, Novellas/Short Stories, Young Adult Fiction. **Career:** W.W. Norton, reader, editor-in-chief, 1970-, vice-chair. **Publications:** Legacies (short stories), 1996; Montenegro (novel), 1997; Lightning Keeper: A Novel, 2006. Ad-

dress: W. W. Norton & Co., 500 5th Ave., New York, NY 10110, U.S.A. **Online address:** slawrence@aol.com

LAWRENCE, Steven C. Also writes as C. L. Murphy. American (born United States), b. 1924. **Genres:** Westerns/Adventure, History, Military/Defense/Arms Control, Young Adult Fiction. **Career:** Writer, 1950-; South Junior High School, English teacher and head, 1951-87; Stonehill College, instructor in creative writing, 1967. **Publications:** Saddle Justice, 1957; Brand of a Texan, 1958; The Iron Marshal, 1960; Night of the Gunmen, 1960; Gun Fury, 1961; Bullet Welcome for Slattery, 1961; A Noose for Slattery, 1962; Longhorns North, 1962; A Texan Comes Riding, 1966; (as C.L. Murphy) Buffalo Grass (juvenile), 1966; That Man from Texas, 1972; Edge of the Land, 1974; Six-Gun Junction, 1974; Walk a Narrow Trail, 1975; Bullet Welcome, 1975; North to Montana, 1975; A Northern Saga: The Account of the North Atlantic-Murmansk, Russia, Convoys, 1976; Day of the Comancheros, 1977; Gun Blast, 1977; Slattery Stands Alone, 1979; The Lynchers, 1987; With Blood in Their Eyes, 1989; Trial for Tennihan, 1989; The Naked Range, 1990; Slattery's Gun Says No, 1990; Slattery Stands Alone, 1991. **Address:** 30 Mercedes Rd., Brockton, MA 02301-6716, U.S.A.

LAWRENCE-LIGHTFOOT, Sara. American (born United States), b. 1944. **Genres:** Education, Biography, Human Relations/Parenting. **Career:** Harlem Hospital, research associate, 1966; Yeshiva University, Albert Einstein School of Medicine, research assistant in psychiatry, 1967-68; Harvard University, Harvard Graduate School of Education, assistant professor, 1972-76, associate professor, 1976-80, professor, 1980-98, Emily Hargroves Fisher professor of education, 1998-. Writer. **Publications:** Worlds Apart: Relationships between Families and Schools, 1978; Beyond Bias: Perspectives on Classrooms, 1979; The Good High School: Portraits of Character and Culture, 1983; Balm in Gilead: Journey of a Healer (biography), 1988; I've Known Rivers: Lives of Loss and Liberation, 1994; Art and Science of Portraiture, 1997; Respect: An Exploration, 1999; The Essential Conversation: What Parents and Teachers Can Learn from Each Other, 2003; The Third Chapter: Passion, Risk and Adventure in the Twenty-Five Years after Fifty, 2009. Contributor to periodicals and books. **Address:** Harvard Graduate School of Education, Harvard University, 6 Appian Way, Cambridge, MA 02138, U.S.A. **Online address:** wendy_angus@gse.harvard.edu

LAWSON, Dorie McCullough. American (born United States), b. 1968?. **Genres:** Adult Non-fiction, Novels, Young Adult Non-fiction. **Career:** Soldier Creek Associates (lecture agency), founder and owner. Writer. **Publications:** NON-FICTION: Posterity: Letters of Great Americans to Their Children, 2004. NOVEL: Along Comes a Stranger, 2007. OTHERS: Tex, 2011. Contributor to periodicals. **Address:** Soldier Creek Associates, PO Box 477, Rockport, ME 04856-0477, U.S.A. **Online address:** dorie@soldiercreek.com

LAWSON, James. American (born United States), b. 1938. **Genres:** Novels, Plays/Screenplays, Documentaries/Reportage, Advertising/Public Relations, Literary Criticism And History, Young Adult Fiction. **Career:** McCann-Marschalk, copywriter, 1962-63; J. Walter Thompson, copywriter, 1963-64; Aspen Times, reporter, 1963; Al Paul Lefton, copywriter, 1964-65; Doyle Dane Bernbach, vice president, 1966-78; Doremus and Co., senior vice president and director of creative services, 1978-80; Cunningham and Walsh Advertising, vice president and creative director, 1980-82; DDB Needham Worldwide, senior vice president and creative director, 1982-93; freelance writer, 1993-95; Jordan McGrath Case & Partners, writer, 1996-98; Lord Group, writer, 1998-2001; Draftfcb, writer, 2002-07; freelancer writer, 2007-. **Publications:** NOVELS: XXX, 1963, Disconnections, 1968; The American Book of the Dead, 1972; Crimes of the Unconscious, 1974; The Girl Watcher, 1976; The Copley Chronicles, 1980; The Fanatic, 1980; Forgeries of the Heart, 1982; The Madman's Kiss, 1988; The Reluctant God, 1993; The Last Day of Petter Grenager, 2005; Acid Rains of Fortune, 2010. **Address:** 151 Charles St., New York, NY 10014-2539, U.S.A. **Online address:** emailawson@aol.com

LAWSON, JonArno Burhans. Canadian (born Canada), b. 1968. **Genres:** Novels, Poetry, Children's Fiction. **Career:** Beth Tikvah Group Home, group home counselor, 1992-96; McCarthy-Tetrault Law Firm, library clerk, 1996-97; University of Toronto, information services technician, 1997; Humber College, instructor, 2002-. Writer. **Publications:** Love Is an Observant Traveller, 1997; Inklings, 1999; Man in the Moon-Fixer's Mask, 2004; Black Stars in a White Night Sky, 2008. Contributor to periodicals. **Address:** Pedlar

Press, PO Box 26, Sta. P, Toronto, ON M5S 2S6, Canada. **Online address:** jonarnol@yahoo.com

LAWSON, Laura J. American (born United States), b. 1966. **Genres:** Homes/Gardens, Architecture, Art/Art History. **Career:** Louisiana State University, assistant professor, 2000-02; University of Illinois, assistant professor, associate professor, 2002-. Writer and academic. **Publications:** (with G. Eckbo, W. Hood and C. Sullivan) People in a Landscape, 1997; City Bountiful: A Century of Community Gardening in America, 2005. Contributor to books and journals. **Address:** Department of Landscape Architecture, University of Illinois, MC-620, 101 Temple Hoyne Buell Hall, 611 Lorado Taft Dr., Champaign, IL 61820-6921, U.S.A. **Online address:** ljlawson@illinois.edu

LAWSON, Linda. American (born United States), b. 1952. **Genres:** Writing/Journalism, Communications/Media, Business/Trade/Industry, Law. **Career:** Michigan Consumers Council, director of information, 1976-81; Ferris State University, instructor, 1981-82; Indiana University, assistant professor, 1988-95, associate professor, 1995-. Writer. **Publications:** Truth in Publishing: Federal Regulation of the Press's Business Practices, 1880-1920, 1993. Contributor to periodicals. **Address:** School of Journalism, Indiana University, 200 Ernie Pyle Hall, 940 E 7th St., Bloomington, IN 47405-7108, U.S.A.

LAWSON, Philip. *See* **BISHOP, Michael.**

LAWSON, Philip. *See* **DI FILIPPO, Paul.**

LAWTON, Barbara (Perry). American (born United States), b. 1930. **Genres:** Horticulture, Sciences. **Career:** Missouri Botanical Garden, manager of publications, editor of Bulletin, 1967-72; St. Louis Post-Dispatch, weekly columnist, 1972-90; Gary Ferguson, public relations counselor and partner, 1972-81; Daniel J. Edelman (public relations), account supervisor, 1981-84; Lawton and Associates, public relations counselor and writer, 1984-; Kirkwood Planning and Zoning Commission, staff, 1986-92; St. Louis Press Club, newsletter editor, 1986-89; Cottage Review, editor. **Publications:** Improving Your Garden Soil, 1992; (with G.F. Van Patten) Organic Gardener's Basics, 1993; Seasonal Guide to the Natural Year-Illinois, Missouri and Arkansas, 1994; The Magic of Irises, 1998; Mints: A Family of Herbs and Ornamentals, 2002; Hibiscus: Hardy and Tropical Plants for the Garden, 2004; Parsleys, Fennels, and Queen Anne's Lace: Herbs and Ornamentals from the Umbel Family, 2007. **Address:** 1430 Timberbrook Dr., Kirkwood, MT 63122-6734, U.S.A.

LAWTON, John. British (born England), b. 1949?. **Genres:** Novels, Mystery/Crime/Suspense. **Career:** British Broadcasting Corp., filmmaker. Novelist. **Publications:** FREDERICK TROY SERIES: Black Out, 1995; Old Flames, 1997; A Little White Death, 1998; Riptide, 2001 as Bluffing Mr. Churchill, 2004; Blue Rondo as Flesh Wounds, 2005; Second Violin, 2007; A Lily of the Field, 2010. NOVELS: Sweet Sunday, 2002. **Address:** Viking Books Publicity, 375 Hudson St., New York, NY 10014, U.S.A.

LAX, Eric. American/Canadian (born Canada), b. 1944?. **Genres:** Film, Medicine/Health, Biography, Documentaries/Reportage. **Career:** Peace Corps, School Partnership Program, director, 1968-70; freelance writer, 1970-; PEN Foundation Intl., trustee and treasurer; PEN Center USA, vice president, 1994-95, president, 1996-2000. **Publications:** The U.S. Overseas: Pinpoints on the Pacific, 1969; On Being Funny: Woody Allen and Comedy, 1975; Life and Death on 10 West, 1984; Woody Allen: A Biography, 1991; Paul Newman, 1996; (with A.M. Sperber) Bogart, 1997; The Mold in Dr. Florey's Coat: The Story of the Penicillin Miracle, 2004; Conversations with Woody Allen: His Films, The Movies and Moviemaking, 2007; Faith, Interrupted: A Spiritual Journey, 2010. Contributor to periodicals. **Address:** 609 Trenton Dr., Beverly Hills, CA 90210-3102, U.S.A.

LAXDAL, Vivienne. Canadian (born Canada), b. 1962. **Genres:** Plays/Screenplays, Theatre, Art/Art History. **Career:** Playwright and actor. **Publications:** Goose Spit, 1988; Karla and Grif: A Play in Two Acts, 1999; Personal Convictions, 1999; (contrib.) TYA5: Theatre for Young Audience, 2000. Contributor to periodicals. **Address:** RR 2, PO Box 206, Masham, QC J0X 2W0, Canada. **Online address:** laxdal@msn.com

LAXER, James. American (born United States), b. 1941. **Genres:** Autobiography/Memoirs. **Career:** Waffle Group (New Left political movement), co-founder, 1969; TV Ontario, host of a public affairs television program, 1978-81; New Democratic Party, research director, 1981-83; York University,

professor. Writer. **Publications:** The Energy Poker Game: The Politics of the Continental Resources Deal, 1970; Canada's Energy Crisis, 1974; (ed. with A. Martin) The Big Tough Expensive Job: Imperial Oil and the Canadian Economy, 1976; (with R. Laxer) The Liberal Idea of Canada: Pierre Trudeau and the Question of Canada's Survival, 1977; Canada's Economic Strategy, 1981; Oil and Gas: Ottawa, the Provinces, and the Petroleum Industry, 1983; Rethinking the Economy: The Laxer Report on Canadian Economic Problems and Policies, 1984; Leap of Faith: Free Trade and the Future of Canada, 1986; Decline of the Superpowers: Winners and Losers in Today's Global Economy, 1989; False God: How the Globalization Myth Has Impoverished Canada, 1993; In Search of a New Left: Canadian Politics after the Neoconservative Assault, 1997; The Undeclared War: Class Conflict in the Age of Cyber Capitalism, 1998; Stalking the Elephant: My Discovery of America, 2000; Discovering America: Travels in the Land of Guns, God, and Corporate Gurus, 2001; The Border: Canada, the U.S. and Dispatches from the 49th Parallel, 2003; Red Diaper Baby: A Boyhood in the Age of McCarthyism (memoir), 2004; Empire, 2006; Mission of Folly: Canada and Afghanistan, 2008; Oil, 2008; Beyond the Bubble: Imagining a New Canadian Economy, 2009; Democracy, 2009. **Online address:** jameslaxer@sympatico.ca

LAY, Carol. American (born United States), b. 1952. **Genres:** Autobiography/Memoirs. **Career:** WayLay, author. Cartoonist. **Publications:** The Oz-Wonderland Wars, 1985; Now, Endsville and Other Stories, 1993; Joy Ride and Other Stories, 1996; Strip Joint, 1998; Wonder Woman: Mythos, 2002; Goodnight, Irene: The Collected Stories of Irene Van De Kamp, 2007; The Big Skinny: How I Changed My Fattitude (memoir), 2008. Illustrator of books by others. Contributor to periodicals. **Address:** Los Angeles, CA, U.S.A. **Online address:** lay@waylay.com

LAYBOURN, Keith. British (born England), b. 1946?. **Genres:** Politics/Government, Humanities. **Career:** Huddersfield Polytechnic (now University of Huddersfield), assistant lecturer, 1971-72, lecturer, 1972-74, senior lecturer, 1974-91, professor of history; Open University, tutor, 1981-91, professor of history, 1991-; Arts and Humanities Research Council, peer reviewer, 2004-. Writer. **Publications:** (Ed. with G. Firth and J. O'Connell) Yorkshire Labour Movements c. 1780-1926: A Guide to Historical Sources and Their Uses, 1980; (ed. with G. Firth and J. Hagerty) Yorkshire at Play: A Guide to Historical Sources and Their Uses, 1982; (with J. Reynolds) Liberalism and the Rise of Labour, 1890-1918, 1984; (with J. Reynolds) Labour Heartland: The Labour Party in West Yorkshire during the Inter-War Years, 1918-1939, 1987; (ed. with D. James) Philip Snowden, 1987; Philip Snowden: A Biography, 1864-1937, 1988; The Rise of Labour: The History of the British Labor Party, 1890-1979, 1988; The Labour Party 1890-1951: A Reader in History, 1988; Britain on the Breadline: A History of Britain during the Inter-War Years, 1990; British Trade Unionism, 1770-1990: A Reader in History, 1991; A History of British Trade Unionism, c. 1770-1990, Alan Sutton, 1992; (ed. with D. James and T. Jowitt) The Centennial History of the Independent Labour Party: A Collection of Essays, 1992; The General Strike of 1926, 1993; The Guild of Help and the Changing Face of Edwardian Philanthropy: The Guild of Help, Voluntary Work and the State, 1904-1919, 1994; The Evolution of British Social Policy and the Welfare State, c. 1800-1993, 1995; The General Strike Day by Day, 1996; The Rise of Socialism in Britain, c. 1881-1951, 1997; (ed.) Social Conditions, Status and Community, 1860-1920, 1997; Modern Britain since 1906: A Reader, 1999; (ed. with K. Dockray) Representations and Reality of War: The British Experience, 1999; (with D. Murphy) Under the Red Flag: Communism in Britain, 1999; A Century of Labour: A History of the Labour Party, 1900-2000, 2000; (ed.) British Political Leaders: A Biographical Dictionary, 2001; Unemployment and Employment Policies Concerning Women in Britain, 1900-1951, 2002; Fifty Key Figures in Twentieth-Century British Politics, 2002; (ed. with C. Collette) Modern Britain since 1979: A Reader, 2003; Marxism in Britain: Dissent, Decline and Re-Emergence 1945-c. 2000, 2006; (with J. Shepherd) Britain's First Labour Government, 2006; Working-Class Gambling in Britain, c. 1906-1960s: The Stages of the Political Debate, 2007; (ed. with J. Lancaster, B. Evans and B. Haigh) The Sons and Daughters of Labour: The Labour Movement in the West Riding of Yorkshire, 2007; (with D. Taylor) Policing in England and Wales, 1918-39: The Fed, Flying Squads and Forensics, 2011. Contributor to books and journals. **Address:** School of Music, Humanities and Media, University of Huddersfield, WG/22, West Bldg., Queensgate, Huddersfield, WY HD1 3DH, England. **Online address:** k.laybourn@hud.ac.uk

LAYDEN, Elmer. *See* **LYDEN, Jacki.**

LAYNE, Christopher. American (born United States), b. 1949. **Genres:** Military/Defense/Arms Control, History. **Career:** U.S. District Judge Richard A. Gadbois, Jr., law clerk, 1982-83; Danning, Gill Gould, Joseph, and Diamond, associate, 1982; Blecher and Collins, partner, 1983-89; Kaye, Scholer, Fierman, Hays, & Handler, associate, 1989-90; University of California, visiting lecturer, 1991-95, Center for Social Theory and Comparative History fellow, 2000-01; Harvard University, Center for Science and International Affairs research fellow, 1995-96; Naval Postgraduate School, research fellow, 1996-98; University of Miami, associate professor of international studies, 2001-02; Texas A&M University, associate professor, 2005-07, Mary Julia and George R. Jordan Professorship of International Affairs, 2007-; Cato Institute, visiting fellow in foreign policy studies; University of Southern California, Center for International Studies, fellow; California Institute of Technology, Arroyo Center, professional staff; Independent Institute, Center on Peace and Liberty, research fellow; NATO/Western Europe, foreign policy analyst. Writer. **Publications:** (with J.A. Isaacson and J. Arquilla) Predicting Military Innovation, 1999; The Peace of Illusions: American Grand Strategy from 1940 to the Present, 2006; (with B.A. Thayer) American Empire: A Debate, 2007. Contributor to journals. **Address:** Bush School of Government and Public Service, Texas A&M University, 4220 TAMU, College Station, TX 77843-4220, U.S.A. **Online address:** clayne@bushschool.tamu.edu

LAYNE, Steven L. American (born United States) **Genres:** Children's Fiction, Poetry. **Career:** Judson College, associate professor of education and literature, 2004-, professor, Master of Education in Literacy, director; national literacy consultant, motivational speaker. Writer and educator. **Publications:** Thomas's Sheep and the Great Geography Test, 1998; This Side of Paradise (young-adult novel), 2001; The Teacher's Night before Christmas, 2001; Life's Literary Lessons: Poems for Teachers, 2001; Life's Literacy Lessons, 2002; My Brother Dan's Delicious, 2003; The Principal's Night before Christmas, 2004; Thomas's Sheep and the Spectacular Science Project, 2004; Verses for Dad's Heart, 2004; Over Land and Sea: A Story of International Adoption, 2005; (with wife, D.D. Layne) T is for Teachers: A School Alphabet, 2005; Verses for Mom's Heart, 2005; The Preacher's Night before Christmas, 2006; Mergers (young-adult novel), 2006; Love the Baby, 2007; (with D.D. Layne) P is for Princess: A Royal Alphabet, 2007; (with D.D. Layne) Number 1 Teacher: A School Counting Book, 2008; Teachers' Night before Halloween, 2008; Igniting a Passion for Reading: Successful Strategies for Building Lifetime Readers, 2009; (with D.D. Layne) W is for Windy City: A Chicago Alphabet, 2010; Paradise lost, 2011; Share with Brother, 2011; Stay with Sister, 2012; Building Lifetime Readers: Steps to Success for America's Schools, forthcoming. **Address:** Department of Education, Judson College, 1151 N State St., Creekside South, Ste. 125, Elgin, IL 60123-1498, U.S.A. **Online address:** slayne@judsonu.edu

LAYTON, Bentley. American (born United States), b. 1941?. **Genres:** Theology/Religion, Humanities. **Career:** Ecole Biblique Et Archéologique Française, visiting professor, 1971-76; Yale University, assistant professor, 1976-78, associate professor, 1978-83, professor of religious studies (ancient Christianity), professor of near eastern languages and civilizations (Coptic), 1983-, Frederick and Laura Goff professor of religious studies, 2001-, Department of Classics, affiliated faculty; Department of History, affiliated faculty. Writer. **Publications:** Catalogue of Coptic Literary Manuscripts in the British Library Acquired since the Year 1906, 1987; The Gnostic Scriptures: A New Translation With Annotations and Introductions, 1987; Coptic Grammar: With Chrestomathy and Glossary: Sahidic Dialect, 2000, 2nd ed., 2004; Coptic Gnostic Chrestomathy: A Selection of Coptic Texts with Grammatical Analysis and Glossary, 2004; Coptic in 20 Lessons: Introduction to Sahidic Coptic with Exercises & Vocabularies, 2006. EDITOR: (trans.) The Gnostic Treatise on Resurrection from Nag Hammadi, 1979; Rediscovery of Gnosticism: Proceedings of the International Conference on Gnosticism at Yale, New Haven, Connecticut, March 28-31, 1978, 1980; Nag Hammadi Codex II, 2-7: Together with XIII, 2, 1989, 2nd ed., 1991. **Address:** Department of Religious Studies, Yale University, 451 College St., PO Box 208287, New Haven, CT 06520-8287, U.S.A. **Online address:** bentley.layton@yale.edu

LAYTON, Clare. See WRIGHT, Daphne.

LAZAR, Lance Gabriel. American (born United States), b. 1945?. **Genres:** History, Theology/Religion. **Career:** Assumption College, assistant professor, 2005-. Writer. **Publications:** Working in the Vineyard of the Lord: Jesuit Confraternities in Early Modern Italy, 2005. Contributor to books and journals. **Address:** Department of History, Assumption College, 500 Salisbury St., Worcester, MA 01609-1265, U.S.A. **Online address:** llazar@assumption.edu

LAZARUS-BLACK, Mindie. American (born United States) **Genres:** Anthropology/Ethnology, Law. **Career:** New York Historical Society, The Horatio Gates Project, editorial assistant, 1976-77; Mountain View Community College, adjunct lecturer in anthropology, 1978; El Centro Community College, adjunct lecturer in sociology, 1981; American Bar Foundation, research assistant, 1988-90, research associate, 1990-92; University of Illinois at Chicago Circle, adjunct lecturer, 1990, assistant professor of criminal justice and affiliate assistant professor of anthropology, 1990-, associate professor, director of graduate studies, professor of criminology, law, and justice, affiliate professor of anthropology; Temple University, Department of Anthropology, professor and chair, 2008-. **Publications:** Legitimate Acts and Illegal Encounters: Law and Society in Antigua and Barbuda, 1994; Rite of Domination: Tales from Domestic Violence Court, 2002; Everyday Harm: Domestic Violence, Court Rites and Cultures of Reconciliation, 2007. EDITOR: (with P. Lange) Family Business in Dallas: A Matter of Values, 1982; (with S. Hirsch) Contested States: Law, Hegemony and Resistance, 1994. Contributor to books and periodicals. **Address:** Department of Anthropology, Temple University, Gladfelter Hall, 2nd Fl., 1115 W Berks St., Philadelphia, PA 19122, U.S.A. **Online address:** mindielb@uic.edu

LAZEBNIK, Claire Scovell. American (born United States) **Genres:** Education, Novels, Young Adult Non-fiction, Human Relations/Parenting. **Career:** Writer. **Publications:** Same As It Never Was (novel), 2003; Olivia's Sister, 2003; (with L.K. Koegel) Overcoming Autism: Finding the Answers, Strategies, and Hope That Can Transform a Child's Life, 2004; (contrib.) American Girls about Town, 2004; Knitting Under the Influence (novel), 2006; The Smart One and the Pretty One, 2008; (with L.K. Koegel) Growing Up on the Spectrum: A Guide to Life, Love, and Learning for Teens and Young Adults with Autism and Asperger's, 2009; If You Lived Here, You'd be Home Now, 2010; Families and Other Nonreturnable Gifts, 2011; Epic Fail, 2011. Contributor to periodicals. **Address:** Viking Press, 375 Hudson St., New York, NY 10014-3658, U.S.A. **Online address:** cslazebnik@aol.com

LAZENBY, Edith P. American (born United States), b. 1945. **Genres:** Theology/Religion, Novels. **Career:** Writer. **Publications:** Tabernacle in the Wilderness: As It Relates to Jesus Christ, 1997. **Address:** PO Box 300928, JFK Airport Sta., Jamaica, NY 11430-0928, U.S.A. **Online address:** exelsie@aol.com

LAZENBY, J(ohn) F(rancis). British/Indian (born India), b. 1934. **Genres:** Classics, Military/Defense/Arms Control, History. **Career:** Newcastle University, lecturer in ancient history, 1959-71, senior lecturer in ancient history, 1971-79, reader in ancient history, 1979-94, Department of Classics, head, 1982-87, School of Humanities, head, 1988-94, professor of ancient history, 1994-99, emeritus professor, 1999-, historian. Writer. **Publications:** (With R.H. Simpson) The Catalogue of the Ships in Homer's Iliad, 1970; Hannibal's War: A Military History of the Second Punic War, 1978; The Spartan Army, 1985; The Defence of Greece, 490-479 B.C., 1993; The First Punic War, 1996; The Peloponnesian War: A Military Study, 2003. **Address:** Department of Classics, School of Historical Studies, Newcastle University, Armstrong Bldg., Claremont Rd., Newcastle upon Tyne, TW NE1 7RU, England.

LAZENBY, Roland. American (born United States), b. 1952. **Genres:** Sports/Fitness. **Career:** Virginia Polytechnic Institute, instructor; State University, faculty. Writer. **Publications:** NONFICTION SPORTS BOOKS: (with B. Packer) Hoops! Confessions of a College Basketball Analyst, 1985; (with E. Green and D. Meador) Championship Basketball: Top College Coaches Present Their Winning Strategies, Tips and Techniques for Players and Coaches, 1987; (with B. Packer) Fifty Years of the Final Four: Golden Moments of the NCAA Basketball Tournament, 1987, rev. ed. as Golden Moments of the Final Four: A Retrospective of the NCAA Basketball Tournament, 1989; 100 Greatest Quarterbacks, 1988; (with B. Packer) College Basketball's 25 Greatest Teams, 1989; The NBA Finals: The Official Illustrated History, 1990; (with J. Denberg and T. Stinson) From Sweet Lou to 'Nique, 1992; The Lakers: A Basketball Journey, 50th anniversary ed., 1993; (with D. Doughty) 'Hoos 'n' Hokies: The Rivalry: 100 Years of Virginia/Virginia Tech Football, 1995; And Now, Your Chicago Bulls! A Thirty Year Celebration!, 1995; Airballs! Notes from the NBA's Far Side, 1996; Bull Run! The Story of the 1995-96 Chicago Bulls: The Greatest Team in Basketball History, 1996; The NBA Finals: A Fifty-Year Celebration, 1996; Yo, Baby, It's Attitude! The New Bad Boyz of the NBA Take the Jordan Test, 1997; Chicago Bulls: The Authorized

Pictorial, 1997; Smashmouth: Attitude between the Lines, 1997; Blood on the Horns: The Long Strange Ride of Michael Jordan's Chicago Bulls, 1998; The Unofficial Chicago Bulls Pocket Primer, 1998; Stockton to Malone: The Rise of the Utah Jazz, 1998; Bird: Portrait of a Competitor, 1998; (with B. Packer) Why We Win: Great American Coaches Offer Their Strategies for Success in Sports and Life, 1999; Love at First Light: Michael Jordan and the Romance of Golf, 1999; Mad Game: The NBA Education of Kobe Bryant, rev. ed., 2000; (ed.) Chicago Sport Century, 2000; Mindgames: Phil Jackson's Long, Strange Journey, 2001; The Pictorial History of Football, 2002; Johnny Unitas: The Best There Ever Was, 2002; Ichiro: The Making of an American Hero, 2002; (with B. Schron) Tom Brady: Sudden Glory, 2002; (with M. Ashley) Emmitt Smith: Record-Breaking Rush to Glory, 2002; The Show: The Inside Story of the Spectacular Los Angeles Lakers in the Words of Those Who Lived It, 2006; (ed.) April 16th: Virginia Tech Remembers, 2007; Jerry West: the Life and Legend of a Basketball Icon, 2009. OTHER: (contrib.) Michael Jordan Scrapbook, 1998. **Address:** Virginia Polytechnic Institute, Department of Communication, 106 Shanks Hall, PO Box 0311, Blacksburg, VA 24061, U.S.A. **Online address:** rllazenby@aol.com

LAZER, Hank. (Henry Alan Lazer). American (born United States), b. 1950. **Genres:** Poetry. **Career:** University of Virginia, Department of English, instructor in English, 1975-77, professor; University of Alabama, professor of American literature, 1977-, assistant dean for humanities and fine arts, 1991-97, Undergraduate Programs and Service, assistant vice president, 1997-2006, vice president, associate provost. Writer. **Publications:** Lyric and Spirit: Selected Essays, 1996-2008, 2008. POETRY: Mouth to Mouth, 1977; INTER(R)RUPTIONS, 1992; Doublespace: Poems 1971-1989, 1992; Negation, 1994; Early Days of the Lang Dynasty, 1996; 3 of 10: H's Journal, Negation, and Displayspace, 1996; Opposing Poetries, 1996; As It Is, 1999; Simple Harmonic Motions: Poem, 2001; Days: Poems, 2002. EDITOR: On Equal Terms: Poems, 1984; What Is a Poet? Essays from the Eleventh Alabama Symposium on English and American Literature, 1987; On Louis Simpson: Depths beyond Happiness, 1988. Works appear in anthologies. Contributor to magazines. **Address:** Department of English, University of Alabama, Maxwell Hall, PO Box 870244, Tuscaloosa, AL 35487-0114, U.S.A. **Online address:** hlazer@bama.ua.edu

LAZER, Henry Alan. See LAZER, Hank.

LAZERSON, Joshua N(athaniel). American (born United States), b. 1959. **Genres:** History, Reference, Biography, Social Sciences, Adult Non-fiction. **Career:** American Bar Association, project manager, 1990-92; Northside HIV Treatment Center, project administrator, 1991-92; Urban Corps of San Diego, program developer, 1992-94; writer, 1993-. **Publications:** Against the Tide: Whites in the Struggle Against Apartheid, 1994; (with K. Irvine) Dictionary of African Biography, vol. III: Southern Africa, 1995. **Address:** 1985 Country Grove Ln., Encinitas, CA 92024-1930, U.S.A.

LAZIN, Fred A. Israeli/American (born United States), b. 1943. **Genres:** Politics/Government, History, Social Sciences. **Career:** Loop College, assistant professor, 1970-71; City University of New York, assistant professor of government, 1971-75, Hunter College, visiting professor, 1998-2000, Queens College, visiting professor, 1999-2000; Ben Gurion University, lecturer, 1975-79, senior lecturer, 1980-86, associate professor, 1986-96, professor, 1996-, Lynn and Lloyd Hurst Family professor of local government, now professor emeritus, Urban Studies Program, head, 1976-84, Hubert H. Humphrey Center for Social Ecology, director, 1981-86, Department of Behavioral Science, chair, 1989-91, Overseas Students Program, director, 1991-96, Distinguished Visitors Program, director, 1996-98, Department of Politics and Government, chair, 2005-08; Hebrew University, visiting senior lecturer, 1981-82; University of California-Los Angeles, visiting associate professor, 1986-87; Cornell University, visiting professor, 1989, 1991; Tufts University, visiting associate professor, 1994; George Washington University, visiting professor, 1995; Rutgers University, visiting fellow, 1996; University of California-San Diego, research associate, 2000-; Sciences Po Bordeaux, visiting professor, 2005, 2008; Southwest University of Political Science & Law, research fellow, 2008; New York University, visiting professor, 2008-09; American University, Center for Israel Studies, visiting professor, 2010-11, Schusterman visiting professor. Writer. **Publications:** (Ed. with D. Soen and Y. Neumann) Cities, Communities, and Planning in the 1980's, 1984; (with S. Aroni) How Successful Was Section 8 in Los Angeles? A Case-Study of a Housing Subsidy Program, 1986; Policy Implementation of Social Welfare in the 1980's, 1987; (ed. with S. Aroni and Y. Gradus) The Policy Impact of Universities in Developing Regions, 1988; (ed. with R.E. Isralowitz, I. Light and C.T. Logan) Immigration and Absorption: Issues in a Multicultural Perspective: Proceedings of the UCLC/BGU Conference on Immigration, May 1991, 1994; Politics and Policy Implementation: Project Renewal in Israel, 1994; (ed. with G.S. Mahler) Israel in the Nineties: Development and Conflict, 1996; The Struggle for Soviet Jewry in American Politics: Israel versus the American Jewish Establishment, 2005; (ed. with V. Hoffmann-Martinot and M. Evans) Local Government Reforms in Countries in Transition: A Global Perspective, 2007; (ed. with M. Evans and N. Jayaram) Higher Education and Equality of Opportunity: Cross-National Perspectives, Lexington Books, 2010. Contributor to periodicals and journals. **Address:** Department of Politics and Government, Ben Gurion University, Beersheva, 84105, Israel. **Online address:** lazin@bgu.ac.il

LAZUTA, Gene. Also writes as Alex Kane, Daniel Raven, Leo Axler. American (born United States), b. 1959. **Genres:** Mystery/Crime/Suspense, Novels, Horror, Literary Criticism And History. **Career:** Kolodiy-Lazuta Funeral Home, funeral director, 1982-. Writer. **Publications:** (As Alex Kane) The Shinglo, 1989; (as Daniel Raven) Happy Cage, 1989; Blood Flies, 1990; Bleeder, 1991; Vyrmin, 1992; Forget Me Not, 1992; BILL HAWLEY UNDERTAKING MYSTERY NOVELS AS LEO AXLER: Final Viewing, 1994; Double Plot, 1994; Grave Matters, 1995; Separated at Death, 1996. **Address:** Kolodiy-Lazuta Funeral Home, 5677 State Rd., Parma, OH 44134-2201, U.S.A.

LE, Nam. Australian/Vietnamese (born Vietnam), b. 1979. **Genres:** Novellas/Short Stories, Novels. **Career:** University of Melbourne, Farrago (student newspaper), editor, 2001; Iowa Writers' Workshop, Truman Capote fellow, 2004; Fine Arts Work Center, Grace Paley fellow, 2006; Phillips Exeter Academy, George Bennett fellow, 2007; University of East Anglia, David T.K. Wong fellow, 2009; Harvard Review, editor. Attorney. **Publications:** The Boat, 2008. Works appear in anthologies. Contributor to periodicals and journals. **Address:** Penguin Group Inc., 250 Camberwell Rd., Camberwell, VI 3124, Australia. **Online address:** namletheboat@gmail.com

LEA, James F(ranklin). American (born United States), b. 1945. **Genres:** Politics/Government, Essays, Engineering. **Career:** Livingston University, assistant professor of political science, 1971-75; University of Southern Mississippi, assistant professor, 1975-77, associate professor, 1977-81, professor of political science, 1981-; University of Wales of Swansea, visiting research professor, 1987; registered professional engineer. Writer. **Publications:** Kazantzakis: The Politics of Salvation, 1979; Political Consciousness and American Democracy, 1982; (ed. and contrib.) Contemporary Southern Politics, 1989; (with H.V. Nickens and M. Wells) Gas Well Deliquification: Solutions to Gas Well Liquid Loading Problems, 2003. Contributor to journals and periodicals. **Address:** Department of Political Science, University of Southern Mississippi, PO Box 5108, Southern Sta., Hattiesburg, MS 39406, U.S.A.

LEAB, Daniel Josef. American/German (born Germany), b. 1936. **Genres:** History, Writing/Journalism, Bibliography, Young Adult Non-fiction, Education, Reference. **Career:** Columbia University, instructor, 1966-68, assistant professor of history, 1969-74, Columbia College, associate dean, 1969-71, graduate seminar in American studies, lecturer, 1970, 1972, 1975, assistant dean of faculties, 1971, special assistant, 1973-74; Bancroft Parkman Corp., director, 1973-; Seton Hall University, associate professor, 1974-79, director of American studies, 1974-79, professor of history, 1979-; Labor History, managing editor, 1974-2000; American Communist History, managing editor, 2001-. **Publications:** (Contrib.) History of the Twentieth Century, 1969; A Union of Individuals: The Formation of the American Newspaper Guild, 1933-36, 1970; (contrib.) Harper Encyclopedia of the Modern World: A Concise Reference History from 1760 to the Present, 1970; From Sambo to Superspade: The Black Experiences in Motion Pictures, 1975; (with K.K. Leab) The Auction Companion, 1981; (with M.F. Neufield and D. Swanson) American Working Class History: A Representative Bibliography, 1983; George Orwell: An Exhibition at the Grolier Club: Selections from the Collection of Daniel J. Leab, 1996; I Was a Communist for the F.B.I.: The Unhappy Life and Times of Matt Cvetic, 2000; Orwell Subverted: The CIA and the Filming of Animal Farm, 2007. EDITOR: The Labor History Reader, 1985; Federal Bureau of Investigation Confidential Files: Communist Activity in the Entertainment Industry: FBI Surveillance Files on Hollywood, 1942-1958, 1991; (with P.P. Mason) Labor History Archives in the United States: A Guide for Researching and Teaching, 1992; Great Depression and the New Deal: A Thematic Encyclopedia, 2009. Contributor to journals. **Address:** Tamiment Library, American Communist History, PO Box 1236, Washington, DC 06793, U.S.A. **Online address:** leabdani@shu.edu

LEACH, Neil. British (born England) **Genres:** Architecture. **Career:** University of Bath, professor of architectural theory; University of Southern California, professor; SCI-Arc, faculty; Architectural Association, faculty; Columbia GSAPP, faculty; Cornell University, faculty; Dessau Institute of Architecture, faculty; IaaC, faculty; London Consortium, faculty; Royal Danish School of Fine Arts, faculty; ESARQ, faculty; University of Nottingham, faculty; University of Brighton, faculty. Writer. **Publications:** (Trans.) On the Art of Building in Ten Books, 1988; (ed.) Rethinking Architecture: A Reader in Cultural Theory, 1997; (ed.) Architecture and Revolution: Contemporary Perspectives on Central and Eastern Europe, 1999; The Anaesthetics of Architecture, 1999; Millennium Culture, 1999; (ed.) Architecture and Revolution, 1999; (with O.F. Lewis and N. Worton) Mars Pants with Oliver Froome, 2000; (ed.) The Hieroglyphics of Space: Reading and Experiencing the Modern Metropolis, 2001; (ed.) Designing for a Digital World, 2002; (ed. with D. Turnbull and C. Williams) Digital Tectonics, 2004; (ed. with X.W. Guo) Hot Spots, Brain Cells, 2004; China, 2004; Camouflage, 2006; (ed. with X.W. Guo) Emerging Talents, Emerging Technologies: Architects, 2006; (ed. with X.W. Guo) Emerging Talents, Emerging Technologies: Students, 2006; Forget Heidegger, 2006; (contrib.) Rapids: Layered Fabrication Technologies for Façades and Building Construction, 2010. Contributor to periodicals. **Address:** University of Bath, Bath, SM BA2 7AY, England. **Online address:** neil@neilleach.com

LEACH, Penelope (Jane). British (born England), b. 1937. **Genres:** Psychology, Social Commentary, Medicine/Health. **Career:** British Home Office, Criminological Research Unit, research officer, 1960-61; Medical Research Council, Unit for the Study of Child Development, research officer, 1964-70; University of London, lecturer, 1965-67; Penguin Books Ltd., outside medical editor, 1973-; University of Bristol, International Centre for Child Studies, research consultant, 1980-90; End Physical Punishment Of Children (EPOCH), founder and parent education coordinator, 1989-; Child Magazine, consulting editor, 1995-; Families, Children and Childcare Study, director; Canadian Society for the Prevention of Cruelty to Children, international officer. **Publications:** Babyhood: Infant Development from Birth to Two Years, 1974 in US Babyhood: Stage By Stage, From Birth To Age Two: How Your Baby Develops Physically, Emotionally, Mentally, 1976, 2nd ed., 1983; Baby and Child, 1977 in US as Your Baby and Child From Birth to Age Five, 1978, rev. ed., 2010; Who Cares? A New Deal for Mothers and Their Small Children, 1979; The Parents A-Z: A Handbook for Children's Health Growth and Happiness, as The Child Care Encyclopedia: A Parents' Guide to the Physical and Emotional Well-Being of Children from Birth through Adolescence, 1984 in US as Your Growing Child: From Babyhood through Adolescence, 1986; The First Six Months: Getting Together with Your Baby, 1987; The Baby Pack, 1990; The Baby Kit, 1990; Children under Stress, 1992; Children First: What Society Must Do and Is not Doing-For Children Today, 1994; Bebe Nino, 2001; Child Care Today: Getting It Right for Everyone, 2009; Your Baby and Child, 2010; Your Baby, 2010; The Essential First Year, 2010. CO-AUTHOR: Joyful and Confident Parenting, 2002; Teaching Your Child Positive Discipline: Your Guide to Joyful and Confident Parenting, 2002; How Your Baby & Child Learns: Give Your Baby & Child the Best Start, 2002; Your Baby and Child's Emotional and Social Development: Your Guide to Joyful and Confident Parenting, 2002. Contributor to periodicals. **Address:** Canadian Society for the Prevention of Cruelty to, Children, 362 Midland Ave., PO Box 700, Midland, ON L4R 4P4, Canada.

LEACH, William. American (born United States), b. 1944. **Genres:** History, Literary Criticism And History, Biography, Business/Trade/Industry. **Career:** New York University, faculty; University of California, faculty; Columbia University, professor of history, 1999-. Writer. **Publications:** True Love and Perfect Union: The Feminist Reform of Sex and Society, 1980, 2nd ed., 1989; Edith Wharton (biography), 1987; (contrib.) The Wonderful Wizard of Oz, 1991; Land of Desire: Merchants, Power and the Rise of a New American Culture, 1993; Country of Exiles: The Destruction of Place in American Life, 1999; Butterfly People: An American Encounter with the Beauty of the World, 2012. **Address:** Department of History, Columbia University, 325 Fayerweather Hall, PO Box 2527, New York, NY 10027-6902, U.S.A. **Online address:** wrl3@columbia.edu

LEACOCK, Elspeth. American (born United States), b. 1946. **Genres:** Geography, History, Children's Fiction, Travel/Exploration. **Career:** Writer and educator. **Publications:** Hands-On Geography, 1993; Geography Brain Quest, 1997; (with S. Buckley) Journeys in Time: A New Atlas of American History, 2001; (with S. Buckley) Places in Time: A New Atlas of American History, 2001; The West, 2002; Children in Time: A New Atlas of American History, 2003; The Exxon Valdez Oil Spill, 2005; (with S. Buckley) Journeys for Freedom: A New Look at America's Story, 2006; (with S. Buckley) Kids Make History: A New Look at America's Story, 2006. **Address:** 319 Bedford Ave., Brooklyn, NY 11211-5203, U.S.A. **Online address:** elleacock@aol.com

LEADER, Darian. British/American (born United States), b. 1965?. **Genres:** Psychology, Young Adult Non-fiction, Social Sciences. **Career:** Centre for Freudian Analysis and Research, co-founder; Leeds Metropolitan University, lecturer. Psychoanalyst and writer. **Publications:** (With J. Groves) Lacan for Beginners, 1994; (with J. Groves) Introducing Lacan, 1996; Why Do Women Write More Letters Than They Post?, 1997; Why Do Women Write More Letters than They Send?: A Meditation on the Loneliness of the Sexes, 1997; Promises Lovers Make When It Gets Late, 1998; Freud's Footnotes, 2000; Stealing the Mona Lisa: What Art Stops Us from Seeing, 2002; Why Do People Get Ill?, 2007; New Black: Mourning, Melancholia and Depression, 2008. Contributor of articles to periodicals. **Address:** Centre for Freudian Analysis and Research, 571 Finchley Rd., Ste. 56, London, GL NW3 7BN, England. **Online address:** darian@cfar.demon.co.uk

LEADER, Mary. American (born United States), b. 1948. **Genres:** Poetry. **Career:** Oklahoma Attorney General, assistant, 1980-81; Oklahoma Supreme Court, referee, 1982-91; Emory University, creative writing fellow for poetry and lecturer in literature and law; University of Memphis, assistant professor of English; Louisiana State University, faculty; Warren Wilson Program for Writers, faculty; Purdue University, Department of English, associate professor, professor. Writer. **Publications:** POETRY: Red Signature, 1997; The Penultimate Suitor, 2001. Contributor to journals. **Address:** Department of English, Purdue University, HEAV 314C, 500 Oval Dr., West Lafayette, IN 47907-2038, U.S.A. **Online address:** mleader@purdue.edu

LEADER, Zachary. British/American (born United States), b. 1946. **Genres:** Literary Criticism And History, Writing/Journalism, Psychology, Essays, Poetry, Education, Humanities. **Career:** Trinity Hall College, faculty; Downing College, faculty; Roehampton University, Digby Stuart College, reader in English, 1977-, professor of English literature, 1983-; California Institute of Technology, visiting professor, 1991-93. Writer. **Publications:** Reading Blake's Songs, 1981; Writer's Block, 1991; Revision and Romantic Authorship, 1996; (ed. with I. Haywood) Romantic Period Writings, 1798-1832: An Anthology, 1998; (ed.) Letters of Kingsley Amis, 2001; (ed.) On Modern British Fiction, 2002; (ed. and intro. with M. O'Neill) Major Works, 2003; Life of Kingsley Amis, 2006; (ed.) The Movement Reconsidered: Essays on Larkin, Amis, Gunn, Davie, and Their Contemporaries, 2009. Contributor to periodicals. **Address:** Department of English and Creative Writing, Digby Stuart College, Roehampton University, Roehampton Ln., London, GL SW15 5PU, England. **Online address:** z.leader@roehampton.ac.uk

LEAHY, James E. American (born United States), b. 1919. **Genres:** Law, Reference. **Career:** Cupler, Tenneson, Serkland & Leahy, attorney, 1949-56; Merchants National Bank and Trust Co., trust department, managing officer and vice president, 1956-64; California Western School of Law, professor of law, 1964-84, professor emeritus, 1984-; American Bar Foundation, Probate Research Study, director. Writer. **Publications:** The First Amendment, 1791-1991: Two Hundred Years of Freedom, 1991; Liberty, Justice, and Equality: How These Constitutional Guarantees Have Been Shaped by United States Supreme Court Decisions Since 1789, 1992; Freedom Fighters of The United States Supreme Court, 1996; Supreme Court Justices who Voted with the Government: Nine who Favored the Individual Rights, 1999; The North Dakota State Constitution: A Reference Guide, 2003. Contributor to journals. **Address:** California Western School of Law, 225 Cedar St., San Diego, CA 92101, U.S.A. **Online address:** firstamend@att.net

LEAHY, Robert L. American (born United States) **Genres:** Psychology, Adult Non-fiction, Medicine/Health, Psychiatry, Social Sciences. **Career:** American Institute for Cognitive Therapy, founder, director; Cornell University Medical School, professor of psychology; Vassar College, instructor; New York University, instructor; University of British Columbia, instructor; Hofstra University, instructor; New School for Social Research, instructor; Yale University, visiting fellow; New York-Presbyterian Hospital, attending psychologist. Writer. **Publications:** NONFICTION: (ed.) The Child's Construction of Social Inequality, 1983; (ed.) The Development of the Self, 1985; Cognitive Therapy: Basic Principles and Applications, 1996; (ed.) Practicing Cognitive Therapy: A Guide to Interventions, 1997; Overcoming Resistance in Cognitive Therapy, 2001; (ed. with E.T. Dowd) Clinical Advances in Cognitive Psychotherapy: Theory and Application, 2002; Psychology and the Economic Mind: Cognitive Processes and Conceptualization, 2003; Cognitive Therapy Techniques: A Practitioner's Guide, 2003; (ed.) Roadblocks in Cognitive Behavioral Therapy: Transforming Challenges into Opportunities for Change, 2003; (ed. with S.L. Johnson) Psychological Treatment of Bipolar Disorder, 2004; (ed.) Contemporary Cognitive Therapy: Theory, Research and Practice, 2004; The Worry Cure: Seven Steps to Stop Worry from Stopping You, 2005; (ed. with P. Gilbert) Therapeutic Relationship in the Cognitive Behavioral Psychotherapies, 2007; Anxiety Free: Unravel Your Fears Before They Unravel You, 2009; (ed. with D. Sookman) Treatment Resistant Anxiety Disorders: Resolving Impasses to Symptom Remission, 2009; Beat the Blues Before they Beat you: How to Overcome Depression, 2010. **Address:** American Institute for Cognitive Therapy, 136 E 57th St., Ste. 1101, New York, NY 10022, U.S.A. **Online address:** rol2001@med.cornell.edu

LEAK, Andrew N. British (born England), b. 1956. **Genres:** Young Adult Non-fiction, Mythology/Folklore, History, Autobiography/Memoirs, Humanities. **Career:** University College London, Department of French, professor and head. Writer. **Publications:** NONFICTION: The Perverted Consciousness: Sexuality and Sartre, 1989; Barthes: Mythologies, 1994; (ed. with G. Paizis) The Holocaust and the Text: Speaking the Unspeakable, 2000; (ed. with A. van den Hoven) Sartre Today: A Centenary Celebration, 2005; Jean-Paul Sartre, 2006. **Address:** University College London, Gower St., London, GL WC1E 6BT, England. **Online address:** a.leak@ucl.ac.uk

LEAKE, John. Austrian/American (born United States), b. 1970. **Genres:** Criminology/True Crime, Autobiography/Memoirs, Biography. **Career:** Freelance writer and translator. **Publications:** Entering Hades: The Double Life of a Serial Killer, 2007. **Address:** Phenix & Phenix Literary Publicists, 2100 Kramer Ln., Ste. 300, Austin, TX 78758, U.S.A.

LEAKEY, Richard (Erskine Frere). Kenyan (born Kenya), b. 1944. **Genres:** Anthropology/Ethnology, Autobiography/Memoirs, Adult Non-fiction, Archaeology/Antiquities, Natural History. **Career:** Anthropological Expeditions, co-leader, 1963-64, 1966-67; Koobi Fora (formerly E. Rudolf) Research Project, leader, 1968-; National Museums of Kenya, administrative director, 1968-74, director, 1974-89; Nakali/Suguta Valley Expedition, leader and coordinator, 1978-; East African Wildlife Society, vice-chairman, 1980-; Anthropology Museum of the People of New York, chairman, 1980-; West Turkana Research Project, leader and coordinator, 1982-, leader, 1984-; Kenya Wildlife Conservation and Management Department, director, 1989-90; Kenya Wildlife Service, director, 1989-94, 1998-99, Public Service and Secretary to the Cabinet, head, 1999-2001; Richard Leakey & Associates Ltd., consultant, 2001-. Writer. **Publications:** (Ed. and contrib.) Fossil Vertebrates of Africa, 1969; (co-ed.) Earliest Man and Environments in the Lake Rudolf Basin: Stratigraphy, Palaeoecology and Evolution, 1976; (ed. with M. Leakey) Koobi For a Research Project, vol. I: The Fossil Hominids and an Introduction to Their Context, 1978; (ed. with G. Isaac) Human Ancestors: Readings from Scientific American, 1979; (ed. and intro.) The Illustrated Origin of Species, 1979; The Making of Mankind, 1981; Human Origins, 1982; One Life (autobiography), 1983; Man-Ape, Ape-Man: The Quest for Human's Place in Nature and Dubois' Missing Link, 1993; (ed. with A. Walker) The Nariokotome Homo Erectus Skeleton, 1993; The Origins of Human Kind, 1994; Wildlife Wars: My Fight to Save Africa's Natural Treasures, 2001; Southeast Africa: 1880 to The Present: Reclaiming a Region of Natural Wealth, 2002; (with F.E. Grine and J.G. Fleagle) First Humans: Origin and Early Evolution of the Genus Homo, 2009; (foreword) Africa's Big Five and Other Wildlife Filmmakers. A Centenary of Wildlife Filming in Kenya, 2010. WITH R. LEWIN: Origins: What New Discoveries Reveal about the Emergence of Our Species and Its Possible Future, 1977; People of the Lake: Mankind and Its Beginnings, 1978; Origins Reconsidered: In Search of What Makes Us Human, 1992; The Sixth Extinction: Patterns of Life and the Future of Humankind, 1995. Contributor to books, journals and periodicals. **Address:** Twaweza Communications Ltd., Twaweza House, Parklands Rd., Westlands, Nairobi, 66872-0800, Kenya. **Online address:** leakey@skyweb.co.ke

LEAL, David L. American (born United States), b. 1968. **Genres:** Politics/Government. **Career:** State University of New York, Department of Political Science, assistant professor, 1997-2002; University of Texas, Department of Government, assistant professor, 2002-05, Mike Hogg professorship in community affairs, 2002-04, associate professor, 2005-, dean's fellow, 2007, Center for Mexican-American Studies, faculty associate, 2002-, Public Policy Institute, director, 2003-. Writer. **Publications:** Democratization and the Ghost of Zapata: Mexico from 1959 to 1991, 1996; Electing America's Governors: The Politics of Executive Elections, 2006; (ed. with R. Espino and K.J. Meier) Latino Politics: Identity, Mobilization and Representation, 2007; (ed. with T.E. Givens and G.P. Freeman) Immigration Policy and Security: U.S., European and Commonwealth Perspectives, 2009; (edited by R.O. de la Garza and L. DeSipio) Beyond the Barrio: Latinos in the 2004 Election, 2010; (ed. with K.J. Meier) Politics of Latino Education, 2011. **Address:** Department of Government, University of Texas at Austin, Austin, TX 78712, U.S.A. **Online address:** dleal@austin.utexas.edu

LEAMAN, Celia A. (Anne Graham). Canadian/British (born England), b. 1948. **Genres:** Novels, Young Adult Non-fiction. **Career:** Fraser Valley Regional Library, assistant librarian. Writer and librarian. **Publications:** Unraveled, 2002; Mary's Child, 2005; Past Present I: A Web of Lies, 2008; The Winnowed Woman: Declarations from a Woman's Heart; Deceitful Hags, 2008. FORTHCOMING: Past Present I: Awareness; Past Present II: Resolution; The Bowerman. **Address:** c/o Author Mail, Twilight Times Books, PO Box 3340, Kingsport, TN 37664-0340, U.S.A. **Online address:** novelist@uniserve.com

LEAMAN, Oliver. American (born United States), b. 1950. **Genres:** Philosophy, Theology/Religion, History. **Career:** University of Kentucky, professor of philosophy and Zantker Professor of Judaic Studies, 2000-. Writer and academic. **Publications:** An Introduction to Medieval Islamic Philosophy, 1985 as An Introduction to Classic Islamic Philosophy, 2002; Averroes and His Philosophy, 1988, rev. ed., 1998; Moses Maimonides, 1990; Evil and Suffering in Jewish Philosophy, 1995; Death and Loss: Compassionate Approaches in the Classroom, 1995; (ed.) Friendship East and West: Philosophical Perspectives, 1996; (ed. with S.H. Nasr) History of Islamic Philosophy, 1996; (ed. with D.H. Frank) History of Jewish Philosophy, 1997; (ed.) The Future of Philosophy: Towards the Twenty-first Century, 1998; Key Concepts in Eastern Philosophy, 1999; A Brief Introduction to Islamic Philosophy, 1999; Eastern Philosophy: Key Readings, 2000; (ed. with D.H. Frank and C.H. Manekin) The Jewish Philosophy Reader, 2000; (ed.) Encyclopedia of Asian Philosophy, 2001; (ed.) Companion Encyclopedia of Middle Eastern and North African Film, 2001; (ed. with G. Howarth) Encyclopedia of Death and Dying, 2002; (ed. with D.H. Frank) The Cambridge Companion to Medieval Jewish Philosophy, 2003; Islamic Aesthetics: An Introduction, 2004; Jewish Thought: An Introduction, 2006; (ed.) The Qur'an: An Encyclopedia, 2006; (ed.) The Biographical Encyclopedia of Islamic Philosophy, 2006; (with K. Ali) Islam: The Key Concepts, 2007; (trans.) M. Campanini, The Qur'an: The Basics, 2007; (with P.S. Groff) Islamic Philosophy A-Z, 2007; (with N. Smart) World Philosophies, 2nd ed., 2008. **Address:** Department of Philosophy, University of Kentucky, 1415 Patterson Office Twr., Lexington, KY 40506-0027, U.S.A. **Online address:** oleaman@uky.edu

LEANING, Jennifer. American (born United States), b. 1945. **Genres:** Medicine/Health, Politics/Government, Military/Defense/Arms Control, Sciences. **Career:** Massachusetts General Hospital, intern and resident, 1975-78; Harvard University, School of Public Health, Department of Global Health and Population, instructor in medicine, 1978-94, assistant professor of medicine, 1994, Francois-Xavier Bagnoud professor of the practice of international health and human Rights, 1994-, Francois-Xavier Bagnoud Center for Health and Human Rights, director, 2010-, Medical School, associate professor of medicine; Harvard Community Health Plan, chief of emergency services, 1984-; Radcliffe Institute for Advanced Study, senior advisor in international and policy studies; Brigham and Women's Hospital, Emergency Department, attending physician. Writer. **Publications:** (Ed. with L. Keyes) The Counterfeit Ark: Crisis Relocation for Nuclear War, 1984; (with R.A. Barron and B.H. Rumack) Bloody Sunday: Trauma in Tbilisi: The Events of April 9, 1989 and Their Aftermath: Report of a Medical Mission to Soviet Georgia, 1990; (ed. with S.M. Briggs and L.C. Chen) Humanitarian Crises: The Medical and Public Health Response, 1999; (ed. with L.C. Chen and V. Narasimhan) Global Health Challenges for Human Security, 2003. **Address:** Department of Global Health and Population, School of Public Health, Harvard University, 651 Huntington Ave., 7th Fl., Boston, MA 02115-6009, U.S.A. **Online address:** jleaning@hsph.harvard.edu

LEAR, James. *See* **SMITH, Rupert.**

LEAR, Linda J(ane). American (born United States), b. 1940. **Genres:** Biography, Bibliography, History. **Career:** Vail Deane School, Department of History, chair, 1963-65; National Cathedral School, Department of History, chair, 1965-68; New Mexico State University, assistant professor, 1974-76; American Association of Retired Persons, Humanities Program, project director and special assistant, 1976-78; George Washington University, assistant director of experimental programs and associated professor, 1978-, research professor of environmental history; Smithsonian Institution, senior fellow, 1993, research associate, 1993-98, senior research associate; Yale University, Beinecke fellow, 1994; University of Maryland, faculty. Writer. **Publications:** Harold L. Ickes: The Aggressive Progressive, 1874-1933, 1981; (comp. with P.G. Fisher) A Selected Bibliography For Washington Studies and Descriptions of Major Local Collections, 1981; (co-ed.) Exploring the Unknown: Selected Documents in the History of the U.S. Civil Space Program, 1995; Rachel Carson: Witness for Nature, 1997; (ed. and intro.) Lost Woods: The Discovered Writing of Rachel Carson, 1998; (intro.) Introduction to The Sense of Wonder, 1998; (intro.) Introduction to the 40th Anniversary Edition of Silent Spring, 2002; Beatrix Potter, A Life in Nature, 2007. **Address:** University of Maryland, 1000 Hilltop Cir., Baltimore, MD 21250, U.S.A. **Online address:** lear.linda@gmail.com

LEAR, Patricia. American (born United States), b. 1944. **Genres:** Novellas/Short Stories, Young Adult Fiction. **Career:** Vogue, editorial assistant, 1971-73. **Publications:** Stardust, 7-Eleven, Route 57, A & W and So Forth: Stories, 1992. Contributor to journals. Works appear in anthologies. **Address:** c/o Amanda Urban, International Creative Management Inc., 730 5th Ave., New York, NY 10019, U.S.A.

LEAR, Peter. *See* **LOVESEY, Peter (Harmer).**

LEARY, Ann (Lembeck). American (born United States), b. 1962?. **Genres:** Plays/Screenplays, Novels, Biography, Humor/Satire. **Career:** Writer. **Publications:** An Innocent, a Broad, 2004; Outtakes from a Marriage, 2008. **Address:** Maria Massie, Lippincott Massie McQuilkin, 27 W 20th St., New York, NY 10011, U.S.A. **Online address:** ann@annleary.com

LEASK, Nigel. British/Scottish (born Scotland), b. 1958. **Genres:** Literary Criticism And History, Travel/Exploration. **Career:** Cambridge University, lecturer in English, 1989-, reader in romantic literature, Queens' College, fellow; University Glasgow, Regius chair in English language and literature, 2004-, Regius professor of English language and literature; Queen's College, fellow. Writer. **Publications:** The Politics of Imagination in Coleridge's Critical Thought, 1988; British Romantic Writers and the East: Anxieties of Empire, 1992; Curiosity and the Aesthetics of Travel Writing, 1770-1840: From an Antique Land, 2002; (ed. with D. Simpson and P. de Bolla) Land, Nation and Culture, 1740-1840: Thinking the Republic of Taste, 2004; (ed. with P. Connell) Romanticism and Popular Culture in Britain and Ireland, 2009; Robert Burns and Pastoral: Poetry and Improvement in Late Eighteenth-Century Scotland, 2010. **Address:** Department of English Literature, University of Glasgow, Rm. 304, 4 University Gardens, Glasgow, G12 8QQ, England. **Online address:** n.leask@englit.arts.gla.ac.uk

LEATHERBARROW, W(illiam) J(ohn). British (born England), b. 1947. **Genres:** Literary Criticism And History, Biography, History, Social Sciences, Humanities. **Career:** University of Sheffield, reader, professor of Russian, 1970-, dean of the faculty of arts, 1997-99, personal chair, 1994, School of Modern Languages, chair, 2001-04, 2005-06. Writer. **Publications:** Fedor Dostoevsky, 1981; (trans. and ed. with D.C. Offord) A Documentary History of Russian Thought: From the Enlightenment to Marxism, 1987; Fedor Dostoevsky: A Reference Guide, 1990; Fyodor Dostoyevsky: The Brothers Karamazov, 1992; (ed.) Crime and Punishment, 1992; (contrib.) Dostoevsky: The Idiot, 1992; (ed.) Dostoevskii and Britain, 1995; (ed.) Dostoevsky's The Devils: A Critical Companion, 1999; (contrib.) Dostoevsky Short Stories: White Nights; A Gentle Creature; The Dream of a Ridiculous Man, 1999; (ed.) The Cambridge Companion to Dostoevskii, 2002; Devil's Vaudeville: The Demonic in Dostoevsky's Major Fiction, 2005; (intro.) Idiot, 2008; (intro.) White Nights; A Gentle Creature; The Dream of a Ridiculous Man, 2009; (ed. with D. Offord) A History of Russian Thought, 2010. **Address:** Russian and Slavonic Studies, University of Sheffield, Jessop West, 1 Upper Hanover St., Sheffield, DU S3 7RA, England. **Online address:** w.leatherbarrow@sheffield.ac.uk

LEAVELL, Linda. American (born United States), b. 1954. **Genres:** Literary Criticism And History, Art/Art History, Biography. **Career:** Rhodes College, visiting assistant professor of English, 1985-86; Oklahoma State University, assistant professor, 1986-91, associate professor, 1991-2008, professor of English, 2008-10. Writer. **Publications:** Marianne Moore and the Visual Arts: Prismatic Color, 1995; (ed. with C. Miller and R.G. Schulze) Critics and Poets on Marianne Moore: A Right Good Salvo of Barks, 2005. Contributor to periodicals. **Address:** 2566 E Frontier Elm Dr., Fayetteville, AR 72703, U.S.A. **Online address:** linda.leavell@okstate.edu

LEAVITT, Caroline. American (born United States), b. 1952. **Genres:** Novels, Children's Non-fiction, Young Adult Fiction, Reference, Medicine/Health, Literary Criticism And History. **Career:** The Boston Globe, columnist; Dame Magazine, columnist. **Publications:** NOVELS: Meeting Rozzy Halfway, 1980; Lifelines, 1982; Jealousies, 1983; Family, 1987; Into Thin Air, 1993; Living Other Lives, 1995; Haunted Clubhouse, 1997; Prince and the Pooch, 1997; Robinhound Crusoe, 1997; Coming Back to Me, 2001; Girls in Trouble, 2004; Kids Family Tree Book, 2005; Samurai, 2007; Pictures of You, 2011. **Address:** c/o Gail Hochman, Brandt and Hochman Literary Agents Inc., 1501 Broadway, Ste. 2310, New York, NY 10036, U.S.A. **Online address:** carleavitt@hotmail.com

LEAVITT, David. American (born United States), b. 1961. **Genres:** Novels, Mathematics/Statistics. **Career:** Viking-Penguin Inc., editorial assistant, reader and educational assistant, 1983-84; University of Florida, professor of creative writing, 2000-, co-director of creative writing, 2006-; Subtropics, editor, 2006-; Princeton University, faculty. **Publications:** Family Dancing, 1984; The Lost Language of Cranes, 1986; Equal Affections, 1989; A Place I've Never Been, 1990; While England Sleeps, 1993; (ed. with M. Mitchell) The Penguin Book of Gay Short Stories, 1994; (with M. Mitchell) Italian Pleasures, 1996; (ed. and intro. with M. Mitchell) Pages Passed from Hand to Hand, 1997; Arkansas, 1997; The Page Turner, 1998; Martin Bauman: Or, A Sure Thing, 2000; The Marble Quilt, 2001; (ed. and intro. with M. Mitchell) Selected Stories, 2001; (with M. Mitchell) In Maremma, 2001; Florence, a Delicate Case, 2002; Collected Stories, 2003; The Body of Jonah Boyd, 2004; (co-author) The M Word, 2004; The Man Who Knew Too Much: Alan Turing and the Invention of the Computer, 2005; The Indian Clerk, 2007; (intro.) A Room with a View, 2009. **Address:** Department of English, University of Florida, 4101 Turlington Hall, PO Box 117310, Gainesville, FL 32611-7310, U.S.A. **Online address:** dleavitt@ufl.edu

LEAVITT, Judith Walzer. American (born United States), b. 1940. **Genres:** History, Medicine/Health, Social Sciences. **Career:** University of Wisconsin, assistant professor, 1975-81, associate professor, 1981-86, Department of the History of Medicine, chair, 1981-93, professor, 1986-, Evjue-Bascom professor of women's studies, 1990-95, School of Medicine, associate dean of faculty, 1996-99, History of Science and Women's Studies, Ruth Bleier WARF professor in the history of medicine, 1997-, Rupple-Bacom professor, 2004-, interim chair, 2007-08, now Rupple Bascom and Ruth Bleier professor emeritus; University of Texas Medical Branch, visiting professor, 1977; State University of New York, Center for Photographic Images in Medicine, project associate, 1979-83; Loma Linda University, William Frederick Norwood lecturer in the history of medicine, 1986; University of California, Charles E. Culpepper Foundation lecturer in the history of medicine, 1988; Duke University, lecturer, 1988; Medical College of Pennsylvania, Kate Hurd Mead lecturer, 1989; Yale University, John F. Fulton Fellow and John F. Fulton lecturer, 1990; Medical College of Wisconsin, Milwaukee Academy of Medicine, lecturer, 1992; Emory University, James Harvey Young lecturer, 1999; Foundation for the History of Women in Medicine, board director, 2000-; University of Minnesota, Sally and Bruce Kentar lecturer, 2001; University of Kansas, Peete lecturer, 2001. Writer. **Publications:** The Healthiest City: Milwaukee and the Politics of Health Reform, 1982; Brought to Bed: Childbearing in America, 1750-1950, 1986; Typhoid Mary: Captive to the Public's Health, 1996; Make Room for Daddy: The Journey from Waiting Room to Birthing Room, 2009. EDITOR: (with R.L. Numbers) Medicine Without Doctors: Home Health Care in American History, 1977; (with R.L. Numbers and G.B. Risse) Sickness and Health in America: Readings in the History of Medicine and Public Health, 1978, 3rd ed. (with R.L. Numbers), 1997; (with R.L. Numbers) Wisconsin Medicine: Historical Perspectives, 1981; Women and Health in America: Historical Readings, 1984, 2nd ed., 1999. Contributor to books. **Address:** Department of Medical History & Bioethics, University of Wisconsin, 1410 Med Sci Ctr., 1300 University Ave., Madison, WI 53706-1532, U.S.A. **Online address:** jwleavit@wisc.edu

LEAVY, Barbara Fass. American (born United States), b. 1936. **Genres:** Literary Criticism And History, Social Sciences, Mystery/Crime/Suspense. **Career:** City University of New York, Queens College, professor of English, now professor emeritus; Cornell University, DeWitt Wallace Institute for the History of Psychiatry, adjunct professor of English in psychiatry. Writer. **Publications:** La Belle Dame sans Merci and the Aesthetics of Romanticism, 1974; (with P.S. Jacobsen) Ibsen's Forsaken Merman: Folklore in the Late Plays, 1988; To Blight with Plague: Studies in a Literary Theme, 1992; In Search of the Swan Maiden: A Narrative on Folklore and Gender, 1994; The Fiction of Ruth Rendell, 2010. Contributor of articles to journals. **Address:** Department of English, Queens College, City University of New York, 65-30 Kissena Blvd., Flushing, NY 11367, U.S.A.

LEBEAU, Roy. See **SMITH, Mitchell.**

LEBOEUF, Michael. American (born United States), b. 1942. **Genres:** Business/Trade/Industry, Self Help, Industrial Relations, Marketing, Administration/Management. **Career:** University of New Orleans, assistant professor, 1969-73, associate professor, 1973-83, professor of management, through 1983, now professor emeritus; Michael LeBoeuf and Associates, founder. **Publications:** Working Smart: How to Accomplish More in Half the Time, 1979; Imagineering: How to Profit from Your Own Creative Powers, 1980; The Productivity Challenge: How to Make it Work for America and You, 1982; The Greatest Management Principle in the World, 1985; How to Win Customers and Keep Them for Life, 1987; Getting Results: The Secret to Motivating Yourself and Others, 1989; Fast Forward: How to Win a Lot More Business in a Lot Less Time, 1993; The Perfect Business: How to Make a Million from Home with No Payroll, No Employee Headaches, No Debts, and No Sleepless Nights!, 1996; The Millionaire in You: Ten Things You Need to Do Now to Have Money and the Time to Enjoy It, 2002; (with T. Larimore and M. Lindauer) Bogleheads' Guide to Investing, 2006, rev. ed., 2007. **Address:** c/o Inkwell Management, 521 5th Ave., 26th Fl., New York, NY 10175, U.S.A. **Online address:** mikelebuf@aol.com

LEBOR, Adam. Hungarian/British (born England), b. 1961?. **Genres:** Novels, History, Literary Criticism And History, Young Adult Non-fiction. **Career:** Independent, reporter, 1991-; London Times, journalist, 1991-, central European correspondent; The Economist, literary critic; Sunday Telegraph, literary critic; Literary Review, literary critic. **Publications:** Hitler's Secret Bankers: The Myth of Swiss Neutrality during the Holocaust, 1997; A Heart Turned East: Among the Muslims of Europe and America, 1997; (with R. Boyes) Surviving Hitler: Choice, Corruption and Compromise in the Third Reich, 2000; (with R. Boyes) Seduced by Hitler: The Choices of a Nation and the Ethics of Survival, 2000; Milosevic: A Biography, 2002; City of Oranges: Arabs and Jews in Jaffa, 2006 in US as City of Oranges: An Intimate History of Arabs and Jews in Jaffa, 2007; Complicity with Evil: The United Nations in the Age of Modern Genocide, 2006; The Believers: How America Fell For Bernard Madoff's 65 Billion Investment Scam, 2009; The Budapest Protocol, 2009. Contributor to journals. **Address:** c/o Elizabeth Sheinkman, Curtis Brown Group, Haymarket House, 28-29 Haymarket, London, GL SW1 4SP, England. **Online address:** mail@adamlebor.com

LEBOVICS, Herman. American/Czech (born Czech Republic), b. 1935. **Genres:** History. **Career:** Brooklyn College, instructor in European history, 1962-65; Oberlin College, visiting assistant professor, 1965-66; State University of New York, Department of History, assistant professor, 1966-69, associate professor of European history, 1969-, professor, board of trustees distinguished professor, 2006-; Columbia University, visiting associate professor, 1972. Writer and historian. **Publications:** Social Conservatism and the Middle Classes in Germany, 1914-1933, 1969; The Alliance of Iron and Wheat in the Third French Republic, 1860-1914: Origins of the New Conservatism, 1988; True France: The Wars over Cultural Identity, 1900-1945, 1992; Mona Lisa's Escort: André Malraux and the Reinvention of French Culture, 1999; Bringing the Empire Back Home: France in the Global Age, 2004; Imperialism and the Corruption of Democracies, 2006; To Preserve a Certain Idea of the Cultural Heritage, forthcoming; John Locke on America, forthcoming. **Address:** Department of History, State University of New York, S-323, Social and Behavioral Sciences Bldg., 3rd Fl., Stonybrook, NY 11794-4348, U.S.A. **Online address:** herman.lebovics@stonybrook.edu

LEBOW, Eileen F. American/Panamanian (born Panama), b. 1925. **Genres:** Air/Space Topics, Education, History, Military/Defense/Arms Control, Transportation, Women's Studies And Issues, Technology, Engineering, Biography.

Career: Teacher, 1964-. Writer. **Publications:** Cal Rodgers and the Vin Fiz: The First Transcontinental Flight, 1989; A Grandstand Seat: The American Balloon Service in World War I, 1998; The Bright Boys: A History of Townsend Harris High School, 2000; Before Amelia: Women Pilots in the Early Days of Aviation, 2002. Contributor to periodicals. **Address:** 2821 29th St. NW, Washington, DC 20008, U.S.A.

LEBOW, Jeanne. American (born United States), b. 1951. **Genres:** Poetry, Natural History. **Career:** Junior high school teacher of English and drama, 1973-77; Memphis State University, instructor in English, 1982-84; University of Southern Mississippi, graduate instructor, 1984-87, adjunct professor and visiting professor, 1992-95; University of Ouagadougou, Fulbright lecturer, 1987-88; Northeast Missouri State University, assistant professor of English, 1988-91; Birdwatchers Digest, writer, 1999-; Mississippi School of the Arts, literary arts instructor. **Publications:** The Outlaw James Copeland and the Champion-Belted Empress (poems), 1991. **Address:** Mississippi School of the Arts, Whitworth College, 355 West Monticello St., Brookhaven, MS 39601-3205, U.S.A.

LEBOWITZ, Albert. American (born United States), b. 1922. **Genres:** Novels, Law, Literary Criticism And History, Young Adult Fiction. **Career:** Morris, Schneider and Lebowitz, partner, 1955-58; Crowe, Schneider, Shanahan and Lebowitz, partner, 1958-66; Perspective, editor, 1961-75; Murphy and Roche, counsel, 1966-67; Murphy and Schlapprizzi, partner, 1969-81; Murphy, Schlapprizzi and Lebowitz, partner, 1981-86; Donald L. Schlapprizzi, counsel, 1986-. Attorney and writer. **Publications:** Laban's Will, 1966; The Man Who Wouldn't Say No, 1969; A Matter of Days, 1989. Contributor to periodicals. **Address:** Gateway One on the Mall, 701 Market St., Ste. 1550, St. Louis, MO 63101-1861, U.S.A.

LE BRETON, Binka. Brazilian/British (born England), b. 1942. **Genres:** Children's Non-fiction, Civil Liberties/Human Rights, Environmental Sciences/Ecology, Autobiography/Memoirs. **Career:** Writer, 1974-; educator and pianist, 1974-89; Amigos de Iracambi, president, Iracambi Rainforest Research Center, director, 1999-. **Publications:** Voices from the Amazon, 1993; The Rainforest, 1997; A Land to Die For, 1997; Todos Sabiam, 2000; Somebody Knows My Name, 2002; Vidas Roubadas, 2002; Trapped: Modern-Day Slavery in the Brazilian Amazon, 2003; Le Piege, 2003, Vite Rubate 2003; The Greatest Gift: The Courageous Life and Death of Sister Dorothy Stang, 2007; A Maior Dádiva, 2008; Where the Road Ends: A Home in the Brazilian Rainforest: A Memoir, 2010. **Address:** Fazenda Iracambi, Caixa Postal Ste. 1, Rosário da Limeira, Muriaé, MI 36878-000, Brazil. **Online address:** binka@iracambi.com

LEBRETON, J(ean) D(ominique). French (born France), b. 1950. **Genres:** Biology, Animals/Pets, Sciences. **Career:** Centre d'Ecologie Fonctionnelle et Evolutive, director of research, 1985-, head. Writer. **Publications:** (Coauthor) Mathematiques Pour Biologistes: Exercices et Problemes Commentes, 1981; (ed. with C. Millier) Modèles Dynamiques Déterministesen Biologie, 1982; (co-ed.) Population Biology of Passerine Birds: An Integrated Approach, 1990; (ed. with C.M. Perrins and G.J.M. Hirons) Bird Population Studies: Their Relevance to Conservation and Management, 1991; (ed. with P.M. North) Marked Individuals in the Study of Bird Population, 1992; (ed. with B. Asselain) Biometrieet Environment, 1993. **Address:** Centre for Functional and Evolutionary Ecology, 1919 route de Mende, Montpellier, 5, France. **Online address:** jean-dominique.lebreton@cefe.cnrs.fr

LEBSOCK, Suzanne (Dee). American (born United States), b. 1949. **Genres:** Mystery/Crime/Suspense, History, Women's Studies And Issues, Essays. **Career:** Rutgers University, assistant professor of history, 1977-, professor of history, 1977-93, acting director of women's studies, 1986-87, board of governors professor of history, 2003-, Women and Gender Studies, affiliate; Woodrow Wilson International Center for Scholars, fellow, 1985; University of North Carolina at Chapel Hill, staff, 1992-95; University of Washington, professor of history, 1995-. Writer. **Publications:** (Contrib.) A Share of Honour: Virginia Women, 1600-1945 (essays), 1984; The Free Women of Petersburg: Status and Culture in a Southern Town, 1784-1860, 1984; Virginia Women, 1600-1945: A Share of Honour, 1987; (with A.F. Scott) Virginia Women: The First Two Hundred Years, 1988; (ed. with N.A. Hewitt) Visible Women: New Essays on American Activism, 1993; A Murder in Virginia: Southern Justice on Trial, 2003. Contributor to periodicals. **Address:** Department of History, Rutgers University, 107 Van Dyck Hall, 16 Seminary Pl., New Brunswick, NJ 08901, U.S.A. **Online address:** lebsock@history.rutgers.edu

LE CARRÉ, John. British (born England), b. 1931. **Genres:** Novels, Mystery/Crime/Suspense, Young Adult Non-fiction, Literary Criticism And History. **Career:** Millfield Junior School, teacher, 1954-55; Eton College, tutor, 1956-58; British Foreign Office, secretary, 1960-63, consultant, 1963-64. Writer. **Publications:** Call for the Dead, 1960; A Murder of Quality, 1962; The Spy Who Came in from the Cold, 1963; The Incongruous Spy: Two Novels of Suspense, 1964; The Looking Glass War, 1965; A Small Town in Germany, 1968; The Naive and Sentimental Lover, 1971; Tinker, Tailor, Soldier, Spy, 1974; The Honourable Schoolboy, 1977; Smiley's People, 1979; The Quest for Karla, 1982; Three Complete Novels, 1983; The Little Drummer Girl, 1983; A Perfect Spy, 1986; John Le Carré: Three Complete Novels, 1986; The Clandestine Muse, 1986; (with G.H. Davies) Vanishing England, 1987; (and intro.) The Russia House, 1989; The Secret Pilgrim, 1991; The Night Manager: A Novel, 1993; Our Game: A Novel, 1995; The Tailor of Panama, 1996; Single & Single: A Novel, 1999; The Constant Gardener: A Novel, 2001; Absolute Friends, 2003; The Mission Song, 2006; (co-author) Not One More Death, 2006; A Most Wanted Man: A Novel, 2008; (co-author) Ox-Tales: Fire, 2009; Our Kind of Traitor: A Novel, 2010; The Collected George Smiley Radio Dramas, 2010. Contributor to periodicals. **Address:** Curtis Brown Group Ltd., Haymarket House, 28-29 Haymarket, 5th Fl., London, GL SW1Y 4SP, England.

LECESNE, James. American (born United States), b. 1954. **Genres:** Novels, Young Adult Fiction, Mystery/Crime/Suspense. **Career:** New York University, teacher; Trevor Hotline, co-founder; After the Storm Foundation, founder. Writer. **Publications:** (With M. Long) My First Car, 1993; Absolute Brightness, 2008; Virgin Territory, 2010; (ed. with S. Moon) The Letter Q: Queer Writers Notes To Their Younger Selves, 2012. **Address:** Your Neighborhood Office, 332 Bleecker St., New York, NY 10014, U.S.A. **Online address:** james@jameslecesne.com

LECKEY, Andrew A. American (born United States), b. 1949. **Genres:** Money/Finance, Law, Business/Trade/Industry. **Career:** Oregon Statesman, finance editor, 1975-76; Phoenix Gazette, state house reporter, 1976-78; The Chicago Sun-Times, finance columnist and reporter, 1980-85; WBEZ Public Radio, finance commentator, 1981-83, on-air commentator, 1983-85; Los Angeles Times Syndicate, syndicated investment columnist, 1983-85; WLS-TV, finance commentator, 1983, business reporter, 1983-93; New York Daily News, finance columnist, 1985; The Chicago Tribune, finance columnist, 1985-; CNBC-TV, financial anchor and reporter, 1995-99; University of California, instructor of business journalism, Graduate School of Journalism, Bloomberg Business Reporting Program, director, 1999-2002; Quicken.com Money Reports, television reporter and contributing editor, 2000-01; CNX Media, on-air reporter, 2000-01; Boston University, College of Communication, visiting professor, 2002-03; Arizona State University, Walter Cronkite School of Journalism and Mass Communication, Donald W. Reynolds National Center for Business Journalism, president and director, 2003-, Donald W. Reynolds endowed chair in business journalism, 2008-. **Publications:** Make Money with the New Tax Laws, 1987; The 20 Hottest Investments for the 21st Century, 1994; The Morningstar Approach to Investing: Wiring into the Mutual Fund Revolution, 1997; Global Investing: A Guide to the 50 Best Stocks in the World, 1999; (ed. with M. Loeb) The Best Business Stories of the Year, 2001, (with J. Bogle) 4th ed., 2004; (with J.C. Bogle and L.L. Budd) The Lack of Money Is the Root of All Evil: Mark Twain's Timeless Advice on Money, Wealth and Investing, 2001. Contributor to periodicals. **Address:** Tribune Media Services, 435 N Michigan Ave., Ste. 1500, Chicago, IL 60611-4066, U.S.A. **Online address:** andrew.leckey@businessjournalism.org

LECKIE, Keith (Ross). Canadian (born Canada), b. 1952. **Genres:** Novels, Plays/Screenplays. **Career:** Scriptwriter and director, 1979-; novelist, 1987-. Educator. **Publications:** The Seventh Gate (novel), 1989; Coppermine, 2010; The Coco River, forthcoming. **Address:** The Alpern Group, 585 Bloor St. W, Toronto, ON M6G 1K5, Canada. **Online address:** krleckie@hotmail.com

LECKIE, Ross. Scottish (born Scotland), b. 1957. **Genres:** Romance/Historical, Adult Non-fiction, Novels. **Career:** Freelance journalist and copywriter, 1986-96; Martin Currie Investment Management, director of corporate communications, 1996-. **Publications:** NON-FICTION: The Bluffer's Guide to the Classics: Bluff Your Way in the Classics, 1989; Grampian, 1991; The Gourmet's Companion, 1994. NOVELS: Hannibal, 1995; Scipio Africanus: The Man Who Defeated Hannibal, 1998; Carthage: A Novel, 2001. **Address:** Shiel Land Associates Ltd., 43 Doughty St., Greator London, WC1N 2LF, England.

LECKIE, Shirley A(nne). American (born United States), b. 1937. **Genres:** History, Biography, Autobiography/Memoirs. **Career:** University of Toledo, academic advisor, 1972-77, coordinator of adult liberal studies, 1974-77, director of external affairs and adult liberal studies, 1977-80, assistant dean of continuing education for business and professional seminars, 1980-81; Millsaps College, assistant professor of history and associate dean of continuing education, 1981-82; University of North Carolina, director of continuing education and special programs, 1983-85; University of Central Florida, assistant professor, 1985-88, associate professor of history, 1988-95, professor of history, 1995-, College of Arts and Science, assistant dean, 1997-98, graduate program coordinator, now professor emeritus; Orlando Metropolitan Women's Political Caucus, secretary, 1988-89. Writer. **Publications:** (With S.A. Leckie) Unlikely Warriors: General Benjamin H. Grierson and His Family, 1984; (ed.) The Colonel's Lady on the Western Frontier: The Correspondence of Alice Kirk Grierson, 1989; Elizabeth Bacon Custer and the Making of a Myth, 1993; Angie Debo: Pioneering Historian, 2000; (with W.H. Leckie) Buffalo Soldiers: A Narrative of the Black Cavalry in the West, 2003; (ed. with B.J. Dinges) Just and Righteous Cause: Benjamin H. Grierson's Civil War Memoir, 2008; (ed. and intro. with N.J. Parezo) Their Own Frontier: Women Intellectuals Re-Visioning the American West, 2008. Work appears in anthologies. Contributor of articles and reviews to journals. **Address:** Department of History, University of Central Florida, 4000 Central Florida Blvd., Orlando, FL 32816-1350, U.S.A. **Online address:** sleckie@cfl.rr.com

LECKY-THOMPSON, Guy W. American/Chinese/British (born England), b. 1974. **Genres:** Information Science/Computers, Technology, Education. **Career:** Computer programmer and author. **Publications:** (With M. DeLoura) Games Programming Gems, 2000; Infinite Games Universe: Mathematical Techniques, 2001; Infinite Game Universe: Level Design, Terrain and Sound, 2002; Corporate Software Project Management, 2005; Video Game Design Revealed, 2007; Just Enough C/C plus plus Programming, 2008; Just Enough Web Programming with XHTML, PHP and MYSQL, 2008; AI and Artificial Life in Video Games, 2008; Fundamentals of Network Game Development, 2009. **Address:** c/o Author Mail, Charles River Media, 10 Downer Ave., Hingham, MA 02043, U.S.A. **Online address:** Guy_W@Lecky-Thompson.net

LECLAIRE, Anne D(ickinson). American (born United States), b. 1942. **Genres:** Novels, Essays, Medicine/Health, Young Adult Non-fiction. **Career:** Cape Cod Illustrated, writer and associate editor, 1974-76; WVLC-Radio, news reporter, 1974-76; Cape Cod Times, reporter, editor and writer, 1976-82; Boston Globe, correspondent, 1979-82; freelance writer, 1982-. **Publications:** NOVELS: Land's End, 1985; Every Mother's Son, 1987; Grace Point, 1992; Sideshow, 1994; Entering Normal, 2001; Leaving Eden, 2002; The Law of Bound Hearts, 2004; The Lavender Hour, 2007. NON-FICTION: Listening Below the Noise: A Meditation on the Practice of Silence, 2009. Works appear in anthologies. Contributor to magazines and newspapers. **Address:** HarperCollins Publishers, 10 E 53rd St., New York, NY 10022, U.S.A. **Online address:** anne@anneleclaire.com

LECOMPTE, Jane. See LECOMPTE, N(ancy) Jane.

LECOMPTE, Mary Lou. American (born United States), b. 1935. **Genres:** History, Recreation, Sports/Fitness. **Career:** Saint Mary's College of Maryland, head of health, physical education and recreation department, 1958-60; University of Texas, instructor, assistant professor, 1960-93, associate professor of kinesiology and health education, 1993-96, retired, 1996; Physical Educator, reviewing editor, 1982-87; American Alliance for Health, Physical Education, Recreation, and Dance, newsletter editor, 1992. **Publications:** (With M.B. Alderson) Step Right In: Making Dance Fun for Boys and Girls, 1973; Cowgirls of the Rodeo: Pioneer Professional Athletes, 1993. Works appear in anthologies. Contributor of articles to journals. **Address:** 12609 Dessau, Ste. A-143, Austin, TX 78754, U.S.A.

LECOMPTE, N(ancy) Jane. Also writes as Jane Lecompte, Jane Ashford. American (born United States), b. 1948. **Genres:** Novels, Romance/Historical, inspirational/Motivational Literature, Literary Criticism And History. **Career:** Writer. **Publications:** AS JANE ASHFORD: Gwendeline, 1980; Bluestocking, 1980; (with V. Myers and R. Swan) Come November/Bluestocking/Hidden Spring, 1980; Man of Honour, 1981; Rivals of Fortune, 1981; The Three Graces, 1982; The Marchington Scandal, 1982; The Headstrong Ward, 1983; A Radical Arrangement, 1983; First Season, 1984; The Impetuous Heiress, 1984; Cachet, 1984 as First Impressions, 1992; The Repentant Rebel,

1984; The Irresolute Rivals, 1985; The Reluctant Rake, 1987; Meddlesome Miranda, 1988; The Marriage Wager, 1996; The Bargain, 1997; Charmed and Dangerous, 1998; Bride to Be, 1999. AS JANE LECOMPTE: Mirage, 1986; Moon Passage, 1989; Sistren, 2006. **Address:** c/o Jean V. Naggar, Jean V. Naggar Literary Agency Inc., 216 E 75th St., Ste. 1E, New York, NY 10021, U.S.A. **Online address:** jane_lecompte@hmco.com

LEDBETTER, Suzann. American (born United States), b. 1953. **Genres:** Biography, Novels, Humor/Satire, Adult Non-fiction, Young Adult Fiction, Mystery/Crime/Suspense, History. **Career:** Quassare Femina Inc., president; Southwest Missouri State University, Department of Continuing Education, instructor; Family Circle Magazine, columnist, contributing editor. Novelist, educator and public speaker. **Publications:** NONFICTION: Nellie Cashman: Prospector and Trailblazer, 1993; Shady Ladies: Seventeen Surprising and Rebellious American Women, 2006. HUMOR: The Toast Always Lands Jelly-Side Down and Other Tales of Suburban Life, 1993; I Have Everything I Had Twenty Years Ago Except Now It's All Lower, 1995. FICTION: On the Edge of Forever, 1992; Trinity Strike, 1996; Redemption Trail, 1996; Deliverance Drive, 1996; Colorado Reverie, 1997; Pure Justice, 1997; Klondike Fever, 1997; East of Peculiar, 2000; North of Clever, 2001; South of Sanity, 2001; West of Bliss, 2002; A Lady Never Trifles with Thieves, 2003; In Hot Pursuit, 2003; Ahead of the Game, 2004; Once A Thief, 2006; Deadly Housewives, 2006; Halfway to Half Way, 2007; Let Sleeping Dogs Lie, 2009; Not the Marryin' Kind, forthcoming. Contributor to magazines. **Address:** Dave Ellingsworth, PO Box 1032, Nixa, MO 65714, U.S.A. **Online address:** suzann@suzannledbetter.com

LEDDY, Mary Jo. Canadian (born Canada), b. 1946. **Genres:** History, Novels. **Career:** High school teacher, 1968-70; Catholic New Times, founding editor, 1973, founding member, 1977, editor, 1977-79, editorial team, 1981-85; Newman Center, campus minister, 1976-77; Toronto Star, columnist, 1979-86; University College, lecturer; Frye Publishing Shalom Institute, honorary director; University of Toronto, Regis College, lecturer in religion and society, adjunct professor, Romero House Community for Refugees, director; Maryknoll Seminary, lecturer; CBC TV, commentator. **Publications:** (Ed. with M.A. Hinsdale) Faith that Transforms: Essays in Honor of Gregory Baum, 1987; Say to the Darkness We Beg to Differ, 1988; Memories of War: Promises of Peace, 1989; Reweaving Religious Life: Beyond the Liberal Model, 1990; (with R. De Roo and D. Roche) In the Eye of the Catholic Storm: The Church Since Vatican II, 1992; At the Border Called Hope: Where Refugees are Neighbours, 1997; Radical Gratitude, 2002; Our Friendly Local Terrorist, 2010; The Other Face of God, 2011. Contributor to periodicals. **Address:** Regis College, Rm. 35, 100 Wellesley St. W, Toronto, ON M5S 2Z5, Canada. **Online address:** m.leddy@utoronto.ca

LEDERER, Katy. American (born United States), b. 1972?. **Genres:** Poetry, Autobiography/Memoirs. **Career:** Explosive, founder and editor, 1997-2007; Poetry Project Newsletter, editor, 1998-99; Fence Magazine, poetry editor. **Publications:** Winter Sex: Poems, 2002; Poker Face: A Girlhood among Gamblers (memoir), 2003; The Heaven-Sent Leaf: Poems, 2008. Works appear in anthologies. Contributor to periodicals. **Address:** BOA Editions Ltd., 250 N. Goodman St., Ste 306, Rochester, NY 14607, U.S.A. **Online address:** katylederer@gmail.com

LEDERER, Richard. American (born United States), b. 1938. **Genres:** Language/Linguistics, Humor/Satire, Animals/Pets, Reference, Education. **Career:** St. Paul's School, English teacher and chair of department, 1962-89; writer, 1987-; San Diego Public Radio, broadcaster. Humorist, linguist and public speaker. **Publications:** (Ed. with P. Burnham) Basic Verbal Skills, rev. ed., 1975; Anguished English: An Anthology of Accidental Assaults upon Our Language, 1987, rev. ed., 2006; Get Thee to a Punnery: Pun and Games with the English Language, 1988, rev. ed., 2006; Crazy English: The Ultimate Joy Ride through Our Language, 1989, rev. ed., 1998; The Play of Words: Fun & Games for Language Lovers, 1990; The Miracle of Language, 1991; More Anguished English: An Expose of Embarrassing, Excruciating, and Egregious Errors in English, 1993; Adventures of a Verbivore, 1994; (with M. Gilleland) Literary Trivia: Fun and Games for Book Lovers, 1994; Building Bridge, 1994; Nothing Risqué Nothing Gained: Ribald Riddles, Lascivious Limericks, Carnal Corn, and Other Good, Clean Dirty Fun, 1995, rev. ed. as The Cunning Linguist: Ribald Riddles, Lascivious Limericks, Carna lCorn, and Other Good, Clean, Dirty Fun!, 2003; (with R. Dowis) The Write Way:

The S.P.E.L.L. Guide to Real-Life Writing, 1995; Pun and Games: Jokes, Riddles, Daffynitions, Tairy Fales, Rhymes, and More Wordplay for Kids, 1996; Fractured English: A Pleasury of Bloopers and Blunders, Fluffs and Flubs, and Gaffes and Goofs, 1996; (intro.) Disorder in the Court: Lega Laughs, Court Jests, and Just Jokes Culled from the Nation's Justice System, 1996; The Word Circus: A Letter-Perfect Book, 1998; (with R. Dowis) Sleeping Dogs Don't Lay: Practical Advice for the Grammatically Challenged, 1999; The Bride of Anguished English: A Bonus of Bloopers, Blunders, Botches, and Boo-Boos, 2000; The Circus of Words, 2001; (with G. Dean) Merriam-Webster's Word Play Crosswords, vol. I, 2001, vol. II, 2002; A Man of My Words: Reflections on the English Language, 2003; (with J.Shore) Comma Sense: A Fundamental Guide to Punctuation, 2005; Revenge of Anguished English: More Accidental Assaults Upon Our Language, 2005; (with J.D. Ertner) Giant Book of Animal Jokes: Beastly Humor for Grownups, 2006; Word Wizard: Super Bloopers, Rich Reflections, and Other Acts of Word Magic, 2006; Have Yourself A Punny Little Christmas: Word Play for the Holidays, 2006; Pun Spooken Here: Word Play for Halloween, 2006; Richard Lederer's Classic Trivia, 2007; Presidential Trivia: The Feats, Fates, Families, Foibles, and Firsts of Our American Presidents, 2007, rev. ed., 2009; Richard Lederer's Literary Trivia, 2007; A Treasury for Dog Lovers, 2009; A Treasury for Cat Lovers, 2009; The Gift of Age: Wit and Wisdom, Information and Inspiration for the Chronologically Endowed, and Those Who Will Be, 2011; A Tribute to Teachers, 2011; (J. Ertner) Wild and Wacky Animal Jokes, 2011; (with J. Ertner) Super Funny Animal Jokes, 2011; (with C. McCullagh) American Trivia, 2012. **Address:** Verbivore Inc., 9974 Scripps Ranch Blvd., Ste. 201, San Diego, CA 92131, U.S.A. **Online address:** richard.lederer@pobox.com

LEDGIN, Stephanie P. American (born United States), b. 1952. **Genres:** Music, Cultural/Ethnic Topics. **Career:** Pickin' Magazine, assistant editor, 1975-77; Hadassah, Women's Zionist Organization of America, writer and production assistant for national promotions department, 1979-81; Hadassah Magazine, editorial assistant, 1981-82; Convenience Store Merchandiser, associate editor, 1982-83; L.F. Kimball Research Institute of the New York Blood Center, editorial administrative assistant, 1984-88; The Traditional Music Line, editor and publisher, 1987-2004; CityFolk, WFUV-FM, radio host, 1989-90; Rutgers University, lecturer in American studies, 1998-2003, New Jersey Folk Festival, director, 1994-2003; Mine Street Coffeehouse, volunteer publicity coordinator, 1996-99. Author. **Publications:** (Co-ed.) Hot Licks for Bluegrass Fiddle, 1984; Homegrown Music: Discovering Bluegrass, 2004; (contrib.) Encyclopedia of New Jersey, 2004; From Every Stage: Images of America's Roots Music, 2005; Discovering Folk Music, 2010. Contributor to periodicals. **Address:** PO Box 628, Pittstown, NJ 08867, U.S.A. **Online address:** ledgin@ledgin.com

LE DOEUFF, Michèle. French (born France), b. 1948. **Genres:** Philosophy, Essays, Translations. **Career:** High school philosophy teacher, 1971-73; Ecole Normale Superieure de Fontenay, lecturer, assistant professor, 1973-80, maitre assistante, 1980-86; Centre National de la Recherche Scientifique, researcher, 1986-93; Oxford University, Weidenfeld visiting professor, 2005-06; University of Geneva, professor. Writer. **Publications:** (With V.G. Pin and Y.J. Echeverría) Conocer Descartes y su obra, 1979; Recherches sur l'imaginaire philosophique, 1980; (with M. Llasera) Francis Bacon: La Nouvelle Atlantide, 1983; (trans.) Shakespeare: Venus et Adonis, 1986; L'Etude et le rouet: Des femmes, de la philosophie, etc., 1989; Philosophical Imaginary, 1989; Francis Bacon: Du Progres et de la promotion des savoirs, 1991; Hipparchia's Choice: Aan Essay Concerning Women, Philosophy, etc., 1991; Sexe du Savoir, 1998; Sex of Knowing, 2003; L'étude et le rouet: des femmes, de la philosophie, etc, 2008. Contributor to periodicals. **Address:** 34 rue de Poitou, Paris, 75003, France.

LEDOUX, Joseph E. American (born United States), b. 1949. **Genres:** Psychology, Sciences. **Career:** Cornell University, NIH postdoctoral fellow, 1977-79, instructor, 1979-80, assistant professor, 1980-86, associate professor, 1986-89; New York University, Center for Neural Science, associate professor, 1989-91, professor of neural science and psychology, 1991-96, Henry and Lucy Moses professor of science, 1996-, university professor, 2005-, Center for the Neuroscience of Fear and Anxiety, director; Nathan Kline Institute, Emotional Brain Institute, director, 2007-. Writer and neurobiologist. **Publications:** (With M.S. Gazzaniga) Integrated Mind, 1978; (ed. with W. Hirst) Mind and Brain: Dialogues in Cognitive Neuroscience, 1986; The Emotional Brain: The Mysterious Underpinnings of Emotional Life, 1996;

Synaptic Self: How Our Brains Become Who We Are, 2002; (ed. with J. De-biec and H. Moss) Self: From Soul to Brain, 2003; (ed. with P.J. Shiromani and T.M. Keane) Post-Traumatic Stress Disorder: Basic Science and Clinical Practice, 2009. Contributor of articles to periodicals. **Address:** Center for Neural Science, New York University, Rm. 809, 4 Washington Pl., New York, NY 10003, U.S.A. **Online address:** ledoux@cns.nyu.edu

LEDWIDGE, Michael. American (born United States), b. 1971?. **Genres:** Novels. **Career:** Writer, 1999-. **Publications:** The Narrowback, 1999; Bad Connection, 2001; Before the Devil Knows You're Dead, 2002; (with J. Patterson) Step on a Crack, 2007; (with J. Patterson) The Quickie, 2007; (with J. Patterson) Dangerous Days of Daniel X, 2008; Run for Your Life, 2009; Worst Case, 2009; Tick Tock, 2011; (with J. Patterson) Now You See Her, 2011. **Address:** Pocket Books, 1230 Ave. of the Americas, 13th Fl., New York, NY 10020, U.S.A.

LEE, Ang. Taiwanese (born Taiwan), b. 1954. **Genres:** Plays/Screenplays, Art/Art History. **Career:** Writer and director. **Publications:** (With N. Peng and J. Schamus) The Wedding Banquet, 1993; (with H.L. Wang and J. Schamus) Eat Drink Man Woman, 1994; (with J. Schamus) Crouching Tiger, Hidden Dragon: A Portrait of the Ang Lee Film, 2000. **Address:** c/o CAA, 9830 Wilshire Blvd., Beverly Hills, CA 90212-1804, U.S.A.

LEE, Anthony W. American (born United States), b. 1960?. **Genres:** Art/Art History, Photography, Literary Criticism And History. **Career:** Mount Holyoke College, associate professor of art history, professor, American Studies Program, chair, 1998-; Defining Moments in American Photography, founder and editor. **Publications:** Painting on the Left: Diego Rivera, Radical Politics, and San Francisco's Public Murals, 1999; Picturing Chinatown: Art and Orientalism in San Francisco, 2001; (with J. Pultz) Diane Arbus: Family Albums, 2003; (ed.) Yun Gee: Poetry, Writings, Art, Memories, 2003; (with E. Young) On Alexander Gardner's Photographic Sketch Book of the Civil War, 2007; (with R. Meyer) Weegee and Naked city, 2008; A Shoe-Maker's Story: Being Chiefly about French Canadian Immigrants, Enterprising Photographers, Rascal Yankees and Chinese Cobblers in a Nineteenth-Century Factory Town, 2008. **Address:** Department of Art, Mount Holyoke College, Rm. 209, Art Bldg., 50 College St., South Hadley, MA 01075, U.S.A. **Online address:** awlee@mtholyoke.edu

LEE, A(rthur) Robert. British (born England), b. 1941. **Genres:** Novels, Novellas/Short Stories, Poetry, Area Studies, Humanities, Literary Criticism And History, Autobiography/Memoirs, Biography, Essays. **Career:** Princeton University, lecturer in American literature, 1965-66, fellow of English-speaking union, 1965-66; University of Virginia, visiting lecturer in English and American literature, 1966-67; California State University, visiting assistant professor of English, 1967-68; University of Kent, lecturer, 1967-87, senior lecturer in English and American literature, 1987-96; Bryn Mawr College, visiting lecturer, 1971-72; University of Louisville, visiting professor, 1973; Governors State University, visiting professor, 1975; Northwestern University, visiting lecturer, 1975-76, visiting associate professor, 1978; Nihon University, chair of American literature, 1997-, professor of English, 1997-; Sunderland University, annual visiting professor in American studies, 2000-07; University of Colorado, visiting professor; University of California, visiting professor; University of New Mexico, visiting professor; BBC radio, broadcaster; Spanish Open University, broadcaster; ORF, broadcaster; NPR, broadcaster; PBS, broadcaster. Writer. **Publications:** Black American Fiction Since Richard Wright, 1983; James Baldwin: Climbing to the Light, 1990; Designs of Blackness: Mappings in the Literature and Culture of Afro-America, 1998; (with G. Vizenor) Postindian Conversations, 1998; Ethnics Behaving Badly, 2001; Multicultural American Literature: Comparative Black, Native, Latino/a and Asian American Fictions, 2003; United States: Re-viewing American Multicultural Literature, 2009; Modern American Counter Writing: Beats, Outriders, Ethnics, 2010; Gerald Vizenor, 2010; Native American Writing, 2011. EDITOR AND CONTRIBUTOR: Moby-Dick, 1975, 3rd ed., 1993; Black Fiction: New Studies in the Afro-American Novel Since 1945, 1980; Nathaniel Hawthorne: New Critical Essays, 1982; Ernest Hemingway: New Critical Essays, 1983; Herman Melville: Reassessments, 1984; Nineteenth-Century American Poetry, 1985; The Nineteenth-Century American Short Story, 1985; Edgar Allan Poe: The Design of Order, 1986; William Faulkner: The Yoknapatawpha Fiction, 1987; First Person Singular: Studies in American Autobiography, 1988; Scott Fitzgerald: The Promises of Life, 1989; The Modern American Novella, 1989; (with M. Irwin and M. Kinkead-Weekes) Tensions and Transitions 1869-1990: The Mediating Imagination for

Ian Gregor, 1990; After Ellison: New Studies in African-American Fiction, 1990; A Permanent Etcetera: Cross-Cultural Perspectives on Post-war America, 1993; Typee, 1993; Billy Budd and Other Stories, 1993; Shadow Distance, 1994; Other British, Other Britain: Contemporary Multicultural Fiction, 1995; (with W.M. Verhoeven) Making America, Making American Literature: Franklin to Cooper, 1996; The Beat Generation Writers, 1996; Loosening the Seams: Interpretations of Gerald Vizenor, 2000; Herman Melville: Critical Assessments, 2001. CONTRIBUTOR: New Perspectives on Melville, 1978; Reading the Victorian Novel: Detail Into Form, 1980; Introduction to American Studies, 1981, rev. ed., 1989; Makers of Modern Culture, 1981; Makers of Nineteenth-Century Culture, 1982; American Fiction: New Readings, 1983; Mark Twain: A Sumptuous Variet, 1985; Essays on Contemporary British Fiction, 1985; Essays on Contemporary American Fiction, 1985; The American City: Literary and Cultural Perspectives, 1988; American Studies in Spain: Proceedings of the University of Valencia International Conference, 1988; American Horror Fiction: From Brockden Brown to Stephen King, 1989; Critical Essays on The Catcher in the Rye, 1989; Post-War Literatures in English: A Lexicon of Contemporary Authors, 1989; Spy Thrillers: From Buchan to Le Carre, 1990; Twentieth-Century Suspense, 1990; The New American Writing: Essays on American Literature Since 1970, 1990. Contributor to books and journals. **Address:** Department of English, College of Humanities and Sciences, Nihon University, 3-25-40 Sakurajosui, Setagaya-ku, Tokyo, 156-8550, Japan. **Online address:** arobertlee@hotmail.com

LEE, Barbara. American (born United States), b. 1946. **Genres:** Autobiography/Memoirs. **Career:** Congressman Ron Dellums, staff, chief of staff. Writer. **Publications:** Renegade for Peace and Justice: Congresswoman Barbara Lee Speaks for Me (memoir), 2008. **Address:** 2444 Rayburn House Office Bldg., Washington, DC 20515, U.S.A.

LEE, Bernie. American (born United States), b. 1926. **Genres:** Mystery/Crime/Suspense, Plays/Screenplays, Literary Criticism And History. **Career:** KMOX-Radio, writer, 1949-53; Cole & Weber Advertising, writer and producer, 1970-72; freelance writer, 1972-. **Publications:** MYSTERY NOVELS: Murder at Musket Beach, 1990; Murder Without Reservation, 1991; Murder Takes Two, 1992. Contributor to magazines. **Address:** 4626 NW Seblar Terr., Portland, OR 97210, U.S.A.

LEE, Chae-Jin. American (born United States), b. 1936. **Genres:** Social Sciences. **Career:** University of Kansas, assistant professor, professor of political science and East Asian Studies, 1965-86, Center for East Asian Studies, co-director, 1976- 82, Department of East Asian languages and Cultures, co-chair, 1976-82, College of Liberal Arts and Sciences, associate dean, 1982-86; Fulbright-Hays visiting scholar in Japan and Korea, 1967-68; California State University, professor of political science & dean of the School of Social and Behavioral Studies, 1986-89; Claremont McKenna College, professor of government, 1989-, Bank of America Professor of Pacific Basin Studies, Keck Center for International and Strategic Studies, director, 1989; University of Washington, visiting associate professor, 1970-71; University of California, visiting professor, 1994; Seoul National University, Fulbright-Hays visiting scholar, 1994, 1995, 2002; U.S. Army Command, faculty; General Staff College, faculty. Writer. **Publications:** Communist China's Policy toward Laos: A Case Study, Center for East Asian Studies, 1970; (ed. with D.S. Suh) Political Leadership in Korea, 1976; Japan Faces China: Political and Economic Relations in the Postwar Era, Johns, 1976; (with G.C. Hurst) The Park Chung Hee Presidency in Historical Perspective, 1980; (with H. Sato) U.S. Policy toward Japan and Korea: A Changing Influence Relationship, 1982; China and Japan: New Economic Diplomacy, 1984; China's Korean Minority: The Politics of Ethnic Education, 1986; The Korean War: 40-year Perspectives, 1991; The United States and China: Changing Relations and Regional Implications, 1991; (ed.) The United States and Japan: Changing Relations, 1992 ; (ed. with J. Speakman) The Prospects for Korean Reunification, 1993; (ed. with H. Sato) U.S. Japan Partnership in Conflict Management: The Case of Korea, 1993; Zhou Enlai: The Early Years, 1994; (with D.B. Park) China and Korea: Dynamic Relations, 1996; (ed. with D.S. Suh) North Korea after Kim Il Sung, Lynne, 1998 ; (ed. with A.L. Rosenbaum) The Cold War Reassessments, 2000; (ed.) The Changing Asia-Pacific Region: Strategic and Economic Issues, 2001; (ed.) U.S. Security Policy under Clinton and Bush: Continuity and Change, 2005; A Troubled Peace: U.S. Policy and the Two Koreas, 2006. Contributor of articles to journals. **Address:** Keck Ctr. for International & Strategic Studies, Claremont McKenna College, 850 Columbia Ave., Claremont, CA 91711, U.S.A. **Online address:** cjlee@claremontmckenna.edu

LEE, Chang-rae. American/Korean (born Korea (South)), b. 1965. **Genres:** Novels. **Career:** University of Oregon, assistant professor of creative writing, 1993-; Hunter College of City University of New York, professor of writing; Princeton University, faculty, 2002-, Lewis Center for the Arts, director and professor of creative writing; Wall Street Journal, financial analyst. Writer. **Publications:** Native Speaker, 1995; Gesture Life, 1999; Aloft, 2004; The Surrendered, 2010. **Address:** c/o Amanda Urban, International Creative Management, 40 W 57th St., New York, NY 10019-4001, U.S.A. **Online address:** changlee@princeton.edu

LEE, Chin-Chuan. Taiwanese/American (born United States), b. 1946. **Genres:** Communications/Media, Writing/Journalism. **Career:** Chinese University of Hong Kong, lecturer, 1978-82, chair professor of journalism and communication, 1994-98; University of Minnesota, professor of journalism and mass communication, 1982-2004, China Times Center for Media and Social Studies, director, professor emeritus, 2004-; Chinese Communication Association, founding president, 1990-94; Chinese University of Hong Kong, professor of journalism and communication, chair, 1994-98; City University of Hong Kong, Department of English and Communication, head, 2002-05, Department of Media and Communication, chair professor and head, 2002-, Center for Communication Research, director, 2005-. Writer. **Publications:** Media Imperialism Reconsidered: The Homogenizing of Television Culture, 1980; Da zhong chuan bo xue: she hui, mei jie, ren, 1981; Lin Yun da shizhe ge ren, 1987; Mi zong hei jiao kan ren sheng, 1987; Chuan bo di guozhu yi, 1987; Tun tun tu tu di wen zhang: xin wen quan yu xue shu jie, 1987; Xin wen di zheng zhi, zheng zhi di xin wen, 1987; Voices of China: The Interplay of Politics and Journalism, 1990; (with J.M. Chan) Mass Media and Political Transition: The Hong Kong Press in China's Orbit, 1991; Zhongguo, zai li shi de zhuan zhe dian shang, 1994; China's Media, Media's China, 1994; (with J.M. Chan and P.S.N. Lee) Hong Kong Journalists in Transition, 1996; Money, Media, Power: Communication Patterns in Cultural China, 2000; (ed.) Power, Money, and Media: Communication Patterns and Bureaucratic Control in Cultural China, 2000; (co-author) Global Media Spectacle: News War over Hong Kong, 2002; (ed.) Chinese Media, Global Contexts, 2003; Beyond the Western Hegemony: Media and Chinese Modernity, 2004; Scholars on Governance, 2008. **Address:** Department of English & Communication, City University of Hong Kong, Tat Chee Ave., Kowloon, 55455, Hong Kong. **Online address:** encclee@cityu.edu.hk

LEE, Dennis (Beynon). Canadian (born Canada), b. 1939. **Genres:** Children's Fiction, Poetry, Literary Criticism And History, Picture/Board Books, inspirational/Motivational Literature, Young Adult Fiction, Science Fiction/Fantasy. **Career:** University of Toronto, Victoria College, English teacher, 1963-67, writer-in-residence, 1978-79; Rochdale College, resource person, 1967-69; House of Anansi Press, co-founder, 1967-, editorial director, through 1972; Macmillan of Canada, editorial consultant, 1974-79; Trent University, writer-in-residence, 1975; University of Edinburgh, Scottish-Canadian exchange fellow, 1980-81; McClelland & Stewart, director of the poetry programme, 1981-84; Canadian Broadcasting Corp., songwriter, 1982-86. **Publications:** Kingdom of Absence, 1967; Civil Elegies, 1968; Wiggle to the Laundromat, 1970; Civil Elegies and Other Poems, 1972; Alligator Pie, 1974; Nicholas Knock and Other People, 1974; Not Abstract Harmonies But, 1974; The Death of Harold Ladoo, 1976; Garbage Delight, 1977; Miscellany, 1977; Savage Fields: An Essay in Literature and Cosmology, 1977; The Gods, 1978; The Ordinary Bath (juvenile), 1979; Jelly Belly, 1983; Lizzy's Lion, 1984; The Dennis Lee Big Book, 1985; The Difficulty of Living on Other Planets, 1987; The Ice Cream Store, 1991; Ping and Pong, 1993; Riffs, 1993; Nightwatch: New and Selected Poems, 1968-1996, 1996; Dinosaur Dinner with a Slice of Alligator Pie, 1997; Body Music (essays), 1998; Bubblegum Delicious: Poems, 2000; The Cat and the Wizard, 2001; Un, 2003; Garbage Delight: Another Helping, 2002; So Cool, 2004; Yesno: Poems, 2007; The Bard of the Universe, 2007; (with M. Lackey, C. Martin and V. Giguere) World Divided, 2012. EDITOR: (with R.A. Charlesworth) An Anthology of Verse, 1964, rev. ed. as A New Anthology of Verse, 1989; (with R.A. Charlesworth) The Second Century Anthologies of Verse: Book 2, 1967; (with H. Adelman) The University Game, 1968; T.O. Now: The Young Toronto Poets, 1968; The New Canadian Poets, 1970-1985, 1985. Works appear in anthologies. Contributor to periodicals. **Address:** Westwood Creative Artists, 94 Harbord St., Toronto, ON M5S 1G6, Canada.

LEE, Don. American (born United States), b. 1959. **Genres:** Novels. **Career:** Emerson College, adjunct instructor, 1984-89, Ploughshares, principal editor, 1989-2007; Macalester College, associate professor of creative writing,

2007-08; Western Michigan University, associate professor, 2008-09; Temple University, professor, 2009-. Writer. **Publications:** COLLECTION: Yellow: Stories, 2001. NOVELS: Country of Origin, 2004; Wrack and Ruin, 2008; The Collective, 2012. Contributor to periodicals. **Address:** Creative Writing Program, Temple University, Dept. of English, 1114 W Berks St., Philadelphia, PA 19122-6090, U.S.A. **Online address:** somewind@gmail.com

LEE, Donald (Lewis). British (born England), b. 1931. **Genres:** Zoology, Biology. **Career:** Cambridge University, Christ's College, research fellow, 1958-63, fellow, 1963-71; Houghton Poultry Research Station, Department of Parasitology, head, 1966-71; University of Hong Kong, Kan Tong Po professor, 1989-90; University of Leeds, Department of Biology, professor, retired, 1996; Rice University, postdoctoral fellow; Brunel University, associate senior research fellow; Slovak Academy of Sciences, visiting fellow. Writer. **Publications:** The Physiology of Nematodes, 1965, (with H.J. Atkinson) 2nd ed., 1976; (ed. with D.H. Jennings) Symbiosis, 1976; (ed.) The Biology of Nematodes, 2002. **Address:** Taylor & Francis Group, Mortimer House, 37-41 Mortimer St., London, GL W1T 3JH, England. **Online address:** pab6dll@leeds.ac.uk

LEE, Donald L(uther). See MADHUBUTI, Haki R.

LEE, Dorothy. See LEE, Dorothy A.

LEE, Dorothy A. (Dorothy Lee). Australian (born Australia), b. 1953?. **Genres:** Theology/Religion, Self Help. **Career:** University of Melbourne, united faculty of theology, faculty; Trinity College, Frank Woods distinguished lecturer in Biblical studies, associate chaplain, chair of field B, professor of New Testament in the uniting church theological hall, Theological School, dean, united faculty of theology; Christ Church Anglican Church, honorary assistant curate, associate curate. Theologian, educator and writer. **Publications:** Women Disciples at the Last Supper: Last Supper Project Paper, Uniting Church in Australia, 1992; The Last Days of Jesus: Mark 11 to 16, 1993; (with J. Honner) Wisdom and Demons: Meditations on Scripture, 1993; The Symbolic Narratives of the Fourth Gospel: The Interplay of Form and Meaning, 1994; (ed. with M. Confoy and J. Nowotny) Freedom and Entrapment: Women Thinking Theology, 1995; The Easy Yoke: Studies in Matthew's Spirituality, 1996; Flesh and Glory: Symbol, Gender and Theology in the Gospel of John, 2002; Transfiguration, 2004. CONTRIBUTOR: Feminist Poetics of the Sacred: Creative Suspicions, 2001; In Many and Diverse Ways: In Honor of Jacques Dupuis, 2003; Jesus in History, Thought and Culture: An Encyclopedia, 2003; Hope: Challenging the Culture of Despair, 2004; Theodicy and Eschatology, 2005; Transcending Boundaries: Contemporary Readings of the New Testament, 2005; What We Have Heard from the Beginning: The Past, Present and Future of Johannine Studies, 2007. Contributor to periodicals. **Address:** Trinity College, Royal Parade, Parkville, VI 3052, Australia. **Online address:** dorothylee@trinity.unimelb.edu.au

LEE, Frances E. American (born United States), b. 1968. **Genres:** Politics/Government. **Career:** Brookings Institution, research fellow, 1997-98; Case Western Reserve University, assistant professor of political science, 1997-2002, associate professor, 2002-04; University of Maryland, associate professor of political science, 2004-10, professor of political science, 2010-. **Publications:** (With B.I. Oppenheimer) Sizing Up the Senate: The Unequal Consequences of Equal Representation, 1999; Beyond Ideology: Politics, Principles, and Partisanship in the U.S. Senate, 2009; (ed. with E. Schickler) The Oxford Handbook of the American Congress, 2011. Contributor of articles to periodicals. **Address:** Department of Government and Politics, University of Maryland, 3140 Tydings Hall, College Park, MD 20742, U.S.A. **Online address:** flee@gvpt.umd.edu

LEE, Helen Elaine. American (born United States), b. 1959. **Genres:** Novels, Young Adult Non-fiction, Literary Criticism And History. **Career:** Massachusetts Institute of Technology, Program in Writing and Humanistic Studies, assistant professor, associate professor. Attorney and novelist. **Publications:** NOVELS: The Serpent's Gift, 1994; Water Marked: A Novel, 1999; Life Without, forthcoming. **Address:** Program in Writing and Humanistic Studies, Massachusetts Institute of Technology, Rm. 14N-425, 77 Massachusetts Ave., Cambridge, MA 02139, U.S.A. **Online address:** helee@mit.edu

LEE, Henry C. American/Chinese (born China), b. 1938. **Genres:** Criminology/True Crime. **Career:** Forensic scientist; Taipei Police Department, lieutenant, 1960, captain, 1960-63; journalist, 1963-64; New York University, research scientist, 1966-75; University of New Haven, faculty, 1973-, assistant professor, 1975-76, associate professor and director of forensic science, 1976-78, professor of forensic science, 1978-2000, distinguished chair professor, 2000-, Center of Applied Research, director, 1976-80, Forensic Science Laboratory, director, 1977-79; Northeastern University, visiting professor, 1977-79; Seton Hall University, faculty, 1978; State of Connecticut's State Forensic Science Laboratory, director, 1979-; University of Connecticut, visiting professor, 1993, research professor, 2000; Central Connecticut University, visiting professor, distinguished professor of criminology, 2000; Connecticut State Police, Forensic Science Laboratory, director, 1975-2000, chief criminalist, Department of Public Safety, commissioner, 1998-2000, chief emeritus, 2000-; Forensic Research and Training Center, director and chairman of the board, 2000-; Wesleyan University, visiting professor; Institute of Forensic Science, visiting professor; National Criminal Police College, visiting professor; University of China, visiting professor. Writer, Educator and consultant. **Publications:** (With P.R. De Forest and R.E. Gaensslen) Forensic Science: An Introduction to Criminalistics, 1983; (with R.E. Gaensslen) Procedures and Evaluations of Antisera for the Typing of Antigens in Bloodstains: ABH, Rh, MNSs, Kell, Duffy and Kidd Blood Group Antigens and Gm/Km Serum Group Antigens, 1984; Dr. Henry C. Lee on Crime Scene Investigation and Reconstruction, 1988; (ed. with R.E. Gaensslen) DNA and Other Polymorphisms in Forensic Science, 1990; (ed. with R.E. Gaensslen) Advances in Fingerprint Technology, 1991, 2nd ed., 2001; Crime Scene Investigation, 1995; Dr. Henry C. Lee on Crime Scene Investigation and Reconstruction: Criminal Law Expert in Residence '98, 1998; (with H.A. Harris) Physical Evidence in Forensic Science, 2000, 3rd ed., 2011; (with T. Palmbach and M.T. Miller) Henry Lee's Crime Scene Handbook, 2001; (with J. Labriola) Famous Crimes Revisited: From Sacco-Vanzetti to O.J. Simpson, 2001; (with F. Tirnady) Blood Evidence: How DNA is Revolutionizing the Way We Solve Crimes, 2002; (with T.W. O'Neil) Cracking Cases: The Science of Solving Crimes, 2002; (with T.W. O'Neil) Cracking More Cases: The Forensic Science of Solving Crimes, 2004; (with J. Labriola) Dr. Henry Lee's Forensic Files: Five Famous Cases-Scott Peterson, Elizabeth Smart, and More, 2006; (with J. Labriola) Budapest Connection, 2006; (with G.M. Taft and K.A. Taylor) Forensic Science Today, 2006, (co-author) 2nd ed., 2009; (with R.E. Gaensslen, H.A. Harris) Introduction to Forensics & Criminalistics, 2008; (with E.M. Pagliaro and K. Ramsland) Real World of a Forensic Scientist: Renowned Experts Reveal What It takes to Solve Crimes, 2009; (with J. Labriola) Shocking Cases from Dr. Henry Lee's Forensic Files, 2010. **Address:** Department of Public Safety, Division of Scientific Services, University of New Haven, 278 Colony St., Meriden, CT 06451, U.S.A. **Online address:** hlee@newhaven.edu

LEE, J. Ardian. (Julianne Ardian Lee). American (born United States), b. 1956?. **Genres:** Young Adult Fiction, Novels. **Career:** Journalist. **Publications:** Son of the Sword, 2001; Outlaw Sword, 2002; Sword of King James, 2003; Sword of the White Rose, 2004. AS JULIANNE LEE: Knight Tenebrae, 2006; Knight's Blood, 2007; Knight's Lady, 2008; A Question of Guilt: A Novel of Mary, Queen of Scots, and the Death of Henry Darnley, 2008; Her Mother's Daughter, 2009. Contributor to periodicals and magazines. **Address:** 192 E Main St., Ste. 170-D, Hendersonville, TN 37075, U.S.A. **Online address:** jules@julianneardianlee.com

LEE, Jeanne M. American/Vietnamese (born Vietnam), b. 1943. **Genres:** Mythology/Folklore, Literary Criticism And History. **Career:** Writer and illustrator. **Publications:** Bà-Năm, 1987; Silent Lotus, 1991; The Song of Mu Lan, 1995; I Once was a Monkey: Stories Buddha Told, 1999; Bitter Dumplings, 2002. Illustrator of books by L. Yep. Contributor to periodicals. **Address:** Farrar Straus & Giroux, 19 Union Sq. W, New York, NY 10003, U.S.A. **Online address:** lee@frontstreetbooks.com

LEE, Jennifer. American/Korean (born Korea (South)), b. 1968. **Genres:** Sociology, Theology/Religion. **Career:** Columbia University, graduate research assistant, 1993-96, university professor's fellow, 1993-95, president's fellow, 1996-98, Paul F. Lazarsfeld Center for the Social Sciences, fellow, 1997; Harvard University, John F. Kennedy School of Government, project director, 1997-98; University of California-Los Angeles, president's postdoctoral fellow, 1998-2000; University of California-Irvine, assistant professor, 2000-03, associate professor of sociology, 2003-, director of graduate studies, 2007-, Center for Research on Immigration, Population and Public Policy, faculty affiliate, 2007-, principal investigator, School of Social Sciences, pro-

fessor of sociology; Center for Advanced Study in the Behavioral Sciences, fellow, 2002-03; University of Chicago, Center for the Study of Race, Politics and Culture, fellow and visiting associate professor, 2006-07. Writer. **Publications:** Civility in the City: Blacks, Jews, and Koreans in Urban America, 2002; (ed. with M. Zhou) Asian American Youth: Culture, Identity, and Ethnicity, 2004; (with F.D. Bean) Diversity Paradox: Immigration and the Color Line in 21st Century America, 2010. **Address:** Department of Sociology, University of California, 3253 Social Sciences Plz. B, PO Box 5100, Irvine, CA 92697-5100, U.S.A. **Online address:** jenlee@uci.edu

LEE, Jennifer. (Li Jing). American (born United States), b. 1976. **Genres:** Novels. **Career:** New York Times, reporter & technology reporter, 2001-02; Washington correspondent, 2002-03; Metro section reporter & blogger, 2004-. Writer. **Publications:** The Fortune Cookie Chronicles: Adventures in the World of Chinese Food, 2008. **Address:** New York, NY , U.S.A. **Online address:** jenny8lee@fortunecookiechronicles.com

LEE, Jid. American/Korean (born Korea (South)), b. 1955. **Genres:** Autobiography/Memoirs. **Career:** Middle Tennessee State University, associate professor of English. Writer. **Publications:** From the Promised Land to Home: Trajectories of Selfhood in Asian-American Women's Autobiography, 1998; To Kill a Tiger: A Memoir of Korea, 2010. Contributor to books and journals. **Address:** Murfreesboro, TN , U.S.A. **Online address:** lee@mtsu.edu

LEE, Joann Faung Jean. American/Hong Kong (born Hong Kong) **Genres:** Cultural/Ethnic Topics, Area Studies. **Career:** Chinese News, freelance writer, 1972; China Lantern, editor, 1972-73; KABC TV News, news writer intern, 1974-75; KXTV News, general assignment reporter, 1975-76; WLS TV News, general assignment reporter and newswriter, 1976-, WCAU TV News, general assignment reporter, 1977-79; WNEW TV News, general assignment reporter, 1979; Cable News Network, correspondent, 1980-81; Columbia University, Graduate School of Journalism, assistant professor; City University of New York, Queen's College, associate professor, journalism director, 1991-95, 1997-; University of Nevada, Reynolds School of Journalism, dean; William Paterson University, Communications Department, professor and chair; American Broadcasting Co., Asian American television reporter; Canadian Broadcasting Corp., American television reporter. **Publications:** Asian American Experiences in the United States, 1991; Asian Americans: Oral Histories of First to Fourth Generation Americans from China, the Philippines, Japan, India, the Pacific Islands, Vietnam, and Cambodia, 1992; Asian American Actors, 2000; Asian Americans in the Twenty-First Century, 2008. **Address:** Queens College, City University of New York, 65-30 Kissena Blvd., Flushing, NY 11367, U.S.A. **Online address:** joann_lee@qc.edu

LEE, J(oseph) Edward. American (born United States), b. 1953. **Genres:** History. **Career:** Adult Education Evening School, instructor, 1975-81; Carolina Community Actions, personnel director, 1981-82; Winthrop University, Department of Archives and Special Collections, graduate assistant, 1981-83, director of teacher education, senior research associate, assistant professor of history, associate professor of history, 1994-, professor of history; University of South Carolina, teaching assistant, 1983-85, adjunct professor of history, 1985-88; Belmont Abbey College, adjunct professor of history, 1988-95; University of North Carolina, senior lecturer and director of teacher education, professor of history, 1985-94, R. Means Davis fellow in southern history. Writer. **Publications:** (Ed. with T. Haynsworth) Yorkville to York, 1998; White Christmas in April: The Collapse of South Vietnam, 1999; Gateway to the New South, 1999; Along the Catawba River, 1999; The Making of a Southern Eden, 2000; (ed. with R. Chepesiuk) South Carolina in the Civil War: The Confederate Experience in Letters and Diaries, 2000; (ed. with T. Haynsworth) White Christmas in April: The Collapse of South Vietnam, 1975, 2000; (with J.L. West) York and Western York County, SC: The Story of a Southern Eden, 2001; (with H.C.T. Haynsworth) Nixon, Ford and the Abandonment of South Vietnam, 2002; John Gary Anderson and His Maverick Motor Company: The Rise and Fall of Henry Ford's Rock Hill Rival, 2007. **Address:** Department of History, Winthrop University, 364 Bancroft Hall, 701 Oakland Ave., Rock Hill, SC 29733, U.S.A. **Online address:** leee@winthrop.edu

LEE, Josephine (D.). American (born United States) **Genres:** Theatre, Race Relations, History. **Career:** Princeton University, lecturer in English, 1984-87; California State University, assistant professor of English, 1987-89; Smith College, assistant professor of English, 1989-94; University of Minnesota, associate professor of English, 1994-97, professor of English and Asian American studies, 1997-, director of graduate studies, 2001-04, Asian American Studies Program, founding director, 2004-06, Asian American Studies Consortium, director, 2007-10; Association for Asian American Studies, president, 2008-10. Writer. **Publications:** Performing Asian America: Race and Ethnicity on the Contemporary Stage, 1997; (ed. with I.L. Lim and Y. Matsukawa) Re/collecting Early Asian America: Essays in Cultural History, 2002; Japan of Pure Invention: Gilbert and Sullivan's The Mikado, 2010. Contributor to books and periodicals. **Address:** Department of English, University of Minnesota, 310D Lind Hall, 207 Church St. SE, Minneapolis, MN 55455, U.S.A. **Online address:** jolee@umn.edu

LEE, Judith Yaross. American (born United States), b. 1949. **Genres:** Area Studies, Cultural/Ethnic Topics, Humanities, Literary Criticism And History, Speech/Rhetoric. **Career:** Field Enterprises Educational Corp., traffic analyst for business research, 1971-73; University Of Chicago, teaching intern in humanities, 1976; Illinois Institute of Technology, instructor in humanities, 1978; Long Island University, adjunct instructor, adjunct assistant professor of English and media arts, 1978-86, faculty admissions coordinator, 1980-81; University of Helsinki, visiting lecturer of English Philology, 1986-87; City University of New York, Fiorello H. LaGuardia Community College, assistant professor of English, 1988-90; Ohio University, assistant professor of journalism and interpersonal communication, 1990-95, associate professor, 1995-2000, professor of interpersonal communication studies, 2000-, COMS Honors Tutorial Program, director of studies, 1999-, Central Region Humanities Center, co-director, 2001-, School of Interdisciplinary Arts, graduate faculty affiliate, 2003-; Bangkok University, visiting professor, 1994. Writer. **Publications:** (Ed. with J.W. Slade) Beyond the Two Cultures: Essays on Science, Technology, and Literature, 1990; Garrison Keillor: A Voice of America, 1991; Defining New Yorker Humor, 2000; (ed. with J.W. Slade) Midwest, 2004; Twain's Brand: Humor in Contemporary American Culture, forthcoming. Works appear in anthologies. Contributor to periodicals. **Address:** School of Communication Studies, Ohio University, 113 Lasher Hall, Athens, OH 45701-2979, U.S.A. **Online address:** leej@ohio.edu

LEE, Julianne Ardian. *See* **LEE, J. Ardian.**

LEE, Leslie (E.). American (born United States), b. 1935?. **Genres:** Plays/Screenplays, Novellas/Short Stories, Young Adult Fiction. **Career:** La Mama E.T.C, staff, 1969-70; College of Old Westbury, instructor in play writing, 1975-76, assistant professor; University of Pennsylvania, playwright-in-residence, 1980-; New York University, Tisch School of the Arts, instructor in dramatic writing; New York State Commission on the Arts, theater panelist, 1982-84; Negro Ensemble Co., coordinator for play writing workshop, 1985; Frederick Douglass Creative Arts Center, instructor in play writing; Valley Forge Army Hospital, medical technician; Pennsylvania Department of Health, bacteriologist. **Publications:** PLAYS: Elegy to a Down Queen, 1969; Cops and Robbers, 1970; As I Lay Dying, a Victim of Spring, 1972; The Night of the No-Moon, 1973; The War Party, 1974; The Day after Tomorrow, 1974; The First Breeze of Summer, 1974; The Book of Lambert, 1977; The American Short Story, 1977; Colored People's Time: A History Play, 1983; Between Now and Then, 1984; The Rabbit Foot, 1990; Black Eagles, 1992; (ed. with C. Smith) Best Black Plays: The Theodore Ward Prize For African American Playwriting, 2007. Contributor to periodicals. **Address:** Tisch School of the Arts, New York University, 721 Broadway, 12th Fl., New York, NY 10003, U.S.A. **Online address:** ll15@nyu.edu

LEE, Lily Xiao Hong. Australian/Chinese (born China), b. 1939. **Genres:** Women's Studies And Issues, History, Humanities. **Career:** University of Hong Kong, Library Serials Department, head, 1965-71; University of Sydney, faculty, 1982-, lecturer, 1993-98, coordinator of M.A. course in translation and interpreting, honorary associate. Writer. **Publications:** Virtue of Yin: Studies on Chinese Women, 1994; (ed. with A.D. Stefenowska) Biographical Dictionary of Chinese Women: The Qing Period, 1644-1911, 1998; (with S. Wiles) Women of the Long March, 1999; (ed.) Biographical Dictionary of Chinese Women: The Twentieth Century, 1912-2000, 2003; Biographical Dictionary of Chinese Women: The Qing Period, Antiquity to Sui, 16th Century BCE to 617, 2007; Zhongguofunu zhuanji cidian (in Chinese), 2010. **Address:** Department of Chinese Studies, University of Sydney, A18 Brennan Bldg., Sydney, NW 2006, Australia. **Online address:** l.lee@sydney.edu.au

LEE, Li Young. American/Indonesian (born Indonesia), b. 1957. **Genres:** Poetry. **Career:** Northwestern University, faculty; University of Iowa, faculty; University of Oregon, faculty; University of Texas at Austin, faculty.

Writer. **Publications:** POETRY: Rose, 1986; The City in Which I Love You, 1990; Book of My Nights, 2001; From Blossoms: Selected Poems, 2007. OTHERS: The Winged Seed, 1995; Breaking The Alabaster Jar: Conversations with Li-Young Lee, 2006; Behind My Eyes, 2008. **Address:** Simon & Schuster, 1230 Ave. of the Americas, New York, NY 10020, U.S.A.

LEE, Marie G. (Marie Myung-Ok Lee). American (born United States), b. 1964. **Genres:** Novels, Young Adult Fiction, Adult Non-fiction, Essays. **Career:** Data Resources/Standard and Poor's, consultant, 1986-88; Goldman Sachs & Co., editor and equity researcher, 1988-90; Yale University, lecturer in literature and creative writing, 1997-98; Brown University, Center for the Study of Race and Ethnicity in America, visiting lecturer in ethnic studies, 2006-. Writer. **Publications:** Finding My Voice, 1992; If It Hadn't Been for Yoon Jun, 1993; Saying Goodbye, 1994; Necessary Roughness, 1996; (contrib.) New year, New Love, 1996; Night of the Chupacabras, 1998; F Is for Fabuloso, 1999; (as Marie Myung-Ok Lee) Somebody's Daughter, 2005. Works appear in anthologies. Contributor to journals and periodicals. **Address:** Center for the Study of Race & Ethnicity in, America, Brown University, Dyer House, 150 Power St., PO Box 1886, Providence, RI 02912-9074, U.S.A.

LEE, Marie Myung-Ok. *See* **LEE, Marie G.**

LEE, Mark. American (born United States), b. 1950?. **Genres:** Military/Defense/Arms Control, Novels, Young Adult Fiction. **Career:** Writer. **Publications:** The Lost Tribe, 1998; The Canal House, 2003. Contributor to periodicals. **Address:** c/o Author Mail, Algonquin Books, PO Box 2225, Chapel Hill, NC 27515-2225, U.S.A.

LEE, Mona. American (born United States), b. 1939. **Genres:** Novels, Science Fiction/Fantasy, Literary Criticism And History, Young Adult Fiction. **Career:** State of Washington, Division of Vocational Rehabilitation, lead counselor; Seattle Local People's Assembly, co-founder; Global Peoples' Assembly, co-chair of service council. Writer. **Publications:** NOVELS: Alien Child, 1999; The Messenger, forthcoming; A Different Place, forthcoming; One Less Car: How to Escape the Prison of the Car Culture, forthcoming. Contributor of short stories to magazines. **Address:** 3600 S Graham St., Seattle, WA 98118, U.S.A.

LEE, M. Owen. Canadian/American (born United States), b. 1930. **Genres:** Classics, Music, Novellas/Short Stories, Autobiography/Memoirs, Art/Art History, Photography. **Career:** University of Toronto, St. Michael's College, lecturer, 1960-63, assistant professor of classics, 1963-68, associate professor of classics, professor of classics, 1975-95, professor emeritus of classics, 1995-; University of St. Thomas, associate professor, 1968-70, professor of classics, 1970-72; Loyola University, associate professor of classics, 1972-75. Writer. **Publications:** (Co-ed.) The New Saint Basil Hymnal, 1958; Word, Sound, and Image in the Odes of Horace, 1969; Top Ten: A Personal Approach to the Movies, 1973; Fathers and Sons in Virgil's Aeneid: Tum Genitor Natum, 1979; Death and Rebirth in Virgil's Arcadia, 1989; Wagner's Ring: Turning the Sky Round, 1990; First Intermissions: Twenty-One Great Operas Explored, Explained and Brought to Life from the Met, 1995; Virgil as Orpheus: A Study of the Georgics, 1996; The Olive-Tree Bed and Other Quests, 1997; A Season of Opera: From Orpheus to Ariadne, 1998; Wagner: The Terrible Man and His Truthful Art, 1999; Father Lee's Opera Quiz Book, 2000; The Operagoer's Guide: One Hundred Stories and Commentaries, 2001; First Intermissions: Commentaries from the Met Broadcasts, 2002; Athena Sings: Wagner and the Greeks, 2003; A Book of Hours: Music, Literature and Life: A Memoir, 2004; The Great Instrumental Works, 2005; The Best Films of Our Years, 2007; Wagner and the Wonder of Art: An Introduction to Die Meistersinger, 2007. Contributor of articles to journals. **Address:** St. Michael's College, University of Toronto, 81 St. Mary St., Toronto, ON M5S 1J4, Canada.

LEE, Pamela M. American (born United States), b. 1967. **Genres:** Art/Art History, History. **Career:** Stanford University, associate professor of art history, 2000-, professor. Writer. **Publications:** NONFICTION: Souvenir of Siteseeing: Travel and Tourism in Contemporary Art, 1991; (with C. Mehring) Drawing Is Another Kind of Language: Recent American Drawings from a New York Private Collection, 1997; Object to Be Destroyed: The Work of Gordon Matta-Clark, 2000; (with N. Baume and J. Flatley) Sol LeWitt: Incomplete Open Cubes, 2001; Josephine Pryde: Serena, 2001; Chronophobia: On Time in the Art of the 1960s, 2004; (with M. Higgs and J.G. Rolfe) Uta Barth, 2004; Nancy Holt: Sightlines, 2011; Forgetting the Art World, 2012.

Contributor to journals. **Address:** Department of Art and Art History, Stanford University, 435 Lasuen Mall, Nathan Cummings Art Bldg., Stanford, CA 94305-2018, U.S.A. **Online address:** plee1@stanford.edu

LEE, Peter H. American (born United States), b. 1929. **Genres:** Literary Criticism And History, Translations. **Career:** Columbia University, assistant professor, 1960-62; University of Hawaii, assistant professor, professor, 1962-87; University of California, professor of Korean and comparative literature, 1987-2007. Writer. **Publications:** Studies in Old Korean Poetry, 1959; Korean Literature: Topics and Themes, 1965; (trans.) Lives of Eminent Korean Monks, 1969; (ed.) Flowers of Fire, 1974, rev. ed., 1986; Songs of Flying Dragons: A Critical Reading, 1975; Celebration of Continuity: Themes in Classic East Asian Poetry, 1979; The Silence of Love: Twentieth Century Korean Poetry, 1980; Anthology of Korean Literature: From Early Times to the Nineteenth Century, 1981; A Korean Storyteller's Miscellany, 1989; Modern Korean Literature: An Anthology, 1990; Pine River and Lone Peak, 1991; Sourcebook of Korean Civilization, 2 vols., 1993-96; Sources of Korean Tradition, 2 vols., 1997-2000; The Record of the Black Dragon Year, 2000; Myths of Korea, 2000; The Columbia Anthology of Traditional Korean Poetry, 2002; A History of Korean Literature, 2003; Echoing Song: Contemporary Korean Women Poets, 2005; Oral Literature of Korea, 2005. TRANSLATOR AND EDITOR: Kranich am Meer, 1959; Anthology of Korean Poetry, 1964; Poems from Korea, 1974. **Address:** Department of Asian Languages & Cultures, University of California, 290 Royce Hall, PO Box 951540, Los Angeles, CA 90095-1540, U.S.A. **Online address:** lee@humnet.ucla.edu

LEE, Rachel. Also writes as Rachel Hagan Lee, Sue Civil-Brown. American (born United States) **Genres:** Romance/Historical, Novels. **Career:** Writer. **Publications:** NOVELS: An Officer and a Gentleman, 1991; A Fateful Choice, 1996; Sins of the Past, 1996; Caught, 1997; Before I Sleep, 1999; When I Wake, 1999; Snow in September, 2000; After I Dream, 2000; A January Chill, 2001; Under Suspicion, 2001; July Thunder, 2002; In The Arms of a Stranger, 2003; Millionaire to Marry, 2003; With Malice, 2003; Last Breath, 2003; Something Deadly, 2004; (with D. Schulze) Breaking Through, 2004; The Hunted, 2008; Guardian in Disguise, 2012. OTHERS: Serious Risks, 1991; Imminent Thunder, 1993; Cowboy Cop, 1995; Destination, 1996; (with K. Freiman, S. Lewis and K. Sutcliffe) Secret Valentines, 1998; (with C. Asaro and M. Lackey) Charmed Destinies, 2003; (with D. Young) A Bodyguard for Christmas, 2010. CONARD COUNTY SERIES: Exile's End, 1992; Cherokee Thunder, 1992; Miss Emmaline and the Archangel, 1993; Ironheart, 1993; Lost Warriors, 1993; Point of No Return, 1994; Thunder Mountain, 1994; A Question of Justice, 1994; A Conard County Reckoning, 1996; Nighthawk, 1997; Cowboy Comes Home, 1998; The Catch of Conard County, 1998; Boots and Badges, 1999; Involuntary Daddy, 1999; A Soldier's Christmas, 2004; A Soldier's Homecoming, 2008; Protector of One, 2009; The Unexpected Hero, 2009; The Man from Nowhere, 2010; The Final Mission, 2011; Just a Cowboy, 2011. AS SUE CIVIL-BROWN: Carried Away, 1997; Letting Loose, 1998; Chasing Rainbow, 1999; Catching Kelly, 2000; Tempting Mr. Wright, 2000; Next Stop, Paradise, 2001; Breaking All the Rules, 2002; The Prince Next Door, 2005; Hurricane Hannah, 2006; (with C. Mann) Holiday Heroes, 2007; The Life of Reilly, 2007. ILDUIN SERIES: Shadows of Myth, 2005; Shadows of Prophecy, 2006; Shadows of Destiny, 2007. OFFICE 119 SERIES: Wildcard, 2005; The Crimson Code, 2006; The Jericho Pact, 2007. CIONARD COUNTY: THE NEXT GENERATION SERIES: Her Hero in Hiding, 2010; A Soldier's Redemption, 2010; No Ordinary Hero, 2011; The Rescue Pilot, 2011. CLAIMING SERIES: Claim the Night, 2011; Claimed by a Vampire, 2012; Forever Claimed, 2012. **Address:** c/o Author Mail, Warner Books Inc., 1271 Ave. of the Americas, New York, NY 10020, U.S.A.

LEE, Rachel Hagan. See **LEE, Rachel.**

LEE, Sally. American (born United States), b. 1943. **Genres:** Children's Non-fiction, Young Adult Non-fiction, Children's Fiction, Picture/Board Books. **Career:** Special School District, teacher, 1965-68; Spring Branch School District, teacher, 1968-71; Sugarland Properties Inc., executive secretary, 1990-. Writer. **Publications:** Donor Banks: Saving Lives with Organ and Tissue Transplants, 1988; Predicting Violent Storms, 1989; New Theories on Diet and Nutrition, 1990; The Throwaway Society, 1990; Pesticides, 1991; San Antonio, 1992; Hurricanes, 1993; (ed.) Parents Magazine's the Best Advice I Ever Got, 2001; Gloria Estefan: Superstar of Song, 2005; Arnold Schwarzenegger: From Superstar to Governor, 2006; Sam Walton: Business Genius of Wal-Mart, 2008; Freddie Prinze, Jr.: From Shy Guy to Movie Star, 2009; The Pebble First Guide to Dinosaurs, 2009; Martha Washington, 2011;

Hillary Clinton, 2011; Eleanor Roosevelt, 2011; Abigail Adams, 2011; Laura Bush, 2011; Delicious Dairy Group, 2012; Healthy Snacks, Healthy You!, 2012; Food Safety, 2012; Staying Safe Online, 2012; Powerful Protein Group, 2012. Contributor of articles to magazines. **Address:** 3111 E Hickory Park Cir., Sugar Land, TX 77479-2616, U.S.A.

LEE, Sandra. See **CUSICK, Heidi Haughy.**

LEE, Sharon. American (born United States), b. 1952. **Genres:** Science Fiction/Fantasy, Writing/Journalism, Mystery/Crime/Suspense. **Career:** University of Maryland, School of Social Work, administrative aide to dean, 1976-78; Book Castle (a book store), founder and owner, 1978-80; Science Fiction and Fantasy Writers of America Inc., executive director, vice president and president, 1997-2003. Writer. **Publications:** CHAPBOOKS WITH S. MILLER: The Naming of Kinzel, 1987; Two Tales of Korval, 1999; Quiet Magic, 1999; Fellow Travelers, 1999; Changeling, 2000; Duty Bound, 2001; Certain Symmetry, 2001; Loose Cannon, 2001; Trading in Futures, 2001; The Cat's Job, 2002; Shadows and Shades, 2002; Master Walk, 2003; With Stars Underfoot, 2004; Necessary Evils, 2005; Calamity's Child, 2006; Crystal Variation, 2011. LIADEN UNIVERSE NOVELS: WITH S. MILLER: Agent of Change, 1988; Conflict of Honors, 1988; Carpe Diem, 1989; Plan B, 1999; Partners in Necessity, 2000; Pilots Choice, 2001; I Dare, 2002; Local Custom, 2002; Scout's Progress, 2002; Balance of Trade, 2004; Crystal Soldier, 2005; (with S. Miller) Crystal Dragon, 2006; Gunshy, 2006; (with S. Miller) Fledgling, 2007; Ghost Ship, 2011; Dragon Ship, 2011. CHAPBOOKS: (with R. Edghill) Variations Three, 1996; Endeavors of Will, 2006. OTHER NOVELS: Barnburner, 2002; (with S. Miller) The Tomorrow Log, 2003; (ed. with S. Miller) Low Port, 2003; (with S. Miller) Sword of Orion, 2005; Liaden Universe Companion, 2007 (with S. Miller) Duainfey, 2008; (with S. Miller) Longeye, 2009; Saltation: A Novel of the Liaden Universe, 2010; (with S. Miller) Mouse and Dragon: A Novel of the Liaden universe, 2010; (with S. Miller) Dragon Variation, 2010; Carousel Tides, 2010; (with S. Miller) Korval's Game, 2011; (with S. Miller) The Agent Gambit, 2011. Contributor to periodicals. **Address:** SRM Publisher Ltd., PO Box 0179, Unity, ME 04988-0179, U.S.A. **Online address:** sharonlee@korval.com

LEE, Sky. Canadian (born Canada), b. 1952. **Genres:** Novellas/Short Stories, Novels, Children's Fiction, Literary Criticism And History, Young Adult Fiction. **Career:** Nurse and writer. **Publications:** (With P. Yee) Teach Me to Fly, Skyfighter! and Other Stories, 1983; Disappearing Moon Cafe (novel), 1991; Bellydancer: Stories, 1994. Contributor to periodicals. **Address:** c/o Seal Press, 3131 Western Ave., Ste. 410, Seattle, WA 98121, U.S.A.

LEE, Tommy W. American (born United States), b. 1971. **Genres:** Theology/Religion, Young Adult Fiction, Adult Non-fiction. **Career:** Circle of Friends Ministries, president, 2001-. Writer. **Publications:** Christ Returns, 2004; The Diaries of a Forced Conspiracy, 2005. **Address:** Circle of Friends Ministries, PO Box 670096, Houston, TX 77267, U.S.A.

LEE, Tonya Lewis. American (born United States) **Genres:** Children's Fiction, Novels, Travel/Exploration. **Career:** Writer, producer and lawyer. **Publications:** (With S. Lee) Please, Baby, Please, 2002; (intro.) Double Dutch, 2002; (with C.M. Anthony) Gotham Diaries, 2004; (with S. Lee) Please, Puppy, Please, 2005; (with S. Lee) Giant Steps to Change the World, 2011. **Address:** c/o Author Mail, Simon Schuster, 1230 Ave. of the Americas, New York, NY 10020, U.S.A. **Online address:** tll@tonyalewislee.com

LEE, Wei-chin. American/Taiwanese (born Taiwan), b. 1956. **Genres:** Politics/Government. **Career:** University of Oregon, postdoctoral research fellow, 1987; Wake Forest University, Department of Political Science, assistant professor of political science, 1987-93, associate professor of political science, 1993-2002, professor, 2002-, Asian Studies Program, coordinator, 1996-2000, Conference Group on Taiwan Studies, assistant coordinator, 1995-97, coordinator, 1997-99, SASASAAS China Program, coordinator, 2003-06, American Association of Chinese Studies, coordinator, 2010; Journal of Asian and African Studies, editor, 1993-2000. **Publications:** Taiwan, 1990; (ed.) Taiwan in Perspective, 2000; (ed. with T.Y. Wang) Sayonara to the Lee Teng-hui Era: Politics in Taiwan 1988-2000, 2003; (ed.) Taiwan's Politics in the 21st Century: Changes and Challenges, 2010. Contributor of articles to periodicals. **Address:** Department of Political Science, Wake Forest University, Tribble C-310, PO Box 7568, Reynolda Sta., Winston-Salem, NC 27109, U.S.A. **Online address:** leewei@wfu.edu

LEE, Wendy. (Wendy Wang Lee). American (born United States), b. 1976. Genres: Novels. Career: Hwa Nan Women's College, English teacher. Writer. Publications: Happy Family, 2008. Address: c/o Claudia Ballard, William Morris Agency, 1325 Ave. of the Americas, New York, NY 10019-6026, U.S.A. Online address: wendy@wendyleebooks.com

LEE, Wendy Wang. See LEE, Wendy.

LEEB, Donna. American (born United States), b. 1948?. Genres: Economics, Money/Finance, Business/Trade/Industry. Career: Leeb Capital Management Inc., secretary, vice president and director. Writer. Publications: (With S. Leeb) Getting in on the Ground Floor, 1986; (with S. Leeb) Defying the Market: Profiting in the Turbulent Post-Technology Boom, 1999; (with S. Leeb) The Oil Factor: Protect Yourself and Profit from the Coming Energy Crisis, 2004; (co-author) Game Over: How You Can Prosper in a Shattered Economy, 2009. Address: Business Plus, 237 Park Ave., New York, NY 10017, U.S.A.

LEEB, Stephen. American (born United States), b. 1946?. Genres: Economics, Money/Finance, Business/Trade/Industry. Career: Leeb Capital Management Inc., chairman of leeb group, president; The Complete Investor, editor; Personal Finance, editor. Publications: (With D. Leeb) Getting in on the Ground Floor, 1986; (with R.S. Conrad) Marketing Timing for the Nineties: The Five Key Signals for When to Buy Hold and Sell, 1993; (with R.S. Conrad) The Agile Investor: Profiting from the End of Buy and Hold, 1997; (with D. Leeb) Defying the Market, 1999; (with D. Leeb) The Oil Factor: Protect Yourself and Profit from the Coming Energy Crisis, 2004; (with G.C. Strathy) The Coming Economic Collapse: How You Can Thrive When Oil Costs $200 a Barrel, 2006; (co-author) Game Over: How You Can Prosper in a Shattered Economy, 2009; (with G. Dorsey) Red Alert: How China's Road to Prosperity Threatens the American Way of Life, 2011. Contributor to periodicals. Address: Leeb Capital Management, 500 5th Ave., 57th Fl., New York, NY 10110, U.S.A. Online address: lcminfo@leeb.net

LEECH, Geoffrey Neil. British (born England), b. 1936. Genres: Language/Linguistics. Career: Clarendon School, assistant schoolmaster, 1960-61; University of London, University College, assistant lecturer in English, 1962-65, lecturer, 1965-69, fellow, 1989-; Massachusetts Institute of Technology, Harkness fellow, 1964-65; Lancaster University, reader in English, 1969-74, professor of linguistics, 1974-96, research professor in English linguistics, 1997-2001, professor emeritus, 2002-, Unit for Computer Research on the English Language, joint director, 1984-95, Institute for English Language Education, chairman, 1985-90, University Centre for Computer Corpus Research on Language, chair, 1995-2002, honorary fellow, 2009-; Beijing Foreign Studies University, honorary professor, 1994-. Writer. Publications: English in Advertising: A Linguistic Study of Advertising in Great Britain, 1966; A Linguistic Guide to English Poetry, 1969; Towards a Semantic Description of English, 1969; Meaning and the English Verb, 1971, 3rd ed., 2004; (co-author) A Grammar of Contemporary English, 1972; Semantics, 1974, 2nd ed., 1981; (with J. Svartvik) A Communicative Grammar of English, 1975, 3rd ed., 2002; Explorations in Semantics and Pragmatics, 1980; (with M.H. Short) Style in Fiction: A Linguistic Introduction to English Fictional Prose, 1981, 2nd ed., 2007; (with M. Deuchar and R. Hoogenraad) English Grammar for Today, 1982, 2nd ed., 2005; Principles of Pragmatics, 1983; (with R. Quirk, S. Greenbaum and J. Svartvik) A Comprehensive Grammar of the English Language, 1985; An A-Z of English Grammar and Usage, 1989, 2nd ed., 2001; Introducing English Grammar, 1992; (co-author) Longman Grammar of Spoken and Written English, 1999; Word Frequencies in Written and Spoken English, 2001; (with D. Biber and S. Conrad) Longman Student Grammar of Spoken and Written English and Workbook, 2002; (with J. Svartvik) English: One Tongue, Many Voices, 2006; Language in Literature: Style and Foregrounding, 2008; Change in Contemporary English: A Grammatical Study, 2009; Selected Writings in English Applied Linguistics, 2011; Politeness in English, 2012. EDITOR: (with S. Greenbaum and J. Svartvik) Studies in English Linguistics, 1980; (with C.N. Candlin) Computers in English Language Teaching and Research: selected Papers from the 1984 Lancaster Symposium Computers in English Language Education and Research, 1986; (with R. Garside and G. Sampson) The Computational Analysis of English: A Corpus-Based Approach, 1987; (with E. Black and R. Garside) Statistically-Driven Computer Grammars of English, 1993; (with G. Myers and J. Thomas) Spoken English on Computer: Transcription, Markup and Application, 1995; (ed. with M. Short) Using Corpora for Language Research: Studies in Honour of Geoffrey Leech, 1996; (with R. Garside and

A. McEnery) Corpus Annotation: Linguistic Information from Computer Text Corpora, 1997; (with P. Rayson and S. Hofmann) Corpus Linguistics, 2011; (with J. Close, S. Wallis and B. Aarts) The English Verb Phrase, 2012. Address: Department of Linguistics & English Language, Lancaster University, C09, County South, University House, Lancaster, LC LA1 4YT, England. Online address: g.leech@lancaster.ac.uk

LEECH, John. British/German (born Germany), b. 1925. Genres: International Relations/Current Affairs, Military/Defense/Arms Control, Politics/Government, Third World. Career: L.G. Mouchel and Partners Ltd., trainee to special assistant to the chair, 1942-52; Bird and Company Ltd., general manager, 1953-57; Indian Patent Stone Co., chief engineer, 1953-57; Britain in Europe/Europe House, director of activities for British membership of the European Community, 1958-61; International Federation of Europe Houses, president, 1961-65; Joint Industrial Exports Ltd., director, 1963-65; Commonwealth Development Corp., general manager, 1965-67; Tanganyika Development Finance Co., general manager, 1965-67, head of external relations; Rural Investment Overseas Ltd., chair, 1985-2000, European co-ordinator, West-West Agenda, 1988-2010; Farm Services Co., director, 1988-; Thapar Industrial Finance, director, 1992-; The Keyboard Charitable Trust, chairman of trustees. Writer. Publications: The NATO Parliamentarians' Conference, 1955-59, 1960; Europe and the Commonwealth, 1961; Aid and the Community, 1972; Halt! Who Goes Where? The Future of NATO in the New Europe, 1991; Asymmetries of Conflict: War Without Death, 2002; (ed.) Whole and Free: NATO, EU Enlargement and Transatlantic Relations, 2002. Contributor to periodicals. Address: The Keyboard Charitable Trust, 8 Chester Sq. Mews, London, GL SW1W 9DS, England. Online address: jleechvr@aol.com

LEECH, Kenneth. British (born England), b. 1939. Genres: Medicine/Health, Sociology, Theology/Religion. Career: Holy Trinity Church, assistant curate, 1964-67; St. Anne's Church, assistant curate, 1967-71; St. Augustines College, chaplain, 1971-74; St. Matthew's Bethnal Green, rector, 1974-81; Church of England, race relations field officer, 1981-87; Runnymede Trust, director, 1987-90; St. Botolph's Church, M.B. Reckitt urban fellow, 1991-, community theologian; King's College, associate. Writer. Publications: (With B. Jordan) Drugs for Young People: Their Use and Misuse, 1967, 2nd ed., 1974; (contrib.) For Christ and the People, 1968; The Drug Subculture: A Christian Analysis, 1969; Pastoral Care and the Drug Scene, 1970, rev. ed. as A Practical Guide to the Drug Scene, 1974; The Real Jesus Revolution, 1972; Keep the Faith Baby, 1973; Youthquake: The Growth of a Counter-Culture Through Two Decades, 1973; Action for Revival, 1974; The Resurrection of the Catholic Social Voice, 1976; Believing in the Incarnation and Its Consequences, 1977; The Charismatic Movement and the Demons, 1977; Soul Friend: A Study of Spirituality, 1977; Brick Lane, 1978; (ed.) The Book of the Lover and the Beloved, 1978; Contemplation and Resistance: As Seen in the Spirituality of Thomas Merton, 1978; Catholic Theology and Social Change, 1978; True Prayer: An Introduction to Christian Spirituality, 1980; The Social God, 1981; What Everyone Should Know about Drugs, 1983; Experiencing God: Theology as Spirituality, 1985; True God, 1985; Spirituality and Pastoral Care, 1986; Struggle in Babylon, 1988; Care and Conflict, 1990; The Eye of the Storm: Living Spirituality in the Real World, 1992; Soul Friend: An Invitation to Spiritual Direction, 1992, rev. ed. as Soul Friend: Spiritual Direction in the Modern World, 2001; Subversive Orthodoxy: Traditional Faith and Radical Commitment, 1992; We Preach Christ Crucified, 1994, new. ed., 2006; The Sky is Red, 1997, rev. ed., 2003; Drugs and Pastoral Care, 1998; Through Our Long Exile, 2001; Race, 2005; Doing Theology in Altab Ali Park: A Project in Whitechapel, East London, 1990-2004, 2006. Contributor to journals and newspapers. Address: St. Botolph's Church, Aldgate High St., London, GL EC3N 1AB, England. Online address: kenleech@aol.com

LEEDER, Elaine J. American (born United States), b. 1944. Genres: Biography, Social Work, Sociology, Social Sciences. Career: Sheltering Arms Children's Service, caseworker, 1969-70; Elmira Psychiatric Center, psychiatric social worker, 1972-73; St. Joseph Hospital, Southern Tier Alcoholism Rehabilitation Service, intake worker and group leader, 1973-77; Chemung County Mental Health Clinic, psychiatric social worker, 1973-80; Ithaca College, professor of sociology and social work, 1977-2001, Social Work Program, coordinator, 1977-2001, head; Economic Opportunities Corp., board director, 1980-83; Tompkins County Task Force for Battered Women, board director, 1986-91, head, 1989-91; Sonoma State University, Department of Sociology, professor of sociology, 2001-, School of Social Sciences, dean, 2001-; Tompkins Cortland Community College, lecturer. Writer. Publications: The Gentle Warrior: Rose Pesotta, Anarchist and Labor Organizer,

1985; The Gentle General: Rose Pesotta, Anarchist and Labor Organizer, 1993; Treating Abuse in Families: A Feminist and Community Approach, 1994; The Family in Global Perspective: A Gendered Journey, 2004; (ed.) Inside and Out: Women, Prison, and Therapy, 2006. Works appear in anthologies. Contributor of articles to journals. **Address:** School of Social Sciences, Sonoma State University, 2078 Stevenson Hall, 1801 E Cotati Ave., Rohnert Park, CA 94928, U.S.A. **Online address:** leeder@sonoma.edu

LEEDS, Barry H. American (born United States), b. 1940. **Genres:** Literary Criticism And History. **Career:** New York Times, credit checker, 1963; City University of New York, lecturer, 1963-64; University of Texas, instructor in English, 1964-65; El Paso Herald Post, drama critic, 1965; Ohio University, teaching fellow, 1965-67; Choice Magazine, consultant and reviewer, 1968-; Central Connecticut State University, assistant professor, 1968-71, associate professor, 1971-76, professor of English, 1976-, CSU distinguished professor of English, 1991-2003, CSU distinguished professor emeritus, 2003-; Connecticut Review, editor, 1989-92. **Publications:** The Structured Vision of Norman Mailer, 1969; Ken Kesey, 1981; The Enduring Vision of Norman Mailer, 2002. Contributor to periodicals. Works appear in anthologies. **Address:** Department of English, Central Connecticut State University, 212 Willard Hall, 1615 Stanley St., New Britain, CT 06050, U.S.A. **Online address:** leeds@ccsu.edu

LEEGANT, Joan. American (born United States), b. 1951?. **Genres:** Writing/Journalism, Novels, Young Adult Fiction. **Career:** Harvard University, writing instructor; Hebrew College, writing instructor; Bar-Ilan University, visiting writer. **Publications:** An Hour in Paradise: Stories, 2003; Wherever You Go: A Novel, 2010. Contributor to periodicals. Works appear in anthologies. **Address:** c/o Jessica Purcell, W. W. Norton & Company Inc., 500 5th Ave., New York, NY 10110-0002, U.S.A. **Online address:** leegant@rcn.com

LEEMAN, Richard W. American (born United States), b. 1955. **Genres:** Communications/Media, History, inspirational/Motivational Literature. **Career:** University of North Carolina at Charlotte, Department of Communication Studies, instructor, 1985-89, lecturer, 1989-90, assistant professor, 1990-95, associate professor, 1995-2000, graduate coordinator of communication studies, 2000, professor, 2000-, chair, 2001-10. Writer. **Publications:** The Rhetoric of Terrorism and Counterterrorism, 1991; Do Everything Reform: The Oratory of Frances E. Willard, 1992; (ed.) African-American Orators: A Biocritical Sourcebook, 1996; (with B. Hill) The Art and Practice of Argumentation and Debate, 1996; (ed. with B.K. Duffy) American Voices: An Encyclopedia of Contemporary American Orators, 2005; (ed. with B.K. Duffy) Will of a People, 2011. Contributor to journals. **Address:** Department of Communication Studies, University of North Carolina, Colvard 5019, 9201 University City Blvd, Charlotte, NC 28223, U.S.A. **Online address:** rwleeman@uncc.edu

LEEN, Jeff. American (born United States), b. 1957?. **Genres:** Biography, Social Sciences. **Career:** St. Louis County Star, journalist, 1979; Columbia Daily Tribune, journalist, 1980-82; Columbia Missourian, journalist; Miami Herald, reporter, 1982-97; Washington Post, reporter, 1997-, Investigative Unit, deputy editor, 1999-2003, editor-in-charge, 2003-, assistant managing editor. **Publications:** (With G. Gugliotta) Kings of Cocaine: Inside the Medellín Cartel, an Astonishing True Story of Murder, Money, and International Corruption, 1989; The Queen of the Ring: Sex, Muscles, Diamonds, and the Making of an American Legend (biography), 2009. Contributor to periodicals. **Address:** Gail Ross Literary Agency, 1666 Connecticut Ave. NW, Ste. 500, Washington, DC 20009, U.S.A. **Online address:** leenj@washpost.com

LEERBURGER, Benedict A. American (born United States), b. 1932. **Genres:** Librarianship, Self Help, Technology, Marketing, Sciences, Business/Trade/Industry, Economics. **Career:** Grolier Inc., staff, 1956-61; McGraw-Hill Book Co., staff, 1961-63, Webster Division, editor-in-chief, 1977-79; Cowles Magazines and Broadcasting Inc., Cowles Encyclopedia of Science, Industry, and Technology, managing editor, 1963-68; Look Magazine, science editor, 1964-69; Crowell, Collier and Macmillan Information Corp., editor and director, 1968-70; National Micropublishing Corp., vice-president and editorial director, 1970-; New York Times, director of publications, 1972-74; Kraus-Thomson Organization Ltd., editor and publisher, 1974-77; Film Review Digest, publisher, 1975-77; Chatham Press, editorial consultant. Freelance writer, 1979-. **Publications:** Josiah W. Gibbs: American Theoretical Physicist, 1963; (ed.) Cowles Encyclopedia of Science, Industry, and Technology, 1967; Marketing the Library, 1982; The Complete Consum-

er's Guide to the Latest Telephones, 1985; Insider's Guide to Foreign Study: Everything You Need to Know about More Than 400 Academic Adventures Abroad, 1987; Promoting and Marketing the Library, 1989; The Complete Guide to Overseas Employment, 1991; (with D. Lay) Jobs Worldwide, 1996. Contributor to journals. **Address:** Impact Publications, 9104 Manassas Dr., Ste. N, Manassas Park, VA 20111, U.S.A. **Online address:** leerbs@cs.com

LEESE, Jennifer L. B. (J. V. Harlee). American (born United States), b. 1970. **Genres:** Children's Fiction, Young Adult Fiction, Children's Non-fiction, Poetry, Novels, History, Mystery/Crime/Suspense. **Career:** Picket News, managing editor and feature writer. **Publications:** Michael's Drawing, 2000; Beetle Bug Adventures: The Castle, 2000; Two Spots Cafe, 2001; Jordie's School Day Adventure, 2002; Notes on the Windowsill (fiction), 2002; (as J.V. Harlee) Gargoyle Tears, 2002; Sounds I Can Hear: In a Car, 2003; Bows for Pigel's Nose, 2003; I am Me, 2004; Two Spots Bakery, 2004; Uniquely Maryland, 2004. POETRY: When I First Heard Your Voice, 1999; Our Mom, 2000; Terror in the Flames & Goodbye Lost Ones Goodbye, 2001. Works appear in anthologies. Contributor to periodicals. **Address:** c/o Author Mail, Heinemann Library, 100 N La Salle, Ste. 1200, Chicago, IL 60602, U.S.A. **Online address:** astoryweaver@aol.com

LEESE, Peter. Danish/British (born England), b. 1962. **Genres:** Adult Non-fiction, History. **Career:** University of Copenhagen, Department of English, Germanic and Romance Studies, associate professor of British history and contemporary Britain; Jagiellonian University, senior lecturer in social and cultural history, assistant professor of English. Writer. **Publications:** (With C. Cook) St. Martin's Guide to Sources in Contemporary British History, as The Longman Guide to Sources in Contemporary British History, 1994; (trans. with E. Wójcik-Leese) W. Szturc, A Short History of Polish Literature, 1998; Shell Shock: Traumatic Neurosis and the British Soldiers of the First World War, 2002; (ed. and intro. with B. Pia̧tek and I. Curyłło-Klag) The British Migrant Experience, 1700-2000: An Anthology, 2002; (ed. with W. Witalisz and contrib.) PASE Papers in Cultural Literature, 2003; Britain Since 1945: Aspects of Identity, 2006. Contributor of articles to books. **Address:** Department of English, Germanic and Romance, Studies, University of Copenhagen, Rm. 24.2, Njalsgade 128, Copenhagen, DK-2300, Denmark. **Online address:** leese@hum.ku.dk

LEE SIX, Abigail (Etta). British (born England), b. 1960. **Genres:** Literary Criticism And History. **Career:** Cambridge University, Sidney Sussex College, research fellow in Spanish, 1986-88; University of London, Queen Mary and Westfield College, professor in Hispanic studies, 1988-, lecturer, 1988-97, senior lecturer in Hispanic studies, 1997-2000, Royal Holloway College, professor of Spanish, 2000-, Institute of Germanic and Romance Studies, associate director. Writer. **Publications:** Juan Goytisolo: The Case for Chaos, 1990; Juan Goytisolo: Campos de Nijar, Critical Guides to Spanish Texts, 1995; (trans.) B.P. Galdós, Inferno (title means: 'Tormento'), 1998; Upgrade Your Spanish, 2001; Gothic Fiction of Adelaida García Morales: Haunting Words, 2006; Gothic Terrors: Incarceration, Duplication, and Bloodlust in Spanish Narrative, 2010; (with H. Thompson) From Hideous to Hedonist: The Changing Face of the Nineteenth-Century Monster, 2011. Contributor of articles to journals and newspapers. **Address:** Department of Hispanic Studies, Royal Holloway, University of London, Egham Hill, Egham, SR TW20 0EX, England. **Online address:** a.leesix@rhul.ac.uk

LEESON, R. A. See **LEESON, Robert (Arthur).**

LEESON, Robert (Arthur). (R. A. Leeson). British (born England), b. 1928. **Genres:** Children's Fiction, Children's Non-fiction, History, Literary Criticism And History, Novels, Business/Trade/Industry, Education, Genealogy/Heraldry, Genealogy/Heraldry. **Career:** Journalist, 1944-56; Morning Star, reporter, 1956-58, parliamentary correspondent, 1958-61, feature writer, 1961-69, literary editor, 1961-80, children's editor, 1969-84; freelance writer and editor, 1969-. **Publications:** (As R.A. Leeson) United We Stand: An Illustrated Account of Trade Union Emblems, 1971; (as R.A. Leeson) Strike: A Live History 1887-1971, 1973; Beyond the Dragon Prow, 1973; Maroon Boy, 1974; The Third Class Genie, 1975; Bess, 1975; The Demon Bike Rider, 1976; The White Horse, 1977; Children's Books and Class Society: Past and Present, 1977; Silver's Revenge, 1978; The Cimaroons, 1978; Challenge in the Dark, 1978; (as R.A. Lesson) Travelling Brothers: The Six Centuries Road from Craft Fellowship to Trade Unionism, 1979; Grange Hill Goes Wild, 1980; Harold and Bella, Jammy and Me, 1980; It's My Life, 1980; Grange Hill for Sale, 1981; Grange Hill Home and Away, 1982; The People's

Dream, 1982; Mum and Dad's Big Business, 1982; Forty Days of Tucker J, 1983; Candy for King, 1983; Genieon the Loose, 1984; Reading and Righting: The Past, Present, and Future of Fiction for the Young, 1985; Reversible Giant, 1986; Wheel of Danger, 1986; Slambash Wangs of a Compo Gormer, 1987; Never Kiss Frogs, 1988; Hey, Robin!, 1989; Burper, 1989; Right Royal Kidnap, 1989; Jan Alone, 1990; Coming Home, 1990; One Frog Too Many, 1991; Landing in Cloud Valley, 1991; Pancake Pickle, 1991; (co-author) Silver Jackanory, 1991; April Fool at Hob Lane School, 1992; No Sleep for Hob Lane, 1992; Ghosts at Hob Lane, 1993; Karlo's Tale, 1993; The Last Genie, 1993; Smart Girls, 1993; Swapper, 1994; The Story of Robin Hood, 1994; The Dog Who Changed the World, 1994; Amazing Adventures of Idle Jack, 1995; Geraldine Gets Lucky, 1995; All the Gold in the World, 1995; Red White and Blue, 1996; Smart Girls Forever, 1996; Lucky Lad, 1997; Doomwater, 1997; Tom's Private War, 1998; Why's the Cow on the Roof?, 1998; Liar, 1999; (ed.) Collected Works in Contemporary Perspective, 2000; (with E. Gaskell) Ruth (play, adaptation), 2000; Song of Arthur, 2000; My Sister Shahrqzad, 2000; Tom's War Patrol, 2001; Onda, Wind Rider, 2003; Partners in Crime, 2003. ZARNIA EXPERIMENT SERIES: Phase 1: Landing, 1993; Phase 2: Fire!, 1993; Phase 3: Deadline, 1993; Phase 4: Danger Trail, 1993; Phase 5: Hide and Seek, 1993; Phase 6: Blast Off!, 1993. TIME ROPE SERIES: Time Rope, 1986; Three Against the World, 1986; The Metro Gangs Attack, 1986; At War With Tomorrow, 1986. **Address:** 18 McKenzie Rd., Broxbourne, HF EN10 7JH, England.

LEESON, Ted. American (born United States), b. 1954. **Genres:** Novels, Adult Non-fiction, Young Adult Fiction. **Career:** Oregon State University, Department of English, senior instructor, 1984-. Writer. **Publications:** The Habit of Rivers: Reflections on Trout Streams and Fly Fishing, 1994; (ed.) The Gift of Trout, 1996; Jerusalem Creek: Journeys into Driftless Country, 2002; Orvis Guide to Tackle Care and Repair: Solid Advice for In-Field or At-Home Maintenance, 2006; Inventing Montana: Dispatches from the Madison Valley, 2009. WITH J. SCHOLLMEYER: Fly Tiers Benchside Reference to Techniques and Dressing Styles, 1998; Trout Flies of the West: Best Contemporary Patterns From the Rockies, West, 1998; Trout Flies of the East: Best Contemporary Patterns From East of the Rockies, 1999; Inshore Flies: Best Contemporary Patterns From the Atlantic and Gulf Coasts, 2000; (with J. Schollmeyer) Tying Emergers, 2004; The Benchside Introduction to Fly Tying, 2006; Flies for Western Super Hatches, 2011. Contributer to periodicals. **Address:** Department of English, Oregon State University, 306 Moreland Hall, Corvallis, OR 97331, U.S.A. **Online address:** tleeson@oregonstate.edu

LE FANU, James. British (born England), b. 1950?. **Genres:** Medicine/Health, Food And Wine. **Career:** Royal Free Hospital, Renal Transplant Unit, associate, Department of Cardiology, associate; St. Mary's Hospital, Renal Transplant Unit, associate, Department of Cardiology, associate; Sunday Telegraph, medical columnist; Daily Telegraph, medical columnist. Writer and physician. **Publications:** Eat Your Heart Out: The Fallacy of the Healthy Diet, 1987; Healthwise: An Intelligent Guide for the Over 60s, 1991, rev. ed. as How to Live to Ninety: With a Bit of Luck, 2000; (ed.) Preventionitis: The Exaggerated Claims of Health Promotion, 1994; (ed.) Food, 1994; Doctor's Diary, 1996; The Daily Telegraph Complete Home Remedies: A Handbook of Treatments for All the Family, 1997, 2nd ed., 1999; (with R.M. Youngson) The Family Encyclopedia of Baby, Toddler, and Childcare, 1998; The Rise and Fall of Modern Medicine, 1999; They Don't Know What's Wrong: Does Your Illness Baffle the Doctors?, 2001; Why Us? How Science Rediscovered the Mystery of Ourselves, 2009. Contributor to periodicals and journals. **Address:** c/o Caroline Dawnay, Peters Fraser and Dunlop Group Ltd., Drury House, 34-36 Russell St., London, GL WC2B 5HA, England.

LEFCOURT, Peter. American (born United States), b. 1941. **Genres:** Novels, Plays/Screenplays. **Career:** Producer and writer. **Publications:** NOVELS: The Deal, 1991; The Dreyfus Affair, 1992; Di and I, 1994; Abbreviating Ernie, 1997; Woody, 1998; Eleven Karens, 2003; The Manhattan Beach Project, 2005. EDITOR: (with L.J. Shapiro) The First Time I Got Paid for It, 2000. **Address:** Ken Cross Management, Los Angeles, CA , U.S.A. **Online address:** lefcourt@earthlink.net

LEFEBURE, Leo D. American (born United States), b. 1952. **Genres:** Theology/Religion. **Career:** Archdiocese of Chicago, Roman Catholic priest, 1978-. St. Stephen Protomartyr Church, associate pastor, 1978-82; Our Lady Help of Christians Parish, associate pastor, 1982-87; University of St. Mary of the Lake, Department of Systematic Theology, instructor of systematic theology, 1987-89, assistant professor, 1989-91, chair, 1989-92, associate profes-

sor, 1991-94, dean of ecclesiastical faculty, 1992-98, professor of systematic theology, 1994-99; Civitas Dei Foundation, president, 1999-2003; Fordham University, Department of Theology, visiting associate professor, 1999-2001, associate professor, 2001-05, professor, 2005-06; Chicago Studies, editor, 1999-2003, associate chair, 2001-03, chair, 2004-05; Georgetown University, visiting Matteo Ricci, S.J. professor of theology, 2005-06, Matteo Ricci S.J. professor of theology, 2006-; University of Hong Kong, The Centre for Catholic Studies of the Chinese, honorary research fellow and advisor, 2010-. **Publications:** Toward a Contemporary Wisdom Christology: A Study of Karl Rahner and Norman Pittenger, 1988; Life Transformed: Meditations on the Christian Scriptures in Light of Buddhist Perspectives, 1989; The Buddha and the Christ: Explorations in Buddhist-Christian Dialogue, 1993; Revelation, the Religions, and Violence, 2000; (with P. Feldmeier) The Path of Wisdom: A Christian Commentary on the Dhammapada, 2010. Contributor of articles to journals and periodicals. **Address:** Department of Theology, Georgetown University, 119 New North, PO Box 571135, Washington, DC 20057-1135, U.S.A. **Online address:** ll253@georgetown.edu

LEFEBURE, Molly. British (born England) **Genres:** Novels, Criminology/True Crime, Geography, Biography, History. **Career:** Newspaper reporter, 1939-41; freelance writer, 1945-; Local Education Authority, counselor, 1950-. **Publications:** Evidence for the Crown, 1955; Murder with a Difference, 1958; English Lake District, 1964; Scratch and Co., 1969; Cumberland Heritage, 1970; The Hunting of Wilberforce Pike, 1972; The Loona Balloona, 1974; Samuel Taylor Coleridge: A Bondage of Opium, 1974; Cumbrian Discovery, 1977; The Bondage of Love: A Life of Mrs. Samuel Taylor Coleridge, 1986; The Illustrated Lake Poets, 1987; Blitz!, 1988; (ed. with R. Gravil) Coleridge Connection: Essays for Thomas McFarland, 1990; Thunder in the Sky, 1991; Thomas Hardy's World, 1996; Private Lives of the Ancient Mariner, forthcoming. Contributor to journals. **Address:** Watson, Little Ltd., 48-56 Bayham Pl., London, GL NW1 0EU, England.

LEFEBVRE, Mario. Canadian (born Canada), b. 1957?. **Genres:** Sciences, Mathematics/Statistics, Technology. **Career:** école Polytechnique de Montréal, Department of Mathematics and Industrial Engineering, professor; Bank of Canada, economist, 1991-97; Conference Board of Canada, Centre for Municipal Studies, director, senior research associate. Writer. **Publications:** Applied Probability and Statistics, 2006; Applied Stochastic Processes, 2007. Contributor to periodicals. **Address:** Ecole Polytechnique de MontrEal, C.P. 6079, Succ. Centre-ville, Montreal, QC H3C 3A7, Canada. **Online address:** mario.lefebvre@polymtl.ca

LEFENS, Tim. American (born United States), b. 1953. **Genres:** Art/Art History, Adult Non-fiction. **Career:** Artistic Realizations Technologies (A.R.T.), director, founder and executive director, 1995-. Author, painter and art instructor. **Publications:** Flying Colors: The Story of a Remarkable Group of Artists and the Transcendent Power of Art, 2002. Contributor to books. **Address:** Artistic Realizations Technologies, 11 Whippoorwill Way, Belle Mead, NJ 08502, U.S.A. **Online address:** a.r.tlefens@artrealization.org

LEFF, David K. American (born United States), b. 1955. **Genres:** Writing/Journalism. **Career:** Office of Legislative Research, senior attorney; Connecticut Department of Environmental Protection, environmental conservation, deputy commissioner; Collinsville Historic District Commission, chair; Connecticut Forest and Park Association and Audubon Connecticut, director. Writer. **Publications:** The Last Undiscovered Place, 2004; The Price of Water: Prose Poems, 2008; Deep Travel: In Thoreau's Wake on the Concord and Merrimack, 2009. **Address:** Collinsville, CT , U.S.A. **Online address:** authordavidkleff@gmail.com

LEFF, Gordon. British (born England), b. 1926. **Genres:** Intellectual History, Philosophy, History, Theology/Religion. **Career:** Cambridge University, King's College, fellow, 1955-59; Manchester University, lecturer, senior lecturer, 1956-65; University of York, reader, 1965-69, professor of history, 1969-, emeritus professor, 1988-. Writer. **Publications:** Bradwardine and the Pelagians, 1957; Medieval Thought: St. Augustine to Ockham, 1958; Gregory of Rimini, 1961; The Tyranny of Concepts, 1961; Richard Fitzralph, 1963; Heresy in the Later Middle Ages, vol. II, 1967; Paris and Oxford Universities in 13th and 14th Centuries, 1968; History and Social Theory, 1969; William of Ockham: The Metamorphosis of Scholastic Discourse, 1975; The Dissolution of the Medieval Outlook, 1976; Medieval Church: Universities, Heresy and the Religious Life: Essays in Honour of Gordon Leff, 1999; Heresy, Philosophy and Religion in the Medieval West, 2002; The Concept of Man in the

Middle Ages, forthcoming. Contributor to periodicals. **Address:** Department of History, University of York, Hestington, York, NY Y01 500, England.

LEFKOWITZ, Mary (Rosenthal). American (born United States), b. 1935. **Genres:** Classics, Biography, Social Sciences. **Career:** Wellesley College, instructor, 1959-63, assistant professor, 1963-69, associate professor, 1969-75, professor of Greek and Latin, 1975-79, chairman, 1970-72, 1975-78, 1981-87, 1991-94, 1997-2004, director of educational research, 1978-79, Andrew W. Mellon professor in the humanities, 1979-2005, Andrew W. Mellon professor emeritus, 2005-; University of California, visiting professor, 1978; St. Hilda's College, Sacher visiting fellow, 1979-80, honorary fellow, 1994-. Writer. **Publications:** The Victory Ode: An Introduction, 1976; Heroines and Hysterics, 1981; The Lives of the Greek Poets, 1981; Women in Greek Myth, 1986, 2nd ed., 2007; First-Person Fictions: Pindar's Poetic I, 1991; Not Out of Africa, 1996; Greek Gods, Human Lives, 2003; History Lesson, 2008. EDITOR: (with M.B. Fant) Women in Greece and Rome, 1977 as Women's Life in Greece and Rome, 1982, 3rd ed., 2005; (with G.M. Rogers) Black Athena Revisited, 1996. Contributor to periodicals. **Address:** 15 W Riding St., Wellesley, MA 02482-6914, U.S.A. **Online address:** mlefkowitz@wellesley.edu

LEGATO, Marianne J. American (born United States), b. 1935. **Genres:** Medicine/Health, Biology. **Career:** Columbia University, College of Physicians and Surgeons, visiting fellow in cardiology, 1965-68, instructor, 1968-69, associate, 1969-70, assistant clinical professor, 1970-73, assistant professor, 1973-77, associate professor of clinical medicine, 1977-98, professor of clinical medicine, 1998-, Partnership for Women's Health, founder and director, Partnership for Gender-Specific Medicine, founder, 1997-; Foundation for Gender-Specific Medicine, founder, 2008-; Journal of Gender-Specific Medicine, founder and editor; Johns Hopkins Medical School, adjunct professor of medicine. **Publications:** The Myocardial Cell for the Clinical Cardiologist, 1973; (with C. Colman) The Female Heart: The Truth about Women and Coronary Artery Disease, 1991; Gender-Specific Aspects of Human Biology for the Practicing Physician, 1997; (with C. Colman) What Women Need to Know: From Headaches to Heart Disease and Everything in Between, 1997; Eve's Rib, 2002; (with L. Tucker) Why Men Never Remember and Women Never Forget, 2005; Why Men Die First: How to Lengthen Your Lifespan, 2008. EDITOR: The Developing Heart: Clinical Implications of Its Molecular Biology and Physiology, 1985; The Stressed Heart, 1987; Pravastatin Sodium: Over 10 Years of Experience: A Worldwide Review of Clinical Articles from the Scientific Literature, 2002; Principles of Gender-Specific Medicine, 2004. Contributor to journals, books and newspapers. **Address:** 962 Park Ave., New York, NY 10028-0313, U.S.A.

LEGG, Gerald. British (born England), b. 1947. **Genres:** Zoology, Biology, Botany, Animals/Pets. **Career:** University of Sierra Leone, Fourah Bay College, lecturer in zoology and researcher, 1971-74; Booth Museum of Natural History, keeper of natural sciences and biologist, 1974-. Writer. **Publications:** FOR ADULTS: (with R.E. Jones) Pseudoscorpions (Arthropoda, Arachnida): Keysand Notes for the Identification of the Species, 1988. FOR CHILDREN: Amazing Tropical Birds, 1991; The X-Ray Picture Book of Amazing Animals, 1993; Minibeasts, 1993; (with K. Barnham) Flyers Animals: Minibeasts, 1994; Monster Animals, 1994; The X-Ray Picture Book of Incredible Creatures, 1995; (with R. Matthews) Amazing Animal Facts, 1997; Sharks, 1997; Creepy Critters, 1997; Dragons, 1998; Bugs, 1998; Find out about Minibeasts, 2003; Birds of Prey, 2004; Octopuses and Squid, 2004; Life in the Desert, 2005. LIFECYCLES SERIES: From Caterpillar to Butterfly, 1997; From Egg to Chicken, 1997; From Seed to Sunflower, 1997; From Tadpole to Frog, 1997. HOW IT WORKS SERIES: The World of Animal Life, 1998; The World of Plant Life, 2000; The World of Insect Life, 2002. SCARY CREATURES SERIES: Bears, 2002; Alligators and Crocodiles, 2002; Rats, 2003. Contributor to periodicals and journals. **Address:** Booth Museum of Natural History, 194 Dyke Rd., Brighton, ES BN1 5AA, England. **Online address:** gerald@natura.uklinux.net

LEGGATT, Alexander. Canadian (born Canada), b. 1940. **Genres:** Theatre, Literary Criticism And History. **Career:** University of Toronto, University College, lecturer, 1965-67, assistant professor, 1967-71, associate professor, 1971-75, professor of English, 1975-2006, professor emeritus, 2006-. Writer. **Publications:** Citizen Comedy in the Age of Shakespeare, 1973; Shakespeare's Comedy of Love, 1974; Ben Jonson: His Vision and His Art, 1981; English Drama: Shakespeare to the Restoration 1590-1660, 1988; King Lear,

1988; Shakespeare's Political Drama, 1988; Harvester Twayne New Critical Introductions to Shakespeare: King Lear, 1988; (comp. with L. Norem) Coriolanus: An Annotated Bibliography, 1989; Shakespeare in Performance: King Lear, 1991; Jacobean Public Theatre, 1992; English Stage Comedy 1490-1990, 1998; Introduction to English Renaissance Comedy, 1999; (ed. with K. Bamford) Approaches to Teaching English Renaissance Drama, 2002; (ed.) The Cambridge Companion to Shakespearean Comedy, 2002; Shakespeare's Tragedies: Violation and Identity, 2005; (ed.) William Shakespeare's Macbeth: A Sourcebook, 2006. **Address:** 2593 St. Clair Ave. E, Toronto, ON M4B 1M2, Canada. **Online address:** alexander.leggatt@utoronto.ca

LEGGE, John David. Australian (born Australia), b. 1921. **Genres:** History, Politics/Government, Biography. **Career:** University of Western Australia, lecturer, 1946-54, senior lecturer, 1955-59, reader in history, 1960; Monash University, foundation chair in history, 1960-77, professor of history, 1960-78, professor emeritus, 1978-, Centre of Southeast Asian Studies, chairman, 1964-86, honorary research associate, Faculty of Arts, dean, 1977-86; Singapore Institute of Southeast Asian Studies, director, 1969-70; Academy of the Social Sciences in Australia, fellow. Writer. **Publications:** (With F. Alexander and F.K. Crowley) The Origins of the Eastern Goldfields Water Scheme in Western Australia, 1954; Australian Colonial Policy, 1956; Problems of Regional Autonomy in Contemporary Indonesia, 1957; Britain in Fiji, 1858-1880, 1958; Central Authority and Regional Autonomy in Indonesia, 1961; Indonesia, 1964, 3rd ed., 1980; Sukarno: A Political Biography, 1972, 3rd ed., 2003; Intellectuals and Nationalism in Indonesia, 1988; (co-ed.) Indonesian Democracy: 1950s-1990s, 1994; (ed. with J. Drakard) Indonesian Independence Fifty Years On, 1945-1995, 1996; Australian Outlook: A History of the Australian Institute of International Affairs, 1999. **Address:** Department of History, Monash University, Rm. W604, Menzies Bldg., Wellington Rd., Clayton, VI 3800, Australia.

LEGGETT, Richard G. Canadian/British (born England), b. 1953. **Genres:** Theology/Religion. **Career:** University of Denver, Department of Foreign Languages and Literatures, teaching assistant in German, 1976-77; Regis High School, teacher of German and French, 1977-78; Diocese of Colorado, diocesan staff, 1981-82; anglican priest, 1981-87; Diocese of Colorado, Bishop's School of Theology, instructor in church history, 1981-83; Christ Episcopal Church, curate, 1982-83, assistant rector, 1983-84; Living the Good News Christian Education Curriculum, theological consultant, 1983-87; Regis College, special lecturer in history, 1983; Cathedral Church of Saint James, coordinator of youth ministry and adult education, 1985-87; Diocese of Northern Indiana, Lay School of Theology and Ministry, instructor in church history, 1985-87; University of Notre Dame, graduate assistant, 1985-86; St. George's Episcopal Mission, priest-in-charge, 1985-86; Episcopal Church Foundation, fellow, 1986-; Vancouver School of Theology, assistant professor of liturgics and church history, 1987-96, associate professor of liturgics and church history, 1996-2001, professor of liturgical studies, 2001-, associate dean. Writer. **Publications:** A Companion to the Waterloo Declaration, 2000. Contributor of articles and reviews to periodicals. **Address:** Vancouver School of Theology, 6000 Iona Dr., Vancouver, BC V6T 1L4, Canada. **Online address:** rleggett@vst.edu

LEGGIERE, Michael V. American (born United States), b. 1969. **Genres:** History. **Career:** Florida State University, Institute on Napoleon and the French Revolution, research assistant, 1991-92, teaching assistant, 1992-93; Hillsborough Community College, adjunct history professor, 1996-98; Louisiana State University, Department of History and Social Sciences, assistant professor of history, 1998-2003, associate professor of history, 2003-08, chair, 2005-08; U.S. Naval War College, College of Distance Education, adjunct professor of strategy and policy, 2001-; Hawaii Pacific University, visiting assistant professor of history, 2002, 2004; University of North Texas, assistant professor of history, 2008-. Historian and writer. **Publications:** Napoleon and Berlin: The Franco-Prussian War in North Germany, 1813, 2002; The Fall of Napoleon: The Allied Invasion of France, 1813-1814, vol. I, 2007. Contributor of articles to books and journals. **Address:** Department of History, University of North Texas, 1601 Kittyhawk Dr., Little Elm, TX 75068, U.S.A. **Online address:** michael.leggiere@unt.edu

LEGGO, Carl Derek. Canadian (born Canada), b. 1953?. **Genres:** Education, Poetry. **Career:** University of British Columbia, Department of Language and Literacy Education, professor, 1990-. Writer. **Publications:** Teaching to Wonder: Responding to Poetry in the Secondary Classroom, 1998; (ed. with R. Kelly) Creative Expression, Creative Education: Creativity as a Primary Rationale for Education, 2008; (with E. Hasebe-Ludt and C.M. Chambers) Life Writing and Literary Métissage as an Ethos for Our Time, 2009. POETRY: Growing Up Perpendicular on the Side of a Hill, 1994; View from My Mother's House, 1999; Come-by-Chance, 2006. Contributor to books and periodicals. **Address:** Department of Language and Literacy Education, University of British Columbia, 215 PonE, 2125 Main Mall, Vancouver, BC V6T 1Z4, Canada. **Online address:** carl.leggo@ubc.ca

LEGGS, Johnny. *See* **LEGUIZAMO, John.**

LEGRAIN, Philippe. British/American (born United States), b. 1973. **Genres:** Business/Trade/Industry, Social Sciences, Economics. **Career:** Independent Economic Analysis (IDEA), new media writer, 1996; SBC Warburg Dillon Read, economic researcher, 1996-97; The Economist, correspondent, 1997-2000; World Trade Organization (WTO), special adviser to the director-general, 2000-01; World Link, editor, 2002; Britain in Europe, chief economist and director of policy, 2003-05; full-time writer, 2005-. **Publications:** Open World: The Truth about Globalisation, 2002; Immigrants: Your Country Needs Them, 2007; Aftershock: Reshaping the World Economy After the Crisis, 2010. Contributor to magazines. **Address:** C/o Ivan R. Dee, 1332 N Halsted St., Chicago, IL 60642-2624, U.S.A. **Online address:** mail@philippelegrain.com

LEGRO, Jeffrey W. American (born United States), b. 1960. **Genres:** Adult Non-fiction, History, Military/Defense/Arms Control, Politics/Government. **Career:** University of Virginia, Randolph P. Compton professor of world politics, Woodrow Wilson Department of Politics, chairman, Miller Center of Public Affairs, Governing America in a Global Era Program, co-founder and faculty associate, Government and Foreign Affairs, associate professor; University of Minnesota, faculty; China Foreign Affairs University, professor, Fulbright professor, 2002-03; American Political Science Association, chairman. Consultant and writer. **Publications:** NONFICTION: Cooperation under Fire: Anglo-German Restraint during World War II, 1995; Rethinking the World: Great Power Strategies and International Order, 2005; (ed. with M.P. Leffler) To Lead the World: American Strategy after the Bush Doctrine, 2008; (ed. with M.P. Leffler) In Uncertain Times: American Foreign Policy after the Berlin Wall and 9/11, 2011. Contributor to periodicals. **Address:** Department of Politics, University of Virginia, PO Box 400787, Charlottesville, VA 22904-4787, U.S.A. **Online address:** jwl4x@virginia.edu

LE GUIN, Elisabeth. American (born United States), b. 1957. **Genres:** Adult Non-fiction, Biography, Music. **Career:** University of California, Department of Musicology, associate professor of musicology and cello and director of undergraduate studies, 1997-; freelance cellist; Philharmonia Baroque Orchestra, founding member; Artaria String Quartet, founding member. Writer. **Publications:** (Contrib.) Beyond Structural Hearing, 2005; (contrib.) Culture of the Horse: Status, Discipline and Identity in the Early Modern World, 2005; (contrib.) In Vivo: Embodying Information, 2005; (ed. with M. Mangani and J. Tortella) Luigi Boccherini: Estudios sobre Fuentes, recepción e historiografía, 2006; Boccherini's Body: An Essay in Carnal Musicology, 2006; (contrib.) Boccherini Studies, 2006. Contributor to periodicals. **Address:** Department of Musicology, University of California, 2539 Schoenberg Music Bldg., 445 Charles E Young Dr. E, Los Angeles, CA 90095-1616, U.S.A. **Online address:** leguin@humnet.ucla.edu

LE GUIN, Ursula K(roeber). American (born United States), b. 1929. **Genres:** Novels, Novellas/Short Stories, Science Fiction/Fantasy, Children's Fiction, Young Adult Fiction, Poetry, Literary Criticism And History, Young Adult Non-fiction, Picture/Board Books, inspirational/Motivational Literature. **Career:** Mercer University, instructor in French, 1954-55; University of Idaho, instructor in French, 1956; Portland State University, visiting lecturer and writer-in-residence; University of California, Revelle College, visiting lecturer and writer-in-residence; University of Reading, visiting lecturer and writer-in-residence; Kenyon College, visiting lecturer and writer-in-residence; Tulane University, Mellon lecturer and writer-in-residence; Emory University, department secretary. Writer. **Publications:** SERIES: HAINISH: Planet of Exile, 1966; Rocannon's World, 1966; City of Illusions, 1967; The Left Hand of Darkness, 1969; The Word for World Is Forest, 1972; The Dispossessed, 1974; Four Ways to Forgiveness, 1995; Worlds of Exile and Illusion, 1996; The Telling, 2000. EARTH SEA: A Wizard of Earthsea, 1968; The Tombs of Atuan, 1970; The Farthest Shore, 1972; The Earthsea Trilogy, 1977; Tehanu, 1990; Earthsea Revisioned, 1993; The Other Wind, 2001; Tales from Earthsea, 2001. ADVENTURES IN KROY: The Adventure of

Cobbler's Rune, 1982; Solomon Leviathan's Nine-Hundred and Thirty-First Trip Around the World, 1983. CATWINGS: Catwings, 1988; Catwings Return, 1989; Jane On Her Own, 1992; Wonderful Alexander and the Catwings, 1994; Tales of the Catwings, 1996; More Tales of the Catwings, 2000; Cat Dreams, 2009. CHRONICLES OF THE WESTERN SHORE: Gifts, 2004; Voices, 2006, Powers, 2007. NOVELS: The Lathe of Heaven, 1971; Very Far Away from Anywhere Else, 1976; The Eye of the Heron, 1978; Malafrena, 1979; The Beginning Place, 1980 in UK as Threshold, 1980; Always Coming Home, 1985; Searoad: Chronicles of Klats, 1991; A Ride on the Red Mare's Back, 1992; Changing Planes, 2003; Lavinia, 2008. COLLECTIONS: Wild Angels, 1974; Orsinian Tales, 1975; The Wind's Twelve Quarters, 1975; Walking in Cornwall, 1976; Hard Words: And Other Poems (poems), 1981; The Compass Rose, 1982; In the Red Zone (poems), 1983; Wild Oats and Fireweed: New Poems (poems), 1987; Buffalo Gals and Other Animal Presences, 1987; (with S.R. Sanders) The Visionary, Wonders Hidden, 1988; The Earthsea Quartet, 1993; Blue Moon over Thurman Street (poems), 1993; Going Out With Peacocks: And Other Poems, (poems), 1994; A Fisherman of the Inland Sea, 1994; Science Fiction Stories, 1994; Unlocking the Air: And Other Stories, 1996; Sixty Odd: New Poems (poems), 1999; The Birthday of the World: And Other Stories, 2002; Incredible Good Fortune: New Poems (poems), 2006; Out Here: Poems and Images from Steens Mountain Country, 2010. CHAPBOOKS: The Water Is Wide, 1976; Leese Webster, 1979; Gwilan's Harp, 1981; The Adventure of Cobbler's Rune, 1982; Solomon Leviathan's 931st Trip Around the World, 1983; The Visionary: The Life Story of Flicker of the Serpentine of Telina-Na, 1984; The Ones Who Walk Away from Omelas, 1991; Nine Lives, 1992; Buffalo Gals: Won't You Come Out Tonight, 1994; The Shobies' Story, 1998. PICTURE BOOKS: A Visit from Dr. Katz, 1988; Fire and Stone, 1989; Fish Soup, 1992; Tom Mouse, 2002. NONFICTION: From Elfland to Poughkeepsie, 1973; Dreams Must Explain Themselves, 1975; The Language of the Night: Essays on Fantasy and Science Fiction, 1979; Steering the Craft: Exercises and Discussions on Story Writing for the Lone Navigator or the Mutinous Crew, 1984; Dancing at the Edge of the World: Thoughts on Words, Women, Places, 1989; The Way of the Water's Going: Images of the Northern California Coastal Range, 1989; (with J.P. Scaton) Lao Tzu: Tao Te Ching: A Book About the Way and the Power of the Way, 1997; The Wave in the Mind: Talks and Essays on the Writer, the Reader, and the Imagination, 2004; (ed. and intro.) Selected Stories of H.G. Wells, 2004; Cheek by Jowl, 2009; Cat Dreams, 2009. OTHERS: (with G. Wolfe and J. Tiptree, Jr.) New Atlantis and Other Novellas of Science Fiction, 1975; (co-author) The Altered I: An Encounter with Science Fiction, 1976; The Birthday of the World and other Stories, 2002; (trans.) Selected poems of Gabriela Mistral, 2003; Kalpa Imperial, 2003; (with K. Kerr, V.N. McIntyre and S. Smith) Dragon Lords and Warrior Women, 2010; The Wild Girls, 2011; Finding My Elegy, 2012. Works appear in anthologies. Contributor to periodicals. **Address:** Virginia Kidd Agency Inc., PO Box 278, Milford, PA 18337-0278, U.S.A.

LEGUIZAMO, John. Also writes as Johnny Leggs. American/Colombian (born Colombia), b. 1965. **Genres:** Plays/Screenplays, Humor/Satire, Literary Criticism And History. **Career:** Writer. **Publications:** PLAYS: Spic-O-Rama, 1992; Mambo Mouth: A Savage Comedy, 1993; Freak: A Semi-Demi-Quasi-Pseudo Autobiography, 1997. OTHERS: Pimps, Hos, Playa Hatas, and All the Rest of My Hollywood Friends: My Life, 2006; The Works of John Leguizamo, 2008. **Address:** Rebel Productions Inc., 268 E 7th St., Ground Fl., New York, NY 10009, U.S.A.

LEHANE, Cornelius. American (born United States) **Genres:** Novels. **Career:** Rockland Community College, assistant professor of English, professor of English; National Education Association, publications editor and writer, senior writer editor. **Publications:** Beware the Solitary Drinker, 2002; What Goes Around Comes Around, 2005; Death at the Old Hotel, 2007. **Address:** National Education Association, 1201 16th St. NW, Washington, DC 20036, U.S.A. **Online address:** clehane@nea.org

LEHANE, Dennis. American (born United States), b. 1965. **Genres:** Mystery/Crime/Suspense, Novels, Young Adult Fiction. **Career:** Florida International University, instructor in English, 1991-93; Harvard University, teacher. Writer and counselor. **Publications:** MYSTERIES: A Drink Before the War, 1994; Darkness, Take My Hand, 1996; Sacred, 1997; Gone, Baby, Gone, 1998; Prayers for Rain, 1999; Mystic River, 2001; Shutter Island, 2003. OTHERS: Coronado: Stories, 2006; The Given Day: A Novel, 2008; Sour Lemon Score: A Parker Novel, 2010; (ed.) Boston Noir, 2010; Moonlight Mile, 2010;

(foreword) The Green Eagle Score, 2010. Contributor to periodicals. **Address:** c/o Ann Rittenberg, Ann Rittenberg Literary Agency Inc., 15 Maiden Ln, Ste. 206, New York, NY 10038, U.S.A.

LEHFELDT, Elizabeth A. American (born United States), b. 1966. **Genres:** Theology/Religion. **Career:** Cleveland State University, associate professor & interim director of general education, 1995-. Historian, educator, writer and editor. **Publications:** (ed. and intro.) The Black Death, 2005; Religious Women in Golden Age Spain: The Permeable Cloister, 2005. **Address:** Department of History, Cleveland State University, 2121 Euclid Ave., Cleveland, OH 44115-2214, U.S.A. **Online address:** e.lehfeldt@csuohio.edu

LEHMAN, Yvonne. American (born United States), b. 1936. **Genres:** Novels, Young Adult Fiction, Novellas/Short Stories. **Career:** Blue Ridge Christian Writers Annual Conference, founder and director, 1976-93, planner and director, 2001-; Montreat College, School of Professional and Adult Studies, teacher of English. **Publications:** NOVELS: Red Like Mine, 1970; Dead Men Don't Cry, 1973; Fashions of the Heart, 1981; In Shady Groves, 1983; Smokey Mountain Sunrise, 1984; Taken by Storm, 1985; More Than a Summer's Love, 1985; Drums of Shelomoh, 1993; Southern Gentleman, 1994; Mountain Man, 1995; A Whole New World, 1996; Painting: A Timeless Treasure of Four All-New Novellas, 1996; A la Mode Hawaiian Heartbeat, 1997; Name that Tune, 2003; Coffee Rings, 2004; Aloha Love, 2009; Picture Bride, 2009; Aloha Brides, 2011. YOUNG ADULT FICTION: Tornado Alley, 1996; Secret Storm, 1996; Mirror of Dreams, 1996; Picture Perfect, 1996; A Fighting Chance, 1997; After the Storm, 1998; Swept Away, 1998; Something Old Something New, 1998; The Gold Star, 1998; Call of the Mountain, 1998; Somewhere a Rainbow, 1999; Dear Jane, 1999; Whiter Than Snow, 1999; Going Home Again, 1999; Never Say Never, 1999; Catch of a Lifetime, 2000; Scrambled Eggs, 2000; Secret Ballot, 2000; Lily's Plight, 2000; The Stranger's Kiss, 2001; Carolina, 2001; South Carolina, 2002; Past the P's Please, 2002; On a Clear Day, 2003; His Hands: A Story of Renewed Hope, 2003. OTHER: (with V.B. Jones, T. Peterson and K. Yapp) Summer Dreams, 1997; (with J. Baer) Heartless Hero/Picture Perfect, 1997; (ed.) Winter Wishes: Four New Inspirational Romances from Christmas Present, 1999; Lessons of the Heart: Four Novellas in which Modern Teachers Learn about Love, 2000; (with G. Aiken, L.A. Coleman and B. Huston) Strings of the Heart, 2003; Moving the Mountain, 2006; Bride Idea, 2007; By Love Acquitted, 2007; Carolina Carpenter Brides: Four Couples Find Tools for Building Romance in a Home Improvement Store, 2007; (with L. Bliss and I. Brand) Kentucky Brides, 2008; North Carolina Weddings, 2008; Moving the Mountain: Romance Complicates a Simple Way of Historic Life, 2009. **Address:** PO Box 188, Black Mountain, NC 28711, U.S.A. **Online address:** ylehman@bellsouth.net

LEHMANN, Geoffrey (John). Australian (born Australia), b. 1940. **Genres:** Novels, Poetry. **Career:** C.R. Wilcox and Lehmann, principal, 1969-76; Price Waterhouse (now Price Waterhouse Coopers) partner, 1990-2000, tax counsel, 2000-, corporate tax lawyer, now retired; University of New South Wales, lecturer in taxation law, academic lawyer. Writer. **Publications:** POETRY: (with L.A. Murray) The Ilex Tree, 1965; A Voyage of Lions and Other Poems, 1968; Conversation with a Rider, 1972; From an Australian Country Sequence, 1973; Selected Poems, 1976; Ross' Poems, 1978; Nero's Poems: Translations of the Public and Private Poems of the Emperor Nero, 1981; Spring Forest, 1992; Collected Poems, 1997. OTHERS: (ed.) Comic Australian Verse, 1972; A Spring Day in Autumn, 1974; Australian Primitive Painters, 1977; (ed. with R. Gray) The Younger Australian Poets, 1983; (with C. Coleman) Taxation Law in Australia, 1989, 5th ed., 1998; Children's Games, 1990; (ed.) The Flight of the Emu: Contemporary Light Verse, 1990; (ed. with R. Gray) Australian Poetry in the Twentieth Century, 1991; The Balloon Farmer, 1994; Sky Boy, 1996; (ed. with R. Gray) Australian Poetry since 1788, 2011. **Address:** 8 Highfield Rd., Lindfield, NW 2070, Australia.

LEHMANN, Wolfgang. Canadian (born Canada), b. 1965?. **Genres:** Sociology, Social Sciences. **Career:** University of Western Ontario, Department of Sociology, assistant professor, associate professor. Writer. **Publications:** Choosing to Labour?: School-Work Transitions and Social Class, 2007; (contrib.) Introduction to Sociology: A Canadian Focus, 9th ed., 2007. Contributor to books and journals. **Address:** Department of Sociology, University of Western Ontario, 5430 Social Science Ctr., 1151 Richmond St., London, ON N6A 5C2, Canada. **Online address:** wlehmann@uwo.ca

LEHMANN-HAUPT, Rachel. American (born United States), b. 1969?. **Genres:** Human Relations/Parenting, Psychology, Autobiography/Memoirs. **Career:** F magazine, founding editor; Plum magazine, editor; The Felker Magazine Center, assistant editor. **Publications:** Airplane Yoga, 2003; In Her Own Sweet Time: Unexpected Adventures in Finding Love, Commitment, and Motherhood, 2009. Contributor of articles to books and magazines. **Address:** c/o Lydia Wills, Paradigm, 360 Park Ave. S, 16th Fl., New York, NY 10010, U.S.A. **Online address:** rachel@lehmannhaupt.com

LEHMBERG, Stanford Eugene. American (born United States), b. 1931. **Genres:** History, Architecture, Biography. **Career:** University of Texas, instructor, 1956-59, assistant professor, 1959-63, associate professor, 1963-67, professor of history, 1967-69; University of Minnesota, Department of History, professor of history, 1969-99, department chairman, 1978-85, professor emeritus, 1999-. Writer. **Publications:** Sir Thomas Elyot, Tudor Humanist, 1960; (ed.) Sir Thomas Elyot, The Book Named the Governor, 1962; Sir Walter Mildmay and Tudor Government, 1964; The Reformation Parliament 1529-1536, 1970; The Later Parliaments of Henry VIII, 1536-1547, 1977; The Reformation of Cathedrals: Cathedrals in English Society, 1485-1603, 1988; The Peoples of the British Isles: A New History, 1992, (with S.A. Meigs and T.W. Heyck) 3rd ed., 2008; Cathedrals under Siege: Cathedrals in English Society, 1600-1700, 1996; (with A.M. Pflaum) The University of Minnesota, 1945-2000, 2001; English Cathedrals: A History, 2005; Churches for the Southwest: The Ecclesiastical Architecture of John Gaw Meem, 2005. **Address:** Department of History, University of Minnesota, 1110 Heller Hall, 271 19th Ave. S, Minneapolis, MN 55455, U.S.A. **Online address:** lehmberg@earthlink.net

LEHNE, Judith Logan. American (born United States), b. 1947. **Genres:** Children's Fiction, Plays/Screenplays, Children's Non-fiction, How-to Books, Animals/Pets, Crafts. **Career:** Allstate Insurance, rate clerk, 1967; McGraw-Hill Publishers, clerk, 1968; Mettler Instruments, research and customer file coordinator, 1968-70; Geico Insurance, sales and service supervisor, 1970-72; Schneider Transport, customer coordinator, 1978-79; Circle M Corral, copywriter and advertising design coordinator for all publicity, 1988-91; Institute of Children's Literature, instructor, 1991-. **Publications:** FOR CHILDREN: The Never-Be-Bored Book: Quick Things to Make When There's Nothing to Do, 1992; When the Ragman Sings, 1993; Coyote Girl, 1995; Kangaroos for Kids (nonfiction), 1997; KANGAROOS, Kangaroo Magic for Kids, 2000; (with P. Lantier) The Wonder of Kangaroos, 2001; Busy Mom's Book of Quick Crafts for Kids, 2004. Contributor to children's magazines. **Address:** c/o Kendra Marcus, Book Stop Literary Agency, 67 Meadow View Rd., Orinda, WI 94563, U.S.A. **Online address:** scribe@newnorth.net

LEHNER, Lyndsay Farber. American (born United States), b. 1980?. **Genres:** Novels. **Career:** Writer and actress. **Publications:** Dust and Shadow: An Account of the Ripper Killings by Dr. John H. Watson, 2009. Contributor to books. **Address:** New York, NY , U.S.A. **Online address:** lyndsayfaye@hotmail.com

LEHR, Jennifer. American (born United States), b. 1969?. **Genres:** Art/Art History, Sex, Autobiography/Memoirs. **Career:** Private Edition Celebration Books (publishing company specializing in coffee-table books), publisher, 1998-. Designer and writer. **Publications:** 78 Drawings of My Face, 1998; Ill-equipped for a Life of Sex: A Memoir, 2004. Contributor to periodicals. **Address:** Susan Golomb Literary Agency, 875 6th Ave., Ste. 2302, New York, NY 10011, U.S.A. **Online address:** jennifer@jenniferlehr.com

LEHRER, James (Charles). (Jim Lehrer). American (born United States), b. 1934. **Genres:** Novels, Plays/Screenplays, Autobiography/Memoirs. **Career:** MacNeil-Lehrer Productions, co-partner; Dallas Morning News, political reporter, 1959; Dallas Times Herald, court reporter, 1959-66, political columnist, 1966-68, city editor, 1968-69; KERA-TV, consultant, 1970, executive director of public affairs, 1970-72, editor and host of nightly news program; PBS, first public affairs coordinator, 1972-73; National Public Affairs Center for Television, PBS News Service, correspondent, 1973; The Robert MacNeil Report, co-anchor, 1975-76; The MacNeil/Lehrer Report, co-anchor and associate editor, 1976-83; The MacNeil/Lehrer NewsHour, co-anchor, 1983-95; The NewsHour with Jim Lehrer, anchor and executive editor, 1995-; Dallas College, instructor in creative writing; Southern Methodist University, instructor in creative writing. **Publications:** MEMOIRS: (as James Lehrer) We Were Dreamers, 1975; A Bus of My Own, 1992. OTHERS: (as James Lehrer) Viva Max!, 1966; Kick the Can, 1988; Crown Oklahoma, 1989; The

Sooner Spy, 1990; Lost and Found, 1991; Short List, 1992; Bus of My Own, 1992; Blue Hearts: A Novel, 1993; Fine Lines, 1994; The Last Debate, 1995; White Widow, 1997; Purple Dots: A Novel, 1998; The Special Prisoner: A Novel, 2000; No Certain Rest: A Novel, 2002; Flying Crows: A Novel, 2004; The Franklin Affair: A Novel, 2005; Phony Marine: A Novel, 2006; Eureka: A Novel, 2007; Mack to the Rescue, 2008; Oh, Johnny: A Novel, 2009; Super: A Novel, 2010; Tension City: Inside the Presidential Debates, 2011. Contributor to periodicals. **Address:** NewsHour, 3620 27th St. S, Arlington, VA 22206, U.S.A. **Online address:** newshour@pbs.org

LEHRER, Jim. See **LEHRER, James (Charles).**

LEHRER, Jonah. American (born United States), b. 1981. **Genres:** Sciences, Art/Art History, Medicine/Health, Business/Trade/Industry, Sports/Fitness. **Career:** Seed Magazine, editor-at-large; National Public Radio, Radio Lab, contributing editor; Scientific American, contributing editor; Columbia University, research assistant; Wired, contributing editor. Journalist. **Publications:** Proust Was a Neuroscientist, 2007; How We Decide, 2009; Decisive Moment: How the Brain Makes up Its Mind, 2009; Imagine: How Creativity Works, 2012. Contributor to journals and periodicals. **Address:** Houghton Mifflin Harcourt Publishing Co., 222 Berkeley St., Boston, MA 02116-3748, U.S.A. **Online address:** jonah.lehrer@gmail.com

LEHRER, Kate. American (born United States), b. 1939. **Genres:** Novels, Literary Criticism And History. **Career:** Writer. **Publications:** NOVELS: Best Intentions, 1987; When They Took Away the Man in the Moon, 1993; Out of Eden, 1996; Confessions of a Bigamist, 2004. **Address:** c/o Ron Goldfarb, Goldfarb & Associates, 721 Gibbon St., Alexandria, VA 22314, U.S.A. **Online address:** kate@katelehrer.com

LEHRER, Stanley. American (born United States), b. 1929. **Genres:** Education, History, Sociology, Theology/Religion, Biography, Cultural/Ethnic Topics, Politics/Government. **Career:** Crossroads Publishing Associates, president and editor, 1948-50; Open Road-American Boy Magazine, youth service editor, 1950-51; School and Society Magazine, vice-president and managing editor, 1953-68, publisher, 1968-72; Society for the Advancement of Education Inc., treasurer, 1953-, trustee, 1963-, president, 1968-99; School and Society Books, publisher, 1963-; Intellect Magazine, founder and publisher, 1972-78; USA Today Magazine, founder, publisher and editorial director, 1978-99; Newsview, publisher and editorial director, 1978-; Your Health, publisher and editorial director, 1980-. **Publications:** Leaders, Teachers, and Learners in Academe: Partners in the Educational Process, 1970; (co-author) Titanic: Fortune & Fate: Catalogue from the Mariners' Museum Exhibition, 1998. EDITED WITH W.W. BRICKMAN: John Dewey: Master Educator, 1959; The Countdown on Segregated Education, 1960; Religion, Government, and Education, 1961; A Century of Higher Education: Classical Citadel to Collegiate Colossus, 1962; Automation, Education, and Human Values, 1966; Conflict and Change on the Campus: The Response to Student Hyperactivism, 1970; Education and the Many Faces of the Disadvantaged: Cultural and Historical Perspectives, 1972; Religion, Government and Education, 1977. Contributor to magazines and journals. **Address:** 82 Shelbourne Ln., New Hyde Park, NY 11040-1044, U.S.A.

LEHRING, Gary L. American (born United States), b. 1966?. **Genres:** Gay And Lesbian Issues, Politics/Government, Military/Defense/Arms Control, History. **Career:** Smith College, Department of Government, assistant professor of government, associate professor of government, Study of Women & Gender, faculty. Writer. **Publications:** Officially Gay: The Political Construction of Sexuality by the U.S. Military, 2003. **Address:** Department of Government, Smith College, 10 Prospect St., Ste. 105, Northampton, MA 01063-6312, U.S.A. **Online address:** glehring@email.smith.edu

LEIB, Franklin A(llen). American (born United States), b. 1944. **Genres:** Novels, Young Adult Non-fiction, Literary Criticism And History, Mystery/Crime/Suspense. **Career:** Bankers Trust Co., vice-president and head of loan syndication, 1971-83; writer, 1985-; Mariner Capital Corp., president. **Publications:** NOVELS: Fire Arrow, 1988; The Fire Dream, 1989; Sea Lion, 1990; Valley of the Shadow, 1991; The House of Pain, 1999; Behold a Pale Horse, 2000. Contributor to periodicals. **Address:** Tor Books, 175 5th Ave., 14th Fl., New York, NY 10010, U.S.A.

LEIBLUM, Sandra R. American (born United States) **Genres:** Medicine/Health, Psychology, Psychiatry. **Career:** University of Medicine and Dentistry of New Jersey, Internship Program in Clinical Psychology, director, Robert Wood Johnson Medical School, professor of psychiatry, 1988-2007, Center for Sexual and Relationship Health, director, Community Mental Health Center, team leader, Postgraduate Program in Sex Therapy, director; Rutgers University, Graduate School of Applied and Professional Psychology, faculty; Worcester State Hospital, psychology intern; Worcester Youth Guidance Center, child-clinical psychology intern; Worcester Polytechnic Institute, counseling psychologist; University Center for Reproductive Endocrinology and Fertility, Infertility Programs, consultant. Writer. **Publications:** AS SANDRA RISA LEIBLUM: (With Mark) Viagra and You: New Treatments for Potency and Sexual Health, 1999; (with J. Sachs) Getting the Sex You Want: A Woman's Guide to Becoming Proud, Passionate and Pleased in Bed, 2002. EDITOR: (with J. Gottman) How to Do Psychotherapy and How to Evaluate It: A Manual for Beginners, 1974; (with L. Pervin) Principles and Practices of Sex Therapy, 1980, 2nd ed. (with R.C. Rosen) as Principles and Practice of Sex Therapy: An Update for the 1990s, 1989, 4th ed., 2007; (with R.C. Rosen and contrib.) Sexual Desire Disorders, 1988; (with R.C. Rosen and contrib.) Erectile Disorders: Assessment and Treatment, 1992; (with R.C. Rosen) Case Studies in Sex Therapy, 1995; (ed.) Infertility: Psychological Issues and Counseling Strategies, 1997; Treating Sexual Desire Disorders: A Clinical Casebook, 2010. Contributor to books and periodicals. **Address:** Department of Psychiatry, Robert Wood Johnson Medical School, University of Medicine and Dentistry of New Jersey, 675 Hoes Ln., Piscataway, NJ 08854, U.S.A. **Online address:** sleiblum@gmail.com

LEIBY, Bruce R. American (born United States), b. 1947. **Genres:** Reference, Biography, Music, Humanities, Communications/Media. **Career:** School teacher, 1970-2006; Delaware County Community College, instructor, 1974. Writer. **Publications:** Gordon MacRae: A Bio-Bibliography, 1991; Howard Keel: A Bio-Bibliography, 1995; (with L.F. Leiby) A Reference Guide to Television's Bonanza: Episodes, Personnel, and Broadcast History, 2001. **Address:** 13 E 6th St., Media, PA 19063, U.S.A. **Online address:** leiby66@msn.com

LEIDER, Richard J. American (born United States) **Genres:** Ethics, Industrial Relations. **Career:** The Inventure Group, founding partner, founder and chairman; Dorobo Fund, founder; University of Minnesota, Carlson Schools Executive Development Center, faculty. Consultant and writer. **Publications:** (With J. Hagberg) The Inventurers: Excursions in Life and Career, 1978; Life Skills: Taking Charge of Your Personal and Professional Growth, 1994; (with D.A. Shapiro) Repacking Your Bags: Lighten Your Load for the Rest of Your Life, 1995, 2nd ed., 2002; The Power of Purpose: Creating Meaning in Your Life and Work, 1997, 2nd ed., 2010; Working Naturally: A New Way to Maximize Individual and Organizational Effectiveness, 1999; (with D.A. Shapiro) Whistle While You Work: Heeding Your Life's Calling, 2001; (with D.A. Shapiro) Claiming Your Place at the Fire: Living the Second Half of Your Life on Purpose, 2004; Something to Live For: Finding Your Way in the Second Half of Life, 2008. Contributor to books. **Address:** The Inventure Group, 23505 Smithtown Rd., Ste. 240, Excelsior, MN 55331, U.S.A. **Online address:** inventuregrp@aol.com

LEIDNER, Alan C. American (born United States) **Genres:** Literary Criticism And History, Theatre, Young Adult Fiction. **Career:** University of Louisville, Department of Classical and Modern Languages, professor of German and chairman; Colloquia Germanica, associate editor. **Publications:** The Impatient Muse: Germany and the Sturm und Drang, 1994; (with K.A. Wurst) Unpopular Virtues: The Critical Reception of J.M.R. Lenz, 1999. EDITOR: Sturm und Drang, 1992; (with H.S. Madland) Space to Act: The Theater of J.M.R. Lenz, 1993. Contributor to periodicals. **Address:** Department of Classical and Modern Languages, University of Louisville, 327 Humanities, Louisville, KY 40292, U.S.A. **Online address:** alan.leidner@louisville.edu

LEIDNER, Gordon. American (born United States), b. 1954. **Genres:** History, inspirational/Motivational Literature. **Career:** Lincoln Group of the District of Columbia, president, 2002-04; Abraham Lincoln Institute, board director. Writer. **Publications:** (Comp. and ed.) A Commitment to Honor: A Unique Portrait of Abraham Lincoln in His Own Words, 2000; Lincoln on God and Country, 2000; Abraham Lincoln: The Complete Book of Facts, Quizzes, and Trivia, 2001; Abraham Lincoln: Quotes, Quips, And Speeches, 2009. Contributor to periodicals. **Address:** White Mane Publishing Company Inc., 73 W Burd St., PO Box 708, Shippensburg, PA 17257, U.S.A. **Online address:** gordonleidner@yahoo.com

LEIER, James Mark. *See* **LEIER**, Mark.

LEIER, **Mark.** (James Mark Leier). Canadian (born Canada), b. 1956. **Genres:** History, Politics/Government, Organized Labor. **Career:** Simon Fraser University, professor of history. Writer. **Publications:** Where the Fraser River Flows: The Industrial Workers of the World in British Columbia, 1990; Red Flags and Red Tape: The Making of a Labour Bureaucracy, 1995; (as James Mark Leier) Rebel Life: The Life and Times of Robert Gosden, Revolutionary, Mystic, Labour Spy, 1999; Bakunin: The Creative Passion, 2006. **Address:** Department of History, Simon Fraser University, AQ 6010, 8888 University Dr., Burnaby, BC V5A 1S6, Canada. **Online address:** leier@sfu.ca

LEIFER, **Carol.** American (born United States), b. 1956. **Genres:** Humor/Satire, Biography. **Career:** Writer and producer. **Publications:** When You Lie about Your Age, the Terrorists Win: Reflections on Looking in the Mirror, 2009. Contributor to periodicals. **Address:** c/o Sonya Rosenfeld, 2000 Ave. of the Stars, Los Angeles, CA 90067, U.S.A.

LEIGH, Amy. *See* **BEAGLEY**, Brenda E.

LEIGH, **Ana.** American (born United States) **Genres:** Novels, Young Adult Fiction, Romance/Historical. **Career:** Writer, 1994-. **Publications:** ROMANCE FICTION: Love's Long Journey, 1981; Paradise Redeemed, 1989; Sweet Enemy Mine, 1991; Proud Pillars Rising, 1991; Angel Hunter, 1992; The Golden Spike, 1994; Tender Is the Touch, 1994; Forever, My Love, 1995; The Law and Lady Justice, 2003; Clay (The Frasers series), 2004; Face of Deception (Bishop's Heroes series), 2004; Reconcilable Differences (Bishop's Heroes series), 2005; The Lawman Said I Do (The Frasers series), 2006. KIRKLAND CHRONICLES SERIES ROMANCE NOVELS: A Question of Honor, 1986; Oh, Promised Destiny, 1986; A Kindled Flame, 1987; These Hallowed Hills, 1991. THE MACKENZIES SERIES; ROMANCE NOVELS: Luke, 1996; Flint, 1996; Cleve, 1997; David, 1998; Peter, 1998; Jared, 1999; Jake, 1999; Josh, 2000; Zach, 2001; Cole, 2002. OTHER: Frontier Christmas, 2003; Frasers Clay, 2004; His Boots under Her Bed: The Frasers, 2007; One Night with a Sweet-Talking Man, 2008; Holding Out for a Hero, 2009; Heart at Risk, 2009. **Address:** c/o Author Mail, Pocket Star Books, 1230 Ave. of the Americas, New York, NY 10020, U.S.A. **Online address:** aleigh@theromanceclub.com

LEIGH, **David.** British (born England), b. 1946. **Genres:** Documentaries/Reportage, Politics/Government. **Career:** Scotsman, staff journalist, 1970-74; Times, staff journalist, 1974-78; Guardian, staff journalist, 1978-82, comment editor, assistant editor, investigations executive editor; Observer, chief investigative reporter, 1980-; City University London, Department of Journalism, Anthony Sampson professor of reporting, 2006-. **Publications:** (With P. Chippindale) The Thorpe Committal, 1979; The Frontiers of Secrecy: Closed Government in Britain, 1980; (with S. Hoggart) Michael Foot: A Portrait, 1981; High Time: The Life and Times of Howard Marks, 1984, rev. ed. as Drug Traffic in Cannabis: Howard Marks, 1988; (co-author) The Worst Accident in the World: Chernobyl, the End of the Nuclear Dream, 1986; (with M. Linklater) Not with Honour: The Inside Story of the Westland Scandal, 1986; The Wilson Plot: How the Spycatchers and Their American Allies Tried to Overthrow the British Government in UK as The Wilson Plot: The Intelligence Services and the Discrediting of a Prime Minister, 1988; (with R. Norton-Taylor) Betrayed: The Real Story of the Matrix Churchill Trial, 1993; (contrib.) Fergie: The Very Private Life of the Duchess of York, 1996; (with E. Vulliamy) Sleaze: The Corruption of Parliament, 1997; The Liar, 1999; (co-author) Wikileaks: Inside Julian Assange's War on Secrecy, 2011. **Address:** The Guardian, Kings Pl., 90 York Way, London, GL N1 9GU, England. **Online address:** david.leigh@guardian.co.uk

LEIGH, Jackie. *See* **SMITH**, Deborah.

LEIGH, Sally. *See* **BIGGS**, John Burville.

LEIGH, **Stephen.** Also writes as Lee Stevens, S. L. Farrell. American (born United States), b. 1951. **Genres:** Science Fiction/Fantasy. **Career:** Vocalist and bassist in groups, 1969-; professional musician, 1970-87; Eastern Hills Camera, sales representative, 1982-85; Kelly Temporary Services, word processing trainer, 1986-88; office automation manager, 1988-; Northern Kentucky University, faculty for creative writing; Kelly Services, sales manager, 1988-. Aikido instructor and writer. **Publications:** Slow Fall to Dawn, 1981;

Dance of the Hag, 1983; A Quiet of Stone, 1984; The Bones of God, 1986; Crystal Memory, 1987; Aces Abroad: A Wild Cards Mosaic Novel, 1988; Dr. Bones and The Secret of the Lona, 1988; Robots and Aliens: Changling, 1989; The Abraxas Marvel Circus, 1989; Alien Tongue, 1991; Jokertown Shuffle: A Wild Cards Mosaic Novel, 1991; Ray Bradbury Presents Dinosaur World, 1992; Ray Bradbury Presents Dinosaur Planet: A Novel, 1993; Dinosaur and Samura, 1993; Dinosaur Warriors, 1994; (with J.J. Miller) Dinosaur Empire, 1995; Dinosaur Conquest, 1996; Dark Water's Embrace, 1998; Dark Water's Edge, 1998; Speaking Stones, 1999; (as Matheew Farrell) Thunder Rift, 2001. AS S.L. FARRELL: Holder of Lightning, 2003; Mage of Clouds, 2004; Heir of Stone, 2005; A Magic of Twilight, 2008; (co-author) Busted Flush: A Wild Cards Mosaic Novel, 2008; A Magic of Nightfall, 2009; A Magic of Dawn, 2010. Contributor to periodicals. **Address:** c/o Merrilee Heifetz, Writers House Inc., 21 W 26th St., New York, NY 10010, U.S.A. **Online address:** sleigh@livejournal.com

LEIKEN, **Robert S.** American (born United States), b. 1939. **Genres:** International Relations/Current Affairs, Politics/Government. **Career:** Educational Services Inc., consultant, 1964-65; Massachusetts Institute of Technology, assistant professor of humanities, 1968-71; Centro Investigacion y Documentacion, professor of European history, 1971-72; National Agricultural University of Mexico, professor of Mexican economic history, 1973; Centro Investigaciones y Docencias Economicas, researcher and professor, 1977-78; National Agricultural University of Mexico, professor of economics, 1978-80; National Endowment for the Humanities, reviewer of media program, 1981-; Georgetown University, Center for Strategic and International Studies, director of Soviet-Latin American project, 1981-; author and editor, 1982-; Carnegie Endowment for International Peace, senior associate, 1983-; Brookings Institution, senior fellow, 1999-, nonresident fellow; Center for the National Interest, Immigration and National Security Program, director, Mexico Program, director; Boston University, visiting professor of communications, Boston College, visiting professor of political science. **Publications:** Soviet Strategy in Latin America, 1982; The Melting Border, 2000; Why Nicaragua Vanished, 2003; Bearers of Global Jihad: Immigration and National Security after 9/11, 2004; Europe's Angry Muslims, 2011. EDITOR: Central America: Anatomy of Conflict, 1984; (with B. Rubin) The Central American Crisis Reader, 1987; A New Moment in the Americas, 1994. Contributor of articles to periodicals. **Address:** Center for the National Interest, 1615 L St., Ste. 1250, Washington, DC 20036, U.S.A. **Online address:** rsleiken@erols.com

LEINER, **Katherine.** American (born United States), b. 1949. **Genres:** Novels, Children's Fiction, Dance/Ballet, Politics/Government, Social Sciences. **Career:** Writer. **Publications:** Ask Me What My Mother Does, 1978; The Real Flash Gordon, 1980; The Greatest Show on Earth, 1980; The Steam Engine Lady, 1981; Both My Parents Work, 1986; Between Old Friends, 1987; The New Adventures of Pippi Longstocking, 1988; Something's Wrong in My House, 1988; (with A. Lindgren) Pippi Longstocking, VII, 1991; Halloween, 1993; First Children: Growing up in the White House, 1995; Mama Does the Mambo, 2001. FOR ADULTS: Digging Out, 2004; Growing Roots: The New Generation of Sustainable Farmers, Cooks and Food Activists, 2010. Contributor to periodicals. **Address:** Baywood Management, 11812 San Vicente Blvd., Ste. 210, Los Angeles, CA 90049, U.S.A. **Online address:** katherine@katherineleiner.com

LEIRA, **Arnlaug.** Norwegian (born Norway) **Genres:** Social Sciences. **Career:** Institute for Social Research, research director and senior research fellow; University of Oslo, Department of Sociology and Human Geography, professor, 1995-, now professor emeritus. Writer. **Publications:** (With S. Bergh) Hå har et kvinnfolk å sia, da! Samtaler med kvinner I eiØstlandsbygd, 1974; Day Care for Children in Denmark, Norway, and Sweden, 1987; Welfare States and Working Mothers: The Scandinavian Experience, 1992; (ed. with T.P. Boje) Gender, Welfare State, and the Market: Towards a New Division of Labour, 2000; Working Parents and the Welfare State: Family Change and Policy Reform in Scandinavia, 2002; (ed. with A.L. Ellingsæter) Velferdsstaten og familien, 2004; (ed. with A.L. Ellingsæter) Politicising Parenthood in Scandinavia: Gender Relations in Welfare States, 2006; (co-ed.) Gendering Citizenship in Western Europe, 2007; (ed. with C. Saraceno) Childhood: Changing Contexts, 2008. **Address:** Department of Sociology and Human Geography, University of Oslo, Rm. 432, Moltke Moes vei 31, Harriet Holters hus, 2 etg., PO Box 1096, Oslo, 0851, Norway. **Online address:** arnlaug.leira@sosiologi.uio.no

LEISER, **Gary.** American (born United States), b. 1946. **Genres:** Area Studies, History, Autobiography/Memoirs. **Career:** Cabrini College, visiting lecturer in Middle Eastern history, 1976; University of Utah, visiting instructor in Middle Eastern history, 1976-77; Food Development Corp., Middle East consultant, 1978; U.S. Department of Defense, staff interpreter and technical liaison office, Middle East specialist, 1980-83, Arabic linguist and analyst, 1983-84; U.S. Air Force, civilian historian, 1984-89; University of Maryland, instructor, 1981; Air University, instructor, 1995; Brightstar Inc., consultant; Travis Air Force Base, civilian historian, 1989-96, Travis Air Museum, curator, 1996-. Writer and lecturer. **Publications:** A History of Travis Air Force Base, 1943-1996, 1996; (with T.M. Cross) A Brief History of Ankara, 2000. EDITOR: Papers and Discussions: Turkiye Is Bankasi, 1984; (trans. and intro.) A History of the Seljuks, 1988; (and trans.) M.F. Koprulu, Origins of the Ottoman Empire, 1992; (and trans.) M.F. Koprulu, Seljuks of Anatolia, 1992; (trans. and intro.) Koprulu, Islam in Anatolia after the Turkish Invasion (Prolegomena), 1993; (and trans.) Vetluga Memoir: A Turkish Prisoner of War in Russia, 1995; (trans. and intro.) Koprulu, Some Observations on the Influence of Byzantine Institutions on Ottoman Institutions, 1999; (and co-trans.) Questions and Answers for Physicians: A Handbook for Students, 2004. Contributor to periodicals. **Address:** 400 Brennan Cir., Travis Air Force Base, Fairfield, CA 94535, U.S.A. **Online address:** gleiser@juno.com

LEISTYNA, Pepi. American (born United States), b. 1963. **Genres:** Adult Non-fiction, Language/Linguistics, Cultural/Ethnic Topics. **Career:** Berlitz International Language School, teacher of French, 1988-89; Brookline Adult and Community Education, teacher of English, 1989-91; English Language Center, teacher of English, 1989-94; Boston Conservatory, teacher of English, 1990; Salem State College, visiting lecturer in English, 1995; University of Massachusetts-Boston, lecturer, 1995-97, assistant professor, 1998-2004, associate professor, 2004-, coordinator of research program of applied linguistics graduate studies; Arizona State University, Educational Policy Research Unit, research fellow, 2001-; Citizens Media Corp., director, 2001-03; Action Coalition for Media Education, vice president of curriculum development, 2004-. Writer. **Publications:** (Ed. with A. Woodrum and S. Sherblom) Breaking Free: The Transformative Power of Critical Pedagogy, 1996; Presence of Mind: Education and the Politics of Deception, 1999; Defining & Designing Multiculturalism: One Public School System's Efforts, 2002; (ed. with C. Meyer) Corpus Analysis: Language Structure and Language Use, 2003; (ed.) Cultural Studies: From Theory to Action, 2005. Contributor to books and periodicals. **Address:** Department of Applied Linguistics, University of Massachusetts, Rm. 78, Fl. 06, Wheatley Hall, 100 Morrissey Blvd., Boston, MA 02125-3393, U.S.A. **Online address:** pepi.leistyna@umb.edu

LEITCH, Donovan. *See* DONOVAN.

LEITCH, Donovan P. *See* DONOVAN.

LEITCH, Maurice. British/Irish (born Ireland), b. 1933. **Genres:** Novels, Novellas/Short Stories, Plays/Screenplays. **Career:** Antrim Primary School, instructor of general subjects, 1954-62; British Broadcasting Corp., features producer, 1962-70, radio drama producer, 1969-89, Radio Four, editor, 1977-89; full-time writer, 1989-. **Publications:** The Liberty Lad, 1967; Poor Lazarus, 1969; Stamping Ground, 1975; The Hands of Cheryl Boyd and Other Stories, 1987; Chinese Whispers, 1987; Burning Bridges, 1989; Gilchrist: A Novel, 1994; Silver's City, 1995; The Smoke King, 1998; The Eggman's Apprentice, 2001; Dining at the Dunbar, 2009. Contributor to periodicals. **Address:** Deborah Rogers Ltd., 20 Powis Mews, London, GL W11 1JN, England.

LEITCH, Will. (J. More). American (born United States), b. 1975. **Genres:** Novels. **Career:** Deadspin, founding editor, 2005-08, editor emeritus, 2008-; New York Magazine, contributing editor, 2008-. **Publications:** Catch (novel), 2005; (as J. More) The Anti-Valentine's Handbook, 2005; God Save the Fan: How Preening Sportscasters, Athletes Who Speak in the Third Person, and the Occasional Convicted Quarterback Have Taken the Fun out of Sports (and How We Can Get It Back), 2008; (contrib.) Reality Matters: 19 Writers Come Clean About the Shows We Can't Stop Watching, 2010; Are We Winning?: Fathers and Sons in the New Golden Age of Baseball, 2010. Contributor to periodicals. **Address:** New York Magazine, 75 Varick St., New York, NY 10013, U.S.A. **Online address:** will@deadspin.com

LEITH, Linda Jane. Canadian/Irish (born Ireland), b. 1949. **Genres:** Novels, Literary Criticism And History, Translations, Young Adult Fiction, Reference. **Career:** John Abbott College, instructor in English, 1975-; Matrix Magazine,

publisher and editor, 1988-94; Vehicule Press, fiction editor, 1989-94; Blue Metropolis Foundation, founder, 1997-; Concordia University, adjunct professor of English, part-time faculty. **Publications:** (Ed.) Telling Differences: New English Fiction from Quebec, 1988; Introducing Hugh Mac Lennan's Two Solitudes, 1990; Birds of Passage (novel), 1993; The Tragedy Queen (novel), 1995; (trans.) Travels with an Umbrella: An Irish Journey, 1999; Desert Lake, 2007; Deux Solitudes, 2008; Marrying Hungary, 2008; Writing in the Time of Nationalism, 2010. Contributor to periodicals. **Address:** Blue Metropolis Foundation, 661 Rose De Lima St., Ste. 201, Montreal, QC H4C 2L7, Canada. **Online address:** info@blue-web.bleu.com

LEITHAUSER, Brad (Edward). American (born United States), b. 1953. **Genres:** Novels, Poetry, Essays. **Career:** Kyoto Comparative Law Center, research fellow, 1980-83; Asahi Culture Center, lecturer, 1982-83; Amherst College, visiting writer, 1984-85; Mount Holyoke College, lecturer, 1987-95, Emily Dickinson senior lecturer in the humanities, 1995-2007; Columbia University School of the Arts, instructor in fiction, 1990-91; Time Magzine, theatre critic, 1995; Johns Hopkins University, Department of Writing Seminars, professor, 2008-. Novelist. **Publications:** POETRY: Hundreds of Fireflies, 1982; A Seaside of Mountain: Eight Poems from Japan, 1985; Cats of the Temple, 1986; Between Leaps: Poems 1972-1985, 1987; The Mail from Anywhere, 1990; The Odd Last Thing She Did: Poems, 1998; Lettered Creatures: Light Verse, 2004; Curves and Angles, 2006; Toad to a Nightingale, 2007. NOVELS: Equal Distance, 1985; Hence, 1989; Seaward, 1993; The Friends of Freeland, 1997; A Few Corrections, 2001; Darlington's Fall: A Novel in Verse, 2002; The Art Student's War, 2009. OTHERS: The Line of Ladies, 1975; (ed.) The Norton Book of Ghost Stories, 1994; Penchants & Places, 1995; (ed. and intro.) No Other Book: Selected Essays, 1995. **Address:** The Writing Seminars, Johns Hopkins University, 603A Dell House, 081 Gilman Hall, 3400 N Charles St., Baltimore, MD 21218, U.S.A. **Online address:** bleithau@jhu.edu

LELCHUK, Alan. American (born United States), b. 1938. **Genres:** Novels, Novellas/Short Stories, Literary Criticism And History, Social Sciences. **Career:** Brandeis University, assistant professor of English, 1966-77, writer-in-residence, 1978-81; Modern Occasions Literary Quarterly, associate editor, 1970-72; Amherst College, writer-in-residence, 1982-84; Dartmouth College, professor liberal studies, 1985-, adjunct professor of liberal studies; Haifa University, writer-in-residence, 1986-87; Steerforth Press, co-founder and literary editor, 1994-; Eotvos Lorand University (ELTE), Otto Salgo professor of American literature and writing, chair in American studies and writing, 1999-2000; International University of Moscow, Fulbright professor and writer, 2003; Moscow State University, Fulbright senior specialist professor, 2005-; University of Napoli, Fulbright professor and writer, 2005-; The Free University in Berlin, Fulbright professor and writer, 2005-. **Publications:** NOVELS: American Mischief, 1973; Miriam at Thirty-Four, 1974; Shrinking: The Beginning of My Own End, 1978; Miriam in Her Forties, 1985; On Home Ground, 1987; Brooklyn Boy, 1990; Playing the Game, 1995; Ziff: A Life?, 2003. OTHERS: (contrib.) Images and Ideas in American Culture, 1979; (ed. with G. Shaked) 8 Great Hebrew Short Novels, 1983, 2nd ed., 2005; (contrib.) Congregations: Contemporary Writers Read the Jewish Bible, 1987; (contrib.) Testimony: Contemporary Writers Make the Holocaust Personal, 1989; (contrib.) Facing America: Multikulturelle Literatur Der Heutigen U.S.A., 1994. Contributor to books. **Address:** Master of Arts in Liberal Studies, Dartmouth College, Wentworth Hall, 316 Thornton Hall, Hanover, NH 03755, U.S.A. **Online address:** alan.lelchuk@dartmouth.edu

LELEUX, Robert. American (born United States), b. 1980?. **Genres:** Novels. **Career:** Writer. **Publications:** The Memoirs of a Beautiful Boy, 2008. **Address:** Gail Hochman, Brandt & Hochman Literary Agents, Inc., 1501 Broadway, New York, NY 10036, U.S.A. **Online address:** janeaustentexas@gmail.com

LELLENBERG, Jon L. American (born United States), b. 1946. **Genres:** Mystery/Crime/Suspense, Literary Criticism And History, Biography, Adult Non-fiction. **Career:** Office of the Secretary of Defense, strategist; Defense policy analyst, national security strategist, writer. **Publications:** Nova 57 Minor: The Waxing and Waning of the 61st Adventure of Sherlock Holmes, 1990; Irregular Proceedings of the Mid 'Forties: An Archival History of the Baker Street Irregulars, March 1944-June 1947, 1995; The New Adventures of Sherlock Holmes: Original Stories, rev. ed., 1999; (with D. Stashower and M.H. Greenberg) Sherlock Holmes in America, 2009. EDITOR: (intro.) Sherlock Homes: His Posthumous Memoirs, 1973; The Quest for Sir Arthur

Conan Doyle: Thirteen Biographers in Search of a Life, 1987; (with J. Nieminski) Dear Starrett-Dear Briggs: A Compendium of Correspondence between Vincent Starrett and Gray Chandler Briggs, 1930-1934: Together with Various Appendices, Notes, and Embellishments, 1989; Irregular Memories of the Thirties: An Archival History of the Baker Street Irregulars' First Decade: 1930-1940, 1990; Irregular Records of the Early 'Forties: An Archival History of the Baker Street Irregulars, January 1941-March 1944, 1991; (with M.H. Greenberg and C. Waugh) Holmes for the Holidays, 1996; Irregular Crises of the Late 'Forties: An Archival History of the Baker Street Irregulars, June 1947-December 1950, 1999; (with M.H. Greenberg and C. Waugh) The New Adventure of Sherlock Holmes: Original Stories, 1999; (with M.H. Greenberg and C. Waugh) More Holmes for the Holidays, 1999; (with M.H. Greenberg and D. Stashower) Murder in Baker Street: New Tales of Sherlock Holmes, 2001; (with M.H. Greenberg and D. Stashower) Murder, My Dear Watson: New Tales of Sherlock Holmes, 2002; (with M.H. Greenberg and D. Stashower) Ghosts in Baker Street, 2006; (with D. Stashower and C. Foley) Arthur Conan Doyle: His Life in Letters, 2008; Baker Street Irregular, 2010. Contributor to periodicals. **Address:** c/o Suzanne Gluck, William Morris Agency, 1325 Ave. of the Americas, New York, NY 10019, U.S.A. **Online address:** jlellenb@dgsys.com

LEMANN, Nicholas. American (born United States), b. 1954. **Genres:** Adult Non-fiction, Essays, History, Biography, Essays, Social Sciences, Photography. **Career:** Washington Monthly, managing and associate editor, 1976-; Texas Monthly, associate, editor, executive editor, 1978-; The Washington Post, national staff reporter, 1979-81; Vieux Carre Courier, staff; The Atlantic Monthly, national correspondent, 1983-; The New Yorker, staff writer, Washington correspondent, 1999-; Harvard Crimson, president; Columbia University, Graduate School of Journalism, dean and Henry R. Luce professor, 2003-. **Publications:** (Ed. with C. Peters) Inside the System, 1979; The Fast Track: Texans and Other Strivers (essays), 1981; Out of the Forties (nonfiction), 1983; The Promised Land: The Great Black Migration and How It Changed America (nonfiction), 1991; The Big Test: The Secret History of the American Meritocracy, 1999, rev. ed., 2000; (intro.) Redemption: The Last Battle of the Civil War, 2006; (intro.) The photographs of Russell Lee, 2008. Contributor to periodicals. **Address:** Columbia University Graduate School of Journalism, 2950 Broadway, 116th St., New York, NY 10027, U.S.A. **Online address:** nl2124@columbia.edu

LEMASTER, Carolyn Gray. American (born United States) **Genres:** Local History/Rural Topics, Biography, Reference. **Career:** University of Arkansas, Forum, editor, 1976-77, Office of Internal Communication, writer, editor and director, 1978-81, research assistant in archives, 1981-83; Arkansas Methodist Newspaper, writer and editor's assistant, 1977; Arkansas Jewish History, researcher and writer, 1981-. **Publications:** A Corner of the Tapestry: A History of the Jewish Experience in Arkansas, 1820s-1990s, 1994; The Ottenheimers of Arkansas, 1995. Contributor to books and periodicals. **Address:** 24424 Maranatha Ln., Little Rock, AR 72223, U.S.A.

LEMASTER, J. R. American (born United States), b. 1934. **Genres:** Poetry, Literary Criticism And History. **Career:** Defiance College, instructor, 1962-65, assistant professor, 1965-69, associate professor, 1969-70, professor of English, 1970-77; Indiana University (Indiana University/Purdue University), part-time instructor, 1965-66; Baylor University, professor of English and director of American studies, 1977-2006, professor emeritus, 2006-. Writer. **Publications:** The Heart is a Gypsy, 1967; Children of Adam, 1971; Weeds and Wildflowers, 1975; (with M.W. Clarke) Jesse Stuart: Essays on His Work, 1977; Jesse Stuart: A Reference Guide, 1979; Jesse Stuart: Kentucky's Chronicler-Poet, 1980; First Person, Second, 1983; (with E.H. Long) The New Mark Twain Handbook, 1985; Purple Bamboo, 1986; Journey to Beijing, 1992; Journeys Around China, 2004; China Teacher: An Intimate Journal, 2005, Walt Whitman and the Persian Poets, 2009 (with S. Jahan). EDITOR: Poets of the Midwest, 1966; Morning in the Sun, 1968; (with S. Sternlicht) Symposia Poets, 1969; (with W. Chaney) There Comes a Time, 1971; (with C. Perrin) Certain Reconciliations, 1972; (with J. O'Kelley) On Weighing a Pound of Flesh, 1973; (with C. Winzeler) The Poem as Unidentified Flying Object, 1974; (with M.W. Clarke) The World of Jesse Stuart, 1975; (intro.) Jesse Stuart: Selected Criticism, 1978; The Keeper of Juno's Swans, 1979; (intro.) Making Sense of Grammar, 1980; The Builder and the Dream, 1980; Jesse Stuart on Education, 1992; (with J.D. Wilson) The Mark Twain Encyclopedia, 1993; (with D.D. Kummings) Walt Whitman: An Encyclopedia, 1998. Contributor to journals. **Address:** Department of English, Baylor University, 1 Bear Pl., Ste. 97404, Waco, TX 76798-7404, U.S.A. **Online address:** j_r_lemaster@baylor.edu

LE MAY, G(odfrey) H. L(ancelot). British/South African (born South Africa), b. 1920?. **Genres:** History, Politics/Government. **Career:** The Sudan Star, assistant editor, 1942-44; The Star, sub-editor, 1944-46; Rhodes University, lecturer, 1947-48; Balliol College, lecturer, 1952-53; University of the Witwatersrand, professor, 1953-68; Worcester College, dean, fellow and senior tutor, 1968-90, emeritus fellow in history. **Publications:** British Government 1914-1953, 1955, 1964; British Supremacy in South Africa 1899-1907, 1965; Black and White in South Africa, 1973; The Victorian Constitution, 1979; (ed. with C.S. Nicholls) The Dictionary of National Biography. Missing Persons, 1994; The Afrikaners, 1995. **Address:** Department of History, Worcester College, Oxford, OX OX1 2HB, England.

LEMAY, Shawna. Canadian (born Canada), b. 1966. **Genres:** Poetry, Essays, Autobiography/Memoirs, Politics/Government. **Career:** Edmonton Public Library, part-time staff. Writer. **Publications:** Calm Things, 2008. POETRY: All the God-sized Fruit, 1999; Against Paradise, 2001; Still, 2003; Blue Feast, 2005; Red Velvet Forest, 2009. **Address:** 470 Ormsby Rd., Edmonton, AB T5T 6B1, Canada. **Online address:** slemay@planet.eon.net

LEMIEUX, A(nne) C(onnelly). American (born United States), b. 1954. **Genres:** Children's Fiction, Young Adult Fiction, Science Fiction/Fantasy, Children's Non-fiction. **Career:** Freelance journalist, 1982-87; writer, 1987-; America Online, Children's Writer's Chat, co-founder and co-moderator. **Publications:** The TV Guidance Counselor, 1993; Super Snoop Sam Snout: The Case of the Yogurt Poker, 1994; The Case of the Stolen Snowman, 1994; The Case of the Missing Marble, 1994; Fruit Flies, Fish and Fortune Cookies, 1994; Do Angels Sing the Blues?, 1995; (contrib.) New Year, New Love, 1996; Dare to Be, M.E.!, 1997; Fairy Lair: A Special Place, 1997; A Hidden Place, 1998; A Magic Place, 1998; All the Answers!, 2000. Works appear in anthologies. **Address:** 1455 Durham Rd., Madison, CT 06443-1657, U.S.A. **Online address:** swan522@aol.com

LEMIRE, Beverly. Canadian (born Canada), b. 1950?. **Genres:** History, Fash Ion/Costume, Women's Studies And Issues, Business/Trade/Industry. **Career:** Wilfrid Laurier University, instructor, 1985; University of Guelph, instructor, 1985; University of Lethbridge, assistant professor, 1986-87; University of New Brunswick, assistant professor, 1987-91, associate professor, 1991-96, professor of history, 1996-2003, university research professor; University of Alberta, Department of History and Classics, professor of history, 2003-, Henry Marshall Tory chair, Material Culture Institute, founding director. Writer. **Publications:** Fashion's Favourite: The Cotton Trade and the Consumer in Britain, 1660-1800, 1991; Dress, Culture, and Commerce: The English Clothing Trade before the Factory, 1660-1800, 1997; (ed. with R. Pearson and G. Campbell) Women and Credit: Researching the Past, Refiguring the Future, 2002; The Business of Everyday Life: Gender, Practice and Social Politics in England, 2005; The British Cotton Trade, 1660-1815, 2009; (ed.) The Force of Fashion in Politics and Society: Global Perspectives from Early Modern to Contemporary Times, 2010; Cotton, 2011. Contributor of articles to journals. Works appear in anthologies. **Address:** Department of History and Classics, University of Alberta, 2-19 Tory Bldg., HM, Edmonton, AB T6G 2H4, Canada. **Online address:** beverly.lemire@ualberta.ca

LEMIRE, Jeff. Canadian (born Canada), b. 1976?. **Genres:** Ghost Writer, Graphic Novels. **Career:** Writer. **Publications:** ESSEX COUNTY TRILOGY GRAPHIC NOVEL SERIES: Tales from the Farm, vol. I, 2007; Ghost Stories, vol. II, 2007; The Country Nurse, vol. III, 2008. **Address:** Toronto, ON , Canada. **Online address:** jeff@jefflemire.com

LEMLIN, Jeanne. American (born United States), b. 1953. **Genres:** Food And Wine, Medicine/Health. **Career:** New York Cooking Center, cooking teacher, 1980-85; cookbook writer, 1985-; Cooking Light, columnist. **Publications:** Vegetarian Pleasures: A Menu Cookbook, 1986; Quick Vegetarian Pleasures, 1992; Main-Course Vegetarian Pleasures, 1995; Simple Vegetarian Pleasures, 1998; Vegetarian Classics: Original and Updated Versions of Tried and True Favorites, 2000; Vegetarian Classics: 300 Essential Recipes for Every Course and Every Meal, 2001. Contributor to journals and periodicals. **Address:** c/o Susan Lescher, Lescher and Lescher Ltd., 67 Irving Pl., New York, NY 10003, U.S.A.

LEMON, Alex. American (born United States), b. 1978. **Genres:** Autobiography/Memoirs, Poetry. **Career:** Texas Christian University, professor of creative writing; Luna: A Journal of Poetry and Translation, co-editor; Macalester College, visiting professor. Poet. **Publications:** Mosquito, 2006;

Hallelujah Blackout, 2008; Happy: A Memoir, 2009. Contributor to books. **Address:** Fort Worth, TX , U.S.A. **Online address:** alxlemon@yahoo.com

LEMON, Rebecca. American (born United States), b. 1968. **Genres:** Literary Criticism And History, Law, Theology/Religion. **Career:** University of Southern California, assistant professor, 2000-06, associate professor of English, 2006-; Huntington Library, research fellow, 2003; American Council of Learned Societies, fellow, 2003-04; Stanford Humanities Center, postdoctoral fellow, 2003-04. Writer. **Publications:** Treason by Words: Literature, Law, and Rebellion in Shakespeare's England, 2006; (co-ed.) The Blackwell Companion to the Bible and English Literature, 2009. Contributor to journals. **Address:** Department of English, College of Letters, Arts & Sciences, University of Southern California, 404 Taper Hall of Humanities, 3501 Trousdale Pkwy., Los Angeles, CA 90089-0354, U.S.A. **Online address:** rlemon@usc.edu

LEMONCHECK, Linda. American (born United States), b. 1954. **Genres:** Women's Studies And Issues, Sex, Philosophy. **Career:** University of Southern California, Gender Studies Program, lecturer; California State University, faculty; Occidental College, faculty; University of California, faculty; West End Family Counseling Services, consultant; Old Town Picture Show (art gallery), owner, 1983-86. Writer. **Publications:** Dehumanizing Women: Treating Persons as Sex Objects, 1985; (with M. Hajdin) Sexual Harassment: A Debate, 1997; Loose Women, Lecherous Men: A Feminist Philosophy of Sex, 1997; (ed. with J.P. Sterba) Sexual Harassment: Issues and Answers, 2001. Contributor to books and periodicals. **Address:** Oxford University Press, 198 Madison Ave., New York, NY 10016-4314, U.S.A. **Online address:** llemon@msn.com

LEMONICK, Michael D. American (born United States), b. 1953. **Genres:** Sciences, Astronomy, Biography. **Career:** Science Digest, writer, senior editor; Discover, executive editor; Time, senior science writer; Climate Central, senior writer. **Publications:** The Light at the Edge of the Universe: Leading Cosmologists on the Brink of a Scientific Revolution, 1993 as The Light at the Edge of the Universe: Dispatches from the Front Lines of Cosmology, 1995; Other Worlds: The Search for Life in the Universe, 1998; Echo of the Big Bang, 2003; The Georgian Star: How William and Caroline Herschel Revolutionized Our Understanding of the Cosmos, 2009. Contributor to journals. **Address:** Princeton University Press, 41 William St., Princeton, NJ 08540-5237, U.S.A. **Online address:** mlemonick@aol.com

LEMONS, James Stanley. American (born United States), b. 1938. **Genres:** Cultural/Ethnic Topics, History, Social Sciences, Women's Studies And Issues. **Career:** Ohio State University, instructor in history, 1965-67; Rhode Island College, assistant professor, 1967-71, associate professor, 1971-76, professor of history, 1976-, professor emeritus of history. Writer. **Publications:** The Woman Citizen: Social Feminism in the 1920s, 1973; (ed.) Aspects of the Black Experience, 1975; (with G.H. Kellner) Rhode Island: The Independent State, 1982; The First Baptist Church in America, 1988; (with E.S. Adler) The Elect: Rhode Island's Women Legislators, 1922-1990, 1990; First: The History of the First Baptist Church in America, 2001; (with G.H. Kellner) Rhode Island: The Ocean State: An Illustrated History, 2004. **Address:** Department of History, Rhode Island College, Gaige Hall, 600 Mount Pleasant Ave., Providence, RI 02908-1991, U.S.A. **Online address:** jlemons@ric.edu

LEMOV, Rebecca. American (born United States) **Genres:** Novels, History, Sciences, Young Adult Fiction. **Career:** University of Washington, instructor in anthropology, Humanities Center, Woodrow Wilson postdoctoral fellow; Harvard University, Department of science, technology and society, postdoctoral fellow, Department of the History of Science, assistant professor. Writer. **Publications:** World As Laboratory: Experiments with Mice, Mazes, and Men, 2005; Database of Dreams: Making a Science of the Human 1942-1961, forthcoming. **Address:** Department of the History of Science, Harvard University, Science Ctr. 371, 1 Oxford St., Cambridge, MA 02138-2901, U.S.A. **Online address:** rlemov@fas.harvard.edu

LEMUS, Felicia Luna. American (born United States), b. 1975?. **Genres:** Civil Liberties/Human Rights. **Career:** The New School, faculty; University of California, faculty; Antioch University, associate faculty. Writer. **Publications:** NOVEL: Trace Elements of Random Tea Parties, 2003; Like Son, 2007. Contributor to magazines. **Address:** Department of Creative Writing, Antioch University, 400 Corporate Pt., Culver City, CA 90230, U.S.A. **Online address:** felicialunalemus@hotmail.com

LENAIL, Laura. See **ANDRE, Michael.**

LENCIONI, Patrick. American (born United States), b. 1965?. **Genres:** Adult Non-fiction. **Career:** Sybase, vice president of organizational development; Oracle Corp., staff; Bain and Co., staff; The Table Group (consulting firm), founder and president, 1997-; Make-A-Wish Foundation of America, board director, 2000-03. Writer. **Publications:** The Five Temptations of a CEO: A Leadership Fable, 1998; Obsessions of an Extraordinary Executive: The Four Disciplines at the Heart of Making Any Organization World Class, 2000; The Five Dysfunctions of a Team: A Leadership Fable, 2002; Death by Meeting: A Leadership Fable about Solving the Most Painful Problem in Business, 2004; Overcoming the Five Dysfunctions of a Team: A Field Guide for Leaders, Managers, and Facilitators, 2005; Silos, Politics and Turf Wars: A Leadership Fable about Destroying the Barriers that Turn Colleagues into Competitors, 2006; Five Dysfunctions of a Team: Facilitator's Guide, 2007; Three Signs of a Miserable Job: A Fable for Managers, 2007; 3 Big Questions for a Frantic Family: A Leadership Fable about Restoring Sanity to the Most Important Organization in Your Life, 2008; Getting Naked: A Business Fable About Shedding the Three Fears that Sabotage Client Loyalty, 2010. Contributor of articles to periodicals. **Address:** The Table Group Inc., 3640 Mt. Diablo Blvd., Ste. 202, Lafayette, CA 94549, U.S.A. **Online address:** patricklencioni@tablegroup.com

LENDE, Heather. American (born United States), b. 1959. **Genres:** Essays, Homes/Gardens, Animals/Pets, Autobiography/Memoirs, Social Sciences, Travel/Exploration. **Career:** Chilkat Valley News, obituary writer; Anchorage Daily News, columnist. **Publications:** If You Lived Here, I'd Know Your Name: News from Small-Town Alaska, 2005; Take Good Care of the Garden and the Dogs: Family, Friendships, and Faith in Small-Town Alaska, 2010. **Address:** Pyramid Island Press, PO Box 936, Haines, AK 99827-0936, U.S.A. **Online address:** heather@heatherlende.com

LENDON, J. E. American/Lebanese (born Lebanon) **Genres:** History, Politics/Government, Military/Defense/Arms Control. **Career:** Massachusetts Institute of Technology, assistant professor, 1991-95, associate professor, 1995-99; University of Virginia, associate professor of ancient history, 1998-2006, professor of ancient history, 2006-. Writer. **Publications:** Empire of Honour: The Art of Government in the Roman World, 1997; Soldiers and Ghosts: A History of Battle in Classical Antiquity, 2005; How the Peloponnesian War Really Broke Out and What it Means for Our Own Time, 2010; Song of Wrath: The Peloponnesian War Begins, 2010. **Address:** Corcoran Department of History, University of Virginia, 323 Nau Hall - S Lawn, 1540 Jefferson Park Ave., PO Box 400180, Charlottesville, VA 22904-4180, U.S.A. **Online address:** lendon@virginia.edu

LENDVAI, Paul. Austrian/Hungarian (born Hungary), b. 1929. **Genres:** History, Politics/Government, Biography. **Career:** Journalist, 1947-56; Financial Times, Vienna correspondent, 1960-82; Europaeische Rundschau, editor-in-chief, 1973-; Radio Austria Intl., director, 1987; österreichischer Rundfunk, Department of Eastern Europe, editor-in-chief, 1982; Radio österreich Intl., staff, 1987; MTI (Hungarian news agency), chief of foreign reporting. **Publications:** Egypt, 1952; Greece, 1954; Eagles in Cobwebs: Nationalism and Communism in the Balkans, 1969; Anti-Semitism without Jews: Communist Eastern Europe, 1971, trans. as Antisemitism in Eastern Europe, 1972; (with K.H. Ritschel) Kreisky: Porträt of a Staatsmannes, 1972; National Tensions in Yugoslavia, 1972; The Limits to Change in the Danubian Region, 1977; Die Grenzen des Wandels: Spielarten des Kommunismus im Donauraum, 1977; (with I. Reuter-Hendrichs) Die Sowjetische Jugoslawienpolitik, 1972-1976, 1977; The Bureaucracy of Truth: How Communist Governments Manage the News, 1981; Religionsfreiheit und Menschenrechte: Bilanz und Aussicht, 1983; The Lonely Albania, 1985; Das einsame Albanien: Reportage aus dem Land der Skipetaren, 1985; Das eigenwillige Ungarn: Innenansichten eines Grenzgängers, 1986; Hungary: The Art of Survival, 1988; Magyarország kivülről, avagy, A túlélés müvészete, 1990; Between Hope and Disenchantment: Reflections on the Change in Eastern Europe, 1994; Zwischen Hoffnung und Ernüchterung: Reflexionen über den Wandel in Osteuropa, 1994; Honnan-hová?: gondolatok a közép és kelet-európai változásokról, 1995; Blacklisted-Memoirs of a Central European Journalist, 1996; Auf schwarzen Listen: Erlebnisse eines Mitteleuropäers, 1996, trans. as Blacklisted: A Journalist's Life in Central Europe, 1998; The Hungarians: Thousand Years of Victory in Defeat, 2002; A világ egy kritikus európai szemével, 2005; Der Ungarnaufstand 1956: eine Revolution und ihre Folgen, 2006; One Day that Shook the Communist World: The 1956 Hungarian Uprising and its Legacy, 2008; Magyarok: gyözelmek és kudarcok, 2009; (with R. Bretschneider) Is der Eiserne Vorhang fiel, 2009; (with R. Bretschneider) Als der Eiserne Vorhang fiel, 2009; Inside Austria: New Challenges, Old Demons, 2010; Mein verspieltes Land, 2010. **Address:** ORF-Zentrum, Kuniglberg, Vienna, 1010, Austria.

LENG, Russell J. American (born United States), b. 1938. **Genres:** Politics/Government, History. **Career:** Middlebury College, Congressional Research Service, Library of Congress, foreign policy analyst, 1965-66, professor of political sciences, 1966-, chairman of political science, 1968-73, 1988-91, dean of sciences, 1975-82, Division of Social Sciences, acting chairman, 1984-85, International Politics and Economics, co-director, 1986-88, F.C. Dirks professor of political science and economics, 1987-89, William R. Kenan, Jr. professor of political science, 1990-93, International Politics and Economics Program, director, 1994-95, Political Economy and International Law, James Jermain professor, retired, 2007, now James Jermain professor emeritus; University of Michigan, visiting associate professor, 1976; Peace Science Society, president, 1997-78. Writer. **Publications:** Interstate Crisis Behavior, 1816-1980: Realism vs. Realpolitik, 1993; Bargaining and Learning in Recurring Crises: The Soviet-American, Egyptian-Israeli and Indo-Pakistan Rivalries, 2000. Contributor to periodicals. **Address:** Department of Political Science, Middlebury College, 355 Davis Family Library, 427 College St., Middlebury, VT 05753, U.S.A. **Online address:** leng@middlebury.edu

LENGEL, Edward G. American (born United States), b. 1968. **Genres:** History, Bibliography, Biography. **Career:** University of Virginia, associate professor of history, professor, Papers of George Washington, associate editor, editor-in-chief; Historian. **Publications:** (Co-ed.) George Washington, The Papers of George Washington, 1985; The Irish through British Eyes: Perceptions of Ireland in the Famine Era, 2002; World War I Memories: An Annotated Bibliography of Personal Accounts Published in English since 1919, 2004; General George Washington: A Military Life, 2005; To Conquer Hell: The Meuse-Argonne, 1918, 2008; (ed.) This Glorious Struggle: George Washington's Revolutionary War Letters, 2008; Inventing George Washington: America's founder in Myth and Memory, 2011. **Address:** University of Virginia, Alderman Library 504, PO Box 400117, Charlottesville, VA 22904, U.S.A. **Online address:** eg12r@virginia.edu

LENNARD, John (Chevening). Jamaican/British (born England), b. 1964. **Genres:** Poetry, Literary Criticism And History, Theatre, Essays, Illustrations, Young Adult Non-fiction, Criminology/True Crime, Mystery/Crime/Suspense, E-books, Science Fiction/Fantasy, Romance/Historical, Children's Fiction, Young Adult Fiction. **Career:** University of London, Royal Holloway and Bedford New College, tutor in English, 1990-91; Open University, faculty, 1990-92; Cambridge University, fellow and director of studies in English, 1991-98, Newton Trust Lecturer, faculty of English, 1993-98; University of Notre Dame, assistant professor, 1998-2004; British American Drama Academy, professor, 1998-2004, Shakespeare Program, dean, 2002-03; Fairleigh Dickinson University, global visiting professor, virtual faculty; University of the West Indies, professor of British and American literature, 2005-09, chair; Humanities-Ebooks L.L.P., general editor, Universities of Oxford, faculty. **Publications:** But I Digress: The Exploitation of Parentheses in English Printed Verse, 1991; The Poetry Handbook: A Guide to Reading Poetry for Pleasure and Practical Criticism, 1996, 2nd ed., 2005; (with M. Luckhurst) The Drama Handbook: A Guide to Reading Plays, 2002. Contributor of articles to periodicals. **Address:** 4 Riverside Hts., Apt. 5, Gordon Town, Saint Andrew, JMAAW10, Jamaica. **Online address:** john.lennard@uwimona.edu.jm

LENNEY, Dinah. American (born United States), b. 1956. **Genres:** Film, How-to Books, Autobiography/Memoirs, Young Adult Non-fiction. **Career:** University of California, acting arts instructor; Pepperdine University, acting arts instructor; University of Southern California, Master of Professional Writing Program, lecturer; Bennington Writing Seminars, core faculty; Rainier Writing Workshop, core faculty. Writer and actor. **Publications:** (With M.L. Belli) Acting for Young Actors: The Ultimate Teen Guide, 2006; Bigger Than Life: A Murder, a Memoir, 2007. **Address:** Dana and David Dornsife College of Letters, Arts, and Sciences, University of Southern California, PED 130, 3560 Watt Way, Los Angeles, CA 90089-0656, U.S.A. **Online address:** dinah@dinahlenney.com

LENNON, Donald R. American (born United States), b. 1938. **Genres:** History, Adult Non-fiction, Social Commentary. **Career:** Archives and History (North Carolina division), archivist, 1964-67; East Carolina University, as-

sociate professor of history, now associate professor emeritus, East Carolina Manuscript Collection, director, Joyner Library, coordinator of special collections, 1967-2001, head of special collections. Writer. **Publications:** (Ed. with I.B. Kellam) The Wilmington Town Book, 1743-1779, 1973; (with A.D. Watson and D.R. Lawson) Harnett, Hooper & Howe: Revolutionary Leaders of the Lower Cape Fear, 1979; (with C.E. Bennett) A Quest for Glory: Major General Robert Howe and the American Revolution, 1991. **Address:** Joyner Library, East Carolina University, E 5th St., Greenville, NC 27858-4353, U.S.A. **Online address:** donlen7@cs.com

LENNON, Joan. Scottish/Canadian (born Canada), b. 1953. **Genres:** Novels, Children's Fiction, Young Adult Fiction. **Career:** Writer and educator. **Publications:** CHILDREN'S AND YOUNG ADULT FANTASY: The Bad-Tempered Dragon, 1998; There's a Kangaroo in My Soup!, 2000; Questors, 2007; Ely Plot: Book I of The Wickit Chronicles, 2008; Fen Gold, 2008; The Seventh Tide, 2008; (with S. Anderson) Tales from the Keep: The Ferret Princess, 2008; Ice Road: The Wickit Chronicles, 2009. OTHERS: (co-author) WOW! 366, 2008; Wag and the King, 2009; Witch Bell, 2009; The Mucker's Tale, 2010; Case of the London Dragonfish, 2010; The Night of the Kelpies, 2010; The Case of the Glasgow Ghoul, 2011. **Address:** c/o Lindsey Fraser, Fraser Ross Associates, 6 Wellington Pl., Edinburgh, EH6 7EQ, Scotland. **Online address:** joanlennon@clara.co.uk

LENNON, J. Robert. American (born United States), b. 1970. **Genres:** Novels. **Career:** University of Montana, lecturer, visiting writer, 1993-95; Cornell University, lecturer, 1998-99, visiting professor, 1997-98, Department of English, assistant professor, 2006-, associate professor and graduate faculty; Wells College, visiting writer, 1999-2000, lecturer, 2000-01; Syracuse University, visiting writer, 2001-02. Writer. **Publications:** NOVELS: The Light of Falling Stars, 1997; The Funnies, 1999; On the Night Plain, 2001; Mailman, 2003; Pieces for the Left Hand: 100 Anecdotes, 2005; Happyland, 2006; (contrib.) So, What Kept You?, 2006; The Flash, 2007; Castle: A Novel, 2009. **Address:** Riverhead Books, 375 Hudson St., New York, NY 10014-3657, U.S.A. **Online address:** jrl24@cornell.edu

LENNOX, John. Canadian (born Canada), b. 1945. **Genres:** Literary Criticism And History, Young Adult Fiction, Biography, Autobiography/Memoirs, Art/Art History, Humanities, Education. **Career:** York University, lecturer in English, 1970-77, associate professor, 1977-90, director of graduate program, 1987-90, professor, 1991-, associate dean for faculty of graduate studies, 1996-99, acting dean, 1999-2000, dean, 2000-05, associate vice-president graduate, 2004-05; Robarts Centre for Canadian Studies, director, 1985-88. Writer. **Publications:** (With C. Thomas) William Arthur Deacon: A Canadian Literary Life, 1982. EDITOR: (with M. Lacombe) Dear Bill: The Correspondence of William Arthur Deacon, 1988; (with J.M. Paterson) Challenges, Projects, Texts: Canadian Editing: Twenty-fifth Conference on Editorial Problems, 1993; Margaret Laurence-Al Purdy: A Friendship in Letters, 1993; (co-author) Voyages: Real and Imaginary, Personal and Collective, 1994; (with R. Panofsky) Selected Letters of Margaret Laurence and Adele Wiseman, 1997. **Address:** Department of English, York University, 4700 Keele St., 237 FC, Toronto, ON M3J 1P3, Canada. **Online address:** jlennox@yorku.ca

LENNOX, Judith. *See* **LENNOX-SMITH, Judith (Elizabeth).**

LENNOX, Terry. *See* **HARVEY, John.**

LENNOX-SMITH, Judith (Elizabeth). (Judith Lennox). British (born England), b. 1953. **Genres:** Romance/Historical, Travel/Exploration, Literary Criticism And History. **Career:** Civil Service, executive officer, 1975-76. Writer. **Publications:** (As Judith Lennox-Smith) Reynardine (novel), 1989; Till the Day Goes Down (novel), 1991; The Glittering Strand (historical novel), 1991; The Italian Garden (historical novel), 1993; The Secret Years, 1994; The Winter House, 1996; Some Old Lover's Ghost, 1997; Footprints on the Sand, 1998; Shadow Child, 1999; The Dark-eyed Girls, 2000; Written On Glass, 2002; Middlemere, 2004; All My Sisters, 2005; Step In The Dark, 2006; Before the Storm, 2008; The Heart of the Night, 2010. **Address:** Hodder Headline, 338 Euston Rd., London, GL NW1 3BH, England.

LENO, James Douglas Muir. *See* **LENO, Jay.**

LENO, Jay. (James Douglas Muir Leno). American (born United States), b. 1950. **Genres:** Humor/Satire. **Career:** Good Times, writer, 1974. **Publications:** (Comp.) Headlines: Real But Ridiculous Samplings from America's

Newspapers, 1989; (comp.) Headlines III: Not the Movie, Still the Book: Real But Ridiculous Samplings from America's Newspapers, 1991; (comp.) Headlines IV: The Next Generaton: More Out-Of-This World Headlines from The Bestselling Series, 1992; Jay Lenos Headlines. Books I, II, III, 1992; Jay Lenos Police Blotter: Real-Life Crime Headlines from The Tonight Show with Jay Leno, 1994; (with B. Zehme) Leading with My Chin, 1996; How to be the Funniest Kid in the Whole Wide World (or Just in Your Class), 2005. **Address:** 3000 W Alameda Ave., PO Box 7885, Burbank, CA 91510-7885, U.S.A.

LENOIR, Janice. See **ROMACK, Janice Reed.**

LENSKI, Noel. (Noel Emmanuel Lenski). American (born United States), b. 1965. **Genres:** History. **Career:** Princeton University, teaching fellow, 1992-93, 1994-95; University of Colorado, Department of Classics, assistant professor, 1995-2002, associate professor, 2002-. Writer. **Publications:** Failure of Empire: Valens and the Roman State in the Fourth Century A.D., 2002; (ed.) The Cambridge Companion to the Age of Constantine, 2006, rev. ed., 2011; (ed. with) The Power of Religion in Late Antiquity, 2009. Works appear in anthologies. Contributor to journals. **Address:** Department of Classics, University of Colorado, Rm. 340, Eaton Humanities, 248 UCB, Boulder, CO 80309-0248, U.S.A. **Online address:** noel.lenski@colorado.edu

LENSKI, Noel Emmanuel. See **LENSKI, Noel.**

LENSKYJ, Helen Jefferson. Australian/Canadian (born Canada), b. 1943. **Genres:** Social Sciences, Autobiography/Memoirs, History, Gay And Lesbian Issues, Sports/Fitness, Recreation, Education, Women's Studies And Issues, Women's Studies And Issues. **Career:** Ontario Ministry of Culture and Recreation, supervisor of parents' and pre-school English and orientation programs, 1972-77, instructor, 1975-77; Townsville College of Advanced Education, lecturer in pre-service and graduate programs, 1978; University of Toronto, Ontario Institute for Studies in Education, part-time instructor, 1986-91, senior research officer, 1987-90; Resources for Feminist Research, co-editor, 1987-90; associate professor, 1991-97, professor of sociology and equity studies, physical education and community health, 1997-2008, Centre for Urban and Community Studies, research associate, 2003-, professor emerita, 2008-. Writer. **Publications:** Out of Bounds: Women, Sport, and Sexuality, 1986; Women, Sport, and Physical Activity: Research and Bibliography, rev. ed., 1988; Women, Sport, and Physical Activity: Selected Research Themes, 1994; Inside the Olympic Industry: Power, Politics, and Activism, 2000; The Best Ever Olympics: Social Impacts of Sydney 2000, 2002; Out on the Field: Gender, Sport, and Sexualities, 2003; A Lot to Learn: Women and Education in Twentieth Century Australia and Canada, 2005; Olympic Industry Resistance: Challenging Olympic Power and Propaganda, 2008. **Address:** Ontario Institute for Studies in Education, University of Toronto, 252 Bloor St. W, Toronto, ON M5S 1V6, Canada. **Online address:** helen.lenskyj@utoronto.ca

LENT, John. Canadian (born Canada), b. 1948. **Genres:** Novels. **Career:** University of Notre Dame, professor; Okanagan University College, professor of literature and creative writing, 1979-; The Kalamalka Institute For Working Writers, Kalamalka Press, founding member, Commercial Creative Writing Certificate, faculty. Writer. **Publications:** A Rock Solid, 1978; Wood Lake Music, 1982; Frieze, 1984; The Face in the Garden (juvenile novel), 1990; Monet's Garden, 1996; Black Horses, Cobalt Suns: New Poems, 2000; So it Won't Go Away, 2005; (with R. Kroetsch) Abundance: The Mackie House Conversations About the Writing Life, 2007; Cantilevered Songs, 2009. **Address:** Okanagan University College, 7000 College Way, Vernon, BC V1B 2N5, Canada. **Online address:** johnlent@uniserve.com

LENT, John A. (John A(nthony) Lent). American (born United States), b. 1936. **Genres:** Area Studies, Communications/Media, Film, Third World, Women's Studies And Issues, Writing/Journalism, Bibliography, Cartoons, Humor/Satire, Reference. **Career:** West Virginia Institute of Technology, instructor and director of public relations, 1960-62, 1965-66; De La Salle College, lecturer, 1964-65; Wisconsin State University, assistant professor of journalism, 1966-67; Marshall University, assistant professor, 1967-69; University of Wyoming, visiting associate professor, 1969-70; University of Iowa, teaching assistant, 1970-72; Universiti Sains Malaysia, Mass Communications Program, organizer and first coordinator, 1972-74; Temple University, associate professor, 1974-76, Department of Journalism, professor, 1976-95, Department of Broadcasting, Telecommunications and Mass Media, professor, 1995-; Third World Media Associates, director, 1986-; WittyWorld,

managing editor, 1987-; University of Western Ontario, Rogers distinguished professor, 2000; Asian Cinema Studies Society, chair. **Publications:** Philippine Mass Communications, 1966; Newhouse, Newspapers, Nuisances (biography), 1966; (co-author) Pied Type, a Load of Coal and the Laser Beam (filmstrip), 1969; Philippine Mass Communications, 1971; (ed.) Asian Newspapers' Reluctant Revolution, 1971; Third World Mass Media and Their Search for Modernity, 1977; Asian Mass Communications, 1974, Supplement, 1978; (ed.) Broadcasting in Asia and the Pacific: A Continental Survey of Radio and Television, 1978; Malaysian Studies: Present Knowledge and Research Trends, 1979; Caribbean Mass Communications, 1981; New World and International Information Order, 1982; Newspapers in Asia, 1982; Comic Art, 1986; Global Guide to Media & Communications, 1987; Videocassettes in the Third World, 1989; Asian Film Industry, 1990; Caribbean Popular Culture, 1990; Mass Communications in the Caribbean, 1990; Women and Mass Communications, 1991; Transnational Communications, 1991; Bibliographic Guide to Caribbean Mass Communications, 1992; Bibliography of Cuban Mass Communications, 1992; Animation, Caricature, Gag and Political Cartoons in the United States and Canada 1994; Cartoonometer, 1994; Comic Books and Comic Strips in the United States, 1994; Comic Art of Europe, 1994; (ed.) Asian Popular Culture, 1995; (ed.) A Different Road Taken, 1995; Comic Art in Africa, Asia, Australia and Latin America, 1996; Global Productions, 1998; (ed.) Themes and Issues in Asian Cartooning, 1999; (ed.) Pulp Demons, 1999; (ed.) Animation in Asia and the Pacific, 2001; (ed.) Illustrating Asia, 2001; Comic Art of Europe through 2000, 2003; Comic Art in Africa, Asia, Australia and Latin America through 2000, 2004; Comic Art of the United States Through 2000, Animation and Cartoons, 2005; (ed.) Cartooning in South America, 2005; (co-ed.) One Hundred Years of Chinese Cinema, 2005; Cartoonists, Works and Characters in the United States Through 2005, 2006; Comic Books and Comic Strips in the United States Through 2005, 2006; (ed.) Cartooning in Africa, 2009; First One Hundred Years of Philippine Komiks and Cartoons, 2009. **Address:** Department of Broadcasting,, Telecommunication & Mass Media, Temple University, Philadelphia, PA 19122, U.S.A. **Online address:** jlent@temple.edu

LENT, John A(nthony). See **LENT, John A.**

LENTIN, Ronit. Israeli/Irish (born Ireland), b. 1944. **Genres:** Novels, Adult Non-fiction, Women's Studies And Issues, Race Relations, Social Sciences. **Career:** Israel Television, production assistant, 1968-69; Irish National Television, researcher, 1969-72; freelance newspaper journalist, 1972-93; University of Limerick, lecturer in women's studies, 1993-95; Trinity College, Centre for Women's Studies, lecturer, 1995-97, lecturer in sociology, 1997-2005, course coordinator for graduate degree in ethnic and racial studies and director of the MPhil in ethnic and racial studies, 1997-, senior lecturer, 2006-. Writer. **Publications:** (With G. Niland) Who's Minding the Children?, 1981; Sihot im Nashim Palestiniyot (title means: Conversations with Palestinian Women), 1982; Triad: Modern Irish Fiction, 1986; Night Train to Mother (novel), 1990; Songs on the Death of Children (novel), 1996; Israel and the Daughters of the Shoah: Reoccupying the Territories of Silence, 2000. EDITOR AND CONTRIBUTOR: In From the Shadows: The UL Women's Studies Collection, vol. I, 1995, vol. II, 1996; Gender and Catastrophe, 1997; (with A. Byrne) (Re)searching Women: Feminist Research and Practice in the Social Sciences in Ireland, 2000; (with N. Abdo) Women and the Politics of Military Confrontation: Palestinian and Israeli Gendered Narratives of Dislocation, 2002; Colore Sulla Pelle: Attitudini e Aspettativedi Minoranze Etniche Femminili in Europa, 2002; (with R. McVeigh) Racism and Anti-racism in Ireland, 2002; Re-Presenting the Shoah for the Twenty-First Century, 2004; (with A. Lentin) Race and State, 2006; (with K. Fricker) Performing Global Networks, 2007; Thinking Palestine, 2008. Contributor to books and periodicals. **Address:** Department of Sociology, Trinity College, Dublin, DU 2, Ireland. **Online address:** rlentin@tcd.ie

LENTZ, Harris M(onroe). American (born United States), b. 1955. **Genres:** Communications/Media, Biography. **Career:** Tennessee State General Assembly, legislative assistant, 1972-76; St. Agnes Academy, librarian, 1973-74; freelance writer and researcher, 1979-; WMC-AM (radio station), co-host, 1991-94. **Publications:** (Comp.) Science Fiction, Horror, and Fantasy Film and Television Credits, 1983, 2nd ed., 2001; Assassinations and Executions: An Encyclopedia of Political Violence, 1865-1986, 1988, rev. ed. as Assassinations and Executions: An Encyclopedia of Political Violence, 1900 through 2000, 2002; Heads of States and Governments: A Worldwide Encyclopedia of Over 2,300 Leaders, 1945 through 1992, 1994; (comp.) Western and Frontier Film and Television Credits: 1903-1995, 1996; Biographical Dictionary of Professional Wrestling, 1997, 2nd ed., 2003; Television Westerns Episode Guide, 1997; Encyclopedia of Heads of States and Governments, 1900 through 1945, 1999; The Volcano Registry, 1999; Obituaries in the Performing Arts, 1999: Film, Television, Radio, Theatre, Dance, Music, Cartoons and Pop Culture, 2000; Feature Films, 1960-1969, 2001; Popes and Cardinals of the 20th Century: A Biographical Dictionary, 2001; American Government Leaders: Major Elected And Appointed Officials, Federal, State And Local, 1776-2005, 2006. **Address:** 3925 Appling Rd., Bartlett, TN 38135, U.S.A. **Online address:** hmliii@aol.com

LENTZ, John C(layton). American (born United States), b. 1957. **Genres:** Theology/Religion. **Career:** Presbyterian Church-Winchester, associate pastor, 1989-94, Presbyterian church-Cleveland Heights, pastor and head of staff, 1994-. Writer. **Publications:** Luke's Portrait of Paul, 1993. **Address:** 3031 Monticello Blvd., Cleveland Heights, OH 44118-1250, U.S.A.

LENZ, Elinor. American (born United States), b. 1928. **Genres:** Education, Women's Studies And Issues, Politics/Government. **Career:** University of California, Department of Humanities and Social Sciences, coordinator of special programs, 1960-71, Western Humanities Center, director, 1971-77. Writer. **Publications:** (Ed. with A. LeBel) Land and the Pursuit of Happiness: A Bicentennial Anthology, 1975; (with M.H. Shaevitz) So You Want to Go Back to School: Facing the Realities of Reentry, 1977; (with L. Adams) Effectiveness Training for Women: E.T.W., 1979; Creating and Marketing Programs in Continuing Education, 1980; Once My Child, Now My Friend, 1981; The Art of Teaching Adults, 1982; (with B.G. Myerhoff) The Feminization of America: How Women's Values Are Changing Our Public and Private Lives, 1985; Be Your Best: Personal Effectiveness in Your Life and Your Relationships, 1989; Rights of Passage: How Women Can Find a New Freedom in Their Midyears, 1992. Contributor to periodicals. **Address:** c/o Michael Hamilburg, Mitchell J. Hamilburg Agency, 149 S Barrington Ave., Ste. 732, Los Angeles, CA 90049-2930, U.S.A.

LEO, Mabel R. American (born United States), b. 1937. **Genres:** Novels, Novellas/Short Stories, Mystery/Crime/Suspense, Romance/Historical, Children's Fiction, Autobiography/Memoirs, Biography, Sports/Fitness, Sports/Fitness. **Career:** Writer. **Publications:** The Saga of Jack Durant (biography), 1996; America: The Italian Dream: Life the Italian Way in the U.S.A. (biography), 1998; Yahoodywho (for children), 2001; Because We Are Friends (short stories), 2001. NOVELS: Dear Sweetheart, 2001; Deadly Choices, 2002; Dark Secrets, 2004. OTHERS: Jack's World, 2005; Mob Mole, 2008. Contributor to periodicals. **Address:** 1274 E Avenida Hermosa, PO Box 17413, Phoenix, AZ 85014-2910, U.S.A. **Online address:** mibbles1274@msn.com

LEO, Richard A. American (born United States), b. 1963. **Genres:** Law, Criminology/True Crime. **Career:** University of Colorado, assistant professor of sociology and adjunct professor of law, 1994-99; Nankai University, visiting professor of sociology, 1996; University of California-Irvine, assistant professor, 1997-2001, associate professor of criminology, law and society and associate professor of psychology and social behavior, 2001-06; University of California-Berkeley, Boalt Hall School of Law, Criminal Justice Program, fellow; University of San Francisco, associate professor of law, 2006-. Writer, attorney and legal consultant. **Publications:** (Ed.) The American Criminal Justice System, 1997; (with G.C. Thomas, III) The Miranda Debate: Law, Justice, and Policing, 1998; Police Interrogation and American Justice, 2008; (with T. Wells) The Wrong Guys: Murder, False Confessions, and the Norfolk Four, 2008; (with G.C. Thomas, III) Confessions of Guilt: From Torture to Miranda and Beyond, 2012. Contributor to books, periodicals and journals. **Address:** School of Law, University of San Francisco, 2130 Fulton Ave., San Francisco, CA 94117, U.S.A. **Online address:** rleo@usfca.edu

LEO, Teresa. American (born United States) **Genres:** Poetry. **Career:** Franklin and Marshall College, visiting writer, 2003; Temple University, instructor of composition; University of Pennsylvania, Kelly Writers House, instructor and acting director; Philadelphia Inquirer, columnist; Painted Bride Quarterly, editor-in-chief; American Poetry Review, contributing editor; Musehouse, treasurer and board director. **Publications:** The Halo Rule (poems), 2008. Contributor to books and periodicals. **Address:** Musehouse, 7924 Germantown Ave., Philadelphia, PA 19118, U.S.A. **Online address:** leo1313@gmail.com

LEON, Nick. See **GRANT, Graeme.**

LEON, Sharon. (Sharon Heerboth). American (born United States), b. 1959. **Genres:** Film, Biography. **Career:** Ralph Wilson Plastics, draftsperson, 1987-90; freelance writer, 1990-; Siecor Corp., draftsperson, 1991-. **Publications:** (With D. Hitzeroth) Sir Isaac Newton, 1992; (with D. Hitzeroth) Thurgood Marshall, 1997. AS SHARON HEERBOTH: (with D. Hitzeroth) Movies: The World on Film, 1991; (with D. Hitzeroth) Galileo Galilei, 1992. **Address:** 6332 Old Mill Cir., Watauga, TX 76148, U.S.A. **Online address:** emandliz@flash.net

LEONARD, Amy Elmore. American (born United States), b. 1966. **Genres:** Theology/Religion, History, Politics/Government. **Career:** Georgetown University, Department of History, assistant professor, 1999-2006, associate professor, 2006-. Writer. **Publications:** Nails in the Wall: Catholic Nuns in Reformation Germany, 2005; (ed. with K. Nelson) Attending to Early Modern Women and Men, 2008; (ed. with K.L. Nelson) Masculinities, Childhood, Violence: Attending to Early Modern Women and Men: Proceedings of the 2006 Symposium, 2011. Contributor to books. **Address:** Department of History, Georgetown University, 628 ICC,, 37th & O St. NW, Washington, DC 20057-1035, U.S.A. **Online address:** ael3@georgetown.edu

LEONARD, Annie. American (born United States), b. 1964?. **Genres:** Natural History, Medicine/Health. **Career:** Funders Workgroup for Sustainable Production and Consumption, coordinator; Global Alliance for Incinerator Alternatives (GAIA), staff; Health Care without Harm, staff; Essential Action, staff; Greenpeace Intl., staff; National Wildlife Federation, staff; The Story of Stuff Project, producer and director. Writer and environmental activist. **Publications:** (With A. Conrad) The Story of Stuff: How Our Obsession with Stuff Is Trashing the Planet, Our Communities, and Our Health-and a Vision for Change, 2010. **Address:** Berkeley, CA , U.S.A. **Online address:** info@storyofstuff.org

LEONARD, Bill J. American (born United States), b. 1946. **Genres:** Theology/Religion, History. **Career:** Northridge Baptist Church, youth minister, 1965-72; Federal War on Poverty Program, coordinator, 1968-69; First Community Church, pastor, 1971-75; Southern Baptist Theological Seminary, professor of religion, 1975-92, William Walker Brookes professor of American Christianity, 1990-91, associate dean, Faculty Association, president; Yale University, visiting lecturer, 1980-81; Foxfire 7, contributing editor, 1982; Seinan Gakuin University, visiting professor, 1988-89; Berea College, Appalachian Ministries Educational Resource Center, faculty, 1989-95, dean, 1991-92, vice chair of executive board, 2001-06; Review & Expositor, managing editor, 1991; Samford University, professor of religion and chair of department, 1992-96; Wake Forest University, School of Divinity, founding dean, 1996-2010, professor of church history, 1996-, Department of Religion, professor of religion, 1996-. **Publications:** (Ed.) Early American Christianity, 1979; Word of God across the Ages: Using Christian History in Preaching, 1981; Out of One, Many: American Religion and American Pluralism, 1984; The Nature of the Church, 1986; God's Last and Only Hope: The Fragmentation of the Southern Baptist Convention, 1990; (ed.) Community in Diversity: A History of Walnut Street Baptist Church, 1990; (ed.) Becoming Christian: Dimensions of Spiritual Formation, 1990; (ed.) Dictionary of Baptists in America, 1994; Risk the Journey: Answering God's Call to Proclaim His Word, 1995; (ed. with G.H. Shriver) Encyclopedia of Religious Controversies in the United States, 1997; (ed.) Christianity in Appalachia: Profiles in Regional Pluralism, 1999; Baptist Ways: A History, 2003; An Introduction to Baptist Principles, 2005; Baptists in America, 2005; Baptist Questions, Baptist Answers, 2009; Challenge of being Baptist, 2010; Baptist Confessions of Faith, rev. ed., 2011. Contributor to books. **Address:** School of Divinity, Wake Forest University, 1834 Wake Forest Rd., PO Box 7719, Reynolda Sta., Winston-Salem, NC 27106, U.S.A. **Online address:** leonabj@wfu.edu

LEONARD, Constance. American (born United States), b. 1923. **Genres:** Mystery/Crime/Suspense, Children's Fiction, Novels, Horror. **Career:** Writer. **Publications:** NOVELS: The Great Pumpkin Mystery, 1971; (with L.H.G. Coxe) Detective Book Club: Woman with a Gun, The Other Maritha, The Mirrow of Hell, 1972; The Other Maritha, 1972; Steps to Nowhere: A Novel of Suspense, 1974; Hostage in Illyria: A Novel of Suspense, 1976; Shadow of a Ghost, 1978. TRACY JAMES MYSTERY SERIES: The Marina Mystery, 1981; Stowaway, 1983; Aground, 1984; Strange Waters, 1985. **Address:** 49 Kaufmann Dr., Peterborough, NH 03458, U.S.A.

LEONARD, Dorothy. (Dorothy Leonard-Barton). American (born United States), b. 1942. **Genres:** Administration/Management, Business/Trade/Industry. **Career:** Freelance journalist in Thailand, 1971-72; Djakarta Business Bulletin, founder and manager, 1972-75; Stanford University, research assistant, 1975-78, research associate, 1978-79; SRI Intl., policy analyst, 1979-80; Massachusetts Institute of Technology, Sloan School of Management, assistant professor, 1981-83; Harvard University, Harvard Business School, assistant professor, 1983-89, associate professor, 1989-93, professor, 1993-94, William J. Abernathy professor of business administration, 1994-2004, director of research, now William J. Abernathy professor of business administration emerita; American Management Systems, board director, 1992-2004; Gannett Communications, board director, 1997-99. Writer. **Publications:** Wellsprings of Knowledge: Building and Sustaining Core Technological Capabilities, 1995; When Sparks Fly: Igniting Creativity in Groups, 1999; (with W.C. Swap) Deep Smarts: How to Cultivate and Transfer Enduring Business Wisdom, 2005; (with W.C. Swap) When Sparks Fly: Harnessing the Power of Group Creativity, 2005; Managing Knowledge Assets, Creativity and Innovation, 2011. Contributor to books and journals. **Address:** Graduate School of Business Administration, Harvard Business School, Soldiers Field Rd., Boston, MA 02163, U.S.A. **Online address:** dleonard@hbs.edu

LEONARD, Elmore. American (born United States), b. 1925. **Genres:** Novels, Mystery/Crime/Suspense, Westerns/Adventure, Plays/Screenplays, Young Adult Non-fiction, inspirational/Motivational Literature, Novellas/Short Stories. **Career:** Campbell Ewald Advertising Agency, copywriter, 1950-61; full-time writer, 1961-; Elmore Leonard Advertising Co., director, 1963-66. **Publications:** The Bounty Hunters, 1953; The Law at Randado, 1955; Escape from Five Shadows, 1956; Last Stand at Saber River in UK as Lawless River, 1959, 2nd ed. as Stand on the Saber, 1960; Hombre, 1961; Valdez Is Coming, 1969; The Big Bounce, 1969; The Moonshine War, 1969; Joe Kidd, 1972; Forty Lashes Less One, 1972; Mr. Majestyk, 1974; Fifty-Two Pickup, 1974; Swag, 1976 as Ryan's Rule, 1976; The Hunted, 1977; Unknown Man No. 89: A Novel, 1977; The Switch, 1978; Gunsights, 1979, 2nd ed., 1988; City Primeval: High Noon in Detroit, 1980; Gold Coast, 1980; Split Images, 1981; Cat Chaser, 1982; (intro.) Willy Remembers, 1983; Stick, 1983; La Brava, 1983; Elmore Leonard's Dutch Treat: 3 Novels, 1985; Glitz, 1985; Bandits, 1987; Touch, 1987; Freaky Deaky, 1988; Killshot, 1989; (intro.) Sprinkled with Ruby Dust, 1989; Get Shorty, 1990; Maximum Bob, 1991; Elmore Leonard Three Complete Novels, 1992; Rum Punch, 1992; Pronto, 1993; Riding the Rap, 1995; Out of Sight, 1998; Cuba Libre, 1998; The Tonto Woman: And Other Western Stories, 1998; Be Cool, 1999; Pagan Babies, 2000; (intro.) The Friends of Eddie Coyle, 2000; Tishomingo Blues, 2002; When the Women Come Out to Dance (stories), 2002; Mr. Paradise, 2004; The Complete Western Stories of Elmore Leonard, 2004; A Coyote's in the House, 2004; The Hot Kid: A Novel, 2005; Comfort to the Enemy, 2005; Blood Money and Other Stories, 2006; Three-ten to Yuma: And Other Stories, 2006; Moment of Vengeance: And Other Stories, 2006; Elmore Leonard's 10 Rules of Writing, 2007; Trail of the Apache and Other Stories, 2007; Up In Honey's Room, 2007; Road Dogs, 2009; Djibouti, 2010; Comfort to the Enemy and Other Carl Webster Stories, 2009; Raylan, 2012; Fire in the Hole, 2012. Contributor to books and periodicals. **Address:** Random House Inc., 1745 Broadway, New York, NY 10019, U.S.A.

LEONARD, Frances. American (born United States), b. 1939?. **Genres:** Money/Finance, Business/Trade/Industry, Economics, Young Adult Nonfiction. **Career:** Attorney, 1979-88; Older Women's League, legal counsel, 1980-88. Writer. **Publications:** Women and Money: The Independent Woman's Guide to Financial Security for Life, 1991; Money and the Mature Woman: How to Hold on to Your Income, Keep Your Home, Plan Your Estate, 1993; Time is Money: A Million Dollar Investment Plan for Today's Twenty and Thirty Somethings, 1996. Contributor to periodicals. **Address:** c/o Sandra Dijkstra, 1155 Camino del Mar, Ste. 515, Del Mar, CA 92014, U.S.A.

LEONARD, Gerald F. American (born United States), b. 1960. **Genres:** History, Social Sciences. **Career:** University of Michigan, teaching assistant, 1986-90, lecturer in History, 1991; Labor Arbitrator Sol Elkin, assistant, 1993; Bodman, Longley and Dahling, law clerk, 1994; Institute of Government, law clerk, 1995; U.S. Court of Appeals for the Fourth Circuit, law clerk to Judge J. Dickson Phillips, Jr., 1995-96; Boston University, professor of law, 1996-; U.S. Supreme Court, law clerk to Justice David Souter, 1996-97; Boston University School of Law, associate professor of law, 1996-2003, professor of law, 2003-, associate dean for academic affairs, 2006-. Writer. **Publications:** The Invention of Party Politics: Federalism, Popular Sovereignty, and Constitutional Development in Jacksonian Illinois, 2002. Contributor to books and journals. **Address:** School of Law, Boston University, 765 Commonwealth

Ave., Boston, MA 02215-1401, U.S.A. **Online address:** gleonard@bu.edu

LEONARD, James S. American (born United States), b. 1947. **Genres:** Literary Criticism And History. **Career:** Bost Engineering Co., city planner, 1968-70; Community Environment Consultants, vice president, 1970-73; City of Morristown, city planning director, 1974-79; University of Tennessee, teaching assistant, 1978-79; Clemson University, visiting assistant professor, 1980; Brown University, teaching assistant, 1981-83; The Citadel, assistant professor, 1983-88, associate professor, 1988-93, professor of English, 1993-, Graduate Program in English, director, department of English, head, 1998-; College of Charleston, Joint M.A. Program in English, director. Writer. **Publications:** (As J.S. Leonard with C.E. Wharton) The Fluent Mundo: Wallace Stevens and the Structure of Reality, 1988; Afterword, A Tramp Abroad (The Oxford Mark Twain), 1996. EDITOR: (with T.A. Tenney and T.M. Davis) Satire or Evasion? Black Perspectives on Huckleberry Finn, 1992; (co-ed.) Authority and Textuality: Current Views of Collaborative Writing, 1994; Making Mark Twain Work in the Classroom, 1999; (ed. with G. McMichael) Anthology of American Literature, 2 vols., 2004, 10th ed., 2011; (ed. with G. McMichael) Concise Anthology of American Literature, 2006, 7th ed., 2010; Mark Twain Circular, 1987-2008. **Address:** Department of English, The Citadel, 119D Capers Hall, 171 Moultrie St., Charleston, SC 29409-6310, U.S.A. **Online address:** leonardj@citadel.edu

LEONARD, Karen Isaksen. American (born United States), b. 1939. **Genres:** Anthropology/Ethnology, History, Social Sciences. **Career:** University of Michigan, Center for South and Southeast Asian Studies, associate, 1967-68, visiting lecturer in history, 1968; University of San Diego, lecturer in history, 1969; University of California, lecturer in history, 1969-70, assistant professor, 1972-78, associate professor, 1978-85, professor of anthropology, 1985-, director of women's studies, 1978-79; University of Virginia, visiting assistant professor, 1978. Writer and anthropologist. **Publications:** Social History of an Indian Caste: The Kayasths of Hyderabad, 1978; Making Ethnic Choices: California's Punjabi-Mexican-Americans, 1992; Finding One's Own Place: Asian Landscapes Re-Visioned in Rural California, in Culture, Power, Place: Explorations in Critical Anthropology, 1997; South Asian Americans, 1997; Muslims in the United States: The State of Research, 2003; (ed.) Immigrant Faiths: Transforming Religious Life in America, 2005; Locating Home: India's Hyderabadis Abroad, 2007; (ed. with G. Reddy and A.G. Gold) Histories of Intimacy and Situated Ethnography, 2010; (ed. with A. Patel) Indo-Muslim Cultures in Transition, 2012. Contributor to books and professional journals. **Address:** Department of Anthropology, University of California, 3151 Social Science Plz., Irvine, CA 92697-5100, U.S.A. **Online address:** kbleonar@uci.edu

LEONARD, Mark. British (born England), b. 1974. **Genres:** History, Politics/Government. **Career:** Demos, researcher; Foreign Policy Centre, founding director, 1998-2004; Centre for European Reform, director of foreign policy, 2004-07; European Council on Foreign Relations, executive director, 2007-; German Marshall Fund of the United States, transatlantic fellow; European Council, legal service trainee. Writer and foreign policy expert. **Publications:** Britain TM: Renewing Our Identities, 1997; Politics without Frontiers: The Role of Political Parties in Europe's Future, 1997; Making Europe Popular: The Search for European Identity, 1998; Rediscovering Europe, 1998; (with T. Hames) Modernising the Monarchy, 1998; The Future Shape of Europe, 2000; Going Public: Diplomacy for the Information Age, 2000; Next Generation Democracy: Legitimacy in Network Europe, 2001; (ed. with T. Arbuthnott) Winning the Euro Referendum: A Guide to Public Opinion and the Issues That Affect It, 2001; (with C. Stead and C. Smewing) Public Diplomacy, 2002; Can Brussels Earn the Right to Act?, 2002; Re-ordering the World: The Long-term Implications of 11 September, 2002; (ed. with P. Griffith) Reclaiming Britishness: Living Together after 11 September and the Rise of the Right, 2002; (ed. with D. Leonard) The Pro-European Reader, 2002; (with C. Smewing) Public Diplomacy and the Middle East, 2003; (with C. Grant) Georgia and the EU: Can Europe's Neighbourhood Policy Deliver?, 2005; (with A. Small and M. Rose) British Public Diplomacy in the Age of Schisms, 2005; Can EU Diplomacy Stop Iran's Nuclear Programme?, 2005; (with K. Barysch and C. Grant) Embracing the Dragon: The EU's Partnership with China, 2005; Why Europe Will Run the 21st Century, 2005; (with C. Grant) The EU's Awkward Neighbour: Time for a New Policy on Belarus, 2006; (with C. Grant) How to Strengthen EU Foreign Policy, 2006; Divided World: The Struggle for Primacy in 2020, 2007; What Does China Think?, 2008. Contributor to periodicals and journals. **Address:** Chalk Farm, GL , England. **Online address:** mark.leonard@ecfr.eu

LEONARD, Richard James. Australian (born Australia), b. 1963?. **Genres:** Race Relations. **Career:** University of Melbourne, visiting lecturer in Australian cinema, Australian Catholic Office for Film Broadcasting, director; United Faculty of Theology, lecturer in cinema and theology; Pontifical Gregorian University, visiting professor; Australian Catholic University, honorary fellow. Writer. **Publications:** Beloved Daughters: 100 Years of Papal Teaching on Women, 1995; Movies That Matter: Reading Film Through the Lens of Faith, 2006; Preaching to the Converted Throughout the Sundays and Feast Days of the Year, 2006; (comp. with J.L. Sundberg) A Glimpse of Heaven: Through the Eyes of Heaven, 2007; Where the Hell is God?, 2010. Contributor to periodicals. **Address:** Australian Catholic Office for Film Broadcasting, Newman College, University of Melbourne, 887 Swanston St., Parkville, VI 3052, Australia. **Online address:** richard.leonard@bigpond.com

LEONARD, Stephen J. American (born United States), b. 1941. **Genres:** Local History/Rural Topics, Biography, Autobiography/Memoirs, History, Art/Art History, Reference. **Career:** Metropolitan State College of Denver, History Department, assistant professor, 1966-74, associate professor, 1974-77, professor of history, chair, 1977-. Writer. **Publications:** (With C. Abbott and D. McComb) Colorado: A History of the Centennial State, 1982, 4th ed., (with C. Abbott and T.J. Noel), 2005; (with T.J. Noel) Denver: From Mining Camp to Metropolis, 1990; Trials and Triumphs: A Colorado Portrait of the Great Depression With FSA Photographs, 1993; (with D. Dines and S.L. Cuba) The Art of Charles Partridge Adams, 1993; (ed. with R.C. Baron and T.J. Noel) Thomas Hornsby Ferril and the American West, 1996; (with K.E. Rucker and T.J. Noel) Colorado Givers: A History of Philanthropic Heroes, 1998; Lynching in Colorado, 1859-1919, 2002; (with T.J. Noel and D.L. Walker Jr.) Honest John Shafroth: A Colorado Reformer, 2003. Contributor to periodicals. **Address:** Department of History, Metropolitan State College, Central Classroom 211B, PO Box 27, Denver, CO 80217-3362, U.S.A. **Online address:** leonards@mscd.edu

LEONARD-BARTON, Dorothy. See LEONARD, Dorothy.

LEONARDI, Susan J. American (born United States), b. 1946. **Genres:** Gay And Lesbian Issues, Women's Studies And Issues, Autobiography/Memoirs, Literary Criticism And History, Humanities. **Career:** University of California, lecturer in English, 1986-87; University of Maryland, assistant professor, 1987-90, associate professor of English, 1990-98, professor, 1999-, now professor emeritus. Writer. **Publications:** Dangerous by Degrees: Women at Oxford and the Somerville College Novelists, 1989; (with R.A. Pope) The Diva's Mouth: Body, Voice, Prima Donna Politics, 1996; And Then They Were Nuns, 2003. Contributor of articles to periodicals. **Address:** Department of English, University of Maryland, 4135 Susquehanna Hall, College Park, MD 20742, U.S.A. **Online address:** sl18@umail.umd.edu

LEONG, Russell (C.). American (born United States), b. 1950. **Genres:** Novellas/Short Stories, Poetry, Literary Criticism And History, History, Politics/Government. **Career:** Pacifica Public Radio, editor, 1975-76; Rockefeller American Generations Fellowship Program, coordinator, 1991-93; University of California, adjunct professor of Asian American studies, Department of English, adjunct professor, Amerasia Journal, editor. **Publications:** The Country of Dreams and Dust (poems), 1993; Phoenix Eyes and Other Stories, 2000. EDITOR: (with J.P. Yip) A History Reclaimed: An Annotated Bibliography of Chinese Language Materials on the Chinese of America, 1986; (contrib. with G. Nomura, R. Endo and S. Sumida) Frontiers of Asian American Studies: Writing, Research and Criticism, 1989; (and intro.) Moving the Image: Independent Asian Pacific American Media Arts, 1970-1990, 1991; (with R. Leong) Los Angeles- Struggles Toward Multiethnic Community: Asian American, African American & Latino perspectives, 1994; Asian American Sexualities: Dimensions of the Gay and Lesbian Experience, 1996; (with D.T. Nakanishi) Asian Americans on War & Peace, 2002; (with V. Lal and D.T. Nakanishi) The Other Indians: A Political and Cultural History of South Asians in America, 2008. Works appear in anthologies. Contributor of articles to periodicals. **Address:** Asian American Studies Center, University of California, 3230 Campbell Hall, 405 Hilgard Ave., Los Angeles, CA 90095-1546, U.S.A. **Online address:** rleong@ucla.edu

LEONHARDT, Alice. See HART, Alison.

LEONI, Giulio. Italian (born Italy), b. 1951. **Genres:** Novels. **Career:** Writer. **Publications:** NOVELS: La donna sulla luna, 2001; E trentuno con la morte, 2003; Il trionfo della volontà, 2005; The Mosaic Crimes,

2006; La compagnia dei serpenti: Il deserto degli spettri, 2006; La compagnia dei serpenti: Il sepolcro di Gengis Khan, 2007; The Kingdom of Light, 2009; La ladra di Cagliostro, 2010. **Address:** Rome, Italy. **Online address:** giulio.leoni@istruzione.it

LEOPOLD, Terry Ann Mood. (Terry Ann Mood). American (born United States), b. 1945. **Genres:** Bibliography, Reference. **Career:** Denver Public Library, librarian, 1969-70; Metropolitan State College, periodicals librarian, 1970-75; University of Colorado, periodicals librarian, 1975-81, English teacher, 1978-79, associate professor, language and literature librarian, 1981-91, humanities bibliographer, 1991-97, head of collection development, 1997-2002, now professor emeritus; Southeast Metropolitan Board of Cooperative Services, teacher in adult education program, 1977-79. Writer. **Publications:** AS TERRY ANN MOOD: (comp. with C.M. Joy) Colorado Local History: A Directory, 1975; Distance Education: An Annotated Bibliography, 1995; (ed. with R.L. Wick) ARBA Guide to Biographical Resources, 1986-1997, 1998; American Regional Folklore: A Sourcebook and Research Guide, 2004. Contributor to journals. **Address:** 6954 E Heritage Pl. N, Centennial, CO 80111, U.S.A. **Online address:** tal954@hotmail.com

LEPAGE, Robert. Canadian (born Canada), b. 1957. **Genres:** Plays/Screenplays, Art/Art History, Theatre. **Career:** Theatre Repere, artistic co-director, 1986-89; Robert Lepage Inc., founder and president, 1988; National Arts Centre, French Theatre, artistic director, 1989-93; Ex Machina (theatre Co.), founder and artistic director, 1994-; In Extremis Images Inc., founder and artistic director, 1994; La Caserne Dalhousie, founder, 1997; Ex Aqueo Films Inc., vice president, 2004. Actor, director and playwright. **Publications:** (With R. Charest) Robert Lepage: Connecting Flights, 1998; Face cachée de la lune, 2007; Projet Andersen, 2007; Stéphan Bureau rencontre Robert Lepage, 2008; (with M. Michaud) The Blue Dragon, 2011. **Address:** c/o Mrs Lynda Beaulieu, 103 Dalhousie St., Quebec City, QC G1K 4B9, Canada. **Online address:** roleinc@attglobal.com

LEPLIN, Jarrett. American (born United States), b. 1944. **Genres:** Philosophy. **Career:** Illinois Institute of Technology, instructor, 1967-70; University of Maryland, instructor, 1970-71; University of North Carolina, Department of philosophy, assistant professor, 1971-76, associate professor, 1976-82, professor, 1982-. Writer. **Publications:** (Ed. with intro.) Scientific Realism, 1984; (ed.) Creation of Ideas in Physics: Studies for a Methodology of Theory Construction, 1995; A Novel Defense of Scientific Realism, 1997; Theory of Epistemic Justification, 2009; Review of Eric Barnes, The Paradox of Predictivism, The Review of Metaphysics, 2010; Review of Brian Ellis, The Metaphysics of Scientific Realism, forthcoming. Contributor to journals. **Address:** Department of Philosophy, University of North Carolina, 216 Foust Bldg., PO Box 26170, Greensboro, NC 27402, U.S.A. **Online address:** j_leplin@uncg.edu

LEPORE, Jill. American (born United States), b. 1966. **Genres:** History, Young Adult Fiction, Children's Non-fiction, Psychology, Military/Defense/Arms Control. **Career:** Yale University, acting instructor in American studies, 1993-95; University of California, assistant professor of history, 1995-96; Boston University, assistant professor of history, 1996-2001, associate professor of history and American studies, 2001-; Harvard University, Department of History, professor, 2004-, David Woods Kemper '41 professor of American history, History and Literature Program, chair; The New Yorker, staff writer, 2005-. **Publications:** The Name of War: King Philip's War and the Origins of American Identity, 1998; (ed.) Encounters in the New World: A History in Documents, 2000; A is for American: Letters and Other Characters in the Newly United States, 2002; New York Burning: Liberty, Slavery, and Conspiracy in Eighteenth-Century Manhattan, 2005; Websterisms: Choice Words from the Original American Dictionary, 2008; (with J. Kamensky) Blindspot: By a Gentleman in Exile and a Lady in Disguise, 2008; The Whites of Their Eyes: The Tea Party's Revolution and the Battle Over American History, 2010; The Mansion of Happiness: A History of Life and Death, 2012; The Story of America: Essays on Origins, forthcoming. Contributor of articles to books, journals and periodicals. **Address:** Department of History, Harvard University, Rm. 209, Robinson Hall, 35 Quincy St., Cambridge, MA 02138-3880, U.S.A. **Online address:** jill_lepore@harvard.edu

LEPPEK, Christopher. American (born United States), b. 1954. **Genres:** Mystery/Crime/Suspense, Horror. **Career:** New Lyons Recorder, reporter, 1977; Intermountain Jewish News, assistant editor, 1977-. **Publications:** The Surrogate Assassin (mystery novel), 1998; (with E. Isler) Chaosicon (horror novel), 2001; (with E. Isler) Dark Seed, forthcoming; Apollonia, forthcoming; Seed of Oblivion, forthcoming; Abattoir, forthcoming. Contributor of articles to magazines and newspapers. **Address:** 1016 S Washington St., Denver, CO 80209, U.S.A. **Online address:** redraven75@aol.com

LERANGIS, Peter. Also writes as Artie Sprengle, A. L. Singer. American (born United States), b. 1955. **Genres:** Novels, Young Adult Fiction, Plays/Screenplays, Adult Non-fiction. **Career:** Freelance copy editor, 1979-85; City University, New York Graduate Center, faculty, 1985-86; freelance writer, 1986-. **Publications:** YOUNG ADULT FICTION: Foul Play (Three Investigators Crimebusters Series), 1990; (as A.L. Singer) Dick Tracy, 1990; The Yearbook, 1994; Driver's Dead, 1994; Spring Fever, 1996; Spring Break, 1996; It Came from the Cafeteria, 1996; Attack of the Killer Potatoes, 1997; Antarctica No. 1: Journey to the Pole, 2000; Antarctica No. 2: Escape from Disaster, 2000; Smiler's Bones, 2005; Tunnel Vision, 2005; WTF, 2007; Summer Stars, 2008; Sword Thief, 2008; Viper's Nest, 2009. WATCHERS SERIES: Last Stop, 1998; Rewind, 1998; I.D., 1999; War, 1999; Lab 6, 1999. ABRA CADABRA! SERIES: Poof! Rabbits Everywhere!, 2001; Boo! Ghosts in the School!, 2001; Presto! Magic Treasure!, 2002; Zap! Science Fair Surprise!, 2002; Yeeps! Secret in the Statue!, 2002; Whoa! Amusement Park Gone Wild!, 2003; Wow! Blast from the Past!, 2003. X ISLE SERIES: X Isle, 2003; Return to X Isle, 2003. SPYX SERIES: The Code, 2004; Hide and Seek, 2004; Proof Positive, 2005; Tunnel Vision, 2005. PUZZLE BOOKS: Puzzles and Games, 1984; Mickey's Drill-a Days: Letters and Words, 1985; Star Trek Puzzle Book, 1986; Star Trek Activity Book, 1986; Super Puzzle No. 1: Going Batty, 1988; Super Puzzle No. 3: Camp Craziness, 1988. SCREENPLAY NOVELIZATIONS: Young Sherlock Holmes, 1985; Star Trek IV: The Voyage Home, 1986; (as A.L. Singer) License to Drive, 1988; (as A.L. Singer) Little Monsters, 1989; (as A.L. Singer) Sing, 1989; (as A.L. Singer) Rescuers Down Under, 1990; (as A.L. Singer) Dick Tracy, 1990; (as A.L. Singer) Disney's Beauty and the Beast, 1991; (as A.L. Singer) Davy Crockett and the Pirates at Cave-In Rock, 1991; (as A.L. Singer) Bingo, 1991; (adapted as A.L. Singer) Disney's Aladdin, 1992; (as A.L. Singer) Home Alone II: Lost in New York, 1992; (as A.L. Singer) Robin Hood, 1992; (as A.L. Singer) Young Indiana Jones Chronicles: Safari Sleuth, 1992; (as A.L. Singer) Little Mermaid, 1993; (as A.L. Singer) Sleeping Beauty, 1993; (as A.L. Singer) Surf Warriors, 1993; (as A.L. Singer) The Swan Princess, 1994; (as A.L. Singer) Miracle on Thirty-fourth Street, 1994; (as A.L. Singer) Mufasa's Little Instruction Book, 1994; (as A.L. Singer) Jumanji (picture book), 1995; (as George Spelvin) Jumanji (young adult), 1995; (as A.L. Singer) The Amazing Panda Adventure, 1995; (as A.L. Singer) Baby-Sitters Club, 1995; (adapted as A.L. Singer) Anastasia, 1997; Sleepy Hollow: A Novelization, 1999; M. Night Shyamalan's The Sixth Sense, 2000; The Road to El Dorado, 2000; Batman Begins, 2005. OTHER MOVIE TIE-IN BOOKS: (as A.L. Singer) Star Wars-Episode One Adventure and Game Books, 2000; (as R.E. Volting) Shrek Gag Book, 2001; (as Artie Sprengle) Madagascar Joke Book, 2005. INTERACTIVE: The Amazing Ben Franklin, 1987; In Search of a Shark, 1987; The Last of the Dinosaurs, 1988; World War II Codebreakers, 1989. NONFICTION: A Kid's Guide to New York City, 1988; Teacher Guide to Square One TV Show, 1989; (with P. Dodson) Dinosaur Bookshelf: Giant Dinosaurs, 1990; (with P. Dodson) Dinosaur Bookshelf: Baby Dinosaurs, 1990; Drama Club, Book 1: The Fall Musical, 2007; Drama club, Book 2: The Big Production, 2007; Drama Club, Book 3: Too Hot!, 2008. AS FRANKLIN W. DIXON: The Genius Thieves, 1987; The Borgia Dagger, 1988; A Killing in the Market, 1988; Danger Zone, 1990. AS CAROLYN KEENE: A Crime for Christmas, 1988; Shock Waves, 1989; Buried in Time, 1990. AS A.L. SINGER: The Sultan's Secret, 1988; Ninja Gaiden, 1990; Blaster Master, 1990; Dick Tracy Catch-a-Crook Adventure, 1990; Bases Loaded 2, 1991; Davy Crockett and the King of the River, 1991; Infiltrator, 1991; Danger on Naboo, 2000. AS MORGAN BURKE: The Party Room No. 1: Get It Started, 2005; After Hours, 2005; The Party Room No. 3: Last Call, 2005. OTHERS: (as Alison Blair) Campus Fever, 1988; (as M.E. Cooper) Falling for You, 1988; Island, 1999; Yikes! It's Alive!, 2003; (with R. Riordan, G. Korman and J. Watson) Vespers Rising, 2011; (with H. Mazer) Somebody Please Tell me Who I Am, 2012; (contrib.) The Dead of Night, 2012. **Address:** c/o George Nicholson, Sterling Lord Literistic, 65 Bleecker St., New York, NY 10012-2420, U.S.A. **Online address:** info@peterlerangis.com

LERCH, Patricia Barker. American (born United States), b. 1947?. **Genres:** Anthropology/Ethnology, Cultural/Ethnic Topics, Anthropology/Ethnology. **Career:** University of North Carolina, professor of anthropology. Writer and anthropologist. **Publications:** Waccamaw Legacy: Contemporary Indians Fight for Survival, 2004. Contributor to books. **Address:** University of North

Carolina, 601 S College Rd., Wilmington, NC 28403-3297, U.S.A. **Online address:** lerch@uncw.edu

LERER, Seth. American (born United States), b. 1955. **Genres:** History, Literary Criticism And History. **Career:** Princeton University, assistant professor of English, professor, 1981-90, director of undergraduate studies, 1986-89; University of California-Berkeley, visiting professor of comparative literature and classics, 1988, visiting professor of comparative literature, 2006; Stanford University, faculty, professor of English, 1990-96, director of graduate studies, 1992-93, 2002-05, professor of English and comparative literature, 1996-2008, director of undergraduate studies, comparative literature, 1996-97, 1998-2000, chair of comparative literature, 1997-2000, 2001-08, Avalon Foundation professor in the humanities, 2001-08, Stanford Humanities Fellows Program, director, 2001-, Stanford History of the Book Workshop, director, 2002-03, vice-chair in English, 2003-05, Graduate Placement, co-director, 2004-05, director of graduate studies, comparative literature, 2005-06, university senate, 2005-06; Washington University-St. Louis, Hurst visiting professor, 1996; University of California, Department of Literature, distinguished professor, dean of arts and humanities, 2009-. Writer. **Publications:** Boethius and Dialogue: Literary Method in the Consolation of Philosophy, 1985; Literacy and Power in Anglo-Saxon Literature, 1991; Chaucer and His Readers: Imagining the Author in Late-Medieval England, 1993; (ed. and contrib.) Reading from the Margins: Textual Studies, Chaucer and Medieval Literature, 1996; (ed.) Literary History and the Challenge of Philology: The Legacy of Erich Auerbach, 1996; Courtly Letters in the Age of Henry VIII: Literary Culture and the Arts of Deceit, 1997; Error and the Academic Self: The Scholarly Imagination, Medieval to Modern, 2002; (ed. and contrib.) The Yale Companion to Chaucer, 2006; Inventing English: A Portable History of the Language, 2007; Children's Literature: A Reader's History from Aesop to Harry Potter, 2008; The Wind in the Willows, 2009. **Address:** Division of Arts and Humanities, University of California, Rm. 410, Literature Bldg., 9500 Gilman Dr., Ste. 0406, La Jolla, CA 92093, U.S.A. **Online address:** slerer@ucsd.edu

LERMAN, Rhoda. American (born United States), b. 1936. **Genres:** Novels, Young Adult Fiction. **Career:** Syracuse University, instructor in English and parapsychology; Rock and Roll Band, manager. Writer. **Publications:** Call Me Ishtar, 1972; Girl That He Marries, 1976; Eleanor: A Novel, 1979; Book of the Night, 1984; God's Ear, 1989; Animal Acts: A Novel, 1994; In the Company of Newfies, 1996. **Address:** 135 Potter Hill Rd., Port Crane, NY 13833-1734, U.S.A.

LERNER, Barron H. American (born United States), b. 1960. **Genres:** Medicine/Health, History. **Career:** Columbia University, instructor, 1989-91, Mailman School of Public Health, assistant professor of medicine and public health, 1993-, associate professor of sociomedical sciences, College of Physicians and Surgeons, Angelica Berrie-Gold Foundation associate professor of medicine and public health, associate professor of medicine; Presbyterian Hospital, assistant physician, 1989-91, attending physician, 1993-; University of Washington, instructor, 1991-93; Department of Medicine Housestaff, director of ethics fellowship. Writer. **Publications:** Contagion and Confinement: Controlling Tuberculosis along the Skid Row, 1998; The Breast Cancer Wars: Hope, Fear and the Pursuit of a Cure in Twentieth-Century America, 2001; (intro.) Journal: A Mother and Daughter's Recovery from Breast Cancer, 2004; When Illness Goes Public: Celebrity Patients and How We Look at Medicine, 2006; One for The Road: Drunk Driving Since 1900, 2011. Contributor to journals and newspapers. **Address:** School of Public Health, Columbia University, 722 W 168th St., 9th Fl., New York, NY 10022, U.S.A. **Online address:** bhl5@columbia.edu

LERNER, Edward M. American (born United States), b. 1949?. **Genres:** Science Fiction/Fantasy. **Career:** Bell Labs, staff; Hughes Aircraft, staff; Honeywell, staff; Northrop Grumman, staff. Writer, physicist and computer specialist. **Publications:** On-line Filing (OLF) a Program Package for Student Records, 1973; Probe, 1991; Moonstruck, 2005; Fools' Experiments, 2008; Small Miracles, 2009. KNOWN SPACE SERIES: (with L. Niven) Fleet of Worlds, 2007; (with L. Niven) Juggler of Worlds, 2008; (with L. Niven) Destroyer of Worlds, 2009; (with L. Niven) Betrayer of Worlds, 2010. COLLECTIONS: Creative Destruction, 2006. Contributor to magazines. Works appear in anthologies. **Address:** Tom Doherty Associates L.L.C., 175 5th Ave., New York, NY 10010, U.S.A. **Online address:** e_lerner@yahoo.com

LERNER, Eric. American (born United States) **Genres:** Novels, Young Adult

Fiction. **Career:** Critical Condition, producer, 1987; Buddhist journal Zero, editor. Producer. **Publications:** Journey of Insight Meditation: A Personal Experience of the Buddha's Way, 1977; Pinkerton's Secret (novel), 2008. **Address:** c/o Eleanor Jackson, Queen Literary Agency, 850 7th Ave., Ste. 704, New York, NY 10019, U.S.A. **Online address:** info@pinkertonssecret.com

LERNER, Eric J. (Eric John Lerner). American (born United States), b. 1947. **Genres:** Novels. **Career:** Colliers Encyclopedia, assistant editor, 1972-74; Lerner Associates, president, 1974; High Tech, contributing editor, 1979-80; IEEE Spectrum, contributing editor, 1980-84; Aerospace America, electronics editor, 1984-90; Lawrenceville Plasma Physics Inc., president, 1985-; Focus Fusions Society, executive director, 2002; European Southern Observatory, visiting astronomer, 2006. **Publications:** The Big Bang Never Happened: A Startling Refutation of the Dominant Theory of the Universe, 1992; (ed. with J.B. Almeida) 1st Crisis in Cosmology Conference, CCC-I, Monao, Portugal, 23-25 June 2005, 2006. Contributor of articles. **Address:** Lawrenceville Plasma Physics, 9 Tower Pl., Lawrenceville, NJ 08648, U.S.A. **Online address:** elerner@igc.org

LERNER, Eric John. *See* **LERNER, Eric J.**

LERNER, Harriet. American (born United States), b. 1944. **Genres:** Children's Non-fiction, Human Relations/Parenting, Psychology, Self Help, Women's Studies And Issues. **Career:** Menninger Clinic, staff psychologist and psychotherapist, 1972-2001. Writer. **Publications:** FOR CHILDREN: (with S. Goldhor) What's So Terrible about Swallowing an Apple Seed?, 1996; (with S. Goldhor) Franny B. Kranny, There's a Bird in Your Hair!, 2001. FOR ADULTS: The Dance of Anger: A Woman's Guide to Changing the Patterns of Intimate Relationships, 1985; Women in Therapy, 1989; The Dance of Intimacy: A Woman's Guide to Courageous Acts of Change in Key Relationships, 1990; The Dance of Deception: Pretending and Truth-Telling in Women's Lives, 1993; Life Preservers: Good Advice When You Need It Most, 1997; The Mother Dance: How Children Change Your Life, 1998; The Dance of Connection: How to Talk to Someone When You're Mad, Hurt, Scared, Frustrated, Insulted, Betrayed or Desperate, 2001; The Dance of Fear: Rising Above Anxiety, Fear and Shame to Be Your Best and Bravest Self, 2005. Contributor of articles to journals. **Address:** Worley Shoemaker Literary Management, 6665 Milhaven Dr., Mission, MO 66202, U.S.A. **Online address:** jolynne.worley@gmail.com

LERNER, Henry M. American (born United States) **Genres:** Medicine/Health, Psychology. **Career:** Newton-Wellesley Obstetrics & Gynecology P.C., founder, president; Women's Urinary Continence Center, director; Pro-Mutual Insurance Co., board directors; Lms Medical Systems Inc., head of clinical development; Harvard Medical School, clinical instructor. Physician and author. **Publications:** Miscarriage: A Doctor's Guide to the Facts: Why It Happens and How Best to Reduce Your Risks, 2003. **Address:** Newton-Wellesley Obstetrics & Gynecology P.C., 2000 Washington St., Ste. 768, Newton, MA 02462, U.S.A. **Online address:** hmlerner@henrylerner.com

LERNER, Laurence (David). British/South African (born South Africa), b. 1925. **Genres:** Novels, Poetry, Literary Criticism And History, Humor/Satire, Romance/Historical. **Career:** Grammar school teacher, 1946-47; University College (now University of Ghana), lecturer in English, 1949-53; Queens University, lecturer in English, 1953-62; Earlham College, visiting professor of English, 1960-61; University of Connecticut, visiting professor of English, 1960-61; University of Sussex, lecturer, professor of English, 1962-84; University of Illinois, visiting professor of English, 1964; University of Dijon, visiting professor of English, 1967; University of Munich, visiting professor of English, 1968-69, 1974-75; University of Paris III, visiting professor of English, 1983; University of Ottawa, visiting professor of English, 1983; Vanderbilt University, Kenan professor of English, Edwin Mims professor of English, 1985-95. Writer. **Publications:** The Englishmen, 1959; Domestic Interior and Other Poems, 1959; The Truest Poetry: An Essay on the Question, What Is Literature?, 1960; The Directions of Memory: Poems 1958-63, 1963; The Truthtellers: Jane Austen, George Eliot and D.H. Lawrence, 1967; A Free Man: A Novel, 1968; Selves: Poems, 1969; The Uses of Nostalgia: Studies in Pastoral Poetry, 1972; An Introduction to English Poetry: Fifteen Poems Discussed by Laurence Lerner, 1974; A.R.T.H.U.R.: The Life and Opinions of a Digital Computer, 1975; Thomas Hardys The Mayor of Casterbridge: Tragedy or Social History?, 1975; Love and Marriage: Literature in Its Social Context, 1979; The Man I Killed, 1980; A.R.T.H.U.R. and M.A.R.T.H.A.:

Or The Loves of the Computers, 1980; The Literary Imagination: Essays on Literature and Society, 1982; A Dialogue, 1983; Chapter and Verse: Bible Poems, 1984; Selected Poems, 1984; My Grandfathers Grandfather, 1985; Rembrandts Mirror, 1987; The Frontiers of Literature, 1988; Angels & Absences: Child Deaths in the 19th Century, 1997; Philip Larkin, 1997; (trans.) Baudelaire: Selected Poems, 1999; Wandering Professor, 1999; Reading Womens Poetry, 2009. EDITOR: Selected Poems, 1953; English Literature: An Interpretation for Students Abroad, 1954; Shakespeares Tragedies: A Selection of Modern Criticism, 1963 in US as Shakespeares Comedies: An Anthology of Modern Criticism, 1967; (with J. Holmstrom) George Eliot and Her Readers: A Selection of Contemporary Reviews, 1966; Shakespeares Comedies, 1967; (with J. Holmstrom) Thomas Hardy and His Readers: A Selection of Contemporary Reviews, 1968; The Context of English Literature: The Victorians, 1978; Reconstructing Literature, 1983; (with V. Bell) On Modern Poetry: Essays Presented to Donald Davie, 1988. OTHER: (trans.) Spleen: Poems, 1967. Contributor of articles to periodicals and magazines. **Address:** Abinger, 1-b Gundreda Rd., Lewes, ES BN7 1PT, England. **Online address:** laurencelerner@tiscali.co.uk

LERNER, Martin. American (born United States), b. 1936. **Genres:** Art/Art History, Travel/Exploration, Photography. **Career:** University of California, assistant professor, 1965-66; Cleveland Museum of Art, assistant curator of oriental art, 1966-72; Case Western Reserve University, adjunct assistant professor, 1968-72; Metropolitan Museum of Art, vice chair in charge of far Eastern art, 1972-75, curator, 1978-; Columbia University, adjunct professor, 2004-. Writer. **Publications:** Indian Miniatures from the Jeffrey Paley Collection: August 6-September 30, 1974, 1974; Bronze Sculptures from Asia, 1975; Blue and White: Early Japanese Export Ware, 1978; The Flame and the Lotus: Indian and Southeast Asian Art from the Kronos Collections, 1984; (with W. Felten) Thai and Cambodian Sculpture from the Sixth to the Fourteenth Centuries, 1989; (with W. Felten) Entdeckungen: Skulpturen der Khmer und Thai, 1989; (with S. Kossak) The Lotus Transcendent: Indian and Southeast Asian Art from the Samuel Eilenberg Collection, 1991; Ancient Khumer Sculpture, 1994. **Address:** Metropolitan Museum of Art, 1000 5th Ave., New York, NY 10028, U.S.A.

LERNER, Michael A. American (born United States) **Genres:** History, Social Sciences. **Career:** Bard High School Early College Manhattan, associate dean of studies, social studies faculty, principal, dean of studies. Writer. **Publications:** Dry Manhattan: Prohibition in New York City, 2007. **Address:** Bard High School Early College, 525 E Huston St., New York, NY 10002, U.S.A. **Online address:** lerner@bard.edu

LERNER, Robert E(arl). American (born United States), b. 1940. **Genres:** History, Theology/Religion. **Career:** Princeton University, instructor in history, 1963-64; Western Reserve University, assistant professor of history, 1964-67; Northwestern University, assistant professor, 1967-71, associate professor, 1971-76, professor of history, 1976-2008, emeritus professor of history, 2008-, Humanities Program, director, 1981-83, Peter B. Ritzma professor in the humanities, 1993-2008, Ritzma emeritus professor in the humanities, 2008-. Writer. **Publications:** The Age of Adversity: Europe in the Fourteenth Century, 1968; The Heresy of the Free Spirit in the Later Middle Ages, 1972, 2nd ed., 1991; (contrib.) One Thousand Years: Western Europe in the Middle Ages, 1974; (co-author) Western Civilizations: Their History and Their Culture, 9th ed., 1980, 15th ed., 2005; The Powers of Prophecy: The Cedar of Lebanon Vision from the Mongol Onslaught to the Dawn of the Enlightenment, 1983; (co-author) Johannes de Rupescissa, 1994; (intro.) Liber Secretorum Eventuum, 1994; Refrigerio dei Santi: Gioacchino da Fiore e L'escatologia Medievale, 1995; Neue Richtungen in der hochund Spätmittelalterlichen Bibelexegese, 1996; The Feast of Saint Abraham: Medieval Millenarians and the Jews, 2001; Scrutare il futuro, 2008. Contributor to periodicals. **Address:** Department of History, Northwestern University, Harris Hall, Ste. L20, Evanston, IL 60201, U.S.A. **Online address:** rlerner@northwestern.edu

LERNER, Steve. American (born United States), b. 1946. **Genres:** Environmental Sciences/Ecology, Natural History, Economics. **Career:** Village Voice, staff writer, 1968-69; Commonweal, research director, 1975-. **Publications:** The CYA Report: Conditions of Life at the California Youth Authority, 1982; Bodily Harm: The Pattern of Fear and Violence at the California Youth Authority, 1986; State-raised: Kids No One Wants: Acting-out Adolescents in New York City's Group Foster-Care Facilities, 1988; The Good News about Juvenile Justice, 1990; The Geography of Foster Care: Keeping Children in the Neighborhood, 1990; Earth Summit: Conversations with Architects of an

Ecologically Sustainable Future, 1991; Beyond the Earth Summit: Conversations with Advocates of Sustainable Development, 1992; Eco-pioneers: Practical Visionaries Solving Today's Environmental Problems, 1997; (with W. Poole) The Economic Benefits of Parks and Open Space: How Land Conservation Helps Communities Grow Smart and Protect the Bottom Line, 1999; Diamond: A Struggle for Environmental Justice in Louisiana's Chemical Corridor, 2005; Sacrifice Zones: The Front Lines of Toxic Chemical Exposure in the United States, 2010. Contributor to periodicals. **Address:** Commonweal, PO Box 316, Bolinas, CA 94924-0316, U.S.A. **Online address:** sdlerner@aol.com

LEROI, Armand Marie. Dutch/New Zealander (born New Zealand), b. 1964. **Genres:** Documentaries/Reportage, Sciences, Genealogy/Heraldry. **Career:** Imperial College London, lecturer, 1996-2001, reader in evolutionary developmental biology, 2001-, professor of evolutionary developmental biology. Writer. **Publications:** Mutants: On Genetic Variety and the Human Body, 2003; Mutants: On the Form, Varieties and Errors of the Human Body, 2003. Contributor to periodicals and journals. **Address:** Department of Life Sciences, Imperial College London, S Block, Silwood Park Campus, Buckhurst Rd., Ascot, BR SL5 7PY, England. **Online address:** a.leroi@imperial.ac.uk

LEROUX-HUGON, Hélène. French (born France), b. 1955. **Genres:** Children's Fiction, Art/Art History, Illustrations, Animals/Pets. **Career:** Madeleine (private art school), teacher, 1978-86; writer and illustrator, 1983-; Lycée St. Pierre la Joliverie, art teacher, 1999-; Ravensburger (publisher), graphic artist and design director, 2000-; Artkids (children's art magazine), production supervisor, 2001-. **Publications:** J'AIME DESSINER SERIES IN ENGLISH AS I CAN DRAW ANIMALS SERIES: J'aime dessiner les animaux d'Afrique, 1997; J'aime dessiner les animaux de nos régions, 1997; J'aime dessiner les animaux de la forêt, 1998; J'aime dessiner les animaux sauvage, 1998; J'aime dessiner les animaux du froid, 1999; J'aime dessiner les animaux de la campagne, 2001; I Can Draw Polar Animals, 2001; I Can Draw Forest Animals, 2001; I Can Draw Country Animals, 2001; I Can Draw Wild Animals, 2001; Art Foam Fun, 2006; (with J. Vicart) Paper Cutouts, 2007. SELF-ILLUSTRATED IN FRENCH: Petits ateliers au fil des saisons, 1993; Gouache: jeux et décors peints, 1994; Fleurs fruits et couronnes, 1994; Masques en papiers pour jouer, 1996; Collages, 1996; Pochoirs: premiers pas, 1997; Vite on se déguise, 1997; Douces mousses, 1997; Ma ferme pâte à modeler, 1998; (with N. Seret) Déguisements pour tous, 1998. Contributor to books. **Address:** 12 rue des Martyrs, Nantes, 44100, France. **Online address:** helene.lerouxhugon@caramail.com

LEROY, Greg. American (born United States) **Genres:** Adult Non-fiction, Business/Trade/Industry. **Career:** Good Jobs First, founder, 1998, director, executive director. Writer. **Publications:** NONFICTION: Research Centers: The Pentagon Moves the High-Tech Battlefield on Campus, 1988; Pantex: Practices, Policy, and Environmental Impact of the Final Assembly Point for all U.S. Nuclear Weapons, 1988; No More Candy Store: States and Cities Making Job Subsidies Accountable, 1994; The Great American Jobs Scam: Corporate Tax Dodging and the Myth of Job Creation, 2005. **Address:** Good Jobs First, 1616 P St. NW, Ste. 210, Washington, DC 20036, U.S.A. **Online address:** goodjobs@goodjobsfirst.org

LEROY, Margaret. American (born United States) **Genres:** Novels, Young Adult Fiction, Young Adult Non-fiction. **Career:** Music therapist, teacher and writer. **Publications:** NONFICTION: Miscarriage, 1987; Trust, 1999; Alysson's Shoes, 2002. FICTION: Aristotle Sludge: A Modern-Day Dinosaur (juvenile), 1991; Pleasure: The Truth about Female Sexuality, 1993; Some Girls Do: Why Women Do and Don't Make the First Move, 1997. NOVELS: Postcards from Berlin: A Novel, 2003; The River House: A Novel, 2005; The Soldier's Wife, 2011. OTHER: Yes, My Darling Daughter, 2009; The Perfect Mother, 2010; The Collaborator, 2011. **Address:** c/o Kathleen Anderson, Anderson Literary Management, 12 W 19th St., 2nd Fl., New York, NY 10011, U.S.A. **Online address:** info@margaretleroy.com

LESCH, David W. American (born United States), b. 1960. **Genres:** Politics/Government, History, Biography. **Career:** Northeastern University, instructor in history, 1987; Johns Hopkins University, instructor in history at extension school, 1988, 1989; University of Maryland, instructor, 1990, adjunct professor of history, 1991; St. Mary's College, visiting assistant professor of Middle East history, 1991-92; Johns Hopkins University, adjunct professor of Middle East history, 1992; Trinity University, Department of History, Middle East History, associate professor, 1992-, professor, John Rogers fac-

ulty fellow, 1995-97, Middle East Concentration, International Studies Program, coordinator; National Public Radio, commentator; Christian Science Monitor Radio, commentator; BBC, commentator; CBS Radio, commentator; Middle East International Business Associates Inc., president. Writer. **Publications:** Syria and the United States: Eisenhower's Cold War in the Middle East, 1992; (ed.) The Middle East and the United States: A Historical and Political Reassessment, 1996, (with M.L. Haas) 5th ed. as The Middle East and the United States: History, Politics, and Ideologies, 2011; 1979: The Year that Shaped the Modern Middle East, 2001; New Lion of Damascus: Bashar al-Asad and Modern Syria, 2005; Arab-Israeli Conflict: A History, 2008. Contributor of articles to journals. **Address:** Department of History, Trinity University, 1 Trinity Pl., San Antonio, TX 78212-7200, U.S.A. **Online address:** dlesch@trinity.edu

LESCH, John E(mmett). American (born United States), b. 1945. **Genres:** History, Sciences, Medicine/Health. **Career:** University of California, Department of History, assistant professor, associate professor, 1977-95, professor, 1995-, now professor emeritus. Writer. **Publications:** Science and Medicine in France: The Emergence of Experimental Physiology, 1790-1855, 1984; (ed.) German Chemical Industry in the 20th Century, 2000; First Miracle Drugs: How the Sulfa Drugs Transformed Medicine, 2007. Contributor to journals and periodicals. **Address:** Department of History, University of California, Berkeley, CA 94720-2550, U.S.A. **Online address:** jlesch@berkeley.edu

LESCROART, John T. American (born United States), b. 1948. **Genres:** Mystery/Crime/Suspense, Novels, Horror. **Career:** Professional singer and guitarist, 1972-77; Guitar Player, editor and advertising director, 1977-79; Guardians of the Jewish Homes for the Aging, associate director, 1979-83; A.T. Kearney Inc., technical writer and associate consultant, 1982-85; Pettit & Martin, word processor and legal administrator, 1985-91; writer, 1991-; CrowArt Records, founder and owner. **Publications:** NOVELS: Sunburn, 1982; Dead Irish, 1989; The Vig, 1990; The 13th Juror, 1994; A Certain Justice, 1995; The Mercy Rule, 1998; (co-author) Natural Suspect, 2001; (with L.D. Estleman) Writing the Popular Novel, 2004; Betrayal: A Novel, 2008; A Plague of Secrets: A Novel, 2009; Treasure Hunt, 2010; The Hunter, 2012. CRIME AND MYSTERY: Son of Holmes: A Fiction, 1986; Rasputin's Revenge: The Further Startling Adventures of Auguste Lupa Son of Holmes, 1987; Hard Evidence, 1993; Son of Holmes and Rasputin's Revenge: The Early Works of John T. Lescroart, 1995; Guilt, 1997; Nothing but the Truth, 1999; The Hearing, 2001; The Oath, 2002; The First Law, 2003; The Second Chair, 2004; The Motive, 2005; Hunt Club, 2006; The Suspect, 2007; Damage, 2011. **Address:** 426 D St., Davis, CA 95616-4131, U.S.A. **Online address:** john_lescroart@mail.vresp.com

LESEUR, Geta. American/Jamaican (born Jamaica) **Genres:** Anthropology/Ethnology, Literary Criticism And History, Third World, Women's Studies And Issues. **Career:** Indiana University, Afro-American Studies, associate instructor, 1975-82; Arizona State University, writing instructor, 1978; Colgate University, assistant professor of English and Africana studies, 1984-85; University of Arizona, adjunct professor of black studies, 1986-87; University of California, African-American Studies, fellow, 1987-88; University of Missouri, assistant professor, 1988-94, Wakonse fellow, 1991, associate professor of English, women's studies and adjunct faculty in black studies, 1994-, Black Arts Ensemble, founding faculty, 1994-; Midwest Modern Language Association, African-American Literature Section, chair, 1992; University of Western Cape, visiting professor, 1993, 1997; Spelman College, visiting professor, 1995. Writer. **Publications:** Ten Is the Age of Darkness: The Black Bildungsroman (literary criticism), 1995; Not All Okies Are White: The Lives of Black Cotton Pickers in Arizona, 2000; Decolonization, Developing Selves: Youth Literature and Fictions of Childhood in South Africa and Developing Nations, forthcoming. Contributor of articles to periodicals. **Address:** Department of Africana Studies, University of Arizona, Rm. 223, Learning Services Bldg., PO Box 210105, Tucson, AZ 85721-0105, U.S.A. **Online address:** getal@email.arizona.edu

LESIKAR, Raymond Vincent. American (born United States), b. 1922. **Genres:** Writing/Journalism. **Career:** Douglas Aircraft Co., department clerk, 1941-42; Sears, Roebuck & Co., management trainee, 1947; Texas Christian University, instructor, 1948-49; University of Texas, assistant professor, 1949-54; Louisiana State University, associate professor, 1954-59, professor 1960-77, emeritus professor of management, 1977-; University of North Texas, professor, 1979-87, head; University of International Business and Economics, professor, 1983; Association for Business Communication, president; International Society for General Semantics, president; Southwest Social Science Association, president; Southwestern Association for Administrative Disciplines, director; educator, consultant and writer. **Publications:** Development of a Statistical Procedure for Estimating Farm Cash Income & Texas Farm Cash Income, 1927-1953, 1954; (with R.D. Hay) Business Report Writing, 1957; (with W.P. Boyd) Productive Business Writing, 1959; Needs of Education for Small Business, Based on a 1959 Survey of Louisiana Businessmen, 1961; Report Writing for Business, 1961, 10th ed., 1998; Business Communication: Theory and Application, 1968, (with M.E. Flatley and K. Rentz) 11th ed. as Business Communication: Making Connections in a Digital World, 2008; (with W. Perlick) Introduction to Business: A Societal Approach, 1972, 3rd ed., 1979; How to Write a Report your Boss will Read and Remember, 1974, rev. ed., 1984; How to Write a Report, 1974; Lesikar's Basic Business Communication, 1979, (with J.D. Pettit and M.E. Flatley) 8th ed., 1999; Basic business communication, 1979, (with M.E. Flatley) 10th ed. as Basic Business Communication: Skills for Empowering the Internet Generation, 2005. **Address:** PO Box 7912, Horseshoe Bay, TX 78657, U.S.A. **Online address:** lesikar@tstar.net

LESJAK, Carolyn. Canadian (born Canada), b. 1963. **Genres:** Literary Criticism And History, History. **Career:** Swarthmore College, associate professor of English; Simon Fraser University, Department of English, associate professor and graduate chair. Writer. **Publications:** (Contrib.) The Edinburgh Encyclopedia of Modern Criticism and Theory, 2002; Working Fictions: A Genealogy of the Victorian Novel, 2006. Contributor to periodicals. **Address:** Department of English, Simon Fraser University, AQ 6118, 8888 University Dr., Burnaby, BC V5A 1S6, Canada. **Online address:** clesjak@sfu.ca

LESLIE, John. American (born United States), b. 1944. **Genres:** Mystery/Crime/Suspense, Romance/Historical. **Career:** Writer. **Publications:** NOVELS: Blood on the Keys, 1988; Bounty Hunter Blues, 1989; Killer in Paradise, 1991; Damaged Goods, 1993; Havana Hustle, 1993; GIDEON LOWRY CRIME NOVELS: Killing Me Softly: A Gideon Lowry Mystery, 1994; Night and Day: A Gideon Lowry Mystery, 1995; Love for Sale: A Gideon Lowry Mystery, 1996; Blue Moon: A Gideon Lowry Mystery, 1998. **Address:** Loretta Barrett Books Inc., 101 5th Ave., 11th Fl., New York, NY 10003, U.S.A.

LESLIE, Kent A. American (born United States), b. 1942. **Genres:** Biography, Autobiography/Memoirs, Adult Non-fiction. **Career:** City University of New York, Queens College, instructor in biology, 1961-64; Emory University, instructor in preventive medicine, 1967-68, teacher, 1991-92; Oglethorpe University, assistant professor of women's studies, 1993-, administrative director of women's studies, 1994-. Writer. **Publications:** Woman of Color, Daughter of Privilege: Amanda America Dickson, 1849-1893, 1995. Contributor to books and journals. **Address:** Oglethorpe University, 4484 Peachtree Rd. NE, Atlanta, GA 30319-2797, U.S.A. **Online address:** kleslie@igc.org

LESLIE, Roger (James). American (born United States), b. 1961. **Genres:** Novels, Adult Non-fiction, Biography, Education. **Career:** Galena Park Independent School District, teacher, 1985-96, librarian, 1996-2000, 2002-. Freelance writer, writing coach and public speaker. **Publications:** (With S.E. Edwards) Galena Park: The Community that Shaped Its Own History, 1993; (with P.P. Wilson) Premiere Events: Library Programs that Inspire Elementary School Patrons, 2001; (with P.P. Wilson) Igniting the Spark: Library Programs that Inspire High School Patrons, 2001; (with P.P. Wilson) Center Stage: Library Programs that Inspire Middle School Patrons, 2002; Drowning in Secret, 2002; Isak Dinesen, Gothic Storyteller, 2004; Success Express for Teens: 50 Activities that Will Change Your Life, 2004; Film Stars and Their Awards: Who Won What for Movies, Theater and Television, 2008; (with P.P. Wilson) Eagle on Ice: Eagle Scout Paul Siple's Antarctic Adventures with Commander Byrd, 2008; Five Minutes from Home, forthcoming. Contributor to periodicals. **Address:** c/o Author Mail, Bayou Publishing, 2524 Nottingham St., Houston, TX 77005-1412, U.S.A. **Online address:** roger@rogerleslie.com

LESLIE, Ward S. See **WARD, Elizabeth Honor.**

LESOURNE, Jacques. French (born France), b. 1928. **Genres:** Economics, History, International Relations/Current Affairs, Social Sciences, Politics/Government. **Career:** Charbonnages de France, Economic Department, chief, 1954-57; SEMA and METRA International Group, chief executive officer and chairman, 1958-75; Conservatoire National des Arts et Métiers (CNAM), chair of economics and industrial statistics, 1974-98, professor of

economics, 1974-98, now professor emeritus; Organization for Economic Cooperation and Development, Interfutures Project, director, 1976-79; French Association of Economics, chairman, 1981-83; Le Monde, chief executive officer, 1991-94. Writer. **Publications:** Technique économique et gestion industrielle, 1958; Economic Technique and Industrial Management, 1959; Le calcul économique, 1964; Du bon usage de l'étude économique dans l'entreprise, 1966; étude économique dans l'entreprise, 1968; (with R. Armand and R. Lattès) Matière grise, année zéro: Essai, 1970; (with R. Armand and R. Lattès) The Management Revolution: Management Consultancy and Computer-Aided Decision Making, 1972; Modèles de croissance des entreprises, 1973; Systèmes du destin, 1976; A Theory of the Individual for Economic Analysis, 1977; Notion de système et les sciences sociales: une prudente espérance: Communication, 1977; (with R. Loué) L'analyse des décisions d'aménagement régional, 1979; Demain, la France dans le monde, 1980; Colloque CNRS Analyse de systeme, 1980; Les mille sentiers de L'avenir, 1981; Soirs et lendemains de fête: journal d'un homme tranquille, 1981-1984, 1984; (with M. Godet) Fin des habitudes, 1985; Gestion des villes: analyse des décisions d'économie urbaine, 1985; Entreprise et ses futurs: comment la voient les chefs d'entreprise, comment l'imagine la prospective, 1985; World perspectives, 1986; Education et société: les défis de l'an 2000, 1988; (co-author) Europe and Japan Facing High Technologies: From Conflict to Cooperation?, 1989; (with B. Lecomte) De l'Atlantique à l'Oural: l'après communism, 1990; Economie de L'ordre et du désordre, 1991; (with B. Lecomte) After Communism, 1991; Economics of Order and Disorder: The Market as Organizer and Creator 1992; Où va l'Etat?: la souveraineté économique et politique enquestion, 1992; (co-author) Scénarios pour l'emploi, 1995; Vérités et mensonges sur le chômage, 1995; Modèle français: grandeur et décadence, 1998; Homme de notre siècle: de Polytechnique à la prospective et au journal Le Mond, 2000; Ces avenirs qui n'ont pas eu lieu: une relecture du XXe siècle contemporain, 2001; (co-author) Leçons de microécunomie évolutionniste, 2002; Démocratie, marché, gouvernance: quels avenirs?, 2004; (ed. with A. Bravo and D. Randet) Avenirs de la recherche et de l'innovation en France, 2004; (co-author) Evolutionary Microeconomics, 2006; Les Crises et le XXIe Siècle, 2009; Un temps d'immobilité, 2009. **Address:** Conservatoire National des Arts et Métiers, 2 Rue Conté, Paris, 75003, France. **Online address:** jolesourne@wanadoo.fr

LESSER, Wendy. American (born United States), b. 1952. **Genres:** Literary Criticism And History, Novels, Essays, Biography, Autobiography/Memoirs. **Career:** Lesser & Ogden Associates, partner, 1977-81; Threepenny Review, founding editor, 1980-. Consultant. **Publications:** The Life Below the Ground: A Study of the Subterranean in Literature and History, 1987; His Other Half: Men Looking at Women Through Art, 1991; (ed. and intro.) Hiding in Plain Sight: Essays in Criticism and Autobiography, 1993; Pictures at an Execution: An Inquiry into the Subject of Murder, 1993; A Director Calls, 1997; The Amateur: An Independent Life of Letters, 1999; (contrib. with J. Acocella) Mark Morris's L'allegro, il penseroso ed il moderato: A Celebration (essays), 2001; Nothing Remains the Same: Rereading and Remembering, 2002; (ed. and intro.) Genius of Language: Fifteen Writers Reflect on Their Mother Tongues, 2004; The Pagoda in the Garden: A Novel in Three Parts, 2005; Room for Doubt, 2007; Music for Silenced Voices: Shostakovich and His Fifteen Quartets, 2011. Contributor to periodicals. **Address:** Threepenny Review, PO Box 9131, Berkeley, CA 94709, U.S.A. **Online address:** wlesser@threepennyreview.com

LESSING, Doris (May). (Jane Somers). British/Iranian (born Iran), b. 1919. **Genres:** Novels, Novellas/Short Stories, Science Fiction/Fantasy, Plays/Screenplays, Poetry, Autobiography/Memoirs, Young Adult Non-fiction, Literary Criticism And History, Essays, Education. **Career:** Writer. **Publications:** NOVELS: The Grass is Singing, 1950; Martha Quest, 1952; A Proper Marriage, 1954; Retreat to Innocence, 1956; A Ripple from the Storm, 1958; The Golden Notebook, 1962; Children of Violence, 1964; Landlocked, 1965; The Four-Gated City, 1969; Briefing for a Descent into Hell, 1971; The Summer Before The Dark, 1973; The Memoirs of a Survivor, 1974; Doris Lessing, 1976; Stories, 1978; Re Colonised Planet 5, Shikasta, 1979; A Garland for Jack Lindsay, 1980; The Marriages between Zones Three, Four, and Five, 1980; The Sirian Experiments: The Report By Ambien II, Of The Five, 1981; The Making of the Preresentative for Planet 8, 1982; Documents Relating to the Sentimental Agents in the Volyen Empire, 1983; The Good Terrorist, 1985; The Fifth Child, 1988; Through The Tunnel, 1990; Canopus in Argos: Archives, 1992; Love Again, 1996; Mara and Dann, 1999; Ben, in the World:

The Sequel to The Fifth Child, 2000; The Old Age of El Magnifico, 2000; The Sweetest Dream, 2001; The Grandmothers: Four Short Novels, 2003; A Home For The Highland Cattle: And The Antheap, 2003; Time Bites: Views and Reviews, 2004; The Story Of General Dann and Mara's Daughter, Griot and the Snow Dog: A Novel, 2005; The Cleft, 2007; Alfred and Emily, 2008; On Cats, 2008. SHORT STORIES: This Was The Old Chief's Country, 1952; Five: Short Novels, 1953; The Habit of Loving, 1957; A Man and Two Women, 1963; African Stories, 1965; Winter in July, 1966; The Story of a Non-Marrying Man and Other Stories, 1972; The Temptation of Jack Orkney and Other Stories, 1972; The Sun between Their Feet, 1973; The Black Madonna, 1974; Sunrise on the Veld, 1975; A Mild Attack of the Locusts, 1977; To Room Nineteen, 1978; London Observed: Stories and Sketches in US as The Real Thing, 1992. NON-FICTION: Going Home, 1957, rev. ed., 1998; In Pursuit of the English, 1960; Particularly Cats, 1967; Prisons We Choose to Live Inside, 1987; The Wind Blows Away Our Words, 1987; Particularly Cats and More Cats, 1989; Particularly Cats.and Rufus, 1991; African Laughter: Four Visits to Zimbabwe, 1992; Under My Skin, 1994; Walking in the Shade, 1997. OTHERS: Fourteen Poems, 1959; A Small Personal Voice (essays and interviews), 1974; The Making of the Representative for Planet 8 (libretto for opera), 1988; Doris Lessing Reader, 1988; Putting the Questions Differently: Interviews with Doris Lessing, 1964-1994, 1996. AS JANE SOMERS: The Diary of a Good Neighbour, 1983; If the Old Could, 1984. **Address:** Jonathan Clowes Ltd., 10 Iron Bridge House, Bridge Approach, London, GL NW1 8BD, England.

LESSNOFF, Michael. Scottish (born Scotland), b. 1940. **Genres:** Politics/Government, Philosophy, Social Sciences, Humanities. **Career:** University of Glasgow, faculty, 1966-86, reader in politics, 1986-2005. Writer. **Publications:** The Structure of Social Science: A Philosophical Introduction, 1974; Social Contract, 1986; (ed.) Social Contract Theory, 1990; The Spirit of Capitalism and the Protestant Ethic, 1994; (with W.L. Miller and A.M. Timpson) Political Culture in Contemporary Britain: People and Politicians, Principles and Practice, 1996; Political Philosophers of the Twentieth Century, 1999; Ernest Gellner and Modernity, 2002. **Address:** Department of Politics, University of Glasgow, Adam Smith Bldg., Glasgow, G12 8QQ, Scotland. **Online address:** michael.lessnoff@glasgow.ac.uk

LESTER, Connie L. American (born United States), b. 1946?. **Genres:** Agriculture/Forestry, History. **Career:** Middle Tennessee State University, adjunct instructor, 1996-98, visiting assistant professor of history, 1998; Mississippi State University, assistant professor of history, 1999-2005; University of Central Florida, assistant professor of history; Florida Historical Quarterly, editor, 2005-. **Publications:** Up from the Mudsills of Hell: The Farmers' Alliance, Populism, and Progressive Agriculture in Tennessee, 1870-1915, 2006. Works appear in anthologies. Contributor of articles to journals. **Address:** Department of History, University of Central Florida, 551 Colbourn Hall (CNH), 4000 Central Florida Blvd., Orlando, FL 32816-1350, U.S.A. **Online address:** clester@mail.ucf.edu

LESTER, David. American/British (born England), b. 1942. **Genres:** Psychiatry, Psychology, Humanities. **Career:** Wellesley College, instructor, 1967-68, assistant professor of psychology, 1968-69; Suicide Prevention and Crisis Service, research director, 1969-71, advisor; Richard Stockton College, associate professor, 1971-74, professor of psychology, 1975-, chair of department, 1971-74, coordinator of criminal justice program, 1977-78, distinguished professor of psychology; Center for the Study of Suicide, executive director, 1993-; International Association for Suicide Prevention, president. Writer. **Publications:** Explorations in Exploration, 1969; (with G. Lester) Suicide: The Gamble with Death, 1971; Why People Kill Themselves, 1972, 4th ed., 2000; Comparative Psychology, 1973; A Physiological Basis for Personality Traits, 1974; Unusual Sexual Behavior, 1975; (with G. Lester) Crime of Passion, 1975; The Use of Alternative Modes for Communication in Psychotherapy, 1977; The Psychological Basis for Handwriting Analysis, 1980; (with B. Sell and K. Sell) Suicide: A Guide to Information Sources, 1980; Psychotherapy for Offenders, 1981; (with M. Murell) Introduction to Juvenile Delinquency, 1981; The Structure of the Mind, 1982; (with A. Levitt) Insanity and Incompetence, 1984; Gun Control, 1984; The Murderer and His Murder, 1986; The Death Penalty, 1987, 2nd ed., 1998; Suicide as a Learned Behavior, 1987; The Biochemical Basis of Suicide, 1988; Suicide from a Psychological Perspective, 1988; Why Women Kill Themselves, 1988; Can We Prevent Suicide?, 1989; Questions and Answers about Suicide, 1989; Suicide from a Sociological Perspective, 1989; (with R.V. Clarke) Suicide: Closing

the Exits, 1989; Understanding and Preventing Suicide, 1990; Questions and Answers about Murder, 1991; Psychotherapy for Suicidal Clients, 1991; (with M. Braswell) Correctional Counseling, 1987, (with M. Braswell and P. Van Voorhis) 7th ed. as Correctional Counseling Rehabilitation, 2009; (with B.L. Danto) Suicide behind Bars, 1993; The Cruelest Death, 1993; Suicide in Creative Women, 1993; Understanding Suicide, 1993; Patterns of Suicide and Homicide in America, 1994; Theories of Personality, 1995; Serial Killers, 1995; Patterns of Suicide and Homicide in the World, 1996; An Encyclopedia of Famous Suicides, 1996; Making Sense of Suicide, 1997; (with B. Yang) The Economy and Suicide, 1997; Suicide in American Indians, 1997; Suicide in African Americans, 1998; (with B. Yang) Suicide and Homicide in the 20th Century, 1998; Crime and the Native American, 1999; By Their Own Hand, 2000; Fixin' to Die, 2003; Mass Murder, 2004; (with M. Lindsay) Suicide by Cop, 2004; Thinking about Suicide, 2004; Is There Life after Death?, 2005; Suicide and the Holocaust, 2005; Exit Weeping: Understanding Suicide Through the Study of Famous Suicides, 2008; (with C. Tartaro) Suicide and Self-Harm in Prisons and Jails, 2009; Preventing Suicide: Closing the Exits Revisited, 2009; Multiple Self Theory of Personality, 2010. EDITOR: Crisis Intervention and Counseling by Telephone, 1973, 2nd ed., 2003; Gambling Today, 1979; The Elderly Victim of Crime, 1981; Suicide, 1988-95; Current Concepts of Suicide, 1990; (with M. Tallmer) Now I Lay Me Down, 1994; Emile Durkheim: Le Suicide 100 Years Later, 1994; (with S. Canetto) Women and Suicidal Behavior, 1995; (with A. Leenaars) Suicide and the Unconscious, 1996; Suicide Prevention, 2001; Katie's Diary, 2004; (with R. Yufit) Assessment, Treatment and Prevention of Suicidal Behavior, 2005; (with S. Stack) Suicide and the Creative Arts, 2009; (with D.A. Lamis) Understanding and Preventing College Student Suicide, 2011. **Address:** Psychology Program, Richard Stockton College, Rm. H251, Jimmie Leeds Rd., Pomona, NJ 08240-0195, U.S.A. **Online address:** lesterd@stockton.edu

LESTER, Julius. American (born United States), b. 1939. **Genres:** Children's Fiction, Poetry, History, Literary Criticism And History, Music, Mythology/Folklore, Autobiography/Memoirs, Novellas/Short Stories, Young Adult Fiction, Novels, Adult Non-fiction, Ghost Writer. **Career:** Sing Out, associate editor, 1964-70; Broadside of New York, contributing editor, 1964-70; Newport Folk Festival, director, 1966-68; WBAI-FM, show host, 1966-73; New School for Social Research, teacher, 1968-70; WNET, talk show host, 1969-71; University of Massachusetts, professor of Afro-American studies, 1971-88, faculty, 1988, Department of Judaic and Near Eastern Studies, professor, 1982-84, Institute for Advanced Studies in Humanities, acting director, associate director, 1982-84, adjunct professor of history, professor of Judaic studies, 1971-2003, professor emeritus of Judaic studies, 2003-; Vanderbilt University, writer-in-residence, 1985. **Publications:** (With P. Seeger) The 12-String Guitar as Played by Leadbelly: An Instructional Manual, 1965; The Mud of Vietnam, 1967; Revolutionary Notes, 1969, Look Out Whitey! Black Power's Gon 'Get Your Mama! 1968, To Be a Slave, 1968; Black Folktales, 1969; Search for the New Land Country: History As Subjective Experience, 1969, Essays of a Black Socialist, 1970; (comp.) Young and Black in America, 1971; The Knee-High Man and Other Tales, 1972, The Long Journey Home: Stories from Black History, 1972; Two Love Stories, 1972; Who I Am, 1974; All Is Well: An Autobiography, 1976; This Strange New Feeling, 1982; Do Lord Remember Me, 1984, The Tales of Uncle Remus: The Adventures of Brer Rabbit, 1987; Lovesong: Becoming a Jew (autobiography), 1988; Many Spots How Does a Leopard Have? And Other Tales, 1989, Further Tales of Uncle Remus, 1990; Falling Pieces of the Broken Sky, 1990, The Last Valley of Uncle Remus, 1994; And All Our Wounds Forgiven, 1994, John Henry, 1994; The Man Who Knew Too Much, 1994; Othello: A Novel, 1995, Sam and the Tigers: A New Telling Of Little Black Sambo, 1996; What a Truly Cool World, 1998, From Slave Ship to Freedom Road, 1998; Black Cowboy, Wild Horses: A True Story, 1998; When the Beginning Began: Stories About God, The Creatures, And Us, 1999, Uncle Remus, 1999; Pharaoh's Daughter: A Novel of Ancient Egypt, 2000; Albidaro and the Mischievous Dream, 2000; Ackamarackus Julius Lester's Sumptuously Silly Fantastically Funny Fables, 2001; When Dad Killed Mom, 2001; (with L. Cohen) The Blues Singers: Ten Who Rocked the World, 2001; Why Heaven is Far Away, 2002; Shining, 2003; Autobiography of God: A Novel, 2004; On Writing For Children & Other People, 2004; Day of Tears: A Novel in Dialogue, 2005; The Old African, 2005; Let's Talk about Race, 2005; Time's Memory, 2006; Cupid: A Tale of Love and Desire, 2007; Guardian, 2008, Hungry Ghosts, 2009. EDITOR: (with M. Varela) To Praise Our Bridges: An Autobiography by Fanny Lou Hamer, 1967; (with M. Varela) Our Folk Tales, 1967; (and intro.) The Seventh Son: The Thought and Writings of WEB Du Bois, vol. II, 1971; (with S. Couch) Is Not No Ambulances For No NIGGUH Tonight, 1972. Contributor to magazines and newspapers. **Address:** Department of Judaic & Near Eastern Studies, University of Massachusetts, Herter 7th Fl., 744 Herter Hall, 161 Presidents Dr., Amherst, MA 01003-9312, U.S.A. **Online address:** lester@judnea.umass.edu

LESTER, June. American (born United States), b. 1942. **Genres:** Information Science/Computers. **Career:** University of Tennessee, assistant professor and cataloger, 1971-73; Emory University, Division of Library and Information Management, librarian and lecturer, 1973-76, assistant professor, 1976-80, associate professor, 1980-87; American Library Association, accreditation officer, 1987-91, Office for Accreditation, director, 1987-91; University of North Texas, School of Library and Information Sciences, associate professor and associate dean, 1991-93; University of Oklahoma, School of Library and Information Sciences, director, 1993-2000, professor, 1993-. Writer. **Publications:** Guidelines for Making a Job Decision: Questions a Prospective Employee Should Have Answers to Beforehand, 1978; (with W.C. Koehler, Jr.) Fundamentals of Information Studies: Understanding Information and Its Environment, 2003, 2nd ed., 2007. Contributor to books. **Address:** School of Library and Information Studies, University of Oklahoma, Rm. 120, 401 W Brooks St., Norman, OK 73019-0528, U.S.A. **Online address:** jlester@ou.edu

LESTER, Margot Carmichael. American (born United States), b. 1962. **Genres:** Self Help, Adult Non-fiction. **Career:** Blue Cross Blue Shield of North Carolina, editorial and administrative assistant, 1984-87, public affairs coordinator, 1987-88; University of North Carolina, publications director, 1989-90, marketing director, 1990-93; Gurley Communications, founder and president, 1993-95; Universal Communications, managing partner, 1995-97; Glaxo Wellcome Inc., communications specialist, 1994-95; Word Factory, founder and president, 1997-; LIPS Inc., investor relations/venture capital consultant, 1999-2000; Sciquest, ir/corporate communications consultant, 1999-2001; Match.com, advise columnist, 2001-11; Hanley Wood Business Media, contributing editor, 2003-11; Teaching That Makes Sense Inc., chief operating officer, 2003-11; Monster, freelance writer, 2004-11; The Carrboro Citizen, staff, 2008-11. **Publications:** The Real Life Guide to Life after College, 1998; The Real Life Guide to Starting Your Career, 1998. Contributor to magazines. **Address:** The Word Factory, 314 Bolin Forest Dr., Carrboro, NC 27510, U.S.A. **Online address:** margot@thewordfactory.com

LESTER, Richard K. American (born United States), b. 1954?. **Genres:** Economics, Business/Trade/Industry. **Career:** Massachusetts Institute of Technology, faculty, 1979, Industrial Performance Center, founding director, Department of Nuclear Science and Engineering, associate professor, 1986, Japan steel industry professor and head, Industrial Performance Center, faculty co-chair and founding director. Writer. **Publications:** (Co-author) Radioactive Waste Management and Regulation, 1977; (with M.L. Dertouzos and R.M. Solow) Made in America: Regaining the Productive Edge, 1989; (ed. with S. Berger) Made by Hong Kong, 1997; The Productive Edge: How U.S. Industries are Pointing the Way to a New Era of Economic Growth, 1998; (with J. Deutch) Making Technology Work: Applications in Energy and the Environment, 2004; (with M.J. Piore) Innovation, the Missing Dimension, 2004; (ed. with S. Berger) Global Taiwan: Building Competitive Strengths in a New International Economy, 2005; Unlocking Energy Innovation: How America can Build a Low-Cost, Low-Carbon Energy System, 2011. **Address:** Department of Nuclear Science and Engineering, Massachusetts Institute of Technology, 24-107, 77 Massachusetts Ave., Cambridge, MA 02139, U.S.A. **Online address:** rklester@mit.edu

LESTEWKA, Patrick. *See* **DAVIDSON, Craig.**

L'ESTRANGE, Anna. *See* **ELLERBECK, Rosemary.**

LESY, Michael. American (born United States), b. 1945?. **Genres:** History, Social Sciences. **Career:** Hampshire College, professor of literary journalism, 1990-. Writer. **Publications:** Wisconsin Death Trip, 1973; Real Life: Louisville in the Twenties, 1976; Time Frames: The Meaning of Family Pictures, 1980; Bearing Witness: A Photographic Chronicle of American Life, 1860-1945, 1982; Visible Light, 1985; The Forbidden Zone, 1987; Rescues: The Lives of Heroes, 1991; Dreamland: America at the Dawn of the Twentieth Century, 1997; Long Time Coming: A Photographic Portrait of America, 1935-1943, 2002; Angel's World: The New York Photographs of Angelo Rizzuto, 2006; Murder City: The Bloody History of Chicago in the Twenties, 2007. **Address:** Hampshire College, 210 Adele Simmons Hall,

893 West St., PO Box CS, Amherst, MA 01002, U.S.A. **Online address:** malha@hampshire.edu

LETCHER, Andy. British (born England), b. 1968?. **Genres:** History, Cultural/Ethnic Topics, Medicine/Health. **Career:** Oxford Brookes University, lecturer. Writer and musician. **Publications:** Shroom: A Cultural History of the Magic Mushroom, 2007. **Address:** Ecco Press, 10 E 53rd St., New York, NY 10022-5244, U.S.A. **Online address:** info@andyletcher.co.uk

LETCHFORD, Stanley. British (born England), b. 1924?. **Genres:** Mathematics/Statistics, Economics, Education, Business/Trade/Industry. **Career:** New College, Oxford University, junior lecturer, 1950-52; Collier Macmillan Schools, director of mathematics studies, 1962-82. Writer. **Publications:** Modern Arithmetic, 1970; Business Mathematics and Statistics, 1974, 3rd ed., 1984; The Economic System: An Introduction for Business Students, 1975; Statistics: A Foundation Course, 1980; Statistics Workbook, 1982; (ed.) Quantitative Methods in Business, 1985; Statistics for Accountants, 1994. **Address:** 21 Gorringe Dr., Lower Willingdon, Lower Willingdon, Eastbourne, ES BN20 9ST, England.

LETELLIER, Robert Ignatius. British/South African (born South Africa), b. 1953. **Genres:** Literary Criticism And History, Music, Bibliography. **Career:** University of Cambridge, tutor. Writer. **Publications:** An Intensifying Vision of Evil: The English Gothic Novel (1764-1820) as a Self-Contained Literary Cycle, 1980; Kindred Spirits: An Assessment of the Interrelationship between the Romantic Novels of England and Germany, 1790-1820, 1982; A Bibliography of the English Novel from the Restoration to the French Revolution: A Checklist of Sources and Critical Materials, 1995; Sir Walter Scott and the Gothic Novel, 1995; Day in Mamre, Night in Sodom: A Study of Abraham and Lot in Genesis 18 and 19, 1995; The English Novel, 1660-1700: An Annotated Bibliography, 1997; (ed.) The Diaries of Giacomo Meyerbeer, vol. I, 1999, vol. II, 2001, vol. III, 2002, vol. IV, 2003; The English Novel, 1700-1740: An Annotated Bibliography, 2002; Meyerbeer Studies, 2005; (intro.) Giacomo Meyerbeer, 2007; Ballets of Ludwig Minkus, 2008; (comp. and intro.) Fiammetta/Néméa, 2010; (comp. and intro.) Paquita, 2010; Daniel-Francois-Esprit Aube, 2010; Opéra-Comique, 2010. **Address:** 7 Parker St., Cambridge, CB CB1 1JL, England. **Online address:** r.letellier@ntlworld.com

LETESSIER, Dorothée. French (born France), b. 1953. **Genres:** Novels, Plays/Screenplays, Autobiography/Memoirs. **Career:** Writer, 1980-. **Publications:** NOVELS: Voyage á Paimpol, 1980; Loïca, 1983; Breath of Air, 1985; La belle Atlantique, 1986; Jean-Baptiste, ou, L'education vagabonde, 1988; La reine des abeilles, 1989; Coach, 1993; L'autocar, 1994; Symptoms, 2009. **Address:** Editions du Seuil, 27 rue Jacob, Paris, 75006, France.

LETHBRIDGE, Robert (David). British/American (born United States), b. 1947. **Genres:** Literary Criticism And History, Art/Art History, Philosophy. **Career:** Cambridge University, staff member, 1973-94, Department of French, lecturer, through 1994, honorary professor; Fitzwilliam College, lecturer in French and fellow senior tutor, 1982-94, master 2005-, honorary professor of nineteenth-century French literature; University of London, chair of French language and literature, 1994, professor of French language and literature, 1999-2003, director, 2003-05, emeritus professor, 2003-; Gates Cambridge Trust, provost, 2010; University of California, visiting professor; University of Melbourne, visiting professor. Writer. **Publications:** Maupassant Pierre et Jean, 1984. EDITOR: (with T. Keefe) Zola and the Craft of Fiction, 1990; (with P. Collier) Artistic Relations: Literature and Visual Arts in Nineteenth-Century France, 1994; (with C. Lloyd) Maupassant, Conteur et Romancier, 1994. AUTHOR OF INTRODUCTION: L'Assommoir, 1995; La Debacle, 2000; Bel-Ami, 2001; Pierre et Jean, 2001. Contributor to periodicals. **Address:** Fitzwilliam College, 9-11, rue de Constantine, Cambridge, CB3 0DG, England. **Online address:** rdl11@cam.ac.uk

LETHEM, Jonathan (Allen). American (born United States), b. 1964. **Genres:** Novels, Novellas/Short Stories, Young Adult Non-fiction. **Career:** Brazen Head Books, bookseller, 1977-80; Gryphon Books, bookseller, 1982-84; Pegasus Books, bookseller, 1985-90; Moe's Books, bookseller, 1990-94. Writer. **Publications:** Gun, with Occasional Music, 1994; Amnesia Moon, 1995; Wall of the Sky, the Wall of the Eye, 1996; As She Climbed across the Table, 1997; Girl in Landscape, 1998; (with C. Scholz) Kafka Americana, 1999; Motherless Brooklyn, 1999; (ed.) The Vintage Book of Amnesia: An Anthology, 2000; (with P.J. Kelly and J. Kessel) Ninety Percent of Everything, 2001; This Shape We're In, 2001; (ed.) Da Capo Best Music Writing 2002: The Year's Finest Writing on Rock, Pop, Jazz, Country & More, 2002; The Fortress of Solitude, 2003; Men and Cartoons: Stories, 2004; The Disappointment Artist and Other Essays, 2005; How We Got Insipid, 2006; Patchwork Planet, 2006; You Don't Love Me Yet, 2007; (ed.) Philip K. Dick: Five Novels of the 1960's and 1970's, 2008; Omega: The Unknown Premiere, 2008; Chronic City: A Novel, 2009; (ed.) Philip K. Dick: Valis and Other Late Novels, 2009; They Live, 2010; (ed. with P. Jackson) The Exegesis of Philip K. Dick, 2011; The Ecstasy of Influence: Nonfictions, etc., 2011. Contributor to periodicals. **Address:** Richard Parks Agency, 138 E 16th St., Ste. 5B, New York, NY 10003, U.S.A.

LETNANOVA, Elena. Slovak (born Slovakia), b. 1942. **Genres:** Music, Humanities. **Career:** Piano soloist and accompanist, 1966-74, 1985-; University of Jan Amos Komensky, lecturer, assistant professor, 1968-70; Slovconcert Agency, concert pianist, 1970-74; State Conservatory of Music, professor of music, 1974-75; University of Jan Amos Komensky, Department of Musicology, assistant professor, associate professor, 1974-84; Barnes Constructural Engineers, draftsperson, 1985; teacher and concert performer, 1985-87; University of Dayton, associate professor of piano and head of piano area, 1987-92; University of Jan Amos Komensky, assistant professor of English, 1992-93; Writer. **Publications:** (Trans.) A.I. Solzhenitsyn, Message from Exile, 1979; Piano Interpretation in the Seventeenth, Eighteenth and Nineteenth Centuries: A Study of Theory and Practice Using Original Documents, 1991; Beginner's Slovak, 2001. **Address:** Slovak Literary Agency, Partizansk 21, Bratislava, 81351, Slovakia.

LETO, Julie Elizabeth. American (born United States) **Genres:** Romance/Historical, Novels. **Career:** Writer, 1988-; teacher, through 1996. **Publications:** Seducing Sullivan, 1998; Private Lessons, 1999; Good Girls Do!, 2000; Pure Chance, 2001; Insatiable, 2001; Exposed, 2001; What's Your Pleasure?, 2002; Just Watch Me, 2002; Double the Pleasure, 2002; Brazen and Burning, 2002; (contrib.) Impetuous, 2003; Up to No Good, 2003; Looking for Trouble, 2003; Undeniable, 2004; (with J. Kenner and S. Kearney) Essence of Midnight, 2004; (with L. Foster) Lip Service, 2004; Line of Fire, 2004; Dirty Little Secrets, 2005; Making Waves, 2005; Signet Eclipse, 2005; (with J Shalvis and C. Adair) Dare Me, 2005; Dirty Little Lies, 2006; (with L. Kelly and K. Raye) Boys of Summer, 2006; (contrib.) I'll Be Home for Christmas, 2006; The Domino Effect, 2006; New Orleans Nights, 2006; Stripped, 2007; Phantom Pleasures, 2008; Josie's Story, 2008; Phantom's Touch, 2008; Kiss of the Phantom, 2009; Something Wicked, 2009; (with L. Kelly) More Blazing Bedtime Stories, 2009; Hard to Hold, 2010; 3 Seductions and a Wedding, 2010; Too Wicked to Keep, 2011; Too Wild to Hold, 2011; Title TBA, 2011; Too Hot to Touch, 2011. Contributor to books. Works appear in anthologies. **Address:** Harlequin.com, PO Box 5190, Buffalo, NY 14240-5190, U.S.A. **Online address:** julie@julieleto.com

LETTS, Billie. American (born United States), b. 1938. **Genres:** Novels, Young Adult Fiction, Young Adult Non-fiction. **Career:** Southeastern Oklahoma State University, instructor, 1975-95, professor. Novelist. **Publications:** NOVELS: Where the Heart Is, 1995; The Honk and Holler Opening Soon, 1998; Shoot the Moon, 2004; Made in the U.S.A, 2008. NON-FICTION: You've Got Mail, Billie Letts, 1999. Contributor to periodicals and magazines. **Address:** c/o Elaine Markson, Markson Thoma Literary Agency, 44 Greenwich Ave., New York, NY 10011, U.S.A.

LEUPP, Gary P. American (born United States), b. 1956. **Genres:** History, Young Adult Non-fiction, Gay And Lesbian Issues. **Career:** Tufts University, assistant professor, 1988-95, associate professor of history, 1995-98, adjunct professor of comparative religion, 1998-, professor of history, 2003-. Writer. **Publications:** Servants, Shophands, and Laborers in the Cities of Tokugawa Japan, 1992; Male Colors: The Construction of Homosexuality in Tokugawa Japan, 1995; Interracial Intimacy in Japan: Western Men and Japanese Women, 1543-1900, 2003; The Weavers of Nishijin: Wage-Labor in Tokugawa Japan, forthcoming. **Address:** Department of History, Tufts University, 101 Rm. East Hall, 11 Talbot Ave., Medford, MA 02155, U.S.A. **Online address:** gary.leupp@tufts.edu

LEV, Peter. American (born United States), b. 1948. **Genres:** Film. **Career:** University of Texas, visiting assistant professor, 1980-82; Towson University, assistant professor, professor of mass communication, professor of electronic media and film, 1983-. Writer. **Publications:** Claude Lelouch, Film Director, 1983; The Euro-American Cinema, 1993; American Films of the '70s: Conflicting Visions, 2000; Transforming the Screen, 1950-1959, 2003; History of

the American Cinema: Twilight Gods, Hollywood 1950-59, vol. VII, 2003; (ed. with J.M. Welsh) Literature/Film Reader: Issues of Adaptation, 2007. Contributor to periodicals. **Address:** Department of Electronic Media and Film, Towson University, Rm. 206, Media Ctr., 8000 York Rd., Baltimore, MD 21252-0001, U.S.A. **Online address:** plev@towson.edu

LEVAY, Simon. American/British (born England), b. 1943. **Genres:** Biology, Gay And Lesbian Issues, Sex, Science Fiction/Fantasy, Sciences. **Career:** University of Gottingen, instructor in neuroanatomy, 1970-72; Harvard Medical School, lecturer in neurobiology, 1972-74, instructor, 1974-75, assistant professor of neurobiology, 1975-80, associate professor of neurobiology, 1980-84, Neurobiology 710: Introduction to the Nervous System, co-director, 1975-84, Neurobiology 208: Advanced Neurobiology: Physiology of the Central Nervous System, director, 1975-84; Salk Institute for Biological Studies, associate professor, 1984-93; University of California, lecturer in neurobiology, 1984-92, Biology 156, co-director, 1984-92, adjunct associate professor of biology, 1985-93; Institute of Gay and Lesbian Education, instructor, 1992-97, co-founder and chair, 1992-98; Stanford University, lecturer, 2003, Human Biology 10, director, 2003. Writer. **Publications:** The Sexual Brain, 1993; (with E. Nonas) City of Friends: A Portrait of the Gay and Lesbian Community in America, 1995; Queer Science: The Use and Abuse of Research into Homosexuality, 1996; Albrick's Gold (novel), 1997; (with K. Sieh) The Earth in Turmoil, Earthquakes, Volcanoes and Their Impact on Humankind, 1998; (with D. Koerner) Here Be Dragons: The Scientific Quest for Extraterrestrial Life, 2000; (with S.M. Valente) Human Sexuality, 2002, 4th ed., 2012; (with C. Freed) Healing the Brain: A Doctor's Controversial Quest for a Cell Therapy to Cure Parkinson's Disease, 2002; (contrib.) Mount St. Helens: Photographs, 2005; When Science Goes Wrong: Twelve Tales from the Dark Side of Discovery, 2008; (with J. Baldwin and J. Baldwin) Discovering Human Sexuality, 2009, 2nd ed., 2012; Gay, Straight and the Reason Why: The Science of Sexual Orientation, 2011. Contributor of articles to periodicals. **Address:** 9003 Norma Pl., West Hollywood, CA 90069, U.S.A. **Online address:** slevay@aol.com

LEVE, Ariel. American (born United States), b. 1968. **Genres:** Autobiography/Memoirs, Biography. **Career:** Sunday Times Magazine, journalist and columnist, 2003-. **Publications:** The Cassandra Chronicles in US as It Could Be Worse, You Could Be Me, 2009. Contributor to books and periodicals. **Address:** U.S.A. **Online address:** ariel@ariel-leve.com

LEVELT, Willem J(ohannes) M(aria). Dutch (born Netherlands), b. 1938. **Genres:** Language/Linguistics, Psychology. **Career:** Institute for Perception, staff, 1962-65; Harvard University, Center for Cognitive Studies, research fellow, 1965-66; University of Illinois, Center for Comparative Psycholinguistics, visiting assistant professor, 1966-67; Louvain University, visiting professor of psycholinguistics, 1967-70; University of Groningen, associate professor of experimental psychology, 1967-68, professor of experimental psychology and of psycholinguistics, 1969-70; University of Nijmegen, professor of experimental psychology, 1971-79, professor of psycholinguistics, 1980-2006; Max Planck Institute for Psycholinguistics, founder, director, 1980-2006, director emeritus, 2006-; Royal Netherlands Academy of Arts and Sciences, president, 2002-05. Writer. **Publications:** On Binocular Rivalry, 1968; Formal Grammars in Linguistics and Psycholinguistics, 3 vols., 1974; (ed. with G.B.F. D'Arcais) Studies in the Perception of Language, 1978; (ed. with A. Sinclair and R.J. Jarvella) Child's Conception of Language, 1978; Speaking: From Intention to Articulation, 1989; (ed.) Lexical Access in Speech production, 1993; An Introduction to the Theory of Formal Languages and Automata, 2008. Contributor to journals and anthologies. **Address:** Max Planck Institute for Psycholinguistics, Wundtlaan 1, PO Box 310, Nijmegen, 6525 XD, Netherlands. **Online address:** willem.levelt@mpi.nl

LEVENE, Mark. British (born England), b. 1953. **Genres:** History, International Relations/Current Affairs, Politics/Government, Biography, Social Sciences, Humanities, Adult Non-fiction. **Career:** University of Warwick, lecturer in history, 1988-; University of Southampton, School of Humanities, reader in comparative history, Jewish History and Culture Board of Studies, chair; Parkes Institute for the Study of Jewish/Non-Jewish Relations, staff. Writer. **Publications:** War, Jews and the New Europe: The Diplomacy of Lucien Wolf, 1914-1919, 1992; (ed. with P. Roberts) The Massacre in History, 1999; Genocide in the Age of the Nation State, vol. I: The Meaning of Genocide, 2005, vol. II, The Rise of the West and the Coming of Genocide, 2005; Meaning of Genocide, 2005; (ed. with D. Cromwell) Surviving Climate Change: The Struggle to Avert Global Catastrophe, 2007. Contributor to professional journals. **Address:** Department of History, School of Humanities, University of Southampton, Rm. 65/2055, Highfield, Southampton, HM S017 1BJ, England. **Online address:** ml1@soton.ac.uk

LEVENTHAL, Bennett (L.). American (born United States), b. 1949. **Genres:** Psychology, Medicine/Health, Psychiatry. **Career:** Charity Hospital at New Orleans, house officer, 1974; Duke University, junior faculty, resident in general psychiatry, 1974-78, senior fellow in pediatric psychiatry, 1976-77, chief fellow of division of child psychiatry, 1976-77, chief resident in psychiatry, 1977-78, clinical associate of medical center, 1978-80; University of Illinois at Chicago, assistant professor, 1978-85, director of child psychiatry clinic, 1978-85, director of child and adolescent psychiatry, 1982-, John Dewey lecturer, 1982, associate chair of department, 1985, associate professor, 1985-90, professor of psychiatry and pediatrics and adjunct professor of psychology and biopsychology, 1990, now Irving B. Harris professor of child and adolescent psychiatry emeritus, Center for Child Mental Health and Developmental Neurosciences, director, Department of Psychiatry, interim chair, Center of Excellence on Autism, co-investigator, Statewide Autism Program, co-director; New York University, Child Study Center, faculty, deputy director of research, Department of Child and Adolescent Psychiatry, vice-chair, Langone Medical Center, professor and vice-chair; Smith College, clinical assistant professor, 1981-83; Wyler Children's Hospital, medical director of childlife and family education program, 1983-, Harris Center for Developmental Studies, director, 1983-89, acting director of student mental health service, 1986-87; University of Illinois, visiting professor, 1984; Chicago Lakeshore Hospital, director of child and adolescent programs, 1986-; Caledonia State Prison, psychiatric consultant; Butner Federal Correctional Institute, psychiatric consultant; Nathan S. Kline Institute for Psychiatric Research, deputy director. Writer. **Publications:** (Ed. with N.L. Stein and T. Trabasso) Psychological and Biological Approaches to Emotion, 1990; (ed.) Bibliography for Training in Child and Adolescent Mental Health: For Training in Child Psychiatry, Child Psychology, Social Work, and Child and Adolescent Psychiatric Nursing, 3rd ed., 1991; (with B. Rubin) Report of the Autism Task Force: Findings and Recommendations, 2005. Contributor of articles. **Address:** Department of Psychiatry, University of Illinois, Rm. 155, 1747 W Roosevelt Rd., Chicago, IL 60608, U.S.A. **Online address:** bll@uic.edu

LEVENTHAL, Judith. American (born United States), b. 1958. **Genres:** Reference, Theology/Religion, History, Education. **Career:** Writer and educator. **Publications:** SMALL MIRACLES SERIES WITH Y. HALBERSTAM: Small Miracles: Extraordinary Coincidences from Everyday Life, 1997; Small Miracles II: Heartwarming Gifts of Extraordinary Coincidences, 1998; Small Miracles of Love and Friendship: Remarkable Coincidences of Warmth and Devotion, 1999; Small Miracles for Women: Extraordinary Coincidences of Heart and Spirit, 2000; Small Miracles for the Jewish Heart: Extraordinary Coincidences from Yesterday and Today, 2002; Small Miracles for Families: Extraordinary Coincidences That Reaffirm Our Deepest Ties, 2003; Small Miracles of the Holocaust: Extraordinary Coincidences of Faith, Hope and Survival, 2008. **Address:** Lyons Press, 246 Goose Ln., PO Box 480, Guilford, CT 06437, U.S.A. **Online address:** jgleventhal@aol.com

LEVER, Christopher. British (born England), b. 1932. **Genres:** Zoology, Biology, Environmental Sciences/Ecology, History, Natural History, Animals/Pets, Sciences. **Career:** John Barran and Sons Ltd., director, 1956-64; Tusk Trust, chairman, through 2005, honorary life president; Linnean Society, fellow; Royal Geographical Society, fellow. Writer. **Publications:** Goldsmiths and Silversmiths of England, 1975; The Naturalized Animals of the British Isles, 1977; Naturalized Mammals of the World, 1985; Naturalized Birds of the World, 1987; The Mandarin Duck, 1990; They Dined on Eland: The Story of the Acclimatisation Societies, 1992; Naturalized Animals: The Ecology of Successfully Introduced Species, 1994; Naturalized Fishes of the World, 1996; The Cane Toad: The History and Ecology of a Successful Colonist, 2001; Naturalized Reptiles and Amphibians of the World, 2003. Contributor to books. **Address:** Newell House, Winkfield, Windsor, BR SL4 4SE, England.

LEVERE, Trevor H(arvey). Canadian/British (born England), b. 1944. **Genres:** Sciences, History, Chemistry. **Career:** University of Toronto, Institute for the History and Philosophy of Science and Technology, assistant professor, 1969-74, associate professor, 1974-81, professor of the history of science, 1981-2006, director, 1981-86, 1993-98, university professor, 2006-07, university professor emeritus, 2007-, Museum Studies Program, director, 1982, Victoria College, fellow, 1982; Cambridge University, Clare Hall,

visiting fellow, 1983; Massachusetts Institute of Technology, Dibner Institute, resident fellow, 1995; Annals of Science, editor, 1999-. **Publications:** Affinity and Matter, 1971; (with G.L.E. Turner) Martinus Van Marum, vol. IV, 1973; Poetry Realized in Nature: Samuel Taylor Coleridge and Early Nineteenth-Century Science, 1981; Science and the Canadian Arctic: A Century of Exploration, 1818-1918, 1993; Chemists and Chemistry in Nature and Society, 1770-1878, 1994; Transforming Matter: A History of Chemistry from Alchemy to the Buckyball, 2001; (with G.L.E. Turner) Discussing Chemistry and Steam: The Minutes of a Coffee House Philosophical Society, 1780-1787, 2002. EDITOR: (with R.A. Jarrell) A Curious Field-Book, 1974; Editing Texts in the History of Science and Medicine, 1982; (with W.R. Shea) Nature, Experiment, and the Sciences, 1990; (and intro. With N.M. Swerdlow) Essays on Galileo and the History and Philosophy of Science, 1999; (with F.L. Holmes) Instruments and Experimentation in the History of Chemistry, 2000. **Address:** Institute for the History and Philosophy of, Science and Technology, University of Toronto, Rm. 316, Victoria College, 91 Charles St. W, Toronto, ON M5S 1K7, Canada. **Online address:** trevor.levere@utoronto.ca

LEVERITT, Thomas. British/Scottish (born Scotland), b. 1976. **Genres:** Novels. **Career:** Writer and portrait painter. **Publications:** The Exchange-Rate between Love and Money 2009. Contributor to periodicals. **Address:** London, GL , England. **Online address:** 24hourcallcentre@leveritt.com

LEVESQUE, John. Canadian (born Canada), b. 1953. **Genres:** Novels, Essays, Young Adult Fiction, Humor/Satire, Autobiography/Memoirs. **Career:** North Bay Nugget, reporter, editor, columnist, 1974-80; Hamilton Spectator, writer, 1981-86, humor columnist, 1984-, film critic, 1986-93; Seattle Post-Intelligencer, columnist. Writer. **Publications:** Rosseter's Memory (novel), 1991; Waiting for Aquarius (columns), 1992; Stranded on the Information Highway (columns), 1996; Geneva Farewell(novel), 1998; Sometime Soon, 2000. **Address:** 5 Pine St., Hamilton, ON L8P 2A2, Canada. **Online address:** johnlevesque@seattlepi.com

LEVI, Barbara Goss. American (born United States), b. 1943. **Genres:** Physics. **Career:** American Institute of Physics, assistant editor, 1969-70, consulting editor, 1971-87, associate editor, 1987-88, senior associate editor, 1989-92, senior editor, 1992-; Princeton University, research staff, Center for Energy and Environmental Studies, 1981, 1983-87; Rutgers University, visiting professor, 1988-89; University of California, journalist-in-residence, American Physical Society, chair. **Publications:** EDITOR: (with D. Hafemeister and H. Kelly) Energy Sources: Conservation and Renewables, 1985; (with M. Sakitt and A. Hobson) The Future of Land-Based Strategic Missiles, 1989; (with D. Hafemeister and R. Scribner) Global Warming: Physics and Facts, 1992. **Address:** American Institute of Physics, 1 Physics Ellipse, Kohn Hall, College Park, MD 20740, U.S.A.

LEVI, Jan Heller. American (born United States), b. 1954. **Genres:** Poetry, Literary Criticism And History, Young Adult Fiction. **Career:** Dell Publications, assistant editor, 1977-78; personal assistant to poet Muriel Rukeyser, 1978-80; Sarah Lawrence College, director of public relations, 1981-83; ArtForum Magazine, associate editor, 1988-90; New York Times, advertising account sales manager, 1990-96; freelance writer and teacher, 1997-; Hunter College, MFA Program in Creative Writing, faculty. **Publications:** (Ed.) A Muriel Rukeyser Reader, 1994; Once I Gazed at You in Wonder: Poems, 1999; (ed. with J.E. Kaufman and A.F. Herzog) Collected Poems of Muriel Rukeyser, 2005; (ed. with S. Miles) Directed by Desire: The Collected Poems of June Jordan, 2005; Skyspeak: Poems, 2005. Contributor of fiction and poetry to journals. **Address:** University of Pittsburgh Press, Eureka Bldg., 5th Fl., 3400 Forbes Ave., Pittsburgh, PA 15260, U.S.A.

LEVIANT, Curt. American/Austrian (born Austria), b. 1932?. **Genres:** Novels, Translations, Young Adult Fiction. **Career:** State University of New Jersey, Rutgers University, professor of Hebrew and Yiddish literature, 1960-, retired, now professor emeritus of Hebrew literature. Writer. **Publications:** NOVELS: The Yemenite Girl, 1977; Passion in the Desert, 1980; The Man Who Thought He was Messiah, 1990; Partita in Venice, 1999; Diary of an Adulterous Woman, 2001; Ladies and Gentlemen, the Original Music of the Hebrew Alphabet, and, Weekend in Mustara: Two Novellas, 2002; A Novel of Klass, 2008. EDITOR: (intro.) Masterpieces of Hebrew Literature: A Treasury of 2000 Years of Jewish Creativity, 1969; (intro.) Masterpieces of Hebrew Literature: Selections from 2000 Years of Jewish Creativity, 2008. TRANSLATOR: S. Aleichem, The Song of Songs, 1996; I.B. Singer, More Stories from My Father's Court, 2000; S. Aleichem, My First Love Affair and

Other Stories, 2002. EDITOR and TRANSLATOR: (and intro.) S. Aleichem, Old Country Tales, 1966; (and intro.) S. Aleichem, Some Laughter, Some Tears: Tales from the Old World and the New, 1968; King Artus: A Hebrew Arthurian Romance of 1279, 1969; (and intro.) S. Aleichem, From the Fair: The Autobiography of Sholom Aleichem, 1985; (and intro.) A. Reisen, The Heart-stirring Sermon: And Other Stories, 1992; S. Aleichem, Happy New Year! and Other Stories, 2000; (and intro.) E. Shtaynbarg, Jewish Book of Fables: Selected Works, 2003; (and intro.) Y. Rosenberg, The Golem and the Wondrous Deeds of the Maharal of Prague, 2007. Contributor to periodicals. **Address:** Rutgers University, State University of New Jersey, 57 US Highway 1, New Brunswick, NJ 08901-8554, U.S.A.

LEVIEUX, Eleanor. French/American (born United States), b. 1937. **Genres:** Language/Linguistics, Translations, Reference. **Career:** René Julliard (publisher), English adviser, 1960-64; International Chamber of Commerce, translator and editor, 1966-86; British Institute in Paris, assistant professor, 1984-; Sciences Po (political science institute), lecturer of English, 1985-88; University of Oregon, professor in French department, 1987, 1989-90, 1992-93, 1995, 1998. **Publications:** WITH M. LEVIEUX: Cassell's Beyond the Dictionary in French, 1967; Beyond the Dictionary in French, 1967, rev. ed. as Cassell's Colloquial French: A Handbook of Idiomatic Usage, 1980, 2nd rev. ed., 1990; Année Bac: Anglais 83, 1983; Année Bac: anglais 85, 1984; Insiders' French: Beyond the Dictionary, 1999. TRANSLATOR: (with D. Coltman and P. Knight) Le Corbusier, The Radiant City, 1967; (with F. Rosset) Sir K. Clark, Léonard de Vinci, 1967; Le Corbusier, The Nursery Schools, 1968; A.Memmi, The Scorpion, 1971; J. Soustelle, The Four Suns, 1971; LeCorbusier, Looking at City Planning, 1972; S. Alexandrian, Man Ray, 1973; S. Alexandrian and P. Waldberg, Max Ernst, 1973; P. Rossi, An Evening in Pisa, 1973; A. Terrasse, P. Delvaux, 1973; R.F. Bruckberger, God and Politics, 1973; A. Memmi, Jews and Arabs, 1975; P. Gauguin, Oviri, 1977; V. Segalen, The Great Statuary of China, 1978; (with B. Thompson) G. Duby, The Age of the Cathedrals, 1981; C. Derouet, Kandinsky: 1934-44 (catalogue), 1985; J.M. Guillaud, Rembrandt, 1986; J.M. Guillaud, Fra Angelico, 1986; D. Abadie, Jean Dubuffet: The First Two Decades, 1986; (with B. Shuey) D. Marchesseau, The Intimate World of Alexander Calder, 1989; (with B. Shuey) J-P. Molinier, Private Gardens in Town, 1991; Emile Zola, The Dreyfus Affair: J'accuse! and Other Writings, 1996. Contributor to periodicals. **Address:** British Institute in Paris, University of London, 9-11 rue de Constantine, Paris, 75340, France.

LEVI-MONTALCINI, Rita. American/Italian (born Italy), b. 1909. **Genres:** Medicine/Health. **Career:** University of Turin, Institute of Anatomy, assistant professor of anatomy, 1945-47; Washington University, Institute of Zoology, resident associate, 1947-56, associate professor, 1956-58, professor, 1958-77, professor emeritus of neurobiology, 1977-, head of zoology department; European Brain Research Institute, founder, president. Italian National Council of Research, Institute of Cell Biology, director, 1969-79; Institute of Neurobiology, National Research Council, founder and director; Italian Senate, senator for life, 2001-. Writer. **Publications:** (Ed.) Semaine, 1980; (co-ed.) Molecular Aspects of Neurobiology, 1986; Elogio dell'imperfezione (autobiography), 1987; In Praise of Imperfection: My Life and Work, 1988; NGF: apertura di una nuova frontiera nella neurobiologia, 1989; (co-author) Reti: Scienza, cultura, economia, 1993; Il tuo futurom, 1993; Science Citoyenne, 1994; Saga of the Nerve Growth Factor: Preliminary Studies, Discovery, Further Development, 1997; Bibliotheca encyclopaedica, 1997; Asso nella manica a brandelli, 1998; Elogio dell'imperfezione, 1999; Galassia Mente, 1999; Cantico di una vita, 2000; Universo inquieto: vita e opere di Paola Levi Montalcini, 2001; Tempo di Mutamenti, 2002; Tempo di azione, 2004; Abbi il coraggio di conoscere, 2005; Nuovi magellani nell'er digitale, 2006; Clessidra della vita di Rita Levi-Montalcini, 2008; Altra parte del mondo, 2009; Cronologia di una scoperta, 2009. **Address:** Washington University in St. Louis, 1 Brookings Dr., St. Louis, MO 63130, U.S.A.

LEVIN, Amy K. American (born United States), b. 1957. **Genres:** Literary Criticism And History, Women's Studies And Issues, Gay And Lesbian Issues. **Career:** Scarsdale High School, English teacher, 1978-80, 1982-88; University of Colorado, senior instructor of English, 1989-90; Central Missouri State University, assistant/associate professor of English, coordinator of Women's Studies, 1990-; University of Pennsylvania, Center for the Study of Black Literature and Culture, Ford Foundation Fellow, 1992; Northern Illinois University, Women Studies, director, professor of English, College of Liberal Arts and Sciences, acting dean, 2009-10. Writer. **Publications:** The

Suppressed Sister: A Relationship in Novels by Nineteenth and Twentieth-Century British Women, 1992; Africanism and Authenticity in African-American Women's Novels, 2003; (ed.) Defining Memory: Local Museums and the Construction of History in America's Changing Communities, 2007; (ed.) Gender, Sexuality and Museums: A Routledge Reader, 2010. **Address:** Women's Studies, Northern Illinois University, RH 103, DeKalb, IL 60115-2825, U.S.A. **Online address:** alevin@niu.edu

LEVIN, Betty (Lowenthal). American (born United States), b. 1927. **Genres:** Children's Fiction, Novels, Animals/Pets. **Career:** Museum of Fine Arts, research assistant, 1951-52; Harvard Graduate School of Education, part-time teaching fellow, 1953; Radcliffe Institute, creative writing fellow, 1968-70; McCarthy Historical Archive, massachusetts coordinator, 1969; Pine Manor Open College, instructor, 1970-75; Minute Man Publications, feature writer, 1972; Emmanuel College, instructor, 1975; Massachusetts Institute of Technology, faculty; Simmons College, Center for the Study of Children's Literature, special instructor, 1975-77, adjunct professor, 1977-87; Bunting Institute, Radcliffe College, fellow, instructor, 1976-. Novelist. **Publications:** The Sword of Culann, 1972; The Zoo Conspiracy, 1973; A Griffon's Nest, 1975; The Forespoken, 1976; Landfall, 1979; The Beast on the Brink, 1980; The Keeping Room, 1981; A Binding Spell, 1984; Put on My Crown, 1985; The Ice Bear, 1986; Julia MacRae Books, 1987; The Trouble with Granary, 1988; Brother Moose, 1990; Mercy's Mill, 1992; Starshine and Sunglow, 1994; Away to Me, Moss!, 1994; Fire in the Wind, 1995; Gift Horse, 1996; Island Bound, 1997; Look Back, Moss: A Novel, 1998; Creature Crossing, 1999; The Banished, 1999; Shadow Catcher, 2000; That'll Do, Moss, 2002; Shoddy Cove, 2003; Thorn, 2005; Unmaking of Duncan Veerick, 2007; The Forbidden Land, 2010. **Address:** Old Winter St., Lincoln, MA 01773, U.S.A.

LEVIN, Doron P. American/Israeli (born Israel), b. 1950. **Genres:** Engineering, Biography, Transportation, Young Adult Non-fiction. **Career:** St. Petersburg Times, reporter, 1977-81; Wall Street Journal, reporter, 1981-87; New York Times, Detroit bureau chief, 1988-. **Publications:** Irreconcilable Differences: Ross Perot vs. General Motors, 1989; Behind the Wheel at Chrysler: The Iacocca Legacy, 1995. **Address:** John Farquharson Ltd., 250 W 57th St., New York, NY 10107, U.S.A.

LEVIN, Gerald. American (born United States), b. 1929. **Genres:** Speech/Rhetoric, Biography, Literary Criticism And History, Self Help, Theology/Religion. **Career:** University of Michigan, instructor in English, 1955-56; University of Colorado, instructor in English, 1956-57; Eastern Illinois University, assistant professor of English, 1957-60; University of Akron, assistant professor, 1960-65, associate professor, 1965-68, professor, 1969-85, director of English composition, 1967-69, professor emeritus of English, 1986-. Writer. **Publications:** Prose Models: An Inductive Approach to Writing, 1964, (comp.) 11th ed. 2001; A Brief Handbook of Rhetoric, 1966; (ed.) The Short Story: An Inductive Approach, 1967; (ed.) The Art of Rhetoric, 1968; (with F. Connolly) Rhetoric Case Book, 1969; Styles for Writing: A Brief Rhetoric, 1972; Sigmund Freud, 1975; Short Essays: Models for Composition, 1977, (ed.) 7th ed., 1995; Richardson the Novelist: The Psychological Patterns, 1978; Writing and Logic, 1982; The Macmillan College Handbook, 1987, 2nd ed., 1991; The Educated Reader, 1988; (intro.) God, the Universe, and Where I Fit In, 2009. **Address:** Departmentt of English, University of Akron, 301 Olin Hall, 302 Buchtel Common, Akron, OH 44325-1901, U.S.A.

LEVIN, Igor. American/Russian (born Russia), b. 1931. **Genres:** Theatre, Art/Art History. **Career:** Scientific researcher, 1954-65; educator, 1965-75; computer-based systems for aerospace applications developer, 1978-. Writer. **Publications:** WITH I. LEVIN: Methodology of Working on the Play and the Role: On the Example of the Cherry Orchard, 1990; Working on the Play and the Role: The Stanislavsky Method for Analyzing the Characters in a Drama, 1992; The Stanislavsky Secret: Not a System, Not a Method But a Way of Thinking, 2002. Contributor to journals. **Address:** 3315 Wisconsin Ave. NW, Apt. 102, Washington, DC 20016, U.S.A.

LEVIN, Irina. American/Russian (born Russia), b. 1937. **Genres:** Theatre, Plays/Screenplays, Young Adult Non-fiction. **Career:** Theatre of Drama and Comedy, actress, 1958-73; solo performer in dramatic readings, 1969-75; Theatre-Studio, drama teacher and director, 1970-75; Catholic University of America, lecturer in acting and scene study, 1981-82. Writer. **Publications:** WITH I. LEVIN: Methodology of Working on the Play and the Role: On the Example of The Cherry Orchard, 1990; Working on the Play and the Role:

The Stanislavsky Method for Analyzing the Characters in a Drama, 1992; The Stanislavsky Secret: Not a System, Not a Method But a Way of Thinking, 2002. **Address:** 3315 Wisconsin Ave. NW, Apt. 102, Washington, DC 20016, U.S.A.

LEVIN, Linda Lotridge. (Linda Lotridge Levin). American (born United States), b. 1940. **Genres:** Novels. **Career:** Providence Journal, photo editor & reporter, 1962- 68; Rhode Island Historical Society, director, 1980-82; University of Rhode Island, professor of journalism, 1983-, chair of department of journalism, 2001-. **Publications:** Providence: From Provincial Village to Prosperous Port, 1750-1790: Lectures, 1978; Federal Rhode Island: The Age of the China Trade, 1790-1820: Lectures Presented at the Second Annual Forum on Rhode Island History, January, 1976, 1978; (with G.H. Kellner and J.S. Lemons) Rhode Island: The Independent State, 1982; Mass Communication Law in Rhode Island, 1993; To Understand: A 10-Year History of Exchanges between Soviet and New England Editors, 1993; The Making of FDR: The Story of Stephen T. Early, America's First Modern Press Secretary, 2007. **Address:** Department of Journalism, University of Rhode Island, Kingston, RI 02881, U.S.A. **Online address:** lllevin@uri.edu

LEVIN, Mark. Also writes as Mark Reed Levin, Mark R. Levin. American (born United States), b. 1957. **Genres:** Novels, Adult Non-fiction. **Career:** Landmark Legal Foundation, director of legal policy, president; U.S. Government, Department of Education, deputy assistant secretary, Department of Interior, deputy solicitor; WABC Radio, host; National Review Online, contributing editor, 2006-07. Attorney. **Publications:** Men in Black: How the Supreme Court is Destroying America, 2005; Rescuing Sprite: A Dog Lover's Story of Joy and Anguish, 2007; Liberty and Tyranny: A Conservative Manifesto, 2009; (intro.) Abraham Lincoln's Gettysburg Address illustrated, 2010. **Address:** Regnery Publishing Inc., 1 Massachusetts Ave. NW, Washington, DC 20001, U.S.A. **Online address:** marklevin.show@citcomm.com

LEVIN, Mark R. See **LEVIN, Mark.**

LEVIN, Mark Reed. See **LEVIN, Mark.**

LEVIN, Michael Eric. American (born United States), b. 1943. **Genres:** Sciences, Women's Studies And Issues. **Career:** Columbia University, preceptor in philosophy, 1966-67, instructor in philosophy, 1968-69; City University of New York, City College, instructor, assistant professor, associate professor, professor of philosophy, 1969-, Graduate Center, faculty. Writer. **Publications:** Metaphysics and the Mind-Body Problem, 1979; Feminism and Freedom, 1987; Why Race Matters: Race Differences and What They Mean, 1997; (with H. Bros) Sexual Preference and Human Rights, 1998; (with L.M. Thomas) Sexual Orientation and Human Rights, 1999. Contributor to journals. **Address:** The Graduate CEnter, City University of New York, 365 5th Ave., New York, NY 10016, U.S.A. **Online address:** meglev@nyc.rr.com

LEVIN, Michael (Graubart). American (born United States), b. 1958. **Genres:** Novels, Theology/Religion, Autobiography/Memoirs, Adult Non-fiction, Politics/Government, Sex, Biography, History, History. **Career:** Columbia Broadcasting System (CBS-TV), news researcher and writer, 1980-81; University of Southern California, teacher in writer's program, 1990-2001; New York University, faculty, 1997-2000; Writer2Author Inc., writing coach, co-chair; Business Ghost Inc., founder. **Publications:** NON-FICTION: Journey To Tradition: The Odyssey of a Born-Again Jew, 1986; Guide to the Jewish Internet, 1996; What Every Jew Needs to Know About God, 1997; Writer's Internet Sourcebook, 1997; Welcome to the Jungle! The Unauthorized Biography of Jim Rome, 1998; Where There's Smoke, There's Salmon: The Book of Jewish Proverbs, 2001; (with J. Bryant) Banking on Our Future: A Program for Teaching You and Your Kids about Money, 2002; Complete Idiot's Guide to Jewish Spirituality and Mysticism, 2002; (with R. Hollander and F. Homberger) Boomer's Guide to Sex That (Still) Sizzles, 2003; (with J. Cateau) Complete Idiot's Guide to the Pentagon, 2003; Complete Idiot's Guide to Your Civil Liberties, 2003; (with D. Winfield) Dropping the Ball: Baseball's Troubles and How We can and Must Solve Them, 2007; (with D. Christie and J. Christie) No Ordinary Love: A True Story of Marriage and Basketball!, 2007; (with J. Garcia) Making Jack Falcone: An Undercover FBI Agent Takes Down a Mafia Family, 2008; (with D. Winfield) Making the Play: How to Get the Best of Baseball Back, 2008; (with H. Bragman) Where's My Fifteen Minutes?: Get Your Company, Your Cause, or Yourself the Recognition You Deserve, 2008. NOVELS: Socratic Method, 1987; Set-

tling the Score, 1989; Alive and Kicking, 1993; Sam and Derek, Derek and Sam, 1997; Janine and Alex, Alex and Janine, 1997; The Shidduch Diaries, 2005; (ed.) Born To Win, 2012; (with D. Oliphant) When All Else Fails, Sell!: How Learning to Sell Can Change Your Life, 2012. Contributor to periodicals. **Address:** Writer2Author Inc., 4199 Campus Dr., Ste. 550, Irvine, CA 92612, U.S.A. **Online address:** michael@celebrityghost.com

LEVIN, Miriam (Ramsfelder). American (born United States), b. 1962. **Genres:** Novels, Children's Fiction, Young Adult Fiction. **Career:** Writer and educator. **Publications:** In the Beginning, 1996. **Address:** 42-39 Herold Dr., Fair Lawn, NJ 07410, U.S.A. **Online address:** amejr999@optonline.net

LEVIN, Ted. American (born United States), b. 1948. **Genres:** Environmental Sciences/Ecology, Zoology, Natural History, Biology. **Career:** New York Zoological Society, educator, 1971-72, 1974; Antioch New England Graduate School, adjunct faculty, 1976-97; Montshire Museum of Science, adjunct naturalist, 1977-92; New England College, part-time faculty, 1978-90; Community of Thetford, justice of the peace, 1996-2000. Write and photographer. **Publications:** Backtracking: The Way of a Naturalist, 1987; Blood Brook: A Naturalist's Home Ground, 1992; Everglades National Park, 1995; (with L. Levin) Creepy Crawly Creatures, 1995; (with S. Lehmer) Up River, 1995; (with F. Asch) Cactus Poems, 1998; Liquid Land: A Journey through the Florida Everglades, 2003. **Address:** University of Georgia Press, 330 Research Dr., Athens, GA 30602-4901, U.S.A. **Online address:** ted.levin@valley.net

LEVIN, Yuval. American (born United States), b. 1977. **Genres:** Politics/Government, Social Sciences, Theology/Religion. **Career:** President's Council on Bioethics, executive director, 2003-05; White House, Domestic Policy Council, associate director; Ethics and Public Policy Center, director of bioethics and American democracy. Writer. **Publications:** Tyranny of Reason: The Origins and Consequences of the Social Scientific Outlook, 2001; Imagining the Future: Science and American Democracy, 2008; (ed. with C. DeMuth) Religion and the American Future, 2008. Contributor to newspapers and periodicals. **Address:** Ethics and Public Policy Center, 1015 15th St. NW, Ste. 900, Washington, DC 20005-2605, U.S.A. **Online address:** ylevin@eppc.org

LEVINE, Alan J. American (born United States), b. 1950. **Genres:** History, Military/Defense/Arms Control, Politics/Government, Mythology/Folklore, Social Sciences. **Career:** Writer, 1989-. **Publications:** British, American and Soviet Political Aims and Military Strategies, 1941-1945: A Study in the Beginnings of the Cold War, 1979; The Soviet Union, the Communist Movement, and the World: Prelude to the Cold War, 1990; The Strategic Bombing of Germany, 1940-1945, 1992; The Missile and Space Race, 1994; The Pacific War, 1995; The United States and the Struggle for Southeast Asia, 1945-1973, 1995; Race Relations within Western Expansion, 1996; The War against Rommel's Supply Lines, 1942-1943, 1999; Captivity, Flight, and Survival in World War II, 2000; From the Normandy Beaches to the Baltic Sea: The Northwest Europe Campaign, 1944-1945, 2000; Stalin's Last War: Korea and the Approach to World War III, 2005; Bad Old Days: The Myth of the 1950s, 2008. **Address:** 138-21 77th Ave., Kew Gardens Hills, NY 11367-2824, U.S.A.

LEVINE, Allan. Canadian (born Canada), b. 1956. **Genres:** Mystery/Crime/Suspense, History, Biography. **Career:** University of Manitoba, instructor in education, 1983-84; St. John's-Ravenscourt School, teacher of history, 1984- ; Camp Massad, board directors, 1986-96; Winnipeg Board of Jewish Education, board directors, 1995-97. Writer. **Publications:** The Exchange: One Hundred Years of Trading Grain in Winnipeg, 1987; (ed. and contrib.) Your Worship: The Lives of Eight of Canada's Most Unforgettable Mayors, 1989; Scrum Wars: The Prime Ministers and the Media, 1993; Fugitives of the Forest: The Heroic Story of Jewish Resistance and Survival during the Second World War, 1998, 2nd ed. 2009; Scattered among the Peoples: The Jewish Diaspora in Ten Portraits, 2002; The Devil in Babylon: Fear of Progress and the Birth of Modern Life, 2005; Coming of Age: A History of the Jewish People of Manitoba, 2009; William Lyon Mackenzie King: A Life Guided By The Hand of Destiny, 2011. HISTORICAL MYSTERIES: The Blood Libel, 1997; Sins of the Suffragette, 2000; The Bolshevik's Revenge, 2002; Evil of the Age, 2008. **Address:** St. Johns-Ravenscourt School, 400 South Dr., Winnipeg, MB R3T 3K5, Canada. **Online address:** aglevine@shaw.ca

LEVINE, Amy-Jill. American (born United States), b. 1956?. **Genres:** Theology/Religion. **Career:** Smith College, teaching assistant, 1976-78; Duke University Divinity School and Trinity College, W.D. Davies instructor in Biblical studies, 1982-83, visiting instructor, 1984-85; University of North Carolina, visiting instructor, 1984-85; Swarthmore College, Department of Religion, assistant professor, 1985-91, acting chair, 1989-90, associate professor, 1991-94, chair, 1991-94, Sara Lawrence Lightfoot associate professor of religion, 1993-94; Vanderbilt University Divinity School, professor of New Testament studies, 1994-, E. Rhodes and Leona B. Carpenter professor of New Testament studies and Carpenter program in religion, gender and sexuality, director, 1996-, College of Arts and Science, professor of Jewish studies, 2010-, university professor, 2010-; Texas Christian University, Brite Divinity School, visiting professor of New Testament, 2005. Writer. **Publications:** The Social and Ethnic Dimensions of Matthean Salvation History, 1988; (ed. with J. Neusner and E.S. Frerichs) Religious Writings and Religious Systems-Systemic Analysis of Holy Books in Christianity, Islam, Buddhism, Greco-Roman Religions, Ancient Israel, and Judaism, vol. I: Islam, Buddhism, Greco-Roman Religions, Ancient Israel and Judaism, 1989; (ed.) Women Like This: New Perspectives on Jewish Women in the Greco-Roman World, 1991; Threatened Bodies, 1997; The Misunderstood Jew: The Church and the Scandal of the Jewish Jesus, 2006; (ed. with D.C. Allison, Jr. and J.D. Crossan) The Historical Jesus in Context, 2006; (contrib.) Cambridge Companion to the Bible, 2007; (with D. Knight) Scriptures of Israel, 2010; Hearing the Jewish Jesus: (with D. Knight) The Parables, 2011; (with D. Knight) An Essential Guide To Second Temple Judaism, 2011; (with D. Knight) The Meaning of the Bible, 2011; (ed. with M. Brettler) Jewish Annotated New Testament, 2011. EDITOR WITH M. BLICKENSTAFF: A Feminist Companion to the Deutero-Pauline Epistles, 2003; A Feminist Companion to John, 2003; Feminist Companion to the Acts of the Apostle, 2004; Feminist Companion to the Catholic Epistles and Hebrews, 2004; A Feminist Companion to Luke, 2004; A Feminist Companion to Mariology, 2005; Feminist Companion to the New Testament Apocrypha, 2006; Feminist Companion to Patristic Literature, 2008; Feminist Companion to the Apocalypse of John, 2009. **Address:** Divinity School and College of Arts and Science, Vanderbilt University, 411 21st Ave. S, Nashville, TN 37240-1121, U.S.A. **Online address:** amy-jill.levine@vanderbilt.edu

LEVINE, Barbara Hoberman. American (born United States), b. 1937. **Genres:** Human Relations/Parenting, Psychology, Self Help, Medicine/Health, Sports/Fitness. **Career:** Renaissance Book Services Corp., owner; Aslan Publishing, owner. Writer. **Publications:** Your Body Believes Every Word You Say: The Language of the Body/Mind Connection, 1991, 2nd ed., 2000. **Address:** Aslan Publishing, 2490 Black Rock Tpke., Ste. 342, Fairfield, CT 06825, U.S.A. **Online address:** barbara1@aslanpublishing.com

LEVINE, Bruce C. American (born United States), b. 1949?. **Genres:** History, Social Sciences. **Career:** University of Illinois, James G. Randall professor of history; University of Cincinnati, faculty; University of California, faculty. Writer. **Publications:** (With others) Who Built America? Working People and the Nation's Economy, Politics, Culture and Society, vol. I: From Conquest and Colonization through Reconstruction and the Great Uprising of 1877, vol. II: From the Centennial Celebration of 1876 to the Great War of 1914, 1989, 3rd ed. as Who Built America? Working People and the Nation's History, 2007; Half Slave and Half Free: The Roots of Civil War, 1992; The Migration of Ideology and the Contested Meaning of Freedom: German-Americans in the Mid-Nineteenth Century, 1992; The Spirit of 1848: German Immigrants, Labor Conflict, and the Coming of the Civil War, 1992; Confederate Emancipation: Southern Plans to Free and Arm Slaves during the Civil War, 2006. **Address:** IL , U.S.A. **Online address:** blevine3@illinois.edu

LEVINE, Gail Carson. American (born United States), b. 1947. **Genres:** Children's Fiction, Young Adult Fiction, Novels, Poetry. **Career:** New York State Department of Labor, employment interviewer, 1970-82; New York State Department of Commerce, administrative assistant, 1982-86; New York State Department of Social Services, welfare administrator, 1986-96; New York State Department of Labor, welfare administrator, 1986-97. Writer. **Publications:** SERIES: For Biddle's Sake, 2002. NOVELS: Ella Enchanted, 1997; Dave at Night, 1999; The Wish, 1999; The Princess Test, 1999; The Fairy's Mistake, 1999; Princess Sonora and the Long Sleep, 1999; Cinderellis and the Glass Hill, 2000; The Two Princesses of Bamarre, 2001; Betsy Who Cried Wolf, 2002; The Fairy's Return, 2002; Fairy Dust and the Quest for the Egg, 2005; Fairest, 2006; Fairy Haven and the Quest for the Wand, 2007;

Ever, 2008; Fairies and the quest for Never Land, 2010; Betsy Red Hoodie, 2010. NON FICTION: Writing Magic: Creating Stories that Fly, 2006. OTHERS: The Princess Tales: vol. I, 2002, vol. II, 2004; The Fairy's Return and Other Princess Tales, 2006; A Tale of Two Castles, 2011; This is Just to Say: Poems, 2012; Beloved Elodie, forthcoming. **Address:** c/o Author Mail, HarperCollins Publishers, 10 E 53rd St., New York, NY 10022, U.S.A. **Online address:** gclevine@cloudq.net

LEVINE, Gustav. American (born United States), b. 1926. **Genres:** Mathematics/Statistics, Psychology. **Career:** Creedmoor Institute for Psychobiologic Studies, research scientist, 1958-66; James McKeen Cattell Fund fellow, 1966-67; Arizona State University, associate professor of psychology, 1967-92. Writer. **Publications:** (With C.J. Burke) Mathematical Model Techniques for Learning Theories, 1972; Introductory Statistics for Psychology: The Logic and the Methods, 1981; A Guide to SPSS for Analysis of Variance, 1991, 2nd ed., 2003; (with S. Parkinson) Experimental Methods in Psychology, 1994. **Address:** 585 Indian Acres Ct., Tucker, GA 30084-1625, U.S.A. **Online address:** guslevine@comcast.net

LEVINE, Jeffrey P. American (born United States), b. 1957. **Genres:** Business/Trade/Industry, Reference. **Career:** U.S. Department of Labor, budget analyst, 1980-81; Ross Associates, manufacturer's representative, 1981-82; JPL Enterprises, owner, 1982-87; writer, 1988-. **Publications:** (With T.E. Crain) Doing Business in New York City, 1989; Doing Business in Chicago, 1990; Doing Business in Boston, 1994, 3rd ed., 1998; Pittsburgh Business Directory, 1995, 3rd ed., 2000; Ingram's Business Directory of Kansas City, 1997; Central Penn Business Directory, 1998, 2nd ed., 2002. **Address:** 10531 Cedar Lake Rd., Ste. 512, Minnetonka, MN 55305, U.S.A. **Online address:** jplauthor@hotmail.com

LEVINE, Joel S. American (born United States), b. 1942. **Genres:** Air/Space Topics, Technology. **Career:** National Aeronautics and Space Administration, Langley Research Center, Atmospheric Science Division, senior research scientist, 1970-, founder and director; College of William and Mary, adjunct professor of applied science and physics, 1992-, visiting professor of environmental science and policy, 1997-. Writer. **Publications:** (Ed. with D.R. Schryer) Man's Impact on the Troposphere: Lectures in Tropospheric Chemistry, 1978; (ed.) The Photochemistry of Atmosphere: Earth, the Other Planets, and Comets, 1985; (ed.) Global Biomass Burning: Atmospheric, Climatic, and Biospheric Implications, 1991; Biomass Burning and Global Change vol. I-II, 1996; (co-author) Wildland Fires and the Environment, 1999. **Address:** Atmospheric Sciences Competency, NASA Langley Research Ctr., Hampton, VA 23681-0001, U.S.A. **Online address:** j.s.levine@larc.nasa.gov

LEVINE, John R. American (born United States), b. 1954. **Genres:** Information Science/Computers, Technology, Politics/Government. **Career:** Interactive Systems Corp., principal developer, 1979-84; Javelin Software, senior engineer, DP director, senior staff, 1984-87; Taughannock Networks, writer, lecturer, consultant., 1987-; Segue Software, co-founder, 1989-2007, senior engineer, 1989-90, director, 1992-2007; The Journal of C Language Translation, editor, 1993-96; Village of Trumansburg, mayor, 2004-07; Blackvine Consulting, partner, 2005-07, staff, 2005-. Writer. **Publications:** (With M.L. Young and J.M. Young II) Understanding Javelin PLUS, 1987; (with D.C. Kay) Graphics File Formats, 1992, 2nd ed., 1994; (with M.L. Young) UNIX for Dummies, 1993; Lex & Yacc, 2nd ed., 2000; (with C. Baroudi and M.L. Young) The Internet for Dummies, 1993, (with M.L. Young and R. Muller) 13th ed., 2012; (with L. Young) More Internet for Dummies, 1994, rev. ed., 1996; (ed.) Internet, 1994; (with M.L. Young) UNIX for Dummies Quick Reference, 1995; Programming for Graphic Files in C and C++, 1994; (co-author) The Internet for Dummies Quick Reference, 1994, rev. ed., 2000; (with M.L. Young) Internet FAQs, 1995; (with C. Baroudi) Internet Secrets, 1995, 2nd ed., 2000; (with M.L. Young) More UNIX for Dummies, 1995; (co-author) Internet E-Mail for Dummies, 1996, 2nd ed., 1998; (co-author) The UNIX Dictionary of Commands, Terms, and Acronyms, 1996; (co-author) E-mail for Dummies, 1997; (co-author) Windows 98: The Complete Reference, 1998; (with C. Baroudi and M.L. Young) The Internet for Dummies Starter Kit, 7th ed., 2000; (co-author) The Internet for Microsoft Windows Me Millennium Edition for Dummies, 2000; (with M.L. Young) Poor Richard's Building Online Communities, 2000; Linkers and Loaders, 2000; (co-author) Windows Millennium Edition: The Complete Reference, 2001; (with R. Everett-Church and G. Stebben) Internet Privacy for Dummies, 2002; (with M. Levine-Young) Windows XP Home Edition, 2002; (with R. Everett-Church and M.L. Young) Spam Fighting for Dummies, 2003; Qmail, 2004; (with

M.L. Young and R. Everett-Church) Fighting Spam for Dummies, 2004; La Internet Para Dummies, 2006; (with M.L. Young) Windows Vista: The Complete Reference, 2007; (with M.J. O'Farrell and J. Algroy) Mobile Internet for Dummies, 2008. **Address:** Taughannock Networks, PO Box 727, Trumansburg, NY 14886-0727, U.S.A. **Online address:** writdir@johnlevine.com

LEVINE, Kristin. American (born United States), b. 1974?. **Genres:** Novels. **Career:** Writer and educator. **Publications:** The Best Bad Luck I Ever Had, 2009; The Lions of Little Rock, 2012. **Address:** G.P. Putnam's Sons, 375 Hudson St., New York, NY 10014-3657, U.S.A. **Online address:** kslevine@cox.net

LEVINE, Laura (Sue). American (born United States), b. 1943. **Genres:** Mystery/Crime/Suspense. **Career:** Reporter and writer. **Publications:** (With D. Chodkowski) Mr. Wrong, A Guide to the Least-Eligible Bachelors in America, 1984; Killer Blonde, 2004; Shoes to Die For, 2005; The PMS Murder, 2006; Death by Pantyhose, 2007; Candy Cane Murder, 2007; Killing Bridezilla, 2008; Killer Cruise, 2009; Troubadours, 2009; Death of a Trophy Wife, 2010; (with L. Meier and J. Fluke) Gingerbread Cookie Murder, 2010. JAINE AUSTEN MYSTERY SERIES: This Pen for Hire, 2002; Last Writes, 2003. **Address:** c/o Author Mail, Kensington Books, 850 3rd Ave., New York, NY 10022, U.S.A. **Online address:** jaineausten@aol.com

LEVINE, Mark. American (born United States), b. 1966. **Genres:** Theology/Religion, Humanities. **Career:** Lund University, Center for Middle Eastern Studies, distinguished visiting professor; University of California, Department of History, professor, 2001-. Writer and musician. **Publications:** (Ed. with V. Mortensen and P. Perez) Twilight of Empire: Responses to Occupation, 2003; Why They Don't Hate Us: Lifting the Veil on the Axis of Evil, 2005; (ed. with A. Salvatore) Religion, Social Practice and Contested Hegemonies: Reconstructing the Public Sphere in Muslim Majority Societies, 2005; Overthrowing Geography: Jaffa, Tel Aviv and the Struggle for Palestine, 1880-1948, 2005; (ed. with S. Sufian) Reapproaching Borders: New Perspectives on the Study of Israel-Palestine, 2007; Heavy Metal Islam: Rock, Resistance, and the Struggle for the Soul of Islam, 2008; Impossible Peace: Israel/ Palestine since 1989, 2009. **Address:** Department of History, University of California, 220 Murray Krieger Hall, Irvine, CA 92697-3275, U.S.A. **Online address:** mlevine@uci.edu

LEVINE, Paul. (Paul Jacob Levine). American (born United States), b. 1948. **Genres:** Novels, Mystery/Crime/Suspense, Plays/Screenplays, Law. **Career:** Miami Herald, reporter, 1969-70; attorney, 1973-77; Los Angeles Times, stringer, 1972; Bartel, Levine and Shuford, trial and appellate attorney and partner, 1977-78; University of Miami, School of Law, adjunct faculty of communications law, 1978-80; Morgan, Lewis and Bockius, attorney and partner, 1978-87; Spence, Payne, Masington, Grossman and Needle, counsel, 1987-88; Grossman and Roth, counselor, 1988-91; CBS-TV, JAG, executive story editor, 1999-2001, First Monday, co-creator/co-executive producer, 2002; WPLG-TV News, legal commentator; AM South Florida, legal commentator; Pennsylvania State University, School of Communications, Alumni Board, director. **Publications:** What's Your Verdict?, 1980; To Speak for the Dead, 1990; Night Vision, 1992; False Dawn, 1993; Mortal Sin, 1994; Slashback, 1995; Fool Me Twice, 1996; Flesh and Bones, 1997; Nine Scorpions, 1998; Solomon vs. Lord, 2005; The Deep Blue Alibi, 2006; Kill All the Lawyers, 2006; Trial & Error, 2007; Illegal, 2009; Lassiter, 2011. Contributor to periodicals. **Address:** c/o Albert Zuckerman, Writers House, 21 W 26th St., New York, NY 10010, U.S.A. **Online address:** paul@paul-levine.com

LEVINE, Paul Jacob. See **LEVINE, Paul.**

LEVINE, Philip. American (born United States), b. 1928. **Genres:** Poetry, Essays, Young Adult Fiction. **Career:** University of Iowa, instructor, 1955-57; California State University, professor of English, 1958-, now professor emeritus; University of Cincinnati, Elliston professor of poetry, 1976; Princeton University, visiting professor, 1978; Columbia University, visiting professor, 1978, 1981, 1984; University of California, visiting professor, 1980; Brown University, visiting professor, 1984; New York University, adjunct professor, 1984; Brown University, university professor, 1985; New York University, Creative Writing Program, distinguished poet-in-residence. **Publications:** POETRY: On the Edge, 1963; Not this Pig, 1968; 5 Detroits, 1970; Thistles, 1970; Pili's Wall, 1971; Red Dust, 1971; They Feed They Lion, 1972; 1933, 1974; New Season, 1975; The Names of the Lost, 1976; Ashes: Poems New & Old, 1979; 7 Years from Somewhere, 1979; One for the Rose,

1981; Selected Poems, 1984; Sweet Will, 1985; (ed.) The Essential Keats, 1987; A Walk with Tom Jefferson, 1988; What Work Is, 1991; New Selected Poems, 1991; The Simple Truth, 1994; The Mercy, 1999; Breath, 2004; News of the World, 2009. ESSAYS: Don't Ask, 1981; The Bread of Time: Toward an Autobiography, 1994; So Ask, 2002. OTHERS: (ed.) Character and Crisis, 1966; On the Edge & Over, 1976; (ed. and trans. with E. Trejo) Tarumba: The Selected Poems of Jaime Sabines, 1979; (ed. and trans. with A. Long) Off the Map: Selected Poems, 1984; (O. Patterson and N. Rush) Earth, Stars and Writers, 1992; (ed. and foreword) Elegy, 1997; Unselected Poems, 1997; So Ask: Essays, Conversations, and Interviews, 2002; Detroit Disassembled, 2010. **Address:** California State University, 5241 N Maple Ave., Fresno, CA 93740, U.S.A.

LEVINE, Stuart George. American (born United States), b. 1932. **Genres:** Novellas/Short Stories, Literary Criticism And History. **Career:** University of Kansas, instructor, 1958-61, assistant professor, 1961-63, associate professor, 1963-69, Department of American Studies, founding chairman, 1965-70, professor, 1969-92, professor emeritus of English, 1994-; University of La Plata, Fulbright lecturer, 1962; University of Costa Rica, Fulbright lecturer, 1965, 1967; California State University, visiting professor, 1969, 1971; National Autonomous University of Mexico, Fulbright lecturer, 1972. Writer. **Publications:** Materials for Technical Writing, 1963; (contrib.) American Culture in the Sixties, 1964; (ed. with N.O. Lurie) The American Indian Today, 1968, rev. ed., 1970; (ed.) The Story of American Painting, 1970; Edgar Poe: Seer and Craftsman, 1972; (ed. with S.F. Levine) The Short Fiction of Edgar Allan Poe, 1976; The Monday-Wednesday-Friday Girl and Other Stories, 1994; (intro. and contrib. with S.F. Levine) Thirty-Two Stories, 2000; (ed. and intro. with S.F. Levine) Eureka, 2004; (ed., intro. and contrib. with S.F. Levine) Critical Theory: The Major Documents, 2009. Contributor to journals. **Address:** Department of English, University of Kansas, Rm. 3001, 1445 Jayhawk Blvd., Lawrence, KS 66045, U.S.A. **Online address:** slevine@ku.edu

LEVINSON, Alan. British (born England), b. 1943. **Genres:** Novellas/Short Stories, Young Adult Fiction. **Career:** Supreme Court of England, solicitor, 1967-; Underwriter for Lloyd's, 1983-; William Sturges & Co., partner. Writer. **Publications:** Table for Four (short stories), 1995. **Address:** William Sturges & Co., Burwood House, 14-16 Caxton St., Westminster, GL SW1H 0QY, England. **Online address:** alan.levinson@williamsturges.co.uk

LEVINSON, David M. American (born United States), b. 1967. **Genres:** Money/Finance, Transportation, Politics/Government. **Career:** Hayes Microcomputer Products, engineering technician, 1985-86; Georgia Institute of Technology, City Planning Program, graduate research assistant, 1988-89; Maryland-National Capital Park and Planning Commission, Montgomery County Planning Department, transportation planner, 1989-94; consultant, 1994-97; University of California, Institute of Transportation Studies, graduate student assistant, 1994-97, PATH Program, post-doctoral researcher, 1998-99; University of Minnesota, Department of Civil Engineering, assistant professor, 1999-2005, associate professor, 2005-, Richard P. Braun/CTS chair in transportation engineering, 2006-, Networks, Economics and Urban Systems Research Group (NEXUS), director, Graduate Studies Certificate in Transportation Studies, director, 2007-. Writer. **Publications:** Financing Transportation Networks, 2002; (ed. with D. Gillen) Assessing the Benefits and Costs of ITS: Making the Business Case for ITS Investments, 2004; (ed. with K.J. Krizek) Access to Destinations, 2005; (with W.L. Garrison) The Transportation Experience: Policy, Planning, and Deployment, 2006; (with K.J. Krizek) Planning for Place and Plexus: Metropolitan Land Use and Transport, 2008; (with F. Xie) Evolving Transportation Networks, 2011; (ed. with H.X. Liu and M. Bell) Network Reliability in Practice, 2011. **Address:** Department of Civil Engineering, University of Minnesota, Rm. 138, 500 Pillsbury Dr. SE, Minneapolis, MN 55455-0116, U.S.A. **Online address:** levin031@umn.edu

LEVINSON, Harry. American (born United States), b. 1922. **Genres:** Administration/Management, Psychology, Medicine/Health. **Career:** Topeka Veterans Administration Hospital, psychological intern, 1946-50; Topeka State Hospital, coordinator of professional education, 1950-54; Menninger Foundation, psychologist, 1954-55, Division of Industrial Mental Health, director, 1954-68; Massachusetts Institute of Technology, Sloan School of Management, visiting professor, 1961-62; University of Kansas, visiting professor, 1967; Levinson Institute, founder and chairman emeritus, 1968-; Harvard University, Thomas Henry Carroll-Ford Foundation, distinguished visiting professor, 1968-72, Medical School, lecturer, 1972-85, clinical professor, 1985-90, professor emeritus, 1990-; Boston University, adjunct professor,

1972-74; Pace University, adjunct professor, 1973-84; Texas A&M University, visiting centennial professor, 1976; Harvard Medical School, Department of Psychiatry, clinical professor of psychology, now professor emeritus. Writer and consultant. **Publications:** A National Perpective on Industrial Human Relations, 1954; (with W.C. Menninger) Human Understanding in Industry: A Guide for Supervisors, 1956; (ed.) Toward Understanding Men, 1956; (co-author) Men, Management and Mental Health, 1962; Emotional Health in the World of Work, 1964, rev. ed., 1980; (co-author) Are You Nobody?, 1966; The Exceptional Executive: A Psychological Conception., 1968, rev. ed. as Executive, 1981; Executive Stress, 1970, rev. ed., 1975; (with A.G. Spohn and J. Molinari) Organizational Diagnosis, 1972; The Great Jackass Fallacy, 1973; Psychological Man, 1976; (with C. Lang) Executive, 1981; Casebook for Psychological Man: Instructor's Guide, 1982; (with S. Rosenthal) CEO: Corporate Leadership in Action, 1984; Ready, Fire, Aim: Avoiding Management by Impulse, 1986; (ed.) Designing and Managing Your Career, 1989; Career Mastery: Keys to Taking Charge of Your Career Throughout Your Work Life, 1992; Organizational Assessment: A Step-by-Step Guide to Effective Consulting, 2002; Harry Levinson on the Psychology of Leadership, 2006; Consulting Psychology: Selected Articles, 2009; Bearding the Lion that Roared: The Levinson Cornerstones, 2010. Contributor to professional journals and popular periodicals. **Address:** Levinson Institute, 28 Main St., Ste. 100, Jaffrey, NH 03452, U.S.A. **Online address:** levinson@levinsoninst.com

LEVINSON, Jay. Israeli/American (born United States), b. 1949. **Genres:** Criminology/True Crime, Travel/Exploration, Law, Theology/Religion. **Career:** U.S. Central Intelligence Agency, questioned document examiner, 1972-81; Israeli Police, questioned document examiner, 1981-85, head of disaster victim identification unit, 1985-97; John Jay College of Criminal Justice, adjunct professor; freelance writer and speaker, 2001-. **Publications:** (Trans. and intro.) A. Levinsohn, Aspects of Disaster Victim Identification in Jewish Law, 1999; Questioned Documents: A Lawyer's Handbook, 2001; (with H. Granot) Terror Bombing: The New Urban Threat: Practical Approaches for Response Agencies and Security, 2002; (with H. Ganot) Transportation Disaster Response Handbook, 2002; Jewish Community of Cuba Until the Castro Revolution, 2005; Jewish Community of Cuba: The Golden Years: 1906-1958, 2006; Jewish Journeys in Jerusalem: A Tourist's Guide, 2010. Contributor to books and journals. **Address:** PO Box 23067, Jerusalem, 91230, Israel. **Online address:** jay_levinson@hotmail.com

LEVINSON, Jay Conrad. American (born United States), b. 1933?. **Genres:** Marketing, Business/Trade/Industry, Economics. **Career:** University of California, lecturer; Leo Burnett Advertising, creative director; J. Walter Thompson, senior vice president; Guerrilla Marketing Intl., co-founder and chairman. Writer. **Publications:** Earning Money without a Job: The Economics of Freedom, 1979, rev. ed. as Earning Money without a Job: Revised for the '90s, 1991; 555 Ways to Earn Extra Money, 1982, rev. ed. as 555 Ways to Earn Extra Money: Revised for the '90s, 1991; Guerrilla Marketing: Secrets for Making Big Profits from Your Small Business, 1984; An Earthling's Guide to Satellite TV, 1985; Quit Your Job: Making the Decision, Making the Break, Making It Work, 1987; Guerrilla Marketing Attack: New Strategies, Tactics and Weapons for Winning Big Profits from Your Small Business, 1989; Guerrilla Marketing Weapons: One Hundred Affordable Marketing Methods for Maximizing Profits from Your Small Business, 1990; The Ninety-Minute Hour, 1990; (with B.J. Blechman) Guerrilla Financing: Alternative Techniques to Finance Any Small Business, 1991; (with B. Gallagher and O.R. Wilson) Guerrilla Selling: Unconventional Weapons and Tactics for Increasing Your Sales, 1992; Guerrilla Marketing Excellence: The Fifty Golden Rules for Small-Business Success, 1993; Guerrilla Marketing for the '90s: The Newest Secrets for Making Big Profits from Your Small Business, 1993; Guerrilla Advertising: Cost-Effective Techniques for Small-Business Success, 1994; (with S. Godin) The Guerrilla Marketing Handbook, 1994; (with C. Rubin) Guerrilla Marketing Online: The Entrepreneur's Guide to Earning Profits on the Internet, 1995; Guerrilla Marketing for the Home-Based Business, 1995; (with C. Rubin) Guerrilla Marketing Online Weapons: One Hundred Low-Cost, High-Impact Weapons for Online Profits and Prosperity, 1996; The Way of the Guerrilla: Achieving Success and Balance as an Entrepreneur in the 21st Century, 1996; (with S. Godin) Get What You Deserve: How to Guerrilla Market Yourself, 1997; (with O.R. Wilson and M.S.A. Smith) Guerrilla Trade Show Selling: New Unconventional Weapons and Tactics to Meet More People, Get More Leads and Close More Sales, 1997; (with O.R. Wilson and M.S.A. Smith) Guerrilla Teleselling: New Unconventional Weapons and Tactics to Sell When You Can't Be There in Person, 1998; (with Mark S.A. Smith and O.R. Wilson) Guerrilla Negotiating:

Unconventional Weapons and Tactics to Get What You Want, 1999; Mastering Guerrilla Marketing: 100 Profit-Producing Insights You Can Take to the Bank, 1999; (with K. Tyler) Guerrilla Saving: Secrets for Keeping Profits in Your Home-Based Business, 2000; (with R. Frishman and M. Larsen) Guerrilla Marketing for Writers, 2001; Guerrilla Marketing: The Best of Guerrilla Marketing, 2001; Guerrilla Creativity: Make Your Message Irresistible, 2001; Guerilla Marketing: Make Your Message Irresistible with the Power of Memes, 2001; Marketing de Guerrilla, 2000; (with J. Lublin, R. Frishman and M. Steisel) Guerrilla Publicity: Hundreds of Sure-Fire Tactics to Maximum Sales for Minimum Dollars, 2002; (with G.W. Hicks) Guerrilla Marketing for Financial Advisors, 2003; Guerrilla Marketing for Free: One Hundred No-Cost Tactics to Promote Your Business and Energize Your Profits, 2003; (with T. Brandt-Sarif) Guerrilla Travel Tactics: Hundreds of Simple Strategies Guaranteed to Save Road Warriors Time and Money, 2004; (foreword) Career Guide for the High-Tech Professional: Where the Jobs Are Now and How to Land Them, 2004; (with A. Lautenslager) Guerrilla Marketing in 30 Days: How to Obtain More Customers and Increase Profits One Day at a Time, 2004, 2nd ed., 2009; (with E. Valas and O.R. Wilson) Guerrilla Retailing: Unconventional Ways to Make Big Profits from Your Retail Business, 2004; (with M.W. McLaughlin) Guerrilla Marketing for Consultants: Breakthrough Tactics for Winning Profitable Clients, 2005; (with D.E. Perry) Guerrilla Marketing for Job-hunters: 400 Unconventional Tips, Tricks and Tactics for Landing Your Dream Job, 2005; (with P.R.J. Hanley) The Guerrilla Marketing Revolution: Precision Persuasion of the Unconscious Mind, 2006; The Guerrilla Entrepreneur: Achieving Success and Balance Now and In the Future, 2007; (with J. Levinson and A. Levinson) Guerrilla Marketing: Easy and Inexpensive Strategies for Making Big Profits from Your Small Business, 4th ed., 2007; (with A. Hernandez) Guerrilla Marketing Success Secrets: 52 Weeks of Marketing & Management Wisdom, 2007; (with M. Meyerson and M.E. Scarborough) Guerrilla Marketing on the Internet: The Definitive Guide from the Father of Guerrilla Marketing, 2008; (with S. Burkow) Guerrilla Profits: 10 Powerful Strategies to Increase Cashflow, Boost Earnings & Get More Business, 2008; (with M. Mann) Guerrilla Networking: A Proven Battle Plan to Attract the Very People You Want to Meet, 2008; (with B. Lovejoy) Guerrilla Street Team Guide, 2008; (with J. Levinson) Startup Guide to Guerrilla Marketing: A Simple Battle Plan for First-time Marketers, 2008; (with R.J. Kaden and G. Linda) MORE Guerrilla Marketing Research: Asking the Right People, the Right Questions, the Right Way and Effectively Using the Answers to Make More Money, 2009; (with S. Savage) Guerrilla Business Secrets: Fifty-Eight Ways to Start, Build and Sell Your Business: A True Story by a True Guerrilla!, 2009; (with D.E. Perry) Guerrilla Marketing for Job Hunters 2.0: 1,001 Unconventional Tips, Tricks and Tactics for Landing Your Dream Job, 2009; (with F. Adkins and C. Forbes) Guerrilla Marketing for Nonprofits, 2009; (with S. Horowitz) Guerrilla Marketing Goes Green: Winning Strategies to Improve Your Profits and Your Planet, 2010; (with S. Gibson) Guerrilla Social Media Marketing: 100+ Weapons to Grow Your Online Influence, Attract Customers, 2010; (with A. Neitlich) Guerrilla Marketing for a Bulletproof Career: How to Attract Ongoing Opportunities in Perpetually Gut-Wrenching Times, for Entrepreneurs, Employees and Everyone In Between, 2011; (with D.E. Perry) Guerrilla Marketing for Job Hunters 3.0, 2011; (with J. Levinson) Guerrilla Marketing Remix, 2011; (with A. Neitlich) Guerrilla Marketing Job Escape Plan, 2012. Contributor to periodicals. **Address:** Guerrilla Marketing Intl., 260 Cascade Dr., PO Box 1336, Mill Valley, CA 94941-1714, U.S.A. **Online address:** jayview@aol.com

LEVINSON, Jerrold. American (born United States), b. 1948. **Genres:** Essays, Philosophy, Art/Art History. **Career:** State University of New York, visiting assistant professor, 1974-75; University of Maryland, assistant professor, associate professor, 1976-91, professor, 1991-, distinguished university professor of philosophy; University of London, visiting professor, 1991; National Endowment for Humanities, Summer Institute, co-director, 1991, director, 2002; Johns Hopkins University, visiting professor, 1993; Universite de Rennes, visiting professor, 1998; University of Canterbury, Erskine Fellow, 1999; Columbia University, visiting professor, 2000; Conservatorio della Svizzera Italiana, philosopher-in-residence, 2004; Universite Libre de Bruxelles, Chaire Chaim Perelman, 2006; University of Kent, Leverhulme visiting professor, 2008-09; University of Leuven, Chaire Francqui, 2010-. Writer. **Publications:** Music, Art, and Metaphysics: Essays in Philosophical Aesthetics, 1990; The Pleasures of Aesthetics: Philosophical Essays, 1996; Music in the Moment, 1998; L'art, La Musique, et L'histoire, 1998; (ed.) Aesthetics and Ethics: Essays at the Intersection, 1998; (co-ed.) Aesthetic Concepts: Essays, 2001; (ed.) Oxford Handbook of Aesthetics, 2003; Contemplating Art: Essays in Aesthetics, 2006. **Address:** Department of Philosophy, University of Maryland, Skinner Bldg., College Park, MD 20742, U.S.A. **Online address:** august@umd.edu

LEVINSON, Marc. American (born United States), b. 1953. **Genres:** Economics, Business/Trade/Industry. **Career:** Time, reporter on business, 1978-83; BNA Publishing, reporter, staff correspondent, 1979-83; Dun's Business Monthly, senior editor, 1985-87; Journal of Commerce, editorial director, 1987-90; Newsweek, senior writer, 1990-; Economist, finance and economics editor, through 1999; J.P. Morgan Chase, economist, 1999-. **Publications:** (With C.M. Aho) After Reagan: Confronting the Changed World Economy, 1988; Beyond Free Markets: The Revival of Activist Economics, 1988; Guide to Financial Markets, 3rd ed., 2003, 5th ed., 2010; The Box: How the Shipping Container Made the World Smaller and the World Economy Bigger, 2006; The Great A&P and the Struggle for Small Business in America, 2011. Contributor of articles to periodicals. **Address:** Newsweek, 251 W 57th St., New York, NY 10019-1802, U.S.A. **Online address:** marclevinson1@gmail.com

LEVITIN, Daniel J. Canadian/American (born United States), b. 1957. **Genres:** Psychology, Education, Music, Sciences, Adult Non-fiction, Songs/Lyrics And Libretti, Anthropology/Ethnology, Biology, Young Adult Non-fiction. **Career:** Pacific Bell, data analysis manager, 1981-84; consultant, 1982-92; Columbia Records, staff engineer, arranger and producer, 1984-85; director of artists and repertory, 1985-88; Daniel Levitin Production, president; Stanford University, Technology and Society, Program in Values, instructor, 1991, Department of Anthropology, instructor, 1994, Department of Music, instructor, 1992-93, lecturer, 1992-98, lecturer in music, 1993-2000, Department of Psychology, visiting lecturer, 1998, Department of Computer Science, visiting lecturer, 1998, Lokey visiting professor of human biology, 2009; University of Oregon, instructor, 1995; Interval Research Corp., postdoctoral research fellow, 1996-98; University of California, Department of Psychology, visiting assistant professor, 1999-2000, Department of Cognitive Science, visiting assistant professor, 1999-2000; McGill University, assistant professor of psychology, 2000-04, Bell professor of psychology of electronic communication, 2002-, associate professor, 2004-, James McGill professor of psychology and neuroscience, 2007-. Writer. **Publications:** From Demo to Deal, 1992; (co-ed.) Billboard Encyclopedia of Record Producers, 1999; (ed.) Foundations of Cognitive Psychology: Core Readings, 2002, 2nd ed., 2011; This Is Your Brain on Music: The Science of a Human Obsession, 2006; The World in Six Songs: How the Musical Brain Created Human Nature, 2008. Contributor to books and journals. **Address:** Department of Psychology, McGill University, 1205 Dr. Penfield Ave., Montreal, QC H3A 1B1, Canada. **Online address:** daniel.levitin@mcgill.ca

LEVITIN, Sonia (Wolff). American/German (born Germany), b. 1934. **Genres:** Novels, Children's Fiction, Animals/Pets, History, Picture/Board Books. **Career:** Junior high school teacher, 1956-57; adult education teacher, 1962-64; Acalanes Adult Center, teacher, 1965-72; Teacher Writer's Program, creative writing teacher, 1973-76, 1978-; University of California, Los Angeles Extension Writers Program, instructor, 1976-. Writer. **Publications:** Journey to America, 1970, 2nd ed., 1993; Rita the Weekend Rat, 1971; Who Owns the Moon?, 1973; Roanoke: A Novel of the Lost Colony, 1973; Jason and the Money Tree, 1974; A Single Speckled Egg, 1976; The Mark of Conte, 1976; Beyond Another Door, 1977; The No-Return Trail, 1978; Reigning Cats and Dogs, 1978; A Sound to Remember, 1979; Nobody Stole the Pie, 1980; (as Sonia Wolff) What They Did to Miss Lily, 1981; The Fisherman and the Bird, 1982; All the Cats in the World, 1982; The Year of Sweet Senior Insanity, 1982; Smile like a Plastic Daisy, 1984; A Season for Unicorns, 1986; The Return, 1987; Incident at Loring Groves, 1988; Silver Days, 1989; The Man Who Kept His Heart in a Bucket, 1991; The Golem and the Dragon Girl, 1993; Annie's Promise, 1993; Adam's War, 1994; Escape from Egypt: A Novel, 1994; Evil Encounter, 1996; A Piece of Home, 1996; Nine for California, 1996; Yesterday's Child, 1997; Boom Town, 1998; The Singing Mountain, 1998; The Cure, 1999; Taking Charge, 1999; Dream Freedom, 2000; Clem's Chances, 2001; When Elephant Goes to a Party, 2001; When Kangaroo Goes to School, 2001; Room in the Heart, 2003; The Goodness Gene, 2005; Strange Relations, 2007; Junk Man's Daughter, 2007. Contributor to periodicals. **Address:** Los Angeles Extension Writers Program, University of California, 10995 Le Conte Ave., Ste. 440, Los Angeles, CA 90024, U.S.A. **Online address:** slevitin@ucla.edu

LEVITT, Matthew. American (born United States), b. 1970?. **Genres:** Civil Liberties/Human Rights, Economics, Politics/Government, Military/Defense/Arms Control. **Career:** U.S. Department of State, lecturer; Federal Bureau of Investigation, counterterrorism intelligence analyst; Washington Institute for Near East Policy, Terrorism Research Program(now Stein Program on Counterterrorism and Intelligence), founding director, 2001-05, fellow and director, 2007-, senior fellow and director; Johns Hopkins University, Paul H. Nitze School of Advanced International Studies, lecturer, 2005-07, adjunct professor, Zanvyl Krieger School of Arts and Sciences, lecturer; U.S. Department of Treasury, deputy assistant secretary for intelligence and analysis, 2005-07; Office of Intelligence and Analysis, deputy chief; U.S. Military Academy, Combating Terrorism Center, fellow, adjunct fellow. Author and intelligence analyst. **Publications:** Targeting Terror: U.S. Policy toward Middle Eastern State Sponsors and Terrorist Organizations, Post-September 11, 2002; Hamas: Politics, Charity and Terrorism in the Service of Jihad, 2006; Negotiating Under Fire: Preserving Peace Talks in the Face of Terror Attacks, 2008; (with M. Jacobson) Combating the Financing of Transnational Threats, 2009. Contributor to books and periodicals. **Address:** Washington Institute for Near East Policy, 1828 L St. NW, Ste. 1050, Washington, DC 20036, U.S.A. **Online address:** mattl@washingtoninstitute.org

LEVITT, Steven D. American (born United States), b. 1967. **Genres:** Economics. **Career:** Corporate Decisions Inc., management consultant, 1989-91; American Bar Foundation, Research fellow, 1997-; University of Chicago, assistant professor, 1997-98, associate professor, 1998-99, professor, 1999-2002, Alvin H. Baum professor of economics, 2002-, Initiative on Chicago Price Theory, director, 2004-; Quarterly Journal of Economy, editor, associate editor, 1998-99; Journal of Political Economy, editor, 1999-. **Publications:** Market Distortions When Agents Are Better Informed: The Value of Information in Real Estate Transactions, 2005; (with R.G. Fryer) The Black-White Test Score Gap through Third Grade, 2005; (with S.J. Dubner) Freakonomics: A Rogue Economist Explores the Hidden Side of Everything, 2005; (ed. with T.J. Miles) Economics of Criminal Law, 2008; (with S.J. Dubner) Superfreakonomics: Global Cooling, Patriotic Prostitutes and Why Suicide Bombers Should Buy Life Insurance, 2009; (with S.J. Dubner) Superfreakonomics: Global Cooling, Patriotic Prostitutes and Why Suicide Bombers Should Buy Life Insurance, 2010; The Role of Skill Versus Luck in Poker, 2011. Contributor to journals. **Address:** Department of Economics, University of Chicago, 1126 E 59th St., Chicago, IL 60637, U.S.A. **Online address:** slevitt@midway.uchicago.edu

LEVOY, Myron. American (born United States), b. 1930. **Genres:** Novels, Children's Fiction, Novellas/Short Stories, Young Adult Fiction, Westerns/Adventure. **Career:** Writer. **Publications:** A Necktie in Greenwich Village (novel), 1968. FOR CHILDREN: Penny Tunes and Princesses, 1972; The Witch of Fourth Street and Other Stories, 1972; Alan and Naomi, 1977; A Shadow Like a Leopard, 1981; Three Friends, 1984; The Hanukkah of Great-Uncle Otto, 1984; Pictures of Adam, 1986; The Magic Hat of Mortimer Wintergreen, 1988; Kelly 'n' Me, 1992. **Address:** c/o Susan Cohen, Writers House Inc., 21 W 26th St., New York, NY 10010, U.S.A.

LEVY, Adrian. British (born England), b. 1965?. **Genres:** History, Young Adult Non-fiction. **Career:** Bolton Evening News, staff; Yorkshire Post, chief reporter; Sunday Times, investigative reporter, 1994, Investigative Insight Section, deputy editor, foreign correspondent, 1998; The Guardian, staff, 2001-. **Publications:** (With C. Scott-Clark) The Stone of Heaven: Unearthing the Secret History of Imperial Green Jade, 2001; (with C. Scott-Clark) Amber Room: The Fate of the World's Greatest Lost Treasure, 2004; (with C. Scott-Clark) Deception: Pakistan, the United States and the Secret Trade in Nuclear Weapons, 2007. Contributor to periodicals. **Address:** c/o Author Mail, Little Brown and Co., 1271 Ave. of the Americas, New York, NY 10020, U.S.A. **Online address:** adrian@secrets-and-lies.co.uk

LEVY, Allison. American (born United States), b. 1968. **Genres:** Art/Art History, History, Humanities. **Career:** Wheaton College, assistant professor of art history; Institute at Palazzo Rucellai, lecturer. Writer. **Publications:** (Ed.) Widowhood and Visual Culture in Early Modern Europe, 2003; Re-Membering Masculinity in Early Modern Florence: Widowed Bodies, Mourning and Portraiture, 2006; (ed.) Sex Acts in Early Modern Italy, 2010. **Address:** Department of Art and Art History, Wheaton College, 26 E Main St., Norton, MA 02766-2322, U.S.A.

LEVY, Andrew (Gordon). American (born United States), b. 1962. **Genres:** Literary Criticism And History, Poetry. **Career:** Edgewood Teleservices, systems analyst and software designer, 1984-86; Philadelphia College of Pharmacy and Science, adjunct professor, 1989-92; Butler University, assistant professor, 1992-96, associate professor, 1996-98, professor, Edna Cooper professor of English, 1998-, Writers Studio, co-director, 1992-, Fellows Program, director, 1993-. Writer. **Publications:** The Culture and Commerce of the American Short Story (monograph), 1993; Curve, 1994; (with F. Leebron) Creating Fiction: A Writer's Companion, 1995; (ed. with F.G. Leebron and P. Geyh) Postmodern American Fiction: A Norton Anthology, 1997; Continuous Discontinuous: Curve 2, 1997; Paper Head Last Lyrics, 2000; First Emancipator: The Forgotten Story of Robert Carter, The Founding Father Who Freed His Slaves, 2005; Brain Wider than the Sky: A Migraine Diary, 2009. Contributor to books and periodicals. **Address:** Department of English, Butler University, Jordan Hall 320D, 4600 Sunset Ave., Indianapolis, IN 46208, U.S.A. **Online address:** alevy@butler.edu

LEVY, Barrie. American (born United States) **Genres:** Human Relations/ Parenting, Social Sciences, Women's Studies And Issues, Adult Non-fiction. **Career:** University of California, Department of Women's Studies, lecturer of social welfare, professor; Westside Domestic Violence Network, consultant. Writer and psychotherapist. **Publications:** NONFICTION: Skills for Violence-Free Relationships: Curriculum for Young People, Ages 13-18, 1984; (ed.) Dating Violence: Young Women in Danger, 1991; In Love and in Danger: A Teen's Guide to Breaking Free of Abusive Relationships, 1993; (with P.O. Giggans) What Parents Need to Know about Dating Violence, 1995; (with P.O. Giggans) 50 Ways to a Safer World: Everyday Actions You Can Take to Prevent Violence in Neighborhoods, Schools and Communities, 1997; Women and Violence, 2008. **Address:** Department of Women's Studies, University of California, 1120 Rolfe Hall, PO Box 951504, Los Angeles, CA 90095-1504, U.S.A. **Online address:** levyb@ucla.edu

LEVY, Constance. American (born United States), b. 1931. **Genres:** Poetry, Children's Fiction. **Career:** Webster Groves School District, teacher, 1952-53; Ritenour School District, teacher, 1953-54; Washington University, supervisor of student teachers, 1974-75; Missouri Arts Council, Writers in the Schools Program, children's poet, 1975-81; Harris-Stowe State College, adjunct instructor of children's literature, 1980-82; freelance poet, 1981-92. **Publications:** I'm Going to Pet a Worm Today and Other Poems, 1991; A Tree Place and Other Poems, 1994; When Whales Exhale, and Other Poems, 1996; A Crack in the Clouds and Other Poems, 1998; Splash!: Poems of Our Watery World, 2002; The Story of Red Rubber Ball, 2004. Contributor to periodicals. **Address:** 58 Frontenac Estates Dr., St. Louis, MO 63131-2602, U.S.A. **Online address:** constlevy@hotmail.com

LEVY, Daniel S. American (born United States), b. 1959?. **Genres:** Biography, Autobiography/Memoirs, History, Romance/Historical. **Career:** Time Magazine, staff reporter. **Publications:** Two-Gun Cohen: A Biography, 1997; (co-author) Shuang qiang Makun: Sun Zhongshan de wai guo bao biao, 1999. Contributor of articles to periodicals. **Address:** Time Magazine, 1271 Ave. of the Americas, New York, NY 10020, U.S.A.

LEVY, David H. Canadian (born Canada), b. 1948. **Genres:** Astronomy. **Career:** Planetary Science Institute, observer, 1982-92; International Halley Watch, assistant discipline specialist, 1985-89; Palomar Asteroid and Comet Survey, observer, 1989-96; Flandrau Planetarium, adjunct scientist, 1991-; University of Arizona, instructional specialist, 1992-96, senior instructional specialist, 1993-96; Parade, contributing editor, 1997-98, science editor, 1998-; Jarnac Observatory, director, 2004-; Arizona State University, Public Policy and American Institutions, Senator John Rhodes chair, 2004. Speaker and amateur astronomer. **Publications:** The Joy of Gazing, 1982; The Universe for Children: How Astronomy minded Adults Can Teach Children to Love the Sky, 1985; (with S.J. Edberg) Observe Comets, 1985; (with S.J. Edberg) Observe Meteors, 1986; Observing Variable Stars: A Guide for the Beginner, 1989; The Sky: A Users Guide, 1991; Clyde Tombaugh: Discoverer of Planet Pluto, 1991; The Man Who Sold the Milky Way: A Biography of Bart Bok, 1993; The Quest for Comets: An Explosive Trail of Beauty and Danger, 1994; Skywatching, 1994; Impact Jupiter: The Crash of Comet Shoemaker-Levy 9, 1995; Stars and Planets, 1995; More Things in Heaven and Earth: Poets and Astronomers Read the Night Sky, 1997; Comets: Creators and Destroyers, 1998; Observing Variable Stars: A Guide for the Beginner, 1998; An Encyclopedia of the Universe, 1998; Shoemaker by Levy: The Man Who Made an Impact, 2000; (ed.) The Scientific American Book of the Cosmos, 2000; Starry Night: Astronomers and Poets Read the Sky, 2001; David Levy's Guide to the Night Sky, 2001. CO-AUTHOR: (with S.J. Edberg) Observe-Comets, 1985; (with S.J. Edberg) Observe-Meteors, 1986; (with G.E. Tomlinson and R. Horgan) Astronomy Day: Bringing Astronomy to the People, 1993; (with

T.B. Hunter) Medical Devices, Abbreviations, Acronyms and Eponyms: A Pocket Guide, 1993; Comet Shoemaker-Levy 9 Slide Set, 1994; (with S.J. Edberg) Observing Comets, Asteroids, Meteors and the Zodiacal Light, 1994; (with L.A. Lebofsky and N.R. Lebofsky) Sharing the Sky: A Parent's and Teachers Guide to Astronomy, 1997; (with S.J. O'Meara) Deep-Sky Companions: The Messier Object, 2000; (with W. Wallach-Levy) Exploring the Universe with Our Children: A Guide for Teachers and Parents, 2001; (with W. Wallach-Levy) Cosmic Discoveries: The Wonders of Astronomy, 2001; Making Friends with the Stars: A Guide for Teachers and Parents, rev. ed., 2001; David Levys Guide to Observing and Discovering Comets, 2003; Deep Sky Objects: The Best and Brightest From Four Decades of Comet Chasing, 2005; David Levy's Guide to Variable Stars, 2nd ed., 2005; Star Trails: 50 Favorite Columns From Sky and Telescope, 2007; David Levys Guide to Observing Meteor Showers, 2008; David Levy's Guide to Eclipses, Transits and Occultations, 2010. Contributor to books and periodicals. **Address:** Prometheus Books, 59 John Glenn Dr., Amherst, NY 14228-2197, U.S.A. **Online address:** david@jarnac.org

LEVY, Deborah. British/South African (born South Africa), b. 1959?. **Genres:** Novels, Novellas/Short Stories. **Career:** Trinity College, Creative Arts, fellow, 1989-91; MANACT Theatre Co., director and writer, through 1992. **Publications:** NOVELS: Beautiful Mutants, 1989; Swallowing Geography, 1993; The Unloved, 1994; Billy and Girl, 1996, rev. ed., 1998; Diary of a Steak, 1998; City A -Z, 2000; 6 Small Acts for Big Women or 6 Big Acts for Small Women, 2001; Pillow Talk in Europe and Other Places, 2004; Swimming Home, 2011. OTHER: Heresies & Eva and Moses: Two Plays, 1987; Ophelia and the Great Idea (short stories), 1989; An Amorous Discourse in the Suburbs of Hell, 1990; (intro.) Walks on Water: Five Performance Texts, 1992; (ed.) Enhanced Performance, 1998; (intro.) Plays 1, 2000. Contributor to books and periodicals. **Address:** c/o Victoria Hobbs, A.M. Heath, 6 Warwick Ct., London, GL WC1R 5DJ, England.

LEVY, Elizabeth. American (born United States), b. 1942. **Genres:** Children's Fiction, Young Adult Non-fiction, Young Adult Fiction, Novels, Mystery/Crime/Suspense. **Career:** American Broadcasting Co., News Department, editor and researcher, 1964-66; Macmillan Publishing Co., assistant editor, 1967-69; New York Public Library, writer in public relations, 1969; JPM Associates (urban affairs consultants), staff writer, 1970-71. Writer, 1971-. **Publications:** FOR CHILDREN. FICTION: Nice Little Girls, 1974; Lizzie Lies a Lot, 1976; Frankenstein Moved in on the Fourth Floor, 1979; The Tryouts, 1979; Running Out of Time, 1980; Running Out of Magic with Houdini, 1981; The Computer that Said Steal Me, 1983; The Shadow Nose, 1983; Dracula Is a Pain in the Neck, 1983; Keep Ms. Sugarman in the Fourth Grade, 1992; Cheater, Cheater, 1993; Gorgonzola Zombies in the Park, 1993; Cleo and the Coyote, 1996; Wolfman Sam, 1996; My Life as a Fifth-Grade Comedian, 1997; Third Grade Bullies, 1997. SOMETHING QUEER MYSTERY SERIES: Something Queer Is Going On, 1973; Something Queer at the Ballpark, 1975; Something Queer at the Library, 1977; Something Queer on Vacation, 1980; Something Queer at the Haunted School, 1982; Something Queer at the Lemonade Stand, 1982; Something Queer in Rock n Roll, 1987; Something Queer at the Birthday Party, 1990; Something Queer in Outer Space, 1993; Something Queer in the Cafeteria, 1994; Something Queer at the Scary Movie, 1995; Something Queer in the Wild West, 1997; Something Queer Under the Sea, 1999. MAGIC MYSTERIES SERIES: The Case of the Gobbling Squash, 1988; The Case of the Mind-Reading Mommies, 1989; The Case of the Tattletale Heart, 1990; The Case of the Dummy with Cold Eyes, 1991. THE GYMNASTS SERIES: The Beginners, 1988; First Meet, 1988; Nobody's Perfect, 1988; The Winner, 1989; Trouble in the Gym, 1989; Bad Break, 1989; Tumbling Ghosts, 1989; Captain of the Team, 1989; Crush on the Coach, 1990; Boys in the Gym, 1990; Mystery at the Meet, 1990; Out of Control, 1990; First Date, 1990; World Class Gymnast, 1990; Nasty Competition, 1991; Fear of Falling, 1991; Gymnasts Commandos, 1991; The New Coach, 1991; Tough at the Top, 1991; The Gymnast Gift, 1991; Go for the Gold, 1992; Team Trouble, 1992. BRIAN AND PEA BRAIN SERIES: Rude Rowdy Rumors, 1994; School Spirit Sabotage, 1994; A Mammoth Mix-Up, 1995. INVISIBLE INC. SERIES: The Schoolyard Mystery, 1994; The Mystery of the Missing Dog, 1995; The Snack Attack Mystery, 1995; The Creepy Computer Mystery, 1996; The Karate Class Mystery, 1996; Parents' Night Fright, 1998. FOR YOUNG ADULTS FICTION: Come Out Smiling, 1981; Double Standard, 1984; The Dani Trap, 1984; Night of Nights, 1984; All Shook Up, 1986; Cold as Ice, 1988; The Drowned, 1995. JODY AND JAKE MYSTERY SERIES: The Case of the Frightened Rock Star, 1980; The Case of the Counterfeit Race Horse, 1980; The Case of the Fired-Up Gang, 1981;

The Case of the Wild River Ride, 1981; The Case of the Mile High Race, 1982. NONFICTION: The People Lobby: The SST Story, 1973; Lawyers for the People, 1974; By-Lines: Profiles in Investigative Journalism, 1975; (with R.H. Harris) Before You Were Three: How You Began to Walk, Talk, Explore, and Have Feelings, 1977; (with M. Miller) Doctors for the People: Profiles of Six Who Serve, 1977; (with E. Hammond and L. Hammond) Elephants in the Living Room, Bears in the Canoe: The Story of the Incredible Family Who Raise and Train Wild Animals in Their Home, 1977; (with T. Richards) Struggle and Lose, Struggle and Win: The United Mineworkers Story, 1977; (with E. Hammond and L. Hammond) Our Animal Kingdom, 1977; Politicians for the People: Six Who Stand for Change, 1979; If You Were There When They Signed the Constitution, 1988. OTHERS: Marco Polo: The Historic Adventure Based on the Television Spectacular, 1982; Father Murphy's First Miracle, 1983; (adaptor) Return of the Jedi, 1983; A Different Twist, 1984; The Bride, 1985; (ed.) Greenberg Van Doren Gallery Selected Works, 1998; Seven Minutes in Heaven, 2000; Seventh-Grade Tango, 2000; Who Are You Calling a Woolly Mammoth?: Prehistoric America, 2000; Our Awesome Ancient Ancestors, 2001; Night of the Living Gerbil, 2001; Big Trouble in Little Twinsville, 2001; Are We There Yet?: Europeans Meet the Americans, 2001; Vampire State Building, 2002; The Principal's On the Roof, 2002; A Hare-Raising Tail, 2002; Cranky Colonials: Pilgrims, Puritans, Even Pirates, 2002; Take Two, They're Small, 2002; Westward, Ha-Ha! 1800-1850, 2003; Revolting Revolutionaries, 1750s-1790s, 2003; The Mystery of Too Many Elvises, 2003; The Mixed-Up Mask Mystery, 2003; The Cool Ghoul Mystery, 2003; Tackling Dad, 2005; Danger and Diamonds: a Mystery at Sea, 2010; Parrots & Pirates: A Mystery at Sea, 2011. FAT ALBERT AND THE COSBY KIDS SERIES: The Shuttered Window, 1981; Mister Big Time, 1981; Spare the Rod, 1981; Mom or Pop, 1981; The Runt, 1981. **Address:** Elaine Markson Literary Agency Inc., 44 Greenwich Ave., New York, NY 10011, U.S.A. **Online address:** elizlevy@elizabethlevy.com

LEVY, Evonne. Canadian (born Canada), b. 1961. **Genres:** Art/Art History, Essays, Biography. **Career:** University of Toronto, associate professor of visual and media culture, Department of Art, associate professor of art. Writer. **Publications:** (Contrib.) Struggle for Synthesis: The Total Work of Art in the 17th and 18th Centuries, 1999; (contrib.) La Basilica di San Pietro, 2000; (contrib.) Die Jesuiten in Wien: Zur Kunst-und Kulturgeschichte der österreichischen Ordensprovinz der Gesellschaft Jesu im 17. und 18. Jahrhundert, 2003; (contrib.) Spirit, Style, Story: Essays Honoring John W. Padberg, S.J., 2003; Propaganda and the Jesuit Baroque, 2004; (ed. with M. Delbeke and S.F. Ostrow) Bernini's Biographies: Critical Essays, 2006; Barock: Architectural History and Politics from Burckhardt to Hitler (1844-1945), forthcoming; (ed. with K. Mills) Lexikon of the Hispanic Baroque: Technologies of a Transantlantic Culture, forthcoming. Contributor to periodicals. **Address:** Department of Art, University of Toronto, Rm. 6036, Sidney Smith Hall, 100 St. George St., Toronto, ON M5S 3G3, Canada. **Online address:** elevy@utm.utoronto.ca

LEVY, Harry. American (born United States), b. 1944. **Genres:** Human Relations/Parenting, Young Adult Fiction. **Career:** PES Inc., founder and president, 1977-90; Health Opinion Research Inc., founder and president, 1984-91; Cyberounds, executive editor, 1996-. Writer. **Publications:** (With D. Caplovitz) Interreligious Dating Among College Students, 1966; Chain of Custody: A Novel, 1998. Contributor to periodicals. **Address:** Random House Inc., 1745 Broadway, Ste. B1, New York, NY 10019-4305, U.S.A. **Online address:** levy@cyberounds.com

LEVY, Helen Fiddyment. American (born United States), b. 1937. **Genres:** Literary Criticism And History, Young Adult Fiction, Travel/Exploration, Women's Studies And Issues. **Career:** University of Michigan, Honors Program, assistant director, 1982-85; George Mason University, instructor in English, 1987-. Writer. **Publications:** Fiction of the Home Place: Jewett, Cather, Glasgow, Porter, Welty, and Naylor, 1992. Contributor to journals. **Address:** Department of English, George Mason University, 4400 University Dr., PO Box 3E4, Fairfax, VA 22030-4422, U.S.A.

LEVY, Jill Meryl. American (born United States) **Genres:** Writing/Journalism, Reference, How-to Books, Civil Liberties/Human Rights. **Career:** MediShare, safety trainer, 1982-86; Hewlett-Packard Co., environmental health and safety trainer, 1986-93; Firebelle Productions, owner, publisher and writer, 1993-. **Publications:** The First Responder's Pocket Guide to Hazardous Materials Emergency Response, 1996, 4th ed. as The The First Responder's Field Guide to Hazmat & Terrorism Emergency Response, 2003; Take Command of Your Writing, 1998; Hazmat Chemistry Study Guide, 2002; The Hazmat Chemistry Mini Review, 2005; The First Responder's Pocket Guide To Radiation Incidents, 2006; Hazmat Chemistry Pocket Pal, 2009; Test Writer's Guide to Crafting Good Questions, 2010. **Address:** Firebelle Productions, 2 Timber Cove Dr., PO Box 110848, Campbell, CA 95008-4106, U.S.A. **Online address:** jill@firebelleproductions.com

LEVY, JoAnn. American (born United States), b. 1941. **Genres:** Novels, History, Women's Studies And Issues, Biography, Money/Finance. **Career:** Writer. **Publications:** Behind the Western Skyline, 1981; They Saw the Elephant: Women in the California Gold Rush, 1992; Unsettling the West: Eliza Farnham and Georgiana Bruce Kirby in Frontier California (biography), 2004. NOVELS: Daughter of Joy, 1998; For California's Gold, 2000; The Sutter Creek Chronicles: A Love Story, 2011. Contributor to magazines. **Address:** PO Box 1809, Sutter Creek, CA 95685-1809, U.S.A. **Online address:** joann@goldrush.com

LEVY, Marc. American/French (born France), b. 1961. **Genres:** Novels. **Career:** Novelist. **Publications:** Et si Cétait vrai, 1999, trans. as If Only it Were True, 2000; Where are You?, 2001; Où es-tu?, 2001; Seven Days for an Eternity, 2003; The Next Time, 2004; Just like Heaven: A Novel, 2005; Mes Amis Mes Amours: Roman, 2006; Lesenfants de la liberté: Roman, 2007; Children of Freedom, 2007; Toutes Ces Choses Qu'on Ne S'est Pas Dites: Roman, 2008; Le Premier Jour, 2009; Première Nuit: Roman, 2009; Le Voleur d'ombres, 2010; L'étrange voyage de monsieur Daldry: Roman, 2011. Contributor to periodicals. **Address:** Editions Robert Laffont, 24 Avenue Marceau, Paris, 75008, Spain.

LEVY, Matthys. American/Swiss (born Switzerland), b. 1929. **Genres:** Architecture, Children's Non-fiction, Earth Sciences, Engineering, Sciences. **Career:** Consultant, 1951-55; 453rd Engineering Construction Battalion, assistant operations officer, 1952-54; Consulting Engineers, 1956-2006; Yale University, visiting critic in architecture, 1960-65; Columbia University, School of Architecture, adjunct professor, 1962-80; Weidlinger Associates, principal, 1964-, chairman, 2002, chairman emeritus, 2006-; Pratt Institute, distinguished professor, 1980-81. Writer. **Publications:** (With M. Salvadori) Structural Design in Architecture, 1967, 2nd ed., 1981; (with M. Salvadori) Why Buildings Fall Down: How Structures Fail, 1992; (with M. Salvadori) Why the Earth Quakes, 1995; (with Salvadori) Earthquake Games: Earthquakes and Volcanoes Explained by Thirty-two Games and Experiments, 1997; (with R. Panchyk) Engineering the City: How Infrastructure Works: Projects and Principles for Beginners, 2000; (with N. Abboud) World Trade Center Structural Engineering Investigation: Rebuttal Report, 2002; Why the Wind Blows: A History of Weather and Global Warming, 2007; Earthquakes, Volcanoes and Tsunamis: Projects and Principles for Beginning Geologists, 2009. **Address:** 40 College St., Apt. 702, Burlington, VT 05401, U.S.A. **Online address:** levy@wai.com

LEVY, Peter B. American (born United States), b. 1956. **Genres:** History, Social Sciences, Politics/Government, Civil Liberties/Human Rights. **Career:** Rutgers University, visiting assistant professor of history, 1986-88; York College, Department of History and Political Science, associate professor, 1989-, chairman, professor of history. **Publications:** (Ed.) Documentary History of the Modern Civil Rights Movement, 1992; (ed.) Let Freedom Ring: A Documentary History of the Modern Civil Rights Movement, 1992; The New Left and Labor in the 1960s, 1994; (ed.) 100 Key Documents in American Democracy, 1994; Encyclopedia of the Reagan-Bush Years, 1996; The Civil Rights Movement, 1998; (ed.) America in the Sixties: Right, Left, and Center: A Documentary History, 1998; Encyclopedia of the Clinton Presidency, 2002; Civil War on Race Street: The Civil Rights Movement in Cambridge, Maryland, 2003. **Address:** Department of History & Political Science, York College, Rm. 304, Life Science Bldg., York, PA 17405, U.S.A. **Online address:** plevy@ycp.edu

LEVY, Philip. American (born United States), b. 1963. **Genres:** History. **Career:** University of South Florida, associate professor. Writer. **Publications:** Fellow Travelers: Indians and Europeans Contesting the Early American Trail, 2007. **Address:** Department of History, University of South Florida, SOC 107, 4202 E Fowler Ave., Tampa, FL 33620-8100, U.S.A. **Online address:** plevy@cas.usf.edu

LEVY, Robert A. American (born United States), b. 1941?. **Genres:** Marketing, Business/Trade/Industry, Law, Politics/Government. **Career:** CDA

Investment Technologies, founder and chief executive officer, through 1991; Georgetown University, adjunct professor of law, 1997-2004; Cato Institute, senior fellow in constitutional studies and chair, 1997-. Educator, entrepreneur, businessperson, administrator and writer. **Publications:** The Relative Strength Concept of Common Stock Price Forecasting: An Evaluation of Selected Applications of Stock Market Timing Techniques, Trading Tactics, and Trend Analysis, 1968; Shakedown: How Corporations, Government, and Trial Lawyers Abuse the Judicial Process, 2004; (with W.H. Mellor) The Dirty Dozen: How Twelve Supreme Court Cases Radically Expanded Government and Eroded Freedom, 2008. Contributor to periodicals. **Address:** Cato Institute, 1000 Massachusetts Ave. NW, Washington, DC 20001-5403, U.S.A. **Online address:** rlevy@cato.org

LEVY, Steven. American (born United States), b. 1951. **Genres:** Information Science/Computers, Sciences, Business/Trade/Industry. **Career:** Freelance writer, critic and publisher, 1975-; MacWorld, columnist, 1985-; Wired, contributing writer, 1993-; Freedom Forum Media Studies Center, fellow, 1994-95; Newsweek, staff, 1995-, senior editor and chief technology writer. **Publications:** Hackers: Heroes of the Computer Revolution, 1984, rev. ed., 1994; The Unicorn's Secret: Murder in the Age of Aquarius, 1988; Artificial Life: The Quest for a New Creation, 1992; Artificial Life: A Report from the Frontier Where Computers Meet Biology, 1993; Insanely Great: The Life and Times of Macintosh, the Computer That Changed Everything, 1994; Crypto: How the Code Rebels Beat the Government, 2001; The Perfect Thing: How the iPod Shuffles Commerce, Culture and Coolness, 2006; (ed.) The Best of Technology Writing 2007, 2007; In the Plex: How Google Thinks, Works and Shapes Our Lives, 2011. Contributor to periodicals. **Address:** Columbia University, Freedom Forum Media Studies Ctr., 2950 Broadway, New York, NY 10027-7004, U.S.A. **Online address:** steven@echonyc.com

LEVY, Thomas. American (born United States), b. 1950. **Genres:** Medicine/Health, Adult Non-fiction, Sciences. **Career:** Charity Hospital of New Orleans, supervisor, 1980-83; American College of Cardiology, fellow, 1983-; Tulane University, Medical School, assistant professor of medicine, 1981-83, instructor in radiology, 1983-84, clinical assistant professor of medicine, 1983-86; Iberia General Hospital, staff, 1984-91; Memorial Hospital, staff, 1991-; International Tesla Society, medical technical advisor, 1994-98; Denver General Hospital, staff, 1995-96; Capital University of Integrative Medicine, associate professor, 1999-2006. Writer. **Publications:** (With H.A. Huggins) Uninformed Consent: The Hidden Dangers in Dental Care, 1999; Optimal Nutrition for Optimal Health, 2001; Vitamin C, Infectious Diseases, and Toxins: Curing the Incurable, 2002; (with R. Kulacz) The Roots of Disease: Connecting Dentistry and Medicine, 2002; Stop America's Number One Killer!: Reversible Vitamin Deficiency Found To Be Origin Of All Coronary Heart Disease, 2006; Journey To The Copper Age: Archaeology In The Holy Land, 2007; Curing The Incurable: Vitamin C, Infectious Diseases, And Toxins, 2009; Master Defender Against Disease, Toxins, and Aging, 2009; Primal Panacea, 2011. Contributor to journals. **Address:** 1585 Mesa Rd., Colorado Springs, CO 80904-2820, U.S.A. **Online address:** televymd@yahoo.com

LEWES, Darby. American (born United States), b. 1946. **Genres:** Literary Criticism And History. **Career:** Oxford University, fellow of English-speaking union, 1985; Saint Xavier University, lecturer in English, 1986-90; University of Chicago, course assistant, 1988, resident head, 1988-91, instructor in literature, 1991-93; Loyola University, visiting assistant professor of English, lecturer, 1991-92, visiting assistant professor of English, 1991-93; Lycoming College, Department of English, assistant professor, 1993-95, associate professor, 1995-, department chair, 1999-2000, professor, 2007-, vice-Chair, 2000, chair, 2000-01; Sigma Tau Delta Honor Society, faculty advisor, 1994-2006; Lycoming English Society, faculty advisor, 1994-2006. Writer. **Publications:** Dream Revisionaries: Genre and Gender in Women's Utopian Fiction, 1870-1920, 1995; Nudes from Nowhere: Utopian Sexual Landscape, 2000; (ed.) A Brighter Morn: The Shelley Circle's Utopian Project, 2003; (ed.) Auto-Poetica: Representations of the Creative Process in Nineteenth-Century British and American Fiction, 2006; (ed.) Double Vision: Literary Palimpsests of the Eighteenth and Nineteenth Centuries, 2008. Contributor to books and periodicals. **Address:** Department of English, Lycoming College, 700 College Pl., Williamsport, PA 17701-5192, U.S.A. **Online address:** lewes@lycoming.edu

LEWICKI, Roy J. American (born United States), b. 1942. **Genres:** Business/Trade/Industry. **Career:** Yale University, assistant professor, 1968-72; Dartmouth College, adjunct associate professor, 1972-77; Duke University,

Fuqua School, associate professor, 1978-84, associate dean, assistant dean and director of the MBA program, 1979-84; Ohio State University, Fisher College of Business, associate professor, 1984-87, associate dean, 1984-91, professor, 1987-, dean's distinguished professor, 1998-2007, Abramowitz Memorial professor of business ethics, 2007-; Tuck School, visiting professor, 1995. Writer. **Publications:** (With M. Bazerman) Negotiating in Organizations, 1983; (with D. Saunders, J. Minton and B. Barry) Negotiation, 1985, 6th ed., 2010; (with D. Saunders, J. Minton and B. Barry) Essentials of Negotiation, 1992, 5th ed., 2010; (with D. Saunders, J. Minton and B. Barry) Negotiation: Readings, Exercises and Cases, 1985, 6th ed., 2010; (with D.T. Hall, D. Bowen and F. Hall) Experiences in Management and Organizational Behavior, 5th ed., 1988; (with B. Sheppard and J. Minton) Organizational Justice: The Search for Fairness in the Workplace, 1992; (with A. Hiam and K.W. Olander) Think before You Speak: The Complete Guide to Strategic Negotiation, 1996; (with A. Hiam) The Fast-forward MBA in Negotiating and Deal Making, 1999; (ed. with B. Gray and M. Elliott) Making Sense of Intractable Environmental Conflicts: Concepts and Cases, 2003; (with A. Hiam) Mastering Business Negotiation: A Working Guide to Making Deals and Resolving Conflict, 2006. **Address:** Fisher College of Business, Ohio State University, 756 Fisher Hall, 2100 Neil Ave., Columbus, OH 43210, U.S.A. **Online address:** lewicki_1@fisher.osu.edu

LEWIN, Leif. Swedish (born Sweden), b. 1941. **Genres:** Business/Trade/Industry, Novels, Politics/Government. **Career:** University of Uppsala, Johan Skytte professor of eloquence and government, 1972-, now professor emeritus, Social Science Faculty, dean, 1991-99, vice rector, 1999-2005. Writer. **Publications:** Planhushallningsdebatten, 1967; Folket och eliterna, 1970; (with B. Jansson and D. Sorbom) The Swedish Electorate, 1887-1968, 1972; Statskunskapen, ideologierna och den olitiska verkligheten, 1973; Asiktsjournalistiken och den fackliga demokratin, 1977; Hur styrs facket? Om demokratin inom fackforeningsrorelsen, 1977, trans. as Governing Trade Unions in Sweden, 1980; Det politiska spelet, 1979; (ed. with E. Vedung) Politics as Rational Action: Essays in Public Choice and Policy Analysis, 1980; Ideologi och strategi: 1984; Misstaget (novel), 1986; Festskrift till professor skytteanus Carl Arvid Hessler: Utgiven till 80-arsagen den 10 Februari 1987, 1987; Det gemensamma basta: Om egenintresset och allmanintresset i vasterlandsk politik, 1988; Upptackten av framtiden, 1990; (ed.) Politiskt ledarskap: Sex forskningsprojekt om konsten att leda ett land, 1994; Votera eller forhandla? Om den svenska parlamentarismen, 1996; (ed. with S. Gustavsson) The Future of the Nation State: Essays on Cultural Pluralism and Political Integration, 1996; Braka inte! Om var tids demokratisyn, 1998; (ed.) Svenskt kynne: En konferens anordnad av Humanistisk-Samhallsvetenskapliga Vetenskapsomradet vid Uppsala Universitet den 29 februari 2000, 2000; (ed.) Svenskt okynne: Att underminera det auktoritara samhället: En konferens anordnad av Humanistisk-Samhallsvetenskapliga Vetenskapsomradet vid UppsalaUniversitet den 14 februari 2002, 2002; Osvenskt kynne: forskare med utländsk bakgrund om sin syn på upsaliensisk humaniora och samhallsvetenskap, 2005; Democratic Accountability: Why Choice in Politics Is Both Possible and Necessary, 2007, Stavstenskapens grunder, 2007; Prime Minister Arvid Lindman, 2010. **Address:** Department of Government, University of Uppsala, PO Box 514, Uppsala, SE-751 20, Sweden. **Online address:** leif.lewin@statsvet.uu.se

LEWIN, Michael Z. British/American (born United States), b. 1942. **Genres:** Novellas/Short Stories, Mystery/Crime/Suspense, Plays/Screenplays, Adult Non-fiction, Novels, Poetry, Young Adult Fiction. **Career:** Central High School, physics teacher, 1966-68; George Washington High School, science teacher, 1968-69. Writer. **Publications:** How to Beat College Tests: A Practical Guide to Ease the Burden of Useless Courses, 1970; Ask the Right Question, 1971; The Way We Die Now, 1973; The Enemies Within, 1974; The Next Man, 1975; Night Cover, 1976; The Silent Salesman, 1978; Outside In, 1980; Missing Woman, 1981; Hard Line, 1982; Out of Season in UK as Out of Time, 1984; Late Payments, 1986; And Baby Will Fall in UK as Child Proof, 1988; Called by a Panther, 1991; Underdog, 1993; (co-ed.) 1st Culprit, 1992; 2nd Culprit, 1993; 3rd Culprit, 1994; Telling Tails, 1994; Family Business, 1995; Rover's Tales, 1998; Cutting Loose, 1999; Family Planning, 1999; The Reluctant Detective and Other Stories, 2001; Eye Opener, 2004; Oh Joe, 2008. **Address:** 15 Bladud Bldg., Bath, SM BA1 5LS, England. **Online address:** readermail@michaelzlewin.com

LEWIN, Rhoda G. American (born United States), b. 1929. **Genres:** History, Literary Criticism And History, Local History/Rural Topics, Race Relations, Writing/Journalism. **Career:** Freelance writer, 1956-; University of Wisconsin, lecturer in journalism; University of Minnesota Extension Division, instructor in communications, humanities and creative writing, 1964-83; Minneapolis Federation for Jewish Service, director, 1972-78, 1986-90, chair, 1990-91; Human Development Task Force, director, 1980-82; Minnesota Independent Scholars' Forum, founder, 1982, president, 1983-84; Jewish chaplaincy at Mayo Clinic and Hospitals, vice-chair, 1988-91; University of Minnesota, Elder Learning Institute, teacher, 2002-. Historian. **Publications:** Security: Everything You Need to Know about Household Alarm Systems, 1982; Temple Israel: A Brief History, 1878-1987, 1987; (ed.) Witnesses to the Holocaust: An Oral History, 1990; Images of America: Jews of North Minneapolis, 2001; Reform Jews of Minneapolis, 2004. Contributor of articles to periodicals. **Address:** U.S.A.

LEWIN, Roger A. American (born United States), b. 1946. **Genres:** Psychology, Human Relations/Parenting, Medicine/Health. **Career:** Sheppard and Enoch Pratt Hospital, resident, 1981-85, psychiatrist, 1985-91, teacher and supervisor, 1991-; Building Systems Inc., housing developer; Quaker School, teacher and director. Writer. **Publications:** (With C. Schultz) Losing and Fusing: Borderline Transitional Object and Self Relations, 1992; Lamentations, 1993; Compassion: The Core Value That Animates Psychotherapy, 1996; New Wrinkles (poems), 1996; Creative Collaboration in Psychotherapy: Making Room for Life, 1997; Spring Fed Pond, 2003; The Mouse and the Unicorn, forthcoming. **Address:** 6525 N Charles St., Towson, MD 21204, U.S.A. **Online address:** lewin.roger@gmail.com

LEWIS, Adrian R. American (born United States), b. 1952. **Genres:** Military/Defense/Arms Control. **Career:** United States Military Academy, Department of History, assistant professor of military and American history, 1987-90, course group director, 1990-91; University of California at Berkeley, assistant professor of military science, 1991-93, professor of military science and department chair, 1993-94; University of North Texas, Department of History, assistant professor of military history, 1995-2001, honor professor, 2000-01, associate professor of military and American history, 2005-08; Naval War College, professor, 2005-; University of Kansas, Department of History, professor, 2008-, Office of Professional Military Graduate Education, director, 2008-; School of the Art Institute of Chicago, consultant, 2009-. Writer.. **Publications:** Omaha Beach: A Flawed Victory, 2001; American Culture of War: The History of U.S. Military Force from World War II to Operation Iraqi Freedom, 2007; The American Culture of War: The History of the U.S. Military Force from World War II to Operation Enduring Freedom, 2011. Contributor to books and journals. **Address:** Department of History, University of Kansas, 1445 Wescoe Hall,, Jayhawk Blvd., Lawrence, KS 66045, U.S.A. **Online address:** alewis@unt.edu

LEWIS, Andrew B. American (born United States), b. 1967. **Genres:** History. **Career:** Harvard University, fellow; National Academy of Education, fellow. Academic, writer and historian. **Publications:** (Ed. with M.D. Lassiter) The Moderates' Dilemma: Massive Resistance to School Desegregation in Virginia, 1998; (with J. Bond) Gonna Sit at the Welcome Table, 2000; The Shadows of Youth: The Remarkable Journey of the Civil Rights Generation, 2009. Contributor to magazines. **Address:** Hornfischer Literary Management, PO Box 50544, Austin, TX 78763, U.S.A.

LEWIS, Arnold. American (born United States), b. 1930. **Genres:** Architecture, Art/Art History, Photography, Homes/Gardens. **Career:** Wells College, educator and art historian. 1962-64; College of Wooster, professor, 1964-96, professor emeritus of art history, 1996-. Writer. **Publications:** (Intro.) American Victorian Architecture: A Survey of the 70's and 80's in Contemporary Photographs, 1975; (ed.) Wooster in 1876, 1976; (contrib.) American Country Houses of the Gilded Age (Sheldon's Artistic Country Seats), 1982; (with J. Turner and S. McQuillin) Opulent Interiors of the Gilded Age: All 203 Photographs from Artistic Houses?: With New Text, 1987; An Early Encounter with Tomorrow: Europeans, Chicago's Loop and the World's Columbian Exposition, 1997. **Address:** College of Wooster, 1189 Beall Ave., Wooster, OH 44691, U.S.A. **Online address:** alewis@wooster.edu

LEWIS, Carol F. Ra. (Carol F. Ra). American (born United States), b. 1939. **Genres:** Poetry, Children's Non-fiction. **Career:** Richmond City Schools, elementary school teacher, 1961-62; Vigo County Schools, elementary school teacher, 1962-64; Champaign Unit 4 Schools, teacher of gifted children, 1964-68; St. James Episcopal, preschool director, 1973-74; Hollins College, lecturer in early childhood education and children's literature, 1974-87; Herald News, editor and columnist, 1990-. **Publications:** AS CAROL F. RA: (comp.) Trot, Trot to Boston: Play Rhymes for Baby, 1987; (with W.J. Smith)

Behind the King's Kitchen: A Roster of Rhyming Riddles, 1992; (with Smith) The Sun Is Up, 1993. Contributor to books. **Address:** 3654 W Mecca Rd., Rockville, IN 47872, U.S.A.

LEWIS, Earl. American (born United States) **Genres:** Race Relations, History. **Career:** University of California, Afro-American Studies Department, assistant professor, 1985-89; University of Michigan, Department of History, Center for Afro-American and African Studies, associate professor, 1989-95, interim director, 1990-91, director, 1991-93, professor, 1995-, Horace H. Rackham School of Graduate Studies, interim dean, 1997-98, dean, 1998-2004, vice provost for academic affairs and graduate studies, 1998-2004, Elsa Barkley Brown and Robin D.G. Kelley Collegiate professor of history and African American and African studies; Emory University, provost and executive vice president for academic affairs, 2004-, professor, Asa Griggs Candler professor of history and African American studies, 2004-; American Academy of Arts and Sciences, fellow, 2008. Writer and consultant. **Publications:** In Their Own Interests: Race, Class and Power in Twentieth-Century Norfolk, 1991; (with R.D.G. Kelley and V. Harding) We Changed the World: African Americans, 1945-1970, 1997; (with H. Ardizzone) Love on Trial: An American Scandal in Black and White, 2001; (co-author) Defending Diversity, 2004. EDITOR: (with R.D.G. Kelley) The Young Oxford History of African Americans, 11 vols., 1997; (with J.W. Trotter) African Americans in the Industrial Age: A Documentary History, 1915-1945, 1996; (with R.D.G. Kelley) To Make Our World Anew: A History of African Americans, 2000; (with T.W. Hunter and J.W. Trotter) African American Urban Experience: Perspectives from the Colonial Period to the Present, 2004. **Address:** Department of History, Emory University, Rm. 1004, 404 Admin Bldg., 561 S Kilgo Cir., 201 Dowman Dr., Atlanta, GA 30322, U.S.A. **Online address:** earl.lewis@emory.edu

LEWIS, Gregg (Allan). American (born United States), b. 1951. **Genres:** Adult Non-fiction, Autobiography/Memoirs, Medicine/Health, Children's Fiction, Biography. **Career:** David C. Cook Publishers, associate editor of youth publications, 1973-76; freelance writer, 1976-77, 1987-; Campus Life, Carol Stream, associate editor, 1977-79, editor, 1980-84, senior editor, 1984-87, editor at large, 1987-; UPI Religious Radio Service, commentator, 1984-85; Marriage Partnership, Carol Stream, senior editor, 1987-88, senior writer, 1988-. **Publications:** Telegarbage, 1977; (with M.M. Lewis) The Hurting Parent, 1980, rev. ed. as The Hurting Parent: Help and Hope for Parents of Prodigals, 2009; (with R.L. Lewis) Inductive Preaching: Helping People Listen, 1983; (with S. Purl) Am I Alive?: A Surviving Flight Attendant's Struggle and Inspiring Triumph Over Tragedy, 1986; (ed. with T. Stafford) You Call This a Family?, 1986; Caught, 1987; (with B. Tirabassi) Just One Victory, 1987; (with M. Wazeter) Dark Marathon: The Mary Wazeter Story: The Ongoing Struggles of a World-Class Runner, 1989; (with S. Perry) In Sickness and in Health: A Story of Love in the Shadow of AIDS, 1989; (with D.S. Lewis) Motherhood Stress: Finding Encouragement in the Ultimate Helping Profession, 1989; (with R.L. Lewis) Learning to Preach Like Jesus, 1989; The Waters Run Deep, 1989; Beyond a Broken Promise, 1989; (with B. Tirabassi) The Life of the Party: A True Story of Teenage Alcoholism, 1990; (with T. Landry) Tom Landry, 1990; (ed.) Hudson Taylor's Spiritual Secret, 1990; (with R.A. Seiple) A Missing Peace: Vietnam: Finally Healing the Pain, 1992; (with C. Wedemeyer and L. Wedemeyer) Charlie's Victory, 1993; (with D.S. Lewis) Did I Ever Tell You about When You Were Little?, 1994; (with D.S. Lewis) Did I Ever Tell You about When Your Parents Were Children?, 1994; (with D.S. Lewis) Did I Ever Tell You about When Your Grandparents Were Young?, 1994; (with D.S. Lewis) Did I Ever Tell You about How Our Family Got Started?, 1994; (with T. and C. Burke) Major League Dad, 1994; (with B. Thomas) Good Sports: Making Sportsa Positive Experience for Everyone, 1994; (with C. Martin) I Can't Walk, So I'll Learn to Dance, 1994; (with D.S. Lewis) When You Were a Baby, 1995; Power of a Promise Kept: Life Stories, 1995; (with D. Gray) Yes, You Can, Heather!: The Story of Heather Whitestone, Miss America 1995, 1995; (with D. Gray) Heather Whitestone, 1995; (with D. Jordan) Family First: Winning the Parenting Game, 1996; (with H.F. Phillips) What Does She Want from Me, Anyway?: Honest Answers to Questions Men Ask About Women, 1997; (with B. and K. McCaughey and D.S. Lewis) Seven from Heaven: The Miracle of the McCaughey Septuplets, 1998; (with D. Morris) Forgiving the Dead Man Walking, 1998; (with B. Carson) Big Picture: Getting Perspective on What's Really Important in Life, 1999; (with B. McCaughey and D.S. Lewis) Celebrating the Wonder of Motherhood: Intimate Moments With My Daughter Mikayla and the Septuplets, 1999; (with M. Akers) The Game and the Glory: An Autobiography, 2000; (with H.G. Koenig) Healing Connection: A World-Renowned Medical

Scientist Discovers the Powerful Link Between Christian Faith and Health, 2000; (with B. Muzikowski) Safe at Home: The True and Inspiring Story of Chicago's Field of Dreams, 2001; (with D. Stevens) Jesus, M.D.: A Doctor Examines the Great Physician, 2001; (with D.S. Lewis) Ben Carson, 2002; (with D.S. Lewis) Brother Andrew, 2002; (with D.S. Lewis) Colin Powell, 2002; (with D.S. Lewis) Dave Dravecky, 2002; (with D.S. Lewis) David Robinson, 2002; (with D.S. Lewis) Joni Eareckson Tada, 2002; (with J. Sonnenberg) Joel, 2004; Miracle at Tenwek: The Life of Dr. Ernie Steury, 2007; (with B. Carson) Take the Risk: Learning to Identify, Choose and Live with Acceptable Risk, 2008; (with D.S. Lewis) Gifted Hands: The Ben Carson Story, 2009. Contributor of articles to journals. **Address:** c/o Zondervan, 5300 Patterson SE, Grand Rapids, MI 49530, U.S.A.

LEWIS, Herbert S. American (born United States), b. 1934. **Genres:** Anthropology/Ethnology, History, Humanities, Politics/Government. **Career:** The City College, Department of Sociology And Anthropology, departmental fellow and assistant, 1956-57; American Museum of Natural History, Department of Public Instruction, instructor, 1957-58; Columbia University, School of General Studies, lecturer in anthropology, 1961; Northwestern University, Departments of Anthropology and Political Science, instructor, 1961-63; University of Wisconsin, Department of Anthropology, assistant professor of anthropology, 1963-67, associate professor of anthropology, 1967-73, professor of anthropology, 1973-96, professor emeritus of anthropology, 1996-, chair, 1978-81, Junior Year Abroad Program, resident director, 1989-90, African Studies Program, chair and director, 1993-95; The Hebrew University, visiting associate professor, 1969-70. Writer. **Publications:** A Galla Monarchy: Jimma Abba Jifar, Ethiopia, 1830-1932, 1965; Leaders and Followers: Some Anthropological Perspectives, 1974; (with B. Wisner) Refugee Rehabilitation in Somalia: Report of a Mission, March 1981, 1981; (with C. Kerven and N. Southerland) Urbanization and Outmigration in Somalia: Final Report, 1983; After the Eagles Landed: The Yemenites of Israel, 1989; The Misrepresentation of Anthropology and Its Consequences, 1998; Boas, Darwin, Science and Anthropology, 2001; Jimma Abba Jifar, an Oromo Monarchy: Ethiopia, 1830-1932, 2001; (ed. with L.G. McLester III) Oneida Lives: Long-Lost Voices of the Wisconsin Oneidas, 2005; Aspects of Oromo Culture and History, 2005; Toward Reconstruction in Anthropology, forthcoming. **Address:** Department of Anthropology, University of Wisconsin, 5135 Sewell Social Science Hall, 5240 Sewell Soc Sci Bldg., 1180 Observatory Dr., Madison, WI 53706-1320, U.S.A. **Online address:** hslewis@wisc.edu

LEWIS, Jack Pearl. American (born United States), b. 1919. **Genres:** Theology/Religion, Archaeology/Antiquities. **Career:** Harding University, Graduate School of Religion (now Harding School of Theology), associate professor, 1954-57, professor of Bible, 1957-89, professor emeritus, 1989-; University Christian Center, director, 1966. Writer. **Publications:** The Minor Prophets, 1966; The Interpretation of Noah and the Flood in Jewish and Christian Literature, 1968; Historical Backgrounds of Bible History, 1971; Archaeology and the Bible, 1975; The Gospel According to Mathew (commentary), 2 vols., 1976; Archeological Background to Bible People, 1981; The English Bible from the KJV to the NIV, 1981, 2nd ed., 1991; Leadership Questions Confronting the Church, 1985; (contrib.) Biblical Interpretation: Principles and Practice: Studies in Honor of Jack Pearl Lewis, Professor of Bible, Harding Graduate School of Religion, 1986; (with B. Flatt, E. West and E. Ferguson) Instrumental Music Issue, 1987; Exegesis of Difficult Passages, 1988; Questions You've Asked about Bible Translations, 1990; Major Prophets, 1999; The Ethics of the Prophets, 2001. EDITOR: Last Things: Essays Presented by His Students to Dr. W. B. West, Jr., Upon the Occasion of his Sixty-fifth Birthday, 1972; Interpreting 2 Corinthians 5: 14-21: An Exercise in Hermeneutics, 1989. **Address:** Harding School of Theology, 1000 Cherry Rd., Memphis, TN 38117, U.S.A. **Online address:** jackplewis@juno.com

LEWIS, James R. American (born United States), b. 1949. **Genres:** Theology/Religion, Philosophy, Reference, Cultural/Ethnic Topics. **Career:** University of Wisconsin, lecturer in religious studies, 1999-; DePaul University, Department of Religious Studies, instructor; Association of World Academics for Religious Edication, executive director. Writer. **Publications:** Yoga for Couples, 1979; (with J.G. Melton) Sex, Slander, and Salvation, 1994; Seeking the Light, 1998; Encyclopedia of UFOs: Abductions, Crashes, Cover-Ups, and More, 1998; Doomsday Prophecies, 2000; Legitimating New Religions, 2003; Astrology Book: The Encyclopedia of Heavenly Influences, 2003; (with J. Petersen) Contemporary Religious Satanism, 2009; Cults 101, 3rd ed., 2012. REFERENCE WORKS: The Astrology Encyclopedia, 1994; Encyclopedia of Afterlife Beliefs and Phenomena, 1994; The Dream Encyclo-

pedia, 1995, (with E.D. Oliver), 2nd ed., 2009; (with E. Oliver) Angels, A to Z, 1996; The Encyclopedia of Cults, Sects, and New Religions, 1998; Encyclopedia of New Religions, Cults, and Sects, 1998; Cults in America, 1998; Peculiar Prophets, 1999; Witchcraft Today, 1999; UFOs and Popular Culture, 2000; (with C. Skutsch) The Human Rights Encyclopedia, 2001; Satanism Today: An Encyclopedia of Religion, Folklore, and Popular Culture, 2001; Cults: A Reference Handbook, 2005; (with E.D. Oliver) Angels A to Z, 2nd ed., 2008; (with N.M. Levine) Children of Jesus and Mary: The Order of Christ Sophia, 2010. EDITOR: The Inner Life of Theosophy, 1990; (and intro.) Theosophy, 1990; The Unification Church, vol. III: Outreach, 1990; (and intro.) The Beginnings of Astrology in America, 1990; (with J.G. Melton) Perspectives on the New Age, 1992; (with J.G. Melton) Church Universal and Triumphant, 1994; From the Ashes, 1994; The Gods Have Landed, 1995; Magical Religion and Modern Witchcraft, 1996; Odd Gods, 2001; The Encyclopedic Sourcebook of UFO Religions, 2003; Oxford Handbook of New Religious Movements, 2004; (with J. Petersen) Controversial New Religions, 2005; The Order of the Solar Temple, 2006; (with D. Kemp) Handbook of New Age, 2007; (with O. Hammer) Invention of Sacred Tradition, 2007; (with J.A. Petersen) The Encyclopedic Sourcebook of Satanism, 2008; (with M. Pizza) Handbook of Contemporary Paganism, 2008; Scientology, 2009; (with S.M. Lewis) Sacred Schisms: How Religions Divide, 2009; (with O. Hammer) Handbook of Religion and the Authority of Science, 2011; Violence and New Religious Movements, 2011. Contributor of articles to books and journals. **Address:** Department of Religious Studies, DePaul University, LOOP Lewis, 1 E Jackson Blvd., Chicago, IL 60604-2201, U.S.A. **Online address:** jlewis@uwsp.edu

LEWIS, Jeremy. British (born England), b. 1942. **Genres:** Essays, Biography, Adult Non-fiction. **Career:** Chatto & Windus, editor, director, 1979-89; freelance writer, 1989-; London Magazine, deputy editor, 1990-94; Peters, Fraser & Dunlop, reader, 1994-2001; The Oldie Magazine, commissioning editor, 1997-; Literary Review, editor-at-large, 2004-; Andre Deutsch Publishers, literary agent; Oxford University Press, editor and literary agent; AP Watt Ltd., literary agent. **Publications:** Playing for Time, 1987; (ed. and intro.) The Chatto Book of Office Life, or, Love Among the Filing Cabinets, 1992; Who Cares about Cyril Connolly?, 1994; Kindred Spirits: Adrift in Literary London, 1995; (ed. with S. Lewis) Work-Family Challenge: Rethinking Employment, 1996; Cyril Connolly: A Life, 1997; The Vintage Book of Office Life, 1998; (intro.) Three Men in a Boat: To Say Nothing of the Dog! And Three Men on the Bummel, 1999; Whistle Blowing: The New Law, 1999; Tobias Smollett, 2003; Penguin Special: The Life and Times of Allen Lane, 2005; Shades of Greene: One Generation of an English Family, 2010. Contributor to periodicals. **Address:** Literary Review, 44 Lexington St., London, GL W1F 0LW, England. **Online address:** jeremy.lewis5@btinternet.com

LEWIS, Johanna Miller. American (born United States), b. 1961. **Genres:** Art/Art History, History. **Career:** College of William and Mary, instructor, 1988; University of Arkansas-Little Rock, assistant profesor of history, 1991-95, associate professor, 1995-2005, professor of history, 2000-, chair and associate coordinator of Public History Program; Clinch Valley State College, lecturer; University of North Carolina-Greensboro, lecturer; National Dunbar History Project, co-director, 1993-. Writer. **Publications:** Artisans in the North Carolina Backcountry, 1995. Contributor to books and periodicals. **Address:** Department of History, University of Arkansas, SH 601 E, 2801 S University, Little Rock, AR 72204-1099, U.S.A. **Online address:** jmlewis@ualr.edu

LEWIS, J(ohn) Parry. British/Welsh (born Wales), b. 1927?. **Genres:** Economics, Mathematics/Statistics, Regional/Urban Planning, History. **Career:** Teacher, 1948-51; University of Wales, University College, lecturer in economic statistics, 1951-59; Victoria University of Manchester (now University of Manchester), lecturer in economic statistics, 1959-64, senior lecturer in mathematical economics, 1964, professor of economics of regions and towns, 1967-82, professor emeritus, 1982-, Centre for Urban and Regional Research, director, 1968-82; University of Exeter, professor of economics, 1965-67. Writer. **Publications:** Introduction to Mathematics for Students of Economics, 1959, 2nd ed., 1969; Building Cycles and Britain's Growth, 1965; Statistical Study of Urban Change, 1967; (with D.F. Medhurst) Urban Decay: An Analysis and a Policy, 1969; A Study of the Cambridge Sub-Region, 1974; Professional Fees in the Building Industry, 1975; (ed.) Urban Economics: A Set Approach, 1979; Freedom to Drink, 1985; (with A. Traill) Statistics Explained, 1999. **Address:** University of Manchester, Oxford Rd., Manchester, GM M13 9PL, England. **Online address:** jparrylewis@riter.freeserve.co.uk

LEWIS, J(ohn) P(aul) Lewis. (J. P. Sinclair Lewis). American (born United States) **Genres:** Novels, History, Military/Defense/Arms Control. **Career:** ViviSphere Publishing, Epaulet Books Division, head. Writer and publisher. **Publications:** AS J.P. SINCLAIR LEWIS: Buffalo Gordon: The Extraordinary Life and Times of Nate Gordon from Louisiana Slave to Buffalo Soldier, 2001; Buffalo Gordon on the Plains, 2003. **Address:** ViviSphere Publishing, 675 Dutchess Tpke., Poughkeepsie, NY 12603-6436, U.S.A.

LEWIS, J(ohn) R(oyston). Also writes as David Springfield, J. R. Lewis, Roy Lewis. British/Welsh (born Wales), b. 1933. **Genres:** Mystery/Crime/Suspense, Law, Novels, Ghost Writer. **Career:** Okehampton Secondary School, English teacher, 1957-59; Cannock Chase Technical College, lecturer, 1959-61; Cornwall Technical College, lecturer, 1961-63; Plymouth College of Technology, lecturer, 1963-67; Her Majesty's Inspector of Schools, teacher, 1967-75; New College, vice-principal, 1975-81; Wigan College of Technology, principal, 1981-2005; Templar North Publications Ltd., managing director; Casdec Ltd., managing director; Felton Press, managing director. Writer. **Publications:** AS J.R. LEWIS: Law for the Retailer, 1964, 3rd ed. as Law for the Retailer and Distributor, 1979; Cases for Discussion, 1965; An Introduction to Business Law, 1965; Law in Action, 1965; Questions and Answers on Civil Procedure, 1966; Building Law, 1966; Democracy: The Theory and the Practice, 1966; Managing within the Law, 1967; (with J.A. Holland) Principles of Registered Land Conveyancing, 1967; Company Law, 1967; Revision Notes for Ordinary Level British Construction, 1967; Civil and Criminal Procedure, 1968, 2nd ed., 1976; Landlord and Tenant, 1968, 2nd ed., 1978; Outlines of Equity, 1968; (with A. Redish) Mercantile and Commercial Law, 1969; (as David Springfield) The Company Executive and the Law, 1970, 2nd ed., 1977; Law for the Construction Industry, 1976; Administrative Law for the Construction Industry, 1976; (with C. Himsworth) The Teaching of Public Administration Teaching in Further and Higher Education, 1979; The Victorian Bar 1837-1882, 1980; Certain Private Incidents, 1980; The Maypole, 1983. MYSTERY NOVELS AS ROY LEWIS: Evolution Man, 1963; A Lover too Many, 1969; A Wolf by the Ears, 1970; Error of Judgment, 1971; The Fenokee Project, 1971; A Fool for a Client, 1972; A Secret Singing, 1972; Blood Money, 1973; Of Singular Purpose, 1973; A Question of Degree, 1974; Double Take, 1975; A Part of Virtue, 1975; Witness My Death, 1976; A Distant Banner, 1976; Nothing but Foxes, 1977; An Uncertain Sound, 1978; An Inevitable Fatality, 1978; A Violent Death, 1979; A Certain Blindness, 1980; Seek for Justice, 1981; A Relative Distance, 1981; Dwell in Danger, 1982; A Gathering of Ghosts, 1982; A Limited Vision, 1983; Once Dying, Twice Dead, 1984; Most Cunning Workmen, 1984; A Blurred Reality, 1985; A Trout in the Milk, 1986; Premium on Death, 1986; Men of Subtle Craft, 1987; The Salamander Chill, 1988; The Devil is Dead, 1989; A Necessary Dealing, 1990; A Kind of Transaction, 1991; A Wisp of Smoke, 1991; A Secret Dying, 1992; Bloodeagle, 1993; The Cross Bearer, 1994; A Short Lived Ghost, 1995; Angel of Death, 1996; Suddenly as a Shadow, 1997; The Shape Shifter, 1998; The Ghost Dancers, 1999; An Assumption of Death, 2000; A Form of Death, 2000; Dead Secret, 2001; The Nightwalker, 2002; Phantom, 2002; The Ways of Death, 2003; Phantom, 2003; Dead Man Running, 2004; Headhunter, 2004; Grave Error, 2005; Embers Of The Dead, 2005; Death Squad, 2006; Dragon Head, 2007; Guardians of the Dead, 2008; Shadowmaker, 2009; Design for Murder, 2010; Dead Ringer, 2011. **Address:** South Stainmore, Old Pk., Westmoreland, CA17 4DY, England. **Online address:** lewisr@tesco.net

LEWIS, John S. American (born United States), b. 1941. **Genres:** Meteorology/Atmospheric Sciences, Environmental Sciences/Ecology, Sciences, Chemistry, Air/Space Topics, Astronomy. **Career:** Massachusetts Institute of Technology, Department of Chemistry and Department of Earth and Planetary Sciences, assistant professor, 1968-72, associate professor, 1972-79, professor of earth and planetary science, 1979-81; University of Arizona, Lunar and Planetary Lab, professor of planetary science, 1981-, Space Engineering Research Center, co-director, 1988-, now professor emeritus of cosmochemistry and planetary atmospheres; American Rocket Co., director, 1988-96; ASPERA Corp., vice president for research and director, 1989; Arizona State Space Commission, commissioner. Writer. **Publications:** (With R.G. Prinn) Planets and Their Atmospheres: Origin and Evolution, 1984; (with R.A. Lewis) Space Resources: Breaking the Bonds of Earth, 1987; (ed. with M.S. Matthews and M.L. Guerrieri) Resources of Near-Earth Space, 1993; Physics and Chemistry of the Solar System, 1995, 2nd ed., 2004; Mining the Sky: Untold Riches from the Asteroids Comets and Planets, 1996; Rain of Iron and Ice: The Very Real Threat of Comet and Asteroid Bombardment, 1996; Worlds without End: The Exploration of Planets Known and Unknown, 1998;

Comet and Asteroid Impact Hazards on a Populated Earth: Computer Modeling, 2000. **Address:** Lunar and Planetary Laboratory, University of Arizona, Kuiper Space Sciences 513, 1629 E University Blvd., Tucson, AZ 85721-0092, U.S.A. **Online address:** jsl@u.arizona.edu

LEWIS, Jon Samuel. *See* **LEWIS, J. S.**

LEWIS, J. Patrick. American (born United States), b. 1942. **Genres:** Children's Fiction, Poetry, Military/Defense/Arms Control, Women's Studies And Issues. **Career:** Otterbein College, professor of economics, 1974-98, professor emeritus, 1998-. Writer. **Publications:** FOR CHILDREN: The Tsar & the Amazing Cow, 1988; The Hippopotamusn't and Other Animal Verses, 1990; Two-legged, Four-legged, No-legged Rhymes, 1991; Earth Verses and Water Rhymes, 1991; The Moonbows of Mr. B. Bones, 1992; One Dog Day, 1st ed., 1993; The Fat-Cats at Sea, 1994; July Is a Mad Mosquito, 1994; (reteller) The Frog Princess: A Russian Folktale, 1994; The Christmas of the Reddle Moon, 1994; Black Swan/White Crow, 1995; Ridicholas Nicholas, 1995; Riddleicious, 1996; The Boat of Many Rooms, 1997; The La-Di-Da Hare, 1997; Long Was the Winter Road They Traveled, 1997; The Little Buggers, 1998; Boshblobberbosh: Runcible Poems for Edward Lear, 1998; Doodle Dandies: Poems That Take Shape, 1998; The House of Boo, 1998; Riddle-Lightful: Oodles of Little Riddle-poems, 1998; The Bookworm's Feast, 1999; Night of the Goat Children, 1999; At the Wish of the Fish: An Adaptation of a Russian Folktale, 1999; Earth & Sea and You & Me, 1999; Freedom Like Sunlight: Praise Songs for Black Americans, 2000; Isabella Abnormella and the Very, Very Finicky Queen of Trouble, 2000; Earth and Us Continuous: Earth's Past and Future, 2000; Good Mousekeeping: An Even Number of Odd Riddle-Rhymes, 2001; A Burst of Firsts, 2001; Earth and You, a Closer View: Nature's Features, 2001; The Shoe Tree of Chagrin Falls: A Christmas Story, 2002; Arithmetickle, 2002; A World of Wonders: Geographic Travels in Verse and Rhyme, 2002; Earth and Me: Our Family Tree, 2002; Earth and Me, Our Family Tree: Nature's Creatures, 2002; Arithme-Tickle: An Even Number of Odd Riddle-Rhymes, 2002; The Last Resort, 2002; The Snowflake Sisters, 2003; Swan Songs: Poems of Extinction, 2003; Galileo's Universe, 2003; Vherses: For Outstanding Females, 2003; Crystal and Ivory: The Snowflake Sisters, 2003; Clickety Clickety Electrickety: Science Riddles, 2004; Scien-trickery: Riddles in Science, 2004; Please Bury Me in the Library: Poems About Books and Reading, 2004; Stolen Smile, 2004; Heroes and She-roes: Poems of Amazing and Everyday Heroes, 2005; Vherses: A Celebration of Outstanding Women, 2005; Monumental Verses, 2005; Once Upon a Tomb: Gravely Humorous Verses, 2005; Please Bury Me in the Library, 2005; Blackbeard, the Pirate King: Several Yarns Detailing The Legends, Myths, And Real-Life Adventures Of History's Most Notorious Seaman, 2006; (with P.B. Janeczko) Wing Nuts: Screwy Haiku, 2006; (with R.K. Dotlich) Castles: Old Stone Poems, 2006; Black Cat Bone, 2006; Blackbeard, the Pirate King, 2006; Wing Nuts: Screwy Haiku, 2006; Big is Big (and Little Little): A Book of Contrasts, 2007; Under the Kissletoe: Christmastime Poems, 2007; Tulip at the Bat, 2007; Michelangelo's World, 2007; Poems for Teaching in the Content Areas, 2007; Good Mornin', Ms. America: The U.S.A. in Verse, 2007; The Brothers' War: Civil War Voices in Verse, 2007; (with P.B. Janeczko) Birds on a Wire or A Jewel Tray of Stars, 2008; (with K. Graves) World's Greatest: Poems, 2008; (with P.B. Janeczko) Birds on a Wire: Renga 'Round Town, 2009; (with B. Zappitello) First Dog, 2009; The Underwear Salesman, 2009; Countdown to Summer: A Poem for Every Day of the School Year, 2009; Spot the Plot! A Riddle Book of Book Riddles, 2009; (with R. Innocenti) The House, 2009; Skywriting: Poems to Fly, 2009; (with J. Yolen) Self-portrait with Seven Fingers: The Life of Marc Chagall in Verse, 2010; Fantastic 5 & 10 [cent] Store: A Rebus Adventure, 2010; Mr. Nickel & Mrs. Dime, 2010; The Kindergarten Cat, 2010; (with B. Zappitello) First Dog's White House Christmas, 2010; (with J. Yolen) Twinspiration: A Double Dose of Poems, 2011; Tugg and Teeny, 2011; Tugg and Teeny: That's What Friends Are For, 2011; Tugg and Teeny: Jungle Surprises, 2011; And the Soldiers Sang, 2011; (with J. Yolen) Double Delivery, 2012. OTHER: (comp. with J.S. Adams and M.W. Curran) The U.S.S.R. Today: Current Readings From The Soviet Press: Selections From The Current Digest of the Soviet Press, From May 16, 1973, to June 25, 1975, 1975; (with J. Yolen) Last Laughs, 2011; When Thunder Comes, 2012; What's Looking at You, Kid, 2012; (with J. Yolen) Take Two!, 2012; Edgar Allan Poe's Apple Pie, 2012; (with D. Florian) Beep! Beep! Poems about Imaginary Cars, 2013. Contributor of articles to periodicals and journals. **Address:** c/o Ginger Knowlton, Curtis Brown Ltd., 10 Astor Pl., New York, NY 10003, U.S.A. **Online address:** info@jpatricklewis.com

LEWIS, J. P. Sinclair. *See* **LEWIS, J(ohn) P(aul) Lewis.**

LEWIS, J. R. *See* **LEWIS, J(ohn) R(oyston).**

LEWIS, J. S. (Jon Samuel Lewis). American (born United States), b. 1972?. **Genres:** Novels. **Career:** Video game development, animation; news reporting; radio production; multimedia design; mural painting; speechwriting; marketing and advertising. Writer. **Publications:** "GREY GRIFFINS" SERIES; YOUNG ADULT FANTASY NOVELS: (with D. Benz) The Revenge of the Shadow King, 2005; (with D. Benz) The Rise of the Black Wolf, 2007; (with D. Benz) The Fall of the Templar, 2008; (with D. Benz) Brimstone Key, 2010; (with D. Benz) Relic Hunters, 2011; (with D. Benz) Paragon Prison, 2012. **Address:** Orchard Books, 338 Euston Rd., London, GL NW1 3BH, England. **Online address:** jslewis@greygriffins.com

LEWIS, Julinda. *See* **LEWIS-FERGUSON, Julinda.**

LEWIS, Linda (Joy). American (born United States), b. 1946. **Genres:** Novels, Children's Fiction, Business/Trade/Industry, Young Adult Fiction. **Career:** Broward County Schools, school teacher, 1972-81; Simon & Schuster, writer, 1985-. **Publications:** LINDA SERIES: We Hate Everything but Boys, 1985; Is There Life after Boys?, 1987; We Love Only Older Boys, 1988; 2 Young 2 Go 4 Boys, 1988; My Heart Belongs to That Boy, 1989; All for the Love of That Boy, 1989; Want to Trade Two Brothers for a Cat?, 1989; Dedicated to That Boy I Love, 1990; Loving Two Is Hard to Do, 1990; Tomboy Terror in Bunk 109, 1991; Preteen Means in Between, 1993. NOVEL: The Road Back to Heaven (adult), 2007. Contributor to newspapers and magazines. **Address:** 812 Hawks Bluff, Clermont, FL 34711, U.S.A. **Online address:** linlewis22@aol.com

LEWIS, Margaret (B.). British/Irish (born Ireland), b. 1942. **Genres:** Biography. **Career:** Open University, tutor, 1970-93; University of Newcastle upon Tyne, public relations officer, 1984-96; tutor in English, 1989-99; Flambard Press, co-founder and co-publisher. Writer. **Publications:** Ngaio Marsh: A Life, 1991; Edith Pargeter: Ellis Peters, 1994, rev. ed., 2003; Josefina de Vasconcellos: Her Life and Art, 2002. **Address:** Flambard Press, Holy Jesus Hospital, City Rd., Newcastle upon Tyne, TW NE1 2AS, England.

LEWIS, Mark Edward. American (born United States), b. 1954?. **Genres:** History, Social Sciences. **Career:** University of Cambridge, Faculty of Oriental Studies, reader; Stanford University, Department of East Asian Languages and Cultures, Kwoh-Ting Li professor in Chinese culture, 2002-. Writer. **Publications:** Sanctioned Violence in Early China, 1990; Writing and Authority in Early China, 1999; The Construction of Space in Early China, 2005; The Flood Myths of Early China, 2006; The Early Chinese Empires: Qin and Han, 2007; China's Cosmopolitan Empire: The Tang Dynasty, 2009; China between Empires: The Northern and Southern Dynasties, 2009. Contributor to books. **Address:** Department of East Asian Languages and Cultures, Stanford University, Rm. 240, 450 Serra Mall, PO Box 2000, Stanford, CA 94305-2024, U.S.A. **Online address:** mel1000@stanford.edu

LEWIS, Mervyn. *See* **FREWER, Glyn.**

LEWIS, Michael. American (born United States), b. 1960. **Genres:** International Relations/Current Affairs, Money/Finance, Politics/Government, Essays. **Career:** The Spectator, editor and columnist; The New Republic, senior editor and campaign correspondent; New York Times Magazine, columnist; University of California, visiting fellow; Vanity Fair, contributing editor, 2009-; Bloomberg, columnist; Slate, columnist. **Publications:** Liar's Poker: Rising Through the Wreckage on Wall Street, 1989; Pacific Rift: Adventures in the Fault Zone Between the U.S. and Japan, 1991; The Money Culture, 1991; Trail Fever: Spin Doctors, Rented Strangers, Thumb Wrestlers, Toe Suckers, Grizzly Bears, and Other Creatures on the Road to the White House, 1997; New New Thing: A Silicon Valley Story, 1999; Losers: The Road to Everyplace but the White House, 2000; Next: The Future Just Happened, 2001; Moneyball: The Art of Winning an Unfair Game, 2003; Coach: Lessons on the Game of Life, 2005; The Blind Side: Evolution of a Game, 2006; (ed. and intro.) The Real Price of Everything: Rediscovering the Six Classics of Economics, 2008; (ed.) Panic: The Story of Modern Financial Insanity, 2008; Home Game: An Accidental Guide to Fatherhood, 2009; The Big Short: Inside the Doomsday Machine, 2010; Boomerang, 2011. Contributor to periodicals. **Address:** c/o Albert Zuckerman, Writers House L.L.C., 21 W 26th St., New York, NY 10010-1003, U.S.A.

LEWIS, Minty. American (born United States), b. 1978. **Genres:** Humor/

Satire. **Career:** Shonen Jump Magazine, graphic designer; Cartoon Network, storyboard artist, 2010-. Writer. **Publications:** PS Comics, 2009. Works appear in anthologies. **Address:** Berkeley, CA , U.S.A. **Online address:** mintylewis@gmail.com

LEWIS, Myron. American (born United States), b. 1968. **Genres:** Ethics, Human Relations/Parenting, Medicine/Health. **Career:** Catholic Social Services, counselor, 1994-96; Northern Michigan Hospital, manager of Rehabilitation services, 1998-; Hansyd Publishing, affiliate; Petoskey/ Harbor Springs Chamber of Commerce, leadership trainer. Writer. **Publications:** Making Right Turns in Your Relationship, 2004. **Address:** Hansyd Publishing, 4630 Cottontail Ln., PO Box 557, Harbor Springs, MI 49740, U.S.A. **Online address:** hansydpublishing@tm.net

LEWIS, Norah L. Canadian (born Canada), b. 1935. **Genres:** Novels, Biography. **Career:** Queen Park School, teacher, 1954-56; Federal Indian Schools, teacher, principal, classroom supervisor, 1956-74; University of British Columbia, sessional lecturer, 1974-84, 1986-93; Jiaotong University, faculty of English; Zhongshan University, faculty of English; Vancouver School of Theology, Elders Institute, chair of advisory council, 1999-. Writer and historian. **Publications:** I Want to Join Your Club: Letters from Rural Children, 1900-1920, 1996; Dear Editor and Friends: Letters from Rural Women of the North-West, 1900-1920, 1998; Freedom to Play: We Made Our Own Fun, 2002. Contributor to periodicals. **Address:** Wilfrid Laurier University Press, 75 University Ave. W, Waterloo, ON N2L 3C5, Canada.

LEWIS, (Norman) Douglas. British/Welsh (born Wales), b. 1940. **Genres:** Law, Politics/Government, Civil Liberties/Human Rights, Public/Social Administration, Regional/Urban Planning, Administration/Management. **Career:** University of Sheffield, professor of public law, 1978-. Writer. **Publications:** (With B. Gateshill) The Commission for Local Administration: A Preliminary Appraisal, 1978; (co-author) Picketing, 1983; (with I. Harden) Noble Lie: The British Constitution and the Rule of Law, 1986; Complaints Procedures in Local Government, 1987; The Private Agents of the State: Beyond Corporatism, 1988; (with P. Burkinshaw and I. Harden) Government by Moonlight: The Hybrid Parts of the State, 1990; (ed. with C. Graham and D. Beyleveld) Happy and Glorious: The Constitution in Transition, 1990; Inner City Regeneration: The Demise of Regional and Local Government, 1992; (with P. Burkinshaw) When Citizens Complain: Reforming Justice and Administration, 1993; (ed. with S.S. Singh) Ombudsmen: India and the World Community, 1995; Choice and the Legal Order: Rising above Politics, 1996; (with D. Campbell) Promoting Participation, 1999; (co-author) Global Governance and the Quest For Justice, 2004. **Address:** Faculty of Law, University of Sheffield, Winter St., Sheffield, DU S3 7ND, England.

LEWIS, Paeony. British (born England), b. 1960. **Genres:** Children's Fiction, Picture/Board Books. **Career:** Children's book writer. **Publications:** CHILDREN'S BOOKS: I'll Always Love You, 2002; No More Biscuits!, 2005 as No More Cookies!, 2005; Hurry Up, Birthday!, 2006; No More Yawning!, 2008; Best Friends or Not?, 2008. SHOOTING STARS SERIES: Cinderella's Wedding, 1999; The Castle Awakes, 2001. **Address:** c/o Hilary Delamere, The Agency, 24 Pottery Ln., Holland Park, London, GL W11 4LZ, England. **Online address:** webpaeony@ntlworld.com

LEWIS, Peter (Elvet). (Peter Elvet Elfed Lewis). British (born England), b. 1937. **Genres:** Communications/Media, Literary Criticism And History, Mystery/Crime/Suspense. **Career:** University of Durham, lecturer, senior lecturer, reader in English, 1964-, professor emeritus, 1964; University of Clermont, visiting professor, 1974-75; Macquarie University, visiting fellow, 1982; Flambard Press, managing director, 1991-. Writer. **Publications:** John Gay: The Beggar's Opera (criticism), 1976. EDITOR: The Beggar's Opera, 1973; Poems '74, 1974; (with G. Cumming) Implosions, 1977. AS PETER LEWIS: (ed.) Radio Drama, 1981; John Le Carre, 1985; Fielding's Burlesque Drama: Its Place in the Tradition, 1987; (ed. with N. Wood) John Gay and the Scriblerians, 1988; Eric Ambler, 1990; Papers of the Radio Literature Conference, 1977, 1978; Enduring to the End, 1990; The National: A Dream Made Concrete, 1990. Works appear in anthologies. Contributor to periodicals. **Address:** Flambard Press, Stable Cottage, E Fourstones, Hexham, NM NE47 5DX, England.

LEWIS, Peter Elvet Elfed. *See* **LEWIS, Peter (Elvet).**

LEWIS, Richard. Indonesian (born Indonesia), b. 1956?. **Genres:** Novels.

Career: Author. **Publications:** The Flame Tree, 2004; The Killing Sea, 2006; The Demon Queen, 2008; Monster's Proof, 2009. **Address:** c/o Scott Miller, Trident Media Group, 41 Madison Ave., 36th Fl., New York, NY 10010, U.S.A. **Online address:** richard@richardlewisauthor.com

LEWIS, Robert W. American (born United States), b. 1930. **Genres:** Literary Criticism And History, Young Adult Fiction. **Career:** University of Nebraska, instructor in English, 1955-58; University of Texas, assistant professor of English, 1963-69; University of North Dakota, associate professor, 1969-71, professor, 1971-90, Chester Fritz distinguished professor of English, 1990-, now Chester Fritz distinguished professor emeritus of English, North Dakota Quarterly, editor, 1982-; University of Catania, Fulbright professor, 1967-68; Ain Shams University, Fulbright professor, 1975-76; North Dakota Humanities Council, chair, 1982-84; North Dakota Museum of Art, president, 1990-92; Ernest Hemingway Foundation, president, 1987-92. **Publications:** Hemingway on Love, 1965; (ed.) Antigenic Variation: Molecular and Genetic Mechanisms of Relapsing Disease, 1987; (ed.) Hemingway in Italy and Other Essays, 1990; A Farewell to Arms: The War of the Words, 1992; (ed. with R.E. Fleming) Under Kilimanjaro, 2005. Contributor to periodicals. **Address:** Depatment of English, University of North Dakota, Rm. 17, Merrifield Hall, 276 Centennial Dr., PO Box 7209, Grand Forks, ND 58202-7209, U.S.A. **Online address:** robert.lewis@und.edu

LEWIS, Roy. *See* **LEWIS, J(ohn) R(oyston).**

LEWIS, Rupert. (Rupert Charles Lewis). Jamaican/American (born United States), b. 1947. **Genres:** History, Politics/Government, Biography, Autobiography/Memoirs. **Career:** University of the West Indies, lecturer, 1972-, reader in political thought, 1992-, professor in FSS-government. Writer. **Publications:** Readings in Government and Politics of the West Indies, 1972; (ed. with M. Warner-Lewis) Garvey: Africa, Europe, the Americas, 1976; Marcus Garvey: Anti-Colonial Champion, 1988; (ed. with P. Bryan) Garvey: His Work and Impact, 1988, rev. ed., 1991; (as Rupert Charles Lewis) Walter Rodney's Intellectual and Political Thought, 1998; (ed. with F. Baptiste) George Padmore: Pan-African Revolutionary, 2009. **Address:** Department of Government, University of the West Indies, Mona Campus, Kingston, 7, Jamaica. **Online address:** rupert.lewis@uwimona.edu.jm

LEWIS, Rupert Charles. *See* **LEWIS, Rupert.**

LEWIS, Sarah Katherine. American (born United States), b. 1972?. **Genres:** Sex, Social Sciences. **Career:** Author. **Publications:** Indecent: How I Make It and Fake It as a Girl for Hire, 2006; Sex and Bacon: Why I Love Things That Are Very, Very Bad for Me, 2008. **Address:** Ann Arbor, MI , U.S.A. **Online address:** sarah@sarahkatherinelewis.com

LEWIS, Shannon. *See* **LLYWELYN, Morgan.**

LEWIS, Sherry. American (born United States) **Genres:** Mystery/Crime/Suspense, Romance/Historical, Travel/Exploration, inspirational/Motivational Literature, Young Adult Fiction. **Career:** Novelist and musician. **Publications:** Call Me Mom, 1995; No Place for Secrets, 1995; This Montana Home, 1996; No Place for Death, 1996; Keeping Her Safe, 1997; No Place For Tears, 1997; No Place for Sin, 1997; Let It Snow, 1998; A Man for Mom, 1999; Time to Dream, 1999; No Place for Memories, 1999; Whispers Through Time, 2000; For the Baby's Sake, 2000; (co-author) Family Matters, 2001; That Woman In Wyoming, 2001; Echo in Time, 2001; Mr. Congeniality, 2002; Christmas Wife, 2003; Only Time Will Tell, 2003; Children's Cop, 2004; High Mountain Home, 2005; Her Secret Family, 2005. **Address:** Berkley Publishing Group, 375 Hudson St., New York, NY 10014, U.S.A. **Online address:** sherrylewis@slbwrites.com

LEWIS, Simon. British/Welsh (born Wales), b. 1971?. **Genres:** Novels, Young Adult Fiction, Young Adult Non-fiction, Mystery/Crime/Suspense. **Career:** Writer. **Publications:** FICTION: Go, 1999; Bad Traffic: An Inspector Jian Novel, 2008. NONFICTION: China: The Rough Guide, 2000; The Rough Guide to Shanghai, 2008; The Rough Guide to Beijing 3, 2008; NOVELS: Border Run, 2012. **Address:** c/o Katherine Monaghan, Scribner Publicity, 1230 Ave. of the Americas, New York, NY 10030, U.S.A. **Online address:** info@simonlewiswriter.com

LEWIS, Stephen (C.). American (born United States), b. 1942. **Genres:** Romance/Historical, Mystery/Crime/Suspense. **Career:** Suffolk Community College, professor of English, 1966-2001, professor emeritus of English, 2001-. Writer. **Publications:** (With E.E. Eriksson, Jr.) Focus on the Written Word, 1972; (with R.D. Cox) The Student Critic: Thinking and Writing about Literature, 1974; (with M.C. Forte) Writing through Reading, 1983; (with M.C. Forte) Discovering Process: Meaning and Form in Reading and Writing, 1985; (with L. Kleiman) Philosophy: An Introduction Through Literature, 1990; The Monkey Rope, 1990; And Baby Makes None, 1991; NoloContendere, 1998; Threnody for a Moth, forthcoming; Two Sisters, forthcoming. HISTORICAL MYSTERIES: The Dumb Shall Sing, 1999; The Blind in Darkness, 2000; The Sea Hath Spoken, 2001; Murder On Old Mission, 2005; Stone Cold Dead, 2007. **Address:** Suffolk County Community College, 533 College Rd., Selden, NY 11784, U.S.A. **Online address:** stevelew@charter.net

LEWIS, Sydney. American (born United States), b. 1952?. **Genres:** Documentaries/Reportage, Education, Social Sciences, Business/Trade/Industry. **Career:** WBEZ, producer of personal essays series, 1997-. Journalist and writer. **Publications:** Hospital, 1994; Totally Alien Life-Form: Teenagers, 1996; Help Wanted, 2000. Contributor to periodicals. **Address:** The New Press, 38 Greene St., 4th Fl., New York, NY 10013, U.S.A.

LEWIS, Thomas H. (Thomas Howard Lewis). American (born United States), b. 1919. **Genres:** Anthropology/Ethnology, Medicine/Health, Psychiatry, Young Adult Non-fiction. **Career:** Writer and Physician. **Publications:** Forgotten Bottles along the Yellowstone, 1985; The Medicine Men: Oglala Sioux Ceremony and Healing, 1990. Contributor articles to journals. **Address:** 87 Columbia Rd., PO Box 162, Boyd, MT 59013, U.S.A.

LEWIS, Thomas Howard. *See* **LEWIS, Thomas H.**

LEWIS, Thomas P(arker). American (born United States), b. 1936. **Genres:** Children's Fiction, Music, Mystery/Crime/Suspense, Art/Art History, Reference. **Career:** Harper & Row Publishers Inc., School and Library Promotion Department, assistant manager, 1964-80, Institutional and Corporate Marketing Departments, coordinator, 1980-82; Pro/Am Music Resources, president, 1982-. Writer. **Publications:** Hill of Fire, 1971; The Dragon Kite, 1973; Clipper Ship, 1978; A Call for Mr. Sniff, 1981; Mr. Sniff and the Motel Mystery, 1983; The Blue Rocket Fun Show, or, Friends Forever!, 1986; The Pro/Am Guide to U.S. Books about Music: Annotated Subject Guide to Current and Backlist Titles, 1987; Frida's Office Day, 1989; Something about the Music, 1990; A Source Guide to the Music of Percy Grainger, 1991; The Pro/Am Book of Music and Mythology, 1991; Village Tales, forthcoming. **Address:** Pro/Am Music Resources, 63 Prospect St., White Plains, NY 10606, U.S.A.

LEWIS, Trudy. American (born United States), b. 1961. **Genres:** Novels, Novellas/Short Stories, Young Adult Fiction, Literary Criticism And History. **Career:** Saint Vincent Academy, English instructor, 1987-88; University of Missouri, Department of English, assistant professor, 1992-98, associate professor, 1998-2004, professor, 2004-. Writer. **Publications:** Private Correspondences (novel), 1994; The Bones of Garbo: A Collection of Short Stories, 2003; Pilgrim's Companion to Alexandria: The Luck of the Loom, forthcoming. Contributor of articles to periodicals. **Address:** Department of English, University of Missouri, 83 McReynolds, Columbia, MO 65211-1500, U.S.A. **Online address:** lewistr@missouri.edu

LEWIS, Ward B. American (born United States), b. 1938. **Genres:** Literary Criticism And History, Bibliography, Reference, Young Adult Fiction. **Career:** University of Iowa, assistant professor of German, 1968-71; University of Georgia, assistant professor, 1971-73, associate professor of German, professor, 1973-2001; University of South Carolina at Columbia, lecturer, 1976; University of Houston, lecturer, 1977; University of Florida, lecturer, 1982, 1986. Writer. **Publications:** Poetry and Exile: An Annotated Bibliography of the Works and Criticism of Paul Zech, 1975; Eugene O'Neill: The German Reception of America's First Dramatist, 1984; (contrib.) German and International Perspectives on the Spanish Civil War: The Aesthetics of Partisanship, 1992; (ed.) The Bird in Langfoot's Belfry, 1993; The Ironic Dissident: Frank Wedekind in the View of His Critics, 1997. Contributor of articles to journals. **Address:** Department of Germanic and Slavic Languages, University of Georgia, Athens, GA 30602, U.S.A. **Online address:** wlewis@arches.uga.edu

LEWIS-FERGUSON, Julinda. (Julinda Lewis). American (born United States), b. 1955. **Genres:** Dance/Ballet, Young Adult Fiction, Autobiography/Memoirs, Biography. **Career:** New York State Council on the Arts, consultant, 1979-, dance program panelist, 1987-91; teacher, 1980-; National Endowment for the Arts, consultant, 1989-; Girl Scouts of the United States of America, National delegate, 1993-96; Girl Scout Council of Greater New York, troop leader, delegate; New York City Board of Education, coordinator of supplemental services. Writer. **Publications:** (Ed.) Black Choreographers Moving: A National Dialogue, 1991; Alvin Ailey, Jr.: A Life in Dance, 1994. Contributor of articles to periodicals. **Address:** Walker & Co., 175 5th Ave., New York, NY 10010, U.S.A.

LEWTON, J. V. *See* **GRESHAM, Stephen.**

L'HEUREUX, John (Clarke). American (born United States), b. 1934. **Genres:** Novels, Novellas/Short Stories, Poetry, Autobiography/Memoirs. **Career:** Entered Society of Jesus (Jesuits), 1954; Georgetown University, writer-in-residence, 1964-65; ordained priest, 1966; Regis College, writer-in-residence, 1968-69; Atlantic, staff editor, 1968-69, contributing editor, 1969-83; Hamline University, visiting professor of American literature, 1971; Tufts College, visiting professor of American literature, 1971-73; Harvard University, visiting assistant professor, 1973; Stanford University, assistant professor, 1973-79, associate professor, 1979-81, professor of English, 1981, director of creative writing program, 1976-89, 1993-94, 1996, Lane professor of humanities, 1985-90, now professor emeritus. Writer. **Publications:** NOVELS: Tight White Collar, 1972, rev. ed., 1993; The Clang Birds, 1972, rev. ed., 1993; Jessica Fayer, 1976; A Woman Run Mad, 1988, rev. ed., 2000; An Honorable Profession, 1991, rev. ed., 2002; The Shrine at Altamira, 1992, rev. ed., 1999; The Handmaid of Desire, 1996; Having Everything, 1999; Lies, 1999; The Miracle, 2002. POETRY: Quick as Dandelions: Poems, 1964; Rubrics for a Revolution, 1967; One Eye and a Measuring Rod: Poems, 1968; No Place for Hiding: Poems, 1971. STORIES: Family Affairs, 1974, rev. ed., 1994; Desires, 1981; Comedians, 1990. OTHER: Picnic in Babylon: A Priest's Journal, 1963-1967 (autobiography), 1967; Uncommon Touch: Fiction and Poetry from the Standard Writing Workshop, 1989; Conversations with John L'Heureux, 2010. **Address:** Department of English, Stanford University, 223A, Margaret Jacks Hall, Bldg. 460, Stanford, CA 94305, U.S.A. **Online address:** jlx@stanford.edu

L. HIGHFIELD, J. R. *See* **HIGHFIELD, (John) Roger (Loxdale).**

LI, Guofang. American/Chinese (born China), b. 1972. **Genres:** Writing/Journalism, Education. **Career:** University of Saskatchewan, Faculty of Education, research assistant, 1977-99, adjunct faculty, 1998-2000, Centre for Second Language Instruction, faculty, 1999-2000, College of Arts and Science, adjunct faculty, 1999-2000; Zhong Shan College, lecturer, 1994; Wuhan University, English Department, lecturer, 1994; Business Foreign Language Training Center, lecturer, 1995; University of British Columbia, Language and Literacy Education, post-doctoral teaching fellow, 2000-01; State University of New York, Department of Learning and Instruction, assistant professor, 2001-06; Michigan State University, Department of Teacher Education, associate professor, 2006-. Writer. **Publications:** East Is East, West Is West?: Home Literacy, Culture and Schooling, 2002; (ed. with G. Beckett) Strangers of the Academy: Asian Women Scholars in Higher Education, 2006; Culturally Contested Pedagogy: Battles of Literacy and Schooling Between Mainstream Teachers and Asian Immigrant Parents, 2006; Culturally Contested Literacies: America's Rainbow Underclass and Urban Schools, 2008; (ed. with L. Wang) Model Minority Myth Revisited: An Interdisciplinary Approach to Demystifying Asian American Educational Experiences, 2008; 21st Century Education: An Encyclopedia, 2008; Multicultural Families, Home Literacies and Mainstream Schooling, 2009; (ed. with P.A. Edwards) Best Practices in ELL Instruction, 2010. Contributor to periodicals. **Address:** Department of Teacher Education, Michigan State University, 350 Erickson Hall, East Lansing, MI 48824, U.S.A. **Online address:** guofang.li1@gmail.com

LI, Joyce H.S. American/Chinese (born China), b. 1972?. **Genres:** Social Sciences, Technology, Information Science/Computers, Adult Non-fiction, Politics/Government. **Career:** Freelance copy editor and proofreader. **Publications:** The Center for Democracy and Technology and Internet Privacy in the U.S.: Lessons of the Last Five Years, 2003. Contributor to books and periodicals. **Address:** c/o Author Mail, Scarecrow Press Inc., 4501 Forbes Blvd., Ste. 200, Lanham, MD 20706-4346, U.S.A.

LI, Leslie. (Leslie Denise Li). American (born United States), b. 1945. **Genres:** Novels, Autobiography/Memoirs, Adult Non-fiction, Film, The-

atre, Travel/Exploration, Women's Studies And Issues, Writing/Journalism, Documentaries/Reportage, Essays, Children's Fiction, Cultural/Ethnic Topics, Autobiography/Memoirs. **Career:** Writer and filmmaker. **Publications:** Bittersweet, 1992; Enter the Dragon, 2002; Daughter of Heaven: A Memoir with Earthly Recipes, 2005; Just Us Girls: The Kim Loo Sisters, forthcoming. Contributor to periodicals. **Address:** 15 E 36th St., Apt. 6D, New York, NY 10016, U.S.A. **Online address:** lesliedli@gmail.com

LI, Leslie Denise. *See* **LI, Leslie.**

LI, Moying. (Moying Li-Marcus). American/Chinese (born China), b. 1954. **Genres:** Autobiography/Memoirs. **Career:** International Department of the Massachusetts Port Authority, assistant director; Marcus Capital Management, senior vice president and equity analyst, 1994-. Writer, administrator, analyst and educator. **Publications:** (As Moying Li-Marcus) Beacon Hill: The Life & Times of a Neighborhood, 2002; Snow Falling in Spring: Coming of Age in China during the Cultural Revolution (memoir), 2008. Contributor of articles to periodicals. **Address:** c/o Wendy Strothman, Strothman Agency LLC, Flagship Wharf, 197 8th St., Ste. 611, Charlestown, MA 02129, U.S.A. **Online address:** wendy@strothmanagency.com

LIA, Brynjar. Norwegian (born Norway), b. 1966. **Genres:** History. **Career:** Norwegian Defense Research Est. (FFI), research professor. Writer. **Publications:** The Society of the Muslim Brothers in Egypt, 1928-1942, 1998; Globalisation and the Future of Terrorism: Patterns and Predictions, 2005; A Police Force without a State: A History of the Palestinian Security Forces in the West Bank and Gaza, 2006; Building Arafat's Police: The Politics of International Police Assistance in the Palestinian Territories after the Oslo Agreement, 2007; Architect of Global Jihad: The Life of Al-Qaida Strategist Abu Mus'ab Al-Suri, 2008. Contributor to periodicals. **Address:** FFI, PO Box 25, Kjeller, NO-2027, Norway. **Online address:** brynjar.lia@ffi.no

LIATSOS, Sandra Olson. American (born United States), b. 1942. **Genres:** Poetry, Children's Fiction, Education. **Career:** Teacher, 1962-73; author, 1973-. **Publications:** FOR CHILDREN: Poems to Count On: 30 Terrific Poems and Activities to Help Teach Math Concepts, 1995; Bicycle Riding and Other Poems, 1997. Contributor of poetry to books and magazines. Works appear in anthologies. **Address:** c/o Marian Reiner, 20 Cedar St., New Rochelle, NY 10801, U.S.A.

LIAZOS, Ariane. American (born United States), b. 1976. **Genres:** Race Relations, History. **Career:** Harvard University, post-doctoral lecturer, 2008-10, instructor, 2010-. Historian and author. **Publications:** (With T. Skocpol and M. Ganz) What a Mighty Power We Can Be: African American Fraternal Groups and the Struggle for Racial Equality, 2006. **Address:** Department of History, Harvard University, Rm. 113, Robinson Hall, 35 Quincy St., Cambridge, MA 02138, U.S.A. **Online address:** liazos@fas.harvard.edu

LIBBY, Alisa M. American (born United States) **Genres:** Novels, History, Romance/Historical. **Career:** Author. **Publications:** The Blood Confession, 2006; The Kings Rose, 2009. **Address:** Zachary Shuster Harmsworth, 535 Boylston St., 11th Fl., Boston, MA 02116, U.S.A. **Online address:** author@alisalibby.com

LIBBY, Ronald T(heodore). American (born United States), b. 1941. **Genres:** Medicine/Health, Politics/Government, International Relations/Current Affairs. **Career:** University of Botswana, lecturer in political science, 1973-75; University of Malawi, lecturer in political science, 1975-76; University of Zambia, lecturer in political science, 1976-79; University of Notre Dame, visiting assistant professor of political science, 1981-83; University of the West Indies, senior lecturer in political science, 1983-85; Northwestern University, visiting associate professor of political science, 1985-86; Australian National University, senior research fellow, 1986-87; Victoria University of Wellington, senior lecturer in political science, 1987-89; Southwest State University, professor of political science and head of department, 1989; Minnesota State University, Department of Political Science, professor and chair, 1989-96; St. Joseph's University, Department of Political Science, professor and chairman, 1996-2000; University of North Florida, professor of political science and public administration, 2000-, Blue Shield Ethics Center, senior fellow. Writer. **Publications:** Toward an Africanized U.S. Policy for Southern Africa: A Strategy for Increasing Political Leverage, 1980; The Politics of Economic Power in Southern Africa, 1987; Hawke's Law: The Politics of

Mining and Aboriginal Land Rights in Australia, 1989, 2nd ed., 1992; Protecting Markets: U.S. Policy and the World Grain Trade, 1992; Eco-Wars: Political Campaigns and Social Movements, 1999; Treating Doctors as Drug Dealers: The DEA's War on Prescription Painkillers, 2005; Criminalization of Medicine: America's War on Doctors, 2008. Contributor to books and journals. **Address:** Department of Political Science, University of North Florida, 4567 St. Johns Bluff Rd., Jacksonville, FL 32224-2665, U.S.A. **Online address:** rlibby@unf.edu

LIBERA, Antoni. Polish (born Poland), b. 1949. **Genres:** Plays/Screenplays, Novels, Translations. **Career:** Dramatic Theatre, literary manager, 1996-2001.Translator and novelist. **Publications:** TRANSLATOR: Samuel Beckett: Pisma Proza, 1982; Waiting for Godot, 1985; (contrib.) Zimy i podróze, 1997; Madame, 1999; Blogoslawieństwo Becketta I Inne Wyznania Literackie, 2004; Godot I Jego Cień, 2009, (with S. Brańczak) Zimy I Podróze, 2009. **Address:** Farrar Straus & Giroux, 19 Union Sq. W, New York, NY 10003, U.S.A.

LIBERMAN, Rosette B. American/Iranian (born Iran) **Genres:** Writing/Journalism, Essays, Business/Trade/Industry, Education. **Career:** University of Connecticut, Amity Regional High School, Co-op Program, English teacher, administrator and college advisor, 1985-. Writer. **Publications:** Guide to Decision-making in Compliance with Section 504, 1988; (with G. Heyworth) The Writing and Revision Stylebook, 2000, 2nd ed., 2005; (with G. Heyworth) The Cooper Hill Stylebook a Guide to Writing & Revision, 2002; The Cooper Hill College Application Essay Bible, 2004. Contributor to books. **Address:** 141 Ramsdell St., New Haven, CT 06515, U.S.A. **Online address:** rbliberman@snet.net

LIBO, Kenneth (Harold). American (born United States), b. 1937. **Genres:** Cultural/Ethnic Topics, History, Biography, Adult Non-fiction, Film. **Career:** City College of the City University of New York, assistant professor of English, 1971-78; independent researcher and writer, 1978-80, 1981-86; Jewish Daily Forward, editor, 1980-81; National Museum of American Jewish History, curator, 1986-89; Museum of Jewish Heritage, curator, 1989-92; Hunter College, adjunct professor of history. **Publications:** (With I. Howe) World of Our Fathers, 1976 in UK as The Immigrant Jews of New York, 1881 to the Present; (ed. with I. Howe) How We Lived: A Documentary History of Immigrant Jews in America, 1880-1930, 1979; (with I. Howe) We Lived There, Too: In Their Own Words and Pictures-Pioneer Jews and the Westward Movement of America, 1984; (with J.L. Loeb and F.L. Loeb) All in a Lifetime, 1996; (with A.K. Hoffman) Seixas-Kursheedts and the Rise of Early American Jewry, 2001; Lots of Lehmans, 2007; From Inside to Outside Our Crowd: The Lehman Family from Bavaria to Alabama to Wall Street to the U.S. Senate, 2007; (with M. Feldberg) The Obermayers: A History of a Jewish Family in Germany and America, 1618-2009, 2009. **Address:** 40 Harrison St., Apt. 12B, 695 Park Ave., New York, NY 10013-2700, U.S.A. **Online address:** kenlibo@aol.com

LIBOV, Charlotte Ann. American (born United States), b. 1950. **Genres:** Medicine/Health, Food And Wine, Travel/Exploration, Writing/Journalism, Popular Culture, Film, Art/Art History. **Career:** Milford Citizen, reporter, 1974-76; Journal Inquirer, general assignment reporter, 1980-81; Springfield Daily News, bureau chief, 1981-84; University of Connecticut, School of Journalism, lecturer, 1982-83; Courant, restaurant reviewer, 1985-92; The New York Times, contributing journalist, 1986-93; Connecticut Public Television, writer and producer, 1988-90; freelance writer, 1992-; Heritage Villager Newspaper, managing editor, 2002-04; Neurology Now, managing editor, 2004-05; Women's Health Hot Line, founding editor. **Publications:** (With F.J. Pashkow) The Women's Heart Book: The Complete Guide to Keeping a Healthy Heart, 1993; (with F.J. Pashkow) 50 Essential Things to Do if the Doctor Says It's Heart Disease, 1995; Migraine: 50 Essential Things to Do, 1998; Beat Your Risk Factors: A Woman's Guide to Reducing Her Risk for Cancer, Heart Disease, Stroke, Diabetes and Osteoporosis, 1999; (with H.M. Kramer) Woman's Guide to Heart Attack Recovery: How to Survive, Thrive and Protect Your Heart, 2007. Contributor to magazines and books. **Address:** 745 Meridian Ave., Ste. 7, Miami Beach, FL 33139, U.S.A. **Online address:** char@libov.com

LICHBACH, Mark Irving. American (born United States), b. 1951. **Genres:** Politics/Government, Sociology. **Career:** Brown University, teaching assistant, 1975; Northwestern University, instructor, 1977, teaching assistant, 1977-78; University of Illinois at Chicago, assistant professor, 1978-

84, associate professor of political science, 1984-91; University of Colorado, associate professor, 1991-94, professor of political science, 1994-98, chair, 1995-98; University of California-Riverside, chair and professor of government and politics, 1998-2001; University of Maryland, professor of political science, 2001-, chair. Writer. **Publications:** Regime Change and the Coherence of European Governments, 1984; The Rebel's Dilemma, 1995; The Cooperator's Dilemma, 1996; (ed. with A.S. Zuckerman) Comparative Politics: Rationality, Culture and Structure, 1997, 2nd ed., 2009; (ed. with J. Kopstein) Comparative Politics: Interests, Identities and Institutions in a Changing Global Order, 2000, 3rd ed., 2009; (with A.B. Seligman) Market and Community: The Bases of Social Order, Revolution and Relegitimation, 2000; Is Rational Choice Theory All of Social Science?, 2003; (ed. with R.N. Lebow) Social Inquiry and Political Knowledge, 2007. Contributor to books and periodicals. **Address:** Department of Government & Politics, University of Maryland, 3140 Tydings Hall, College Park, MD 20742, U.S.A. **Online address:** mlichbach@gvpt.umd.edu

LICHT, H. William (Bill). Also writes as William Licht, L. William Hermann. American (born United States), b. 1915. **Genres:** Novels, Theology/Religion, Natural History. **Career:** Pan American World Airlines, engineer, flight engineer and co-pilot, 1942-53; Radio Corporation of America, manufacturing design engineer, 1953-81. Writer. **Publications:** (As William Licht) Air Pollution Control Engineering: Basic Calculations for Particulate Collection, 1980, 2nd ed., 1988; NOVELS: (as L. William Hermann) The Firestorm, 1993; (as Bill Licht) Kingdom Age: Angels and Demons, 2000; Watchers: Kingdom Justice, 2000. OTHER: (ed. with R.L. Byers and D.W. Cooper) Control and Dispersion of Air Pollutants, 1978; (ed. with A.J. Engel and S.M. Slater) Control of Emissions from Stationary Combustion Sources, 1979; (ed.) Implications of the Clean Air Amendments of 1977 and of Energy Considerations for Air Pollution Control, 1980; The Last 1260 Days, 2002. FORTHCOMING: Scenario of the Last Days; Commentary, Revelation. **Address:** 240 Brazil Ct., Sanford, FL 32771, U.S.A.

LICHT, William. *See* **LICHT, H. William (Bill).**

LICHTBLAU, Eric. American (born United States), b. 1965?. **Genres:** Law, Politics/Government. **Career:** Los Angeles Times, staff member, 1987-99; Justice Department, staff writer, 1999-2002; New York Times, Justice Department, correspondent, 2002-; Cornell University, lecturer; Syracuse University, lecturer; Mensa University, lecturer. Journalist. **Publications:** Bush's Law: The Remaking of American Justice, 2008. **Address:** Washington Bureau, New York Times, 1627 I St., 7th Fl., Washington, DC 20006-4007, U.S.A. **Online address:** ericl@nytimes.com

LICHTENBERG, Jacqueline. (Daniel R. Kerns). American (born United States), b. 1942. **Genres:** Science Fiction/Fantasy, Young Adult Fiction, Horror, Novels. **Career:** Writer, 1968-; Star Trek Wel Committee, founder and policy adviser; Science Fiction Writers of America, Speakers Bureau, chairman; Monthly Aspectarian, science fiction review columnist, 1993-; Sime-Gen Inc., co-founder. **Publications:** House of Zeor, 1974, 3rd ed., 1981; (with S. Marshak and J. Winston) Star Trek Lives!, 1975; Unto Zeor, Forever, 1978; (with J. Lorrah) First Channel, 1980; Mahogany Trinrose: A Sime/Gen Novel, 1981; Molt Brother, 1982; (with J. Lorrah) Channel's Destiny, 1982, Ren Sime, 1984; City of a Million Legends, 1985; Dushau, 1985; Farfetch, 1985; Outreach, 1986; (with J. Lorrah) Zelerod's Doom, 1986; Those of My Blood, 1988; Dreamspy, 1989; Never Cross a Palm With Silver: The Bible Tarot Series, 1997; (with J. Lorrah) To Kiss or To Kill, 2004; Science Is Magic Spelled Backwards: And Other Stories, 2011; Through the Moon Gate: And Other Tales of Vampirism, 2011. AS DANIEL R. KERNS: Hero, 1993; Border Dispute, 1994. **Address:** Richard Curtis Associates Inc., 171 E 74th St., 2nd Fl., New York, NY 10021, U.S.A. **Online address:** jl@simegen.com

LICHTENBERG, Peter A. American (born United States), b. 1959. **Genres:** Psychology, Gerontology/Senior Issues. **Career:** Western State Hospital, director of geriatric psychology, 1986-90; University of Virginia Medical School, Department of Behavioral Medicine and Psychiatry, assistant professor, 1987-91; Wayne State University, Department of Physical Medicine and Rehabilitation, assistant professor, 1991-95, associate professor, 1995-2002, Rehabilitation Institute of Michigan, associate director, 1991-, training director, 1991-98, associate chief, 1993-98, professor of psychology, psychiatry and behavioral neuroscience and physical medicine and rehabilitation, 2002-, Institute of Gerontology, director, 1998-, Merrill Palmer Skillman Institute, interim director, 2008-09, director, 2009-; Mental Health and Aging Interest Group, coordinator, 1994-96, director, 2009-; Psychologists in Long-Term Care, director, 1996-98; Lifespan Alliance, founding director, 2009. Writer. **Publications:** A Guide to Psychological Practice in Geriatric Long-Term Care, 1994; (ed. with K. Anchor, J.T. Barth and S. Hinderer) Advances in Medical Psychotherapy, vol. VII, 1994, vol. VIII, 1995; Mental Health Practice in Geriatric Health Care Settings, 1998; (co-author) Depression in Geriatric Medical and Nursing Home Patients: A Treatment Manual, 1998; (ed.) Handbook of Assessment in Clinical Gerontology, 1999, 2nd ed., 2010; (ed. with D.L. Murman and A.M. Mellow) Handbook of Dementia: Psychological, Neurological and Psychiatric Perspectives, 2003. Contributor to journals. **Address:** Institute of Gerontology, University of Wayne, 87 E Ferry St., 226 Knapp, Detroit, MI 48202, U.S.A. **Online address:** p.lichtenberg@wayne.edu

LICHTENBERG, Philip. American (born United States), b. 1926. **Genres:** Human Relations/Parenting, Psychiatry, Psychology, Social Work. **Career:** Harvard University, research fellow in clinical psychology, 1951-52; New York University, assistant professor, 1952-54; Michael Reese Hospital, research psychologist, 1954-57; New York State Mental Health Research Unit, research psychologist (social), 1957-61; Bryn Mawr College, associate professor, 1961-68, professor, 1968-96, Mary Hale Chase professor emeritus of social science and social work and social research and professor emeritus of social work and social research, 1996-; Gestalt Therapy Institute of Philadelphia, faculty, 1984-. Writer. **Publications:** (With R. Kohrman and H. MacGregor) Motivation for Child Psychiatry Treatment, 1960; Psychoanalysis: Radical and Conservative, 1969; (with D.G. Norton) Cognitive and Mental Development in the First Five Years of Life, 1970; Lectures in Psychoanalysis for Social Workers, 1978; Getting Even: The Equalizing Law of Relationships, 1988; Undoing the Clinch of Oppression, 1990 as Community and Confluence, 1994; (with J.V. Beusekom and D. Gibbons) Encountering Bigotry: Befriending Projecting Persons in Everyday Life, 1997. Contributor to periodicals. **Address:** Gestalt Therapy Institute of Philadelphia, PO Box 961, Bryn Mawr, PA 19010-0961, U.S.A. **Online address:** phl.els.lichtenberg@gmail.com

LICHTENSTEIN, Alex. American (born United States), b. 1962. **Genres:** History, Economics. **Career:** Florida International University, Department of History, assistant professor, 1990-97, associate professor, 1997-2002, 2007-; North Caroliniana Society, Archie K. Davis fellow, 1991; National Endowment for the Humanities, fellow, 1994-95; American Friends Service Committee., consultant; University of the Western Cape, visiting Fulbright lecturer in American history, 2000; Rice University, associate professor of history, 2002-07; University of Pennsylvania, associate professor. Writer. **Publications:** Twice the Work of Free Labor: The Political Economy of Convict Labor in the New South, 1996. Contributor to books and periodicals. **Address:** Department of History, Florida International University, DM397, PO Box 1892, Miami, FL 33199, U.S.A. **Online address:** lichtens@fiu.edu

LICHTENSTEIN, Alice. American (born United States), b. 1958?. **Genres:** Adult Non-fiction, Novels, Literary Criticism And History. **Career:** Boston University, faculty, fellow in creative writing; Wheaton College, faculty; Lesley College, faculty; Harvard University Summer School, faculty; Hartwick College, faculty of creative writing and lecturer in English. Writer. **Publications:** The Genius of the World: A Novel, 2000; Lost: A Novel, 2010. Contributor to periodicals. **Address:** c/o Miriam Altshuler Literary Agency, 53 Old Post Rd. N, Red Hook, NY 12571-2262, U.S.A. **Online address:** lichtensteina@hartwick.edu

LICHTENSTEIN, Nelson. American (born United States), b. 1944. **Genres:** History, Biography, Organized Labor. **Career:** Catholic University of America, assistant professor, associate professor, 1981-89; National Endowment for the Humanities, junior fellow, 1982, senior fellow, 1993; University of Virginia, professor, 1989-2001; University of California, professor, 2001-, MacArthur Foundation professor of history, 2010, Center for the Study of Work, Labor and Democracy, director; Society of American Historians, fellow. Writer. **Publications:** Labor's War at Home: The CIO in World War II, 1982; Major Problems in the History of American Workers: Documents and Essays, 1991, 2nd ed., 2003; The Most Dangerous Man in Detroit: Walter Reuther and the Fate of American Labor, 1995; Walter Reuther: The Most Dangerous Man in Detroit, 1997; What's Next for Organized Labor?: Report of the Century Foundation Task Force on the Future of Unions, 1999; (co-author) Who Built America? Working People and the Nation's Economy, Politics, Culture, and Society, 2nd ed., 2000; State of the Union: A Century of American Labor, 2002; Retail Revolution: How Wal-Mart Created a Brave

New World of Business, Transformed the Global Economy, And Put Politics In Every Store, 2009. EDITOR: Political Profiles: The Johnson Years, 1976; Political Profiles: The Kennedy Years, 1976; (with S. Meyer) On the Line: Essays in the History of Auto Work, 1989; (with H.J. Harris) Industrial Democracy in America: The Ambiguous Promise, 1993; Wal-Mart: The Face of Twenty-First-Century Capitalism, 2006; American Capitalism: Social Thought and Political Economy in the Twentieth Century, 2006. The Retail Revolution: How Wal-Mart Created a Brave New World of Business, 2009. **Address:** Department of History, University of California, HSSB 4256, Santa Barbara, CA 93106, U.S.A. **Online address:** nelson@history.ucsb.edu

LICHTERMAN, Paul. American (born United States), b. 1959. **Genres:** Adult Non-fiction, Anthropology/Ethnology. **Career:** University of Wisconsin, Department of Sociology, assistant professor, 1992-2004, associate professor, 2004-06; Princeton University, Center for the Study of Religion, visiting fellow, 2001-02; American Journal of Sociology, consulting editor, 2004-06; University of Southern California, Dana and David Dornsife College of Letters, Arts and Sciences, Department of Sociology, associate professor, 2004-08, professor, 2008-, School of Religion, associate professor, 2004-08, professor, 2008-. **Publications:** NONFICTION: The Search for Political Community: American Activists Reinventing Commitment, 1996; Elusive Togetherness: Church Groups Trying to Bridge America's Divisions, 2005; (ed. with C.B. Potts) The Civic Life of American Religion, 2009. **Address:** Department of Sociology, University of Southern California, 352 Kaprielian Hall, 3620 S Vermont Ave., Los Angeles, CA 90089-2539, U.S.A. **Online address:** lichterm@usc.edu

LICKLIDER, Roy. (Roy E. Licklider). American (born United States), b. 1941. **Genres:** International Relations/Current Affairs. **Career:** Yale University, assistant in research, grader and teaching assistant, 1964-67; Tougaloo College, assistant professor of political science, 1967-68; Rutgers University, Douglass College, assistant professor, 1968-72, associate professor, 1972-89, chair of department, 1974-77, professor of political science, 1989-; Exxon Education Foundation, program officer, 1977-78; New School for Social Research, Center for the Study of Social Change, visiting researcher, 1990-91. Writer. **Publications:** (As Roy E. Licklider) The Private Nuclear Strategists, 1971; Political Power and the Arab Oil Weapon: The Experience of Five Industrial Nations, 1988; Stopping the Killing: How Civil Wars End, 1993; (ed. with Mia Bloom) Living Together After Ethnic Killing: Debating the Kaufmann Thesis, 2007. Contributor to journals. **Address:** Department of Political Science, Rutgers University, 89 George St., New Brunswick, NJ 08901-1411, U.S.A. **Online address:** licklide@rci.rutgers.edu

LICKLIDER, Roy E. See **LICKLIDER, Roy.**

LIDCHI, Maggi. See **GRASSI, Maggi Lidchi.**

LIDDINGTON, Jill. British (born England), b. 1946. **Genres:** Gay And Lesbian Issues, History, Local History/Rural Topics, Women's Studies And Issues, Biography. **Career:** Leeds University, School of Continuing Education, lecturer, 1982-2003, reader, 1999-, Centre for Interdisciplinary Gender Studies, honorary research fellow, 2006-; Royal Historical Society, fellow; Royal Society of Arts, fellow; Historian, biographer, reader and writer. **Publications:** (With J. Norris) One Hand Tied behind Us: The Rise of the Women's Suffrage Movement, 1978, rev. ed., 2000; The Life and Times of a Respectable Rebel: Selina Cooper, 1864-1946, 1984; The Long Road to Greenham: Feminism and Anti-Militarism in Britain since 1820, 1989; Presenting the Past: Anne Lister of Halifax, 1791-1840, 1994; Female Fortune: Land, Gender and Authority: The Anne Lister Diaries, 1833-36, 1998; Nature's Domain: Anne Lister and the Landscape of Desire, 2003; Rebel Girls: Their Fight for the Vote, 2006. **Address:** Centre for Interdisciplinary Gender Studies, University of Leeds, The Coach House, 5 Hillary Pl., Leeds, LS2 9JT, England. **Online address:** j.r.liddington@leeds.ac.uk

LIDDLE, Peter (Hammond). British (born England), b. 1934. **Genres:** History, Military/Defense/Arms Control, International Relations/Current Affairs, Adult Non-fiction. **Career:** Havelock School, history teacher, 1957-58; Gateacre Comprehensive School, history department, teacher and head, 1958-67; Notre Dame College of Education, lecturer in history, 1967; Sunderland Polytechnic, lecturer, 1967-70, senior lecturer, 1970-87; Sunderland Industrial Archaeological Society, chairman, 1969, Conference and Exhibition on World War I, Sunderland Polytechnic, chair, 1984, 1994; University of Leeds, keeper of Liddle collection, 1988-99, School of History, associate lecturer,

1995-99; The Poppy and the Owl, founder, editor and contributor, 1990-99; Second World War Experience Center, director, 1999-, Life President; Everyone's War, founder, editor and contributor, 1999-; collector of archival records pertaining to World Wars I and II; British Audio-Visual Trust, vice president. **Publications:** Men of Gallipoli, 1976 in US as Men of Gallipoli: The Dardanelles and Gallipoli Experience, August 1914 to January 1916, 1988; World War I Archive: Personal Experience Material for Use in Schools, 1977; (ed.) Testimony of War 1914-18, 1979; Sailor's War 1914-18, 1985; Gallipoli 1915: Pens, Pencils and Cameras at War, 1985; 1916: Aspects of Conflict, 1985; (ed. and contrib.) Home Fires and Foreign Fields: British Social and Military Experience in the First World War, 1985; The Airman's War 1914-18, 1987; The Soldier's War 1914-18, 1988; Voices of War: Front Line and Home Front, 1988; The 1916 Battle of the Somme: A Reappraisal, 1992; The Worst Ordeal: Britons at Home and Abroad, 1994; (ed. with H. Cecil and contrib.) Facing Armageddon: The First World War Experienced, 1996; (ed.) Passchendaele in Perspective: The Third Battle of Ypres, 1997; (ed. with H. Cecil) At the Eleventh Hour: Reflections, Hopes and Anxieties at the Close of the Great War, 1918, 1998; (ed. with R.C. Begg) For Five Shillings a Day: Experiencing War 1939-1945, 2000; (ed. with J. Bourne and I. Whitehead and contrib.) The Great World War 1914-1945, vol. I: Lightning Strikes Once, 2000, vol. II, Who Won? Who Lost, 2001; (ed. and comp.) D-Day by Those Who Were There, 2004; Captured Memories 1900-1918: Across the Threshold of War, 2010. Contributor to periodicals. **Address:** The Second World War Experience Centre, 1A Rudgate Ct., Walton, Wetherby, WY LS23 7BF, England. **Online address:** enquires@war_experience.org

LIDE, David R. American (born United States), b. 1928. **Genres:** Chemistry, Physics, Sciences, Information Science/Computers. **Career:** National Bureau of Standards, physicist, 1954-63, Molecular Spectroscopy Section, chief, 1963-69, Office of Standard Reference Data, director, 1969-88; freelance editor and consultant, 1988-. **Publications:** (With R.P. Nelson and A.A. Maryott) Selected Values of Electric Dipole Moments for Molecules in the Gas Phase, 1967; (co-author) Property Index to NSRDS Data Compilations, 1964-1972, 1975; Basic Laboratory and Industrial Chemicals, 1993; (ed. with G.W.A. Milne) Handbook of Data on Organic Compounds, 3rd ed., 1994; (with H.V. Kehiaian) CRC Handbook of Thermophysical and Thermochemical Data, 1994; (ed.) CRC Handbook of Chemistry and Physics, 71st ed., 1990, 90th ed., 2009; Handbook of Organic Solvents, 1995; (ed. with G.W.A. Milne) Names, Synonyms and Structures or Organic Compounds, 1995; A Century of Excellence in Measurements, Standards, and Technology, 2001; (with G.L. Trigg and E.R. Cohen) AIP Physics Desk Reference, 3rd ed., 2003. Contributor to books. **Address:** 13901 Riding Loop Dr., North Potomac, MD 20878, U.S.A. **Online address:** drlide@post.harvard.edu

LIDE, Mary. Also writes as Mary Clayton, Mary Lomer. American/British (born England) **Genres:** Novels, History, Mystery/Crime/Suspense, Young Adult Fiction. **Career:** International Monetary Fund, administrative assistant, 1981-84; The Writer's Center, teacher of writing workshop, 1989-90; University of Michigan, Fulbright English-speaking union fellow. Writer. **Publications:** Ann of Cambray, 1984; Gifts of the Queen, 1985; A Royal Quest, 1987 in UK as Hawks of Sedgemont, 1988; Isobelle, 1988 in US as Diary of Isobelle, 1988; Tregaran, 1989; Command of the King, 1990; The Legacy of Tregaran, 1991; The Homecoming in US as the Sea Scape, 1992; Polmena Cove, 1994. AS MARY CLAYTON: Our Town: History of Willenhall, 1991; (with H. Magennis) The Old English Lives of St. Margaret, 1994; Pearls before Swine, 1995; Dead Men's Bones, 1995; The Seafarer, 1996; The Prodigal's Return, 1997; The Word Is Death, 1997; Death Is the Inheritance, 1998; The Apocryphal Gospels of Mary in Anglo-Saxon England, 1999; The Cult of the Virgin Mary in Anglo-Saxon England, 2003. AS MARY LOMER: The Bait, 1961; Robert of Normandy, 1991; Fortune's Knave: The Making of William the Conqueror, 1992. **Address:** Goodman Associates, 500 W End Ave., New York, NY 10024-4338, U.S.A.

LIE, John. American/Korean (born Korea (South)), b. 1959. **Genres:** Sociology, Area Studies, Food And Wine, Music, History, Social Sciences. **Career:** Yonsei University, visiting associate professor, 1988-89; University of Hawai, visiting assistant professor, 1988; University of Oregon, assistant professor of sociology, 1989-92; University of Illinois, assistant professor of sociology, 1992-95, associate professor of sociology, 1995-98, Department of Sociology, head, 1996-2001, Asian American Studies Program, director, 1996-97, professor of sociology, 1998-2001; Keio University, visiting associate professor, 1993; National Taiwan University, visiting professor, 1997; University of Waikato, visiting professor, 1998; Harvard University, visiting professor,

2000-01; University of Michigan, professor of sociology, 2001-03, Korea Foundation professor, 2001-03, Center for Japanese Studies, director, 2002-03, Korean Studies Program, director, 2002-03; University of California, Institute of East Asian Studies, professor of sociology, 2003-, C.K. Cho professor, 2003-04, Center for Korean Studies, chair, 2003-04, dean of international and area studies and Class of 1959 Professor, 2004-09, Senior International Leaders' Council, chair, 2005-09. Writer. **Publications:** (With A. Giddens) Readings and Study Guide: Introduction to Sociology, 1991; (ed. and trans.) The Impoverished Spirit in Contemporary Japan: Selected Essays of Honda Katsuichi, 1993; (ed.) Global Sociology, 1994; (with N. Abelman) Blue Dreams: Korean Americans and the Los Angeles Riots, 1995; Han Unbound: The Political Economy of South Korea, 1998; Multiethnic Japan, 2001; (with R. Brym) Sociology: Your Compass for a New World, 2003, 3rd ed., 2007; Modern Peoplehood, 2004; Multiethnic Japan, 2004; Zainichi (Koreans in Japan): Diasporic Nationalism and Postcolonial Identity, 2008; (ed. with S. Ryang) Diaspora without Homeland: Being Korean in Japan, 2009; The Crisis of Scholarly Publication, forthcoming. **Address:** Institute of East Asian Studies, Department of Sociology, University of California, 360 Stephens Hall, 2223 Fulton St., Ste. 2318, Berkeley, CA 94720-2318, U.S.A. **Online address:** johnlie@berkeley.edu

LIEBER, Keir A. (Keir Alexander Lieber). American (born United States), b. 1970. **Genres:** Young Adult Non-fiction. **Career:** Slovak Technical University, visiting lecturer, 1990; Carnegie Endowment for International Peace, editorial assistant, Foreign Policy journal, 1993; Henry L. Stimson Center, research assistant, 1993-94; University of Chicago, Department of Political Science, research assistant, 1995-96, teaching assistant, 1996-97, Program on International Security Policy Workshop coordinator, 1997-98; Georgetown University, School of Foreign Service, Security Studies Program, visiting assistant professor, 2000-01; University of Notre Dame, assistant professor of political science, 2001-; Joan B. Kroc Institute for International Peace Studies, fellow; Nanovic Institute for European Studies, fellow. **Publications:** NONFICTION: War and the Engineers: The Primacy of Politics over Technology, 2005. Contributor to journals. **Address:** Joan B. Kroc Inst. for Intl. Peace Studies, University of Notre Dame, 100 Hesburgh Center for International Studies, PO Box 639, Notre Dame, IL 46556, U.S.A. **Online address:** klieber@nd.edu

LIEBER, Keir Alexander. See **LIEBER, Keir A.**

LIEBER, Robert J. American (born United States), b. 1941. **Genres:** International Relations/Current Affairs, Politics/Government. **Career:** Harvard University, Department of Government, teaching fellow, 1966-68, Center for International Affairs, research associate, 1974-75; University of California, assistant professor, 1968-72, associate professor, 1972-77, chairman, 1975-76, 1977-80, professor of political science, 1977-81; St. Antony's College, visiting fellow, 1969-70; Atlantic Institute, research associate, 1978-79, visiting fellow; Woodrow Wilson International Center for Scholars, fellow, 1980-81; Georgetown University, Department of Government, professor of government and international affairs, 1982-, chairman, 1990-96, Department of Psychology, interim chair, 1997-99; Brookings Institution, visiting fellow; Fudan University, visiting fellow. Writer. **Publications:** British Politics and European Unity: Parties, Elites, and Pressure Groups, 1970; Theory and World Politics, 1972; Oil and the Middle East War: Europe in the Energy Crisis, 1976; (with A.J. Groth and N.I. Lieber) Contemporary Politics: Europe, 1976; The Oil Decade, 1983; No Common Power: Understanding International Relations, 1988, 4th ed., 2001; The American Era: Power and Strategy for the 21st Century, 2005; (co-author) Mediniyut ha-ḥuts shel Artsot ha-Berit liḳrat kehunato ha-sheniyah shel ha-naśi Bush, 2007. EDITOR: (with K.A. Oye and D. Rothchild) Eagle Entangled: U.S. Foreign Policy in a Complex World, 1979; (with K.A. Oye and D. Rothchild) Eagle Defiant: United States Foreign Policy in the 1980s, 1983; Will Europe Fight for Oil?: Energy Relations in the Atlantic Area, 1983; (with K.A. Oye and D. Rothchild) Eagle Resurgent?: The Reagan Era in American Foreign Policy, 1987; (with K.A. Oye and D. Rothchild) Eagle in a New World: American Grand Strategy in the Post-Cold War Era, 1992; Eagle Adrift: American Foreign Policy at the End of the Century, 1997; Eagle Rules?: Foreign Policy and American Primacy in the Twenty-first Century, 2002; Foreign Policy, 2008. Contributor to periodicals. **Address:** Department of Government, Georgetown University, 664 Intercultural Ctr., 37th & O St. NW, PO Box 571034, Washington, DC 20057-1034, U.S.A. **Online address:** lieberr@georgetown.edu

LIEBERMAN, Ben. See **LIEBERMAN, Benjamin.**

LIEBERMAN, Benjamin. (Ben Lieberman). American (born United States), b. 1962?. **Genres:** Politics/Government, History, Economics. **Career:** Fitchburg State College, faculty. Writer. **Publications:** (As Ben Lieberman) From Recovery to Catastrophe: Municipal Stabilization and Political Crisis in Weimar, Germany, 1998; Terrible Fate: Ethnic Cleansing in the Making of Modern Europe, 2006. **Address:** Fitchburg State College, 303 Miller Hall, 160 Pearl St., Fitchburg, MA 01420-2697, U.S.A. **Online address:** blieberman@fitchburgstate.edu

LIEBERMAN, Herbert. American (born United States), b. 1933. **Genres:** Novels, Plays/Screenplays, Literary Criticism And History. **Career:** Jamaica High School, teacher of English, 1957-59; New York Times, writer, 1959-60; Macmillan Publishing Co., associate editor, 1960-63; McCormick-Mathers Publishing Co., senior editor, 1963-67; Reader's Digest Association, senior editor, 1967-77, Reader's Digest Condensed Book Club, executive editor of condensed book projects, 1977-. **Publications:** PLAYS: Matty and the Moron and Madonna, 1964. NOVELS: The Adventures of Dolphin Green, 1967; Crawlspace, 1971; The Eighth Square, 1973; Brilliant Kids, 1975; City of the Dead, 1976; The Climate of Hell, 1978; Night Call from a Distant Time Zone, 1982; Nightbloom, 1984; The Green Train, 1986; Shadow Dancers, 1989; Sandman, Sleep, 1993; The Girl with the Botticelli Eyes, 1996; The Concierge, 1998; Widdershims, 2002; Le Vagabond De Holmby Park, 2003. **Address:** Georges Borchardt Inc., 136 E 57th St., New York, NY 10022-2707, U.S.A.

LIEBERMAN, Laurence (James). American (born United States), b. 1935. **Genres:** Poetry, Literary Criticism And History. **Career:** Orange Coast College, teacher, 1960-64; College of the Virgin Islands, assistant professor, 1964-66, associate professor of English, 1966-68; University of Illinois, associate professor of English, 1968-70, professor of English, 1970-, now professor emeritus of English; University of Illinois Press, poetry editor, 1971-; Orange County Illustrated, poetry editor. **Publications:** POETRY: The Unblinding: Poems, 1968; The Osprey Suicides, 1973; God's Measurements, 1980; Eros at the World Kite Pageant: Poems 1979-82, 1983; The Mural of Wakeful Sleep, 1985; The Creole Mephistopheles, 1988; New and Selected Poems: 1962-92, 1993; The St. Kitts Monkey Feuds, 1995; Dark Songs: Slave House and Synagogue, 1996; Compass of the Dying, 1998; The Regatta in the Skies: Selected Long Poems, 1999; Flight from the Mother Stone (poems), 2000; Hour of the Mango Black Moon, 2004; Carib's Leap: Selected and New Poems of the Caribbean, 2005. OTHERS: (intro.) The Achievement of James Dickey: A Comprehensive Selection of His Poems with a Critical Introduction, 1968; Unassigned Frequencies: American Poetry in Review 1964-77, 1977; Beyond the Muse of Memory: Essays on Contemporary American Poets, 1995. **Address:** Department of English, University of Illinois, Rm. 208 MC 718, 608 S Wright St., Urbana, IL 61801-3630, U.S.A. **Online address:** llieberm@illinois.edu

LIEBERMAN, Leanne. Canadian (born Canada), b. 1974?. **Genres:** Novels. **Career:** Writer and educator. **Publications:** Gravity, 2008. Contributor to periodicals. **Address:** Kingston, ON , Canada. **Online address:** leanne@leannelieberman.com

LIEBERMAN, Richard K. American (born United States) **Genres:** Novels, Music, History. **Career:** City University of New York, LaGuardia Community College, faculty, 1972-, professor and archivist, LaGuardia and Wagner Archives, director. Writer. **Publications:** (With J.E. Lieberman) City Limits: A Social History of Queens, 1983; Steinway & Sons, 1995. Contributor to periodicals. **Address:** LaGuardia and Wagner Archives, LaGuardia Community College, City University of New York, Rm. E-238C, 31-10 Thomson Ave., Long Island City, NY 11101, U.S.A. **Online address:** richardli@lagcc.cuny.edu

LIEBERMAN, Robert C. American (born United States), b. 1964. **Genres:** Biography, Autobiography/Memoirs. **Career:** Columbia University, assistant professor of political science; Russell Sage Foundation, visiting scholar. Writer. **Publications:** Shifting the Color Line: Race and the American Welfare State, 1998; Shaping Race Policy: The United States in Comparative Perspective, 2005. Contributor to journals. **Address:** Department of Political Science, Columbia University, International Affairs Bldg., 420 W 118th St., 7th Fl., New York, NY 10027, U.S.A. **Online address:** rcl15@columbia.edu

LIEBERMAN, Susan (Abel). American (born United States), b. 1942. **Genres:** Human Relations/Parenting, Fash Ion/Costume, Psychology. **Ca-reer:** Super Summers Inc., executive director, 1993-; Rice University, director of leadership rice, 1998-2006; executive coach, 2006-09; Y Collaborative, founding partner, 2010-. Writer. **Publications:** Let's Celebrate: Creating New Family Traditions, 1984; The KIDFUN Activity Book, 1990; (with S. Feldscher) The KIDFUN Activity Book, 1990, new ed., 1995; New Traditions: Redefining Celebrations for Today's Family, 1990; The Real High School Handbook: How To Survive, Thrive, and Prepare for What's Next, 1997; (with N.A. Bartle) Venus in Blue Jeans: Why Mothers and Daughters Need to Talk About Sex, 1998; The Mother-In-Law's Manual: Proven Strategies for Creating and Maintaining Healthy Relationships With Married Children, 2009. **Address:** Leadership Rice, Rice University, MS-200, 6100 Main St., PO Box 1892, Houston, TX 77251, U.S.A. **Online address:** susan@lieberman.net

LIEBERT, Elizabeth. American (born United States), b. 1944. **Genres:** Theology/Religion, Young Adult Non-fiction, Essays. **Career:** Fort Wright College, director, 1977-79; St. Thomas Theological Seminary, assistant professor of pastoral care, 1982-87, department chair, 1985-87; San Francisco Theological Seminary, director of the program in christian spirituality, 1987-2001, associate professor, 1987-93, professor of spiritual life, 1993-, dean of the seminary and vice president for academic affairs, 2009-. Writer. **Publications:** NONFICTION: Changing Life Patterns: Adult Development in Spiritual Direction, 1992; (with J.C. Endres) A Retreat with the Psalms: Resources for Personal and Communal Prayer, 2001; (with K. Dyckman and M. Garvin) The Spiritual Exercises Reclaimed: Uncovering Liberating Possibilities for Women, 2001; Exploring Christian Spirituality: Essays in Honor of Sandra M. Schneiders, 2006; The Way of Discernment: Spiritual Practices for Decision Making, 2008. Contributor of articles to periodicals. **Address:** San Francisco Theological Seminary, 105 Seminary Rd., San Anselmo, CA 94960-2905, U.S.A. **Online address:** eliebert@sfts.edu

LIEBERTHAL, Kenneth G. American (born United States), b. 1943. **Genres:** History, Politics/Government. **Career:** Swarthmore College, instructor, 1972, assistant professor, 1972-75, associate professor, 1976-82, professor of political science and chairman of social science division, 1982-83; University of Michigan, Center for Chinese Studies, visiting associate research scientist, 1977, research associate, 1983-, visiting professor, 1983, professor of political science, 1983-2009, director, 1986-89, Russian and East European Center, faculty associate, 1984-, Arthur F. Thurnau professor of political science and William Davidson professor of business administration, 1995-2009; professor emeritus of political science and of business administration, 2009-; WUOM-Radio, Foreign Affairs commentator, 1989-98; William Davidson Institute, faculty associate, 1996-2009, distinguished fellow, director; Center for Advanced Study in the Behavioral Sciences, fellow, 1998-99, senior fellow; RAND Corp., social scientist, 1975-76; National Security Council, special assistant, 1998-2000; Brookings Institution, visiting fellow, 2000, 2004-05, 2008-09, John L. Thornton China Center, senior fellow and director, 2009-. Writer. **Publications:** Research Guide to Central Party and Government Meetings in China, 1949-1976, 1976; The Foreign Policy Debate in Peking as Seen through Allegorical Articles, 1973-1976, 1977; Central Documents and Politburo Politics in China, 1978; Sino-Soviet Conflict in the 1970s: Its Evolution and Implications for the Strategic Triangle, 1978; The Strategic Triangle: Can the U.S. Play the China Card?, 1979; Revolution and Tradition in Tientsin, 1949-52, 1980; (with M. Oksenberg) Bureaucratic Politics and Chinese Energy Development, 1986; (with M. Oksenberg) Policy Making in China: Leaders, Structures and Processes, 1988; China's Changing Petroleum Industry, 1988; (co-author) Paths to Sino-U.S. Cooperation in the Automotive Sector, 1989; (with B. Dixon) Research Guide to Central Party and Government Meetings in China, 1949-1986, 1989; (with D.M. Lampton) Bureaucracy, Politics and Decision Making in Post-Mao China, 1992; The Future of United States-China Relations: A Proposal for a Sustainable, Bipartisan Policy, 1994; Governing China: From Revolution through Reform, 1995, rev. ed. 2004; (ed. with Shuen-fu Lin and E. Young) Constructing China: The Interaction of Culture and Economics, 1997; (with Mikkal Herberg) Chinas Search For Energy Security and Implications for U.S. Policy, 2006; (with C.K. Prahalad) End of Corporate Imperialism, 2008; (with D. Sandalow) Overcoming Obstacles to U.S. China Cooperation on Climate Change, 2009; The Intelligence Community and U.S. Foreign Policy: Getting Analysis Right, 2009; Managing the China Challenge, 2011; (with M.S. Indyk and M.E. O'Hanlon) Bending History, 2012. CONTRIBUTOR: Disarmament and Soviet Policy, 1964-68, 1969; Agenda for the Nation, 1980; The Sino-Soviet Conflict: A Global Perspective, 1982; (ed. with N. Lardy) Chen Yun's Strategy for China's Development: A Non-Maoist Alternative, 1982; China's New Social Fabric, 1983; China's Foreign Relations in the 1980's,

1984; The Cambridge History of China, vol. XIV, 1987; Asean and China: An Evolving Relationship, 1988; (ed. with D.M. Lampton) Bureaucracy, Politics and Policy-Making in Post-Mao China, 1991; (co-ed.) Perspectives on Modern China: Four Anniversaries, 1991; Culture and Negotiation, 1993; Hong Kong under Chinese Rule: The Economic and Political Implications of Reversion, 1997; Living with China: U.S. China Relations in the Twenty First Century, 1997; North Korea in the World Economy, 2003; The New Chinese Leadership: Challenges and Opportunities after the 16th Party Congress, 2004; Strategic Asia 2007-08, 2007; Power Realignments in Asia: China, India and the United States, 2009. **Address:** The Brookings Institution, 1775 Massachusetts Ave. NW, Washington, DC 20036, U.S.A. **Online address:** klieberthal@brookings.edu

LIEBESCHUETZ, John Hugo W. G. British/German (born Germany), b. 1927?. **Genres:** Archaeology/Antiquities, History, Theology/Religion. **Career:** Heanor Grammar School, school teacher, 1957-63; University of Leicester, lecturer, 1963-74, senior lecturer, 1974-78, reader in classics, 1978-79; University of Nottingham, professor of classical and archaeological studies, 1979-92, professor emeritus, 1992-; University College London, fellow. Writer. **Publications:** Antioch: City and Imperial Administration in the Later Roman Empire, 1972; Continuity and Change in Roman Religion, 1979; Barbarians and Bishops: Army, Church, and State in the Age of Arcadius and Chrysostom, 1990; From Diocletian to the Arab Conquest: Change in the Late Roman Empire, 1990; The Decline and Fall of the Roman City, 2001; Ambrose of Milan: Political Letters and Speeches, 2005; Decline and Change in Late Antiquity: Religion, Barbarians and Their Historiography, 2006; Wolf Liebeschuetz Reflected: Essays Presented By Colleagues, Friends & Pupils, 2007; Ambrose and John Chrysostom: Clerics between Desert and Empire, 2011. Contributor to journals. **Address:** Department of Classics, University of Nottingham, Archaeology and Classics Bldg., University Pk., Nottingham, NT NG7 2RD, England. **Online address:** abzwl@exmail.nottingham.ac.uk

LIEBICH, Andre. Swiss/British (born England), b. 1948. **Genres:** International Relations/Current Affairs, History, Politics/Government. **Career:** Harvard University, teaching fellow, 1971-72, professor; Oxford University, St. Antony's College, junior associate, 1972-73; Universite du Quebec a Montreal, lecturer, 1973-74, assistant professor, 1974-78, associate professor, 1978-82, professor of political science, 1982-91; Université de Montréal, lecturer, 1975; Graduate Institute of International Studies, professor of international history and politics, 1989-; Institute of Historical Research, visiting research fellow, 2002-03; IHP section, head, 1991-93, 1998-2001; director of graduate studies, 2005-08; Modern European History Research Centre, senior research associate, 2010. Writer. **Publications:** Between Ideology and Utopia, 1979; Mencheviks en exil face à l Union soviétique, 1982; Les Minorites Nationales en Europe Centrales et Orientale, 1997; From the Other Shore: Russian Social Democracy after 1921, 1997. EDITOR/CO-EDITOR: The Future of Socialism in Europe?, 1979; Selected Writings of August Cieszkowski, 1979; Le Liberalisme Classique, 1986; Les Minorites en Europe Centrale: Vers une Solution Europeenne?, 1993; Citizenship, East and West, 1995; Dilemmas of Democratization after Communism, 1997; Construire l Europe: mélanges en hommage à Pierre du Bois, 2008. OTHERS: Must Nations Become States? The Birth of Self-Determination, forthcoming; Henry Wickham Steed (1871-1956), forthcoming. **Address:** International & Development Studies, Graduate Institute, PO Box 136, CP 36, Geneva, CH 1211-21, Switzerland. **Online address:** liebich@hei.unige.ch

LIEBLER, M. L. American (born United States), b. 1953. **Genres:** Poetry, inspirational/Motivational Literature. **Career:** Ridgeway Press, founding editor and publisher, 1974-; Wayne State University, senior lecturer in English, 1980-, Intern Program, faculty, 1985-, Minority Task Force on Education, director, 1990-97; Poetry Resource Center of Michigan, president, 1985-92; Center for Creative Studies, adjunct professor of English, 1985-90; Young Men's Christian Association, director of arts and humanities for Detroit association, 1994-, Mid-America field coordinator for national organization, 1997-, director of National Writer's Voice Project in Detroit; Broadside Press, director of poet in the libraries program, 1995-2000, poet-in-residence, 1996-99; WDTR-FM, host/producer, 1995-99; Columbia Broadcasting System (CBS) TalkRadio, weekly literary host/ segment producer, 1997-99; Northern Michigan University, poet-in-residence, 2000; Springfed Literary Arts of Metro Detroit, director, 2004-. **Publications:** POETRY: Measuring Darkness, 1980; Whispers by the Lawn, vol. I, 1985, vol. II, 1987; Breaking the Voodoo, 1990; (ed.) The Vision of Words, 1992; Deliver Me, 1992; Stripping the Adult Century Bare, 1995; Brooding the Heartlands, 1998; Written in Rain:

New & Selected Poems, 2000; (ed. with M.J. Boyd) Abandon Automobile: Detroit City Poetry 2001, 2001; Breaking the Voodoo & Other Poems, 2001; The China Journal, 2002; The Moon a Box: Poems of This World, 2004; The Fragrant Benediction of Life, 2004; Greatest Hits 1980-2005, Wide Awake in Someone Else's Dreams, 2008; (ed. and intro.) Working Words, 2010. **Address:** Department of English, Wayne State University, Rm. 10201.2, 5057 Woodward Ave., Ste. 9408, Detroit, MI 48202, U.S.A. **Online address:** mlliebler@wayne.edu

LIEBMAN, Herbert. American (born United States), b. 1935. **Genres:** Plays/Screenplays, Literary Criticism And History, Biography, Autobiography/Memoirs. **Career:** College of Staten Island, professor of English, 1966-, now emeritus; State University of New York, fiction fellow, 1974; National Endowment for the Arts, fellow; 1979; MacDowell Colony, fellow, 1979; Ragdale Foundation, fellow; Helene Wurlitzer Foundation, fellow; playwright and director. **Publications:** The Dramatic Art of David Storey: The Journey of a Playwright, 1996. Contributor of short stories to periodicals. **Address:** Department of English, College of Staten Island, 2800 Victory Blvd., Staten Island, NY 10314, U.S.A. **Online address:** hlieb35@aol.com

LIEBMANN, George W. American (born United States), b. 1939. **Genres:** Law. **Career:** University of Chicago, law review managing editor, 1962-63; Law clerk, 1963-64; Frank, Bernstein, Conaway and Goldman, partner, 1964-67, 1969-79; Maryland State Law Department, assistant attorney general, 1967-69; Library Company of the Baltimore Bar, president, 1975-77; Governor Hughes of Maryland, executive assistant, 1979-80; Liebmann and Shively, principal and lawyer, 1980-; University of Manchester, fellow, 1993-94; Cambridge University, Wolfson College, visiting fellow, 1996, 1998; Lincoln Institute of Land Policy, faculty associate, 1997. Writer. **Publications:** Maryland District Court Law and Practice, 1976; Civil Procedure Forms, 1984; Maryland Circuit CourtForms, 1984; The Gallows in the Grove, 1995, rev. ed., 1997; The Little Platoons, 1995; Solving Problems Without Large Government: Devolution, Fairness, and Equality, 2000; Six Lost Leaders, 2001; Neighborhood Futures: Citizen Rights and Local Control, 2004; Common Law Tradition: A Collective Portrait of Five Legal Scholars, 2005; (ed. with O.R. Shively) Trimmer's Almanac: Ten Years of the Calvert Institute, 1996-2006, 2007; Diplomacy Between the Wars: Five Diplomats and the Shaping of the Modern World, 2008; (ed.) Prohibition in Maryland, 2011. **Address:** Liebmann & Shively, 8 W Hamilton St., Baltimore, MD 21201, U.S.A. **Online address:** liebmann@erols.com

LIEBOVICH, Louis W. American (born United States) **Genres:** Politics/Government, Writing/Journalism. **Career:** Champaign-Urbana Courier, reporter, 1971-72; Rockford Register Republic, reporter and acting city editor, 1972-76; Milwaukee Sentinel, reporter and assistant city editor, 1976-80; University of Wisconsin-Milwaukee, instructor in journalism, 1978-81; University of Wisconsin-Whitewater, instructor in journalism, 1982-85; University of Illinois, assistant professor, 1985-91, associate professor, 1991-97, Institute of Communications Research, professor of journalism and research professor, 1997-, director of graduate studies in journalism, 1997-2004, professor of communication, professor of media studies. **Publications:** The Press and the Origins of the Cold War, 1944-1947, 1988; (ed.) The Last Jew from Wegrow, 1991; Bylines in Despair: Herbert Hoover, the Great Depression and the U.S. News Media, 1994; The Press and the Modern Presidency: Myths and Mindsets from Kennedy to Clinton, 1998, 2nd ed. as The Press and the Modern Presidency: Myths and Mindsets from Kennedy to Election 2000, 2001; Richard Nixon, Watergate and the Press: A Historical Retrospective, 2003; Abraham's Rhyme: The Story of an American Family, 2007. Contributor to books. **Address:** Department of Journalism, College of Media, University of Illinois, 334 Gregory Hall, 810 S Wright St., Urbana, IL 61801, U.S.A. **Online address:** liebovic@illinois.edu

LIEBREICH, Karen. British (born England) **Genres:** Novels, Adult Nonfiction, Sports/Fitness. **Career:** French Institute, cultural assistant; British Broadcasting Corp., producer and documentary researcher; History Channel, producer and documentary researcher; The Baby Directory, founder, 2005-06. Writer and historian. **Publications:** Doing Business in Eastern Europe, 1991; (with M. Liebreich) Complete Skier: A Practical Guide for Skiers, 1993; UneXplained, 1997; Fallen Order: Intrigue Heresy and Scandal in the Rome of Galileo and Caravaggio, 2004; The Letter in the Bottle, 2006; (with J. Wagner and A. Wendland) The Family Kitchen Garden: How to Plant, Grow, and Cook Together, 2009. **Address:** c/o Author Mail, Grove/Atlantic Inc., 841 Broadway, 4th Fl., New York, NY 10003-4704, U.S.A. **Online address:**

assistant@karenliebreich.com

LIEF, Judith L. American (born United States), b. 1946. **Genres:** inspirational/Motivational Literature, Self Help, Medicine/Health, Art/Art History, Psychology, Theology/Religion. **Career:** Shambhala Intl., teacher, 1975-; Vajradhatu Publications, editor-in-chief, 1975-; Naropa Institute, dean, president, 1980-85, trustee, 1986-; Shambhala Publications, editor, 1985-; Shambhala Intl., teacher of Buddhist. **Publications:** Making Friends with Death: A Buddhist Guide to Encountering Mortality, 2001. EDITOR: Heart of the Buddha, 1991; Transcending Madness, 1992; Training the Mind and Cultivating Loving Kindness, 1993; The Art of Calligraphy, 1994; Dharma Art, 1996; Glimpses of Shunyata, 1996; Glimpses of Space, 1999; Glimpses of Mahayana, 2001; Glimpses of Realization, 2003; The Teacup and the Skullcup, 2006; True Perception, the Path of Dharma Art, 2008; The Truth of Suffering and the Path to Liberation, 2009. **Address:** Shambhala International, 1084 Tower Rd., Halifax, NS B3H 2Y5, Canada. **Online address:** garudalake@hotmail.com

LIENESCH, Michael. American (born United States), b. 1948. **Genres:** Politics/Government, Theology/Religion. **Career:** University of North Carolina, Department of Political Science, instructor, 1977, assistant professor, 1978-84, associate professor, 1985-92, professor, 1992-, Bowman and Gordon Gray professor, 1995-98, adjunct professor of American studies, 1996-, professor of distinguished teaching, 2010-. Writer. **Publications:** New Order of the Ages: Time, the Constitution, and the Making of Modern American Political Thought, 1988; (ed. with M.A Gillespie) Ratifying the Constitution, 1989; Redeeming America: Piety and Politics in the New Christian Right, 1993; In the Beginning: Fundamentalism, The Scopes Trial, and The Making of the Antievolution Movement, 2007. **Address:** Department of Political Science, University of North Carolina, 370A, 361 Hamilton Hall, PO Box 3265, Chapel Hill, NC 27599-3265, U.S.A. **Online address:** lienesch@email.unc.edu

LIEVEN, D. C. B. See **LIEVEN, Dominic.**

LIEVEN, Dominic. (D. C. B. Lieven). British (born England) **Genres:** History, Local History/Rural Topics, Social Commentary, Military/Defense/Arms Control. **Career:** London School of Economics, professor of Russian history and politics, MSc Comparative Politics, coordinator, head of department; Tokyo University, visiting professor; Harvard University, visiting professor; Göttingen University, Humboldt fellow; Munich University, Humboldt fellow. Writer. **Publications:** (As D.C.B. Lieven) Russia and the Origins of the First World War, 1983; (ed.) British Documents on Foreign Affairs: Reports and Papers from the Foreign Office Confidential Print. Part I, from the Mid-Nineteenth Century to the First World War. Series A, Russia, 1859-1914, 1983; (ed. with D.C. Watt) British Documents on Foreign Affairs: Reports and Papers from the Foreign Office Confidential Print: The Soviet Union, 1917-1939, 1985-86; Issues of Conflict in the Contemporary World: Ten Essays by Members of the Institute for the Study of Conflict to Mark the Publication of Conflict Study No. 200, 1987; Russia's Rulers Under the Old Regime, 1989; The Soviet Crisis, 1991; The Aristocracy in Europe, 1993; Nicholas II: Emperor of All the Russias, 1993 in US as Nicholas II: Twilight of the Empire, 1994; Empire: The Russian Empire and Its Rivals, 2000; Empire's Aftermath: A Comparative Perspective, 2002; The Cambridge History of Russia, 2006; Russia Against Napoleon: The True Story of the Campaigns of War and Peace, 2010. **Address:** Department of International History, London School of Economics, Office E603, Houghton St., London, GL WC2A 2AE, England. **Online address:** d.lieven@lse.ac.uk

LIFSHIN, Lyn. American (born United States), b. 1942. **Genres:** Poetry. **Career:** State University of New York, English instructor, 1968, 1970; New York State Mental Health Department, writing consultant, 1969; Empire State College, writing consultant, 1973; Mansfield State College, poet-in-residence, 1974; Albany Public Library Poetry Workshop, director; Glenwood College, poet-in-residence, 1991, 1994. **Publications:** Why Is the House Dissolving?: Poems, 1968; Black Apples, 1970; Leaves and Night Things, 1971; Femina Two, 1972; Moving by Touch, 1972; Merchurochrome Sun Poems, 1972; Tentacles, Leaves, 1972; Love Poems, 1972; The Old House on the Croton, 1973; Museum, 1974; Forty Days, Apple Nights, 1974; The Croton, 1974; The Old House, 1974; Wild Flowers Smoke, 1974; Green Bandages, 1974; All the Women Poets, 1974; Audley End Poems, 1974; Old House Poems, 1975; Upstate Madonna: Poems, 1970-1974, 1975; Some Madonna Poems, 1976; Leaning South, 1976; Plymouth Women, 1976; North Poems, 1976; Shaker House Poems, 1976; Glass, 1978; Paper Apples, 1978; Crazy Arms,

1979; 35 Sundays, 1979; Colors of Cooper Black, 1981; Hotel Lifshin, 1982; Mad Girl Poems, 1982; Blue Dust New Mexico, 1982; Reading Lips, 1982; Want Ads, 1982; In the Dark with Just One Star, 1982; Madonna Who Shifts for Herself, 1983; Naked Charm, 1984; Kiss the Skin Off, 1985; Blue Horses Nuzzle Thursday, 1985; Raw Opals, 1987; Many Madonnas: Poems, 1988; Red Hair and the Jesuit, 1988; Unsealed Lips, 1989; (with B. Subraman) Skin Divers, 1989; Rubbed Silk, 1989; Not Made of Glass, 1989; The Doctor Poems, 1990; More Naked Charm, 1990; The Innocents, 1991; Reading Lips, 1992; Marilyn Monroe: Poems by Lyn Lifshin, 1994; Parade, 1994; Shooting Kodachromes, 1994; Appleblossoms, 1994; Feathers in the Wind, 1994; The 375 Poem about Me Comes in the Mail, 1994; Pointe Shoes, 1995; Blue Tattoo: Poems of the Holocaust, 1995; The Mad Girl Drives in a Daze, 1995; Color and Light, 1996; Mad Girls, Dead Men, 1996; More Mad Girls, 1996; My Mother's Fire, 1996; Autobiography, 1996; Jesus Alive and in the Flesh, 1997; Cold Comfort: Selected Poems, 1970-1996, 1997; Caught in the Act, 1997; Flesh Dress, 1997; Before It's Light: New Poems, 1999; Licorice Daughter: My Year with Ruffian, 2005; The Daughter I Don't Have, 2005; Another Woman Who Looks Like Me: Poems, 2006; An Unfinished Story, 2006; Nutley Pond, 2008; 92 Rapple Drive, 2008; Light at the End: The Jesus Poems, 2008; Persephone, 2008; Lost in the Fog, 2008; Barbaro: Beyond Brokenness, 2008; Ballet Madonnas, 2010; Katrina, 2010; Lost Horses, 2010; Chiffon, 2010; Ballroom, 2010; All the Poets Who Have Touched Me, Living And Dead: All True: Especially the Lies, 2011. EDITOR: Tangled Vines: A Collection of Mother and Daughter Poems, 1978; Ariadne's Thread: A Collection of Contemporary Women's Journals, 1982; Lips Unsealed: Confidences from Contemporary Women Writers, 1990. **Address:** 2719 Baronhurst Dr., Vienna, VA 22181-6158, U.S.A. **Online address:** onyxvelvet@aol.com

LIGHT, Alison Elizabeth. British (born England), b. 1955. **Genres:** Young Adult Non-fiction. **Career:** Writer and educator. University of Newcastle upon Tyne, professor of modern English literature and culture, 2006-; University of East London, Raphael Samuel History Center, part-time professor; British Broadcasting Corp., staff; Royal Holloway College, lecturer; University College, lecturer; London University, lecturer. Writer. **Publications:** NONFICTION: Forever England: Femininity, Literature and Conservatism between the Wars, 1991; (ed. with S. Alexander and G.S. Jones) Island Stories: Unravelling Britain, 1998; Composing One's Self: Virginia Woolf's Diaries and Memoirs, 2007; (ed. and intro.) Raphael Samuel, The Lost World of British Communism, 2007; Mrs. Woolf and the Servants, 2007 in US as Mrs. Woolf and the Servants: An Intimate History of Domestic Life in Bloomsbury, 2008. OTHERS: (ed. and intro.) Virginia Woolf, Flush, 2000. Contributor to books and periodicals. **Address:** School of English Lit., Language, Linguistics, University of Newcastle upon Tyne, Newcastle upon Tyne, NE1 7RU, United Kingdom. **Online address:** alison.light@ncl.ac.uk

LIGHTFOOT, Deborah J. See **LIGHTFOOT SIZEMORE, Deborah.**

LIGHTFOOT, D. J. See **LIGHTFOOT SIZEMORE, Deborah.**

LIGHTFOOT, Gordon. Canadian (born Canada), b. 1938. **Genres:** Songs/Lyrics And Libretti, Music. **Career:** Writer. **Publications:** Sit Down Young Stranger, 1970; If you Could Read my Mind, 1970; Summer Side of Life, 1971; Don Quixote, 1972; The Pony Man, 1972; Old Dan's Records, 1973; Sundown, 1974; Cold on the Shoulder, 1975; Summertime Dream, 1976; Gord's Gold, 1976; Dream Street Rose, 1980; The Best of Gordon Lightfoot, 1980; East of Midnight, 1986; Guitar Anthology, 1996; The New Best of Gordon Lightfoot, 1998. **Address:** 1365 Yonge St., Ste. 207, Toronto, ON M4T 2P7, Canada.

LIGHTFOOT, Kent G. American (born United States), b. 1953. **Genres:** History, Politics/Government, Social Sciences. **Career:** University of California, Department of Anthropology, professor. Writer. **Publications:** Prehistoric Political Dynamics: A Case Study from the American Southwest, 1984; (with R. Kalin and J. Moore) Prehistoric Hunter-Gatherers of Shelter Island, New York: An Archaeological Study of the Mashomack Preserve, 1987; Indians, Missionaries and Merchants: The Legacy of Colonial Encounters on the California Frontiers, 2005; (with O. Parrish) California Indians and Their Environment: An Introduction, 2009. EDITOR: (with S. Upham and R.A. Jewett) The Sociopolitical Structure of Prehistoric Southwestern Societies, 1989; (with T.A. Wake and A.M. Schiff) The Archaeology and Ethnohistory of Fort Ross, California, 1991; (with L.S. Cordell and G.R. Milner) Archaeology in America: An Encyclopedia, 2008. **Address:** Department of Anthropology,

University of California, Rm. 213, 2251 College Bldg., 232 Kroeber Hall, Berkeley, CA 94720-3710, U.S.A. **Online address:** klightfoot@berkeley.edu

LIGHTFOOT SIZEMORE, Deborah. Also writes as D. J. Lightfoot, Deborah J. Lightfoot. American (born United States), b. 1956. **Genres:** Science Fiction/Fantasy, Children's Non-fiction, History, Writing/Journalism, Biography. **Career:** Texas Agricultural Extension Service, writer, 1976-77; Abilene Reporter-News, copy editor, 1978; Motheral Printing Co., customer service representative, 1978-79; Graphic Arts Inc., production co-ordinator, 1980-81; freelance writer and editor, 1981-; Boy Scouts of America, National Publishing Division, freelance writer and editor, 1981-; Dairymen's Digest Magazine, contributing editor, 1981-89, 1995-97; Tarrant County Junior College, writing instructor, 1993; Boys' Life Magazine, acting associate editor, 1995; Seven Rivers Publishing, managing editor, 2003-. **Publications:** (Ed.) In and By: The Fort Worth Stockyards, 1945-1955, 1987; Your Future with the BSA: A Career Guide for Scouting Professionals, 1989; The LH7 Ranch In Houston's Shadow: The E.H. Marks' Legacy from Longhorns to the Salt Grass Trail, 1991; (as D.J. Lightfoot) Trail Fever: The Life of a Texas Cowboy (juvenile), 1992, rev. ed., 2003; (with S.W. Freese) A Century in the Works: Freese and Nichols Consulting Engineers, 1894-1994, 1994; Waterspell (fiction) forthcoming. Contributor to magazines. **Address:** PO Box 682, Crowley, TX 76036, U.S.A. **Online address:** djls@djlightfoot.com

LIGHTMAN, Alan P. American (born United States), b. 1948. **Genres:** Novels, Sciences. **Career:** Cornell University, postdoctoral fellow in astrophysics, 1974-76; Harvard University, assistant professor of astronomy, 1976-79, lecturer in astronomy and physics, 1979-89; Smithsonian Astrophysical Observatory, staff astrophysicist, 1979-89; Massachusetts Institute of Technology, John E. Burchard professor of science and writing and senior lecturer in physics, 1989-2001, head of program in writing and humanistic studies, 1991-97, adjunct professor of humanities, 2001-; American Academy of Arts and Sciences, fellow, 1996. Writer. **Publications:** Problem Book in Relativity and Gravitation (textbook), 1975; Radioactive Processes in Astrophysics (textbook), 1979; (ed. with J. Cornell) Revealing the Universe: Prediction and proof in Astronomy, 1982; Time Travel and Papa Joe's Pipe: Essays on the Human Side of Science, 1984; A Modern Day Yankee in a Connecticut Court and Other Essays on Science, 1986; (with R. Brawer) Origins: The Lives and Worlds of Modern Cosmologists, 1990; Ancient Light: Our Changing View of the Universe, 1991; Time for the Stars: Astronomy in the 1990s, 1992; Great Ideas in Physics, 1992, 3rd ed. as Great Ideas in Physics: The Conservation of Energy, The Second Law of Thermodynamics, The Theory of Relativity and Quantum Mechanics, 2000; Einstein's Dreams, 1993; Good Benito, 1995; Dance for Two: Selected Essays, 1996; The Diagnosis, 2000; Reunion, 2003; (ed. with D. Sarewitz and C. Desser) Living with the Genie: Essays on Technology and The Quest for Human Mastery, 2003; Heart of the Horse, 2004; A Sense of the Mysterious: Science and The Human Spirit, 2005; The Discoveries, 2005; Ghost, 2007; Song of Two Worlds, 2009; Mr. G: A Novel About the Creation, 2011. Contributor to periodicals. **Address:** Program in Writing & Humanistic Studies, Massachusetts Institute of Technology, Rm. 14E-303, Cambridge, MA 02139, U.S.A.

LIGON, Samuel. American (born United States) **Genres:** Sex, Novels, Novellas/Short Stories. **Career:** Eastern Washington University, associate professor of creative writing; Willow Springs, editor, 2004-. **Publications:** Safe in Heaven Dead: A Novel, 2003; Drift and Swerve, 2009. Contributor to periodicals. **Address:** c/o Author Mail, HarperCollins Publishers, 10 E 53rd St., New York, NY 10022, U.S.A. **Online address:** sam@samuelligon.net

LIH, Andrew. American (born United States), b. 1968?. **Genres:** Information Science/Computers, Technology. **Career:** AT&T Bell Laboratories, engineer, 1990-93; Mediabridge Infosystems, staff; Columbia University, Graduate School of Journalism, adjunct professor, 1995, Center for New Media, director of technology, 1995, Interactive Design Lab, principal investigator, 1999; University of Hong Kong, Journalism and Media Studies Center, assistant professor, 2003; Wikipedia, editor and administrator, 2003-; The Wall Street Journal, video and multimedia reporter, 2008. Entrepreneur and engineer. **Publications:** The Wikipedia Revolution: How a Bunch of Nobodies Created the World's Greatest Encyclopedia, 2009. Contributor to periodicals. **Address:** U.S.A. **Online address:** andrew@andrewlih.com

LILA, Kim. American (born United States), b. 1966. **Genres:** Food And Wine, Business/Trade/Industry. **Career:** Kleinschmidt, staff, 1997-. Writer. **Publications:** Simply Casseroles, 1998. **Address:** Kleinschmidt, 550 Amherst Dr.,

Lake Villa, IL 60046, U.S.A. **Online address:** kimmmerly@hotmail.com

LILES, Maurine Walpole. American (born United States), b. 1935. **Genres:** Children's Fiction, Children's Non-fiction, Mythology/Folklore, Novellas/Short Stories. **Career:** Writer and educator. **Publications:** (With M. Fields) Rebecca of Blossom Prairie: Grandmother of a Vice-President, 1990; Kitty of Blossom Prairie, 1992; The Boy of Blossom Prairie Who Became Vice-President, 1993; Sam and the Speaker's Chair: The Story of Sam Rayburn, Speaker of the U.S. House of Representatives, 1994; Willer and the Piney Woods Doctor, 1995; The Littlest Vaquero: Texas First Cowboys and How They Helped Win the American Revolution, 1996; Doña María, La Ranchera: Woman Rancher in Spanish Texas, 2000. **Address:** 1405 S 3rd St., PO Box 546, Floresville, TX 78114-0546, U.S.A. **Online address:** willer2@aol.com

LILIENFELD, Jane. American (born United States), b. 1945?. **Genres:** Literary Criticism And History, Novels, Humanities. **Career:** Chicago State College, affiliate, 1968-69; Lincoln University, associate professor of English, professor. Writer. **Publications:** (Intro.) Virginia Woolf: Emerging Perspectives, 1994; (ed. with J. Oxford) The Languages of Addiction, 1999; Reading Alcoholisms: Theorizing Character and Narrative in Selected Novels of Thomas Hardy, James Joyce, and Virginia Woolf, 1999. Contributor to periodicals. **Address:** Department of English, Lincoln University, 432 Martin Luther King Hall, 820 Chestnut St., Jefferson City, MO 65101-3537, U.S.A. **Online address:** lilienfeldj@lincolnu.edu

LILIENFELD, Scott O. American (born United States), b. 1960. **Genres:** Psychology, Sciences. **Career:** State University of New York, Department of Psychology, assistant professor, 1990-94; Emory University, associate professor of psychology, 1994-, professor of psychology. Writer. **Publications:** Seeing Both Sides: Classic Controversies in Abnormal Psychology, 1995; Looking into Abnormal Psychology, 1998; (ed. with S.J. Lynn and J.M. Lohr) Science and Pseudoscience in Clinical Psychology, 2003; (with J.M. Wood, M.T. Nezworski and H.N. Garb) What's Wrong with the Rorschach?, 2003; (with M.R. Widows) PPI-R: Psychopathic Personality Inventory- Revised, 2005; (ed. with W.T. O'Donohue) Great Ideas of Clinical Science: 17 Principles that Every Mental Health Professional Should Understand, 2007; (ed. with W. O'Donohue and K.A. Fowler) Personality Disorders: Toward the DSM-V, 2007; (ed. with J. Ruscio and S.J. Lynn) Navigating the Mindfield: A Guide to Separating Science from Pseudoscience in Mental Health, 2008; (ed. with J.L. Skeem and K.S. Douglas) Psychological Science in the Courtroom: Consensus and Controversy, 2009; (with S.J Lynn, L.L. Namy and N.J. Woolf) Psychology: From Inquiry to Understanding, 2009, 2nd ed., 2011; (with S.J Lynn, L.L. Namy and N.J. Woolf) 50 Great Myths of Popular Psychology: Shattering Widespread Misconceptions about Human Behavior, 2009; (co-author) Psychology: A Framework for Everyday Thinking, 2010; (ed. with W.T. O'Donohue) Great Readings in Clinical Science, 2012; Introductory Psychology: A Critical Thinking Approach, forthcoming. **Address:** Department of Psychology, Emory University, 473 Psychology Bldg., 36 Eagle Row, Atlanta, GA 30322, U.S.A. **Online address:** slilien@emory.edu

LILIENTHAL, David E. See **ELY, David.**

LILLA, Mark. American (born United States), b. 1956?. **Genres:** Politics/Government, Social Sciences. **Career:** The Public Interest, editor, 1984; New York University, faculty; University of Chicago, professor; Columbia University, Department of History, professor of the humanities and religion, 2007-. Writer. **Publications:** (Ed. with N. Glazer) The Public Face of Architecture: Civic Culture and Public Spaces, 1987; G.B. Vico: The Making of an Anti-Modern, 1993; (ed.) New French Thought: Political Philosophy, 1994; (ed. with R. Dworkin and R. Silvers) The Legacy of Isaiah Berlin, 2001; The Reckless Mind: Intellectuals in Politics, 2001; (ed. with L. Wieseltier) For Daniel Bell, 2005; The Stillborn God: Religion, Politics, and the Modern West, 2007; Ignorance and Bliss, forthcoming. **Address:** Department of History, Columbia University, 512 Knox Hall, 1180 Amsterdam Ave., PO Box 2527, New York, NY 10027-7039, U.S.A. **Online address:** mlilla@columbia.edu

LILLER, William. American (born United States), b. 1927. **Genres:** Astronomy, Sciences. **Career:** Harvard University, Department of Astronomy, professor, 1960-83, head, now retired. Writer and astronomer. **Publications:** Space Astrophysics, 1961; (with B. Mayer) The Cambridge Astronomy Guide: A Practical Introduction to Astronomy, 1985; (ed. with P.M. Lugger) Asteroids to Quasars: A Symposium Honouring William Liller, 1991; The Cambridge Guide to Astronomical Discovery, 1992; The Ancient Solar Observatories of Rapanui: The Archaeoastronomy of Easter Island, 1993; (with A.B.H. Rapahango) Speak Rapanui!, 1996. **Address:** Center for Nova Research, Casilla 5022, Renaca, Vina del Mar, CL 23457, Chile. **Online address:** wliller@compuserve.com

LILLEY, Stephen R(ay). American (born United States), b. 1950. **Genres:** Children's Non-fiction, History, Biography, Education, Reference. **Career:** Schoolteacher, 1972-74; Lincoln County Schools, teacher, 1974-; Northeast Missouri State University, adjunct faculty, 1977; Hannibal LaGrange College, adjunct faculty, 1989-92. Writer. **Publications:** Hernando Cortes, 1996; The Conquest of Mexico, 1997; Fighters Against American Slavery, 1999. Contributor to periodicals. **Address:** 274 Lilley Ln., Elsberry, MO 63343-3199, U.S.A. **Online address:** trumpeter@lincolnco.net

LIM, Elvin T. American (born United States), b. 1976. **Genres:** Politics/Government. **Career:** University of Tulsa, associate professor; Wesleyan University, assistant professor of government. Writer, historian and researcher. **Publications:** The Anti-Intellectual Presidency: The Decline of Presidential Rhetoric from George Washington to George W. Bush, 2008. Contributor to books, periodicals and journals. **Address:** Department of Government, Wesleyan University, 308 Public Affairs Ctr., 238 Church St., Middletown, CT 06459-0019, U.S.A. **Online address:** elim@wesleyan.edu

LIM, Shirley Geok-lin. American/Malaysian (born Malaysia), b. 1944. **Genres:** Novels, Novellas/Short Stories, Poetry, Literary Criticism And History, Autobiography/Memoirs, Social Sciences. **Career:** University of Malaya, lecturer, 1967-69; Brandeis University, teaching assistant, 1970-72; City University of New York, Queens College, teaching fellow, 1972-73, Hostos Community College, assistant professor, 1973-76, Graduate Center, Mellon Fellow, 1983; State University of New York, Westchester College, associate professor, 1976-90; National University of Singapore, visiting fellow, 1982, writer-in-residence, 1985; Institute of Southeast-Asian Studies, fellow, 1985-86; Institute of Southeast-Asian Studies East-West Center, writer-in-residence, 1988; Centre for Advanced Studies, Asia Foundation fellow, 1989; University of California, professor of Asian American studies, 1990-94, professor of women's studies and English, 1993-; Nanyang Technological University, Fulbright distinguished lecturer, 1996; University of Hong-Kong, chair professor, Department of English, head, 1999-2002. Writer. **Publications:** POETRY: Crossing the Peninsula, 1980; No Man's Grove, 1985; Modern Secrets, 1989; Monsoon History, 1994. OTHERS: Another Country and Other Stories, 1982; Nationalism and Literature: English-Language Writers from the Philippines and Singapore, 1993; Writing South/East Asia in English, 1994; Life's Mysteries, 1995; Among the White Moon Faces (memoir), 1996; Two Dreams (stories), 1997; What the Fortune Teller Didn't Say, 1998; Joss and Gold, 2001; Sister Swing, 2006. EDITOR: (and intro.) The Forbidden Stitch, 1989; Approaches to Teaching Kingston's The Woman Warrior, 1991; Reading Asian American Literatures, 1992; (with A. Ling) Reading the literatures of Asian America, 1992; (with N.A. Spencer) One World of Literature, 1992; Asian American Literature, 1999; Transnational Asia Pacific Gender, Representations and the Public Sphere, 1999; Power, Race and Gender in Academe, 2000; Tilting the Continent, 2000; Moving Poetry, 2001; (co-ed.) Transnational Asian American Literature: Sites and Transits, 2006; (with A. Poon and P. Holden) Writing Singapore: An Historical Anthology of Singapore Literature, 2009. Contributor to periodicals. **Address:** Department of English, University of California, SH 2719, Santa Barbara, CA 93106-3170, U.S.A. **Online address:** slim@english.ucsb.edu

LIM, Walter S. H. Singaporean (born Singapore), b. 1959. **Genres:** Politics/Government, History. **Career:** National University of Singapore, associate professor, deputy head (literature). Writer. **Publications:** The Arts of Empire: The Poetics of Colonialism from Ralegh to Milton, 1998; John Milton, Radical Politics, and Biblical Republicanism, 2006; (ed. with D. Johanyak) The English Renaissance, Orientalism, and the Idea of Asia, 2010. Contributor to books, journals and periodicals. **Address:** Singapore. **Online address:** elllimw@nus.edu.sg

LIMA, Patrick. Canadian (born Canada) **Genres:** Horticulture, Art/Art History, Homes/Gardens. **Career:** Writer. **Publications:** The Harrowsmith Perennial Garden: Flowers for Three Seasons, 1987; The Harrowsmith Herb Handbook, 1989; The Natural Food Garden: Growing Vegetables and Fruits Chemical-Free, 1992; (contrib.) Herbs: The Complete Gardener's Guide, 2001; The Organic Home Garden: How to Grow Fruits & Vegetables Naturally, 2004. **Address:** Larkwhistle Garden, 191 Lindsay Rd. 40, Dyers Bay, Miller

Lake, ON N0H 1Z0, Canada. **Online address:** larkwhistle@amtelecom.net

LIMA, Robert (F.). American/Cuban (born Cuba), b. 1935. **Genres:** Plays/Screenplays, Poetry, Literary Criticism And History, Bibliography, Biography, Translations. **Career:** City University of New York, Hunter College, lecturer in Romance literatures, 1962-65; Pennsylvania State University, assistant professor, 1965-68, associate professor, 1968-73, professor of Spanish and comparative literature, 1973-2002, Department of Comparative Literature, chairman, 1970-75, Institute for the Arts and Humanistic Studies, fellow, 1986-2002, professor emeritus, 2002-; Modern International Drama, editorial associate, 1967-81; University de San Marcos, Peru, poet-in-residence. **Publications:** The Theatre of Garcia Lorca, 1963; Ramon del Valle-Inclan, 1972; An Annotated Bibliography of Ramon del Valle-Inclan, 1972; (co-author) Poems of Exile and Alienation, 1976; Fathoms (poetry), 1981; (co-author) Dos Ensayos Sobre Teatro Espanol de Los Veinte, 1984; The Olde Ground (poetry), 1985; Valle-Inclan: The Theatre of His Life, 1988; Mayaland (poetry), 1992; Dark Prisms: Occultism in Hispanic Drama, 1995; Valle-Inclan: El Teatro De Su Vida, 1995; Ramon Del Valle-Inclan: An Annotated Bibliography, vol. I: Works, 1999; Sardinia/Sardegna (prose, poetry), 2000; Tracking the Minotaur (poetry), 2003; The Dramatic World of Valle-Inclan, 2003; Stages of Evil: Occultism in Western Theater and Drama, 2005; The International Bibliography of Studies on the Life and Works of Ramón del Valle-Inclan, 2 vols., 2008; The Pointing Bone (poetry), 2008; Prismas Oscuros: El ocultismo en el teatro hispanico, 2010; The Rites of Stone (prose, poetry), 2010. EDITOR/CO-EDITOR: Seventh Street Anthology: Poems of Les Deux Megots, 1961; The Readers Encyclopedia of American Literature, rev. ed., 1962; Anthology of Festival Poetry, 1962; McGraw-Hill Encyclopedia of World Drama, 1972; Surrealism: A Celebration, 1975; Borges and the Esoteric, 1993; (with P. Zatlin) Tribute to Martha T. Halsey, 1995; The Alchemical Art of Leonora Carrington, 2001; Texts and Contexts: A Tribute to Beno Weiss, 2001. EDITOR AND TRANSLATOR: A.M. Barrenechea, Borges the Labyrinth Maker, 1965; Valle-Inclan: Autobiography, Aesthetics, Aphorisms, 1966; R. Valle-Inclan, The Lamp of Marvels, 1986; Savage Acts: Four Plays by Valle-Inclan, 1991. **Address:** Department of Spanish, Italian & Portuguese, Pennsylvania State University, 211 Burrowes Bldg., University Park, PA 16802-6203, U.S.A. **Online address:** rxl2@psu.edu

LI-MARCUS, Moying. See **LI, Moying.**

LIMON, Jerzy. Polish (born Poland), b. 1950. **Genres:** Novels, Literary Criticism And History, Theatre. **Career:** Adam Mickiewicz University, Department of English, instructor, 1975-79, lecturer, 1979-80; University of Gdansk, Department of English, assistant professor, 1980-85, associate professor, 1985-93, professor, 1993-. Writer. **Publications:** Munchhauseniada (novel), 1980; Gentlemen of a Company: English Players in Central and Eastern Europe, 1590-1660, 1985; Dangerous Matter: English Drama and Politics in 1623-24, 1986; The Masque of Stuart Culture, 1990; Wieloryb (novel), 1998; Koncert niedzwiedzicy (novel), 1999; Miedzy niedem a scena, 2002; Trzy teatry: scena-telewizja-radio, 2003; Piaty wymiar teatru, 2006; The Chemistry of the Theatre: Performativity of Time, 2010. EDITOR: (with J.L. Halio) Shakespeare and His Contemporaries: Eastern and Central European Studies, 1993; (with M. Gibinska) Hamlet East and West, 1998. **Address:** Department of English, University of Gdansk, ul. Wita Stwosza 55, Gdansk-Oliwa, 80-824, Poland.

LIMON, Martin. American (born United States), b. 1948?. **Genres:** Mystery/Crime/Suspense, Novels, Young Adult Fiction, Criminology/True Crime. **Career:** Freelance writer, 1992-. **Publications:** NOVELS: Jade Lady Burning, 1992; Slicky Boys, 1997; Buddha's Money, 1998; The Door to Bitterness, 2005; The Wandering Ghost: A Novel, 2007; G.I. Bones, 2009; Mr. Kill, 2011. Contributor to periodicals. **Address:** c/o Bantam Books, 1540 Broadway, New York, NY 10036, U.S.A.

LIMONOV, Éduard. French/Russian (born Russia), b. 1943. **Genres:** Novels, Poetry, Autobiography/Memoirs, Biography. **Career:** Writer, 1980-. **Publications:** Russkoe (poems), 1979; Journal d'un rate, 1982; Dnevnik neudachnika, ili, sekretnaia tetrad, 1982; Eto ia: Edichka, 1982; Molodoi negodiai, 1986; Palach, 1986; Le petit Salaud, 1988; Memoir of a Russian Punk, 1990; Inostranets: Smutnoe vremia, 1992; Disappearance of Barbarians, 1992; Podrostok Savenko: Povest, 1992; Stranac u rodnom gradu, 1993; Ubiistvo Chasovogo, 1993; U nas bylavelikaia epokha, 1994; Limonov protiv Zhirinovskogo, 1994; Kon'iak Napoleon, 1995; Limonov: v fotografiiakh s kommentariiami, napisannymi imsamim!, 1996; 316, punkt V (novel), 1998; Sobranie sochinenii v trekhtomakh, 1998; Okhota na Bykova, 2001; Kniga mërtvykh, 2001; Moiapoliticheskaia biografiia, 2002; Palach, 2002; Dnevnik neudachnika, 2002; Amerikanskie Kanikuly: Rasskazy, 2002; Devochka-zver: rasskazy, 2002; Drugaia Rossiia Ochertaniia Budushchego, 2003; Drugaia Rossiia Revoliutsiia prodolzhaetsia, 2004; Po tiur mam, 2004; Kak My Stroili Budushchee Rossii, 2004; Torzhestvo Metafiziki, 2005; Eresi: Ocherki Natural'noi Filosofii, 2008; Poslednie dni Supermena, 2008; Smert' Sovremennykh Geroev, 2008; Mal'chik, begi!: Stikhotvoreniia, 2009; Nekrologi, 2010; Putin, 2011; A Young Scoundrel; My Political Biography; Another Russia; Russian Psycho; Control Shot; The Holy Monsters; Imprisoned by Dead Men; The Book of Water; The Wild Girl; American Vacation; The Great Mother of Love; Anatomy of a Hero. Contributor to books and periodicals. **Address:** c/o Mary Kling, La Nouvelle Agence, 7 rue Corneille, Paris, 75006, France.

LIN, Grace. American (born United States), b. 1974. **Genres:** Picture/Board Books, Illustrations, Novels. **Career:** Freelance illustrator and author, 1997- . **Publications:** SELF-ILLUSTRATED PICTURE BOOKS: The Ugly Vegetables, 1999; Dim Sum for Everyone!, 2001; Kite Flying, 2002; Okie-dokie, 2003; Olvina Flies, 2003; Robert's Snow, 2004; Jingle Bells, 2004; Fortune Cookie Fortunes, 2004; Deck the Halls, 2004; The Twelve Days of Christmas, 2004; Merry Christmas! Let's All Sing!, 2005; Our Seasons, 2006; Olvina Swims, 2007; The Red Thread: An Adoption Fairy Tale, 2007; Lissy's Friends, 2007; Bringing in the New Year, 2008. JUVENILE NOVELS: The Year of the Dog, 2006; The Year of the Rat, 2007; Where the Mountains Meet the Moon, 2009. OTHER: (comp. with R. Mercer) Robert's Snowflakes: Artists' Snowflakes for Cancer's Cure, 2005. **Address:** PO Box 401036, North Cambridge, MA 02140-0011, U.S.A. **Online address:** gracelin@concentric.com

LIN, Jami. American (born United States), b. 1956. **Genres:** Homes/Gardens. **Career:** Earth Design Inc., president, 1983-; Consultant and interior designer. Writer. **Publications:** Feng Shui Today: Earth Design, the Added Dimension, 1995; The Feng Shui Anthology: Contemporary Earth Design, 1997; The Essence of Feng Shui: Balancing Your Body, Home, and Life with Fragrance, 1998; Basic Energy, 2001; Earth Energy, 2001; Heaven Energy, 2001; Yearly + Monthly Energies, 2001; Tantric Feng Shui: Scoring a Perfect Ten with Your Lover, 2003. **Address:** Earth Design Inc., PO Box 530725, Miami Shores, FL 33153, U.S.A. **Online address:** gp@jamilin.com

LIN, Tan (Anthony). American/Chinese (born China), b. 1957. **Genres:** Poetry, Food And Wine, Photography, How-to Books, Horticulture, Information Science/Computers, Librarianship, Race Relations, Race Relations, Novels, Literary Criticism And History, E-books, Art/Art History, Zoology, Paranormal, Law, Architecture, Bibliography. **Career:** Whitney Museum of American Art, assistant for rights and reproductions, 1980-83; Martell and Co., writer and researcher, 1984-86; Atlantic Center for the Arts, associate artist-in-residence, 1992; Centre College, poet-in-residence, 1997; Maryland Institute, College of Art, visiting artist-in-residence; University of Virginia, assistant professor of English, 1993-99; California Institute of the Arts, 1999; New Jersey City University, associate professor of English, 2000-. **Publications:** Lotion Bullwhip Giraffe, 1996; Blipsoak01, 2003; (intro.) Alice's Adventures in Wonderland; and, Through the Looking-glass and What Alice Found There, 2003; Ambience is a Novel with a Logo, 2007; Heath: Plagiarism/Outsource, 2008; Seven Controlled Vocabularies and Obituary. 2004. The Joy of Cooking, 2010; Insomnia and the Aunt, 2011. Works appear in anthologies. **Address:** Department of English, New Jersey City University, Karnoutsos Hall, Jersey City, NJ 07305, U.S.A. **Online address:** tananthonylin@hotmail.com

LINCECUM, Jerry Bryan. American (born United States), b. 1942. **Genres:** Autobiography/Memoirs, History. **Career:** Austin College, Department of English, assistant professor, 1967-71, associate professor, 1972-77, professor, 1977-, chair, 1995-99, Henry L. and Laura H. Shoap professor of English, 1997-2006, professor emeritus of English, 2006-; Telling Our Stories (autobiography writing project), director, 1990-; Center for Excellence in Liberal Arts Teaching and Faculty Development, director, 2002-06. Writer. **Publications:** EDITOR: (with E.H. Phillips and intro.) Adventures of a Frontier Naturalist: The Life and Times of Dr. Gideon Lincecum, 1994; (with E.H. Phillips and P.A. Redshaw) Science on the Texas Frontier: Observations of Dr. Gideon Lincecum, 1997; (with E.H. Phillips and P.A. Redshaw) Gideon Lincecum's Sword: Civil War Letters from the Home Front, 2001; (with F.E. Abernethy and F.B. Vick) The Family Saga: A Collection of Texas Family Legends, 2003. **Address:** 1603 Moreland Dr., Sherman, TX 75090, U.S.A. **Online address:** jlincecum@austincollege.edu

LINCOLN, Don. American (born United States), b. 1964?. **Genres:** Sciences. **Career:** Rice University, research assistant, 1986-94, lab instructor, 1986-88; Triton College, adjunct assistant professor, 1993-99; University of Michigan, research fellow, 1994-98; Fermi National Accelerator Laboratory, research associate, 1998-99, associate scientist, 1999-2004, scientist, 2004-10, senior scientist, 2010-; North Central College, adjunct assistant professor, 1999-2002; University of Notre Dame, Department of Physics, adjunct associate professor, 2005-10, adjunct professor, 2010-. Physicist and writer. **Publications:** Understanding the Universe: From Quarks to the Cosmos, 2004; The Quantum Frontier: The Large Hadron Collider, 2009. Contributor to periodicals. **Address:** Department of Physics, University of Notre Dame, Fermilab MS352 D0, 225 Nieuwland Science Hall, Notre Dame, IL 46556, U.S.A. **Online address:** lucifer@fnal.gov

LINCOLN, Edward J. American (born United States), b. 1949. **Genres:** Economics. **Career:** Center for Japan-U.S. Business and Economic Studies, director; New York University, Stern School of Business, faculty; Johns Hopkins University, School for International Studies, faculty; Council on Foreign Relations, senior fellow; Brookings Institution, senior fellow; American Embassy, special economic advisor ambassador Walter Mondale. Writer. **Publications:** (With D.E. Rosenthal) Legal Aspects of Doing Business in Japan, 1983, 1983; Japan's Economic Role in Northeast Asia, 1987; Japan, Facing Economic Maturity, 1988; (ed.) Japan and the Middle East, 1990; Japan's Unequal Trade, 1990., Japan's Rapidly Emerging Strategy toward Asia, 1992; Japan's New Global Role, 1993; Troubled Times: U.S.-Japan Trade Relations in the 1990s, 1999; Arthritic Japan: The Slow Pace of Economic Reform, 2001; East Asian Economic Regionalism, 2004; Winners without Losers: Why Americans Should Care More about Global Economic Policy, 2007. Contributor to periodicals. **Address:** Leonard N. Stern School of Business, Kaufman Management Center, Rm. 7-89, 44 W 4th St., New York, NY 10012, U.S.A. **Online address:** elincoln@stern.nyu.edu

LIND, Michael. American (born United States), b. 1962. **Genres:** Politics/Government, Social Sciences. **Career:** The National Interest, executive editor, 1991-94; Harper's Magazine, senior editor, 1994-98, Washington editor, 1998-; New America Foundation, co-founder, 1998-, American Strategy Project, director, Whitehead Senior Fellow, Economic Growth Program, policy director; Harvard University, faculty; Johns Hopkins University, faculty; Virginia Polytechnic Institute and State University, faculty; The New Yorker, staff; The New Republic, staff. **Publications:** The Next American Nation: The New Nationalism and the Fourth American Revolution, 1995; (intro.) The New Republic Guide to the Issues: The '96 Campaign, 1996; Powertown, 1996; Up from Conservatism: Why the Right is Wrong for America, 1996; (ed. and intro.) Hamilton's Republic: Readings in the American Democratic Nationalist Tradition, 1997; The Alamo: An Epic, 1997; Vietnam, the Necessary War: A Reinterpretation of America's Most Disastrous Military Conflict, 1999; (with T. Halstead) The Radical Center: The Future of American Politics, 2001; When You are Someone Else, 2002; Bluebonnet Girl, 2003; Made in Texas: George W. Bush and the Southern Takeover of American Politics, 2003; Poems, 2005; What Lincoln Believed: The Values and Convictions of America's Greatest President, 2005; American Way of Strategy, 2006; Parallel Lives, 2007. Contributor to periodicals. **Address:** New America Foundation, 1899 L St. NW, Ste. 400, Washington, DC 20036, U.S.A. **Online address:** lind@newamerica.net

LINDBECK, (K.) Assar (E.). Swedish (born Sweden), b. 1930. **Genres:** Economics. **Career:** Treasury Department, staff, 1953-54, Economic Secretariat, staff, 1955-56; University of Michigan, visiting assistant professor, 1958; University of Stockholm, lecturer, 1959-60, reader, 1962-63, acting professor of economics, 1963, professor of economics, 1964-71, Institute for International Economic Studies, director and professor of international economics, 1971-95, professor emeritus; Stockholm School of Economics, professor of economics, 1964-71; Bank of Sweden, economic adviser, 1964-68, 1972-74; Columbia University, Wesley Clair Mitchell research professor, 1968-69; University of California, Ford rotating research professor, 1969; Yale University, Irving Fisher visiting professor, 1976-77; Hoover Institution, visiting fellow, 1977; The World Bank, visiting researcher, 1986-87; University of Singapore, Lee Kuan Yew distinguished professor, 1987; International Monetary Fund, visiting researcher, 1990; University of Munich, Center for Economic Studies, visiting researcher, 1996. Consultant and writer. **Publications:** The New Theory of Credit Control in the United States: An Interpretation and Elaboration, 1959; A Study of Monetary Analysis, 1963; Monetary-Fiscal Analysis and General Equilibrium, 1967; Jordbrukspolitikens mål och medal, 1968; Jordbrusknäringens ekonomi, 1969; Den nya vänsterns politiska ekonomi, 1970; Samhällsekonomisk politik, 1971; (with Gulbrandsen) The Economics of the Agriculture Sector, 1971; The Political Economy of the New Left: An Outsider's View, 1971, 2nd ed., 1977; Søkelys på menneske og stat, 1972; Hyreskontroll och bostadsmarknad, 1972; Inflation and Employment in Swedish Economic Policy, 1972; (with J. Herin and J. Myhrman) Flexible Exchange Rates and Stabilization Policy, 1977; Fondfrågan, 1979; Inflation: Global, International and National Aspects, 1980; Ekonomi och mångfald, 1980; Makt och ekonomi: om fondfrågan, 1982; Hur mycket politik tål ekonomin?: högskattesamhällets problem, 1986; (with Snower) The Insider-Outsider Theory of Employment and Unemployment, 1988; Unemployment and Macroeconomics, 1993; Selected Essays of Assar Lindbeck, 1993; (co-author) Turning Sweden Around, 1994; West European Employment Problem, 1996; The Swedish Experiment, 1997; (co-author) Politisk makt med oklart ansvar: Ekonomirådets rapport 2000, 2000; European Social Model: Lessons for Developing Countries, 2002. **Address:** Institute for International Economic Studies, Stockholm University, Stockholm, 106 91, Sweden. **Online address:** assar@iies.su.se

LINDBERG, Staffan I. Swedish (born Sweden), b. 1969. **Genres:** Politics/Government. **Career:** Future of Civil Society Organisations, Ministry of Domestic Affairs, youth advisor, 1990; Lund University, researcher, 1997-98, Department of Political Science, research assistant, 1999, PGA/Parliament of Ghana, parliamentary fellow, 1999-2001, assistant professor, 2005; University College, lecturer, 1998-99; Kent State University, Department of Political Science, assistant professor, 2005-06; University of Florida, Department of Political Science, Center for African Studies, assistant professor, 2006-10, associate professor, 2010-; University of Gothenburg, Quality of Government Institute, research fellow, 2010-, Department of Political Science, research director, 2010-. Writer. **Publications:** (Ed. with Arni Sverrisson) Social Movements in Development: The Challenge of Globalization and Democratization, 1997; Democracy and Elections in Africa, 2006; (ed.) Democratization by Elections: A New Mode of Transition, 2009. Contributor of chapters and articles. **Address:** Department of Political Science, University of Florida, 234 Anderson Hall, PO Box 117325, Gainesville, FL 32611, U.S.A. **Online address:** lindberg@polisci.ufl.edu

LINDBERGH, Judith. American (born United States), b. 1963. **Genres:** Young Adult Fiction, Novels, Romance/Historical. **Career:** Writer and photographer. **Publications:** The Thrall's Tale, 2006. Contributor to periodicals. **Address:** c/o Author Mail, Viking Publicity, Penguin Group, 375 Hudson St., New York, NY 10014-3658, U.S.A. **Online address:** judith@judithlindbergh.com

LINDE, Paul R. American (born United States), b. 1961. **Genres:** Psychiatry. **Career:** San Francisco County Jails, contract psychiatrist, 1989-92; San Francisco General Hospital, Psychiatric Emergency Services, attending psychiatrist, 1992-93, 1995-; University of California, School of Medicine, clinical instructor, 1992-94, assistant clinical professor, 1994-2000, associate clinical professor, 2000-; Santa Clara Valley Medical Center, Consulting Psychiatrist Emergency Psychiatric Services, staff, 1993; Harare Central Hospital, consulting psychiatrist, 1994-95; University of Zimbabwe, honorary lecturer of psychiatry, 1994-95; California Pacific Medical Center, attending psychiatrist, 1997-99; STOP Clinic/Stonewall Project, attending psychiatrist, 2005-07, medical director, 2007-. Writer. **Publications:** Of Spirits and Madness: An American Psychiatrist in Africa, 2001; Danger to Self: On the Front Line with an ER Psychiatrist, 2010. Contributor to periodicals. **Address:** c/o Jane Dystel, Dystel and Goderich Agency, 1 Union Sq. W, New York, NY 10003, U.S.A. **Online address:** prlinde@hotmail.com

LINDELL, Colleen. American (born United States), b. 1963. **Genres:** Medicine/Health. **Career:** St. Croix Valley Memorial Hospital, registered nurse, 1984-85, director of surgical services and coordinator of Diabetes Program, 1987-96; St. John's Northeast Hospital, registered nurse, 1985-87; Med-Legal.net, president and consultant, 1996-, founder, 1996-; Medwave Inc., clinical coordinator, 1996-97; Magellan Medical Services, nurse consultant, 1996-97; Fairview Lakes Regions Medical Center, registered nurse, 1996-2001. Writer. **Publications:** Internet Medical and Health, Searching and Sources Guidebook, 1998. Contributor to periodicals. **Address:** Med-Legal.net Inc., 1828 45th Ave., Ste. 104, Osceola, WI 54020-5403, U.S.A. **Online address:** lindell@med-legal.net

LINDEMANN, Mary. American (born United States), b. 1949. **Genres:** History, Literary Criticism And History, Medicine/Health. **Career:** Carnegie Mellon University, professor of history; University of Miami, Department of History, professor, chair; Netherlands Institute for Advanced Study in the Humanities and Social Sciences, fellow-in-residence, 2002-03; Herzog August Bibliothek, fellow, 2006-07. Writer. **Publications:** 140 Jahre israelitisches Krankenhaus in Hamburg: Vorgeschichte und Entwicklung, 1981; Patriots and Paupers: Hamburg, 1712-1830, 1990; Health and Healing in Eighteenth-Century Germany, 1996; Medicine and Society in Early Modern Europe, 1999, 2nd ed. 2010; (ed.) Ways of Knowing: Ten Interdisciplinary Essays, 2004; Liaisons Dangereuses: Sex, Law and Diplomacy in the Age of Frederick the Great, 2006; Charlotte's Web: The Guyard Incest Case as History and Literature, forthcoming. **Address:** Department of History, University of Miami, Rm. 605, Ashe Administration Bldg., Coral Gables, FL 33124, U.S.A. **Online address:** mlindemann@miami.edu

LINDEN, David J. American (born United States), b. 1961. **Genres:** Sciences. **Career:** Johns Hopkins University School of Medicine, Department of Neuroscience, professor; Journal of Neurophysiology, chief editor, 2008-. **Publications:** The Accidental Mind: How Brain Evolution Has Given Us Love, Memory, Dreams and God, 2007; The Compass of Pleasure: How Our Brains Make Fatty Foods, Orgasm, Exercise, Marijuana, Generosity, Vodka, Learning and Gambling Feel So Good, 2011. **Address:** Solomon H. Snyder Department of Neuroscience, School of Medicine, Johns Hopkins University, 916 Hunterian Bldg., 725 N Wolfe St., Baltimore, MD 21205, U.S.A. **Online address:** dlinden@jhmi.edu

LINDENBAUM, Pija. Swedish (born Sweden), b. 1955. **Genres:** Children's Fiction, Illustrations, Science Fiction/Fantasy, Social Sciences. **Career:** Writer and illustrator. **Publications:** Elsi-Marie och småpapporna, 1991; Boken om Bodil, 1991; Else-Marie and her Seven Little Daddies, 1991; Boodil, My Dog, 1992; Britten och Prins Benny, 1996; Starke Arvid, 1997; Glossas Café, 1998; Gittan och gråvargarna, 2000; Gittan och färskallarna, 2001; Gittan och älgborsorna, 2003; Boken om Gittan, 2005; Nür åkes mamma glümde bort, 2005; Lill-Zlatan och morbror raring, 2006; When Owen's Mom Breathed Fire, 2006; Kenta och barbisarna, 2007; Mini Mia and her Darling Uncle, 2007; Ken and the Barbies, 2008; Siv sover vilse, 2009; Gittans hörihop-ett slags memoryspel, 2010; Gittan gömmer bort sej, 2011; Gittan-pussel och citat, 2011. **Address:** 3A Bjurholmsg, Stockholm, 116 38, Sweden.

LINDENMEYER, Kriste. (Kriste A. Lindenmeyer). American (born United States), b. 1955. **Genres:** History, Women's Studies And Issues, Politics/Government. **Career:** University of Cincinnati, adjunct assistant professor, 1991; Tennessee Technological University, assistant professor, 1991-96, associate professor of history, 1996-2000; Vanderbilt University, adjunct associate professor, 1997-98; University of Maryland, associate professor, 2000-06, professor of history, 2006-, department chair, 2005-, Kauffman Entrepreneurship Fellow, 2007-10. Writer, academic and historian. **Publications:** A Right to Childhood: The U.S. Children's Bureau and Child Welfare, 1912-46, 1997; (ed.) Ordinary Women, Extraordinary Lives: Women in American History, 2000; (ed. with A.E. Kersten) Politics and Progress: American Society and the State since 1865, 2001; The Greatest Generation Grows Up: American Childhood in the 1930s, 2005. Contributor to periodicals and journals. **Address:** Department of History, University of Maryland, Administration Bldg., 7th Fl., 1000 Hilltop Cir., Baltimore, MD 21250-0001, U.S.A. **Online address:** lindenme@umbc.edu

LINDENMEYER, Kriste A. See **LINDENMEYER, Kriste.**

LINDENMUTH, Kevin J. American (born United States), b. 1965. **Genres:** Plays/Screenplays, Film, How-to Books. **Career:** B Productions Inc., production manager, 1989-98; Brimstone Media Productions L.L.C., owner, 1992-, director and producer of PBS documentaries, 1998-2010; Independent genre films, director, 1992-2003. Writer. **Publications:** Making Movies on Your Own: Practical Talk from Independent Filmmakers, 1998; The Independent Film Experience: Interviews with Directors and Producers, 2002; The Documentary Moviemaking Course: The Starter Guide to Documentary Filmmaking, 2010. **Address:** Brimstone Media Productions L.L.C., 7900 State St., Brighton, MI 48116, U.S.A. **Online address:** kjlindenmuth@aol.com

LINDER, Marc. American (born United States), b. 1946?. **Genres:** Economics, Law, Translations, History, Politics/Government, Industrial Relations, Sociology, Novels, Novellas/Short Stories, Business/Trade/Industry. **Career:** Hohenheim University, research associate of project on the industrialization of agrarian regions, 1973-74; Roskilde University Center, lecturer in division of social sciences, 1974-77; National Autonomous University of Mexico, professor of economics, 1977; translator of German, Danish, Swedish, Norwegian, Polish, Dutch, Italian, French and Spanish, 1977-80; Texas Rural Legal Aid, attorney in farmworker division, 1983-90; University of Iowa, College of Law, visiting associate professor, 1990-92, associate professor of labor, 1992-94, professor, 1994-. Writer. **Publications:** (Trans.) J. Bobrowski, I Taste Bitterness (stories), 1970; Der Anti-Samuelson, 4 vols., 1974, trans. as Anti-Samuelson, 2 vols., 1977; Reification and the Consciousness of the Critics of Political Economy, 1975; (trans.) F. Wander, The Seventh Well (novel), 1976; European Labor Aristocracies, 1985; The Supreme Labor Court in Nazi Germany, 1987; The Employment Relationship in Anglo-American Law, 1989; Farewell to the Self-Employed: Deconstructing a Socioeconomic and Legal Solipsism, 1992; Migrant Workers and Minimum Wages: Regulating the Exploitation of Agricultural Labor in the United States, 1992; Projecting Capitalism: A History of the Internationalization of the Construction Industry, 1994; Labor Statistics and Class Struggle, 1994; The Dilemmas of Laissez-Faire Population Policy in Capitalist Societies, 1997; (with I. Nygard) Void Where Prohibited: Rest Breaks and the Right to Urinate on Company Time, 1998; (with L.S. Zacharias) Of Cabbages and Kings County: Agriculture and the Formation of Modern Brooklyn, 1999; Wars of Attrition: Vietnam, the Business Round Table and the Decline of the Construction Unions, 1999, 2nd ed., 2000; (trans., contrib. and intro.) H. Kirk, Fiskerne (title means: 'The Fisherman'), 1999, 2nd ed., 2000; Moments Are the Elements of Profit: Overtime and the Deregulation of Working Hours Under the Fair Labor Standards Act, 2000; (trans. and intro.) H. Kirk, Slaven (title means: 'The Slave'), 2000; (trans., contrib. and intro.) H. Kirk, Daglejerne (title means: 'The Day Laborers: The New Times'), 2001; (trans., contrib. and intro.) M. Klitgaard, Der sidder enmand I en sporvogn (title means: 'There's a Man Sitting on a Trolley'), 2001; (trans., contrib. and intro.) M. Klitgaard, Gud mildner luften for de klippedefaar (title means: 'God Tempers the Wind to Shorn the Lamb'), 2002; The Autocratically Flexible Workplace: A History of Overtime Regulation in the United States, 2002; Void Where Prohibited Revisited: The Trickle-Down Effect of OSHA's At-Will Bathroom-Break Regulation, 2003; Time and a Half's the American Way: A History of the Exclusion of White-Collar Workers from Overtime Regulation, 1868-2004, 2004. Works appear in anthologies. Contributor of articles to journals. **Address:** College of Law, University of Iowa, 458 Boyd Law Bldg., Iowa City, IA 52242-1113, U.S.A. **Online address:** marc-linder@uiowa.edu

LINDER, Robert D. American (born United States), b. 1934. **Genres:** History, Humanities, Politics/Government. **Career:** William Jewell College, assistant professor of history, 1963-65; Kansas State University, associate professor, 1965-73, professor of history, 1973-2003, university distinguished professor of history, 2003-. Writer. **Publications:** The Political Ideas of Pierre Viret, 1964; (co-ed.) Protest and Politics: Christianity and Contemporary Affairs, 1968; (ed. with R.M. Kingdon) Calvin and Calvinism: Sources of Democracy?, 1970; (ed.) God and Caesar: Case Studies in the Relationship of Christianity and the State, 1971; (contrib.) The Westminster Dictionary of Church History, 1971; (ed. with R.G. Clouse and R.V. Pierard) The Cross and the Flag, 1972; (with R.V. Pierard) Politics: A Case for Christian Action, 1973; (contrib.) A Dictionary of Christian Ethics, 1973; (co-ed.) Eerdman's Handbook to the History of Christianity, 1977; (with R.V. Pierard) Twilight of the Saints: Biblical Christianity and Civil Religion in America, 1978; (with R.V. Pierard) Civil Religion and the Presidency, 1988; (co-ed.) A Dictionary of Christianity in America, 1990; (co-ed.) The History of Christianity, 1990; (co-ed.) A Concise Dictionary of Christianity in America, 1995; (co-ed.) Introduction to the History of Christianity, 2002, rev. ed., 2006; (ed. with G.R. Treloar) Making History for God: Essays on Evangelicalism, Revival and Mission: In Honour of Stuart Piggin, Master of Robert Menzies College, 1990-2004, 2004; The Reformation Era, 2008. Contributor to books and journals. **Address:** Department of History, Kansas State University, 205 Eisenhower Hall, Manhattan, KS 66506-1000, U.S.A. **Online address:** rdl@ksu.edu

LINDGREN, Barbro. Swedish (born Sweden), b. 1937. **Genres:** Children's Fiction, Poetry. **Career:** Commercial artist and designer; writer, 1965-. **Publications:** FOR CHILDREN: Mattias sommar (title means: 'Mattias's Summer'), 1965, trans. as Hilding's Summer, 1967; Mera om Mattias, 1966; Hej, hej Mattias, 1967; I Vaestan Grind, 1968; Loranga, Masarin och Dartanjang, 1969; Loranga, Loranga, 1970; Nu har Kalle faat en liten syster, 1970; Jaettehemligt, 1971; Goda goda: Dikter, 1971, rev. ed., 1976; Nu aer vi gorillor lassas vi, 1971, trans. as Let's Be Gorillas!, 1976; Vaerldshemligt, 1972; Alban: popmuffa foer sma hundar, 1972, rev. ed., 2004, trans. as Alban, 1974;

Bladen brinner, 1973, rev. ed., 1978; Groengoelingen aer paa vaeg: Dikter foer barn och andra, 1974; Barbros pjaeser foer barn och andra, 1975, rev. ed., 1978; Molnens bröder, 1975; Vad tycker du?, 1976; Lilla Sparvel, 1976; Rapporter från marken, 1976; Stora Sparvel, 1977; (with L. Westman) Hemliga Laadans Hemlighet, 1978; (with Westman) Jag har en tam myra, 1978; (with Westman) Kom ner fraan traedet, 1978; (with Westman) Var aer mina byxor?, 1978; (with Westman) Vaerldens laengsta korv, 1978; (with Westman) Laesa med varandra, 1978; Garderobsbio, 1978; Bara Sparvel, 1979; Sagan om den lilla farbrorn, 1979, trans. as The Story of the Little Old Man, 1991; Nils Pantaloni Penell, 1980; Fotograf Jag, 1980; Mamman och den vilda bebin, 1980; Max nalle, 1981, trans. as Sam's Teddy Bear, 1982 in UK as Sam's Teddy, 1984; Max bil, 1981, trans. as Sam's Car, 1982; Max kaka, 1981, trans. as Sam's Cookie, 1982 in UK as Sam's Biscuit, 1984; Den vilda bebiresan, 1982 in UK as The Wild Baby's Boat Trip, 1983; Max Boll, 1982, trans. as Sam's Ball, 1983; Max Lampa, 1982, trans. as Sam's Lamp, 1983 in UK as Bad Sam!, 1983; Max Balja, 1982, trans. as Sam's Bath, 1983; Pompe badar I en a, 1982; Pompe gar I skogen, 1982; OBS! Viktigt!, 1983, 2nd ed., 1990; Sagan om Karlknut, 1985, trans. as A Worm's Tale, 1988; Vilda bebin får en hund, 1985, trans. as The Wild Baby's Dog, 1986; Max Potta, 1986, trans. as Sam's Potty, 1986; Max Dockvagn, 1986, trans. as Sam's Wagon, 1986 in UK as Sam's Cart, 1986; Vems lilla moessa flyger, 1987; Pellerell, 1987; Sunkan flyger, 1989, trans. as Shorty Takes Off, 1990; Korken Flyger, 1990; Stackars Allan, 1990; Pojken och stjarnan, 1991; Titta Max grav, 1991; Jam-Jam Jb-Jb, 1992; Stora Syster, Lille Bror, 1992; Bara Boerje, 1992, trans. as Louie, 1994; Puss Puss Sant Sant, 1993; Jag säjer bara Elitchoklad: prosastycken, 1993; Gomorron Gud, 1994; Har ar Det Lilla Huset, 1994; Max Napp, 1994; Max Bloja, 1994; Svempa vill ha manga nappar, 1995; Lilla Lokomotivet Rosa, 1995, trans. as Rosa, Perpetual Motion Machine, 1996; Rosa Flyttar Till Stan, 1996; Loranga: del ett & två: en samlingsvolym, 1996; Rosa Pa Bal, 1997; Na ar vi jobbarkaniner, 1997; (with A. Höglund) Nu är vi jobbarkaniner, 1997; Andrejs langtan, 1997, trans. as Andrei's Search, 2000; Namen Benny, 1998, trans. as Benny's Had Enough, 1999; Per och Pompe, 1998; Rosa pa dagis, 1999, trans. as Rosa Goes to Daycare, 2000; Prinsessan Rosa, 1999; Angeln Gunnar dimper ner, 2000; Vi leker att du ar en humla, 2000; Jamen Benny, 2001, trans. as Benny and the Binky, 2002; Tre fugor av Bach, 2001; Graddbullarna Bulle och Rulle, Julia vill ha ett djur, 2002, trans. as Julia Wants a Pet, 2003; Rosas sanger (Songs of Rosa), 2004. FOR ADULTS: Genom Ventilerna, 1967. OTHERS: Felipe, 1970; Eldvin, 1972; Çîroka apoyê hûrik, 2000; Julia Wants a Pet, 2003; Nöff nöff Benny, 2007; Oink, Oink Benny, 2008; Om sorgen och den lilla glädjen, 2009; Apans ABC, 2010. Contributor to periodicals. **Address:** Raben & Sjoegren, Tryckerigatan 4, PO Box 2052, Stockholm, 103 12, Sweden. **Online address:** info@eriksson-lindgren.se

LINDGREN, David T(readwell). American (born United States), b. 1939. **Genres:** Technology. **Career:** Central Intelligence Agency, imagery analyst, 1964-66; Dartmouth College, professor of geography and department head, 1966-2001, now professor emeritus; Central Intelligence Agency, consultant; National Aeronautics and Space Administration, consultant; U.S. Department of the Interior, consultant. Writer. **Publications:** (With R.B. Simpson and W. Goldstein) Land Use Change Detection in the Boston and New Haven Areas, 1970-72, 1974; Land Use Planning and Remote Sensing, 1985; Trust but Verify: Imagery Analysis in the Cold War, 2000; In All Good Conscience, 2007; No Ordinary Summer, forthcoming. **Address:** Department of Geography, Dartmouth College, 6017 Fairchild, Hanover, NH 03755, U.S.A. **Online address:** david.lindgren@dartmouth.edu

LINDGREN, James M. American (born United States), b. 1950. **Genres:** History. **Career:** Old Dominion University, instructor in history, 1978-79, 1980; State University of New York, Department of History, assistant professor, 1984-91, associate professor, 1991-94, professor of history, 1994-, chair, 2001-04. Writer. **Publications:** Preserving the Old Dominion: Historic Preservation and Virginia Traditionalism, 1993; Preserving New England: Preservation, Progressivism and the Remaking of Memory, 1995. Contributor to journals. Works appear in anthologies. **Address:** Department of History, State University of New York, 322 Champlain Valley Hall, Plattsburgh, NY 12901, U.S.A. **Online address:** lindgrjm@plattsburgh.edu

LINDHOLDT, Paul J. American (born United States), b. 1954. **Genres:** Literary Criticism And History, Environmental Sciences/Ecology, Poetry, Language/Linguistics, Intellectual History, Essays, Autobiography/Memoirs, Communications/Media, Writing/Journalism. **Career:** Western Washington University, Fairhaven College, lecturer, 1980-81, 1987-90; Pennsylvania State University, teaching assistant, 1981-84; Idaho State University, lecturer in English, 1984-87; University of Idaho, visiting assistant professor of English, 1990-94; Eastern Washington University, lecturer, 1994-97, assistant professor, 1997-2003, associate professor, 2003-07, Department of English, professor, 2007-. Writer. **Publications:** (Ed. and intro.) John Josselyn, Colonial Traveler: A Critical Edition of Two Voyages to New-England, 1988; (ed. with M. Friedman) Cascadia Wild: Protecting an International Ecosystem, 1993; (ed. and intro.) History and Folklore of the Cowichan Indians, by Martha Douglas Harris, 2004; (ed. and intro. with D. Knowles) Holding Common Ground: The Individual and Public Lands in the American West, 2005; (ed. and intro.) The Canoe and the Saddle: A Critical Edition, 2006; In Earshot of Water: Notes from the Columbia Plateau, 2011. **Address:** Department of English, Eastern Washington University, 250 PAT, Cheney, WA 99004, U.S.A. **Online address:** plindholdt@mail.ewu.edu

LINDISFARNE, Nancy. *See* **LINDISFARNE-TAPPER, Nancy.**

LINDISFARNE-TAPPER, Nancy. Also writes as Nancy Starr Self, Nancy Lindisfarne, Nancy Tapper. British/American (born United States), b. 1944. **Genres:** Novellas/Short Stories, Anthropology/Ethnology, Adult Non-fiction, Social Sciences. **Career:** University of London, King's College, Department of History and Philosophy of Religion, faculty. Writer. **Publications:** (As Nancy Tapper) Bartered Brides: Politics, Gender and Marriage in an Afghan Tribal Society, 1991; (ed. as Nancy Lindisfarne with A. Cornwall) Dislocating Masculinity: Comparative Ethnographies, 1994; (ed. as Nancy Lindisfarne-Tapper with B. Ingham) Languages of Dress in the Middle East, 1997; (as Nancy Lindisfarne) Dancing in Damascus, 2000; (as Nancy Lindisfarne) Elhamdülillah laikiz: cinsiyet, Islâm ve Türk cumhuriyetçiligi=Thank God, We're Secular: Gender, Islam and Turkish Republicanism, 2002. Contributor to journals. Works appear in anthologies. **Address:** Department of Anthropology & Sociology, London School of Oriental & African Studies, University of London, Thornhaugh St., Russell Sq., London, GL WC1H 0XG, England.

LINDNER, Koenraad J(an). Chinese/Dutch (born Netherlands), b. 1941. **Genres:** Medicine/Health. **Career:** State University of New York College, assistant professor, 1973-74; University of Manitoba, assistant professor, associate professor, 1974-96; University of Hong Kong, sport psychology, lecturer, senior lecturer, 1993-, associate professor, now retired. Writer. **Publications:** (Ed. with D.J. Caine and C.G. Caine) Epidemiology of Sports Injuries, 1996; (with J.H. Kerr and M. Blaydon) Exercise Dependence, 2007. **Address:** Physical Education & Sports Science Unit, University of Hong Kong, 111 Pokfulam Rd., Hong Kong, 1, China. **Online address:** klindner@hku.hk

LINDQUIST, N(ancy) J(ane). Canadian (born Canada), b. 1948. **Genres:** Mystery/Crime/Suspense, Young Adult Fiction, Plays/Screenplays, Young Adult Non-fiction, Novels. **Career:** Teacher, 1970-72; Markham Economist-Sun, writer, editor and columnist, 1989-; The Word Guild, co-founder and executive director, 2001-; Joy Equipping Ministries, co-director; LoveJoy Ministries, co-director; That's Life! Communications, partner; motivational speaker, 2005-. **Publications:** MANZIUK AND RYAN MYSTERY SERIES: Shaded Light, 1999; Glitter of Diamonds, 2007. NOVELS FOR YOUNG ADULTS: The Best of Friends, 1991, rev. ed., 2000; In Time of Trouble, 1999; Friends Like These, 2000; Friends in Need, 2001; More Than Friends, 2004. NONFICTION: The Bridge, vol. I, 1998, vol. II, 1999; (co-author) The New You, 2000; Behind the News: Report from Bethlehem, 2001; (ed. with W.E. Nelles) Hot Apple Cider: Words to Stir the Heart and Warm the Soul, 2008; (ed. with W.E. Nelles) A Second Cup of Hot Apple Cider: Words to Stimulate the Mind and Delight the Spirit, 2011. Contributor articles to magazines. **Address:** The Word Guild, PO Box 487, Markham, ON L3P 3R1, Canada. **Online address:** author@njlindquist.com

LINDSAY, D. Michael. American (born United States), b. 1971?. **Genres:** Theology/Religion. **Career:** George H. Gallup International Institute, consultant for religion and culture, 1998-2003; Princeton Theological Seminary, visiting professor, 2003; New Brunswick Theological Seminary, visiting assistant professor, 2005; Rice University, assistant professor of sociology, 2006-, faculty associate of Leadership Rice, 2006-, Center on Race, Religion and Urban Life, assistant director, 2006-09, Kinder Institute for Urban Research, director, 2010-. Writer. **Publications:** (With G. Gallup) Surveying the Religious Landscape: Trends in U.S. Beliefs, 1999; (with G.H. Gallup) The Gallup Guide: Reality Check for 21st Century Churches, 2002; Faith in the Halls of Power: How Evangelicals Joined the American Elite, 2007. Contributor of articles to journals. **Address:** Department of Sociology, Rice University, MS-28, 6100 Main St., PO Box 1892, Houston, TX 77005-1827, U.S.A. **Online**

address: mlindsay@rice.edu

LINDSAY, Frederic. Scottish (born Scotland), b. 1933. **Genres:** Novels, Plays/Screenplays, Poetry, Young Adult Fiction, Children's Fiction, Mystery/Crime/Suspense. **Career:** Annan Academy, instructor in English, 1960-66; Hamilton College of Education, lecturer in English and applied linguistics, 1966-78; writer, 1979-; Scottish PEN, vice-president. **Publications:** And Be the Nation Again (poems), 1975. NOVELS: Brond, 1984; Jill Rips, 1987; A Charm Against Drowning, 1988; After the Stranger Came, 1992; Kissing Judas, 1997; A Kind of Dying, 1998; Idle Hands, 1999; Death Knock, 2000; Darkness in My Hand, 2001; The Endings Man, 2005; My Life As A Man, 2006; Tremor of Demons, 2007; The Stranger from Home, 2008. Contributor to periodicals. **Address:** 28 The Green, Pencaitland, East Lothian, EH34 5HE, Scotland. **Online address:** frederic.lindsay@hotmail.com

LINDSAY, Geoff. British (born England) **Genres:** Education, How-to Books. **Career:** British Psychological Society, president and honorary treasurer; Sheffield Local Education Authority, senior educational psychologist; University of Warwick, Institute of Education, inaugural chair of special needs education and educational psychology, 1995-, professor, Centre for Educational Development, Appraisal and Research, director, 1999-, Special Educational Needs, coordinator, Psychology and Special Needs Research Unit, director, Centre for Education and Industry, director, 2010-. Writer. **Publications:** (With L. Pearson) Special Needs in the Primary School: Identification and Intervention, 1986; (with P. Clough) Integration and the Support Service: Changing Roles in Special Education, 1991, (co-author) Ethics for European psychologists, 2008. EDITOR: Problems of Adolescence in the Secondary School, 1983; Screening for Children with Special Needs: Multidisciplinary Approaches, 1984; (with A. Miller) Psychological Services for Primary Schools, 1991; (with D. Thompson) Values into Practice in Special Education, 1997; (with M. Desforges) Baseline Assessment: Practice, Problems and Possibilities, 1998; (with A. Lewis) Researching Children's Perspectives, 2000. **Address:** Institute of Education, University of Warwick, Rm. WE145, Coventry, WM CV4 7AL, England. **Online address:** geoff.lindsay@warwick.ac.uk

LINDSAY, James. (James M. Lindsay). American (born United States), b. 1959. **Genres:** Novels, Cultural/Ethnic Topics, Politics/Government, Philosophy. **Career:** University of Iowa, Department of Political Science, instructor, 1987-88, assistant professor, 1988-92, associate professor, 1992-95, professor of political science, 1995-99; National Security Council, director for global issues and multilateral affairs, 1996-97; Brookings Institution, Foreign Policy Studies Program, senior fellow, 1999-2003, deputy director, 2003; United States Commission on National Security/21st Century, consultant, 2000-01; Council on Foreign Relations Inc., vice president, director of studies and Maurice R. Greenberg Chair, 2003-06, senior vice president, director of studies and Maurice R. Greenberg Chair, 2009-; United States Institute of Peace, Task Force on United Nation Reform, staff expert, 2005; University of Texas, Lyndon B. Johnson School of Public Affairs, Tom Slick chair for international affairs, 2006-09, Robert S. Strauss Center for International Security and Law, director, 2006-09. Writer. **Publications:** AS JAMES M. LINDSAY: Congress and Nuclear Weapons, 1991; Great Philosophical Problems, 1992; (ed. with R.B. Ripley) Congress Resurgent: Foreign and Defense Policy on Capitol Hill, 1993; Congress and the Politics of U.S. Foreign Policy, 1994; (with P. Squire, C.R. Covington and E.R. Smith) Dynamics of Democracy, 1995, 6th ed., 2009; (ed. with R.B. Ripley) U.S. Foreign Policy after the Cold War, 1997; (with M.E. O'Hanlon) Defending America: The Case for Limited National Missile Defense, 2001; America Abroad: American Foreign Policy, 2002; (co-author) Protecting the American Homeland: One Year On, 2003; (ed.) American Politics after September 11, 2003, 2nd ed., 2004; (with I.H. Daalder) America Unbound: The Bush Revolution in Foreign Policy, 2003; (ed. with H.J. Aaron and P.S. Nivola) Agenda for the Nation, 2003. **Address:** Council on Foreign Relations, 1777 F St. NW, Washington, DC 20006, U.S.A. **Online address:** jlindsay@cfr.org

LINDSAY, James M. *See* **LINDSAY, James.**

LINDSAY, John. *See* **LADELL, John L.**

LINDSAY, Sarah. American (born United States), b. 1958. **Genres:** Poetry. **Career:** Pace Communications, copy editor. **Publications:** POETRY: Bodies of Water, 1986; Insomniac's Lullaby, 1989; Primate Behavior, 1997; Mount Clutter, 2000; Twigs & Knucklebones, 2008. Contributor to books and periodicals. **Address:** Copper Canyon Press, PO Box 271, Port Townsend, WA 98368, U.S.A. **Online address:** sarah.lindsay@paceco.com

LINDSAY, William. British (born England), b. 1956?. **Genres:** Children's Fiction, Animals/Pets. **Career:** Writer. **Publications:** The Great Dinosaur Atlas, 1991; Tyrannosaurus, 1992; Barosaurus, 1992; Corythosaurus, 1993; Triceratops, 1993; Prehistoric Life, 1994; Dinosaurs, 1995, 2nd ed., 2003; On the Trail of Incredible Dinosaurs, 1998; (with N. Clark) 1,001 Facts about Dinosaurs, 2002. **Address:** c/o Author Mail, Dorling Kindersley Ltd., 80 Strand, London, GL WC2R ORL, England.

LINDSAY-POLAND, John. American (born United States), b. 1960. **Genres:** Civil Liberties/Human Rights, Adult Non-fiction, Social Commentary. **Career:** Peace Brigades Intl., peace team staff, Colombia Project, co-founder; Fellowship of Reconciliation, Task Force on Latin America and the Caribbean, research and advocacy director, 1989-, Colombia Update, editor. **Publications:** (With T. Barry, Gandásegui and P. Simonson) Inside Panama: The Essential Guide to Its Politics, Economy, Society, and Environment, 1995; Emperors in the Jungle: The Hidden History of the U.S. in Panama, 2003; Poligonos de tiro: pasado, presente y futuro del proceso de saneamiento de bases militares y otras areas y bienes utilizados por Estados Unidos en la republica de Panama, 2007; Military Assistance and Human Rights: Colombia, U.S. Accountability and Global Implications, 2010. Contributor to periodicals. **Address:** Fellowship of Reconciliation, PO Box 271, Nyack, NY 10960, U.S.A. **Online address:** johnlp@forusa.org

LINDSEY, Brink. American (born United States) **Genres:** Economics, Adult Non-fiction, Social Commentary, Money/Finance, Politics/Government. **Career:** Regulation (magazine), senior editor; Cato Institute, director of regulatory studies, Center for Trade Policy Studies, director, 1998-2004, vice president for research, 2004-; Cato Unbound, senior editor and founder, 2005-. Political scientist and attorney. **Publications:** Against the Dead Hand: The Uncertain Struggle for Global Capitalism, 2002; (with D.J. Ikenson) Antidumping Exposed: The Devilish Details of Unfair Trade Law, 2003; The Age of Abundance: How Prosperity Transformed America's Politics and Culture, 2007; Paul Krugman's Nostalgianomics: Economic Policies, Social Norms, and Income Inequality, 2009. Contributor to periodicals. **Address:** Cato Institute, 1000 Massachusetts Ave. NW, Washington, DC 20001-5403, U.S.A. **Online address:** blindsey@cato.org

LINDSEY, Johanna. American/German (born Germany), b. 1952. **Genres:** Romance/Historical, Young Adult Fiction. **Career:** Writer, 1975-. **Publications:** Captive Bride, 1977; A Pirate's Love, 1978; Fires of Winter, 1980; Paradise Wild, 1981; Glorious Angel, 1982; So Speaks the Heart, 1983; Heart of Thunder, 1983; A Gentle Feuding, 1984; Brave the Wild Wind, 1984; Love Only Once, 1985; Tender is the Storm, 1985; A Heart So Wild, 1986; When Love Awaits, 1986; Hearts Aflame, 1987; Secret Fire, 1987; Tender Rebel, 1988; Silver Angel, 1988; Defy not the Heart, 1989; Savage Thunder, 1989; Warrior's Woman, 1990; Gentle Rogue, 1990; Once a Princess, 1991; Prisoner of My Desire, 1991; Man of My Dreams, 1992; Angel, 1992; The Magic of You, 1993; Keeper of the Heart, 1993; Surrender My Love, 1994; You Belong to Me, 1994; Until Forever, 1995; Love Me Forever, 1995; Say You Love Me, 1996; All I Need is You 1997; Pirate's Love, 1997; The Present: A Malory Holiday Novel, 1998 as The Holiday Present, 2003; Joining, 1999; The Heir, 2000; Home for the Holidays, 2000; Heart of a Warrior, 2001; Prisoner of my Desire, 2002; The Pursuit, 2002; A Man to Call My Own, 2003; A Loving Scoundrel: A Malory Novel, 2004; Marriage Most Scandalous, 2005; Captive of My Desires, 2006; The Devil Who Tamed Her, 2007; No Choice But Seduction, 2008; Rogue of my Own, 2009; That Perfect Someone, 2010; When Passion Rules, 2011. **Address:** c/o Author Mail, Publicity Department, Atria Books, 1230 Ave. of the Americas, New York, NY 10020, U.S.A.

LINDSKOLD, Jane M. American (born United States), b. 1962. **Genres:** Novels, Biography, Novellas/Short Stories, Young Adult Fiction. **Career:** Lynchburg College, assistant professor, 1989-94; writer, 1994-. **Publications:** NONFICTION: Roger Zelazny, 1993; Chronomaster: The Official Strategy Guide, 1996. NOVELS: Brother to Dragons, Companion to Owls, 1994; Marks of Our Brothers, 1995; Pipes of Orpheus, 1995; Roger Zelazny and Jane Lindskold's Chronomaster: A Novel, 1996; Smoke and Mirrors, 1996; Roger Zelazny and Jane Lindskold's Chronomaster: The Offical Strategy Guide, 1996; (with R. Zelazny) Donnerjack, 1997; Changer: A Novel of the Athanor, 1998; (with R. Zelazny) Lord Demon, 1999; Legends Walking: A Novel of the Athanor, 1999; The Buried Pyramid, 2004; Child of a Rainless Year,

2005; Thirteen Orphans, 2008; Nine Gates, 2009; Five Odd Honors, 2010. THROUGH WOLF'S EYES SERIES: Through Wolf's Eyes, 2001; Wolf's Head, Wolf's Heart, 2002; The Dragon of Despair, 2003; Wolf Captured, 2004; Wolf Hunting, 2006; Wolf's Blood, 2007. CAPTAIN AH-LEE SERIES: Endpoint Insurance, 2011; Here to There, 2011; Star Messenger, 2011; Winner Takes Trouble, 2011. Works appear in anthologies. **Address:** c/o Kay McCauley, Pimlico Agency Inc., PO Box 20490, Dag Hammarskjold Sta., New York, NY 10017, U.S.A. **Online address:** janel@janelindskold.com

LINDSTROM, Lamont (Carl). American (born United States), b. 1953. **Genres:** Anthropology/Ethnology, Autobiography/Memoirs. **Career:** Southwestern at Memphis, visiting assistant professor, 1981-82; University of Tulsa, assistant professor, 1982-88, associate professor, 1988-92, professor of anthropology, 1992-, Kendall professor of anthropology, department chair, 1991-95, Department of Sociology, acting chair, 1991-92; East-West Center, Institute of Culture and Communication, fellow, 1987-88; National Endowment for the Humanities, seminar director, 1991, 1993; University of California, visiting professor of anthropology, 1999. Writer. **Publications:** Kwamera Dictionary: Nikukua Savai Nagkiariien Nininife, 1986; Drugs in Western Pacific Societies: Relations of Substance (monograph), 1987; (ed. with G.M. White and contrib.) The Pacific Theater: Island Representations of World War II, 1989; (with G.M. White) Island Encounters: Black and White Memories of the Pacific War, 1990; Knowledge and Power in a South Pacific Society, 1990; (with V. Lebot and M. Merlin) Kava: The Pacific Drug, 1992; Cargo Cult: Strange Stories of Desire From Melanesia and Beyond, 1993; (ed. with G.M. White) Chiefs Today: Traditional Pacific Leadership and the Postcolonial State, 1997; (ed. with J. Gwero) Big Wok: Storian Blong Wol Wo Tu long Vanuatu, 1998. Contributor of articles to journals. **Address:** Department of Anthropology, University of Tulsa, Harwell Hall, 2nd Fl., 600 S College Ave., Tulsa, OK 74104, U.S.A. **Online address:** lamont-lindstrom@utulsa.edu

LINDVALL, Michael L(loyd). American (born United States), b. 1947. **Genres:** Theology/Religion, Documentaries/Reportage, Novels, Literary Criticism And History, Young Adult Fiction. **Career:** Drayton Avenue Presbyterian Church, associate pastor, 1974-79; First Presbyterian Church of Northport, pastor, 1979-92; First Presbyterian Church of Ann Arbor, senior pastor, 1992-; Brick Presbyterian Church, pastor, 2002-, senior pastor. Writer. **Publications:** The Good News from North Haven: A Year in the Life of a Small Town, 1991; Leaving North Haven, 2001; The Christian Life: A Geography of God, 2001; What did Jesus Do?: A Crash Course in his Life and Times, 2006; Geography of God: Exploring the Christian Journey, 2007; Knowing God's Triune Story, 2010. Contributor of short stories to periodicals. **Address:** The Brick Presbyterian Church, 62 E 92nd St., New York, NY 10128-1398, U.S.A.

LINDVALL, Terence R. *See* **LINDVALL, Terry R.**

LINDVALL, Terry R. (Terence R. Lindvall). American/Swiss (born Switzerland), b. 1948. **Genres:** Theology/Religion. **Career:** CBN/Regent University, film faculty, 1978-, president, 1993-94, distinguished chair of visual communication; William and Mary, faculty, Walter Mason Fellow of Religious Studies; Duke University, faculty; Virginia Wesleyan University, faculty, C.S. Lewis Chair of Communication and Christian Thought. Army chaplain, ordained congregational minister and writer. **Publications:** Surprised by Laughter: The Comic World of C.S. Lewis, 1996; (comp.) The Silents of God: Selected Issues and Documents in Silent American Film and Religion, 1908-1925, 2001; The Mother of All Laughter: Sarah & the Genesis of Comedy, 2003; Sanctuary Cinema: Origins of the Christian Film Industry, 2007. **Address:** VA , U.S.A. **Online address:** tlindvall@vwc.edu

LINEBAUGH, Peter. American (born United States), b. 1942?. **Genres:** Social Sciences. **Career:** University of Massachusetts, faculty; Harvard University, faculty; Tufts University, faculty; Franconia College, history professor, 1973-; University of Rochester, history faculty, 1976-82; Trinity College, history faculty, 1993-94; University of Toledo, professor of history, 1994-; Bard College, visiting professor of history, 2000-05. Writer. **Publications:** (Co-ed.) Albion's Fatal Tree: Crime and Society in Eighteenth-Century England, 1975; The London Hanged: Crime and Civil Society in the Eighteenth Century, 1992, 2nd ed., 2006; (with M. Rediker) The Many-Headed Hydra: Sailors, Slaves, Commoners, and the Hidden History of the Revolutionary Atlantic, 2000; The Magna Carta Manifesto: Liberties and Commons for All, 2008; (intro.) Peter Linebaugh Presents Thomas Paine: Common Sense, Rights of Man and Agrarian Justice, 2009. Contributor to periodicals. **Address:** Department of History, University of Toledo, 2801 Bancroft, Toledo, OH 43606-3390, U.S.A. **Online address:** plineba@yahoo.com

LING, Peter J(ohn). British (born England), b. 1956. **Genres:** Civil Liberties/Human Rights, History, Race Relations, Technology, Transportation. **Career:** Lancashire Polytechnic, lecturer in history, 1984-86; Leicester Polytechnic, lecturer in history, 1986-88; Edge Hill College of Higher Education, lecturer in history, 1988-89; University of Nottingham, lecturer, 1989-96, senior lecturer in American studies, 1996-, professor of American studies. Writer. **Publications:** America and the Automobile: Technology, Reform, and Social Change, 1990; (ed. with S. Monteith) Gender in the Civil Rights Movement, 1999; TransAtlantic Encounters, 2000; Martin Luther King, Jr., 2002; Democratic Party: A Photographic History, 2003. Contributor of articles to professional journals. **Address:** Department of American Studies, University of Nottingham, Rm. B66 Trent, University Park, Nottingham, NG7 2RD, England. **Online address:** peter.ling@nottingham.ac.uk

LING, Roger (John). British (born England), b. 1942. **Genres:** Archaeology/Antiquities, Architecture, Art/Art History, Classics. **Career:** University of Wales, University College of Swansea, lecturer in classics, 1967-71; University of Manchester, lecturer, senior lecturer, 1971-83, reader in history of art, 1983-92, Department of History of Art, head, 1988-91, professor of classical art and archaeology, 1992-2010, professor emeritus 2010-, Archaeological Society, president, 1999-2004; British School at Rome, faculty member, 1974-78, 1981-85; Association Internationale pour la Peinture Murale Antique, president, 2001-02; Association for the Study and Preservation of Roman Mosaics, chairman, 2000-11. Writer. **Publications:** The Greek World, 1976; (with N. Davey) Wall-Painting in Roman Britain, 1982; (ed.) The Hellenistic World to the Coming of the Romans, 1984; Romano-British Wall Painting, 1985; Classical Greece, 1988; Roman Painting, 1991; The Insula of the Menander at Pompeii, vol. I: The Structures, 1997, (with L.A. Ling) vol. II: The Decorations, 2005; Ancient Mosaics, 1998; Stuccowork and Painting in Roman Italy, 1999; (ed.) Making Classical Art: Process and Practice, 2000; Pompeii: History, Life and Afterlife, 2005. Contributor to books and journals. **Address:** Department of Archaeology & Art History, School of Arts, Histories & Cultures, University of Manchester, Mansfield Cooper Bldg. 3.21, Manchester, GM M13 9PL, England. **Online address:** roger.ling@manchester.ac.uk

LINGARD, Jeanette. Australian (born Australia) **Genres:** Literary Criticism And History, Philosophy, History. **Career:** University of Sydney, Southeast Asian Studies, associate lecturer. Writer and translator. **Publications:** (Trans. and intro.) Diverse Lives: Contemporary Stories from Indonesia, 1995. **Address:** Department of Southeast Asian Studies, University of Sydney, City Rd., Sydney, NW 2006, Australia.

LINGARD, Joan (Amelia). Scottish/British (born England), b. 1932. **Genres:** Novels, Children's Fiction, Plays/Screenplays, Adult Non-fiction, Picture/Board Books, Young Adult Fiction, Horror. **Career:** Educator, 1948-61; writer, 1963-. **Publications:** NOVELS: Liam's Daughter, 1963; The Prevailing Wind, 1964; The Tide Comes In, 1966; The Headmaster, 1967; A Sort of Freedom, 1969; The Lord on Our Side, 1970; The Second Flowering of Emily Mountjoy, 1979; Greenyards, 1981; Sisters by Rite, 1984; Reasonable Doubts, 1986; The Women's House, 1989; Clever Clive, 1993; After Colette, 1993; Slow Flo, 1994; The Kiss, 2002. JUVENILE NOVELS: Frying as Usual, 1973; No Place for Love, 1976; Snake among the Sunflowers, 1977; The Gooseberry, 1978 in US as The Odd Girl Out, 1979; The File on Fraulein Berg, 1980; The Winter Visitor, 1983; Strangers in the House, 1983; The Freedom Machine, 1986; The Guilty Party, 1987; Rags and Riches, 1988; Glad Rags, 1990; Hands off Our School!, 1992; Night Fires, 1993; Lizzie's Leaving, 1995; Dreams of Love and Modest Glory, 1995. KEVIN AND SADIE JUVENILE SERIES: The Twelfth Day of July, 1970; Across the Barricades, 1972; Into Exile, 1973; A Proper Place, 1975; Hostages to Fortune, 1977. MAGGIE JUVENILE SERIES: The Clearance, 1974; The Resettling, 1975; The Pilgrimage, 1976; The Reunion, 1978. LATVIAN PETERSONS JUVENILE SERIES: Tug of War, 1990; Between Two Worlds, 1991. TILLY SERIES: Tilly and the Wild Goats, 2005; Tilly and the Badgers, 2006. OTHERS: Can You Find Sammy the Hamster?, 1990; (with P. Casey) Morag and the Lamb, 1990; Secrets, 1991; Sulky Suzy, Jittery Jack, 1996; A Secret Place, 1998; Dark Shadows, 1998; John and the Treehouse, 1998; Tom and the Tree House, 1998; The Egg Thieves, 1999; Natasha's Will, 2000; River Eyes, 2000; Me and My Shadow, 2001; The Same Only Different, 2001; Tortoise Trouble, 2002; Tell the Moon to Come Out, 2003; The Sign of the

Black Dagger, 2005; Encarnita's Journey, 2005; After You've Gone, 2007; The Eleventh Orphan, 2008; What to Do about Holly, 2009; The Chancery Lane Conspiracy, 2010; The Stolen Sister, 2011. Contributor to periodicals. **Address:** David Higham Associates Ltd., 5-8 Lower John St., Golden Sq., London, GL W1F 9HA, England.

LINGEMAN, Richard. Also writes as William Randolph, Niles Chignon. American (born United States), b. 1931. **Genres:** History, Literary Criticism And History, Medicine/Health, Biography. **Career:** Monocle, co-founder and executive editor, 1960-66; New York Times Book Review, columnist, associate editor, assistant editor, 1969-78; The Nation, executive editor, 1978-95, senior editor, 1995-; PEN, director. **Publications:** (Ed. with V. Navasky) Monocle Peep Show, 1965; (as Niles Chignon) The Camp Followers' Guide, 1965; Drugs from A to Z: A Dictionary, 1969; Don't You Know There's a War On? (history), 1970; Small Town America: A Narrative History, 1620-the Present, 1980; Theodore Dreiser: At the Gates of the City, 1871-1907, 1986; Theodore Dreiser: An American Journey, 1908-1945, 1990; Sinclair Lewis: Rebel from Main Street, 2002; (ed.) Sinclair Lewis: Arrowsmith, Elmer Gantry, Dodsworth, 2002; Don't You Know There's a War On?: The American Home Front, 1941-1945, 2003; Double Lives: American Writers' Friendships, 2006; The Nation Guide to the Nation, 2008. Contributor to periodicals. **Address:** The Nation, 33 Irving Pl., 8th Fl., New York, NY 10003, U.S.A.

LINGENFELTER, Richard Emery. American (born United States), b. 1934. **Genres:** Astronomy, History, Mythology/Folklore, Bibliography. **Career:** Lawrence Radiation Laboratory, physicist, 1957-62; University of California-Los Angeles, Institute of Geophysics and Planetary Physics, research geophysicist, 1962-68, Department of Astronomy, professor-in-residence, 1969-79, Department of Planetary and Space Science, professor-in-residence, 1969-79; University of California-San Diego, Center for Astrophysics, research physicist, 1979-. Writer. **Publications:** (With R.A. Dwyer) The Nonpareil Press of T.S. Harris, 1957; First Through the Grand Canyon, 1958; The Newspapers of Nevada, 1858-1958: A History and Bibliography, 1964; The Rush of '89: The Baja California Gold Fever & Captain James Edward Friend's Letters from the Santa Clara Mines, 1967; Presses of the Pacific Islands, 1817-1867: A History of the First Half Century of Printing in the Pacific Islands, 1967; The Hardrock Miners: A History of the Mining Labor Movement in the American West, 1863-1893, 1974; Steamboats on the Colorado River, 1852-1916, 1978; (with H. Hudson and D. Worrall) Gamma Ray Transients and Related Astrophysical Phenomena, 1982; (with K. Gash) Newspapers of Nevada: A History and Bibliography 1854-1979, 1984; (with R. Dwyer) Lying on the Eastern Slope: James Townsend's Comic Journalism on the Mining Frontier, 1984; Death Valley and the Amargosa: A Land of Illusion, 1986; (with R.A. Dwyer) Dan DeQuille: The Washoe Giant: A Biography and Anthology, 1990; Bonanzas and Borrascas: Gold Lust and Silver Sharks, 1848-1884, 2012; Bonanzas and Borrascas: Copper Kings and Stock Frenzies, 1885-1918, 2012. EDITOR: The Cement Hunters, 1960; Washoe Rambles, 1963; (with R.A. Dwyer and D. Cohen) The Songs of the Gold Rush, 1964; (comp. with R.A. Dwyer and D. Cohen) Songs of the American West, 1968; (with H. Hudson and D. Worrall) Gamma Ray Transients and Related Astrophysical Phenomena, 1982; (with R.A. Dwyer) Death Valley Lore: Classic Tales of Fantasy, Adventure, and Mystery, 1988; (with R.A. Dwyer) Sagebrush Trilogy: Ida Meacham Strobridge and Her Works, 1990; (with R. Rothschild) High Velocity Neutron Stars and Gamma Ray Bursts, 1996; The Mining West: A Bibliography and Guide to the History and Literature of Mining in the American and Canadian West, 2002. **Address:** Center for Astrophysics, University of California, SERF 402, 9500 Gilman Dr., La Jolla, CA 92093-0424, U.S.A. **Online address:** rlingenfelter@ucsd.edu

LINK, Kelly. American (born United States), b. 1969. **Genres:** Novellas/Short Stories. **Career:** Lady Churchill's Rosebud Wristlet, co-founder and co-editor, 1996-; Small Beer Press, co-founder, 2000-; Smith College, faculty. **Publications:** 4 Stories, 2000; Stranger Things Happen (short stories), 2001; Catskin: A Swaddled Zine, 2002; (ed.) Trampoline: An Anthology, 2003; Magic for Beginners, 2005; (ed. with G.J. Grant) The Best of Lady Churchill's Rosebud Wristlet, 2007; (ed. with E. Datlow and G.J. Grant) The Year's Best Fantasy and Horror 2007: 20th Annual Collection, 2007; (co-author) The Restless Dead: Ten Original Stories of the Supernatural, 2007; Pretty Monsters: Stories, 2008. Works appear in anthologies. **Address:** Small Beer Press, 150 Pleasant St., Ste. 306, Easthampton, MA 01027, U.S.A. **Online address:** info@kellylink.net

LINK, William A. (William Allen Link). American (born United States), b. 1954. **Genres:** History, Education, Politics/Government. **Career:** University of North Carolina, assistant professor, 1981-86, associate professor, 1986-92, professor of history, 1992-2004, head of the history department, 1998-2004, College of Arts and Sciences, associate dean, 1995-98; University of Florida, Richard J. Milbauer Professor of History, 2004-. Writer. **Publications:** (with A.S. Link) The Twentieth Century: An American History, 1983, 2nd ed. as The Twentieth Century: A Brief American History in Two Volumes, 1992; A Hard Country and a Lonely Place: Schooling, Society, and Reform in Rural Virginia, 1870-1920, 1986; (with A.S. Link and W.B. Catton) American Epoch: A History of the United States since 1900, 1987; The Paradox of Southern Progressivism, 1880-1930, 1992; (with A.S. Link) American Epoch: A History of the United States since 1900, 1993; William Friday: Power, Purpose, and American Higher Education, 1995; (ed. and intro.) The Rebuilding of Old Commonwealths: And Other Documents of Social Reform in the Progressive Era South, 1996; (with M.S. Wheeler) The South in the History of the Nation: A Reader, 1999; Roots of Secession: Slavery and Politics in Antebellum Virginia, 2003; Righteous Warrior: Jesse Helms and the Rise of Modern Conservatism, 2008; North Carolina: Change and Tradition in a Southern State, 2009. **Address:** Department of History, University of Florida, 231 Keene-Flint Hall, PO Box 117320, Gainesville, FL 32611-7320, U.S.A. **Online address:** linkwa@ufl.edu

LINK, William Allen. See **LINK, William A.**

LINKLATER, Magnus (Duncan). Scottish (born Scotland), b. 1942. **Genres:** History, Politics/Government. **Career:** London Evening Standard, editor, 1966-69; Sunday Times, reporter and column editor, 1967-69, editor, 1969-72, editor, 1972-75, news editor, 1975-79, features editor, 1979-83; Observer, managing editor, 1983-86; London Daily News, editor, 1986-87; The Scotsman, editor, 1988-94; The Times, columnist, 1994-; Scotland on Sunday, columnist, 1998-. **Publications:** (With L. Chester and S. Fay) Hoax: The Inside Story of the Howard Hughes-Clifford Irving Affair, 1972; (with L. Chester and D. May) Jeremy Thorpe: A Secret Life, 1979 as The Secret Life of Jeremy Thorpe, 1980; Massacre: The Story of Glencoe, 1982; (and ed. with P. Eddy and P. Gillman) The Falklands War, 1982; (co-author) The Fourth Reich: Klaus Barbie and the Neo-Fascist Connection, 1984 in US as The Nazi Legacy: Klaus Barbie and the International Fascist Connection, 1985; Scotland, 1984, 2nd ed., 2000; (with D. Leigh) Not with Honour: The Inside Story of the Westland Scandal, 1986; (with C. Hesketh) John Graham of Claverhouse: Bonnie Dundee: For King and Conscience, 1992; (ed. with R. Denniston) Anatomy of Scotland, 1992; (contrib.) Highland Wilderness, 1993; People in a Landscape, 1997. **Address:** c/o Caradoc King, AP Watt Ltd., 20 John St., London, GL WC1N 2DR, England. **Online address:** magnus.linklater@thetimes.co.uk

LINKS, Bo. American (born United States), b. 1949. **Genres:** Novels, Novellas/Short Stories, Law. **Career:** Jacobs, Blanckenburg, May & Colvin, attorney, 1974-79; Colvin, Martin & Links, attorney, 1979-84; Dobbs, Berger, Molinari, attorney, 1985-94; Berger, Nadel & Vannelli, attorney, 1994-; California Lawyer Magazine, legal editor, 2008-09. **Publications:** Follow the Wind (fiction), 1995; Riverbank Tweed & Roadmap Jenkins: Tales from the Caddie Yard, 2001; The End of the Line, forthcoming; The Lion Sleeps Tonight, forthcoming. AS ROBERT D. LINKS: (ed.) Toward Social Change, 1971; (ed.) Bancroft-Whitney California Civil Practice, 1993; (ed.) California Civil Practice Civil Rights Module, 1994; (with H.E. Kahn) California Civil Practice. Civil Rights Litigation, 2003. **Address:** c/o Jacques de Spoelberch, 9 Shagbark Rd., Wilson Pt., South Norwalk, CT 06854, U.S.A. **Online address:** bolinks@aol.com

LIN-LIU, Jen. Chinese/American (born United States), b. 1977?. **Genres:** Food And Wine, Travel/Exploration. **Career:** TimeOut Beijing, food editor; Zagat Survey, restaurant editor; Black Sesame Kitchen, founder, 2008-. Journalist. **Publications:** Serve the People: A Stir-Fried Journey through China, 2008; (with S. Pham) Frommer's Beijing, 5th ed., 2008. Contributor to books and journals. **Address:** Beijing, China. **Online address:** servethepeoplebook@gmail.com

LINN, Karen. American (born United States), b. 1957. **Genres:** Cultural/Ethnic Topics, Music, Social Sciences, Young Adult Non-fiction. **Career:** Smithsonian Institution, National Museum of American History, researcher, 1988-91; Library of Congress, archivist, 1991-. Writer. **Publications:** Register of the Sam DeVincent Collection of Illustrated American Sheet Music, 3 vols., 1989; That Half-Barbaric Twang: The Banjo in American Popular Culture, 1991. Contributor to journals. **Address:** Library of Congres, 101 Independence Ave. SE, Washington, DC 20540, U.S.A.

LINNEA, Ann. (Ann L. Schimpf). American (born United States), b. 1949. **Genres:** Environmental Sciences/Ecology, Travel/Exploration, Theology/Religion, Autobiography/Memoirs. **Career:** Schoolteacher, forest service naturalist and journalist, 1971-82; Sense of Wonder Workshops, co-founder, 1981-92; Peer Spirit Inc., co-founder, 1994-. Writer. **Publications:** Deep Water Passage: A Spiritual Journey at Midlife, 1995; A Journey through the Maxwelton Watershed, 2002; Keepers of the Trees: A Guide to Re-Greening North America, 2010; (with C. Baldwin) The Circle Way: A Leader in Every Chair, 2010. AS ANN L. SCHIMPF: (with M. Davis) Cache Trails (hiking guide), 1974; (with S. Datwyler) Cache Tours (skiing guide), 1977; (with M. Herman, J. Passineau and P. Treuer) Teaching Kids to Love the Earth, 1990. **Address:** Peer Spirit Inc., PO Box 550, Langley, WA 98260, U.S.A. **Online address:** linnea@peerspirit.com

LINNELL, David. British/Zimbabwean (born Zimbabwe), b. 1928. **Genres:** Literary Criticism And History, Art/Art History, Photography. **Career:** Actor, 1950-54; Minster Theatre Guild, co-director, 1950-54; Elmira Little Theatre, co-director, 1954-55; advertising copywriter, 1956-67; Curtain Theatre, manager and administrator, 1967-89. Writer. **Publications:** Blake, Palmer, Linnell and Co.: The Life of John Linnell, 1994. **Address:** 6 Godstalls Ln., Steyning, WS BN44 3NE, England.

LINSKY, Leonard. American (born United States), b. 1922. **Genres:** Language/Linguistics, Philosophy. **Career:** University of Illinois at Urbana-Champaign, assistant professor, professor of philosophy, 1948-67; University of Wisconsin-Madison, visiting professor, 1951; University of Michigan, visiting professor, 1956; University of Amsterdam, visiting professor, 1960-61; University of Chicago, visiting professor, 1964 and 1966, professor of philosophy, 1967-93, chairman of department, 1968-74, professor emeritus, 1993-; Tel Aviv University, Bar Hillel Memorial Lecturer, 1978; University of California, faculty. Writer. **Publications:** Referring, Humanities, 1967; Names and Descriptions, 1977; Oblique Contexts, 1983; (contrib.) Early Analytic Philosophy: Frege, Russell, Wittgenstein: Essays in Honor of Leonard Linsky, 1997. EDITOR: Semantics and the Philosophy of Language: A Collection of Readings, 1952; Reference and Modality, 1971. Contributor to periodicals. **Address:** Department of Philosophy, University of Chicago, 5801 Ellis Ave., Chicago, IL 60637, U.S.A.

LINSON, Art. American (born United States), b. 1942?. **Genres:** Film, Biography, Engineering. **Career:** Spin Dizzy Records, owner. Writer and producer. **Publications:** American Hot Wax, 1978; The Wild Life, 1984; A Pound of Flesh: Perilous Tales of How to Produce Movies in Europe, 1993; What Just Happened?: Bitter Hollywood Tales from the Front Line, 2002. **Address:** William Morris Agency, 151 El Camino Dr., Beverly Hills, CA 90212-2775, U.S.A.

LINTNER, Bertil. Thai/Swedish (born Sweden), b. 1953. **Genres:** Politics/Government, Travel/Exploration. **Career:** Freelance journalist, 1979-88; Far Eastern Economic Review, Burma correspondent, 1988-2004; Politiken, Southeast Asia correspondent, 1995-2003; Svenska Dagbladet, East Asia correspondent, 1995-; Asia Pacific Media Services Ltd., writer, 2003-; Jane's Information Group, senior analyst, 2004-. **Publications:** NONFICTION: (co-author) Miraklet i Asean: Fup eller fakta?, 1984; Outrage: Burma's Struggle for Democracy, 1989; Rejsen til jadelandet, Mellemfolkeligt Samvirke, 1989; Aung San Suu Kyi and Burma's Unfinished Renaissance, 1990; Land of Jade: A Journey through Insurgent Burma, 1990, 2nd ed. as Land of Jade: A Journey from India through Northern Burma to China, 1996; The Rise and Fall of the Communist Party of Burma (CPB), 1990; Cross-border Drug Trade in the Golden Triangle (S.E. Asia), 1991; Burma in Revolt: Opium and Insurgency since 1948, 1994, 2nd ed., 1999; The Kachin: Lords of Burma's Northern Frontier, 1997; (contrib.) The Right to Know: Access to Information in Southeast Asia, 2001; Blood Brothers: Crime, Business, and Politics in Asia, 2002 in US as Blood Brothers: The Criminal Underworld of Asia, 2003; Great Leader, Dear Leader: Demystifying North Korea under the Kim Clan, 2005; Aung San Suu Kyi and Burma's Struggle for Democracy, 2007; (with M. Black) Merchants of Madness, 2009. Contributor to books and periodicals. **Address:** Asia Pacific Media Services Ltd., PO Box 79, Chiang Mai, 50000, Thailand. **Online address:** lintner@asiapacificms.com

LINTON, Harold. American (born United States), b. 1947. **Genres:** Architecture, Design. **Career:** Lawrence Technological University, College of Architecture and Design, assistant dean, 1991-98, department chair; Bradley University, professor of art and department chair, 1998-2005; University of Art and Design, professor; ColorDesign 3D, chief executive officer, founder; Harley Ellis Architecture, color and design consultant; George Mason University, Department of Art and Visual Technology, professor and chair. Writer. **Publications:** Color Model Environments: Color and Light in Three-Dimensional Design, 1985; (with R. Rochon) Color in Architectural Illustration, 1989; (with R.J. Strickfaden) Architectural Sketching in Markers, 1991; Color Consulting: A Survey of International Color Design, 1991; (with S. Sutton) Sketching the Concept: Perspective Illustration for Architects, Designers and Artists, 1993; Color Forecasting: A Survey of International Color Marketing, 1994; Portfolio Design, 1996, 3rd ed., 2003; Color in Architecture: Design Methods for Buildings, Interiors and Urban Spaces, 1999; (with L. Clary and S. Rost) Marketing for Architects and Designers, 2005; (with R. Rowe and G. Will) Graphic Design Portfolio Strategies for Print and Digital Media, 2010. **Address:** Department of Art and Visual Technology, College of Visual and Performing Arts, George Mason University, Rm. 2050, Art and Design Bldg., 4400 University Dr., MSN 1C3, Fairfax, VA 22030, U.S.A. **Online address:** linton@gmu.edu

LINTON, Simi. American (born United States), b. 1947?. **Genres:** Autobiography/Memoirs, Social Sciences, Sports/Fitness. **Career:** Baruch College, Department of Psychology, assistant professor, 1985-88; City University of New York, Hunter College, Department of Educational Foundations and Counseling Programs, assistant professor, associate professor, 1988-98, Disability/Arts, president; Columbia University, University Seminar on Disability Studies, co-director, 2003-. Writer. **Publications:** Claiming Disability: Knowledge and Identity, 1998; My Body Politic: A Memoir, 2006. **Address:** Lescher and Lescher Ltd., 47 E 19th St., New York, NY 10003-1323, U.S.A. **Online address:** disabilityarts@yahoo.com

LINTREY, Alan R. See GORDON, W. Terrence.

LINZER, Anna. American (born United States), b. 1950?. **Genres:** Novels, Novellas/Short Stories, Poetry, Money/Finance, Business/Trade/Industry, Young Adult Fiction. **Career:** Author and consultant. **Publications:** Ghost Dancing, 1998; (with R. Linzer) It's Simple!: Money Matters for the Nonprofit Board Member, 1999; (with R. Linzer) It's Easy!: Money Matters for Nonprofit Managers, 2001; (with R. Linzer) Cash Flow Solution: The Nonprofit Board Member's Guide To Financial Success, 2007; (with R. Linzer) Cash Flow Strategies: Innovation In Nonprofit Financial Management, 2008; Blind Virgil: A Novel In Many Voices, forthcoming. Contributor to periodicals. **Address:** 391 Beach Dr., Quilcene, WA 98376, U.S.A. **Online address:** rslinzer@earthlink.net

LINZEY, Andrew. British (born England), b. 1952. **Genres:** Animals/Pets, Theology/Religion, Politics/Government. **Career:** St. Augustine's College, deacon, 1975; ordained a priest of the Anglican Church, 1976; University of Essex, chaplain, 1981, Centre for the Study of Theology, director of studies, 1987-92; Mansfield College, senior research fellow, 1992-2000; Oxford University, faculty of theology, 1992, faculty, 2000-06, director; University of Prince Edward Island, visiting lecturer, 1992; University of Madrid summer school, co-director, 1992; University of Winchester, honorary professor; University of Nottingham, special professor in theology, 1992-96; Saint Xavier University, visiting professor, 1994, special professor, 1996-; University of Birmingham, honorary professor, 1996-2007; Koret School of Veterinary Medicine, Hebrew University of Jerusalem, visiting professor, 1998; Oxford Centre for Animal Ethics, faculty of theology, director, 2006. Writer. **Publications:** Animal Rights: A Christian Assessment of Man's Treatment of Animals, 1976; (co-author) Animals and Ethics, 1980; (ed. with P.J. Wexler) Heaven and Earth: Essex Essays in Theology and Ethics, 1986; Christianity and the Rights of Animals, 1987; (with P.A.B. Clarke) Research on Embryos: Politics, Theology and Law, 1988; (ed. with Clarke) Theology, the University and the Modern World, 1988; (ed. with T. Regan) Animals and Christianity: A Book of Readings, 1988; (ed. with T. Regan) Love the Animals: Meditations and Prayers, 1989; (ed. with Regan) Compassion for Animals, 1989; (ed. with Regan) Song of Creation, 1989; (ed. with P.A.B. Clarke) Political Theory and Animal Rights, 1990; (ed.) The Sayings of Jesus, 1991; (ed. with Wexler) Fundamentalism and Tolerance: An Agenda for Theology and Society, 1991; Animal Theology, 1995; (ed. with P.B. Clarke) Dictionary of Ethics, 1996; (with D. Cohn-Sherbok) After Noah, 1997; (ed. with D. Yamamoto)

Animals on the Agenda: Questions about Animals for Theology and Ethics, 1998; Animal Gospel, 2000; Animal Rites: Liturgies of Animal Care, 1999; (ed. with P.B. Clarke) Animal Rights: A Historical Anthology, 2004; (ed. with R. Kirker) Gays and the Future of Anglicanism: Responses to the Windsor Report, 2005; Creatures of the Same God: Explorations in Animal Theology, 2007; (ed.) Link between Animal Abuse and Human Violence, 2009; Why Animal Suffering Matters: Philosophy, Theology and Practical Ethics, 2009; (ed. with T. Regan) Other Nations: Animals in Modern Literature, 2010. Contributor to books and periodicals. **Address:** The Ferrater Mora Oxford Centre for Animal Ethics, 91 Iffley Rd., Oxford, OX OX4 1EG, England. **Online address:** volinzey@aol.com

LIOU, K(uo-)N(an). American/Taiwanese (born Taiwan), b. 1943. **Genres:** Meteorology/Atmospheric Sciences. **Career:** Columbia University, Goddard Institute for Space Studies, research associate, 1970-72; University of Washington, assistant professor, 1972-74; University of Utah, Department of Meteorology, associate professor, 1975-80, professor, 1980-97, chair, 1996-97, adjunct professor, 1997-, Center for Atmospheric and Remote Sounding Studies, director, 1987-97, research professor, 1992-, adjunct professor of physics, 1992-96, adjunct professor of geology and geophysics, 1992-97; University of California, visiting professor, 1981, Institute of Radiation and Remote Sensing, director, 1997-2006, Department of Atmospheric and Oceanic Sciences, professor, 1997-, chair, 2000-04, distinguished professor, 2004-, Mechanical and Aerospace Engineering, professor, 2003-, Joint Institute for Regional Earth System Science and Engineering (JIFRESSE), founding director, 2006-. Writer. **Publications:** An Introduction to Atmospheric Radiation, 1980, 2nd ed., 2002; (ed.) Atmospheric Radiation: Progress and Prospects, 1987; Radiation and Cloud Processes in the Atmosphere: Theory, Observation, and Modeling (monograph), 1992; (ed. with M.D. Chou) Recent Progress in Atmospheric Sciences: Applications to the Asia-Pacific Region, 2008. Contributor to journals. **Address:** Department of Atmospheric & Oceanic Sciences, University of California, 405 Hilgard Ave., 7127 Math Sciences Bldg., Los Angeles, CA 90095-1565, U.S.A. **Online address:** knliou@atmos.ucla.edu

LIPARTITO, Kenneth. American (born United States), b. 1957?. **Genres:** History, Sciences. **Career:** Middlebury College, visiting instructor in history, 1985-86; Rice University, visiting professor of history, 1987-88; University of Houston, Department of History, assistant professor, 1988-90, associate professor, 1991-98; Florida International University, Department of History, professor, 1998-, chair. Historian and writer. **Publications:** The Bell System and Regional Business: The Telephone in the South, 1877-1920, 1989; (with J. Pratt) Baker & Botts in the Development of Modern Houston, 1991; (with C.H. Peters) Investing for Middle America: John Elliott Tappan and the Origins of American Express Financial Advisors, 2001; (ed. and contrib. with D.B. Sicilia) Constructing Corporate America: History, Politics, Culture, 2004; (with O.R. Butler) A History of the Kennedy Space Center, 2007. Contributor to books. **Address:** Department of History, Florida International University, University Pk., 11200 SW 8th St., PO Box 397, Miami, FL 33174, U.S.A. **Online address:** lipark@fiu.edu

LIPIN, Lawrence M. American (born United States), b. 1956. **Genres:** Politics/Government. **Career:** Pacific University, professor of history; United States History Exam, Educational Testing Service, reader, 2004-05; Oregon Historical Society, Sterling Fellowships in Pacific Northwest History, member of awards committee, 2001-. Writer. **Publications:** Producers, Proletarians and Politicians: Workers and Party Politics in Evansville and New Albany, Indiana, 1850-87, 1994; Workers and the Wild: Conservation, Consumerism and Labor in Oregon, 1910-30, 2007. Contributor to journals. **Address:** Department of History, Pacific University, 2043 College Way, Forest Grove, OR 97116, U.S.A. **Online address:** lipinlm@pacificu.edu

LIPKIN, Randie. American (born United States), b. 1953. **Genres:** Novels. **Career:** Writer. **Publications:** Untitled (A Skier): A Novel, 1995; Without, 1998. **Address:** New York, NY, U.S.A. **Online address:** miffyskates@gmail.com

LIPMAN, Elinor. American (born United States), b. 1950. **Genres:** Novels, Novellas/Short Stories, Humor/Satire. **Career:** Massachusetts Labor Relations Commission, public information officer, 1974-75; Massachusetts Teachers Association, managing editor, 1975-81; Simmons College, special instructor in communications, 1984-85; Hampshire College, visiting assistant professor of creative writing, 1988-89; writer, 1989-; Smith College, instructor, 1997, Elizabeth Drew chair in creative writing. **Publications:** NOVELS:

Then She Found Me, 1990; The Way Men Act, 1992; Isabel's Bed, 1995; The Ladies' Man, 1998; The Inn at Lake Devine, 1999; The Dearly Departed, 2001; The Pursuit of Alice Thrift, 2003; My Latest Grievance, 2006; The Family Man, 2009. OTHER: Into Love and Out Again (stories), 1987. Works appear in anthologies. Contributor to periodicals. **Address:** c/o Suzanne Gluck, William Morris Endeavor Entertainment, 1325 Ave. of the Americas, New York, NY 10019, U.S.A. **Online address:** author@elinorlipman.com

LIPMAN, Victoria M. American (born United States), b. 1949. **Genres:** Novels, Young Adult Fiction. **Career:** Writer. **Publications:** NOVEL: Leaving Alva, 1998. **Address:** Simon and Schuster Inc., 1230 Ave. of the Americas, New York, NY 10020, U.S.A. **Online address:** victorialipman@cox.net

LIPMAN-BLUMEN, Jean. American (born United States), b. 1933. **Genres:** Business/Trade/Industry, Economics, Social Sciences, Humanities, Politics/Government. **Career:** National Institute of Education Women's Research Program, assistant director, 1973-78; Office of the Assistant Secretary for Education, special assistant; Center for Advanced Study in the Behavioral Sciences, fellow, 1978-79; LBS Intl., president, 1979-84; University of Connecticut, visiting professor of sociology and organizational behavior; University of Maryland, visiting professor of sociology and organizational behavior; Claremont University, professor of public policy, Peter F. Drucker Graduate School of Management, Institute for Advanced Studies in Leadership, Thorton F. Bradshaw professor of public policy, professor of organizational behavior, co-founder and director; Achieving Styles Institute (consulting group), director. Writer. **Publications:** Sex Roles and Social Policy: A Complex Social Science Equation, 1979; Gender Roles and Power, 1984; The Connective Edge: Leading in an Interdependent World, 1996; (with H.J. Leavitt) Hot Groups: Seeding Them, Feeding Them, and Using Them to Ignite Your Organization, 1999; Connective Leadership: Managing in a Changing World, 2000; (with G. Gabe) Step Wars: Overcoming the Perils and Making Peace in Adult Stepfamilies, 2004; Allure of Toxic Leaders: Why We Follow Destructive Bosses and Corrupt Politicians-And How We Can Survive Them, 2005; (ed. with R.E. Riggio and I. Chaleff) The Art of Followership: How Great Followers Create Great Leaders and Organizations, 2008. Contributor to periodicals. **Address:** Drucker Graduate School of Management, Claremont Graduate University, 1021 N Dartmouth Ave., Claremont, CA 91711, U.S.A. **Online address:** jeanlipman28@gmail.com

LIPPER, Joanna. American (born United States) **Genres:** Documentaries/ Reportage, Illustrations, Human Relations/Parenting. **Career:** Sea Wall Entertainment, owner; Harvard University, Sheila Biddle Ford Foundation fellow, 2008-, Department of African and African American Studies, lecturer. Writer and filmmaker. **Publications:** SELF-ILLUSTRATED: Growing Up Fast, 2003. OTHERS: (with A. Lipper) Baby Stuff: A No-Nonsense Shopping Guide for Every Parent's Lifestyle, 1997, rev. ed., 2002. **Address:** Department of African and African American Studies, Du Bois Inst for African & African American Res, Harvard University, 104 Mount Auburn St., 3R, Cambridge, MA 02138, U.S.A. **Online address:** info@joannalipper.com

LIPPERT, Randy K. Canadian (born Canada), b. 1966?. **Genres:** Law. **Career:** University of Windsor, associate professor of criminology. Writer. **Publications:** Sanctuary, Sovereignty, Sacrifice: Canadian Sanctuary Incidents, Power and Law, 2005. Contributor to books and journals. **Address:** Department of Sociology and Anthropology, University of Windsor, Windsor, ON N9B 3P4, Canada. **Online address:** lippert@uwindsor.ca

LIPPI, Ronald D. (Ronald David Lippi). American (born United States), b. 1949. **Genres:** Social Sciences, History, Anthropology/Ethnology, Biology, Sociology, Archaeology/Antiquities. **Career:** University of Wisconsin-Marathon County, Department of Anthropology and Sociology, associate professor, professor, 1989-, chair, associate campus dean. Writer. **Publications:** La primera revolución ecuatoriana: El desarrollo de la vidaagrícola en el antiguo Ecuador, 1996; Una exploración arqueológica del Pichincha Occidental, Ecuador, Museo Jacinto Jijón y Caamaño, Pontificia Universidad Católica del Ecuador, 1998; Tropical Forest Archaeology in Western Pichincha, Ecuador, 2004. Contributor to periodicals. **Address:** Department of Anthropology and Sociology, University of Wisconsin-Marathon County, Rm. 143, 518 S 7th Ave., Wausau, WI 54401-5362, U.S.A. **Online address:** rlippi@uwc.edu

LIPPI, Ronald David. See **LIPPI, Ronald D.**

LIPPI(-GREEN), Rosina. (Sara Donati). American (born United States),

b. 1956. **Genres:** Novels, Language/Linguistics. **Career:** Western Washington University, associate professor; University of Michigan, faculty. Writer. **Publications:** NOVELS: Homestead, 1998; Tied to the Tracks, 2006; Pajama Girls of Lambert Square, 2008. AS ROSINA LIPPI-GREEN: (ed.) Recent Developments in Germanic Linguistics, 1992; Language Ideology and Language Change in Early Modern German: A Sociolinguistic Study of the Consonantal System of Nuremberg, 1994; (ed. with J.C. Salmons) Germanic Linguistics: Syntactic and Diachronic, 1996; English with an Accent: Language, Ideology, and Discrimination in the United States, 1997, 2nd ed., 2011. AS SARA DONATI: Into the Wilderness, 1998; Dawn on a Distant Shore, 2000; Lake in the Clouds, 2002; Fire Along the Sky, 2004; Queen of Swords, 2006; Endless Forest, 2010. Contributor of articles to periodicals. **Address:** c/o Jill Grinberg, Jill Grinberg Literary Management L.L.C., 16 Court St., Ste. 3306, Brooklyn, NY 11241-1013, U.S.A. **Online address:** rosinalippi@pobox.com

LIPPMAN, Thomas W. American (born United States), b. 1940. **Genres:** Documentaries/Reportage. **Career:** Washington Post, reporter and foreign correspondent, 1965-99, Middle East bureau chief; freelance writer, 1999-; National Defense University, lecturer on middle eastern affairs; Brookings Institution, lecturer on middle eastern affairs; Council on Foreign Relations, adjunct senior fellow. **Publications:** Islam-Politics and Religion in the Muslim World, 1982; Understanding Islam, 1982, rev. ed., 1995; Egypt after Nasser: Sadat, Peace, and the Mirage of Prosperity, 1989; Washington Post Deskbook on Style, 1989; Madeleine Albright and the New American Diplomacy, 2000; Inside the Mirage: America's Fragile Partnership with Saudi Arabia, 2004; Arabian Knight: Col. Bill Eddy USMC and the Rise of American Power in the Middle East, 2008; Saudi Arabia on the Edge: The Uncertain Future of an American Ally, 2012. Contributor of articles and reviews to periodicals. **Address:** Middle East Institute, 1761 North St. NW, Washington, DC 20036-2882, U.S.A. **Online address:** tw122@columbia.edu

LIPPY, Charles H(oward). American (born United States), b. 1943. **Genres:** Theology/Religion, Bibliography. **Career:** Oberlin College, assistant professor of religion, 1972-74; Miami University, visiting assistant professor of religion and American studies, 1974-75; West Virginia Wesleyan College, assistant professor of Bible, religion and humanities, 1975-76; Clemson University, assistant professor, 1976-80, associate professor, 1980-85, professor of religion, 1985-94, professor of history, 1985-88, acting head of department, 1988-89, Program in Philosophy and Religion, director, 1987-88; University of Tennessee at Chattanooga, LeRoy A. Martin distinguished professor of religious studies, 1994-, now retired; Emory University, visiting professor, 1990-91. Writer. **Publications:** Seasonable Revolutionary: The Mind of Charles Chauncy, 1981; A Bibliography of Religion in the South, 1985; The Christadelphians in North America, 1989; (with R. Choquette and S. Poole) Christianity Comes to the Americas, 1492-1776, 1992; Being Religious, American Style, 1994; Modern America Popular Religion: A Critical Assessment and Annotated Bibliography, 1996; (with R. Krapohl) The Evangelicals: A Historical, Thematic, and Biographical Guide, 1999; Pluralism Comes of Age: American Religious Culture in the Twentieth Century, 2000; Do Real Men Pray?: Images of the Christian Man and Male Spirituality in White Protestant America, 2005; Introducing American Religions, 2009. EDITOR and CONTRIBUTOR: Religious Periodicals of the United States: Academic and Scholarly Journals, 1986; (with P.W. Williams) Encyclopedia of the American Religious Experience: Studies of Traditions and Movements, 3 vols., 1988; Twentieth-Century Shapers of American Popular Religion, 1989; Religion in South Carolina, 1993; (with P.M. Fackler) Popular Religious Magazines of the United States, 1995; (with J. Topolewski and N. Topolewski) Where Rivers Run and Mountains Rise: Essays in Celebration of the Sesquicentennial of the Wyoming Annual Conference of The United Methodist Church, 2002; (with S.S. Hill) Encyclopedia of Religion in the South, 2005; Faith in America: Changes, Challenges, New Directions, 2006; Introducing American Religion, 2009; (with P.W. Williams) Encyclopedia of Religion in America, 2010. **Address:** 711 Hurricane Creek Rd., Chattanooga, TN 37421, U.S.A. **Online address:** charles-lippy@utc.edu

LIPSKY, David. American (born United States), b. 1965. **Genres:** Novels, Travel/Exploration, Money/Finance, Young Adult Fiction. **Career:** New York University, creative writing instructor; Rolling Stone Magazine, contributing editor. **Publications:** Three Thousand Dollars: Stories, 1989; (with A. Abrams) Late Bloomers: Coming of Age in Today's America: The Right Place at the Wrong Time, 1994; The Pallbearer, 1996; The Art Fair, 1996; Absolutely American: Four Years at West Point, 2003; Although Of Course You End Up Becoming Yourself: A Road Trip with David Foster Wallace,

2010. Contributor of articles and short fiction to periodicals. Works appear in anthologies. **Address:** c/o Author Mail, Vintage Books, 1745 Broadway, New York, NY 10019-4368, U.S.A.

LIPSYTE, Robert (Michael). American (born United States), b. 1938. **Genres:** Novels, Children's Fiction, Sports/Fitness, Medicine/Health, Music, Autobiography/Memoirs, Young Adult Non-fiction. **Career:** New York Times, sports reporter, 1959-67, sports columnist, 1967-71, 1991-2002; New York Post, columnist, 1977; Columbia Broadcasting System Inc., Sunday Morning Program, sports essayist, 1982-86; National Broadcasting Company Inc., correspondent, 1986-88; Public Broadcasting Service, The Eleventh Hour, host, 1989-90, PBS Show, host, 2009-11. **Publications:** (With D. Gregory) Nigger: An Autobiography, 1964; The Masculine Mystique, 1966; The Contender, 1967; Assignment: Sports, 1970, rev. ed., 1984; (with S. Cady) Something Going, 1973; Liberty Two, 1974; Sportsworld: An American Dreamland, 1975; One Fat Summer, 1977; Free to Be Muhammad Ali, 1978; (ed. with G. Brown) Sports and Society, 1980; Summer Rules: A Novel, 1981; Jock and Jill: A Novel, 1982; The Summerboy: A Novel, 1982; The Brave, 1991; The Chemo Kid, 1992; The Chief, 1993; Arnold Schwarzenegger: Hercules in America, 1993; Jim Thorpe: 20th-Century Jock, 1993; Michael Jordan: A Life Above The Rim, 1994; Joe Louis: A Champ for All America, 1994; (with P. Levine) Idols of the Game: A Sporting History of the American Century, 1995; In the Country of Illness: Comfort and Advice for the Journey, 1998; Jock Culture: Writing And Fighting, 2001; Robert Lipsyte Teacher's Guide, 2003; Warrior Angel, 2003; Heroes of Baseball: The Men Who Made It America's Favorite Game, 2005; Raiders Night, 2006; Yellow Flag, 2007; Center Field, 2010; An Accidental Sportswriter: A Memoir, 2011; Twinning Project, 2012. Contributor to periodicals. **Address:** Clarion Books, 215 Park Ave. S, New York, NY 10003, U.S.A. **Online address:** robert@robertlipsyte.com

LIPTON, Eunice. American (born United States), b. 1941?. **Genres:** Autobiography/Memoirs, History, Art/Art History, Women's Studies And Issues, Biography, Social Commentary, Writing/Journalism, Essays, Essays. **Career:** University of Rhode Island, instructor in art history, 1965-67; Bard College, instructor in art history, 1970-72; Hunter College of the City University of New York, lecturer to assistant professor of art history, 1973-78; Parsons School of Design, lecturer in art history, 1978-80; State University of New York, associate professor of art history, 1980-88; Williams College and Clark Art Institute, Robert Sterling Clark visiting professor, 1986; School of the Art Institute of Chicago, visiting artist, 1988; non-fiction writer and journalist, 1988-; Fantastic Coalition of Women in the Arts, founding member, 1989. **Publications:** PICASSO CRITICISM, 1901-1939: The Making of an Artist-Hero, 1976; LOOKING INTO DEGAS: Uneasy Images of Women and Modern Life, 1986; ALIAS OLYMPIA: A Woman's Search for Manet's Notorious Model and Her Own Desire, 1992, rev. ed., 1994; FRENCH SEDUCTION: An American's Encounter with France, Her Father, and the Holocaust, 2007. **Address:** Carroll & Graf publishers, New York, NY 10011, U.S.A. **Online address:** info@eunicelipton.com

LIPTON, James. American (born United States), b. 1926. **Genres:** Business/Trade/Industry, Economics, Photography. **Career:** Inside the Actors Studio, host, 1994-; New School University, Actors Studio Drama School, founding dean, 1994-2004, dean emeritus, 2004-. Writer, producer and actor. **Publications:** An Exaltation of Larks: or The Venereal Game, 1968, 2nd ed., Viking, 1977; Mirrors, 1981; An Exaltation of Business and Finance, 1993; An Exaltation of Home and Family, 1993; An Exaltation of Romance & Revelry, 1994; Inside Inside, 2007. Contributor to periodicals. **Address:** The Actors Studio Drama School, 1 Pace Plz., New York, NY 10038, U.S.A.

LIQUORI, Martin William. *See* LIQUORI, Marty.

LIQUORI, Marty. (Martin William Liquori). American (born United States), b. 1949. **Genres:** Sports/Fitness. **Career:** Athletic Attic (retail sporting goods store), founder and president, 1971-; I.T.A. ProTrack, master of ceremonies, 1971-73; ABC Sports, commentator, 1971-; Brooks Shoe Co., designer and promotional director, 1974-78; ESPN-TV, Running and Racing, producer, 1986-; ML Productions, founder and owner, 1989-; Marty Liquori Sportswear Inc., president; Le Coq Sportif, marketing consultant; Le Cog Sportif, marketing consultant; Athletic Lady, vice-president. Writer. **Publications:** (With S. Myslenski) On the Run: In Search of the Perfect Race, 1977; (with J.L. Parker, Jr.) Marty Liquori's Guide for the Elite Runner, 1980; (with J.L. Parker, Jr.) Real Running, 1982; (with G.S. Couzens) Marty Liquori's Home Gym Workout, 1986. **Address:** 2915 NW 58th Blvd., Gainesville, FL 32606-

8517, U.S.A.

LISANDRELLI, Elaine Slivinski. American (born United States), b. 1951. **Genres:** Education, Young Adult Non-fiction, Biography, Children's Fiction. **Career:** North Pocono Middle School, English teacher, 1973-; Marywood University, adjunct faculty, 1986-; International Correspondence School, proofreader, 1991. Writer and consultant. **Publications:** (Co-author) Easywriter, 1987; (with S.C. Bartoletti) The Study Skills Workout, 1988. YOUNG ADULT NONFICTION: Maya Angelou: More Than a Poet, 1996; Bob Dole: Legendary Senator, 1997; Ida B. Wells-Barnett: Crusader against Lynching, 1998; Ignacy Jan Paderewski: Polish Pianist and Patriot, 1999; Jack London: A Writer's Adventurous Life, 1999. Contributor to magazines and periodicals. **Address:** North Pocono Middle School, 701 Church St., Moscow, PA 18444, U.S.A.

LISBOA, Maria Manuel. British/Mozambiquian (born Mozambique), b. 1963. **Genres:** Literary Criticism And History, Art/Art History. **Career:** University of Newcastle, Newcastle upon Tyne, lecturer in Portuguese and Brazilian literature, 1988-93; Cambridge University, St. John's College, lecturer in Portuguese, Brazilian, and African (Lusopaone) literature, 1993-, Department of Spanish and Portuguese, professor of Portuguese literature and culture. Writer. **Publications:** Machado de Assis and Feminism: Re-Reading the Heart of the Companion, 1996; Teu Amor Fez de Mim Um Lago Triste: Ensaios Sobre Os Maias, 2000; Paula Rego's Map of Memory: National and Sexual Politics, 2003; Uma Mãe Desconhecida: Ensaios sobre Eça de Queirós, 2008; Afterwards: The Way Worlds End in Fiction, Film and Art, forthcoming. Contributor of articles to periodicals. **Address:** St. John's College, Cambridge University, St John's St., Cambridge, CB2 1TP, United Kingdom. **Online address:** mmgl100@cam.ac.uk

LISCHER, Sarah Kenyon. American (born United States), b. 1970. **Genres:** Humanities, Military/Defense/Arms Control, Civil Liberties/Human Rights, Young Adult Non-fiction. **Career:** Sweet Briar College, Department of Government, assistant professor, 2003-05; Wake Forest University, Department of Political Science, associate professor, 2005-. Writer. **Publications:** Dangerous Sanctuaries: Refugee Camps, Civil War, and the Dilemmas of Humanitarian Aid (nonfiction), 2005. Contributor to periodicals. **Address:** Department of Political Science, Wake Forest University, Tribble A-308C, PO Box 7568, Winston-Salem, NC 27106, U.S.A. **Online address:** lischesk@wfu.edu

LISCOMB, Kathlyn Maurean. Canadian/American (born United States), b. 1950. **Genres:** Art/Art History, Cultural/Ethnic Topics, Travel/Exploration. **Career:** School of the Art Institute of Chicago, visiting lecturer in art history and aesthetics, 1985; University of Victoria, Department of History in Art, assistant professor, 1986-91, associate professor, 1991-2000, professor, 2000-. Writer. **Publications:** Learning from Mount Hua: A Chinese Physician's Illustrated Travel Record and Painting Theory, 1993; (with E.J. Markus) China and Beyond: The Legacy of a Culture, 2002. Contributor to periodicals and journals. **Address:** Department of History in Art, University of Victoria, PO Box 1700, Victoria, BC V8W 2Y2, Canada. **Online address:** kliscomb@finearts.uvic.ca

LISK, Jill (Rosina Ann). British (born England), b. 1938. **Genres:** History, Area Studies. **Career:** Taunton School, head of history department; Barr's Hill Girls Grammar School, history mistress; La Sainte Union Convent Grammar School, history mistress; Bridgewater Girls Grammar School, history mistress. Writer. **Publications:** The Struggle for Supremacy in the Baltic 1600-1725, 1967. **Address:** 26 Northfield, Bridgwater, SM TA6 4DA, England.

LISLE, Holly. American (born United States), b. 1960. **Genres:** Novels, Science Fiction/Fantasy, Adult Non-fiction. **Career:** Writer, 1993-. Nurse. **Publications:** ARHEL NOVELS: Fire in the Mist, 1992; Bones of the Past, 1993; Mind of the Magic, 1995. GLENRAVEN NOVELS: (with M.Z. Bradley) Glenraven, 1996; (with M.Z. Bradley) In the Rift, 1998; (with M.Z. Bradley) In the Rift Glenraven II, 1999. DEVIL'S POINT NOVELS: Sympathy for the Devil, 1996; (with W. Spence) The Devil & Dan Cooley, 1996; (with T. Nolan) Hell on High, 1997. BARD'S TALE NOVELS: (with A. Allston) Thunder of the Captains, 1996; (with A. Allston) Wrath of the Princes, 1997; Curse of the Black Heron, 1998. SECRET TEXTS SERIES: Diplomacy of Wolves, 1998; Vengeance of Dragons, 1999; Courage of Falcons, 2000; Vincalis the Agitator, 2002; The Secret Texts, 2002. WORLD GATES SERIES: Memory of Fire, 2002; The Wreck of Heaven, 2003; Gods Old and Dark, 2004. WORLD

OF KORRE SERIES: Talyn: A Novel of Korre, 2005. OTHERS: (with M. Lackey) When the Bough Breaks, 1993; Minerva Wakes, 1994; (with S.M. Stirling) The Rose Sea, 1994; (with C. Guin) Mall, Mayhem and Magic, 1995; Hunting the Corrigan's Blood, 1997; (with M. Lackey and M. Shepherd) The Otherworld, 2000; Midnight Rain, 2004; Last Girl Dancing, 2005; I See You, 2006; Night Echoes, 2007; Ruby Key, 2008; Hawkspar: A Novel of Korre, 2008; Silver Door, 2009; Invisible Warrior, forthcoming. **Address:** c/o Russell Galen, Scovil Chichak Galen Literary Agency, 276 5th Ave., Ste. 708, New York, NY 10001, U.S.A. **Online address:** holly@hollylisle.com

LISLE, Janet Taylor. American (born United States), b. 1947. **Genres:** Children's Fiction, Children's Non-fiction, Young Adult Fiction, Classics. **Career:** Writer. **Publications:** FOR CHILDREN: The Dancing Cats of Applesap, 1984; Sirens and Spies, 1985; The Great Dimpole Oak, 1987; Afternoon of the Elves, 1989; The Lampfish of Twill, 1991; Forest, 1993; The Gold Dust Letters, 1994; Looking for Juliette, 1994; A Message from the Match Girl, 1995; Angela's Aliens, 1996; The Lost Flower Children, 1999; The Art of Keeping Cool, 2000; How I Became a Writer and Oggie Learned to Drive, 2002; The Crying Rocks, 2003, 2nd ed., 2005; Black Duck, 2006; Highway Cats, 2008. **Address:** c/o Penguin Putnam, Books for Young Readers, 345 Hudson St., New York, NY 10014, U.S.A. **Online address:** janetlisle@hotmail.com

LISLE, Laurie. American (born United States), b. 1942. **Genres:** Autobiography/Memoirs, Biography, Essays, Autobiography/Memoirs, Biography, Autobiography/Memoirs, Women's Studies And Issues, Art/Art History, Art/Art History. **Career:** Providence Journal and Evening Bulletin, reporter, critic, 1965-66; Newsweek, researcher and reporter, 1970-77; freelance writer, 1978-; The East Hampton Star, staff; Long Island University, Southampton College, associate professor of English, 1981-82. Writer. **Publications:** Portrait of an Artist: A Biography of Georgia O'Keeffe, 1980, rev. ed., 1986; Louise Nevelson: A Passionate Life, 1990; Without Child: Challenging the Stigma of Childlessness, 1996; Four Tenths of an Acre: Reflections on a Gardening Life, 2005; Westover: Giving Girls a Place of Their Own, 2009. Contributor of articles to periodicals. **Address:** PO Box 1067, Sharon, CT 06069, U.S.A. **Online address:** readermail@laurielisle.com

LISLE, Rebecca. British (born England) **Genres:** Children's Fiction, Novels, Picture/Board Books. **Career:** Author, artist and educator. **Publications:** SELF-ILLUSTRATION: Sparks Will Fly, 1988; Shrubbery Skulduggery, 1990; The Weatherstone Eleven, 1992; Finders, Keepers, 1995; Copper, 2002; Planimal Magic, 2003; The Curse of the Toads, 2006; Amethyst, 2006; The Curse of the Ravens, 2007; Practical Princess, 2008; The Gnome with the Knobbly Knees, 2009; Wizard Dog, 2009; Crystal, 2010. OTHERS: Petrified, 1996; Mr. Cool Cat, 1999; The Empty Grave, 2000; The Bear Pit, 2001; (reteller) Romeo and Juliet, 2002; Rocky, 2003; Dogs Don't Do Dishes, 2004; The Toad Prince, 2005; The Dog in the Diamond Collar, 2006; The Boy In the Big Black Box, 2007. **Address:** c/o Caroline Walsh, David Higham Associates Ltd., 5-8 Lower John St., Golden Sq., London, GL W1R 4HA, England. **Online address:** rebecca.lisle@blueyonder.co.uk

LISS, David. American (born United States), b. 1966. **Genres:** Adult Non-fiction, Young Adult Fiction, Novels, Graphic Novels. **Career:** Writer. **Publications:** BENJAMIN WEAVER SERIES: A Conspiracy of Paper, 2000; A Spectacle of Corruption, 2004; The Devil's Company, 2009. COLLECTION: (with P. Bronson and A. Parsons) Men Seeking Women: Love and Sex Online, 2001. NOVELS: The Coffee Trader, 2003; The Ethical Assassin, 2006; The Whiskey Rebels, 2008; The Darkening Green, 2011. GRAPHIC NOVEL: Black Panther: The Man Without Fear, vol. I, 2011. OTHERS: Minesweeper, 2001; The Double Dealer, 2006; The Thoughtful Assassin, 2006; Twelfth Enchantment, 2011. Works appear in anthologies. **Address:** Random House Inc., 1745 Broadway, New York, NY 10019-4368, U.S.A. **Online address:** davidliss@sbcglobal.net

LISTER, R(ichard) P(ercival). British (born England), b. 1914. **Genres:** Novels, Novellas/Short Stories, Poetry, Travel/Exploration, History, Theology/Religion, Westerns/Adventure. **Career:** United Steel Companies Ltd., trainee, 1937-39; Royal Naval Torpedo Factory, metallurgist, 1940; Royal Aircraft Establishment, metallurgist, 1941-43; Ministry of Aircraft Production, scientific officer, 1943-47; British Non-Ferrous Metals Research Association, liaison officer, 1947-49; freelance writer, 1949-54, 1959-; Macdonald & Evans Ltd. (publishers), general editor, 1954-57. **Publications:** The Way Backwards, 1950; The Oyster and the Torpedo, 1951; Rebecca Redfern, 1953;

The Idle Demon: A Collection of Verses, 1958; The Rhyme and the Reason, 1963; The Questing Beast, 1965; A Journey in Lapland: The Hard Way to Haparanda, 1965 in US as The Hard Way to Haparanda, 1966; The Secret History of Genghis Khan in US as Genghis Khan, 1969; One Short Summer, 1974; Marco Polo's Travels in Xanadu with Kublai Khan, 1976; (ed. and intro.) Letters to Frank Harris and other Friends, 1980; (contrib.) Allotments, 1985; The Albatross and Other Poems, 1986; Nine Legends, 1991; Two Northern Stories, 1996; Glimpses of a Planet, 1997; Me and the Holy Spirit, 1999. SELF-ILLUSTRATED: A Muezzin from the Tower of Darkness Cries: Travels in Turkey in UK as Turkey Observed, 1967; The Travels of Herodotus, 1979. Contributor of articles to periodicals. **Address:** 42-46 St. James's Gardens, London, GL W11 4RQ, England.

LITAN, Robert E(li). American (born United States), b. 1950. **Genres:** Economics, History, Sciences, Money/Finance. **Career:** The Brookings Institution, research assistant, 1972-73, Economic Studies Program, senior fellow, 1984-87, 2003-, Center for Economic Progress and Employment, director, 1987-92, Center for Law, Economics, and Politics, director, 1992-93, Cabot Family chair in economics, vice president and director, 1996-2003, The Brookings-Wharton Papers on Financial Services, co-editor, 1997-2003, AEI-Brookings Joint Center on Regulatory Studies, director, 1998-2007, Economic Studies Program, senior fellow, 2003-; Regulatory Analysis Review Group, principal staff, 1977-79; Arnold & Porter, associate, 1979-82; Powell, Goldstein, Frazer & Murphy, senior associate, 1982-84, partner, 1984, of counsel, 1984-90; United States Department of Justice, Antitrust Division, deputy assistant attorney general, 1993-95; United States Office of Management Budget, associate director, 1995-96; Economists Inc., special consultant, 1996-2002; Analysis Group, special consultant, 1999-2002; Charles River Associates, senior consultant, 2002-; Ewing Marion Kauffman Foundation, vice president for research and policy, 2003-; Inc Magazine, contributing editor, 2005; Criterion Associates, senior consultant, 2006-08; Empiris L.L.C., senior consultant, 2008. **Publications:** Energy Modeling for an Uncertain Future, 1978; (with W.D. Nordhaus) Reforming Federal Regulation, 1983; (with R.Z. Lawrence) Saving Free Trade: A Pragmatic Approach, 1986; What Should Banks Do?, 1987; (ed. with R.Z. Lawrence and C.L. Schultze) American Living Standards: Threats and Challenges, 1988; (ed. with C. Winston) Liability: Perspectives and Policy, 1988; (ed. with P. Huber) The Liability Maze: The Impact of Liability Law on Safety and Innovation, 1991; (ed. with R. Boltuck) Down in the Dumps: Administration of the Unfair Trade Laws, 1991; The Revolution in U.S. Finance: The Frank M. Engle Lecture in Economic Security Presented on April 30, 1991, at the American College, Bryn Mawr, Pa, 1992; (co-author) Physical Damage and Human Loss: The Economic Impact of Earthquake Mitigation Measures, 1992; (with J.R. Barth and R.D. Brumbaugh) The Future of American banking, 1992; (with M. Baily and G. Burtless) Growth with Equity: Economic Policymaking for the Next Century, 1993; (ed.) Verdict: Assessing the Civil Jury System, 1993; (ed. with G.G. Kaufman) Assessing Bank Reform: FDICIA One Year Later, 1993; (with R.J. Herring) Financial Regulation in the Global Economy, 1995; (with R.W. Hahn) Improving Regulatory Accountability, 1997; (with J. Rauch) American Finance for the 21st Century, 1998; None of Your Business: World Data Flows, Electronic Commerce, and the European Privacy Directive, 1998; (with W. Niskanen) Going Digital!: A Guide to Policy in the Digital Age, 1998; (ed. with A. Harwood and M. Pomerleano) Financial Markets and Development: The Crisis in Emerging Markets, 1999; (co-author) Community Reinvestment Act After Financial Modernization, 2000; (ed. with C. Adams and M. Pomerleano) Managing Financial and Corporate Distress: Lessons from Asia, 2000; (with P.J. Wallison) GAAP Gap, 2000; (with A.M. Rivlin) Beyond the Dot.coms: The Economic Promise of the Internet, 2001; Community Reinvestment Act after Financial Modernization: A Baseline Report, 2001; (ed. with A.M. Rivlin) Economic Payoff from the Internet Revolution, 2001; (ed. with P. Masson and M. Pomerleano) Open Doors: Foreign Participation in Financial Systems in Developing Countries, 2001; (ed. with P. Hakim) The Future of North American Integration: Beyond NAFTA, 2002; (ed. with M. Pomerleano and V. Sundararajan) Financial Sector Governance: The Roles of the Public and Private Sectors, 2002; (with Y. Kop) Sticking Together: The Israeli Experiment in Pluralism, 2002; (ed. with E.J. Dionne, Jr. and K.M. Drogosz) United We Serve: National Service and the Future of Citizenship, 2003; (ed. with M. Pomerleano and V. Sundararajan) The Future of Domestic Capital Markets in Developing Countries, 2003; (ed. with G. Caprio and J.A. Hanson) Financial Crises: Lessons from the Past, Preparation for the Future, 2005; (ed. with Y. Fuchita) Financial Gatekeepers: Can they Protect Investors?, 2006; (with B. Steil) Financial Statecraft: The Role of Financial Markets in American Foreign Policy, 2006; (with W.J. Baumol and C.J. Schramm) Good Capitalism, Bad Capitalism, and the Economics of Growth and Prosperity, 2007; (with P.J. Wallison) Competitive Equity: A Better way to Organize Mutual Funds, 2007; (ed. with Y. Fuchita) New Financial Instruments and Institutions: Opportunities and Policy Challenges, 2007; (ed. with M.S. Barr and A. Kumar) Building Inclusive Financial Systems: A Framework for Financial Access, 2007; (ed. with Y. Fuchita) Pooling Money: The Future of Mutual Funds, 2008; (ed. with Y. Fuchita and R.J. Herring) Prudent Lending Restored: Securitization After the Mortgage Meltdown, 2009; (ed. with M.N. Baily) Moving Money: The Future of Consumer Payments, 2009; (ed. with D.B. Audretsch and R.J. Strom) Entrepreneurship and Openness, 2009; (ed. with Y. Fuchita and R.J. Herring) After the Crash: The Future of Finance, 2010. Contributor to periodicals and journals. **Address:** The Brookings Institution, 1775 Massachusetts Ave. NW, Washington, DC 20036-2103, U.S.A. **Online address:** rlitan@brookings.edu

LITHGOW, John (Arthur). American (born United States), b. 1945. **Genres:** Children's Fiction, Education, Adult Non-fiction. **Career:** Actor, director and writer. **Publications:** Under the Gun, 1972-1973; The Prodigal Daughter, 1973; My Fat Friend, 1974; Kaufman at Large (solo show), 1981; Babysongs Presents John Lithgow's Kid-size Concert (video), 1990; Singin' in the Bathtub (children's musical album), 1999; The Remarkable Farkle McBride (children's book), 2000; Marsupial Sue (children's book), 2001; Farkle and Friends (children's musical album), 2002; Micawber (children's book), 2002; I'm a Manatee (children's book), 2003; Carnival of the Animals, 2004; Lithgow Palooza!: 101 Ways to Entertain and Inspire Your Kids, 2004; Marsupial Sue Presents the Runaway Pancake, 2005; Lithgow Party Paloozas: 52 Unexpected Ways to Make a Birthday, Holiday, or Any Day A Celebration for Kids, 2005; Boredom Blasters Home Sick Edition, 2005; (with M. Slack) Boredom Blasters Halloween Edition, 2005; Boredom Blasters: Holiday Fun Edition, 2006; Mahalia Mouse Goes to College, 2007; I Got Two Dogs, 2008; Drama, 2011. **Address:** Creative Artists Agency, 9830 Wilshire Blvd., Beverly Hills, CA 90212-1825, U.S.A.

LITHMAN, Yngve Georg. Swedish/Norwegian (born Norway), b. 1943. **Genres:** Anthropology/Ethnology, Area Studies. **Career:** University of Stockholm, Department of Anthropology, faculty, 1978-; University of London, visiting fellow of anthropology, 1985; University of Manitoba, professor, 1989-90; University of Bergen, International Migration and Ethnic Relations Research Unit (IMER), director, 1996-, now director emeritus, Department of Sociology, professor of sociology, 1996-. Writer. **Publications:** Two Papers on Canadian Indians, 1973; The Community Apart: A Case Study of a Canadian Indian Reserve Community, 1978, 3rd ed., 1986; The Practise of Underdevelopment and the Theory of Development, 1983; (co-author) People and Land in Northern Manitoba, 1992. EDITOR: Nybyggarna I Sverige, 1986; (with W.T. Gerholm) The New Islamic Presence in Western Europe, 1988; (with H.G. Sicakkan) Diversity and Citizenship: The European Union, Citizens, Minorities, and Migrants, 2003; (with H.G. Sicakkan) Changing the Basis of Citizenship in the Modern State: Political Theory and the Politics of Diversity, 2005; (with M. Andersson and O. Sernhede) Youth, Otherness, and the Plural City: Modes of Belonging and Social Life, 2005; (with H.G. Sicakkan) What Happens When a Society is Diverse?: Exploring Multidimensional Identities, 2006. Contributor to journals. **Address:** International Migration and Ethnic Relations, Research Unit, University of Bergen, Nygårdsgaten 5, 5th Fl., PO Box 7800, Bergen, 5015, Norway. **Online address:** yngve.lithman@sos.uib.no

LITMAN, Ellen. American/Russian (born Russia), b. 1973?. **Genres:** Novels. **Career:** Syracuse University, graduate instructor, 2001-04; Union Institute and University, Vermont College, faculty, 2004-05; University of Wisconsin, James C. McCreight fellow in fiction, 2004-05; Babson College, lecturer in rhetoric, 2005-06; Grub Street Inc., instructor, 2005-07; University of Connecticut, Creative Writing, assistant professor and associate director. Writer. **Publications:** The Last Chicken in America: A Novel in Stories, 2007. Work appears in anthologies. Contributor of articles to periodicals. **Address:** Department of English, University of Connecticut, 215 Glenbrook Rd., Ste. 4025, Storrs, CT 06269-4025, U.S.A. **Online address:** ellen.litman@uconn.edu

LITTELL, Robert. French/American (born United States), b. 1935. **Genres:** Novels, Young Adult Fiction, Literary Criticism And History. **Career:** Newsweek magazine, Eastern Europe and Soviet Union editor. **Publications:** (With R.Z. Chesnoff and E. Klein) If Israel Lost the War, 1967; (ed.) The Czech Black Book, 1969; Left and Right with Lion and Ryan, 1970; The Defection of A.J. Lewinter: A Novel of Duplicity, 1973; Sweet Reason, 1974; The October Circle, 1976; Mother Russia, 1978; The Debriefing: A Novel, 1979; The Amateur: A Novel of Revenge, 1981; The Sisters: A Novel of Betrayal, 1986; The Revolutionist, 1988; The Once and Future Spy: A Novel of Obsession, 1990; An Agent in Place, 1991; The Visiting Professor, 1994; Walking Back the Cat, 1997; (with S. Peres) For the Future of Israel, 1998; The Company: A Novel of the CIA, 2002; Agent in Place, 2005; Legends: A Novel of Dissimulation, 2005; Vicious Circle: A Novel of Mutual Distrust, 2006; Stalin Epigram: A Novel, 2009. **Address:** Overlook Press, 1 Overlook Dr., Woodstock, NY 12498, U.S.A.

LITTEN, Harold. See BAHR, Robert.

LITTEN, Julian. British (born England), b. 1947. **Genres:** Art/Art History, History, Social Sciences. **Career:** Victoria and Albert Museum, museum assistant, 1966-74, senior museum assistant, 1974-82, research assistant, 1983-88, curator, 1988-98; Canterbury Christ Church University College, visiting lecturer, 1999, 2004; Portsmouth cathedral, chairman. Writer. **Publications:** St. Mary's Church, Woodford, Essex, 1977; Sir Gilbert Scott, 1978; Land for the Living: The Cremation Movement (film), 1989; The English Way of Death: The Common Funeral since 1450, 1991; (intro.) The Eucharistic Year: Seasonal Devotions for the Sacrament, 2002; English Church Furnishings, 1919-1939, forthcoming. **Address:** John Pawsey Literay Agency, 60 High St., Tarring, Worthing, WS BN14 7NR, England.

LITTLE, Amanda. American (born United States), b. 1974?. **Genres:** Social Sciences. **Career:** Feedmag.com, reporter, 1996-; Village Voice, columnist; Grist.org, columnist, 2003-07; Salon.com, columnist, 2003-07; Outside Magazine, contributing editor and columnist. **Publications:** Power Trip: From Oil Wells to Solar Cells-Our Ride to the Renewable Future, 2009. **Address:** Nashville, TN , U.S.A. **Online address:** info@amandalittle.com

LITTLE, Anne Colclough. American (born United States), b. 1944. **Genres:** Literary Criticism And History, Poetry, Social Sciences. **Career:** Auburn University, assistant professor, 1989-95, associate professor of English, 1995-, director of Learning Center, 1995-99, director of composition, 1999-, now professor emeritus. Writer. **Publications:** (Ed. with R.C. Evans) The Muses Females Are: Martha Moulsworth and Other Women Writers of the English Renaissance, 1995; (with R.C. Evans and B. Wiedemann) Short Fiction: A Critical Companion, 1997; (ed. with S. Paul) Denise Levertov: New Perspectives, 2000. Contributor to periodicals. **Address:** Department of English and Philosophy, Auburn University, 7041 Senator's Dr., PO Box 244023, Montgomery, AL 36124, U.S.A. **Online address:** alittle@mail.aum.edu

LITTLE, Benerson. American (born United States), b. 1959?. **Genres:** History, Military/Defense/Arms Control, Travel/Exploration, International Relations/Current Affairs. **Career:** Writer, consultant and educator. **Publications:** The Sea Rover's Practice: Pirate Tactics and Techniques, 1630-1730, 2005; The Buccaneer's Realm: Pirate Life on the Spanish Main, 1674-1688, 2007; Pirate Hunting: The Fight Against Pirates, Privateers, and Sea Raiders from Antiquity to the Present, 2010; How History's Greatest Pirates Pillaged, Plundered, and Got Away With It, 2010. **Address:** Huntsville, AL , U.S.A. **Online address:** readermail@benersonlittle.com

LITTLE, Bentley. (Phillip Emmons). American (born United States), b. 1960. **Genres:** Horror, Mystery/Crime/Suspense, Novels, Novellas/Short Stories. **Career:** Radical Environmental Group, founder. Writer. **Publications:** HORROR NOVELS: The Revelation, 1990; The Mailman, 1991; (as Phillip Emmons) Death Instinct, 1992 in UK as Bentley Little as Evil Deeds, 1994; The Summoning, 1993; Night School, 1994 in US as University, 1995; Dark Dominion, 1995 in US as Dominion, 1996; The Store, 1996; Houses, 1997 in US as The House, 1998; The Ignored, 1997; Guests, 1997 in US as The Town, 2000; The Walking, 2000; The Association, 2001; The Return, 2002; The Policy, 2003; the Resort, 2004; Dispatch, 2005; The Burning, 2006; Hunting, 2006; The Mall, 2006; The Vanishing, 2007; The Academy, 2008; His Father's Son, 2009; The Disappearance, 2010; Ghost Story, 2012. OTHER: Murmurous Haunts, 1997; The Collection (short stories), 2002; (with D. Clegg, C. Golden and T. Piccirilli) Four Dark Nights, 2002. Contributor to periodicals. Works appear in anthologies. **Address:** Dominick Abel, 146 W 82nd St., Ste. 1B, New York, NY 10024, U.S.A.

LITTLE, Cynthia. (Cynthia M. Little). American (born United States) **Genres:** Human Relations/Parenting, Self Help, Romance/Historical. **Ca-**

reer: Writer and real estate agent. **Publications:** Life Lessons before I Do: Things I Wish I Knew!, 2005. Contributor to periodicals. **Address:** c/o Author Mail, Sleepless Warrior Publishing, 14989 Grassy Knoll Ct., Woodbridge, VA 22193, U.S.A.

LITTLE, Cynthia M. *See* **LITTLE, Cynthia.**

LITTLE, Douglas. Australian (born Australia), b. 1942. **Genres:** Animals/Pets, Education. **Career:** Architect, 1966-2002; AFS Student Exchange Program, chapter president, 1985-88. Writer. **Publications:** Ten Little Known Facts About Hippopotamuses: And More Little Known Facts and a Few Fibs About Other Animals, 1994. Contributror to periodicals. **Address:** 2/355 Maroubra Rd., Maroubra, NW 2035, Australia.

LITTLE, (Flora) Jean. Canadian/Taiwanese (born Taiwan), b. 1932. **Genres:** Children's Fiction, Poetry, Picture/Board Books, Novellas/Short Stories, Animals/Pets, Young Adult Non-fiction, Novels. **Career:** University of Guelph, Department of English, adjunct professor, 1992-; Beechwood School for Crippled Children, specialist teacher; Institute of Special Education, visiting instructor; Florida University, visiting instructor. Writer. **Publications:** It's a Wonderful World (poems), 1947; Mine for Keeps, 1962; Home from Far, 1965; One to Grow On, 1965; Spring Begins in March, 1966; Take Wing, 1968; When the Pie Was Opened: Poems, 1968; One to Grown On, 1969; Look through My Window, 1970; Kate, 1971; From Anna, 1972; Stand in the Wind, 1975; Listen for the Singing, 1977; Zephyr, 1983; Mama's Going to Buy You a Mockingbird, 1984; Mama's Going to Buy You a Mockingbird, 1984; Lost and Found, 1985; Different Dragons, 1986; Little by Little, 1987; Hey World, Here I Am: Poems, 1989; Invitations to Joy: A Celebration of Canada's Young Readers and the Books They Love, 1989; Stars Come Out Within, 1990; Once upon a Golden Apple, 1991; Jess Was the Brave One, 1991; The Revenge of the Small Small, 1992; His Banner over Me, 1995; Bats about Baseball, 1995; Jenny and the Hanukkah Queen, 1995; Gruntle Piggle Takes Off, 1996; The Belonging Place, 1997; Emma's Magic Winter, 1998; What Will the Robin Do Then? (poetry), 1998; I Know an Old Laddie, 1999; Willow and Twig, 2000; Emma's Yucky Brother, 2000; The Jean Little Collection, 2001; Orphan at My Door: The Home Child Diary Of Victoria Cope, 2001; (contrib.) When I Went to the Library: Writers Celebrate Books and Reading, 2001; Birdie for Now, 2002; Brothers Far from Home: The World War I Diary of Eliza Bates, 2003; I Gave My Mom a Castle (poetry), 2003; Emma's Strange Pet, 2003; Pippin the Christmas Pig, 2004; Birthday Girl, 2004; Rescue Pup, 2004; Forward, Shakespeare!, 2005; Somebody Else's Summer, 2005; Dancing Through the Snow, 2007; Elle danse dans la tourmente, 2007; If I Die before I Wake: The Flu Epidemic Diary of Fiona Macgregor, 2007; Sweetest One of All, 2008; Exiles from the War: The War Guests Diary of Charlotte Mary Twiss, 2010; Emma's Worm Club, 2011. Contributor to periodicals. **Address:** Viking Canada, 90 Eglinton Ave. E, Ste. 700, Toronto, ON M4P 2Y3, Canada. **Online address:** jeanlittle@nospamrogers.com

LITTLE, J. I. Canadian (born Canada), b. 1947. **Genres:** History, Cultural/Ethnic Topics, Economics. **Career:** Simon Fraser University, Department of History, faculty, 1976-, professor and chair. Writer and historian. **Publications:** Colonizing an Eastern Frontier: Compton County, Quebec, National Museum of Man, 1981; Nationalism, Capitalism, and Colonization in Nineteenth-Century Quebec: The Upper St. Francis District, 1989; Ethno-Cultural Transition and Regional Identity in the Eastern Townships of Quebec, 1989; Crofters and Habitants: Settler Society, Economy, and Culture in a Quebec Township, 1848-1881, 1991; (contrib.) The Immigrant Experience, 1992; (ed.) The Child Letters: Public and Private Life in a Canadian Merchant-Politician's Family, 1841-1845, 1995; State and Society in Transition: The Politics of Institutional Reform in the Eastern Townships, 1838-1852, 1997; (ed.) Love Strong as Death: Lucy Peel's Canadian Journal, 1833-1836, 2001; (contrib.) On the Margins of the Family, 2003; Borderland Religion: The Emergence of an English-Canadian Identity, 1792-1852, 2004; The Other Quebec: Microhistorical Essays on Nineteenth-Century Religion and Society, 2006; Loyalties in Conflict: A Canadian Borderland in War and Rebellion, 1812-1840, 2008. Contributor to periodicals. **Address:** Department of History, Simon Fraser University, AQ 6234, 8888 University Dr., Burnaby, BC V5A 1S6, Canada. **Online address:** jlittle@sfu.ca

LITTLE, Katherine C. American (born United States), b. 1969?. **Genres:** Literary Criticism And History. **Career:** Fordham University, associate professor. Writer and academic. **Publications:** Confession and Resistance: Defining the Self in Late Medieval England, 2006. Contributor to periodicals. **Address:** Fordham University, 441 E. Fordham Rd., Bronx, NY 10458-5149, U.S.A. **Online address:** kalittle@fordham.edu

LITTLE, Terra. American (born United States), b. 1973. **Genres:** Literary Criticism And History. **Career:** Writer. **Publications:** Running from Mercy, 2008; Where There's Smoke, 2009. **Address:** U.S.A. **Online address:** writeterralittle@yahoo.com

LITTLEFIELD, Bill. (William E. Littlefield). American (born United States), b. 1948. **Genres:** Novels, Sports/Fitness, Biography. **Career:** Curry College, writer-in-residence, professor of humanities, 1976-; Harvard University, Summer School, faculty of sports writing, John F. Kennedy School Summer Program, faculty, 1981-87; National Public Radio, host and commentator, 1984-. **Publications:** Prospect, 1989; Champions: Stories of Ten Remarkable Athletes, 1993; Baseball Days: From the Sandlots to the Show, 1993; Keepers: Radio Stories From Only a Game & Elsewhere, 1998; The Circus in the Woods (novel), 2001; (ed. with R.A. Johnson) Fall Classics: The Best Writing about the World Series' First 100 Years (anthology), 2003; Only a Game, 2007; (contrib.) Succeeding in Business with Microsoft Office Excel 2007: a Problem-Solving Approach, 2007. Contributor to periodicals. **Address:** c/o Only a Game, WBUR, 890 Commonwealth Ave., 3rd Fl., Boston, MA 02215, U.S.A. **Online address:** blittlef@wbur.bu.edu

LITTLEFIELD, Holly. American (born United States), b. 1963. **Genres:** Novels, Travel/Exploration, Adult Non-fiction, Education, Picture/Board Books. **Career:** Park Center Senior High School, teacher, 1986-93; University of Minnesota, Carlson School of Management, researcher and teacher of communication, 1992-, instructor, 1993-99, Department of Strategic Management and Organization, senior lecturer, 1999-. Writer. **Publications:** FICTION: Fire at the Triangle Factory, 1996. COLORS OF THE WORLD SERIES: The Colors of Germany, 1997; The Colors of Japan, 1997; Colors of Ghana, 1999; Colors of India, 2000. PICTURE THE AMERICAN PAST SERIES: Children of the Trail West, 1999; Children of the Indian Boarding Schools, 2001; Children of the Orphan Trains, 2001. OTHERS: (with L. Bridwell-Bowles and K.S. DeVore) Identity Matters: Rhetorics of Difference, 1998; Rooftop Adventure of Minnie and Tessa, Factory Fire Survivors, 2011. Contributor to periodicals. **Address:** Carlson School of Management, University of Minnesota, 4-233, 321 19th Ave. S, Minneapolis, MN 55455-0438, U.S.A. **Online address:** littl009@umn.edu

LITTLEFIELD, William E. *See* **LITTLEFIELD, Bill.**

LITTLEJOHN, Duffy. American (born United States), b. 1953. **Genres:** Travel/Exploration, Social Sciences. **Career:** McCarthy, Flowers, and Roberts (law firm), attorney, 1983-84; Meadows and Doris (law firm), attorney, 1984-85; San Francisco District Attorney's Office, assistant district attorney, 1985-87; Alameda County District Attorney's Office, senior deputy district attorney, 1987-89; criminal defense attorney, 1989-90, 1992-. Writer. **Publications:** Hopping Freight Trains in America, 1993; Cindertrail Tales, 1994; The Anomaly, 1995; Flight from Paradise, 1995; Lonesome Whistle, 2002; Ridin' Free, 2002. **Address:** Zephyr Rhoades Press, PO Box 1999, Silver City, NM 88062-1999, U.S.A. **Online address:** dlittlejohnzrp@zianet.com

LITTLETON, Darryl. American (born United States) **Genres:** Sociology, Humor/Satire, Biography, Autobiography/Memoirs. **Career:** Writer. **Publications:** Black Comedians on Black Comedy: How African-Americans Taught Us to Laugh, 2006. **Address:** Applause Theatre & Cinema Books, 19 W 21st St., Ste. 201, New York, NY 10010-6883, U.S.A. **Online address:** darryllittleton@blackcomedycompetition.com

LITTLETON, Mark (R.). American (born United States), b. 1950. **Genres:** Novels, Adult Non-fiction, Children's Fiction, Young Adult Fiction, Children's Non-fiction, Young Adult Non-fiction. **Career:** Author and pastor. **Publications:** NONFICTION: A Place to Stand: When Life Throws You off Balance, 1986; When God Seems Far Away: Biblical Insight for Common Depression, 1987; Lies We Like to Hear: Satan's Everyday Strategies, 1988; Submission is for Husbands, Too (adult), 1988; Cool Characters with Sweaty Palms, 1989; What To Do When God Doesn't Follow Your Plan, 1989; The Terrible Plight of Oliver B., 1990; Delighted by Discipline, 1990; Escaping the Time Crunch, 1990; Battle Ready: Winning the War with Temptation, 1992; (with B. and A. Kelley) Stasia's Gift, 1993; The Storm Within, 1994; (with F. Minirth) You Can!, 1994. ADULT FICTION: Tales of the Neverending, 1990; Death Trip: A Novel, 1992; Before Eden, 1995. YOUNG ADULT

NONFICTION: When They Invited Me to Fellowship I Thought They Meant a Cruise, 1992; The Basics: Nailing down What Builds You up, 1994. UP SERIES (young adult nonfiction): Beefin' Up: Daily Feed for Amazing Grazing, 1989; Tunin' Up: Daily Jammin' for Tight Relationships, 1991; Fillin' Up, 1993; Pairin' Up, 1995. ROCKY CREEK ADVENTURES SERIES (young adult fiction): The Adventure at Rocky Creek, 1993; Tree Fort Wars, 1993; Trouble down the Creek, 1994. CRISTA CHRONICLES SERIES (young adult fiction): The Secret of Moonlight Mountain, 1992; Winter Thunder, 1992; Robbers on Rock Road, 1993; Escape of the Grizzly, 1994; Danger on Midnight Trail, 1994; Friends No Matter What, 1994. SPORTS HEROES SERIES: Baseball, 1995; Basketball, 1995; Football, 1995; Track and Field, 1995; Soccer, 1996; Summer Olympics, 1996; Baseball 2, 1996; Basketball 2, 1996; Olympics 2002, 2002; Extreme Sports, 2002; Auto Racing, 2002; Baseball Three, 2002. OTHERS: Basics: Nailing Down What Builds You Up, 1994; Track & Field, 1995; Before Eden, 1995; God Is!, 1997; Truth About Rock, 1998; NIrV kids' Book of Devotions: A 356-Day Adventure in God's Word, 1998; (with J.G. Littleton) Light the Torch, Pass the Flame: Lessons from Our Fathers, 1998; (with J.G. Littleton) What's in the Bible for Teens, 2000, rev. ed., 2007; (with J.C. Maxwell) Leading Your Sports Team, 2001; (with J.C. Maxwell) Leading in Your Youth Group, 2001; (with J.C. Maxwell) Leading as a Friend, 2001; Tracks in the Sand, 2001; Sarah's Secret, 2001; Jesus: Everything You Need to Know to Figure Him Out, 2001; 101 Amazing Truths about Jesus That You Probably Didn't Know, 2001; Hoofbeats on the Trail, 2002; Getting Honest with God: Praying as if God Really Listens, 2003; (contrib.) The Edge Devotional Bible, 2003; (with V. Armitage) Living Life to the Max: Solomon's Wisdom for Christian Living, 2004; Through the Bible Devotions, 2004; (with C. Wright) Doc: Heroic Stories of Medics, Corpsmen and Surgeons in Combat, 2005; (with J.G. Littleton) What's in the Bible for Teens: Life's Questions, God's Answers, 2007; The Ten-Second Prayer Principle: Praying Powerfully As You Go, 2007; The Bible Bathroom Book: Information for Those Who Have Only Minutes to Read, 2008; Big Bad God of the Bible, 2008; My Impossible Year, 2009; The War in Heaven, 2009; The Get-A-Clue Devotions: The Case of the Howling Dog and 51 More Mysteries, 2010; 365 The New Testament Devotions for Kids, 2010. **Address:** Thomas Nelson Inc., 501 Nelson Pl., PO Box 141000, Nashville, TN 37214, U.S.A. **Online address:** mlittleton@earthlink.net

LITTLEWOOD, Clayton. British (born England), b. 1963?. **Genres:** Biography, Autobiography/Memoirs. **Career:** Writer. **Publications:** Dirty White Boy: Tales of Soho, 2008. **Address:** London, GL , England. **Online address:** clayuk@aol.com

LITTMAN, Jonathan (Russell). American (born United States), b. 1958. **Genres:** Information Science/Computers, Medicine/Health, Psychology. **Career:** PC World (magazine), contributing editor, 1983-84; PC Week (magazine), staff reporter, 1984-86; Mac World (magazine), contributing editor, 1987-. **Publications:** Once upon a Time in Computer Land: The Amazing, Billion-Dollar Tale of Bill Millard, 1987; The Fugitive Game: Online with Kevin Mitnick, 1996; Watchman: The Twisted Life and Crimes of Serial Hacker Kevin Poulsen, 1997; Beautiful Game: Sixteen Girls and the Soccer Season that Changed Everything, 1999; (with T. Kelley) Art of Innovation: Lessons in Creativity from IDEO, America's Leading Design Firm, 2001; (with C. Sandys) We Shall not Fail: The Inspiring Leadership of Winston Churchill, 2003; (with T. Kelley) Ten Faces of Innovation: IDEO's Strategies for Beating the Devil's Advocate & Driving Creativity Throughout your Organization, 2005; (with M. Hershon) I Hate People!: Kick Loose from the Overbearing and Underhanded Jerks at Work and Get What You Want Out of Your Job, 2009. Contributor of articles to magazines. **Address:** Little Brown & Company Inc., 1271 Ave. of the Americas, New York, NY 10020, U.S.A.

LITWACK, Leon. Also writes as Leon Frank Litwack, Leon F. Litwack. American (born United States), b. 1929. **Genres:** History, Race Relations. **Career:** University of Wisconsin, instructor, 1958-59, assistant professor, 1959-63, associate professor, 1963-65; University of California, Department of History faculty, 1965-, assistant professor, professor, 1971-, Alexander F. and May T. Morrison professor, 1987-, now Alexander F. and May T. Morrison professor emeritus; Organization of American Historians, president, distinguished lecturer. Writer. **Publications:** North of Slavery: The Negro in the Free States 1790-1860, 1961; (co-author) The United States, 1982, 4th ed., 1994; Been in the Storm So Long: The Aftermath of Slavery, 1979; (co-author) Before the Point of No Return: An Exchange of Views on the Cold War, the Reagan Doctrine, and What Is to Come, 1986; (with A. Meier) Black Leaders of the Nineteenth Century, 1988; Trouble in Mind: Black Southerners

in the Age of Jim Crow, 1998; (co-author) Without Sanctuary: Lynching Photography in America, 2000. EDITOR: The American Labor Movement, 1962; (with K. Stampp) Reconstruction: An Anthology of Revisionist Writings, 1969; (with A. Meier) Black Leaders of the Nineteenth Century, 1988; (with D.C. Hine) The Harvard Guide to African-American History, 2001; How Free is Free?: The Long Death of Jim Crow, 2009. **Address:** Department of History, University of California, 3229 Dwinelle Hall, Berkeley, CA 94720-2550, U.S.A. **Online address:** llitwack@berkeley.edu

LITWACK, Leon F. *See* **LITWACK, Leon.**

LITWACK, Leon Frank. *See* **LITWACK, Leon.**

LITWAK, Robert S. American (born United States), b. 1953. **Genres:** Military/Defense/Arms Control, History, Economics. **Career:** London School of Economics, Department of International Relations, lecturer, 1977-81, tutor, 1978-80; London International Institute for Strategic Studies, research associate, 1979-81; RAND Corp., Department of Political Science, consultant, 1981-82; Harvard University, Center for International Affairs, Olin postdoctoral fellow, 1981-83, Russian Research Center, Olin post-doctoral fellow, 1981-83; Wellesley College, Barnette Miller visiting assistant professor, 1982-83; Woodrow Wilson International Center for Scholars, international security studies senior program associate and research associate, 1983-88, director of international security studies, 1988-, vice president for programs, 2009-; American University, professorial lecturer, 1988; White House, National Security Council, nonproliferation director, 1995-96; Georgetown University, Edmund A. Walsh School of Foreign Service, Security Studies Program, adjunct professor, 2000-; Los Alamos National Laboratory, consultant, 2006-. Writer. **Publications:** Security in the Persian Gulf, 1981; (with S. Chubin and A. Plascov) Security in the Gulf, 1982; Détente and the Nixon Doctrine: American Foreign Policy and the Pursuit of Stability, 1969-1976, 1984; (with T. George and S. Chubin) India and the Great Powers, 1984; (ed. with S.F. Wells, Jr.) Strategic Defenses and Soviet-American Relations, 1987; (ed. with S.F. Wells, Jr.) Superpower Competition and Security in the Third World, 1988; (ed. with M.B. Bullock) The United States and the Pacific Basin: Changing Economic and Security Relationships, 1991; (ed. with M. Reiss) Nuclear Proliferation after the Cold War, 1994; Rogue States and U.S. Foreign Policy: Containment after the Cold War, 2000; Regime Change: U.S. Strategy through the Prism of 9/11, 2007. Contributor to periodicals and journals. **Address:** Woodrow Wilson International Center for Scholars, Ronald Reagan Bldg. and International Trade Ctr., 1 Woodrow Wilson Plz., 1300 Pennsylvania Ave. NW, Washington, DC 20004-3027, U.S.A. **Online address:** robert.litwak@wilsoncenter.org

LIU, Eric. American (born United States), b. 1968. **Genres:** Literary Criticism And History, Translations, Autobiography/Memoirs. **Career:** Next Progressive, founder, 1991, editor, 1991-96; National Security Council, Clinton Speech writer, 1993-94; White House, deputy domestic policy adviser, 1999-2000; Real Networks, vice president, 2000-02; The New America Foundation, fellow, 2002-. Writer. **Publications:** (Ed.) Next: Young American Writers on the New Generation, 1994; The Accidental Asian: Notes of a Native Speaker (memoir), 1998; Guiding Lights: The People Who Lead Us Toward Our Purpose in Life, 2004; The True Patriot, 2008; (with S. Noppe-Brandon) Imagination First: Unlocking the Power of Possibility, 2009; (with V. Pellatt) Thinking Chinese Translation: A Course in Translation Method: Chinese to English, 2010; Gardens of Democracy: A New American Story of Citizenship, The Economy and the Role of Government; (trans.) Travels of Lao Can. Contributor to periodicals. **Address:** c/o Raphael Sagalyn, Sagalyn Literary Agency, 7201 Wisconsin Ave., Ste. 675, Bethesda, MD 20814, U.S.A. **Online address:** liu@newamerica.net

LIU, Hsiao-yuan. *See* **LIU, Xiaoyuan.**

LIU, Lydia H. American (born United States), b. 1957. **Genres:** Literary Criticism And History, Cultural/Ethnic Topics. **Career:** Tsinghua University, School of Journalism and Communication, executive dean; University of California, Catherine and William L. Magistretti Distinguished Professor of East Asian Languages and Cultures; University of Michigan, faculty member and chair of the Helmut Stern Professorship in Chinese Studies; Columbia University, Wun Tsun Tam Professor in the Humanities, 2006-. Writer. **Publications:** Translingual Practice: Literature, National Culture, and Translated Modernity-China, 1900-1937, 1995; (ed.) Tokens of Exchange: The Problem of Translation in Global Circulations, 1999; (ed. with J.T. Zeitlin and E. Widmer) Writing and Materiality in China: Essays in Honor of Patrick Hanan, 2003; The Clash of Empires: The Invention of China in Modern World Making, 2004. Contributor to books and periodicals. **Address:** Department of East Asian Languages & Cultures, Columbia University, 407 Kent Hall, PO Box 3907, New York, NY 10027, U.S.A. **Online address:** ll2410@columbia.edu

LIU, Timothy. American (born United States), b. 1965. **Genres:** Poetry, Literary Criticism And History. **Career:** Cornell College, assistant professor, 1994-98; University of California, Holloway lecturer, 1997-; William Paterson University, Department of English, assistant professor, associate professor, professor, 1998-; Bennington College Graduate Writing Seminars, core faculty, 2005-. Writer. **Publications:** A Zipper of Haze, 1988; Vox Angelica: Poems, 1992; Burnt Offerings, 1995; Say Goodnight, 1998; (ed.) Word of Mouth: An Anthology of Gay American Poetry, 2000; Hard Evidence, 2001; A Mighty Fortress, 2001; Of Thee I Sing, 2004; For Dust Thou Art, 2005; (with G. Drasler) Polytheogamy, 2009; Bending the Mind Around the Dream's Blown Fuse, 2009; (with H. Bergwall) The Thames & Hudson Project, 2011. Contributor to journals. **Address:** Department of English, William Paterson University, 300 Pompton Rd., Atrium 250, Wayne, NJ 07470, U.S.A. **Online address:** liut@wpunj.edu

LIU, Xiaoyuan. (Hsiao-yuan Liu). Chinese/American (born United States), b. 1952?. **Genres:** History. **Career:** Iowa State University, professor of history. Historian, educator, writer and editor. **Publications:** A Partnership for Disorder: China, the United States, and Their Policies for the Postwar Disposition of the Japanese Empire, 1941-1945, 1996; (ed. with C.X.G. Wei) Chinese Nationalism in Perspective: Historical and Recent Cases, 2001; (ed. with C.X.G. Wei) Exploring Nationalisms of China: Themes and Conflicts, 2002; (ed. with V. Mastny) China and Eastern Europe, 1960s-1980s: Proceedings of the International Symposium: Reviewing the History of Chinese-East European Relations from the 1960s to the 1980s, Beijing, 24-26 March 2004, 2004; Frontier Passages: Ethnopolitics and the Rise of Chinese Communism, 1921-1945, 2004; Reins of Liberation: An Entangled History of Mongolian Independence, Chinese Territoriality and Great Power Hegemony, 1911-1950, 2006. Contributor to journals. **Address:** Department of History, Iowa State University, 623 Ross Hall, Ames, IA 50011, U.S.A. **Online address:** xyliu@iastate.edu

LIVELY, Adam. British/Welsh (born Wales), b. 1961. **Genres:** Novels, Politics/Government, Young Adult Non-fiction, Literary Criticism And History. **Career:** Critic, novelist, broadcaster and teacher. **Publications:** NOVELS: Blue Fruit, 1988; The Burnt House, 1989; The Snail, 1991; Sing the Body Electric, 1993. NONFICTION: Parliament: The Great British Democracy Swindle, 1990; (ed. with J. Lively) Democracy in Britain: A Reader, 1994; Masks: Blackness, Race and the Imagination, 1998. **Address:** c/o Derek Johns, A. P. Watt Ltd., 20 John St., London, GL WC1N 2DR, England. **Online address:** adamlively89@gmail.com

LIVELY, Penelope. British/Egyptian (born Egypt), b. 1933. **Genres:** Novels, Novellas/Short Stories, Children's Fiction, Plays/Screenplays, Young Adult Non-fiction, History. **Career:** British Broadcasting Corp., acting presenter. Writer. **Publications:** CHILDREN'S FICTION: Astercote, 1970; The Whispering Knights, 1971; The Wild Hunt of Hagworthy, 1971 in US as The Wild Hunt of the Ghost Hounds, 1972; The Driftway, 1972; The Ghost of Thomas Kempe, 1973; The House in Norham Gardens, 1974; Going Back, 1975; The Boy without a Name, 1975; A Stitch in Time, 1976; Fanny's Sister, 1976; The Stained Glass Window, 1976; The Voyage of QV 66, 1978; Fanny and the Monsters, 1978; Fanny and the Battle of Potter's Piece, 1980; The Revenge of Samuel Stokes, 1981; Fanny and the Monsters and Other Stories, 1982; Uninvited Ghosts and Other Stories, 1984; Dragon Trouble, 1984; Debbie and the Little Devil, 1987; A House Inside Out, 1987; Judy and the Martian, 1992; The Cat, the Crow, and the Banyan Tree, 1994; Good Night, Sleep Tight, 1995; Two Bears and Joe, 1995; A Martian Comes to Stay, 1995; Goldilocks and the Three Bears, 1997; Ghostly Guests, 1997; One, Two, Three Jump!, 1998; In Search of a Homeland: The Story of the Aeneid, 2001. ADULT NOVELS: The Road to Lichfield, 1977; Treasures of Time, 1979; Judgement Day, 1980; Next to Nature, Art, 1982; Perfect Happiness, 1983; According to Mark, 1984; Moon Tiger, 1988; Passing On, 1989; City of the Mind, 1991; Cleopatra's Sister, 1993; Heat Wave, 1996; The Five Thousand and One Nights, 1997; Spiderweb, 1999; The Photograph, 2003; Making It Up, 2005; Consequences, 2007; Family Album, 2009; How It All Began, 2011. STORIES: Nothing Missing but the Samovar and Other Stories, 1978; Corruption and Other Stories, 1984; Pack of Cards: Stories 1978-86, 1986;

Lost Dog and Other Stories, 1996; Beyond the Blue Mountains, 1997; (co-author) Stories for 6-Year-Olds, 1997; (with M. Hoffman and G. Cross) Spooky Stories: Three Stories in One, 2008. OTHERS: The Presence of the Past: An Introduction to Landscape History, 1976; (intro.) Father and His Fate, 1984; (intro.) Manservant and Maidservant, 1987; (intro.) The Age of Innocence, 1988; (intro.) Alice's Adventures in Wonderland, 1993; Oleander, Jacaranda: A Childhood Perceived (memoir), 1994; (intro.) My Antonia, 1996; (intro.) The Mythical Quest, 1996; A House Unlocked, 2001; (ed.) New Writing, 2001. Contributor to books and periodicals. **Address:** David Higham Associates Ltd., 5-8 Lower John St., Golden Sq., London, GL W1F 9HA, England.

LIVINGSTON, Gordon (S.). American (born United States), b. 1938. **Genres:** Medicine/Health, Human Relations/Parenting, Adult Non-fiction, Autobiography/Memoirs, Essays, Philosophy, Politics/Government, Psychiatry, Social Commentary. **Career:** Columbia Medical Plan, psychiatrist, 1971-; Johns Hopkins University, Department of Psychiatry, assistant professor, professor, chairman; Patuxent Medical Group, chief of psychiatry; The Family Center, staff. Writer. **Publications:** Only Spring: On Mourning the Death of My Son, 1995; Too Soon Old, Too Late Smart: Thirty True Things You Need to Know Now, 2004; And Never Stop Dancing: Thirty More True Things You Need to Know Now, 2006; How to Love, 2009. Contributor to journals. **Address:** The Family Center, 4785 Dorsey Hall Dr., Ste. 109, Ellicott City, MD 21042, U.S.A. **Online address:** gslcvk@aol.com

LIVINGSTON, James. American (born United States), b. 1949. **Genres:** Politics/Government, Economics. **Career:** Rutgers University, professor of history; New York Public Library, Cullman Center for Scholars and Writers, fellow. Writer. **Publications:** Origins of the Federal Reserve System: Money, Class, and Corporate Capitalism, 1890-1913, 1986; Pragmatism and the Political Economy of Cultural Revolution, 1850-1940, 1994; Pragmatism, Feminism, and Democracy: Rethinking the Politics of American History, 2001; The World Turned Inside Out: American Thought and Culture at the End of the 20th Century, 2010. Contributor to periodicals. **Address:** Department of History, Rutgers University, 307 Van Dyck Hall, New Brunswick, NJ 08901, U.S.A. **Online address:** jameslivingston49@hotmail.com

LIVINGSTON, Robert Henry. American (born United States), b. 1934. **Genres:** Songs/Lyrics And Libretti, Plays/Screenplays, Music, Young Adult Fiction. **Career:** Gateway Playhouse, stage manager, 1953-56; Booth Theater, assistant stage manager, 1956-59; Columbia Broadcasting System, production assistant, 1959, assistant director, director, 1960-63; writer, 1963-. Freelance director. **Publications:** The Me Nobody Knows: Libretto, 1971; Taking My Turn, 1984; Finkel's Follies, 1990. **Address:** c/o David Hatfield, Carid Management, 1641 3rd Ave., New York, NY 10028, U.S.A.

LIVOTI, Carol. American (born United States) **Genres:** Women's Studies And Issues, Medicine/Health. **Career:** New York Medical College, assistant professor, 1973-76; Playgirl Magazine, columnist, 2005-; Seventeen Magazine, columnist, 2005-. Writer and gynecologist. **Publications:** (With E. Topp) Vaginas: An Owner's Manual, 2004; (with E. Topp) The Stress-Free Pregnancy Guide: A Doctor Tells You What to Really Expect, 2008. **Address:** c/o Author Mail, Avalon Publishing Group, 1400 65th St., Ste. 250, Emeryville, CA 94608-1077, U.S.A. **Online address:** carol@vaginas411.com

LL COOL J. American (born United States), b. 1968. **Genres:** Autobiography/Memoirs, Music, How-to Books, Self Help. **Career:** Rapper, actor and writer. **Publications:** All Change, 1996; Phenomenon and Beef with Canibus, 1997; (with K. Hunter) I Make My Own Rules, 1997; And the Winner Is ..., 2002; 10, 2002; (with D. Honig and J. O'Connell) LL Cool J's Platinum Workout, 2007; (with J. Stoppani, C. Palmer and D. Honig) LL Cool J's Platinum 360 Diet and Lifestyle: A Full-Circle Guide to Developing Your Mind, Body and Soul, 2010. **Address:** c/o Jason Barrett, Alchemy Entertainment, 73 Market St., Venice, CA 90291, U.S.A.

LLEWELLYN, Kate. Australian (born Australia), b. 1936. **Genres:** Novels, Poetry, Travel/Exploration, Autobiography/Memoirs, Essays. **Career:** Gawler District Hospital, nurse, 1954-58; Royal Adelaide Hospital, trainee nurse, 1958-60; Llewellyn Galleries, co-owner and director, 1968-75; Bonython Galleries, owner and co-director, 1971-72. Writer. **Publications:** POETRY: Trader Kate and the Elephants, 1983; Luxury, 1985; Honey, 1988; Mountain, 1989; Figs, 1990; Selected Poems, 1992; Crosshatched, 1994; So False and Other Poems, 1999. OTHERS: (ed. with S. Hampton) The Penguin Book of Australian Women Poets, 1986; The Waterlily, 1986; Dear You,

1987; Angels and Dark Madonnas-Travels in Italy and India, 1991; Lilies, Feathers and Frangipani, 1993; The Floral Mother and Other Essays, 1995; Gorillas, Tea, and Coffee: An African Sketchbook, 1996; Sofala and Other Poems, 1999; Playing with Water, 2005; The Dressmaker's Daughter, 2008; Kate Llewellyn, 2010. **Address:** Curtis Brown Australia, PO Box 19, Paddington, NW 2021, Australia.

LLEWELLYN, Sam. British (born England), b. 1948. **Genres:** Novels, Mystery/Crime/Suspense, Romance/Historical, Children's Fiction, Marine Sciences/Oceanography, Mythology/Folklore, History, Local History/Rural Topics, Local History/Rural Topics. **Career:** New Hat Publishing, director of Arch Books; The Marine Quarterly, writer, columnist and editor. **Publications:** THRILLERS: Dead Reckoning, 1988; Blood Orange, 1989; Death Roll, 1990; Deadeye, 1991; Blood Knot, 1992; Riptide, 1994; Clawhammer, 1994; Maelstrom, 1995; Storm Force from Navarone, 1996; The Shadow in the Sands, 1998; Black Fish, 2010. CHILDREN'S BOOKS: Pegleg, 1989; Pig in the Middle, 1989; The Rope School, 1994; The Magic Boathouse, 1995; The Polecat Cafe, 1996; Little Darlings, 2005; Bad Bad Darlings, 2006; Desperado Darlings, 2007; The Return of Death Eric, 2007; The Haunting of Death Eric, 2007; Abbot Dagger's Academy and the Quest for the Holy Grail, 2008; Lyonesse: The Well Between the Worlds, 2009, Lyonesse: Darksolstice, 2010. OTHER: Gurney's Revenge, 1978; Gurney's Reward, 1979; Gurney's Release, 1979; Hell Bay(novel), 1980; The Last Will and Testament of Robert Louis Stevenson, 1981; Yacky dar Moy Bewty!: A Phrasebook for the Regions of Britain (with Irish Supplement), 1985; Small Parts in History (nonfiction), 1985; The Worst Journey in the Midlands (nonfiction), 1985; Great Circle, 1987; The Sea Garden, 2001; The Malpas Legacy, 2002; Nelson (nonfiction), 2004; Emperor Smith, the Man Who Built Scilly (nonfiction), 2005, The Minimum Boat (collected columns) 2010. **Address:** Araminta Whitley, 14 Vernon St., London, GL W14 ORJ, England. **Online address:** sam@samllewellyn.com

LLITERAS, D. S. American (born United States), b. 1949. **Genres:** Novels, Poetry, Young Adult Fiction, Romance/Historical, History. **Career:** Norfolk Fire Department, firefighter, 1986-. Writer. **Publications:** LLEWELLYN TRILOGY: In the Heart of Things, 1992; Into the Ashes, 1993; Half Hidden by Twilight, 1994. NOVELS: In a Warrior's Romance, 1991; The Thieves of Golgotha, 1998; Judas the Gentile, 1999; 613 West Jefferson, 2001; Jerusalem's Rain, 2003; Silence of John, 2005; The Master of Secrets, 2007. Works appear in anthologies. Contributor to periodicals. **Address:** PO Box 5216, Virginia Beach, VA 23471-0216, U.S.A.

LLOBERA, Josep R. See Obituaries.

LLOYD, A(lan) R(ichard). British (born England), b. 1927. **Genres:** Novels, Science Fiction/Fantasy, Animals/Pets, History, Biography, Military/Defense/Arms Control, Young Adult Fiction. **Career:** Jersey Evening Post, journalist; freelance magazine writer; full-time author, 1962-. **Publications:** NOVELS: The Last Otter, 1984 in US as The Boy and the Otter, 1985; The Farm Dog, 1986; Wingfoot, 1993. FANTASY NOVELS: Kine, 1982 in UK as Marshworld, 1990; Witchwood, 1989; Dragonpond, 1990. AS ALAN LLOYD: The Drums of Kumasi: The Story of the Ashanti Wars, 1964; The Making of the King, 1066 in UK as The Year of the Conqueror, 1966; The Spanish Centuries, 1968 as The Spanish Centuries: A Narrative History of Spain from Ferdinand and Isabella to Franco, 2002; Franco, 1969; The King Who Lost America: A Portrait of the Life and Times of George III in UK as The Wickedest Age: The Life and Times of George III, 1971; The Eighteenth Concubine, 1972; The Maligned Monarch: A Life of King John of England, 1972 in UK as King John, 1973; Marathon: The Story of Civilizations on Collision Course, 1973 as Marathon: The Crucial Battle That Created Western Democracy, 2006; The Scorching of Washington: The War of 1812, 1974; The Taras Report on the Last Days of Pompeii, 1975; The War in the Trenches, 1975; The Hundred Years War, 1977; Destroy Carthage!: The Death Throes of an Ancient Culture, 1977; The Great Prize Fight, 1977; Trade Imperial, 1979; The Gliders: The Story of the Wooden Chariots of World War II, 1982. OTHER: Zulu War, 1879, 1973. **Address:** c/o Author Mail, HarperCollins, 77-85 Fulham Palace Rd., London, GL W6 8JB, England.

LLOYD, Elisabeth A. (Elisabeth Anne Lloyd). American (born United States), b. 1956. **Genres:** Biology, Philosophy, Sciences, Sex, Women's Studies And Issues. **Career:** University of California, visiting lecturer, 1984-85; assistant professor of philosophy, 1985-88; University of California at Berkeley, assistant professor, 1988-90; associate professor of philosophy, 1990-97,

program in logic and methodology of science, associate professor, 1997-99; Harvard University, Museum of Comparative Zoology, research associate, 1989; University of California at Davis, program in history and philosophy of science, associate faculty, 1990-; Stanford University, consulting faculty, 1990; University of Auckland, visiting senior lecturer, 1990; Indiana University, department of biology, professor, 1998-, department of philosophy, adjunct professor, 1998-, history and philosophy of science, Arnold and Maxine Tanis chair, 2001-, Center of Integrative Study of Animal Behavior, adjunct faculty, 2003-, Kinsey Institute for Research in Sex, Gender and Reproduction, affiliated faculty, 2005-; University of Pittsburgh, Pitzer College, lecturer; Rutgers University, lecturer; University of Western Ontario, lecturer; University of Pennsylvania, lecturer; Ohio State University, lecturer; Haverford College, lecturer. Writer and photographer. **Publications:** The Structure and Confirmation of Evolutionary Theory, 1988; (ed. with E.F. Keller and contrib.) Keywords in Evolutionary Biology, 1992; The Case of the Female Orgasm: Bias in Evolutionary Science, 2005; Science, Politics and Evolution, 2008. Contributor to journals. **Address:** History & Philosophy of Science Department, Indiana University, 1011 E 3rd St., Goodbody Hall 130, Bloomington, IN 47405-2401, U.S.A. **Online address:** ealloyd@indiana.edu

LLOYD, Elisabeth Anne. See **LLOYD, Elisabeth A.**

LLOYD, Geoffrey Ernest Richard. British (born England), b. 1933. **Genres:** Philosophy, History. **Career:** Cambridge University, assistant lecturer, 1965-67, lecturer, 1967-74, King's College, senior tutor, 1969-73, reader, 1974-83, professor of ancient philosophy and science, 1983-2000, master of Darwin College, 1989-2000, retired, 2000; Cornell University, White professor at large, 1990-96; East Asian History of Science Trust, chairman, 1992-2002. Writer. **Publications:** Polarity and Analogy: Two Types of Argumentation in Early Greek Thought, 1966; Aristotle: The Growth and Structure of His Thought, 1968; Early Greek Science: Thales to Aristotle, 1970; Greek Science after Aristotle, 1973; Magic, Reason and Experience, 1979; Science, Folklore and Ideology, 1983; Science and Morality in Greco-Roman Antiquity, 1985; The Revolutions of Wisdom, 1987; Demystifying Mentalities, 1990; Methods and Problems in Greek Science, 1991; Adversaries and Authorities, 1996; Aristotelian Explorations, 1996; Greek Thought, 2000; The Ambitions of Curiosity, 2002; (with N. Sivin) The Way and the Word, 2002; In the Grip of Disease, 2003; Ancient Worlds, Modern Reflections, 2004; The Delusions of Invulnerability: Wisdom and Morality in Ancient Greece, China and Today, 2005; Principles and Practices in Ancient Greek and Chinese Science, 2006; Cognitive Variations: Reflections on the Unity and Diversity of the Human Mind, 2007, (with N.W. Yi) Gu dai shi jie de xian dai si kao, 2008; Disciplines in the Making: Cross-cultural Perspectives on Elites, Learning and Innovation, 2009. EDITOR: Hippocratic Writings, 1978; Aristotle on Mind and the Senses, 1978; (with J. Brunschwig) Le Savoir Grec, 1996; (with J. Brunschwig) Greek Thought: A Guide to Classical Knowledge, 2000; (with J. Brunschwig) A Guide to Greek Thought, 2003; (with J. Brunschwig) The Greek Pursuit of Knowledge, 2003. **Address:** Needham Research Institute, University of Cambridge, 8 Sylvester Rd., Cambridge, CB3 9AF, England. **Online address:** gel20@cam.ac.uk

LLOYD, Margaret Glynne. American/British (born England), b. 1946. **Genres:** Poetry, Literary Criticism And History, Young Adult Fiction. **Career:** Springfield College, faculty, 1987-, Department of Humanities, chair, associate professor of English, professor of English, distinguished Springfield professor of humanities, 1996-97; University of Connecticut, faculty; University of Massachusetts, faculty; Westfield State College, faculty. Writer. **Publications:** William Carlos Williams's Paterson: A Critical Reappraisal, 1980; This Particular Earthly Scene (poetry), 1993; Moment in the Field: Voices from Arthurian Legend: Poems, 2006. Contributor of articles to journals, periodicals and magazines. **Address:** Springfield College, 263 Alden St., Springfield, MA 01109-3797, U.S.A. **Online address:** mlloyd@spfldcol.edu

LLOYD, P(eter) C. See **LLOYD, Peter Cutt.**

LLOYD, Peter Cutt. (P(eter) C. Lloyd). British (born England), b. 1927. **Genres:** Anthropology/Ethnology, Gerontology/Senior Issues, History, Sociology, Third World, Urban Studies. **Career:** West African Institute of Social and Economic Research, research fellow, 1949-56; Western Nigerian Ministry of Lands, lands research officer, 1956-59; University of Ibadan, Department of Sociology, head, 1959-64, lecturer, 1959-62, senior lecturer, 1962-64; University of Birmingham, senior lecturer, 1964-66, reader in West African sociology, 1966-67; University of Sussex, reader, 1967-78, professor, 1978-

92, emeritus professor of social anthropology, 1992-; International African Institute, honorary director, 1988-91. Writer. **Publications:** Yoruba Land Law, 1962; Africa in Social Change, 1967; Classes, Crises and Coups: Themes in the Sociology of Developing Countries, 1971; The Political Development of Yoruba Kingdoms in the Eighteenth and Nineteenth Centuries, 1971; Power and Independence: Urban Africans' Perception of Social Inequality, 1974; Slums of Hope?: Shanty Towns of the Third World, 1979; The Young Towns of Lima: Aspects of Urbanization in Peru, 1980; A Third World Proletariat?, 1982. EDITOR: (intro.) The New Elites of Tropical Africa, 1966; (with A.L. Mabogunje and B. Awe) The City of Ibadan, 1967; (with P. Amis) Housing Africa's Urban Poor, 1990. **Address:** School of Social Sciences and Cultural Studies, University of Sussex, Arts D D421, Brighton, ES BN1 9SJ, England. **Online address:** p.c.lloyd@sussex.ac.uk

LLOYD, P(eter) J(ohn). Australian/New Zealander (born New Zealand), b. 1937. **Genres:** Economics, Business/Trade/Industry. **Career:** New Zealand Department of Statistics, research officer, 1959; Victoria University of Wellington, lecturer, 1962-64, senior lecturer, 1964-65; Michigan State University, assistant professor, 1965-68, associate professor of economics, 1969; Australian National University, Australian Capital Territory, senior research fellow, 1969, senior fellow, 1970-81, professorial fellow, 1981-83, Research School of Pacific Studies, faculty chair, 1976-77; University of Melbourne, professor, 1983-2003, Institute of Applied Economic and Social Research, acting director, 1992, 1995, Ritchie professor of economics, 1995-2002, Faculty of Economics and Commerce, dean, 1988-93, Asian Business Centre, director, 1994-96, Asian Economics Centre, director, 1997-99, Centre of Financial Studies, acting director, 2000-01, emeritus professor, 2003-. Writer. **Publications:** Economic Development of the Tourist Industry in New Zealand, 1964; International Trade Problems of Small Nations, 1968; New Zealand Manufacturing Production and Trade with Australia, 1971; Non-Tariff Distortions of Australian Trade, 1973; (with H. Grubel) Intra-Industry Trade: The Theory and Measurement of International Trade in Differentiated Products, 1974; Economic Relationships between Australia and New Zealand, 1976; Anti-Dumping Actions and the GATT System, 1977; Future of CER: A Single Market for Australia and New Zealand, 1991; Measuring and Modelling Non-Tariff Distortions with Special Reference to Trade in Agricultural Commodities, 1991; Aggregation by Industry in General Equilibrium Models with International Trade, 1991; (with K. Vautier) International Trade and Competition Policy: CER, APEC and the WTO, 1997; (with L. Cameron and M. Dowling) Australia and Asia: A Study of Comparative Economic Performance, 1998; International Trade Opening and the Formation of the Global Economy: Selected Essays, 1999; (with K. Vautier) Promoting Competition in Global Markets: A Multi-national Approach, 1999; Economic Importance of East Asia to Australia, 2000; (with B. Bora and M. Pangestu) Industrial Policy and the WTO, 2000; Intra-Industry Trade: Critical Writings in Economics, 2002. EDITOR: Mineral Economics in Australia, 1984; (with L. Chong-Yah) Singapore: Resources and Growth, 1986; (with L. Pasinetti) Structural Change, Economic Interdependence and World Development, 1987; (with S. King) Economic Rationalism: Dead End or Way Forward?, 1993; (with L. Williams) International Trade and Migration in the APEC Region, 1996; (with X. Zhang) China in the Global Economy, 2000; (with X. Zhang) Models of the Chinese Economy, 2001; (with J. Nieuwenhuysen and M. Mead) Growth with Equity, 2001; (with J. Nieuwenhuysen and M. Mead) Reshaping Australia's Economy: Growth with Equity and Sustainability, 2001; (with H. Lee) Frontiers of Research in Intra-Industry Trade, 2002; (with H.G. Grubel) Intra-Industry Trade, 2003. Contributor to books and journals. **Address:** Department of Economics, Faculty of Economics and Commerce, University of Melbourne, Rm. 514, Economics and Commerce Bldg., Parkville, VI 3010, Australia. **Online address:** pjlloyd@unimelb.edu.au

LLOYD, Richard Douglas. American (born United States), b. 1967?. **Genres:** Social Sciences. **Career:** Saint Xavier University, visiting assistant professorial lecturer, 2000-03, Department of Sociology, Anthropology and Criminal Justice, student advisor, 2000-03; University of Chicago, Collegiate Division of the Social Sciences, Collegiate Division of the Social Sciences, lecturer, 2003; Vanderbilt University, Department of Sociology, undergraduate advisor, 2003-, assistant professor of sociology, 2003-10, associate professor of sociology, 2010-, Peabody College, Community Research and Action, affiliated faculty, 2004-, Program in American Studies, affiliated faculty, 2006-; American Journal of Sociology, consulting editor, 2007-09. **Publications:** Neo-Bohemia: Art and Commerce in the Postindustrial City, 2005, 2nd ed., 2010. Contributor to books and periodicals. **Address:** Department of Sociology, Vanderbilt University, 201D Garland Hall, PO Box 351811, Nash-

ville, TN 37235-1811, U.S.A. **Online address:** r.d.lloyd@vanderbilt.edu

LLOYD, Rosemary. American/Australian (born Australia), b. 1949. **Genres:** Literary Criticism And History, Translations. **Career:** Cambridge University, New Hall, fellow, 1978-90, university lecturer, 1979-90; Indiana University, Rudy professor of French and Italian, professor of gender studies, adjunct professor of comparative literature and English, 1990-, now Rudy professor emerita of French. Writer. **Publications:** Baudelaire et Hoffmann: Affinités et influences, 1979; Baudelaire's Literary Criticism, 1981; Mallarme: Poesies, 1984; Flaubert's Madame Bovary, 1990; The Land of Lost Content: Children and Childhood in Nineteenth-Century French Literature, 1992; Closer and Closer Apart: Jealousy in Literature, 1995; Mallarmé: The Poet and His Circle, 1999; Baudelaire's World, 2002; Shimmering in a Transformed Light: Writing the Still Life, 2005. EDITOR: (with L. Watson) Patterns of Evolution in Nineteenth-Century French Poetry, 1991; (co-ed.) Oeuvres Completes, vol. II, 1996; Banville, Roses de Noel, 1998; Cambridge Companion to Baudelaire, 2005. TRANSLATOR: (and ed.) Selected Letters of Charles Baudelaire, 1986; (and ed.) Selected Letters of Stéphane Mallarmé, 1988; (and intro.) C. Baudelaire, Prose Poems and La Fanfarlo, 1991; (and intro.) G. Sand, The Master Pipers, 1994; (and ed.) Revolutions in Writing: Nineteenth-Century French Prose, 1996. Contributor to periodicals and journals. **Address:** Department of French and Italian, Indiana University, 642 Ballantine Hall, 1020 E Kirkwood Ave., Bloomington, IN 47405-7103, U.S.A. **Online address:** rolloyd@indiana.edu

LLOYD, Saci. British (born England), b. 1967. **Genres:** Novels, Young Adult Fiction. **Career:** Camouflage Films, script editor; Newham Sixth Form College, head of media. **Publications:** The Carbon Diaries 2015 (young-adult novel), 2009; The Carbon Diaries 2017 (young-adult novel), 2010; Momentum, 2012. **Address:** c/o Veronique Baxter, David Higham Associates, 5-8 Lower John St., Golden Sq., London, GL W1F 9HA, England. **Online address:** saci@sacilloyd.com

LLOYD, Seth. American (born United States), b. 1960. **Genres:** Sciences, Information Science/Computers. **Career:** Stanford Linear Accelerator Center, research scientist, 1979; Brookhaven National Laboratory, research scientist, 1980; Institute Laue-Langevin, research scientist, 1981; European Center for Nuclear Research (CERN), research scientist, 1982; Columnist Harvard Review, editor, 1985-87; Santa Fe Institute, adjunct faculty, 1987-; California Institute of Technology, research fellow, 1988-91, postdoctoral fellow; Los Alamos National Laboratory, research fellow, 1991-94, postdoctoral fellow; Massachusetts Institute of Technology, assistant professor of mechanical engineering, 1994-98, Finmeccanica Career Development professorship, 1996-, associate professor of mechanical engineering, 2001-02, professor of mechanical engineering, 2002-, principal investigator of research laboratory electronics; Quantum Technologies, consultant, 1996-; Hewlett Packard, consultant, 1998-; Microsoft, consultant, 2000-; Santa Fe Institute, adjunct faculty. Physicist and writer. **Publications:** Programming the Universe: A Quantum Computer Scientist Takes on the Cosmos, 2006. Contributor to journals. **Address:** Massachusetts Institute of Technology, Rm. 3-160, 77 Massachusetts Ave., Cambridge, MA 02139-4307, U.S.A. **Online address:** slloyd@mit.edu

LLOYD, T(revor) O(wen). Canadian/British (born England), b. 1934. **Genres:** History, Politics/Government, International Relations/Current Affairs, Autobiography/Memoirs. **Career:** University of Toronto, Department of History, lecturer, 1959-63, assistant professor, 1963-67, associate professor, 1967-71, professor, 1971-97, professor emeritus, 1997-. Writer. **Publications:** The General Election of 1880, 1968; Canada in World Affairs, 1957-59, 1968; (ed. with J.T. McLeod) Agenda: 1970, 1968; Empire to Welfare State: English History 1906-1967, 1970, 5th ed. as Empire, Welfare State, Europe: History of the United Kingdom, 1906-2001, 2002; Suffragettes International: The World-Wide Campaign for Women's Rights, 1971; The Growth of Parliamentary Democracy in Britain, 1973; (ed.) Lay Presidency at the Eucharist?, 1977; Evangelicals, Obedience, and Change, 1977; The British Empire, 1558-1983, 1984, 2nd ed. as The British Empire, 1558-1995, 1996; Empire: The History of the British Empire, 2001. **Address:** Department of History, University of Toronto, Rm. 2074, Sidney Smith Hall, 100 St. George St., University of Toronto, Toronto, ON M5S 3G3, Canada.

LLYWELYN, Morgan. (Shannon Lewis). British/Irish/American (born United States), b. 1947. **Genres:** Novels, Romance/Historical, Biography, History. **Career:** Fashion model and dance instructor, 1954-56; secretary in

Denver, 1956-59; riding instructor, 1959-61; amateur equestrian, 1961-76; writer, 1974-. **Publications:** The Wind from Hastings, 1978; Lion of Ireland: The Legend of Brian Boru, 1980; The Horse Goddess, 1982; (as Shannon Lewis) Personal Habits, 1982; Bard: The Odyssey of the Irish, 1984; Grania: She-King of the Irish Seas, 1986; Xerxes, 1987; The Isles of the Blest, 1989; Red Branch, 1989; Druids, 1991; On Raven's Wing, 1991; Last Prince of Ireland: A Novel, 1992; O'Sullivan's March, 1992; Strongbow: The Story of Richard and Aoife, 1992, rev. ed., 1996; The Elementals, 1993; Finn Mac Cool, 1994; (with M. Scott) Ireland: A Graphic History, 1995; (with M. Scott) Silverhand, 1995; Cold Places, 1995; Brian Boru, Emperor of the Irish, 1995; Pride of Lions, 1996; Vikings in Ireland, 1996; Silver light, 1996; 1916: A Novel Of The Irish Rebellion, 1998; Essential Library for Irish Americans, 1999; A Pocket History of Irish Rebels, 2000; The Earth Is Made Of Stardust, 2000; (with M. Scott) Etruscans, 2000; 1921, 2001; 1949: A Novel of the Irish Free State, 2003; 1972: A Novel of Ireland's Unfinished Revolution, 2005; The Greener Shore: A Novel Of The Druids Of Hibernia, 2006; Pirate Queen, 2006; The Young Rebels, 2006; Druids, 2006; 1999: A Novel Of The Celtic Tiger And The Search For Peace, 2008; Brendan, 2010; Cave of Secrets, 2012. **Address:** c/o Abner Stein, 10 Roland Gardens, London, GL SW7 3PH, England. **Online address:** morganllywelyn@gmail.com

LO, Malinda. American/Chinese (born China), b. 1974?. **Genres:** Science Fiction/Fantasy, Novels. **Career:** Ballantine Books, editorial assistant; AfterEllen.com, managing editor and writer, through 2008. Entertainment journalist. **Publications:** Ash, 2009; Huntress, 2010. Contributor to periodicals. **Address:** Laura Langlie Agency, 63 Wyckoff St., Brooklyn, NY 11201, U.S.A. **Online address:** mlo@malindalo.com

LO, Shiu-Hing. Canadian (born Canada), b. 1963. **Genres:** Politics/Government, History. **Career:** University of East Asia, lecturer, 1989-90; Lignan College, assistant lecturer, 1990-91; Murdoch University, Asia Research Center, research fellow, 1991-92; University of Hong Kong, assistant professor, 1993-96, associate professor of political science, 1996-2004; University of Waterloo, associate professor, 2004-09, professor of political science, 2009-. Writer. **Publications:** Political Development in Macau, 1995; (ed. with J. Cheng) From Colony to SAR: Hong Kong's Challenges Ahead, 1995; (with B. Sautman) The Tibet Question and the Hong Kong Experience, 1995; (with D.H. McMillen) Images and Perceptions of the Pro-China Hong Kong Elite, 1995; The Politics of Democratization in Hong Kong, 1997; Jiu qi guo du: xianggang di tiao zhan, 1997; (with W. Yu) Election and Democracy in Hong Kong: The 1998 Legislative Council Election, 1999; Governing Hong Kong: Legitimacy, Communication, and Political Decay, 2001; Dong Jianhua zheng fu: guan zhi wei ji yu chu lu, 2002; (co-ed.) The Tung Chee-hwa Government: Crisis and Solutions, 2002, 2nd ed., 2003; Hong Kong, 1 July 2003': Half a Million Protestors: The Security Law, Identity Politics, Democracy, and China, 2004; (with M.K. Chan) Historical Dictionary of the Hong Kong SAR and the Macao SAR, 2006; The Dynamics of Beijing-Hong Kong Relations: A Model for Taiwan?, 2008; Political Change in Macao, 2008; The Politics of Cross- border Crime in Greater China: Case Studies of Mainland China, Hong Kong, and Macao, 2009; Competing Chinese Political Visions: Hong Kong vs. Beijing on Democracy, 2010; Chinese Politics from Mao to Hu, 2010. Contributor to books, periodicals and journals. **Address:** University of Waterloo, Rm. 313, Hagey Hall, 200 University Ave. W, Waterloo, ON N2L 3G1, Canada. **Online address:** sonny@watarts.uwaterloo.ca

LOADES, David. See **LOADES, David Michael.**

LOADES, David Michael. Also writes as David Loades, D. M. Loades. British (born England), b. 1934. **Genres:** History, Biography, Politics/Government. **Career:** University of St. Andrews, lecturer in political science, 1961-63; University of Durham, lecturer, 1963-71, senior lecturer, 1971-77, reader in modern history, 1977-80; University of Wales, professor of history, 1980-96, now professor emeritus; British Academy, John Foxe Project, literary director, 1993-2004; University of Sheffield, honorary research professor, 1996-2008. Writer. **Publications:** Two Tudor Conspiracies, 1965; The Oxford Martyrs, 1970, 2nd ed., 1992; Politics and the Nation 1450-1660: Obedience, Resistance and Public Order, 1973, 5th ed., 1999; The Bibliography of the Reform, 1450-1648, Relating to the United Kingdom and Ireland for the Years 1955-70, 1975; The Reign of Mary Tudor: Politics, Government, and Religion in England, 1553-1558, 1979, 2nd ed. 1991; (with J.C.H. Aveling and H.R. McAdoo) Rome and the Anglicans: Historical and Doctrinal Aspects of Anglican-Roman Catholic Relations, 1982; The Tudor Court, 1987, rev. ed., 1992; Mary Tudor: A Life, 1990; Politics, Censorship and the English

Reformation, 1991; Cranmer and The English Reformation, 1991; The Tudor Navy: An Administrative, Political, and Military History, 1992; The Mid-Tudor Crisis, 1545-1565, 1992; Revolution in Religion: The English Reformation, 1530-1570, 1992; Essays in European History 1453-1648, 1993, rev. ed., 2003; The Politics of Marriage, 1994; Essays on the Reign of Edward VI, 1994; John Dudley, Duke of Northumberland, 1504-1553, 1996; John Dudley, Duke of Northumberland, Lord President of the Council, 1996; Henry VIII and His Queens, 1996; Power in Tudor England, 1997; Tudor Government: Structures of Authority in the Sixteenth Century, 1997; England's Maritime Empire: Seapower, Commerce, and Policy, 1490-1690, 2000; Chronicles of the Tudor Queens, 2002; Elizabeth I: The Golden Reign of Gloriana, 2003; Essays in Tudor History, 2003; Intrigue and Treason: The Tudor Court, 1547-1558, 2004; The Cecils: Privilege and Power behind the Throne, 2007; Henry VIII: Court, Church and Conflict, 2007; Life and Career of William Paulet (c. 1475-1572), Lord Treasurer and First Marquis of Winchester, 2008; The Princes of Wales, 2008; Making of the Elizabethan Navy, 1540-1590: From the Solent to the Armada, 2009; The Six Wives of Henry VIII, 2009; Tudor Queens of England, 2009; The Fighting Tudors, 2009; Henry VIII: King and Court, 2009; The Religious Culture of Marian England, 2010; Tudors for Dummies, 2010; Henry VIII, 2011. EDITOR/CO-EDITOR: The Papers of George Wyatt Esquire, of Boxley Abbey in the County of Kent, 1968; The End of Strife: Papers Selected From the Proceedings of the Colloquium of the Commission Internationale d'histoire Ecclésiastique Comparée Held at the University of Durham, 2 to 9 September 1981, 1984; (with C. Cross and J.J. Scarisbrick) Law and Government under the Tudors: Essays Presented to Sir Geoffrey Elton, Regius Professor of Modern History in the University of Cambridge, on the Occasion of His Retirement, 1988; (with K. Walsh) Faith and Identity: Christian Political Experience: Papers Read at the Anglo-Polish Colloquium of the British Sub-Commission of the Commission Internationale d'histoire Ecclésiastique Comparée, 9-13 September 1986, 1990; The Tudor Chronicles-the Kings, 1990; John Foxe and the English Reformation, 1997; John Foxe: An Historical Perspective, 1999; (with C.S. Knighton) Anthony Roll of Henry VIII's Navy: Pepys Library 2991 and British Library Additional MS 22047 with Related Documents, 2000; Reader's Guide to British History, 2003; Letters from the Mary Rose, 2003; John Foxe: At Home and Abroad, 2004; (with E. Duffy) Church of Mary Tudor, 2006; (ed. with C.S. Knighton) Navy of Edward VI and Mary I, 2011. **Address:** The Cottage, Priory Ln., Burford, OX OX18 4SG, England.

LOADES, D. M. See **LOADES, David Michael.**

LOBANOV-ROSTOVSKY, Sergei. (Kenneth Abel). American (born United States) **Genres:** Novels. **Career:** Kenyon College, associate professor of English, 1993-, professor of English, 2008-. Writer. **Publications:** Bait, 1994; The Blue Wall, 1996; Cold Steel Rain, 2000; The Burying Field, 2002; Down in the Flood, 2009. Contributor to periodicals. **Address:** Department of English, Kenyon College, Lentz House and Sunset Cottage 103, Gambier, OH 43022-9623, U.S.A. **Online address:** lobanovrosto@kenyon.edu

LOBBAN, Richard A. American (born United States), b. 1943. **Genres:** Anthropology/Ethnology, Area Studies, History. **Career:** Rhode Island College, professor of anthropology and African studies, 1972-, Program of African and Afro-American Studies, director, 1985-94, Department of Anthropology and African Studies, chair, professor emeritus of anthropology; Bucknell University, professor; Dartmouth College, professor; University of Pittsburgh, professor; American University in Cairo, Urban Development Unit at Social Research Center, head, 1982-84; Sudan Studies Association, executive director, founder; Rhode Island Black Heritage Society, vice president. Writer. **Publications:** Eritrean Liberation Front: A Close-Up View, 1972; Three Studies on National Integration in the Arab World, 1974; Historical Dictionary of the Republics of Guinea-Bissau and Cape Verde, 1979, (with P.K. Saucier) 4th ed. as Historical Dictionary of the Republic of Cape Verde, 2007; (ed.) Urban Research Strategies for Egypt, 1983; (with J. Forrest) Historical Dictionary of Guinea-Bissau, 3rd ed., 1988, (with P.K. Mendy), 1997; (with C. Fluehr-Lobban and J.O. Voll) Historical Dictionary of the Sudan, 1992, 3rd ed. (with C. Fluehr-Lobban and R. Kramer), 2002; Cape Verde: Crioulo Colony to Independent Nation, 1995; (ed.) Middle Eastern Women in the Invisible Economy, 1998; Historical Dictionary of Ancient and Medieval Nubia, 2004. **Address:** Department of Anthropology & African Studies, Rhode Island College, 600 Mount Pleasant Ave., Providence, RI 02908-1991, U.S.A. **Online address:** rlobban@ric.edu

LOBEL, Jules. American (born United States), b. 1951. **Genres:** Law,

Politics/Government. **Career:** Rabinowitz, Boudin, Standard, Krinsky & Lieberman (law firm), associate, 1978-83; South Brooklyn Area Policy Board, president, 1979-80; University of Pittsburgh, assistant professor, 1983-86, associate professor, 1986-89, professor of law, 1989-, Bessie McKee Wathour endowed chair; Nicaragua National Assembly, consultant, 1985. Writer. **Publications:** (Ed.) Civil Rights Handbook, 1985; (ed.) Alternative Views of the Constitution, 1988; (ed.) A Less Than Perfect Union: Alternative Perspectives on the U.S. Constitution, 1988; Success without Victory: Lost Legal Battles and the Long Road to Justice in America, 2003; (with D. Cole) Less Safe, Less Free: Why America Is Losing the War on Terror, 2007. Contributor to periodicals. **Address:** School of Law, University of Pittsburgh, 505 Barco Law Bldg., 3900 Forbes Ave., Pittsburgh, PA 15260, U.S.A. **Online address:** jll4@pitt.edu

LOBENSTINE, Margaret. American (born United States), b. 1943?. **Genres:** Young Adult Non-fiction, Psychology. **Career:** Alternative Approaches (coaching and consulting business), founder; University of Massachusetts, Family Business Center, facilitator; STAPLES, resident expert. Writer and educator. **Publications:** The Renaissance Soul: Life Design for People with Too Many Passions to Pick Just One, 2006. **Address:** 442 Warren Wright Rd., Belchertown, MA 01007-9364, U.S.A. **Online address:** mlobenstine@togetunstuck.com

LOCHTE, Dick. American (born United States), b. 1944. **Genres:** Novels, Novellas/Short Stories, Mystery/Crime/Suspense, Plays/Screenplays. **Career:** Playboy Enterprises, promotional copywriter, 1966-70; Playboy Enterprises West Coast, promotional manager, 1970-73; Los Angeles Free Press, film critic, 1971-74; freelance writer, 1973-; Los Angeles Times, book columnist, 1974-85; Los Angeles Magazine, theater critic, 1975-96; Los Angeles Times, Book Review, mystery fiction reviewer, 1996-2009. **Publications:** Sleeping Dog, 1985; Laughing Dog, 1988; Blue Bayou, 1992; The Neon Smile, 1995; (with C. Darden) The Trials of Nikki Hill, 1999; Lucky Dog and Other Tales of Murder, 2000; (with C. Darden) L.A. Justice, 2001; (with C. Darden) Last Defense, 2002; (with C. Darden) Lawless, 2004; Croaked!, 2007; (with A. Roker) Morning Show Murders: A Novel, 2009; (with A. Roker) Midnight Show Murders, 2010; (with A. Roker) Talk Show Murders, 2011; Blues in the Night, 2012. **Address:** William Morris Endeavor Entertainment L.L.C., 1350 Ave. of the Americas, New York, NY 10019, U.S.A. **Online address:** dlochte@gmail.com

LOCK, Charles (John Somerset). Danish/British (born England), b. 1955. **Genres:** Literary Criticism And History. **Career:** Hoegskolan i Karlstad, lecturer, 1980-82; University of Toronto, assistant professor, 1983-88, associate professor, 1988-93, professor of English, 1993-; University of Copenhagen, professor of English literature, 1996-. **Publications:** Criticism in Focus: Thomas Hardy, 1992. Contributor to periodicals. **Address:** Department of English, Germanic & Romance Studies, Faculty of Humanities, University of Copenhagen, Njalsgade 128, Copenhagen S, DK-2300, Denmark. **Online address:** lock@hum.ku.dk

LOCK, Joan. British (born England), b. 1933. **Genres:** Novels, Novellas/Short Stories, Mystery/Crime/Suspense, Plays/Screenplays, Children's Non-fiction, Criminology/True Crime, History, Women's Studies And Issues, Women's Studies And Issues, Young Adult Non-fiction, Autobiography/Memoirs. **Career:** Queen Elizabeth Hospital, student nurse, 1950-54; Metropolitan Police, policewoman, 1954-60; British European Airways, reservations clerk, 1961-66; John Lewis Partnership, in-house journalist, 1973-93. Writer. **Publications:** Lady Policeman, 1968; Reluctant Nightingale, 1970; The British Policewoman: Her Story, 1979; Marlborough Street: The Story of a London Court, 1980; Tales from Bow Street, 1982; Blue Murder, 1986; Dreadful Deeds and Awful Murders: Scotland Yard's First Detectives, 1829-1878, 1990; Scotland Yard Casebook: The Making of the CID 1865-1935, 1993; Dead Image, 2000; Death in Perspective, 2001; Dead Born, 2002; Dead Letters, 2003; Famous Trials, 2003; Famous Prisons, 2003; Protecting Yourself against Criminals, 2003; Dead End, 2004; Dead Fall, 2005; Dead Loss, 2005; Dead Centre, 2008. Contributor to magazines, journals and newspapers. **Address:** c/o Juliet Burton, Juliet Burton Literary Agency, 2 Clifton Ave., London, GL W12 9DR, England. **Online address:** message@joanlock.co.uk

LOCKE, Attica. American (born United States), b. 1974?. **Genres:** Novels. **Career:** Sundance Institute, Feature Filmmaker's Lab, fellow. Writer. **Publications:** Black Water Rising (novel), 2009. **Address:** Los Angeles, CA , U.S.A. **Online address:** attica@atticalocke.com

LOCKE, Christopher. American (born United States), b. 1947. **Genres:** Business/Trade/Industry, Marketing, Money/Finance. **Career:** Fujitsu International Engineering, technical editor; Ricoh Software Research Center, technical editor; Elsevier Science Publishers, technical editor; Institute for New Generation Computer Technology, technical editor, 1983-85; Carnegie Group, director of corporate communications, 1985-91; Intelligent Technology Group, vice president of corporate communications, 1985-91; Carnegie Mellon University, Robotics Institute, director of industrial relations, 1985-91; CIMLINC, director of corporate communications, 1991-92; Avalanche Development, vice president of business development, 1992-93; CMP Publications, Internet Business Report, editor, 1993; MecklerWeb Corp., president, 1994; internetMCI, editor and publisher, 1995; IBM, program director of online community development, 1995-96; Entropy Web Consulting, president, 1996-; Entropy Gradient Reversals, editor and publisher, 1995-; Displaytech, vice president of business development, 1996-97; personalization.com, editor-in-chief, 1999-2000; Highbeam Research, chief blogging officer, 2003-04; Krugle, blog wrangler, 2006. **Publications:** Gonzo Marketing: Winning Through Worst Practices, 2001; The Bombast Transcripts: Rants and Screeds of Rage Boy, 2002. Contributor to periodicals. **Address:** 930-D W Moorhead Cir., Boulder, CO 80305, U.S.A. **Online address:** clocke@gmail.com

LOCKE, Hillary Bell. *See* **BOWEN, Michael.**

LOCKE, Hubert G. American (born United States), b. 1934. **Genres:** History, Theology/Religion, Politics/Government. **Career:** Downtown Detroit Young Men's Christian Association, associate youth work secretary, 1956-57; Wayne State University, Center for Urban Studies, fellow, director of religious affairs, 1959-62, adjunct assistant professor, 1967-72, Leo M. Franklin Memorial professor in human relations, 1969-70; Detroit Commissioner of Police, administrative assistant, 1966-67; Wayne State University, adjunct assistant professor of urban education, Center for Urban Studies, fellow, 1967-72; University of Nebraska, College of Public Affairs and Community Service, dean, 1972-75, associate professor of urban studies, 1972-76; University of Washington, assistant dean, associate dean of arts and science, 1976-77, Daniel J. Evans School of Public Affairs, professor, 1976-99, vice provost academic affairs, 1977-82, professor public affairs, 1982-, dean, 1982-87, dean emeritus, 1999-, Marguerite Corbally emeritus professor of public service; Conant Gardens, Church of Christ, minister. **Publications:** The Detroit Riot of 1967, 1969; The Care and Feeding of White Liberals, 1970; (ed. with Franklin H. Littell) The German Church Struggle and the Holocaust, 1974; The Impact of Affirmative Action and Civil Service on American Policy Systems, 1979; (ed.) The Church Confronts the Nazis, 1984; (ed.) Exile in the Fatherland: The Prison Letters of Martin Niemöller, 1986; (ed.) Barmen Confession, 1986; (ed. with A.L. Berger and F.H. Littell) What Have We Learned?: Telling the Story and Teaching the Lessons of the Holocaust, 1993; The Black Antisemitism Controversy: Protestant Views and Perspectives, 1994; (ed. with M.S. Littell) Holocaust and Church Struggle, 1996; (ed. with M.S. Littell) Remembrance and Recollection: Essays on the Centennial Year of Martin Niemoller and Reinhold Neibuhr, and the Fiftieth Year of the Wannsee Conference, 1996; Learning from History: A Black Christian's Perspective on the Holocaust, 2000; Groping for God, 2002; Searching for God in Godforsaken Times and Places, 2003. CONTRIBUTOR: The Urban Crisis, 1969; Students, Religion and the University Community, 1970. **Address:** University of Washington, 109 Parrington Hall, PO Box 353055, Seattle, WA 98195-3055, U.S.A.

LOCKE, Juliane Poirier. (Juliane Poirier). American (born United States), b. 1959. **Genres:** Earth Sciences, Biography, Sciences, Reference. **Career:** St. Helena Star, editor; California Academy of Sciences, science editor; California Academy of Sciences, science editor; Community Pulse, managing editor; Four Springs, program leader; Napa City-County Library, literacy and volunteer services supervisor. **Publications:** Vineyards in the Watershed: Sustainable Winegrowing in Napa County, 2002; England's Jane: The Story of Jane Austen, 2006. Contributor to publications and magazines. **Address:** Four Springs, 14598 Sheveland Rd., Middletown, CA 95461, U.S.A. **Online address:** juliane1@sbcglobal.net

LOCKE, Robert R. American (born United States), b. 1932. **Genres:** Adult Non-fiction, Administration/Management, Autobiography/Memoirs, History, Industrial Relations, Social Commentary, Education, Business/Trade/Industry, Business/Trade/Industry. **Career:** University of Hawaii, professor of history, business and management, 1974-98, professor emeritus, 1999-; European Institute for Advanced Studies in Management, visiting professor,

1982-84; University of London, London School of Economics and Political Science, visiting professor, 1986-88; University of Reading, visiting professor, 1989-2002; Queens University, visiting professor. Writer. **Publications:** French Legitimists and the Politics of Moral Order in the Early Third Republic, 1974; Les Fonderies Et Forges D'Alais: À Lépoque Des Premiers Chemins De Fer: La Création D'une Entreprise Moderne, 1978; The End of the Practical Man: Entrepreneurship and Higher Education in Germany, France, and Great Britain, 1880-1940, 1984; Management and Higher Education Since 1940: The Influence of America and Japan on West Germany, Great Britain, and France, 1989; The Collapse of the American Management Mystique, 1996; (ed.) Management Education, 1998; (with K.E. Schone) The Entrepreneurial Shift: Americanization in European High-Technology Management Education, 2004; (with V. Locke) Discovering Vera, 2007; (with J.C. Spender) Confronting Managerialism, 2011. **Address:** Department of History, University of Hawaii, 2530 Dole St., Honolulu, HI 96822, U.S.A. **Online address:** blocke@hawaii.edu

LOCKERBIE, D(onald) Bruce. American/Canadian (born Canada), b. 1935. **Genres:** Plays/Screenplays, Administration/Management, Education, History, Literary Criticism And History, Theology/Religion, Biography. **Career:** Wheaton College, visiting professor of English; visiting consultant, 1974-; PAIDEIA Inc., chief executive officer, chairman, 1984-. Writer. **Publications:** Billy Sunday, 1965; Patriarchs and Prophets, 1969; Hawthorne, 1970; Melville, 1970; Twain, 1970; Major American Authors, 1970; (with L. Westdahl) Success in Writing, 1970; Purposeful Writing, 1972; The Way They Should Go, 1972; The Liberating Word, 1974; Education of Missionaries Children: The Neglected Dimension of World Mission, 1975; The Cosmic Center: The Apostle's Creed, 1977, rev. ed., 1986; Apostle's Creed: Do you Really Believe It?, 1977; A Man under Orders: Lt. General William K. Harrison, 1979; The Timeless Moment, 1980; Asking Questions, 1980; Who Educates Your Child?, 1981; Fatherlove, 1981; In Peril on the Sea, 1984; (ed.) The Christian, The Arts, and Truth, 1985; Thinking and Acting like a Christian, 1989; College: Getting In and Staying In, 1990; Take Heart, 1990; A Passion for Learning: A History of Christian Thought on Education, 1994, 2nd ed., 2007; From Candy Sales to Committed Donors, 1996; Dismissing God: Modern Writers' Struggle against Religion, 1998; Thinking-and-Acting Like a Christian, 2001; Christian Paideia: The Habitual Vision of Greatness, 2005. Contributor to periodicals. **Address:** PAIDEIA Inc., PO Box 26, Stony Brook, NY 11790, U.S.A. **Online address:** dbl@paideia-inc.com

LOCKHART, Paul Douglas. American (born United States), b. 1963. **Genres:** History, Social Sciences. **Career:** Wright State University, professor and director of graduate program, 1989-; Odense Universitet, Kultur og Samfundsbeskrivelse, Institut for Historie, visiting lecturer, 1997; State University of New York, National Endowment for the Humanities, visiting distinguished professor, 2000; Potsdam College, NEH visiting distinguished professor of history. Writer. **Publications:** Denmark in the Thirty Years' War, 1618-1648: King Christian IV and the Decline of the Oldenburg State, 1996; Sweden in the Seventeenth Century, 2004; Frederik II and the Protestant Cause: Denmark's Role in the Wars of Religion, 1559-1596, 2004; Denmark, 1513-1660: The Rise and Decline of a Renaissance Monarchy, 2007; The Drillmaster of Valley Forge: The Baron De Steuben and the Making of the American Army, 2008; The Whites of Their Eyes, 2011. **Address:** Department of History, Wright State University, 370 Millett Hall, 3640 Colonel Glenn Hwy., Dayton, OH 45435, U.S.A. **Online address:** paul.lockhart@wright.edu

LOCKLIN, Gerald Ivan. American (born United States), b. 1941. **Genres:** Novels, Novellas/Short Stories, Plays/Screenplays, Poetry, Literary Criticism And History, Bibliography. **Career:** University of Arizona, teaching assistant, 1961-64; California State University-Los Angeles, instructor, 1964-65; California State University-Long Beach, assistant professor, professor, 1965-2003, professor emeritus, 2003-, part-time lecturer, Master of Professional Program, part-time lecturer. Writer. **Publications:** POETRY: Sunset Beach, 1967; (with R. Koertge and C. Stetler) Tarzan and Shane Meet the Toad, 1970; The Toad Poems, 1970; Poop and Other Poems, 1972; Son of Poop, 1973; Toad's Europe, 1973; The Criminal Mentality, 1976; Toad's Sabbatical, 1978; Frisco Epic, 1978; Pronouncing Borges, 1978; Two Summer Sequences (and prose), 1979; Two Weeks on Mr. Stanford's Farm, 1980; The Last Toad, 1980; Two for the Seesaw and One for the Road, 1980; Scenes from a Second Adolescence and Other Poems, 1981; By Land, Sea, and Air, 1982; Why Turn a Perfectly Good Toad into a Prince? (and story), 1984; Gringo and Other Poems, 1985; (with R. Zepeda) We Love L.A.: The Olympic Boxing Poems, 1985; The Clubfoot Midget Shoots Pool, 1986; The English Mini-Tour, 1987;

A Constituency of Dunces, 1988; The Death of Jean-Paul Sartre and Other Poems, 1988; (co-author) Toad Comes to Cleveland, 1988; Return to Ronnie Scott's, 1988; On the Rack, 1988; Lost and Found, 1989; The Rochester Poems, 1990; The Illegitimate Son of Mr. Madman, 1991; The Return of the Prodigal Father, 1991; A Yank at Bangor, 1991; (with R. Zepeda) The Lincoln, Nebraska Poems, 1991; The Firebird Poems, 1992; Outtakes, 1992; (with R. Zepeda) The Yellow Ford of Texas, 1993; Toad Writes Short Shorts, 1993; Big Man on Canvas, 1994; The Old Mongoose and Other Poems, 1994; (with R. Zepeda) The Durango Poems, 1994; (with R. Zepeda) Buying a Cabin: The Big Bear Poems, 1995; The Pittsburgh Poems, 1996; The Last Round-up, 1996; The Art Farmer Suite, and Other Poems, 1997; The Active Ingredient and Other Poems, 1997; More Jazz Poems, 1998; The Hospital Poems, 1998; Go West Young Toad, 1999; The Firebird Poems, 1999; The Back East Poems, 1999; This Sporting Life and Other Poems, 1999; Running into Ger, 1999; The Face of Chet Baker, 1999; The Iceberg Theory and Other Poems, 2000; Art and Life, 2000; Familiarities, 2001; Duke, Lester, Charles: The Sixth Jazz Chap, 2001; The Mystical Exercycle, 2002; The Life Force Poems, 2002; Young Chet, 2002; The Author's Not Quite Dead, 2002; Takes on Bill Evans, 2002; More Takes, 2003; Retirement Blues, 2003; The Modigliani/Montparnasse, Poems, 2003; 2 Jazz Poems, 2003; Music and Imagination, 2003; The Dorset Poems, 2003; The Ultimate Pessimist and Other Poems, 2003. SHORT STORIES/NOVELLAS: Locked In, 1973; The Four-Day Work Week and Other Stories, 1977; A Weekend in Canada, 1979; The Case of the Missing Blue Volkswagen, 1984; The Gold Rush and Other Stories, 1989; The Conference, 1990; Candy Bars: Selected Stories, 2000; The Pocket Book, 2003. OTHER: The Chase: A Novel, 1976; The Cure: A Novel for Speedreaders, 1979; Gerald Haslam, 1987; Children of a Lesser Demagogue, 1988; Locklin Biblio, 1991; (comp. and ed. with E. Field and C. Stetler) A New Geography of Poets, 1992; Women Trouble (chapbook), 1994; The Cabo Conference, 1995; Two Jazz Sequences, 1995; The New Male, 1996; Charles Bukowski: A Sure Bet, 1996; The Macao/Hong Kong Trip, 1996; The First Time He Saw Paris, 1997; Two Novellas, 1998; Down and Out: A Novel, 1999; Hemingway Colloquium: The Poet Goes to Cuba, 1999; A Simpler Time, a Simpler Place, 2000; Four Jazz Women: Toshiko, Claudia, June, and Jane, 2000. Contributor to periodicals. **Address:** Department of English, California State University, MHB 511, 1250 Bellflower Blvd., Long Beach, CA 90840-0004, U.S.A. **Online address:** glocklin@csulb.edu

LOCKRIDGE, Larry. (Laurence S(hockley) Lockridge). American (born United States), b. 1942. **Genres:** Novels, Literary Criticism And History, Philosophy, Biography, Autobiography/Memoirs. **Career:** Harvard University, teaching fellow, 1967-68; Rutgers University, assistant professor of English, 1969-76; Northwestern University, visiting lecturer in English, 1977-78; New York University, associate professor, 1978-89, professor of English, 1989-. Writer. **Publications:** Coleridge the Moralist, 1977; The Ethics of Romanticism, 1989; Shade of the Raintree: The Life and Death of Ross Lockridge, Jr., 1994. EDITOR: (with J. Maynard and D. Stone) Nineteenth-Century Lives: Essays Presented to Jerome Hamilton Buckley, 1989; Raintree County, 1994. **Address:** Department of English, New York University, 19 University Pl., Rm. 525, New York, NY 10003, U.S.A. **Online address:** ll3@nyu.edu

LOCKRIDGE, Laurence S(hockley). See **LOCKRIDGE, Larry.**

LOCKSLEY, Rebecca. See **ROUTLEY, (Bernarra) Jane.**

LOCKWOOD, David. British (born England), b. 1929?. **Genres:** Sociology. **Career:** London School of Economics, lecturer, 1953-60; Cambridge University, St. John's College, faculty, 1958, lecturer, faculty and fellow, 1960-68; University of Essex, professor of sociology, 1968-2001, chair, 1968, pro-vice chancellor, 1989-92, Institute of Social and Economic Research, visiting professor. Writer and social determinist. **Publications:** The Blackcoated Worker: A Study in Class Consciousness, 1958, 2nd ed., 1989; (co-author) The Affluent Worker: Industrial Attitudes and Behaviour, 1968; The Affluent Worker: Political Attitudes and Behaviour, 1968; The Affluent Worker in the Class Structure, 1969; There is a Gate, 1973; Francis Kilvert, 1990; Solidarity and Schism: The Problem of Disorder in Durkheimian and Marxist Sociology, 1992. **Address:** Institute for Social and Economic Research, University of Essex, Rm. 2N2.5A.07, Level 5A, Wivenhoe Pk., Colchester, EX CO4 3SQ, England. **Online address:** lockd@essex.ac.uk

LOCKWOOD, Gilly. See **LANAGAN, Margo.**

LOCKWOOD, Glenn. See **WHITEHEAD, David (Henry).**

LOCKWOOD, Jane. *See* **MULLANY, Janet.**

LOCKWOOD, Jeffrey A(lan). American (born United States), b. 1960?. **Genres:** Adult Non-fiction. **Career:** Louisiana State University, LSU Alumni research fellow, 1982-86, postdoctoral associate, 1985-86; Commonwealth Scientific and Industrial Research Organization, Division of Entomology, visiting scientist, 1993-94; Australian National University, visiting fellow, 1993-94; University of Wyoming, assistant professor of entomology, 1986-91, associate professor of entomology, 1991-96, professor of entomology, 1996-, adjunct professor of natural sciences, 1996-, professor of natural sciences and humanities 1996-, Association for Applied Acridology Intl., director, 1998, affiliate professor of philosophy, 2003-. Writer. **Publications:** Project and Report, Development of High Mountain Plant Communities as Wetland Mitigation Systems for Copper Mine Effluent, 1993; Ethical Issues in Biological Control, 1997; Biology and Recommendations for Use of Nosema Locustae Canning, Biological Control Agent of Grasshoppers, 1998; Grasshoppers and Grassland Health: Managing Grasshopper Outbreaks without Risking Environmental Disaster, 2000; Grasshopper Dreaming: Reflections on Killing and Loving, 2002; Locust: The Devastating Rise and Mysterious Disappearance of the Insect That Shaped the American Frontier, 2004; Prairie Soul: Finding Grace in the Earth beneath My Feet, 2004; Guest of the World: Meditations, 2006; Six-Legged Soldiers: Using Insects as Weapons of War, 2009. Contributor to periodicals. **Address:** Department of Philosophy, University of Wyoming, 1000 E University Ave., PO Box 3354, Laramie, WY 82071, U.S.A. **Online address:** lockwood@uwyo.edu

LOCKYER, Judith (Ann). American (born United States), b. 1949. **Genres:** Literary Criticism And History, Humanities. **Career:** University of Michigan, instructor and associate director of composition, 1985; Albion College, associate professor of English, 1985-, professor and chair of English. Writer. **Publications:** Ordered by Words: Language and Narration in the Novels of William Faulkner, 1991. **Address:** Department of English, Albion College, 611 E Porter St., Albion, MI 49224, U.S.A. **Online address:** jlockyer@albion.edu

LODATO, Victor. American (born United States), b. 1968. **Genres:** Novels. **Career:** Writer and actor. **Publications:** Mathilda Savitch (novel), 2009. Contributor to periodicals. **Address:** c/o David McCormick, McCormick & Williams, 37 W 20th St., New York, NY 10011, U.S.A. **Online address:** dm@mccormickwilliams.com

LODGE, David. British (born England), b. 1935. **Genres:** Novels, Plays/Screenplays, Literary Criticism And History, Young Adult Non-fiction, Essays, Novellas/Short Stories, Young Adult Non-fiction. **Career:** British Council, staff assistant, 1959-60; University of Birmingham, lecturer, 1960-71, senior lecturer, 1971-73, reader, 1973-76, professor of modern English literature, 1976-87, professor emeritus of English literature, 1987-; University of California, visiting associate professor, 1969; University of East Anglia, Henfield creative writing fellow, 1977. Writer. **Publications:** About Catholic Authors, 1958; The Picturegoers, 1960; Ginger, You're Barmy, 1962; The British Museum Is Falling Down, 1965; Language of Fiction: Essays in Criticism and Verbal Analysis of the English Novel, 1966; Graham Greene, 1966; Out of the Shelter, 1970, rev. ed., 1989; The Novelist at the Crossroads and Other Essays on Fiction and Criticism, 1971; Evelyn Waugh, 1971; Changing Places: A Tale of Two Campuses, 1975; The Modes of Modern Writing: Metaphor, Metonymy and the Typology of Modern Literature, 1977; Modernism, Antimodernism and Postmodernism, 1977; How Far Can You Go?, 1980 as Souls and Bodies, 1982; Working with Structuralism, 1981; Small World: An Academic Romance, 1984; (intro.) The Best of Ring Lardner, 1984; Write On: Occasional Essays 1965-1985, 1986; Nice Work, 1988; After Bakhtin: Essays on Fiction and Criticism, 1990; The Writing Game: A Comedy (play), 1991; Paradise News, 1992; The Art of Fiction: Illustrated from Classic and Modern Texts, 1992; Therapy (novel), 1995; Surprised by Summer, 1996; The Practice of Writing, 1997; The Man Who Wouldn't Get Up: And Other Stories, 1998; Home Truths: A Novella, 1999; Thinks, 2001; Consciousness & the Novel: Connected Essays, 2002; Author, Author, 2004; Scenes of Academic Life: Selected from His Own Novels, 2005; The Year of Henry James: The Story of a Novel, 2006; Deaf Sentence, 2008; A Man of Parts, 2011; Campus Trilogy, 2011; Secret Thoughts, 2011. EDITOR: Jane Austen's Emma: A Casebook, 1968, rev. ed., 1991; Emma, 1971, rev. ed., 1990; 20th Century Literary Criticism: A Reader, 1972; Scenes of Clerical Life, 1973; The Woodlanders, 1974; The Spoils of Poyton, 1987; Modern Criticism and

Theory: A Reader, 1988, 3rd ed., 2008. Contributor to periodicals. **Address:** Curtis Brown Group Ltd., Haymarket House, 28-29 Haymarket, London, GL SW1Y 4SP, England.

LODGE, Jeff. American (born United States), b. 1952. **Genres:** Novels, Mystery/Crime/Suspense, Young Adult Fiction. **Career:** Virginia Commonwealth University, Department of English, graduate teaching assistant, 1992-, adjunct instructor in English, 1995-, coordinator of graduate programs in English, 1996-2006, assistant professor of English, 2006-; Johns Hopkins University, instructor at Center for Talented Youth, 1994-95; University of Richmond, adjunct instructor, 1995-96. Writer. **Publications:** Where This Lake Is (fiction), 1997; A Wailing over Us, forthcoming; The History of My Misfortunes, forthcoming. **Address:** Department of English, Virginia Commonwealth University, Al Luqta St., PO Box 8095, Doha, 1, Qatar. **Online address:** jalodge@vcu.edu

LODISH, Leonard M. American (born United States), b. 1943. **Genres:** Advertising/Public Relations. **Career:** University of Pennsylvania, Wharton School, Department of Marketing, assistant professor, 1968-71, associate professor, 1971-76, professor, 1976-, chair, 1984-88, 1991-92, Samuel R. Harrell professor, 1987-, Global Consulting Practicum, founder and leader, 1978-, Sales Force Management Executive Program, co-director, 1994-, Wharton West, vice dean, 2001-09, Program for Social Impact, vice dean, 2009-, Wharton San Francisco, senior advisor, 2009-; Procter & Gamble, advertising and promotion decision support, marketing research and strategy staff, 1984-96; Information Resources Inc., director of packaged goods marketing and strategy decision support, 1985-2003; Franklin Electronic Publishing Corp., director, 1987-; Anheuser Busch, marketing strategy and decision support staff, 1989-93; J&J Snack Food Corp., director, 1992-; Walsh PDS, pharmaceutical marketing analysis staff, 1992-99; Tropicana, marketing strategy and tactics staff, 1995-99; ConAgra, consultant, 2000-. Writer and consultant. **Publications:** The Advertising and Promotion Challenge: Vaguely Right or Precisely Wrong?, 1986; (with H.L. Morgan and A. Kallianpur) Entrepreneurial Marketing: Lessons from Wharton's Pioneering MBA Course, 2001; (with H.L. Morgan and S. Archambeau) Marketing That Works: How Entrepreneurial Marketing Can Add Sustainable Value to Any Sized Company, 2007. Contributor of articles to journals. **Address:** Department of Marketing, Wharton School, University of Pennsylvania, 772 Jon M. Huntsman Hall, 3730 Walnut St., Philadelphia, PA 19104-6371, U.S.A. **Online address:** lodish@wharton.upenn.edu

LOEB, Jeph. American (born United States), b. 1958. **Genres:** Cartoons. **Career:** Public Broadcasting Service (PBS), writer and producer. **Publications:** PLOTS AND SCRIPTS; SELECTED TITLES: Batman: Haunted Knight: The Legends of the Dark Knight Halloween Specials: Three Tales of Halloween in Gotham City, 1994; X-Men: The Age of Apocalypse, 1995; X-Men: Dawn of the Age of Apocalypse, 1996; Onslaught: To the Victor, 1997; Wolverine Gambit Victims, 1997; Batman: The Long Halloween (contains thirteen issues of the miniseries), 1998; Superman for All Seasons, 1999; Superman: No Limits, 2000; The Witching Hour, 2000; Batman: Dark Victory, 2001; Superman: Endgame, 2001; Superman: 'Til Death Do Us Part, 2002; Superman: Our Worlds at War, 2002; Superman: The Ultimate Guide, 2002; Superman: President Lex, 2003; Daredevil: Yellow, 2003; Spider-Man: Blue, 2003; Batman: Hush, vol. I, 2003, vol. II, 2004; Hulk: Gray, 2004; Superman, Batman, 2004; Challengers of the Unknown must Die, 2004; Catwoman: When in Rome, 2005; (with D. Cooke) Spirit, 2007; Superman, Batman: Vengeance, 2008; Hush, 2009; (contrib.) Batman Beyond: Hush Beyond, 2011. Contributor to periodicals. **Address:** c/o Author Mail, DC Comics, 1700 Broadway, New York, NY 10019, U.S.A.

LOEB, Karen. American (born United States), b. 1946. **Genres:** Literary Criticism And History, Novellas/Short Stories, Poetry, Young Adult Fiction. **Career:** Columbia College, instructor in English, 1968-74; Eckerd College, instructor in writing and composition, 1979-88; University of Wisconsin, associate professor of English, 1988-. Writer. **Publications:** Jump Rope Queen and Other Stories, 1992. Work appears in anthologies. Contributor of articles to magazines and newspapers. **Address:** Department of English, University of Wisconsin, Rm. 405, Hibbard Hall, 105 Garfield Ave., Eau Claire, WI 54702-4004, U.S.A.

LOEFFELHOLZ, Mary. American (born United States), b. 1958?. **Genres:**

Women's Studies And Issues, Literary Criticism And History, Young Adult Fiction. **Career:** University of Illinois, assistant professor of English, women's studies, criticism and interpretive theory, 1986-88; Northeastern University, assistant professor of English, 1988-93, associate professor of English, 1993-2002, department chair, 2001-06, professor of English, 2002-, associate dean for faculty affairs and director of the Graduate School in the College of Arts and Sciences, 2006-07, special advisor to the president for faculty affairs, 2007-08, vice provost for academic affairs. Writer. **Publications:** Dickinson and the Boundaries of Feminist Theory, 1991; Experimental Lives: Women and Literature, 1900-1945, 1992; From School to Salon: Reading Nineteenth-century American Women's Poetry, 2004; The Norton Anthology of American Literature, 2007; (ed. with M.N. Smith) A Companion to Emily Dickinson, 2008; The Blackwell Companion to Emily Dickinson, 2008. **Address:** Department of English, Northeastern University, 360 Huntington Ave., 406 Holmes, 405 NI, Boston, MA 02115, U.S.A. **Online address:** m.loeffelholz@neu.edu

LOEHR, Davidson. American (born United States), b. 1942?. **Genres:** Theology/Religion, History. **Career:** U.S. Army-Vietnam, photographer; Unitarian Universalist minister, 1986-2009, retired; First Unitarian Universalist Church of Austin, minister, 2000-. Writer and musician. **Publications:** The Legitimate Heir to Theology: A Study of Ludwig Wittgenstein, 1988; America, Fascism, and God: Sermons from a Heretical Preacher, 2005; The Rise of Secular Religion in America, forthcoming. **Address:** First Unitarian Universalist Church of Austin, 4700 Grover Ave., Austin, TX 78756-3108, U.S.A.

LOEN, Raymond O(rdell). American (born United States), b. 1924. **Genres:** Administration/Management, Business/Trade/Industry, Economics. **Career:** Uarco Inc., sales representative, sales trainer and city sales manager, 1949-53; H.B. Maynard and Company Inc., staff consultant and senior consultant, 1953-59; Fibreboard Corp., sales training manager and director of management services, 1959-63; R.O. Loen Co., management consultant to large and small businesses, 1963-, president; Loen Brandt Inc., founder and director, 1965-70; Swift Energy Co., founding director and board director, 1979-2000, director emeritus, 2000-; Validity Inc., director, 2002-, president; United Medical Laboratories Inc., chair and director; Lancet Medical Industries Inc., founder and director; Graphic Software Systems Inc., director. Writer and consultant. **Publications:** Personnel Management, 1969; Manage More by Doing Less, 1971; Supervising by Objectives, 1971; Superior Supervision: The 10 Percent Solution, 1994. Contributor to journals. **Address:** R.O. Loen Co., 16 Becket St., Lake Oswego, OR 97035-1034, U.S.A.

LOENGARD, John. American (born United States), b. 1934. **Genres:** Illustrations, Photography, Art/Art History. **Career:** Freelance photographer, 1956-61, 2000-; LIFE, photographer, 1961-72, picture editor, 1978-87, contributing photographer, 1987-2000; Time Inc., Magazine Development Group, picture editor, 1972-; People, founding picture editor, 1973-74; International Center of Photography, faculty; writer, 2000-. **Publications:** Pictures Under Discussion (photographs), 1987; Life Classic Photographs: A Personal Interpretation, 1988; Faces/Life, 1991; Celebrating the Negative (photographs), 1994; Georgia O'Keeffe at Ghost Ranch (photographs), 1995; Life Photographers: What They Saw, 1998; As I See It, 2005; (with G. O'Keeffe) Georgia O'Keeffe/John Loengard: Paintings & Photographs: A Visit to Abiquiu and Ghost Ranch, 2006 as Image and Imagination: Georgia O'Keeffe by John Loengard, 2007; Age of Silver: Encounters with Great Photographers, 2011. **Address:** 20 W 86th St., New York, NY 10024, U.S.A. **Online address:** loenpics@aol.com

LOEVY, Robert D(ickinson). American (born United States), b. 1935. **Genres:** Politics/Government, History, Social Sciences. **Career:** Goucher College, assistant professor of political science, 1960-68; Colorado College, professor of political science, 1968-. Writer. **Publications:** (Co-author) American Government: We Are One, 1986; To End All Segregation: The Politics of the Passage of the Civil Rights Act of 1964, 1990; (with T.E. Cronin) Colorado Politics and Government: Governing the Centennial State, 1993; The Flawed Path to the Presidency, 1992: Unfairness and Inequality in the Presidential Selection Process, 1995; The Flawed Path to the Governorship, 1994: The Nationalization of a Colorado Statewide Election, 1996; (ed. and contrib.) The Civil Rights Act of 1964: The Passage of the Law That Ended Racial Segregation, 1997; The Manipulated Path to the White House 1996: Maximizing Advantage in the Presidential Selection Process, 1998; Colorado College: A Place of Learning, 1874-1999, 1999; On the Forward Edge: American Government and the Civil Rights Act of 1964, 2005. **Address:** Department of Political Science, Colorado College, Rm. 22G, Palmer Hall, 14 E Cache La Poudre St., Colorado Springs, CO 80903, U.S.A. **Online address:** bloevy@coloradocollege.edu

LOEWE, M. A. N. *See* **LOEWE, Michael.**

LOEWE, Michael. (M. A. N. Loewe). British (born England), b. 1922. **Genres:** History, Bibliography. **Career:** British Government Communications, specialist officer, 1942-56; University of London, lecturer in history of the Far East, 1956-63; Cambridge University, lecturer in Chinese studies, 1963-90; European Association of Chinese Studies, president, 1984-86; Needham Research Institute, deputy director; Queen's College, director of studies; Sidney Sussex College, director of studies; Lucy Cavendish College, director of studies; Wolfson College, director of studies. Writer. **Publications:** Military Operations in the Han Period, 1961; Imperial China: The Historical Background to the Modern Age, 1966; Records of Han Administration, vol. I: Historical Assessment, 1967, vol. II: Documents, 1967; Everyday Life in Early Imperial China during the Han Period, 202 B.C.-A.D. 220, 1968; Crisis and Conflict in Han China, 104 B.C. to A.D. 9, 1974; Ways to Paradise: The Chinese Quest for Immortality, 1979; Chinese Ideas of Life and Death: Faith, Myth and Reason in the Han Period (202 B.C.-A.D. 220), 1982; The Pride That was China (Great Civilizations series), 1990; Divination, Mythology and Monarchy in Han China, 1994; A Biographical Dictionary of the Qin, Former Han and Xin Periods (221 B.C.-A.D. 24), 2000; The Men Who Governed Han China: Companion to A Biographical Dictionary of the Qin, Former Han and Xin Period, 2004; Faith, Myth and Reason in Han China, 2005; (contrib.) Recarving China's Past: Art, Archaeology, and Architecture of the Wu Family Shrines, 2005; Government of the Qin and Han Empires: 221 B.C.E.-220 C.E., 2006; Dong Zhongshu, a Confucian Heritage and the Chun qiu fan lu, 2011; Bing: From Farmer's Son to Magistrate in Han China, 2011; Supplementary Volume to the Cambridge History of China, vol. I, forthcoming. EDITOR: (with C. Blacker) Ancient Cosmologies, 1975; (with C. Blacker) Oracles and Divination, 1981; (with D. Twitchett) The Cambridge History of China, vol. I: The Ch'in and Han Empires, 221 B.C.-A.D. 220, 1986; Early Chinese Texts: A Bibliographical Guide, 1993; (with E.L. Shaughnessy) The Cambridge History of Ancient China: From the Origins of Civilization to 221 B.C., 1999; (with M. Nylan) China's Early Empires: A Re-Appraisal, 2010. Contributor to periodicals. **Address:** Willow House, Grantchester, Cambridge, CB3 9NF, England.

LOEWER, (Henry) Peter. American (born United States), b. 1934. **Genres:** Horticulture, Homes/Gardens, Young Adult Fiction, Illustrations, Natural History, Sciences, Young Adult Fiction. **Career:** Graphos Studio, owner and art director, 1963-; Upper Delaware, art director, 1979-80; Sullivan County Democrat, editor, 1979-81; Warwick Photo Advertiser, production manager, 1983-86; WCQS, host. Freelance artist. **Publications:** SELF-ILLUSTRATED: The Indoor Water Gardener's How-to Handbook, 1973; Bringing the Outdoors In, 1974, 2nd ed., 1990; Seeds and Cuttings, 1975; Wildflower Perennials for Your Garden, 1976; Growing and Decorating with Grasses, 1977; Growing Plants in Water, 1980; Evergreens: A Guide for Landscape, Lawn, and Garden, 1981; The Month-by-Month Garden Almanac, 1983; Gardens by Design, 1986; The Annual Garden, 1987; American Gardens, 1988; A Year of Flowers, 1989; The Indoor Window Garden, 1990; The Wild Gardener, 1991; Tough Plants for Tough Places, 1992; Rodale's Annual Garden, 1992; The Evening Garden, 1993; (with C. Tufts) The National Wildlife Federations Guide to Gardening for Wildlife, 1995; (with J. Loewer) The Moonflower, 1997. OTHERS: (contrib.) A World of Plants: The Missouri Botanical Garden, 1988; Letters to Sarah (juvenile), 1989; The Inside-Out Stomach (juvenile), 1990; (with A. Halpin) Secrets of the Great Gardeners: The Brooklyn Botanic Garden, 1991; (contrib.) Perennials, 1992; The New Small Garden, 1994; Step-by-Step Annuals, 1994; Wildflowers & Native Plants, 1995; Ornamental Grasses, 1995; Seeds, 1995; Thoreau's Garden, 1996; Pond Water Zoo: An Introduction to Microscopic Life, 1996; (with L. Mellichamp) The Winter Garden: Planning and Planting for the Southeast, 1997; Fragrant Gardens: How to Select and Make the Most of Scented Flowers and Leaves, 1999; Solving Weed Problems, 2001; Outwitting Weeds, 2001; Solving Deer Problems: How to Keep Them out of the Garden, Avoid Them on the Road, and Deal with Them Anywhere!, 2003; Small-Space Gardening: How to Successfully Grow Flowers and Vegetables in Containers and Pots, 2003; Jefferson's Garden, 2004; Ornamental Grasses for the Southeast, 2004; Native Perennials for the Southeast, 2006; Gardens of North Carolina: A Traveler's Guide, 2007. EDITOR: Taylor's Guide to Annuals, 1986; Garden Ornaments, 1987. **Address:** c/o Dominick Abel, Dominick Abel Literary

Agency Inc., 146 W 82nd St., New York, NY 10024, U.S.A. **Online address:** thewildgardener@earthlink.net

LOEWER, Jean. *See* **JENKINS, Jean.**

LOEWY, Erich H. American/Austrian (born Austria), b. 1927. **Genres:** Ethics, Medicine/Health. **Career:** Boston City Hospital, intern, 1954-55; Case Western Reserve University, resident, 1957-60, demonstrator, 1960-64, clinical instructor, 1964-70, senior clinical instructor in medicine, 1970-77; Union University, Albany Medical College, clinical assistant professor of cardiology, 1977-81; Adirondack Community College, lecturer, 1979-81; University of Connecticut, School of Medicine, assistant professor of medicine, 1981-84; University of Illinois, assistant professor, 1984-89, associate professor of ethics, 1989-, College of Medicine, assistant professor, 1987-89, associate professor of clinical medicine, 1989-93, professor of medicine (ethics), 1993-; University of Aarhus, visiting professor, 1989, 1991, 1992; Nordic School of Public Health, visiting professor, 1990; University of Marburg, visiting professor, 1990, 1992; Free University of Amsterdam, visiting professor, 1992; Converse College, visiting professor, 1992; Erskine College, visiting professor, 1992; Johns Hopkins University, lecturer; University of Florida, lecturer; Medical College of Ohio, lecturer; University of Tennessee, lecturer; University of California, Davis Health System, professor of medicine and founding chair of bioethics program, now professor emeritus of medicine, Department of Philosophy, associate faculty. Writer. **Publications:** Ethical Dilemmas in Modern Medicine, 1986; A Textbook of Medical Ethics, 1989; Suffering and the Beneficent Community: Beyond Libertarianism, 1991; Freedom and Community: The Ethics of Interdependence, 1993; Ethische Fragen in der Medizin, 1995; Textbook of Healthcare Ethics, 1996, (with R.S. Loewy) 2nd ed., 2004; Moral Strangers, Moral Acquaintance, and Moral Friends: Connectedness and its Conditions, 1997; (with R.S. Loewy) The Ethics of Terminal Care: Orchestrating the End of Life, 2000; (co-ed.) Dokumentation des ersten Giessener Symposiums vom 10. bis 12. Dezember 1999 zum Thema die Hospizbewegung im internationalen Vergleich, 2nd ed., 2000; (ed. with R.S. Loewy) Changing Health Care Systems from Ethical, Economic, and Cross Cultural Perspectives, 2001; (ed. with R. Gronemeyer) Wohin mit den Sterbenden?: Hospiz in Europa, 2001. Works appear in anthologies. Contributor of articles to journals. **Address:** University of California, Patient Support Services Bldg., Ste. 2500, 4150 V St., Sacramento, CA 95817, U.S.A. **Online address:** ehloewy@ucdavis.edu

LOFAS, Jeannette. American (born United States), b. 1940. **Genres:** Human Relations/Parenting, Psychology, Social Sciences, Romance/Historical. **Career:** Atlas Magazine, co-founder and associate editor, 1959-61; Radio Free Europe, reporter, on-air reporter, 1961-69; ABC-TV, reporter and film critic, on-air reporter, 1969; NBC, reporter and film critic; CBS, reporter and film critic; Ivan Tors Films, producer, 1970; Snowmass Arts Foundation, executive director, 1971-72; Family Matters, host, 1972-73; Stepfamily Foundation Inc., founder and president, 1975-; KWTV, television reporter and film critic; Metro Media, on-air reporter; Whitney Museum of American Art, New American Film Series, co-founder. **Publications:** (With R. Roosevelt) Living in Step (nonfiction), 1976; (with D.B. Sova) Stepparenting (nonfiction), 1985, rev. ed., 2004; (with J. MacMillan) He's OK, She's OK: Honoring the Differences between Men and Women (psychology), 1995; Family Rules: Helping Stepfamilies and Single Parents Build Happy Homes, 1998. **Address:** The Stepfamily Foundation Inc., 310 W 85th St., Ste. 1B, New York, NY 10024, U.S.A. **Online address:** stepfamily@aol.com

LOFTON, Ramona. (Sapphire Lofton). American (born United States), b. 1950. **Genres:** Novels, Poetry, Theology/Religion. **Career:** New School University, faculty; State University of New York, faculty; Trinity College, faculty; Fairleigh Dickinson University, faculty; Brooklyn College, faculty. Writer. **Publications:** Meditations on the Rainbow: Poetry, 1987; (ed. with D. Eiker) Keep Simple Ceremonies: The Feminist Spiritual Community of Portland, Maine, 1993, 2nd ed., 1995; American Dreams, 1994; Push: A Novel, 1996; Black Wings & Blind Angels: Poems, 1999, Kid, 2011. Works appear in anthologies. Contributor to periodicals. **Address:** The New School, 55 W 13th St., New York, NY 10011-7958, U.S.A.

LOFTON, Rodney. American (born United States), b. 1968?. **Genres:** Autobiography/Memoirs. **Career:** Speaker and freelance writer. **Publications:** The Day I Stopped Being Pretty: A Memoir, 2007. Contributor to books and magazines. **Address:** Richmond, VA , U.S.A. **Online address:** rodlofton@aol.com

LOFTON, Sapphire. *See* **LOFTON, Ramona.**

LOGAN, Anne. *See* **COLLEY, Barbara.**

LOGAN, Cait. *See* **KLEINSASSER, Lois.**

LOGAN, Chuck. American (born United States), b. 1942. **Genres:** Mystery/Crime/Suspense, Novels, Young Adult Fiction. **Career:** St. Paul Pioneer Press, staff artist, 1975-; writer, 1985-. **Publications:** Hunter's Moon, 1996; The Price of Blood, 1997; The Big Law, 1998; Absolute Zero, 2002; Vapor Trail, 2003; After the Rain, 2004; Homefront, 2005; South of Shiloh: A Thriller, 2008. **Address:** c/o Sloan Harris, International Creative Management Inc., 825 8th Ave., New York, NY 10019, U.S.A.

LOGAN, George M(eredith). Canadian/American (born United States), b. 1941. **Genres:** Literary Criticism And History, Music, Philosophy, History, Essays. **Career:** Queen's University, assistant professor, 1967-74, associate professor, 1974-83, professor of English, 1983-95, head of department, 1985-94, James Cappon professor of English, 1995-, now professor emeritus; University of Toronto, Massey College, senior fellow. Writer. **Publications:** The Meaning of More's Utopia, 1983; The Indiana University School of Music: A History, 2000. EDITOR: (co-ed.) The Norton Anthology of English Literature, 5th ed., 1986, 8th ed., 2005; (with R.M. Adams) Utopia, 1989, 2nd ed., 2002; (with G. Teskey) Unfolded Tales: Essays on Renaissance Romance, 1989; (with R.M. Adams and C.H. Miller) Utopia: Latin Text and English Translation, 1995; The History of King Richard the Third, 2005; Utopia: A Norton Critical Edition, 3rd ed., 2011; The Cambridge Companion to Thomas More, 2011. **Address:** Massey College, 4 Devonshire Pl., Toronto, ON M5S 2E1, Canada. **Online address:** logang@queensu.ca

LOGAN, Jake. *See* **SMITH, Martin Cruz.**

LOGAN, Matt. *See* **WHITEHEAD, David (Henry).**

LOGAN, Michael F. American (born United States), b. 1950. **Genres:** Regional/Urban Planning, Urban Studies. **Career:** University of Arizona, history teacher, 1990-94; Pima Community College, teacher, 1992-94; Oklahoma State University, Department of History, assistant professor of history, 1994-, associate professor, professor and department head, 1994-, secretary, 1995-2000, U.S. survey coordinator, 1997-2000, director of graduate studies, 2003-06; Certificate Program in Environmental Studies, director, 2005-. Writer. **Publications:** Fighting Sprawl and City Hall: Resistance to Urban Growth in the Southwest, 1995; Lessening Stream: An Environmental History of the Santa Cruz River, 2002; Desert Cities: The Environmental History of Phoenix and Tucson, 2006; (co-ed.) Visions of America's Heritage: Readings in United States History, 2008. Contributor of articles to periodicals. **Address:** Department of History, Oklahoma State University, 501D Life Science W, Stillwater, OK 74078, U.S.A. **Online address:** michael.logan@okstate.edu

LOGAN, Shirley Wilson. American (born United States), b. 1943. **Genres:** Literary Criticism And History. **Career:** School teacher, 1964-67, 1970-74; Howard University, instructor in English, 1967-70, 1975-77; University of Maryland, instructor, 1980-92, Professional Writing Program Computer Laboratory, coordinator, 1986-92, assistant professor of English, 1992-, Professional Writing Program, director, 1992-99, advisor, associate professor of English, professor of English, Rhetoric Minor chair. Writer. **Publications:** (Ed. and intro.) With Pen and Voice: A Critical Anthology of Nineteenth-Century African-American Women, 1995; We are Coming: The Persuasive Discourse of Nineteenth-Century Black Women, 1999; Liberating Language: Sites of Rhetorical Education in Nineteenth Century Black America, 2008. Contributor to books and periodicals. **Address:** Department of English, University of Maryland, 3114 Tawes Hall, College Park, MD 20742, U.S.A. **Online address:** slogan@umd.edu

LOGAN, William. American (born United States), b. 1950. **Genres:** Poetry, Adult Non-fiction. **Career:** University of Florida, director of creative writing program, 1983-2000, assistant professor, 1983-87, associate professor, 1987-91, professor of English, 1991-, alumni professor of English, 1996-99. Writer. **Publications:** POETRY: Dream of Dying, 1980; Sad-Faced Men, 1982; Moorhen, 1984; Difficulty, 1985; Sullen Weedy Lakes, 1988; Vain Empires,

1998; Night Battle, 1999; Macbeth in Venice, 2003; The Whispering Gallery, 2005; Strange Flesh, 2008; Deception Island: Selected Earlier Poems, 1974-1999, 2011. NONFICTION: (ed. with D. Gioia) Certain Solitudes: On the Poetry of Donald Justice, 1997; All the Rage, 1998; Reputations of the Tongue, 1999; (ed.) Randall Jarrell, Poetry and the Age, 2000; Desperate Measures, 2002; The Undiscovered Country, 2005; Our Savage Art, 2009; (intro.) Guy Vernon: A Novelette in Verse, 2012. Contributor to periodicals. **Address:** Department of English, University of Florida, 4211H Turlington Hall, PO Box 117310, Gainesville, FL 32611-7310, U.S.A. **Online address:** wlogan@english.ufl.edu

LOGSTON, Anne. American (born United States), b. 1962. **Genres:** Science Fiction/Fantasy. **Career:** Writer. **Publications:** Shadow, 1991; Shadow Dance, 1992; Greendaughter, 1993; Dagger's Edge, 1994; Dagger's Point, 1995; Wild Blood, 1995; Guardian's Key, 1996; Firewalk, 1997; Waterdance, 1999; Exile, 1999; Shadow Hunt, 2005. Contributor to periodicals. **Address:** Ace Books, 200 Madison Ave., New York, NY 10016, U.S.A.

LOGUE, Christopher. (Christopher John Logue). British (born England), b. 1926. **Genres:** Novellas/Short Stories, Young Adult Fiction, Plays/Screenplays, Poetry, Documentaries/Reportage, Translations. **Career:** Private Eye, columnist, 1962-. Actor. **Publications:** Wand and Quadrant, 1953; Devil, Maggot and Son, 1955; The Man Who Told His Love: Twenty Poems Based on Pablo Neruda's Los Cantos d'Amores, 1958; The Trial of Cob and Leach: A News Play, 1959; Songs, 1959; Trials by Logue (Antigone and Cob and Leach), 1960; Songs from The Lily-White Boys, 1960; Patrocleia: Book 16 of Homer's Iliad Freely Adapted into English, 1962; Patrocleia of Homer, 1963; True Stories, 1966; Selections from a Correspondence between an Irishman and a Rat, 1966; Logue's A.B.C., 1966; How to Find Poetry Everywhere, 1969; The Girls, 1969; Ring a Dumb Carillon, 1969; New Numbers, 1969; Isles of Jessamy, 1971; (contrib.) For Talitha, 1941-1971, 1971; Twelve Cards, 1972; Duet for Mole and Worm, 1972; Singles, 1973; Mixed Rushes, 1974; Puss-in-Boots Pop-Up, 1976; Ratsmagic (juvenile), 1976; The Crocodile (juvenile), 1976; Abecedary: Verse, 1977; Red Bird: Love Poems, 1979; The Magic Circus (juvenile), 1979; Bumper Book of True Stories, 1980; Ode to the Dodo: Poems 1953-1978, 1981; War Music: An Account of Books 16-19 of the Iliad, 1981; Arrival of the Poet in the City: A Melodrama for Narrator and Seven Musicians, 1983; Fluff, 1984; Meridian, 1987; Kings: An Account of Books 1-2 of Homer's Iliad, 1991; The Husbands, An Account of Books 3-4 of Homer's Iliad, 1995; War Music: An Account of Books 1-4 and 16-19 of Homer's Iliad, 1997; Prince Charming: A Memoir, 1999; All Day Permanent Red: The First Battle Scenes of Homer's Iliad Rewritten, 2003; Cold Calls: War Music Continued, 2005. EDITOR: True Stories from Private Eye, 1973; The Children's Book of Comic Verse, 1979; London in Verse, 1982; Sweet & Sour: An Anthology of Comic Verse, 1983; The Oxford Book of Pseuds, 1983; (comp.) The Children's Book of Children's Rhymes, 1986. Contributor to magazines and newspapers. **Address:** 41 Camberwell Grove, London, GL SE5 8JA, England.

LOGUE, Christopher John. *See* **LOGUE, Christopher.**

LOGUE, Mary. American (born United States), b. 1952. **Genres:** Novels, Children's Fiction, Children's Non-fiction, Mystery/Crime/Suspense. **Career:** The Village Voice, copy-editor, 1981-83; Simon & Schuster, copy-editor, 1983-85; Graywolf Press, editor, 1986-88; The Creative Co., editor, 1995-2000; Mid-List Press, freelance editor, 2002-; Loft Literary Center, teacher; Hamline University, Children's Literature MFA program, faculty. **Publications:** A House in the Country, 1994; (trans.) B. Gandiol-Coppin, Ancient Civilizations, 2001; Wolf Who Loved Music, 2003; Bone Harvest, 2004; Sea Stars, 2005; Sponges, 2005; Sea Jellies, 2005; Meticulous Attachment (poems), 2005; Poison Heart, 2005; Snatched, 2006; (contrib.) Courthouses of Minnesota, 2006; (with P. Hautman) Skullduggery, 2007; (with P. Hautman) Doppelganger, 2008; Frozen Stiff, 2010; Sleep Like a Tiger, 2012. FOR ADULTS: (ed.) The Thief of Sadness/Nor Haven Poetry Collective, 1979; (ed. with L. Sutin) Believing Everything, An Anthology of New Writing, 1980; Discriminating Evidence (poetry), 1990; Halfway Home: A Granddaughter's Biography, 1996; Settling (poetry), 1997; (ed. with J.C. Mitchell) Over the Waves, 1999; Hand Work: Poems, 2009; New Year's Eve, forthcoming. MYSTERY NOVELS FOR ADULTS: Red Lake of the Heart (mystery), 1987; Still Explosion: A Laura Malloy Mystery, 1993; Blood Country: A Claire Watkins Mystery, 1999; Dark Coulee: A Claire Watkins Mystery, 2000; Glare Ice: A Claire Watkins Mystery, 2001. FICTION FOR CHILDREN: The Missing Statue of Minnehaha, 1993; The Haunting of Hunter House, 1993;

Dancing with an Alien, 2000; Maiden Rock, 2007; Point No Point, 2008. NON-FICTION FOR CHILDREN: Forgiveness: The Story of Mahatma Gandhi, 1996; Elizabeth Barrett Browning: Love, 1996; A Life of Love: The Story of Elizabeth Barrett Browning, 1998; Trust: The Story of Helen Keller, 1999; Imagination: The Story of Walt Disney, 1999. **Address:** MidList Press, 4324 12th Ave. S, Minneapolis, MN 55407-3218, U.S.A. **Online address:** marylogue@comcast.net

LOH, Sandra Tsing. American (born United States), b. 1962. **Genres:** Plays/Screenplays, Novels, Autobiography/Memoirs, Humor/Satire, Biography. **Career:** Buzz magazine, columnist, 1992-96; KCRW-Radio, commentator, 1997-; National Public Radio (NPR), commentator; The Atlantic Monthly, contributing editor. **Publications:** Depth Takes a Holiday: Essays from Lesser Los Angeles, 1996; Aliens in America (monologue), 1997; If You Lived Here, You'd Be Home by Now (novel), 1997; A Year in Van Nuys (humor), 2001; Mother on Fire, 2008. Contributor to periodicals. **Address:** c/o Sloan Harris, International Creative Management, 40 W 57th St., New York, NY 10019, U.S.A.

LOHANS, Alison. Canadian/American (born United States), b. 1949. **Genres:** Novels, Children's Fiction, Young Adult Fiction, Science Fiction/Fantasy, Poetry, E-books, Picture/Board Books, Novellas/Short Stories, Novellas/Short Stories. **Career:** Argenta Friends School, teacher, 1973-74; writer, 1976-; Regina Public Board of Education, instrumental music teacher, 1976-79; University of Regina, Faculty of Education, research assistant, teaching assistant, project associate, 1986-88, 2001-05, University of Regina Extension, instructor, 1990-95, Center for Continuing Education, instructor, 2004, 2006; Saskatchewan Writers Guild, instructor, 1995-2000, 2012; Regina Public Library, writer-in-residence, 2002-03. **Publications:** FOR YOUNG ADULTS: Who Cares about Karen?, 1983; Can You Promise Me Spring?, 1986; Foghorn Passage, 1992, rev. ed., 1997; Laws of Emotion, 1993; Don't Think Twice, 1997, rev. ed., 2009; This Land We Call Home, 2007; River Rat, 2008; Collapse of the Veil, 2010; Crossings, 2012. FOR CHILDREN: Mystery of the Lunchbox Criminal, 1990, rev. ed., 1999; Germy Johnson's Secret Plan, 1992, rev. ed., 2008; Nathaniel's Violin, 1996; Getting Rid of Mr. Ribitus, 1998; Sundog Rescue, 1999; No Place for Kids, 1999; Skateboard Kids, 1999; Waiting for the Sun, 2001; The Raspberry Room, 2006; Old, Tired Dog, 2006; Germy Johnson's Piano War, 2010; Doppelganger, 2010; Dog Alert, 2011; Picturing Alyssa, 2011; The Break, 2012; Stop That Pup!, 2012. TRANSLATIONS: Y a-t-il un voleur dans l'ecole?, 1990; Le plan secret de Jeremie Jalbert, 1992; Far jag en puss?, 2002; Hvem bryr seg om Karen?, 2002. **Address:** 76 Dolphin Bay, Regina, SK S4S 4Z8, Canada. **Online address:** lohans@sasktel.net

LÖHR, Robert. German (born Germany), b. 1973. **Genres:** Novels, Romance/Historical, Young Adult Fiction. **Career:** Writer. **Publications:** Das Erlkönig-Manöver: Historischer Roman (historical novel), 2007. **Address:** Above the Line Agency, Wieland Strasse 5, Berlin, 10625, Germany.

LOMAS, Herbert. British (born England), b. 1924. **Genres:** Poetry, Translations, Adult Non-fiction. **Career:** The Anargyrios School, teacher, 1950-51; University of Helsinki, lecturer, senior lecturer, 1952-65; West London Institute of Higher Education, lecturer, principal lecturer, 1966-83. Writer. **Publications:** POETRY: Chimpanzees are Blameless Creatures, 1969; Private and Confidential, 1974; Public Footpath, 1981; Fire in the Garden, 1984; Letters in the Dark, 1986; Trouble, 1992; Selected Poems, 1995; A Useless Passion, 1999; The Vale of Todmorden, 2003; Casual Knack of living: Collected Poems, 2009. TRANSLATOR: (and ed.) Territorial Song: Contemporary Writing from Finland, 1981; (and ed.) Contemporary Finnish Poetry, 1991; E. Stenberg, Wings of Hope and Daring (poems), 1992; K. Nieminen, Fugue (poems), 1992; I. Tiihonen, Black and Red (poems), 1993; I. Tiihonen, The Black and the Red, 1993; L. Krohn, The Eyes of the Fingertips Are Opening (poems), 1993; R. Ahti, Narcissus in Winter (poems), 1994; L. Otonkoski, Two Sequences for Kuhmo, 1994; A. Paasilinna, The Year of the Hare (novel), 1995; J. Rinnemaa, In Wandering Hall, 1995; Selected Poems: Eeva-Liisa Manner, 1997; Three Finnish Poets: Melleri, Ahti, Stenberg, 1999; Pentti Holappa: A Tenant Here: Selected Poems, 1999; Ilpo Tiihonen: Gaia, a Musical for Children, 2001; Not before Sundown (novel), 2003 in US as Troll: A Love Story, 2004; A. Paasilinna, Year of the Hare, 2006. OTHERS: (co-author) A Handbook of Modern English for Finnish Students, 1957; Who Needs Money? (nonfiction), 1972. Contributor to periodicals. **Address:** N Gable, 30 Crag Path, Aldeburgh, SU IP15 5BS, England. **Online address:** herbert@hlomas.freeserve.co.uk

LOMAX, Marion. *See* **BOLAM, Robyn.**

LOMAZOW, Steven. American (born United States), b. 1948?. **Genres:** Writing/Journalism. **Career:** Mount Sinai School of Medicine, assistant professor of neurology; Freedom Forum Newseum, consultant. Writer and neurologist. **Publications:** American Periodicals: A Collector's Manual and Reference Guide: An Annotated Catalog of a Collection, 1996; (with E. Fettmann) FDR's Deadly Secret, 2009. **Address:** Mount Sinai School of Medicine, 1 Gustave L. Levy Pl., New York, NY 10029-6574, U.S.A.

LOMBARDO, Billy. American (born United States), b. 1962. **Genres:** Novels. **Career:** Latin School of Chicago, teacher of English literature and creative writing; University of California, Extension Program, teacher of fiction; Polyphony H.S. (student-run national literary magazine for high school writers and editors), co-founder and artistic director. Writer. **Publications:** Meanwhile, Roxy Mourns (poetry), 2009. FICTION: The Logic of a Rose: Chicago Stories, 2005; How to Hold a Woman (novel), 2009; The Man with Two Arms (novel), 2010. Contributor to periodicals. **Address:** Forest Park, IL , U.S.A. **Online address:** polyphonyhs@gmail.com

LOMBARDO, Mary A. American (born United States), b. 1938. **Genres:** Mathematics/Statistics, Language/Linguistics, Poetry, inspirational/Motivational Literature, Education. **Career:** Albuquerque Teachers Federation, negotiator, newspaper editor and director of staff, 1984-94; Albuquerque Public Schools, reading teacher, 1994-2000; Vintage Players (volunteer drama troupe), performer, 1996-2000. Writer. **Publications:** The Really Red School House, 1969; Mastering Math Through Magic: Grades 4-6, 2002; Mastering Math Through Magic: Grades 2-3, 2003; Mastering Math Through Magic: Grades 6-8, 2003; Poetry and Pop-Ups, 2003; Rhymes, Writing, and Role-Play: Quick and Easy Lessons for Beginning Readers, 2004; Monthly Mini-Lessons: Forty Projects for Independent Study, Grades 4-6, 2005; Monthly Mini-Lessons: Forty Projects for Independent Study, Grades 2 and 3, 2005; Easy-Does-It Grammar for Grades 4-12, 2007; Two Minute Meditations: A Daily Walk with the Saints, 2009. **Address:** 1820 Lester Dr. NE, Albuquerque, NM 87112-2847, U.S.A. **Online address:** willgo2nm@aol.com

LOMBORG, Bjørn. Danish (born Denmark), b. 1965. **Genres:** Environmental Sciences/Ecology. **Career:** University of Aarhus, assistant professor, 1994-96, associate professor of statistics, 1997-2005; Environmental Assessment Institute, director, 2002-04; Copenhagen Business School, adjunct professor of management, politics, and philosophy, 2005-; Copenhagen Consensus Center, director, 2006-. Writer. **Publications:** Verdens sande tilstand, 1998, trans. as The Skeptical Environmentalist: Measuring the Real State of the World, 2001; (ed.) Global Crises, Global Solutions, 2004, 2nd ed., 2009; (ed.) How to Spend $50 Billion to Make the World a Better Place, 2006; Cool It: The Skeptical Environmentalist's Guide to Global Warming, 2007; (ed.) Solutions for the World's Biggest Problems: Costs and Benefits, 2007; (ed.) Latin American Development Priorities: Costs and Benefits, 2009. Contributor to periodicals. **Address:** Copenhagen Consensus Center, Copenhagen Business School, Solbjerg Plads 3, Frederiksberg, DK-2000, Denmark.

LOMER, Mary. *See* **LIDE, Mary.**

LOMNITZ, Cinna. Mexican (born Mexico), b. 1925. **Genres:** Earth Sciences, Sciences, Natural History. **Career:** University of Chile, Institute (now Department) of Geophysics, director, 1957; University of California, Seismological Stations, chief, 1964-68; National University of Mexico, Institute of Geophysics, professor of seismology, 1968, now professor emeritus of seismology; Geofisica Internacional, editor. Writer. **Publications:** Investigaciones Gravimétricas En La Región De Chillán, 1959; Global Tectonics and Earthquake Risk, 1974; (ed. with E. Rosenblueth) Seismic Risk and Engineering Decisions, 1976; (co-author) Terremoto de la Zona Centro-Nororiente del Ecuador, 5 de Marzo de 1987, 1987; Fundamentals of Earthquake Prediction, 1994. Contributor to journals. **Address:** Institute of Geophysics, National University of Mexico, Mexico City, DF 04510, Mexico. **Online address:** cinna@prodigy.net.mx

LOMNITZ, Larissa Adler. Mexican/Chilean (born Chile), b. 1932. **Genres:** Anthropology/Ethnology, Sociology, Politics/Government, Sciences. **Career:** Universidad Nacional Autonoma de Mexico, professor of socio-cultural anthropology, 1973-, Institute of Mathematics, senior researcher, researcher emeritus of socio-cultural anthropology, 1996-; Columbia University, Tinker professor, 1985-86; City University of New York, distinguished visiting professor, 1987-88; American University, distinguished professor, 1989-90; Escuela Nacional de Antropologia y Historia, staff, 1994-96; University of Notre Dame, Gustavo Garza visiting professor, 2000-01. Writer. **Publications:** Cómo Sobreviven Los Marginados, 1975; Networks and Marginality: Life in a Mexican Shantytown, 1977; (with M. Perez-Lizaur) A Mexican Elite Family, 1820-1980: Kinship, Class and Culture, 1987; (with A. Melnick) Chile's Middle Class: A Struggle for Survival in the Face of Neoliberalism, 1991; (with J. Fortes) Becoming a Scientist in Mexico, 1994; Redes Sociales Cultura y Poder: Ensayos de Antropologia Latinoamericana, 1994; (with A. Melnick) Cultura Política Chilena Y Los Partidos De Centro, 1998; (with A. Melnick) Neoliberalismo y Clase Media, 1998; (with A. Melnick) Chile's Political Culture and Parties: An Anthropological Explanation, 2000; (with R.S. Elena and I. Adler) Simbolismo y Ritual en la Política Mexicana, 2004; Redes, Comunidades, Grupos y Trabajo Entre Pares en la Investigación Educative, 2009; (with R.S. Elena and I. Adler) Symbolism and Ritual in a One-party Regime: Unveiling Mexico's Political Culture, 2010. **Address:** Delegacion Alvaro Obregon, Universidad Nacional Autonoma de Mexico, PO Box 20-726, Admon. 20, Mexico City, DF DF 01000, Mexico. **Online address:** larissa@unam.mx

LOMONACO, Palmyra. American (born United States), b. 1932. **Genres:** Children's Fiction, Education, Young Adult Fiction. **Career:** Teacher and writer, 1954-84; New Mexico Department of Human Services, child-care specialist; Bernalillo County Mental Health-Mental Retardation Center, child care trainer; Albuquerque-Bernalillo County Economic Opportunity Board, director of child development and child care centers; University of New Mexico, adjunct instructor in on-site programs for Navajo and Apache early childhood education; University of Albuquerque, adjunct assistant professor of education; Duke University, Department of Pediatrics, play therapist; Durham Technical Community College, Early Childhood Associate Program, program director and instructor; Durham Nursery, director; Pre-School Inc., director; Carolina Wren Press, director; Lollipop Press, director. Consultant. **Publications:** Music and Motion: The Rhythmic Language of Children, 1976; Up from the Classroom, 1977; Halloween: Its Place in the Curriculum, 1988; Joey's Blanket, 1994; Night Letters, 1995. Contributor to magazines. **Address:** 4100 Five Oaks Dr., Ste. 41, Durham, NC 27707, U.S.A.

LONCRAINE, Rebecca. British (born England), b. 1974. **Genres:** Poetry, Biography. **Career:** Writer. **Publications:** The Book of Repulsive Women and Other Poems, 2003; The Real Wizard of Oz: The Life and Times of L. Frank Baum, 2009. Contributor of articles to periodicals. **Address:** c/o James Gill, United Agents, Lexington House, 12-26 Lexington St., London, GL W1F 0LE, England. **Online address:** mailme@rebeccaloncraine.com

LONDON, Cait. *See* **KLEINSASSER, Lois.**

LONDON, Charles. American (born United States), b. 1980?. **Genres:** Military/Defense/Arms Control, Theology/Religion, Sociology. **Career:** New York Public Library, young adult librarian; Refugees Intl., research associate. Writer. **Publications:** One Day the Soldiers Came: Voices of Children in War, 2007; Far from Zion: In Search of a Global Jewish Community, 2009. Contributor to journals. **Address:** Brooklyn, NY , U.S.A. **Online address:** charles@calondon.com

LONDON, Herbert I. American (born United States), b. 1939. **Genres:** Education, Politics/Government, Social Sciences, Young Adult Non-fiction. **Career:** New School for Social Research, instructor in American studies, 1966; Australian National University, research associate, 1966-67; New York University, assistant professor, 1967-69, associate professor, 1969-76, professor of social studies, 1976-, professor emeritus, University without Walls, director, 1971-76, Gallatin Division, dean, 1972-92, John M. Olin professor of humanities; Hudson Institute, consultant, 1969-, president, 1997-2011, president emeritus, 2011-. Writer. **Publications:** Non-White Immigration and the White Australia Policy, 1970; Fitting In: Crosswise at Generation Gap, 1974; The Overheated Decade, 1976; The Seventies: Counterfeit Decade, 1979; Myths That Rule America, 1981; Closing the Circle: A Cultural History of the Rock Revolution, 1984; Why are They Lying to Our Children?, 1984; Military Doctrine and the American Character, 1984; Armageddon in the Classroom, 1986; The Broken Apple: Notes on New York in the 1980s, 1989; From the Empire State to the Vampire State: New York in a Downward Transition, 1994; Decade of Denial: A Snapshot of America in the 1990s, 2001; America's Secular Challenge: The Rise of a New National Religion, 2008; Decline and Revival in Higher Education, 2010. EDITOR and CONTRIBUTOR: Education in the

Twenty-First Century, 1969; (co-ed.) Social Science Theory, Structure and Application, 1975; A Strategy for Victory without War, 1988; (with J.F. Cooper and L. Jarvick) The National Endowments: A Critical Symposium, 1995; (with T.J. Duesterberg) Riding the Next Wave: Why this Century will be a Golden Age for Workers, the Environment, and Developing Countries, 2001. **Address:** Hudson Institute, 90 Broad St., New York, NY 10004, U.S.A. **Online address:** herb@hudson.org

LONDON, Joan. Australian (born Australia), b. 1948. **Genres:** Novels, Novellas/Short Stories, History. **Career:** Writer. **Publications:** Sister Ships and Other Stories, 1986; Letter to Constantine (short stories), 1993; (with E. Jolley) Sunburnt Country: Stories of Australian Life, 2000; Gilgamesh: A Novel, 2001; The New Dark Age, (collected stories), 2004; Letter to Constantine, 2005; Good Parents, 2009. Works appear in anthologies. **Address:** c/o Barbara Mobbs, PO Box 126, Edgecliff, New South Wales, NW 2027, Australia.

LONDON, Lawrence Steven. *See* **STEVENS, Lawrence L.**

LONDON, Mark. American (born United States), b. 1952. **Genres:** Novels, Young Adult Non-fiction, Social Sciences. **Career:** London & Mead, partner. Lawyer and writer. **Publications:** (With B. Kelly) Amazon, 1983; Masonry: How to Care for Old and Historic Brick and Stone, 1988; (with B. Kelly) The Four Little Dragons: Inside Korea, Taiwan, Hong Kong and Singapore at the Dawn of the Pacific Century, 1989; (with B. Kelly) The Last Forest: The Amazon in the Age of Globalization, 2007. **Address:** London & Mead, 1225 19th St. NW, Ste. 320, Washington, DC 20009, U.S.A. **Online address:** shark@londonandmead.com

LONEY, Glenn Meredith. American (born United States), b. 1928. **Genres:** Photography, Literary Criticism And History, Theatre, Travel/Exploration, Art/Art History, Music, Dance/Ballet, Young Adult Fiction, Young Adult Fiction. **Career:** San Francisco State College (now University), instructor in language arts, 1955-56; Nevada Southern University (now University of Nevada, Las Vegas), instructor in English and theater, 1955-56; University of Maryland Overseas, professor of English and speech, 1956-59; Hofstra University, instructor in theater, 1959-61; Adelphi University, instructor in theater, 1959-61; Brooklyn College of the City University of New York, assistant professor, 1961-67, associate professor, 1967-70, professor of theater, 1970-, now professor emeritus; www.ModernTheatre.Info, founder/advisor. Writer. **Publications:** Briefing and Conference Techniques, 1959; Theater Crafts Book of Costume, 1973; Theater Crafts Book of Make-Up, Masks and Wigs, 1974; (with P. McKay) The Shakespeare Complex: A Guide to Summer Festivals and Year-round Repertory in North America, 1975; The Young Vic Scapino, 1975; (with L.S. Epstein) Your Future in the Performing Arts, 1980; California Gold Rush Dramas, 1983; 20th Century Theater, 2 vols., 1983; Unsung Genius: The Passion of Dancer-Choreographer Jack Cole, 1984; (with W. Boswell) Creating Careers in Music Theatre, 1988. EDITOR: (and intro.) Dramatic Soundings: Evaluations and Retractions Culled from 30 Years of Dramatic Criticism, 1968; (with R. Corrigan) Tragedy: A Critical Anthology, 1971; (and intro. with R. Corrigan) Comedy, 1971; (and intro. with R. Corrigan) The Forms of Drama, 1972; Peter Brook's RSC Production of Midsummer Night's Dream, 1974; Peter Brook's Production of William Shakespeare's a Midsummer Night's Dream for the Royal Shakespeare Company, 1974; The Frank Dunlop Young Vic Production of Scapino!: A Long Way off from Moliere, 1975; (and intro.) The House of Mirth: The Play of the Novel, 1981; Musical Theater in America: Papers and Proceedings of the Conference on the Musical Theatre in America, 1984; Staging Shakespeare: Seminars on Production Problems, 1990; (with R. Helfer) Peter Brook: From Oxford to Orghast, 1998. Contributor to periodicals. **Address:** University Graduate Center, Brooklyn College, The City University of New York, 365 5th Ave., New York, NY 10016-4309, U.S.A. **Online address:** glenn.loney@verizon.net

LONG, Alecia P. American (born United States), b. 1966?. **Genres:** History. **Career:** Louisiana State Museum, Department of Education and Research, division director and museum historian, 1998-2001, historian and writer, 2001-04; Georgia State University, assistant professor of history; Louisiana State University, assistant professor of history, 2007-; Caleidoscop, program chair. **Publications:** The Great Southern Babylon: Sex, Race and Respectability in New Orleans, 1865-1920, 2004; (ed. with L.A. Whites and contrib.) Occupied Women: Gender, Military Occupation and the American Civil War, 2009. Contributor to journals. **Address:** Department of History, Louisiana State University, 223B Himes Hall, 3357 Highland Rd., Baton Rouge, LA 70803-0001, U.S.A. **Online address:** aplong@lsu.edu

LONG, A(nthony) A(rthur). American/British (born England), b. 1937. **Genres:** Classics, Philosophy. **Career:** University of Otago, lecturer in classics, 1961-64; University of Nottingham, lecturer in classics, 1964-66; University of London, lecturer, 1966-71, University College, reader in Greek and Latin, 1971-73; University of Munich, visiting professor of classical philology, 1973; University of Liverpool, Department of Greek, Gladstone professor of Greek and chair, 1973-83; Princeton University, old dominion fellow in classics, 1978; University of California, Department of Classics, visiting professor of classics, 1982, professor, 1982-, chair, 1986-90, Irving G. Stone professor of literature, 1991-, Department of Rhetoric, adjunct faculty, 1995-, Department of Philosophy, adjunct faculty, 2006-; University of Leiden, Department of Classics, visiting professor, 1991; Ecole Normale Supérieure, visiting professor of classics and philosophy, 1993, 2001; University of Otago, William Evans fellow, 1995; University of Harare, visiting professor of classics, 1996; University of Texas, Brackenridge distinguished professor in the humanities, 2003; University of Utrecht, Belle van Zuylen professor of philosophy, 2003. Writer. **Publications:** Language and Thought in Sophocles: A Study of Abstract Nouns and Poetic Technique, 1968; (ed.) Problems in Stoicism, 1971, 2nd ed., 1996; Hellenistic Philosophy: Stoics, Epicureans, Sceptics, 1974, 2nd ed., 1986; Soul and Body in Stoicism: Protocol of the Thirty-Sixth Colloquy, 3 June 1979, 1980; (ed. with W.W. Fortenbaugh and P.M. Huby) Theophrastus of Eresus: On His Life and Work, 1985; (with D.N. Sedley) The Hellenistic Philosophers, 1987; (ed. with J.M. Dillon) Question of Eclecticism: Studies in Later Greek Philosophy, 1988; Stoic Studies, 1996; (ed.) The Cambridge Companion to Early Greek Philosophy, 1999; Epictetus: A Stoic and Socratic Guide to Life, 2002; From Epicurus to Epictetus: Studies in Hellenistic and Roman Philosophy, 2006; (ed.) A Free Will: Origins of the Notion in Ancient Thought, 2011. Contributor to books and journals. **Address:** Department of Classics, University of California, 7218 Dwinelle Hall, Ste. 2520, Berkeley, CA 94720-2520, U.S.A. **Online address:** aalong@berkeley.edu

LONG, Benjamin. American (born United States), b. 1967. **Genres:** Travel/Exploration, Sciences, Animals/Pets. **Career:** Idaho Statesman, reporter, 1988; Daily Idahonian, reporter, 1989-92; Daily Inter Lake, reporter, 1992-98. **Publications:** Backtracking by Foot, Canoe, and Subaru along the Lewis and Clark Trail, 2000. **Address:** c/o Author Mail, Sasquatch Books, 119 S Main, Ste. 400, Seattle, WA 98104, U.S.A. **Online address:** karenben@montanasky.net

LONG, Carolyn Morrow. American (born United States), b. 1940. **Genres:** History, Theology/Religion, Biography, Autobiography/Memoirs, Social Sciences. **Career:** Vermont State Craft Center, artist-in-residence, 1973-80; Smithsonian Institution, National Museum of American History, conservator, 1983-2001; writer, 2001-. **Publications:** Spiritual Merchants: Religion, Magic, and Commerce, 2001; A New Orleans Voudou Priestess: The Legend and Reality of Marie Laveau, 2006; Madame Lalaurie, Mistress of the Haunted House, 2012. **Address:** 3815 Alton Pl. NW, Washington, DC 20016, U.S.A. **Online address:** carolynlong@earthlink.net

LONG, Cathryn J. American (born United States), b. 1946. **Genres:** Children's Non-fiction, Archaeology/Antiquities, Young Adult Non-fiction, Education, How-to Books, Politics/Government, Sciences, Technology, Technology. **Career:** Freelance writer, 1976-; University of Cincinnati, co-founder of U-Kids, 1981-82, Center for the Electronic Reconstruction of Historic and Archaeological Sites, writer and educational consultant, 1996-; Curriculum Design for Tomorrow's World Inc., associate, 1982-. **Publications:** (With R.W. Tretten) The Future of American Government: What Will It Be?, 1978; (with D.C. King) Themes for Teaching U.S. History: Conflict and Change, 1979; (with R.W. Tretten and M.S. Branson) Work in Tomorrow's World, 1979; (with M.J. Turner, J.S. Bowes and E.J. Lott) Civics: Citizens in Action, 1986, rev. ed., 1990; The Middle East in Search of Peace, 1994, rev. ed., 1996; Ohio: Past and Present, 1995; Crossword America, 4 vols., 1999; The Cherokee, 2000; Ancient America, 2002; Westward Expansion, 2003; The Agricultural Revolution, 2004. Contributor to books. **Address:** Center for the Electronic Reconstruction of, Historical and Archaeological Sites, University of Cincinnati, PO Box 210016, Cincinnati, OH 45221, U.S.A. **Online address:** cjlong2@yahoo.com

LONG, Christopher. American (born United States), b. 1957?. **Genres:** Biography, Adult Non-fiction, Money/Finance. **Career:** University of Texas,

School of Architecture, assistant professor, associate professor, chair of architectural history and theory, professor. Writer. **Publications:** (With R. Fraser) The World Financial System, 1992; (contrib.) Western European Economic Organizations: A Comprehensive Guide, 1992; Josef Frank: Life and Work, 2002; Paul T. Frankl and Modern American Design, 2007; The Looshaus, 2011. Contributor to books. **Address:** School of Architecture, University of Texas, SUT 4.104, 1 University Sta. B7500, Austin, TX 78712-0222, U.S.A. **Online address:** chrlong@mail.utexas.edu

LONG, D. Stephen. American (born United States), b. 1960. **Genres:** Theology/Religion, inspirational/Motivational Literature, Cultural/Ethnic Topics. **Career:** Duke Divinity School, director of continuing education, 1990-95; St. Joseph's University, assistant professor of theology, 1995-98; Garrett-Evangelical Theological Seminary, assistant professor of systematic theology, 1998-2001, associate professor of systematic theology, 2001-07; Garrett-Evangelical's Center for Ethics and Values, co-director, 1998-2000; Marquette University, professor of systematic theology, 2007-. Writer. **Publications:** Living the Discipline: United Methodist Theological Reflections on War, Civilization and Holiness 1991; Tragedy, Tradition, Transformism: The Ethics of Paul Ramsey, 1993; Divine Economy: Theology and the Market, 2000; The Goodness of God: Theology, Church and the Social Order, 2001; John Wesley's Moral Theology: The Quest for God and Goodness, 2005; (with N. Fox) A Calculated Futures: Theology, Ethics and the Politics of Faith, 2007; Theology and Culture, 2007; (ed.with G. Kalantzis) God's Sovereignty: An Evangelical and Catholic Exploration, 2008; (ed. with G. Kalantzis) Sovereignty of God Debate, 2009; (with W.B. Eerdmanns) Speaking of God: Theology, Language and Truth, 2009; Theology and Culture: A Guide to the Discussion, 2010; Christian Ethics: A Very Short Introduction, 2010; Hebrews, 2011. **Address:** Department of Theology, Marquette University, 212 Coughlin Hall, 607 N 13th St., PO Box 1881, Milwaukee, WI 53201-1881, U.S.A. **Online address:** d.stephen.long@marquette.edu

LONG, Edward Leroy. American (born United States), b. 1924. **Genres:** Ethics, Theology/Religion. **Career:** Union Seminary, tutor-assistant in Christian ethics, 1950-51; Virginia Polytechnic Institute, part-time associate professor of philosophy and ethics, 1951-54, associate professor and head of department of philosophy and religion, 1955-57; Blacksburg Presbyterian Church, minister to students, 1951-55; Oberlin College, associate professor, 1957-65, professor of religion, 1965-76; Drew University, professor of Christian ethics, 1976-82, professor of Christian ethics and theology of culture, 1982-84, James W. Pearsall professor of Christian ethics and theology of culture, 1984-86, professor emeritus, 1986-; General Theological Seminary, visiting professor of Christian ethics, 1977-78; Union Theological Seminary, visiting lecturer, 1980-981; Princeton Theological Seminary, visiting lecturer, 1980-81; Purdue University, Eli Lilly visiting professor of science; Society for Religion in Higher Education, fellow. Writer. **Publications:** Science and Christian Faith, 1950; The Christian Response to the Atomic Crisis, 1950; Religious Beliefs of American Scientists, 1952; Conscience and Compromise: An Approach to Protestant Casuistry, 1954; Christians are Citizens: The Role of the Responsible Christian Citizen in an Era of Crisis, 1957; (with J.T. Stephens) The Christian as a Doctor, 1960; The Role of the Self in Conflicts and Struggle, 1962; A Survey of Christian Ethics, 1967; War and Conscience in America, 1968; (ed. with R.T. Handy) Theology and Church in Times of Change: Essays in Honor of John Coleman Bennett, 1970; A Survey of Recent Christian Ethics, 1982; Peace Thinking in a Warring World, 1983; Academic Bonding and Social Concern, 1984; Higher Education as a Moral Enterprise, 1992; To Liberate and Redeem: Moral Reflections on the Biblical Narrative, 1997; Patterns of Polity: Varieties of Church Governance, 2001; Facing Terrorism: Responding as Christian, 2004. **Address:** Drew University, 36 Madison Ave., Madison, NJ 07940, U.S.A.

LONG, Elliot. *See* **BENNETT, R.G. Stephen.**

LONG, Eugene Thomas. American (born United States), b. 1935. **Genres:** Philosophy, Theology/Religion. **Career:** Randolph-Macon College, assistant professor of philosophy, 1964-66, associate professor of philosophy, 1966-68, professor of philosophy, 1968-70; University of South Carolina, associate professor of philosophy, 1970-73, Department of Philosophy, chair, 1972-87, professor of philosophy, 1973-2002, distinguished professor emeritus 2002-. Writer. **Publications:** Jaspers and Bultmann: A Dialogue between Philosophy and Theology in the Existentialist Tradition, 1968; Existence, Being and God, 1985; Twentieth Century Western Philosophy of Religion 1900-2000, 2000. EDITOR AND CONTRIBUTOR: God, Secularization and History: Essays

in Memory of Ronald Gregor Smith, 1974; Experience, Reason and God, 1980; (co-ed.) God and Temporality, 1984; (co-ed.) Being and Truth, 1986; Prospects for Natural Theology, 1992; God, Reason and Religions, 1995; Issues in Contemporary Philosophy of Religion, 2001; Self and Others, 2007; (with P. Horn) Ethics of Belief, 2009. **Address:** Department of Philosophy, University of South Carolina, Columbia, SC 29208, U.S.A. **Online address:** longg@mailbox.sc.edu

LONG, Jeff. American (born United States), b. 1951. **Genres:** Westerns/Adventure, History, Novels, Literary Criticism And History. **Career:** Witness Inc., founder. Writer. **Publications:** Outlaw: The True Story of Claude Dallas, 1985; (foreword) Mountain Journeys: Stories of Climbers and Their Climbs, 1989. NOVELS: Angels of Light, 1987; Duel of Eagles: The Mexican and U.S. Fight for the Alamo, 1990; The Ascent, 1992; Empire of Bones: A Novel of Sam Houston and the Texas Revolution, 1993; The Descent, 1999; Year Zero, 2002; Reckoning, 2004, rev. ed., 2005; The Wall: A Thriller, 2006; Deeper, 2007. Contributor to periodicals. **Address:** c/o Author Mail, Simon & Schuster-Pocket Books, 1230 Ave. of the Americas, New York, NY 10020, U.S.A.

LONG, Michael G. American (born United States) **Genres:** Biography, Autobiography/Memoirs. **Career:** Elizabethtown College, associate professor of religious studies and peace and conflict studies. Writer. **Publications:** Against Us, but for Us: Martin Luther King, Jr. and the State, 2002; Have the Time of Your Life: Living for God in Each Moment, 2003; Martin Luther King, Jr. on Creative Living, 2004; Billy Graham and the Beloved Community, 2006; (ed. with T.W. Sadd) God and Country? Diverse Perspectives on Christianity and Patriotism, 2007; (ed.) First Class Citizenship: The Civil Rights Letters of Jackie Robinson, 2007; Resist! Christian Dissent for the 21st Century, 2008; (ed.) The Legacy of Billy Graham: Critical Reflections on America's Greatest Evangelist, 2008. **Address:** Elizabethtown College, 1 Alpha Dr., Elizabethtown, PA 17022-2298, U.S.A. **Online address:** longm@etown.edu

LONG, Pamela O. American (born United States) **Genres:** History, Technology, Sciences. **Career:** Barnard College, visiting assistant professor of history, 1981-82; Library of Congress, copyright examiner, 1983-86; St. Mary's College of Maryland, visiting assistant professor of history, 1989-90; St. John's College, part-time tutor, 1991-92; Johns Hopkins University, Department of the History of Science, Medicine and Technology, visiting assistant professor of history of science, 1995-98. Writer. **Publications:** (Ed.) Science and Technology in Medieval Society, 1985; Technology, Society and Culture in Late Medieval and Renaissance Europe, 1300-1600, 2000; Openness, Secrecy, Authorship: Technical Arts and the Culture of Knowledge from Antiquity to the Renaissance, 2001; Technology and Society in the Medieval Centuries: Byzantium, Islam and the West, 500-1300, 2003; (with B. Curran, A. Grafton and B. Weiss) Obelisk: A History, 2009; (ed. with D. McGee and A.M. Stahl) The Book of Michael of Rhodes: A Fifteenth-century Maritime Manuscript, 2009; Artisan/Practitioners and the Rise of the New Sciences, 1400-1600, 2011. Contributor of articles to books and periodicals. **Address:** 3100 Connecticut Ave. NW, Ste. 137, Washington, DC 20008-5100, U.S.A. **Online address:** pamlong@pamelaolong.com

LONG, Thomas G. American (born United States), b. 1946. **Genres:** Theology/Religion. **Career:** Emory University, Candler School of Theology, Bandy professor of preaching, coordinator of the initiative in religious practices and practical theology; Princeton Theological Seminary, professor of preaching and worship. Writer and minister. **Publications:** Shepherds and Bathrobes: Sermons for Advent, Christmas and Epiphany (Sundays in Ordinary Time): Cycle B Gospel Texts, 1987; The Senses of Preaching, 1988; (ed. with N.D. McCarter) Preaching and the Literary Forms of the Bible, 1989; The Witness of Preaching, 1989, 2nd rev. ed., 2005; Preaching in and Out of Season, 1990; (ed. with G.R. O'Day) Listening to the Word: Studies in Honor of Fred B. Craddock, 1993; (ed. with C. Plantinga) A Chorus of Witnesses: Model Sermons for Today's Preacher, 1994; Whispering the Lyrics: Sermons for Lent and Easter: Cycle A: Gospel Texts, 1995; (ed. with E. Farley) Preaching as a Theological Task: World, Gospel, Scripture: In Honor of David Buttrick, 1996; Something Is about to Happen: Sermons for Advent and Christmas, 1996; Hebrews, 1997; Matthew, 1997; Beyond the Worship Wars: Building Vital and Faithful Worship, 2001; Testimony: Talking Ourselves into Being Christian, 2004; (ed. with L.T. Tisdale) Teaching Preaching as a Christian Practice: A New Approach to Homiletical Pedagogy, 2008. **Address:** Emory University, Candler School of Theology, 1531 Dickey Dr., Atlanta, GA 30322, U.S.A. **Online address:** tglong@emory.edu

LONGFELLOW, Layne (A.). (Layne Allen Longfellow). American (born United States), b. 1937. **Genres:** Children's Fiction, Poetry, Environmental Sciences/Ecology, Young Adult Non-fiction, Humor/Satire. **Career:** Prescott College, assistant professor of psychology, 1970-71, academic vice president, 1972-74; Menninger Foundation, director of executive seminars, 1975-78; Banff Centre, wilderness seminars director, 1978-85; Lecture Theatre Inc., president, 1983-; National Center for Preventive and Stress Medicine, seminar collaborator, 1983-86; Institute for Human Skills, director, 1985-. Writer. **Publications:** (As Layne Allen Longfellow) Visual Feast, 1995; Imaginary Menagerie, 1997. Contributor to books and periodicals. **Address:** Lecture Theatre Inc., 1134 W Haining St., Ste. D, Prescott, AZ 86305-1693, U.S.A.

LONGFELLOW, Layne Allen. *See* **LONGFELLOW, Layne (A.).**

LONGLEY, Kyle. American (born United States), b. 1963. **Genres:** Politics/Government, Mythology/Folklore, Military/Defense/Arms Control. **Career:** Centre College, visiting assistant professor, 1993-94; The Citadel, visiting assistant professor of history, 1994-95; Arizona State University, professor of history, Snell Family dean's distinguished professor, director of graduate studies and chair of department of history, 1995-, College of Liberal Arts and Sciences, dean faculty fellow. Writer and historian. **Publications:** The Sparrow and the Hawk: Costa Rica and the United States during the Rise of José Figueres, 1997; In the Eagle's Shadow: The United States and Latin America, 2002, 2nd ed., 2009; Senator Albert Gore, Sr.: Tennessee Maverick, 2004; (co-author) Deconstructing Reagan: Conservative Mythology and America's Fortieth President, 2007; Grunts: The American Combat Soldier in Vietnam, 2008; (ed.) Encyclopedia of U.S.-Latin American relations, 2012. Contributor to books and periodicals. **Address:** Department of History, Arizona State University, 4488 Coor Hall, PO Box 4302, Tempe, AZ 85287-4302, U.S.A. **Online address:** kyle.longley@asu.edu

LONGLEY, Michael. Irish (born Ireland), b. 1939. **Genres:** Poetry, Autobiography/Memoirs, Literary Criticism And History. **Career:** Avoca School, assistant master, 1962-63; Belfast High School, staff, 1963-64; Erith Secondary School, staff, 1963-64; Royal Belfast Academical Institution, staff, 1964-69; teacher, 1970-91; Arts Council of Northern Ireland, assistant director, director for literature and the traditional arts, 1970-91; Trinity College, writer fellow, 1993, professor of poetry, 2007-10. Writer. **Publications:** Ten Poems, 1965; (with S. Heaney and D. Hammond) Room to Rhyme, 1968; Secret Marriages: Nine Short Poems, 1968; (with B. Tebb and I. Crichton Smith) Three Regional Voices, 1968; No Continuing City: Poems 1963-68, 1969; Lares, 1972; An Exploded View: Poems, 1968-1972, 1973; Fishing in the Sky, 1975; Man Lying on a Wall, 1976; The Echo Gate: Poems 1975-1978, 1979; Selected Poems, 1963-1980, 1981; Patchwork, 1981; Poems, 1963-1983, 1985; Gorse Fires, 1991; Baucis and Philemon, 1993; Tuppeny Stung: Autobiographical Chapters, 1994; Birds and Flowers, 1994; The Ghost Orchid, 1995; The Ship of the Wind: Eight Poems, 1997; Broken Dishes, 1998; Selected Poems, 1998; (with S. Longley) Out of the Cold: Drawings & Poems for Christmas, 1999; The Weather in Japan, 2000; Snow Water, 2004; Collected Poems, 2006; A Hundred Doors, 2011. EDITOR: Causeway: The Arts in Ulster, 1971; Under the Moon, Over the Stars: Young People's Writing from Ulster, 1971; Selected Poems of Louis MacNeice, 1990; (and intro.) Poems, 1993. Contributor to magazines. **Address:** Wake Forest University Press, PO Box 7333, Winston-Salem, NC 27109-7333, U.S.A. **Online address:** wfupress@wfu.edu

LONGMAN, Jere. American (born United States), b. 1954. **Genres:** Sports/Fitness, Documentaries/Reportage, History. **Career:** New York Times, sports writer. **Publications:** The Girls of Summer: The U.S. Women's Soccer Team and How It Changed the World, 2000; Among the Heroes: United Flight 93 and the Passengers and Crew Who Fought Back, 2002; If Football's a Religion, Why Don't We have a Prayer?: Philadelphia, its Faithful and the Eternal Quest for Sports Salvation, 2005; The Hurricanes: One High School Team's Homecoming After Katrina, 2008; (with N. Schuyler) Not Without Hope, 2010. Contributor to periodicals. **Address:** New York Times, 229 W 43rd St., New York, NY 10036, U.S.A.

LONGMATE, Norman Richard. British (born England), b. 1925. **Genres:** Mystery/Crime/Suspense, Education, History, Autobiography/Memoirs, Biography, Military/Defense/Arms Control, Medicine/Health. **Career:** Fleet Street, journalist, 1952-57; Daily Mirror, feature writer, 1953-57; Electricity Council, administrator in industrial relations department, 1957-63; British Broadcasting Corp., radio producer, 1963-65, administrator in secretariat, 1965-83; Worcester College, reader in modern history; full-time writer, 1983-

. **Publications:** HISTORY: King Cholera: The Biography of a Disease, 1966; The Waterdrinkers: A History of Temperance, 1968; Alive and Well: Medicine and Public Health 1830 to the Present Day, 1970; How We Lived Then: A History of Everyday Life during the Second World War, 1971; (and intro.) If Britain Had Fallen, 1972; The Workhouse, 1974; Milestones in Working Class History, 1975; The GI's: The Americans in Britain 1942-45, 1975; Real Dad's Army: The Story of the Home Guard, 1974; Air-Raid: The Bombing of Coventry 1940, 1976; When We Won The War: The Story of Victory in Europe 1945, 1977; The Hungry Mills: The Story of the Lancashire Cotton Famine 1861-1865, 1978; The Doodlebugs: The Story of the Flying-Bombs, 1981; The Bombers: The RAF Offensive against Germany 1939-1945, 1983; The Breadstealers: The Fight against the Corn Laws 1838-1846, 1984; Hitler's Rockets: The Story of the V-2s, 1985; Defending the Island: From Caesar to the Armada, 1989; Island Fortress: The Defense of Great Britain 1603-1945, 1991. DETECTIVE STORIES: Death Won't Wash, 1957; A Head for Death, 1958; Strip Death Naked, 1959; Vote for Death, 1960; Death in Office, 1961. EDITOR: A Socialist Anthology and the Men Who Made it, 1953; (comp.) Writing for the BBC: A Guide for Professional and Part-Time Freelance Writers on Possible Markets for Their Work Within the British Broadcasting Corporation, 1966; The Home Front: An Anthology of Personal Experience, 1938-1945, 1981. OTHER: Oxford Triumphant, 1954; Keith in Electricity, 1961; Electricity Supply, 1961; Electricity as a Career, 1964; The Real Dad's Army: The Story of the Home Guard, 1974; Childhood and Schooldays, 2000. **Address:** Random House UK Ltd., 20 Vauxhall Bridge Rd., London, GL SW1V 2SA, England. **Online address:** anharr@cybertours.com

LONGWORTH, Philip. British (born England), b. 1933. **Genres:** History, Military/Defense/Arms Control. **Career:** Central Asian Research Centre, researcher, 1962-65; Commonwealth War Graves Commission, historian, 1965-67; University of Birmingham, lecturer in Russian history, 1970; University of London, School of Slavonic and East European Studies, visiting fellow, 1973-74; McGill University, professor of history, 1984-2003, now professor emeritus of history. Writer. **Publications:** (Trans.) M.Y. Lermontov, A Hero of Our Time, 1962; The Art of Victory: The Life and Achievements of Generalissimo Suvorov, 1729-1800, 1965; The Unending Vigil: A History of the Commonwealth War Graves Commission, 1917-1967, 1967, 3rd ed. as The Unending Vigil: A History of the Commonwealth War Graves Commission, 2003; (ed.) Confrontations with Judaism: A Symposium, 1967; The Cossacks, 1969; The Three Empresses: Catherine I, Anne, and Elizabeth of Russia, 1972; The Rise and Fall of Venice, 1974; Alexis, Tsar of All the Russias, 1984; The Making of Eastern Europe, 1992, 2nd ed. as The Making of Eastern Europe: From Prehistory to Postcommunism, 1997; Russia: The Once and Future Empire from Pre-history to Putin, 2006; Russia's Empires, 2006. Contributor to books. **Address:** A.M. Heath & Company Ltd., 79 St. Martin, London, GL WC2N 4AA, England.

LONGYARD, William H(enry). American (born United States), b. 1958?. **Genres:** Air/Space Topics, History, How-to Books, Language/Linguistics. **Career:** Writer. **Publications:** (Ed.) How to Build and Fly Hydrogen and Hot Air Balloons, 1985; Who's Who in Aviation History: 500 Biographies, 1994; Writer's Quick Fix, 2000; A Speck on the Sea: Epic Voyages in the Most Improbable Vessels, 2003; Bugatti Blue (novel), forthcoming. **Address:** 2913 Bradenton Dr., Winston-Salem, NC 27103, U.S.A. **Online address:** longyard@ix.netcom.com

LONGYEAR, Barry B. American (born United States), b. 1942. **Genres:** Novels, Novellas/Short Stories, Mystery/Crime/Suspense, Science Fiction/Fantasy, Self Help, Writing/Journalism, Humor/Satire. **Career:** Madison Corp., production manager, 1967-68; Sol III Publications, editor, publisher and ghostwriter, 1968-72, freelance writer, 1977-. Teacher and writer. **Publications:** City of Baraboo, 1980; Manifest Destiny (stories), 1980; Circus World (stories), 1980; Science Fiction Writer's Workshop I: An Introduction to Fiction Mechanics, 1980; Elephant Song, 1981; The Tomorrow Testament, 1983; It Came from Schenectady, 1984; (with D. Gerrold) Enemy Mine, 1985; Sea of Glass, 1986; Saint Mary Blue, 1988; Naked Came the Robot, 1988; The God Box, 1989; The Homecoming, 1989; Infinity Hold, 1990; The Change, 1994; Slag Like Me, 1994; The Last Enemy, 1997; The Enemy Papers, 1998; Yesterday's Tomorrow, 1997; Silent Her, 2001; Kill All The Lawyers, 2010; Keep The Law, 2010; ABC is for Artificial Beings Crimes: Jaggers & Shad, 2010; Butterfly and the Witch Boy, 2010. Contributor to magazines. Works appear in anthologies. **Address:** PO Box 100, New Sharon, ME 04955-0100, U.S.A. **Online address:** barrylongyear@hciwireless.net

LOO, Tina. (Tina Merrill Loo). Canadian (born Canada), b. 1962?. **Genres:** Law, History, Essays, Criminology/True Crime. **Career:** University of British Columbia, associate professor. Writer and historian. **Publications:** Making Law, Order and Authority in British Columbia, 1821-1871, 1994; Essays in the History of Canadian Law, vol. V: Crime and Criminal Justice, 1996; (with C. Strange) Making Good: Law and Moral Regulation in Canada, 1867-1939, 1997; (with C. Strange) True Crime, True North: The Golden Age of Canadian Pulp Magazines, 2004; States of Nature: Conserving Canada's Wildlife in the Twentieth Century, 2006. Contributor of articles to periodicals. **Address:** Department of History, University of British Columbia, 1297-1873 East Mall, Vancouver, BC V6T 1Z1, Canada. **Online address:** tina.loo@ubc.ca

LOO, Tina Merrill. See **LOO, Tina.**

LOOBY, Christopher. American (born United States) **Genres:** Literary Criticism And History. **Career:** University of Chicago, teacher, 1987-96; University of Pennsylvania, associate professor of English and graduate chair, 1996-; University of California, Department of English, professor. Writer. **Publications:** NONFICTION: Benjamin Franklin, 1990; Voicing America: Language, Literary Form, and the Origins of the United States, 1996; (ed.) The Complete Civil War Journal and Selected Letters of Thomas Wentworth Higginson, 2000; (intro.) Sheppard Lee: Written By Himself, 2008. **Address:** Department of English, University of California, 186 Humanities Bldg., PO Box 951530, Los Angeles, CA 90095-1530, U.S.A. **Online address:** clooby@humnet.ucla.edu

LOOKINGBILL, Brad D. (Brad Darren Lookingbill). American (born United States), b. 1969. **Genres:** Military/Defense/Arms Control, History. **Career:** Independence Community College, instructor in history, 1995-96; Columbia College, professor of history, 1996-. Writer, historian and public speaker. **Publications:** Dust Bowl, USA: Depression America and the Ecological Imagination, 1929-1941, 2001; War Dance at Fort Marion: Plains Indian War Prisoners, 2006; American Military History: A Documentary Reader, 2011. Contributor to books and periodicals. **Address:** Department of History, Columbia College, 209 St. Clair Hall, 1001 Rogers St., Columbia, MO 65201-4580, U.S.A. **Online address:** bdlookingbill@ccis.edu

LOOKINGBILL, Brad Darren. See **LOOKINGBILL, Brad D.**

LOOMES, Brian. British (born England), b. 1938?. **Genres:** Crafts, Biography, Genealogy/Heraldry, Natural History, Antiques/Furnishings. **Career:** Antiques dealer, 1966-. Writer and genealogist. **Publications:** Yorkshire Clockmakers, 1972; Westmorland Clocks and Clockmakers, 1974; The White Dial Clock, 1974; Lancashire Clocks and Clockmakers, 1975; Country Clocks and their London Origins, 1976; Watch and Clock Makers of the World, vol. II, 1976; Complete British Clocks, 1978; Clocks: Guide to Dating and Valuation, 1980; White Dial Clocks: The Complete Guide, 1981; The Early Clockmakers of Great Britain, 1982; Grandfather Clocks and Their Cases, 1985; Antique British Clocks: A Buyer's Guide, 1991; Antique British Clocks Illustrated, 1991; The Concise Guide to British Clocks, 1992; British Clocks Illustrated, 1992; The Concise Guide to Tracing Your Ancestry, 1992; Bird Gardening, 1993; Painted Dial Clocks, 1995; The Clockmakers of Northern England, 1997; Brass Dial Clocks, 1998; Watchmakers and Clockmakers of the World 21st Century Edition, 2006; Lantern Clocks 2008. **Address:** Calf Haugh Farm, Pateley Bridge, Harrogate, NY HG3 5HW, England. **Online address:** brian@brianloomes.com

LOOMIS, Christine. American (born United States) **Genres:** Children's Fiction, Travel/Exploration, Picture/Board Books. **Career:** Parents' Magazine, travel editor; Family Life, travel editor. **Publications:** My New Baby-Sitter, 1991; At the Laundromat, 1993; In the Diner, 1993; At the Library, 1993; The Cleanup Surprise, 1993; At the Mall, 1994; One Cow Coughs: A Counting Book for the Sick and Miserable, 1994; We're Going on a Trip, 1994; The Hippo Hop, 1995; Fodor's Family Adventures, 1996, 2nd ed., 1998; Rush Hour, 1996; Cowboy Bunnies, 1997; Simplify Family Travel, 1998; Across America, I Love You, 2000; Astro Bunnies, 2001; Scuba Bunnies, 2004; The 10 Best Things About My Dad, 2004; Hattie Hippo, 2006; Best Father's Day Present Ever, 2007. Contributor to magazines and periodicals. **Address:** 4230 Gilpin Dr., Boulder, CO 80303-2530, U.S.A.

LOOMIS, Jennifer A. American (born United States), b. 1942. **Genres:** Zoology, Medicine/Health, Photography. **Career:** Writer. **Publications:** A Duck in a Tree, 1996; (with H. Kugiya) Portraits of Pregnancy: The Birth of a

Mother, 2009. Contributor to periodicals. **Address:** Stemmar House Publishers, 4 White Brook Rd., PO Box 89, Gilsum, NH 03448, U.S.A.

LOOMIS, Susan Herrmann. American (born United States), b. 1955. **Genres:** Food And Wine, Travel/Exploration. **Career:** Wenatchee World, reporter, 1977; North Central Washington Museum, director of public relations, 1978; Cabrini Hospital, assistant director of public relations, 1979-80; Ecole de Cuisine La Varenne, editorial staff, 1981-82; Village Voice Cafe-Librairie, chef and manager, 1982-83; free-lance writer, 1983-84, 1986-; International Association of Cooking Professionals, editor, 1985-86. **Publications:** (With P. Wells) The Food Lover's Guide to Paris, 1984 4th ed. 1999; Paris in Your Pocket, 1985; Food Lover's Guide to France, 1987; The Great American Seafood Cookbook, 1988; Farmhouse Cookbook, 1991; Seafood Celebrations, 1993; Clambakes & Fish Fries, 1994; French Farmhouse Cookbook, 1996; Italian Farmhouse Cookbook, 2000; On Rue Tatin: Living and Cooking in a French Town, 2001; Tarte Tatin, 2003; Cooking at Home on Rue Tatin, 2005; Nuts in the Kitchen: More than 100 Recipes for Every Taste and Occasion, 2010. Contributor to periodicals. **Address:** c/o Angela Miller, 1 Sheridan Sq., Ste. 7B, New York, NY 10014, U.S.A.

LOON See **Martien, Jerry.**

LOONEY, Dennis (Oscar). American (born United States), b. 1955. **Genres:** Literary Criticism And History, History, Adult Non-fiction, Translations. **Career:** Boston University, research assistant in Greek lexicography, 1978-80; University of North Carolina, assistant, 1981; City University of New York, Latin/Greek Institute, instructor, 1984-85, 1987; University of Pittsburgh, assistant professor of Italian, 1986-92, adjunct associate professor of classics, 1994-, Pitt Summer Program in Italy, director, 1991-, associate professor of Italian, 1993-, professor of Italian, Program in Medieval and Renaissance Studies, director, 1994-96, Department of French and Italian, chair, 1996-2003, 2006-, Semester at Sea, academic dean, 2000, Center for West European Studies/European Union Center, acting director, 2003, assistant dean, 2004-06, Departments of Classics and Philosophy, faculty. Writer. **Publications:** Compromising the Classics: Romance Epic Narrative in the Italian Renaissance, 1996; (ed. with D. Shemek) Phaethon's Children: The Este Court and Its Culture in Early Modern Ferrara, 2005; (ed.) The Quest for Epic: From Ariosto to Tasso, 2006; (trans. and intro.) My Muse Will Have a Story to Paint, 2010; Freedom Readers: The African American Reception of Dante Alighieri and the Divine Comedy, 2011. FORTHCOMING: (ed. and intro.) Parva sed apta mihi: The Poet's Other Voice: Ariosto's Prose. **Address:** Department of French and Italian, University of Pittsburgh, 1317 H Cathedral of Learning, Pittsburgh, PA 15260, U.S.A. **Online address:** looney@pitt.edu

LOONEY, Douglas S. (Don Yaeger). American (born United States), b. 1942. **Genres:** Sports/Fitness. **Career:** Nashville Banner, general assignment reporter, 1965-68; Omaha World-Herald, bureau chief, 1968-70; Better Homes & Gardens, special assignments editor, 1970; National Observer, staff writer, 1970-75; Sports Illustrated, senior writer, 1975-2002, retired, 2002; University of Colorado, School of Journalism and Mass Communication (SJMC), chairman, adjunct instructor of journalism; National Broadcasting Co. (NBC-TV), sports commentator. **Publications:** (With D. Yaeger) Under the Tarnished Dome: How Notre Dame Betrayed Its Ideals for Football Glory, 1993; (ed.) All for the Love of a Child: A Memoir, 1997. Works appear in anthologies. Contributor to books and periodicals. **Address:** School of Journalism and Mass Communication, University of Colorado, 1480 30th St., Boulder, CO 80303-1010, U.S.A.

LOOSER, Devoney. American (born United States), b. 1967. **Genres:** Literary Criticism And History, Humanities, Women's Studies And Issues, History, Intellectual History, Gerontology/Senior Issues, Biography, Adult Non-fiction, Adult Non-fiction. **Career:** State University of New York, instructor in English, 1989-92, Writing Program, assistant to the director, 1992-93; Indiana State University, assistant professor of English and and women's studies, 1993-98, acting director of women's studies, 1997-98; Terre Haute Council on Domestic Abuse, board director, 1997-98; University of Wisconsin, Center for 20th-Century Studies, research associate, 1996-97, assistant professor of women's studies, 1998-2000; University of California, William Andrews Clark Memorial Library, fellow, 1997; Newberry Library, lecturer, 1997, fellow, 2005; Tulane University, Newcomb Center for Research on Women, lecturer, 1998; Arizona State University, visiting assistant professor of English, 2000-01; Louisiana State University, assistant professor of English, 2001-02, James Smith Noel Collection, fellow, 2002; University of Missouri, assistant professor, 2002-04, associate professor of English, 2004-09, professor of English, 2009-, literature coordinator, 2006-08; Huntington Library, fellow, 2004; King's College London Special Collections, fellow, 2004; University of Kansas Spencer Library, fellow, 2004, 2006. Writer. **Publications:** British Women Writers and the Writing of History, 1670-1820, 2000; Women Writers and Old Age in Great Britain, 1750-1850, 2008. EDITOR: Jane Austen and Discourses of Feminism, 1995; (with E.A. Kaplan and contrib.) Generations: Academic Feminists in Dialogue, 1997. Contributor to books and periodicals. **Address:** Department of English, University of Missouri, 107 Tate Hall, Columbia, MO 65211, U.S.A. **Online address:** looserd@missouri.edu

LOPACH, James J. American (born United States), b. 1942. **Genres:** Politics/Government. **Career:** John Adams High School, teacher in English, 1967-68; Pacific Telephone Co., assistant manager, manager, 1968-69; University of Notre Dame, instructor and director of sophomore program, 1972-73; University of Montana, Bureau of Government Research, director of research, 1973-75, Department of Political Science, assistant professor, 1975-78, associate professor, 1978-83, professor, 1983-, Bureau of Government Research, chair of department and director, 1977-84, 1985-87, 2006-08, Maureen and Mike Mansfield Center, acting director, 1984-85, College of Arts and Science, associate dean, 1987-88, special assistant, 1988-92, associate provost, 1992-95, special assistant, 1995-96, professor of American government and public law. Writer. **Publications:** (With L.S. McKinsey) Handbook of Montana Forms of Local Government, 1975; (with R.E. Eagle) Changing Governments in Great Falls: Transition Amid Dissent, 1975; (with P. Koehn) Profile of Montana Local Government Study Commissioners, 1976; (with P. Koehn) Montana Local Government Review: An Analysis and Summary, 1977; (ed. with M.H. Brown and K. Jackson) Tribal Constitutions, Their Past-Their Future: Proceedings of a Conference Held at Billings, Montana, August 12-13, 1977, 1978; (with L.S. McKinsey) A State Mandates Local Government Review: The Montana Experience, 1979; (co-author) We the People of Montana: The Workings of a Popular Government, 1983; (with K. Ford and D. O'Donnell) Planning Small Town America: Observations, Sketches and a Reform Proposal, 1990; (with M.H. Brown and R.L. Clow) Tribal Government Today: Politics on Montana Indian Reservations, 1990, rev. ed., 1998; (with J.A. Luckowski) Jeannette Rankin: A Political Woman, 2005. Works appear in anthologies. Contributor to journals. **Address:** Department of Political Science, University of Montana, 349 Liberal Arts, 32 Campus Dr., Missoula, MT 59812-0004, U.S.A. **Online address:** james.lopach@umontana.edu

LOPES, Dominic (M. McIver). Canadian/Scottish (born Scotland), b. 1964. **Genres:** Philosophy, Humor/Satire, Photography, Art/Art History. **Career:** Indiana University, associate professor of philosophy, 1992; University of British Columbia, Faculty of Arts, associate dean, Department of Philosophy, professor; Ritsumeikan University, visiting professor; University of Modena and Reggio Emilia, visiting professor; École des Hautes Études en Sciences Sociales, visiting professor. Writer. **Publications:** Understanding Pictures, 1996; (ed. with D. Lopes) A Handful of Grams: Goan Proverbs, 1996; (ed. with B. Gaut) The Routledge Companion to Aesthetics, 2001, 2nd ed., 2005; (ed. with M. Kieran) Imagination, Philosophy, and the Arts, 2003; (ed. with E. John) Philosophy of Literature: Contemporary and Classic Readings: An Anthology, 2004; Sight and Sensibility: Evaluating Pictures, 2005; (ed. with M. Kieran) Knowing Art: Essays in Aesthetics and Epistemology, 2006; A Philosophy of Computer Art, 2009; (ed. with D. Costello) The Media of Photography, 2012; Beyond Art: Foundations of Appreciation, forthcoming; Four Arts of Photography, forthcoming. **Address:** Department of Philosophy, University of British Columbia, E367 Buchanan, 1866 Main Mall, Vancouver, BC V6T 1Z1, Canada. **Online address:** dom.lopes@ubc.ca

LOPEZ, Jack. American (born United States), b. 1950. **Genres:** Essays. **Career:** Orange Coast College, instructor, 1987; University of Redlands, instructor, 1988; California State University, professor of English, 1989-. Writer. **Publications:** Cholos and Surfers: A Latino Family Album, 1998; Snapping Lines: Stories, 2001; In the Break: A Novel, 2006. Work represented in anthologies. contributor to periodicals. **Address:** Department of English, California State University, Rm. 810, Sierra Twr., 18111 Nordhoff St., Northridge, CA 91330, U.S.A. **Online address:** jack.lopez@csun.edu

LOPEZ, Jonathan. American (born United States), b. 1969?. **Genres:** History. **Career:** Art historian and writer. **Publications:** The Man Who Made Vermeers: Unvarnishing the Legend of Master Forger Han van Meegeren, 2008. **Address:** c/o Rob McQuilkin, Lippincott, Massie & McQuilkin, 27 W 20th St., Ste. 305, New York, NY 10011, U.S.A. **Online address:** contact@jonathanlopez.net

LOPEZ, Josefina. Mexican/American (born United States), b. 1969. **Genres:** Plays/Screenplays, Novels. **Career:** Playwright, screenwriter and actress. **Publications:** PLAYS: Food for the Dead and La Pinta: Two One-Act Plays, 1996; Simply Maria, or, the American Dream: A One-Act Play, 1996; Real Women Have Curves, 1996; Confessions: A One Woman Show, 1997; Confessions of Women from East L.A., 1997. OTHER: Hungry Woman in Paris (novel), 2009. **Address:** Marilyn Atlas Management, 8899 Beverly Blvd., Ste. 704, Los Angeles, CA 90048, U.S.A.

LÓPEZ, Lorraine. American (born United States), b. 1956?. **Genres:** Young Adult Fiction, Novellas/Short Stories. **Career:** University of Georgia, Georgia Center for Continuing Education, instructor, 1977-2000, Department of English, teaching assistant, 1996-99; The Georgia Review, editorial assistant, 1999-2000; Brenau University, Department of Humanities, assistant professor, 2000-02; Vanderbilt University, Department of English, associate professor, 2002-; Institute for Violence Prevention, co-founder and director of education programs. **Publications:** Soy la Avon Lady and Other Stories, 2002; Call Me Henri: A Novel, 2006; The Gifted Gabaldón Sisters, 2008; (ed.) An Angle of Vision: Women Writers and Their Poor and Working-Class Roots, 2009; Homicide Survivors Picnic, 2009; The Realm of Hungry Spirits, 2011. Contributor to books and periodicals. **Address:** Department of English, Vanderbilt University, 425 Benson Hall, 2301 Vanderbilt Pl., PO Box 351654, Nashville, TN 37235, U.S.A. **Online address:** lorraine.lopez@vanderbilt.edu

LOPEZ, Steve. American (born United States), b. 1953. **Genres:** Novels, Adult Non-fiction. **Career:** Oakland Tribune, news reporter, columnist, 1977-83; San Jose Mercury News, columnist, 1983-85; Philadelphia Inquirer, columnist, 1985-96; Time Inc., columnist and writer-at-large, 1997-; Los Angeles Times, columnist, 2001-. **Publications:** Third and Indiana: A Novel, 1994; Land of Giants: Where No Good Deed Goes Unpunished, 1995; The Sunday Macaroni Club, 1997; In the Clear, 2002; Soloist: A Lost Dream, an Unlikely Friendship and the Redemptive Power of Music, 2008; Dreams and Schemes: My Decade of Fun in the Sun, 2010. **Address:** Los Angeles Times, 202 W 1st St., Los Angeles, CA 90012, U.S.A. **Online address:** steve.lopez@latimes.com

LOPEZ-LUJAN, Leonardo. Mexican (born Mexico), b. 1964. **Genres:** Archaeology/Antiquities, History. **Career:** Instituto Nacional de Antropologia e Historia, archaeologist and researcher, 1988-; Proyecto Templo Mayor, director, 1991-; Escuela Nacional de Antropologia e Historia, professor; Museo del Templo Mayor, senior researcher in archaeology, Writer. **Publications:** The Offerings of the Templo Mayor of Tenochtitlan, 1994, rev. ed., 2005; (with A.L. Austin) Mexico's Indigenous Past, 2001; (with E.M. Moctezuma) Monumental Mexica Sculpture=Monumental Aztec Sculpture, 2009. IN SPANISH: Nómadas Y Sedentarios: El Pasado Prehispánico De Zacatecas, 1989; La Recuperación Mexico Del Pasado Teotihuacano, 1989; Las Ofrendas Del Templo Mayor De Tenochtitlán, 1993; (with L. Manzanilla) Historia Antigua De México, 1994; Xochicalco Y Tula, 1995; (with A.L. Austin) El Pasado Indígena, 1996; (with A.L. Austin) Mito Y Realidad De Zuyuá: Serpiente Emplumada Y Las Transformaciones Mesoamericanas DelClásico Al Posclásico, 1999; (with M. Fauvet-Berthelot) Aztèques: La Collection De Sculptures Du Musée du Quai Branly, 2005; (with J. Levin) Tenochtitlán, 2005; La Casa De Las águilas: Un Ejemplo De La Arquitectura Religiosa De Tenochtitlan, 2006; (with D.Carrasco and E.M. Moctezuma) Breaking through Mexico's Past: Digging the Aztecs with Eduardo Matos Moctezuma, 2007. EDITOR: Atlas Historico De Mesoamerica, 1989; (with W.L. Fash, Jr.) The Art of Urbanism: How Mesoamerican Kingdoms Represented Themselves in Architecture and Imagery, 2009; Sacrificio Humano En La Tradición Religiosa Mesoamericana, 2010; Tlaltecuhtli, 2010. Contributor to archeology journals. **Address:** Museo del Templo Mayor, Instituto Nacional de Antropologia e Historia, Guatemala 60, Centro, Mexico City, ME 06060, Mexico. **Online address:** peterlourie@gmavt.net

LOPREATO, Joseph. American/Italian (born Italy), b. 1928. **Genres:** Sociology, Human Relations/Parenting, Demography, Sex, Psychology, Social Sciences. **Career:** University of Massachusetts, assistant professor of sociology, 1960-62; University of Rome, visiting lecturer, 1962-64; University of Connecticut, associate professor of sociology, 1964-66; University of Texas, professor of sociology, 1966-, chair of department, 1969-72. Writer. **Publications:** (With E. Jackson) Italian Made Simple, 1960; Vilfredo Pareto, 1965; Peasants No More: Social Class and Social Change in an Underdeveloped

Society, 1967; Italian Americans, 1970; (with L.E. Hazelrigg) Class, Conflict, and Mobility: Theories and Studies of Class Structure, 1972; (comp. with L.S. Lewis) Social Stratification: A Reader, 1974; The Sociology of Vilfredo Pareto, 1975; Human Nature and Biocultural Evolution, 1984; Evoluzione e Natura Umana, 1990; Mai Più Contadini, 1990; (with T. Crippen) Crisis in Sociology: The Need for Darwin, 1999. **Address:** 1801 Lavaca St., Ste. 10A, Austin, TX 78701, U.S.A. **Online address:** lopreato@mail.la.utexas.edu

LOPRESTI, Robert. American (born United States), b. 1954. **Genres:** Mystery/Crime/Suspense, Librarianship, Young Adult Non-fiction, Young Adult Fiction, Romance/Historical. **Career:** Wayne Public Library, librarian, 1977-81; William Paterson College of New Jersey, instructor, assistant professor, librarian, 1981-87; Western Washington University, assistant professor, librarian, interim map librarian, 1987-. Writer. **Publications:** (Ed.) Thurber on Crime, 1991; Such a Killing Crime, 2005. Contributor to periodicals. Works appear in anthologies. **Address:** Western Libraries, Western Washington University, 229 Haggard Hall, 516 High St., Bellingham, WA 98225-9103, U.S.A. **Online address:** rob.lopresti@wwu.edu

LOPRETE, Kimberly A. Irish (born Ireland), b. 1955?. **Genres:** History. **Career:** National University of Ireland, lecturer in medieval history. Writer. **Publications:** Adela of Blois: Countess and Lord (c. 1067-1137), 2007. **Address:** National University of Ireland, Rm. 404, University Rd., Galway, GL 1, Ireland. **Online address:** kim.loprete@nuigalway.ie

LORBER, Judith. American (born United States), b. 1931. **Genres:** Medicine/Health, Sociology, Women's Studies And Issues, Social Sciences. **Career:** New York State Pharmacist, assistant editor, 1953-55; Montefiore Hospital and Medical Center, project director in health services research, 1966-68; Bellevue Hospital, Psychiatric Division, assistant research sociologist, 1969-70; Fordham University, instructor, assistant professor, 1970-72; City University of New York, Brooklyn College, assistant professor, associate professor, professor, 1972-95, professor emeritus, 1995-, Graduate Center of the City University of New York, professor, 1981-95, Women's Studies Certificate Program, coordinator, 1988-91, professor emeritus of sociology and women's studies, 1995-; Mount Sinai Medical Center, adjunct associate professor, 1978-95; Bar Ilan University, lecturer, 1992-93; Ruhr University, Bochum, Germany, Marie Jahoda Professor, 1997; Dortmund University, visiting professor, 2003; Carl von Ossietzky University, Fulbright senior specialist, 2004. **Publications:** Women Physicians: Careers, Status, and Power, 1984; Paradoxes of Gender, 1994; Gender and the Social Construction of Illness, 1997, (with L.J. Moore) 2nd ed., 2002; Gender Inequality: Feminist Theories and Politics, 1998, 4th ed., 2010; Breaking the Bowls: Degendering and Feminist Change, 2005; Gendered Bodies: Feminist Perspectives, 2007, 2nd ed., 2011. EDITOR: (with E. Freidson) Medical Men and Their Work, 1972; (with S.A. Farrell) The Social Construction of Gender, 1991; (with M.M. Ferree and B.B. Hess) Revisioning Gender, 1998; (with K. Davis and M. Evans) Handbook of Gender and women's Studies, 2006; (with E. Freidson) Medical Professionals and the Organization of Knowledge, 2008. Contributor to books. **Address:** City University of New York Graduate Center, 365 Fifth Ave., Rm. 6112.04, New York, NY 10016, U.S.A. **Online address:** jlorber@rcn.com

LORD, Carnes. American (born United States) **Genres:** Politics/Government. **Career:** Office of the Vice President of the United States, assistant for national security affairs, 1989-91; U.S. Naval War College, professor of military and naval strategy, Naval War College Press, strategic researcher; National Defense University, distinguished fellow, 1991-93; Naval War College Press, director; Naval War College Review, editor; Yale University, faculty; University of Virginia, faculty; Adelphi University, faculty; Fletcher School of Law and Diplomacy, faculty. **Publications:** (Trans. and intro. with D.A. Trafton) Tassos Dialogues: A Selection with the Discourse on the Art of the Dialogue, 1982; Education and Culture in the Political Thought of Aristotle, 1982; (trans. and intro.) The Politics, 1984; The Presidency and the Management of National Security, 1988; (ed. with F.R. Barnett) Political Warfare and Psychological Operations: Rethinking the U.S. Approach, 1989; (ed. with D.K. O'Connor) Essays on the Foundations of Aristotelian Political Science, 1991; (trans.) L. Strauss, Xenophon's Socratic Discourse, 1998; The Modern Prince: What Leaders Need to Know Now, 2003; Losing Hearts and Minds?: Public Diplomacy and Strategic Influence in the Age of Terror, 2006; (ed.) Reposturing the Force: U.S. Overseas Presence in the Twenty-first Century, 2006; (ed. with A.S. Erickson and L.J. Goldstein) China goes to Sea: Maritime Transformation in Comparative Historical Perspective,

2009. **Address:** Strategic Research Department, U.S. Naval War College, 686 Cushing Rd., PO Box 231, Newport, RI 02841, U.S.A. **Online address:** carnes.lord@nwc.navy.mil

LORD, Jeffrey. See NELSON, Ray.

LORD, John Vernon. British (born England), b. 1939. **Genres:** Children's Fiction, Illustrations. **Career:** Freelance book illustrator, 1960-; University of Brighton, College of Art, faculty, 1961-70, 1992-99, teacher, 1968, Brighton Polytechnic, Faculty of Art and Design, principal lecturer in drawing and illustration, 1961-, staff, 1970-92, Department of Visual Communication, head, 1974-81, 1984, professor of illustration, 1986-99, Department of Graphic Arts, head, 1989-91, School of Design, head, 1997-98, professor emeritus, 1999-. Writer. **Publications:** SELF-ILLUSTRATED: The Runaway Roller Skate, 1974; Miserable Aunt Bertha, 1980; (ed. and intro.) Aesop's Fables, 1989; Dreams Experienced and Jotted Down From the Diaries of John Vernon Lord, 1994. OTHERS: Mr. Mead and His Garden, 1975; (ed. and intro.) The Nonsense Verse of Edward Lear, 1984, 3rd ed., 1992; Giant Jam Sandwich, 2007; Drawing Upon Drawing, 2007. Illustrator of books by others. **Address:** c/o Upwell, 4 Orchard Ln., Ditchling, Hassocks, WS BN6 8TH, England.

LORD, Nancy J. American (born United States), b. 1952. **Genres:** Novellas/Short Stories, Local History/Rural Topics, Natural History, Essays, Humanities, Marine Sciences/Oceanography, Sciences, Social Commentary, Travel/Exploration, Writing/Journalism, Essays, Adult Non-fiction, Environmental Sciences/Ecology. **Career:** State of Alaska, legislative aide, 1979-89; independent writer 1984-; University of Alaska, instructor, adjunct professor, visiting professor, associate professor of writing, 1991-. **Publications:** The Compass Inside Ourselves: Short Stories, 1984; Survival: Stories, 1991; Darkened Waters: A Review of the History, Science, and Technology Associated with the Exxon Valdez Oil Spill and Cleanup, 1992; Fishcamp: Life on an Alaskan Shore (nonfiction), 1997; Green Alaska: Dreams from the Far Coast (nonfiction), 2000; The Man Who Swam with Beavers: Stories, 2001; Beluga Days: Tracking a White Whale's Truths (nonfiction), 2004; Beluga Days: Tales of an Endangered White Whale, 2007; Rock, Water, Wild: An Alaskan Life, 2009; Early Warming: Crisis and Response in the Climate-Changed North, 2011. **Address:** PO Box 558, Homer, AK 99603, U.S.A. **Online address:** njl@alaskawriters.com

LORD, Sheldon. See BLOCK, Lawrence.

LORD, Tom. See BRAUN, Matt(hew).

LORD, Tony. British (born England), b. 1949?. **Genres:** Homes/Gardens, Horticulture. **Career:** National Trust, gardens adviser, 1979-89; Royal Horticultural Society, Plant Finder, principal editor. Research chemist and consultant. **Publications:** (Comp.) Small Period Gardens: A Practical Guide to Design and Planting, 1992; New Wines of Spain, 1992; Gardening at Sissinghurst, 1995 as Planting Schemes from Sissinghurst, 2003; Best Borders, 1996; Designing with Roses, 1999; Versatile Roses, 1999; Chocolate, 2000; Encyclopedia of Planting Combinations: The Ultimate Visual Guide to Successful Plant Harmony, 2002, rev. ed., 2008; Sissinghurst: Classic Garden Inspirations, 2002; Dictionary of French Wines, 2002; (contrib.) Flora: The Gardener's Bible: More Than 20,000 Garden Plants from Around the World, 2003. Contributor to periodicals. **Address:** c/o Author Mail, Frances Lincoln Ltd., 4 Torriano Mews, Torriano Ave., London, GL NW5 2RZ, England.

LORDAN, Beth. See LORDAN, (Ellenora) Beth.

LORDAN, (Ellenora) Beth. (Beth Lordan). American (born United States), b. 1948. **Genres:** Novels, Novellas/Short Stories. **Career:** Cornell University, teaching assistant, 1984-86, lecturer, 1986-88; Southern Illinois University, assistant professor of English, 1991-94, associate professor, 1994-99, professor, 1999-, Irish and Irish Immigration Studies, director; National Endowment for the Arts, fiction fellow, 1993; National University of Ireland, visiting professor, 1998. Writer. **Publications:** August Heat: A Novel, 1989; And Both Shall Row: A Novella and Stories, 1998; But Come Ye Back 2004. Contributor to periodicals. **Address:** Department of English, Southern Illinois University, Faner Hall 2284, 1000 Faner Dr., PO Box 4503, Carbondale, IL 62901-4503, U.S.A. **Online address:** lordan@siu.edu

LORDON, Randye. American (born United States) **Genres:** Mystery/Crime/Suspense, Novels. **Career:** Writer. **Publications:** Brotherly Love, 1993; Sisters Keeper, 1994; Father Forgive Me, 1997; Mother May I, 1998; Say Uncle, 1999; East of Niece, 2001; Son of a Gun, 2005. Contributor to periodicals. **Address:** c/o Author Mail, St. Martins Press, 175 5th Ave., New York, NY 10010, U.S.A. **Online address:** randye@randyelordon.com

LORENZ, Lee (Sharp). American (born United States), b. 1932. **Genres:** Illustrations, Children's Fiction, Cartoons, Young Adult Fiction. **Career:** New Yorker, staff cartoonist, 1958-, art editor, 1973-98, retired, 1998. Writer, artist and musician. **Publications:** ADULT BOOKS: Here It Comes: A Collection of Cartoons, 1968; Now Look What You've Done!, 1977; Real Dogs Don't Eat Leftovers: A Guide to All that is Truly Canine, 1983; The Golden Age of Trash: Cartoons for the Eighties, 1987. CHILDREN'S BOOKS: SELF-ILLUSTRATED: Pinchpenny John (adapted from The Miller's Tale in Geoffrey Chaucer's Canterbury Tales), 1981; Dinah's Egg, 1990. CHILDREN'S BOOKS: The Feathered Ogre, 1981; Big Gus and Little Gus, 1982; Hugo and the Spacedog, 1983; A Weekend in the Country, 1985. COMPILER AND EDITOR: (and comp.) The Essential George Booth, 1998; (and comp.) The Essential Charles Barsotti, 1998; (and comp.) The Essential Jack Ziegler, 2000. OTHERS: Teddy Bear Habit, 1967; The Art of the New Yorker, 1925-1995, 1995; The World of William Steig, 1998; Pig and Duck Buy a Truck, 2000; Old Farts are Forever, 2009. Illustrator of books by others. **Address:** PO Box 131, Easton, CT 06612-0131, U.S.A.

LORENZ, Ralph. American/Scottish (born Scotland), b. 1969. **Genres:** Engineering, Air/Space Topics, Crafts, Astronomy. **Career:** University of Surrey, UOSAT Spacecraft Engineering Research Unit, engineer; European Space Agency, Cassini-Huygens Project, engineer; Jet Propulsion Laboratory, engineer; University of Arizona, Lunar and Planetary Laboratory, research associate; Johns Hopkins University, Applied Physics Laboratory, instructor. Writer and astronomer. **Publications:** (With J. Mitton) Lifting Titan's Veil: Exploring the Giant Moon of Saturn, 2002; (ed. with A. Kleidon) Non-equilibrium Thermodynamics and the Production of Entropy: Life, Earth, and Beyond, 2005; (with D.M. Harland) Space Systems Failures: Disasters and Rescues of Satellites, Rockets and Space Probes, 2005; Spinning Flight: Dynamics of Frisbees, Boomerangs, Samaras, and Skipping Stones, 2006; (with A. Ball, J. Garry and V. Kerzhanovich) Planetary Landers and Entry Probes, 2007; (with J. Mitton) Titan Unveiled: Saturn's Mysterious Moon Explored, 2008. **Address:** Department of Space, Applied Physics Lab, Johns Hopkins University, MP3-E104, 11100 Johns Hopkins Rd., Laurel, MD 20723-6099, U.S.A. **Online address:** ralph.lorenz@jhuapl.edu

LOREY, Dean. American (born United States), b. 1967. **Genres:** Novels. **Career:** My Wife and Kids, ABC, co-executive producer, 2001-03, executive producer, 2003-05, director, 2003-05; Arrested Development, co-executive producer, 2005-06. Screenwriter, producer, director and author. **Publications:** NIGHTMARE ACADEMY SERIES: Nightmare Academy, 2008; Nightmare Academy, Book Two: Monster Madness, 2008. **Address:** William Morris Agency, 151 El Camino Dr., Beverly Hills, CA 90212, U.S.A. **Online address:** dean@deanlorey.com

LORIGA, Ray. Spanish (born Spain), b. 1967. **Genres:** Plays/Screenplays, Novels. **Career:** Writer. **Publications:** Lo peor de todo, 1992; Héroes, 1993; Días extraños, 1994; Caídos del cielo, 1995; Carne tremula, 1997; La pistola de mi hermano, 1997; Tokio ya no nos quiere, 1999; Trífero, 2000; El hombre que inventó Manhattan, 2004; The Seventh Day, 2004; Teresa, El Cuerpo de Cristo, 2007; Ya Slo Habla de Amor, 2008; Oficiales y El Destino de Cordelia, 2009; Sombrero Y Mississippi, 2010. **Address:** c/o Author Mail, St. Martins Press, 175 5th Ave., New York, NY 10010, U.S.A. **Online address:** info@rayloriga.com

LORING, Kevin. Canadian (born Canada), b. 1974. **Genres:** Theatre. **Career:** Playhouse Theatre Co., artist-in-residence, 2006; National Arts Centre English Theatre, playwright-in-residence, 2009-10; Savage Society, founder. **Publications:** Where the Blood Mixes, 2009. **Address:** Playhouse Theatre Co., 127 E 2nd Ave., Vancouver, BC V5T 1B4, Canada. **Online address:** kevilor@hotmail.com

LORRIMER, Claire. Also writes as Patricia Robins, Susan Patrick, Susan Patrick. British (born England), b. 1921. **Genres:** Novellas/Short Stories, Romance/Historical, Children's Fiction, Young Adult Fiction, Poetry, Biography, Novels, Autobiography/Memoirs, Autobiography/Memoirs. **Career:** Woman's Illustrated Magazine, sub-editor, 1938-40. Writer. **Publications:** A Voice in the Dark, 1967; The Shadow Falls, 1974; Chatelaine, 1978; Re-

lentless Storm, 1979; The Garden (cameo), 1980; The The Wilderling, 1982; Last Year's Nightingale, 1984; Frost in the Sun, 1986; House of Tomorrow (biography), 1987; The Secret of Quarry House, 1988; Ortolans, 1990; The Spinning Wheel, 1991; Variations (stories), 1991; The Silver Link, 1993; Eleanor, 1994; Sophia, 1994; Emma, 1994; Fool's Curtain, 1994; Connie's Daughter, 1995; Beneath the Sun, 1996; The Reunion, 1997; The Reckoning, 1998; The Woven Thread, 1998; Second Chance, 1998; An Open Door, 1999; Never Say Goodbye, 2000; Search for Love, 2000; For Always, 2001; The Faithful Heart, 2002; Deception, 2003; Over My Dead Body, 2003; Troubled Waters, 2004; Dead Centre, 2005; Infatuation, 2007; Truth to Tell, 2007; You Never Know: An Autobiography, 2007; Emotions, 2008; Dead Reckoning, 2009; Scarlett, 2011; Antoinette, 2011. MAVREEN SERIES: Mavreen, 1976; Tamarisk, 1978; Chantal, 1980. AS SUSAN PATRICK: Statues of Snow (novel), 1948. NOVELS AS PATRICIA ROBINS: To the Stars, 1944; See No Evil, 1945; Three Loves, 1949; Awake My Heart, 1950; Beneath the Moon, 1951; Leave My Heart Alone, 1951; The Fair Deal, 1952; Heart's Desire, 1953; So This Is Love, 1953; Heaven in Our Hearts, 1954; One Who Cares, 1954; Love Cannot Die, 1955; The Foolish Heart, 1956; Give All to Love, 1956; Where Duty Lies, 1957; He Is Mine, 1957; Love Must Wait, 1958; Lonely Quest, 1959; Lady Chatterley's Daughter, 1961; The Last Chance, 1961; The Long Wait, 1962; The Runaways, 1962; Seven Loves, 1962; With All My Love, 1963; The Constant Heart, 1964; Second Love, 1964; The Night Is Thine, 1964; There Is But One, 1965; No More Loving, 1965; Topaz Island, 1965; Love Me Tomorrow, 1966; The Uncertain Joy, 1966; The Man behind the Mask, 1967; Forbidden, 1967; Sapphire in the Sand, 1967; Return to Love, 1968; Laugh on Friday, 1969; No Stone Unturned, 1969; Cinnabar House, 1970; Under the Sky, 1970; The Crimson Tapestry, 1972; Play Fair with Love, 1972; None But He, 1973; No More Loving, 1986; Topaz Island, 1988; Forever, 1991; Forbidden, 1992; Fulfillment, 1993; Forsaken, 1993; The Legend, 1997. JUVENILES AS PATRICIA ROBINS: The Adventures of the Three Baby Bunnies, 1934; Tree Fairies, 1945; Sea Magic, 1946; The Heart of a Rose, 1947; The One Hundred Pound Reward, 1966. **Address:** Chiswell Barn, Christmas Mill Ln., Marsh Green, Edenbridge, KT TN8 5PR, England. **Online address:** info@clairelorrimer.co.uk

LOSADA (GOYA), Jose Manuel. Spanish/British (born England), b. 1962. **Genres:** Literary Criticism And History. **Career:** Spanish teacher, 1986-88; University of Navarre, associate professor of French, 1991-, Department of Modern Languages, assistant director, 1992-93; Complutense University of Madrid, associate professor, 1992-96, professor of French literature, 2006, university professor, 2009; University of Montreal, visiting fellow, 1995, visiting professor. Writer. **Publications:** L'Honneur au Théâtre: La Conception de l'Honneur dans le Théâatre Espagnol et Francais du XVIIe Siècle, 1994; Tristán y su ángel: Diez Ensayos de Literatura General y Comparada, 1995; Los Violines de Viena (novel), 1996; Romancero General, 1998; Bibliographie Critique de la Litterature Espagnole en France au XVIIe Siecle: Presence et Influence, 1999. EDITOR: (with P. Brunel and contrib.) Don Juan: Tirso, Molière, Pouchkine, Lenau; Analyses et Synthèses sur un Mythe Litteraire, 1993; (and contrib.) Poéticas Francesas del Siglo XX: Poetiques Francaises du XXE Siecle, 1994; (and trans.) V. Hugo, La Leyenda de los Siglos, 1994; (with K. Reichenberger and A. Rodriguez and contrib.) De Baudelaire a Lorca, 1996; Don Juan y Sus Fantasmas, 1997; Bibliography of the Myth of Don Juan in Literary History, 1997; Métamorphoses du roman français, 2010; Mito y mundo contemporáneo, 2010. Contributor to books and periodicals. **Address:** Complutense University of Madrid, Ciudad Universitaria, Avenida Seneca 2, Rectorado, Madrid, 28040, Spain. **Online address:** josemanuellosada@wanadoo.es

LO SCALZO, Jim. American (born United States), b. 1967?. **Genres:** Novels, Autobiography/Memoirs, Biography. **Career:** U.S. News and World Report, staff photographer, 1994-; George Washington University, faculty of photojournalism. Writer. **Publications:** Evidence of My Existence (memoir), 2007. **Address:** Washington, DC , U.S.A. **Online address:** jloscalzo@usnews.com

LOSCH, Richard R. American (born United States), b. 1933. **Genres:** Theology/Religion. **Career:** Episcopal priest, 1959-69; Trinity Episcopal Church, curate, 1959-61; St. John's Episcopal Church, rector, 1961-66; secondary school teacher, 1966-85; Camp Pomperaug, B.S.A., assistant camp director, 1966-69; Watkinson School, English and Humanities master/chaplain, 1966-69; Saint Michael's Episcopal Church, assistant to rector, 1966-86; Tower School, assistant headmaster and science/math master, 1969-81, assistant to the rector, 1969-86; Indian Pond Scout Reservation, camp director, 1970, 1973-79; Danvers High School, instructor, 1981-85; computer programmer and consultant, 1985-86; Saint Timothy's Episcopal Church, assistant to rector, 1986-89; Saint Timothy's School, principal, 1986-88, math instructor and coordinator, 1988-89; Cape Fear Academy, math instructor and department head, 1989-93; University of West Alabama, math instructor, 1994-2000, assistant professor of statistics, 2001-06; Saint James' Episcopal Church, rector, 1994-2003, priest-in-charge, 2003-08; St. Paul's Episcopal Church, priest-in-charge, 2005-08, retired, 2009. Writer. **Publications:** The Many Faces of Faith: A Guide to World Religions and Christian Traditions, 2001; The Uttermost Part of the Earth: A Guide to Places in the Bible, 2005; All the People in the Bible: An A-Z Guide to the Saints, Scoundrels and Other Characters in Scripture, 2008. **Address:** 102 W Monroe St., PO Box 1560, Livingston, AL 35470, U.S.A. **Online address:** loschr@bellsouth.net

LOSHITZKY, Yosefa. Israeli (born Israel) **Genres:** Film, Art/Art History. **Career:** Israeli television, production assistant, 1977-78; U.S. Department of State, Middle Eastern fellow, 1980; Indiana University, associate instructor in comparative literature, 1982-85; Israel's National Council of Culture and Art, fellow, 1983; Bowling Green State University, visiting professor of radio, television, and film, 1985-86; Hebrew University of Jerusalem, Department of Communication, lecturer, senior lecturer, 1987-2002; Jerusalem Cinematheque, lecturer, 1987-88; University of London, visiting professor, 1995-96; King's College, Department of Film Studies, visiting professor, 2003-04; University of London, School of Advanced Study, Institute of Romance Studies, visiting research fellow, 2003-05, School of Oriental and African Studies, Centre for Media and Film Studies, professorial research associate; University College London, Leverhulme Trust visiting professor, 2004-05; University of East London, School of Humanities and Social Sciences, professor of film and media studies; Tel-Aviv University, external lecturer; University of Sussex, lecturer; University of Sheffield, lecturer; University of Warwick, lecturer; University of Lancaster, lecturer. Writer. **Publications:** The Radical Faces of Godard and Bertolucci, 1995; (ed.) Spielberg's Holocaust: Critical Perspectives on Schindlers List, 1997; Identity Politics on the Israeli Screen, 2001; Screening Strangers: Migration and Diaspora in Contemporary European Cinema, 2010; Just Jews? Antisemitism and Islamophobia in Contemporary Culture and Beyond, forthcoming. Contributor to books and periodicals. **Address:** School of Humanities and Social Sciences, University of East London, EB.2.53, Docklands Campus, 4-6 University Way, London, GL E16 2RD, England. **Online address:** y.loshitzky@uel.ac.uk

LOSSE, Deborah N(ichols). American (born United States), b. 1944. **Genres:** Literary Criticism And History, Novels, History. **Career:** Arizona State University, assistant professor, 1973-80, associate professor, 1980-92, professor of French, 1992-, now professor emeritus, Faculte Libre des Scienceet Lettres Humaines, director of study abroad program, 1983, 1986, Academic Senate, president, 1994-95, College of Liberal Arts and Sciences, Department of Languages and Literatures, chair, 2001-04, divisional dean of humanities, 2004-; Graduate College, associate dean of academic programs, 1995-2001. Writer. **Publications:** Rhetoric at Play: Rabelais and Satirical Eulogy, 1980; Sampling the Book: Renaissance Prologues and the French Conteurs, 1994. Contributor of articles to books and journals. **Address:** Department of Languages and Literatures, Arizona State University, PO Box 6505, Tempe, AZ 85287-0202, U.S.A. **Online address:** dlosse@asu.edu

LOTCHIN, Roger W. American (born United States), b. 1935. **Genres:** Local History/Rural Topics, History, Urban Studies. **Career:** University of North Carolina, assistant professor, 1966-74, associate professor, 1974-79, professor of history, 1979-; Urban History Association, president, 2005-. Writer. **Publications:** San Francisco, 1846-1856: From Hamlet to City, 1974; (ed.) The Martial Metropolis: U.S. Cities in War and Peace, 1984; Fortress California, 1910-1961: From Warfare to Welfare, 1992; (ed.) The Way We Really Were: The Golden State in the Second Great War, 2000; The Bad City in the Good War: San Francisco, Los Angeles, Oakland and San Diego, 2003. **Address:** Department of History, University of North Carolina, 562 Hamilton Hall, PO Box 3520, Chapel Hill, NC 27599-3195, U.S.A. **Online address:** rlotchin@email.unc.edu

LOTRIDGE LEVIN, Linda. See **LEVIN**, Linda Lotridge.

LOTT, Bret. American (born United States), b. 1958. **Genres:** Novels, Novellas/Short Stories, Adult Non-fiction, Young Adult Fiction. **Career:** Big

Yellow House Inc., cook's trainer, 1977-79; RC Cola, salesman, 1979-80; Daily Commercial News, reporter, 1980-81; Ohio State University, instructor in remedial English, 1984-86; College of Charleston, professor of English, 1986-2004, writer-in-residence, 1986-2004, faculty, 2007-; Vermont College of Norwich, M.F.A. Program, faculty, 1994-2000; Louisiana State University, Southern Review, editor and director, 2004-08. **Publications:** NOVELS: The Man Who Owned Vermont, 1987; A Stranger's House, 1988; Jewel, 1991; Reed's Beach, 1993; The Hunt Club, 1998; Song I Knew by Heart, 2004; Ancient Highway, 2008; Dead Low Tide, 2012. SHORT STORY COLLECTIONS: A Dream of Old Leaves, 1989; How to Get Home, 1996; Difference between Women and Men, 2005. NONFICTION: Fathers, Sons and Brothers: The Men in My Family, 1997; Before We Get Started: A Practical Memoir of the Writer's Life, 2005. OTHER: (ed. with W.S. Olsen) Year in Place, 2001; (ed. and intro.) Not Safe, but Good, 2006; (ed. and intro.) Best Christian Short Stories, 2006; (ed.) Eyes to See, 2008. Works appear in anthologies. Contributor to periodicals. **Address:** Department of English, College of Charleston, 66 George St., Charleston, SC 29424, U.S.A. **Online address:** lottb@cofc.edu

LOTT, Eric. American (born United States), b. 1959. **Genres:** History, Humanities, Music, Race Relations, Theatre. **Career:** Manhattan Community College, instructor, 1983-87; Columbia University, President's fellow, 1984, 1985; Columbia University, instructor, 1985-86; University of Virginia, instructor, 1988-89, assistant professor of English, 1990-96, associate professor, 1996-2000, professor of English, 2000-. Writer. **Publications:** (Contrib.) The Cambridge Handbook of American Literature, 1986; Love and Theft: Blackface Minstrelsy and the American Working Class, 1993; The Disappearing Liberal Intellectual, 2006; Tangled Up in Blue: The Cultural Contradictions of American Racism, forthcoming. Works appear in anthologies. Contributor to periodicals. **Address:** Department of English, University of Virginia, 214 Bryan Hall, 1215 Lee St., PO Box 400121, Charlottesville, VA 22904-4121, U.S.A. **Online address:** ewl4p@virginia.edu

LOTT, Jeremy. American (born United States), b. 1978. **Genres:** History. **Career:** Cato Institute, assistant managing editor, manager of editorial services; American Spectator, assistant managing editor, managing editor; Capital Research Center, Labor Watch, editor; RealClearReligion, editor; Books & Culture, contributing editor. Educator. **Publications:** In Defense of Hypocrisy: Picking Sides in the War on Virtue, 2006; The Warm Bucket Brigade: The Story of the American Vice Presidency, 2007; William F. Buckley Jr.: Christian Encounters, 2010. Contributor to books and periodicals. **Address:** Thomas Nelson Inc., PO Box 141000, Nashville, TN 37214, U.S.A. **Online address:** jlott@realclearpolitics.com

LOTT, John R. American (born United States), b. 1958. **Genres:** Economics, Essays, Law. **Career:** California State University, Department of Economics, lecturer, 1983-84; Texas A&M University, visiting assistant professor, 1984-86; Stanford University, Hoover Institution, The John M. Olin National Fellow, 1986-87; Rice University, visiting assistant professor, 1987-88; United States Sentencing Commission, chief economist, 1988-89; University of California, John E. Anderson Graduate School of Management, visiting assistant professor, 1989-91; University of Pennsylvania, Wharton School, Carl D. Covitz Term Assistant Professor, 1991-95; Cornell University, Law School, John M. Olin Visiting Fellow, 1994; University of Chicago, George J. Stigler Center for the Study of the Economy and the State, John M. Olin Visiting Assistant Professor 1994-95, John M. Olin Law and Economics Fellow, 1995-99; Economic Inquire, co-editor, 1996-98; Federal Trade Commission, consultant, 2002-; University of Maryland, College Park Foundation, visiting senior research scientist, 2003-; Fox News, columnist. Economist. **Publications:** (ed.) Uncertainty and Economic Evolution: Essays in Honor of Armen A. Alchian, 1997; More Guns, Less Crime: Understanding Crime and Gun-Control Laws, 1998, 2nd ed., 2000; Are Predatory Commitments Credible? Who Should the Courts Believe?, 1999; The Bias against Guns: Why Almost Everything You've Heard about Gun Control Is Wrong, 2003; Straight Shooting: Guns, Economics, and Public Policy, 2006; Freedomnomics: Why the Free Market Works and Other Half-Baked Theories Don't, 2007. Contributor of articles to journals. **Address:** University of Maryland, 3209 A.V. Williams Bldg., College Park, MD 20742, U.S.A. **Online address:** johnrlott@aol.com

LOTTMAN, Herbert. (Herbert R. Lottman). French/American (born United States), b. 1927. **Genres:** Intellectual History, Biography, Military/Defense/Arms Control, Politics/Government, Law. **Career:** Farrar, Straus & Giroux, editor, agent and representative, 1956-69; freelance writer, 1960-; Publishers Weekly, contributing editor, 1972-79, international correspondent, 1979-.

Publications: Flaubert: A Biography, 1989. AS HERBERT R. LOTTMAN: Detours from the Grand Tour, 1970; How Cities Are Saved, 1976; Albert Camus: A Biography, 1979; The Left Bank: Writers, Artists, and Politics from the Popular Front to the Cold War, 1982; Pétain, Hero or Traitor: the Untold Story, 1985; The Purge: The Purification of French Collaborators after World War II in UK as People's Anger: Justice and Revenge after the Liberation of France, 1986; Colette: A Life, 1991; The Fall of Paris: June 1940, 1992; The French Rothschilds: The Great Banking Dynasty through Two Turbulent Centuries, 1995; Jules Verne: An Exploratory Biography, 1996; Michelin, 100 ans d'aventures, 1998; Man Ray's Montparnasse, 2001; Albert Camus in New York, 2001; (co-author) Theatre de la Mode: Fashion Dolls: The Survival of Haute Couture, 2nd ed., 2001; L'Ecrivain Engage et ses Ambivalences, 2003; The Michelin Men: Driving an Empire, 2003; Oscar Wilde in Paris, 2009. Contributor to magazines and newspapers. **Address:** Palgrave Macmillan Ltd., 175 5th Ave., New York, NY 10010, U.S.A.

LOTTMAN, Herbert R. *See* **LOTTMAN, Herbert.**

LOTZ, Anne Graham. American (born United States), b. 1948. **Genres:** Theology/Religion, Self Help, inspirational/Motivational Literature, Reference. **Career:** Bible study instructor, 1976-88; AnGeL Ministries, founder and president, 1988-; evangelist speaker. Writer. **Publications:** The Vision of His Glory: Finding Hope through the Revelation of Jesus Christ, 1996; The Glorious Dawn of God's Story: Finding Meaning for Your Life in Genesis, 1997; Daily Light for Every Day, 1998; God's Story: Finding Meaning for Your Life Through Knowing God, 1999; Just Give Me Jesus, 2000; The Daily Light Journal: Evening Readings, 2000; Heaven: My Father's House, 2001; My Heart's Cry, 2002; Why? Trusting God When You Don't Understand, 2004; Joy of My Heart: Meditating Daily on God's Word, 2004; I Saw the Lord: A Wake-Up Call for Your Heart, 2005; My Jesus is...Everything, 2005; Life is Just Better-with Jesus, 2007; Magnificent Obsession: Embracing the God-filled Life, 2009; Expecting to See Jesus: A Wake-up Call for God's People, 2011; Heaven, God's Promise for Me, 2011. **Address:** AnGeL Ministries, 5115 Hollyridge Dr., Raleigh, NC 27612-3111, U.S.A. **Online address:** angelmnsty@aol.com

LOUD, G(raham) A(nthony). British (born England), b. 1953. **Genres:** History. **Career:** University of Leeds, lecturer in history, 1978-92, senior lecturer, 1992-2000, reader in medieval Italian history, 2000-, professor of medieval Italian history, Institute of Medieval Studies, director; McMaster University, Liri Valley Archaeological Survey, consultant, 1978-80. Writer. **Publications:** Church and Society in the Norman Principality of Capua, 1058-1197, 1985; (trans. with T.E.J. Wiedemann) The History of the Tyrants of Sicily by Hugo Falcandus 1154-69, 1998; Conquerors and Churchmen in Norman Italy, 1999; Montecassino and Benevento in the Middle Ages: Essays in South Italian Church History, 2000; The Age of Robert Guiscard: Southern Italy and the Norman Conquest, 2000; Latin Church in Norman Italy, 2007; (trans.) The Crusade of Frederick Barbarossa, 2009. EDITOR: (with I.N. Wood) Church and Chronicle in the Middle Ages: Essays Presented to John Taylor, 1991; (with A. Metcalfe) The Society of Norman Italy, 2002. **Address:** School of History, University of Leeds, History Staff Common Rm. 330, Michael Sadler Arts Bldg., Leeds, LS2 9JT, England. **Online address:** g.a.loud@leeds.ac.uk

LOUD, Patricia Cummings. American (born United States), b. 1930. **Genres:** Art/Art History, Institutions/Organizations, Architecture, History, Photography, Adult Non-fiction. **Career:** University of Texas at Austin, teacher of children's art courses, 1949-51; Frederick County Board of Education, teacher in public school system, 1951-53; Radcliffe College, resident fellow, 1954-56; Brown University, Ford fellow in college teaching, 1956-57, teaching associate in art history, 1957-60; Connecticut College, lecturer and instructor in modern art and slide librarian, 1970-72; University of Connecticut, lecturer in art history, 1970-71; Texas Christian University, instructor in art history and humanities, 1972-76; Van Cliburn Foundation, executive assistant and coordinator of volunteers, 1980-81; Kimbell Art Museum, slide librarian and architectural historian, 1981-92, curator of architecture and visual resources, 1993, curator of architecture and archivist, 1994-, curator emeritus of architecture and archivist. Writer. **Publications:** In Pursuit of Quality: The Kimbell Art Museum, A History of Its Art and Architecture, 1987; (and ed.) The Art Museums of Louis I. Kahn, 1989. Contributor to books. **Address:** Kimbell Art Museum, 3333 Camp Bowie Blvd., Fort Worth, TX 76107, U.S.A.

LOUDEN, Robert B. American (born United States), b. 1953. **Genres:** Philosophy, Politics/Government, Translations, Essays. **Career:** Indiana University Northwest, adjunct lecturer, 1977-80; Barat College, adjunct lecturer, 1979-80; Iowa State University, visiting assistant professor of philosophy, 1980-82; University of Southern Maine, assistant professor, 1982-88, associate professor, 1988-96, chairman of department, 1988-89, 1992-96, 1998-2000, professor of philosophy, 1996-; Gottingen University, visiting associate professor, 1992; Emory University, visiting associate professor, 1995. Writer. **Publications:** Morality and Moral Theory: A Reappraisal and Reaffirmation, 1992; Kant's Impure Ethics: From Rational Beings to Human Beings, 2000; The World We Want: How and Why the Ideals of the Enlightenment Still Elude Us, 2007. EDITOR: (with P. Schollmejer and contrib.) The Greeks and Us: Essays in Honor of Arthur Adkins, 1996; (trans.) Anthropology from a Pragmatic Point of View, 2006; (trans. with G. Zöller) I. Kant, Anthropology, History and Education, 2007; Kant's Human Being: Essays on His Theory of Human Nature, 2011. Contributor to books, journals and newspapers. **Address:** Department of Philosophy, University of Southern Maine, 47 Exeter St., Portland, ME 04104-9300, U.S.A. **Online address:** louden@maine.edu

LOUDON, David L. American (born United States), b. 1944. **Genres:** Marketing, Economics, Administration/Management, Business/Trade/Industry. **Career:** Louisiana State University, instructor in marketing, 1969-71; University of Rhode Island, assistant professor, associate professor of marketing, 1971-80; University of Louisiana (formerly Northeast Louisiana University), Department of Management and Marketing, associate professor, professor of marketing and head, 1980-2005, chair, 2001-05; Professional Marketing Systems, partner; ABSCAN Inc., president; Samford University, professor of marketing; Services Marketing Quarterly, editor. **Publications:** (With A. Della Bitta) Consumer Behavior, 1979, 4th ed., 1993; (with R. Stevens) Legal Services Marketing: A Planning Guide, 1989; (with R. Stevens and B. Warren) Marketing Planning Guide, 1991, 2nd ed. (and with B. Wrenn), 1997; (with R. Stevens) Marketing for Churches and Ministries, 1992; Strategic Planning for Not-for-Profit Organizations, 1994; (with R.H. Migliore and R.E. Stevens) Church and Ministry Strategic Planning: From Concept to Success, 1994; Fundamentals of Strategic Planning for Healthcare Organizations, 1997; Strategic Planning for Collegiate Athletics, 2000; (with B. Wrenn and R. Stevens) Marketing Research: Text and Cases, 2002, 2nd ed., 2007. **Address:** Department of Mangement, Brock School of Business, Samford University, Rm. 305, Dwight M. Beeson Hall, 800 Lakeshore Dr., Birmingham, AL 35229, U.S.A. **Online address:** dlloudon@samford.edu

LOUDON, Mary. British (born England), b. 1966. **Genres:** Adult Non-fiction, Young Adult Fiction, Theology/Religion. **Career:** Poet and journalist. **Publications:** (Ed.) Unveiled: Nuns Talking, 1992; Revelations: The Clergy Questioned, 1994; Secrets and Lives: Middle England Revealed, 2000; Relative Stranger: A Life after Death (memoir), 2006; Relative Stranger: Piecing Toether A Life Plagued by Madness, 2006. Contributor of articles and book reviews to periodicals. **Address:** Capel & Land Ltd., 29 Wardour St., London, GL W1D 6PS, England.

LOUËR, Laurence. French (born France), b. 1972?. **Genres:** Politics/Government, History, Social Sciences, Theology/Religion. **Career:** Centre for International Studies and Research, researcher, 2003-, Critique Internationale, co-editor-in-chief, 2006-; French Ministry of Foreign Affairs, Direction of Prospective, consultant, 2004-09. **Publications:** Les Citoyens Arabes d'Israël, 2003, rev. ed., 2007; Chiisme et politique au Moyen-Orient: Iran, Irak, Liban, monarchies du Golfe, 2008; Transnational Shia Politics: Religious and Political Networks in the Gulf, 2008. **Address:** Centre for International Studies and Research, 56 Rue Jacob, Paris, 75006, France. **Online address:** louer@ceri-sciences-po.org

LOUGHERY, John. (John Francis Loughery). American (born United States), b. 1953. **Genres:** Adult Non-fiction, Gay And Lesbian Issues, History, Biography, Essays. **Career:** Columbia Grammar and Preparatory School, English teacher, 1977-93; freelance journalist and art critic, 1985-; Hudson Review, art critic, 1990-; full-time writer, 1993. Biographer and historian. **Publications:** Alias S.S. Van Dine: The Man Who Created Philo Vance, 1992; (ed.) First Sightings: Stories of American Youth, 1993; (ed.) Into the Widening World: International Coming-of-Age Stories, 1995; John Sloan: Painter and Rebel, 1995; (with S. Gechtoff) Sonia Gechtoff: Four Decades, 1956-1995, 1995; The Other Side of Silence: Men's Lives and Gay Identities, A Twentieth-Century Hisotry, 1998; (ed. and intro.) Eloquent Essay: An Anthology of Classic and Creative Nonfiction, 2000. **Address:** 2600 Netherland Ave., Riverdale, NY 10463, U.S.A.

LOUGHERY, John Francis. *See* **LOUGHERY**, John.

LOUGHLIN, **James**. Irish (born Ireland), b. 1948. **Genres:** History, International Relations/Current Affairs, Politics/Government. **Career:** Teacher, 1982-83; University of Ulster, lecturer in modern European and British history, 1984-86, Magee College, lecturer in history, 1988-97, senior lecturer in history, 1997-99, reader in history, 1999-; Queen's University, Institute of Irish Studies, junior research fellow, 1985, adjunct lecturer in modern history and politics, 1985-86, research associate, 1986-87, senior research fellow, 1987-88. Writer. **Publications:** Gladstone, Home Rule and the Ulster Question, 1882-93, 1986; Ulster Unionism and British National Identity since 1885, 1995; The Ulster Question since 1945, 1995, 2nd ed., 2004; British Monarchy and Ireland: 1800 to the Present, 2007. Contributor to books and periodicals. **Address:** Arts and Humanities Research Institute, School of English, History and Politics, University of Ulster, Rm. MA101 Magee Campus, Londonderry, BT48 7JL, Northern Ireland. **Online address:** jp.loughlin@ulster.ac.uk

LOUIE, **Andrea**. American (born United States), b. 1966. **Genres:** Novels, Young Adult Fiction. **Career:** Boston Globe, copyediting intern, 1987; San Jose Mercury News, reporting intern, 1988; Akron Beacon Journal, reporter, 1989-92; Market News Service, freelance editor, 1995-2000; Brooklyn College, adjunct writer, 1995-; The Chicago Tribune, literary critic, 1997-; Asian American Writers' Workshop, publications director, 1998-2000; Banchet Bianca Floral Design, designer, 2000-; Michigan State University, associate professor of anthropology, Asian Pacific American Studies Program, director. Novelist and journalist. **Publications:** Moon Cakes: A Novel, 1995; Chineseness across Borders: Renegotiating Chinese Identities in China and the United States, 2004; (ed. with J. Lew) Topography of War: Asian American Essays, 2006. **Address:** Prince Street Sta., PO Box 582, New York, NY 10012-4017, U.S.A. **Online address:** louie@msu.edu

LOUIE, **David Wong**. American (born United States), b. 1954?. **Genres:** Novels, Novellas/Short Stories, Young Adult Fiction. **Career:** University of California-Berkeley, teacher of creative writing and literature, 1988, associate professor of humanities, 1992-; Vassar College, faculty, 1988-92; University of California-Los Angeles, Department of Asian American Studies, assistant professor, associate professor and faculty adviser, 1992-, Department of English, assistant professor, associate professor, 1992-. Writer. **Publications:** STORIES: Pangs of Love, and Other Stories, 1991; The Barbarians Are Coming, 2000. Work appears in anthologies. Contributor to periodicals. **Address:** Department of Asian American Studies, University of California, 3336 Rolfe Hall, PO Box 957225, Los Angeles, CA 90095-7225, U.S.A. **Online address:** louie@humnet.ucla.edu

LOUIS, **Cindi**. American (born United States), b. 1962. **Genres:** Romance/Historical, Novels. **Career:** Romance Noir Book Club, founder, 1999-. Romance novelist. **Publications:** Crazy Thing Called Love, 2001; Mad 'Bout You, 2002; (with B. Jackson, F. Mason and K. Perrin) The Best Man, 2003; Texas Heat, forthcoming. Contributor to periodicals. **Address:** PO Box 411366, Dallas, TX 75241, U.S.A. **Online address:** reader@cindilouis.com

LOUIS, **Laura Glen**. American/Chinese (born China) **Genres:** Novellas/Short Stories, Young Adult Fiction. **Career:** Writer. **Publications:** Talking in the Dark: Stories, 2001; Some, like Elephants, 2010. Works appear in anthologies. **Address:** c/o Author Mail, Harcourt Inc., 6277 Sea Harbor Dr., Orlando, FL 32887, U.S.A. **Online address:** info@lauraglenlouis.com

LOUIS, **Pat**. *See* **FRANCIS**, Dorothy Brenner.

LOUIS, **William Roger**. American (born United States), b. 1936. **Genres:** History, Military/Defense/Arms Control. **Career:** Yale University, assistant professor, associate professor, 1962-70; University of Texas, professor of history, 1970-85, British Studies Program, director, 1975-, Kerr chair of English history and culture, 1985-, distinguished teaching professor, 1999-; St. Antony's College, fellow, 1986-; American Historical Association, National History Center, founding director, 2001; Library of Congress, Kluge chair, 2010-. Writer and historian. **Publications:** OXFORD PRESS HISTORICAL SURVEYS: (ed. with M. Howard) The Oxford History of the Twentieth Century, 1998; (ed.) The Oxford History of the British Empire, 1998. ADVENTURES WITH BRITANNIA: (ed.) Adventures with Britannia: Personalities, Politics and Culture in Britain, 1995; (ed.) More Adventures with Britannia: Personalities, Politics, and Culture in Britain, 1998; (ed.) Still More Adventures with Britannia: Personalities, Politics, and Culture in Britain, 2003; (ed.) Yet More Adventures with Britannia: Personalities, Politics, and Culture in Britain, 2005; (ed.) Penultimate Adventures with Britannia, 2007; (ed.) Ultimate Adventures with Britannia, 2009. IMPERIALISM: (ed.) Imperialism: The Robinson and Gallagher Controversy, 1976; Imperialism at Bay 1941-1945: The United States and the Decolonization of the British Empire, 1977 in US as Imperialism at Bay: The United States and the Decolonization of the British Empire, 1941-1945, 1978. COLONIALISM IN AFRICA: Ruanda-Urundi, 1884-1919, 1963, 2nd ed. in US as Ruanda-Urundi, 1884-1919, 1979; Great Britain and Germany's Lost Colonies, 1914-1919, 1967; (ed. with P. Gifford and A. Smith) Britain and Germany in Africa: Imperial Rivalry and Colonial Rule, 1967; (ed. with J. Stengers) E.D. Morel's History of the Congo Reform Movement, 1968; (ed. with P. Gifford) France and Britain in Africa: Imperial Rivalry and Colonial Rule, 1971; (ed. with P. Gifford) The Transfer of Power in Africa: Decolonization, 1940-1960, 1982; (ed. with P. Gifford) Decolonization and African Independence: The Transfers of Power, 1960-1980, 1988. COLONIALISM IN THE MIDDLE EAST: The British Empire in the Middle East, 1945-1951: Arab Nationalism, the United States, and Postwar Imperialism, 1984; (ed. with R.W. Stookey) The End of the Palestine Mandate, 1986; (ed. with J.A. Bill) Musaddiq, Iranian Nationalism, and Oil, 1988; (ed. with R. Owen) Suez 1956: The Crisis and Its Consequences, 1989; (ed. with R.A. Fernea) The Iraqi Revolution of 1958: The Old Social Classes Revisited, 1991; (ed. with R. Owen) A Revolutionary Year: The Middle East in 1958, 2002; Ends of British Imperialism: The Scramble for Empire, Suez and Decolonization: Collected Essays, 2006. BRITISH POLICY IN THE PACIFIC: British Strategy in the Far East, 1919-1939, 1971; (ed.) National Security and International Trusteeship in the Pacific, 1972; (ed. with W.S. Livingston) Australia, New Zealand, and the Pacific Islands since the First World War, 1979. WWII AND THE CHURCHILL ERA: (ed.) The Origins of the Second World War: A.J.P. Taylor and His Critics, 1972; (ed. with H. Bull) The Special Relationship: Anglo-American Relations since 1945, 1986; In the Name of God, Go! Leo Amery and the British Empire in the Age of Churchill, 1992; (ed. with R. Blake) Churchill, 1993; (ed.) Burnt Orange Britannia, 2005. OTHERS: (ed.) Resurgent Adventures with Britannia, 2011; (ed. with A. Shlaim) 1967 Arab-Israeli War, 2012. Contributor of articles to journals. **Address:** Department of History, University of Texas, 1 University Sta. F9400, Austin, TX 78712-0527, U.S.A. **Online address:** britishstudies@mail.utexas.edu

LOUNDAGIN, **Choeleen N.** American (born United States), b. 1967. **Genres:** Novels, Sports/Fitness. **Career:** Ice skating coach and performance enhancement consultant, 1992-; InnerChamp Books, affiliate; Santa Rosa Figure Skating Club, coach liaison. Writer. **Publications:** The Inner Champion, 1997, 2nd ed. as The Inner Champion: A Mental Toughness Training Manual for Figure Skaters, 2004. Contributor to periodicals. **Address:** InnerChamp Books, PO Box 11362, Santa Rosa, CA 95406-1362, U.S.A. **Online address:** inrchamp@aol.com

LOUNSBERRY, **Barbara**. American (born United States), b. 1946. **Genres:** Adult Non-fiction, Humanities, Writing/Journalism, Biography, Documentaries/Reportage, Essays, Politics/Government, Mystery/Crime/Suspense, Literary Criticism And History. **Career:** University of Northern Iowa, Office of Public Information, news and feature writer, 1965-72, instructor of journalism, 1973-74, Department of English, assistant professor of English, 1976-82, associate professor, 1983-89, professor of English, 1990-2006, professor emeritus, 2006-; KUNI-Radio, drama critic, 1973-; Iowa Humanities Board, president, 1990-91. Writer. **Publications:** The Art of Fact: Contemporary Artists of Nonfiction, 1990; (comp.) The Writer in You: A Writing Process Reader, 1992; (ed. with G. Talese) Writing Creative Nonfiction: The Literature of Reality, 1996; (co-ed.) The Tales We Tell: Perspectives on the Short Story, 1998; Time and Chance: An Iowa Murder Mystery, 1998; (ed.) 16, 000 Suspects: A Ragbrai Mystery, 1999; (ed.) Politics Is Murder: An Iowa Mystery, 2000; (intro.) The Gay Talese Reader: Portraits and Encounters, 2003. Contributor to periodicals. Works appear in anthologies. **Address:** Department of English, University of Northern Iowa, 117 Baker Hall, Cedar Falls, IA 50614-0502, U.S.A. **Online address:** barbara.lounsberry@uni.edu

LOURIE, **Richard**. American (born United States), b. 1940?. **Genres:** Novels, Novellas/Short Stories, Area Studies, Translations, Biography, Autobiography/Memoirs, Children's Fiction, Young Adult Fiction, Young Adult Fiction. **Career:** New York Times, Mikhail Gorbachev's translator; The Moscow Times, correspondent. **Publications:** NOVELS: Sagittarius in Warsaw, 1973; First Loyalty, 1985; Zero Gravity, 1987; The Autobiography of Joseph Stalin, 2000. TRANSLATOR FROM RUSSIAN: U. Shulevitz, Soldier and Tsar in the Forest: A Russian Tale (for children), 1972; V. Voinovich, The Life and Extraordinary Adventures of Private Ivan Chonkin, 1977; V. Voinovich, In Plain Russian: Stories, 1979; Pretender to the Throne, 1981; E. Sevela, Why There Is No Heaven on Earth, 1982; A. Likhanov, Shadows across the Sun, 1983; (with D. Arthur and B. Barrett) E. Sevela, The Standard Bearer, 1983; V. Voinovich, The Anti-Soviet Soviet Union, 1986; V. Voinovich, Moscow 2042, 1987; A. Lvov, The Courtyard, 1988; (and intro.) A. Tertz, Goodnight, 1989; Autobiography of Joseph Stalin, 1999; A. Sakharov, Memoirs, 1990, 2002. TRANSLATOR FROM POLISH: C. Milosz, Visions from San Francisco Bay, 1982; T. Konwicki, The Polish Complex, 1982; T. Konwicki, A Minor Apocalypse, 1983; K. Brandys, A Warsaw Diary 1978-81, 1984; R. Spasowski, The Liberation of One: The Autobiography of R. Spasowski, Polish Ambassador to the United States, 1986; E. Czarnecka and A. Fiut, Conversations with C. Milosz, 1987; (with J. Neugroschel) L. Dobroszycki, ed., The Chronicle of the Lodz Ghetto, 1941-1944, 1987; T. Konwicki, Moonrise, Moonset, 1987; A. Hertz, The Jews in Polish Culture, 1988; T. Konwicki, Bohin Manor, 1990; (and ed.) A. Wat, My Century: The Odyssey of a Polish Intellectual, 1988, 2003; J. Korczak, King Matt the First (for children), 1986, 2004. OTHERS: Letters to the Future, 1975; Russia Speaks: An Oral History from the Revolution to the Present, 1991; Predicting Russia's Future, 1991; Hunting the Devil, 1993; H. Grynberg, Jewish War and the Victory, 2001; Sakharov: A Biography, 2002; Hatred for Tulips, 2007; Joop: A Novel of Anne Frank, 2008. Contributor to periodicals. **Address:** 533 Canal St., Ste. 6, New York, NY 10013-1328, U.S.A.

LOURY, Glenn C(artman). American (born United States), b. 1948. **Genres:** Race Relations, Essays, Economics, Social Sciences. **Career:** Northwestern University, assistant professor of economics, 1976-79; University of Michigan, associate professor, 1979-80, professor of economics, 1980-82; Harvard University, professor of economics and Afro-American studies, 1982-84, John F. Kennedy School of Government, professor of political economy, 1984-91; Boston University, Institute on Race and Social Division, founder and director, 1997-2003, professor of economics, 1991-2005, University professor, 1994-2005; Brown University, Merton P. Stoltz professor of the social sciences and professor of economics, 2005-. Writer. **Publications:** (Ed. with J.Q. Wilson and contrib.) From Children to Citizens, vol. III: Families, Schools, and Delinquency Prevention, 1987; One by One, from the Inside Out: Essays and Reviews on Race and Responsibility in America, 1995; (contrib.) Mending Fences: Renewing Justice between Government and Civil Society, 1998; Anatomy of Racial Inequality, 2002; Racial Justice: The Superficial Morality of Colour-blindness in the United States, 2004; (ed. with T. Modood and S.M. Teles) Ethnicity Social Mobility and Public Policy: Comparing the U.S.A. and U.K., 2005; Race, Incarceration and American Values, 2008. Contributor of articles to journal. **Address:** Department of Economics, Brown University, 64 Waterman St., PO Box B, Providence, RI 02912, U.S.A. **Online address:** glenn_loury@brown.edu

LOUV, Richard. American (born United States), b. 1949. **Genres:** Human Relations/Parenting, Sciences. **Career:** San Diego Union-Tribune, columnist, 1984-2007; Parents Magazine, contributing editor; Monitor Radio Network, commentator; Children & Nature Network, chairman and co-founder, 2005; National Forum on Children and Nature, co-chair; National Civic League, senior associate. **Publications:** The Mexican Migration, Southwind, 1980; America II, 1983; Childhood's Future, 1990; FatherLove: What We Need, What We Seek, What We Must Create, 1993; 101 Things You Can Do for Our Children's Future, 1994; The Web of Life: Weaving the Values that Sustain Us, 1996; Fly-Fishing for Sharks: An American Journey, 2000; Last Child in the Woods: Saving Our Children from Nature-Deficit Disorder, 2005; The Nature Principle, 2011. Contributor to periodicals and newspapers. **Address:** c/o Jacqueline Green, 2515 Astral Dr., Los Angeles, CA 90046, U.S.A. **Online address:** rlouv@cts.com

LOUX, Ann Kimble. American (born United States), b. 1943. **Genres:** Autobiography/Memoirs, Sociology, Biography. **Career:** St. Mary's College, faculty, professor emeritus of English. Writer. **Publications:** The Limits of Hope: An Adoptive Mother's Story, 1997. **Address:** Department of English, St. Mary's College, 400 Main Bldg., Notre Dame, IN 46556, U.S.A. **Online address:** aloux@saintmarys.edu

LOVE, D. Anne. American (born United States), b. 1949. **Genres:** Children's Fiction, Children's Non-fiction, Self Help. **Career:** School administrator, 1974-88; University of North Texas, professor, 1989-91; full-time writer, 1989-; Western Hills Area Education Agency, consultant, 1994-96. **Publica-**

tions: JUVENILE FICTION: Bess's Log Cabin Quilt, 1995; Dakota Spring, 1995; My Lone Star Summer, 1996; Three against the Tide, 1998; I Remember the Alamo, 1999; A Year without Rain, 2000; The Puppeteer's Apprentice, 2003; The Secret Prince, 2005; Semiprecious, 2006; of Numbers and Stars: The Story of Hypatia, 2006; Picture Perfect, 2007; Defying the Diva, 2008. **Address:** Simon & Schuster Children's Publishing, 1230 Ave. of the Americas, New York, NY 10020, U.S.A.

LOVE, Douglas. American (born United States), b. 1967. **Genres:** Children's Fiction, Plays/Screenplays, Children's Non-fiction, Theatre. **Career:** Walden Media, senior vice president of television and live entertainment; Family Stage San Francisco, producing artistic director; Walden Family Playhouse, producing artistic director; Love Letters Ltd., owner; World Book Encyclopedia, creative consultant. Writer. **Publications:** PLAYS: Free To Be You And Me: 1987; Be Kind to Your Mother (Earth): 1993; Blame It on the Wolf, 1993; So You Want to Be a Star, 1993; Holiday in the Rain Forest, 1994; Kabuki Gift, 1994; Angelita, 1995; The Little House Christmas Theater Kit, 1995. OTHERS: Imagination Station: 99 Games to Spark Your Imagination, 1995; Great American Kids Slumber Party Book, 1997; Great American Kids Backyard Campout Book, 1997; Disney Do-It-Yourself Costume & Face Painting Book, 1997; Disney's Face Painting and Costume Kit, 1997; Organic Valley Presents the Earth Dinner by Douglas Love, 2005. **Address:** c/o Ken Meyer, Ken Meyer & Associates, 8840 Wilshire Blvd., Ste. 200, Beverly Hills, CA 90211, U.S.A. **Online address:** info@douglaslove.com

LOVE, Eric T. L. American (born United States), b. 1965. **Genres:** History, Social Sciences. **Career:** University of Colorado, assistant professor, associate professor, professor. Historian and writer. **Publications:** Race Over Empire: Racism and U.S. Imperialism, 1865-1900, 2004. **Address:** Department of History, University of Colorado, Rm. HLMS 346, 234 UCB, Hellems, Boulder, CO 80309-0234, U.S.A. **Online address:** eric.love@colorado.edu

LOVE, (Kathleen) Ann. Canadian (born Canada), b. 1947. **Genres:** Environmental Sciences/Ecology, Children's Non-fiction, Young Adult Non-fiction, Young Adult Fiction, Natural History. **Career:** Pollution Probe, founder and education coordinator, 1969-72; Stroke, American Heart Association Journal, managing editor, 1980-86; teacher, 1972-75, 1991-2003. **Publications:** (With J. Drake) Take Action: An Environmental Book for Kids, 1992; (with J. Drake) The Kids' Cottage Book, 1993 in US as The Kids' Summer Handbook, 1994; Grizzly Dance (fiction), 1994; Taking Control, 1997; (with J. Drake) Mining, 1997; Ice Cream at the Castle, 1999; Kid Book of the Far North, 2000; (with J. Drake) Cool Woods: A Trip Around the World's Boreal Forest, 2003; (with J. Drake) Snow Amazing: Cool Facts and Warm Tales, 2004; (with J. Drake) Trash Action: A Fresh Look at Garbage, 2006; (with J. Drake) Sweet!: The Delicious Story of Candy, 2007; (with J. Drake) Alien Invaders: Species that Threaten Our World, 2008; (with J. Drake) Talking Tails: The Incredible Connection Between People and Their Pets, 2010. **Address:** c/o Author Mail, Ticknor & Fields, 215 Park Ave. S, New York, NY 10003, U.S.A.

LOVE, Susan M. American (born United States), b. 1948. **Genres:** Medicine/Health. **Career:** Beth Israel Hospital, assistant in surgery, 1980-87, Breast Clinic, director, 1980-88, associate surgeon, 1987-92, Faulkner Breast Center, director of research, 1992; Dana Farber Cancer Institute, clinical associate, 1981-92; Fenway Community Health Center, board director, 1986-88; National Breast Cancer, founder and member, 1991-; Lesbian Health Foundation, board director, 1992-; University of California, associate professor of clinical surgery, 1992-96, adjunct associate professor, 1996-97, adjunct professor of general surgery, 1997-, Revlon chair in women's health, 1995-96, Revlon/UCLA Breast Center, director, 1992-96; Santa Barbara Breast Cancer Institute, director of research, 1995-, medical director, 1996-, president. Writer. **Publications:** (With K. Lindsey) Dr. Susan Love's Breast Book, 1990, 5th ed., 2010; (co-author) The Wellness Community Guide to Fighting for Recovery from Cancer, 1995; (with W. Silen and W.E. Matory) Atlas of Techniques in Breast Surgery, 1996; (with K. Lindsey) Dr. Susan Love's Hormone Book: Making Informed Choices about Menopause, 1997; (co-author) Breast Cancer: Society Shapes an Epidemic, 2000; (with K. Lindsey) Dr. Susan Love's Menopause and Hormone Book: Making Informed Choices, 2003; (with A.D. Domar and L.A. Hirschman) Live a Little!: Breaking the Rules won't Break Your Health, 2009. Contributor to medical textbooks. Contributor of articles to journals. **Address:** 2811 Wilshire Blvd., Ste. 500, Santa Monica, CA 90403, U.S.A. **Online address:** slove@earthlink.net

LOVEGROVE, James (Matthew Henry). (J. M. H. Lovegrove). British (born England), b. 1965. **Genres:** Novels, Novellas/Short Stories, Young Adult Fiction, Children's Fiction. **Career:** Writer, 1990-. **Publications:** NOVELS: The Hope, 1990; (with P. Crowther) Escardy Gap, 1996; (as J.M.H. Lovegrove) The Guardians: Krilov Continuum, 1998; Days, 1998; (as J.M.H. Lovegrove) The Guardians: The Berserker, 1999; (contrib.) Web 2028, 1999; Leningrad Nights, 2000; The Foreigners, 2000; Imagined Slights, 2001; United Kingdom, 2003; Worldstorm, 2004; Provender Gleed, 2005; The Age Of Ra, 2009; The Age Of Zeus, 2010. CHILDREN'S BOOKS: The Web: Computopia, 1998; Wings, 2001; House of Lazarus, 2003; Ant God, 2005; Cold Keep, 2006; Kill Swap, 2007; Freerunner, 2009; The 5 Lords Of Pain, 2010. NOVELLAS: (with P. Crowther) The Hand That Feeds, 1999; How the Other Half Lives, 1999; Gig, 2004; Dead Brigade, 2007. OTHERS: Redlaw, 2011; The Age of Odin, 2011. Contributor to periodicals. **Address:** c/o Jonathan Oliver, Rebellion Publishing Ltd., Riverside House, Osney Mead, Oxford, OX OX2 0ES, England.

LOVEGROVE, J. M. H. *See* **LOVEGROVE, James (Matthew Henry).**

LOVELACE, Earl. Trinidadian (born Trinidad and Tobago), b. 1935. **Genres:** Novels, Novellas/Short Stories, Plays/Screenplays, Picture/Board Books, Social Sciences, Sociology. **Career:** Trinidad Guardian, proofreader, 1953-54; Department of Forestry, staff, 1954-56; Jamaican Civil Service, Department of Agriculture, agricultural assistant, 1956-66, Department of Forestry, forest ranger, 1956-66; Federal City College, (University of the District of Columbia), instructor, 1971-73; University of the West Indies, lecturer in literature and creative writing, 1977-87; University of Iowa, International Writing Program, visiting writer, 1980; Hartwick College, writer-in-residence, 1986; Johns Hopkins University, visiting novelist-in-residence; Wellesley College, visiting lecturer, 1996-97; Dragon Productions, producer; Pacific Lutheran University, Department of English, distinguished novelist, 1999-2004; Trinidad Express, columnist; University of Trinidad and Tobago, Board of Governors, staff, 2005. **Publications:** While Gods Are Falling, 1965; The Schoolmaster, 1968; The Dragon Can't Dance, 1979; The Wine of Astonishment, 1982; Jestina's Calypso & Other Plays, 1984; A Brief Conversion and Other Stories, 1988; Salt (novel), 1997; Crawfie the Crapaud, 1997; Growing in the Dark, 2003; (contrib.) A Place in the World, 2008; Is Just a Movie, 2011. Contributor to periodicals. **Address:** c/o André Deutsch, Carlton Publishing Group, 20 Mortimer St., London, GL W1T 3JW, England.

LOVELACE, Merline (A.). American (born United States), b. 1946. **Genres:** Romance/Historical, Westerns/Adventure, Mystery/Crime/Suspense, Novels, Military/Defense/Arms Control. **Career:** Novelist, 1991-; lecturer. **Publications:** ROMANCE NOVELS: Bits and Pieces, 1993; Maggie and Her Colonel (novella), 1994; Alena, 1994; Sweet Song of Love, 1994; Dreams and Schemes, 1994; Siren's Call, 1994; Somewhere in Time, 1994; His Lady's Ransom, 1995; Lady of the Upper Kingdom, 1996; Line of Duty, 1996; Beauty and the Bodyguard, 1996; Halloween Honeymoon, 1996; Thanksgiving Honeymoon, 1996; Valentine's Honeymoon, 1997; Duty and Dishonor, 1997; Above and Beyond, 1997; Countess in Buckskin, 1997; White Tiger/Green Dragon, 1997; Return to Sender, 1998; The Tiger's Bride, 1998; The Mercenary and the New Mom, 1999; A Savage Beauty, 2003; Untamed, 2004; Mind Games, 2008; The Duke's New Year Resolution, 2008; The Executive's Valentine Seduction, 2009; The Hello Girl, 2009; Crusader Captive, 2011; Desert Fire. DANGER SERIES: Night of the Jaguar, 1995; Cowboy and the Cossack, 1995; Undercover Man, 1996; Perfect Double, 1996; Hot as Ice, 2002; Texas Hero, 2002; To Love a Thief, 2003; Closer Encounters, 2006; Devlin and the Deep Blue Sea, 2006; Diamonds Can Be Deadly, 2006; Stranded with a Spy, 2007; Match Play, 2008; Undercover Wife, 2008; Risky Engagement, 2010; Danger in the Desert, 2011; Strangers When We Meet, 2011; Double Deception, 2011. HOLIDAY HONEYMOONS SERIES: Wrong Bride, Right Groom, 1996; Halloween Honeymoon, 1996; The 14th and Forever, 1997. MILITARY THRILLER SERIES: Line of Duty, 1996; Duty and Dishonor, 1997; Call of Duty, 1998; River Rising, 1999; Dark Side of Dawn, 2001; After Midnight, 2003; Eye of the Beholder, 2005. MEN OF THE BAR-H SERIES: If a Man Answers, 1998; A Man of His Word, 1999; Mistaken Identity, 2000; The Harder They Fall, 2000; Twice in One Lifetime, 2001. GARRETTS OF WYOMING SERIES: The Horse Soldier, 2001; The Colonel's Daughter, 2002; The Captains Woman, 2003. OTHERS: (co-author) Officer's Bride, 2001; The Spy Who Loved Him, 2001; (co-author) At the Edge, 2002; A Question of Intent, 2003; Full Throttle, 2004; The Right Stuff, 2004; The First Mistake, 2005; The Middle Sin, 2005; The Last Bullet, 2005; Ex Marks the Spot, 2007; Risky Business, 2008; The CEO's Christmas Proposition,

2008; All the Wrong Moves, 2009; Protector, 2009; Seduced by the Operative, 2009; (with J. Greene and C. Myers) Baby, it's Cold Outside, 2010; Now You See Her, 2010; Christmas with a Vampire, 2010; Catch Her If You Can, 2011. Works appear in anthologies. **Address:** c/o Pam Hopkins, Elaine Davie Literary Agency, 620 Park Ave., Rochester, NY 14607, U.S.A. **Online address:** merline@swbell.net

LOVELL, (Alfred Charles) Bernard. British (born England), b. 1913. **Genres:** Astronomy, Physics, Autobiography/Memoirs, Economics, Sciences. **Career:** University of Manchester, assistant lecturer in physics, 1936-39, lecturer in physics, 1945-47, senior lecturer, 1947, reader in physics, 1949-51, professor of radio astronomy, 1951-80, professor emeritus, 1980-, Jodrell Bank Observatory, founder, director, 1951-80; Order of the British Empire, officer, 1946, 1964; Telecommunications Research Establishment, staff, 1939-45; University of Edinburgh, Visiting Montague Burton Professor of International Relations, 1973; Oxford University, Bickley lecturer, 1977. Writer. **Publications:** Science and Civilization, 1939; World Power Resources and Social Development, 1945; Electronics and Their Application in Industry and Research, 1947; (with J.A. Clegg) Radio Astronomy, 1952; Radio Astronomiia, 1953; Meteor Astronomy, 1954; (with R.H. Brown) The Exploration of Space by Radio, 1957; The Individual and the Universe, 1959; The Exploration of Outer Space, 1962; (with M.J. Lovell) Discovering the Universe, 1963; Impact of Modern Astronomy on the Problems of the Origins of life and the Cosmos, 1963; The Solar System, 1964; Our Present Knowledge of the Universe, 1967; (ed. with T. Margerison) The Explosion of Science, 1967; The Physical Universe, 1967; (co-author) The New Universe, 1968; The Story of Jodrell Bank, 1968, rev. ed. as Voice of the Universe: Building the Jodrell Bank Telescope, 1987; (ed.) Astronomy, 2 vols., 1970; Out of the Zenith: Jodrell Bank, 1957-70, 1973; The Origins and International Economics of Space Exploration, 1973; Man's Relation to the Universe, 1975; P.M.S. Blackett, 1976; In the Center of Immensities, 1978; Whence and Wherefore: The Cosmological Destiny of Man Scientifically and Philosophically Considered, 1978; Emerging Cosmology, 1981; The Jodrell Bank Telescopes, 1985; Voice of the Universe, 1987; (with F.G. Smith) Pathways to the Universe, 1988; Astronomer by Chance, 1990; Echoes of War, 1991; The Effect of Science on the Second World War, 2000. **Address:** Jodrell Bank Observatory, School of Physics & Astronomy, The University of Manchester, Macclesfield, CH SK11 9DL, England.

LOVELL, Glenville. American/Barbadian (born Barbados), b. 1955?. **Genres:** Novels, Young Adult Fiction, Mystery/Crime/Suspense, Literary Criticism And History. **Career:** Writer and actor. **Publications:** Fire in the Canes, 1995; Song of Night, 1998; Too Beautiful to Die, 2003; Love and Death in Brooklyn, 2004. **Address:** Soho Press, 853 Broadway, New York, NY 10003, U.S.A. **Online address:** glenville@glenvillelovell.com

LOVELL, Julia. British (born England), b. 1975?. **Genres:** History. **Career:** University of London, department of history, lecturer; Cambridge, Queen's College, professor of modern chinese literature. Writer. **Publications:** The Great Wall: China against the World, 1000 B.C.-A.D. 2000, 2006; The Politics of Cultural Capital: China's Quest for a Nobel Prize in Literature, 2006. TRANSLATOR: Han Shaogong, A Dictionary of Maqiao, 2003; (with E. Tyldesley) Xinran, Sky Burial, 2004; Nan Talese/Doubleday, 2005; I Love Dollars and Other Stories of China, 2006; Yan Lianke, Serve the People!, 2007; Eileen Chang, Lust, Caution: The Story, 2007. Contributor to journals. **Address:** School of History, Classics, and Archaeology, Birkbeck College, University of London, Rm. 320, 27 Russell Sq,, London, GL WC1B 5DQ, England. **Online address:** j.lovell@bbk.ac.uk

LOVELL, Marc. *See* **MCSHANE, Mark.**

LOVELL, Margaretta M. American (born United States), b. 1944. **Genres:** Art/Art History. **Career:** Yale Art Gallery, American Arts Department, curatorial assistant, 1972-75; Yale University, Department of Art History, acting assistant professor, 1978-80, assistant professor, 1980-81; University of California, Department of Art History, assistant professor, 1981-90, associate professor, 1992-2003, professor, 2003-, Jay D. McEvoy Jr. professor of American art and architecture, 2007-, American Studies Program, co-director, 1995-98, 1999-2000, director, 2003-04, American Studies Summer Institute, director, 2000; Fine Arts Museums of San Francisco, curator of American art, 1981-85; College of William & Mary, Duane A. and Virginia S. Dittman professor of American studies, 1991-92. Writer. **Publications:** Venice: The American View, 1860-1920, 1984; A Visitable Past: Views of Venice by American Artists, 1860-1915, 1989; Art in a Season of Revolution: Painters, Artisans, and Patrons in Early America, 2005; (contrib.) American Encounters: Art, History, and Cultural Identity, 2008. **Address:** Department of History of Art, University of California, 421A Doe Library, Ste. 6020, Berkeley, CA 94720, U.S.A. **Online address:** mmlovell@berkeley.edu

LOVELL, Mary S(ybilla). British (born England), b. 1940?. **Genres:** Novels, History, Local History/Rural Topics, Travel/Exploration, Biography. **Career:** Accountant and business director, 1963-83; technical writer and documentation manager, 1983-86; writer, 1986-. **Publications:** A Hunting Pageant, 1981; Cats as Pets, 1982; Straight on till Morning: The Biography of Beryl Markham, 1987; (ed.) The Splendid Outcast (stories), 1987; The Sound of Wings: The Life of Amelia Earhart, 1989; Cast No Shadow: The Life of the American Spy Who Changed the Course of World War II, 1992; Rebel Heart, the Biography of Jane Digby, 1995; A Rage to Live: Biography of Sir Richard F. Burton and Isabel (Lady) Burton, 1998; The Sisters (biography), 2001; The Mitford Girls: The Biography of an Extraordinary Family, 2005; Bess of Hardwick: First Lady of Chatsworth, 1527-1608, 2005; Churchills: In Love and War, 2011; One More Spring, forthcoming; Deadlier than the Male: Women Adventurers (anthology), forthcoming. **Address:** c/o Robert Ducas, The Barn House, 244 Westside Rd., Norfolk, CT 06058, U.S.A. **Online address:** mlovell2002@yahoo.com

LOVELY, Stephen. American (born United States), b. 1966. **Genres:** Novels, Mystery/Crime/Suspense. **Career:** Cell, editorial staff; University of Iowa Hospital, Pediatric Intensive Care Unit, night clerk; University of Iowa, Interdisciplinary Program in Literature, administrator, Center for Media Production, accountant, Iowa Young Writers' Studio, director, 2005-. **Publications:** Irreplaceable, 2009. **Address:** Iowa Young Writers' Studio, University of Iowa, C215 Seashore Hall, Iowa City, IA 52242-1402, U.S.A. **Online address:** stephenlovelynovel@gmail.com

LOVESEY, Peter (Harmer). (Peter Lear). British (born England), b. 1936. **Genres:** Novellas/Short Stories, Mystery/Crime/Suspense, Sports/Fitness, Young Adult Fiction. **Career:** Thurrock Technical College, senior lecturer, 1961-69; Hammersmith College, Department of General Education, head, 1969-75. Writer. **Publications:** The Kings of Distance: A Study of Five Great Runners, 1968 as Five Kings of Distance, 1981; (with T. McNab) The Guide to British Track and Field Literature, 1275-1968, 1969; Wobble to Death, 1970, rev. ed., 1999; The Detective Wore Silk Drawers, 1971; Abracadaver, 1972; Mad Hatter's Holiday: A Novel of Murder in Victorian Brighton, 1973; Invitation to a Dynamite Party in US as The Tick of Death, 1974; A Case of Spirits, 1975; Swing, Swing Together, 1976; Waxwork, 1978; The Official Centenary History of the Amateur Athletic Association, 1979; The False Inspector Dew, 1982; Keystone, 1983; Butchers and Other Stories of Crime, 1985; Rough Cider, 1986; Bertie and the Tinman, 1988; The Black Cabinet: Stories Based on True Crimes, 1989; On the Edge, 1989; The Staring Man and Other Stories, 1989; Bertie and the Seven Bodies, 1990; The Last Detective, 1991; Diamond Solitaire, 1992; Bertie and the Crime of Passion, 1993; The Crime of Miss Oyster Brown and Other Stories, 1994; (co-author) A Dead Giveaway, 1995; The Summons, 1995; Bloodhounds, 1996; Upon a Dark Night, 1997; Do Not Exceed the Stated Dose, 1998; The Vault, 2000; The Reaper, 2000; The Kiss of Death: A Peter Diamond Mystery, 2000; In Suspense, 2001; (comp. with T. McNab and A. Huxtable) An Athletics Compendium: A Guide to the Literature of Track and Field, 2001; The Sedgemoor Strangler and Other Stories of Crime, 2001; Dead Gorgeous, 2002; Diamond Dust, 2002; The House Sitter, 2003; The Circle, 2005; The Secret Hangman, 2007; The Headhunters, 2008; Murder on the Short List, 2008; Skeleton Hill, 2009; Stagestruck, 2011; Cop to Corpse, 2012. AS PETER LEAR: Goldengirl, 1977; Spider Girl, 1980; The Secret of Spandau, 1986. Contributor to periodicals. Works appear in anthologies. **Address:** Vanessa Holt Ltd., 59 Crescent Rd., Leigh-on-Sea, EX SS9 2PF, England. **Online address:** p.lovesey@virgin.net

LOVETT, Bobby L. American (born United States), b. 1943. **Genres:** Intellectual History, Biography, Autobiography/Memoirs, Theology/Religion. **Career:** White State High School, teacher, 1969-70; Eureka College, assistant professor of history, 1970-73; Tennessee State University, professor of history, 1973-, dean of arts and sciences, 1983-. Writer and historian. **Publications:** A Black Man's Dream: The First 100 Years: Richard Henry Boyd and the National Baptist Publishing Board, 1993; (ed. with L.T. Wynn) Profiles of African Americans in Tennessee, 1996; The African-American History of Nashville, Tennessee, 1780-1930: Elites and Dilemmas, 1999; (contrib.) The Southern Elite and Social Change: Essays in Honor of Willard B. Gatewood,

Jr. and The Art of William Edmondson, 2000; The Civil Rights Movement in Tennessee: A Narrative History, 2005; How It Came to Be: The Boyd Family's Contribution to African American Religious Publishing from the 19th to the 21st Century, 2007. Contributor to journals. **Address:** Department of History, Geography, and Political Sc, Tennessee State University, 320 Crouch Hall, 3500 John A. Merritt Blvd., Nashville, TN 37209-1561, U.S.A. **Online address:** blovett@tnstate.edu

LOVETT, Sarah. American (born United States), b. 1953?. **Genres:** Travel/Exploration, Children's Non-fiction, Zoology, Mystery/Crime/Suspense. **Career:** Office of the Attorney General, legal researcher; New Mexico State Penitentiary, forensic researcher; writer, 1989-; theater director and playwright. **Publications:** TRAVEL BOOKS: Kidding around London: A Family Guide to the City, 1989; Kidding around London: A Young Person's Guide to the City, 1989; Kidding around NYC: A Young Person's Guide to the City, 1989; Kidding around the Hawaiian Islands: A Young Person's Guide, 1990; Kidding around the National Parks of the Southwest: A Young Person's Guide, 1990; Unique Colorado: A Guide to the State's Quirks, Charisma, and Character, 1993; Unique Florida: A Guide to the State's Quirks, Charisma and Character, 1993; Unique New Mexico: A Guide to the State's Quirks, Charisma and Character, 1993; Unique New England: A Guide to the Region's Quirks, Charisma and Character, 1994; Unique Texas: A Guide to the State's Quirks, Charisma and Character, 1994. OTHERS: Kidding around New York City: A Young Person's Guide to the City, 1989; (contrib.) Primates, 1991; (contrib.) Fishes, 1992; (contrib.) Mammals, 1996; (contrib.) Bats, 1996; (contrib.) Reptiles, 1996; (contrib.) Insects, 1996; Animal Hunter, 1997; Dark Alchemy, 2003. EXTREMELY WEIRD SERIES: Extremely Weird Reptiles, 1991, 2nd ed., 1992; Extremely Weird Primates, 1991; Extremely Weird Birds, 2nd ed., 1992; Extremely Weird Endangered Species, 1992, 2nd ed., 1996; Extremely Weird Fishes, 1992; Extremely Weird Insects, 1992; Extremely Weird Sea Creatures, 2nd ed., 1992; Extremely Weird Mammals, 1993, 2nd ed., 1996; Extremely Weird Micro Monsters, 1993; Extremely Weird Snakes, 1993; Extremely Weird Spiders, 1996; Extremely Weird Bats, 2nd ed., 1996; Extremely Weird Frogs, 2nd ed., 1996; Encyclopedia of Extremely Weird Animals, 1997; Extremely Weird Animal Defenses, 1997; Extremely Weird Animal Disguises, 1997; Extremely Weird Animal Hunters, 1997. MYSTERIES: Dangerous Attachments, 1995; Acquired Motives, 1996; A Desperate Silence, 1997; Dantes' Inferno, 2001. Contributor to periodicals. **Address:** Theresa Pk., Sanford J. Greenburger Associates Inc., 55 5th Ave., New York, NY 10003, U.S.A. **Online address:** sarah@sarahlovett.com

LOVRIC, Michelle. Australian (born Australia), b. 1959?. **Genres:** Novels, Cultural/Ethnic Topics, Language/Linguistics, Medicine/Health, Humor/Satire, Classics, Animals/Pets, Translations, Translations. **Career:** Courtauld Institute of Art, Royal Literary Fund Fellow, 2010-. Novelist. **Publications:** (Comp.) Birds: An Illustrated Treasury, 1992; (comp.) Cats: An Illustrated Treasury, 1992; (comp.) Love: An Illustrated Treasury, 1992; (comp.) Women: An Illustrated Treasury, 1993; (comp.) Friends: An Illustrated Treasury of friendship, 1993; (comp.) Seasons: An Illustrated Treasury, 1993; Mothers: An Illustrated Treasury of Motherhood, 1993; (with M. Philo) Victorian Decoupage: Sourcebook with 10 Projects, 1994; (comp.) Horses: An Illustrated Treasury, 1994; (comp.) Kittens: An Illustrated Treasury, 1994; Love Letters: An Illustrated Treasury, 1994; (comp.) Christmas: An Illustrated Treasury, 1994; Roses: An Illustrated Treasury, 1995; (with M. Philo) Victorian Christmas: Sourcebook with 10 Projects, 1995; (comp.) The Countryside: An Illustrated Treasury, 1995; How to Write Love Letters, 1996; (with N.D. Mardas) The Sweetness of Honey and the Sting of Bees: A Book of Love from the Ancient Mediterranean, 1997; (with M. Philo) Victorian Cats, 1997; Bleeding Hearts: Love Poems for the Nervous & Highly Strung, 1998; (with N.D. Mardas) How to Insult, Abuse, & Insinuate in Classical Latin, 1998; (with L. Chambers) Latin Stuff & Nonsense, 1999; (ed.) Weird Wills & Eccentric Last Wishes, 2000; (ed.) Eccentric Epitaphs: Gaffes from beyond the Grave, 2000; Cleopatra's Face: Fatal Beauty, 2001; Women's Wicked Wit: From Jane Austen to Roseanne Barr, 2000; Carnevale, 2001; Insult and Curse Book, 2002; (intro.) The Virago Book of Christmas, 2002; Venice: Tales of the City, 2003; The Floating Book, 2003; (with J. Quickfall) How to Seduce, Pleasure, & Titillate in Classical Latin, 2003; The World's Greatest Letters: From Ancient Greece to the Twentieth Century, 2004; Women's Wicked Wisdom, 2004; More Women's Wicked Wit, 2004; Ladies Bits, 2004; The Remedy: A Novel of London and Venice, 2005; Cowgirls, Cockroaches and Celebrity Lingerie, The World's Most Unusual Museums, 2008; Book of Human Skin, 2010; The Mourning Emporium, 2010; The Undrowned Child (children's novel), 2011. Contributor to periodicals. **Address:** c/o Victoria Hobbs, A.M.

Heath, 6 Warwick Ct., London, GL WC1R 5DJ, England. **Online address:** ml@michellelovric.com

LOW, Anthony. American (born United States), b. 1935. **Genres:** Literary Criticism And History, Poetry. **Career:** Seattle University, assistant professor of English, 1965-68; New York University, assistant professor, 1968-71, associate professor, 1971-78, Department of English, professor, 1978-2006, chairman, 1989-95, professor emeritus, 2006-; Conference on Christianity and Literature, president, 1996-2000. Writer. **Publications:** Augustine Baker, 1970; The Blaze of Noon: A Reading of Samson Agonistes, 1974; Love's Architecture: Devotional Modes in Seventeenth-Century English Poetry, 1978; (ed.) Urbane Milton: The Latin Poems, 1984; The Georgic Revolution, 1985; The Reinvention of Love: Poetry, Politics and Culture from Sidney to Milton, 1993; Aspects of Subjectivity: Society and Individuality from the Middle Ages to Shakespeare and Milton, 2003. Contributor to journals. **Address:** Department of English, New York University, 19 University Pl., New York, NY 10003, U.S.A. **Online address:** al2@nyu.edu

LOW, Brian J. Canadian (born Canada), b. 1950. **Genres:** History, Social Sciences, Education, Film, Adult Non-fiction. **Career:** University of British Columbia, instructor, 1994-98; National Hua Qiao University, instructor, 1999-2002; Brock University, instructor, 2002; Oxbridge University, instructor, 2002-03. Writer. **Publications:** NFB Kids: Portrayals of Children by the National Film Board of Canada, 1939-1989, 2002; The New Generation?: Mental Hygiene and the Portrayals of Children by the National Film Board of Canada, 1946-1967, 2003; Lessons in Living: Film Propaganda and Progressive Education, 2003; The Hand that Rocked the Cradle: A Critical Analysis of Rockefeller Philanthropic Funding, 1920-1960, 2004; English Intensive Reading 5, 2008. **Address:** Wilfrid Laurier University Press, 75 University Ave. W, Waterloo, ON N2L 3C5, Canada. **Online address:** bjlow99@yahoo.com

LOW, Kathleen. American (born United States) **Genres:** Librarianship, History. **Career:** University of California, copy cataloger, 1980-83, Shields Library, student assistant, King Hall School of Law Library, student assistant; CLASS, online coordinator, 1983-84; California State Library, online reference librarian, 1984-88, database specialist, 1988-89, outreach services manager, 1989-92, principal librarian, 1992, Library Development Services Bureau, library programs consultant, 1992-. Writer. **Publications:** Electronic Access to Government and Government Information: A Selective Bibliography, 1991; Legislative Reference Services and Sources, 1995; (ed.) Roles of Reference Librarians: Today and Tomorrow, 1996; Recruiting Library Staff: A How-to-Do-It Manual for Librarians, 1999; Casanova was a Librarian: A Light-Hearted Look at the Profession, 2007. Contributor to magazines. **Address:** Library Development Services Bureau, California State Library, Rm. 100, Library and Courts Bldg. II, 900 North St., 4th Fl., Sacramento, CA 95814-4800, U.S.A. **Online address:** klow@library.ca.gov

LOW, Robert. Scottish/British (born England), b. 1949. **Genres:** Novels. **Career:** Sunday Post, staff journalist, 1967-68; freelance journalist, 1968-70; Daily Record, features writer, 1971-2003; freelance journalist and author, 2003-. **Publications:** OATHSWORN SERIES: The Whale Road, 2007; The Wolf Sea, 2008; The White Raven, 2009; The Prow Beast, 2010. KINGDOM TRILOGY: The Lion Wakes, 2011; The Lion at Bay, 2012. OTHERS: (with M. Bles) The Kidnap Business, 1987; (ed.) The Observer Book of Profiles, 1991. **Address:** HarperCollins Publishers, 10 East 53rd St., New York, NY 10022-5244, U.S.A. **Online address:** robert@robert-low.com

LOW, Setha M. American (born United States), b. 1948. **Genres:** Cultural/ Ethnic Topics, Social Sciences, Architecture, Anthropology/Ethnology, Psychology. **Career:** San Francisco State College (now University), instructor in anthropology, 1971; University of Pennsylvania, assistant professor, 1976-82, associate professor of landscape architecture and regional planning, anthropology and city planning, 1982-88, Center for the Study of Aging, associate faculty, 1982-87, Leonard Davis Institute of Health Economics, associate faculty, 1984-87, visiting lecturer, 1992-95; Universidad de Costa Rica, honorary professor, 1986-87; City University of New York, Graduate School and University Center, professor of environmental psychology and anthropology, 1987-, Public Space Research Group, director, 1988-; York University, visiting professor, 1991; New York University, visiting professor, 1995. Writer. **Publications:** Culture, Politics, and Medicine in Costa Rica: An Anthropological Study of Medical Change, 1985; (with F. Johnston) Children of the

Urban Poor: The Sociocultural Environment of Growth, Development, and Malnutrition in Guatemala City, 1995; On the Plaza: The Politics of Public Space and Culture, 2000; Behind the Gates: Life, Security, and the Pursuit of Happiness in Fortress America, 2003; (with D. Taplin and S. Scheld) Rethinking Urban Parks: Public Space and Cultural Diversity, 2005. EDITOR: (with E. Chambers) Housing, Culture, and Design: A Comparative Perspective, 1989; (with D.L. Davis) Gender, Health, and Illness: The Case of Nerves, 1989; (with I. Altman) Place Attachment, 1992; Theorizing the City: The New Urban Anthropology Reader, 1999; (with D. Lawrence-Zúñiga) Anthropology of Space and Place: Locating Culture, 2003; (with N. Smith) Politics of Public Space, 2006. Contributor of books to articles. **Address:** Graduate Center, City University of New York, 365 5th Ave., New York, NY 10016-4309, U.S.A. **Online address:** slow@gc.cuny.edu

LOW, Shari. Scottish (born Scotland), b. 1967?. **Genres:** Young Adult Non-fiction, Novels. **Career:** Sheraton Hotel-Shanghai, manager of hotel nightclub, 1989; Sheraton Hotel-Hong Kong, manager of leisure complex, 1990-91; Hilton Hotel, manager, 1991. Daily Record, columnist; Pinewood Studios, satellite communications salesperson, 2000. **Publications:** What If?, 2001 in German as Torschlusspanik, 2003; Double Trouble in German as Marchen Prinz Auf Abruf, 2004; Why Not? in German as Saure Gurken Zeit, 2004; Freunde, Sex und Alibis, 2006; The Motherhood Walk of Fame in German as Happy Ohne Ende, 2007; My Best Friend's Life in German as Treuesprünge, 2008; A Brand New Me in German as Sternschnuppern, 2008; Herzfinsternis, 2009; Temptation Street, 2010. **Address:** c/o Sheila Crowley, A.P. Watt Ltd., 20 John St., London, GL WC1N 2DR, England. **Online address:** readers@sharilow.com

LOWDEN, Desmond Scott. British (born England), b. 1937. **Genres:** Mystery/Crime/Suspense, Plays/Screenplays, Novels, Young Adult Fiction, Horror. **Career:** Pinewood-Shepperton Studios, movie assistant director and assistant editor, 1956-60; television and film writer, 1963-70; novelist, 1970-. **Publications:** NOVELS: Bandersnatch, 1969; The Boondocks, 1972; Bellman and True, 1975; Boudapesti 3, 1979; Sunspot, 1981; (co-author) Winter's Crimes 14, 1982; Cry Havoc, 1984; The Shadow Run, 1989; Once in Royal, 1989; The Chain, 1990. **Address:** Rogers, Coleridge and White, 20 Powis Mews, London, GL W11 1JN, England.

LOWE, Ben(no P.). American (born United States), b. 1956. **Genres:** History, Intellectual History, Theology/Religion, Area Studies. **Career:** Barry University, assistant professor of history, 1990-93; Florida Atlantic University, assistant professor, 1993-96, associate professor of history, 1996-2011, professor of history, 2011-; Graduate Program, director; Religious Studies, director. Historian and writer. **Publications:** Imagining Peace: A History of Early English Pacifist Thought, 1340-1560, 1997; Commonwealth and the English Reformation: Protestantism and the Politics of Religious Change in the Gloucester Vale, 1483-1560, 2010. Contributor to books. **Address:** Department of History, Florida Atlantic University, 777 Glades Rd., Boca Raton, FL 33431, U.S.A. **Online address:** bplowe@fau.edu

LOWE, Helen. New Zealander (born New Zealand), b. 1961?. **Genres:** Novels. **Career:** Women on Air (monthly poetry feature on New Zealand public radio 96.9FM), host. Novelist. **Publications:** Thornspell (novel), 2009. Works appear in anthologies. Contributor to periodicals. **Address:** c/o Robin Rue, Writers House Literary Agency, 21 W 26th St., New York, NY 10010, U.S.A.

LOWE, Jack Phillips. American (born United States), b. 1969. **Genres:** Poetry, Novellas/Short Stories. **Career:** Roosevelt University, teacher's assistant, 1996; freelance copy editor and proofreader, 1998-2003, 2006-10. Writer. **Publications:** So Much for Paradise, 2000; Long Form, 2003; Pariah Tales, 2007; Revolt at the Internet Cafe, 2010. **Address:** PO Box 39, Addison, IL 60101, U.S.A. **Online address:** jlowe169@hotmail.com

LOWE, Joy L. American (born United States), b. 1939. **Genres:** Adult Non-fiction, Education. **Career:** Opelousas-Eunice Public Library, administrative librarian, 1967-70; Glenbrook School, librarian, 1973-75; Louisiana Tech University, associate professor, 1977-2003, senate chair, 1994-95. Writer. **Publications:** WITH K.I. MATTHEW: Neal-Schuman Guide to Recommended Children's Books and Media for Use with Every Elementary Subject, 2002, 2nd ed., 2010; Colonial America in Literature for Youth: A Guide and Resource Book, 2003; Discoveries and Inventions in Literature for Youth: A Guide and Resource Book, 2004; Neal-Schuman Guide to Celebrations and

Holidays around the World: The Best Books, Media, and Multicultural Learning Activities, 2004; Puppet Magic, 2007. **Address:** 9712 Hwy. 146, Ruston, LA 71270-7021, U.S.A. **Online address:** joyjlowe@bellsouth.net

LOWE, Keith. British (born England), b. 1970?. **Genres:** Novels, History, Military/Defense/Arms Control. **Career:** Cassell, non-fiction editor. **Publications:** Tunnel Vision (novel), 2001; New Free Chocolate Sex (novel), 2005; Inferno: The Fiery Destruction of Hamburg, 1943, 2007. Contributor to periodicals. **Address:** Peters Fraser and Dunlop Group Ltd., Drury House, 34-43 Russell St., London, GL WC2B 5HA, England.

LOWE, Mick. Canadian/American (born United States), b. 1947. **Genres:** Adult Non-fiction. **Career:** Daily Nebraskan, staff writer and columnist, 1966-68; Lincoln Daily Star, staff writer, 1967-68; Georgia Straight, staff writer and columnist, 1970-72; The Grape, co-founder, 1972; Gauntlet, editor, 1973-74; Globe and Mail, freelance correspondent, 1974-76, 1979-87; CBC Radio News, staff reporter, 1977-78; CBC Radio Morning North Sudbury, founding producer, 1978; Cambrian College, lecturer in journalism, 1988-90. **Publications:** Conspiracy of Brothers: A True Story of Murder, Bikers, and the Law, 1989; One Woman Army: The Life of Claire Culhane, 1992; Premature Bonanza: Standoff at Voisey's Bay, 1998. Contributor of articles to periodicals. **Address:** c/o Seal Books, 105 Bond St., Toronto, ON M5B 1Y3, Canada.

LOWE, Rodney. British (born England), b. 1946. **Genres:** History, Politics/Government, Public/Social Administration, Economics. **Career:** Heriot-Watt University, lecturer in history, 1972-78; University of Bristol, honorary research fellow, professor of contemporary history, 1979-, now professor emeritus; Australian National University, visiting research fellow, 1994; British Government, Cabinet Office, official historian, through 2008. Writer. **Publications:** Conflict and Consensus in British Industrial Relations, 1916-1948: A Listing and Guide to the Harvester Microfilm Collection: Selected from PRO Classes Lab 2, Lab 10, Lab 27, Lab 31, Lab 34, PRO 30/69, T1, T162, 1985; Adjusting to Democracy: The Role of The Ministry of Labour in British Politics, 1916-1939, 1986; (with B.W.E. Alford and N. Rollings) Economic Planning 1943-51: A Guide to Documents in the Public Record Office, 1992; (with A. Land and N. Whiteside) Development of the Welfare State, 1939-51: A Guide to Documents in the Public Record Office, 1992; The Welfare State in Britain since 1945, 1993, 3rd ed., 2005; (with P. Bridgen) Welfare Policy Under the Conservatives, 1951-1964: A Guide to Documents in the Public Record Office, 1998; (ed. with H. Fawcett) Welfare Policy in Britain: The Road From 1945, 1999; (with M. Jones) From Beveridge to Blair: The First Fifty Years of Britain's Welfare State, 2002; Official History of the British Civil Service: Reforming the Civil Service, 2011. **Address:** Department of Historical Studies, University of Bristol, 11 Woodland Rd., Bristol, BS8 1TB, England. **Online address:** r.lowe@bristol.ac.uk

LOWE, Sheila. British (born England) **Genres:** Mystery/Crime/Suspense, Novels, Adult Non-fiction, How-to Books, Psychology, E-books. **Career:** Sheila Lowe & Associates, owner. Writer. **Publications:** The Complete Idiot's Guide to Handwriting Analysis, 1999, 2nd ed., 2007; Handwriting of the Famous and Infamous, 2000, 2nd ed., 2009; Poison Pen, 2007; Written in Blood: A Forensic Handwriting Mystery, 2008; Dead Write: A Forensic Handwriting Mystery, 2009; Last Writes: A Forensic Handwriting Mystery, 2009. **Address:** Sheila Lowe & Associates, Ventura, CA 93004, U.S.A. **Online address:** sheila@sheilalowe.com

LOWE, Stephen. British (born England), b. 1947. **Genres:** Plays/Screenplays, Young Adult Fiction, Translations. **Career:** Stephen Joseph Theatre-in-the-Round, actor and director, 1975-78; Dartington College of Arts, senior lecturer, 1978-82; Meeting Ground Theatre Co., co-artistic director, 1984-; Meeting Ground Theatre Co., director; Royal Court Theatre, resident playwright; Riverside Studios, resident playwright; Dartington College of Arts, resident playwright; Arts Council England, chair. Artistic director. **Publications:** Touched, 1977, 1981; The Ragged Trousered Philanthropists, 1978, rev. ed., 1983; Tibetan Inroads, 1981; Cards, 1983; Moving Pictures: Four Plays, 1985; (ed. and intro.) Peace Plays, 2 vols., 1985, 1989; Divine Gossip, 1989; (trans.) William Tell, 1989; Old Big 'Ead in the Spirit of the Man, 2005; Empty Bed Blues, 2010. **Address:** c/o Howard Gooding, Judy Daish Associates, 2 St. Charles Pl., London, GL W10 6EG, England. **Online address:** steph@stephenlowe.co.uk

LOWE, Tom. American (born United States), b. 1952. **Genres:** Novels. Ca-

reer: Writer. **Publications:** A False Dawn (novel), 2009. **Address:** c/o Phyllis Wesyberg, Harold Ober Associates Literary Agency, 425 Madison Ave., New York, NY 10017, U.S.A. **Online address:** tomlowebooks@gmail.com

LOWE-EVANS, Mary. American (born United States), b. 1941. **Genres:** Literary Criticism And History, Essays, Young Adult Fiction. **Career:** University of West Florida, assistant professor, 1987-91, associate professor, 1991-94, Women Faculty Equity Commission, chair, 1991-, College of Arts and Sciences, associate dean, 1993-96, Women's Studies Program, director, 1993-96, chair of the department, professor of English and foreign languages, 1994-, now professor emeritus; American Association of University Women, vice president, 1993-94. Writer. **Publications:** Crimes Against Fecundity: Joyce and Population Control, 1989; Frankenstein: Mary Shelley's Wedding Guest, 1993; (ed.) Critical Essays on Mary Wollstonecraft Shelley, 1998; Catholic Nostalgia in Joyce and Company, 2008. Contributor to books and periodicals. **Address:** College of Arts & Social Sciences, University of West Florida, Bldg. 50, Rm. 247, 11000 University Pkwy., Pensacola, FL 32514, U.S.A. **Online address:** mevans@uwf.edu

LOWELL, Pamela. American (born United States) **Genres:** Young Adult Fiction, Women's Studies And Issues, Novels. **Career:** Author and therapist. **Publications:** Survival Meditations for Parents of Teens, 2004; Returnable Girl (young-adult novel), 2006; Spotting for Nellie, 2009. Contributor to periodicals. **Address:** c/o Susan Schulman, 454 W 44th St., New York, NY 10036-5205, U.S.A. **Online address:** palwrites@aol.com

LOWENBERG, Anton D(avid). American/South African (born South Africa), b. 1957. **Genres:** Economics, Social Sciences, Business/Trade/Industry, International Relations/Current Affairs, Politics/Government. **Career:** California State University, assistant professor, 1984-92, professor of economics, 1992-. Writer. **Publications:** WITH W.H. KAEMPFER: International Economic Sanctions: A Public Choice Perspective, 1992; The Origins and Demise of South African Apartheid: A Public Choice Analysis, 1998. **Address:** Department of Economics, California State University, Juniper Hall JH4238, 18111 Nordhoff St., Northridge, CA 91330-8374, U.S.A. **Online address:** anton.lowenberg@csun.edu

LOWENBERG, Susan. American (born United States), b. 1957. **Genres:** Literary Criticism And History, Reference, Novels, Romance/Historical. **Career:** Bradley University, librarian, 1981-86; California State University Library, chair of circulation department, 1986-89; University of Colorado, head of access services department, 1989-90, science librarian and curator of Map Library, 1991-92; California Institute of the Arts, librarian of information resources and theatre/dance, 1993-99, associate dean, 1999-. Writer. **Publications:** C.S. Lewis: A Reference Guide, 1972-1988, 1993; Alaric's Song, 2008. **Address:** California Institute of the Arts Library, 24700 McBean Pkwy., Valencia, CA 91355-2397, U.S.A. **Online address:** susan.lowenberg@susanlowenberg.com

LOWENSTEIN, Michael W. American (born United States), b. 1942. **Genres:** Business/Trade/Industry, Administration/Management, Marketing, Industrial Relations. **Career:** Customer Retention Associates, managing director, 1995-; ROI Systems, consultant; Market Probe Inc., executive vice president. Writer. **Publications:** Customer Retention: An Integrated Process for Keeping Your Best Customers, 1995; (co-author) Redefining Consumer Affairs, 1996; The Customer Loyalty Pyramid, 1997; (with J. Griffin) Customer Winback: How to Recapture Lost Customers and Keep Them Loyal, 2001; One Customer, Divisible: Linking Customer Insight to Loyalty and Advocacy Behavior, 2005; The Customer Advocate and the Customer Saboteur, 2011; Customer Retention Blueprints, forthcoming. Contributor to periodicals. **Address:** Market Probe Inc., 2655 North Mayfair Rd., Milwaukee, WI 53226, U.S.A. **Online address:** lowen1@directtvinternet.com

LOWENTHAL, Cynthia J. American (born United States), b. 1952. **Genres:** Literary Criticism And History, History, Art/Art History. **Career:** Brandeis University, teaching assistant, 1983-87; Tulane University, Department of English and American Literature, assistant professor, 1987-93, associate professor, 1993-2006, faculty associate of women's studies, 1991-2005, graduate faculty, 1994-2005, Liberal Arts and Sciences, associate dean, 1994-2000, Newcomb College, dean, 2000-06; College of Charleston, School of Humanities and Social Sciences, dean and professor of English department, 2006-. Writer. **Publications:** Lady Mary Wortley Montagu and the Eighteenth-Century Familiar Letter, 1994; Performing Identities on the Restoration Stage,

2003. **Address:** Department of English, Tulane University, Newcomb 108, New Orleans, LA 70118, U.S.A. **Online address:** lowenth@tulane.edu

LOWENTHAL, Gary T(obias). American (born United States) **Genres:** Law, Biography, Mystery/Crime/Suspense. **Career:** U.S. Bureau of Prisoners, assistant, 1968; Morrison & Foerster, attorney, 1969; University of California, School of Law, legal writing instructor, 1969-70; Alameda County, assistant public defender, 1970-74; Lowenthal & Zimmerman, partner, 1974-76; Arizona State University, professor of law, 1976-2007, director of clinical programs, 1993-97, Sandra Day O'Connor College of Law, now professor emeritus; Maricopa County Attorney's Office, deputy county attorney, 1977-78; University of Virginia, School of Law, visiting professor, 1979; Stanford Law School, visiting professor, 1984-85; Maricopa County Superior Court, 1998-. Writer. **Publications:** Down and Dirty Justice: A Chilling Journey into the Dark World of Crime and the Criminal Courts, 2003. Contributor to journals. **Address:** College of Law, Arizona State University, PO Box 877906, Tempe, AZ 85287-7906, U.S.A. **Online address:** gary.lowenthal@asu.edu

LOWER, Michael T. American (born United States) **Genres:** History. **Career:** University of Minnesota, Department of History, faculty. Historian, educator and writer. **Publications:** The Barons Crusade: A Call to Arms and Its Consequences, 2005. Contributor to periodicals. **Address:** University of Minnesota, 101 Pleasant St. SE, Minneapolis, MN 55455, U.S.A. **Online address:** mlower@umn.edu

LOWERY, Robert G. American (born United States), b. 1941. **Genres:** Essays, Biography, Reference. **Career:** Sean O'Casey Review, publisher, 1974-82; Irish Literary Supplement, publisher, 1982-. Writer. **Publications:** Sean O'Casey's Autobiographies: An Annotated Index, 1983. EDITOR: (with D. Krause) Sean O'Casey: Centenary Essays, 1980; Essays on Sean O'Casey's Autobiographies, 1981; From Times Past: Brooks Atkinson on Sean O'Casey, 1982; A Whirlwind in Dublin: The Plough Riots and the Star Riots, 1984; (with P. Angelin) My Very Dear Sean: George Jean Nathan on Sean O'Casey-Letters and Reviews, 1985. Contributor of articles to journals. **Address:** 2592 N Wading River Rd., Wading River, NY 11792-1404, U.S.A.

LOWING, Anne. See GEACH, Christine.

LOWNDES, Joseph E. American (born United States), b. 1966. **Genres:** Politics/Government. **Career:** University of Oregon, assistant professor of political science, 2003-. Writer. **Publications:** (With J. Novkov and D. Warren) Race and American Political Development, 2008; From the New Deal to the New Right: Race and the Southern Origins of Modern Conservatism, 2008. Contributor of articles to periodicals. **Address:** Eugene, OR , U.S.A. **Online address:** jlowndes@uoregon.edu

LOWRY, Lois (Hammersberg). American (born United States), b. 1937. **Genres:** Children's Fiction, Young Adult Fiction, Literary Criticism And History, Picture/Board Books, Novels, Education, Sociology, Young Adult Non-fiction, Young Adult Non-fiction. **Career:** Writer and photographer, 1972-. **Publications:** JUVENILE NOVELS: Values and the Family, 1977; A Summer to Die, 1977; Find a Stranger, Say Goodbye, 1978; Anastasia Krupnik, 1979; Autumn Street, 1980; Anastasia Again!, 1981; Anastasia at Your Service, 1982; The One Hundredth Thing about Caroline, 1983; Taking Care of Terrific, 1983; Anastasia, Ask Your Analyst, 1984; Us and Uncle Fraud, 1984; Anastasia on Her Own, 1985; Switcharound, 1985; Anastasia Has the Answers, 1986; Anastasia's Chosen Career, 1987; Rabble Starkey, 1987; All About Sam, 1988; Number the Stars, 1989; Your Move, J.P.!, 1990; Anastasia at This Address, 1991; Attaboy, Sam!, 1992; The Giver, 1993; Anastasia, Absolutely, 1995; See You Around Sam!, 1996; Stay!: Keepers Story, 1997; Looking Back: A Book of Memories, 1998; Zooman Sam, 1999; Gathering Blue, 2000; Gooney Bird Greene, 2002; The Silent Boy, 2003; The Messenger, 2004; Gooney Bird and the Room Mother, 2005; Gossamer, 2006; Gooney, The Fabulous, 2007; The Willoughbys, 2008; Crow Call, 2009; Gooney Bird is so Absurd, 2009; Birthday Ball, 2010; Bless this Mouse, 2011; Like the Willow Tree: The Diary of Lydia Amelia Pierce, 2011. OTHER: Black American Literature, 1973; Literature of the American Revolution, 1974; (intro.) Dear Author: Students Write about the Books That Changed Their Lives, 1998; Looking Back: A Book of Memories, 1998; Gooney Bird on the Map, 2011. Contributor of articles to periodicals. **Address:** c/o Phyllis Westberg, Harold Ober Associates, 425 Madison Ave., New York, NY 10017-1110, U.S.A. **Online address:** info@loislowry.com

LOWRY, Ritchie Peter. American (born United States), b. 1926. **Genres:** Sociology. **Career:** California State University, instructor, associate professor of sociology, 1955-64; American University, Special Operations Research Office, senior research scientist, associate professor of research, 1964-66; Basic Studies Division, acting chair, 1964-65, professorial lecturer in sociology; Boston College, Department of Sociology, professor of sociology, 1966-, chair, 1967-70, now professor emeritus; Good Money Inc., founder, president, 1982-. Writer. **Publications:** Who's Running This Town? Community Leadership and Social Change, 1965; (ed.) Problems of Studying Military Roles in Other Cultures: A Working Conference, 1967; (with R.P. Rankin) Sociology: The Science of Society, 1968, 3rd ed. as Sociology: Social Science and Social Concern, 1977; Social Problems: A Critical Analysis of Theory and Public Policy, 1973; Information Flow in Government Agencies, 1977; Looking Different Ways, 1977; Bridging the Gap: Public, Scientific, and Policy Views of Rape, 1978; A Meta-Analysis of Research Grant Applications Assigned to the NIMH Work and Mental Health Program, 1984; Good Money: A Guide to Socially Responsible Investing for the '90s, 1991. **Address:** Department of Sociology, Boston College, 422 McGuinn Hall, 140 Commonwealth Ave., Chestnut Hill, MA 02467-3807, U.S.A. **Online address:** goodmoney1@aol.com

LOWRY, William R. American (born United States), b. 1953. **Genres:** Politics/Government, Environmental Sciences/Ecology. **Career:** OSCO Drug Stores, assistant manager, 1979-81; The Brookings Institution, research fellow, 1987-88; Washington University, assistant professor, 1988-95, associate professor, 1995-2003, professor, 2003-05, 2006-, director of undergraduate studies for political science, 1995-2000; associate chair, 1999-2001, director of graduate studies, 2001-02, Environmental Studies Program, co-founder. Writer. **Publications:** The Dimensions of Federalism: State Governments and Pollution Control Policies, 1992; The Capacity for Wonder: Preserving National Parks, 1994; Preserving Public Lands for the Future: The Politics of Intergenerational Goods, 1998; Dam Politics: Restoring America's Rivers, 2003; Repairing Paradise: The Restoration of Nature in America's National Parks, 2009. **Address:** Department of Political Science, Washington University, 243 Seigle, 1 Brookings Dr., PO Box 1063, St. Louis, MO 63130-4899, U.S.A. **Online address:** lowry@wustl.edu

LOWY, Jonathan. American (born United States) **Genres:** Novels, Young Adult Fiction, Literary Criticism And History. **Career:** Writer. **Publications:** Elvis and Nixon, 2001; The Temple of Music, 2004. Contributor to periodicals. **Address:** c/o Author Mail, Crown Publishers, 1745 Broadway, New York, NY 10019, U.S.A.

LOXLEY, James. Scottish (born Scotland), b. 1968?. **Genres:** Literary Criticism And History, Theology/Religion. **Career:** University of Edinburgh, lecturer in English literature, senior lecturer in English literature and head of department. Writer. **Publications:** Royalism and Poetry in the English Civil Wars: The Drawn Sword, 1997; The Complete Critical Guide to Ben Jonson, 2002; Performativity, 2006. Contributor to books and journals. **Address:** Department of English Literature, University of Edinburgh, Office 6.14, David Hume Twr., George Sq., Edinburgh, EH8 9JX, Scotland. **Online address:** james.loxley@ed.ac.uk

LOY, Rosetta. Italian (born Italy), b. 1931. **Genres:** Novels. **Career:** Writer. **Publications:** NOVELS: La bicicletta, 1974; La porta dell'acqua, 1976; L'estate di Letuqué, 1982; All'insaputa della notte, 1984; Le strade di polvere, 1987; Sogni d'inverno, 1992; Cioccolata da Hanselmann, 1995; La parola ebreo, 1997; Ahi, Paloma, 2000; Nero è l'albero dei ricordi, azzurra l'aria, 2004; Prima Mano, 2009; Cuori Infranti, 2010. **Address:** c/o Giovanna Cau, via Maria Adelaide 8, Rome, 00196, Italy. **Online address:** r.loy@libero.it

LOZA, Steven (Joseph). American (born United States), b. 1952. **Genres:** Music. **Career:** University of California, associate professor, professor of ethnomusicology, Latin American Center, associate director, research and director of music department, Undergraduate Studies, director, Mexican Arts Series, director, 1986-96; University of Chile, School of Music, staff, 1989; Kanda University of International Studies, faculty, 1996-97; latin jazz performer and producer; University of New Mexico, lecturer III, adjunct professor of music, College of Fine Arts, Arts of Americas Institute, head. Writer. **Publications:** Barrio Rhythm: Mexican American Music in Los Angeles, 1993; (ed.) Selected Reports in Ethnomusicology 10: Musical Aesthetics and Multiculturalism in Los Angeles, 1994; Tito Puente and the Making of Latin Music, 1999; (ed.) Religion as Art: Guadalupe, Orishas, and Sufi, 2009. **Address:** Department of Ethnomusicology, University of California, 445 Charles E. Young Dr. E, 2539 Schoenberg Music Bldg., Los Angeles, CA 90095-1616, U.S.A. **Online address:** sloza@ucla.edu

LU, Ning. Chinese (born China), b. 1955. **Genres:** Politics/Government, Social Work. **Career:** Government of China, analyst, 1975-87; International Center, fellow, 1988-93; Atlantic Council, senior fellow, 1994-95; SPH (newspaper), senior correspondent, 1995-; World Bank, consultant. Writer. **Publications:** Flashpoint Spratlys, 1995; The Dynamics of Foreign-Policy Decision Making in China, 1997, 2nd ed., 2000. **Address:** SPH/BT, 390 Kim Seng Rd., Singapore, 239495, China. **Online address:** luming@sph.com.sg

LU, Suping. American (born United States), b. 1955. **Genres:** History, Politics/Government. **Career:** University of Nebraska, assistant professor, associate professor, 1994-2006, professor, 2006-. Writer and historian. **Publications:** They Were in Nanjing: The Nanjing Massacre Witnessed by American and British Nationals, 2004; (ed. and intro.) Terror in Minnie Vautrin's Nanjing: Diaries and Correspondence, 1937-38, 2008; (ed.) A Mission under Duress: The Nanjing Massacre and Post-Massacre Social Conditions Documented by American Diplomats, 2010. **Address:** University of Nebraska, 225B Love Library, Lincoln, NE 68588-4100, U.S.A. **Online address:** slu@unlnotes.unl.edu

LUBAR, David. American (born United States), b. 1954. **Genres:** Young Adult Fiction, Novels. **Career:** Creative Computing Magazine, editor, 1980-82. **Publications:** (With T. Riley and K. Riley) Computer Controller Cookbook, 1983; (comp.) It's Not a Bug, It's a Feature!: Computer Wit and Wisdom, 1995; The Unwilling Witch (young adult), 1997; The Psychozone: The Witch's Monkey and Other Tales, 1997; The Psychozone: Kidzilla and Other Tales, 1997; The Wavering Werewolf (young adult), 1997; The Vanishing Vampire (young adult), 1997; The Gloomy Ghost (young adult), 1998; Hidden Talents (young adult), 1999; Monster Road (young adult), 1999; The Trouble with Heroes, 2002; Dunk, 2002; Flip, 2003; In the Land of the Lawn Weenies and Other Misadventures, 2003; Wizards of the Game, 2003; Dog Days, 2004; Don't Cramp My Style, 2004; Sleeping Freshmen Never Lie, 2005; Invasion of the Road Weenies: And Other Warped and Creepy Tales, 2005; Punished!, 2006; Curse of the Campfire Weenies and Other Warped and Creepy Tales, 2007; True Talents, 2007; My Rotten Life, 2009; Battle of the Red Hot Pepper Weenies: And Other Warped and Creepy Tales, 2009; Big Stink, 2010; Goop Soup, 2010; Dead Guy Spy, 2010; Enter the Zombie, 2011; Attack of the Vampire Weenies and Other Warped and Creepy Tales, 2011. Works appear in anthologies. **Address:** 4695 Oakwood Ln., Nazareth, PA 18064, U.S.A. **Online address:** david@davidlubar.com

LUBAR, Joel F. American (born United States), b. 1938. **Genres:** Biology, Psychology, Medicine/Health, Sciences. **Career:** University of Rochester, Department of Psychology, assistant professor, 1963-67; University of Tennessee, associate professor, 1967-71, professor of psychology, 1971, now professor emeritus; International Journal of Physiology and Behavior, regional editor, 1969-88; Southeastern Biofeedback Institute, co-director, 1979-; Biofeedback and Self-Regulation, associate editor, 1990-. **Publications:** Biological Foundations of Behavior, 1969; (with R.L. Isaacson, L. Schmaltz and R. Douglas) A Primer of Physiological Psychology, 1971; (ed.) A First Reader in Physiological Psychology, 1972; Readings on Biological Foundations of Behavior, 1975; (with W. Deering) Behavioral Approaches to Neurology, 1981; Physiological Bases of Behaviour, 1982; (ed.) Quantitative Electroencephalographic Analysis (QEEG) Databases for Neurotherapy: Description, Validation and Application, 2003. Contributor to journals. **Address:** Department of Psychology, University of Tennessee, 310 Austin Peay Bldg., Knoxville, TN 37996-0900, U.S.A. **Online address:** jlubar@utk.edu

LUBBOCK, Jules. British (born England), b. 1943. **Genres:** Architecture, Art/Art History, Politics/Government, Education. **Career:** Manchester University, lecturer; University of Essex, professor of art history. Writer and academic. **Publications:** (with M. Crinson) Architecture-Art or Profession? Three Hundred Years of Architectural Education in Britain, 1994; The Tyranny of Taste: The Politics of Architecture and Design in Britain, 1550-1960, 1995; Storytelling in Christian Art from Giotto to Donatello, 2006. **Address:** Department of Art History and Theory, University of Essex, Wivenhoe Pk., Colchester, EX CO4 3SQ, England. **Online address:** lubbj@essex.ac.uk

LÜBBREN, Nina. British/German (born Germany), b. 1962. **Genres:** Cultural/Ethnic Topics, History. **Career:** University of Leeds, faculty; Birkbeck College, faculty; Open University, faculty; Cambridge School of Art, senior lecturer in art history and modern visual culture; Anglia Ruskin University, senior lecturer in art history, 1995-, senior lecturer in film studies and acting programme leader. Writer. **Publications:** Rural Artists' Colonies in Europe, 1870-1910, 2001; (ed. with D. Crouch) Visual Culture and Tourism, 2002; (contrib.) Impressionist Giverny: A Colony of Artists, 1885-1915, 2007; Visual Narrative in European Painting, 1860-1900, forthcoming. Contributor to books. **Address:** Anglia Ruskin University, Rm. Hel 365, East Rd., Cambridge, CB1 1PT, England. **Online address:** nina.lubbren@anglia.ac.uk

LUBET, Steven. American (born United States), b. 1949?. **Genres:** Young Adult Non-fiction. **Career:** Legal Assistance Federation, staff attorney, 1973-75; Northwestern University, School of Law, visiting assistant professor, 1978-81, assistant professor, 1976-78, associate professor, 1978-81, professor of law, 1981-, Williams Memorial professor of law, Fred Bartlit Center for Trial Strategy, director, professor of comparative literary studies; Federal Trade Commission, designated consumer representative, 1977-78; Illinois Office of Education, special education hearing officer, 1978-81; National Institute of Trial Advocacy, instructor, assistant team leader, Midwest Regional Trial Advocacy Program, teaching team leader, 1978-86, Expert Witness Program, director, 1982-98, Midwest Deposition Program, director, 1988-99; DePaul University, lecturer, 1974-75; Emory University School of Law, visiting professor, 1987-88. Association of American Law Schools, director of law teachers, 1993-94. Attorney and writer. **Publications:** NONFICTION: (co-ed.) Chutzpah: A Jewish Liberation Anthology, 1977; Beyond Reproach: Ethical Restrictions on the Extrajudicial Activities of State and Federal Judges, 1984; (with J. Rosenbaum) Financial Disclosure by Judges: Functional Analysis and Critique, 1989; (with J.M. Shaman and J.J. Alfini) Judicial Conduct and Ethics, 1990, 3rd ed., 2000; Vending Operator, Inc. v. Nita Department of Transportation: Problems and Case File, 3rd ed., 1993; Modern Trial Advocacy: Analysis and Practice, 1993 as Modern Trial Advocacy, 2000, 3rd ed. as Modern Trial Advocacy: Analysis and Practice, 2004; Judicial Conduct and Ethics, 1995; (with John W. Cooley) Arbitration Advocacy, 1997, 2nd ed., 2003; Expert Testimony: A Guide for Expert Witnesses and the Lawyers Who Examine Them, 1998; Modern Trial Advocacy: Canada, 2000; Judicial Conduct and Ethics, 2000; Nothing But the Truth: Why Trial Lawyers Don't, Can't, and Shouldn't Have to Tell the Whole Truth, 2001; (with J. Trumbull-Harris) Mock Trials: Preparing, Presenting, and Winning Your Case, 2001; Arbitration Advocacy, 2003; Murder in Tombstone: The Forgotten Trial of Wyatt Earp, 2004; Lawyers' Poker: 52 Lessons That Lawyers Can Learn from Card Players, 2006; The Importance of Being Honest: How Lying, Secrecy, and Hypocrisy Collide with Truth in Law, 2008; (with E.I. Boals) Expert Testimony: A Guide for Expert Witnesses and the Lawyers Who Examine Them, 2009. Contributor to periodicals and journals. **Address:** School of Law, Northwestern University, 375 E Chicago Ave., Chicago, IL 60661, U.S.A. **Online address:** slubet@law.northwestern.edu

LUBLIN, Nancy. American (born United States), b. 1971. **Genres:** Business/Trade/Industry. **Career:** Dress for Success (nonprofit), founder, 1996; Do Something (nonprofit), chief executive officer, 2003-; New York University, adjunct faculty. Writer. **Publications:** Pandora's Box: Feminism Confronts Reproductive Technology, 1998; (with V. Martir and J. Steers) Do Something! A Handbook for Young Activists, 2010; Zilch: The Power of Zero in Business, 2010. Contributor to periodicals. **Address:** Do Something Inc., 24-32 Union Sq. E, 4th Fl., New York, NY 10003, U.S.A.

LUCADO, Max (Lee). American (born United States), b. 1955. **Genres:** inspirational/Motivational Literature, Theology/Religion, Adult Non-fiction, History. **Career:** Central Church of Christ, Miami, associate minister, 1979-82; Tijunca-lareja de Cristo, missionary, 1983-88; Oak Hills Church of Christ, pulpit minister, senior minister, 1988-, Minister of writing and preaching; lecturer on a daily radio program. **Publications:** NONFICTION: On the Anvil, 1985; No Wonder They Call Him the Savior, 1986, 2nd ed., 1987; God Came Near: Chronicles of the Christ, 1987; Six Hours One Friday: Anchoring to the Cross, 1989; Applause of Heaven, 1990; In the Eye of the Storm, 1991; And the Angels Were Silent, 1993; Portions as The Final Week of Jesus, 1994; He Still Moves Stones, 1993, 2nd ed., 1994; Walking with the Savior, 1993; A Gentle Thunder: Hearing God Through the Storm, 1995; In the Grip of Grace, 1996, rev. ed., 2006; (with J. Countryman) God's Inspirational Promise Book, 1996; The Great House of God, 1997; The Cross, 1998; (co-author) The Heart of Christmas, 1998; Just Like Jesus, 1998, rev., 2003; The Gift for All People:

Thoughts on God's Great Grace, 1999; When Christ Comes, 1999; Grace for the Moment: Inspirational Thoughts for Each Day of the Year, 2000; America Looks Up: Reaching Toward Heaven for Hope and Healing, 2001; One Incredible Moment: Celebrating the Majesty of the Manger, 2001; (with F. Rivers and J.B. Jenkins) What the Cross Means to Me, 2002. JUVENILE FICTION: Just in Case You Ever Wonder, 1992; Tell Me the Story, 1992, 2nd ed., 2005; Tell Me the Secrets, 1993; (with J.A. and S. Lucado) The Children of the King, 1994; (with J.A. and S. Lucado) The Crippled Lamb: Highlights From And the Angels were Silent, 1994; The Song of the King, 1995; Alabaster's Song, 1996; Because I Love You, 1998; Jacob's Gift, 1998; All You Ever Need, 2000; Small Gifts in God's Hands, 2000; With You All the Way, 2000; You Are Mine, 2001; If Only I Had a Green Nose, 2002. FICTION: When God Whispers Your Name, 1994; In Search of Wonder: A Call to Worship Renewal, 1995; Cosmic Christmas, 1997; The Christmas Cross: A Story about Finding Your Way Home for the Holidays, Word, 1998. OTHERS: (ed.) Inspirational Bible: Life Lessons From the Inspired Word of God, 1995; You Are Special, 1997, rev. ed., You Are Special: A Story for Everyone, 2002; (co-ed.) Legacy of promises for a Godly Man, 1998; (with C. Swindoll and C. Colson) The Glory of Christmas, 1996; Let the Journey Begin: God's Roadmap for new Beginnings, 1998; Just the Way You Are, 1999; He Did this Just for You, 2000; He Chose the Nails: What God Did to Win Your Heart, 2000; Traveling Light: Releasing the Burdens you were Never Intended to Bear, 2001; Safe in the Shepherd's Arms: Hope and Encouragement from Psalm 23, 2002; Just like Jesus Devotional: A Thirty Day Walk with the Savior, 2002; A Heart like Jesus, 2002; A Love Worth giving to you at Christmas, 2002; A Love Worth Giving: Living in the Overflow of God's Love, 2002; Traveling Light for Mothers, 2002; Hermie: A Common Caterpillar, 2002; (contrib.) Friendship & Kindness, 2002; Shaped by God, 2002; (co-author) The Heart of a Father: True Stories of Inspiration and Encouragement, 2002; Come Together & Worship, 2003; (contrib.) Hermie and the Big Bully Croaker, 2003; Best of all, 2003; (contrib.) Rock, Roll and Run, 2003; (contrib.) Stuck in a Sticky Den, 2003; Experiencing the Heart of Jesus: Knowing His Heart, Feeling His Love, 2003; Next Door Savior, 2003; Numbers, 2004; It's Not about Me: Rescue from the Life We Thought Would make Us Happy, 2004; Flo the Lyin' Fly, 2004; Resurrection Morning, 2004; (contrib.) Punchinello and the most Marvelous Gift: A Story about Giving, 2004; (contrib.) Lucia and the Razzly Dazzly Wemberry Pies, 2004; (contrib.) The 12 Bugs of Christmas, 2004; Hat for Ivan, 2004; Colors, 2004; Everyday Blessings: Inspirational Thoughts From The Published Works Of Max Lucado, 2004; ABCs, 2004; Give it All to Him: A Story of New Beginnings, 2004; Come Thirsty Workbook: Receive what Your Soul Longs for, 2004; Figuras/Shapes; Cure for the Common Life: Living in Your Sweet Spot, 2005, rev. ed., 2008; It's Not About Me: Live Like you Mean It, 2005; Mocha with Max: Friendly Thoughts & Simple Truths from the Writings of, 2005; Way Home: A Princess Story, 2005; God's Mirror: A Modern Parable, 2005; Bug Collection: Four Stories from the Garden, 2005; Turn: Remembering Our Foundations, 2005; The Christmas Candle, 2006; Facing Your Giants: A David And Goliath Story For Everyday People, 2006; The Oak Inside The Acorn, 2006; (ed.) Max Lucado's Daily Devotional Bible: Everyday Encouragement for young Readers, 2006; Your Special Gift, 2006; Stanley the Stinkbug goes to Camp, 2006; In the Beginning, 2006; For These Tough Times: Reaching Toward Heaven For Hope And Healing, 2006; God's Promises For You: Scripture Selections, 2006; 3: 16: The Numbers of Hope, 2007; Coming Home, 2007; (contrib.) Milo, 2007; A Max Lucado Children's Treasury, 2007; Growing the Marriage of Your Dreams, 2007; Gaining a New Attitude on Life: 4 Interactive Bible Studies for Individuals or Small Groups, 2007; Hope, Pure and Simple: 316 Thoughts to Lift Your Soul, 2007; Every Day Deserves A Chance: Wake Up To The Gift Of 24 Little Hours, 2007; Facing Your Giants, 2007; You!: God's Brand-new Idea made to be Amazing, 2007; God's Great Big Love for Me: A 3: 16 Book, 2007; Dealing with Difficult People: 4 Interactive Bible Studies for Individuals or Small Groups, 2007; Becoming Money Smart: 4 Interactive Bible Studies for Individuals or Small Groups, 2007; Becoming a Student of God's Word: 4 Interactive Bible Studies for Individuals or Small Groups, 2007; God Thinks You're Wonderful!, 2007; Cast of Characters: Common People in the Hands of an Uncommon God, 2008; Tallest of Smalls, 2009; Fearless: Imagine Your Life without Fear, 2009; (with J. Lucado) Redefining Beautiful: What God Sees When God Sees You, 2009; Fear Not: For I am with You Always: Promise Book, 2009; His Name is Jesus: The Promise of God's Love Fulfilled, 2009; You can be Everything God Wants You to Be, 2010; Outlive Your Life: You were Made to Make a Difference, 2010; One Hand, Two Hands, 2010; Max on Life: Answers and Inspiration for Life's Questions, 2010; You Changed My Life, 2010; God's Story, Your Story: When His becomes Yours, 2011; (with R. Frazee) Making Room for Neighbors, 2011; Celebrating Christmas with Jesus, 2011; God Thinks You're Wonderful, Mom, 2011; Live Loved: Experiencing God's Presence in Everyday Life, 2011; Lucado Inspirational Reader: Hope and Encouragement for Your Everyday Life, 2011; (with K.D. Hill and R. Fraze) Story for Children, 2011; Thank You, God, For Blessing Me, 2011; Thank You, God, for Loving Me, 2011; Make Every Day Count, 2012; Great Day Every Day: Navigating Life's Challenges With Promise and Purpose, 2012; God Listens When I Pray, 2012; Do you know I love you, God?, 2012; Cast of Characters: Lost and Found, 2012. **Address:** UpWords, PO Box 692170, San Antonio, TX 78269-2170, U.S.A.

LUCAITES, John Louis. American (born United States), b. 1952. **Genres:** History, Politics/Government. **Career:** University of North Carolina, instructor, 1975-76; University of Missouri, instructor, 1981-82; University of Alabama, instructor, 1982-84, assistant professor, 1984-87; Indiana University, assistant professor, 1987-93, associate professor, 1993-2007, professor of rhetoric and public culture, 2007-. Writer. **Publications:** (Ed. with L.M. Bernabo) Great Speakers and Speeches, 1992; (ed. with C. Calloway-Thomas) Martin Luther King, Jr., and the Sermonic Power of Public Discourse, 1993; (ed. with C.M. Condit) Crafting Equality: America's Anglo-African Word, 1993; Contemporary Rhetorical Theory: A Reader, 1999; (with R. Hariman) No Caption Needed: Iconic Photographs, Public Culture, and Liberal Democracy, 2007; (and ed. with B.A. Biesecker) Rhetoric, Materiality, and Politics, 2009. **Address:** Indiana University, Rm. 245, 800 E 3rd St., Bloomington, IN 47405, U.S.A. **Online address:** lucaites@indiana.edu

LUCAS, Celia. Welsh/British (born England), b. 1938. **Genres:** Children's Fiction, Biography, Young Adult Fiction. **Career:** George Rainbird Ltd., editorial assistant, 1962-65; W.H. Allen Ltd., art editor, 1965-66; Daily Mail, researcher, 1966-68, reporter, 1968-71; Welsh Border News Agency, partner, 1971-74, director, 1974-80; Lucas News Agency, director, 1980-; Two's Co. (public relations consultancy), director, 1986-. **Publications:** Prisoners of Santo Tomas, 1974; Steel Town Cats, 1987; (with I. Skidmore) Glyndwr Country, 1988; Anglesey Rambles, 1989; The Adventures of Marmaduke Purr Cat, 1990; The Terrible Tale of Tiggy Two, 1995; Madoc's Prickly Problem, 2000. **Address:** Virgin & Child Cottage, Brynsiencyn, Anglesey, LL61 6PB, Wales.

LUCAS, Craig. American (born United States), b. 1951. **Genres:** Plays/Screenplays, Songs/Lyrics And Libretti. **Career:** Seattle Repertory Theatre, playwright-in-residence, 1998; Intiman Theatre, associate artistic director. Writer. **Publications:** Blue Window: A Comedy, 1985; Reckless, 1985, rev. ed., 1998; Prelude to a Kiss, 1990; Three Postcards, rev. ed., 1995; What I Meant Was: New Plays and Selected One-Acts, 1999; Prelude to a Kiss and Other Plays, 2002; God's Heart: A Play, 2002; Stranger, 2002; Reckless and Other Plays, 2003; (with D. Schulner) This Thing of Darkness, 2003; Small Tragedy, 2005; The Light in the Piazza, 2007; The Dying Gaul and Other Screenplays, 2008; (adapted) Uncle Vanya: A Tragicomedy, 2009; Prayer for My Enemy: A Play, 2009. **Address:** c/o Peter Franklin, William Morris Agency, 1325 Ave. of the Americas, New York, NY 10019, U.S.A.

LUCAS, Eileen. American (born United States), b. 1956. **Genres:** Children's Non-fiction, Biography, Young Adult Fiction, Romance/Historical. **Career:** Teacher and writer. **Publications:** Peace on the Playground: Nonviolent Ways of Problem-Solving, 1991; Water: A Resource in Crisis, 1991; Vincent Van Gogh, 1991; Acid Rain, 1991; Jane Goodall, Friend of the Chimps, 1992; Mind at Work: How to Make it Work Better for You, 1993; Cherokees: People of the Southeast, 1993; Ojibwas: People of the Northern Forests, 1994; Naturalists, Conservationists, and Environmentalists, 1994; The Everglades, 1994; The European Conquest, 1995; Trade, 1995; Civil Rights, the Long Struggle, 1996; The Complete Library of U.S. Presidents: The Eisenhower, Kennedy, Johnson Years, 1997; The Complete History of our Presidents, 1997; The Nixon, Ford, Carter Years, 1997; The Reagan, Bush, Clinton Years, 1997; Contemporary Human Rights Activists, 1997; Cracking the Wall: The Struggles of the Little Rock Nine, 1997; Elizabeth Dole: A Leader in Washington, 1998; The Eighteenth and Twenty-First Amendments, 1998; Our Postal System, 1999; Prudence Crandall: Teacher for Equal Rights, 2001; The Aaron Burr Treason Trial, 2003; More Than the Blues?: Understanding and Dealing With Depression, 2010; The Little Rock Nine Stand Up for Their Rights, 2011. **Address:** 167 Fontana Ave., PO Box 543, Fontana, WI 53125, U.S.A.

LUCAS, Geralyn. American (born United States), b. 1968?. **Genres:** Medicine/Health, Women's Studies And Issues, Fashion/Costume, Biography, Autobiography/Memoirs. **Career:** American Broadcasting Company Inc., ABC

News, 20/20 Magazine, editorial producer; Lifetime Television, director of original programming, executive director of public affairs. Writer. **Publications:** Why I Wore Lipstick To My Mastectomy, 2004. Contributor to periodicals. **Address:** c/o Author Mail, St. Martins Press, 175 5th Ave., New York, NY 10010-7703, U.S.A. **Online address:** geralynlucas@whyiworelipstick.com

LUCAS, John. British (born England), b. 1937. **Genres:** Poetry, Literary Criticism And History, Biography, Young Adult Fiction, Autobiography/Memoirs. **Career:** University of Reading, lecturer in English, 1961-64; University of Nottingham, lecturer, 1964, senior lecturer, 1971-75, reader in English, 1975-77; University of Maryland, visiting professor, 1967-68; University of Indiana, visiting professor, 1967-68; Loughborough University, professor of English, 1977-96, now professor emeritus; Nottingham Trent University, research professor, 1977, now professor emeritus; University of Athens, professor of English literature, 1984-85; La Trobe University, visiting fellow, 1992; Shoestring Press, owner. Writer. **Publications:** (With J. Goode and D. Howard) Tradition and Tolerance in 19th Century Fiction, 1966; The Melancholy Man: A Study of Dickens's Novels, 1970, 2nd ed., 1980; About Nottingham, 1971; Chinese Sequence, 1972; A Brief Bestiary, 1972; Arnold Bennett: A Study of His Fiction, 1974; Tim and the Quarry Affair, 1974; (trans.) Egil's Saga, 1975; The Literature of Change, 1977; The 30's: A Challenge to Orthodoxy, 1978; Hassocks, 1978; The Literature of Change, 1980; Romantic to Modern Literature: Essays on Ideas and Culture 1750-1900, 1982; The Days of the Week, 1983; Moderns & Contemporaries, Novelists, Poets, Critics, 1985; (with B. Haynes) The Trent Bridge Battery, 1985; Modern English Poetry: From Hardy to Hughes, 1986; Studying Grosz on the Bus, 1989; England and Englishness: Poetry and Nationhood 1688-1900, 1989; Charles Dickens: The Major Novels, 1992; Flying to Romania, 1992; John Clare, 1994; One for the Piano, 1997; The Radical Twenties: Aspects of Writing, Politics and Culture, 1997; William Blake, 1998; (with J. Goodridge) Selected Poems of Robert Bloomfield, 1999; Radical Twenties: Writing, Politics and Culture, 1999; On the Track, 2000; The Good That We Do, 2001; Ivor Gurney, 2001; Starting to Explain: Essays on Poetry, 2002; A World Perhaps: New and Selected Poems, 2002; The Long and the Short of It, 2004; 92 Acharnon Street, 2007. EDITOR: Poems of George Crabbe, 1967; Jane Austen's Mansfield Park, 1971; (and intro.) Literature and Politics in the 19th Century, 1971; W.H. Mallock's The New Republic, 1974; The 1930s, 1978; (with I. Fletcher) Poems of G.S. Fraser, 1981; (and with intro. and afterword) Selected Writings, 1988; D.H. Lawrence, 1991; Oliver Goldsmith, 1988; Writing and Radicalism, 1996; (with D. Beldin) Stanley Middleton at Eighty, 1999. **Address:** Nottingham Trent University, Burton St., Nottingham, NT NG1 4BU, England.

LUCAS, John A. American (born United States), b. 1927. **Genres:** Sports/Fitness, Essays. **Career:** Track and field coach, 1949-72; Pennsylvania State University, College of Health & Human Development, senior research and teaching professor of sport history, 1961-93, professor emeritus of exercise and sport science, 1993-. Writer. **Publications:** (With R. Smith) Saga of American Sport, 1978; The Modern Olympic Games, 1980; 30 and More Jogging Trails in State College, Pennsylvania, 1981; Future of the Olympic Games, 1993. Contributor to journals. **Address:** Department of Public Information, College of Health & Human Development, Pennsylvania State University park, 309 Old Main, University Park, PA 16802, U.S.A. **Online address:** jal11@psu.edu

LUCAS, John Randolph. British (born England), b. 1929. **Genres:** Philosophy, Mathematics/Statistics, Essays. **Career:** Oxford University, Merton College, junior research fellow, 1953-56, fellow and tutor, 1960-96, reader in philosophy, 1990-96, University Faculty of Philosophy, now emeritus; Corpus Christi College, fellow and assistant tutor, 1957-58; Princeton University, Jane Eliza Procter Visiting Fellow, 1957-58; University of Leeds, Leverhulme Research Fellow, 1959-60; Oxford Consumer Group, chairperson, 1961-63, 1966-67, vice-chairperson, 1963-66; University of Edinburgh, Gifford Lecturer, 1971-73; University of Dundee, Margaret Harris Lecturer, 1981; Calvin College, Harry Jelema Lecturer, 1987. Writer. **Publications:** The Principles of Politics, 1966; The Concept of Probability, 1970; The Freedom of the Will, 1970; (with A.J.P. Kenny, H.C.L. Higgins and C.H. Waddington) The Nature of Mind, 1972; A Treatise on Time and Space, 1973; (with Kenny, L. Higgins and Waddington) The Development of Mind, 1973; Democracy and Participation, 1976; Freedom and Grace: Essays, 1976; On Justice: Peri Dikaiou, 1980; Space, Time and Causality: An Essay in Natural Philosophy, 1984; The Future: An Essay on God, 1989; (with P.E. Hodgson) Spacetime and Electromagnetism: An Essay on the Foundations of the Special Theory of

Relativity, 1990; Responsibility, 1993; (with M.R. Griffiths) Ethical Economics, 1996; The Roots of Mathematics, 1999; Conceptual Roots of Mathematics: An Essay on the Philosophy of Mathematics, 2000; (with B. Mitchell) An Engagement with Plato's Republic: A Companion to The Republic, 2003; Reason and Reality: An Essay in Metaphysics, 2009. CONTRIBUTOR: Analytical Philosophy, 1962; Justice and Equality, 1971; Education, Equality and Society, 1975; Facts and Values, 1986; The Nature of Time, 1987; Business Ethics, 1998. Contributor to periodicals. **Address:** Merton College, University of Oxford, Merton St., Oxford, GL OX1 4JD, England. **Online address:** john.lucas@merton.ox.ac.uk

LUCAS, Michele Claire. American (born United States), b. 1937?. **Genres:** Novels, Young Adult Fiction, Romance/Historical. **Career:** Time Inc., photo editor. **Publications:** A High and Hidden Place: A Novel, 2005; Long Ago Person Found, forthcoming. **Address:** HarperCollins Publishers, 10 E 53rd St., 7th Fl., New York, NY 10022, U.S.A.

LUCASHENKO, Melissa. Australian (born Australia), b. 1967. **Genres:** Documentaries/Reportage, Novels, Social Commentary, Travel/Exploration. **Career:** Foundation for Aboriginal and Islander Research Action, newspaper editor. **Publications:** Steam Pigs, 1997; Killing Darcy, 1998; Hard Yards, 1999; Too Flash, 2002; The Orphan, forthcoming; Barbed Wire, forthcoming. **Address:** University of Queensland Press, Staff House Rd., PO Box 6042, St. Lucia, QL 4067, Australia. **Online address:** supergin27@bigpond.com.au

LUCERO, Lisa Joyce. American (born United States), b. 1962. **Genres:** History, Social Sciences. **Career:** Santa Monica College, instructor, 1994-95; Loyola Marymount University, instructor, 1995; New Mexico State University, assistant professor, 1997-2003, Center for Latin American Studies, faculty member, 1997-2007, associate professor, 2003-07; University of Pennsylvania, research associate, 2004; University of Illinois, associate professor, 2007-. Writer. **Publications:** (ed. with E.A. Bacus) Complex Polities in the Ancient Tropical World, 1999; Social Integration in the Ancient Maya Hinterlands: Ceramic Variability in the Belize River Area, 2001; Water and Ritual: The Rise and Fall of Classic Maya Rulers, 2006; (ed. with B.W. Fash) Precolumbian Water Management: Ideology, Ritual, and Power, 2006. Contributor of articles to books, periodicals and journals. **Address:** Department of Anthropology, University of Illinois, MC-148, 109 Davenport Hall, 607 S Mathews Ave., Urbana, IL 61801-3635, U.S.A. **Online address:** ljlucero@illinois.edu

LUCEY, Michael. American (born United States), b. 1960. **Genres:** Adult Non-fiction, Gay And Lesbian Issues, History. **Career:** University of California, Department of French, assistant professor of French and comparative literature, 1988-94, associate professor of French and comparative literature, 1994-2002, professor of French and comparative literature, 2002-, chair, 2005-11, Center for the Study of Sexual Culture, director, 2001-05, 2006-07, Bernie H. Williams professor of comparative literature, 2011-. Writer. **Publications:** NONFICTION: Gide's Bent: Sexuality, Politics, Writing, 1995; (contrib.) Gay Histories and Cultures: An Encyclopedia, 2000; The Misfit of the Family: Balzac and the Social Forms of Sexuality, 2003; (contrib.) Dictionnaire des cultures gays et lesbiennes, 2003; (trans.) D. Eribon, Reflexions sur la question gay, (title means: 'Insult and the Making of the Gay Self') 2004; (contrib.) Columbia History of Twentieth Century French Thought, 2005; Never Say I: Sexuality and the First Person in Colette, Gide, and Proust, 2006. Contributor to books and periodicals. **Address:** Departments of French, University of California, 4123 Dwinelle Hall, PO Box 2580, Berkeley, CA 94720-2580, U.S.A. **Online address:** mlucey@berkeley.edu

LUCHETTI, Cathy. American (born United States), b. 1945. **Genres:** Food And Wine, History, Women's Studies And Issues, Social Sciences. **Career:** Writer. **Publications:** (With C. Olwell) Women of the West, 1982; Home on the Range: A Culinary History of the American West, 1983; Under God's Spell: Frontier Evangelists, 1772-1915, 1989; I Do!: Courtship, Love and Marriage on the American Frontier: A Glimpse at America's Romantic Past through Photographs, Diaries and Journals, 1715-1915, 1995; The Hot Flash Cookbook: Delicious Recipes for Health and Well Being through Menopause, 1997; Medicine Women: The Story of Early-American Women Doctors, 1998; Mama Says: Inspiration, Wit and Wisdom from the Mothers in Our Lives, 2000; Children of the West: Family Life on the Frontier, 2001; Men of the West: Life on the American Frontier, 2004. **Address:** c/o Anne Edelstein, Harold Ober Associates, 425 Madison Ave., New York, NY 10017, U.S.A.

Online address: c.luchetti@sbcglobal.net

LUCIAK, Ilja Alexander. Austrian (born Austria), b. 1956. **Genres:** Politics/Government, Social Sciences, History. **Career:** Universidad Centroamerican, visiting professor, 1984-85; Virginia Polytechnic Institute and State University, assistant professor, 1987-94, associate professor, 1994-2002, professor of political science and department chair, 2002-; Swedish International Development Authority, consultant; United Nations Development Fund for Women, consultant. Writer. **Publications:** The Sandinista Legacy: Lessons from a Political Economy in Transition, 1995; After the Revolution: Gender and Democracy in El Salvador Nicaragua and Guatemala, 2001; Gender and Democracy in Cuba, 2007. **Address:** Department of Political Science, Virginia Polytechnic Institute, 531 Major Williams Hall, Blacksburg, VA 24061-0001, U.S.A. **Online address:** iluciak@vt.edu

LUCIE, Doug. British (born England), b. 1953. **Genres:** Plays/Screenplays, Young Adult Fiction, Literary Criticism And History. **Career:** Oxford Playhouse Co., resident playwright, 1979-80; University of Iowa, visiting playwright. Director. **Publications:** Progress & Hard Feelings, 1985; Fashion, 1987; Grace, 1993; Plays, 1998. **Address:** Alan Brodie Representation, 211 Piccadilly, London, GL W1J 9HF, England.

LUCIE-SMITH, (John) Edward (McKenzie). (Peter Kershaw). British/Jamaican (born Jamaica), b. 1933. **Genres:** Poetry, Art/Art History, Photography, Translations, Novellas/Short Stories. **Career:** RAF, education officer, 1954-56; Turret Books, co-founder, 1965; freelance writer, 1966-; Tehran Museum of Contemporary Art, director. **Publications:** A Tropical Childhood and Other Poems, 1961; (with J. Clemo and G. MacBeth) Penguin Modern Poets 6, 1964; Confessions and Histories, 1964; Fir-Tree Song, 1965; Jazz for the NUF, 1965; A Game of French and English, 1965; Three Experiments, 1965; Mystery in the Universe: Notes on an Interview with Allen Ginsberg, 1965; Gallipoli-Fifty Years After (poetry), 1966; Cloud, Fountain, Sun, Statue, 1966; Op Art, 1966; What Is a Painting?, 1966; Silence, 1967; Heureux Qui, Comme Ulysse..., 1967; Borrowed Emblems, 1967; Towards Silence, 1968; Teeth and Bones, 1968; Thinking about Art: Critical Essays, 1968; (as Peter Kershaw) A Beginner's Guide to Auctions, 1968; Snow Poem, 1968; Egyptian Ode, 1969; Six Kinds of Creature, 1969; Movements in Art since 1945 in US as Late Modern: The Visual Arts since 1945, 1969, new ed., 2001; Six More Beasts, 1970; Lovers, 1970; The Rhino, 1971; A Girl Surveyed, 1971; The Yak, The Polar Bear, The Dodo, The Goldfish, The Dinosaur, The Parrot, 1971; A Concise History of French Painting, 1971; Eroticism in Western Art, 1972; Symbolist Art, 1972; The First London Catalogue: All the Appurtenances of a Civilised, Amusing and Comfortable Life, 1974; The Well-Wishers, 1974; The Invented Eye: Masterpieces of Photography, 1839-1914, 1975; Joan of Arc, 1976; (with C. Dars) How the Rich Lived, 1976; (with C. Dars) Work and Struggle, 1977; Art Today, 1977, 3rd ed., 1989; Fantin-Latour, 1977; The Dark Pageant (novel), 1977; Outcasts of the Sea, 1978; A Concise History of French Painting, 1978; Super-Realism, 1979; Furniture: A Concise History, 1979; Cultural Calendar of the Twentieth Century, 1979; Story of Craft: the Craftsman's Role in Society, 1981; The Body, 1981; Bertie and the Big Red Ball (for children), 1982; Jan Vanriet, 1982; A History of Industrial Design, 1983; Art Terms: An Illustrated Dictionary, 1984; Beasts with Bad Morals (poetry), 1984; Art of the 1930's, 1985; American Art Now, 1985; Lives of the Great 20th Century Artists, 1986; (with P.J. Smith) Craft Today: Poetry of the Physical, 1986; Sculpture since 1945, 1987; (with S. Kelly) Self Portrait: a Modern View, 1987; Obsert Lancaster, 1988; (co-author) The New British Painting, 1988; Impressionist Women, 1989; Art in the 1980s, 1990; (with C.L. Carter and J.W. Burnham) Richard Lippold, Sculpture, 1990; Art Deco Painting, 1990; Fletcher Benton, 1990; Jean Rustin, 1990; Harry Holland, 1991; Sexuality in Western Art, 1991; Wendy Taylor, 1992; Andres Nagel, 1992; Alexander, 1992; Art and Civilization, 1992; Latin American Art of the 20th Century, 1993, 2nd ed., 2004; Race, Sex and Gender in Contemporary Art, 1994; Elisabeth Frink: A Portrait, 1994; John Kirby, 1994; American Realism, 1994; Visual Arts in the 20th Century, 1996; The Art of Albert Paley, 1996; Lin Emery, 1996; Art Erotica, 1997; Adam, 1998; Zoo, 1998; (with J. Chicago) Women and Art, 1999; (contrib.) Paul Pletka, 1999; Women in Art, 1999; Judy Chicago: An American Vision, 2000; (contrib.) Olga de Amaral, 2000; Sergio Ceccotti, 2001; Flora: Gardens and Plants in Art and Literature, 2001; (contrib.) Dino Valls, 2001; Albert Huie: Father of Jamaican Painting, 2001; (with G. O'Brien and K. Scarlett) Chris Booth: Sculpture in Europe, Australia & New Zealand, 2001; Artists of the Ideal: Nuovo Classicismo, 2002; Changing Shape: New and Selected Poems, 2002; (contrib.)

Paolo Borghi, 2002; (contrib.) Stefano Di Stasio, 2002; Art Tomorrow, 2002; Julio Larraz, 2003; Thames & Hudson Dictionary of Art Terms, 2004; Peeter Mudist, 2004; (contrib.) Art of Robyn Kahukiwa, 2005; (contrib.) Gargallo, 2006; Elias Rivera, 2006; (with V. Combalía) Pedro Moreno Meyerhoff, 2006; Censoring the Body, 2007; (with W. Wickiser) Ralph L. Wickiser, the Reflected Stream: The Early Years, 1975-1985, 2009; (with C. Hunter and A.F. Burgess) Seven Bridges Collection: The First Fifteen Years, 1993-2008, 2009; (contrib.) La punta dell'iceberg, 2009; Lives of the Great Modern Artists, 2009; Glory of Angels, 2009; (contrib.) Bacon: I disegni, 2010; Face of Jesus, 2011. EDITOR: Rubens, 1961; Raphael, 1961; (with P. Hobsbaum) A Group Anthology, 1963; The Penguin Book of Elizabethan Verse, 1965; The Liverpool Scene, 1967; A Choice of Browning's Verse, 1967; The Penguin Book of Satirical Verse, 1967; Holding Your Eight Hands: A Book of Science Fiction Verse, 1969; (with P. White) Art in Britain, 1969-1970, 1970; British Poetry since 1945, 1970; (with S. Watson-Taylor) French Poetry Today: A Bi-Lingual Anthology, 1971; Primer of Experimental Poetry, 1870-1922, 1971; Masterpieces from the Pompidou Centre, 1983; The Faber Book of Art Anecdotes, 1992; (co-author) Ludmila Armata, 2003. TRANSLATOR: Manet, 1962; Jonah: Selected Poems of Jean-Paul de Dadelsen, 1967; (with P. Claudel) Five Great Odes, 1970; The Muses, 1967. **Address:** Rogers, Coleridge and White, 20 Powis Mews, London, GL W11 1JN, England. **Online address:** edward@edwardlucie-smith.com

LUCIRE, Yolande. Australian (born Australia) **Genres:** Sciences, Medicine/Health, Sports/Fitness. **Career:** University of New South Wales, senior lecturer. Writer and psychiatrist. **Publications:** Constructing RSI: Belief and Desire, 2003. Contributor of articles to journals. **Address:** Level 5, Edgecliff Center, 203-233 New South Head Rd., PO Box 3004, Edgecliff, NW 2027, Australia. **Online address:** lucire@ozemail.com.au

LUCIUK, Lubomyr Y(aroslav). Canadian (born Canada), b. 1953. **Genres:** Area Studies, Geography, History, Military/Defense/Arms Control. **Career:** Royal Ontario Museum, field research assistant, 1967-71; Ontario Ministry of Natural Resources, researcher, 1972-77; Queen's University, Department of Geography, graduate teaching assistant, 1975-78, graduate research assistant, 1979-80, assistant professor of geography and Canada research fellow of social sciences and humanities Research Council of Canada, 1988-90, adjunct professor, 1990-92; University of Alberta, research assistant in geography, 1979-80, Canadian Institute of Ukrainian Studies, research assistant in oral history, 1982-84; University of Toronto, Department of Geography, Neporany postdoctoral fellow, 1984-88, adjunct professor and chair, 1984-88; Royal Military College of Canada, Department of Politics and Economics, assistant professor, 1990-92, associate professor, 1993-98, professor, 1999-, chairman, Ethnic and Immigration Studies Program, fellow; University of British Columbia, Department of History, adjunct professor, 1997; Ukrainian Canadian Civil Liberties Association, chairman, 2007-10, director of research; York University, Refugee Documentation Centre, fellow; Ukrainian Canadian Centennial Committee Inc., chair. Writer. **Publications:** Ukrainians in the Making, 1980; (comp. with B.S. Kordan) Anglo-American Perspectives on the Ukrainian Question, 1938-1951, 1987; A Time for Atonement, 1988; (with B.S. Kordan and G.J. Matthews) Creating a Landscape: A Geography of Ukrainians in Canada, 1989; (with A. Chyczij) Memorial, 1989; Welcome to Absurdistan, 1994; (with R. Sorobey) Konowal, 1995; Roll Call, 1999; Searching for Place, 2000; Konowal: A Canadian Hero, 2000; In Fear of the Barbed Wire Fence, 2001; Without just Cause: Canada's First National Internment Operations and the Ukrainian Canadians, 1914-1920, 2006; (with V. Humeniuk) Their Just War: Images of the Ukrainian Insurgent Army, 2007; (comp. with L. Szwaluk) Recalling Canada's First National Internment Operations, 2009. EDITOR: (intro.) Heroes of Their Day: The Reminiscences of Bohdan Panchuk, 1983; (with B.S. Kordan) A Delicate and Difficult Question, 1986; (with N. Hillmer and B.S. Kordan) On Guard For Thee, 1988; (with M. Carynnyk and B.S. Kordan) The Foreign Office and the Famine, 1988; (with M. Carrynnyk) Between Two Worlds: The Memoirs of Stanley Frolick, 1990; (with S.M. Hryniuk) Canada's Ukrainians, 1991; (with S.M. Hryniuk) Multiculturalism and Ukrainian Canadians: Identity, Homeland Ties and the Community's Future, 1993; Righting an Injustice, 1994; Not Worthy: Walter Duranty's Pulitzer Prize and the New York Times, 2004; (with L. Grekul) Holodomor: Reflections on the Great Famine of 1932-1933 in Soviet Ukraine, 2008. **Address:** Department of Politics & Economics, Royal Military College of Canada, PO Box 17000, Sta. Forces, Kingston, ON K7K 7B4, Canada. **Online address:** luciuk-l@rmc.ca

LUCKETT, Dave. Australian (born Australia), b. 1951. **Genres:** Children's

Fiction, Science Fiction/Fantasy, Young Adult Fiction, Novels, Novellas/ Short Stories, Sports/Fitness. **Career:** Teacher, 1974-75; federal public servant, 1977-97. Writer. **Publications:** CHILDRENS NOVELS: The Adventures of Addam, 1995; Night Hunters, 1995; The Best Batsman in the World, 1996; The Wizard and Me, 1996; The Last Eleven, 1997; A Dark Winter, 1998; A Dark Journey, 1999; A Dark Victory, 1999; Cricket Australia: Kids' Ultimate Fan Handbook, 2004; The Truth About Magic, 2005; Iron Soldiers: A Story of Arms and Armour, 2005; (with M. Fatchen) Howzat!: A Celebration of Cricket, 2005; The Return of Rathalorn, 2005. TENABRAN SERIES: A Dark Winter, 1998; A Dark Journey, 1999; A Dark Victory, 1999. RHIANNA CHRONICLES SERIES: Rhianna and the Wild Magic, 2000 in US as The Girl, the Dragon, and the Wild Magic, 2003; Rhianna and the Dogs of Iron, 2002 in US as Girl, the Apprentice and the Dogs of Iron, 2004; Rhianna and the Castle of Avalon, 2002 in US as Girl, the Queen and the Castle, 2004. Contributor to periodicals. **Address:** Omnibus Books, 175-177 Young St., Parkside, SA 5063, Australia. **Online address:** home@daveluckett.com

LUCSKO, David. American (born United States), b. 1976. **Genres:** Business/Trade/Industry. **Career:** University of Detroit Mercy, instructor, 2005-10; Auburn University, assistant professor of history, 2010-. Writer. **Publications:** The Business of Speed: The Hot Rod Industry in America, 1915-1990, 2008. **Address:** Department of History, Auburn University, 310 Thach Hall, Auburn, AL 36849, U.S.A.

LUDBROOK, John. Australian/New Zealander (born New Zealand), b. 1929?. **Genres:** Medicine/Health, Sciences. **Career:** University of Otago, senior lecturer in surgery, 1959-63; University of New South Wales, professor of surgery, 1964-68; University of Adelaide, professor, 1969-80; professor emeritus of surgery, 1980-; Baker Medical Research Institute, associate director, 1981-88; University of Melbourne, statistical consultant. Writer. **Publications:** (With G.J. Fraenkel and H.A.F. Dudley) Guide to House Surgeons on the Surgical Unit, 1961, 5th ed., 1974; Aspects of Venous Function in the Lower Limbs, 1966; (with R.G. Elmslie) Introduction to Surgery: 100 Topics, 1976; Analysis of the Venous System, 1972; (ed. with V.C. Marshall) Clinical Science for Surgeons, 1988. **Address:** University of Adelaide, Level 6, Wills Bldg., Adelaide, SA 5005, Australia. **Online address:** ludbrook@unimelb.edu.au

LUDDY, Karon. American (born United States), b. 1955?. **Genres:** Novels, Children's Fiction. **Career:** Honeywell Corp., staff; Apple Computer, staff; University of North Carolina, writing instructor, Department of American Studies, adjunct professor. Writer. **Publications:** Spelldown: The Big-Time Dreams of a Small-Town Word Whiz (novel), 2007; Wolf Heart (poetry), 2007. **Address:** Department of English, University of North Carolina, 9201 University City Blvd., Charlotte, NC 28223-0001, U.S.A. **Online address:** karonluddy1@mac.com

LUDWICKSON, John. American (born United States), b. 1948. **Genres:** Archaeology/Antiquities, Social Sciences, History. **Career:** North Dakota Historical Society, archaeologist, 1976-77; Nebraska State Historical Society, curator of anthropology, archaeologist, 1978-. Writer. **Publications:** (With G.H. Smith) Fort Manuel: The Archaeology of an Upper Missouri Trading Post of 1812-1813, 1981; (with D. Blakeslee and J. O'Shea) Missouri National Recreational River: Native American Cultural Resources, 1987; (with J.M. O'Shea) Archaeology and Ethnohistory of the Omaha Indians: The Big Village Site, 1992; (with J.R. Bozell) Archeology of the Patters on Site: Native American Life in the Lower Platte Valley, A.D. 1000-1300, 1999. **Address:** Nebraska State Historical Society, 1500 R St., PO Box 82554, Lincoln, NE 68501, U.S.A. **Online address:** john.ludwickson@nebraska.gov

LUDWIG, Jack. American/Canadian (born Canada), b. 1922. **Genres:** Novels, Novellas/Short Stories, Plays/Screenplays, Sports/Fitness. **Career:** Williams College, instructor, 1949-53; Bard College, assistant professor, associate professor, Division of Language and Literature, chairman, 1953-58; University of Minnesota, instructor, 1958-61; Stony Brook University, professor of English, 1961-, now professor emeritus, Stony Brook Poetry Center, director, 1993-94; Commission on College Physics Film Project, consultant, 1965-66; University of Toronto, writer-in-residence, 1968-69; Stratford (Ontario) Shakespeare Festival, resident playwright, 1970; Banff Centre, writer-in-residence, 1974; University of California, visiting professor, 1976. **Publications:** NOVELS: Confusions, 1963; Above Ground, 1968; A Woman of Her Age, 1973; The Rites of Leo Spring, forthcoming; The November May Day of Doba Montreal, forthcoming. SPORTS: Hockey Night in Moscow,

1974, rev. ed. as The Great Hockey Thaw, or The Russians Are Here!, 1974; Five Ring Circus: The Montreal Olympics, 1976; Games of Fear and Winning: Sports with an Inside View, 1976; The Great American Spectaculars: The Kentucky Derby, Mardi Gras and the Other Days of Celebration, 1976. EDITOR: (as Jack Barry Ludwig) (with W.R. Poirier) Stories: British and American, 1953; (with S. Bellow and K. Botsford) The Noble Savage, 1960-62; (with A. Wainwright) Soundings: New Canadian Poets, 1970. OTHERS: Recent American Novelists, 1962; Requiem for Bibul (short story), 1967; Homage to Zolotova (poetry), 1974; General Agamemnon, forthcoming. Works appear in anthologies. Contributor to books and periodicals. **Address:** Stony Brook University, 100 Nicolls Rd., Stony Brook, NY 11794, U.S.A. **Online address:** jack.ludwig@stonybrook.edu

LUDWIKOWSKI, Rett R. American/Polish (born Poland), b. 1943. **Genres:** Law, Politics/Government, Theology/Religion, Language/Linguistics. **Career:** Jagiellonian University, senior lecturer in political science, 1967-71, adjunct professor, 1971-76, assistant professor of politics, 1976-81, associate professor of law, 1981, Division of Business, chairman, 1976-80, Department of Modern Political Movements and Ideas, chair, 1976-82, Division of Law, chair, 1980-81; Marguerite Wilbur Foundation, senior fellow, 1981-82; Alfred University, visiting professor, 1983-; Elizabethtown College, visiting professor, 1983-; Catholic University of America, visiting professor, 1984-85; Columbus School of Law, professor of law, 1985-, Institute of Comparative and International Law, director, 1987-; CUA International Trade and Business Summer Program-Poland, director, 1992-; Oceana Publications Inc., managing editor, 2001-03. **Publications:** Murzynski Radykalizm w USA: Czarni Muzulmani Czarna Wladza, Czarne Pantery, 1976; Konserwatyzm Krolestwa Polskiego w Okresie Miedzypowstaniowym: Z Rozwazan Nad Ideologia I Polityka, 1976; The Conservatism of the Kingdom of Poland during the Inter-Insurrectional Period: Considerations on Ideology and Politics, 1976; Black Radicalism in the United States, 1976; (with J. Wolenski) J.S. Mill, 1979; Essays on Galician Political Movements, 1848-1892, 1980; Szkice Na Temat Galicyjskich Ruchów I Myśli Politycznej, 1848-1892, 1980; Polska Kultura Polityczna: Mity, Tradycje I Współczesność, 1980; Main Currents of Polish Political Thought, 1815-1890, 1982; Główne Nurty Polskiej Myśli Politycznej, 1815-1890, 1982; Will the Crisis of Communism Begin in Poland?, 1983; The Crisis of Communism: Its Meaning, Origins and Phases, 1986; Continuity and Change in Poland: Conservatism in Polish Political Thought, 1991; (ed. with K. Thompson) Constitutionalism and Human Rights: America, Poland and France: A Bicentennial Colloquium at the Miller Center, 1991; America and the World of Business, 1991; I-God (in Polish), 1992; (with W. Fox Jr.) The Beginning of the Constitutional Era: A Bicentennial Comparative Analysis of the First Modern Constitutions, 1993; International Trade and Business Regulations (in Polish), vol. I, 1996, vol. II: (ed. and co-author) International Trade and Business Transactions, 1998; Constitution-Making in the Region of Former Soviet Dominance, 1996; Regulacje Handlu i Biznesu Miedzynarodowego, 1996; Comparative Constitutional Law, 2002; (ed.) Comparative Human Rights and Fundamental Freedoms, vol. I, 2002; Mafia, 2005, vol. II, 2006, vol. III, 2008; International Trade, 2006; The Courts in the United States, TNOIK, Torun?, 2008; (with A. Ludwikowski) Wyboty Prezydenckie w USA, 2009. Contributor to journals. **Address:** Columbus School of Law, Catholic University of America, 3600 John McCormack Rd. NE, Washington, DC 20064, U.S.A. **Online address:** ludwikowski@law.edu

LUEBBERMANN, Mimi. American/Venezuelan (born Venezuela), b. 1945. **Genres:** Horticulture, How-to Books, Food And Wine. **Career:** Tasting of Summer Produce, development director, 1988-90; Organic Farming Research Foundation, coordinator of celebration of the organic harvest, 1992; Sonoma County Chefs' Tasting, coordinator, 1998. Writer. **Publications:** (With G. Brennan) Beautiful Bulbs: Simple Secrets for Glorious Gardens-Indoors and Out, 1993; (with G. Brennan) Little Herb Gardens: Simple Secrets for Glorious Gardens-Indoors and Out, 1993; Paydirt: How to Raise Herbs and Produce for Serious Cash, 1994, rev. ed., 1997; Miscarriage Grief, 1994; Terrific Tomatoes: Simple Secrets for Glorious Gardens-Indoors and Out, 1994; Climbing Vines: Simple Secrets for Glorious Gardens-Indoors and Out, 1995; Coping with Miscarriage: A Simple, Reassuring Guide to Emotional and Physical Healing, 1995; Easy Orchids: Simple Secrets for Glorious Gardens-Indoors and Out, 1996; Salad Gardens: Simple Secrets for Glorious Gardens-Indoors and Out, 1996; The Williams-Sonoma Wedding Planner, 1996; Bread Baking with Herbs: Delicious Breads, Muffins, Focaccia, and More, 1996; The Country Baker's Book of Baking with Herbs, 1996; Heirloom Gardens: Simple Secrets for Old-Fashioned Flowers and Vegetables, 1997; Cactus and Succulent Gardens: Simple Secrets for Glorious Gardens-Indoors and Out,

1997; Little Potted Gardens: Simple Secrets for Glorious Gardens-Indoors and Out, 1998; Homegrown Fruit: Simple Secrets for Glorious Gardens-Indoors and Out, 1998; The Art of Arranging Silk Flowers, 1998; Shade Gardens, 1999; Vegetable Gardens, 1999; Sonoma: A Food and Wine Lovers? Journey, 2003; Beautiful Gardens of the Wine Country, 2004; The Heirloom Tomato Cookbook, 2006. EDITOR: (with J. Bennett) Where the Heart Is: A Celebration of Home, 1995; (contrib.) Smith and Hawken's Book of Outdoor Gardening, 1997. **Address:** Windrush Farm, 2263 Chileno Valley Rd., Petaluma, CA 94952, U.S.A.

LUEBKE, Frederick Carl. American (born United States), b. 1927. **Genres:** History. **Career:** Concordia University Nebraska, assistant professor, associate professor of history, 1961-68; University of Nebraska-Lincoln, associate professor, 1968-72, professor, 1972-87, Center for Great Plains Studies, director, 1983-88, Charles J. Mach distinguished professor of history, 1987-94, professor emeritus, 1994-, now retired, 1994. Writer. **Publications:** Immigrants and Politics: The Germans of Nebraska, 1880-1900, 1969; Bonds of Loyalty: German Americans and World War I, 1974; Germans in Brazil: A Comparative History of Cultural Conflict During World War I, 1987; Germans in the New World: Essays in the History of Immigration, 1990; A Harmony of the Arts: The Nebraska State Capitol, 1990; Nebraska: An Illustrated History, 1995, 2nd ed., 2005. EDITOR: Ethnic Voters and the Election of Lincoln, 1971; (co-ed.) The Great Plains: Environment and Culture, 1979; Ethnicity on the Great Plains, 1980; Vision and Refuge: Essays on the Literature of the Great Plains, 1981; (co-ed.) Mapping the North American Plains, 1987; European Immigrants in the American West, 1998. **Address:** 4650 Crescent Ridge Ln., Eugene, OR 97405, U.S.A. **Online address:** fredluebke@comcast.net

LUELLEN, Valentina. *See* **POLLEY**, Judith Anne.

LUFT, Lya Fett. Brazilian (born Brazil), b. 1938. **Genres:** Poetry, Novels, Essays, Biography, Autobiography/Memoirs, Young Adult Fiction. **Career:** Translator, poet, essayist and educator, 1964-. **Publications:** POETRY AND ESSAYS: Canções de limiar, 1964; Canções delimiar, 1967; Flauta doce: Tema e variacões (1965-1969), 1972; Matéria do cotidiano, 1978; Mulher no palco, 1984; O lado fatal, 1988. NOVELS: Asparceiras, 1980; A asa esquerda do anjo, 1981; Reunião de familia, 1982; O quarto fechado, 1984. OTHERS: Exílio, 1987; A Sentinela, 1994; O Rio do Meio, 1996; Romance Das Palavras: Uma história Etimológica e semântica, 1996; Secreta Mirada, 1997; O Ponto Cego, 1999; Historias do Tempo, 2000; Perdas & Ganhos, 2003; Pensar é transgredir, 2004; Histórias de bruxa boa, 2004; Para nãodizer adeus, 2005; Em outras palavras, 2006; Losses and Gains: Reflections on a Life, 2007; Silêncio dos amantes, 2008; Crise Global e o Novo Papel Mundial Dos BRICs, 2009; Múltipla Escolha, 2010; Riqueza do mundo, 2011. **Address:** Carcanet Press, Alliance House, 30 Cross St., 4th Fl., Manchester, LC M2 7AQ, England.

LUHRMANN, T(anya) M(arie). American (born United States), b. 1959. **Genres:** Anthropology/Ethnology, Psychiatry, Psychology, Medicine/Health. **Career:** Cambridge University, Christ's College, research fellow, 1985-89; University of California, assistant professor, 1989-92, associate professor, 1992-98, chair, 1997-98, professor of anthropology, 1998-2000; University of Chicago, Department of Anthropology, associate, 2000-, Department of Comparative Human Development, Max Palevsky professor, 2004-07; Stanford University, Department of Anthropology, professor, 2007-; Watkins University, professor, 2010-. Writer. **Publications:** Persuasions of the Witch's Craft: Ritual Magic in Contemporary England in UK as Persuasions of the Witch's Craft: Ritual Magic and Witchcraft in Present-Day England, 1989; The Good Parsi: The Fate of a Colonial Elite in a Postcolonial Society, 1996; Of Two Minds: An Anthropologist looks at American Psychiatry, 2000; When God Talks Back: Understanding the American Evangelical Relationship with God, 2012; Other Minds: Essays on the Complex Construction of Subjective Experience, forthcoming; Uptown: Living on the Street with Psychosis, forthcoming. Contributor to periodicals. **Address:** Department of Anthropology, Stanford University, 50 Anthropology Bldg., Stanford, CA 94305-2034, U.S.A. **Online address:** luhrmann@stanford.edu

LUI, Mary Ting Yi. American (born United States), b. 1967?. **Genres:** History, Criminology/True Crime. **Career:** Yale University, American Studies and History, associate professor of American studies and history, professor of American studies and history. Historian and writer. **Publications:** The Chinatown Trunk Mystery: Murder, Miscegenation and Other Dangerous Encounters in Turn-of-the-Century New York City, 2005. **Address:** Department of

History, Yale University, HGS 106, PO Box 208324, New Haven, CT 06520-8324, U.S.A. **Online address:** mary.lui@yale.edu

LUIS, William. American (born United States) **Genres:** Literary Criticism And History, Adult Non-fiction. **Career:** Cornell University, teaching assistant, 1976-78; Dartmouth College, instructor, 1979-80, assistant professor, 1980-85, associate professor, 1985-88; State University of New York, visiting associate professor, 1988-89, associate professor, 1989-91, Latin American and Caribbean Area Studies Program, acting director, 1988-89, director, 1989-90; Vanderbilt University, associate professor, 1991-96, professor, 1996-, Chancellor's professor of Spanish, 2006, professor of English, 2001; Afro-Hispanic Review, editor, 2004-. **Publications:** Literary Bondage: Slavery in Cuban Narrative, 1990; Dance Between Two Cultures: Latino-Caribbean Literature Written in the United States, 1997; Culture and Customs of Cuba, 2001; Lunes de Revolucion: Literatura y cultura en los primeros anos de la Revolucion Cubana, 2003; Bibliografa y antologia critica de las vanguardias literarias: El Caribe, 2010. EDITOR: (with E. Desnoes) Los Dispositivos en la flor: Cuba, literatura desde la Revolucion, 1981; Voices from Under: Black Narrative in Latin America and the Caribbean, 1984; (with J. Rodriguez-Luis and contrib.) Translating Latin America: Culture as Text, 1991; Dictionary of Literary Biography, vol. CXIII: Modern Latin American Fiction Writers, First Series, 1992, (with A. Gonaez) vol. CXLV: Modern Latin American Fiction Writers, Second Series, 1994; Boletin de la Fundacion Federico Garcia Lorca, 1995; (and intro.) Autobiografia del esclavo Poeta y otros escritos, 2007; (and intro.) Tato Laviera: Mix(ing) t(hro)u(gh) ou(t), 2008; Exile and Return in Chango, el gran putas, 2010; Latino Identify and the Desiring Machine, 2011. Contributor to books and journals. **Address:** Department of Spanish and Portuguese, Vanderbilt University, 323 Furman Hall, PO Box 1617, Sta. B, Nashville, TN 37235, U.S.A. **Online address:** william.luis@vanderbilt.edu

LUKACS, John (Adalbert). (John R. Lukacs). American/Hungarian (born Hungary), b. 1924. **Genres:** History. **Career:** Chestnut Hill College, associate professor of history, professor of history, chair, 1947-74, now professor emeritus; Columbia University, visiting professor, 1954-55; University of Pennsylvania, visiting professor, 1964; University of Toulouse, Fulbright professor, 1964-65; Johns Hopkins School of Advanced International Studies, visiting professor, 1970-71; Fletcher School of Law and Diplomacy, visiting professor, 1971, 1972. Writer and historian. **Publications:** The Great Powers and Eastern Europe, 1953; (ed. and trans.) European Revolution and Correspondence with Gobineau, by Alexis de Tocqueville, 1959; A History of the Cold War, 1962, 3rd ed. as A New History of the Cold War, 1966; Decline and Rise of Europe, 1965; Historical Consciousness: Or the Remembered Past, 1968; The Passing of the Modern Age, 1970; The Last European War: September 1939-December 1941, 1976; 1945: Year Zero, 1978; Philadelphia: Patricians and Philistines, 1900-1950, 1981; Outgrowing Democracy: A History of the United States in the Twentieth Century, 1984; The People of South Asia, 1984; Immigration and Migration, 1986; Excavations at Inamgaon, 1988; Budapest 1900: A Historical Portrait of a City and Its Culture, 1988; Confessions of an Original Sinner, 1990; The Struggle between Churchill and Hitler, 1991; The End of the 20th Century and the End of the Modern Age, 1993; Destinations Past: Traveling Through History with John Lukacs, 1994; The Duel: May 10-July 31, 1994; Europai Vilaghaboru, 1939-1941, 1995; (with G.F. Kennan) George F. Kennan and the Origins of Containment, 1944-1946, 1997; The Hitler of History, 1997; A Thread of Years, 1998; A Student's Guide to European History, 1999; Five Days in London, May 1940, 1999; A Student's Guide to the Study of History, 2000; Churchill: Visionary, Statesman, Historian, 2002; At the End of an Age, 2002; New Republic: A History of the United States in the Twentieth Century, 2004; Democracy and Populism: Fear and Hatred, 2005; Remembered Past: John Lukacs on History, Historians and Historical Knowledge, 2005; June 1941: Hitler and Stalin, 2006; George Kennan: A Study of Character, 2007; Magyar Irasok, 2007; Blood, Toil, Tears and Sweat: The Dire Warning, 2008; (ed.) American Austen: The Forgotten Writing of Agnes Repplier, 2009; Last Rites, 2009; The Legacy of the Second World War, 2010; Through the History of the Cold War, 2010; Future of History, 2011; History and the Human Condition: A Historian's Pursuit of Knowledge, 2012. **Address:** Department History and Political, School of Undergraduate Studies, Chestnut Hill College, 9601 Germantown Ave., Philadelphia, PA 19118, U.S.A.

LUKACS, John D. American (born United States), b. 1977?. **Genres:** History, Military/Defense/Arms Control. **Career:** Writer and historian. **Publications:** Escape from Davao: The Forgotten Story of the Most Daring Prison Break of the Pacific War, 2010. Contributor of articles to periodicals. **Ad-**

dress: AZ , U.S.A. **Online address:** john@johndlukacs.com

LUKACS, John R. *See* **LUKACS, John (Adalbert).**

LUKAS, Christopher. (C. W. Lukas). American (born United States), b. 1935. **Genres:** Film, Autobiography/Memoirs, Medicine/Health. **Career:** WNET, director of cultural programming, director of programming, 1963-71; Public Broadcasting Service, head writer, 1973-74; KQED, producer, director of national programming, head writer, 1974-79, producer, writer, director, 2005-; City College of New York, professor, chair of department of film and video, 1979-86; Alvin H. Perlmutter Inc., producer, director, writer, 1987-97; Independent video producer, writer and director, 1997-. **Publications:** Directing for Film and Television, 1985, rev. ed., 2001; (with H.M. Seiden) Silent Grief: Living in the Wake of Suicide, 1987, rev. ed., 2007; (with K.O. Kaplan) Staying in Charge: Practical Plans for the End of Your Life, 2004; The First Year-Prostate Cancer: An Essential Guide for the Newly Diagnosed, 2005; Blue Genes: A Memoir of Loss and Survival, 2008. **Address:** NY , U.S.A. **Online address:** lukandluk@optonline.net

LUKAS, C. W. *See* **LUKAS, Christopher.**

LUKER, Nicholas (John Lydgate). (N. J. L. Luker). British (born England), b. 1945. **Genres:** Literary Criticism And History, Translations. **Career:** University of Nottingham, lecturer, 1970-88, senior lecturer in Russian, 1988-, Department of Russian and Slavonic Studies, associate professor; Victoria University of Wellington, visiting lecturer, 1976; Dartmouth College, visiting lecturer, George Washington University, visiting lecturer, Luther College, visiting lecturer; University of Auckland, visiting lecturer, 1993; University of Wellington, visiting lecturer, 1996; University of Otago, visiting lecturer, 1998. Writer. **Publications:** (As N.J.L. Luker) Alexander Grin, 1973; (trans. with B. Scherr) A. Grin, The Seeker of Adventure (selected stories), 1978; Alexander Kuprin, 1978; (As N.J.L. Luker) Aleksandr Grin, the Forgotten Visionary, 1980; The Forgotten Visionary, 1982; (with S. O'Dell) Mikhail Artsybashev: A Comprehensive Bibliography, 1983; In Defence of a Reputation: Essays on the Early Prose of Mikhail Artsybashev, 1990; (with B.P. Scherr and S. Ellis) The Shining World: Exploring Aleksandr Grin's Grinlandia, 2007. EDITOR: (trans. and intro.) An Anthology of Russian Neo-Realism: The Znanie School of Maxim Gorky, 1982; (and intro.) Fifty Years On: Gorky and His Time (critical essays), 1987; (trans. and intro.) Alexander Grin: Selected Short Stories, 1987; (trans. and intro.) From Furmanov to Sholokhov: An Anthology of the Classics of Socialist Realism, 1988; (and contrib.) The Russian Short Story, 1900-1917 (critical essays), 1991; (co-trans. and intro.) Y. Miloslavsky, Urban Romances and Other Stories, 1994; (and contrib.) After the Watershed, Russian Prose, 1917-1927 (critical essays), 1996; (and contrib.) Out of the Shadows (critical essays), 2003. Contributor to books. **Address:** Department of Russian and Slavonic Studies, University of Nottingham, University Pk., Nottingham, NG7 2RD, England. **Online address:** nicholas.luker@nottingham.ac.uk

LUKER, N. J. L. *See* **LUKER, Nicholas (John Lydgate).**

LUKES, Steven M. American/British (born England), b. 1941. **Genres:** Philosophy, Politics/Government, Sociology, Social Sciences. **Career:** Oxford University, Worcester College, lecturer in politics, 1964-66, Nuffield College, fellow, 1964-66, Balliol College, fellow and tutor in politics and sociology, 1966-87; University of Paris, visiting lecturer, associate professor of public law, 1974; University of Sao Paolo, visiting professor, 1975; Witwatersrand University, Hofmeyer fellow, 1979; Harvard University, visiting lecturer; University of California, visiting lecturer; Princeton University, visiting lecturer; Hebrew University, visiting lecturer; European University Institute, professor of social and political theory, 1987-95, director, 1995-96; British Academy, fellow, 1989-; University of Siena, professor of moral philosophy, 1996-2000; New York University, professor of sociology, 1998-2003; London School of Economics, Department of Sociology, visiting centennial professor, 2001-03; Wissenschaftskolleg zu Berlin Institute, advanced study fellow, 2009-10; Oxford University Press, editor; Groupe d'Etudes Durkheimiennes, founding member. **Publications:** Émile Durkheim, His Life and Work: An Historical and Critical Study, 1972; Individualism, 1973; Power: A Radical View, 1974, 2nd ed., 2004; Essays in Social Theory, 1977; (with I. Galnoor) No Laughing Matter: A Collection of Political Jokes, 1985; Marxism and Morality, 1985; Moral Conflict and Politics, 1991; The Curious Enlightenment of Professor Carilat: A Comedy of Ideas, 1995, 2nd ed., 2009; Liberals and Cannibals: The Implications of Diversity, 2003; Moral Relativism, 2008;

Sketch for a Historical Picture of the Progress of the Human Mind and other Writings, forthcoming. EDITOR: (with A. Arblaster) The Good Society: A Book of Readings, 1970; (with M. Hollis) Rationality and Relativism, 1982; (and intro.) Rules of Sociological Method, 1982; (with A. Scull) Durkheim and the Law, 1983; (with M. Carrithers and S. Collins) Category of the Person: Anthropology, Philosophy, History, 1985; Power, 1986; (with C. Joppke) Multicultural Questions, 1999. Contributor to books. **Address:** Department of Sociology, New York University, Rm. 4125, 295 Lafayette St., PO Box 1464, New York, NY 10003, U.S.A. **Online address:** steven.lukes@nyu.edu

LUKKEN, Miriam. (Miriam Willingham Lukken). American (born United States), b. 1960. **Genres:** Adult Non-fiction, Human Relations/Parenting, Young Adult Non-fiction, Education. **Career:** Teacher, 1983-92; educator and writer, 1992-. **Publications:** Read This Book Before Your Child Starts School, 1994; (ed.) Southern Born and Bread (cookbook), 1996; Mrs. Dunwoody's Excellent Instructions for Homekeeping: Timeless Wisdom and Practical Advice, 2003. **Address:** c/o Joann Davis, Redbridge Inc., 700 Washington St., New York, NY 10014, U.S.A. **Online address:** mimilukken@charter.net

LUKKEN, Miriam Willingham. *See* **LUKKEN, Miriam.**

LUMER, Christoph. German (born Germany), b. 1956. **Genres:** Philosophy, Adult Non-fiction. **Career:** University of Osnabrück, assistant professor, 1987-93, associate professor, 1993-99, leading researcher, 2000-02; University of Urbino, Department of Philosophy, visiting professor, 1990; University of Siena, contract professor, 1999-2002, associate professor of moral philosophy, 2002-. Writer. **Publications:** Practical Theory of Argumentation: Theoretical Foundations, Practical Justification, and Rules of Some Important Types of Arguments (in German), 1990; Rational Altruism: A Prudential Theory of Rationality and Altruisms (in German), 2000, 2nd ed., 2009; The Greenhouse: A Welfare Assessment and Some Morals, 2002; (ed. with S. Nannini) Intentionality, Deliberation and Autonomy: The Action-Theoretic Basis of Practical Philosophy, 2007; (ed.) Normative Ethics-Principles of Acting Morally (in Italian), 2008; (ed. with C. Fehige and U. Wessels) Meaningful and Violent Actions: Philosophical Essays for Georg Meggle (in German), 2009; (ed. with U. Meyer) Mind and Morals: Analytical Reflections for Wolfgang Lenzen (in German), 2011. **Address:** Department of Philosophy, University of Siena, Via Roma 47, Siena, 53100, Italy. **Online address:** lumer@unisi.it

LUMPKIN, Aaron. American (born United States), b. 1951. **Genres:** Self Help, Social Work, inspirational/Motivational Literature. **Career:** United States Department of Veterans Affairs, program supporter, 1985-. Writer and motivational speaker. **Publications:** You Can Be Positive, Confident, and Courageous, 2001; You Get One Shot at Life-Aim for Success, 2006; Secrets of Life: Insights into the Meaning of Life, forthcoming. **Address:** Winning Publications, 1020 Preston Dr., Nashville, TN 37206-1323, U.S.A. **Online address:** jaaronlump@aol.com

LUMPKIN, Betty S(tewart). American (born United States), b. 1934. **Genres:** Librarianship, Education, Information Science/Computers. **Career:** Elementary schoolteacher, 1966-67; junior high school English teacher and curriculum coordinator, 1967-74; middle school librarian, 1974-75; teacher, 1975-79; Ooltewah High School, head of library department, 1979-; Freedoms Foundation, vice-president of education. Writer. **Publications:** (With B.H. Sorrow) CD-ROM for Librarians and Educators: A Resource Guide to over 300 Instructional Programs, 1993, 2nd ed., 1996. **Address:** 7718 Mahan Gap Rd., PO Box 659, Ooltewah, TN 37363-9751, U.S.A.

LUMRY, Amanda (R.). American (born United States) **Genres:** Adult Non-fiction, Travel/Exploration. **Career:** Photographer, writer and publisher. **Publications:** (Contrib.) MalaMala: Pathway to an African Eden, 1999; (with L. Hurwitz) Tigers in Terai, 2003, 2nd ed., 2007; (with L. Hurwitz) Mission to Madagascar, 2005; (with L. Hurwitz) Survival of the Salmon, 2006; (with L. Hurwitz) South Pole Penguins, 2007; (with L. Hurwitz) Polar Bear Puzzle, 2007; (with L. Hurwitz) Operation Orangutan, 2007; (with L. Hurwitz) Project Panda, 2008. ADVENTURES OF RILEY SERIES: (with L. Hurwitz) Safari in South Africa, 2003; (with L. Hurwitz) Amazon River Rescue, 2004; (with L. Hurwitz) Dolphins in Danger, 2005; (with L. Hurwitz) Outback Odyssey, 2009. **Address:** Eaglemont Press, 1309 114th Ave. SE, Ste. 200, Bellevue, WA 98004, U.S.A.

LUMSDEN, Linda J. American (born United States), b. 1953. **Genres:** History. **Career:** Hartford Courant, reporter-intern, 1975; Hartford Times, reporter, 1975-76; Journal Inquirer, reporter, 1976-79; Lake Placid News, reporter, 1980-81; Adirondack Daily Enterprise, sports editor, 1980-81; Middletown Times Daily Record, assistant sunday editor, 1981-82; Adirondack Daily Enterprise, features editor, 1983-87; Western Kentucky University, Bowling Green, associate professor of journalism and director of mass communication sequence, 1996-2006; University of Arizona, School of Journalism, assistant professor, 2006-, director of graduate studies. Writer. **Publications:** Rampant Women: Suffragists and the Right of Assembly, 1997; The Inez: The Life and Times of Inez Milholland, 2004. **Address:** Department of Journalism, University of Arizona, Rm. 338, Marshall Bldg., Tucson, AZ 85721, U.S.A. **Online address:** lumsden@email.arizona.edu

LUNAN, Duncan. British/Scottish (born Scotland), b. 1945. **Genres:** Science Fiction/Fantasy, Air/Space Topics, Astronomy, Sciences. **Career:** Association in Scotland to Research into Astronautics (ASTRA), treasurer, 1965-66, 1977-78, 1990-91, 1997-, president, 1966-72, 1978-85, 1991-97, vice-president, 1972-76, secretary, 1985-89; Glasgow SF Circle, chairman, 1969-75, co-chairman, 1986-92; Glasgow Herald, science fiction critic, 1971-85; European Space Association, vice-president, 1977-79; Glasgow Parks Department, Astronomy Project, manager, 1978-79; Airdrie Observatory, acting curator, 1979-80, assistant curator, 1987-97, curator, 2002-; International Correspondence Schools, tutor in English literature and language, 1995-; Traditional Music and Song Association of Scotland, founding member. Writer. **Publications:** Man and the Stars: Contact & Communication with other Intelligence, 1974; Interstellar Contact, 1975; New Worlds for Old, 1979, 2nd ed. as The Fold of the Sun, forthcoming; Man and the Planets: The Resources of the Solar System, 1983, 2nd ed., forthcoming; (ed.) Starfield, Science Fiction by Scottish Writers, 1989; Search Among the Stars, forthcoming. Contributor of articles to books and periodicals. **Address:** Flat 65, Dalriada House, 56 Blythswood Ct., Anderston, Glasgow, ST G2 7PE, Scotland. **Online address:** astra@dlunan.freeserve.co.uk

LUND, Gerald N. (Gerald Niels Lund). American (born United States), b. 1939. **Genres:** Novels, Romance/Historical, Theology/Religion. **Career:** Teacher in Mormon schools, 1965-74; Church of Jesus Christ of Latter-Day Saints, Church Education System, zone administrator, instructor, curriculum writer and director, 1965-99, general authority, 2002-08, now retired; Walnut Institute of Religion, director, 1971-74; Mormon Church, director of college curriculum, 1974-82, director of in-service training, 1982-; Brigham Young University, president. **Publications:** The Coming of the Lord, 1971; This is Your World, 1973; One in Thine Hand, 1982; The Alliance, 1983; (with R. Hendrix) Leverage Point, 1985; The Freedom Factor, 1987; The Work and the Glory (series): vol. I: Pillar of Light, 1990, vol. II: Like a Fire is Burning, 1991, vol. III: Truth Will Prevail, 1992, vol. IV: Thy Gold to Refine, 1993, vol. V: A Season of Joy, 1994, vol. VI: Praise to the Man, 1995, vol. VII: No Unhallowed Hand, 1996, vol. VIII: So Great a Cause, 1997, vol. IX: All is Well, 1998; Three Adventure Novels, 1994; Jesus Christ: Key to the Plan of Salvation, 1991; Fire of the Covenant: A Novel of the Willie and Martin Handcart Companies, 1999; Kingdom and the Crown, vol. I: Fishers of Men, 2000, vol. II: Come Unto Me, 2001, vol. III: Behold the Man, 2002; Hearing the Voice of the Lord: Principles and Patterns of Personal Revelation, 2007; Undaunted: The Miracle of the Hole-in-the-Rock Pioneers, 2009; Divine Signatures: The Confirming Hand of God, 2010. **Address:** LDS Church, 50 NE Temple St., Fl. 4, Salt Lake City, UT 84150, U.S.A.

LUND, Gerald Niels. See LUND, Gerald N.

LUND, Michael. American (born United States), b. 1945?. **Genres:** Novels, Literary Criticism And History, Young Adult Fiction. **Career:** Longwood University, instructor, 1974-76, assistant professor, 1976-83, associate professor, 1983-90, professor of English, 1990-, now professor emeritus; Cormier Honors College, assistant director. Writer. **Publications:** Reading Thackeray, 1988; (with L.K. Hughes) The Victorian Serial, 1991; America's Continuing Story: An Introduction to Serial Fiction, 1850-1900, 1993; (with L.K. Hughes) Victorian Publishing and Mrs. Gaskell's Work, 1999; Growing Up on Route 66 (novel), 2000; Route 66 Kids, 2002; Left-hander on Route 66, 2003; Miss Route 66, 2004; Route 66 to Vietnam: A Draftee's Story, 2004; Route 66 Spring, 2004; Route 66 Chapel, 2006; Route 66 Choir, 2010; Route 66 Sweetheart, 2011. Works appear in anthologies. Contributor of articles to journals. **Address:** Department of English and Modern Languages, Longwood University, 201 High St., Farmville, VA 23909-1800, U.S.A. **Online address:** lundmc@longwood.edu

LUNDBERG, George D. American (born United States), b. 1933. **Genres:** Medicine/Health, How-to Books. **Career:** University of Southern California Medical Center, professor of pathology and associate director of laboratories; University of California, professor and chair of pathology; American Medical Association, Journal of the American Medical Association (JAMA), editor, American Medical News, editor, Scientific Information and Multimedia Group, editor-in-chief, 1982-99; Medscape (online medical information), founding editor, emeritus editor-in-chief, 2002-, Medscape General Medicine, editor-in-chief, 1999-2009; WebMD, special advisor, 2002-; CBS HealthWatch.com, founder and editor-in-chief; Northwestern University, adjunct professor; Harvard School of Public Health, adjunct professor; Stanford University, consulting professor; American Society of Clinical Pathologists, president. **Publications:** (With J. Stacey) Severed Trust: Why American Medicine Hasn't Been Fixed, 2001. EDITOR: (and contrib.) Managing the Patient-focused Laboratory, 1975; (with B.H. Woolley) Pathology for the Practicing Pharmacist, 1976; The Professional and Community Role of the Pathologist in Alcohol Abuse, 1976; Using the Clinical Laboratory in Medical Decision-making, 1983; (with H.S. Meyer) Fifty-one Landmark Articles in Medicine: The JAMA Centennial Series, 1985; (with H.M. Cole) AIDS, from the Beginning, 1986. **Address:** Medscape L.L.C., 76 9th Ave., Ste. 719, New York, NY 10011, U.S.A. **Online address:** glundberg@webmd.net

LUNDE, David (Eric). American (born United States), b. 1941. **Genres:** Poetry, Science Fiction/Fantasy, Translations, Romance/Historical. **Career:** State University of New York College, instructor, 1967-69, assistant professor, 1969-72, associate professor, 1972-78, professor of English, 1978-2001, professor emeritus, 2001-; Drama and Theatre, managing editor, 1968-71; Basilisk Press, editor and publisher, 1970-85. Poet and translator. **Publications:** POETRY: Ironic Holidays, 1965; Les Papillons, 1967; Sludge Gulper 1, 1971; Calibrations, 1981; Blues for Port City (science fiction poems), 1995; Heart Transplants & Other Misappropriations, 1996; Nightfishing in Great Sky River (poems), 1999; (trans.) B. Zhilin, The Carving of Insects, 2006; Instead (poems), 2007; (trans.) Breaking the Willow, 2008; (trans.) 300 Tang Poems, 2011. **Address:** 2218 Mcpherson Ave., North Bend, OR 97459, U.S.A. **Online address:** davelunde@earthlink.net

LUNDE, Paul. British/American (born United States), b. 1943?. **Genres:** Adult Non-fiction, Theology/Religion, History, Translations. **Career:** Writer and historian. **Publications:** (With J. Wintle) A Dictionary of Arabic and Islamic Proverbs, 1984; (trans. and ed. with C. Stone) The Meadows of Gold, 1989; (with L. Maby and J.A. Sabini) Saudi ARAMCO and Its World: Arabia and the Middle East, 1995; Islam: Faith, Culture, History, 2002; Islam: Gegenwart und Geschichte, 2002; Organized Crime: An Inside Guide to the World's Most Successful Industry, 2004; (ed. with A. Porter) Trade and Travel in the Red Sea Region: Proceedings of Red Sea Project I Held in The British Museum, October 2002, 2004; (ed.) The Book of Codes: Understanding the World of Hidden Messages, 2009. Contributor to periodicals. **Address:** c/o Author Mail, Dorling Kindersley Ltd., 80 Strand, London, GL WC2R 0RL, England. **Online address:** paullunde@hotmail.com

LUNDEBERG, Philip (Karl). (Philip Karl Boraas Lundeberg). American (born United States), b. 1923. **Genres:** History, Bibliography, Sciences. **Career:** U.S. Navy Department, Division of Naval History, U.S. Naval Operations, assistant to the historian, 1950-53; St. Olaf College, assistant professor of history, 1953-55; U.S. Naval Academy, faculty, 1955-59; Smithsonian Institution, National Museum of American History, Museum of History and Technology, Department of Armed Forces History, consultant, 1959, associate curator, 1959-61, curator, 1961-84, Division of Transportation, curator, 1984, curator emeritus of naval history, 1984-; American Military Institute, president; United States Commission on Military History, president; International Congress of Maritime Museums, chairman; International Council of Museums, secretary; Council of American Maritime Museums, president. Writer. **Publications:** The Continental Gunboat Philadelphia and the Northern Campaign of 1776, 1966, 2nd ed., 1995; (ed.) Bibliographie de l'Histoire des Grandes Routes Maritimes: Etats-Unis d'Amerique, 1971; Samuel Colt's Submarine Battery, 1974; (co-author) Sea Power, A Naval History, 1960, 1981; Gunboat Philadelphia and the Defense of Lake Champlain in 1776, 1995; American Anti-Submarine Operations in the Atlantic, 1943-1945, 1998. **Address:** Armed Forces History Collections, National Museum of American History, Smithsonian Institution, Washington, DC 20560, U.S.A.

LUNDEBERG, Philip Karl Boraas. See LUNDEBERG, Philip (Karl).

LUNDESTAD, Geir. Norwegian (born Norway), b. 1945. **Genres:** Politics/Government, Military/Defense/Arms Control. **Career:** University of Oslo, Department of History, research fellow, 1970-73, adjunct professor of international history, 1991-, professor of history; University of Tromsø, associate professor of history, 1974-79, professor of American civilization, 1979-88, professor of history, 1988-90; Harvard University, Department of History, Charles Waren fellow, 1978-79, Center for International Affairs, visiting professor, 1983; Woodrow Wilson International Center, fellow, 1988-89; Norwegian Nobel Institute, director. Writer. **Publications:** (With K.E. Eriksen) Norsk utenrikspolitikk, 1972; The American Non-Policy towards Eastern Europe, 1943-1947, 1975; Hovedlinjer i norsk historie 1945-ca. 1965, 1975; USAs politikk overfor Norge 1945-1948, 1976; America, Scandinavia, and the Cold War, 1945-1959, 1980; øst, vest, nord, sør, 1985; The American Empire and Other Studies of US Foreign Policy in a Comparative Perspective, 1990; Empire by Integration: The United States and European Integration, 1945-1997, 1998; The United States and Western Europe since 1945: From Empire by Invitation to Transatlantic Drift, 2003; East, West, North, South: Major Developments in International Relations since 1945, 6th ed., 2010. EDITOR: (with O.A. Westad) Beyond the Cold War: New Dimensions in International Relations, 1993; The Fall of Great Powers, Peace, Stability, and Legitimacy, 1994; No End to Alliance: The United States and Western Europe: Past, Present, and Future, 1998; The Nobel Peace Prize, 2001; (ed. with O. Njølstad) War and Peace in the 20th Century and Beyond, 2002; Just Another Major Crisis?: The United States and Europe since 2000, 2008. Contributor to journals and newspapers. **Address:** Norwegian Nobel Institute, Henrik Ibsens gate 51, Oslo, NO-0255, Norway. **Online address:** gl@nobel.no

LUNDIN, Anne. American (born United States), b. 1944. **Genres:** Cultural/Ethnic Topics, Literary Criticism And History, Theology/Religion. **Career:** Ellis School, English teacher, 1969-74; University of Southern Mississippi, assistant curator of the Grummond collection, 1987-93; University of Wisconsin, School of Library and Information Studies, assistant professor, 1993-98, associate professor, 1999-2003, professor of English, 2004-08, professor emeritus, 2008-. Writer. **Publications:** (With C.W. Cubberley) Teaching Children's Literature: A Resource Guide with a Directory of Courses, 1995; (ed. with G.E. Lundin) Contemporary Religious Ideas: Bibliographic Essays, 1996; Victorian Horizons: The Reception of the Picture Books of Walter Crane, Randolph Caldecott, and Kate Greenaway, 2001; (ed. with W.A. Wiegand) Defining Print Culture for Youth: The Cultural Work of Children's Literature, 2003; Constructing the Canon of Children's Literature: Beyond Library Walls and Ivory Towers, 2004. Contributor to periodicals. **Address:** School of Library and Information Studies, University of Wisconsin, Rm. 4217, Helen C. White Hall, 600 N Park St., Madison, WI 53706-1403, U.S.A. **Online address:** alundin@wisc.edu

LUNDIN, Roger. American (born United States), b. 1949. **Genres:** History, Language/Linguistics, Literary Criticism And History, Theology/Religion. **Career:** Wheaton College, faculty, 1978-, Blanchard professor of English, Clyde S. Kilby professor of English, Arthur F. Holmes professor of faith and learning. Writer. **Publications:** (With A.C. Thiselton and C. Walhout) The Responsibility of Hermeneutics, 1985; (ed. with M.A. Noll) Voices from the Heart: Four Centuries of American Piety, 1987; (with S.V. Gallagher) Literature through the Eyes of Faith, 1989; The Culture of Interpretation: Christian Faith and the Postmodern World, 1993; (ed.) Disciplining Hermeneutics: Interpretation in Christian Perspective, 1997; Emily Dickinson and the Art of Belief, 1998, 2nd rev. ed., 2004; (with C. Walhout and A.C. Thiselton) The Promise of Hermeneutics, 1999; From Nature to Experience: The American Search for Cultural Authority, 2005; (contrib.) Catholic Universities in the New Europe, 2005; (contrib.) In American History through Literature, 1820-1870, 2006; (contrib.) Hermeneutics at the Crossroads, 2006; (ed. and intro.) There before Us: Religion, Literature and Culture from Emerson to Wendell Berry, 2007; (ed. with D.J. Treier and M. Husbands) The Beauty of God: Theology and the Arts, 2007; Believing Again: Doubt and Faith in a Secular Age, 2009; (ed.) Invisible Conversations: Religion in the Literature of America, 2009. Contributor to periodicals. **Address:** Department of English, Wheaton College, 314 Blanchard Hall, 501 College Ave., Wheaton, IL 60187-5593, U.S.A. **Online address:** roger.lundin@wheaton.edu

LUNDIN, Steve. Also writes as Steven Erikson. Canadian (born Canada), b. 1959. **Genres:** Novels, Science Fiction/Fantasy, Sports/Fitness, Novellas/Short Stories. **Career:** Writer, archaeologist and anthropologist. **Publications:** AS STEVEN ERIKSON: Fishin' with Grandma Matchie, 2004; The Devil Delivered, 2004; Revolvo, 2008; Forge of Darkness, 2012; This River Awakens, 2012; The Devil Delivered and Other Tales, 2012. MALAZAN BOOK OF THE FALLEN SERIES AS STEVEN ERIKSON: Gardens of the Moon, 1999; Deadhouse Gates, 2000; Memories of Ice, 2001; House of Chains, 2002; Midnight Tides, 2004; The Bonehunters, 2005; Reaper's Gale, 2007; Toll the Hounds, 2008; Dust of Dreams, 2009; The Crippled God, 2010. BAUCHELAIN AND KORBAL BROACH SERIES AS STEVEN ERIKSON: Blood Follows, 2002; The Healthy Dead, 2004; The Lees of Laughter's End, 2007; Bauchelain and Korbal Broach: The Collected Stories, vol. I, 2007; Crack'd Pot Trail, 2009. OTHERS: A Ruin of Feathers, 1992; Stolen Voices, 1993; Revolvo and Other Canadian Tales, 1997; This River Awakens, 1998; When She's Gone, 2004; Closest Governments to the People: A Complete Reference Guide to Local Government in Washington State, 2007. **Address:** c/o Author Mail, Bantam Press, 20 Vauxhall Bridge Rd., London, GL SW1V 2SA, England.

LUNDMAN, Richard J. American (born United States), b. 1944. **Genres:** Sociology, Organized Labor, Administration/Management, Industrial Relations. **Career:** University of Delaware, assistant professor of sociology, 1972-75; Ohio State University, assistant professor, associate professor of sociology, 1975-84, professor of sociology, 1984-, chairperson of graduate studies, 1985-89, alumni distinguished teaching professor. Writer. **Publications:** (Ed. with M.D. Ermann) Corporate and Governmental Deviance: Problems of Organizational Behavior in Contemporary Society, 1978, 6th ed., 2002; Police and Policing, 1980; (ed. and contrib.) Police Behavior: A Sociological Perspective, 1980; (with M.D. Ermann) Corporate Deviance, 1982; Prevention and Control of Juvenile Delinquency, 1984, 3rd ed., 2001; In the Company of Cops, 2004. **Address:** Department of Sociology, Ohio State University, 106 Townshend Hall, 1885 Neil Ave Mall, Columbus, OH 43210, U.S.A. **Online address:** lundman.1@osu.edu

LUNDSTROM, John B(ernard). American (born United States), b. 1948. **Genres:** History, Military/Defense/Arms Control, Biography. **Career:** Milwaukee Public Museum, curator of history, 1974-86, assistant curator of Americana, 1986-89, curator of American and military history, 1989-2004, senior curator, 2004-, now curator emeritus. Writer. **Publications:** The First South Pacific Campaign: Pacific Fleet Strategy, December 1941-June 1942, 1976; The First Team: Pacific Naval Air Combat from Pearl Harbor to Midway, 1984, rev. ed., 1990; The First Team and the Guadalcanal Campaign: Naval Fighter Combat from August to November 1942, 1994; (with S. Ewing) Fateful Rendezvous: The Life of Butch O'Hare, 1997; Black Shoe Carrier Admiral: Frank Jack Fletcher at Coral Sea, Midway, and Guadalcanal, 2006. Contributor to periodicals. **Address:** Milwaukee Public Museum, 800 W Wells St., Milwaukee, WI 53233-1478, U.S.A. **Online address:** jl@mpm.edu

LUNDVALL, Bengt-Åke. Danish/Swedish (born Sweden), b. 1941. **Genres:** Social Work, Economics, Business/Trade/Industry. **Career:** GLOBELICS, coordinator; University of Ålborg, associate professor, 1973, IKE-group, coordinator, 1977-, docent, 1989, Department for Business Studies, professor in economics, 1995-; University of Sussex, Science Policy Research Unit, visiting research fellow, 1983-84; Stanford University, Department of Economics, visiting research fellow, 1984; Organisation for Economic Cooperation and Development, deputy director, 1992-95; Danish Research Unit for Industrial Dynamics, research manager, 1995-2001, Danish network, coordinator, 1996-2001; Tsinghua University, special term professor, 2003-06. Writer. **Publications:** (Intro. with P. Dencik and L. Herlitz) Marxismens politiska ekonomi, 1969; (Ed.) Product Innovation and User-Producer Interaction, 1985; (ed. with C. Freeman) Small Countries Facing the Technological Revolution, 1988; (ed.) National Systems of Innovation: Toward a Theory of Innovation and Interactive Learning, 1992; (ed. with D. Archibugi) The Globalizing Learning Economy, 2001; Innovation, Growth and Social Cohesion: The Danish Model, 2002; (ed. with P. Conceição and M.V. Heitor) Innovation, Competence Building and Social Cohesion in Europe: Towards a Learning Society, 2003; (ed. with M. and P. Gammeltoft) Putting Africa First: The Making of African Innovation Systems, 2003; Product Innovation, Interactive Learning and Economic Performance, 2004; (ed. with E. Lorenz) How Europe's Economies Learn, 2006; (ed. with P. Intarakumnerd and J. Vang-Lauridsen) Asia's Innovation Systems in Transition, 2006; (ed.) Handbook of Innovation Systems and Developing Countries, 2009. **Address:** University of Alborg, Fibigersstraede 4, Aalborg, 9000, Denmark. **Online address:** bal@business.auc.dk

LUNGE-LARSEN, Lise. American/Norwegian (born Norway), b. 1955. **Genres:** Mythology/Folklore, Children's Fiction, Literary Criticism And History, Classics. **Career:** College of St. Catherine, instructor in English and director of English as a second language program, 1981-87; Hamline University, adjunct faculty, 1982-90; University of Minnesota, instructor in children's literature, 1990, 1994. Writer. **Publications:** (Reteller with M. Preus) The Legend of the Lady Slipper: An Ojibwe Tale, 1999; (reteller) The Troll with No Heart in His Body, and Other Tales of Trolls from Norway, 1999; The Race of the Birkebeiners, 2001; The Hidden Folk: Stories of Fairies, Dwarves, Selkies, and Other Secret Beings, 2004; Noah's Mittens: The Story of Felt, 2006; (reteller) Adventures of Thor the Thunder God, 2007; Gifts from the Gods: Ancient Words and Wisdom from Greek and Roman Mythology, 2011. **Address:** Houghton Mifflin Harcourt, 222 Berkeley St., Boston, MA 02116, U.S.A. **Online address:** liselungelarsen@gmail.com

LUNN, Janet (Louise Swoboda). Canadian/American (born United States), b. 1928. **Genres:** Children's Fiction, History, Young Adult Fiction, Picture/Board Books, Humor/Satire, Reference, Adult Non-fiction. **Career:** Ginn and Co., children's book consultant, 1968-78; Clarke Irwin Publishers, children's editor, 1972-75; Regina Public Library, writer-in-residence, 1982-83; Writers' Union of Canada, chairwoman, 1984-85; Kitchener Public Library, writer-in-residence, 1988; University of Ottawa, writer-in-residence, 1993. **Publications:** PICTURE BOOKS: The Twelve Dancing Princesses, 1979; Amos's Sweater, 1988; Duck Cakes for Sale, 1989; Come to the Fair, 1997; The Umbrella Party, 1998; Charlotte, 1998. NOVELS: Double Spell, 1968 in US as Twin Spell, 1969; The Root Cellar, 1981; Shadow in Hawthorn Bay, 1986; The Hollow Tree, 1997. NON-FICTION: (with R. Lunn) The County: The First Hundred Years In Loyalist Prince Edward, 1967; Larger Than Life, 1979; (with C. Moore) The Story of Canada, 1990, rev. ed., 2000; Laura Secord: A Story of Courage, 2001; Maud's House of Dreams: The Life of Lucy Maud Montgomery, 2002; A Rebel's Daughter: The 1837 Rebellion Diary of Arabella Stevens, 2006; The Unexplained: A Haunted Canada Book, 2008. OTHERS: One Hundred Shining Candles, 1991; (foreword) The Canadian Children's Treasury, 1994; (ed.) The Unseen: Scary Stories, 1997; (co-author) Dear Canada, 2006. Contributor of articles to periodicals. **Address:** Barnes and Noble Booksellers Inc., 122 5th Ave., New York, NY 10011-5605, U.S.A. **Online address:** janetlunn@sympatico.ca

LUONGO, F. Thomas. American (born United States) **Genres:** Politics/Government, History, Biography, Autobiography/Memoirs. **Career:** Tulane University, Department of History, Eva-Lou Joffrion Edwards professor, associate dean, Medieval and Early Modern Studies Program, co-director, Honors Program, director. Writer. **Publications:** The Saintly Politics of Catherine of Siena, 2006. **Address:** Tulane University, 6823 St. Charles Ave., Herbert Hall, Ste. 105, New Orleans, LA 70118-5698, U.S.A. **Online address:** tluongo@tulane.edu

LUONGO-ORLANDO, Katherine. Canadian (born Canada), b. 1969. **Genres:** How-to Books, Adult Non-fiction, Education. **Career:** Middle-school teacher and music director, 1992-97; John D. Parker Junior Public School, teacher, 1997-. Writer and consultant. **Publications:** A Project Approach to Language Learning: Linking Literary Genres and Themes in Elementary Classrooms, 2001; Authentic Assessment: Designing Performance-based Tasks, 2003; The Cornerstones to Early Literacy, 2010. **Address:** c/o Author Mail, Pembroke Publishers Ltd., 538 Hood Rd., Markham, ON L3R 3K9, Canada. **Online address:** k.luongo-orlando@rogers.com

LUPER, Steven. (Steven Dennis Luper-Foy). American (born United States), b. 1956. **Genres:** Philosophy, Adult Non-fiction, Social Commentary. **Career:** Trinity University, Department of Philosophy, assistant professor, 1982-88, associate professor, 1988-94, chair, 1988-94, 2005-, professor, 1994-. Writer. **Publications:** Invulnerability: On Securing Happiness, 1996; Living Well: Introductory Readings in Ethics, 2000; A Guide to Ethics, 2002; Philosophy of Death, 2009. EDITOR: The Possibility of Knowledge: Nozick and His Critics, 1987; Problems of International Justice, 1988; (with C. Brown) The Moral Life, 1992, 2nd ed., 1999; Social Ideals and Policies: Readings in Social and Political Philosophy, 1999; (with C. Brown) Drugs, Morality and the Law, 1994; Existing: An Introduction to Existential Thought, 2000; The Skeptics: Contemporary Essays, 2002; Essential Knowledge: Readings in Epistemology, 2003. **Address:** Department of Philosophy, Trinity University, 1 Trinity Pl., San Antonio, TX 78212-7200, U.S.A. **Online address:** sluper@trinity.edu

LUPER-FOY, Steven Dennis. See **LUPER, Steven.**

LUPICA, Mike. American (born United States), b. 1952. **Genres:** Mystery/Crime/Suspense, Sports/Fitness, Autobiography/Memoirs, Novels, Young Adult Non-fiction. **Career:** Boston Globe, correspondent, 1970-74; Boston Phoenix, columnist, 1971-75; Boston magazine, columnist, 1974-75; Washington Star, feature writer, 1974-75; World Tennis, writer, 1974-81; New York Post, basketball writer and columnist, 1975-76; New York News, columnist, 1977-81; New York Daily News, columnist, 1980-; CBS Morning News, broadcast sports journalist, 1982-84, Entertainment and Sports Programming Network (ESPN), sports journalist, 1982-83; The Sports Reporters, panelist, 1983; WCBS-TV, sports journalist, 1983; WNBC Radio, sports journalist. **Publications:** (With R. Jackson) Reggie: The Autobiography, 1984; (with B. Parcells) Parcells: Autobiography of the Biggest Giant of Them All, 1987; Shooting from the Lip: Essays, Columns, Quips, and Gripes in the Grand Tradition of Dyspeptic Sports Writing (non-fiction), 1988; (with W. Goldman) Wait Till Next Year: The Story of a Season When What Should've Happened Didn't and What Could've Gone Wrong Did, 1988; Jump, 1995; Jump (novel), 1995; Mad as Hell: How Sports Got Away from the Fans-and How We Get It Back, 1996; (with F. Imus) The Fred Book, 1998; Summer of '98: When Homers Flew, Records Fell and Baseball Reclaimed America, 1999; Bump and Run (novel), 2000; Full Court Press, 2001; Wild Pitch, 2002; New York, 2003; Too Far, 2004; Travel Team, 2004; Heat, 2006; Miracle on 49th Street, 2006; Hot Hand, 2007; Two-minute Drill, 2007; Summer Ball, 2007; The Big Field, 2008; Safe at Home: A Comeback Kids Novel, 2008; Long Shot: A Comeback Kids Novel, 2008; Million-Dollar Throw, 2009; Shoot-out: A Comeback Kids Novel, 2010; The Batboy, 2010; Game Changers, 2012. PETER FINLEY MYSTERIES: Dead Air, 1986; Extra Credits, 1988; Limited Partner, 1990; Red Zone, 2003. OTHER: Shooting from the Lip (nonfiction), 1988; (with W. Goldman) Wait till Next Year, 1988; Mad as Hell: How Sports Got Away from the Fans and How We Got It Back, 1996; (intro.) Fathers & Sons & Sports: Great Writing, 2009; Hero, 2010; The Underdogs, 2011. Contributor to periodicals. **Address:** New York Daily News, 450 W 33rd St., Fl. 3, New York, NY 10001-2681, U.S.A. **Online address:** mike@lupica.com

LUPOFF, Richard A(llen). American (born United States), b. 1935. **Genres:** Novellas/Short Stories, Mystery/Crime/Suspense, Science Fiction/Fantasy, Young Adult Fiction, Literary Criticism And History, Young Adult Non-fiction, Graphic Novels. **Career:** Sperry Univac, technical writer, 1958-63; Canaveral Press, editor, 1962-70; International Business Machines Corp., writer and director of technical films, 1963-70; Algol, book editor and reviewer, 1968-79; Crawdaddy, west coast editor, 1970-71; fulltime writer, 1970-82, 1986-; Changes, west coast editor, 1971-72; Organ, editor, 1972; KPFA-FM, broadcaster and interviewer, 1977-; Canyon Press, editor, 1985-; editor for numerous magazines. **Publications:** NONFICTION: (ed.) The Reader's Guide to Barsoom and Amtor, 1963; Edgar Rice Burroughs: Master of Adventure, 1965, rev. ed., 1975; (ed. as Dick Lupoff with D. Thompson) All in Color for a Dime, 1970; (ed. with D. Thompson as Dick O'Donnell) The Comic-Book Book, 1974; Barsoom: Edgar Rice Burroughs and the Martian Vision, 1976; (ed. with G. Davis) The Investigations of Avram Davidson, 1999; Great American Paperback: An Illustrated Tribute to Legends of the Book, 2001; Master of Adventure: The Worlds of Edgar Rice Burroughs, 2005. FICTION: One Million Centuries, 1967, rev. ed., 1981; (ed. with D. Thompson) Sacred Locomotive Flies, 1971; (with T. Carr and R. Silverberg) No Mind of Man: Three Original Novellas of Science Fiction, 1973; Into the Aether, 1974; The Crack in the Sky, 1976 in UK as Fool's Hill, 1978; The Triune Man, 1976; Sandworld, 1976; Lisa Kane: A Novel of the Supernatural, 1976; (with R.E. Howard) The Return of Skull-Face, 1977; Sword of the Demon, 1977; Space War Blues, 1978; The Ova Hamlet Papers, 1979; (ed.) What If? Stories That Should Have Won the Hugo, vol. I, 1980, vol. II, 1981; Stroka Prospekt, 1982; The Digital Wristwatch of Philip K. Dick, 1985; (comp.) Lovecraft's Book, 1985; The Forever City, 1987; The Black Tower, 1988; The Final Battle, 1990; Professor Thintwhistle, 1991; Night of the Living Gator, 1992; The Digital Wristwatch of Philip K. Dick: Hyperprism, 1993; Hyperprism, 1994. CHAPBOOKS: Nebogipfel at the End of Time, 1979. SUN'S END SERIES: Sun's End, 1984; Galaxy's End, 1988. TWIN PLANETS SERIES: Circumpolar!, 1984; Countersolar!, 1987. LINDSEY AND PLUM SERIES: The Comic Book Killer, 1988; The Classic Car Killer, 1991; The Bessie Blue Killer, 1994; The Sepia Siren Killer, 1994; The Cover Girl Killer, 1995; The Silver Chariot Killer, 1996; The Radio Red Killer, 1997; The Tinpan Tiger Killer, 1998; One Murder At A Time, 2001. COLLECTIONS: Before. 12: 01. and After, 1996; Claremont Tales, 2001; Claremont Tales II, 2002; Errors, 2005. Quintet: The Cases of Chase and Delacroix, 2008; Deep Space, 2009.

OTHERS: The Case of the Doctor Who Had No Business; or, The Adventure of the Second Anonymous Narrator, 1966; (with S. Stiles) The Adventures of Professor Thintwhistle and His Incredible Aether Flyer, 1991; The Emerald Cat Killer, 2010. Works appear in anthologies. **Address:** Henry Morrison Inc., PO Box 235, Bedford Hills, NY 10507, U.S.A.

LURAGHI, Raimondo. Italian (born Italy), b. 1921. **Genres:** History, Politics/Government. **Career:** Junior College, professor of history, 1954-64; University of Genoa, professor of American history, 1964-96, professor emeritus, 1996-; Harvard University, visiting professor; University of Richmond, visiting professor; University of Georgia, visiting professor; New York University, visiting professor. Writer. **Publications:** Ascesa e tramonto del colonialismo, 1964; Histoire du colonialisme, desgrandes découvertes aux mouvements d'indépendance, 1967; Stati Uniti, 1974; The Rise and Fall of the Plantation South, 1976; (ed.) La Guerra Civile Americana, 1976; (co-author) Economia e società degli Stati Unititra Ottocento e Novecento, 1977; Stati Uniti nell'età della guerracivile, 1978; John F. Kennedy, 1978; Storia della Guerra Civile Americana, 1984, rev. ed., 1994; (co-ed.) NATO and the Mediterranean, 1985; (contrib.) Opere di Raimondo Montecuccoli, 1988; Marinai del Sud: Storia della Marina confederata nella Guerra Civile Americana, 1861-1865, 1993; Storia della guerra civile Americana, 1994; (contrib.) Resistenza: Album della guerra di liberazione, 1995; A History of the Confederate Navy, 1996; Cinque lezioni sulla Guerra Civile americana (1861-1865), 1997; Sul sentiero di guerra: Storia delle guerre indiane del Nordamerica, 2000; Eravamo Partigiani: Ricordi del Tempo di Guerra, 2005; Spada e le magnolie: il Sud nella storia degli Stati Uniti, 2007. **Address:** 155 Corso Regina Margherita, Torino, 10122, Italy.

LURIA, Keith P. American (born United States), b. 1953. **Genres:** Theology/Religion, Cultural/Ethnic Topics, History, Social Sciences, Politics/Government. **Career:** North Carolina State University, professor of history. Academic and historian. **Publications:** Territories of Grace: Cultural Change in the Seventeenth-Century Diocese of Grenoble, 1991; Sacred Boundaries: Religious Coexistence and Conflict in Early-Modern France, 2005. **Address:** Department of History, North Carolina State University, 470 Withers Hall, 2101 Hillsborough St., PO Box 8108, Raleigh, NC 27695-8108, U.S.A. **Online address:** keithluria@ncsu.edu

LURIE, Alison. American (born United States), b. 1926. **Genres:** Novels, Fash Ion/Costume, Literary Criticism And History, Mythology/Folklore, Picture/Board Books, Young Adult Non-fiction, Novellas/Short Stories. **Career:** Cornell University, Department of English, lecturer in English, 1970-73, associate professor, 1973-76, professor of English, 1976-, Frederic J Whiton professor of American literature, 1989-, now Frederic J. Whiton professor emeritus of American literature. Writer. **Publications:** Love and Friendship, 1962; The Nowhere City, 1965; Imaginary Friends, 1967; Real People, 1969; The War between the Tates, 1974; Poems and Plays, 1976; Only Children, 1979; The Heavenly Zoo: Legends And Tales of the Stars, 1979; Clever Gretchen and Other Forgotten Folktales (juvenile), 1980; Fabulous Beasts (juvenile), 1981; The Language of Clothes, 1981, 2nd ed., 1991; Foreign Affairs, 1984; The Truth about Lorin Jones, 1988; Don't Tell the Grown-Ups: Subversive Children's Literature, 1990; Not in Front of the Grown-ups, 1991; Women and Ghosts, 1994; The Last Resort, 1998; (reteller) The Black Geese: A Baba Yaga Story from Russia, 1999; Familiar Spirits: A Memoir of James Merrill and David Jackson, 2001; Boys and Girls Forever: Children's Classics from Cinderella to Harry Potter, 2003; Truth and Consequences, 2005; Baba Yaga and the Stolen Baby, 2007; (contrib.) Glorious Sky: Herbert Katzman's New York, 2010. EDITOR: Oxford Book of Modern Fairy Tales, 1993; (and intro.) The Secret Garden, 1999. Contributor of articles to periodicals. **Address:** Department of English, Cornell University, 250 Goldwin Smith Hall, Ithaca, NY 14853-3201, U.S.A. **Online address:** al28@cornell.edu

LURIE, April. American (born United States), b. 1962?. **Genres:** Novels, Young Adult Non-fiction, Young Adult Fiction. **Career:** Writer. **Publications:** YOUNG ADULT: Dancing in the Streets of Brooklyn, 2002; Brothers, Boyfriends, & Other Criminal Minds, 2007; The Latent Powers of Dylan Fontaine, 2008; Less-Dead, 2010. **Address:** Delacorte Press, 1745 Broadway, New York, NY 10019, U.S.A. **Online address:** a-lurie@sbcglobal.net

LURIE, Jonathan. American (born United States), b. 1939. **Genres:** History, Law, Politics/Government, Military/Defense/Arms Control. **Career:** Rutgers University, instructor, 1969-70, assistant professor, 1970-76, associate professor of history and law, 1976-84, Graduate School of Newark, associate dean, 1976-80, adjunct professor of law, professor of history, 1985-, now professor emeritus; U.S. Court of Military Appeals, historian, 1987-2001; U.S. Military Academy, visiting professor of law, 1994-95. Writer. **Publications:** The Chicago Board of Trade, 1859-1905: The Dynamics of Self Regulation, 1979; Law and the American Nation, 1865-1912, 1983; The Constitution and Economic Change, 1988; Arming Military Justice: The Origins of the U.S. Court of Military Appeals, 1775-1950, 1992; Pursuing Military Justice: The History of the Court of Military Appeals, 1951-1980, 1998; Military Justice in America: The U.S. Court of Appeals for the Armed Forces, 1775-1980, 2001; (with R.M. Labb) Slaughterhouse Cases: Regulation, Reconstruction and the Fourteenth Amendment, 2003; The Chase Court: Justices, Rulings and Legacy, 2004; William Howard Taft: Progressive Conservative, 2011. Contributor to journals. **Address:** Department of History, Rutgers University, 330 Conklin Hall, 175 University Ave., Newark, NJ 07102-1814, U.S.A. **Online address:** jlurie@andromeda.rutgers.edu

LURIE, Morris. Australian (born Australia), b. 1938. **Genres:** Novels, Novellas/Short Stories, Children's Fiction, Plays/Screenplays, Essays, Young Adult Fiction. **Career:** Full-time writer, 1973-. **Publications:** NOVELS: Rappaport, 1966; The London Jungle Adventures of Charlie Hope, 1968; Rappaport's Revenge, 1973; Flying Home, 1978; Seven Books for Grossman, 1983; Madness, 1991; To Light Attained: A Novel, 2008. SHORT STORIES: Happy Times, 1969; Inside the Wardrobe: 20 Stories, 1975; Running Nicely, 1979; Dirty Friends, 1981; Outrageous Behaviour, 1984; The Night We Ate the Sparrow: A Memoir and 14 Stories, 1985; Two Brothers, Running, 1988; The String, 1995; Welcome to Tangier, 1997; The Secret Strength of Children, 2001. FOR CHILDREN: The 27th Annual African Hippopotamus Race, 1969; Arlo the Dandy Lion, 1971; Toby's Millions, 1982; The Story of Imelda, Who Was Small, 1984; Night-Night!, 1986; What's That Noise? What's That Sound?, 1991; Racing the Moon 1993; Boy in a Storm at Sea, 1997; Zeeks Alive!, 1997. ESSAYS: The English in Heat, 1972; Hack Work, 1977; Public Secrets: Blowing the Whistle on Australia, England, France, Japan, the U.S. and Places Worse, 1981; Snow Jobs, 1985; My Life as a Movie and Other Gross Conceits, 1988. OTHER: Waterman: Three Plays, 1979; Whole Life (autobiography), 1987; When and How to Write Short Stories and What They Are (textbook), 2000; 17 Versions of Jewishness: 20 Examples, 2001. Contributor to periodicals. Works appear in anthologies. **Address:** Penguin Books, 487 Maroondah Hwy., PO Box 257, Ringwood, VI 3134, Australia. **Online address:** MorrisLurie@commonground.com.au

LURQUIN, Paul F. American (born United States), b. 1942. **Genres:** Sciences, Biology, History, Technology, Engineering. **Career:** Washington State University, School of Molecular Biosciences, professor of genetics, now professor emeritus. Writer. **Publications:** (Ed. with A. Kleinhofs) Genetic Engineering in Eukaryotes, 1983; The Green Phoenix: A History of Genetically Modified Plants, 2001; High Tech Harvest: Understanding Genetically Modified Food Plants, 2002; The Origins of Life and the Universe, 2003; (with C.K. Omoto) Genes and DNA: A Beginner's Guide to Genetics and Its Applications, 2004; (with L. Stone) A Genetic and Cultural Odyssey: The Life and Work of L. Luca Cavalli- Sforza, 2005; (with L. Stone) Genes, Culture and Human Evolution: A Synthesis, 2007; (with L. Stone) Evolution and Religious Creation Myths: How Scientists Respond, 2007. **Address:** School of Molecular Biosciences, Washington State University, PO Box 647520, Pullman, WA 99164-7520, U.S.A. **Online address:** lurquin@wsu.edu

LUSANE, Clarence. American (born United States), b. 1953?. **Genres:** History, Adult Non-fiction, Politics/Government, Race Relations. **Career:** Howard University, Center for Drug Abuse Research, faculty; Columbia University, Institute for Research in African American Studies, faculty; American University, School of International Service, associate professor of political science, Comparative and Regional Studies Program, director; Black Political Agenda Journal, editor. **Publications:** Pipe Dream Blues: Racism and the War on Drugs, 1991; The Struggle for Equal Education, 1992; New Beginnings and a Cautious Celebration: African Americans and the 1992 Election, 1994; African Americans at the Crossroads: The Restructuring of Black Leadership and the 1992 Elections, 1994; No Easy Victories: Black Americans and the Vote, 1996; Race in the Global Era: African Americans at the Millennium, 1997; Hitler's Black Victims: The Historical Experiences of Afro-Germans, European Blacks, Africans, and African Americans in the Nazi Era, 2003; (with K. Chouhan) Black Voluntary and Community Sector Funding: Its Impact on Civic Engagement and Capacity Building, 2004; Colin Powell and Condoleezza Rice: Foreign Policy, Race, and the New American Century, 2006; Black History of the White House, 2011. **Address:**

School of International Service, American University, Rm. 335 A, 4400 Massachusetts Ave. NW, Washington, DC 20016-8071, U.S.A. **Online address:** clusane@american.edu

LUSBY, Jim. (James Kennedy). Irish/British (born England), b. 1951?. **Genres:** Novels. **Career:** Writer and novelist. **Publications:** (With M. Dungan) Snuff, 1992; (with H. Ciglic) Philip Marlowe in Macbethovi umori: Zabavna radijska igra, 1993; Making the Cut, 1995; Flashback, 1996; (as James Kennedy) Armed and Dangerous, 1996; Kneeling at the Altar, 1998; (as James Kennedy) Silent City, 1998; Crazy Man Michael, 2000; A Waste of Shame, 2001; Serial: A Confession, 2002. **Address:** c/o Author Mail, Eve White Literary Agent, 54 Gloucester St., London, GL SW1V 4EG, England.

LUSK, John. American (born United States), b. 1969?. **Genres:** Novels, Natural History, Biography. **Career:** Ernst & Young Information Technology Group, senior consultant; Platinum Concepts Inc., co-founder, 1999-. Writer. **Publications:** (With K. Harrison) The Mouse Driver Chronicles: The True-Life Adventures of Two First-Time Entrepreneurs, 2002. **Address:** c/o Author Mail, Perseus Books Group, 387 Park Ave. S, 12th Fl., New York, NY 10016-8810, U.S.A.

LUSTBADER, Eric Van. American (born United States), b. 1946. **Genres:** Novels, Mystery/Crime/Suspense, Westerns/Adventure, Science Fiction/Fantasy. **Career:** CIS-TRANS Productions (music producers), owner, 1963-67; teacher, 1968-70; Cashbox (music trade journal), associate editor, 1970-72; Elektra Records, director of international artists and repertory and assistant, 1972-73; Dick James Music, director of publicity and creative services, 1974-75; Sweet Dream Productions, owner, 1975-76; NBC-TV, writer and field producer of news film on Elton John, 1976; CBS Records, designer of publicity and album covers and manager of media services, 1976-78; Writer, 1978-. **Publications:** SUNSET WARRIOR CYCLE: The Sunset Warrior, 1977; Shallows of Night, 1978; Dai-San, 1978; Beneath an Opal Moon, 1980; Dragons on the Sea of Night, 1997. NICHOLAS LINNEAR SERIES: The Ninja, 1980; The Miko, 1984; White Ninja, 1990; Kaisho: A Nicholas Linnear Novel, 1993; Floating City, 1994; Second Skin, 1995. NOVELS: Sirens, 1981; Black Heart, 1983; Zero, 1988; French Kiss, 1989; Angel Eyes, 1991; Black Blade, 1993; Batman: The Last Angel, 1994; Dark Homecoming, 1997; Pale Saint, 1998; Art Kills, 2002; The Testament, 2006; Blood Trust, 2011. CHINA MAROC SERIES: Jian, 1985; Shan, 1986. PEARL SAGAS SERIES: The Ring of Five Dragons, 2001; The Veil of a Thousand Tears, 2002; Mistress of the Pearl, 2004. BOURNE SERIES WITH R. LUDLUM: The Bourne legacy, 2004; The Bourne Betrayal, 2007; The Bourne Sanction, 2008; The Bourne Deception, 2009; The Bourne Objective, 2010; The Bourne Reality, 2011; The Bourne Dominion, 2011; The Bourne Upset, 2012; The Bourne Imperative, 2012. JACK MCCLURE SERIES: First Daughter, 2008; Last Snow, 2010. **Address:** Henry Morrison Inc., 105 S Bedford Rd., PO Box 235, Mt. Kisco, NY 10549, U.S.A. **Online address:** evl@ericvanlustbader.com

LUSTED, Marcia Amidon. American (born United States), b. 1962. **Genres:** Novels, Architecture, History. **Career:** Freelance writer, 2002-; Institute of Children's Literature, instructor, 2004-; Cobblestone Publishing, assistant editor. **Publications:** Time's Passage (fiction), 2000; Building History: The Holy City of Jerusalem, 2002; Building History: Hoover Dam, 2003; Building History: The Canals of Venice, 2003; Building History: A Nuclear Power Plant, 2004; Building History: The Empire State Building, 2005; Chunnel, 2005; International Space Station, 2006; National Mall, 2006; 2004 Indian Ocean Tsunami, 2008; Revolution and the New Nation, 2008; Obesity and Food Policing, 2008; Advertising to Children, 2009; Cosmetic Surgery, 2009; Iowa: The Hawkeye State, 2010; Oregon: The Beaver State, 2010; Alabama: The Heart of Dixie, 2010; Ohio: The Buckeye State, 2010; Virginia: The Old Dominion, 2010; Pennsylvania: The Keystone State, 2010; Georgia: The Peach State, 2010; Illinois: The Prairie State, 2010; Tiananmen Square Protests, 2010; Wisconsin: The Badger State, 2010; How to Analyze the Works of Stephen King, 2010; Arizona: The Grand Canyon State, 2010; Poverty, 2010; Maryland: The Old Line State, 2010; Missouri: The Show-Me State, 2010; Technology Pioneers: Social Networking: Myspace, Facebook & Twitter, 2011; District Of Columbia: The Nation's Capital, 2011; Women's Roles In Religion, 2011; Alaska: The Last Frontier, 2011; Puerto Rico: The Isle Of Enchantment, 2011; Utah: The Beehive State, 2011; Idaho: The Gem State, 2011; Montana: The Treasure State, 2011; Wyoming: The Equality State, 2011; Nevada: The Silver State, 2011; Hawaii: The Aloha State, 2011; North Dakota: The Peace Garden State, 2011; Entertainment, 2011; The Chernobyl Disaster, 2011; America's Colonization and Settlement, 2011; The Oregon

Trail, 2012; The Chilean Miners' Rescue, 2012; The Fight for Women's Suffrage, 2012; Mark Zuckerberg, 2012; The Capture and Killing of Osama Bin Laden, 2012; The 2011 Japan Disasters, 2012. **Address:** Cobblestone Publishing, 30 Grove St., Ste. C, Peterborough, NH 03458, U.S.A. **Online address:** nfwriter@worldpath.net

LUSTIG, Nora Claudia. American/Argentine (born Argentina), b. 1951. **Genres:** Business/Trade/Industry, Economics, Adult Non-fiction. **Career:** El Colegio de Mexico, professor of economic studies, 1975-91, Masters Program in Economics, academic coordinator, 1975-76, 1986-88; Government of Mexico, consultant, 1975-; Inter-American Development Bank, consultant, 1975-, Poverty and Inequality Unit, senior advisor and chief, 1997-2001; United Nations Development Programme, consultant, 1975-, Poverty Group, director, 2006-07; World Bank, consultant, 1975-, World Development Report, deputy director and director, 2000-01; University of California, visiting professor, 1984; Mexican National System of Research, fellow, 1987-91; Brookings Institution, visiting fellow, 1989-93, Foreign Policy Studies Program, senior fellow, 1989-97, non-resident senior fellow, 1997-2004; Washington Exchange, co-director, 1990-; International Food Policy Research Institute, board director, 1994-98; Universidad de las Américas, president and professor of economics, 2001-05; George Washington University, Elliott School of International Affairs, J.B. and Maurice C. Shapiro visiting professor of international affairs, 2007-09; Tulane University, Department of Economics, Samuel Z. Stone professor of Latin American economics, 2009-. Writer. **Publications:** IN SPANISH: (ed.) Panorama y Perspectivas de la Economía Mexicana, 1980; Distribucion del ingreso y crecimiento en México: Un análisis de ideas estructuralistas, 1981; (ed. with R. Bouzas) Liberalización Comercial e Integración Regional: De NAFTA a MERCOSUR, 1992; (co-author) México, 1992; (co-ed.) Mexico: Auge, crisis y ajuste, 3 vols., 1993; (ed. with M. Cárdenas) Pobreza y desigualdad en América Latina, 1999. NONFICITON: Mexico: The Remaking of an Economy, 1992, 2nd ed., 1998. EDITOR: (with B.P. Bosworth and R.Z. Lawrence) North American Free Trade: Assessing the Impact, 1992; Coping with Austerity, 1995; (with B.P. Bosworth and S.M. Collins) Coming Together?: Mexico-United States Relations, 1997; (with S. Edwards) Labor Markets in Latin America: Combining Social Protection with Market Flexibility, 1997; Shielding the Poor: Social Protection in the Developing World, 2000; (with F. Bourguignon and F.H.G. Ferreira) Microeconomics of Income Distribution Dynamics in East Asia and Latin America, 2004; (with L.F. Lopez-Calva) Declining Inequality in Latin America: A Decade of Progress?, 2010. OTHERS: (co-author) Social Protection for Equity and Growth, 2000; (contrib.) Attacking Poverty, 2000. Contributor to books. **Address:** Department of Economics, Tulane University, 204 Tilton Hall, 6823 St. Charles Ave., New Orleans, LA 70118, U.S.A. **Online address:** nlustig@tulane.edu

LUSTIG, T(imothy) J(ohn). British (born England), b. 1961. **Genres:** Novels, Area Studies, Literary Criticism And History, Novellas/Short Stories, Classics. **Career:** University of Keele, lecturer in American literature, 1993-, Programme director. Writer. **Publications:** Doubled Up, 1990; (ed. and intro.) The Turn of the Screw and Other Stories, 1992; Henry James and the Ghostly, 1994. **Address:** c/o Carol Smith, Carol Smith Literary Agency, 25 Hornton Ct., Kensington High St., London, GL W8 7RT, England. **Online address:** t.j.lustig@ams.keele.ac.uk

LUST-OKAR, Ellen. American (born United States), b. 1966. **Genres:** Politics/Government. **Career:** Yale University, associate professor of political science. Political scientist, educator and writer. **Publications:** Structuring Conflict in the Arab World: Incumbents, Opponents and Institutions, 2005; (with S. Zerhouni) Political Participation in the Middle East, 2008. Contributor to books and periodicals. **Address:** Department of Political Science, Yale University, New Haven, CT 06520, U.S.A. **Online address:** ellen.lust-okar@yale.edu

LUTTWAK, Edward (Nicolae). American/British/Italian (born Italy), b. 1942. **Genres:** History, International Relations/Current Affairs, Military/Defense/Arms Control, Politics/Government, Economics. **Career:** University of Bath, lecturer, 1965-67; Washington Center of Foreign Policy Research, associate director, 1972-75; Johns Hopkins University, research professor, 1975-78; Georgetown University, Center for Strategic and International Studies, senior fellow, 1976-87, research professor in international security affairs, 1978-82, Arleigh Burke chair, 1987-, director of geo-economics, 1991-; University of California-Berkeley, Nimitz lecturer, 1987; Yale University, Tanner lecturer, 1989. Writer. **Publications:** A Dictionary of Modern War, 1971; The Strategic Balance, 1972; The Political Uses of Sea Power, 1974; The U.S.-U.S.S.R. Nuclear Weapons Balance, 1974; Coup d'etat: A Practical Handbook, 1979; Sea Power in the Mediterranean: Political Utility and Military Constraints, 1979; The Israeli Army, 1983; The Grand Strategy of the Soviet Union, 1983; The Pentagon and the Art of War, 1984; Strategy and History, 1985; Strategy: The Logic of War and Peace, 1987, rev. ed., 2001; The Endangered American Dream: How to Stop the United States from being a Third World Country and How to Win the Geo-Economic Struggle for Industrial Supremacy, 1993; Turbo-capitalism: Winner and Losers in the Global Ecomony, 1999; Virtual American Empire: War, Faith and Power, 2009; Grand Strategy of the Byzantine Empire, 2009; Rise of China and the Logic of Strategy, 2012. **Address:** Center for Strategic and International Studies, Georgetown University, 1800 K St. NW, Washington, DC 20006-2202, U.S.A. **Online address:** eluttwak@gmail.com

LUTZ, Catherine A. American (born United States), b. 1952. **Genres:** Anthropology/Ethnology. **Career:** Harvard University, assistant professor, 1980-81; State University of New York, assistant professor, 1981-89, associate professor of anthropology, 1989-92; University of North Carolina, associate professor, 1992-96, professor of anthropology, 1996-2003; Brown University, Watson Institute for International Studies and Anthropology, professor, research professor, 2003-, chair, Thomas J. Watson Jr. Family professor of anthropology and international studies, chair; American Ethnological Society, president, 2001-05; Radcliffe Institute for Advanced Study, Matina S. Horner distinguished visiting professor, 2007-08. Writer. **Publications:** Unnatural Emotions: Everyday Sentiments on a Micronesian Atoll & their Challenge to Western Theory, 1988; (with J.L. Collins) Reading National Geographic, 1993; Homefront: A Military City and the American Twentieth Century, 2001; (with A.L. Fernandez) Carjacked, 2010; (with M. Gutmann) Breaking Ranks, 2010. EDITOR: Micronesia as Strategic Colony: The Impact of U.S. Policy on Micronesian Health and Culture, 1984; (with L. Abu-Lughod) Language and the Politics of Emotion, 1990; (with T. Schwartz and G.M. White) New Directions in Psychological Anthropology, 1992; Bases of Empire: The Global Struggle Against U.S. Military Posts, 2009. **Address:** Watson Institute for International Studies, Brown University, 111 Thayer St., PO Box 1970, Providence, RI 02912, U.S.A. **Online address:** catherine_lutz@brown.edu

LUTZ, John Sutton. Canadian (born Canada), b. 1959?. **Genres:** Essays, History. **Career:** University of Victoria, Victoria, associate professor in history, 1997-; University of British Columbia, postdoctoral fellow; University of Washington, postdoctoral fellow; University of Victoria, postdoctoral fellow. Academic, writer and historian. **Publications:** (Ed. with J. Lee) Situating Race and Racisms in Space, Time, and Theory: Critical Essays for Activists and Scholars, 2005; (ed.) Myth and Memory: Stories of Indigenous-European Contact, 2007; (ed. with B. Neis) Making and Moving Knowledge: Interdisciplinary and Community- Based Research in a World on the Edge, 2008; Makúk: A New History of Aboriginal-White Relations, 2008. Contributor to books and journals. **Address:** Department of History, University of Victoria, Rm. B245, Clearihue Bldg., 3800 Finnerty Rd., Victoria, BC V8W 3P4, Canada.

LUTZ, John (Thomas). American (born United States), b. 1939. **Genres:** Novellas/Short Stories, Mystery/Crime/Suspense, Plays/Screenplays, Writing/Journalism, Novels. **Career:** Private Eye Writers of America, president, 1987-88; Mystery Writers of America, president, 1991. Writer. **Publications:** NOVELS: The Truth of the Matter, 1971; Buyer Beware, 1976; Bonegrinder, 1977; Lazarus Man, 1979; Jericho Man, 1980; The Shadow Man, 1981; (with S. Greene) Exiled, 1982; (with B. Pronzini) The Eye, 1984; Nightlines, 1984; The Right to Sing the Blues, 1986; Tropical Heat, 1986; Ride the Lightning, 1987; Scorcher, 1987; Dancer's Debt, 1988; Kiss, 1988; Shadowtown, 1988; Time Exposure, 1989; Flame, 1989; SWF Seeks Same, 1990; Diamond Eyes, 1990; Bloodfire, 1991; Hot, 1992; Dancing with the Dead, 1992; Spark, 1993; Thicker than Blood, 1993; Torch, 1994; Burn, 1995; Death by Jury, 1995; The Ex, 1996; Lightning, 1996; Oops! A Nudger Mystery, 1998; (with D. August) Final Seconds, 1998; The Night Caller, 2001; The Night Watcher, 2002; The Night Spider, 2003 as Night Victims, 2009; Darker Than Night, 2004; Fear the Night, 2005; Chill of Night, 2006; In for the Kill, 2007; Night Kills, 2008; Urge to Kill, 2009; Mister X, 2010; Serial, 2011; Pulse, 2012. SHORT STORIES: Better Mousetraps: The Best Mystery Stories of John Lutz, 1988; Shadows Everywhere, 1994; Until You are Dead, 1998; The Nudger Dilem-

mas, 2001, Arful, 2006; Chop Survey, 2006; The Laundry Room, 2006. OTHERS: Endless Road, and Other Stories, 2003; Darker Than Night, 2004; Fear the Night, 2005; Chill the Night, 2006; In for the Kill, 2008; Night Kills, 2008. Contributor to books and periodicals. **Address:** 880 Providence Ave., St. Louis, MO 63131, U.S.A. **Online address:** jlutz65151@aol.com

LUTZ, Lisa. American (born United States), b. 1970. **Genres:** Mystery/Crime/Suspense, Romance/Historical. **Career:** Writer. **Publications:** The Spellman Files, 2007; Curse of the Spellmans, 2008; Revenge of the Spellmans, 2009; The Spellmans Strike Again, 2010; (with D. Hayward) Heads You Lose, 2011. **Address:** Levine Greenberg Literary Agency, 307 7th Ave., Ste. 2407, New York, NY 10001, U.S.A. **Online address:** contactlisa@lisalutz.com

LUTZ, Tom. American (born United States) **Genres:** History, Adult Nonfiction, Literary Criticism And History. **Career:** University of Iowa, associate professor of English, professor, 1989-2004; California Institute of the Arts, staff, 2004-05; University of California, Department of Creative Writing, professor and chair, 2005-, Palm Desert MFA in Creative Writing, director, Writing for the Performing Arts, director; Stanford University, faculty; University of Copenhagen, faculty. Writer. **Publications:** American Nervousness, 1903: An Anecdotal History, 1991; (ed. with S. Ashton) These Colored United States: African American Essays from the 1920s, 1996; Crying: The Natural and Cultural History of Tears, 1999; Cosmopolitan Vistas: American Regionalism and Literary Value, 2004; Doing Nothing: A History of Loafers, Loungers, Slackers and Bums in America, 2006; (with B. Fern) Ashes to Gold, 2011. **Address:** Department of Creative Writing, University of California, 4147 INTS Bldg., 900 University Ave., Riverside, CA 92521, U.S.A. **Online address:** tom.lutz@ucr.edu

LUX, Maureen K. Canadian (born Canada), b. 1956. **Genres:** Adult Non-fiction, Medicine/Health, History. **Career:** Federation of Saskatchewan Indian Nations, historical consultant, 1999-2002; Brock University, Department of History, assistant professor, 2002-, associate professor. Writer. **Publications:** Medicine That Walks: Disease, Medicine and Canadian Plains Native People, 1880-1940, 2001. Contributor to periodicals. **Address:** Department of History, Brock University, Rm. GL 219, 500 Glenridge Ave., St. Catharines, ON L2S 3A1, Canada. **Online address:** mlux@brocku.ca

LUXON, Thomas H. American (born United States), b. 1954. **Genres:** Literary Criticism And History. **Career:** University of Chicago, William Rainey Harper instructor, 1984-85; St. Lawrence University, visiting assistant professor of English, 1985-86; Franklin and Marshall College, assistant professor of English, 1987-88; Dartmouth College, Department of English, associate professor of English, 1988-, professor of English, vice chair, 1994-96, Dartmouth Center for the Advancement of Learning, Cheheyl professor and director. Day Care Center, director. Writer. **Publications:** Literal Figures: Puritan Allegory and the Reformation Crisis in Representation, 1995; Single Imperfection: Milton, Marriage, and Friendship, 2005. Contributor to books. **Address:** Department of English, Dartmouth College, 6247 Baker Library, 6032 Sanborn House, Hanover, NH 03755, U.S.A. **Online address:** thomas.h.luxon@dartmouth.edu

LUX-STERRITT, Laurence. See **STERRITT, Laurence Lux.**

LUXTON, Donald. Canadian (born Canada), b. 1954. **Genres:** History, Architecture. **Career:** Donald Luxton & Associates, heritage consultant, 1983. Writer. **Publications:** (With L.D. Acres) Lions Gate, 1999; Vancouver General Hospital: 100 Years of Care and Service, 2006; (ed.) Building the West: The Early Architects of British Columbia, 2nd ed., 2007. **Address:** Donald Luxton & Associates, 1030-470 Granville St., Vancouver, BC V6C 1V5, Canada. **Online address:** donald@donaldluxton.com

LUYENDIJK, Joris. Dutch (born Netherlands), b. 1971. **Genres:** Reference, Biography, Autobiography/Memoirs. **Career:** University of Tilburg, Leonardo Chair, 2010. Writer. **Publications:** People Like Us: Misrepresenting the Middle East, 2009. Contributor to newspapers. **Address:** Susijn Agency Ltd., 64 Great Titchfield St., 3rd Fl., London, GL W1W 7QH, England.

LUZ, Ulrich. Swiss (born Switzerland), b. 1938. **Genres:** Theology/Religion. **Career:** International Christian University, professor, 1969-71; University of Göttingen, professor of New Testament, 1972-80; University of Bern, professor of New Testament studies, 1980-2003, professor emeritus of New Testament, 2003-. Theologian and writer. **Publications:** Das Geschichtsverständnis des Paulus, 1968; (with Seiichi Yagi) Gott in Japan: Anstösse Zum Gespräch mit japanischen Philosophen, Theologen, Schriftstellern, 1973; (with P. Lapide) Der Jude Jesus: Thesen eines Juden: Antworten eines Christen, 1979; (contrib.) Eschatologie Und Friedenshandeln: Exegetische Beitrage Zur Frage Christlicher Friedensverantwortung, 1981; (with R. Smend) Gesetz, 1981; (ed. with H. Weder) Die Mitte Des Neuen Testaments: Einheit Und Vielfalt Neutestamentlicher Theologie: Festschrift Fur Eduard Schweizer Zum Siebzigsten Geburtstag, 1983; (with C. Link and L. Vischer) Sie aber hielten fest an der Gemeinschaft: Einheit der Kirche als Prozess im Neuen Testament und heute, 1988; Das Evangelium nach Matthäus (Mt 1-7), 1985; Matthew: A Commentary, 1989; Das Evangelium nach Matthäus (Mt 8-17), 1990; (contrib.) Zankapfel Bibel: Eine Bibel, Viele Zugänge: Ein theologisches Gesprach, 1992; Die Jesusgeschichte Des Matthäus, 1993; Matthew in History: Interpretation, Influence, and Effects, 1994; (ed. with U. Neuenschwander and J. Zurcher) Reich Gottes Und Christentum, 1995; Das Evangelium nach Matthäus (Mt 18-25) 1997; (contrib.) Antijudaismus-christliche Erblast, 1999; Matthew 8-20: A Commentary, 2001; (ed. with W. Dietrich) The Bible in a World Context: An Experiment in Contextual Hermeneutics, 2002; Das Evangelium nach Matthäus (Mt 26-28), 2002; (with A. Michaels) Jesus Oder Buddha: Leben Und Lehre Im Vergleich, 2002; (ed. with C. Gunzler and J. Zurcher) Vorträge, Vorlesungen, Aufsatze, 2003; (ed. with I.Z. Dimitrov, J.D.G. Dunn and K.W. Niebuhr) Das Alte Testament als christliche Bibel in orthodoxer und westlicher Sicht, 2004; (contrib.) Die pragende Kraft der Texte, 2005; Studies in Matthew, 2005; Matthew 21-28: A Commentary, 2005; Matthew 1-7: A Commentary, 2007; (contrib.) Neutestamentliche Exegese im Dialog, 2008; (with L. Vischer and C. Link) ökumene im Neuen Testament und heute, 2010; (ed. with J. Zürcher) Die Weltanschauung der indischen Denker, 2010. **Address:** University of Bern, Langgassstrasse 51, Bern, CH-3000, Switzerland. **Online address:** ulrich.luz@theol.unibe.ch

LWIN, Nanda Layos. Canadian (born Canada), b. 1971. **Genres:** Music, Art/Art History, Photography. **Career:** Music Data Research, founder and president, 1995-; Seneca College, professor of civil engineering technology, 2004; Humber College, lecturer. Journalist. **Publications:** The Record 1994; Chart Almanac, 1995; The Canadian Singles Chart Book, 1996; Canada's Top Hits of the Year, 1997; The 1996 Country Chart Yearbook, 1997; Canada's Top 1000 Singles, 1998; Top 40 Hits: The Essential Chart Guide, 1999; Top Albums: The Essential Chart Guide, 2003; The Essential 2002 Chart Yearbook, 2003; (contrib.) Top 10 of Everything, 1998-2005; (contrib.) The Top 100 Canadian Singles, 2010. **Address:** Music Data Research, Sheppard Centre Postal Sta., PO Box 43225, Toronto, ON M2N 6N1, Canada. **Online address:** lwin@look.ca

LY, Many. American/Cambodian (born Cambodia), b. 1977?. **Genres:** Children's Fiction, Young Adult Non-fiction. **Career:** Greater Pittsburgh Literacy Council, program services manager. Writer and educator. **Publications:** Home Is East, 2005; Roots and Wings, 2008. **Address:** Greater Pittsburgh Literacy Council, Center-Whitehall Pl., Apt. 18, 1450 Maple Dr.,, Pittsburgh, PA 15227, U.S.A. **Online address:** many.ly@hotmail.com

LYCETT GREEN, Candida. British/Irish (born Ireland), b. 1942. **Genres:** Homes/Gardens, Horticulture, Plays/Screenplays, Children's Fiction. **Career:** Vogue Magazine, contributing editor, 1987-; Churches Conservation Trust, vice president. **Publications:** The Adventure of Hadrian Hedgehog, 1970; Hadrian in the Orient, 1971; (with C. Booker) Goodbye London: An Illustrated Guide to Threatened Buildings, 1972; The Front Garden, 1979; (with T. Evans) English Cottages, 1982; Brilliant Gardens, 1989; The Perfect English Country House, 1991; Dangerous Edge of Things, 1995; England: Travels through an Unwrecked Landscape, 1996; Country Life's One Hundred Favorite Houses, 1999; (with H.R.H. The Prince of Wales) The Garden at Highgrove, 2000; Over the Hills and Far Away: An English Odyssey, 2003; Unwrecked England, 2009. EDITOR: (and intro.) John Betjeman: Letters, vol. I: 1926-1951, 1994, vol. II: 1951-1984, 1995; (and intro.) Coming Home: An Anthology of His Prose, 1920-1977, 1997; Betjeman's Britain: An Anthology of Prose and Verse, 1999. Contributor to periodicals. **Address:** c/o Aitken Alexander, Aitken Alexander Associates Ltd, 18-21 Cavaye Pl., London, GL SW10 9PT, England.

LYDECKER, John. *See* **GALLAGHER, Stephen.**

LYDEN, Jacki. Also writes as Elmer Layden, Anthony Laden. American (born United States), b. 1954. **Genres:** Autobiography/Memoirs, Biography. **Career:** National Public Radio, journalist, 1979; reporter, 1981-, senior correspondent, reporter from Chicago bureau, middle east and European correspondent from London bureau; University of Chicago, Benton fellow, 1991-92. **Publications:** (With C. Jakus) Landmarks and Legends of Uptown, 1980; Daughter of the Queen of Sheba (memoir), 1997; (contrib. with T. Bahrampour, E. Gheytanchi) Project Misplaced: The Rise and Fall of Simon Ordoubadi, 2004. Contributor to magazines. **Address:** National Public Radio, 635 Massachusetts Ave. NW, Washington, DC 20001-3740, U.S.A.

LYFTOGT, Kenneth L. American (born United States), b. 1951. **Genres:** Local History/Rural Topics. **Career:** University of Northern Iowa, Department of History, lecturer; Iowa Public School System and Iowa Humanities Board, lecturer; Northeast Iowa Civil War Association, founding member. Writer. **Publications:** Road Freaks of Trans-Amerika, 1975; (with A. Sunseri) The Sullivan Family of Waterloo (booklet), 1988; (ed.) Left for Dixie: The Civil War Diary of John Rath, 1991; Highway 13, 1991; From Blue Mills to Columbia: Cedar Falls and the Civil War, 1993; Iowa's Forgotten General: Matthew Mark Trumbull, 2005. **Address:** Department of History, University of Northern Iowa, 203 Seerley Bldg., Cedar Falls, IA 50614, U.S.A. **Online address:** ken.lyftogt@uni.edu

LYKINS, Jenny. American (born United States) **Genres:** Romance/Historical, Young Adult Fiction, Novels, Science Fiction/Fantasy. **Career:** Writer. **Publications:** NOVELS: Lost Yesterday, 1997; Echoes of Tomorrow, 1997; Waiting for Yesterday, 1997; Distant Dreams, 1998; River of Dreams, 1999. OTHER: (with E. Bevarly, C. Claybourne and L. Kurland) Christmas Spirits, 1997. Contributor to books. **Address:** Jove Books, 375 Hudson St., New York, NY 10014-3658, U.S.A. **Online address:** jenlykins@aol.com

LYNCH, Allen C. American (born United States), b. 1955. **Genres:** Politics/Government, International Relations/Current Affairs, History. **Career:** Institute for East-West Security Studies, research associate, 1984-87, deputy director of studies, 1987-89; Columbia University, W. Averill Harriman Institute for Advanced Study of the Soviet Union, assistant director, 1989-92; University of Virginia, Department of Government and Foreign Affairs, associate professor, 1992-2001, Department of Politics, professor, 2001-, Cummings Memorial Professor of International Affairs, 2002-08, Hugh S. & Winifred B. Cumming memorial chair in international affairs, Center for Russian and East European Studies, director, 1993-2008; RFE-RL Research Institute, visiting fellow, 1993-94; Feris Foundation of America Inc., executive vice-president, 1988-94; Free University, JFK Institute for North American Studies, visiting professor, 2001; Institut des Hautes Etudes Internationales, Albert Gallatin Fellow in International Affairs. Writer. **Publications:** (Ed. with F.S. Larrabee and R.B. Byers) Confidence-Building Measures and International Security, 1986; Political and Military Implications of the Nuclear Winter Theory, 1987; (ed. with K.S. McNamara) Changing Dimensions of East-West Relations, 1987; The Soviet Study of International Relations, 1987, rev. ed., 1989; Gorbachev's International Outlook: Intellectual Origins and Political Consequences, 1989; The Soviet Breakup and U.S. Foreign Policy, 1992; The Cold War Is Over-Again, 1992; (ed. with K.W. Thompson) Soviet and Post-Soviet Russia in a World of Change, 1994; (with F.S. Larrabee) Russia, Ukraine and European Security: Implications for Western Policy, 1994; (with R. Lukic) Europe from the Balkans to the Urals: The Disintegration of Yugoslavia and the Soviet Union, 1996; Does Russia have a Democratic Future?, 1997; How Russia is Not Ruled: Reflections on Russian Political Development, 2005; Vladimir Putin and Russian Statecraft, 2011. **Address:** Department of Politics, University of Virginia, S397 Gibson Hall, 1540 Jefferson Park Ave., PO Box 400787, Charlottesville, VA 22904, U.S.A. **Online address:** al4u@virginia.edu

LYNCH, Chris. Scottish/American (born United States), b. 1962. **Genres:** Young Adult Fiction, Novels. **Career:** Emerson University, teacher of writing, 1995; Vermont College, teacher of writing, 1997-. Writer. **Publications:** Shadow Boxer, 1993; Iceman, 1994; Gypsy Davey, 1994; Slot Machine, 1995; Political Timber, 1996; Ladies' Choice, 1997; Scratch and the Sniffs, 1997; Johnny Chesthair, 1997; Wolf Gang, 1998; Whitechurch, 1999; Extreme Elvin, 1999; Gold Dust, 2000; Freewill, 2001; All the Old Haunts, 2001; Who the Man, 2002; Gravedigger's Cottage, 2004; Inexcusable, 2005; Me, Dead Dad & Alcatraz, 2005; Sins of the Fathers, 2006; The Big Game of Everything, 2008; Cyberia, 2008; Monkey See, Monkey Don't, 2009; Hothouse, 2010; Doing Your Research Project in Sport, 2010; Prime Evil, 2010; Angry Young Man, 2011; Kill Switch, 2012. BLUE-EYED SON SERIES: Mick, 1996; Blood Relations, 1996; Dog Eat Dog, 1996. HE-MAN WOMAN-HAT-

ERS CLUB SERIES (for young readers): Johnny Chest Hair, 1997; Babes in the Woods, 1997. Contributor to articles. **Address:** c/o Fran Lebowitz, Writers House, 21 W 26th St., New York, NY 10010, U.S.A.

LYNCH, Daniel. American (born United States), b. 1946. **Genres:** Novels, Biography, Military/Defense/Arms Control. **Career:** New Jersey Air National Guard, staff, 1969-75, sergeant; Philadelphia Inquirer, political writer, 1970-74; Newsday, Queens editor, 1974-79; Times Union, managing editor and columnist, 1979-2000; New York State Associated Press, president, 1994-95, director. **Publications:** Deadly Ernest, 1986; A Killing Frost, 1987; Deathly Pale, 1988; Brennan's Point, 1988; Bad Fortune, 1989; Yellow: A Novel, 1992; Running with the Machine: A Journalist's Eye-Opening Plunge into Politics, 2001; (with P. Rutherford) Into the Dragon's Teeth: Warriors' Tales of the Battle of the Bulge, 2004. Contributor to periodicals. **Address:** Whitston Publishing Company Inc., PO Box 38263, Albany, NY 12203-8263, U.S.A.

LYNCH, Frances. See COMPTON, D(avid) G(uy).

LYNCH, Jack. American (born United States) **Genres:** Language/Linguistics, Literary Criticism And History. **Career:** Rutgers University, Department of English, assistant professor, 1998-2004, associate professor of English, 2004-10, professor of English, 2010-, Faculty of Arts and Sciences, acting senior associate dean. Writer. **Publications:** (Ed.) The Age of Johnson: A Scholarly Annual, vol. VI, 1994, vol. XX, 2010; A Bibliography of Johnsonian Studies, 1986-1998, 2000; (contrib.) Encyclopedia of Computer Science, 4th ed., 2000; (ed.) Samuel Johnson's Dictionary: Selections from the 1755 Work That Defined the English Language, 2002; (contrib.) Literature and Digital Technologies: W.B. Yeats, Virginia Woolf, Mary Shelley, and William Gass, 2003; The Age of Elizabeth in the Age of Johnson, 2003; (ed.) Samuel Johnson's Insults: A Compendium of Snubs, Sneers, Slights, and Effronteries from the Eighteenth Century Master, 2004; (ed. with A. McDermott) Anniversary Essays on Johnson's Dictionary, 2005; Becoming Shakespeare: The Unlikely Afterlife That Turned a Provincial Playwright into the Bard, 2007; (contrib.) Comparative Excellence: New Essays on Shakespeare and Johnson, 2007; Deception and Detection in Eighteenth-century Britain, 2008; English Language, 2008; Lexicographer's Dilemma, 2009; (ed.) Benjamin Franklin, 2010; (ed.) Nathaniel Hawthorne, 2010; (ed.) Dracula, 2010; (ed.) Jane Austen, 2010; Don't Quit your Day Job, 2010; (ed.) Canterbury Tales, 2011; Samuel Johnson in Context, 2011. Contributor to journals and periodicals. **Address:** Department of English, Rutgers University, 360 Martin Luther King Blvd., 249 University Ave., Newark, NJ 07102, U.S.A. **Online address:** jlynch@andromeda.rutgers.edu

LYNCH, Janet Nichols. American (born United States), b. 1952. **Genres:** Music, Biography, Novellas/Short Stories, Children's Fiction, Novels. **Career:** Pianist, 1970-; private piano teacher, 1972-90; De Anza College, instructor in music, 1980-90; Skyline College, instructor in music, 1981-90; Divisadero Middle School, English teacher 2000-05; El Diamante High School, English and history teacher; College of the Sequoias, professor of music and English. Writer. **Publications:** FOR YOUNG READERS: American Music Makers: An Introduction to American Composers, 1990; (as Janet Nichols) Women Music Makers: An Introduction to Women Composers, 1992; (as Janet Nichols) Casey Wooster's Pet Care Service, 1993; Peace is a Four-Letter Word, 2005; Messed Up, 2009; Addicted to Her, 2010. FOR ADULTS: Chest Pains: A Novel, 2009. Contributor to journals and periodicals. **Address:** 123 S Cottonwood Ct., Visalia, CA 93291-5112, U.S.A. **Online address:** jnicholslynch@gmail.com

LYNCH, John. British (born England), b. 1927. **Genres:** History. **Career:** University of Liverpool, lecturer in history, 1954-61; University of London, University College, lecturer, reader and professor of Latin American history, 1961-74, professor of Latin American history, Institute of Latin American Studies, director, 1974-87, emeritus professor, 1987-. Writer. **Publications:** Spanish Colonial Administration, 1782-1810: The Intendant System in the Viceroyalty of the Rio de la Plata, 1958; Spain Under the Habsburgs, 2 vols., 1964-69; (ed. with R.A. Humphreys) The Origins of the Latin American Revolutions 1808-1826, 1965; The Spanish American Revolutions 1808-1826, 1973; Argentine Dictator: Juan Manuel de Rosas 1829-1852, 1981; (ed.) Andrés Bello: The London Years, 1982; España bajo los Austrias, 1982; Past and Present in the Americas: A Compendium of Recent Studies, 1984; (co-author) The Cambridge History of Latin America, vol. III, 1985, vol. IV, 1986; Spanish American Revolutions, 1808-1826, 1986; Hispanoamérica, 1750-1850: Ensayos sobre la sociedad y el estado, 1987; Bourbon Spain 1700-1808, 1989;

Caudillos in Spanish America 1800-1850, 1992; Spain, 1516-1598: From Nation State to World Empire, 1992; Latin American Revolutions, 1808-1826: Old and New World Origins, 1994; Massacre in the Pampas, 1872: Britain and Argentina in the Age of Migration, 1998; Latin America between Colony and Nation, 2001; Argentine caudillo: Juan Manuel de Rosas, 2001; Simón Bolívar: A Life, 2006; San Martín: Argentine Soldier, American Hero, 2009. **Address:** 8 Templars Cres., London, GL N3 3QS, England. **Online address:** johnlynch53@msn.com

LYNCH, Michael. Scottish (born Scotland), b. 1946. **Genres:** History, Theology/Religion, Genealogy/Heraldry. **Career:** University College of North Wales, lecturer in history, 1971-79; University of Edinburgh, lecturer, 1979-88, senior lecturer in Scottish history, 1988-92, Sir William Fraser professor of Scottish history and paleography, 1992-2005, professor emeritus, 2005-, research fellow. Writer. **Publications:** Edinburgh and the Reformation, 1981; Scotland: A New History, 1991, 2nd ed., 1992; Lloyd George and the Liberal Dilemma, 1993; The People's Republic of China Since 1949, 1998; An Introduction to Modern British History, 1900-1999, 2001; Interregnum, 2002; (with R.D. Anderson and N. Phillipson) University of Edinburgh: An Illustrated History, 2003; Britain, 1900-51, 2008; From Autocracy to Communism: Russia 1894-1941, 2008; Sixteenth-Century Scotland: Essays in Honour of Michael Lynch, 2008. EDITOR: The Early Modern Town in Scotland, 1986; (with G. Stell and M. Spearman) The Scottish Medieval Town, 1988; Mary Stewart, Queen in Three Kingdoms, 1988; (with A.A. MacDonald and I.B. Cowan) The Renaissance in Scotland: Studies in Literature, Religion, History, and Culture Offered to John Durkhan, 1994; (with D. Broun and R.J. Finlay) Image and Identity: The Making and Re-making of Scotland Through the Ages, 1998; (with J. Goodare) The Reign of James VI, 2000; (with H.T. Dickinson) The Challenge to Westminster: Sovereignty, Devolution and Independence, 2000; Oxford Companion to Scottish History, 2001; (with E.P. Dennison and D. Ditchburn) Aberdeen Before 1800: A New History, 2002. **Address:** School of History, Classics and Archaeology, University of Edinburgh, Rm. 1, 18 Buccleuch Pl., Old College S Bridge, Edinburgh, BR EH8 9LN, Scotland. **Online address:** m.lynch@ed.ac.uk

LYNCH, Michael. American (born United States), b. 1951. **Genres:** Sciences, Mathematics/Statistics, Genealogy/Heraldry. **Career:** University of Illinois, assistant professor, 1977-, professor, through 1989; University of Oregon, professor of biology, 1989-2001, Ecology and Evolution Program, director, 1989-93, 1996-2000; University of Indiana, professor of biology, 2001-04, distinguished professor, 2005-; Indiana University Center for Genomics and Bioinformatics, associated investigator, 2007-; public speaker. Writer. **Publications:** (With B. Walsh) Genetics and Analysis of Quantitative Traits, 1998; The Origins of Genome Architecture, 2007. Contributor to journals. **Address:** Department of Biology, Indiana University, 1001 E 3rd St., Bloomington, IN 47405-3700, U.S.A. **Online address:** milynch@indiana.edu

LYNCH, Michael P(atrick). American (born United States), b. 1966?. **Genres:** Philosophy, History. **Career:** University of Mississippi, assistant professor, 1995-2000; Connecticut College, Department of Philosophy, assistant professor, 2000-01, associate professor, 2002-04, chair, 2003-04, freshman advisor, 2001-04; University of Connecticut, associate professor of philosophy, 2004-07, professor of philosophy, 2007-; University of St. Andrews, Arché Centre for Logic, Language, Metaphysics and Epistemology, associate fellow, 2007-; University of Aberdeen, Northern Institute of Philosophy, associate fellow, 2007-. Writer. **Publications:** Truth in Context: An Essay on Pluralism and Objectivity, 1998; True to Life: Why Truth Matters, 2004; Truth as One and Many, 2009; Faith in Reason, forthcoming. EDITOR: The Nature of Truth: Classic and Contemporary Perspectives, 2001; (with H. Battaly) Perspectives on the Philosophy of William P. Alston, 2005; (with P. Greenough) Truth and Realism, 2006. Contributor to periodicals. **Address:** Department of Philosophy, University of Connecticut, U-2054, 205 Manchester Hall, 344 Mansfield Rd., Storrs, CT 06269-2054, U.S.A. **Online address:** mplynch@uconn.edu

LYNCH, Patrick. See GEARY, Joseph.

LYNCH, Patrick. See SINGTON, Philip.

LYNCH, Peter S. Scottish/American (born United States), b. 1944. **Genres:** Economics, Money/Finance, Business/Trade/Industry. **Career:** University of Stirling, senior lecturer in politics, 1944-; Fidelity Investments Inc., research analyst, 1969-74, research director, 1974-77, Fidelity Magellan Fund, manager, 1977-90, trustee, 1990-, Fidelity Management & Research Co., vice-chairman, 2007-, research consultant. Writer. **Publications:** (With J. Rothchild) On Up on Wall Street: How to Use What You Already Know to Make Money in the Market, 1989; (with J. Rothchild) Beating the Street: How to Pick Winning Stocks and Develop a Strategy for Mutual Funds, 1993; (with J. Rothchild) Learn to Earn: A Beginner's Guide to the Basics of Investing and Business, 1996; Minority Nationalism and European Integration, 1996. Contributor to periodicals. **Address:** University of Stirling, Stirling, FK9 4LA, Scotland. **Online address:** p.a.lynch@stir.ac.uk

LYNCH, Thomas. American (born United States), b. 1948?. **Genres:** Poetry, Essays, Novellas/Short Stories, Young Adult Fiction. **Career:** University of Michigan, adjunct professor in the graduate creative writing program; Lynch and Sons, funeral director. **Publications:** Skating with Heather Grace, 1986; Grimalkin and Other Poems, 1994; The Undertaking: Life Studies from the Dismal Trade, 1997; Still Life in Milford: Poems, 1998; Bodies in Motion and at Rest, 2000; Booking Passage: We Irish & Americans, 2005; Apparition & Late Fictions, 2010; Walking Papers: Poems 1999-2009, 2010; The Sin Eater-A Breviary, 2011. **Address:** Lynch & Sons, 404 E Liberty St., Milford, MI 48381, U.S.A. **Online address:** thoslynch@aol.com

LYNCH, Timothy J. British (born England), b. 1969. **Genres:** History. **Career:** Boston College Centre, director, 2000-03; University of Leicester, lecturer in U.S. foreign policy, 2003-05; University of London, faculty, 2005-; U.S. foreign policy, senior lecturer; U.S. Presidency Centre, deputy director, 2008-; Oxford Encyclopedia of American Military and Diplomatic History, editor-in-chief, 2010-. Contributor to periodicals. **Publications:** Turf War: The Clinton Administration and Northern Ireland, 2004. (with R.S. Singh) After Bush: The Case for Continuity in American Foreign Policy, 2008. Contributor to books and periodicals. **Address:** Institute for the Study of the Americas, School of Advanced Study, University of London, Senate House, Malet St., London, GL WC1E 7HU, England. **Online address:** timothy.lynch@sas.ac.uk

LYNCH, Wayne. Canadian (born Canada), b. 1948. **Genres:** Animals/Pets. **Career:** Science writer and photographer, 1979-. **Publications:** AUTHOR AND PHOTOGRAPHER: Married to the Wind, 1984; Bears: Monarchs of the Northern Wilderness, 1993, rev. ed., 1995; Bears, Bears, Bears, 1995; A Is for Arctic: Natural Wonders of a Polar World, 1996; Arctic Alphabet: Exploring the North from A to Z, 1999; Penguins!, 1999; Wild Birds across the Prairies, 1999; (with A. Lang) Loons, 2000; The Great Northern Kingdom: Life in the Boreal Forest, 2001; The Scoop on Poop! The Fascinating Science of How Animals Use Poop, 2002; Seals, 2002; Hawks, 2004; (with A. Lang) Windswept: A Passionate View of the Prairie Grasslands, 2004; (with A. Lang) Wild Alberta: A Visual Celebration, 2005; Owls of the United States and Canada: A Complete Guide to Their Biology and Behavior, 2007; Penguins of the World, 2007; Arctic A to Z, 2009; Planet Arctic: Life at the Top of the World, 2010. CRITTER QUIZ SERIES: Whose Baby Is This?, 2003; Whose Bottom Is This?, 2003; Whose Feet Are These?, 2003; Whose House Is This?, 2003; Whose Nose Is This?, 2003; Whose Teeth Are These?, 2003. OUR WILD WORLD SERIES: (with L. Evert) Birds of Prey: Explore the Fascinating Worlds of Eagles, Falcons, Owls, Vultures, 2005; Falcons, 2005; Owls, 2005; Vultures, 2005. OUR WILD WORLD ECOSYSTEMS SERIES: (with A. Lang) Prairie Grasslands, 2006; (with A. Lang) Rocky Mountains, 2006; (with A. Lang) The Arctic, 2007; The Everglades, 2007; Sonoran Desert, 2008. NATURE BABY SERIES WITH A. LANG PHOTOGRAPHER: Baby Penguin, 2002; The Adventures of Baby Bear, 2002; Baby Fox, 2003; Baby Elephant, 2003; Baby Lion, 2003; Baby Seal, 2004; Baby Ground Squirrel, 2005; Baby Koala, 2005; Baby Owl, 2005; Baby Sloth, 2005; Baby Grizzly, 2006; Baby Porcupine, 2006; Baby Sea Turtle, 2007; Baby Mountain Sheep, 2008; Baby Polar Bear, 2008. Contributor to books. **Online address:** lynchandlang@shaw.ca

LYND, Staughton (Craig). American (born United States), b. 1929. **Genres:** History, Novellas/Short Stories, Essays, Young Adult Non-fiction. **Career:** University Settlement House, tenant organizer and community worker, 1957-58; Spelman College, history instructor, 1961-64; Yale University, assistant professor of history, 1964-67; Chicago State College, associate professor of history, 1967-68; Legal Services Corp., attorney, 1978-96. Writer. **Publications:** NONFICTION: Anti-Federalism in Dutchess County, New York: A Study of Democracy and Class Conflict in the Revolutionary Era, 1962; (ed.) Nonviolence in America: A Documentary History, 1966, (ed. with A. Lynd) rev. ed., 1995; (with T. Hayden) The Other Side, 1967; Reconstruction, 1967;

Class Conflict, Slavery and the United States Constitution (essays), 1968; Intellectual Origins of American Radicalism, 1968; (with M. Ferber) The Resistance, 1971; (ed.) Personal Histories of the Early C.I.O., 1973; (with G. Alperovitz) Strategy and Two Essays Towards a New Program: American Socialism, 1973; (ed.) American Labor Radicalism: Testimonies and Interpretations, 1973; (ed. with A. Lynd) Rank and File: Personal Histories by Working-Class Organizers, 1973; Labor Law for the Rank and Filer, 1978, 2nd ed., 2011; The Fight Against Shutdowns: Youngstown's Steel Mill Closings, 1982; (ed. with S. Bahour and A. Lynd) Homeland: Oral Histories of Palestine and Palestinians, 1994; (ed.) We Are All Leaders: The Alternative Unionism of the Early 1930s, 1996; (with A. Lynd) Liberation Theology for Quakers, 1996; Living inside Our Hope: A Steadfast Radical's Thoughts on Rebuilding the Movement, 1997; (ed. with A. Lynd) The New Rank and File, 2000; Lucasville: The Untold Story of a Prison Uprising, 2004, 2nd ed., 2011; (with A. Grubacic) Wobblies & Zapatistas: Conversations on Anarchism, Marxism and Radical History, 2008; (with A. Lynd) Stepping Stones: Memoir of a Life Together, 2009; (ed.) From Here to There: The Staughton Lynd Reader, 2010; (with D. Gross) Solidarity Unionism at Starbucks, 2011. **Address:** 1694 Timbers Ct., Niles, OH 44446-3941, U.S.A. **Online address:** Salynd@aol.com

LYNDS, Gayle (Hallenbeck). American (born United States) **Genres:** Novels, Mystery/Crime/Suspense, Literary Criticism And History. **Career:** Arizona Republic, reporter; General Electric TEMPO, editor; Santa Barbara magazine, editor-in-chief; Prime magazine, editor; International Thriller Writers Inc., co-founder and co-president, 2004-. **Publications:** Masquerade (thriller), 1996; Mosaic, 1998; Mesmerized, 2001; The Coil, 2004; I'd Kill For That: A Serial Novel, 2004; The Last Spymaster, 2006; The Book of Spies, 2010. WITH R. LUDLUM: The Hades Factor, 2000; The Paris Option, 2002; The Altman Code, 2003. NONFICTION AS GAYLE STONE: (with C.E. Crowther) Intimacy: Strategies for Successful Relationships, 1986. JUVENILE FICTION AS G.H. STONE: Rough Stuff, 1989; Reel Trouble, 1989; Fatal Error, 1990. **Address:** International Thriller Writers Inc., PO Box 311, Eureka, CA 95502, U.S.A.

LYNN, Adele B. American (born United States), b. 1953. **Genres:** Human Relations/Parenting, Psychology, Administration/Management, Business/Trade/Industry. **Career:** Federal Reserve Bank, trainer, 1980-82; The Adele Lynn Leadership Group (formerly Lynn Learning Labs), founder and owner, 1982-. Writer. **Publications:** Mentoring: Passing on the Torch, 1997; In Search of Honor: Lessons from Workers on How to Build Trust, 1998; The Emotional Intelligence Activity Book: 50 Activities for Developing EQ at Work, 2002; EQ Difference: A Powerful Program for Putting Emotional Intelligence to Work, 2005; Quick Emotional Intelligence Activities for Busy Managers: 50 Team Exercises that Get Results in Just 15 Minutes, 2007; EQ Interview: Finding Employees with High Emotional Intelligence, 2008. Contributor to periodicals and journals. **Address:** The Adele Lynn Leadership Group, 609 Broad Ave., Belle Vernon, PA 15012, U.S.A. **Online address:** lynnlabs@westol.com

LYNN, David H. American (born United States) **Genres:** Young Adult Fiction, Literary Criticism And History. **Career:** Kenyon College, professor of English, 1994-; Kenyon Review, editor, 1994-. **Publications:** The Hero's Tale: Narrators in the Early Modern Novel, 1989; Fortune Telling, 1998; Wrestling with Gabriel, 2002; (ed.) The Best of the Kenyon Review, 2003; Year of Fire, 2006. Contributor to periodicals. **Address:** Department of English, Kenyon College, Lentz House and Sunset Cottage, Finn House 114, Gambier, OH 43022, U.S.A. **Online address:** lynnd@kenyon.edu

LYNN, Jackie. See HINTON, Lynne.

LYNN, John A(lbert). American (born United States), b. 1943. **Genres:** History, Military/Defense/Arms Control, Politics/Government, Social Sciences. **Career:** Indiana University, visiting assistant professor of history, 1972-73; University of Maine, assistant professor of history, 1973-77; University of Illinois, faculty, 1981-, assistant professor of history, 1978-83, Program in Arms Control, Disarmament and International Security, faculty, 1981-, associate professor of history, 1983-91, professor of history, 1991, Military Education Council, chair, 2001-, now professor emeritus; Marine Corps University, Oppenheimer chair, 1994-95; The Ohio State University, adjunct professor of history, 1998-. Writer. **Publications:** The Bayonets of the Republic: Motivation and Tactics in the Army of Revolutionary France, 1791-94, 1984; (ed.) The Tools of War: Instruments, Ideas and Institutions of Warfare, 1445-

1871, 1990; (with G. Satterfield) A Guide to Sources in Early Modern European Military History in Midwestern Research Libraries, 1991, 2nd ed., 1994; (ed.) Feeding Mars: Logistics in Western Warfare from the Middle Ages to the Present, 1993; (co-author) Don't Blame God!: A Biblical Answer to the Problem of Evil, Sin, and Suffering, 1993; Giant of the Grand siècle: The French Army, 1610-1715, 1997; Wars of Louis XIV, 1664-1714, 1999; French Wars 1667-1714: The Sun King at War, 2002; The Mind of War: A History of Combat and Culture, 2002; Battle: A History of Combat and Culture, 2003, rev. ed., 2004; Women, Armies and Warfare in Early Modern Europe, 2008. **Address:** Department of History, University of Illinois at Urbana-Champaign, 309 Gregory Hall, 810 S Wright St., PO Box 466, Urbana, IL 61801, U.S.A. **Online address:** johnlynn@illinois.edu

LYNN, Jonathan. American/British (born England), b. 1943. **Genres:** Novels, Plays/Screenplays, Mystery/Crime/Suspense, Film, Art/Art History, Politics/Government, Humor/Satire. **Career:** Cambridge Theatre Co., director, 1977-81. Actor, writer and producer. **Publications:** A Proper Man (novel), 1976; (ed. with A. Jay) The Complete Yes Minister: The Diaries of a Cabinet Minister, 1984; (ed. with A. Jay) The Complete Yes Prime Minister: The Diaries of the Right Hon. James Hacker, 1986; Nuns On The Run, 1990; Mayday (novel), 1993; (contrib.) Ji Mantriji, 2001; Ji Pradhanmantriji, 2002; (with A. Jay) Yes Prime Minister, 2010. **Address:** c/o Anthony Jones, United Agents, 12-26 Lexington St., London, GL W1F 0LE, England. **Online address:** jonathan@jonathanlynn.com

LYNN, Karyl Charna. See ZIETZ, Karyl Lynn.

LYNN, Richard. British (born England), b. 1930. **Genres:** Psychology, History, Economics, Social Sciences. **Career:** University of Exeter, lecturer, 1956-67; Economic and Social Research Institute, professor of psychology, 1967-72; University of Ulster, professor of psychology, 1972, now professor emeritus. Writer. **Publications:** Attention, Arousal, and the Orientation Reaction, 1966; The Irish Brain Drain, 1968; The Universities and the Business Community, 1969; Personality and National Character, 1971; National Differences in Anxiety, 1971; Introduction to the Study of Personality, 1971; The Entrepreneur: Eight Case Studies, 1974; (ed.) Dimensions of Personality: Papers in Honour of H.J. Eysenck, 1981; Educational Achievement in Japan: Lessons for the West, 1988; The Secret of the Miracle Economy, 1991; Dysgenius: Genetic Deterioration in Modern Populations, 1996; Eugenics: A Reassessment, 2001; Science of Human Diversity: A History of the Pioneer Fund, 2001; (with T. Vanhanen) IQ and the Wealth of Nations, 2002; Race Differences in Intelligence: An Evolutionary Analysis, 2006; IQ and Global Inequality, 2006; The Global Bell Curve, 2008. Contributor to journals. **Address:** University of Ulster, Cromore Rd., Coleraine, BT52 1SA, Northern Ireland. **Online address:** richard@rlynn.co.uk

LYNN, Tracy. See BRASWELL, Elizabeth.

LYON, Andrea D. American (born United States), b. 1952?. **Genres:** Biography, Autobiography/Memoirs. **Career:** Cook County Public Defender's Office, staff, 1976-90, Homicide Task Force, assistant defender, 1979-90, Homicide Task Force, chief; Illinois Capital Resource Center, founder and director, 1990-95; University of Michigan Law School, assistant clinical professor of law, 1995-2000; De; Paul University College of Law, Center for Justice in Capital Cases, director, 2000-, associate clinical professor, 2000-06, clinical professor of law and associate dean for clinical programs, 2006-; University of Michigan Law School, visiting clinical professor, 2010, 2011. Lawyer and writer. **Publications:** (With E. Hughes and M. Prosser) Federal Habeas Corpus: Cases and Materials, 2005; Angel of Death Row: My Life as a Death Penalty Defense Lawyer, 2009. Contributor to periodicals. **Address:** DePaul College of Law, 14 E Jackson Blvd., 1st Fl., 1E, Chicago, IL 60604, U.S.A. **Online address:** andrea@andrealyon.com

LYON, Annabel. Canadian (born Canada), b. 1971. **Genres:** Novellas/Short Stories, Novels, Children's Fiction. **Career:** Writer. **Publications:** Oxygen, 2000; The Best Thing for You, 2004; Saturday Night Function, 2005; All-Season Edie, 2008; The Golden Mean, 2009; Encore Edie, 2010. **Address:** New Westminster, BC, Canada. **Online address:** annabellyon@telus.net

LYON, Bentley. American (born United States), b. 1929. **Genres:** Mystery/Crime/Suspense, Novels, Young Adult Fiction. **Career:** U.S. Forest Service, staff, 1947-85. Writer. **Publications:** (Ed. and comp.) Wildland Fire Management Terminology, 1985; White Crow, 1989; Summer Stalk, 1992. **Address:**

PO Box 1900, Porterville, CA 93258-1900, U.S.A.

LYON, David. Canadian/British (born England), b. 1948. **Genres:** Philosophy, Sociology, Technology, Theology/Religion, Ethics, Politics/Government. **Career:** Teacher, 1972-74, 1975-90; Wilfrid Laurier University, visiting assistant professor, 1976-77, visiting professor, 1984; Regent College, visiting lecturer, 1976; Calvin College, research fellow, 1981-82; University of Leeds, Television Research Centre, visiting research fellow, 1984-85; London Institute for Contemporary Christianity, associate faculty, 1985-90; New College, visiting professor, 1986; Open University, course tutor in sociology of technology, 1987-90; Queen's University, associate professor, 1991-94, professor of sociology and head of department, 1994-, Queen's research chair, Canada Council Killam research fellow, 2008-10; Ecole Des Hautes Etudes en Sciences Sociales, professor, 1996; Institute for Social and Economic Change, visiting professor, 2004; Universidad Autonoma del Estado de Mexico, visiting professor, 2009. Writer. **Publications:** Christians and Sociology: Towards a Christian Perspective, 1975; Christians & Sociology: The Challenge of Sociology, a Christian Response, 1976; Karl Marx: A Christian Appreciation of His Life and Thought, 1979; Karl Marx: A Christian Assessment of His Life & Thought, 1981; Sociology and the Human Image, 1983; Future Society, 1984; The Silicon Society, 1986; The Steeple's Shadow: On the Myths and Realities of Secularization, 1987; The Information Society: Issues and Illusions, 1988; Postmodernity, 1994, 2nd ed., 1999; The Electronic Eye: The Rise of Surveillance Society, 1994; Living Stones: St. James' Church, Kingston, 1845-1995: From Stuartville to Queen's Campus, 1995; (ed. with E. Zureik) Computers, Surveillance and Privacy, 1996; Jesus in Disneyland: Religion in Postmodern Times, 2000; (ed. with M.V. Die) Rethinking Church, State and Modernity: Canada Between Europe and America, 2000; Surveillance Society: Monitoring Everyday Life, 2002; (ed.) Surveillance as Social Sorting: Privacy, Risk and Digital Discrimination, 2003; Surveillance after September 11, 2003; (ed.) Theorizing Surveillance: The Panopticon and Beyond, 2006; Surveillance Studies: An Overview, 2007; (ed. with C.J. Bennett) Playing the Identity Card, 2008; Identifying Citizens: ID Cards as Surveillance, 2009; (ed. with E. Zureik and Y. Abu-Laban) Surveillance and Control in Israel/Palestine: Population, Territory and Power, 2010; (ed. with K. Ball and K. Haggerty) Handbook of Surveillance Studies, 2012; (ed. with A. Doyle and R. Lippert) Eyes Everywhere: The Global Growth of Camera Surveillance, 2012. Contributor of articles to journals and magazines. **Address:** Department of Sociology, Queen's University, Mac-Corry D526, Kingston, ON K7L 3N6, Canada. **Online address:** lyond@queensu.ca

LYON, Elizabeth. American (born United States), b. 1950?. **Genres:** Adult Non-fiction, Novels, Young Adult Fiction, How-to Books, Humanities, Medicine/Health, Self Help, Psychology, Writing/Journalism, E-books, Autobiography/Memoirs. **Career:** Lyon's Literary Services, founder and operator, 1988-2002; Editing Intl., president, 2002-04, operator, 2004-. Writer and educator. **Publications:** Mabel: The Story of One Midwife, 1981; Nonfiction Book Proposals Anybody Can Write: How to Get a Contract and Advance Before Writing Your Book, 1995, rev. ed., 2002; The Sell-Your-Novel Tool Kit: Everything You Need to Know about Queries, Synopses, Marketing, and Breaking In, 2002; Writer's Guide to Nonfiction, 2003; A Writer's Guide to Fiction, 2004; National Directory of Editors and Writers: Freelance Editors, Copyeditors, Ghostwriters, and Technical Writers, and Proofreaders for Individuals, Businesses, Nonprofits, and Government Agencies, 2005; Manuscript Makeover: Revision Techniques No Fiction Writer Can Afford to Ignore, 2008. Contributor to periodicals. Works appear in anthologies. **Address:** Editing Intl., 3530 E Game Farm Rd, Ste 39, Springfield, OR 97477, U.S.A. **Online address:** elyon123@comcast.net

LYON, George Ella. American (born United States), b. 1949. **Genres:** Novels, Children's Fiction, Young Adult Fiction, Picture/Board Books, Young Adult Non-fiction. **Career:** University of Kentucky, instructor in English and creative writing, 1977-, visiting assistant professor, 1991-92; Centre College of Kentucky, visiting assistant professor, 1979-80, writer-in-residence, 1985; Transylvania University, lecturer in humanities and creative writing, 1984-86; Sayre School, writer-in-residence, 1986; Radford University, visiting faculty, 1986; Shepherdstown College, writer-in-residence, 2001. **Publications:** POETRY: Mountain, 1983; Growing Light, 1987; Catalpa, 1993, 2nd ed., 2007; Back, 2010; All the Water in the World, 2011. YOUNG ADULT NOVELS: Borrowed Children, 1988; Red Rover, Red Rover, 1989; Here and Then, 1994; With a Hammer for My Heart, 1997; Don't You Remember, 2007; My Friend, the Starfinder, 2008; Sleepsong, 2008; (with S. Anderson) You and Me and Home Sweet Home, 2009; The Pirate of Kindergarten, 2010; Holding On to Zoe, 2012; She Let Herself Go, 2012. PICTURE BOOKS: Father Time and the Day Boxes, 1985; A Regular Rolling Noah, 1986; A B Cedar: An Alphabet of Trees, 1989; Together, 1989; Come a Tide, 1990; Basket, 1990; Cecil's Story, 1991; The Outside Inn, 1991; Who Came Down That Road?, 1992; Dreamplace, 1993; Mama is a Miner, 1994; Five Live Bongos, 1994; A Day at Damp Camp, 1996; Ada's Pal, 1996; A Wordful Child, 1996; A Sign, 1998; Counting on the Woods, 1998; A Traveling Cat, 1998; Book, 1999; One Lucky Girl, 2000; Gina. Jamie. Father. Bear, 2002; Mother to Tigers, 2003; Weaving the Rainbow, 2004; Sonny's House of Spies, 2004; When You Get Little and I Get Big, 2006; No Dessert Forever!, 2006; Trucks Roll!, 2007. OTHERS: Braids (play), 1985; Choices: Stories for Adult New Readers, 1989; Looking Back for the Words, 1989; (ed. with J.W. Miller and G. Norman) A Gathering at the Forks, 1993; (ed. with B.H. Baber and G. Norman) Old Wounds, New Words: Poems from the Appalachian Poetry Project, 1994; Where I'm from, Where Poems Come From, 1999; (ed. with L. Kendrick) Crossing Troublesome: Twenty-five Years of the Appalachian Writers Workshop, 2002; (ed.) Kentucky Christmas, 2003; Which Side Are You On?: The Story of a Song, 2011. Contributor to books and periodicals. **Address:** Atheneum Books, 1230 Ave. of the Americas, New York, NY 10020-1513, U.S.A. **Online address:** ginalyon2001@yahoo.com

LYON, Janet. American (born United States) **Genres:** Literary Criticism And History. **Career:** University of Illinois, teacher of English and women's studies; Penn State University, associate professor of English, women's studies and science, technology and society, Disability Studies Minor, faculty-in-charge, English honors adviser, Summer Study Abroad Program, faculty; Journal of Modern Literature, editor. **Publications:** Manifestoes: Provocations of the Modern, 1999; The Perfect Hostess: Salons in Modernity, forthcoming. Contributor to books and journals. **Address:** Department of English, College of Liberal Arts, Penn State University, 19 Burrowes Bldg., 3451 Walnut St., University Park, PA 16802, U.S.A. **Online address:** jwl12@psu.edu

LYON, Jeff(rey R.). American (born United States), b. 1943. **Genres:** Medicine/Health, Sciences, Sports/Fitness. **Career:** Miami Herald, reporter, 1964-66; Chicago Today, reporter, 1966-74; Chicago Tribune Magazine, political correspondent, columnist and feature writer, 1974-, deputy editor; Columbia College Chicago, coordinator, creative writing teacher, 1987, director of science communication program, 1988-, Department of Journalism, senior lecturer. **Publications:** Playing God in the Nursery, 1985; (with P. Gorner) Altered Fates: Gene Therapy and the Retooling of Human Life, 1995. Contributor to periodicals. **Address:** Department of Journalism, Columbia College Chicago, Rm. 201 C, 33 E Congress Pkwy., 600 S Michigan Ave., Chicago, IL 60605-1900, U.S.A. **Online address:** jlyons@colum.edu

LYONS, Dan. American (born United States), b. 1956. **Genres:** Transportation. **Career:** Amoco Motor Club, RoadSmart magazine, road test editor; Car Collector magazine, feature editor; Car Classics magazine, feature editor; Times Union, Automotive Weekly section, road test columnist, 1992-; Motor Matters group, automotive columnist; AutoMedia.com, staff, road test reviewer; Kelley Blue Book, staff, road test reviewer. Writer and photographer. **Publications:** (Co-author) Cars of 1957, 1997; Sixties American Cars, 1998; (with J. Scott and contrib.) Muscle Car Milestones, 2001; (with P. Paternie and contrib.) Modern American Muscle, 2001; (co-author) Cars of 1965, 2002; (with J.F. Katz) Corvette: An American Classic, 2001, rev. ed., 2003; Cars of the Fantastic '50s, 2005; Cars of the Sensational 60s, 2006. Contributor to books and magazines. **Address:** 8 Colonie Ave., Latham, NY 12110-3104, U.S.A. **Online address:** info@lyonsonwheels.com

LYONS, Daniel. *See* **JOBS, Daniel Steve.**

LYONS, David (Barry). American (born United States), b. 1935. **Genres:** Philosophy, Law. **Career:** Machinist, 1954-56; engineering draftsman and designer, 1956-58; Cornell University, Sage School of Philosophy, assistant professor, 1964-67, associate professor, 1967-71, professor of philosophy, 1971-90, chairman, 1978-84, Susan Linn Sage professor of philosophy, 1990-95, professor emeritus of philosophy, 1995-, Law School, professor of law, 1979-95, professor emeritus of law, 1995-; Boston University, professor of law, 1995-, professor of philosophy, 1998-. Writer. **Publications:** Forms and Limits of Utilitarianism, 1965; In the Interest of the Governed: A Study in Bentham's Philosophy of Utility and Law, 1973, rev. ed., 1991; Ethics and the Rule of Law, 1984; Moral Aspects of Legal Theory, 1993; Rights, Welfare, and Mill's Moral Theory, 1994. EDITOR: Rights, 1979; Mill's Utilitarianism: Critical Essays, 1998. **Address:** Department of Philosophy, Boston University, 765 Commonwealth Ave., Boston, MA 02215, U.S.A. **Online address:** dbl@bu.edu

LYONS, Gabe. American (born United States), b. 1975?. **Genres:** Theology/Religion. **Career:** Catalyst, co-founder; Q, founder. Writer. **Publications:** (With D. Kinnaman) Unchristian: What a New Generation Really Thinks about Christianity ... and Why It Matters, 2007; (with C.W. Colson) The Faith: What Christians Believe, Why They Believe It, and Why It Matters, 2008; The Next Christians: The Good News About the End of Christian America, 2010. **Address:** Crown Publishing Group, 1745 Broadway, New York, NY 10019, U.S.A. **Online address:** glyons@fermiproject.com

LYONS, Louis. British (born England), b. 1937. **Genres:** Mathematics/Statistics, Physics, Sciences, Novels. **Career:** Oxford University, Jesus College, tutor and fellow, 1969-, university lecturer in nuclear physics, 1970-, senior tutor, 1980-83, vice-principal, 1992-95, professor of physics, emeritus fellow; Imperial College London, Department of Physics, visiting professor. Editor. **Publications:** Statistics for Nuclear and Particle Physicists, 1986; A Practical Guide to Data Analysis for Physical Science Students, 1991; All You Wanted to Know about Mathematics but Were Afraid to Ask, 1995; (ed. with M.K. Unel) Statistical Problems in Particle Physics, Astrophysics and Cosmology: Proceedings of PHYSTAT05, Oxford, UK, 12-15 September 2005, 2006. Contributor to journals. **Address:** Department of Particle & Nuclear Physics, Oxford University, Rm. 510, Blackett Lab, Prince Consort Rd., London, GL SW7 2AZ, England. **Online address:** l.lyons1@physics.ox.ac.uk

LYONS, Martyn. Australian/British (born England), b. 1946. **Genres:** History. **Career:** University of New South Wales, professor, 1977-, School of History, head, 1991-94. Writer and historian. **Publications:** France under the Directory, 1975; Revolution in Toulouse: An Essay on Provincial Terrorism, 1978; The Totem and the Tricolour: A Short History of New Caledonia since 1774, 1986; (with L. Taksa) Australian Readers Remember: An Oral History of Reading 1890-1930, 1992; Napoleon Bonaparte and the Legacy of the French Revolution, 1994; (ed. with R. Aldrich) The Sphinx in the Tuileries and Other Essays in Modern French History, 1999; Readers and Society in Nineteenth-Century France: Workers, Women, Peasants, 2001; (ed. with J. Arnold) A History of the Book in Australia, 1891-1945: A National Culture in a Colonised Market, 2001; (ed. with P. Russell) Australia's History: Themes and Debates, 2005; Post-Revolutionary Europe, 1815-1856, 2006; (ed.) Ordinary Writings, Personal Narratives: Writing Practices in 19th and Early 20th-Century Europe, 2007; Reading Culture and Writing Practices in Nineteenth-Century France, 2008; A History of Reading and Writing: In the Western World, 2010. **Address:** School of History and Philosophy, University of New South Wales, Rm. MB349, C20-Morven Brown Bldg., Sydney, NW 2052, Australia. **Online address:** m.lyons@unsw.edu.au

LYONS, Nick. American (born United States), b. 1932. **Genres:** Literary Criticism And History, Sports/Fitness, Business/Trade/Industry, Animals/Pets. **Career:** University of Michigan, faculty; City University of New York, Hunter College, professor of English, 1961-88; Crown Publishers, executive editor, 1964-74; The Lyons Press, president and founder, 1978-99. **Publications:** (Ed.) Jones Very: Selected Poems, 1966; Fisherman's Bounty, 1970; The Seasonable Angler: The Adventures and Misadventures of an Angling Addict, 1970; Fishing Widows, 1974; The Sony Vision, 1976; (with H. Tanzer) Your Pet isn't Sick, 1977; Bright Rivers, 1977; Locked Jaws: The Tragical-Historical-Comical Journal of a Dieter in Quest of a Youthful Figure, 1979; Confessions of a Fly-Fishing Addict, 1989; Spring Creek, 1992; A Flyfisher's World, 1996; (ed. and foreword) In Praise of Wild Trout, 1998; (comp.) Quotable Fisherman, 1998; My Secret Fishing Life, 1999; Full Creel: A Nick Lyons Reader, 2000; (ed. and intro.) Hemingway on Fishing, 2000; (ed. and foreword) Traver on Fishing: A Treasury of Robert Traver's Finest Stories and Essays About Fishing for Trout, 2001; (ed. and intro.) Classic Fishing Stories, 2002; (comp. and intro. with N. Lyons) Quotable Dad, 2003; (intro.) Hatches II, 2004; (ed. and intro.) The Gigantic Book of Fishing Stories, 2007; (ed. and intro.) The Best Fishing Stories Ever Told, 2010; (ed. with T. Lyons) Little Red Book of Dad's Wisdom, 2011. Contributor to periodicals. **Address:** 342 W 84th St., New York, NY 10024-4255, U.S.A.

LYONS, Thomas Tolman. American (born United States), b. 1934. **Genres:** Civil Liberties/Human Rights, History, Race Relations, Politics/Government, Law, Social Sciences. **Career:** Mount Hermon School for Boys, teacher of history, 1958-63; Phillips Academy, teacher of American history and urban studies, 1963-79, professor, visiting fellow, 1969-, John Mason Kemper

Instructor in History, 1979-, chairman of department, 1979-, now faculty emeritus; Dartmouth College, visiting fellow in history, 1968-69. Writer. **Publications:** (With E.C. Rozwenc) Realism and Idealism in Wilson's Peace Program, 1965; (with E.C. Rozwenc) Reconstruction and the Race Problem, 1968; Black Leadership in American History, 1971; Supreme Court and Individual Rights in Contemporary Society, 1975; America, 1975; The Expansion of the Federal Republic, 1800-1848, 1978; (with A.C. Ganley and G.T. Sewall) After Hiroshima: America since 1945, 1979; (with A.C. Ganley and G.T. Sewall) U.S.A. Since 1945: After Hiroshima, 1993. EDITOR: (with E.C. Rozwenc) Presidential Power in the Era of the New Deal, 1963; (with E.C. Rozwenc) Realism and Idealism in Wilson's Peace Program, 1965; The President: Preacher, Teacher, Salesman: Selected Presidential Speeches, 1933-1983, 1985. **Address:** 8 Oak St., Newburyport, MA 01950, U.S.A. **Online address:** lyons.et@comcast.net

LYONS, William (Edward). Australian (born Australia), b. 1939. **Genres:** Philosophy. **Career:** University of Glasgow, lecturer in philosophy, 1973-85; Trinity College Dublin, fellow, now emeritus fellow, School of Mental and Moral Science, head, 1985-95, professor of moral philosophy, 1985-2004, professor emeritus, 2004-. Writer. **Publications:** Gilbert Ryle: An Introduction to His Philosophy, 1980; Emotion, 1980; The Disappearance of Introspection, 1986; (ed.) Modern Philosophy of Mind, 1995; Approaches to Intentionality, 1995; Matters of the Mind, 2001; The Crooked Roads of Genius, 2005. **Address:** Department of Philosophy, Trinity College Dublin, College Green, Dublin, DU D2, Ireland. **Online address:** wlyons@tcd.ie

LYSAUGHT, Jerome P. American (born United States), b. 1930. **Genres:** Education, Medicine/Health, Sciences, Technology. **Career:** University of Kansas, Eberhardt fellow, 1953-; Eastman Kodak Co., training specialist, 1954-60; Educational Microfilm Systems, assistant manager, 1954-61; Eastman Kodak Co., assistant manager, 1954-61; Rochester Junior Chamber of Commerce, director, 1957-; Recordak Corp., assistant product manager, 1960-62; University of Rochester, Warner School, associate lecturer in education, 1962-63, assistant professor, 1963-66, research associate in medical education, 1964-, associate professor, 1966-69, professor of education, 1969-, School of Medicine and Dentistry, professor of pediatrics, Graduate School of Education and Human Development, professor of curriculum and teaching, Health Professions Education, coordinator, Graduate Programs in Higher Education, coordinator, University College of Liberal and Applied Studies, Graduate Programs in Adult Learning, coordinator, National Commission for the Study of Nursing and Nursing Education, director; Rochester Clearinghouse for Information on Self-Instruction, coordinator, 1964-; National Commission for the Study of Nursing and Nursing Education, past director, 1967-73; John Wiley & Sons Inc., editorial consultant; McGraw-Hill Book Co., editorial consultant; American Hospital Association, consultant; American Society of Clinical Pathologists, consultant; Harvard University School of Public Health, consultant; Rush University of the Health Sciences, consultant. Writer. **Publications:** (With C.M. Williams) A Guide to Programmed Instruction, 1963; An Abstract for Action: Report of the National Commission for the Study of Nursing and Nursing Education, 1970; Appendices, 1971; Action in Nursing: Progress in Professional Purpose, 1974; A Luther Christmas Anthology, 1978; Trends and Issues in American Nursing: An Independent View, 1979; Action in Affirmation: Toward an Unambiguous Profession of Nursing, 1981. EDITOR: Programmed Learning: Evolving Principles and Industrial Applications, 1961; Programmed Instruction in Medical Education, 1965; (with H. Jason) Self-Instruction in Medical Education: Proceedings of the Second Rochester Conference, June 24-26, 1965, 1967; (with S.A. Sutherland and P.A. Mullen) Individualized Instruction in Medical Education: Proceedings, 1968; Instructional Systems in Medical Education: Proceedings, 1970; Instructional Technology in Medical Education, 1973; From Abstract into Action: Implementation of the Recommendations of the National Commission for the Study of Nursing and Nursing Education, 1973. Contributor to books and journals. **Address:** 17 Bretton Woods Dr., Rochester, NY 14618, U.S.A. **Online address:** jlys@son.rochester.edu

LYSSIOTIS, Tes. Australian (born Australia) **Genres:** Plays/Screenplays. **Career:** Teacher, 1975-81; Filiki Players, co-founder, 1984-. Writer. **Publications:** The Forty Lounge Cafe, 1990; A White Sports Coat & Other Plays, 1996. **Address:** Currency Press, 164 James St., PO Box 2287, Redfern, Sydney, NW 2016, Australia. **Online address:** after_after_life08@hotmail.com

LYSTRA, Karen. American (born United States) **Genres:** History, Adult Non-fiction, Biography, Autobiography/Memoirs, Humanities. **Career:** California State University, professor of American studies. Writer. **Publications:** Searching the Heart: Women, Men and Romantic Love in Nineteenth-Century America, 1989; Dangerous Intimacy: The Untold Story of Mark Twain's Final Years, 2004; The Funniest Joke in the World: The Untold Story of Mark Twain, forthcoming. Contributor to periodicals. **Address:** Department of American Studies, California State University, UH-412, 800 N State College Blvd., PO Box 34080, Fullerton, CA 92834-6868, U.S.A. **Online address:** klystra@fullerton.edu

LYTLE, Elizabeth Stewart. American (born United States), b. 1949. **Genres:** Children's Non-fiction, Homes/Gardens, How-to Books. **Career:** Freelance magazine writer, 1984-; News-Herald, feature writer and consumer editor, 1971-86; English teacher, 1990-; Meridian Intl., magazine contributing editor, 1993-. Communications consultant. **Publications:** Careers in the Construction Industry, 1992, 2nd ed., 1994; Careers as an Electrician, 1993, rev. ed., 1999; Careers in Plumbing, Heating, and Cooling, 1995; Careers in Cosmetology, 1999. Contributor of articles to magazines. **Address:** Rosen Publishing Group Inc., 29 E 21st St., New York, NY 10010, U.S.A. **Online address:** lizlytle@usa.choice.com

LYTLE, Mark H. (Mark Hamilton Lytle). American (born United States), b. 1945. **Genres:** History, Politics/Government, Biography, Autobiography/Memoirs. **Career:** Bard College, professor of history and environmental studies, Lyford Paterson Edwards and Helen Gray Edwards professor of historical studies, American Studies Program, chair, Master of Arts in Teaching Program, director, faculty, 1974-, Environmental and Urban Studies Program, coordinator; Dublin University College, Mary Ball professor of American history, 2000, 2004; University of Nottingham, external examiner; University of Limerick, external examiner. Writer. **Publications:** (With J.W. Davidson) After the Fact: American Historians and Their Methods, 1981; (with J.W. Davidson) The United States: A History of the Republic, 1981, 5th ed., 1990; (with J.W. Davidson as Mark Hamilton Lytle) After the Fact: The Art of Historical Detection, 1982, 6th ed., 2010; (with D.M. Merkt) Shang: A Biography of Charles E. Wheeler, 1984; (contrib.) A History of the Republic, 1986, 2nd ed., 1990; (as Mark Hamilton Lytle) The Origins of the Iranian-American Alliance, 1941-1953, 1987; (with J.W. Davidson and M.B. Stoff) American Journey: The Quest for Liberty since 1865, 1992; (as Mark Hamilton Lytle) America's Uncivil Wars: The Sixties Era: From Elvis to the Fall of Richard Nixon, 2006; (as Mark Hamilton Lytle) The Gentle Subversive: Rachel Carson, Silent Spring, and the Rise of the Environmental Movement, 2007; Nation of Nations: A Narrative History of the American Republic, 6th ed., 2007. **Address:** Bard College, PO Box 5000, Annandale-On-Hudson, NY 12504-5000, U.S.A. **Online address:** lytle@bard.edu

LYTLE, Mark Hamilton. *See* **LYTLE, Mark H.**

LYTTON, Deborah. American (born United States), b. 1966. **Genres:** Novels. **Career:** Kelly Lytton & Williams L.L.P., attorney. Writer, photographer, actress and singer. **Publications:** Jane in Bloom (novel), 2009. Contributor to periodicals. **Address:** c/o Stacey Kendall Glick, Dystel & Goderich Literary Management, 1 Union Sq. W, Ste. 904, New York, NY 10003, U.S.A. **Online address:** deborah@deborahlytton.com